S0-AFX-338

YEARBOOK OF THE UNITED NATIONS 2008

Volume 62

YEARBOOK OF THE UNITED NATIONS, 2008

Volume 62

The United Nations Department of Public Information is dedicated to communicating the ideals and work of the United Nations to the world; to interacting and partnering with diverse audiences; and to building support for peace, development, and human rights for all. Based on official documents, although not an official record, the *Yearbook of the United Nations* stands as the most authoritative reference work on the Organization and an indispensable tool for anyone seeking information on the UN system.

The *Yearbook of the United Nations* is produced by the Yearbook Unit of the Publications and Editorial Cluster in the Outreach Division of the Department of Public Information.

Chief Editor: Orrin F. Summerell

Managing Editor: Edoardo Bellando

Senior Editors: Lawri Moore, Anthony Paterniti, John R. Sebesta

Associate Editors: Udy Bell, Meghan Lynn, Shiyun Sang

Copy Editor: Sunita Chabra

Typesetter: Galina Brazhnikova

Researcher: Mary Lee Kortes

Administrative Assistant: Sheila Poinesette

Copy Coordinator: Marc Bender

Editorial Assistant: David Haken

Yearbook of the United Nations
Room 910B
300 East 42nd Street
New York, New York 10017
United States of America

e-mail: **unyearbook@un.org**

All volumes of the *Yearbook of the United Nations* from the 1946–47 edition (Vol. 1) to the 2007 edition (Vol. 61) can be accessed in full online on the *Yearbook* website: **unyearbook.un.org**.

For more information on the United Nations, please visit the website of the Organization: **un.org**.

YEARBOOK OF THE UNITED NATIONS 2008

Volume 62

Department of Public Information
United Nations, New York

Yearbook of the United Nations, 2008
Volume 62

Published by the United Nations Department of Public Information
New York, New York 10017, United States of America

ISBN: 978-92-1-101227-9
eISBN: 978-92-1-054459-7
ISSN: 0082-8521
United Nations publication
Sales No. E.10.I.1 H

Jacket Design: Graphic Design Unit, United Nations, New York

Printed in the United States of America

Foreword

Multiple crises in 2008 demanded immediate, concrete results from the United Nations. Severe economic recession challenged global solidarity and threatened to compromise efforts to combat climate change. A food crisis endangered the fight against poverty and hunger, putting at risk the world's poorest and most vulnerable people. Natural disasters, most notably in China, Haiti and Myanmar, caused more than 235,000 deaths, affected some 214 million people, and resulted in an estimated $190 billion in economic damage—further exacerbating already dire humanitarian situations and placing the utmost strains on aid delivery and relief assistance.

In a year that marked the sixtieth anniversary of United Nations peacekeeping, outbreaks of hostilities in the Democratic Republic of the Congo, the Georgian province of Abkhazia, the Sudan and elsewhere tested the mettle of United Nations forces and the efficacy of United Nations diplomacy. Although we were not always able to protect innocent people from harm, and suffered losses among our own, we helped deliver solutions that avoided further catastrophe and turned the tide in favour of peace and recovery.

The situation in Israel and the Occupied Palestinian Territory remained difficult. Little progress was made on nuclear safeguard issues in Iran or on proliferation issues in the Democratic People's Republic of Korea, and terrorism remained a global threat, although the Counter-Terrorism Committee reported significant progress by Member States in implementing the Global Counter-Terrorism Strategy.

The United Nations continued to support the efforts of post-conflict countries and those in transition. The Organization provided assistance to successful democratic elections in Nepal and Sierra Leone, and buttressed progress in Bangladesh, Côte d'Ivoire and Liberia. The Peacebuilding Commission expanded its involvement to a fourth country emerging from conflict: the Central African Republic. In the face of a worsening humanitarian situation in Afghanistan, the United Nations helped strengthen institutions and facilitated international civilian efforts. We promoted calm in a potentially explosive situation in Kosovo, and searched for ways to deal with piracy and issues of humanitarian access in Somalia.

I have always emphasized that human rights must be a core principle in the pursuit of the global good. The sixtieth anniversary of the Universal Declaration of Human Rights saw the launch of the Universal Periodic Review mechanism for examining the human rights record of all Member States. The struggle for gender equality and the empowerment of women is a central part of our efforts for human rights, and the year saw several initiatives, including the launch of the UNiTE to End Violence Against Women campaign and the adoption of Security Council resolution 1820(2008), which broke new legal ground in stating that "rape and other forms of sexual violence can constitute war crimes, crimes against humanity or a constitutive act with respect to genocide".

This *Yearbook* highlights these and many other issues on which the United Nations was active. As I stated in my annual report on our work in 2008, the rising demand for our services is daunting, yet I am convinced that with dedication, focus and commitment we can live up to the hopes of all peoples who look to us to build a more peaceful, prosperous and just world. By promoting an informed understanding of the work and purposes of the United Nations among the peoples of the world, this volume, like its predecessors, contributes to building support for peace, development, human rights and the rule of law for all.

Ban Ki-moon
Secretary-General of the United Nations
New York, April 2012

Table of contents

Part Three: Economic and social questions

Part Four: Legal questions

Part Five: Institutional, administrative and budgetary questions

Appendices

Indices

About the 2008 edition of the *Yearbook*

This sixty-second volume of the *Yearbook of the United Nations* continues the tradition of providing the most comprehensive coverage available of the activities and concerns of the United Nations. The present volume highlights the attention given by the United Nations in 2008 to conflicts in the Democratic Republic of the Congo, the Georgian province of Abkhazia and the Sudan, along with the challenges posed by severe economic recession, the food security crisis, climate change and natural disasters, piracy and terrorism. It features UN accomplishments in supporting democracy in post-conflict countries, championing human rights and the rule of law, fighting for gender equality and strengthening international cooperation in countering the world drug problem.

The user can locate information contained in this volume by using the Table of contents, the Subject index, the Index of resolutions and decisions and the Index of Security Council presidential statements. The volume also features six appendices: Appendix I comprises a roster of Member States; Appendix II reproduces the Charter of the United Nations and the Statute of the International Court of Justice; Appendix III presents the structure of the principal organs of the United Nations; Appendix IV provides the agenda for each session of the principal organs in 2008; Appendix V gives the addresses of United Nations information centres and services worldwide; and Appendix VI lists the addresses of the specialized agencies and other related organizations of the UN system.

Structure and scope of articles

The *Yearbook* is subject-oriented and divided into five parts covering political and security matters; human rights issues; economic and social questions; legal issues; and institutional, administrative and budgetary matters. Chapters present summaries of pertinent UN activities, including those of intergovernmental and expert bodies, as well as major reports, Secretariat activities and, in selected cases, the views of States in written communications.

Activities of UN bodies. All resolutions, decisions and other major activities of the principal organs and, on a selective basis, those of subsidiary bodies are either reproduced or summarized in the appropriate chapter. The texts of all resolutions and decisions of a substantive nature adopted in 2008 by the General Assembly, the Security Council and the Economic and Social Council are reproduced or summarized under the relevant topic. These texts are preceded by procedural details giving date of adoption, meeting number and vote totals (in favour–against–abstaining), if any, and an indication of their approval by a sessional or subsidiary body prior to final adoption. The texts are followed by details of any recorded or roll-call vote.

Major reports. Most reports of the Secretary-General in 2008, along with selected reports from other UN sources, such as seminars and working groups, are summarized.

Secretariat activities. The operational activities of the United Nations for development and humanitarian assistance in 2008 are described under the relevant topics. For major activities financed outside the UN regular budget, selected information is given on contributions and expenditures.

Views of States. Written communications sent to the United Nations by Member States and circulated as documents of the principal organs have been summarized, in selected cases, under the relevant topics. Substantive actions by the Security Council have been analysed and brief reviews of the Council's deliberations given, particularly in cases where an issue was taken up but no resolution was adopted.

Multilateral treaties. Information on signatories and parties to multilateral treaties and conventions has been taken from the series *Multilateral Treaties Deposited with the Secretary-General* (ST/LEG/SER/E) (see **treaties.un.org**).

Terminology

Formal titles of bodies, organizational units, conventions, declarations and officials are given in full on first mention in each main section. They are also used in resolution/decision texts, as well as in the Subject index under the key word of the title. Short titles may be used in subsequent references.

Acknowledgements

The Yearbook Unit would like to express its appreciation to the following persons for their contribution to the *Yearbook of the United Nations, 2008*:

Contributing Editors/Writers: Luisa Balacco, Elizabeth Baldwin-Penn, Kathryn Gordon, Helen Graham, Peter Jackson, T. Vishnu Jayaraman, Christine Koerner, Bojana Matic, Benedicta Obodoruku, Mebrak Tareke

Researcher: Nilton Sperb

Copy Editors: Alison Koppelman, Karen Sholto

Proofreaders: June Chesney, Judith Goss

Interns: Dante Cotton, Inna Tsyrlin, Daniel Zugna

Indexer: Maria A. Sullivan

Web Consultant: Belal Hassan

Abbreviations commonly used in the *Yearbook*

ACABQ Advisory Committee on Administrative and Budgetary Questions
AU African Union
BINUB United Nations Integrated Office in Burundi
BONUCA United Nations Peacebuilding Support Office in the Central African Republic
CARICOM Caribbean Community
CEB United Nations System Chief Executives Board for Coordination
CIS Commonwealth of Independent States
CPC Committee for Programme and Coordination
DPKO Department of Peacekeeping Operations
DPRK Democratic People's Republic of Korea
DRC Democratic Republic of the Congo
ECA Economic Commission for Africa
ECE Economic Commission for Europe
ECLAC Economic Commission for Latin America and the Caribbean
ECOWAS Economic Community of West African States
ESCAP Economic and Social Commission for Asia and the Pacific
ESCWA Economic and Social Commission for Western Asia
EU European Union
FAO Food and Agriculture Organization of the United Nations
HIV/AIDS human immunodeficiency virus/acquired immunodeficiency syndrome
IAEA International Atomic Energy Agency
ICAO International Civil Aviation Organization
ICC International Criminal Court
ICJ International Court of Justice
ICRC International Committee of the Red Cross
ICSC International Civil Service Commission
ICTR International Criminal Tribunal for Rwanda
ICTY International Tribunal for the Former Yugoslavia
IDPs internally displaced persons
IFAD International Fund for Agricultural Development
IFC International Finance Corporation
ILO International Labour Organization
IMF International Monetary Fund
IMO International Maritime Organization
ITU International Telecommunication Union
JIU Joint Inspection Unit
LDC least developed country
MDGs Millennium Development Goals
MINURCAT United Nations Mission in the Central African Republic and Chad
MINURSO United Nations Mission for the Referendum in Western Sahara
MINUSTAH United Nations Stabilization Force in Haiti
MONUC United Nations Organization Mission in the Democratic Republic of the Congo
NEPAD New Partnership for Africa's Development
NGO non-governmental organization
NPT Treaty on the Non-Proliferation of Nuclear Weapons
NSGT Non-Self-Governing Territory
OAS Organization of American States
OCHA Office for the Coordination of Humanitarian Affairs
ODA official development assistance
OECD Organisation for Economic Co-operation and Development
OHCHR Office of the United Nations High Commissioner for Human Rights
OIOS Office of Internal Oversight Services
OSCE Organization for Security and Cooperation in Europe
PA Palestinian Authority
UNAIDS Joint United Nations Programme on HIV/AIDS
UNAMA United Nations Assistance Mission in Afghanistan
UNAMI United Nations Assistance Mission for Iraq
UNAMID African Union-United Nations Hybrid Operation in Darfur
UNCTAD United Nations Conference on Trade and Development
UNDOF United Nations Disengagement Observer Force
UNDP United Nations Development Programme
UNEP United Nations Environment Programme
UNESCO United Nations Educational, Scientific and Cultural Organization
UNFICYP United Nations Peacekeeping Force in Cyprus
UNFPA United Nations Population Fund
UN-Habitat United Nations Human Settlements Programme
UNHCR Office of the United Nations High Commissioner for Refugees
UNICEF United Nations Children's Fund
UNIDO United Nations Industrial Development Organization
UNIFIL United Nations Interim Force in Lebanon
UNIOSIL United Nations Integrated Office in Sierra Leone
UNIPSIL United Nations Integrated Peacebuilding Office in Sierra Leone
UNMEE United Nations Mission in Ethiopia and Eritrea
UNMIK United Nations Interim Administration Mission in Kosovo
UNMIL United Nations Mission in Liberia
UNMIS United Nations Mission in the Sudan
UNMIT United Nations Integrated Mission in Timor-Leste
UNOCI United Nations Operation in Côte d'Ivoire
UNODC United Nations Office on Drugs and Crime
UNOGBIS United Nations Peacebuilding Support Office in Guinea-Bissau
UNOMIG United Nations Observer Mission in Georgia
UNOPS United Nations Office for Project Services
UNOWA Office of the Special Representative of the Secretary-General for West Africa
UNRWA United Nations Relief and Works Agency for Palestine Refugees in the Near East
UNTSO United Nations Truce Supervision Organization
UNWTO World Tourism Organization
WFP World Food Programme
WHO World Health Organization
WIPO World Intellectual Property Organization
WMDs weapons of mass destruction
WMO World Meteorological Organization
WTO World Trade Organization
YUN Yearbook of the United Nations

Explanatory note on documents

The following is a guide to the principal United Nations document symbols appearing in this volume:

A/- refers to documents of the General Assembly, numbered in separate series by session. Thus, A/63/- refers to documents issued for consideration at the sixty-third session, beginning with A/63/1. Documents of special and emergency special sessions are identified as A/S and A/ES-, followed by the session number.

A/C.- refers to documents of the Assembly's Main Committees. For example, A/C.1/- identifies documents of the First Committee, A/C.6/- documents of the Sixth Committee. A/BUR/- refers to documents of the General Committee. A/AC.- documents are those of the Assembly's ad hoc bodies and A/CN.- of its commissions. For example, A/AC.105/- identifies documents of the Assembly's Committee on the Peaceful Uses of Outer Space, A/CN.4/- of its International Law Commission. Assembly resolutions and decisions since the thirty-first (1976) session have been identified by two Arabic numerals: the first indicates the session of adoption, the second the sequential number in the series. Resolutions are numbered consecutively from 1 at each session. Decisions since the fifty-seventh (2002) session are numbered consecutively from 401 for those concerned with elections and appointments and from 501 for all other decisions. Decisions of special and emergency special sessions are numbered consecutively from 11 for those concerned with elections and appointments and from 21 for all other decisions.

E/- refers to documents of the Economic and Social Council, numbered in separate series by year. Thus, E/2008/- refers to documents issued for consideration by the Council at its 2008 sessions, beginning with E/2008/1. E/AC.-, E/C.- and E/CN.-, followed by identifying numbers, refer to documents of the Council's subsidiary ad hoc bodies, committees and commissions. For example, E/CN.5/- refers to documents of the Council's Commission for Social Development, E/C.2/- to documents of its Committee on Non-Governmental Organizations. E/ICEF/- documents are those of the United Nations Children's Fund (UNICEF). Symbols for the Council's resolutions and decisions, since 1978, consist of two Arabic numerals: the first indicates the year of adoption and the second the sequential number in the series. There are two series: one for resolutions, beginning with 1 (resolution 2008/1), and one for decisions, beginning with 201 (decision 2008/201).

S/- refers to documents of the Security Council. Its resolutions are identified by consecutive numbers followed by the year of adoption in parentheses, beginning with resolution 1(1946).

ST/-, followed by symbols representing the issuing department or office, refers to documents of the United Nations Secretariat.

Documents of certain bodies bear special symbols, including the following:

CD/-	Conference on Disarmament
CERD/-	Committee on the Elimination of Racial Discrimination
DC/-	Disarmament Commission
DP/-	United Nations Development Programme
HSP/-	United Nations Human Settlements Programme
ITC/-	International Trade Centre
TD/-	United Nations Conference on Trade and Development
UNEP/-	United Nations Environment Programme

Many documents of the regional commissions bear special symbols, which are sometimes preceded by the following:

E/ECA/-	Economic Commission for Africa
E/ECE/-	Economic Commission for Europe
E/ECLAC/-	Economic Commission for Latin America and the Caribbean
E/ESCAP/-	Economic and Social Commission for Asia and the Pacific
E/ESCWA/-	Economic and Social Commission for Western Asia

Various other document symbols include the following:

L.- refers to documents of limited distribution, such as draft resolutions.

CONF.- refers to conference documents.

INF- refers to general information documents.

SR.- refers to summary records and is followed by a meeting number.

PV.- refers to verbatim records and is followed by a meeting number.

United Nations sales publications each carry a sales number with the following components separated by periods: a capital letter indicating the language(s) of the publication; two Arabic numerals indicating the year; a Roman numeral indicating the subject category; a capital letter indicating a subdivision of the category, if any; and an Arabic numeral indicating the number of the publication within the category. Examples: E.06.II.A.2; E/F/R.05.II.E.8; E.08.II.C.2.

All documents cited in the text in square brackets may be obtained through the UN Official Document System website: **documents.un.org**.

Report of the Secretary-General on the work of the Organization

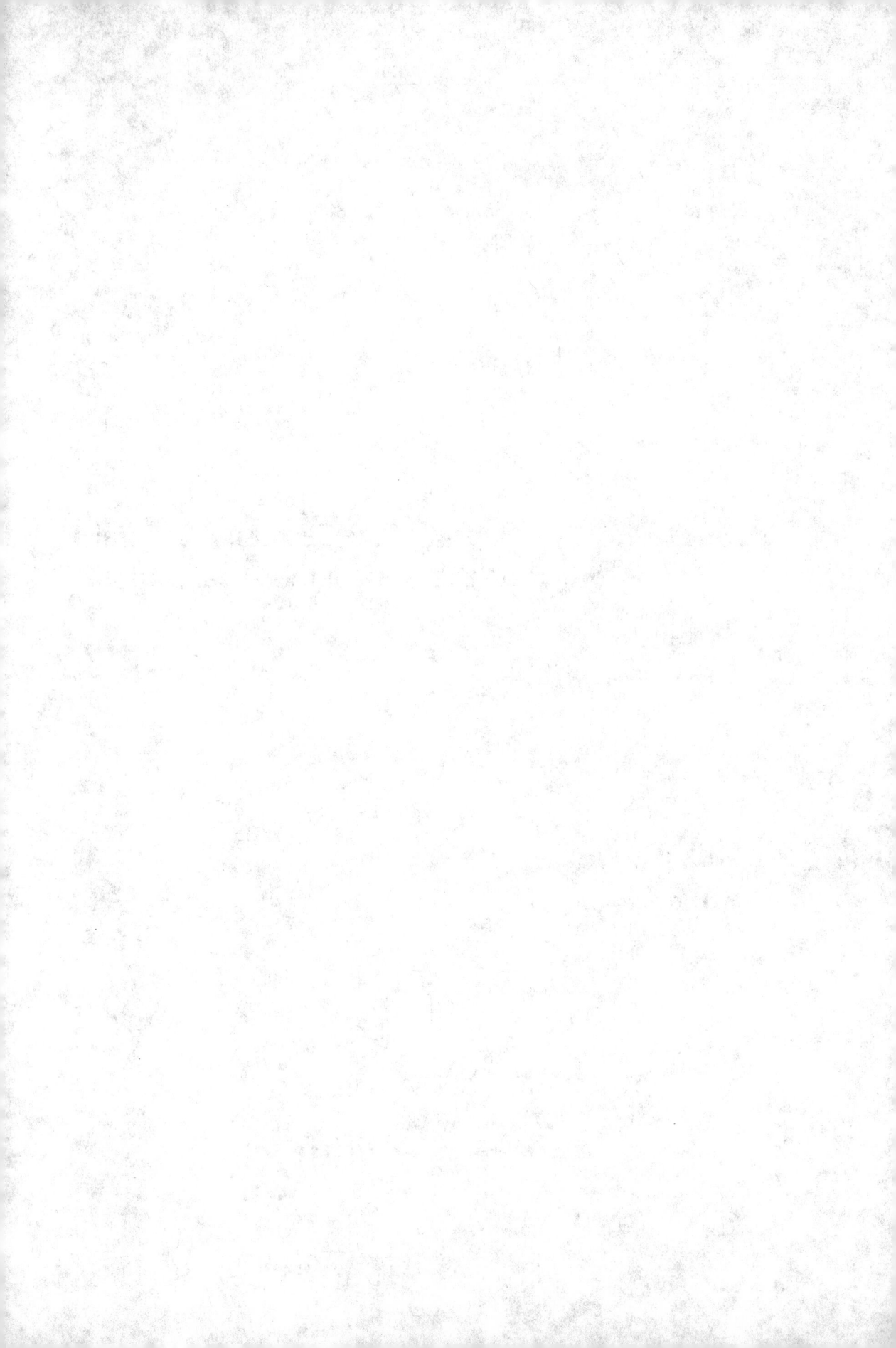

Report of the Secretary-General on the work of the Organization

Following is the Secretary-General's report on the work of the Organization **[A/63/1]**, *dated 12 August 2008, submitted to the sixty-third session of the General Assembly. The Assembly took note of it on 6 October* **(decision 63/504)**.

Chapter I

Introduction

1. As I come to the end of my second year at the helm of the United Nations, I am inspired by the commitment and energy of the people who serve this Organization; at the same time, I am acutely aware of the increasing weight of responsibility that lies on our collective shoulders. This past year we experienced a huge increase in the intensity of engagement across the entire spectrum of development, security, humanitarian affairs and human rights issues. The international community turned to us for assistance which ranged from helping victims of conflict and disaster and addressing the needs of the poor and hungry to restoring peace between warring parties and mobilizing the global community to address a new generation of global challenges like climate change and terrorism.

2. The rising demand for our services is daunting, and yet I am convinced that with dedication, focus and commitment we can live up to the hopes of all peoples who look to us to build a more peaceful, prosperous and just world.

3. To achieve this necessary focus, in 2008 and for the rest of my tenure, we must dedicate our effort to three key areas: delivering results for people most in need, securing global goods, and creating a stronger United Nations through full accountability.

4. The United Nations has had a long and proud history of establishing norms and principles that govern international relations. That history can and must continue. But in this new era where the world is increasingly turning to the United Nations to deliver a wide range of services in just about every corner of the Earth, the biggest challenge we face is to deliver concrete results for people most in need, wherever they are. To meet these growing needs and high expectations, we must enhance our operational delivery. This means concentrating our resources where the Organization can make the biggest difference. We cannot just make promises or call on others to act; we cannot wait for solutions to emerge. We need to seize opportunities to show results now that justify the hopes for a better future.

5. The second area requiring our focus is securing global goods. The United Nations is uniquely placed to lead the effort to address global threats that endanger every person everywhere in the world, and to secure the corresponding goods. Challenges like climate change and global health know no borders and cannot be addressed by a single State or groups of States. As the only universal organization with a comprehensive mandate, ours has a strong comparative advantage with respect to catalysing action by all countries, and building new multi-stakeholder alliances. The United Nations must rise to this challenge, since there is no other forum that can legitimately address these issues on a global scale as effectively.

6. My message is clear: we will rise or fall together depending on the effectiveness of our common response. Strategies to address these new challenges will need to be developed globally, but the locus of action and responsibility will be primarily the national level. I appeal to Governments to take action, as the consequences of inaction will spare none.

7. To deliver results for a better world, we must work to strengthen the United Nations through full accountability. Only full accountability will enable us to achieve optimal outcomes. We must look at accountability not as a narrow technical issue, but as a fundamental organizing principle and operational guideline for our Organization, and must encourage Member States to adopt the same principle. An organization where all are held accountable for upholding their responsibilities will be a significantly stronger one.

8. Working together, we can improve the nature and quality of life of the world's population and we can prevent both national and global threats from escalating to catastrophic proportions. As enshrined in the Charter of the United Nations, we, the peoples of the United Nations, have this obligation and responsibility.

Chapter II

Delivering results for people most in need

9. One of the most important roles that the United Nations can play is that of champion of the powerless, the forgotten and the marginalized. Our greatest responsibility is to ensure that we improve the welfare of these populations—that we deliver results to those most in need. This means that we must help Member States deliver on their Millennium Development Goal commitments, that we must use all the resources and expertise we have gained in the field of preventive diplomacy, peacekeeping and peacebuilding to establish and preserve a secure and peaceful world, and that we must provide relief and rehabilitation assistance to victims of conflicts and disaster. It also means that we must work with the international community to ensure respect for human rights; support States in establishing rule of law, preventing genocide and delivering on their responsibility to protect; and assist them in establishing good governance and democracy.

A. Development

10. We must deliver results for a more prosperous and healthy world. Development should not be the privilege of a handful but a right for all. Yet, half of the world's adult population owns barely 1 per cent of global wealth. Although we have made significant gains towards the global goal of halving extreme poverty by 2015, many countries, particularly in Africa, are off-track with respect to achieving the Millennium Development Goals. We must build on existing real and measurable progress, and scale up action and financing. But addressing the Millennium Development Goals is not enough: we must tackle the food crisis, climate change, natural disasters and violent conflicts, which threaten to turn back the clock on development advances. And we must give priority to mitigating the impact of these forces on those most in need—the poor, women, and children, who are almost always the first and hardest hit.

11. To deliver leadership in development in the face of today's global challenges, the United Nations will need a more coherent, focused and reinvigorated approach, building on the integration of the normative and operational strengths of the Organization as a whole. This is the thrust of the proposal I put forward in my report on strengthening the development pillar of the Secretariat (A/62/708), specifically its ability to deliver effectively and efficiently on its development mandates, to improve its strategic position in dealing with major development issues and processes, and to provide important benefits to Member States. I have encouraged Member States to act on the proposal during the forthcoming session of the General Assembly. In the past year, I have also undertaken initiatives in a number of related priority areas: better linking normative, analytical and operational functions; strengthening global to regional, regional to national, and interregional linkages; furthering synergies among the work of the Secretariat, the United Nations funds and programmes and the United Nations system as a whole; and forging partnerships with key stakeholders who can complement our work in the development arena.

1. The Millennium Development Goals and the other internationally agreed development goals

12. As we pass the halfway point on the path to reaching the Millennium Development Goals by 2015, critical action is needed to meet all of them. The outlook for the education, health and environmental Millennium Development Goals is mixed. Across the board, gains in education seem to be most encouraging, while those linked to maternal health are least on track. We must deliver on commitments already made as well as scale up existing successes and replicate them in other countries. I am calling on the United Nations system and Member States to make addressing the needs of the poorest, with a special focus on Africa, a central priority.

13. While the number of people living in extreme poverty has declined over the years, 1.2 billion—most of whom are living in the least developed countries, especially in Africa—are still stuck in the poverty trap. Without immediate humanitarian aid and robust long-term investments in agriculture, the food crisis is expected to drive an additional 100 million people into extreme poverty. The effects of climate change will be no less severe.

14. Many countries are close to delivering universal primary education. We must continue to build on and seek out innovative measures, such as school feeding programmes and school fee waivers, which have contributed to these advances. For example, the fact that countries like Malawi, Kenya and the United Republic of Tanzania abolished primary school fees has resulted in dramatic increases in enrolment rates. Many other countries, however, still face enormous challenges. For example, in sub-Saharan Africa, about 41 million primary school-age children are out of school; and in South Asia, 31.5 million remain out of school.

15. Women are integral members of society and significant drivers of development. We must continue to fight for gender equality and to empower women. While women's status has improved in some areas like education, gender gaps remain pervasive. Women are underrepresented in politics and positions of power and are often paid less and subjected to far worse working conditions than men. Violence against

women remains widespread, ranging from domestic violence to purposeful victimization in war, and constitutes a severe obstacle to the achievement of all global development goals. In January 2008, I launched a campaign to end violence against women, which aims at mobilizing public opinion, securing political will and ensuring increased resources to tackle this issue.

16. Perhaps the worst gender disparities are seen in the area of health, where women make up more than half of adults living with HIV in sub-Saharan Africa and every year more than 500,000 women continue to die from complications of pregnancy and childbirth. Progress continues to be slowest in improving maternal health compared with all Millennium Development Goal targets, and the provision of adequate and reliable data at the national, regional and international levels disaggregated by sex remains a challenge. This is unacceptable. I am strongly committed to advancing progress on maternal health and I urge all Member States to allocate more attention and resources to this Goal.

17. Not only is promoting and securing health for all ethical, but it also builds a foundation for prosperity, stability and poverty reduction. We must move forward in areas such as infant mortality and under-five mortality, measles and immunization, poliomyelitis and guinea worm eradication and scaling-up of malaria control tools, and in that of HIV antiretroviral treatment.

18. The AIDS epidemic continues to require an urgent response. While we have expanded access to antiretroviral treatment to 3 million people, infections continue apace, with 2.5 million newly infected in 2007 alone. The importance of prevention has never been clearer. With an estimated 33.2 million people now living with HIV, combating stigma and discrimination is equally important. The 2008 high-level meeting on AIDS reviewed progress achieved in implementing the 2001 Declaration of Commitment on HIV/AIDS and the 2006 Political Declaration on HIV/AIDS and reminded us of our responsibilities in combating the scourge of HIV/AIDS.

19. I am committed to advancing action on infectious diseases. About 1.2 billion of the world's poorest populations suffer from the crippling effects of neglected tropical diseases. Malaria kills more than 1 million people every year. These numbers are unacceptable. The first HIV/Tuberculosis Global Leaders' Forum, held at the margin of the high-level meeting on AIDS this year, called for increased collaboration on the issue of HIV and tuberculosis co-infection. We must replicate proved strategies to combat these diseases. By 2010, I intend to ensure universal coverage against malaria through ensuring that all people at risk, especially women and children in Africa, are fully covered by indoor residual spraying and long-lasting insecticide-treated bednets. Our global efforts also start at home: this year I launched UN Cares, a programme to provide services such as training, counselling and testing for HIV-positive United Nations personnel and their families.

20. Strengthening health systems provides the base for the dramatic scale-up of high-impact interventions needed to reach the health Goals. A comprehensive human resources strategy is key, particularly building up a cadre of community health workers who can provide basic services to the poor.

21. Meeting the water and sanitation targets is also of critical importance. Almost 1 billion people lack access to safe drinking water and 2.6 billion do not have access to adequate sanitation. We must double the current annual investment by the international community to about $30 billion.

22. The impacts of climate change, as seen through deforestation, soil erosion, desertification and land degradation, are aggravating poverty and threatening livelihoods. We must prioritize action to prevent a further loss in biodiversity and ensure that development efforts are environmentally sustainable.

23. A global partnership for development is critical to revitalize efforts towards achieving the Goals. I urged world leaders to deliver on the official development assistance commitments made at the 2005 World Summit, at the International Conference on Financing for Development in Monterrey, Mexico, and in Gleneagles and Heiligendamm. I call for quick and concrete progress to achieve the goal of $50 billion per year by 2010.

24. Developing open, rule-based, predictable and non-discriminatory trading and financial systems is integral to achieving the Goals. I am heartened by the Accra Accord adopted by the United Nations Conference on Trade and Development at its twelfth session (UNCTAD XII). We must seek to implement its ambitious agenda and make globalization a powerful means to achieve poverty eradication.

25. We must also aim for a successful outcome of the Doha round of trade negotiations this year. The continued deadlock poses a significant risk to the multilateral trading system and to the ability to achieve the Goals. Key World Trade Organization members must redouble efforts to produce a meaningful and significant development package. The food crisis is a grave sign of the need to break the impasse on agricultural trade liberalization.

26. This year, we are at a turning point in the achievement of the Goals. The High-level Event on the Millennium Development Goals on 25 September 2008 will be critical to catalysing the action needed to bridge the implementation gap. I urge Member States to provide strong leadership. The Doha Follow-up International Conference on Financing for Develop-

ment to Review the Implementation of the Monterrey Consensus at the end of 2008 will offer another important opportunity to review many of the critical issues at stake. Let us ensure that the coming year is a "year of action"—one in which we translate our promises into food, shelter, education and health for those most in need.

2. The special needs of Africa

27. During my tenure, I have made a special commitment to addressing Africa's peace, security and development needs. The Office of the Special Adviser on Africa has played an important role in forwarding this agenda, as has the Millennium Development Goals Africa Steering Group composed of multilateral development partners, which presented in June 2008 a set of practical costed recommendations for achieving the Millennium Development Goals by 2015 in Africa. I urge all countries to work with me in implementing these important recommendations.

28. It is encouraging that the overall economic performance of Africa remains strong, with a 5.7 per cent growth of gross domestic product (GDP) and a 3.7 per cent per capita income increase in 2007, owing to improved macroeconomic management, and increased private capital flows, as well as better governance in many parts of the continent. Good governance and democracy are central to promoting overall prosperity, stability and peace, as acknowledged by African leaders themselves in the Constitutive Act establishing the African Union. I commit the United Nations to supporting efforts of Africa to improve and safeguard its young democracies.

29. However, while overall growth rates are positive, they are extremely unequal throughout the continent, with a number of countries experiencing negligible, if not negative, GDP growth rates. In countries where there has been positive growth, there is little evidence that the poorest are seeing an improvement in their circumstances. Scaling up public and private sector investments and exploiting regional resources are vital.

30. Progress requires peace and security. I have been greatly encouraged by the Security Council's support for African regional peace processes and initiatives, as well as the progress made by the Security Council and the African Union Peace and Security Council in implementing their shared goal of developing a more structured relationship. The Peacebuilding Commission's engagement in Burundi, Sierra Leone and Guinea-Bissau should assist in stabilizing their fragile economic and political environments. I encourage the General Assembly, Security Council and the Peacebuilding Commission to continue to place the special needs of Africa at the forefront of their agenda.

31. I am committed to ensuring that the United Nations is optimally configured to help Member States make progress towards reaching their development goals. Throughout 2008, I took important steps to strengthen the development pillar of the Organization. The reinvigorated campaign under my leadership to attain the Millennium Development Goals, and other internationally agreed development goals, is one dimension of my strategy. Introducing managerial reforms that strengthen the Organization's ability to deliver effective programming is a second important dimension which is discussed later in the report. Working to strengthen greater linkages across the development activities of the larger United Nations system, particularly through the work of my Policy Committee, which has provided recommendations for addressing policy and programme gaps in the United Nations development initiatives, is a third dimension of my strategy. Finally, I have encouraged the United Nations system to forge stronger partnerships with key stakeholders who can complement our work in the development arena, including new and emerging development partners. These also include the business community, civil society, and other charitable groups, as well as regional organizations, all of which are discussed below.

B. Peace and security

32. We must deliver results for a more secure world. Once again, during this past year, in too many places around the world, children bore arms instead of holding textbooks, the earth was scorched instead of cultivated, and national revenues were diverted to arms instead of being spent on education and health care. Every life lost and every penny spent on war was stolen from future generations.

33. The United Nations was called upon to assist in the search for peace or to promote dialogue and reconciliation on multiple fronts, including in the Sudan, Somalia, Iraq, Myanmar, the Middle East, Nepal, Sri Lanka, northern Uganda, the Central African Republic, Chad, Western Sahara and elsewhere. Our efforts took many forms. In addition to development assistance and humanitarian aid, we engaged in preventive diplomacy and peace negotiations, conducted peacekeeping missions and supported peacebuilding efforts in the aftermath of war.

1. Preventive diplomacy and support to peace processes

34. Where fighting has erupted or has the potential to do so, lasting peace rests ultimately on finding political solutions to the issues that are the source of conflict. The scale and complexity of the political, preventive and peacemaking tasks before us have grown, while a commensurate strengthen-

ing of the relevant machinery of the United Nations is long overdue. The rationale and the proposals for strengthening the Department of Political Affairs of the United Nations Secretariat were expressed in detail in my report to the General Assembly (A/62/521 and Corr.1), issued on 2 November 2007. I view those proposals as a vital complement to the earlier reforms of United Nations peacekeeping operations and as one of my top priorities. The United Nations needs to become more effective not only at stabilizing conflict situations and dealing with their humanitarian side effects, but at preventing and resolving them through political means. In the area of conflict prevention and resolution, which are Charter responsibilities, we need to do better, and the proposals to strengthen the Department of Political Affairs are fundamental to achieving a more effective role for the United Nations in this important area. Those proposals respond, in particular, to the call for a more effective use of tools such as preventive diplomacy, mediation and my "good offices" in the service of Member States and our partners in regional organizations.

35. With voluntary support, we have already taken important strides in implementing the 2005 decision of Member States to strengthen my good offices capacity, including in the mediation of disputes. We now have a fully operational Mediation Support Unit and a rapidly deployable Standby Team of Mediation Experts which are at the service of United Nations envoys, Member States and regional organizations. We have increasingly solid partnerships with regional organizations and can call upon an array of experts to assist in peacefully resolving and preventing disputes.

36. This past year, the Organization was able in many instances to assist Member States with preventive diplomacy and to provide concrete support to peace processes. For example, Nepal, with the support of the United Nations, held a historic election for a Constituent Assembly and has now embarked on the transition to a new political future. In the Central African Republic, we supported the preparatory process for a national dialogue. Following the outbreak of post-electoral violence in Kenya, the United Nations supported the African Union-led mediation by former Secretary-General Kofi Annan, which enabled the people of Kenya to avoid a larger tragedy. In the search for a political solution in Darfur, my Special Envoy continued to work closely with the African Union to try to encourage cohesion, build trust and make progress on key issues such as security, while broadening the national, regional and international bases of support. In Somalia, despite deteriorating security on the ground, my Special Representative made determined efforts to move the political process forward, as contingency planning continued for a possible stabilization force and, subsequently, conditions permitting a peacekeeping operation. In Cyprus, with renewed impetus and political will on the part of the Cypriots and their leaders, the United Nations assisted in the launch and facilitation of a preparatory process intended to lead to full-fledged negotiations.

37. With the establishment of the International Commission against Impunity in Guatemala (CICIG), we are involved in an innovative attempt to dismantle criminal groups whose actions threaten to erode hard-fought gains in the peace process. At the request of the Governments of Central Asia, we opened in Ashgabat the United Nations Regional Centre for Preventive Diplomacy in Central Asia, with a mandate to assist them in managing shared threats peacefully. In Iraq, we took up the challenge of a strengthened mandate calling for a greater United Nations role in forging political dialogue and reconciliation between Iraqis, encouraging regional dialogue and assisting in the resolution of disputed internal boundaries.

38. In the Middle East, I worked through the Quartet and with my envoys in the region to continue to push for comprehensive peace and security. An agreement to achieve the election of a president in Lebanon and indirect talks between Israel and the Syrian Arab Republic gave some reason to hope that the dynamics might change, and I continue to strive for the attainment of a peace agreement between Israelis and Palestinians as soon as possible.

2. Peacekeeping

39. Peacekeeping is a core function of the United Nations. Peacekeeping operations constitute a critical step towards achieving sustainable peace. They have an important role in assisting national actors in the development and implementation of peacebuilding strategies and work in partnership with the United Nations country team, the international financial institutions and other international partners.

40. In this sixtieth anniversary year of United Nations peacekeeping, the Department of Peacekeeping Operations of the United Nations Secretariat leads 19 missions with more than 130,000 women and men, including troop and police contributions from 117 Member States, supported by a budget of some $7 billion.

41. In order to ensure that the current demands on our peacekeeping operations are met in such a way as to encompass their scale and complexity, I initiated the restructuring of the Department of Peacekeeping Operations. This included the creation of a new Department of Field Support, the establishment of the Office of the Rule of Law and Security Institutions in the Department of Peacekeeping Operations, Integrated Operational Teams, and a number of new shared mechanisms. The Department finalized several essential doctrine documents this past year including,

notably, the "capstone" doctrine contained in "United Nations Peacekeeping Principles and Guidelines". The Department also continues to make progress on the Peace Operations 2010 reform agenda.

42. During this reporting period, peacekeeping operations provided wide-ranging support to peace. In Haiti, Afghanistan and the Democratic Republic of the Congo, our operations played a key role in supporting political processes, some of which hovered precariously between conflict and peace. In Kosovo, the role of the United Nations remained key to ensuring a safe and secure environment and stability in the region, and our operations adapted to the evolving situation on the ground so as to allow regional organizations such as the European Union to play a greater operational role within the status-neutral framework of Security Council resolution 1244(1999) and under the overall authority of the United Nations.

43. Peacekeeping operations also supported the efforts of State institutions to fully restore their authority. In Lebanon, for example, the United Nations Interim Force in Lebanon (UNIFIL) is playing a key role in facilitating the return of the Lebanese Armed Forces to the area south of the Litani River, and in creating conditions within its area of responsibility needed to enable governing structures to function normally.

44. Peacekeeping operations are working with key partners to provide more holistic support to national efforts in policing, the building of justice and corrections capacity, the removal of landmines and explosive remnants of war, and the design and conduct of demobilization, disarmament and reintegration programmes. For example, in mid-March, an expert mission comprising various United Nations entities and external parties visited Timor-Leste and issued a report (S/2008/329, annex) that made comprehensive recommendations on policing and broader rule-of-law and security sector reform issues. Reflecting the need to ensure early deployment of the police component, a Standing Police Capacity was established and deployed to the United Nations Mission in the Central African Republic and Chad (MINURCAT) to assist the Chadian law enforcement agencies in establishing and training a special Chadian police element.

45. In 2008, peacekeeping operations also reinforced States' capacities to protect human rights through translating international human rights standards into national laws, regulations and policies. Missions advised on laws aimed at providing human rights protection in Burundi and Sierra Leone, and also assisted in strengthening domestic judicial processes in Liberia.

46. In addition to support for our current operations, the past year saw the deployment of two of our most complex operations to date, namely, to Darfur and to Chad and the Central African Republic. The ongoing deployment of these operations has been supported by recent peacekeeping innovations. The first Integrated Operational Team at the Department of Peacekeeping Operations Headquarters provided support to the African Union-United Nations Hybrid Operation in Darfur in developing and implementing an integrated deployment plan. It also supported the African Union and United Nations Special Envoys in their efforts to bring the parties to the negotiating table. To assist in our work in Chad, we developed innovative partnership arrangements with the European Union.

47. Unfortunately, our many successes to date are challenged by two key issues: a number of unacceptable cases of sexual misconduct by some of our own peacekeepers and a mismatch between mandates and resources.

48. Extensive activities have been undertaken at Headquarters and in the field to prevent and address sexual exploitation and abuse by United Nations personnel. These include: training, streamlined and strengthened reporting mechanisms, awareness-raising and outreach activities both for United Nations personnel and for the host populations, a pilot campaign to address prostitution/transactional sex, and the establishment of welfare and recreation activities. The Secretariat and Member States have also agreed to a new model memorandum of understanding with troop-contributing countries that provides the United Nations with more reliable leverage for addressing sexual exploitation. Member States have also adopted a comprehensive strategy on assistance to victims. We need to ensure that the Secretariat and Member States are serious about the issue and that action is taken as we strive towards zero impunity.

49. Given the increased complexity and range of our operations and the difficult political and security environments in which many operations are deployed, now more than ever the international community must strengthen its commitment to them. Troop and police contributions are limited. Many Member States are already overstretched. Yet, at the same time, the demands being placed upon troop and police contributors and the Secretariat continue to rise. I urge Member States to maintain a common purpose behind peacekeeping. This requires sustained political engagement with relevant parties so that there is a peace to keep, and the provision of necessary resources to ensure that United Nations peacekeeping can live up to the expectations of it held by those most vulnerable.

3. Peacebuilding

50. Countries emerging from conflict face a unique set of challenges and unless they are identified and effectively addressed, these countries incur a high risk of relapsing into violence. Peacebuilding activities help promote peace agreements, lay the foundation for sustainable peace and development, and address the special needs of conflict-affected States. In 2006, Member States established a new peacebuilding architecture, comprising the Peacebuilding Commission, the Peacebuilding Support Office and the Peacebuilding Fund. In the past year, these institutions further developed their methods of extending support to countries emerging from conflict.

51. The Peacebuilding Commission, supported by the Peacebuilding Support Office, has demonstrated its added value in providing sustained attention to the countries under its consideration. The first two cases under its consideration were Burundi and Sierra Leone, followed by Guinea-Bissau and the Central African Republic, which were referred to the Commission in December 2007 and June 2008, respectively. In Sierra Leone, it played an important role in assisting with the election process, while in Burundi, it assisted in averting a major crisis by facilitating a dialogue between key stakeholders who had reached a deadlock in Parliament. The Commission has further developed its peacebuilding tools for strategic engagement, including a monitoring and tracking mechanism to measure progress made against the commitments contained in country-specific strategic frameworks.

52. This past year, the Peacebuilding Fund continued to provide a crucial funding mechanism supporting early peacebuilding initiatives. It enjoyed strong financial support from Member States and recorded pledges of $267 million, derived from a diverse base of some 44 individual donor countries. Significant progress has been made in strengthening the linkages between the Fund and the integrated strategic approaches to peacebuilding taken by the Commission. For instance, the designation of an initial funding envelope for Guinea-Bissau has provided immediate support while allowing for a better alignment in the long term between the Fund and the integrated peacebuilding strategy under deliberation in the Commission.

53. In addition to providing financial support to the countries under consideration by the Commission, I have made active use of the Fund in support of peacebuilding efforts in countries that are not in the current agenda of the Commission, including the Central African Republic, Liberia and Nepal. I have commissioned, through the Peacebuilding Support Office, an external evaluation of the Fund for the purpose of reflecting on lessons learned during its first two years of operation and further enhancing both its strategic and its catalytic role.

54. Peacebuilding is not just about "bricks and mortar": it is a transformative process involving changing attitudes about how to manage conflict. As dealing with the aftermath of war can be costly, strengthening our capacity to resolve conflicts earlier rather than later is among the smartest investments we can make. For this reason, I am deeply committed to strengthening our peacebuilding institutions and ensuring that they are optimally configured to meet evolving needs.

C. Humanitarian affairs

55. Some of the most vulnerable and "in need" populations around the world are those that have been affected by conflicts and natural disasters. In spite of increasing global challenges, the humanitarian community has made significant strides in delivering accountable, predictable and timely assistance. Nevertheless, these efforts must be strengthened even further with additional resources and continued reforms.

56. The unprecedented increases in food prices, compounded by a decades-long decline in investment in agriculture, have reduced access to food for hundreds of millions of people. In response to the recent crisis, I created a High-level Task Force on the Global Food Security Crisis which has developed a Comprehensive Framework for Action giving us a clear road map regarding how to address the crisis. The Framework has been welcomed by many Member States. United Nations organizations are meanwhile responding to the urgency of the situation. For example, the World Food Programme has raised $3 billion of the $6 billion needed for 2008. I have set aside a reserve of $100 million from the Central Emergency Response Fund to help fund new humanitarian needs related to soaring food prices. In addition, the Food and Agriculture Organization of the United Nations has launched a $1.7 billion appeal to provide low-income countries with seeds and other agricultural support.

57. The rise in the number and intensity of extreme weather events has also been striking, with an increasing number of the poor being affected by drought, floods and cyclones. In 2007, the United Nations launched an unprecedented 15 Flash Appeals, 14 of which were in response to extreme weather events in Africa, Asia and Latin America.

58. One of the largest disasters in 2008 was Cyclone Nargis, which hit Myanmar in May and claimed the lives of tens of thousands of people, with millions severely affected. This disaster and the initial access problems for international relief workers highlighted the need to strengthen our partnership with regional organizations and to work with Gov-

ernments to create operating environments conducive to their receiving effective assistance. The earthquake in Sichuan Province, China, also in May 2008, illustrated how disaster events can surpass even the disaster response capacities of major countries. These events underscored vividly once again the importance of working closely with Governments to reduce disaster risk through the implementation of the Hyogo Framework for Action 2005–2015.

59. Despite the consolidation of peace and relative stability in Côte d'Ivoire, Nepal and Timor-Leste, a number of major internal conflicts continue, with large numbers of civilians requiring urgent humanitarian assistance and protection. Forced displacement, violations of the rules of international humanitarian law governing conduct of hostilities, sexual violence and ensuring safe and unhindered humanitarian access remain significant challenges for the humanitarian community.

60. For some 36 million people affected by armed conflict, flight is the only option, either within or across borders. At the end of 2007, the world's refugee population had reached 9.9 million people, more than half of them children. The overall global population of internally displaced persons was about 26 million and rising.

61. The United Nations and its partners have increased their efforts to address the humanitarian situations in Afghanistan, Iraq and the Occupied Palestinian Territories where insecurity hinders access to many vulnerable people. For example, 12 months of restrictions imposed on the movement of commercial and humanitarian goods and people in and out of Gaza have had severe consequences for the well-being of the population, 75 per cent of whom rely on international assistance. Notwithstanding rising insecurity in Afghanistan, particularly in the southern provinces, the World Food Programme was able to reach close to 6.8 million beneficiaries in 2007.

62. The humanitarian community remains actively engaged in a number of countries in Africa, with some of the largest operations in the Democratic Republic of the Congo, Somalia and the Sudan. Darfur remains the world's largest humanitarian operation, with 14,700 humanitarian aid workers delivering assistance to 4.27 million affected individuals. While the situation remains fragile between the North and the South, approximately 1 million displaced persons and refugees have returned to the Southern Sudan.

63. The Central Emergency Response Fund, which had provided predictable funding to sudden-onset and neglected crises since its inception in 2006, exceeded the $1 billion mark in pledges at the donor conference in December 2007, and will be close to its annual grant element target of $450 million in 2008. Pledges have been received from over 90 Member States. The Fund has distributed over $800 million in over 60 countries. I encourage all Member States to continue to contribute to this effective multilateral relief capacity.

D. Human rights, rule of law, genocide prevention and the responsibility to protect, and democracy and good governance

64. Respecting human rights, providing justice and the rule of law, preventing genocide and delivering on the responsibility to protect, and establishing democracy and good governance are core responsibilities of all Member States and of the United Nations itself. They define what it means to deliver results for a more just world. 2008 is a pivotal year for human rights: it is the sixtieth anniversary of the adoption of the Universal Declaration of Human Rights. I have called on the entire United Nations family to strengthen their advocacy efforts and take concrete steps to integrate human rights into all aspects of the Organization's work. The responsibility falls on us to advance the original vision of the Declaration—a vision encompassing one indivisible set of rights, inalienable to all humankind.

1. Human rights

65. This past year, I was pleased to witness the positive impact of recent institutional reforms in the human rights machinery, including the strengthening of the Human Rights Council, the bolstering of the United Nations rapid response capacity, the streamlining of existing institutions and the adoption of new human rights instruments.

66. The Human Rights Council launched the Universal Periodic Review this year, and examined the record of 32 States. The process is an important advance for the future of the Council and its role in the Organization's human rights machinery. The Council must ensure that assessments are fair, that review processes and methods are transparent and that nations are held accountable for progress, stagnation or regression in the implementation of human rights standards. Failure to do so could lead to distrust and disillusionment, as arose in the final years of the Commission on Human Rights. Given the range and scope of allegations of human rights violations throughout the world, the Council must address all such situations to ensure full credibility.

67. Thanks to the continued strengthening of the Peace Missions Support and Rapid Response Units established in 2006, the Organization was also able to carry out more robust emergency missions to address unforeseen human rights situations in the field. Most recently, it conducted a three-week fact-finding mission to assess allegations of grave human rights

violations committed in the post-election period in Kenya and to gather first-hand information from diverse sources.

68. The Rapid Response Unit is one reflection of the increasing human rights presence of the United Nations on the ground. As at December 2007, the Office of the United Nations High Commissioner for Human Rights supported 8 regional offices, 11 country offices and 17 human rights components of peace missions with 400 international human rights officers and national staff. The importance of this field presence should not be underestimated, as our experience is showing that the presence of United Nations human rights officers in conflict-prone environments may act as a deterrent to would-be human rights violators.

69. The human rights treaty bodies worked towards further harmonizing their respective working methods, adopting changes that would also complement the Human Rights Council's Universal Periodic Review mechanism. To further ensure streamlining, the Committee on the Elimination of Discrimination against Women was moved from New York to Geneva.

70. On 13 September 2007, in a milestone move, the General Assembly adopted the United Nations Declaration on the Rights of Indigenous Peoples. In May 2008, the Convention on the Rights of Persons with Disabilities and the Optional Protocol thereto entered into force, providing a full range of reporting, complaint and inquiry mechanisms.

71. We are embarking on a new era in human rights. Never before have we generated such wide international acceptance of and consensus on human rights standards. We have expanded and strengthened our tools and mechanisms for monitoring and encouraging compliance. Now, let us use our institutions and tools to deliver results for all people, everywhere.

2. Rule of law

72. The United Nations has reaffirmed repeatedly the centrality of the rule of law to human development and the maintenance of peace and security. The demand for our assistance in this area continues to grow, with the United Nations system now working in over 80 countries to help States translate international legal standards into national legislation and to support the development of constitutions, justice institutions and legal frameworks. Yet, we continue to face numerous challenges. For example, in many countries, the culture of impunity and lack of accountability, even for the most serious international crimes, gravely undermines the rule of law.

73. This year, the United Nations system made progress in strengthening its rule-of-law capacity, and in enhancing system-wide coordination and coherence, particularly in conflict and post-conflict environments. I have also sought to strengthen the Organization's policy development and coordination capacity by establishing a Rule of Law Unit to support the Rule of Law Coordination and Resource Group, which ensures coherence of rule-of-law activities within the United Nations system. I am pleased to observe that Member States, in General Assembly resolution 62/70, expressed their support for the new rule-of-law arrangements and I anticipate that the reinvigorated common approach that they advance will improve the quality of the rule-of-law assistance that we provide to Member States.

3. Genocide prevention and the responsibility to protect

74. The concept of the responsibility to protect was embraced by the 2005 World Summit and has been endorsed by both the General Assembly and the Security Council. It is sustained by the positive and affirmative vision of sovereignty as responsibility and rests on three pillars: the affirmation of Member States that they have a primary and continuing legal obligation to protect their populations from genocide, war crimes, ethnic cleansing and crimes against humanity, and from their incitement; the acceptance by Member States of their responsibility to respond in a timely and decisive manner, in accordance with the Charter of the United Nations, to help protect populations from the four types of crimes described above; and the commitment of the United Nations system to assist States in meeting these obligations. This past year, I instructed the Organization to begin to take the initial steps to ensure that the system has the flexibility and capacity to help Member States meet their commitments. I look forward to seeing this capacity institutionalized towards the end of the year.

4. Democracy and good governance

75. While democracy has made gains in many regions, there have been important setbacks, as witnessed by the failure of some States to conduct free and fair elections, the adoption of states of emergency, increased restrictions on the independence of the media, and crackdowns on political and civil liberties. Experience has shown us that disregard for democratic principles poses serious security, economic and social challenges which often transcend national borders. For this reason, the role of the United Nations in strengthening democratic institutions and practices is inseparable from its work in promoting peace and security, development and human rights.

76. Highlights in the past year of the work of the United Nations in this area included support to the Constituent Assembly process in Nepal and to the electoral authorities of Sierra Leone. Of course, just

as democracy entails more than elections, so is electoral assistance only one means by which the United Nations helps promote democracy. The Organization also provided support through programmes fostering good governance practices and democratic institutions.

77. The United Nations Democracy Fund (UNDEF) provides assistance to governmental, non-governmental, national, regional and international organizations, including relevant United Nations departments, offices, funds, programmes and agencies, in funding projects that build and strengthen democratic institutions, promote human rights and ensure the participation of all groups in democratic processes. The Fund has received approximately $90 million to date. It had launched its second call for project proposals in 2007 and received a total of 1,873 applications from 137 countries, 85.9 per cent of which were submitted by civil society organizations. In mid-May 2008, 86 projects were approved.

78. I call on Member States to recommit themselves to promoting democracy on 15 September, the newly established International Day of Democracy at the United Nations.

E. System-wide coherence

79. In the past year, Member States—through the 2007 triennial comprehensive policy review—have renewed their guidance to the United Nations system with a view to its becoming more coherent, efficient and effective at country, regional and global levels. This and other guidance from Member States, including through the ongoing informal consultations in the General Assembly on system-wide coherence, continue to direct our work in this area.

80. I am pleased to report that the "Delivering as one" initiative—launched in January 2007 upon the request of Governments in eight pilot countries—has started to yield some important results and lessons. It has reaffirmed that national ownership and leadership are essential components of increased coherence. It is clear that the United Nations system can maximize its support for national priorities only through the process of working together, leveraging more effectively its respective capacities and expertise. There are encouraging signs that, in the pilot countries, Governments have experienced improved United Nations delivery of programmes and reduced transaction costs.

81. At Headquarters level, the United Nations Development Group continued to develop guidance on national ownership in the programming process, harmonized policies and procedures, training to upgrade the skills of United Nations country teams, and improvement in the selection and accountability of, and support provided to, resident coordinators. It also significantly enhanced coherence of response in post-crisis situations. Another major step towards improved United Nations system coordination was the decision in 2007 to formally make the United Nations Development Group a third pillar of the United Nations System Chief Executives Board for Coordination in order to ensure complementarity and reduce overlap between the two coordination bodies. This streamlining will result in important improvements in United Nations internal coordination and system-wide coherence, and will ultimately improve United Nations support to Member States.

82. Finally, as part of a continuing effort to ensure efficiency and coherence in communications, the United Nations Communications Group (UNCG) brings together United Nations system organizations, including funds, programmes and specialized agencies, with the Department of Public Information of the United Nations Secretariat and the Executive Office of the Secretary-General. The Groups exist at the country level in over 80 countries. Over the past year, this Group contributed to developing and implementing communications strategies, including the crafting and dissemination of coherent messages and information products, on the Millennium Development Goals, climate change and the sixtieth anniversary of the Universal Declaration of Human Rights, among other concerns.

Chapter III

Securing global goods

83. The United Nations is uniquely placed to lead the world in responding to twenty-first century threats that transcend borders, threatening all nations and all peoples. As I scan the immediate horizon, I perceive four issues that fall within this category of challenges: climate change, counter-terrorism, disarmament and non-proliferation, and global health. I am convinced that the United Nations, with its global reach, legitimacy and unique ability to convene both State and non-State actors, has a vital role to play in ensuring that nations come together to secure the associated global goods for future generations.

A. Climate change

84. Climate change has been among my top priorities since I became Secretary-General. I am delighted to report that last year, the United Nations Intergovernmental Panel on Climate Change shared the Nobel Peace Prize with Al Gore, former Vice-President of the United States of America. The Nobel Prize Committee recognized this important body's long-standing commitment to improving our knowledge concerning man-made climate change, and its efforts towards laying the foundations for the measures that are needed to counteract such change.

85. On 24 September 2007, I convened a high-level event on climate change in New York on the margins of the General Assembly, which brought together 80 world leaders to discuss how to address climate change and galvanize support for advancing the negotiations.

86. This meeting set the tone for the United Nations-sponsored climate talks in December of last year where Member States reached an important agreement on climate change, including the adoption of the Bali Road Map setting out the process for developing a new global agreement to help confront climate change. Subsequent negotiations have been designed to develop a shared vision for a long-term global goal of reducing emissions; promote national/international action on mitigation and adaptation; encourage technology development and transfer; and provide developing countries with the financial resources and investment required for addressing environmental challenges. The negotiating process continues this year with an important session of the Conference of the Parties to the United Nations Framework Convention on Climate Change to be held in Poznań, Poland, in December, and is set to culminate in an agreed outcome in Copenhagen in 2009.

87. The Clean Development Mechanism (CDM) provides a good example of how the United Nations can harness the power of the market. The total traded volume in the global carbon market rose from $31 billion in 2006 to $64 billion in 2007. The Clean Development Mechanism now boasts over 1,000 registered projects in 49 countries all over the world. Various United Nations organizations are supporting countries in broadening the geographical reach of the Mechanism, and in increasing the sustainable development benefits in addition to that of producing reductions in emissions.

88. I am pleased to observe the coordinated way in which the United Nations has come together to work with nations on adaptation and on helping to mainstream climate change into policy and development plans. One good example of our work to date is the Nairobi Work Programme on impacts, vulnerability and adaptation to Climate Change coordinated by the secretariat of the United Nations Framework Convention on Climate Change. This programme, launched by the intergovernmental process, brings together over 100 United Nations entities and other organizations to promote adaptation assessment and planning, to incorporate adaptation into all relevant policy areas and to foster assistance to developing countries in line with their needs.

89. Another example is the Nairobi Framework to support developing countries' participation in the Clean Development Mechanism (CDM). This joint effort of the United Nations Environment Programme, the United Nations Development Programme, the secretariat of the United Nations Framework Convention on Climate Change, the Economic Commission for Africa, the African Development Bank and the World Bank has made substantial progress. Partner agencies are also working together on the organization of the first-ever African Carbon Forum, which will be held in Dakar in September 2008, providing an excellent opportunity to keep up the positive momentum of the Clean Development Mechanism in Africa.

90. At the United Nations, I have determined that the plan for renovating our New York Headquarters should follow strict environmental guidelines, including the reduction of our carbon footprint. I have asked the chief executives of all United Nations programmes, funds and specialized agencies to move swiftly towards climate neutrality in their operations.

91. We are also redoubling our efforts to communicate the messages on climate change to the public. The message of World Environment Day for 2008, bearing the slogan "Kick the habit! towards a low-carbon economy", has been that our world is in the grip of a dangerous carbon habit which is causing the build-up of significant greenhouse gases in the atmosphere. These in turn are contributing to climate change. The solution requires widespread changes in the behaviour and action of individuals, business and Governments.

B. Global health

92. There is growing political awareness that health is fundamental to economic growth and development, and that threats to health can compromise a country's stability and security.

93. In recent years, there has been an unprecedented rise in public and private funding directed towards health challenges. Bilateral aid has increased substantially, and so have the budgets of major health-related United Nations organizations such as the World Health Organization, the United Nations Children's Fund, the United Nations Population Fund, the Joint United Nations Programme on HIV/AIDS (UNAIDS) and the World Bank, as well as those of major global health partnerships. Private philanthropy and the corporate sector have scaled up action and become full partners with Governments and non-governmental organizations in the delivery of care in poor countries. Numerous country-led initiatives have been set in motion, spearheaded primarily by Norway, the United Kingdom of Great Britain and Northern Ireland, France and Canada.

94. Within this new global health sphere, the United Nations system has been able to make sig-

nificant progress on several fronts. As highlighted in Chapter II, section A, above, these include the fight against diseases like measles and poliomyelitis and specific tropical diseases, as well as malaria and HIV/AIDS. However, significant challenges remain. Inadequate advancements in meeting the health Goals have been largely due to deficient health systems, threats to health security posed by pandemic influenza and other emerging diseases, and profound inequities in health, as well as the failure to protect the poor from ill health and insufficient health expenditures.

95. The growing number of initiatives and partnerships, which offer a critical new opportunity and challenge, are welcome but have thus far failed to generate cohesive and coherent action. The United Nations health-related organizations, namely, the World Health Organization, the United Nations Children's Fund, the United Nations Population Fund and UNAIDS, have reached out and partnered with the World Bank, the Global Fund to Fight AIDS, Tuberculosis and Malaria, the Global Alliance for Vaccines and Immunization and the Bill and Melinda Gates Foundation to enhance dialogue and coordination. The creation of this group, the so-called H8, represents an encouraging step towards achieving increased coherence among key players inside and outside the United Nations system.

96. In order to push for decisive and coherent action, I have convened the leaders of United Nations-related entities and prominent non-United Nations figures from foundations, the private sector, civil society and academia to explore new opportunities in global health, discuss the strategic role of the United Nations in shaping the future of global health, and focus on critical priorities, in particular building functioning and affordable health systems, advancing progress on women's health, especially maternal health, and pushing for action on addressing neglected tropical diseases.

97. Upcoming intergovernmental meetings such as the High-level Event on the Millennium Development Goals and the Follow-up International Conference on Financing for Development to Review the Implementation of the Monterrey Consensus, to be held at Doha in November–December 2008, will offer opportunities to push for action on this front, and I encourage all stakeholders to continue to build on the current momentum in order to finally end the senseless suffering.

C. Countering terrorism

98. The threat of terrorism to international peace, security and development is significant and affects people in every part of the world. The United Nations has itself suffered terrorism-related losses, most recently in the wake of the 11 December 2007 attack on the United Nations offices in Algiers. My thoughts are with the victims and their loved ones, whose sacrifice will be remembered.

99. The two-year review of the implementation of the United Nations Global Counter-Terrorism Strategy, which will be held in September 2008, provides us with an opportunity to recommit ourselves to combating this scourge. The Strategy, drafted and adopted by the General Assembly in 2006, lays out concrete measures for responding to the conditions conducive to the spread of terrorism, preventing and combating terrorism in all its forms, strengthening the individual and collective capacity of States and the United Nations to do so, and ensuring the protection of human rights and the rule of law. The adoption of the Strategy has demonstrated the important role that the United Nations can play in curbing this threat, but only its implementation will solidify our relevance in this area. The positive reports coming out of the various meetings of the Assembly on the Strategy inspire me with confidence in our ability to succeed.

100. The main responsibility for implementing the Strategy falls on Member States. Nonetheless, various Secretariat departments, specialized agencies and United Nations funds and programmes contribute to this important endeavour—individually, collectively and with partners. In Tunis, in November 2007, the United Nations, in partnership with the Organization of the Islamic Conference and its Islamic Educational, Scientific and Cultural Organization, held an International Conference on Terrorism: Dimensions, Threats and Countermeasures. The United Nations also collaborated with Member States and regional organizations in holding, in May 2007, the Vienna Symposium to Discuss Practical Measures to Implement the United Nations Global Counter-Terrorism Strategy.

101. The United Nations Counter-Terrorism Implementation Task Force, which brings together 24 entities of the United Nations system, has worked on system-wide implementation efforts and provided implementation support to Member States. The Task Force has established nine working groups in areas of the Strategy where coordination and cooperation across the United Nations system can add value. The topic areas include the link between conflict prevention/resolution and terrorism, radicalization and extremism that lead to terrorism, victims of terrorism, prevention/response to attacks involving weapons of mass destruction, financing of terrorism, use of the Internet for terrorist purposes, protection of vulnerable targets, and protection of human rights while countering terrorism. In addition, the Task Force is also working to enhance the ability of the United Nations to help, upon their request, interested Mem-

ber States implement the Strategy in an integrated manner via a user-friendly interface with the United Nations system.

102. I have also asked the Department of Safety and Security to focus on prevention and mitigation measures relating to United Nations personnel operating in hostile environments. At the same time, preventive measures depend on the effective cooperation of Member States. In its resolution 59/276 (of 23 December 2004), the General Assembly emphasized that "the primary responsibility for ensuring the safety and security of United Nations staff and premises rests with the host country". Accordingly, the United Nations is engaged in renewed dialogue to determine where enhanced cooperation and coordination with host-country authorities can be achieved. This work has been given additional impetus by the recurrent statements of extremist groups threatening to target humanitarian organizations. In February of this year, I appointed an Independent Panel on Safety and Security of United Nations Personnel and Premises Worldwide, headed by Lakhdar Brahimi and composed of international experts in the field. Its report, released in June, recognizes that risk management is not consistently understood or applied by all actors. It calls for a review of the size of the United Nations staff presence and the manner in which the system does business in light of security considerations. I am carefully examining the report and will be taking follow-up action. As a first step, and on the recommendation of the report, I have suggested establishing an independent accountability procedure to review the responsibilities of the key individuals and offices concerned in the Algiers attack. I am committed to working towards ensuring a safer and better environment for this Organization in the pursuit of its noble tasks.

103. Strategic partnerships among Member States, the United Nations system, regional and subregional organizations and civil society remain crucial in the fight against terrorism. We must continue to work together to implement the United Nations Global Counter-Terrorism Strategy and, through our efforts, to create a more secure world.

D. Disarmament and non-proliferation

104. The risks inherent in the very existence of weapons of mass destruction, especially nuclear weapons, are universally recognized. I welcome recent initiatives aimed at achieving a world free of nuclear weapons, as well as reductions of nuclear arsenals and reduced reliance on nuclear weapons. However, further reductions in strategic and non-strategic stockpiles, greater transparency, de-alerting and a diminished role for nuclear weapons in security policies are needed.

105. The year 2008 marks the fortieth anniversary of the opening for signature of the Treaty on the Non-Proliferation of Nuclear Weapons. The Treaty must be strengthened and trust in it must be rebuilt, as part of a broader process of reaffirming the rule of law as well as the importance of multilateralism. Preparations for the 2010 Review Conference of the Parties to the Treaty are proceeding satisfactorily.

106. I support efforts for a peaceful political solution regarding concerns over the nuclear programme of the Islamic Republic of Iran and urge the implementation of all measures to build confidence in its exclusively peaceful nature.

107. I am encouraged by the continued determination and efforts by States to bring the Comprehensive Nuclear-Test-Ban Treaty into force as soon as possible. I am pleased to report progress in the implementation of the Convention on the Prohibition of the Development, Production and Stockpiling of Bacteriological (Biological) and Toxin Weapons and on Their Destruction. States parties have developed a focused programme on national, regional and international measures to improve biosafety and biosecurity. To support these activities, an Implementation Support Unit has been set up within the Office for Disarmament Affairs of the United Nations Secretariat.

108. Efforts continue in the Conference on Disarmament to overcome the long-standing deadlock over its priorities. In January 2008, I urged Members to forestall arms races, reduce tensions and free resources for achieving the Millennium Development Goals. Successful negotiations on a fissile material ban and substantive discussions on preventing the placement of weapons in outer space, nuclear disarmament and security assurances depend on high-level leadership and political support.

109. Controlling conventional weapons remains central to United Nations disarmament efforts. I have reinforced the United Nations Coordinating Action on Small Arms mechanism under which standards on small arms control are now being developed. Strong calls to address the humanitarian impact of cluster munitions have been answered with the adoption in May of the Convention on Cluster Munitions.

110. The revitalization of multilateral disarmament efforts is within reach. Full implementation of existing multilateral disarmament and non-proliferation agreements and the achievement of their universality remain a major challenge. Strengthening existing regional mechanisms and developing effective partnerships, in accordance with chapter VIII of the Charter of the United Nations, would help bolster progress and unlock the current disarmament stalemate.

111. The establishment of the Office for Disarmament Affairs of the United Nations Secretariat in 2007 increased the advocacy potential of the Or-

ganization. Under the leadership of its High Representative, the Office has effectively promoted greater awareness of the challenges posed by disarmament and non-proliferation and has enhanced its engagement and cooperation with Member States, intergovernmental organizations and civil society.

Chapter IV

Creating a stronger United Nations through full accountability

112. In order to deliver on the increasing demands for our services, we need a stronger, more effective and modern Organization. Based on mandates agreed by world leaders at the 2005 World Summit and subsequent General Assembly mandates and changes made by the Secretary-General, a large number of wide-ranging reforms are now being implemented.

113. In order to strengthen the Organization's overall accountability framework, I have called for the establishment of a new accountability compact with senior managers. I am committed to ensuring that there is accountability within the Secretariat, flowing both ways between me, to senior managers, and staff. I am also taking steps to strengthen the Secretariat's accountability to Member States for ensuring that the Organization is well managed, upholding individual and collective integrity, and delivering results.

114. I am asking Member States to be accountable to the Organization and to each other, by providing sufficient political, financial and human resources to implement the mandates given and by living up to their intergovernmental commitments.

115. Further, I hope that over the next few years we will all work, the Secretariat and Member States included, on increasing our accountability to the global public, in whose name we all serve, and to those we are assisting at the country level. Accountability goes beyond answering to those who have delegated authority to us: it also means taking into account the interests of those affected by our actions.

A. The Secretariat, the intergovernmental machinery, regional organizations, and global constituencies

116. When I took my oath of office, I promised to breathe new life into the Secretariat. In my address to the General Assembly last September, I spoke of building a stronger United Nations for a better world. I am taking steps to reform the Secretariat, and I am also committed to working with Member States to ensure that our intergovernmental machinery meets the changing and growing demands on the United Nations today.

1. The Secretariat

117. To enable us to do the job expected of us, we must have a strong, empowered Secretariat that has a management infrastructure built around achieving results. For this reason, I proposed a new accountability architecture, including the full implementation of results-based management and enterprise risk management. A results-based management approach requires managers to state clearly what they intend to achieve and to align their staff and financial resources with these goals. It will also require managers themselves to monitor and evaluate their programmes regularly and systematically in order to identify problems and take corrective actions so as to increase the likelihood of delivering the intended results. To this end, the senior managers' compacts, which are shared with staff, continue to provide a transparent means for reflecting goals, highlighting priorities and assessing whether results have been achieved.

118. As the Secretariat becomes less Headquarters-based and more operational, it will require different skill sets among its staff. Anticipated retirements—for example, 23.3 per cent of staff at the Director level will retire in the next three years—offer an opportunity to update the staff profile to better meet emerging needs. To this end, the Secretariat is proactively conducting workforce planning, improving its recruitment processes, and proposing contract terms and conditions of service that will increase the likelihood of attracting and retaining high-calibre staff. Staff mobility is essential to producing a more versatile and multi-skilled workforce which can rise to today's complex challenges. I am committed to ensuring that gender equality is given high priority in our staffing policies.

119. The Secretariat is also making itself more responsive to the needs of the field by reforming its procurement policies and procedures. Comprehensive guidelines and controls will be implemented. Professionalism is being enhanced through intensified training and better use of technology, with strengthened emphasis on ethics and transparency.

120. The new system of the administration of justice approved by the General Assembly in 2007 will further advance the goal of accountability and better management in dealing with internal employment-related disputes. A strengthened, integrated Office of the Ombudsman, which includes a Mediation Division, will form a critical "informal" pillar in this system, identifying and resolving problems at the earliest opportunity, thereby averting time-consuming and costly formal adjudication. The new internal justice system is anticipated to be in place by January 2009.

121. Taking full advantage of information and communications technology (ICT) is central to improving efficiency and effectiveness and strengthening

accountability. Since August 2007, the Chief Information Technology Officer has spearheaded the drive for a strong and unified ICT strategy. One important effort under way entails introducing an enterprise resource planning (ERP) system to replace the current Integrated Management Information System. The goal is to build an integrated global information system that supports the effective management of human, financial and physical resources, while also incorporating streamlined processes and best practices. The ERP system, when implemented, will also enable the Organization's planned adoption of, and compliance with, the International Public Sector Accounting Standards.

122. To further enhance performance and responsiveness, I have also placed greater Secretariat-wide emphasis on documentation delivery in a timely, cost-effective manner. In its pursuit of greater efficiencies, the Department for General Assembly and Conference Management of the United Nations Secretariat chaired a meeting of conference managers from the United Nations system in June to explore the feasibility of applying the "Delivering as one" concept to the area of conference servicing and management. In order to meet our multilingual mandate, maximize cost-effectiveness and ensure the highest standards of quality in the delivery of language and conference services, it is crucial for us to join forces with our United Nations system partners to pool scarce conference-servicing resources and to coordinate efforts in the area of recruitment of language staff.

123. Although many of these management reforms are in an early stage and have not yet had time to bear full fruit, the Secretariat is in fact already seeing positive results. For example, the Department of Management's 2007 client satisfaction staff survey showed substantial increases in favourable responses to questions regarding improvements in efficiency of delivery of services (up 11 per cent from 2006), the streamlining and simplification of rules and processes (up 10 per cent from 2006) and the ability to access information from the Department of Management in a timely manner (up 11 per cent from 2006).

2. Intergovernmental machinery

124. The international political environment has changed significantly since the United Nations was founded, and in this context I attach great importance to the reform of the Security Council. I share Member States' growing recognition that there is no perfect solution and welcome their discussions on the possibility of intermediate or interim solutions.

125. I am following with interest efforts by the General Assembly aimed at modernization and at increasing its effectiveness. Holding interactive debates on current issues of critical importance to the international community like climate change, the Millennium Development Goals, management reform, human security and human trafficking has succeeded in stimulating valuable discussion and underscoring the importance of this universal forum.

126. In order to provide more opportunity for direct exchange, in the past year I began to brief the General Assembly periodically on my most recent activities. These informal meetings of the plenary have allowed for an interactive engagement with Member States, thereby providing an important additional tool for enhancing dialogue, transparency and accountability. I intend to continue this important practice.

127. Reforms proposed by Member States at the 2005 World Summit to strengthen the effectiveness of the Economic and Social Council in promoting a global partnership for development continued to be institutionalized in 2008. Most notably, during the high-level segment of its substantive session, the Council held its first Development Cooperation Forum and its second annual ministerial review. The Development Cooperation Forum discussed "how to make development cooperation more coherent and more effective" and developed valuable strategic input to the Doha Review Conference on Financing for Development and the Accra High-level Forum on Aid Effectiveness. During the annual ministerial review, eight countries—developing and developed—reported on the progress they had made towards achieving the goals and targets of the United Nations development agenda. Ministerial round tables addressed the question of how to put the world on a sustainable development path. I welcome and encourage an energized Council and look forward to its recommendations on measures that the international community can take to improve implementation of agreed development goals and promote sustainable development.

3. Cooperation with regional organizations

128. From the highest political level on down to the field, the United Nations and regional organizations are strengthening their partnerships and working more closely than ever in responding to the challenges of peacekeeping, peacemaking and post-conflict peacebuilding.

129. The Ten-Year Capacity-Building Programme frames our growing partnership with the African Union, the importance of which was also reflected in the debate in the Security Council on my report on the relationship between the United Nations and regional organizations in the maintenance of international peace and security (S/2008/186). An important illustration is provided today in Darfur, where joint efforts are under way with the African Union both in peacekeeping and in promoting the political process.

130. In Asia, the United Nations and the Association of Southeast Asian Nations joined forces to respond to the emergency needs of Myanmar following tropical cyclone Nargis. In November 2007, the United Nations and the Organization of the Islamic Conference undertook a joint effort to further the fight against terrorism. The Tunis Conference, mentioned in paragraph 100 above, provided an excellent opportunity to discuss and build understanding of the United Nations Global Counter-Terrorism Strategy as implementation efforts pick up. The United Nations also cooperated with the European Commission in implementing the European Union and Central Asia Strategy for a New Partnership, as well as with the Ibero-American General Secretariat in organizing the policy dialogue of Heads of State on social cohesion during the Seventeenth Ibero-American Summit held in Santiago in November 2007.

131. There is clear political recognition that regionalism as a component of multilateralism is necessary and feasible. I am optimistic that an effective sharing of responsibilities for peace and security between international and regional organizations, particularly in Africa, is now within reach.

B. Global constituencies

1. Strengthening partnerships with civil society

132. I am happy to report that not only has civil society's engagement with the work of the United Nations increased but it may also become more results-oriented, as reflected in targeted engagement on key thematic issues like development, human rights and climate change. It has become a well-established practice for the General Assembly to conduct interactive hearings with representatives of non-governmental organizations, civil society and the private sector during all major United Nations conferences.

133. The number of civil society organizations involved in development work that were granted consultative status with the Economic and Social Council increased by 136 over the past year, from 3,051 in 2007 to 3,187 at the present time in 2008. Their active participation in multi-stakeholder dialogues on financing for development and sustainable development enriched both discussions and was reflected in the outcomes of intergovernmental meetings in these areas. There are 1,664 non-governmental organizations associated with the Department of Public Information of the United Nations Secretariat that support its mission to make the public around the world better aware of the work of the Organization.

134. Human rights were a major focus of innovative partnerships initiated with civil society. For the first time, the annual DPI/NGO Conference is scheduled to be held outside United Nations Headquarters; the Conference will be held in Paris, home to the signing of the Universal Declaration of Human Rights. The theme of the September 2008 event is "Reaffirming Human Rights for All: the Universal Declaration at 60". The Holocaust and the United Nations Outreach Programme initiated groundbreaking collaboration with public institutions in arranging four regional seminars designed to enhance the capacity of local staff at United Nations information centres worldwide to help "mobilize civil society for Holocaust remembrance and education, in order help prevent future acts of genocide".

135. A new outreach programme on "Remembrance of Victims of Slavery and the Transatlantic Slave Trade" has been established, featuring participation by a number of civil society groups, including academic institutions, collaboration with which is also the focus of initiatives launched this year to invigorate partnership.

136. Collaboration between civil society and the United Nations continued in support of internationally agreed development goals. In the "Stand Up and Speak Out against Poverty" initiative, United Nations information centres worked with the Millennium Campaign Office and civil society to promote awareness of the Millennium Development Goals. An estimated 43 million people participated worldwide.

2. Engaging the business community

137. The business community is an increasingly important partner in achieving United Nations goals, particularly those related to sustainable development, including climate change and peace and conflict. For example, in February 2008, the Organization hosted the Third Investor Summit on Climate Risk, through which public treasuries, institutional investors and financial services firms pledged to invest $10 billion over two years in clean technologies.

138. Almost all United Nations organizations, funds and programmes have staff dedicated to working with business in a wide range of engagements. Additionally, the United Nations Global Compact, through its thousands of business participants located in over 120 countries, is a source of significant avenues for the advancement of United Nations principles in business communities globally, particularly in developing countries.

139. The United Nations has taken concrete steps to increase the effectiveness and accountability of the Organization's growing relationships with business. This February, the Organization launched a review of the "Guidelines between the United Nations and the Business Community" to reflect experiences across the Organization. Also under way is the development of a new United Nations-business website which will better facilitate identification of partners. Additionally, the "Partnership Assessment

Tool" and the *Business Guide to Partnering with NGOs and the United Nations: Report 2007/2008* were both released in the past year.

140. Achieving United Nations goals, especially the Millennium Development Goals, will require more and deeper collaboration with the private sector. The September 2008 High-level Event on the Goals will include the business community in discussions on necessary steps to be taken to accelerate their achievement. Additional opportunities to increase and enhance engagement with the private sector must be explored at the broad organizational level and also within individual organizations, funds and programmes.

Chapter V

Conclusion

141. The United Nations is situated at the nexus of some of the most important and complex issues facing the world at present. Today, more than ever, thanks to its universal membership and global reach, the United Nations can effect positive global change, making the world a safer, more prosperous and more just place for all people. During my tenure, I am committed to seizing this opportunity and ensuring that we work with all partners to not only deliver results to those most in need but also help the world address global threats through securing global goods. These goals will not be reached, however, unless full accountability becomes both our organizing principle and our operational guideline. We must take decisive action and allow the good of humanity to be our beacon call. I believe we can deliver a better world to future generations, and, indeed, to this generation. I look forward to working with all Member States towards meeting this awesome and crucial challenge.

ANNEX

Millennium Development Goals, targets and indicators, 2008: statistical tables

GOAL 1
Eradicate extreme poverty and hunger

Target 1.A
Halve, between 1990 and 2015, the proportion of people whose income is less than one dollar a day

Indicator 1.1
Proportion of population living below $1 purchasing power parity (PPP) per day (no new global or regional data are yet available)

Indicator 1.2
Poverty gap ratio (no new global or regional data are yet available)

Indicator 1.3
Share of poorest quintile in national consumption
(Percentage)

	2005[a]
Northern Africa	6.1
Sub-Saharan Africa	3.6
Latin America and the Caribbean	2.9
Eastern Asia	4.3
Southern Asia	7.4
South-Eastern Asia	5.7
Western Asia	6.2
Commonwealth of Independent States	7.0
Transition countries in South-Eastern Europe	8.2

[a] High-income economies, as defined by the World Bank, are excluded.

Target 1.B
Achieve full and productive employment and decent work for all, including women and young people

Indicator 1.4
Growth rate of gross domestic product (GDP) per person employed

(*a*) Annual growth rate of GDP per person employed
(Percentage)

	1997	*2007*[a]
World	2.5	3.3
Developing regions	3.6	5.5
Northern Africa	−1.4	2.6
Sub-Saharan Africa	0.5	3.5
Latin America and the Caribbean	1.4	2.9
Eastern Asia	7.1	8.5
Southern Asia	2.2	5.4
South-Eastern Asia	2.4	3.6
Western Asia	2.8	2.2
Oceania	−5.8	1.2
Commonwealth of Independent States	2.9	6.4
Commonwealth of Independent States, Asia	1.3	9.8
Commonwealth of Independent States, Europe	3.4	6.1
Developed regions	2.2	2.1
Transition countries in South-Eastern Europe	−3.6	6.4
Least developed countries	1.8	4.5
Landlocked developing countries	1.4	4.8
Small island developing States	2.0	3.2

[a] Preliminary data.

(*b*) GDP per person employed
(2000 United States dollars (PPP))

	1997	*2007*[a]
World	16 223	20 489
Developing regions	8 126	11 837
Northern Africa	14 495	16 487
Sub-Saharan Africa	4 544	5 348
Latin America and the Caribbean	17 906	19 459
Eastern Asia	6 795	13 667
Southern Asia	6 067	8 974
South-Eastern Asia	8 267	9 789
Western Asia	23 022	25 850
Oceania	6 822	6 733
Commonwealth of Independent States	11 143	18 465
Commonwealth of Independent States, Asia	5 480	10 982
Commonwealth of Independent States, Europe	12 739	20 965
Developed regions	53 109	63 292
Transition countries in South-Eastern Europe	11 010	18 332

	1997	2007[a]
Least developed countries	2 775	3 598
Landlocked developing countries	3 618	4 842
Small island developing States	14 963	18 645

[a] Preliminary data.

Indicator 1.5

Employment-to-population ratio

(a) Total

(Percentage)

	1997	2000	2007[a]
World	62.6	62.2	61.7
Developing regions	64.8	64.1	63.2
Northern Africa	43.6	43.2	45.9
Sub-Saharan Africa	67.8	67.1	66.8
Latin America and the Caribbean	59.0	59.3	60.0
Eastern Asia	74.9	73.9	71.9
Southern Asia	57.6	57.2	56.4
South-Eastern Asia	67.2	66.7	66.4
Western Asia	48.1	47.7	48.3
Oceania	68.2	68.9	70.0
Commonwealth of Independent States	54.9	53.9	56.2
Commonwealth of Independent States, Asia	57.0	57.3	58.7
Commonwealth of Independent States, Europe	54.3	52.9	55.4
Developed regions	56.1	56.6	56.3
Transition countries in South-Eastern Europe	54.3	52.3	49.8
Least developed countries	70.5	70.1	69.4
Landlocked developing countries	67.7	67.9	68.5
Small island developing States	56.2	57.8	58.6

[a] Preliminary data.

(b) Men, women and youth, 2007[a]

(Percentage)

	Men	Women	Youth
World	74.3	49.1	47.8
Developing regions	77.1	49.1	48.9
Northern Africa	70.0	22.1	27.8
Sub-Saharan Africa	78.9	55.1	54.8
Latin America and the Caribbean	73.7	47.1	44.4
Eastern Asia	78.4	65.2	63.0
Southern Asia	77.6	34.1	41.9
South-Eastern Asia	78.2	54.9	47.0
Western Asia	69.9	24.9	33.9
Oceania	73.8	66.2	56.3
Commonwealth of Independent States	63.0	50.4	35.0
Commonwealth of Independent States, Asia	65.6	52.4	37.4
Commonwealth of Independent States, Europe	62.1	49.8	33.9
Developed regions	63.9	49.0	44.1
Transition countries in South-Eastern Europe	56.1	44.0	26.6
Least developed countries	82.2	57.7	58.7
Landlocked developing countries	77.7	59.6	57.0
Small island developing States	72.1	45.5	42.5

[a] Preliminary data.

Indicator 1.6

Proportion of employed people living below $1 (PPP) per day

(Percentage)

	1997	2007[a]
World	24.2	16.4
Developing regions	30.6	20.4
Northern Africa	3.0	1.3
Sub-Saharan Africa	55.5	51.4
Latin America and the Caribbean	11.6	8.0
Eastern Asia	18.8	8.7
Southern Asia	51.5	31.5
South-Eastern Asia	24.1	13.3
Western Asia	2.9	5.4
Oceania	22.9	21.6
Commonwealth of Independent States	6.5	1.5
Commonwealth of Independent States, Asia	11.0	5.8
Commonwealth of Independent States, Europe	5.2	0.0
Developed regions	0.2	0.1
Transition countries in South-Eastern Europe	3.8	2.3
Least developed countries	51.8	47.0
Landlocked developing countries	43.5	37.1
Small island developing States	18.7	20.3

[a] Preliminary data.

Indicator 1.7

Proportion of own-account and contributing family workers in total employment

(a) Both sexes

(Percentage)

	1997	2007[a]
World	52.8	49.9
Developing regions	64.4	59.9
Northern Africa	35.2	32.9
Sub-Saharan Africa	76.1	71.2
Latin America and the Caribbean	31.4	33.0
Eastern Asia	63.2	55.7
Southern Asia	79.2	75.8
South-Eastern Asia	63.4	59.3
Western Asia	37.1	29.1
Oceania	62.3	68.5
Commonwealth of Independent States	13.9	15.3
Commonwealth of Independent States, Asia	33.4	31.3
Commonwealth of Independent States, Europe	8.4	10.0
Developed regions	11.4	9.5
Transition countries in South-Eastern Europe	31.6	26.4
Least developed countries	82.6	77.2
Landlocked developing countries	70.5	68.7
Small island developing States	33.4	36.7

[a] Preliminary data.

(b) Men

(Percentage)

	1997	2007[a]
World	50.7	48.7
Developing regions	60.6	57.0
Northern Africa	31.8	30.4
Sub-Saharan Africa	70.1	64.3
Latin America and the Caribbean	32.1	33.3
Eastern Asia	57.9	52.3
Southern Asia	75.8	72.9
South-Eastern Asia	59.0	56.0
Western Asia	32.3	26.2
Oceania	56.1	62.7
Commonwealth of Independent States	14.7	15.7
Commonwealth of Independent States, Asia	32.8	30.1
Commonwealth of Independent States, Europe	9.2	10.6
Developed regions	11.6	10.3
Transition countries in South-Eastern Europe	29.8	26.9
Least developed countries	77.8	72.4
Landlocked developing countries	67.8	65.7
Small island developing States	33.8	37.5

[a] Preliminary data.

(*c*) **Women**
(Percentage)

	1997	2007[a]
World	56.1	51.7
Developing regions	70.7	64.4
Northern Africa	46.8	40.6
Sub-Saharan Africa	84.4	80.6
Latin America and the Caribbean	30.1	32.5
Eastern Asia	69.6	60.1
Southern Asia	87.5	82.6
South-Eastern Asia	69.6	63.8
Western Asia	52.9	37.7
Oceania	69.4	75.0
Commonwealth of Independent States	13.1	14.9
Commonwealth of Independent States, Asia	34.0	32.6
Commonwealth of Independent States, Europe	7.6	9.3
Developed regions	11.1	8.4
Transition countries in South-Eastern Europe	33.9	25.7
Least developed countries	89.1	83.9
Landlocked developing countries	73.9	72.4
Small island developing States	32.7	35.4

[a] Preliminary data.

Target 1.C

Halve, between 1990 and 2015, the proportion of people who suffer from hunger

Indicator 1.8

Prevalence of underweight children under 5 years of age

(*a*) **Total**
(Percentage)

	1990	2006
Developing regions	33	26
Northern Africa	11	6
Sub-Saharan Africa	32	28
Latin America and the Caribbean	13	8
Eastern Asia	17	7
Southern Asia	54	46
South-Eastern Asia	37	25
Western Asia	14	13
Oceania	—	—

(*b*) **By sex**[a]
(Percentage)

	Boys	Girls	Boy-to-girl ratio
Developing regions	27	27	1.00
Northern Africa	7	6	1.16
Sub-Saharan Africa	29	27	1.07
Latin America and the Caribbean	9	9	1.00
Eastern Asia	10	11	0.91
Southern Asia	41	42	0.98
South-Eastern Asia	26	26	1.00
Western Asia	14	14	1.00
Oceania	—	—	—

[a] 1998–2006.

Indicator 1.9

Proportion of population below minimum level of dietary energy consumption[a]
(Percentage)

	1990–1992	2001–2003
Developing regions	20	17
Northern Africa	4	4
Sub-Saharan Africa	33	31
Latin America and the Caribbean	13	10
Eastern Asia	16	12
Southern Asia	25	21
South-Eastern Asia	18	12
Western Asia	6	9
Oceania	15	12
Commonwealth of Independent States	7[b]	7
Commonwealth of Independent States, Asia	16[b]	20
Commonwealth of Independent States, Europe	4[b]	3
Developed regions	<2.5[b]	<2.5
Least developed countries	22	19
Landlocked developing countries	38	36
Small island developing States	23	19

[a] No new global or regional data are available. Data presented are from the 2006 report (A/61/1).

[b] Data referring to the period 1993–1995.

GOAL 2
Achieve universal primary education

Target 2.A

Ensure that, by 2015, children everywhere, boys and girls alike, will be able to complete a full course of primary schooling

Indicator 2.1

Net enrolment ratio in primary education

(*a*) **Total**[a]

	1991	2000	2006
World	82.0	84.9	88.5
Developing regions	79.6	83.3	87.5
Northern Africa	82.8	91.3	95.0
Sub-Saharan Africa	53.5	58.0	70.7
Latin America and the Caribbean	86.7	94.4	95.5
Eastern Asia	98.0	99.1	94.3
Southern Asia	71.9	80.1	89.8
South-Eastern Asia	95.6	94.3	95.0
Western Asia	80.4	84.8	88.3
Oceania	—	—	—
Commonwealth of Independent States	90.0	89.9	93.3
Commonwealth of Independent States, Asia	88.3	92.4	93.9
Commonwealth of Independent States, Europe	90.8	88.0	92.8
Developed regions	97.9	97.4	96.4
Least developed countries	53.0	60.2	74.9
Landlocked developing countries	53.7	63.0	76.3
Small island developing States	67.3	81.5	75.1

[a] Primary- and secondary-level enrolees per 100 children of primary-education enrolment age. Ratios correspond to school years ending in the years for which data are presented.

(*b*) **By sex**[a]

	1991		2000		2006	
	Boys	Girls	Boys	Girls	Boys	Girls
World	87.2	76.7	87.7	81.9	89.9	87.0
Developing regions	85.7	73.3	86.4	79.9	89.1	85.8
Northern Africa	89.7	75.5	94.0	88.4	96.8	93.1
Sub-Saharan Africa	57.5	49.5	61.3	54.7	73.5	67.8
Latin America and the Caribbean	87.5	86.3	95.1	93.6	95.3	95.7
Eastern Asia	100.0	97.3	98.5	99.8	94.0	94.7
Southern Asia	85.7	57.0	86.7	73.0	92.0	87.3
South-Eastern Asia	97.8	94.0	95.5	93.0	95.8	94.1
Western Asia	87.0	73.3	89.1	80.4	91.7	84.8
Oceania	—	—	—	—	—	—
Commonwealth of Independent States	90.2	89.8	90.3	89.6	93.3	93.2

	1991		2000		2006	
	Boys	Girls	Boys	Girls	Boys	Girls
Commonwealth of Independent States, Asia	88.6	88.0	92.6	92.2	94.5	93.3
Commonwealth of Independent States, Europe	91.0	90.6	88.5	87.5	92.4	93.1
Developed regions	97.7	98.1	97.5	97.4	96.0	96.8
Least developed countries	58.6	47.2	63.7	56.7	77.7	72.1
Landlocked developing countries	58.2	49.2	67.4	58.5	79.0	73.6
Small island developing States	63.6	71.1	82.8	80.1	76.2	74.0

[a]Primary- and secondary-level enrolees per 100 children of primary-education enrolment age. Ratios correspond to school years ending in the years for which data are presented.

Indicator 2.2

Proportion of pupils starting grade 1 who reach last grade of primary[a]

	1999			2006		
	Total	Boys	Girls	Total	Boys	Girls
World	82.1	84.8	79.2	86.3	88.2	84.4
Developing regions	79.4	82.6	75.9	84.7	86.9	82.5
Northern Africa	86.6	90.4	82.6	91.9	94.0	89.8
Sub-Saharan Africa	49.0	53.1	45.0	59.8	64.7	54.9
Latin America and the Caribbean	96.6	96.1	97.1	100.4	99.7	101.1
Eastern Asia	101.7	101.4	102.0	98.1	98.5	97.8
Southern Asia	68.8	75.3	61.7	81.3	83.9	78.5
South-Eastern Asia	89.2	89.9	88.4	95.4	95.4	95.4
Western Asia	80.4	86.8	73.8	88.9	94.3	83.2
Oceania	62.8	65.7	59.7	66.1	69.9	62.1
Commonwealth of Independent States	96.0	96.4	95.5	98.3	98.5	98.1
Commonwealth of Independent States, Asia	95.7	96.2	95.1	100.9	101.7	100.0
Commonwealth of Independent States, Europe	96.1	96.5	95.6	96.4	96.1	96.7
Developed regions	99.2	98.6	99.9	97.0	96.5	97.5
Least developed countries	47.2	51.2	43.1	57.2	60.9	53.4
Landlocked developing countries	53.1	58.4	47.8	61.0	65.3	56.6
Small island developing States	73.9	73.9	74.0	73.3	73.4	73.1

[a]Primary completion rates correspond to school years ending in the years for which data are presented. The primary completion rate is calculated using the gross intake rate at the last grade of primary, which is defined as follows: "Total number of new entrants in the last grade of primary education, regardless of age, expressed as a percentage of the population of the theoretical entrance age to the last grade". (*Global Education Digest 2004: Comparing Education Statistics Across the World* (Montreal, Canada, United Nations Educational, Scientific and Cultural Organization (UNESCO) Institute for Statistics (UIS), 2004), annex B, p. 148).

Indicator 2.3

Literacy rate of 15–24 year-olds, women and men

(*a*) Total

(Percentage who can both read and write)

	1985–1994	1995–2004[a]	2007
World	83.5	87.0	89.1
Developing regions	80.2	84.6	87.2
Northern Africa	68.4	79.4	86.5
Sub-Saharan Africa	64.4	70.2	72.1
Latin America and the Caribbean	93.7	96.2	97.0
Eastern Asia	94.5	98.9	99.2
Southern Asia	60.6	72.8	79.9
South-Eastern Asia	94.5	96.1	95.6
Western Asia	88.6	91.7	92.8
Oceania	72.9	73.1	70.6
Commonwealth of Independent States	99.7	99.7	99.7
Commonwealth of Independent States, Asia	99.6	99.6	99.6
Commonwealth of Independent States, Europe	99.7	99.7	99.7
Developed regions	99.4	99.4	99.4
Least developed countries	55.5	64.7	68.0
Landlocked developing countries	60.8	67.8	70.4
Small island developing States	86.9	87.8	89.8

[a]The regional averages presented in this table are calculated using a weighted average of the latest available observed data point for each country or territory for the reference period. UNESCO Institute for Statistics estimates have been used for countries with missing data.

(*b*) By sex[a]

(Percentage who can both read and write)

	1985–1994		1995–2004		2007	
	Men	Women	Men	Women	Men	Women
World	87.8	79.2	90.2	83.8	91.3	86.8
Developing regions	85.3	75.0	88.3	80.8	89.8	84.6
Northern Africa	77.8	58.6	85.3	73.3	90.8	82.2
Sub-Saharan Africa	70.8	58.6	76.0	65.0	77.2	67.3
Latin America and the Caribbean	93.2	94.2	95.7	96.7	96.5	97.4
Eastern Asia	97.1	91.8	99.2	98.5	99.4	99.1
Southern Asia	71.5	49.1	80.6	64.5	84.5	75.0
South-Eastern Asia	95.4	93.5	96.3	96.0	95.3	95.8
Western Asia	93.9	82.9	95.5	87.9	96.1	89.3
Oceania	75.0	70.7	75.0	71.1	69.8	71.5
Commonwealth of Independent States	99.7	99.7	99.7	99.7	99.7	99.7
Commonwealth of Independent States, Asia	99.6	99.6	99.6	99.6	99.6	99.6
Commonwealth of Independent States, Europe	99.7	99.8	99.7	99.8	99.7	99.8
Developed regions	99.5	99.4	99.4	99.4	99.4	99.3
Least developed countries	63.0	48.5	71.5	58.3	73.4	62.9
Landlocked developing countries	66.3	55.8	74.3	61.9	76.5	64.7
Small island developing States	86.6	87.2	86.8	88.9	88.4	91.3

[a]The regional averages presented in this table are calculated using a weighted average of the latest available observed data point for each country or territory for the reference period. UNESCO Institute for Statistics estimates have been used for countries with missing data.

GOAL 3

Promote gender equality and empower women

Target 3.A

Eliminate gender disparity in primary and secondary education, preferably by 2005, and in all levels of education no later than 2015

Indicator 3.1

Ratios of girls to boys in primary, secondary and tertiary education

(*a*) Primary[a]

	1991	2000	2006
World	0.89	0.92	0.95
Developing regions	0.87	0.92	0.94
Northern Africa	0.82	0.91	0.93
Sub-Saharan Africa	0.83	0.85	0.89
Latin America and the Caribbean	0.97	0.97	0.97
Eastern Asia	0.94	1.01	0.99
Southern Asia	0.77	0.84	0.95
South-Eastern Asia	0.97	0.97	0.97
Western Asia	0.83	0.88	0.91
Oceania	0.90	0.90	0.89
Commonwealth of Independent States	0.99	0.99	0.99
Commonwealth of Independent States, Asia	0.99	0.99	0.98
Commonwealth of Independent States, Europe	1.00	0.99	1.00
Developed regions	0.99	0.99	1.00
Least developed countries	0.79	0.86	0.90
Landlocked developing countries	0.82	0.83	0.90
Small island developing States	0.96	0.95	0.95

[a] Using gross enrolment ratios.

(*b*) Secondary[a]

	1991	2000	2006
World	—	0.93	0.95
Developing regions	—	0.90	0.94
Northern Africa	0.79	0.95	0.99
Sub-Saharan Africa	—	0.82	0.80
Latin America and the Caribbean	1.09	1.07	1.07
Eastern Asia	—	0.97	1.01
Southern Asia	0.60	0.77	0.85
South-Eastern Asia	0.90	0.98	1.02
Western Asia	—	0.80	0.84
Oceania	0.82	0.91	0.88
Commonwealth of Independent States	1.03	1.00	0.97
Commonwealth of Independent States, Asia	0.98	0.97	0.96
Commonwealth of Independent States, Europe	1.06	1.02	0.98
Developed regions	1.01	1.01	1.00
Least developed countries	—	0.82	0.82
Landlocked developing countries	0.85	0.86	0.83
Small island developing States	1.05	1.04	1.03

[a] Using gross enrolment ratios.

(*c*) Tertiary[a]

	1991	2000	2006
World	—	0.96	1.06
Developing regions	—	0.78	0.93
Northern Africa	0.54	0.68	1.00
Sub-Saharan Africa	—	0.62	0.68
Latin America and the Caribbean	—	1.13	1.16
Eastern Asia	—	0.55	0.93
Southern Asia	—	0.67	0.76
South-Eastern Asia	0.83	0.95	0.98
Western Asia	—	0.82	0.90
Oceania	—	0.68	0.86
Commonwealth of Independent States	1.16	1.21	1.29
Commonwealth of Independent States, Asia	1.04	0.90	1.07
Commonwealth of Independent States, Europe	1.20	1.27	1.33
Developed regions	1.07	1.20	1.28
Least developed countries	—	0.65	0.62
Landlocked developing countries	0.86	0.75	0.83
Small island developing States	—	1.21	1.54

[a] Using gross enrolment ratios.

Indicator 3.2

Share of women in wage employment in the non-agricultural sector

(Percentage of employees)

	1990	1995	2000	2006
World	35.5	36.5	37.7	39.0
Northern Africa	20.9	21.0	19.3	21.3
Sub-Saharan Africa	25.3	26.9	28.5	30.8
Latin America and the Caribbean	36.4	38.6	40.5	42.3
Eastern Asia	38.0	38.8	39.6	41.1
Southern Asia	13.2	14.9	16.7	18.6
South-Eastern Asia	37.7	37.1	38.6	37.8
Western Asia	17.0	17.6	19.2	20.3
Oceania	33.2	34.7	35.8	36.4
Commonwealth of Independent States	49.2	49.6	50.4	51.4
Commonwealth of Independent States, Asia	44.7	45.3	46.2	47.9
Commonwealth of Independent States, Europe	50.1	50.5	51.2	52.2
Developed regions	43.3	44.5	45.3	46.3

Indicator 3.3

Proportion of seats held by women in national parliament[a]

(Percentage)

	1990	1997	2002	2008[b]
World	12.8	11.4	13.8	18.0
Developing regions	10.4	10.1	12.1	16.5
Northern Africa	2.6	1.8	2.2	8.3
Sub-Saharan Africa	7.2	9.0	12.0	17.3
Latin America and the Caribbean	11.9	12.4	15.7	22.2
Eastern Asia	20.2	19.3	20.2	19.8
Southern Asia	5.7	5.9	4.9	12.9
South-Eastern Asia	10.4	10.8	13.9	17.4
Western Asia	4.6	3.0	5.2	9.1
Oceania	1.2	1.6	2.4	2.5
Commonwealth of Independent States	—	6.2	8.6	13.9
Commonwealth of Independent States, Asia	—	7.0	8.8	13.9
Commonwealth of Independent States, Europe	—	5.4	8.4	13.9
Developed regions	16.3	15.6	19.1	22.6
Least developed countries	7.3	7.3	10.4	17.0
Landlocked developing countries	14.0	6.6	10.7	18.6
Small island developing States	15.2	11.3	14.2	21.0

[a] Single or lower house only.

[b] As of 31 January 2008.

GOAL 4

Reduce child mortality

Target 4.A

Reduce by two thirds, between 1990 and 2015, the under-five mortality rate

Indicator 4.1

Under-five mortality rate[a]

	1990	2000	2006
World	93	80	72
Developing regions	103	88	80
Northern Africa	82	48	35
Sub-Saharan Africa	184	167	157
Latin America and the Caribbean	55	35	27
Eastern Asia	45	36	24
Southern Asia	120	94	81
South-Eastern Asia	77	47	35

	1990	2000	2006
Western Asia	69	47	40
Oceania	85	73	66
Commonwealth of Independent States	47	41	30
Commonwealth of Independent States, Asia	79	64	47
Commonwealth of Independent States, Europe	27	23	17
Developed regions	11	8	6
Transition countries of South-Eastern Europe	30	19	15

[a]Deaths of children before reaching age 5 per 1,000 live births.

Indicator 4.2

Infant mortality rate[a]

	1990	2000	2006
World	64	55	49
Developing regions	70	60	54
Northern Africa	62	39	30
Sub-Saharan Africa	109	100	94
Latin America and the Caribbean	43	29	22
Eastern Asia	36	29	20
Southern Asia	86	69	61
South-Eastern Asia	53	35	27
Western Asia	54	38	32
Oceania	62	54	49
Commonwealth of Independent States	39	34	26
Commonwealth of Independent States, Asia	64	54	40
Commonwealth of Independent States, Europe	22	20	15
Developed regions	9	6	5
Transition countries of South-Eastern Europe	23	16	13

[a]Deaths of children under age 1 per 1,000 live births.

Indicator 4.3

Proportion of 1-year-old children immunized against measles[a]

(Percentage)

	1990	2000	2006
World	72	72	80
Developing regions	71	69	78
Northern Africa	84	93	96
Sub-Saharan Africa	56	55	72
Latin America and the Caribbean	76	92	93
Eastern Asia	98	85	93
Southern Asia	57	57	66
South-Eastern Asia	72	81	82
Western Asia	79	87	88
Oceania	70	68	70
Commonwealth of Independent States	85	97	97
Commonwealth of Independent States, Asia	—	96	95
Commonwealth of Independent States, Europe	85	97	99
Developed regions	84	91	93
Transition countries of South-Eastern Europe	91	93	93

[a]Children aged 12–23 months who received at least one dose of measles vaccine.

GOAL 5

Improve maternal health

Target 5.A

Reduce by three quarters, between 1990 and 2015, the maternal mortality ratio

Indicator 5.1

Maternal mortality ratio[a]

	1990	2005
World	430	400
Developing regions	480	450
Northern Africa	250	160
Sub-Saharan Africa	920	900
Latin America and the Caribbean	180	130
Eastern Asia	95	50
Southern Asia	620	490
South-Eastern Asia	450	300
Western Asia	190	160
Oceania	550	430
Commonwealth of Independent States	58	51
Developed regions	11	9
Least developed countries	900	870

[a]Maternal deaths per 100,000 live births.

Indicator 5.2

Proportion of births attended by skilled health personnel

(Percentage)

	Around 1990	Around 2006
World	49	62
Developing regions	47	61
Northern Africa	45	79
Sub-Saharan Africa	42	47
Latin America and the Caribbean[a]	68	86
Eastern Asia	71	98
Southern Asia	27	40
South-Eastern Asia	48	73
Western Asia	60	75
Oceania	—	—
Commonwealth of Independent States	96	98
Commonwealth of Independent States, Asia	92	97
Commonwealth of Independent States, Europe	99	99
Developed regions	—	—
Transition countries of South-Eastern Europe	99	98

[a]For deliveries in health-care institutions only.

Target 5.B

Achieve, by 2015, universal access to reproductive health

Indicator 5.3

Contraceptive prevalence rate[a]

(Percentage)

	1990	2005
World	52.8	62.2
Developing regions	50.2	61.2
Northern Africa	44.0	59.8
Sub-Saharan Africa	12.0	20.6
Latin America and the Caribbean	62.0	71.5
Eastern Asia	77.5	86.4
Southern Asia	38.5	52.7
South-Eastern Asia	47.9	58.3
Western Asia	43.3	54.8
Oceania	—	28.8[b]
Commonwealth of Independent States	61.2[c]	67.0
Commonwealth of Independent States, Asia	54.5[c]	56.8
Commonwealth of Independent States, Europe	63.4	71.3
Developed regions	66.5	67.3
Transition countries of South-Eastern Europe	56.0	55.3
Least developed countries	16.1	30.3

	1990	2005
Landlocked developing countries	22.6	32.2
Small island developing States	46.8	52.9

[a]Among women aged 15–49 who are married or in union.

[b]Data from 2000.

[c]Data from 1995.

Indicator 5.4
Adolescent birth rate[a]

	1990	2005
World	61.0	48.6
Developing regions	66.5	53.1
Northern Africa	42.9	31.5
Sub-Saharan Africa	130.6	118.9
Latin America and the Caribbean	77.4	73.1
Eastern Asia	21.3	5.0
Southern Asia	90.1	53.7
South-Eastern Asia	50.4	40.4
Western Asia	63.6	50.2
Oceania	82.3	63.5
Commonwealth of Independent States	52.1	28.4
Commonwealth of Independent States, Asia	44.8	28.9
Commonwealth of Independent States, Europe	55.2	28.1
Developed regions	34.7	23.6
Transition countries of South-Eastern Europe	48.2	29.0
Least developed countries	129.3	117.6
Landlocked developing countries	104.5	105.3
Small island developing States	80.4	69.7

[a]Births per 1,000 women aged 15–19 years.

Indicator 5.5
Antenatal care coverage (at least one visit and at least four visits)

(*a*) At least one visit[a]
(Percentage)

	Around 1990	Around 2005
World	55	75
Developing regions	54	74
Northern Africa	47	70
Sub-Saharan Africa	68	75
Latin America and the Caribbean	77	95
Eastern Asia	—	—
Southern Asia	39	65
South-Eastern Asia	71	93
Western Asia	54	76
Oceania	—	—
Commonwealth of Independent States, Asia	89	98

[a]Proportion of women aged 15–49 years who received antenatal care during pregnancy from skilled health personnel, at least once.

Indicator 5.6
Unmet need for family planning[a]
(Percentage)

	1995	2005
Northern Africa	16.3	10.4
Sub-Saharan Africa	25.7	24.1
Latin America and the Caribbean	12.4	10.5
Southern Asia	19.1	14.8
South-Eastern Asia	12.8	11.1
Western Asia	16.4	12.2
Commonwealth of Independent States	15.0	13.9[b]
Transition countries of South-Eastern Europe	14.7	15.0

[a]Among married women of reproductive age (aged 15–49 years).

[b]Latest available data pertain, approximately, to 2000.

GOAL 6
Combat HIV/AIDS, malaria and other diseases

Target 6.A
Have halted by 2015 and begun to reverse the spread of HIV/AIDS

Indicator 6.1
HIV prevalence among population aged 15–24 years
(Percentage)

	1990		2002		2007	
	Estimated adult (15–49) HIV prevalence	Adults (15+) living with HIV who are women	Estimated adult (15–49) HIV prevalence	Adults (15+) living with HIV who are women	Estimated adult (15–49) HIV prevalence	Adults (15+) living with HIV who are women
Developing regions	0.3	51	1.0	57	0.9	58
Northern Africa	<0.1	20	<0.1	27	0.1	29
Sub-Saharan Africa	2.1	54	5.4	59	4.9	59
Latin America and the Caribbean	0.2	27	0.5	35	0.6	35
Eastern Asia	<0.1	19	0.1	26	0.1	28
Southern Asia	<0.1	35	0.3	38	0.3	38
South-Eastern Asia	0.2	15	0.4	32	0.4	34
Western Asia	<0.1	41	0.1	46	0.1	47
Oceania	<0.1	27	0.4	36	1.3	39
Commonwealth of Independent States, Asia	<0.1	10	<0.1	21	0.1	25
Commonwealth of Independent States, Europe	<0.1	a	0.7	27	1.2	31
Developed regions	0.2	14	0.3	21	0.3	23

[a]Data not available: epidemics in this region are recent and no data are available for earlier years.

Indicator 6.2
Condom use at last high-risk sex[a], 2000–2006[b]

	Women		Men	
	Number of countries covered by surveys	Percentage who used a condom at last high-risk sex	Number of countries covered by surveys	Percentage who used a condom at last high-risk sex
Sub-Saharan Africa	35	31	24	46
Latin America and the Caribbean	11	47	—	—
Southern Asia	1	22	2	38
Commonwealth of Independent States, Asia	3	52	—	—

[a]Proportion of young women and men aged 15–24 years reporting the use of a condom during sexual intercourse with a non-regular sexual partner in the last 12 months, among those who had such a partner in the last 12 months.

[b]Data refer to the most recent year available during the period specified.

Indicator 6.3
Proportion of population aged 15–24 years with comprehensive correct knowledge of HIV/AIDS[a], 2000–2006[b]
(Percentage)

	Women		Men	
	Number of countries covered by surveys	Percentage who have comprehensive knowledge	Number of countries covered by surveys	Percentage who have comprehensive knowledge
Developing regions	62	26	—	—
Northern Africa	3	8	—	—

	Women		Men	
	Number of countries covered by surveys	Percentage who have comprehensive knowledge	Number of countries covered by surveys	Percentage who have comprehensive knowledge
Sub-Saharan Africa	39	25	24	30
Southern Asia	3	23	2	43
South-Eastern Asia	4	23	—	—
Commonwealth of Independent States, Europe	10	24	—	—
Commonwealth of Independent States, Asia	7	20	—	—
Transition countries of South-Eastern Europe	7	19	2	6

[a] Proportion of young women and men aged 15–24 who correctly identify the two major ways of preventing the sexual transmission of HIV (using condoms and limiting sex to one faithful, uninfected partner), who reject two common local misconceptions and who know that a healthy-looking person can transmit the AIDS virus.

[b] Data refer to the most recent year available during the period specified.

Indicator 6.4

Ratio of school attendance of orphans to school attendance of non-orphans aged 10–14 years[a], 2000–2006[b]

	Number of countries with data	School attendance ratio
Sub-Saharan Africa	40	0.81

[a] Ratio of the current school attendance rate of children aged 10–14 years both of whose biological parents have died, to the current school attendance rate of children aged 10–14 years both of whose parents are still alive and who currently live with at least one biological parent.

[b] Data refer to the most recent year available during the period specified.

Target 6.B

Achieve, by 2010, universal access to treatment for HIV/AIDS for all those who need it

Indicator 6.5

Proportion of population with advanced HIV infection with access to antiretroviral drugs[a]

(Percentage)

	2006	2007
Developing regions	22	31
Northern Africa	24	32
Sub-Saharan Africa	21	30
Latin America and the Caribbean	57	62
Eastern Asia	18	18
Southern Asia	10	16
South-Eastern Asia	32	44
Oceania	25	38
Commonwealth of Independent States	9	14

[a] Receiving antiretroviral therapy.

Target 6.C

Have halted by 2015 and begun to reverse the incidence of malaria and other major diseases

Indicator 6.6

Incidence and death rates associated with malaria (no global or regional data are available)

Indicator 6.7

Proportion of children under age 5 sleeping under insecticide-treated bed nets[a]

(Percentage)

Sub-Saharan Africa (36 countries)	7
South-Eastern Asia (5 countries)	2

[a] 2000–2006.

Indicator 6.8

Proportion of children under age 5 with fever who are treated with appropriate antimalarial drugs

(Percentage)

Developing regions (49 countries)	20
Sub-Saharan Africa (38 countries)	36
South-Eastern Asia (5 countries)	2

Indicator 6.9

Incidence, prevalence and death rates associated with tuberculosis

(a) Incidence

(Number of new cases per 100,000 population excluding HIV-infected)

	1990	2000	2006
World	123	127	128
Developing regions	150	150	151
Northern Africa	54	50	44
Sub-Saharan Africa	157	253	291
Latin America and the Caribbean	99	67	53
Eastern Asia	119	105	100
Southern Asia	172	168	165
South-Eastern Asia	271	229	210
Western Asia	54	43	38
Oceania	201	191	183
Commonwealth of Independent States	48	104	105
Commonwealth of Independent States, Asia	60	104	117
Commonwealth of Independent States, Europe	44	104	101
Developed regions	25	19	15
Transition countries of South-Eastern Europe	61	84	76

(b) Prevalence

(Number of existing cases per 100,000 population, excluding HIV-infected)

	1990	2000	2006
World	293	268	214
Developing regions	369	324	256
Northern Africa	60	52	45
Sub-Saharan Africa	352	493	521
Latin America and the Caribbean	152	94	67
Eastern Asia	319	266	197
Southern Asia	529	435	287
South-Eastern Asia	475	333	264
Western Asia	92	63	51
Oceania	590	470	371
Commonwealth of Independent States	78	152	124
Commonwealth of Independent States, Asia	100	138	140
Commonwealth of Independent States, Europe	71	156	118
Developed regions	29	22	15
Transition countries of South-Eastern Europe	101	123	84

(c) Deaths

(Number per 100,000 population, excluding HIV-infected)

	1990	2000	2006
World	27	26	22
Developing regions	34	32	26

	1990	2000	2006
Northern Africa	5	4	4
Sub-Saharan Africa	39	55	59
Latin America and the Caribbean	13	9	6
Eastern Asia	24	20	15
Southern Asia	44	40	29
South-Eastern Asia	65	46	31
Western Asia	8	6	6
Oceania	52	42	34
Commonwealth of Independent States	8	17	16
Commonwealth of Independent States, Asia	9	15	17
Commonwealth of Independent States, Europe	8	17	15
Developed regions	3	2	2
Transition countries of South-Eastern Europe	9	11	11

Indicator 6.10

Proportion of tuberculosis cases detected and cured under directly observed treatment short course

(*a*) New cases detected under directly observed treatment short course (DOTS)

(DOTS smear-positive case detection rate: percentage)

	2000	2006
World	28	61
Developing regions	29	62
Northern Africa	85	88
Sub-Saharan Africa	35	45
Latin America and the Caribbean	40	69
Eastern Asia	30	78
Southern Asia	14	63
South-Eastern Asia	39	77
Western Asia	34	54
Oceania	12	26
Commonwealth of Independent States	12	51
Commonwealth of Independent States, Asia	36	55
Commonwealth of Independent States, Europe	4	49
Developed regions	22	57
Transition countries of South-Eastern Europe	13	78

(*b*) Patients successfully treated under directly observed treatment short course

(Percentage)

	2000	2005
World	82	85
Developing regions	82	85
Northern Africa	88	82
Sub-Saharan Africa	72	76
Latin America and the Caribbean	81	79
Eastern Asia	94	94
Southern Asia	83	86
South-Eastern Asia	86	89
Western Asia	80	81
Oceania	76	75
Commonwealth of Independent States	76	66
Commonwealth of Independent States, Asia	78	75
Commonwealth of Independent States, Europe	68	59
Developed regions	76	73
Transition countries of South-Eastern Europe	85	83

GOAL 7

Ensure environmental sustainability

Target 7.A

Integrate the principles of sustainable development into country policies and programmes and reverse the loss of environmental resources

Indicator 7.1

Proportion of land area covered by forest[a]

(Percentage)

	1990	2000	2005
World	31.3	30.6	30.3
Northern Africa	1.3	1.5	1.5
Sub-Saharan Africa	29.2	27.3	26.5
Latin America and the Caribbean	49.9	47.2	46.0
Caribbean	23.4	24.9	26.1
Latin America	50.3	47.5	46.3
Eastern Asia	16.5	18.1	19.8
Southern Asia	14.0	14.3	14.2
South-Eastern Asia	56.3	49.9	46.8
Western Asia	3.3	3.4	3.5
Oceania	68.3	65.0	63.4
Commonwealth of Independent States	38.6	38.7	38.6
Commonwealth of Independent States, Asia	3.9	3.9	3.9
Commonwealth of Independent States, Europe	46.6	46.7	46.7
Developed regions	30.4	30.7	30.8

[a] No new global or regional data are available; data presented are from 2006 report (A/61/1).

Indicator 7.2

Carbon dioxide emissions, total, per capita and per $1 GDP (PPP)

(*a*) Total[a]

(Millions of metric tons)

	1990	1995	2000	2005[b]
World	21 345	22 188	23 605	27 661
Developed regions	10 812	11 063	11 650	12 026
Developing regions	6 695	8 596	9 614	13 096
Northern Africa	227	280	377	437
Sub-Saharan Africa	461	486	549	652
Latin America and the Caribbean	1 048	1 157	1 287	1 408
Eastern Asia	2 923	3 869	3 895	6 132
Southern Asia	989	1 307	1 651	2 044
South-Eastern Asia	419	674	808	1 183
Western Asia	622	817	1 039	1 229
Oceania	6	6	7	10
Commonwealth of Independent States[c]	3 181	2 354	2 132	2 293
Commonwealth of Independent States, Asia[c]	481	347	327	391
Commonwealth of Independent States, Europe[c]	2 700	2 007	1 805	1 902
Annex I countries[d,e]	11 638	11 872	12 594	13 007

(*b*) Per capita

(Metric tons)

	1990	1995	2000	2005[b]
World	4.1	3.9	3.9	4.3
Developed regions	11.8	11.5	11.8	11.9
Developing regions	1.6	1.9	2.0	2.5
Northern Africa	1.9	2.2	2.7	2.9
Sub-Saharan Africa	0.9	0.8	0.8	0.8
Latin America and the Caribbean	2.4	2.4	2.5	2.5
Eastern Asia	2.4	3.0	2.9	4.4
Southern Asia	0.8	1.0	1.1	1.3
South-Eastern Asia	1.0	1.4	1.6	2.1
Western Asia	4.6	5.3	5.9	6.3
Oceania	1.0	0.9	1.0	1.2
Commonwealth of Independent States[c]	11.2	8.3	7.6	8.2
Commonwealth of Independent States, Asia[c]	7.1	5.0	4.6	5.3
Commonwealth of Independent States, Europe[c]	12.5	9.3	8.6	9.3
Annex I countries[d,e]	12.0	11.8	12.2	12.2

(*c*) Per $1 GDP (PPP)
(Kilograms)

	1990	1995	2000	2005[b]
World	0.48	0.55	0.50	0.49
Developed regions	0.47	0.45	0.40	0.38
Developing regions	0.65	0.64	0.59	0.62
Northern Africa	0.46	0.51	0.60	0.57
Sub-Saharan Africa	0.57	0.56	0.54	0.50
Latin America and the Caribbean	0.34	0.32	0.31	0.30
Eastern Asia	1.45	1.17	0.87	0.91
Southern Asia	0.59	0.62	0.61	0.55
South-Eastern Asia	0.41	0.45	0.48	0.55
Western Asia	0.56	0.60	0.66	0.63
Oceania	0.33	0.25	0.26	0.38
Commonwealth of Independent States[c]	1.48	1.49	1.25	0.97
Commonwealth of Independent States, Asia[c]	2.28	2.16	1.68	1.30
Commonwealth of Independent States, Europe[c]	1.40	1.42	1.20	0.93
Annex I countries[d, e]	0.51	0.48	0.43	0.40

[a]Total CO_2 emissions from fossil fuels include emissions from: solid fuel consumption, liquid fuel consumption and gas fuel consumption; cement production; and gas flaring (United States Carbon Dioxide Information Analysis Center (CDIAC)).

[b]Preliminary data.

[c]The 1990 column shows 1992 data.

[d]Based on the annual national emission inventories of annex I countries (with the exception of Belarus, the Russian Federation and Ukraine, which are included in Commonwealth of Independent States) which report to the Conference of the Parties to the United Nations Framework Convention on Climate Change; non-annex I countries do not have annual reporting obligations.

[e]Excluding emissions/removals from land use, land-use change and forestry.

Indicator 7.3

Consumption of ozone-depleting substances
(Tons of ozone depletion potential)

	1990	2000	2006
Developing regions	247 501	212 466	71 269
Northern Africa	6 203	8 129	2 586
Sub-Saharan Africa	23 449	9 561	2 425
Latin America and the Caribbean	76 048	31 087	11 527
Eastern Asia	103 217	105 762	38 040
Southern Asia	3 338	28 161	7 598
South-Eastern Asia	21 108	16 809	4 608
Western Asia	11 435	11 855	4 272
Oceania	47	129	14
Commonwealth of Independent States	139 454	27 585	1 494
Commonwealth of Independent States, Asia	2 738	928	193
Commonwealth of Independent States, Europe	136 716	26 657	1 301
Developed Regions[a]	826 801	24 060	10 528
Transition countries of South-Eastern Europe	6 239	966	373
Least developed countries	1 463	4 766	1 706
Landlocked developing countries	3 354	2 386	799
Small island developing States	7 162	2 125	1 043

[a]Including transition countries of South-Eastern Europe.

Indicator 7.4

Proportion of fish stocks within safe biological limits
(Percentage)

	1990	2000	2004
Total	81	72	75
Fully exploited	50	47	52
Under- and moderately exploited	31	25	23

Indicator 7.5

Proportion of total water resources used[a], around 2000
(Percentage)

Developing regions	6.75
Northern Africa	76.60
Sub-Saharan Africa	2.16
Latin America and the Caribbean	1.44
Eastern Asia	21.87
Southern Asia	26.61
South-Eastern Asia	4.68
Western Asia	47.42
Oceania	0.02
Commonwealth of Independent States	5.62
Developed regions	9.10
Transition countries of South-Eastern Europe	11.10
Least developed countries	3.45
Landlocked developing countries	8.43
Small island developing States	1.23

[a]Surface water and groundwater withdrawal as a proportion of total actual renewable water resources.

Target 7.B

Reduce biodiversity loss, achieving, by 2010, a significant reduction in the rate of loss

Indicator 7.6

Proportion of terrestrial and marine areas protected

(*a*) Terrestrial and marine[a]
(Percentage)

	Excluding undated protected areas			Including undated protected areas (total)
	1990	2000	2007	
World[b]	6.0	8.6	9.9	12.4
Developing regions	6.1	9.6	11.3	13.0
Northern Africa	2.1	3.1	3.4	3.7
Sub-Saharan Africa	8.5	9.0	9.5	11.6
Latin America and the Caribbean	7.3	14.4	18.8	21.0
Eastern Asia	7.0	9.9	10.9	14.0
Southern Asia	4.3	5.1	5.4	5.6
South-Eastern Asia	2.6	5.3	6.0	7.5
Western Asia	3.7	17.8	17.8	17.9
Oceania	0.4	0.9	7.1	8.2
Commonwealth of Independent States	1.7	2.8	2.8	7.6
Developed regions	10.3	12.8	14.5	18.0
Least developed countries	7.5	8.3	9.5	10.8
Landlocked developing countries	8.1	10.6	10.7	11.5
Small island developing States	3.1	13.9	16.8	17.8

[a]Ratio of protected area (terrestrial and marine combined) to total territorial area. Differences between these figures and those of the statistical annex of the 2007 report of the Secretary-General (A/62/1) are due to the availability of new data and revised methodologies.

[b]Including territories that are not considered in the calculations of regional aggregates and of aggregates of developed and developing regions.

(*b*) **Terrestrial**[a]

(Percentage)

	Excluding undated protected areas			Including undated protected areas (total)
	1990	2000	2007	
World	6.3	9.0	10.0	12.9
Developing regions	7.1	11.0	12.6	14.7
Northern Africa	2.1	3.1	3.4	3.7
Sub-Saharan Africa	9.1	9.6	10.1	12.4
Latin America and the Caribbean	8.2	15.5	20.2	22.7
Eastern Asia	7.4	10.5	11.5	14.7
Southern Asia	4.5	5.3	5.6	5.9
South-Eastern Asia	5.4	11.0	11.8	15.0
Western Asia	4.0	19.1	19.1	19.2
Oceania	1.8	2.5	2.6	8.8
Commonwealth of Independent States	1.7	2.6	2.6	7.7
Developed regions	10.0	12.1	12.7	16.9
Least developed countries	8.3	9.2	9.6	11.1
Landlocked developing countries	8.1	10.6	10.7	11.6
Small island developing States	5.4	26.4	26.6	28.3

[a] Ratio of terrestrial protected area to total surface area.

(*c*) **Marine**[a]

(Percentage)

	Excluding undated protected areas			Including undated protected areas (total)
	1990	2000	2007	
World	3.9	6.4	9.6	9.8
Developing regions	0.6	2.2	4.3	4.5
Northern Africa	0.3	2.6	3.4	4.9
Sub-Saharan Africa	0.5	1.4	1.8	1.8
Latin America and the Caribbean	1.5	7.3	10.0	10.5
Eastern Asia	0.4	0.6	0.6	0.6
Southern Asia	1.2	1.3	1.3	1.3
South-Eastern Asia	0.3	0.7	1.3	1.5
Western Asia	0.6	1.7	1.7	1.8
Oceania	0.1	0.6	8.1	8.1
Commonwealth of Independent States	2.3	5.6	5.6	5.9
Developed regions	11.9	16.6	23.5	23.5
Least developed countries	0.4	1.1	8.7	8.8
Landlocked developing countries[b]	0.0	0.0	0.0	0.0
Small island developing States	0.9	1.8	7.2	7.6

[a] Ratio of marine protected area to total territorial waters.

[b] Some landlocked developing countries have territorial water claims within inland seas.

Indicator 7.7

Proportion of species threatened with extinction[a]

(Percentage of species not expected to become extinct in the near future)

	1994	2008
World	92.19	91.86
Developed regions	93.50	93.10
Developing regions	92.54	92.20
Northern Africa	97.60	97.12
Sub-Saharan Africa	93.75	93.61
Latin America and the Caribbean	93.10	92.96
Eastern Asia	96.16	95.78
Southern Asia	95.95	95.52
South-Eastern Asia	93.37	92.66
Western Asia	97.53	96.99
Oceania	91.86	91.41
Commonwealth of Independent States	96.36	95.71

[a] International Union for Conservation of Nature (IUCN) Red List Index values for birds plus the number of non-Data Deficient species.

Target 7.C

Halve, by 2015, the proportion of people without sustainable access to safe drinking water and basic sanitation

Indicator 7.8

Proportion of population using an improved drinking water source

(Percentage)

	1990			2006		
	Total	Urban	Rural	Total	Urban	Rural
World	77	95	63	87	96	78
Developing regions	71	93	59	84	94	76
Northern Africa	88	95	82	92	96	87
Sub-Saharan Africa	49	82	35	58	81	46
Latin America and the Caribbean	84	94	61	92	97	73
Eastern Asia	68	97	55	88	98	81
Southern Asia	74	91	68	87	95	84
South-Eastern Asia	73	92	64	86	92	81
Western Asia	86	95	70	90	95	80
Oceania	51	92	39	50	91	37
Commonwealth of Independent States	93	97	84	94	99	86
Commonwealth of Independent States, Asia	87	95	80	88	98	79
Commonwealth of Independent States, Europe	95	98	87	97	99	91
Developed regions	98	100	95	99	100	97

Indicator 7.9

Proportion of population using an improved sanitation facility

(Percentage)

	1990			2006		
	Total	Urban	Rural	Total	Urban	Rural
World	54	78	36	62	79	45
Developing regions	41	66	28	53	71	39
Northern Africa	62	82	44	76	90	59
Sub-Saharan Africa	26	40	20	31	42	24
Latin America and the Caribbean	68	81	35	79	86	52
Eastern Asia	48	61	43	65	74	59
Southern Asia	21	53	10	33	57	23
South-Eastern Asia	50	74	40	67	78	58
Western Asia	79	93	56	84	94	64
Oceania	52	80	44	52	80	43
Commonwealth of Independent States	90	95	81	89	94	81
Commonwealth of Independent States, Asia	95	97	93	93	95	92
Commonwealth of Independent States, Europe	89	94	77	88	94	75
Developed regions	99	100	96	99	100	96

Target 7.D

By 2020, to have achieved a significant improvement in the lives of at least 100 million slum-dwellers

Indicator 7.10

Proportion of urban population living in slums[a,b]
(Percentage)

	1990	2001	2005
Developing regions	46.5	42.7	36.5
Northern Africa	37.7	28.2	14.5
Sub-Saharan Africa	72.3	71.9	62.2
Latin America and the Caribbean	35.4	31.9	27.0
Eastern Asia	41.1	36.4	36.5
Southern Asia	63.7	59.0	42.9
South-Eastern Asia	36.8	28.0	27.5
Western Asia	26.4	25.7	24.0
Oceania	24.5	24.1	24.1
Commonwealth of Independent States, Asia	30.3	29.4	29.4
Commonwealth of Independent States, Europe	6.0	6.0	6.0

[a]No new global or regional data are available; data presented are from the 2007 report (A/62/1).

[b]Represented by the urban population living in households with at least one of the four characteristics: lack of access to improved drinking water, lack of access to improved sanitation, overcrowding (three or more persons per room) and dwellings made of non-durable material.

The decrease in the percentage of populations living in slum conditions is mostly due to a change in the definition of adequate sanitation. In 2005, only a proportion of households using pit latrines were considered slum households, whereas in 1990 and 2001, all households using pit latrines had been counted as slum households. The change affects estimates mostly in those countries where the use of pit latrines is more widespread, such as those in Sub-Saharan Africa.

GOAL 8
Develop a global partnership for development

Target 8.A

Develop further an open, rule-based, predictable, non-discriminatory trading and financial system

Includes a commitment to good governance, development and poverty reduction—both nationally and internationally

Target 8.B

Address the special needs of the least developed countries

Includes: tariff- and quota-free access for the least developed countries' exports; enhanced programme of debt relief for heavily indebted poor countries (HIPC) and cancellation of official bilateral debt; and more generous official development assistance (ODA) for countries committed to poverty reduction

Target 8.C

Address the special needs of landlocked Developing countries and Small Island Developing States (through the Programme of Action for the Sustainable Development of Small Island Developing States and the outcome of the twenty-second special session of the General Assembly)

Target 8.D

Deal comprehensively with the debt problems of developing countries through national and international measures in order to make debt sustainable in the long term

Official development assistance (ODA)

Indicator 8.1

Net ODA, total and to the least developed countries, as a percentage of Organization for Economic Cooperation and Development/Development Assistance Committee donors' gross national income

(*a*) Annual total assistance[a]
(Billions of United States dollars)

	1993	2002	2003	2004	2005	2006	2007[b]
All developing countries	56.1	58.3	69.1	79.4	107.1	104.4	103.7
Least developed countries	14.0	15.9	22.6	23.5	24.6	29.4	—

[a]Including non-ODA debt forgiveness but excluding forgiveness of debt for military purposes.

[b]Preliminary data.

(*b*) Share of OECD/DAC donors' gross national income
(Percentage)

	1993	2002	2003	2004	2005	2006	2007[a]
All developing countries	0.30	0.23	0.25	0.26	0.33	0.31	0.28
Least developed countries	0.07	0.06	0.08	0.08	0.08	0.09	—

[a]Preliminary data.

Indicator 8.2

Proportion of total bilateral, sector-allocable ODA of OECD/DAC donors to basic social services (basic education, primary health care, nutrition, safe water and sanitation)

	1997	2000	2002	2004	2006
Percentage	6.8	14.1	18.0	15.9	21.6
Billions of United States dollars	2.1	4.3	5.6	7.7	12.0

Indicator 8.3

Proportion of bilateral official development assistance of OECD/DAC donors that is untied[a]

	1990	2003	2004	2005	2006
Percentage	67.6	91.8	91.3	92.3	94.5
Billions of United States dollars	16.3	30.1	30.8	48.9	53.8

[a]Based on only about 40 per cent of total ODA commitments from OECD/DAC countries, as it excludes technical cooperation and administrative costs, as well as all ODA from Austria, Luxembourg, New Zealand and the United States of America which do not report the tying status of their ODA.

Indicator 8.4

ODA received in landlocked developing countries as a proportion of their gross national incomes

	1990	2003	2004	2005	2006
Percentage	6.4	8.0	7.9	7.0	6.3
Billions of United States dollars	6.9	11.8	13.8	14.7	16.1

Indicator 8.5

ODA received in small island developing States as a proportion of their gross national incomes

	1990	2003	2004	2005	2006
Percentage	2.6	2.7	2.8	2.8	2.7
Billions of United States dollars	2.1	1.8	2.0	2.5	2.5

Market access

Indicator 8.6

Proportion of total developed-country imports (by value and excluding arms) from developing countries and least developed countries, admitted free of duty
(Percentage)

	1996	1998	2000	2003	2006[a]
(*a*) *Excluding arms*					
Developing countries	53	54	63	71	81
Least developed countries	68	81	75	81	89
(*b*) *Excluding arms and oil*					
Developing countries	54	54	65	71	77
Least developed countries	78	78	70	78	79

[a] Preliminary data.

Indicator 8.7

Average tariffs imposed by developed countries on agricultural products and textiles and clothing from developing countries
(Percentage)

	1996	1998	2000	2003	2006
(*a*) *Agricultural goods*					
Developing countries	10.5	10.0	9.3	9.4	8.6
Least developed countries	4.0	3.6	3.7	2.8	2.8
(*b*) *Textiles*					
Developing countries	7.3	7.0	6.6	5.8	5.2
Least developed countries	4.5	4.3	4.1	3.5	3.2
(*c*) *Clothing*					
Developing countries	11.4	11.2	10.8	9.7	8.2
Least developed countries	8.1	8.0	7.8	7.0	6.4

Indicator 8.8

Agricultural support estimate for OECD countries as a percentage of their gross domestic product

	1990	2003	2004	2005	2006[a]
Percentage	2.02	1.17	1.15	1.07	0.99
Billions of United States dollars	321	352	388	382	372

[a] Preliminary data.

Indicator 8.9

Proportion of ODA provided to help build trade capacity[a]
(Percentage)

	2001	2002	2003	2004	2005	2006
World	3.3	3.2	3.6	2.5	3.0	3.2

[a] Trade-related technical assistance/capacity-building as a proportion of total sector-allocable ODA.

Debt sustainability

Indicator 8.10

Total number of countries that have reached their HIPC decision points and number that have reached their HIPC completion points (cumulative)

	2000[a]	2008[b]
Reached completion point	1	23
Reached decision point but not completion point	21	10
Yet to be considered for decision point	13	8
Total eligible countries	**35**	**41**

[a] As of March 2001; including only countries that are heavily indebted poor countries (HIPC) in 2008.

[b] As of June 2008.

Indicator 8.11

Debt relief committed under HIPC and Multilateral Debt Relief initiatives[a]
(Billions of United States dollars, cumulative)

	2000	2008
To countries that reached decision or completion point	28	69

[a] Expressed in end-2006 net present value terms; commitment status as of June 2008.

Indicator 8.12

Debt service as a percentage of exports of goods and services[a,b]

	1990	1995	2000	2006
Developing regions	18.6	14.3	12.5	6.6
Northern Africa	39.9	22.7	15.4	8.3
Sub-Saharan Africa	11.4	10.5	9.4	5.4
Latin America and the Caribbean	20.6	18.7	21.8	14.8
Eastern Asia	10.5	9.0	5.1	0.8
Southern Asia	17.7	26.9	13.7	4.4
South-Eastern Asia	16.7	7.9	6.5	5.6
Western Asia	24.2	18.4	14.2	12.5
Oceania	14.0	7.8	5.9	1.4
Commonwealth of Independent States	0.6[c]	6.1	8.1	7.3
Commonwealth of Independent States, Asia	0.6[c]	3.8	8.4	1.4
Commonwealth of Independent States, Europe	0.6[c]	6.2	8.1	8.2
Transition countries of South-Eastern Europe	9.4	11.7	11.8	5.7
Least developed countries	16.7	13.3	11.6	6.8

[a] Debt service as a proportion of exports of goods and services and net income from abroad.

[b] Including countries reporting to the World Bank Debtor Reporting System, Aggregates are based on available data and, for some years, might exclude countries that do not have data on exports of goods and services and net income from abroad.

[c] Data for 1993.

Target 8.E

In cooperation with pharmaceutical companies, provide access to affordable, essential drugs in developing countries

Indicator 8.13

Proportion of population with access to affordable essential drugs on a sustainable basis (no global or regional data are available)

Target 8.F

In cooperation with the private sector, make available the benefits of new technologies, especially information and communications

Indicator 8.14

Telephone lines[a] per 100 population

	1990	2000	2006
World	9.7	15.9	19.3
Developing regions	2.4	8.0	13.4
Northern Africa	2.9	7.5	11.0
Sub-Saharan Africa	1.0	1.4	1.6
Latin America and the Caribbean	6.3	14.7	17.5
Eastern Asia	1.9	13.0	28.3
Southern Asia	0.7	3.3	4.6
South-Eastern Asia	1.3	4.8	10.6
Western Asia	9.8	17.7	17.9
Oceania	3.4	5.4	5.2

	1990	2000	2006
Commonwealth of Independent States	12.4	18.5	24.9
Commonwealth of Independent States, Asia	7.9	8.9	11.1
Commonwealth of Independent States, Europe	13.9	21.8	30.0
Transition countries of South-Eastern Europe	13.5	21.7	23.0
Developed regions	42.9	55.3	49.9
Least developed countries	0.3	0.5	0.9
Landlocked developing countries	2.3	2.7	3.2
Small island developing States	7.1	12.6	12.4

[a] Fixed telephone lines.

Indicator 8.15
Cellular subscribers per 100 population

	1990	2000	2006
World	0.2	12.3	40.6
Developing regions	0.0	5.2	30.8
Northern Africa	—	2.9	42.6
Sub-Saharan Africa	—	1.8	17.6
Latin America and the Caribbean	0.0	12.2	54.4
Eastern Asia	0.0	8.7	36.5
Southern Asia	—	0.4	15.7
South-Eastern Asia	0.1	4.3	33.8
Western Asia	0.1	14.8	57.6
Oceania	0.0	2.5	9.4
Commonwealth of Independent States	0.0	1.8	81.1
Commonwealth of Independent States, Asia	0.0	1.3	23.4
Commonwealth of Independent States, Europe	0.0	2.0	102.3
Transition countries of South-Eastern Europe	0.0	11.3	81.0
Developed regions	1.1	47.9	92.2
Least developed countries	0.0	0.3	8.8
Landlocked developing countries	0.0	1.1	10.6
Small island developing States	0.2	10.1	35.9

Indicator 8.16
Internet users per 100 population

	1990	2000	2006
World	0.1	6.6	18.5
Developing regions	—	2.0	10.8
Northern Africa	0.0	0.8	10.4
Sub-Saharan Africa	0.0	0.5	3.4
Latin America and the Caribbean	0.0	3.9	18.7
Eastern Asia	—	3.3	12.5
Southern Asia	0.0	0.5	9.7
South-Eastern Asia	0.0	2.4	9.9
Western Asia	—	3.9	13.5
Oceania	0.0	1.9	5.2
Commonwealth of Independent States	0.0	1.4	16.4
Commonwealth of Independent States, Asia	0.0	0.5	6.0
Commonwealth of Independent States, Europe	0.0	1.7	20.2
Transition countries of South-Eastern Europe	0.0	3.9	44.2
Developed regions	0.3	29.5	58.4
Least developed countries	0.0	0.1	1.4
Landlocked developing countries	0.0	0.3	2.8
Small island developing States	0.0	4.8	15.8

Sources: United Nations Inter-Agency and Expert Group on Millennium Development Goals Indicators and MDG Indicators Database (http://mdgs.un.org).

Notes: Except where indicated, regional groupings are based on United Nations geographical regions, with some modifications necessary to create, to the extent possible, homogeneous groups of countries for analysis and presentation. The regional composition adopted for 2008 reporting on MDG indicators is available at http://mdgs.un.org, under "Data".

Commonwealth of Independent States (CIS) comprises Belarus, Moldova, Russian Federation and Ukraine in Europe, and Armenia, Azerbaijan, Georgia, Kazakhstan, Kyrgyzstan, Tajikistan, Turkmenistan and Uzbekistan in Asia.

Where shown, "Developed regions" comprises Europe (except CIS countries), Australia, Canada, Japan, New Zealand and the United States of America. In the tables, developed regions always include transition countries in Europe, unless the latter are presented separately as "Transition countries of South-Eastern Europe".

PART ONE

Political and security questions

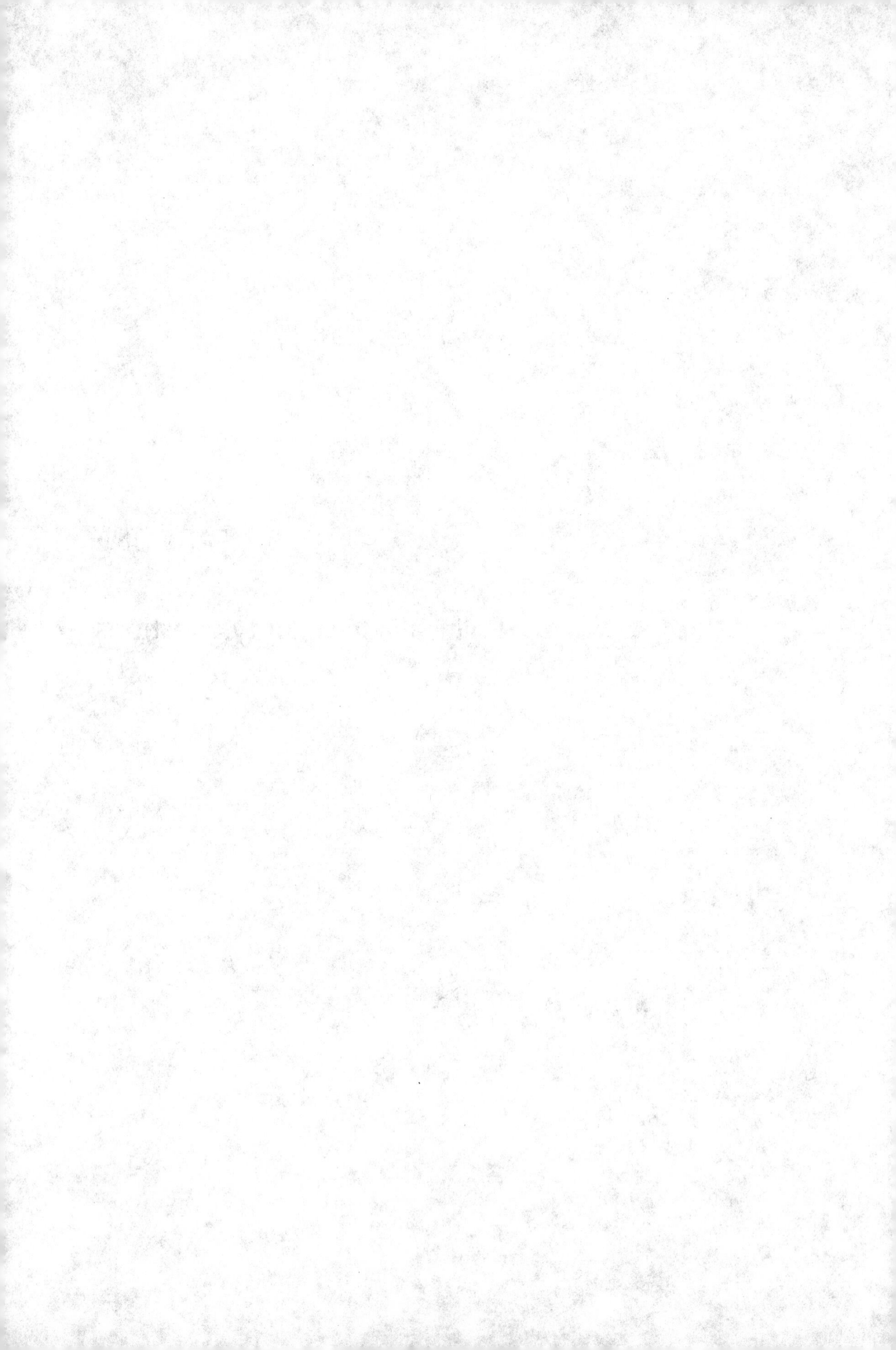

Chapter I

International peace and security

The year 2008 brought new challenges for international peace and security, as the United Nations worked to address several conflict situations, mainly in Africa, and further incidents of international terrorism, while supporting the efforts of post-conflict countries to sustain peace and stability, rebuild national institutions, and restore economic development. The Security Council debated ways to strengthen collective security, stressing the importance of an effective multilateral system to better address global threats. It also reviewed UN assistance in helping States in conflict reform their security sector within the framework of the rule of law, and strengthening the Organization's role in mediation and settlement of disputes. The Council took measures to strengthen the Department of Political Affairs so as to make it more effective in supporting UN peace efforts in countries emerging from conflict. The Peacebuilding Commission enhanced its involvement in that regard by establishing a country-specific configuration for the Central African Republic, bringing to four the number of countries emerging from conflict under consideration by the Commission. The Commission also conducted biannual reviews of the Burundi and Sierra Leone configurations and conducted missions to Guinea-Bissau to assess that country's needs. During the year, the United Nations maintained 12 political and peacebuilding missions and offices.

The scale and frequency of international terrorist acts increased during the year, especially in Pakistan and Afghanistan, and reached countries previously untouched by the scourge. Concerned at the escalating situation, the Security Council, on 9 December, held a debate on threats to international peace and security caused by terrorist attacks around the world. The Council called upon all Member States to redouble efforts to tackle global terrorism by dedicating attention to bringing to justice the perpetrators, facilitators and masterminds of terrorist acts. The Council pledged to continue following developments in order to organize as efficiently as possible its efforts in combating terrorism, reaffirmed the importance of its resolutions and statements on terrorism, and stressed the need for implementing them. The Counter-Terrorism Committee reported significant progress by Member States in implementation of the Global Counter-Terrorism Strategy, adopted by the General Assembly in 2006.

The year marked the sixtieth anniversary of UN peacekeeping. The General Assembly, at a special commemorative session on 7 November to observe that event, adopted the Declaration on the Occasion of the Sixtieth Anniversary of United Nations Peacekeeping, in which it paid tribute to the hundreds of thousands of men and women who, in the past 60 years, had served under the UN flag in more than 60 peacekeeping operations, and honoured the memory of more than 2,400 of them who had died in the cause of peace. To strengthen its peacekeeping capacity, the Organization considered strategies for conducting complex peacekeeping operations. It stepped up efforts to enhance the safety and security of peacekeeping personnel, and considered a comprehensive report by the Secretary-General on conduct and discipline among UN peacekeeping personnel and initiatives to improve their welfare. A decrease of 64 per cent in allegations of sexual exploitation and abuse by peacekeeping personnel reflected the Organization's concerted efforts to address that issue. At the end of 2008, there were 16 peacekeeping missions, served by 112,307 uniformed and civilian personnel.

Regarding the financial position of UN peacekeeping operations, expenditures increased by 21.7 per cent to $6,265.8 million for the 2007–2008 financial year, compared to $5,148.1 million for the previous reporting period; the increase was due mainly to the start-up of two missions and the rapid expansion of another.

Promotion of international peace and security

Maintenance of international peace and security

Security sector reform

Special Committee on Peacekeeping Operations consideration. The Special Committee on Peacekeeping Operations, at its 2008 substantive session (New York, 10 March–4 April and 3 July) [A/62/19], emphasized that security sector reform was an important aspect of multidimensional peacekeeping operations. The establishment of an effective, professional and accountable security sector was one of the critical elements in the transition from UN peacekeeping to sustainable peace and development, including economic recovery. The Special Committee stressed that the sustainability of security sector reform depended on national ownership, sustained international community support, including bilateral donors, and the engagement and commitment of the host countries and societies involved. The United Nations and the international community should avoid imposing external models of security sector reform and concentrate on strengthening the capacity of the host country to develop, manage and implement reform through inclusive consultation processes at all stages of transition from peacekeeping to peacebuilding and sustainable development. The UN approach to security sector reform should be flexible, adaptable and tailored to the country concerned.

The Special Committee acknowledged the leading role of the Department of Peacekeeping Operations (DPKO) in carrying out security sector reform activities in peacekeeping missions, and the significant contribution the Committee itself could make to security sector reform issues in UN peacekeeping operations. It noted efforts to develop a UN approach to security sector reform, as it pertained to peacekeeping operations, outlined in the Secretary-General's report on the subject (see below), and recognized the need for such an approach to be holistic, coherent and better coordinated to ensure comprehensive implementation in line with national strategies and good distribution of resources and activities, and to avoid duplication.

A security sector reform unit should be established in the Office of Rule of Law and Security Institutions, and the Secretariat should elaborate guidelines and advise on the implementation of an integrated approach to security sector reform in peacekeeping missions in consultation with Member States. The Committee stressed the importance of lessons learned and best practices in that regard.

The Special Committee believed that security sector reform should take place within a broad framework of the rule of law, contribute to the overall strengthening of UN rule-of-law activities in peacekeeping operations, and not be duplicative. To that end, it underlined the importance of coordination to ensure consistency and coherence.

The Special Committee requested that the work on clarifying the relationship between security sector reform and disarmament, demobilization and reintegration be completed. It reiterated the importance of incorporating gender perspectives in security sector reform programmes.

Security Council consideration. On 12 May [meetings 5889 & 5890], the Security Council held a debate on the maintenance of international peace and security: the Council's role in supporting security sector reform. It had before it the Secretary-General's report on the role of the United Nations in supporting this reform [A/62/659-S/2008/39], submitted in response to presidential statement S/PRST/2007/3 [YUN 2007, p. 39] and General Assembly resolution 61/291 [ibid., p. 75]. The report described the evolution of the UN approach to security and the role security sector reform played in contributing to a vision of security based on the rule of law. It reviewed UN system experience in supporting security sector reform and key lessons that had emerged. The report also set out principles that should guide a UN approach to such reform, outlined specific ways in which the Organization might best be placed to support those reforms, and highlighted the centrality of partnerships in that regard.

According to the report, States and societies defined and pursued security according to their particular contexts, histories, cultures and needs; no single model of a security sector existed. Effective and accountable security sectors, however, had a number of common features: a legal and/or constitutional framework providing for the legitimate and accountable use of force in accordance with universally accepted human rights norms and standards, including sanctioning mechanisms for the use of force and setting out the roles and responsibilities of different actors; an institutionalized system of governance and management with mechanisms for the direction and oversight of security, including systems for financial management and review, as well as the protection of human rights; capacities, including structures, personnel, equipment and resources, to provide effective security; mechanisms for interaction among security actors, including modalities for coordination and cooperation among different actors, based on their respective constitutional/legal roles and responsibilities; and a culture of service, which promoted unity, integrity, discipline, impartiality and respect for human rights among security actors and shaped the manner in which they carried out their duties.

The United Nations existed to support the maintenance of international peace and security and to assist Governments and peoples in building a world in which freedom from fear and want was a reality for all. The lessons of the past 60 years had illustrated that those goals were fundamentally intertwined; security, development and human rights were preconditions for sustainable peace. While Member States were the primary providers of security, the UN task was to support national actors in achieving their security, peace and development goals. To that end, the development of effective and accountable security institutions, on the basis of non-discrimination, full respect for human rights, and the rule of law, was essential. The United Nations had been involved for many years in assisting national actors in enhancing or re-establishing security, particularly in the aftermath of conflict. Despite that extensive experience, support for security sector reform remained largely an ad hoc undertaking. The Organization had not elaborated principles and standards to guide its support for national actors in enhancing or re-establishing security. It lacked a system-wide approach for delivering coherent assistance, and its capacity and resources to support national authorities were relatively weak.

A holistic and coherent UN approach to security sector reform was vital to provide a basis for a transparent framework for reform, establish international principles consistent with the UN Charter and human rights laws and standards, and facilitate assistance to national authorities and their international partners engaged in security sector reform. It would also better position the Organization to support national and regional authorities in the facilitation, mobilization and coordination of assistance and resources for security sector reform. Such an approach would increase the effectiveness and efficiency of UN efforts, thereby contributing to the timely withdrawal of UN peacekeeping operations, facilitating early recovery from conflict, and helping build the conditions necessary for sustainable peace and development. It would also ensure that personnel in the field received professional and timely guidance.

Following a review of the lessons learned from the UN system and Member States' experience in supporting national security sector reform, the report set out core principles to guide a UN approach to such reform. The goal should be to support States and societies in developing effective, inclusive and accountable security institutions so as to contribute to international peace and security, sustainable development and the enjoyment of human rights; reform should be undertaken on the basis of a national decision, a Council mandate and/or an Assembly resolution, the UN Charter and human rights laws and standards; support for reform should be anchored on national ownership and the commitment of involved States and societies; and the UN approach should be made flexible, country-, region- and/or environment- and stakeholder-specific, gender-sensitive, and address and prevent sexual and gender-based violence. In addition, a security sector reform framework and a clearly defined strategy were essential in planning and implementing post-conflict activities. The effectiveness of international support for security sector reform would be shaped by the integrity of motive, the level of accountability, the amount of resources provided, coordination of national and international partners' efforts, monitoring and regular evaluation, and specific benchmarks to track and maintain progress.

A number of immediate priorities were recommended for the development of a UN approach to security sector reform in support of national actors: developing UN policies and guidelines; strengthening strategic advisory and specialist capacities; strengthening field capacity for security sector reform; assessing gaps and resource requirements; designating lead entities; enhancing the coordination and delivery of support; building partnerships to provide effective support, expertise and adequate resources to national security sector reform processes; and establishing a UN inter-agency security sector reform support unit to deliver on those priorities.

SECURITY COUNCIL ACTION

On 12 May [meeting 5890], following consultations among Security Council members, the President made statement **S/PRST/2008/14** on behalf of the Council:

> The Security Council recalls the statement by its President of 20 February 2007 and emphasizes that security sector reform is an essential element of any stabilization and reconstruction process in post-conflict environments. The Council recognizes that the establishment of an effective, professional and accountable security sector is one of the necessary elements for laying the foundations for peace and sustainable development.
>
> The Council welcomes the efforts of the Secretary-General on security sector reform and takes note of his report entitled "Securing peace and development: the role of the United Nations in supporting security sector reform" of 23 January 2008.
>
> The Council commends Slovakia and South Africa for their joint initiative in holding the workshop entitled "International Workshop on Enhancing United Nations Support for Security Sector Reform in Africa: Towards an African Perspective" in Cape Town, South Africa, on 7 and 8 November 2007 and takes note of the letter dated 20 November 2007 from the Permanent Representatives of Slovakia and South Africa to the United Nations addressed to the Secretary-General. The Council encourages further similar activities.
>
> The Council recognizes that security sector reform is a long-term process and reiterates that it is the sovereign right and primary responsibility of the country concerned to determine its national approach and priorities for security sector reform. It should be a nationally owned process that is rooted in the particular needs and conditions of the country in question.
>
> The Council underlines that the strong support of the United Nations and the international community is also critical in strengthening national capacities, thereby reinforcing national ownership, which is crucial for the sustainability of the process.
>
> The Council recognizes the important role that the United Nations has played in supporting national security sector reform efforts and underlines the need for its continued engagement. In this regard, the Council emphasizes the need to develop a holistic and coherent United Nations approach to security sector reform as recommended by the Secretary-General, in close consultation with Member States.
>
> The Council underlines that United Nations support to security sector reform must take place within a broad framework of the rule of law and should contribute to the overall strengthening of the United Nations rule of law activities as well as wider reconstruction and devel-

opment efforts. This will require coordination with all relevant United Nations actors, in particular the Rule of Law Coordination and Resource Group, to ensure coherence of approach.

The Council emphasizes the important role that the Peacebuilding Commission, through its integrated peacebuilding strategies, can play in ensuring continuous international support to countries emerging from conflict. The Council also recognizes the importance of continued close cooperation and partnerships with non-United Nations actors, in particular regional, subregional and other intergovernmental organizations, including international financial institutions and bilateral donors, as well as non-governmental organizations.

The Council requests the Secretary-General to continue to include, wherever appropriate, recommendations related to security sector reform in his periodic reports on United Nations operations mandated by the Council.

Strengthening collective security

On 19 November [meeting 6017], the Security Council considered the issue of strengthening collective security, having before it a concept paper submitted by Costa Rica [S/2008/697] entitled "Strengthening collective security through general regulation and reduction of armaments: the safest road to peace and development". Outlining the objectives and challenges, the paper stated that the world would not enjoy development without security, nor security without development, and neither without respect for human rights. Unless those goals were simultaneously advanced, none would succeed. Despite their reaffirmation in the 2005 World Summit Outcome contained in Assembly resolution 60/1 [YUN 2005, p. 48], multilateralism, the notion of collective security and the authority of the Security Council as its primary guarantor had seen their foundations eroded. The international system needed to develop a common vision and recommit to multilateralism and the rule of law. Collective security depended on effective cooperation among the United Nations and regional organizations. Regional arrangements and organizations played a pivotal role in promoting and maintaining international peace and security. A constructive and proactive interaction between regional arrangements and the Council should be developed further. An enhanced system of regional arrangements, duly coordinated, mandated and supported by the United Nations—in particular by the Council—could help prevent and address conflict, including its root causes and triggers. The Council's responsibility and mandate went beyond maintenance of international peace and security, and included the obligation to promote its establishment and maintenance. Current developments required that consensus on major threats should be built and translated into concrete action, including addressing the root causes of those challenges.

The Council President expressed the view that members had an obligation to reflect upon the role entrusted to the Council to promote international peace and security, and the current meeting provided an opportunity to consider the instruments that could be used to achieve the Charter objectives, including the strengthening of both regional and global multilateral mechanisms and arms control and regulation. The dialogue should also focus on action that would lead to a more rational use of resources, without undermining security, to ensure greater development. It was a particularly opportune moment, as arms races were developing around the world and crises, such as the food, environmental, energy and economic crises, were impeding efforts to improve the lives of those condemned to poverty, ignorance and ill-health. The time had come to recognize the link between the squandering of resources on arms and the need for those resources to advance to greater levels of human development.

Sergio Duarte, the High Representative for Disarmament Affairs, in addressing the Council, said that achieving a sense of collective security was a vital step towards preventing conflict. The strengthening of collective security could build trust between States and pave the way for agreements and cooperation in other fields, steadily tying countries together in shared interests, better understanding and mutual support. No serious discussion on the limitation or elimination of armaments could avoid the topic of improving transparency. Predictable and transparent State behaviour could build confidence and thereby promote collective security. He welcomed the Council's recognition that progress in disarmament and the regulation of armaments could make important contributions to strengthening international security.

On 19 November, the Security Council, in presidential statement **S/PRST/2008/43** (see p. 592), stressed the vital importance of an effective multilateral system for better addressing the multifaceted and interconnected challenges and threats confronting the world and achieving progress in peace and security, development and human rights—the pillars of the UN system and the foundations for collective security and well-being. It expressed its support for multilateralism as one of the most important means for resolving security concerns in accordance with international law.

Mediation and settlement of disputes

On 23 September [meeting 5979], the Security Council, as part of its consideration on the maintenance of international peace and security, discussed the mediation and settlement of disputes. The Council extended an invitation, under rule 39 of its provisional rules of procedure, to former Special Adviser Lakhdar Brahimi to attend the meeting.

The Council had before it a concept paper [S/2008/590] submitted by Burkina Faso, which stated that the settlement of disputes by peaceful means had always been a major concern of the international community. Over time, the increasingly frequent recourse to mediation, conducted by actors with widely varying backgrounds, had made it one of the principal alternatives for the settlement of contemporary conflicts. With over a half century of experience, the United Nations had established effective mechanisms for the prevention and settlement of conflicts through mediation. At the subregional and regional levels, initiatives, mechanisms and institutions were also in place for the governance of the actions of organizations and States in mediation and other peaceful dispute settlement methods. Mediation had a greater likelihood of success at those levels, as the parties to the dispute and the mediator shared the same geographical, historical, economic, social, cultural and demographic background. Therefore, the international community, including the United Nations, should provide support for local processes, especially financial and logistical support. Several non-State structures also offered expertise in mediation and settlement of conflicts. However, while the several actors, mechanisms, structures and activities enriched the conduct of mediation, they could cause complications or even stall the mediation owing to lack of coordination.

In addition to promoting mediation as a method of dispute settlement, the high-level meeting of the Council aimed to: evaluate UN activities and mechanisms in mediation and review the implementation of resolution 1625(2005) [YUN 2005, p. 155] on conflict prevention, particularly in Africa, as well as the effectiveness of other relevant Council resolutions and declarations; examine ways to make UN mediation more effective at the operational and institutional levels; evaluate the functioning and contribution to conflict resolution of subregional and regional mediation mechanisms, and make proposals for enhancing their effectiveness; explore ways to improve the coordination of mediation activities, such as the appointment of joint mediators; provide a forum for exchanging experiences in mediation among key figures, civil society, and specialized centres; and assess the influence of sociocultural factors and ownership of the process. The discussions could also focus on the role, especially of the Council and the Secretary-General, in conducting mediation, and how it could be enhanced; the contribution of regional and subregional organizations; support for regional mediation initiatives conducted by Member States and regional and subregional bodies; and the role of women and civil society in the mediation process.

During the debate, the Council President said that mediation required confidence and coordination between the mediator, the parties to the conflict, local actors and all partners. In crisis mediation, three essential elements should be highlighted: ownership by the major parties of the process to resolve the crisis; a final document satisfying each protagonist and providing answers to fundamental questions regarding the onset of the crisis, while remaining even-handed; and appropriate follow-up mechanisms to allow the parties to overcome obstacles and to strengthen dialogue and confidence.

The Secretary-General, addressing the Council, said that pursuant to the 2005 World Summit Outcome contained in General Assembly resolution 60/1 [YUN 2005, p. 48], a small Mediation Support Unit (MSU) had been established in the Department of Political Affairs to provide operational support to peace processes and be a repository of knowledge for mediators. During 2008, MSU established a standby team of mediation experts that could be deployed anywhere in the world in a matter of days. In the first half of the year, MSU provided support to some 15 peace processes, as well as to the Southern Africa Development Community, the Economic Community of Central African States and the African Union to strengthen their mediation capacities. However, its funding in the regular budget was meagre, with no funds for programme activities. The Secretary-General urged the Council to ensure that mediation efforts had the requisite resources. As past experience suggested that an effective mediation effort throughout the conflict cycle was necessary for effective peacekeeping and peacebuilding, it was critical that the Council provide the same support to enhance the structures, processes, tools and resources required for mediation as for peacekeeping and peacebuilding activities.

Mr. Brahimi told the Council that a mediator should include in the peace process all parties to the conflict. He or she should never act to placate his or her own ego; rather, the person should put the concerns and aspirations of all the people of the country concerned at the forefront. In the case of Afghanistan, the interests of the Afghan people should override those of the United Nations, the North Atlantic Treaty Organization, neighbours and any other country. However, there should be no misunderstanding: mediation that was inclusive and involved dialogue with all parties did not mean that any offence, by anyone, should be condoned or ignored. The mediators' hand would be significantly strengthened when the principles and approaches they adhered to in conducting the mediation were seen to be supported by all Council and UN Members as a whole. That meant, in particular, that there had to be only one channel of communication with the parties. The mediator, particularly a UN mediator, needed all the help possible, especially from the Council. That help should begin with giving the mediator the time and space needed to work out solutions, overcome prejudices and reconcile competing narratives of the conflict. It meant resisting pressure to initiate competing mediating efforts and standing firm against predetermined or hastily conducted agreements that were imposed from outside or did not address the core issues. The credibility of the United Nations and the world's faith in its relevance suffered greatly when the mediation of conflicts was left unattended for long periods or ignored altogether, as well as when the Council was perceived to be more concerned about the suffering of some than others, selective in the enforcement of its resolutions, or employing double standards. The damage to that credibility on some issues would affect its mediation efforts everywhere. Mr. Brahimi concluded that the Organization's universality, impartiality and consistent adherence to the principles enshrined in its Charter were the most powerful weapons in a UN mediator's arsenal. If the Organization equipped and supported its mediators well, they would be more likely to provide the help the victims of war demanded and achieve the peace the Council sought.

SECURITY COUNCIL ACTION

On 23 September [meeting 5979], following consultations among Security Council members, the President made statement **S/PRST/2008/36** on behalf of the Council:

> The Security Council recalls the purposes and principles of the Charter of the United Nations and reaffirms its commitment to the pacific settlement of disputes, including through mediation, in conformity with the Charter, in particular Chapter VI thereof. The Council recalls all its relevant previous statements and resolutions.
>
> The Council underlines the importance of mediation as a means of pacific settlement of disputes and encourages the further use of this mechanism in the settlement of disputes. The Council reaffirms the crucial role of the United Nations in this regard.
>
> The Council affirms that, as the organ with the primary responsibility for the maintenance of international peace and security, it has a responsibility to promote and support mediation as an important means for the pacific settlement of disputes.
>
> The Council emphasizes the importance of the actions undertaken by the Secretary-General, in using his good offices and his representatives and special envoys, and United Nations mediators in promoting mediation and in the pacific settlement of disputes. The Council takes note of the establishment of the Mediation Support Unit of the Department of Political Affairs of the Secretariat, which provides expertise for supporting the mediation efforts of the United Nations and regional and subregional organizations.
>
> The Council requests the Secretary-General to continue to ensure that mediation processes conducted by or under the auspices of the United Nations are guided by the purposes and principles of the Organization and that mediators are experienced, impartial, have a good knowledge of all the stakeholders, facts and circumstances of any dispute to which they have been assigned, and are provided with the necessary support and flexibility to approach mediation according to the specificities of the disputes; to this end, the Council encourages the Secretary-General to consider ways to strengthen the capabilities of the Secretariat.
>
> The Council notes the important contribution of regional and subregional organizations, civil society and other stakeholders to the pacific settlement of disputes, in particular through mediation, and commends them for their efforts. The Council is resolved to strengthen United Nations support to such mediation efforts through improved cooperation, in particular in Africa; the Council encourages other bilateral and multilateral partners to do likewise.
>
> The Council underlines the importance of engaging the potential and the existing capacities and capabilities of regional and subregional organizations in mediation efforts, and welcomes the promotion of regional approaches to the pacific settlement of disputes.
>
> The Council notes that women have an important role to play in the settlement of disputes, stresses the importance of their equal participation and full involvement in all efforts for the maintenance and promotion of peace and security, and calls upon the Secretary-General and the heads of regional and subregional organizations to take into account the gender aspect during the selection of mediators, as well as the approach and perspective that women can render in mediation processes.
>
> The Council highlights the importance of considering peacebuilding and recovery requirements in the mediation process to help to build the foundations for sustainable peace, and stresses that the Peacebuilding Commission has a role to play in the promotion of mediation.
>
> The Council emphasizes the need to ensure the coherence of mediation processes by or under the auspices of the United Nations, through the improved coordination of efforts with other actors, including regional and subregional organizations, in order to enhance the effectiveness of international efforts.
>
> The Council also stresses that no mediation initiative can be viable without the ownership and full involvement of all relevant parties to the dispute throughout the process. The Council reaffirms that conflict prevention and the pacific settlement of disputes should be at the core of mediation efforts.
>
> The Council requests the Secretary-General to submit, within six months of the adoption of the present statement, a report on mediation and its support activities which takes into account experiences of the United Nations and other key actors and makes recommendations for enhancing the effectiveness of United Nations mediation.

Natural resources and conflict

On 25 July [A/63/191], Belgium requested that the item entitled "Natural resources and conflict" be included in the agenda item on the maintenance of international peace and security by the sixty-third session of the General Assembly. Belgium stated that the link between natural resources and conflict was well-documented both at the conceptual level and in the context of specific conflict situations. It referred to the 2007 thematic debate on the issue by the Security Council [YUN 2007, p. 41], and the similar discussion by the Working Group on Lessons Learned of the Peacebuilding Commission on 8 May 2008 [A/63/92-S/2008/417]. Belgium noted that the policy debate on the issue had long been focused on particular countries or narrowed down to specific dimensions. An approach to better understand the different aspects of the issue was to make a distinction between the successive phases of a (potential) conflict. Belgium was convinced that the question of natural resources and conflict was multifaceted and deserved a broad debate. In that regard, the General Assembly offered an inclusive and comprehensive forum for such a debate, the aim of which would be to: stimulate further reflection on how the exploitation of natural resources could play a role in certain conflicts, and on how to ensure that natural resources became a source of development; better understand what the international community could do to assist Governments in that area, and what the responsibilities of the various concerned actors were, including the private sector and regional organizations; and take stock of ongoing initiatives and explore how their effectiveness could be strengthened.

In September [A/63/250], the Assembly's General Committee decided to postpone to a later date its consideration of the question of the inclusion of the item entitled "Natural resources and conflict" in the Assembly's draft agenda.

Conflict prevention

The General Assembly, by **decision 62/554** of 15 September, deferred consideration of the item entitled "Prevention of armed conflict" and decided to include it in the draft agenda of its sixty-third (2008) session. On 24 December, the Assembly, by **decision 63/552**, decided that the item "Prevention of armed conflict" would remain for consideration during its resumed sixty-third (2009) session.

Review Summit on armed violence and development. In a 16 October letter [A/63/494], Switzerland transmitted to the Secretary-General the Geneva Declaration on Armed Violence and Development adopted in June 2006 and the Summit Statement adopted at the Review Summit of the Declaration (Geneva, 12 September 2008). The Declaration acknowledged that armed violence and conflict impeded realization of the Millennium Development Goals (MDGS) [YUN 2000, p. 51] and that conflict prevention, conflict resolution, violence reduction, human rights, good governance, and peacebuilding were key steps towards reducing poverty, promoting economic growth and improving people's lives.

On 17 November, the General Assembly adopted **resolution 63/23** (see p. 635), which took note of the Declaration and the resolve expressed in the Summit Statement to develop goals, targets and measurable indicators on armed violence and development as a complement to the MDGS.

Peacekeeping and prevention of armed conflict

Parliamentary hearing. The 2008 Parliamentary Hearing (New York, 20–21 November) [A/63/729] considered "Towards effective peacekeeping and the prevention of conflict: Delivering on our commitments". The hearing, attended by some 200 parliamentarians from over 60 countries, was conducted in four sessions on the responsibility to protect (Session I), sexual violence against women and children in conflict (Session II), integrating a human security approach into the work of the United Nations (Session III) and major challenges facing UN peacekeeping operations (Session IV). In **resolution 63/24** of 18 November (see p. 1536), the General Assembly requested its President to submit a summary of the Hearing to its next session.

Implementation of Security Council resolution 1625(2005)

In response to Security Council presidential statement S/PRST/2007/31 [YUN 2007, p. 45], the Secretary-General submitted a January report [S/2008/18] on the implementation of Security Council resolution 1625(2005) [YUN 2005, p. 155] on conflict prevention, particularly in Africa. The report examined the Council's role in prevention, including preventive initiatives in Africa and more effective use of sanctions, as well as that of the Secretary-General through such measures as good offices, information-sharing regarding potential conflicts, mediation support and preventive field presence. It also reviewed national preventive capacity-building, including electoral assistance and building capacities for conflict management, building the capacity of regional organizations, and further developing system coherence and coordination on prevention.

The Secretary-General stated that, in recognition of its multidimensional nature, the United Nations was developing increasingly multifaceted approaches to conflict prevention, drawing on the cooperation of different actors. That comprehensive approach included structural prevention to address the root causes of conflict; operational prevention to ensure the effectiveness of early warning mechanisms, mediation, humanitarian access and response, the protection of civilians, and targeted sanctions in the face of immediate crises; and systemic prevention to prevent conflicts from spilling over into other States. The recognition that those different approaches should be linked so as to create a comprehensive conflict-prevention strategy had allowed for a more holistic and systemized approach to the maintenance of international peace and security and international collective security mechanisms. The Council's endorsement of the comprehensive approach to prevention was reflected in its focused activities in Africa, which was indicative of its intention to play a more proactive role in addressing conflict there. As for of the more effective use of sanctions, the Secretary-General stated that greater attention should be paid to implementing the recommendations of arms embargo monitoring groups and holding violators responsible.

It was also imperative that the Council broaden its responses and adopt a more comprehensive approach, including the development of norms and frameworks for ensuring that the activities of the business sector did not exacerbate or fuel conflicts. In that regard, the UN system had been working with private sector partners through the Global Compact [YUN 2000, p. 989] to promote corporate social responsibility. The Compact had developed instruments such as a conflict impact assessment and a risk-management tool to enable companies to measure their impact on the environment and make the requisite positive changes. The Council played a role in advancing that agenda, but more needed to be done to strengthen the international regulatory framework and encourage States to forcefully and constructively promote conflict-sensitive practices in their business sectors. The hardware used in conflict, including guns, tanks and landmines, was cheaply produced and widely sold, making it a hazard to peace. General Assembly recommendations aimed at reducing trafficking in small arms and light weapons had been unevenly and inadequately implemented. The Secretary-General called on Member States to renew their commitment in that regard.

Regarding his role in conflict prevention, the Secretary-General said that he relied on the Department of Political Affairs (DPA), as the operational arm of his mission of good offices, to keep him informed of potential conflict situations and provide strategies to keep tensions from escalating. He had submitted proposals to the Assembly for strengthening DPA, including its regional coverage, through the establishment of regional offices, and he suggested a Regional Office for the Great Lakes and Central Africa. He also proposed enhancing DPA's policy-planning capacity and mediation support function to assist Member States in responding to cross-cutting global issues, such as transnational organized crime networks, corruption and terrorism.

The Council and the Assembly continued to take parallel and supportive action for conflict prevention, but mechanisms needed to be enhanced to ensure regular, systematic briefings of the Council by the Secretariat on disputes or situations likely to endanger international peace and security. The oversight role of the Economic and Social Council was relevant to system coordination in matters of development cooperation and humanitarian assistance. The Security Council should continue to engage the Economic and Social Council and the Human Rights Council in facilitating the flow of information to it from UN funds, programmes and agencies.

The Secretary-General concluded that the United Nations was making progress in conflict prevention, particularly in Africa, including through a better-defined role for the Council. Those efforts had made the UN preventive system more attentive to early signs of rising tensions of potential conflict and more effective at transmitting that information to the Council. However, the gap between the rhetoric and the employment of effective preventive mechanisms had to be closed in order to operationalize prevention throughout the UN system, provide an adaptive system to respond to requests from Member States and regional organizations, support preventive efforts of the Assembly and the Council, and fulfil Member States' preventive mandates.

To enhance its preventive action capacity, the Secretary-General called on the Council to dispatch timely missions to assess situations in the field; increase use of the Arria Formula (Security Council informal consultative arrangement) or similar arrangements for informal discussions; maintain its focus on addressing cross-border threats to peace and security, notably the illicit trade in small arms and drugs and human trafficking; ensure the constructive use of sanctions and use reports of experts to motivate parties to resolve conflicts without violence; broaden the use of sanctions to non-state actors, and in that regard continue its 2007 debate on natural resources and conflict [YUN 2007, p. 41]; and develop a more structured relationship with the African Union (AU) Peace and Security Council, as called for in their 2007 joint communiqué [ibid., p. 110].

The Secretary-General called upon Member States to: strengthen UN preventive diplomacy and mediation support capacities, in particular, initiatives to strengthen DPA, including through expansion of regional field presences in Africa; combat cross-border and transnational threats to stability, including efforts to control the arms trade; and consider the deployment of integrated offices charged with building national capacities for conflict prevention in the aftermath of the drawdown of peacekeeping operations. Member States and the international community were urged to continue to address gender-based violence. Member States should enhance support for the Peacebuilding Commission to ensure that it had the resources to assist all countries eligible to be on its agenda. African States and the international community should fully cooperate in developing the capacities of African regional and subregional organizations to deploy civilian and military assets quickly when needed, including the development of the AU African Standby Force.

Among his proposals, the Secretary-General mentioned: strengthening the Secretariat's capacity to analyse conflict situations and develop recommendations; enhancing the UN regional field presence in support of prevention, particularly in Africa; providing the Council with regular reports and analyses of developments in regions of potential armed conflict, particularly in Africa; instructing the UN system to build on current collaborations, strengthen frameworks and deploy expertise on prevention; enhancing UN cooperation and coordination with regional organizations; presenting specific proposals on regional coordination in a report as requested by the Council in presidential statement S/PRST/2007/7 [ibid., p. 109]; ensuring that the UN system worked closely with the African Peace and Security Architecture, including the Panel of the Wise, and help build long-term AU capacity; supporting UN system efforts to build national and regional capacity, notably in Africa, to address the root causes of conflict, while strengthening institutions that provided channels for peaceful conflict resolution; strengthening the UN ability to promote preventive diplomacy and mediation capability; and strengthening the Secretariat's ability to promote fairness and transparency in electoral processes and other means of supporting the development of post-conflict institutions.

The Council, in **resolution 1809(2008)** of 16 April (see p. 109) , encouraged the continuing involvement of regional and subregional organizations in the peaceful settlement of disputes, including through conflict prevention, confidence-building and mediation efforts. It expressed its determination to strengthen and enhance cooperation between the United Nations and regional organizations, particularly the AU, in conflict prevention, resolution and management, including good offices, mediation support, effective use of sanctions, electoral assistance and preventive field presence, and in the case of Africa, focusing on support to the AU Panel of the Wise, among others.

United Nations and regional organizations

On 16 April [meeting 5868], the Security Council, during consideration of peace and security in Africa, held a debate on the relationship between the United Nations and regional organizations, in particular the AU, in the maintenance of international peace and security. It had before it a concept paper by South Africa [S/2008/229] and an April report [S/2008/186] by the Secretary-General on the subject, as requested by the Council in presidential statement S/PRST/2007/7 [YUN 2007, p. 109].

The Secretary-General's report highlighted the issues that defined the nature of the collaborative partnership in international peace and security between the United Nations and regional organizations, in particular the AU; the division of responsibilities under Chapter VIII of the UN Charter on regional arrangements; the multifaceted nature and levels of cooperation with regional organizations; and the challenges and opportunities created by such partnerships. According to the report, the need for greater involvement by regional organizations with the United Nations in conflict prevention, management and resolution in all regions had been recognized. Enhancing that relationship under Chapter VIII should be based on a clearer definition of the basis and processes of such cooperation, as well as understanding and appreciating how such partnerships should be framed to avoid misunderstanding and misperception of their meaning and scope. The challenge was finding ways to replace the current approach with more planned, consistent and reliable arrangements, including sustainable, flexible and predictable funding for long-term planning, deployment and sustainment of a peacekeeping operation undertaken by a regional organization and authorized by the Council.

The Secretary-General made a number of recommendations for addressing common security challenges and for expanding dialogue and cooperation between the UN Security Council and regional organizations, in particular the AU Peace and Security Council. He recommended that the UN Security Council define the role of regional organizations in the maintenance of peace and security, in particular the prevention, management and resolution of conflicts; distinguish between regional organizations for Chapter VIII activities and all other regional organizations' activities, and develop a structure for identifying regional security mechanisms; continue the desk-to-desk dialogues on conflict prevention between the United Nations and regional organizations on cross-cutting issues and extend such a mechanism to the AU; and increase consultations among regional organizations. The United Nations should improve and better coordinate African peacekeeping training initiatives, including through the development of regional centres for military and civilian aspects of conflict prevention and peace support, and the enhancement of the capacity of the AU and subregional organizations in the financial and administrative management of peacekeeping operations. To enhance the predictability, sustainability and flexibility of financing regional organizations undertaking peacekeeping under a UN mandate, an AU-UN panel would be set up within three months to make recommendations on support for regional organizations' peacekeeping operations.

In the field of disarmament and non-proliferation, the United Nations and intergovernmental, regional and subregional organizations should: intensify coordination and cooperation in strengthening national, regional and international capacities in implementing the Global Counter-Terrorism Strategy contained in Assembly resolution 60/288 [YUN 2006, p. 66]; and encourage regional and subregional organizations, in particular the AU, to enhance exchange of information and pursue joint planning and implementation of regional and subregional initiatives to address the issue of small arms and light weapons. On conflict prevention and mediation, the Secretary-General recalled his recommendation to strengthen DPA (see p. 47). With regard to peacebuilding support and post-conflict reconstruction, he recommended that the United Nations establish a standing collaborative working group to develop an agenda of consultations on linking UN peacebuilding processes and the Peacebuilding Commission with the work of regional organizations; and ensure, during the peacekeeping phase, that the foundations were laid for sustainable post-conflict peacebuilding, with a focus on strengthening the national reconciliation process and managing the economy. In the area of human rights, the Secretary-General recommended continuing support for establishing human rights components in peacekeeping and political missions, and implementing the provisions of Assembly resolution 61/296 [YUN 2007, p. 304] calling on the United Nations to assist in developing a strategy and policies to support the AU. On humanitarian action, he recommended the incorporation of protection of civilians in armed conflict through the development of an AU policy framework and guidance, and enhancing AU early warning methodology and systems through the development of a multirisk early warning tool.

The Council, in **resolution 1809(2008)** of 16 April (see p. 109), recognizing the need to enhance the predictability, sustainability and flexibility of financing regional organizations undertaking United Nations-mandated peacekeeping operations, welcomed the Secretary-General's proposal to set up within three months an AU-UN panel to consider ways of supporting such peacekeeping operations and lessons learned.

Conflict diamonds

Kimberley Process. At its 2008 session, the plenary meeting of the Kimberley Process (New Delhi, India, 3–6 November) reviewed the Kimberley Process Certification Scheme (KPCS), established in 2003 [YUN 2003, p. 55] to stop the trade in conflict diamonds from fuelling armed conflict, protect the legitimate diamond industry and ensure implementation of UN resolutions on trade in conflict diamonds. In accordance with General Assembly resolution 62/11 [YUN 2007, p. 48], India transmitted to the Secretary-General the report of the plenary meeting on behalf of the Chair of the Kimberley Process [A/63/560].

The plenary welcomed Mexico as a KPCS participant. In 2008, Congo resumed trade in rough diamonds, after having been readmitted to KPCS in 2007. As at 6 November 2008, the total number of KPCS participants stood at 49, representing 75 countries. Algeria, Bahrain, Burkina Faso, Cameroon, Cape Verde, Egypt, Gabon, Kuwait, Mali, Panama, the Philippines, Qatar and Swaziland had expressed interest in joining the Kimberley Process, while Burkina Faso and Panama confirmed their intention to do so. Venezuela voluntarily separated from the Kimberley Process for two years and ceased certifying diamonds for export. It retained the right to participate in Kimberley Process meetings and working groups, and the obligation to report on rough diamond production during that period. KPCS would continue to report on Venezuela's compliance with its minimum standards, and to support Venezuela in developing a plan to implement those standards and to fully reintegrate in KPCS.

Peer review visits were undertaken to five diamond producing and trading centres (Central African Republic, Guinea, Israel, Liberia, United Arab Emirates). The situation in Côte d'Ivoire continued to be monitored, and a joint UN-Kimberley Process mission in April confirmed the continued production of diamonds, particularly at the Bobi-Seguela site, and that Ivorian diamonds seemed to be effectively controlled and "taxed" by elements of the rebel movement Forces nouvelles. The Security Council, in **resolution 1842(2008)** of 29 October (see p. 194), renewed until 31 October 2009 the measures preventing importation by any State of rough diamonds from Côte d'Ivoire. The Kimberley Process would continue to pursue dialogue with Ivorian authorities regarding preparations for a certification scheme. The Kimberley Process and Ghana continued their constructive engagement. An update review mission concluded that Ghana had made significant progress in addressing weaknesses in internal controls, particularly with regard to the registration of miners and the collection of reliable production statistics. The Kimberley Process continued to mobilize technical assistance to assist Ghana in registering artisanal miners and providing accurate assessment of diamond production. It was also finalizing the footprinting (size frequency distribution diagram) exercise in respect of West African diamond-producing participants. Production footprints had been prepared for Côte d'Ivoire, Togo and Zimbabwe. Statistical protocols were developed to allow comparison of the export footprints with the participants' production footprint. Information technology linkage between participants to improve the quality of KPCS data was also initiated.

KPCS provided technical assistance and funding to develop participants' capacities to implement the Scheme. Kimberley Process participants, industry and civil society supported projects in Angola, the Central African Republic, Ghana, Guinea, Liberia, Sierra Leone and the United Republic of Tanzania. Funding was also received for specific activities, such as statistical training, satellite monitoring, and the participation of observers in peer review visits. KPCS developed guidelines that recommended interim measures in cases of serious non-compliance with its minimum requirements, listing the guiding principles for determining serious non-compliance and an indicative list of escalating measures, such as targeted statistical analysis, enhanced monitoring and additional verification measures, mobilization of technical assistance, and suspension of export and import operations. Rules and criteria for the selection of the Kimberley Process Vice-Chair, rules and procedures for readmission of former participants, and guiding principles on participation of guests of the Chair in the Kimberley Process were also developed. The Process was working on greater cooperation on implementation and enforcement of issues such as fake certificates, the handling of suspicious shipments, and infringements of KPCS.

GENERAL ASSEMBLY ACTION

On 11 December [meeting 67], the General Assembly adopted **resolution 63/134** [draft: A/63/L.52 & Add.1] without vote [agenda item 11].

The role of diamonds in fuelling conflict: breaking the link between the illicit transaction of rough diamonds and armed conflict as a contribution to prevention and settlement of conflicts

The General Assembly,

Recognizing that the trade in conflict diamonds continues to be a matter of serious international concern, which can be directly linked to the fuelling of armed conflict, the activities of rebel movements aimed at undermining or overthrowing legitimate Governments and the illicit traffic in and proliferation of armaments, especially small arms and light weapons,

Recognizing also the devastating impact of conflicts fuelled by the trade in conflict diamonds on the peace, safety and security of people in affected countries, and the systematic and gross human rights violations that have been perpetrated in such conflicts,

Noting the negative impact of such conflicts on regional stability and the obligations placed upon States by the Charter of the United Nations regarding the maintenance of international peace and security,

Recognizing, therefore, that continued action to curb the trade in conflict diamonds is imperative,

Recalling that the elimination of illicit diamonds from legitimate trade is the primary objective of the Kimberley Process,

Acknowledging that the diamond sector is an important catalyst for achieving poverty reduction and meeting the requirements of the Millennium Development Goals in producing countries,

Bearing in mind the positive benefits of the legitimate diamond trade to producing countries, and underlining the need for continued international action to prevent the problem of conflict diamonds from negatively affecting the trade in legitimate diamonds, which makes a critical contribution to the economies of many of the producing, exporting and importing States, especially developing States,

Noting that the vast majority of rough diamonds produced in the world are from legitimate sources,

Recalling the Charter and all the relevant resolutions of the Security Council related to conflict diamonds, and determined to contribute to and support the implementation of the measures provided for in those resolutions,

Recalling also Security Council resolution 1459(2003) of 28 January 2003, in which the Council strongly supported the Kimberley Process Certification Scheme as a valuable contribution against trafficking in conflict diamonds,

Welcoming the important contribution of the Kimberley Process, which was initiated by African diamond-producing countries,

Noting with satisfaction that the implementation of the Kimberley Process Certification Scheme continues to have a positive impact in reducing the opportunity for conflict diamonds to play a role in fuelling armed conflict and would help to protect legitimate trade and ensure the effective implementation of the relevant resolutions on trade in conflict diamonds,

Acknowledging that lessons learned from the Kimberley Process are useful for the work of the Peacebuilding Commission in its consideration of the countries included in its agenda, as appropriate,

Recalling its resolutions 55/56 of 1 December 2000, 56/263 of 13 March 2002, 57/302 of 15 April 2003, 58/290 of 14 April 2004, 59/144 of 15 December 2004, 60/182 of 20 December 2005, 61/28 of 4 December 2006 and 62/11 of 26 November 2007, in which it called for the development and implementation as well as a periodic review of proposals for a simple, effective and pragmatic international certification scheme for rough diamonds,

Welcoming, in this regard, the implementation of the Kimberley Process Certification Scheme in such a way as not to impede the legitimate trade in diamonds or impose an undue burden on Governments or industry, particularly smaller producers, nor hinder the development of the diamond industry,

Welcoming also the decision of forty-nine Kimberley Process Participants, representing seventy-five countries, including the twenty-seven members of the European Union represented by the European Commission, to address the problem of conflict diamonds by participating in the Process and implementing the Kimberley Process Certification Scheme,

Noting the consensual outcomes of the plenary meeting of the Kimberley Process, held in New Delhi from 3 to 6 November 2008,

Welcoming the important contributions made and that continue to be made by civil society and the diamond industry, in particular the World Diamond Council which represents all aspects of the diamond industry, to assist international efforts to stop the trade in conflict diamonds,

Welcoming also the voluntary self-regulation initiatives for the diamond industry announced by the World Diamond Council, and recognizing that a system of such voluntary self-regulation contributes, as described in the Interlaken Declaration of 5 November 2002 on the Kimberley Process Certification Scheme for Rough Diamonds, to ensuring the effectiveness of national systems of internal control for rough diamonds,

Noting with appreciation that the Kimberley Process has pursued its deliberations on an inclusive basis, involving concerned stakeholders, including producing, exporting and importing States, the diamond industry and civil society, as well as applicant States and international organizations,

Recognizing that State sovereignty should be fully respected and that the principles of equality, mutual benefits and consensus should be adhered to,

Recognizing also that the Kimberley Process Certification Scheme, which came into effect on 1 January 2003, will be credible only if all Participants have requisite national legislation coupled with effective and credible internal systems of control designed to eliminate the presence of conflict diamonds in the chain of producing, exporting and importing rough diamonds within their own territories, while taking into account that differences in production methods and trading practices, as well as differences in institutional controls thereof, may require different approaches to meeting minimum standards,

Welcoming the efforts of the Kimberley Process to elaborate new rules and procedural norms for regulating the activities of its working bodies, Participants and observers,

1. *Reaffirms its strong and continuing support* for the Kimberley Process Certification Scheme and the Kimberley Process as a whole;

2. *Recognizes* that the Kimberley Process Certification Scheme can help to ensure the effective implementation of relevant resolutions of the Security Council containing sanctions on the trade in conflict diamonds and act as a mechanism for the prevention of future conflicts, and calls for the full implementation of existing Council measures targeting the illicit trade in rough diamonds, particularly conflict diamonds which play a role in fuelling conflict;

3. *Also recognizes* the important contributions that the international efforts to address the problem of conflict diamonds, including the Kimberley Process Certification Scheme, have made to the settlement of conflicts and the consolidation of peace in Angola, Liberia and Sierra Leone;

4. *Notes* the decision of the General Council of the World Trade Organization of 15 May 2003 granting a waiver with respect to the measures taken to implement the Kimberley Process Certification Scheme, effective from 1 January 2003 to 31 December 2006, and the decision of the General Council of 17 November 2006 granting an extension of the waiver until 31 December 2012;

5. *Takes note* of the report of the Chair of the Kimberley Process submitted pursuant to resolution 62/11, and congratulates the participating Governments, the regional economic integration organization, the diamond industry and civil society organizations involved in the Process for contributing to the development, implementation and monitoring of the Kimberley Process Certification Scheme;

6. *Acknowledges* the progress made by Kimberley Process working groups, Participants and observers during 2008 in fulfilling the objectives set by the Chair to strengthen implementation of the peer review system, increase the transparency and accuracy of statistics, promote research into the traceability of diamonds, promote inclusiveness by broadening the level of involvement by both Governments and civil society in the Certification Scheme, foster a sense of ownership by Participants, improve information and communication flows and enhance the capacity of the Certification Scheme to respond to emerging challenges;

7. *Stresses* that the widest possible participation in the Kimberley Process Certification Scheme is essential, and encourages all Member States to contribute to the work of the Kimberley Process by seeking membership, participating actively in the Certification Scheme and complying with its undertakings;

8. *Welcomes* the admission in 2008 of Mexico to the Kimberley Process and the resumption of trade in rough diamonds by the Congo, and recognizes the increased involvement of civil society organizations, in particular those from producer countries, in the Process;

9. *Also welcomes* the guidelines endorsed by the New Delhi plenary meeting that recommend interim measures for serious non-compliance with Kimberley Process minimum requirements, set out the guiding principles for determination of serious non-compliance and include an indicative list of escalating measures, namely, targeted statistical analysis, enhanced monitoring and additional verification measures, mobilization of technical assistance, and suspension and resumption of export and import operations;

10. *Notes with satisfaction* that, in line with paragraph 14 of its resolution 62/11, a visit led by the representative of the Chair of the Kimberley Process was undertaken to the Bolivarian Republic of Venezuela, which helped to provide a better understanding of the challenges being experienced by the Bolivarian Republic of Venezuela in the diamond mining sector and led to the recommendation that the Process should continue to engage with the Bolivarian Republic of Venezuela, which has voluntarily separated from the

Kimberley Process Certification Scheme for a period of two years, and to assist and support the Bolivarian Republic of Venezuela in developing a plan of action to implement the minimum standards of the Certification Scheme and fully reintegrate into the Scheme;

11. *Notes with appreciation* the willingness of the Kimberley Process to support and provide technical assistance to those Participants experiencing temporary difficulties in complying with the requirements of the Kimberley Process Certification Scheme, and welcomes the recommendations in this regard of the Process plenary meeting held in New Delhi, which include a provision that such Participants would, if the Participation Committee so determined, retain membership and participate in the Process activities, and continue to be subject to all other obligations under the Certification Scheme;

12. *Notes with satisfaction* the systematization of the work of the Kimberley Process with respect to continuing to develop transparent and uniform rules and procedures, introducing a mechanism for consultations and coordination within the Process, and adoption by the New Delhi plenary meeting of the rules and criteria for selection of the Vice-Chair of the Process, rules and procedures for readmission of a former Process Participant, and guiding principles on participation of the guests of the Process Chair in the Process;

13. *Notes with appreciation* the cooperation of the Kimberley Process with the United Nations on the issue of diamonds from Côte d'Ivoire, by participating in a joint United Nations-Kimberley Process field mission to Côte d'Ivoire and by pursuing the monitoring of diamond activity in Côte d'Ivoire, welcomes plans by Côte d'Ivoire to re-establish Government control over diamond mining and trade, and encourages continued cooperation between the Process and the United Nations in tackling this issue, with the ultimate objective of meeting the preconditions for the lifting of United Nations sanctions on the trading of rough diamonds from Côte d'Ivoire;

14. *Acknowledges* the progress made by Ghana in 2008 in strengthening its internal controls in follow-up to the administrative decision on Ghana adopted by the plenary meeting of the Kimberley Process, held in Gaborone from 6 to 9 November 2006, and agrees that continued implementation of the action plan by Ghana would greatly enhance the effectiveness of the Process;

15. *Notes with satisfaction* the publication for the first time of Kimberley Process rough diamond trade and production sub-annual data for 2004 to 2007, welcomes the progress made towards the collection and submission of complete and accurate statistical reports on the production of and trade in rough diamonds, and encourages all of the Process Participants to continue to enhance the quality of data, and to respond promptly to Process analyses of these data;

16. *Also notes with satisfaction* the development, in line with paragraph 7 of its resolution 60/182 and paragraph 7 of its resolution 61/28, of "footprints", size-frequency distribution diagrams, that characterize the diamond production of Côte d'Ivoire, the Marange diamond field in Zimbabwe and Togo and the continued work undertaken for Ghana, and the development of statistical protocols to allow comparison of the export footprints with the established production footprint of the Participants;

17. *Notes with appreciation* the publication of a consolidated matrix of inventories of Participants engaged in artisanal alluvial diamond production and the continued efforts to follow up on the effective implementation of the Moscow declaration on improving internal controls over alluvial diamond production;

18. *Stresses* the importance of implementing the declaration on internal controls in diamond trading and manufacturing centres endorsed by the plenary meeting of the Kimberley Process, held in Brussels from 5 to 8 November 2007, and encourages all such centres to carry out effective enforcement measures, including those set out in the guidance on internal controls for Participants engaged in trading and manufacturing, as part of their own internal controls for ensuring adequate Government oversight over the trade in rough diamonds;

19. *Notes with appreciation* the assistance and capacity-building efforts extended by various donors, and encourages other donors to provide financial and technical expertise to Kimberley Process Participants to help them to develop tighter monitoring and control measures;

20. *Acknowledges with great appreciation* the important contribution that India, as Chair of the Kimberley Process in 2008, has made to the efforts to curb the trade in conflict diamonds, and takes note that the Process has selected Namibia as Chair and Israel as Vice-Chair of the Process for 2009;

21. *Requests* the Chair of the Kimberley Process to submit to the General Assembly at its sixty-fourth session a report on the implementation of the Process;

22. *Decides* to include in the provisional agenda of its sixty-fourth session the item entitled "The role of diamonds in fuelling conflict".

Strengthening the Department of Political Affairs in conflict prevention

Report of Secretary-General. The Secretary-General, in a report [A/62/521 & Corr.1] on revised estimates relating to the proposed programme budget for the biennium 2008–2009 under sections 1, 3, 28D and 35, related to the strengthening of DPA, stated that preventive diplomacy was a core function of the United Nations and was central to its role. The relevance of the Organization would be judged by how well that central role was performed. Within the United Nations, DPA had primary responsibility for carrying out preventive diplomacy and supporting the Secretary-General's good offices function. While there was strong demand to step up and systematize the Organization's work on prevention, prospects for success were slim unless the chronic under-resourcing of that strategic part of the Secretariat was redressed. The current level of resources for DPA constrained the Organization's ability to deliver on its mandates. The Secretary-General proposed to reconfigure the current structure to make DPA more field-oriented. The unsustainable trend for DPA towards increased responsibilities without an increase in human or financial resources had to be reversed. The growing demand for conflict prevention, preventive diplomacy and the Secretary-General's good offices, as well as the demands on the Department for political advice and a coordinating political role, had overstretched the Department's staff and leadership. Strengthening DPA to better support a more proactive United Nations in conflict prevention would require both additional resources and new ways of working when confronting potential conflict situations, particularly through greater mobility and presence in the field. It would also require improved management and oversight mechanisms.

The Secretary-General proposed: building the capability of the Department's regional Divisions to allow sufficient capacity for improved monitoring and analysis, effective policy formulation, rapid dispatch of assets to support early resolution of conflicts and support for the Secretary-General's good offices; strengthening its policy-planning capacity and mediation support function through the establishment of a Policy, Partnerships and Mediation Support Division to assist Member States on cross-cutting global issues such as transnational organized crime, corruption, democracy and terrorism; increasing the resources of the Electoral Assistance Division to cope with the demand for its services, and the increasing number and complexity of requests for technical assistance and advice; and supporting the Security Council with its expanding workload, as well as certain General Assembly committees, by providing for some Office of Internal Oversight Services positions to support the increased demands placed on the sanctions committees, under the Security Council Affairs Division. Other proposals included the establishment of a network of regional offices to assist Member States and regional organizations with their preventive diplomacy efforts, providing a more agile platform to support preventive diplomacy by the Special Envoys of the Secretary-General, strengthening relations with regional organizations, building local capacity and encouraging regional approaches to conflict prevention. Each office would work closely with UN missions, agencies and programmes, providing a localized hub for conflict prevention activities by the UN system and other regional partners. They would replace single country political missions, which had a more limited focus. Management, executive and oversight functions needed to be tightened by refocusing the work of the Office of the Under-Secretary-General and by reinforcing the capabilities of the Department's Executive Office.

The Secretary-General requested the Assembly to approve the establishment of 96 new posts and the reclassification of four posts under section 3, Political affairs; the establishment of five new posts and the reclassification of one post from D-1 to D-2 under section 1, Overall policymaking, direction and coordination, for the United Nations Liaison Office at Addis Ababa; and appropriate a total amount of $21,036,100, comprising $439,200 under section 1, Overall policymaking, direction and coordination, $14,276,100 under section 3, Political affairs, $4,184,700 under section 28D, Office of Central Support Services, and $2,136,100 under section 35, Staff assessment, offset by a corresponding amount under income section 1, Income from staff assessment, under the proposed programme budget for the biennium 2008–2009.

Report of ACABQ. In January [A/62/7/Add. 32], the Advisory Committee on Administrative and Budgetary Questions (ACABQ) recommended approval of the establishment of 56 additional posts, including the reclassification of four posts (one D-1 to D-2, one P-5 to D-1, one P-3 to P-4 and one P-2 to P-3) under section 3; the establishment of four additional posts, including the reclassification of one post from D-1 to D-2 under section 1, for the United Nations Liaison Office at Addis Ababa; and a reduction of $8,142,700 from the additional estimate of $21,036,100 proposed by the Secretary-General.

Communications. On 7 March [A/C.5/62/24], Antigua and Barbuda and Cuba transmitted to the Secretary-General a letter sent to the Under-Secretary-General for Political Affairs conveying the views of the Joint Coordination Committee (Group of 77 and China and the Non-Aligned Movement) on the Secretary-General's proposals for strengthening DPA. The Committee, while supporting some elements of the proposals, had important concerns. It was disappointed that the views, priorities and role of developing countries, including their contribution to conflict prevention and resolution, were not adequately reflected in the report. They had particular concerns regarding the establishment and nature of the proposed regional offices, stressing that those offices could only be established with the full support and consent of the host country and all Member States concerned, and with an appropriate mandate by the Assembly. A regional office could not have an extraterritorial mandate (i.e. a mandate extending beyond the countries of that region), and there was no uniform formula for the establishment of the regional offices. The Committee requested the Secretariat to issue a corrigendum to the report, reflecting the comments and concerns of the Member States.

On 12 March [A/C.5/62/25], the Secretary-General conveyed the clarifications to those concerns as provided by the Under-Secretary-General for Political Affairs, which he endorsed. Additional questions raised could be addressed through the Fifth Committee, and the Secretariat would provide information as required.

GENERAL ASSEMBLY ACTION

On 24 December [meeting 74], the General Assembly, on the recommendation of the Fifth (Administrative and Budgetary) Committee [A/63/648/Add.2], adopted **resolution 63/261** without vote [agenda item 118].

Strengthening of the Department of Political Affairs

The General Assembly,

Recalling its resolution 62/236 of 22 December 2007,

Having considered the report of the Secretary-General on the revised estimates under section 1, Overall policy-making, direction and coordination, section 3, Political affairs, section 28D, Office of Central Support Services, and section 35, Staff assessment, of the proposed programme budget for the biennium 2008–2009, relating to the strengthening of the Department of Political Affairs, the report of the Office of Internal Oversight Services on the audit of the management of special political missions by the Department of Political Affairs, the letter dated 7 March 2008 from the Permanent Representatives of Antigua and Barbuda and Cuba to the United Nations addressed to the Secretary-General, the letter dated 12 March 2008 from the Secretary-General to the Permanent Representatives of Antigua and Barbuda and Cuba to the United Nations and the related report of the Advisory Committee on Administrative and Budgetary Questions,

Reaffirming its rules of procedure,

Recalling the Regulations and Rules Governing Programme Planning, the Programme Aspects of the Budget, the Monitoring of Implementation and the Methods of Evaluation and the Financial Regulations and Rules of the United Nations,

Stressing the intergovernmental, multilateral and international character of the United Nations,

Reaffirming the role of the General Assembly and its relevant intergovernmental and expert bodies, within their respective mandates, in planning, programming, budgeting, monitoring and evaluation,

Recognizing that the prevention of armed conflict and the peaceful settlement of disputes are central to the mandate of the United Nations,

Recognizing also that preventive diplomacy is a core function of the United Nations and is central to the role of the Secretary-General and that the Department of Political Affairs has primary responsibility for carrying out preventive diplomacy and supporting the good offices function of the Secretary-General,

Recognizing further the important role of the good offices of the Secretary-General, including in the mediation of disputes,

1. *Takes note* of the report of the Secretary-General;

2. *Stresses* that any activity by the Department of Political Affairs related to preventive diplomacy and conflict resolution must be carried out in accordance with the principles of sovereignty, territorial integrity and political independence of States;

3. *Also stresses* that improvement in the capacity of the United Nations to prevent and resolve conflicts is a better investment than dealing with the cost of armed conflict and its aftermath;

4. *Recognizes* the important role women play in the area of preventive diplomacy;

5. *Also recognizes* that the root causes of armed conflict are multidimensional in nature, thus requiring a comprehensive and integrated approach to the prevention of armed conflict;

6. *Notes* that the objective of strengthening and rationalizing the Department of Political Affairs, including its supportive role regarding preventive diplomacy and resolution of conflict, is to improve the Department's effectiveness and efficiency in fulfilling its mandate;

7. *Reaffirms* that the Fifth Committee is the appropriate Main Committee of the General Assembly entrusted with responsibilities for administrative and budgetary matters;

8. *Also reaffirms* its role in carrying out a thorough analysis and approval of human and financial resources and policies, with a view to ensuring full, effective and efficient implementation of all mandated programmes and activities and the implementation of policies in this regard;

9. *Further reaffirms* its role with regard to the structure of the Secretariat, and stresses that proposals to amend the overall departmental structure, as well as the format of the programme budget and the biennial programme plan, are subject to its review and prior approval;

10. *Reaffirms* its resolution 55/231 of 23 December 2000, and requests the Secretary-General to ensure that in presenting the programme budget, expected accomplishments and indicators of achievement are included to measure achievements in the implementation of the programmes of the Organization and not those of individual Member States;

11. *Requests* the Secretary-General to explore potential synergies and complementarities among special political missions, where possible, in order to avoid duplication and overlap, bearing in mind the autonomous nature of each legislative mandate;

12. *Underlines* the continued importance of the role of the Secretary-General in ensuring, when appointing his special representatives and envoys, the highest standards of integrity, competency, impartiality and professionalism;

13. *Emphasizes* the sensitivity of the mandates of special political missions, and in this regard recalls Article 2, paragraph 7, of the Charter of the United Nations;

14. *Recalls* that the Secretary-General may nominate special representatives and envoys, and in this respect notes the intention of the Secretary-General to continuously consult with Member States concerned on these matters;

15. *Also recalls* the role of the Secretary-General as the Chief Administrative Officer of the Organization, in accordance with the provisions of Article 97 of the Charter;

16. *Reiterates* that the delegation of authority on the part of the Secretary-General should be in order to facilitate the better management of the Organization, but stresses that the overall responsibility for management of

the Organization rests with the Secretary-General as the Chief Administrative Officer;

17. *Also reiterates* the importance of strengthened accountability in the Organization and of ensuring greater accountability of the Secretary-General to Member States, inter alia, for the effective and efficient implementation of legislative mandates and the use of human and financial resources;

18. *Recalls* the letter dated 7 March 2008 from the Permanent Representatives of Antigua and Barbuda and Cuba to the United Nations addressed to the Secretary-General and the letter dated 12 March 2008 from the Secretary-General to the Permanent Representatives of Antigua and Barbuda and Cuba to the United Nations, stresses the strong concerns of some Member States contained therein, and requests the Secretary-General to ensure that there is sufficient knowledge within the Department of Political Affairs of the political situation in all regions and to abide strictly by the principles enshrined in the Charter;

19. *Requests* the Secretary-General, in this regard, to ensure that, in the submission of future budget documents, the narrative parts are based solely on factual information;

20. *Stresses* the importance of the role of the Department of Political Affairs in providing appropriate political guidance in the context of its involvement in United Nations trust funds to which it provides such guidance, in accordance with the principles enshrined in the Charter and the relevant resolutions of the General Assembly;

21. *Endorses* the conclusions and recommendations contained in the report of the Advisory Committee on Administrative and Budgetary Questions, subject to the provisions of the present resolution;

22. *Recalls* section V, paragraph 8, of its resolution 62/238 of 22 December 2007, takes note of the report of the Office of Internal Oversight Services and stresses the importance of its full implementation;

23. *Emphasizes* the importance of the integration of effort, policy coherence and efficiency in the use of resources;

24. *Reiterates its request* to the Secretary-General to address systemic issues that hamper good management of the Organization, including the work processes and procedures, and in that context stresses that structural change is no substitute for managerial improvement;

25. *Requests* the Secretary-General to identify, where possible, means to achieve greater complementarities and synergies between the Department of Political Affairs and other departments and offices of the United Nations Secretariat as well as other relevant actors of the United Nations system;

26. *Stresses* the importance of clear reporting lines and accountability between the special political missions and Headquarters;

27. *Decides* to establish the Middle East and West Asia Division and, in this regard, not to divide it into sections and units, and stresses the need to continue the current arrangement;

28. *Recalls* all United Nations resolutions related to the situation in the Middle East and the question of Palestine, and notes the responsibilities of the Middle East and West Asia Division in this regard;

29. *Decides* that the Asia and Pacific Division shall be composed of two sections, as follows:

(*a*) Asia-Pacific I Section (Central, South and North-East Asian countries);

(*b*) Asia-Pacific II Section (South-East Asia and the Pacific countries);

30. *Also decides* that the Americas Division shall comprise four sections, as follows:

(*a*) North America;

(*b*) Central America;

(*c*) The Caribbean;

(*d*) South America;

31. *Stresses* the importance of the Department of Political Affairs continuing to pay adequate attention to the situation in Haiti in support of the Department of Peacekeeping Operations, together with the Department of Economic and Social Affairs, the Economic Commission for Latin America and the Caribbean and other relevant United Nations entities;

32. *Decides* that the Caribbean Section shall be headed at the P-5 level;

33. *Stresses* the importance of the Department of Political Affairs continuing to pay adequate attention to regional and subregional organizations;

34. *Decides* not to establish a Policy, Partnerships and Mediation Support Division and not to approve the reclassification of a post for a director of that division from the D-1 to the D-2 level, and requests the Secretary-General to resubmit his proposals, taking fully into account the mandate of the Department of Political Affairs as stipulated in the strategic framework;

35. *Also decides* not to establish a Special Political Missions Support Unit until a report on the management and administration of special political missions by the Department of Political Affairs is considered by the General Assembly;

36. *Stresses* the need for the Secretary-General to consider the status of the existing field presence of the United Nations entities engaged in promoting peace and security, taking into account their respective mandates, before proposing the establishment of regional offices;

37. *Recalls* paragraph 23 of the report of the Advisory Committee on Administrative and Budgetary Questions, and stresses that the establishment of any future regional political affairs office requires the concurrence of all concerned Member States covered by the relevant mandate approved by the appropriate legislative bodies;

38. *Encourages* the Secretary-General to continue to regularly brief Member States on issues related to the work of the Department of Political Affairs and to keep ensuring appropriate interaction between the Department and the principal bodies of the Organization;

39. *Requests* the Secretary-General to entrust the Office of Internal Oversight Services with conducting an audit of the management of special political missions by the Department of Political Affairs, as a follow-up to the report of the Office, and to submit a report on the audit to the General Assembly for consideration at the main part of its sixty-fourth session;

40. *Also requests* the Secretary-General to submit a comprehensive report to the General Assembly at its sixty-fifth session on the efficiency and effectiveness of the new structure in the implementation of mandates as well as programmatic delivery and improvements in the administrative and management processes and efficiency gains;

41. *Decides* to establish the posts as contained in the annex to the present resolution.

Annex

Department of Political Affairs: posts to be established under the programme budget for the biennium 2008–2009

Organizational unit		*Number of posts*	*Post level*
United Nations Liaison Office	New	3	1 P-5, 1 P-3, 1 LL
	Reclassification		1 D-1 to D-2
Office of the Under-Secretary-General	Reclassification		1 P-3 to P-4
	Redeployment		D-2 from Americas Division
Office of the Assistant Secretary-General (Africa)	New	1	1 P-4
Africa I Division	New	8	3 P-4, 2 P-3, 1 P-2, 2 GS (OL)
Africa II Division	New	6	1 P-3, 4 P-2, 1 GS (OL)
Middle East and West Asia Division	New	5	1 P-5, 1 P-4 (Iraq), 2 P-3, 1 P-2
Asia and Pacific Division	New	4	3 P-3, 1 P-2
Americas Division	New	3	1 P-5, 2 P-2
	Redeployment		D-2 to the Office of the Under-Secretary-General
Europe Division	New	1	1 P-4 (Cyprus)
	Reclassification		1 D-1 to D-2
Mediation Support Unit	New	7	1 P-4, 3 P-3, 2 P-2, 1 GS (OL)
Electoral Assistance Division	New	8	1 P-5, 3 P-4, 4 GS (OL)
	Reclassification		1 P-2 to P-3
Security Council Affairs Division	New	2	2 P-2
Executive Office	New	1	1 P-4
	Reclassification		1 P-5 to D-1
	Total	**49**	**2 D-2, 1 D-1, 3 P-5, 12 P-4, 12 P-3, 12 P-2, 8 GS (OL), 1 LL**

Abbreviations: GS (OL), General Service (Other Level); LL, Local level.

Peacemaking and peacebuilding

Post-conflict peacebuilding

Post-conflict stabilization

On 20 May [meeting 5895], the Security Council, at the United Kingdom's request, considered the issue of post-conflict peacebuilding, in particular post-conflict stabilization: peace after war. It had before it a concept paper on the subject submitted by the United Kingdom [S/2008/291], which sought to identify the challenges facing the international community in stabilizing countries recovering from conflict and delivering sustainable peace. It stated that nearly 30 per cent of conflicts that ended through negotiated settlements restarted within five years, often because the international community did not get its act together in the critical period immediately following a ceasefire and peace agreement. At that point, crucial needs had to be met, including rapid implementation of the peace agreement to maintain the commitment of the parties, re-establishment of stability and the rule of law, and a demonstrable improvement in the lives of local people. The international community needed to support national and local State institutions in taking responsibility for the recovery effort, but their efforts were often too little, too late and too fragmented. Three gaps were identified that hampered international efforts to help countries emerging from conflict to stabilize: leadership and how to ensure that the actors operated effectively and coherently, building legitimate and competent national ownership and capacity as quickly as possible; putting in place rapidly deployable and skilled civilian capacity; and the provision of more rapid and flexible funding.

The Secretary-General, in his address to the Council, said that lessons from many countries demonstrated that, while each context was different, there were three common and immediate priorities to be addressed: establishing viable political processes to buttress peace agreements and to put in place legitimate national authorities; restoring security and the rule of law, including early development of accountable security services and justice systems; and delivering immediate benefits to the affected population and creating conditions for longer-term development. To strengthen the collective response in the immediate aftermath of conflict and deliver on those priorities, the Organization needed to be coherent and put in place structures, planning and monitoring processes to support that effort throughout the transition to longer-term peacebuilding. Coordination and clarity of leadership were critical to ensuring that each partner brought its distinctive strength to the collective effort. The United Nations also needed sufficient capacity and expertise. The Secretary-General's Special Representatives should be empowered to lead on the ground, including having the means to identify strategic priorities, elaborate plans and mobilize funds with others, in particular development partners. The creation of the Office of Rule of Law and Security Institutions in DPKO reflected the commitment to a team approach to upholding the rule of law, security sector reform and respect for human rights, but there remained a shortage of judges, prison wardens, State administrators and managers—particularly those with knowledge of the countries and systems in which the Organization operated. Not only should they be well equipped when deployed, but should also have start-up funding at their disposal. The Organization had to do better in delivering early peace dividends by scaling up relief and development capacities to enable national authorities to pay their civil servants, restoring agricultural life and initiating employment programmes. Ultimately, all of that depended on early and flexible funding. Bold and innovative steps were required to meet critical priority needs. To facilitate rapid delivery in the earliest phase, the international community should explore approaches such as a common start-up fund. Many of those issues had been identified by the Peacebuilding Commission, which had a key role to play in supporting national actors in achieving their long-term objectives for sustainable peace and development.

The representative of the World Bank said that over the previous 15 years, the World Bank had expanded its work on conflict and fragility, both operationally and analytically, focusing more on peacebuilding, State-building, institutional reforms and partnerships. The Bank had approved a new State-building and peacebuilding fund to address the needs of State and local governance and peacebuilding in fragile situations, with the aim to complement the UN Peacebuilding Fund and other efforts. It had commissioned applied research in areas such as conflict and development and natural resources and conflict, in collaboration with renowned research institutions. Overcoming the problems of countries coming out of conflict or seeking to avoid the breakdown of the State was crucial to the Bank's development mission. With regard to more rapid and flexible funding, large-scale post-conflict multi-donor trust funds could play a critical role during the reconstruction process, as the Afghanistan Reconstruction Trust Fund and the Trust Fund for Timor-Leste had done. The Bank believed that the fiduciary principles accord being prepared by the United Nations Development Group and the Bank would significantly improve the administration of such trust funds and deliver results more rapidly. To be strategic, large-scale post-conflict trust funds should be built upon post-conflict needs assessments, transitional results matrices and sector analysis, but they did not always cater to the start-up phase. A number of other funds, such as the Peacebuilding Fund, could cover that phase without the need for a separate assessment.

SECURITY COUNCIL ACTION

On 20 May [meeting 5895], following consultations among Security Council members, the President made statement **S/PRST/2008/16** on behalf of the Council:

> The Security Council recalls its primary responsibility for the maintenance of international peace and security and emphasizes the critical importance of post-conflict peacebuilding in laying the foundation for sustainable peace and development after the scourge of war.
>
> The Council recognizes that supporting States to recover from conflict and build sustainable peace is a major challenge facing the international community, and that an effective response requires political, security, humanitarian and development activities to be integrated and coherent, including in the first phase of integrated mission planning.
>
> The Council emphasizes the importance of national ownership and the primary responsibility of national authorities emerging from conflict for peacebuilding and sustainable development, expresses its intention to support those efforts and encourages other actors to do the same.
>
> The Council recalls its resolution 1645(2005) and welcomes the work of the Peacebuilding Commission in advising on the coordination of international peacebuilding activities and resources, and expresses its support for enhancing the role of the Peacebuilding Commission, the Peacebuilding Support Office and the Peacebuilding Fund.
>
> The Council recognizes that, in particular in the immediate aftermath of conflict, affected countries have urgent needs including, but not limited to, the re-establishment of the institutions of government, disarmament, demobilization and reintegration of armed forces, security sector reform, transitional justice, reconciliation, re-establishing the rule of law and respect for human rights and economic revitalization. The Council underlines that civilian expertise in post-conflict peacebuilding is essential in helping to meet these needs.
>
> The Council encourages efforts to address the urgent need for rapidly deployable civilian expertise and stresses that the critical role for such expertise is working in cooperation with national authorities to strengthen national capacities.
>
> The Council highlights the need for the United Nations to play a leading role in the field in coordinating international efforts in post-conflict situations. The Council stresses that coordination between national authorities and others involved in longer-term reconstruction and development, including organs of the United Nations system in accordance with their respective mandates, the international financial institutions, as well as with civil society and the business sector, is vital for the success of United Nations and international engagement in post-conflict situations.
>
> The Council stresses the need to ensure that finance is available from the outset for recovery and peacebuilding activities to meet immediate needs, and to lay a solid foundation for longer-term reconstruction and development.
>
> The Council reaffirms the role of regional organizations in the prevention, management and resolution of conflicts in accordance with Chapter VIII of the Charter of the United Nations, and the need to strengthen the capacity of regional organizations in helping countries to recover from conflict.
>
> The Council encourages the Secretary-General, the Peacebuilding Commission, international and regional organizations and Member States to consider how to support national efforts in affected countries to secure a sustainable peace more rapidly and effectively, includ-

ing in the areas of coordination, civilian deployment capabilities and financing. The Council invites the Secretary-General to provide advice within 12 months to the relevant United Nations organs on how best to take forward these issues within the United Nations system and, taking into consideration the views of the Peacebuilding Commission, how to coordinate peacebuilding activities and encourage the mobilization and most effective use of resources for urgent peacebuilding needs.

Communication. In response to the Council's request to advise relevant UN bodies on how to take forward the issues pertaining to securing sustainable peace, the Secretary-General, in a 19 September letter [A/63/374-S/2008/620] to the Peacebuilding Commission Chairperson, indicated his intention to dedicate the requisite efforts and capacities towards that end. In that regard, he had appointed the Assistant Secretary-General for Peacebuilding Support, Jane Holl Lute, to coordinate the exercise, indicate the appropriate timing for the Commission's contribution to that exercise, and represent him at all related Commission deliberations. He hoped that by addressing critical gaps in the UN response to post-conflict situations, the Commission's advisory role would assume greater significance for all UN and non-UN operational activities in the countries concerned.

Disarmament, demobilization and reintegration

Special Committee on Peacekeeping Operations consideration. The Special Committee on Peacekeeping Operations, at its 2008 substantive session (New York, 10 March–4 April and 3 July) [A/62/19], requested DPKO to ensure that disarmament, demobilization and reintegration (DDR) programmes were tailored to the specific context, carried out within a broad peacebuilding strategy, including institution-building, and consistent with the host country's national strategies. Together with other UN partners, it should ensure that DDR programmes were developed in line with the integrated DDR standards. The Special Committee noted the Secretariat's efforts to provide support and guidance to DDR programmes in the field, and in piloting integrated DDR units, with the intention of reviewing lessons learned from those units. The Special Committee requested a briefing on progress made on the implementation of DDR standards and programmes, as well as on the activities of the inter-agency working group on those issues. It recognized that the reintegration of ex-combatants was especially challenging and should be planned from the outset in conjunction with disarmament and demobilization programmes, as well as socio-economic development and job creation. It encouraged the inter-agency working group to further develop integrated DDR standards on assessment, planning and the implementation of social and economic reintegration programmes, and called upon donors to provide long-term, timely and sustained support to DDR programmes, ensuring that sufficient funds were allocated to the entire process. The Special Committee stressed the importance of ensuring that all women and children associated with armed forces and groups were included in DDR programmes, and reiterated the importance of including special measures to ensure the early release of children from armed groups and to prevent their re-recruitment.

Other peacebuilding issues

Special Committee on Peacekeeping Operations consideration. The Special Committee on Peacekeeping Operations, at its 2008 substantive session [A/62/19], reaffirmed the need for DPKO to plan and conduct UN peacekeeping activities in such a manner as to facilitate post-conflict peacebuilding, the prevention of recurrence of armed conflicts and progress towards sustainable peace and development. The Special Committee underlined the importance of coordination between DPKO, the Peacebuilding Support Office, UN funds, programmes and agencies and non-UN partners in peacebuilding efforts. It emphasized the need for a coherent and coordinated approach, building on the strengths of various actors, including UN bodies. The Special Committee underlined the need to formulate peacebuilding strategies and programmes that were integrated with host-nation strategies and programmes to ensure national ownership, and recommended that DPKO explore opportunities for partnerships in post-conflict situations with international financial institutions, such as the World Bank and the International Monetary Fund, and regional arrangements, such as the European Union, with a view to establishing effective cooperation.

The Special Committee underlined the role of the Peacebuilding Commission in developing integrated peacebuilding strategies and marshalling resources for their implementation, ensuring fulfilment of mutual commitments on the part of stakeholders, and promoting dialogue on cross-cutting peacebuilding issues and lessons learned. It welcomed the establishment of inter-agency coordination mechanisms to ensure coordination among UN actors involved in peacebuilding, and encouraged regular interaction among UN partners and with Member States to increase the sharing of knowledge and best practices. It requested DPKO to ensure that lessons learned in the transition from UN peacekeeping operations to integrated offices were applied elsewhere.

The Special Committee recognized that creating and sustaining stability in a post-conflict environment required that the causes of the conflict be addressed and that local rule-of-law capacities be established from the beginning of a UN peacekeeping operation and strengthened. Recognizing the need for greater clarity and specificity in UN peacekeeping mandates on rule-of-law issues, it requested that DPKO ensure that rule-of-law and transitional justice were integrated into the planning of peacekeeping operations. The Special Committee welcomed the progress made in assessing lessons learned and options for rule-of-law strategies in the field for ongoing and future UN peacekeeping operations. It welcomed the development of guidance material for operational rule-of-law issues, and requested the Secretariat to brief Member States whenever guidance material was initiated and to provide information on progress. It called upon DPKO to ensure cooperation and coordination among all mission components in the context of rule of law, underlining the importance of a holistic and coherent UN approach.

The General Assembly, in **resolution 63/128** of 11 December (see p. 1450), decided to include in the provisional agenda of its sixty-sixth (2011) session the item "Rule of law and transitional justice in conflict and post-conflict situations".

Peacebuilding Commission

In accordance with Security Council resolutions 1645(2005) and 1646(2005) [YUN 2005, p. 94] and General Assembly resolution 60/180 [ibid.], the Peacebuilding Commission submitted a June report [A/63/92-S/2008/417] on its second session for the period from 23 June 2007 to 22 June 2008. During the session, the Commission consolidated its achievements in Burundi and Sierra Leone and instituted a joint monitoring and tracking mechanism to allow it to review progress in those two countries. It was able to apply some of the lessons learned in the two countries and to build some innovations into the new Guinea-Bissau process, such as dispatching a field mission by the Chair of the Guinea-Bissau configuration, immediately following the country's referral to the Commission and the adoption of a two-track approach on the use of the Peacebuilding Fund. Those initiatives were observed in all configurations and demonstrated the Commission's ability to provide a flexible response as the situation warranted. While progress had been achieved in its existing configurations, the evolving challenges before the Commission required additional and targeted efforts by its members, partners and relevant actors. The Commission would chart the way forward in its engagement with the countries on its agenda and in further refining its role and added value.

The Commission's Working Group on Lessons Learned, at eight informal meetings, focused on the lessons and good practices associated with: the design and monitoring of peacebuilding strategic frameworks in fragile States; constraints placed on fiscal capacities in post-conflict countries; the challenges to local governance and decentralization in post-war contexts; opportunities for enhancing women's participation in peacebuilding; promotion of justice during transition; risks from failing to address internal displacement in post-war settings; and the interplay between the environment, natural resources, conflict and peacebuilding. The Working Group targeted its findings and policy recommendations at the work of the country-specific configurations. In June, the Working Group reviewed the major principles and best practices collected to date within the broader peacebuilding perspective, and its Chair reported to the Organizational Committee on the findings.

To provide integrated strategies for peacebuilding, the Commission continued to pay attention to the countries under its consideration and to support national efforts in the areas of dialogue, reconciliation, capacity-building, institutional reforms, economic recovery and human rights. It intended to enhance its standing by building on its accomplishments and by consolidating efforts in the countries under its consideration so as to minimize the risk of their lapse or relapse into conflict. It would refine the Integrated Peacebuilding Strategy concept, as well as options for future engagement, tailored to the specific country situations. With the assistance of the Peacebuilding Support Office, it would research support for peacebuilding activities in the countries under its consideration. In that context, it noted the need for the Secretariat to support the mapping exercise on peacebuilding activities in those countries, and invited all stakeholders to provide information to the Peacebuilding Support Office.

The Commission, at its first informal ambassadorial-level retreat (18–19 January), discussed the added value of the Commission in addressing peacebuilding challenges and gaps in the overall peace continuum and the development of an understanding on the way forward at the conceptual, methodological and strategic levels. It agreed to continue the peacebuilding strategy and policy discussion to strengthen its capacity to implement its mandates and enhance impact on the ground.

In terms of marshalling resources and enhancing coordination, the Commission acknowledged the importance of official development assistance and trade and investment in post-conflict countries, and was encouraged that several bilateral Commission partners had increased their commitments towards countries under consideration or initiated a new engagement. It would continue to develop methods for mobilizing international and domestic resources and related instruments, such as the early mapping exercise and systematic monitoring and tracking mechanisms. It would also strengthen its involvement in the mobilization of non-financial resources, and cooperation with the World Bank, the International Monetary Fund, regional development banks and regional or subregional organizations in addressing the specific needs of countries by building on expertise within the United Nations and other organizations. The Commission would create closer strategic ties between its engagements and the use of the Peacebuilding Fund and explore ways to engage in the General Assembly's review of the Fund's terms of reference.

As for enhancing collaboration and outreach, the Commission Chairperson would continue to hold regular meetings with the Presidents of UN principal organs and the Secretary-General, and keep the Organizational Committee informed of those discussions. The Commission would continue to promote implementation of Integrated Peacebuilding Strategies and seek support of relevant actors to that effect. To enhance its convening role, the Commission would encourage inputs from Member States, international and regional organizations and civil society, and disseminate the outcome of its work and lessons learned, including through its website, the Peacebuilding Community of Practice and the Peacebuilding Initiative project of the Program on Humanitarian Policy and Conflict Research.

On 25 April, Côte d'Ivoire's request for placement on the Commission's agenda was conveyed to the Security Council for consideration. The request was also brought to the attention of the Assembly, the Economic and Social Council and the Secretary-General.

During the year, the Commission carried out activities relevant to countries on its agenda: Burundi (see p. 152), the Central African Republic (see p. 158), Guinea-Bissau (see p. 228) and Sierra Leone (see p. 214).

Organizational Committee

The Peacebuilding Commission's Organizational Committee held formal meetings on 12, 19 and 23 June [PBC/2/OC/SR.6, PBC/2/OC/SR.7 & Add.1]. The Committee discussed at its first meeting the letter from the Security Council President conveying the Council's acceptance of the request by the Central African Republic that the country be placed on the Commission's agenda and inviting the Commission to advise it on the situation there. At subsequent meetings, the Committee considered the Commission's revised draft report on its second session. The Committee also held informal meetings on 16 January, 19 February, 24 March, 17 April, 13 May, 2, 12 and 19 June, 15 September, 29 October, 19 November and 17 December. Among the subjects discussed were: the role of the private sector in peacebuilding; harmonizing Peacebuilding Commission and Peacebuilding Fund activities; forging synergies for peacebuilding; the construction of capable States in Africa, with reports from the task force on the private sector and the Working Group on Lessons Learned; cooperation with the United Nations Development Programme (UNDP); employment/income generation and private sector development in post-conflict countries; and preparations for the review of the terms of reference of the Peacebuilding Fund and for the Secretary-General's report on post-conflict peacebuilding and early recovery.

The Committee considered letters from the Commission Chairperson and Acting Chairperson of 1 February [PBC/2/OC/9] inviting a number of States, UN agencies and intergovernmental bodies to participate in the Guinea-Bissau configuration, and of 24 March [PBC/2/OC/10] concerning the participation of Benin in that configuration; letters of 30 June [PBC/3/OC/5], 20 August [PBC/3/OC/6] and 9 September [PBC/3/OC/7] concerning the participation of States and organizations in the Central African configuration; letters of 27 June [PBC/3/OC/3] concerning the participation of Norway in the Burundi configuration and of 17 July [PBC/3/OC/2] concerning the election of Sweden as Chair of that configuration; and letters of 17 June [PBC/2/OC/13] concerning the participation of Burkina Faso in the Sierra Leone configuration, and of 27 June [PBC/3/OC/4] on the participation of Italy in the Guinea-Bissau and Sierra Leone configurations.

Organizational Committee membership

Security Council. On 3 January [A/62/684-S/2008/84 & Corr.1], the Security Council President informed the Secretary-General that, following informal consultations conducted on the same date, the Council had selected Belgium and South Africa to participate in the Organizational Committee for a term of one year, until the end of 2008.

Economic and Social Council. On 14 January, the Economic and Social Council re-elected Brazil to the Organizational Committee until 22 June (**decision 2008/201 A**). On 20 June, the Council extended until 11 July the terms of office of Angola, Brazil, the Czech Republic, Guinea-Bissau, Indonesia, Luxembourg and Sri Lanka (**decision 2008/201 D**). On 11 and 16 July, it further extended those terms of office until 31 December (**decision 2008/201 E**).

ECONOMIC AND SOCIAL COUNCIL ACTION

On 19 December [meeting 47], the Economic and Social Council adopted **resolution 2008/38** [draft: E/2008/L.7/Rev.1] without vote [agenda item 1].

Membership of the Economic and Social Council on the Organizational Committee of the Peacebuilding Commission

The Economic and Social Council,

Recalling General Assembly resolution 60/180 of 20 December 2005 and Security Council resolution 1645(2005) of 20 December 2005, concurrently establishing the Peacebuilding Commission,

Recalling also, in particular, paragraphs 12 *(b)*, 13 and 17 of General Assembly resolution 60/180 and Security Council resolution 1645(2005), establishing the institutional relationship between the Economic and Social Council and the Peacebuilding Commission,

Recalling further its resolution 2006/3 of 8 May 2006 on the membership of the Council on the Organizational Committee of the Peacebuilding Commission,

Recalling General Assembly resolution 63/145 of 18 December 2008, in which the Assembly, inter alia, invited other bodies with members elected to the Organizational Committee of the Peacebuilding Commission to adjust the term of office of their respective members so that the term of office of all members of the Organizational Committee could start on 1 January instead of 23 June,

Recognizing the important role to be performed by the Peacebuilding Commission towards recovery, reintegration and reconstruction in countries emerging from conflict, particularly in Africa,

Recalling that due consideration is to be given to countries that have experienced post-conflict recovery in the composition of the Organizational Committee of the Peacebuilding Commission,

1. *Decides* that, starting in 2009, the two-year term of office of the members of the Economic and Social Council elected to the Organizational Committee of the Peacebuilding Commission shall begin on 1 January, instead of on 23 June, with the possibility, as applicable, of their sharing the term within the concerned regional group for the seats allocated to it, subject to the concurrence of the Council;

2. *Also decides* that the distribution of the seven seats allocated to the Economic and Social Council on the Organizational Committee of the Peacebuilding Commission shall be as follows:

(a) One seat for each of the five regional groups, namely, African States, Asian States, Eastern European States, Latin American and Caribbean States and Western European and other States;

(b) In the election of members of the Economic and Social Council to the Organizational Committee whose term of office shall start on 1 January 2009, the two remaining seats shall be allocated to the regional group of African States;

3. *Further decides* that the established practice of the Economic and Social Council regarding members elected to its subsidiary bodies who are not able to complete their term of office shall apply to members elected to the Organizational Committee by the Council.

Also on 19 December, the Council elected Algeria, El Salvador, Guinea-Bissau, Luxembourg, Morocco, Poland and the Republic of Korea to a term of office on the Committee, beginning on 1 January 2009, of two years or until the expiration of their membership in the Council, whichever was earlier (**decision 2008/201 G**).

General Assembly. On 20 June, the General Assembly decided, as an interim measure, to extend the term of office of the members of the Assembly on the Organizational Committee, namely, Burundi, Chile, Egypt, El Salvador and Fiji, which was due to expire on 22 June, until 11 July (**decision 62/419 A**). On 11 July, the Assembly decided, as an interim measure, to further extend the term of office the members of the Assembly on the Committee until 31 December (**decision 62/419 B**).

GENERAL ASSEMBLY ACTION

On 18 December [meeting 70], the General Assembly adopted **resolution 63/145** [draft: A/63/L.58] without vote [agenda item 104 *(b)*].

Election by the General Assembly of seven members of the Organizational Committee of the Peacebuilding Commission: term of office

The General Assembly,

Recalling its resolution 60/180 and Security Council resolution 1645(2005), both of 20 December 2005, in which the General Assembly and the Security Council concurrently operationalized the decision by the 2005 World Summit to establish the Peacebuilding Commission as an intergovernmental advisory body,

Recalling in particular paragraphs 4 *(a)* to *(e)* and 5 of the above-mentioned resolutions setting out the arrangements for the composition of the Organizational Committee of the Peacebuilding Commission,

Recalling its resolution 60/261 of 8 May 2006 on the arrangements for the election by the General Assembly of seven members of the Organizational Committee of the Peacebuilding Commission,

Recalling also General Assembly decision 62/419 B of 11 July 2008, whereby the term of office of the members of the General Assembly on the Organizational Committee of the Peacebuilding Commission due to expire on 22 June 2008 was extended until 31 December 2008,

1. *Decides* that, beginning with the election to be held during the sixty-third session, the term of office of the members of the General Assembly on the Organizational Committee of the Peacebuilding Commission shall begin on 1 January instead of 23 June;

2. *Also decides* that the term of office of the two members of the General Assembly on the Organizational Committee of the Peacebuilding Commission due to expire on 22 June 2009, namely Georgia and Jamaica, shall be extended until 31 December 2009;

3. *Invites* other bodies with members on the Organizational Committee of the Peacebuilding Commission that have not yet done so to adjust the term of office of their respective members so that the term of office of all members of the Organizational Committee can start on 1 January.

On 22 December, the Assembly elected Benin, Chile, South Africa, Thailand and Uruguay as members of the Committee for a two-year term beginning on 1 January 2009 to fill the vacancies occurring on the expiration of the terms of office of Burundi, Chile, Egypt, El Salvador and Fiji (**decision 63/415**).

Troop and financial contributors. On 4 April [A/62/795], Ghana informed the General Assembly President that, on the basis of informal consultations held on 26 March, the top 10 contributing countries of military personnel and civilian police had selected Bangladesh, India, Pakistan, Nepal and Nigeria to serve on the Organizational Committee for a two-year term starting on 23 June.

On 30 April [A/62/825], the United States, as facilitator of the group of 10 leading financial contributors to the United Nations, informed the Assembly President that Canada, Germany, Japan, the Netherlands and Sweden, from among the 10, would serve for a second term on the Organizational Committee. On 18 December [A/63/632], the United States informed the Secretary-General that the group had decided to extend the term of the five members by six months, from 23 June to 31 December 2010.

On 20 June, the Assembly was informed that the term of office of the members of the troop-contributing countries on the Commission's Organizational Committee, which was due to expire on 22 June, had been extended until 11 July (**decision 62/419 A**). On 11 July, the Assembly was informed, by a letter dated 10 July to the President of the General Assembly, that the term of office of the current members of the troop-contributing countries on the Organizational Committee had been extended until 31 December (**decision 62/419 B**).

On 19 December [A/63/631], Ghana, referring to its 10 July letter confirming that Bangladesh, India, Nepal, Nigeria and Pakistan would represent the top 10 troop-contributing countries on the Committee, stated that it was Ghana's understanding that the question of allocation of regional seats in the General Assembly and the Economic and Social Council in respect of Committee membership had been resolved, thus paving the way for the election of new members from those bodies by 22 December. It therefore informed the Secretary-General that it had been decided that the term of office of the five countries from the troop-contributing country category would be from 1 January 2009 until 31 December 2009.

Financing of Peacebuilding Commission field missions

In 2007, the Commission's Organizational Committee considered the question of the financing of field missions of the Commission [YUN 2007, p. 54] and mandated its Chairman [A/62/493] to inform the Secretary-General of its request that the agenda item of the General Assembly's sixty-second session entitled "Report of the Peacebuilding Commission" be also allocated to the Fifth Committee for the sole purpose of considering the question of financing field missions of the Commission.

To facilitate the Fifth Committee's review, the Secretary-General submitted a January 2008 note [A/62/670] containing preliminary estimates of field visits to be undertaken by the Commission in 2008 and 2009. It was anticipated that visits would be undertaken to each of the three countries under consideration, in addition to one country in Asia and one in the Americas. Given the potential increase in the number of countries on the Commission's agenda, the Assembly might wish to consider more stable funding for those visits. The preliminary cost estimate was $676,300 for the 2008–2009 biennium. Any future requirements would be considered in the context of the proposed programme budget for the relevant biennium.

The Advisory Committee on Administrative and Budgetary Questions (ACABQ), in a February report [A/62/7/Add.33], recommended that the Assembly concur with the Secretary-General's proposal. The Assembly did so in section II of **resolution 62/245** of 3 April (see p. 1551).

Peacebuilding Fund

In response to General Assembly resolution 60/287 [YUN 2006, p. 58], the Secretary-General submitted the second annual report [A/63/218-S/2008/522 & Corr.1] on the Peacebuilding Fund, established in 2006 [ibid.] as a mechanism for extending critical support at the early stages of a peace process. The report provided an update on the Fund's activities and achievements from 1 July 2007 to 30 June 2008, and highlighted the achievements and emerging lessons that required the attention of the UN system in order to enhance its effectiveness as a strategic instrument for consolidating peace in post-conflict countries.

As at 30 June, the Fund had received pledges of $269.9 million from 44 donors, a $43 million (19 per cent) increase over the 2007 figure, exceeding the $250 million funding target. Of that amount, $238.5 million had been received. The top eight contributors to the Fund were Sweden ($42.3 million), the United Kingdom ($36 million), Norway ($32.1 million), Japan ($20 million), Canada ($18.8 million), the Netherlands ($18.5 million), Ireland ($12.6 million) and Germany ($10 million). Over 20 developing countries had also contributed to the Fund, illustrating its broad donor base. The Fund also benefited from its first private donation, in the amount of $18,933 by a single individual, as well as an additional $8.4 million in interest and investment income as at 31 December 2007. A total of $106.9 million or 44.8 per cent of total Fund deposits had been allocated to support Fund activities in the four countries on the Peacebuilding Commission's agenda (window I countries), one of the five countries declared eligible for window II funding (countries designated by the Secretary-General) and for seven emergency projects under window III funding (emergency projects). The balance of unprogrammed funds available for new Fund countries and pipeline projects stood at $131.6 million (55.2 per cent of total deposits).

Since the creation of the Fund, 37 projects had been approved to support priority plan and emergency window activities in nine post-conflict countries: Burundi, the Central African Republic, Côte d'Ivoire, Guinea, Guinea-Bissau, Haiti, Kenya, Liberia and Sierra Leone. Under windows I and II, the level of allocated funds transferred to recipient UN organizations was as follows: Burundi (89 per cent), Guinea-Bissau (98 per cent), Liberia (0.6 per cent) and Sierra Leone (46 per cent). Under the emergency window, seven projects amounting to $5.9 million had been approved.

Under window I funding, Guinea-Bissau was declared eligible for Fund Support on 11 March. Under window II funding, the Central African Republic was declared eligible to receive the Fund's support in January, Comoros on 25 June, Côte d'Ivoire on 19 June, and Guinea on 25 June. The Fund's emergency window supported projects in seven countries (Côte d'Ivoire, the Central African Republic, Guinea, Liberia, Burundi, Haiti, Kenya), with a focus on supporting political dialogue (2 projects), national reconciliation (2 projects), security support (1 project) and support for peace agreements (2 projects).

The thematic priority areas of the Fund included promoting good governance and the rule of law, security sector reform, justice delivery and reforms, promoting and protecting human rights, youth empowerment and employment, tackling poverty and land dispute, return and resettlement of refugees, promoting inclusive national political dialogue, support for peace agreements and ceasefires, democratization and electoral reform, and promoting reconciliation and conflict prevention. The Fund's Advisory Group, at its second meeting in March, reviewed the Fund's first year of full operations and emerging challenges and lessons. The Advisory Group provided guidance on the use of the Fund's windows, funding allocations criteria, emerging challenges and opportunities, the independent evaluation of the Fund in 2008, and ways to improve project performance and delivery. In proposing the Office of Internal Oversight Services as the independent evaluator, the Advisory Group stressed the importance of early evaluation to help strengthen the Fund's methodology, operational capabilities and scope. The evaluation, commissioned in March, would propose enhancements to its modus operandi and functions. On the basis of that evaluation, the Secretary-General planned to review the Fund's terms of reference, in consultation with the Advisory Group and with the advice of the Commission and the General Assembly.

The Secretary-General concluded that the Fund had shown its ability to function as a flexible, stand-alone mechanism. That ability should be preserved while ensuring performance accountability. Frequent interaction with the Commission, in the form of quarterly progress reports and communications, was needed to ensure optimum synergies and that lessons learned from operations were factored into Commission discussions. The Fund's methodology should be flexible enough to provide for a broad range of post-conflict early recovery situations, including those where local capacities needed initial strengthening prior to decentralized resource allocation. Although the emergency window had worked well, it did not meet the demand for larger-scale stand-alone projects. That window's scope, size and use might need to be reviewed to allow the Fund to support larger-scale operations on a case-by-case basis, without the need for setting up an entire window II infrastructure.

UN agency programming modalities and procedures had been key causes of delays in project implementation. Agencies should develop more appropriate mechanisms for early recovery interventions and adapt procedures in line with the Fund's uniqueness. Simplification of national Fund coordination structures, described as too cumbersome in Sierra Leone and Burundi, might be needed. The capacity of the Peacebuilding Support Office to monitor and backstop the Fund at the country level was limited. In view of the rapidly expanding number of Fund countries, additional staff capacity was required to address crucial programme management and planning, monitoring and evaluation needs. In addition, resources were required to build surge capacity to support new and ongoing programmes, monitoring visits, technical advisory services, global training and monitoring and evaluation systems. In-country capacity to manage the Fund portfolio needed to be reviewed to ensure sound project design and implementation. To better support the national steering committees and implementing partners, in-country support budgets should include provision for staff, monitoring and evaluation, training, technical support services and transport. As many new programmes had initial delays due to the workload during Fund start-up, surge capacity should be provided to ensure appropriate in-country capacity to implement the Fund. Such surge capacity should be funded from the Fund's overhead or from other surge mechanisms for early recovery, such as the UNDP Bureau for Crisis Prevention and Recovery. The current policy of covering operational costs entirely from the overhead should be reviewed, in particular for countries with smaller funding envelopes, because it limited the Fund's ability to set up appropriate secretariats to build local capacity. The Fund's Advisory Group should be strengthened by expanding its membership to include the appointment, by the Secretary-General, of additional independent expertise on peacebuilding and early recovery programming. In recognition of the growing importance of regional and subregional organizations in facilitating, brokering and consolidating peace, and in national peacebuilding efforts, consideration should be given to direct Fund support for such activities. An annual pledging conference, as stipulated in the terms of reference, should be held to ensure longer-term donor support.

With regard to the overall activities of its third session [A/64/341-S/2009/444], the Commission reported that, in December, in compliance with the terms of reference of the Fund, the Peacebuilding Support Office initiated a consultative process leading to the revision of those terms of reference.

Special political missions

Evaluation of special political missions

OIOS report. The Office of Internal Oversight Services (OIOS) submitted an April report [E/AC.51/2008/2] on the in-depth evaluation of political affairs: field special political missions led by the Department of Political Affairs (DPA) but supported by the Department of Field Support (DFS). The evaluation examined the efficiency, effectiveness and impact of 10 field special political missions and their activities.

OIOS found that stakeholders generally acknowledged that special political missions played an important role in conflict prevention and peacebuilding. However, it was difficult to ascertain their relative contribution to their mandates or areas of activity due to a number of factors, including the lack of a clear definition and vision of the role of special political missions in UN peacebuilding and conflict prevention efforts, and insufficient coordination and cooperation in their work with other UN actors. There was only limited monitoring, review and self-evaluation by DPA of special political mission performance, with little assessment of their contribution to peacebuilding and conflict prevention. Also hindering the impact of special political missions were poor systems and processes for administrative and substantive support, which were not sufficiently responsive and tailored to each mission's needs and circumstances. Strategic planning and mission deployment were also in need of improvement.

OIOS made four recommendations for enhancing the contribution of special political missions to peacebuilding and conflict prevention. It recommended that DPA, working with other Secretariat departments and the Secretary-General, develop clear guidelines that defined special political missions, their role in UN peacebuilding and conflict prevention, and the responsibilities of Secretariat departments with respect to leadership and support to those missions. DPA was called on to improve initial strategic planning, preparation and deployment of special political missions by ensuring that a clear mission strategy was developed for each mission. DPA and DFS should agree and prepare terms of reference or guidelines that improved cooperation and coordination in special political mission planning and support and that outlined the respective roles, responsibilities and standards for interaction between the Departments to ensure that mission resources were better tailored to circumstances and need. Mechanisms were needed for stronger overall management of DPA, coordination and oversight of special political missions, including policies or processes within the Department for more formalized coordination and knowledge-sharing in mission planning and support, as well as clarification of overall responsibility and accountability within the Department for special political mission performance and results. All relevant departments agreed or agreed in principle with the recommendations.

CPC consideration. The Committee for Programme and Coordination, at its forty-eighth session (9 June–3 July) [A/63/16], recommended that the General Assembly endorse the OIOS recommendations as revised by the Committee. It noted the need to improve the overall management of the special political missions, as well as the intended overall role and goals, the expected mission activities and how those activities would contribute to achieving the mission mandate, and the expected time to achieve the mandate or criteria that might be used in measuring progress and in determining whether the mission accomplished its mandate. The Committee recommended that the Assembly request the Secretary-General to ensure that special political missions and other local actors strengthen their cooperation and coordination in order to achieve the expected outcomes and to enhance the effectiveness and efficiency of the work of the United Nations.

By **decision 62/545 B** of 3 April, the Assembly deferred until its sixty-third (2008) session the agenda item on "Report of the Office of Internal Oversight Services on the audit of the management of special political missions by the Department of Political Affairs".

Roster of 2008 political missions and offices

On 1 January 2008, 12 UN political missions and offices were in operation: 6 in Africa, 4 in Asia and the

Pacific, and 2 in the Middle East. During the year, one mission (the United Nations Integrated Office in Sierra Leone (UNIOSIL)) was closed and one new mission (the United Nations Integrated Peacebuilding Office in Sierra Leone (UNIPSIL)) was launched; thus, 12 missions and offices were in operation at the end of the year.

In Africa, the mandate of the United Nations Peacebuilding Support Office in Guinea-Bissau was extended until 30 June 2009. On 4 August, the Security Council requested the Secretary-General to establish UNIPSIL, beginning 1 October 2008, for a period of 12 months, replacing UNIOSIL, whose mandate ended on 31 July. The Council noted the Secretary-General's recommendation to extend the mandate of the United Nations Support Office in the Central African Republic until 31 December 2009, and looked forward to receiving his recommendation regarding the establishment of an integrated UN office in the Central African Republic. The Council extended, until 31 December 2009, the mandate of the United Nations Integrated Office in Burundi. In addition, on 29 December [S/2008/827], the Council President informed the Secretary-General that the Council had noted his recommendation [S/2008/826] that the mandate of the temporary Liaison Office of the Special Envoy of the Secretary-General for the Lord's Resistance Army (LRA)-affected areas be extended through 31 December 2009 and the Office upgraded to a special political mission (see p. 170).

With regard to Asia and the Pacific, the Council renewed the mandates of the United Nations Mission in Nepal until 23 January 2009 and the United Nations Assistance Mission in Afghanistan until 23 March 2009, and that of the United Nations Assistance Mission for Iraq for a 12-month period beginning on 7 August 2008. In the Democratic People's Republic of Korea, the United Nations Command continued to implement the maintenance of the 1953 Armistice Agreement [YUN 1953, p. 136].

(For financing of UN political and peacebuilding missions, see PART FIVE, Chapter II.)

UNPOS

United Nations Political Office for Somalia

Established: 15 April 1995.

Mandate: To monitor the situation in Somalia and keep the Security Council informed, particularly about developments affecting the humanitarian and security situations, repatriation of refugees and impacts on neighbouring countries.

Special Representative of the Secretary-General: Ahmedou Ould-Abdallah (Mauritania).

Strength: 32 international civilian staff, 16 local civilian staff.

UNOGBIS

United Nations Peacebuilding Support Office in Guinea-Bissau

Established: 3 March 1999.

Mandate: To support efforts to consolidate constitutional rule, enhance political dialogue and promote national reconciliation, respect for the rule of law and human rights; assist in strengthening the capacity of national institutions; and support security sector reform.

Representative of the Secretary-General: Shola Omoregie (Nigeria).

Strength: 9 international civilian staff, 2 military advisers, 1 police adviser, 14 local civilian staff.

UNSCO

Office of the United Nations Special Coordinator for the Middle East

Established: 1 October 1999.

Mandate: To act as the focal point for the UN contribution to the implementation of the peace agreements and to enhance UN assistance.

Special Coordinator for the Middle East Peace Process and Personal Representative of the Secretary-General to the Palestine Liberation Organization and the Palestinian Authority: Robert H. Serry (Netherlands).

Strength: 29 international civilian staff, 24 local civilian staff.

BONUCA

United Nations Peacebuilding Office in the Central African Republic

Established: 15 February 2000.

Mandate: To support efforts to consolidate peace and promote national reconstruction and economic recovery.

Representative of the Secretary-General: François Lonseny Fall (Guinea).

Strength: 24 international civilian staff, 5 military advisers, 6 police, 54 local civilian staff, 3 UN volunteers.

UNSCOL

Office of the United Nations Special Coordinator for Lebanon (formerly known as the Office of the Personal Representative of the Secretary-General for Southern Lebanon)

Established: 16 February 2007.

Mandate: To represent the Secretary-General politically and coordinate UN work in Lebanon.

Special Coordinator for Lebanon: Michael C. Williams (United Kingdom).

Strength: 14 international civilian staff, 28 local civilian staff.

UNOWA

Office of the Special Representative of the Secretary-General for West Africa

Established: 29 November 2001.

Mandate: To enhance the contribution of the United Nations towards the achievement of peace and security priorities in West Africa.

Special Representative of the Secretary-General: Said Djinnit (Algeria).

Strength: 10 international civilian staff, 11 local civilian staff.

UNAMA

United Nations Assistance Mission in Afghanistan

Established: 28 March 2002.

Mandate: To fulfil the tasks and responsibilities entrusted to the United Nations in the Bonn Agreement; promote national reconciliation and rapprochement; manage all UN humanitarian relief, recovery and reconstruction activities; and assist in the promotion of the political process.

Special Representative of the Secretary-General: Kai Eide (Norway).

Strength: 250 international civilian staff, 16 military observers, 5 civilian police, 1,163 local civilian staff, 41 UN volunteers.

UNAMI

United Nations Assistance Mission for Iraq

Established: 14 August 2003.

Mandate: To advise, support and assist the Government and people of Iraq in advancing inclusive political dialogue and national reconciliation, and the Government and the Independent High Electoral Commission in the development of processes for holding elections and referenda; promote, support and facilitate the delivery of humanitarian assistance and the voluntary return of refugees and displaced persons; promote the protection of human rights and judicial and legal reform; and conduct related activities under Security Council resolution 1770(2007) [YUN 2007, p. 346].

Special Representative of the Secretary-General: Staffan de Mistura (Sweden).

Strength (staff based in Iraq, Jordan and Kuwait)*:* 296 international civilian staff, 389 local civilian staff, 222 troops, 6 military advisers.

UNIPSIL

United Nations Integrated Peacebuilding Office in Sierra Leone

Established: 1 October 2008.

Mandate: To provide political support for identifying and resolving tensions and threats of potential conflict; monitor and promote human rights, democratic institutions and the rule of law, including efforts to counter transnational organized crime and drug trafficking; consolidate good governance reforms, with a focus on anti-corruption instruments; support decentralization, reviewing the 1991 Constitution and the enactment of legislation; and coordinate with and support the work of the Peacebuilding Commission, as well as implementation of the Sierra Leone Cooperation Framework and projects supported by the Peacebuilding Fund.

Executive Representative of the Secretary-General: Michael von der Schulenburg (Germany).

Strength: 13 international civilian staff, 1 local civilian staff, 9 UN volunteers.

BINUB

United Nations Integrated Office in Burundi

Established: 1 January 2007.

Mandate: To support the Government of Burundi in its efforts towards long-term peace and stability, focusing on activities related to peace consolidation and democratic governance; disarmament, demobilization and reintegration; security sector reform; promotion and protection of human rights and measures to end impunity; and donor and UN agency coordination.

Executive Representative of the Secretary-General: Youssef Mahmoud (Tunisia).

Strength: 117 international civilian staff, 213 local civilian staff, 8 military observers, 12 civilian police, 50 UN volunteers.

UNMIN

United Nations Mission in Nepal

Established: 23 January 2007.

Mandate: To support the peace process in Nepal by: monitoring the management of arms and armed personnel of the Nepal Army and the Maoist Army; assisting the parties, through a Joint Monitoring Coordinating Committee, in implementing the agreement on the management of arms and armed personnel; assisting in the monitoring of ceasefire agreements; and providing technical assistance to the Election Commission.

Special Representative of the Secretary-General: Ian Martin (United Kingdom).

Strength: 104 international civilian staff, 158 local civilian staff, 61 military observers, 33 UN volunteers.

UNRCCA

United Nations Regional Centre for Preventive Diplomacy for Central Asia

Established: 10 December 2007.

Mandate: To liaise with Governments of the region and other parties on preventive diplomacy issues; monitor and analyse the situation on the ground and provide the Secretary-General with information related to conflict prevention efforts; facilitate coordination and information exchange with regional organizations; and support the efforts of regional coordinators and the UN system in promoting an integrated approach to preventive development and humanitarian assistance.

Special Representative of the Secretary-General: Miroslav Jenča (Slovakia).

Strength: 2 international civilian staff.

Threats to international peace and security

International terrorism

On 9 December [meeting 6034], the Security Council held a debate on threats to international peace and security caused by terrorist acts. According to Croatia, which submitted a concept paper on the subject [S/2008/738], the goal of the debate was to revitalize and strengthen international security in combating the threat of terrorism, including the UN leading role in global counter-terrorism efforts. The paper stated that although important strategic counter-terrorism guidance had been adopted, it was clear that specific follow-up had not occurred in the desired time frame. In that regard, many speakers referred to the lack of guidance and coherence within the United Nations.

The Secretary-General, addressing the Council, said that terrorism was a global scourge, inflicting appalling and morally reprehensible carnage, fomenting distrust between States and peoples, tearing societies apart, undermining institutions and weakening bonds between communities. The attacks in Mumbai, India (see p. 66), were the most recent example of misguided individuals run amok. Terrorism was a leading threat to international peace and security, and combating it had to be one of the main priorities of the international community. The United Nations had a responsibility to lead the international community's efforts to confront that menace. Indeed, the Security Council and the General Assembly had strongly condemned terrorism time and again, and had sought to promote the universal norm that terrorism was never acceptable.

SECURITY COUNCIL ACTION

On 9 December [meeting 6034], following consultations among Security Council members, the President made statement **S/PRST/2008/45** on behalf of the Council:

The Security Council, underlining that peace and security in the world are indivisible and taking into account the interconnection and interdependence of the world, reaffirms that terrorism in all its forms and manifestations constitutes one of the most serious threats to international peace and security and that any acts of terrorism are criminal and unjustifiable regardless of their motivations, whenever and by whomsoever committed. It further reaffirms its determination to combat threats to international peace and security caused by acts of terrorism by all possible means in accordance with the Charter of the United Nations.

The Council welcomes recent statements by intergovernmental organizations condemning all forms of terrorism, including suicide bombing and hostage-taking, which build upon the universal condemnation by the international community of unlawful acts of terrorism, including against civilians, that cannot be justified or excused under any circumstances or pursuant to any political, philosophical, ideological, racial, ethnic, religious or other consideration, and reaffirms the need for Member States to work together urgently to prevent and suppress such acts.

The Council emphasizes the central role of the United Nations in the global struggle against terrorism.

The Council reaffirms the importance of all its resolutions and statements on terrorism, in particular resolutions 1373(2001) and 1624(2005), and stresses the need for their full implementation.

The Council renews its call upon States to become parties as soon as possible to all relevant international conventions and protocols relating to terrorism and to implement those to which they are party.

The Council believes that terrorist safe havens continue to be a significant concern and reaffirms the need for States to strengthen cooperation in order to find, deny safe haven to and bring to justice, on the basis of the principle of extradite or prosecute, any person who supports, facilitates, participates or attempts to participate in the financing, planning, preparation or commission of terrorist acts or provides safe havens.

The Council reaffirms the importance of the work of the committees established pursuant to resolutions 1267(1999), 1373(2001) and 1540(2004) and continues its support and guidance to the committees.

The Council particularly expresses its support for, and commitment to contributing to the implementation of, the United Nations Global Counter-Terrorism Strategy of 8 September 2006 and welcomes the adoption by the General Assembly of resolution 62/272 of 5 September 2008, in which it reaffirmed the Strategy and its four pillars and called for its implementation in an integrated manner and in all its aspects.

The Council emphasizes that enhancing dialogue and broadening understanding among civilizations, in an effort to prevent the indiscriminate targeting of different religions and cultures, and addressing unresolved regional conflicts and the full range of global issues, including development issues, will contribute to international cooperation, which by itself is necessary to sustain the broadest possible fight against terrorism.

The Council condemns in the strongest terms the incitement of terrorist acts and repudiates attempts at the justification or glorification of terrorist acts that may incite further terrorist acts. It reaffirms the importance of countering radicalization and extremism that may lead to terrorism and preventing the exploitation of young people by violent extremists.

The Council, reaffirming that the promotion and protection of human rights for all and the rule of law are essential to an effective counter-terrorism strategy and that effective counter-terrorism measures and the protection of human rights are complementary and mutually reinforcing, reminds States that they must ensure that any measures taken to combat terrorism comply with all their obligations under international law, in particular international human rights, refugee and humanitarian law.

The Council emphasizes the importance of technical assistance aimed at increasing the capabilities of Member States in the fight against terrorism by addressing their counter-terrorism needs.

The Council believes that the strengthening of mutual trust among States Members of the United Nations will facilitate the creation of conditions for a successful fight against terrorism, and that success in that fight will positively reinforce peace and security in the world.

The Council, deeply concerned at the continuous terrorist attacks around the world, calls upon all States Members of the United Nations to renew the degree of solidarity manifested immediately after the tragic event of 11 September 2001, and to redouble efforts to tackle global terrorism, dedicating significant attention to bringing to justice the perpetrators, facilitators and masterminds of terrorist acts while expressing deep compassion with all victims of terrorism.

The Council will continue to follow developments in order to organize as efficiently as possible its efforts in combating terrorism.

Global Counter-Terrorism Strategy

Review of implementation

On 4 September [meeting 117] and 5 September [meeting 120], the General Assembly conducted the first review of the Global Counter-Terrorism Strategy, adopted in 2006 in resolution 60/288 [YUN 2006, p. 66]. It had before it a July report [A/62/898] of the Secretary-General on the United Nations Global Counter-Terrorism Strategy: activities of the UN system in implementing the Strategy, submitted in accordance with Assembly resolution 60/228. The report highlighted efforts of the Counter-Terrorism Implementation Task Force and provided a partial picture of the Strategy's implementation to date. The report described measures to: address the conditions conducive to terrorism; prevent and combat terrorism; build State capacity to prevent terrorism and strengthen the UN role in that regard; and ensure respect for human rights and the rule of law as the fundamental basis of the fight against terrorism.

The UN system had contributed to implementation in two ways: its departments, specialized agencies, funds and programmes had taken action within their own workplans, both individually and in partnerships; and the system's 24 entities and Interpol had provided a forum for discussing strategic issues and coordinating action. The Task Force had created nine working groups in areas that could benefit from engagement by more than one UN entity.

Within the UN system, the Department of Political Affairs (DPA), the United Nations Development Programme (UNDP), the United Nations Educational, Scientific and Cultural Organization (UNESCO) and the Department of Peacekeeping Operations (DPKO) had contributed to the implementation of the work outlined in the Strategy's first pillar (measures to address conditions conducive to the spread of terrorism), as had the three Task Force working groups on preventing and resolving conflicts, on supporting and highlighting victims of terrorism, and on addressing radicalization and extremism that lead to terrorism. As the lead UN department for peacemaking and preventive diplomacy, DPA had a wide range of activities for reducing conflicts around the world. Since the adoption of the Strategy, it had established the United Nations Regional Centre for Preventive Diplomacy for Central Asia, which began operations in June, to assist the Governments of that region in responding more proactively to cross-border challenges and threats such as terrorism, drug trafficking and organized crime. It also promoted a culture of peace, justice and human development; ethnic, national and religious tolerance; and respect for all religions, beliefs or cultures, as called for in the Strategy. UNESCO supported programmes that advanced human rights and respect for diversity; fostered dialogue and tolerance among civilizations, cultures and peoples; and promoted mutual knowledge and respect. In January, UNESCO and the Alliance of Civilizations signed a memorandum of understanding to promote joint programming and cooperation on outreach activities. In the previous year, 90 countries had received support from UNDP for the rule of law, access to justice and human rights. UNDP had prepared two programmes on global rule of law and justice, and introduced an initiative focusing on the link between poverty and governance. DPKO sought to reduce opportunities for terrorists to sustain their criminal activities through programmes designed to ensure the adoption of fair and accountable criminal justice systems, the promotion of public safety, and the establishment of the rule of law. The Task Force working group on preventing and resolving conflicts undertook efforts to integrate counter-terrorism objectives into UN system work on the prevention and resolution of armed conflict. To date, the working group had drafted initial guidance on counter-terrorism for use by representatives of the Secretary-General and other peacemakers.

In the area of measures to combat terrorism, the UN system had helped Member States draft legal instruments and guidelines establishing standards for preventative action; compiled rosters and databases to centralize information about resources available to prevent and respond to terrorist acts; and assessed the counter-terrorism capacities of Member States. Through its working group on tackling the financing of terrorism, the Task Force was analysing the effectiveness of the measures in a number of countries to combat terrorist-financing and to identify new approaches to address the issue. The working group had convened seven round tables in Vienna and New York to explore views and proposals with outside experts in the areas of banking, intelligence (including financial intelligence), regulation, law enforcement and criminal justice.

In his recommendations for the way forward, the Secretary-General stated that four briefings to the Assembly on the work of the Counter-Terrorism Implementation Task Force in connection with the Global Counter-Terrorism Strategy had taken place since 2007, the latest on 4 May 2008 in New York. Member States had expressed interest in greater systematization in order to guide the Task Force on its activities and to provide a stronger communication channel with the membership. The UN system would welcome such an agreement, should Member States so agree. The decision regarding the systematization of their interface with the Task Force rested with the membership, but the Secretary-General could provide advice based on the UN system's support capacity. Two aspects were pertinent: systematization should be commensurate with the resources provided by the Assembly, both personnel and financial; and the process of systematization should not constitute the greater share of the Task Force's work, if its coordination and coherence function was to be adequately maintained. Those needs could be met by a number of mechanisms, including regular briefings by the Task Force to the Assembly.

In an effort to operate within existing resources, the Secretary-General relied on voluntary contributions and temporary staff support. However, current arrangements were not sustainable. The Secretary-General would continue to address staffing requirements from within existing resources. Among the requests noted by the Task Force was increased engagement between the UN system and global, regional and subregional organizations, and civil society on the implementation of the Strategy. Global, regional and subregional organizations and civil society provided a resource that had not been tapped by the UN system. Member States, through the governing bodies of those organizations, should encourage cross-regional assistance and cooperation in counter-terrorism so that global, regional and subregional bodies that had developed procedures and expertise in that area could assist those still developing related capacities. The UN system, through the Task Force, if adequately staffed and resourced, could provide a strategic interface with global, regional and subregional bodies and civil society on the Strategy.

The Secretary-General concluded that initial successes in implementing the Counter-Terrorism Strategy should not blur the fact that much remained to be done to dissuade people from resorting to terrorism, deny terrorists the means to carry out their attacks, deter States from supporting terrorism, develop State capacity to defeat terrorism, and defend human rights. Only persistent, concerted and coordinated efforts would provide the opportunity to fully implement the United Nations Counter-Terrorism Strategy and secure a more peaceful world.

On 20 August [A/62/943-S/2008/575], the Permanent Observer of Palestine forwarded to the Security Council President and the Secretary-General a position paper submitted by the Arab Group on the subject. The Group encouraged the establishment of an International Counter-Terrorism Centre under the UN umbrella as envisaged in the Strategy. It stressed the importance of following up on the implementation of the Strategy in a comprehensive and non-selective manner and the pivotal role of the Assembly in addressing the issue of combating terrorism in all its aspects. The Group considered that the institutionalization of the Task Force within the Secretariat with the necessary resources would provide a basis for an organized, constructive and integrated contribution to Member States' efforts in achieving the Strategy's objectives.

The Secretary-General, addressing the Assembly on 4 September, urged Member States to take multilateral counter-terrorism further, guided by three main principles. First, the Organization should be innovative in developing its tools, and not shy away from non-traditional approaches to promoting security. Multilateral counter-terrorism cooperation should be undertaken in an integrated manner across the four pillars of the Strategy and range of actors. The UN system, through the Task Force, was developing that capacity. Second, multilateral counter-terrorism efforts had to be undertaken in partnership with regional and subregional organizations and with civil society. Third, at the international level, those efforts should leverage the Organization's comparative strengths. Bilateral actions might be insufficient to face the needs, whereas the UN collective approach gave multilateral efforts an advantage that should be maximized. The Secretary-General said that he was working to institutionalize the Task Force within the Secretariat and would convene a symposium in New York on supporting victims of terrorism.

GENERAL ASSEMBLY ACTION

On 5 September [meeting 120], the General Assembly adopted **resolution 62/272** [draft: A/62/L.48] without vote [agenda item 118].

The United Nations Global Counter-Terrorism Strategy

The General Assembly,

Reaffirming the United Nations Global Counter-Terrorism Strategy, contained in General Assembly resolution 60/288 of 8 September 2006, which called for, inter alia, an examination in two years of progress made in the implementation of the Strategy and for consideration to be given to updating it to respond to changes, as provided for in paragraph 3 *(b)* of that resolution,

Recalling the pivotal role of the General Assembly in following up the implementation and the updating of the Strategy,

Renewing its unwavering commitment to strengthen international cooperation to prevent and combat terrorism in all its forms and manifestations,

Recognizing that international cooperation and any measures undertaken by Member States to prevent and combat terrorism must fully comply with their obligations under international law, including the Charter of the United Nations and relevant international conventions and protocols, in particular human rights law, refugee law and international humanitarian law,

Convinced that the General Assembly is the competent organ with universal membership to address the issue of international terrorism,

Mindful of the need to enhance the role of the United Nations and the specialized agencies, within their mandates, in the implementation of the Strategy,

Stressing that the Counter-Terrorism Implementation Task Force shall carry out its activities within the framework of its mandate, with policy guidance offered by Member States through interaction with the General Assembly on a regular basis,

Recognizing the importance of institutionalizing the Task Force within the Secretariat,

1. *Reiterates its strong condemnation* of terrorism in all its forms and manifestations, committed by whomever, wherever and for whatever purposes, as it constitutes one of the most serious threats to international peace and security;

2. *Reaffirms* the United Nations Global Counter-Terrorism Strategy and its four pillars, which constitute an ongoing effort, and calls upon Member States, the United Nations and other appropriate international, regional and subregional organizations to step up their efforts to implement the Strategy in an integrated manner and in all its aspects;

3. *Takes note* of the report of the Secretary-General entitled "United Nations Global Counter-Terrorism Strategy: activities of the United Nations system in implementing the Strategy";

4. *Also takes note* of the measures that Member States as well as appropriate international, regional and subregional organizations have adopted within the framework of the Strategy, as presented at the first biennial review of the Strategy, on 4 and 5 September 2008, all of which strengthen cooperation to fight terrorism, in particular through the exchange of best practices;

5. *Reaffirms* the primary responsibility of Member States to implement the Strategy while further recognizing the need to enhance the important role the United Nations plays, in coordination with other international, regional and subregional organizations, as appropriate, in facilitating coherence in the implementation of the Strategy at the national, regional and global levels and in providing assistance, especially in the area of capacity-building;

6. *Encourages* non-governmental organizations and civil society to engage, as appropriate, on how to enhance efforts to implement the Strategy, including through interaction with Member States and the United Nations system;

7. *Calls upon* the United Nations entities involved in supporting counter-terrorism efforts to continue to facilitate the promotion and protection of human rights and fundamental freedoms while countering terrorism;

8. *Calls upon* States that have not done so to consider becoming parties in a timely manner to the existing international conventions and protocols against terrorism, and upon all States to make every effort to conclude a comprehensive convention on international terrorism, and recalls the commitments of Member States with regard to the implementation of General Assembly and Security Council resolutions relating to international terrorism;

9. *Notes with appreciation* the continued contribution of United Nations entities and subsidiary bodies of the Security Council to the Counter-Terrorism Implementation Task Force;

10. *Reaffirms* the need to enhance international cooperation in countering terrorism, and in this regard recalls the role of the United Nations system in promoting international cooperation and capacity-building as one of the elements of the Strategy;

11. *Urges* the Secretary-General to make the necessary arrangements to carry out the institutionalization of the Task Force, in accordance with resolution 60/288, in order to ensure overall coordination and coherence in the counter-terrorism efforts of the United Nations system;

12. *Decides* to interact with the Task Force on a regular basis, in order to receive briefings and reports on its current and future work, assess the work being undertaken on the Strategy implementation efforts, including the work of the Task Force, and to offer policy guidance;

13. *Requests* the Secretary-General to submit to the General Assembly at its sixty-fourth session a report on progress made in the implementation of the Strategy, which could contain suggestions for its future implementation by the United Nations system, as well as in the implementation of the present resolution;

14. *Decides* to include in the provisional agenda of its sixty-fourth session the item entitled "The United Nations Global Counter-Terrorism Strategy" in order to undertake in two years an examination of the report of the Secretary-General requested in paragraph 13 above, as well as the implementation of the Strategy on the part of Member States and to consider updating the Strategy to respond to changes.

Terrorist attacks in 2008

In 2008, terrorist attacks continued worldwide with increased intensity and frequency, resulting in the deaths of hundreds of innocent civilians and injuries to many others. Those attacks were condemned by the Security Council, Member States and the Secretary-General, who called for increased efforts to combat the threat they posed to international peace and security.

Afghanistan

The Security Council, in a 17 February press statement [SC/9251], condemned the suicide attack in Kandahar, Afghanistan, on the same day, causing numerous deaths. Council members noted with dismay that the attack was one of the deadliest in Afghanistan in recent years and targeted civilians. They urged States to cooperate with the Afghan authorities in bringing the perpetrators to justice. Council members reiterated their concern at the increasing threat to the local population, national security forces, international military and international assistance efforts posed by the Taliban, Al-Qaida, illegal armed groups, criminals and those involved in the narcotics trade.

Council members also condemned the suicide attack on 7 July on the Indian Embassy in Kabul. Council members, in a press statement of the same day [SC/9386], reaffirmed their determination to combat terrorism in all its forms. They urged States to cooperate with the authorities to bring the perpetrators to justice.

Algeria

On 19 August, a terrorist attack occurred in Les Issers (east of Algiers), Algeria, at a gendarmerie training academy, killing 43 persons, including civilians, most of whom were between 18 and 20 years of age. In a statement issued the same day [SG/SM/11755], the Secretary-General condemned the attack and added that violence would not deter Algerians from the path of peace and national reconciliation. He urged the international community to support the Government in combating terrorism. In another statement issued the next day [SG/SM/11756], the Secretary-General condemned the two car bomb attacks in the city of Bouira, which reportedly killed 11 people.

SECURITY COUNCIL ACTION

On 19 August [meeting 5962], following consultations among Security Council members, the President made statement **S/PRST/2008/31** on behalf of the Council:

> The Security Council condemns in the strongest terms the suicide terrorist attack that occurred in Les Issers, Algeria, on 19 August 2008, causing numerous deaths and injuries at a gendarmerie training academy. It expresses its deep sympathy and condolences to the victims of this heinous act of terrorism and to their families, and to the people and Government of Algeria.
>
> The Council underlines the need to bring the perpetrators, organizers, financers and sponsors of this reprehensible act of terrorism to justice, and urges all States, in accordance with their obligations under international law and resolution 1373(2001) and consistent with resolution 1624(2005), to cooperate actively with the Algerian authorities in this regard.
>
> The Council reaffirms that terrorism in all its forms and manifestations constitutes one of the most serious threats to international peace and security, and that any acts of terrorism are criminal and unjustifiable, regardless of their motivation, wherever, whenever and by whomsoever committed.
>
> The Council further reaffirms the need to combat by all means, in accordance with the Charter of the United Nations, threats to international peace and security caused by terrorist acts. The Council reminds States that they must ensure that any measures taken to combat terrorism comply with all their obligations under international law, in particular international human rights, refugee and humanitarian law.
>
> The Council reiterates its determination to combat all forms of terrorism, in accordance with its responsibilities under the Charter.

Guinea-Bissau

On 23 November, an armed attack was perpetrated on the official residence of Guinea-Bissau President Bernardo João Vieira in Bissau. The Secretary-General, in a 24 November press statement [SG/SM/11947], condemned the attack, expressed concern at reports of alleged involvement of elements of the Armed Forces of Guinea-Bissau and called upon them to refrain from any measures that could further destabilize the country. That action, coming soon after the 16 November legislative elections, could have a devastating impact on the country's fragile stability. The Secretary-General called on the authorities to re-establish law and order and to conduct a thorough investigation, with a view to ensuring respect for the rule of law and human rights.

India

On 26 November, the city of Mumbai, India, was hit by a rash of shootings and blasts that killed and wounded a large number of people. In a statement issued the same day [SG/SM/11956], the Secretary-General condemned the attacks, reiterating his conviction that no cause or grievance could justify indiscriminate attacks against civilians. He called for the perpetrators to be brought to justice swiftly. Two days later, the Security Council issued a press statement [SC/9513] calling for those responsible to be brought to justice and reiterating that all acts of terrorism were criminal and unjustifiable. On 2 December [SG/SM/11976], the Secretary-General, after speaking with Indian Prime Minister Manmohan Singh, again expressed his sympathy to the families of the victims and reaffirmed his determination to play a lead role for the United Nations in dealing with that global menace.

The State Duma of the Russian Federation, in a 23 December statement [A/63/660-S/2008/811] transmitted to the Secretary-General, said that its members were appalled by that monstrous act directed against the people of India. They said that there could be no justification for atrocities of terrorist organizations, in whatever ethnic or religious guise. The counter-terrorist coalition of leading world powers should secure the unconditional implementation by all members of the international community of the Global Counter-Terrorism Strategy.

Lebanon

On 13 August, a terrorist attack occurred in the Lebanese town of Tripoli, causing numerous deaths and injuries, including of members of the Lebanese Armed Forces. In a press statement of the same day [SC/9422], the Security Council condemned the attack, called for those responsible to be brought to justice, commended the Government's commitment to do so, and called for international cooperation with the Government to that end.

On 11 September, the Secretary-General [SG/SM/11785] and the Security Council [SC/9444] condemned the attack that occurred the previous day in Lebanon, killing Saleh Aridi, a member of the Lebanese Democratic Party, and injuring several others. On 29 September [SG/SM/11840], the Secretary-General condemned the terrorist attack that took place that day in Tripoli, reportedly killing four people, including three members of the Lebanese Armed Forces. The Secretary-General was encouraged by the measures taken in recent weeks by the Lebanese to resume national dialogue and called upon them not to be deterred by the new attack.

Pakistan

On 2 June, a terrorist car bomb attack occurred outside the Danish Embassy in Islamabad, Pakistan, causing numerous deaths, injuries and damage to nearby buildings, including one housing UNDP. The attack was condemned that day by the Security Council President (see below) and the Secretary-General [SG/SM/11608].

SECURITY COUNCIL ACTION

On 2 June [meeting 5903], following consultations among Security Council members, the President made statement **S/PRST/2008/19** on behalf of the Council:

> The Security Council condemns in the strongest terms the terrorist attack that occurred outside the Danish Embassy in Islamabad on 2 June 2008, causing numerous deaths, injuries and damage to nearby buildings, including a building housing the United Nations Development Programme. It expresses its deep sympathy and condolences to the victims of this heinous act of terrorism and to their families, and to the people and Governments of Pakistan and Denmark.
>
> The Council underlines the need to bring the perpetrators, organizers, financers and sponsors of this reprehensible act of terrorism to justice, and urges all States, in accordance with their obligations under international law and resolution 1373(2001) and consistent with resolution 1624(2005), to cooperate actively with the Pakistani authorities in this regard.
>
> The Council reaffirms that terrorism in all its forms and manifestations constitutes one of the most serious threats to international peace and security, and that any acts of terrorism are criminal and unjustifiable, regardless of their motivation, wherever, whenever and by whomsoever committed.
>
> The Council further reaffirms the need to combat by all means, in accordance with the Charter of the United Nations, threats to international peace and security caused by terrorist acts. The Council reminds States that they must ensure any measures taken to combat terrorism comply with all their obligations under international law, in particular international human rights, refugee and humanitarian law.
>
> The Council reiterates its determination to combat all forms of terrorism, in accordance with its responsibilities under the Charter.

Another terrorist suicide attack on 6 July in front of a police station near the Red Mosque in Islamabad caused numerous deaths and injuries among civilians and police personnel. The next day, a series of terrorist attacks in parts of Karachi caused multiple casualties. In a 7 July statement [SG/SM/11687], the Secretary-General condemned the attacks. He urged all political forces to unite against the scourge of terrorism. The Council, in an 8 July press statement [SC/9389], condemned the attacks in Islamabad and Karachi, and reiterated its concern at the threats posed by the Taliban, Al-Qaida and illegal armed groups to peace and security in the region. The Council members reaffirmed the need to combat by all means, in accordance with the UN Charter, threats to international peace and security caused by terrorist acts, and they reminded States that they had to ensure that measures taken to combat terrorism complied with all obligations under international law. A further two suicide attacks occurred in Wah Cantt, Pakistan, on 21 August, causing numerous deaths and injuries.

SECURITY COUNCIL ACTION

On 21 August [meeting 5964], following consultations among Security Council members, the President made statement **S/PRST/2008/32** on behalf of Council members:

The Security Council condemns in the strongest terms the twin suicide terrorist attacks that occurred in Wah Cantt, Pakistan, on 21 August 2008, causing numerous deaths and injuries. It expresses its deep sympathies and condolences to the victims of these heinous acts of terrorism and to their families, and to the people and Government of Pakistan.

The Council underlines the need to bring the perpetrators, organizers, financers and sponsors of these reprehensible acts of terrorism to justice, and urges all States, in accordance with their obligations under international law and resolution 1373(2001) and consistent with resolution 1624(2005), to cooperate actively with the Pakistani authorities in this regard.

The Council reaffirms that terrorism in all its forms and manifestations constitutes one of the most serious threats to international peace and security, and that any acts of terrorism are criminal and unjustifiable, regardless of their motivation, wherever, whenever and by whomsoever committed.

The Council further reaffirms the need to combat by all means, in accordance with the Charter of the United Nations, threats to international peace and security caused by terrorist acts. The Council reminds States that they must ensure that any measures taken to combat terrorism comply with all their obligations under international law, in particular international human rights, refugee and humanitarian law.

The Council reiterates its determination to combat all forms of terrorism, in accordance with its responsibilities under the Charter.

On 20 September, a terrorist attack against the Marriot Hotel in Islamabad reportedly killed and injured a large number of people, including foreign diplomats. On the same day [SG/SM/11800], the Secretary-General condemned that attack and reiterated that no cause could justify the indiscriminate targeting of civilians.

SECURITY COUNCIL ACTION

On 22 September [meeting 5978], following consultations among Security Council members, the President made statement **S/PRST/2008/35** on behalf of Council members:

The Security Council condemns in the strongest terms the terrorist attack that occurred in Islamabad on 20 September 2008, causing numerous deaths and injuries, including among foreign diplomats. It expresses its deep sympathy and condolences to the victims of this heinous act of terrorism and to their families, and to the people and Government of Pakistan.

The Council underlines the need to bring the perpetrators, organizers, financers and sponsors of this reprehensible act of terrorism to justice, and urges all States, in accordance with their obligations under international law and resolution 1373(2001) and consistent with resolution 1624(2005), to cooperate actively with the Pakistani authorities in this regard.

The Council reaffirms that terrorism in all its forms and manifestations constitutes one of the most serious threats to international peace and security, and that any acts of terrorism are criminal and unjustifiable, regardless of their motivation, wherever, whenever and by whomsoever committed.

The Council further reaffirms the need to combat by all means, in accordance with the Charter of the United Nations, threats to international peace and security caused by terrorist acts. The Council reminds States that they must ensure that any measures taken to combat terrorism comply with all their obligations under international law, in particular international human rights, refugee and humanitarian law.

The Council reiterates its determination to combat all forms of terrorism, in accordance with its responsibilities under the Charter.

Somalia

On 29 October, multiple bomb attacks occurred in the northern Somali towns of Boosasso and Hargeysa, where a suicide car bombing at the UNDP compound killed two UN staff and seriously injured six others, two of them critically. In a statement of the same date [SG/SM/11893], the Secretary-General deplored those outrageous acts of violence deliberately targeting innocent civilians and UN personnel. He stressed the neutrality of the United Nations, as well as humanitarian personnel, and urged all parties to support and facilitate the delivery of assistance to the Somali population.

SECURITY COUNCIL ACTION

On 30 October [meeting 6009], following consultations among Security Council members, the President made statement **S/PRST/2008/41** on behalf of the Council:

The Security Council condemns in the strongest terms the terrorist suicide attacks that occurred in the towns of Hargeysa and Boosasso in Somalia on 29 October 2008. These heinous attacks, which caused numerous deaths and injuries and appear to have been coordinated, targeted the compound of the United Nations Development Programme and an Ethiopian Government office, as well as local government offices.

The Council expresses its deepest sympathy and condolences to the victims of these attacks and to their families, and to the people and authorities of Somalia and Ethiopia. It notes with appreciation that some of the victims are being treated at the French medical centre in Djibouti.

The Council commends United Nations personnel for their action on the ground in Somalia, in support of the Somali population.

The Council underlines the need to bring the perpetrators, organizers, financers and sponsors of these reprehensible acts of terrorism to justice and urges all States, in accordance with their obligations under international law and resolution 1373(2001) and consistent with resolution 1624(2005), to cooperate actively with the authorities of Somalia in this regard.

The Council reaffirms that terrorism in all its forms and manifestations constitutes one of the most serious threats to international peace and security, and that any acts of terrorism are criminal and unjustifiable, regardless of their motivation, wherever, whenever and by whomsoever committed.

The Council further reaffirms the need to combat by all means, in accordance with the Charter of the United Nations, threats to international peace and security caused by terrorist acts. The Council reminds States that they must ensure that any measures taken to combat terrorism comply with all their obligations under international law, in particular international human rights, refugee and humanitarian law.

The Council reiterates its determination to combat all forms of terrorism, in accordance with its responsibilities under the Charter.

Sri Lanka

On 7 October, a suicide attack in Anuradhpura, Sri Lanka, wounded and killed scores of people, including retired army General Janaka Perera. The Secretary-General condemned the attack in a statement of the same day [SG/SM/11850] and expressed his condolences to the Government and people of Sri Lanka and sympathies to the victims and their families.

Other incidents

On 10 July [SC/9394], the Security Council condemned the terrorist attack on Turkish police protecting the United States Consulate in Istanbul on 9 July, causing death and injury to Turkish police personnel.

On 17 September [SC/9446], the Council condemned the terrorist attack that occurred at the entrance of the United States Embassy in Sana'a, Yemen, which caused the death of Yemeni security personnel, as well as numerous injuries.

On 24 September [SC/9455], the Council condemned terrorist attacks in Spain that caused death and injuries.

On 27 September [SC/9460], the Council condemned the terrorist attack in Damascus, Syrian Arab Republic, which caused numerous deaths and injuries.

On 12 December [SG/SM/12000], the Secretary-General condemned the bomb attack in Kirkuk, Iraq, which took the lives of many civilians, including children. He said that the attack was particularly troubling because it targeted a meeting to promote dialogue and reconciliation between different communities in the region. He called on the Iraqi people and their leaders not to be deterred by such acts.

Measures to eliminate international terrorism

In 2008, the United Nations strengthened its efforts to combat and eliminate international terrorism. The General Assembly, having considered the Secretary-General's report [A/63/173 & Add.1] on measures to eliminate international terrorism, requested, in **resolution 63/129** of 11 December (see p. 1441), the Terrorism Prevention Branch of the United Nations Office on Drugs and Crime (UNODC) to enhance UN capabilities in preventing terrorism, and recognized, in the context of the United Nations Global Counter-Terrorism Strategy [YUN 2006, p. 66] and Security Council resolution 1373(2001) [YUN 2001, p. 61], its role in assisting States in becoming parties to and implementing the relevant international conventions and protocols relating to terrorism and in strengthening international cooperation mechanisms in criminal matters related to terrorism. In **resolution 63/60** of 2 December (see p. 589), having considered the Secretary-General's report on measures to prevent terrorists from acquiring weapons of mass destruction [A/63/153], the Assembly called upon Member States to support international efforts to prevent terrorists from acquiring such weapons and their means of delivery.

Communications. On 27 February [A/62/711-S/2008/133], Turkey brought to the attention of the Secretary-General the judgement of the Antwerp Court of Appeals in Belgium, acquitting several members of the terrorist Revolutionary People's Liberation Army-Front, which had perpetrated numerous violent acts in Turkey and other European countries. The Turkish authorities were exploring the possibility of appeal. Turkey believed that the conclusions of the Court contradicted the fundamental principles of the global fight against terrorism.

On 23 April [S/2008/296], the League of Arab States forwarded to the Secretary-General resolutions issued at the twentieth session of its Council, including one on ways of combating international terrorism, by which Arab States resolved to support UN counter-terrorism efforts and affirmed the continuation of Arab support to monitor implementation of the Global Counter-Terrorism Strategy.

On 30 May [A/62/853-S/2008/358], the Russian Federation forwarded to the Secretary-General a communiqué on the outcome of the 15 May meeting of the Foreign Ministers of China, India and the Russian Federation, in which they affirmed that anti-terrorism cooperation should be supported within both the UN system and regional organizations. They called upon all UN Member States to comply with international terrorism conventions and related protocols, as well as Security Council resolutions on counter-terrorism. On the same date [A/62/854-S/2008/359], a joint communiqué of the 16 May meeting of the Foreign Ministers of Brazil, China, India and the Russian Federation, in which they emphasized the importance of implementing the UN Global Counter-Terrorism Strategy in all its aspects and considered that UN Member States should take concerted efforts towards the speedy finalization under UN auspices of a comprehensive convention on international terrorism.

On 14 August [A/62/939-S/2008/567], Morocco forwarded to the Secretary-General the Rabat Declaration adopted by the Fifth Conference of Ministers of Justice of the French-speaking African Countries (Rabat, Morocco, 12–16 May) on the implementation of international counter-terrorism instruments. The Conference adopted the Convention on Extradition and Mutual Legal Assistance in Counter-Terrorism, which was annexed to the Declaration.

The Panama Declaration, adopted by Colombia, Costa Rica, the Dominican Republic, El Salvador, Guatemala, Honduras, Mexico, Nicaragua, Panama and Peru at the Second Ministerial Conference on International Cooperation against Terrorism and Transnational Organized Crime (Panama, 26–29 May) [A/62/947-S/2008/585] and transmitted to the Secretary-General on 15 August, called on UNODC and the Organization of American States General Secretariat to continue providing technical assistance to participating States for implementing universal counter-terrorism instruments, and UNODC, including the Terrorism Prevention Branch and its regional offices, to implement the Global Counter-Terrorism Strategy in coordination with regional bodies.

On 23 October [A/63/507-S/2008/675], Iran protested the action taken by the United Kingdom, following a verdict by the British Court of Appeal on 7 May, to remove the name of the so-called "People's Mojahedin Organization of Iran", which Iran described as a terrorist group, from Britain's list of proscribed groups.

On 29 December [S/2008/833], the Philippines requested that the statement made by its representative at the Security Council's 9 December meeting be circulated as a Council document. In the statement, the Philippines said that delays in the prosecution, trials and judgement of terrorists would send the wrong signal to them and their co-conspirators, and embolden them. It urged the United Nations to take action.

Counter-Terrorism Committee

CTC report on implementation of resolution 1624(2005)

In January [S/2008/29], the Chairman of the Committee established pursuant to Security Council resolution 1373(2001) [YUN 2001, p. 61], known as the Counter-Terrorism Committee (CTC), submitted to the Security Council the Committee's second report on the implementation of resolution 1624(2005) [YUN 2005, p. 102], which called on States to combat terrorism, including prohibiting by law and preventing incitement to commit terrorist acts. As at 16 July 2007, 88 States had reported to CTC on their implementation of the resolution. Of the 19 States reporting between 7 September 2006 and 16 July 2007, 10 had introduced legal provisions expressly criminalizing incitement, three had established terrorist acts as criminal offences and had introduced provisions criminalizing incitement to commit any offence, and four had no provisions specific to terrorist acts, although such acts generally fell under other criminal offences, to which general anti-incitement provisions applied. Two of those four States were in the process of drafting specific counter-terrorism legislation. Fewer than half of reporting States had expressly criminalized incitement, although most professed to address the problem through general criminal provisions.

The reports indicated that steps were taken to address other aspects of the resolution, including measures to deny safe haven, strengthen the security of international borders, promote dialogue and understanding among civilizations, and counter incitement motivated by extremism and intolerance. Many States described steps taken to ensure that their measures to implement the resolution complied with all obligations under international law. On the basis of the reports received from States and information gathered through visits, the Committee would explore the needs of States for technical assistance on all aspects of the resolution and would facilitate assistance.

CTC reports on implementation of resolution 1373(2001)

In 2008, the CTC Chairman submitted on 20 March and 18 July CTC's work programmes for the periods from 1 January to 30 June [S/2008/187] and 1 July to 31 December [S/2008/471], respectively. CTC was assisted in its work by the Counter-Terrorism Committee Executive Directorate (CTED).

Report of CTED Executive Director (March). The Executive Director of CTED, reporting to the Council on 19 March [meeting 5855], said that, as requested in resolution 1787(2007) [YUN 2007, p. 66], he had reviewed CTED's organization and methods of work, in consultation with CTC members, the UN membership, CTED staff, UN agencies and outside experts. The revised organizational plan [S/2008/80] was endorsed by CTC on 24 January and was before the Council. Part of the review included general progress made in the implementation of resolution 1373(2001). The review was informed by three priorities: the consistency of judgements across various countries and regions; facilitation of technical assistance; and communication. There was a clear need to explain, particularly to the wider UN membership, CTC work and how it could help countries confront terrorism. The principal organizational change to CTED was the establishment, within the Assessment and Technical Assistance Office, of five cross-cutting functional groups in the areas of technical assistance; terrorist financing; border control, arms trafficking and law enforcement; general legal issues; and issues raised by resolution 1624(2005), as well as the human rights aspects of counter-terrorism. Additionally, two smaller units were created: a quality control unit to review CTED documents and to ensure that they were consistent in style and format; and a communications and outreach unit to develop more proactive communications strategies. Regarding methods of work, the revised organizational plan suggested several innovations: a more flexible approach to country visits to allow for focused visits tailored to the situation of the country concerned; a more comprehensive engagement with donors to better match their capabilities with the vulnerabilities identified in CTC dialogue with countries; more active involvement by CTED in the work of the Counter-Terrorism Implementation Task Force; and strengthened collaboration and cooperation with the experts of the Security Council Committees established pursuant to resolutions 1267(1999) [YUN 1999, p. 265] and 1540(2004) [YUN 2004, p. 544]. The report also highlighted the usefulness of strengthened relations with international, regional and subregional organizations.

The Director was confident that implementing those changes in CTED structure and work would improve its credibility and usefulness. He pointed to two significant Directorate activities: the finalization of the Preliminary Implementation Assessments (PIAs), one for each Member State, on the implementation of resolution 1373(2001)—some 160 of which had been adopted by the Committee and sent to the capitals of the States concerned; and the finalization of the revised "Survey of the implementation of Security Council resolution 1373(2001)", which examined the progress of counter-terrorism efforts in all regions and subregions, difficulties encountered and gaps and vulnerabilities to be addressed.

SECURITY COUNCIL ACTION

On 20 March [meeting 5856], the Security Council unanimously adopted **resolution 1805(2008)**. The draft [S/2008/182] was submitted by Belgium, Burkina Faso, China, Costa Rica, Croatia, France, Italy, Panama, the Russian Federation, the United Kingdom and the United States.

The Security Council,

Reaffirming that terrorism in all its forms and manifestations constitutes one of the most serious threats to international peace and security and that any acts of terrorism are criminal and unjustifiable regardless of their motivation, whenever and by whomsoever committed, and remaining determined to contribute further to enhancing the effectiveness of the overall effort to fight this scourge on a global level,

Recalling its resolution 1373(2001) of 28 September 2001, pursuant to which it established the Counter-Terrorism Committee, and recalling also its other resolutions concerning threats to international peace and security caused by terrorist acts,

Recalling in particular its resolutions 1535(2004) of 26 March 2004 and 1787(2007) of 10 December 2007, which pertain to the Counter-Terrorism Committee Executive Directorate,

Recalling its previous reviews of the Executive Directorate contained in the statements by its President of 21 December 2005 and 20 December 2006, and reaffirming its conclusions contained therein,

Welcoming the revised organizational plan for the Executive Directorate submitted by its Executive Director and the recommendations contained therein,

Noting with appreciation the emphasis by the Executive Directorate on the guiding principles of cooperation, transparency and even-handedness, and its stated intention to adopt a more proactive communications strategy,

Underscoring the central role of the United Nations in the global fight against terrorism, and welcoming the adoption by the General Assembly of the United Nations Global Counter-Terrorism Strategy on 8 September 2006 and the creation of the Counter-Terrorism Implementation Task Force to ensure overall coordination and coherence in the counter-terrorism efforts of the United Nations system,

Reminding States that they must ensure that any measures taken to combat terrorism comply with all their obligations under international law, and should adopt such measures in accordance with international law, in particular international human rights, refugee and humanitarian law, and recalling that the Executive Directorate should continue, in accordance with its mandate, to advise the Counter-Terrorism Committee on issues relating to such law in connection with the identification and implementation of effective measures to implement resolution 1373(2001) and resolution 1624(2005) of 14 September 2005,

1. *Underlines* that the overarching goal of the Counter-Terrorism Committee is to ensure the full implementation of resolution 1373(2001), and recalls the crucial role of the Counter-Terrorism Committee Executive Directorate in supporting the Committee in the fulfilment of its mandate;

2. *Decides* that the Executive Directorate shall continue to operate as a special political mission under the policy guidance of the Counter-Terrorism Committee for the period ending 31 December 2010, and further decides to conduct an interim review by 30 June 2009 and a comprehensive consideration of the work of the Executive Directorate prior to the expiration of its mandate;

3. *Welcomes and affirms* the endorsement by the Counter-Terrorism Committee of the recommendations contained in the revised organizational plan for the Executive Directorate;

4. *Urges* the Executive Directorate to continue strengthening its role in facilitating technical assistance for the implementation of resolution 1373(2001) aimed at increasing the capabilities of Member States in the fight against terrorism by addressing their counter-terrorism needs;

5. *Stresses* the importance of a tailored dialogue among the Executive Directorate, the Counter-Terrorism Committee and Member States, including for the development of relevant implementation strategies by Member States, and encourages the Committee and the Executive Directorate to arrange meetings with Member States in various formats;

6. *Urges* the Executive Directorate also to intensify cooperation with relevant international, regional and subregional organizations with a view to enhancing the capacity of Member States to fully implement resolution 1373(2001) and to facilitate the provision of technical assistance;

7. *Encourages* the Executive Directorate to continue providing the necessary support for the work of the Counter-Terrorism Committee with Member States towards comprehensive implementation of resolution 1624(2005), as set out in paragraph 6 of that resolution;

8. *Welcomes* the briefing by the Executive Director of the Executive Directorate, looks forward to the global survey of the implementation of resolution 1373(2001), and directs the Counter-Terrorism Committee to submit an annual report on the implementation of the present resolution, with its observations and recommendations;

9. *Requests* the Counter-Terrorism Committee, in addition to the report requested in paragraph 8 above, to report orally, through its Chairman, at least every one hundred and eighty days to the Security Council on the overall work of the Committee and the Executive Directorate, and, as appropriate, in conjunction with the reports by the Chairmen of the Security Council Committee established pursuant to resolution 1267(1999) and the Security Council Committee established pursuant to resolution 1540(2004), and encourages informal briefings for all interested Member States;

10. *Reiterates* the need to enhance ongoing cooperation among the Counter-Terrorism Committee, the Committee established pursuant to resolution 1267(1999) and the Committee established pursuant to resolution 1540(2004), as well as their respective groups of experts, including through, as appropriate, enhanced information-sharing, coordinated visits to countries, technical assistance and other issues of relevance to all three Committees, and expresses its intention to provide guidance to the Committees on areas of common interest in order better to coordinate counter-terrorism efforts;

11. *Welcomes and emphasizes* the importance of the readiness of the Executive Directorate to participate actively in and support all relevant activities under the United Nations Global Counter-Terrorism Strategy, including within the Counter-Terrorism Implementation Task Force established to ensure overall coordination and coherence in the counter-terrorism efforts of the United Nations system.

Report of CTC Chairman (May). On 6 May [meeting 5886], the CTC Chairman, in his briefing to the Council, said that the three subsidiary bodies of the Council established pursuant to resolutions 1267(1999), 1373(2001) and 1540(2004) had continued to jointly implement their common strategy through ongoing cooperation, mostly through their expert groups. He reported on the two major initiatives of CTC's work: the adoption of the new CTED organizational plan by the Council in March (see above) and the adoption of PIAS aimed at intensifying dialogue with Member States on implementing resolution 1373(2001). To date, the Committee had adopted 167 of the 192 PIAS. The Committee also adopted its work programme for 1 January to 30 June. Within the first category of its activities, implementation of resolution 1373(2001), besides adopting the PIAS, CTC commenced consideration of the revised survey of Member States' implementation of that resolution. The survey examined the implementation of counter-terrorism efforts in all regions and subregions, pinpointed areas for further improvements and identified shortfalls and vulnerabilities that needed to be addressed either regionally or globally. CTC organized visits to Member States, a fundamental component in monitoring and promoting implementation of resolution 1373(2001), allowing CTED to gain firsthand experience on the ground. The Committee had concluded on-site visits to Bosnia and Herzegovina, the Niger and Saudi Arabia, and was currently visiting Cambodia, to be followed by the Lao People's Democratic Republic. The visits resulted in a comprehensive assessment of all counter-terrorism measures, enhancing the Committee's understanding of the counter-terrorism measures in place, including challenges, best practices and technical assistance needs or programmes, and strengthening its cooperation with other international organizations.

Regarding the facilitation of technical assistance, CTC and CTED were engaged in dialogue with Member States. CTED reviewed strategies and mechanisms for facilitating technical assistance, with a view to strengthening the Committee's contribution and recording its impact. Its future challenge would be to devise more creative approaches so that the Committee, through CTED, could exercise its brokering role as effectively as possible. The Committee posted on its website the technical assistance matrix to help donors guide their assistance programmes and decision-making, and a directory of assistance enabling recipients to view and identify the programmes that best suited their needs.

With respect to the implementation of resolution 1624(2005), CTC submitted to the Council its second report on progress made by Member States in its implementation (see below). The Committee agreed to explore the technical assistance needs of States for implementation, and to facilitate provision of such assistance, while encouraging States that had not yet reported to do so. The Committee continued to play its part in implementing the United Nations Global Counter-Terrorism Strategy, and CTED was participating in the work of the Counter-Terrorism Implementation Task Force. The Committee continued to cooperate with other parts of the UN system, and in particular with the two other Security Council committees dealing with counter-terrorism.

Report of CTC Chairman (June). In June [S/2008/379], the CTC Chairman, in accordance with Council resolution 1805(2008) (see p. 71), submitted the CTC report on the survey of the implementation of resolution 1373(2001). The purpose for the survey was to present current trends in implementing the resolution, with a view to identifying regional vulnerabilities or areas where groups of States were facing particular implementation difficulties and might benefit from a regional or subregional approach to terrorism. The survey focused on the areas addressed by the resolution, notably counter-terrorism legislation and policies pertaining to counter-terrorist financing, border control, law enforcement, international cooperation and the protection of human rights. It also assessed implementation of the resolution by regions and subregions, and drew conclusions about global progress in key thematic areas.

Report of CTC Chairman (November). On 12 November [meeting 6015], the CTC Chairman, in his briefing to the Security Council, reported that since his June briefing, CTC had accomplished several key initiatives. In May, it adopted a document entitled "Survey of the implementation of Security Council resolution 1373(2001)" (see p. 72), which it submitted to the Council. The report, prepared on the basis of evaluations contained in PIAS, contained priority recommendations for the Committee's future action. The Committee continued to analyse PIAS, and had so far adopted 188 of them. As the first deadlines for Member States to respond to PIAS had expired, the Committee endorsed a proposal for conducting the stocktaking of each Member State's implementation of resolution 1373(2001). That process had already started and would be carried out in stages at the subcommittee and Committee levels.

The CTED reorganization plan (see p. 71) established five cross-cutting technical working groups, covering major areas of implementation of resolution 1373(2001), as well as implementation of resolution 1624(2005). The groups presented to the Committee the first results of their work, aimed at revising and harmonizing criteria for technical judgements of elements of resolution 1373(2001), and were completing a document to assist CTED in that task. The Committee continued organizing visits to Member States to monitor and promote implementation of resolution 1373(2001), and had concluded on-site visits to Cambodia, the Lao People's Democratic Republic, South Africa and Egypt, and a focused visit to Madagascar. It was also engaged in a follow-up visit to Kenya, to be followed by visits to Uganda and the United Kingdom. The Committee approved a new list of visits for the period ending 2010. Member States to be visited would be invited to meet with CTC members informally to present their views on the visit and its outcome before finalization of the report.

The Committee reminded Member States to ensure that any measures taken to combat terrorism should comply with international obligations. The Committee explored the technical assistance needs of States to implement resolution 1624(2005), and how to facilitate the provision of such assistance. It encouraged those States that had not yet reported to do so. It also encouraged Member States to become party to and implement the 16 international counter-terrorism instruments, and to play their part in implementing the United Nations Global Counter-Terrorism Strategy, including participation in the Counter-Terrorism Implementation Task Force.

Reports of States. Between February and July, the CTC Chairman transmitted to the Council President reports submitted by Member States on action they had taken or planned to take to implement resolutions 1373(2001) and 1624(2005), and letters from the Committee requesting follow-up information [S/2008/58–59, S/2008/76–77, S/2008/121, S/2008/314–315 & Corr.1, S/2008/336–337, S/2008/385–386].

Counter-Terrorism Committee Executive Directorate

Extension of CTED mandate. On 20 March, the Security Council, in resolution 1805(2008) (see p. 71), extended the cted mandate until 31 December 2010, and asked it to conduct a review by 30 June 2009 and a comprehensive consideration of its work prior to the expiration of its mandate.

Appointment of CTED Executive Director. On 13 November [S/2008/711], the Secretary-General informed the Security Council President of his intention to extend the appointment of Mike Smith (Australia) as CTED Executive Director until 31 December 2009. The Council approved the appointment on 17 November [S/2008/712].

IAEA action

The General Conference of the International Atomic Energy Agency, at its fifty-second session (Vienna, 29 September–4 October), adopted resolution GC(52)/RES/10 on measures to protect against nuclear terrorism, in which it called upon Member States to provide political, financial and technical support, including in-kind contributions, to improve nuclear and radiological security and prevent nuclear and radiological terrorism, and to provide the Nuclear Security Fund the political and—on a voluntary basis—financial support it needed, in a manner which enabled flexibility.

Peacekeeping operations

In 2008, United Nations peacekeeping reached the milestone of its sixtieth anniversary. To commemorate that event, the General Assembly held a special session on 7 November, at which it adopted a Declaration paying tribute to those who had given their lives in the service of humankind.

During the year, the Assembly and the Security Council continued to oversee the management and operation of UN peacekeeping missions. The Council addressed key issues pertaining to the overall conduct of those operations, reviewed the individual mandates of several ongoing operations and created new ones to deal with new security concerns. The Assembly took action on a number of financial and administrative matters.

The Department of Peacekeeping Operations (DPKO) continued to implement the recommendations of the Special Committee on Peacekeeping Operations, whose mandate was to review the whole question of peacekeeping operations in all its aspects.

Sixtieth anniversary of UN peacekeeping

The Special Committee on Peacekeeping Operations, at its 2008 substantive session (New York, 10 March–4 April and 3 July) [A/62/19], recommended to the General Assembly that it hold a commemorative meeting during its sixty-third (2008) session for the sixtieth anniversary of peacekeeping. The Special Committee recommended a draft declaration for adoption by the Assembly.

On 7 November [meeting 41], the General Assembly held the commemorative meeting. The Assembly President said that current peacekeeping operations—all 20 of them, requiring more than 110,000 personnel—were characterized by their unprecedented scale and complexity. They remained a key measure of the ability of the United Nations to meet its Charter mandate and the expectations of the world's peoples. The annual UN peacekeeping budget was approximately $5.6 billion, representing one half of 1 per cent of global military spending. Because a peacekeeping mandate was not specifically spelled out in the Charter, that work had to evolve through innovative partnerships nurtured by different UN organs. Noting the interaction among different areas of UN responsibilities, he said that the Security Council, the Assembly and the Secretariat enjoyed a close partnership that had grown and responded to ever-changing circumstances over the decades. The broad-based participation had helped to assure the credibility of each intervention. The principles of neutrality, transparency and universality gave them legitimacy and should be defended by all. The restructuring of peacekeeping operations, arising from catastrophic failures in the 1990s and highlighted in the groundbreaking report of the Chairman of the Panel on United Nations Peace Operations (Brahimi report) [YUN 2000, p. 83], should enhance the UN ability to identify, coordinate and sustain increasingly complex operations. The Assembly had the responsibility to ensure that operations were equipped with the tools needed to fulfil their mandates, but, almost without exception, they were still being sent into harm's way with insufficient resources. Troop-contributing countries should have more of a say in determining the resources required to minimize the risk and maximize the chances of success of the operations where their troops were sent. Troop-contributing countries also should be involved at the earliest stage when the Security Council mandated an operation, and in any changes in that mandate. That closer involvement would create more reality checks to ensure that operations were well conceived and administered from the outset.

The Deputy Secretary-General recalled that, sixty years earlier, the Council had dispatched a small group of international military observers to the Middle East to supervise an uneasy ceasefire between the new State of Israel and its neighbours. That first peacekeeping mission was an experiment that the founders of the United Nations had not foreseen. The model proved to be a great success. Peacekeeping had evolved into one of the cornerstones of international diplomacy. Currently, there were more than 100,000 UN peacekeepers deployed in 18 missions across the globe. That scale was unprecedented. Peacekeeping operations had also evolved to meet the changing nature of conflict. Beyond monitoring ceasefires, peacekeepers had wide-ranging mandates: helping post-conflict societies to rebuild; nurturing democratic governance; protecting civilians; disarming ex-combatants; supervising elections; and strengthening institutions. The evolution of peacekeeping did not come without cost. Peacekeepers operated in some of the most austere and challenging environments. Peacekeepers needed clear and achievable mandates, political will and material resources. The Deputy Secretary-General asked the Assembly to pay tribute to the more than 2,500 peacekeepers and other personnel who had given their lives while serving the United Nations.

GENERAL ASSEMBLY ACTION

On 7 November [meeting 41], the General Assembly adopted **resolution 63/16** [draft: A/63/L.16 & Add.1] without vote [agenda item 31].

Sixtieth anniversary of United Nations peacekeeping

The General Assembly

Adopts the Declaration on the Occasion of the Sixtieth Anniversary of United Nations Peacekeeping, as set out in the annex to the present resolution.

ANNEX

Declaration on the Occasion of the Sixtieth Anniversary of United Nations Peacekeeping

We, the States Members of the United Nations, recall with pride the awarding of the 1988 Nobel Peace Prize to the United Nations peacekeeping forces. Today, peacekeeping is the flagship activity of the United Nations, helping to restore peace and stability and bringing hope to millions of people in various regions around the world affected by conflicts. We pay tribute to the hundreds of thousands of men and women who, in the past sixty years, have served under the United Nations flag in more than sixty peacekeeping operations around the world, and we honour the memory of more than 2,400 United Nations peacekeepers who gave their lives in the cause of peace. We also commend the efforts made by United Nations and related personnel who are currently performing their duties in peacekeeping operations.

We reiterate our strong support for all measures undertaken to effectively promote the safety and security of United Nations peacekeeping personnel. We, the States Members of the United Nations, reaffirm our commitment and willingness to provide full support to United Nations peacekeepers, to ensure that they are able to successfully and safely fulfil the tasks entrusted to them.

General aspects of UN peacekeeping

Strengthening operational capacity

The Special Committee on Peacekeeping Operations, at its 2008 substantive session (New York, 10 March–4 April and 3 July) [A/62/19], stated that there should be adequate capabilities and clear guidelines for peacekeeping missions to carry out their mandated tasks. The Special Committee welcomed the establishment of the post of the Military Adviser at the Assistant Secretary-General level, and requested the Secretary-General to appoint the Adviser urgently. He should also ensure that the military function within DPKO was appropriately and adequately staffed and structured. That matter should be considered in conjunction with reviews of the organization of DPKO and the Department of Field Support (DFS) to avoid duplication and maximize capacity. The Special Committee urged transparency in the recruitment of staff for senior positions in the Office of Military Affairs. The Secretariat should study and review, in consultation with troop-contributing countries, the requirements for generating military police units and personnel from countries providing troops to a mission.

The Special Committee noted the incorporation of the Police Division in the Office of the Rule of Law and Security Institutions, and reaffirmed its support for the inclusion of the Police Adviser as a permanent member of the DPKO senior management team. It looked forward to receiving by July the report on the review of all aspects of the Standing Police Capacity's first year of operation. It noted the Secretariat's intention to relocate the Standing Police Capacity to the UN Logistics Base at Brindisi, Italy, and looked forward to the consideration of that matter by the General Assembly's Fifth Committee. Recognizing the need to recruit qualified personnel for police components of UN peacekeeping operations, the Special Committee encouraged the Secretariat to improve recruitment procedures and guidance.

To overcome the contingent-owned equipment and sustainability shortfalls faced by some troop-contributing countries, the Special Committee recommended that DPKO and DFS continue to facilitate enabling arrangements, including through other Member States and bilateral arrangements.

Concerning the need for enhanced, rapidly deployable capacities for UN peacekeeping missions in crisis, the Special Committee decided to reconvene its informal open-ended working group on those capacities to prepare a comprehensive report on feasible options for consideration by the Special Committee at its next substantive session.

The Special Committee reiterated the need for the full implementation of the integrated mission planning process and called for periodic briefings by the Secretariat on the status of the implementation. The integrated mission planning process guidelines should be completed as quickly as possible, and the Secretary-General should designate a high-ranking official to oversee and steer the process.

The Special Committee noted the change in subordination of the Situation Centre. It recognized that several divisions and sections of DPKO and DFS might need seconded military and police expertise to increase efficiency and improve communication between the Secretariat, troop-contributing countries and field missions. The Special Committee noted the internal publication entitled "United Nations peacekeeping operations: principles and guidelines", bearing in mind that it did not create legal obligations for Member States or their contingents. It believed that further work on the publication should take into account the views of Member States, best practices and lessons learned in the field and be done in an inclusive and transparent manner.

Strategies for complex peacekeeping operations

The Special Committee on Peacekeeping Operations, at its 2008 substantive session [A/62/19], stressed that the UN system and the international community, in particular donor countries, in cooperation with national authorities, should develop and engage in coordination systems focused on immediate needs, as well as long-term reconstruction and poverty reduction. It recognized that better coordination with UN country teams and development actors was important in ensuring greater efficiency in development efforts and addressing urgent development problems.

The Special Committee recognized the specific needs of children in armed conflict, which should be taken into account in peace negotiations and peace arrangements. It recommended the inclusion of specific child protection provisions in the mandates of peacekeeping operations and the deployment of child protection advisers in peacekeeping operations. DPKO should elaborate the role and responsibilities of the advisers within peacekeeping missions and outline modalities for cooperation with UN agencies, funds and programmes, to ensure a comprehensive strategy of prevention and response with respect to violence against children. The Special Committee recommended the designation of a focal point in DPKO to liaise with the Special Representative of the Secretary-General for Children and Armed Conflict and the Special Representative of the Secretary-General on violence against children in order to further the action of peacekeeping in the area of child protection.

The Special Committee urged the Secretariat and troop-contributing countries to continue harmonizing predeployment awareness programmes and applying UN guidelines on medical clearance and medical conditions that precluded deployment. It recommended that full use be made of opportunities for adequately resourced peer education training programmes. The Special Committee commended outreach efforts by peacekeeping operations, in collaboration with the United Nations Population Fund and the Joint United Nations Programme on HIV/AIDS, to raise awareness among host communities, and the collaborative efforts to integrate HIV issues in disarmament, demobilization and reintegration programmes.

Safety and security

The Special Committee on Peacekeeping Operations, at its 2008 substantive session [A/62/19], expressed grave concern at the security environment in many peacekeeping missions. It stated that the liaison arrangements of UN field operations, which were to maintain contact with the parties, should be improved at appropriate levels, especially tactical and operational levels, so as to establish effective immediate responses to safety and security issues. Some troops were being stretched to cover geographic areas that exceeded their capacities, which threatened their security and adversely affected their performance, discipline, and command and control. It called upon DPKO to ensure that UN peacekeeping personnel were deployed in accordance with agreed concepts of operation.

The Special Committee expressed concern over the quality of local security personnel and its possible impact on the safety and security of peacekeeping personnel. It requested DPKO and the Department of Safety and Security to improve the quality of those personnel and to present a policy for screening and verification before hiring. The Special Committee underlined the importance of assuring that all military and police officers deployed in UN peacekeeping missions were under UN security arrangements, including the UN security management system. It requested the Secretariat to report on steps taken to address the issue.

The Special Committee requested DPKO to report before its next session on the use of advanced monitoring and surveillance technologies in UN peacekeeping operations, and the Secretariat to develop modalities for their use with due attention to legal, operational, technical and financial considerations, as well as the consent of the countries concerned with regard to their application in the field.

The Special Committee welcomed the Secretariat's steps to analyse the factors and circumstances contributing to fatalities of UN peacekeeping personnel. It recommended that the Secretariat improve the collection and processing of data from field missions to allow for more thorough analysis of fatalities and serious injuries, and report annually to Member States. The Special Committee stressed the need for the Secretariat to improve relevant policies and procedures to enhance the mechanism for managing crisis situations in peacekeeping operations in a well-coordinated and effective manner. It requested the Secretariat to develop security procedures with regard to setting up UN positions in peacekeeping missions.

Conduct and discipline

Report of Secretary-General. In March [A/62/758], the Secretary-General, responding to section XVI of General Assembly resolution 61/276 [YUN 2007, p. 83] on peacekeeping issues, submitted a comprehensive report on conduct and discipline, including justification of all posts. The Special Committee on Peacekeeping Operations, at its resumed 2005 session [YUN 2005, p. 120], had adopted the framework for a comprehensive strategy to address sexual exploitation and abuse and other forms of serious misconduct in peacekeeping missions. The strategy was intended to address and eliminate all forms of misconduct in peacekeeping missions, particularly sexual exploitation and abuse, by taking measures aimed at: enforcement action in cases of reported misconduct; provision of assistance to victims of sexual exploitation and abuse; and prevention of misconduct. To enable action in relation to each of the three elements, Member States showed commitment to implementing systemic changes relating to the fundamental paradigm that governed such action. The Conduct and Discipline Unit at Headquarters and those Units in peacekeeping missions had been, since their establishment in 2005, the focal point in DPKO, DFS and the missions for the progressive implementation of the comprehensive strategy to address sexual exploitation and abuse. The report reviewed the functions assigned to the Units, the extent to which their performance of those functions had assisted in implementing the strategy, and elements of the strategy. In addition, a set of operational functions resulting from the strategy was identified, the successful performance of which was dependent on adequate personnel capacity.

While the Conduct and Discipline Unit at Headquarters had made progress in the development of a regulatory framework, new guidelines and Standard Operating Procedures were required to address policies recently adopted and changes in implementation modalities of some processes. None of the special political missions had a Conduct and Discipline Unit per se, but had single Conduct and Discipline Officers, since those missions were small in number of personnel and usually lacked police or military components. All Conduct and Discipline Units had international and national support staff to assist in database management, translation of documents, and provision of administrative and logistical support.

The functions performed by the Units at Headquarters and in the field reflected on their role as mechanisms for internal oversight of conduct, discipline and accountability within DPKO/DFS and peacekeeping missions. Their presence and performance of those functions had contributed to the Organization's progress in establishing aspects of a framework of operational policies and procedures that made for coherent and effective responses to misconduct by peacekeepers. Progress had been made to bring about systemic changes, such as revisions to the model memorandum of understanding and victim assistance strategy. While involved in deliberations for strengthening the criminal accountability of UN personnel, legislative bodies were set to consider a framework for providing minimum levels of welfare and recreation facilities to all categories of peacekeeping personnel and adopt a common code of conduct. At the operational level, the establishment of Conduct and Discipline Units was a distinct improvement on former arrangements, which were fragmented and ad hoc. Those Units, as mechanisms for internal monitoring of conduct and discipline answering to heads of mission and DPKO/DFS, had enhanced the ability of heads of mission to take a "holistic approach" to issues of misconduct, and effectively discharge their disciplinary responsibilities. In peacekeeping missions, the more vigorous, coherent and consistent operational activity in disciplinary matters since 2005 had begun to show some signs of improvement. A comparative review of the available records on the total annual number of reports alleging sexual exploitation and abuse suggested that the strategy might be beginning to bear fruit.

The report provided justification of staffing levels, functions, and their impact on conduct and discipline for the Conduct and Discipline Units at Headquarters and in the field. It proposed converting into posts all general temporary assistance positions at Headquarters and in the field for the 2008–2009 budget period, as the functions performed were ongoing and fully integrated into the mandate and operations of DPKO/DFS and the missions, and not temporary in nature. It also proposed the use of uniform nomenclature, (i.e. "Conduct and Discipline Units").

Pending consideration by the Assembly of those suggestions, the proposed 2008–2009 peacekeeping operations support account budget and individual peacekeeping operations budgets included conduct and discipline staffing requirements. Should the Assembly approve the conversion of all conduct and discipline general temporary assistance positions to posts, there would be no financial implications for 2008–2009 for the peacekeeping operations support account or individual peacekeeping missions.

The Secretary-General recommended that the General Assembly take note of the report and approve the conversion of posts for 2008–2009, as well as uniform nomenclature.

The Assembly, by **decision 62/545 C** of 20 June, deferred until its sixty-third (2008) session the agenda item "Comprehensive report of the Secretary-General on conduct and discipline, including full justification of all posts".

Special Committee on Peacekeeping Operations consideration. The Special Committee on Peacekeeping Operations, at its 2008 substantive session [A/62/19], affirmed that any kind of misconduct by peacekeeping personnel was detrimental to the missions and the Organization's image, and had adverse effects on the population of host countries. All peacekeeping personnel had to adhere to all applicable UN rules, regulations, provisions and guidelines for peacekeepers, as well as to national laws and regulations. All acts of misconduct should be investigated and punished in accordance with due process of law, as well as with memorandums of understanding concluded between the United Nations and Member States. The Special Committee requested that the United Nations take appropriate measures to prevent unsubstantiated allegations of misconduct from damaging the credibility of any UN peacekeeping mission or troop-contributing country or UN peacekeeping personnel, and ensure that steps were taken to restore their image and credibility when allegations of misconduct were found to be legally unproven. The Special Committee welcomed the finalization of the revised model memorandum of understanding [YUN 2007, p. 69] and urged its implementation by the Secretariat in respect of existing and new memorandums of understanding.

The Special Committee noted the Secretary-General's 2007 report on strengthening investigations [ibid., p. 1473] and looked forward to the outcome of the Assembly deliberations on it. It noted the Secretary-General's report on the comprehensive review of the welfare and recreation needs of all categories of peacekeeping personnel [A/62/663] (see p. 100), and requested a further report on the matter, detailing the implications of the proposals. The Special Committee was concerned at the delays in housing peacekeeping personnel in appropriate accommodations with adequate protection against the elements, and requested the Secretariat to improve the situation pursuant to the Contingent-Owned Equipment Manual.

Sexual exploitation and abuse in UN peacekeeping operations

OIOS report. In a February report on peacekeeping operations in 2007 [A/62/281 (Part II & Add.1)], OIOS reported a 64 per cent decrease over 2006 in allegations of sexual exploitation and abuse. While the numbers still underscored the need for strengthening efforts to prevent misconduct, particularly sexual exploitation and abuse, the decline in allegations reflected positively on the Organization's efforts, following the report of the Secretary-General's Special Adviser on Sexual Exploitation and Abuse by United Nations Peacekeeping Personnel on a comprehensive strategy to eliminate sexual exploitation and abuse in UN peacekeeping operations [YUN 2005, p. 119]. Many variables contributed to an environment conducive to behaviour specifically discouraged under the Secretary-General's bulletin [ST/SGB/2003/13] on sexual exploitation and abuse [YUN 2004, p. 107] and other misconduct. Therefore, while progress was being made, because of the complex and evolving nature of the environment in which the Organization operated, there was no guarantee that status quo efforts would lead to a further decline in misconduct. Any allegation of misconduct, regardless of the type, was an allegation that might adversely impact the credibility and reputation of the Organization and hence its ability to discharge its mandate. For its part, OIOS, in its 2007 report on strengthening investigations [YUN 2007, p. 1473], highlighted proposals for restructuring and strengthening its investigation function to better meet the demand for investigations.

Report of Secretary-General. The Secretary-General, in a June report on special measures for protection from sexual exploitation and sexual abuse [A/62/890], submitted in response to General Assembly resolution 57/306 [YUN 2003, p. 1237], indicated that 127 allegations of sexual exploitation and abuse involving DPKO personnel were reported to OIOS in 2007, a substantial decrease from the 357 cases reported in 2006. The highest number of allegations reported (59) originated at the United Nations Organization Mission in the Democratic Republic of the Congo, down from the 176 cases reported in 2006.

As at 31 December, investigations of allegations made in 2007 involving 136 UN peacekeeping personnel were completed. Of the 118 investigations of allegations involving military personnel, 113 were determined to be substantiated and 5 unsubstantiated. One Member State reported ongoing criminal proceedings following the repatriation of 111 military personnel, while three others reported action taken against 21 military personnel, comprising three dismissals from service, six reprimands, seven imprisonments, one reduction in rank and imprisonment, and four dismissals from service and imprisonment. Investigations of allegations involving nine civilian personnel determined six to be substantiated and three unsubstantiated. Investigations of allegations were conducted involving nine police and corrections personnel, two of which were determined to be substantiated and seven unsubstantiated.

Special Committee on Peacekeeping Operations consideration. The Special Committee on Peacekeeping Operations, at its 2008 substantive session [A/62/19], called on the United Nations to continue to implement its policy of zero tolerance of sexual exploitation and abuse in UN peacekeeping operations. Underlining the importance of eliminating all forms of misconduct, the Special Committee remained concerned about new cases of misconduct reported, including sexual exploitation and abuse, and about the number of outstanding allegations still awaiting investigation, and encouraged continued efforts to address that backlog, in accordance with the provisions of the new model memorandum of understanding. It welcomed progress made towards the elimination and prevention of misconduct, including sexual exploitation and abuse, and noted that OIOS had reported a decrease in the number of allegations of sexual exploitation and abuse it had received (see p. 78). It suggested that such data should be disaggregated according to type of misconduct alleged. It welcomed the Assembly's adoption of the strategy on assistance to victims of sexual exploitation by UN personnel [YUN 2007, p. 1519].

Cooperation with troop-contributing countries

The Special Committee on Peacekeeping Operations, at its 2008 substantive session [A/62/19], expressed the view that the relationship between those who planned, mandated and managed UN peacekeeping operations and those who implemented the operations' mandates should be enhanced. Troop-contributing countries, through their experience and expertise, could contribute to the planning process and assist the Security Council in making effective and timely decisions. It called upon the Secretariat to improve information-sharing with troop-contributing countries and to ensure that the Secretary-General's reports on specific operations were circulated to those countries in time for holding meetings with them before discussions among Council members. It encouraged all troop-contributing countries to participate in meetings with the Council and the Secretariat in order to achieve meaningful outcomes, and underscored the importance of better interaction between the Council's Working Group on Peacekeeping Operations and troop-contributing countries, so that the experience and expertise of those countries could be drawn upon when implementing and extending peacekeeping mandates. It encouraged the Working Group to implement the recommendations contained in its 2006 report [YUN 2006, p. 86].

The Special Committee urged the Secretariat to consult with the troop-contributing countries when planning changes in the tasks, rules of engagement, operational concepts or command and control structure that impacted the personnel, equipment, training and logistics requirements, in order to enable them to give advice in the planning process and to ensure that their troops had the capacity to meet the new demands. The Secretariat should also consult with those countries when planning a drawdown of troops in any peacekeeping operation. The drawdown should take place only after consideration of inputs from the troop-contributing countries and bearing in mind the situation on the ground. Existing procedures for interaction between troop-contributing countries, the Secretariat and the Council should be used to their fullest extent.

The Special Committee recognized progress by the Secretariat in increasing cooperation and consultations with troop-contributing countries and looked forward to continued and improved cooperation, including easy access to briefing material in written form. It requested the Secretariat to produce predeployment threat assessments and share them with potential troop-contributing countries. It also recognized the possible benefit from potential troop-contributing countries making reconnaissance visits to new missions before presenting their pledges to those missions, and the need for more cooperation in that regard between DPKO, DFS and the Department of Safety and Security, and more interactions with potential troop-contributing countries from the early stages of planning.

Cooperation with regional organizations

The Special Committee on Peacekeeping Operations, at its 2008 substantive session [A/62/19], noted the Secretariat's establishment of a capacity for partnerships, other than that dedicated to the African Union, to serve as a coordination point for all issues related to cooperation with regional arrangements and other multilateral partners engaged in matters relating to peacekeeping operations. The Committee believed that the new capacity could avoid duplication or competition of efforts among multilateral institutions. It looked forward to continued dialogue with the Secretariat on making the best use of the possibilities for employing regional arrangements' capacities under appropriate circumstances, as envisaged in the 2005 World Summit Outcome [YUN 2005, p. 49]. It reiterated its support for the Secretary-General's proposal to implement modalities for operational cooperation in peacekeeping within regional arrangements.

Women in peacekeeping

The Special Committee on Peacekeeping Operations, at its 2008 substantive session [A/62/19], encouraged DPKO to support local women's peace initiatives and the involvement of women and women's groups in all activities related to the peace process and conflict resolution. In that regard, it recognized the importance of gender advisers to UN missions. The Special Committee underlined the gravity of all acts of sexual and gender-based violence, including sexual exploitation and abuse, and stressed the importance of addressing the needs of all victims of such acts. It emphasized the need for regular training of UN staff and related personnel in gender-sensitive approaches in the context of their responsibilities and mandate, and for responding to cases of sexual and gender-based violence in a culturally sensitive manner and the deployment of UN gender advisers to missions. The Special Committee noted the continuing under-representation of women at senior management levels and among uniformed personnel in peacekeeping missions. It urged DPKO to develop a comprehensive strategy for increasing women's participation in all aspects and at all levels of UN peacekeeping operations, pursuant to General Assembly resolution 59/164 on the improvement of the status of women in the UN system [YUN 2004, p. 1429] and Security Council resolution 1325(2000) on women and peace and security [YUN 2000, p. 1113].

Communication. On 16 June [S/2008/402], the United Kingdom transmitted to the Council President the summary report of the Wilton Park conference on "Women targeted or affected by armed conflict: what role for military peacekeepers", organized by the United Nations Development Fund for Women, UN Action Against Sexual Violence in Conflict and DPKO, with the assistance of Canada and the United Kingdom.

On 19 June, the Security Council, in **resolution 1820(2008)** (see p. 1265), expressed concern about the persistent obstacles and challenges to the participation and full involvement of women in the prevention and resolution of conflict as a result of violence, intimidation and discrimination, which eroded women's capacity and legitimacy to participate in post-conflict public life. It urged the Secretary-General and his Special Envoys to invite women to participate in discussions pertinent to the prevention and resolution of conflict, the maintenance of peace and security, and post-conflict peacebuilding, and encouraged all parties to facilitate the equal and full participation of women at decision-making levels.

Report of Secretary-General. The Secretary-General, in his September report on women and peace and security [S/2008/622] (see also p. 1264), stated that, as at July 2008, women constituted 2.2 per cent of military personnel in UN peacekeeping operations compared to 1 per cent in July 2004, and 7.6 per cent of civilian police personnel compared to 5 per cent in 2004. In those settings where peacekeeping missions were supporting the restructuring of police services (Kosovo, Timor-Leste, Sierra Leone), women civilian police represented more than 15 per cent. As at 30 June 2008, women's representation in DPKO in civilian posts in the Professional and higher categories reached 28.6 per cent, and 26.3 per cent at the D-1 level and above, up from 27.5 and 12 per cent respectively in 2004. In DFS, women accounted for 36.4 per cent of all Professional and higher-level personnel. In field-based operations, women's representation accounted for 23 per cent. The Secretary-General had stepped up efforts to increase the number of women in peacekeeping, in particular at the senior leadership level. As at September 2008, there was one woman Head of Mission (Liberia) and seven Deputy Heads of Mission (Burundi, Chad, Democratic Republic of the Congo, Lebanon, Liberia, Nepal, the Sudan).

The Secretary-General stated that the deployment of women in peacekeeping forces, in police forces and among civilian personnel facilitated engagement with local women, enhanced their access to social and psychological services, including trauma counselling, information-sharing on sexual harassment, abuse and rape, and lowered the incidence of sexual violence and abuse, particularly in camps of internally displaced persons and refugees. Member States endeavoured to enlarge the pool of qualified women eligible for secondment to peacekeeping and peacebuilding missions. Training of military police and civilian peacekeeping personnel on the protection, rights and particular needs of women, as well as the importance of involving women in all peacekeeping functions, received attention from Member States, the United Nations and civil society. DPKO led UN efforts to provide training and improve training materials and tools. The International Research and Training Institute for the Advancement of Women developed an interactive website highlighting gender training opportunities for UN peacekeepers. Thirteen full-time gender advisers in UN peacekeeping operations, including integrated missions, provided technical guidance to heads of mission to increase women's participation in implementing the operation's mandate. Five missions had a gender focal point, a staff member who had the gender portfolio in addition to other tasks. DPKO developed guidelines to ensure that gender advisers were serving as catalysts for gender mainstreaming. The United Nations Volunteers programme increased the number of gender specialists from 3 in 2004 to 19 in 2008. DFS and DPKO increased the representation of women among UN uniformed personnel, including by strengthening their outreach to Member States, particularly troop- and police-contributing countries.

In statement **S/PRST/2008/39** of 29 October (see p. 1264), the Council President said that the Council remained concerned about the underrepresentation of women at all stages of peace processes and in peacebuilding, and called upon the Secretary-General to appoint more women to pursue good offices on his behalf, particularly as Special Representatives and Special Envoys. It urged Member States and international, regional and subregional organizations to take measures to increase women's participation in conflict prevention, conflict resolution and peacebuilding, and to strengthen the role of women as decision makers in those areas. The Council also requested the Secretary-General to report on the obstacles and challenges to strengthening the participation of women in those areas, including recommendations to address those issues, by October 2009.

Oversight activities

OIOS reported in February [A/62/281 (Part II)] on its peacekeeping oversight activities from 1 January to 31 December 2007. The Office issued 154 oversight reports related to peace operations, which accounted for 54 per cent of all OIOS recommendations. The recommendations highlighted four risk areas: governance, compliance, and financial and operational risks. While overall resources dedicated to peace operations remained at a similar level in 2007 as the year before, a new OIOS presence was established in the United Nations Interim Force in Lebanon and the United Nations Integrated Mission in Timor-Leste, while the presence of the Office in the United Nations Operation in Burundi (ONUB) was phased out. OIOS also expanded its presence in the United Nations Organization Mission in the Democratic Republic of the Congo (MONUC). The scope of OIOS audits varied widely from relatively routine to complex global or horizontal audits in areas such as fuel management, procurement and management, and direction of special political missions. During the reporting period, the resident audit offices conducted comprehensive risk assessments of mission activities, which would serve as the basis for the 2008 Internal Audit Division audit workplan.

In 2007, the OIOS Investigations Division received 469 allegations pertaining to staff involved in peace operations, comprising 65 per cent of all allegations received by the Division that year. In total, 87 investigation reports were issued in 2007.

In the area of governance risk, OIOS assessed impact on mission operations arising from failure to inform, direct, manage and monitor UN activities. An audit of occupational safety and health in the United Nations Mission in Liberia (UNMIL) found that DPKO needed to work with the Department of Safety and Security to develop guidelines for the occupational safety and health of civilian personnel in that Mission. The lack of direction provided to the Mission resulted in fragmentation of safety and health programmes. Overall, UNMIL programmes did not meet international standards, nor did they adequately mitigate occupational safety and health risks. As a result, personnel were exposed to high risk of accidents and health problems that could have been averted by meeting minimum standards. In an audit of UNIFIL, OIOS found that the Mission needed to formulate indicators of achievement and performance measures for the political and civilian affairs components of its operations, which were critical to evaluating the effectiveness of operations. Reviews of four missions noted that, while the practice of results-based budgeting was evolving, several areas needed improvement to enhance its utility in peacekeeping missions. Two main issues hindered its full utilization: it was not fully utilized as a management tool in most missions because it was not linked to or integrated into the mission implementation plans; and there was a lack of results-based budgeting capacity at the missions due to staff turnover and a lack of useful results-based budgeting guidance.

As to compliance risk, OIOS, based on its comprehensive audit of the United Nations Mission in Nepal, concluded that policies and procedures on human resources, procurement and logistical support that were specific to launching short-term political missions needed to be developed, considering the limited duration of their mandates and the associated political and reputational risks to the Organization. The absence of such policy adversely affected the deployment of political missions and their mandate implementation. There were also serious internal control shortcomings in the Mission's operational areas, particularly administrative and logistical planning, procurement and asset management. Other examples of compliance risk were found in UNMIL, the United Nations Mission in Ethiopia and Eritrea, ONUB, MONUC, the United Nations Disengagement Observer Force (UNDOF), the United Nations Interim Administration Mission in Kosovo and the United Nations Stabilization Mission in Haiti.

Among examples of financial risk, the report noted the OIOS Procurement Task Force's examination of some 40 complaints involving corruption and procurement irregularities in MONUC. The Task Force found numerous cases of vendors and companies having to pay staff as a prerequisite for the award of business contracts, or offering to pay money in exchange for assistance in the procurement process. The Task Force identified extensive efforts by several procurement staff members to solicit payments and bribes from vendors in exchange for preferential treatment and benefits. It also found extensive corruption in the Mission's procurement and an overall collapse of ethical culture. A lack of continuity at the managerial level on the one hand, improper ethics and procurement training, and little rotation of staff on the other, contributed to that development. The Task Force concluded that the Mission should overhaul its procurement operations and provide ethics training, or divest responsibility for procurement to Headquarters or an independent third party. An audit of the management of systems contracts for peacekeeping operations identified various internal control weaknesses, from the planning stage to vendor performance evaluation and payments, which represented high risk of inefficiency and ineffectiveness in operations.

Operational risk involved impact on the mandate arising from failure of internal processes. In an audit of UNDOF, OIOS found that there was little rotation of procurement staff, while good management practice called for periodic rotation to minimize the risk of collusion with vendors. In an audit of air operations of the United Nations Mission in the Sudan, OIOS found that the Mission's air assets, comprising 42 aircraft, were underutilized. OIOS recommended that the Mission conduct a comprehensive review of its air asset requirements and adjust its fleet to ensure cost-effectiveness.

In an April addendum to the report [A/62/281 (Part II)/Add.1], the Secretary-General provided his comments on the OIOS findings.

By **decision 62/545 C** of 20 June, the Assembly deferred until its sixty-third (2008) session the item on "Report on the activities of the Office of Internal Oversight Services for the period from 1 January to 31 December 2007, and the Secretary-General's note transmitting his comments thereon".

Public information in peacekeeping operations

The General Assembly, in Part III of **resolution 63/100 B** of 5 December (see p. 702) on the role of the Department of Public Information (DPI) in UN peacekeeping operations, commended the DPI role and its network of UN information centres in commemorating the sixtieth anniversary of UN peacekeeping (see p. 74). It requested the Secretariat to ensure the Department's involvement from the planning stage of future peacekeeping operations through interdepartmental consultations and coordination with other Secretariat departments, in particular DPKO and DFS. It requested DPI, DPKO and DFS to continue their cooperation in raising awareness of the new realities, successes and challenges faced by peacekeeping operations, especially multidimensional and complex ones, and the recent surge in UN peacekeeping activities, and welcomed efforts by the three Departments to develop and implement a comprehensive communications strategy on current challenges facing UN peacekeeping. The Assembly also asked DPI and DPKO to cooperate in implementing an outreach programme to explain the Organization's zero-tolerance policy regarding sexual exploitation and abuse and to inform the public of the outcome of all such cases involving peacekeeping personnel.

Comprehensive review of peacekeeping

Special Committee on Peacekeeping Operations

As requested by the General Assembly in resolution 61/291 [YUN 2007, p. 75], the Special Committee on Peacekeeping Operations and its Working Group continued their comprehensive review of peacekeeping operations in all their aspects [A/62/19]. In response to the Committee's request, the Secretary-General submitted a December report [A/63/615 & Add.1] on the implementation of the Committee's recommendations.

The Special Committee held its 2008 session from 10 March to 4 April and 3 July in New York. The Special Committee discussed guiding principles, definitions and implementation of mandates, restructuring of peacekeeping, safety and security, conduct and discipline, strengthening operational capacity, strategies for complex peacekeeping operations, cooperation with troop-contributing countries, enhancement of African peacekeeping capabilities, cooperation with regional arrangements, best practices, training, personnel issues and financial matters.

GENERAL ASSEMBLY ACTION

On 11 September [meeting 121], the General Assembly, on the recommendation of the Fourth (Special Political and Decolonization) Committee [A/62/406/Add.1], adopted **resolution 62/273** without vote [agenda item 34].

Comprehensive review of the whole question of peacekeeping operations in all their aspects

The General Assembly,

Recalling its resolution 2006(XIX) of 18 February 1965 and all other relevant resolutions,

Recalling in particular its resolutions 61/267 A of 16 May 2007 and 61/267 B and 61/291 of 24 July 2007,

Affirming that the efforts of the United Nations in the peaceful settlement of disputes, including through its peacekeeping operations, are indispensable,

Convinced of the need for the United Nations to continue to improve its capabilities in the field of peacekeeping and to enhance the effective and efficient deployment of its peacekeeping operations,

Considering the contribution that all States Members of the United Nations make to peacekeeping,

Noting the widespread interest in contributing to the work of the Special Committee on Peacekeeping Operations expressed by Member States, in particular troop-contributing countries,

Bearing in mind the continuous necessity of preserving the efficiency and strengthening the effectiveness of the work of the Special Committee,

1. *Welcomes* the report of the Special Committee on Peacekeeping Operations and its Working Group;

2. *Endorses* the proposals, recommendations and conclusions of the Special Committee, contained in paragraphs 15 to 199 of its report;

3. *Urges* Member States, the Secretariat and relevant organs of the United Nations to take all necessary steps to implement the proposals, recommendations and conclusions of the Special Committee;

4. *Reiterates* that those Member States that become personnel contributors to the United Nations peacekeeping operations in years to come or participate in the future in the Special Committee for three consecutive years as observers shall, upon request in writing to the Chairman of the Special Committee, become members at the following session of the Special Committee;

5. *Decides* that the Special Committee, in accordance with its mandate, shall continue its efforts for a comprehensive review of the whole question of peacekeeping operations in all their aspects and shall review the implementation of its previous proposals and consider any new proposals so as to enhance the capacity of the United Nations to fulfil its responsibilities in this field;

6. *Requests* the Special Committee to submit a report on its work to the General Assembly at its sixty-third session;

7. *Decides* to include in the draft agenda of its sixty-third session the item entitled "Comprehensive review of the whole question of peacekeeping operations in all their aspects".

On 5 December, the Assembly, by **decision 63/523**, took note of the report of the Fourth Committee on the comprehensive review peacekeeping [A/63/402].

Operations in 2008

As at 1 January 2008, there were 17 peacekeeping missions in operation—8 in Africa, 1 in the Americas, 2 in Asia, 3 in Europe and the Mediterranean and 3 in the Middle East. During the year, one mission was completed: the United Nations Mission in Ethiopia and Eritrea, bringing the total number of missions in operation at year's end to 16.

Africa

In Africa, the Security Council extended the mandates of the United Nations Mission for the Referendum in Western Sahara until 30 April 2009, and of the United Nations Mission in Ethiopia and Eritrea until 31 July 2008. On 30 July, it decided to terminate the latter's mandate as at 31 July 2008. The Council also extended the mandates of the United Nations Mission in Liberia until 30 September 2009; and the United Nations Mission in the Sudan until 30 April 2009. The Council twice renewed the mandate of the United Nations Operation in Côte d'Ivoire—first, until 30 July 2008 and second, until 31 January 2009. It extended the deployment of the United Nations Organization Mission in the Democratic Republic of the Congo (MONUC) until 31 December 2009; the mandate of the African Union-United Nations Hybrid Operation in Darfur until 31 July 2009; and the mandate of the United Nations Mission in the Central African Republic and Chad until 15 March 2009.

Americas

In the Americas, the Security Council extended the mandate of the United Nations Stabilization Mission in Haiti until 15 October 2009.

Asia

In Asia, the United Nations Military Observer Group in India and Pakistan, established in 1949, continued to monitor the ceasefire in Jammu and Kashmir.

The Security Council extended the mandate of the United Nations Integrated Mission in Timor-Leste until 26 February 2009.

In September, the Council extended the authorization of the International Security Assistance Force in Afghanistan for a further period of 12 months beyond 13 October 2008.

Europe and the Mediterranean

In Europe and the Mediterranean, the Security Council twice extended the mandate of the United Nations Observer Mission in Georgia: until 15 October 2008 and 15 February 2009; and that of the United Nations Peacekeeping Force in Cyprus until 15 December 2008 and 15 June 2009. The United Nations Interim Administration Mission in Kosovo, Serbia, remained in place. On 21 November 2007, the Council authorized the Member States acting through or in cooperation with the European Union to establish, for a further period of 12 months, a multinational stabilization force (EUFOR) in Bosnia and Herzegovina (**resolution 1845(2008)**) (see p. 431).

Middle East

Three long-standing operations continued in the Middle East. The United Nations Truce Supervision Organization continued to monitor ceasefires, supervise armistice agreements and assist other peacekeeping operations in the region. The mandate of the United Nations Disengagement Observer Force was twice renewed, until 31 December 2008 and until 30 June 2009; and that of the United Nations Interim Force in Lebanon was renewed until 31 August 2009.

Roster of 2008 operations

UNTSO

United Nations Truce Supervision Organization

Established: May 1948.

Mandate: To monitor ceasefires, supervise armistice agreements and assist other peacekeeping operations in the Middle East.

Strength as at December 2008: 151 military observers.

UNMOGIP

United Nations Military Observer Group in India and Pakistan

Established: January 1949.

Mandate: To supervise the ceasefire between India and Pakistan in Jammu and Kashmir.

Strength as at December 2008: 44 military observers.

UNFICYP

United Nations Peacekeeping Force in Cyprus

Established: March 1964.

Mandate: To prevent the recurrence of fighting between the two Cypriot communities.

Strength as at December 2008: 859 troops, 68 police.

UNDOF

United Nations Disengagement Observer Force

Established: June 1974.

Mandate: To supervise the ceasefire between Israel and the Syrian Arab Republic and the disengagement of Israeli and Syrian forces in the Golan Heights.

Strength as at December 2008: 1,039 troops.

UNIFIL

United Nations Interim Force in Lebanon

Established: March 1978.

Mandate: To restore peace and security and assist the Lebanese Government in ensuring the return of its effective authority in the area; expanded in 2006 to include monitoring the cessation of hostilities in Lebanon and Israel [YUN 2006, p. 584], supporting the deployment of the Lebanese Armed Forces throughout southern Lebanon, and helping to ensure humanitarian access to civilian populations and the safe return of displaced persons.

Strength as at December 2008: 12,435 troops.

MINURSO

United Nations Mission for the Referendum in Western Sahara

Established: April 1991.

Mandate: To monitor and verify the implementation of a settlement plan for Western Sahara and assist in the holding of a referendum in the Territory.

Strength as at December 2008: 20 troops, 197 military observers, 6 civilian police.

UNOMIG

United Nations Observer Mission in Georgia

Established: August 1993.

Mandate: To verify compliance with a ceasefire agreement between the parties to the conflict in Georgia and investigate ceasefire violations; expanded in 1994 to include monitoring the implementation of an agreement on a ceasefire and separation of forces and observing the operation of a multinational peacekeeping force.

Strength as at December 2008: 136 military observers, 20 civilian police.

UNMIK

United Nations Interim Administration Mission in Kosovo

Established: June 1999.

Mandate: To promote the establishment of substantial autonomy and self-government in Kosovo, perform basic civilian administrative functions, organize and oversee the development of provisional institutions, facilitate a political process to determine Kosovo's future status, support reconstruction of key infrastructure, maintain civil law and order, protect human rights and assure the return of refugees and displaced persons.

Strength as at December 2008: 841 civilian police, 22 military observers.

MONUC

United Nations Organization Mission in the Democratic Republic of the Congo

Established: November 1999.

Mandate: To establish contacts with the signatories to the Ceasefire Agreement, provide technical assistance in the implementation of the Agreement, provide information on security conditions, plan for the observation of the ceasefire, facilitate the delivery of humanitarian assistance and assist in the protection of human rights; expanded in 2007 to include assisting the Government in establishing a stable security environment [YUN 2007, p. 119] and supporting the strengthening of democratic institutions and the rule of law.

Strength as at December 2008: 16,603 troops, 740 military observers, 1,079 civilian police.

UNMEE

United Nations Mission in Ethiopia and Eritrea

Established: July 2000.

Mandate: To establish and put into operation the mechanism for verifying the cessation of hostilities and to assist the Military Coordination Commission in tasks related to demining and in administrative support to its field offices.

Terminated: 31 July 2008.

UNMIL

United Nations Mission in Liberia

Established: 19 September 2003.

Mandate: To support the implementation of the ceasefire agreement and the peace process; protect UN staff, facilities and civilians; support humanitarian and human rights activities; and assist in national security reform, including national police training and the formation of a new, restructured military.

Strength as at December 2008: 10,607 troops, 180 military observers, 1,066 civilian police.

UNOCI

United Nations Operation in Côte d'Ivoire

Established: April 2004.

Mandate: To monitor the implementation of the 3 May 2003 comprehensive ceasefire agreement and the movement of armed groups; assist in disarmament, demobilization, reintegration, repatriation and resettlement; protect UN personnel, institutions and civilians; support humanitarian assistance; support implementation of the peace process; and assist in the promotion of human rights, public information, and law and order. The mandate was expanded in 2007 [YUN 2007, p. 170] to include assisting in disarming and dismantling militias; identifying the population and organizing elections; reforming the security sector; monitoring the arms embargo; and supporting the redeployment of State administration.

Strength as at December 2008: 7,830 troops, 197 military observers, 1,163 civilian police.

MINUSTAH

United Nations Stabilization Mission in Haiti

Established: June 2004.

Mandate: To ensure a secure and stable environment in support of the Transitional Government; support the constitutional and political process; support the Transitional Government in bringing about national dialogue, conducting free and fair elections, and extending State authority throughout the country; promote and protect human rights and coordinate with the Transitional Government in the provision of humanitarian assistance.

Strength as at December 2008: 7,036 troops, 2,053 civilian police.

UNMIS

United Nations Mission in the Sudan

Established: March 2005.

Mandate: To support the implementation of the Comprehensive Peace Agreement signed between the Government of the Sudan and the Sudan People's Liberation Movement/Army on 9 January 2005; facilitate and coordinate the voluntary return of refugees and internally displaced persons (IDPs), and humanitarian assistance; assist with demining; and protect human rights. The mandate was expanded in 2006 to support implementation of the 2006 Darfur Peace Agreement [YUN 2006, p. 274] and the 2004 N'djamena Agreement on Humanitarian Ceasefire on the Conflict in Darfur [YUN 2004, p. 235].

Strength as at December 2008: 8,726 troops, 620 military observers, 679 civilian police.

UNMIT

United Nations Integrated Mission in Timor-Leste

Established: August 2006.

Mandate: To support the Government of Timor-Leste in consolidating stability; enhancing a culture of democratic governance; facilitating political dialogue; conducting the 2007 electoral process; establishing a continuous presence in the three border districts, alongside UN police officers; reviewing the role and needs of the security sector; building the capacity of State and Government institutions and strengthening capacity and mechanisms for monitoring, promoting and protecting human rights; and promoting justice and reconciliation.

Strength as at December 2008: 33 military observers, 1,517 civilian police.

UNAMID

African Union-United Nations Hybrid Operation in Darfur

Established: July 2007.

Mandate: To contribute to the restoration of security conditions necessary for the safe provision of humanitarian assistance throughout Darfur; contribute to the protection of threatened populations; observe compliance with and verify the implementation of ceasefire agreements signed since 2004, and assist in the implementation of the 2006 Darfur Peace Agreement [YUN 2006, p. 274] and subsequent agreements; assist the political process to ensure inclusiveness; support joint AU-UN mediation efforts; contribute to a secure environment for economic reconstruction and development, as well as the return of IDPs and refugees; contribute to the protection of human rights; promote the rule of law; and monitor the security situation at Sudan's borders with Chad and the Central African Republic.

Strength as at December 2008: 12,194 troops, 2,767 civilian police, 175 military observers.

MINURCAT

United Nations Mission in the Central African Republic and Chad

Established: September 2007.

Mandate: To select, train, advise and facilitate support to elements of the Police tchadienne pour la protection humanitaire; contribute to the creation of a more secure environment; support the Chadian Government and the Office of the United Nations High Commissioner for Refugees in relocating refugee camps; exchange information with the Sudanese Government, the AU Mission in the Sudan, UNAMID and other regional and international organizations on threats to humanitarian activities in the region; contribute to the monitoring, promotion and protection of human rights; support the strengthening of the capacity of the Governments of Chad and the Central African Republic, and civil society, through training in international human rights standards and efforts to end the recruitment and use of children by armed groups; and assist Chad and the Central African Republic in promoting the rule of law.

Strength as at December 2008: 44 military observers, 235 civilian police.

Financial and administrative aspects of peacekeeping operations

The General Assembly considered a number of issues related to financial and administrative aspects of UN peacekeeping operations, including the financial performance of UN peacekeeping operations; the support account for peacekeeping operations; funds for closed missions; consolidation of peacekeeping accounts; financial reports and audited financial statements; procedures for determining reimbursement to Member States for contingent-owned equipment; best practices, management and financing of the UN Logistics Base at Brindisi, Italy; restructuring; personnel matters; criminal responsibility of UN staff and experts on mission; welfare and recreational needs of peacekeeping staff; death and disability; training; and staffing of field missions.

Financing

Expenditures for UN peacekeeping operations from 1 July 2007 to 30 June 2008 rose by 21.7 per cent, from $5,148.1 million in the previous fiscal year to $6,265.8 million [A/63/5 (Vol. II)]. The net increase was mainly due to the start-up of UNAMID and MINURCAT and the expansion of UNIFIL, which were partially offset by the reduced expenditures for UNMIS.

In terms of the overall financial situation during the year, assessments, unpaid assessments and expenditures all increased, with a corresponding decrease in liquidity in active missions totalling $136.8 million. Outstanding unpaid assessments for active peacekeeping missions increased by 44 per cent, from $707.5 million to $1,018.9 million. Unpaid assessments for closed missions did not change significantly. As at 30 June, total unpaid assessments amounted to $1,576.5 million.

Available cash for active missions totalled $1,891.5 million, while liabilities reached $2,224.7 million. For closed missions, available cash totalled $507.5 million, while liabilities were $481.8 million. Closed missions with cash surpluses continued to be the only available source of lending to active peacekeeping missions. New loans totalling $72 million were made during the reporting period, bringing total loans outstanding as at 30 June to $37.6 million.

Notes of Secretary-General. In a January note [A/C.5/62/23], the Secretary-General, further to the information provided in 2007 [YUN 2007, p. 85] on approved resources for peacekeeping operations, the United Nations Logistics Base (UNLB) at Brindisi, Italy, and the support account for peacekeeping operations from 1 July 2007 to 30 June 2008, provided updated information reflecting financing actions taken by the General Assembly during its sixty-second session in respect of MINURCAT and UNAMID, bringing the total to $6,746,805,700.

In May [A/C.5/62/28], in accordance with General Assembly resolution 49/233 A [YUN 1994, p. 1338], the Secretary-General submitted to the Fifth Committee information on the proposed budgetary requirements of each peacekeeping operation, including budget levels for UNLB and the support account for peacekeeping operations, for 1 July 2008 to 30 June 2009, by category, and with the aggregate total resource requirements amounting to $7,376,102,600.

In August [A/C.5/62/31], the Secretary-General submitted information on approved resources for peacekeeping operations for 1 July 2008 to 30 June 2009, including requirements for UNLB, and the support account for peacekeeping operations, amounting to $7,093,389,000.

Financial performance

In April [A/62/727], the Secretary-General submitted an overview report on the financing of UN peacekeeping operations: budget performance for the period from 1 July 2006 to 30 June 2007 and the budget for 1 July 2008 to 30 June 2009. During the former period, total expenditure amounted to $5,156.9 million, against an approved budget of $5,399.1 million, exclusive of voluntary contributions in kind. The budget for peacekeeping operations for the latter period was estimated at $7,368.3 million.

The Advisory Committee on Administrative and Budgetary Questions (ACABQ), in an April report [A/62/781] on administrative and budgetary aspects of the financing of peacekeeping operations, reviewed and commented on the Secretary-General's overview report on budget performance for 2006–2007 and budgets for 2008–2009, as well as the report of the Board of Auditors on peacekeeping operations.

On 20 June (**decision 62/545 C**), the General Assembly deferred consideration until its sixty-third (2008) session of the Secretary-General's report and the related ACABQ report.

Peacekeeping support account

In March [A/62/766 & Add.1], the Secretary-General submitted the performance report on the budget of the support account for peacekeeping operations for the period from 1 July 2006 to 30 June 2007. Expenditures for the period amounted to $177,695,400, against approved resources of $189,017,400, resulting in an unencumbered balance of $11,322,000, which was attributable primarily to underexpenditure in respect of non-post resources, offset by additional requirements under post, communications and medical expenditures.

The Secretary-General recommended that the General Assembly not transfer the amount of $2,014,000 included in the $7,097,000 previously authorized in resolution 61/279 [YUN 2007, p. 97], representing the excess of the authorized level of the Peacekeeping Reserve Fund used to finance the requirements of the support account for 1 July 2007 to 30 June 2008; apply the total amount of $13,790,000, comprising the unencumbered balance of $5,491,600 and other income of $1,759,000 for the financial year ended 30 June 2007, the support account fund balance from the periods 1996–1997 to 1999–2000 in the amount of $2,138,000, and the excess of the authorized level of the Peacekeeping Reserve Fund for the financial period ended 30 June 2007 in the amount of $4,401,400, to the support account requirements for 1 July 2006 to 30 June 2007; apply the excess of the authorized level of the Peacekeeping Reserve Fund for the financial period ended 30 June 2007 in the amount of $2,014,000 to the support account requirements for 1 July 2007 to 30 June 2008; and apply the amount of $469,600, representing the remaining balance of the excess of the authorized level of the Peacekeeping Reserve Fund for the financial period ended 30 June 2007, to the support account requirements for the following year.

In April [A/62/783 & Corr.1], the Secretary-General submitted the budget for the support account for peacekeeping operations for the period from 1 July 2008 to 30 June 2009, amounting to $287,651,700. It provided for a total of 1,278 posts, comprising 1,122 continuing posts, 76 new posts, including 15 transferred from peacekeeping missions, and 80 general temporary assistance positions converted to posts.

The Independent Audit Advisory Committee submitted in May [A/62/814 & Add.1] its comments on the proposed budget for OIOS under the support account for peacekeeping operations for 1 July 2008 to 30 June 2009, with an emphasis on the proposed restructuring of the Investigations Division.

In June [A/62/855], ACABQ provided its observations and recommendations on the financial performance report for 1 July 2006 to 30 June 2007 and the proposed budget for the support account for peacekeeping operations from 1 July 2008 to 30 June 2009. The report also addressed the proposed additional resources for DPKO's Office of Military Affairs (see p. 95). ACABQ recommended approval of 54 of the 156 posts proposed by the Secretary-General in his report on the support account budget, and 29 of the 92 additional posts proposed for strengthening the Office of Military Affairs. It recommended that the Assembly approve the staffing and non-staffing resources requested by the Secretary-General, subject to its observations and recommendations, and requested that the adjusted amount be provided to the Assembly. It also recommended approval of the recommendations contained in the performance report for 1 July 2006 to 30 June 2007.

GENERAL ASSEMBLY ACTION

On 20 June [meeting 109], the General Assembly, on the recommendation of the Fifth Committee [A/62/600/Add.1], adopted **resolution 62/250** without vote [agenda item 140].

Support account for peacekeeping operations

The General Assembly,

Recalling its resolutions 45/258 of 3 May 1991, 47/218 A of 23 December 1992, 48/226 A of 23 December 1993, 55/238 of 23 December 2000, 56/241 of 24 December 2001, 56/293 of 27 June 2002, 57/318 of 18 June 2003, 58/298 of 18 June 2004, 59/301 of 22 June 2005, 60/268 of 30 June 2006, 61/245 and 61/246 of 22 December 2006, 61/256 of 15 March 2007 and 61/279 of 29 June 2007, its decisions 48/489 of 8 July 1994, 49/469 of 23 December 1994 and 50/473 of 23 December 1995 and its other relevant resolutions,

Having considered the reports of the Secretary-General on the financing of the support account for peacekeeping operations and on the comprehensive analysis of the Office of Military Affairs of the Department of Peacekeeping Operations, the preliminary report of the Secretary-General on the status of implementation of General Assembly resolution 61/279 on strengthening the capacity of the United Nations to manage and sustain peacekeeping operations, the report of the Independent Audit Advisory Committee on the proposed budget for the Office of Internal Oversight Services under the support account for peacekeeping operations for the period from 1 July 2008 to 30 June 2009 and the related report of the Advisory Committee on Administrative and Budgetary Questions,

Recognizing the importance of the ability of the United Nations to respond and deploy rapidly to a peacekeeping operation upon adoption of a relevant resolution of the Security Council, within thirty days for traditional peacekeeping operations and ninety days for complex peacekeeping operations,

Recognizing also the need for adequate support during all phases of peacekeeping operations, including the liquidation and termination phases,

Mindful that the level of the support account should broadly correspond to the mandate, number, size and complexity of peacekeeping missions,

1. *Takes note* of the reports of the Secretary-General on the financing of the support account for peacekeeping operations and on the comprehensive analysis of the Office of Military Affairs of the Department of Peacekeeping Operations, the preliminary report of the Secretary-General on the status of implementation of General Assembly resolution 61/279 on strengthening the capacity of the United Nations to manage and sustain peacekeeping operations, and the report of the Independent Audit Advisory Committee on the proposed budget for the Office of Internal Oversight Services under the support account for peacekeeping operations for the period from 1 July 2008 to 30 June 2009;

2. *Reaffirms* its role with regard to the structure of the Secretariat, and stresses that proposals that amend the overall departmental structure, as well as the format of the budgets of the Organization and the biennial programme plan, are subject to review and approval by the General Assembly;

3. *Also reaffirms* its role in carrying out a thorough analysis and approval of human and financial resources and policies with a view to ensuring the full, effective and efficient implementation of all mandated programmes and activities and the implementation of policies in this regard;

4. *Further reaffirms* that the Fifth Committee is the appropriate Main Committee of the General Assembly entrusted with responsibility for administrative and budgetary matters;

5. *Reaffirms* rule 153 of its rules of procedure;

6. *Emphasizes* that ongoing management reforms must be fully taken into account when presenting additional proposals for reform;

7. *Reaffirms* that the support account funds shall be used for the sole purpose of financing human resources and non-human resource requirements for backstopping and supporting peacekeeping operations at Headquarters, and that any changes in this limitation require the prior approval of the General Assembly;

8. *Also reaffirms* the need for adequate funding for the backstopping of peacekeeping operations, as well as the need for justification for that funding in support account budget submissions;

9. *Recalls* the role of the Secretary-General as the Chief Administrative Officer of the Organization, in accordance with the provisions of Article 97 of the Charter of the United Nations;

10. *Reiterates* that the delegation of authority on the part of the Secretary-General should be in order to facilitate the better management of the Organization, but stresses that the overall responsibility for management of the Organization rests with the Secretary-General as the Chief Administrative Officer;

11. *Affirms* the need for the Secretary-General to ensure that the delegation of authority to the Department of Peacekeeping Operations, the Department of Field Support and field missions is in strict compliance with relevant resolutions and decisions, as well as relevant rules and procedures of the General Assembly on this matter;

12. *Stresses* that heads of departments report to and are accountable to the Secretary-General;

13. *Notes* the unique nature of the reporting line from the head of the Department of Field Support to the Under-Secretary-General for Peacekeeping Operations, and decides that having one head of department (Department of Field Support) report to and take direction from another head of department (Department of Peacekeeping Operations) shall not set a precedent in the Secretariat;

14. *Requests* the Secretary-General to address systemic issues that hamper good management of the Organization, including by improving work processes and procedures, and in that context stresses that structural change is no substitute for managerial improvement;

15. *Reiterates* the importance of strengthened accountability in the Organization and of ensuring greater accountability of the Secretary-General to Member States, inter alia, for the effective and efficient implementation of legislative mandates and the use of human and financial resources;

16. *Recalls its request* to the Secretary-General to specifically define accountability, as well as clear accountability mechanisms, including to the General Assembly, and to propose clear parameters for its application and the instruments for its rigorous enforcement, without exception, at all levels, to ensure effective and efficient operations and management of resources in the Organization;

17. *Emphasizes* the importance of preserving the unity of command in missions at all levels, as well as a coherence in policy and strategy and clear command structures in the field and up to and including Headquarters;

18. *Requests* the Secretary-General to ensure a clear chain of command, accountability, coordination and maintenance of an adequate system of checks and balances;

19. *Emphasizes* the importance of interaction and coordination with troop-contributing countries;

20. *Also emphasizes* the need to ensure the safety and security of United Nations personnel;

21. *Urges* the Secretary-General, within the framework established in its resolutions 52/12 B of 19 December 1997 and 52/220 of 22 December 1997, to define explicitly the role and duties of the Deputy Secretary-General in the reform set out in its resolution 61/279, including in relation to the Department of Peacekeeping Operations, the Department of Field Support, the Department of Political Affairs and the Department of Management;

22. *Recalls* section I, paragraph 6, of its resolution 55/238, paragraph 11 of its resolution 56/241 and paragraph 19 of its resolution 61/279, and requests the Secretary-General to ensure the proper representation of troop-contributing countries in the Department of Peacekeeping Operations and the Department of Field Support, taking into account their contribution to United Nations peacekeeping;

23. *Reiterates* that the Secretary-General, in employing staff, shall ensure the highest standards of efficiency, competence and integrity as the paramount consideration, with due regard for the principle of equitable geographical distribution, in accordance with Article 101, paragraph 3, of the Charter and relevant resolutions of the General Assembly;

24. *Reaffirms* paragraph 67 of its resolution 61/279, and requests the Secretary-General to include detailed information on mechanisms in place and measures taken to address the management challenges which the new organizational structure of the Department of Peacekeeping Operations/Department of Field Support poses, and the improvement that the new structure has brought in ensuring efficiency and effectiveness in the support for peacekeeping operations and special political missions, as well as to coordination with the Department of Political Affairs, in the context of the comprehensive report to be submitted at the second part of its resumed sixty-third session;

25. *Notes with concern* the late submission of the budgets of some peacekeeping operations, which puts considerable strain on the work of the General Assembly and the Advisory Committee on Administrative and Budgetary Questions, and, while recognizing the challenges faced in preparing the budget proposals and related reports on peacekeeping and special factors affecting some missions, requests the Secretary-General to intensify his efforts to improve the quality and timely issuance of peacekeeping documents;

26. *Reiterates its request* in paragraph 13 of its resolution 60/268 and paragraph 32 of its resolution 61/279, and urges the Secretary-General to submit the comprehensive report on the evolution of the support account at the second part of its resumed sixty-third session within the context of his next budget proposal for the support account;

27. *Notes* that the application of an accurate vacancy rate is good budgetary practice and essential for the appropriate assessment on Member States;

28. *Requests* the Secretary-General, when submitting his budget proposals, to include details of the full annual cost of posts for the subsequent budget;

29. *Takes note* of paragraph 48 of the report of the Advisory Committee on Administrative and Budgetary Questions;

30. *Stresses* the importance of complementarity of efforts and avoiding duplication between integrated operational teams and substantive components of the Secretariat, and requests the Secretary-General to report thereon, and to provide a clear definition of the roles and responsibilities of the integrated operational teams, in the comprehensive report to be submitted to the General Assembly at the second part of its resumed sixty-third session;

31. *Affirms* the importance of ensuring that the information and communications technology operations and requirements relating to peacekeeping are fully addressed and properly managed, taking into account the principle of unity of command;

32. *Reaffirms* the need for effective and efficient administration and financial management of peacekeeping operations, and urges the Secretary-General to continue to identify measures to increase the productivity and efficiency of the support account;

33. *Requests* the Secretary-General to ensure the full implementation of the relevant provisions of General Assembly resolutions 59/296 of 22 June 2005, 60/266 of 30 June 2006 and 61/276 of 29 June 2007 and other relevant resolutions;

34. *Endorses* the conclusions and recommendations contained in the report of the Advisory Committee on Administrative and Budgetary Questions, subject to the provisions of the present resolution;

35. *Takes note* of paragraphs 81 to 87 of the report of the Advisory Committee on Administrative and Budgetary Questions, and decides to establish the following posts in the current structure of the Office of Military Affairs:

(*a*) One D-1, two P-5, ten P-4 and four P-3 posts in the Office of the Military Adviser and one P-4 post for a civilian officer;

(*b*) Three P-4 posts and two P-3 posts in the Force Generation Service;

(*c*) Twelve P-4 posts in the Military Planning Service;

(*d*) Four P-4 posts in the Current Military Operations Service;

(*e*) One P-4 and three P-3 posts to be assigned to the Logistics Support Division of the Department of Field Support;

(*f*) One P-4 and one P-3 to be assigned to the Information and Communications Technology Division of the Department of Field Support;

36. *Requests* the Secretary-General to submit for its consideration at its sixty-fourth session a comprehensive report on the implementation of the strengthening of the Office of Military Affairs and its impact on the organization and capacities of the Office;

37. *Requests* the Special Committee on Peacekeeping Operations to consider the report referred to in paragraph 36 above at its 2010 substantive session;

38. *Decides* to approve the following posts:

(*a*) One P-5 post for a Security Focal Point in the Situation Centre, Department of Peacekeeping Operations;

(*b*) Two P-4 posts for a Policy Adviser and a Policy Development Officer in the Police Division, Department of Peacekeeping Operations;

(*c*) One P-3 post for a Programme Officer in the Risk Management Unit of the Office of the Under-Secretary-General for Field Support;

(*d*) One P-3 post for a Finance and Budget Officer in the Budget and Performance Reporting Service of the Field Budget and Finance Division, Department of Field Support;

(*e*) One D-2 post for the Director of the Information and Communications Technology Division, Department of Field Support;

(*f*) One General Service (Other level) post for a Human Resources Assistant (Roster Development) in the Office of Human Resources Management;

39. *Decides* not to approve the following posts:

(*a*) One D-1 post for a Principal Officer and one General Service (Other level) post for an Administrative Assistant in the Asia and Middle East Division, Department of Peacekeeping Operations;

(*b*) One P-3 post in the Engineering Section of the Logistics Support Division, Department of Field Support;

(*c*) One P-4 post in the Property Management Section of the Logistics Support Division, Department of Field Support;

(*d*) One P-4 post for a Technical Information Operations Support Officer, Department of Field Support;

(*e*) One P-4 post for a Management Analyst Officer in the Management Support Service of the Office of the Under-Secretary-General for Management;

(*f*) One General Service (Other level) Finance Assistant (Health and Life Insurance Section) in the Accounts Division, Department of Management;

(*g*) One P-4 and one P-3 post for Procurement Officers in the Procurement Division, Department of Management;

(*h*) One P-4 Legal Officer in the Office of the Legal Counsel, Office of Legal Affairs;

40. *Decides* to convert one P-5 and one General Service general temporary assistance position in the Conduct and Discipline Unit to posts;

41. *Also decides* to approve the following positions as general temporary assistance:

(*a*) One P-4 Human Resources Officer (Outreach and Strategic Staffing Section) in the Office of Human Resources Management, Department of Management;

(*b*) One P-3 Finance Officer in the Treasury Division, Department of Management;

42. *Takes note* of paragraph 130 of the report of the Advisory Committee on Administrative and Budgetary Questions, and decides to continue the four P-3 positions in the Peacekeeping Financing Division, Department of Management;

43. *Decides* to reduce the non-post resources by 1,899,100 United States dollars, and requests the Secretary-General to consider applying the reduction, inter alia, to the consultancy requirements referred to in paragraphs 297 and 354 of the report of the Secretary-General on the budget for the support account for peacekeeping operations for the period from 1 July 2008 to 30 June 2009;

44. *Also decides* to maintain, for the financial period from 1 July 2008 to 30 June 2009, the funding mechanism for the support account used in the current period, from 1 July 2007 to 30 June 2008, as approved in paragraph 3 of its resolution 50/221 B of 7 June 1996;

Financial performance report for the period from 1 July 2006 to 30 June 2007

45. *Takes note* of the report of the Secretary-General on the financial performance of the support account for peacekeeping operations for the period from 1 July 2006 to 30 June 2007;

46. *Decides* not to transfer the amount of 2,014,000 dollars included in the amount of 7,097,000 dollars, previously authorized in its resolution 61/279, representing the excess of the authorized level of the Peacekeeping Reserve Fund utilized to finance the requirements of the support account in respect of the period from 1 July 2007 to 30 June 2008;

47. *Decides* to apply the total amount of 13,790,000 dollars, comprising the unencumbered balance of 5,491,600 dollars and other income of 1,759,000 dollars in respect of the financial period ended 30 June 2007, the support account fund balance in respect of financial periods ended 30 June 1997, 30 June 1998, 30 June 1999 and 30 June 2000 in the total amount of 2,138,000 dollars, and the excess of the authorized level of the Peacekeeping Reserve Fund in respect of the financial period ended 30 June 2007 in the amount of 4,401,400 dollars, to the support account requirements for the period from 1 July 2006 to 30 June 2007;

48. *Also decides* to apply the excess of the authorized level of the Peacekeeping Reserve Fund in respect of the financial period ended 30 June 2007 in the amount of 2,014,000 dollars to the support account requirements for the period from 1 July 2007 to 30 June 2008;

Budget estimates for the financial period from 1 July 2008 to 30 June 2009

49. *Approves* the support account requirements in the amount of 273,922,800 dollars for the financial period from 1 July 2008 to 30 June 2009, including 1,122 continuing and 98 new temporary posts and their related post and non-post requirements;

Financing of the budget estimates

50. *Decides* that the requirements for the support account for peacekeeping operations for the financial period from 1 July 2008 to 30 June 2009 shall be financed as follows:

(*a*) The amount of 469,600 dollars, representing the balance remaining of the excess of the authorized level of the Peacekeeping Reserve Fund in respect of the financial period ended 30 June 2007, to be applied to the resources required for the financial period from 1 July 2008 to 30 June 2009;

(*b*) The balance of 273,453,200 dollars to be prorated among the budgets of the active peacekeeping operations for the financial period from 1 July 2008 to 30 June 2009;

(*c*) The estimated staff assessment income of 26,274,600 dollars, comprising the amount of 26,221,200 dollars for the financial period from 1 July 2008 to 30 June 2009 and the increase of 53,400 dollars in respect of the financial period ended 30 June 2007, to be offset against the balance referred to in subparagraph (*b*) above, to be prorated among the budgets of the individual active peacekeeping operations.

Funds for closed missions

In March [A/62/757], the Secretary-General provided information on the updated financial position of 20 closed peacekeeping missions as at 30 June 2007. The net cash surplus in the accounts of 15 closed missions credited to Member States as at that date amounted to $181,776,000, not including $18,316,000 owed by the United Nations Support Mission in Haiti/United Nations Transition Mission in Haiti/United Nations Civilian Police Mission in Haiti, the United Nations Mission in the Central African Republic and MINURSO. Five of the closed missions reflected cash deficits totalling $88,036,000, owing to outstanding payments of assessed contributions.

The Secretary-General recommended that the General Assembly, subject to its approval of his proposal to consolidate the peacekeeping accounts effective 1 July 2008, in accordance with the framework outlined in his updated report on the consolidation of peacekeeping accounts [A/62/726] (see below), decide to return to Member States credits available as at 30 June 2008 in closed peacekeeping missions with cash surpluses.

In April [A/62/816], ACABQ provided its comments on the Secretary-General's report. It also called for fresh proposals to resolve the problem of debts in cash-deficient closed missions.

Consolidation of peacekeeping accounts

The Secretary-General, in response to General Assembly resolution 61/278 [YUN 2007, p. 87], submitted in March an updated comprehensive report [A/62/726] on the consolidation of peacekeeping accounts, including a simulation of options proposed. The Secretary-General's original proposal [YUN 2006, p. 97] was to consolidate retroactively all peacekeeping accounts, of both active and closed missions, except for the United Nations Emergency Force (UNEF), the United Nations Operation in the Congo (ONUC), the Peacekeeping Reserve Fund and the strategic deployment stocks, to improve cash management and operational flexibility. The Secretariat still considered that to be the preferred approach—the one that would provide the greatest flexibility in the use of peacekeeping resources with increased reimbursements to troop- and police-contributing Member States while simplifying the administrative processes for financing operations. Consideration was given to the consolidation of the accounts of only the active missions, or alternatively only the closed missions, but no significant benefits of such approaches could be identified.

The proposed consolidation framework envisaged the following: the peacekeeping accounts would be consolidated retroactively, effective 1 July 2008, with the four exceptions; peacekeeping assessments would be consolidated quarterly during each peacekeeping period (July, October, January and April) on the basis of the approved appropriation for each peacekeeping mission and its mandate period, with the provision that assessments should also cover any outstanding unassessed appropriations from prior financial periods; and credits from unencumbered balances, interest and other miscellaneous income would be applied to offset the consolidated assessments of the subsequent fiscal period, similar to the practice under the regular budget, and voluntary contributions would be taken into account. Upon consolidation, all outstanding and unpaid balances would be combined, except for the outstanding amounts for UNEF and ONUC, and the arrears of Belarus and Ukraine before 1996. With regard to amounts in suspense in favour of Member States at the effective date, all unapplied credit balances and overpayments to all peacekeeping missions would be combined and offset in total against the outstanding and unpaid balances at that date; remaining unapplied amounts would be carried forward and applied to the consolidated assessments issued after the implementation date.

The Secretary-General's budget proposals for each peacekeeping mission would continue to be prepared separately; however, there would be a single financing resolution showing the breakdown by mission, and there would be no transfer of appropriations between missions. A consolidated performance report would be presented at the overall peacekeeping budget level and would report the consolidated expenditures compared to the overall total appropriations, as well as expenditures and appropriations by mission, focusing on significant issues emerging from the analysis of the most important drivers of expenditure. Results-based budgeting frameworks would continue to be presented for each mission as addenda to the financial performance report. In light of the overall improvement in liquidity, credits available as at 30 June 2008 in closed peacekeeping missions with cash surpluses should be returned to Member States individually prior to consolidation; the credits would first be applied to reduce a Member State's unpaid assessment, if any, and thereafter be used at the discretion of the Member State. Credits available to be returned totalled $181.8 million as at 30 June 2007.

The Secretary-General said that the proposed consolidation of peacekeeping accounts would permit more consistent and timely reimbursements to troop- and police-contributing countries, since cash in the peacekeeping accounts would be commingled, obviating the need to defer payments for cash-poor missions; enable payments in respect of certain liabilities in closed missions currently deferred due to lack of cash in their respective accounts; enable the return of credits in closed peacekeeping missions with cash surpluses to Member States; facilitate planning and administration for Member States, since the total requirements for the entire financial year would be largely known at the beginning of the financial period, thereby reducing the number of peacekeeping assessments from about 40 per financial period to only four; require a single General Assembly resolution rather than 17 separate resolutions on the financing of peacekeeping operations; improve the overall liquidity of peacekeeping operations, resulting in greater flexibility in the use of peacekeeping resources; simplify the administrative processes; and result in a simplified set of financial statements, as a single consolidated expenditure statement combining expenditures for peacekeeping operations would be prepared and another statement would break down expenditures by mission.

The Secretary-General requested the Assembly to consolidate the peacekeeping accounts effective 1 July 2008 in accordance with the proposed framework.

ACABQ, in its comments [A/62/818] on the Secretary-General's report, stated that it continued to believe that it was for Member States to decide on the matter.

Accounts and auditing

At its resumed sixty-second (2008) session, the General Assembly considered the financial report and audited financial statements for UN peacekeeping operations for the period from 1 July 2006 to 30 June 2007 [A/62/5 (Vol. II)], the Secretary-General's report on the implementation of the recommendations of the Board of Auditors [A/62/784], and the related ACABQ report [A/62/823].

GENERAL ASSEMBLY ACTION

On 20 June [meeting 109], the General Assembly, on the recommendation of the Fifth Committee [A/62/534/Add.1], adopted **resolution 62/223 B** without vote [agenda item 125].

Financial reports and audited financial statements, and reports of the Board of Auditors

The General Assembly,

Recalling its resolutions 58/249 B of 18 June 2004, 59/264 B of 22 June 2005, 60/234 B of 30 June 2006, 61/233 B of 29 June 2007 and 62/223 A of 22 December 2007,

Having considered the financial report and audited financial statements for the twelve-month period from 1 July 2006 to 30 June 2007 and the report of the Board of Auditors on the United Nations peacekeeping operations, the report of the Advisory Committee on Administrative and Budgetary Questions on the report of the Board of Auditors on the accounts of the United Nations peacekeeping operations for the financial period ended 30 June 2007 and the report of the Secretary-General on the implementation of the recommendations of the Board of Auditors concerning the United Nations peacekeeping operations for the financial period ended 30 June 2007,

1. *Accepts* the audited financial statements of the United Nations peacekeeping operations for the period from 1 July 2006 to 30 June 2007;

2. *Takes note* of the observations and endorses the recommendations contained in the report of the Board of Auditors;

3. *Reiterates* that the issue of outstanding assessed contributions is a policy matter of the General Assembly, and urges all Member States to make every possible effort to ensure the payment of their assessed contributions in full;

4. *Takes note* of the observations and endorses the recommendations contained in the report of the Advisory Committee on Administrative and Budgetary Questions on the report of the Board of Auditors;

5. *Commends* the Board of Auditors for the quality of its report and the streamlined format thereof;

6. *Takes note* of the report of the Secretary-General on the implementation of the recommendations of the Board of Auditors concerning the United Nations peacekeeping operations for the financial period ended 30 June 2007;

7. *Requests* the Secretary-General to ensure the full implementation of the recommendations of the Board of Auditors, including those relating to the cancellation of unliquidated obligations and the system of assets management, and the related recommendations of the Advisory Committee in a prompt and timely manner, subject to the provisions of the present resolution;

8. *Also requests* the Secretary-General to continue to indicate an expected time frame for the implementation of the recommendations of the Board of Auditors as well as the priorities for their implementation, including the office-holders to be held accountable and measures taken in that regard;

9. *Further requests* the Secretary-General to continue to provide, in future reports on the implementation of the recommendations of the Board of Auditors concerning the United Nations peacekeeping operations, a full explanation for delays in the implementation of all outstanding recommendations of the Board.

Reimbursement issues

Reformed procedures for determining reimbursement for contingent-owned equipment

Report of Working Group. On 22 February [A/C.5/62/26], the Chairman of the 2008 Working Group on Contingent-Owned Equipment transmitted to the Fifth Committee the report on the Group's findings on reimbursement rates for equipment. The Working Group, which was presented with 24 issue papers by various Member States and the Secretariat, addressed the issues for the reimbursement procedure in three areas (major equipment, self-sustainment, medical support services), each dealt with by a subworking group. According to the report, the overall impact of changes in reimbursement rates and the addition of new services would result in an increase of 2.7 per cent of the contingent-owned equipment portion of the UN peacekeeping budget based on memorandums of understanding. The Working Group conducted a comprehensive review of contingent-owned ducted a comprehensive review of contingent-owned equipment reimbursement rates for major equipment and the model/procedures for future reviews. It recommended the adoption of proposed revised rates, and that future triennial reviews be conducted in the form of a comprehensive review, using data provided or elected by troop/police contributors.

Report of Secretary-General. In April [A/62/774 & Corr.1], the Secretary-General, in his report on the subject, set out the cost implications of implementing the Working Group's recommendations estimated at $57,701,993 for the first year, which would be reported with effect from 1 July 2008 in the context of the individual peacekeeping operations' financial performance reports for the 2008–2009 biennium. The Secretary-General said that the proposed revised standards and administrative procedures and the addition of new categories and subcategories would benefit the Secretariat by improving the structure of the contingent-owned equipment system and provide more transparent and enhanced verification tools. The Secretariat requested Member States to submit national cost data no later than two months prior to the next Working Group meeting.

The Secretary-General recommended that the Assembly approve the new reimbursement rates recommended for major equipment, self-sustainment and medical support services, and adopt the revised format for future triennial reviews of contingent-owned equipment reimbursement rates using actual cost data. In regard to "special cases" major equipment, the Assembly should approve the proposed reimbursement rates for new items and new categories of major equipment; agree to an increase in the threshold value of "special cases" from $500 to $1,000; and adopt the addition to the definition of "special cases". It should also approve the increase from 10 per cent to 20 per cent in the provision to deploy major equipment as overstock in accordance with the quantities authorized in the memorandum of understanding; adopt the predeployment training activities proposed by the Integrated Training Service; agree to the revision of the self-sustainment standard under "accommodation"; adopt the revision of the calculation of mission factors; approve the increase in recreational leave allowance for members of military contingents/formed police units from 7 days to 15; agree to the revision of the self-sustainment subcategory "welfare" and inclusion of "Internet access" as a subcategory with a reimbursement rate of $2.76 per person per month; approve the standards and reimbursement rates for provision of "basic firefighting" and "fire detection and alarm" capabilities in field missions at $0.16 and $0.13 per person per month, respectively; adopt the proposed reimbursement method for medical structures; agree to the revision of standards for "basic first aid" and "high-risk areas"; adopt the definition and reimbursement rates of "fee for service" for medical support services; and approve the revised standards of medical facilities and the equipment list of the aero-medical evacuation and forward surgery modules.

In May [A/62/851], ACABQ recommended approval of the 2008 Working Group's proposals. While agreeing with the recommendation that the overstock of major equipment be increased from 10 to 20 per cent, ACABQ noted that the higher ceiling might result in significant financial implications for the Organization.

GENERAL ASSEMBLY ACTION

On 20 June [meeting 109], the General Assembly, on the recommendation of the Fifth Committee [A/62/600/Add.1], adopted **resolution 62/252** without vote [agenda item 140].

Reformed procedures for determining reimbursement to Member States for contingent-owned equipment

The General Assembly,

Recalling its resolutions 55/274 of 14 June 2001 and 59/298 of 22 June 2005,

Having considered the report of the Secretary-General on the reformed procedures for determining reimbursement to Member States for contingent-owned equipment, the report of the 2008 Working Group on Contingent-Owned Equipment, as transmitted by the Chairman of the Working Group to the Chairman of the Fifth Committee, and the related report of the Advisory Committee on Administrative and Budgetary Questions,

1. *Takes note* of the report of the Secretary-General on the reformed procedures for determining reimbursement to Member States for contingent-owned equipment and the report of the 2008 Working Group on Contingent-Owned Equipment, as transmitted by the Chairman of the Working Group to the Chairman of the Fifth Committee;

2. *Endorses* the conclusions and recommendations contained in the report of the Advisory Committee on Administrative and Budgetary Questions, subject to the provisions of the present resolution;

3. *Takes note* of paragraph 6 of the report of the Advisory Committee, and invites the Working Group to reconsider its recommendation at its next meeting;

4. *Recalls* paragraph 8 of its resolution 55/274, and requests the Secretary-General to submit an update of his report, including the arrangements for recreational leave allowance, for its consideration at the second part of its resumed sixty-third session.

Peacekeeping best practices

On 20 June (**decision 62/545 C**), the General Assembly deferred until its sixty-third (2008) session, consideration of the Secretary-General's report on peacekeeping best practices [YUN 2007, p. 87].

Special Committee consideration. The Special Committee on Peacekeeping Operations, at its 2008 substantive session [A/62/19], noted the ongoing review by DPKO of technically feasible options for making guidance materials available to troop-contributing countries in the most efficient manner, steps taken to include a best practices officer or focal point in peacekeeping missions, and the importance of developing best practices materials and integrating them into learning processes in staff members' daily work; and it looked forward to being informed on those issues.

Management of peacekeeping assets

United Nations Logistics Base

The General Assembly, at its resumed sixty-second (2008) session, considered the performance report on the UNLB budget for the period from 1 July 2006 to 30 June 2007 [A/62/669]. Expenditure for the period totalled $32,929,200 gross ($30,688,000 net) against a total appropriation of $35,478,700 gross ($32,943,500 net), resulting in an unencumbered balance of $2,549,500 gross ($2,555,500 net). The total value from strategic deployment of stocks for the period amounted to $88.2 million, including a $21.9 million rollover from the prior-period fund balance, and $66.3 million corresponding to shipments of strategic deployment stocks at replacement values to peacekeeping and special political missions and to other entities, thereby generating funds for replenishment. Strategic stock replenishment expenditures for the period amounted to $36.8 million. The balance of some $51 million was rolled over to the 2007–2008 period.

The Secretary-General requested the Assembly to decide on the treatment of the unencumbered balance and of other income/adjustments for the period amounting to $2,982,600 from interest income ($2,045,000), other/miscellaneous income ($262,200) and savings on or cancellation of prior-period obligations ($675,400).

The Assembly considered the proposed UNLB budget for 1 July 2008 to 30 June 2009 [A/62/769] amounting to $45,827,400, an increase of $5,447,800 or 13.5 per cent over the previous financial period and providing for 59 international staff, 206 national staff and 22 temporary positions.

In May [A/62/781/Add.12], ACABQ recommended that the UNLB proposed budget be reduced by $58,400 and that the Assembly appropriate an amount of $45,769,000 gross for the maintenance of the Base for the period from 1 July 2008 to 30 June 2009.

In June [A/C.5/62/30], the Secretary-General submitted to the Fifth Committee a note reflecting the resources to be approved by the Assembly in respect of each peacekeeping mission, including the prorated shares of the support account for peacekeeping operations and UNLB.

GENERAL ASSEMBLY ACTION

On 20 June [meeting 109], the General Assembly, on the recommendation of the Fifth Committee [A/62/600/Add.1], adopted **resolution 62/251** without vote [agenda item 140].

Financing of the United Nations Logistics Base at Brindisi, Italy

The General Assembly,

Recalling section XIV of its resolution 49/233 A of 23 December 1994 and its resolution 62/231 of 22 December 2007,

Recalling also its decision 50/500 of 17 September 1996 on the financing of the United Nations Logistics Base at Brindisi, Italy, and its subsequent resolutions thereon, the latest of which was resolution 61/277 of 29 June 2007,

Recalling further its resolution 56/292 of 27 June 2002 concerning the establishment of the strategic deployment stocks and its subsequent resolutions on the status of the implementation of the strategic deployment stocks, the latest of which was resolution 61/277,

Having considered the reports of the Secretary-General on the financing of the United Nations Logistics Base and the related report of the Advisory Committee on Administrative and Budgetary Questions,

Reiterating the importance of establishing an accurate inventory of assets,

1. *Notes with appreciation* the facilities provided by the Government of Italy to the United Nations Logistics Base at Brindisi, Italy;

2. *Endorses* the conclusions and recommendations contained in the report of the Advisory Committee on Administrative and Budgetary Questions, and requests the Secretary-General to ensure their full implementation;

3. *Requests* the Secretary-General to ensure the full implementation of the relevant provisions of its resolutions 59/296 of 22 June 2005, 60/266 of 30 June 2006 and 61/276 of 29 June 2007, as well as other relevant resolutions;

Financial performance report for the period from 1 July 2006 to 30 June 2007

4. *Takes note* of the report of the Secretary-General on the financial performance of the United Nations Logistics Base for the period from 1 July 2006 to 30 June 2007;

Budget estimates for the period from 1 July 2008 to 30 June 2009

5. *Approves* the cost estimates for the United Nations Logistics Base amounting to 45,769,000 United States dollars for the period from 1 July 2008 to 30 June 2009;

Financing of the budget estimates

6. *Decides* that the requirements for the United Nations Logistics Base for the period from 1 July 2008 to 30 June 2009 shall be financed as follows:

(*a*) The unencumbered balance and other income in the total amount of 5,532,100 dollars in respect of the financial period ended 30 June 2007 to be applied against the resources required for the period from 1 July 2008 to 30 June 2009;

(*b*) The balance of 40,236,900 dollars to be prorated among the budgets of the active peacekeeping operations for the period from 1 July 2008 to 30 June 2009;

(*c*) The net estimated staff assessment income of 3,179,400 dollars, comprising the amount of 3,473,400 dollars for the period from 1 July 2008 to 30 June 2009 and the decrease of 294,000 dollars in respect of the financial period ended 30 June 2007, to be set off against the balance referred to in subparagraph (*b*) above, to be prorated among the budgets of the individual active peacekeeping operations;

7. *Also decides* to consider at its sixty-third session the question of the financing of the United Nations Logistics Base at Brindisi, Italy.

Restructuring issues

Special Committee consideration. The Special Committee on Peacekeeping Operations, at its 2008 substantive session [A/62/19], noted the restructuring of DPKO and establishment of DFS [YUN 2007, p. 93], acknowledged the ongoing implementation process on integrating the two Departments, and called upon the Secretariat to fully implement General Assembly resolution 61/279 [ibid., p. 97] in a timely manner. The Special Committee emphasized the importance of preserving unity of command in missions at all levels, as well as coherence in policy and strategy and clear command structures in the field and up to and including at Headquarters. It requested the Secretary-General to ensure a clear chain of command, accountability, coordination and maintenance of an adequate system of checks and balances.

Recognizing the intended role of integrated operational teams in facilitating the horizontal coordination and integration of DPKO and DFS activities, the Special Committee acknowledged the work being done to develop the teams' terms of reference. It requested DPKO and DFS to work in a coordinated manner to provide leadership and support to peacekeeping missions, and to work in such a manner in their relationship with Member States, in particular troop-contributing countries. The Special Committee recommended urgent action to fill all posts, particularly those at senior management level, in accordance with resolution 61/279 [YUN 2007, p. 97].

Report of Secretary-General. The Secretary-General, in March [A/62/741], issued a preliminary report on the status of implementation of Assembly resolution 61/279, as requested therein, in which he reviewed progress made in restructuring DPKO, including the establishment of DFS and consequent achievements. The two Departments undertook to complete the restructuring process within 12 months; at the time of the report, the Secretariat was more than halfway through the process. The reform had been shaped by the need for greater focus on strategic issues related to mission planning and mandate implementation, and for more effective coordination in cross-cutting areas of activity, such as mission planning, deployment, management and support, as well as crisis response. The restructuring process had been guided by four principles: giving priority to field missions; ensuring unity of command within UN peacekeeping; maintaining simplicity of approach with a focus on objectives, real needs and results; and ensuring transparency and inclusiveness so as to facilitate decision-making, accountability and engagement of all stakeholders. The restructuring process focused on the priority areas of: recruitment and senior appointments; the establishment of integrated and common structures, policies and processes; information management and technology support; outreach and the dissemination of information to all stakeholders on restructuring; development and conduct of training programmes for integrated operational teams; development and implementation of evaluation mechanisms; and office space and co-location.

Recruitment for the additional 152 authorized positions had been a management priority, and 69 positions had been filled, including most senior appointments. Restructuring had involved the establishment of integrated operational teams for coordination between DFS and DPKO, and six of the seven teams had been created within the regional divisions of the Office of Operations, to be staffed by military, police and support specialists. Integration was also enhanced through shared resources, linking management of budgets and human resources. Public information activities were reformed to ensure outreach to primary stakeholders, including staff from both Departments and field missions, in addition to internal and external partners. Efforts were made to co-locate the two Departments: senior management was co-located in 2007 and priority accorded to co-locating the integrated operational teams.

Office of Military Affairs

In March [A/62/752], the Secretary-General, responding to General Assembly resolution 61/279, submitted a report on the comprehensive analysis of the Office of Military Affairs in DPKO. In that resolution, the Assembly affirmed its support of the reform proposals to deal with the growing volume and complexity of peacekeeping operations, including proposals for strengthening the Office's leadership capacities and management of the exponential growth in peacekeeping operations. Accordingly, the Office's military leadership was strengthened. Further developments in peacekeeping, such as the support required for increasingly complex operations and the higher threat environments, however, had rendered those adjustments inadequate.

That assessment was reinforced by the results of a comprehensive analysis of the Office of Military Affairs, lessons identified from the Strategic Military Cell established in 2006 to provide guidance to a reinforced UNIFIL, and experts in specialized areas. There was a need within the Secretariat for enhanced military oversight and guidance for complex and challenging missions, where military actions on the ground could have major political consequences at a strategic level, and where the threat to UN military personnel was high. Such enhanced oversight and guidance required additional military officers at the headquarters level to monitor military operations and provide an analysis of military threats, as well as additional leadership experience. In addition, specialist military officers were required to carry out more complex operations, including the collation and analysis of military intelligence, the planning, management and oversight of military maritime, air and aviation capabilities, and the provision of advice to DFS on the planning, support, management and oversight of military operations, particularly in military logistics and communications. All of those capacities were currently lacking in the Office of Military Affairs. On the basis of the lessons identified and the increasingly complex nature of peacekeeping missions, a different form of military headquarters in the Secretariat was needed to provide a higher degree of strategic military planning, guidance, support and oversight.

The DPKO Office of Military Affairs should fulfil three critical military functions in support of peacekeeping operations: possess the breadth and depth of rank and experience to provide the best military advice; conduct strategic and operational planning, including field assessments and contingencies for current and new peacekeeping operations and quickly generate, balance, deploy and rotate the military forces required for missions, and produce military directives and orders, including rules of engagement, to guide and direct the military, and components of field operations; and produce, review and amend the policies needed to underpin peacekeeping operations while looking ahead to develop military capabilities to meet future peacekeeping challenges. In an increasingly complex and challenging peacekeeping environment, a much greater degree of military strategic assessment, oversight, guidance and technical direction, including crisis response, was required. To perform those functions, the Office of Military Affairs had a staff of 67 military officers (13 of whom were assigned on a full-time basis to the integrated operational teams in the Office of Operations) and 5 civilian Professionals, supported by 18 General Service staff. In addition, the Office had to maintain a regular dialogue with 119 troop-contributing countries. The Office therefore lacked the rank, capacity and specialist capabilities to fulfil the functions of a strategic military headquarters within DPKO in both routine and crisis situations.

The proposal for a strengthened Office of Military Affairs would add the expert military capacities found in many military headquarters structures. The leadership and senior management would be enhanced with the addition of three one-star generals at the Principal Officer level to reduce the span of command and control of the Military Adviser, increase the level and availability of military advice, improve interaction with Member States and provide stronger oversight of all military staff functions.

Those changes would substantially increase the degree and quality of military strategic advice, support, guidance and oversight provided to field missions, without changing the existing chain of command; strengthen unity of command by allowing the leadership in the Secretariat and at field missions to make better informed, timely and agreed decisions based on common assessments of situations; address critical gaps, including the need for military specialists and mission start-up capability; and increase Member States' confidence in the leadership and management of the military aspects of peacekeeping operations.

The Secretary-General outlined the new services and units envisaged for the expanded Office, their respective duties and the need for 92 additional posts. He recommended that the Assembly approve the proposals and decide to include $6,399,600 in the requirements for the support account for peacekeeping operations for 1 July 2008 to 30 June 2009 (see p. 87).

Standing Police Capacity

Special Committee consideration. At its 2008 substantive session [A/62/19], the Special Committee on Peacekeeping Operations discussed police capacities for peacekeeping missions. It took note of the incorporation of the Police Division in the Office of the Rule of Law and Security Institutions, and supported the inclusion of the Police Adviser in the DPKO senior management team. It noted the rapid expansion of the policing functions in the field.

Report of Panel of Experts. In response to General Assembly resolution 62/273 (see p. 82), the Secretary-General, in December [A/63/630], transmitted the report of the Panel of Experts on the Standing Police Capacity's first year of operation, and expressed support for its recommendations. Outlining issues, the Panel made recommendations on core functions, command and control, structure and personnel, support, financial and material assistance to national authorities, recruitment, and conditions of service. The Panel stated that the Police Capacity's established core functions—start-up of the police component for new peacekeeping operations, assistance to and assessment of police components in existing missions, and conducting investigations as requested—were appropriate. With its current structure and capacity, however, it was only able to meet current demand for its services with difficulty. The Panel believed that a system for prioritizing requests for assistance should be in place. The Standing Police Capacity members should participate in technical assessments for anticipated complex operations, along with other representatives from the Police Division, to build joint knowledge of the mission area. When the Standing Police Capacity moved to UNLB, its Chief should continue to report to the UN Police Adviser. The Panel presented two options for the Standing Police Capacity's structure—one which would require 54 staff, to be supported by budget planners, human resource managers, civil engineers, contract managers, and a New York-based focal point to liaise with Headquarters; and a second option with 40 per cent more staff, which would enable the Standing Police Capacity to cover one major or two smaller new operations per year. The Panel recommended that adequate resources be made available to facilitate immediate financial and material assistance to national law enforcement agencies in conjunction with UN police deployment. Particular attention should be given to recruitment of personnel, ensuring that staff had the necessary background, language abilities, training and weapons proficiency.

Personnel matters

The Special Committee on Peacekeeping Operations, at its 2008 substantive session [A/62/19], expressed concern over the high number of vacancies in peacekeeping missions and requested the Secretariat to accelerate the recruitment of personnel. It underscored the importance of effective interaction between Headquarters and the field to ensure efficient communications and the safety of peacekeeping personnel. In that regard, it encouraged the Secretary-General to employ staff in DPKO and DFS competent in the Secretariat's working languages. Acknowledging the importance of interaction of UN military observers, police and civilian personnel with the local population, it urged DPKO and DFS to make further efforts to recruit staff and experts on mission with language skills relevant to the mission area where they were to be deployed, and to address specific requirements of peacekeeping operations. It affirmed that good command of the official language spoken in the country should be taken into account in selecting and training personnel.

The Special Committee was concerned that the UN death and disability claims process for peacekeeping personnel was overly cumbersome, lengthy and lacking in transparency. It noted that discrepancies existed between the compensation benefits provided to experts on mission and those provided to contingent members.

Criminal accountability of UN staff and experts on mission

Report of Ad Hoc Committee. The Ad Hoc Committee on criminal accountability of United Nations officials and experts on mission, established by the General Assembly in resolution 61/29 [YUN 2006, p. 109], held its second session (New York, 7–9 and 11 April) [A/63/54] to continue consideration of the 2006 report of the Group of Legal Experts [ibid.] on ensuring the accountability of UN staff and experts on mission with respect to criminal acts committed on peacekeeping operations. The Ad Hoc Committee discussed the issues concerning international cooperation contained in the report, in particular facilitating investigations by the host State; facilitating investigations by States other than the host State; administrative investigations by the United Nations; and legislative and other changes. The discussion also addressed specific issues such as timely notification and reporting mechanisms; collecting and securing the integrity of evidence (testimony, material, confidentiality) and use by States of material provided by the United Nations; conduct of on-site investigations (consent and conditions for consent); extradition and mutual legal assistance; the role of the United Nations (independent and professional administrative investigation); the role of experts, including military lawyers and military prosecutors with knowledge of the State's military law; admissibility (of evidence in a foreign jurisdiction); recognition (of administrative investigation by the United Nations); due process; transfer of criminal proceedings; and transfer of prisoners.

Support was expressed for the proposal that States expand their cooperation on the exchange of information, extradition, the serving of sentences and other measures to facilitate the exercise of criminal jurisdiction, including judicial assistance mechanisms. Similarly, cooperation with the United Nations could cover the exchange of information, assistance with respect to procedural issues (such as the gathering of evidence), reporting on the status of investigations and enhancing rule-of-law capacities. Reference was made to the fact that, while criminal investigation remained the primary responsibility of the host State, evidence gathered by the United Nations remained important for subsequent criminal proceedings. Some delegations reiterated the view that it was premature to discuss negotiating an international convention on the topic, as had been proposed by the Group of Legal Experts and supported by the Secretariat in its 2007 note [YUN 2007, p. 101]. Some delegations expressed support, in principle, for a convention requiring Member States to exercise jurisdiction over their nationals participating in UN operations. It was noted that, while bilateral agreements existed, their coverage was incomplete and did not usually address judicial cooperation between States and the United Nations.

The Ad Hoc Committee reiterated the recommendation that the Sixth (Legal) Committee, during the sixty-third (2008) session of the General Assembly, establish a working group to continue consideration of the report of the Group of Legal Experts.

Report of Secretary-General. In an August report on the criminal accountability of UN officials and experts on mission [A/63/260 & Add.1], submitted in response to General Assembly resolution 62/63 [YUN 2007, p. 102], the Secretary-General provided information from 28 Governments on the extent to which their national laws established jurisdiction, particularly over serious crimes committed by their nationals while serving as UN officials or experts on mission, as well as information from 21 Governments on cooperation among States and with the United Nations in the exchange of information and the facilitation of investigations and prosecution of such individuals. The report contained information by the Secretariat on bringing credible allegations that a crime might have been committed by UN officials to the attention of States against whose nationals such allegations had been made. It provided information on Secretariat activities on ensuring that prospective experts on mission were informed of the expectation that they should meet high standards in their conduct and behaviour, as well as regarding taking other practical measures to strengthen training on UN standards of conduct, including through predeployment and in-mission training.

Working Group consideration. On the recommendation of the Ad Hoc Committee on criminal accountability of United Nations officials and experts on mission (see above), the Sixth Committee [A/63/437], on 6 October, established a Working Group to continue consideration of the report of the Group of Legal Experts established by the Secretary-General pursuant to resolution 59/300 [YUN 2005, p. 122], focusing on its legal aspects and taking into account the views expressed in the Ad Hoc Committee. The Working Group met on 14, 15 and 17 October. On 24 October, the Working Group's Chairperson presented to the Sixth Committee an oral report on its work. The Committee adopted a draft resolution on the subject on 29 October [A/C.6/63/L.10], which was adopted by the General Assembly.

GENERAL ASSEMBLY ACTION

On 11 December [meeting 67], the General Assembly, on the recommendation of the Sixth Committee [A/63/437], adopted **resolution 63/119** without vote [agenda item 73].

Criminal accountability of United Nations officials and experts on mission

The General Assembly,

Recalling its resolution 59/281 of 29 March 2005, in which it endorsed the recommendation in paragraph 56 of the report of the Special Committee on Peacekeeping Operations that the Secretary-General make available to the United Nations membership a comprehensive report on the issue of sexual exploitation and abuse in United Nations peacekeeping operations,

Noting that the Secretary-General, on 24 March 2005, transmitted to the President of the General Assembly a report of his Adviser concerning sexual exploitation and abuse by United Nations peacekeeping personnel,

Recalling its resolution 59/300 of 22 June 2005 endorsing the recommendation of the Special Committee on Peacekeeping Operations that a group of legal experts be established to provide advice on the best way to proceed so as to ensure that the original intent of the Charter of the United Nations can be achieved, namely that United Nations staff and experts on mission would never be effectively exempt from the consequences of criminal acts committed at their duty station, nor unjustly penalized without due process,

Recognizing the valuable contribution of United Nations officials and experts on mission towards the fulfilment of the principles and purposes of the Charter,

Reaffirming the need to promote and ensure respect for the principles and rules of international law,

Reaffirming also that the present resolution is without prejudice to the privileges and immunities of United Nations officials and experts on mission and the United Nations under international law,

Reaffirming further the obligation of United Nations officials and experts on mission to respect the national laws of the host State, as well as the right of the host State to exercise, where applicable, its criminal jurisdiction, in accordance with the relevant rules of international law and agreements governing operations of United Nations missions,

Deeply concerned by reports of criminal conduct, and conscious that such conduct, if not investigated and, as appropriate, prosecuted, would create the negative impression that United Nations officials and experts on mission operate with impunity,

Reaffirming the need to ensure that all United Nations officials and experts on mission function in a manner that preserves the image, credibility, impartiality and integrity of the United Nations,

Emphasizing that crimes committed by such persons are unacceptable and have a detrimental effect on the fulfilment of the mandate of the United Nations, in particular with respect to the relations between the United Nations and the local population in the host country,

Conscious of the importance of protecting the rights of victims of criminal conduct, as well as ensuring adequate protection for witnesses, and noting the adoption of its resolution 62/214 of 21 December 2007 on the United Nations Comprehensive Strategy on Assistance and Support to Victims of Sexual Exploitation and Abuse by United Nations Staff and Related Personnel,

Emphasizing the need to enhance international cooperation to ensure the criminal accountability of United Nations officials and experts on mission,

Recalling its resolution 61/29 of 4 December 2006, establishing the Ad Hoc Committee on criminal accountability of United Nations officials and experts on mission,

Having considered the report of the Group of Legal Experts established by the Secretary-General pursuant to resolution 59/300 and the report of the Ad Hoc Committee, as well as the note by the Secretariat and the report of the Secretary-General on criminal accountability of United Nations officials and experts on mission,

Recalling its resolution 62/63 of 6 December 2007,

Convinced of the need for the United Nations and its Member States to urgently take strong and effective steps to ensure criminal accountability of United Nations officials and experts on mission in the interest of justice,

1. *Expresses its appreciation* for the work done by the Ad Hoc Committee on criminal accountability of United Nations officials and experts on mission and the Working Group of the Sixth Committee on the same subject;

2. *Strongly urges* States to take all appropriate measures to ensure that crimes by United Nations officials and experts on mission do not go unpunished and that the perpetrators of such crimes are brought to justice, without prejudice to the privileges and immunities of such persons and the United Nations under international law, and in accordance with international human rights standards, including due process;

3. *Strongly urges* all States to consider establishing to the extent that they have not yet done so jurisdiction, particularly over crimes of a serious nature, as known in their existing domestic criminal laws, committed by their nationals while serving as United Nations officials or experts on mission, at least where the conduct as defined in the law of the State establishing jurisdiction also constitutes a crime under the laws of the host State;

4. *Encourages* all States to cooperate with each other and with the United Nations in the exchange of information and in facilitating the conduct of investigations and, as appropriate, prosecution of United Nations officials and experts on mission who are alleged to have committed crimes of a serious nature, in accordance with their domestic laws and applicable United Nations rules and regulations, fully respecting due process rights, as well as to consider strengthening the capacities of their national authorities to investigate and prosecute such crimes;

5. *Also encourages* all States:

(a) To afford each other assistance in connection with criminal investigations or criminal or extradition proceedings in respect of crimes of a serious nature committed by United Nations officials or experts on mission, including assistance in obtaining evidence at their disposal in accordance with their domestic law or any treaties or other arrangements on extradition and mutual legal assistance that may exist between them;

(b) In accordance with their domestic law, to explore ways and means of facilitating the possible use of information and material obtained from the United Nations for purposes of criminal proceedings initiated in their territory for the prosecution of crimes of a serious nature committed by United Nations officials and experts on mission, bearing in mind due process considerations;

(c) In accordance with their domestic law, to provide effective protection for victims of, witnesses to, and others who provide information in relation to, crimes of a serious nature alleged to have been committed by United Nations officials and experts on mission and to facilitate access by victims to victim assistance programmes, without prejudice to the rights of the alleged offender, including those relating to due process;

(d) In accordance with their domestic law, to explore ways and means of responding adequately to requests by host States for support and assistance in order to enhance their capacity to conduct effective investigations in respect of crimes of a serious nature alleged to have been committed by United Nations officials and experts on mission;

6. *Requests* the Secretariat to continue to ensure that requests to Member States seeking personnel to serve as experts on mission make States aware of the expectation that persons who serve in that capacity should meet high standards in their conduct and behaviour and are aware that certain conduct may amount to a crime for which they may be held accountable;

7. *Urges* the Secretary-General to continue to take such other practical measures as are within his authority to strengthen existing training on United Nations standards of conduct, including through predeployment and in-mission induction training for United Nations officials and experts on mission;

8. *Decides* that the consideration of the report of the Group of Legal Experts, in particular its legal aspects, taking into account the views of Member States and the information contained in the note by the Secretariat, shall be continued during its sixty-fourth session in the framework of a working group of the Sixth Committee;

9. *Requests* the Secretary-General to bring credible allegations that reveal that a crime may have been committed by United Nations officials and experts on mission to the attention of the States against whose nationals such allegations are made, and to request from those States an indication of the status of their efforts to investigate and, as appropriate, prosecute crimes of a serious nature, as well as the types of appropriate assistance States may wish to receive from the Secretariat for the purposes of such investigations and prosecutions;

10. *Requests* the United Nations, when its investigations into allegations suggest that crimes of a serious nature may have been committed by United Nations officials or experts on mission, to consider any appropriate measures that may facilitate the possible use of information and material for purposes of criminal proceedings initiated by States, bearing in mind due process considerations;

11. *Encourages* the United Nations, when allegations against United Nations officials and experts on mission are determined by a United Nations administrative investigation to be unfounded, to take appropriate measures, in the interests of the Organization, to restore the credibility and reputation of such officials and experts on mission;

12. *Urges* the United Nations to continue cooperating with States exercising jurisdiction in order to provide them,

within the framework of the relevant rules of international law and agreements governing activities of the United Nations, with information and material for purposes of criminal proceedings initiated by States;

13. *Emphasizes* that the United Nations, in accordance with the applicable rules of the Organization, should take no action that would retaliate against or intimidate United Nations officials and experts on mission who report allegations concerning crimes of a serious nature committed by United Nations officials and experts on mission;

14. *Takes note with appreciation* of the information provided by Governments in response to its resolution 62/63;

15. *Requests* the Secretary-General to report to the General Assembly at its sixty-fourth session on the implementation of the present resolution, in particular with respect to paragraphs 3, 5 and 9 above, as well as any practical problems in its implementation, on the basis of information received from Governments and the Secretariat;

16. *Also requests* the Secretary-General to include in the report information on the number and types of credible allegations and any actions taken by the United Nations and its Member States regarding crimes of a serious nature committed by United Nations officials and experts on mission;

17. *Decides* to include in the provisional agenda of its sixty-fourth session the item entitled "Criminal accountability of United Nations officials and experts on mission".

Welfare and recreational needs

In January [A/62/663], the Secretary-General, responding to the request of the Special Committee on Peacekeeping Operations at its 2005 resumed session [YUN 2005, p. 120] and endorsed by the General Assembly in resolution 59/300 [ibid., p. 122], submitted a report on the comprehensive review of the welfare and recreational needs of all categories of peacekeeping personnel. The report reviewed the relevant aspects of the conditions of service of various categories of peacekeeping personnel, including international staff members and members of military and police contingents, and described the status of the reforms under consideration or under way, such as classification of duty stations as family or non-family, payment of mission subsistence allowance to staff officers and review of the rates of reimbursement to troop/police contributing countries for, among other things, the welfare category of self-sustainment. It surveyed the current welfare and recreation practices in peacekeeping missions and identified issues concerning the need to improve the welfare of various categories of personnel.

The Secretariat proposed a number of measures to address those issues. It suggested that DFS and DPKO submit Secretariat issue paper No. 8 for the consideration of the Working Group on Contingent-Owned Equipment at its February session (see p. 92), recommending that the recreational leave allowance be made admissible to contingent personnel for the entirety of 15 days of leave allowed in six months of deployment with a peacekeeping mission. The Departments should review the compensatory time off policy in consultation with the Office of Human Resources Management, elaborate it, and promulgate a revised and consistent policy by means of an administrative issuance.

Another recommendation called for the establishment of a post exchange at the mission and, if feasible, the sector headquarters to accommodate the supply needs of staff and to generate dividends from sales that might be used as income for the mission's welfare fund. A post-exchange contract should be opened for bidding prior to deployment, and appropriate space for a post exchange should be provided in initial engineering plans. DFS, in consultation with DPKO, would revise the existing guidance on the subject. In order to facilitate provision of basic utilities, peacekeeping missions should, where such a need existed, offer fuel and generators to staff on a cost-sharing basis. Similarly, the supply of electricity to private accommodations for a monthly flat rate should be among welfare practices.

Provisions in the model memorandum of understanding on Internet availability were not sufficient to provide personal e-mail access for all contingent personnel, and were generally reserved for senior officers. An Internet facility for personal use by all contingent personnel should be made available on each base. In peacekeeping operations where the local communications infrastructure was inadequate, communications could be facilitated by engaging a private, satellite-based service provider, and in cases where the local infrastructure was available, the missions should facilitate the establishment of calling booths using specialized calling cards. DFS would review the feasibility of providing such facilities on a cost-recovery basis. Concerning travel on leave and for recreational purposes, it was found that some lower-paid categories of peacekeeping personnel were unable to participate in welfare flights due to costs. In order to facilitate the charter by personnel of official aircraft for welfare flights, DFS would re-examine the restriction to a maximum of 30 UN civilian personnel allowed on a UN aircraft, as it precluded a reasonable cost per seat. Contingents should be encouraged to establish leave centres inside or outside the mission area where personnel could spend the leave allowed them for rest and recuperation; facilities such as a television lounge, DVD players, books and indoor and outdoor games should be provided at the leave centres.

Another proposed measure was for DFS and DPKO to submit Secretariat issue paper No. 9 for the consideration of the Working Group, recommending the revision of performance standards in the subcategory of welfare with a view to spelling them out in specific terms. Within the framework of the revised minimum standards of welfare provided elsewhere in the Manual, annex G to the model memorandum of understanding, guidelines to troop/police-contributing countries, should include a description of the minimum welfare and recreation facilities that the troop/police-contributing country would be required to furnish for the peacekeeping mission, in order to qualify for reimbursement for the welfare subcategory. DFS and DPKO would submit to the Working Group on Contingent-Owned Equipment an issue paper on the minimum standards of welfare and recreation facilities to be provided by the troop/police-contributing countries' contingent personnel. In terms of facilities for non-contingent personnel, there was clearly a need for minimum welfare and recreation facilities at duty stations in peacekeeping missions, including "welfare kits", comprising generic equipment, such as an indoor gymnasium, a multi-purpose recreation centre to be used as an indoor lounge, an Internet cafe and bar, provided with games such as table tennis, darts, board games and refreshments, a television set with a VCR/DVD player and accessories, and a library and a prayer/meditation room. An eventual need was seen for welfare officers and units in peacekeeping missions.

The Secretary-General recommended that the Assembly take note of the measures to be undertaken by the Secretariat as part of its effort to improve the welfare of all categories of peacekeeping personnel, as described in the report, and endorse the need for welfare and recreation arrangements for non-contingent personnel.

Death and disability

In April [A/62/805 & Corr.1], the Secretary-General, in response to General Assembly resolution 61/276, section X [YUN 2007, p. 81], reported on the status of cases for death and disability for formed police units, military contingents, civilian police officers and military observers processed and currently in process. As at 28 February, 94 cases for military contingents and formed police units (17 for death and 77 for disability) were under processing and 25 cases were under review for civilian police officers and military observers (3 for death and 22 for disability).

The Secretary-General reported on the comprehensive review of the administrative and payment arrangement for such cases. The Secretariat had initiated a review of the procedures for settlement of death and disability claims. As the issues to be discussed were cross-cutting in nature and would impact the work process in several departments, a working group was established to review the current methodology and suggest measures.

The Secretary-General submitted a November report [A/63/550] on the comprehensive review of compensation of death and disability benefits, which updated the status of cases for death and disability for formed police units, military contingents, civilian police officers and military observers processed and in process. As at 30 September, 120 cases for military contingents and formed police units (14 for death and 106 for disability) were being processed, and 23 cases were being reviewed for civilian police officers and military observers (7 for death and 16 for disability). Of those cases, 93 were awaiting further information from Member States, and 50 involved additional information requested from field missions.

In its review of the rules and methodology of the administrative and payment arrangements, the Secretariat examined the issue of equal treatment of members of military contingents, formed police units, military observers and civilian police officers. Under the current system, award for death or disability depended on the nature of deployment of the uniformed personnel. While beneficiaries of deceased military contingent and formed police unit members were awarded a maximum payment of $50,000, beneficiaries of civilian police officers and military observers might receive much more than $50,000, even at the same rank, if their last annual salary less allowances exceeded $25,000. To remedy that situation, the Secretariat recommended an award of $50,000 to all categories of uniformed personnel, and that the General Assembly approve the application of the methodology enumerated in the Secretary-General's 1977 report on death and disability benefits [YUN 1997, p. 61] and followed for contingent/formed police personnel in death and disability cases related to military observers, civilian police officers and other seconded uniformed personnel, so as to standardize the process for all categories of uniformed personnel and enable the quick resolution of most cases.

The Working Group also looked at the possible establishment of a deadline for the completion and submission of board of inquiry reports in cases of suspected gross negligence or wilful misconduct. Death and disability cases for troops/formed police units were processed without waiting for a board of inquiry report when the force commander/police commissioner confirmed that there had been no evidence in the investigation to indicate any gross negligence or wilful misconduct on the part of the contingent/formed police unit member. In such cases, however, a board of inquiry report was mandatory. To standardize the board of inquiry procedures and speed up the process, the Secretariat issued a policy directive and standard operating procedures effective 1 June. Those documents directed the missions to complete the board of inquiry proceedings as soon as possible, preferably within four weeks. In order to ensure the timely completion of board of inquiry proceedings on cases of a highly technical nature or where specialized skills were required, the new policy enabled the Under-Secretaries-Generals of DPKO and DFS to establish a headquarters board of inquiry, drawing on the resources and skills of UN Headquarters and the missions.

The Assembly was requested to approve the application of the methodology and reimbursement rates followed to settle contingent/formed police unit death or disability claims in cases related to the death or disability of military observers/civilian police officers/ other seconded uniformed personnel in peacekeeping missions; to establish a uniform death compensation of $50,000 and a proportionate amount for permanent disability or loss of function; and to allow the Secretariat to request appropriate medical/supporting documentation without placing any limit on the number of requests to Member States.

Training

Note of Secretary-General. In a February note [A/62/676], the Secretary-General reported on the preparation of a comprehensive report on training in peacekeeping, as requested by the General Assembly in resolutions 60/266 [YUN 2006, p. 89] and 60/267 [ibid., p. 102]. The report would cover the efficiency and effectiveness of all DPKO training programmes to be implemented by UNLB, and compare them to those provided by other facilities and UN offices.

Since 1 November 2005, all DPKO training elements at Headquarters (police, military and civilian) had been merged to form the Integrated Training Service. For cost-saving reasons, the Service's Training Delivery Section was relocated to UNLB in the 2006–2007 budget year, and was fully staffed from early 2008. Subsequently, since the creation of DFS, a full review of the Service's priorities and focus had been undertaken and a training strategy formulated within DPKO and DFS, and with Member States. The strategy would be implemented over the next year and would include a review of the training needs of Member States, field missions and Headquarters.

As a result of the refocusing of the efforts of the Integrated Training Service, the Secretary-General was unable to submit a report on training in peacekeeping for consideration in 2008. While much work had been done to improve training for peacekeeping operations, further work was needed to finalize and implement the new Integrated Training Service strategy, conduct a comprehensive training needs analysis and validate the findings and recommendations. It was expected that the complete report on training in peacekeeping operations would be submitted to the Assembly at its resumed sixty-third (2009) session.

The Assembly, by **decision 62/545 C** of 20 June, deferred consideration of the Secretary-General's note on the comprehensive report on training in peacekeeping until its sixty-third (2009) session.

Special Committee consideration. The Special Committee on Peacekeeping Operations, at its 2008 substantive session [A/62/19], reaffirmed the need to ensure that all personnel selected for peacekeeping missions had the required professional background, expertise and training. It noted the Secretariat's work on the development of a UN peacekeeping training strategy, and requested that the strategy be provided to the Special Committee. It also noted the ongoing work of the Integrated Training Service on the development of minimum training standards and training modules, and requested a detailed progress report before its next substantive session. It took note of the recognition process by the Integrated Training Service of courses conducted by peacekeeping and training institutions using the standardized training modules. Noting the suspension of the process, it stressed the need to develop a mechanism for resuming that activity and for expanding and speeding up the recognition process. An integrated mission planning process training package should be put in place and made an integral part of the UN senior mission leadership training. The Special Committee looked forward to receiving more information on steps taken by the Secretariat to enhance predeployment training capacity for police personnel and facilitate bilateral training assistance.

The Special Committee called for the finalization of the first specialized training modules for police and their dissemination to Member States and peacekeeping operations in the six official languages and their distribution, to be supplemented by DPKO training of the trainers courses. It looked forward to receiving a report on the development of the senior mission administrative and resource training.

The Special Committee called upon the Secretariat to develop training standards and operating guidelines for formed police units, in consultation with Member States, and to improve the quality of standardized training modules on the prevention of sexual exploitation and abuse in peacekeeping operations, and called upon the Member States to utilize them. DPKO should continue providing information, training materials and training modules on issues related to preventing the spread of HIV/AIDS to be used during predeployment training of peacekeeping personnel. The Special Committee supported the development of an electronic learning tool for generic peacekeeping lessons to be used by Member States' national or multinational peacekeeping training institutions, and encouraged the Integrated Training Service to evaluate the option of web-based training modules for all peacekeeping mission personnel. The Secretariat was encouraged to further contribute to the development of online peacekeeping programmes available in all UN official languages and easily accessible by candidates from developing countries. The Special Committee urged DPKO and the United Nations Institute for Training and Research to work together to promote existing electronic learning programmes and to ensure that their training materials were complementary, and encouraged continued wide participation by African, Latin American and Caribbean peacekeepers in the relevant programmes. The Special Committee reiterated its request for DPKO to develop a comprehensive gender training strategy, and looked forward to receiving information on the issue.

Staffing of field missions

On 3 April, by **decision 62/545 B**, the General Assembly decided to defer until its sixty-third session the Secretary-General's reports on the staffing of field missions, including the use of 300- and 100-series appointments [YUN 2007, p. 103] and on detailed proposals for streamlining UN contractual arrangements [ibid., p. 1507].

On the same date, the Assembly, in **resolution 62/248** of 3 April (see p. 1615) on human resources management, having considered those reports, as well as the addendum to the report of the International Civil Service Commission for the year 2006 [ibid., p. 1496] and section II of the ACABQ report [ibid., p. 1510], decided to continue consideration of the issue of contractual arrangements and conditions of service, including in UN field operations, at the main part of its sixty-third (2008) session.

On 20 June, the Assembly, by **decision 62/549**, continued the suspension of the application of the four-year maximum limit for appointments of limited duration until 31 December 2008; authorized the Secretary-General to reappoint, under the 100-series of the Staff Rules, those mission staff whose service under 300-series contracts reached the four-year limit by 31 December 2008, provided that their functions were reviewed and found necessary and their performance was confirmed as fully satisfactory; and requested the Secretary-General to continue the practice of using 300-series contracts as the primary instrument for the appointment of new staff.

Chapter II

Africa

During 2008, the United Nations maintained its commitment to promoting peace, stability and development in Africa through six United Nations political and peacebuilding missions and seven peacekeeping operations. The Organization faced daunting challenges in helping the countries in conflict situations and those in transition to post-conflict peacebuilding in Central Africa and the Great Lakes region, West Africa and the Horn of Africa return to peace, stability and prosperity. Many countries faced the complex task of bringing rebel groups into the peace process, concluding disarmament, demobilization and reintegration programmes for ex-combatants, promoting national reconciliation and creating conditions for economic and social development.

The Office of the Special Adviser on Africa and the Office of the Special Representative of the Secretary-General for West Africa brought a regional perspective to issues facing the continent, promoted conflict prevention and raised awareness about subregional problems. The United Nations worked closely with the African Union (AU), the Economic Community of West African States (ECOWAS), the Economic Community of Central African States and other regional organizations and international actors to assist Governments in improving security, ensuring humanitarian access, energizing peace processes and promoting development. The United Nations continued to monitor Security Council-sanctioned arms embargoes in the Democratic Republic of the Congo (DRC), the Darfur region of western Sudan and Somalia.

The United Nations Peacebuilding Commission expanded its work to the Central African Republic in addition to its ongoing efforts in Burundi, Guinea-Bissau and Sierra Leone, where it assisted in electoral processes and facilitated dialogue. By October, 45 Member States had pledged $267 million to the Peacebuilding Fund.

A Security Council mission in June visited Djibouti (for Somalia affairs), the Sudan, Chad, the DRC and Côte d'Ivoire to promote peace and reconciliation.

Central Africa and the Great Lakes region continued to be affected by the activities of armed groups and militias, especially in the eastern part of the DRC. Nonetheless, by year's end, the region made noticeable steps towards resolving long-standing conflicts.

The signing in November 2007 of the Nairobi Communiqué by the DRC and Rwanda and, in January, of the *Actes d'engagement*—known as the Goma Agreements—by the DRC, the rebel Congrès National pour la Défense du Peuple (CNDP) and other armed groups from North and South Kivu in the eastern DRC laid the ground for finally eliminating the regional threat of—in particular foreign—armed groups active there through a separation of forces and their disarming and demobilization or brassage (integration into the national armed forces). Little progress, however, was made by the Mixed Technical Commission on Peace and Security of the Amani programme—the framework for implementing the Goma Agreements. In August, violence flared in the eastern DRC, on the border with Rwanda, where 10,000 UN peacekeepers of the United Nations Organization Mission in the Democratic Republic of the Congo (MONUC) were tasked with protecting 10 million civilians. Following a series of skirmishes, CNDP in late October began a major offensive threatening Goma (the provincial capital of North Kivu), and other ethnic-based rebel groups entered the fray. When CNDP overwhelmed the Forces armées de la République démocratique du Congo, displacing hundreds of thousands of civilians, MONUC reinforced its presence in Goma and surrounding areas. In November, the Security Council authorized an additional 3,085 troops and police for MONUC, including special forces, and increased air assets, so that it might better protect civilians and ensure humanitarian access. As the crisis threatened to spill beyond the borders of the DRC, the Secretary-General met with regional leaders at a special summit in Nairobi in November, also appointing a Special Envoy for the Great Lakes Region to work with the parties and the international community to end the crisis. Following discussions with the Special Envoy, CNDP announced that it would withdraw its forces from the Kanyabayonga-Nyanzale and Kabasha-Kiwanja axes, where fighting had most recently occurred. Meanwhile, the Lord's Resistance Army (LRA), which originated in Uganda, continued to operate in the DRC's Province Orientale, bordering the Sudan. At year's end, the Security Council extended MONUC's mandate by another 12 months.

Burundi continued to face serious peace and security challenges, primarily emanating from the stalled implementation of the 2006 Comprehensive Ceasefire Agreement, enduring mistrust among political actors, increased restrictions on public liberties, slow progress in fighting impunity, persistent human rights violations, insecurity and high levels of poverty. The end of the year, however, brought a breakthrough in the peace process, when, at a Summit of the Heads of State and Government of the Great Lakes Region (Bujumbura, Burundi, 4 December), the Government of Burundi, the Palipehutu-FNL and attending Heads of State signed a declaration calling for the commencement of the disarmament, demobilization and reintegration of Palipehutu-FNL and the political integration of its leadership.

The political situation in the Central African Republic continued to be dominated by preparations for the inclusive political dialogue aimed at ending the recurrent political and security crises in the country—which was finally held in Bangui in December. The overall political, security and socio-economic situation, however, remained fragile, compounded by a weak economy, multifaceted social problems and impunity, with severe security challenges, particularly in the northern and south-eastern parts of the country.

Police and military liaison officers of the United Nations Mission in the Central African Republic and Chad (MINURCAT) worked with their counterparts of the European Union military operation (EUFOR) there to enhance stability and support human rights and the rule of law. The Mission focused on the training and deployment of the Détachement Intégré de Sécurité—the special Chadian police for maintaining law and order in refugee camps and among displaced civilians within a 10-kilometre radius of the camps in eastern Chad. In December, the Secretary-General recommended the concept of a United Nations force of at least 4,900 peacekeepers to take over from EUFOR in early 2009.

As for Uganda, the Special Envoy of the Secretary-General for LRA-affected areas worked to conclude the peace process. However, because the leader of LRA, Joseph Kony, did not sign the final peace agreement, the DRC, Southern Sudan and Uganda launched joint military action against his camps in the eastern DRC. Such military action was intended not to derail the peace process, but rather to pressure LRA into assembling in Ri-Kwangba (Southern Sudan) and signing the final peace agreement.

Welcoming recent steps towards the restoration of peace and stability in the Great Lakes region, the Security Council, in July, terminated several measures imposed in the wake of the 1994 Rwanda genocide to prohibit the sale and supply of arms and related materiel for use in that country. Nonetheless, the border area between Rwanda and the DRC remained a matter of concern due to the violence that reignited in August in the eastern part of the DRC and continued through the following months.

In West Africa, the Secretary-General said that significant progress was made in the consolidation of peace and democratic governance, and UN peace missions in the subregion began to wind down. The United Nations Office for West Africa carried out its revised mandate, including supporting ECOWAS, which was demonstrating increased capacity to address political, social, economic and security issues in the region. However, many challenges remained, such as youth unemployment, rapid urbanization and irregular migration, while others were emerging or increasing in magnitude, including social and economic crises, human and drug trafficking and insecurity in the Sahelian band. Widespread corruption, which weakened State institutions and the rule of law, was a concern. Other threats to stability included the proliferation of small arms and light weapons, the potential eruption of border conflicts, and organized crime, with drug trafficking constituting the most widespread cross-border activity. Furthermore, the scourge of coups d'état had re-emerged in Guinea, Guinea-Bissau and Mauritania. Three high-level missions visited the subregion during the year to assess progress made and challenges facing countries of the subregion.

In Côte d'Ivoire, efforts continued to move the peace process forward through implementation of the 2007 Ouagadougou Agreement and its supplementary accords. The ceasefire monitored by the United Nations Operation in Côte d'Ivoire and the French Licorne forces continued to hold, with no major violations of the arms embargo. The partnership between President Laurent Gbagbo and Prime Minister Guillaume Soro remained strong, and the removal of the Green Line dividing the country allowed political leaders and the general population to move freely throughout the country. Although progress was made in preparations for the presidential elections, logistical and technical delays resulted in their postponement to 2009. A fourth supplementary accord to the Ouagadougou Agreement, which clarified issues relating to key processes that had stalled, was signed in December.

The Government of Liberia continued efforts to improve governance and security, combat corruption, regain control of the country's natural resources and build a stronger economy. With the assistance of the United Nations Mission in Liberia and other organizations, further progress was made in consolidating peace, stability and democracy. The Government finalized its first national poverty reduction strategy, and Liberia reached the completion point under the enhanced Heavily Indebted Poor Countries Initiative. The Truth and Reconciliation Commission began public hearings in January and submitted its first report to the Legislature and President Ellen Johnson-Sirleaf in December. Following his visit to Liberia in April, the Secretary-General recommended adjustments to the second phase of the drawdown of the Mission.

The Government of Sierra Leone continued efforts to implement its agenda for peace consolidation and economic recovery. Developments included the approval of a national anti-corruption strategy and the submission of the Constitutional Review Commission report proposing amendments to the 1991 Constitution. The Secretary-General presented the completion strategy for the United Nations Integrated Office in Sierra Leone, which entailed the transition to a successor integrated political office—the United Nations Integrated Peacebuilding Office in Sierra Leone. The transition resulted in the adoption of a Joint Vision of the United Nations Family for Sierra Leone. In December, President Ernest Bai Koroma issued his Agenda for Change, presenting the Government's priorities for the next three years, including the foundation for peacebuilding efforts.

The Special Court for Sierra Leone continued to try those bearing the greatest responsibility for serious violations of international, humanitarian and Sierra Leonean laws committed in the territory since 1996. The trial of the former President of Liberia, Charles Taylor, resumed in January.

The United Nations Peacebuilding Support Office in Guinea-Bissau assisted the Government in its efforts to promote national reconciliation, conduct legislative elections, and combat drug and human trafficking, and organized crime. The political climate remained fragile, despite the Government stability pact signed by the three main political parties in 2007. In July, the African Party for the Independence of Guinea and Cape Verde withdrew from the pact. Political and institutional tensions over the National Assembly's mandate culminated in August with the appointment of a new Prime Minister and Government. Progress was achieved with the establishment of the National Reconciliation Commission and the National Commission for Human Rights. Nonetheless, instability in the military manifested itself in August, when the authorities uncovered a planned coup d'état, and in November, when unknown assailants attacked the residence of President João Bernardo Vieira, who escaped unharmed. The illicit drug trade remained a concern amid reports that Guinea-Bissau was becoming a strategic link in the transport of illegal narcotics from South America to Europe.

Cameroon and Nigeria continued to cooperate in implementing the 2002 ruling of the International Court of Justice on their land and maritime boundary through the Cameroon-Nigeria Mixed Commission. During the year, the transfer of authority from Nigeria to Cameroon of the remaining zone of the Bakassi peninsula was completed.

Following the death of the President of Guinea, Lansana Conté, a military junta seized power in December. The coup was widely condemned internationally.

The democratic process in Mauritania suffered a setback in August, when the former Chief of Staff of the army seized power from President Sidi Mohamed Ould Cheikh Abdallahi—the first democratically elected president in the history of the country—placing him under house arrest. The Security Council condemned the coup and demanded the immediate release of the President and the restoration of the legitimate, constitutional, democratic institutions.

The political situation in the Horn of Africa continued to be adversely affected by conflicts and other forms of insecurity within and between States. In the Sudan, the Sudanese Armed Forces, the Sudan People's Liberation Army/Movement and the United Nations Mission in the Sudan (UNMIS) made uneven progress in de-escalating tension in the north-south border area and resuming implementation of the security arrangements set out in the 2005 Comprehensive Peace Agreement. In March, President Omar Al-Bashir of the Sudan and President Idriss Déby Itno of Chad signed the Dakar Agreement, by which the two countries committed themselves to ending their differences. In April, the Security Council renewed the UNMIS mandate for a further 12-month period. On 10 May, Justice and Equality Movement fighters from the Darfur region of the Sudan attacked Omdurman, Sudan, but were repelled by Sudanese Government forces. The Sudan accused Chad of supporting the attack and severed diplomatic ties. In May, tensions between the Sudanese armed forces and the Sudan People's Liberation Army in the town of Abyei erupted into full-scale fighting that continued until 20 May. Following several weeks of consultations, the parties finalized a road map agreement to resolve the situation in Abyei, and referred the dispute over the Abyei borders to the Permanent Court of Arbitration in The Hague. The electoral law was adopted by the National Assembly and signed by President Al-Bashir in July. That same month, the Prosecutor of the International Criminal Court requested that the Court issue an arrest warrant against President Al-Bashir on charges of genocide, crimes against humanity and war crimes. Meanwhile, relations between Chad and the Sudan improved, and the two countries exchanged ambassadors in November.

In Northern Darfur, a status-of-forces agreement between the African Union-United Nations Hybrid Operation in Darfur (UNAMID) and the Sudan was signed on 9 February. Nevertheless, UNAMID deployment progressed slowly and faced significant challenges, including insufficient troops and equipment. In July, a UNAMID patrol was attacked in Darfur, resulting in the death of seven peacekeepers, and a

UNAMID officer was killed by unknown gunmen. The Government began a military campaign in September and engaged in further operations in October. Despite a unilateral declaration of a cessation of hostilities by the Government on 12 November, its forces conducted aerial bombings in Northern and Western Darfur during that month. Southern Darfur also experienced an upsurge in violence, as Government patrols were attacked. Inter-tribal fighting continued in Northern and Southern Darfur, and targeted attacks against humanitarian workers hindered the provision of assistance to the civilian population.

In Somalia, coordinated attacks by anti-Government elements took place in Mogadishu, and Ethiopian Army and Transitional Federal Government operations to eradicate those elements increased. In January, an integrated task force headed by the UN Department of Political Affairs deployed an assessment mission to Somalia to develop a comprehensive UN strategy for the country. The assessment outlined a three-track approach consisting of political, security and programmatic dimensions. The Department also led a fact-finding mission to the region in January to update contingency plans for the possible deployment of a UN peacekeeping mission. In March, the Transitional Federal Government of Somalia unveiled its reconciliation strategy, which included proposals to promote peacebuilding and reconciliation between the Government and opposition groups. In May, the Secretary-General's Special Representative initiated the first round of talks in Djibouti between the Transitional Federal Government and the Alliance for the Re-liberation of Somalia. On 19 August, the Government and the Alliance signed the Djibouti agreement for the cessation of hostilities. The Somali parties signed an agreement on the cessation of armed confrontation during a third round of talks in Djibouti on 26 October. On the same date, the Government and the Alliance for the Re-liberation of Somalia adopted a declaration on the establishment of a unity Government.

Despite those developments, insurgent groups increased attacks on troops of the African Union Mission in Somalia (AMISOM) in April and May, resulting in the death of peacekeepers. The acting head of the United Nations Development Programme in Mogadishu was killed by unidentified gunmen on 6 July. On 29 October, suicide bomb attacks targeted the UNDP compound in Hargeysa, as well as the town of Boosasso in northern Somalia; two UN staff members were killed and six others were injured. In June, the Security Council authorized States cooperating with the Transitional Federal Government to enter Somalia's territorial waters to repress acts of piracy and armed robbery.

The Organization's efforts to address the border dispute between Ethiopia and Eritrea changed dramatically during the year. In January, the Secretary-General reported that Eritrea continued to induct troops into the Temporary Security Zone between the two countries and maintained its restrictions on the United Nations Mission in Ethiopia and Eritrea (UNMEE). The Security Council extended the UNMEE mandate until 31 July, and demanded that Eritrea resume fuel shipments to the Mission or allow it to import fuel, which had been restricted since December 2007. In February, the Secretariat informed Eritrea of the decision to relocate Mission personnel to Ethiopia, and requested that it extend to the Mission the necessary cooperation. However, the Eritrean Defence Forces hindered the cross-border movement of personnel and equipment. The Secretary-General instructed UNMEE to begin relocating military personnel to their home countries pending a final decision by the Council on the Mission's future. The Council terminated the UNMEE mandate effective 31 July. No progress was made towards the construction of boundary pillars between the two countries in the manner foreseen by the Eritrea-Ethiopia Boundary Commission. The Commission reported that since it had concluded all administrative matters connected with the termination of its mandate, it considered itself *functus officio*.

On 11 June, Djibouti stated that Eritrean armed forces had launched unprovoked attacks on Djiboutian army positions the previous day. On 12 June, the Security Council condemned Eritrea's military aggression and called on the parties to commit to a ceasefire. A UN fact-finding mission that visited Addis Ababa, Ethiopia, and Djibouti in July and August established that a stalemate had developed between Djibouti and Eritrea that could only be resolved by diplomatic means. It recommended renewing as a matter of priority the Secretary-General's offer of good offices to defuse tensions.

The two parties to the dispute concerning the Territory of Western Sahara—Morocco and the Frente Polisario para la Liberación de Saguía el-Hamra y de Río de Oro (Frente Polisario)—met with the Secretary-General's Personal Envoy for Western Sahara in January and March for the third and fourth rounds of talks, respectively. The parties remained far apart on ways to achieve a solution, but agreed to explore the establishment of family visits by land route, in addition to the programme of air visits, and reiterated their commitment to continue negotiations. In April, the Security Council extended the mandate of the United Nations Mission for the Referendum in Western Sahara until 30 April 2009.

The United Nations also addressed the political and humanitarian crises that followed the elections of December 2007 in Kenya and the elections of March 2008 in Zimbabwe.

Promotion of peace in Africa

In 2008, the United Nations remained engaged in the search to resolve the root causes of conflict in Africa and encourage peace and sustainable development on the continent. In April, the Security Council, during consideration of the item on peace and security in Africa, held a debate on the relationship between the United Nations and regional organizations, in particular the African Union (AU), in the maintenance of international peace and security. In June, the Council sent a mission to five African countries. The General Assembly took action on assistance to refugees, returnees and displaced persons in Africa in December.

Working Group. The Ad Hoc Working Group on Conflict Prevention and Resolution in Africa, established in 2002 [YUN 2002, p. 93] to monitor the implementation of Security Council recommendations relating to its role in conflict prevention and resolution in Africa, continued to contribute to the Council's work by promoting a better understanding of ways to address crises on the continent.

On 30 December [S/2008/836], the Chairman of the Working Group, Dumisani S. Kumalo, transmitted the report on its activities in 2008. At its meeting on 6 March, the Group heard a briefing by the Under-Secretary-General for Political Affairs, B. Lynn Pascoe, on the proposal to strengthen the Department of Political Affairs (DPA). The briefing provided the Group with an opportunity to understand how DPA saw its role in conflict prevention and resolution, and it proposed steps to strengthen the Department. On 1 December, the Group addressed the concept of "responsibility to protect" in order to highlight conflict prevention, a critical component of the responsibility to protect; contribute to the debate on the upcoming report of the Secretary-General on responsibility to protect; and propose recommendations to the Security Council to enhance cooperation in conflict prevention and resolution between the United Nations and regional and subregional organizations.

On 18 December [S/2008/795], the Council agreed that the Group would continue its work until 31 December 2009.

Relationship between the United Nations and regional organizations

On 16 April [meeting 5868], the Security Council met to consider the agenda item on peace and security in Africa, including the relationship between the United Nations and regional organizations, in particular the AU, in maintaining international peace and security. Before the Council was an 8 April concept paper [S/2008/229], submitted by South Africa; the report of the Secretary-General on the relationship between the United Nations and regional organizations, in particular the AU, in the maintenance of international peace and security [S/2008/186]; and the report of the Secretary-General on the implementation of Security Council resolution 1625(2005) [YUN 2005, p. 155] on conflict prevention, particularly in Africa [S/2008/18] (see p. 43). The meeting was addressed by 24 countries and two international organizations.

The Security Council President, Thabo Mbeki, President of South Africa, speaking in his national capacity, stated that the AU had shown its commitment to resolving African conflicts. The operationalization of the AU Peace and Security Council and the continental early warning systems, post-conflict reconstruction and development, the Panel of the Wise and the African Standby Force were clear indications of that commitment and the basic architecture for addressing peace and security issues on the continent. The availability of resources, however, remained the most important constraint limiting Africa's capacity to give effect to those commitments and help resolve its own conflicts. Because the funding of regional peacekeeping operations was central to defining and streamlining the relationship between the United Nations and the AU, he welcomed the proposal of the Secretary-General to establish an AU-UN panel of distinguished persons to consider the modalities of financing and supporting in other ways the peacekeeping operations undertaken by regional organizations. He also called for a comprehensive review of UN peacekeeping missions in order to improve their effectiveness.

The Secretary-General stated that the African Peace and Security Architecture was being developed through concrete steps ranging from good offices and mediation on border issues to early warning, conflict prevention and building operational capacity. A dedicated team had been established to help operationalize the concept of an African standby force, and the establishment of the secretariat of the AU Panel of the Wise and the launch of the UN mediation standby team of experts had better equipped both organizations for the critical task of mediation.

The Under-Secretary-General for Political Affairs noted that conflict prevention remained the most cost-effective and efficient way to promote international peace and security, and the Secretary-General had proposed strengthening DPA to work in that area. To implement Security Council resolution 1625(2005), the Secretary-General had called on the Council to increase its use of the "Arria Formula", which enabled Council members to discuss matters with invited personalities in an informal and closed setting; dispatch missions to the field; carry out lessons-learned exercises to motivate parties to resolve conflicts; and develop a stronger and more structured relationship with the AU Peace and Security Council. He had called for full cooperation in developing the capacities of African regional organizations to deploy both civilian and military assets quickly, including developing an African standby force. As for the relationship between the United Nations and regional organizations, in particular the AU, in the maintenance of international peace and security, the Secretary-General had proposed better support arrangements for further cooperation, and suggested setting up a panel of distinguished persons from the United Nations and the AU to make recommendations on how to help finance peacekeeping operations undertaken by regional organizations.

The Chairperson of the AU Commission, Alpha Oumar Konaré, stressed the importance of building African capacities through consolidating the continental peace and security architecture; strengthening planning capacities; helping develop an early warning system; establishing standby forces capable of deploying a standing rapid intervention force; and refusing to allow lawless zones to exist. In total, some 45 speakers addressed the day-long debate.

SECURITY COUNCIL ACTION

On 16 April [meeting 5868], the Security Council unanimously adopted **resolution 1809(2008)**. The draft [S/2008/252] was submitted by South Africa.

The Security Council,

Reaffirming all its previous resolutions and the statements by its President on cooperation between the United Nations and regional organizations, in particular resolutions 1625(2005) of 14 September 2005 and 1631(2005) of 17 October 2005, and the statements of 20 July 2004, 19 November 2004, 28 March 2007, 28 August 2007 and 6 November 2007,

Reaffirming also its resolutions 1325(2000) of 31 October 2000, 1612(2005) of 26 July 2005 and 1674(2006) of 28 April 2006,

Recalling its primary responsibility for the maintenance of international peace and security, and recognizing that cooperation with regional and subregional organizations in matters relating to the maintenance of peace and security and consistent with Chapter VIII of the Charter of the United Nations can improve collective security,

Welcoming the role of the African Union in efforts to settle conflicts on the African continent, and expressing its support for the peace initiatives conducted by the African Union and through subregional organizations,

Emphasizing the need to strengthen the role of the United Nations in the prevention of armed conflicts, and stressing the utility of developing effective partnerships between the United Nations and regional organizations, in particular the African Union, in order to enable early responses to disputes and emerging crises in Africa, and in this regard noting with interest the proposal made by the Secretary-General of conducting joint reviews by the United Nations and regional organizations of the state of peace and security and of mediation endeavours, particularly in Africa, where joint mediation is being undertaken,

Recognizing that regional organizations are well positioned to understand the root causes of armed conflicts owing to their knowledge of the region, which can be a benefit for their efforts to influence the prevention or resolution of those conflicts,

Stressing the importance of further strengthening cooperation with the African Union in order to assist in building its capacity to deal with common collective security challenges in Africa, including through the commitment by the African Union of rapid and appropriate responses to emerging crisis situations and the development of effective strategies for conflict prevention, peacekeeping and peacebuilding,

Recalling the resolve of Heads of State and Government at the 2005 World Summit to expand, as appropriate, the involvement of regional organizations in the work of the Security Council and to ensure that regional organizations that have a capacity for the prevention of armed conflict or peacekeeping consider the option of placing such capacity in the framework of the United Nations Standby Arrangements System,

Recognizing the importance of strengthening the capacity of regional and subregional organizations in conflict prevention and crisis management and in post-conflict stabilization,

Taking note of lessons learned from practical cooperation between the United Nations and the African Union, in particular the transition from the African Mission in Burundi to the United Nations Operation in Burundi and from the African Union Mission in the Sudan to the African Union-United Nations Hybrid Operation in Darfur (UNAMID),

Acknowledging the contribution of the United Nations Liaison Office at Addis Ababa in strengthening coordination and cooperation between the United Nations and the African Union, as well as the need to consolidate it so as to enhance its performance,

Recognizing that regional organizations have the responsibility in securing human, financial, logistical and other resources for their organizations, including by obtaining contributions from their members and soliciting contributions from donors to fund their operations, and recognizing the challenges in accessing United Nations assessed contributions for funding regional organizations,

Recognizing also that one major constraint facing some regional organizations, in particular the African Union, in effectively carrying out the mandates of maintaining regional peace and security is securing predictable, sustainable and flexible resources,

Taking note of both the report of the Secretary-General on the relationship between the United Nations and regional organizations, in particular the African Union, in the maintenance of international peace and security and the report of the Secretary-General on conflict prevention, particularly in Africa,

1. *Expresses its determination* to take effective steps to further enhance the relationship between the United Nations and regional organizations, in particular the African

Union, in accordance with Chapter VIII of the Charter of the United Nations;

2. *Encourages* the continuing involvement of regional and subregional organizations in the peaceful settlement of disputes, including through conflict prevention, confidence-building and mediation efforts;

3. *Welcomes* regional dialogue and the promotion of shared experiences as well as common regional approaches to the settlement of disputes and other issues relating to peace and security;

4. *Welcomes and further encourages* the ongoing efforts of the African Union and the subregional organizations to strengthen their peacekeeping capacity and to undertake peacekeeping operations on the continent, in accordance with Chapter VIII of the Charter, and to coordinate with the United Nations, through the Peace and Security Council of the African Union, as well as ongoing efforts to develop a continental early warning system, response capacity such as the African Standby Force and enhanced mediation capacity, including through the Panel of the Wise of the African Union;

5. *Welcomes* recent developments regarding cooperation between the United Nations, the African Union and the European Union, including the contribution of the European Union to the enhancement of African Union capacities;

6. *Encourages* regional and subregional organizations to strengthen and increase cooperation among them, in particular cooperation between the African Union, the Organization of American States, the League of Arab States, the Association of Southeast Asian Nations and the European Union, including efforts to enhance their respective capacities, in the maintenance of international peace and security;

7. *Expresses its determination* to strengthen and make more effective its cooperation with relevant organs of regional organizations, in particular the Peace and Security Council;

8. *Also expresses its determination* to strengthen and enhance cooperation between the United Nations and regional organizations, in particular the African Union, in conflict prevention, resolution and management, including good offices, mediation support, effective use of sanctions as mandated by the Security Council, electoral assistance and preventive field presence; and in the case of Africa, focusing on support to the Panel of the Wise, among others;

9. *Stresses* that common and coordinated efforts undertaken by the United Nations and regional organizations, in particular the African Union, in matters of peace and security, should be based on their complementary capacities, making full use of their experience in accordance with the Charter and the relevant statutes of the regional organizations;

10. *Underlines* the importance of the implementation of the Ten-Year Capacity-Building Programme for the African Union mainly focusing on peace and security, in particular the operationalization of the African Standby Force;

11. *Encourages* the increased engagement of the African Union Peacekeeping Support Team within the Department of Peacekeeping Operations of the United Nations Secretariat as a coordinating point aimed at providing the necessary expertise and transfer of technical knowledge to enhance the capacity of the Peace Support Operations Division of the African Union, including in mission planning and management, as well as the deployment of staff of the Department of Political Affairs of the Secretariat to work with the African Union on the operationalization of the Panel of the Wise and other mediation programmes;

12. *Calls upon* the Secretariat, in coordination with the African Union Commission, to develop a list of needed capacities and recommendations on ways in which the African Union can further develop military, technical, logistical and administrative capabilities;

13. *Encourages* closer cooperation between the Secretariat and the African Union Commission, including by supporting regular follow-up missions by Secretariat staff to African Union headquarters to provide further assistance and share experiences;

14. *Expresses its determination* to further consider how to strengthen the capacity of the United Nations in the prevention of armed conflict, particularly in Africa;

15. *Recognizes* the important role of the good offices of the Secretary-General in Africa, and encourages the Secretary-General to continue to use mediation as often as possible to help to resolve conflicts peacefully, working in coordination and closely with the African Union and other subregional organizations in that regard, as appropriate;

16. *Recognizing* the need to enhance the predictability, sustainability and flexibility of financing regional organizations when they undertake peacekeeping under a United Nations mandate, welcomes the proposal by the Secretary-General to set up within three months an African Union-United Nations panel consisting of distinguished persons to consider in depth the modalities of how to support such peacekeeping operations, in particular start-up funding, equipment and logistics, and to consider in depth lessons from past and current African Union peacekeeping efforts;

17. *Requests* the Secretary-General to include in his regular reporting to the Council assessments of progress on the cooperation between the United Nations and relevant regional organizations;

18. *Decides* to remain seized of the matter.

Cooperation between the AU and the UN system

On 17 April, the UN Security Council and the AU Peace and Security Council held a meeting in New York, during which they explored ways and means of developing a stronger working relationship. Following an exchange of views, the two bodies issued a joint communiqué [S/2008/263] in which they reaffirmed their determination to strengthen AU conflict prevention, management and resolution capacities and post-conflict stabilization capacities.

In a letter of 3 October [A/63/515], the United Republic of Tanzania, in its capacity as AU Chair, forwarded to the General Assembly documents containing decisions, declarations and resolutions adopted by the eleventh ordinary session of the AU Assembly (Sharm el-Sheikh, Egypt, 30 June–1 July); and decisions adopted by the AU Executive Council at its thirteenth ordinary session (Sharm el-Sheikh, 24–28 June).

By identical letters of 24 December [A/63/666-S/2008/813], the Secretary-General transmitted to the General Assembly and Security Council the report of the AU-UN panel on modalities for support to AU peacekeeping operations. The panel was established on 12 September in response to Council resolution 1809(2008) (see p. 109). To enhance the predictability, sustainability and flexibility of the financing of United Nations-mandated peace operations undertaken by the AU, the panel recommended the establishment of two new financial mechanisms. The first would be based on United Nations-assessed funding and designed to support specific operations; that should be on a case-by-case basis to support Council-authorized AU peacekeeping operations for a period of up to six months. Initially, at least, that support should be provided mainly in kind. The second, a voluntarily funded multi-donor trust fund, should focus on comprehensive capacity-building for conflict prevention and resolution, as well as for institution-building, and should be designed to attract new and existing donors, while fostering African ownership. The panel also recommended that the AU develop its logistics capacity and explore innovative options, including commercial multifunction contracts.

Security Council mission to Africa

By a letter dated 30 May [S/2008/347], the Security Council President informed the Secretary-General that the Council would send a mission to Africa from 31 May to 10 June to visit Djibouti (on Somalia), the Sudan, Chad, the Democratic Republic of the Congo (DRC) and Côte d'Ivoire.

Mission report. Following a briefing given to the Council on 18 June [meeting 5915] by the four leaders of the mission—Michel Kafando (Burkina Faso), Jean-Maurice Ripert (France), Dumisani Kumalo (South Africa) and John Sawers (United Kingdom)—the mission issued its report [S/2008/460] on 15 July.

In Djibouti for Somalia affairs, the mission's visit reaffirmed the international community's commitment to a comprehensive and lasting settlement of the situation in Somalia through the Transitional Federal Charter, and stressed the importance of broad-based and representative institutions reached through a political process ultimately inclusive of all. The mission was briefed by the Special Representative of the Secretary-General for Somalia and the Chief Security Adviser before meeting with the President of Somalia and the delegation of the Transitional Federal Government; the AU delegation; the opposition group Alliance for the Re-liberation of Somalia; the UN country team; and members of Somali civil society. The mission recommended, among other things, that the Council continue to consider how it could best support the Secretary-General's Special Representative in his efforts to provide practical assistance to furthering the political progress already made; that the Council consider how it could best lend its support to the agreement initialled by the Transitional Federal Government and the Alliance for the Re-liberation of Somalia; and that the Council should consider ways to enhance the international security presence in Somalia, including a peacekeeping operation to take over from the African Union Mission in Somalia, at an appropriate time, subject to continued progress in the political process and improvement in the security situation on the ground, as indicated by resolution 1814(2008) (see p. 275).

In the Sudan, the mission reaffirmed the international community's determination to ensure the implementation of the 2005 Comprehensive Peace Agreement [YUN 2005, p. 301], and the resolution of the situation in Darfur. The mission met in Juba with the First Vice-President; in Darfur with internally displaced persons, representatives of the humanitarian community and the Wali (Governor) of Northern Darfur; and in Khartoum with the Minister for Foreign Affairs, the Presidential Adviser, the Minister for Investment, representatives of opposition parties, the Chairperson of the Assessment and Evaluation Commission established to monitor the Agreement, and the President of the Sudan. Among its recommendations, the mission proposed that the Council should continue to support the parties in implementing the Agreement, including by improving security arrangements between the parties; that the United Nations Mission in the Sudan (UNMIS) should begin preparations to support the conduct of national elections, in close collaboration with the United Nations Development Programme and the parties to the Agreement; that UNMIS should, consistent with its mandate and in accordance with resolution 1812(2008) (see p. 235), robustly deploy peacekeeping personnel in and around Abyei to support the implementation of the Agreement, including protecting civilians; that the Council should begin consideration of a new resolution to extend the mandate of the United Nations-African Union Hybrid Operation in Darfur after it expired on 31 July; and that the United Nations should urgently appoint a chief mediator to spearhead the UN and AU efforts on Darfur.

In Chad, the mission stressed the Council's commitment to help the authorities protect Darfur refugees, internally displaced persons and other vulnerable populations, and facilitate the delivery of humanitarian assistance in eastern Chad and the north-eastern

Central African Republic through the deployment of a multidimensional presence there. It also demonstrated the Council's support for the United Nations Mission in the Central African Republic and Chad (MINURCAT) and the European Union military operation in Chad and the Central African Republic (EUFOR). The mission met with the Governor of Goz Beida, humanitarian agencies and non-governmental organizations, along with the Prime Minister. It also visited two camps, one hosting refugees from Darfur and the other hosting Chadian internally displaced persons. The mission recommended, among other things, that the Council reaffirm its full support to MINURCAT and EUFOR, and encourage the Secretary-General to deploy MINURCAT as quickly as possible; that when the Council examined the arrangements for following up EUFOR, including a possible UN operation, it take fully into account the call from the people in Chad for increased security in the eastern part of the country; that the Council encourage the Government to build upon the 2007 Political Agreement for the reinforcement of the democratic process [YUN 2007, p. 155]; and that the Council continue to call on Chad and the Sudan to implement their commitments under the Dakar Agreement (see p. 268), severing ties with rebel groups operating on both sides of the border.

In the DRC, the mission reaffirmed the Council's support to the Government in its efforts to consolidate peace and stability in the east, promote recovery and development, and implement the Goma and Nairobi processes. It also expressed the Council's concern regarding the humanitarian situation in the east, the continuing prevalence of gender-based violence and human rights abuses, and the recruitment of children, especially by armed groups.

The mission met in Kinshasa with the President, the Government and parliamentary institutions, including opposition representatives; and in Goma with the Governor of North Kivu and the National Coordinator of the Amani Programme for the security, pacification, stabilization and reconstruction of North and South Kivu in line with the Goma Agreements (see p. 120). It visited there as well as the Mugunga II camp of internally displaced persons, and met with civil society representatives. Among its recommendations, the mission proposed that the Council, while continuing to prepare for a future gradual drawdown, should keep the capabilities of the United Nations Organization Mission in the Democratic Republic of the Congo under review to ensure that they supported the Mission with the necessary force enablers, tactical intelligence and, where feasible, standby special forces to assist the DRC with the implementation of the Goma and Nairobi processes and address the challenges posed by other foreign armed groups; that the Mixed Technical Commission on Peace and Security—the framework for implementing the Goma Agreements—should make rapid progress on reaching an agreement on the modalities and timelines for disengagement and brassage, with the full cooperation of the Congolese armed groups; and that the Forces démocratiques de libération du Rwanda, ex-Rwandan Armed Forces/Interahamwe and other Rwandan armed groups should present themselves without any further delay or preconditions for disarmament, demobilization, repatriation, resettlement and reintegration. The mission also encouraged the Governments of the DRC and Rwanda to continue implementing their commitments under the Nairobi Communiqué [YUN 2007, p. 127] to make sure that all conditions were in place to allow that process to advance. The Government and the judiciary should take appropriate measures against the armed groups that continued to prey on the local population and perpetrate acts of sexual violence; and the Government should take further steps to end the recruitment of children, in particular by armed groups.

In Côte d'Ivoire, the mission acknowledged the progress made in implementing the Ouagadougou Political Agreement [YUN 2007, p. 175] under the Facilitation of the President of Burkina Faso. It noted a relaxed political and security environment marked by renewed confidence of all stakeholders in the Agreement, and a significant acceleration of the preparations for the elections. The mission met with the President; a delegation from the Forces nouvelles; the Special Representative of the Facilitator; the Chairman of the Independent Electoral Commission; the Chiefs of Staff of the Defence and Security Forces and of the Forces nouvelles; and others from Government and civil society. The mission recommended, among other things, that the Council continue to support the implementation of the Ouagadougou Political Agreement, as well as the role of the Facilitator and the Special Representative of the Secretary-General for Côte d'Ivoire, including for the certification of all stages of the electoral process; and that the Council encourage all parties to adhere to the agreed timeline leading to open, free, fair and transparent elections on 30 November, and implement in earnest all outstanding tasks under the Ouagadougou Agreement.

Office of the Special Adviser on Africa

In 2008, the Office of the Special Adviser on Africa (OSAA), established by General Assembly resolution 57/7 [YUN 2002, p. 910], continued to enhance international support for Africa's development and security through its advocacy and analytical work; assist the Secretary-General in improving coherence and coordination of UN system support to Africa; and facilitate global intergovernmental deliberations on Africa, in particular relating to the New Partnership for Africa's Development (NEPAD) [YUN 2001, p. 900]. At a conference in May in New York on "The governance dimension of the Millennium Development Goals in Africa", OSAA organized a panel discussion on the "Challenges of Increased Aid to Africa". At issue were measures for African and donor countries and international organizations that would help ensure the effective use of scaled-up aid and strengthen its positive impact on growth and poverty reduction. Also in May, at the Tokyo International Conference on Africa's Development (TICAD IV) (Yokohama, Japan) (see p. 1015), the Office chaired the group on peace and good governance. In September, OSAA organized a high-level meeting in New York on Africa's development to recommit the international community to development and review the implementation of all commitments made to and by Africa. It also co-organized a side event on "Governance Challenges in Africa". The Office also issued studies on small-scale enterprise development and foreign direct investment in Africa and on the private sector's institutional response to NEPAD.

African peacekeeping capacity

At its 2008 substantive session (New York, 10 March–4 April and 3 July) [A/62/19], the Special Committee on Peacekeeping Operations discussed the enhancement of African peacekeeping capacities. Stressing the need for coherent and effective coordination of support to the AU, the Committee reiterated the AU lead and ownership of its 10-year capacity-building plan [YUN 2006, p. 340], including donor coordination, and requested the Secretariat to continue to assist in such coordination and help broaden the donor base. The Committee reaffirmed that the provision of logistical and financial reserves to facilitate the AU's rapid deployment capabilities was of primary importance. It also emphasized the importance of implementing the joint action plan for UN support to the AU in peacekeeping in the short, medium and long terms, focusing primarily on collaboration in the areas of conflict prevention and peacekeeping, in particular assistance to the development of an African standby force. The Committee reiterated its recommendation that the Department of Peacekeeping Operations (DPKO) continue to support the AU in ensuring commonality of procedures for joint planning and coordination with subregional economic communities. Finally, it requested that the established multidisciplinary AU peacekeeping support team continue to serve as a coordinating point for all issues in DPKO related to cooperation with the AU, and that the Committee be informed regularly about its functioning and mandate, particularly with regard to providing technical support to the regional and subregional capacities.

Implementation of Secretary-General's 1998 recommendations on promotion of peace

Report of Secretary-General. In response to General Assembly resolution 61/230 [YUN 2006, p. 117], the Secretary-General in August submitted a report [A/63/212] on the implementation of the recommendations contained in his 1998 report on the causes of conflict and promotion of durable peace and sustainable development in Africa [YUN 1998, p. 66]. The report reviewed major peace and security developments in Africa during the past year, underlining the concerns being addressed by Africa and the international community in order to restore and maintain peace and rebuild post-conflict countries. It also reviewed progress in relation to the short-term steps and actions proposed in the previous report [YUN 2007, p. 112] to support efforts towards a conflict-free Africa, pending a substantive review of new challenges and threats to long-term peace and sustainable development. The report focused on the international response to conflict situations through prevention and mediation; peacekeeping (in Chad and the Central African Republic, Côte d'Ivoire, the Darfur region in the Sudan, the DRC, Ethiopia and Eritrea, Liberia, Somalia and Western Sahara); and peacebuilding (in Burundi, the Central African Republic, Guinea-Bissau and Sierra Leone). It also discussed strengthening the response of the UN system to peace and security needs through support for African regional and subregional organizations, including enhanced capacity-building in support of the AU, cooperation with subregional organizations and cooperation between the Security Council and the AU Peace and Security Council; reducing the proliferation of small arms and ending the culture of violence; and generating employment in post-conflict countries. The report concluded that despite a decade of achievements, the international community would have to press forward with increased dedication, together with African regional organizations, to assure lasting peace and development in the face of growing global challenges.

GENERAL ASSEMBLY ACTION

On 11 September [meeting 121], the General Assembly adopted **resolution 62/275** [draft A/62/L.47 & Add.1] without vote [agenda item 64 *(b)*].

Implementation of the recommendations contained in the report of the Secretary-General on the causes of conflict and the promotion of durable peace and sustainable development in Africa

The General Assembly,

Recalling the report of the Open-ended Ad Hoc Working Group on the Causes of Conflict and the Promotion of Durable Peace and Sustainable Development in Africa and its resolutions 53/92 of 7 December 1998, 54/234 of 22 December 1999, 55/217 of 21 December 2000, 56/37 of 4 December 2001, 57/296 of 20 December 2002, 57/337 of 3 July 2003, 58/235 of 23 December 2003, 59/255 of 23 December 2004, 60/223 of 23 December 2005 and 61/230 of 22 December 2006, as well as its resolutions 62/179 of 19 December 2007 on the New Partnership for Africa's Development and 59/213 of 20 December 2004 on cooperation between the United Nations and the African Union,

Recalling also, in this context, Security Council resolutions 1809(2008) of 16 April 2008 on peace and security in Africa, 1325(2000) of 31 October 2000 and 1820(2008) of 19 June 2008 on women and peace and security, 1366(2001) of 30 August 2001 on the role of the Council in the prevention of armed conflicts, 1612(2005) of 26 July 2005 on children and armed conflict, 1625(2005) of 14 September 2005 on strengthening the effectiveness of the Council's role in conflict prevention, particularly in Africa, and 1631(2005) of 17 October 2005 on cooperation between the United Nations and regional and subregional organizations in maintaining international peace and security,

Recalling further the 2005 World Summit Outcome, through which world leaders reaffirmed their commitment to addressing the special needs of Africa,

Recognizing that development, peace, security and human rights are interlinked and mutually reinforcing,

Recalling the creation by the Economic and Social Council, by its resolution 2002/1 of 15 July 2002, of ad hoc advisory groups on African countries emerging from conflict,

Stressing that the responsibility for peace and security in Africa, including the capacity to address the root causes of conflict and to resolve conflicts in a peaceful manner, lies primarily with African countries, while recognizing the need for support from the international community,

Recognizing, in particular, the importance of strengthening the capacity of the African Union and subregional organizations to address the causes of conflict in Africa,

Noting that despite the positive trends and advances in obtaining durable peace in Africa, the conditions required for sustainable development have yet to be consolidated throughout the continent and that there is therefore an urgent need to develop African human and institutional capacities, particularly in countries emerging from conflict,

Noting also that conflict prevention and the consolidation of peace would benefit from the coordinated, sustained and integrated efforts of the United Nations system and Member States, and regional and subregional organizations, as well as international and regional financial institutions,

Reaffirming the need to strengthen the synergy between Africa's economic and social development programmes and its peace and security agenda,

Reaffirming also the importance of the Peacebuilding Commission as a dedicated mechanism to address, in an integrated manner, the special needs of countries emerging from conflict towards recovery, reintegration and reconstruction and to assist them in laying the foundation for peace and sustainable development,

Underlining the need to address the negative implications of the illegal exploitation of natural resources in all its aspects for peace, security and development in Africa, and underlining also the fact that the illicit trade in natural resources is a matter of serious international concern, which can be directly linked to the fuelling of armed conflicts and the illicit trade in and proliferation of arms, especially small arms and light weapons,

1. *Takes note* of the progress report of the Secretary-General on the implementation of the recommendations contained in his report on the causes of conflict and the promotion of durable peace and sustainable development in Africa, and welcomes recent institutional developments in addressing such causes and other efforts in conflict prevention, peacemaking, peacekeeping and peacebuilding undertaken by African countries, African regional organizations and the United Nations system;

2. *Welcomes* the progress made, in particular by the African Union and the subregional organizations, in the prevention, management and resolution of conflict and in post-conflict peacebuilding in a number of African countries, and calls for intensified efforts and a coordinated approach between national Governments, the African Union, subregional organizations, the United Nations system and partners with a view to achieving further progress towards the goal of a conflict-free Africa;

3. *Recognizes* that international and regional efforts to prevent conflict and consolidate peace in Africa should be channelled towards the sustainable development of Africa and human and institutional capacity-building of African countries and organizations, particularly in priority areas identified at the continental level;

4. *Calls upon* the United Nations system to continue to mainstream the special needs of Africa in all its normative and operational activities;

5. *Welcomes* efforts to enhance practical cooperation, within the framework of an effective partnership, between the United Nations and the African Union in the realm of conflict prevention and resolution, crisis management, peacemaking, peacekeeping and post-conflict peacebuilding in Africa, and in this context urges the United Nations system and the international community to increase, coordinate and sustain their efforts aimed at assisting African countries in addressing the full range of causes of conflict in Africa;

6. *Recalls* the signing of the declaration on enhancing cooperation between the United Nations and the African Union, in Addis Ababa, on 16 November 2006, and the ongoing efforts in this regard, and underlines the importance of the implementation of the ten-year capacity-building programme for the African Union, mainly focusing on peace and security, in particular the operationalization of the African Standby Force, urges all stakeholders to support the full implementation of the ten-year programme for the African Union, and requests the Secretary-General to include in his next annual report on the implementation of the recommendations contained in his 1998 report, a detailed account of the progress achieved in this regard;

7. *Welcomes* the ongoing efforts of the African Union and the subregional organizations to strengthen their peacekeeping capacity and to take the lead in peacekeeping operations in the continent, in accordance with Chapter VIII of the Charter of the United Nations and in close coordination with the United Nations, through the Peace and Security Council of the African Union, as well as ongoing efforts to develop a continental early warning system, response capacity, such as the African Standby Force, and

enhanced mediation capacity, including through the Panel of the Wise;

8. *Notes with appreciation* the establishment of the multidisciplinary African Union Peacekeeping Support Team within the Department for Peacekeeping Operations at the Secretariat, and reaffirms the need for the United Nations and other development partners to increase their support for the African Union, including through existing forums for cooperation with Africa, in order to enhance its capacity and effectiveness in the planning, deployment and management of peacekeeping operations, including in the advanced training of African peacekeepers, and in peacebuilding activities, and encourages the donor community to provide further support to the African Union, including through the replenishment of its Peace Fund;

9. *Calls for* a holistic and coordinated approach at the national, subregional, regional and international levels to improve the effectiveness of mechanisms for conflict prevention and resolution, crisis management, peacemaking, peacekeeping and post-conflict peacebuilding efforts in Africa, and reaffirms the need for observing such an approach in the design and implementation of all programmes within the context of the ten-year capacity-building programme;

10. *Stresses* the critical importance of a regional approach to conflict prevention, in particular with respect to cross-border issues such as disarmament, demobilization and reintegration programmes, the prevention of illegal exploitation of natural resources and trafficking in high-value commodities and the illicit trade in small arms and light weapons in all its aspects, and in this regard emphasizes the central role of the African Union and the subregional organizations in addressing such issues;

11. *Reaffirms its commitment* to address the special needs of Africa, where some progress can be noted but where some countries remain off track in meeting the Millennium Development Goals by 2015, in order to enable it to enter the mainstream of the world economy, and to strengthen cooperation with the New Partnership for Africa's Development by providing coherent support for the programmes drawn up by African leaders within that framework, including by mobilizing internal and external financial resources and facilitating approval of such programmes by the multilateral financial institutions;

12. *Welcomes* the adoption of Security Council resolution 1809(2008) on peace and security in Africa;

13. *Notes with concern* that violence against women and children everywhere continues and often increases, even as armed conflicts draw to an end, urges further progress in the implementation of policies and guidelines relating to the protection of and assistance to women and children in conflict and post-conflict situations, and notes the adoption of Security Council resolution 1820(2008) on women and peace and security;

14. *Calls upon* the United Nations system and Member States to support the African Union in its effort to effectively integrate training in international humanitarian law and international human rights law, with particular emphasis on the rights of women and children, in the training of civilian and military personnel of national standby contingents at both the operational and tactical levels, as set out in article 13 of the Protocol Relating to the Establishment of the Peace and Security Council of the African Union;

15. *Welcomes* the ongoing efforts of the African Union to ensure protection of the rights of women in conflict and post-conflict situations, recalls, in this regard, the adoption of the Protocol to the African Charter on Human and Peoples' Rights on the Rights of Women in Africa and the Solemn Declaration on Gender Equality in Africa by the Assembly of Heads of State and Government of the African Union at their second and third ordinary sessions, held in Maputo in July 2003 and Addis Ababa in July 2004, and their entry into force, stresses the significance of those instruments for all countries in Africa in strengthening the role of women in peace and conflict prevention in the continent, and strongly urges the United Nations and all parties to redouble their efforts and support in this regard;

16. *Calls for* the enhancement of the role of women in conflict prevention, conflict resolution and post-conflict peacebuilding consistent with Security Council resolution 1325(2000);

17. *Notes with concern* the tragic plight of children in conflict situations in Africa, in particular the phenomenon of child soldiers, as well as other grave violations against children, and stresses the need for the protection of children in armed conflicts, post-conflict counselling, rehabilitation and education, with due regard to the relevant resolutions of the General Assembly and the Security Council;

18. *Takes note* of the conclusions of the expert group meeting on "Youth in Africa: participation of youth as partners in peace and development in post-conflict countries", held in Namibia in November 2006, and calls upon the United Nations system and Member States to adopt strategies to include youth as central stakeholders and key actors in the rehabilitation, reconciliation and rebuilding of war-torn communities and in contributing to sustainable development in their countries;

19. *Recognizes* the important role of the good offices of the Secretary-General in Africa, and encourages the Secretary-General to continue to use mediation as often as possible to help to solve conflicts peacefully, taking due consideration of the work performed by the African Union and the subregional organizations in that regard;

20. *Notes* the efforts of the Mediation Support Unit, newly established in the Department of Political Affairs of the Secretariat, in particular the establishment of a standby team of mediation experts who will be on call to assist in peacemaking efforts around the world;

21. *Invites* the United Nations and the donor community to increase efforts to support ongoing regional efforts to build African mediation and negotiation capacity;

22. *Welcomes* African-led initiatives to strengthen political, economic and corporate governance, such as the African Peer Review Mechanism, encourages even more African countries to join this process, and calls upon the United Nations system and Member States to assist African Member States and regional and subregional organizations in their efforts to enhance good governance, including the promotion of the rule of law and the holding of free and fair elections;

23. *Recognizes* the role of the Peacebuilding Commission in ensuring that national ownership of the peacebuilding process in countries emerging from conflict is observed

and that nationally identified priorities are at the core of international and regional efforts in post-conflict peacebuilding in the countries under consideration, notes the important steps taken by the Commission in engaging with Sierra Leone, Burundi, Guinea-Bissau and the Central African Republic through integrated peacebuilding strategies, calls for sustained regional and international commitment to the implementation of these strategies and their design process, recalls the adoption of the Sierra Leone Peacebuilding Cooperation Framework and the Strategic Framework for Peacebuilding for Burundi, and calls for their implementation;

24. *Calls upon* the United Nations system and invites Member States to assist African countries emerging from conflict in their efforts to build national capacities of governance, including the rehabilitation of the security sector, disarmament, demobilization and the reintegration of ex-combatants, provision for the safe return of internally displaced persons and refugees, the launch of income-generation activities, particularly for youth and women, and the delivery of basic public services;

25. *Stresses* the importance of effectively addressing challenges that continue to hamper the achievement of peace, stability and sustainable development on the continent, inter alia, the increased prevalence of infectious disease such as HIV/AIDS, the effects of global warming and climate change, the extremely high rates of youth unemployment, human trafficking, massive displacements of people, the illegal exploitation of natural resources, the illicit trade in small arms and light weapons, the emergence of terrorist networks and the increased activity of transnational organized crime, and in this regard encourages the United Nations system and Member States to assist African countries to effectively address these challenges;

26. *Also stresses* the importance of creating an environment conducive to national reconciliation and social and economic recovery in countries emerging from conflict;

27. *Encourages* African Governments to establish appropriate structures and policies to create an environment conducive to attracting direct foreign investment, calls upon African Member States and regional and subregional organizations to assist African countries emerging from conflict in devising national natural resources and public revenue management structures, and invites the international community to assist in that process by providing adequate financial and technical assistance, as well as by renewing its commitment to efforts aimed at combating the illegal exploitation of the natural resources of those countries;

28. *Welcomes* the various important initiatives of Africa's development partners in recent years, inter alia, the Africa Partnership Forum, the New Asian-African Strategic Partnership, the China-Africa Partnership, the European Union-Africa Strategic Partnership, the Group of Eight-Africa Partnership, the Millennium Challenge Account, the Emergency Plan for AIDS Relief of the President of the United States of America and the Tokyo International Conference on African Development, and emphasizes, in this regard, the importance of coordination in such initiatives on Africa and the need for their effective implementation;

29. *Requests* the Secretary-General to consider the need to submit to the General Assembly at its sixty-fifth session a report on the outcome of the review of his 1998 report;

30. *Decides* to continue to monitor the implementation of the recommendations contained in the 1998 report of the Secretary-General;

31. *Requests* the Secretary-General to submit to the General Assembly at its sixty-third session a progress report on the implementation of the present resolution.

Central Africa and Great Lakes region

Great Lakes region

Political and security situation

In 2008, Central Africa and the Great Lakes region continued to be affected by armed groups and militias. Despite the signing of the Nairobi communiqué in November 2007 [YUN 2007, p. 127], which set out a common approach to ending the threat to peace and security in both countries, and in the Great Lakes region, relations between the Democratic Republic of the Congo (DRC) and Rwanda remained challenging. In March, the Security Council took action to address the presence of armed groups and militias in the eastern DRC, which was perpetuating a climate of insecurity. It demanded that Rwandan armed groups operating in that area, including the Forces démocratiques de libération du Rwanda and ex-Rwandan Armed Forces (ex-FAR)/Interahamwe turn themselves in to Congolese authorities and the United Nations Organization Mission in the Democratic Republic of the Congo (MONUC) for disarmament, demobilization, repatriation, resettlement and reintegration.

SECURITY COUNCIL ACTION

On 13 March [meeting 5852], the Security Council unanimously adopted **resolution 1804(2008)**. The draft [S/2008/171] was prepared in consultations among Council members.

The Security Council,

Recalling its previous resolutions, in particular resolutions 1649(2005) of 21 December 2005, 1771(2007) of 10 August 2007, 1794(2007) of 21 December 2007 and 1797(2008) of 30 January 2008, and the statements by its President concerning the Democratic Republic of the Congo and the Great Lakes region,

Reaffirming its commitment to respect for the sovereignty, territorial integrity and political independence of the Democratic Republic of the Congo and the Republic of Rwanda as well as all States in the region,

Expressing its grave concern at the continued presence of the Forces démocratiques de libération du Rwanda, the ex-Rwandan Armed Forces/Interahamwe and other Rwandan armed groups referred to in the joint communiqué of the Governments of the Democratic Republic of the Congo and the Republic of Rwanda signed at Nairobi on 9 November 2007 ("the Nairobi communiqué") operating in the eastern part of the Democratic Republic of the Congo, which continues to pose a serious threat to the peace and security of the entire Great Lakes region,

Deploring the persistence of violations of human rights and international humanitarian law carried out by the Forces démocratiques de libération du Rwanda, the ex-Rwandan Armed Forces/Interahamwe and other Rwandan armed groups operating in the eastern part of the Democratic Republic of the Congo, condemning in particular sexual violence perpetrated by those groups, and recalling its resolution 1325(2000) of 31 October 2000 on women and peace and security, its resolution 1612(2005) of 26 July 2005 on children and armed conflict and the conclusions on children and armed conflict in the Democratic Republic of the Congo endorsed by it,

Recognizing the commitment and sustained efforts of the Democratic Republic of the Congo, the Republic of Rwanda, other countries of the region and their international partners to solve their common security concerns and achieve and sustain regional peace and stability, as expressed in particular in the Nairobi communiqué and the conclusions of the high-level meeting of the Tripartite Plus Joint Commission, held in Addis Ababa on 4 and 5 December 2007,

Recalling the signing at Nairobi on 15 December 2006 of the Pact on Security, Stability and Development in the Great Lakes Region, and underscoring the commitments not to support rebel armed groups and to cooperate with a view to disarming and dismantling existing rebel armed groups,

Welcoming the decision of the Government of the Democratic Republic of the Congo to hold a meeting in Kisangani to address the issue of the presence of the Forces démocratiques de libération du Rwanda, the ex-Rwandan Armed Forces/Interahamwe and other Rwandan armed groups in the Democratic Republic of the Congo,

Supporting the ongoing efforts of the United Nations Organization Mission in the Democratic Republic of the Congo to promote the voluntary disarmament, demobilization, repatriation, resettlement and reintegration of these groups,

Expressing its grave concern at the continued presence of other armed groups and militias in the eastern part of the Democratic Republic of the Congo, which perpetuates a climate of insecurity in the whole region, underscoring that the statements of commitment (*Actes d'engagement*) signed at Goma on 23 January 2008, together with the Nairobi communiqué, represent a major step towards the restoration of lasting peace and stability in the Great Lakes region, calling upon the signatories to the Goma statements of commitment to take immediate action in support thereof, and expressing its intention to continue to monitor closely their implementation,

1. *Demands* that all members of the Forces démocratiques de libération du Rwanda, the ex-Rwandan Armed Forces/Interahamwe and other Rwandan armed groups operating in the eastern part of the Democratic Republic of the Congo immediately lay down their arms and present themselves without any further delay or preconditions to the Congolese authorities and the United Nations Organization Mission in the Democratic Republic of the Congo for their disarmament, demobilization, repatriation, resettlement and reintegration;

2. *Demands also* that the Forces démocratiques de libération du Rwanda, the ex-Rwandan Armed Forces/Interahamwe and other Rwandan armed groups operating in the eastern part of the Democratic Republic of the Congo immediately stop recruiting and using children, release all children associated with them and put an end to gender-based violence, particularly rape and other forms of sexual abuse, and all other forms of violence, and stresses the need for those responsible to be brought to justice;

3. *Recalls* the mandate of the Mission to facilitate the voluntary demobilization and repatriation of disarmed foreign combatants and their dependants, and to use all necessary means, within the limits of its capacity and in the areas where its units are deployed, to support operations led by the integrated brigades of the Armed Forces of the Democratic Republic of the Congo with a view to disarming the recalcitrant armed groups in order to ensure their participation in the disarmament, demobilization, repatriation, resettlement and reintegration process;

4. *Calls upon* the Governments of the Democratic Republic of the Congo and the Republic of Rwanda to intensify their cooperation to implement their commitments under the Nairobi communiqué, in particular with a view to creating the conditions conducive to the repatriation of demobilized combatants;

5. *Recalls* that the targeted measures, including a travel ban and an asset freeze imposed by paragraphs 13 and 15 of resolution 1596(2005) of 18 April 2005 were extended by resolution 1649(2005) and resolution 1698(2006) of 31 July 2006 to apply, in particular, to political and military leaders of armed groups operating in the Democratic Republic of the Congo who impede the disarmament and the voluntary repatriation or resettlement of combatants belonging to those groups, and stresses that those measures are applicable to leaders of the Forces démocratiques de libération du Rwanda, the ex-Rwandan Armed Forces/Interahamwe and other Rwandan armed groups designated in accordance with the provisions of those resolutions;

6. *Undertakes* to consider, in its forthcoming review of the measures described in paragraph 5 above, expanding their applicability, as appropriate and taking into account participation in or contribution to the disarmament, demobilization, repatriation, resettlement and reintegration process, to other members of the Forces démocratiques de libération du Rwanda, the ex-Rwandan Armed Forces/Interahamwe or other Rwandan armed groups operating in the territory of the Democratic Republic of the Congo or to persons providing other forms of assistance to them;

7. *Stresses* that the arms embargo imposed by resolution 1493(2003) of 28 July 2003, as expanded by resolution 1596(2005), prohibits the provision of arms and any related materiel or technical training and assistance to all foreign armed groups and illegal Congolese militias in the Democratic Republic of the Congo, including the Forces démocratiques de libération du Rwanda, the ex-Rwandan

Armed Forces/Interahamwe and other Rwandan armed groups;

8. *Calls upon* Member States to consider taking the measures necessary to prevent the provision by their nationals or from their territories of any financial, technical or other forms of support to or for the benefit of the Forces démocratiques de libération du Rwanda, the ex-Rwandan Armed Forces/Interahamwe or other Rwandan armed groups operating in the territory of the Democratic Republic of the Congo;

9. *Reiterates its call upon* all States to intensify cooperation with and render all necessary assistance to the International Criminal Tribunal for the Prosecution of Persons Responsible for Genocide and Other Serious Violations of International Humanitarian Law Committed in the Territory of Rwanda and Rwandan Citizens Responsible for Genocide and Other Such Violations Committed in the Territory of Neighbouring States between 1 January and 31 December 1994;

10. *Decides* to remain actively seized of the matter.

Communication. In a letter of 14 March [S/2008/180] to the Security Council, Rwanda welcomed the fact that at last, 14 years after the 1994 genocide, the Security Council had adopted resolution 1804(2008), targeting the authors of that genocide—the ex-FAR/Interahamwe, currently known as the Forces démocratiques de liberation du Rwanda (FDLR), and the Rassemblement Uni pour la Démocratie-Urunana (RUD-Urunana), among others. Rwanda welcomed the Council's determination to end the threat posed by those groups to the security and sovereignty of Rwanda, the DRC and the entire Great Lakes region. Rwanda expressed its determination to continue cooperation with the DRC and other partners in ending the threat posed by those armed groups; reiterated its welcome and encouragement to all members of Rwandan armed groups who wished to repatriate; and called on the DRC and MONUC to help them do so safely and expeditiously. Rwanda would continue to guarantee returnees safety, security and the enjoyment of all the rights to which Rwandans were constitutionally entitled.

Meanwhile, relations between the DRC and Uganda continued to improve. The Joint Permanent Commission established by the two countries met regularly. On 11 May, at a meeting in Dar-es-Salaam, United Republic of Tanzania, the President of the DRC, Joseph Kabila, and the President of Uganda, Yoweri Museveni, agreed to maintain the status quo along their common border while the Joint Border Remarking Committee carried out its work. They also agreed to consider elevating their diplomatic representation to the ambassadorial level, and renewed their determination to end the threat posed by the Allied Democratic Forces and the National Army for the Liberation of Uganda (ADF/NALU).

Following those and subsequent discussions, as well as a meeting of the Chiefs of Staff from the DRC, Uganda and Southern Sudan in Kampala, Uganda, on 2 June, the DRC indicated its intention to conduct military operations against the Ugandan rebel group the Lord's Resistance Army (LRA). On 30 May, MONUC and the DRC armed forces (FARDC) had signed a joint directive for operations against LRA, which focused on protecting civilians, containing LRA, and facilitating the voluntary disarmament, demobilization, repatriation, resettlement and reintegration of LRA elements.

Follow-up to second International Conference on the Great Lakes Region

At the second International Conference on the Great Lakes Region (Nairobi, December 2006) [YUN 2006, p. 124], 11 countries signed the Pact on Security, Stability and Development in the Great Lakes Region, pledging to pursue peace, security, political stability and development.

Communication. In a letter dated 22 February [S/2008/125], Uganda, in its capacity as Chair of the Great Lakes Region Initiative, communicated to the Security Council a 15 December 2007 statement of Liberata Mulamula, Executive Secretary of the International Conference on the Great Lakes Region—the intergovernmental organization coordinating the implementation of the Pact—on the first anniversary of the signing of the Pact, commemorating positive developments and outlining remaining challenges.

The Executive Secretariat of the International Conference on the Great Lakes Region held the second meeting of parliamentarians of the Great Lakes region (Bujumbura, Burundi, 3–4 March), during which it was decided to formalize the establishment of a regional forum of parliamentarians before the next meeting in November. The Executive Secretariat also organized a regional workshop (Bujumbura, 25–28 March) on the integration of gender in the implementation of the Pact. In April, the Conference Secretariat launched a series of planning workshops in the region to review the Pact's programmes of action and protocols, and to develop road maps for implementation.

The Pact entered into force on 21 June following ratification by eight of the 11 core countries of the International Conference on the Great Lakes Region. Under the terms of the Pact, Governments committed themselves to addressing the key security, governance, development, humanitarian and social challenges from a regional perspective.

At the second Regional Inter-Ministerial Committee Meeting of the International Conference on the Great Lakes Region (Brazzaville, Congo, 21–22 May), the Ministers commended the Government of the DRC for its efforts to implement the Nairobi Communiqué, and called on the ex-FAR/Interahamwe to seize the opportunity to voluntarily disarm and return to Rwanda.

Special Envoy on the Great Lakes region

Appointment and activity. Following large-scale hostilities in the latter half of the year between the Government of the DRC and the rebel group Congrès national pour la défense du people (CNDP), led by Laurent Nkunda, the Secretary-General, on 9 December, appointed former Nigerian President Olusegun Obasanjo as his Special Envoy on the Great Lakes region. The Extraordinary Summit of the AU and the International Conference on the Great Lakes Region (Nairobi, Kenya, 7 November), which endorsed the appointment, proposed that the Special Envoy should also represent the AU and the Great Lakes region as a facilitator and be joined in those tasks by former Tanzanian President Benjamin Mkapa—a choice that the Secretary-General endorsed. In November and December, the two facilitators met with the presidents of Angola, the Congo, the DRC, Kenya, Rwanda, Uganda and the United Republic of Tanzania, as well as with the leader of CNDP. Following those meetings, a dialogue between the DRC and CNDP opened on 8 December in Nairobi. Relations between the DRC and Rwanda warmed, and their cooperation was enhanced. Although CNDP had threatened Goma in November, the prospect of a military takeover of the town had considerably receded. CNDP remained unwilling at the end of the year, however, to sign a formal recommitment to its unilateral cessation of hostilities. CNDP also accused the DRC of incursions into areas that it had called on MONUC to occupy after it had vacated them. (For more information on the situation in the eastern DRC, see p. 125.)

Standing Advisory Committee on Security Questions

At its twenty-seventh ministerial meeting (Luanda, Angola, 13–15 May) [A/63/82-S/2008/360], the 11-member United Nations Standing Advisory Committee on Security Questions in Central Africa reviewed the geopolitical and security situation in Burundi, Cameroon, the Central African Republic, Chad and the DRC. The persistence of tensions, the deterioration of the security situation and the resurgence of armed confrontations, along with the corresponding humanitarian and human rights situation, gave the Committee cause for concern.

The Committee condemned the attacks in Burundi perpetrated by the Parti pour la libération du peuple hutu-Forces nationales de libération (Palipehutu-FNL) against innocent populations in the capital, Bujumbura, in violation of the 2006 ceasefire agreement [YUN 2006, p. 153], and urged the Government, Palipehutu-FNL and all other political actors to give priority to dialogue with a view to finding solutions to all outstanding problems and take all steps necessary for the full implementation of the agreement.

Social tensions in Cameroon had reduced due to improvements in the population's purchasing power following the reduction of tariffs on essential commodities and the increase in Government employees' salaries. The Committee expressed concern, however, at criminal "roadblocking" in some border areas, and called on security forces to continue to combat that phenomenon, in concert with neighbouring countries. It also welcomed Cameroon's contribution to the deployment of the European Union operation (EUFOR) and the Central African Multinational Force in the Republic of Chad and the Central African Republic. It appealed to donors to provide Cameroon with the support needed to deal with the refugee influx in the north, as a result of developments in Chad, and in order to ensure that refugees could return promptly to their home countries.

Regarding the Central African Republic, the Committee noted with satisfaction the ceasefire and peace agreement of 9 May between the Government and the Armée populaire pour la restauration de la démocratie. It expressed concern, however, at the insecurity caused by ongoing banditry in the north, and at acts of violence against civilians, as well as at the presence of Ugandan rebel LRA elements in the south-east, along with the use of that region of the country as a crossing to neighbouring countries. The Committee encouraged the Government to pursue its efforts to combat impunity and reduce the number of extrajudicial killings, as recommended to the United Nations Human Rights Council by the Special Rapporteur on extrajudicial, summary or arbitrary executions following his visit to the country (see p. 803).

The Committee expressed concern at the deterioration of relations between Chad and the Sudan, and called on both nations to re-establish dialogue towards implementing the Dakar Agreement of 13 March (see p. 268). In cooperation with Chad, the Committee appealed to the international community to resolve the Darfur crisis, and requested the United Nations to reactivate the United Nations Development Programme Small Arms Project, a disarmament project that ceased to operate in 2006. It also called for measures to strengthen the capacity of security services in the subregion to combat the proliferation of small arms and light weapons, and for the establishment of appropriate border patrol mechanisms in the subregion.

The Committee welcomed the Goma statement of commitment and the Amani programme for peace, pacification, stability and development in the provinces of North and South Kivu, signed by the Government of the DRC and rebel armed groups on 23 January, and urged all parties to work towards their prompt implementation (see below). It also welcomed the Nairobi Communiqué signed on 9 November 2007 by the DRC and Rwanda [YUN 2007, p. 127], as well as the round table held in Kinshasa from 18 to 20 February 2008 on security sector reform in the DRC and the start of judicial reform. The Committee expressed concern at the deteriorating security situation in the eastern DRC, particularly in the Ituri region, and called on the armed groups to turn in their weapons and participate unconditionally in the disarmament, demobilization, reintegration and rehabilitation process.

On 2 December, by **resolution 63/78** (see p. 647), the General Assembly reaffirmed its support for efforts aimed at promoting confidence-building measures at the regional and subregional levels in order to ease tensions and conflicts in Central Africa and to further peace, stability and sustainable development in the subregion.

(For information on the Committee's review of the promotion of disarmament and arms limitation in Central Africa and the report of the Secretary-General on the Committee's activities, see p. 646.)

Democratic Republic of the Congo

The year began with renewed hope when the Government of the Democratic Republic of the Congo (DRC), the rebel Congrès national pour la défense du peuple (CNDP) and other armed groups from the Kivus in the eastern DRC signed in January statements of commitment—the *Actes d'engagement,* known as the Goma Agreements—providing for a ceasefire and the separation of forces, and for the rebels to either disarm and demobilize or be integrated into the national armed forces through brassage (intermixing). However, little progress was made in disarming the many disparate armed groups plaguing the region.

In August, the largest UN peacekeeping operation, the United Nations Organization Mission in the Democratic Republic of the Congo (MONUC), found itself challenged when violence reignited in the volatile eastern region, on the border with Rwanda. The situation worsened in late October, when CNDP, led by Laurent Nkunda, undertook a major offensive threatening Goma, the provincial capital of North Kivu. Mr. Nkunda's forces quickly overwhelmed the Armed Forces of the Democratic Republic of the Congo (FARDC) and displaced hundreds of thousands of civilians. MONUC peacekeepers, finding themselves lodged between warring groups, protected civilians where they could, while the Government army they were there to support was virtually incapacitated.

The United Nations set in motion a series of actions to address the conflict. MONUC quickly reconfigured its forces throughout the east, reinforcing its presence in Goma and surrounding areas. In November, following a visit to the DRC, the Under-Secretary-General for Peacekeeping Operations urged the Security Council to send more troops to the Mission. The Council agreed to authorize an additional 3,100 troops and police. The Secretary-General also called for the deployment of a multinational force as a bridging measure until MONUC could be reinforced. He met with regional leaders in Nairobi in November, as the crisis threatened to spill beyond the borders of the DRC; and he appointed Olusegun Obasanjo, the former President of Nigeria, as his Special Envoy on the Great Lakes Region to work with the parties on finding a lasting peace. The Security Council, on 22 December, extended the mandate of MONUC by one year, and called on the Mission to make protecting civilians a priority.

Political developments and MONUC activities

The Conference on Peace, Security and Development in North and South Kivu was held in Goma, DRC, from 6 to 25 January with the engagement of and support from MONUC and international partners. In all, 1,250 delegates attended, including representatives of Congolese armed groups, local communities, local authorities, political parties and civil society. They worked in two seminars, one for North Kivu and one for South Kivu. At each seminar, four committees were set up to consider issues relating to peace, security, social and humanitarian affairs and development. A key outcome of the Conference was the adoption, on 23 January, of two statements of commitment (*Actes d'engagement*) for North and South Kivu signed by all participating Congolese armed groups, including CNDP and Banyamulenge insurgents from South Kivu, represented by the Forces républicaines fédéralistes. The statements—the so-called Goma Agreements—committed the armed groups to accepting a ceasefire monitored by MONUC; agreeing that all militias should undergo disarmament, demobilization and reintegration; and facilitating the return of refugees and internally displaced persons. The Government committed itself to presenting to Parliament a measure renewing the amnesty law, which had expired in 2003, and extending it to cover recent acts of war and insurrection. The amnesty would not, however, apply to war crimes, crimes against humanity or genocide. The statements did not address several key issues, including the timeline for disarming the armed groups and modalities for brassage. The signatories agreed to establish a Mixed Technical Commission on Peace and Security to address those issues and to monitor implementation. It was agreed that the Commission would comprise representatives of the Government, the armed groups and international partners.

Secretary-General statement (January). On 23 January, the Secretary-General, in a press statement [SG/SM/11385-AFR/1647], congratulated the Government of the DRC as well as the organizers and participants in the Conference on Peace, Security and Development in North and South Kivu on its successful conclusion. The commitment of the armed groups of North and South Kivu to end all hostilities, as outlined in the statements of commitment signed by those groups and the Government on 23 January, represented an important step towards restoring lasting peace and stability in the Great Lakes region, and a complement to the Nairobi Communiqué of 9 November 2007 [YUN 2007, p. 127].

MONUC electoral assistance. On 30 January, by resolution 1797(2008) (see below), the Security Council authorized MONUC to provide assistance to the authorities of the DRC, including the National Independent Electoral Commission, in the organization, preparation and conduct of local elections. The Council had before it the twenty-fourth report of the Secretary-General on MONUC [YUN 2007, p. 125] and a letter of the Secretary-General of 30 November 2007 [ibid., p. 126] to the Council President providing preliminary estimates on the cost and financial requirements for MONUC's support to the elections, expected to be held in the latter half of 2008.

SECURITY COUNCIL ACTION

On 30 January [meeting 5828], the Security Council unanimously adopted **resolution 1797(2008)**. The draft [S/2008/50] was prepared in consultations among Council members.

The Security Council,

Recalling its resolutions and the statements by its President concerning the Democratic Republic of the Congo, in particular resolutions 1756(2007) of 15 May 2007 and 1794(2007) of 21 December 2007,

Reaffirming its commitment to continue to contribute to the consolidation of peace and stability in the Democratic Republic of the Congo in the post-transition period, in particular through the United Nations Organization Mission in the Democratic Republic of the Congo,

Recalling the importance of elections, including the forthcoming local elections, for the longer-term restoration of peace and stability, national reconciliation and the establishment of the rule of law in the Democratic Republic of the Congo,

Encouraging international partners to continue to support the electoral process in the Democratic Republic of the Congo,

Welcoming the letter of the Secretary-General dated 11 October 2007 and the letter dated 30 November 2007 and the recommendations contained in the twenty-fourth report of the Secretary-General on the Mission, of 14 November 2007 with respect to assistance by the Mission to the Congolese authorities in the organization, preparation and conduct of local elections,

1. *Authorizes* the United Nations Organization Mission in the Democratic Republic of the Congo, in close coordination with international partners and the United Nations country team, to provide assistance to the Congolese authorities, including the National Independent Electoral Commission, in the organization, preparation and conduct of local elections, as recommended in the letter of the Secretary-General dated 11 October 2007 and the letter dated 30 November 2007;

2. *Decides* to remain actively seized of the matter.

At the same meeting, following consultations among Security Council members, the President made statement **S/PRST/2008/2** on behalf of the Council:

The Security Council congratulates President Kabila and the Government of the Democratic Republic of the Congo, as well as the organizers of and participants in the Conference on Peace, Security and Development in North and South Kivu, on the success of the Conference, held in Goma from 6 to 23 January 2008.

The Council is particularly pleased that the armed groups in North and South Kivu have undertaken to observe a complete and immediate ceasefire, to begin the withdrawal of their forces with a view to their brassage or their disarmament, demobilization and reintegration under the national programme for that process, and to abide strictly by the rules of international humanitarian and human rights law, set out in the statements of commitment (*Actes d'engagement*) which they signed with the Government of the Democratic Republic of the Congo on 23 January 2008.

The Council commends the Government of the Democratic Republic of the Congo for ordering a ceasefire in accordance with the statements of commitment. Within the framework of the fight against impunity, while noting the Government's pledge to seek parliamentary approval of an amnesty law covering acts of war and insurrection, the Council welcomes the exclusion of genocide, war crimes and crimes against humanity from the scope of this amnesty.

The Council urges all the parties to the agreements to respect the ceasefire and to implement the other commitments they have undertaken effectively and in good faith. In this connection, it emphasizes the importance of the work to be carried out by the joint commissions provided for in the statements of commitment, and encourages the international community, including the United Nations Organization Mission in the Democratic Republic of the Congo, to support that process. It also encourages the Mission to support the implementation of the statements of commitment, within the limits of its capacity and in accordance with its mandate, including with regard to the protection of civilians.

The Council also welcomes the resolutions adopted at the Goma Conference and calls upon the appropriate authorities to act on the recommendations addressed to them. It underscores the need for the Congolese authorities and all political and social stakeholders in North and South Kivu to continue, through dialogue, to seek long-term and comprehensive ways to address the root causes of instability.

The Council reiterates the importance of the commitments undertaken by the Government of the Democratic Republic of the Congo and the Government of the Republic of Rwanda in their joint communiqué on a common approach to end the threat posed by illegal armed groups in the eastern part of the Democratic Republic of the Congo to peace and stability in both countries and the Great Lakes region, signed at Nairobi on 9 November 2007. It calls upon the two Governments to continue to implement fully the joint communiqué, in particular by promptly taking appropriate measures to induce the Forces démocratiques de libération du Rwanda and other foreign armed groups to lay down their arms without preconditions and return to their home countries.

The Council encourages the international community, in particular the eastern neighbours of the Democratic Republic of the Congo in the Great Lakes region, to fully support the new dynamic launched by the Goma Conference and the Nairobi joint communiqué, which together represent a major step towards the restoration of lasting peace and stability in the Great Lakes region.

Arrest on ICC warrant. On 6 February, Mathieu Ngudjolo Chui, a colonel in FARDC, alleged former leader of the Front des nationalistes et intégrationnistes (FNI) and war criminal, was arrested in connection with crimes against humanity in Ituri and transferred to the International Criminal Court—the first time that the Congolese authorities, at the Court's request, made an arrest.

Report of Secretary-General (April). In an April report [S/2008/218] on MONUC submitted to the Security Council pursuant to resolution 1794(2007) [YUN 2007, p. 128], the Secretary-General said that important steps had been taken towards achieving the benchmarks outlined in his previous report [ibid., p. 125] regarding the elimination of the threat posed by national and foreign armed groups to the eastern part of the DRC and neighbouring countries, and the stabilization of sensitive areas, particularly in the east.

To support the work of the Mixed Technical Commission on Peace and Security, an ad hoc ceasefire monitoring mechanism, chaired by MONUC, became operational on 10 February. As at 15 March, the mechanism had received 108 reports of violations, of which 64 had been verified, 30 had been confirmed as non-violations and 14 remained under investigation. Most violations were reported in North Kivu, involving FARDC, CNDP, the Coalition of Congolese Patriotic Resistance and Mayi-Mayi groups. In February, President Kabila issued executive orders which established the framework for "Amani", the Government programme created following the Goma Agreements for the security, pacification, stabilization and reconstruction of North and South Kivu. He issued additional executive orders on 24 March outlining the composition and structure of the commission on peace and security, which would be jointly chaired by the Government and the International Facilitation (AU, International Conference on the Great Lakes Region, European Union, United Nations, United States).

In accordance with the Nairobi Communiqué signed by the Governments of the DRC and Rwanda on 9 November 2007 [YUN 2007, p. 127], President Kabila, on 11 February 2008, issued a presidential decree creating a steering committee for the implementation of the Government's plan to eradicate foreign armed groups from the territory of the DRC. The Nairobi Communiqué had led to a renewed focus on disarmament, demobilization, reintegration and resettlement or repatriation. MONUC was assisting the Government in developing its implementation plan in that regard and supporting the efforts of the DRC and Rwanda towards their common goal of repatriating or relocating the estimated 6,000 ex-Rwandan Armed Forces (FAR)/Interahamwe elements in the DRC. MONUC had relocated its disarmament, demobilization, repatriation, resettlement or reintegration section to Goma, and was supporting the efforts of the DRC to sensitize the political and military leadership of the ex-FAR/Interahamwe.

The political and security situation in Bas-Congo had sharply deteriorated. Tensions in the province increased early in January, following clashes between the national police and the Bundu Dia Kongo (BDK) politico-religious movement, which had challenged State authority throughout the province, calling for greater fiscal decentralization, regional autonomy and self-determination, while also reviving residual electoral disputes and demanding that the Government respect its right to cultural and religious freedoms. BDK, which had a record of threatening and attacking public officials, staging violent demonstrations and taking other provocative actions, had called for the holding of a conference on peace and development in Bas-Congo. The Government considered BDK to be seditious, and believed that its activities were intended to undermine the Constitution. During a visit to Matadi on 27 February, the Special Representative of the Secretary-General, Alan Doss, urged local authorities and BDK to exercise restraint and work towards a peaceful resolution of the tensions.

Three days after the Government launched operations to restore State authority in the most sensitive areas in Bas-Congo on 28 February, MONUC dispatched a formed police unit together with an infantry company and several teams of military observers to assess the situation, protect civilians and cooperate with provincial authorities.

Progress towards institutional reform was slow, and the Government made little headway in implementing its programme for 2007–2011 or the governance contract. Little was achieved in the decentralization process mandated by the Constitution, or in the President's five declared priority areas of health, education, water and electricity, infrastructure and employment.

The overall security situation remained fragile. Kinshasa and other provinces witnessed a surge in violent crime, attributed in large part to unpaid demobilized former combatants along with military and police personnel. The security situation in Ituri improved following the third phase of the disarmament, demobilization and reintegration process, which targeted elements of the Forces de résistance patriotique d'Ituri (FRPI), FNI and the Mouvement révolutionnaire congolais. In Djugu and Irumu territories, however, FNI and FRPI splinter groups that refused to disarm were creating insecurity. MONUC and FARDC continued joint operations against FRPI, which was reportedly recruiting new combatants and being resupplied with weapons, while the movement of CNDP and Mayi-Mayi combatants from North Kivu into the brassage centre in Kamina complicated the security situation in Katanga.

The humanitarian situation in the Kivus remained a source of concern. With a displaced population of some 800,000, North Kivu continued to have the highest concentration of internally displaced persons in the DRC. The Goma process notwithstanding, insecurity persisted among internally displaced persons and local communities. As at 15 March, only tentative population returns had been observed. Forced recruitment by all armed groups signatories to the statements of commitment had deepened the sense of insecurity and led to additional displacements. A series of earthquakes in the region in February further aggravated the situation.

Meanwhile, MONUC developed a security and stabilization strategy to lay the groundwork for the Mission's eventual orderly withdrawal, in particular from the eastern part of the DRC. To implement the strategy, MONUC had strengthened its civilian, police and military presence in the east. The strategy focused on political and military actions to encourage remaining armed groups to disband; political measures to encourage the fulfilment of commitments made within the Goma process; basic first steps to ensure the return of State authority to areas formerly controlled by armed groups; and support for the return and reintegration of war-affected populations.

MONUC continued to provide operational support to FARDC aimed at stabilizing sensitive areas and expanding State authority, both of which were critical elements of the benchmarks. The extent of that support was undermined, however, by the ad hoc nature of the requests of FARDC, which were routinely incomplete and delivered with limited warning and usually without preparatory liaison. The Mission also provided security for the delivery of humanitarian assistance and for the return and the reintegration of refugees and internally displaced persons.

The human rights situation remained precarious and a cause for concern. Elements of Congolese and foreign armed groups, as well as members of the national security forces, continued to carry out arbitrary executions and commit acts of rape, torture and cruel, inhuman and degrading treatment. A MONUC human rights investigative team concluded that on 16 and 17 January, in the vicinity of Kalonge, North Kivu, CNDP elements executed at least 30 civilians. On 2 January, in Musizero, North Kivu, soldiers of the FARDC second integrated brigade allegedly killed eight people, including three children. MONUC was hindered in its monitoring of the intelligence services, however, by systematic refusal to grant access to many detention centres, as a state of almost total impunity for serious offences continued to prevail.

Sexual violence—prevalent throughout the DRC—and gender-based violence remained major areas of concern for MONUC and the UN country team. MONUC concentrated on reinforcing the Congolese capacity to prevent sexual violence, assist victims and end impunity for perpetrators. Progress in security sector reform, however, had been modest.

The Secretary-General observed that while the statements of commitment that emerged from the Goma conference were an important step forward, the significant number of verified ceasefire violations was a matter of concern. He encouraged the Governments of the DRC and Rwanda, as well as the international community, to maintain momentum in implementing the Nairobi Communiqué and the provisions of Security Council resolution 1804(2008) (see p. 116) in order to jointly address the problems posed by Rwandan armed groups in the eastern part of the DRC. He also urged the Congolese authorities to refrain from disproportionate use of force, which contributed to instability and posed the risk of grave humanitarian consequences. The Secretary-General further urged the Government, assisted by its international partners, to redouble its efforts to consolidate democracy, enhance governance, combat corruption, respect human rights and establish the rule of law at the national and local levels.

Report of Secretary-General (July). Reporting on major developments [S/2008/433] since his last report, the Secretary-General stated that the overall security situation remained tenuous. In North Kivu, there was a reduction in the number of ceasefire violations documented by MONUC, but attacks against civilian targets—including non-governmental organizations (NGOs) and UN agencies, funds and programmes—increased. FDLR and the coalition of Patriotes résistants congolais (PARECO) continued to attack FARDC positions near Lake Edward in the Northern Rutshuru area. Other security incidents were reportedly linked to efforts by armed groups to extend areas under their control before disengagement. CNDP had allegedly continued recruitment and training of combatants, while the prospects of reintegration benefits appeared to have resuscitated or prompted the emergence of little-known or insignificant groups, who had stepped up recruitment. In Goma, attacks on individuals, armed robberies and assassinations had increased.

Insecurity in South Kivu increased, notably in outlying territories, and armed robberies of international NGOs and transport vehicles had taken place. The Mission's increased patrols and escorts for humanitarian actors and NGOs helped stem the increase in armed attacks; however, the re-recruitment of demobilized ex-combatants and other elements by armed groups continued to contribute to instability.

Elsewhere in the east, attacks by LRA on local populations had increased in and around the Garamba Park area as well as along the DRC-Southern Sudan-Central African Republic border areas, where the population had been subjected to looting, rape and abduction. In Orientale Province, seasonal cross-border movement of M'Bororo tribes into the DRC, and their increasingly aggressive posture, had further strained relations with local populations.

In Bas-Congo, the security situation had improved since the violent clashes between the national police and BDK members in February and March. In Burundi, large-scale hostilities resumed in April between the Burundian National Defence Forces and Palipehutu-FNL, raising concerns of a possible spill-over effect into South Kivu, especially in light of unconfirmed reports of collaboration between FNL and FDLR.

As for the implementation of the Goma and Nairobi processes, the Secretary-General reported that the Mixed Technical Commission on Peace and Security had been inaugurated in Goma on 3 April by the Minister of State for the Interior in the presence of the Special Representative and representatives of the International Facilitation. Co-chaired by the Government and MONUC, the Commission focused initially on procedural issues, adopting a calendar setting out its objectives and agreeing on its provincial structures. The Amani programme had launched a comprehensive sensitization campaign to inform combatants and civilian populations about the Goma Agreements, as well as to prepare armed elements for the brassage or disarmament, demobilization and reintegration phases. Important issues remained to be resolved, however, and practical arrangements needed to be put in place. Armed groups, in particular CNDP, had insisted that those phases take place in the Kivus, while the Government maintained that they should be carried out outside the Kivus.

Encouraging progress had been made in implementing the Nairobi Communiqué. In line with its commitments, the Government had adopted a multidimensional approach to encourage the disarmament, demobilization, repatriation, resettlement and reintegration or relocation of FDLR elements away from the DRC-Rwanda border area. The approach combined direct dialogue with certain ex-FAR/Interahamwe leaders—including leaders of the Rassemblement Uni pour la Démocratie-Urunana (RUD-Urunana)—with other sensitization efforts and increased military pressure. On 26 May, the Government convened a conference in Kisangani with leaders of the RUD faction of FDLR and the Rassemblement Populaire Rwandais (RPR). The discussions secured agreement on a road map in which FDLR-RUD and RPR recognized the Nairobi Communiqué as a framework for the peaceful repatriation of their combatants and confirmed their commitment to voluntary disarmament, repatriation or relocation under security guarantees from the Government and the international community. The FDLR-FOCA (Forces combattantes abacunguzi)—reportedly under the control of radical, Europe-based leaders such as Callixte Mbarushimana and Ignace Murwanashyaka—however, rejected both the Kisangani Conference and the road map. The Government also faced difficulties due to resistance from the provinces to the temporary resettlement of FDLR elements.

The UN strategy for security and stabilization of the eastern DRC involved supporting the Congolese follow-up to the Goma conference; the extension of State authority in the east and eventual return and reintegration of ex-combatants; and—in terms of security—increasing patrolling and monitoring of the ceasefire. It also involved increasing military pressure on FDLR in areas where the latter controlled commercial activities and the illegal exploitation of natural resources. Efforts to encourage the voluntary disarmament, demobilization, repatriation, resettlement and reintegration of FDLR elements had been revitalized. MONUC also supported Government efforts to encourage FDLR leaders in Europe to agree to disarmament, demobilization, repatriation, resettlement and reintegration. That appeared to have yielded some progress with respect to the group's RUD-Urunana faction, but extremist FDLR leaders continued to resist peaceful resolution of the problem posed by FDLR's continued presence in the DRC.

With regard to the deployment and military posture of the Mission, the Secretary-General reported that former UN Military Adviser General Maurice Baril, accompanied by a small team from the Department of Peacekeeping Operations and the Department of Field Support, undertook a military evaluation mission of MONUC from 19 to 29 April. It concluded that the Division Headquarters in Kisangani no longer provided an optimal command and control structure, particularly with respect to the Mission's military action to support the Nairobi and Goma processes in the Kivus. Consequently, the Division Headquarters would be reconfigured to establish a forward Force headquarters in Goma, as operational demands in the Kivus represented the Force's main effort. The Baril mission also concluded that the Force's robust rules of engagement and the measures outlined in the Secretary-General's third special report [YUN 2004, p. 127] remained fully applicable to the current situation; acknowledged that, to fulfil its mandate, MONUC required a high degree of mobility and flexibility on the part of its contingents; and affirmed that a willingness to use appropriate force in accordance with the rules of engagement was also required, both to protect civilians and to support the Nairobi and Goma processes, including through joint military operations with FARDC.

The Secretary-General observed that despite considerable effort invested in the Mixed Technical Commission on Peace and Security, the lack of progress on core issues and increased tensions on the ground risked paralysing the Goma process. There was a need for the parties to take concrete action consistent with the spirit of the Goma conference. While the ceasefire had largely held, recent clashes were a growing source of concern, along with continued recruitment by armed groups. He urged the Governments of the DRC and Rwanda, as well as the international community, to maintain momentum in implementing the Nairobi Communiqué and the provisions of resolution 1804(2008). The outcome of the Kisangani conference had provided an opportunity for diminishing the threat posed by FDLR through peaceful means. An effective FARDC, respectful of human rights and international humanitarian law, was essential for peace and stability throughout the country, and the establishment of a rapid reaction force, as foreseen by the Government, would help to enhance the operational capacity of FARDC in addressing the threat posed by the armed groups. The Secretary-General urged the Government and its international partners to recognize the Nairobi and Goma processes and the establishment of a rapid reaction force as mutually reinforcing actions. He also stated his concern at the growing threat to regional security posed by LRA, which had recently resumed abductions and attacks on civilians along the DRC-Southern Sudan-Central African Republic border areas. While MONUC would continue to work with the Government of the DRC to protect civilians and undertake to contain LRA in the Garamba Park area within the limits of its present capacities, the Mission would require additional capacity if tasked with further support to FARDC, beyond the current activities envisaged to respond to the threat posed by LRA.

Appointment. On 2 September [S/2008/591], the Secretary-General informed the Security Council of his intention to appoint Lieutenant General Vicente Diaz de Villegas (Spain) as Force Commander of MONUC to replace Lieutenant General Babacar Gaye (Senegal), whose tour of service was ending on 22 September, of which the Council took note on 3 September [S/2008/592].

Resurgence of violence in eastern DRC

Midway through the year, efforts to stabilize the eastern DRC witnessed significant setbacks. In June, CNDP, together with the Forces républicaines fédéralistes (FRF), withdrew from the Mixed Technical Commission on Peace and Security. CNDP indicated that its demands were not being addressed, including guarantees for the protection of the Tutsi community once CNDP forces had been dismantled; the security of CNDP soldiers going into brassage; and the safe return of refugees from Burundi, Rwanda and Tanzania. Large-scale hostilities between FARDC and CNDP erupted on 28 August. The fighting, which spread throughout North Kivu, exacerbated the humanitarian crisis, displacing over 250,000 people and bringing the number of internally displaced persons in the eastern part of the country to more than 1.35 million. Throughout the fighting from August to November, MONUC, in accordance with its mandate, supported the efforts of FARDC to repel CNDP offensives, and sought to secure major population centres and axes. In the face of the major CNDP offensive, however, FARDC abandoned positions held jointly with MONUC.

In September, seven members of the UN family were killed in the crash of a humanitarian aircraft in South Kivu.

Security Council statement (September). In a press statement of 12 September [SC/9445], the Security Council expressed concern over the fighting between FARDC and armed elements of CNDP as a violation of the Goma Agreements, by which CNDP and other armed groups in North and South Kivu had undertaken to observe a complete and immediate ceasefire; begin the withdrawal of their forces with a view to their brassage or their disarmament, demobilization and reintegration; and abide strictly by the rules of international humanitarian and human rights law. The Council urged CNDP to immediately cease its offensive operations; return to its positions held until 28 August; surrender military equipment taken from FARDC in the fighting; and re-engage constructively in the Goma peace process, including participation in the Mixed Technical Commission. The Council also condemned acts of hostility against MONUC.

Hostilities and ceasefire (September–October). In September, following CNDP advances around Sake, MONUC supported FARDC in pushing CNDP back to its pre-28 August positions. By mid-October, FARDC succeeded in recapturing Ntamugenga and captured Tongo, which had been in CNDP-controlled territory. At the same time, CNDP launched attacks on FARDC positions along the Goma-Rutshuru axis and captured the military camp of Rumangabo. MONUC applied immediate pressure on both sides, after which FARDC pulled back from Tongo, and CNDP withdrew temporarily from Rumangabo.

On 2 October, CNDP leader Laurent Nkunda called for the "liberation" of the Congo, further heightening anxieties, for which he was condemned by the international community, national actors and the population. Exchanges of fire across the border between Rwanda and the DRC further compounded the crisis in the area.

SECURITY COUNCIL ACTION

On 21 October [meeting 5998], following consultations among Security Council members, the President made statement **S/PRST/2008/38** on behalf of the Council:

> The Security Council expresses its grave concern at the resurgence of violence in the eastern provinces of the Democratic Republic of the Congo and its potential regional implications. It is alarmed by the humanitarian consequences of the recent fighting and urges all parties to immediately respect a ceasefire.
>
> The Council expresses its deep concern over continued threats to the safety of the civilian population and to the conduct of humanitarian operations. The Council strongly condemns the continuing recruitment and use of children by armed groups as well as the continued prevalence of sexual and gender-based violence in the eastern region of the Democratic Republic of the Congo. It urges all parties to comply fully with their obligations under international law, including international humanitarian law, human rights law and refugee law.
>
> The Council reiterates the need to respect the sovereignty and territorial integrity of the Democratic Republic of the Congo. It once again calls upon all armed groups to immediately lay down their arms and present themselves without any further delay or preconditions to Congolese authorities and the United Nations Organization Mission in the Democratic Republic of the Congo for their disarmament, repatriation, resettlement and/or reintegration, as appropriate.
>
> The Council reaffirms that the Goma and Nairobi processes constitute the framework within which long-term stability in the eastern region of the Democratic Republic of the Congo should be pursued. The Council urges all the parties to the Goma and Nairobi agreements to implement their commitments effectively and in good faith. In this respect, the Council strongly condemns the recent declarations by Mr. Laurent Nkunda calling for a national rebellion.
>
> The Council reiterates its strong support for the Mission in helping to restore peace in the Kivus and encourages the Mission to reinforce its action to ensure the protection of civilians. The Council expresses its full support for the disengagement plan elaborated by the Mission and accepted by the Government of the Democratic Republic of the Congo and urges all parties to abide by it.
>
> The Council welcomes the intention of the Mission to reconfigure its forces and optimize their deployment so as to enhance its efficiency within the existing mandate and troop ceiling. The Council takes note of the additional capacities for the Mission requested by the Special Representative of the Secretary-General for the Democratic Republic of the Congo. The Council requests the Secretary-General to present a full analysis of the situation and recommendations in his next report to the Council.
>
> The Council urges the Government of the Democratic Republic of the Congo to take effective steps to ensure that there is no cooperation between elements of the Armed Forces of the Democratic Republic of the Congo and the Forces démocratiques de libération du Rwanda. The Council also calls upon the Governments in the region to cease all support to the armed groups in the eastern region of the Democratic Republic of the Congo.
>
> The Council urges the Government of the Democratic Republic of the Congo and the Government of the Republic of Rwanda to urgently engage in efforts to settle their differences, including by reactivating the Joint Verification Mechanism, and calls upon them to implement fully the Nairobi communiqué of 9 November 2007. The Council encourages the Secretary-General to step up his efforts to facilitate dialogue between Rwanda and the Democratic Republic of the Congo.
>
> The Council strongly condemns the recent attacks by the Lord's Resistance Army, including the abduction by the Lord's Resistance Army of 159 schoolchildren in villages in Orientale Province. The Council recalls the International Criminal Court indictments against members of the Lord's Resistance Army leadership on charges of, among other things, enlistment of children through abduction, as a war crime.

In a major offensive operation that started on 26 October, CNDP recaptured the FARDC camp at Rumangabo and took control of Rugari, Kalengera, Burare, Rutshuru and the main road between Goma and Rutshuru, advancing to within a few kilometres of Goma before declaring a unilateral ceasefire on 29 October. Retreating rogue elements of FARDC, however, caused major insecurity within Goma following the unilateral ceasefire declaration of CNDP. In response, MONUC began to reinforce its military presence in Goma and the surrounding area in order to protect civilians. In view of the near total disintegration of FARDC in the face of advancing CNDP troops, MONUC was the only organized force in Goma and was compelled to step in to substitute for the role of the national security forces.

SECURITY COUNCIL ACTION

On 29 October [meeting 6006], following consultations among Security Council members, the President made statement **S/PRST/2008/40** on behalf of the Council:

The Security Council condemns the recent offensive by the Congrès national pour la défense du peuple in the eastern region of the Democratic Republic of the Congo and demands that it bring its operations to an end. The Council welcomes the announcement by Mr. Laurent Nkunda of an immediate ceasefire and looks to Mr. Nkunda to ensure its effective and durable implementation, and the re-engagement of the Congrès national pour la défense du peuple in the Goma process. The Council expresses its grave concern about the dramatic humanitarian consequences of the recent fighting. The Council urges all parties to respect fully their obligations under international law to protect civilians, to ensure access to the population in need and to guarantee the safety and security of humanitarian personnel. The Council affirms that any attack against the civilian population, including at major population centres, is totally unacceptable.

The Council urges all the signatories to the Goma and Nairobi processes to implement their commitments effectively and in good faith. In this respect, the Council calls upon the authorities of the Democratic Republic of the Congo and Rwanda to take concrete steps to defuse tensions and to restore stability in the region. The Council strongly supports the efforts of the Secretary-General to facilitate the dialogue between the leaders of the two countries and encourages him to send a special envoy tasked with this mission as soon as possible.

The Council urges the Government of the Democratic Republic of the Congo to take effective steps to ensure that there is no cooperation between elements of the Armed Forces of the Democratic Republic of the Congo and the Forces démocratiques de libération du Rwanda. The Council also calls upon the Governments of the region to cease all support to the armed groups in the eastern region of the Democratic Republic of the Congo. The Council expresses its concern at the reports of heavy weapons fire across the Democratic Republic of the Congo-Rwanda border. The Council reiterates its determination to continue to monitor closely the implementation of the arms embargo and other measures as set out in its resolution 1807(2008).

The Council expresses its full support for the United Nations Organization Mission in the Democratic Republic of the Congo and condemns all attacks, regardless of their perpetrators, launched against the Mission in the past days. The Council calls upon the Mission to continue to implement fully its mandate, in all its aspects, in particular by robust actions to protect civilians at risk and to deter any attempt by any armed group to threaten the political process.

The Council duly notes the reinforcement of the Mission requested by the Secretariat. The Council will study expeditiously that request in view of the developments of the situation on the ground.

Appointments. On 31 October [S/2008/681], in light of events unfolding in the MONUC area and upon the resignation of Lieutenant General Diaz de Villegas, the Secretary-General informed the Council of his intention to reappoint Lieutenant General Babacar Gaye (Senegal) as Interim Force Commander of MONUC for a period of up to six months, of which the Council took note that same day [S/2008/682].

On 3 November [S/2008/684], to facilitate dialogue between the leaders of the DRC and Rwanda, the Secretary-General informed the Council of his intention to appoint Olusegun Obasanjo (Nigeria) his Special Envoy for the eastern DRC, of which the Council took note on 5 November [S/2008/685].

Continuation of hostilities

The unilateral ceasefire declared by CNDP on 29 October remained in place until 4 November, when the coalition of Congolese Patriotic Resistance (PARECO) and Mayi-Mayi militia launched an attack against CNDP at Kiwanja, north of Rutshuru. CNDP captured Kiwanja after intense fighting on 4 and 5 November. MONUC later conducted a preliminary investigation of the reported killing of civilians during the fighting, and ascertained that a number of people had been killed during the crossfire between CNDP and PARECO/Mayi-Mayi. There were also indications that, following the withdrawal of PARECO/Mayi-Mayi, many more civilians were killed when CNDP took control of Kiwanja.

On 11 November, clashes between CNDP and FARDC occurred in and around Kibati, north of Goma. Also on 11 November, fighting between FARDC and CNDP began further north, in Rutshuru territory, with CNDP forces gaining control of Ndeko and Rwindi. Meanwhile, MONUC itself was directly targeted by retreating FARDC elements in Ntamugenga and Rwindi on 27 and 28 October, and in the Kanyabayonga area on 12 and 13 November.

Together with international partners, the United Nations undertook intensive political efforts to arrest the deterioration of the situation. On 7 November, the Secretary-General travelled to Nairobi to participate in a regional summit on the situation, convened under the auspices of the AU and the International Conference on the Great Lakes Region. In a joint statement adopted on 7 November, summit participants called on all armed groups in North Kivu to observe an immediate ceasefire. On 16 November, the Secretary-General's Special Envoy, Mr Obasanjo, met with Laurent Nkunda, and insisted on the importance of an immediate return to a durable ceasefire, backed by an effective monitoring mechanism. He secured the latter's agreement with respect to the recommendations of the Nairobi joint statement, and his recommitment to the principles of the Goma statements of commitment and the 2007 Nairobi Communiqué. On 18 November, CNDP announced that it was withdrawing its forces from the Kanyabayonga-Nyanzale and Kabasha-Kiwanja axes, where fighting had most recently occurred, and requested MONUC to deploy in those areas.

Reinforcement of MONUC. By a letter of 31 October [S/2008/703], the Secretary-General provided to the Security Council an explanatory note by the Department of Peacekeeping Operations on the additional requirements for MONUC in light of the persistent crisis in the eastern DRC, particularly around the city of Goma, which was deteriorating rapidly, with the humanitarian situation increasingly dire. The additional capacities, which would entail an increase of 2,785 troops in the MONUC authorized military strength and 300 police officers in its formed police unit strength, were intended to give MONUC the quick-response capability that it lacked; adequate mobility to enable it to move troops to any crisis point in a timely manner; the capability to carry out essential engineering work in sensitive areas where civilian engineering contractors could not operate; and necessary surveillance capabilities in terms of equipment and personnel.

By resolution 1843(2008) of 20 November (see below), the Council authorized the increase of troops and police officers until 31 December 2008.

SECURITY COUNCIL ACTION

On 20 November [meeting 6018], the Security Council unanimously adopted **resolution 1843(2008)**. The draft [S/2008/716] was submitted by Belgium, Costa Rica, Croatia, France, Italy, South Africa, the United Kingdom and the United States.

The Security Council,

Recalling its previous resolutions and the statements by its President concerning the Democratic Republic of the Congo, in particular resolutions 1756(2007) of 15 May 2007 and 1794(2007) of 21 December 2007 and the statement by its President of 29 October 2008,

Expressing its strong support for the United Nations Organization Mission in the Democratic Republic of the Congo in its efforts to restore peace in the Kivus, and taking note of the letter dated 31 October 2008 from the Secretary-General to the President of the Security Council requesting additional capacities for the Mission in order to ensure the effective implementation of its mandate,

Recalling that, under resolution 1794(2007), the mandate of the Mission expires on 31 December 2008, and looking forward to the report and recommendations of the Secretary-General regarding the mandate and reconfiguration of the Mission,

Reaffirming its commitment to respect the sovereignty, territorial integrity and political independence of the Democratic Republic of the Congo,

Reiterating its condemnation of the resurgence of violence in the eastern region of the Democratic Republic of the Congo, and demanding that all parties immediately respect a ceasefire,

Welcoming the appointment of the former President of Nigeria, Mr. Olusegun Obasanjo, by the Secretary-General as his Special Envoy for the Great Lakes Region, and calling upon all parties to the conflict to cooperate with him in finding an urgent political solution to the crisis,

Expressing its extreme concern at the deteriorating humanitarian situation and, in particular, the targeted attacks against the civilian population, sexual violence, recruitment of child soldiers and summary executions, and considering that this situation should be addressed as a matter of urgency,

Urging all parties to ensure timely, safe and unhindered access of all humanitarian actors and to comply fully with their obligations under international law, including international humanitarian law, human rights law and refugee law,

Determining that the situation in the Democratic Republic of the Congo continues to pose a threat to international peace and security in the region,

Acting under Chapter VII of the Charter of the United Nations,

1. *Decides* to authorize, as recommended by the Secretary-General in his letter dated 31 October 2008 to the President of the Security Council, a temporary increase of the authorized military strength of the United Nations Organization Mission in the Democratic Republic of the Congo of up to 2,785 military personnel, and the strength of its formed police unit of up to 300 personnel;

2. *Authorizes* the immediate deployment of those additional capacities until 31 December 2008, and expresses its intention to extend this authorization on the occasion of the renewal of the mandate of the Mission, underlining that the duration of stay of the additional forces will depend on the security situation in the Kivus;

3. *Stresses* that this temporary increase in personnel aims at enabling the Mission to reinforce its capacity to protect civilians, to reconfigure its structure and forces and to optimize their deployment;

4. *Underscores* the importance of the Mission implementing its mandate in full, including through robust rules of engagement;

5. *Emphasizes* that the Mission will be reviewed in view of the recent developments by 31 December 2008;

6. *Decides* to remain actively seized of the matter.

Further developments

The implementation of the 2007 Nairobi Communiqué also stalled in regard to the continued presence of FDLR in the eastern part of the DRC. The repatriation of FDLR elements dropped significantly as a result of the deteriorating situation there. On 17 September, MONUC and FARDC approved a new plan of military operations against FDLR, targeting its sources of revenue, such as road barriers and mines under its control. FARDC earmarked 10 of the 12 battalions trained by MONUC for that operation. With the resumption of hostilities, however, the Government redeployed the 10 battalions for operations against CNDP.

In Ituri there was a resurgence of armed groups, while further north, in Haut Uélé Orientale province, the security situation deteriorated markedly following LRA attacks against civilians. A MONUC investigation in the province revealed that, from 17 September to 4 October, LRA abducted some 177 children and killed an estimated 76 adults. MONUC also provided logistical support, training and planning assistance to FARDC-led operations aimed at containing and isolating LRA in the Garamba Park area.

Communications. By a letter of 8 October [S/2008/641], the DRC transmitted to the Security Council a report of resumption of hostilities on the part of Rwanda. By a 10 October letter [S/2008/644], the DRC transmitted to the Council an information note allegedly proving the presence of Rwandan troops in Rumangabo and a series of photographs allegedly proving Rwanda's involvement in clashes in North Kivu. By a letter of 13 October [S/2008/646], the DRC transmitted to the Council an inventory of objects allegedly abandoned by elements of the Rwandan Defence Forces at the Rumangabo theatre of operations and a series of photographs allegedly proving the involvement of Rwanda. In all instances, the DRC called on the Council to take action.

By a letter of 14 October [S/2008/649], Rwanda brought to the Council's attention a note from Rwanda to the DRC of the same date including a detailed account of collaboration of FARDC and ex-FAR/Interahmawe/FDLR. That collaboration was said to be unacceptable and tantamount to arming and therefore strengthening those genocidal forces, contrary to the letter and spirit of the Lusaka Agreement, the Pretoria Agreement, the Nairobi Communiqué, resolution 1804(2008) and the Pact on Security, Stability and Development in the Great Lakes Region, as well as contrary to the Tripartite Plus arrangements to which both countries subscribed. The letter expressed concern about reported atrocious acts by DRC security agencies in the form of abducting, torturing and even killing innocent Rwandans in the eastern DRC, and demanded that the association with the very forces that were the root cause of instability in the region cease. By a letter of 15 October [S/2008/652], Rwanda requested the Council to condemn alleged FARDC collaboration, co-location, rearmament and combined military operations with ex-FAR/Interahamwe/FDLR, to sanction FARDC commanders and to stop all MONUC support to FARDC until there was a verified end to FARDC/FDLR co-location and collaboration.

By a letter of 4 November [S/2008/686] to the Council, Rwanda brought to its attention a statement on efforts to resolve the crisis in the eastern DRC. The key issue that needed to be dealt with by the international community and that could not be handled by Rwanda and the DRC alone was the continued presence of ex-FAR/Interahamwe/FDLR on Congolese soil. The two Governments had agreed to participate in a regional meeting bringing together all stakeholders to review solutions to the root causes of the crisis; and within that regional framework Rwanda remained committed to contributing to a lasting solution in order to achieve a peaceful and stable region.

Report of Secretary-General (November). In November, in his fourth special report on MONUC to the Security Council [S/2008/728], the Secretary-General set forth major developments since July, most significantly the escalation of violence in the eastern DRC. He also reviewed the implementation of the Mission's mandate pursuant to resolution 1794(2007) [YUN 2007, p. 128], and made recommendations on the configuration of the Mission and the additional resources it required in order to effectively carry out its mandate.

While the security situation remained stable in the DRC apart from the violence in the east, little progress had been achieved in the key peace consolidation tasks, including the delivery of basic services and the extension of State authority. Preparations for local elections continued, but key legislation, without which the necessary preparatory work could not proceed, had yet to be adopted, risking further delays in the conduct of the elections. Despite some improvement in cooperation between MONUC and national authorities on human rights issues, the human rights situation in the DRC remained a cause for concern. FARDC and national police elements had been responsible for many serious human rights violations, including arbitrary executions, rape, torture and other cruel, inhuman or degrading treatment. Congolese and foreign armed groups, in particular CNDP, PARECO, Mayi-Mayi Mongol, FDLR and LRA, had also perpetrated serious human rights abuses with impunity, including mass killings, torture, abductions, the forced recruitment of children, forced displacement, the destruction of camps for internally displaced persons, forced labour and sexual slavery and other forms of sexual violence. The overall humanitarian situation remained fragile, with vital health, nutrition and food security indicators still at emergency thresholds in many parts of the country.

The Secretary-General observed that deficiencies of FARDC and the challenges encountered by an overstretched MONUC attempting to address the renewed hostilities in the Kivus had opened a debate among many stakeholders about the Mission's mandate. After discussing how MONUC deployment and reconfiguration, with units from other sectors reinforcing those in the Kivus, were addressing its capacity constraints, the Secretary-General outlined the additional capabilities that would give MONUC the force reserve and quick-response capacity that it lacked; ensure that it was able to move troops to any crisis point in a timely manner; enable it to carry out essential engineering work in sensitive areas where civilian engineering contractors could not operate; and provide it with the necessary surveillance capabilities in terms of equipment and personnel. Acknowledging that the situation in the eastern part of the DRC would have been far worse without the presence of the Mission and its role in the protection of tens of thousands of civilians, the facilitation of humanitarian assistance and the prevention of major human rights abuses, the Secretary-General recommended that the Security Council extend the MONUC mandate until 31 December 2009.

Extension of MONUC mandate. By resolution 1856(2008) (see below), the Security Council extended the mandate of the Mission until 31 December 2009, while reinforcing its strength and refocusing its mandate. It authorized the continuation until that date of up to 19,815 military personnel, 760 military observers, 391 police personnel and 1,050 personnel of formed police units. MONUC would also have the mandate of protecting civilians, humanitarian personnel and UN personnel and facilities; disarming, demobilizing and monitoring resources of foreign and Congolese armed groups; training and mentoring FARDC in support of security sector reform; helping to secure the territory of the DRC; and supporting the strengthening of democratic institutions and the rule of law.

SECURITY COUNCIL ACTION

On 22 December [meeting 6055], the Security Council unanimously adopted **resolution 1856(2008)**. The draft [S/2008/800] was submitted by Belgium, France and the United Kingdom.

The Security Council,

Recalling its resolutions and the statements by its President concerning the Democratic Republic of the Congo, in particular resolutions 1794(2007) of 21 December 2007 and 1843(2008) of 20 November 2008 and the statements by its President of 21 October 2008 and 29 October 2008,

Reaffirming its commitment to the sovereignty, territorial integrity and political independence of the Democratic Republic of the Congo,

Stressing the primary responsibility of the Government of the Democratic Republic of the Congo for ensuring security in its territory and protecting its civilians with respect for the rule of law, human rights and international humanitarian law,

Condemning the repeated offensive military actions by the Congrès national pour la défense du peuple in the past months, which have caused massive displacement of populations in North Kivu as well as cross-border movements of refugees and which have also involved the Coalition des patriotes résistants congolais and other illegal armed groups, and condemning also the attacks by the Lord's Resistance Army in Orientale Province, as well as the resumption of hostilities by illegal armed groups in Ituri,

Underlining that a major obstacle to lasting peace in the Kivus is the presence and activities of illegal armed groups on Congolese territory, including the Forces démocratiques de libération du Rwanda, as acknowledged in its resolution 1804(2008) of 13 March 2008, which represent one of the primary causes for the conflict in the region,

Taking note of the final declaration of the Nairobi summit organized on 7 November 2008 by President Mwai Kibaki, acting Chairman of the International Conference on the Great Lakes Region, and President Jakaya Kikwete, President-in-office of the African Union, and the communiqué of the extraordinary summit of the Heads of State and Government of the Southern African Development Community, held in Sandton, South Africa, on 9 November 2008, welcoming the appointment of facilitators, including the Special Envoy of the Secretary-General for the Great Lakes Region, the former President of Nigeria, Mr. Olusegun Obasanjo, and the former President of the United Republic of Tanzania, Mr. Benjamin Mkapa, inviting these facilitators to keep the Security Council informed of their activities, and encouraging the countries of the region to maintain this high level of commitment on the crisis in the eastern part of the Democratic Republic of the Congo, and to act to assist efforts to resolve the conflict,

Recalling the joint communiqué of the Government of the Democratic Republic of the Congo and the Government of the Republic of Rwanda signed at Nairobi on 9 November 2007 and the Acte d'engagement which emerged from the Conference on Peace, Security and Development in North and South Kivu, held in Goma from 6 to 23 January 2008, and reaffirming that the Goma and Nairobi processes are the appropriate framework for stabilizing the situation in the eastern part of the Democratic Republic of the Congo,

Emphasizing the responsibility of the Government of the Democratic Republic of the Congo and the Governments of the region to prevent the use of their respective territories in support of violations of the arms embargo imposed by Council resolution 1807(2008) of 31 March 2008 or in support of activities of armed groups present in the region in accordance with the Pact on Security, Stability and Development in the Great Lakes Region, urging them to take effective measures to prevent cross-border support to any illegal armed group in the eastern region of the Democratic Republic of the Congo, and welcoming the progress made in high-level bilateral talks between the Governments of the Democratic Republic of the Congo and Rwanda,

Recalling the importance of urgently carrying out comprehensive and lasting security sector reform and of permanently disarming, demobilizing, resettling or repatriating, as appropriate, and reintegrating Congolese and foreign armed groups for the long-term stabilization of the Democratic Republic of the Congo, and the contribution made by international partners in this field,

Recognizing the link between the illegal exploitation of natural resources, the illicit trade in such resources and the proliferation of and trafficking in arms as one of the major factors fuelling and exacerbating conflicts in the Great Lakes region of Africa, and in particular in the Democratic Republic of the Congo,

Expressing its extreme concern at the deteriorating humanitarian and human rights situation, condemning in particular the targeted attacks against the civilian population, sexual violence, recruitment of child soldiers and summary executions, stressing the urgent need for the Government of the Democratic Republic of the Congo, in cooperation with the United Nations Organization Mission in the Democratic Republic of the Congo and other relevant actors, to end those violations of human rights and international humanitarian law, in particular those carried out by the militias and armed groups and by elements of the Armed Forces of the Democratic Republic of the Congo, the Congolese National Police and other security and intelligence services, and to bring the perpetrators, as well as the senior commanders under whom they serve, to justice, and calling upon Member States to assist in this regard and to continue to provide medical, humanitarian and other assistance to victims,

Recalling its resolutions 1325(2000) of 31 October 2000 and 1820(2008) of 19 June 2008 on women and peace and security, its resolution 1502(2003) of 26 August 2003 on the protection of United Nations personnel, associated personnel and humanitarian personnel in conflict zones, its resolution 1674(2006) of 28 April 2006 on the protection of civilians in armed conflict and its resolution 1612(2005) of 26 July 2005 on children and armed conflict, and recalling the conclusions of the Security Council Working Group on Children and Armed Conflict pertaining to parties to the armed conflict of the Democratic Republic of the Congo,

Condemning the continuing illicit flow of weapons within and into the Democratic Republic of the Congo, and declaring its determination to continue to monitor closely the implementation of the arms embargo and other measures set out in its resolution 1807(2008),

Underscoring the long-term, sustainable efforts needed from the Government of the Democratic Republic of the Congo and its international partners to consolidate democracy and promote the rule of law, good governance, recovery and development,

Expressing its full support for the Mission, condemning all attacks against United Nations peacekeepers and humanitarian personnel, regardless of the perpetrators, and emphasizing that those responsible for such attacks must be brought to justice,

Recalling that the temporary increase of the capacities of the Mission authorized by its resolution 1843(2008) aims at enabling the Mission to reorganize and, in particular, reconfigure its structure and forces and optimize their deployment, allowing the constitution of a quick-reaction capability to provide greater flexibility to deploy as needed to strengthen efforts to protect civilians and provide additional security in the eastern part of the Democratic Republic of the Congo,

Recognizing that effective coordination between the Government of the Democratic Republic of the Congo and the Mission on security matters in the areas of conflict, as well as the accelerated building of credible, cohesive and disciplined Congolese armed forces, is essential for the implementation of the mandate of the Mission,

Taking note of the fourth special report of the Secretary-General on the Mission, of 21 November 2008, and of the recommendations contained therein,

Determining that the situation in the Democratic Republic of the Congo continues to pose a threat to international peace and security in the region,

Acting under Chapter VII of the Charter of the United Nations,

1. *Decides* to extend the deployment of the United Nations Organization Mission in the Democratic Republic of the Congo until 31 December 2009, and authorizes the continuation until that date of up to 19,815 military personnel, 760 military observers, 391 police personnel and 1,050 personnel of formed police units;

2. *Requests* the Mission to attach the highest priority to addressing the crisis in the Kivus, in particular the protection of civilians, and to concentrate progressively during the coming year its action in the eastern part of the Democratic Republic of the Congo;

3. *Decides* that the Mission shall, from the adoption of the present resolution, have the following mandate, in this order of priority, working in close cooperation with the Government of the Democratic Republic of the Congo:

Protection of civilians, humanitarian personnel and United Nations personnel and facilities

(a) To ensure the protection of civilians, including humanitarian personnel, under imminent threat of physical violence, in particular violence emanating from any of the parties engaged in the conflict;

(b) To contribute to the improvement of the security conditions in which humanitarian assistance is provided and assist in the voluntary return of refugees and internally displaced persons;

(c) To ensure the protection of United Nations personnel, facilities, installations and equipment;

(d) To ensure the security and freedom of movement of United Nations and associated personnel;

(e) To carry out joint patrols with the national police and security forces to improve security in the event of civil disturbance;

Disarmament, demobilization, and monitoring of resources of foreign and Congolese armed groups

(f) To deter any attempt at the use of force to threaten the Goma and Nairobi processes from any armed group, foreign or Congolese, particularly in the eastern part of the Democratic Republic of the Congo, including by using cordon and search tactics and undertaking all necessary operations to prevent attacks on civilians and disrupt the military capability of illegal armed groups that continue to use violence in that area;

(g) To coordinate operations with the integrated brigades of the Armed Forces of the Democratic Republic of the Congo deployed in the eastern part of the Democratic Republic of the Congo and support operations led by and jointly planned with these brigades in accordance with international humanitarian, human rights and refugee law with a view to:

—Disarming the recalcitrant local armed groups in order to ensure their participation in the disarmament, demobilization and reintegration process and the release of children associated with those armed groups;

—Disarming the foreign armed groups in order to ensure their participation in the disarmament, demobilization, repatriation, resettlement and reintegration process and the release of children associated with those armed groups;

—Preventing the provision of support to illegal armed groups, including support derived from illicit economic activities;

(h) To facilitate the voluntary demobilization and repatriation of disarmed foreign combatants and their dependants;

(i) To contribute to the implementation of the national programme of disarmament, demobilization and reintegration of Congolese combatants and their dependants, with particular attention to children, by monitoring the disarmament process and providing, as appropriate, security in some sensitive locations, as well as supporting reintegration efforts pursued by the Congolese authorities in cooperation with the United Nations country team and bilateral and multilateral partners;

(j) To use its monitoring and inspection capacities to curtail the provision of support to illegal armed groups derived from illicit trade in natural resources;

Training and mentoring of the Armed Forces of the Democratic Republic of the Congo in support of security sector reform

(k) To provide military training, including in the area of human rights, international humanitarian law, child protection and the prevention of gender-based violence, to various members and units of the integrated brigades of the Armed Forces of the Democratic Republic of the Congo deployed in the eastern part of the Democratic Republic of the Congo, as part of international broader efforts to support security sector reform;

(l) In coordination with international partners, including the European Union Mission of Assistance for Security Sector Reform and the European Union Police Mission, to contribute to the efforts of the international community to assist the Government of the Democratic Republic of the Congo in the initial planning process of the security sector reform, to build credible, cohesive and disciplined Congolese armed forces and to develop the capacities of the Congolese National Police and related law enforcement agencies;

Territorial security of the Democratic Republic of the Congo

(m) To observe and report in a timely manner on the position of armed movements and groups and the presence of foreign military forces in the key areas of volatility, especially by monitoring the use of landing strips and the borders, including on the lakes;

(n) To monitor the implementation of the measures imposed by paragraph 1 of resolution 1807(2008), in cooperation, as appropriate, with the Governments concerned and with the Group of Experts established pursuant to resolution 1533(2004) of 12 March 2004, including by inspecting, as it deems necessary and without notice, the cargo of aircraft and of any transport vehicle using the ports, airports, airfields, military bases and border crossings in North and South Kivu and in Ituri;

(o) To seize or collect, as appropriate, the arms and any related materiel whose presence in the territory of the Democratic Republic of the Congo violates the measures imposed by paragraph 1 of resolution 1807(2008) and to dispose of such arms and related materiel as appropriate;

(p) To provide assistance to the competent customs authorities of the Democratic Republic of the Congo in implementing the provisions of paragraph 8 of resolution 1807(2008);

(q) To assist the Government of the Democratic Republic of the Congo in enhancing its demining capacity;

4. *Decides also* that the Mission shall also have the mandate, in close cooperation with the Congolese authorities, the United Nations country team and donors, to support the strengthening of democratic institutions and the rule of law and, to that end:

(a) To provide advice to strengthen democratic institutions and processes at the national, provincial, regional and local levels;

(b) To promote national reconciliation and internal political dialogue, including through the provision of good offices, and support the strengthening of civil society and multi-party democracy, and give the necessary support to the Goma and Nairobi processes;

(c) To assist in the promotion and protection of human rights, with particular attention to women, children and vulnerable persons, investigate human rights violations and publish its findings, as appropriate, with a view to putting an end to impunity, assist in the development and implementation of a transitional justice strategy, and cooperate in national and international efforts to bring to justice perpetrators of grave violations of human rights and international humanitarian law;

(d) In close coordination with international partners and the United Nations country team, to provide assistance to the Congolese authorities, including the National Independent Electoral Commission, in the organization, preparation and conduct of local elections;

(e) To assist in the establishment of a secure and peaceful environment for the holding of free and transparent local elections that are expected to be held by the end of June 2009;

(f) To contribute to the promotion of good governance and respect for the principle of accountability;

(g) In coordination with international partners, to advise the Government of the Democratic Republic of the Congo on strengthening the capacity of the judicial and correctional systems, including the military justice system;

5. *Authorizes* the Mission to use all necessary means, within the limits of its capacity and in the areas where its units are deployed, to carry out the tasks listed in paragraphs 3 *(a)* to *(g)*, *(i)*, *(j)*, *(n)* and *(o)* and in paragraph 4 *(e)* above;

6. *Emphasizes* that the protection of civilians, as described in paragraphs 3 *(a)* to *(e)*, must be given priority in decisions about the use of available capacity and resources,

over any of the other tasks described in paragraphs 3 and 4 above;

7. *Requests* the Secretary-General to present recommendations in his next three-monthly report on the progressive handover of those tasks listed in paragraph 4 from the Mission to the United Nations country team and bilateral and multilateral partners, as far as the western part of the country is concerned, with a view to reinforcing the action of United Nations peacebuilding mechanisms in the Democratic Republic of the Congo and in order to permit the Mission to concentrate its efforts on the eastern part of the country;

8. *Underscores* the importance of the Mission implementing the mandate described in the present resolution in full, including through robust rules of engagement, and requests the Secretary-General to ensure that the concept of operations and rules of engagement of the Mission are updated by 31 January 2009 to bring them fully in line with the provisions of the present resolution and to report to the Security Council and troop-contributing countries;

9. *Requests* the Secretary-General to continue to report regularly, and at least every three months, on the situation in the Democratic Republic of the Congo and on the activities of the Mission, and to provide to the Council, with the same regularity, a specific update on the military situation;

10. *Requests in particular* the Secretary-General, in his next report under paragraph 9 above, to inform the Council on the development of a strategic workplan with appropriate benchmarks to measure and track progress on the implementation of the mandate described in paragraphs 3 and 4 above;

11. *Requests* the Secretary-General to include in his next report a comprehensive assessment of the Mission's disarmament, demobilization and reintegration and disarmament, demobilization, repatriation, resettlement and reintegration programmes and, in close coordination with his Special Envoy for the Great Lakes Region, to make recommendations on possible adjustments needed to increase their effectiveness, resourcing and coordination with the military component of the Mission;

12. *Demands* that all parties cooperate fully with the operations of the Mission and that they ensure the security of, as well as unhindered and immediate access for, United Nations and associated personnel in carrying out their mandate, throughout the territory of the Democratic Republic of the Congo, demands in particular that all parties provide full access to the military observers of the Mission, including in all ports, airports, airfields, military bases and border crossings, and, in addition, that the human rights observers of the Mission be granted access to detention centres and *brassage* centres, and requests the Secretary-General to report without delay any failure to comply with these demands;

13. *Requests* the Mission, in view of the scale and severity of sexual violence committed especially by armed elements in the Democratic Republic of the Congo, to strengthen its efforts to prevent and respond to sexual violence, including through training for the Congolese security forces in accordance with its mandate, and to regularly report, including in a separate annex if necessary, on actions taken in this regard, including data on instances of sexual violence and trend analyses of the problem;

14. *Emphasizes* that operations led by the Armed Forces of the Democratic Republic of the Congo against illegal foreign and Congolese armed groups should, consistent with the mandate set forth in paragraph 3 *(g)* above, be planned jointly with the Mission and in accordance with international humanitarian, human rights and refugee law and should include appropriate measures to protect civilians;

15. *Takes note* of the measures taken by the Mission to address instances of sexual exploitation and abuse and of the zero-tolerance policy, and requests the Secretary-General to continue to investigate fully the allegations of sexual exploitation and violence by civilian and military personnel of the Mission, and to take the appropriate measures set out in the Secretary-General's bulletin on special measures for protection from sexual exploitation and sexual abuse;

16. *Encourages* the Mission to enhance its interaction with the civilian population, in particular internally displaced persons, to raise awareness and understanding about its mandate and activities;

17. *Demands* that all the parties to the Goma and Nairobi processes respect the ceasefire and implement their commitments effectively and in good faith, and calls upon all armed groups to immediately lay down their arms and present themselves without any further delay or preconditions to Congolese authorities and the Mission for their disarmament, repatriation, resettlement and/or reintegration, as appropriate;

18. *Requests* the Secretary-General and his Special Envoy for the Great Lakes Region to intensify their good offices, in close consultation with the Special Representative of the Secretary-General for the Democratic Republic of the Congo, in facilitating a political solution to address the underlying causes of the crisis in the Kivus, and calls upon the Government of the Democratic Republic of the Congo, the Government of the Republic of Rwanda and other Governments of the region, international partners and all regional and Congolese parties to cooperate with the Special Envoy and with the Special Representative;

19. *Urges* the Government of the Democratic Republic of the Congo and the Government of the Republic of Rwanda to take concrete steps to defuse tensions, including by reactivating the Joint Verification Mechanism, and to step up their cooperation in order to implement fully the commitments undertaken in their joint communiqué signed at Nairobi on 9 November 2007, in particular to address as a priority the disarmament and repatriation of the Forces démocratiques de libération du Rwanda, working in close cooperation with the Special Envoy and the Mission;

20. *Urges* all Governments in the region, in particular those of Burundi, the Democratic Republic of the Congo, Rwanda and Uganda, to resolve in a constructive manner their shared security and border problems, to prevent the use of their respective territories in support of violations of the arms embargo reaffirmed by resolution 1807(2008) or in support of activities of armed groups present in the region, and to abide by their commitments to establish bilateral diplomatic relations made at the meeting of the Tripartite Plus Joint Commission of September 2007;

21. *Urges* all States, especially those in the region, to take appropriate steps to end the illicit trade in natural resources, including, if necessary, through judicial means, and, where necessary, to report to the Council, encourages, in particular, the Government of the Democratic Republic of the Congo to work with specialist organizations, international financial institutions and the Mission, as well as the countries of the region, to establish a plan for an effective and transparent control over the exploitation of natural resources, including by conducting a mapping exercise of the main sites of illegal exploitation;

22. *Requests* the Government of the Democratic Republic of the Congo, with the support of the international community and the Mission, to develop and implement as a matter of urgency a comprehensive national security sector reform strategy, including based on the outcome of the round table on the security sector, held in February 2008, in order to establish professional security organizations in the areas of defence, police and the administration of justice that protect civilians, are well managed, and act in accordance with the Constitution and with respect for the rule of law, human rights and international humanitarian law, urges the Government to ensure the sustainability of the support given by its partners in this area, in particular by giving priority to the reform of the administration and command structures of the Armed Forces of the Democratic Republic of the Congo and all its other security forces, and reiterates its call upon the Congolese authorities to establish a vetting mechanism to take into account, when they select candidates for official positions, including key posts in the armed forces, national police and other security services, the past actions of the candidates in terms of respect for international humanitarian law and human rights;

23. *Demands* that all parties ensure timely, safe and unhindered access of all humanitarian actors and comply fully with their obligations under international law, including international humanitarian law, human rights law and refugee law;

24. *Demands also*, recalling its resolution 1698(2006) of 31 July 2006, that all armed groups, in particular the forces of Mr. Laurent Nkunda, the Forces démocratiques de libération du Rwanda and the Lord's Resistance Army immediately stop recruiting and using children and release all children associated with them;

25. *Recalls* the utmost importance of the fight against impunity, notably in the eastern part of the Democratic Republic of the Congo, by bringing to justice those who have committed crimes and atrocities;

26. *Requests* the Secretary-General, through his Special Representative, to continue to coordinate all the activities of the United Nations system in the Democratic Republic of the Congo;

27. *Decides* to remain actively seized of the matter.

Communications. By a letter of 10 November [S/2008/701], the DRC transmitted to the Security Council statistics on the repatriation of Rwandan refugees to North Kivu for 2008 and a record of repatriation of Rwandan refugees to North Kivu from January 1999 to November 2008. By a letter of 20 November [S/2008/724], the DRC transmitted to the Secretary-General and the Council an inquiry concerning relieving General Karake Karenzi, commander of the Rwandan contingent operating under the African Union-United Nations Hybrid Operation in Darfur (UNAMID), of his duties. The DRC held him responsible for the massacres perpetrated in Manono, Katanga Province, in 1999, and for the clashes in the town of Kisangani, Eastern Province, in 2000.

Year-end developments. In a later report [S/2009/160], the Secretary-General noted that developments in the eastern part of the DRC and the Great Lakes region had significantly reshaped the political and military landscape in North Kivu. Although the situation remained fragile, concerted actions by the Government of the DRC and neighbouring countries had presented opportunities for effectively addressing the issue of armed groups, one of the main causes of conflict in the eastern part of the country. On 5 December, at the conclusion of the third meeting of the "Four plus Four" Commission—a bilateral mechanism established in October by the DRC and Rwanda aimed at normalizing their relations—the two countries announced their agreement on a joint military plan to address the continued presence of FDLR in the eastern part of the DRC. They also pledged to take concrete steps towards the restoration of full-fledged mutual diplomatic relations.

On 14 December, FARDC, the Ugandan armed forces and the Sudan People's Liberation Army (SPLA) launched a joint operation in Haut Uélé against LRA. Ugandan and Congolese officials announced that the operation was effective in destroying several LRA bases, cutting off food and ammunition supplies and disrupting the movement's command-and-control structure. In Ituri, the situation remained volatile in November, with the launch of several attacks against FARDC by FRPI in Irumu territory. In December, however, FARDC, supported by MONUC, was able to reoccupy some of the villages that had been captured by FRPI.

Following the Extraordinary Summit of the leaders of the Great Lakes region (Nairobi, 7 November), at which it was agreed that the Special Envoy for the Great Lakes Region and his co-facilitator would focus on a comprehensive peace in the eastern part of the DRC and the root causes of the conflict (see p. 119), the co-facilitation launched, on 8 December, a dialogue between the Government and CNDP in Nairobi that served as a confidence-building mechanism between the parties.

Children and armed conflict

In November, as requested by resolution 1612(2005) [YUN 2005, p. 863], the Secretary-General submitted to the Security Council a report [S/2008/693] on children and armed conflict in the DRC, conveying progress in ending the recruitment and use of children and other grave violations being committed against war-affected children. Covering major developments since the previous report [YUN 2007, p. 130], the report noted a decrease in the number of allegations of grave violations against children, but indicated that children were still the primary victims of the ongoing conflict in affected areas. Recruitment and use of children by armed forces and groups continued, particularly in connection with outbreaks of hostilities. The report also raised concerns about the re-recruitment of children, due in part to insufficient support from earlier disarmament, demobilization and reintegration processes.

Widespread incidents of rape and other sexual violence against girls and boys remained a concern. Both State and non-State parties were responsible for violations. There had been some progress in implementing a national action plan on disarmament, demobilization and reintegration of children, as well as follow-up and a programmatic response to the most grave violations—killing or maiming children; recruiting or using child soldiers; attacks against schools or hospitals; rape or other grave sexual violence against children; abducting children; and denying humanitarian access for children. The Government was committed to addressing impunity for violations against children, as demonstrated by the prosecutions of perpetrators by military and civil judicial mechanisms. The Secretary-General urged all parties to implement the recommendations of his previous reports along with the conclusions and recommendations of the Security Council Working Group on Children and Armed Conflict [YUN 2006, p. 920; YUN 2007, pp. 131, 790].

In December, the Working Group established by resolution 1612(2005) [YUN 2005, p. 863] submitted its conclusions on children and armed conflict in the DRC [S/AC.51/2009/3], which contained the Group's exchange of views on the Secretary-General's report. The Group recommended that the Council urge the Government to ensure that the integration of forces from CNDP, the Mayi-Mayi militias and other armed groups into FARDC did not lead to any new recruitment and use of children in FARDC, and that it was used as an opportunity to obtain the release of all children associated with those armed groups; and to adopt and implement a comprehensive national strategy to prevent, respond to and combat sexual violence. The Group also agreed that letters should be addressed to the World Bank and donors requesting funding to support reintegration activities for child soldiers; prioritizing the situation of girls; and urging support for the Government in implementing a comprehensive national strategy to prevent, respond to and combat sexual violence.

Arms embargo

The Security Council Committee on the DRC, established pursuant to resolution 1533(2004) [YUN 2004, p. 137] to review and monitor the arms embargo on armed groups imposed by resolution 1493(2003) [YUN 2003, p. 130], reported [S/2008/832] on its activities from 1 January to 31 December 2008, during which it held six informal consultations. In February, by resolution 1799(2008) (see p. 136), the Council extended the arms embargo and releated sanctions until 31 March 2008. Pursuant to resolution 1807(2008) (ibid.), by which the Council in March extended the arms embargo and related sanctions until 31 December 2008, the Committee received seven notifications from States in advance of the shipment of arms or related materiel for the DRC, or the provision of assistance, advice or training related to military activities in the DRC.

Group of Experts

The Group of Experts on the DRC, established pursuant to Security Council resolution 1533(2004) to gather and analyse information on the flow of arms and related materiel, as well as arms networks, in violation of the measures imposed by paragraph 20 of resolution 1493(2003), submitted three reports during the year [S/2008/43, S/2008/772, S/2008/773].

As requested by resolution 1799(2008) (see p. 136) and resolution 1807(2008) (ibid.), respectively, the Secretary-General, on 20 February [S/2008/120], reappointed the Group of Experts for a period expiring on 31 March; while on 9 May [S/2008/312], he appointed five new experts to constitute the Group for a period ending on 31 December 2008, replacing two of those with new appointments on 6 August [S/2008/526].

Report of Group of Experts (February). In February [S/2008/43], the Security Council Committee on the DRC submitted to the Council the final report of the Group of Experts, as requested in resolution 1771(2007) [YUN 2007, p. 133]. The report presented two case studies concerning the illegal armed groups that posed the most serious threat to peace and security in the eastern DRC—the Forces démocratiques de libération du Rwanda-Forces combattantes abacunguzi (FDLR-FOCA) and the military wing of CNDP, respectively. At issue were their leadership structure, arms supplies, cross-border recruitment, financing, and recruitment and use of children, as well as associated illegal armed groups. In addition, the report conveyed the results of investigations concerning potential violations of the arms embargo by the Government of the DRC and UN Member States. It discussed the monitoring of targeted travel and financial sanctions imposed against individuals and entities.

It also outlined the role of the exploitation of natural resources in the financing of illegal armed groups.

The Group recommended that the Security Council Committee inform the Group and MONUC of notifications that the Committee received pursuant to paragraph 4 of Security Council resolution 1771(2007) concerning the supplies of arms and related materiel for the DRC as well as technical training and assistance; that the Committee request the Government of the DRC to enhance the arms embargo monitoring capacity of MONUC by notifying MONUC of all incoming shipments of military supplies in a timely fashion; and that the Security Council request the Government and its international cooperation partners to reactivate an effective process of disarmament, demobilization and reintegration of members of illegal armed groups. It also recommended that the Committee encourage the Government of the DRC and its international cooperation partners to establish sufficient customs storage facilities and equip its customs administration and law-enforcement institutions with appropriate operational equipment; encourage the Governments of the DRC and neighbouring States to establish closer cooperation among their respective customs authorities with a view to improving implementation of the arms embargo and targeted travel and finance measures; request the Governments of the DRC and regional States to prevent cross-border recruitment of child soldiers; request child protection organizations in the Great Lakes region to strengthen their cooperation in the field to prevent cross-border recruitment of child soldiers; request Member States to circulate to their relevant authorities the list of individuals and entities subject to targeted sanctions; and request Member States to ensure that individuals and entities under their jurisdiction that purchased minerals and precious stones from districts in the DRC with a strong rebel presence conduct due diligence to ensure that their purchases did not profit illegal armed groups.

SECURITY COUNCIL ACTION

On 15 February [meeting 5836], the Security Council unanimously adopted **resolution 1799(2008)**. The draft [S/2008/97] was prepared in consultations among Council members.

The Security Council,

Recalling its previous resolutions, in particular resolutions 1771(2007) of 10 August 2007 and 1794(2007) of 21 December 2007, and the statements by its President concerning the Democratic Republic of the Congo,

Condemning the continuing illicit flow of weapons within and into the Democratic Republic of the Congo, and declaring its determination to continue to monitor closely the implementation of the arms embargo and other measures set out in its resolutions,

Reiterating its serious concern regarding the presence of armed groups and militias in the eastern part of the Democratic Republic of the Congo, particularly in the provinces of North and South Kivu and the Ituri district, which perpetuates a climate of insecurity in the whole region,

Recalling its intention to review the measures set forth in resolution 1771(2007), with a view to adjusting them, as appropriate, in light of consolidation of the security situation in the Democratic Republic of the Congo, in particular progress in security sector reform, including the integration of the armed forces and the reform of the national police, and in disarming, demobilizing, repatriating, resettling and reintegrating, as appropriate, Congolese and foreign armed groups,

Determining that the situation in the Democratic Republic of the Congo continues to constitute a threat to international peace and security in the region,

Acting under Chapter VII of the Charter of the United Nations,

1. *Decides* to extend until 31 March 2008 the measures on arms imposed by paragraph 20 of resolution 1493(2003) of 28 July 2003 as amended and expanded by paragraph 1 of resolution 1596(2005) of 18 April 2005;
2. *Decides also* to extend, for the period specified in paragraph 1 above, the measures on transport imposed by paragraphs 6, 7 and 10 of resolution 1596(2005);
3. *Decides further* to extend, for the period specified in paragraph 1 above, the financial and travel measures imposed by paragraphs 13 and 15 of resolution 1596(2005), paragraph 2 of resolution 1649(2005) of 21 December 2005 and paragraph 13 of resolution 1698(2006) of 31 July 2006;
4. *Decides* to extend, for the period specified in paragraph 1 above, the mandate of the Group of Experts referred to in paragraph 9 of resolution 1771(2007);
5. *Decides also* to remain actively seized of the matter.

On 31 March [meeting 5861], the Security Council unanimously adopted **resolution 1807(2008)**. The draft [S/2008/213] was submitted by Belgium, Costa Rica, Croatia, France, Italy, the United Kingdom and the United States.

The Security Council,

Recalling its previous resolutions, in particular resolution 1794(2007) of 21 December 2007, and the statements by its President concerning the Democratic Republic of the Congo,

Reaffirming its commitment to the sovereignty, territorial integrity and political independence of the Democratic Republic of the Congo as well as all States in the region,

Reiterating its serious concern regarding the presence of armed groups and militias in the eastern part of the Democratic Republic of the Congo, particularly in the provinces of North and South Kivu and the Ituri district, which perpetuates a climate of insecurity in the whole region,

Stressing the primary responsibility of the Government of the Democratic Republic of the Congo for ensuring security in its territory and protecting its civilians with respect for the rule of law, human rights and international humanitarian law,

Recalling the joint communiqué of the Government of the Democratic Republic of the Congo and the Government of the Republic of Rwanda signed at Nairobi on 9 November 2007 and the outcome of the Conference on Peace, Security and Development in North and South Kivu, held in Goma from 6 to 23 January 2008, which together represent a major step towards the restoration of lasting peace and stability in the Great Lakes region, and looking forward to their full implementation,

Recalling also its resolution 1804(2008) of 13 March 2008 and its demand that the Rwandan armed groups operating in the eastern part of the Democratic Republic of the Congo lay down their arms without any further delay or preconditions,

Reiterating the importance of urgently carrying out security sector reform and of disarming, demobilizing, repatriating, resettling and reintegrating, as appropriate, Congolese and foreign armed groups for the long-term stabilization of the Democratic Republic of the Congo, and welcoming in this regard the round table on the reform of the security sector that was held in Kinshasa on 25 and 26 February 2008,

Taking note of the final report of the Group of Experts on the Democratic Republic of the Congo established pursuant to resolution 1771(2007) of 10 August 2007 ("the Group of Experts") and of the recommendations contained therein,

Condemning the continuing illicit flow of weapons within and into the Democratic Republic of the Congo, and declaring its determination to continue to monitor closely the implementation of the arms embargo and other measures set out in its resolutions concerning the Democratic Republic of the Congo,

Stressing that improved exchange of information between the Security Council Committee established pursuant to resolution 1533(2004) ("the Committee"), the Group of Experts, the United Nations Organization Mission in the Democratic Republic of the Congo, other United Nations offices and missions in the region, within their respective mandates, and the Governments of the region can contribute to the prevention of arms shipments to non-governmental entities and individuals subject to the arms embargo,

Recognizing the linkage between the illegal exploitation of natural resources, illicit trade in such resources and the proliferation of and trafficking in arms as one of the factors fuelling and exacerbating conflicts in the Great Lakes region of Africa,

Recalling its resolution 1612(2005) of 26 July 2005 and its previous resolutions on children and armed conflict, and strongly condemning the continued recruitment, targeting and use of children, in violation of applicable international law, in the hostilities in the Democratic Republic of the Congo,

Recalling also its resolution 1325(2000) of 31 October 2000 on women and peace and security, and strongly condemning the continuing violence, in particular sexual violence, directed against women in the Democratic Republic of the Congo,

Calling upon the donor community to continue to provide urgent assistance needed for the reform of the administration of justice in the Democratic Republic of the Congo,

Recalling the measures on arms imposed by paragraph 20 of resolution 1493(2003) of 28 July 2003, as amended and expanded by paragraph 1 of resolution 1596(2005) of 18 April 2005,

Recalling also the measures on transport imposed by paragraphs 6, 7 and 10 of resolution 1596(2005),

Recalling further the financial and travel measures imposed by paragraphs 13 and 15 of resolution 1596(2005), paragraph 2 of resolution 1649(2005) of 21 December 2005 and paragraph 13 of resolution 1698(2006) of 31 July 2006,

Determining that the situation in the Democratic Republic of the Congo continues to constitute a threat to international peace and security in the region,

Acting under Chapter VII of the Charter of the United Nations,

A

1. *Decides*, for a further period ending on 31 December 2008, that all States shall take the necessary measures to prevent the direct or indirect supply, sale or transfer, from their territories or by their nationals, or using their flag vessels or aircraft, of arms and any related materiel, and the provision of any assistance, advice or training related to military activities, including financing and financial assistance, to all non-governmental entities and individuals operating in the territory of the Democratic Republic of the Congo;

2. *Decides also* that the measures on arms previously imposed by paragraph 20 of resolution 1493(2003) and paragraph 1 of resolution 1596(2005), as renewed in paragraph 1 above, shall no longer apply to the supply, sale or transfer of arms and related materiel, and the provision of any assistance, advice or training related to military activities to the Government of the Democratic Republic of the Congo;

3. *Decides further* that the measures in paragraph 1 above shall not apply to:

(a) Supplies of arms and related materiel as well as technical training and assistance intended solely for the support of or use by the United Nations Organization Mission in the Democratic Republic of the Congo;

(b) Protective clothing, including flak jackets and military helmets, temporarily exported to the Democratic Republic of the Congo by United Nations personnel, representatives of the media and humanitarian and development workers and associated personnel, for their personal use only;

(c) Other supplies of non-lethal military equipment intended solely for humanitarian or protective use, and related technical assistance and training, as notified in advance to the Committee in accordance with paragraph 5 below;

4. *Decides* to terminate the obligations set out in paragraph 4 of resolution 1596(2005) and paragraph 4 of resolution 1771(2007);

5. *Decides also*, for the period referred to in paragraph 1 above, that all States shall notify in advance to the Committee any shipment of arms and related materiel for the Democratic Republic of the Congo, or any provision of assistance, advice or training related to military activities in the Democratic Republic of the Congo, except those re-

ferred to in paragraphs 3 *(a)* and *(b)* above, and stresses the importance of such notifications containing all relevant information, including, where appropriate, the end-user, the proposed date of delivery and the itinerary of shipments;

B

6. *Decides further* that, for a further period ending on the date referred to in paragraph 1 above, all Governments in the region, and in particular those of the Democratic Republic of the Congo and of States bordering Ituri and the Kivus, shall take the necessary measures:

(a) To ensure that aircraft operate in the region in accordance with the Convention on International Civil Aviation, signed at Chicago, United States of America, on 7 December 1944, in particular by verifying the validity of documents carried in aircraft and the licences of pilots;

(b) To prohibit immediately in their respective territories the operation of any aircraft inconsistent with the conditions in the Convention or the standards established by the International Civil Aviation Organization, in particular with respect to the use of falsified or out-of-date documents, and to notify the Committee of the measures they take in this regard;

(c) To ensure that all civilian and military airports or airfields on their respective territories will not be used for a purpose inconsistent with the measures imposed by paragraph 1 above;

7. *Recalls* that, pursuant to paragraph 7 of resolution 1596(2005), each Government in the region, in particular those of States bordering Ituri and the Kivus, as well as that of the Democratic Republic of the Congo, must maintain a registry for review by the Committee and the Group of Experts of all information concerning flights originating in their respective territories en route to destinations in the Democratic Republic of the Congo, as well as flights originating in the Democratic Republic of the Congo en route to destinations in their respective territories;

8. *Decides* that, for a further period ending on the date referred to in paragraph 1 above, the Government of the Democratic Republic of the Congo on the one hand, and those of States bordering Ituri and the Kivus on the other hand, shall take the necessary measures:

(a) To strengthen, as far as each of them is concerned, customs controls on the borders between Ituri or the Kivus and the neighbouring States;

(b) To ensure that all means of transport on their respective territories will not be used in violation of the measures taken by Member States in accordance with paragraph 1 above, and notify the Committee of such actions;

C

9. *Decides* that, during the period of enforcement of the measures referred to in paragraph 1 above, all States shall take the necessary measures to prevent the entry into or transit through their territories of all persons designated by the Committee pursuant to paragraph 13 below, provided that nothing in the present paragraph shall obligate a State to refuse entry into its territory to its own nationals;

10. *Decides also* that the measures imposed by paragraph 9 above shall not apply:

(a) Where the Committee determines in advance and on a case-by-case basis that such travel is justified on the grounds of humanitarian need, including religious obligation;

(b) Where the Committee concludes that an exemption would further the objectives of the resolutions of the Security Council, that is, peace and national reconciliation in the Democratic Republic of the Congo and stability in the region;

(c) Where the Committee authorizes in advance, and on a case-by-case basis, the transit of individuals returning to the territory of the State of their nationality, or participating in efforts to bring to justice perpetrators of grave violations of human rights or international humanitarian law;

11. *Decides further* that all States shall, during the period of enforcement of the measures referred to in paragraph 1 above, immediately freeze the funds, other financial assets and economic resources which are on their territories from the date of adoption of the present resolution, which are owned or controlled, directly or indirectly, by persons or entities designated by the Committee pursuant to paragraph 13 below, or that are held by entities owned or controlled, directly or indirectly, by them or by any persons or entities acting on their behalf or at their direction, as designated by the Committee, and decides that all States shall ensure that no funds, financial assets or economic resources are made available by their nationals or by any persons within their territories to or for the benefit of such persons or entities;

12. *Decides* that the provisions of paragraph 11 above do not apply to funds, other financial assets and economic resources that:

(a) Have been determined by relevant States to be necessary for basic expenses, including payment for foodstuffs, rent or mortgage, medicines and medical treatment, taxes, insurance premiums and public utility charges, or for payment of reasonable professional fees and reimbursement of incurred expenses associated with the provision of legal services, or fees or service charges, in accordance with national laws, for routine holding or maintenance of frozen funds, other financial assets and economic resources, after notification by the relevant States to the Committee of the intention to authorize, where appropriate, access to such funds, other financial assets and economic resources and in the absence of a negative decision by the Committee within four working days of such notification;

(b) Have been determined by relevant States to be necessary for extraordinary expenses, provided that such determination has been notified by the relevant States to the Committee and has been approved by the Committee; or

(c) Have been determined by relevant States to be the subject of a judicial, administrative or arbitration lien or judgement, in which case the funds, other financial assets and economic resources may be used to satisfy that lien or judgement, provided that the lien or judgement was entered prior to the date of the present resolution, is not for the benefit of a person or entity designated by the Committee pursuant to paragraph 13 below, and has been notified by the relevant States to the Committee;

13. *Decides also* that the provisions of paragraphs 9 and 11 above shall apply to the following individuals and, as appropriate, entities, as designated by the Committee:

(a) Persons or entities acting in violation of the measures taken by Member States in accordance with paragraph 1 above;

(b) Political and military leaders of foreign armed groups operating in the Democratic Republic of the Congo who impede the disarmament and the voluntary repatriation or resettlement of combatants belonging to those groups;

(c) Political and military leaders of Congolese militias receiving support from outside the Democratic Republic of the Congo who impede the participation of their combatants in disarmament, demobilization and reintegration processes;

(d) Political and military leaders operating in the Democratic Republic of the Congo and recruiting or using children in armed conflicts in violation of applicable international law;

(e) Individuals operating in the Democratic Republic of the Congo and committing serious violations of international law involving the targeting of children or women in situations of armed conflict, including killing and maiming, sexual violence, abduction and forced displacement;

14. *Decides further* that, for a further period ending on the date referred to in paragraph 1 above, the measures in paragraphs 9 and 11 above shall continue to apply to individuals and entities already designated pursuant to paragraphs 13 and 15 of resolution 1596(2005), paragraph 2 of resolution 1649(2005) and paragraph 13 of resolution 1698(2006), unless the Committee decides otherwise;

D

15. *Decides* that the Committee shall, from the date of adoption of the present resolution, have the following mandate:

(a) To seek from all States, and particularly those in the region, information regarding the actions taken by them to implement effectively the measures imposed by paragraphs 1, 6, 8, 9 and 11 above and to comply with paragraphs 18 and 24 of resolution 1493(2003), and thereafter to request from them whatever further information it may consider useful, including by providing States with an opportunity, at the request of the Committee, to send representatives to meet with the Committee for more in-depth discussion of relevant issues;

(b) To examine, and to take appropriate action on, information concerning alleged violations of the measures imposed by paragraph 1 above and information on alleged arms flows highlighted in the reports of the Panel of Experts on the Illegal Exploitation of Natural Resources and Other Forms of Wealth in the Democratic Republic of the Congo, identifying, where possible, individuals and entities reported to be engaged in such violations, as well as aircraft or other vehicles used;

(c) To present regular reports to the Council on its work, with its observations and recommendations, in particular on the ways to strengthen the effectiveness of the measures imposed by paragraph 1 above;

(d) To receive notifications in advance from States made under paragraph 5 above, to inform the Mission and the Government of the Democratic Republic of the Congo of every notification received, and to consult with the Government of the Democratic Republic of the Congo and/or the notifying State, if appropriate, to verify that such shipments are in conformity with the measures set forth in paragraph 1 above, and to decide, if need be, upon any action to be taken;

(e) To designate, pursuant to paragraph 13 above, persons and entities as subject to the measures set forth in paragraphs 9 and 11 above, including aircraft and airlines, in light of paragraphs 6 and 8 above, and regularly to update its list;

(f) To call upon all States concerned, and particularly those in the region, to provide the Committee with information regarding the actions taken by them to investigate and prosecute, as appropriate, individuals and entities designated by the Committee pursuant to subparagraph *(e)* above;

(g) To consider and decide on requests for the exemptions set out in paragraphs 10 and 12 above;

(h) To promulgate guidelines as may be necessary to facilitate the implementation of paragraphs 1, 6, 8, 9 and 11 above;

16. *Calls upon* all States, in particular those in the region, to support the implementation of the arms embargo and to cooperate fully with the Committee in carrying out its mandate;

E

17. *Requests* the Secretary-General to extend, for a period expiring on 31 December 2008, the mandate of the Group of Experts established pursuant to resolution 1771(2007);

18. *Requests* the Group of Experts to fulfil the following mandate:

(a) To examine and analyse information gathered by the Mission in the context of its monitoring mandate and share with the Mission, as appropriate, information that might be of use in the fulfilment of the Mission's monitoring mandate;

(b) To gather and analyse all relevant information in the Democratic Republic of the Congo, countries of the region and, as necessary, in other countries, in cooperation with the Governments of those countries, on flows of arms and related materiel, as well as networks operating in violation of the measures imposed by paragraph 1 above;

(c) To consider and recommend, where appropriate, ways of improving the capabilities of interested States, in particular those of the region, to ensure that the measures imposed by paragraph 1 above are effectively implemented;

(d) To update the Committee on its work, as appropriate, and report to the Council in writing, through the Committee, by 15 August 2008 and again before 15 November 2008, on the implementation of the measures set forth in paragraphs 1, 6, 8, 9 and 11 above, with recommendations in this regard, including information on the sources of financing, such as from natural resources, which are funding the illicit trade in arms;

(e) To keep the Committee frequently updated on its activities;

(f) To provide the Committee, in its reports with a list, with supporting evidence, of those found to have violated the measures imposed by paragraph 1 above, and

those found to have supported them in such activities, for possible future measures by the Council;

(g) Within its capabilities and without prejudice to the execution of the other tasks in its mandate, to assist the Committee in the designation of the individuals referred to in of paragraphs 13 *(b)* to *(e)* above, by making known to the Committee without delay any useful information;

19. *Requests* the Mission, within its existing capabilities and without prejudice to the performance of its current mandate, and the Group of Experts to continue to focus their monitoring activities in North and South Kivu and in Ituri;

20. *Requests* the Government of the Democratic Republic of the Congo, other Governments in the region as appropriate, the Mission and the Group of Experts to cooperate intensively, including by exchanging information regarding arms shipments with a view to facilitating the effective implementation of the arms embargo on non-governmental entities and individuals, regarding the illegal trafficking in natural resources, and regarding the activities of individuals and entities designated by the Committee pursuant to paragraph 13 above;

21. *Reiterates its demand*, expressed in paragraph 19 of resolution 1596(2005), that all parties and all States, particularly those in the region, cooperate fully with the work of the Group of Experts, and that they ensure:

(a) The safety of its members;

(b) Unhindered and immediate access, in particular to persons, documents and sites that the Group of Experts deems relevant to the execution of its mandate;

F

22. *Decides* that, when appropriate and no later than 31 December 2008, it shall review the measures set forth in the present resolution, with a view to adjusting them, as appropriate, in light of consolidation of the security situation in the Democratic Republic of the Congo, in particular progress in security sector reform, including the integration of the armed forces and the reform of the national police, and in disarming, demobilizing, repatriating, resettling and reintegrating, as appropriate, Congolese and foreign armed groups;

23. *Decides also* to remain actively seized of the matter.

Report of Group of Experts (July). In August [S/2008/772], the Security Council Committee on the DRC submitted to the Council the interim (July) report of the Group of Experts, as requested in resolution 1807(2008). The report presented two case studies concerning FDLR-FOCA and CNDP, respectively. It focused on their military support and recruitment, along with their financing. The report also addressed other armed groups and their recruitment of children; human rights violations involving the targeting of children and women; natural resources and the financing of illegal armed groups; flights into the DRC carrying weapons; and the monitoring of targeted sanctions against listed individuals and entities. The Group expressed its concern that if sufficient safeguards were not put in place, funding from the Amani programme could be used for recruitment and weapons purchases. FARDC remained one of the main suppliers of weapons and ammunition to armed groups in the region, and numerous sources had informed the Group of arms transfers from FARDC to illegal armed groups. It had received numerous reports indicating that problems with the national demobilization process had allowed militia to re-recruit and rearm demobilized combatants. The Group believed that reforms were needed in both taxation and in the revenue-collecting bodies active along the borders, since prohibitive taxes and tariffs, combined with weak State institutions, had driven a large part of all trade—both inside and outside the DRC—underground, generating large amounts of bribes for administrative officials at all border posts in the country. The Group recommended that greater accountability by the Government for arms storage be incorporated into security sector reform; that customs posts be electronically linked and that the Government boost the structure of its Office de gestion du fret maritime, which registered customs declarations in Mombasa, Kenya, for goods being imported to or exported from the DRC; and that dry ports in Bunagana as well as Ishasha and Kasindi—other important customs posts in North Kivu—be completed. The Group was working with MONUC to raise awareness of its monitoring mandate with respect to the arms embargo, and to obtain documents from Member States regarding bank transfers, phone records and arms exports.

Report of Group of Experts (November). In December [S/2008/773], the Security Council Committee on the DRC submitted to the Council the final (November) report of the Group of Experts, as requested in resolution 1807(2008). The report continued with its case-study approach, focusing on the North and South Kivu provinces, in analysing CNDP with regard to its political support, financing, military support and recruitment, Bunagana border post control, individual financiers, exploitation of natural resources, and support by the Government of Rwanda; and on FDLR-FOCA with regard to its political leadership in Europe, financing through natural resources and collaboration with FARDC. The report also discussed other armed groups; the role of natural resources in contributing to the financing of illegal armed groups; arms supply to non-governmental armed groups; civil aviation and logistics; the recruitment and use of children by armed groups; serious violations of international law targeting women and children; and compliance with the sanctions regime.

Among its recommendations, the Group proposed that the Sanctions Committee enforce compliance with the arms embargo by writing officially to Member States that had not responded to the requests and questions of the Group, and note their compliance status; consider political leadership in non-governmental armed groups as inherent support to those groups; request the authorities of the DRC to issue clear directives to its troops that collaboration and cohabitation with FDLR and PARECO were prohibited; and remind the Government of Rwanda of its obligations under the Nairobi Communiqué to prevent any form of support to CNDP and the entry into and exit from its territory and that of its members. The Group also recommended that the Security Council clarify the role that MONUC should play with regard to collecting information on the support of armed groups. Further, it proposed that the Committee encourage the Department of Peacekeeping Operations to provide clear guidance to the civilian staff and contingents of MONUC on their obligations regarding the arms embargo; request the Government of the DRC to promote stockpile security, accountability and management of arms and ammunition; and request MONUC to improve its database of small arms and light weapons. The Group further recommended that the Security Council consider requesting MONUC to establish border-monitoring teams, in particular at the Bunagana and Kasindi border crossings. It also proposed that the Committee address a letter to the Government of the DRC requesting the full implementation of child protection verification procedures; encourage MONUC and the United Nations Children's Fund (UNICEF) to increase coordination among child protection partners, with a view to creating a unified database on demobilized children; call on MONUC to share information with the Group on child recruitment and the targeting of women and children in situations of armed conflict; call on Member States to work with local and international NGOs to develop a map of mineral-rich zones and armed groups in order to create awareness and remove uncertainty among commercial entities with respect to the origin of minerals purchased from areas controlled by armed groups; urge Member States to ensure that exporters and consumers of Congolese mineral products under their jurisdiction conducted due diligence on their suppliers regarding the origin of their products; and request the DRC to take concrete steps towards improving the safety and security of its airspace.

In response to the report, the Security Council extended the arms embargo and related sanctions until 30 November 2009.

Communication. By a letter of 15 December [S/2008/791] to the Security Council, Rwanda responded to allegations contained in the final report of the Group of Experts [S/2008/773] concerning the Government's support of CNDP.

SECURITY COUNCIL ACTION

On 22 December [meeting 6056], the Security Council unanimously adopted **resolution 1857(2008)**. The draft [S/2008/801] was submitted by Belgium and France.

The Security Council,

Recalling its previous resolutions, in particular resolutions 1804(2008) of 13 March 2008 and 1807(2008) of 31 March 2008, and the statements by its President concerning the Democratic Republic of the Congo,

Reaffirming its commitment to the sovereignty, territorial integrity and political independence of the Democratic Republic of the Congo as well as all States in the region,

Reiterating its serious concern regarding the presence of armed groups and militias in the eastern part of the Democratic Republic of the Congo, particularly in the provinces of North and South Kivu and the Ituri district, which perpetuates a climate of insecurity in the whole region, and demanding that all the parties to the Goma and Nairobi processes respect the ceasefire and implement their commitments effectively and in good faith,

Stressing the primary responsibility of the Government of the Democratic Republic of the Congo for ensuring security in its territory and protecting its civilians, with respect for the rule of law, human rights and international humanitarian law,

Taking note of the interim and final reports of the Group of Experts on the Democratic Republic of the Congo ("the Group of Experts") established pursuant to resolution 1771(2007) of 10 August 2007 and extended pursuant to resolution 1807(2008) and of the recommendations contained therein,

Condemning the continuing illicit flow of weapons within and into the Democratic Republic of the Congo, and declaring its determination to continue to monitor closely the implementation of the arms embargo and other measures set out in its resolutions concerning the Democratic Republic of the Congo,

Stressing the obligation of all States to abide by the notification requirements set out in paragraph 5 of resolution 1807(2008),

Reiterating the importance of the Government of the Democratic Republic of the Congo and the Governments of the region taking effective steps to ensure that there is no support, in and from their territories, for the armed groups in the eastern part of the Democratic Republic of the Congo,

Supporting the decision of the Democratic Republic of the Congo to work towards enhancing revenue transparency in its extractive industries,

Recognizing the linkage between the illegal exploitation of natural resources, illicit trade in such resources and the proliferation of and trafficking in arms as one of the major factors fuelling and exacerbating conflicts in the Great Lakes region of Africa,

Recalling its resolutions 1325(2000) of 31 October 2000 and 1820(2008) of 19 June 2008 on women and peace and security, its resolution 1502(2003) of 26 August 2003 on the protection of United Nations personnel, associated personnel and humanitarian personnel in conflict zones, its resolution 1612(2005) of 26 July 2005 on children and armed conflict and its resolution 1674(2006) of 28 April 2006 on the protection of civilians in armed conflict,

Determining that the situation in the Democratic Republic of the Congo continues to constitute a threat to international peace and security in the region,

Acting under Chapter VII of the Charter of the United Nations,

1. *Decides* to renew until 30 November 2009 the measures on arms imposed by paragraph 1 of resolution 1807(2008), and reaffirms the provisions of paragraphs 2, 3 and 5 of that resolution;

2. *Decides also* to renew, for the period specified in paragraph 1 above, the measures on transport imposed by paragraphs 6 and 8 of resolution 1807(2008), and reaffirms the provisions of paragraph 7 of that resolution;

3. *Decides further* to renew, for the period specified in paragraph 1 above, the financial and travel measures imposed by paragraphs 9 and 11 of resolution 1807(2008), and reaffirms the provisions of paragraphs 10 and 12 of that resolution;

4. *Decides* that the measures referred to in paragraph 3 above shall apply to the following individuals and, as appropriate, entities, as designated by the Security Council Committee established pursuant to resolution 1533(2004):

(*a*) Persons or entities acting in violation of the measures taken by Member States in accordance with paragraph 1 above;

(*b*) Political and military leaders of foreign armed groups operating in the Democratic Republic of the Congo who impede the disarmament and the voluntary repatriation or resettlement of combatants belonging to those groups;

(*c*) Political and military leaders of Congolese militias receiving support from outside the Democratic Republic of the Congo who impede the participation of their combatants in disarmament, demobilization and reintegration processes;

(*d*) Political and military leaders operating in the Democratic Republic of the Congo and recruiting or using children in armed conflicts in violation of applicable international law;

(*e*) Individuals operating in the Democratic Republic of the Congo and committing serious violations of international law involving the targeting of children or women in situations of armed conflict, including killing and maiming, sexual violence, abduction and forced displacement;

(*f*) Individuals obstructing access to or the distribution of humanitarian assistance in the eastern part of the Democratic Republic of the Congo;

(*g*) Individuals or entities supporting the illegal armed groups in the eastern part of the Democratic Republic of the Congo through illicit trade in natural resources;

5. *Decides also* that, for a further period ending on the date referred to in paragraph 1 above, the measures in paragraph 3 above shall continue to apply to individuals and entities already designated pursuant to paragraphs 13 and 15 of resolution 1596(2005) of 18 April 2005, paragraph 2 of resolution 1649(2005) of 21 December 2005, paragraph 13 of resolution 1698(2006) of 31 July 2006 and paragraphs 9 and 11 of resolution 1807(2008), unless the Committee decides otherwise;

6. *Decides further* to expand the mandate of the Committee as set out in paragraph 8 of resolution 1533(2004) of 12 March 2004 and expanded upon in paragraph 18 of resolution 1596(2005), paragraph 4 of resolution 1649(2005) and paragraph 14 of resolution 1698(2006) and reaffirmed in paragraph 15 of resolution 1807(2008) to include the following tasks:

(*a*) To review regularly the list of individuals and entities designated by the Committee pursuant to paragraphs 4 and 5 above with a view to keeping the list as updated and accurate as possible and to confirm that listing remains appropriate and to encourage Member States to provide any additional information whenever such information becomes available;

(*b*) To promulgate guidelines in order to facilitate the implementation of the measures imposed by the present resolution and keep them under active review as may be necessary;

7. *Calls upon* all States, in particular those of the region, to support the implementation of the measures specified in the present resolution, to cooperate fully with the Committee in carrying out its mandate and to report to the Committee, within forty-five days of the date of adoption of the present resolution, on the actions they have taken to implement the measures imposed by paragraphs 1 to 5 above, and encourages all States to send representatives, at the Committee's request, to meet with the Committee for more in-depth discussion of relevant issues;

8. *Requests* the Secretary-General to extend, for a period expiring on 30 November 2009, the mandate of the Group of Experts established pursuant to resolution 1771(2007), and requests the Group of Experts to fulfil its mandate as set out in paragraph 18 of resolution 1807(2008) and to report to the Council in writing, through the Committee, by 15 May 2009 and again before 15 October 2009;

9. *Decides* that the mandate of the Group of Experts referred to in paragraph 8 above shall also include the tasks outlined below:

(*a*) To include in its reports to the Committee any information relevant to the designation by the Committee of the individuals and entities described in paragraphs 4 and 5 above;

(*b*) To assist the Committee in updating the publicly available reasons for listing and identifying information for individuals and entities referenced in paragraph 5 above and in compiling the narrative summaries referred to in paragraph 18 below;

10. *Requests* the Group of Experts to continue to focus its activities in North and South Kivu and in Ituri;

11. *Requests* the Government of the Democratic Republic of the Congo, other Governments in the region as appropriate, the United Nations Organization Mission in the Democratic Republic of the Congo and the Group of Experts to cooperate intensively, including by exchanging information regarding arms shipments, illegal trafficking in natural resources and activities of individuals and entities designated by the Committee pursuant to paragraphs 4 and 5 above;

12. *Requests in particular* that the Mission share information with the Group of Experts, especially on the support received by armed groups, on the recruitment and use of children and on the targeting of women and children in situations of armed conflict;

13. *Demands* that all parties and all States ensure cooperation with the Group of Experts by individuals and entities within their jurisdiction or under their control;

14. *Reiterates its demand*, expressed in paragraph 21 of resolution 1807(2008), that all parties and all States, particularly those in the region, cooperate fully with the work of the Group of Experts, and that they ensure:

(a) The safety of its members;

(b) Unhindered and immediate access, in particular to persons, documents and sites that the Group of Experts deems relevant to the execution of its mandate;

15. *Encourages* Member States to take measures, as they deem appropriate, to ensure that importers, processing industries and consumers of Congolese mineral products under their jurisdiction exercise due diligence on their suppliers and on the origin of the minerals they purchase;

16. *Also encourages* Member States to submit to the Committee for inclusion on its list of designees names of individuals or entities who meet the criteria set out in paragraph 4 above, as well as any entities owned or controlled, directly or indirectly, by the submitted individuals or entities or individuals or entities acting on behalf of or at the direction of the submitted entities;

17. *Decides* that, when proposing names to the Committee for listing, Member States shall provide a detailed statement of case, together with sufficient identifying information to allow for the positive identification of individuals and entities by Member States, and decides further that for each such proposal Member States shall identify those parts of the statement of case that may be publicly released, including for use by the Committee for the development of the summary described in paragraph 18 below or for the purpose of notifying or informing the listed individual or entity, and those parts which may be released upon request to interested States;

18. *Directs* the Committee, in coordination with the relevant designating States and with the assistance of the Group of Experts referred to in paragraph 8 above, after a name is added to the list, to make accessible on the Committee website a narrative summary of reasons for listing, and further directs the Committee, with the assistance of the Group of Experts and in coordination with the relevant designating States, to update the publicly available reasons for listing and identifying information for the individuals and entities referred to in paragraph 5 above;

19. *Decides* that the Secretariat shall, after publication but within one week after a name is added to the list of individuals and entities, notify the permanent mission of the country or countries where the individual or entity is believed to be located and, in the case of individuals, the country of which the person is a national (to the extent this information is known) and to include with this notification a copy of the publicly releasable portion of the statement of case, any information on reasons for listing available on the Committee website, a description of the effects of designation as provided in the relevant resolutions, the procedures of the Committee for considering de-listing requests, and the provisions regarding available exemptions;

20. *Demands* that Member States receiving notification as in paragraph 19 above take, in accordance with their domestic laws and practices, all possible measures to notify or inform in a timely manner the listed individual or entity of the designation, together with the information provided by the Secretariat as set out in paragraph 19 above;

21. *Welcomes* the establishment within the Secretariat, pursuant to resolution 1730(2006) of 19 December 2006, of the Focal Point that provides listed individuals, groups, undertakings or entities with the option to submit a petition for de-listing directly to the Focal Point;

22. *Urges* designating States and States of citizenship and residence to review de-listing petitions received through the Focal Point, in accordance with the procedures outlined in the annex to resolution 1730(2006), in a timely manner and to indicate whether they support or oppose the request in order to facilitate review by the Committee;

23. *Directs* the Committee to consider requests, in accordance with its guidelines, for the removal from the Committee's list of designees of those who no longer meet the criteria pursuant to the present resolution;

24. *Decides* that the Secretariat shall, within one week after a name is removed from the Committee's list of designees, notify the permanent mission of the country or countries where the individual or entity is believed to be located and, in the case of individuals, the country of which the person is a national (to the extent this information is known), and demands that States receiving such notification take measures, in accordance with their domestic laws and practices, to notify or inform the individual or entity concerned of the de-listing in a timely manner;

25. *Encourages* the Committee to ensure that fair and clear procedures exist for placing individuals and entities on the Committee's list of designees and for removing them as well as for granting humanitarian exemptions;

26. *Decides* that, when appropriate and no later than 30 November 2009, it shall review the measures set forth in the present resolution, with a view to adjusting them, as appropriate, in light of the consolidation of the security situation in the Democratic Republic of the Congo, in particular progress in security sector reform, including the integration of the armed forces and the reform of the national police, and in disarming, demobilizing, repatriating, resettling and reintegrating, as appropriate, Congolese and foreign armed groups;

27. *Decides also* to remain actively seized of the matter.

MONUC

The United Nations Organization Mission in the Democratic Republic of the Congo (MONUC), established by Security Council resolution 1279(1999) [YUN 1999, p. 92], continued to discharge its mandate, as enhanced by Council resolutions 1565(2004) [YUN 2004, p. 129], 1756(2007) [YUN 2007, p. 119] and 1856(2008) (p. 130). MONUC, headquartered in the DRC capital, Kinshasa, was headed by Alan Doss (United Kingdom), the Special Representative of the Secretary-General for the DRC.

Sexual exploitation and abuse. In the context of its peace operations oversight activities during the year, the Office of Internal Oversight Services (OIOS) [A/63/302 (Part II)] substantiated reports that four members of a national contingent in MONUC sexually exploited and abused local minors and young women, and that one contingent member had assaulted a civilian. OIOS found that the contingent commander had failed to exercise appropriate command and control responsibilities, which directly contributed to the sexual exploitation and abuse. While OIOS could not substantiate misconduct reports against 29 contingent members, it recommended that the concerned troop-contributing country further investigate reports against 32 other contingent members. Following the recommendations of OIOS, the Department of Field Support referred the case to the concerned troop-contributing country for appropriate action.

Financing

In June, the General Assembly considered the performance report [A/62/737] on the MONUC budget for the period 1 July 2006–30 June 2007, which showed expenditures of $1,085,127,900 against an appropriation of $1,091,242,800, leaving an unencumbered balance of $6,114,900. The Assembly also had before it the proposed budget [A/62/755] for MONUC for the period 1 July 2008–30 June 2009, amounting to $1,191,372,300. The Advisory Committee on Administrative and Budgetary Questions (ACABQ) recommended [A/62/781/Add.8] that the unencumbered balance of $6,114,900, as well as other income and adjustments of $55,462,400 for the period 2006–2007, be credited to Member States in a manner to be determined by the Assembly. ACABQ further recommended a reduction of $3,695,900 in the proposed 2008–2009 budget, with an appropriation of $1,187,676,400 for that period.

GENERAL ASSEMBLY ACTION

On 20 June [meeting 109], the General Assembly, on the recommendation of the Fifth (Administrative and Budgetary) Committee [A/62/869], adopted **resolution 62/256** without vote [agenda item 144].

Financing of the United Nations Organization Mission in the Democratic Republic of the Congo

The General Assembly,

Having considered the reports of the Secretary-General on the financing of the United Nations Organization Mission in the Democratic Republic of the Congo and the related report of the Advisory Committee on Administrative and Budgetary Questions,

Recalling Security Council resolutions 1258(1999) of 6 August 1999 and 1279(1999) of 30 November 1999 regarding, respectively, the deployment to the region of the Democratic Republic of the Congo of military liaison personnel and the establishment of the United Nations Organization Mission in the Democratic Republic of the Congo, and the subsequent resolutions by which the Council extended the mandate of the Mission, the latest of which was resolution 1794(2007) of 21 December 2007, by which the Council extended the mandate of the Mission until 31 December 2008,

Recalling also its resolution 54/260 A of 7 April 2000 on the financing of the Mission and its subsequent resolutions thereon, the latest of which was resolution 61/281 of 29 June 2007,

Recalling further its resolution 58/315 of 1 July 2004,

Reaffirming the general principles underlying the financing of United Nations peacekeeping operations, as stated in General Assembly resolutions 1874(S-IV) of 27 June 1963, 3101(XXVIII) of 11 December 1973 and 55/235 of 23 December 2000,

Noting with appreciation that voluntary contributions have been made to the Mission,

Mindful of the fact that it is essential to provide the Mission with the financial resources necessary to enable it to fulfil its responsibilities under the relevant resolutions of the Security Council,

1. *Requests* the Secretary-General to entrust the Head of Mission with the task of formulating future budget proposals in full accordance with the provisions of General Assembly resolutions 59/296 of 22 June 2005, 60/266 of 30 June 2006 and 61/276 of 29 June 2007, as well as other relevant resolutions;

2. *Takes note* of the status of contributions to the United Nations Organization Mission in the Democratic Republic of the Congo as at 31 March 2008, including the contributions outstanding in the amount of 343.6 million United States dollars, representing some 7 per cent of the total assessed contributions, notes with concern that only thirty-six Member States have paid their assessed contributions in full, and urges all other Member States, in particular those in arrears, to ensure payment of their outstanding assessed contributions;

3. *Expresses its appreciation* to those Member States which have paid their assessed contributions in full, and urges all other Member States to make every possible effort to ensure payment of their assessed contributions to the Mission in full;

4. *Expresses concern* at the financial situation with regard to peacekeeping activities, in particular as regards the reimbursements to troop contributors that bear additional burdens owing to overdue payments by Member States of their assessments;

5. *Also expresses concern* at the delay experienced by the Secretary-General in deploying and providing adequate resources to some recent peacekeeping missions, in particular those in Africa;

6. *Emphasizes* that all future and existing peacekeeping missions shall be given equal and non-discriminatory treatment in respect of financial and administrative arrangements;

7. *Also emphasizes* that all peacekeeping missions shall be provided with adequate resources for the effective and efficient discharge of their respective mandates;

8. *Reiterates its request* to the Secretary-General to make the fullest possible use of facilities and equipment at the United Nations Logistics Base at Brindisi, Italy, in order to minimize the costs of procurement for the Mission;

9. *Endorses* the conclusions and recommendations contained in the report of the Advisory Committee on Ad-

ministrative and Budgetary Questions, subject to the provisions of the present resolution, and requests the Secretary-General to ensure their full implementation;

10. *Decides* to establish two P-3 posts for the Conduct and Discipline Team and one P-3 position to be funded from general temporary assistance;

11. *Also decides* not to abolish the eight P-3 posts and two National Officer posts of the Child Protection Section, and requests the Secretary-General to make every effort to fill all vacancies in the Section;

12. *Notes with concern* that the Mission continues to experience high vacancy and staff turnover rates, and urges the Secretary-General to ensure expeditious recruitment for all positions to ensure mandate delivery, including for the upcoming elections;

13. *Acknowledges with appreciation* that the use of the logistics hub in Entebbe, Uganda, has been cost-effective and has resulted in savings for the United Nations, and welcomes the expansion of the logistics hub to provide logistical support to peacekeeping operations in the region and to contribute further to their enhanced efficiency and responsiveness, taking into account the ongoing efforts in this regard;

14. *Notes* that there has been cooperation among the missions to explore new avenues for achieving greater synergies in the use of the resources of the Organization, including the concept of a regional support base in Entebbe for the United Nations Organization Mission in the Democratic Republic of the Congo, the United Nations Integrated Office in Burundi and the United Nations Mission in the Sudan, bearing in mind that individual missions are responsible for the preparation and implementation of their own budgets and for controlling their assets and logistical operations;

15. *Decides* to establish the post of Coordination Assistant (Field Service) for the Office of the Deputy Special Representative;

16. *Also decides* to establish the post of Administrative Officer (P-3) in the Office of the Special Representative;

17. *Underlines* the fact that the temporary positions required for the local elections shall serve solely for that purpose and that the deployment shall be aligned to the schedule of the election;

18. *Requests* the Secretary-General to ensure close coordination with the United Nations country team in order to ensure integration of efforts in the support of the forthcoming local elections in the Democratic Republic of the Congo;

19. *Takes note* of paragraph 23 of the report of the Advisory Committee, and recalls paragraph 17, section II, of its resolution 61/244 of 22 December 2006, in which it acknowledged that the interaction of United Nations personnel with the local population in the field is essential and that language skills constitute an important element of the selection and training processes and therefore affirmed that a good command of the official language(s) spoken in the country of residence should be taken into account as an additional asset during those processes;

20. *Requests* the Secretary-General to ensure the full implementation of the relevant provisions of its resolutions 59/296, 60/266 and 61/276;

21. *Also requests* the Secretary-General to take all necessary action to ensure that the Mission is administered with a maximum of efficiency and economy;

22. *Further requests* the Secretary-General, in order to reduce the cost of employing General Service staff, to continue efforts to recruit local staff for the Mission against General Service posts, commensurate with the requirements of the Mission;

Financial performance report for the period from 1 July 2006 to 30 June 2007

23. *Takes note* of the report of the Secretary-General on the financial performance of the Mission for the period from 1 July 2006 to 30 June 2007;

Budget estimates for the period from 1 July 2008 to 30 June 2009

24. *Decides* to appropriate to the Special Account for the United Nations Organization Mission in the Democratic Republic of the Congo the amount of 1,242,729,000 dollars for the period from 1 July 2008 to 30 June 2009, inclusive of 1,187,676,400 dollars for the maintenance of the Mission, 47,991,000 dollars for the support account for peacekeeping operations and 7,061,600 dollars for the United Nations Logistics Base;

Financing of the appropriation

25. *Also decides* to apportion among Member States the amount of 621,364,500 dollars for the period from 1 July to 31 December 2008, in accordance with the levels updated in General Assembly resolution 61/243 of 22 December 2006, and taking into account the scale of assessments for 2008, as set out in its resolution 61/237 of 22 December 2006;

26. *Further decides* that, in accordance with the provisions of its resolution 973(X) of 15 December 1955, there shall be set off against the apportionment among Member States, as provided for in paragraph 25 above, their respective share in the Tax Equalization Fund of the amount of 14,584,200 dollars, comprising the estimated staff assessment income of 11,999,600 dollars approved for the Mission, the prorated share of 2,305,600 dollars of the estimated staff assessment income approved for the support account and the prorated share of 279,000 dollars of the estimated staff assessment income approved for the United Nations Logistics Base;

27. *Decides* to apportion among Member States the amount of 621,364,500 dollars for the period from 1 January to 30 June 2009 at a monthly rate of 103,560,750 dollars, in accordance with the levels updated in resolution 61/243, and taking into account the scale of assessments for 2009, as set out in resolution 61/237, subject to a decision of the Security Council to extend the mandate of the Mission;

28. *Also decides* that, in accordance with the provisions of its resolution 973(X), there shall be set off against the apportionment among Member States, as provided for in paragraph 27 above, their respective share in the Tax Equalization Fund of the amount of 14,584,200 dollars, comprising the estimated staff assessment income of 11,999,600 dollars approved for the Mission, the prorated share of 2,305,600 dollars of the estimated staff assessment income approved for the support account and the prorated share of 279,000

dollars of the estimated staff assessment income approved for the United Nations Logistics Base;

29. *Further decides* that, for Member States that have fulfilled their financial obligations to the Mission, there shall be set off against their apportionment, as provided for in paragraph 25 above, their respective share of the unencumbered balance and other income in the total amount of 61,577,300 dollars in respect of the financial period ended 30 June 2007, in accordance with the levels updated in resolution 61/243, and taking into account the scale of assessments for 2007, as set out in resolution 61/237;

30. *Decides* that, for Member States that have not fulfilled their financial obligations to the Mission, there shall be set off against their outstanding obligations their respective share of the unencumbered balance and other income in the total amount of 61,577,300 dollars in respect of the financial period ended 30 June 2007, in accordance with the scheme set out in paragraph 29 above;

31. *Also decides* that the increase of 1,225,500 dollars in the estimated staff assessment income in respect of the financial period ended 30 June 2007 shall be added to the credits from the amount of 61,577,300 dollars referred to in paragraphs 29 and 30 above;

32. *Emphasizes* that no peacekeeping mission shall be financed by borrowing funds from other active peacekeeping missions;

33. *Encourages* the Secretary-General to continue to take additional measures to ensure the safety and security of all personnel participating in the Mission under the auspices of the United Nations, bearing in mind paragraphs 5 and 6 of Security Council resolution 1502(2003) of 26 August 2003;

34. *Invites* voluntary contributions to the Mission in cash and in the form of services and supplies acceptable to the Secretary-General, to be administered, as appropriate, in accordance with the procedure and practices established by the General Assembly;

35. *Decides* to include in the provisional agenda of its sixty-third session the item entitled "Financing of the United Nations Organization Mission in the Democratic Republic of the Congo".

On 22 December, by **decision 63/552**, the Assembly decided that the agenda item on MONUC financing would remain for consideration during its resumed sixty-third (2009) session.

Burundi

In 2008, Burundi continued to face serious peace and security challenges, primarily emanating from the stalled implementation of the 2006 Comprehensive Ceasefire Agreement, enduring mistrust among political actors, increased restrictions on public liberties, slow progress in fighting impunity, persistent human rights violations, insecurity and high levels of poverty. The end of the year, however, brought a significant breakthrough in the peace process, when, at a Summit of the Heads of State and Government of the Great Lakes Region (Bujumbura, Burundi, 4 December), the Government of Burundi, the rebel Party for the Liberation of the Hutu People-Forces nationales de Libération (Palipehutu-FNL) and attending Heads of State signed a Declaration calling for the commencement of the disarmament, demobilization and reintegration of Palipehutu-FNL and the political integration of its leadership. The United Nations Integrated Office in Burundi (BINUB) continued to support the country in efforts to achieve sustainable peace.

Political and security situation

The overall political, security and humanitarian situation in Burundi deteriorated significantly in the first months of the year. Large-scale hostilities resumed in April between the national security forces and Palipehutu-FNL, while renewed friction between political parties led to another political crisis, paralysing the work of Parliament and the broad-based Government appointed in November 2007 [YUN 2007, p. 141]. Additional causes for concern included population displacements as a consequence of the hostilities; continued widespread violations of human rights perpetrated by the national security forces; lack of progress on transitional justice; and potential food insecurity.

Steps towards ending the stalemate in the peace process initially gained momentum early in the year, as the South African Facilitator convened a meeting (Cape Town, South Africa, 22–23 February) of regional and international bilateral and multilateral stakeholders to discuss the Burundi peace process. The meeting agreed on a common approach to support the conclusion of the peace process, based on a road map of sequenced steps: the Programme of Action to Take Further the Peace Process in Burundi. The Programme of Action envisaged the implementation of the 2006 Comprehensive Ceasefire Agreement [YUN 2006, p. 153] and the conclusion of the peace process by the end of 2008. The first phase entailed the conclusion of disarmament and demobilization following the return of FNL by 1 April to the Joint Verification and Monitoring Mechanism established to implement the Agreement [ibid., p. 148], and the return of the FNL leadership to Burundi by 1 May. The second phase envisaged the integration of FNL members into national institutions as well as their socio-economic reintegration at the community level.

The Programme of Action was endorsed by the Government of Burundi late in February and by FNL on 1 March. On 16 March, the FNL leadership, Government representatives and the Political Directorate (comprising the Executive Representative of the Secretary-General for Burundi, representatives of the Facilitation and the Regional Peace Initiative, representatives of the AU and the EU, and the Ambassadors of South Africa and the United Republic of Tanzania to Burundi) met and reaffirmed their commitment to the implementation of the Agreement of Principles of June 2006 and the Comprehensive Ceasefire Agreement. Following technical negotiations, an agreement was concluded by FNL and the AU on 17 March outlining the security and logistical arrangements to be provided by the AU Special Task Force in Burundi to returning FNL members. FNL did not, however, return to the Joint Verification and Monitoring Mechanism on 1 April as stipulated in the Programme of Action, arguing that the existing legal framework granting its members provisional immunity was not sufficient and that a new law, to be adopted by Parliament, was required as a precondition for their return. Public assurances given by the President on 11 March and at meetings with the Political Directorate, to the effect that the law and decree were still valid, did not convince FNL leaders.

On 17 April, FNL issued a communiqué stating that it reserved the right to defend itself should the Government attack its positions. Fighting broke out on the same day, as FNL reportedly carried out attacks on positions of the Forces de défense nationale in the capital. Subsequent aerial bombings conducted by the national defence forces reportedly destroyed FNL bases north of Bujumbura and repelled further attacks on the capital. FNL rejected responsibility for the violence, blaming the Government for the attacks and underlining its commitment to the Comprehensive Ceasefire Agreement. The Government considered the attacks a deliberate breach of the ceasefire, and on 18 April issued a communiqué accusing FNL of using the question of provisional immunity as a pretext for thwarting the peace process. National actors and international stakeholders expressed concern over unconfirmed reports that FNL was receiving support from the Forces démocratiques de libération du Rwanda (FDLR).

Even before the resumption of hostilities, the security situation had progressively deteriorated, with Bujumbura particularly affected by increased banditry. The political consensus that had led to the formation of a broad-based Government in November 2007 faced numerous challenges. Those included contestations by the Front pour la démocratie au Burundi (FRODEBU) of the distribution of responsibilities among the members of the new Government and the exclusion of several party members by the ruling party, the Conseil national pour la défense de la démocratie-Forces pour la défense de la démocratie (CNDD-FDD). On 8 March, simultaneous grenade attacks targeted the residences of four signatories of an open letter, including the recently excluded former First Vice-President of the National Assembly, who had requested of the Secretary-General political and security assistance in light of what they had perceived to be credible threats to their lives from alleged militias established by the national security services. The work of the National Assembly remained paralysed throughout the parliamentary session that concluded on 30 April.

SECURITY COUNCIL ACTION

On 24 April [meeting 5876], following consultations among Security Council members, the President made statement **S/PRST/2008/10** on behalf of the Council:

> The Security Council expresses its serious concern at the recent confrontations between the Parti pour la libération du peuple hutu-Forces nationales de libération and the National Defence Forces of Burundi, following attacks by the Parti pour la libération du peuple hutu-Forces nationales de libération, and the resulting loss of lives.
>
> The Council condemns the use of violence, and again calls upon the two parties to scrupulously respect the ceasefire concluded on 7 September 2006. It urges the Parti pour la libération du peuple hutu-Forces nationales de libération to return immediately and without preconditions to the Joint Verification and Monitoring Mechanism and calls upon both parties to resume their dialogue to overcome the obstacles that hinder the implementation of the Comprehensive Ceasefire Agreement and delay the conclusion of the peace process in Burundi.
>
> The Council reiterates its support for the Regional Peace Initiative on Burundi, the South African Facilitation and other partners of Burundi, and encourages them to sustain their commitment to bring the parties to overcome the current crisis and implement the Programme of Action to Take Further the Peace Process in Burundi, adopted at the meeting held in Cape Town, South Africa, on 22 and 23 February 2008. It supports a proactive role of the Political Directorate in that regard.
>
> The Council requests the Secretary-General to play a robust political role in support of the peace process and to keep the Council closely informed of developments in Burundi, including in the context of his reports to the Council on the United Nations Integrated Office in Burundi.
>
> The Council stresses that any attempt to jeopardize peace in Burundi through violent means is unacceptable, and expresses its intention to consider possible additional measures, as appropriate, in support of peace and stability in Burundi.

On 6 May, in a letter to the Tanzanian Foreign Minister, FNL indicated its intention to return to the Joint Verification and Monitoring Mechanism and the Political Directorate within 10 days. FNL also requested protection from Tanzanian troops that were part of the African Union Special Task Force upon their return to Burundi.

Report of Secretary-General (May). In his third report on BINUB [S/2008/330], submitted pursuant to Security Council resolution 1791(2007) [YUN 2007,

p. 142], the Secretary-General reviewed developments since his last report [ibid., p. 140]. He summarized peace consolidation challenges, including efforts to enhance democratic governance despite the deterioration in the political and security situation; tensions between the Government and the media; security sector reform and disarmament, demobilization and reintegration; lack of progress in implementing civilian disarmament; the human rights situation, including escalating violations committed by the police and new cases of torture and summary executions attributed to the national intelligence services, as well as widespread sexual violence against women and children; justice sector reform; transitional justice mechanisms; grave violations of children's rights; and structural poverty and stagnating development standards.

The Secretary-General observed that unless the implementation of the Comprehensive Ceasefire Agreement was put back on track, the new cycle of violence could undo all the gains since the signing of the Arusha Agreement in 2000 [YUN 2000, p. 143]. The resumed fighting and the ongoing political instability were raising concerns among national and international stakeholders about possible spillover into neighbouring countries. The Secretary-General stated that in the event of further delays in the implementation of the Programme of Action, the Security Council should consider taking additional measures in consultation with the Regional Peace Initiative, the AU and other regional mechanisms. As a precautionary measure, and in accordance with paragraph 4 of resolution 1719(2006) [YUN 2006, p. 153], he had requested BINUB and MONUC to undertake contingency planning should the situation deteriorate further. Considering that the Tripartite Steering Committee for National Consultations on Transitional Justice Mechanisms was facing internal difficulties, particularly the Burundian members' non-compliance with the framework agreement governing its work—another cause for concern—and that corrective actions were needed to permit the Committee to credibly implement its mandate, the Secretary-General intended to revert shortly to the Security Council with a separate report on the implementation of resolution 1606(2005) [YUN 2005, p. 207].

Security Council press statement. Following a 22 May briefing [meeting 5897] on the situation in Burundi by the Executive Representative of the Secretary-General, Youssef Mahmoud, the Security Council reiterated [SC/9339-AFR/1703] its concern at the confrontation between Palipehutu-FNL and the national defence forces, following attacks by FNL in violation of the Comprehensive Ceasefire Agreement. It stressed the need for a cessation of hostilities and urged the parties to implement fully the Agreement. The Council noted with satisfaction that an FNL delegation had returned to Bujumbura and that the Joint Verification and Monitoring Mechanism had resumed its work. It expressed support and encouragement for the efforts of the Political Directorate of the Facilitator, and of the regional initiative to back the peace process, but emphasized its concern at the political tension and the paralysis of the National Assembly. The Council called on all political parties to find a solution to the impasse and return to the spirit of reconciliation and dialogue that had led to a successful transition. It urged the Government to fulfil its commitment to protect all Burundians, regardless of their political affiliation, and to prevent impunity for perpetrators of violence and violations of human rights, while adhering to the rule of law.

Report of Secretary-General (November). In his fourth report on BINUB [S/2008/745], the Secretary-General said that the Political Directorate and the Joint Verification and Monitoring Mechanism convened on 19 May in Bujumbura. Although the Government and Palipehutu-FNL issued a joint declaration on 26 May, in which they agreed to put an end to the hostilities that had erupted in April, the peace process drifted towards a deepening stalemate.

On 2 June, Government and Palipehutu-FNL delegates to the Joint Verification and Monitoring Mechanism adopted a joint operational plan outlining the demobilization and integration calendar for Palipehutu-FNL combatants. Also in June, the Political Directorate, including representatives of the Government and Palipehutu-FNL, met with the Group of Special Envoys for Burundi in Magaliesberg. The parties and the Group issued the Magaliesberg Communiqué, in which the Government and Palipehutu-FNL reaffirmed their commitment to seek common and comprehensive solutions to the impediments that had stymied past efforts towards the implementation of the peace process. By 21 July, about 2,100 Palipehutu-FNL elements had arrived at the first assembly area, in Rugazi commune, Bubanza Province; however, the Government publicly deplored the extremely low ratio of weapons to combatants and the absence of a list verifying the 21,000 combatants that Palipehutu-FNL claimed to have. Controversy ensued after Palipehutu-FNL Chairman Agathon Rwasa—who had returned to Burundi at the end of May— made public his letter of 27 July addressed to the South African Facilitator requesting that approximately half of all senior civilian and military positions in Government institutions be allocated to Palipehutu-FNL.

On 18 August, President Nkurunziza and Palipehutu-FNL Chairman Rwasa met in the presence of the Facilitator of the Burundi Peace Process, South African Minister of Defence Charles Nqakula, and committed to biweekly closed-door meetings. On 18 and 19 August, however, the President issued two decrees, establishing a commission to examine the combatant status of the alleged Palipehutu-FNL dissidents at Randa and Buramata communes, Bubanza Province, and officially recognizing them as Palipehutu-FNL deserters. That prompted Palipehutu-FNL, which had disowned the group, to publicly accuse the Government of sabotaging the peace process. Meanwhile, Chairman Rwasa sent a letter to the President on 26 August accusing the ruling party, CNDD-FDD, of assassination plots against himself and other senior Palipehutu-FNL leaders.

Despite those tensions, the Palipehutu-FNL Chairman met the President in Ngozi on 29 August, accompanied by the Facilitator and the Political Directorate. Their meeting resulted in the Ngozi Declaration, in which the responsibility of both leaders in resolving outstanding issues was clarified. Three issues were judged as potentially inconsistent with the Constitution, and the help of the Political Directorate was sought: recognition of Palipehutu-FNL as a political party under its current name; participation of Palipehutu-FNL as a parliamentary observer; and accommodation of Palipehutu-FNL members in the executive branch of the Government.

On 17 September, the Palipehutu-FNL Chairman submitted a memorandum to the Political Directorate stating that his movement would not comply with demobilization requirements prior to being registered as a political party under its current name. He proposed to exempt Palipehutu-FNL from having to comply with the Constitution regarding its name until after the 2010 elections, at which time a constitutional reform might be undertaken that would allow it to maintain its name. Separate Political Directorate meetings with President Nkurunziza and Chairman Rwasa on 26 September confirmed that the leaders remained deadlocked on the issues of political accommodation and military integration. No progress was made despite messages from the Regional Peace Initiative conveyed to President Nkurunziza and Chairman Rwasa on 6 November that the 31 December deadline for completing the implementation of the Comprehensive Ceasefire Agreement would have to be observed; the Government would have to accommodate Palipehutu-FNL in national institutions in conformity with the law; Palipehutu-FNL should spare no effort to send its combatants to assembly areas for the disarmament, demobilization and reintegration process; and Palipehutu-FNL would have to forgo the ethnic connotation in its name. In a disturbing development, reports of both Palipehutu-FNL and Government defence forces taking up new military positions were confirmed, contributing to public fears in western provinces about possible renewed armed clashes.

In other political developments, the paralysis affecting the work of the executive and legislative branches of Government over the previous year ended with the exclusion of 22 dissenting CNDD-FDD parliamentarians from the National Assembly, as the Constitutional Court ruled on 6 June that the continued presence in Parliament of those parliamentarians was unconstitutional because they no longer represented any elected political group or party. Their replacement by parliamentarians loyal to CNDD-FDD re-established the ruling party's simple majority. As a result, legislative activities resumed and an unprecedented number of laws were adopted, although the political opposition and some international observers questioned the Constitutional Court's ruling, and raised questions about the independence of the judiciary.

On 18 June, President Nkurunziza established by decree the Permanent National Independent Electoral Commission, which was welcomed by the country's political actors who, however, deplored the lack of consultation. The second parliamentary plenary session, which took place from June to August, was productive, adopting 20 laws, including two related directly to peace consolidation: the laws on the establishment of the National Security Council and the National Council on Unity and Reconciliation. In July, however, two of the 22 former CNDD-FDD parliamentarians who had been removed from their seats were arrested for allegedly threatening State security; a third was arrested in October on charges of assaulting a magistrate. On 6 October, the Ministry of the Interior issued an order regulating meetings and demonstrations of political parties and other associations. Between August and November, a number of members of the political opposition were arrested, along with several civil society and media representatives.

The Secretary-General urged the Government and Palipehutu-FNL to spare no efforts in making the necessary difficult compromises on issues that had hindered the implementation of the Agreement; called on both parties to heed the recent messages of the leaders of the Regional Peace Initiative; and urged Palipehutu-FNL to release the children associated with the movement immediately and unconditionally. Expressing concern about the increasing number of arrests of members of the political opposition and representatives of civil society and the media, the Secretary-General urged the authorities to respect the right to freedom of expression and assembly enshrined in the Constitution; and called on the authorities to allow peaceful assemblies, to desist from detaining persons for expressing their beliefs or opinions, and to guarantee due process and fair judicial review for all detainees. Finally, he recommended that the Security Council extend BINUB's mandate for an additional 12-month period following the expiration of its current mandate on 31 December 2008, while stressing that in light of the evolving situation on the ground, it would be important for the Council to conduct a review of the mandate by June 2009. By resolution 1858(2008), the Council followed this recommendation (see below).

Year-end developments. A later report [S/2009/270] of the Secretary-General covered significant breakthroughs in the peace process towards the end of the year. At the Summit of the Heads of State and Government of the Great Lakes Region (Bujumbura, Burundi, 4 December), the Government of Burundi, Palipehutu-FNL and attending Heads of State signed a Declaration in which Palipehutu-FNL agreed to consult its membership, by 31 December, on changing the movement's name in compliance with Burundian law. The Declaration also called for the commencement of the disarmament, demobilization and reintegration of Palipehutu-FNL and the political integration of its leadership. The President of Burundi, who committed himself to reserving 33 civil service posts for senior members of the movement, also reiterated his commitment to release FNL prisoners.

The Presidency requested the Palipehutu-FNL Chairman to submit by 24 December a list of members of the movement to be considered for the proposed posts, although Palipehutu-FNL maintained that the Government should first consult it on the level of those posts. On 12 December, the President issued a decree outlining the mandate and organization of the Electoral Commission that superseded the initial decree issued in June. The new decree introduced measures significantly increasing the prerogatives of the Executive over the Commission.

Despite the repeal in November of the order by the Minister of the Interior significantly limiting the activities of political parties and associations, restrictions on the freedom of assembly of opposition political parties imposed by local administrators affiliated with the ruling CNDD-FDD party persisted.

Security Council consideration. On 11 December [meeting 6037], the Security Council was briefed by Charles Nqakula, Facilitator of the Burundi Peace Process, and Anders Lidén, Chairman of the Burundi configuration of the Peacebuilding Commission.

SECURITY COUNCIL ACTION

On 22 December [meeting 6057], the Security Council unanimously adopted **resolution 1858(2008)**. The draft [S/2008/802] was submitted by Belgium and France.

The Security Council,

Recalling its resolutions and the statements by its President on Burundi, in particular resolutions 1719(2006) of 25 October 2006 and 1791(2007) of 19 December 2007,

Reaffirming its strong commitment to the sovereignty, independence, territorial integrity and unity of Burundi,

Welcoming the Declaration of the Summit of the Heads of State and Government of the Great Lakes Region on the Burundi Peace Process, which took place in Bujumbura on 4 December 2008, and the agreements reached between the Government of Burundi and the Parti pour la libération du peuple hutu-Forces nationales de libération,

Paying tribute to the Regional Peace Initiative on Burundi, the South African Facilitation, the African Union and the Political Directorate for their sustained engagement in support of Burundi's peace consolidation efforts to promote the full implementation of the Comprehensive Ceasefire Agreement signed on 7 September 2006 at Dar-es-Salaam, United Republic of Tanzania, by the Government of Burundi and the Parti pour la libération du peuple hutu-Forces nationales de libération,

Taking note of the progress achieved by Burundi in key peace consolidation areas, as well as the remaining challenges, in particular implementing the Comprehensive Ceasefire Agreement with the Parti pour la libération du peuple hutu-Forces nationales de libération, consolidating democratically elected institutions, strengthening good governance, completing the disarmament, demobilization and reintegration process, and taking forward the reform of the security sector, including ensuring that the security forces and justice institutions effectively protect human rights and the rule of law,

Welcoming the establishment of the Permanent National Independent Electoral Commission, recalling the need for nominations of its members to be through an independent and inclusive process, and recalling the importance that the elections scheduled in 2010 are prepared in the spirit of reconciliation and dialogue enshrined in the Constitution of Burundi that had led to a successful transition,

Emphasizing the need for the United Nations system and the international community to maintain their support for peace consolidation and long-term development in Burundi, welcoming the continued engagement of the Peacebuilding Commission on Burundi and the recent visit of the delegation led by the Chairperson of the Burundi configuration of the Commission, and taking note of the June 2008 biannual review of progress in the implementation of the Strategic Framework for Peacebuilding in Burundi and of the briefing by the Chairperson of the Burundi configuration of the Commission on 11 December 2008,

Recognizing the importance of transitional justice in promoting lasting reconciliation among all the people of Burundi, and welcoming progress in the preparations for national consultations on the establishment of transitional justice mechanisms, including through the establishment of a technical follow-up committee and a forum of civil society representatives,

Noting with concern the continuing human rights violations and restrictions on civil liberties, including arrests of members of the political opposition and representatives of civil society, the media and trade unions, and welcoming the decision of the Government of Burundi to rescind its order to regulate meetings and demonstrations of political parties and associations,

Welcoming the efforts of the Burundian authorities to fight impunity, in particular the trial and conviction of some of the perpetrators of the Muyinga massacre,

Recalling its resolutions 1325(2000) of 31 October 2000 and 1820(2008) of 19 June 2008 on women and peace and security, its resolution 1674(2006) of 28 April 2006 on the protection of civilians in armed conflict and its resolution 1612(2005) of 26 July 2005 on children and armed conflict,

Having considered the fourth report of the Secretary-General on the United Nations Integrated Office in Burundi,

1. *Decides* to extend until 31 December 2009 the mandate of the United Nations Integrated Office in Burundi, as set out in resolution 1719(2006) and renewed in resolution 1791(2007);

2. *Urges* the Government of Burundi and the Parti pour la libération du peuple hutu-Forces nationales de libération to make every effort to implement, before 31 December 2008, the agreements they reached on 4 December 2008 so as to bring this last phase of the peace process to a successful conclusion, and calls upon both parties to desist from any action that may create tension or bring about the resumption of hostilities and to resolve outstanding issues through dialogue and in a spirit of cooperation;

3. *Calls upon* the Parti pour la libération du peuple hutu-Forces nationales de libération to work with the Government of Burundi, the Joint Verification and Monitoring Mechanism and all international partners in order to encourage all its combatants to move without conditionalities to assembly areas and to fully implement the disarmament, demobilization and reinsertion process;

4. *Encourages* the leaders of the Regional Peace Initiative on Burundi, the African Union, the South African Facilitation, the Political Directorate and other international partners to sustain their efforts in order to assist the parties in the implementation of the Declaration of 4 December 2008 and to remain actively engaged on the ground to monitor the process and to ensure its sustainability;

5. *Reiterates its request* for the Secretary-General, including through the United Nations Integrated Office in Burundi, to play a robust political role in support of all facets of the peace process, in full coordination with subregional, regional and international partners;

6. *Encourages* the Government of Burundi to take the necessary measures to create an environment conducive to the holding of free, fair and peaceful elections in 2010, and welcomes the readiness of the United Nations to assist in the process;

7. *Requests* the Executive Representative of the Secretary-General for Burundi to facilitate and promote dialogue among national and international stakeholders, in particular in the context of the upcoming elections, while continuing to support their efforts to sustain peace and stability;

8. *Encourages* the Government of Burundi to pursue its efforts regarding peace consolidation challenges, in particular democratic governance, justice, security reforms and the protection of human rights;

9. *Encourages* the Government of Burundi, the Peacebuilding Commission and national and international partners to honour the commitments they have made under the Strategic Framework for Peacebuilding in Burundi, and requests the Commission, with support from the United Nations Integrated Office in Burundi and the United Nations country team, to continue to assist the Government in laying the foundations for sustainable peace and security and long-term development in Burundi and in mobilizing the resources needed to achieve these aims, including for the coming elections;

10. *Underscores* the importance of the disarmament, demobilization and reintegration process, and urges all international partners, in particular the United Nations Integrated Office in Burundi, the United Nations Development Programme and the World Bank, to ensure that there are no gaps in resources and capacities during the interim period between the Multi-country Demobilization and Reintegration Programme and the establishment of the Burundi-specific trust fund mechanism;

11. *Encourages*, in this regard, the Government of Burundi, in collaboration with all international partners, to elaborate a disarmament, demobilization and reintegration strategy and to lay the foundations for the sustainable socio-economic reintegration of demobilized soldiers, ex-combatants, returning refugees, the displaced and other vulnerable groups affected by the conflict, particularly women and children, in accordance with Security Council resolutions 1325(2000), 1612(2005), 1674(2006) and 1820(2008);

12. *Also encourages* the Government of Burundi, with the support of the United Nations Integrated Office in Burundi and other partners, to ensure that national consultations on the establishment of transitional justice mechanisms are begun as soon as possible, without further delay;

13. *Further encourages* the Government of Burundi to pursue its efforts to broaden respect for and protection of human rights, including through the establishment of a National Independent Human Rights Commission, bearing in mind the Paris Principles outlined in the annex to General Assembly resolution 48/134 of 20 December 1993, and further encourages it to end impunity and to take the necessary measures to ensure that its citizens fully enjoy their civil, political, social, economic and cultural rights without fear or intimidation, as enshrined in the Constitution of Burundi and provided for by international human rights instruments, including those ratified by Burundi;

14. *Expresses, in particular, its concern* at the continuing sexual and gender-based violence, and urges the Government of Burundi to take the necessary steps, including through specific legislation, to prevent further violations and to ensure that those responsible are brought to justice, in accordance with international law;

15. *Demands* that the Parti pour la libération du peuple hutu-Forces nationales de libération and other armed groups release unconditionally and without further delay all children associated with them, and emphasizes the need for their sustainable reintegration and reinsertion;

16. *Urges* the United Nations Integrated Office in Burundi to strengthen current provisions for cooperation with the United Nations Organization Mission in the Democratic Republic of the Congo, within the limits of their respective capacities and current mandates;

17. *Encourages* the Executive Representative to pursue his action to enhance the integration and effectiveness of United Nations efforts on the ground in support of the implementation of the Strategic Framework for Peacebuilding in Burundi and of the recovery and development priorities of the Government and people of Burundi;

18. *Requests* the Secretary-General to report to the Council by May 2009 on the implementation of the mandate of the United Nations Integrated Office in Burundi, including on the results of the technical assessment mission that he intends to conduct early in 2009, and to incorporate in his report any recommendations that may guide the Council in deciding on the future direction of the Integrated Office;

19. *Decides* to remain actively seized of the matter.

Peacebuilding Commission

Reporting on its second session [A/63/92-S/2008/417], the Peacebuilding Commission said that on 6 February, the Burundi configuration agreed on an annual workplan, focusing on fulfilling the engagements reflected in the Strategic Framework for Peacebuilding in Burundi [YUN 2007, p. 52] and in the Monitoring and Tracking Mechanism, monitoring the peacebuilding process, and providing advice to relevant stakeholders. The Chair of the configuration participated in a meeting (Cape Town, South Africa, 22–23 February) of special envoys for Burundi, which agreed on the Programme of Action to Take Further the Burundi Peace Process. In March [A/62/760-S/2008/192], the Chairpersons of the Peacebuilding Commission and the Commission's Burundi configuration transmitted to the General Assembly, the Security Council and the Economic and Social Council the conclusions and recommendations adopted by the Burundi configuration [PBC/2/BDI/7] at its Cape Town meeting. In discussions held on 28 and 29 February, the Chair of the configuration sensitized the World Bank Group and the International Monetary Fund on the objectives of the Strategic Framework and the engagement between Burundi and the Commission. A configuration delegation travelled to Burundi (10–15 May) on a field mission to obtain information about the situation and to review preparations for the first biannual review of the Strategic Framework.

Among its conclusions, the Commission expressed concern over the withdrawal of Palipehutu-FNL from the Joint Verification and Monitoring Mechanism. It commended the renewed efforts of the South African Facilitation to get Palipehutu-FNL to resume its participation in the Mechanism. The Commission also noted the establishment of a Political Directorate, to be based in Bujumbura, to facilitate dialogue on political obstacles during implementation of the Agreement, promote trust between the parties and help implement political arrangements. The Commission recommended that the Government explore ways to resolve politically its differences with Palipehutu-FNL leaders, take measures to build confidence, and create conditions for the return of Palipehutu-FNL, its reintegration into national institutions, and the resumption of its participation in the Mechanism and in the Directorate. The Government and stakeholders should continue dialogue to resolve differences and work through national democratic institutions to ease tensions. The South African Facilitation, the Regional Peace Initiative, the AU and the Political Directorate should continue to help ensure the implementation of the Agreement within the 30 June time frame, and allow the Directorate to monitor political and socio-economic reintegration, as stipulated in the programme of action for July–December. The Secretary-General should play a robust political role in support of the peace process, in coordination with regional and international partners. The Security Council should monitor the situation, in particular implementation of the Agreement, and consider appropriate actions for its effective implementation. The Assembly and the Economic and Social Council should support the programme of action and the efforts by the Facilitation and the Regional Peace Initiative. Donors and other partners should support the Government's efforts, including the financing of incentives for the socio-economic reintegration of FNL and other demobilized combatants.

Biannual review of Strategic Framework (June). On 23 June, the Commission considered the first report [PBC/2/BDI/10] reviewing progress in the implementation of the Strategic Framework. The report analysed trends and evaluated progress in the five main challenge areas: promotion of good governance; implementation of the Comprehensive Ceasefire Agreement; the security sector; justice, promotion of human rights and action to combat impunity; and the land-use issue and socio-economic recovery. It also assessed mutual commitments as defined in the Strategic Framework. According to the report, the Government, the Commission and stakeholders had made a considerable effort to implement the commitments and contributions to peacebuilding. However, the complexity and dynamic character of the challenge required a more continuous commitment to overcome the principal peacebuilding risks. It made a number of recommendations (see below) for strengthening commitments and set out actions to be taken by different stakeholders.

The Commission, in its review [PCB/2/BDI/9] of the first biannual report, welcomed the progress made in the priority areas set out in the Strategic Framework and the matrix of the Mechanism, in particular steps taken to reinforce governance, including the establishment of the framework for dialogue and the operationalization of the Anti-Corruption Brigade and Court. Among its recommendations, the Government was requested to submit a draft law on succession to the National Assembly. It should seek assistance to address the deficiencies in the electoral legal framework observed in 2005 [YUN 2005, p. 208] and present by December a revised draft legal framework reflecting

Burundi's political reality, consensus and support. The electoral commission should be operational by early 2009 in order to manage the 2010 and subsequent elections. The international community should help the Government identify resources and provide financial and technical support. The Government should develop a comprehensive security sector reform plan, including independent parliamentary oversight of the national defence and police forces and the intelligence service, with emphasis on professionalism and political neutrality. It should ensure that the defence force was provided for and that personnel requirements were commensurate with defence needs. In the area of disarmament, demobilization and reintegration, the Government should ensure that economic and social opportunities, including community-based programmes, were available to former combatants to enable them to reintegrate into communities. The Government should work with BINUB, civil society and other stakeholders to assist the Tripartite Steering Committee in launching national consultations on establishing transitional justice mechanisms. The Government should pursue perpetrators of violence against women and children and submit to the National Assembly a comprehensive law to eradicate gender-based violence, as well as a draft law establishing a national human rights commission. The National Assembly should adopt, as a priority, the revised draft criminal code. Concerning land use and socio-economic recovery, the Government should facilitate dialogue and consultation on land reform, the mechanisms for resolving land disputes and the harmonization of approaches. The Commission would continue to mobilize the required international support. The Government should implement integrated community-based strategies for refugees and returnees, with a focus on women and children, and coordinate international assistance through the Partners Coordination Group. The Commission would give priority to socio-economic recovery; it would focus on the possible effects of the global food crisis and rising fuel costs on the country's already fragile socio-economic situation to ensure that it did not undermine the peace consolidation efforts.

On 23 June [A/62/888-S/2008/442], the Acting Chairperson of the Peacebuilding Commission and the Chairman of the Burundi configuration drew the attention of the Presidents of the General Assembly, the Security Council and the Economic and Social Council to the recommendations of the biannual review, particularly the recommendation pertaining to the mobilization and coordination of international assistance.

The Commission, reporting on its third session [A/64/341-S/2009/444], stated that, following the mission (21–23 October) to Burundi by the Chair of the Burundi configuration to discuss with stakeholders opportunities for and challenges of mutual engagement, the configuration adopted a workplan focusing on support to the peace process, notably in the disarmament, demobilization and reintegration of Palipehutu-FNL; assistance to Burundi in creating an environment for free, fair and transparent national elections in 2010; support to refugees; and land issues and the socio-economic reintegration of ex-combatants. The Commission agreed to give priority to improving its impact on the ground, and efficient communication on the Strategic Framework and its relationship with complementary tools, such as support from the Peacebuilding Fund and the Burundi poverty reduction strategy paper. On 12 December, the Burundi configuration addressed developments in the peace process with the participation of the Facilitator of the peace process, who briefed members on the outcome of the Great Lakes Region Summit meeting (4 December) (see p. 150) and on the challenges relating to disarmament, demobilization and reintegration and the political integration of Palipehutu-FNL. Members of the configuration confirmed their support for efforts to address those challenges and their readiness to contribute to funding for disarmament.

The Commission, on 16 December [PBC/3/BDI/1], adopted the conclusions of the Burundi configuration, welcoming the setting-up by the Government and the World Bank of the Transitional Demobilization and Reintegration Project for Disarmament, Demobilization and Reintegration, and calling for additional contributions to the Project's Trust Fund. It called on the international community to extend logistical, material and financial support for establishing designated assembly areas for cantonment and other preparatory tasks for the immediate commencement of the disarmament, demobilization and reintegration process. It urged Palipehutu-FNL to release all children associated with it, and called for international support for speedy reunification with their families and their reintegration and rehabilitation. The Commission encouraged the Government to develop a longer-term strategy for the sustainable socio-economic reintegration of combatants and others, including previously demobilized combatants, soldiers and police.

On 22 December, the Security Council, in resolution 1858(2008) (see p. 150), took note of the June biannual review of the implementation of the Strategic Framework.

(For further information on the Peacebuilding Commission, see p. 54.)

Children and armed conflict

In February [S/AC.51/2008/6], the Chairman of the Security Council Working Group on Children and Armed Conflict transmitted the conclusions adopted by the Group with respect to the Secretary-General's 2007 report on children and armed conflict in Burundi [YUN 2007, p. 144]. The Group expressed concern regarding delays in implementing the Comprehensive Ceasefire Agreement; the suspension of participation of Palipehutu-FNL in the Joint Verification and Monitoring Mechanism; the failure to formally release children associated with Palipehutu-FNL, and reports of further child recruitment and use by Palipehutu-FNL; and the alarming increase in cases of rape and other grave sexual violence committed against children, especially girls, and the prevailing impunity concerning those cases, despite positive steps taken by the Government to address the situation and prosecute perpetrators. The Group insisted on the need for further international support to assist disarmament, demobilization and reintegration programmes for children and other programmes designed to improve child protection and awareness-raising on the rights of the child.

BINUB

The United Nations Integrated Office in Burundi (BINUB), established by Security Council resolution 1719(2006) [YUN 2006, p. 153] to support the Government in its effort towards long-term peace and stability and coordinate the work of the UN agencies in the country, focused on peace consolidation and democratic governance; disarmament, demobilization and reintegration of ex-combatants; security sector reform; promotion and protection of human rights; measures to end impunity through a truth and reconciliation commission and special tribunal; and donor and UN agency coordination. Headquartered in the capital, Bujumbura, BINUB was headed by the Secretary-General's Executive Representative for Burundi, Youssef Mahmoud (Tunisia).

Financing

In December, the General Assembly considered the Secretary-General's October report [A/63/346/Add.3] on proposed resource requirements for BINUB totalling $37,898,400 for 2009, as well as the related ACABQ report [A/63/593]. On 24 December, in section XI of **resolution 63/263** (see p. 1548), the Assembly endorsed ACABQ's recommendations and approved budgets totalling $429,497,600 for the 27 special political missions, including BINUB.

ONUB

The United Nations Operation in Burundi (ONUB), established in 2004 by Security Council resolution 1545(2004) [YUN 2004, p. 145], concluded its mandate on 31 December 2006 [YUN 2006, p. 157] and was replaced by BINUB on 1 January 2007.

Financing

In January, the Secretary-General submitted the performance report [A/62/668] on the ONUB budget for the period 1 July 2006–30 June 2007, with expenditures of $118,534,100 against an appropriation of $128,536,700, making for an unencumbered balance of $10,002,600, together with other income of $20,727,200. In April, ACABQ recommended [A/62/781/Add.2] that the amount of $24,337,000, representing net cash available in the Special Account of the Operation as at 30 June 2007, be credited to Member States in a manner to be determined by the General Assembly, and endorsed the recommendation of the Secretary-General that a decision be deferred to the sixty-third session of the Assembly on the treatment of the amount of $6,392,800, representing a cash shortfall in the Special Account of the Operation as at 30 June 2007 from the total amount of $30,729,800.

GENERAL ASSEMBLY ACTION

On 20 June [meeting 109], the General Assembly, on the recommendation of the Fifth Committee [A/62/866], adopted **resolution 62/253** without vote [agenda item 141].

Financing of the United Nations Operation in Burundi

The General Assembly,

Having considered the report of the Secretary-General on the financing of the United Nations Operation in Burundi, the related report of the Advisory Committee on Administrative and Budgetary Questions and the statements made by the representative of the Secretary-General and the Chairperson of the Advisory Committee,

Recalling Security Council resolution 1545(2004) of 21 May 2004, by which the Council authorized, for an initial period of six months as from 1 June 2004, with the intention to renew it for further periods, the deployment of a peacekeeping operation called the United Nations Operation in Burundi, and the subsequent resolutions by which the Council extended the mandate of the Operation, the last of which was resolution 1692(2006) of 30 June 2006, by which the Council extended the mandate of the Operation until 31 December 2006,

Recalling also its resolution 58/312 of 18 June 2004 on the financing of the Operation and its subsequent resolutions thereon, the latest of which was resolution 61/9 B of 29 June 2007,

Reaffirming the general principles underlying the financing of United Nations peacekeeping operations, as stated in General Assembly resolutions 1874(S-IV) of 27 June 1963, 3101(XXVIII) of 11 December 1973 and 55/235 of 23 December 2000,

1. *Takes note* of the status of contributions to the United Nations Operation in Burundi as at 31 March 2008, including the credits in the amount of 27.5 million United States dollars;

2. *Endorses* the conclusions and recommendations contained in the report of the Advisory Committee on Administrative and Budgetary Questions, subject to the provisions of the present resolution, and requests the Secretary-General to ensure their full implementation;

Financial performance report for the period from 1 July 2006 to 30 June 2007

3. *Takes note* of the report of the Secretary-General on the financial performance of the Operation for the period from 1 July 2006 to 30 June 2007;

4. *Also takes note* of paragraphs 14 and 15 of the report of the Advisory Committee;

5. *Decides* that Member States that have fulfilled their financial obligations to the Operation shall be credited with their respective share of the unencumbered balance and other income in the amount of 30,729,800 dollars in respect of the financial period ended 30 June 2007, in accordance with the levels updated in General Assembly resolution 61/243 of 22 December 2006, and taking into account the scale of assessments for 2007, as set out in its resolution 61/237 of 22 December 2006;

6. *Also decides* that, for Member States that have not fulfilled their financial obligations to the Operation, their share of the unencumbered balance and other income in the amount of 30,729,800 dollars in respect of the financial period ended 30 June 2007 shall be set off against their outstanding obligations, in accordance with the scheme set out in paragraph 5 above;

7. *Further decides* that the decrease of 378,700 dollars in the estimated staff assessment income in respect of the financial period ended 30 June 2007 shall be set off against the credits from the amount of 30,729,800 dollars referred to in paragraphs 5 and 6 above;

8. *Decides* to include in the provisional agenda of its sixty-third session the item entitled "Financing of the United Nations Operation in Burundi".

In November, the Secretary-General submitted a report [A/63/551] on ONUB financing providing details on the final disposition of its assets, with a total inventory value of $59,152,442 as at 3 November. Of that amount, $51,336,500 in assets had been transferred to other missions or for temporary storage at the United Nations Logistics Base at Brindisi, Italy; $1,936,200 in assets had been sold; $2,799,400 in assets had been donated to the Government of Burundi; and $3,080,300 in assets had been written off or lost. The Secretary-General requested that the General Assembly take note of the report.

On 24 December (**decision 63/552**), the General Assembly decided that the agenda item on ONUB financing would remain for consideration during its resumed sixty-third (2009) session.

Central African Republic

The political situation in the Central African Republic in 2008 continued to be dominated by intensified preparations for the inclusive political dialogue, aimed at ending the recurrent political and security crises in the country, which was held in the capital, Bangui, in December. The overall political, security and socio-economic situation, however, remained fragile, and was compounded by a weak economy, multifaceted social problems and impunity, along with severe security challenges, particularly in the northern and south-eastern parts of the country. The United Nations Peacebuilding Support Office in the Central African Republic (BONUCA) continued to assist the Government in its efforts to consolidate peace in the country. In June, the Peacebuilding Commission added the country to its agenda and established the Central African Republic configuration.

Political and security situation

Report of Secretary-General (June). In his report [S/2008/410] on the situation in the Central African Republic and on BONUCA activities from January to June, submitted in response to Security Council presidential statement S/PRST/2001/25 [YUN 2001, p. 156], the Secretary-General noted that the Dialogue Preparatory Committee had completed its work and, on 25 April, submitted its report to President François Bozizé. Facilitated by BONUCA and the International Organization of la Francophonie, and presided over by the Centre for Humanitarian Dialogue, the Committee brought together the country's main political, social and rebel groups for substantive discussions on political and governance issues, the security situation and political-military groups, and socio-economic development. In line with the Committee's recommendations, President Bozizé, on 8 June, set up a 15-member committee to help organize the dialogue.

On 9 May, the Government concluded a peace agreement with the Armée populaire pour la restauration de la démocratie (APRD) rebel movement, the last of the country's three major rebel groups to sign a peace agreement. The agreement, signed in Libreville under the auspices of President Omar Bongo Ondimba of Gabon, provided for an immediate cessation of hostilities, the cantonment of APRD fighters in their current positions, the rehabilitation of conflict-affected areas, and the creation of security conditions for the holding of the inclusive political dialogue. It also foresaw the adoption of a general amnesty law.

The Special Representative of the Secretary-General in the Central African Republic, François Lonseny Fall, continuing his efforts to facilitate preparations for the dialogue, met with the APRD leadership in February to persuade APRD to participate in the Preparatory Committee. The Special Representative also continued to consult closely with the Committee of External Partners, based in Bangui, and with the leadership of the subregional peacekeeping force for the Central African Republic, the Multinational Force of the Central African Economic and Monetary Community (FOMUC). BONUCA organized training on dialogue and negotiation for members of the Dialogue Preparatory Committee, and facilitated the establishment of the operations of the United Nations Mission in the Central African Republic and Chad (MINURCAT).

The security situation remained relatively stable in Bangui, despite isolated cases of criminal activity. Elsewhere, apart from localized clashes, there was a decrease in the intensity of conflict between Government forces and rebel groups in the north. However, acts of indiscipline and lawlessness among defence and security forces, especially in their relations with the general population, continued to increase. Two new security phenomena were vigilante groups defending against highway bandits in the north-western provinces of Ouham, Ouham-Pendé and Nana-Grébizi; and well-armed and -equipped poachers active in the Vakaga and Haute-Kotto prefectures. A new zone of tension emerged in the south-east of the country, into which armed elements—believed to be renegades from Uganda's LRA—had reportedly infiltrated from their bases in southern Sudan. The security situation improved significantly in the north-eastern provinces of Vakaga and Bamingui-Bangoran following the deployment, in March, of the European Union Force (EUFOR) and the peace agreement signed in 2007 between the Government and the rebel group Union des forces démocratiques pour le rassemblement (UFDR) [YUN 2007, p. 146].

Overall political and operational command for FOMUC was scheduled to be transferred from the Economic and Monetary Community of Central Africa (CEMAC) to the Economic Community of Central African States (ECCAS) as at 1 July 2008, pursuant to the decision of the ECCAS Council of Ministers taken at its meeting in Libreville, Gabon, on 25 and 26 February.

The majority of the population in the north-west and north-east continued to live in fear and insecurity owing to the activities of Government armed forces, rebel groups and criminal gangs. Crime had also become a major impediment to social and economic stability, engendering massive population displacements and inhibiting the free movement of persons and humanitarian operations. Following attacks against the relatively peaceful south-eastern region in February and early March, reportedly by LRA infiltrators, the Office for the Coordination of Humanitarian Affairs organized a joint assessment mission from 22 to 25 March with UNICEF, BONUCA and the UN Department of Safety and Security to evaluate the security and human rights situation, as well as the status of protection of civilians.

Following meetings with the Special Representative of the Secretary-General for Children and Armed Conflict, who visited the country from 27 to 31 May, APRD and UFDR leaders agreed to release all children participating in their movements for eventual reintegration in communities. BONUCA also continued to provide civic education training, promoting the ideals of peace, democratic values and fundamental rights and freedoms.

The Secretary-General observed that Government efforts to improve respect for human rights needed to be intensified and made irreversible as a first step in curbing the culture of impunity. Urging the authorities to do more to strengthen respect for the rule of law through the promotion and protection of human rights and fundamental freedoms, and to deal decisively with impunity, the Secretary-General also called on the international community to provide assistance to the country in restoring its judicial sector.

Comprehensive Peace Agreement. On 21 June, the Central African Republic, APRD and UFDR signed the Comprehensive Peace Agreement in Libreville.

On 27 June, following a briefing by the Secretary-General's Special Representative on the situation in the Central African Republic, the Security Council, in a press statement [SC/9380-AFR/1721], welcomed that agreement and called on all other political-military groups in the country to join it. The Council commended President Bongo of Gabon and Colonel Muammar Al-Qadhafi of the Libyan Arab Jamahiriya for the assistance they provided to the parties in order to reach the comprehensive peace agreement and the agreements of Sirte (February 2007) [YUN 2007, p. 146], Birao (April 2007) [ibid.] and Libreville (June 2008). It called on the Government and the rebel movements to implement fully those agreements and to convene, as soon as possible, the inclusive political dialogue.

Report of Secretary-General (November). In his report [S/2008/733] covering the June to November period, the Secretary-General stated that the political situation had been dominated by efforts to create a conducive environment for the convening of an inclusive political dialogue as a crucial first step towards national reconciliation and stabilization. The Libreville Comprehensive Peace Agreement signed on 21 June between the Government and the APRD and UFDR rebel groups called for disarmament, demobilization and reintegration, along with amnesty for rebel fighters and their leaders. The withdrawal of APRD and the coalition of opposition parties, Union des forces vives de la nation (UFVN), from the dialogue process in response to the draft amnesty laws tabled by the Government before an extraordinary session of the National Assembly, however, prompted the Secretary-General's Special Representative to engage in intensive consultations with national stakeholders and regional and international partners, with a view to breaking the deadlock and reviving the stalled peace process. To facilitate the resolution of the political deadlock, the Secretary-General met twice with President Bozizé to encourage him to take the necessary measures to facilitate the holding of the dialogue as soon as possible.

On 29 September, the National Assembly adopted a single consolidated general amnesty law covering offences committed by Government security and defence forces and rebel elements from 15 March 2003 to the date of the promulgation of the law by President Bozizé on 13 October—except for crimes falling within the jurisdiction of the International Criminal Court. APRD and UFVN, however, rejected the law, describing the conditions set out therein as unrealistic and unhelpful for the reconciliation process. The Follow-up Committee to the Libreville Comprehensive Peace Agreement referred the matter to President Bongo of Gabon, in his capacity as mediator of the Central African Republic peace process. Meanwhile, President Bozizé expanded the membership of the Dialogue Organizing Committee to include opposition and rebel movements; and the Government released from prison 12 rebel leaders and fighters in compliance with the Amnesty Law—a gesture welcomed by the President of APRD, who instructed his field commanders to identify sites for cantonment of rebel fighters. Despite the progress made towards the holding of the dialogue, the Secretary-General remained concerned that new rebel groups, including splinter factions from existing groups, had emerged; they considered themselves as being left out of the peace process and could constitute a new threat to peace and stability.

The security situation in Bangui and its surrounding areas remained relatively calm, as in the north-eastern prefectures of Vakaga and Bamingui-Bangoran—traditional strongholds of UFDR—where, however, splinter groups had emerged. Intermittent clashes occurred in the north-western and north-central parts of the country between Government forces and various rebel groups, especially APRD. While bandit activity decreased with the beginning of the rainy season, vigilante activities in Ouham-Pendé Prefecture evolved into armed militias supporting the Government, giving rise to reprisal attacks by APRD against local populations. The absence of State authority in the south-eastern prefecture of Haut-Mbomou was a concern, as were poachers in the eastern and north-eastern prefectures of Vakaga and Haute-Kotto.

In July, the operational responsibilities for the subregional peace force in the Central African Republic, FOMUC, were transferred from the six-member CEMAC to the 10-member ECCAS. Its regional peace force, the Mission de consolidation de la paix en Centrafrique (MICOPAX), was mandated in September by the Follow-up Committee to the Libreville Comprehensive Peace Agreement to supervise the implementation of an immediate ceasefire. Among other training initiatives, BONUCA provided capacity-building support to enhance the operational capabilities of 87 police officers and 40 gendarmes through training in criminal investigations, information-gathering, professional standards and ethics. It also continued to support MINURCAT in implementing its mandate in the Central African Republic.

In June, the Peacebuilding Fund approved for funding a priority plan addressing the immediate needs of the country in security sector reform, good governance and the rule of law, and revitalization of communities affected by conflict. The Secretary-General reported that he had allocated $10 million from the Fund for those priorities. The Peacebuilding Support Office and the Multi-Donor Trust Fund of the United Nations Development Programme fielded two missions to support implementation. A National Steering Committee, co-chaired by the Minister of State for Planning, the Economy and International Cooperation and the Special Representative, selected nine projects for a total amount of over $5.4 million to be implemented with national partners.

The Secretary-General renewed his appeal to all national stakeholders, in particular the Government and the armed groups, to work together within the framework of the signed peace agreements and to address their differences by peaceful means. BONUCA having published its first public report on the human rights situation in the country in October, the Secretary-General also urged the authorities to strengthen the rule of law and promote good governance by ensuring the promotion and protection of human rights and addressing the culture of impunity, with a view to its eradication.

Security Council consideration. On 2 December [meeting 6027], the Secretary-General's Special Representative, Mr. Fall, and the Chair of the Peacebuilding Commission's Central African Republic configuration, Jan Grauls, briefed the Security Council on the situation in the country.

Year-end developments. The inclusive political dialogue was held in Bangui from 8 to 20 December with the participation of representatives of the presidential majority, the democratic opposition, other political parties, civil society, Government authorities and the armed political groups. UN representatives and regional and international partners of the Central African Republic also attended. The dialogue provided an occasion for reviewing the main problems that had afflicted the country since independence and for proposing solutions aimed at breaking the cycle of crises that the country had been experiencing. Three committees focused on: political matters and governance; the security situation and armed groups; and socio-economic development. Recommendations adopted in a plenary session included establishing a new Government gathering the entities participating in the dialogue; an independent electoral commission to prepare the 2010 elections; a steering committee on disarmament, demobilization and reintegration; a high court of justice; and a follow-up committee on implementing the recommendations of the dialogue.

BONUCA

The mission of the United Nations Peacebuilding Support Office in the Central African Republic (BONUCA), established by the Security Council in 2000 [YUN 2000, p. 162], was to support Government efforts to consolidate peace and national reconciliation, strengthen democratic institutions and facilitate international mobilization of political support and resources for national reconstruction and economic recovery. In addition, the Office was tasked with promoting public awareness of human rights and monitoring developments in that field. BONUCA was headed by the Special Representative of the Secretary-General, François Lonseny Fall (Guinea).

Extension of mandate. In his November report [S/2008/733], the Secretary-General recommended to the Security Council that the mandate of BONUCA be extended for an additional year, from 1 January to 31 December 2009, considering it crucial for the authorities of the Central African Republic to receive the necessary support in implementing the conclusions of the forthcoming inclusive political dialogue. He also announced his intention to prepare proposals for an integrated UN presence in the country.

On 23 December [S/2008/809], the Council took note of the Secretary-General's recommendation. It also acknowledged the need to establish an integrated UN office in the Central African Republic, and looked forward to the Secretary-General's recommendations in that regard by 28 February 2009.

Financing

In October [A/63/346/Add.3], the Secretary-General submitted requirements for BONUCA for 2009 amounting to $8,818,100, as well as estimated overexpenditures in 2008 in the amount of $490,200. In December [A/63/593], ACABQ endorsed the resources requested, subject to its observations and recommendations. On 24 December, in section XI of **resolution 63/263** (see p. 1548), the General Assembly endorsed the ACABQ recommendations and approved budgets totalling $429,497,600 for the 27 special political missions, including BONUCA.

Peacebuilding Commission

The President of the Security Council, on 30 May [A/62/864-S/2008/383], referred the Peacebuilding Commission's Chairperson to the 6 March request by the Minister of Foreign Affairs, Regional Integration and Francophonie of the Central African Republic that the country be placed on the Commission's agenda. The President stated that the Council supported the request, and invited the Commission to provide advice and recommendations on: the situation in the Central African Republic, particularly in the establishment and conduct of an inclusive political dialogue; action by national authorities and support from the international community to develop an effective, accountable and sustainable national security sector system; and the restoration of the rule of law, including respect for human rights and good governance. The Commission could play a critical role in enhancing coordination and coherence within the UN system and among the wider international community in consolidating the Central African Republic's peacebuilding efforts.

Responding on 17 June [A/62/889-S/2008/419], the Commission Chairperson informed the Council President that the Commission's Organizational Committee had agreed both to the request and to establish a country-specific configuration, to be chaired by Belgium. The Commission would establish, in consultation with the country's authorities, the priorities and programme of work of the Central African Republic configuration, and would inform the Council of its preliminary findings and any progress in its consideration of the situation in the country.

In a 27 June press statement [SC/9380], the Security Council welcomed the inclusion of the Central African Republic in the Commission's agenda and the creation of a country-specific configuration. To support that work, the Council requested the Secretary-General to make recommendations on how the mandate of BONUCA and the Secretary-General's Special Representative, as well as the configuration of BONUCA and the UN country team, should be revised.

In the overall report on its third session [A/64/341-S/2009/444], the Commission stated that, in July, the Central African Republic configuration Chairperson conducted an exploratory mission to Bangui to establish contacts with national authorities and other stakeholders. The Commission endorsed the peacebuilding priorities set out by the Central African Republic at the 8 October meeting of the Central African Republic configuration: reform of the security sector, including disarmament, demobilization and reintegration (DDR); good governance and the rule of law; and socio-economic advancement through the implementation of development hubs. The Commission also identified the successful conclusion of the inclusive political dialogue and the implementation of its recommendations as a cross-cutting priority.

Report of Commission mission. The Commission undertook a mission to the Central African Republic (30 October–6 November) to discuss with the Government and other stakeholders the main peacebuilding priorities and challenges, the actions being undertaken by the Government to address those challenges, and the nature and scope of international support needed. It visited sites of ongoing projects that were relevant to peacebuilding and exchanged views on the activities of the Peacebuilding Fund with the National Steering Committee.

The mission, in its December report [PBC/3/CAF/3], found that expectations remained high with regard to the engagement of the Central African Republic with the Commission, and the Commission's role in focusing international attention on the country's needs. However, the relationship between the activities of the Peacebuilding Fund and those of the Commission remained confusing for many interlocutors. The delegation clarified the difference between them, particularly as the $10 million allocated by the Fund for the country was financing programmes and activities on the ground. The delegation emphasized the Government's primary responsibility for achieving progress on the peacebuilding priorities and the need for concurrent progress on all of them to avoid additional tensions among the population. The delegation realized the importance of concurrently addressing the priority areas, and highlighted the Commission's challenge to coordinate the action of all stakeholders to ensure not only progress, but also careful sequencing of the various actions and projects. All three priorities were either covered or about to be covered by individual frameworks and/or programmes. In the area of security sector reform, a detailed timeline of implementable actions was established. UNDP finalized a DDR plan and launched a comprehensive project to strengthen the rule of law through justice and security. The delegation concluded that integration of the UN presence on the ground would ensure better coherence among the actors and support the Commission in fulfilling the objectives of better coordination and sequencing. The delegation agreed to discuss with UNDP the Government's request that the remainder of the first allocation from the Peacebuilding Fund be used for implementing the DDR strategy. The delegation was struck by the overarching need to strengthen support for national capacity-building through additional assistance and other innovative ways, as a shortage of qualified personnel at all levels was hampering the transition from humanitarian intervention to sustainable development, which could jeopardize the Government's capacity to deliver basic social and other services throughout the country.

(For further information on the Peacebuilding Commission, see p. 54.)

Chad and Central African Republic

In Chad and the Central African Republic, the police and military liaison officers of the United Nations Mission in the Central African Republic and Chad (MINURCAT) in 2008 worked with the EU-led military force (EUFOR Chad/Central African Republic) to enhance stability and support human rights and the rule of law. The Mission focused on the training and deployment of the Détachement Intégré de Sécurité (DIS), the special Chadian police for maintaining law and order in refugee camps and among displaced civilians within a 10-kilometre radius of the camps in eastern Chad. The fragility of the situation in Chad was demonstrated in February, when a coalition of Chadian rebel groups operating under the name Résistance nationale launched an attack on the capital. In December, the Secretary-General recommended the concept of a UN force of at least 4,900 peacekeepers to take over from EUFOR by 15 March 2009.

Political and security situation

Security Council press statement. In September 2007, by resolution 1778(2007) [YUN 2007, p. 153], the Security Council authorized the deployment of MINURCAT and EUFOR Chad/Central African Republic in eastern Chad and north-eastern Central African Republic to contribute to the protection of civilian populations and facilitate the provision of humanitarian assistance. On 7 January [SC/9221-AFR/1643], following a briefing by the Secretariat on the preparations for deploying those missions, the Council welcomed the progress made and encouraged contributors to make available to MINURCAT and EUFOR the personnel and resources required for implementing their mandates.

Appointment. By a letter of 25 January [S/2008/52], the Secretary-General informed the Security Council that he intended to appoint Victor da Silva Angelo (Portugal) as his Special Representative and Head of MINURCAT. The Council took note of that intention on 29 January [S/2008/53]. He took up his duties on 7 March.

Attack on N'Djamena. Following rising tensions at the end of 2007 between Chad and the Sudan [YUN 2007, p. 156], the situation in the area along the border with Darfur further deteriorated on 30 January following reports that a Chadian National Armed Forces (FANT) aircraft had been shot down in Western Darfur by members of Chadian armed opposition groups. At the same time, Chadian military helicopters reportedly bombed suspected rebel positions in eastern Chad. Subsequently, the rebel movements claimed that they had seized control of Oum Hadjer, located between Abéché and the capital, N'Djamena.

On 31 January, Résistance nationale forces advanced from bases in the Chadian-Sudanese border region in a column of an estimated 200 to 300 vehicles. That same day, all non-essential UN personnel were evacuated to Douala, Cameroon, with the support of France and the logistical assistance of MONUC. On the night of 1–2 February, the rebel forces entered N'Djamena and surrounded the presidential palace and other strategic locations throughout the city. Heavy fighting erupted, but Government troops managed to push the rebel forces back, consolidating their positions in the capital by 5 February.

Communication. In a letter of 3 February [S/2008/69] to the Security Council, Chad solicited the support of the Council in the face of an attempt to overthrow the Government.

SECURITY COUNCIL ACTION

On 4 February [meeting 5830], following consultations among Security Council members, the President made statement **S/PRST/2008/3** on behalf of the Council:

The Security Council expresses its grave concern regarding the situation in Chad.

The Council supports the decision of the African Union of 2 February 2008 strongly condemning the attacks perpetrated by armed groups against the Government of Chad, demanding to put an immediate end to the violence and calling upon all the countries of the region to respect the unity and territorial integrity of the member States of the African Union.

The Council welcomes in particular the decision of the African Union to mandate the Leader of the Libyan Arab Jamahiriya, Colonel Muammar Al-Qadhafi, and President Denis Sassou Nguesso of the Republic of the Congo to engage the Chadian parties with a view to ending the fighting and to initiate efforts aimed at seeking a lasting solution to the crisis.

The Council strongly condemns these attacks and all attempts at destabilization by force, and recalls its commitment to the sovereignty, unity, territorial integrity and political independence of Chad.

The Council urges all States in the region to abide fully by the obligations they have entered into with regard to respect for and securing of their common border, in particular under the Tripoli Agreement of 8 February 2006, the Riyadh Agreement of 3 May 2007 and the Sirte Agreement of 25 October 2007.

The Council calls upon the States of the region to deepen their cooperation with a view to putting an end to the activities of armed groups and their attempt to seize power by force.

The Council calls upon Member States to provide support, in conformity with the Charter of the United Nations, as requested by the Government of Chad.

The Council expresses its concern regarding the direct threat that the combats pose for the safety of the civilian population, including internally displaced persons and refugees.

The Council reaffirms its full support for the United Nations Mission in the Central African Republic and Chad and the European Union operation (EUFOR Chad/Central African Republic), whose deployment in eastern Chad and the north-eastern Central African Republic was authorized by resolution 1778(2007), to contribute to the protection of vulnerable civilian populations and to facilitate the provision of humanitarian assistance.

The Council expresses its concern over the safety and security of humanitarian personnel, United Nations personnel and European Union personnel and material deployed in Chad. It underlines that all parties have a responsibility to ensure the protection of all these personnel and of the diplomatic personnel present in Chad.

Communication. By a letter of 4 March [S/2008/139], the United Republic of Tanzania transmitted to the Security Council a communiqué on the situation in Chad adopted by the AU Peace and Security Council at its 110th meeting (Addis Ababa, Ethiopia, 18 February). The AU called on all the Chadian parties to unconditionally renounce the use of force and engage in constructive dialogue to find a peaceful solution to the problems facing the country. It also stressed the need for the urgent deployment of MINURCAT and EUFOR in order to facilitate humanitarian efforts.

Report of Secretary-General (April). In his April report on MINURCAT [S/2008/215], submitted pursuant to Security Council resolution 1778(2007) [YUN 2007, p. 153], the Secretary-General covered major events since his last report [ibid., p. 155].

By 22 February, all MINURCAT international staff had redeployed to the capital from Cameroon and resumed their normal activities. On 13 March, during the eleventh summit of the Organization of the Islamic Conference (Dakar, Senegal, 13–14 March), which was attended by the Secretary-General, President Idriss Déby of Chad and President Omar al-Bashir of the Sudan signed a new agreement in which they agreed to reconcile, normalize their relations and contribute to peace and stability in the two countries and in the region. They asked the international community to take all necessary measures to put in place a peace and security force in order to guarantee and observe the mixed operations aimed at securing their common border. In addition, the parties agreed to the establishment of a contact group to monitor the implementation of the agreement; to cease supporting the activities of armed groups; and to ensure that their respective territories were not used for the destabilization of one or the other State.

Also on 13 March, however, Chad issued a communiqué stating that rebel groups supported by the Sudan had crossed the border from the Sudan into Chad, near Moudeina. On 14 March, a second group was reported closer to Abéché, with FANT units reportedly redeploying in anticipation of movements in the Sudan in the border area near Adré. Nonetheless, on the same day, Chad lifted the state of emergency it had imposed in mid-February.

Meanwhile, MINURCAT and EUFOR further consolidated their relationship with the Government of Chad through the Coordination nationale d'appui à la force internationale, headed by the Special Representative of President Déby for MINURCAT and EUFOR. In late January, MINURCAT, jointly with Chadian police authorities and EUFOR, identified potential sites for the police headquarters in Abéché, six stations in the main towns, 12 posts and the respective infrastructure and equipment needs. A police familiarization programme to initiate a continuous MINURCAT police presence in Abéché started on 25 February with a team of eight officers deployed on a rotating basis, and contributed to enhancing MINURCAT visibility in eastern Chad.

From 18 to 24 January, the Department of Peacekeeping Operations (DPKO) conducted a mission to N'Djamena to discuss with the authorities, the UN country team, the EU and other partners potential MINURCAT justice and corrections activities and their planning and implementation. The Mission determined that there was a need to harmonize formal and traditional justice mechanisms, and to build the capacities of traditional and formal justice officials. Also identified as key issues were the training of prison staff and the improvement of correction infrastructure.

Of the authorized MINURCAT strength of 50 military liaison officers, 15 were deployed, focusing their activities on establishing a comprehensive liaison network with key stakeholders. While the EU Council launched the military bridging operation EUFOR Chad/Central African Republic on 28 January, the security situation and delays related to EUFOR force generation did not allow the planned deployment in that month of up to 25 military liaison officers. However, the senior military liaison officer and an advance military liaison officer team deployed to the EUFOR operational headquarters in Paris and EUFOR headquarters in Abéché. As at 15 March, more than 1,500 EUFOR personnel were present in Chad and the Central African Republic, including 200 in north-eastern Central African Republic, constituting almost half of the total authorized strength. The Secretary-General observed that the attainment of full EUFOR initial operational capacity would enable MINURCAT to deploy and undertake its mandated activities.

The Secretary-General said that the attempt by Chadian armed groups to capture N'Djamena, the continuing instability in the Chad/Sudan border area, as well as the cross-border movement of armed groups, underscored the need for a comprehensive approach in addressing the situation in Chad. The internal crisis in Chad, the situation facing refugees and internally displaced persons in eastern Chad and the Central African Republic, the tensions between Chad and the Sudan and the situation in Darfur needed to be addressed simultaneously in a coordinated effort that took into account the root causes and regional aspects of the internal conflicts. Neither MINURCAT nor EUFOR, however, were ideally mandated to address those issues. The parties themselves would have to demonstrate the political will and commitment necessary to resolve the underlying political and security challenges. The Secretary-General also expressed concern about the highly volatile security situation in Chad and the Central African Republic, which would continue to have an impact on the much-needed assistance provided by the humanitarian community to the populations at risk.

Attacks by armed groups. The security situation in the border areas of Chad and the Central African Republic with Darfur remained fragile and unpredictable. On 11 June, following reports that Chadian rebel groups had crossed the border in Moudeina, FANT bombed suspected rebel groups. Fighting erupted between FANT and Chadian rebel groups around the Koukou Angarana and Goz Amer refugee camps on 12 June. The following day, Chadian rebel groups briefly took control of Goz Beida. They looted offices of aid agencies, including the premises of the Office of the United Nations High Commissioner for Refugees (UNHCR), and set ablaze a fuel depot. Aid workers sought refuge in the EUFOR camp during the attack. On 15 June, Chadian rebel groups briefly took control of Am Dam, some 120 kilometres south of Abéché. On 16 June, rebel groups briefly took the town of Biltine, 90 kilometres north of Abéché. The next day, they attacked several towns during their retreat towards the Chad-Sudan border. Also on 17 June, Chad reported that Sudanese army helicopters had attacked the town of Adé, a charge that the Sudan denied.

SECURITY COUNCIL ACTION

On 16 June [meeting 5913], following consultations among Security Council members, the President made statement **S/PRST/2008/22** on behalf of the Council:

> The Security Council condemns in the strongest terms the attacks conducted by Chadian armed groups since 11 June 2008.
>
> The Council condemns all attempts at destabilization by force, and reiterates its commitment to the sovereignty,

unity, territorial integrity and political independence of Chad. It demands that armed groups cease violence immediately and urges all parties to respect the Sirte Agreement of 25 October 2007.

The Council calls upon States in the region to implement their commitments under the Dakar Agreement of 13 March 2008 and prior agreements, and to cooperate with a view to putting an end to the activities of armed groups in the region and their attempts to seize power by force.

The Council conveys its deep concern at the direct threat that the activities of armed groups pose for the safety of the civilian population and the conduct of humanitarian operations, and urges all parties to comply fully with their obligations under international humanitarian law.

The Council expresses its full support for the United Nations Mission in the Central African Republic and Chad and the European Union operation (EUFOR Chad/Central African Republic) deployed in Chad and the Central African Republic to contribute to the protection of vulnerable civilian populations and to facilitate the provision of humanitarian assistance, and calls upon all parties to guarantee the security and freedom of movement of their personnel and associated personnel.

The Council encourages the Chadian authorities to persevere in promoting political dialogue, with respect for the constitutional framework, as initiated by the agreement of 13 August 2007.

The Council stands ready to consider appropriate measures against those groups and individuals that constitute a threat to the stability of the region or violate international humanitarian law.

Report of Secretary-General (July). In his July report [S/2008/444] on MINURCAT, the Secretary-General said that while the dialogue between the Government and the political parties had been revived within the framework of the 13 August 2007 agreement [YUN 2007, p. 155], no progress had been made towards the opening of similar dialogue with the Chadian Armed Opposition Group, which continued to pursue the military option. Members of the opposition coalition—the Coordination des partis politiques pour la défense de la Constitution—expressed doubts about President Déby's intention to begin an inclusive political dialogue. In April, the President designated a new Government, including four former political opponents appointed as the Ministers of Justice, Defence, Agriculture and Territorial Administration. Those positive steps towards a broad-based Government enjoyed considerable national support. In May, Prime Minister Saleh Abbas announced that Government emissaries had entered into direct negotiations with Chadian armed opposition groups to bring them back into the framework of the peace agreement signed on 25 October 2007 in Sirte, Libyan Arab Jamahiriya between the Government and the main such groups, including the Union des forces pour le développement et la démocratie (UFDD), the Rassemblement des forces pour le changement (RFC) and the Union des forces pour la démocratie et le développement fondamental (UFDDF) [YUN 2007, p. 156].

In the Central African Republic, MINURCAT continued to work closely with BONUCA and the UN country team to support police sector reform and the restoration of State authority in the Vakaga region in the north-eastern part of the country. Challenges in Chad affecting the full deployment of UN police and Integrated Security Detachment (DIS) officers included the absence of infrastructure for office and living space; inadequate logistical support for the training facilities and delays in refurbishing of the National Police Academy; limited ground and air transportation; the absence of a legal framework establishing DIS due to the delay in signing the memorandum of understanding between Chad and MINURCAT on DIS; and the delay in selecting the first batch of 220 police officers and gendarmes that would integrate with DIS.

From 15 to 23 April, an inter-agency planning mission led by DPKO visited Chad to assess the justice and corrections system as it related to the mandated activities of MINURCAT. The mission included representatives of UNHCR, UNDP, the Office of the United Nations High Commissioner for Human Rights (OHCHR), UNICEF and the European Commission. The team noted that eastern Chad was marked by barely functioning justice institutions, with a lack of judges and prosecutors and serious gaps in court infrastructure, as well as an almost complete absence of defence lawyers. With regard to arrests and detention-related activities of DIS, the team outlined a three-pronged approach including tracking of the cases of those detained or arrested by DIS, support for Chad's mobile court system and support to key prisons. Following the planning mission, MINURCAT undertook three joint assessment exercises with the prison authorities to consider cost-effective ways to improve the prison infrastructure and the general prison conditions in some areas. It also developed four quick-impact projects to address needs in terms of general infrastructure, security, improved accommodation, sanitary facilities and health service delivery in the Abéché, Goz Beida and N'Djamena prisons.

The Secretary-General remained concerned by the repeated cycles of rebel incursions into Chad and the continuing insecurity, which had impeded humanitarian access, particularly since the killing of the Director of Save the Children on 1 May.

Report of Secretary-General (September). In September [S/2008/601], the Secretary-General reported that progress had been achieved in regard to the 13 August 2007 agreement on electoral reforms. In June, the Committee established to follow up the implementation of that agreement submitted to the Government draft bills on the electoral law and the establishment of the independent electoral commission. In July, the Ministry of Economy and Planning began a cartographic census, to be completed in early 2009 and followed by a demographic census for updating the voter registration list. Also in that month, eight additional political parties signed the 13 August agreement, bringing the number of signatory parties to 91 out of 101 registered political parties in Chad. Five of the new signatory parties belonged to the presidential majority and three to opposition parties. Progress in the implementation of the Sirte Agreement, however, remained limited.

On 18 August, the Libyan Arab Jamahiriya brokered an agreement between Chad and RFC dissidents under which the latter signed the Sirte Agreement. Despite progress on that front, in August, the Mouvement pour la justice et la démocratie au Tchad, an armed group from the northern part of the country, joined the Alliance Nationale under the UFDD leader, Mahamat Nouri. Also that month, Timan Erdimi, the leader of RFC, reportedly announced that contacts were under way with other armed opposition groups to reinforce the Alliance's military capacity.

In August, the National Commission of Inquiry submitted its report on the February attack on N'Djamena. It found that both rebel groups and FANT were responsible for violating human rights during the attack, including through arbitrary execution, torture, rape and the disproportionate use of force. The Commission recommended establishing a committee, to include the international community, to follow up on its findings and recommendations. On 15 August, a Chadian court sentenced former President Hissène Habré to death in absentia for allegedly providing financial, material and moral support to rebels who attacked the capital in February. Eleven rebel leaders involved in the February attacks were also sentenced to death in absentia.

The Secretary-General noted that the security situation, particularly in eastern Chad, remained volatile. The number of skirmishes between FANT and armed opposition groups decreased, but carjackings, armed robberies and crime targeting national and international humanitarian staff continued.

The MINURCAT Police Commissioner, Major General Gerardo Chaumont (Argentina), took up his duties in Chad on 9 August. MINURCAT rehabilitated the DIS training centre at the National Police Academy and conducted a training course for 231 DIS elements. The memorandum of understanding between the Government and MINURCAT on UN support for DIS was signed on 14 August, although the presidential decree establishing the Detachment had yet to be signed. MINURCAT judicial advisory and corrections units established relations with national counterparts, and carried out four needs assessments in Abéché, Goz Beida and N'Djamena prisons. MINURCAT initiated a high-level visit to Kerfi with the Governor of the region of Dar Sila, and representatives of the Coordination nationale d'appui à la force internationale au Tchad, UN agencies and NGOs. The team met with local authorities and representatives to assess the situation following inter-ethnic clashes in July. As a result of the visit, leaders of the Mouro and Dadjo ethnic groups, which participated in the clashes, agreed to work together in developing the region.

In view of Security Council resolution 1325(2000) [YUN 2000, p. 1113], and **resolution 1820(2008)**, (see p. 1265), MINURCAT undertook a number of sensitization activities for UN police and DIS personnel to combat violence against women and girls, especially with regard to their protection in refugee camps and internally displaced persons sites. It conducted similar activities for civil society organizations, local authorities and law enforcement agencies. The Mission also drafted a code of conduct for the prevention of gender-based violence.

The Secretary-General also reported that the deployment of EUFOR had been completed and the force comprised 3,300 troops, of whom approximately 200 were located in the Central African Republic. Patrols across the area and high-visibility operations were being carried out.

UN-EU midterm review. Regarding arrangements for following up the EUFOR presence at the end of its one-year mandate, including a possible UN operation, the Secretary-General reported, as requested by the Security Council in resolution 1778(2007) [YUN 2007, p. 153], that a UN-EU team visited Chad and the Central African Republic from 18 to 24 June. The team consisted of representatives of DPKO, the Departments of Field Support, Political Affairs and Safety and Security, the Office for the Coordination of Humanitarian Affairs (OCHA), UNHCR, OHCHR and MINURCAT, as well as the EU, the European Commission and EUFOR.

In Chad, while EUFOR was beginning to have a positive effect in deterring security threats, MINURCAT was still at the early stages of its deployment into the eastern part of the country, and DIS had not yet begun to deploy. Humanitarian access had decreased as security conditions had forced aid workers to limit operations. Some parties had called on the United Nations to create a border-monitoring mechanism to deter the cross-border activities of armed opposition groups. After careful assessment, the Secretariat concluded that monitoring—let alone securing—the border between Chad, the Sudan and the Central African Republic was a virtually impossible task. It would be extremely manpower-intensive, and there would be no guarantee that monitoring cross-border activities in one area would not simply push them to another area. The only solution to insecurity created by the Chadian armed opposition groups was for those groups to give up their quest to take power by force and to engage in dialogue with the Government to address their grievances.

In the Central African Republic, the main security threats consisted of common and petty crimes, roadblocks and banditry; the team did not assess an immediate threat of spillover of the Darfur conflict into the area. EUFOR activities included limited patrolling in and around Birao and securing the airstrip. Nonetheless, Government representatives requested that the United Nations take over from EUFOR in order to address possible cross-border violence from Darfur.

Expanded MINURCAT mandate. The Secretary-General also reported that the Secretariat had developed recommendations for an enhanced MINURCAT mandate that would include a military force to take over from EUFOR at the end of its mandate on 15 March 2009, along with others for the use of the Mission's good offices to assist the Government and relevant stakeholders in addressing the underlying causes of insecurity in eastern Chad related to the safe and voluntary return of refugees and internally displaced persons. The enhanced mandate of MINURCAT would concentrate on eastern Chad, with a limited military contingent in the north-eastern part of the Central African Republic. The Secretary-General outlined the conceived Mission's force and support requirements, support of DIS, peace aspects and financial implications.

The Secretary-General had dispatched the Assistant Secretary-General for Peacekeeping Operations, Edmond Mulet, to Chad and the Central African Republic to discuss the possible UN operation. In Chad, President Déby had agreed to the deployment of a military UN follow-on operation to replace EUFOR, and requested that such an operation remain within the framework of Security Council resolution 1778(2007) to address the spillover of the Darfur crisis and help create conditions for the return of refugees and internally displaced persons. In the Central African Republic, President Bozizé had requested that such an operation replace EUFOR, highlighted the peculiar security situation in the northern part of the country and stated that the operation could play a deterrent role and minimize the possibility of a security vacuum that could derail the peace processes.

The Secretary-General recommended that the Security Council consider establishing a UN military force of up to 6,000 troops and logistic enablers to take over from EUFOR. He also called on Member States with the necessary capabilities to work with DPKO in establishing an "over the horizon" standby presence with appropriate support capability that could be deployed expeditiously to back up the Mission's mandate should the security situation exceed the capabilities of a UN peacekeeping operation. He further recommended that the Council consider leaving in draft form the resolution authorizing the deployment of the force until such time as the Secretariat had firm commitments of troops and other critical mission support elements from Member States. In the meantime, the United Nations would explore with the EU the possibility of a limited extension of EUFOR to cover any potential gap between the end of its mandate and the arrival of the new UN force, should the United Nations face force-generation difficulties.

On 24 September, by resolution 1834(2008) (see below), the Security Council extended the mandate of MINURCAT until 15 March 2009, and stated its intention to authorize the deployment of a UN military force to follow up EUFOR in Chad and the Central African Republic.

SECURITY COUNCIL ACTION

On 24 September [meeting 5981], the Security Council unanimously adopted **resolution 1834(2008)**. The draft [S/2008/616] was submitted by Belgium, Costa Rica, Croatia, France, the Libyan Arab Jamahiriya and the United States.

The Security Council,

Recalling its resolutions and the statements by its President concerning Chad, the Central African Republic and the subregion, including resolution 1778(2007) of 25 September 2007, and its resolutions 1769(2007) of 31 July 2007 and 1828(2008) of 31 July 2008,

Reaffirming its commitment to the sovereignty, unity, territorial integrity and political independence of Chad and the Central African Republic, and to the cause of peace in the region,

Reiterating its concern at the humanitarian and security repercussions in eastern Chad and the north-eastern Central African Republic of the ongoing violence in Darfur,

Deeply concerned at the activities of armed groups and other attacks in eastern Chad, the north-eastern Central African Republic and western Sudan, which threaten the security of the civilian population, the conduct of humanitarian operations in those areas and the stability of those countries, and which result in serious violations of human rights and international humanitarian law,

Stressing that a proper settlement of the Darfur issue and an improvement of relations between the Sudan, Chad and the Central African Republic will contribute to long-term peace and stability in the region,

Reiterating its full support for the efforts of the Secretary-General and of the African Union, through the Joint African Union-United Nations Chief Mediator for Darfur, Mr. Djibrill Yipènè Bassolé, to revive the peace process begun by the Darfur Peace Agreement, consolidate the ceasefire and reinforce the peacekeeping presence in Darfur,

Reaffirming that any attempt at destabilization through violent means or seizing power by force is unacceptable,

Reaffirming also its resolutions 1325(2000) of 31 October 2000 and 1820(2008) of 19 June 2008 on women and peace and security, its resolution 1502(2003) of 26 August 2003 on the protection of humanitarian and United Nations personnel and its resolution 1674(2006) of 28 April 2006 on the protection of civilians in armed conflict,

Reaffirming further its resolution 1612(2005) of 26 July 2005 on children and armed conflict, taking note of the report of the Secretary-General on children and armed conflict in Chad and the recommendations contained therein, and recalling the conclusions regarding Chad adopted by its Working Group on Children and Armed Conflict,

Recognizing that the Governments of Chad and the Central African Republic bear primary responsibility for ensuring the security of civilians in their territories,

Bearing in mind the Convention relating to the Status of Refugees of 28 July 1951 and the Protocol thereto, of 31 January 1967, along with the Organization of African Unity Convention governing the specific aspects of refugee problems in Africa of 10 September 1969,

Emphasizing the need to respect international refugee law, preserve the civilian and humanitarian nature of refugee camps and internally displaced persons sites and prevent any recruitment of individuals, including children, which might be carried out in or around the camps by armed groups,

Welcoming the deployment by the European Union of its operation in eastern Chad and Central African Republic (EUFOR Chad/Central African Republic), noting that the European Union declared the initial operational capacity of its operation on 15 March 2008, and recalling that, according to resolution 1778(2007), the mandate of EUFOR Chad/Central African Republic therefore runs until 15 March 2009,

Welcoming also the selection and training by the United Nations Mission in the Central African Republic and Chad of the first group of police and gendarmerie officers of the Détachement intégré de sécurité (previously referred to as the Police tchadienne pour la protection humanitaire), and stressing the need to expedite the deployment of the Détachement intégré de sécurité,

Having examined the report of the Secretary-General of 12 September 2008 and the recommendations contained therein on the arrangements for following up EUFOR Chad/Central African Republic at the end of its mandate,

Determining that the situation in the region of the border between the Sudan, Chad and the Central African Republic constitutes a threat to international peace and security,

1. *Decides* to extend until 15 March 2009 the mandate of the United Nations Mission in the Central African Republic and Chad, as set out in resolution 1778(2007);

2. *Calls upon* the Secretary-General to complete the deployment of the Mission as soon as possible, and upon the Government of Chad, with the support of the Mission according to its mandate, to carry out the full deployment of the Détachement intégré de sécurité expeditiously;

3. *Invites* donors to continue to contribute to the Mission trust fund, established to support the Détachement intégré de sécurité;

4. *Expresses its intention* to extend beyond the date referred to in paragraph 1 above the multidimensional presence established in Chad and the Central African Republic to help to create the security conditions conducive to a voluntary, secure and sustainable return of refugees and displaced persons, and to this end expresses its intention to authorize the deployment of a United Nations military component to follow up EUFOR Chad/Central African Republic in both Chad and the Central African Republic, taking fully into account the recommendations contained in the report of the Secretary-General referred to in paragraph 8 below and in consultation with the Governments of those countries;

5. *Requests* the Secretary-General, in close cooperation with the European Union, to continue planning and to initiate the force generation and logistical, administrative, financial and other necessary arrangements with a view to a transfer of authority, including in the north-eastern Central African Republic, between EUFOR Chad/Central African Republic and the United Nations military component referred to in paragraph 4 above on 15 March 2009, subject to a new decision of the Security Council;

6. *Encourages* the Governments of Chad and the Central African Republic to continue to cooperate with the United Nations and the European Union to facilitate the smooth transition from EUFOR Chad/Central African Republic to the United Nations military component;

7. *Encourages* troop-contributing countries to pledge the necessary force requirements and, in particular, the helicopters, reconnaissance units, engineers, logistics and medical facilities;

8. *Requests* the Secretary-General to submit a new report by 15 November 2008 on progress towards the full deployment of the Mission and the Détachement intégré de sécurité and on updating the planning and conducting preparations referred to in paragraphs 4 and 5 above, including options on the size, structure and mandate of the proposed United Nations military presence in the north-eastern Central African Republic to take over the EUFOR Chad/Central African Republic presence;

9. *Also requests* the Secretary-General to continue to report regularly, and at least every three months, on the security and humanitarian situation, including movements of refugees and internally displaced persons, in eastern Chad, the north-eastern Central African Republic and the region, on progress towards the objective of helping to create the security conditions conducive to a voluntary, secure and sustainable return of refugees and displaced persons and on the implementation of the mandate of the Mission;

10. *Expresses its intention* to adopt the decision referred to in paragraphs 4 and 5 above by 15 December 2008;

11. *Encourages* the respective Governments of the Sudan, Chad and the Central African Republic to ensure that their territories are not used to undermine the sovereignty of others, to cooperate actively with a view to implementing the Dakar Agreement of 13 March 2008 and previous agreements, and to cooperate with a view to putting an end to the activities of armed groups in the region and their attempts to seize power by force, looks forward to the implementation of the commitment of the Sudan and Chad to restore diplomatic ties with a view to fully normalizing their relations, and welcomes the role played in particular by the regional contact group, the Governments of the Libyan Arab Jamahiriya and the Republic of the Congo as African co-mediators, as well as the African Union and

the United Nations, including through the Special Representative of the Secretary-General for the Central African Republic and Chad and Head of the Mission, in support of the Dakar process;

12. *Demands* that armed groups cease violence immediately, and urges all parties in Chad and the Central African Republic respectively to respect and implement the Sirte Agreement of 25 October 2007 and the comprehensive peace agreement signed at Libreville on 21 June 2008;

13. *Encourages* the authorities and political stakeholders in Chad and the Central African Republic to continue to pursue their efforts at national dialogue, with respect for the constitutional frameworks, notes the positive efforts of the Government of Gabon to support a national dialogue in the Central African Republic, emphasizes also the importance of the political agreement for the reinforcement of the democratic process, signed at N'Djamena on 13 August 2007, and encourages the parties to proceed with its implementation;

14. *Decides* to remain actively seized of the matter.

Communication. In a letter of 28 October [S/2008/679] to the Security Council, Chad asserted that certain passages in the September report of the Secretary-General did not accurately reflect its viewpoints on the question of an extended MINURCAT operation with a military component. Chad held that the mandate of the operation was essentially humanitarian, aimed at protecting civilians and improving security for the delivery of humanitarian assistance. The operation was not a conventional peacekeeping one implying some kind of "neutrality", "impartiality" or "good offices" within the framework of any type of peace agreement; its main objective was to respond to the hopes for security placed in it by the humanitarian organizations that were at the origin of the appeal for that operation and by the affected populations in eastern Chad: refugees, displaced persons and host civilian populations. The force should not exceed 3,000 troops and, to effectively implement its mandate, it should be better equipped than EUFOR.

Report of Secretary-General (December). In his December report [S/2008/760] on MINURCAT, the Secretary-General said that on 15 September, President Idriss Déby issued a decree reappointing or reassigning new governors in all 22 regions of the country, and appointing new préfets and secrétaires généraux in all 60 departments. On 9 October, the President issued a decree restructuring the territorial administration, including the establishment of four new administrative regions. Limited progress was made towards the implementation of electoral reforms. The Government had yet to approve and submit to the Parliament, for its formal consideration, draft bills related to the electoral law and the establishment of the National Electoral Commission, as provided for under the agreement of 13 August on electoral reform.

Although there were no major political developments related to the mandate of MINURCAT in the north-eastern part of the Central African Republic, the Sam Oundja refugee camp in that region, with a population of some 3,000 refugees from Darfur, was attacked on 8 November by an unidentified armed group. Subsequently, EUFOR evacuated nine humanitarian workers to Birao.

In Chad, the security situation remained unchanged. Carjackings, armed robberies and crimes targeting humanitarian workers, Chadian citizens and refugees continued. On 15 November, EUFOR reported that two Sudanese helicopters had fired on its road patrol, near Birak in eastern Chad, destroying two vehicles. In an effort to mitigate the continuing threat from unexploded ordnance and other explosive remnants of war scattered across eastern Chad as a result of conflicts going back to the 1980s, a UN mine-action team was deployed to MINURCAT headquarters in midyear to coordinate and monitor clearance of those devices. Eastern Chad faced a humanitarian challenge—exacerbated by attacks of heavily armed bandits—with over 290,000 Sudanese refugees, more than 180,000 internally displaced persons and a further 700,000 individuals among the host communities who were in need of food, water and health care.

As at 24 November, MINURCAT comprised 863 personnel, including 236 UN police officers and 46 military liaison officers. On 27 September, President Déby signed the decree formally establishing DIS. Shortly thereafter, the Chadian authorities presented to MINURCAT a list appointing 71 DIS commanders and specifying their assignments. On 16 October, the President signed a second decree appointing the Commander of DIS together with two Deputy Commanders (for operations and administration). MINURCAT completed the training of 109 new DIS officers. The major logistical challenge affecting UN police and DIS deployment having been the acute shortage of suitable accommodation and infrastructure, and skilled labour to undertake construction work, MINURCAT built four of five planned police stations for UN police and DIS.

(For information on Chad and the Sudan, see p. 267.)

Children and armed conflict

Pursuant to Security Council resolution 1612(2005) [YUN 2005, p. 863], the Secretary-General in August presented to the Security Council the second country report on children and armed conflict in Chad [S/2008/532]. The report, covering the period from July 2007 to June 2008, focused on six grave violations perpetrated against children in Chad, namely: recruiting or using child soldiers; killing and maiming of children; rape or other grave sexual violence against children; denial of humanitarian access to children;

attacks against schools and hospitals; and the abduction of children. Those violations were situated in the volatile political, military and security context of continued armed conflict between the armed forces and rebel groups, the presence in eastern Chad of foreign rebel groups, cross-border raids by the Janjaweed, and continuing inter-ethnic tensions mainly between Arab and non-Arab communities.

All parties reportedly continued to recruit and use children. Unexploded ordnance and landmines were of concern, especially in the north. Rape and other sexual violence were said to be common, girls being the major victims. A significant and increasing number of incidents targeting humanitarian personnel and assets by parties to the conflict was reported. No direct attacks on schools were said to have occurred, but there were two attacks against schoolteachers in the Goz Beida area. Children had also been abducted as a result of the conflict.

The beginning of disarmament, demobilization and reintegration activities was seen as a positive step in addressing violations of child rights. All parties were urged to implement the recommendations set out in the Secretary-General's first report, along with the subsequent conclusions and recommendations of the Security Council Working Group on Children and Armed Conflict [YUN 2007, p. 157], and to comply with the resolutions of the Council on children and armed conflict to halt the child rights violations and abuses for which they had been cited. They were also urged to develop action plans to identify and release children from their ranks, in the framework of resolution 1612(2005) [YUN 2005, p. 863] and on the basis of the criteria established for action plans.

MINURCAT

The mandate of the United Nations Mission in the Central African Republic and Chad (MINURCAT), established by Security Council resolution 1778(2007) [YUN 2007, p. 153], was to help create the security conditions conducive to a voluntary, secure and sustainable return of refugees and displaced persons, including by contributing to the protection of refugees, displaced persons and civilians in danger; to facilitate the provision of humanitarian assistance in eastern Chad and the north-eastern Central African Republic; and to create favourable conditions for the reconstruction and development of those areas. Victor da Silva Angelo (Portugal) was the Special Representative of the Secretary-General and Head of MINURCAT.

Expanded MINURCAT mandate. In resolution 1834(2008) (see p. 164), the Security Council requested an update on the planning and preparations for the transfer of authority from EUFOR—of which 3,300 troops were deployed in the area of operation—to a UN military force on 15 March 2009, including options on the size, structure and mandate of the proposed military presence in the Central African Republic. For that purpose, a UN technical assessment mission comprising representatives of DPKO, the Departments of Field Support and Safety and Security, as well as OCHA, UNHCR, OHCHR and MINURCAT, visited Chad and the Central African Republic from 6 to 13 October, in consequence of which the proposed plan for the force was further refined.

In view of concerns expressed by Chad regarding the UN force structure and composition and its areas of deployment, the Military Adviser for Peacekeeping Operations, Lieutenant General Chikadibia Obiakor, visited Chad from 12 to 14 November to consult the national authorities on the refined concept of operations for the new force. Meeting with the Secretary-General in Doha on 29 November, President Déby agreed to the deployment of a UN force of some 4,900 troops.

As the most immediate and constant threat to the civilian population and humanitarian operations lay in attacks by heavily armed bandits, the UN force would comprise some 4,900 troops, including three battalions in eastern Chad and a battalion-size mobile reserve force supported by 18 helicopters. In the Central African Republic, the Secretary-General recommended a small military liaison team of approximately 15 officers.

In consultation with the Headquarters Integrated Mission Task Force, including OCHA, UNDP, UNHCR, OHCHR and MINURCAT, the following benchmarks were developed for the exit strategy of MINURCAT: voluntary return and resettlement in secure conditions of a critical mass of internally displaced persons; demilitarization of refugee and internally displaced person camps; capacity of local authorities to provide the necessary security for refugees, internally displaced persons, civilians and humanitarian workers; ability of national law enforcement agencies to maintain law and order with respect for international human rights standards; progress of an independent and effective judiciary in eastern Chad helping to end impunity; and a strengthened prison system in eastern Chad based on a human rights approach to prison management. The benchmarks would be reviewed as the situation evolved and would form basis of the Mission's implementation plan.

Underscoring that the minimum requirement for the follow-on UN force was some 4,900 troops, the Secretary-General submitted to the Security Council for its consideration and authorization his proposals for the UN force presence in Chad and north-eastern Central African Republic.

The financial implications for establishing the force on a full-cost basis for a 12-month period were estimated at some $530.1 million [S/2008/760/Add.1].

Financing of MINURCAT

In April [A/62/804], the Secretary-General submitted the budget for MINURCAT for the period from 1 July 2008 to 30 June 2009 in the amount of $307,835,700. In June [A/62/781/Add.15], ACABQ recommended a reduced amount of $301,124,200.

GENERAL ASSEMBLY ACTION

On 20 June [meeting 109], the General Assembly, on the recommendation of the Fifth Committee [A/62/602/Add.1], adopted **resolution 62/233 B** without vote [agenda item 164].

Financing of the United Nations Mission in the Central African Republic and Chad

The General Assembly,

Having considered the report of the Secretary-General on the financing of the United Nations Mission in the Central African Republic and Chad and the related report of the Advisory Committee on Administrative and Budgetary Questions,

Recalling Security Council resolution 1778(2007) of 25 September 2007, by which the Council approved the establishment in Chad and the Central African Republic, in consultation with the authorities of Chad and the Central African Republic, of a multidimensional presence and decided that the multidimensional presence should include, for a period of one year, a United Nations Mission in the Central African Republic and Chad,

Recalling also its resolution 62/233 A of 22 December 2007,

Reaffirming the general principles underlying the financing of United Nations peacekeeping operations, as stated in General Assembly resolutions 1874(S-IV) of 27 June 1963, 3101(XXVIII) of 11 December 1973 and 55/235 of 23 December 2000,

Mindful of the fact that it is essential to provide the Mission with the financial resources necessary to enable it to fulfil its responsibilities under the resolution of the Security Council,

Noting with appreciation that voluntary contributions have been made to the Mission,

1. *Requests* the Secretary-General to entrust the Head of Mission with the task of formulating future budget proposals, in full accordance with the provisions of General Assembly resolutions 59/296 of 22 June 2005, 60/266 of 30 June 2006 and 61/276 of 29 June 2007, as well as other relevant resolutions;

2. *Takes note* of the status of contributions to the United Nations Mission in the Central African Republic and Chad as at 30 April 2008, including the contributions outstanding in the amount of 45 million United States dollars, representing some 25 per cent of the total assessed contributions, notes with concern that only fifty-six Member States have paid their assessed contributions in full, and urges all other Member States, in particular those in arrears, to ensure payment of their outstanding assessed contributions;

3. *Expresses its appreciation* to those Member States which have paid their assessed contributions in full, and urges all other Member States to make every possible effort to ensure payment of their assessed contributions to the Mission in full;

4. *Expresses concern* at the financial situation with regard to peacekeeping activities, in particular as regards the reimbursements to troop contributors that bear additional burdens owing to overdue payments by Member States of their assessments;

5. *Also expresses concern* at the delay experienced by the Secretary-General in deploying and providing adequate resources to some recent peacekeeping missions, in particular those in Africa;

6. *Emphasizes* that all future and existing peacekeeping missions shall be given equal and non-discriminatory treatment in respect of financial and administrative arrangements;

7. *Also emphasizes* that all peacekeeping missions shall be provided with adequate resources for the effective and efficient discharge of their respective mandates;

8. *Reiterates its request* to the Secretary-General to make the fullest possible use of facilities and equipment at the United Nations Logistics Base at Brindisi, Italy, in order to minimize the costs of procurement for the Mission;

9. *Endorses* the conclusions and recommendations contained in the report of the Advisory Committee on Administrative and Budgetary Questions, and requests the Secretary-General to ensure their full implementation;

10. *Recalls* paragraph 14 of the report of the Advisory Committee on Administrative and Budgetary Questions, and encourages the United Nations Mission in the Central African Republic and Chad and other United Nations missions in the region to continue, where possible, their efforts to achieve greater synergy, while bearing in mind that individual missions are responsible for the preparation and implementation of their own budgets and for controlling their own assets and logistical operations;

11. *Requests* the Secretary-General to include in future budget submissions details of the mechanisms that exist at Headquarters and in the field for ensuring coordination and collaboration among all United Nations actors active in the relevant mission area;

12. *Also requests* the Secretary-General to ensure the full implementation of the relevant provisions of its resolutions 59/296, 60/266 and 61/276;

13. *Further requests* the Secretary-General to take all action necessary to ensure that the Mission is administered with a maximum of efficiency and economy;

14. *Requests* the Secretary-General, in order to reduce the cost of employing General Service staff, to continue efforts to recruit local staff for the Mission against General Service posts, commensurate with the requirements of the Mission;

Budget estimates for the period from 1 July 2008 to 30 June 2009

15. *Decides* to appropriate to the Special Account for the United Nations Mission in the Central African Re-

public and Chad the amount of 315,083,400 dollars for the period from 1 July 2008 to 30 June 2009, inclusive of 301,124,200 dollars for the maintenance of the Mission, 12,168,700 dollars for the support account for peacekeeping operations and 1,790,500 dollars for the United Nations Logistics Base;

Financing of the appropriation for the period from 1 July 2008 to 30 June 2009

16. *Also decides* to apportion among Member States the amount of 73,519,456 dollars for the period from 1 July to 24 September 2008, in accordance with the levels updated in General Assembly resolution 61/243 of 22 December 2006, and taking into account the scale of assessments for 2008, as set out in its resolution 61/237 of 22 December 2006;

17. *Further decides* that, in accordance with the provisions of its resolution 973(X) of 15 December 1955, there shall be set off against the apportionment among Member States, as provided for in paragraph 16 above, their respective share in the Tax Equalization Fund of the amount of 1,742,182 dollars, comprising the estimated staff assessment income of 1,436,352 dollars approved for the Mission, the prorated share of 272,838 dollars of the estimated staff assessment income approved for the support account and the prorated share of 32,992 dollars of the estimated staff assessment income approved for the United Nations Logistics Base;

18. *Decides* to apportion among Member States the amount of 241,563,944 dollars for the period from 25 September 2008 to 30 June 2009 at a monthly rate of 26,256,950 dollars, in accordance with the levels updated in General Assembly resolution 61/243, and taking into account the scale of assessments for 2008 and 2009, as set out in its resolution 61/237, subject to a decision of the Security Council to extend the mandate of the Mission;

19. *Also decides* that, in accordance with the provisions of its resolution 973(X), there shall be set off against the apportionment among Member States, as provided for in paragraph 18 above, their respective share in the Tax Equalization Fund of the amount of 5,724,318 dollars, comprising the estimated staff assessment income of 4,719,448 dollars approved for the Mission, the prorated share of 896,462 dollars of the estimated staff assessment income approved for the support account and the prorated share of 108,408 dollars of the estimated staff assessment income approved for the United Nations Logistics Base;

20. *Emphasizes* that no peacekeeping mission shall be financed by borrowing funds from other active peacekeeping missions;

21. *Encourages* the Secretary-General to continue to take additional measures to ensure the safety and security of all personnel under the auspices of the United Nations participating in the Mission, bearing in mind paragraphs 5 and 6 of Security Council resolution 1502(2003) of 26 August 2003;

22. *Invites* voluntary contributions to the Mission in cash and in the form of services and supplies acceptable to the Secretary-General, to be administered, as appropriate, in accordance with the procedure and practices established by the General Assembly;

23. *Decides* to include in the provisional agenda of its sixty-third session the item entitled "Financing of the United Nations Mission in the Central African Republic and Chad".

Uganda

Political and security situation

In March, the Chief Mediator of the peace process between the Government of Uganda and the Lord's Resistance Army (LRA), Riek Machar Teny, Vice-President of the Government of Southern Sudan, and the Special Envoy of the Secretary-General for the LRA-affected areas, former President of Mozambique Joaquim Albert Chissano, helped the parties conclude their negotiations and sign agreements on all the various agenda items. However, because the leader of LRA, Joseph Kony, did not sign the final peace agreement providing the capstone for the various agreements, the DRC, Southern Sudan and Uganda launched joint military action against his camps in the eastern DRC. According to the three countries, that military action was not intended to derail the peace process, but rather to pressure Mr. Kony into assembling, with his rebel forces, in Ri-Kwangba (Southern Sudan), and signing the final peace agreement.

By a letter of 23 June [S/2008/414] to the Security Council, the Secretary-General transmitted a communication from the Chief Mediator transmitted to him by the Special Envoy. In that communication, which reported on the status of the peace talks, the Chief Mediator stated that: efforts should continue to bring LRA back to the peace process; a door should be left open for diplomatic action that would restore dialogue with LRA in Juba even if other actions were contemplated; implementation of certain aspects of the Juba Agreements [YUN 2007, pp. 160 & 161], especially humanitarian and socio-economic interventions in LRA-affected areas, should begin; work should continue on establishing new justice institutions; the mediation process and certain mechanisms that had already been established should be sustained; and the process should continue to be adequately resourced to ensure that those affected by the conflict were assisted in returning to their communities. That would also enable the Mediator, the Facilitator and other stakeholders to ensure their preparedness to deal with the demobilization of LRA when the group returned to the process.

SECURITY COUNCIL ACTION

On 22 December [meeting 6058], following consultations among Security Council members, the President made statement **S/PRST/2008/48** on behalf of the Council:

The Security Council is grateful for the efforts undertaken by Mr. Joaquim Chissano, former President of Mozambique, as the Special Envoy of the Secretary-General for the Lord's Resistance Army-affected areas. The Council expresses its appreciation for his briefing of 17 December 2008, and agrees with his recommendation that the peace efforts should continue. The Council welcomes President Chissano's readiness to continue in his role for a further period.

The Council reiterates its welcome of the Final Peace Agreement, negotiated between the Government of Uganda and the Lord's Resistance Army and reached through the Juba peace process. The Council commends the Government of Uganda for its continued commitment to the Agreement and its investment in the peace process.

The Council condemns the repeated failure of Mr. Joseph Kony to sign the Final Peace Agreement. It calls upon the Lord's Resistance Army to sign and honour the Agreement immediately and to begin the process of disarmament, demobilization and reintegration to ensure a peaceful, political solution.

The Council strongly condemns the recent attacks by the Lord's Resistance Army in the Democratic Republic of the Congo and Southern Sudan, which pose a continuing threat to regional security. It demands that the Lord's Resistance Army cease its recruitment and use of children and that it release immediately all women, children and other non-combatants, in accordance with Council resolution 1612(2005). The Council reiterates its deep concern at the long-running and brutal insurgency by the Lord's Resistance Army, which has caused the death, abduction and displacement of thousands of innocent civilians in Uganda, the Sudan and the Democratic Republic of the Congo.

The Council recalls the International Criminal Court arrest warrants for certain leaders of the Lord's Resistance Army on charges of, among other things, war crimes and crimes against humanity, including murder, rape and the enlistment of children through abduction. The Council recalls the statement by its President of 22 June 2006, and reaffirms that it attaches vital importance to promoting justice and the rule of law, including respect for human rights, as an indispensable element for lasting peace. The Council reaffirms that ending impunity is essential for a society recovering from conflict to come to terms with past abuses committed against civilians and to prevent their recurrence.

The Council commends the States in the region for their increased cooperation and welcomes the joint efforts they have made to address the security threat posed by the Lord's Resistance Army. The Council calls upon these States to ensure that all actions are carried out in accordance with international humanitarian, human rights and refugee law and to take appropriate measures to protect civilians. The Council encourages these States to keep the United Nations missions in the region informed about their actions.

The Council welcomes the re-establishment of peace and security in northern Uganda. It encourages the Government of Uganda, with the support of international partners, to honour its commitment to accelerate reconciliation, recovery and development in that region through rapid implementation of its Peace, Recovery and Development Plan for Northern Uganda and relevant agenda items in the Final Peace Agreement and to disburse anticipated financing for the Peace, Recovery and Development Plan without delay.

The Council will continue to monitor the situation closely.

Extension of Special Envoy. In a letter of 23 December [S/2008/826] to the Security Council, the Secretary-General reported that the political process, suspended in early December by the Chief Mediator, might resume shortly. Uganda remained committed to the continuation of the peace process, and the door remained open for Mr. Kony to sign the final peace agreement. In the meantime, as a direct result of the successes in the peace process, security had returned to northern Uganda, economic activities had gradually been resumed, and internally displaced persons had returned home. Consequently, the Secretary-General recommended that the mandate of the Office of the Special Envoy be extended for an additional year, until 31 December 2009, to allow him to continue his efforts towards achieving a durable peace in northern Uganda.

The Office would continue to: assist the Special Envoy in developing a relationship of mutual trust among the parties and the mediation and in building their confidence in the political process; assist the Special Envoy in coordinating the efforts of the regional players, donors and civil society organizations involved; follow up on the peace talks on behalf of the Special Envoy and promote a peaceful agreement between Uganda and LRA through the support of African ambassadors; coordinate the activities of the five African ambassadors/guarantors of the peace process (DRC, Kenya, Mozambique, South Africa, United Republic of Tanzania); serve as a focal point for the Special Envoy's regional activities, including the coordination of all international activities in support of the talks; liaise with all stakeholders in Uganda and in the region; monitor and analyse internal and regional political and security developments in Uganda and neighbouring countries; coordinate the activities of the unit in Juba; and maintain close consultation with MONUC and UNMIS on security and military issues in connection with the Special Envoy's mandate.

In a letter of 29 December [S/2008/827] to the Secretary-General, the Security Council took note of that information and recommendation.

Children and armed conflict

In June, in response to the request of the Security Council Working Group on Children and Armed Conflict for an update on the implementation of the recommendation contained in paragraph 11 of its conclusions issued pursuant to his 2007 report on children and armed conflict in Uganda [YUN 2007, p. 161], the Secretary-General submitted to the Council an additional report on children and armed conflict in Uganda [S/2008/409] that also highlighted recent incidents of cross-border recruitment and the use of children from the Central African Republic, the DRC and Southern Sudan by LRA.

Owing to the apparent absence of LRA from Ugandan territory, there had been no recent cases of recruitment and use of Ugandan children, or other grave violations against children attributable to LRA. Children and women, however, were still present in LRA ranks, and there had been no movement on their release. There were reports alleging that LRA had been recruiting children from the Central African Republic, the DRC and Southern Sudan, abducting them from school and even killing them. Further discussions on how best to monitor and report on the violations committed against children by LRA would be held with the United Nations Task Forces on Monitoring and Reporting in Uganda, the DRC, the Central African Republic and the Sudan, taking into account the regional cross-border dimension of the problem. The Task Forces should be requested to develop, in cooperation with MONUC, a strategy for increased regional joint capability to monitor and report on cross-border recruitment and the use of children by LRA. The latter was urged to provide a complete list of names and ages of the women and children remaining in its ranks for verification, and to effect their immediate release.

Rwanda

Political and security situation

The border area between Rwanda and the DRC remained an area of concern, as violence reignited in August in the volatile eastern region of the DRC, on the border with Rwanda, and a cross-border incident between the two countries highlighted the threat of a wider regional conflict (see p. 126). In addition, the Security Council, by resolution 1804(2008), took action to address the presence of Rwandan armed groups in the DRC (see p. 116).

End of arms embargo

Welcoming recent steps towards the restoration of peace and stability in the Great Lakes region, the Security Council terminated several measures imposed in the wake of the devastating 1994 Rwanda genocide to prohibit the sale and supply of arms and related materiel for use in that country. It also dissolved, by resolution 1823(2008) (below), the Security Council Committee established pursuant to resolution 918(1994) [YUN 1994, p. 285] to monitor the arms embargo concerning Rwanda.

SECURITY COUNCIL ACTION

On 10 July [meeting 5931], the Security Council unanimously adopted **resolution 1823(2008)**. The draft [S/2008/432] was prepared in consultations among Council members.

The Security Council,

Recalling its resolutions 918(1994) of 17 May 1994, 1005(1995) of 17 July 1995, 1011(1995) of 16 August 1995, 1013(1995) of 7 September 1995, 1053(1996) of 23 April 1996, 1161(1998) of 9 April 1998 and 1749(2007) of 28 March 2007,

Having considered the report of 31 December 2007 of the Security Council Committee established pursuant to resolution 918(1994) concerning Rwanda and the oral report of 22 May 2008 by the Chairman of the Committee,

Stressing the importance of the cooperation of all States, in particular those in the region, with the Security Council Committee established pursuant to resolution 1533(2004) concerning the Democratic Republic of the Congo and with the Group of Experts established pursuant to resolution 1533(2004) of 12 March 2004, while carrying out its mandate as renewed by resolution 1807(2008) of 31 March 2008,

Stressing also the need for States in the region to ensure that arms and related materiel delivered to them are not diverted to or used by illegal armed groups,

Recalling the joint communiqué of the Government of the Democratic Republic of the Congo and the Government of the Republic of Rwanda signed at Nairobi on 9 November 2007 and the outcome of the Conference on Peace, Security and Development in North and South Kivu, held in Goma, Democratic Republic of the Congo, from 6 to 23 January 2008, which together represent a major step towards the restoration of lasting peace and stability in the Great Lakes region, and looking forward to their full implementation,

Welcoming the entry into force of the Pact on Security, Stability and Development in the Great Lakes Region, and stressing the importance of its full implementation,

Reiterating its call upon the States of the region to deepen further their cooperation with a view to consolidating peace in the region,

Acting under Chapter VII of the Charter of the United Nations,

1. *Decides* to terminate the prohibitions imposed by paragraphs 9 and 10 of resolution 1011(1995);

2. *Decides also* to dissolve the Security Council Committee established pursuant to resolution 918(1994) concerning Rwanda.

West Africa

Regional issues

Peace consolidation in West Africa

Report of Secretary-General. In response to a Security Council request to report on the fulfilment of the revised mandate of the United Nations Office for West Africa (UNOWA) every six months [YUN 2007, p. 168], the Secretary-General in June submitted a report [S/2008/426] covering the period from 1 January to 30 June 2008, which also addressed the recommendations made in his March 2007 report on cross-border issues in West Africa [YUN 2007, p. 165]. The Secretary-General said that significant progress was made in West Africa in the consolidation of peace and democratic governance, and UN peace missions had begun to wind down. Two countries in the subregion—Guinea-Bissau and Sierra Leone—had been placed on the agenda of the United Nations Peacebuilding Commission, and the Economic Community of West African States (ECOWAS) was demonstrating increased capacity to tackle political, social, economic and security problems. However, many challenges remained, such as youth unemployment, rapid urbanization and irregular migration, while others were emerging or increasing in proportion, including social and economic crises, human and drug trafficking, and insecurity in the Sahelian band. In order to assess and raise awareness of progress made and challenges facing countries of the subregion, particularly with regard to electoral processes, rising food prices and climate change, three high-level missions were undertaken: the Secretary-General embarked on a four-nation visit to Burkina Faso, Côte d'Ivoire, Ghana and Liberia (19–23 April); the Assistant Secretary-General for Political Affairs visited eight countries in the subregion (9–21 May); and the Secretary-General's Special Adviser on conflict visited the Sahel region (Burkina Faso, Mali, the Niger) from 1 to 6 June.

The Secretary-General said that the socio-economic landscape of West Africa was becoming a growing threat to peace and security. Half of the population was living below the poverty line, and with an annual growth rate of 2.3 per cent, the population in the subregion was expected to double by 2050, further exacerbating pressure on land and other resources and leading to greater social and political instability. Youth unemployment, with 65 per cent of some 270 million people under the age of 30 years either unemployed or underemployed, remained a concern. Meanwhile, the food crisis had become a security risk which, if not effectively addressed, could trigger violent demonstrations, strikes and other manifestations of civil unrest, such as the street protests in Burkina Faso, Cameroon, Côte d'Ivoire, Guinea and Senegal, or destabilize countries struggling to recover from conflict or experiencing political difficulties. The report also highlighted the vulnerability of the subregion to climate change and disruptive weather patterns; rapid urbanization of cities; pollution of the urban environment; toxic waste; and rising food prices.

Significant advances with regard to governance had been made, and democracy and peace were slowly yet firmly taking root. However, that progress was jeopardized by widespread corruption, which contributed to weakening State institutions and the rule of law, and in its worst form led to human rights abuses and the outbreak of conflict. New corruption practices had flourished with the discovery of natural resources, and transparent and accountable oversight of resource management was needed if all segments of society were to reap the benefits of national wealth. The resolution of long-standing conflicts had put an end to mass human rights violations, but those continued on a smaller scale due largely to the prevailing culture of impunity. The establishment of transitional justice mechanisms had borne results, yet more work was needed to ensure accountability for past and ongoing human rights violations. Elections were highlighted as potentially destabilizing processes that threatened fragile countries. In light of the elections scheduled during the year in Côte d'Ivoire, Ghana, Guinea and Guinea-Bissau, efforts needed to be made to ensure credible electoral processes and to avoid violence and instability.

A key challenge for many post-conflict and transitional countries in the subregion was security sector reform. Despite efforts to improve oversight of the security sector, restructure and train security forces, and increase engagement of the international community, security forces in a number of West African countries continued to be a source of aggravation for the population. Widespread bribery and extortion at illegal checkpoints and roadblocks restricted the free movement of goods and people, impeding economic development and integration. Persisting discontent over poor living conditions, inadequate compensation and limited employment opportunities for former combatants had led disgruntled security forces to engage in more lucrative criminal activity.

On cross-border issues, the Secretary-General said that due to their fragile economies and weak Governments, West African societies were particularly vulnerable to corruption and lawlessness. Some countries of the Sahel region, such as Guinea and Guinea-Bissau, had become fertile ground for organized crime. Drug trafficking constituted the most widespread cross-border activity, and in some cases, drug trafficking networks had permeated Government structures and security forces. Other areas of concern included human trafficking, which affected women, children and migrants and was a growing trend; the estimated 10 million light weapons circulating throughout the region and the continuing proliferation of small arms; the potential eruption of border conflicts, particularly where international borders had yet to be delimited and demarcated; and the crisis in the Sahel region, particularly northern Niger and Mali, which was emerging as one of the most pressing threats to peace and security in West Africa. In addition to being home to rebel activity, the region had proven to be a breeding ground for cross-border crime. Drug trafficking, arms smuggling and irregular migration, particularly along the trans-Saharan caravan routes, were on the rise. The increasingly blurred lines between criminal, rebel and terrorist activities further complicated efforts to address the situation.

The Secretary-General observed that most West African countries were in a period of transition from conflict to peace consolidation, and remained fragile and vulnerable to outbreaks of renewed violence. UNOWA would continue to play an active role in mobilizing support to the subregion, focusing its activities on capacity-building, peace consolidation and cross-border challenges. In particular, the Office would engage in building the capacity of countries and their institutions in areas such as security sector reform, good governance and the rule of law, with attention given to cooperation with the Economic Community of West African States (ECOWAS) to facilitate peaceful electoral processes. On security sector reform, UNOWA would undertake consultations to facilitate the adoption of an ECOWAS strategy by emphasizing the importance of a subregional approach to the issue. UNOWA would strengthen its collaboration with ECOWAS to enhance the effectiveness of early warning systems and other conflict-prevention mechanisms; raise awareness on cross-border threats to peace and security; and, with regard to sensitive border areas, promote the peaceful settlement of disputes and recommend confidence-building measures such as joint military patrols and regular consultations with affected populations to minimize violent incidents. The Office would also intensify its efforts, in cooperation with the United Nations Office on Drugs and Crime (UNODC) and other institutions, to combat cross-border crime. On the food crisis, UNOWA would raise awareness of the problem and promote concerted solutions addressing short- and long-term needs through sustained engagement with Governments, UN agencies and civil society.

Year-end developments. In a later report [S/2009/39], the Secretary-General said that the problems of youth unemployment, food insecurity and rapid urbanization, as well as the challenges posed by corruption, irregular migration, human and drug trafficking, and the proliferation of small arms and light weapons had been compounded by the adverse impact of the global financial and food crises on West African countries. Large segments of the population were forced to reduce consumption or exclude certain food items from their diets. The financial crisis and threat of a global recession raised concerns about its impact on African economies, prospects for meeting the Millennium Development Goals and the potential reduction in foreign direct investment and remittances from abroad. Transnational organized crime, particularly drug trafficking, was becoming a major concern. Several countries had reported important seizures of narcotics on their territory, unauthorized aeroplane landings most likely linked to drug trafficking, and arrests of European, Latin American and West African nationals involved in illicit trafficking. In a positive development, in Liberia, national law enforcement agencies and United Nations Mission in Liberia police conducted an operation that resulted in the eradication of some 400,000 cannabis plants. Meanwhile, the scourge of coups d'état had re-emerged, as evidenced by the 6 August military coup against the President of Mauritania, Sidi Mohamed Ould Cheikh Abdellahi; the 23 November attack on the residence of the President of Guinea-Bissau, João Bernardo Vieira; and the move by a group of military officers in Guinea on 23 December to seize power after the death of President Lansana Conté. West Africa was also affected by severe flooding in the course of the rainy season, resulting in hundreds of deaths and damage to infrastructure, property and crops in several countries.

UNOWA

UNOWA was established by the Secretary-General in 2001 [YUN 2001, p. 162] and extended for three years from 1 January 2005 to 31 December 2007 on the recommendation of the Secretary-General [YUN 2004, p. 170] and the concurrence of the Security Council [YUN 2005, p. 224]. Following a 2006 midterm review of the Office [YUN 2006, p. 175], and subsequent recommendations by an independent consultant, the functions and activities of UNOWA were revised in December 2007 [YUN 2007, p. 168], and the Council extended its mandate until 31 December 2010 [ibid.]. General Lamine Cissé (Senegal) continued to serve as Officer-in-Charge for UNOWA through March 2008. UNOWA maintained its headquarters in Dakar, Senegal.

Appointment. In February, by an exchange of letters with the Security Council President [S/2008/127, S/2008/128], the Secretary-General appointed Said Djinnit (Algeria) as his Special Representative for West Africa and Head of UNOWA. He took up his functions on 1 April, replacing Mr. Cissé.

Activities

During the year, UNOWA activities focused on eight main areas: strengthening the capacity of ECOWAS; subregional cooperation; UN inter-institutional cooperation; governance; cross-border issues; human rights and gender; food security and humanitarian assistance; and support to the Cameroon–Nigeria Mixed Commission. The Office convened high-level meetings with the heads of UN peace missions in West Africa to exchange views on the situation in the subregion and emerging threats to peace, including the food crisis, developments in the Sahelian band in light of increasing cross-border organized crime, deteriorating security in northern areas of the subregion, and the situation in Guinea and its potential impact on the Mano River region.

Strengthening the capacity of ECOWAS to help prevent, manage and resolve conflicts remained a UNOWA priority. UNOWA–ECOWAS cooperation advanced and was evidenced by a joint mission (Conakry, Guinea, 4–6 February) to attend a meeting of the national electoral commissions of ECOWAS member States, which led to the establishment of a subregional network of electoral commissions; joint missions to several West African countries to address threats to peace and security; and the participation of UNOWA military advisers in planning conferences for a command post exercise of the ECOWAS standby force (Bamako, Mali, 15–21 June). UNOWA organized the first meeting of the task force of the ECOWAS Gender Development Centre (Dakar, 31 January–1 February), which adopted the task force's workplan and terms of reference. UNOWA also worked to engage ECOWAS on the ongoing food crisis, and encouraged the adoption by West African countries of an integrated approach to the problem. In a tripartite effort, UNOWA, ECOWAS and UNODC worked to address the threat of cross-border crime and drug trafficking, and organized the Ministerial Conference on Drug Trafficking as a Security Threat to West Africa (Praia, Cape Verde, 28–29 October) (see p. 228).

In other activities, UNOWA led a Department of Political Affairs assessment mission to Guinea (14–21 March); attended the meeting of the Mano River Union (MRU) Council of Ministers and the summit of MRU Heads of State and Government (14–15 May); facilitated the visit of a delegation from the Office of the United Nations High Commissioner for Human Rights (OHCHR) to operationalize OHCHR's new regional office for West Africa in Dakar; and organized an experts' workshop (26–27 June) to facilitate a harmonized and integrated approach to human rights and gender. The Office continued to host the West African office of the Youth Employment Network [YUN 2007, p. 167], which resumed its study of youth employment initiatives in West African countries. UNOWA participated in an experts' meeting (Dakar, 7–9 October) to assist the ECOWAS early warning system in designing a Web-based forum for the exchange of information among key subregional stakeholders, including political and human rights experts. It also facilitated linkages among UN system institutions in the subregion, and on 10 July and 6 October, convened information-sharing and coordination meetings of heads of Dakar-based UN agencies.

In support of the Cameroon–Nigeria Mixed Commission, UNOWA chaired the March and June meetings of the Commission, which resulted in the finalization of the maritime boundary line between Cameroon and Nigeria; an agreement to provide information on offshore oil and gas resources; plans for the upcoming transfer of authority in the Zone of the Bakassi peninsula; and a discussion on further confidence-building measures.

Financing

In a report issued in October [A/63/346/Add.3] dealing with estimated requirements for special political missions grouped under thematic cluster III (United Nations offices, peacebuilding support offices, integrated offices and commissions), the Secretary-General proposed resource requirements for UNOWA in the amount of $5,788,600 for the period 1 January to 31 December 2009, which ACABQ recommended for approval [A/63/593].

On 24 December, in section XI of **resolution 63/263**, the Assembly endorsed the recommendations of ACABQ and approved the budgets for 27 special political missions, including the UNOWA budget, under section 3, Political affairs, of the programme budget for the 2008–2009 biennium (see p. 1548).

Other regional developments

During the year, ECOWAS continued efforts to realize its peace consolidation strategy, particularly in improving regional security, controlling small arms proliferation and drug trafficking, and articulating a conflict prevention framework as envisaged during the 2004 Security Council mission to the region [YUN 2004, p. 169]. Other priority areas included general aspects of development and the creation of an ECOWAS Emergency Strategic Intervention Unit to address natural disasters and other emergency humanitarian situations. At a meeting of the ECOWAS Mediation and Security Council (Ouagadougou, Burkina Faso, 16 January), members adopted the ECOWAS Conflict Prevention Framework, which would provide the ECOWAS Commission and its member States with a common mechanism for early reaction to issues relating to good governance, conflict prevention and resolution, and the inclusion of those themes in ECOWAS programmes. On 7 February, the heads of institutions responsible for managing elections in ECOWAS member States met in Conakry, Guinea, and established the ECOWAS Network of Electoral Commissions for cooperation in improving electoral laws and practices, the exchange of experiences and best practices, and the pooling and sharing of electoral resources to ensure cost-effectiveness. In May, ECOWAS convened meetings of its Small Arms Programme

(ECOSAP) to improve collaboration among member States on border management to control the movement of small arms and light weapons. At the end of a seven-day ECOWAS Command Post Exercise to assess the status of the troops pledged for the 6,500-strong ECOWAS Standby Force (ESF), and their operational readiness, equipment and training level (Bamako, Mali, 21 June), organizers and partners said that the exercise had achieved the set objectives. In October, ECOWAS approved a 10-day field-training exercise in 2009 for the logistic component of ESF to evaluate its capacity to support peace operations. In other activities, the ECOWAS Heads of State and Government, at their thirty-third ordinary summit (Ouagadougou, Burkina Faso, 18 January), adopted a poverty reduction strategy document and the ECOWAS Common Approach on Migration, a regional mechanism for addressing the challenges of intra-community mobility and migration to third countries; ECOWAS co-hosted a conference on "African Youth and Employment" (Accra, Ghana, 5 September); and it convened an experts meeting on Drug Trafficking as a Security Threat to West Africa (Praia, Cape Verde, 26–27 October). In other developments, the Security Council, on 16 April, held a debate on the "Relationship between the United Nations and regional organizations, in particular the African Union, in the maintenance of international peace and security".

Côte d'Ivoire

In 2008, the United Nations, the Economic Community of West African States, the African Union and the international community supported Government efforts to move the peace process forward in Côte d'Ivoire through implementation of the 2007 Ouagadougou Agreement and its supplementary accords [YUN 2007, pp. 174 & 184]. The United Nations Operation in Côte d'Ivoire assisted the Government in the removal of the Green Line (former zone of confidence), the completion of the mobile courts operations, preparations for the presidential elections scheduled for 30 November, and the continued stability of the political and security environment. The partnership between President Laurent Gbagbo and Prime Minister Guillaume Soro remained strong. The lifting of the Green Line allowed political party leaders and the general population to move freely throughout the country. The Security Council mission that visited the country in June noted a relaxed political and security environment marked by a renewed confidence in the Agreement. However, obstacles hampered progress in the disarmament of former combatants, the dismantling of militias and other key aspects of the peace process. Due to accumulated logistical and technical delays, the authorities postponed the elections until 2009. In December, a fourth supplementary accord to the Agreement was signed, which clarified issues related to security sector reform and the restoration of State administration throughout the country.

The Panel of Experts continued to monitor implementation of the arms, travel and diamond sanctions imposed on Côte d'Ivoire. In October, the Security Council decided to renew the sanctions on arms and diamonds, as well as the travel measures, for a further 12 months.

Implementation of the Ouagadougou Agreement

In 2008, efforts continued to move the peace process forward through implementation of the 2007 Ouagadougou Agreement, its supplementary agreements and resolution 1721(2006) [YUN 2006, p. 197], which provided a road map for the transition period. The lifting of the Green Line, which replaced the abolished zone of confidence that had separated troops belonging to the National Armed Forces of Côte d'Ivoire—deployed in the Government-controlled south of the country—from those of the rebel movement (Forces nouvelles)—deployed in the north [YUN 2007, p. 176]—continued under the control of the Integrated Command Centre (CCI) [ibid., p. 182], established to implement the military and security aspects of the Agreement and manned by Government and Forces nouvelles personnel. The United Nations Operation in Côte d'Ivoire (UNOCI) carried out the functions under its revised mandate [YUN 2007, p. 170] and was supported by the Licorne (French forces), whose deployment was endorsed by Security Council resolution 1464(2003) [YUN 2003, p. 168].

Report of Secretary-General (January). In his January report [S/2008/1] on UNOCI, the Secretary-General said that the overall security situation in the country had improved owing to the favourable political environment engendered by the Ouagadougou Agreement, which addressed issues that had blocked the identification of the population, the preparation of the voter list, the disarmament process, the restructuring of the armed forces and the restoration of State authority throughout the country. The national armed forces and the armed forces of the Forces nouvelles had demonstrated a willingness to collaborate, providing security for confidence-building events, such as the visits of President Gbagbo to the northern part of the country and of Prime Minister Soro to the presidential stronghold of Gagnoa. Since the establishment of the Green Line (former zone of confidence), no violations had been recorded and the overall risk of a resumption of hostilities between the two forces was assessed as low. The performance of CCI had improved and Ivorian mixed police units continued to maintain law and order with the support of UNOCI police officers. Eight of the 17 observation points along the Green Line had been removed in accordance with the Agreement to halve the number of posts every two months. However, the Centre faced difficulties in fulfilling its mandate, as a result of financial constraints and its limited planning and operational capacities. Other factors of instability remained a threat to the peace process, such as the lack of progress towards the unification of the national defence and security forces and the dismantling and disarmament of militias in the western part of the country. Criminality was on the rise in several areas of the country, and incidents of extortion and denial of freedom of movement perpetrated by both the national armed forces and the Forces nouvelles continued to be reported.

Despite those challenges, the Secretary-General noted that the November 2007 signing of the second and third agreements [YUN 2007, p. 184] supplementary to the Ouagadougou Agreement—one designating the technical operator for the identification of the population and the other establishing new timelines for implementing the Agreement—gave new impetus to the peace process. With regard to voter registration, it was expected that the Government would be able to expedite the process once a consensual modus operandi for identification and the establishment of the voter rolls had been finalized. UNOCI set up a small certification support cell that was developing criteria and benchmarks for the conduct of the certification exercise, to be agreed upon with the Facilitator and Burkina Faso President Blaise Compaoré, in consultation with other partners. The mobile courts operations to identify the population, which commenced in September 2007 [ibid., p. 182], progressed without any major security incidents. As at 24 December, the mobile courts had granted 93,027 duplicate birth certificates nationwide. However, of the 55 technical teams deployed, only 33 were operational, and the geographical coverage of the mobile teams was limited to 47 of the country's 727 communes. Meanwhile, the redeployment of UNOCI forces from the former zone of confidence was ongoing. The force would be spread throughout the country to support CCI in providing security for the redeployment of State administration; the identification of the population; the disarmament and dismantling of militias; the disarmament, demobilization and reintegration of ex-combatants; and preparations for the elections. In order to increase the mobility of its troops, UNOCI would reduce the number of its camps from 44 to 24. Six camps had already been dismantled, and 18 more were expected to be vacated in early 2008. Four new camps would be established at Divo and Issia in the west, Dabakala in the north and Adzope, near Abidjan, in the south. UNOCI's police component continued to provide advice and training to the national police and gendarmerie in the Government-controlled areas, and would assist CCI in conducting an assessment of their needs in the context of the envisaged reform of the security sector. The Licorne (French forces) continued to maintain its full, quick-reaction capacity to support UNOCI, and France reaffirmed its commitment to maintaining the force in the country.

The Secretary-General said that the direct involvement of President Gbagbo and Prime Minister Soro in resolving key issues demonstrated the value of their partnership and the importance of a consensual approach and Ivorian ownership of the peace process. He took note of their efforts to consult with members of the political opposition on implementation of the Ouagadougou Agreement, and the intention of the Facilitator to convene more frequent meetings of the standing consultative forum to encourage dialogue. He also called on the international consultative organ established by resolution 1765(2007) [YUN 2007, p. 180] to play a more proactive role in supporting the parties in the implementation of the Agreement, including by providing advice and helping to overcome obstacles. On the conduct of the elections, he stated that while the United Nations would not organize the elections as it had done in other countries, his Special Representative would conduct the certification of all stages of the electoral process in an impartial manner, in consultation with the parties, the Facilitator and international partners. As only limited progress was made in restoring State authority and disarming militias and combatants, he recommended that the Security Council extend the UNOCI mandate for a 12-month period, until 15 January 2009, and that the strength of the Operation be maintained until the benchmarks set out in his May 2007 report [ibid., p. 176] were achieved.

On 15 January, by resolution 1795(2008) (see below), the Security Council renewed the mandates of UNOCI and the French forces supporting it until 30 July, and requested the Secretary-General to report on the implementation of key steps of the peace process three weeks prior to that date.

SECURITY COUNCIL ACTION

On 15 January [meeting 5820], the Security Council unanimously adopted **resolution 1795(2008)**. The draft [S/2008/15] was submitted by France.

The Security Council,

Recalling its previous resolutions, in particular resolutions 1739(2007) of 10 January 2007 and 1765(2007) of 16 July 2007, and the statements by its President relating to the situation in Côte d'Ivoire,

Reaffirming its strong commitment to respect for the sovereignty, independence, territorial integrity and unity of Côte d'Ivoire, and recalling the importance of the principles of good-neighbourliness, non-interference and regional cooperation,

Recalling that it endorsed the agreement signed by President Laurent Gbagbo and Mr. Guillaume Soro at Ouagadougou on 4 March 2007 ("the Ouagadougou Political Agreement"), and that it has supported the appointment of Mr. Soro as Prime Minister,

Expressing again its appreciation to the Chairperson of the Economic Community of West African States, President Blaise Compaoré of Burkina Faso ("the Facilitator"), for his continued efforts to facilitate the inter-Ivorian direct dialogue that led, in particular, to the signing of the Ouagadougou Political Agreement, commending and encouraging the continued efforts of the African Union and the Economic Community of West African States to promote peace and stability in Côte d'Ivoire, and reiterating its full support for them,

Reiterating its strong condemnation of any attempt to destabilize the peace process by force, in particular the attack committed on 29 June 2007 in Bouaké against the Prime Minister of Côte d'Ivoire, Mr. Guillaume Soro, that resulted in several deaths, and stressing that the perpetrators of such criminal acts must be brought to justice,

Having taken note of the report of the Secretary-General of 2 January 2008,

Reiterating its firm condemnation of all violations of human rights and international humanitarian law in Côte d'Ivoire,

Recalling its resolution 1612(2005) of 26 July 2005 on children and armed conflict and the subsequent conclusions of the Security Council Working Group on Children and Armed Conflict pertaining to parties to the armed conflict in Côte d'Ivoire,

Recalling also its resolution 1325(2000) of 31 October 2000 on women and peace and security and its resolution 1674(2006) of 28 April 2006 on the protection of civilians in armed conflict,

Welcoming the establishment, as agreed by the parties at the meeting of the Evaluation and Monitoring Committee of 11 May 2007 and the Facilitator, of an international consultative organ to accompany the Ivorian political forces and the Facilitator in the implementation of the Ouagadougou Political Agreement, stressing the importance of this organ participating in the meetings of the Committee as an observer, and recalling that it may be consulted at any time by the Facilitator,

Welcoming also the success of the donors' round table of 18 July 2007, and emphasizing the importance of the continuing support of the United Nations system and the international community for strengthening the capacity of the Government of Côte d'Ivoire and of the electoral bodies in order to organize the presidential and legislative elections,

Determining that the situation in Côte d'Ivoire continues to pose a threat to international peace and security in the region,

Acting under Chapter VII of the Charter of the United Nations,

1. *Welcomes* the second and third agreements supplementary to the Ouagadougou Political Agreement ("the supplementary agreements") signed by President Laurent Gbagbo and Mr. Guillaume Soro at Ouagadougou on 28 November 2007 under the facilitation of President Blaise Compaoré of Burkina Faso;

2. *Takes note* of the recommendations of the African Union in this regard, endorses the supplementary agreements, calls upon the Ivorian parties to implement the supplementary agreements and the Ouagadougou Political Agreement fully, in good faith and within the amended time frame set out in the agreements, which will require the Ivorian parties to redouble their efforts, and encourages the international community to bring continued support to this effect;

3. *Commends* the Facilitator for his continued efforts to support the peace process, and encourages the Ivorian parties to make further concrete progress, in particular in the identification of the Ivorian population and the registration of voters, the disarmament and dismantling of militias, the disarmament, demobilization and reintegration programme, the unification and restructuring of the defence and security forces and the restoration of State authority throughout the country;

4. *Decides* to renew the mandates of the United Nations Operation in Côte d'Ivoire and of the French forces supporting it, as determined in resolution 1739(2007), until 30 July 2008, in order to support the organization in Côte d'Ivoire of free, open, fair and transparent elections within the time frame set out in the Ouagadougou Political Agreement and the supplementary agreements;

5. *Requests* the United Nations Operation in Côte d'Ivoire, within its existing resources and mandate, to support the full implementation of the Ouagadougou Political Agreement and of the third supplementary agreement;

6. *Calls upon* all parties concerned to ensure that the protection of women and children is addressed in the implementation of the Ouagadougou Political Agreement as well as in the post-conflict reconstruction and recovery phases, including continued monitoring and reporting of the situation of women and children;

7. *Invites* the signatories to the Ouagadougou Political Agreement to take the necessary steps to protect vulnerable civilian populations, including by guaranteeing the voluntary return, reinstallation, reintegration and security of displaced persons, with the support of the United Nations system, and to fulfil in this regard their commitments in accordance with the Agreement and their obligations under international humanitarian law;

8. *Expresses its intention* to review by 30 July 2008 the mandates of the United Nations Operation in Côte d'Ivoire and of the French forces supporting it, as well as the troop level of the United Nations Operation in Côte d'Ivoire, in light of the progress achieved in the implementation of the key steps of the peace process, and requests the Secretary-General to provide to the Security Council a report on these key steps three weeks before that date;

9. *Gives its full support* to the efforts of the Special Representative of the Secretary-General for Côte d'Ivoire, and recalls that he shall certify that all stages of the electoral process provide all the necessary guarantees for the holding of open, free, fair and transparent presidential and legislative elections in accordance with international standards;

10. *Requests* the Secretary-General to keep the Council regularly informed, in particular on the preparation of the electoral process, including the registration of voters, and

notably by providing to the Council a report in this regard no later than 15 April 2008, and welcomes the establishment by the United Nations Operation in Côte d'Ivoire of a certification support cell to assist the Special Representative in fulfilling this task;

11. *Also requests* the Secretary-General to continue to take the necessary measures to ensure full compliance in the United Nations Operation in Côte d'Ivoire with the United Nations zero-tolerance policy on sexual exploitation and abuse and to keep the Council informed, and urges troop-contributing countries to take appropriate preventive action, including predeployment awareness training, and other action to ensure full accountability in cases of such conduct involving their personnel;

12. *Recalls* the importance of the provisions of the Ouagadougou Political Agreement and of the supplementary agreements, including paragraph 8.1 of the Ouagadougou Political Agreement and paragraphs 8 and 9 of the third supplementary agreement, and urges the Ivorian political forces to rely on the mediation of the Facilitator for any major difficulty concerning the electoral process;

13. *Encourages* the Facilitator to continue to support the process to settle the crisis in Côte d'Ivoire, and requests the United Nations Operation in Côte d'Ivoire to continue to assist him and his Special Representative in Abidjan, Mr. Boureima Badini, in the conduct of the facilitation, including by helping the Facilitator, as appropriate and upon his request, to carry out his arbitration role in accordance with the provisions of paragraph 8.1 of the Ouagadougou Political Agreement and paragraphs 8 and 9 of the third supplementary agreement;

14. *Decides* to remain actively seized of the matter.

Technical assessment mission (March)

The Secretary-General reported [S/2008/250] that at the request of his Special Representative, a technical assessment mission visited Côte d'Ivoire from 3 to 12 March to assess the progress made towards preparing for the elections and to assist UNOCI in developing proposals on the role the Operation should play in supporting the remaining tasks of the Ouagadougou Agreement. The assessment mission, comprising UN representatives from the Department of Peacekeeping Operations, the Department of Political Affairs and the Office of the UN High Commissioner for Human Rights, met with international and Ivorian stakeholders, including President Gbagbo, Prime Minister Soro, the Chiefs of Staff of the Ivorian defence and security forces and of the Forces nouvelles, representatives of political parties, and the heads of national institutions responsible for implementing key processes under the Agreement. The mission noted an improvement in the overall political and security environment. It confirmed that all parties were interested in holding national elections in 2008, were convinced that the Agreement had ended the armed conflict and believed that the lingering political crisis could be resolved only through the holding of elections. The road to the elections, on the other hand, was fraught with technical challenges and security and political risks. In addition, most of the key election-related processes were plagued by funding gaps. At the technical level, the electoral timelines were problematic. The third supplementary agreement envisaged that presidential elections would be held by the end of the first semester of 2008; all parties recognized that that was no longer technically feasible. There were also concerns that the identification of the population might become contentious. Although feedback on the mobile court operations from Ivorian stakeholders was positive, the opposition party Rassemblement des républicains complained that many Ivorians had not been able to access the mobile courts—primarily in the west—owing to the presence of militias, even if they were dormant. On security aspects, most parties insisted that disarmament must precede the elections. The Forces nouvelles maintained that they would canton their combatants and place their weapons in storage, in accordance with the third supplementary agreement, once the civic service and reintegration programmes were in place. However, the civic service programme was still only a concept, and donors insisted that they would fund reintegration programmes only if they were involved in their design and implementation. While the Chiefs of Staff of the defence and security forces and of the Forces nouvelles had developed a proposal for a unified transition army that would be composed of mixed units responsible for providing security to the electoral process, the proposal had yet to be approved by the President and Prime Minister. Moreover, decisions on the ranks and salaries of the Forces nouvelles elements that would rejoin the army were still pending. Meanwhile, reintegration of the Forces nouvelles elements into the national police and gendarmerie stalled following the police and gendarmerie commanders' rejection of the proposal by the Facilitator to include 4,000 Forces nouvelles personnel in those forces. Other security concerns included the possibility of civil unrest emanating from the population's frustration with the slow progress of the peace process; the continuing exploitation by armed groups in the north; and the threat of dormant militias being mobilized during the elections. In that regard, the Chief of Staff of the defence and security forces, along with the police and gendarmerie commanders, reiterated the request for the Security Council to grant an exception to the arms embargo to allow the import of riot control gear and side weapons for the police and of spare parts for the military transport helicopter.

On the role of UNOCI in supporting the remaining tasks under the Agreement, the assessment mission identified seven areas on which UNOCI would focus: helping the parties address challenges and minimize risks identified in the report; supporting efforts by the parties and the Facilitator to keep the peace process on track; contributing to a secure environment for the elections; contributing to enhancing the credibility of the electoral process; providing logistical support for the elections; assisting national institutions in carrying out key tasks that had to be completed before the elections; and devising a public information strategy to sensitize the Ivorian players about the UNOCI role in the peace process. The UNOCI military and police components would devise, respectively, contingency plans for stabilization interventions to prevent acts of violence aimed at disrupting the peace process and for the redeployment of the UNOCI riot control capabilities to high-risk areas, including the western part of the country, Bouaké and Abidjan. On disarmament, UNOCI would support an accelerated implementation of the cantonment of forces and work with the Facilitator to encourage the parties to agree on an arrangement for the control of weapons placed under storage. The assessment mission also reported on support to persons affected by the conflict, efforts to create a positive political environment through the media, the monitoring of the human rights situation, the economic recovery process and financial support for the implementation of the Ouagadougou Agreement.

Other political and security developments

Report of Secretary-General (April). In his April report [S/2008/250] on Côte d'Ivoire, the Secretary-General said that the security situation remained stable yet fragile, owing to the lack of progress in disarming the Forces nouvelles and in dismantling the militias in the west. Violent crimes, particularly armed robberies in the western part of the country, were a major concern. Several individuals were arrested in association with a December 2007 attack against Forces nouvelles personnel in Bouaké. Supporters of Sergeant Ibrahim Coulibaly, a former member of the Forces nouvelles, were accused of the attacks, and criminal investigations were ongoing. In another incident, 11 individuals allegedly associated with Mr. Coulibaly were arrested in Abidjan for plotting a coup. On 30 January 2008, the prosecutor of the military court in Abidjan issued an international arrest warrant against Mr. Coulibaly, who was accused of conspiracy against the State. Although demonstrations in Abidjan and San Pedro on 31 March and 1 April against the rising cost of living turned violent and disrupted the mobile courts operations, the demonstrations stopped after the Government announced emergency measures to curb taxes on food and basic services for a three-month period.

As the security and political climate continued to improve, political parties increased their activities throughout the country. On 1 February, the Rassemblement des républicains held its convention in Abidjan and designated its leader, Alassane Ouattara, as the party's candidate for the presidential elections. The ruling party, the Front populaire ivoirien, held a rally in Bouaké, the stronghold of the Forces nouvelles, with the participation of the Minister for Defence, who was also the chairman of President Gbagbo's campaign for the presidential election. The party also started a campaign tour in the north on 31 March. During a two-day visit to Abidjan (5-6 March), the ECOWAS Commission President announced that his organization would support the electoral process financially and deploy electoral observers. The partnership between President Gbagbo and Prime Minister Soro remained strong and they continued to consult with regional leaders on progress made in the implementation of the Ouagadougou Agreement.

On 14 January and 21 March, the Facilitator of the peace process, President Compaoré, convened meetings of the Evaluation and Monitoring Committee (CEA) of the Ouagadougou Agreement established to monitor the implementation of the Agreement and address any obstacles. The international consultative organ, comprising the international partners of Côte d'Ivoire, including UNOCI, participated in the meetings. In January, participants stressed the need to prioritize the electoral process and for the United Nations to elaborate, in consultation with the Government, the parameters and modus operandi of the Secretary-General's Special Representative in the certification of all stages of the electoral process. At the March meeting, participants recommended that the decrees related to the modalities for voter registration and for the collaboration between the technical operator (the French company SAGEM) and the National Institute of Statistics, as well as the SAGEM contract to produce national identity cards and voter cards, be concluded as soon as possible in order to facilitate announcing a date for the elections. They also recommended the acceleration of the cantonment of combatants; the immediate start of the disarmament and dismantling of militias; and the Government's provision of appropriate funding for the cantonment operations and reintegration of ex-combatants.

The report also summarized the status of implementation of the Ouagadougou Agreement, including building the capacity of CCI, which stood at 544 out of the authorized maximum of 568 Forces nouvelles and national defence and security personnel. UNOCI continued redeploying its troops from the former zone of confidence in order to reinforce its presence in the west and the north and to make additional troops available to support CCI; UNOCI had removed all except 2 of the 17 observation posts it had established along the Green Line. The commanders of the two armed forces made efforts to begin their respective cantonment. On 24 January, the Chief of Staff of the defence and security forces announced that 12,000 of his soldiers had been cantoned and registered, and had deposited their weapons in storage. The cantonment of Forces nouvelles, however, had not progressed significantly. As at 1 April, only 109 elements had been cantoned due to logistical and financial constraints, as well as the lack of a clearly defined reintegration programme. While the national programme for reinsertion and community rehabilitation, which was expected to absorb 6,000 ex-combatants, had facilitated the registration and profiling of Forces nouvelles personnel, the programme faced funding and operational challenges. The civic service programme, intended to absorb 20,000 former combatants and 20,000 youth at risk, had yet to be launched and would cost approximately $90 million. The Government requested CCI to start the disarmament and dismantling of militias by 18 February, and UNOCI built and equipped four weapons collections points, which were handed over to the authorities on 17 March. The process remained stalled due to the absence of arrangements for conducting the operation and lack of an agreement between the Government and militia leaders on the payment of salaries and reintegration arrangements for the militia. On 20 February, President Gbagbo signed a decree establishing a working group to develop a framework for the organization, composition and functioning of the new national defence and security forces. On 5 January, the Facilitator presented a proposal on the numbers of Forces nouvelles to be integrated into the new national defence forces, which included 5,000 to join the armed forces, 600 security auxiliaries trained by UNOCI to be integrated into the police and gendarmerie, and 3,400 additional personnel to be assigned to CCI. Although the parties had not formally responded to the Facilitator's proposals, they formed the basis for discussion by the working group.

The restoration of State administration throughout the country was hampered by various constraints. Out of the 24,437 civil servants who had been displaced during the conflict, only 6,094 had yet to return to their posts, but a funding shortfall of some $20.7 million to complete the redeployment exercise hindered progress. The redeployment of finance and customs officials faced challenges, such as the absence of a comprehensive plan for redeploying the law enforcement, legal, judicial and corrections personnel needed to provide support to the officials. In addition, the judiciary could not be redeployed prior to the completion of the mobile courts operations, as 50 per cent of the country's judges were involved in that exercise. In that connection, the mobile courts were expected to complete their operations by the end of April. Some 111 mobile courts were involved in the identification of the population, and as at 8 April, the number of duplicate birth certificates issued since the first wave of mobile courts operations in 2006 totalled 565,854. On 20 February, the Government adopted the technical specifications for the issuing of identity cards and voter cards; the contract between the Government and SAGEM was signed on 27 March. However, the division of responsibilities between SAGEM and the National Institute of Statistics, which traditionally produced the cards and was expected to conduct the identification and registration process jointly with SAGEM, had yet to be defined.

In other aspects of the electoral process, the Independent Electoral Commission (IEC), with assistance from UNOCI, completed the mapping of 90 per cent of the 10,453 proposed polling stations using global positioning technology. The Secretary-General's Special Representative elaborated a framework for certifying all stages of the electoral process that included benchmarks to assess the existence of a secure environment during the period leading to the elections; the full participation of the population and the candidates in the process; the inclusiveness of the electoral process; the equitable access of all candidates to the media and media neutrality; the credibility of the electoral lists and their acceptance by all parties; and the results of the election, as determined through a transparent counting process and accepted by all or challenged peacefully through appropriate channels. The benchmarks were defined in consultation with all national and international partners. The legal framework for the electoral process, along with an ordinance modifying the electoral code and a decree on the modalities for the establishment of the new voters list, had yet to be finalized. The Secretary-General observed that the Ouagadougou Agreement had built upon the progress made by previous agreements, bringing Côte d'Ivoire closer to national elections. Its most significant achievement included the positive, albeit fragile, political and security environment that prevailed throughout the country, the incipient recovery of the economy and the advances made in the identification of the population. He welcomed the consensus among the parties to hold the elections in 2008 and said that the UN system would continue to put at the disposal of the national stakeholders and institutions resources such as technical expertise, logistical assistance and capacity-building support.

Electoral process

The Secretary-General reported [S/2008/451] that on 14 April, on the recommendation of the IEC and agreed to by all political parties and civil society, President Gbagbo issued a decree setting 30 November as the date of the first round of presidential elections. As the lifting of the zone of confidence allowed political party leaders and the general population to move freely throughout the country, significant efforts were made to reinvigorate political party structures and increase outreach activities in preparation for the elections, including rallies by political parties throughout Côte d'Ivoire. The political parties and civil society discussed the implementation of key aspects of the Ouagadougou Agreement and supplementary agreements. The ruling party, the Front populaire ivoirien, advocated for the disarmament of combatants and the transfer of administrative authority to the préfets, sous-préfets and customs officers redeployed in the north, while the opposition alliance, the Rassemblement des houphouétistes pour la démocratie et la paix, dispatched teams throughout the country to sensitize the population on the identification process and the upcoming registration of voters. The President of Côte d'Ivoire's Economic and Social Council, Laurent Dona Fologo, previously a member of former President Henri Konan Bédié's Parti démocratique de Côte d'Ivoire, formed a new political party, the Rassemblement pour la paix, le progrès et le partage, and announced his support for President Gbagbo in the elections.

During his visit to Côte d'Ivoire (23–24 April), the Secretary-General welcomed the consensus reached by the parties on the election date and witnessed the signing of two documents that advanced the electoral process: an agreement between the Government and international donors, under which the latter committed $43 million to support the electoral process, and the Code of Good Conduct during the electoral period, endorsed by 37 political parties.

SECURITY COUNCIL ACTION

On 29 April [meeting 5880], following consultations among Security Council members, the President made statement **S/PRST/2008/11** on behalf of the Council:

The Security Council recalls that it endorsed the Ouagadougou Political Agreement as well as its supplementary agreements.

The Council warmly welcomes the approval by the Ivorian authorities of the proposal by the Independent Electoral Commission to organize presidential elections on 30 November 2008. It underlines that this announcement, supported by all Ivorian parties, and the signing by President Laurent Gbagbo of related decrees, constitute an important step forward. The Council encourages the Ivorian parties to redouble their efforts to meet this commitment, and the international community to bring continued support to this effect.

The Council commends the Facilitator, President Blaise Compaoré of Burkina Faso, for his continued efforts to support the peace process in Côte d'Ivoire, in particular through the Ouagadougou Political Agreement follow-up and consultation mechanisms. This support to the actions of President Laurent Gbagbo and Prime Minister Guillaume Soro, with the active engagement of the Special Representative of the Secretary-General for Côte d'Ivoire, Mr. Choi Young-Jin, has been instrumental towards achieving the establishment of a consensus among all political parties to hold presidential elections in 2008.

The Council reaffirms its full support to the Special Representative and recalls that he shall certify that all stages of the electoral process provide all the necessary guarantees for the holding of open, free, fair and transparent presidential and legislative elections in accordance with international standards, consistent with paragraph 9 of resolution 1795(2008). It fully supports, in particular, the five-criteria framework elaborated by Mr. Choi in this regard and welcomed by the Ivorian parties.

The Council welcomes the visit of the Secretary-General to Burkina Faso and Côte d'Ivoire from 22 to 24 April 2008 and is encouraged by the signing, under the auspices of the Secretary-General, of a Code of Good Conduct for elections by all political parties.

The Council welcomes the report of the Secretary-General of 15 April 2008. It encourages the Ivorian parties to build on the ongoing mobile courts process for the identification of the Ivorian population and the registration of voters. The Council looks forward to the publication of the electoral list as a crucial step in the electoral process.

The Council calls upon the parties to make concrete progress to promote political stability and security, in particular in the context of the forthcoming presidential elections, in such key areas as the disarmament and dismantling of militias, the disarmament, demobilization and reintegration programme, the storage of weapons, the unification and restructuring of the defence and security forces and the full restoration of State authority throughout the country.

The Council takes note with appreciation of the support of bilateral and multilateral donors, in particular the Economic Community of West African States, the African Union and the European Union. It calls upon donors and the Government of Côte d'Ivoire to make further efforts to finance the electoral process, including through the trust fund established by the United Nations Development Programme to that effect, and calls upon the authorities of Côte d'Ivoire to engage fully with the donors. It also encourages the international community to enhance its financial support for the facilitation.

The Council expresses its appreciation for the role played by the United Nations Operation in Côte d'Ivoire, supported by the French forces, in contributing to bring the security needed for the peace process and the logistical support required for the preparation of the elections. It welcomes the assessment made by the Secretary-General on the troop level of the United Nations Operation in Côte d'Ivoire in his report. The Council will review by 30 July 2008 the mandates of the United Nations Operation in Côte d'Ivoire and the French forces supporting it, as well as the troop level of the United Nations Operation in Côte d'Ivoire, in accordance with paragraph 8 of resolution 1795(2008).

The Council requests the Secretary-General to keep it regularly informed of the situation, including on the logistical support that the United Nations Operation in Côte d'Ivoire will provide for the elections.

Following the confirmation of the 30 November date for the presidential election, IEC announced an electoral timetable that conformed to the Constitution and the revised electoral code. The provisional electoral list would be published on 31 August, with the definitive list for both the presidential and legislative elections published on 15 November. IEC would submit the polling report within three days of the first round of elections to the Constitutional Council, which would have up to seven days to issue a statement on the election results. If no presidential candidate won decisively, a second round of elections would take place within 15 days of the proclaimed results. Legislative elections would take place 45 days after the announced results of the presidential elections.

In other preparatory activity, local electoral commissions, which would play a critical role in supervising the identification process and in organizing the elections, were being installed throughout the country and, as at 1 July, some 369 out of 415 commissions had been established. UNOCI assisted IEC with a review of the 11,000 polling stations that were used during the 2000 elections, and was using its geographic information system technology in the planning process. The UNOCI certification support cell developed a modus operandi for the certification process. Field reports, together with formal and informal consultations with the Facilitator and national and international partners, would serve as the basis for the certification of the electoral process.

Permanent Consultative Framework meeting (May). On 9 May, the Facilitator convened the third meeting of the Permanent Consultative Framework of the Ouagadougou Agreement, comprising the main political leaders: President Gbagbo, Prime Minister Soro and the opposition leaders, Mr. Bédié and Alassane Dramane Ouattara, President of the Rassemblement des républicains. The final communiqué called for a rapid launch of the identification operation and reconstitution of civil registers, the immediate dismantling of the militias and commencement of the civic service programme. The meeting decided that the mobile court operations would continue beyond the 15 May deadline.

Security Council mission

The Security Council mission in Côte d'Ivoire was led by Ambassador Michel Kafando (Burkina Faso), who briefed the Security Council on the mission on 18 June [meeting 5915] (see p. 111). On 15 July, the mission reported [S/2008/460] that it met with the main political players, including President Gbagbo, and with military and administrative authorities, the facilitators of the political process, the leadership of UNOCI and other representatives of the UN system, civil society, the IEC Chairman and representatives of the National Institute of Statistics and of SAGEM, the technical operator for the identification and voter registration. The mission noted a relaxed political and security environment in Côte d'Ivoire, marked by a renewed confidence by all stakeholders in the Ouagadougou Agreement and a significant acceleration of the preparations for the elections. The mission stressed the responsibility of IEC, SAGEM and the National Institute of Statistics in ensuring the transparency of the voter lists and, in order to support the Special Representative in his task, requested the two technical operators involved in the preparation of the voters' lists to submit on a regular basis, through IEC, all information and documentation that could inform the Special Representative's certification mandate. It also encouraged the Special Representative to continue to sensitize Ivorians on his framework for the certification of the electoral process.

On security aspects, progress was made with the completion of the cantonment of the national defence and security forces and the launching of the process in the areas controlled by the Forces nouvelles. It was estimated that the cantonment process would be completed within five months and in time for the elections. Other positive developments included the lifting of the zone of confidence, the gradual removal of observation points along the Green Line, and the free movement of parties throughout the territory, conducting electoral campaigns and sensitization in the peace process. However, the likely impact of the disarmament of former combatants, dismantling of the militias and reunification of the army on the overall security of the electoral process was a concern. In light of the limited progress achieved in those areas, the Rassemblement des républicains and civil society urged the Security Council to maintain the sanctions regime and the arms embargo until the peace process had become irreversible and the key processes of disarmament, demobilization and reintegration, dismantling of the militias and reunification of the army were completed. On the other hand, the four Generals representing the impartial forces (Licorne and UNOCI), the national defence and security forces and the Forces nouvelles emphasized the excellent working relations among their units since the signing of the Ouagadougou Agreement; stressed the progress made by CCI in overseeing the process of disarmament, demobilization and reintegration, dismantling of militias and reunification of the army; and minimized the security risks facing the electoral process. A security plan for the electoral process was being developed by the leadership of the national defence and security forces, the Forces nouvelles, CCI and the impartial forces, based on a thorough threat assessment, and provided for an enhanced cooperation with the defence and security forces of neighbouring States. The Licorne Force Commander pointed to the responsibility of the political leaders, who had yet to agree on the quotas for reintegrating former Forces nouvelles elements into the new army and on the modus operandi for reinserting former combatants, including the civic service programme. All interlocutors concurred that it would be appropriate to defer any decision on the reunification of the army to the new President and administration. They also called for the Security Council to maintain the troop levels of UNOCI and the Licorne until the elections.

During his meeting with the Security Council mission, President Gbagbo reiterated his intention to organize the presidential election on 30 November, despite the difficulties encountered, mainly resulting from a lack of funding. He stressed the need for the technical operators to ensure that they meet the deadline for the elections, and as the relevant decrees had been adopted and the Government at the end of May had made a first payment to SAGEM, he considered that the onus was on them to expedite the preparation of the elections. He was confident that security was no longer an issue for the electoral process, given the presence on the ground of UNOCI and the Licorne forces, and stressed that the focus should be on mobilizing financial resources to assist the Government to meet its obligations to SAGEM and to support the cantonment of former combatants.

The Security Council mission urged the State media to play a greater role in supporting the peace process by promoting dialogue and organizing political debates ahead of the elections. It encouraged key political leaders and the Facilitator to ensure that the peace process remained inclusive, and in particular, to consider the concerns expressed by civil society regarding the transparency of the Ouagadougou political process, while also urging civil society to assume ownership of the process. On the human rights situation, it urged the national defence and security forces, the Forces nouvelles and the impartial forces to address the trend of sexual and gender-based violence in the country. The mission concluded the report with a series of recommendations addressed to the Security Council, to UNOCI and the Licorne forces and to the Ivorian parties.

Extension of UNOCI mandate

Report of Secretary-General (July). In his July report [S/2008/451] on UNOCI and the status of implementation of the Ouagadougou Agreement, the Secretary-General said that significant progress had been made in identifying the population when the mobile courts operation ended in May. Some 627,923 declaratory judgements in lieu of birth certificates had been issued, including 533,789 documents to Ivorian nationals, which would serve as identity papers for registration on the voter's roll. In addition, the decree on the modus operandi for the production and issuance of national identity cards and the registration of voters, which clarified the modalities of cooperation between the two operators, SAGEM and the National Institute of Statistics, was promulgated on 19 June.

On the disarmament, demobilization and reintegration process, the cantonment of the Forces nouvelles continued. As at 1 July, some 6,285 Forces nouvelles elements had been cantoned, out of which 3,980 chose to be demobilized and 1,305 volunteered to join the new national armed forces. However, only 86 weapons, of which 10 were serviceable, had been collected and stored under the custody of the Forces nouvelles. In June, the Ministry of Defence established a disarmament monitoring committee to address obstacles facing the cantonment process, such as the absence of reintegration programmes for foreign combatants and the inability of the Government to pay the agreed $214 monthly allowance to each cantoned combatant for a three-month period. Meanwhile, both the national programme for reinsertion and community rehabilitation and the national civic service programme faced financial challenges, with the latter expected to cost $80 million in 2008, of which the Government had budgeted $24 million. No progress was made in the disarmament and dismantling of militias. Militia leaders rejected the Government proposal that the 1,019 armed militia elements remaining in the west would be absorbed by the national civic service programme, and continued to demand payment of the safety net package received by the first group of militias disarmed in Guiglo in July 2006. The unification of the armed forces remained stalled over the issue of the ranks and numbers of the Forces nouvelles to be integrated into the new national armed forces.

While the overall security situation remained stable, recurrent protests by cantoned Forces nouvelles combatants underscored the risks of setbacks if adequate resources were not provided to support key aspects of the peace process. Other security concerns included increasing criminality in the area of the country controlled by the Forces nouvelles and the instability of the western part of the country. Redeployment of the UNOCI military force from the former zone of confidence continued, with efforts to consolidate its camps from 44 to 24 and increase force mobility. Twenty out of the planned 24 camps had been dismantled. A new deployment location was established in the north, while efforts were continuing to establish three new camps in Divo and Issia in the west and Adzopé in the south, where there had been no UNOCI presence.

The Secretary-General observed that notwithstanding the positive developments, Côte d'Ivoire still faced significant challenges. The continued existence of militias and the lack of credibility of the cantonment of former combatants with weapons stored under secure and verifiable arrangements could pose risks to the electoral process. In view of the parties' decision to defer until after the elections key aspects of the Ouagadougou Agreement, including the unification of the armed forces and effective disarmament, he encouraged the national defence and security forces and the Forces nouvelles to jointly develop a comprehensive plan for the security of the elections, in consultation with the Facilitator and the impartial forces. In order to ensure that demobilized combatants were constructive participants in the electoral process, he encouraged all stakeholders to expedite projects for reinserting ex-combatants, ex-militias and youth-at-risk in the months leading to the elections. He added that UNOCI, with the Ivorian authorities and the Licorne force, was assessing the security threats that might impact the electoral process and was moving forward on comprehensive security contingency planning. In that connection, and as the key benchmarks to trigger the beginning of the withdrawal of UNOCI remained incomplete, he recommended the extension of the UNOCI mandate, at its current strength, for a six-month period until 31 January 2009. A comprehensive assessment and further recommendations on troop levels would be submitted after the announcement of the results of the elections.

SECURITY COUNCIL ACTION

On 29 July [meeting 5945], the Security Council unanimously adopted **resolution 1826(2008)**. The draft [S/2008/486] was submitted by Belgium, Burkina Faso, France and South Africa.

The Security Council,

Recalling its previous resolutions, in particular resolutions 1739(2007) of 10 January 2007, 1765(2007) of 16 July 2007 and 1795(2008) of 15 January 2008, and the statements by its President relating to the situation in Côte d'Ivoire, and resolution 1777(2007) of 20 September 2007 on the situation in Liberia,

Reaffirming its strong commitment to the sovereignty, independence, territorial integrity and unity of Côte d'Ivoire, and recalling the importance of the principles of good-neighbourliness, non-interference and regional cooperation,

Recalling that it endorsed the agreement signed by President Laurent Gbagbo and Mr. Guillaume Soro at Ouagadougou on 4 March 2007 ("the Ouagadougou Political Agreement"), and the following supplementary agreements, as recommended by the African Union,

Recalling also that it welcomed the announcement by the Ivorian authorities of the organization on 30 November 2008 of the first round of the presidential elections and that it encouraged the Ivorian parties to redouble their efforts to meet this commitment, and the international community to bring continued support to this effect,

Expressing again its appreciation to President Blaise Compaoré of Burkina Faso ("the Facilitator") for his continued efforts to support the peace process in Côte d'Ivoire, in particular through the Ouagadougou Political Agreement follow-up mechanisms, commending and encouraging the continued efforts of the African Union and the Economic Community of West African States to promote peace and stability in Côte d'Ivoire, and reiterating its full support for them,

Stressing again the importance of the international consultative organ participating in the meetings of the Evaluation and Monitoring Committee, as an observer, and recalling that it may be consulted at any time by the Facilitator,

Reiterating its strong condemnation of any attempt to destabilize the peace process by force, and expressing its intention to examine without delay the situation after any such attempt, on the basis of a report of the Secretary-General,

Having taken note of the report of the Secretary-General of 10 July 2008,

Noting with concern, in spite of the sustained improvement of the overall human rights situation, the persistence of cases of human rights violations against civilians, including numerous acts of sexual violence, stressing that the perpetrators must be brought to justice, and reiterating its firm condemnation of all violations of human rights and international humanitarian law in Côte d'Ivoire,

Recalling its resolution 1612(2005) of 26 July 2005 on children and armed conflict and the subsequent conclusions of the Security Council Working Group on Children and Armed Conflict pertaining to parties to the armed conflict in Côte d'Ivoire,

Recalling also its resolutions 1325(2000) of 31 October 2000 and 1820(2008) of 19 June 2008 on women and peace and security, and its resolution 1674(2006) of 28 April 2006 on the protection of civilians in armed conflict, condemning any sexual violence, and encouraging the Secretary-General to mainstream a gender perspective in the implementation of the mandate of the United Nations Operation in Côte d'Ivoire,

Emphasizing the importance of the continuing support of the United Nations system and the international community for strengthening the capacity of the Government of Côte d'Ivoire and of the electoral bodies to organize the electoral process,

Determining that the situation in Côte d'Ivoire continues to pose a threat to international peace and security in the region,

Acting under Chapter VII of the Charter of the United Nations,

1. *Decides* to renew the mandates of the United Nations Operation in Côte d'Ivoire and of the French forces supporting it, as determined in resolution 1739(2007), until 31 January 2009, in particular to support the organization in Côte d'Ivoire of free, open, fair and transparent elections;

2. *Requests* the United Nations Operation in Côte d'Ivoire, within its existing resources and mandate, to support the full implementation of the Ouagadougou Political Agreement and its supplementary agreements, and in particular to contribute to bringing the security needed by the peace process and by the electoral process and to provide logistical support to the Independent Electoral Commission for the preparation and the holding of the elections;

3. *Strongly encourages* the Defence and Security Forces of Côte d'Ivoire and the Forces nouvelles to jointly develop a comprehensive plan for the security of the elections, in close coordination with the Facilitator, with the technical

and logistical support of the United Nations Operation in Côte d'Ivoire, which is supported by the French forces;

4. *Encourages* the Ivorian parties to make further concrete progress, in particular in removing the remaining logistical obstacles that impede the identification of the population, the registration of voters, the disarmament and dismantling of militias, the cantonment and disarmament, demobilization and reintegration programme, the unification and restructuring of defence and security forces and the restoration of State authority throughout the country;

5. *Urges* the political parties to comply fully with the Code of Good Conduct for elections which they signed under the auspices of the Secretary-General, and in particular urges the Ivorian authorities to allow equitable access to public media;

6. *Calls upon* all concerned parties to ensure that the protection of women and children is addressed in the implementation of the Ouagadougou Political Agreement as well as the post-conflict reconstruction and recovery phases, including continued monitoring and reporting of the situation of women and children;

7. *Stresses* the importance of ensuring the equal protection of and respect for the human rights of every Ivorian as they relate to the electoral system, and in particular of removing obstacles and challenges to the participation and full involvement of women in public life;

8. *Invites* the signatories to the Ouagadougou Political Agreement to take the necessary steps to protect vulnerable civilian populations, including by guaranteeing the voluntary return, reinstallation, reintegration and security of displaced persons, with the support of the United Nations system, and to fulfil in this regard their commitments in accordance with the Agreement and their obligations under international humanitarian law;

9. *Expresses its intention* to review by 31 January 2009 the mandates of the United Nations Operation in Côte d'Ivoire and the French forces supporting it, as well as the troop level of the United Nations Operation in Côte d'Ivoire, in light of the progress achieved in the implementation of the key steps of the peace process and of the progress of the electoral process, and requests the Secretary-General to provide to the Security Council a report in this regard three weeks before that date, including some benchmarks for a possible phased drawdown of the troop level of the United Nations Operation in Côte d'Ivoire, taking into consideration the electoral process and the situation on the ground and in particular the security conditions;

10. *Reiterates its full support* to the efforts of the Special Representative of the Secretary-General for Côte d'Ivoire, recalls that he shall certify that all stages of the electoral process provide all the necessary guarantees for the holding of open, free, fair and transparent presidential and legislative elections in accordance with international standards, and reaffirms its support to the five-criteria framework elaborated by the Special Representative and referred to in the report of the Secretary-General of 15 April 2008;

11. *Recalls* that the publication of the electoral list is a crucial step in the electoral process, calls upon the Independent Electoral Commission, the technical operators, the authorities of Côte d'Ivoire and the political parties to redouble their efforts in this regard, and requests the Special Representative to certify it explicitly;

12. *Welcomes* the financial assistance provided by donors to the Independent Electoral Commission, which made it possible to finance the electoral process;

13. *Calls upon* the donors to increase, in particular, their financial support to the cantonment, disarmament and reintegration of former combatants and militia and to the redeployment of State administration throughout the country;

14. *Commends* the Special Representative for his efforts to facilitate the reinsertion of former combatants through the launching of one thousand microprojects, and encourages donors to contribute to their financing;

15. *Requests* the Secretary-General to continue to take the necessary measures to ensure full compliance in the United Nations Operation in Côte d'Ivoire with the United Nations zero-tolerance policy on sexual exploitation and abuses and to keep the Council informed, and urges troop-contributing countries to take appropriate preventive action, including predeployment awareness training, and other action to ensure full accountability in cases of such conduct involving their personnel;

16. *Recalls* the importance of the provisions of the Ouagadougou Political Agreement and of the supplementary agreements, including paragraph 8.1 of the Ouagadougou Political Agreement and paragraphs 8 and 9 of the third supplementary agreement, and urges the Ivorian political forces to rely on the mediation of the Facilitator for any major difficulty concerning the electoral process;

17. *Commends* the Facilitator for continuing to support the process to settle the crisis in Côte d'Ivoire, and requests the United Nations Operation in Côte d'Ivoire to continue to assist him and his Special Representative in Abidjan, Mr. Boureima Badini, in the conduct of the facilitation, including by helping the Facilitator, as appropriate and upon his request, to carry out his arbitration role in accordance with the provisions of paragraph 8.1 of the Ouagadougou Political Agreement and paragraphs 8 and 9 of the third supplementary agreement;

18. *Requests* the Secretary-General to keep the Council regularly informed of the situation and of the preparation of the electoral process, including the process of the establishment of the electoral list, and notably by providing to it a report in this regard, no later than 15 October 2008;

19. *Decides* to remain actively seized of the matter.

Further political and security developments

Report of Secretary-General (October). In his eighteenth report on UNOCI [S/2008/645], the Secretary-General said that the political atmosphere in Côte d'Ivoire remained positive and, in preparation for the elections, political parties intensified their information and sensitization campaign activities throughout the country. In August, at its national convention in Yamoussoukro, the ruling Front populaire ivoirien political party nominated President Gbagbo as its candidate for the presidential election. The opposition Parti démocratique de Côte d'Ivoire conducted a one-week sensitization campaign in the Vallée du Bandama region, while the party's leader and presidential candidate, former President Bédié, toured the north for six days. The Rassemblement des républicains held its national convention in Yamoussoukro in October and designated Alassane Ouattara as the party's presidential candidate. Civil society groups intensified their activities, including the adoption of a code of conduct to govern their activities during the electoral period and the creation of a mechanism for monitoring implementation of the Ouagadougou Agreement. On 10 July and 15–17 September, the Facilitator convened meetings of CEA. In July, the meeting discussed ways of addressing the logistical constraints impeding the launch of the identification and voter registration processes, and in September participants focused on measures to resolve the long-standing issue of the ranks and numbers of Forces nouvelles personnel to be integrated into the new army.

While the overall security situation remained stable, worrying security concerns included demonstrations by disgruntled personnel of the Forces nouvelles and the national defence and security forces; tensions between communities over land and other issues, especially in the west; and strikes and demonstrations to protest against the rising cost of living in urban areas. An atmosphere of insecurity remained in the western part of the country, as well as in parts of the former zone of confidence, owing to continuing indiscriminate attacks by highway robbers, coupled with violence, including the rape of women. UNOCI prepared a comprehensive assessment of the security situation in the electoral period, including a detailed threat analysis, as well as measures to minimize election-related security risks and threats. Existing resources and arrangements would contribute towards minimizing those security risks and threats. Nonetheless, UNOCI indicated that, should the need arise, it would recommend resorting to the inter-mission reinforcement arrangements provided under resolution 1609(2005) [YUN 2005, p. 236] during the period before or after the elections. In consultation with the leadership of the defence and security forces and the Forces nouvelles, UNOCI developed a security plan for the elections. UNOCI troops continued to patrol in the country and, jointly with the United Nations Mission in Liberia (UNMIL), along the Ivorian-Liberian border.

On the status of implementation of the Ouagadougou Agreement, UNOCI, on 30 July, dismantled the last observation post along the Green Line, and thereby the Green Line that replaced the zone of confidence ceased to exist. Mixed police units patrolled the former zone of confidence, even though their operational capacity remained limited due to inadequate equipment and financial support. CCI built up its capacity with support from UNOCI and the Licorne force. Out of an authorized strength of 668 personnel, CCI comprised 458 Government and Forces nouvelles military personnel: 214 elements based at the headquarters in Yamoussoukro, and 244 deployed in the former zone of confidence as part of the mixed police units and supporting elements. On the cantonment, demobilization and reintegration of combatants, as at 1 October, 11,364 Forces nouvelles personnel had been cantoned, out of a total of 34,678 combatants declared by the group; only 10 weapons and some ammunition were collected. Ongoing financial problems compelled the national programme for reinsertion and community rehabilitation to scale down its programmes and close most of its offices around the country. In addition, while the national civic service programme had increased its capacity, it would be unable to absorb the expected caseload of 15,000 former combatants by the end of October owing to a lack of agreement between the Government and the Forces nouvelles. Positive developments included the launch by several donors of programmes for reinserting former combatants and youth at risk and the approval by the Peacebuilding Support Office of $4 million to fund 1,000 microprojects for the short-term reinsertion of more than 5,000 combatants. On disarming and dismantling the militias, the registration and profiling of the militias in the western part of the country were completed, but the Government had not yet determined the arrangements for disarming, dismantling and reintegrating militia personnel. Progress was made in redeploying Government officials who were displaced from the north during the conflict. Challenges such as Forces nouvelles zone commanders reluctant to relinquish their authority in the areas under their control, logistical and financial constraints, and delays in re-establishing the judicial system and an adequate police presence, however, hampered the work of redeployed State officials.

On the electoral process, several decrees were issued in September, including those outlining the modalities of the voting exercise and specifications for electoral materials, as well as a 14 September presidential decree stipulating that voter registration would be conducted over a 45-day period. Supplementary mobile courts, deployed in August to issue duplicate birth certificates to applicants in areas not adequately covered during the main operation, concluded their work on 25 September. The identification of the population and the voter registration processes were launched on 15 September and, as at 1 October, some 5,849 voters had been registered. Although the pace of voter registration and identification was expected to increase as more teams were deployed throughout the country, the process was not likely to be completed within the 45-day period as stipulated by the decree. Tasks to be accomplished included the setting-up of coordination centres; the establishment of registration sites; the operationalization of identification kits; the selection, training and deployment of identification agents; and the launching of a sensitization campaign. As at 1 October, IEC reported that 43 of the 70 coordination centres were operational, and all 35,000 identification agents had been recruited and were being trained and deployed. UNOCI and UN agencies supported the registration process by providing technical expertise, logistical assistance and equipment. The UNOCI certification cell was closely monitoring key aspects of the electoral process and collecting information that would enable the Special Representative to exercise his certification mandate. UNOCI also established a small cell to coordinate the deployment of international observers. Delays in voter identification and registration had proven greater than expected, with a potential impact on the electoral timeline.

The Secretary-General said that with the launching of the voter registration process the peace process had crossed a critical milestone. Highlighting the success of the mobile courts operations and the consensus reached by the parties to resolve arising issues, he observed that it was imperative to carry out the issuance of identity cards and voter registration in an equally credible and transparent manner. He added that the Special Representative, in the exercise of his certification mandate, would not be focusing on finding fault with the process, but would pursue a constructive approach aimed at anticipating problems and assisting the parties and the electoral authorities to address them in a manner that would preserve the credibility of the elections. He expressed concern about the lack of progress in the redeployment of State authority in the north, the disappointing results of efforts to collect and store the weapons of former combatants, the stalled process of the dismantling and disarming the militias, and the continued existence of youth groups that tended to resort to politically motivated violence.

Security Council consideration. On 27 October [meeting 6001], the Secretary-General's Special Representative, Choi Young-Jin, briefed the Security Council on the identification of the population and the elections, particularly the challenges facing the identification process.

SECURITY COUNCIL ACTION

On 7 November [meeting 6014], following consultations among Security Council members, the President made statement **S/PRST/2008/42** on behalf of the Council:

> The Security Council notes that, as mentioned in the report of the Secretary-General of 13 October 2008, the peace process has crossed a critical milestone with the launching of the identification and voter registration operations on 15 September 2008. However, it also notes that the delays that have occurred since the launch of the identification and voter registration processes on 15 September 2008 have proven greater than expected. It notes that the Special Representative of the Secretary-General for Côte d'Ivoire indicated on 27 October 2008 that, if the elections scheduled for 30 November 2008 were delayed, they were likely to be delayed by several months, due mainly to logistical difficulties. The Council expresses its deep concern about a possible third consecutive delay since the signing of the Ouagadougou Political Agreement, which could put the entire Ivorian peace process at risk.
>
> The Council commends the Facilitator for convening a meeting of the Permanent Consultative Framework of the Ouagadougou Political Agreement on 10 November 2008, in order for the Ivorian political actors to address all the main difficulties of the electoral process, and, in particular, with a view to finding an agreement on the new electoral time frame. It urges all the Ivorian political actors to cooperate fully with the Facilitator, with the support of the Special Representative of the Secretary-General, and to demonstrate their political determination to fulfil the commitments made in the Ouagadougou Political Agreement and within the framework of its follow-up mechanisms.
>
> The Council further urges, to this end, the President of the Independent Electoral Commission, which is in charge of the organization of the elections, to share publicly this new timeline, including, in particular, the full roll-out of the identification process and certain other stages, such as the publication of the provisional and final versions of the electoral list, the production and distribution of identity and voter cards and the date of the presidential elections. It emphasizes that all political actors must pay particular attention to the accumulating logistical delay.
>
> The Council urges the Ivorian parties to take immediately and as a priority the concrete steps necessary to complete the identification and voter registration operations in a credible and transparent manner before the end of January 2009. It expresses its determination to bring its full support to a credible electoral process in Côte d'Ivoire, on the understanding that the presidential elections will be organized before the end of spring 2009. The Council recalls that all political parties agreed to abide by the Code of Good Conduct for Elections that they signed under the auspices of the Secretary-General on 24 April 2008.
>
> The Council recalls that, pursuant to resolutions 1572(2004) and 1842(2008), any threat to the electoral process in Côte d'Ivoire shall constitute a threat to the peace and national reconciliation process and it reaffirms its determination to impose targeted measures against any person designated by its sanctions committee concerning Côte d'Ivoire as being responsible for these threats. The Council expresses its willingness to review the sanctions regime at the latest three months after the presidential elections.
>
> The Council requests the Secretary-General to keep it informed of the evolution of the situation. It reaffirms its full support for the efforts of the Special Representative of the Secretary-General and his certification mandate, including the explicit certification of the electoral list. It expresses its intention to take the progress of the electoral process fully into consideration when it reviews

the mandate of the United Nations Operation in Côte d'Ivoire and the French forces supporting it, before 31 January 2009.

Postponement of elections (November). On 10 November, the Facilitator convened the fourth meeting of the Permanent Consultative Framework of the Ouagadougou Agreement, which determined that it was no longer feasible to hold presidential elections by 30 November due to the accumulated logistical and technical delays. The Consultative Framework requested IEC to establish, before 31 December, a timeline for the identification of the population and voter registration, on the basis of which the parties would agree on a new date for the first round of the presidential elections. In a letter dated 11 November [S/2008/694], Burkina Faso, as the Facilitator, transmitted to the Security Council the press statement on the meeting.

Year-end developments

Technical assessment mission (December)

The Secretary-General reported [S/2009/21] that a technical assessment mission, which visited Côte d'Ivoire from 10 to 14 December to review UNOCI's role in the peace process, received briefings from UNOCI, the UN country team and the French Licorne force, and consulted with the Facilitator and a wide spectrum of national and international stakeholders. It also consulted with senior French officials in Paris on 15 December. On the electoral process, the mission was informed that the completion of the voter registration process by the end of February 2009 would depend on the ability of the Government to immediately disburse $15 million, required to deploy the remaining 4,000 identification and voter registration teams throughout Côte d'Ivoire. At the end of the identification and voter registration process, IEC would produce a provisional list of voters, following which a new election date would be set. All stakeholders assessed that, once IEC produced the final list of voters, an incompressible period of two to three months should be added to the election timeline for producing and distributing identification and voter cards. Consequently, the assessment mission determined that, while all parties remained committed to holding the elections in the first half of 2009, additional delays could not be excluded. In support of the electoral process, UNOCI would call upon IEC to share a new electoral timeline with the parties and the international community, outlining all stages of the process. UNOCI would also monitor compliance by the parties with the code of good conduct for the elections; support civil society organizations in holding national consensus days in early 2009; safeguard the peace process and the result of the elections; mobilize the donor community to provide financial support for Government efforts to implement the remaining electoral tasks; advocate for the Government to disburse the funds needed by the institutions involved in the electoral process in a timely manner; assist the parties to develop an integrated security plan for the elections, delineating the responsibilities of the national defence and security forces, the Forces nouvelles and the impartial forces; provide technical and logistical support for the electoral process; and monitor the progress made.

On security-related issues, all stakeholders agreed that the parties should—prior to the elections—expedite the disarmament of former combatants and the dismantling of the militias and launch the reunification and restructuring of the national defence and security forces, including through the reintegration of eligible elements of the Forces nouvelles. However, the assessment mission confirmed that the operational capabilities of the institutions responsible to plan and implement those processes—CCI, the national programme for reinsertion and community rehabilitation and the civic service programme—depended on enhanced support from the Government and international partners. It also noted that 300 Forces nouvelles elements assigned in November to the mixed police units to provide security for the identification and voter registration process in Abidjan returned to Bouaké on 3 December citing non-payment of their allowances by CCI, and that the 600 police auxiliaries trained by UNOCI had neither been integrated into the national security services nor equipped to assist in securing the north of the country. The assessment mission called for the establishment of mechanisms to control the weapons surrendered by former combatants and the development of a more comprehensive framework governing the future of the security sector.

While all stakeholders were of the view that UNOCI's capabilities should be retained in order for it to contribute to maintaining a secure environment for the implementation of the Ouagadougou Agreement, the assessment mission and UNOCI agreed that it would be possible to adjust the UNOCI troop level and posture, taking into account the security threats, such as the existence of armed militias and violent youth; the absence of effective disarmament of former combatants; the uncompleted redeployment of State administration; the risk of localized clashes in the north and the west; the limited freedom of movement due to checkpoints and roadblocks; and the fact that the elections could be a catalyst for violence. The assessment mission proposed a reduction of UNOCI by one battalion, from 8,115 to 7,450 troop personnel, on the understanding that the force's mobility would be enhanced with adequate air capabilities, and taking into account the continued support of the French forces to UNOCI in terms of quick-reaction capabilities. The UNOCI force would be positioned in fewer, yet more concentrated positions, from which sufficient troop numbers could be rapidly deployed as airborne quick-reaction detachments. The assessment mission proposed benchmarks as preconditions for a more substantial drawdown of the force, which included the completion of credible disarmament, demobilization and reintegration of former combatants and dismantling of militias; successful completion of the elections; commencement of security sector reform; and restoration of State authority throughout the country.

Fourth supplementary accord to Ouagadougou Agreement

The Secretary-General reported [S/2009/21] that on 22 December President Gbagbo and Prime Minister Soro had signed a fourth supplementary accord to the Ouagadougou Agreement, which clarified the modalities and timeline for conducting, before the elections, the disarmament of the former combatants of the Forces nouvelles and the dismantling of the militias; the launching of the reunification of the defence and security forces; and the completion, by 15 January 2009, of the redeployment of State administration throughout the country, including the *corps préfectoral* (local authorities), the judiciary and the fiscal and customs administrations. Under the agreement, some 4,000 Forces nouvelles personnel were expected to immediately, but temporarily, join the police and gendarmerie to provide security during the electoral process, while 5,000 Forces nouvelles elements would join the unified army within two years. The agreement also provided for the disarmament of Forces nouvelles former combatants and pro-Government militias at least two months before the elections, with payment by the Government of a $1,000 demobilization package to those declared eligible by CCI. As most of the key processes under the Ouagadougou Agreement remained plagued by considerable funding gaps, the agreement also provided for the immediate redeployment of the tax and customs administration in the Centre-North-West zone on the basis of a single exchequer in order to give the Government access to the tax revenue that was not being collected in the north to finance some elements of the peace process. On 30 December, Burkina Faso transmitted to the Security Council the text of the agreement, together with a press release issued from the Facilitator's office on 22 December [S/2008/834].

On the electoral process, the Secretary-General said that the identification and voter registration process expanded to Abidjan on 29 September, Bouaké on 18 November and 57 additional districts in December. The process was completed in Abidjan on 14 December, where nearly 2.1 million people were identified. Nationwide, approximately 2.8 million people were identified and by late December some 3,000 sites had opened. Nonetheless, the process continued to be hindered by logistical, financial and procedural challenges. The inventory of 351,888 civil registers identified thus far was published on 15 December, and the reconstitution of the registers was scheduled to conclude in February 2009.

Although the security situation remained generally stable, frequent demonstrations by military units demanding payment of allowances were reported both in areas controlled by the Forces nouvelles and by the Government. Disruptions of the identification of the population and voter registration operations were also reported. Meanwhile, inter-community clashes over land issues between returning internally displaced persons and local communities were reported in Abidjan district, Bondoukou, Yocoboué and several villages in the Bas Sassandra region, which resulted in at least 19 persons killed, 43 injured and 400 displaced. Other reported security incidents included roadside robberies, killings, ambushes, burglaries and sexual violence, including rape. Efforts by law enforcement agencies to curb criminality continued to be hampered by logistical, financial and human resource constraints and by the proliferation of arms in the country. In a positive development, UNOCI, on 14 November, received a visit from the leadership of the Student Federation, which confirmed its commitment to support the peace process. UNOCI would continue its dialogue with the Federation and other youth groups.

As at 15 December, the strength of CCI was 518 military personnel drawn from Government forces and the Forces nouvelles. Although the Centre's communications capacity and mobility improved somewhat, its operations continued to be hampered by financial and logistical constraints. In order to secure the identification and voter registration operations, more than 220 Government forces were deployed to the north, while Forces nouvelles elements deployed to the south returned to their bases in the north on 3 December. UNOCI and the Licorne force continued to maintain a support capacity within CCI to provide logistical support and assist the Centre in its planning and coordination activities. Progress in dismantling the militias remained slow, and the institutions in charge of the reintegration and reinsertion of former combatants and militias continued to face financial and logistical constraints. In other activity, a joint assessment between UNMIL, UNOCI and the United Nations Development Programme, focusing on militias in Liberia, concluded that between 1,500 and 2,000 Liberian ex-combatants remained at the border with Liberia and needed to be closely monitored.

As at 15 December, UNOCI military strength stood at 8,020 personnel, including 7,741 troops, 191 military observers and 88 staff officers, against an authorized strength of 8,115. Licorne, with 1,800 personnel, continued to maintain a quick-reaction capability to support UNOCI. The ongoing redeployment process of UNOCI troops at 24 camps would be completed in February 2009. UNOCI's police strength stood at 1,137 personnel against an authorized ceiling of 1,200, including 387 officers and 750 personnel in six formed police units.

The Secretary-General observed that timely implementation of the fourth supplementary agreement was critical to avoid further delays to the presidential elections, which were linked to the completion of the disarmament of the former combatants of the Forces nouvelles and the dismantling of militias. In order to safeguard the progress achieved by the parties, it was necessary to address the accumulated technical and logistical delays. He urged IEC to make public, as soon as possible, a new and realistic electoral timeline.

Children and armed conflict

The Security Council Working Group on Children and Armed Conflict, established by resolution 1612(2005) [YUN 2005, p. 863], submitted in February its conclusions on children and armed conflict in Côte d'Ivoire [S/AC.51/2008/5 & Corr.1], which contained the Group's exchange of views on the Secretary-General's 2007 report [YUN 2007, p. 185]. The Group noted that the parties to the conflict in Côte d'Ivoire were no longer mentioned in the annexes to the report of the Secretary-General on children and armed conflict [ibid., p. 790] as recruiting or using children and expressed its intent to pay further attention to the adherence of the parties to their commitments to halt the recruitment and use of children. The Group made recommendations addressed to the Ivorian President and Prime Minister, the UN Secretary-General, the Secretary-General of the Forces nouvelles and the leaders of the Front pour la libération du Grand Ouest, the Alliance patriotique de l'ethnie Wé, the Union patriotique de résistance du Grand Ouest and the Mouvement ivoirien de libération de l'ouest de la Côte d'Ivoire. It also requested that the World Bank and donors provide resources to strengthen reintegration programmes for demobilized children, and support the Government in preparing and implementing a national action plan to fight violence against children, including rape and other sexual violence. The Working Group submitted a report on its activities to the Security Council in July [S/2008/455] (see p. 852). The Secretary-General reported [S/2009/21] that UNOCI continued to incorporate child protection concerns across the Operation. During 2008, UNOCI conducted 204 training and sensitization sessions targeting a variety of partners within Côte d'Ivoire and benefiting 6,068 UNOCI personnel. UNOCI also intensified its advocacy with the parties to the conflict to move forward on measures to address sexual violence against children, including the adoption of a national action plan for children in armed conflict.

UN Peacebuilding Fund

In his April report [S/2008/250], the Secretary-General said that a $700,000 assistance package was provided through the emergency window of the United Nations Peacebuilding Fund to support the facilitation efforts of President Blaise Compaoré (Burkina Faso), in his capacity as Chairman of ECOWAS. On 30 April [S/2008/451], the Fund approved an extension of the emergency project to support the Ivorian direct dialogue and increased the contribution from $700,000 to $1 million. The Fund was established in 2006 [YUN 2006, p. 58] as a mechanism for extending critical support at the early stages of a peace process. Its "three-window architecture" comprised window I for countries on the agenda of the Peacebuilding Commission; window II for countries designated by the Secretary-General; and window III, or the emergency window, for urgent peacebuilding activities. On 19 June, the Secretary-General declared Côte d'Ivoire eligible to receive funds under the second window of the Fund. Consequently, the United Nations and the Government developed a priority plan to address urgent peacebuilding needs. On 14 July, some $5 million was approved, with $4 million allocated to support reinsertion projects, while $1 million would sustain the facilitation efforts by the Office of the Special Representative of the Facilitator in Abidjan [S/2008/645].

Peacebuilding Commission action. On 25 April [A/63/92-S/2008/417], the Peacebuilding Commission conveyed to the Security Council for consideration the Government's request for placement on the Commission's agenda. The request was also brought to the attention of the General Assembly, the Economic and Social Council and the Secretary-General.

Sanctions

The Security Council Committee established pursuant to resolution 1572(2004) [YUN 2004, p. 187] concerning Côte d'Ivoire continued to monitor implementation of the arms embargo, travel restrictions and assets freeze on designated individuals and entities imposed by that resolution, and the ban on the import of all rough diamonds from Côte d'Ivoire, pursuant to resolution 1643(2005) [YUN 2005, p. 251], as renewed by resolution 1782(2007) [YUN 2007, p. 188]. In 2008, the Committee held five informal consultations. In June [S/2008/366], Security Council members elected Jan Grauls (Belgium) to serve as the Committee's Chairman, and Italy and South Africa to continue to serve as Vice-Chairmen for the period ending 31 December 2008.

In a report on its 2008 activities [S/2008/829], the Committee Chairman said that on 16 June, the Committee approved an arms embargo exemption request pursuant to resolution 1572(2004), and on 21 October updated the list of individuals subject to the travel ban and assets freeze imposed by resolutions 1572(2004) and 1643(2005). The Committee also considered 10 monthly arms embargo and media monitoring reports prepared by UNOCI; the midterm and final reports of the Group of Experts on Côte d'Ivoire, which assessed compliance with the sanctions; and four quarterly UNOCI human rights reports. On 30 October, the Committee received a report from Mali on the implementation of Security Council resolutions 1572(2004) and 1643(2005).

Appointments. On 16 December [S/2008/793], the Secretary-General, as requested in resolution 1842(2008) (see p. 194), informed the Council of the appointment of Grégoire Bafouatika (Congo), James Bevan (United Kingdom), Noora Jamsheer (Bahrain) and El Hadi Salah (Algeria) to the Group of Experts on Côte d'Ivoire. He later informed the Council of the appointment of Joel Hernando Salek (Colombia) as the fifth expert [S/2009/5].

Report of Group of Experts (April). In accordance with resolutions 1572(2004) and 1782(2007), the Group of Experts monitoring the effectiveness of the sanctions, in a midterm report issued in April [S/2008/235], examined cooperation with stakeholders; monitoring of the embargo; verification of the air fleet capacity; military assistance; arms; defence-related expenditures and natural resources; the diamond embargo; and individual sanctions. On the embargo inspections, the Group observed that there was a decrease in the number of denials for access by the national armed forces and the Forces nouvelles, and an increase in the number of inspections over the course of each month, even though access to some strategic sites, such as port areas, remained limited. Since the establishment of the inspection mechanism, none of the sites held by the Republican Guard had ever been inspected by UNOCI because the authorities had systematically denied access to the sites, claiming that UNOCI had no mandate to perform the inspections. Experts were also concerned by the modus operandi adopted by UNOCI, particularly the notice given to the military authorities of inspections by UNOCI, which varied between 72 hours and six days. The Group believed that the effectiveness of the monitoring of the embargo on arms and related materiel had been, and continued to be, diminished by the inability to perform spontaneous inspections.

The Group identified other concerns, including the fact that national legislation had not been adopted, nor had any administrative measures been prescribed, to ensure compliance with the sanctions; national authorities had not sensitized customs staff to be vigilant and not allow the export and import of prohibited goods; UNOCI had not informed Ivorian customs of the items subject to the embargo—which was a prerequisite for instituting checks on the nature of embargoed materials; and between 2000 and 2006, there had been a significant amount of transit cargo—defined by the Group as cargo not intended for domestic consumption in Côte d'Ivoire, yet passing through its territory directed to neighbouring countries—totalling some 6.1 million tons. The Group also noted, with regard to transit cargo, that no customs authorities had been deployed to the borders of Côte d'Ivoire within the territories under the control of the Forces nouvelles; cargo declared to customs authorities as "in transit" to another country was manifested and declared in customs documentation for transit, yet not inspected by customs authorities upon arrival in Côte d'Ivoire; and there was no monitoring or inspection by the customs authority at border areas to determine whether any seals remained intact at the point of export. Consequently, the Group was concerned that transit cargo might be diverted for domestic use in Côte d'Ivoire.

The Group pursued its enquiries on the use of aircraft belonging to the air force, monitored the possible presence of foreign technicians who could provide technical assistance, and verified movement of aircraft on international and domestic routes. It also deemed it necessary to sensitize UNOCI Air Operations personnel and the UNOCI Togolese battalion posted at the Abidjan air force base to exercise vigilance on the activities at that location and notify the Group of any suspicious activity. On military assistance, the Group gathered credible information indicating that since the establishment of the sanctions regime in 2004, members of the national defence and security forces and Forces nouvelles had been receiving military training in other States, in violation of Security Council resolution 1572(2004). The training courses were ongoing, ranging in duration from five months to four years.

On the arms embargo, the Group said that the evolution of the general situation in Côte d'Ivoire, the lack of strategic needs for new military equipment and the investigations of the Group into the issue could explain the absence of information on recent imports of military equipment. However, the possibility of such violations could not be ruled out. The Group indicated that it was not in a position to reach any conclusions regarding cases of possible embargo violations directly involving the security forces, and that it would conduct further investigations. With regard to deliveries by air to Côte d'Ivoire of items classified as "10.43 kg of dynamite/explosive", although the consignee was a company involved in the oil exploration/production industry, the Group deemed that such imports constituted a violation of the sanctions regime. The Group provided updates on the cases dealing with Tusk Trading Pty Ltd, Imperial Armour and the inspections of goods shipped by Yssouf Diabaté, who was arrested in 2006 [YUN 2006, p. 205].

On the diamond embargo, the Group sought to identify as many case studies as possible in the diamond-producing countries and in the trading centres, because Ivorian diamonds continued to be exported through the neighbouring countries and surfaced through the major trading centres. On the status of internal controls applied by Ghana, particularly the registration of galamsey (illegal miners), in discussions with the Precious Minerals Marketing Company Limited and the Minerals Commission, the Group found that no progress had been made on the identification and registration of galamsey. As a result, there could be no assurances that illegally mined foreign diamonds were not entering the Ghanaian system and subsequently sent to the international trading centres. Mali remained a concern as one of the probable major exit points for Ivorian diamonds in violation of the sanctions regime. The Malian authorities could not provide the Group with any production data nor detail any measures to monitor production. In addition, the Government had not taken any measures to prevent diamonds of foreign origin from entering the country in spite of the sanctions. However, Malian customs authorities informed the Group of a consignment of 31 rough diamonds, which they seized after an individual applied in December 2007 to export them through Bamako airport, purporting that they were of Malian origin. In other activity, the Group collected information that led it to identify individuals linked to illicit trade in rough diamonds in the major diamond-trading centre in Antwerp, Belgium, and was in possession of information that conflict diamonds from Côte d'Ivoire were transiting through Dubai, United Arab Emirates.

The Group made recommendations pertaining to customs, arms and military assistance, and diamonds, including, among others, the dissemination of information specific to embargoed goods to Ivorian customs inspection staff on the part of UNOCI and the Ivorian customs management; the establishment by UNOCI of a specific monitoring unit; the dedication by UNOCI and Ivorian authorities of special monitoring procedures specific to transit cargo, maximizing the utilization of the X-ray container scanner at the port of Abidjan; and the diligent inspection by the UNOCI embargo cell of the seized ammunition related to the case of Mr. Diabaté. The Group also urged the Kimberley Process (see p. 44) to send its Technical Group to Bamako to examine the seized diamond shipment and provide its opinion about their origin.

Report of Group of Experts (October). In October, the Chairman of the Security Council Committee established pursuant to resolution 1572(2004) transmitted to the Council President the final report of the Group of Experts [S/2008/598] on the situation in Côte d'Ivoire, in accordance with resolution 1782(2007). The report examined cooperation with stakeholders; the situation in Côte d'Ivoire; embargo inspections; customs; aviation; military assistance; arms; defence-related expenditures and natural resources; the diamond embargo; and individual sanctions. Although the Group reported that meetings with various Ivorian authorities were conducted in a cordial atmosphere, it also observed that the requisite information was not always readily forthcoming from the customs and the Ministries of Economy and Finance, Defence and the Interior. During its visits, the Group received full cooperation from some States, yet experienced reluctant cooperation or refusals to share information from others. None of the neighbouring States clearly articulated to the Group measures taken to implement the sanctions. Investigations were hampered by the lack of responses from States and private individuals and entities, while private companies, banking institutions and State institutions investigating financial crimes were often reluctant to share information with the Group, despite assurances of confidentiality. The report listed the States, international agencies and private companies that did not respond to the Group's request for information.

On customs matters, the Group found that the capacity of the UNOCI embargo cell was limited because only one customs officer was employed as a consultant in the cell, and efforts to track the movement of imported sanctioned goods were ineffective and labour-intensive. The Group concluded that the embargo cell had conducted no substantive inspections within the customs environment, and that embargo controls could be easily circumvented by determined individuals and companies. The Group recommended that UNOCI accept the Ivorian customs' offer to form a joint "special monitoring unit", and that UNOCI communicate information about a wider range of embargoed goods—particularly those which had a potential dual use in the military environment—to the embargo staff performing the inspections and to Ivorian customs.

Despite the low ratio of denials for weapons inspections—three out of 572 between January and August—the Group said that the effectiveness of inspections remained limited. The list of scheduled inspections was still communicated to the military authorities in advance, no attempts to conduct unannounced inspections were recorded in 2008, and no inspection of sensitive sites, such as those of the "presidential perimeter", had been scheduled by UNOCI since January. Moreover, UNOCI inspection statistics did not properly reflect the state of monitoring of the embargo. Inspections deemed "successful" were based on permitted access and whether the operations were undertaken without any expression of hostility. No qualitative consideration of the state or quantities of the equipment presented to the inspection unit were taken into account, and no mention other than "successful" or "denied" was used to define the result of the inspections.

On transit cargo, no significant progress had been made on the Group's request for UNOCI to implement procedures to utilize the scanner for transit goods travelling by road and no X-ray scanning of transit cargo was being carried out. Concerned that goods imported for transit through Côte d'Ivoire were not inspected in any way, the Group concluded that the potential for importation and diversion of sanctioned cargo continued to pose a great risk. In addition, Ivorian customs had made no visible effort to adapt the transit system in the context of the sanctions, or to mitigate risks associated with the geographical challenges.

On the redeployment of Ivorian customs authorities to the borders, the Group travelled to northern Côte d'Ivoire in June and noted a limited deployment of 13 customs officers and an equivalent number of Forces nouvelles personnel designated as customs officers at the border crossing of Ouangolodougou, on the border of Burkina Faso. Members of the Forces nouvelles previously posted in the border area remained there and continued to exercise the same level of authority they had prior to the redeployment, preventing the Ivorian customs authorities from performing their duties, including inspections and examinations. The Forces nouvelles personnel had little or no customs knowledge, were insufficiently trained and were unqualified to work as customs officers. The remaining border crossings with neighbouring countries in the centre, north and west region remained under the control of the Forces nouvelles, with no Ivorian customs authorities present. In July, the Group had requested a written status report on their redeployment, yet had not received any response. Meanwhile, exploitation of natural resources in the centre, north and west zone by various companies, mostly foreign, continued at a regular pace.

On the arms embargo, the Group was unable to conclude whether there had been any violation of the sanctions regime by the two parties. However, it gathered several indications that movements of small volumes of weapons occurred, and due to their frequency, the possibility of violations could not be excluded. The Group obtained confirmation that explosive goods were regularly imported into the country, reportedly for industrial purposes, as relevant Ivorian authorities had granted import licences without informing the importing company that such transfers were prohibited under the embargo on military equipment and related materiel. The Group considered the need for law enforcement and riot control equipment expressed by the national police, the gendarmerie and CCI. More detailed elements were needed to establish the veracity of figures provided by the Director-General of the national police on estimated equipment requirements, and the Group believed that the equipment needs prepared by the gendarmerie were excessive, especially the Kalashnikov assault rifles and ammunition, which should be limited to military activities.

On the diamond embargo, the Group invited the experts of the Kimberley Process to conduct a joint mission to assess the production and illicit export of diamonds from Côte d'Ivoire. The Ministry of Mines estimated that between 5,000 and 10,000 miners were active in Séguéla, while less than 5,000 miners were in the village of Tortiya. Following the mission, the report of the Kimberley Process estimated total production capacity in Côte d'Ivoire at between 114,000 and 188,500 carats per year, and the Group estimated its annual value at between $12.5 million and $20.7 million. The Group also established that most of the diamonds produced in Séguéla and Tortiya left the country via Sikasso to Bamako, Mali.

In conclusion, the Group recommended the strengthening of the UNOCI monitoring capacity by adding to the embargo cell a significant number of international customs officers with sanctions experience; surveillance by the impartial forces of all airports, landing strips and heliports capable of receiving flights originating in foreign countries; the establishment by UNOCI of standard operating procedures for securing any previously unaccounted-for military equipment recovered; and the organization by UNOCI of sensitization sessions for private companies that used in their commercial and industrial activities non-military goods subject to the embargo. On diamonds, the Group recommended that the Kimberley Process assist the Ivorian Government in instituting a basic control mechanism to govern the diamond trade and assist the Guinean Government in strengthening its internal control systems, including enhanced customs vigilance at the borders and ports of entry. It also urged the Malian authorities to seize the diamonds under detention by Malian customs at Bamako airport, conduct a comprehensive investigation of the case and sensitize their officials to be vigilant about the cross-border trade of diamonds.

SECURITY COUNCIL ACTION

On 29 October [meeting 6004], the Security Council unanimously adopted **resolution 1842(2008)**. The draft [S/2008/672] was submitted by France.

The Security Council,

Recalling its previous resolutions and the statements by its President relating to the situation in Côte d'Ivoire, in particular resolutions 1782(2007) of 29 October 2007 and 1826(2008) of 29 July 2008,

Reaffirming its strong commitment to respect for the sovereignty, independence, territorial integrity and unity of Côte d'Ivoire, and recalling the importance of the principles of good-neighbourliness, non-interference and regional cooperation,

Taking note of the report of the Secretary-General of 13 October 2008 and the reports of the Group of Experts on Côte d'Ivoire transmitted on 9 April and 8 October 2008,

Emphasizing the continued contribution to Côte d'Ivoire's stability, in particular in the context of the forthcoming presidential elections, of the measures imposed by resolutions 1572(2004) of 15 November 2004 and 1643(2005) of 15 December 2005,

Recalling that in its resolution 1782(2007), it welcomed the initial measures to implement the Ouagadougou Political Agreement, and recalling also that in its resolution 1826(2008), it encouraged, in particular, the Ivorian parties to remove the remaining logistical obstacles that impeded the identification of the population and the registration of voters,

Welcoming, in this regard, the official launching of the identification and voter registration operations on 15 September 2008, and urging the Ivorian parties to take all the necessary steps to complete these operations,

Noting again with concern, in spite of the sustained improvement in the overall human rights situation, the persistence of cases of human rights violations against civilians, including numerous acts of sexual violence, stressing that the perpetrators must be brought to justice, reiterating its firm condemnation of all violations of human rights and international humanitarian law in Côte d'Ivoire, and recalling its resolutions 1325(2000) of 31 October 2000 and 1820(2008) of 19 June 2008 on women and peace and security, its resolution 1612(2005) of 26 July 2005 on children and armed conflict and its resolution 1674(2006) of 28 April 2006 on the protection of civilians in armed conflict,

Recalling that the Security Council Committee established pursuant to paragraph 14 of resolution 1572(2004) ("the Committee") will consider and decide upon requests for the exemptions set out in paragraphs 8, 10 and 12 of resolution 1572(2004) which are submitted in accordance with the guidelines adopted by the Committee, and expressing the availability of the Committee and of the Group of Experts to give technical explanations as may be needed,

Determining that the situation in Côte d'Ivoire continues to pose a threat to international peace and security in the region,

Acting under Chapter VII of the Charter of the United Nations,

1. *Decides* to renew until 31 October 2009 the measures on arms and the financial and travel measures imposed by paragraphs 7 to 12 of resolution 1572(2004) and the measures preventing the importation by any State of all rough diamonds from Côte d'Ivoire imposed by paragraph 6 of resolution 1643(2005);

2. *Decides also* to review the measures renewed in paragraph 1 above in light of the progress achieved in the implementation of the key steps of the peace process and of the progress of the electoral process, as referred to in resolution 1826(2008), by the end of the period mentioned in paragraph 1 above, and decides further to carry out during the period mentioned in paragraph 1 above:

(a) A review of the measures renewed in paragraph 1 above no later than three months after the holding of open, free, fair and transparent presidential elections in accordance with international standards; or

(b) A midterm review no later than 30 April 2009 if no review has been scheduled on the basis of paragraph 2 *(a)* of the present resolution at that date;

3. *Calls upon* the Ivorian parties to the Ouagadougou Political Agreement and all States, in particular those in the subregion, to fully implement the measures renewed in paragraph 1 above, including, as appropriate, by making the necessary rules and regulations, and calls also upon the United Nations Operation in Côte d'Ivoire and the French forces supporting it to bring their full support, in particular, to the implementation of the measures on arms renewed in paragraph 1 above, within their capacities and respective mandates, as determined in resolution 1739(2007) of 10 January 2007 and renewed in resolution 1826(2008);

4. *Reiterates its demand*, in particular, that the Ivorian authorities take the necessary measures to put an immediate end to any violation of measures imposed by paragraph 11 of resolution 1572(2004), including those violations mentioned by the Group of Experts on Côte d'Ivoire in its reports of 21 September 2007 and 8 October 2008;

5. *Also reiterates its demand* that the Ivorian parties to the Ouagadougou Political Agreement, in particular the Ivorian authorities, provide unhindered access, particularly to the Group of Experts established pursuant to paragraph 9 of resolution 1643(2005), to equipment, sites and installations referred to in paragraph 2 *(a)* of resolution 1584(2005) of 1 February 2005, when appropriate without notice and including those under the control of Republican Guard units, and to the United Nations Operation in Côte d'Ivoire and the French forces supporting it in order to enable them to carry out their respective mandates as set out in paragraphs 2 and 8 of resolution 1739(2007) and renewed in resolution 1826(2008);

6. *Decides* that any threat to the electoral process in Côte d'Ivoire, in particular any attack or obstruction of the action of the Independent Electoral Commission in charge of the organization of the elections or the action of the operators mentioned in paragraphs 1.3.3 and 2.1.1 of the Ouagadougou Political Agreement shall constitute a threat to the peace and national reconciliation process for the purposes of paragraphs 9 and 11 of resolution 1572(2004);

7. *Decides also* that any serious obstacle to the freedom of movement of the United Nations Operation in Côte d'Ivoire and of the French forces supporting it, or any attack or obstruction of the action of the United Nations Operation in Côte d'Ivoire, of the French forces, of the Special Representative of the Secretary-General for Côte

d'Ivoire, of the Facilitator mentioned in paragraph 10 of resolution 1765(2007) of 16 July 2007 or his Special Representative in Côte d'Ivoire shall constitute a threat to the peace and national reconciliation process for the purposes of paragraphs 9 and 11 of resolution 1572(2004);

8. *Requests* the Secretary-General and the Government of France to report to the Security Council immediately, through the Committee, any serious obstacle to the freedom of movement of the United Nations Operation in Côte d'Ivoire and of the French forces supporting it, including the names of those responsible, and requests the Secretary-General and the Facilitator to report to the Council immediately, through the Committee, any attack or obstruction of their action or the action of the Special Representatives mentioned in paragraph 7 above;

9. *Requests* all States concerned, in particular those in the subregion, to cooperate fully with the Committee, and authorizes the Committee to request whatever further information it may consider necessary;

10. *Decides* to extend the mandate of the Group of Experts as set out in paragraph 7 of resolution 1727(2006) of 15 December 2006 until 31 October 2009, and requests the Secretary-General to take the necessary administrative measures;

11. *Requests* the Group of Experts to provide a midterm report to the Committee by 15 April 2009 and to submit a final written report to the Council, through the Committee, fifteen days before the end of its mandated period, on the implementation of the measures imposed by paragraphs 7, 9 and 11 of resolution 1572(2004) and paragraph 6 of resolution 1643(2005), as well as recommendations in this regard;

12. *Requests* the Secretary-General to communicate, as appropriate, to the Council, through the Committee, information gathered by the United Nations Operation in Côte d'Ivoire and, where possible, reviewed by the Group of Experts, concerning the supply of arms and related materiel to Côte d'Ivoire;

13. *Requests* the Government of France to communicate, as appropriate, to the Council, through the Committee, information gathered by the French forces and, where possible, reviewed by the Group of Experts, concerning the supply of arms and related materiel to Côte d'Ivoire;

14. *Requests* the Kimberley Process to communicate, as appropriate, to the Council, through the Committee, information which, where possible, has been reviewed by the Group of Experts, concerning the production and illicit export of diamonds;

15. *Urges* all States, relevant United Nations bodies and other organizations and interested parties, including the Kimberley Process, to cooperate fully with the Committee, the Group of Experts, the United Nations Operation in Côte d'Ivoire and the French forces, in particular by supplying any information at their disposal on possible violations of the measures imposed by paragraphs 7, 9 and 11 of resolution 1572(2004) and paragraph 6 of resolution 1643(2005) and reiterated in paragraph 1 above;

16. *Underlines* that it is fully prepared to impose targeted measures against persons to be designated by the Committee who are determined to be, among other things:

(a) A threat to the peace and national reconciliation process in Côte d'Ivoire, in particular by blocking the implementation of the peace process as referred to in the Ouagadougou Political Agreement;

(b) Attacking or obstructing the action of the United Nations Operation in Côte d'Ivoire, of the French forces supporting it, of the Special Representative of the Secretary-General, of the Facilitator or of his Special Representative in Côte d'Ivoire;

(c) Responsible for obstacles to the freedom of movement of the United Nations Operation in Côte d'Ivoire and of the French forces supporting it;

(d) Responsible for serious violations of human rights and international humanitarian law committed in Côte d'Ivoire;

(e) Publicly inciting hatred and violence;

(f) Acting in violation of the measures imposed by paragraph 7 of resolution 1572(2004);

17. *Decides* to remain actively seized of the matter.

UNOCI

The United Nations Operation in Côte d'Ivoire (UNOCI) was established in 2004 by Security Council resolution 1528(2004) [YUN 2004, p. 173] to replace the United Nations Mission in Côte d'Ivoire and ECOWAS forces. Its mandate was to monitor the ceasefire and the movement of armed groups; assist in disarmament, demobilization, reintegration, repatriation and resettlement; protect UN personnel and civilians; support implementation of the peace process; and provide assistance in the monitoring of human rights, public information and law and order. The UNOCI mandate was revised in 2007 [YUN 2007, p. 170] to include supporting the work of the Integrated Command Centre (CCI), monitoring the cessation of hostilities and movement of armed groups, and providing other security-related assistance. UNOCI was supported by the French Licorne forces. Headquartered in Abidjan, UNOCI was headed by the Special Representative of the Secretary-General, Choi Young-Jin (Republic of Korea). The Security Council, by resolution 1826(2008) (see p. 184), extended the UNOCI mandate until 31 January 2009.

During 2008, the Secretary-General submitted reports to the Security Council on developments in Côte d'Ivoire and the activities of UNOCI in January [S/2008/1], April [S/2008/250], July [S/2008/451], and October [S/2008/645], with a later report covering the remainder of the year [S/2009/21]. In addition to political and security aspects, the reports summarized UNOCI activities in addressing the humanitarian and human rights situation in the country, as well as other issues such as economic recovery, reconstruction and development, HIV/AIDS, media monitoring and public information, the promotion of gender mainstreaming, child protection and the safety and security of personnel.

On personnel conduct and discipline matters, investigations continued with regard to the 2007 allegations of sexual exploitation and abuse by UNOCI military personnel stationed in the Bouaké area [YUN 2007, p. 190]. The Secretary-General reported in January that, in the interim, the contingent concerned was redeployed to Duékoué, in the western part of the country. In a press conference on 30 May, following the release of a Save the Children, United Kingdom report entitled *No One to Turn To*, which focused on the underreporting of sexual exploitation and abuse of children committed by peacekeepers and humanitarian workers in peacekeeping operations, including in Côte d'Ivoire, the Secretary-General's Special Representative emphasized the need for all allegations to be brought immediately to the attention of UNOCI so that full investigations could take place and those found guilty could face appropriate sanctions. A preliminary investigation by the United Nations Office of Internal Oversight Services to assess the credibility of the allegations in the report, which concerned the rape of a 12-year-old girl, was ongoing. UNOCI continued to sensitize its military, police and civilian personnel on the Secretary-General's zero-tolerance policy for sexual exploitation and abuse, and to consult with staff on the prohibition of discrimination, harassment—including sexual harassment—and abuse of authority [ST/SGB/2008/5].

Financing

In June, at its resumed sixty-second (2008) session, the General Assembly considered the performance report on the UNOCI budget for the period from 1 July 2006 to 30 June 2007 [A/62/642], showing actual expenditures of $450,769,600 against a total appropriation of $472,889,300, as well as the proposed UNOCI budget for the period from 1 July 2008 to 30 June 2009 [A/62/750] in the amount of $477,058,000, gross, together with the related ACABQ report [A/62/781/Add.13]. The proposed budget provided for the deployment of 200 military observers, 7,915 military contingent personnel, 450 UN police officers, 750 formed police unit personnel, 498 international staff, 709 national staff, 301 United Nations Volunteers and 8 Government-provided personnel, as well as 5 international and 7 national temporary positions. ACABQ recommended reductions in the amount of $98,100 and the approval of an amount of $476,959,900.

On 20 June, the General Assembly took note of the performance report on the 2006–2007 UNOCI budget and appropriated $497,455,100 for the period from 1 July 2008 to 30 June 2009 (resolution 62/254) (below).

GENERAL ASSEMBLY ACTION

On 20 June [meeting 109], the General Assembly, on the recommendation of the Fifth (Administrative and Budgetary) Committee [A/62/867], adopted **resolution 62/254** without vote [agenda item 142].

Financing of the United Nations Operation in Côte d'Ivoire

The General Assembly,

Having considered the reports of the Secretary-General on the financing of the United Nations Operation in Côte d'Ivoire and the related report of the Advisory Committee on Administrative and Budgetary Questions,

Recalling Security Council resolution 1528(2004) of 27 February 2004, by which the Council established the United Nations Operation in Côte d'Ivoire for an initial period of twelve months as from 4 April 2004, and the subsequent resolutions by which the Council extended the mandate of the Operation, the latest of which was resolution 1795(2008) of 15 January 2008, by which the Council extended the mandate of the Operation until 30 July 2008,

Recalling also its resolution 58/310 of 18 June 2004 on the financing of the Operation and its subsequent resolutions thereon, the latest of which was resolution 61/247 B of 29 June 2007,

Reaffirming the general principles underlying the financing of United Nations peacekeeping operations, as stated in General Assembly resolutions 1874(S-IV) of 27 June 1963, 3101(XXVIII) of 11 December 1973 and 55/235 of 23 December 2000,

Mindful of the fact that it is essential to provide the Operation with the financial resources necessary to enable it to fulfil its responsibilities under the relevant resolutions of the Security Council,

1. *Requests* the Secretary-General to entrust the Head of Mission with the task of formulating future budget proposals in full accordance with the provisions of General Assembly resolutions 59/296 of 22 June 2005, 60/266 of 30 June 2006 and 61/276 of 29 June 2007, as well as other relevant resolutions;

2. *Takes note* of the status of contributions to the United Nations Operation in Côte d'Ivoire as at 30 April 2008, including the contributions outstanding in the amount of 67 million United States dollars, representing some 3.5 per cent of the total assessed contributions, notes with concern that only fifty-two Member States have paid their assessed contributions in full, and urges all other Member States, in particular those in arrears, to ensure payment of their outstanding assessed contributions;

3. *Expresses its appreciation* to those Member States which have paid their assessed contributions in full, and urges all other Member States to make every possible effort to ensure payment of their assessed contributions to the Operation in full;

4. *Expresses concern* at the financial situation with regard to peacekeeping activities, in particular as regards the reimbursements to troop contributors that bear additional burdens owing to overdue payments by Member States of their assessments;

5. *Also expresses concern* at the delay experienced by the Secretary-General in deploying and providing adequate re-

sources to some recent peacekeeping missions, in particular those in Africa;

6. *Emphasizes* that all future and existing peacekeeping missions shall be given equal and non-discriminatory treatment in respect of financial and administrative arrangements;

7. *Also emphasizes* that all peacekeeping missions shall be provided with adequate resources for the effective and efficient discharge of their respective mandates;

8. *Reiterates its request* to the Secretary-General to make the fullest possible use of facilities and equipment at the United Nations Logistics Base at Brindisi, Italy, in order to minimize the costs of procurement for the Operation;

9. *Endorses* the conclusions and recommendations contained in the report of the Advisory Committee on Administrative and Budgetary Questions, subject to the provisions of the present resolution, and requests the Secretary-General to ensure their full implementation;

10. *Takes note* of paragraph 22 (*b*) of the report of the Advisory Committee and decides to establish a national Professional post for an Engineer to be responsible for local environmental protection;

11. *Requests* the Secretary-General to ensure the full implementation of the relevant provisions of its resolutions 59/296, 60/266 and 61/276;

12. *Also requests* the Secretary-General to take all necessary action to ensure that the Operation is administered with a maximum of efficiency and economy;

13. *Further requests* the Secretary-General, in order to reduce the cost of employing General Service staff, to continue efforts to recruit local staff for the Operation against General Service posts, commensurate with the requirements of the Operation;

Financial performance report for the period from 1 July 2006 to 30 June 2007

14. *Takes note* of the report of the Secretary-General on the financial performance of the Operation for the period from 1 July 2006 to 30 June 2007;

Budget estimates for the period from 1 July 2008 to 30 June 2009

15. *Decides* to appropriate to the Special Account for the United Nations Operation in Côte d'Ivoire the amount of 497,455,100 dollars for the period from 1 July 2008 to 30 June 2009, inclusive of the amount of 475,402,600 dollars for the maintenance of the Operation, 19,223,800 dollars for the support account for peacekeeping operations and 2,828,700 dollars for the United Nations Logistics Base;

Financing of the appropriation

16. *Also decides* to apportion among Member States the amount of 40,117,347 dollars for the period from 1 to 30 July 2008, in accordance with the levels updated in General Assembly resolution 61/243 of 22 December 2006, and taking into account the scale of assessments for 2008, as set out in its resolution 61/237 of 22 December 2006;

17. *Further decides* that, in accordance with the provisions of its resolution 973(X) of 15 December 1955, there shall be set off against the apportionment among Member States, as provided for in paragraph 16 above, their respective share in the Tax Equalization Fund of 953,605 dollars, comprising the estimated staff assessment income of 786,613 dollars approved for the Operation, the prorated share of 148,960 dollars of the estimated staff assessment income approved for the support account and the prorated share of 18,032 dollars of the estimated staff assessment income approved for the United Nations Logistics Base;

18. *Decides* to apportion among Member States the amount of 457,337,753 dollars for the period from 31 July 2008 to 30 June 2009, at a monthly rate of 41,454,592 dollars, in accordance with the levels updated in resolution 61/243, and taking into account the scale of assessments for 2008 and 2009, as set out in resolution 61/237, subject to a decision of the Security Council to extend the mandate of the Operation;

19. *Also decides* that, in accordance with the provisions of its resolution 973(X), there shall be set off against the apportionment among Member States, as provided for in paragraph 18 above, their respective share in the Tax Equalization Fund of 10,871,095 dollars, comprising the estimated staff assessment income of 8,967,387 dollars approved for the Operation, the prorated share of 1,698,140 dollars of the estimated staff assessment income approved for the support account and the prorated share of 205,568 dollars of the estimated staff assessment income approved for the United Nations Logistics Base;

20. *Further decides* that, for Member States that have fulfilled their financial obligations to the Operation, there shall be set off against their apportionment, as provided for in paragraph 16 above, their respective share of the unencumbered balance and other income in the total amount of 38,685,500 dollars in respect of the financial period ended 30 June 2007, in accordance with the levels updated in resolution 61/243, and taking into account the scale of assessments for 2007, as set out in resolution 61/237;

21. *Decides* that, for Member States that have not fulfilled their financial obligations to the Operation, there shall be set off against their outstanding obligations their respective share of the unencumbered balance and other income in the total amount of 38,685,500 dollars in respect of the financial period ended 30 June 2007, in accordance with the scheme set out in paragraph 20 above;

22. *Also decides* that the decrease of 422,200 dollars in the estimated staff assessment income in respect of the financial period ended 30 June 2007 shall be set off against the credits from the amount of 38,685,500 dollars referred to in paragraphs 20 and 21 above;

23. *Emphasizes* that no peacekeeping mission shall be financed by borrowing funds from other active peacekeeping missions;

24. *Encourages* the Secretary-General to continue to take additional measures to ensure the safety and security of all personnel participating in the Operation under the auspices of the United Nations, bearing in mind paragraphs 5 and 6 of Security Council resolution 1502(2003) of 26 August 2003;

25. *Invites* voluntary contributions to the Operation in cash and in the form of services and supplies acceptable to the Secretary-General, to be administered, as appropriate, in accordance with the procedure and practices established by the General Assembly;

26. *Decides* to include in the provisional agenda of its sixty-third session the item entitled "Financing of the United Nations Operation in Côte d'Ivoire".

Liberia

In 2008, the Government of Liberia continued efforts to improve governance and security, combat corruption, regain control and management over the country's natural resources and build a stronger economy. With the assistance of the United Nations Mission in Liberia and other international and regional organizations, further progress was made in consolidating peace, stability and democracy. In March, the Government finalized its first national poverty reduction strategy, and Liberia reached the decision point under the enhanced Heavily Indebted Poor Countries Initiative. Implementation of the new poverty reduction strategy, addressing high unemployment, and reform of rule-of-law institutions and the security sector, in particular the Liberian National Police, were identified as critical areas to be addressed. The Truth and Reconciliation Commission began public hearings in January. At the opening of the hearings, President Ellen Johnson-Sirleaf apologized to the people of Liberia on behalf of all Governments of Liberia for the acts that contributed to the conflict. The Commission sent its first report to the Legislature and President in December. Following his visit to Liberia in April and a review by a technical assessment team in May, the Secretary-General recommended adjustments to the second phase of the drawdown of the Mission.

The Panel of Experts established to assess implementation of the arms and travel measures imposed on Liberia removed 10 individuals from the travel-ban list. In December, the Security Council renewed the travel and arms restrictions for a further 12 months. The trial of former President Charles Taylor resumed in The Hague, Netherlands, on 7 January, after a six-month delay to allow time for counsel to prepare his defence.

Peacebuilding efforts and UNMIL activities

Report of Secretary-General (March). In his sixteenth progress report on the United Nations Mission in Liberia (UNMIL) [S/2008/183], the Secretary-General reviewed developments in the country and progress made in the drawdown phase of the Mission's consolidation, drawdown and withdrawal plan since his August 2007 report [YUN 2007, p. 195]. He said that the Government continued to focus on priorities such as ensuring economic recovery; obtaining forgiveness of the country's debt; fighting corruption; implementing its interim poverty reduction strategy; revitalizing the agricultural sector; restoring basic services; rehabilitating basic infrastructure; and renovating and building schools, clinics, hospitals and administrative buildings. The Government also made progress in implementing the Governance and Economic Management Assistance Programme, reforming the security sector, regaining control and efficient management of its natural resources, strengthening the capacity of its institutions, and consolidating State authority throughout the country.

The overall political situation remained stable and, in further efforts to foster political and ethnic reconciliation, President Johnson-Sirleaf attended a national peace festival in Monrovia on 2 January, where together with George Weah, the former presidential candidate for the Congress for Democratic Change, she highlighted the need for national reconciliation. On 28 January, the President announced her intention to pardon George Koukou, former Speaker of the National Transitional Legislative Assembly, who was on trial for treason. On the same date, in her State of the Republic address to the legislature, the President stated that the country had an economic growth rate of 9 per cent and that revenue collection for the first 11 months of 2007 totalled $163.3 million, which surpassed the projected annual target of $152.5 million. In addition, the World Bank and the African Development Bank had cleared over $671 million of Liberia's $4.8 billion debt arrears, and the International Monetary Fund (IMF) had agreed to a financing arrangement that would forgive $920 million of the country's debts. During his visit to Liberia in February, United States President George W. Bush pledged the continued support of his Government for peacekeeping and reconstruction efforts, as well as the security sector reform programme. His Government would also provide 1 million textbooks for schoolchildren and desks and chairs for 10,000 students for the next academic year. In other activity, UNMIL supported Government efforts to restructure the political party system. On 18 and 19 March, in collaboration with other partners, the Mission facilitated a two-day workshop on political party system reform for representatives of political parties and members of the legislature. Meanwhile, at the Special Court for Sierra Leone in The Hague, the trial of former Liberian President Charles Taylor resumed on 7 January after a six-month delay to allow him to prepare his defence (see p. 219).

Relations between the executive branch of the Government and the legislature continued to improve. The legislature passed several important bills, including the Governance Commission Act, and four other Acts were under review. The Judiciary Committee of the House of Representatives began public hearings to investigate allegations made by former House Speaker Edwin Snowe that members of the House had received $5,000 inducements from the executive branch of Government to sign a resolution calling for his removal. At the hearing of 3 March, Mr. Snowe provided audio recordings in which four legislators allegedly admitted receiving such funds. The trials of both Mr. Snowe, indicted for the theft of $1 million of public funds from the Liberia Petroleum Refining Company during his tenure as Managing Director, and of Charles Gyude Bryant, former Chairman of the National Transitional Government charged with economic sabotage for misappropriating $1.3 million, were ongoing. In March, the Minister of Justice announced that the Government had failed to reach an out-of-court settlement with Mr. Bryant to discontinue his trial in exchange for the return of the misappropriated funds.

The overall security situation remained generally calm and stable; however, violent protests by various groups and civil disturbances on rubber plantations continued. The Mission assisted the National Security Council with the development of a national security strategy and operational plan. The strategy focused on coordinating information among law enforcement and security agencies, as well as strengthening community and police cooperation through information-sharing. The security situation along the borders with Côte d'Ivoire, Guinea and Sierra Leone remained stable. UNMIL conducted several operations to deter the cross-border movement of weapons and recruitment of mercenaries, to reassure the local population and to foster better coordination among security agencies deployed along the border areas. The Mission continued to provide security to the Special Court for Sierra Leone.

Efforts to rebuild the national police continued, and some 3,662 officers had graduated from the national police academy. Several advanced programmes designed to strengthen the supervisory and specialized capacities of personnel of the national police and the Bureau of Immigration and Naturalization were completed. Although 90 per cent of national police officers authorized to be deployed to the counties had been deployed, county operations were hampered by the lack of basic infrastructure and police equipment. Assistance from UNMIL quick-impact projects supported the reconstruction and rehabilitation of 11 police stations and the construction of a new immigration office. The United States continued to lead international support for the training and restructuring of the 2,000-strong armed forces; as at 11 January, the number of trained recruits totalled 1,124.

On the reintegration of ex-combatants, the United Nations Development Programme (UNDP) and the National Commission on Disarmament, Demobilization, Reintegration and Rehabilitation, in collaboration with UNMIL, continued to implement a one-year reintegration and rehabilitation programme for a final group of 8,700 ex-combatants that had commenced in December 2007 [YUN 2007, p. 199]. Since 2005, UNMIL had collected and destroyed 884 weapons, 1,754 pieces of unexploded ordnance, 108,838 rounds of ammunition and 12,002 assorted spares and miscellaneous parts.

Progress in restoring and consolidating State authority throughout the country was slow. Logistical and capacity constraints of implementing parties led to delays in rehabilitating county administrative buildings. The UN country team and UNMIL were assisting the Institute for Statistics and Geo-Information Services with its preparations to conduct a national census in March, which would be the first census conducted by the Government since 1984. UNMIL would also provide logistical support to facilitate the census process.

In efforts to regain control over and efficiently manage the country's natural resources, the Forestry Development Authority signed a management contract with a Swiss firm aimed at discouraging the illegal production of timber and ensuring that exported forest products met international standards. In order to reorganize the diamond sector, the Government converted the Government Diamonds Office into the Office of Precious Minerals, and the Presidential Task Force on Diamonds became the Liberian Diamond Board. It also completed a draft mineral policy and was working towards the establishment of a mining cadastre system. UNMIL supported Government efforts to re-establish its control and provide social services on Liberia's rubber plantations.

While the human rights situation improved, efforts to promote and protect human rights were hindered by deficiencies in the justice system such as recurring absenteeism and reports of corrupt practices involving judicial and law enforcement officials; detention facilities that were below minimum human rights standards; large numbers of pretrial detainees awaiting trial for extended periods; and insufficient numbers of qualified corrections officers. The reform of the judicial and corrections system continued to be slow owing to the lack of infrastructure, inadequate numbers of qualified officers, lack of capacity to process cases, poor case management, inadequately trained court staff, low salaries, lack of a legal and judicial reform policy framework, and a legal regime that allowed only Liberian citizens to be legal practitioners or judges. UNMIL worked with the Ministry of Justice and the Supreme Court to address those deficiencies.

The Secretary-General observed that despite encouraging developments, a number of tasks critical to the sustainability of peace and stability remained to be fully implemented, including the reform of the legal and judicial system, the reintegration of war-affected populations and the extension of the rule of law throughout the country. In addition to significant challenges such as pervasive poverty, food insecurity, high unemployment, massive illiteracy, poor infrastructure and the inadequate delivery of basic services, corruption was still a major concern. He appealed to donors to support the equipment and deployment needs of the national police, to international partners to support the Government in its efforts to overhaul the judicial and corrections system and to the international community to provide funding for the Truth and Reconciliation Commission to complete its work. On the diamond industry, he urged the Government to establish a computerized data bank for mining licences, to review incentives and remuneration for the field staff of the Ministry of Lands, Mines and Energy and to ensure that banking channels were used for all diamond transactions. With regard to the drawdown of UNMIL, the Secretary-General noted that the Mission would continue to monitor progress in meeting the benchmarks and indicators.

Security Council consideration (April). In her briefing of 14 April to the Security Council on the situation in Liberia [meeting 5864], the Secretary-General's Special Representative, Ellen Margrethe Løj, highlighted three critical areas that needed to be addressed for further progress in the country and to enable UNMIL to successfully draw down: the reform of the security sector, not least the reform of the national police; the reform of rule-of-law institutions; and the effective implementation of the new poverty reduction strategy and task of addressing high unemployment. She said that the incidence of gender-based violence, particularly rape, was unacceptable, yet she was encouraged that with the support of UNMIL and the UN country team, the Government was finalizing the national gender policy. It had also established a special court to prosecute rape cases and developed a national action plan against gender-based violence to deter rape.

Report of Secretary-General (August). In his seventeenth report [S/2008/553] on UNMIL, the Secretary-General, who visited Liberia on 21 and 22 April, reviewed major developments in the country and presented recommendations for adjustments to the second phase of the UNMIL drawdown. The political situation remained stable and key economic and social indicators continued to improve.

The security situation remained stable yet fragile, as the prevalence of law-and-order incidents, including mob justice and random violence, underlined the tenuous state of the security environment. Other threats to sustained peace and stability included violent disturbances in many of the rubber plantations; demonstrations by former personnel of the security forces; student protests; violent criminal activities, particularly armed robbery and rape; and the high number of young people who were unemployed. Frequent ethnic tensions and land disputes between communities, as well as between communities and commercial enterprises, continued to be of concern. Other potential sources of instability included the illegal exploitation of resources by ex-combatants in economic enclaves and inaccessible mining areas, and drug and light weapons trafficking in the subregion. In May, UNMIL, the national police, the Drug Enforcement Agency and other national security agencies began a joint operation aimed at combating the cultivation and trafficking of marijuana. The drug posed a threat to internal security, since some of it was consumed by individuals who would go on to commit crimes, while the rest was believed to be trafficked across the porous borders into neighbouring countries. In that connection, the control and management of the borders remained a concern; of the 176 points of entry into the country, only 36 were considered official.

Further progress was made in the reform of the security sector. The President approved the national security strategy, which incorporated the country's security architecture with a regulatory framework. Basic training for the last batch of 500 recruits and training for 29 officer candidates for the armed forces began in June. It was hoped that the training tempo would be sustained in order for the new army to be fully trained before late 2009 to enable it to begin joint exercises and training with UNMIL troops. Training and development of the national police also continued, yet was hampered by various challenges. It became evident due to funding challenges that the first 200 officers of the planned 500-strong emergency response unit might not be fully operational by July 2009 as indicated in the Mission's benchmark. Disciplinary problems and misconduct within the national police force also raised concerns and led to the establishment of a Professional Standards Division. On the administration of justice countrywide, a positive development was the launch on 17 June of a Judicial Institute to provide sustained training for judicial officials.

The plan for the drawdown of UNMIL proposed in the Secretary-General's August 2007 report [YUN 2007, p. 195] provided for a three-year implementation time frame with built-in hold and review periods to assess the security situation and core benchmarks, and to adjust the pace or depth of the troop and police adjustments as necessary. As part of the review, from 12 to 24 May, the Government, UNMIL and the UN country team conducted a joint security assessment in all 15 counties to determine the level of security threats and evaluate the capacity of national and local institutions to respond. The joint security assessment teams confirmed that in most of the counties there had been no significant change in the security threat level since the Secretary-General's August 2007 report, while in a few counties the security situation had deteriorated. It was only in the north-western counties that the situation was assessed as relatively benign. The main threats to peace and stability emanated from law and order maintenance issues, such as the weak operational capacity of the security and rule-of-law institutions and the public's loss of confidence in those institutions. Other factors were the competition over natural resources, the potential regional instability and food insecurity, which was a new element. Consequently, none of the assessment teams recommended the total withdrawal of UNMIL military or police personnel from their locations. On the basis of those findings and taking into account progress made in the core benchmarks, UNMIL, together with a technical assessment mission led by the UN Department of Peacekeeping Operations, undertook a detailed review of phase 2 of the UNMIL force and police drawdown plans.

Following consultations with UNMIL and the technical assessment mission, the Secretary-General recommended that phase 2 of the drawdown of the military component, which would run from October 2008 to September 2009, should involve the repatriation of a further 1,460 military personnel, thereby reducing UNMIL troop strength to 10,231 personnel by September 2009. While the troop reduction represented a larger number than in his previous proposal for the second stage, the Secretary-General was confident that UNMIL would be able to continue to discharge its mandate of providing the necessary security umbrella throughout the country to enable the Government to continue its reform and restructuring programme. During phase 3, which would run from October 2009 to December 2010, a further reduction of 2,100 troops was envisaged, bringing the strength of UNMIL to 8,131 troops in December 2010. The plan also took cognizance of the Mission's security responsibilities along the borders, providing contingency plans for dealing with potential fallouts from external developments, as well as UNMIL's obligations under resolution 1609(2005) [YUN 2005, p. 236] to reinforce the United Nations Operation in Côte d'Ivoire if necessary. The Mission would continue to provide security to the Special Court for Sierra Leone.

On the police component, the Secretary-General said that the strengthening of the national police and the establishment of the emergency response unit had not progressed as well as envisaged. Therefore, it was not possible to reduce the tasks being undertaken by UNMIL formed police units in the Monrovia area and transfer those units to other key "hotspots", such as Harper, Lofa, Sinoe and Zwedru. The inability to fulfil the core assumptions meant that more support would be needed from UN police advisers during the next mandate period than previously envisaged. Additional support was required to provide the necessary strategic advice, training, mentoring and institutional capacity-building in specialized policing fields to the national police, which would still need support from UN police for its regular activities, including joint patrolling.

In view of those developments, and the increasing challenges related to the maintenance of law and order, the Secretary-General proposed an increase in the number of formed police units from five to seven (from 605 to 845 personnel), with effect from September 2008; no reductions should be made to the police advisory component between September 2008 and September 2009. He added that he intended to make internal adjustments in the strength of the UN police to accommodate eight additional correction officers, which would bring the police component strength to 1,375 personnel (845 formed police unit personnel, 32 correction officers and 498 police advisers). For the period from October 2009 to December 2010, a reduction of 132 UN police advisers was proposed, bringing the police strength to 1,243 personnel at the end of the drawdown period in December 2010. The Secretary-General recommended the extension of UNMIL for a 12-month period, until 30 September 2009.

SECURITY COUNCIL ACTION

On 29 September [meeting 5985], the Security Council unanimously adopted **resolution 1836(2008)**. The draft [S/2008/613] was prepared in consultations among Council members.

The Security Council,

Recalling its resolutions and the statements by its President concerning the situation in Liberia and the subregion, in particular resolutions 1509(2003) of 19 September 2003, 1626(2005) of 19 September 2005, 1750(2007) of 30 March 2007 and 1777(2007) of 20 September 2007,

Welcoming the report of the Secretary-General of 15 August 2008, and taking note of the recommendations contained therein,

Further welcoming the continuing efforts of the Government of Liberia to improve governance and security and combat corruption, as well as the important measures taken by the Government to consolidate its control over Liberia's natural resources and build a stronger economy,

Commending the Government of Liberia for the adoption of its first national poverty reduction strategy, for 2008–2011, and calling upon the international community to collaborate with the Government in the implementation of the strategy,

Noting with appreciation the steps being taken to facilitate national reconciliation and conflict management, with the support of the Peacebuilding Fund,

Noting the progress made in rebuilding, equipping and deploying the Liberian National Police and restructuring the Armed Forces of Liberia, and in developing a national security architecture, acknowledging the challenges that remain, and encouraging the Government of Liberia, in cooperation with the international community, to expedite its efforts in these fields,

Noting also the continuing need for support from United Nations police advisers to the Liberian National Police, as reflected in the report of the Secretary-General,

Expressing its appreciation for the continuing support of the international community, the Economic Community of West African States and the African Union,

Commending the work of the United Nations Mission in Liberia, under the leadership of the Special Representative of the Secretary-General for Liberia, for its continuing and significant contribution to maintaining peace and stability in Liberia, and welcoming the close cooperation between the Mission and the United Nations Operation in Côte d'Ivoire, as well as with neighbouring Governments, in coordinating security activities in the border areas in the subregion,

Noting with appreciation the progress made to date in the reintegration of ex-combatants, welcoming the contribution being made by the United Nations Development Programme, the Mission, international partners and the National Commission on Disarmament, Demobilization, Reintegration and Rehabilitation, and recognizing that there continues to be a need for formal sector employment,

Recognizing the significant challenges that remain in the consolidation of Liberia's post-conflict transition, including consolidation of State authority, massive development and reconstruction needs, the reform of the judiciary, extension of the rule of law throughout the country, and the further development of the Liberian security forces and security architecture, in particular the Liberian National Police, and noting that crimes of corruption and violence, in particular with regard to the exploitation of Liberia's natural resources, threaten to undermine progress towards those ends,

Welcoming the progress achieved on the broad benchmarks laid down in the report of the Secretary-General of 12 September 2006 and the core benchmarks presented in the reports of the Secretary-General of 8 August 2007 and 19 March 2008, welcoming the continuing efforts of the Mission to promote and protect, in cooperation with the Government of Liberia, the rights of civilians, in particular children and women, calling upon the Liberian authorities to continue to cooperate with the United Nations country team and civil society in order to achieve further progress in these areas and, in particular, to combat violence against children and women, including gender-based violence, sexual exploitation and abuse, and recalling its resolutions 1674(2006) of 28 April 2006 and 1612(2005) of 26 July 2005, as well as its resolutions 1325(2000) of 31 October 2000 and 1820(2008) of 19 June 2008 on women and peace and security,

Reiterating the continuing need for support by the Mission for the security of the Special Court for Sierra Leone,

Determining that the situation in Liberia continues to constitute a threat to international peace and security in the region,

Acting under Chapter VII of the Charter of the United Nations,

1. *Decides* that the mandate of the United Nations Mission in Liberia shall be extended until 30 September 2009;

2. *Reaffirms its intention* to authorize the Secretary-General to redeploy troops, as may be needed, between the Mission and the United Nations Operation in Côte d'Ivoire on a temporary basis in accordance with the provisions of resolution 1609(2005) of 24 June 2005;

3. *Endorses* the recommendation of the Secretary-General for a reduction of an additional 1,460 personnel deployed as part of the military component of the Mission and for the streamlining of the current four sectors into two, and authorizes the Secretary-General to implement this recommendation during the period from October 2008 to March 2009;

4. *Also endorses*, with immediate effect, the recommendation of the Secretary-General for an increase of 240 in the authorized number of personnel deployed as part of the police component of the Mission in order to provide strategic advice and expertise in specialized fields, provide operational support to regular policing activities and react to urgent security incidents, as well as his plans for internal adjustments in the composition of the police component within the overall ceiling, including an increase in the number of formed police units;

5. *Requests* the Secretary-General to continue to monitor progress on the core benchmarks detailed in paragraph 66 of his report of 8 August 2007 and in his report of 19 March 2008, and any subsequent refinements of the benchmarks that may be recommended by the Secretary-General or his Special Representative for Liberia, to report on that progress to the Security Council by 15 February 2009 and, in view of the extent of that progress, to recommend to the Council no later than 15 February 2009 any further adjustments in the military and police components of the Mission, as appropriate, and to include in his report, in consultation with the Government of Liberia, long-range scenarios for a phased drawdown and withdrawal of the troop contingent of the Mission, as the situation permits and without compromising the security of Liberia;

6. *Also requests* the Secretary-General, in consultation with the Government of Liberia, to develop further detailed benchmarks to measure and track progress towards the achievement of security in Liberia, and in that context to include in his report of 15 February 2009 and in subsequent reports a comprehensive assessment both of the progress made towards building the capacity of the Liberian National Police and of the contribution of the Mission towards that goal, and to make recommendations on possible adjustments needed to Mission police training or concept of operations, as appropriate;

7. *Expresses its intention* to review by 31 March 2009 the recommendations of the Secretary-General described in paragraph 5 above;

8. *Requests* the Secretary-General to provide by 15 August 2009 a report covering progress made on the issues addressed in paragraphs 5 and 6 above during the period from February to August 2009;

9. *Decides* to remain seized of the matter.

Year-end developments. The Secretary-General reported [S/2009/86] that the relationship between the legislative and executive branches continued to improve, allowing for the adoption of several key bills, including the Defence Act and the Anti-Corruption Commission Act. However, other important draft bills were pending, due to the suspension of the Senate's President pro tempore. The leadership dispute in the Senate hampered the work of the legislature during the second half of the year. The allocation of $15 million from the UN Peacebuilding Fund was fully programmed in support of the priority projects of the Government, and a peacebuilding office was established in December within the Ministry of Internal Affairs to develop national capacity and ownership of the peacebuilding process.

The security situation remained stable, yet was characterized by an underlying fragility. In October, UNMIL quelled violent disturbances involving ex-combatants in Grand Cape Mount, Grand Gedeh and Nimba counties caused by misunderstandings regarding reintegration benefits and the intended beneficiaries of a programme to assist the final caseload of former combatants who had not benefited from reintegration opportunities. The situation along the borders remained calm yet unpredictable. The death of President Lansana Conté in December and the subsequent military coup in Guinea (see p. 231) contributed to the uncertainty of the security environment, owing to the long-standing cross-border relationships and ethnic affinities between the peoples of the two countries, which had played a significant role during the Liberian civil conflict. The postponement of the elections in Côte d'Ivoire and limited progress in the Ivorian disarmament process, including the dismantling of the militias in the west of that country, also exacerbated the fragile situation in the region. A joint assessment by the United Nations Operation in Côte d'Ivoire (UNOCI), UNMIL and UNDP concluded that approximately 1,500 to 2,000 Liberian ex-combatants remained in Côte d'Ivoire near the Liberian border and needed to be closely monitored. The level of border monitoring was increased, including through joint operations of UNMIL with the security forces of Sierra Leone and Guinea, as well as with UNOCI.

On security sector reform, the United States continued to lead international support for the building of the new armed forces, which reached their planned strength of 2,000 troops in August, when the last batch of recruits completed basic training. The first battalion was activated at the same time, followed by the second in December. Meanwhile, there had been a number of incidents of indiscipline and failure to respect the rule of law by soldiers of the armed forces. Progress was also made in the reform and strengthening of the national police, in particular with the formulation of a five-year national police strategic plan, providing a comprehensive development framework. Although many challenges remained, development of the 500-strong police emergency response unit progressed. On strengthening the judicial, legal and corrections institutions, the convening of the National Rule of Law Retreat in September was a major step forward, as it was the first time the three branches of Government engaged in dialogue regarding rule-of-law issues. While the launch of the Judicial Training Institute in June was an important step in addressing the shortage of qualified staff, particularly public defenders, the Institute had yet to become fully operational, primarily because of lack of funding. The corrections sector was still characterized by weak infrastructure and low budgetary allocation. The sector was additionally strained by massive overcrowding in most facilities, and there were several incidents of prison breaks. The most serious was the riot and subsequent escape in December of 163 prisoners from Monrovia Central Prison, of which 85 remained at large.

Truth and Reconciliation Commission

The Secretary-General reported [S/2008/183] that the Truth and Reconciliation Commission, established by the Transitional Government in 2005 [YUN 2005, p. 263], made significant progress in implementing its mandate. The Commission began nationwide public hearings in Monrovia on 8 January to inquire into human rights violations during the country's 14-year civil war. President Johnson-Sirleaf addressed the opening of the hearings, apologized to the people of Liberia on behalf of all Governments of Liberia for the acts that contributed to the conflict, and called on Liberians to respond positively to Commission requests to attend hearings and provide truthful testimonies. The Commission completed public hearings in Monrovia on 31 January and began holding hearings in the counties. UNMIL worked closely with the Commission to ensure the successful completion of its mandate, and organized a series of outreach events and radio programmes to promote reconciliation and support the Commission's work. The Commission also held public hearings (St. Paul, Minnesota, United States, 10–14 June) at Hamline University, which focused on the experience of Liberians in the diaspora.

The Secretary-General subsequently reported [S/2008/553] that the Commission had completed its public hearings in all 15 counties and commenced thematic hearings in July. Although the Commission had previously requested a three-month extension of its mandate, on 15 July it asked the legislature for nine months, until 30 June 2009. On 11 and 12 August, Alhaji G.V. Kromah, the former head of the disbanded United Liberation Movement appeared before the Commission, testifying under the theme "Understanding the Conflict Through its Principal Events and Actors". He expressed remorse for his role in the conflict.

In later developments [S/2009/86], the Commission on 13 October released the findings of its conflict mapping survey, which identified land and property disputes as key threats to Liberia's fragile peace. The first volume of its report, containing an overview of the root causes of the conflict, was sent to the Legislature and the President in December.

Other developments. In the trial of Mr. Taylor, the Special Court for Sierra Leone began hearing the testimony of a prominent witness in the case, former Liberian Vice-President Moses Blah, on 14 May. On 1 September, the Special Court received a request from the Truth and Reconciliation Commission for an audience with former Liberian President Charles Taylor, who refused the request. On 30 October, Mr. Taylor's son, the United States national Charles Taylor Jr., was convicted by a jury in Miami, Florida, United States, for torture committed when he was the head of an anti-terrorist unit in Liberia during his father's presidency.

UNMIL

The United Nations Mission in Liberia (UNMIL), established by Security Council resolution 1509(2003) [YUN 2003, p. 194], was mandated to support the implementation of the 2003 Agreement on Ceasefire and Cessation of Hostilities [ibid., p. 189] and the peace process; protect UN staff, facilities and civilians; support humanitarian and human rights activities; and assist in national security reform, including national police training and the formation of a new, restructured military. By resolution 1638(2005) [YUN 2005, p. 267], the Council enhanced the mandate to include the apprehension and detention of former President Charles Taylor in the event of his return to Liberia, as well as his transfer to the Special Court for Sierra Leone. By resolution 1750(2007) [YUN 2007, p. 194], the Council decided that the Mission's mandate should include the provision of administrative and related support and security, on a cost-reimbursable basis, for activities conducted in Liberia by the Special Court for Sierra Leone with the consent of the Liberian Government. By resolution 1836(2008) (see p. 201), the Council approved the Secretary-General's recommendation to reduce the military component of UNMIL by an additional 1,460 personnel between October 2008 and March 2009 and to immediately increase its police component by 240 officers.

During 2008, the Secretary-General submitted reports to the Security Council on developments in Liberia and the activities of UNMIL in March [S/2008/183] and in August [S/2008/553], with a later report covering the remainder of the year [S/2009/86]. In addition to political and security aspects, the reports summarized UNMIL activities to address the humanitarian and human rights situation, as well as efforts to assist in national recovery, reconstruction and development. Throughout the year, the Mission also provided HIV/AIDS awareness training and sensitization to its personnel and promoted gender mainstreaming in its activities. UNMIL continued to be headed by the Special Representative of the Secretary-General for Liberia, Ellen Margrethe Løj (Denmark), maintaining its headquarters in the capital, Monrovia.

Appointment. In an exchange of letters with the Security Council President on 16 October [S/2008/665] and 20 October [S/2008/666], the Secretary-General appointed Lieutenant General A. T. M. Zahirul Alam (Bangladesh) as Force Commander of UNMIL to replace Lieutenant Chikadibia Obiakor (Nigeria), whose tour ended on 18 July.

Financing

In June, at its resumed sixty-second (2008) session, the General Assembly considered the performance report on the UNMIL budget for 1 July 2006 to 30 June 2007 [A/62/648], showing actual expenditures amounting to $676,202,000 against a total appropriation of $714,613,300 and the proposed budget for 1 July 2008 to 30 June 2009 [A/62/764] of $603,708,000, gross, together with the related ACABQ report [A/62/781/Add.10]. The proposed budget provided for the deployment of 215 military observers, 11,602 military contingent personnel, 582 UN police officers, 605 formed police unit personnel, 549 international staff, 1,049 national staff inclusive of 57 national officers, and 251 United Nations Volunteers. ACABQ recommended approving the proposed budget for 2008–2009 in the amount of $603,708,000.

GENERAL ASSEMBLY ACTION

On 20 June [meeting 109], the General Assembly, on the recommendation of the Fifth Committee [A/62/876], adopted **resolution 62/263** without vote [agenda item 152].

Financing of the United Nations Mission in Liberia

The General Assembly,

Having considered the reports of the Secretary-General on the financing of the United Nations Mission in Liberia and the related report of the Advisory Committee on Administrative and Budgetary Questions,

Recalling Security Council resolution 1497(2003) of 1 August 2003, by which the Council declared its readiness to establish a United Nations stabilization force to support the transitional government and to assist in the implementation of a comprehensive peace agreement in Liberia,

Recalling also Security Council resolution 1509(2003) of 19 September 2003, by which the Council decided to establish the United Nations Mission in Liberia for a period of twelve months, and the subsequent resolutions by which the Council extended the mandate of the Mission, the latest of which was resolution 1777(2007) of 20 September 2007, by which the Council extended the mandate of the Mission until 30 September 2008,

Recalling further its resolution 58/315 of 1 July 2004,

Recalling its resolution 58/261 A of 23 December 2003 on the financing of the Mission and its subsequent resolutions thereon, the latest of which was resolution 61/286 of 29 June 2007,

Reaffirming the general principles underlying the financing of United Nations peacekeeping operations, as stated in General Assembly resolutions 1874(S-IV) of 27 June 1963, 3101(XXVIII) of 11 December 1973 and 55/235 of 23 December 2000,

Noting with appreciation that voluntary contributions have been made to the Mission,

Mindful of the fact that it is essential to provide the Mission with the financial resources necessary to enable it to fulfil its responsibilities under the relevant resolutions of the Security Council,

1. *Requests* the Secretary-General to entrust the Head of Mission with the task of formulating future budget proposals in full accordance with the provisions of General Assembly resolutions 59/296 of 22 June 2005, 60/266 of 30 June 2006 and 61/276 of 29 June 2007, as well as other relevant resolutions;

2. *Takes note* of the status of contributions to the United Nations Mission in Liberia as at 30 April 2008, including the contributions outstanding in the amount of 71 million United States dollars, representing some 2 per cent of the total assessed contributions, notes with concern that only sixty-five Member States have paid their assessed contributions in full, and urges all other Member States, in particular those in arrears, to ensure payment of their outstanding assessed contributions;

3. *Expresses its appreciation* to those Member States which have paid their assessed contributions in full, and urges all other Member States to make every possible effort to ensure payment of their assessed contributions to the Mission in full;

4. *Expresses concern* at the financial situation with regard to peacekeeping activities, in particular as regards the reimbursements to troop contributors that bear additional burdens owing to overdue payments by Member States of their assessments;

5. *Also expresses concern* at the delay experienced by the Secretary-General in deploying and providing adequate resources to some recent peacekeeping missions, in particular those in Africa;

6. *Emphasizes* that all future and existing peacekeeping missions shall be given equal and non-discriminatory treatment in respect of financial and administrative arrangements;

7. *Also emphasizes* that all peacekeeping missions shall be provided with adequate resources for the effective and efficient discharge of their respective mandates;

8. *Reiterates its request* to the Secretary-General to make the fullest possible use of facilities and equipment at the United Nations Logistics Base at Brindisi, Italy, in order to minimize the costs of procurement for the Mission;

9. *Endorses* the conclusions and recommendations contained in the report of the Advisory Committee on Administrative and Budgetary Questions, and requests the Secretary-General to ensure their full implementation;

10. *Recalls* paragraph 13 of its resolution 60/121 B of 30 June 2006, and reiterates, in view of the importance of ensuring coordination and collaboration of efforts with the United Nations agencies and programmes, its request to the Secretary-General to report to the General Assembly on the progress made in the development of a collaboration framework and the efforts towards developing an integrated workplan in the context of his budget submission at the sixty-third session of the Assembly;

11. *Requests* the Secretary-General to review the staffing structure of the Mission and its related costs and to report thereon in his next budget proposal;

12. *Also requests* the Secretary-General to ensure the full implementation of the relevant provisions of its resolutions 59/296, 60/266 and 61/276;

13. *Further requests* the Secretary-General to take all necessary action to ensure that the Mission is administered with a maximum of efficiency and economy;

14. *Requests* the Secretary-General, in order to reduce the cost of employing General Service staff, to continue efforts to recruit local staff for the Mission against General Service posts, commensurate with the requirements of the Mission;

Financial performance report for the period from 1 July 2006 to 30 June 2007

15. *Takes note* of the report of the Secretary-General on the financial performance of the Mission for the period from 1 July 2006 to 30 June 2007;

Budget estimates for the period from 1 July 2008 to 30 June 2009

16. *Decides* to appropriate to the Special Account for the United Nations Mission in Liberia the amount of 631,689,100 dollars for the period from 1 July 2008 to 30 June 2009, inclusive of 603,708,000 dollars for the maintenance of the Mission, 24,392,000 dollars for the support account for peacekeeping operations and 3,589,100 dollars for the United Nations Logistics Base;

Financing of the appropriation

17. *Also decides* to apportion among Member States the amount of 157,922,278 dollars for the period from 1 July to 30 September 2008, in accordance with the levels updated in General Assembly resolution 61/243 of 22 December 2006, and taking into account the scale of assessments for 2008, as set out in its resolution 61/237 of 22 December 2006;

18. *Further decides* that, in accordance with the provisions of its resolution 973(X) of 15 December 1955, there shall be set off against the apportionment among Member States, as provided for in paragraph 17 above, their respective share in the Tax Equalization Fund of 3,567,150 dollars, comprising the estimated staff assessment income of 2,910,325 dollars approved for the Mission, the prorated share of 585,925 dollars of the estimated staff assessment income approved for the support account and the prorated share of 70,900 dollars of the estimated staff assessment income approved for the United Nations Logistics Base;

19. *Decides* to apportion among Member States the amount of 473,766,822 dollars for the period from 1 October 2008 to 30 June 2009, at a monthly rate of 52,640,758

dollars, in accordance with the levels updated in resolution 61/243, and taking into account the scale of assessments for 2008 and 2009, as set out in resolution 61/237, subject to a decision of the Security Council to extend the mandate of the Mission;

20. *Also decides* that, in accordance with the provisions of its resolution 973(X), there shall be set off against the apportionment among Member States, as provided for in paragraph 19 above, their respective share in the Tax Equalization Fund of 10,701,450 dollars, comprising the estimated staff assessment income of 8,730,975 dollars approved for the Mission, the prorated share of 1,757,775 dollars of the estimated staff assessment income approved for the support account and the prorated share of 212,700 dollars of the estimated staff assessment income approved for the United Nations Logistics Base;

21. *Further decides* that, for Member States that have fulfilled their financial obligations to the Mission, there shall be set off against their apportionment, as provided for in paragraph 17 above, their respective share of the unencumbered balance and other income in the total amount of 84,508,500 dollars in respect of the financial period ended 30 June 2007, in accordance with the levels updated in resolution 61/243, and taking into account the scale of assessments for 2007, as set out in resolution 61/237;

22. *Decides* that, for Member States that have not fulfilled their financial obligations to the Mission, there shall be set off against their outstanding obligations their respective share of the unencumbered balance and other income in the total amount of 84,508,500 dollars in respect of the financial period ended 30 June 2007, in accordance with the scheme set out in paragraph 21 above;

23. *Also decides* that the increase of 758,400 dollars in the estimated staff assessment income in respect of the financial period ended 30 June 2007 shall be added to the credits from the amount of 84,508,500 dollars referred to in paragraphs 21 and 22 above;

24. *Emphasizes* that no peacekeeping mission shall be financed by borrowing funds from other active peacekeeping missions;

25. *Encourages* the Secretary-General to continue to take additional measures to ensure the safety and security of all personnel participating in the Mission under the auspices of the United Nations, bearing in mind paragraphs 5 and 6 of Security Council resolution 1502(2003) of 26 August 2003;

26. *Invites* voluntary contributions to the Mission in cash and in the form of services and supplies acceptable to the Secretary-General, to be administered, as appropriate, in accordance with the procedure and practices established by the General Assembly;

27. *Decides* to include in the provisional agenda of its sixty-third session the item entitled "Financing of the United Nations Mission in Liberia".

Sanctions

The Security Council received several reports on the implementation of sanctions imposed on Liberia, pursuant to Council resolutions 1521(2003) [YUN 2003, p. 208] and 1792(2007) [YUN 2007, p. 206], which banned arms and related materiel, military training and international travel by individuals who constituted a threat to the peace process in Liberia and the subregion. Financial sanctions were also imposed on the former President of Liberia, Charles Taylor, his immediate family and senior officials of the former Taylor regime by resolution 1532(2004) [YUN 2004, p. 204]. The Council terminated the sanctions on round logs and timber products in 2006 by resolution 1689(2006) [YUN 2006, p. 226] and on diamonds in 2007 by resolution 1753(2007) [YUN 2007, p. 202].

Appointments. In a letter dated 8 February [S/2008/85], the Secretary-General, as requested in resolution 1792(2007), informed the Council of the re-appointment of Wynet V. Smith (Canada) to the Panel of Experts concerning Liberia, as well as the appointment of Guy Lamb (South Africa) and Thomas R. Creal (United States) to replace two of the panellists previously appointed, Dimieari Von Kemedi and Rajiva Bushan [YUN 2007, p. 202], who were unable to continue their service. On 14 July [S/2008/459], the Secretary-General informed the Council of the appointment of Ms. Smith, Nelson Alusala (Kenya) and Mr. Creal to the Panel of Experts. Under resolution 1792(2007), the Panel was mandated to conduct an assessment mission to Liberia and neighbouring States in order to report on the implementation of resolution 1521(2003) and any violations of the sanctions imposed by that resolution and by resolution 1532(2004); the impact and effectiveness of the measures imposed; the implementation of forestry legislation; the Government's compliance with the Kimberley Process Certification Scheme; and the progress in the timber and diamond sectors since the lifting of the sanctions.

Implementation of sanctions regime

Report of Expert Panel (June). In June, the Chairman of the Security Council Committee established pursuant to resolution 1521(2003) [YUN 2003, p. 208] concerning Liberia transmitted to the Council a report [S/2008/371] of the Panel of Experts concerning Liberia that contained an assessment of the arms embargo, as well as the travel-ban and asset-freeze measures on designated individuals and entities. On the arms embargo, the Panel found that while there were no serious violations, a series of minor violations took place, mainly involving the small-scale transfer of ammunition and single-barrel rifles by individuals from Côte d'Ivoire and Guinea into Liberia. A related problem was Liberia's antiquated and transient approach to firearms control. On 23 January, the Committee established pursuant to resolution 1521(2003) approved an application from the United States and Liberian Governments for an exemption from the embargo for arms, ammunition and equipment to train the newly established emergency response unit of the national police. The delivery of Chinese arms, ammunition and policing equipment to the special security services were completed in the early part of the year. However, further deliveries of exempted arms and related materiel by China and the United States took place without notification to the sanctions Committee upon delivery of those consignments, as required by resolution 1792(2007). Moreover, the Liberian Government had not marked the arms and ammunition in question, as required by resolution 1683(2006). The Panel made recommendations for the Ministry of Justice to resolve the uncertainty surrounding the status of its firearms-control policy and legislation; the Government to make arrangements for marking the firearms received from China and the United States; the sanctions Committee to stipulate the manner in which arms and ammunition were to be marked, as no standardized approach was being employed; the United States Embassy in Monrovia to permit the UNMIL Firearm Inspection Team to periodically inspect the exempted arms and related materiel that had been transferred to Liberia; and the Government to ensure that officers required to carry firearms were trained and vetted and border control officials were provided with improved training and resources to enable them to effectively carry out their duties. In addition, all ammunition transferred to the Government of Liberia under exemptions should be marked during the manufacturing stage.

On the travel ban, the Panel visited Monrovia's Roberts International Airport and scrutinized passenger ledgers for the period from 1 September 2007 to 5 May 2008, finding no evidence of violations. It noted that the existence of the Security Council travel ban against certain Liberians and foreign nationals was widely acknowledged, yet was also subject to some criticism among Liberians. The names on the current lists, however, were not so widely known. Officials at many points of entry indicated that, where appropriate, they sought to enforce the travel ban. Yet many Government officials did not understand that Liberia's role in implementing the ban was only to prevent the entry into Liberia of foreign nationals on the list, not to prevent the departure of Liberian citizens. In addition, there were resource, administrative and technical challenges to the enforcement of the travel ban, including out-of-date and missing information, such as valid passport numbers. The Panel also found that the Bureau of Immigration and Naturalization was not provided with updated versions of the travel-ban list. Five individuals were removed from the travel-ban list during the reporting period. The Panel recommended the safe storage of the passenger ledgers at Roberts International Airport and the introduction of quality-control processes with respect to recording passenger data. It also recommended that States provide the sanctions Committee with complete and up-to-date information, including photographs, of all individuals on the travel-ban list. The Liberian Government should distribute the list throughout Liberia, thus contributing to a more effective implementation of the travel ban.

The Panel reported that the Government cited the 1986 Constitution as the reason Liberia had not frozen any assets as required by Council resolution 1532(2004). Several high-ranking Liberian legislators and legal scholars, as well as legal advisers to the Ministry of Justice, however, said that Liberian laws provided for such action in accordance with due process, and that the asset-freeze measure of resolution 1532(2004) could be executed without new legislation or executive order. The Panel conducted an investigation of the financial records of parties named on the asset-freeze list and proved that there were assets available for freezing. Tracing of the flow of funds indicated that Gus Kouwenhoven received at least $7 million, yet only $51,692 had been frozen; Edwin Snowe received more than $1 million, yet no assets had been frozen; and Joseph Wong Kiia Tai received more than $8.5 million, with no assets frozen. Funds traced via diverted tax revenues to former President Taylor, as a sample test only, were approximately $20 million, with no assets frozen. The Panel received responses from seven of 25 States and territories requested to provide an update on frozen assets of persons on the list. As at 15 May, the aggregate worldwide assets frozen totalled just over $8.37 million, which was far short of the several hundred million dollars noted by some investigative reporters and the Prosecutor of the Sierra Leone Special Court. It was the Panel's opinion that techniques were available for States to move forward with a more comprehensive implementation of resolution 1532(2004). The Panel recommended a review of the asset-freeze list and modification of the names, with an emphasis on the parties related to Charles Taylor and individuals that had served or were serving as alter egos for him, or had been unjustly enriched. A revision of the business list that was more reflective of companies that had received monies was also recommended, as well as the establishment of a strong team of technical experts to assist Liberia.

On the diamond sector, the Panel said that diamond exploration and mining activities were on the increase. Ten companies had licences for diamond exploration; five applications for new diamond-related mineral exploration licences had been forwarded to the Inter-Ministerial Concessions Committee for consideration; and three of nine existing mineral development agreements were for diamond exploration companies. The Government made significant progress in implementing the Kimberley Process Certification Scheme and its own system of internal controls. Overall, the Government Diamond Office was functioning well. Since the lifting of sanctions on rough diamonds, the Office had issued 43 Kimberley Process certificates, and 39 shipments of rough diamonds had been legally exported as at 15 May. However, a number of challenges and causes for concern remained. Office staff had issued one certificate to an unlicensed exporter, and of the two imports of rough diamonds processed, neither had proceeded properly through the system of internal controls. In addition, statistics gathered by the Office indicated the absence of large and valuable stones from exported shipments, and there were concerns that diamonds were being exported without entering the official system. A setback occurred in February, when a fire at the building housing the Office left it without a roof, and the ensuing rains that flooded the database room damaged the computers that stored the database, affecting the functioning of the Office for a month. Meanwhile, the system of Regional Diamond Offices was not operating as effectively as it could and there was a need for customs, the Ministry of Lands, Mines and Energy and the national police to cooperate more fully to improve the enforcement of mining law and internal controls. The Panel made a series of recommendations addressed to the Ministry of Lands, Mines and Energy, the Government Diamond Office, the Kimberley Process and its working groups, donors and the Government, including to request another Kimberley Process review visit within the next year given the challenges it faced in implementation.

The Forestry Development Authority (FDA) continued to make progress in implementing the National Forestry Reform Law, including approval by the FDA Board of Directors of the National Forest Management Strategy, the preparation of forest management guidelines and the development of the code of forest harvesting practices. Nonetheless, some areas required improvement and others were causes for concern. The Panel did not have sufficient information on the protected-area network to assess progress, and the demarcation of East Nimba Reserve in February had led to conflict between FDA staff and local residents. On the process of awarding contracts for commercial logging concessions, some 44 logging companies had been pre-qualified for bidding on contracts, six timber sales contracts had been tendered and FDA had forwarded recommendations for awarding contracts to three companies to the Inter-Ministerial Concessions Committee. Three forest management contracts had been advertised and bids submitted, and evaluation and due diligence of the 13 bids were under way. The chain-of-custody contract was signed. The Panel made several recommendations for implementation by FDA and for the Government to make a decision about the outstanding recommendation of the third-phase Forest Concession Review Committee and the pre-qualification panel regarding debarment of logging companies. It called on the Liberia Forest Initiative to establish benchmarks for evaluating the willingness and capacity of FDA to implement the new legal framework in order to help it determine where funding needs might be required.

SECURITY COUNCIL ACTION

On 18 June [meeting 5914], the Security Council unanimously adopted **resolution 1819(2008)**. The draft [S/2008/394] was prepared in consultations among Council members.

The Security Council,

Recalling its previous resolutions and the statements by its President on the situation in Liberia and West Africa,

Welcoming the sustained progress made by the Government of Liberia since January 2006 in rebuilding Liberia for the benefit of all Liberians, with the support of the international community,

Recalling its decision not to renew the measures in paragraph 10 of resolution 1521(2003) of 22 December 2003 regarding round logs and timber products originating in Liberia, and stressing that Liberia's progress in the timber sector must continue with the effective implementation and enforcement of the National Forestry Reform Law signed into law on 5 October 2006, including the resolution of land and tenure rights, the conservation and protection of biodiversity and the process for the awarding of contracts for commercial forestry operations,

Recalling also its decision to terminate the measures in paragraph 6 of resolution 1521(2003) regarding diamonds,

Welcoming the participation of the Government of Liberia in the Kimberley Process Certification Scheme, noting the implementation by Liberia of the necessary internal controls and other recommendations of the Kimberley Process, and calling upon the Government to continue to work diligently to ensure the effectiveness of these controls,

Stressing the continuing importance of the United Nations Mission in Liberia in improving security throughout Liberia and helping the Government of Liberia to establish its authority throughout the country, particularly in the diamond- and timber-producing regions and border areas,

Urging all parties to support the Government of Liberia in identifying and implementing measures that will ensure progress towards meeting the conditions set out in paragraph 5 of resolution 1521(2003),

Welcoming the report of the Panel of Experts on Liberia, including on the issues of diamonds, timber, targeted sanctions, and arms and security,

Determining that, despite significant progress having been made in Liberia, the situation there continues to constitute a threat to international peace and security in the region,

Acting under Chapter VII of the Charter of the United Nations,

1. *Requests* that the Secretary-General renew the mandate of the Panel of Experts appointed pursuant to paragraph 1 of resolution 1760(2007) of 20 June 2007 for a further period, until 20 December 2008, and requests that the Panel of Experts report to the Security Council through the Committee established pursuant to paragraph 21 of resolution 1521(2003) ("the Committee") by 1 December 2008 on all issues listed in paragraph 5 of resolution 1792(2007) of 19 December 2007, and to provide informal updates to the Committee, as appropriate, before that date;

2. *Also requests* the Secretary-General to reappoint the Panel of Experts and to make the necessary financial and security arrangements to support the work of the Panel;

3. *Calls upon* all States and the Government of Liberia to cooperate fully with the Panel of Experts in all the aspects of its mandate;

4. *Encourages* the Government of Liberia to implement the recommendations of the most recent Kimberley Process review and to work closely with the Kimberley Process to continue to strengthen Liberian controls on rough diamond trade;

5. *Encourages* the Kimberley Process to inform, as appropriate, the Council, through the Committee, about its assessment of progress made by the Government of Liberia in implementing the Kimberley Process Certification Scheme;

6. *Reiterates* the importance of continuing assistance by the United Nations Mission in Liberia to the Government of Liberia, the Committee and the Panel of Experts, within its capabilities and areas of deployment, and without prejudice to its mandate, including in monitoring the implementation of the measures in paragraphs 2 and 4 of resolution 1521(2003), and in this regard recalls its request that the Mission inspect inventories of weapons and ammunition obtained in accordance with paragraphs 1 and 2 of resolution 1683(2006) of 13 June 2006 to ensure that all such weapons and ammunition are accounted for, and make periodic reports to the Committee on its findings;

7. *Reiterates its request* to the United Nations Operation in Côte d'Ivoire, within its capabilities and areas of deployment, and without prejudice to its mandate, to assist the Committee and the Panel of Experts by passing to the Committee and the Panel any information relevant to the implementation of the measures in paragraphs 2 and 4 of resolution 1521(2003) in the context of enhanced coordination among United Nations missions and offices in West Africa;

8. *Decides* to remain actively seized of the matter.

Report of Expert Panel (December). On 12 December, the sanctions Committee Chairman transmitted the report of the Panel of Experts [S/2008/785] to the Security Council. On the diamond industry, the Panel reported that between 5 September 2007 and 30 September 2008, the Government of Liberia authorized exports of over 64,000 carats of rough diamonds valued at $11.9 million. Between 1 January and 30 September 2008, it earned more than $277,000 in export fees and more than $663,150 in licence fees. The Ministry of Lands, Mines and Energy had undertaken more awareness-raising activities and worked with customs officials to ensure that export and import controls functioned more effectively. However, the Government Diamond Office had yet to put in place a system for protecting its digital data files. Regional harmonization efforts were under way and were crucial to addressing common challenges of countries in the subregion. The Panel reiterated its recommendation for the Kimberley Process to develop and adopt guidelines regarding problematic and suspicious shipments. It also urged the Security Council to direct UNMIL to provide support to the Government in its efforts to complete security sector reforms and re-establish control over its natural resources—including diamonds and timber.

Although gains were made in implementing the National Forestry Reform Law, including the FDA's submission to the National Legislature of legislation on community rights regarding forest lands, progress in the commercial sector was more uneven. The Panel found that FDA actions did not comply with some important requirements of the National Forestry Reform Law and with its regulations on the awarding of contracts for commercial timber concessions. A major concern was the change made to the payment terms for three forest-management contracts after the conclusions of negotiations, which could result in the loss of $50 million in revenue for the Government over the course of the 25-year period of the contracts. The Panel observed that concerted efforts would be required to ensure that the forestry reform process continued and the forestry sector could contribute to development on a long-term basis. It urged the Government to reassess its strategy for allocating commercial timber concessions, and to ensure that FDA and other ministries and agencies followed the legal framework that was meant to ensure that financially and technically capable companies applied for timber concessions.

The sanctions Committee on Liberia delisted Charles Bright, Moussa Cisse and Montgomery Dolo from the travel-ban list in May. Charles Taylor Jr. was convicted in October in a federal court in Miami, United States, on torture, firearms and conspiracy charges. Allegations were made that a number of individuals travelled in contravention of the travel ban, and the Panel was attempting to verify that information. Officials in some States in the region continued to claim that they were unaware of the travel-ban list and stressed that their ability to enforce it was limited, due to the porosity of their borders and lack of capacity. The Panel recommended that the Government and other States in the region be more diligent in their application of the travel ban, particularly given the allegations of designated individuals being engaged in recruitment.

The sanctions Committee on Liberia delisted Charles Bright from the asset-freeze list, while another designated individual submitted a request for delisting. The Panel anticipated more petitions for delisting. In their discussions on targeted sanctions, experts and Government implementers recognized the need for the asset-freeze sanctions to evolve. The Panel recommended that the Security Council task an appropriate UN body to serve as the central depository and hub of all asset information and tracing of monies related to Council sanctions. The United Nations could also be tasked with maintaining a repository of information and expertise to assist in tracing the movement of assets from State to State. It also recommended following up with scheduled visits to each of the States that approved the Panel's conducting an on-site visit to banks for a review of the financial records.

As Liberia's borders remained porous and had multiple informal entry points, the Panel noted that the potential for trafficking in arms and ammunition between Côte d'Ivoire and Liberia was great. On the border between Guinea and Liberia, minor cases of transfers of single-barrel ammunition continued. Previously approved exemptions of arms and ammunition for training of the emergency response unit and for the armed forces were delivered, and the sanctions Committee approved an exemption for more materials for the police emergency response unit. Although all imported weapons were marked in conformity with Security Council resolution 1683(2006), the markings were of inferior quality because of the tool used and were susceptible to rust. The Panel recommended that States given exemptions to export weapons notify the Committee in advance of the consignment reaching the port of entry in Liberia, thereby allowing for inspection to take place before the consignment was transferred into storage. It also called for the Government to strengthen the capacity of its law enforcement agencies responsible for monitoring the country's borders, the close monitoring by the authorities of allegations of recruitment of potential fighters along the border between Côte d'Ivoire and Liberia, and the acquisition of more effective weapon-marking machines, preferably of the laser-marking type, whose marks could withstand weathering and obliteration.

SECURITY COUNCIL ACTION

On 19 December [meeting 6051], the Security Council unanimously adopted **resolution 1854(2008)**. The draft [S/2008/797] was submitted by the United States.

The Security Council,

Recalling its previous resolutions and the statements by its President on the situation in Liberia and West Africa,

Welcoming the sustained progress made by the Government of Liberia since January 2006 in rebuilding Liberia for the benefit of all Liberians, with the support of the international community,

Recalling its decision not to renew the measures in paragraph 10 of resolution 1521(2003) of 22 December 2003 regarding round logs and timber products originating in Liberia, and stressing that Liberia's progress in the timber sector must continue with the effective implementation and enforcement of the National Forestry Reform Law signed into law on 5 October 2006, including the resolution of land and tenure rights, the conservation and protection of biodiversity and the process for the awarding of contracts for commercial forestry operations,

Recalling also its decision to terminate the measures in paragraph 6 of resolution 1521(2003) regarding diamonds, welcoming the participation of the Government of Liberia in the Kimberley Process Certification Scheme, noting the implementation by Liberia of the necessary internal controls and other requirements of the Kimberley Process, and calling upon the Government to continue to work diligently to ensure the effectiveness of these controls,

Recalling further the statement by its President of 25 June 2007 recognizing the role of voluntary initiatives aimed at improving revenue transparency, such as the Extractive Industries Transparency Initiative, and, taking note of General Assembly resolution 62/274 of 11 September 2008 on strengthening transparency in industries, supporting Liberia's decision to, inter alia, take part in the Initiative and other extractive industry transparency initiatives and encouraging Liberia's continued progress in implementing its Initiative workplan to improve revenue transparency,

Stressing the continuing importance of the United Nations Mission in Liberia in improving security throughout Liberia and helping the Government of Liberia to establish its authority throughout the country, particularly in the regions producing diamonds, timber and other natural resources, and border areas,

Taking note of the report of the Panel of Experts on Liberia, including on the issues of diamonds, timber, targeted sanctions, and arms and security, submitted on 12 December 2008,

Having reviewed the measures imposed by paragraphs 2 and 4 of resolution 1521(2003) and paragraph 1 of resolution 1532(2004) of 12 March 2004 and the progress towards meeting the conditions set out in paragraph 5 of resolution 1521(2003), and concluding that insufficient progress has been made towards that end,

Underlining its determination to support the Government of Liberia in its efforts to meet those conditions, and encouraging donors to do likewise,

Urging all parties to support the Government of Liberia in identifying and implementing measures that will ensure progress towards meeting the conditions set out in paragraph 5 of resolution 1521(2003),

Determining that, despite significant progress having been made in Liberia, the situation there continues to constitute a threat to international peace and security in the region,

Acting under Chapter VII of the Charter of the United Nations,

1. *Decides*, on the basis of its assessment of progress made to date towards meeting the conditions for lifting the measures imposed by resolution 1521(2003):

(*a*) To renew the measures on arms imposed by paragraph 2 of resolution 1521(2003) and modified by paragraphs 1 and 2 of resolution 1683(2006) of 13 June 2006 and by paragraph 1 (*b*) of resolution 1731(2006) of 20 December 2006 and to renew the measures on travel imposed by paragraph 4 of resolution 1521(2003) for a further period of twelve months from the date of adoption of the present resolution;

(*b*) That Member States shall notify the Security Council Committee established pursuant to paragraph 21 of resolution 1521(2003) ("the Committee") upon delivery of all arms and related materiel supplied in accordance with paragraph 2 (*e*) or paragraph 2 (*f*) of resolution 1521(2003), paragraph 2 of resolution 1683(2006) or paragraph 1 (*b*) of resolution 1731(2006);

(*c*) To review any of the above measures at the request of the Government of Liberia, once the Government reports to the Council that the conditions set out in resolution 1521(2003) for terminating the measures have been met and provides the Council with information to justify its assessment;

2. *Recalls* that the measures imposed by paragraph 1 of resolution 1532(2004) remain in force, notes with concern the findings of the Panel of Experts on Liberia on the lack of progress in this regard, and calls upon the Government of Liberia to continue to make all necessary efforts to fulfil its obligations;

3. *Reconfirms its intention* to review the measures imposed by paragraph 1 of resolution 1532(2004) at least once a year, and directs the Committee, in coordination with the relevant designating States and with the assistance of the Panel of Experts, to update as necessary the publicly available reasons for listing for entries on the travel ban and assets freeze lists as well as the Committee guidelines, particularly with regard to listing and de-listing procedures;

4. *Decides* to extend the mandate of the current Panel of Experts appointed pursuant to paragraph 1 of resolution 1819(2008) of 18 June 2008 for a further period, until 20 December 2009, to undertake the following tasks:

(*a*) To conduct two follow-up assessment missions to Liberia and neighbouring States, in order to investigate and compile a midterm report and a final report on the implementation, and any violations, of the measures imposed by resolution 1521(2003) and renewed in paragraph 1 above, including any information relevant to the designation by the Committee of the individuals described in paragraph 4(*a*) of resolution 1521(2003) and paragraph 1 of resolution 1532(2004), and including the various sources of financing, such as from natural resources, for the illicit trade in arms;

(*b*) To assess the impact and effectiveness of the measures imposed by paragraph 1 of resolution 1532(2004), including, in particular, with respect to the assets of former President Charles Taylor;

(*c*) To assess the implementation of forestry legislation passed by the Liberian Congress on 19 September 2006 and signed into law by President Johnson-Sirleaf on 5 October 2006;

(*d*) To assess compliance by the Government of Liberia with the Kimberley Process Certification Scheme, and to coordinate with the Kimberley Process in assessing compliance;

(*e*) To provide a midterm report to the Council, through the Committee, by 1 June 2009 and a final report to the Council, through the Committee, by 20 December 2009 on all the issues listed in the present paragraph, and to provide informal updates to the Committee, as appropriate, before those dates, especially on progress in the timber sector since the lifting of the measures imposed by paragraph 10 of resolution 1521(2003) in June 2006, and in the diamond sector since the lifting of the measures imposed by paragraph 6 of resolution 1521(2003) in April 2007;

(*f*) To cooperate actively with other relevant groups of experts, in particular the Group of Experts on Côte d'Ivoire re-established pursuant to paragraph 10 of resolution 1842(2008) of 29 October 2008, and with the Kimberley Process Certification Scheme;

(*g*) To identify and make recommendations regarding areas where the capacity of States in the region can be strengthened to facilitate the implementation of the measures imposed by paragraph 4 of resolution 1521(2003) and paragraph 1 of resolution 1532(2004);

(*h*) To assist the Committee in updating the publicly available reasons for listing for entries on the travel ban and assets freeze lists;

5. *Requests* the Secretary-General to reappoint the current members of the Panel of Experts and to make the necessary financial and security arrangements to support the work of the Panel;

6. *Calls upon* all States and the Government of Liberia to cooperate fully with the Panel of Experts in all the aspects of its mandate;

7. *Encourages* the Government of Liberia to continue to implement the recommendations of the 2008 Kimberley Process review team to strengthen internal controls over diamond mining and export;

8. *Encourages* the Kimberley Process to continue to cooperate with the Panel of Experts and to report on developments regarding implementation by Liberia of the Kimberley Process Certification Scheme;

9. *Decides* to remain actively seized of the matter.

Security Council Committee. The Security Council Committee established pursuant to resolution 1521(2003) concerning Liberia submitted a report [S/2009/236] on its activities in 2008. During the year, the Committee held one formal meeting and 10 informal consultations. The Committee considered and approved five requests for exceptions to the arms embargo: to transfer ammunition from UNMIL formed police units to UN police trainers for the firearms training of vetted officers of the police training academy; to enable the United States Government to provide training to the Liberian Special Security Service, and equipment and training to the emergency response unit; to ship weapons and ammunition for training national police officers recruited to serve in the emergency response unit; and to ship equipment for the repair and maintenance of previously approved arms used for training the armed forces.

The Committee considered five requests for travel-ban waivers, of which one was granted. It also received and approved two notifications, regarding the intention of the Italian Government to authorize access to hitherto frozen funds in order to recover expenses of an entity included on the asset-freeze list. The Committee considered 11 requests for delisting from its travel-ban list and asset-freeze list. Three of those requests were received from States (in connection with seven individuals), and four were submitted through the focal point process as set out in resolution 1730(2006). The Committee agreed to delist 10 individuals and observed that the removal of the names was illustrative of the continuing trend towards the conditioned removal of sanctions related to Liberia, which began with the termination of sanctions on timber imports from Liberia in June 2006 and on rough diamond imports from Liberia in April 2007. The delistings were effected through requests from both States and the focal point for delisting, which demonstrated the effectiveness of both channels to pursue delistings set out in the Committee's guidelines. The Committee did not consider two de-listing requests received from the focal point, as the designating State did not support the requests. The Committee removed the tenth individual, Gus Kouwenhoven, from its travel-ban and asset-freeze lists on 15 December [SC/9538], retaining the names of 47 of the 57 persons listed as at 31 December 2007.

The Committee did not receive any additional replies from States on actions taken to implement the sanctions in resolution 1521(2003); thus the number of replies received remained at 17. No additional replies were received from States on action taken to trace and freeze funds, other financial assets and economic resources described in resolution 1532(2004); the number of replies remained at 15.

Sierra Leone

In 2008, the Government of Sierra Leone continued efforts to implement its agenda for peace consolidation and economic recovery. At his first presidential retreat, President Ernest Bai Koroma discussed his vision and strategies for moving the country forward and secured the commitment of each minister to allow their performance to be periodically monitored and assessed. Other developments included the appointment of a public service reform Director, the launch of the Justice Sector Reform Strategy and Investment Plan, the approval of a national anti-corruption strategy and the submission of the Constitutional Review Commission report, which proposed 136 amendments to the 1991 Constitution. Successful local council elections were conducted in July. The United Nations Integrated Office in Sierra Leone continued to support Government efforts to consolidate peace. The Secretary-General presented the completion strategy for the Office, including the gradual drawdown of the mission, termination of its mandate by 30 September and transition to a successor integrated political office. His recommendations on the mandate, structure and strength of the United Nations Integrated Peacebuilding Office in Sierra Leone were endorsed by the Security Council in August and the transition culminated in the adoption of a Joint Vision of the United Nations Family for Sierra Leone that brought together the political mandate of the Office with the development and humanitarian mandates of other UN system bodies. In December, President Koroma issued his Agenda for Change, which presented the priorities of the Government over the next three years and set out the foundation for peacebuilding. A high-level stakeholders' consultation was held in May to garner support for the Sierra Leone Peacebuilding Cooperation Framework. During the year, some 47 per cent of the $35 million allocated to Sierra Leone through the Peacebuilding Fund had been committed through seven projects.

The Special Court for Sierra Leone continued to try those bearing the greatest responsibility for serious violations of international humanitarian and Sierra Leonean laws committed in the territory of Sierra Leone since 1996. Two cases were ongoing during the year, including the trial of former Liberian President Charles Taylor.

Peacebuilding efforts

Peace consolidation process and UNIOSIL activities

UNIOSIL completion strategy. In response to Security Council resolution 1793(2007) [YUN 2007, p. 214], the Secretary-General, in a letter of 31 January [S/2008/63], outlined the completion strategy for the United Nations Integrated Office in Sierra Leone (UNIOSIL), which entailed a 20 per cent reduction in staff by 31 March; a continued mission at 80 per cent of the strength as at 21 December 2007 until 30 June 2008; and the termination of the UNIOSIL mandate by 30 September 2008. To determine the number of staff required to perform the remaining tasks, UNIOSIL conducted a section-by-section assessment of the personnel required to implement those tasks, which included assisting the Government in its efforts to reform the Constitution; enhance democratic governance; strengthen the security, judicial and corrections sectors; promote human rights; strengthen women's participation in the political process; and address the root causes of the conflict as identified by the report of the Truth and Reconciliation Commission [YUN 2004, p. 219].

On the basis of the mission-wide review, it was determined that UNIOSIL could be downsized by 62 posts, including 15 international staff members, 43 national staff and 4 UN Volunteers, which represented 20 per cent of its authorized staffing complement. UNIOSIL was streamlining tasks within each section to ensure that the mission retained the requisite capacity to effectively perform its tasks. The mission would also transfer some of its activities to relevant UN agencies. Until the expiration of its mandate on 30 September, UNIOSIL would implement the following key tasks: assist the Government in conducting local government elections scheduled for 5 July; monitor the security situation and strengthen the capacity of the national security sector; promote transparency and accountability, including good governance, and combat corruption; monitor and promote human rights and the rule of law; promote a culture of peace, dialogue and participation through UN Radio; implement resolution 1325(2000) [YUN 2000, p. 1113] and promote the empowerment of women and their participation in decision-making; and facilitate the work of the Peacebuilding Commission.

Following the local government elections in July, UNIOSIL would gradually draw down its remaining personnel, beginning with substantive personnel, while the administrative and logistical staff needed to complete the liquidation process would withdraw last. Any additional proposals on the mission's drawdown, as well as on the mandate, structure and strength of the follow-on integrated political office discussed in the Secretary-General's December 2007 report [YUN 2007, p. 211] would be submitted in his April report on UNIOSIL.

On 28 February [S/2008/137], the Security Council took note of the UNIOSIL completion strategy and requested the Secretary-General to provide further information in his April report on the planned drawdown of UNIOSIL between the local elections in July and their completion in September; specific proposals on the mandate, structure and strength of the successor integrated political office; and plans for the UN police/military adviser team element.

Report of Secretary-General (April). In his sixth report on UNIOSIL [S/2008/281], the Secretary-General said that the Government of Sierra Leone made efforts to implement its agenda for peace consolidation and economic recovery. On 12 and 13 January, at his first presidential retreat for cabinet Ministers, deputy Ministers and other key Government officials, President Koroma discussed his vision and strategies for moving the country forward, focusing on six priority areas: energy and water supply; transportation by road, air and water; youth unemployment; economic growth sectors, including agriculture, mining, tourism, and fisheries and marine resources; social services, including education, health care and housing; and capacity development in the public and private sectors, in local government and in the justice system.

Political tension between supporters of the ruling All People's Congress party (APC) and the Sierra Leone People's Party (SLPP) continued to be a concern. In January, SLPP adopted a resolution calling on the Government to immediately dissolve the National Electoral Commission and remove the Chairperson before the local council elections on 5 July. It also condemned the dismissal by the APC Government of public officials perceived to be supporters of SLPP. On 13 February, the High Court of Sierra Leone dismissed the case brought by SLPP in December 2007, which challenged the decision of the National Electoral Commission to invalidate votes cast in 477 polling stations during the presidential run-off elections on 8 September 2007. The Court ruled that it had no jurisdiction under the 1991 Constitution to consider any proceedings concerning the election of a president. On 5 April, the National Electoral Commission announced that APC had won all four seats in the parliamentary by-elections held on 29 March to fill vacancies that had arisen following the appointment of the incumbents to ministerial posts. The by-elections were well organized and ran smoothly.

The security situation in the country, including along the borders with Guinea and Liberia, remained calm. Although the territorial dispute between Guinea and Sierra Leone over the border town of Yenga was still not settled, the Sierra Leonean Government expressed its commitment to resolve the issue. The main threats to stability included the high numbers of unemployed young people, poor economic and social conditions exacerbated by the rising price of food commodities and gasoline, and unresolved political and ethnic tensions. UNIOSIL worked with the United Kingdom Department for International Development (DFID) to strengthen the Sierra Leone police by providing it with training, mentoring, management development, and technical and policy advice. The mission had supported the police election planning secretariat to prepare for the March by-elections and was assisting the police in developing a security operational plan and budget for the local council elections in July.

UNIOSIL continued to support the efforts of the United Kingdom, through the International Military Advisory and Training Team and DFID, to reform and restructure the Sierra Leone Armed Forces. Following a comprehensive review undertaken by the Ministry of Defence, the Government approved a further reduction of the armed forces, from 10,500 to 8,500 troops, to be completed by 2010. Meanwhile, the armed forces continued to face financial and logistical challenges, including the inadequate supply of fuel to operate vehicles and generators. In addition, military personnel and their families were still living in overcrowded, substandard conditions at the main barracks in Freetown, with limited access to safe drinking water and proper sanitation. Efforts were under way to upgrade the three military barracks in Freetown with funds from the UN Peacebuilding Fund.

In preparation for the local council elections on 5 July, UNIOSIL provided technical assistance to the National Electoral Commission. The elections would cover the five city councils of Bo, Freetown, Kenema, Koidu-New Sembehun and Makeni, the Bonthe Township Municipal Council, and 13 district councils. In efforts to enhance the role of women in the political process, UNIOSIL encouraged political parties to promote gender equality and youth empowerment by increasing the number of women candidates in the elections. It also convened a series of meetings with a wide range of stakeholders to explore ways to increase women's representation in the elections, which resulted in the establishment of a national steering committee and a five-month workplan with benchmarks. UNIOSIL facilitated the establishment of a working group to coordinate technical and capacity-building support to Parliament, while the development of a capacity development programme for parliamentarians was also under way. President Koroma appointed a Director for Public Service Reform, and on 19 February launched the Sierra Leone Justice Sector Reform Strategy and Investment Plan 2008–2010, which focused on creating safe communities, providing access to justice, strengthening the rule of law and improving the delivery of justice. A Justice Sector Coordination Office was established to facilitate the day-to-day implementation of the strategy. UNDP set up temporary courts to assist in clearing long-outstanding cases and helped to refurbish and equip court facilities.

On efforts to fight corruption, the Anti-Corruption Commission developed a strategic workplan, established a Department of Investigation, Intelligence and Prosecution and relocated anti-corruption prosecutors from the Office of the Attorney General to the Commission. In February, the Cabinet approved a national anti-corruption strategy, which was supported by UNIOSIL and other international partners. On 17 April, the Commission arrested Francis Gabbidon for alleged offences under the Anti-Corruption Act of 2000 during his tenure as Ombudsman from 2000 to 2007.

On 10 January, the Constitutional Review Commission, established by the Government in 2006 [YUN 2006, p. 234] to revise the Constitution, submitted to President Koroma its report, which proposed 136 amendments, 15 of which were amendments to "entrenched" provisions that would require approval by national referendum. Several recommendations made by the Truth and Reconciliation Commission and provisions relating to the protection and promotion of human rights and fundamental freedoms were not included. In promoting respect for human rights, gains were made in building the capacity of the national Human Rights Commission to monitor, protect and promote human rights and to review the status of implementation of the recommendations of the Truth and Reconciliation Commission. Some progress was also made in building the capacity of State institutions to address the root causes of the conflict.

On the drawdown of UNIOSIL, the Secretary-General said that the 20 per cent reduction of the mission had been completed, bringing its staffing strength from 309 to 247 civilian staff. UNIOSIL would reduce its remaining civilian staff through attrition, including reassignment of personnel to other peacekeeping operations and expiration of staff contracts. It was estimated that 60 support personnel would be needed to complete the liquidation of UNIOSIL, which was expected to take place between October and December. He observed that UNIOSIL had made significant progress in supporting Government efforts to consolidate peace, including strengthening the capacity of the security sector, promoting respect for human rights and the rule of law, building the capacity of the National Electoral Commission to conduct elections and making arrangements for the handover of UN Radio. As the sustained commitment of the United Nations in Sierra Leone would continue to be required following the drawdown of UNIOSIL in September, he recommended that the Security Council approve the establishment of an integrated UN peacebuilding office to succeed UNIOSIL for an initial one-year period. The mandate, structure and strength of the office were outlined in the report (see below).

Security Council consideration (May). Briefing the Security Council on the situation in Sierra Leone on 7 May [meeting 5887], the Assistant Secretary-General for Rule of Law and Security Institutions in the Department of Peacekeeping Operations, Dmitry Titov, focused on the preparations for the local elections, the challenges facing the security sector, the socio-economic conditions in the country, human rights and rule-of-law issues, peacebuilding support activities and the proposed mandate, structure and strength of the post-UNIOSIL office.

The Chairman of the Peacebuilding Commission's country-specific meetings on Sierra Leone, Frank Majoor, briefed the Council on the advocacy and resource-mobilization efforts of the Commission and the findings of his visit to Sierra Leone (21–25 April). He said that the Commission's engagement with Sierra Leone focused on three objectives: generating support for the implementation of the commitments contained in the Peacebuilding Cooperation Framework, broadening the donor base, and triggering new activities or scaling up existing ones in peacebuilding priority areas.

Appointment. On 27 May, the Secretary-General appointed Michael von der Schulenburg (Germany) as the Acting Executive Representative in Sierra Leone and Head of UNIOSIL.

Establishment of UN Peacebuilding Office

In response to Security Council resolution 1793(2007), the Secretary-General, in his April report [S/2008/281], submitted proposals on the mandate, structure and strength of the United Nations Integrated Peacebuilding Office in Sierra Leone (UNIPSIL), which would succeed UNIOSIL in October following the expiration of its mandate. The UNIPSIL mandate included assisting Government efforts in the following areas: providing political support to national and local efforts for identifying and resolving tensions and threats of potential conflict; completing and consolidating good governance reforms; reviewing the 1991 Constitution and key legislation; strengthening the justice sector, Parliament and key governance institutions; supporting security sector reform; promoting the effective functioning of local government; implementing the Peacebuilding Cooperation Framework and the work of the Peacebuilding Commission and the Peacebuilding Fund; observing and analysing the human rights situation with a view to strengthening national human rights institutions and practices, including implementation of the recommendations of the Truth and Reconciliation Commission; sustaining efforts for the political and economic empowerment of youth and women; supporting gender mainstreaming into peace consolidation efforts; promoting collaboration and coordination among all partners; promoting a culture of peace and dialogue, including by providing support to the envisaged independent public broadcasting station; and continuing cooperation with other peace operations in the subregion to promote regional peace.

UNIPSIL would be led by the UN Department of Political Affairs (DPA), with UNDP support, in close consultation with the UN country team, the Peacebuilding Support Office and other stakeholders. The Office would be headed by the Secretary-General's Executive Representative, with a staff of 19 professional officers, assisted by 3 national administrative assistants, 24 operational support staff (16 international and 8 national) and 20 helicopter support staff (4 international and 16 national). The helicopter service was particularly important given that local means of transport from the international airport at Lungi to the mainland in Freetown did not comply with international or UN standards and that an air capacity for medical evacuation would continue to be a requirement. UNIPSIL would comprise a small front office and three substantive sections focusing on the key areas of the mandate: peace and governance; human rights and the rule of law; and youth and gender empowerment. Its structure would allow for the co-location of UN political and development personnel, who would utilize the joint resources of the integrated office and the UN country team to implement the UNIPSIL mandate. The Secretary-General indicated that the ability of UNIPSIL to effectively implement its mandate would be contingent on the availability of requisite logistical capacity and resources, as well as operational support from the Department of Field Support.

SECURITY COUNCIL ACTION

On 4 August [meeting 5948], the Security Council unanimously adopted **resolution 1829(2008)**. The draft [S/2008/512] was prepared in consultations among Council members.

The Security Council,

Recalling its previous resolutions and the statements by its President concerning the situation in Sierra Leone,

Commending the valuable contribution that the United Nations Integrated Office in Sierra Leone has made to the recovery of Sierra Leone from conflict and to the country's peace, security and development,

Welcoming the report of the Secretary-General of 29 April 2008 and his recommendations on the United Nations Integrated Peacebuilding Office in Sierra Leone,

Welcoming also the holding of peaceful and democratic local elections in July 2008 as another important milestone in consolidating a sustainable peace in Sierra Leone,

Emphasizing the importance of the continued support of the United Nations system and the international community for the long-term peace, security and development of Sierra Leone, particularly through the strengthening of the capacity of the Government of Sierra Leone,

Stressing the importance of a smooth transition between the United Nations Integrated Office in Sierra Leone and the new United Nations Integrated Peacebuilding Office in Sierra Leone, and of the effective and efficient operation of that Office,

Welcoming the progress in the implementation of the Sierra Leone Peacebuilding Cooperation Framework, and encouraging the Government of Sierra Leone to continue its close engagement with the Peacebuilding Commission by implementing the recommendations of the first biannual review of the Framework,

Welcoming also the progress made in reforming the security sector in Sierra Leone and, in particular, the developing professionalism of the Republic of Sierra Leone Armed Forces and the Sierra Leone Police, and underlining the importance of the planned further strengthening and rationalizing of the security architecture so that the Armed Forces and the Police are sustainable in the long term and able to carry out their tasks effectively,

Reiterating its appreciation for the work of the Special Court for Sierra Leone and its vital contribution to reconciliation, peacebuilding and the rule of law in Sierra Leone, reiterating its expectation that the Court will finish its work expeditiously, and recognizing that further arrangements will be needed to address residual matters after trials and appeals are completed,

Welcoming the role played by the Economic Community of West African States, and encouraging the member States of the Mano River Union and other organizations to continue their efforts aimed at building regional and subregional peace and security,

1. *Requests* the Secretary-General to establish the United Nations Integrated Peacebuilding Office in Sierra Leone, as recommended in his report, for a period of twelve months beginning on 1 October 2008, with the key tasks as specified in paragraphs 3, 4, 5 and 8 below;

2. *Welcomes* the recommendation of the Secretary-General in his report that the United Nations Integrated Peacebuilding Office in Sierra Leone should be headed by an Executive Representative of the Secretary-General who would also serve as the Resident Representative of the United Nations Development Programme and United Nations Resident Coordinator, and underlines the need for appropriate expertise and adequate material resources so that the Office can effectively and efficiently implement its mandate;

3. *Requests* that the United Nations Integrated Peacebuilding Office in Sierra Leone focus on and support the Government of Sierra Leone in the following areas:

(a) Providing political support to national and local efforts for identifying and resolving tensions and threats of potential conflict, whatever the source;

(b) Monitoring and promoting human rights, democratic institutions and the rule of law, including efforts to counter transnational organized crime and drug trafficking;

(c) Consolidating good governance reforms, with a special focus on anti-corruption instruments such as the Anti-Corruption Commission;

(d) Supporting decentralization, reviewing the 1991 Constitution and the enactment of relevant legislation;

(e) Closely coordinating with and supporting the work of the Peacebuilding Commission, as well as the implementation of the Sierra Leone Peacebuilding Cooperation Framework and projects supported through the Peacebuilding Fund;

4. *Underlines* the importance of establishing a fully integrated office with effective coordination of strategy and programmes among the United Nations agencies, funds and programmes in Sierra Leone, and emphasizes the need for the United Nations system to support and cooperate fully with the United Nations Integrated Peacebuilding Office in Sierra Leone, in accordance with the Executive Representative's function as Resident Representative and Resident Coordinator;

5. *Stresses* the need for close cooperation between the United Nations Integrated Peacebuilding Office in Sierra Leone, the Economic Community of West African States, the Mano River Union, international partners and other United Nations missions in the region;

6. *Emphasizes* that the Government of Sierra Leone bears the primary responsibility for peacebuilding, security and long-term development in the country, and encourages the Government to continue its close engagement with the Peacebuilding Commission in this regard, including through the regular monitoring of progress in the implementation of the Sierra Leone Peacebuilding Cooperation Framework, and further encourages international partners to continue to provide support to the Government and to cooperate with the Commission;

7. *Calls upon* the Government of Sierra Leone and all other stakeholders in the country to increase their efforts to promote good governance, including through the effective functioning of local government and continued measures to combat corruption and improve accountability; promote the development of the private sector to generate wealth and employment opportunities, in particular for young people; strengthen the judiciary; and advance human rights, including through the implementation of the recommendations of the Truth and Reconciliation Commission;

8. *Emphasizes* the important role of women in the prevention and resolution of conflicts and in peacebuilding, as recognized in resolutions 1325(2000) of 31 October 2000 and 1820(2008) of 19 June 2008, underlines that a gender perspective should be taken into account in implementing all aspects of the mandate of the United Nations Integrated Peacebuilding Office in Sierra Leone, and encourages the Office to work with the Government of Sierra Leone in this regard;

9. *Requests* that the Secretary-General keep the Security Council informed, every four months, on the implementation of the mandate of the United Nations Integrated Peacebuilding Office in Sierra Leone and the present resolution, with the first report due by 31 January 2009;

10. *Decides* to remain actively seized of the matter.

In his first report on UNIPSIL [S/2009/59], the Secretary-General said that the transition from UNIOSIL to UNIPSIL proceeded as planned, with extensive consultations among UN system entities, culminating in the adoption of a Joint Vision of the United Nations Family for Sierra Leone. The Joint Vision brought together the political mandate of UNIPSIL with the development and humanitarian mandates of UN agencies, funds and programmes, and defined the contribution of the UN system in the implementation of the President's Agenda for Change and the Sierra Leone poverty reduction strategy. In addition to the overall objective of assisting the Government in consolidating peace, the Joint Vision identified four priorities: the economic integration of the rural areas; the engagement of unemployed youth; equitable access to health care; and the enhancement of good governance.

Further peace process developments

The Secretary-General reported [S/2009/59] that the political situation remained stable. The interaction between the two major parties, SLPP and APC, was largely constructive. The Government made the fight against corruption a key element in its reform platform. On 15 October, it established a Commission of Inquiry to examine the use of donor funds by the previous SLPP administration. UNIPSIL encouraged the resumption of political dialogue through the revival of the All Political Parties Association and the rejuvenation of the Political Parties Registration Commission. Chieftaincy disputes remained a major challenge for the political and legal processes.

On 1 December, President Koroma issued his Agenda for Change, which presented the policies and priorities of the Government for a three-year period and set out the foundation for peacebuilding. Funding required to achieve the objectives outlined in the Agenda was estimated at $2.1 billion. To enhance democratic institutions, UNIPSIL, UNDP and other partners formed a working group that coordinated international assistance to Parliament. Eight regional retreats were organized for 124 parliamentarians and paramount chiefs between October and December. UNDP and the Inter-Parliamentary Union sponsored a meeting of African parliamentarians and support staff from neighbouring countries on the role of Parliament. Meanwhile, decentralization frameworks and institutions were in place and successful local council elections were held in July. UNDP and the UN Capital Development Fund also supported local capacity-building efforts.

Cocaine trafficking represented the greatest single threat to security. An immediate concern was the increasing use of Sierra Leone as a trans-shipment point for the trafficking of illegal narcotics from South America to Europe. Another security challenge was piracy. The Government planned to work with its neighbours to establish joint sea patrols.

In other developments, the Government and UNIPSIL agreed on a road map for the transfer of UN Radio to an independent public broadcaster. UNIPSIL provided technical support for draft legislation establishing the new broadcast service. It also continued to assist the Government in implementing the Truth and Reconciliation Commission recommendations. In December, the Child Rights Act was formally launched. The Secretary-General appealed to States and the international community to extend support to Sierra Leone, in particular to the implementation of the President's Agenda for Change.

Peacebuilding Commission

Reporting on its second session [A/63/92-S/2008/417], the Peacebuilding Commission stated that, on 17 January, the Sierra Leone configuration agreed on a workplan for resource mobilization, outreach and advocacy for the Peacebuilding Cooperation Framework adopted in 2007 [YUN 2007, p. 53]. The Chair of the configuration visited Washington, D.C., London, Brussels, Berlin and The Hague and later met with representatives of the private sector, foundations and international financial institutions about the Framework. On 7 May, the Chair briefed the Security Council on recent developments and made recommendations for continuing the UN integrated presence in the country.

Stakeholder consultation. A high-level consultation on Sierra Leone (New York, 19 May) [PBC/2/SLE/5] underscored the importance of providing international support through direct budget support, sector-wide programmes and multi-donor funding mechanisms to ensure national ownership. It made recommendations related to aid coordination policy and a national youth employment and empowerment strategy, along with initiatives to foster national reconciliation, inter-party dialogue and participation of youth and women in the electoral process in the lead-up to the 5 July elections (see p. 214).

Mission to Sierra Leone (June). The Commission sent a delegation to Sierra Leone headed by the Chair of the configuration (1–7 June) [PBC/2/SLE/7]. The mission addressed youth employment and empowerment, local elections, the 2008–2010 poverty reduction strategy paper (PRSP) and donor coordination, energy sector development, justice and security sector reform, capacity-building and subregional issues. It recommended that the next PRSP be conflict-sensitive, linked to the Framework, and have clear objectives. The Government was urged to hold consultations with stakeholders on the report of the Constitutional Review Commission; follow up on the decisions of the Presidential Summit of the Mano River Union (14–15 May); convene ministerial and sectoral meetings on issues of common concern, especially security; finalize decisions on aid coordination and develop an aid policy; increase domestic revenue-generation to reduce aid dependency; and strengthen national ownership and sustainability of reform initiatives. The United Nations and international partners were called on to strengthen support for implementing the Truth and Reconciliation Commission's recommendations and establishing the Commission's Follow-up Committee within the National Human Rights Commission. The Peacebuilding Commission should support the Ministry of Foreign Affairs in coordinating Government leadership in the peacebuilding process; provide greater support for Government advocacy and resource mobilization; and advocate with UN bodies to ensure support for the Commission.

Biannual reviews of Cooperation Framework. The Sierra Leone configuration held biannual reviews of the implementation of the Framework on 19 June and 15 December. It had before it June [PBC/2/SLE/9 & PBC/2/SLE/8] and December reports [PBC/3/SLE/3 & PBC/3/SLE/2] containing conclusions and recommendations concerning the Framework.

In identical letters of 20 June [A/62/887-S/2008/416] to the General Assembly, Security Council and Economic and Social Council, and a 15 December [A/63/802-S/2008/850] to the Assembly and Security Council, the Chairs of the Peacebuilding Commission and the Sierra Leone configuration drew attention to the recommendations addressed to the international community for follow-up. In a later report [A/64/341-S/2009/444], the Commission confirmed that the recommendations and conclusions on the implementation of the Framework were transmitted to all stakeholders.

(For further information on the Peacebuilding Commission, see p. 54).

UNIOSIL

The United Nations Integrated Office in Sierra Leone (UNIOSIL), established by Security Council resolution 1620(2005) [YUN 2005, p. 282], was mandated to assist the Government in strengthening the capacity of State institutions, rule of law, human rights and the security sector; developing economic empowerment initiatives for youth; improving transparency and good governance and building capacity to hold free and fair elections in 2007, as well as to liaise with the Sierra Leonean security sector; coordinate with UN missions and regional organizations in West Africa to address cross-border issues; and coordinate with the Special Court for Sierra Leone. The United Nations Integrated Peacebuilding Office in Sierra Leone succeeded UNIOSIL in October following the expiration of its mandate on 30 September 2008. In 2008, the Secretary-General submitted to the Security Council the UNIOSIL completion strategy [S/2008/63] and an April report on developments in Sierra Leone and the activities of UNIOSIL [S/2008/281]. In addition to political and security aspects, the report summarized UNIOSIL activities relating to humanitarian issues, human rights and the rule of law, public information/UN Radio, socio-economic matters, implementation of Security Council resolution 1325(2000) and gender mainstreaming, and support to the Special Court for Sierra Leone, as well as the Peacebuilding Commission.

Financing of missions

UNIPSIL

In an October report [A/63/346/Add.3] dealing with estimated requirements for special political missions grouped under thematic cluster III (United Nations offices, peacebuilding support offices, integrated offices and commissions), the Secretary-General proposed resource requirements for UNIPSIL in the amount of $15,204,000 for the period 1 January to 31 December 2009, which ACABQ recommended for approval [A/63/593]. The requirements of some $3,451,000 for UNIPSIL start-up operations for the period 1 October to 31 December 2008 were accommodated by utilizing the estimated unencumbered balance of the appropriation for UNIOSIL.

On 24 December, in section XI of **resolution 63/263**, the Assembly endorsed the recommendations of ACABQ and approved the budgets for 27 special political missions, including the UNIPSIL budget, under section 3, Political affairs, of the programme budget for the 2008–2009 biennium (see p. 1548).

UNAMSIL

In June, the General Assembly considered a report of the Secretary-General providing details on the final disposition of the assets of the United Nations Mission in Sierra Leone (UNAMSIL) [A/62/756], which had a total inventory value of $61,909,000 and were disposed of as at 31 December 2007. ACABQ [A/62/781/Add.4] noted that the final closure of UNAMSIL accounts would take place in 2009, at which time the final performance report would be submitted for consideration by the Assembly. It recommended that the Assembly take note of the Secretary-General's report on the final disposition of UNAMSIL assets.

GENERAL ASSEMBLY ACTION

On 20 June [meeting 109], the General Assembly, on the recommendation of the Fifth Committee [A/62/879], adopted **resolution 62/266** without vote [agenda item 154].

Financing of the United Nations Mission in Sierra Leone

The General Assembly,

Having considered the report of the Secretary-General on the financing of the United Nations Mission in Sierra Leone and the related report of the Advisory Committee on Administrative and Budgetary Questions,

Bearing in mind Security Council resolution 1270(1999) of 22 October 1999, by which the Council established the United Nations Mission in Sierra Leone, and the subsequent resolutions by which the Council revised and extended the mandate of the Mission, the latest of which was resolution 1610(2005) of 30 June 2005, by which the Council extended the mandate of the Mission for a final period of six months until 31 December 2005,

Recalling its resolution 53/29 of 20 November 1998 on the financing of the United Nations Observer Mission in Sierra Leone and subsequent resolutions on the financing of the United Nations Mission in Sierra Leone, the latest of which was resolution 61/288 of 29 June 2007,

Reaffirming the general principles underlying the financing of United Nations peacekeeping operations, as stated in General Assembly resolutions 1874(S-IV) of 27 June 1963, 3101(XXVIII) of 11 December 1973 and 55/235 of 23 December 2000,

Noting with appreciation that voluntary contributions have been made to the Mission,

1. *Takes note* of the status of contributions to the United Nations Observer Mission in Sierra Leone and the United Nations Mission in Sierra Leone as at 31 March 2008, including the credits in the amount of 89.5 million United States dollars;

2. *Endorses* the conclusions and recommendations contained in the report of the Advisory Committee on Administrative and Budgetary Questions, and requests the Secretary-General to ensure their full implementation;

Disposition of assets of the United Nations Mission in Sierra Leone

3. *Takes note* of the report of the Secretary-General on the financing of the Mission;

4. *Encourages* Member States that are owed credits for the closed peacekeeping mission accounts to apply those credits to any accounts where the Member State concerned has outstanding assessed contributions;

5. *Decides* to include in the provisional agenda of its sixty-third session the item entitled "Financing of the United Nations Mission in Sierra Leone".

Special Court for Sierra Leone

The Special Court for Sierra Leone, jointly established by the Government of Sierra Leone and the United Nations in 2002 [YUN 2002, p. 164], pursuant to Security Council resolution 1315(2000) [YUN 2000, p. 205], continued in 2008 to try those bearing the greatest responsibility for violations of international humanitarian and Sierra Leonean laws committed in the territory of Sierra Leone since November 1996. The trials of two cases were ongoing during the year: the Revolutionary United Front (RUF) trial, in the first trial chamber, and the trial of former Liberian President Charles Taylor in the second trial chamber. In addition, the Appeals Chambers delivered judgements pertaining to the Armed Forces Revolutionary Council (AFRC) and the Civil Defence Forces (CDF) trials, which were completed in 2007.

On 21 and 22 February 2008, the Special Court convened an international meeting of experts at its Freetown headquarters to discuss residual issues that required consideration with regard to the Special Court's dissolution in 2010. The conference was attended by representatives of the Special Court's Management Committee, the Government of Sierra Leone, UN Member States, international tribunals, national and international non-governmental organizations, and the international donor community. A conference report highlighted issues requiring action. In December, an updated Completion Strategy was presented to the Management Committee. As the Special Court neared the completion of its mandate, it continued downsizing its personnel and would remain reliant on the contribution of gratis personnel to fill key positions.

RUF trial. In the Revolutionary United Front (RUF) trial, which had adjourned in June 2007 to allow Trial Chamber I to focus on the CDF Trial Judgement [YUN 2007, p. 219], the Issa Sesay defence recommenced and continued through two additional trial sessions, from 4 October to 27 November 2007 and from 10 January to 13 March 2008. Although it closed its case on 13 March, the Sesay defence was permitted to call one additional witness as the Chamber granted the defence application to issue a subpoena for Ahmad Tejan Kabbah, former President of Sierra Leone. Mr. Kabbah testified publicly on 16 May. On 10 April, Morris Kallon commenced his defence case and testified personally from 11 to 21 April. The defence case for Augustine Gbao began on 2 June and concluded on 24 June after calling eight witnesses. Final trial briefs were submitted by Mr. Gbao, Mr. Kallon and the Prosecution on 29 July, and by Mr. Sesay on 31 July. The Trial Chamber heard closing arguments on 5 August. During the 2007–2008 reporting period, Trial Chamber I issued 63 decisions and orders in the RUF trial, bringing the number of decisions and orders issued by the Chamber since the commencement of the trial to 217.

Trial of Charles Taylor. The hearing of evidence in the trial of former Liberian President Charles Taylor commenced on 7 January, after the Chamber in August 2007 had granted his counsel additional time to prepare the case [ibid.]. During the first trial session from January to March, the Prosecution presented the testimony of 21 witnesses, including 4 experts, 7 victims and 10 insider witnesses. In total, the Prosecution called some 91 witnesses.

AFRC appeal. In the Armed Forces Revolutionary Council (AFRC) trial, Alex Tamba Brima, Brima Bazzy Kamara and Santigie Borbor Kanu appealed the Court's 2007 judgement [ibid., p. 218], which found them guilty of seven counts of war crimes and four counts of crimes against humanity, imposing sentences of 50 years of imprisonment for Mssrs. Brima and Kanu and 45 years for Mr. Kamara. On 22 February 2008, the Appeals Chamber issued its judgement, dismissing the appeals of the convicted persons, granting the Prosecution's appeal that acts of forced marriage constituted "other inhumane acts"—a crime against humanity—and upholding the sentences.

CDF appeal. In the Civil Defence Forces (CDF) trial, the judgement issued in August 2007 [ibid., p. 219] found Mssrs. Moinina Fofana and Allieu Kondewa guilty of four counts of murder, cruel treatment, pillage and collective punishment, and Mr. Kondewa also guilty of enlisting children under the age of 15 into an armed group. In October, Mssrs. Fofana and Kondewa were sentenced to six years and eight years of imprisonment, respectively. On 28 May 2008, the Appeals Chamber delivered its judgment after hearing oral arguments on 12 and 13 March. The Appeals Chamber reversed the acquittal of Mssrs. Fofana and Kondewa on murder and other inhumane acts as crimes against humanity, found them guilty of those crimes, revised the concurrent sentences imposed by the Trial Chamber and entered new concurrent sentences for a total term of imprisonment of 15 years for Mr. Fofana and 20 years for Mr. Kondewa.

Sanctions

The Security Council Committee established pursuant to resolution 1132(1997) [YUN 1997, p. 135] concerning Sierra Leone submitted a report [S/2009/94] covering its 2008 activities in monitoring and implementing the 1998 embargo on the sale or supply of arms to Sierra Leone and the travel ban on leading members of the former military junta in Sierra Leone and of the Revolutionary United Front (RUF), imposed by resolution 1171(1998) [YUN 1998, p. 169].

During 2008, the Committee held one session of informal consultations. On 30 May it considered a letter dated 1 May from Sierra Leone with recommendations for the revision of the Committee's travel-ban list in light of the overall security, judicial, political and other developments in the country. It also urged the Committee, in its review of the notification provision for arms exports imposed by resolution 1171(1998), to consider the ECOWAS Convention on Small Arms and Light Weapons, Their Ammunition and Other Related Materials, which Sierra Leone had ratified; the adoption by the General Assembly of the International Instrument to Enable States to Identify and Trace, in a Timely and Reliable Manner, Illicit Small Arms and Light Weapons [YUN 2005, p. 621]; and the UN Register of Conventional Arms, to which Sierra Leone had been contributing. Subsequently, on 9 June, the Committee decided to delist 24 individuals from the travel ban [SC/9350]. In a reply of 25 June, the Chairman informed Sierra Leone of the Committee's decision to remove the names. With regard to the review of the notification requirements for the delivery of arms or related materiel to Sierra Leone, Committee members were of the view that decisions on the arms embargo fell within the purview of the Security Council, and therefore had decided to convey the 1 May 2008 letter to the Council. During the reporting period, no violations or alleged violations of the sanctions regime were brought to the attention of the Committee.

In other activity, the Chairman, on 7 January, informed the Registrar of the Special Court for Sierra Leone that, pursuant to Security Council resolution 1793(2007) [YUN 2007, p. 214], the travel of any witnesses required to appear at trial before the Special Court was exempt from the travel-ban restrictions. In that connection, with regard to the Registrar's 31 December 2007 request for a waiver of the travel restrictions for a witness in the trial of Charles Taylor, advance approval by the Committee was not required. The Chairman had also sought the agreement of the Special Court on notification procedures for the travel of listed individuals pursuant to paragraph 8 of resolution 1793(2007). In a reply of 15 January 2008, the Registrar confirmed to the Committee the notification procedures to be followed in connection with the travel of any individuals included on the Committee's travel-ban list whose presence was required before the Special Court.

The Committee observed that six individuals remained on the travel-ban list: the former leader of the Armed Forces Revolutionary Council (AFRC) junta and five others who had been indicted by the Special Court. The delisting of 24 individuals was made possible in part by the improved security situation in Sierra Leone and by the prevailing stability in the subregion due to the commitment of leaders of the Mano River Union countries to a peaceful resolution of issues. In light of those developments and Sierra Leone's suggestion on the review of the notification provision for arms exports, the Committee Chairman encouraged members of the Committee and the Security Council to continue consultations to determine the appropriate time to streamline the legal basis for the sanctions.

Guinea-Bissau

In 2008, the United Nations Peacebuilding Support Office in Guinea-Bissau continued to assist the Government in its efforts to promote national reconciliation, organize legislative elections and combat drug and human trafficking and organized crime. The political climate remained fragile, despite the political and government stability pact signed by the three main political parties in 2007. Political and institutional tensions between President João Bernardo Vieira and the National Assembly concerning the mandate of the Assembly culminated in August with the appointment of a new Prime Minister and Government. An amnesty bill passed in April exempted those involved in political-military crimes prior to October 2004 from legal prosecution, and established the National Reconciliation Commission. Progress was achieved with the establishment of the National Commission for Human Rights; a financial agreement between the European Community and the United Nations Office on Drugs and Crime, which supported the creation of a special anti-narcotics unit within the judiciary police; and the calm and orderly conduct of legislative elections in November. Nonetheless, relations between two of the three signatories to the stability pact continued to deteriorate, and in July, the African Party for the Independence of Guinea and Cape Verde withdrew from the pact. Instability in the military manifested itself in August, when the authorities uncovered a planned coup d'état, and in November, when unknown assailants attacked the residence of President Vieira, who escaped unharmed. The illicit drug trade remained a concern amid reports that Guinea-Bissau was becoming a strategic link in the transport of illegal narcotics from South America to Europe. The Economic Commission of West African States convened a ministerial conference on drug trafficking to help design a regional action plan and prepare a draft political declaration. In light of the work of the Peacebuilding Commission in Guinea-Bissau, the Economic and Social Council terminated the mandate of the Ad Hoc Advisory Group on Guinea-Bissau.

Political and security developments and UNOGBIS activities

Report of Secretary-General (March). In his report [S/2008/181] on developments in the country and activities of the United Nations Peacebuilding Support Office in Guinea-Bissau (UNOGBIS), the Secretary-General noted that the political climate continued to be fragile, despite the political and government stability pact signed by the three main political parties in March 2007 [YUN 2007, p. 222] and the National Assembly's approval of the Government programme and the 2007 and 2008 budgets in December 2007 [ibid., p. 230]. On 29 February, the President of the African Party for the Independence of Guinea and Cape Verde (PAIGC), Carlos Gomes Jr., announced the withdrawal of the Party's political confidence in the Prime Minister, Martinho N'Dafa Cabi, over issues of internal discipline. Following the Assembly's unanimous approval of draft legislation granting amnesty to those involved in political-military motivated crimes against the security of the State up to 6 October 2004 [ibid.], proponents of the law, including President João Bernardo Vieira and the Chief of the General Staff, General Batista Tagme Na Waie, argued that it would facilitate reconciliation and pave the way for security sector reform. Civil society organizations, while recognizing the positive impact it might have on national reconciliation, stated that there should have been broader involvement of civil society in the debate and that the issues of truth and restorative justice were not sufficiently addressed. The draft law was submitted for review to the parliamentary permanent special commission on human rights, legal and constitutional affairs. Controversy also surrounded the re-election on 26 January of the President of the Supreme Court, Maria do Céu Monteiro, by an electoral college consisting of nine Supreme Court judges, due to the interpretation of two pieces of legislation, one of which provided for a restricted electoral college, while the other, a more recent law of 2002, provided for a wider electoral college consisting of 100 judges from the various judicial institutions. Ms. Monteiro's main rival, Supreme Court Judge Emílio Kafft Kosta, boycotted the election, but his protest to the election commission was rejected. Critics stated that the election was a blow to the rule of law and complained of political interference in the process.

On UN electoral assistance, UNDP finalized a project document to provide support for the 2008–2010 electoral cycle, including the 2008 legislative elections and presidential elections scheduled for 2010. UNDP proposed a budget of $4.7 million for the legislative elections, of which some $1.2 million had been secured. However, the budget did not include the payment of arrears ($1.7 million) owed to electoral commissions from past elections, the cost of voter registration in the diaspora and salaries of Government officials in charge of the electoral process, amounting to $2 million. Although the authorities had yet to set a date for the legislative elections, in comments broadcasted at the end of January, General Na Waie warned politicians to respect the results of the elections or face arrest. The National Civil Society Movement for Peace, Democracy and Development urged the military not to interfere in political and legal matters and called on the international community to closely follow political and social developments in the country. Under the capacity-building programme for parliamentarians, the Netherlands Development Organization (SNV) and UNOGBIS organized training in conflict transformation skills for 15 parliamentarians, while 14 parliamentarians attended a leadership training workshop facilitated by SNV. In February, UNOGBIS and SNV facilitated a workshop on conflict transformation for 11 senior political and military advisers nominated by the Offices of the President and the Prime Minister, the leaders of the parliamentary parties—PAIGC, the Social Renewal Party (PRS) and the United Social Democratic Party (PUSD)—and General Na Waie.

On military and security aspects, the security sector reform programme was launched on 23 January. General Na Waie expressed support for the restructuring and modernization of the armed forces, yet warned that the reforms should not result in the impoverishment of the beneficiaries, as such a situation could make them vulnerable to manipulation. A €7.7 million financial convention between the European Commission and the Government for the security sector reform/disarmament, demobilization and reintegration project was signed on 22 January. The Lisbon International Conference on Drug Trafficking in December 2007 [YUN 2007, p. 228] raised $6.7 million of the $19 million required for the anti-narcotics programme developed by the Government with the assistance of the United Nations Office on Drugs and Crime (UNODC), which would allow for the implementation of emergency action plans for 2008. On 22 January, at a debriefing and follow-up meeting organized by UNOGBIS and attended by Government representatives, international partners and UNODC representatives, it was agreed that the Minister of Justice and UNODC should urgently find an efficient strategic framework for implementing the narcotics programme. The judicial police, UNODC and UNOGBIS experts visited a number of facilities in Bissau and in the surrounding areas to identify suitable venues for the installation of a temporary detention centre. In addition to the two senior advisers assigned to Bissau in November 2007, UNODC would appoint a project manager by March 2008 to coordinate its expanding activities in Guinea-Bissau. Meanwhile, the International Federation for Human Rights dispatched a team to Guinea-Bissau (7–16 January) to look into reports of a deteriorating environment for human rights and press freedom, particularly with regard to reporting on drug issues, following allegations that journalists had been threatened for reporting on suspected drug trafficking activities in the country. In other security developments, a mission from the UN Department of Economic and Social Affairs visited Guinea-Bissau (21–25 January) to assess the progress made by the National Commission against the Proliferation of Small Arms and Light Weapons towards developing a plan of action, which included a pilot project. In January, the authorities arrested two Mauritanians in Bissau who were wanted by Mauritania for the alleged murder of four French citizens in Mauritania. The Mauritanians, who claimed to be members of Al-Qaida, were extradited to Mauritania. On 25 February, Guinea-Bissau and Spain signed an agreement to jointly conduct air and sea patrols along Guinea-Bissau's maritime borders with a view to combating human trafficking.

The Secretary-General observed that the Government had made tangible progress in engaging the international community in its efforts to implement reforms necessary for sustainable political and economic stabilization. As Guinea-Bissau had been placed on the Peacebuilding Commission's agenda and declared eligible for funding from the Peacebuilding Fund, he urged the Government and its partners to move the process forward, particularly in setting up the national steering committee and implementing quick-impact projects. On the legislative elections, he encouraged the authorities to set a date for the polls as a first step towards creating a climate of confidence in the credibility of the process and urged the international community to provide resources for the elections, including resources to cover the arrears from past elections. He further appealed to the international community to provide enhanced support and training for Guinea-Bissau's law enforcement and criminal justice system within the wider framework of security sector reform and the fight against organized crime, drug trafficking and terrorism.

Security Council consideration (March). Briefing the Security Council on 26 March [meeting 5860], the Secretary-General's Special Representative, Shola Omoregie (Nigeria), said that the previous evening, President Vieira had announced that the legislative elections would be held on 16 November, but preparations for the elections were moving forward slowly.

The Chair of the Guinea-Bissau Configuration of the Peacebuilding Commission, Maria Luiza Ribeiro Viotti, briefed the Council on progress made by the Commission and on the way forward. In order to develop the strategic framework, the Commission would conduct a field mission to the country in April.

Report of Secretary-General (June). In his report [S/2008/395] on Guinea-Bissau and UNOGBIS activities, the Secretary-General said that the political environment was marked by tensions between President Vieira and the National Assembly over the mandate of the Assembly, which was expected to end on 21 April. The Constitution provided for a four-year mandate for the Assembly beginning on the date of the announcement of the results of legislative elections, while the electoral law set the dates for the elections between 23 October and 25 November of the year when the legislature's mandate ended. If elections were held on 16 November, as was promulgated by a 25 March decree by President Vieira, and the mandate of the 2004–2008 legislature ended on 21 April in accordance with the Constitution, there would be an institutional vacuum of more than six months between the end of the Assembly's mandate and the elections. At the request of PRS, the National Assembly convened a debate on 27 March and adopted a resolution to extend the Assembly's mandate until the results of the legislative elections were announced. Supporters invoked a National Assembly internal regulation stipulating that the mandate of parliamentarians commenced with the first session after the elections and ended after the announcement of the results of the following elections; those opposed considered the resolution's adoption unconstitutional and sought the legal opinion of the Supreme Court of Justice. President Vieira and other political actors questioned the resolution's legality as it passed without the mandatory two-thirds majority and would come into effect without the President's assent, thereby usurping his constitutional powers of promulgation. The President held separate consultations with members of political parties, followed on 15 April by a meeting of the Council of State aiming to seek a consensual solution. On 16 April, an extraordinary session of the National Assembly adopted an exceptional transitional constitutional bill extending the mandate of the Assembly until the announcement of the results of the elections, which President Vieira promulgated on 18 April. However, opposition parties and civil society expressed concerns that the President had signed the bill under pressure from the military, and decried continued interference in politics by the armed forces. Following a 28 April request by parliamentarians for an advisory opinion on the exceptional transitional constitutional bill, the Supreme Court confirmed on 17 May that legal consultations were taking place with, among others, the Prosecutor General and the Speaker of the National Assembly. On 18 April, President Vieira signed the amnesty bill exempting those involved in political-military crimes prior to October 2004 from legal prosecution, restoring the political and civil rights of those who lost them as a consequence of past crises, and formalizing the creation of a National Reconciliation Commission, which among its other functions would provide monetary compensation to those who had incurred injuries or material losses due to past political-military conflicts.

Following the announcement of the date of the elections and the presentation of the electoral budget, estimated at $8.6 million, the mobilization of financial resources became a major challenge. In April, the European Union (EU) announced a contribution of €600,000 towards the elections, while ECOWAS agreed in June to contribute $500,000. However, after UNDP presented a revised electoral budget of $15.6 million, it was decided that the option to use biometric voter registration was too expensive and no longer feasible if the 16 November election date was to be maintained. In June it was announced that the Government would use manual voter registration in the 2008 elections, and that preparations for biometric voter registration for the 2010 presidential elections could start as early as January 2009. Meanwhile, UNOGBIS produced 13 radio programmes focused on the elections, reconciliation, gender issues and the fight against drug trafficking. In June, a series of programmes were broadcast on Security Council resolution 1325(2000) [YUN 2000, p. 1113] and the participation of women in the electoral process.

The security situation was affected by the political instability and the presence of armed groups involved in robbing entire villages, although paradoxically the crime rate remained low. In a 13 April incident, however, the headquarters of the judicial police in Bissau was attacked and vandalized by approximately 20 agents of the public order police, which led to 21 prison inmates being set free. One judicial police officer, in custody for the killing of a public order police officer, was led away and killed, and his body was put on public display. Prime Minister Cabi and the Ministers of Justice and of the Interior condemned the incident and announced the creation of a commission of inquiry to investigate and hold those responsible accountable. The Secretary-General's Special Representative met with the authorities to ensure that the incident did not trigger further crises and to promote a quick resolution of the situation, in part to prevent compromising the anti-narcotics operations of the judicial police. On 5 May, the International Contact Group on Guinea-Bissau met in Praia, condemned the clashes between the security forces and called on the Government to put in place strong law enforcement mechanisms to fight impunity. The Group also agreed to establish a local contact group comprising its representatives in Bissau, under the co-presidency of Portugal and ECOWAS. In other security developments, the UNODC Special Adviser on anti-narcotics and organized crime assumed his duties in Bissau in May; the first meeting of the national committee for the implementation of the anti-narcotics operational plan was held in the Ministry of Justice on 23 May; and the Deputy Prosecutor General interviewed the Prime Minister on 14 May about his public claim that he was aware of the involvement of several people in drug trafficking activities.

The Government released the results of the UNDP-financed census of the armed forces, which resulted in the issuance of identity cards to all 4,458 active personnel. The security sector reform programme envisaged a reduction of the size of the armed forces to 3,440 personnel. Preparations were under way with EU assistance to conduct a census in June of veterans of the liberation war. In April, an EU civilian and military team of security and defence experts arrived in Guinea-Bissau to prepare the logistical and technical conditions for the deployment of 15 EU civilian and military personnel in the country, which would provide technical assistance in security sector reform to the security and defence services. A delegation from the ECOWAS Committee of Chiefs of Defence Staff undertook a fact-finding mission (14–16 April) to Guinea-Bissau to ascertain the state of the military barracks and the living condition of military personnel, and to meet with national authorities to discuss the political and socio-economic situation and the status of the security sector reform effort. The delegation called on ECOWAS and the United Nations to scale up their mobilization of donor support for the implementation of programmes to benefit civilian and military segments of the population. In that connection, a resource-mapping exercise on donor support for the security sector was organized (New York, 22–23 May). Discussions highlighted the need to further support the Government financially, materially and technically and to fill gaps in the areas of law enforcement and criminal justice.

The Secretary-General said that the disclosure by the authorities of knowledge of individuals involved in drug trafficking and organized crime underscored the need for the international community to take strong action in support of the Government to address those issues. He urged the authorities to take advantage of international instruments to tackle the phenomenon, which had regional and international implications. He renewed his appeal to the international community to provide budgetary assistance to Guinea-Bissau, particularly for the legislative elections, and recommended the strengthening of the resources and capacity of UNOGBIS and the UN country team to enable them to support the peacebuilding process fully and effectively.

Security Council consideration (June). In his briefing to the Council of 25 June [meeting 5925], the Special Representative said that the country had seen a slight improvement in its economic performance indicators and that it could become eligible for IMF debt relief instruments if the indicators continued to improve, which would reduce the volume of the country's debt-service payments.

The UNODC Executive Director said that drug trafficking was not only a serious issue in Guinea-Bissau, but also an acute threat that transnational organized crime posed to security in West Africa. He provided an update on UNODC assistance to Guinea-Bissau and Government efforts to strengthen the legal basis for fighting drugs and crime and to establish management structures for the implementation of the anti-narcotic and organized crime emergency plan.

Report of Secretary-General (September). In his report [S/2008/628] on developments in Guinea-Bissau and UNOGBIS activities, the Secretary-General said that the political situation was marked by a deepening political malaise, as well as military tension and instability. Relations between PAIGC and PRS—two of the three signatories to the political and government stability pact—continued to deteriorate, with both seeking to control key ministerial posts. Relations between the leaders of PAIGC, Carlos Gomes Jr., and Prime Minister Cabi also deteriorated as both contested the leadership of the party during its congress, won by Mr. Gomes. Tensions mounted when Prime Minister Cabi in July signed a decree, without reference to the Finance Minister or PAIGC, appointing PRS candidates to the posts of Directors-General of the Treasury, Revenue and Taxes and Customs, which prompted allegations among his critics in his party that he was favouring PRS. PAIGC withdrew from the stability pact on 28 July, while PRS and PUSD, the other two signatories, decided to remain in the pact. On 1 August, the Supreme Court ruled that the exceptional transitional constitutional law extending the National Assembly's mandate beyond 21 April was unconstitutional. Consequently, President Vieira dissolved Parliament on 5 August, dismissed the Government and appointed a new Prime Minister, Carlos Correia, to set up a caretaker Government. The Government was drawn largely from PAIGC, yet included two PUSD ministers, five PRS members and one member of the United People's Alliance. PRS distanced itself from the new Government, arguing that it had not been consulted about the appointment of its members, whom it considered dissidents.

On the electoral process, President Vieira and Prime Minister Correia gave assurances that legislative elections would be held on 16 November as scheduled. The manual voter registration exercise was carried out between 3 and 29 July. Despite the difficulties posed by the rainy season and logistical problems, the results were excellent. Some 578,974 of an estimated electorate of 611,875 were registered, corresponding to 94.6 per cent of the estimated total. The provisional lists would be published at various polling sectors, and voters would be allowed two weeks to file amendments and complaints; the definitive list was expected to be ready by 17 October. A European electoral observer mission that visited Guinea-Bissau in June to assess the political, logistical and security conditions in advance of the November polls noted that the conditions were in place to deploy an estimated 50 EU electoral observers. The AU sent an assessment mission from 18 to 21 August, while ECOWAS would be sending a team of observers. UNOGBIS would be coordinating those international observers who would not operate under the EU umbrella.

Instability in the military emerged in August when the authorities reported that they had uncovered an attempted coup d'état, allegedly organized by the Navy Chief of Staff, Rear Admiral José Américo Bubo Na Tchuto, that was to be carried out on 1 August. Although the Rear Admiral was suspended and kept under house arrest, he escaped and was arrested on 12 August in the Gambia. The Gambian authorities requested UN assistance to return him to Guinea-Bissau. The leader of PRS, former President Kumba Yalá, returned to Guinea-Bissau on 7 July after a one-year absence and announced that he had converted to Islam, assuming the name Mohamed Yalá Embaló, yet left the country on 8 August in the wake of the discovery of the coup attempt. Meanwhile, progress was made in security sector reform on 20 August, when 30 senior military officers were transferred from active service to reserve status at a ceremony marking the start of the security sector reform programme. The 30 officers would attend briefings in Nigeria before taking part in a one-year reinsertion programme in Brazil financed by ECOWAS. UNOGBIS, UNDP and other partners organized a workshop for public law-and-order institutions aimed at strengthening collaboration and working relationships among them.

The World Bank announced a $5 million grant from the Global Food Crisis Response Programme trust funds to mitigate the losses to the budget resulting from tax exemptions on rice and fuel imports and as a contribution to the Government's emergency plan for the 2008–2009 agricultural campaign. Another concern was the health sector, as a cholera epidemic that had been affecting the country since May had resulted in 6,126 reported cases, with 119 deaths as at 14 September. WHO and UNICEF were working with the Ministry of Health to combat the epidemic.

The Secretary-General reiterated his call to the Security Council to take strong action and to consider establishing a panel of experts to investigate the identity and activities of those involved in drug trafficking and organized crime in Guinea-Bissau, with the possibility of punitive, targeted sanctions that would reverse the growth in drug trafficking. On the reports of a coup plot by elements in the military, he called on all political actors not to use the military to advance their individual agendas and on the military to continue to honour its professional and republican tradition to protect and defend the State.

Security Council consideration (October). In his briefing of 7 October [meeting 5988] to the Council, the Under-Secretary-General for Political Affairs, B. Lynn Pascoe, said that preparations for the polls were on track as 23 parties and two coalitions had submitted applications to the Supreme Court by the 18 September deadline, which meant that 27 of the 34 registered parties would be participating in the elections.

SECURITY COUNCIL ACTION

On 15 October [meeting 5995], following consultations among Security Council members, the President made statement **S/PRST/2008/37** on behalf of the Council:

> The Security Council recalls its previous statements on Guinea-Bissau and takes note of the latest report of the Secretary-General on developments in Guinea-Bissau and on the activities of the United Nations Peacebuilding Support Office in Guinea-Bissau. The Council reaffirms its support for the continuing efforts to consolidate peace in that country.
>
> The Council welcomes the commitment of the Government of Guinea-Bissau to hold legislative elections on 16 November 2008, as well as the technical and financial support towards the elections provided by the international community, including by Angola, Brazil, Portugal, the Economic Community of West African States, the European Union, the Peacebuilding Fund and the United Nations Development Programme. It calls upon donors to continue to provide financial resources to support the electoral process.
>
> The Council calls upon the Government of Guinea-Bissau and all actors, including political parties, the security forces and civil society, to ensure an environment conducive to transparent, free and fair elections and to respect the results of the polls.
>
> The Council notes with satisfaction the adoption of the Strategic Framework for Peacebuilding in Guinea-Bissau by the Guinea-Bissau configuration of the Peacebuilding Commission on 1 October 2008, and notes the importance of the rapid and effective implementation of quick-impact projects financed by the Peacebuilding Fund. The Council looks forward to the establishment of the monitoring and tracking mechanism of the Strategic Framework.
>
> The Council reiterates the importance of security sector reform in Guinea-Bissau, encourages the Government of Guinea-Bissau to sustain its efforts in implementing the national security sector reform programme, and underscores the need for the international community to provide further coordinated assistance for its implementation.
>
> The Council remains seriously concerned by the continued growth in drug trafficking as well as organized crime, which threatens peace and security in Guinea-Bissau and in the subregion. The Council underlines the responsibility that the Government of Guinea-Bissau has for tackling this issue and calls upon the international community to cooperate actively with Guinea-Bissau in this regard, particularly in providing continued support for building the capacity of national law enforcement and judicial authorities. The Council requests that the Secretary-General provide in his next report further details of the measures required to deal with these challenges.
>
> The Council welcomes the initiative of the Economic Community of West African States to convene a regional conference on combating drug trafficking in Praia on 28 and 29 October 2008, and looks forward to the resulting regional plan of action.
>
> The Council expresses its concern about the consequences of rising food and fuel prices and welcomes the support of the World Bank to address this crisis. The Council encourages the Government of Guinea-Bissau to continue its dialogue and cooperation with the international financial institutions. The Council is also concerned about the cholera epidemic and calls upon the Government and its partners to continue and strengthen the efforts to secure its eradication.
>
> The Council recognizes and commends the important role played by the Representative of the Secretary-General in Guinea-Bissau and the staff of the United Nations Peacebuilding Support Office in Guinea-Bissau, as well as by the United Nations country team, towards helping to consolidate peace, democracy, the rule of law and development, and expresses its appreciation for their activities. The Council looks forward to receiving recommendations from the Secretary-General on how the United Nations presence in Guinea-Bissau should be reconfigured to support peacebuilding more effectively.

Elections. The Secretary-General reported [S/2008/751] that preparations for the elections were generally smooth. On 4 October, the Supreme Court announced its approval of the candidates of 21 political parties and 2 political coalitions. The official political campaign commenced on 25 October and ended on 14 November. During the first few days, the most notable campaign activity was that of the Republican Party for Independence and Development (PRID), a new party launched in September by former Prime Minister Aristides Gomes, which was supported mainly by former members of the breakaway wing of PAIGC. PAIGC launched its political campaign on a platform of commitment to moving Guinea-Bissau forward through reform programmes, including security sector reform, with an emphasis on downsizing, restructuring and modernizing the armed forces. The leader of PRS, former President Mohamed Yalá Embaló, returned to Guinea-Bissau from Morocco amid popular support at rallies in the east of the country, where he made his first campaign stop. Of the 21 registered parties and two coalitions, only nine parties actively participated in the campaign, while the others, mainly due to lack of funding, appeared to restrict their campaigns to the officially sanctioned media of radio and television. UNOGBIS, in partnership with the Faculty of Law, trained 36 representatives of 20 political parties on electoral law and supported the drafting of a Women's Political Platform Declaration signed by women of the various political parties. The platform developed a policy statement identifying the major concerns and constraints affecting women. UNOGBIS also organized a three-day seminar for local journalists to provide them with technical information and skills on the coverage of the electoral process.

On 16 November, the voting took place in a calm and orderly manner in almost all 2,705 polling stations. There was a high voter turnout, around 72 per cent according to the observers, who applauded the fairly equal participation of male and female voters. The voting and counting processes were also considered transparent and followed the established guidelines in 92 per cent of the observed procedures. On 26 November, the Electoral Commission announced the provisional results of the elections. PAIGC gained the most overall support, securing 227,036 votes and 67 of the 100 seats in the National Assembly, while PRS won 115,409 votes and obtained 28 seats; and PRID won 34,305 votes and 3 seats. The New Democracy Party and the Democratic Alliance won 10,721 and 6,321 votes respectively, and obtained one seat each. The Electoral Commission noted that only 10 women were elected as compared to the 12 elected in 2004.

On 20 November, the Security Council welcomed the holding of the elections, as scheduled, in an orderly and peaceful manner, and called on political parties and leaders to respect the results and to resolve any concerns through peaceful means [SC/9506].

Attack against residence of the President

During the early hours of 23 November, unknown assailants attacked the residence of President Vieira with rocket-propelled grenades and gunfire [S/2008/751]. The residence sustained considerable damage, particularly the President's living quarters, indicating that the violence was aimed at assassinating him. While the President and his family escaped unhurt, tensions mounted as fears for his security increased dramatically. Within hours of the attack, the Special Representative consulted with the President, Prime Minister Correia, the Ministers of the Interior and Defence and other officials on immediate measures to ensure the security of the President and to stabilize the situation. He convened a meeting of the Ambassadors and representatives of international organizations accredited to Guinea-Bissau, which resulted in the issuance of a strongly worded press statement declaring the solidarity of the international community with the President and warning the armed forces against any further destabilizing act. Later in the day, the Chief of the General Staff arrested five members of the military on suspicion of being implicated in the attack, while investigations continued.

On the same day [SG/SM/11947], the Secretary-General condemned the attack, noted with concern reports of the alleged involvement of elements of the armed forces and called for the authorities to re-establish law and order and to conduct a thorough investigation.

On 25 November [SC/9510], the Security Council condemned the attack, called on the Government to bring to justice those responsible for the attack, and urged all parties to resolve any disputes through political and peaceful means.

Communication. In a letter dated 26 November [S/2008/740], Portugal transmitted to the Security Council, on behalf of the Community of Portuguese-speaking Countries (CPLP), the Declaration on Guinea-Bissau adopted by CPLP in Lisbon on 25 November, which condemned the attack against the residence of the President and encouraged the local formation of the International Contact Group for Guinea-Bissau to convene as soon as possible, with the objective of assessing the views of the various national and international actors in Guinea-Bissau. CPLP further proposed the adoption of a CPLP programme for the stability of Guinea-Bissau based on three main pillars: a decisive and effective fight against drug trafficking; the deepening of the security sector reform; and the mobilization of international resources for the development of Guinea-Bissau.

Further political and security developments

Report of Secretary-General (December). In his report on developments in Guinea-Bissau and UNOGBIS activities [S/2008/751], the Secretary-General said that the period under review was marked by an increase in the tempo of preparations for the legislative elections and heightened military and security tensions. In September and October, a number of security incidents were reported that were linked to foreign residents allegedly involved in organized crime, one of which led to the death of a Nigerian citizen who was assassinated in one of Bissau's most popular commercial centres. The incidence of general petty theft and crime registered a slight increase, although the overall crime rate, especially targeting foreigners, remained minimal. During the weekend of 17 to 19 October, a reshuffle in the presidential security team and a simultaneous change in the security guards assigned to the Chief of the Defence Staff took place in the wake of speculation about an alleged interference in military matters by the former Navy Chief of Staff, Rear Admiral Na Tchuto, who had fled to the Gambia after being accused of leading a failed coup in August. By 20 October, the situation was brought back under control by General Na Waie. On 27 October, the non-governmental organization Landmine Action launched its report on the landmine impact survey, which provided the basis for elaborating the Guinea-Bissau strategic anti-mine action plan for 2009–2011. According to the study, 80 of the 264 communities visited were mined, with 11, 13 and 56 of them being considered of high, medium and low priority, respectively.

Following a request from the Minister of Defence for a strengthening of UN technical support and backstopping on security sector reform, the Secretary-General deployed an inter-agency assessment mission to Guinea-Bissau (13–24 October) to assess the context of security sector reform and assist the Special Representative in formulating a response to the Government's request. The mission noted that the security sector reform process, while rooted in a participatory process between national counterparts and international partners, lacked clear strategic vision in the medium to long term, which raised questions about the long-term sustainability and ownership of the reform processes beyond the leadership and policy level of the Ministries of Defence, Interior and Justice. The mission was concerned by the lack of sensitization and involvement of civil society, the media and other key stakeholders. It noted that weak Government capacity and the lack of institutional infrastructure and planning resources constrained the process. The mission made recommendations for the review and formulation of existing and new legislation and the strengthening of national and international coordination.

In October, the Minister of Justice and the UNODC Executive Director launched a project aimed at strengthening the capacity of the justice sector in fighting drug trafficking through the creation of a specialized pool of prosecutors and judges. In a 13 November discussion with the Special Representative, Prime Minister Correia expressed his conviction that the anti-narcotics effort should not only take account of Guinea-Bissau as a transit point, but should also focus on tackling the points of origin and destination of drug-trafficking activities. He supported the view that tougher measures, including targeted sanctions against proven drug traffickers, drug-trafficking syndicates and their accomplices, would be a significant step forward.

Progress was made in the human rights sector on 6 November, when the Council of Ministers approved the law establishing the National Commission for Human Rights, a Government body that would be responsible for vigilance, early warning, monitoring and investigation of human rights issues. The Commission would comprise 30 members drawn from public and private entities, headed by a president, and would have as observers representatives of the Ministries of Justice and the Interior, the Prosecutor General's office, civil society, religious bodies, political parties, the Institute for Women and Children, the media and trade unions.

In other activity, UNOGBIS, in collaboration with other UN system entities and its partners from the Forum for the Humanitarian Situation in Prisons, visited detention centres in Bissau on 7 October to raise awareness on the rights of detainees and to support the national authorities in ensuring respect for the dignity inherent in human beings even if deprived of freedom. During the visits, several human rights violations were verified, namely the existence of detention centres with inadequate facilities and lacking minimum living standards. Several recommendations were made, including the creation and promotion of weekly medical assistance for detainees in all prison facilities in the country; the establishment of additional centres and specific measures for vulnerable groups such as women, children and adolescents; the adoption of mechanisms for the provision of water and food in the prison centres of the judicial police; and the closure of the underground detention cells of the Primeira and Segunda Esquadra police stations in Bissau.

In response to the Security Council's request [YUN 2007, p. 227] for recommendations on the reconfiguration of the UN presence, the Secretary-General said that a Headquarters-based integration task force on Guinea-Bissau was established in October to begin discussions on an integrated UN presence in the country. Since the legislative elections had been successfully held, a technical mission would be conducted in early 2009 for consultation with national authorities, regional and international partners and members of the UN system operating in Bissau, with a view to proposing options for an integrated UN presence. He commended the Government's commitment to implementing a reform agenda and recommended that the Council continue to support the implementation of the security sector reform programme. On the fight against drug trafficking, he appealed to ECOWAS member States, as well as Security Council members and the international community, to monitor and support the timely implementation of the regional action plan that resulted from the Ministerial Conference on Drug Trafficking (see below). He also called on the international community to enhance its support and assistance to the Government to reinforce the national capacity to combat drug trafficking. In response to a request from the Government on 21 November, the Secretary-General recommended the extension of the UNOGBIS mandate for an additional year, until 31 December 2009.

Ministerial Conference on Drug Trafficking. ECOWAS, with the support of UNODC, UNOWA and UNOGBIS, and the facilitation of the Government of Cape Verde, convened the Ministerial Conference on Drug Trafficking as a Threat to West Africa (Praia, 28–29 October), which brought together experts and policymakers, as well as regional, international and UN system entities, to help design a regional action plan and prepare a draft political declaration. The draft action plan presented a comprehensive set of actions and mechanisms to combat drug trafficking in West Africa. The action plan and political declaration were adopted on 19 December by the thirty-fifth ordinary session of the ECOWAS Authority of Heads of State and Government.

Year-end developments. In a later report [S/2009/169], the Secretary-General said that while the country had taken modest steps to improve its democratic and governance profile, the political and security environment remained tense. Following the armed attack against the residence of President Vieira on 23 November, the challenges of securing and protecting the President remained a major source of concern internally and for regional and international partners. An ECOWAS mission (25 November), the President of Cape Verde and the Special Envoy of the President of Angola (14 December), and the Special Envoy of the AU Chairman (9–11 December) visited Bissau for talks with stakeholders, including the Secretary-General's former Special Representative, and to assess the political and security situation. After the attack, Prime Minister Correia established a Commission of Inquiry to carry out a parallel investigation into the case. It was reported that military authorities in Bissau had handed over to the civilian authorities seven military personnel alleged to have been involved in the 23 November attack. The Government requested the extradition of the alleged ringleader, Navy Sergeant N'tchami Yalá, who was detained in Senegal. The UNOGBIS human rights unit monitored and reported on the hearings for the suspects allegedly involved in the attack with regard to the rule of law and human rights standards conducive to a fair trial. Although UNOGBIS had been invited to participate as an observer, it did not attend the hearings as there was no provision for observers in the national penal code. A joint delegation of the Defence and Security Reconciliation Committee and the Political Platform for Women began a series of visits to all barracks in the country to discuss peace and reconciliation.

The economic situation remained fragile and the country faced severe cash flow difficulties. In December, IMF extended the emergency post-conflict assistance programme, running from January to December 2008, until the end of June 2009.

Ad Hoc Advisory Group. In its May report [E/2008/55], the Ad Hoc Advisory Group on Guinea-Bissau provided an overview of its work since its establishment in 2002 [YUN 2002, p. 920], highlighted its main accomplishments and key recommendations, and concluded with observations about Guinea-Bissau that might be useful to the Peacebuilding Commission. The Group also recommended the termination of its mandate. The Economic and Social Council, in **resolution 2008/30** of 25 July (see p. 1019), terminated the Group's mandate and invited the Peacebuilding Commission to consider the Group's work and to draw upon the lessons learned from that experience.

Peacebuilding Commission

The Organizational Committee of the Peacebuilding Commission, in December 2007 [YUN 2007, p. 230], decided to place Guinea-Bissau on the Commission's agenda, and established a country-specific configuration under the leadership of Brazil [A/62/686-S/2008/87]. On 25 March [A/62/768-S/2008/208], the Commission Chairperson reported on action taken, including the conduct of an exploratory mission to Guinea-Bissau [PBC/2/GNB/6]; a mapping of resources and gaps for peacebuilding in the country; and a presentation by the Government on the country's priorities for peacebuilding. After being advised by the Guinea-Bissau configuration, the Secretary-General announced the eligibility of Guinea-Bissau to the Peacebuilding Fund. On 2 April, the Commission presented a background note [PBC/2/GNB/5] on the situation in Guinea-Bissau to assist in the discussions on the development of the Strategic Framework for Peacebuilding in the country.

Report of Peacebuilding Commission. In a report of 15 May [PBC/2/GNB/7] on its mission to Guinea-Bissau (6–11 April), the Peacebuilding Commission found that many problems faced by the country stemmed from the prevailing institutional fragility of the State, constraining the Government from effectively managing key aspects of public, political, security and development policies and from delivering basic services to its population, which set the conditions for political instability and increased vulnerability of the already fragile State. The delegation identified the following key areas for priority action: elections; security sector reform; rule of law and the fight against drug trafficking; illegal migration and other forms of transnational organized crime activities; public administration reform; reactivation of the economy; and rebuilding of the infrastructure, particularly in the energy sector. Given the urgency and magnitude of the problems faced by Guinea-Bissau, the mission concluded that the peacebuilding strategy should be based on a two-track approach, combining strategic planning with quick-impact projects. The delegation specified three criteria for assistance: contribution to promoting stability; contribution to sustained socio-economic growth and development; and contribution to job creation.

Peacebuilding Fund. Following the approval of an interim priority plan, the Secretary-General, on 28 April, allocated a Peacebuilding Fund funding envelope of $6 million to Guinea-Bissau [A/63/92-S/2008/417]. That initial disbursement, in support of projects in the fields of judicial police, army barracks, youth employment and elections, was the first tranche of the Fund allocation. A second tranche would be allocated after the adoption of the strategic framework. On 31 July, the Commission informally adopted the Strategic Framework [PBC/3/GNB/3], subject to a final review by the Government.

Conclusions and recommendations. Following the change of Government in August, the Chair of the Guinea-Bissau configuration undertook a fact-finding visit to the country (10–12 September) to gain a perspective on the political developments and explore options for the Commission's engagement, including the timing for the adoption of the Strategic Framework for Peacebuilding. On the basis of that visit and a meeting of the Commission (New York, 17 September), the Commission provided its conclusions and recommendations on the situation in Guinea-Bissau on 24 September [PBC/3/GNB/1]. On 5 December, the Chairperson of the Peacebuilding Commission transmitted in identical letters to the General Assembly and Security Council [A/63/597-S/2008/762] the conclusions and recommendations of the Commission on the situation in Guinea-Bissau [PBC/3/GNB/4], which referred to the successful holding of legislative elections on 16 November, the Commission's contribution to the electoral process, and threats to the consolidation of peace and democracy following the attack against the residence of the President on 23 November. After extensive consultations with members of the Guinea-Bissau configuration, Government authorities, civil society and international and regional organizations, the Strategic Framework for Peacebuilding in the country was adopted on 1 October. Consultations were under way on creating a monitoring mechanism to assess progress in the implementation of the Framework.

UNOGBIS

The United Nations Peacebuilding Support Office in Guinea-Bissau (UNOGBIS), a political mission established in 1999 by decision of the Secretary-General and supported by Security Council resolution 1233(1999) [YUN 1999, p. 140], was extended until 31 December 2008 [YUN 2007, p. 231]. Its mandate was revised by resolution 1580(2004) [YUN 2004, p. 229] in the face of intensified political turmoil and uncertainty, and in 2007 [YUN 2007, p. 230] to allow the Office to contribute to mobilizing international support for national efforts to eliminate drug trafficking. The Office was headed by the Special Representative of the Secretary-General, Shola Omoregie (Nigeria). During 2008, the Secretary-General submitted reports on developments in Guinea-Bissau and UNOGBIS in March [S/2008/181], June [S/2008/395], September [S/2008/628] and December [S/2008/751].

Revision of mandate. In a letter dated 10 December [S/2008/777], the Secretary-General said that UNOGBIS continued to support national efforts to stabilize the country, focusing on efforts to promote peacebuilding and national reconciliation, and cooperated with national authorities in addressing the growing threat of drug trafficking and organized crime. Activities leading up to the holding of elections on 16 November included resource mobilization, civic education and the strengthening of the capacities of women's groups. UNOGBIS coordinated the work of international electoral observers and played a lead role in coordinating the country's engagement with the Peacebuilding Commission. A UNDP-financed census of the armed forces carried out in March was a milestone in the security sector reform process. UNOGBIS also facilitated an inter-agency security sector reform assessment mission in October aimed at proposing a UN integrated action plan to support the implementation of the security sector reform programme.

Following a request by the Government on 21 November for an additional year of assistance from the Office to support national efforts to consolidate peace, the Secretary-General recommended the extension of the UNOGBIS mandate until 31 December 2009, with a slightly revised mandate. Accordingly, UNOGBIS activities for 2009 would focus on: assisting the Peacebuilding Commission in its engagement with Guinea-Bissau; strengthening the capacities of national institutions; supporting an inclusive national reconciliation and political dialogue; supporting the implementation of security sector reform; extending cooperation to national authorities in their efforts to combat drug trafficking and organized crime; assisting with the promotion and institutionalization of respect for the rule of law and human rights; incorporating a gender perspective into peacebuilding; facilitating efforts to curb the proliferation of small arms and light weapons and contributing to the collection of those held illicitly; and enhancing cooperation with the AU, CPLP, ECOWAS, the EU and other partners in efforts towards the stabilization of Guinea-Bissau.

In follow-up to his letter of 28 November 2007 [YUN 2007, p. 230], in which he indicated his intention to submit recommendations to the Security Council on transforming UNOGBIS into an integrated mission after the holding of successful legislative elections, the Secretary-General said that a technical assessment mission would be deployed to Guinea-Bissau in the first quarter of 2009 to consult with the Government and the UN country team on integration-related strategies. Following the mission, he would submit recommendations to the Council for action. On 22 December [S/2008/778], the Council extended the UNOGBIS mandate until 30 June 2009, took note of the information and proposal in the Secretary-General's letter and requested that he submit recommendations on the establishment of an integrated UN Office by 15 June 2009.

Financing

In an October report [A/63/346/Add.3], dealing with estimated requirements for special political missions grouped under thematic cluster III (United Nations offices, peacebuilding support offices, integrated offices and commissions), the Secretary-General proposed resource requirements for UNOGBIS in the amount of $4,833,000 for the period 1 January to 31 December 2009, which ACABQ recommended for approval [A/63/593].

On 24 December, in section XI of **resolution 63/263**, the Assembly endorsed the recommendations of ACABQ and approved the budgets for 27 special political missions, including the UNOGBIS budget, under section 3, Political affairs, of the programme budget for the 2008–2009 biennium (see p. 1548).

Cameroon–Nigeria

In 2008, Cameroon and Nigeria continued to cooperate to advance progress in implementing the 2002 ruling of the International Court of Justice (ICJ) [YUN 2002, p. 1265] on the land and maritime boundary between them through the Cameroon-Nigeria Mixed Commission.

Cameroon-Nigeria Mixed Commission

The Cameroon-Nigeria Mixed Commission—the mechanism established by the Secretary-General in 2002 at the request of the Presidents of Cameroon and Nigeria to facilitate the peaceful implementation of the ICJ ruling of 10 October 2002 on the border dispute between them [YUN 2003, p. 8]—was chaired by the new Special Representative of the Secretary-General for West Africa, Said Djinnit (Algeria). The Commission was responsible for the demarcation of the land and maritime boundaries between the two countries; the withdrawal of civil administration, military and police forces and transfer of authority in relevant areas along the boundary; the demilitarization of the Bakassi peninsula; the protection of the rights of the affected populations; the development of projects to promote joint economic ventures and cross-border cooperation; and the reactivation of the five-member Lake Chad Basin Commission (Cameroon, Central African Republic, Chad, Niger, Nigeria), created in 1964 for the regulation and planning of the uses of the Lake and other natural resources of the conventional basin. By the end of 2007, all four sections of the ICJ ruling—comprising the withdrawal and transfer of authority in the Lake Chad area in December 2003, the withdrawal and transfer of authority along the land border in July 2004, the agreement on the modalities of withdrawal and transfer of authority in the Bakassi peninsula in June 2006, and the agreement on the delineation of the maritime boundary in May 2007—had been resolved to the satisfaction of the two countries [YUN 2007, p. 232]. A UN team based in Dakar, Senegal, provided substantive, technical and logistical support to the Commission and its subsidiary bodies. The United Nations Office for West Africa also provided support to the work of the Mixed Commission.

In 2008, the activities of the Commission focused on: supporting the demarcation of the land boundary and delineation of the remaining maritime boundary, including the determination of the maritime tripoint between Cameroon, Equatorial Guinea and Nigeria; accelerating the land demarcation exercise and addressing the needs of affected populations; completing the withdrawal and transfer of authority from all relevant areas in the Bakassi peninsula, as per the Greentree Agreement [YUN 2006, p. 252]; and recommending confidence-building measures and environmental safeguards necessary to ensure the sustainability of good relations of neighbourliness.

Activities

Progress report. In a letter dated 3 December [S/2008/756], the Secretary-General informed the Security Council of the latest activities undertaken by the Mixed Commission as it continued to support and facilitate the peaceful implementation of the ICJ ruling. He said that since his previous report [YUN 2007, p. 232], the Commission had been able to facilitate the process smoothly and peacefully, and to keep an open dialogue between the two countries. In follow-up to the delineation of the maritime boundary in 2007, the boundary line was transposed onto an agreed map in March 2008. On 14 August, the transfer of authority from Nigeria to Cameroon of the remaining "Zone" of the Bakassi peninsula was successfully completed, marking a milestone in the implementation of the ICJ ruling and the peaceful resolution of the boundary dispute. In preparation for the handover, the follow-up Committee, which was established to monitor the implementation of the Greentree Agreement, held regular meetings preceded by field visits. The UN civilian observers monitoring the situation in areas of withdrawal and transfer of authority in the Lake Chad area, along the boundary, and in the Bakassi peninsula concluded that the prevailing situation concerning the rights of affected populations was satisfactory. Meanwhile, the Commission supported the formulation of confidence-building measures to ensure the security and welfare of those populations and promote initiatives to enhance trust between the two Governments and their people. Initiatives on social amenities within the Lake Chad area continued to be promoted, and support for resource mobilization for the Lake Chad Basin Commission was provided during the year.

On the demarcation of the 1,950 kilometre land boundary, the Commission expected to complete two of four field assessments along the boundary by the end of 2008, amounting to a total assessed boundary length of approximately 1,250 kilometres, at least 180 kilometres of which required further clarification. With regard to the physical demarcation, the majority of preliminary mapping and preliminary large-scale mapping through satellite imagery had been completed, as had the contract that provided survey control stations used to carry out the final survey of the constructed pillars. The first quality assurance contract was completed in 2008. The Secretary-General expressed his intention to continue the activities of the Mixed Commission and to request resources from the regular budget for the support team of the Commission to help advance implementation of the ICJ ruling.

On 9 December [S/2008/757], the Security Council took note of the Secretary-General's letter and urged Commission members to work with international donors to seek voluntary contributions.

Financing

In an October report [A/63/346/Add.3] dealing with estimated requirements for special political missions grouped under thematic cluster III (United Nations offices, peacebuilding support offices, integrated offices and commissions), the Secretary-General proposed resource requirements for the Mixed Commission in the amount of $8,099,800 for the period 1 January to 31 December 2009, which ACABQ recommended for approval [A/63/593].

On 24 December, in section XI of **resolution 63/263**, the Assembly endorsed the recommendations of ACABQ and approved the budgets for 27 special political missions, including the Commission's budget, under section 3, Political affairs, of the programme budget for the 2008–2009 biennium (see p. 1548).

Guinea

Following the death on 22 December of the President of Guinea, General Lansana Conté, who had ruled the country since 1984, the Secretary-General on 23 December extended his condolences and respect to the family of the President and to the Government and people of Guinea [SG/SM/12018]. He acknowledged President Conté's long-standing commitment to the maintenance of peace and unity in Guinea and the promotion of stability and regional cooperation in the Mano River Basin. He also stressed the need for a peaceful and democratic transfer of power in accordance with the Constitution and urged the armed forces and all stakeholders to respect the democratic process.

Nonetheless, on the same date, a military junta—the National Council for Democracy and Development—led by Captain Moussa Dadis Camara seized power in Guinea. The coup was widely condemned internationally.

Mauritania

In 2008, the democratic process in Mauritania suffered a major setback. In a 6 August coup, General Mohamed Ould Abdel Aziz, the former army Chief of Staff and head of the Presidential Guard, took power from Sidi Mohamed Ould Cheikh Abdallahi, who in 2007 had become the first democratically elected president in the history of the country. President Abdallahi was held under house arrest at the presidential palace in the capital, Nouakchott. The Secretary-General on the same day regretted the overthrow of the Government of President Abdallahi, noted that the Government was elected in a multi-party democratic election, and called for respect for the rule of law and for the immediate restoration of constitutional order [SG/SM/11732].

Security Council consideration. On 19 August [meeting 5960], the representative of Mauritania briefed the Council on the situation in the country and the conditions under which the 6 August "corrective change" took place, including: abuses and terrorist attacks; corruption, underhanded dealings, vote-buying and the diversion of public funds; a dispute with the majority party in Parliament on carrying out duties that were recognized by the Constitution; and the firing of all the country's military leaders. He asserted that the change could not be qualified as a coup d'état.

SECURITY COUNCIL ACTION

On 19 August [meeting 5960], following consultations among Security Council members, the President made statement **S/PRST/2008/30** on behalf of the Council:

> The Security Council condemns the overthrow by the Mauritanian military of the democratically elected Government of Mauritania and welcomes the statements condemning the coup by the African Union, the European Union and other members of the international community.
>
> The Council opposes any attempt to change government through unconstitutional means.
>
> The Council condemns the actions of the State Council, in particular its move to seize the powers of the presidency.
>
> The Council demands the immediate release of President Sidi Mohamed Ould Cheikh Abdallahi and the restoration of the legitimate, constitutional, democratic institutions immediately.
>
> The Council recognizes the important role played by the African Union as well as the support of regional and international partners, including the Secretary-General of the United Nations, through his Special Representative for West Africa, Mr. Said Djinnit, and calls upon all to assist in restoring constitutional order in Mauritania.
>
> The Council will monitor developments in this situation.

Statement by Secretary-General. On 22 December [SG/SM/12017], the Secretary-General welcomed the release of President Abdallahi from house arrest and called again for the prompt restoration of constitutional order.

Horn of Africa

Sudan

In 2008, uneven progress was made in implementing the 2005 Comprehensive Peace Agreement between the Sudan People's Liberation Movement/Army (SPLM/A) and the Government of National Unity. Redeployment of Sudanese Armed Forces (SAF) north of the 1956 boundary line and of the SPLA south of the line remained incomplete. On 14 May, tensions between the two forces in Abyei erupted into full-scale fighting that continued until 20 May. Following several weeks of consultations, the parties finalized a road map agreement for the peaceful resolution of the situation, which was endorsed by the presidency of the Government on 8 June. The dispute over the Abyei borders was referred to the Permanent Court of Arbitration at The Hague. On 10 May, Justice and Equality Movement (JEM) fighters from the Darfur region of the Sudan attacked the city of Omdurman, across the Nile from the Sudanese capital, Khartoum, and were repelled by Government forces. The fifth national census in the Sudan was conducted from 22 April to 6 May. The electoral law was adopted by the National Assembly on 7 July and was signed by President Omar Al-Bashir on 14 July. On the same date, the Prosecutor of the International Criminal Court requested that the Court issue an arrest warrant against the President on charges of genocide, crimes against humanity and war crimes. The Prosecutor's request affected the political landscape within the Sudan, as well as regional politics and the role of the United Nations in the country. The United Nations Mission in the Sudan (UNMIS), however, continued to support implementation of the Peace Agreement, facilitate the return of refugees and internally displaced persons, assist in humanitarian and demining operations, and promote human rights. In April, the Security Council renewed the UNMIS mandate until 30 April 2009 and asked the Mission to provide technical and logistical support to the parties in demarcating the north-south border.

Relations between Chad and the Sudan remained volatile. On 13 March, President Idriss Déby Itno of Chad and President Al-Bashir signed the Dakar Agreement, by which the two countries committed to ending their differences. On 10 May, however, the Sudan accused Chad of supporting the JEM attack on Omdurman and severed diplomatic ties. Relations between Chad and the Sudan later improved, and the two countries exchanged ambassadors on 9 November.

Implementation of Comprehensive Peace Agreement

Report of Secretary-General (January). In his January report on the Sudan [S/2008/64], submitted pursuant to Security Council resolution 1590(2005) [YUN 2005, p. 304] and covering developments since his October 2007 report [YUN 2007, p. 240], the Secretary-General said that the Sudanese Armed Forces (SAF), the Sudan People's Liberation Army (SPLA) and the United Nations Mission in the Sudan (UNMIS) made progress on de-escalating tension in the north-south border area and resuming implementation of the security arrangements set out in the 2005 Comprehensive Peace Agreement [YUN 2005, p. 301]. On 9 January, SAF announced that it had completed its redeployment from the south in accordance with the agreed deadline. According to figures verified by UNMIS, however, 88 per cent of some 46,000 SAF troops had been redeployed as at 15 January, including voluntarily demobilized soldiers, who made up 16.2 per cent of the total. SPLA troops continued their redeployment from Blue Nile and Southern Kordofan states; redeployment remained at 8.5 per cent of the stated strength of some 59,000. SPLA-aligned forces at Debab and Abu Matariq also began redeployment towards Southern Sudan, but stopped in contested areas around the disputed line of 1 January 1956. The strength of the Joint Integrated Units, composed of members of SAF and SPLA, reached 82.2 per cent of the authorized 39,000 personnel.

UNMIS continued to provide technical support to the Government of National Unity and the Government of Southern Sudan to enhance their human rights capacity; monitor the human rights situation and developments regarding the rule of law; and monitor and follow up on reports of threats against civilians. With regard to electoral assistance, UNMIS continued to track preparations for a census and met regularly with international partners on planning for such assistance, but operational planning was hampered by a lack of progress in enacting the electoral law. UNMIS increased its engagement with the Northern and Southern Disarmament, Demobilization and Reintegration Commissions. The first phase of the National Disarmament, Demobilization and Reintegration Plan, signed by the Presidency in November 2007, would begin in 2008 and cover 45,000 ex-combatants each from SAF and SPLA. To date, UNMIS mine-action teams had opened more than 21,000 kilometres of roads; cleared 15.5 million square metres of suspected dangerous areas; and destroyed some 5,300 anti-personnel mines, 2,400 anti-tank mines, 637,000 pieces of unexploded ordnance and 360,000 small arms and ammunition. As at 14 January, 95 per cent of the authorized UNMIS force strength (9,267 of a total of 9,716) was deployed, including 544 military observers, 191 staff officers and 8,532 troops. UNMIS police advisers numbered 645 and were deployed in 21 sites in the Mission area.

The Secretary-General observed that major challenges to the full implementation of the Comprehensive Peace Agreement remained. He urged the parties to begin the demarcation of the north-south boundary and to advance the formation of Joint Integrated Units. The strategic assessment of UNMIS, which was requested by the Council in resolution 1784(2007) [YUN 2007, p. 241], indicated the need for a review of the strength of the Mission's military component; clarification of its mandate with regard to border demarcation, census and elections, as well as a review of resources to meet those needs; greater integration of activities in the area of rule of law and security institutions, and reliable funding for those activities; and consideration of a new security sector reform mandate. The assessment also pointed to a need to review disarmament, demobilization and reintegration, and returns issues. It recommended a review of Mission functions related to humanitarian coordination to ensure a smooth transition to the recovery and development phase.

Communication. On 15 February [S/2008/119], the Sudan requested the Security Council to retain on the list of matters of which it was seized the item entitled "Letter dated 20 February 1958 from the representative of the Sudan addressed to the Secretary-General (S/3963)" [YUN 1958, p. 83], which dealt with the issue of the Sudan-Egypt border.

Report of Secretary-General (April). In his report of 22 April on the Sudan [S/2008/267], the Secretary-General said that in order to complete the interim period of the Comprehensive Peace Agreement in a timely manner, a number of remaining milestones needed to be met, including final redeployment of armed forces; the formation of Joint Integrated Units; disarmament, demobilization and reintegration of ex-combatants; border demarcation; the resolution of the Abyei issue; preparations for the upcoming census and elections; and wealth-sharing concerns, including division of the oil revenues derived from the disputed area of Abyei. The Technical Ad Hoc Border Committee established new timelines, stating that its demarcation work in the western and eastern sectors of the border would start by the end of June, while work in the central sector would not start before September. Differences between the parties in the interpretation of the north-south border line continued to hamper the monitoring and verification of redeployed forces, with disagreement over the status of SAF at Abyei, and SPLA forces at Kharasana and the assembly area at White Lake/Jau. Although the formation and training of Joint Integrated Units continued, recurring security incidents highlighted their fragile cohesion. Following clashes in Kapoeta in Eastern Equatoria state on 11 and 12 March, the SAF element of the local Joint Integrated Unit was relocated to Torit. However, in Khorflus in Upper Nile state on 7 and 8 March, the local Unit stabilized a tense situation after fighting occurred between SPLA and Southern Sudan Police elements. The failure of the Presidency to resolve the Abyei issue, including the appointment of a local administration, continued to mar overall implementation of the Agreement.

On 11 February, the Presidency decreed 15–30 April as the dates for the national census; public information campaigns about the census began in February, with uneven coverage. On 13 April, the Government of Southern Sudan announced a delay in the census, citing inadequate refugee return and the exclusion of religion and ethnicity from the questionnaire. Following emergency consultations in the Government of National Unity, the Presidency decided that the census would begin on 22 April.

The overall security situation in the UNMIS area of responsibility remained relatively calm, but the continued presence of SAF and SPLA military personnel around the oilfields and other areas along the disputed 1956 borderline remained a source of tension. A road accident on 7 February in Balom involving an SAF truck and vehicles carrying the Commissioner from Abeimnom and his escort resulted in a firefight between SPLA and local Misseriya tribal militia, injuring several people. Both sides in the Abyei region imposed restrictions on UNMIS, including denial of security clearances for air patrols, making monitoring or verification of reported incidents difficult. The two parties lifted UN movement restrictions for 14 days, beginning on 5 April, but the lifting of restrictions was only applied to limited locations and did not allow verification of troops in critical areas such as Muglad, Grinti/Meiram or Heglig. The frequency of incursions into Southern Sudan by splinter groups of the Lord's Resistance Army (LRA) increased during the reporting period. The groups attacked villages and local populations in Western Equatoria state, sometimes resulting in deaths.

In response to resolution 1784(2007), in February a joint technical assessment mission composed of representatives from UNMIS, the UN Department of Peacekeeping Operations (DPKO) and other departments and agencies conducted a review of the UNMIS mandate. The mission found that the mandate was sufficiently broad to allow UNMIS to support the peace process in a wide range of tasks. The major challenges for UNMIS in supporting implementation of the Peace Agreement were related to the need for the parties to demonstrate the political will necessary to move forward in implementing their commitments. In that regard, UNMIS should enhance its efforts to build trust with the parties and broaden consent for its role.

UNMIS completed a number of its core monitoring and verification tasks, but conditions were not yet in place to reduce its military presence. The Mission established a Joint Integrated Unit support cell to assist the Joint Defence Board—the national body responsible for Joint Integrated Unit development—in identifying requirements and to coordinate international assistance to the Units. It made significant progress in the establishment of electoral capacity at its headquarters in Khartoum and at the Juba field office, and its international partners continued to meet on planning for electoral assistance. The Secretary-General requested UNMIS and the UN country team to jointly develop a conflict management strategy for the 1 January 1956 border areas, and directed that the Assistance Liaison Unit be restructured to reflect the transition to recovery and development, while maintaining support for humanitarian activities.

Regarding disarmament, demobilization and reintegration, the Secretary-General said that SAF and SPLA forces were unlikely to be significantly reduced until greater confidence was established between the parties. The Northern and Southern Disarmament, Demobilization and Reintegration Commissions indicated their intent to demobilize and reintegrate, in 2008, up to 50,000 personnel, mainly veterans and special needs groups; and demobilize, between 2008 and 2011, approximately 132,000 combatants who had been absorbed into SAF and SPLA since the signing of the Peace Agreement. The Secretary-General proposed a number of prerequisites that might serve as benchmarks to be met before the United Nations began operations to support the disarmament, demobilization and reintegration of SAF and SPLA.

The Secretary-General welcomed recent cooperation between the Governments of National Unity and of Southern Sudan in preparing an agenda for economic recovery and development, but remained concerned that progress in key areas of the Peace Agreement was still lacking. He urged both parties to resolve remaining differences and enable a peaceful census with maximum coverage. He observed that the next phase of the Agreement's implementation required a reorientation of UNMIS priorities and activities, including increased exercise of the Mission's good offices, confidence-building and conflict management; reorientation for peacekeeping activities around the 1 January 1956 border area; reallocation of resources to anticipated hot spots; support for a visible peace dividend throughout the country; and a stronger engagement with state authorities in Southern Sudan. He recommended that the Security Council, in its renewal of the UNMIS mandate, authorize the Mission to: provide technical and logistical support to the border demarcation process; provide support to the corrections system and authorize the deployment of up to 40 seconded corrections officers; monitor the activities of LRA elements in Southern Sudan; and liaise with the African Union-United Nations Hybrid Operation in Darfur (UNAMID), the AU-UN Joint Mediation Support Team and neighbouring UN missions to ensure their support for implementing the Agreement.

SECURITY COUNCIL ACTION

On 30 April [meeting 5882], the Security Council unanimously adopted **resolution 1812(2008)**. The draft [S/2008/283] was submitted by Belgium, Costa Rica, Croatia, France, Italy, the United Kingdom and the United States.

The Security Council,

Recalling all its resolutions and the statements by its President concerning the situation in the Sudan,

Recalling also its resolution 1674(2006) of 28 April 2006 on the protection of civilians in armed conflict, in which it reaffirms, inter alia, the relevant provisions of the 2005 World Summit Outcome, its resolution 1612(2005) of 26 July 2005 on children and armed conflict, its resolution 1502(2003) of 26 August 2003 on the protection of humanitarian and United Nations personnel and its resolution 1325(2000) of 31 October 2000 on women and peace and security,

Reaffirming its commitment to the sovereignty, unity, independence and territorial integrity of the Sudan and to the cause of peace,

Commending the work of the United Nations Mission in the Sudan in support of the Comprehensive Peace Agreement of 9 January 2005, commending also the continued commitment of troop-contributing countries in support of the Mission, and commending further the efforts of the Mission in assisting in the transition of the African Union Mission in the Sudan to the African Union United Nations Hybrid Operation in Darfur (UNAMID),

Recognizing that successful implementation of the Comprehensive Peace Agreement is essential to the resolution of the crisis in Darfur and to sustainable peace and stability in the region, and condemning acts of violence perpetrated by all sides,

Taking note of the report of the Secretary-General of 22 April 2008 on the Sudan, including his recommendations, taking note also of the report of the Secretary-General of 29 August 2007 on children and armed conflict in the Sudan, and recalling the conclusions on children and armed conflict in the Sudan endorsed by the Security Council,

Welcoming the appointment of Sir Derek Plumbly as the new Chairman of the Assessment and Evaluation Commission,

Recalling the commitment of the international community to support the Comprehensive Peace Agreement process, including through development aid, and urging donors to support the implementation of the Agreement and to honour all pledges to this end,

Recalling also the need for the United Nations Mission in the Sudan to make full use of its current mandate and capabilities with regard to the activities of militias and armed groups such as the Lord's Resistance Army in the Sudan, as stated in resolution 1663(2006) of 24 March 2006,

Welcoming the mediation efforts of the Government of Southern Sudan to bring an end to the 22-year conflict between the Lord's Resistance Army and the Government of Uganda, and urging the parties to reach a resolution,

Welcoming also the start of the national census on 22 April 2008 as a significant milestone in the implementation of the Comprehensive Peace Agreement, and urging the continued support of a fair and inclusive census and acceptance of the results by all the parties,

Determining that the situation in the Sudan continues to constitute a threat to international peace and security,

1. *Decides* to extend the mandate of the United Nations Mission in the Sudan until 30 April 2009, with the intention to renew it for further periods;

2. *Requests* the Secretary-General to report to the Security Council every three months on the implementation of the mandate of the Mission, progress on implementation of the Comprehensive Peace Agreement and respect for the ceasefire, and to provide an assessment and recommendations on measures that the Mission might take to further support elections and to advance the peace process;

3. *Stresses* the importance of full and expeditious implementation of all elements of the Comprehensive Peace Agreement, the Darfur Peace Agreement and the Eastern Sudan Peace Agreement of 14 October 2006, and calls for all the parties to respect their commitments to these agreements without delay;

4. *Welcomes* the sustained commitment of the parties to work together in the Government of National Unity, and urges the cooperation of the National Congress Party and the Sudan People's Liberation Movement in carrying out their responsibilities to further implement the Comprehensive Peace Agreement;

5. *Stresses* the critical role of the Assessment and Evaluation Commission in overseeing and reporting on the implementation of the Comprehensive Peace Agreement, calls for strengthening of the Commission's autonomy, and urges all parties to cooperate fully with the Commission and to implement its recommendations;

6. *Calls for* all parties to cooperate with full unrestricted monitoring and verification by the Mission in the Abyei region, without prejudice to the final agreement on the actual borders between the two sides, and urges the Mission to consult with the parties, and to deploy, as appropriate, personnel to the Abyei region, including areas of Kordofan;

7. *Calls upon* the parties to address and find a mutually agreeable solution to the Abyei issue, and further urges all parties to redeploy their forces away from the disputed border of 1 January 1956 and fully establish an interim administration in Abyei in accordance with the Comprehensive Peace Agreement;

8. *Requests* the Mission, acting within its current mandate and within its current means and capabilities, to provide technical and logistical support, as requested, to help the parties in the process of demarcation of the north/south border of 1956, in accordance with the Comprehensive Peace Agreement;

9. *Stresses* the important role of the Joint Integrated Units for the full implementation of the Comprehensive Peace Agreement, and urges donors to offer support, both materiel and training, coordinated by the Mission in consultation with the Joint Defence Board, to enable the full establishment and operational effectiveness of the Joint Integrated Units as soon as possible;

10. *Welcomes* the adoption of the National Strategic Plan for Disarmament, Demobilization and Reintegration, encourages the parties to agree swiftly on a date to launch its implementation, takes note of the benchmarks proposed

by the Secretary-General in this regard, and urges the Mission, consistent with its mandate, to assist in voluntary disarmament and weapons collection and destruction efforts in implementation of plans under the Comprehensive Peace Agreement for disarmament, demobilization and reintegration;

11. *Requests* the Mission, consistent with its mandate and in coordination with the relevant parties, and taking into account the need to pay particular attention to the protection, release and reintegration of all children associated with armed forces and armed groups, to increase its support for the National Disarmament, Demobilization and Reintegration Coordination Council and the Northern and Southern Sudan Disarmament, Demobilization and Reintegration Commissions;

12. *Further urges* donors to respond to calls for assistance from the joint United Nations Disarmament, Demobilization and Reintegration Unit;

13. *Encourages* the Mission, consistent with its mandate, and within authorized levels of civilian police, to continue efforts to assist the parties to the Comprehensive Peace Agreement in promoting the rule of law and in restructuring the police and corrections services in the Sudan, including in Southern Sudan, and to assist in the training of civilian police and corrections officers;

14. *Urges* the Government of National Unity to complete the conduct of an inclusive national census and to prepare expeditiously for the conduct of free and fair elections in all of the Sudan;

15. *Urges* the Mission, consistent with its mandate, to begin immediate preparations to support the conduct of national elections, including support for the development of a national strategy for the conduct of elections in close collaboration with the United Nations Development Programme and the parties to the Comprehensive Peace Agreement, and further urges the international community to provide technical and material assistance for electoral preparations;

16. *Encourages* the Mission, consistent with its mandate, to assist the parties to the Comprehensive Peace Agreement in addressing the need for a national inclusive approach towards reconciliation and peacebuilding, emphasizing, in particular, the role of women in the prevention and resolution of conflicts and in peacebuilding, as recognized in resolution 1325(2000), and of civil society, and to take this need into account in implementing all aspects of its mandate;

17. *Calls upon* the parties to the Comprehensive Peace Agreement and the communiqué signed by the United Nations and the Government of National Unity in Khartoum on 28 March 2007 to support, protect and facilitate all humanitarian operations and personnel in the Sudan;

18. *Welcomes* the continuing organized returns of internally displaced persons from Khartoum to Southern Kordofan and Southern Sudan and of refugees from countries of asylum to Southern Sudan, and encourages the promotion of efforts, including the provision of necessary resources to the Office of the United Nations High Commissioner for Refugees and implementing partners, to ensure that such returns are voluntary and sustainable, and further requests the Mission, within its capabilities and areas of deployment, to coordinate with partners to facilitate sustainable returns, including by helping to establish the necessary security conditions;

19. *Expresses its concern* at the persistence of localized conflict and violence, especially in the border area, mostly affecting civilians and with the potential for escalation; urges in this regard full cooperation of the National Congress Party and the Sudan People's Liberation Movement in carrying out the obligations of the Government of National Unity for the protection of civilians in armed conflict, in accordance with resolution 1674(2006); and supports the intention of the Mission to strengthen its conflict management capacity by developing and executing an integrated strategy to support local conflict resolution mechanisms, in order to maximize protection of civilians;

20. *Notes* that conflict in one area of the Sudan affects conflict in other areas in the Sudan and in the region, and therefore urges the Mission to coordinate closely with UNAMID, the African Union-United Nations Joint Mediation Support Team and other stakeholders to ensure complementary implementation of the mandates of those bodies in support of the implementation of the Comprehensive Peace Agreement and of the overall objective of peace in the Sudan;

21. *Requests* the Mission to coordinate with humanitarian, recovery and development agencies, within its capabilities and areas of deployment, to facilitate the provision of recovery and development assistance, which is essential to deliver a peace dividend to the people of the Sudan;

22. *Calls upon* the Government of National Unity to cooperate fully with all the United Nations operations within its territory in the implementation of their mandates;

23. *Requests* the Secretary-General to submit for the consideration of the Security Council a report on possible measures that the Mission could take to assist with the implementation of a future final peace agreement between the Government of Uganda and the Lord's Resistance Army;

24. *Reiterates its concern* over the restrictions and all impediments placed on the movements of Mission personnel and materiel in the Sudan, and the adverse impact that such restrictions and impediments have on the ability of the Mission to perform its mandate effectively and on the ability of the humanitarian community to reach affected persons; and in this regard calls for all parties to cooperate fully with the Mission and facilitate the performance of its mandate, and to abide by their obligations under international humanitarian law;

25. *Requests* the Secretary-General to continue to take the necessary measures to ensure full compliance in the Mission with the United Nations zero tolerance policy on sexual exploitation and abuse and to keep the Council informed, and urges troop-contributing countries to take appropriate preventive action, including predeployment awareness training, and other action to ensure full accountability in cases of such conduct involving their personnel;

26. *Decides* to remain actively seized of the matter.

Attack on Omdurman. On 9 May, the Sudan informed the diplomatic community in Khartoum that the Justice and Equality Movement (JEM) was advancing with some 200–300 armed vehicles from Northern Darfur towards the city of El Obeid in Northern

Kordofan, aiming to attack the capital. On 10 May, JEM fighters, crossing 1,200 kilometres from Darfur, attacked Omdurman, adjacent to Khartoum. Media and local sources reported that JEM elements took over the Omdurman police station, killing six police officers. After a day of skirmishes, Government forces repelled the JEM fighters. According to the National Intelligence and Security Service of the Sudan, 79 members of Government security forces, 57 civilians and 329 JEM members were killed in the fighting. The Government also reported that 20–30 JEM vehicles were destroyed and some 200 JEM personnel were arrested. It imposed a curfew on 10 May in Omdurman and Khartoum; the curfew was lifted on 11 May in Khartoum but remained in place until 12 May in Omdurman, as Government forces conducted house-to-house searches for JEM fighters and weapons.

The Sudan accused Chad of supporting the JEM attack, and on 10 May severed diplomatic ties with Chad. Chad issued a statement on 11 May denying any involvement. On 13 May, the National Assembly convened an extraordinary session to condemn the attack. SPLM, the National Umma Party (NUP) and the Democratic Unionist Party (DUP) also condemned it, calling for a political solution in Darfur and a fair trial for all those arrested in connection with the attack.

SECURITY COUNCIL ACTION

On 13 May [meeting 5891], following consultations among Security Council members, the President made statement **S/PRST/2008/15** on behalf of the Council:

> The Security Council strongly condemns the attacks of 10 May perpetrated by the Justice and Equality Movement (JEM) against the Sudanese Government in Omdurman, and urges all parties to cease violence immediately, respect their obligations under international humanitarian law and commit to a peaceful resolution of all outstanding issues.
>
> The Security Council urges restraint by all parties, and in particular, warns that no retaliatory action should be taken against civilian populations, or that has an impact on stability in the region.
>
> The Security Council reiterates the urgent need for all parties to engage fully and constructively in the political process. The Security Council calls upon the States of the region to implement their commitments under the Dakar Accord, and to cooperate with a view to putting an end to the activities of armed groups and their attempts to seize power by force.
>
> The Security Council strongly condemns all attempts at destabilization by force, and reaffirms its commitment to the sovereignty, unity, independence and territorial integrity of Sudan.

Clashes in Abyei. On 14 May, long-standing tensions in the disputed town of Abyei erupted into full-scale fighting following the killing of an SAF soldier at an SPLA checkpoint on 13 May. The fighting, which ended on 20 May, resulted in 89 fatalities, the displacement of more than 50,000 civilians, the destruction of most of Abyei town and the evacuation of UN and NGO civilian staff from the area. Representatives of both parties characterized the clashes as the most serious crisis since the signing of the Comprehensive Peace Agreement in 2005.

Security Council mission

The Security Council mission to Africa (see p. 111) briefed the Council on 18 June [meeting 5915]. In its report of 15 July [S/2008/460], the mission to the Sudan (3–5 June) stated that it met with President Omar Al-Bashir, First Vice-President Salva Kiir Mayardit, Foreign Affairs Minister Deng Alor, Presidential Adviser Nafie Ali Nafie, representatives of opposition parties and of the humanitarian community in Northern Darfur, and a delegation of internally displaced persons in Northern Darfur.

In Juba, the First Vice-President stressed that the Sudan should be considered from a strategic perspective, and that allowing the Comprehensive Peace Agreement to collapse would endanger the entire continent of Africa. He suggested steps that the United Nations could take to improve the implementation of the Agreement, protection of civilians by UNMIS, the functionality of institutions established under the Agreement and the disarmament, demobilization and reintegration process. The mission stated its willingness to consider the issue of a strengthened mandate for UNMIS when it returned to New York.

Government officials informed the mission that a subcommittee had been established to determine the way forward with regard to Abyei. The subcommittee agreed on four key areas, dealing with the return of displaced persons, granting UNMIS full access to the Abyei area, the establishment of a temporary administration in Abyei and engaging an international body to overcome the impasse regarding border demarcation. The mission stressed the urgency of resolving the Abyei crisis and making decisive progress on other outstanding areas of the Peace Agreement. It stated that the Abyei incident would not have occurred if the Agreement had been implemented on schedule.

President Al-Bashir reaffirmed his Government's commitment to the implementation of the Peace Agreement and stated that all the institutions necessary to implement the Agreement had been formed. He indicated that the resolution of the Abyei issue was the top priority with respect to the Agreement, and said that it would soon be settled through ongoing consultations between the National Congress Party (NCP) and SPLM. The mission was encouraged to hear that progress was being made but expressed concern over the continuing violence in Darfur (see p. 244), which was affecting the humanitarian situation. It reiterated its condemnation of the 10 May attack by JEM, and urged the President to exercise restraint in responding to the attack. The President stressed that the Government had a right to self-defence in the context of the attack on Omdurman, and stated that Chad had allowed JEM to gather in Chad and cross the border to attack the Sudanese capital. In a letter of 9 June [S/2008/373], the President transmitted to the Security Council his statement of 5 June to the mission.

The mission recommended that the Council continue to support the parties in implementing the Comprehensive Peace Agreement, including by improving security arrangements between the parties. UNMIS should begin preparations to support the conduct of national elections, in close collaboration with UNDP and the parties to the Agreement. Consistent with its mandate and in accordance with Security Council resolution 1812(2008) (see p. 235), UNMIS should robustly deploy peacekeeping personnel in and around Abyei to support implementation of the Agreement, including protection of civilians.

Further developments

Abyei road map. Following several weeks of consultations, the parties finalized a road map agreement on Abyei, which was endorsed by the Presidency of the Government of National Unity on 8 June. The road map comprised four points. First, the parties agreed to the deployment of new Joint Integrated Units and police units, the subsequent redeployment of SAF and SPLA forces out of the Abyei area and freedom of movement for UNMIS within the area. Secondly, they agreed that the civilian population should return to the area once security arrangements were in place, and a civil administration headed by SPLM and deputized by NCP should be set up within the agreed interim boundaries. Thirdly, oil revenues from the Abyei area were to be shared according to the provisions of the Peace Agreement, with both parties contributing an agreed percentage to a fund for the development of the areas along the north-south border. Finally, the parties agreed to resort to arbitration to resolve the dispute over the findings of the Abyei Boundaries Commission, and committed themselves to implement the decision of an international arbitration tribunal.

A presidential decree of 15 June established the administration within the agreed provisional geographical boundaries, gave the Abyei area special status under the Presidency, and defined its administrative parameters and powers. By 18 June, the deployment of Joint Integrated Units to Abyei, made up of 613 SAF and SPLA troops, was completed, and preparations for police deployment were under way.

SECURITY COUNCIL ACTION

On 24 June [meeting 5923], following consultations among Security Council members, the President made statement **S/PRST/2008/24** on behalf of the Council:

> The Security Council welcomes the road map for the return of internally displaced persons and the implementation of the Abyei Protocol ("the road map") signed by the National Congress Party and the Sudan People's Liberation Movement on 8 June 2008. The Council emphasizes that the peaceful resolution of the situation in Abyei is vital to the effective implementation of the Comprehensive Peace Agreement and peace in the region. The Council welcomes the agreements in the road map, including its provisions regarding revenue-sharing and the interim boundaries in Abyei. The Council urges the parties to use the opportunity created by the signing of the road map to resolve all outstanding issues related to implementation of the Agreement and welcomes the commitment of the parties to take unresolved issues to arbitration as necessary.
>
> The Council deeply regrets the recent outbreak of fighting in Abyei, the ensuing displacement of civilians and the obstruction to the freedom of movement of the United Nations Mission in the Sudan. The Council urges the parties to facilitate immediate humanitarian support for the displaced citizens and support for their voluntary return as soon as an interim administration and the agreed security arrangements are in place.
>
> The Council encourages the parties to fully implement the road map within the agreed timelines, in particular with the establishment of an Abyei Area Administration; deployment of a new Joint Integrated Unit battalion; ensuring free movement for forces of the Mission in the Abyei area and access to the north and south of the Abyei area to carry out its mandate to support implementation of the Agreement; and redeployment of the Sudanese Armed Forces and Sudan People's Liberation Movement troops outside the interim Abyei administrative area agreed to by the parties.
>
> The Council calls upon the Mission, within its mandate and in accordance with Council resolution 1812(2008), to robustly deploy, as appropriate, peacekeeping personnel in and around Abyei to help to reduce tensions and prevent the escalation of conflict in support of implementation of the Agreement. The Council requests the Secretary-General to examine the root causes of and the role played by the Mission in connection with the violence between the parties in Abyei in May 2008 and to consider what follow-up steps may be appropriate for the Mission.

Report of Secretary-General (July). In July [S/2008/485], the Secretary-General reported that SPLA and SAF began withdrawing from the Abyei area on 30 June and 4 July, respectively, and UNMIS enjoyed freedom of movement throughout the area. The parties decided to refer the dispute over the boundaries of Abyei to the Permanent Court of Arbitration at The Hague. UNMIS was supporting the implementation of the road map, and core UN civilian staff in Abyei were providing good offices and planning for the return of an expanded UN presence. Despite those positive developments, tensions in the Abyei area remained high. One UN military observer was shot on 7 July during an altercation between an SAF monitor and SPLA at a market located 30 kilometres south of Abyei, and was in critical condition.

The second SPLM National Convention was held in Juba from 15 to 21 May. On 20 May President Al-Bashir and NUP leader Sadiq Al-Mahdi signed a national agreement covering issues such as democratic transformation, civil liberties and Darfur. On 14 July, International Criminal Court (ICC) Prosecutor Luis Moreno Ocampo requested that the Court issue an arrest warrant for President Al-Bashir on charges of genocide, crimes against humanity and war crimes; the request would be reviewed by the Court's Pretrial Chamber (see p. 259).

As at 8 July, the total redeployment of SAF troops verified by UNMIS and accepted by the Ceasefire Joint Monitoring Commission stood at 97 per cent of the 46,403 troops initially stated as being present south of the current borderline. For SPLA, verified and accepted redeployment stood at 10 per cent of 59,168 troops initially stated as being present north of the line. The low percentage of SPLA forces redeployed, especially from Southern Kordofan, continued to be a source of tension, as its forces remained in areas that SAF contended were north of the 1 January 1956 line. UNMIS verified 33,385 Joint Integrated Unit troops, representing 90.5 per cent of the stated strength of 36,866 and 84.2 per cent of the total authorized strength of 39,639.

The Sudan's fifth national census was conducted from 22 April to 6 May, with public support in most parts of the country. Government officials reported a coverage rate of 85 per cent in Western Darfur and 90 per cent in Northern and Southern Darfur. The Director of the National Bureau for Statistics claimed, on 6 May, that most states had achieved a 100 per cent completion rate, with a coverage rate of 90 per cent throughout the Sudan. Throughout the process, UNMIS provided extensive logistical and transportation support, and assisted in retrieving census forms from the states. Census results were expected to be released by the fourth quarter of 2008. The Cabinet finally approved the electoral law on 27 June and forwarded it to the National Assembly, which adopted it on 7 July. The President signed the law on 14 July. The National Elections Commission was to be established within one month of the enactment of the law.

UNMIS worked closely with officials of Greater Equatoria to facilitate peace and reconciliation talks between the Bari and the Mundari tribes and facilitated the implementation of an agreed transfer of the Wanding area from Jonglei to Upper Nile. Progress was made towards achieving the benchmarks for disarmament, demobilization and reintegration set out by the Secretary-General in his April report. Following approval of the national reintegration policy by the National Council for Disarmament, Demobilization and Reintegration Coordination, the parties signed a national multi-year project document on disarmament, demobilization and reintegration at a conference co-chaired by Japan and UNDP (Geneva, 25 June). The Northern and Southern Sudan Disarmament, Demobilization and Reintegration Commissions established technical coordination committees to develop joint operations plans. The two Commissions began joint programme activities in Blue Nile state, resulting in the demobilization of 88 children formerly associated with SPLA. Despite those achievements, many challenges remained, including the need for the Sudanese authorities and UNMIS to finalize the joint operational plan.

The Secretary-General urged both parties to complete their redeployment out of the interim Abyei area as quickly as possible. He appealed to the parties to agree quickly on their nomination of the new civil administration and to work together to ensure the conditions necessary for the return of displaced persons. Regarding the demarcation of the 1 January 1956 boundary, the Secretary-General expressed concern about the high degree of militarization along the border and reports of troop movements by both parties in the three transitional areas of Abyei, Blue Nile, and Southern Kordofan. He urged both sides to expedite the redeployment of forces in accordance with the Peace Agreement; begin demarcation of the 1 January 1956 boundary line; and resolve the status of disputed areas.

Report of Secretary-General (October). In October [S/2008/662], the Secretary-General reported progress in implementing the security arrangements under the Abyei road map agreement. As at 4 October, almost all SAF and SPLA personnel had left the road map area as required, with two exceptions: a small, unverified group of SAF personnel providing security at Diffra oilfields in the outer ring; and SPLA military police patrolling the Agok area. UNMIS pressed the parties to withdraw those forces in accordance with the Comprehensive Peace Agreement and the road map. The new Abyei Joint Integrated Unit, composed of 640 personnel trained by UNMIS, became operational in August and was assuming control of military positions as SAF and SPLA departed. Preparations for the deployment of two further companies to Diffra and Agok were ongoing. The Joint Integrated Police Unit was deployed and was policing Abyei town. The first group of 168 personnel of the Unit arrived in early August, comprising 150 regular police (103 from the south and 47 from the north) and 18 officers (2 from the south and 16 from the north). UNMIS provided transport and supplies, and conducted a basic training course for the Unit's personnel. The arrival of the second group, consisting of 33 Government police personnel and 49 Southern Sudan police personnel, brought the strength of the Police Unit to 250.

On 8 August, the Presidency appointed Arop Mayak Mony Tock of SPLM as Chief Administrator for the Abyei Interim Administration and Rahama Abdelrahman al-Nour (NCP) as his Deputy, in accordance with the road map and the Peace Agreement. On 6 October, President Al-Bashir appointed the remaining members of the Abyei Executive and Area Councils. As at 1 October, between 12,000 and 16,000 persons out of some 50,000 displaced had returned to the Abyei area. The UNMIS Force Commander led an inquiry into the events in Abyei in May, as requested by the Ceasefire Political Commission, and produced a draft report. The Secretary-General urged the parties to finalize the report and, based on its findings, take action against those responsible for the violence, looting and displacement of the civilian population of Abyei and the surrounding area.

As at 4 October, total redeployment of SAF troops verified by UNMIS and accepted by the Ceasefire Joint Monitoring Commission stood at 96.9 per cent of the 46,403 troops initially stated as being present south of the current border line. For SPLA, redeployment stood at 10.6 per cent of the 59,168 troops initially stated as being present north of the line. The Joint Integrated Units reached 84.7 per cent of their mandated strength of 39,639 troops, with SAF soldiers comprising 52.4 per cent and SPLA 47.6 per cent of the total. However, the Units still lacked communication equipment, transport, administrative facilities, habitation, water and sanitation; and financial and logistical supply lines had yet to be unified.

Despite the adoption of the electoral law in July, other electoral preparations made little progress. The Political Parties Affairs Council had not been formed, and aspects of the broader legal framework needed to be brought into conformity with the Bill of Rights of the National Constitution of the Sudan.

The security situation in the UNMIS area of operations improved during the reporting period. In Abyei, the situation stabilized as road map implementation continued. In Southern Kordofan, reports of inter-ethnic violence declined, but the build-up of SAF and SPLA forces in the north-south border area remained a concern. Renewed clashes with LRA were reported, ending a period of relative calm. On 18 September, suspected LRA elements allegedly attacked an SPLA detachment near Yambio in Western Equatoria. It was reported that one SPLA soldier and three LRA rebels were killed, villagers were abducted and houses were looted and burned.

Restrictions on UNMIS freedom of movement were lifted in many areas and monitoring and verification denials decreased significantly, but some limitations remained, particularly in Sector VI (Abyei). In August, DPKO and the Department of Field Support (DFS) conducted a joint review of UNMIS military capabilities. Subject to budgetary approval, the study recommended the deployment of one additional company in Sector I (Juba), three in Sector IV (Kadugli) and two in Sector VI (Abyei). Sector V (Damazin) would be downsized from a four-company to a three-company battalion, with the fourth company being redeployed to protect the El Obeid Logistics Base. Implementation of the review would require an increase in the strength of UNMIS from 9,375 to 9,975 troops, which was within the mandated strength of 10,000 under Security Council resolution 1590(2005) [YUN 2005, p. 304].

A DPKO fact-finding team visited the Sudan from 9 to 12 August in the wake of questions regarding UNMIS actions during the Abyei crisis in May. The team found that, while most of Abyei's population left before the fighting reached its peak, UNMIS protected a large group of people inside its compound. It recommended that the Mission review its overall deployment, with a view to reinforcing Sector VI (Abyei) and other possible flashpoints, and develop an effective conflict-management strategy. The team's recommendations were incorporated into planning and reflected in the military capability review.

UNMIS continued to work with the parties to advance plans for starting the disarmament, demobilization and reintegration programme. On 9 September, the National Disarmament, Demobilization and Reintegration Coordination Council agreed to conduct a pilot programme for 700 to 1,000 beneficiaries. UNMIS, through the United Nations Children's Fund (UNICEF), began reintegration activities for 88 children who were demobilized in May. Reintegration activities were ongoing for children previously demobilized in Khartoum, Gedaref and Southern Kordofan states. In eastern Sudan, UNDP supported the demobilization of 1,700 former combatants.

Sporadic spontaneous returns continued, but organized repatriation of refugees and internally displaced persons (IDPs) came to a complete halt as hazardous road conditions, incompatible school calendars in asylum countries and the beginning of the planting season contributed to an unfavourable climate for further returns. By mid-September, the Office of the United Nations High Commissioner for Refugees (UNHCR) reported a total for organized and assisted refugee repatriation of 137,620 people, of whom 60,655 arrived in 2008. Since the signing of the Peace Agreement in 2005, the grand total, including spontaneous returns, had reached 294,450.

Humanitarian programmes progressed in the areas of road construction, mine clearance, vaccination and the training of teachers, lawyers, police and Government officials. More than 85,000 IDPs were assisted in the first half of the year, and 3.4 million received food assistance. The Government in July signed the United Nations Development Assistance Framework (UNDAF) 2009–2012, and UN agencies were translating it into programmes that would start in 2009. On 16 August, UNMIS received a written request for electoral assistance from the Government of Southern Sudan and confirmed its intention to provide assistance in line with its mandate. A parallel request from authorities in Khartoum was expected, and assistance would be forthcoming. To date, UNMIS mine-action teams had cleared 2,107 of the 3,956 areas identified as dangerous, and opened 27,155 kilometres of road.

The Secretary-General observed that the lack of mutual trust and confidence between NCP and SPLM remained the main challenge to the implementation of the Comprehensive Peace Agreement, and urged the leaders to improve their relationship in the spirit of the Agreement. He urged the Presidency to agree on the Border Commission's technical report, which was expected to be submitted by mid-October to ensure the start of the demarcation process. He urged the parties to lift all remaining restrictions of movement for UNMIS, and urged close coordination between the Ceasefire Political Commission and the Joint Defence Board to ensure that the Commission's decisions were implemented without delay. The Government was urged to cooperate with ICC and put in place an effective national judicial and political process.

Year-end developments. In a later report [S/2009/61], the Secretary-General said that the overall security situation in the UNMIS area of operations was relatively stable, but remained fragile and unpredictable in certain areas. On 12 December, a firefight broke out between members of the Joint Integrated Unit and the Joint Integrated Police Unit in Abyei town, killing one and injuring nine. The situation was calmed following immediate intervention by the commanders of the Units, the Chief Administrator, the Secretary-General's Special Representative and the Area Joint Military Committee. The Joint Integrated Unit redeployed to its new headquarters north of Abyei town. The personnel of both Units were disarmed, except for those on duty, and UNMIS began patrolling the town with armoured personnel carriers. Following the refusal by LRA leader Joseph Kony to sign the Juba Final Peace Agreement on 29 November, Ugandan, Congolese and Southern Sudanese forces launched a joint operation on 14 December against LRA positions in the northern Democratic Republic of the Congo. SPLA subsequently deployed forces along the border to prevent spillover from the fighting.

Tribal conflict remained a security problem throughout Southern Sudan. In Warrab state, 16 died in clashes between Lou Areik and Apuk Padoy on 20 October. On 8 December, Dinka Lou Areik and Dinka Apuk Bol clashed in Adhaul village, killing six. On 10 November, a dispute among armed civilians in Unbill escalated into widespread fighting among clans, displacing more than 7,500 households.

Regarding the implementation of the Comprehensive Peace Agreement, the Secretary-General reported that the Chief Administrator of Abyei, Arop Moyak Monytoc, the Deputy Chief Administrator, Rahama Abderahman Al-Nour, and five other members of the Abyei Area Administration took office on 11 November. The return of some 50,000 civilians displaced during fighting in the Abyei area in May was slow, with up to 10,000 returning to the Abyei area north of the Kiir River, and about 5,000 each to Abyei town and villages north of the river between July and December. An estimated two thirds of the returned population fled again during the incident of 12 December in Abyei.

SAF and SPLA failed to meet the deadline of 12 December agreed by the Ceasefire Joint Monitoring Commission for the withdrawal of their remaining forces in Diffra and Agok. At the Commission meeting of 17 December, the parties agreed to 15 January 2009 as the new deadline. On 19 December, 39 SPLA military police were withdrawn from Agok to the south of the Abyei road map area, along with some 226 armed personnel of various Southern Sudan security forces. On 1 November, 30 personnel of the Joint Integrated Unit from Balom deployed to Banjideed to provide security along migration routes. Following the incident of 12 December, all Units were withdrawn from Abyei town and 257 Joint Integrated Police Unit personnel were tasked with maintaining law and order there.

On 30 October, the presiding officer of the Permanent Court of the Arbitration Tribunal for the Abyei dispute accepted his appointment, thereby formally establishing the Tribunal. On 19 November, the Ceasefire Political Commission and the Joint Defence Board held their first joint session, attended by the Secretary-General's Special Representative. On 26 November, the UNMIS Force Commander presented to the Ceasefire Political Commission the report of the Ceasefire Joint Monitoring Commission on the May violence in Abyei; the co-chairpersons of the Ceasefire Political Commission vowed to implement the recommendations of the report. The National Elections Commission was sworn in on 25 November, but more time would be required for it to reach the operational capacity to complete election preparations. The Political Parties Affairs Council, required to register political parties, was established in late November.

Regarding the political situation, SPLM and nine southern political parties met in Juba from 8 to 13 November, the first south-south dialogue since 2005. The parties reserved the right to reject census results; reiterated the importance of adhering to the elections schedule set by the Peace Agreement; urged the Government of National Unity to provide the logistics and funding necessary to complete border demarcation before the general elections; and called for the National Assembly to enact the Southern Sudan Referendum Law immediately. On 16 October, NCP, SPLM, the Umma Party, the Democratic Unionist Party (DUP) and other national parties attended the first session of the Sudan People's Forum in Khartoum, with hopes of resolving the Darfur conflict and other major national issues. The meeting reconvened the following day in Kenana (White Nile state) under the chairmanship of President Al-Bashir and established a 13-member presidential council and seven subcommittees chaired by eminent political and civil society actors.

In November, UNMIS facilitated the first round table of political parties in Western Equatoria state. Nine parties participated, including SPLM and NCP, marking the first time the parties discussed the electoral law, the political parties act and the role of political parties throughout the election cycle. UNMIS also facilitated a Dinka Malual/Misseriya Humr reconciliation conference in Northern Bahr el Ghazal (11–14 November); participants agreed that unarmed Misseriya pastoralists should have unhindered access to grazing areas and water points in the south. As at 17 December, 99.7 per cent of UNMIS military personnel (9,346 out of 9,375) were deployed in the Sudan, including 622 military observers, 190 staff officers and 8,534 troops. Movement restrictions continued to hamper UNMIS monitoring and verification in some parts of its area of operation. As at 1 December, UNMIS had deployed 84 per cent of its mandated police strength (677 police advisers, including 60 women) to 22 sites throughout the mission area.

Spontaneous returns of IDPs and refugees declined towards the end of the year, as major religious holidays and impassable overland routes discouraged extensive relocation. In 2008, 129,950 IDPs and refugees returned through United Nations or other organized programmes, and 325,438 returned spontaneously.

Children and armed conflict

In February [S/AC.51/2008/7], the Security Council Working Group on Children and Armed Conflict submitted its conclusions on parties in the armed conflict in the Sudan, having examined the Secretary-General's 2007 report on children and armed conflict in the Sudan [YUN 2007, p. 244] on 18 September 2007. The Group recommended that the Security Council address letters on that issue to the Government of National Unity, the Secretary-General and the President of the AU Peace and Security Council. It issued a public statement in which it condemned the recruitment of children and other violations and abuses, especially gender-based and sexual violence against children in the Sudan. It urged all parties to protect the civilian population, especially children; release all children within their ranks; refrain from new child recruitment; respect the neutrality of refugee camps, IDP settlements, schools and medical facilities; end and prevent rape and other gender-based violence by members of their groups; and allow unimpeded and secure access for humanitarian assistance to children. The Group further agreed to address letters to the UNICEF Executive Director, the World Bank and donors.

UNMIS

The United Nations Mission in the Sudan (UNMIS), established by Security Council resolution 1590(2005) [YUN 2005, p. 304], continued to support implementation of the Comprehensive Peace Agreement signed by the Government of the Sudan and SPLM/A; facilitate and coordinate the voluntary return of refugees and IDPs, and humanitarian assistance; assist with demining; and protect and promote human rights. UNMIS was headed by the Special Representative of the Secretary-General in the Sudan, Ashraf Jehangir Qazi (Pakistan). In April, the Council extended the UNMIS mandate until 30 April 2009.

As at 31 December, UNMIS comprised 8,726 troops, 620 military observers and 679 police personnel.

Appointment. By an exchange of letters between the Secretary-General and the Security Council on 20 and 23 May [S/2008/339, S/2008/340], Major General Paban Thapa (Nepal) was appointed UNMIS Force Commander, replacing Lieutenant General Jasbir Singh Lidder (India).

Financing

In March [A/62/749], the Secretary-General submitted the performance report on the UNMIS budget for the period from 1 July 2006 to 30 June 2007. In April [A/62/785 & Corr.1], he submitted the proposed UNMIS budget for the period from 1 July 2008 to 30 June 2009, which amounted to $838,265,900.

In June [A/62/781/Add.16], ACABQ recommended that the General Assembly appropriate $820,720,600 for the 12-month period from 1 July 2008 to 30 June 2009, $17,545,300 less than the amount proposed by the Secretary-General.

GENERAL ASSEMBLY ACTION

On 20 June [meeting 109], the General Assembly, on the recommendation of the Fifth Committee [A/62/880], adopted **resolution 62/267** without vote [agenda item 155].

Financing of the United Nations Mission in the Sudan

The General Assembly,

Having considered the reports of the Secretary-General on the financing of the United Nations Mission in the Sudan and the related report of the Advisory Committee on Administrative and Budgetary Questions,

Recalling Security Council resolution 1590(2005) of 24 March 2005, by which the Council established the United Nations Mission in the Sudan for an initial period of six months as from 24 March 2005, and the subsequent resolutions by which the Council extended the mandate of the Mission, the latest of which was resolution 1812(2008) of 30 April 2008, by which the Council extended the mandate of the Mission until 30 April 2009,

Recalling also its resolution 59/292 of 21 April 2005 on the financing of the Mission and its subsequent resolutions thereon, the latest of which was resolution 61/289 of 29 June 2007,

Recalling further its resolution 58/315 of 1 July 2004,

Reaffirming the general principles underlying the financing of United Nations peacekeeping operations, as stated in General Assembly resolutions 1874(S-IV) of 27 June 1963, 3101(XXVIII) of 11 December 1973 and 55/235 of 23 December 2000,

Noting with appreciation that voluntary contributions have been made to the trust fund in support of the peace process in the Sudan,

Mindful of the fact that it is essential to provide the Mission with the financial resources necessary to enable it to fulfil its responsibilities under the relevant resolutions of the Security Council,

1. *Requests* the Secretary-General to entrust the Head of Mission with the task of formulating future budget proposals in full accordance with the provisions of General Assembly resolutions 59/296 of 22 June 2005, 60/266 of 30 June 2006 and 61/276 of 29 June 2007, as well as other relevant resolutions;

2. *Takes note* of the status of contributions to the United Nations Mission in the Sudan as at 30 April 2008, including the contributions outstanding in the amount of 167.3 million United States dollars, representing some 5 per cent of the total assessed contributions, notes with concern that only thirty Member States have paid their assessed contributions in full, and urges all other Member States, in particular those in arrears, to ensure payment of their outstanding assessed contributions;

3. *Expresses its appreciation* to those Member States which have paid their assessed contributions in full, and urges all other Member States to make every possible effort to ensure payment of their assessed contributions to the Mission in full;

4. *Expresses concern* at the financial situation with regard to peacekeeping activities, in particular as regards the reimbursements to troop contributors that bear additional burdens owing to overdue payments by Member States of their assessments;

5. *Also expresses concern* at the delay experienced by the Secretary-General in deploying and providing adequate resources to some recent peacekeeping missions, in particular those in Africa;

6. *Emphasizes* that all future and existing peacekeeping missions shall be given equal and non-discriminatory treatment in respect of financial and administrative arrangements;

7. *Also emphasizes* that all peacekeeping missions shall be provided with adequate resources for the effective and efficient discharge of their respective mandates;

8. *Reiterates its request* to the Secretary-General to make the fullest possible use of facilities and equipment at the United Nations Logistics Base at Brindisi, Italy, in order to minimize the costs of procurement for the Mission;

9. *Endorses* the conclusions and recommendations contained in the report of the Advisory Committee on Administrative and Budgetary Questions, subject to the provisions of the present resolution, and requests the Secretary-General to ensure their full implementation;

10. *Reaffirms* section XX of resolution 61/276, and encourages the Secretary-General, where feasible, to enhance regional and inter-mission cooperation with a view to achieving greater synergies in the use of the resources of the Organization and the implementation of mandates of the missions, while bearing in mind that individual missions are responsible for the preparation and implementation of their own budgets and for controlling their own assets and logistical operations;

11. *Also reaffirms* paragraph 32 of its resolution 62/232 of 22 December 2007;

12. *Requests* the Secretary-General to ensure that future budget submissions contain sufficient information, explanation and justification of the proposed resource requirements relating to operational costs in order to allow Member States to take well-informed decisions;

13. *Decides* to approve 20 of the 28 United Nations Volunteers for property management proposed by the Secretary-General in paragraph 101 of his report;

14. *Takes note* of paragraphs 45 and 50 of the report of the Advisory Committee;

15. *Requests* the Secretary-General, in his next overview report, to include information on the environmental policy, guidelines and pilot study as referred to in paragraph 174 of the report of the Secretary-General;

16. *Also requests* the Secretary-General to ensure the full implementation of the relevant provisions of its resolutions 59/296, 60/266 and 61/276;

17. *Further requests* the Secretary-General to take all necessary action to ensure that the Mission is administered with a maximum of efficiency and economy;

18. *Requests* the Secretary-General, in order to reduce the cost of employing General Service staff, to continue efforts to recruit local staff for the Mission against General Service posts, commensurate with the requirements of the Mission;

Financial performance report for the period from 1 July 2006 to 30 June 2007

19. *Takes note* of the report of the Secretary-General on the financial performance of the Mission for the period from 1 July 2006 to 30 June 2007;

Budget estimates for the period from 1 July 2008 to 30 June 2009

20. *Decides* to appropriate to the Special Account for the United Nations Mission in the Sudan the amount of 858,771,200 dollars for the period from 1 July 2008 to 30 June 2009, inclusive of 820,720,600 dollars for the maintenance of the Mission, 33,169,900 dollars for the support account for peacekeeping operations and 4,880,700 dollars for the United Nations Logistics Base;

Financing of the appropriation

21. *Also decides* to apportion among Member States the amount of 715,642,666 dollars for the period from 1 July 2008 to 30 April 2009, in accordance with the levels updated in General Assembly resolution 61/243 of 22 December 2006, and taking into account the scale of assessments for 2008, as set out in its resolution 61/237 of 22 December 2006;

22. *Further decides* that, in accordance with the provisions of its resolution 973(X) of 15 December 1955, there shall be set off against the apportionment among Member States, as provided for in paragraph 21 above, their respective share in the Tax Equalization Fund of 18,685,833 dollars, comprising the estimated staff assessment income of 15,708,583 dollars approved for the Mission, the prorated share of 2,655,917 dollars of the estimated staff assessment income approved for the support account and the prorated share of 321,333 dollars of the estimated staff assessment income approved for the United Nations Logistics Base;

23. *Decides* to apportion among Member States the amount of 143,128,534 dollars for the period from 1 May to 30 June 2009, at a monthly rate of 71,564,267 dollars, in accordance with the levels updated in resolution 61/243, and taking into account the scale of assessments for 2008 and 2009, as set out in resolution 61/237, subject to a decision of the Security Council to extend the mandate of the Mission;

24. *Also decides* that, in accordance with the provisions of its resolution 973(X), there shall be set off against the apportionment among Member States, as provided for in paragraph 23 above, their respective share in the Tax Equalization Fund of 3,737,167 dollars, comprising the estimated staff assessment income of 3,141,717 dollars approved for the Mission, the prorated share of 531,183 dollars of the estimated staff assessment income approved for the support account and the prorated share of 64,267 dollars of the estimated staff assessment income approved for the United Nations Logistics Base;

25. *Further decides* that, for Member States that have fulfilled their financial obligations to the Mission, there shall be set off against their apportionment, as provided for in paragraph 21 above, their respective share of the unencumbered balance and other income in the total amount of 159,505,000 dollars in respect of the financial period ended 30 June 2007, in accordance with the levels updated in resolution 61/243, and taking into account the scale of assessments for 2007, as set out in resolution 61/237;

26. *Decides* that, for Member States that have not fulfilled their financial obligations to the Mission, there shall be set off against their outstanding obligations their respective share of the unencumbered balance and other income in the total amount of 159,505,000 dollars in respect of the financial period ended 30 June 2007, in accordance with the scheme set out in paragraph 25 above;

27. *Also decides* that the decrease of 1,662,100 dollars in the estimated staff assessment income in respect of the financial period ended 30 June 2007 shall be set off against the credits from the amount of 159,505,000 dollars referred to in paragraphs 25 and 26 above;

28. *Emphasizes* that no peacekeeping mission shall be financed by borrowing funds from other active peacekeeping missions;

29. *Encourages* the Secretary-General to continue to take additional measures to ensure the safety and security of all personnel participating in the Mission under the auspices of the United Nations, bearing in mind paragraphs 5 and 6 of Security Council resolution 1502(2003) of 26 August 2003;

30. *Invites* voluntary contributions to the Mission in cash and in the form of services and supplies acceptable to the Secretary-General, to be administered, as appropriate, in accordance with the procedure and practices established by the General Assembly;

31. *Decides* to include in the provisional agenda of its sixty-third session the item entitled "Financing of the United Nations Mission in the Sudan".

The Assembly, by **decision 63/552** of 24 December, decided that the agenda item on UNMIS financing would remain for consideration during its resumed sixty-third (2009) session.

Darfur

The security situation in the Darfur region of the Sudan deteriorated, even as deployment of the African Union-United Nations Hybrid Operation in Darfur (UNAMID) continued. In January, Chadian regular forces targeted Chadian rebels in Darfur in air attacks, and a convoy of vehicles carrying rations for UNAMID personnel in Western Darfur was attacked by the Sudanese Armed Forces (SAF). In February, SAF and allied militia attacked Abu Suruj, a former Justice and Equality Movement (JEM) stronghold, and other areas in Western Darfur. The Government started a military campaign in Northern Darfur in September and engaged in further military operations in October. Despite a unilateral declaration of a cessation of hostilities by the Government on 12 November, its forces conducted aerial bombings in Northern and Western Darfur during that month. Southern Darfur also experienced an upsurge in violence, as Government patrols were attacked. Inter-tribal fighting continued in Northern and Southern Darfur, and targeted attacks against humanitarian workers and their assets hindered the provision of assistance to the civilian population.

On 16 November, the Sudan extended until 31 January 2010 fast-track measures facilitating humanitarian aid to Darfur based on a joint communiqué between the Sudan and the United Nations. A status-of-forces agreement between UNAMID and the Sudan was signed on 9 February. Nevertheless, UNAMID deployment progressed slowly and faced significant challenges, including insufficient troops and equipment. In July, a UNAMID patrol was attacked in Darfur, resulting in the death of seven peacekeepers, and a UNAMID officer was killed by unknown gunmen. At year's end, UNAMID strength stood at 63 per cent of the authorized total of military personnel. On 30 June, the Secretary-General appointed Djibrill Yipènè Bassolé (Burkina Faso) as the Joint African Union-United Nations Chief Mediator for Darfur.

On 1 February [S/2008/130], the Secretary-General informed the Security Council that he had extended the appointment of his Special Envoy for Darfur, Jan Eliasson, until 30 June.

Political and security situation

Security Council consideration. On 9 January [meeting 5817], the Under-Secretary-General for Peacekeeping Operations, Jean-Marie Guéhenno, briefed the Security Council on challenges and impediments to the deployment of UNAMID, established in 2007 [YUN 2007, p. 251], and on the security situation in Darfur. He reported that a number of outstanding issues undermining UNAMID deployment were directly dependent on the outcome of discussions with the Government of the Sudan. Regarding the composition of the UNAMID military component, the Government expressed its objections to the deployment of units from Thailand and Nepal, and verbally rejected a combined Nordic engineering unit. The Government had agreed that it would be ready to begin consultations on the status-of-forces agreement on 13 December 2007, but no interlocutor had been made available for such discussions. UNAMID was also unable to finalize the agreement with the Government on a suitable piece of land in El Geneina for the Operation. However, the Government released impounded communications equipment and was permitting UNAMID to use the El Obeid logistics hub as a staging area.

Mr. Guéhenno stated that UNAMID was functioning as a 're-hatted' version of the African Union Mission in the Sudan (AMIS), with few additional troops or police having arrived in the mission area since the transfer of authority from AMIS to UNAMID on 31 December 2007 [ibid., p. 259]. New UNAMID units needed to be deployed more rapidly if the Operation was to have an impact on the Darfur situation in the first half of 2008. Advance parties of Egyptian and Ethiopian infantry battalions were expected to be in Darfur by the end of February, pending the resolution of outstanding issues, and the remainder of the Chinese engineering unit was expected by March. Most of the enabling units were expected to deploy before June, and five remaining battalions were scheduled to deploy in the latter half of the year. Deployment challenges were compounded by shortfalls in critical areas, including the provision of transportation and aviation assets.

As UNAMID deployment accelerated, the security situation in Darfur deteriorated dramatically. On 2 January, JEM seized the Government-controlled towns of Sirba and Abu Suruj. In the press and in discussions with UN officials in the field, JEM leader Khalil Ibrahim repeatedly threatened to attack the Western Darfur state capital, El Geneina. The Secretary-General had condemned the acts of aggression by JEM.

On 7 January, a UNAMID convoy of more than 20 clearly marked vehicles carrying rations for UNAMID personnel in Western Darfur was attacked by SAF using light weapons and rocket-propelled grenades as it travelled from Um Baru to Tine; the convoy's movements had been confirmed with the Government and rebel movements in advance. A civilian Sudanese driver suffered gunshot wounds. UNAMID troops elected not to return fire and took up a defensive position. The convoy reached Tine and the driver received medical treatment there.

Statement by Secretary-General. In a press statement of 8 January [SG/SM/11362], the Secretary-General condemned the attack of 7 January and stressed that, for the Operation to be able to perform its mandated functions, the Government had to provide unequivocal guarantees that there would be no recurrence of such activities by its forces.

SECURITY COUNCIL ACTION

On 11 January [meeting 5818], following consultations among Security Council members, the President made statement **S/PRST/2008/1** on behalf of the Council:

> The Security Council condemns in the strongest possible terms the attack on 7 January 2008 by elements of the Sudanese Armed Forces, as confirmed by the African Union United Nations Hybrid Operation in Darfur (UNAMID), on a UNAMID supply convoy. The Council stresses that any attack on or threat against UNAMID is unacceptable, and demands that there be no recurrence of attacks on UNAMID. The Council welcomes the commitment of the Government of the Sudan to undertake a complete and full investigation into the incident, together with the United Nations and the African Union.
>
> The Council welcomes the transition of authority from the African Union peacekeeping operation, the African

Union Mission in the Sudan, to UNAMID, which occurred on 31 December 2007. The Council commends the Mission for its prompt action to begin to re establish peace and security in Darfur.

The Council calls upon the Government of the Sudan to expedite full compliance with Council resolution 1769(2007), including by concluding all the necessary arrangements for the expeditious deployment of an effective UNAMID force.

The Council further urges the Government of the Sudan and all armed groups to respect an immediate and complete ceasefire and demands that all parties cooperate fully with the deployment of UNAMID and respect its security and freedom of movement.

The Council reiterates that an inclusive political settlement and the successful deployment of UNAMID are essential for re-establishing peace and stability in Darfur. The Council urges all parties, including rebel groups, to engage fully and constructively in the political process under the leadership of the United Nations Special Envoy for Darfur, Mr. Jan Eliasson, and the African Union Special Envoy for Darfur, Mr. Salim Ahmed Salim, who have the full support of the Council. The Council expresses its readiness to take action against any party that impedes the peace process, humanitarian aid or the deployment of UNAMID. The Council also recognizes that due process must take its course.

The Council expresses concern about the deterioration of security and humanitarian conditions in Darfur and calls upon the United Nations and all Member States to facilitate the rapid and complete deployment of UNAMID. The Council urges capable Member States to contribute the helicopter and transportation units necessary to ensure the successful implementation of the mandate of UNAMID.

Report of Secretary-General (February). The Secretary-General, in his February report on UNAMID deployment [S/2008/98], said that during a visit to the Sudan in January by his Special Envoy and the AU Special Envoy, Salim Ahmed Salim, two of the five major movement groupings—the United Resistance Front (URF) and SLM/A-Unity—expressed their readiness to enter pre-negotiation talks under UN and AU auspices. The Special Envoys were consulting with representatives of SLM/A-Abdul Shafie, JEM-Khalil Ibrahim and SLM/A-Abdul Wahid in an effort to obtain a similar commitment. The format for the participation of Minni Minawi, a signatory of the 2006 Darfur Peace Agreement [YUN 2006, p. 274], remained unresolved.

Regarding the security situation, the Secretary-General reported that Chadian regular forces targeted Chadian rebels in Darfur in air attacks early in January. On 6 January, the Chadian Air Force bombed the villages of Gokar and Wadi Rady, about 25 kilometres south of El Geneina; six Chadian rebels were killed and four were seriously wounded. A total of 283 humanitarian staff based in the areas north and south of El Geneina that were affected by the fighting were forced to relocate to El Geneina and other areas in Darfur, effectively halting aid to the civilian population. Government forces on 13 January arrested a member of the JEM splinter faction Collective Leadership. On 17 January, following dialogue between UNAMID and the Sudanese authorities, all JEM members were released.

The top UNAMID leadership was fully deployed with the arrival in the Sudan on 18 January of the Deputy Joint Special Representative for Operations and Management. On 31 January, the strength of UNAMID stood at 9,126 uniformed personnel, including 7,476 military personnel, 1,510 police officers, and one formed police unit. A total of 1,256 civilians, representing 23 per cent of the authorized strength, were deployed. Eighty per cent of the force headquarters staff positions were filled, and 80 to 90 per cent of sector headquarters staffing, military observer posts and liaison officer posts were filled. UNAMID police absorbed 1,380 police officers from AMIS as well as 124 light and heavy support package personnel. Due to lack of office space at the current headquarters, UNAMID personnel were split over four sites across El Fasher, impeding efficiency. Reconfiguration of the force to be able to meet its mandated tasks was hampered by the slow pace of transfer of equipment from AMIS; in that regard, the AU liquidation team was working with UNAMID to ensure the transfer of key assets. Negotiations between UNAMID and the Government on the status-of-forces agreement resumed on 14 January in Khartoum; the agreement was signed by the AU-UN Joint Special Representative for Darfur, Rodolphe Adada, and the Sudanese Foreign Minister, Deng Alor, on 9 February.

The deployment of UNAMID continued to face challenges in generating critical capabilities and securing land and clearance for goods and equipment. The Operation was still short of pledges for one heavy and one medium ground transport unit; three military utility aviation units, consisting of 18 helicopters; and two attack helicopters in addition to the four pledged by Ethiopia. Many countries that were willing to contribute formed police units did not have the logistical capabilities required to fulfil the mandated tasks. At the same time, the United Nations and the AU were working with troop- and police-contributing countries to accelerate the pace of pre-deployment preparations.

The Under-Secretary-General for Peacekeeping Operations visited the region (21–29 January) to discuss with Government officials the outstanding issues related to UNAMID deployment and to survey development conditions. On 27 January, he met with the AU Commissioner for Peace and Security, Said Djinnit, and the Under-Secretary of State of the Sudan, Mutrif Siddiq, in Addis Ababa, Ethiopia. The meeting confirmed the need for enhanced cooperation between the AU and the United Nations and the Government with respect to UNAMID deployment.

Hostilities between Government and JEM-Khalil Ibrahim forces in Western Darfur and the continued build-up of their forces in the area severely undermined humanitarian conditions and access to civilians in need of assistance. The Secretary-General urged all parties to cooperate with the efforts of the Special Envoys to convene negotiations as soon as possible; reiterated his call on all parties to refrain from the use of force and begin negotiations; condemned cross-border attacks; and urged Chad and the Sudan to respect each other's territorial sovereignty and implement existing non-aggression agreements. He appealed to all UNAMID troop and police contributors to expedite the deployment of the units and assets pledged to the Operation. Member States were urged to provide the outstanding enabling units, including air assets, to permit UNAMID to achieve full operating capability.

Attacks in Western Darfur. On 8 February, SAF and allied militia attacked Abu Suruj, a former JEM stronghold located north of El Geneina in Western Darfur. The Government-led attack included hundreds of militia, over 130 vehicles, three attack helicopters, and at least one Antonov aircraft. Much of Abu Suruj was burned down during the attack, and thousands of civilians fled the fighting towards Chad and other areas. In an assessment conducted by UNAMID and humanitarian agencies on 12 February, Abu Suruj residents informed the assessment team that approximately 28 civilians had been killed in the attack, and that JEM forces had fled prior to the hostilities. Also on 8 February, a joint Government and militia force attacked Sirba, near Abu Suruj, killing approximately 42 civilians, including a tribal leader. Local residents reported that several thousand civilians fled Sirba during the attack, and indicated that almost half of the town was burned to the ground. Seleia, located north-east of Sirba, was bombed by Government aircraft that evening. In a press statement of 9 February [SG/SM/11406], the Secretary-General said that UNAMID had received preliminary reports confirming that an estimated 200 casualties resulted from the fighting. Condemning the attacks, he stressed that all parties had to adhere to international humanitarian law, which prohibited attacks against civilians.

The Government offensive resumed on 18 February, when SAF and allied militia attacked JEM and SLM/A-Abdul Wahid positions in Aro Sharow, Kandare and Kurlongo, situated in the Jebel Moon area of Western Darfur. During the attacks, SAF aircraft dropped at least five bombs in Aro Sharow and an additional eight bombs on Kandare and Kurlongo. Those areas hosted displaced civilians from the offensive of 8 February. A major build-up of Government forces around Jebel Moon followed the attacks of 18 February, including SAF, allied militia, heavy artillery and aircraft. Heavy fighting ensued for several days, with the Government directing its assault at the JEM and SML/A-Abdul Wahid forces that controlled the area. On 22 February, JEM and SLM/A-Abdul Wahid commanders called UNAMID senior leadership and humanitarian agencies, seeking UNAMID intervention to provide safe passage to civilians trapped by the fighting. Government officials subsequently indicated to the Joint Special Representative that they would be willing to identify a staging area in one of their controlled areas from which women and children could proceed to a safe area. The United Nations Humanitarian Coordinator for the Sudan estimated that there were nearly 20,000 civilians in the area. Although direct confrontation between the parties had largely ended by 25 February, reported troop movements to the area suggested that renewed violence was likely.

Reports of Secretary-General (March–May). In March [S/2008/196], the Secretary-General reported that on 29 February, a Government patrol was ambushed at Amr Gedid, approximately 80 kilometres north of Nyala, by SLM/A-Unity forces. Five Government soldiers were reportedly killed and eight injured. On the same day, a Government police patrol was attacked by a group of militia in Domaya, 7 kilometres north-west of Nyala, resulting in the deaths of two Government soldiers and the wounding of 14 others. On 1 March, a commercial convoy of 43 trucks and fuel tankers accompanied by a Government police escort was ambushed by SLM/A-Unity forces near Gabat Hamada, 85 kilometres north of Nyala; six Government soldiers were reportedly killed and six wounded. Government authorities in Nyala stated that a military and police convoy dispatched to the area recovered one of the four stolen tankers.

Incidents of inter-tribal fighting occurred in both Northern and Southern Darfur. On 27 February, a group of approximately 160 men on horses and camels from the Rizeigat and Salamat tribes attacked Habbaniya tribesmen in the town of El Sunita in Southern Darfur. Twenty-one people were reported killed, a number of civilians were injured, and parts of El Sunita were set ablaze. Six of the attackers were also reported to have been killed, and 21 captured. On 28 February, the Habbaniya retaliated, killing 60 people east of Gereida. In Northern Darfur, fighting between the Zaghawa and Beni Hussein tribes was reported to have displaced approximately 300 people.

Targeted attacks against humanitarian workers and their assets continued to constrain humanitarian operations. During the first two months of 2008, 54 vehicles were hijacked, including two UNAMID vehicles and 32 trucks contracted to the World Food Programme (WFP); 18 WFP-contracted drivers remained missing. During the same period, 14 humanitarian premises were attacked by armed persons and four humanitarian compounds were destroyed and looted during the surge in violence north of El Geneina. Since JEM's attack on the northern corridor of Western Darfur in December 2007 [YUN 2007, p. 259], the Government had denied humanitarian agencies access to areas north of Seraf Jidad, cutting off assistance to some 160,000 people. The Government indicated that access would not be granted until it regained control. An estimated 12,000 civilians, including humanitarian workers, fled into Chad as a result of the attacks of 8 February on Abu Suruj, Sirba and Seleia, and one aid worker was killed. During the attacks of 18 February, the Government banned all humanitarian flights to the north of El Geneina. As fighting subsided in some areas, humanitarian missions were able to visit Kondobe, Sirba, Abu Suruj, Seraf Jidad and Seleia.

With the deployment of the senior UNAMID leadership and a sizeable portion of international and civilian staff in place, a number of substantive units began their work. Mine-action teams began their operations in the Kutum area in Northern Darfur, clearing two bombs dropped by aircraft, followed by a mine-action assessment of approximately 40 square kilometres. The lack of sufficient military engineer units hindered construction of the Operation's infrastructure. With limited means, UNAMID was upgrading, expanding or relocating 32 camps in Darfur and establishing two additional camps. The 135-person advance party of the Chinese engineer company was permanently based at the UNAMID supercamp in Nyala, where it was developing the infrastructure for the Operation. The military component conducted several hundred short- and long-range patrols throughout Darfur on a monthly basis. Core elements of the Joint Operations, Mission Analysis and Logistics Centres were established in February.

The consultations of the AU-UN Special Envoys and the Joint Mediation Support Team saw an increased engagement of the five Darfur movement groups—JEM, SLM/A-Abdul Shafie, SLM/A-Abdul Wahid, SLM/A-Unity and the United Resistance Front (URF)—and the Government of National Unity. However, the security situation in Chad and in Western Darfur limited the ability of the mediators to conduct consultations with the movements, and the movements' ability to hold consultations among themselves. The Joint Mediation Support Team, UNAMID and the Darfur-Darfur Dialogue and Consultation worked together to finalize a plan of action and strategy for including civil society organizations, IDPs and tribal leaders in the political process. The Special Envoys held informal consultations with partners on 17 and 18 March in Geneva on the way forward.

The Secretary-General observed that tensions between Chad and the Sudan were having a destabilizing effect on Darfur. He called on both countries to stop supporting the other's rebel groups and address instability in the border area. He urged all parties to abandon military confrontation, commit themselves to the political process and provide full support and cooperation to the efforts led by the Special Envoys.

In response to Security Council resolution 1769(2007) [YUN 2007, p. 251], by which the Council authorized the establishment of UNAMID, the Secretary-General in April submitted a report [S/2008/249] on developments in Darfur, progress made in the implementation of the Operation, and the status of the political process between January and March. He said that at the end of the reporting period, SAF was still engaging JEM and elements of SLM/A in and around Jebel Moon. On 19 March, JEM reportedly ambushed an SAF convoy 65 kilometres north of El Geneina, killing 19 Government soldiers. Hostilities between rebel factions also occurred. Heavy fighting was reported on 19 March in Shurum, located 80 kilometres south-east of Nyala, between members of the SLM/A-Minni Minawi and SLM-Free Will factions, during which nine people were killed. UNAMID increased its patrol presence in the northern corridor of Western Darfur state, and plans were made to deploy a permanent contingent as soon as possible. On 19 March, the Deputy Joint Special Representative and the military Chief of Staff visited Seleia to explore options for a more permanent UNAMID deployment in the area.

Military operations conducted by SAF and militias in the northern corridor of Western Darfur during the first three months of the year caused dozens of civilian fatalities and the displacement of an estimated 60,000 people. More than 90,000 people had been displaced across Darfur. By the end of March, thousands of people had returned to their places of origin, especially in Abu Suruj and Sirba, but many more remained displaced. Humanitarian access was constrained by insecurity, restrictions created by the parties and subsequent limitations on the use of air assets. Operations were also constrained by targeted attacks against humanitarian workers and their assets. During the reporting period, 73 vehicles were hijacked, including 3 UNAMID vehicles and 45 trucks contracted by WFP.

Regarding UNAMID deployment, the equipment and vehicles of the Bangladesh multi-role logistics company and Nigerian level II hospital arrived in the Sudan and were expected to reach Nyala and El Geneina, respectively, in April, with their personnel following in May. The Secretary-General and President Al-Bashir discussed UNAMID deployment on the margins of the eleventh summit of the Organization of the Islamic Conference (OIC) (Dakar, Senegal, 13–14

March). They agreed that UNAMID would accept one additional battalion from Egypt and another from Ethiopia, following which the deployment of the Thai and Nepalese units would be expedited. The Force Commander made clear the priority of bringing the 10 UNAMID battalions up to UN standards in terms of troop numbers and self-sustainment capability. While the contributing countries were able to generate the required number of troops, many were finding it difficult to procure the necessary equipment. The Government agreed in principle to the right of UNAMID to conduct night flights, but it continued to restrict the Operation's flying hours.

In May [S/2008/304], the Secretary-General reported that significant clashes occurred between the rebel movements and Government forces, as well as armed factions of the rebel movements, especially in the states of Western and Southern Darfur. On 12 April, JEM attacked an SAF post at Kush Kush, located 15 kilometres north-west of Seleia; SAF retaliated by conducting air attacks and shelling JEM positions near Seleia. Sixty-two civilians were killed in the attacks. On the same day, SLM/A-Abdul Wahid attacked SAF in the Kass area south of Jebel Marra, reportedly killing 17 Government police officers. On 16 April, SLM/A-Minni Minawi and SLM/A-Free Will clashed east of Nyala, resulting in three reported fatalities. Tribal fighting over livestock continued between the Habbaniya and Salamat in Southern Darfur. On 17 April, several hundred Habbaniya on horseback and 31 vehicles clashed with the Salamat, resulting in 31 Habbaniya fatalities. Six Salamat were reportedly killed. Tension arose in El Fasher between SAF and Government-allied militia, reportedly due to the Government's failure to pay the militia their expected salaries. The militia looted the El Fasher market on 6 April, resulting in one civilian death. On 29 April, one woman was killed and property and livestock were destroyed during SAF aerial attacks and fighting between Government and rebel forces in the SLM/A-controlled area of El Hashim and Heles, north of Kutum in Northern Darfur. On 2 May, UNAMID airlifted eight civilians wounded in an SAF air attack on the village of Umm Sidir in Northern Darfur the previous day, which had also left two men dead. On 4 May, three people were killed and one was seriously injured when an unidentified aircraft bombed the villages of Ein Bessar and Hatan in Northern Darfur. The same day, an unidentified aircraft bombed Shegeg Karo village, killing 12 people and wounding 27. On 5 May, the Government denied UNAMID permission to evacuate the wounded civilians from Shegeg Karo.

On 29 April, a convoy of three commercial vehicles carrying two UNAMID containers of equipment from El Obeid to Nyala was hijacked near Abu Karinka, Southern Darfur, by 30 unidentified armed men in two vehicles. UNAMID immediately notified the Government and began patrols and an aerial search for the missing trucks and cargo. UNAMID leadership requested the assistance of the Government in addressing the backlog of UNAMID cargo at Port Sudan, streamlining the customs clearance process and ensuring security along the main transportation routes. UNAMID was augmenting inland road transport with cargo airlifts from El Obeid to El Fasher. Regarding recruitment, 40 international staff selected for UNAMID appointment declined the offer and many short-listed candidates failed to confirm interest in being interviewed for posts, citing reasons related to the harsh living and working conditions in Darfur. A team from DPKO and the Department of Field Support (DFS) visited the Sudan in April to identify ways to expedite deployment. The team and UNAMID developed an enhanced deployment plan, which aimed at achieving 80 per cent deployment of the authorized strength of the Operation by the end of 2008. To achieve that target, the rotations of the 10 infantry battalions already deployed had to meet the UN standard for strength and equipment; six new battalions—including two from Ethiopia, two from Egypt, one from Senegal and one from Thailand—and two new companies from Nepal would have to deploy; vital enabling units, including engineer, transportation, logistics and medical units, should deploy before the rainy season; and 11 additional formed police units should deploy. Agreements for land were finalized for building supercamps at El Fasher, Nyala, Zalingei and El Geneina, as well as a camp for substantive personnel at El Geneina. The schedule for AMIS liquidation was developed, verification of assets continued, and a coordination mechanism for land and other third-party claims was established. It was anticipated that the handover of former AMIS equipment and assets to UNAMID would be completed in June, but other AMIS liquidation processes, including land and claims issues, were likely to continue beyond that date.

UNAMID increased significantly its patrolling and investigation activities, including joint military and police patrols in Western Darfur's northern corridor, where large numbers of civilians were displaced during the fighting in February. UNAMID police entered the second phase of a three-phase patrolling plan for the camps for internally displaced persons, expanding the duration of its daily patrols to cover the period from 8 a.m. to midnight. At the end of April, UNAMID was implementing more than 50 quick-impact projects, totalling more than $1 million, in cooperation with community partners, universities, the UN country team and international agencies.

The Special Envoys undertook two missions to the Sudan in April, during which they urged the parties to cease hostilities, improve the security environment, and intensify their preparations for substantive talks.

Security Council mission. The Security Council mission (see p. 111) that visited five African countries from 31 May to 10 June [S/2008/460] met with the Governor of Northern Darfur and with representatives of the humanitarian community there. It also met with representatives of internally displaced persons living in the Zam Zam camp in Northern Darfur, and assured them that the Council would do everything in its power to improve their circumstances. In a meeting with the mission on 4 June, the Sudanese Minister for Foreign Affairs, Deng Alor, indicated that the Government remained committed to the ceasefire and to resolving the situation through the political process, and asked for the international community's continued assistance in bringing the parties to the negotiating table. The mission stated that the Darfur crisis was its principal focus, and asked that the understanding reached between the Secretary-General and President Al-Bashir with regard to the deployment of Thai and Nepalese troops under UNAMID be confirmed in writing. It stressed the need for the Government of National Unity to abide by the agreements reached with the Darfur humanitarian community, particularly the 2007 joint communiqué on the facilitation of humanitarian activities [YUN 2007, p. 248], and the importance of the Government's full cooperation with ICC.

Presidential Adviser Nafie Ali Nafie informed the mission that the Government had shown flexibility in the implementation of resolution 1769(2007) [YUN 2007, p. 251]. The mission welcomed the Government's improved coordination with UNAMID, but stressed that there were still areas in which greater cooperation was needed. In particular, the mission asked for the removal of all limitations on the freedom of movement of UNAMID, including its ability to use Darfur airports 24 hours per day. The Adviser confirmed the understanding reached by President Al-Bashir and the Secretary-General on the deployment of the Thai and Nepalese units following the arrival of the Ethiopian and Egyptian battalions.

President Al-Bashir reiterated to the mission his Government's commitment to the political process, as well as his conviction that the military option could not lead to a durable solution. The Government had delivered on its commitment regarding UNAMID deployment, and he urged all stakeholders to contribute to the assets still missing in the UNAMID force. He confirmed the Sudan's commitment to facilitating the work of the humanitarian community in Darfur, and indicated that the joint communiqué on the issue was being implemented. The President also confirmed that the Government was willing to provide escorts for UNAMID supply convoys if so requested. As to allowing UNAMID flights to operate at night, he encouraged the United Nations to improve the airports and road infrastructure in Darfur, which the Government could not afford to do.

The mission recommended that the Council renew its demand that all parties in Darfur cease hostilities and engage in the political process, and stand ready to take action against any party that undermined the peace process. The United Nations should take forward President Al-Bashir's agreements regarding the deployment of the Thai and Nepalese troops as soon as Egyptian and Ethiopian troops arrived; the protection of UN land convoys; the upgrading of Darfur airports; and the operation of UN flights 24 hours per day. The United Nations should appoint a chief mediator to spearhead AU-UN efforts on Darfur. The Government and all other parties to the conflict should cooperate with ICC, consistent with resolution 1593(2005) [YUN 2005, p. 324] and bearing in mind presidential statement S/PRST/2008/21 (see p. 259).

Report of Secretary-General (June). In June [S/2008/400], the Secretary-General said that following the JEM attack on Omdurman on 10 May, UNAMID reported movement of JEM personnel throughout Darfur, including 19 JEM vehicles arriving in El Daein in Southern Darfur on 12 May and 27 vehicles moving from the Dar El Salam area to Daba Tuga in Northern Darfur on 12 and 13 May. On 15 May, the Government issued a decree, initiated and signed by Minni Minawi, to establish a committee to "remove the negative consequences of the Omdurman attack on Darfur civilians" in cooperation with legal and security bodies. The Government pursued JEM elements in Darfur, and at least 11 civilians were reportedly arrested in El Geneina and surrounding IDP camps by the National Intelligence and Security Service at the end of May.

Clashes continued between tribal groups, between rebel movements, and between rebel movements and the Government and its affiliated forces. On 8 and 15 May, fighting broke out between Zaghawa and Birgit groups south-east of Nyala, resulting in the deaths of at least seven people. On 15 and 19 May, fighting between SLA-Minni Minawi and SLA-Free Will factions reportedly resulted in the deaths of five SLA-Minni Minawi combatants and 13 civilians. On 21 May, Janjaweed militia members attacked a vehicle transporting SLA-Minni Minawi soldiers near the Kabkabiya market in Northern Darfur, killing one SLA-Minni Minawi combatant. SLA-Unity expressed support for the JEM attack on Omdurman and, on 26 May, made a public threat to attack Khartoum.

Regarding UNAMID deployment, the Secretary-General said that the plan to achieve 80 per cent of deployment by the end of 2008 was based on the assumption that the Operation's engineering capability would be reinforced immediately. To that end, a multi-pronged strategy was being pursued, consisting of the accelerated deployment of engineer units; the temporary transfer of UNMIS engineer assets to UNAMID; a request for UNAMID troop contributors to swap one company from each incoming battalion with a pioneer company with light engineering capability; and building the capacity of local Sudanese construction companies. The JEM attack on Omdurman on 10 May delayed the deployment of new troops to Darfur and rotations of troops already present. Nevertheless, the rotation of the South African battalion was completed on 16 May; a Nigerian battalion also completed rotation on 20 May, but not at the UN standard strength. The slow movement of equipment from Port Sudan to Darfur was due largely to insecurity, in addition to lengthy customs clearances and the limited number of local contractors. The deployment of formed police units and their equipment was also delayed.

The Special Envoys held informal consultations (Geneva, 4–5 June) with regional and international partners to assess the political situation and discuss ways to take the mediation process forward. The Envoys called for the parties to exercise maximum restraint, abstain from further military action and engage in the political process. They stressed the need for the normalization of relations between Chad and the Sudan and for progress on implementation of the Comprehensive Peace Agreement [YUN 2005, p. 301].

Appointment. On 30 June [S/2008/438], the Secretary-General informed the Security Council that he, jointly with the AU Commission Chairperson, had appointed Djibrill Yipènè Bassolé (Burkina Faso) as the Joint African Union-United Nations Chief Mediator for Darfur. Mr. Bassolé would conduct full-time mediation efforts; the Special Envoys would remain available for advice and engagement. The Security Council took note of the appointment on 3 July [S/2008/439].

Report of Secretary-General (July). In July [S/2008/443], the Secretary-General reported on progress made in the implementation of UNAMID and the status of the political process in Darfur between April and June. In response to the instability in Western Darfur, UNAMID developed a plan to conduct at least three long- and short-range patrols, together with two night patrols to IDP camps throughout the sector each week. UNAMID was patrolling IDP camps from 8 a.m. to 6 p.m., with a view to providing a 24-hour presence. Progress was hampered, however, by the lack of reliable personal radios and the limited presence of formed police units.

Clashes between SLA-Minni Minawi and SLA-Free Will forces in Northern and Southern Darfur resulted in the displacement of more than 90,000 civilians during the reporting period. Shootings and the burning of the market and IDP dwellings in Tawila by Government troops on 13 May, in retaliation for the killing of a soldier, temporarily displaced some 20,000 persons. Owing to the violence targeting the humanitarian community, food aid was halved starting on 1 May. In addition, a very poor crop harvest in Southern and Northern Darfur led to an expanded 'hunger season', with the supply of cereals and other food items dramatically reduced. Bureaucratic restrictions also hindered the 16,500 aid workers in Darfur in providing essential humanitarian assistance.

Following the signing of the status-of-forces agreement on 9 February, the UNAMID leadership met regularly with senior Government officials and engaged them on issues related to UNAMID deployment. On 16 June, the Government agreed to extend airport operations by two hours; create a local technical committee to address technical problems; cooperate on the security of convoys and supply routes; and expedite customs clearances and issuance of visas. The Assistant Secretaries-General for Peacekeeping Operations and Field Support, joined by the AU-UN Joint Special Representative for Darfur, met with the AU Commissioner for Peace and Security, Ramtane Lamamra, to discuss deployment issues in the margins of the thirteenth Ordinary Session of the Executive Council of the African Union (Sharm el-Sheikh, Egypt, 24–28 June). Those officials then met jointly with a team from the Government of the Sudan. During the discussions, the Sudanese representatives reiterated the Government's commitment to UNAMID deployment. The AU-UN team emphasized the importance of Government cooperation and support in the following key areas: expeditious movement of contingent-owned equipment into Darfur, including the provision of security for convoys; the provision of land for camps; and the facilitation of engineering activities. UNAMID contingent-owned equipment convoys would be permitted to take place every 24 hours from El Obeid to Darfur, an increase from the previous provision for one convoy every 48 hours.

Despite the efforts of the two Special Envoys, the 2007 road map for the political process in Darfur [YUN 2007, p. 251] reached an impasse. The prospect for peace talks decreased due to the fragmentation of the movements, including the dissolution of URF into three separate groups; the deteriorating security situation; the absence of trust and cohesion between and within the parties; the renewed crisis between Chad and the Sudan (see p. 267); and the absence of political will to cease hostilities and resume negotiations. Implementation of the 2006 Darfur Peace Agreement [YUN 2006, p. 274] continued to be largely ignored by the parties on the ground, and was further hindered by the refusal of non-signatories to recognize the mechanisms put in place by the Agreement.

The Secretary-General observed that UNAMID deployment was far behind schedule, and sexual and gender-based violence continued with impunity. Heightened insecurity and banditry hampered the provision of humanitarian assistance to nearly 2.5 million people, and the international community struggled to perform even the most basic work to protect civilians.

Attacks against UNAMID. On 8 July, a UNAMID patrol was attacked near Shangil Tobaya, Northern Darfur, resulting in the death of seven peacekeepers and the wounding of 22. The deliberate and well-organized attack was the most serious since the start of the Operation. In a 9 July press statement [SG/SM/11690], the Secretary-General condemned the attack and called on the Government to do its utmost to identify the perpetrators and bring them to justice. He called on all parties to respect their agreements, redouble efforts to ensure the safety of the peacekeeping force, and reach a settlement to the Darfur crisis.

On 10 July, a UNAMID night patrol was struck by hostile fire 4 kilometres from the UNAMID company site in Masteri; there were no casualties. On 11 July, rocket-propelled grenades were fired near the UNAMID camp in Zam Zam. On 16 July, a UNAMID officer commanding the For Baranga protection force southwest of El Geneina was shot and killed by unknown armed men.

SECURITY COUNCIL ACTION

On 16 July [meeting 5935], following consultations among Security Council members, the President made statement **S/PRST/2008/27** on behalf of the Council:

> The Security Council condemns in the strongest possible terms the attack on 8 July 2008 on a military and police convoy of the African Union-United Nations Hybrid Operation in Darfur (UNAMID) in Um Hakibah by 200 fighters on horses and in 40 vehicles, using sophisticated weaponry and tactics, which resulted in the death of 7 peacekeepers and a further 22 United Nations/African Union personnel being wounded. This unacceptable act of extreme violence is the largest attack on UNAMID since the transfer of authority from the African Union Mission in the Sudan on 31 December 2007. The Council is particularly concerned that the attack was premeditated, deliberate and intended to inflict casualties.
>
> The Council welcomes the United Nations investigation under way and the Government of the Sudan's statement that it would assist the United Nations investigation. It calls upon the Government of the Sudan to do its utmost to ensure that the perpetrators of the attack are swiftly identified and brought to justice. The Council underlines its determination to take action against those responsible after hearing the outcome of the investigation by UNAMID.
>
> The Council expresses its condolences to the Governments of Rwanda, Ghana and Uganda for the deaths of their peacekeepers and to the families of the victims. It commends the dedication of UNAMID personnel. The Council stresses that any attack or threat against UNAMID is unacceptable, and demands that there be no reoccurrence. It underlines that attacks on United Nations peacekeepers during an armed conflict can constitute war crimes under applicable international law and calls upon all parties to comply with their obligations under international humanitarian law.
>
> The Council calls upon all parties to agree to a cessation of hostilities, to engage fully and constructively in the political process under the leadership of the new Joint African Union United Nations Chief Mediator for Darfur, Mr. Djibrill Yipènè Bassolé, and to cooperate fully with the deployment of UNAMID and respect its security and freedom of movement.
>
> The Council further calls upon the United Nations and all parties to facilitate the rapid and complete deployment of UNAMID, and upon capable Member States to contribute the helicopter and transportation units necessary to ensure the successful implementation of the mandate of UNAMID.

On 31 July [meeting 5947], the Security Council adopted **resolution 1828(2008)** by vote (14-0-1). The draft [S/2008/506] was submitted by the United Kingdom.

> *The Security Council,*
>
> *Reaffirming* all its previous resolutions and the statements by its President concerning the situation in the Sudan,
>
> *Reaffirming* its strong commitment to the sovereignty, unity, independence and territorial integrity of the Sudan and its determination to work with the Government of the Sudan, in full respect of its sovereignty, to assist in tackling the various challenges in the Sudan,
>
> *Recalling* its resolutions 1325(2000) of 31 October 2000 and 1820(2008) of 19 June 2008 on women and peace and security, resolution 1502(2003) of 26 August 2003 on the protection of humanitarian and United Nations personnel, resolution 1612(2005) of 26 July 2005 on children and armed conflict and the subsequent conclusions on the Sudan of the Security Council Working Group on Children and Armed Conflict, as approved by the Council, and resolution 1674(2006) of 28 April 2006 on the protection of civilians in armed conflict, in which it reaffirms, inter alia, the relevant provisions of the 2005 World Summit Outcome, as well as the report of its mission to the Sudan from 3 to 6 June 2008,
>
> *Welcoming* the report of the Secretary-General of 7 July 2008, and recalling the confirmation of President Bashir during his meeting with the Council that the African Union United Nations Hybrid Operation in Darfur (UNAMID) shall be deployed in full,
>
> *Deploring*, one year after the adoption of resolution 1769(2007) on 31 July 2007, the deterioration in the security and humanitarian situation in Darfur,
>
> *Stressing* the need to enhance the safety and security of UNAMID personnel,
>
> *Noting* with strong concern ongoing attacks on the civilian population and humanitarian workers and continued and widespread sexual violence, including as outlined in the reports of the Secretary-General,

Emphasizing the need to bring to justice the perpetrators of such crimes and urging the Government of the Sudan to comply with its obligations in this respect, and reiterating its condemnation of all violations of human rights and international humanitarian law in Darfur,

Taking note of the communiqué issued by the Peace and Security Council of the African Union at its one hundred and forty second meeting, held on 21 July 2008, having in mind concerns raised by members of the Council regarding potential developments subsequent to the application by the Prosecutor of the International Criminal Court of 14 July 2008, and taking note of their intention to consider these matters further,

Reaffirming its concern that the ongoing violence in Darfur might further negatively affect the stability of the Sudan as a whole, as well as the region, noting with concern the ongoing tensions between the Governments of the Sudan and Chad, and reiterating that a reduction in these tensions and rebel activity in both countries must be addressed to achieve long-term peace in Darfur and in the region,

Expressing its determination to promote and support the political process in Darfur, especially the new Chief Mediator, and deploring the fact that some groups refuse to join the political process,

Reiterating its deep concern for the decreasing security of humanitarian personnel, including killings of humanitarian workers, in Darfur and the hindering of their access to populations in need, condemning the parties to the conflict who have failed to ensure the full, safe and unhindered access of relief personnel as well as the delivery of humanitarian assistance, further condemning all instances of banditry and carjackings, and recognizing that, with many civilians in Darfur having been displaced, humanitarian efforts remain a priority until a sustained ceasefire and an inclusive political process are achieved,

Demanding an end to attacks on civilians, from any quarter, including by aerial bombing, and the use of civilians as human shields,

Determining that the situation in Darfur, Sudan, continues to constitute a threat to international peace and security,

1. *Decides* to extend the mandate of the African Union United Nations Hybrid Operation in Darfur (UNAMID), as set out in resolution 1769(2007), for a further twelve months, to 31 July 2009;

2. *Welcomes* the agreement of the Government of the Sudan, during its meeting with the Security Council on 5 June 2008, to the African Union United Nations troop deployment plan, commends the contribution made by troop and police contributing countries and donors to UNAMID, and in order to facilitate the full and successful deployment of UNAMID and to enhance the protection of its personnel:

(a) Calls for the rapid deployment, as planned by the Secretary-General, of force enablers, including the heavy support package's engineer, logistical, medical and signal units, and of additional troops, police and civilian personnel, including contractors; and

(b) Calls upon States Members of the United Nations to pledge and contribute the helicopter, aerial reconnaissance, ground transport, engineering and logistical units and other force enablers required;

3. *Underlines* the importance of raising the capability of those UNAMID battalions formerly deployed by the African Union Mission in the Sudan and other incoming battalions, requests the continuing assistance of donors in ensuring that these battalions are trained and equipped to United Nations standards, and further requests the Secretary-General to include this in his next report to the Council;

4. *Welcomes* the intention of the Secretary-General to deploy 80 per cent of UNAMID by 31 December 2008, and urges the Government of the Sudan, troop contributors, donors, the Secretariat and all stakeholders to do all they can to facilitate this;

5. *Also welcomes* the signing of the status of forces agreement, demands that the Government of the Sudan comply with it fully and without delay, and further demands that the Government of the Sudan and all armed groups in the territory of the Sudan ensure the full and expeditious deployment of UNAMID and remove all obstacles to the proper discharge of its mandate, including by ensuring its security and freedom of movement;

6. *Underlines*, with a view to strengthening cooperation with troop and police contributors, as well as their safety and security, the need for enhanced guidelines, procedures and information-sharing;

7. *Underlines also* the need for UNAMID to make full use of its current mandate and capabilities with regard to the protection of civilians, ensuring humanitarian access and working with other United Nations agencies;

8. *Reiterates its condemnation* of previous attacks on UNAMID, stresses that any attack on or threat against UNAMID is unacceptable, demands that there be no recurrence of such attacks, and further requests the Secretary-General to report to the Council on the result of United Nations investigations and with recommendations to prevent a recurrence of such attacks;

9. *Reiterates* that there can be no military solution to the conflict in Darfur and that an inclusive political settlement and the successful deployment of UNAMID are essential to re establishing peace in Darfur;

10. *Welcomes* the appointment of Mr. Djibrill Yipènè Bassolé as the Joint African Union United Nations Chief Mediator for Darfur, who has its full support, calls upon the Government of the Sudan and rebel groups to engage fully and constructively in the peace process, including by entering into talks under the mediation of Mr. Bassolé, demands that all the parties, in particular rebel groups, finalize their preparations for and join the talks, and underlines also the need for the engagement of civil society, including women and women led organizations, community groups and tribal leaders;

11. *Demands* an end to violence by all sides, to attacks on civilians, peacekeepers and humanitarian personnel, and to other violations of human rights and international humanitarian law in Darfur; further demands that all parties cease hostilities and immediately commit themselves to a sustained and permanent ceasefire; and encourages the mediation to consult with all relevant parties on security issues with a view to a more effective Ceasefire Commission working closely with UNAMID to monitor the cessation of hostilities;

12. *Calls upon* the Sudan and Chad to abide by their obligations under the Dakar Agreement, the Tripoli Agreement and subsequent bilateral agreements, including by ending support for rebel groups, welcomes the creation of the Dakar Agreement Contact Group and the consideration being given to improved monitoring of the border between the Sudan and Chad; and takes note of the agreement of the Sudan and Chad on 18 July 2008 to restore diplomatic relations;

13. *Demands* the full implementation of the joint communiqué between the Government of the Sudan and the United Nations on the facilitation of humanitarian activities in Darfur, and that the Government of the Sudan, all militias, armed groups and all other stakeholders ensure the full, safe and unhindered access of humanitarian organizations and relief personnel;

14. *Requests* the Secretary-General to ensure *(a)* continued monitoring and reporting of the situation of children, and *(b)* continued dialogue with the parties to the conflict towards the preparation of time-bound action plans to end the recruitment and use of child soldiers and other violations against children;

15. *Demands* that the parties to the conflict immediately take appropriate measures to protect civilians, including women and children, from all forms of sexual violence, in line with resolution 1820(2008), and requests the Secretary-General to ensure, as appropriate, that resolutions 1325(2000) and 1820(2008) are implemented by UNAMID and to include information on this in his report requested in paragraph 17 below;

16. *Demands* that the parties to the conflict in Darfur fulfil their international obligations and their commitments under relevant agreements, the present resolution and other relevant Council resolutions;

17. *Requests* the Secretary-General to report to the Council every sixty days after the adoption of the present resolution on developments on UNAMID, the political process, the security and humanitarian situation, and compliance by all parties with their international obligations;

18. *Reiterates* its readiness to take action against any party that impedes the peace process, humanitarian assistance or the deployment of UNAMID, and recognizes that due process must take its course;

19. *Decides* to remain seized of the matter.

VOTE ON RESOLUTION 1828(2008):

In favour: Belgium, Burkina Faso, China, Costa Rica, Croatia, France, Indonesia, Italy, Libyan Arab Jamahiriya, Panama, Russian Federation, South Africa, United Kingdom, Viet Nam.

Against: None.

Abstaining: United States.

Speaking after the vote, the United States said that it had abstained because the language added to the resolution would send the wrong signal to President Al-Bashir and undermine efforts to bring him and others to justice.

Report of Secretary-General (August). In August [S/2008/558], the Secretary-General reported that a series of deadly attacks against UNAMID peacekeepers, a decline in the overall security situation and uncertainty regarding the implications of the request of 14 July by the ICC Prosecutor for an arrest warrant against President Al-Bashir led the United Nations to take heightened security precautions, including the classification of Darfur as a phase IV security environment and a temporary relocation of non-essential staff. Nevertheless, UNAMID stepped up patrols in rural areas of Sector West to reduce threats and boost the confidence of the population, particularly farmers.

Aerial bombardments increased in Darfur following the attack of 10 May on Omdurman by JEM. On 19 July, 15 bombs were reportedly dropped on the villages surrounding Jebel Moon, where JEM forces were reportedly stationed; further air attacks were reported on 22 July. Aerial attacks were also reported in the area controlled by SLM/A-Abdul Wahid 40 kilometres south-west of El Fasher, including bombings of Gollo on 5 and 21 July. On 15, 17 and 20 July, air attacks on SLM/A-Unity and JEM positions were conducted in Jebel Adulla in Southern Darfur. The attacks marked an escalation in the intensity of the conflict between the Government and the rebel factions not signatories to the Darfur Peace Agreement.

From 2 to 5 July, a 35-vehicle convoy staffed by 20 UNAMID police advisers and 18 UNAMID transport staff and technicians delivered vehicles, fuel and equipment from the El Obeid Logistics Base to El Fasher with an escort provided by the Government, the second such convoy to leave El Obeid in July. UNAMID policing activities were temporarily suspended in mid-July due to the security situation and the move to security phase IV. The situation later stabilized, however, and on 20 July, the UNAMID Police Commissioner authorized a return to normal activities.

Following the crash of an IL-76 aircraft in Khartoum on 30 June, the Government banned all flights of Ilyushin and Antonov aircraft, with the exception of UNAMID and UNMIS flights, provided the aircraft were not more than 20 years old and were contracted from outside the Sudan. Despite the UNAMID exception, the ban resulted in some delays in the movement of cargo, including emergency food rations for UNAMID personnel. The transportation of equipment required by contractors to complete work in the supercamps was also delayed until 24 July, when the Government provided authorization to move the materials. The Sudanese Civil Aviation Authority visited Darfur airports late in July, paving the way for UNAMID to expand parking and apron spaces, as well as undertake other rehabilitation work at the three airports in Darfur.

Further developments

Report of Secretary-General (October). In response to resolution 1828(2008), the Secretary-

General in October submitted a report [S/2008/659] on UNAMID deployment, the political process, the security and humanitarian situation, and compliance by all parties with their international obligations. The report covered the period from August to early October.

The security and humanitarian situation remained precarious, especially in Northern Darfur and in IDP camps. On 12 August, the SLA-Abdul Wahid faction reported a Government offensive in the Wadi Atrun area of Northern Kordofan, allegedly resulting in seven deaths. The Government acknowledged the deployment of its forces to the area but said that no fighting had occurred. On 16 August, the faction again reported a Government attack on rebel bases in Abu Hamra and Kafod, allegedly resulting in the death of two combatants. On 25 August, heavily armed Government security forces surrounded the Kalma IDP camp south of Nyala, which accommodated some 80,000 people, with approximately 60 vehicles; the Government launched the operation to search for weapons and other contraband. The security forces were confronted by a crowd of internally displaced persons and opened fire. In the ensuing skirmish, 32 people were killed and at least 85 were injured. UNAMID deployed a team of military, police and medical personnel that evacuated the wounded to a medical facility in Nyala. Following the incident, 18 SPLM officials in the Government of National Unity and four local legislators resigned from their posts in protest. UNAMID took up the incident with Government agencies and the Humanitarian Aid Commission. On 10 September, the Government announced the establishment of a ministerial-level Security Task Force on Darfur to improve the humanitarian and security situation in IDP camps, and requested the participation of UNAMID and the UN Resident/Humanitarian Coordinator.

The Government began a new military campaign in Northern Darfur in September. On 6 and 7 September, it launched air strikes, followed by ground operations north of Kutum and east of Jebel Marra, respectively, involving attack helicopters and 50 to 100 vehicles. The Government stated that the operations were an effort to secure the main convoy routes for humanitarian access; nevertheless, its forces engaged SLA-Unity, SLA-Abdul Wahid, and the URF (JEM Collective) groups in combat. On 13 and 14 September, combined SAF, militia and Central Reserve Police forces in up to 150 vehicles launched another major offensive into eastern Jebel Marra. The Government also bombed suspected rebel strongholds, including in Karbala, Jebel Adoula, and the Umo and Jebel Moon areas, reportedly killing 12 people. Clashes between the SLA-Minni Minawi and the SLA-Free Will factions—both signatories of the Darfur Peace Agreement—continued north of El Fasher. Tribal conflict dominated the security situation in Southern Darfur, with up to 150 casualties reported as a result of fighting between the Rezeigat and Messerayah tribes.

The newly appointed AU-UN Joint Chief Mediator for Darfur, Djibrill Bassolé, arrived in the Sudan on 25 August. The Government pledged to cooperate with the Chief Mediator and expressed its determination to seek a speedy political solution to the Darfur crisis. The Chief Mediator met with representatives of rebel movements, IDPs, tribal leaders, and NGOs in El Fasher, Nyala and El Geneina. He urged the parties to lay down their arms and engage in dialogue, and encouraged the Government to take forward the Sudan People's Initiative announced in July. The Chief Mediator also met with the leaders of rebel groups and discussed measures to improve security and resume peace talks with the Government. Movement representatives, IDPs and tribal leaders reiterated their demands for power-sharing and security. On 19 September, UNAMID facilitated a meeting between Vice-President Osman Taha and Minni Minawi; they agreed on a cessation of hostilities and reaffirmed their commitment to the Darfur Peace Agreement.

Regarding UNAMID deployment, the Secretary-General said that a considerable number of military units, as well as two formed police units, would be deployed to Darfur during the remainder of the year. The units expected to deploy in October would include the 348-strong main body of the Bangladeshi multi-role logistics company; 148 members of the Egyptian Transport Unit; the 40-personnel advance party of the Pakistani engineer company; and most of the first Ethiopian and Egyptian battalions, composed of 440 and 632 troops, respectively. Deployment of formed police units from Nepal and Indonesia was also expected to be completed in October. The 10 infantry battalions already deployed would begin their rotations in October. In addition, three formed police units would be deployed by the end of the year.

UNAMID put in place additional commercial contracts for road, rail, and air transportation of contingent-owned and UN equipment directly into Darfur from Port Sudan. DFS and DPKO worked with the Friends of UNAMID group to arrange airlifts of troops and contingent-owned equipment directly from troop-contributing countries into Darfur. In addition, selected contributors were asked to undertake either self-deployment of all contingent-owned equipment and personnel in the region or the direct airlift of such equipment to Darfur. In response to a DFS request, the Government, in a letter of 26 September, agreed to provide blanket clearance for arriving flights carrying contingent-owned equipment. The arrangement would first be applied to airlift equipment for the Pakistani Level III Hospital, which would be operational before the end of the year. In the progress report submitted by the Government to the AU Commission on 17 September, the Sudanese authorities confirmed in writing their acceptance of the Thai battalion and Nepalese units that were expected to deploy in 2009.

Restrictions imposed by the Government and the various movements repeatedly undermined the Operation's freedom of movement. On 11 August, a UNAMID helicopter came under fire while flying from El Geneina to Kulbus, sustaining minor damage; another UNAMID helicopter came under fire south of Jebel Moon. JEM apologized for the second incident, acknowledging that it mistakenly identified the white helicopter as a Government aircraft. On 14 September, a UNAMID helicopter was fired upon by unknown perpetrators while flying from Shangil Tobayi to Tawilla. On 29 September, a helicopter operated by a UNAMID contractor crashed near Nyala, resulting in the death of the four people on board.

A tripartite meeting between the Government, the AU Commission and the United Nations (Khartoum, 7 October), attended by the Under-Secretary-General for Field Support, Susana Malcorra, discussed the steps taken by each of the parties to expedite UNAMID deployment and ensure its functioning. The parties agreed to address issues related to freedom of movement; air operations and flight clearances; railway rehabilitation; visa processing; customs clearance; Government liaison; military deployment; and the use of local construction capacity. The Government instructed the armed forces and civil aviation authorities to ensure that Government helicopters were no longer painted white, in order to distinguish them from UNAMID helicopters and those used for international humanitarian activities. It was agreed that UNAMID and the Sudanese Civil Aviation Authority would contribute to the review of the crash on 29 September of a helicopter operated by a UNAMID contractor. The Government approved the rehabilitation of the El Fasher and Nyala airports and the new airport in El Geneina, and the United Nations committed itself to expediting those efforts. The Government approved the use of Darfur airports by UNAMID from 7 a.m. to 7 p.m., and circulated instructions to that effect to the Civil Aviation and National Security authorities, as well as the walis, or governors, in Darfur. It was agreed to gradually implement operations taking place around the clock, with UNAMID contributing the necessary equipment and support. Regarding UNAMID convoys, the Government confirmed that it would escort any such convoy as frequently as every 48 hours; that the frequency of convoys would be increased to one every 24 hours as long as they comprised at least 30 vehicles; and that the frequency would be increased to one every 24 hours in due course. The United Nations agreed to support Government efforts to rehabilitate portions of the railway. The Government agreed that UNAMID equipment, goods and materials would undergo customs clearance one time only, at their point of entry. It confirmed the establishment of a liaison office in El Fasher that would ensure local implementation of national-level decisions. The United Nations, the AU and the Government agreed to support the possible self-deployment of the second battalions from Egypt and Ethiopia.

The high-level committee on the facilitation of humanitarian activities in Darfur met on 20 August and reaffirmed the imperative to continue to deliver services in accordance with humanitarian principles. Despite an assurance from the Government to facilitate humanitarian access, local Sudanese authorities continued to impose bureaucratic constraints on humanitarian organizations.

Government decree. On 25 November [S/2008/739], the Sudan transmitted to the Security Council the decision of 16 November of its Ministry of Humanitarian Affairs to extend until 31 January 2010 fast-track measures facilitating humanitarian aid.

Report of Secretary-General (December). In his December report on UNAMID deployment [S/2008/781], the Secretary-General said that in October, Government forces, supported by militia, launched operations aimed at reinforcing their positions and driving SLA-Unity forces from their areas of control. Those operations led UNAMID to identify "no go areas" for UN personnel, particularly east of Jebel Marra in Northern Darfur. In Muhajeria and surrounding areas in Southern Darfur, seven armed tribal clashes reportedly took place from 5 to 11 October pitting Ma'aliya, Messeriya and Birgid tribes against members of the Zaghawa tribe. At least 41 men and three children were killed, seven women were reportedly raped, cultivated land was burned and livestock was looted. Despite the unilateral declaration of a cessation of hostilities by the Government on 12 November (see below), aerial bombings were reportedly conducted in different locations in Northern Darfur between 12 and 15 November and in Western Darfur on 17 November. On 16 November, Government troops were ambushed in the Graida area in Southern Darfur. On the same day, Government police forces came under gunfire while conducting routine patrols between the cities of Buram and Joghana, resulting in the death of two officers. UNAMID investigated reports of aerial attacks by the Government carried out on 21 and 22 November in Abu Dangal, Southern Darfur, and confirmed the presence of unexploded ordnance. In addition to conducting its mandated tasks, UNAMID was implementing a security enhancement plan designed to mitigate security risks to staff. The Darfur Integrated Security Task Force, created following the incident of 25 August at Kalma camp, met for the first time on 26 November in Khartoum. UNAMID and the Government agreed to hold regular monthly meetings, starting in January 2009.

The Sudan People's Forum (SPF) was launched by President Al-Bashir in October. It was attended by senior leaders of all main political parties, with the exception of the Popular Congress Party and the Sudan Communist Party, and included representatives from Darfur, with the exception of Darfur armed movements. Among the issues discussed were security, power-sharing and wealth-sharing. The Forum concluded on 12 November with the President's announcement of an immediate unilateral ceasefire subject to the establishment of a ceasefire-monitoring mechanism, as well as a programme for disarming militia groups and a community police service for IDP camps. The President agreed in principle to compensation for the victims of the conflict. He also agreed to end hostile propaganda and to discuss with the people of Darfur an increase in the number of states in Darfur from the current three. The issues of a single Darfur region and a Vice-President for Darfur were deferred. Some armed movements, including JEM, rejected the SPF conclusions, including the unilateral ceasefire.

The Joint Chief Mediator conducted extensive consultations with the parties. The Government and the rebel movements pledged to work closely with him on a framework agreement that would encompass the timing, venue, format and agenda for talks, as well as a commitment to a cessation of hostilities. In October and November, the Joint Chief Mediator also met with other stakeholders, including the Government of Qatar and the countries of the region. On 15 November, he briefed the AU Peace and Security Council, stressing the importance of improved relations between Chad and the Sudan. The Chief Mediator emphasized the need for all Member States to influence the parties to move towards a solution to the conflict. On 10 October, a joint delegation of Qatar, the AU and the League of Arab States (LAS) visited Darfur to discuss the possibility of peace talks in Doha, Qatar.

On 13 October, SAF and SLA-Minni Minawi signed a memorandum of understanding on political and military coordination in El Fasher. Referred to as the El Fasher Declaration, the memorandum outlined joint activities with a view to looking into possible compensation for the deaths and damage resulting from the hostilities in East Jebel Marra; coordinating security arrangements in Darfur; encouraging and protecting trade and humanitarian access; and bringing non-signatories of the Darfur Peace Agreement into the political process. In line with the memorandum, President Al-Bashir issued a decree incorporating the Peace Agreement into the interim Constitution, which was to be finalized and submitted for adoption by the National Assembly.

UNAMID continued to operate in a phase IV security environment, characterized by high levels of banditry, carjacking, military engagements and deadly attacks on UNAMID forces. In an attack on 29 October, a UNAMID peacekeeper was killed and another injured while guarding a water-point near the Kassab IDP camp in Kutum, Northern Darfur. On 9 November, one peacekeeper was injured and a vehicle was taken in an ambush of a UNAMID convoy. UNAMID continued to provide a round-the-clock presence near the Kalma IDP camp and established a mission-wide integrated approach to IDP protection. The Operation approved 56 quick-impact projects totalling $1.2 million. It continued to face some restrictions on its freedom of movement. On 24 October, a Government patrol stopped a UNAMID patrol in El Geneina and subsequently ordered UNAMID to stop conducting night patrols in the town.

As at 30 November, the strength of UNAMID uniformed personnel stood at 12,482, including 9,941 military and 2,541 police personnel. The number of civilian personnel totalled 2,962, or 53 per cent of full capacity, consisting of 770 international staff, 1,933 national staff and 259 United Nations Volunteers (UNVs). Since 1 January, 58 staff had left UNAMID through resignations, reassignments and expiration of appointments, and 98 selected candidates had rejected recruitment offers. A total of 1,363 military and police personnel arrived in Darfur in October and November. In mid-October, 325 members of the Bangladeshi multirole logistics unit arrived in Nyala. In mid-November, 148 members of the Egyptian transport unit also arrived in Nyala. In Northern Darfur, 490 personnel of the first Egyptian battalion were deployed to Um Kadada in late November. Two formed police units, consisting of 140 personnel each from Nepal and Indonesia, arrived in October and were deployed to Nyala and El Fasher, respectively. The rotation of the 10 former AMIS infantry battalions would be completed in January 2009. Of those battalions, two were deployed at the UN standard strength of 800 personnel, six would reach UN standard strength by the end of December and two would be upgraded to standard strength in early 2009. With the deployment of additional IL-76 aircraft, it was anticipated that UNAMID would clear the backlog of contingent-owned equipment at the logistics base in El Obeid by January 2009. DFS and UNAMID were deploying additional L100-class aircraft to speed up the delivery of contingent-owned equipment to the airfield in El Geneina. Engineering work for the Nyala supercamp was scheduled to be completed by the end of 2008, and the El Fasher and El Geneina supercamps were scheduled to be completed by the end of January 2009.

At the second meeting of the Tripartite Committee (Khartoum, 16 November) [S/2008/714], UNAMID informed the Government that the four tactical helicopters pledged by Ethiopia might be deployed sooner than previously anticipated. The Government agreed to work with UNAMID to put in place any interim arrangements and undertake any preparation required for the deployment of the helicopters. It also agreed to meet with UNAMID to discuss the allocation of a frequency for a UN broadcast radio system for Darfur.

The Secretary-General observed that the Operation continued to face enormous challenges. Pledges for a multirole logistics unit, a medium transport unit, a heavy transport unit, an aerial reconnaissance unit, light tactical helicopters and 18 medium-utility helicopters were still outstanding. He appealed again to those in a position to provide mission-critical capabilities to do so. He welcomed President Al-Bashir's unilateral declaration of a cessation of hostilities, but was disappointed that military activity by the Government continued. He called on all parties to use restraint and renew their commitment to an immediate and unconditional cessation of hostilities. He welcomed the Government's extension of the joint communiqué on humanitarian access and urged it to do more to ensure that the agreements were fulfilled. He called on the Government to comply with its obligations under international human rights and humanitarian law, particularly with regard to civilians. Regarding the application of 14 July by the ICC Prosecutor for an arrest warrant against President Al-Bashir (see p. 259), the Secretary-General said that the United Nations respected the independence of the Court and its judicial process, and stressed the importance of full compliance by all parties with the Court's actions.

Year-end developments. In a later report on UNAMID deployment [S/2009/83], the Secretary-General described the security and humanitarian situation in Darfur in December. The Government reported that two large columns of JEM rebels crossed the border from Chad into Northern Darfur on 11 December, precipitating SAF troop reinforcements and aerial bombardments of strategic locations intended to avert a JEM offensive into Southern Darfur and beyond. Tribal fighting remained a key destabilizing factor in Southern Darfur. On 4 December, 20 Fallata men were allegedly killed by Habbaniya tribesmen in Al-Tomat. On 11 December, 28 members of the Habbaniya tribe were reportedly killed when approximately 700 armed men from the Salamat and Fallata tribes launched a counter-attack on Wad Hagam in Southern Darfur. On 25 December, 150 armed men believed to be from the Salamat and Fallata tribes attacked the Habbaniya and Abu Darak nomadic communities in Wad Hagam; five civilians were reportedly killed during the attack. From 25 December, UNAMID provided support to the reconciliation conference between the tribes initiated by local government. Clashes between the North Gimir and South Gimir tribes in Antakina village, Southern Darfur, between 6 and 8 December resulted in the death of approximately 20 people. The clashes arose from long-standing disputes over land jurisdiction and local authority between the groups.

In Zalingei, Western Darfur, tension increased between armed nomads and IDPs around the Hassa Hissa IDP camp. On 1 December, two internally displaced persons were shot and injured by an armed nomad, who was then beaten by IDPs and killed. The reaction of armed nomads resulted in the shooting of three IDPs, including one child, on 2 December. The rapid deployment of UNAMID and SAF, and close cooperation between UNAMID and the local authorities, contributed to the resolution of the conflict and prevented its further escalation. Incidents involving unexploded ordnance injured two children in Gokar, Western Darfur, on 14 December; and killed one child and injured two others in Kera, Northern Darfur, on 16 December.

In 2008, some 317,000 people were displaced in Darfur, compared with 300,000 in 2007, bringing the total number of displaced individuals in Darfur above 2.7 million. As a result of continued violence, humanitarian organizations had to rely increasingly on air assets; restrictions on air operations, however, prevented the free movement of life-saving assistance. The number of attacks on humanitarian aid workers nearly doubled in 2008 compared with the previous year: 277 humanitarian vehicles were hijacked, compared with 137 in 2007; 218 humanitarian personnel were abducted, compared with 147 in 2007; 192 humanitarian premises were attacked, compared with 93 in 2007; and 36 staff members were wounded, compared with 24 the previous year. In 2008, 11 UNAMID staff members were killed and four remained missing. On 27 December, a UNAMID staff member lost his life due to injuries sustained during a carjacking incident in El Fasher. The Secretary-General reported that, despite enormous difficulties, including the volatile security situation, UNAMID reached the goal of 60 per cent of military deployment on 31 December.

Activities of ICC Prosecutor

Briefing by ICC Prosecutor (June). In his briefing to the Security Council on 5 June [meeting 5905], the Prosecutor of the International Criminal Court (ICC), Luis Moreno-Ocampo, said that three years after the Security Council, by resolution 1593(2005) [YUN 2005, p. 324], referred the Darfur situation to the Court, massive crimes were still being committed in Darfur. The Prosecutor had collected compelling evidence that would identify those most responsible for crimes against civilians in Darfur, and would present a second case to the ICC judges in July. Despite claims by the Sudan that it would investigate and prosecute perpetrators, the Office of the Prosecutor found no trace of Sudanese proceedings in relation to crimes in Darfur over the previous three years. Although the Sudan had the legal obligation and the ability to arrest and surrender Ahmad Harun and Ali Kushayb, for whom ICC in 2007 issued arrest warrants for crimes against humanity and war crimes [YUN 2007, p. 259], the Government did not recognize the Court's jurisdiction and was not complying with resolution 1593(2005). Mr. Harun was attacking people in IDP camps; as Minister of State for Humanitarian Affairs, he was hindering humanitarian aid; and as a member of the UNAMID oversight committee, he was affecting the deployment and safety of peacekeepers. The Council had to make clear that the two fugitive indictees and those who protected them would not benefit from leniency from the international community. In a new investigation, the Prosecutor's Office collected evidence showing a pattern of attacks against civilians, particularly the 2.5 million forcibly displaced into camps. Evidence showed an organized campaign by Sudanese officials to attack civilians, with the objective of destroying entire communities. In IDP camps, crimes and insecurity were organized. Instead of being disarmed, Janjaweed militias were integrated into the Sudanese security apparatus and stationed near camps, where rapes of women and usurpation of land was systematic. Sudanese officials were facilitating the settlement of groups affiliated with Janjaweed militias on Fur, Masalit and Zaghawa land. The evidence showed that the commission of crimes on such a scale throughout Darfur over a five-year period required the sustained mobilization of the entire Sudanese State apparatus. A third investigation into crimes committed against peacekeepers and aid workers focused on the 2007 attacks on AMIS peacekeepers in Haskanita, Southern Darfur [ibid., p. 255]. In July, the Prosecutor would present to the ICC judges his evidence on those most responsible for the crimes committed in Darfur. He asked the Security Council to issue a presidential statement requesting the Government to stop the crimes, to arrest Messrs. Harun and Kushayb, and to comply with resolution 1593(2005).

SECURITY COUNCIL ACTION

On 16 June [meeting 5912], following consultations among Security Council members, the President made statement **S/PRST/2008/21** on behalf of the Council:

> The Security Council takes note of the seventh briefing by the Prosecutor of the International Criminal Court on 5 June 2008 pursuant to resolution 1593(2005).
>
> The Council recalls its decision, under Chapter VII of the Charter of the United Nations, taken in resolution 1593(2005), that the Government of the Sudan and all other parties to the conflict in Darfur shall cooperate fully with and provide any necessary assistance to the International Criminal Court and the Prosecutor pursuant to that resolution, while stressing the principle of complementarity of the Court.
>
> The Council takes note of the efforts made by the Prosecutor to bring to justice the perpetrators of war crimes and crimes against humanity in Darfur and, in particular, notes the follow-up by the Court with the Government of the Sudan, including the transmittal by the Registry of the Court to the Government of the Sudan of arrest warrants on 16 June 2007 and the opening by the Prosecutor of other investigations on crimes committed by various parties in Darfur.
>
> In this respect, the Council urges the Government of the Sudan and all other parties to the conflict in Darfur to cooperate fully with the Court, consistent with resolution 1593(2005), in order to put an end to impunity for the crimes committed in Darfur.

Application for arrest warrant. The Secretary-General reported on 23 July [S/2008/485] that on 14 July, the ICC Prosecutor requested that the Court issue an arrest warrant for President Al-Bashir on charges of genocide, crimes against humanity and war crimes under the Statute of the Court. The request would be reviewed by the Court's Pretrial Chamber.

On 16 July, President Al-Bashir tasked a committee chaired by First Vice-President Salva Kiir to develop the Sudan's diplomatic and legal position on the crisis. A Special Prosecutor was appointed by the Ministry of Justice on 3 August to investigate allegations of human rights abuses committed in Darfur since 2003. Also in August, the President launched the Sudan People's Initiative, which sought to form a national position on resolving the Darfur crisis by reaching out to all political parties. The Government assured the United Nations that it would continue to cooperate with both UNMIS and UNAMID. However, senior Government officials issued public warnings of possible serious consequences for UNMIS if the President was indicted; the Secretary-General and his Special Representative received similar warnings directly. The United Nations reiterated to the Government that it would respect the independence of the judicial process and that UNMIS would remain committed to implementing its mandate in support of the peace process.

Communications. In a letter of 14 July [S/2008/465] to the Security Council, the AU forwarded a decision adopted by the eleventh ordinary session of the AU Assembly of Heads of State and Government (Sharm el-Sheikh, Egypt, 30 June–1 July) on the report of the Commission on the Abuse of the Principle of Universal Jurisdiction. The Assembly resolved, among other things, that the abuse of the principle of universal jurisdiction could endanger international law, order and security; the political nature and abuse of the principle by judges from some non-African States against African leaders, particularly Rwanda, was a violation of the sovereignty and territorial integrity of those States; the misuse of indictments against African leaders had a destabilizing effect; and such warrants should not be executed in AU member States. It requested the AU Chairperson to present the matter to the Security Council and General Assembly for consideration, and asked UN Member States to impose a moratorium on the execution of warrants until all related legal and political issues were fully discussed between the AU, the European Union (EU) and the United Nations.

On 16 July, the National Assembly of the Sudan adopted two resolutions that were transmitted to the Security Council on 24 July [S/2008/488]: resolution No. 1, by which the Assembly rejected the indictment by the ICC Prosecutor against Sudanese senior officials, including the President; and resolution No. 2, by which it rejected the ratification of the 1998 Rome Statute of the International Criminal Court establishing the Court [YUN 1998, p. 1209] and the Sudan's signing of the Statute in 2000.

An extraordinary session of the LAS Council (Cairo, Egypt, 19 July) adopted a resolution concerning the ICC Prosecutor's application for an arrest warrant for President Al-Bashir. In the resolution, which was transmitted to the Security Council on 25 July [S/2008/505], the LAS Council affirmed its respect for the sovereignty of the Sudan and the competence and independence of its judiciary. It rejected the "unbalanced position" of the ICC Prosecutor and any attempt to politicize the principles of international justice and use them to diminish the sovereignty, unity, security, stability or national symbols of States. The UN Security Council was asked to not allow any party, operation or process the opportunity to undermine efforts to resolve the Darfur crisis by political means or create a climate of instability in the Sudan.

On 21 July [S/2008/481], the AU forwarded to the Security Council a communiqué adopted by the one hundred and forty-second meeting of the AU Peace and Security Council, held the same day in Addis Ababa, in relation to the ICC Prosecutor's application. The Peace and Security Council expressed its conviction that approval of the application by the Court's Pre-Trial Chamber could undermine ongoing efforts to resolve the Darfur conflict and promote peace and reconciliation in the Sudan, and might lead to further suffering for the people of the Sudan and greater destabilization, with far-reaching consequences for the country and the region. It requested the UN Security Council, in accordance with article 16 of the Rome Statute, to defer the process initiated by ICC. The Peace and Security Council invited the AU Commission to set up an independent, high-level panel, composed of distinguished Africans, to examine the situation and make recommendations to the Council on how to address the issues of accountability and impunity, as well as reconciliation. It urged the Government of the Sudan to investigate human rights violations in Darfur and bring perpetrators to justice. The Peace and Security Council extended the UNAMID mandate for a further 12-month period and requested the UN Security Council to do the same (see p. 252). It also urged the Government to extend unreserved cooperation to UNAMID and the international community to provide the necessary support for the Operation. The Peace and Security Council expressed its support to the Joint AU-UN Chief Mediator and urged all Sudanese parties to cooperate with him.

On the same date, the Sudanese Minister of Justice, Abdulbasit Sabdarat, made a statement before the AU Peace and Security Council in connection with the application of 14 July; the statement was transmitted to the Secretary-General and the Security Council in identical letters of 29 July [S/2008/500]. The Minister said that the application for the arrest warrant was based on false pretences and hearsay, and was politically motivated and unjustified. The accusations against the President undermined, pre-empted and endangered the efforts of the AU, the United Nations and the Sudanese Government to resolve the Darfur conflict and implement the Comprehensive Peace Agreement and the 2006 Eastern Sudan Peace Agreement [YUN 2006, p. 264]. The Prosecutor had compromised the principles of international law, including the principle of complementarity enshrined in the Rome Statute, and his actions represented a flagrant intervention into the internal affairs of the Sudan. The Government asked the Peace and Security Council to condemn and reject the application of 14 July and the unfounded accusations made by the ICC Prosecutor; reaffirm the decision of the eleventh ordinary session of the AU Assembly of Heads of State and Government (see above); and call on the UN Security Council to halt the process before ICC and give full effect to the principle of complementarity.

In a letter of 22 July to the Security Council [S/2008/483], Uganda, on behalf of the Organization of the Islamic Conference (OIC) Group in New York, stated that OIC was concerned about the effect of the Chief Prosecutor's request on the peace and reconciliation efforts in the Sudan. The action to indict President Al-Bashir would adversely affect the ongoing peace initiatives, including Security Council resolution 1769(2007) [YUN 2007, p. 251], by which UNAMID was established, and would complicate the implementation of the 2005 Comprehensive Peace Agreement [YUN 2005, p. 301] in Southern Sudan and the stabilization of Darfur. OIC therefore sought the intervention of the Security Council under article 16 of the Rome Statute to defer any possible indictment against President Al-Bashir.

On 5 August, Senegal transmitted to the Security Council [S/2008/525] and to the Secretary-General and the General Assembly [A/63/230] the final communiqué of the emergency expanded ministerial meeting of the OIC Executive Committee (Jeddah, Saudi Arabia, 4 August), which discussed the ICC Prosecutor's attempt to seek the indictment of President Al-Bashir. The meeting expressed its solidarity with the Sudan under President Al-Bashir's leadership and considered the Prosecutor's application for indictment unwarranted and unacceptable. It urged the Security Council to suspend the application indefinitely, and called on OIC member States and the international community to intensify their engagement for peacebuilding efforts in Darfur and to reinforce UNAMID.

On 18 August [S/2008/559], LAS transmitted to the Security Council a package of measures aimed at finding a political settlement of the Darfur issue. The package, which was agreed to between the Government of the Sudan and the LAS Secretary-General in Khartoum on 21 July, stated that efforts to implement the political solution initiative of the Sudanese national forces had to be reactivated. The role of UNAMID should be enhanced and its mandated duty of protecting civilians should be facilitated. The package stated that the Sudanese judiciary should continue to consider criminal cases on the basis of investigations by existing or future judicial committees. The Government affirmed its commitment to dealing with the remnants of conflict in Darfur in accordance with the law. Under the package, the Security Council would halt the proceedings taken under resolution 1593(2005) [YUN 2005, p. 324], by which it referred the situation in Darfur since 1 July 2002 to the ICC Prosecutor.

On 15 October [S/2008/656], Lebanon, in its capacity as Chairman of the Arab Group, and on behalf of LAS, transmitted to the Security Council the resolution adopted by the Special Session of the LAS Council of Ministers of Justice (Cairo, Egypt, 12 October) regarding the ICC Prosecutor's application. The Council of Ministers maintained that the application had no sound legal basis. It rejected any attempt to politicize the principles of international justice, as well as double standards in the application of legal principles derived from international law.

A letter of 13 November [S/2008/713] contained five decisions issued by the Sudanese Minister of Justice regarding the legal process concerning Darfur. By a decision of 3 August, General Counsel Nimr Ibrahim Muhammad was appointed Special Prosecutor for the crimes committed in Darfur beginning in 2003; three Senior Counsels were appointed to a committee to assist him. By decisions Nos. 20, 21 and 22 of 16 September, Committees of the Wise to assist the Special Prosecutor were established in Southern, Northern and Western Darfur states, respectively. By decision No. 23 of 16 September, a 12-member High-level National Committee to assist the Special Prosecutor was established.

Briefing by ICC Prosecutor (December). Briefing the Security Council on 3 December [meeting 6028], the ICC Prosecutor discussed, among other matters, his request for an arrest warrant against President Al-Bashir. The evidence showed that in March 2003, President Al-Bashir ordered attacks against the Fur, Masalit and Zaghawa ethnic groups and triggered attacks in villages and IDP camps; at least 35,000 people were killed, and thousands of women and girls were raped. The 2.5 million people in camps were being subjected to living conditions calculated to bring about their destruction. In response to the application, Presidential Adviser Bona Malwal said on 25 July that with the indictment of President Al-Bashir, the Government could not be responsible for the well-being of foreign forces in Darfur; other officials, including the President, made statements threatening the victims and against the men and women deployed under the authority of the Council. The Prosecutor said that such threats should be seen as a confirmation of criminal intentions.

On 20 November, the Prosecutor said, he had presented to ICC Pre-Trial Chamber I the case against three rebel commanders allegedly responsible for the war crime of directing attacks against AMIS peacekeepers in Haskanita, Southern Darfur, in 2007 [YUN 2007, p. 255], which killed 12 peacekeepers. In response to the application, five rebel groups stated that they were ready to collaborate with ICC and hand over any member requested by the Court. The Government, however, had not heeded the Council President's statement S/PRST/2008/21 of 16 June (see p. 259). Genocide and rape in and around IDP camps continued, villages continued to be bombed, humanitarian assistance was still hindered, and more than 5,000 displaced persons died each month. On 10 September, the Office of the Prosecutor sent a letter to the Government requesting information on national investigations or prosecutions planned or under way concerning the attacks of 25 August on the Kalma IDP camp, but no response was received. On 7 October, President Al-Bashir publicly stated that mass rape did not exist. A Government report of 17 September circulated to the AU and the United Nations confirmed that there had been no national proceedings in the Sudan in relation to the crimes being investigated by the Court. Over the previous five years, the Sudan tried and completed only seven cases. Mr. Harun, for whom an arrest warrant was issued in 2007 [YUN

2007, p. 259], continued to hold the post of Minister of State for Humanitarian Affairs, in charge of the people he had displaced; President Al-Bashir publicly declared that he would not hand over the Minister to ICC because Mr. Harun was implementing his instructions.

The Prosecutor stated that so-called suspected ICC witnesses were being arrested and tried for treason. President Al-Bashir continued to implement his plan to destroy entire ethnic groups, and his criminal behaviour included providing immunity and concealing crimes. He was using the diplomatic apparatus to campaign against ICC, and was trying to convince organizations and the Security Council that they had to protect him. If the ICC judges decided to issue an arrest warrant against President Al-Bashir, united and consistent action would be needed to ensure the execution of the warrant. The President's criminal actions should not be ignored, and the international community could not be part of any cover-up of genocide or crimes against humanity.

Following the Prosecutor's briefing, South Africa said that in light of the steps being taken by the AU, as described in the communiqué of 21 July of the AU Peace and Security Council, and others to ensure that peace and justice were mutually reinforcing in Darfur, it continued to hope that the Security Council would take the necessary time to discuss and decide on deferment of the potential case against President Al-Bashir under article 16 of the Rome Statute. It reaffirmed the appeal expressed in presidential statement S/PRST/2008/21 that all parties to the Darfur conflict cooperate fully with ICC. South Africa also asked whether Security Council discussion of article 16 as it applied to the case would be understood as an attempt by the Council to protect those involved or cover up what was happening in the Sudan. The Prosecutor responded to South Africa by providing further details about his investigation of the crimes committed in Darfur.

Sanctions

The Security Council, by resolution 1556(2004) [YUN 2004, p. 240], imposed an arms embargo on all non-governmental entities and individuals, including the Janjaweed, operating in Darfur. By resolution 1591(2005) [YUN 2005, p. 319], the Council imposed a travel ban and assets freeze, and established a Committee to oversee implementation of the sanctions against individuals to be designated by the Committee. The Secretary-General was requested to appoint a Panel of Experts for six months to assist the work of the Council and the Committee. The Panel of Experts, established in June 2005 [ibid., p. 322], was mandated to assist the Committee in monitoring implementation of the arms embargo and sanctions; make recommendations to the Committee on possible Council actions; and provide information on individuals who impeded the peace process, committed violations of international law, or were responsible for offensive military overflights.

Appointment. On 28 January [S/2008/48], the Secretary-General appointed a fifth expert to serve on the Panel of Experts established pursuant to resolution 1591(2005) until 15 October. The four other members of the Panel were appointed in 2007 [YUN 2007, p. 262].

Extension of Panel of Experts. On 15 October, by resolution 1841(2008) (see below), the Security Council extended until 15 October 2009 the mandate of the Panel of Experts and requested it to submit during 2009 an interim report and a final report with its findings and recommendations.

SECURITY COUNCIL ACTION

On 15 October [meeting 5996], the Security Council unanimously adopted **resolution 1841(2008)**. The draft [S/2008/648] was submitted by the United States.

The Security Council,

Recalling its previous resolutions concerning the situation in the Sudan, in particular resolutions 1556(2004) of 30 July 2004, 1591(2005) of 29 March 2005, 1651(2005) of 21 December 2005, 1665(2006) of 29 March 2006, 1672(2006) of 25 April 2006, 1713(2006) of 29 September 2006, 1769(2007) of 31 July 2007, 1779(2007) of 28 September 2007 and 1828(2008) of 31 July 2008, and the statements by its President concerning the Sudan,

Reaffirming its commitment to the sovereignty, unity, independence and territorial integrity of the Sudan, and recalling the importance of the principles of good neighbourliness, non-interference and cooperation in the relations among States in the region,

Stressing again its firm commitment to the cause of peace throughout the Sudan, full implementation of the Comprehensive Peace Agreement of 9 January 2005, full implementation of the framework agreed between the parties for a resolution of the conflict in Darfur (the Darfur Peace Agreement), and an end to the violence and atrocities in Darfur,

Reiterating the importance of promoting a political process to restore peace and stability in Darfur, and strongly urging those parties that have not yet agreed to participate in negotiations to do so immediately and all parties to the conflict to engage fully and constructively in the process and to cooperate with the Joint African Union United Nations Chief Mediator for Darfur, Mr. Djibrill Yipènè Bassolé,

Reiterating its belief in the basis provided by the Darfur Peace Agreement for a lasting political solution and sustained security in Darfur, and deploring that the Agreement has not been fully implemented by the signatories and has not been signed by all parties to the conflict in Darfur,

Noting with strong concern the ongoing violence, impunity and consequent deterioration of the humanitarian situation, reiterating its deep concern about the security of civilians and humanitarian aid workers and about humanitarian access to populations in need, and calling upon all parties in Darfur to cease offensive actions immediately and to refrain from further violent attacks,

Demanding that there should be no aerial bombings nor use in Darfur, by any party to the conflict, of white aircraft or aircraft with markings resembling those on United Nations aircraft, and demanding that the parties to the conflict exercise restraint and cease military action,

Commending the efforts of, and reiterating its full support for, the Joint African Union-United Nations Chief Mediator, the United Nations Secretary-General, the League of Arab States and the leaders of the region to promote peace and stability in Darfur, looking forward to the full and rapid deployment of the African Union-United Nations Hybrid Operation in Darfur (UNAMID), and expressing its strong support for the political process under the African Union-United Nations-led mediation,

Recalling the midterm report of 27 May 2008 of the Panel of Experts appointed by the Secretary-General pursuant to paragraph 3 *(b)* of resolution 1591(2005) and extended by resolutions 1651(2005), 1665(2006), 1713(2006) and 1779(2007), taking note of the final report of the Panel, and expressing its intent to study the recommendations of the Panel further and to consider appropriate next steps,

Emphasizing the need to respect the provisions of the Charter of the United Nations concerning privileges and immunities and the Convention on the Privileges and Immunities of the United Nations, as applicable to United Nations operations and persons engaged in such operations,

Determining that the situation in the Sudan continues to constitute a threat to international peace and security in the region,

Acting under Chapter VII of the Charter,

1. *Decides* to extend until 15 October 2009 the mandate of the current Panel of Experts, originally appointed pursuant to resolution 1591(2005) and previously extended by resolutions 1651(2005), 1665(2006), 1713(2006) and 1779(2007), and requests the Secretary-General to take the necessary administrative measures;

2. *Requests* the Panel of Experts to provide, no later than 29 March 2009, a midterm briefing on its work and, no later than ninety days after the adoption of the present resolution, an interim report to the Security Council Committee established pursuant to paragraph 3 *(a)* of resolution 1591(2005), and a final report no later than thirty days prior to the termination of its mandate to the Security Council, with its findings and recommendations;

3. *Also requests* the Panel of Experts to coordinate its activities, as appropriate, with the operations of the African Union United Nations Hybrid Operation in Darfur (UNAMID) and with international efforts to promote the political process in Darfur, and to assess in its interim and final reports progress towards reducing violations by all parties of the measures imposed by paragraphs 7 and 8 of resolution 1556(2004) and paragraph 7 of resolution 1591(2005) and progress towards reducing impediments to the political process, threats to stability in Darfur and the region and other violations of the above mentioned resolutions;

4. *Urges* all States, relevant United Nations bodies, the African Union and other interested parties to cooperate fully with the Committee and the Panel of Experts, in particular by supplying any information at their disposal on the implementation of the measures imposed by resolutions 1556(2004) and 1591(2005);

5. *Decides* to remain actively seized of the matter.

Report of Panel of Experts. On 7 November [S/2008/647], the Chairman of the Security Council Committee established pursuant to resolution 1591(2005) transmitted to the Council the final report of the Panel of Experts on the Sudan, in response to Security Council resolution 1779(2007) [YUN 2007, p. 261]. The report, which was presented to the Committee on 10 October, contained the Panel's findings and recommendations for the period from 28 September 2007 to 19 September 2008. The Panel noted that flagrant violations of the arms embargo by all Darfur parties continued, allowing both the Government and the armed groups to conduct offensive military operations inside and outside Darfur. Attempts to bring the warring parties to the negotiating table or to broker ceasefires had failed. The Darfur armed groups had further fragmented and insecurity had increased. Offensive military overflights continued with impunity and both the major armed groups and the Sudanese army continued to carry out attacks. The replacement of AMIS peacekeeping forces with the new UNAMID force did not produce the security dividends expected. Ten months into its deployment, UNAMID proved incapable of defending itself or the civilian population, and it could not fulfil its obligations to monitor the arms embargo.

Within the context of continued violations of the embargo, the Darfur conflict expanded into the wider region. Armed groups from Darfur reached the capitals of both Chad and the Sudan, and a proxy war was being carried out between the Sudan and Chad through non-State actors in and around Darfur. Opposition groups were armed on their respective territories with the support and encouragement of the two Governments and their respective military and intelligence branches. Arms and military materiel delivered to Chad and the Sudan outside of the provisions of the embargo were diverted into Darfur and fuelled the conflict. The consequences of the violations and regional escalation of the conflict most acutely affected the civilian population. Humanitarian access continued to decrease across the three Darfur states as insecurity increased. Violations of international human rights and humanitarian law continued and violators operated in a culture of impunity. The civilian population displaced into refugee and IDP camps as a result of the conflict continued to grow, and attacks escalated in the camps themselves.

In its recommendations, the Panel reiterated its 2006 recommendation [YUN 2006, p. 294] that the Security Council expand the arms embargo to all of the Sudan, and that it also include Chad and northern parts of the Central African Republic. Monitoring should be carried out at airports, seaports and road links throughout the territory subject to an extended embargo comprising additional territory in Chad and the Central African Republic. Limitations imposed by the Sudan on the access of UNMIS, UNAMID and the Panel of Experts to material, including flight logs, should be removed, and the system should allow for unanticipated cargo spot checks. Arms embargo monitoring should be incorporated within UNAMID, UNMIS, the United Nations Mission in the Central African Republic and Chad (MINURCAT) and the European Union-led military force in Chad and the Central African Republic (EUFOR); dedicated arms embargo cells should be created within those missions; and cooperation mechanisms among the missions should be created for embargo monitoring and verification. The Panel reiterated its recommendation that countries trading military goods and services with the Sudan implement a requirement for end-use certification, and recommended the voluntary cessation of sales of arms and related materiel to the Sudan where it could be proven that the end use of previous deliveries had violated the embargo. It also recommended imposing targeted sanctions on SAF and Ministry of Defence leaders when military equipment supplied with end-user certification was proven to have been used in Darfur. The Sudan should be required to remove from the region all identified post-embargo military equipment, weapons and munitions, and aircraft transported into Darfur in violation of the embargo. The Council should enhance the Panel's capacity to conduct in-depth investigations into violations of an extended embargo and to liaise with regional peacekeeping missions.

Appointment. On 26 November [S/2008/743], the Secretary-General appointed five persons to serve on the Panel of Experts until 15 October 2009.

Report of Sanctions Committee. On 31 December [S/2008/840], the Sanctions Committee Chairman transmitted to the Security Council a report on activities in 2008. The Committee held eight informal consultations and submitted four reports to the Council. It received no additional replies from Member States on steps taken to implement the sanctions; thus, the total number of replies received remained 13. During its informal consultations on 10 October, the Committee discussed with members of the Panel of Experts the findings and recommendations contained in the Panel's final report under resolution 1779(2007) [YUN 2007, p. 260] and agreed to implement some of the recommendations or elements thereof. On 20 November, the Chairman sent a letter to the Sudan concerning arms embargo notification and compliance; offensive military overflights; Government aircraft that could be confused with aircraft owned by international organizations, including the United Nations; the Panel's work on the ground; and the travel ban and assets freeze. The Government responded on 22 December.

UNAMID

The African Union-United Nations Hybrid Operation in Darfur (UNAMID) was established in 2007 by Security Council resolution 1769(2007) [YUN 2007, p. 251] as the first AU-UN hybrid operation. It incorporated the African Union Mission in the Sudan (AMIS), which had been deployed in Darfur since 2004. The core mandate of UNAMID was to protect civilians, but other tasks included contributing to security for humanitarian assistance, monitoring the implementation of agreements, assisting the political process, promoting human rights and the rule of law, and monitoring the situation along the Sudan's borders with Chad and the Central African Republic. UNAMID deployment continued to be hindered by a deteriorating security situation, poor transportation infrastructure within the Sudan, and a range of diplomatic and political issues. The Operation lacked a number of key assets, including transport units, aircraft and, in some cases, basic accommodations. As at 31 December, UNAMID strength stood at 12,369 military personnel—63 per cent of the authorized total—and 2,767 police. In July, the Security Council, by resolution 1828(2008), extended the UNAMID mandate for a further 12-month period ending on 31 July 2009 (see p. 252).

Financing

In April [A/62/791 & Corr.1, 2], the Secretary-General submitted the proposed UNAMID budget for the period from 1 July 2008 to 30 June 2009, amounting to $1,699,710,000. The budget provided for the deployment of 240 military observers, 19,315 military contingent personnel, 3,772 UN police officers, 2,660 formed police unit personnel, 1,554 international staff and 3,455 national staff. In May [A/62/781/Add.14], ACABQ recommended that the General Assembly approve the appropriation in the amount proposed by the Secretary-General, subject to the submission of a report by the Secretary-General no later than 30 November on progress in the implementation of the budget. It also recommended assessment of $849,855,000 for the period from 1 July to 31 December 2008.

GENERAL ASSEMBLY ACTION

On 20 June [meeting 109], the General Assembly, on the recommendation of the Fifth Committee [A/62/601/Add.1], adopted **resolution 62/232 B** without vote [agenda item 161].

Financing of the African Union-United Nations Hybrid Operation in Darfur

B

The General Assembly,

Having considered the report of the Secretary-General on the financing of the African Union-United Nations Hybrid Operation in Darfur and the related report of the Advisory Committee on Administrative and Budgetary Questions,

Recalling Security Council resolution 1769(2007) of 31 July 2007, by which the Council established the African Union-United Nations Hybrid Operation in Darfur for an initial period of twelve months as from 31 July 2007,

Recalling also its resolution 62/232 A of 22 December 2007 on the financing of the Operation,

Reaffirming the general principles underlying the financing of United Nations peacekeeping operations, as stated in its resolutions 1874(S IV) of 27 June 1963, 3101(XXVIII) of 11 December 1973 and 55/235 of 23 December 2000,

Mindful of the fact that it is essential to provide the Operation with the financial resources necessary to enable it to fulfil its responsibilities under the resolution of the Security Council,

Noting the hybrid nature of the Operation, and in that regard stressing the importance of ensuring full coordination of efforts between the African Union and the United Nations at the strategic level, unity of command at the operational level and clear delegation of authority and accountability lines,

1. *Requests* the Secretary-General to entrust the Head of Mission with the task of formulating future budget proposals in full accordance with the provisions of General Assembly resolutions 59/296 of 22 June 2005, 60/266 of 30 June 2006 and 61/276 of 29 June 2007, as well as other relevant resolutions;

2. *Takes note* of the status of contributions to the African Union-United Nations Hybrid Operation in Darfur as at 30 May 2008, including the contributions outstanding in the amount of 345.1 million United States dollars, representing some 27 per cent of the total assessed contributions, notes with concern that only sixty-four Member States have paid their assessed contributions in full, and urges all other Member States, in particular those in arrears, to ensure payment of their outstanding assessed contributions;

3. *Expresses its appreciation* to those Member States that have paid their assessed contributions in full, and urges all other Member States to make every possible effort to ensure payment of their assessed contributions to the Operation in full;

4. *Expresses concern* at the financial situation with regard to peacekeeping activities, in particular as regards the reimbursements to troop contributors that bear additional burdens owing to overdue payments by Member States of their assessments;

5. *Also expresses concern* at the delay experienced by the Secretary-General in deploying and providing adequate resources to some recent peacekeeping missions, in particular those in Africa;

6. *Emphasizes* that all future and existing peacekeeping missions shall be given equal and non-discriminatory treatment in respect of financial and administrative arrangements;

7. *Also emphasizes* that all peacekeeping missions shall be provided with adequate resources for the effective and efficient discharge of their respective mandates;

8. *Reiterates its request* to the Secretary-General to make the fullest possible use of facilities and equipment at the United Nations Logistics Base at Brindisi, Italy, in order to minimize the costs of procurement for the Operation;

9. *Endorses* the conclusions and recommendations contained in the report of the Advisory Committee on Administrative and Budgetary Questions, subject to the provisions of the present resolution, and requests the Secretary-General to ensure their full implementation;

10. *Requests* the Secretary-General to ensure the full implementation of the relevant provisions of its resolutions 59/296, 60/266 and 61/276;

11. *Also requests* the Secretary-General to take all necessary action to ensure that the Operation is administered with a maximum of efficiency and economy;

12. *Further requests* the Secretary-General to include in his future budget submission details of the mechanisms that exist at Headquarters and in the field for ensuring coordination and collaboration among all United Nations actors active in the relevant mission area;

13. *Requests* the Secretary-General to ensure that future budgets for the Operation contain sufficient information, explanation and justification of the proposed resource requirements relating to its operational costs in order to allow Member States to take well-informed decisions;

14. *Also requests* the Secretary-General, in order to reduce the cost of employing General Service staff, to continue efforts to recruit local staff for the Operation against General Service posts, commensurate with the requirements of the Operation;

Budget estimates for the period from 1 July 2008 to 30 June 2009

15. *Decides* to appropriate to the Special Account for the African Union-United Nations Hybrid Operation in Darfur the amount of 1,569,255,200 dollars for the period from 1 July 2008 to 30 June 2009, inclusive of 1,499,710,000 dollars for the maintenance of the Operation, 60,624,500 dollars for the support account for peacekeeping operations and 8,920,700 dollars for the United Nations Logistics Base;

Financing of the appropriation

16. *Also decides* to apportion among Member States the amount of 147,437,934 dollars for the period from 1 to 31 July 2008, in accordance with the levels updated in General Assembly resolution 61/243 of 22 December 2006, and taking into account the scale of assessments for 2008, as set out in its resolution 61/237 of 22 December 2006;

17. *Further decides* that, in accordance with the provisions of its resolution 973(X) of 15 December 1955, there

shall be set off against the apportionment among Member States, as provided for in paragraph 16 above, their respective share in the Tax Equalization Fund of 2,242,000 dollars, comprising the estimated staff assessment income of 1,697,825 dollars approved for the Operation, the prorated share of 485,408 dollars of the estimated staff assessment income approved for the support account and the prorated share of 58,767 dollars of the estimated staff assessment income approved for the United Nations Logistics Base;

18. *Decides* to apportion among Member States the amount of 771,962,266 dollars, comprising the amount of 708,212,500 dollars for the maintenance of the Operation for the period from 1 August to 31 December 2008 at a monthly rate of 141,642,500 dollars and the amount of 63,749,766 dollars for the support account and the United Nations Logistics Base for the period from 1 August 2008 to 30 June 2009 at the monthly rate of 5,795,433 dollars, in accordance with the levels updated in General Assembly resolution 61/243, and taking into account the scale of assessments for 2008 and 2009, as set out in its resolution 61/237, subject to a decision of the Security Council to extend the mandate of the Operation;

19. *Also decides* that, in accordance with the provisions of its resolution 973(X), there shall be set off against the apportionment among Member States, as provided for in paragraph 18 above, their respective share in the Tax Equalization Fund of 14,475,050 dollars, comprising the estimated staff assessment income of 8,489,125 dollars approved for the Operation, the prorated share of 5,339,492 dollars of the estimated staff assessment income approved for the support account and the prorated share of 646,433 dollars of the estimated staff assessment income approved for the United Nations Logistics Base;

20. *Emphasizes* that no peacekeeping mission shall be financed by borrowing funds from other active peacekeeping missions;

21. *Encourages* the Secretary-General to continue to take additional measures to ensure the safety and security of all personnel participating in the Operation under the auspices of the United Nations, bearing in mind paragraphs 5 and 6 of Security Council resolution 1502(2003) of 26 August 2003;

22. *Invites* voluntary contributions to the Operation in cash and in the form of services and supplies acceptable to the Secretary-General, to be administered, as appropriate, in accordance with the procedure and practices established by the General Assembly;

23. *Decides* to include in the provisional agenda of its sixty-third session the item entitled "Financing of the African Union-United Nations Hybrid Operation in Darfur".

In November [A/63/535], the Secretary-General submitted the UNAMID performance report for the period from 1 July 2007 to 30 June 2008. The report discussed the UNAMID mandate and resource performance, and provided an analysis of variances. Expenditures for the period from 1 July 2007 to 30 June 2008 totalled $1,056,478,600 gross ($1,049,786,300 net) against an apportionment of $1,275,653,700 gross ($1,264,273,500 net). The resulting unencumbered balance of $219,175,100 gross ($214,487,200 net) represented, in gross terms, 17.2 per cent of the total apportionment. The Secretary-General recommended that the General Assembly decide on the treatment of the unencumbered balance with respect to the period from 1 July 2007 to 30 June 2008 and of other income for the period ended 30 June 2008 in the amount of $6,268,100.

In a November progress report on the 2008–2009 UNAMID budget [A/63/544], the Secretary-General provided information on the status of budget implementation as at 30 September, including progress in the implementation of requests made by the General Assembly and ACABQ recommendations endorsed by the Assembly; and updated information on resource requirements, including the revised UNAMID deployment plan and projected expenditures for the period ending 30 June 2009. The projected expenditure for the period from 1 July 2008 to 30 June 2009 amounted to $1,499,710,000 gross. The Secretary-General recommended that the Assembly assess $649,855,000 for the maintenance of the Operation for the period from 1 January to 30 June 2009, in addition to the amount of $849,855,000 assessed for the period from 1 July to 31 December 2008 under Assembly resolution 62/232 B (see above).

ACABQ, in a December report [A/63/606 & Corr.1], set out recommendations that would entail a reduction of $100 million in the amount to be assessed on Member States for the maintenance of UNAMID for the period from 1 January to 30 June 2009. Accordingly, it recommended that the Assembly assess $549,855,000 for the maintenance of the Operation for that period. With regard to UNAMID financing for the period from 1 July 2007 to 30 June 2008, ACABQ recommended that the unencumbered balance of $219,175,100 and other income/adjustments in the amount of $6,268,100 be credited to Member States in a manner to be determined by the Assembly.

GENERAL ASSEMBLY ACTION

On 24 December [meeting 74], the General Assembly, on the recommendation of the Fifth Committee [A/63/647], adopted **resolution 63/258 A** without vote [agenda item 148].

Financing of the African Union-United Nations Hybrid Operation in Darfur

The General Assembly,

Having considered the reports of the Secretary-General on the African Union-United Nations Hybrid Operation in Darfur and the related report of the Advisory Committee on Administrative and Budgetary Questions,

1. *Endorses* the conclusions and recommendations contained in the report of the Advisory Committee on Administrative and Budgetary Questions, subject to the provisions of the present resolution, and requests the Secretary-General to ensure their full implementation;

Financial performance report for the period from 1 July 2007 to 30 June 2008

2. *Takes note* of the report of the Secretary-General on the financial performance of the Operation for the period from 1 July 2007 to 30 June 2008;

Progress report for the period from 1 July 2008 to 30 June 2009

3. *Also takes note* of the progress report of the Secretary-General on the budget of the Operation for the period from 1 July 2008 to 30 June 2009;

4. *Reaffirms* the provisions of paragraph 15 of its resolution 62/232 B of 20 June 2008;

Financing of the appropriation for the period from 1 July 2008 to 30 June 2009

5. *Decides* to apportion among Member States the amount of 449,855,000 United States dollars for the period from 1 January to 30 June 2009, in accordance with the updated levels approved by the General Assembly in its resolution 61/243 of 22 December 2006, and taking into account the scale of assessments for 2009 as set out in its resolution 61/237 of 22 December 2006, in addition to the amount of 919,400,200 dollars already apportioned among Member States under the terms of resolution 62/232 B, comprising the amount of 849,855,000 dollars for the maintenance of the Operation for the period from 1 July to 31 December 2008, the amount of 60,624,500 dollars for the support account for peacekeeping operations for the period from 1 July 2008 to 30 June 2009, and the amount of 8,920,700 dollars for the United Nations Logistics Base at Brindisi, Italy, for the period from 1 July 2008 to 30 June 2009;

6. *Also decides* that, in accordance with the provisions of its resolution 973(X) of 15 December 1955, there shall be set off against the apportionment among Member States, as provided for in paragraph 5 above, their respective share in the Tax Equalization Fund of 6,373,050 dollars, representing the estimated staff assessment income approved for the Operation for the period from 1 January to 30 June 2009;

7. *Authorizes* the Secretary-General, upon the advice of the Controller, to assess on Member States, as required, a further amount of up to 200 million dollars for the maintenance of the Operation for the period from 1 January to 30 June 2009;

8. *Decides* that, for Member States that have fulfilled their financial obligations to the Operation, their respective share of the unencumbered balance and other income in the total amount of 225,443,200 dollars in respect of the financial period ended 30 June 2008, shall, on an exceptional basis, and in the light of the submission of a progress report during the budget period, be offset against either their apportionment as provided for in paragraph 5 above or the apportionment for the Operation effective for the period from 1 July 2009 to 30 June 2010, according to the preference of the relevant Member State, in accordance with the updated levels approved by the General Assembly in its resolution 61/243, taking into account the scale of assessments for 2008, as set out in its resolution 61/237, and requests the Secretary-General to implement such an approach;

9. *Also decides* that, for Member States that have not fulfilled their financial obligations to the Operation, there shall be set off against their outstanding obligations their respective share of the unencumbered balance and other income in the total amount of 225,443,200 dollars in respect of the financial period ended 30 June 2008, in accordance with the scheme set out in paragraph 8 above;

10. *Further decides* that the decrease of 4,687,900 dollars in staff assessment income in respect of the financial period ended 30 June 2008 shall be set off against the credits from the amount of 225,443,200 dollars referred to in paragraphs 8 and 9 above;

11. *Decides* to keep under review during its sixty-third session the item entitled "Financing of the African Union-United Nations Hybrid Operation in Darfur".

The Assembly, by **decision 63/552** of 24 December, decided that the agenda item on UNAMID financing would remain for consideration during its resumed sixty-third (2009) session.

Chad–Sudan

In a press statement of 7 January [SC/9221], the Security Council expressed its concern at the recent upsurge of activities of illegal armed groups in western Darfur and in eastern Chad, and at the resulting tension between the two countries. The Council called on the Sudan and Chad to exercise restraint and pursue dialogue and cooperation, and called on all parties in the Sudan and Chad to respect their commitments, in particular in the 2006 Tripoli Agreement [YUN 2006, p. 297], the 2007 Riyadh Agreement [YUN 2007, p. 266] and the 2007 Sirte Agreement [ibid., p. 156].

Communications (January–March). In a letter of 9 January to the Security Council [S/2008/20], the Sudan said that the President of Chad, Idriss Déby Itno, in a speech delivered on 5 January in N'Djamena, Chad, publicly declared that Chadian forces would attack positions inside the Sudan. On 6 January, the Chadian air force bombed the Sudanese villages of Juwkar and Wadi Rati 35 kilometres from Geneina, injuring seven people, five of whom later died. The Sudan described previous Chadian violations of Sudanese airspace, including those that took place on 6 and 20 October 2007; 19, 27 and 28 November 2007; 28 December 2007; and 1 January 2008. The Sudan emphasized that allowing Chad to continue its aggression would undermine efforts to resolve the question of Darfur and would jeopardize the security and peace of the entire region.

On 15 January [S/2008/21], Chad denied Sudanese allegations that sought to portray Chad as an aggressor against the Sudan, where in fact the Sudan was disregarding its commitments with respect to dialogue, peace and security, particularly those contained in the 2006 Tripoli Agreement and the 2007 Riyadh Agreement. Chad had the right to defend itself under Article 51 of the UN Charter. The Sudan had not stopped organizing and arming hostile groups in its territory to destabilize Chad, and was secretly plotting to install a compliant regime in N'Djamena prior to the deployment of the EU operation (EUFOR) there.

On 5 February [S/2008/75], Chad stated that the situation in the country could be further aggravated by new armed attacks from the Sudan aimed at overthrowing democratically established institutions. The attacks, which began on 3 February in Adé and Adré from the direction of the Sudanese border, threatened to compromise efforts to find a solution to acts of aggression against Chad.

On 5 March [S/2008/160], the Sudan stated that, on 3 March, a military jeep carrying non-African soldiers crossed the Sudanese border from Chad and opened fire on the Sudanese observer unit in the village of Umm Jaradil in Western Darfur. The observer unit returned fire, hitting the vehicle; the people on board fled on foot into Chadian territory. Later, three other jeeps supported by a military helicopter arrived from Chad. A soldier and a number of civilians were wounded in the ensuing confrontation with the Sudanese military unit.

Dakar Agreement. On 13 March, President Déby of Chad and President Al-Bashir of the Sudan, under the auspices of President Abdoulaye Wade of Senegal, signed an agreement in Dakar, Senegal, in which they committed to ending the differences between the two countries, normalizing relations and helping to achieve peace and stability in their countries and the region. The parties also agreed to form a Contact Group under the joint chairmanship of the Congo, Eritrea and the Libyan Arab Jamahiriya to follow up on and implement the provisions of the Agreement and monitor any breaches. On 14 March [SG/SM/11464], the Secretary-General commended the Governments of Chad and the Sudan on the Agreement and called on the two countries to remain steadfast in their resolve to restore peace and stability along their shared border.

Communications (March–May). In a letter of 19 March to the Security Council [S/2008/207], the Sudan stated that on 18 March, Chad facilitated the entry of Bahr Idris Abu Girda of the Justice and Equality Movement (JEM) into the Sudan from N'Djamena to engage in military and subversive operations against the Sudan. Chad was providing Sudanese rebel groups with weapons, including anti-aircraft guns, missile launchers and 500 vehicles. Chadian authorities were also coordinating various movements and groups to launch an attack, including coordination and liaison between JEM officials in Chad and Ahmad Mojan of the SLA-Unity group. The Sudan said that on 18 March, SAF members were ambushed by JEM elements travelling from Chadian territory in an area near Gradia, north-east of El Geneina in Western Darfur; a number of SAF members were wounded or killed.

On 21 March [S/2008/193], Chad categorically denied the information contained in the Sudan's letter, and regretted such disinformation, intended to undermine the implementation of the Dakar Agreement. Preparations were being made to revitalize heavily rearmed groups supported by the Janjaweed to engage again in acts to destabilize and overthrow the legitimate authorities of Chad.

On 27 March [S/2008/212 & Corr.1], the Sudan stated that Chad had violated the Dakar Agreement and previous agreements by sponsoring, between 22 and 24 March, a meeting of Darfur rebel groups in the Abu Nabaq area, 15 kilometres west of the Sudanese city of Kubus; participants included JEM head Khalil Ibrahim and Chadian General 'Abd al-Rahim Bahr. The meeting's objective was to tighten coordination between the Government of Chad and rebel movements in Darfur. On 25 March, Chad began to supply vehicles and ammunition through rebel movement leaders in the Chadian cities of Abashi and Gereida in preparation for attacks against locations in Darfur and Kordofan. In response, Chad, on 28 March [S/2008/217], expressed its indignation that the Sudan had seized upon the pretext described in the letter to reactivate its campaign of destabilization and aggression against Chad, in disregard of the Dakar Agreement.

On 31 March [S/2008/216], the Sudan stated that President Déby was personally supervising coordination with JEM in order to attack Dongola and other cities in the northern province of the Sudan. To that end, JEM received from Chad 156 vehicles, ammunition and heavy weapons, including air defence missiles. The Sudan said that plans included attacks in Western Darfur.

On 1 April [S/2008/222], Chad stated that on that day heavily equipped armed groups with allegiance to the Sudan and supported by the Janjaweed had crossed the border from the Sudan and attacked Adé in Chad. Chad said that it would be judicious to strengthen the United Nations Mission in the Central African Republic and Chad (MINURCAT) to increase its security impact in the area.

On 14 April [S/2008/255], the Sudan informed the Security Council that on 12 April, a JEM force launched an attack from inside Chadian territory on the area of Jabal Kushkush, situated 5 kilometres inside Sudanese territory, with 50 vehicles, infantry and horsemen. Other groups from Chad launched a second attack the same day. Three members of the Sudanese armed forces were killed and 31 were wounded in the attacks.

On 5 May [S/2008/305], the Sudan said that Chad gave direct military aid, consisting of three large trucks loaded with military equipment, three fuel tankers and three vehicles, to JEM in Darfur. On 7 May [S/2008/308], Chad replied that the Sudan repeated baseless accusations intended to excuse action by the Sudan to destabilize Chad, which had no involvement whatsoever in any action by Darfur rebels.

Attack on Omdurman. On 10 May, JEM fighters travelling in 300 armed pickup trucks attacked Omdurman, adjacent to the Sudanese capital, Khartoum. The attack was repelled by Government forces (see p. 236). The Sudan accused Chad of supporting the JEM attack, and President Al-Bashir announced on State television that the Sudan had severed diplomatic ties with Chad. Chad issued a statement on 11 May denying any involvement.

In a letter of 11 May to the Security Council [S/2008/325], the Sudan stated that the JEM attack on Omdurman was planned, financed and carried out by Chad, using a proxy force of mercenaries and foreigners, and was irrefutable confirmation of the information that the Sudan had conveyed to the Council in previous letters.

The Sudan boycotted a meeting of the Dakar Agreement Contact Group (Tripoli, Libya, 12–13 May). Members of the group in attendance (Chad, Congo, Eritrea, Gabon, Libya, Senegal) issued a communiqué on 12 May calling on all parties to exercise restraint. The Security Council, in presidential statement S/PRST/2008/15 of 13 May (see p. 237), condemned the attacks, urged all parties to cease violence and called on the States of the region to implement their commitments under the Dakar Agreement.

In a letter of 15 May [S/2008/332], Chad, referring to the Sudan's letter of 11 May, stressed that Chad was in no way implicated in the attack on Omdurman by JEM, a movement in Darfur struggling against the Government.

Communication. On 17 June [S/2008/398], Chad informed the Security Council that the Sudan had that day launched a ground and air attack on Adé and Bakout, situated near the Chad-Sudan border. Chad asked the Council to condemn the belligerent and unacceptable conduct of the Sudan and urge it to stop its aggression against Chad.

Further developments

In July [S/2008/443], the Secretary-General reported that tensions remained high along the Chad-Sudan border, particularly in the period following the attack of 10 May on Omdurman. On 13 June, forces of the Chadian Armed Opposition Groups (CAOG) seized the towns of Goz Beida and Adé in Chad, but were driven out by Chadian regular forces the following day. The efforts of the Dakar Agreement Contact Group to lessen tensions between the Sudan and Chad, as well as the work of the Chairman of the AU Commission, Jean Ping, were vital in promoting dialogue between the two countries. The group last met on 9 June in Brazzaville, Congo, and would meet again on 17 July in Dakar, Senegal.

In August [S/2008/558], the Secretary-General said that relations between Chad and the Sudan had improved. During a meeting of the Dakar Agreement Contact Group (Dakar, 17 July), it was announced that, in response to an appeal made by President Wade of Senegal, President Al-Bashir had accepted a resumption of diplomatic relations with Chad. In resolution 1828(2008) of 31 July (see p. 252), the Security Council called on Chad and the Sudan to abide by their obligations under the Dakar Agreement, the 2006 Tripoli Agreement [YUN 2006, p. 297] and subsequent bilateral agreements, including by ending support for rebel groups.

In October [S/2008/659], the Secretary-General reported that the resumption of diplomatic relations between the Sudan and Chad was announced at the 12 September meeting of the Contact Group (Asmara, Eritrea). In December [S/2008/781], he stated that Chad and the Sudan exchanged ambassadors on 9 November, and both countries sent representatives to participate in the Dakar Agreement Contact Group meeting in N'Djamena on 15 November.

Somalia

The security situation remained volatile throughout Somalia in 2008, despite some progress on the political front. In January, a UN assessment mission to Somalia outlined an approach for a comprehensive UN strategy for the country including political, security and programmatic dimensions. The Department of Peacekeeping Operations led a fact-finding mission to the region in January to update contingency plans for the possible deployment of a UN peacekeeping mission in Somalia. In February, AU Chairperson Alpha Oumar Konaré requested the United Nations to provide a support package for the African Union Mission in Somalia (AMISOM) amounting to some $817.5 million. In response, the Secretary-General's Special Representative and the country team increased political mediation and programmatic support to the Transitional Federal Government and Somali stakeholders. In May, the Special Representative initiated talks in Djibouti between the Government of Somalia and the Alliance for the Re-liberation of Somalia. On 9 June, the parties signed the Djibouti agreement on the cessation of hostilities. During a third round of talks in Djibouti on 26 October, the parties signed an agreement on the cessation of armed confrontation. On the same date, the Government and the Alliance adopted a declaration on the establishment of a unity Government and an inclusive Parliament.

Despite those positive developments, insurgent groups increased attacks on AMISOM troops in April and May, resulting in the death of peacekeepers. The acting head of the United Nations Development Programme (UNDP) in Mogadishu was killed by unidentified gunmen on 6 July. On 29 October, suicide bomb attacks targeted the UNDP compound in Hargeysa and the town of Boosasso, killing two UN staff members and wounding six others. Meanwhile, piracy off the Somali coast greatly increased. In June, the Security Council authorized States cooperating with the Transitional Federal Government to enter Somalia's territorial waters to repress acts of piracy and armed robbery. In November, the Council imposed financial sanctions on individuals engaging in acts that threatened Somalia's peace, security and stability.

National reconciliation process and security situation

Political and security developments

AU Peace and Security Council decision. The one hundred and fifth meeting of the AU Peace and Security Council (Addis Ababa, Ethiopia, 18 January) issued a communiqué containing its decision on the situation in Somalia. Among other measures, the Council extended the mandate of the African Union Mission in Somalia (AMISOM), which was authorized in 2007 by the AU Peace and Security Council [YUN 2007, p. 268] and the UN Security Council by resolution 1744(2007) [ibid., p. 269], for a further six months. It appealed to AU member States to provide the required troops and other personnel to reach the authorized strength of the Mission, as well as financial and logistical support to facilitate its deployment. The Peace and Security Council stressed the need for the deployment of a UN peacekeeping operation in Somalia that would take over AMISOM and support the long-term stabilization and post-conflict reconstruction of the country, and reiterated its appeal to the Security Council to take steps for the early deployment of such an operation. AU member States and the international community were called on to provide support to enhance the capacity of Somali institutions, including the Transitional Federal Government and its security and defence forces. The UN Security Council was urged to review the arms embargo imposed by resolution 733(1992) [YUN 1992, p. 199] in order to enable the Government to establish effective security and defence forces, while maintaining the embargo on elements aiming to undermine peace and reconciliation in Somalia.

Briefing by AU Permanent Observer. The AU Permanent Observer, Lila Ratsifandrihamanana, addressing the Security Council on 15 February [meeting 5837], said that despite constraints facing AMISOM, it continued to provide medical services and water to the population residing near its headquarters in Mogadishu, Somalia, and to receive for storage and destruction weapons surrendered by various armed elements. The AMISOM budget amounted to $622 million per year, but little more than $32 million had been contributed, mainly from China, the EU, Italy, LAS and Sweden. The United States continued to provide significant logistical support to the Ugandan contingent, as well as communications equipment for the Mission's strategic headquarters in Addis Ababa. Of 8,000 troops authorized by the AU Peace and Security Council, only two Ugandan battalions and an advance team of 192 Burundian soldiers were on the ground in Mogadishu. The AU would convene a high-level international meeting to refocus international attention on Somalia and mobilize support for the reconciliation process.

Following the Permanent Observer's briefing, Somalia urged the Council to accelerate the implementation of presidential statement S/PRST/2007/49 [YUN 2007, p. 280], in which the Council reiterated its request that the Secretary-General develop contingency plans for the possible deployment of a UN peacekeeping operation to succeed AMISOM, as set out in resolution 1772(2007) [ibid., p. 276].

SECURITY COUNCIL ACTION

On 20 February [meeting 5842], the Security Council unanimously adopted **resolution 1801(2008)**. The draft [S/2008/113] was submitted by the United Kingdom.

The Security Council,

Recalling its previous resolutions concerning the situation in Somalia, in particular resolutions 733(1992) of 23 January 1992, 1356(2001) of 19 June 2001, 1425(2002) of 22 July 2002, 1725(2006) of 6 December 2006, 1744(2007) of 20 February 2007 and 1772(2007) of 20 August 2007, and the statements by its President, in particular those of 13 July 2006, 22 December 2006, 30 April 2007, 14 June 2007 and 19 December 2007,

Reaffirming its respect for the sovereignty, territorial integrity, political independence and unity of Somalia,

Reiterating its commitment to a comprehensive and lasting settlement of the situation in Somalia through the Transitional Federal Charter, stressing the importance of broad-based and representative institutions reached through a political process ultimately inclusive of all, as envisaged in the Transitional Federal Charter, and reiterating its support for Somalia's transitional federal institutions,

Welcoming the appointment by President Abdullahi Yusuf Ahmed of Prime Minister Nur "Adde" Hassan Hussein, the subsequent appointment of a new Cabinet under the Transitional Federal Government, and the relocation of the Transitional Federal Government to Mogadishu,

Commending the work of the Special Representative of the Secretary-General for Somalia, Mr. Ahmedou Ould-Abdallah, and affirming its strong support for his efforts,

Underlining the importance of providing and maintaining stability and security throughout Somalia, and underscoring the importance of disarmament, demobilization and reintegration of militia and ex-combatants in Somalia,

Condemning all acts of violence and extremism inside Somalia, and expressing its concern regarding the continued violence inside Somalia,

Stressing its concern at the upsurge in piracy off the Somali coast described in paragraph 22 of the report of the Secretary-General of 7 November 2007, and recalling the joint communiqué of the International Maritime Organization and the World Food Programme of 10 July 2007,

Reiterating its appreciation of the efforts of the international community, in particular the African Union, as well as the League of Arab States, the Intergovernmental Authority on Development and the European Union, to promote peace, stability and reconciliation in Somalia, and welcoming their continued engagement,

Recalling that cooperation between the United Nations and the regional arrangements in matters relating to the maintenance of peace and security, as are appropriate for regional action, is an integral part of collective security as provided for in the Charter of the United Nations,

Welcoming the communiqué of the Peace and Security Council of the African Union of 18 January 2008, which states that the African Union will extend the mandate of its mission to Somalia for an additional six months,

Emphasizing the contribution that the African Union Mission in Somalia and its Ugandan and Burundian contingents are making to lasting peace and stability in Somalia, including the important work that the Ugandan forces have carried out in providing medical care for Somali citizens, condemning any hostility towards them, and urging all parties in Somalia and the region to support and cooperate with the Mission, *Welcoming* the sustained commitment of the Government of Uganda to supporting the efforts of the Mission over the last year and the Government of Burundi for its recent deployment,

Taking note of the report of the Secretary-General on the situation in Somalia, in particular paragraph 32 thereof, and expressing its appreciation for his support of the Mission,

Underlining that the full deployment of the Mission will help to facilitate the full withdrawal of other foreign forces from Somalia and help to create the conditions for lasting peace and stability there,

Noting that the communiqué of the Peace and Security Council of 18 January 2008 calls for the United Nations to deploy a peacekeeping operation to Somalia that will support the long-term stabilization and post-conflict restoration in the country,

Recalling the request made in the statement by its President of 19 December 2007 that the Secretary-General report to the Security Council on the development of contingency plans for the possible deployment of a United Nations peacekeeping operation to succeed the Mission, as set out in resolution 1772(2007),

Determining that the situation in Somalia continues to constitute a threat to international peace and security in the region,

Acting under Chapter VII of the Charter,

1. *Decides* to renew the authorization of member States of the African Union to maintain a mission in Somalia for a further period of six months, which shall be authorized to take all necessary measures, as appropriate, to carry out the mandate set out in paragraph 9 of resolution 1772(2007), and underlines, in particular, that the African Union Mission in Somalia is authorized to take all necessary measures, as appropriate, to provide security for key infrastructure and to contribute, as may be requested and within its capabilities, to the creation of the necessary security conditions for the provision of humanitarian assistance;

2. *Affirms* that the provisions set out in paragraphs 11 and 12 of resolution 1772(2007) shall continue to apply to the mission referred to in paragraph 1 above;

3. *Urges* member States of the African Union to contribute to the Mission in order to help to facilitate the full withdrawal of other foreign forces from Somalia and help to create the conditions for lasting peace and stability there;

4. *Urges* Member States to provide financial resources, personnel, equipment and services for the full deployment of the Mission;

5. *Reaffirms its intention* to take measures against those who seek to prevent or block a peaceful political process, or those who threaten the transitional federal institutions or the Mission by force, or take action that undermines stability in Somalia or the region;

6. *Looks forward* to the forthcoming report of the Secretary-General, due on 10 March 2008, including on specific options to strengthen the ability of the United Nations Political Office for Somalia to support further the full deployment of the Mission, and to prepare for the possible deployment of a United Nations peacekeeping operation to succeed the Mission, and affirms its intention to meet again promptly following the release of the report to consider what further action it might take in the light of options and recommendations contained therein;

7. *Requests* the Secretary-General to continue and intensify his efforts to promote an ongoing political process which is ultimately inclusive of all, including by assisting the transitional federal institutions' role in delivering this and services to the Somali people and by working together with the international community, including the African Union, the League of Arab States, the Intergovernmental Authority on Development, the European Union and the International Contact Group on Somalia and its members;

8. *Calls upon* all international organizations and Member States to support the Special Representative of the Secretary-General for Somalia in his work in order to enhance security and bring a comprehensive and lasting peace to Somalia, and requests that they work through him at all times so that a coordinated effort can be attained;

9. *Urges* the transitional federal institutions and all parties in Somalia to respect the conclusions of the National Reconciliation Congress and to sustain an equally inclusive ongoing political process thereafter, ultimately involving all stakeholders, including political leaders, clan leaders, religious leaders, the business community and representatives of civil society such as women's groups, and encourages them to unite behind the efforts to promote such an inclusive dialogue;

10. *Welcomes* the efforts of the Transitional Federal Government towards producing a plan for implementing the conclusions of the National Reconciliation Congress, including the completion of the constitutional process, and

reiterates the need for agreement on a comprehensive and lasting cessation of hostilities and a road map of the critical path for the remainder of the transitional process, including free and democratic elections in 2009 as set out in Somalia's Transitional Federal Charter;

11. *Emphasizes* the continued contribution made to Somalia's peace and security by the arms embargo imposed by resolution 733(1992), as elaborated and amended by subsequent resolutions, demands that all Member States, in particular those of the region, comply fully with it, and reiterates its intention to consider ways to strengthen its effectiveness;

12. *Encourages* Member States whose naval vessels and military aircraft operate in international waters and airspace adjacent to the coast of Somalia to be vigilant to any incidents of piracy therein and to take appropriate action to protect merchant shipping, in particular the transportation of humanitarian aid, against any such act, in line with relevant international law, and welcomes the contribution made by France to protect the World Food Programme naval convoys and the support now provided by Denmark to this end;

13. *Reaffirms* its resolution 1325(2000) of 31 October 2000 on women and peace and security, and its resolutions 1674(2006) of 28 April 2006 and 1738(2006) of 23 December 2006 on the protection of civilians in armed conflict, and stresses the responsibility of all parties and armed groups in Somalia to take appropriate steps to protect the civilian population in the country, consistent with international humanitarian, human rights and refugee law, in particular by avoiding any indiscriminate attacks on populated areas;

14. *Strongly supports and encourages* the ongoing humanitarian relief efforts in Somalia, recalls its resolution 1502(2003) of 26 August 2003 on the protection of humanitarian and United Nations personnel, calls upon all parties and armed groups in Somalia to take appropriate steps to ensure the safety and security of Mission and humanitarian personnel, and to grant timely, safe and unhindered access for the delivery of humanitarian assistance to all those in need, and urges the countries in the region to facilitate the provision of humanitarian assistance by land or via airports and seaports;

15. *Reaffirms* its previous resolution 1612(2005) of 26 July 2005 on children and armed conflict, and recalls the subsequent conclusions of the Security Council Working Group on Children and Armed Conflict pertaining to parties to the armed conflict in Somalia;

16. *Decides* to remain actively seized of the matter.

Communication. In a letter of 20 February to the Secretary-General annexed to the Secretary-General's March report on the situation in Somalia (see below), the AU Chairperson, Alpha Oumar Konaré, requested that the United Nations put in place a financial, logistical and technical support package for AMISOM, amounting to some $817,500,000. The letter contained a note detailing immediate requirements that were not funded, and described the deployment situation: only three battalions out of nine authorized had deployed; the fourth was not expected to be fully deployed until the end of May. The AU was not certain that troops pledged by Ghana and Nigeria would deploy in the required time frame without a more robust Mission support package. The United Nations was requested to consider providing logistical support in procurement and project management for the upgrading of AMISOM mission headquarters to UN minimum operating safety standard criteria; establishment of a main logistics base in Mombasa, Kenya, in Djibouti, or in Dar es Salaam, United Republic of Tanzania, and a forward base in Mogadishu; procurement and provision of long-term fuel and ration contracts; enhancement of voice and data communications systems; establishment of a transit camp near Mogadishu airport; provision of essential AU police communications equipment, armoured vehicles and accommodation infrastructure; transportation and deployment of AMISOM troops and equipment; provision of one fixed-wing aircraft to transport personnel within the mission area and to Nairobi, Kenya; and enhancement of the AMISOM hospital to UN level II standard. As the AU administration was not resourced to cope with the operational tempo required for peacekeeping on such a large scale, the AU was seeking UN assistance in the area of mission support. Specifically, the United Nations was asked to provide staff on loan in the critical areas of Chief of Mission support, procurement, budget, finance, internal oversight, contingent-owned equipment, contract management, and a security adviser to the Head of Mission.

Report of Secretary-General (March). In response to presidential statement S/PRST/2001/30 [YUN 2001, p. 210], the Secretary-General in March submitted a report [S/2008/178 & Corr.1,2] on the situation in Somalia, covering developments since his previous report [YUN 2007, p. 278]. On 6 January, Prime Minister Nur Hassan Hussein announced the appointment of a new cabinet comprising 18 Ministers and 5 Deputy Ministers. Of the 18 ministerial posts, nine were selected from within Parliament. The other nine Ministers were to be selected from outside Parliament; six of those Ministers had been appointed and the remaining three were left to the opposition in exile. Following the relocation of the Government from Baidoa to Mogadishu on 20 January, the Prime Minister made public statements on his Government's willingness to restore security, uphold press freedom, and promote national reconciliation. On 10 January, Parliament endorsed the Cabinet and its proposed programme of work, which focused on reconciliation, peace and security, strengthening institutions, the Constitution and electoral issues. The Government hoped to establish a Somali State with functional governance institutions and a multiparty system. Before the end of the transition period, it intended to enact an electoral bill; set up a national census commission; establish a national electoral commission; enact a bill regulating the formation and registration of political parties; and establish a commission for the delimitation of regional, State and district boundaries. The Secretary-General's Special Representative for Somalia, Ahmedou Ould-Abdallah, focused his efforts on building greater cohesion among members of the international community involved in Somalia. The EU and other international partners, together with the UN country team and the United Nations Political Office for Somalia (UNPOS), intensified efforts to strengthen coordination for international assistance to the Transitional Federal Government. A six-month start-up package worth $14 million was developed to strengthen the transitional federal institutions.

The security situation remained volatile throughout Somalia, despite significant regional variations. Criminal elements engaged in trafficking in human beings, weapons and drugs; unauthorized collection of taxes and levies; and abduction, kidnapping and extortion. In the north, the border dispute between the self-declared independent republic of Somaliland and the semi-autonomous region of Puntland remained a security concern, aggravated by kidnappings and acts of piracy, especially in Puntland. In southern and central Somalia, the Union of Islamic Courts (UIC) and other anti-Government elements continued to conduct insurgency operations in Mogadishu, Kismaayo, Baidoa and other areas, targeting mainly the Ethiopian armed forces and the forces of the Transitional Federal Government, police stations and Government authorities. The security situation in Mogadishu was characterized by coordinated attacks by anti-Government elements and an increase in Ethiopian army and Transitional Federal Government operations to eradicate those elements. Insurgents occasionally targeted AMISOM and the United Nations.

An 850-strong Burundian battalion completed its deployment in Mogadishu on 20 January. Mission strength stood at 2,613 personnel. AMISOM continued to provide security and conduct patrols for the protection of the airport, seaport and presidential palace. The AU continued to face serious constraints, particularly with regard to finance, logistics and force generation. Sweden pledged to provide the mission with a level-II hospital. Other financial support came from the EU, China, Italy, LAS and the United Kingdom. The United States and the North Atlantic Treaty Organization (NATO) pledged to provide airlift facilities to troop-contributing countries, and Nigeria pledged a contribution of $2 million. The pledges, however, fell short of projected requirements. The United Nations deployed a team of military and civilian experts to AU headquarters to increase AMISOM planning and implementation capacity.

Two complementary missions to Somalia were conducted during the reporting period, and their findings were annexed to the report. A task force on Somalia, headed by the UN Department of Political Affairs (DPA), was established in New York and deployed an assessment mission to Somalia in January to develop a comprehensive UN strategy for Somalia. The task force's assessment set out the most critical factors driving the conflict and outlined an integrated, three-track approach including political, security and programmatic (humanitarian, recovery and development) dimensions that could form the basis for a strategy led by the Special Representative. It included recommendations for integrating the three tracks; strengthening the capacity of UNPOS and the UN country team; developing a viable security component; establishing a mechanism linking the United Nations, international partners and Somali authorities; relocating the UN headquarters for activities in Somalia to the country; and improving UN human rights capacity.

In accordance with presidential statement S/PRST/2007/49 [YUN 2007, p. 280] and resolution 1772(2007) [ibid., p. 276], DPKO led an interdepartmental fact-finding mission to the region (7–25 January) to consult with stakeholders and assess the security situation on the ground, with a view to updating contingency plans for the possible deployment of a UN peacekeeping operation in Somalia, and provide recommendations for further UN support to AMISOM. The mission developed four scenarios leading to the deployment of a possible UN peacekeeping operation. Under scenario 1, UN political and programmatic support to Somalia would be facilitated through a substantial relocation of UN staff from Nairobi to Somalia. The Secretary-General had requested the UN Department of Safety and Security to develop viable options to meet that objective, and the Security Council could consider establishing a maritime task force to formalize the unilateral initiatives being undertaken by individual States. Under scenario 2, UNPOS headquarters would be relocated to Mogadishu to strengthen UN political support to the peace process. Under scenario 3, an impartial stabilization force composed of an estimated 8,000 troops and police officers would be deployed to allow the withdrawal of Ethiopian forces, prevent a security vacuum and provide impetus to the political dialogue. Under scenario 4, a UN peacekeeping operation would be deployed. A force of 15 to 21 infantry battalions would be required, and the number of military personnel could total 27,000, with a police component of up to 1,500 officers.

On 10 January, the Secretary-General's Special Representative met with the leadership of the Alliance for the Re-liberation of Somalia (ARS) in Asmara, Eritrea; ARS expressed its support for an approach that addressed the grievances of the parties to the conflict.

As a follow-up to the December 2007 briefing by the Special Representative to the Security Council [YUN 2007, p. 280], the United Kingdom facilitated a meeting on security challenges and options for Somalia (London, 9 January 2008). The meeting considered options for the strengthening of AMISOM; the deployment of a UN peacekeeping force; the possible deployment of a multinational force as a bridging mechanism between the current situation and a UN peacekeeping mission; and a political settlement without the need for an international force.

Regarding the humanitarian situation, the Secretary-General said that nearly 300,000 people had left the capital since October 2007 following an upsurge of fighting between the Transitional Federal Government and anti-Government elements. The delivery of humanitarian assistance was confronted with access and operational challenges. A major relief effort continued in a key centre of the crisis along the Mogadishu-Afgooye corridor, where 200,000 internally displaced persons lived. The effort included food distribution, the transportation of 2 million litres of clean water per day, construction of latrines, vaccination campaigns and the setting-up of schools.

The Secretary-General observed that the political situation in the country provided a unique opportunity for proactive international engagement to support domestic initiatives. The security situation, however, remained a concern, as did the dire humanitarian condition of the Somali people. He reiterated his call for the leaders of the Transitional Federal Government to implement the recommendations of the National Reconciliation Congress of 2007 [YUN 2007, p. 275], including the development of a road map for the completion of the tasks provided for in the Transitional Federal Charter [YUN 2003, pp. 247 & 248] and the implementation of the National Security and Stabilization Plan. The Secretary-General called on all parties to cease hostilities, engage in the search for peace, protect the civilian population and abstain from harming humanitarian workers and other expatriates. He called on Somalis to renounce violence and adhere to the Transitional Federal Charter.

The Secretary-General endorsed the three-track approach of the strategic assessment as the basis for UN engagement. He had asked the Department of Safety and Security, in consultation with DPKO and the Department of Field Support (DFS), to develop security options for relocating UNPOS and the country team headquarters from Nairobi to Mogadishu. In addition to AMISOM and a possible UN peacekeeping force, the international community should consider other options, including the deployment of a robust multinational force for a specific period to secure a specific area, which could pave the way for the withdrawal of foreign forces. The Secretary-General called for the establishment of a capacity within UNPOS to monitor and enhance human rights protection.

Reconciliation strategy. On 14 March, the Transitional Federal Government unveiled its reconciliation strategy, which included two components: promoting peacebuilding at the community level and proposing reconciliation between the Government and the opposition based within and outside Somalia. On 23 March, Prime Minister Hussein met with the leadership of the Hawiye Traditional and Unity Council to present a proposed strategy paper detailing the reconciliation programme and invited civil society representatives to play a role in the reconciliation process. With the exception of the Al-Shabaab group, which stated that it would not engage with the Government, the strategy was met with mostly positive reactions from other Somali stakeholders, particularly ARS. The Special Representative invited ARS leaders to engage in preliminary discussions on their role in the peace process as a prelude to face-to-face talks with the Government. In a letter of 6 May, he informed members of the Somali diaspora of his efforts to secure peace and called for their support. A high-level ARS delegation, including its Chairman, Sheikh Sharif Sheikh Ahmed, and the Chairman of its Central Committee, Sharif Hassan Sheikh Aden, met with the Special Representative and other members of the international community (Nairobi, 28 March–5 April). The delegation agreed to discuss the peace agenda advocated by the Government. It welcomed the UN facilitation role and signed a related memorandum of understanding on 4 April. Opposition leaders stressed the need for the international community to give priority to achieving sustainable peace in Somalia and recognize the responsibility to deploy a neutral force that would be accepted by Somalis. They identified the presence of Ethiopian forces in Somalia and ongoing human rights violations as key areas to be addressed by the international community. Following the meeting, ARS leaders consulted with their constituents within Somalia and abroad to secure their support for further talks with the Government.

Communication. On 23 April [S/2008/309], the Secretary-General responded to the letter of 20 February from the AU Chairperson (see p. 272) setting out the requirements for enhancing AMISOM deployment and requesting further UN support to the AU in meeting those requirements. The Secretary-General said that the United Nations firmly supported the AU view that significant progress had been made in facilitating a credible and inclusive political process, and that the international community could do more to support Somali efforts to bring lasting peace and security. The Special Representative and the UN country team were stepping up the provision of the political mediation and programmatic support necessary for the Transitional Federal Government and Somali stakeholders to engage in a viable process towards a political agreement, while building up the necessary governance and security infrastructure. Once sufficient progress was made in the political and security agreements necessary for the deployment of a UN operation, the Secretary-General would be in a position to make the appropriate recommendations to the Security Council. In the meantime, the Secretariat would continue to provide technical planning support to the AU for AMISOM deployment and to update contingency planning for such an operation. The United Nations agreed that the AU required additional international assistance to enhance AMISOM effectiveness. As requested in the letter of 20 February, the first area of UN assistance would focus on building AU capacity to address the support challenges related to the deployment and sustainment of AMISOM through the provision of additional UN technical advisers to the AMISOM planning team in Addis Ababa, particularly in the areas of procurement, finance and logistics. Attached to the Secretary-General's letter was a list of additional technical advisers that the United Nations would be ready to provide to the AU, pending budgetary approval by the General Assembly.

The second area of assistance would focus on enhancing coordination between the AU, donors and troop-contributing countries to ensure that sufficient funding and support was secured for the requirements of AMISOM and for those of troop-contributing countries. The Secretary-General suggested that the AU and the United Nations hold a high-level donor conference to highlight the needs of AMISOM and solicit additional donor contributions. He also suggested that, at the time of the conference, the two organizations establish a standing coordination mechanism to ensure the continuous updating of the AMISOM concept of operations and requirements, and develop a programme of meetings with troop-contributors and donors to follow up on outstanding requirements. The Secretary-General believed that his proposals represented the most effective way in which the United Nations could help the AU meet its challenges in supporting AMISOM.

Air strike. On 1 May, the United States launched an air strike on Dhusamareeb in the Galgaduud region, killing Sheikh Aden Hashi Ayrow, the military commander of Al-Shabaab. On 4 May, residents of Galgaduud demonstrated against the air strike and Al-Shabaab issued threats of revenge. Following the incident, aid workers were interrogated on suspicion of being spies for the United States, and the United Nations was obliged to introduce restrictions on the movement of United States citizens employed by the United Nations in Somalia.

SECURITY COUNCIL ACTION

On 15 May [meeting 5893], the Security Council unanimously adopted **resolution 1814(2008)**. The draft [S/2008/327] was prepared in consultations among Council members.

The Security Council,

Recalling its previous resolutions concerning the situation in Somalia, in particular resolutions 733(1992) of 23 January 1992, 1356(2001) of 19 June 2001, 1425(2002) of 22 July 2002, 1725(2006) of 6 December 2006, 1744(2007) of 20 February 2007, 1772(2007) of 20 August 2007, 1801(2008) of 20 February 2008 and 1811(2008) of 29 April 2008, and the statements by its President, in particular those of 13 July 2006, 22 December 2006, 30 April 2007, 14 June 2007 and 19 December 2007,

Reaffirming its respect for the sovereignty, territorial integrity, political independence and unity of Somalia,

Reiterating its commitment to a comprehensive and lasting settlement of the situation in Somalia through the Transitional Federal Charter, stressing the importance of broad-based and representative institutions reached through a political process ultimately inclusive of all, as envisaged in the Transitional Federal Charter, and reiterating its support for Somalia's transitional federal institutions to take this forward,

Reiterating the need for agreement on a comprehensive and lasting cessation of hostilities and a road map for the remainder of the transitional process, including free and democratic elections in 2009 as set out in the Transitional Federal Charter,

Welcoming the continued efforts of Prime Minister Nur "Adde" Hassan Hussein and his Cabinet, under the leadership of President Abdullahi Yusuf Ahmed and supported by the Transitional Federal Parliament, to advance the political process and implement the transitional period, as required by the Transitional Federal Charter, in particular the agreement to prepare a timetable for the constitutional process leading to a referendum in 2009, the presentation of the reconciliation strategy of the Transitional Federal Government, engagement with clan and local leaders across the country, and efforts to implement the National Security and Stabilization Plan and to improve public finance management, including budgetary and fiscal processes, and supporting efforts to make further progress in all these areas,

Welcoming also the commitment of all Somali parties that have agreed to engage in dialogue with each other with a view to establishing peace and security in Somalia, urging all Somali parties to honour these commitments and to resort to peaceful means only to resolve their disputes, further welcoming the supporting role of the United Nations, in particular the practical support of the Special Representative of the Secretary-General for Somalia and the United Nations Political Office for Somalia to help to progress this dialogue, and supporting in this regard the start of discussions between the parties in Djibouti on 12 May 2008,

Welcoming further the report of the Secretary-General of 14 March 2008 on the situation in Somalia, in particular the assessment that the political situation in Somalia currently provides a renewed opportunity for the international community to give practical support to domestic initiatives, including an increased presence of United Nations personnel and, subject to broad-based political and security agreements and conditions on the ground, the deployment of a United Nations peacekeeping operation to succeed the African Union Mission in Somalia,

Welcoming the support of the Secretary-General for a comprehensive United Nations strategic approach for peace and stability in Somalia, aligning and integrating political, security and programmatic efforts in a sequenced and mutually reinforcing way, and endorsing ongoing work by the United Nations to support the political process in Somalia and to determine options for relocating United Nations staff to Somalia,

Commending the work of the Special Representative of the Secretary-General, Mr. Ahmedou Ould-Abdallah, and of the United Nations Political Office for Somalia, reaffirming its strong support for the work of the Special Representative, in particular his leading role in coordinating international efforts, and requesting that all parties, as well as international organizations, the United Nations country team and Member States support and work in close coordination with him at all times,

Reaffirming its condemnation of all acts of, and incitement to, violence inside Somalia, expressing its concern at all acts intended to prevent or block a peaceful political process, and expressing its further concern at such acts and incitement continuing,

Underlining the importance of providing and maintaining stability and security throughout Somalia, and underscoring the importance of the disarmament, demobilization and reintegration of militia and ex-combatants in Somalia,

Emphasizing the contribution that the Mission is making to lasting peace and stability in Somalia, welcoming in particular the continuing commitment of the Governments of Uganda and Burundi, regretting the recent loss of a Burundian soldier, condemning any hostility towards the Mission, and urging all parties in Somalia and the region to support and cooperate with the Mission,

Underlining that the full deployment of the Mission will help to facilitate the full withdrawal of other foreign forces from Somalia and help to create the conditions for lasting peace and stability there,

Taking note of the letter dated 20 February 2008 from the Chairperson of the African Union Commission to the Secretary-General, annexed to the report of the Secretary-General, and of the reply from the Secretary-General dated 23 April 2008,

Emphasizing the continued contribution made to Somalia's peace and security by the arms embargo imposed by resolution 733(1992), as elaborated and amended by resolutions 1356(2001), 1425(2002), 1725(2006), 1744(2007) and 1772(2007), and reiterating its demand that all Member States, in particular those in the region, comply fully with it,

Expressing its deep concern at the human rights situation in Somalia, and taking note of the resolution on Somalia adopted by the Human Rights Council at its seventh session, and of the renewal by that Council of the mandate of the independent expert on the situation of human rights in Somalia,

Expressing its serious concern at the worsening humanitarian situation in Somalia and the continuing difficulties for humanitarian organizations operating in Somalia, including humanitarian access and security for humanitarian personnel, and reaffirming the humanitarian principles of humanity, neutrality, impartiality and independence,

Determining that the situation in Somalia continues to constitute a threat to international peace and security in the region,

Acting under Chapter VII of the Charter of the United Nations,

1. *Requests* the Secretary-General to continue and intensify his efforts, working together with the international community, to promote an ongoing political process which is ultimately inclusive of all, including by assisting the transitional federal institutions in this regard and in delivering services to the Somali people;

2. *Strongly supports* the approach proposed by the Secretary-General in his report of 14 March 2008, welcomes his intention to provide an updated comprehensive, integrated United Nations strategy for peace and stability in Somalia, aligning and integrating political, security and programmatic efforts in a sequenced and mutually reinforcing way, and to include an assessment of the capacity of the United Nations Political Office for Somalia to implement the strategy, and requests that he submit the updated version to the Security Council within sixty days of the adoption of the present resolution;

3. *Approves* the proposal made by the Secretary-General in his report to establish a joint planning unit in the office of the Special Representative of the Secretary-General for Somalia to facilitate effective and efficient implementation of the integrated strategy;

4. *Welcomes* the recommendation of the Secretary-General, as set out in his report, to relocate the United Nations Political Office for Somalia and the country team headquarters from Nairobi to Mogadishu or an interim location in Somalia in order to help to deliver the comprehensive, integrated United Nations strategy in Somalia, and requests the Secretary-General to establish the necessary security arrangements for such a relocation, and to update the Council when he submits the strategy, referred to in paragraph 2 above;

5. *Decides* that the United Nations Political Office for Somalia and the United Nations country team shall, in promoting a comprehensive and lasting settlement in Somalia and through the promotion of the ongoing political process, enhance their support to the transitional federal institutions with the aim of developing a constitution and holding a constitutional referendum and free and democratic elections in 2009, as required by the Transitional Federal Charter, and facilitating coordination of the support of the international community to these efforts, and requests the Secretary-General, within sixty days of the adoption of the present resolution, to report on progress with this work;

6. *Recalls its intention* to take measures against those who seek to prevent or block a peaceful political process, or those who threaten the transitional federal institutions or the African Union Mission in Somalia by force, or take action that undermines stability in Somalia or the region, and therefore requests the Security Council Committee established pursuant to resolution 751(1992) (hereinafter

"the Committee") to provide, within sixty days of the adoption of the present resolution, recommendations on specific targeted measures to be imposed against such individuals or entities;

7. *Also recalls its intention* to strengthen the effectiveness of the United Nations arms embargo on Somalia, states its intention to take measures against those who breach the arms embargo and those who support them in doing so, and therefore requests the Committee to provide, within sixty days of the adoption of the present resolution, recommendations on specific targeted measures to be imposed against such individuals or entities;

8. *Requests* the Secretary-General to continue his contingency planning for the possible deployment of a United Nations peacekeeping operation in Somalia to succeed the Mission, including of possible additional scenarios, in close contact with the United Nations Political Office for Somalia, the United Nations country team and other United Nations stakeholders, taking account of all relevant conditions on the ground, and considering additional options for the size, configuration, responsibility and proposed area of operations of the mission, depending on different conditions on the ground, requests the Secretary-General to provide an update on progress in his planning in the report referred to in paragraph 5 above, and expresses its willingness to consider, at an appropriate time, a peacekeeping operation to take over from the Mission, subject to progress in the political process and improvement in the security situation on the ground;

9. *Welcomes* the undertaking by the Secretary-General, as set out in his letter dated 23 April 2008 to the Chairperson of the African Union Commission, to provide additional United Nations technical advisers to the African Union Strategic Planning and Management Unit in Addis Ababa, and encourages the Secretary-General to continue to explore with the Chairperson of the African Union Commission, in coordination with donors, ways and means to strengthen United Nations logistical, political and technical support for the African Union, to build the institutional capacity of the African Union to carry out its commitments in addressing the challenges it faces in supporting the Mission, and to assist the full deployment of the Mission, to the extent possible and as appropriate, with the goal of achieving United Nations standards, and to update the Council in the report referred to in paragraph 5 above;

10. *Reiterates its call upon* Member States to provide financial resources, personnel, equipment and services for the full deployment of the Mission, and upon States members of the African Union to contribute to the Mission in order to facilitate the withdrawal of other foreign forces from Somalia and help to create the conditions for lasting peace and stability there, urges those Member States which have offered to contribute to the Mission to fulfil such commitments, recognizes that more needs to be done to harness increased support for the Mission, and takes note of the proposals of the Secretary-General for harnessing such support, as set out in his letter dated 23 April 2008;

11. *Reiterates its support* for the contribution made by some States to protect the World Food Programme maritime convoys, calls upon States and regional organizations, in close coordination with each other and as notified in advance to the Secretary-General, and at the request of the Transitional Federal Government, to take action to protect shipping involved with the transportation and delivery of humanitarian aid to Somalia and United Nations-authorized activities, calls upon troop-contributing countries to the Mission, as appropriate, to provide support to this end, and requests the Secretary-General to provide his support to this effect;

12. *Strongly supports and encourages* the ongoing humanitarian relief efforts in Somalia, recalls its resolution 1502(2003) of 26 August 2003 on the protection of humanitarian and United Nations personnel, calls upon all parties and armed groups in Somalia to take appropriate steps to ensure the safety and security of Mission personnel and United Nations and humanitarian personnel, demands that all parties ensure timely, safe and unhindered access for the delivery of humanitarian assistance to all those in need, wherever they may be, and urges the countries in the region to facilitate the provision of humanitarian assistance, including the timely, safe and unhindered passage of essential relief goods into Somalia by land or via airports and seaports;

13. *Requests* the Secretary-General to strengthen ongoing efforts for establishing a United Nations-led mechanism for bringing together and facilitating consultations between humanitarian organizations operating in Somalia, the Transitional Federal Government, donors and other relevant parties in order to help to resolve issues of access, security and provision of humanitarian relief throughout Somalia, and further requests the Secretary-General to report on progress in the report referred to in paragraph 5 above;

14. *Also requests* the Secretary-General to establish an effective capacity within the United Nations Political Office for Somalia to monitor and enhance the protection of human rights in Somalia, and to ensure coordination, as appropriate, between the United Nations Political Office for Somalia, the Office of the United Nations High Commissioner for Human Rights and the independent expert of the Human Rights Council on the situation of human rights in Somalia, and further requests the Secretary-General to report on progress in achieving this in the report referred to in paragraph 5 above;

15. *Supports* the ongoing efforts of the United Nations, the African Union and interested Member States, in close cooperation with the Transitional Federal Government, to develop security sector institutions in Somalia, and requests the Special Representative of the Secretary-General to enhance his coordination role in this area, aligning relevant United Nations programmes and activities of Member States;

16. *Condemns* all and any violations of human rights and international humanitarian law, calls upon all parties in Somalia to respect fully their obligations in this regard, and calls for those responsible for such violations in Somalia to be brought to justice;

17. *Reaffirms* its resolution 1325(2000) of 31 October 2000 on women and peace and security and its resolutions 1674(2006) of 28 April 2006 and 1738(2006) of 23 December 2006 on the protection of civilians in armed conflict, and stresses the responsibility of all parties and armed

groups in Somalia to take appropriate steps to protect the civilian population in the country, consistent with international humanitarian, human rights and refugee law, in particular by avoiding any indiscriminate attacks on populated areas;

18. *Also reaffirms* its resolution 1612(2005) of 26 July 2005 on children and armed conflict, and recalls the subsequent conclusions of the Security Council Working Group on Children and Armed Conflict pertaining to parties to the armed conflict in Somalia;

19. *Recalls* that, pursuant to Article 65 of the Charter of the United Nations, the Economic and Social Council may furnish information to the Security Council and shall assist the Security Council upon its request;

20. *Decides* to remain actively seized of the matter.

Djibouti talks (May–June). On 12 May, the Special Representative initiated a first round of talks in Djibouti between the Transitional Federal Government and ARS. On 15 May, the two sides committed to a peaceful resolution of the conflict and signed a joint declaration calling on their supporters to facilitate unhindered humanitarian access and the delivery of assistance. The ARS Chairman acknowledged Eritrea's support for ARS but accused it of attempting to divide the group. He urged the Eritrean Government to engage with the true leadership of ARS and restated the ARS call for the withdrawal of Ethiopian troops, whom he accused of violating human rights. A second round of talks began in Djibouti on 31 May, coinciding with the visit of the Security Council mission to Africa. Council members encouraged the parties to engage in credible dialogue and reiterated their readiness to support any agreement.

On 9 June, the Transitional Federal Government and ARS reached a political agreement that was initialled by both parties and provided for a cessation of hostilities for an initial 90-day period, starting 30 days from the signing of the agreement. It also provided for submission of a joint request to the Security Council to authorize and deploy, within four months, an international stabilization force from non-neighbouring friendly States. Under the agreement, the Government would act in accordance with Ethiopia's decision to withdraw its troops following the deployment of a sufficient number of UN forces; ARS would dissociate itself from any armed groups or individuals that did not adhere to the agreement; and both parties would ensure unhindered humanitarian access. The parties decided to establish, within 15 days of the signing of the agreement, a joint security committee, chaired by the United Nations, to follow up on the implementation of agreed security arrangements; and a high-level committee, also chaired by the United Nations, to address political, justice and reconciliation issues. The agreement called for the convening of a conference before the end of July to further discuss those issues, and of an international conference within the next six months to support the reconstruction and development of Somalia. While hardliners within the opposition condemned the agreement, ARS leaders reiterated their commitment to it and expressed a desire for an early withdrawal of Ethiopian troops. Prime Minister Hussein invited opposition leaders who had not participated in the Djibouti talks to join the political process.

Statement by Secretary-General. Welcoming the agreement, the Secretary-General, in a press statement of 10 June [SG/SM/11629], said that he would remain engaged through the efforts of his Special Representative, and called on the international community to provide diplomatic and financial support for the implementation of the agreement.

Security Council mission

The Security Council mission to Africa (see p. 111) briefed the Council on 18 June [meeting 5915]. In its report of 15 July [S/2008/460], the mission stated that in Djibouti for talks on Somalia (2–3 June) it received briefings by the Special Representative, Ahmedou Ould Abdallah, and the Chief Security Adviser, Jean Lausberg. It met with the President of Somalia, Abdullahi Yusuf Ahmed, and the delegation of the Transitional Federal Government, including the Minister for Foreign Affairs, Ali Ahmed Jama; an AU delegation, led by the Commissioner for Peace and Security, Ramtane Lamamra; ARS, led by its Chairman, Sheikh Sharif Sheikh Ahmed; the UN country team; and members of civil society.

President Yusuf reiterated his commitment to the ongoing dialogue in Djibouti (see above) and stressed that he wanted to lead his country to peace and stability. He appealed to the Security Council to lift the arms embargo on Somalia to allow the Transitional National Government to build its security apparatus; deploy a UN peacekeeping operation to take over from AMISOM; and assist in addressing piracy. Regarding the remaining steps anticipated in the transitional road map, the President appealed for assistance in drafting a new Constitution and conducting a census in preparation for the elections, as stipulated in the Transitional Federal Charter. The mission stressed the need for political and security agreements and the appropriate conditions on the ground before any deployment of a UN peacekeeping mission. It encouraged the participation of women in the political process and stressed the importance of ending impunity, protecting human rights and ensuring unhindered access for humanitarian relief. The Minister for Foreign Affairs stated that the Government was committed to investigating any accusations of human rights abuses and prosecuting guilty parties.

The AU Commissioner for Peace and Security stressed that the situation in Somalia was a threat to international peace and security, owing to piracy, violations of the arms embargo, and the illegal exploitation and abuse of Somalia's natural resources. The mission urged the AU to work closely with the Special Representative on the political front and reach out to the parties that were not yet engaged in the Djibouti dialogue.

ARS set out the principles through which it believed the crisis could be resolved, namely, peace and restoration of Somalia's sovereignty through dialogue; the legitimate right under international law to resist occupation; the withdrawal of Ethiopian forces; peace as a unifying element; rejection of violence and terrorism; Islam as the only guarantee for peace, stability and social justice; and access to humanitarian assistance. It appealed to the Council to ensure the withdrawal of Ethiopian troops; investigate war crimes and establish a war crimes tribunal; end massacres and killings in the country, including in places of worship; and provide emergency relief assistance. The mission stressed that the only basis for withdrawal of Ethiopian troops and the deployment of a UN peacekeeping mission was a political agreement that could be presented to the international community.

The mission recommended that the Security Council continue to consider ways to support the Special Representative in his efforts to further political progress. It also recommended that it consider how best to support the agreement of 9 June between the Transitional Federal Government and ARS (see p. 278); and ways to enhance the international security presence, including the deployment of a peacekeeping operation to take over from AMISOM at an appropriate time.

Further developments

Killing of UNDP official. On 6 July, the acting head of the UNDP office in Mogadishu, Ali Osman Ahmed, was killed by unidentified gunmen as he exited a mosque. Mr. Ahmed's brother and son were among those wounded in the attack. In a press statement of 7 July [SG/SM/11685], the Secretary-General condemned the killing and encouraged all Somalis to work together towards peace and reconciliation.

The Security Council, in a press statement of 8 July [SC/9388], condemned the killing and reaffirmed the imperative to respect the safety and security of UN and humanitarian personnel. The Council called on all Somalis to prevent such attacks from occurring in the future and to work together through peaceful dialogue.

Report of Secretary-General (July). In July [S/2008/466], the Secretary-General reported that the general security situation in Somalia remained volatile. Criminal activities in southern and central areas and in Puntland increased significantly, exacerbated by weak law enforcement capacity. The authorities of Somaliland and Puntland continued to build up their military presence around the disputed area of Las Aanod. The build-up created a security vacuum elsewhere in Puntland, which, along with the lack of payments to police and militias working for the Government, led to increases in piracy along the coastline, kidnapping and threats of hostage-taking. As a result, the security level in Puntland was upgraded to phase IV. Clashes between Union of Islamic Courts (UIC) militants, Al-Shabaab and Ethiopian-backed Government forces became more frequent in and around Baidoa and along the Mogadishu-Afgooye-Baidoa highway. The absence of Government control in Beletweyne and Wajid, held by UIC, permitted banditry and criminality to thrive, leading to the relocation of all international staff. In Baidoa, five incidents involving roadside improvised explosive devices occurred in May. Following reports of the killing of 21 civilians in April, threats of retaliation were made against Ethiopian troops. On 20 May, gunmen kidnapped two Italian nationals and their Somali colleague from an Italian aid organization compound in the Lower Shabelle region. In early April, two Kenyan and two British teachers were executed by anti-Government elements in Beletweyne. Most international non-governmental organizations (NGOs) evacuated their international staff. On 7 June, a British Broadcasting Corporation reporter was killed in Kismaayo by unknown gunmen, bringing to nine the number of journalists killed since 2007.

Insurgent groups increased attacks on AMISOM troops in April and May. On 8 April, a suicide car bomb exploded at an AMISOM position in Mogadishu, killing one Burundian soldier. On 23 May, a roadside bomb exploded in Mogadishu, injuring four Ugandan peacekeepers. The AU continued to face financial, logistical and force-generation constraints in completing the deployment of AMISOM, which consisted of one Burundian and two Ugandan battalions in Mogadishu, totalling 2,650 troops. On 22 June, the AU signed an umbrella memorandum of understanding with UNOPS in Nairobi for the procurement of equipment for its future mission headquarters in Mogadishu. Italy disbursed €10 million in support of AMISOM activities involving the development of a concept of operations for the Somali police.

On 30 April, the International Contact Group on Somalia met in Oslo, Norway, to discuss the political process, as well as the security and humanitarian situations. It called on all parties to respect international humanitarian law, and agreed that the chairmanship of the group should pass to the Special Representative in order to strengthen the UN leadership role in the peace process.

On 20 May, the three political parties of Somaliland—the ruling National Democratic Union Party and the opposition Peace, Unity and Development Party and Justice and Welfare Party—and the newly established Electoral Commission agreed on dates for local and presidential elections, which would be held on 15 December 2008 and 15 March 2009, respectively. International partners, including Denmark, Norway, the United Kingdom, the United States and the EU, expressed their commitment to support democracy in Somaliland and fund the elections. Presidential and parliamentary elections in Puntland were scheduled for January 2009.

Humanitarian conditions worsened dramatically owing to the ongoing conflict, increasing food prices, a deepening drought and civil insecurity. The number of people in need of humanitarian assistance increased by 40 per cent from January, to 2.6 million, representing 35 per cent of the population. At the same time, actions against the aid community were increasing. On 17 May, the Somali head of the NGO Horn Relief was murdered in Kismaayo. Fifteen aid workers had been killed since January.

In response to resolution 1814(2008), the Secretary-General provided an update regarding the establishment of the necessary security arrangement for the relocation of UNPOS and the UN country team to Mogadishu, as recommended in his March report. The United Nations was developing the modalities for establishing an integrated planning team, which would support the work of the Integrated Task Force on Somalia and conduct an interagency security assessment mission to the region by the end of the third quarter of 2008. Deployment of staff to Mogadishu would require the downgrading of the security level there from phase V to phase IV. Increased UN deployment to Baidoa would be possible without a change from the current security phase IV, but would depend on the adoption of robust mitigating measures.

Extension of AMISOM authorization. The AU Peace and Security Council, meeting on 29 June, condemned in a communiqué threats and acts of violence against AMISOM. It extended the AMISOM mandate for an additional six-month period, beginning on 17 July, and decided that the mission would support the implementation of the agreement of 9 June between the Transitional Federal Government and ARS. The Peace and Security Council appealed to member States to provide the troops and other personnel required to enable AMISOM to reach its authorized strength, and reiterated its appeal for financial and logistical support to complete deployment of the Mission.

SECURITY COUNCIL ACTION

On 19 August [meeting 5957], the Security Council unanimously adopted **resolution 1831(2008)**. The draft [S/2008/566] was prepared in consultations among Council members.

The Security Council,

Recalling its previous resolutions concerning the situation in Somalia, in particular resolutions 733(1992) of 23 January 1992, 1744(2007) of 20 February 2007, 1801(2008) of 20 February 2008, 1811(2008) of 29 April 2008 and 1814(2008) of 15 May 2008, and other relevant resolutions, namely resolutions 1325(2000) of 31 October 2000, 1502(2003) of 26 August 2003, 1612(2005) of 26 July 2005, 1674(2006) of 28 April 2006 and 1738(2006) of 23 December 2006, and the statements by its President, in particular those of 14 June 2007 and 19 December 2007,

Reaffirming its respect for the sovereignty, territorial integrity, political independence and unity of Somalia,

Underlining the importance of providing and maintaining stability and security throughout Somalia, and underscoring the importance of disarmament, demobilization and reintegration of militia and ex-combatants in Somalia,

Reaffirming its condemnation of all acts of, and incitement to, violence inside Somalia, expressing its concern at all acts intended to prevent or block a peaceful political process, and expressing its further concern at such acts and incitement continuing,

Recalling that cooperation between the United Nations and the regional arrangements in matters relating to the maintenance of peace and security, as are appropriate for regional action, is an integral part of collective security as provided for in the Charter of the United Nations,

Welcoming the communiqué of the Peace and Security Council of the African Union of 29 June 2008, which states that the African Union will extend from 17 July 2008 the mandate of its mission to Somalia for an additional six months,

Emphasizing the contribution that the African Union Mission in Somalia is making to lasting peace and stability in Somalia, welcoming in particular the continuing commitment of the Governments of Uganda and Burundi, condemning any hostility towards the Mission, and urging all parties in Somalia and the region to support and cooperate with the Mission,

Welcoming the signing on 19 August 2008 of the agreement between the Transitional Federal Government of Somalia and the Alliance for the Re-liberation of Somalia, and noting that this agreement calls for the United Nations to authorize and deploy an international stabilization force from countries that are friends of Somalia, excluding neighbouring States,

Noting that the communiqué of the Peace and Security Council of 29 June 2008 calls for the United Nations to deploy a peacekeeping operation to Somalia that will support long-term stabilization and post-conflict restoration in the country,

Recalling its willingness to consider, at an appropriate time, a peacekeeping operation to take over from the Mission, subject to progress in the political process and improvement in the security situation on the ground,

Underlining that the full deployment of the Mission will help to facilitate the full withdrawal of other foreign forces from Somalia and help to create the conditions for lasting peace and stability there,

Determining that the situation in Somalia continues to constitute a threat to international peace and security in the region,

Acting under Chapter VII of the Charter,

1. *Decides* to renew the authorization of member States of the African Union to maintain a mission in Somalia for a further period of six months, which shall be authorized to take all necessary measures, as appropriate, to carry out the mandate set out in paragraph 9 of resolution 1772(2007) of 20 August 2007, and underlines, in particular, that the African Union Mission in Somalia is authorized to take all necessary measures, as appropriate, to provide security for key infrastructure and to contribute, as may be requested and within its capabilities, to the creation of the necessary security conditions for the provision of humanitarian assistance;

2. *Affirms* that the provisions set out in paragraphs 11 and 12 of resolution 1772(2007) shall continue to apply to the mission referred to in paragraph 1 above;

3. *Urges* member States of the African Union to contribute to the Mission in order to help to facilitate the full withdrawal of other foreign forces from Somalia and help to create the conditions for lasting peace and stability there;

4. *Urges* Member States to provide financial resources, personnel, equipment and services for the full deployment of the Mission;

5. *Encourages* the Secretary-General to continue to explore with the Chairperson of the African Union Commission, in coordination with donors, ways and means to strengthen United Nations logistical, political and technical support for the African Union, to build the institutional capacity of the African Union to carry out its commitments in addressing the challenges it faces in supporting the Mission, and to assist the full deployment of the Mission, to the extent possible and as appropriate, with the goal of achieving United Nations standards, and in this regard takes note of the proposals set out in paragraph 32 of the report of the Secretary-General of 16 July 2008 on the situation in Somalia;

6. *Decides* to remain actively seized of the matter.

Djibouti agreement. The Secretary-General reported [S/2008/709] significant progress in the discussions between the Transitional Federal Government and ARS towards the implementation of the agreement initialled by the two parties on 9 June. From 16 to 19 August, the parties met in Djibouti, where they endorsed the terms of reference of the High-Level Committee and the Joint Security Committee provided for in the agreement. On 19 August, the Djibouti agreement was signed in the presence of members of the international community.

The Joint Security Committee was co-chaired by the United Nations and the AU, and its meetings were attended by commanders of the security forces of the Transitional Federal Government and field commanders of ARS, whose Commander-in-Chief, Omar Hershi, led the delegation. The responsibilities of the Committee included recommending the modalities and time frame of the phased withdrawal of Ethiopian forces and implementing a cessation of armed confrontation between the Government and ARS. It was also responsible for establishing a joint force of the Government and ARS to observe, verify and monitor compliance with the agreement, facilitate humanitarian access and assistance, investigate reported breaches of the agreement and find solutions in the event of a breach. In addition, the Committee would prepare recommendations for the restructuring and reform of the Somali armed forces. It was envisaged that AMISOM, working with the joint Somali security force, would assist in the monitoring and verification of the ceasefire; bridge the gap before the deployment of an international stabilization force; provide protection for both parties; secure the main lines of communication; and build the capacity of the Somali security force, particularly the police. The leaders of the two delegations to the Committee on 18 August signed a final communiqué that called for the deployment of a UN peacekeeping force. The Committee agreed on modalities for the implementation its mandate, including: observing a ceasefire and cessation of hostilities between the Government and ARS and disengaging the parties' combatants; facilitating the deployment of a UN peacekeeping force; establishing liaison between the two parties and preventing armed confrontation; and demolishing illegal checkpoints that hindered humanitarian aid.

SECURITY COUNCIL ACTION

On 4 September [meeting 5970], following consultations among Security Council members, the President made statement **S/PRST/2008/33** on behalf of the Council:

The Security Council welcomes the signing in Djibouti on 19 August 2008 of a peace and reconciliation agreement between the Transitional Federal Government and the Alliance for the Re-liberation of Somalia ("the Djibouti agreement"), the preliminary work undertaken by the High Level Committee and the Joint Security Committee set up under the agreement, as well as recent political developments. The Council expresses its determination that the agreement should provide the basis for lasting peace, security and stability for the people of Somalia, including the ultimate withdrawal of foreign forces. The Council commends the efforts deployed by the Transitional Federal Government and the Alliance for the Re-liberation of Somalia to this end and their commitment to peace.

The Council reaffirms its respect for the sovereignty, territorial integrity, political independence and unity of Somalia.

The Council extends its gratitude to the Special Representative of the Secretary-General for Somalia, Mr.

Ahmedou Ould Abdallah, and to the United Nations Political Office for Somalia for mediating dialogue between the parties and garnering support for the political process. The Council further expresses its gratitude to the Government of Djibouti for hosting talks between the parties.

The Council calls upon the parties to meet all elements of the agreement in full. In particular, the Council underlines the crucial importance of the parties taking all necessary measures to ensure, without delay, unhindered humanitarian access and assistance to the Somali people, and of the parties and their allies terminating all acts of armed confrontation. The Council states its support for the implementation of the agreement and its intention to review that implementation continuously.

The Council reiterates its strong support for the African Union Mission in Somalia and again urges the international community to provide financial resources, personnel, equipment and services for the full deployment of the Mission.

The Council takes note of the parties' request in the Djibouti agreement that the United Nations, within a period of 120 days, authorize and deploy an international stabilization force. The Council further notes, in this regard, the communiqués issued by the Peace and Security Council of the African Union on 29 June, 8 August and 20 August 2008.

The Security Council, acknowledging recent positive political developments in the wake of the Djibouti agreement as confirmed by Mr. Ould Abdallah, reaffirms its willingness, as set out in its resolution 1814(2008), to consider, at an appropriate time, a United Nations peacekeeping operation to take over from the Mission, subject to progress in the political process and improvement in the security situation on the ground.

The Council recalls the Secretary-General's contingency planning for a United Nations integrated peacekeeping mission in Somalia, which recommends that plans be put in place for the deployment of an international stabilization force, within the framework of the approach presented by the Secretary-General in his report of 14 March 2008.

In this regard, the Council requests that the Secretary-General elaborate on his contingency plans and provide, in consultation with the parties and other relevant stakeholders, a detailed and consolidated description of a feasible multinational force, its mandate and derived tasks, to include, inter alia, the size and geographical scope of that force, progressively deployed, and further provide a detailed concept of operations for a feasible United Nations peacekeeping operation.

The Council further requests the Secretary-General urgently to identify and approach States that might contribute the financial resources, personnel, equipment and services required, stands ready to support the Secretary-General in this regard, and calls upon States to respond favourably.

The Council requests the Secretary-General to report on the implementation of the Djibouti agreement by the parties, including an update on the conditions on the ground, as well as on his planning, including discussions with potential contributing States, within 60 days.

Government dismissals and Addis Ababa agreement. On 29 July, Prime Minister Hussein dismissed the Mayor of Mogadishu and Governor of Benadir Region, Mohammed Dheere, on charges of mismanagement of public funds. On 2 August, 10 cabinet members allied with President Yusuf resigned in protest of the dismissal. President Yusuf subsequently reinstated the Mayor, which exacerbated tensions within the Government. On 3 August, the Prime Minister nominated five new ministers and a deputy minister to replace those who had resigned.

On 25 August, the leadership of the Transitional Federal Government—including the President, the Prime Minister and the Speaker of Parliament—met in Addis Ababa and reached an agreement under the auspices of the Ethiopian Government. The agreement provided for the reconstitution of the Benadir regional administration; the proper collection and administration of revenue; capacity-building for the Ministry of Finance and the customs, airport and seaport administrations; and the redeployment of Ethiopian troops outside the capital. A motion of no confidence against the Prime Minister was defeated in Parliament on 1 September. Members of the Transitional Federal Parliament voted on 6 September against reinstating the cabinet members who had resigned; a Parliament committee examined the issue and upheld its earlier decision not to reinstate them.

Terrorist attacks. On 29 October, five suicide bomb attacks occurred in the towns of Hargeysa and Boosasso in northern Somalia. In Hargeysa the attacks targeted the UNDP compound, the Ethiopian consulate and local government offices. Two UN staff members were killed and six others injured. The Security Council, in presidential statement **S/PRST/2008/41** (see p. 68), condemned the attack in the strongest terms.

Report of Secretary-General (November). In November [S/2008/709], the Secretary-General reported on a number of political developments. The second meeting of the Joint Security Committee (Djibouti, 17–19 September), established in August through the Djibouti agreement (see p. 281), focused on planning for the implementation of the cessation of armed confrontation; the time frame and locations of the withdrawal of Ethiopian forces; and the possible formation of a joint security force. The Committee drafted a ceasefire declaration and an implementation document. The parties, however, requested more time to consult their constituencies, particularly the commanders on the ground, before signing the documents. A communiqué issued on 21 September indicated that Committee members were given 15 days to carry out consultations before proceeding with joint sessions to finalize detailed military modalities, pending the issuance of the ceasefire declaration.

The parties signed an agreement on the cessation of armed confrontation during a third round of talks (Djibouti, 26 October). Under the agreement, a ceasefire would become effective on 5 November; the relocation of Ethiopian troops from Mogadishu and Beletweyne would begin on 21 November and would be completed in accordance with the Djibouti agreement; and AMISOM forces, with the assistance of joint Somali security forces, would provide security in areas vacated by Ethiopian troops. The Joint Security Committee would operate from within Somalia by the end of November.

The Special Representative addressed the twenty-ninth Extraordinary Meeting of the Intergovernmental Authority on Development (IGAD) Council of Ministers on the situation in Somalia (Nairobi, 28 October). In a declaration of 29 October, IGAD urged the parties to implement the ceasefire agreement of 26 October. It requested that the Transitional Federal Government appoint a new cabinet and establish a new Benadir administration within 15 days, finalize the drafting of the Constitution and enact an electoral and political parties law. It established a facilitator to help monitor the implementation of its decisions.

In Somaliland, the authorities launched a nationwide media campaign for voter registration in preparation for the presidential elections on 29 March 2009. All registered parties reiterated their commitment to uphold the rule of law and the Constitution, and maintain peace and stability. Presidential and parliamentary elections in Puntland were scheduled for 9 January 2009.

The security situation in south-central Somalia deteriorated dramatically between July and October. The Monitoring Group on Somalia noted persistent violations of the arms embargo in an environment of general lawlessness and lack of accountability. Continuous fighting between anti-Government elements and Government-backed Ethiopian forces occurred in different locations throughout the country, resulting in a heavy loss of civilian lives. Beletweyne was evacuated by the Ethiopian armed forces as a result of discussions with ARS fighters on the ground following the signing of the Djibouti agreement. The Government did not have the capacity to defend and control the entire country, and was unable to pay salaries to the police and troops. As a result, about 40 per cent of the police officers trained by the United Nations left the police force owing to the non-payment of salaries. The international community, which had supported the Government in maintaining its security, withheld support due to allegations of human rights violations by some Government forces, as well as a lack of transparency and accountability for the funding provided. The Secretary-General said that it was essential that security institutions be strengthened through the provision of necessary resources.

The fighting increasingly threatened UN activities. Mortar attacks on airfields and roadblocks within Somalia prevented UN and NGO humanitarian workers from discharging their duties. The risk of UN staff being targeted in another major terrorist attack in the country or at the United Nations Office at Nairobi was growing. The threat of attack issued by Al-Shabaab against all flights into Mogadishu International Airport from 16 September, and the subsequent mortar attack on an aircraft at that airport, pointed to the deterioration of the security situation in Mogadishu.

In response to Security Council presidential statement S/PRST/2008/33 of 4 September (see p. 281), the Secretary-General tasked DPKO to develop the concept of a feasible international stabilization force to support the implementation of the Djibouti agreement, taking into account the presence of AMISOM. In September, a DPKO team visited Addis Ababa to develop a description of such a force jointly with the AU. It was proposed that a feasible stabilization force would be composed of a headquarters and two multinational force brigades, operating under unified command. The force's area of operations would be limited to Mogadishu. It would adopt a phased approach, in which it would be deployed to Mogadishu (Phase One); monitor and verify withdrawal of the Ethiopian armed forces from Mogadishu (Phase Two); and focus on stabilization operations in Mogadishu to create space for the Transitional Federal Government to consolidate its authority, support relocation of the United Nations to Mogadishu and facilitate the conduct of a UN technical assessment mission (Phase Three). In Phase Four, a UN peacekeeping operation would take over from the international stabilization force, subject to political progress and improvements in the security situation, and following a Security Council resolution. DPKO developed a list of countries that were considered to have the capacity to provide a lead contingent, troops, funding or equipment for the envisaged force. The Secretary-General sent letters to the leaders of those countries, appealing to them to take the lead role, or contribute troops, funds or equipment for the force.

In November, AMISOM consisted of two Burundian battalions and two Ugandan battalions, amounting to 3,400 troops in Mogadishu. The second Burundian battalion was deployed to Somalia between 11 and 13 October. AMISOM estimated that to reach its mandated strength, approximately $200 million would be required for 2009, excluding bilateral support to troops.

Meeting for the first time under the chairmanship of the Special Representative (Djibouti, 16 September), the International Contact Group on Somalia urged the parties to agree on measures for implementing the cessation of armed confrontation, and to allow the withdrawal of Ethiopian forces and the deployment of the stabilization force requested in the agreement. The Group expressed its support for the implementation of agreements reached in the meetings of the Committees. It condemned the continuing violence and called on all parties to cease hostilities and allow free and unhindered access for humanitarian aid. The Group urged all parties to join the political process; work through the Committees provided for in the Djibouti agreement; and agree on plans and mechanisms to support the delivery of much-needed humanitarian assistance.

Sweden hosted a preparatory meeting for an International Donor Conference on Recovery and Development for Somalia (Stockholm, Sweden, 20–21 October), as provided for in the Djibouti agreement. The Special Representative chaired the meeting, which was attended by representatives of the Transitional Federal Government, ARS and the donor community. As at 1 October, approximately $164.7 million had been mobilized for recovery and development activities across Somalia, representing 58 per cent of what was required to meet UN transition plan targets for 2008. Meanwhile, the humanitarian situation continued to deteriorate. According to a food security assessment carried out in August, the number of people in need of livelihood and humanitarian support had increased by 77 per cent, from 1.8 million to 3.2 million people since January. The humanitarian crisis was expanding to the north, where at least 350,000 persons were in need of humanitarian assistance or livelihood support.

The Secretary-General urged all Somalis to join the Djibouti process, implement it faithfully and commit unconditionally to peace. He observed that the Addis Ababa agreement of 25 August had to be implemented quickly to establish a credible and efficient administration in Mogadishu and its region.

Joint declaration. At a meeting of the High-Level Committee on 26 October, the Transitional Federal Government and ARS adopted a joint declaration on the establishment of a unity Government and inclusive Parliament, in line with the commitments made under the Djibouti agreement. In November, the High-Level Committee agreed on further modalities to enhance political cooperation, and the two parties established a working group to engage on details of the unity structures. The Joint Security Committee developed detailed proposals to strengthen the work of the High-Level Committee, particularly with regard to the implementation of the agreement on the cessation of armed confrontation, also signed on 26 October. The Joint Security Committee established a working group for the integration and realignment of the police, and agreed to develop plans for the formation of interim joint security forces and command structures. It also agreed to establish a verification and monitoring mission, with headquarters in Mogadishu, to promote a comprehensive ceasefire. Lack of financial and logistical support, however, delayed progress in all areas. In a workshop facilitated by UNDP (Naivasha, Kenya, 20–24 November), the Joint Security Committee decided to develop a 10,000-strong civilian police force under Somali law and with international standards.

Security Council consideration. Addressing the Security Council on 20 November [meeting 6020], the Assistant Secretary-General for Political Affairs, Haile Menkerios, said that the withdrawal of Ethiopian forces from locations in Beletweyne and Mogadishu began on 17 November, as agreed in the cessation of hostilities agreement of 26 October. The Ethiopian command handed over its main base in Mogadishu to AMISOM, and field commanders of both the Transitional Federal Government and ARS were organizing their forces for the implementation of the agreement. Hard-line groups, including Al-Shabaab, expanded their operations within south-central Somalia, and militia groups gained military control in the Lower Juba and Lower Shebelle regions, including the city of Merka, where Government authority was absent.

Raisedon Zenenga, Director of the Africa II Division of DPKO, briefed the Council on actions taken by DPKO with respect to presidential statement S/PRST/2008/33 of 4 September (see p. 281), which asked the Secretary-General to approach States that might contribute financial resources, personnel, equipment and services for the envisaged multinational force. On 18 September, DPKO convened a meeting with Council members to seek their suggestions and support regarding the mobilization of countries that could contribute to the force. The Secretary-General on 24 October wrote to 50 countries identified as potential contributors. Many countries indicated that they would need more time to respond. Seven responses had been received: one Member State offered to contribute equipment, airlift capacity or funding, and four advised that they were unable to contribute troops. Two of the three organizations approached expressed readiness to help facilitate funding from their member States. The remaining 45 countries and one organization approached had yet to respond. On 17 November, the Secretariat convened a meeting of the 50 Member States and three organizations approached, providing additional information based on the inquiries received.

Year-end developments

In a later report [S/2009/132], the Secretary-General said that in November, Ethiopia announced its intention to start withdrawing its forces from Somalia by the end of the year. In early December, ARS members, led by Sheikh Sharif Sheikh Ahmed, returned to Mogadishu for the first time in two years to begin implementation of the Djibouti agreement. The delegation was warmly received by representatives of the Transitional Federal Government, ARS supporters and the local population. In a statement delivered on 29 December before Parliament and cabinet members in Baidoa, President Yusuf announced that he was resigning to avoid being seen as an "obstacle to peace". Following his resignation, the Speaker of Parliament, Sheikh Adan Madobe, became acting President, in line with the Transitional Federal Charter, which empowered Parliament to elect a new President within 30 days.

UNDP suspended mine-action activities in south-central Somalia late in 2008 due to the security situation. Security constraints also continued to hamper humanitarian operations across much of the country. In 2008, 34 aid workers were killed and 26 were abducted. Nevertheless, WFP shipped nearly 260,000 tons of food to Somalia, nearly four times the amount shipped in 2007, reaching more than 1.5 million Somalis with food aid every month.

Communications. In a letter of 19 December [S/2008/804] to the Security Council, the Secretary-General said that only 14 countries out of the 50 approached responded to his request for contributions to the multinational force envisaged in presidential statement S/PRST/2008/33; sufficient troop pledges to allow deployment of such a force were unlikely to materialize. The complex security challenges in Somalia could not be addressed within the capabilities of a typical UN peacekeeping force, and a multinational force was the right tool for stabilizing Mogadishu. The Secretary-General presented alternative options that could be undertaken immediately to support the Djibouti peace process and contribute to the conditions required for deploying a UN peacekeeping operation. That included requesting the AU to maintain AMISOM troops on the ground following the withdrawal of Ethiopian forces at the end of 2008, coupled with measures to reinforce the mission; providing international training for the joint police and military forces of the Government and ARS established by the Djibouti process; building the capacity of rule-of-law and security institutions; establishing a maritime task force or adding to the current anti-piracy operations (see below) a quick-reaction component; and continuing preparations for the deployment of a UN peacekeeping operation at the appropriate time.

In a letter of 31 December [S/2008/846], the Secretary-General informed the Council that the Secretariat had initiated action to provide logistics support for AMISOM. He noted that, given the lead time required to put in place the appropriate servicing arrangements, the United Nations might need to rely on existing arrangements to ensure the uninterrupted provision of logistics support.

Piracy and armed robbery against vessels off the coast of Somalia

Communications. On 23 April [S/2008/271], Spain informed the Security Council that on 20 April, the Spanish fishing boat *Playa de Bakio* was captured by unidentified persons some 230 miles off the coast of Somalia. The vessel carried a crew of 26, of whom 13 were Spanish nationals and the other 13 were from Ghana, Madagascar, Senegal and Seychelles. The assailants used rocket-propelled grenades that damaged the vessel without affecting its seaworthiness or causing injuries. The boat was anchored near the Somali port of Hobyo, and the crew members were being held against their will. Spain immediately contacted the highest authorities of the Transitional Federal Government, who demonstrated their solidarity and cooperation with a view to the prompt release of the abducted sailors and vessel. Spain also contacted the AU and other organizations and Governments, and dispatched a detachment of the Spanish navy to the region to monitor developments. Spain stressed the need for the international community to take joint action under UN auspices in order to prevent and punish such acts, which jeopardized the delivery of humanitarian assistance, contributed to destabilizing the region and threatened the safety of international maritime traffic.

On 1 May [S/2008/292], Spain informed the Council that the *Playa de Bakio* was released on 27 April together with its crew members, all of whom were unharmed. Spain said that it supported the initiatives under discussion in the Council to strengthen cooperation among States and international organizations to combat piracy and armed robbery, in cooperation with the Somali authorities. Any maritime security initiative should be accompanied by a coordinated international technical assistance effort for Somalia and neighbouring States.

In identical letters of 8 May [A/62/841-S/2008/310] addressed to the General Assembly, the Security Council and the Secretary-General, Canada, Denmark, Greece, Japan, the Netherlands, Norway, the Republic of Korea and Spain stated that acts of piracy and armed robbery against commercial and humanitarian ships in the waters off Somalia were jeopardizing the delivery of humanitarian assistance, and contributing to destabilizing the region. They also posed a major threat to the safety of international maritime traffic and, thereby, to international peace and security. Initiatives in place to address the problem were insufficient. In a letter of 27 February to the Council, the Transitional Federal Government requested urgent assistance from the Council in securing the international and territorial waters off the coast of Somalia. In accordance with the UN Charter, the Council was working on initiatives that would entail calling on States and regional organizations to take action to protect shipping involved with the delivery of humanitarian aid and United Nations-authorized activities; stressing respect for the sovereignty and territorial integrity of Somalia; and authorizing States to enter Somalia's territorial waters to deter, prevent and suppress acts of piracy using all means necessary. In the medium- and long-term, the international community should address the challenge of ensuring peace and stability in Somalia itself, without which piracy and armed robbery in the region's waters could not be effectively tackled.

On 12 May [S/2008/323], Somalia said that the Transitional Federal Government did not have the capacity to interdict pirates or secure the waters off its coast. It therefore called on States and regional organizations to take action to protect shipping involved in the transportation of humanitarian aid and United Nations-authorized activities. The Government stressed that Somalia's sovereignty and territorial integrity should be fully respected, and called on States and interested organizations to provide technical assistance. In that regard, the Government had granted a number of States authorization to enter Somali territorial seas in order to deal with threats to shipping. It supported the adoption by the Council of a resolution under Chapter VII of the Charter to authorize States cooperating with the Transitional Federal Government to enter Somalia's territorial sea and use all necessary means to identify, deter, prevent and repress acts of piracy and armed robbery. The Government urged the Council to act favourably and quickly on the draft resolution on piracy (see below).

SECURITY COUNCIL ACTION

On 2 June [meeting 5902], the Security Council unanimously adopted **resolution 1816(2008)**. The draft [S/2008/351] was submitted by 16 Member States.

The Security Council,

Recalling its previous resolutions and the statements by its President concerning the situation in Somalia,

Gravely concerned by the threat that acts of piracy and armed robbery against vessels pose to the prompt, safe and effective delivery of humanitarian aid to Somalia, the safety of commercial maritime routes and to international navigation,

Expressing its concerns at the quarterly reports from the International Maritime Organization since 2005, which provide evidence of continuing piracy and armed robbery, in particular in the waters off the coast of Somalia,

Affirming that international law, as reflected in the United Nations Convention on the Law of the Sea of 10 December 1982 ("the Convention"), sets out the legal framework applicable to combating piracy and armed robbery, as well as other ocean activities,

Reaffirming the relevant provisions of international law with respect to the repression of piracy, including the Convention, and recalling that they provide guiding principles for cooperation to the fullest possible extent in the repression of piracy on the high seas or in any other place outside the jurisdiction of any State, including but not limited to boarding, searching and seizing vessels engaged in or suspected of engaging in acts of piracy, and to apprehending persons engaged in such acts with a view to such persons being prosecuted,

Reaffirming its respect for the sovereignty, territorial integrity, political independence and unity of Somalia,

Taking into account the crisis situation in Somalia and the lack of capacity of the Transitional Federal Government to interdict pirates or patrol and secure either the international sea lanes off the coast of Somalia or Somalia's territorial waters,

Deploring the recent incidents of attacks upon and hijacking of vessels in the territorial waters and on the high seas off the coast of Somalia, including attacks upon and hijackings of vessels operated by the World Food Programme and numerous commercial vessels, and the serious adverse impact of these attacks on the prompt, safe and effective delivery of food aid and other humanitarian assistance to the people of Somalia and the grave dangers they pose to vessels, crews, passengers and cargo,

Taking note of the letters dated 5 July and 18 September 2007 from the Secretary-General of the International Maritime Organization to the Secretary-General of the United Nations regarding the piracy problems off the coast of Somalia, and of resolution A.1002(25) adopted by the Assembly of the International Maritime Organization on 29 November 2007, in which Governments were strongly urged to increase their efforts to prevent and repress, within the provisions of international law, acts of piracy and armed robbery against vessels, irrespective of where such acts occur, and recalling the joint communiqué issued by the International Maritime Organization and the World Food Programme on 10 July 2007,

Taking note also of the letter dated 9 November 2007 from the Secretary-General to the President of the Security Council reporting that the Transitional Federal Government needs and would welcome international assistance to address the problem,

Taking note further of the letter dated 27 February 2008 from the Permanent Representative of Somalia to the United Nations addressed to the President of the Security Council conveying the consent of the Transitional Federal Government to the Council for urgent assistance in securing the territorial and international waters off the coast of Somalia for the safe conduct of shipping and navigation,

Determining that the incidents of piracy and armed robbery against vessels in the territorial waters of Somalia and the high seas off the coast of Somalia exacerbate the situation in Somalia which continues to constitute a threat to international peace and security in the region,

Acting under Chapter VII of the Charter of the United Nations,

1. *Condemns and deplores* all acts of piracy and armed robbery against vessels in territorial waters and the high seas off the coast of Somalia;

2. *Urges* States whose naval vessels and military aircraft operate on the high seas and airspace off the coast of Somalia to be vigilant to acts of piracy and armed robbery, and in this context encourages, in particular, States interested in the use of commercial maritime routes off the coast of Somalia to increase and coordinate their efforts to deter acts of piracy and armed robbery at sea in cooperation with the Transitional Federal Government;

3. *Urges* all States to cooperate with each other, with the International Maritime Organization and, as appropriate, with the relevant regional organizations in connection with, and share information about, acts of piracy and armed robbery in the territorial waters and on the high seas off the coast of Somalia, and to render assistance to vessels threatened by or under attack by pirates or armed robbers, in accordance with relevant international law;

4. *Urges* States to work in cooperation with interested organizations, including the International Maritime Organization, to ensure that vessels entitled to fly their flag receive appropriate guidance and training on avoidance, evasion and defensive techniques and to avoid the area whenever possible;

5. *Calls upon* States and interested organizations, including the International Maritime Organization, to provide technical assistance to Somalia and nearby coastal States, upon their request, to enhance the capacity of these States to ensure coastal and maritime security, including combating piracy and armed robbery off the Somali and nearby coastlines;

6. *Affirms* that the measures imposed by paragraph 5 of resolution 733(1992) of 23 January 1992 and further elaborated upon in paragraphs 1 and 2 of resolution 1425(2002) of 22 July 2002 do not apply to supplies of technical assistance to Somalia solely for the purposes set out in paragraph 5 above, which have been exempted from those measures in accordance with the procedure set out in paragraphs 11 *(b)* and 12 of resolution 1772(2007) of 20 August 2007;

7. *Decides* that, for a period of six months from the date of the present resolution, States cooperating with the Transitional Federal Government in the fight against piracy and armed robbery at sea off the coast of Somalia, for which advance notification has been provided by the Transitional Federal Government to the Secretary-General, may:

(a) Enter the territorial waters of Somalia for the purpose of repressing acts of piracy and armed robbery at sea, in a manner consistent with such action permitted on the high seas with respect to piracy under relevant international law; and

(b) Use, within the territorial waters of Somalia, in a manner consistent with action permitted on the high seas with respect to piracy under relevant international law, all necessary means to repress acts of piracy and armed robbery;

8. *Requests* that cooperating States take appropriate steps to ensure that the activities they undertake pursuant to the authorization in paragraph 7 above do not have the practical effect of denying or impairing the right of innocent passage to the ships of any third State;

9. *Affirms* that the authorization provided in the present resolution applies only with respect to the situation in Somalia and shall not affect the rights or obligations or responsibilities of Member States under international law, including any rights or obligations under the Convention, with respect to any other situation, and underscores in particular that it shall not be considered as establishing customary international law, and affirms further that this authorization has been provided only following receipt of the letter dated 27 February 2008 from the Permanent Representative of Somalia to the United Nations addressed to the President of the Security Council conveying the consent of the Transitional Federal Government;

10. *Calls upon* States to coordinate their actions with other participating States taken pursuant to paragraphs 5 and 7 above;

11. *Calls upon* all States, and in particular flag, port and coastal States, States of the nationality of victims and perpetrators of piracy and armed robbery, and other States with relevant jurisdiction under international law and national legislation, to cooperate in determining jurisdiction and in the investigation and prosecution of persons responsible for acts of piracy and armed robbery off the coast of Somalia, consistent with applicable international law, including international human rights law, and to render assistance by, among other actions, providing disposition and logistics assistance with respect to persons under their jurisdiction and control, such as victims and witnesses and persons detained as a result of operations conducted under the present resolution;

12. *Requests* States cooperating with the Transitional Federal Government to inform the Security Council within three months of the progress of actions undertaken in the exercise of the authority provided in paragraph 7 above;

13. *Requests* the Secretary-General to report to the Council within five months of the adoption of the present resolution on the implementation of the present resolution and on the situation with respect to piracy and armed robbery in territorial waters and the high seas off the coast of Somalia;

14. *Requests* the Secretary-General of the International Maritime Organization to brief the Council on the basis of cases brought to his attention by the agreement of all affected coastal States, and duly taking into account the existing bilateral and regional cooperative arrangements, on the situation with respect to piracy and armed robbery;

15. *Expresses its intention* to review the situation and consider, as appropriate, renewing the authority provided in paragraph 7 above for additional periods upon the request of the Transitional Federal Government;

16. *Decides* to remain seized of the matter.

Report of Secretary-General. In July [S/2008/466], the Secretary-General reported that the authorities of Somaliland and Puntland had built up their military presences around the disputed area of Las Aanod. The build-up had created a security vacuum elsewhere in Puntland, which, along with the lack of payments to police and militias working for the Government, had led to increased piracy. As at 15 July, 14 piracy incidents had taken place off the north-eastern coastline of Somalia in 2008, making its territorial waters one of the most dangerous places in the world. Denmark, France and the Netherlands had provided military escorts for humanitarian vessels, and the United Nations was working with the AU, the EU and other organizations on implementing resolution 1816(2008).

SECURITY COUNCIL ACTION

On 7 October [meeting 5987], the Council unanimously adopted **resolution 1838(2008)**. The draft [S/2008/633] was submitted by 19 Member States.

The Security Council,

Recalling its resolutions 1814(2008) of 15 May 2008 and 1816(2008) of 2 June 2008,

Gravely concerned by the recent proliferation of acts of piracy and armed robbery at sea against vessels off the coast of Somalia, and by the serious threat it poses to the prompt, safe and effective delivery of humanitarian aid to Somalia, to international navigation and the safety of commercial maritime routes, and to fishing activities conducted in conformity with international law,

Noting with concern that increasingly violent acts of piracy are carried out with heavier weaponry, in a larger area off the coast of Somalia, using long-range assets such as mother ships, and demonstrating more sophisticated organization and methods of attack,

Reaffirming that international law, as reflected in the United Nations Convention on the Law of the Sea of 10 December 1982 ("the Convention"), sets out the legal framework applicable to combating piracy and armed robbery at sea, as well as other ocean activities,

Commending the contribution made by some States since November 2007 to protect the World Food Programme maritime convoys, and the establishment by the European Union of a coordination unit with the task of supporting the surveillance and protection activities carried out by some member States of the European Union off the coast of Somalia, and the ongoing planning process towards a possible European Union naval operation, as well as other international or national initiatives taken with a view to implementing resolutions 1814(2008) and 1816(2008),

Noting recent humanitarian reports that as many as three and a half million Somalis will be dependent on humanitarian food aid by the end of the year, and that maritime contractors for the World Food Programme will not deliver food aid to Somalia without naval warship escorts, expressing its determination to ensure long-term security of World Food Programme deliveries to Somalia, and recalling that in resolution 1814(2008) it requested the Secretary-General to provide his support for efforts to protect World Food Programme maritime convoys,

Reaffirming its respect for the sovereignty, territorial integrity, political independence and unity of Somalia,

Taking note of the letter dated 1 September 2008 from the President of Somalia to the Secretary-General expressing the appreciation of the Transitional Federal Government to the Security Council for its assistance and expressing the willingness of the Transitional Federal Government to consider working with other States, as well as regional organizations, to provide advance notifications additional to those already provided, in accordance with paragraph 7 of resolution 1816(2008), to combat piracy and armed robbery at sea off the coast of Somalia,

Recalling that in the statement by its President of 4 September 2008 it welcomed the signing of a peace and reconciliation agreement in Djibouti and commended the Special Representative of the Secretary-General for Somalia, Mr. Ahmedou Ould-Abdallah, for his ongoing efforts, and emphasizing the importance of promoting a comprehensive and lasting settlement in Somalia,

Recalling also that in the statement by its President of 4 September it took note of the parties' request in the Djibouti agreement that the United Nations, within a period of one hundred and twenty days, authorize and deploy an international stabilization force, and looking forward to the report of the Secretary-General, due sixty days from its passage, in particular a detailed and consolidated description of a feasible multinational force, as well as a detailed concept of operations for a feasible United Nations peacekeeping operation,

Emphasizing that peace and stability, the strengthening of State institutions, economic and social development and respect for human rights and the rule of law are necessary to create the conditions for a full eradication of piracy and armed robbery at sea off the coast of Somalia,

Determining that the incidents of piracy and armed robbery against vessels in the territorial waters of Somalia and the high seas off the coast of Somalia exacerbate the situation in Somalia which continues to constitute a threat against international peace and security in the region,

Acting under Chapter VII of the Charter of the United Nations,

1. *Reiterates* that it condemns and deplores all acts of piracy and armed robbery at sea against vessels off the coast of Somalia;

2. *Calls upon* States interested in the security of maritime activities to take part actively in the fight against piracy on the high seas off the coast of Somalia, in particular by deploying naval vessels and military aircraft, in accordance with international law, as reflected in the Convention;

3. *Calls upon* States whose naval vessels and military aircraft operate on the high seas and airspace off the coast of Somalia to use on the high seas and airspace off the coast of Somalia the necessary means, in conformity with international law, as reflected in the Convention, for the repression of acts of piracy;

4. *Urges* States that have the capacity to do so to cooperate with the Transitional Federal Government in the fight against piracy and armed robbery at sea in conformity with the provisions of resolution 1816(2008);

5. *Urges* States and regional organizations, in conformity with the provisions of resolution 1814(2008), to continue to take action to protect the World Food Programme maritime convoys, which is vital to bring humanitarian assistance to the affected populations in Somalia;

6. *Urges* States, as requested, in particular, in International Maritime Organization resolution A.1002(25) of 29 November 2007, to issue to ships entitled to fly their flag, as necessary, advice and guidance on appropriate precaution-

ary measures to protect themselves from attack or actions to take if under attack or the threat of attack when sailing in waters off the coast of Somalia;

7. *Calls upon* States and regional organizations to coordinate their actions pursuant to paragraphs 3, 4 and 5 above;

8. *Affirms* that the provisions of the present resolution apply only with respect to the situation in Somalia and shall not affect the rights or obligations or responsibilities of Member States under international law, including any rights or obligations under the Convention, with respect to any situation, and underscores in particular that the present resolution shall not be considered as establishing customary international law;

9. *Looks forward* to the report of the Secretary-General requested in paragraph 13 of resolution 1816(2008), and expresses its intention to review the situation with respect to piracy and armed robbery at sea against vessels off the coast of Somalia with a view, in particular upon the request of the Transitional Federal Government, to renewing the authority provided in paragraph of resolution 1816(2008) for an additional period;

10. *Decides* to remain seized of the matter.

Further developments

In his November report [S/2008/709], the Secretary-General provided an update on the implementation of resolution 1816(2008) of 2 June (see p. 286). The Secretariat received confirmation from Somalia that Canada, Denmark, France, India, the Russian Federation, Spain and the United States were cooperating with the Transitional Federal Government in fighting piracy. It also received letters from Canada, Denmark, France, Spain and the United States confirming that they had deployed maritime units off the coast of Somalia to fight piracy and armed robbery against ships, in keeping with resolution 1816(2008). On 22 August, the United States led the establishment of a maritime security patrol area in international waters off the Somali coast. The area, which was intended to act as a buffer between the Somali coast and the shipping lanes off southern Yemen, was patrolled by three United States vessels, as well as vessels from Canada, France and the United Kingdom. Meanwhile, Canada and the Netherlands were supporting WFP by providing a naval escort to ships carrying food aid from Mombasa to Mogadishu. NATO deployed seven ships from its Standing Maritime Group 2 to protect ships carrying humanitarian aid and eligible merchant vessels.

On 15 September, the EU General Affairs Council established a coordination unit tasked with supporting the surveillance and protection activities carried out by some EU member States off the coast of Somalia. The Council approved a plan for implementing the military coordination action, which would comprise a coordination cell based in London, as well as a strategic military option for a possible naval operation, which the EU intended to launch by December. The EU also proposed that DPKO play a role in coordinating the growing number of Member States and organizations conducting maritime operations off the Somali coast.

The Secretary-General said that the activities of individuals engaged in piracy and armed robbery were weakening the Transitional Federal Government and the Puntland authorities. Since January, about 65 merchant ships, with about 200 crew members each, had been hijacked, particularly in the sea area bordering Puntland. It was estimated that, since the beginning of 2008, $25–30 million had been paid in ransom to pirates. The Secretary-General called on the international community to address the legal issues relating to persons apprehended while engaged in acts of piracy and armed robbery against ships. The United Nations would continue to work with the International Maritime Organization (IMO) to monitor the implementation of resolutions 1816(2008) and 1838(2008).

Briefing by IMO Secretary-General. On 20 November [meeting 6020], the IMO Secretary-General, Efthimios Mitropoulos, briefed the Security Council on the escalating incidents of piracy and armed robbery in the waters off Somalia and in the Gulf of Aden. More than 120 attacks had been reported in 2008, resulting in more than 35 ships having been seized by pirates and more than 600 seafarers kidnapped and held for ransom. At the time of the briefing, 14 ships and some 280 seafarers were being held hostage in Somalia; two seafarers had lost their lives in similar instances. The concerns of IMO were threefold: protecting seafarers, fishermen and passengers on ships sailing off the coast of Somalia and in the Gulf of Aden; ensuring the delivery of humanitarian aid to Somalia by WFP-chartered ships; and preserving the integrity of the shipping lane through the Gulf of Aden, which served more than 12 per cent of the total volume of oil transported by sea, as well as commodities carried by bulk carriers and finished goods transported by container ships. The IMO Secretary-General said that his organization would appreciate action by the Security Council to: extend the provisions of resolution 1816(2008) that allowed States cooperating with the Transitional Federal Government in the fight against piracy to enter Somalia's territorial waters to repress such acts and use all necessary means to do so; call on interested States to take part in the fight against piracy and armed robbery; strengthen the provisions of resolutions 1816(2008) and 1838(2008) with respect to clear rules of engagement to disrupt pirate activities; and urge States to establish legal jurisdiction to bring alleged offenders to justice. IMO was doing everything possible to increase awareness of the problem; advise ships to take avoidance, evasion and defensive measures; and assist countries in the region in building capacity to contribute to overall efforts, including through legislation. A coordinated international and national response was necessary for the safety and well-being of seafarers, the delivery of humanitarian aid, the protection of the marine environment and the continuation of operation of the shipping industry.

Somalia renewed its request for the Council's help in securing the international and territorial waters off its coast. It urged the renewal for one year of the authorization provided to those cooperating with the Transitional Federal Government, as stipulated in resolution 1816(2008), as well as other assistance that the Council might deem necessary. Somalia appealed to the Council, other nations and international organizations to support anti-piracy efforts.

Communication. In a letter of 26 November [A/63/580] to the General Assembly, Egypt and Yemen stated that they had organized a consultative meeting of Arab coastal countries of the Red Sea to address the issue of piracy off the coast of Somalia (Cairo, 20 November). The meeting was attended by Djibouti, Jordan, Saudi Arabia and the Sudan, as well as representatives of the Transitional Federal Government and LAS.

SECURITY COUNCIL ACTION

On 2 December [meeting 6026], the Security Council unanimously adopted **resolution 1846(2008)**. The draft [S/2008/748] was submitted by 19 Member States.

The Security Council,

Recalling its previous resolutions concerning the situation in Somalia, especially resolutions 1814(2008) of 15 May 2008, 1816(2008) of 2 June 2008 and 1838(2008) of 7 October 2008,

Continuing to be gravely concerned by the threat that piracy and armed robbery at sea against vessels pose to the prompt, safe and effective delivery of humanitarian aid to Somalia, to international navigation and the safety of commercial maritime routes, and to other vulnerable ships, including fishing activities in conformity with international law,

Reaffirming its respect for the sovereignty, territorial integrity, political independence and unity of Somalia,

Further reaffirming that international law, as reflected in the United Nations Convention on the Law of the Sea of 10 December 1982 ("the Convention"), sets out the legal framework applicable to combating piracy and armed robbery at sea, as well as other ocean activities,

Taking into account the crisis situation in Somalia and the lack of capacity of the Transitional Federal Government to interdict pirates or patrol and secure either the international sea lanes off the coast of Somalia or Somalia's territorial waters,

Taking note of the requests of the Transitional Federal Government for international assistance to counter piracy off its coasts, including the letter dated 1 September 2008 from the President of Somalia to the Secretary-General expressing the appreciation of the Transitional Federal Government to the Security Council for its assistance and expressing the willingness of the Transitional Federal Government to consider working with other States and regional organizations to combat piracy and armed robbery at sea off the coast of Somalia, the letter dated 20 November 2008 conveying the request of the Transitional Federal Government that the provisions of resolution 1816(2008) be renewed, and the request made by the Permanent Representative of Somalia to the United Nations before the Council on 20 November 2008 that the renewal be for an additional twelve months,

Taking note also of the letters from the Transitional Federal Government to the Secretary-General providing advance notification with respect to States cooperating with the Transitional Federal Government in the fight against piracy and armed robbery at sea off the coast of Somalia and from other Member States to the Council to inform the Council of their actions, as requested in paragraphs 7 and 12 of resolution 1816(2008), and encouraging those cooperating States, for which advance notification has been provided by the Transitional Federal Government to the Secretary-General, to continue their respective efforts,

Expressing again its determination to ensure the long-term security of World Food Programme maritime deliveries to Somalia,

Recalling that in its resolution 1838(2008) it commended the contribution made by some States since November 2007 to protect the World Food Programme maritime convoys, and the establishment by the European Union of a coordination unit with the task of supporting the surveillance and protection activities carried out by some member States of the European Union off the coast of Somalia, as well as other international or national initiatives taken with a view to implementing resolutions 1814(2008) and 1816(2008),

Emphasizing that peace and stability within Somalia, the strengthening of State institutions, economic and social development and respect for human rights and the rule of law are necessary to create the conditions for a full eradication of piracy and armed robbery at sea off the coast of Somalia,

Welcoming the signing on 19 August 2008 of a peace and reconciliation agreement between the Transitional Federal Government and the Alliance for the Re-liberation of Somalia ("the Djibouti agreement"), as well as their signing of a joint ceasefire agreement on 26 October 2008, noting that the Djibouti agreement calls for the United Nations to authorize and deploy an international stabilization force, and taking note of the report of the Secretary-General of 17 November 2008 on the situation in Somalia, including his recommendations in this regard,

Commending the key role played by the African Union Mission in Somalia in facilitating the delivery of humanitarian assistance to Somalia through the port of Mogadishu and the contribution that the Mission has made towards the goal of establishing lasting peace and stability in Somalia, and recognizing specifically the important contributions of the Governments of Uganda and Burundi to Somalia,

Welcoming the organization of a ministerial meeting of the Council in December 2008 to examine ways to improve international coordination in the fight against piracy and armed robbery off the coast of Somalia and to ensure that the international community has the proper authorities and tools at its disposal to assist it in these efforts,

Determining that the incidents of piracy and armed robbery against vessels in the territorial waters of Somalia and the high seas off the coast of Somalia exacerbate the situation in Somalia, which continues to constitute a threat to international peace and security in the region,

Acting under Chapter VII of the Charter of the United Nations,

1. *Reiterates* that it condemns and deplores all acts of piracy and armed robbery against vessels in territorial waters and the high seas off the coast of Somalia;

2. *Expresses its concern* over the finding contained in the report of the Monitoring Group on Somalia of 20 November 2008 that escalating ransom payments are fuelling the growth of piracy off the coast of Somalia;

3. *Welcomes* the efforts of the International Maritime Organization to update its guidance and recommendations to the shipping industry and to Governments for preventing and suppressing piracy and armed robbery at sea and to provide this guidance as soon as practicable to all Member States and to the international shipping community operating off the coast of Somalia;

4. *Calls upon* States, in cooperation with the shipping industry, the insurance industry and the International Maritime Organization, to issue to ships entitled to fly their flag appropriate advice and guidance on avoidance, evasion and defensive techniques and measures to take if under the threat of attack or attack when sailing in the waters off the coast of Somalia;

5. *Calls upon* States and interested organizations, including the International Maritime Organization, to provide technical assistance to Somalia and nearby coastal States upon their request to enhance the capacity of these States to ensure coastal and maritime security, including combating piracy and armed robbery at sea off the Somali and nearby coastlines;

6. *Welcomes* initiatives by Canada, Denmark, France, India, the Netherlands, the Russian Federation, Spain, the United Kingdom of Great Britain and Northern Ireland and the United States of America and by regional and international organizations to counter piracy off the coast of Somalia pursuant to resolutions 1814(2008), 1816(2008) and 1838(2008), the decision by the North Atlantic Treaty Organization to counter piracy off the Somalia coast, including by escorting vessels of the World Food Programme, and, in particular, the decision by the European Union on 10 November 2008 to launch, for a period of twelve months from December 2008, a naval operation to protect World Food Programme maritime convoys bringing humanitarian assistance to Somalia and other vulnerable ships and to repress acts of piracy and armed robbery at sea off the coast of Somalia;

7. *Calls upon* States and regional organizations to coordinate, including by sharing information through bilateral channels or the United Nations, their efforts to deter acts of piracy and armed robbery at sea off the coast of Somalia in cooperation with each other, the International Maritime Organization, the international shipping community, flag States and the Transitional Federal Government;

8. *Requests* the Secretary-General to submit to it a report, no later than three months after the adoption of the present resolution, on ways to ensure the long-term security of international navigation off the coast of Somalia, including the long-term security of World Food Programme maritime deliveries to Somalia and a possible coordination and leadership role for the United Nations in this regard to rally Member States and regional organizations to counter piracy and armed robbery at sea off the coast of Somalia;

9. *Calls upon* States and regional organizations that have the capacity to do so to take part actively in the fight against piracy and armed robbery at sea off the coast of Somalia, in particular, consistent with the present resolution and relevant international law, by deploying naval vessels and military aircraft, and through seizure and disposition of boats, vessels, arms and other related equipment used in the commission of piracy and armed robbery off the coast of Somalia or for which there are reasonable grounds for suspecting such use;

10. *Decides* that, for a period of twelve months from the date of the present resolution, States and regional organizations cooperating with the Transitional Federal Government in the fight against piracy and armed robbery at sea off the coast of Somalia, for which advance notification has been provided by the Transitional Federal Government to the Secretary-General, may:

(a) Enter into the territorial waters of Somalia for the purpose of repressing acts of piracy and armed robbery at sea, in a manner consistent with such action permitted on the high seas with respect to piracy under relevant international law; and

(b) Use, within the territorial waters of Somalia, in a manner consistent with such action permitted on the high seas with respect to piracy under relevant international law, all necessary means to repress acts of piracy and armed robbery at sea;

11. *Affirms* that the authorizations provided in the present resolution apply only with respect to the situation in Somalia and shall not affect the rights or obligations or responsibilities of Member States under international law, including any rights or obligations under the Convention, with respect to any other situation, and underscores in particular that the present resolution shall not be considered as establishing customary international law, and affirms further that such authorizations have been provided only following receipt of the letter dated 20 November 2008 conveying the consent of the Transitional Federal Government;

12. *Affirms also* that the measures imposed by paragraph 5 of resolution 733(1992) of 23 January 1992 and further elaborated upon in paragraphs 1 and 2 of resolution 1425(2002) of 22 July 2002 do not apply to supplies of technical assistance to Somalia solely for the purposes set out in paragraph 5 above, which have been exempted from those measures in accordance with the procedure set out in paragraphs 11 *(b)* and 12 of resolution 1772(2007) of 20 August 2007;

13. *Requests* that cooperating States take appropriate steps to ensure that the activities they undertake pursuant to the authorization in paragraph 10 above do not have the

practical effect of denying or impairing the right of innocent passage to the ships of any third State;

14. *Calls upon* all States, and in particular flag, port and coastal States, States of the nationality of victims and perpetrators of piracy and armed robbery, and other States with relevant jurisdiction under international law and national legislation, to cooperate in determining jurisdiction and in the investigation and prosecution of persons responsible for acts of piracy and armed robbery off the coast of Somalia, consistent with applicable international law, including international human rights law, and to render assistance by, among other actions, providing disposition and logistics assistance with respect to persons under their jurisdiction and control, such as victims and witnesses and persons detained as a result of operations conducted under the present resolution;

15. *Notes* that the Convention for the Suppression of Unlawful Acts against the Safety of Maritime Navigation of 10 March 1988 provides for parties to create criminal offences, establish jurisdiction and accept delivery of persons responsible for or suspected of seizing or exercising control over a ship by force or threat thereof or any other form of intimidation; urges States parties to the Convention for the Suppression of Unlawful Acts against the Safety of Maritime Navigation to fully implement their obligations under said Convention and cooperate with the Secretary-General and the International Maritime Organization to build judicial capacity for the successful prosecution of persons suspected of piracy and armed robbery at sea off the coast of Somalia;

16. *Requests* States and regional organizations cooperating with the Transitional Federal Government to inform the Council and the Secretary-General within nine months of the progress of actions undertaken in the exercise of the authority provided in paragraph 10 above;

17. *Requests* the Secretary-General to report to the Council within eleven months of the adoption of the present resolution on the implementation of the resolution and on the situation with respect to piracy and armed robbery in territorial waters and the high seas off the coast of Somalia;

18. *Requests* the Secretary-General of the International Maritime Organization to brief the Council on the basis of cases brought to his attention by the agreement of all affected coastal States, and duly taking into account the existing bilateral and regional cooperative arrangements, on the situation with respect to piracy and armed robbery;

19. *Expresses its intention* to review the situation and consider, as appropriate, renewing the authority provided in paragraph 10 above for additional periods upon the request of the Transitional Federal Government;

20. *Decides* to remain seized of the matter.

Communication. In a letter of 12 December to the Security Council [S/2008/786], Cuba, on behalf of the Non-Aligned Movement, condemned all acts of piracy and armed robbery against vessels in the territorial waters and seas off the coast of Somalia, also stressing the need for a political settlement in the country.

SECURITY COUNCIL ACTION

On 16 December [meeting 6046], the Security Council unanimously adopted **resolution 1851(2008).** The draft [S/2008/789] was submitted by Belgium, Croatia, France, Greece, Liberia, the Republic of Korea, Spain and the United States.

The Security Council,

Recalling its previous resolutions concerning the situation in Somalia, especially resolutions 1814(2008) of 15 May 2008, 1816(2008) of 2 June 2008, 1838(2008) of 7 October 2008, 1844(2008) of 20 November 2008 and 1846(2008) of 2 December 2008,

Continuing to be gravely concerned by the dramatic increase in the incidents of piracy and armed robbery at sea off the coast of Somalia in the last six months, and by the threat that piracy and armed robbery at sea against vessels pose to the prompt, safe and effective delivery of humanitarian aid to Somalia, and noting that pirate attacks off the coast of Somalia have become more sophisticated and daring and have expanded in their geographical scope, notably evidenced by the hijacking of the M/V *Sirius Star* 500 nautical miles off the coast of Kenya and subsequent unsuccessful attempts well east of the United Republic of Tanzania,

Reaffirming its respect for the sovereignty, territorial integrity, political independence and unity of Somalia, including Somalia's rights with respect to offshore natural resources, including fisheries, in accordance with international law,

Further reaffirming that international law, as reflected in the United Nations Convention on the Law of the Sea of 10 December 1982, sets out the legal framework applicable to combating piracy and armed robbery at sea, as well as other ocean activities,

Again taking into account the crisis situation in Somalia, and the lack of capacity of the Transitional Federal Government to interdict, or upon interdiction to prosecute pirates or to patrol and secure the waters off the coast of Somalia, including the international sea lanes and Somalia's territorial waters,

Noting the several requests of the Transitional Federal Government for international assistance to counter piracy off the coast of Somalia, including the letter dated 9 December 2008 from the President of Somalia requesting the international community to assist the Transitional Federal Government in taking all necessary measures to interdict those who use Somali territory and airspace to plan, facilitate or undertake acts of piracy and armed robbery at sea, and the letter dated 1 September 2008 from the President of Somalia to the Secretary-General expressing the appreciation of the Transitional Federal Government to the Security Council for its assistance and expressing the willingness of the Transitional Federal Government to consider working with other States and regional organizations to combat piracy and armed robbery off the coast of Somalia,

Welcoming the launching of the European Union operation Atalanta to combat piracy off the coast of Somalia and to protect vulnerable ships bound for Somalia, as well as the efforts of the North Atlantic Treaty Organization and other States acting in a national capacity in cooperation with the Transitional Federal Government to suppress piracy off the coast of Somalia,

Also welcoming the recent initiatives of the Governments of Egypt and Kenya, the Special Representative of the Secretary-General for Somalia and the United Nations Office on Drugs and Crime to achieve effective measures to remedy the causes, capabilities and incidents of piracy and armed robbery off the coast of Somalia, and emphasizing the need for current and future counter-piracy operations to effectively coordinate their activities,

Noting with concern that the lack of capacity, domestic legislation and clarity about how to dispose of pirates after their capture has hindered more robust international action against the pirates off the coast of Somalia and in some cases has led to pirates being released without facing justice, and reiterating that the Convention for the Suppression of Unlawful Acts against the Safety of Maritime Navigation of 10 March 1988 provides for parties to create criminal offences, establish jurisdiction and accept delivery of persons responsible for or suspected of seizing or exercising control over a ship by force or threat thereof or any other form of intimidation,

Welcoming the report of 20 November 2008 of the Monitoring Group on Somalia, and noting the role that piracy may play in financing embargo violations by armed groups,

Determining that the incidents of piracy and armed robbery at sea in the waters off the coast of Somalia exacerbate the situation in Somalia which continues to constitute a threat to international peace and security in the region,

Acting under Chapter VII of the Charter of the United Nations,

1. *Reiterates* that it condemns and deplores all acts of piracy and armed robbery against vessels in waters off the coast of Somalia;

2. *Calls upon* States and regional and international organizations that have the capacity to do so to take part actively in the fight against piracy and armed robbery at sea off the coast of Somalia, in particular, consistent with the present resolution, resolution 1846(2008) and international law, by deploying naval vessels and military aircraft and through seizure and disposition of boats, vessels, arms and other related equipment used in the commission of piracy and armed robbery at sea off the coast of Somalia, or for which there are reasonable grounds for suspecting such use;

3. *Invites* all States and regional organizations fighting piracy off the coast of Somalia to conclude special agreements or arrangements with countries willing to take custody of pirates in order to embark law enforcement officials ("shipriders") from the latter countries, in particular countries in the region, to facilitate the investigation and prosecution of persons detained as a result of operations conducted under the present resolution for acts of piracy and armed robbery at sea off the coast of Somalia, provided that the advance consent of the Transitional Federal Government is obtained for the exercise of third State jurisdiction by shipriders in Somali territorial waters and that such agreements or arrangements do not prejudice the effective implementation of the Convention for the Suppression of Unlawful Acts against the Safety of Maritime Navigation;

4. *Encourages* all States and regional organizations fighting piracy and armed robbery at sea off the coast of Somalia to establish an international cooperation mechanism to act as a common point of contact between and among States, regional organizations and international organizations on all aspects of combating piracy and armed robbery at sea off the coast of Somalia; and recalls that future recommendations on ways to ensure the long-term security of international navigation off the coast of Somalia, including the long-term security of World Food Programme maritime deliveries to Somalia and a possible coordination and leadership role for the United Nations in this regard to rally Member States and regional organizations to counter piracy and armed robbery at sea off the coast of Somalia are to be detailed in a report of the Secretary-General no later than three months after the adoption of resolution 1846(2008);

5. *Also encourages* all States and regional organizations fighting piracy and armed robbery at sea off the coast of Somalia to consider creating a centre in the region to coordinate information relevant to piracy and armed robbery at sea off the coast of Somalia, to increase regional capacity with the assistance of the United Nations Office on Drugs and Crime to arrange effective shiprider agreements or arrangements consistent with the United Nations Convention on the Law of the Sea and to implement the Convention for the Suppression of Unlawful Acts against the Safety of Maritime Navigation, the United Nations Convention against Transnational Organized Crime and other relevant instruments to which States in the region are party, in order to effectively investigate and prosecute piracy and armed robbery at sea offences;

6. In response to the letter dated 9 December 2008 from the Transitional Federal Government, *encourages* Member States to continue to cooperate with the Transitional Federal Government in the fight against piracy and armed robbery at sea, notes the primary role of the Transitional Federal Government in rooting out piracy and armed robbery at sea, and decides that for a period of twelve months from the date of adoption of resolution 1846(2008), States and regional organizations cooperating in the fight against piracy and armed robbery at sea off the coast of Somalia for which advance notification has been provided by the Transitional Federal Government to the Secretary-General may undertake all necessary measures that are appropriate in Somalia, for the purpose of suppressing acts of piracy and armed robbery at sea, pursuant to the request of the Transitional Federal Government, provided, however, that any measures undertaken pursuant to the authority of the present paragraph shall be undertaken consistent with applicable international humanitarian and human rights law;

7. *Calls upon* Member States to assist the Transitional Federal Government, at its request and with notification to the Secretary-General, to strengthen its operational capacity to bring to justice those who are using Somali territory to plan, facilitate or undertake criminal acts of piracy and armed robbery at sea, and stresses that any measures undertaken pursuant to the present paragraph shall be consistent with applicable international human rights law;

8. *Welcomes* the communiqué issued by the International Conference on Piracy around Somalia, held in Nairobi on 11 December 2008, and encourages Member States to work to enhance the capacity of relevant States in the region to combat piracy, including judicial capacity;

9. *Notes with concern* the findings contained in the report of the Monitoring Group on Somalia of 20 November 2008 that escalating ransom payments are fuelling the growth of piracy in waters off the coast of Somalia, and that the lack of enforcement of the arms embargo established by resolution 733(1992) of 23 January 1992 has permitted ready access to the arms and ammunition used by the pirates and driven in part the phenomenal growth in piracy;

10. *Affirms* that the authorization provided in the present resolution applies only with respect to the situation in Somalia and shall not affect the rights or obligations or responsibilities of Member States under international law, including any rights or obligations under the United Nations Convention on the Law of the Sea, with respect to any other situation, and underscores in particular that the present resolution shall not be considered as establishing customary international law, and affirms further that such authorizations have been provided only following the receipt of the letter dated 9 December 2008 conveying the consent of the Transitional Federal Government;

11. *Affirms also* that the measures imposed by paragraph 5 of resolution 733(1992) and further elaborated upon in paragraphs 1 and 2 of resolution 1425(2002) of 22 July 2002 shall not apply to weapons and military equipment destined for the sole use of Member States and regional organizations undertaking measures in accordance with paragraph 6 above;

12. *Urges* States, in collaboration with the shipping and insurance industries, and the International Maritime Organization to continue to develop avoidance, evasion and defensive best practices and advisories to take when under attack or when sailing in waters off the coast of Somalia, and further urges States to make their citizens and vessels available for forensic investigation, as appropriate, at the first port of call immediately following an act or attempted act of piracy or armed robbery at sea or release from captivity;

13. *Decides* to remain seized of the matter.

Following the adoption of the resolution, the Secretary-General said that his Special Representative for Somalia convened an international conference on piracy from 11 to 12 December to further discuss the issue, and his Legal Adviser stood ready to assist States in finding a solution to the practical, legal and jurisdictional issues involved. The Secretariat had designated a focal point in the DPKO Office of Military Affairs for information-sharing on anti-piracy operations. UN anti-piracy efforts had to be appraised in the context of a comprehensive approach that fostered the peace process, helped the parties rebuild security and governance capacity, addressed human rights issues and harnessed economic opportunities throughout Somalia.

The Secretary of State of the United States, Condoleeza Rice, announced that her country intended to work with partners to create a contact group on Somali piracy. The United States envisioned the contact group serving as a mechanism to share intelligence, coordinate activities and reach out to other partners, including those in the shipping and insurance industries.

Children and armed conflict

In response to Security Council resolution 1612(2005) [YUN 2005, p. 863], the Secretary-General, in May [S/2008/352], submitted to the Council and its Working Group on Children and Armed Conflict his second report on the situation of children and armed conflict in Somalia, which covered the period from 16 March 2007 to 15 March 2008. The report stressed that the level of grave violations against children increased over the year, particularly with regard to the recruitment and use of children in armed conflict; the killing, maiming and raping of children; and the denial of humanitarian access to children. Insecurity and violence in central and southern Somalia increased, as Transitional Federal Government and Ethiopian forces continued to battle anti-Government groups. The regional border dispute between Somaliland and Puntland added to the overall insecurity. In the absence of rule of law, crimes against civilians, including children, continued to be committed with impunity. The Government and various factions of the anti-Government forces, including remnants of the Union of Islamic Courts and the Al-Shabaab group, were among the parties cited in the report as responsible for recruiting and using child soldiers and committing violations against children. Children were also being killed and maimed as a result of military actions by Ethiopian forces in the course of confrontations with anti-Government forces and civilian demonstrators. Reported cases of rape and other sexual violence against children also increased. The report described dialogue and action plans to redress violations of children's rights and follow-up and programmatic responses by UNDP, UNICEF and other organizations. It contained recommendations aimed at strengthening child protection action.

In December [S/AC.51/2008/14], the Security Council Working Group on Children and Armed Conflict submitted its conclusions on children and armed conflict in Somalia, which contained the Group's exchange of views on the Secretary-General's report. The Working Group expressed its concern at the high number of children killed and maimed as a result of the conflict, the use of children to plant roadside bombs and other explosive devices, and the indiscriminate use of anti-personnel landmines. The Working Group condemned recent indiscriminate shelling and mortar attacks in Mogadishu and urged all parties to: comply with international humanitarian law; commit to maintaining the neutrality and security of schools and hospitals; allow unimpeded humanitarian access for children; end acts of sexual violence against children and protect children from such violence; halt new deployments of landmines; reflect child protection in ongoing reconciliation efforts and peace processes; release all children present in their ranks; and engage in an action plan to end abuses. The Working Group made recommendations to the Security Council and agreed to address letters to the World Bank, donors, and the Somalia Task Force on Monitoring and Reporting.

United Nations Political Office for Somalia

The United Nations Political Office for Somalia (UNPOS), established in 1995 [YUN 1995, p. 402] and headed by the Secretary-General's Special Representative, Ahmedou Ould-Abdallah (Mauritania), continued to assist in advancing the cause of peace and reconciliation and to monitor the situation in the country. The Security Council, in resolution 1814(2008) of 15 May (see p. 275), approved the Secretary-General's proposal to establish a joint planning unit in the office of the Special Representative to facilitate implementation of an updated, comprehensive, integrated strategy for peace and stability in Somalia, as discussed in the Secretary-General's March report [S/2008/178 & Corr.1,2]. It decided that UNPOS and the UN country team would support the transitional federal institutions in developing a Constitution and holding a constitutional referendum and free and democratic elections in 2009. The Secretary-General was asked to establish the necessary security arrangements for relocating UNPOS and the country team from Nairobi to Mogadishu.

Financing

The Secretary-General, in his February report [A/62/512/Add.6] on estimates in respect of special political missions, good offices and other political initiatives authorized by the General Assembly and/or the Security Council, said that with the upgrading of the level of the UNPOS head to the Under-Secretary-General level in 2007 [YUN 2007, p. 281] and the increased role entrusted to him, including the implementation of an integrated UN approach for Somalia, UNPOS would take over constitutional, electoral and peace education activities from UNDP and legal support activities provided through the United Nations Office at Nairobi. Consequently, the organizational structure would be slightly rearranged. The Secretary-General presented revised estimated requirements for UNPOS for 2008 amounting to $16,233,800 net ($17,155,500 gross). The proposed revised requirements provided for civilian personnel costs amounting to $7,105,300 for 72 positions, including 33 additional positions, for six months in Nairobi and six months in Somalia.

In March [A/62/7/Add.37], ACABQ recommended that the Assembly approve the resources requested by the Secretary-General for the special political missions, including UNPOS.

The General Assembly, in section III of **resolution 62/245** of 3 April (see p. 1550), approved additional budgets for special political missions, including UNPOS, for 2008, totalling $48,954,400 ($53,571,500 gross).

In October [A/63/346/Add.3], the Secretary-General presented the proposed resource requirements for 10 special political missions, including UNPOS, grouped under the thematic cluster of UN offices, peacebuilding support offices, integrated offices and commissions. The resource requirements for UNPOS for the period from 1 January to 30 June 2009 amounted to $5,998,800 net ($6,420,400 gross). The reduction of $9,266,300 in 2009 requirements compared to the 2008 appropriation was attributable to the 2009 requirements being budgeted for six months, compared to the 12-month period in 2008. A supplementary budget for the period from 1 July to 31 December 2009, based on the recommendations of a security assessment mission to be dispatched to Somalia in the fourth quarter of 2008, would be presented to the Assembly at a later stage.

In a December report [A/63/593], ACABQ recommended that the Assembly approve the resources requested by the Secretary-General for the special political missions authorized by the Assembly and/or Security Council, including UNPOS.

The Assembly, in section XI of **resolution 63/263** of 24 December (see p. 1548), approved budgets totalling $429,497,600 for the 27 political missions authorized by the Assembly and/or Council.

Arms embargo

The Security Council, by resolution 751(1992) [YUN 1992, p. 202], established the Committee on sanctions against Somalia to oversee the arms embargo imposed on that country by resolution 733(1992) [ibid., p. 199]. A Panel of experts was established by resolution 1425(2002) [YUN 2002, p. 206] to generate information on arms embargo violations. The Panel of Experts was succeeded by a Monitoring Group established by resolution 1519(2003) [YUN 2003, p. 254] to focus on embargo violations.

Report of Monitoring Group (April). As requested by the Security Council in resolution 1766(2007) [YUN 2007, p. 282], the Nairobi-based Monitoring Group of four experts continued to investigate arms embargo violations, update the draft list of individuals and entities violating the embargo and make recommendations.

In its report of 2 April [S/2008/274], which the Committee transmitted to the Council on 24 April, the Group stated that armed actions between opposition groups and the Transitional Federal Government force increased from October 2007 to April 2008. Opposition groups, particularly the Shabaab, gained control of more territory and limited the deployment of Government troops and their backers, the Ethiopian national defence force. Insurgents carried out sustained attacks using guerrilla warfare, established bases across Somalia, and received regular shipments of arms by sea. Their increased strength and successes contributed to the fragmentation of Government security forces, which commanders started to reinforce with their own militias.

Weapons sent to all parties of the conflict originated in some of the States previously reported, namely Eritrea, Ethiopia and Yemen, and reached Somalia by small vessels or through remote locations along land borders. The Group found that the arms embargo had limited impact on the conflict, as the parties were still able to receive arms. The Government was not able to control its borders against arms arriving in violation of the embargo. Cross-border shipments reached the parties directly or fuelled the seven arms markets that had opened since the Bakaraaha Arms Market in Mogadishu moved underground. The Group received information on arms sales by prominent Government security officials and Ethiopian and Ugandan AMISOM officers at the market in Mogadishu; such arms originated from army stocks or were seized following battles with insurgents. According to arms traders, the biggest suppliers of ammunition to the markets were Ethiopian and Government commanders. The Somali police no longer differed from other actors in the conflict: it purchased arms in Yemen, in violation of the embargo, not having requested an exemption from the Committee. Police commanders were also buying and selling arms at the Mogadishu markets.

The Monitoring Group recommended, among other measures, that the Committee address letters to States found by the Group to have violated the arms embargo, and address a letter to the Transitional Federal Government drawing its attention to the provisions contained in relevant Council resolutions for exemptions to the arms embargo for the development of security institutions. It also recommended that the Committee request the Government, Ethiopia and AMISOM to investigate the information regarding the sale by Government officials and Ethiopian and Ugandan military officers of weapons and ammunition to the Somali arms markets, and send their findings to the Committee within two months of the date of the report. The Group recommended that the Council expand its mandate to include the provision of information on internal arms transactions subject to possible additional measures. It also recommended that the Council impose individual targeted sanctions on embargo violators and their supporters and on elements that threatened by force the transitional federal institutions or AMISOM; and that the Committee designate persons and entities subject to individual measures.

SECURITY COUNCIL ACTION

On 29 April [meeting 5879], the Security Council unanimously adopted **resolution 1811(2008)**. The draft [S/2008/278] was submitted by the United Kingdom.

The Security Council,

Reaffirming its previous resolutions and the statements by its President concerning the situation in Somalia, in particular resolution 733(1992) of 23 January 1992, which established an embargo on all deliveries of weapons and military equipment to Somalia (hereinafter referred to as "the arms embargo"), and resolutions 1519(2003) of 16 December 2003, 1558(2004) of 17 August 2004, 1587(2005) of 15 March 2005, 1630(2005) of 14 October 2005, 1676(2006) of 10 May 2006, 1724(2006) of 29 November 2006, 1744(2007) of 20 February 2007, 1766(2007) of 23 July 2007, 1772(2007) of 20 August 2007 and 1801(2008) of 20 February 2008,

Recalling that, as set out in resolutions 1744(2007) and 1772(2007), the arms embargo on Somalia does not apply to *(a)* weapons and military equipment, technical training and assistance intended solely for the support of or use by the African Union Mission in Somalia, and *(b)* supplies and technical assistance by States intended solely for the purpose of helping to develop security sector institutions, consistent with the political process set out in those resolutions and in the absence of a negative decision by the Security Council Committee established pursuant to resolution 751(1992) (hereinafter referred to as "the Committee") within five working days of receiving an advance notification of such supplies or assistance on a case-by-case basis,

Reaffirming the importance of the sovereignty, territorial integrity, political independence and unity of Somalia,

Reiterating the urgent need for all Somali leaders to take tangible steps to continue political dialogue,

Commending the work of the Special Representative of the Secretary-General for Somalia, Mr. Ahmedou Ould-Abdallah, and reaffirming its strong support for his efforts,

Taking note of the report of the Monitoring Group submitted on 24 April 2008 pursuant to paragraph 3 *(i)* of resolution 1766(2007) and the observations and recommendations contained therein,

Condemning flows of weapons and ammunition supplies to and through Somalia in violation of the arms embargo as a serious threat to peace and stability in Somalia,

Reiterating its insistence that all States, in particular those in the region, should refrain from any action in contravention of the arms embargo and should take all necessary steps to hold violators accountable,

Reiterating and underscoring the importance of enhancing the monitoring of the arms embargo in Somalia through persistent and vigilant investigation into the violations, bearing in mind that strict enforcement of the arms embargo will improve the overall security situation in Somalia,

Determining that the situation in Somalia continues to constitute a threat to international peace and security in the region,

Acting under Chapter VII of the Charter of the United Nations,

1. *Stresses* the obligation of all States to comply fully with the measures imposed by resolution 733(1992);

2. *Reiterates its intention*, in the light of the report of the Monitoring Group of 24 April 2008, to consider specific action to improve implementation of and compliance with measures imposed by resolution 733(1992);

3. *Decides* to extend the mandate of the Monitoring Group referred to in paragraph 3 of resolution 1558(2004), and requests the Secretary-General to take the necessary administrative measures as expeditiously as possible to re-establish the Monitoring Group for a further six months, drawing, as appropriate, on the expertise of the members of the Monitoring Group established pursuant to resolution 1766(2007) and appointing new members as necessary, in consultation with the Committee, the mandate to be as follows:

(*a*) To continue the tasks outlined in paragraphs 3 (*a*) to (*c*) of resolution 1587(2005);

(*b*) To continue to investigate, in coordination with relevant international agencies, all activities, including in the financial, maritime and other sectors, which generate revenues used to commit arms embargo violations;

(*c*) To continue to investigate any means of transport, routes, seaports, airports and other facilities used in connection with arms embargo violations;

(*d*) To continue refining and updating information on the draft list of those individuals and entities who violate the measures implemented by Member States in accordance with resolution 733(1992), inside and outside Somalia, and their active supporters, for possible future measures by the Security Council, and to present such information to the Committee as and when the Committee deems appropriate;

(*e*) To continue making recommendations based on its investigations, on the previous reports of the Panel of Experts appointed pursuant to resolutions 1425(2002) of 22 July 2002 and 1474(2003) of 8 April 2003, and on the previous reports of the Monitoring Group appointed pursuant to resolutions 1519(2003), 1558(2004), 1587(2005), 1630(2005), 1676(2006), 1724(2006) and 1766(2007);

(*f*) To work closely with the Committee on specific recommendations for additional measures to improve overall compliance with the arms embargo;

(*g*) To assist in identifying areas where the capacities of States in the region can be strengthened to facilitate the implementation of the arms embargo;

(*h*) To provide to the Council, through the Committee, a midterm briefing within ninety days of its establishment, and to submit progress reports to the Committee on a monthly basis;

(*i*) To submit, through the Committee, for the consideration of the Council, a final report covering all the tasks set out above, no later than fifteen days prior to the termination of the mandate of the Monitoring Group;

4. *Requests* the Secretary-General to make the necessary financial arrangements to support the work of the Monitoring Group;

5. *Reaffirms* paragraphs 4, 5, 7, 8 and 10 of resolution 1519(2003);

6. *Requests* the Committee, in accordance with its mandate and in consultation with the Monitoring Group and other relevant United Nations entities, to consider the recommendations in the reports of the Monitoring Group of 5 April and 16 October 2006, 17 July 2007 and 24 April 2008 and recommend to the Council ways to improve implementation of and compliance with the arms embargo, in response to continuing violations;

7. *Decides* to remain actively seized of the matter.

Communication. On 6 June [S/2008/370], Uganda responded to allegations made by the Monitoring Group in its April report (see p. 295) of the involvement of some Uganda People's Defence Forces personnel in arms dealing in Somalia. Uganda conducted an investigation into the matter; it found that the allegations were false, and that the rumours concerning such activities were initiated by elements hostile to AMISOM.

Appointment. On 10 June [S/2008/378], the Secretary-General informed the Security Council of the four experts whom he had appointed to the Monitoring Group.

SECURITY COUNCIL ACTION

On 20 November [meeting 6019], the Security Council unanimously adopted **resolution 1844(2008)**. The draft [S/2008/710] was submitted by the United Kingdom.

The Security Council,

Recalling its previous resolutions concerning the situation in Somalia, in particular resolutions 733(1992) of 23 January 1992, 751(1992) of 24 April 1992, 1356(2001) of 19 June 2001, 1425(2002) of 22 July 2002, 1519(2003) of 16 December 2003, 1676(2006) of 10 May 2006, 1725(2006) of 6 December 2006, 1744(2007) of 20 February 2007, 1772(2007) of 20 August 2007, 1801(2008) of 20 February 2008, 1811(2008) of 29 April 2008 and 1814(2008) of 15 May 2008, and the statements by its President, in particular those of 13 July 2006, 22 December 2006, 30 April 2007 and 14 June 2007, and recalling also its resolution 1730(2006) of 19 December 2006 on general issues relating to sanctions,

Reaffirming its respect for the sovereignty, territorial integrity, political independence and unity of Somalia,

Underlining the importance of providing and maintaining stability and security throughout Somalia,

Reaffirming its condemnation of all acts of violence in Somalia and incitement to violence inside Somalia, and expressing its concern at all acts intended to prevent or block a peaceful political process,

Expressing its grave concern over the recent increase in acts of piracy and armed robbery at sea against vessels off the coast of Somalia, and noting the role piracy may play in financing embargo violations by armed groups, as described in the statement of 9 October 2008 by the Chairman of the Security Council Committee established pursuant to resolution 751(1992) (hereinafter "the Committee") to the Council,

Emphasizing the continued contribution made to Somalia's peace and security by the arms embargo imposed by paragraph 5 of resolution 733(1992), as elaborated and amended by resolutions 1356(2001), 1425(2002), 1725(2006), 1744(2007) and 1772(2007), and reiterating its demand that all Member States, in particular those in the region, comply fully with the requirements of these resolutions,

Recalling its intention, outlined in paragraph 6 of resolution 1814(2008), to take measures against those who seek to prevent or block a peaceful political process, or those who threaten the transitional federal institutions of Somalia or the African Union Mission in Somalia by force, or take action that undermines stability in Somalia or the region,

Also recalling its intention, outlined in paragraph 7 of resolution 1814(2008), to strengthen the effectiveness of the United Nations arms embargo on Somalia, and to take measures against those who breach the arms embargo and those who support them in doing so,

Recalling its request to the Committee, outlined in paragraphs 6 and 7 of resolution 1814(2008), to provide recommendations on specific targeted measures to be imposed against such individuals or entities,

Taking note of the letter dated 1 August 2008 from the Vice-Chairman of the Committee to the President of the Security Council,

Determining that the situation in Somalia continues to constitute a threat to international peace and security in the region,

Acting under Chapter VII of the Charter of the United Nations,

1. *Decides* that all Member States shall take the measures necessary to prevent the entry into or transit through their territories of individuals designated by the Committee pursuant to paragraph 8 below, provided that nothing in the present paragraph shall oblige a State to refuse its own nationals entry into its territory;

2. *Decides also* that the measures imposed by paragraph 1 above shall not apply:

(*a*) Where the Committee determines on a case-by-case basis that such travel is justified on the grounds of humanitarian need, including religious obligation; or

(*b*) Where the Committee determines on a case-by-case basis that an exemption would otherwise further the objectives of peace and national reconciliation in Somalia and stability in the region;

3. *Decides further* that all Member States shall freeze without delay the funds, other financial assets and economic resources which are on their territories, which are owned or controlled, directly or indirectly, by the individuals or entities designated by the Committee pursuant to paragraph 8 below, or by individuals or entities acting on their behalf or at their direction, or by entities owned or controlled by them, as designated by the Committee, and further decides that all Member States shall ensure that any funds, financial assets or economic resources are prevented from being made available by their nationals, or by any individuals or entities within their territories, to or for the benefit of such individuals or entities;

4. *Decides* that the measures imposed by paragraph 3 above do not apply to funds, other financial assets or economic resources that have been determined by relevant Member States:

(*a*) To be necessary for basic expenses, including payment for foodstuffs, rent or mortgage, medicines and medical treatment, taxes, insurance premiums and public utility charges or exclusively for payment of reasonable professional fees and reimbursement of incurred expenses associated with the provision of legal services, or fees or service charges, in accordance with national laws, for routine holding or maintenance of frozen funds, other financial assets and economic resources, after notification by the relevant State to the Committee of the intention to authorize, where appropriate, access to such funds, other financial assets or economic resources, and in the absence of a negative decision by the Committee within three working days of such notification;

(*b*) To be necessary for extraordinary expenses, provided that such determination has been notified by the relevant State or Member States to the Committee and has been approved by the Committee; or

(*c*) be the subject of a judicial, administrative or arbitral lien or judgement, in which case the funds, other financial assets and economic resources may be used to satisfy that lien or judgement, provided that the lien or judgement was entered into prior to the date of the present resolution, is not for the benefit of a person or entity designated pursuant to paragraph 3 above, and has been notified by the relevant State or Member States to the Committee;

5. *Decides also* that Member States may permit the addition to the accounts frozen pursuant to the provisions of paragraph 3 above of interest or other earnings due on those accounts or payments due under contracts, agreements or obligations that arose prior to the date on which those accounts became subject to the provisions of the present resolution, provided that any such interest, other earnings and payments continue to be subject to these provisions and are frozen;

6. *Reaffirms* the general and complete arms embargo against Somalia imposed by resolution 733(1992), as elaborated and amended by resolutions 1356(2001), 1425(2002), 1725(2006), 1744(2007) and 1772(2007);

7. *Decides* that all Member States shall take the measures necessary to prevent the direct or indirect supply, sale or transfer of weapons and military equipment and the direct or indirect supply of technical assistance or training, financial and other assistance, including investment, brokering or other financial services, related to military activities or to the supply, sale, transfer, manufacture, maintenance or use of weapons and military equipment, to the individuals or entities designated by the Committee pursuant to paragraph 8 below;

8. *Decides also* that the provisions of paragraphs 1, 3 and 7 above shall apply to individuals, and that the provisions of paragraphs 3 and 7 above shall apply to entities, designated by the Committee:

(*a*) As engaging in or providing support for acts that threaten the peace, security or stability of Somalia, including acts that threaten the Djibouti agreement of 19 August 2008 or the political process, or threaten the transitional federal institutions or the African Union Mission in Somalia by force;

(b) As having acted in violation of the general and complete arms embargo reaffirmed in paragraph 6 above;

(c) As obstructing the delivery of humanitarian assistance to Somalia, or access to, or distribution of, humanitarian assistance in Somalia;

9. *Decides further* that the measures outlined in paragraphs 1, 3 and 7 above cease to apply in respect of such individuals or entities if and at such time as the Committee removes them from the list of designated individuals and entities;

10. *Underlines* the importance of coordination by the Committee with other United Nations sanctions committees and with the Special Representative of the Secretary-General for Somalia;

11. *Decides* to expand the mandate of the Committee as set out in resolution 751(1992) to include the following tasks:

(a) To monitor, with the support of the Monitoring Group established pursuant to resolution 1519(2003), the implementation of the measures imposed in paragraphs 1, 3 and 7 above, in addition to the general and complete arms embargo reaffirmed in paragraph 6 above;

(b) To seek from all Member States, in particular those in the region, information regarding the actions taken by them to implement effectively the measures imposed by paragraphs 1, 3 and 7 above and whatever further information it may consider useful in this regard;

(c) To examine information regarding alleged violations of measures imposed by paragraphs 1, 3 and 7 above, paragraph 5 of resolution 733(1992) and paragraphs 1 and 2 of resolution 1425(2002), and take appropriate action if necessary;

(d) To designate individuals and entities pursuant to paragraphs 3 and 8 above, upon the request of Member States as referred to in paragraph 12 below;

(e) To consider and decide upon requests for exemptions as set out in paragraphs 2 and 4 above;

(f) To review regularly the list of individuals and entities designated by the Committee pursuant to paragraphs 3 and 8 above, with a view to keeping the list as updated and accurate as possible and to confirm that listing remains appropriate, and to encourage Member States to provide any additional information whenever such information becomes available;

(g) To report at least every one hundred and twenty days to the Security Council on its work and on the implementation of the present resolution, with its observations and recommendations, in particular on ways to strengthen the effectiveness of the measures imposed by paragraphs 1, 3 and 7 above;

(h) To identify possible cases of non-compliance with the measures pursuant to paragraphs 1, 3 and 7 above and to determine the appropriate course of action on each case, and requests the Chairman, in periodic reports to the Council pursuant to subparagraph *(g)* above to provide progress reports on the work of the Committee on this issue;

(i) To amend its existing guidelines to facilitate the implementation of the measures imposed by the present resolution and keep these guidelines under active review as may be necessary;

Listing

12. *Encourages* Member States to submit to the Committee for inclusion on its list of designees names of individuals or entities who meet the criteria set out in paragraph 8 above, as well as any entities owned or controlled, directly or indirectly, by the submitted individuals or entities or individuals or entities acting on behalf of or at the direction of the submitted entities;

13. *Decides* that, when proposing names to the Committee for listing, Member States shall provide a detailed statement of case, together with sufficient identifying information to allow for the positive identification of individuals and entities by Member States, and decides further that for each such proposal Member States shall identify those parts of the statement of case that may be publicly released, including for use by the Committee for development of the summary described in paragraph 14 below or for the purpose of notifying or informing the listed individual or entity, and those parts which may be released upon request to interested States;

14. *Directs* the Committee, in coordination with the relevant designating States and with the assistance of the Monitoring Group, after a name is added to the list, to make accessible on the Committee's website a narrative summary of reasons for listing;

15. *Decides* that the Secretariat shall, after publication but within one week after a name is added to the list of individuals and entities, notify the permanent mission of the country or countries where the individual or entity is believed to be located and, in the case of individuals, the country of which the person is a national (to the extent this information is known) and include with this notification a copy of the publicly releasable portion of the statement of case, any information on reasons for listing available on the Committee's website, a description of the effects of designation, the Committee's procedures for considering de-listing requests, and the provisions regarding available exemptions;

16. *Demands* that Member States receiving notification as in paragraph 15 above take, in accordance with their domestic laws and practices, all possible measures to notify or inform in a timely manner the listed individual or entity of the designation, together with the information provided by the Secretariat as set out in paragraph 15 above;

17. *Encourages* Member States receiving notification as in paragraph 15 above to inform the Committee of steps they have taken to implement the measures set out in paragraphs 1, 3 and 7 above;

De-listing

18. *Welcomes* the establishment within the Secretariat of the Focal Point, pursuant to resolution 1730(2006), that provides listed individuals, groups, undertakings or entities with the option to submit a petition for de-listing directly to the Focal Point;

19. *Urges* designating States and States of citizenship and residence to review de-listing petitions received through the Focal Point, in accordance with the procedures outlined in the annex to resolution 1730(2006), in a timely manner and to indicate whether they support or oppose the request in order to facilitate review by the Committee;

20. *Directs* the Committee to consider requests, in accordance with its guidelines, for the removal from the Committee's list of designees of those who no longer meet the criteria pursuant to the present resolution;

21. *Decides* that the Secretariat shall, within one week after a name is removed from the Committee's list of designees, notify the permanent mission of the country or countries where the individual or entity is believed to be located and, in the case of individuals, the country of which the person is a national (to the extent this information is known), and demands that States receiving such notification take measures, in accordance with their domestic laws and practices, to notify or inform the concerned individual or entity of the de-listing in a timely manner;

22. *Encourages* the Committee to ensure that fair and clear procedures exist for placing individuals and entities on the Committee's list of designees and for removing them, as well as for granting humanitarian exemptions;

23. *Decides* that the mandate of the Monitoring Group, as set out in paragraph 3 of resolution 1811(2008), shall also include the tasks outlined below:

(a) To assist the Committee in monitoring implementation of the present resolution by providing any information on violations of the measures imposed in paragraphs 1, 3 and 7 above, in addition to the general and complete arms embargo reaffirmed in paragraph 6 above;

(b) To include in its reports to the Committee any information relevant to the designation by the Committee of the individuals and entities described in paragraph 8 above;

(c) To assist the Committee in compiling the narrative summaries referred to in paragraph 14 above;

24. *Reminds* all Member States of their obligation to implement strictly the measures imposed by the present resolution and all relevant resolutions;

25. *Decides* that all Member States shall report to the Committee within one hundred and twenty days of the adoption of the present resolution on the steps they have taken with a view to implementing effectively paragraphs 1 to 7 above;

26. *Decides also* to review the measures outlined in paragraphs 1, 3 and 7 above within twelve months;

27. *Decides further* to remain actively seized of the matter.

Report of Monitoring Group (December). In response to resolution 1811(2008) (see p. 296), the Monitoring Group issued a report on 20 November [S/2008/769], which the Committee transmitted to the Security Council on 10 December. The Group stated that most serviceable weapons and almost all ammunition available in Somalia had been delivered since 1992 in violation of the embargo. Although provisions existed for exemptions to the embargo to be granted by the Council under resolutions 1725(2006) [YUN 2006, p. 308], 1744(2007), 1772(2007) [YUN 2007, p. 276] and 1816(2008) (see p. 286), no exemption for delivery of arms and ammunition or other lethal support to any Somali armed force or group had ever been granted. Consequently, the Monitoring Group believed that every armed force, group or militia in Somalia, their financiers, supporters and, in some cases, foreign donors, were in violation of the arms embargo. The volume and pattern of arms transfers to Somalia had remained fairly constant since the Ethiopian military intervention and the overthrow of the Council of Somalia Islamic Courts in January 2007 [YUN 2007, p. 270]. The transfer of skills and technology for military and terrorist purposes contributed to an escalation in targeted killings, the use of improvised explosive devices and other types of violence.

Commercial imports, mainly from Yemen, remained the most consistent source of arms, ammunition and military materiel to Somalia. Since June, Yemeni curbs on domestic arms sales had reduced the volume of exports to Somalia and driven up arms prices in Somali markets. Nevertheless, weapons from Yemen continued to feed Somali retail arms sales and armed opposition and criminal groups. Insurgent groups in Ethiopia also procured arms and ammunition from Yemen, which then transited Somalia in violation of the embargo. Arms and ammunition also flowed from Somalia to Yemen, allegedly in support of Yemeni insurgents.

Financing for embargo violations by armed opposition groups was derived from a variety of sources, including the Government of Eritrea, private donors in the Arab and Islamic world, and organized fund-raising among Somali diaspora groups. Armed opposition groups sustained themselves through the use of the Internet, and a number of websites and Internet forums were openly affiliated with one or more groups. Contributions for the armed struggle were increasingly taking the form of commercial goods, which could be resold in Somalia to generate cash.

Another source of arms and materiel to Somalia was external contributions—which were intended to support security and stabilization—to Government forces. Such contributions were eligible for exemption from the embargo, but most were not authorized by the Security Council, and thus constituted violations. As much as 80 per cent of the external support was diverted to private purposes, Somali arms markets or opposition groups. Contributions to the Government security sector thus represented a net source of insecurity and an obstacle to stabilization.

The Monitoring Group recommended, among other measures, that the Security Council require States and international organizations that came into possession of weapons, ammunition or military materiel on Somali territory, destined for Somalia or originating there to record the identifying characteristics of those items and share them with the Group, in accordance with Council resolution 1425(2002)

[YUN 2002, p. 206]. It recommended that the Council establish more precise guidelines for the notification of support to security sector institutions, and extend to international organizations, including UN specialized agencies, the requirement to notify the sanctions Committee of security sector support programmes. The Group also recommended that the Council authorize international naval forces in the Gulf of Aden and the Indian Ocean to seize any weapons encountered in the course of their operations and interdict arms trafficking; and request those naval forces to share with the Group information about weapons seizures.

SECURITY COUNCIL ACTION

On 19 December [meeting 6050], the Security Council unanimously adopted **resolution 1853(2008)**. The draft [S/2008/796] was submitted by the United Kingdom.

The Security Council,

Reaffirming its previous resolutions and the statements by its President concerning the situation in Somalia, in particular resolution 733(1992) of 23 January 1992, which established an embargo on all deliveries of weapons and military equipment to Somalia (hereinafter referred to as "the arms embargo"), and resolutions 1519(2003) of 16 December 2003, 1558(2004) of 17 August 2004, 1587(2005) of 15 March 2005, 1630(2005) of 14 October 2005, 1676(2006) of 10 May 2006, 1724(2006) of 29 November 2006, 1744(2007) of 20 February 2007, 1766(2007) of 23 July 2007, 1772(2007) of 20 August 2007, 1801(2008) of 20 February 2008, 1811(2008) of 29 April 2008 and 1844(2008) of 20 November 2008,

Recalling that, as set out in resolutions 1744(2007) and 1772(2007), the arms embargo on Somalia does not apply to *(a)* weapons and military equipment, technical training and assistance intended solely for the support of or use by the African Union Mission in Somalia, and *(b)* supplies and technical assistance by States intended solely for the purpose of helping to develop security sector institutions, consistent with the political process set out in those resolutions and in the absence of a negative decision by the Security Council Committee established pursuant to resolution 751(1992) (hereinafter referred to as "the Committee") within five working days of receiving an advance notification of such supplies or assistance on a case-by-case basis,

Reaffirming the importance of the sovereignty, territorial integrity, political independence and unity of Somalia,

Reaffirming also that the Djibouti peace agreement and follow-on dialogue process represent the most viable basis for a resolution of the conflict in Somalia, and reiterating its commitment to a comprehensive and lasting settlement of the situation in Somalia based on the Transitional Federal Charter,

Reiterating the urgent need for all Somali leaders to take tangible steps to continue political dialogue,

Commending the work of the Special Representative of the Secretary-General for Somalia, Mr. Ahmedou Ould-Abdallah, and reaffirming its strong support for his efforts,

Taking note of the report of the Monitoring Group of 20 November 2008 submitted pursuant to paragraph 3 *(i)* of resolution 1811(2008) and the observations and recommendations contained therein,

Condemning flows of weapons and ammunition supplies to and through Somalia in violation of the arms embargo as a serious threat to peace and stability in Somalia,

Reiterating its insistence that all States, in particular those in the region, should refrain from any action in contravention of the arms embargo and should take all necessary steps to hold violators accountable,

Reiterating and underscoring the importance of enhancing the monitoring of the arms embargo in Somalia through persistent and vigilant investigation into the violations, bearing in mind that strict enforcement of the arms embargo will improve the overall security situation in Somalia,

Determining that the situation in Somalia continues to constitute a threat to international peace and security in the region,

Acting under Chapter VII of the Charter of the United Nations,

1. *Stresses* the obligation of all States to comply fully with the measures imposed by resolution 733(1992), as well as resolution 1844(2008);

2. *Reiterates its intention* to consider specific action to improve implementation of and compliance with measures imposed by resolution 733(1992), as well as resolution 1844(2008);

3. *Decides* to extend the mandate of the Monitoring Group referred to in paragraph 3 of resolution 1558(2004), and requests the Secretary-General to take the necessary administrative measures as expeditiously as possible to re-establish the Monitoring Group for a period of twelve months, drawing, as appropriate, on the expertise of the members of the Monitoring Group established pursuant to resolution 1811(2008), and with the addition of a fifth expert, in consultation with the Committee, in order to fulfil its expanded mandate, this mandate being as follows:

(a) To continue the tasks outlined in paragraphs 3 *(a)* to *(c)* of resolution 1587(2005);

(b) To carry out additionally the tasks outlined in paragraphs 23 *(a)* to *(c)* of resolution 1844(2008);

(c) To continue to investigate, in coordination with relevant international agencies, all activities, including in the financial, maritime and other sectors, which generate revenues used to commit arms embargo violations;

(d) To continue to investigate any means of transport, routes, seaports, airports and other facilities used in connection with arms embargo violations;

(e) To continue refining and updating information on the draft list of those individuals and entities who violate the measures implemented by Member States in accordance with resolution 733(1992) and paragraphs 8 *(a)* to *(c)* of resolution 1844(2008), inside and outside Somalia, and their active supporters, for possible future measures by the Security Council, and to present such information to the Committee as and when the Committee deems appropriate;

(*f*) To continue making recommendations based on its investigations, on the previous reports of the Panel of Experts appointed pursuant to resolutions 1425(2002) of 22 July 2002 and 1474(2003) of 8 April 2003, and on the previous reports of the Monitoring Group appointed pursuant to resolutions 1519(2003), 1558(2004), 1587(2005), 1630(2005), 1676(2006), 1724(2006), 1766(2007) and 1811(2008);

(*g*) To work closely with the Committee on specific recommendations for additional measures to improve overall compliance with the arms embargo, as well as the measures imposed in paragraphs 1, 3 and 7 of resolution 1844(2008);

(*h*) To assist in identifying areas where the capacities of States in the region can be strengthened to facilitate the implementation of the arms embargo, as well as the measures imposed in paragraphs 1, 3 and 7 of resolution 1844(2008);

(*i*) To provide to the Council, through the Committee, a midterm briefing within six months of its establishment, and to submit progress reports to the Committee on a monthly basis;

(*j*) To submit, through the Committee, for consideration by the Council, a final report covering all the tasks set out above, no later than fifteen days prior to the termination of the mandate of the Monitoring Group;

4. *Requests* the Secretary-General to make the necessary financial arrangements to support the work of the Monitoring Group;

5. *Reaffirms* paragraphs 4, 5, 7, 8 and 10 of resolution 1519(2003);

6. *Requests* the Committee, in accordance with its mandate and in consultation with the Monitoring Group and other relevant United Nations entities, to consider the recommendations in the reports of the Monitoring Group of 5 April and 16 October 2006, 17 July 2007 and 24 April and 20 November 2008 and recommend to the Council ways to improve implementation of and compliance with the arms embargo as well as the measures imposed in paragraphs 1, 3 and 7 of resolution 1844(2008), in response to continuing violations;

7. *Decides* to remain actively seized of the matter.

Report of Committee on sanctions. On 19 December [S/2008/806], the Chairman of the Security Council Committee on sanctions against Somalia submitted a report on activities in 2008. The Committee met seven times in informal consultations. On 25 March, the Committee discussed a request by the Monitoring Group for assistance in eliciting replies from the AU and Member States. Subsequently, on 27 March, it dispatched letters to the AU, Ethiopia, Somalia and the United Arab Emirates. On 25 June, the Committee discussed the request made by the Security Council in resolution 1814(2008) (see p. 275) to provide recommendations on specific measures the Council might impose on individuals and entities that blocked the peace process or breached the arms embargo. On 24 July, it held an exchange of views with the Secretary-General's Special Representative for Somalia in connection with the Council's request for recommendations on specific measures. In a letter of 1 August to the Council, the Committee conveyed its recommendations to the Council concerning the imposition of targeted measures against individuals and entities as designated by the Committee. During the reporting period, the Committee received 14 requests for exemptions to the arms embargo for non-lethal military equipment pursuant to Council resolution 1356(2001) [YUN 2001, p. 212]; one request for an exemption to the embargo pursuant to resolution 1772(2007) [YUN 2007, p. 276]; and a notification pursuant to resolution 1744(2007) [ibid., p. 269]. Denmark and the Netherlands informed the Committee of their decisions to provide naval escort to merchant ships carrying relief cargo at the request of WFP and with the consent of the Transitional Federal Government.

Financing of Monitoring Group

On 11 September [A/63/346/Add.2], the Secretary-General submitted to the General Assembly estimated financial requirements for the Monitoring Group for 2009, amounting to $1,393,800 ($1,414,400 gross). In December [A/63/593], ACABQ recommended that the Assembly approve the resources requested by the Secretary-General for 27 political missions, including the Monitoring Group.

The Assembly, in section XI of **resolution 63/263** of 24 December (see p. 1548), approved budgets totalling $429,497,600 for the 27 political missions authorized by the Assembly and/or Council.

Eritrea–Ethiopia

In 2008, the United Nations maintained its presence in Eritrea and Ethiopia to assist both countries in implementing the June 2000 Agreement on Cessation of Hostilities and the December 2000 Comprehensive Peace Agreement, both signed in Algiers (the Algiers Agreements), which regulated their border dispute that had led to armed conflict in 1998 and subsequent intermittent fighting. The United Nations Mission in Ethiopia and Eritrea (UNMEE) continued to monitor the border region referred to as the Temporary Security Zone—a 25-kilometre-wide buffer zone that marked the formal separation of forces—and to support the work of the Eritrea-Ethiopia Boundary Commission, the neutral body mandated under the terms of the Peace Agreement to delimit and demarcate the colonial treaty border. In January, the Security Council extended the UNMEE mandate until the end of July. However, UN engagement in the border dispute between the two countries changed dramatically during the year. Eritrea maintained its restrictions on the Mission, which had not received any fuel from its suppliers in Eritrea since December 2007 and was forced to reduce its operational activities. Despite demands by the Council for Eritrea to resume fuel shipments to the Mission or allow it to import fuel without restrictions, the situation remained unresolved. Cross-border movement and efforts to relocate UN personnel and equipment to Ethiopia were hindered by Eritrean Defence Forces and the Mission was compelled to activate an alternate plan whereby personnel and equipment were regrouped in Asmara and Assab, Eritrea. As those facilities were inadequate for an extended stay of the regrouped troops, the Mission was instructed by the Secretary-General to begin relocating military personnel to their home countries pending a final decision by the Council on the Mission's future. In June, the Council presented to the President of Eritrea and the Prime Minister of Ethiopia options for future UN engagement, which both countries rejected. Subsequently, the Council terminated the Mission's mandate effective 31 July. No progress was made towards the construction of boundary pillars between the two countries in the manner foreseen in 2006 by the Eritrea-Ethiopia Boundary Commission. In its final report, the Commission said that a copy of the maps illustrating the points of demarcation of the boundary between the two countries was deposited with the Secretary-General on 17 January. The Commission, having terminated its mandate, considered itself *functus officio*.

Implementation of Algiers Agreements

Report of Secretary-General (January). In his January report on Ethiopia and Eritrea [S/2008/40 & Corr.1], submitted pursuant to Security Council resolution 1320(2000) [YUN 2000, p. 176], the Secretary-General said that the Eritrean defence forces continued to induct troops into the Temporary Security Zone. UNMEE observed some 500 newly deployed Eritrean soldiers in the Zone in Sector West, 300 in Sector Centre and 100 in Subsector East. Some 17 new Eritrean camps were established in the Zone and adjacent areas. Eritrea maintained all previously imposed restrictions on the United Nations Mission in Ethiopia and Eritrea (UNMEE). It maintained the 45 permanent restrictions on UNMEE freedom of movement in a number of areas [YUN 2007, p. 288], and banned the Mission from carrying out night patrols. The Mission had not received any fuel from its suppliers in Eritrea since 1 December 2007, forcing UNMEE to reduce important operational activities, including patrols, demining and the provision of administrative support to regional locations and team sites. The Mission repeatedly raised the matter with the Eritrean Commissioner. It also requested permission to import fuel from the United Nations Mission in the Sudan (UNMIS), but did not receive a response. On 15 January, UNMEE reported that if the situation was not resolved through the immediate provision of fuel authorized by Eritrea, the Mission would be compelled to begin relocating its personnel from the country and effectively halt its operations.

The Secretary-General reported that Ethiopia and Eritrea had not complied with Council resolution 1767(2007) [YUN 2007, p. 289], which called on the parties to de-escalate the situation, including by returning to the 16 December 2004 levels of deployment and by avoiding provocative military activities. In an interview broadcast on Eritrean television on 5 January, President Isaias Afwerki of Eritrea reaffirmed his 2007 position that the border issue had been legally resolved, and that Eritrea considered the border demarcated [ibid., p. 293]. In a 15 January letter to the Council, President Afwerki stated that the Eritrea-Ethiopia Boundary Commission [YUN 2000, p. 180] had terminated its functions by completing its work through 'virtual demarcation' and that the boundary was demarcated. He urged the Council to compel the evacuation of the Ethiopian army and institutions occupying sovereign Eritrean territories.

In a letter of 18 January to the Secretary-General, the Minister of Foreign Affairs of Ethiopia said that the Commission's virtual demarcation had no validity in international law, and attempts to equate the status of its 13 April 2002 delimitation decision [YUN 2002, p. 88] and its 27 November 2006 statement [YUN 2006, p. 324], in which the Commission identified the location of points for the placement of border pillars, were unacceptable, and therefore could not be equally binding. Ethiopia fully accepted the 2002 delimitation decision as final and binding and was committed to its implementation and the full demarcation of the border. On the same date, the Minister of Foreign Affairs also sent a letter to the Council, in which he described the Commission's virtual demarcation as "legal fiction". He stressed that Eritrea was in breach of the 2000 Algiers Agreement on Cessation of Hostilities between Ethiopia and Eritrea [YUN 2000, p. 173], as it had violated the Temporary Security Zone, and urged the Council to take appropriate measures against that party.

In early January, the Secretariat informed Ethiopia and Eritrea that the Secretary-General intended to proceed with the appointment of the candidate for the post of the Secretary-General's Special Representative proposed in December 2007. Both countries indicated that they would appreciate it if the Secretary-General did not move forward with the appointment at that time.

The Secretary-General called on the parties to comply with the Council's demands as set out in resolution 1767(2007). In light of the restrictions on UNMEE operations, including the stoppage of fuel supplies, he recommended a one-month technical roll-over of the UNMEE mandate. In the meantime, the Secretary-General would review developments on the ground and the challenges facing UNMEE, and prepare recommendations on the Mission's future direction, including possible withdrawal or relocation.

Report of Boundary Commission (January). Annexed to the Secretary-General's report [S/2008/40 & Corr.1] (see above) was the twenty-sixth report of the Eritrea-Ethiopia Boundary Commission. The Commission stated that, notwithstanding the September 2007 meeting of the two parties [YUN 2007, p. 290], no progress was made towards building boundary pillars in the manner foreseen in the Commission's 27 November 2006 statement. In stipulating that the boundary stood automatically as demarcated by the boundary points listed in the annex to the statement, the Commission considered that it had fulfilled its mandate, and remained in existence to deal with remaining administrative matters.

Communication. In a letter of 29 January to the Security Council [S/2008/54], Eritrea said that the final and binding demarcation of the boundary was expected to be completed within six months of the Boundary Commission's 2002 delimitation decision [YUN 2002, p. 188], but the process had been held hostage by Ethiopia for nearly six years. The final and binding delimitation and demarcation of the boundary was exclusively the mandate of the Boundary Commission, and no State had the right to intervene in the process. Eritrea urged the Council to focus on the fundamental issue of Ethiopia's withdrawal from sovereign Eritrean territory. Eritrea also stated that the Secretary-General's January report was presented by the Secretary-General's Acting Special Representative in total disregard for its previous protests and concerns. It reiterated its protest regarding the Acting Special Representative, about whom Eritrea expressed its disapproval in 2006 [YUN 2006, p. 325] and in February 2007 [YUN 2007, p. 287].

SECURITY COUNCIL ACTION

On 30 January [meeting 5829], the Security Council unanimously adopted **resolution 1798(2008)**. The draft [S/2008/49] was submitted by Belgium.

The Security Council,

Reaffirming all its previous resolutions and the statements by its President pertaining to the situation between Ethiopia and Eritrea (hereinafter referred to as "the parties") and the requirements contained therein, including in particular resolutions 1320(2000) of 15 September 2000, 1430(2002) of 14 August 2002, 1466(2003) of 14 March 2003, 1640(2005) of 23 November 2005, 1681(2006) of 31 May 2006, 1710(2006) of 29 September 2006, 1741(2007) of 30 January 2007 and 1767(2007) of 30 July 2007,

Stressing once again its unwavering commitment to the peace process and to the full and expeditious implementation of the Agreement on Cessation of Hostilities of 18 June 2000 and the Peace Agreement of 12 December 2000 ("the Algiers Agreements") as a basis for peaceful and cooperative relations between the parties, and recalling article 4, paragraph 15, of the Peace Agreement, in which the parties agreed that the delimitation and demarcation determinations of the Eritrea-Ethiopia Boundary Commission shall be final and binding,

Expressing its support for the efforts of the Boundary Commission, welcoming once again the acceptance by the parties of the delimitation decision of the Commission of 13 April 2002, recalling that it acknowledged the statement by the Commission of 27 November 2006, and taking note of the twenty-sixth report of the Commission annexed to the report of the Secretary-General of 23 January 2008,

Stressing that the physical demarcation of the border between Eritrea and Ethiopia would support a comprehensive and lasting settlement of the dispute between the parties and the normalization of their relations,

Expressing its deep concern about the continuing dispute between Ethiopia and Eritrea, and over the continued tense and potentially unstable security situation in the Temporary Security Zone and the adjacent areas, and stressing that it is the primary responsibility of the parties to end this situation by fulfilling expeditiously their obligations under the Algiers Agreements,

Reaffirming once again the integrity of the Temporary Security Zone as provided for in paragraphs 12 to 14 of the Agreement on Cessation of Hostilities, and recalling the objectives of its establishment, in particular to create conditions conducive to a comprehensive and lasting settlement of the conflict, and the commitment of the parties to respect the Temporary Security Zone,

Underlining that the Security Council remains committed to its role, in particular helping to ensure that the parties respect the commitments they made in the Agreement on Cessation of Hostilities and the Peace Agreement, to which the United Nations was one of the witnesses,

Commending the efforts made by the United Nations Mission in Ethiopia and Eritrea and its military and civilian personnel to accomplish its duties, despite the difficult circumstances,

Having considered the report of the Secretary-General,

1. *Decides* to extend the mandate of the United Nations Mission in Ethiopia and Eritrea for a period of six months, until 31 July 2008;

2. *Reiterates its call* for the parties to show maximum restraint and refrain from any threat or use of force against each other, avoid provocative military activities and put an end to the exchange of hostile statements;

3. *Reiterates its call upon* Eritrea and Ethiopia to maintain their full commitment to the Agreement on Cessation of Hostilities of 18 June 2000, and to de-escalate the situation, including by returning to the 16 December 2004 levels of deployment;

4. *Underlines* that Eritrea and Ethiopia bear the primary responsibility for achieving a comprehensive and lasting settlement of the border dispute and normalizing their relations, demands that they take immediately concrete steps in order to complete the process launched by the Peace Agreement of 12 December 2000 by enabling physi-

cal demarcation of the border, and urges them to normalize their relations;

5. *Reiterates its demands* on Eritrea to withdraw immediately all troops and heavy military equipment from the Temporary Security Zone, to provide the Mission with the access, assistance, support and protection required for the performance of its duties and to remove immediately and without preconditions the restrictions on the Mission;

6. *Reiterates its call upon* Ethiopia to reduce the number of military forces in the areas adjacent to the Temporary Security Zone;

7. *Notes with grave concern* the Mission's critical fuel levels, demands that the Government of Eritrea resume immediately fuel shipments to the Mission or allow the Mission to import fuel without restrictions, and requests the Secretary-General to keep the Security Council informed of developments;

8. *Reiterates its call upon* both parties to fully cooperate with the Mission with a view to urgently reactivating the work of the Military Coordination Commission, which remains a unique forum to discuss pressing military and security issues;

9. *Strongly supports* the ongoing efforts of the Secretary-General and the international community to engage with Eritrea and Ethiopia to help them to normalize their relations, to promote stability between the parties and to lay the foundation for a comprehensive and lasting settlement of the dispute, and urges the parties to accept the Secretary-General's good offices;

10. *Welcomes* the ongoing efforts of the Secretary-General towards the earliest appointment of a Special Representative;

11. *Expresses its willingness* to reconsider any changes to the mandate of the Mission in the light of subsequent developments in the implementation of the Algiers Agreements;

12. *Calls upon* Member States to provide contributions to the trust fund, established pursuant to resolution 1177(1998) of 26 June 1998 and referred to in article 4, paragraph 17, of the Peace Agreement;

13. *Expresses its deep appreciation* for the contribution and dedication of the troop-contributing countries to the work of the Mission;

14. *Decides* to remain actively seized of the matter.

Communications. In a statement of 1 February [S/2008/68], Eritrea said that the Boundary Commission's demarcation by coordinates (virtual demarcation) constituted a culmination of the arbitration process and a final and comprehensive settlement of the border issue. The Security Council had no other authority or function other than enforcing the Commission's delimitation and demarcation determinations. As resolution 1798(2008) was in contravention of fundamental premises of the UN Charter and key principles of international law, and distorted fundamental tenets of the Algiers Peace Agreement, Eritrea considered that resolution irrelevant.

In a letter of 1 February to the Council [S/2008/66], the Secretary-General referred to his letter of 21 January to the Council on the fuel crisis facing UNMEE and his appeal for President Afwerki's personal intervention to facilitate the resumption of fuel delivery. The Secretary-General had yet to receive a response from President Afwerki, and UNMEE had not been authorized to import fuel directly or from UNMIS. Consequently, UNMEE operations were coming to a halt. He informed the Council that if the Eritrean authorities did not reinstate the fuel supply by 6 February, he would be compelled to instruct UNMEE to begin relocating personnel and equipment from Eritrea. Under the UNMEE contingency plan, some of the Mission's troops would have to be relocated temporarily to the Ethiopian side until a decision was taken on the longer-term presence of UNMEE, while other troops might be concentrated in Asmara, Eritrea, for temporary evacuation to their home countries. A technical assessment mission led by the UN Department of Peacekeeping Operations (DPKO) would work with UNMEE and the Eritrean and Ethiopian authorities on options for the Mission's future direction. If Eritrea insisted on maintaining restrictions that would endanger UNMEE personnel, the Secretary-General would have to consider the total withdrawal of the Mission and recommend the termination of its mandate.

In a press statement of 4 February [SC/9240], the Security Council expressed its concern about the fact that the restrictions on fuel deliveries had not been lifted, reiterated its demand that Eritrea lift those restrictions without preconditions, and requested Eritrea to facilitate the dispatch of the UN technical assessment mission, which was due to depart for the region on 5 February.

In a statement of 15 February [S/2008/100] on the relocation on UNMEE, Eritrea said that the insinuation of impending danger to UNMEE troops in Eritrea was unfounded, and Eritrea could not acquiesce in temporary relocation or some other new arrangement that was at variance with the provisions of the Agreement. Eritrea called again on the Council to redress the situation and ensure the removal of the Ethiopian occupation of Eritrean territories.

SECURITY COUNCIL ACTION

On 15 February [meeting 5838], following consultations among Security Council members, the President made statement **S/PRST/2008/7** on behalf of the Council:

The Security Council recalls that on 30 January 2008 it adopted resolution 1798(2008) on the United Nations Mission in Ethiopia and Eritrea. The Council is following with the utmost concern the situation confronting the Mission. It expresses its full support for the efforts of the Secretary-General to address this problem.

The Council notes with great concern that, by maintaining restrictions on the Mission despite the numerous demands of the Council and by refusing to reinstate fuel deliveries to the Mission, the Government of Eritrea has created a situation in which a temporary relocation of personnel and equipment from Eritrea has been rendered inevitable. The Council also expresses deep concern about the impediments and logistical constraints put on the Mission in its attempts to organize this temporary relocation. The Council condemns such steps taken by Eritrea.

The Council strongly condemns the lack of cooperation from the Government of Eritrea, which not only gravely contravenes Council resolutions and the Agreement on Cessation of Hostilities of 18 June 2000 but also fails to comply with Eritrea's general obligation to assist forces that have been stationed with its consent. The Council holds Eritrea responsible for the safety and security of the Mission and its personnel.

The Council demands that the Government of Eritrea resume full cooperation with the Mission, including by ending all its restrictions on the Mission, and abide by all its obligations as a State Member of the United Nations.

The Council expresses its determination to closely monitor the situation and to consider further appropriate steps for the safety and protection of the Mission and its personnel.

Relocation of UNMEE

In a March special report [S/2008/145], the Secretary-General said that the situation concerning the non-delivery of fuel to UNMEE remained unresolved at the end of January, forcing the Mission to reduce its daily patrols in the Temporary Security Zone from 60 to 20. UNMEE estimated that if it maintained the minimum level of operations without replenishing its stocks, the fuel supply would be completely exhausted by the end of March. A technical assessment mission, composed of participants from the UN Departments of Peacekeeping Operations, Field Support and Safety and Security, visited Addis Ababa, Ethiopia, from 6 to 11 February; it was not able to travel to Eritrea due to the cancellation of the participants' visas by the Eritrean authorities. In a note of 8 February, the Secretariat informed Eritrea of the decision to relocate UNMEE personnel and requested it to extend the necessary cooperation to the Mission. The technical assessment mission, UNMEE and the Ministry of Defence of Ethiopia agreed to the emergency relocation plan on 10 February. The plan provided for the cross-border movement of 1,375 military personnel and their equipment from the Temporary Security Zone to five sites in Ethiopia. An advance unit of the UNMEE Indian Battalion carrying equipment in five vehicles was allowed to cross the border on 11 February. On 12 February, vehicles of the Mine Action Coordination Centre were stopped by Eritrean soldiers in Sector Centre, and two vehicles of the Indian Battalion were prevented from crossing the border in Subsector East; the Mine Action Coordination Centre vehicles were allowed to cross the border on 13 February. In all, the Eritrean authorities allowed no more than six vehicles to cross into Ethiopia. On 15 February, the commercial company that distributed food rations to UNMEE informed the Mission that it would not be able to distribute the following week's rations, as its sub-contracted Eritrean company had stated that it had no vehicles "to do business for UNMEE". The Department of Field Support raised the issue with the Permanent Representative of Eritrea, informing him that some of the relocating contingents had only two days of emergency rations left. The same day, one month of rations were delivered to UNMEE in Asmara.

Efforts by UNMEE to engage the Eritrean authorities on 12 and 15 February to request them to facilitate the relocation to Ethiopia were unsuccessful: the Eritrean authorities maintained that the relocation was a "unilateral decision" by the United Nations, and the relocation plan had to be abandoned. On 14 and 15 February, the Secretariat briefed countries contributing troops to UNMEE on the developments. All countries considered the situation facing UNMEE and the measures imposed by the Eritrean authorities as unacceptable. They demanded that Eritrea provide the fuel required for relocating the Mission and allow UNMEE peacekeepers to leave Eritrea with their equipment in a dignified and orderly manner.

UNMEE was compelled to activate an alternative contingency plan, under which personnel and equipment from the Temporary Security Zone were regrouped in Asmara and Assab, Eritrea, beginning on 17 February. Following that date, a number of incidents occurred in which Eritrean soldiers prevented the movement of UNMEE personnel and equipment. In a letter of 20 February (see below), Eritrea stated that UNMEE had not informed the Eritrean authorities of its decision to regroup its personnel in Asmara until 19 February. The Secretary-General stated, however, that his Deputy Special Representative met with the Acting Eritrean Commissioner in charge of liaison with UNMEE on 12 February to discuss the relocation arrangements, but the Commissioner maintained that he had no instructions to discuss the relocation. UNMEE also sent notes to the Eritrean authorities on 15 and 18 February informing them of the status of the temporary relocation. On 19 February, the Commissioner informed the Deputy Special Representative that Eritrea would allow the movement of the blocked personnel and equipment to Asmara. Nevertheless, Eritrean soldiers continued to prevent the relocation. On 20 February, UNMEE informed the Commissioner of the difficulties the Mission was facing; the same day, the blocked convoys were allowed to move to Asmara. UNMEE continued to encounter problems, however, including incidents on 23 and 25 February, in which Eritrean soldiers prevented the movement of UNMEE fuel and equipment. All military units were given orders to carry as much of their equipment as the available fuel would allow. The Mission was further instructed to inventory all equipment and materiel that could not be relocated, and to present those inventories to the Eritrean authorities, conveying the expectation that Eritrea would safeguard the materiel until it could be removed. On 22 February, UNMEE informed the Eritrean authorities about the UN equipment that would be left at the vacated sites and requested their cooperation in keeping it safe; it also met with the Eritrean Commissioner to discuss the matter. The Commissioner stated that since UNMEE had decided unilaterally to relocate from the Temporary Security Zone, Eritrea should not be held responsible for any items left behind. Also on 22 February, the Secretariat requested Eritrea to reconsider its position, resume fuel supplies, lift all restrictions, and allow UNMEE to carry on with its mandate. The Eritrean authorities had still not responded. As at 26 February, 681 personnel of the 1,008 stationed in Sectors West and Centre of the Temporary Security Zone had been relocated to Asmara. In Subsector East, 101 troops from the Indian Battalion and the Indian Construction Company, as well as 11 military observers from various countries, were regrouped at Assab. The military personnel deployed on the Ethiopian side were not affected by the fuel crisis and continued to perform their tasks.

The Secretary-General said that there were no adequate facilities in Asmara and Assab for an extended stay of the regrouped troops, and a further relocation from Asmara and Assab to the designated sites in Ethiopia would be a lengthy and complex exercise. He therefore instructed UNMEE to begin relocating the military personnel in Asmara and Assab to their home countries pending a final decision by the Security Council on the Mission's future. The necessary personnel from the Indian, Jordanian and Kenyan contingents would remain in Asmara as a rear party to secure the contingent-owned equipment and facilitate its transportation when a decision was taken. Some 60 international civilian personnel, including the Deputy Special Representative and the Chief of Mission Support, would also remain in Asmara for liaison purposes and to inventory the equipment that would be left behind. The military and civilian personnel deployed on the Ethiopian side would remain in their positions until the Council decided on the future of UNMEE.

The Secretary-General observed that the restrictions imposed on UNMEE were unacceptable and in breach of the fundamental principles of peacekeeping. In view of the untenable situation in which Eritrea placed UNMEE, it was vital to relocate the Mission's personnel to sustainable locations. Once the relocation was completed, he intended to submit a report to the Council providing options and recommendations for any future UN peacekeeping presence in the area. He urged Eritrea and Ethiopia to avoid any action that could exacerbate the situation in the border areas and undermine the Agreement.

Communications (February-March). In letters to the Security Council dated 20 February [S/2008/114], 3 March [S/2008/148] and 4 March [S/2008/156], Eritrea addressed the issue of the UNMEE fuel supply, the regrouping of UNMEE troops and equipment and the safety and security of the troops. In those communications, Eritrea maintained that there was no threat to the safety and security of UN troops in the country and that the issue of the UNMEE fuel supply was technical and could have been resolved without politicizing it. It stated that the United Nations had made unilaterally the decision to regroup UNMEE troops. In that connection, Eritrea had not been adequately notified or provided in advance with the details of any changes in the Mission's status and major movements outside its area of responsibility. Notifications received from UNMEE were incomplete and did not include details on the scope and duration of the relocation, the legal explanation of its implications in terms of the Algiers Agreement, or logistical details. Communications on the regrouping of troops were received after the regrouping had been put into effect or, as in the case of the Mission personnel moved to Asmara, Eritrea was informed when the bulk of the troops had already arrived. Eritrea was also not provided in advance with the plan for the move or the handling of the Mission's heavy equipment. Subsequently, Eritrea had approached DPKO to ascertain UN plans concerning UNMEE, but no information was provided. Eritrea also reiterated its request for a response from the Secretary-General regarding Ethiopia's occupation of Eritrean territories in violation of the UN Charter and Algiers Peace Agreement. It stated that it could not be blamed for a lack of cooperation if its views and concerns as a host country were disregarded.

In a letter of 10 March to the Security Council [S/2008/172], Eritrea stated that it had no role in the major decisions that affected the status of UNMEE in Eritrea. The decision to relocate UNMEE troops from Eritrea to Ethiopia was done through closed consultation between the Secretary-General and Ethiopian Prime Minister Meles Zenawi during the tenth ordinary session of the AU Assembly (Addis Ababa, 31 January–2 February). No consultations were held between the Secretariat and Eritrean authorities concerning the regrouping of UN troops to Asmara, and there remained a lack of clear information from the Secretariat on critical matters pertaining to the future status of UNMEE.

In a letter of 25 March to the Secretary-General [S/2008/200], President Afwerki stated that Eritrea could not accept any arrangements that would legitimize the Ethiopian occupation of sovereign Eritrean territories, and urged the Secretary-General to ensure the evacuation of the occupation. With regard to UNMEE, the President said that Eritrea had no wish to retain UNMEE equipment. When informed fully and clearly on the operational details regarding the evacuation of the Mission, it would not be difficult to put in place appropriate measures towards its smooth implementation.

In a letter of 28 March to the Secretary-General [S/2008/214], Ethiopia referred to President Afwerki's 25 March letter and stated that Eritrea had undermined the core elements of the 2000 Agreement on Cessation of Hostilities [YUN 2000, p. 173], as well as the integrity of the Temporary Security Zone and a fully operational UNMEE. Ethiopia was not in occupation of any Eritrean territory, nor could the issue of occupation arise before demarcation was finalized. Eritrea had increased tension along the border between the two countries as it expanded its takeover of the Zone, and increased restrictions on UNMEE operations to the point where the Mission's effectiveness was destroyed. Those actions were taken in deliberate defiance of the United Nations and the Security Council, as well as the Algiers Agreement, which Eritrea was working to nullify. Ethiopia believed that it was necessary for the Council to impose punitive sanctions on Eritrea to ensure that it fulfilled the international obligations to which it had committed itself in 2000.

Report of Secretary-General (April). In his April special report on Ethiopia and Eritrea [S/2008/226], the Secretary-General said that UNMEE reached a critical turning point with the temporary relocation of the Mission's military personnel and equipment from Eritrea. Following the further temporary relocation of the Eritrea-based military personnel to their home countries, the UNMEE presence in Eritrea consisted of 164 military personnel, who constituted a rear party that would remain in the country to protect contingent-owned equipment until it was shipped. A small number of civilian personnel maintained a liaison with the Eritrean authorities and provided administrative support in handling the remaining equipment. The Mission's military personnel in Ethiopia continued to carry out their mandated tasks. The UNMEE presence in Ethiopia consisted of some 302 military personnel, including 90 military observers, deployed at seven sites along the southern boundary of the Temporary Security Zone and at UNMEE headquarters in Addis Ababa.

Taking into account the views expressed by Council members, together with the positions of Eritrea and Ethiopia, the Secretary-General presented four options that could be considered for the UN peacekeeping presence in Eritrea and Ethiopia: Eritrea could reconsider its position, resume fuel supplies to UNMEE, lift all restrictions and allow the Mission to continue to perform the tasks originally envisaged in the Agreement on Cessation of Hostilities; UNMEE could be terminated, leaving no UN peacekeeping presence in the area; a small observer mission could be deployed in the border area; and liaison offices could be established in Asmara and Addis Ababa to maintain UN readiness to assist the parties in implementing the border demarcation decision of the Boundary Commission, as well as the Comprehensive Peace Agreement.

On 20 March, the Assistant Secretary-General for Peacekeeping Operations, Edmond Mulet, met with the Permanent Representative of Eritrea to seek his Government's views on those options and on the future of UNMEE. The Permanent Representative said that he would not discuss the Mission's future or the options because the United Nations had already taken the decision to relocate the Mission without consulting Eritrea.

Ethiopian authorities had informed the technical assessment mission that Ethiopia would find it extremely difficult to accept the long-term deployment of UNMEE limited to the Ethiopian side of the border. Such a deployment would effectively create a new security zone on Ethiopian territory, with legal implications for the status of the Agreement on Cessation of Hostilities and the Temporary Security Zone. The maximum Ethiopia could agree to would be an emergency relocation of UNMEE for a limited duration to ensure the safety and security of the peacekeepers while the Security Council decided on the future of the Mission. On 25 March, the Under-Secretary-General for Peacekeeping Operations, Jean-Marie Guéhenno, discussed the options with Ethiopia, which informed him that it would continue to cooperate with the United Nations and would consider the proposed options. Ethiopia stressed that the two parties had the primary responsibility to resolve the dispute between them. Ethiopia would support the Secretary-General's good offices and was ready to meet with Eritrea to discuss the dispute.

On 26 March, the Secretary-General's Chef de Cabinet, Vijay Nambiar, met with the Permanent Representative of Eritrea, who stated that the Eritrean authorities were ready to cooperate in the relocation of UNMEE and would facilitate the transportation of the Mission's equipment to the seaports of Assab and Massawa, as requested by UNMEE. In order to transport UN and contingent-owned equipment from the Temporary Security Zone to Asmara and Assab, Eritrea requested that it be provided with an inventory of all equipment left in the Zone. UNMEE and the Secretariat undertook to provide the requested lists.

The Secretary-General observed that the military occupation by Eritrea of the Temporary Security Zone and the restrictions it imposed on UNMEE violated the Agreement on Cessation of Hostilities and undermined the basis of the Mission's mandate. The total withdrawal of UNMEE could result in an escalation of tensions in the border area, with the risk of a resumption of hostilities. The deployment of an observer mission would require the agreement of both countries, but its mere presence might not provide adequate deterrence, especially against the possible accidental resumption of hostilities. The establishment of liaison offices would work only if both parties were prepared to proceed with the implementation of the final and binding decision of the Boundary Commission, with UN support. The Secretary-General recommended that the Council authorize him to explore with the two parties the four options, with the understanding that the resulting arrangements would have to be accompanied by parallel Council efforts to address the fundamental legal and political issues at the heart of the dispute. In the meantime, the Secretary-General would engage the parties on the options and report to the Council before the expiration of the UNMEE mandate on 31 July, setting out specific proposals agreed upon with the parties. Pending a final discussion by the Council on the envisaged recommendations, the temporary relocation of UNMEE from Eritrea and the deployment of the Mission in Ethiopia would remain in place as an interim arrangement. The Secretary-General urged Eritrea and Ethiopia to consider the consequences of the continued stalemate and accept the assistance of the Council and his good offices in implementing the agreements to which they had committed themselves.

Communications (April). In a letter of 15 April to the Security Council [S/2008/254], Eritrea said that it noted several omissions and incorrect assertions and assumptions in the Secretary-General's April report, particularly regarding the circumstances surrounding the departure of UNMEE, the status of the Temporary Security Zone and the completion of the Boundary Commission's work. It highlighted elements taken from the Algiers Agreements and previous reports of the Secretary-General that would complete the special report, and requested that they be read together with the report. Eritrea found the Secretary-General's observation concerning its military occupation of the Zone and restrictions placed on UNMEE unresponsive to, and incongruous with, prevailing reality. The Zone, which lay inside Eritrea, was not created as a permanent buffer zone, and its status changed with the completion of the Commission's work in November 2007 [YUN 2007, p. 293], despite Ethiopia's failure to respect its commitment to the Algiers Peace Agreement. The presence of some Eritrean troops in their own territory could not constitute military occupation.

On 18 April [S/2008/262], Ethiopia said that Eritrea continued to question its acceptance of the Boundary Commission's delimitation decision and appeared to have no interest in resolving the dispute legally and peacefully. Eritrea had consistently violated the Agreement on the Cessation of Hostilities over several years through its incursions into the Temporary Security Zone and the restrictions on UNMEE beginning in 2004. Ethiopia expected the Security Council to take punitive measures against Eritrea for those violations.

SECURITY COUNCIL ACTION

On 30 April [meeting 5883], following consultations among Security Council members, the President made statement **S/PRST/2008/12** on behalf of the Council:

> The Security Council notes that the continuation of Eritrea's obstructions towards the United Nations Mission in Ethiopia and Eritrea has reached a level such as to undermine the basis of the Mission's mandate and has compelled the Mission to temporarily relocate. The Council recalls its previous condemnation of Eritrea's lack of cooperation.
>
> The Council notes the underlying fundamental issues and stands ready to assist the parties to overcome the current stalemate, taking into account the interests and concerns of both parties.
>
> The Council will, in the light of consultations with the parties, decide on the terms of a future United Nations engagement and on the future of the Mission.
>
> The Council stresses, in accordance with its repeated statements, that the primary responsibility for achieving a comprehensive and lasting settlement of the border dispute and normalizing their relations rests with the parties themselves.
>
> The Council urges both sides to show maximum restraint and to refrain from any threat or use of force against each other and calls upon the parties to address forthwith the unresolved issues in accordance with the commitments made in the Agreement on Cessation of Hostilities of 18 June 2000 and the Peace Agreement of 12 December 2000 ("the Algiers Agreements").

Communications (April–July). On 30 April [S/2008/287], Eritrea said that in presidential statement S/PRST/2008/12, the Security Council not only neglected to endorse the Boundary Commission's final delimitation and demarcation decision of 27 November 2006 [YUN 2006, p. 324], but also failed to demand the withdrawal of Ethiopian troops from sovereign Eritrean territories. As the Commission completed its demarcation on 30 November 2007 [YUN 2007, p. 293], the specific condition stated in Council resolution 1320(2000) [YUN 2000, p. 176] concerning the UNMEE mandate and the completion of the delimitation and demarcation process had been met, necessitating the Council to terminate the Mission's mandate.

On 5 June [S/2008/368], the Secretary-General informed the Security Council that the temporary relocation of UNMEE military personnel to their home countries was completed on 19 May. Pending a Council decision on the Mission's future, he proposed that the temporarily relocated troops be considered repatriated. The Council agreed with that proposal on 30 June [S/2008/427].

In a letter of 7 July to the Security Council [S/2008/446], President Afwerki stated that in mid-April, Ethiopia invaded Mount Musa Ali, situated at the borders of Djibouti, Eritrea and Ethiopia, thereby occupying sovereign Eritrean and Djiboutian lands. The Council had not taken any remedial action against Ethiopia's act of aggression. Instead, it issued presidential statement S/PRST/2008/20 (see p. 316) against Eritrea on the basis of a bogus accusation by Djibouti. Eritrea said that the whole affair was concocted to cover up Ethiopia's acts of aggression and repeated violations of the peace agreement and that Ethiopia's new flouting of international law constituted another reminder to the Council to shoulder its legal responsibilities.

In a letter of 15 July [S/2008/463], Eritrea said that it did not report the invasion of Mount Musa Ali by Ethiopia on the date it occurred because it could not consider the act in isolation from Ethiopia's illegal occupation of Eritrea's sovereign territories for the previous six years. The United States misused its leverage in the Council to paralyse implementation of the Boundary Commission during that period; its objective of derailing the legal process continued unabated. Eritrea also called on the Council to examine the acts of destabilization fomented in the region by the United States and seek appropriate remedies.

On 17 July [S/2008/468], Ethiopia, referring to Eritrea's recent communications, including its letter of 15 July, said that there had been no Ethiopian takeover of any Eritrean or Djiboutian territory. Djibouti itself had made no such claim about Musa Ali.

Termination of UNMEE mandate

In a letter of 24 July to the Secretary-General [S/2008/487], Eritrea referred to a DPKO aide-memoire of 22 July detailing options on how the United Nations could most effectively support Eritrea and Ethiopia in implementing the Algiers Agreements. Eritrea said that the options appeared to be geared towards preventing a resumption of hostilities through a permanent presence of a UN observer force, in effect legitimizing Ethiopia's illegal occupation of sovereign Eritrean territories. The idea of a UN special envoy at that stage of the process further accommodated Ethiopia's persistent request for an alternative mechanism to tamper with and modify the Boundary Commission's delimitation and demarcation determinations. Eritrea could not accept that state of affairs. It would have no problem restoring good-neighbourly relations with Ethiopia but for that to happen, Ethiopia had to withdraw its troops from sovereign Eritrean territories. Eritrea called on UN institutions to channel their efforts towards addressing that obstacle.

An addendum to Eritrea's letter of 24 July [S/2008/487/Add.1] contained a letter of 1 July from the Legal Adviser to the Office of the President of Eritrea to the Boundary Commission, stating that Eritrea considered the Commission's mandate fulfilled. Eritrea continued to press the Security Council to exercise its legal authority in enforcing the Commission's delimitation and demarcation determinations.

In a letter of 28 July to the Security Council [S/2008/496], the Secretary-General said that on 22 July, his Acting Special Representative consulted with the Ethiopian Government, and the Assistant Secretary-General for Peacekeeping Operations met with the Permanent Representative of Eritrea to the United Nations to seek their views on the options for future UN engagement in the two countries, which were presented in identical letters of 10 June from the Council President to Ethiopian Prime Minister Zenawi and Eritrean President Afwerki. The options included a small military observer mission in Ethiopia; a small political and military liaison office in Ethiopia; and a Special Envoy of the Secretary-General based in New York. As indicated in a letter of 24 July from Ethiopia, which was annexed to the Secretary-General's letter, and the letter of the same date from Eritrea (see above), both parties rejected those options. The Secretary-General welcomed their earlier declarations that they had no intention of restarting the war, but believed that the risk of escalation of tension in the border area and a resumption of hostilities following the withdrawal of UNMEE remained a reality. He expressed concern over the destabilizing effect for the Horn of Africa of the continuing crisis, as well as the negative impact on prospects for economic development and the welfare of the region's people. The Council should keep the issue on its agenda and remain engaged with the parties to address the legal, political and security issues at the core of the crisis. The Secretary-General intended to continue working closely with the parties through his good offices with a view to normalizing their relations.

SECURITY COUNCIL ACTION

On 30 July [meeting 5946], the Security Council unanimously adopted **resolution 1827(2008)**. The draft [S/2008/491] was submitted by Belgium.

The Security Council,

Reaffirming all its previous resolutions and the statements by its President pertaining to the situation between Ethiopia and Eritrea,

Stressing once again its unwavering commitment to the peace process and to the full and expeditious implementation of the Agreement on Cessation of Hostilities of 18 June 2000 and the Peace Agreement of 12 December 2000 (hereinafter referred to as "the Algiers Agreements") as a basis for peaceful and cooperative relations between Ethiopia and Eritrea,

Considering that Ethiopia and Eritrea bear a shared responsibility in the implementation of the Algiers Agreements, in which they agreed that the delimitation and demarcation determinations of the Eritrea-Ethiopia Boundary Commission shall be final and binding and that their forces shall respect the integrity of the Temporary Security Zone,

Reaffirming that the primary responsibility for achieving a comprehensive and lasting settlement of the border dispute and normalizing their relations rests with Ethiopia and Eritrea, and that the Security Council stands ready to assist them in addressing the underlying fundamental issues, taking into account the interests and concerns of both countries,

Regretting that Eritrea's obstructions towards the United Nations Mission in Ethiopia and Eritrea reached a level so as to undermine the basis of the Mission's mandate and compelled the Mission to temporarily relocate from Eritrea, stressing that this relocation was without prejudice to the Algiers Agreements and to the integrity of the Temporary Security Zone, and recalling the Council's previous condemnation of Eritrea's lack of cooperation,

Commending the efforts made by the Mission and its military and civilian personnel to accomplish its duties, despite the difficult circumstances, and expressing its deep appreciation for the contribution and dedication of the troop-contributing countries to the work of the Mission,

Having considered the special report of the Secretary-General of 7 April 2008, the letters from Ethiopia and Eritrea, dated 17 and 18 June 2008 respectively, in response to the letters dated 10 June 2008 from the President of the Security Council, and the letter dated 28 July 2008 from the Secretary-General in response to the letter dated 3 July 2008 from the President of the Security Council,

1. *Decides* to terminate the mandate of the United Nations Mission in Ethiopia and Eritrea effective on 31 July 2008, emphasizes that this termination is without prejudice to the obligations of Ethiopia and Eritrea under the Algiers Agreements, and calls upon both countries to cooperate fully with the United Nations, including in the process of liquidation of the Mission;

2. *Demands* that Ethiopia and Eritrea comply fully with their obligations under the Algiers Agreements, show maximum restraint and refrain from any threat or use of force against each other, and avoid provocative military activities;

3. *Strongly supports* the ongoing efforts of the Secretary-General and the international community to engage with Ethiopia and Eritrea to help them to implement the Algiers Agreements, to normalize their relations, to promote stability between them and to lay the foundation for a comprehensive and lasting peace between them, and again urges Ethiopia and Eritrea to accept the Secretary-General's good offices;

4. *Requests* the Secretary-General to further explore with Ethiopia and Eritrea the possibility of a United Nations presence in Ethiopia and Eritrea in the context of the maintenance of international peace and security;

5. *Also requests* the Secretary-General to keep the Security Council regularly informed of the situation between Ethiopia and Eritrea and to make recommendations as appropriate;

6. *Decides* to remain actively seized of the matter.

Further developments

Final report of Boundary Commission. In a letter of 2 October [S/2008/630], the Secretary-General informed the Security Council that he would no longer provide regular reports on the situation between Eritrea and Ethiopia. The letter contained the twenty-seventh and final report of the Boundary Commission, covering the period from 1 January to 25 August 2008. The Commission noted that on 17 January, a copy of the maps illustrating the points identified in the annex to the 27 November 2006 statement [YUN 2006, p. 324] was deposited with the Secretary-General; another was retained in the office of the United Nations Cartographer for public reference. Ethiopia continued to be in arrears of its share of the Commission's expenses, in breach of the Algiers Agreement. A final account would be transmitted to the parties and the remaining funds held on deposit would be returned to the United Nations Trust Fund.

The Commission on 18 June 2008 had sent a letter to the parties stating that more than six months had passed since the expiry of the period indicated in the Commission's 27 November 2006 statement. Since there had been no communication from the parties concerning the placing of pillars on the ground, the Commission had to conclude that the boundary stood demarcated in accordance with the coordinates annexed to the 2006 statement; that no further activity on its part was called for; and that it should therefore take the few final steps to wind up its operation. If no reply to the contrary was received within two weeks, the Commission would assume that there was no objection to that procedure.

Eritrea had replied on 1 July 2008, stating that it considered the Commission's mandate as fulfilled, and that it continued to press the Security Council to exercise its authority in enforcing the Commission's determinations. Ethiopia had not responded. Since the Commission had concluded all administrative matters connected with the termination of its mandate, it considered itself *functus officio.*

Communications. In a letter of 24 October to the Secretary-General [S/2008/673], Eritrea referred to the

Boundary Commission's final report (see p. 311), and urged the Council to ensure the eviction of Ethiopia's occupation from its sovereign territories, including the new occupation of its land at Mount Musa Ali since May (see p. 310).

On 4 November [S/2008/690], Eritrea drew the Council's attention to Ethiopia's refusal to withdraw from Badme, Dembe Mengul and other sovereign Eritrean territories, as well as Mount Musa Ali, and said that occupation of those territories constituted a violation of the UN Charter.

In a letter of 10 November to the Council [S/2008/700], President Afwerki stated that Ethiopia continued to occupy the town of Badme and other Eritrean territories in violation of fundamental tenets of international law, and that those acts constituted a flagrant breach of the Algiers Peace Agreement and the UN Charter. In April, Ethiopia had gone one step further and occupied the Eritrean part of Mount Musa Ali on the Ethiopia-Djibouti-Eritrea junction.

UNMEE

The United Nations Mission in Ethiopia and Eritrea (UNMEE) was established by Security Council resolution 1312(2000) [YUN 2000, p. 174] to monitor and verify implementation of the 2000 Algiers Agreement on Cessation of Hostilities between Eritrea and Ethiopia [ibid., p. 173]. Its core operations, which the Council revised in resolution 1320(2000) [ibid., p. 176] and 1430(2002) [YUN 2002, p. 189], were devoted to observation, reporting, analysis, identification of potential flashpoints and preventive action, chairing the Military Coordination Commission and assisting the Boundary Commission. UNMEE monitored the area within and around the 25-kilometre-wide Temporary Security Zone, which separated the two countries and was divided into Sectors West and Centre and Subsector East. The Mission was headquartered in Addis Ababa and Asmara. In resolution 1798(2008) of 30 January (see p. 304), the Council extended the UNMEE mandate until 31 July 2008 and demanded that Eritrea resume needed fuel shipments to the Mission or allow it to import fuel without restrictions. Eritrea's continued obstructions towards UNMEE, however, undermined the Mission's mandate and compelled it to temporarily relocate its personnel from the Eritrean parts of the Zone to Asmara and Assab, and later to their home countries. The temporary relocation of UNMEE military personnel was completed on 19 May. On 5 June, the Secretary-General proposed that the relocated troops be considered repatriated, pending a Council decision on the future of the Mission; the Council agreed with the proposal on 30 June. By resolution 1827(2008) of 30 July (see p. 310), the Council terminated the UNMEE mandate effective 31 July.

The Acting Special Representative of the Secretary-General for Eritrea and Ethiopia, Azouz Ennifar (Tunisia), was appointed in August 2006 [YUN 2006, p. 326] and served as Chief of Mission until the termination of the UNMEE mandate.

Financing

At its resumed sixty-second session, the General Assembly considered the Secretary-General's performance report on the UNMEE budget for the period 1 July 2006 to 30 June 2007 [YUN 2007, p. 295], and the proposed UNMEE budget for the period from 1 July 2008 to 30 June 2009 [A/62/811], which amounted to $100,367,400. It also considered the related ACABQ report [A/62/781/Add.17 & Corr.1], which endorsed the proposed appropriation for 2008–2009.

GENERAL ASSEMBLY ACTION

On 20 June [meeting 109], the General Assembly, on the recommendation of the Fifth Committee [A/62/872], adopted **resolution 62/259** without vote [agenda item 148].

Financing of the United Nations Mission in Ethiopia and Eritrea

The General Assembly,

Having considered the reports of the Secretary-General on the financing of the United Nations Mission in Ethiopia and Eritrea and the related report of the Advisory Committee on Administrative and Budgetary Questions,

Recalling Security Council resolution 1312(2000) of 31 July 2000, by which the Council established the United Nations Mission in Ethiopia and Eritrea, and the subsequent resolutions by which the Council extended the mandate of the Mission, the latest of which was resolution 1798(2008) of 30 January 2008, by which the Council extended the mandate of the Mission until 31 July 2008,

Recalling also its resolution 55/237 of 23 December 2000 on the financing of the Mission and its subsequent resolutions thereon, the latest of which was resolution 61/248 B of 29 June 2007,

Reaffirming the general principles underlying the financing of United Nations peacekeeping operations, as stated in General Assembly resolutions 1874(S-IV) of 27 June 1963, 3101(XXVIII) of 11 December 1973 and 55/235 of 23 December 2000,

Noting with appreciation that voluntary contributions have been made to the Mission,

Mindful of the fact that it is essential to provide the Mission with the financial resources necessary to enable it to fulfil its responsibilities under the relevant resolutions of the Security Council,

1. *Requests* the Secretary-General to entrust the Head of Mission with the task of formulating future budget proposals in full accordance with the provisions of General Assembly resolutions 59/296 of 22 June 2005, 60/266 of

30 June 2006 and 61/276 of 29 June 2007, as well as other relevant resolutions;

2. *Takes note* of the status of contributions to the United Nations Mission in Ethiopia and Eritrea as at 30 April 2008, including the contributions outstanding in the amount of 26.5 million United States dollars, representing some 2 per cent of the total assessed contributions, notes with concern that only sixty-six Member States have paid their assessed contributions in full, and urges all other Member States, in particular those in arrears, to ensure payment of their outstanding assessed contributions;

3. *Expresses its appreciation* to those Member States which have paid their assessed contributions in full, and urges all other Member States to make every possible effort to ensure payment of their assessed contributions to the Mission in full;

4. *Expresses concern* at the financial situation with regard to peacekeeping activities, in particular as regards the reimbursements to troop contributors that bear additional burdens owing to overdue payments by Member States of their assessments;

5. *Also expresses concern* at the delay experienced by the Secretary-General in deploying and providing adequate resources to some recent peacekeeping missions, in particular those in Africa;

6. *Emphasizes* that all future and existing peacekeeping missions shall be given equal and non-discriminatory treatment in respect of financial and administrative arrangements;

7. *Also emphasizes* that all peacekeeping missions shall be provided with adequate resources for the effective and efficient discharge of their respective mandates;

8. *Reiterates its request* to the Secretary-General to make the fullest possible use of facilities and equipment at the United Nations Logistics Base at Brindisi, Italy, in order to minimize the costs of procurement for the Mission;

9. *Endorses* the conclusions and recommendations contained in the report of the Advisory Committee on Administrative and Budgetary Questions, and requests the Secretary-General to ensure their full implementation;

10. *Requests* the Secretary-General to ensure the full implementation of the relevant provisions of its resolutions 59/296, 60/266 and 61/276;

11. *Also requests* the Secretary-General to take all necessary action to ensure that the Mission is administered with a maximum of efficiency and economy;

12. *Further requests* the Secretary-General, in order to reduce the cost of employing General Service staff, to continue efforts to recruit local staff for the Mission against General Service posts, commensurate with the requirements of the Mission;

Financial performance report for the period from 1 July 2006 to 30 June 2007

13. *Takes note* of the report of the Secretary-General on the financial performance of the Mission for the period from 1 July 2006 to 30 June 2007;

Budget estimates for the period from 1 July 2008 to 30 June 2009

14. *Decides* to appropriate to the Special Account for the United Nations Mission in Ethiopia and Eritrea the amount of 105,010,000 dollars for the period from 1 July 2008 to 30 June 2009, inclusive of 100,367,400 dollars for the maintenance of the Mission, 4,047,100 dollars for the support account for peacekeeping operations and 595,500 dollars for the United Nations Logistics Base;

Financing of the appropriation

15. *Also decides* to apportion among Member States the amount of 8,750,833 dollars for the period from 1 to 31 July 2008, in accordance with the levels updated in General Assembly resolution 61/243 of 22 December 2006, and taking into account the scale of assessments for 2008, as set out in its resolution 61/237 of 22 December 2006;

16. *Further decides* that, in accordance with the provisions of its resolution 973(X) of 15 December 1955, there shall be set off against the apportionment among Member States, as provided for in paragraph 15 above, their respective share in the Tax Equalization Fund of the amount of 231,307 dollars for the period from 1 to 31 July 2008, comprising the estimated staff assessment income of 194,983 dollars approved for the Mission, the prorated share of 32,408 dollars of the estimated staff assessment income approved for the support account and the prorated share of 3,916 dollars of the estimated staff assessment income approved for the United Nations Logistics Base;

17. *Decides* to apportion among Member States the amount of 46,075,167 dollars, comprising the amount of 41,819,750 dollars for the maintenance of the Mission for the period from 1 August to 31 December 2008 at a monthly rate of 8,363,950 dollars, and the amount of 4,255,717 dollars for the support account and the United Nations Logistics Base for the period from 1 August 2008 to 30 June 2009 at a monthly rate of 386,883 dollars, in accordance with the levels updated in resolution 61/243, and taking into account the scale of assessments for 2008 and 2009, as set out in resolution 61/237, subject to a decision of the Security Council to extend the mandate of the Mission;

18. *Also decides* that, in accordance with the provisions of its resolution 973(X), there shall be set off against the apportionment among Member States, as provided for in paragraph 17 above, their respective share in the Tax Equalization Fund of the amount of 1,374,493 dollars for the period from 1 August 2008 to 30 June 2009, comprising the estimated staff assessment income of 974,917 dollars approved for the Mission, the prorated share of 356,492 dollars of the estimated staff assessment income approved for the support account and the prorated share of 43,084 dollars of the estimated staff assessment income approved for the United Nations Logistics Base;

19. *Further decides* that, for Member States that have fulfilled their financial obligations to the Mission, there shall be set off against their apportionment, as provided for in paragraph 15 above, their respective share of the unencumbered balance and other income in the total amount of 18,012,400 dollars in respect of the financial period ended 30 June 2007, in accordance with the levels updated in resolution 61/243, and taking into account the scale of assessments for 2007, as set out in resolution 61/237;

20. *Decides* that, for Member States that have not fulfilled their financial obligations to the Mission, there shall be set off against their outstanding obligations their respec-

tive share of the unencumbered balance and other income in the total amount of 18,012,400 dollars in respect of the financial period ended 30 June 2007, in accordance with the scheme set out in paragraph 19 above;

21. *Also decides* that the decrease of 32,900 dollars in the estimated staff assessment income in respect of the financial period ended 30 June 2007 shall be set off against the credits from the amount of 18,012,400 dollars referred to in paragraphs 19 and 20 above;

22. *Emphasizes* that no peacekeeping mission shall be financed by borrowing funds from other active peacekeeping missions;

23. *Encourages* the Secretary-General to continue to take additional measures to ensure the safety and security of all personnel participating in the Mission under the auspices of the United Nations, bearing in mind paragraphs 5 and 6 of Security Council resolution 1502(2003) of 26 August 2003;

24. *Invites* voluntary contributions to the Mission in cash and in the form of services and supplies acceptable to the Secretary-General, to be administered, as appropriate, in accordance with the procedure and practices established by the General Assembly;

25. *Decides* to include in the provisional agenda of its sixty-third session the item entitled "Financing of the United Nations Mission in Ethiopia and Eritrea".

In November [A/63/546 & Corr.1], the Secretary-General submitted the revised UNMEE budget for the period from 1 July 2008 to 30 June 2009, in view of the termination of the Mission's mandate. He proposed that the Assembly reduce the appropriation of $100,367,400 it approved in resolution 62/259 for the maintenance of the Mission to $37,016,400. In a December report [A/63/602], ACABQ recommended approval of the Secretary-General's proposal.

GENERAL ASSEMBLY ACTION

On 24 December [meeting 74], the General Assembly, on the recommendation of the Fifth Committee [A/63/646], adopted **resolution 63/257 A** without vote [agenda item 139].

Financing of the United Nations Mission in Ethiopia and Eritrea

The General Assembly,

Having considered the report of the Secretary-General on the financing of the United Nations Mission in Ethiopia and Eritrea and the related report of the Advisory Committee on Administrative and Budgetary Questions,

Recalling Security Council resolution 1312(2000) of 31 July 2000, by which the Council established the United Nations Mission in Ethiopia and Eritrea, and the subsequent resolutions by which the Council extended the mandate of the Mission, the last of which was resolution 1798(2008) of 30 January 2008, by which the Council extended the mandate of the Mission until 31 July 2008,

Recalling also Security Council resolution 1827(2008) of 30 July 2008, by which the Council terminated the mandate of the Mission effective on 31 July 2008,

Recalling further its resolution 55/237 of 23 December 2000 on the financing of the Mission and its subsequent resolutions thereon, the latest of which was resolution 62/259 of 20 June 2008,

Reaffirming the general principles underlying the financing of United Nations peacekeeping operations, as stated in General Assembly resolutions 1874(S-IV) of 27 June 1963, 3101(XXVIII) of 11 December 1973 and 55/235 of 23 December 2000,

Noting with appreciation that voluntary contributions have been made to the Mission,

Mindful of the fact that it is essential to provide the Mission with the necessary financial resources to enable it to complete its administrative liquidation,

1. *Takes note* of the status of contributions to the United Nations Mission in Ethiopia and Eritrea as at 31 October 2008, including the contributions outstanding in the amount of 17.5 million United States dollars, representing some 1 per cent of the total assessed contributions, notes with concern that only eighty-seven Member States have paid their assessed contributions in full, and urges all other Member States, in particular those in arrears, to ensure payment of their outstanding assessed contributions;

2. *Expresses its appreciation* to those Member States which have paid their assessed contributions in full, and urges all other Member States to make every possible effort to ensure payment of their assessed contributions to the Mission in full;

3. *Expresses concern* at the financial situation with regard to peacekeeping activities, in particular as regards the reimbursements to troop contributors that bear additional burdens owing to overdue payments by Member States of their assessments;

4. *Also expresses concern* at the delay experienced by the Secretary-General in deploying and providing adequate resources to some recent peacekeeping missions, in particular those in Africa;

5. *Emphasizes* that all future and existing peacekeeping missions shall be given equal and non-discriminatory treatment in respect of financial and administrative arrangements;

6. *Also emphasizes* that all peacekeeping missions shall be provided with adequate resources for the effective and efficient discharge of their respective mandates;

7. *Endorses* the conclusions and recommendations contained in the report of the Advisory Committee on Administrative and Budgetary Questions, and requests the Secretary-General to ensure their full implementation;

8. *Requests* the Secretary-General to take all necessary action to ensure that the Mission is administered with a maximum of efficiency and economy;

Revised budget estimates for the period from 1 July 2008 to 30 June 2009

9. *Decides* to reduce the appropriation of 100,367,400 dollars approved for the maintenance of the Mission for the period from 1 July 2008 to 30 June 2009 under the terms of its resolution 62/259 by the amount of 63,351,000 dollars, to 37,016,400 dollars;

10. *Also decides* to reduce the amount of the estimated staff assessment income approved for the maintenance of the Mission for the period from 1 July 2008 to 30 June 2009 under the terms of its resolution 62/259 from 2,339,800 dollars to 1,111,400 dollars;

Financing of the appropriation

11. *Further decides* to apportion among Member States the amount of 28,652,450 dollars for the administrative liquidation of the Mission for the period from 1 August 2008 to 30 June 2009, in addition to the amount of 8,750,833 dollars already apportioned for the period from 1 to 31 July 2008 under the terms of its resolution 62/259, in accordance with the levels updated in its resolution 61/243 of 22 December 2006, and taking into account the scale of assessments for 2008 and 2009, as set out in its resolution 61/237 of 22 December 2006;

12. *Decides* that, in accordance with the provisions of its resolution 973(X) of 15 December 1955, there shall be set off against the apportionment among Member States, as provided for in paragraph 11 above, their respective share in the Tax Equalization Fund of the estimated staff assessment income of 916,417 dollars approved for the Mission for the period from 1 August 2008 to 30 June 2009;

13. *Emphasizes* that no peacekeeping mission shall be financed by borrowing funds from other active peacekeeping missions;

14. *Encourages* the Secretary-General to continue to take additional measures to ensure the safety and security of all personnel participating in the Mission under the auspices of the United Nations, bearing in mind paragraphs 5 and 6 of Security Council resolution 1502(2003) of 26 August 2003;

15. *Decides* to keep under review during its sixty-third session the item entitled "Financing of the United Nations Mission in Ethiopia and Eritrea".

By **decision 63/522** of 24 December, the Assembly decided that the agenda item on UNMEE financing would remain for consideration during its resumed sixty-third (2009) session.

Djibouti and Eritrea

Communications. In a letter of 5 May to the Security Council [S/2008/294], Djibouti stated that it had witnessed since February a progressive increase in Eritrean troops at the border between Djibouti and Eritrea, including the preparation of fortifications and battlements; equipment flows; and well-armed Eritrean soldiers on the Djiboutian side of the promontory of the Ras Doumeira mountain range overlooking Red Sea shipping lanes. Refraining from any forceful action, Djibouti attempted to resolve the issue through diplomacy, which included bilateral contacts at all levels. It sought the advice and intercession of a key Gulf State leader and shared its concerns with the diplomatic community in Djibouti, the AU Peace and Security Council and the League of Arab States (LAS). Djibouti's efforts, however, failed to elicit any credible response. Therefore, it had to maintain a state of preparedness for the possibility of an incursion into its territory by Eritrean forces. Djibouti sensed a danger of being drawn into an unwarranted confrontation with Eritrea and considered Eritrea's move a misguided intimidation that constituted a provocation against its sovereignty and territorial integrity. Any attempts by Eritrea to impede Djibouti's progress and disrupt its peace and tranquillity could not be tolerated. Djibouti called on the Security Council to deploy all necessary measures towards preventing another conflict in the region.

On 9 June [S/2008/381], Djibouti informed the Council that although it had explored all the necessary bilateral and regional avenues to resolve the situation, Eritrea had strengthened its troops and made further incursions into Djibouti's territory. Its efforts to find a solution to the crisis were rejected by the Eritrean authorities. Similar efforts were undertaken by friendly countries, and regional organizations, including the AU, LAS and the Organization of the Islamic Conference (OIC), dispatched good offices missions. Those efforts failed due to the systematic opposition of Eritrea, which categorically denied that the two countries had any border issues. Eritrea insisted that it was not inclined to engage in fabricated problems that were part of external interferences designed to foment crisis in the region.

Djibouti provided an account of the situation on the ground, as reported by its military authorities as well as independent parties. It said that on 9 May, a delegation from the LAS Peace and Security Council visited Djibouti and reported that the Eritrean army was present in Djiboutian territory in several places, and that intensive work was being carried out in Ras Doumeira and Doumeira Island. On 15 May, Djiboutian military authorities attempted to climb to the top of Ras Doumeira, but at the halfway point were arrested by Eritrean soldiers. Djibouti concluded that Eritrean authorities did not recognize the Djiboutian borders and intended to appropriate a strategic part of Djibouti's sovereign territory without justification. Djibouti hoped that the Council would assume its responsibilities by dispatching a field mission to evaluate the situation and demand that troops pull back to their previous positions.

On 11 June [S/2008/387], Djibouti said that on 10 June, Eritrean armed forces launched unprovoked attacks against Djiboutian army positions. It noted that the act of aggression took place at a time when peace negotiations between Somali parties in Djibouti had resulted in the conclusion of a peace agreement (see p. 278). Djibouti requested the convening of an emergency Security Council meeting to end the aggression by Eritrean armed forces.

SECURITY COUNCIL ACTION

On 12 June [meeting 5908], following consultations among Security Council members, the President made statement **S/PRST/2008/20** on behalf of the Council:

The Security Council expresses its strong concern about the serious incidents that occurred on 10 June 2008 along the frontier between Djibouti and Eritrea, which led to several deaths and dozens of wounded.

The Council condemns Eritrea's military action against Djibouti in Ras Doumeira and Doumeira Island.

The Council calls upon the parties to commit to a ceasefire and urges both parties, in particular Eritrea, to show maximum restraint and withdraw forces to the status quo ante.

The Council urges both parties, in particular Eritrea, to cooperate and engage in diplomatic efforts to resolve the matter peacefully and in a manner consistent with international law.

The Council welcomes the efforts of the African Union, the League of Arab States and those States that have offered their assistance and calls upon the parties, in particular Eritrea, to engage fully in efforts to resolve the crisis.

The Council encourages the Secretary-General urgently to use his good offices and reach out to both parties, as appropriate and in coordination with regional efforts, to facilitate bilateral discussions to determine arrangements for decreasing the military presence along the border and to develop confidence-building measures to resolve the border situation.

Security Council consideration. On 24 June [meeting 5924], the Director of the Africa Division of the UN Department of Political Affairs, João Honwana, briefed the Council on the situation on the border between Djibouti and Eritrea, which was described as calm but tense. Military regroupings were taking place on either side of the border but the de facto ceasefire between the two countries, observed since the previous week, continued to hold. Local press and other sources reported that Djiboutian forces had reoccupied lost ground and regrouped near the border, but other reports indicated that those forces had retreated to a position about 4 kilometres from the border to be out of range of Eritrean mortars. LAS called on Eritrea to withdraw its forces from the border area; France and Egypt urged Eritrea to allow mediation; and the AU joined the United Nations in calling for talks between the two countries to end the border clashes. In a meeting on 19 June with the Director, Eritrea acknowledged that skirmishes had occurred, but said that Djibouti had initiated the attack and Eritrea had only reacted in self-defence. Eritrea blamed the United States for creating wars in the Horn of Africa; reiterated Eritrea's peaceful intentions towards Djibouti; and questioned the Council's hastiness in issuing presidential statement S/PRST/2008/20. On the same day, Djibouti said that the situation at the border could ignite into a war. Many soldiers had died in the fighting and numerous troops and heavy equipment were present at the border. Eritrea had failed to explain the reasons for its military presence, refused to resume dialogue with Djibouti and rebuffed offers by the President of Yemen to act as a mediator. Djibouti never intended to wage war but had been forced to respond to the attacks. In a meeting on 23 June, the Secretary-General and the Prime Minister of Djibouti agreed on the need to resolve the situation through dialogue, confidence-building, and a return to the status quo ante.

The Prime Minister of Djibouti, Dileita Mohamed Dileita, said that his country thought that Eritrea was pursuing its confrontation with Ethiopia by means of a conflict with Djibouti, through which transited most of the merchandise headed for Ethiopia. Eritrean authorities were hiding behind a total denial of the dispute. Djibouti military forces had been attacked solely by Eritrean forces, and Djibouti would not hesitate to exercise its right to self-defence, accorded under the UN Charter. It had taken all necessary steps to find a diplomatic way out of the crisis in order to avoid being drawn again into a useless conflict. Eritrea, however, rejected all mediation and persisted in denying the existence of any problem. At the same time, it took advantage of the situation to make further territorial gains and strengthen its army's positions. The peace and security of shipping lanes throughout the region were the key stakes in the conflict. There had been no positive developments since the Council's statement S/PRST/2008/20 (see above), and no sign of goodwill regarding the peaceful settlement of the dispute from the Eritrean authorities. Whereas the Djibouti army had withdrawn several kilometres since 12 June, Eritrean troops had again infiltrated Djiboutian territory. Djibouti was prepared to cooperate with the Council and the Secretary-General in their efforts to resolve the unilateral military adventure, which merited the Council's urgent attention.

Eritrea said that it had made no incursion into Djibouti's territory and had no territorial ambitions. There had been numerous contacts between the two Governments, including at the highest level. The leaders of the two countries decided to address the current development in a calm manner that took into account the need to ensure peace and security in the region. There was no territorial or other dispute between Eritrea and Djibouti, and Djibouti's unwarranted hostile campaign was underpinned by, and synchronized with, ulterior motives and regional developments. On 22 April, Ethiopia set up a military camp on Mount Musa Ali, situated at the intersection of the borders of Djibouti, Eritrea and Ethiopia (see p. 310), and deployed long-range artillery and heavy equipment directed at Eritrea. On 10 June, Djibouti was pushed to launch a military attack on the border, and Eritrea pulled its forces back to avoid the attack. On 12 June,

Djibouti continued its attack, and Eritrea defended itself. Djibouti, however, accused Eritrea of the very acts that it had perpetrated. The underlying objective of the military provocation was to divert Eritrea from its legal pursuit to ensure Ethiopia's eviction from its sovereign territories in accordance with the final and binding determination of the Eritrea-Ethiopia Boundary Commission [YUN 2006, p. 324], and to embroil Eritrea on another front. Eritrea said that it would continue to value close cooperation with Djibouti, and called on countries with global reach and influence in the region to ensure that their policies became a positive force for development, peace and security for the people of the region.

Press statement. In a press statement of 24 June [SC/9376], the Security Council regretted that Eritrea had not answered the calls sent by presidential statement S/PRST/2008/20 and reiterated its call to the parties, in particular Eritrea, to withdraw forces to the status quo ante. The Council requested the Secretary-General to send a fact-finding mission to the border between Djibouti and Eritrea and called on the parties to facilitate the work of the mission. It also asked the Secretary-General to brief the Council on the situation in less than two weeks, if possible.

Fact-finding mission

The Secretary-General directed the Department of Political Affairs (DPA) to dispatch a fact-finding mission to Djibouti and Eritrea to assess the political, security and humanitarian situation in the area; the mission was also scheduled to visit Ethiopia, which shared a common border with both countries in the area of Mount Musa Ali. The mission, led by Sam Ibok, Deputy Director of the Africa II Division of DPA, visited Addis Ababa (28–31 July and 4–6 August) and Djibouti (1–4 August). The mission could not visit Asmara or the Eritrean side of the border because Eritrea refused to issue visas. The mission submitted its report to the Security Council in September [S/2008/602].

In Addis Ababa, the mission discussed the crisis with representatives of the AU, LAS and the Ethiopian Ministries of Defence and Foreign Affairs. In Djibouti, it met with members of the Government and the diplomatic corps, the UN Resident Coordinator and officials from several UN programmes and agencies. It was also received by the President of Djibouti, Ismail Omar Guelleh. The report discussed the history of the Djibouti-Eritrea border and implications for the status of Doumeira; set out a chronology of developments leading to the clashes of 10–12 June (see p. 316); and described initiatives by the AU and other organizations and actors to defuse tension and foster dialogue.

The clashes reportedly caused more than 35 deaths and left dozens wounded on both sides. The mission found that the Djibouti military had withdrawn 4 or 5 kilometres from the disputed area, in accordance with presidential statement S/PRST/2008/20, and adopted a defensive posture beyond the mortar range of the Eritrean defence forces. The mission was unable to identify clearly anti-aircraft weapons or any other weaponry from its observation point south of the disputed zone. It also could not determine whether the Eritrean defence forces had accomplished their deployment in the area. The security situation on the ground was described as stable but tense; it was not clear how long the Eritrean defence forces were prepared to hold the disputed sites. The mission established the incontestable fact that a stalemate had developed between Djibouti and Eritrea and that it could only be resolved through diplomatic means. Since the beginning of the tensions, relations between the two States had significantly deteriorated, prompting Djibouti to recall its ambassador to Eritrea and expel Eritrea's ambassador to Djibouti in June. Diplomatic relations between the two countries were suspended, as Eritrea continued to downplay the gravity of the situation and rebuff all attempts by regional and international organizations, including the United Nations, to help defuse tension. Only a high-level political intervention accepted by Eritrea could de-escalate the tension and persuade the parties to demilitarize their border and return to the status quo ante. Although the number of displaced persons was relatively low, the militarization of the border had a negative impact on the population.

The mission observed that the developments at the border, especially the militarization of Doumeira, constituted a threat to the stability and socio-economic development of Djibouti. The ongoing tension posed a considerable risk to the country's peace and security. The mission identified an interrelation between the Eritrea–Ethiopia conflict (see p. 302) and the Djibouti–Eritrea crisis: a breakthrough in the Eritrea–Ethiopia peace process would help secure Eritrea's cooperation in demilitarizing its border with Djibouti. In the short term, there might be no resolution of the dispute without the full cooperation of both countries, especially Eritrea.

The mission recommended renewing the offer of the Secretary-General's good offices to defuse the tension. To convey the importance attached by the Secretary-General and the Council to a solution to the crisis, the Under-Secretary-General for Political Affairs could return to Asmara to consult with the Eritrean leadership. Eritrea should be given a specific time frame to issue the necessary visas and facilitate the work of such a mission, including visits to the Eritrean side of the deployment in Doumeira. UN efforts to resolve the crisis should focus on providing the two countries with a platform to discuss the border and agree on a fair process that would lead to the demarcation of their frontier. Other recommendations were related to confidence-building through demilitarization of the border and better treatment of deserters of the Eritrean defence forces who crossed into Djibouti between April and June. The mission concluded that a sovereign country was being drawn into a crippling and unaffordable military mobilization to deal with a situation that might ultimately threaten national, regional and international peace. If the Secretary-General's good offices offer was again rebuffed by Eritrea, the matter should be referred to the Council for appropriate action.

Communication. In a letter of 16 September to the Security Council [S/2008/605], Eritrea reiterated its position regarding the report of the UN fact-finding mission, stating that the United States pursued a policy aimed at embroiling the Horn of Africa in an endless conflict, and had instigated the conflict between Djibouti and Eritrea.

Further developments

Security Council consideration. On 3 October [S/2008/635], Djibouti informed the Security Council that President Guelleh wished to address the Council in connection with the Djibouti–Eritrea question. Speaking before the Council on 23 October [meeting 6000], President Guelleh said that following the forceful occupation of part of Djibouti's territory, his country adopted a policy of calm and caution that provided sufficient time for bilateral contacts to resolve the differences between Djibouti and Eritrea amicably and peacefully. Eritrea's military construction on the ground continued, however, and the lack of cooperation on the part of the Eritrean authorities and their failure to respond to Djibouti's initiatives left Djibouti with no choice but to mass troops along the border to protect its territorial integrity. While Djibouti searched tirelessly for a peaceful diplomatic solution, Eritrea continued to reinforce its troops and carried out further incursions into Djiboutian territory. The President reiterated his country's determination to recover all its territory illegally occupied by Eritrea—Ras Doumeira and the Doumeira islands. The provocation and inexplicable invasion of Djibouti's territory were unacceptable, and it was imperative that the Council address the conflict in a timely and comprehensive manner. President Guelleh also alerted the Council to the danger posed by drawing comparisons between the Djibouti–Eritrea conflict and the Eritrea–Ethiopia conflict, as suggesting such a link would encourage Eritrea to indefinitely occupy Djibouti's territory, lead its people into other useless, fratricidal conflicts, and continue its adventurism in the region. The President invited the Council to consider key points that were illustrated in the report of the fact-finding mission. First, Eritrea must be called on to honour its international obligations and cooperate with the United Nations, accepting its good offices to resolve the crisis. Secondly, the priority for Djibouti was the demilitarization of the conflict area and the withdrawal of forces to pre-February 2008 positions. Thirdly, the two countries had to show themselves willing to re-establish mutual trust, particularly by activating bilateral mechanisms and submitting to a legal process or arbitration leading to an agreed demarcation of the border. Given the urgency of the situation, the President called on the Council to require both countries, within approximately three weeks, to devote themselves to resolving the crisis and said that failure to implement such a decision should give rise to Council sanctions. Inaction would encourage and reward Eritrea's attitude, and leave Djibouti with no option but war.

Eritrea said that there had been no new developments since the brief incident in June that was instigated by the unprovoked attack by Djibouti against Eritrea's units inside its own territory. Eritrea had chosen the path of restraint to avoid escalating a crisis not of Djibouti's making, but created by others. Contrary to the claims made, Eritrea had not taken any land belonging to Djibouti and had no territorial ambitions. President Afwerki had called President Guelleh and decided to address the problem calmly. That occurred when Eritrea was approached by the Emir of Qatar, to whom Eritrea showed its openness to solve any real or perceived source of problems. Eritrea desired the restoration of good-neighbourly relations with Djibouti on the basis of full, mutual respect for territorial integrity and sovereignty. It would not, however, allow itself to be dragged into a diversionary and fabricated conflict, or be obliged to have an exchange on a situation designed to foment conflict on the ground.

Communication. On 4 December [S/2008/766], Djibouti transmitted a letter from President Guelleh to the Council, which indicated that regional and international diplomatic efforts made since May to resolve the crisis had been rejected by Eritrea and a stalemate had developed. Sufficient time had elapsed for Eritrea to demonstrate goodwill, interest and peaceful intentions, rather than the outright denial and rebuffs to mediation, facilitation and the establishment of facts. Eritrea continued to link its problem with Djibouti to its long-standing problem with Ethiopia. For Djibouti, any extended entrenchment by Eritrea in Ras Doumeira and Doumeira Island was unacceptable. Consequently, Djibouti was awaiting action by the Council towards the demilitarization and withdrawal of forces from the conflict area and acceptance by Eritrea that it had a border dispute with Djibouti that it had to resolve peacefully, consistent with diplomatic and legal practices.

North Africa

Western Sahara

In 2008, negotiations towards a lasting political solution to the question of Western Sahara continued. Although the two parties to the dispute concerning the Territory—Morocco and the Frente Polisario para la Liberación de Saguía el-Hamra y de Río de Oro (Frente Polisario)—held talks with the Secretary-General's Personal Envoy for Western Sahara in January and March, the parties remained far apart on ways to achieve a solution. Morocco favoured autonomy and Frente Polisario set out arrangements for a State where natural resources were exploited for the benefit of the inhabitants of the Territory and where the interests of Morocco and other neighbouring States were protected. However, they agreed to explore the establishment of family visits by land route in addition to the programme of air visits. The parties also discussed the human rights situation in Western Sahara and in the Tindouf refugee camps in Algeria, and reiterated their commitment to continue negotiations. The Personal Envoy visited the region in February for in-depth consultations with the Prime Minister of Morocco, the Frente Polisario Secretary-General and senior Government officials from other interested countries on ways to move the negotiations into a more intensive and substantive phase. The United Nations Mission for the Referendum in Western Sahara (MINURSO) continued to monitor compliance with the 1991 ceasefire that ended hostilities between the two parties over the governance of the Territory. The situation in the Mission's area of responsibility remained generally calm and the Security Council extended its mandate until 30 April 2009.

Peacemaking efforts

In response to Security Council resolution 1783(2007) [YUN 2007, p. 299], the Secretary-General in January submitted a report [S/2008/45] on the status and progress of the negotiations on Western Sahara, covering developments since his October 2007 report [YUN 2007, p. 298]. Pursuant to resolution 1754(2007) [ibid., p. 297], delegations from Morocco and the Frente Polisario para la Liberación de Saguía el-Hamra y de Río de Oro (Frente Polisario) met in Manhasset, New York, United States (7–9 January), to continue the negotiations that began in 2007 [ibid., p. 298]. The parties held separate meetings with the Secretary-General's Personal Envoy, Peter van Walsum (Netherlands), as well as several face-to-face discussions. Representatives of the neighbouring countries, Algeria and Mauritania, were consulted separately during the meeting. The Personal Envoy underlined that the Council expected the parties to negotiate in good faith and show the political will to ensure the success of the negotiations. The parties reiterated their commitment to negotiations and the implementation of resolutions 1783(2007) and 1754(2007). Nevertheless, their positions remained far apart on ways to achieve a just, lasting and mutually acceptable political solution providing for the self-determination of the people of Western Sahara; as a result, little exchange took place that could be characterized as negotiations. The parties did, however, engage in an extensive exchange of views about the implementation of the two resolutions. They discussed matters related to administration, including competencies and organs. Although the parties replied to queries raised by the Personal Envoy and interacted with each other to some degree, they did not examine specific elements of each other's proposals. The parties agreed to convene again in Manhasset in March for a fourth round of talks. Annexed to the report was the Personal Envoy's communiqué of 9 January, in which the parties reiterated their commitment to show political will and negotiate in good faith, and agreed on the need to move the process into a more intensive and substantive negotiation phase.

March negotiations. The Secretary-General reported that at the fourth round of negotiations (Manhasset, 16–18 March), the parties held several face-to-face discussions, as well as separate meetings with the Personal Envoy; representatives of the neighbouring countries were consulted separately during the meeting. The parties engaged in a broad exchange of views on the implementation of resolutions 1754(2007) and 1783(2007), and on the exercise of the principle of self-determination. They also discussed subjects related to administration, competencies and organs, as well as justice and resources. They were invited to consider strengthening confidence-building measures, as well as a possible expansion of the existing programme. Frente Polisario indicated that it accepted without exception all the proposals made by the Personal Envoy. The parties agreed to explore the establishment of family visits by land route, in addition to the programme of air visits, which would increase the number of Western Saharans who could benefit from such visits. The parties would further examine the issue of visits by land within the framework of the Office of the United Nations High Commissioner for Refugees (UNHCR). The parties also raised matters related to human rights in the Territory and in the Tindouf refugee camps, and reiterated their commitment to continue the negotiations at a date to be determined.

Communications. In a letter of 3 April to the Secretary-General [S/2008/221], Morocco said that Algeria and Frente Polisario sought to conceal their lack of political commitment to the Manhasset negotiation process by diverting the attention of the international community towards alleged human rights violations against indigenous people of the Sahara region and other regions of Morocco. Morocco had refrained from responding to accusations and diversionary tactics, preferring to devote its energy to the success of the negotiations and to the socio-economic development of the region. In order to clear up any ambiguity, however, Morocco provided clarifications regarding the points that had been a recurrent theme in those communications. Those clarifications included reforms undertaken by Morocco and progress achieved in the area of human rights, as well as efforts to improve infrastructure, education, health care and housing in the Sahara region. Through its actions, Morocco had demonstrated its desire to enrich the dynamic launched by the Security Council and pledged to persevere in that vein.

In a letter to the Secretary-General dated 3 April [S/2008/230], Morocco stated that the overall situation and increasingly deplorable living conditions of the people in the Tindouf camps in Algeria were a source of concern to Morocco and the international community. It called on Algeria, as the host country, to allow UNHCR free access to the camps in order to identify and register the persons living there; assess their food-related needs; and determine their wishes concerning voluntary return to their country of origin.

On 11 April [S/2008/241], South Africa transmitted a letter of 10 April from the Frente Polisario Secretary-General, Mohamed Abdelaziz, in which he provided the view of Frente Polisario regarding the negotiations held in March. During those talks, Frente Polisario explained its ideas for future administrative, political, economic, social and security arrangements in the Territory of Western Sahara, in order to elaborate its 2007 proposal for a mutually acceptable political solution that provided for the self-determination of the people of Western Sahara [YUN 2007, p. 296]. It indicated that Morocco's proposal denied the legitimate right of self-determination, and thereby the possibility of a permanent democratic solution. Condemning the human rights abuses of Saharawi civilian populations inside the occupied Territory, Frente Polisario urged the Council to implement the recommendations of the 2006 report of the United Nations High Commissioner for Human Rights [YUN 2006, p. 334], in particular that MINURSO be mandated to monitor the human rights of the inhabitants of Western Sahara. Frente Polisario was ready to continue the negotiating process and elaborate further its constructive ideas for arrangements to govern the Territory, and was willing to take account of Morocco's security concerns, including over its southern border. Frente Polisario also expressed its willingness to begin security cooperation with Morocco to combat security threats in the trans-Sahara region.

Report of Secretary-General (April). In response to resolution 1783(2007) [YUN 2007, p. 299], the Secretary-General in April submitted a report [S/2008/251] on the situation in Western Sahara, covering developments since his October 2007 report [YUN 2007, p. 298] and his January 2008 report on the status and progress of negotiations. On 17 February, Frente Polisario organized elections in the Western Saharan refugee camps near Tindouf for a new 'Saharan parliament'. The 'parliament' held its inaugural meetings as part of official celebrations held by Frente Polisario in Tifariti on 27 February to mark the thirty-second anniversary of the proclamation of the 'Saharan Arab Democratic Republic'. Morocco objected to the events in Tifariti and to construction taking place there, claiming that Frente Polisario was breaching the terms of the military agreements. In a meeting on 3 March with the MINURSO Force Commander, the Moroccan military threatened action by "adequate means", including air strikes, to prevent further construction in the Tifariti area. The Force Commander responded that those civilian activities were taking place some 70 kilometres east of the berm—the buffer strip that separated the Moroccan-administered portion of the Territory (west) from the area controlled by Frente Polisario (east)—in the area of limited restrictions, where such activities did not violate military agreement No. 1 (see p. 323) of 1998 [YUN 1998 p. 194]. From 18 February to 13 March, the Royal Moroccan Army (RMA) conducted a series of pre-scheduled military training exercises in the vicinity of Awsard, involving some 1,200 troops stationed in the Awsard subsector. MINURSO was notified of the exercises in October 2007, and they were deemed to be in accordance with military agreement No. 1. In a letter of 13 March to the UN Secretary-General, the Frente Polisario Secretary-General protested the apparent provocation the military exercises entailed on the eve of the fourth round of the Manhasset negotiations.

The Secretary-General's Personal Envoy held consultations with Morocco and Frente Polisario, as well as Algeria and Mauritania and other interested countries. In addition, he visited the region from 5 to 15 February for in-depth consultations on ways to move the negotiations forward. He met with the Moroccan Prime Minister, Abbes El Fassi (Rabat, Morocco, 6–7 February); the Frente Polisario Secretary-General and its Coordinator with MINURSO, M'Hamed Khadad, as well as other senior Frente Polisario officials and traditional leaders (Tindouf, 9–10 February); the Algerian Prime Minister, Abdelaziz Belkhadem (Algiers, Algeria, 11–13 February); and senior Government officials of Algeria, Mauritania and Morocco. He met with the President of Mauritania, Sidi Mohamed Ould Cheikh Abdellahi, in Nouakchott, Mauritania, on 14 February. The Personal Envoy also visited the El Aaiun refugee camp.

The situation in the MINURSO area of responsibility remained generally calm. The Mission continued to monitor the 6 September 1991 ceasefire [YUN 1991, p. 796]; between 1 October 2007 and 31 March 2008, it performed 4,042 ground patrols and 289 air patrols to visit RMA units and the Frente Polisario armed forces, and monitor adherence to the military agreements. MINURSO continued to enjoy good relations with RMA and the Frente Polisario armed forces. However, both sides continued not to deal directly with each other, and all known contact between them took the form of meetings and written communications with MINURSO. Violations of the military agreement had decreased since the Secretary-General's October 2007 report. MINURSO observed 3 new violations by RMA and 10 by the Frente Polisario armed forces. It recorded a significant decrease in the number of freedom-of-movement violations by both sides, with 139 such violations recorded on the part of RMA and 33 on the part of Frente Polisario. Both parties continued to extend their cooperation to MINURSO in the marking and disposal of mines, unexploded ordnance and expired ammunition. The newly established Mine Action Coordination Centre was working to enhance information on mine contamination and response, raise the level of safety for UN personnel and provide support for mine-action programmes.

UNHCR and WFP continued to provide humanitarian assistance to the most vulnerable Western Saharan refugees in the refugee camps near Tindouf. The UNHCR-led confidence-building programme continued to be implemented in coordination with MINURSO and in cooperation with the parties. Between November 2004 and 28 March 2008, 5,644 Western Saharans benefited from the exchange of family visits; 55 per cent of the beneficiaries were women and 35 per cent were children under the age of 18.

As to human rights, the Frente Polisario Secretary-General wrote to the UN Secretary-General eight times between January and April to protest the arrests and alleged repression of Western Saharan human rights activists by Moroccan authorities throughout the Territory, and to petition the United Nations to broaden the MINURSO mandate to include human rights protection and monitoring. Moroccan media expressed concerns about alleged human rights abuses in the camps near Tindouf and highlighted the allegedly deteriorating human rights and humanitarian situation of Western Saharan refugees in the camps.

Based on the fourth round of talks held in March, and taking into account the Personal Envoy's assessment, the Secretary-General recommended that the Council reiterate its call on the parties to enter into a more intensive and substantive phase of negotiations and to negotiate without preconditions. The Secretary-General believed that the presence of MINURSO remained indispensable for maintaining the ceasefire, and recommended that the Council extend the Mission's mandate until 31 October.

SECURITY COUNCIL ACTION

On 30 April [meeting 5884], the Security Council unanimously adopted **resolution 1813(2008)**. The draft [S/2008/284] was submitted by France, the Russian Federation, Spain, the United Kingdom and the United States.

The Security Council,

Recalling all its previous resolutions on Western Sahara,

Reaffirming its strong support for the efforts of the Secretary-General and his Personal Envoy for Western Sahara to implement resolutions 1754(2007) of 30 April 2007 and 1783(2007) of 31 October 2007,

Reaffirming its commitment to assist the parties to achieve a just, lasting and mutually acceptable political solution which will provide for the self-determination of the people of Western Sahara in the context of arrangements consistent with the principles and purposes of the Charter of the United Nations, and noting the role and responsibilities of the parties in this respect,

Reiterating its call upon the parties and States of the region to continue to cooperate fully with the United Nations and with each other to end the current impasse and to achieve progress towards a political solution,

Taking note of the proposal presented by Morocco to the Secretary-General on 11 April 2007, and welcoming serious and credible Moroccan efforts to move the process forward towards resolution, and taking note also of the proposal presented by the Frente Popular para la Liberación de Saguía el-Hamra y de Río de Oro to the Secretary-General on 10 April 2007,

Taking note also of the four rounds of negotiations held under the auspices of the Secretary-General, and welcoming the progress made by the parties to enter into direct negotiations,

Welcoming the agreement of the parties, expressed in the communiqué of the Personal Envoy of the Secretary-General of 18 March 2008, to explore the establishment of family visits by land, which would be in addition to the existing programme by air, and encouraging them to do so in cooperation with the United Nations High Commissioner for Refugees,

Welcoming also the commitment of the parties to continue the process of negotiations through United Nations-sponsored talks,

Noting the view of the Secretary-General that the consolidation of the status quo is not an acceptable outcome of the current process of negotiations, and noting further that progress in the negotiations will have a positive impact on the quality of life of the people of Western Sahara in all its aspects,

Having considered the report of the Secretary-General of 14 April 2008,

1. *Reaffirms* the need for full respect of the military agreements reached with the United Nations Mission for the Referendum in Western Sahara with regard to the ceasefire;

2. *Endorses* the report's recommendation that realism and a spirit of compromise by the parties are essential to maintain the momentum of the process of negotiations;

3. *Calls upon* the parties to continue to show political will and work in an atmosphere propitious for dialogue in order to enter into a more intensive and substantive phase of negotiations, thus ensuring the implementation of resolutions 1754(2007) and 1783(2007) and the success of negotiations, and affirms its strong support for the commitment of the Secretary-General and his Personal Envoy towards a solution to the question of Western Sahara in this context;

4. *Also calls upon* the parties to continue negotiations under the auspices of the Secretary-General without preconditions and in good faith, taking into account the efforts made since 2006 and subsequent developments, with a view to achieving a just, lasting and mutually acceptable political solution which will provide for the self-determination of the people of Western Sahara in the context of arrangements consistent with the principles and purposes of the Charter of the United Nations, and notes the role and responsibilities of the parties in this respect;

5. *Invites* Member States to lend appropriate assistance to these talks;

6. *Requests* the Secretary-General to keep the Security Council informed on a regular basis on the status and progress of these negotiations under his auspices, and expresses its intention to meet to receive and discuss his report;

7. *Also requests* the Secretary-General to provide a report on the situation in Western Sahara well before the end of the mandate period;

8. *Urges* Member States to provide voluntary contributions to fund confidence-building measures that allow for increased contact between separated family members, especially family visits, as well as for other confidence-building measures that may be agreed between the parties;

9. *Decides* to extend the mandate of the Mission until 30 April 2009;

10. *Requests* the Secretary-General to continue to take the necessary measures to ensure full compliance in the Mission with the United Nations zero-tolerance policy on sexual exploitation and abuse and to keep the Council informed, and urges troop-contributing countries to take appropriate preventive action, including predeployment awareness training, and other action to ensure full accountability in cases of such conduct involving their personnel;

11. *Decides* to remain seized of the matter.

Communication. In a letter of 27 May to the Secretary-General [S/2008/348], Morocco stated that from 19 to 22 May, Frente Polisario, supported by Algeria, again marshalled troops and held political demonstrations in the Tifariti zone east of the berm, in full view of MINURSO personnel, which undermined the ongoing negotiations. Morocco, while reiterating its support for the efforts of the Secretary-General and of his Personal Envoy to reach a political solution, reaffirmed that it could not accept or tolerate any change in the status quo in the zone.

Report of Secretary-General. In a later report [S/2009/200 & Corr.1], the Secretary-General said that King Mohammed VI of Morocco addressed his country on 30 July, the ninth anniversary of his enthronement, to register the need for respect for Morocco's territorial integrity. He called on Algeria to normalize ties between the two countries and reopen their common borders. In a statement on 6 November marking the thirty-third anniversary of Morocco's 'Green March' into Western Sahara [YUN 1975, p. 175], the King announced his Government's intention to transfer power to the regions, including Western Sahara, as part of decentralization reform.

In other developments, the mandate of the Personal Envoy, Peter van Walsum, ended in August. The Under-Secretary-General for Political Affairs, B. Lynn Pascoe, visited Morocco on 14 and 15 October for further discussions. The Secretary-General met in September with the Moroccan Minister for Foreign Affairs and Cooperation, Taïb Fassi Fihri, and with the Frente Polisario Secretary-General on 4 November, reiterating to the parties his commitment to pursuing the negotiation process mandated by the Council. The Consultative Council on Human Rights of the Government of Morocco held a meeting (Laayoune, 29–30 October) with the Royal Advisory Council for Saharan Affairs and a number of Moroccan and local NGOs to discuss the human rights situation in Western Sahara. The meeting highlighted the need to ensure better protection and promotion of human rights, with particular safeguards for union and political freedoms.

GENERAL ASSEMBLY ACTION

The General Assembly, in December, examined the Secretary-General's July report [A/63/131] summarizing his 1 July 2007 to 30 June 2008 reports to the Security Council on the question of Western Sahara and the relevant chapter of the 2008 report of the Special Committee on decolonization [A/63/23].

On 5 December [meeting 64], the Assembly, on the recommendation of the Fourth (Special Political and Decolonization) Committee [A/63/408], adopted **resolution 63/105** without vote [agenda item 37].

Question of Western Sahara

The General Assembly,

Having considered in depth the question of Western Sahara,

Reaffirming the inalienable right of all peoples to self-determination and independence, in accordance with the principles set forth in the Charter of the United Nations and General Assembly resolution 1514(XV) of 14 December 1960 containing the Declaration on the Granting of Independence to Colonial Countries and Peoples,

Recognizing that all available options for self-determination of the Territories are valid as long as they are in accordance with the freely expressed wishes of the people concerned and in conformity with the clearly defined principles contained in General Assembly resolutions 1514(XV) of 14 December 1960 and 1541(XV) of 15 December 1960 and other resolutions of the Assembly,

Recalling its resolution 62/116 of 17 December 2007,

Recalling also all resolutions of the General Assembly and the Security Council on the question of Western Sahara,

Recalling further Security Council resolutions 658(1990) of 27 June 1990, 690(1991) of 29 April 1991, 1359(2001) of 29 June 2001, 1429(2002) of 30 July 2002, 1495(2003) of 31 July 2003, 1541(2004) of 29 April 2004, 1570(2004) of 28 October 2004, 1598(2005) of 28 April 2005, 1634(2005) of 28 October 2005, 1675(2006) of 28 April 2006 and 1720(2006) of 31 October 2006,

Underlining the adoption of Security Council resolutions 1754(2007) on 30 April 2007, 1783(2007) on 31 October 2007 and 1813(2008) on 30 April 2008,

Expressing its satisfaction that the parties have met on 18 and 19 June 2007, on 10 and 11 August 2007, from 7 to 9 January 2008 and from 16 to 18 March 2008 under the auspices of the Personal Envoy of the Secretary-General and in the presence of the neighbouring countries and that they have agreed to continue the negotiations,

Calling upon all the parties and the States of the region to cooperate fully with the Secretary-General and his Personal Envoy and with each other,

Reaffirming the responsibility of the United Nations towards the people of Western Sahara,

Welcoming in this regard the efforts of the Secretary-General and his Personal Envoy in search of a mutually acceptable political solution to the dispute, which will provide for the self-determination of the people of Western Sahara,

Having examined the relevant chapter of the report of the Special Committee on the Situation with regard to the Implementation of the Declaration on the Granting of Independence to Colonial Countries and Peoples,

Having also examined the report of the Secretary-General,

1. *Takes note* of the report of the Secretary-General;

2. *Supports* the process of negotiations initiated by Security Council resolution 1754(2007) and further sustained by Council resolutions 1783(2007) and 1813(2008), with a view to achieving a just, lasting and mutually acceptable political solution, which will provide for the self-determination of the people of Western Sahara, and commends the efforts undertaken by the Secretary-General and his Personal Envoy in this respect;

3. *Welcomes* the commitment of the parties to continue to show political will and work in an atmosphere propitious for dialogue, in order to enter into a more intensive phase of negotiations, in good faith and without preconditions, taking note of efforts and developments since 2006, thus ensuring implementation of Security Council resolutions 1754(2007), 1783(2007) and 1813(2008) and the success of negotiations;

4. *Also welcomes* the ongoing negotiations between the parties held on 18 and 19 June 2007, on 10 and 11 August 2007, from 7 to 9 January 2008 and from 16 to 18 March 2008 in the presence of the neighbouring countries under the auspices of the United Nations;

5. *Calls upon* the parties to cooperate with the International Committee of the Red Cross, and calls upon them to abide by their obligations under international humanitarian law;

6. *Requests* the Special Committee on the Situation with regard to the Implementation of the Declaration on the Granting of Independence to Colonial Countries and Peoples to continue to consider the situation in Western Sahara and to report thereon to the General Assembly at its sixty-fourth session;

7. *Invites* the Secretary-General to submit to the General Assembly at its sixty-fourth session a report on the implementation of the present resolution.

MINURSO

In 2008, the United Nations Mission for the Referendum in Western Sahara (MINURSO), established by Security Council resolution 690(1991) [YUN 1991, p. 794], continued to monitor compliance with the 1991 formal ceasefire [ibid., p. 796] between Frente Polisario and Morocco. The Mission's military observers carried out monitoring through a combination of ground and air patrols and observation posts, and through inspections of larger-than-company-size military units of Frente Polisario and RMA. The main focus was on military activities close to the berm, the defensive sand wall built by RMA between 1981 and 1987 across Western Sahara, extending from the north-east corner to the south-west, near the Mauritanian border.

Military Agreement No. 1, which MINURSO signed separately with the parties [YUN 1998, p. 194], remained the basic legal instrument governing the ceasefire monitoring of the five parts into which, for operational purposes, the disputed territory of Western Sahara was divided: one 5-kilometre-wide buffer strip to the east and south of the berm; two restricted areas—one, 25 kilometres wide east of the berm and the other, 30 kilometres wide west of it; and two areas with limited restrictions that encompassed the remainder of the Territory. Bilateral military agreements Nos. 2 and 3 [YUN 1999, p. 180], committing both parties to cooperating with MINURSO in the exchange of mine-related information, marking of mined areas, and clearance and destruction of mines and unexploded ordnance, remained in force.

At the end of 2008, MINURSO numbered 491 personnel: 197 military observers, 20 troops, 6 police, 97 international civilians, 153 local civilians and 18 United Nations Volunteers. The Mission maintained its headquarters in Laayoune, Western Sahara; a liaison office in Tindouf, Algeria; and nine military-observer team sites located across the Territory: four on the Moroccan-controlled side and five on the Frente Polisario side. In April, the Council extended the MINURSO mandate until 30 April 2009.

Financing

In June, the General Assembly considered the performance report [A/62/611] on the MINURSO budget for the period from 1 July 2006 to 30 June 2007, with expenditures amounting to $41,702,600; the Secretary-General's report [A/62/679] on the MINURSO budget requirements for the period from 1 July 2008 to 30 June 2009, totalling $45,728,400; and the related ACABQ report [A/62/781/Add.3], which recommended reducing that amount to $45,698,200.

In an April note [A/62/817] on financing arrangements for MINURSO for the period from 1 July 2007 to 30 June 2008, the Secretary-General said that resource requirements had increased by $3,870,500 and would be offset by the projected unutilized balance of $2,116,300. The Secretary-General requested the Assembly to appropriate and assess $1,754,200 for the maintenance of the Mission for the period from 1 July 2007 to 30 June 2008, in addition to the $44,321,600 already appropriated for that period under resolution 61/290 [YUN 2007, p. 301].

In a statement of 12 May to the Fifth Committee [A/C.5/62/SR.40], the ACABQ Chairman said that, in light of the Mission's chronically precarious financial situation, ACABQ found that it had no choice but to concur with the Secretary-General's request.

GENERAL ASSEMBLY ACTION

On 20 June [meeting 109], the General Assembly, on the recommendation of the Fifth Committee [A/62/881], adopted **resolution 62/268** without vote [agenda item 156].

Financing of the United Nations Mission for the Referendum in Western Sahara

The General Assembly,

Having considered the reports of the Secretary-General on the financing of the United Nations Mission for the Referendum in Western Sahara, the related report of the Advisory Committee on Administrative and Budgetary Questions, the note by the Secretary-General on the financing arrangements for the Mission and the oral statement by the Chairman of the Advisory Committee on Administrative and Budgetary Questions,

Recalling Security Council resolution 690(1991) of 29 April 1991, by which the Council established the United Nations Mission for the Referendum in Western Sahara, and the subsequent resolutions by which the Council extended the mandate of the Mission, the latest of which was resolution 1813(2008) of 30 April 2008, by which the Council extended the mandate of the Mission until 30 April 2009,

Recalling also its resolution 45/266 of 17 May 1991 on the financing of the Mission and its subsequent resolutions and decisions thereon, the latest of which was resolution 61/290 of 29 June 2007,

Reaffirming the general principles underlying the financing of United Nations peacekeeping operations, as stated in General Assembly resolutions 1874(S-IV) of 27 June 1963, 3101(XXVIII) of 11 December 1973 and 55/235 of 23 December 2000,

Noting with appreciation that voluntary contributions have been made to the Mission,

Mindful of the fact that it is essential to provide the Mission with the financial resources necessary to enable it to fulfil its responsibilities under the relevant resolutions of the Security Council,

1. *Reiterates its request* to the Secretary-General to entrust the Head of Mission with the task of formulating future budget proposals in full accordance with the provisions of General Assembly resolutions 59/296 of 22 June 2005, 60/266 of 30 June 2006 and 61/276 of 29 June 2007, as well as other relevant resolutions;

2. *Takes note* of the status of contributions to the United Nations Mission for the Referendum in Western Sahara as at 31 March 2008, including the contributions outstanding in the amount of 46.8 million United States dollars, representing some 7 per cent of the total assessed contributions, notes with concern that only sixty-eight Member States have paid their assessed contributions in full, and urges all other Member States, in particular those in arrears, to ensure payment of their outstanding assessed contributions;

3. *Expresses its appreciation* to those Member States which have paid their assessed contributions in full, and urges all other Member States to make every possible effort to ensure payment of their assessed contributions to the Mission in full;

4. *Expresses concern* at the financial situation with regard to peacekeeping activities, in particular as regards the reimbursements to troop contributors that bear additional burdens owing to overdue payments by Member States of their assessments;

5. *Also expresses concern* at the delay experienced by the Secretary-General in deploying and providing adequate resources to some recent peacekeeping missions, in particular those in Africa;

6. *Emphasizes* that all future and existing peacekeeping missions shall be given equal and non-discriminatory treatment in respect of financial and administrative arrangements;

7. *Also emphasizes* that all peacekeeping missions shall be provided with adequate resources for the effective and efficient discharge of their respective mandates;

8. *Reiterates its request* to the Secretary-General to make the fullest possible use of facilities and equipment at the United Nations Logistics Base at Brindisi, Italy, in order to minimize the costs of procurement for the Mission;

9. *Endorses* the conclusions and recommendations contained in the report of the Advisory Committee on Administrative and Budgetary Questions and in the oral statement by the Chairman of the Advisory Committee, subject to

the provisions of the present resolution, and requests the Secretary-General to ensure their full implementation;

10. *Decides* not to approve the Field Service post in the Archiving Unit;

11. *Decides* to provide general temporary assistance for the national General Service post in the Archiving Unit for one year, and requests the Secretary-General to rejustify its continuation in the context of the next budget submission;

12. *Requests* the Secretary-General to ensure the full implementation of the relevant provisions of its resolutions 59/296, 60/266 and 61/276;

13. *Also requests* the Secretary-General to take all necessary action to ensure that the Mission is administered with a maximum of efficiency and economy;

14. *Further requests* the Secretary-General, in order to reduce the cost of employing General Service staff, to continue efforts to recruit local staff for the Mission against General Service posts, commensurate with the requirements of the Mission;

Financial performance report for the period from 1 July 2006 to 30 June 2007

15. *Takes note* of the report of the Secretary-General on the financial performance of the Mission for the period from 1 July 2006 to 30 June 2007;

Financing arrangements for the period from 1 July 2007 to 30 June 2008

16. *Also takes note* of the note by the Secretary-General on the financing arrangements for the Mission for the period from 1 July 2007 to 30 June 2008;

17. *Decides* to appropriate to the Special Account for the United Nations Mission for the Referendum in Western Sahara the amount of 1,754,200 dollars for the maintenance of the Mission for the period from 1 July 2007 to 30 June 2008, in addition to the amount of 46,471,700 dollars already appropriated for the Mission for the same period under the terms of resolution 61/290;

Financing of the additional appropriation for the period from 1 July 2007 to 30 June 2008

18. *Also decides*, taking into account the amount of 46,471,700 dollars already apportioned under the terms of resolution 61/290, to apportion among Member States the additional amount of 1,754,200 dollars for the maintenance of the Mission for the period from 1 July 2007 to 30 June 2008, in accordance with the levels updated in General Assembly resolution 61/243 of 22 December 2006, and taking into account the scale of assessments for 2007 and 2008, as set out in its resolution 61/237 of 22 December 2006;

19. *Further decides* that, in accordance with the provisions of its resolution 973(X) of 15 December 1955, the decrease of 235,000 dollars in the estimated staff assessment income in respect of the financial period from 1 July 2007 to 30 June 2008 shall be added to the apportionment among Member States as provided for in paragraph 18 above;

Budget estimates for the period from 1 July 2008 to 30 June 2009

20. *Decides* to appropriate to the Special Account for the Mission the amount of 47,702,500 dollars for the period from 1 July 2008 to 30 June 2009, inclusive of 45,600,800 dollars for the maintenance of the Mission, 1,832,100 dollars for the support account for peacekeeping operations and 269,600 dollars for the United Nations Logistics Base;

Financing of the appropriation for the period from 1 July 2008 to 30 June 2009

21. *Also decides* to apportion among Member States the amount of 39,752,080 dollars for the period from 1 July 2008 to 30 April 2009, in accordance with the levels updated in resolution 61/243, and taking into account the scale of assessments for 2008 and 2009, as set out in resolution 61/237;

22. *Further decides* that, in accordance with the provisions of its resolution 973(X), there shall be set off against the apportionment among Member States, as provided for in paragraph 21 above, their respective share in the Tax Equalization Fund of 1,909,500 dollars, comprising the estimated staff assessment income of 1,745,080 dollars approved for the Mission, the prorated share of 146,670 dollars of the estimated staff assessment income approved for the support account and the prorated share of 17,750 dollars of the estimated staff assessment income approved for the United Nations Logistics Base;

23. *Decides* to apportion among Member States the amount of 7,950,420 dollars for the period from 1 May to 30 June 2009, at a monthly rate of 3,975,208 dollars, in accordance with the levels updated in resolution 61/243, and taking into account the scale of assessments for 2009, as set out in resolution 61/237, subject to a decision of the Security Council to extend the mandate of the Mission;

24. *Also decides* that, in accordance with the provisions of its resolution 973(X), there shall be set off against the apportionment among Member States, as provided for in paragraph 23 above, their respective share in the Tax Equalization Fund of 381,900 dollars, comprising the estimated staff assessment income of 349,020 dollars approved for the Mission, the prorated share of 29,330 dollars of the estimated staff assessment income approved for the support account and the prorated share of 3,550 dollars of the estimated staff assessment income approved for the United Nations Logistics Base;

25. *Further decides* that, for Member States that have fulfilled their financial obligations to the Mission, there shall be set off against their apportionment, as provided for in paragraph 21 above, their respective share of the unencumbered balance and other income in the total amount of 2,903,700 dollars in respect of the financial period ended 30 June 2007, in accordance with the levels updated in resolution 61/243, and taking into account the scale of assessments for 2007, as set out in resolution 61/237;

26. *Decides* that, for Member States that have not fulfilled their financial obligations to the Mission, there shall be set off against their outstanding obligations their respective share of the unencumbered balance and other income in the total amount of 2,903,700 dollars in respect of the financial period ended 30 June 2007, in accordance with the scheme set out in paragraph 25 above;

27. *Also decides* that the decrease of 345,700 dollars in the estimated staff assessment income in respect of the financial period ended 30 June 2007 shall be set off against

the credits from the amount of 2,903,700 referred to in paragraphs 25 and 26 above;

28. *Emphasizes* that no peacekeeping mission shall be financed by borrowing funds from other active peacekeeping missions;

29. *Encourages* the Secretary-General to continue to take additional measures to ensure the safety and security of all personnel participating in the Mission under the auspices of the United Nations, bearing in mind paragraphs 5 and 6 of Security Council resolution 1502(2003) of 26 August 2003;

30. *Invites* voluntary contributions to the Mission in cash and in the form of services and supplies acceptable to the Secretary-General, to be administered, as appropriate, in accordance with the procedure and practices established by the General Assembly;

31. *Decides* to include in the provisional agenda of its sixty-third session the item entitled "Financing of the United Nations Mission for the Referendum in Western Sahara".

By **decision 63/552** of 24 December, the General Assembly decided that the agenda item on MINURSO financing would remain for consideration during its resumed sixty-third (2009) session.

Other issues

Kenya

In 2008, the United Nations supported the efforts of the AU, the EU and the international community to address the political, security and humanitarian crisis that developed in Kenya in the aftermath of presidential, parliamentary and local elections held on 27 December 2007 under allegations of irregularities. On 30 December, the Electoral Commission of Kenya (ECK) announced that Mwai Kibaki of the Party of National Unity (PNU) won the presidential elections and the Orange Democratic Movement (ODM), the party of the opposition leader and presidential candidate Raila Odinga, had obtained the majority in Parliament. EU observers questioned the credibility of the electoral results, citing lack of access to some counting centres in the Central Province, as well as evidence of irregularities. Criticism also emanated from the international community. Demonstrations and ethnically motivated violence ensued—reportedly from supporters of both Government and opposition sides—targeting civilians. Instability was concentrated in central, western and coastal Kenya. An estimated 600,000 people were displaced as numerous reports of abuses against civilians emerged, including killings, rape and arson. Although a mediation initiative was launched in early January 2008 by the AU Chairman, Ghanaian President John Kufuor, in collaboration with other stakeholders, settlement prospects were diminished by the concurrent nomination of supporters of President Kibaki for key cabinet posts. Although talks broke down on 10 January, the parties agreed to mediation by an AU-sponsored Panel of Eminent African Personalities led by former UN Secretary-General Kofi Annan. On 1 February, the parties agreed on a four-point negotiating agenda addressing an end to the violence, the humanitarian situation, the political crisis, and land and historical injustices.

Decision of AU Assembly. The tenth ordinary session of the AU Assembly (Addis Ababa, 31 January–2 February), in a decision on the situation in Kenya following the presidential election, called for an in-depth investigation into the human rights violations that had occurred and urged the parties to build on their agreement of 1 February to end the violence and to commit themselves to a peaceful solution to the crisis through dialogue and in conformity with the rule of law.

SECURITY COUNCIL ACTION

On 6 February [meeting 5831], following consultations among Security Council members, the President made statement **S/PRST/2008/4** on behalf of the Council:

The Security Council welcomes the announcement of progress in the negotiations, overseen by Mr. Kofi Annan, between Mr. Mwai Kibaki and Mr. Raila Odinga on 1 February 2008, including the adoption of an agenda and a timetable for action to end the crisis in Kenya following the disputed elections of 27 December 2007. The Council welcomes the African Union communiqué of 21 January 2008, commends the efforts of the African Union, the President of Ghana, Mr. John Kufuor, and the Secretary-General of the United Nations, Mr. Ban Ki-moon, and emphasizes its full support for the Panel of Eminent African Personalities, led by Mr. Annan, in assisting the parties in finding a political solution. The Council deplores the widespread violence following the elections, which has resulted in extensive loss of life and serious humanitarian consequences.

The Council expresses its deep concern that, despite the commitments made on 1 February 2008, civilians continue to be killed, subjected to sexual and gender-based violence and displaced from their homes. The Council emphasizes that the only solution to the crisis lies through dialogue, negotiation and compromise and strongly urges Kenya's political leaders to foster reconciliation and to elaborate and implement the actions agreed to on 1 February without delay, including by meeting their responsibility to engage fully in finding a sustainable political solution and taking action to end immediately violence, including ethnically motivated attacks, dismantle armed gangs, improve the humanitarian situation and restore human rights. Recalling the need to avoid impunity, the Council calls for those responsible for violence to be brought to justice. It expresses its concern at the political, security and economic impact of the crisis in Kenya on the wider region.

The Council expresses its strong concern at the continuing dire humanitarian situation in Kenya and calls for the protection of refugees and internally displaced persons. The Council further expresses its concern for the safety of humanitarian workers and United Nations personnel and calls upon all parties to facilitate their work and ensure their safety. The Council welcomes the decisions, following consultations with the Government of Kenya, of the United Nations High Commissioner for Human Rights and the Special Adviser of the Secretary-General for the Prevention of Genocide to dispatch missions to Kenya. It calls upon Kenya's political leaders to facilitate the work of these missions and looks forward to being informed by the Secretary-General of their findings.

The Council further requests the Secretary-General to report on how the United Nations can further support the mediation efforts in Kenya and, as necessary, on the impact of the crisis on the wider subregion and United Nations operations in the subregion.

Security Council consideration. On 25 February [meeting 5845], the Under-Secretary-General for Humanitarian Affairs and Emergency Relief Coordinator, John Holmes, briefed the Council on his visit to Kenya (8–10 February) to reaffirm UN support for the people of Kenya and the mediation process led by Mr. Annan, as well as to assess the humanitarian situation on the ground. The violence resulted in approximately 1,000 deaths; at least 300,000 people had been driven from their homes and over 270,000 people from six of Kenya's eight provinces remained in approximately 200 camps and sites in the Nyanza, Rift Valley, Central, Coastal and Western Provinces. An estimated 500,000 people required assistance with shelter, water, food and medical care, while the needs of some 12,000 Kenyan refugees in Uganda were also being addressed. Common threads among all the displaced groups were their need for safety and security, particularly for women and children; disturbing accounts of continuing abuses in and around the camps; and the psychological consequences of the trauma experienced. He heard stories of murder, rape and burning, and said that the ethnic basis of much of what had happened was clear. Meanwhile, heightened ethnic awareness and fears had spread through much of Kenya, fuelling polarization. The effects of ethnic divisions on basic Government services had been dramatic in some areas, as staff quietly left or were afraid to go to work. Consequently, even if a political agreement was reached, the displacement crisis would not disappear quickly, posing a challenge for politicians, Kenyan society and the humanitarian community. There was a lot to be done in terms of rebuilding confidence and providing security before people could return home. He added that there must be accountability for those responsible for the violence, abuses of human rights and multiple failures to protect civilians. He also briefed the Council on the economic impact of the crisis, ongoing activities by UN agencies and NGO partners to address the humanitarian situation and the status of contributions from donors (see p. 1001).

Power-sharing agreement. On 28 February, ODM and PNU signed a power-sharing agreement to resolve the political crisis and thereby enacted the National Accord and Reconciliation Act 2008. The provisions of the "Agreement on the Principles of Partnership of the Coalition Government" established the following: the authority of the Prime Minister to coordinate and supervise the execution of the affairs of the Government; the manner in which the Prime Minister would be nominated and selected; the composition of the Cabinet (President, Vice-President, Prime Minister, two Deputy Prime Ministers and the other Ministers); the processes and conditions for the removal of the Prime Minister and Deputy Prime Ministers, the dissolution of the coalition Government, and the maintenance of the portfolio balance with regard to Government composition; and the entrenchment of the National Accord and Reconciliation Act in the Constitution. In a press statement of 29 February [SC/9265], the Security Council expressed its support to President Kibaki and Mr. Odinga in forming a new Government and called for the Agreement to be implemented without delay.

On 4 March, the two parties reached agreements on a constitutional review process; a commission of inquiry on post-election violence; an independent review committee to look into the conduct and management of the elections; and a truth, justice and reconciliation commission. On 18 March, the National Assembly approved a constitutional amendment and the National Accord and Reconciliation Act, which reflected the provisions of the Agreement. As tensions and divisions between ODM and PNU arose over the appointment of ministers, an agreement on the division of portfolios within the coalition Government was reached, involving an increase in the number of ministries to 40. On 17 April, Raila Odinga was sworn in as Prime Minister.

In March, Justice Johann Kriegler (South Africa) was named to chair the Independent Review Commission on the elections, and in April President Kibaki appointed Appeals Court Justice Philip Waki (Kenya) to chair the commission of inquiry on post-election violence.

Report of Independent Review Commission. In September, the Independent Review Commission on the General Elections held in Kenya on 27 December 2007 submitted its report to President Kibaki and to the Chair of the Panel of Eminent African Personalities. The report found that Kenya's constitutional and legal framework relating to elections contained weaknesses and inconsistencies that reduced its effectiveness and that the electoral management process as a whole needed revision. In the preparation and conduct of the 2007 elections, ECK lacked the necessary independence, capacity and functionality due to weaknesses in its organizational structure, composition and management systems. Other issues included defects in the voter register, which excluded nearly one third of eligible voters, with a bias against women and young people, and included the names of some 1.2 million dead people; abuse of polling; defective data collation, transmission and tallying; and the lack of adequate planning, staff selection and training, public relations and dispute resolution mechanisms. The integrity of the process and credibility of the results were so gravely impaired that the question of whether or not there was actual rigging at the national tally centre was irrelevant, as the results were irretrievably polluted. The report contained recommendations on reforming the electoral management process, including the development and implementation of legislative and political measures to support that process.

OHCHR mission. The Office of the United Nations High Commissioner for Human Rights (OHCHR) deployed a fact-finding mission to Kenya (6–28 February) to look into the violence and allegations of grave human rights violations following the elections. The mission's report included recommendations aimed at contributing to the parties' efforts to achieve sustainable peace through justice and respect for human rights (see p. 863).

Zimbabwe

During 2008, the political situation in Zimbabwe deteriorated owing to a post-election crisis that evolved following the holding of presidential, senatorial, parliamentary and local elections on 29 March. In the House of Assembly, the main opposition party, the Movement for Democratic Change (MDC) won 99 seats, while the ruling party, the Zimbabwe African National Union-Patriotic Front (ZANU-PF) won 97 seats. Another opposition faction that later committed to an alliance with MDC won 10 seats. In the Senate, ZANU-PF and the combined opposition won 30 seats each. The Zimbabwe Electoral Commission (ZEC), however, did not release the results of the presidential election. MDC claimed that its candidate, Morgan Tsvangirai, won the presidency outright.

SADC summit. The Southern African Development Community (SADC) convened the First Extraordinary Summit of Heads of State and Government (Lusaka, Zambia, 13 April) to discuss the political developments in Zimbabwe. Member States, with the exception of Zimbabwe, held informal consultations with presidential candidate Tsvangirai and independent candidate Simba Makoni. Both opposition leaders confirmed that the elections were held in a free, fair and peaceful environment and that they had no problem with the results of the parliamentary, senatorial and local elections. However, they were concerned by the delay in announcing the results of the presidential elections, as well as the lack of their participation in the verification process, which was being conducted by ZEC.

The Summit urged the electoral authorities to expeditiously verify and release the results in accordance with the due process of law, including verification and counting done in the presence of and authenticated by candidates or their agents. SADC offered to send its Election Observer Mission, which would be present throughout the verification and counting. If run-off elections were necessary, the Summit urged the Government to ensure that the elections were held in a secure environment. The Summit further appealed to ZEC to ensure strict compliance with the rule of law and SADC principles and guidelines governing democratic elections.

Security Council consideration (April). On 16 April [meeting 5868], during the Council's high-level debate on peace and security in Africa (see p. 108), the Secretary-General expressed concern at the prolonged non-release of the election results and said that the situation could deteriorate without a transparent solution to the impasse. He urged SADC leaders to continue efforts to address the issue and said that the United Nations stood ready to provide assistance. The President of Tanzania and AU Chairperson, Jakaya Kikwete, commended the work of SADC, stating that its efforts had enabled the people of Zimbabwe to hold peaceful elections and that SADC remained seized with the situation to ensure that the will of the people was respected. Eight members of the Council (Belgium, Costa Rica, Croatia, France, Italy, Panama, United Kingdom, United States) expressed concern about the situation, with several calling for either a free and fair second round or the release of the results of the presidential elections.

Election results. On 2 May, ZEC announced the results of the presidential elections and revealed that neither of the two leading contenders managed an outright win. Mr. Tsvangirai led by obtaining 47.9 per cent of the votes cast, while Robert Mugabe received 43.7 per cent, followed by former Finance Minister Simba Makoni with 8.3 per cent. Meanwhile, in the period leading up to the announcement of the results, the political and security situation had remained tenuous. On 25 April, approximately 185 to 200 opposition supporters were arrested on suspicion of involvement in political violence during a police raid on MDC offices in the capital city of Harare. MDC said that many of those arrested were taking shelter after fleeing intimidation. The following day,

ZEC announced that the results of the parliamentary elections remained unchanged in 18 of 23 constituencies where recounts had taken place; the ZANU-PF loss of parliamentary majority was therefore confirmed. More than 180 of the arrested opposition activists were released without charge on 29 April, after MDC won a High Court order the previous day.

On 22 June, the opposition candidate, Mr. Tsvangirai, withdrew from the presidential run-off of 27 June, citing the absence of conditions for credible elections due to widespread violence and restrictions on his ability to campaign.

Security Council consideration (June). The Security Council held three meetings on 23 June. The first [meeting 5919], in response to a request from Belgium [S/2008/407], heard a briefing on the situation in Zimbabwe from the Under-Secretary-General for Political Affairs, B. Lynn Pascoe. The second [meeting 5920] was held in private and the Council, in a communiqué, indicated that it had an exchange of views with the representative of Zimbabwe. The third [meeting 5921] issued statement S/PRST/2008/23 (see below).

In his briefing to the Council, the Under-Secretary-General said that the withdrawal of Mr. Tsvangirai from the presidential run-off demonstrated that the situation had deteriorated to alarming levels and had reached a new degree of gravity. During the visit to Zimbabwe by Assistant Secretary-General Haile Menkerios to explore ways to improve the political climate, meetings were held with a wide spectrum of actors, including President Mugabe, the Ministers of Foreign Affairs, Justice, Labour and Social Welfare, the Deputy Commander of the army, ZEC, the leaders of MDC, civil society and church organizations, and the leaders of SADC. Based on his observations, Mr. Menkerios informed the Secretary-General that conditions did not exist for free and fair elections and that no outcome of an election run under those conditions could be considered credible. The country had experienced a staggering degree of violence, with the opposition claiming that more than 80 of its supporters had been killed by ZANU-PF supporters and that thousands were displaced from their wards. There was evidence that such violence had been perpetrated by a combination of State agencies—army, police and intelligence—as well as by war veterans and youth militias. The Government claimed that violence had also been perpetrated by MDC activists. While evidence suggested that there had been some retaliatory violence, it was of a much lesser degree than that of the Government and its supporters. The campaign of intimidation and threat had created a climate of fear, while the violence and displacements posed a challenge to the voting process.

The Under-Secretary-General said that it was hoped that the climate would improve with the arrival of a large number of regional and international observers, as their presence could help deter the violence and increase confidence. As at 23 June, some 397 SADC observers had been deployed in Zimbabwe, with 430 SADC observers expected in total (compared to 163 SADC observers for the first round). The AU and ECOWAS had also increased their number of observers. Despite those measures, initial reports by observer missions provided accounts of politically motivated violence. Other concerns included the restrictive provisions imposed on domestic observer groups by the authorities, diminishing their capacity to recruit observers; the situation of the MDC candidate, who had little or no access to Zimbabwean media and was barred from campaigning freely; the arrest and detention of the MDC Secretary-General on charges of treason; and reports that the MDC headquarters had been raided and dozens of supporters were being detained. In light of the above, the Under-Secretary-General said that the conditions for a free and fair run-off election did not exist. He made recommendations for the postponement of the elections, Government action to ensure that conditions were established for a credible process, and dialogue between the parties to determine a period during which conditions for free and fair elections could be created. He reiterated the Secretary-General's call on both parties to resume talks and seek a peaceful resolution of the crisis.

SECURITY COUNCIL ACTION

On 23 June [meeting 5921], following consultations among Council members, the President made statement **S/PRST/2008/23** on behalf of the Council:

> The Security Council condemns the campaign of violence against the political opposition ahead of the second round of the presidential elections scheduled for 27 June 2008, which has resulted in the killing of scores of opposition activists and other Zimbabweans and the beating and displacement of thousands of people, including many women and children.
>
> The Council further condemns the actions of the Government of Zimbabwe that have denied its political opponents the right to campaign freely, and calls upon the Government to stop the violence, to cease political intimidation, to end the restrictions on the right of assembly and to release the political leaders who have been detained. The Council urges the international monitors and observers to remain in Zimbabwe while the crisis continues.
>
> The Council regrets that the campaign of violence and the restrictions on the political opposition have made it impossible for a free and fair election to take place on 27 June. The Council further considers that, to be legitimate, any government of Zimbabwe must take account of the interests of all its citizens. The Council notes that the results of the elections of 29 March 2008 must be respected.

The Council expresses its concern over the impact of the situation in Zimbabwe on the wider region. The Council welcomes the recent international efforts, including those of the leaders of the Southern African Development Community and particularly President Mbeki. The Council calls upon the Zimbabwean authorities to cooperate fully with all efforts, including through the United Nations, aimed at finding a peaceful way forward, through dialogue between the parties, that allows a legitimate government to be formed that reflects the will of the Zimbabwean people.

The Council further expresses its concern at the grave humanitarian situation in Zimbabwe and condemns the suspension by the Government of Zimbabwe of the operations of humanitarian organizations, which has directly affected one and a half million people, including half a million children. The Council calls upon the Government to immediately allow humanitarian organizations to resume their services.

The Council will continue to monitor closely the situation and requests the Secretary-General to report on ongoing regional and international efforts to resolve the crisis.

Run-off election. Despite calls for the election to be postponed until proper conditions were in place, including by the Secretary-General, second-round elections were held on 27 June. Incumbent President Mugabe stood as the only candidate and the official results declared him the winner with 85.5 per cent of the votes. President Mugabe was inaugurated on 29 June.

AU Assembly summit. The AU Assembly, at its eleventh ordinary session (Sharm el-Sheikh, Egypt, 30 June–1 July), adopted a resolution that expressed concern over the situation in Zimbabwe, the negative reports of the observers on the run-off election, and the violence and loss of life that had occurred. The Assembly urged President Mugabe and Mr. Tsvangirai to engage in dialogue with a view to promoting peace, stability, democracy and reconciliation. It supported the establishment of a government of national unity and recommended the continuation of SADC mediation efforts, including the establishment of a mechanism for a negotiated solution. The text of the AU resolution was transmitted to the Council in a letter dated 10 July [S/2008/452].

Security Council consideration (July). On 8 July [meeting 5929], Deputy Secretary-General Asha-Rose Migiro briefed the Council on the situation in Zimbabwe and the discussion of it at the AU Summit in Sharm el-Sheikh (see above). She said that three African observer missions present on the ground—AU, Pan-African Parliament and SADC—issued unequivocal condemnations of the electoral process and its results. Many irregularities were reported, including the requirement of voters to report the serial number of their ballots to ZANU-PF officials, rendering the concept of anonymous voting meaningless. Some people spoiled their ballots in protest, accounting for 5.1 per cent of the total votes. There were no national observers as in the first round, which stripped the elections of a critical measure of transparency and credibility, although regional groups had substantially augmented the number of observers for the second round. The United Nations provided logistic and technical support to SADC efforts to increase observation. The observer missions also indicated that the process leading up to the run-off election did not conform to accepted standards and was seriously flawed.

The Deputy Secretary-General said that the crisis of legitimacy surrounding the re-election of President Mugabe was compounded by the paralysis of State institutions. There was no functioning Parliament and civil society had been silenced and intimidated. Meanwhile, there were severe shortages of food and basic services. There was a need to restore the rule of law and to start building public institutions. She said that MDC and ZANU-PF recognized that Zimbabwe's political future depended on a transitional arrangement promoting national unity. The two parties, therefore, had accepted a dialogue towards a negotiated settlement and talks were ongoing under South African mediation, with President Thabo Mbeki working towards a direct meeting between President Mugabe and Mr. Tsvangirai. At the AU Summit, there was broad support for the creation of a government of national unity as a way forward. She said that the Secretary-General supported the AU recommendation for the continuation of SADC mediation efforts and the establishment of a mediation mechanism. He further called on the Zimbabwe authorities to lift restrictions on humanitarian activities.

On 11 July [meeting 5933], the Security Council considered a draft resolution [S/2008/447] that provided for the imposition of an arms embargo on Zimbabwe, as well as a travel ban and financial freeze against President Mugabe and 13 senior Government officials. Zimbabwe told the Council that the root cause of the crisis was land ownership and that the adverse reports on inter-party violence were overdramatized in the media, as only 10 per cent of the country might have witnessed some sort of violence. The Government would investigate the cases of the people who had claimed to be victims of political violence, and most of the culprits from both parties, including criminal gangs, had already appeared before the courts. Sanctions imposed by the United States in 2001 and the EU in 2002 had put the country's economy under siege and were affecting the vulnerable groups and general population. Meanwhile, political dialogue was ongoing between the contending parties. Zimbabwe welcomed the AU resolution and pointed out that, in line with his SADC mandate and supported by the AU, President Mbeki was in the country over the weekend to consult with President Mugabe and the political parties to chart the way forward. In that regard, Zimbabwe was of the view that any other initiative would be counterproductive and undermine the role of SADC and President Mbeki. He said that the draft resolution was an abuse of Chapter VII of the UN Charter, and its adoption would set a dangerous precedent. Zimbabwe's problems could be solved by Africans working together, and trying to impose a solution from outside would be unfair to Zimbabweans, SADC and the AU.

The result of the voting on the draft resolution was 9 in favour (Belgium, Burkina Faso, Costa Rica, Croatia, France, Italy, Panama, United Kingdom, United States), 5 against (China, Libyan Arab Jamahiriya, Russian Federation, South Africa, Viet Nam) and 1 abstention (Indonesia). Owing to the negative votes of two permanent members of the Council, the draft resolution was not adopted.

On 21 July, MDC and ZANU-PF signed a memorandum of understanding.

Global Political Agreement. On 15 September, under the facilitation of SADC, the Global Political Agreement on resolving the challenges facing Zimbabwe was signed between ZANU-PF and the two MDC formations led by Mr. Tsvangirai and Arthur Mutambara, respectively. The parties agreed to work together to solve the situation and chart a new political direction for the country. Key areas addressed in the 25-article Agreement included the framework for a new Government, humanitarian food assistance, the land question, the rule of law and respect for the constitution and other laws, security of persons and prevention of violence, sanctions and measures, freedom of expression and communication, interim constitutional amendments, implementation mechanisms and periodic review mechanisms.

Libyan Arab Jamahiriya

The twentieth session of the Council of the League of Arab States (LAS) (Damascus, Syrian Arab Republic, 29–30 March) [S/2008/296] adopted a resolution by which it affirmed the right of the Libyan Arab Jamahiriya to seek compensation for the material and human losses caused by the sanctions imposed on it by the Security Council in connection with the terrorist attacks against Pan Am flight 103 on 21 December 1988 and Union de transports aériens flight 772 on 19 September 1989. It also affirmed the demand for the release of Libyan national Abdelbaset al-Megrahi, considering his continued detention to be that of a hostage according to international law. The LAS Council demanded that the United Kingdom release all documents requested by the defence counsel for that Libyan national to the Scottish Criminal Cases Review Commission.

Mauritius–United Kingdom/France

Addressing the General Assembly on 29 September during the general debate [A/63/PV.16], Mauritius said that high-level talks were under way to settle the issue of its sovereignty claim regarding the Chagos Archipelago, including Diego Garcia, which the United Kingdom had excised from the territory of Mauritius prior to its independence, in disregard of Assembly resolutions 1514(XV) [YUN 1960, p. 49] and 2066(XX) [YUN 1965, p. 587]. Mauritius was sensitive to the aspirations of its citizens to return to the islands of their birth in the archipelago, from which they had been forcibly removed. It also urged France to pursue dialogue with Mauritius on the issue of sovereignty over Tromelin Island.

On 3 October [A/63/475], the United Kingdom, in exercise of the right of reply, maintained that the British Indian Ocean Territory was British and had been since 1814. It did not recognize Mauritius' sovereignty claim. However, the British Government recognized Mauritius as the only State that had the right to assert a claim of sovereignty when the United Kingdom relinquished its own sovereignty. The Territory would be ceded when no longer required for defence purposes. The United Kingdom remained open to discussions regarding arrangements governing the Territory or its future, and stated that when the time came for the Territory to be ceded it would liaise closely with Mauritius. It valued its close and constructive cooperation with Mauritius on a wide range of issues and looked forward to continuing such cooperation.

Chapter III

Americas

During 2008, the United Nations continued to advance the cause of lasting peace, human rights, sustainable development and the rule of law in the Americas. In Guatemala, the newly established International Commission against Impunity continued to implement its mandate. In October, the Secretary-General provided the General Assembly with an update on the current state and activities of the Commission, and the UN role in the implementation of its mandate.

In Haiti, continuing challenges relating to the political and security situation hampered progress in the democratic process. In February, internal tensions between the Government and Parliament culminated in Prime Minister Jacques-Edouard Alexis' being summoned to appear before the Chamber of Deputies to respond to questions on the high cost of living, security, justice reform and the development of the country's agriculture. In April, six days of increasingly violent demonstrations in various parts of the country against the high cost of living and increasing cost of basic food commodities exemplified the potential for civil unrest. The United Nations Stabilization Mission in Haiti (MINUSTAH) assisted the Haitian National Police in responding to the security crisis. Nonetheless, the disturbances subsequently led to a vote of censure against the Government of Prime Minister Alexis, which left Haiti without a fully functioning Government for over four months. In August and September, a series of hurricanes and storms struck Haiti, exacerbating an already dire humanitarian situation arising from the food insecurity crisis. Over 800,000 Haitians lost their homes or were directly affected by the disasters. The need to address the problems posed by the hurricanes helped resolve the political standoff and generated a new sense of solidarity. The confirmation process for a new Government was concluded in September and the new Prime Minister was sworn into office. Subsequently, the houses of Parliament passed a law allowing the President to declare a state of emergency and establish a system of flexible disbursement of national funds to assist affected populations.

MINUSTAH provided extensive support to the authorities and the UN country team to facilitate the provision and coordination of humanitarian assistance and access by humanitarian personnel. The Mission also continued to support the training and institutional development of the police. In December, further progress was achieved with the adoption of a legislative agenda for 2009 and the issuance of a decree by the President, together with the new Prime Minister and members of her Government, setting the first and second rounds of the partial senatorial elections for 19 April and 7 June 2009.

In other developments in the region, the General Assembly again called on States to refrain from promulgating laws and measures such as the ongoing embargo against Cuba by the United States. The Assembly also considered activities undertaken by the United Nations to strengthen cooperation with the Caribbean Community.

Central America

In 2008, Central America further consolidated peace and built democratic and equitable societies upon the foundation developed in years of successful UN peacemaking efforts. In that connection, the United Nations continued to assist the region through development programming, the good offices of the Secretary-General and other means.

Guatemala

Four years after the ending of the mandate of the United Nations Verification Mission in Guatemala in 2004 [YUN 2004, p. 287], the country continued to build upon the foundation laid in previous years. In 2008, the International Commission against Impunity in Guatemala (CICIG), established in September 2007 [YUN 2007, p. 308] with the concurrent entry into force of the 2006 agreement between the country and the United Nations [YUN 2006, p. 870], carried on implementing its mandate. Under the terms of the agreement, which set up the Commission as an independent, non-United Nations organ, the main CICIG objective was to assist, strengthen and support State institutions responsible for investigating and prosecuting crimes allegedly committed by illegal security forces and clandestine security organizations, and other criminal conduct related to those entities.

In a letter dated 18 September [A/63/376], Guatemala said that it was timely to inform the General Assembly of the achievements made related to CICIG. It therefore requested that the Assembly, pursuant to its decision 60/508 [YUN 2005, p. 376], accept the letter as notification and include CICIG for consideration at its sixty-third (2008) session, under the agenda item entitled "The situation in Central America: progress in fashioning a region of peace, freedom, democracy and development".

CICIG update. On 27 October [A/63/511], the Secretary-General transmitted to the Assembly an update on CICIG, including its establishment, activities and the UN role in the implementation of its mandate. He noted that the United Nations would be involved in an innovative attempt to dismantle criminal groups whose actions threatened to erode hard-fought gains in the peace process and had taken on the CICIG initiative at the explicit request of Guatemala. In that connection, the Organization had worked with three successive Governments to establish the Commission, most recently, to ensure its effective functioning. The mandated functions of CICIG included: determining the existence of illegal security groups and clandestine security structures; collaborating with the State in dismantling such groups and structures; promoting the investigation, prosecution and punishment of crimes committed by their members; and recommending to the State the adoption of policies for eradicating such groups and structures and preventing their re-emergence. While the Commission was set up as a non-UN organ, with its expenses being met through voluntary contributions from the international community, a trust fund administered by the United Nations Development Programme was established in October 2007 to channel those contributions and ensure transparency and accountability. Guatemala would provide the Commission with office space and other in-kind contributions, as well as ensure the security and protection of Commission staff. Some $26 million had been raised from 12 Member States and the European Union, which would cover 90 per cent of the projected two-year budget, and other Member States had seconded security staff, criminal investigators and legal experts. The Commission was operational with a staffing level of 115 international and Guatemalan staff assigned to both professional and administrative functions.

In the first year of its two-year mandate, CICIG made significant advances. It had received information from numerous sources that permitted progress in mapping clandestine structures. The Commission was investigating 15 high-impact cases, most often in coordination with the Office of the Public Prosecutor. In other activities, CICIG had identified and provided the authorities with the names of civil servants who had been derelict in their duty or had obstructed the work of CICIG; analysed national legislation on security, criminal law and criminal procedure in light of international best practices; identified legal and regulatory changes needed to better protect constitutional rights, remove obstacles and fill legal gaps that interfered with the prompt administration of justice; and submitted reform proposals for transmission as draft laws to the Congress.

The Secretary-General also highlighted challenges the Commission faced, such as those that could arise as investigations and court proceedings advanced in cases that touched powerful criminal interests, as well as the need to strengthen security, reinforce the framework for staff protection and immunities, facilitate the transnational exchange of information pertinent to its cases and create effective mechanisms for witness protection. He expressed the hope that CICIG, the United Nations, Guatemala and other Member States would work together to address those issues with alacrity and creativity.

The Assembly considered the Secretary-General's update on 10 November [A/63/PV.43]. Guatemala observed that the initiative to establish the Commission originated in Guatemala and reflected the country's conviction that international cooperation was needed to confront organized groups that operated with impunity—not to replace national authorities, but to support them and thereby strengthen them in the future. The Secretary-General added that CICIG activities would open new areas of work for the United Nations and provide lessons learned that might be useful to other Member States. The Secretary-General called for the Assembly's continued support for CICIG, without any additional financial or budgetary implications. On the same date, the Assembly adopted resolution 63/19, which took note of the Secretary-General's update and requested that he report on the Commission's work at its sixty-fourth (2009) session.

GENERAL ASSEMBLY ACTION

On 10 November [meeting 43], the General Assembly adopted **resolution 63/19** [draft: A/63/L.18 & Add.1] without vote [agenda item 20].

The situation in Central America: progress in fashioning a region of peace, freedom, democracy and development

The General Assembly,

Recalling its relevant resolutions on the situation in Central America, and particularly resolution 58/239 of 23 December 2003,

Recalling also paragraph 16 of the above-mentioned resolution, in which the General Assembly took note with satisfaction of the intention of the Government of Guatemala to establish a Commission for the Investigation of Illegal Groups and Clandestine Security Apparatuses and urged the Secretary-General to support that initiative with a view to its prompt implementation,

Apprised by the Secretary-General through his periodic reports of the ensuing protracted negotiations to define the nature and characteristics of the Commission in order to comply with norms and policies of both the United Nations and the Government of Guatemala, those of the latter including the need for parliamentary ratification,

Bearing in mind that the Agreement between the United Nations and the State of Guatemala on the establishment of an International Commission against Impunity in Guatemala was, in fact, signed on 12 December 2006, and that it was ratified by the Guatemalan Congress on 1 August 2007 and entered into force on 4 September 2007,

Aware that the Secretary-General, in accordance with the provisions contained in the Agreement on the establishment of the Commission, had proceeded to appoint the Commissioner in September 2007, and that, after an organizational period of three months, the Commission began implementing its mandate in accordance with Guatemalan law and the provisions of its founding Agreement, to support, strengthen and assist institutions of the State of Guatemala responsible for investigating and prosecuting crimes that compromise fundamental human rights of its citizens and the rule of law,

Bearing in mind that the Commission has carried out its activities through voluntary contributions of Member States and other donors from the international community and that the Government of Guatemala has provided additional budgetary allotments to State institutions to support their work in collaboration with the Commission,

Convinced that, pursuant to Articles 55 and 56 of its Charter, the United Nations promotes respect for human rights and fundamental freedoms for all and that Member States pledge themselves to take action in cooperation with the Organization for the achievement of that purpose,

1. *Takes note* of the letter dated 27 October 2008 from the Secretary-General to the President of the General Assembly on the establishment, current state and activities of the International Commission against Impunity in Guatemala and the role that the United Nations has played in its implementation;

2. *Commends* the Government of Guatemala for its commitment to combat impunity and strive to strengthen the institutions that buttress the rule of law and the defence of human rights;

3. *Expresses its appreciation* to those Member States and other donors that have supported the International Commission against Impunity in Guatemala, through voluntary contributions, financial and in kind, and urges them to continue their support;

4. *Also expresses its appreciation* to the Secretary-General for providing effective and efficient assistance to the Commission, and calls upon him to continue to do so in order that the Commission may successfully carry out its mandate and address the challenges that it faces;

5. *Requests* the Secretary-General to report to the General Assembly at its sixty-fourth session on the work of the Commission.

Haiti

During 2008, although the political and security situation in Haiti remained challenging, progress was made in the democratic process with the July adoption of a new electoral law drafted by the Provisional Electoral Council and the installation of a new Prime Minister and Government in September. Following the promulgation of three key laws relating to the independence of the judiciary and the status of magistrates, the United Nations Stabilization Mission in Haiti (MINUSTAH) continued its work with the authorities, donors and other stakeholders to promote the availability of legal assistance to those in need. The first legal aid office opened in Cité Soleil in January, and by August, eight such offices had been established. In March, Haiti was admitted as a member of the Rio Group, marking a further step forward in the country's integration into regional structures. In April, civil unrest in the country was characterized by a series of demonstrations against the high cost of living, which resulted in the evacuation of UN offices in Les Cayes, in the south of the country. Haiti's fragile political consensus was tested following a Senate vote to censure the Government of Prime Minister Jacques-Edouard Alexis. Although four months of negotiations were required to obtain legislative approval for his successor, Michèle Duvivier Pierre-Louis, by year's end gains were made in the political process. In December, representatives of the Government and Parliament, with support from MINUSTAH and donors, participated in a joint workshop that culminated in the adoption of an agreed legislative agenda for 2009. An electoral schedule for the next three years was also completed. With nearly 80 per cent of Haiti's population living on $2 or less per day, extreme poverty remained one of the most far-reaching and complex challenges facing the country. In addition to providing security support, MINUSTAH facilitated the reform of rule-of-law structures, particularly the strengthening of the Haitian National Police (HNP), and the judicial and prison systems. It also monitored the human rights situation and supported humanitarian recovery and development.

Political and security situation

National dialogue and reconciliation

In 2008, the Government continued efforts to reach out to political groups and to strengthen State institutions. Progress was achieved in January with the consensus compromise that allowed the 10 senators whose terms would expire that year to remain in office until the adoption of a new electoral law, and with the Chamber of Deputies and the Senate electing new bureaux, which expressed the intention of enhancing cooperation between the two chambers. President René Préval continued to emphasize the need to reform rule-of-law institutions and to pursue efforts to combat corruption and impunity. In his 14 January address to the Parliament, he stressed that the country should not expect a quick solution to its problems, and called for a partnership between the public and private sectors. While his call for constitutional reform, queries regarding the need for an army, and statements on the high cost of living resulted in some criticism, they also generated reflection on those issues by political leaders, the private sector and civil society.

Despite the advances gained, differences between the branches of Government threatened to undermine effective governance. Tensions between the Government and Parliament culminated in Prime Minister Jacques-Edouard Alexis' being summoned to appear before the Chamber of Deputies on 28 February. During a 10-hour debate, the Prime Minister and Cabinet members responded to a variety of questions, mostly on the high cost of living, but also on security, justice reform and the development of the country's agriculture. The eight deputies who initiated the procedure voted to censure the Government, while 63 voted against and 13 abstained. Although the outcome represented an overall endorsement of the Government's approach, the event underlined the fragility of the political collaboration and the degree to which it was affected by public frustration.

Report of Secretary-General. In his March report [S/2008/202], the Secretary-General said that the political situation remained fragile given the continued political divisions and weak institutions, and the absence of significant improvements in the living conditions of the population. Many Haitians had experienced additional hardship due to an increase in the price of commodities and staple products, and tensions were generated by the public perception of deterioration in security conditions, including a rise in the number of kidnappings. In addition to the February summoning of Prime Minister Alexis, political dynamics were strained due to the ongoing investigation by an ad hoc Senate commission of allegations of dual nationality against senior officials, as dual nationality was forbidden by the Constitution, and a number of public exchanges and media reports suggested that tensions continued to exist between the judicial system and HNP.

Despite those challenges, significant achievements had been realized. The branches of Government worked together to enact critical judicial reform. On 18 February, the Provisional Electoral Council established in December 2007 [YUN 2007, p. 308] submitted a draft electoral law to the Government that was subsequently sent to Parliament for consideration. Meanwhile, MINUSTAH was helping plan the logistical and security aspects of the senatorial elections, and the ongoing updating of the voter rolls by the National Office of Identification, in collaboration with the Organization of American States, had resulted in the registration of more than 450,000 new voters.

On reform of rule-of-law structures, the Secretary-General said that the passage into law of a framework for judicial independence was a significant step forward and that it was essential that plans be translated into action and necessary funding be made available to support reform. The United Nations Development Programme (UNDP), in consultation with the Government, was working towards the establishment of a joint rule-of-law trust fund which could facilitate the mobilization and coordination of international aid. The Government adopted a three-year justice reform plan focusing on five key areas: reorganization of the Ministry of Justice and Public Security; strengthening of the judiciary; improved access to justice and efficiency of the courts; rehabilitation and development of corrections facilities; and modernization of key legislation. In other efforts, MINUSTAH continued to work with the authorities and other stakeholders to promote the availability of legal aid to those in need; a legal aid office was established in Cité Soleil in January, and it was foreseen that five additional offices would be opened throughout the country; and President Préval requested MINUSTAH assistance in ensuring the effective judicial review of high-priority cases related to kidnapping and organized crime.

The institutions of governance continued to suffer from a lack of qualified personnel, poor infrastructure and limited resources. MINUSTAH provided expertise and technical assistance in support of key institutions and assisted efforts by the authorities to strengthen border management. However, the presence of the Government at the land border and key ports fell far short of what was required. The security situation had improved significantly since major operations undertaken against gangs in early 2007 [YUN 2007, p. 309], yet the potential for volatility remained. Since December, several areas of Port-au-Prince had experienced an increase in criminality, and the average number of reported kidnappings per month reached 28 between December 2007 and February 2008—up from 11 six months earlier. Anti-Government demonstrations, with a focus on the rising cost of living, had increased, and there were indications that gangs might be trying to reorganize themselves. In the regions outside the capital, the security situation remained relatively calm, but unrest and occurrences of popular justice had been reported. Illicit trafficking activities along the coast and by air, as well as misunderstandings between local communities in the border region, were also a concern.

MINUSTAH continued to work with national authorities, UNDP and donors in strengthening HNP, which was gradually becoming more effective in apprehending criminals and had made several drug shipment seizures. Nonetheless, the total number of police officers, which stood at 8,444, remained well below the 14,000 identified in the HNP reform plan as necessary for basic policing duties. The Mission continued to provide operational support to HNP with military patrols throughout the country and activities of its formed police units; worked with national authorities to adapt its security profile; provided assistance in HNP efforts to respond to major crimes and kidnapping incidents; secured strategic locations, such as the national penitentiary; and enhanced security in the vicinity of priority ports. MINUSTAH also supported HNP efforts to reform its weapons registration unit and assisted the Government in the revision of legislation on the import and possession of arms and in the implementation of a weapons registry system. The Mission was also strengthening the capacity of the judicial police.

In other developments, the Presidential Commission established in 2007 to undertake a process of reflection on the reinforcement of public security issued in January its first report, which discussed the definition of a defence policy and national security. MINUSTAH continued to implement its community violence reduction programme, including the launch on 1 March of six labour-intensive projects in violence-affected communities, which employed 7,572 individuals. Pursuant to Security Council resolution 1780(2007) [YUN 2007, p. 313], MINUSTAH launched a process of consultations with the authorities to identify benchmarks to measure consolidation of the emerging stability. Suggested critical milestones arising from those discussions included the completion of a cycle of elections; the establishment of a sustainable security structure and of an independent and credible judicial and penal system; and the extension of State authority throughout the country. Lasting stability would also require a tangible improvement in the living standards of the population and the creation of conditions for economic recovery. On 6 March, during the Rio Group Summit held in the Dominican Republic, Haiti was admitted as a member of the Group, marking a step forward in the country's integration into regional structures.

The Secretary-General observed that significant strides had been made in key areas, but the potential for regression remained apparent. He urged the leadership and institutions of Haiti to collaborate with one another and the executive and legislative branches of the Government to persevere in jointly outlining strategies for the future and in implementing them. Strong international involvement was indispensable for continued progress, and institutional reform could not succeed without extensive bilateral support. In that connection, he hoped that the establishment of a rule-of-law trust fund would be a useful vehicle for channelling assistance in that area. On the stability consolidation plan initiated by MINUSTAH, he would provide further details, including relevant benchmarks, in his next report.

Security Council consideration (April). In his 8 April [meeting 5862] briefing to the Security Council, the Special Representative of the Secretary-General and Head of MINUSTAH, Hédi Annabi, said that the political, security and institution-building progress, as well as the initial signs of improvement in the socio-economic situation, were only a first step and that progress remained fragile. The potential for a deterioration of relations was made clear by the February summoning of the Prime Minister before the Chamber of Deputies and the 1 April shooting inside the Parliament during a debate on investigations into alleged spending irregularities by legislators. Further problems could lie ahead related to ongoing inquiries on the possession of double nationality by legislators and Government officials, the question of constitutional reform, the preparation of elections for one third of the Senate, and unrest in various parts of the country, which was characterized by rising anti-Government demonstrations against the high cost of living, yet also appeared to have a political dimension. There were potential security implications in such unrest, such as the demonstrations that required the evacuation of UN offices in Les Cayes, in the south of the country, and similar demonstrations, albeit less violent, that took place in Gonaives, Port-au-Prince and a few other locations.

In order to combat the threat of criminality and violence, MINUSTAH had reinforced its collaboration with the authorities and enhanced sharing of information; stepped up the presence of checkpoints throughout Port-au-Prince, where most of the kidnappings had taken place; worked to enhance the investigative and response capabilities of its police; and reinforced its presence along Haiti's land and maritime borders. MINUSTAH would continue to assist in the professionalization of the police and its institutional development, but complementary bilateral support was needed to meet HNP needs, including in areas such as infrastructure, transport, telecommunications and other equipment. He called for Haiti's democratic structures to be strengthened to facilitate greater institutionalization of dialogue and to break a tradition of politically motivated violence, as well as for the country's basic administrative capacities to be enhanced so that essential services could be provided to the population. The Mission could provide some of the assistance required and would continue to support local authorities. MINUSTAH would also continue to work towards strengthening national capabilities in key areas such as border management. He also urged donor countries, international financial institutions and the private sector to work with the authorities to find creative ways to generate "a stability dividend", an immediate and tangible improvement in socio-economic conditions that could allow the stabilization process to advance.

Escalation of violence and censure of Government

The Secretary-General reported [S/2008/586] that the sense of security crucial for public and investor confidence was seriously tested on 3 April, when a peaceful demonstration in Les Cayes of several hundred people against the rising cost of living turned to violent attacks against the Government and MINUSTAH. In the following six days, the protests spread to other cities, including Port-au-Prince, and became increasingly violent. In the capital, demonstrators erected barricades at crossroads, set tires ablaze and looted businesses and residences, resulting in several deaths, many injuries and significant damage to property. All available Haitian security forces and MINUSTAH military and formed police units in Port-au-Prince and other large cities were mobilized to bring the situation under control. The protests began as an expression of public frustration sparked by the rapid escalation in the global prices of basic commodities, which imposed severe hardship on the country's poor. However, as events unfolded, it became apparent from the level and scale of the demonstrations that they were being deliberately manipulated to serve a variety of political, criminal or financial objectives. The protests largely subsided after an appeal for calm by President Préval on 9 April. Three days later, the Senate voted to censure the Government, alleging that it had failed to control the cost of living. On the same day, President Préval announced a programme of short-term subsidies on imported rice and a medium-term plan to revive agricultural production.

Four months of negotiations were required in order to obtain legislative approval for the successor of Prime Minister Alexis, who remained in a caretaker capacity. During that period, Haiti was left without a fully functioning government. While a group of 16 Senators worked together to censure Prime Minister Alexis, a number of others left the upper house on 8 May, upon the conclusion of their terms of office. The Senate, which had 30 seats, was functioning with just 18 serving members, 16 of whom had to be present to form a constitutionally required quorum. Moreover, no date had been set for senatorial elections, which should have taken place in November 2007. The legislative process was significantly hampered and the Government was unable to submit any draft legislation, including key bills such as the draft 2008 revised budget.

Appointment of Prime Minister. President Préval's third nominee, Michèle Duvivier Pierre-Louis, received the approval of the lower house on 17 July and that of the Senate on 31 July. Nearly five months after the vote of censure of the Government, the new Prime Minister was sworn into office on 5 September [S/2009/129].

Further political and security developments

Report of Secretary-General. In August [S/2008/586], the Secretary-General said that Haiti's fragile political consensus was severely tested following the April Senate vote to censure the Government, which had been preceded by six days of anti-government demonstrations against the rising cost of living (see above). The April crisis had led to the postponement of a high-level donors conference to launch the poverty reduction strategy paper, which had been scheduled for 24 and 25 April in Port-au-Prince. Parliamentary dynamics remained fluid, and while activity in the Chamber of Deputies was characterized by heated debates over allegations of corruption and mismanagement, the Concertation des Parlementaires Progressistes had emerged as a relatively cohesive mechanism and played a significant role in facilitating the Chamber's ratification of Prime Minister Pierre-Louis. The President and Prime Minister were conducting consultations with a broad range of political actors with a view to forming a new government and building support within the Parliament for an eventual Statement of Government Policy, which required approval by an absolute majority in both houses. The parties prepared a "governability pact" for consideration by the executive branch, which outlined a possible formula for reinforced collaboration between all branches of Government and political parties and listed a number of objectives that could be addressed through joint action. Among those was a proposal that a consensus be sought to support the modification of certain provisions within the 1987 Constitution, deemed in some quarters as problematic.

Several electoral events were scheduled to take place in the next three years based on the calendar of the Constitution, including the delayed elections for one third of the Senate; elections in November 2009 to renew the Chamber of Deputies and a second third of the Senate; and elections for municipal and local officials. Presidential elections would take place in November 2010. The new electoral law drafted by the Provisional Electoral Council and submitted to Parliament in February was adopted by the legislature on 9 July and published on 25 July. The law introduced important changes, such as an increase in the number of voting centres; a possible increase in the number of Deputies from 99 to 142; a provision for the inclusion of blank votes in elections results; and measures to increase transparency in the electoral process and improve compliance with the Constitution. The Council began a comprehensive review of its structures and resources, both at central and local levels, in light of the provisions of the new law. The new requirement for at least two voting centres in each communal section necessitated the identification of more than 540 new voting centres throughout the country, beyond the 821 existing centres. MINUSTAH was providing technical, security and logistical support to facilitate those exercises. The ongoing updating of the voter rolls resulted in the registration of over 570,000 voters, from an estimated maximum pool of some 700,000 potential new voters.

Bilateral programmes to strengthen various ministries continued, and the Alexis Government developed a six-year State plan for the implementation of administrative reform. However, limited progress was made on broader projects to modernize the State, and ministries continued to suffer from a lack of resources and qualified personnel. MINUSTAH continued to work with the leadership of both chambers of Parliament in providing expertise and technical assistance to strengthen legislative capacity. It facilitated parliamentary and mayoral outreach programmes in all 10 departments through the organization of countrywide forums on relations between Members of Parliament and elected local officials. At the local level, MINUSTAH assisted the Ministry of Interior and local government in providing technical assistance to municipal councils on public administration. The Mission also supported training programmes, seminars and town hall meetings in communes around the country.

MINUSTAH continued to support the efforts of Haitian authorities to strengthen border management, including facilitating weekly informal coordination meetings with local Haitian and Dominican authorities and assisting in refurbishing customs and immigration facilities at Malpasse. On 18 June, at the meeting of the Presidential Commission on Border Development, the Commission President presented a draft decree to create a national coordinating council for border management, which would play a central role in promoting an integrated and cohesive approach to border management. Meanwhile, new border complexes were under construction at Belladère and Ouanaminthe, with bilateral support.

While there had been no further major incidents of civil disturbance since the April crisis and kidnappings had diminished in July, those events, together with brief incidents involving former military elements, underscored the fragility of the security environment and the need for continued preparedness on the part of MINUSTAH and HNP. As Haiti continued to experience threats that HNP was unable to handle alone, MINUSTAH security forces played an indispensable role in ensuring stability. The kidnappings, which seemed to be primarily motivated by ransom, were confined to the country's larger cities; some appeared to be opportunistic, while others were carried out by organized groups. Collaborative efforts by HNP and MINUSTAH to address the issue led to the arrest of several suspected kidnappers, including apparent organizers, and in July the number of kidnappings dropped to less than half the average monthly figure for the previous six months. During the April demonstrations, Haitian security forces and MINUSTAH military and formed police units contained the violence and averted the risk of an attack on the National Palace, as well as other key installations.

In addition to targeted operations, MINUSTAH's military component maintained regular patrolling throughout the country, including along the coast and land border, and increased its aerial surveillance with an additional aircraft. MINUSTAH also supported the enhancement of the National Commission for Disarmament, Dismantlement and Reinsertion, and along with the Commission, launched seven additional labour-intensive projects in violence-affected areas. A total of 20 such projects had been initiated during the year, with 14 of them ongoing and employing some 30,600 persons. As the composition of the Mission's military and police components had been significantly reconfigured over the previous two years to reflect changing circumstances and priorities, and given the demands placed on MINUSTAH forces in April, no further reconfiguration was advised at the time of the report. It was anticipated that the planned increase in HNP in the upcoming 12 months would lay the groundwork for the beginning of a systematic and progressive assumption of responsibilities by HNP, together with a corresponding reconfiguration of MINUSTAH.

Further progress was made towards reform of rule-of-law structures. Out of the target envisaged in the HNP reform plan of 14,000 trained and vetted officers by 2011, HNP included 8,546 officers—of whom 8.5 per cent were female. Ongoing training continued and it was expected that some 1,200 cadets would graduate from the police school in the first half of 2009. The Government launched a programme for reform of the Central Command of the Judicial Police, and a significant expansion of the police school was completed in June. On implementation of the three-year justice reform plan, the Government established commissions to supervise the election and certification of members of the Superior Council of the Judiciary. All nine members of the Council were selected and began vetting in July. The Government also prepared a draft law calling for the establishment of 160 new courts throughout the country. If adopted, the law would require the training of an additional 350 magistrates beyond the existing figure of 700, as well as of judicial support staff and administration. While the reopening of the School of Magistrates was delayed due to renovations, its overall curriculum and internal rules were finalized, and a training session for justices of the peace began on 7 July, with 25 participants. Another four legal aid offices opened in Port-de-Paix, Jacmel, Les Cayes and Jérémie, bringing the number of such offices to eight, out of a planned total of 18 by the end of 2009. Discussions were ongoing regarding proposals to establish specialized chambers within the Port-au-Prince jurisdiction to cover high-profile cases, including kidnappings and financial crimes. The Government, with support from MINUSTAH and other partners, launched a programme to reorganize and standardize court registration processes and case tracking management. An initiative on juvenile justice was also launched, which foresaw additional specialized judges in several jurisdictions. Progress was also achieved in implementing the 2007–2012 strategic plan of the National Prison Administration. However, much remained to be done in its four main areas of concentration: improvement of infrastructure; procurement of necessary equipment; training of personnel; and enhanced treatment of detainees. MINUSTAH continued to help ensure security and meet the need of detainees, while providing technical support for longer-term planning.

With regard to the consolidation plan, the Secretary-General said that while events that took place during the reporting period had an adverse impact on the timeline for progress in the five key areas, those broad objectives remained valid. In an annex to the report, he provided an elaboration of the initial outline and identified further indicators to measure and track progress, which were developed through MINUSTAH in consultation with the authorities.

The Secretary-General observed that Haiti's stabilization process had suffered a significant setback as a result of the April disturbances, the censure of the Government, and the prolonged difficulties in reaching agreement on a new Prime Minister and Government. Moreover, the delay of the adoption and implementation of State programmes, the continuing paralysis of the legislative process, the undermining of public confidence and the dissuading of internal and external private investment had increased the hardship experienced by the Haitian people and compounded the difficulties created by unfavourable global trends. He highlighted tasks that demanded priority attention, such as the adoption of short-term measures to meet the immediate needs of the Haitian people and help them cope with the global food and fuel crisis; finalization of the planning that was launched with the poverty reduction strategy paper process; the engagement of donors; and continued support for programmes to strengthen the country's rule-of-law structures. Renewed efforts to enhance communication between the authorities and the public, and the engagement of the private sector and civil society, were also crucial for success. As the continued deployment of the Mission remained indispensable in ensuring the country's stability and in contributing to the strengthening of rule-of-law institutions, the Secretary-General recommended that MINUSTAH's mandate be extended for a further year, until 15 October 2009, and that its military and police components be maintained at their existing strength. In addition to the support of MINUSTAH, he said that the engagement of the wider international community would be critical for real progress. Bilateral support through the provision of specialized training and through funding for necessary infrastructure would remain crucial for institution-building efforts. Moreover, the extreme hardship experienced by the country needed to be addressed or further destabilization would occur.

Communication. On 2 September [S/2008/640], Uruguay transmitted to the Security Council a joint communiqué released at the meeting of the Deputy Ministers for Foreign Affairs and Deputy Ministers of Defence of the "2 x 9 Mechanism" on Haiti (Montevideo, Uruguay, 29 August), which included the nine Latin American countries that contributed troops to MINUSTAH. The Ministers welcomed the appointment of Prime Minister Pierre-Louis, urged political leaders to form a new Government as soon as possible, and encouraged continued dialogue and the shaping of democratic consensus that included leaders of the country's productive sector. The Ministers observed that MINUSTAH had made significant progress in helping the Government to restore stability and establish security. They made recommendations for the Mission to envisage a new phase that would focus on helping build Haiti's institutional capacity and making substantial progress in social and economic development, basic services, administration of justice and infrastructure. They called on the international community to maintain and increase its political and financial commitments, as well as its presence on the ground. They also requested the United Nations to establish a system for coordinating international cooperation and donations for Haiti.

Security Council consideration (October). In his 8 October briefing to the Security Council [meeting 5990], the Special Representative reported on significant events in Haiti, including the devastating series of hurricanes that struck the country from mid-August to early September and the nomination and confirmation of the new Government. Over 800,000 Haitians lost their homes or were directly affected by the hurricanes and storms. There was also massive destruction of roads and bridges and large-scale destruction of crops.

MINUSTAH responded by undertaking evacuations, providing emergency medical care, supporting efforts to shore up collapsing infrastructure and helping bring critical relief supplies to those who needed them, in collaboration with national authorities and the UN country team.

The need to respond to the problems posed by the hurricanes helped to unblock a political standoff that had lasted nearly five months and to generate a new sense of solidarity. The lengthy and difficult confirmation process for a new Government was concluded on 5 September. Since then, the Parliament demonstrated a fresh level of interest in working with the executive branch, passing emergency legislation that enabled greater flexibility to provide relief funds, and adopting a supplementary budget as required under the Constitution. Civil society and the private sector worked alongside elected representatives to assist victims of the hurricanes, and the Government was pursuing a policy of informing and engaging the public. In other activity, MINUSTAH was working with the national authorities to prepare for the senatorial elections. Those efforts, however, were complicated by the confusion generated by the hurricanes.

On the stability consolidation plan, the Special Representative provided a summary of MINUSTAH's accomplishments in the five areas of focus and on the challenges that lay ahead. He said that the timelines for those areas were subject to change and that it was essential to measure progress not only by the calendar, but according to the effective achievement of the objectives. The consolidation of stability depended on the engagement of three sets of actors: the Haitian leadership and people; MINUSTAH and the UN system; and the wider international community, whose assistance and resources were indispensable to turn those plans into a reality. He also called for the convening of a discussion of the poverty reduction strategy paper that would take into account the vast extent of damage created by the hurricanes and explore how a large-scale effort might be launched to help Haiti recreate a basic infrastructure.

SECURITY COUNCIL ACTION

On 14 October [meeting 5993], the Security Council unanimously adopted **resolution 1840(2008)**. The draft [S/2008/642] was prepared in consultation among Council members.

The Security Council,

Reaffirming its previous resolutions on Haiti, in particular resolutions 1542(2004) of 30 April 2004, 1576(2004) of 29 November 2004, 1608(2005) of 22 June 2005, 1658(2006) of 14 February 2006, 1702(2006) of 15 August 2006, 1743(2007) of 15 February 2007 and 1780(2007) of 15 October 2007,

Reaffirming its strong commitment to the sovereignty, independence, territorial integrity and unity of Haiti,

Reaffirming its support to the Government of Haiti, and welcoming the recent formation of the Government of Prime Minister Michèle Pierre-Louis and the approval of her Government's General Policy Declaration by the Parliament as steps towards providing governance, stability and democracy in Haiti and as a new opportunity to place the long-term reform process back on track,

Encouraging the Government of Haiti and all the other relevant Haitian political, social and economic actors to strengthen democratic dialogue and forge the widest and most inclusive consensus possible, recognizing that leadership and constant political will of the Government among the relevant Haitian actors is needed to strengthen governance and national capacities to address the highest-priority issues in its national agenda,

Recognizing the devastation that has been suffered by the people of Haiti during the current hurricane season and the immediate, medium-term and long-term damage done to the agricultural and infrastructure sectors as well as its impact on Haiti's stability and security situation,

Acknowledging the challenges facing the Government of Haiti to coordinate the delivery of humanitarian relief and to start the recovery efforts, as well as the need to establish a disaster and risk reduction strategy,

Recognizing that the rapid rise in global food and fuel prices continues to pose a significant threat to the overall process of stabilization in Haiti and has adversely affected the political, security, humanitarian, social, economic and development fields, and encouraging the international community to continue to support Haiti in this regard,

Recognizing also the interconnected nature of the challenges in Haiti, reaffirming that sustainable progress on security, the rule of law and institutional reform, national reconciliation and development are mutually reinforcing, and welcoming the continuing efforts of the Government of Haiti and the international community to address these challenges,

Recognizing further that respect for human rights, due process, addressing the issue of criminality and putting an end to impunity are essential to ensuring the rule of law and security in Haiti,

Commending the United Nations Stabilization Mission in Haiti for continuing to assist the Government of Haiti to ensure a secure and stable environment, and deploring again the violence which took place in April 2008, reiterating its deep regret about the loss of life and the attacks against Mission facilities and United Nations personnel and commending the measures taken by the Mission, expressing its gratitude to the troops and police personnel of the Mission and to their countries, and paying tribute to those injured or killed in the line of duty,

Acknowledging some improvements in the security situation in recent months, but noting that the security situation remains fragile,

Emphasizing the importance of cooperation between Haiti and neighbouring and regional States in effectively managing and securing both Haiti's land and maritime territorial borders, in line with the shared interest to secure those borders,

Underscoring that international illicit trafficking in persons, drugs and arms continues to affect the stability of Haiti,

Emphasizing the role of regional organizations in the ongoing process of stabilization and reconstruction in Haiti, and calling upon the Mission to continue to work closely with the Organization of American States and the Caribbean Community, taking note of the joint communiqué issued by the 2 x 9 Mechanism on Haiti on 29 August 2008,

Stressing the importance of establishing credible, competent and transparent governance, and encouraging the Government of Haiti to further strengthen State institutions,

Welcoming the initial recommendations of the Consultative Commission on Prolonged Pretrial Detention, and expressing its strong support for further efforts on this issue as well as in addressing in an effective and timely manner the issue of prison overcrowding,

Calling upon the Government of Haiti, in coordination with the international community, to continue to advance security sector reform, in particular as was called for in the Haitian National Police Reform Plan adopted by the Government on 8 August 2006, as well as reinforcing the efforts to reform the critical judiciary and correctional systems,

Welcoming the initial steps taken towards strengthening the judicial system in accordance with the national justice reform plan, including judicial institution modernization and improvement in access to justice, which are crucial aspects of the reconstruction and stabilization of Haiti,

Welcoming also the adoption of the new electoral law and looking for its early implementation in view of the forthcoming elections, also welcoming the support of the Organization of American States to update the Haitian voter registry, and calling upon the Haitian authorities, with the continued support of donors and partners of Haiti and regional organizations as well as the Mission and the United Nations system, to establish permanent and effective electoral institutions and to hold elections consistent with Haiti's constitutional and legal requirements,

Underlining the need for the quick implementation of highly effective and visible labour-intensive projects that help to create jobs and deliver basic social services,

Acknowledging the efforts undertaken by the Haitian authorities and the contributions of the international community and the United Nations system, supported by the Mission, to respond to the humanitarian and other needs of disaster-affected people, and stressing the importance for future actions in this regard to be fully coordinated among donors and partners of Haiti, with the Government of Haiti as well as within the United Nations system,

Recognizing the importance of long-term commitment of international donors and partners of Haiti, and encouraging them to continue strengthening their levels of assistance,

Stressing the need to reinforce the capacities of the Government of Haiti and its institutions, in particular in the coordination of international cooperation,

Welcoming the report of the Secretary-General of 27 August 2008,

Determining that the situation in Haiti continues to constitute a threat to international peace and security in the region, despite the progress achieved thus far,

Acting under Chapter VII of the Charter of the United Nations, as described in section I of paragraph 7 of resolution 1542(2004),

1. *Decides* to extend the mandate of the United Nations Stabilization Mission in Haiti, as contained in resolutions 1542(2004), 1608(2005), 1702(2006), 1743(2007) and 1780(2007), until 15 October 2009, with the intention of further renewal;

2. *Expresses its satisfaction* with the reconfiguration of the Mission carried out in accordance with resolution 1780(2007), and endorses the recommendation made by the Secretary-General in paragraph 20 of his report to maintain the current Mission configuration until the planned substantial increase of the Haitian National Police capacity allows for a reassessment of the situation, taking into account the need to adjust the composition of the Mission and realign its activities to reflect the changing circumstances and priorities on the ground, including the need to further strengthen the training of the National Police;

3. *Decides*, therefore, that the Mission will continue to consist of a military component of up to 7,060 troops of all ranks and a police component of a total of 2,091 police;

4. *Recognizes* the ownership and primary responsibility of the Government and the people of Haiti over all aspects of the country's stabilization, recognizes the role of the Mission in supporting the efforts of the Government in this regard, and encourages the Government to continue to take full advantage of international support to enhance its capacity, which is indispensable for the sustainable success of the Mission;

5. *Expresses its full support* for the Special Representative of the Secretary-General for Haiti, notably in his efforts related to improving stability and governance in close cooperation with the Government of Haiti, and reaffirms his authority in the coordination and conduct of all activities of United Nations agencies, funds and programmes in Haiti;

6. *Reaffirms its call upon* the Mission to support the political process under way in Haiti, including through the good offices of the Special Representative, and, in cooperation with the Government of Haiti, to promote an all-inclusive political dialogue and national reconciliation, and to provide logistical and security assistance for the upcoming electoral process, in particular the elections, which were scheduled to take place in November 2007, to fill the Senate seats that were left vacant with the end of the mandate of one third of the senators on 8 May 2008;

7. *Recognizes* the importance of resolving political differences through dialogue, and encourages the Special Representative to facilitate this dialogue between the Government of Haiti and all relevant political actors in order to ensure that the democratically elected political institutions can continue carrying forward the reform work laid down in the national strategy for growth and poverty reduction paper;

8. *Welcomes* the continuing contribution of the Mission to the efforts of the Government of Haiti to build institutional capacity at all levels, and calls upon the Mission, consistent with its mandate, to expand such support to strengthen self-sustaining State institutions, especially outside Port-au-Prince, including through the provision of specialized expertise to key ministries and institutions;

9. *Requests* that the Mission continue its support of the Haitian National Police as deemed necessary to ensure security in Haiti, and encourages the Mission and the Government of Haiti to continue to undertake coordinated deterrent actions to decrease the level of crime and violence;

10. *Recognizes* the need for improving and enhancing efforts in the implementation of the Haitian National Police Reform Plan, and requests the Mission, consistent with its mandate, to remain engaged in assisting the Government of Haiti to reform and restructure the National Police, notably by supporting the monitoring, mentoring, training and vetting of police personnel and the strengthening of institutional and operational capacities, while working to recruit sufficient individual police officers to serve as instructors and mentors of the National Police, consistent with its overall strategy to progressively transfer geographical and functional responsibility for conventional law and order duties to its Haitian counterparts in accordance with the Reform Plan;

11. *Invites* Member States, including neighbouring and regional States, in coordination with the Mission, to engage with the Government of Haiti to address cross-border illicit trafficking in persons, drugs and arms and other illegal activities, and to contribute to strengthening the capacity of the Haitian National Police in these areas;

12. *Requests* the Mission to provide technical expertise in support of the efforts of the Government of Haiti to pursue an integrated border management approach, with emphasis on State capacity-building, and underlines the need for coordinated international support for Government efforts in this area;

13. *Welcomes* the imminent deployment of the Mission's sixteen maritime patrol boats in support of the Haitian National Police's Coast Guard responsibilities in protecting and patrolling the maritime borders of Haiti;

14. *Recognizes* the need for the Mission to continue its efforts to patrol along maritime and land border areas in support of border security activities by the Haitian National Police, and encourages the Mission to continue discussions with the Government of Haiti and Member States to assess the threats along Haiti's land and maritime borders;

15. *Requests* the United Nations country team, and calls upon all actors, to complement security and development operations undertaken by the Government of Haiti with the support of the Mission with activities aimed at effectively improving the living conditions of the populations concerned, and requests the Mission to continue to implement quick-impact projects;

16. *Condemns* any attack against personnel or facilities of the Mission, and demands that no acts of intimidation or violence be directed against United Nations and associated personnel or facilities or other actors engaged in humanitarian, development or peacekeeping work;

17. *Welcomes* the steps taken towards the reform of rule of law institutions, requests the Mission to continue to provide necessary support in this regard, and encourages the Haitian authorities to take full advantage of that support, notably in modernizing key legislation and in the implementation of the justice reform plan, the establishment of the Superior Council of the Judiciary, the reorganization and standardization of court registration processes and the management of cases, and the need to address the issue of prolonged pretrial detentions;

18. *Encourages* the implementation of the strategic plan of the National Prison Administration, and supports the strengthening of the Mission's capacity, as referred to in paragraph 42 of the report of the Secretary-General, in particular to address prison overcrowding, and requests the Mission to remain engaged in supporting the mentoring and training of corrections personnel and strengthening institutional and operational capacities;

19. *Requests* the Mission to continue to pursue its community violence reduction approach, including through support to the National Commission on Disarmament, Dismantlement and Reintegration and concentrating its efforts on labour-intensive projects, the development of a weapons registry, the revision of current laws on importation and possession of arms, the reform of the weapons permit system and the promotion of a national community policing doctrine;

20. *Reaffirms* the human rights mandate of the Mission, calls upon the Haitian authorities to continue their efforts to promote and protect human rights, and calls upon the Mission to continue to provide human rights training to the Haitian National Police and other relevant institutions, including the correctional services;

21. *Strongly condemns* the grave violations against children affected by armed violence, as well as widespread rape and other sexual abuse of girls, and requests the Mission to continue to promote and protect the rights of women and children as set out in Security Council resolutions 1325(2000) of 31 October 2000, 1612(2005) of 26 July 2005 and 1820(2008) of 19 June 2008;

22. *Requests* the Secretary-General to continue to take the measures necessary to ensure full compliance of all Mission personnel with the United Nations zero-tolerance policy on sexual exploitation and abuse and to keep the Council informed, and urges troop-contributing countries to ensure that acts involving their personnel are properly investigated and punished;

23. *Calls upon* the Mission and the United Nations country team to further enhance their coordination and, in concert with the Government of Haiti and international partners, help to ensure greater efficiency in the implementation of the national strategy for growth and poverty reduction paper in order to achieve progress in the area of socio-economic development, which was recognized as essential for the stability of Haiti in the consolidation plan of the Secretary-General, and address urgent development problems, in particular those caused by recent hurricanes;

24. *Recognizes* the need for a high-level donor conference to lend its support to the national strategy for growth and poverty reduction paper, and in this regard calls upon the international community, in particular donor countries and partners of Haiti and multilateral institutions, in cooperation with the Haitian authorities, to devise and implement under the leadership of the Haitian authorities an efficient aid coordination system, based on mutual responsibility, which would focus on short-term immediate needs, as well as medium- and long-term reconstruction requirements, and also encourages donors and partners

of Haiti to accelerate the disbursement of their pledges as a contribution to development and stability in Haiti;

25. *Welcomes* the progress made by the Mission in its communications and public outreach strategy, and requests it to continue these activities;

26. *Also welcomes* the work done by the Secretary-General to develop five benchmarks and indicators to measure progress being made towards the consolidation of stability in Haiti, and requests the Secretary-General to continue updating the consolidation plan on the basis of the outline provided, in consultation with the Government of Haiti, taking into account the national strategy for growth and poverty reduction paper, as appropriate, and to inform the Council accordingly in his reports;

27. *Requests* the Secretary-General to report to the Council on the implementation of the mandate of the Mission semi-annually and no later than forty-five days prior to its expiration;

28. *Also requests* the Secretary-General to include in his reports a comprehensive assessment of threats to security in Haiti, taking into account a review of the activities and composition of the Mission, its coordination with the United Nations country team and other development actors and the need for poverty eradication and sustainable development in Haiti, and to propose, as appropriate, options to reshape the composition of the Mission;

29. *Decides* to remain seized of the matter.

Other developments. In a later report [S/2009/129], the Secretary-General said that there were indications of a new readiness among the political leadership to work together, owing to the crisis created by the series of hurricanes and tropical storms and by renewed tensions related to the senatorial elections. The Senate approved the *Déclaration de politique générale* of Michèle Duvivier Pierre-Louis on 5 September, and she was sworn in as Prime Minister on the same day. The Senate's action occurred against the background of a need to respond to the storms that hit the country in August and September, including tropical storm Hanna, which caused massive flooding and damage on 1 and 2 September, especially in the city of Gonaïves. The following week, the houses of Parliament passed a law allowing the President to declare a state of emergency, and thereby put in place a system of flexible disbursement of national funds to assist affected populations. President Préval drew upon that authority, enabling the Government to disburse $200 million in relief to hurricane victims. The private sector joined relief efforts by raising funds and in-kind assistance, while the international community also provided substantial assistance. On 30 September, the Parliament approved a revised 2007–2008 budget. The installation of the new Government was welcomed by MINUSTAH and the wider international community, which had sought to foster a collaborative approach to resolve the long-standing political impasse.

Despite those collaborative efforts, relations between the executive and legislative branches deteriorated in November, when parliamentarians expressed dissatisfaction with the new Government and questioned its management of post-disaster funds. On 27 November, five senators belonging to Lespwa, the main political formation represented in the Government, initiated the "interpellation" of the Minister of Economy and Finance, holding him responsible for Haiti's economic problems. Although the summons was later postponed, Parliament continued to hold numerous hearings with the Prime Minister and various cabinet ministers. In a positive development, on 9 and 10 December, representatives of the Government and Parliament, with support from MINUSTAH and donors, participated in a joint workshop which culminated in the adoption of an agreed legislative agenda for 2009. The agenda comprised 31 laws and 10 conventions, including measures that could assist in the consolidation of stability, such as legislation to curb corruption, and a draft customs code.

Progress was also made in the preparations for the elections. On 28 November, the Provisional Electoral Council launched the registration process for political parties and candidates for the elections. In order to comply with new requirements for voter access established by electoral law in July, the Council, with support from MINUSTAH, had identified 630 new voting centres throughout the country to supplement the 821 existing centres. Security assessment of the new centres, carried out jointly by HNP and the Mission, began in December and was expected to be completed in February 2009. On 29 December, President Préval, together with Prime Minister Pierre-Louis and members of her Government, issued a decree setting the first and second rounds of the partial senatorial elections for 19 April and 7 June 2009, respectively. MINUSTAH continued to provide technical, logistical and security assistance to the Council and other Haitian authorities in support of the electoral process.

The security situation remained fragile. Persistent poverty and youth unemployment in urban areas, aggravated by the destruction caused by the hurricanes and storms, created an environment that was vulnerable to renewed gang activity and instances of civil unrest. There were also reports of widespread trafficking in drugs and weapons throughout the country. The potential scale and impact of such activity was highlighted by an alleged theft of money linked to drug trafficking that took place in Port-de-Paix in November, which appeared to implicate members of the police and judiciary. MINUSTAH military and police personnel worked with HNP to deter criminal activities in urban areas and to improve information-sharing and collaboration with the general public, which paved the way for the dismantling of a number of kidnapping rings in the second half of the year.

In other activities, in October, MINUSTAH started producing and disseminating for broadcast on Haitian television stations a weekly video programme focusing on economic and social initiatives undertaken by Haitians, as well as on the international community's contributions towards achieving stability. An economist based at Oxford University visited Haiti from 1 to 5 December—at the request of the Secretary-General—to identify measures that could favour long-term economic recovery. He subsequently outlined a number of proposals, focusing in particular on job creation through the revival of export-driven industries. Two new legal aid offices were opened in Croix des Bouquets and Fort-Liberté in October, bringing the number of such offices to nine by the end of the year. On 10 December, the Minister of Justice announced the establishment of a new National Commission on Pretrial Detention to follow up on the recommendations of the previous Consultative Commission on Pretrial Detention.

Programme of support for Haiti

Ad Hoc Advisory Group. The Ad Hoc Advisory Group on Haiti, mandated by Economic and Social Council decision 2004/322 [YUN 2004, p. 939] to follow and advise on the long-term development of the country, submitted a June report [E/2008/90] that analysed the follow-up to recommendations in the Group's 2007 report [YUN 2007, p. 316] on key issues for the long-term development of Haiti, namely, development planning and aid coordination, institutional capacity-building, and levers for economic and social development. Progress was achieved with the finalization of the national growth and poverty strategy paper by the end of 2007, and the ongoing preparation by the UN system of the United Nations Development Assistance Framework. Other developments included the adoption by Parliament of legislation on magistrates and progress made in 2007 in macroeconomic performances, such as a growth rate of 3.2 per cent, reversing the negative trend since 2004. Improvement in economic governance resulted in an increase in remittances and donor flows, as well as debt relief by the Inter-American Development Bank, although negative social indicators, and their impact on the economic situation, persisted. The report also provided information on the food crisis that Haiti had been experiencing in previous months, which had led to an institutional and political vacuum, and on action needed to end the crisis. Observing that political stability was paramount to development work in Haiti and that 2008 was a pivotal year, the Group encouraged the timely installation of a new Government. The report concluded with recommendations aimed at improving the economic and social situation and the impact of development support.

The Economic and Social Council, in **resolution 2008/10** of 23 July (see p. 1021), extended the Group's mandate until July 2009.

MINUSTAH

In 2008, the United Nations Stabilization Mission in Haiti (MINUSTAH), established by Security Council resolution 1542(2004) [YUN 2004, p. 294], maintained its focus on ensuring a secure and stable environment, supporting the electoral process and reform of rule-of-law structures, strengthening State institutions, providing humanitarian and development assistance, and protecting and promoting human rights.

Based in Port-au-Prince, MINUSTAH continued to be headed by the Secretary-General's Special Representative for Haiti, Hédi Annabi (Tunisia), and Major General Carlos Alberto dos Santos Cruz (Brazil) remained in his role as Force Commander. By resolution 1840(2008), the Council extended MINUSTAH's mandate to 15 October 2009.

MINUSTAH activities

During 2008, the Secretary-General reported to the Security Council on MINUSTAH activities and developments in Haiti for the periods from 22 August 2007 to 26 March 2008 [S/2008/202] and 26 March to 27 August 2008 [S/2008/586]. Activities for the remainder of the year were covered in a later report [S/2009/129]. In addition to political and security aspects, the reports summarized MINUSTAH activities dealing with human rights; child protection; the humanitarian and development situation; gender issues; reform of rule-of-law structures; the consolidation plan; strengthening of the State; the conduct and discipline of UN personnel; and Mission support.

Human rights. The situation in the country remained better than that experienced before the February 2006 elections [YUN 2006, p. 345]. Nonetheless, a number of problems persisted, with several due to continuing weaknesses in rule-of-law institutions, such as arrest without valid charges, evidence or proper judicial oversight; detention records and investigation reports that were difficult to track, poor in quality or non-existent; and a judicial system undermined by shortcomings in criminal investigations and delays in implementing decisions, which contributed to the high level of pretrial detentions. Lynching remained a widespread problem. From August 2007 to January 2008, some 66 incidents were reported that resulted in deaths of 30 individuals and injuries to 45 others. MINUSTAH supported the adoption of enabling legislation on the Office of the Ombudsman and worked to improve the Office's visibility through joint programming. It also organized training on human rights, law enforcement and due process standards for police officers, magistrates and national human rights non-governmental organizations (NGOs). In cooperation with the Office of the United Nations High Commissioner for Human Rights, a workshop on reporting to international treaty monitoring bodies was conducted for ministry representatives in advance of the establishment of an inter-ministerial commission to prepare the country's second periodic report to the Committee on the Rights of the Child. The Mission also supported the work of the Office of Citizen Protection, the sole independent human rights institution foreseen by the Constitution. In the wake of the August–September storms, the ability of the Haitian people to enjoy basic economic, social and cultural rights suffered a decline. During her visit to Haiti in November, the UN High Commissioner for Human Rights called for reinforced support for the victims of the hurricanes. The Independent Expert on the situation of human rights in Haiti also visited the country in November and emphasized the link between extreme poverty and instability.

Child protection. The improved security situation resulted in a significant reduction in the number of children affected by armed violence. However, areas of concern remained, including the kidnapping and trafficking of children, the rape of girls, and the number of minors held in pretrial detention, which increased to 266 in February 2008 from 226 in July 2007. Between March and August 2008, children represented 35 per cent of kidnapping victims, while two minors were killed by their captors. MINUSTAH produced radio messages by Haitian musician Wyclef Jean condemning kidnapping and sexual violence against children. The Juvenile Court, which drew on MINUSTAH technical assistance, became increasingly efficient, and the number of minors held in pretrial detention fell to 246 in June. Other areas of concern included the situation of children in institutional care centres; the increase in the trafficking of children to the Dominican Republic for labour and sexual exploitation; and the impact of the 2008 hurricane season on the educational system. Due to the destruction of school structures and the use of schools as temporary shelters, the start of the school year was delayed in various areas. Positive developments included the adoption of an implementation plan for the national Education for All strategy, the appointment of juvenile judges throughout the country between October and December and the establishment of a juvenile tribunal in Cap Haïtien. MINUSTAH and the United Nations Children's Fund (UNICEF) trained HNP officers, while the police appointed 50 regional child protection focal points in all 10 departments of Haiti. The Mission, UNDP and UNICEF worked with the Ministries of Justice and Social Affairs to improve the administration of justice for children in detention and were supporting Government efforts to strengthen the monitoring of institutional care centres.

Humanitarian situation. In 2008, Haiti suffered setbacks owing to rapidly rising global food and fuel prices, food insecurity, inflation and the impact of four successive hurricanes and tropical storms that hit Haiti in August and early September. Progress was undermined in numerous key areas, such as the country's gross domestic product, State revenue, agricultural and industrial production, the delivery of basic services, job creation and the percentage of the population living on less than $1 per day. The increase in food and fuel prices resulted in a food crisis, to which the authorities responded by outlining proposals such as price supports and revenue-generating, labour-intensive activities, together with a longer-term programme to enhance agriculture. National authorities indicated that food insecurity affected some 2.5 million Haitians. The immediate human cost of the hurricanes and storms included 793 deaths, 548 persons injured and 310 persons missing, while the damage or destruction of approximately 100,000 houses and the loss of livelihoods affected more than 165,000 families, especially in the Artibonite, South and South-East Departments. The Government estimated that more than 800,000 people were affected and in need of humanitarian assistance in 9 of the country's 10 departments. Damage to roads and bridges hampered recovery efforts and reduced access to basic services, including health care, water and nutrition. Pockets of malnutrition were identified all over the country, affecting some 210,000 persons. In the immediate aftermath of the hurricanes, MINUSTAH, the UN system, NGOs and bilateral donors supported the authorities by delivering emergency assistance and relief supplies to affected populations, focusing on urgent needs such as shelter, nutrition, water, sanitation and protection. MINUSTAH military, police and logistical components played a key role in undertaking rescue operations; provided immediate security; facilitated the delivery of emergency supplies; and shored up collapsing infrastructure immediately after the hurricanes. Mission efforts were supplemented by bilateral partners, whose swift and generous response made a critical difference in rescue and relief efforts.

Development. In macroeconomic terms, Haiti continued to make progress in stabilizing the economy under the International Monetary Fund (IMF) Poverty Reduction and Growth Facility programme. Following a 3.2 per cent rise in gross domestic product (GDP) and a decline in the inflation rate to 7.6 per cent in 2007, which rose to 11 per cent in January 2008, the IMF, nonetheless, estimated a continued GDP growth rate of 4.3 per cent during the year. With donor support, the MINUSTAH military component completed a series of small-scale projects aimed at delivering a peace dividend to more than 25,000 people in communities most affected by violence. The Mission also pursued, along with the World Bank, the provision of a grant to support infrastructure improvements that would facilitate operational activities and favour local development. In May, the UN country team submitted the first draft of the UN Development Assistance Framework (UNDAF), which outlined development strategies in Haiti for the period 2009–2011 for all UN agencies, funds, and programmes, and most civilian sections of MINUSTAH. However, increasing global food and fuel prices during the first half of 2008 posed a threat to Haiti's stability. Inflation doubled to 15.8 per cent in June and economic growth forecasts for the country were revised downwards from 3.7 per cent to 2.5 per cent. Official estimates indicated that 2008 GDP growth slowed to 1.3 per cent. The 12-month inflation rate peaked at 19.8 per cent in September, yet fell to 10.1 per cent by the end of December. A post-disaster needs assessment, prepared by the Government with the support of the World Bank, the European Commission and the United Nations, outlined a framework for early recovery, rehabilitation and reconstruction; needs were estimated at $763 million. In November, the UNDAF was approved as a UN common response in support of the poverty reduction strategy paper 2008–2010, with requirements of $520 million for its implementation during the next three years.

Gender. In February, in collaboration with the Ministry of Women's Affairs and Rights, MINUSTAH hosted a high-level delegation from the UN Division for the Advancement of Women and supported the validation process of the Government's initial report on the Convention on the Elimination of All Forms of Discrimination against Women. The Mission also worked with other UN system entities to support the National Plan of Action to Combat Violence against Women. According to national findings, there appeared to be an increase in the number of documented cases of physical and sexual violence against women and minors and a decrease in the number of reported gang rapes. It seemed that improved security and access to assistance, as well as public information campaigns, had motivated more victims of violence to seek help. MINUSTAH police assisted the HNP in strengthening its capacity to prevent and respond to violence against women and girls, including through training programmes. The Mission and HNP jointly initiated an information campaign in schools to increase children's awareness of women's rights and of punishable crimes under the Penal Code, such as rape and domestic violence. In June, the Mission conducted a series of regional workshops to identify obstacles to the participation of women in politics. Also in June, the Government submitted its first report to the Committee on the Elimination of All Forms of Discrimination Against Women. The Mission carried out a three-week programme entitled "Women in Action" to commemorate the adoption of Security Council resolution 1325(2000) [YUN 2000, p. 1113], and to mark the International Day for the Elimination of Violence Against Women, on 25 November, bringing together approximately 4,500 participants in 88 activities.

Other activities. In addition to routine tasks, key Mission support activities included the logistical facilitation of the military and police deployment at the four land border crossings with the Dominican Republic. Reconnaissance trips for eight seaport border locations were completed early in the year in preparation for the deployment of maritime assets when they became available, and by August, the development of coastal installations was under way to accommodate the maritime component of the Mission. MINUSTAH continued to integrate HIV/AIDS awareness and training into its activities, and to promote and maintain the availability of voluntary counselling and confidential testing at two permanent sites and through one mobile team. Following the series of storms and hurricanes that struck the country, MINUSTAH provided extensive assistance to Haitian authorities and the UN country team to facilitate the provision and coordination of humanitarian assistance and access by humanitarian personnel, including through large-scale transportation operations. In other efforts, MINUSTAH conducted road infrastructure and rehabilitation projects; undertook construction activity to deploy troops and equipment along the maritime border; extended coverage of Radio MINUSTAH to the Centre Department; began logistical support preparations for the senatorial elections; and supported a countrywide campaign organized jointly by the World Health Organization and UNICEF, by which some 3.7 million children were vaccinated in 2008.

Financing of MINUSTAH

In January [A/62/631], the Secretary-General submitted the performance report on the budget of MINUSTAH for the period from 1 July 2006 to 30 June 2007, in which he recommended that the General Assembly should decide on the treatment of the unencumbered balance of $5,187,000 and other income and adjustments amounting to $34,594,200 for the period ended 30 June 2007.

On 5 March [A/62/720], the Secretary-General submitted to the Assembly the MINUSTAH budget for the period from 1 July 2008 to 30 June 2009, which amounted to $575,103,200 gross and provided for the deployment of 7,060 military personnel, 951 UN police officers, 1,140 formed police personnel, 550 international staff, 1,288 national staff, 220 UN Volunteers and 16 government-provided personnel, including temporary positions.

ACABQ report. In a 7 May report [A/62/781/Add.6], the Advisory Committee on Administrative and Budgetary Questions (ACABQ) identified reductions totalling $186,700. It therefore recommended that the General Assembly appropriate $574,916,500 for the period 1 July 2008 to 30 June 2009; and that the unencumbered balance and the amount resulting from other income and adjustments for the period 1 July 2006 to 30 June 2007 be credited to Member States in a manner to be determined by the Assembly.

GENERAL ASSEMBLY ACTION

On 20 June [meeting 109], the General Assembly, on the recommendation of the Fifth (Administrative and Budgetary) Committee [A/62/874], adopted **resolution 62/261** without vote [agenda item 150].

Financing of the United Nations Stabilization Mission in Haiti

The General Assembly,

Having considered the reports of the Secretary-General on the financing of the United Nations Stabilization Mission in Haiti and the related report of the Advisory Committee on Administrative and Budgetary Questions,

Recalling Security Council resolution 1529(2004) of 29 February 2004, by which the Council declared its readiness to establish a United Nations stabilization force to support continuation of a peaceful and constitutional political process and the maintenance of a secure and stable environment in Haiti,

Recalling also Security Council resolution 1542(2004) of 30 April 2004, by which the Council decided to establish the United Nations Stabilization Mission in Haiti for an initial period of six months, and the subsequent resolutions by which the Council extended the mandate of the Mission, the latest of which was resolution 1780(2007) of 15 October 2007, by which the Council extended the mandate of the Mission until 15 October 2008,

Recalling further its resolution 58/315 of 1 July 2004,

Recalling its resolution 58/311 of 1 June 2004 on the financing of the Mission and its subsequent resolutions thereon, the latest of which was resolution 61/284 of 29 June 2007,

Reaffirming the general principles underlying the financing of United Nations peacekeeping operations, as stated in General Assembly resolutions 1874(S-IV) of 27 June 1963, 3101(XXVIII) of 11 December 1973 and 55/235 of 23 December 2000,

Mindful of the fact that it is essential to provide the Mission with the financial resources necessary to enable it to fulfil its responsibilities under the relevant resolutions of the Security Council,

1. *Requests* the Secretary-General to entrust the Head of Mission with the task of formulating future budget proposals in full accordance with the provisions of General Assembly resolutions 59/296 of 22 June 2005, 60/266 of 30 June 2006 and 61/276 of 29 June 2007, as well as other relevant resolutions;

2. *Takes note* of the status of contributions to the United Nations Stabilization Mission in Haiti as at 31 March 2008, including the contributions outstanding in the amount of 171.5 million United States dollars, representing some 10 per cent of the total assessed contributions, notes with concern that only sixty-three Member States have paid their assessed contributions in full, and urges all other Member States, in particular those in arrears, to ensure payment of their outstanding assessed contributions;

3. *Expresses its appreciation* to those Member States which have paid their assessed contributions in full, and urges all other Member States to make every possible effort to ensure payment of their assessed contributions to the Mission in full;

4. *Expresses concern* at the financial situation with regard to peacekeeping activities, in particular as regards the reimbursements to troop contributors that bear additional burdens owing to overdue payments by Member States of their assessments;

5. *Also expresses concern* at the delay experienced by the Secretary-General in deploying and providing adequate resources to some recent peacekeeping missions, in particular those in Africa;

6. *Emphasizes* that all future and existing peacekeeping missions shall be given equal and non-discriminatory treatment in respect of financial and administrative arrangements;

7. *Also emphasizes* that all peacekeeping missions shall be provided with adequate resources for the effective and efficient discharge of their respective mandates;

8. *Reiterates its request* to the Secretary-General to make the fullest possible use of facilities and equipment at the United Nations Logistics Base at Brindisi, Italy, in order to minimize the costs of procurement for the Mission;

9. *Endorses* the conclusions and recommendations contained in the report of the Advisory Committee on Administrative and Budgetary Questions, subject to the provisions of the present resolution, and requests the Secretary-General to ensure their full implementation;

10. *Decides* to approve the upgrade and redeployment of one P-5 post from the Civil Affairs Section to the Office of the Principal Deputy Special Representative of the Secretary-General;

11. *Also decides* to approve the establishment of fourteen national General Service temporary positions for Drivers;

12. *Requests* the Secretary-General to make every effort for the Mission to comply with United Nations aviation safety standards, in particular regarding meteorological information and firefighting equipment;

13. *Also requests* the Secretary-General to strengthen the coordination between the Mission, the United Nations country team and other United Nations entities, including in addressing the root causes of unexpected emergencies such as the unrest generated by the recent food crisis in Haiti;

14. *Further requests* the Secretary-General to take all necessary steps to address the high vacancy rate in national posts as a matter of urgency;

15. *Decides* to allocate up to 2 million dollars for quick-impact projects for the period from 1 July 2008 to 30 June 2009;

16. *Also decides* that quick-impact projects shall be conducted by the Mission in accordance with the requirements set out in resolution 61/276, and requests the Secretary-General to report thereon to the General Assembly at its sixty-third session;

17. *Requests* the Secretary-General to ensure the full implementation of the relevant provisions of its resolutions 59/296, 60/266 and 61/276;

18. *Also requests* the Secretary-General to take all necessary action to ensure that the Mission is administered with a maximum of efficiency and economy;

19. *Further requests* the Secretary-General, in order to reduce the cost of employing General Service staff, to continue efforts to recruit local staff for the Mission against General Service posts, commensurate with the requirements of the Mission;

Financial performance report for the period from 1 July 2006 to 30 June 2007

20. *Takes note* of the report of the Secretary-General on the financial performance of the Mission for the period from 1 July 2006 to 30 June 2007;

Budget estimates for the period from 1 July 2008 to 30 June 2009

21. *Decides* to appropriate to the Special Account for the United Nations Stabilization Mission in Haiti the amount of 601,580,100 dollars for the period from 1 July 2008 to 30 June 2009, inclusive of 574,916,500 dollars for the maintenance of the Mission, 23,243,500 dollars for the support account for peacekeeping operations and 3,420,100 dollars for the United Nations Logistics Base;

Financing of the appropriation

22. *Also decides* to apportion among Member States the amount of 175,460,862 dollars for the period from 1 July to 15 October 2008, in accordance with the levels updated in General Assembly resolution 61/243 of 22 December 2006, and taking into account the scale of assessments for 2008, as set out in its resolution 61/237 of 22 December 2006;

23. *Further decides* that, in accordance with the provisions of its resolution 973(X) of 15 December 1955, there shall be set off against the apportionment among Member States, as provided for in paragraph 22 above, their respective share in the Tax Equalization Fund of 4,557,495 dollars, comprising the estimated staff assessment income of 3,827,308 dollars approved for the Mission, the prorated share of 651,379 dollars of the estimated staff assessment income approved for the support account and the prorated share of 78,808 dollars of the estimated staff assessment income approved for the United Nations Logistics Base;

24. *Decides* to apportion among Member States the amount of 426,119,238 dollars for the period from 16 October 2008 to 30 June 2009 at a monthly rate of 50,131,675 dollars, in accordance with the levels updated in resolution 61/243, and taking into account the scale of assessments for 2008 and 2009, as set out in resolution 61/237, subject to a decision of the Security Council to extend the mandate of the Mission;

25. *Also decides* that, in accordance with the provisions of its resolution 973(X), there shall be set off against the apportionment among Member States, as provided for in paragraph 24 above, their respective share in the Tax Equalization Fund of 11,068,205 dollars, comprising the estimated staff assessment income of 9,294,892 dollars approved for the Mission, the prorated share of 1,581,921 dollars of the estimated staff assessment income approved for the support account and the prorated share of 191,392 dollars of the estimated staff assessment income approved for the United Nations Logistics Base;

26. *Further decides* that, for Member States that have fulfilled their financial obligations to the Mission, there shall be set off against their apportionment, as provided for in paragraph 22 above, their respective share of the unencumbered balance and other income in the total amount of 39,781,200 dollars in respect of the financial period ended 30 June 2007, in accordance with the levels updated in resolution 61/243, and taking into account the scale of assessments for 2007, as set out in resolution 61/237;

27. *Decides* that, for Member States that have not fulfilled their financial obligations to the Mission, there shall be set off against their outstanding obligations their respective share of the unencumbered balance and other income in the total amount of 39,781,200 dollars in respect of the financial period ended 30 June 2007, in accordance with the scheme set out in paragraph 26 above;

28. *Also decides* that the decrease of 85,200 dollars in the estimated staff assessment income in respect of the financial period ended 30 June 2007 shall be set off against the credits from the amount of 39,781,200 dollars referred to in paragraphs 26 and 27 above;

29. *Emphasizes* that no peacekeeping mission shall be financed by borrowing funds from other active peacekeeping missions;

30. *Encourages* the Secretary-General to continue to take additional measures to ensure the safety and security of all personnel participating in the Mission under the auspices of the United Nations, bearing in mind paragraphs 5 and 6 of Security Council resolution 1502(2003) of 26 August 2003;

31. *Invites* voluntary contributions to the Mission in cash and in the form of services and supplies acceptable to the Secretary-General, to be administered, as appropriate, in accordance with the procedure and practices established by the General Assembly;

32. *Decides* to include in the provisional agenda of its sixty-third session the item entitled "Financing of the United Nations Stabilization Mission in Haiti".

On 24 December, by **decision 63/552**, the Assembly decided that the item on financing of MINUSTAH would remain for consideration during its resumed sixty-third (2009) session.

Other questions

Colombia–Ecuador

In a 3 March letter [S/2008/146] to the Security Council, Ecuador reported that on 1 March, military aircraft and army police personnel from Colombia made incursions into Ecuadorian territory in the Province of Sucumbios. After clashing with members of the Revolutionary Armed Forces of Colombia (FARC), they killed 17 people, including high-ranking leaders of that irregular Colombian group. In the context of those events, Colombian State forces entered the territory of Ecuador, took possession of a number of bodies and transported them back to Colombia. Expressing disappointment over the actions of the Colombian forces and noting the lack of bilateral cooperation in the operations, Ecuador stated that the events constituted a violation of its territorial integrity and that it would make use of all available security resources to prevent any recurrence of those circumstances. Ecuador called for the peaceful solution to Colombia's internal conflict and said that it stood ready to contribute to humanitarian efforts to achieve peace and understanding in Colombia.

On 13 March, in identical letters to the Secretary-General and the Security Council [S/2008/177], Ecuador reiterated its position on the internal conflict in Colombia; stated that it was a victim and not the facilitator of the conflict; and reported on steps taken concerning FARC members who were crossing the border, including the deployment of 11,000 members of the armed forces and police to their shared border. Ecuador also confirmed its non-interference in the internal affairs of Colombia, in accordance with international law.

Cuba–United States

In response to General Assembly resolution 62/3 [YUN 2007, p. 321], the Secretary-General submitted an August report [A/63/93] on information received from 116 States, one non-Member State, the European Union and 22 UN bodies, as at 23 July, on the implementation of that resolution. The resolution had called on States to refrain from the unilateral application of economic and trade measures against other States, and urged them to repeal or invalidate such measures. In October [A/63/93/Add.1], he transmitted information received from one additional State.

GENERAL ASSEMBLY ACTION

On 29 October [meeting 33], the General Assembly adopted **resolution 63/7** [draft: A/63/L.4] by recorded vote (185-3-2) [agenda item 19].

Necessity of ending the economic, commercial and financial embargo imposed by the United States of America against Cuba

The General Assembly,

Determined to encourage strict compliance with the purposes and principles enshrined in the Charter of the United Nations,

Reaffirming, among other principles, the sovereign equality of States, non-intervention and non-interference in their internal affairs and freedom of international trade and navigation, which are also enshrined in many international legal instruments,

Recalling the statements of the Heads of State or Government at the Ibero-American Summits concerning the need to eliminate unilateral application of economic and trade measures by one State against another that affect the free flow of international trade,

Concerned at the continued promulgation and application by Member States of laws and regulations, such as that promulgated on 12 March 1996 known as the "Helms-Burton Act", the extraterritorial effects of which affect the sovereignty of other States, the legitimate interests of entities or persons under their jurisdiction and the freedom of trade and navigation,

Taking note of declarations and resolutions of different intergovernmental forums, bodies and Governments that express the rejection by the international community and public opinion of the promulgation and application of measures of the kind referred to above,

Recalling its resolutions 47/19 of 24 November 1992, 48/16 of 3 November 1993, 49/9 of 26 October 1994, 50/10 of 2 November 1995, 51/17 of 12 November 1996, 52/10 of 5 November 1997, 53/4 of 14 October 1998, 54/21 of 9 November 1999, 55/20 of 9 November 2000, 56/9 of 27 November 2001, 57/11 of 12 November 2002, 58/7 of 4 November 2003, 59/11 of 28 October 2004, 60/12 of 8 November 2005, 61/11 of 8 November 2006 and 62/3 of 30 October 2007,

Concerned that, since the adoption of its resolutions 47/19, 48/16, 49/9, 50/10, 51/17, 52/10, 53/4, 54/21, 55/20, 56/9, 57/11, 58/7, 59/11, 60/12, 61/11 and 62/3, further measures of that nature aimed at strengthening and extending the economic, commercial and financial embargo against Cuba continue to be promulgated and applied, and concerned also at the adverse effects of such measures on the Cuban people and on Cuban nationals living in other countries,

1. *Takes note* of the report of the Secretary-General on the implementation of resolution 62/3;

2. *Reiterates its call upon* all States to refrain from promulgating and applying laws and measures of the kind referred to in the preamble to the present resolution, in conformity with their obligations under the Charter of the United Nations and international law, which, inter alia, reaffirm the freedom of trade and navigation;

3. *Once again urges* States that have and continue to apply such laws and measures to take the necessary steps to repeal or invalidate them as soon as possible in accordance with their legal regime;

4. *Requests* the Secretary-General, in consultation with the appropriate organs and agencies of the United Nations system, to prepare a report on the implementation of the present resolution in the light of the purposes and principles of the Charter and international law and to submit it to the General Assembly at its sixty-fourth session;

5. *Decides* to include in the provisional agenda of its sixty-fourth session the item entitled "Necessity of ending the economic, commercial and financial embargo imposed by the United States of America against Cuba".

RECORDED VOTE ON RESOLUTION 63/7:

In favour: Afghanistan, Albania, Algeria, Andorra, Angola, Antigua and Barbuda, Argentina, Armenia, Australia, Austria, Azerbaijan, Bahamas, Bahrain, Bangladesh, Barbados, Belarus, Belgium, Belize, Benin, Bhutan, Bolivia, Bosnia and Herzegovina, Botswana, Brazil, Brunei Darussalam, Bulgaria, Burkina Faso, Burundi, Cambodia, Cameroon, Canada, Cape Verde, Central African Republic, Chad, Chile, China, Colombia, Comoros, Congo, Costa Rica, Côte d'Ivoire, Croatia, Cuba, Cyprus, Czech Republic, Democratic People's Republic of Korea, Democratic Republic of the Congo, Denmark, Djibouti, Dominica, Dominican Republic, Ecuador, Egypt, Equatorial Guinea, Eritrea, Estonia, Ethiopia, Fiji, Finland, France, Gabon, Gambia, Georgia, Germany, Ghana, Greece, Grenada, Guatemala, Guinea, Guinea-Bissau, Guyana, Haiti, Honduras, Hungary, Iceland, India, Indonesia, Iran, Ireland, Italy, Jamaica, Japan, Jordan, Kazakhstan, Kenya, Kiribati, Kuwait, Kyrgyzstan, Lao People's Democratic Republic, Latvia, Lebanon, Lesotho, Liberia, Libyan Arab Jamahiriya, Liechtenstein, Lithuania, Luxembourg, Madagascar, Malawi, Malaysia, Maldives, Mali, Malta, Mauritania, Mauritius, Mexico, Moldova, Monaco, Mongolia, Montenegro, Morocco, Mozambique, Myanmar, Namibia, Nauru, Nepal, Netherlands, New Zealand, Nicaragua, Niger, Nigeria, Norway, Oman, Pakistan, Panama, Papua New Guinea, Paraguay, Peru, Philippines, Poland, Portugal, Qatar, Republic of Korea, Romania, Russian Federation, Rwanda, Saint Kitts and Nevis, Saint Lucia, Saint Vincent and the Grenadines, Samoa, San Marino, Sao Tome and Principe, Saudi Arabia, Senegal, Serbia, Seychelles, Sierra Leone, Singapore, Slovakia, Slovenia, Solomon Islands, Somalia, South Africa, Spain, Sri Lanka, Sudan, Suriname, Swaziland, Sweden, Switzerland, Syrian Arab Republic, Tajikistan, Thailand, The former Yugoslav Republic of Macedonia, Timor-Leste, Togo, Tonga, Trinidad and Tobago, Tunisia, Turkey, Turkmenistan, Tuvalu, Uganda, Ukraine, United Arab Emirates, United Kingdom, United Republic of Tanzania, Uruguay, Uzbekistan, Vanuatu, Venezuela, Viet Nam, Yemen, Zambia, Zimbabwe.

Against: Israel, Palau, United States.

Abstaining: Marshall Islands, Micronesia.

Communications. On 23 April [A/62/821-S/2008/279], Cuba transmitted a statement on the upcoming one-year anniversary (8 May) of the unconditional release of alleged terrorist Luis Posada Carriles in the United States [YUN 2007, p. 322]. It reiterated its call for the United States to respond to Venezuela's 2005 request for the extradition of Mr. Carriles [YUN 2005, p. 394]; stated that other alleged terrorists had received equally lenient treatment; and observed that, in contrast, on 12 September 2008, five alleged anti-terrorist crusaders would have been detained unjustly in United States prisons for 10 years. Other communications from Cuba addressed the alleged relationship between United States diplomats in Havana, alleged terrorists of Cuban origin in Miami, and mercenary activities in Cuba [A/63/281-S/2008/431] and a request for items to be retained on the list of matters of which the Security Council was seized [S/2008/136].

Cooperation between the United Nations and regional organizations

Caribbean Community

The Secretary-General, in response to General Assembly resolution 58/316 [YUN 2004, p. 1374], submitted, in his August consolidated report [A/63/228-S/2008/531 & Corr.1] on cooperation between the United Nations and regional organizations, a summary of UN/Caribbean Community (CARICOM) collaborative activities, which highlighted consultations with the UN Department of Political Affairs (DPA) aimed at improving bilateral cooperation and the flow of information between its officials and CARICOM's Office of the Assistant Secretary-General for Foreign and Community Relations; the 13 March meeting between the DPA Under-Secretary-General, permanent representatives and other officials of the CARICOM Caucus to discuss the UN Secretary-General's proposals to strengthen the Department; the participation of a joint United Nations Office on Drugs and Crime/DPA delegation in the presentation of a report entitled *Crime, Violence and Development: Trends, Cost and Policy Options in the Caribbean* to the fifth meeting of the Caribbean Council of Ministers Responsible for National Security and Law Enforcement in April; and the organization of a High-level Round Table on International Cooperation for Sustainable Development in Caribbean Small Island Developing States (Bridgetown, Barbados, 25–27 March) by the UN Department of Economic and Social Affairs, in cooperation with Barbados and Iceland. The meeting explored possibilities for the development of new international partnerships, particularly in the area of renewable energy and sustainable fisheries. In other activity, the Department of Public Information and CARICOM organized a series of events in observance of the International Day for the Elimination of Racial Discrimination (21 March) and the International Day of Remembrance of the Victims of Slavery and the Transatlantic Slave Trade (25 March). The report also covered CARICOM activities with various UN system bodies to address issues such as environmental and sustainable development programmes; building South-South linkages between Caribbean small island developing States; climate change; and the situation of children, including adolescents and youths, and other aspects such as early childhood development, education of children and child protection.

GENERAL ASSEMBLY ACTION

On 26 November [meeting 60], the General Assembly adopted **resolution 63/34** [draft: A/63/L.38 & Add.1] without vote [agenda item 114 *(e)*].

Cooperation between the United Nations and the Caribbean Community

The General Assembly,

Recalling its resolutions 46/8 of 16 October 1991, 49/141 of 20 December 1994, 51/16 of 11 November 1996, 53/17 of 29 October 1998, 55/17 of 7 November 2000, 57/41 of 21 November 2002, 59/138 of 10 December 2004 and 61/50 of 4 December 2006,

Bearing in mind the provisions of Chapter VIII of the Charter of the United Nations on the existence of regional arrangements or agencies for dealing with such matters relating to the maintenance of international peace and security as are appropriate for regional action and other activities consistent with the purposes and principles of the United Nations,

Bearing in mind also, in this regard, the cooperation activities undertaken by the United Nations and the Caribbean Community in fields related to prohibiting and restricting the use of certain conventional weapons, preventing and eradicating the illicit trade in narcotic drugs, small arms and light weapons and the proliferation of weapons of mass destruction,

Recalling the fruitful and action-oriented exchanges that have taken place between the two organizations following the signing on 27 May 1997 by the Secretary-General of the United Nations and the Secretary-General of the Caribbean Community of a cooperation agreement between the secretariats of the two organizations,

Bearing in mind that, in its resolutions 54/225 of 22 December 1999, 55/203 of 20 December 2000, 57/261 of 20 December 2002, 59/230 of 22 December 2004 and 61/197 of 20 December 2006, it recognized the importance of adopting an integrated management approach to the Caribbean Sea area in the context of sustainable development,

Bearing in mind also the support that the Caribbean Community has received from the United Nations for its efforts to advance its implementation of the Mauritius Strategy for the Further Implementation of the Programme of Action for the Sustainable Development of Small Island Developing States, including in the areas of exploring possibilities for renewable energy and sustainable fisheries,

Noting the support that the United Nations Environment Programme has been extending to the environmental and sustainable development programmes of the Caribbean Community, including its close collaboration with the Sustainable Development Unit of the Caribbean Community Secretariat, and related national and regional institutions,

Expressing appreciation, in this context, for the technical role of the United Nations Environment Programme in building cooperation linkages among the small island developing States of the Caribbean Community, and in facilitating the assessment by them of the implications of their adaptation to climate change, which will guide future United Nations Environment Programme climate change programmes in the region,

Noting that the World Summit on Sustainable Development considered the specific issues and problems facing small island developing States, taking note in this regard of the Monterrey Consensus of the International Conference on Financing for Development, and noting the outcome of the International Meeting to Review the Implementation of the Programme of Action for the Sustainable Development of Small Island Developing States,

Noting also that the Caribbean region is the second most hazard-prone region in the world and is frequently exposed to devastating hazards including earthquakes, floods, hurricanes and volcanic eruptions,

Noting further that, in recent months, parts of the Caribbean region, in particular Haiti, have been hard hit, and in some cases devastated, by hurricanes, and concerned that their frequency, intensity and destructive power continue to pose a challenge to the development of the region,

Taking note of the report by the Secretary-General on implementation of the Declaration of Commitment on HIV/AIDS and the Political Declaration on HIV/AIDS, in particular his conclusion that while per capita domestic spending on HIV in low-income and lower middle-income countries has continued to increase, the current pace of scale-up will not meet the estimated resources needed to achieve universal access to HIV prevention, treatment, care and support by 2010,

Taking note with appreciation of the joint statement of the fourth general meeting of representatives of the Caribbean Community and the United Nations system, held in Turkeyen, Guyana, on 25 and 26 January 2007,

Taking note with appreciation also of the number of consultations and information exchanges that have been taking place between officials of the two organizations aimed at strengthening their bilateral cooperation in such areas as crime, drug abuse control and violence,

Gravely concerned about the current daunting international environment, characterized by, inter alia, crises in food and energy security, the impact of global warming and an international financial system in turmoil, all of which create enormous challenges for the development efforts of the countries of the Caribbean Community,

Affirming the consequent need to further strengthen the cooperation that already exists between entities of the United Nations system and the Caribbean Community in the areas of economic and social development and of political and humanitarian affairs,

Convinced of the need for the coordinated utilization of available resources to promote the common objectives of the two organizations,

Having considered the report of the Secretary-General on cooperation between the United Nations and regional and other organizations,

1. *Takes note* of the report of the Secretary-General, in particular section II.E on the Caribbean Community, concerning efforts to strengthen and deepen cooperation;

2. *Calls upon* the Secretary-General of the United Nations, in association with the Secretary-General of the Caribbean Community, as well as the relevant regional organizations, to continue to assist in furthering the development and maintenance of peace and security within the Caribbean region;

3. *Invites* the Secretary-General to continue to promote and expand cooperation and coordination between the United Nations and the Caribbean Community in order to increase the capacity of the two organizations to attain their objectives;

4. *Calls for*, in this context, vastly increased efforts by developed countries to strengthen the multilateral develop-

ment framework so that the United Nations development system may respond more effectively to the needs of programme countries, so that they, including the countries of the Caribbean Community, can pursue their development efforts on the basis of secure and predictable funding;

5. *Urges* the specialized agencies and other organizations and programmes of the United Nations system to step up their cooperation with the Secretary-General of the United Nations and the Secretary-General of the Caribbean Community with a view to intensifying their consultations and programmes of cooperation with the Caribbean Community and its associated institutions in the attainment of their objectives, with special attention to the areas and issues identified by the two organizations at their fourth general meeting, held in January 2007, as set out in the report of the Secretary-General, as well as in its resolutions 54/225, 55/2 of 8 September 2000, 55/203 and S-26/2 of 27 June 2001 and the decisions of the World Summit on Sustainable Development, and of the International Meeting to Review the Implementation of the Programme of Action for the Sustainable Development of Small Island Developing States, as well as the Monterrey Consensus of the International Conference on Financing for Development;

6. *Takes note* of the exchanges in progress between the United Nations Industrial Development Organization and the Caribbean Community aimed at the design and implementation of programmes for enhancing the industrial development capacity of the countries of the Caribbean Community;

7. *Also takes note* of the various cooperation activities between the Caribbean Community and the Food and Agriculture Organization of the United Nations designed to increase agricultural output and improve food security in the region by modernizing agricultural production and developing sustainable agricultural strategies;

8. *Invites* the organizations of the United Nations system, as well as Member States, to increase financial and other assistance to the countries of the Caribbean Community to help to implement the priorities of the Caribbean Regional Strategic Framework for HIV/AIDS, which sets out realistic targets for reducing the rate of new infections, raising the quality and coverage of care, treatment and support and building institutional capacity, and to cope with the problems and the burden caused by the HIV/AIDS pandemic;

9. *Stresses* the urgent need for the reopening of the office of the United Nations Office on Drugs and Crime in the region so as to reinforce the efforts of the States of the region in their struggle against the interrelated scourges of drugs, violent crime and the illicit trade in small arms and light weapons;

10. *Expresses appreciation* for the cooperation received from the Department of Public Information of the Secretariat in the implementation of the activities commemorating on 25 March 2007 the two-hundredth anniversary of the abolition of the transatlantic slave trade, the commemoration of which is to be observed on an annual basis;

11. *Also expresses appreciation* for the continuing support and cooperation being received from the Department of Public Information in the preparatory activities for establishing a permanent memorial to the victims of slavery and the transatlantic slave trade, in keeping with General Assembly resolution 62/122 of 17 December 2007;

12. *Invites* the Secretary-General to consider utilizing a strategic programming framework modality to strengthen the coordination and cooperation between the two secretariats as well as between the United Nations field offices and the Caribbean Community;

13. *Calls upon* the United Nations, the specialized agencies and other organizations and programmes of the United Nations system to assist the countries of the Caribbean in addressing the social and economic consequences of the vulnerability of Caribbean economies and the challenges that this poses for achieving the Millennium Development Goals and the goal of sustainable development;

14. *Reaffirms* the objective of strengthening the implementation of the Mauritius Strategy for the Further Implementation of the Programme of Action for the Sustainable Development of Small Island Developing States, including through the mobilization of financial and technological resources, as well as capacity-building programmes;

15. *Welcomes* the extensive work done by the Commission on the Caribbean Sea since the adoption of General Assembly resolution 61/197 entitled "Towards the sustainable development of the Caribbean Sea for present and future generations", including the development of institutional and legal frameworks for Caribbean Sea governance;

16. *Also welcomes* the initiatives of Member States in assisting in the cooperation between the United Nations and the Caribbean Community, and encourages their continuing efforts;

17. *Further welcomes* the convening in New York, on 9 and 10 February 2009, of the fifth general meeting between representatives of the Caribbean Community and its associated institutions on the one hand and of the United Nations system on the other, in order to review and appraise progress in the implementation of the agreed areas and issues and to hold consultations on such additional measures and procedures as may be required to facilitate and strengthen cooperation between the two organizations;

18. *Requests* the Secretary-General to submit to the General Assembly at its sixty-fifth session a report on the implementation of the present resolution;

19. *Decides* to include in the provisional agenda of its sixty-fifth session the sub-item entitled "Cooperation between the United Nations and the Caribbean Community".

Chapter IV

Asia and the Pacific

In 2008, the United Nations continued to face significant political and security challenges in Asia and the Pacific, as it worked to restore peace and stability and to promote economic and social development in the region.

In Afghanistan, 2008 was the most violent year since 2001, with insurgents continning their attempts at destabilization though sophisticated asymmetric attacks. Nevertheless, the capacity of the Afghan national army increased, relations with Pakistan improved, areas under opium cultivation were reduced by 19 per cent and nearly 2 million Afghans were peacefully registered for elections.

The United Nations Assistance Mission in Afghanistan (UNAMA) coordinated international humanitarian and development assistance, fostered political dialogue and helped the Government build institutions. It reached out to the Afghan public, especially those who felt alienated from their Government but were not opposed to the Constitution or targeted by UN sanctions. In March, the Security Council extended UNAMA's mandate by another year.

The International Security Assistance Force (ISAF), a multinational force established by the Council in 2001, continued to assist the Government in maintaining security. In September, the Council extended ISAF's authorization until October 2009. The North Atlantic Treaty Organization maintained its role as lead command for ISAF.

In June, the Security Council adopted resolution 1817(2008) on the fight against illicit drugs in Afghanistan. In November, the General Assembly called upon the Government to continue addressing the threat posed by extremist groups and criminal violence, and urged donors to increase the proportion of assistance channelled directly to Afghanistan's core budget.

In Iraq, 2008 saw a decrease in security incidents and relative stability, even as United States troops deployed for the military surge were withdrawn. The multinational force progressively transferred security responsibilities to the Iraqi army. On 27 November, the Iraqi Council of Representatives approved a bilateral agreement placing United States forces under Iraq's authority and jurisdiction, with a timeline for their withdrawal from Iraq by December 2011. On 22 December, by resolution 1859(2008), the Council took note of the agreed expiration of the mandate of the multinational force on 31 December.

Despite a decrease in violent, high-visibility attacks by militias, insurgents and criminal gangs, indiscriminate attacks by roadside, car or suicide bombs were almost daily occurrences—often with women and occasionally children as suicide bombers. Iraq's efforts to meet internationally agreed development targets, as set forth in the International Compact for Iraq, resulted in cancellation of its debt in December by the Paris Club.

The United Nations Assistance Mission in Iraq (UNAMI) continued to advise the Government on developing civil and social services, foster human rights protection and legal reforms, and contribute to the coordination of development and reconstruction. In August, the Council extended UNAMI's mandate for another year.

The United Nations persisted in following up on issues relating to Iraq's 1990 invasion of Kuwait—including the repatriation of the remains of Kuwaiti and third-country nationals, the return of Kuwaiti property and compensation for losses and damage.

The United Nations Integrated Mission in Timor-Leste (UNMIT) further assisted the country in reforming the security sector, strengthening the rule of law, promoting economic and social development and fostering democratic governance. On 11 February, an armed group led by the former military police commander of the armed forces, Alfredo Reinado, carried out separate attacks against President José Ramos-Horta and Prime Minister Kay Rala Xanana Gusmão. The attacks resulted in the nearly fatal injury of the president and in the death of Mr. Reinado. Nonetheless, for the most part, the leaders and people of Timor-Leste made steady progress in all areas. The unresolved grievances of the 600 "petitioners" dismissed from the armed forces in 2006 were settled in August with the petitioners' acceptance of financial compensation to return to civilian life. The pace of closures of the internally displaced persons camps accelerated as a result of the Government-led National Recovery Strategy, supported by UNMIT; by December, most of the internally displaced had returned to their communities or had been resettled. UNMIT supported the rebuilding of the national police through training and institutional development. The certification process for the majority of police officers was completed in 2008, and preparations were made for a gradual resumption of responsibilities by the Timorese police. In the meantime, UNMIT continued to maintain a robust police presence across the country. The professionalism and internal stability of the national security and defence forces remained a concern, among widespread perceptions that they enjoyed impunity. That perception was further entrenched due to the 94 presidential pardons granted to convicted criminals in May, which, while legal, were considered by many as undermining efforts to promote accountability and to combat impunity.

In March, the Security Council imposed additional sanctions against Iran over its nuclear programme, including the inspection of cargo suspected of carrying prohibited goods, the tighter monitoring of financial institutions and the extension of travel bans and asset freezes. In September, the Council requested Iran to stop uranium enrichment and reprocessing activities and to cooperate with inspectors from the International Atomic Energy Agency.

A major accomplishment of UN peace operations in 2008 was the transition in Nepal, where a political mission, the United Nations Mission in Nepal, run by the Department of Political Affairs, helped the country hold nationwide Constituent Assembly elections, which effectively ended the civil war. After two postponements, the Nepalese people turned out in large numbers on 10 April to elect the Assembly, the most inclusive legislative body in the country's history. Following the election, the Assembly voted to abolish the 239-year-old monarchy. Nepal still faced many challenges, however, including the integration and rehabilitation of some 19,000 former combatants.

The Secretary-General's Special Adviser for Myanmar visited the country in March to encourage the authorities to promote democratization and national reconciliation. He met with senior Government ministers as well as with detained opposition leader Daw Aung San Suu Kyi and members of her party, the National League for Democracy. On 2 May, Cyclone Nargis struck Myanmar, leaving more than 130,000 people dead or missing. The United Nations appealed for $187 million to help provide humanitarian relief, and called on the authorities to grant more access for delivering humanitarian aid to the victims. Secretary-General Ban Ki-moon visited Myanmar in May and met Senior General Than Shwe, who agreed to allow international aid workers into the country, regardless of their nationality. By June, some 1.3 million people had received assistance. In July, the United Nations launched an appeal for $482 million. The Special Adviser visited the country in August, holding talks with the Planning and Health ministers, the Foreign Affairs Minister and senior Government members. In September, the Secretary-General welcomed the release of political prisoners. In November, he called for all political prisoners to be released and for all citizens to be allowed to participate freely in their country's political future.

During the year, the Secretary-General encouraged progress in the six-party talks aimed at the verifiable denuclearization of the Korean Peninsula. In July and October, the Secretary-General urged Cambodia and Thailand to resolve diplomatically their border dispute.

Afghanistan

Political and security situation

In 2008, the international community continued to assist the Government of Afghanistan in laying the foundation for peace and stability and the restoration of economic and social development, through support provided by the United Nations Assistance Mission in Afghanistan (UNAMA), under the direction of the Special Representative of the Secretary-General and Head of Mission, and the International Security Assistance Force (ISAF), led by the North Atlantic Treaty Organization (NATO).

The Secretary-General submitted two progress reports to the General Assembly and the Security Council, in March [A/62/722-S/2008/159] and September [A/63/372-S/2008/617], on the situation in Afghanistan and on UNAMA activities, as well as a later report covering the end of the year [A/63/751-S/2009/135], and a special report to the Council [S/2008/434] on the June 2008 Paris Conference in Support of Afghanistan. The Security Council carried out a mission to Afghanistan in November.

ISAF activities were reported to the Council by the NATO Secretary-General through the UN Secretary-General [S/2008/319, S/2008/597, S/2008/770, S/2009/283]. The Council, by resolution 1806(2008) (see p. 355), extended the UNAMA mandate until 23 March 2009; and by resolution 1833(2008) (see p. 374), it extended the ISAF authorization until 13 October 2009. In March, the Secretary-General appointed Kai Eide (Norway) as his Special Representative for Afghanistan and Head of UNAMA.

Attacks in Kabul, Kandahar. In a press statement of 15 January [SC/9226], Security Council members condemned the suicide attack that occurred at the Hotel Serena in Kabul on 14 January, causing several casualties among security guards, hotel guests and bystanders. Council members noted that the Taliban claimed responsibility for the attack and underlined the need to bring perpetrators, organizers, financiers and sponsors to justice. They reiterated their concern at the increasing threat to the population, national security forces, international military and international assistance efforts posed by the Taliban, Al-Qaida, illegal armed groups, criminals and those involved in the narcotics trade. No terrorist act could reverse the path towards peace, democracy and reconstruction, which was supported by the people and the Government of Afghanistan and the international community.

In a press statement of 17 February [SC/9251], Security Council members condemned the suicide attack that caused numerous deaths in the province of Kandahar on the same day. The attack was one of the deadliest in Afghanistan in recent years and targeted civilians—including children—and police officers.

New Special Representative. On 6 March [S/2008/165], the Secretary-General informed the President of the Security Council of his intention to appoint Kai Eide (Norway) as his Special Representative for Afghanistan and Head of UNAMA. The Council took note of that intention on 7 March [S/2008/166]. Mr. Eide replaced Tom Koenigs (Germany), who served from February 2006 until December 2007.

Report of Secretary-General (March). In a report issued on 6 March [A/62/722-S/2008/159], the Secretary-General said that the Taliban, related armed groups and the drug economy were fundamental threats to Afghanistan's fragile institutions. The country remained divided between the generally more stable west and north, whose problems related to factionalism and criminality, and the south and east, with an increasingly coordinated insurgency. Even within the south, conflict was concentrated in a fairly small area. A worrying trend was the emergence of insurgent activity in the far north-west, including provinces bordering Kabul. Of the country's 376 districts, 36—including most of those in the east, south-east and south—remained largely inaccessible to Afghan officials and to aid workers.

Poor governance and limited development efforts, particularly at provincial and district levels, sustained anti-Government elements by causing political alienation, but efforts to reconnect provincial administrations to central Government structures had begun to bear fruit. Relations between the legislature and the executive branch had improved, and there was a focus on holding the upcoming elections, scheduled for 2009 and 2010.

ISAF had conducted successful operations in unstable areas, but its effectiveness was hampered by insufficient troop strength and national caveats limiting the functions of some troops. The United Nations Mine Action Centre cleared 168 square kilometres of land, destroying 26,401 anti-personnel landmines, 649 anti-tank landmines and 1,659,302 items of unexploded ordnance.

Although counter-narcotics efforts had gained momentum and 12 provinces were expected to remain free of opium cultivation in 2008, Afghanistan was emerging as one of the world's largest suppliers of cannabis.

Progress on human rights remained limited. Freedom of expression faced tactics of intimidation by anti-Government elements and governmental restrictions on journalists and media outlets. Children continued to be the victims of insurgency-related violence, and violence and harmful practices against women and girls remained a concern. Public access to courts and legal aid remained elusive for most Afghans, but there had been slow improvements in the legal infrastructure, and a private corps of lawyers continued to grow.

Afghanistan's per capita gross domestic product (GDP) had nearly doubled to $289, but 34 to 42 per cent of the population lived below the poverty line and much of the economy's impressive growth was indirectly related to the illegal drug industry and the significant amounts of foreign aid. The revenue-to-GDP ratio remained one of the world's lowest, with just enough to meet some two thirds of the Government's operating budget.

Security Council consideration (March). Briefing the Council on 12 March [meeting 5851], the Under-Secretary-General for Peacekeeping Operations, Jean-Marie Guéhenno, said that the Afghan insurgency was more robust and ruthless than had been imagined. Corruption had made governmental institutions even more fragile, and a massive illegal drug economy was thriving in the context of weak State authority. UNAMA was reaching out to the public, especially those who felt alienated from their Government but were not opposed to the Constitution and were not targets of UN sanctions. To be credible, such activities had to be backed up by improved governance, especially at the local level.

Afghanistan said that the Afghan National Army had reached 58,000 troops and assumed a greater role in fighting the terrorists. Afghanistan was continuing its reconstruction, and would soon finalize the Afghan National Development Strategy.

Pakistan said that the key lay in Afghanistan assuming greater ownership of its security, governance and development. Making security a prerequisite for development and assistance could be counter-productive; both should be pursued simultaneously. Pakistan was committed to Afghanistan's sustainable peace and development; their destinies were interlinked.

SECURITY COUNCIL ACTION

On 20 March [meeting 5857], the Security Council unanimously adopted **resolution 1806(2008)**. The draft [S/2008/185] was prepared in consultations among Council members.

The Security Council,

Recalling its previous resolutions on Afghanistan, in particular resolution 1746(2007) of 23 March 2007, in which it extended, until 23 March 2008, the mandate of the United Nations Assistance Mission in Afghanistan, as established by resolution 1662(2006) of 23 March 2006, and recalling also its resolution 1659(2006) of 15 February 2006, in which it endorsed the Afghanistan Compact,

Reaffirming its strong commitment to the sovereignty, independence, territorial integrity and national unity of Afghanistan,

Reaffirming its continued support for the Government and people of Afghanistan as they rebuild their country, strengthen the foundations of sustainable peace and constitutional democracy and assume their rightful place in the community of nations,

Reaffirming in this context its support for the implementation, under the ownership of the Afghan people, of the Afghanistan Compact, the Afghanistan National Development Strategy and the National Drug Control Strategy, and noting that sustained and coordinated efforts by all relevant actors are required to consolidate progress made towards their implementation and to overcome continuing challenges,

Recalling that the Afghanistan Compact is based on a partnership between the Government of Afghanistan and the international community, based on the desire of the parties for Afghanistan to progressively assume responsibility for its own development and security, and with a central and impartial coordinating role for the United Nations,

Stressing the central and impartial role that the United Nations continues to play in promoting peace and stability in Afghanistan by leading the efforts of the international community, including, jointly with the Government of Afghanistan, the coordination and monitoring of efforts in implementing the Afghanistan Compact, and expressing its appreciation and strong support for the ongoing efforts of the Secretary-General, his Special Representative for Afghanistan and the women and men of the Mission,

Recognizing once again the interconnected nature of the challenges in Afghanistan, reaffirming that sustainable progress on security, governance and development, as well as the cross-cutting issue of counter-narcotics, is mutually reinforcing, and welcoming the continuing efforts of the Government of Afghanistan and the international community to address these challenges through a comprehensive approach,

Stressing the importance of a comprehensive approach in addressing the challenges in Afghanistan, noting in this context the synergies in the objectives of the Mission and of the International Security Assistance Force, and stressing the need for strengthened cooperation, coordination and mutual support, taking due account of their respective designated responsibilities,

Reiterating its concern about the security situation in Afghanistan, in particular the increased violent and terrorist activities by the Taliban, Al-Qaida, illegal armed groups, criminals and those involved in the narcotics trade, and the increasingly strong links between terrorism activities and illicit drugs, resulting in threats to the local population, including children, national security forces and international military and civilian personnel,

Stressing the importance of ensuring safe and unhindered access of humanitarian workers, including United Nations staff and associated personnel,

Expressing its concern over the harmful consequences of violent and terrorist activities by the Taliban, Al-Qaida and other extremist groups on the capacity of the Government of Afghanistan to guarantee the rule of law, to provide security and basic services to the Afghan people and to ensure the improvement and protection of their human rights and fundamental freedoms,

Recalling the importance of the Kabul Declaration on Good-neighbourly Relations of 22 December 2002, looking forward to the Third Regional Economic Cooperation Conference on Afghanistan, to be held in Islamabad, and stressing the crucial importance of advancing regional cooperation as an effective means to promote security, governance and development in Afghanistan,

Welcoming the holding of the Afghan-Pakistani Peace Jirga in Kabul in August 2007 and the collective determination expressed at the Jirga to bring sustainable peace to the region, including by addressing the terrorist threat, and expressing its support for the relevant follow-up processes,

Recalling its resolutions 1265(1999) of 17 September 1999, 1296(2000) of 19 April 2000, 1674(2006) of 28 April 2006 and 1738(2006) of 23 December 2006 on the protection of civilians in armed conflict, its resolution 1325(2000) of 31 October 2000 on women and peace and security and its resolution 1612(2005) of 26 July 2005 on children and armed conflict, and taking note with appreciation of the seventh report of the Secretary-General on children and armed conflict, of 21 December 2007,

1. *Welcomes* the report of the Secretary-General of 6 March 2008;

2. *Expresses its appreciation* for the United Nations long-term commitment to work with the Government and the people of Afghanistan;

3. *Decides* to extend the mandate of the United Nations Assistance Mission in Afghanistan, as defined in its resolutions 1662(2006) and 1746(2007), until 23 March 2009;

4. *Decides also* that the Mission and the Special Representative of the Secretary-General for Afghanistan, within their mandate and guided by the principle of reinforcing Afghan ownership and leadership, shall lead the international civilian efforts, inter alia:

(a) To promote, as co-chair of the Joint Coordination and Monitoring Board, more coherent support by the international community to the Government of Afghanistan and the adherence to the principles of aid effectiveness enumerated in the Afghanistan Compact, including through mobilization of resources, coordination of the assistance provided by international donors and organizations and direction of the contributions of United Nations agencies, funds and programmes, in particular for counter-narcotics, reconstruction and development activities;

(b) To strengthen the cooperation with the International Security Assistance Force at all levels and throughout the country, in accordance with their existing mandates, in order to improve civil-military coordination, to facilitate the timely exchange of information and to ensure coherence between the activities of national and international security forces and of civilian actors in support of an Afghan-led development and stabilization process, including through engagement with provincial reconstruction teams and engagement with non-governmental organizations;

(c) Through a strengthened and expanded presence throughout the country, to provide political outreach, promote at the local level the implementation of the Afghanistan Compact, the Afghanistan National Development Strategy and the National Drug Control Strategy, and facilitate inclusion in and understanding of the policies of the Government of Afghanistan;

(d) To provide good offices to support, if requested by the Government of Afghanistan, the implementation of Afghan-led reconciliation programmes, within the framework of the Afghan Constitution and with full respect for the implementation of measures introduced by the Security Council in its resolution 1267(1999) of 15 October 1999 and other relevant resolutions of the Council;

(e) To support efforts, including through the Independent Directorate for Local Governance, to improve governance and the rule of law and to combat corruption, in particular at the subnational level, and to promote development initiatives at the local level with a view to helping to bring the benefits of peace and deliver services in a timely and sustainable manner;

(f) To play a central coordinating role to facilitate the delivery of humanitarian assistance in accordance with humanitarian principles and with a view to building the capacity of the Government of Afghanistan, including by providing effective support to national and local authorities in assisting and protecting internally displaced persons and to creating conditions conducive to the voluntary, safe, dignified and sustainable return of refugees and internally displaced persons;

(g) To continue, with the support of the Office of the United Nations High Commissioner for Human Rights, to cooperate with the Afghan Independent Human Rights Commission, to cooperate also with relevant international and local non-governmental organizations, to monitor the situation of civilians, to coordinate efforts to ensure their protection and to assist in the full implementation of the fundamental freedoms and human rights provisions of the Afghan Constitution and international treaties to which Afghanistan is a State party, in particular those regarding the full enjoyment by women of their human rights;

(h) To support, at the request of the Afghan authorities, the electoral process, in particular through the Afghan Independent Electoral Commission, by providing technical assistance, coordinating other international donors, agencies and organizations providing assistance and channelling existing and additional funds earmarked to support the process;

(i) To support regional cooperation to work towards a stable and prosperous Afghanistan;

5. *Calls upon* all Afghan and international parties to coordinate with the Mission in the implementation of its mandate and in efforts to promote the security and freedom of movement of United Nations and associated personnel throughout the country;

6. *Stresses* the importance of strengthening and expanding the presence of the Mission and other United Nations agencies, funds and programmes in the provinces, and encourages the Secretary-General to pursue current efforts to finalize the necessary arrangements to address the security issues associated with such strengthening and expansion;

7. *Calls upon* the Government of Afghanistan, and the international community and international organizations, to implement the Afghanistan Compact and the annexes thereto in full, and stresses in this context the importance of meeting the benchmarks and timelines of the Compact for progress on security, governance, the rule of law and human rights, and economic and social development, as well as the cross-cutting issue of counter-narcotics;

8. *Reaffirms* the central role played by the Joint Coordination and Monitoring Board in coordinating, facilitating and monitoring the implementation of the Afghanistan Compact, stresses the need to strengthen its authority and capacity to, inter alia, measure progress towards the benchmarks outlined in the Compact and facilitate the coordination of international assistance in support of the Afghanistan National Development Strategy, and calls upon all relevant actors to cooperate with the Board in this regard, including by reporting assistance programmes to the Government of Afghanistan's aid coordination unit and to the Board;

9. *Welcomes* the progress made by the Government of Afghanistan in the finalization of the Afghanistan National Development Strategy, looks forward to its launch, and stresses the importance, in this context, of adequate resource mobilization, including through the fulfilment of the pledges made at the London Conference on Afghanistan, held on 31 January and 1 February 2006, possible new pledges and increased assistance to the core budget;

10. *Notes with interest* the intention, expressed by members of the Joint Coordination and Monitoring Board at the Political Directors Meeting on Afghanistan, held in Tokyo on 5 February 2008, to prepare an international conference to review progress on the implementation of the Afghanistan Compact, welcomes the offer of France to host such a conference in Paris in June 2008, and requests the Secretary-General to report to the Council on its outcome and to include in that report, if necessary, further recommendations concerning the mandate of the Mission;

11. *Calls upon* the Government of Afghanistan, with the assistance of the international community, including the International Security Assistance Force and the Operation Enduring Freedom coalition, in accordance with their respective designated responsibilities as they evolve, to continue to address the threat to the security and stability of Afghanistan posed by the Taliban, Al-Qaida, illegal armed groups, criminals and those involved in the narcotics trade;

12. *Condemns in the strongest terms* all attacks, including improvised explosive device attacks, suicide attacks and abductions, targeting civilians and Afghan and international forces and their deleterious effect on the stabilization, reconstruction and development efforts in Afghanistan, and condemns further the use by the Taliban and other extremist groups of civilians as human shields;

13. *Reiterates its concern* about all civilian casualties, calls for compliance with international humanitarian and human rights law and for all appropriate steps to be taken to ensure the protection of civilians, and recognizes in this context the robust efforts taken by the Force and other international forces to minimize the risk of civilian casualties, notably the continuous review of tactics and procedures and the conduct of after-action reviews in cooperation with the Government of Afghanistan in cases where civilian casualties have reportedly occurred;

14. *Expresses its strong concern* about the recruitment and use of children by Taliban forces in Afghanistan as well as the killing and maiming of children as a result of the conflict, reiterates its strong condemnation of the recruitment and use of child soldiers in violation of applicable international law and all other violations and abuses committed against children in situations of armed conflict and stresses the importance of implementing Council resolution 1612(2005), and in this context requests the Secretary-General to strengthen the child protection component of the Mission, in particular through the appointment of child protection advisers;

15. *Stresses* the importance of increasing, within a comprehensive framework, the functionality, professionalism and accountability of the Afghan security sector through training, mentoring and empowerment efforts, in order to accelerate progress towards the goal of self-sufficient and ethnically balanced Afghan security forces providing security and ensuring the rule of law throughout the country;

16. *Welcomes*, in this context, the continued progress in the development of the Afghan National Army and its improved ability to plan and undertake operations, and encourages sustained training efforts, including through the operational mentoring and liaison teams, and advice in developing a sustainable defence planning process as well as assistance in defence reform initiatives;

17. *Calls for* further efforts to enhance the capabilities of the Afghan National Police in order to reinforce the authority of the Government of Afghanistan throughout the country, welcomes the increasing role played by the International Police Coordination Board in policy setting and coordination, and stresses the importance, in this context, of the contribution of the European Union through the European Union Police Mission in Afghanistan;

18. *Also calls for* further progress in the implementation by the Government of Afghanistan, with support from the international community, of the programme of disbandment of illegal armed groups;

19. *Expresses its concern* at the serious harm that increasing opium cultivation, production and trafficking causes to the security, development and governance of Afghanistan as well as to the region and internationally; calls upon the Government of Afghanistan, with the assistance of the international community, to accelerate the implementation of the National Drug Control Strategy as discussed at the meeting of the Joint Coordination and Monitoring Board held in Tokyo in February 2008, in particular at the local level, and to mainstream counter-narcotics throughout national programmes; and encourages additional international support for the four priorities identified in the Strategy, including through contributions to the Counter-Narcotics Trust Fund;

20. *Calls upon* States to strengthen international and regional cooperation to counter the threat to the international community posed by the illicit production of and trafficking in drugs originating in Afghanistan, including through border management cooperation in drug control and cooperation for the fight against the illicit trafficking in drugs and precursors and against money-laundering linked to such trafficking, taking into account the outcome of the Second Ministerial Conference on Drug Trafficking Routes from Afghanistan, organized by the Government of the Russian Federation in cooperation with the United Nations Office on Drugs and Crime and held in Moscow from 26 to 28 June 2006, within the framework of the Paris Pact initiative;

21. *Welcomes* the adoption by the Afghan authorities, in accordance with the outcome of the Rome Conference on the Rule of Law in Afghanistan, held on 2 and 3 July 2007, of the National Justice Programme launched at the meeting of the Joint Coordination and Monitoring Board held in Tokyo in February 2008, and stresses the importance of its full and timely implementation by all the relevant actors in order to accelerate the establishment of a fair and transparent justice system, strengthen the rule of law throughout the country and eliminate impunity;

22. *Stresses*, in this context, the importance of further progress in the reconstruction and reform of the prison sector in Afghanistan, in order to improve the respect for the rule of law and human rights therein;

23. *Notes with concern* the effects of widespread corruption on security, good governance, counter-narcotics efforts and economic development, and calls upon the Government of Afghanistan, with the assistance of the international community, to vigorously lead the fight against corruption and to enhance its efforts to establish a more effective, accountable and transparent administration;

24. *Encourages* all Afghan institutions, including the executive and legislative branches, to work in a spirit of cooperation, calls upon the Government of Afghanistan to pursue continued legislative and public administration reform in order to ensure good governance, full representation and accountability at both the national and the subnational levels, stresses the need for further international efforts to provide technical assistance in this area, and recalls the role of the Senior Appointments Panel in accordance with the Afghanistan Compact;

25. *Encourages* the international community to assist the Government of Afghanistan in making capacity-building and human resources development a cross-cutting priority;

26. *Notes* the leading role that the Afghan institutions will play in the organization of the next elections, encourages the Government of Afghanistan, with support from the international community, to accelerate the planning and preparation of such elections, stresses the need to establish a permanent civil and voter registry in accordance with the Afghanistan Compact, and emphasizes the importance of free, fair, inclusive and transparent elections in order to sustain the democratic progress of the country;

27. *Calls for* full respect for human rights and fundamental freedoms and international humanitarian law throughout Afghanistan, notes with concern the increasing restrictions on freedom of the media, commends the Afghan Independent Human Rights Commission for its courageous efforts to monitor respect for human rights in Afghanistan as well as to foster and protect those rights and to promote the emergence of a pluralistic civil society, and stresses the importance of full cooperation with the Commission by all relevant actors;

28. *Recognizes* the significant progress achieved on gender equality in Afghanistan in recent years, strongly condemns continuing forms of discrimination and violence

against women and girls, stresses the importance of implementing Council resolution 1325(2000), and requests the Secretary-General to continue to include in his reports to the Council relevant information on the process of integration of women into the political, economic and social life of Afghanistan;

29. *Calls for* enhanced efforts to ensure the full implementation of the Action Plan on Peace, Justice and Reconciliation in accordance with the Afghanistan Compact, without prejudice to the implementation of measures introduced by the Council in its resolution 1267(1999) and other relevant resolutions of the Council;

30. *Welcomes* the cooperation of the Government of Afghanistan and the Mission with the Security Council Committee established pursuant to resolution 1267(1999) in the implementation of resolution 1735(2006) of 22 December 2006, including by identifying individuals and entities participating in the financing or support of acts or activities of Al-Qaida and the Taliban using proceeds derived from illicit cultivation and production of and trafficking in narcotic drugs and their precursors, and encourages the continuation of such cooperation;

31. *Also welcomes* ongoing efforts by the Government of Afghanistan and its neighbouring and regional partners to foster trust and cooperation with each other, including recent cooperation initiatives developed by regional organizations, and stresses the importance of increasing cooperation between Afghanistan and the partners against the Taliban, Al-Qaida and other extremist groups, in promoting peace and prosperity in Afghanistan and in fostering cooperation in the economic and development sectors as a means to achieve the full integration of Afghanistan into regional dynamics and the global economy;

32. *Calls for* the strengthening of the process of regional economic cooperation, including measures to facilitate regional trade, to increase foreign investments and to develop infrastructure, noting Afghanistan's historical role as a land bridge in Asia;

33. *Recognizes* the importance of the voluntary, safe, orderly return and sustainable reintegration of the remaining Afghan refugees for the stability of the country and the region, and calls for continued and enhanced international assistance in this regard;

34. *Requests* the Secretary-General to report to the Council every six months on developments in Afghanistan, in addition to the report requested in paragraph 10 of the present resolution;

35. *Decides* to remain actively seized of the matter.

Attack in Kabul. In a press statement of 28 April [SC/9313], Security Council members condemned the terrorist attack that on 27 April targeted an official ceremony in Kabul attended by Afghan President Hamid Karzai, Afghan authorities, diplomats and international officials. Council members noted that the Taliban had claimed responsibility for the attack and underlined the need to bring perpetrators, organizers, financiers and sponsors to justice. Council members reaffirmed their commitment to further reinforcing Afghan ownership and leadership of the country's development and security.

SECURITY COUNCIL ACTION

On 11 June [meeting 5907], the Security Council unanimously adopted **resolution 1817(2008)**. The draft [S/2008/376] was submitted by Afghanistan, Belgium, Croatia, France, Italy, the Russian Federation, the United Kingdom and the United States.

The Security Council,

Recalling its previous resolutions on Afghanistan, in particular resolutions 1659(2006) of 15 February 2006, 1776(2007) of 19 September 2007 and 1806(2008) of 20 March 2008, and the statement by its President of 17 June 2003,

Recalling also its resolutions 1267(1999) of 15 October 1999 and 1735(2006) of 22 December 2006, and reiterating its support for international efforts to combat terrorism in accordance with international law, including the Charter of the United Nations,

Reaffirming its strong commitment to the sovereignty, independence, territorial integrity and national unity of Afghanistan,

Reaffirming its continued support for the Government and people of Afghanistan as they rebuild their country, strengthen the foundations of sustainable peace and constitutional democracy and assume their rightful place in the community of nations,

Noting with concern the existing links between international security, terrorism and transnational organized crime, money-laundering, trafficking in illicit drugs and illegal arms, and in this regard emphasizing the need to enhance coordination of efforts at the national, subregional, regional and international levels in order to strengthen a global response to this serious challenge,

Reiterating its concern about the security situation in Afghanistan, in particular the continued violent and terrorist activities by the Taliban, Al-Qaida, illegal armed groups, criminals and those involved in the narcotics trade, and the links between illicit drug trafficking and terrorism, and calling upon the Government of Afghanistan, with the assistance of the international community, including the International Security Assistance Force and the Operation Enduring Freedom coalition, in accordance with their respective designated responsibilities as they evolve, to continue to address the threat to the security and stability of Afghanistan posed by the Taliban, Al-Qaida, illegal armed groups, criminals and those involved in the narcotics trade,

Welcoming the ongoing efforts of the Government of Afghanistan in the fight against narcotic drugs and also welcoming the efforts of neighbouring countries to address the impact on the region of the production of illicit drugs in Afghanistan, including through interdiction activities, and encouraging the international and regional organizations to enhance their role in the fight against illicit trafficking in narcotics and precursors, and paying homage to the sacrifice of members of the security forces of Afghanistan and its neighbouring countries in the fight against drug traffickers,

Reiterating its support for the fight against the illicit production of and trafficking in drugs from, and chemical precursors to, Afghanistan, in neighbouring countries, countries on trafficking routes, drug destination countries and precursor-producing countries, encouraging increased cooperation between those countries to strengthen anti-narcotics controls to curb the drug flow, including through border management cooperation, and expressing its support for the Paris Pact initiative, for the outcome of the Second Ministerial Conference on Drug Trafficking Routes from Afghanistan, organized in Moscow from 26 to 28 June 2006, and for the meeting organized in Kabul on 31 October and 1 November 2007 within the framework of the Paris Pact initiative; and stressing the need for Member States to take measures, with the support of relevant international actors, to combat the laundering of proceeds of criminal activity, corruption and illicit trafficking in narcotics and precursors in line with the outcome of the Moscow conference,

Recalling that achieving a sustained and significant reduction in the production of and trafficking in narcotics with a view to eliminating the narcotics industry has been identified as a cross-cutting priority in the Afghanistan Compact adopted in London on 31 January 2006, which provides the framework for the partnership between the Government of Afghanistan and the international community, as well as for the Government's National Drug Control Strategy,

Stressing the importance of a comprehensive approach to address the drug problem of Afghanistan, which, to be effective, has to be integrated into the wider context of efforts carried out in the three areas of security, governance, rule of law and human rights, and economic and social development, stressing that the development of alternative-livelihood programmes is of key importance in the success of the efforts in counter-narcotics in Afghanistan, and reiterating that extensive efforts also have to be made to reduce the demand for drugs globally in order to contribute to the sustainability of the elimination of illicit cultivation in Afghanistan,

Expressing utmost concern at the increase in illegal smuggling, for illicit use, to and within Afghanistan of chemical precursors needed to produce heroin, in particular acetic anhydride, and also hydrochloric acid and acetone, linked to the high level of opium cultivation, production and trafficking, and noting that most of the opium produced in Afghanistan is now processed in the country,

Recalling the Political Declaration adopted by the General Assembly at its twentieth special session, in which Member States decided to establish the year 2008 as a target date for States to eliminate or significantly reduce, inter alia, the diversion of precursors, and recognizing that action against the world drug problem is a common and shared responsibility requiring an integrated and balanced approach in full conformity with the purposes and principles of the Charter and international law,

Acknowledging the role of the Commission on Narcotic Drugs of the Economic and Social Council as the central policymaking and coordinating body within the United Nations system on international drug control issues, and welcoming the intention of the Commission to consider the issue of precursor control as one of the central questions to be discussed during the high-level segment of its fifty-second session,

Acknowledging also the mandate and the leading role played by the International Narcotics Control Board, as an independent treaty body, in the implementation of the United Nations international drug control conventions and the international control of precursors,

Stressing the central role played by the United Nations Office on Drugs and Crime in assisting Member States, notably by providing technical assistance, in the fight against illicit drugs,

1. *Expresses utmost concern* at the high level of opium cultivation, production and trafficking, which involves, in particular, the diversion of chemical precursors, and stresses once again the serious harm that it causes to the security, development and governance of Afghanistan as well as to the region and internationally, and to the success of international efforts;

2. *Calls upon* all Member States to increase international and regional cooperation in order to counter the illicit production of and trafficking in drugs in Afghanistan, including by strengthening the monitoring of the international trade in chemical precursors, notably but not limited to acetic anhydride, and to prevent attempts to divert the substances from licit international trade for illicit use in Afghanistan;

3. *Invites* all Member States, in particular chemical precursor-producing countries, Afghanistan, neighbouring countries, and all countries on the trafficking routes to increase their cooperation with the International Narcotics Control Board, notably by fully complying with the provisions of article 12 of the United Nations Convention against Illicit Traffic in Narcotic Drugs and Psychotropic Substances of 1988, in order to eliminate loopholes utilized by criminal organizations to divert chemical precursors from licit international trade;

4. *Urges* exporting States to ensure the systematic notification of all exports of relevant chemical precursors, upon request from importing States, in accordance with provisions of the 1988 Convention, and encourages importing States to request the systematic notification of such exports; and also urges the Governments that have not yet done so to register with and utilize the online system for the exchange of pre-export notifications (PEN Online);

5. *Calls upon* States that have not done so to consider ratifying or acceding to, and State parties to implement fully, the multilateral treaties whose aim is to fight against the illicit trafficking in narcotic drugs, notably the Single Convention on Narcotic Drugs of 1961 as amended by the Protocol of 25 March 1972 and the United Nations Convention against Illicit Traffic in Narcotic Drugs and Psychotropic Substances of 1988, underlines the importance for all States parties to those treaties to implement them fully, and stresses that nothing in the present resolution will impose on State parties new obligations with regard to those treaties;

6. *Expresses its continued support* to the commitment and efforts of Afghanistan to achieve a sustained and significant reduction in the production of and trafficking in narcotics with a view to complete elimination, expresses also its support to the Afghan National Drug Control Strategy, and calls upon the Government of Afghanistan, with the assistance of the international community, to accelerate its implementation, as discussed at the seventh meeting of the Joint Coordination and Monitoring Board held in To-

kyo in February 2008, and calls for additional international support for the priorities identified in the Strategy;

7. *Calls upon* all Member States, in particular chemical precursor-producing countries, Afghanistan, neighbouring countries and all countries on the trafficking routes, to adopt adequate national legislation, consistent with the requirements of relevant international conventions to which they are parties, where it has not yet been done, and to strengthen their national capacities in the areas of (i) regulation and monitoring of manufacture of and trade in chemical precursors, with a view to controlling the final destination of such chemicals, and (ii) specialized enforcement operations against the diversion of precursors, including for their detection and disposal in Afghanistan and the region, and for strengthening border controls;

8. *Invites* the international community to provide financial and technical assistance and support in building national capacity in the fields referred to in paragraph 7 above to Afghanistan and, where appropriate and upon request, neighbouring countries, including through voluntary contributions to the United Nations Office on Drugs and Crime; stresses in particular the importance of training and equipping law enforcement agencies, including border police and customs officers, so as to allow them to deal efficiently with such tasks as detection, scanning, stockpiling, transportation and destruction of chemical precursors; and encourages Afghanistan and its neighbours to make full use of such assistance;

9. *Reiterates its support* for the Paris Pact initiative aimed at facilitating counter-narcotics cooperation and coordination among countries seriously affected by the trafficking in narcotic drugs produced in Afghanistan, for the outcome of the Second Ministerial Conference on Drug Trafficking Routes from Afghanistan, organized in Moscow from 26 to 28 June 2006 in cooperation with the United Nations Office on Drugs and Crime, and for other international and/or regional relevant initiatives, such as Project Cohesion, and calls upon Paris Pact partners to further promote international and regional initiatives;

10. *Welcomes* the launch, under the guidance of the United Nations Office on Drugs and Crime and the Project Cohesion Task Force, of the Targeted Anti-Trafficking Regional Communication, Expertise and Training initiative targeting precursors used in the manufacture of heroin in Afghanistan, and urges the Paris Pact partners to cooperate closely with a view to achieving its successful implementation;

11. *Recognizes* the legitimate need of industry to have access to precursors and its important role in preventing the diversion of precursors, and encourages all Member States, in particular producing countries, Afghanistan and its neighbours to develop partnerships with the private sector so as to prevent the diversion of precursors;

12. *Looks forward* to the outcome of the international conference in support of Afghanistan, which will be held in Paris on 12 June 2008, and encourages the participants at the conference to make concrete proposals on the ways to address the problem of the diversion of chemical precursors for illicit use, within the wider framework of the discussions on the strengthening of counter-narcotics activities in the Afghanistan National Development Strategy and the National Drug Control Strategy;

13. *Encourages* Member States to submit to the Security Council Committee established pursuant to resolution 1267(1999) for inclusion on the Consolidated List names of individuals and entities participating in the financing or support of acts or activities of Al-Qaida, Osama bin Laden and the Taliban, and other individuals, groups, undertakings and entities associated with them, using proceeds derived from the illicit cultivation and production of and trafficking in narcotic drugs produced in Afghanistan and their precursors, in order to give full effect to the relevant provisions of resolution 1735(2006);

14. *Requests* the Secretary-General to include, as appropriate, in his regular reports to the Security Council and the General Assembly on the situation in Afghanistan, in close consultation with the United Nations Office on Drugs and Crime and the International Narcotics Control Board, observations and recommendations on the fight against drug production and trafficking, notably on the issue of the illicit traffic in chemical precursors to and within Afghanistan;

15. *Invites* the Commission on Narcotic Drugs to consider, in accordance with its mandate, ways to strengthen regional and international cooperation to prevent the diversion and smuggling of chemical precursors to and within Afghanistan, and further opportunities for Member States to support the Government of Afghanistan in developing capacities to tackle precursors and trafficking;

16. *Decides* to remain seized of the matter.

Paris Conference and Declaration

Special report of Secretary-General (July). In a special report dated 3 July [S/2008/434] on the outcome of the Paris Conference in Support of Afghanistan, the Secretary-General said that the Conference, held on 12 June, resulted in pledges of international assistance totalling approximately $20 billion. With the launch of the Afghanistan National Development Strategy in Paris, some 80 international stakeholders agreed to a road map under Afghan leadership to be implemented through a strengthened partnership between the Government and the international community. The Paris Declaration identified the key elements for the security and prosperity of the Afghan people, and underlined an expanded role for the Secretary-General's Special Representative and UNAMA. The February 2006 Afghanistan Compact [YUN 2006, p. 363] remained the basis for that common effort.

The Strategy was the Government's five-year plan for joint action on security, governance, rule of law and human rights, and economic and social development. It was based on the Millennium Development Goals and the Afghanistan Compact.

Since the Secretary-General's March report, insurgent and terrorist activity had increased, particularly in the south and east. In May, there were more recorded security incidents in the country than at any time since the overthrow of the Taliban regime in

2001. The insurgents continued to rely on asymmetric attacks, resulting in high levels of civilian casualties.

For UNAMA to fulfil its mandate and achieve the Paris priorities, greater resources had to be mobilized. Addressing priorities required additional personnel for elections, support for the Afghanistan National Development Strategy, aid effectiveness, institution-building and the delivery of humanitarian assistance. The Secretary-General recommended that UNAMA further expand its field presence by opening six new provincial offices over the next 12 months, adding that any such expansion should be undertaken with staff security as the highest priority.

The Secretary-General recommended that UNAMA focus on free, fair and secure elections in 2009 and 2010; the Afghanistan National Development Strategy; implementing the economic priorities of the Strategy; governance and institution-building; aid effectiveness and increased accountability; humanitarian action; regional cooperation; and such ongoing priorities as protecting human rights, reducing the production and trafficking of narcotics and improving civil-military coordination.

Security Council statement. In a press statement of 16 June [SC/9361], Security Council members welcomed the holding of the Conference, the reaffirmation of the long-term partnership between Afghanistan and the international community, the review of progress in the implementation of the Afghanistan Compact, and the commitment of Conference participants to working more closely together under Afghan leadership to support the Afghanistan National Development Strategy. Council members welcomed the Government's commitment to pursue political and economic reform, to work with the international community and to take leadership for its development. Council members welcomed in particular the commitment by Conference participants to support the central role of the Special Representative and UNAMA in coordinating international efforts, especially with the Government.

Further developments

Attack in Kabul. On 7 July, Security Council members, by a press statement [SC/9386], condemned the terrorist suicide attack that occurred on that day at the Indian Embassy in Kabul, causing numerous deaths among Afghan civilians, Indian diplomats and security personnel, as well as numerous injuries, including at the nearby Indonesian Embassy.

Security Council consideration (July). Briefing the Council on 9 July [meeting 5930], the Secretary-General's Special Representative, Kai Eide, stressed the role of the United Nations in helping the Government implement the National Development Strategy while ensuring an adequate international response. John Holmes, Under-Secretary-General for Humanitarian Affairs and Emergency Relief Coordinator, said that humanitarian access had to be increased by means ranging from days or zones of tranquillity to vaccination campaigns and more lasting access agreements in conflict areas.

Afghanistan's Minister for Foreign Affairs, Rangin Dâdfar Spantâ, said that those who were behind the Taliban and Al-Qaida had enhanced their support to those groups with an elaborate system of terrorist sanctuaries, and the financing, recruiting, arming and training of suicide bombers outside Afghanistan's borders. Welcoming his country's expanded relations with Pakistan's new civilian Government, he said that a joint approach was needed to eliminate the bases of the terrorist networks that threatened both countries.

Pakistan's Minister for Foreign Affairs, Shah Mehmood Qureshi, said that in fighting the threat posed by terrorism and extremist violence, his country had lost more soldiers than any other. Afghanistan and Pakistan could achieve their common objectives by combining military containment with political reconciliation, administrative control and rapid socio-economic development. The military option should be used as the last resort, lest it create more alienation, more opposition and more enemies.

SECURITY COUNCIL ACTION

On 11 July [meeting 5932], following consultations among Security Council members, the President made statement **S/PRST/2008/26** on behalf of the Council:

The Security Council welcomes the special report of the Secretary-General on the International Conference in Support of Afghanistan, held in Paris on 12 June 2008, and on the United Nations Assistance Mission in Afghanistan, as well as the briefing by the Special Representative of the Secretary-General for Afghanistan, Mr. Kai Eide, on 9 July 2008.

The Council welcomes the outcome of the Conference, including the generous financial pledges made in support of the Afghanistan National Development Strategy and the commitment by the Government of Afghanistan to promote security, good governance, the rule of law, human rights and socio-economic development and to pursue political and economic reform, including by taking concrete steps to combat corruption. The Council welcomes the strengthened partnership between the Government and the international community resulting from such mutual pledges and commitments. The Council endorses the key elements identified in the Paris Declaration as essential for the security and prosperity of the Afghan people, including the importance of holding free, fair and secure elections in 2009 and 2010, the importance of ensuring respect for the human rights of all Afghans and the provision of humanitarian assistance, and the need to improve aid effectiveness in order to ensure that the benefits of development are tangible for every Afghan.

The Council also welcomes the review of the Afghanistan Compact presented at the Conference. In this regard, the Council reiterates its call upon the Government of Afghanistan and the international community to implement the Compact and the annexes thereto in full.

The Council recalls the strengthened role of the Mission and the Special Representative in leading and coordinating international civilian efforts in Afghanistan, through an integrated approach and guided by the principle of reinforcing Afghan ownership and leadership. The Council reaffirms in particular the priorities for the Mission and the Special Representative identified in paragraph 4 of its resolution 1806(2008) and endorses the views of the Secretary-General and his Special Representative on the areas that require greater attention. The Council calls upon all relevant actors to give their full support to the Mission's enhanced coordinating role.

The Council endorses the recommendation that, in order for the Mission to fulfil its mandate, much greater substantive, administrative and security resources will need to be expeditiously mobilized in the areas mentioned in the report of the Secretary-General, through the relevant processes and procedures within the United Nations system. The Council welcomes in particular the intention to proceed, pursuant to resolution 1806(2008), with another expansion of the field presence of the Mission through the opening of six new provincial offices over the next 12 months. The Council also welcomes plans to improve the coherence of action of the United Nations country team in support of the priorities of the Mission.

The Council reaffirms once again its strong commitment to the sovereignty, independence, territorial integrity and national unity of Afghanistan. The Council expresses its strong concern about the security situation in Afghanistan and stresses the need to continue to address the threat to the security and stability of Afghanistan posed by the Taliban, Al-Qaida, illegal armed groups, criminals and those involved in the narcotics trade and in the diversion of chemical precursors, including through the implementation of measures introduced in its resolution 1267(1999) and other relevant resolutions of the Council. The Council notes the links between illicit drug trafficking, corruption and terrorism, and stresses the need for full implementation of its resolution 1817(2008) on international cooperation to prevent trafficking in and diversion of chemical precursors of heroin for illicit use in Afghanistan.

Report of Secretary-General (September). In a report of 23 September [A/63/372-S/2008/617], the Secretary-General said that despite the enhanced capabilities of the Afghan army and international forces, the security situation had deteriorated markedly, with the insurgency expanding its influence beyond traditionally volatile areas to provinces neighbouring Kabul.

The insurgency's use of asymmetric tactics had led to a sharp rise in civilian casualties. Civilians were also being killed as a result of military operations by Afghan and international security forces, particularly when insurgents concealed themselves in populated areas. The most pressing humanitarian problems were drought and high global food prices, which had created food shortages affecting one sixth of the population.

On the positive side, the June Paris Conference had launched the Afghanistan National Development Strategy. The number of poppy-free provinces had increased from 13 to 18, and most cultivation was now concentrated in a few provinces; but the cost of eradication in terms of lives lost had been high, and revenues from the illegal opium economy continued to finance the insurgency.

The National Assembly adopted laws on the civil service, public health and political parties, but the lower house was unable to adopt the new electoral law. The Cabinet, however, approved a proposal by the Independent Election Commission to run voter registration in four phases, between 6 October 2008 and 3 February 2009.

Regional cooperation efforts led to an agreement by Afghanistan, India, Pakistan and Turkmenistan to begin constructing a trans-Afghanistan gas pipeline in 2010, and Iran concluded memorandums of understanding with Afghanistan on bilateral trade.

The number of security incidents increased to 983 in August—the highest since the fall of the Taliban in 2001 and a 44 per cent increase compared with August 2007. Of more than 3,800 lives lost in insurgency-related violence through the end of July, over one third were civilians.

In the first eight months of 2008, civilian deaths recorded by UNAMA had increased by 39 per cent, to a total of 1,445. Of those, 55 per cent were attributed to attacks by anti-Government elements, 40 per cent to pro-Government forces and 5 per cent to unknown agents. More than 120 attacks targeted humanitarian and development programmes, with 30 humanitarian aid workers killed and 92 abducted.

UNAMA recorded 142 summary executions by the armed opposition in 2008 and dozens of cases of threats, intimidation and harassment of doctors, teachers, students, tribal elders, Government employees, former police and military personnel, and labourers involved in public-interest construction work.

The number of security incidents in the capital, however, had decreased, reflecting the enhanced capability of Afghan intelligence and security forces. In addition, ISAF, with 55,000 troops, increased its presence in the east and the south, as well as in Kapisa, Logar and Wardak provinces around Kabul.

As for the inflow of chemical precursors for illicit heroin manufacturing, Pakistan, Iran and other neighbouring countries made significant seizures of acetic anhydride—the first such seizures since 2001. The Secretary-General urged Governments to intensify their participation in activities led by the International Narcotics Control Board and the United Nations Office on Drugs and Crime to prevent diversion and trafficking of precursors to Afghanistan and neighbouring States.

With respect to human rights, the atmosphere of impunity perpetuated the notion that crime and the abuse of power was acceptable. That undermined efforts to uphold the rule of law, including redress for victims of human rights violations. The Cabinet in May adopted the National Action Plan for the Women of Afghanistan, and in August, the President and the Ministry of the Interior denounced the high incidence of sexual assaults.

Since the beginning of the year, more than 200,000 Afghan refugees had been repatriated, largely from Pakistan. However, armed conflict in the south, ethnic strife in Behsud and the potential impact of the drought in the northern and western parts of the country had displaced thousands.

Following the Paris Conference, UNAMA undertook to enhance the coordination of donor efforts and to strengthen aid effectiveness. To meet priorities identified in its mandate and at the Conference, UNAMA would require significant staffing increases, some structural changes and an increase in essential security-related equipment. The specifics would be detailed in the upcoming UNAMA budget proposal to the General Assembly.

Security Council consideration (October). Briefing the Council on 14 October [meeting 5994], the Special Representative cited positive developments in Afghanistan, including improved relations with Pakistan and changes to strengthen its Interior and Agriculture Ministries and the police. UNAMA had a better working relationship with ISAF than half a year earlier, but it was still a small mission in need of qualified staff to fulfil its mandate.

Afghanistan said that real security in the country required improvement in the day-to-day lives of people, including governance and the rule of law, humanitarian and counter-narcotics efforts, the upcoming elections, strong army and police forces, and a sustainable economy. Afghanistan had found in the new President of Pakistan, Asif Ali Zardari, a friend and trusted leader with whom it could counter terrorism. An increase in international troops was essential to that task.

Pakistan said that security in Afghanistan must be addressed in all its aspects, including the Taliban insurgency, Al-Qaida, lingering warlordism, factional rivalries, criminal and other illegal armed groups, and the drug trade. Pakistan would press forward on cooperation with Afghanistan and would be hosting a meeting of a mini-jirga in Islamabad on 27 and 28 October.

GENERAL ASSEMBLY ACTION

On 10 November [meeting 42], the General Assembly adopted **resolution 63/18** [draft: A/63/L.17 & Add.1] without vote [agenda item 17].

The situation in Afghanistan

The General Assembly,

Recalling its resolution 62/6 of 5 November 2007 and all its previous relevant resolutions,

Recalling also all relevant Security Council resolutions and statements by the President of the Council on the situation in Afghanistan, in particular resolutions 1659(2006) of 15 February 2006, 1806(2008) of 20 March 2008, 1817(2008) of 11 June 2008 and 1833(2008) of 22 September 2008, as well as the statement by the President of the Council of 11 July 2008,

Reaffirming its strong commitment to the sovereignty, independence, territorial integrity and national unity of Afghanistan, and respecting its multicultural, multi-ethnic and historical heritage,

Reaffirming its continued support for the implementation of the Afghanistan Compact of 31 January 2006, which provides the framework for the partnership between the Government of Afghanistan and the international community, and recalling in this regard the spirit and the provisions of the Bonn Agreement of 5 December 2001 and the Berlin Declaration, including the annexes thereto, of 1 April 2004,

Recognizing once again the interconnected nature of the challenges in Afghanistan, reaffirming that sustainable progress on security, governance and development, as well as the cross-cutting theme of counter-narcotics, is mutually reinforcing, and welcoming the continuing efforts of the Government of Afghanistan and the international community to address these challenges in a coherent manner,

Reiterating the urgent need to tackle the challenges in Afghanistan, in particular the increased violent criminal and terrorist activities by the Taliban, Al-Qaida, illegal armed groups and those involved in the narcotics trade, in particular in the south and east, and the development of Afghan Government institutions, including at the subnational level, the strengthening of the rule of law, the acceleration of justice sector reform, the promotion of national reconciliation, without prejudice to the fulfilment of the measures introduced by the Security Council in its resolution 1267(1999) of 15 October 1999 and other relevant resolutions, and an Afghan-led transitional justice process, the safe and voluntary return of Afghan refugees and internally displaced persons in an orderly and dignified manner, the promotion and protection of human rights and the advancement of economic and social development,

Condemning, in the strongest terms, all attacks, including improvised explosive device attacks, suicide attacks and abductions, targeting civilians and Afghan and international forces, and their deleterious effect on the stabilization, reconstruction and development efforts in Afghanistan, and condemning further the use by the Taliban, Al-Qaida and other extremist and criminal groups of civilians as human shields,

Deeply concerned about the recent increase in violence in Afghanistan, in particular in the south and east, recognizing the increased threats posed by the Taliban, Al-Qaida and other extremist and criminal groups as well as the challenges related to the efforts to address such threats, expressing its serious concern about the high number of civilian casualties, noting relevant statements of Afghan authorities and high-ranking United Nations officials, as well as statements to the press by the President of the Security Council in this regard, and calling for compliance with international humanitarian and human rights law and for all appropriate measures to be taken to ensure the protection of civilians,

Recognizing the efforts made by the International Security Assistance Force and other international forces to minimize the risk of civilian casualties, and calling upon them to make additional robust efforts in this regard, notably by the continuous review of tactics and procedures and the conduct of after-action reviews and investigations in cooperation with the Government of Afghanistan in cases where civilian casualties have occurred and when the Government finds these joint investigations appropriate,

Noting the importance of the national Government being representative of the ethnic diversity of the country and ensuring also the full and equal participation of women,

1. *Stresses* the central and impartial role of the United Nations in promoting peace and stability in Afghanistan, expresses its appreciation and strong support for all efforts of the Secretary-General and his Special Representative in this regard, and welcomes the leading role of the United Nations Assistance Mission in Afghanistan in the coordination of the international civilian effort, guided by the principle of reinforcing Afghan ownership and leadership;

2. *Welcomes* the Declaration of the Paris Conference of 12 June 2008 and the additional international support as pledged, reaffirms that the Afghanistan Compact, including the annexes thereto, remains the agreed basis for the work of both Afghanistan and the international community, welcomes the launching of the Afghanistan National Development Strategy, which reflects, inter alia, increased Afghan ownership and responsibility, and welcomes the Afghan commitment to pursue political and economic reform;

3. *Also welcomes* the reports of the Secretary-General and the recommendations contained therein;

4. *Expresses its strong concern* about the security situation in Afghanistan, stresses the need to continue to address the threat to the security and stability of Afghanistan caused by increased violent and terrorist activity by the Taliban, Al-Qaida and other extremist and criminal groups, including those involved in the narcotics trade, and strongly condemns all acts of violence and intimidation committed in Afghanistan, in particular in the southern and eastern parts, including suicide attacks;

5. *Expresses in this regard deep regret* at the resulting loss of life and physical harm inflicted upon Afghan civilians and civilians of other nationalities, including the personnel of Afghan and international agencies and all other humanitarian workers and the diplomatic corps, as well as upon the personnel of the Afghan National Security Forces, the International Security Assistance Force and the Operation Enduring Freedom coalition;

6. *Stresses* the need for the Government of Afghanistan and the international community to continue to work closely together in countering these challenges of terrorist attacks by the Taliban, Al-Qaida and other extremist and criminal groups, which are threatening the democratic process as well as the reconstruction and economic development of Afghanistan, and reiterates in this regard its call for full implementation of measures introduced in relevant Security Council resolutions, in particular resolution 1267(1999);

7. *Notes with concern* that the security situation is causing some organizations to cease or curtail their humanitarian and development work in some parts of Afghanistan;

8. *Stresses* the importance of the provision of sufficient security, welcomes the presence of the Force throughout Afghanistan, and calls upon Member States to continue contributing personnel, equipment and other resources to the Force and to further develop the provincial reconstruction teams in close coordination with the Government of Afghanistan and the Mission;

9. *Notes*, in the context of the comprehensive approach, the synergies in the objectives of the Mission and the Force;

10. *Also notes* that the responsibility for providing security and law and order throughout the country resides with the Government of Afghanistan supported by the Force and the Operation Enduring Freedom coalition, and recognizes the institutional progress achieved in this respect and the continued coordination between the Force and the coalition;

11. *Stresses* the importance of further extending central government authority, including the presence of Afghan security forces, to all provinces of Afghanistan;

12. *Calls upon* the Government of Afghanistan, with the assistance of the international community, including through the Operation Enduring Freedom coalition and the Force, in accordance with their respective designated responsibilities, to continue to address the threat to the security and stability of Afghanistan;

13. *Commends* the Afghan National Army and the Afghan National Police, the Force and the Operation Enduring Freedom coalition for their efforts to improve security conditions in Afghanistan;

14. *Welcomes* the continued development of the Afghan National Army and the Afghan National Police, recognizes the international support provided, calls for intensified Afghan and international efforts to modernize and strengthen both institutions and related Government departments, with particular attention to the Afghan National Police which continues to face challenges in its development, and welcomes in this regard the continued deployment of the European Union Police Mission in Afghanistan and the focused district development and in-district reform programmes;

15. *Acknowledges*, in this context, that the Afghan National Army and the Afghan National Police require additional support to enhance their capability and professionalism, including through the provision of increased training and mentoring, more modern equipment and infrastructure, and continued salary support;

16. *Urges* the Afghan authorities to take all possible steps to ensure the safety, security and free movement of all

United Nations, development and humanitarian personnel, and their safe and unhindered access to all affected populations, and to protect the property of the United Nations and of development or humanitarian organizations;

17. *Also urges* the Afghan authorities to make every effort, in accordance with General Assembly resolution 60/123 of 15 December 2005, to bring to justice the perpetrators of attacks;

18. *Stresses* the importance of advancing the full implementation of the programme of disbandment of illegal armed groups throughout the country under Afghan ownership, while ensuring coordination and coherence with other relevant efforts, including security sector reform, community development, counter-narcotics, district-level development and Afghan-led initiatives to ensure that entities and individuals do not illegally participate in the political process, including elections in 2009 and 2010, in accordance with adopted laws and regulations in Afghanistan, and calls for adequate support in order for the Ministry of the Interior to increasingly assume its leading role in implementing the programme of disbandment of illegal armed groups;

19. *Welcomes* the commitment of the Government of Afghanistan to stand firm on the disbandment of illegal armed groups and to work actively at national, provincial and local levels to advance this commitment, stresses, in this regard, all efforts to create sufficient legal income-earning opportunities, and calls for continued international support for these efforts;

20. *Remains deeply concerned* about the problem of millions of anti-personnel landmines and explosive remnants of war, which constitute a great danger for the population and a major obstacle to the resumption of economic activities and to recovery and reconstruction efforts;

21. *Welcomes* the progress achieved through the Mine Action Programme for Afghanistan, supports the Government of Afghanistan in its efforts to meet its responsibilities under the Convention on the Prohibition of the Use, Stockpiling, Production and Transfer of Anti-personnel Mines and on Their Destruction, to cooperate fully with the Mine Action Programme coordinated by the United Nations and to eliminate all known or new stocks of anti-personnel landmines, and acknowledges the need for more assistance from the international community in this regard;

22. *Stresses* that regional cooperation constitutes an effective means to promote security and development in Afghanistan;

23. *Pledges its continued support*, after the successful completion of the political transition, to the Government and people of Afghanistan as they rebuild their country, strengthen the foundations of a constitutional democracy and resume their rightful place in the community of nations;

24. *Recalls* the constitutional guarantee of human rights and fundamental freedoms for all Afghans as a significant political achievement, and stresses the need to fully implement the human rights provisions of the Afghan Constitution, including those regarding the full enjoyment by women and children of their human rights;

25. *Calls for* the full respect of the human rights and fundamental freedoms of all, without discrimination of any kind, including on the basis of gender, ethnicity or religion, in accordance with obligations under the Afghan Constitution and international law;

26. *Commends* the achievements and the commitment of the Government of Afghanistan in this respect, and expresses its concern at the harmful consequences of violent and terrorist activities by the Taliban, Al-Qaida and other extremist and criminal groups for the enjoyment of human rights and for the capacity of the Government of Afghanistan to ensure human rights and fundamental freedoms for all Afghans;

27. *Recalls* Security Council resolutions 1674(2006) of 28 April 2006 and 1738(2006) of 23 December 2006 on the protection of civilians in armed conflict, expresses its concern at the high number of civilian casualties, including women and children, as stated in the recent report of the Secretary-General on the situation in Afghanistan, reiterates its call for all feasible steps to be taken to ensure the protection of civilians, and calls for full compliance with international humanitarian and human rights law;

28. *Recognizes* the importance of holding free, fair and secure elections in 2009 and 2010 as a crucial step towards consolidating democracy for all Afghans as identified in the Afghanistan Compact, stresses the responsibility of the Afghan authorities in this regard, and calls upon the international community to continue to provide sustained support, including financial assistance and support to the Government of Afghanistan to ensure the security of the elections;

29. *Welcomes* the steps taken by the Government of Afghanistan on justice sector reform, stresses the need for further accelerated progress towards the establishment of a fair and effective justice system as an important step towards the goal of strengthening the Government, providing security and ensuring the rule of law throughout the country, and urges the international community to continue to support the efforts of the Government in these areas in a coordinated manner;

30. *Also welcomes*, in this regard, the adoption by the Afghan authorities of the National Justice Programme, and stresses the importance of its full and timely implementation by all the relevant actors;

31. *Urges* the Government of Afghanistan and the international community to devote adequate resources to the reconstruction and reform of the prison sector in order to improve respect for the rule of law and human rights therein, while reducing physical and mental health risks to inmates;

32. *Emphasizes* the importance of ensuring access for relevant organizations to all prisons in Afghanistan, and calls for full respect for relevant international law, including humanitarian law and human rights law, where applicable, including with regard to minors, if detained;

33. *Notes with concern* reports of continued violations of human rights and of international humanitarian law, including violent or discriminatory practices, violations committed against persons belonging to ethnic and religious minorities, as well as against women and girls, stresses the need to promote tolerance and religious freedom as guaranteed by the Afghan Constitution, emphasizes the necessity of investigating allegations of current and past violations, and stresses the importance of facilitating the provision of efficient and effective remedies to the victims and of bring-

ing the perpetrators to justice in accordance with national and international law;

34. *Stresses* the need to ensure respect for the right to freedom of expression and the right to freedom of thought, conscience or belief, while noting with concern recent attempts to limit freedom of expression and to intimidate journalists, and condemns cases of the abduction and even killing of journalists by terrorist as well as extremist and criminal groups;

35. *Reiterates* the important role of the Afghan Independent Human Rights Commission in the promotion and protection of human rights and fundamental freedoms, stresses the need to expand its range of operation in all parts of Afghanistan in accordance with the Afghan Constitution, encourages the Government of Afghanistan to take increasing responsibility for the core funding of the Commission, and calls upon the international community for continued support in this regard;

36. *Calls for* the full implementation by the Government of Afghanistan of the Action Plan on Peace, Justice and Reconciliation, in the framework of the Afghan Constitution, without prejudice to the implementation of measures introduced by the Security Council in its resolution 1267(1999), and recalls other relevant resolutions in this regard, including Council resolution 1806(2008);

37. *Recalls* Security Council resolutions 1325(2000) of 31 October 2000 and 1820(2008) of 19 June 2008 on women and peace and security, commends the efforts of the Government of Afghanistan to mainstream gender issues and to protect and promote the equal rights of women and men as guaranteed, inter alia, by virtue of its ratification of the Convention on the Elimination of All Forms of Discrimination against Women, and by the Afghan Constitution, and reiterates the continued importance of the full and equal participation of women in all spheres of Afghan life, and of equality before the law and equal access to legal counsel without discrimination of any kind;

38. *Welcomes* the creation of a special fund for the protection of women at risk, set up by the United Nations Development Fund for Women with the support of the Office of the United Nations High Commissioner for Refugees;

39. *Also welcomes* the implementation of the National Action Plan for Women in Afghanistan and the significant efforts by the Government of Afghanistan to counter discrimination, urges the Government to actively involve all elements of Afghan society, in particular women, in the development and implementation of relief, rehabilitation, recovery and reconstruction programmes, and encourages the collection and use of statistical data on a sex-disaggregated basis to provide information on gender-based violence and accurately track the progress of the full integration of women into the political, economic and social life of Afghanistan;

40. *Applauds* the progress achieved on gender equality and in the empowerment of women in Afghan politics as historic milestones in the political process which will help to consolidate durable peace and national stability in Afghanistan, while noting the need to promote the empowerment of women also at the provincial level;

41. *Strongly condemns* incidents of discrimination and violence against women and girls, in particular if directed against women activists and women prominent in public life, wherever they occur in Afghanistan, including killings, maiming and "honour killings" in certain parts of the country;

42. *Stresses* the need to ensure respect for the human rights and fundamental freedoms of children in Afghanistan, recalls the need for the full implementation of the Convention on the Rights of the Child and the two Optional Protocols thereto by all States parties, as well as Security Council resolution 1612(2005) of 26 July 2005 on children and armed conflict;

43. *Expresses in this regard its concern* about the ongoing recruitment and use of children by illegal armed and terrorist groups in Afghanistan, as described in the report of the Secretary-General on children and armed conflict of 21 December 2007, stresses the importance of ending the use of children contrary to international law, and welcomes the progress achieved by and firm commitment of the Government of Afghanistan in this regard, including the strong condemnation of any exploitation of children;

44. *Welcomes* the adoption by the Government of Afghanistan of the National Plan of Action on Combating Child Trafficking, also welcomes initiatives to pass legislation on human trafficking, guided by the Protocol to Prevent, Suppress and Punish Trafficking in Persons, Especially Women and Children, supplementing the United Nations Convention against Transnational Organized Crime, and stresses the importance of considering becoming a party to the Protocol;

45. *Urges* the Government of Afghanistan to continue to effectively reform the public administration sector in order to implement the rule of law and to ensure good governance and accountability at both national and local levels, and stresses the importance of meeting the respective benchmarks of the Afghanistan Compact, with the support of the international community;

46. *Welcomes* the appointment of officials, as required by the Afghanistan Compact, to the Senior Appointments Panel, and encourages the Government of Afghanistan to make active use of this panel, thus enhancing efficiency and transparency in the appointment of senior officials;

47. *Encourages* the international community, including all donor nations, to assist the Government of Afghanistan in making capacity-building and human resources development a cross-cutting priority;

48. *Welcomes* the ratification by Afghanistan of the United Nations Convention against Corruption, encourages the Government of Afghanistan to vigorously pursue its efforts to establish a more effective, accountable and transparent administration at national, provincial and local levels of Government leading the fight against corruption in accordance with the Afghanistan Compact, and notes with concern the effects of corruption with regard to security, good governance, combating the narcotics industry and economic development;

49. *Applauds* the establishment of the Independent Directorate of Local Governance by the Government of Afghanistan, calls upon Afghan authorities and the international community to actively support the work of the Directorate to establish and strengthen governance institutions at subnational levels and ensure that those institutions play a strong role in facilitating the delivery of national activities and programmes to improve the well-being of the

Afghan people, and welcomes in this regard international support provided, including the agreements the Directorate has signed with India and the Islamic Republic of Iran to expand public service training;

50. *Urges* the Government of Afghanistan to address, with the assistance of the international community, the question of claims for land property through a comprehensive land titling programme, including formal registration of all property and improved security of property rights, and welcomes the steps already taken by the Government in this regard;

51. *Welcomes* the launch of the Afghanistan National Development Strategy, as well as further efforts of the Government of Afghanistan to achieve the Millennium Development Goals;

52. *Also welcomes* the continuing and growing ownership of rehabilitation, reconstruction and development efforts by the Government of Afghanistan, and emphasizes the crucial need to achieve ownership in all fields of governance and to improve institutional capabilities, including at the provincial level, in order to use aid more effectively;

53. *Stresses* the need for a continued strong international commitment to humanitarian assistance and for programmes, under the ownership of the Government of Afghanistan, of recovery, rehabilitation, reconstruction and development, while expressing its appreciation to the United Nations system and to all States and international and non-governmental organizations whose international and local staff continue to respond positively to the humanitarian, transition and development needs of Afghanistan despite increasing security concerns and difficulties of access in certain areas;

54. *Expresses its appreciation* for the humanitarian and development assistance work of the international community in the reconstruction and development of Afghanistan, recognizes the necessity for further improvement in the living conditions of the Afghan people, and emphasizes the need to strengthen and support the capacity of the Government of Afghanistan to deliver basic social services, in particular education and public health services, and to promote development;

55. *Also expresses its appreciation* for the work of the provincial reconstruction teams;

56. *Urgently appeals* to all States, the United Nations system and international and non-governmental organizations to continue to provide, in close coordination with the Government of Afghanistan and in accordance with its national development strategy, all possible and necessary humanitarian, recovery, reconstruction, development, financial, technical and material assistance for Afghanistan, and recalls in this regard the leading role of the Mission in coordinating international efforts;

57. *Urges* the international community, in accordance with the Afghanistan Compact, to increase the proportion of donor assistance channelled directly to the core budget, as agreed bilaterally between the Government of Afghanistan and each donor, as well as through other more predictable core budget funding modalities in which the Government participates, such as the Afghanistan Reconstruction Trust Fund, the Law and Order Trust Fund and the Counter-Narcotics Trust Fund;

58. *Invites* all States and intergovernmental and non-governmental organizations providing assistance to Afghanistan to focus on institution-building in a coordinated manner and to ensure that such work complements and contributes to the development of an economy characterized by sound macroeconomic policies, the development of a financial sector that provides services, inter alia, to microenterprises, small and medium-sized enterprises and households, transparent business regulations and accountability;

59. *Encourages* the international community to support the local economy as a measure for long-term stability and countering narcotics and, in this respect, to explore possibilities for enhancing local procurement;

60. *Welcomes* all efforts to increase regional economic cooperation, and recognizes the important role of the Economic Cooperation Organization and the South Asian Association for Regional Cooperation in promoting Afghanistan's development;

61. *Calls for* strengthening the process of regional economic cooperation, including measures to facilitate regional trade, to increase foreign investments and to develop infrastructure, noting Afghanistan's historic role as a land bridge in Asia;

62. *Reiterates* the necessity of providing Afghan children, especially Afghan girls, with educational and health facilities in all parts of the country, welcomes progress achieved in the sector of public education, recalls the National Education Strategic Plan as a promising basis for further achievements, and reiterates further the need to provide vocational training for adolescents;

63. *Recognizes* the special needs of girls, strongly condemns terrorist attacks on education facilities, especially on those for Afghan girls, and encourages the Government of Afghanistan, with the assistance of the international community, to expand those facilities, to train professional staff and to promote full and equal access to them by all members of Afghan society, including in remote areas;

64. *Welcomes* the continuous return of refugees and internally displaced persons, in a voluntary and sustainable manner, while noting with concern that conditions in parts of Afghanistan are not yet conducive to safe and sustainable returns to some places of origin;

65. *Expresses its appreciation* to those Governments that continue to host Afghan refugees, acknowledging the huge burden they have so far shouldered in this regard, and reminds them of their obligations under international refugee law with respect to the protection of refugees, the principle of voluntary return and the right to seek asylum and to allow international access for their protection and care;

66. *Urges* the Government of Afghanistan, acting with the support of the international community, to continue to strengthen its efforts to create the conditions for the voluntary, safe, dignified and sustainable return and reintegration of the remaining Afghan refugees and internally displaced persons;

67. *Welcomes*, in this regard, the continued constructive work between the countries of the region, and the tripartite agreements between the Office of the United Nations High Commissioner for Refugees, the Government of Afghanistan and the Governments of countries hosting

refugees from Afghanistan, in particular Pakistan and the Islamic Republic of Iran;

68. *Calls for* the provision of continued international assistance to the large numbers of Afghan refugees and internally displaced persons to facilitate their voluntary, safe, dignified and orderly return and sustainable reintegration into society so as to contribute to the stability of the entire country;

69. *Recognizes* that underdevelopment and lack of capacity increase the vulnerability of Afghanistan to natural disasters and to harsh climate conditions, and urges in this regard the Government of Afghanistan, with the support of the international community, to increase its efforts aimed at modernizing the agricultural sector and strengthening its agricultural production, thereby reducing Afghanistan's vulnerability to adverse external conditions such as drought, flooding and the recent steep rise in global food prices;

70. *Expresses its concern* at the worsening humanitarian situation, especially the perilous food security situation, created in particular by high world food and energy prices and continued drought conditions in Afghanistan, and calls for urgent international support for and the early fulfilment, before the approaching winter, of the funding target of the emergency appeal to address the high food price and drought crisis;

71. *Welcomes* the growing number of poppy-free provinces and other positive developments in fighting drug production in Afghanistan, as reported by the United Nations Office on Drugs and Crime in the "Afghanistan Opium Survey 2008", released on 26 August 2008, but reiterates its deep concern about the continued cultivation and production of narcotic drugs in Afghanistan, mainly concentrated in areas where the Taliban, Al-Qaida and other extremist and criminal groups are particularly active, as well as the ongoing drug trafficking, and stresses the need for more coordinated and resolute efforts by the Government of Afghanistan, supported by the international community, to fight this menace;

72. *Notes with great concern* the increasingly strong nexus between the drug trade and terrorist activities by the Taliban, Al-Qaida and other extremist and criminal groups which pose a serious threat to security, the rule of law and development in Afghanistan, and stresses the importance of the implementation of all relevant Security Council resolutions in this regard, including resolution 1735(2006) of 22 December 2006;

73. *Stresses* the need to prevent trafficking in and diversion of chemical precursors used in the illicit manufacturing of drugs, including heroin for illicit use in Afghanistan, and calls for the full implementation of Security Council resolution 1817(2008) in this regard;

74. *Urges* the Government of Afghanistan, supported by the international community, to work to mainstream counter-narcotics throughout all the national programmes and to ensure that counter-narcotics is a fundamental part of the comprehensive approach, as well as to increase its efforts against opium cultivation and drug trafficking in accordance with the balanced eight-pillar plan of the Afghan National Drug Control Strategy;

75. *Commends* the efforts of the Government of Afghanistan in this regard, as well as the efforts to carry out the National Drug Control Strategy, including the Prioritized Implementation Plan, urges the Government and the international community to take decisive action, in particular to stop the processing of and trade in drugs, by pursuing the concrete steps set out in the Strategy and in the Afghanistan Compact and through initiatives such as the Good Performance Initiative established to provide incentives for governors to reduce cultivation in their provinces, and encourages the Afghan authorities to work at the provincial level on elaborating counter-narcotics implementation plans;

76. *Calls upon* the international community to assist the Government of Afghanistan in carrying out its National Drug Control Strategy, aimed at eliminating the cultivation, production, trafficking in and consumption of illicit drugs, including through increased support for Afghan law enforcement and criminal justice agencies, agricultural and rural development, demand reduction, the elimination of illicit crops, increasing public awareness, building the capacity of drug control institutions, care and treatment centres for drug addicts and creating alternative livelihoods for farmers;

77. *Encourages* the international community to increasingly channel counter-narcotics funding through the Government of Afghanistan's Counter-Narcotics Trust Fund, and urges the efficient and timely delivery of the aid provided;

78. *Stresses* the importance of a comprehensive approach to address the drug problem of Afghanistan, which, to be effective, has to be integrated into the wider context of efforts carried out in the areas of security, governance, rule of law and human rights, and economic and social development, stresses that the development of alternative livelihood programmes is of key importance in the success of the efforts in counter-narcotics in Afghanistan, and reiterates that extensive efforts have also to be made to reduce the demand for drugs globally in order to contribute to the sustainability of the elimination of illicit cultivation in Afghanistan;

79. *Urges* the Government of Afghanistan, assisted by the international community, to promote the development of sustainable livelihoods in the formal production sector as well as other sectors, and to improve access to reasonable and sustainable credit and financing in rural areas, thus improving substantially the lives, health and security of the people, particularly in rural areas;

80. *Supports* the fight against the illicit trafficking in drugs from and precursors to Afghanistan and neighbouring States and countries along trafficking routes, including increased cooperation among them in strengthening anti-narcotic controls and the monitoring of the international trade in chemical precursors;

81. *Calls upon* States to strengthen international and regional cooperation to counter the increasing threat to the international community posed by the illicit production of drugs in Afghanistan and trafficking in drugs, recognizes the progress achieved by relevant initiatives within the framework of the Paris Pact, the Second Ministerial Conference on Drug Trafficking Routes from Afghanistan, held in Moscow from 26 to 28 June 2006, the meeting in Kabul in October 2007, and the Tehran agreement on a triangular initiative by Afghanistan, the Islamic Republic

of Iran and Pakistan, and stresses the importance of further progress in the implementation of these initiatives;

82. *Pays homage* to all those who have lost their lives in the fight against drug traffickers, in particular members of the security forces of Afghanistan and its neighbouring countries;

83. *Welcomes* recent initiatives to promote border management cooperation in drug control between Afghanistan and its neighbours;

84. *Stresses* the importance of further, effective cooperative support by relevant international and regional actors, including the United Nations and the Force within its designated responsibilities, to Afghan-led sustained efforts to address the threat posed by the illicit production of and trafficking in drugs;

85. *Expresses its appreciation* for the work of the Mission as mandated by the Security Council in its resolution 1806(2008), and stresses the continued importance of the central and impartial role played by the Mission in promoting and coordinating a more coherent international engagement;

86. *Welcomes* the ongoing extension of the presence of the Mission into additional provinces, which thus ensures that the United Nations fulfils its essential coordinating role, and encourages the Mission to consolidate its presence and to continue its expansion throughout the country, in particular in the south, security conditions permitting;

87. *Stresses* the need to ensure that the Mission is adequately resourced to fulfil its mandate;

88. *Acknowledges* the central role played by the Joint Coordination and Monitoring Board in facilitating and monitoring the implementation of the Afghanistan Compact, stresses the role of the Board to support Afghanistan by, inter alia, coordinating international assistance and reconstruction programmes, and welcomes further efforts to provide appropriate guidance and promote a more coherent international engagement;

89. *Commends* the continuing efforts of the signatories of the Kabul Declaration on Good-neighbourly Relations of 22 December 2002 to implement their commitments under the Declaration, and furthermore calls upon all other States to respect and support the implementation of those provisions and to promote regional stability;

90. *Welcomes* efforts by the Governments of Afghanistan and its neighbouring partners to foster trust and cooperation with each other, and looks forward, where appropriate, to increasing cooperation between Afghanistan and all its neighbouring and regional partners against the Taliban, Al-Qaida and other extremist and criminal groups and in promoting peace and prosperity in Afghanistan, in the region and beyond;

91. *Also welcomes* the important role of Afghanistan's neighbours and regional partners, including the Shanghai Cooperation Organization, in promoting the country's stability and development;

92. *Encourages* the Group of Eight countries to continue to promote cooperation with and assistance for Afghanistan through mutual consultation and agreement, including follow-up projects in areas such as repatriation of refugees, border management and economic development;

93. *Appreciates* the efforts of the members of the Tripartite Commission, namely Afghanistan, Pakistan and the Force, to continue to address cross-border activities and to broaden its cooperation;

94. *Emphasizes* the need to maintain, strengthen and review civil-military relations among international actors, as appropriate, at all levels in order to ensure complementarity of action based on the different mandates and comparative advantages of the humanitarian, development, law enforcement and military actors present in Afghanistan, bearing in mind the central and impartial coordinating role of the United Nations;

95. *Requests* the Secretary-General to report to the General Assembly every six months during its sixty-third session on developments in Afghanistan, as well as on the progress made in the implementation of the present resolution;

96. *Decides* to include in the provisional agenda of its sixty-fourth session the item entitled "The situation in Afghanistan".

Children and armed conflict

In November, pursuant to Security Council resolution 1612(2005) [YUN 2005, p. 863], the Secretary-General submitted a report on children and armed conflict in Afghanistan [S/2008/695], covering the period from 1 July 2007 to 15 August 2008. During that period, 81 children were killed and 332 sustained injuries due to unexploded ordnance and explosive remnants of war. Acts of violence targeted schools as representative of the Government or of perceived foreign interference; the Taliban and its proxies were reportedly responsible. The Taliban had denied nearly all girls the right to attend school while in power, a position they still brutally enforced. Arson was by far the most frequent type of incident carried out on educational facilities.

There were substantive reports of children, especially boys, being sexually abused and exploited by members of the armed forces and armed groups. Most victims did not want their experience to be reported. The report discussed certain incidents involving personnel of the national security forces that had been appropriately dealt with by the authorities.

Children had been used by all parties throughout the 30 years of armed conflict. Internally displaced families reported that the threat of recruitment by armed groups was higher "because the Taliban pay more than the police".

Visiting Afghanistan from 28 June to 3 July, the Secretary-General's Special Representative for Children and Armed Conflict, Radhika Coomaraswamy, expressed her concern about reports of children being used by anti-Government elements, the death and injury of children during fighting, the detention of children, sexual violence against children and continuing attacks on schools, teachers and schoolchildren. She also expressed concern about the unintentional death of children as a result of the operations of international military forces and the Afghan national security forces. She stressed that UN monitoring agents should have unimpeded access to all detention facilities where children were believed to be present. Worrisome allegations about sexual violence against boys by armed actors should be confronted despite their sensitive nature.

The United Nations Children's Fund (UNICEF) in January began a capacity-building initiative for local non-governmental organizations (NGOs) active in the field of human rights, aimed at developing a monitoring system to reduce the unlawful detention of children. In June, UNICEF initiated a dialogue with the National Directorate of Security to ensure due process for all juveniles, and the implementation of the juvenile protection measures in the new anti-terrorist law.

Security Council mission

On 14 November [S/2008/708], the President of the Security Council informed the Secretary-General that the Council had decided to send a mission to Afghanistan from 21 to 28 November. The Mission was to be led by Giulio Terzi di Sant'Agata (Italy). Its terms of reference included reviewing the humanitarian situation, and therewith food security; progress with respect to security, governance, the rule of law, human rights, economic and social development and counter-narcotics; efforts to address the threat posed by the Taliban, Al-Qaida, illegal armed groups and criminals, and therewith the narcotics trade; and implementation of the enhanced coordinating role assigned to UNAMA and the Special Representative by Security Council resolution 1806(2008) (see p. 355). The Mission would assess the cooperation between UNAMA and ISAF, as well as the implementation of the commitments made at the June Paris Conference. It would reaffirm the Security Council's continued support for the Government and people of Afghanistan as they rebuilt their country and the importance of regional cooperation, while underlining the central and impartial role of the United Nations in promoting peace and stability.

Report of Security Council mission (December). The head of the mission briefed the Council on 4 December [meeting 6031]. The report of the mission [S/2008/782], dated 12 December, noted a striking year-to-year increase in the numbers of security incidents since 2003 and in the number of incidents targeting the humanitarian and development community. Interlocutors identified four main reasons: the influx of militants recruited from outside Afghanistan (UNAMA estimated that 20 per cent of insurgents were from outside the country); insufficient integration and coordination of military, political, governance and development efforts; a dearth of reconstruction and employment opportunities combined with a large number of unemployed young men; and frustration with the tactics of the international forces, including civilian casualties caused by their combat operations.

As described to the mission, the overriding objective of the insurgency was to undermine the Government's capacity and legitimacy. The most immediate impediment to improved governance was governmental corruption at both the national and subnational levels. A second major problem was the lack of effective governance at the local level.

The perceived inability of Afghan and international forces to defeat the insurgents had led to calls for talks with insurgent groups. President Karzai restated his readiness to engage in talks with those who would renounce violence and accept the Constitution. According to members of the Afghan human rights community, many Afghans feared that political reconciliation efforts were a 'mask' for an alliance between the Government and Afghanistan's more fundamentalist forces, which could undermine the gains in human rights since 2002.

The mission was informed that perceived inefficiencies in the delivery of international assistance had undermined the confidence of the population in its Government and in the international community. The Secretary-General's Special Representative said that progress in implementing the Afghanistan National Development Strategy was accelerating, but the costing of projects took time, especially given the weak bureaucracy. The Finance Minister noted the reluctance of donors to work through Afghan institutions, which was essential if the Strategy was to be effective.

Report of Secretary-General. In a later report [A/63/751-S/2009/135], the Secretary-General called 2008 the most violent year in Afghanistan since 2001. Two trends had worsened—the insurgents' attempts at destabilization and their increased use of more sophisticated asymmetric attacks with disregard for civilians. Those attacks—including assassinations, intimidation and abductions—increasingly targeted civil servants, religious scholars, the aid community and road construction projects. On 4 September, the Head of the Appeals Court Division of the Central Narcotics Tribunal was assassinated in Kabul. On 26 November, Belqis Mazloomyar, an Afghan contract worker for the United Nations High Commissioner for Refugees (UNHCR), was shot to death at a meeting of local elders in Lower Sheikh Mesri.

Resumption of the death penalty was disquieting, owing to deficiencies in due process and fair trial guarantees. Women in public life were increasingly subjected to threats and intimidation; the most prominent female senior police officer in Kandahar was assassinated in September. Women—particularly those who were victims of sexual violence—still lacked access to legal, medical or psychosocial redress mechanisms.

UNAMA recorded 626 civilian casualties between September and December, and 2,118 for the year—a 40 per cent increase over 2007. Anti-Government elements remained responsible for the largest proportion of those casualties. Civilian casualties also continued to be reported as a result of operations conducted by pro-Government forces, with air strikes accounting for 68 per cent of such fatalities.

Freedom of movement of unarmed civil servants was reduced by the intensified fighting and the increased campaign of intimidation and assassination. As at December, 231 of the country's approximately 400 districts continued to report near-total accessibility, while 10 were considered completely beyond the Government's control, and access to 165 remained difficult or problematic.

Some 275 attacks against schools were reported through November, with 66 dead and 64 injured, mostly children. Children's education, particularly that of girls, was seen as anti-Islamic by the Taliban, turning children into targets. In September, insurgents burned over 100,000 textbooks being transported to Kandahar. In November, Taliban militants attacked a group of girls en route to school, throwing acid in their faces. From June to December, there were 202 incidents of extreme violence directed against the education community, with 83 killed and 164 injured.

Poor rainfall made the 2008 cereal harvest the smallest since 2002, leaving more than 5 million people in need of immediate food assistance. Some 1.2 million children under the age of five and 550,000 pregnant or lactating mothers in 22 provinces remained at high risk of severe malnutrition. Despite repeated rounds of national and subnational polio immunization days, polio remained endemic in Afghanistan because of insecurity and limited access to some communities.

In 2008, some 278,000 registered refugees had returned to Afghanistan and had been assisted by UNHCR, 98.5 per cent of them having returned from Pakistan. Some 10 per cent of returnees were unable to return to their place of origin due to insecurity, socio-economic hardships and land disputes. There were more than 230,000 internally displaced persons at the end of the year, but some 600 families had been able to return to their place of origin in 2008.

Sectoral issues

Judicial system and the rule of law

The rule of law remained insufficiently institutionalized, and respect for international humanitarian law, human rights and accounting for past abuses continued to be treated as secondary matters.

Following the establishment in March of the National Justice Sector Strategy and the National Justice Programme, the three justice institutions—the Ministry of Justice, the Supreme Court and the Office of the Attorney-General—established a programme oversight committee with World Bank assistance. In July, the first general assembly of the Independent Afghan Bar Association met in Kabul to decide on its constitution and elect officials. The number of registered lawyers in Afghanistan tripled from 200 in 2007 to almost 600 in 2008, 130 of whom were women.

The Government enacted laws on terrorism, abduction and human trafficking and on the creation of the High Office of Oversight to combat corruption. Further progress was hampered by the fact that the Supreme Court, the Office of the Attorney-General and the Ministry of Justice suffered from a lack of resources, inadequate infrastructure and a shortage of qualified judges and prosecutors. Corruption and intimidation by officials remained common. Detention centres and prisons remained in a state of neglect.

Security sector reform

The reform and rebuilding of the national police was proceeding at a slow pace. Some 70 per cent of the 82,000-strong force was estimated to be present for duty. Serious inadequacies remained with regard to training and equipment. Since the police composed the only security force that maintained a durable presence in communities across Afghanistan, its shortcomings had serious effects. Border police were almost non-existent along significant parts of the border and were unable to prevent large-scale smuggling and drug trafficking.

While the Afghan army continued to improve, reaching a strength of more than 62,000, insufficient numbers of police officers and lack of training and equipment had contributed to a very high casualty rate: as many as 720 police officers were killed between March and August. Corruption was still a problem, and there were credible reports of police positions being sold for large sums—particularly in lucrative transit and drug-trafficking corridors.

Disarmament, demobilization and reintegration and disbandment of armed groups

Progress was made in disbanding illegal armed groups. Out of 51 targeted districts, 21 had complied with the corresponding programme, and 161 illegal armed groups were disbanded. Over 1,050 individuals were arrested or disarmed and 5,700 weapons confiscated. The Afghanistan New Beginnings Programme, supported by the United Nations Development Programme (UNDP), promoted capacity-building, in particular through the establishment of a dedicated cell for the disbandment of illegal armed groups, within the Ministry of the Interior, to support the transition to full Government control of the disarmament process.

Counter-narcotics activities

In August, the United Nations Office on Drugs and Crime (UNODC) released the *Afghanistan opium survey 2008*, which reported a 19 per cent decrease in opium cultivation and a 6 per cent decline in production. The decrease in cultivation was attributed to a combination of improved governance and poor climatic conditions, including cold and drought. Public awareness campaigns also played a role.

The increase in the number of poppy-free provinces meant that more than half of the country's 34 provinces were poppy-free. Thus, poppy production was no longer a country-wide phenomenon but rather concentrated in areas where insurgent and organized crime groups were particularly active: 98 per cent of the country's opium was grown in seven southern and south-western provinces. Against those achievements, UNODC reported that crop yields actually increased in 2008, and that only 5,480 of the 50,000 hectare eradication target was reached. Achieving that result proved costly: 77 members of the eradication force were killed, a six-fold increase compared with the previous year.

Implementation of the Afghan National Drug Control Strategy [YUN 2006, p. 363] remained slow. A provincial approach was agreed upon and provincial counter-narcotics plans were being prepared; however, agreement had yet to be reached on a funding mechanism for those plans.

On 4 September, Judge Alim Hanif, Head of the Appeals Court Division of the Central Narcotics Tribunal, was assassinated in Kabul. There were strong indications that his murder was related to his anti-narcotics role.

The Economic and Social Council, by **resolution 2008/27** of 24 July (see p. 1366), called upon Afghanistan to intensify its counter-narcotic efforts and upon Member States to provide technical assistance and support to Afghanistan, Iran and Pakistan in their fight against drug trafficking.

Recovery, rehabilitation and reconstruction

Progress continued in several sectors: the basic package of health services covered 82 per cent of the population, and the gross enrolment in schools was estimated to have increased in 2007 to 5.7 million, with girls constituting 35 per cent of that figure. On the other hand, 80 per cent of the population still did not have access to electricity.

There continued to be a significant underinvestment in agriculture. Of the country's total 7.9 million arable hectares, less than half was cultivated, mostly owing to a lack of irrigation. Pre-war irrigation systems were damaged, operating at about 25 per cent efficiency and covering only one third of the pre-war irrigated areas. Poor irrigation impeded the development of the country's agricultural export potential.

Social aspects

Afghanistan continued to face serious human rights deficiencies as a result of the impact of the conflict on civilians, a pervasive atmosphere of impunity, absence of official impetus for the transitional justice process, a weak judicial system and threats to the media from both State and non-State actors. Many of those deficiencies also contributed to very high levels of poverty, affecting 42 per cent of the population.

The Government's awareness of gender in policy implementation had improved, as demonstrated by several initiatives towards gender-sensitive programming. However, the status of women remained one of the lowest in the world, and the maternal mortality rate was one of the highest. In 2007, only 25.7 per cent of pupils who completed primary education were girls, and trends showed that the proportion of girls in school was declining. The participation of women in employment, especially in the civil service, declined from 25.9 per cent in 2005 to 22 per cent in 2007.

In the first half of 2008, the United Nations-managed Mine Action Centre for Afghanistan, with Government support, destroyed 38,297 anti-personnel landmines, 419 anti-tank mines and 957,362 explosive remnants of war, and provided mine-awareness education for 760,434 people. During the second half of the year, over 42,000 anti-personnel mines, 500 anti-tank mines and 1.5 million explosive remnants of war were destroyed, and hundreds of communities had their land freed from the threat of mines. Mine-risk education reached 800,000 Afghans. Advocacy for the rights of landmine survivors and other persons with disabilities continued.

UNAMA

The United Nations Assistance Mission in Afghanistan (UNAMA) was established by Security Council resolution 1401(2002) [YUN 2002, p. 264] to promote, among other things, national reconciliation and the responsibilities entrusted to the United Nations under the 2001 Bonn Agreement [YUN 2001, p. 263]. It comprised the Office of the Special Representative, two substantive pillars—one political in scope

(Pillar I) and one for relief, recovery and reconstruction (Pillar II)—along with an administrative component. The Mission was headquartered in Kabul, with regional offices in Bamyan, Gardez, Herat, Jalalabad, Kabul, Kandahar, Kunduz and Mazar-e-Sharif, and provincial offices in Badakhshan, Badghis, Daikundi, Faryab, Ghor, Khost, Kunar, Nimroz and Zabul. UNAMA was headed by the Special Representative of the Secretary-General, Kai Eide (Norway). By resolution 1806(2008) (see p. 355), the Security Council extended the UNAMA mandate until 23 March 2009.

UNAMA financing

In October [A/63//346/Add.4], the Secretary-General outlined proposed resource requirements for UNAMA from 1 January to 31 December 2009, totalling $168,156,400 net ($179,166,600 gross). In December [A/63/593], the Advisory Committee on Administrative and Budgetary Questions (ACABQ) recommended revised resource requirements of $163,976,500 net ($174,343,000 gross).

On 24 December, the General Assembly, in **resolution 63/263**, section XI (see p. 1548), approved that amount as part of the $429,497,600 budget for the 27 special political missions authorized by the General Assembly and/or the Security Council.

International Security Assistance Force

During the year, the Secretary-General transmitted to the Security Council, in accordance with Council resolutions 1386(2001) [YUN 2001, p. 267] and 1510(2003) [YUN 2003, p. 310], reports from the International Security Assistance Force (ISAF) on its activities for the periods from 1 November 2007 to 31 January 2008 [S/2008/319]; 1 February to 30 April [S/2008/597]; and 1 May to 31 July [S/2008/770]. Activities from August to the end of the year were covered in a later report [S/2009/283].

As at 25 July, ISAF had 49,101 personnel from the 26 NATO nations and 2,215 from 14 non-NATO nations. During the quarter that ended on 31 July, ISAF continued to conduct security operations while supporting governance, reconstruction and development as the Afghan army grew in size and capability.

Dushanbe Declaration. By a 19 September letter [A/63/370-S/2008/614], China, Kazakhstan, Kyrgyzstan, the Russian Federation, Tajikistan and Uzbekistan transmitted to the Secretary-General and the Security Council the Dushanbe Declaration of the Heads of member States of the Shanghai Cooperation Organization (SCO), adopted by the Presidents of those countries at the SCO summit held in Dushanbe, Tajikistan, on 28 August.

Referring to ISAF, the Declaration said that external challenges and threats to security complicated the situation in the region. The situation in Afghanistan, and the expansion in drug trafficking and cross-border organized crime, called for strengthened coordination and the creation of joint mechanisms to assess, prevent and respond to such challenges and threats. ISAF must pay greater attention to countering the production and smuggling of Afghan narcotics, in cooperation with the Afghan Government, its neighbours and other interested countries. That task should be reflected in its mandate when the Security Council next met to consider the situation in Afghanistan. The SCO Heads of State underlined the need to prepare for the convening of a special conference on Afghanistan under the aegis of the organization to discuss collective action against terrorism, illicit drug trafficking and organized crime.

Communication. In a 12 September letter [S/2008/603], the Afghan Foreign Minister expressed appreciation for the role played by ISAF in his country. Afghanistan welcomed the proposal that ISAF continue to operate in Afghanistan until its national security forces were fully able to provide security for their nation.

Extension of ISAF mandate

On 22 September [meeting 5977], the Security Council unanimously adopted **resolution 1833(2008)**. The draft [S/2008/610] was prepared in consultations among Council members.

The Security Council,

Reaffirming its previous resolutions on Afghanistan, in particular resolutions 1386(2001) of 20 December 2001, 1510(2003) of 13 October 2003, 1776(2007) of 19 September 2007 and 1806(2008) of 20 March 2008,

Reaffirming also its resolutions 1267(1999) of 15 October 1999, 1368(2001) of 12 September 2001, 1373(2001) of 28 September 2001 and 1822(2008) of 30 June 2008, and reiterating its support for international efforts to root out terrorism in accordance with the Charter of the United Nations,

Recalling its resolutions 1265(1999) of 17 September 1999, 1296(2000) of 19 April 2000, 1674(2006) of 28 April 2006 and 1738(2006) of 23 December 2006 on the protection of civilians in armed conflict, its resolutions 1325(2000) of 31 October 2000 and 1820(2008) of 19 June 2008 on women and peace and security, and its resolution 1612(2005) of 26 July 2005 on children and armed conflict,

Reaffirming its strong commitment to the sovereignty, independence, territorial integrity and national unity of Afghanistan,

Recognizing that the responsibility for providing security and law and order throughout the country resides with the Afghan authorities, stressing the role of the International Security Assistance Force in assisting the Government of

Afghanistan to improve the security situation, and welcoming the cooperation of the Government with the Force,

Recognizing once again the interconnected nature of the challenges in Afghanistan, reaffirming that sustainable progress on security, governance and development, as well as the cross-cutting issue of counter-narcotics, is mutually reinforcing, and welcoming the continuing efforts of the Government of Afghanistan and the international community to address these challenges through a comprehensive approach,

Stressing the central and impartial role that the United Nations continues to play in promoting peace and stability in Afghanistan by leading the efforts of the international community, noting in this context the synergies in the objectives of the United Nations Assistance Mission in Afghanistan and of the Force, and stressing the need for strengthened cooperation, coordination and mutual support, taking due account of their respective designated responsibilities,

Expressing its strong concern about the security situation in Afghanistan, in particular the increased violent and terrorist activities by the Taliban, Al-Qaida, illegal armed groups, criminals and those involved in the narcotics trade, and the increasingly strong links between terrorism activities and illicit drugs, resulting in threats to the local population, including children, national security forces and international military and civilian personnel,

Encouraging the Force to further effectively support, within its designated responsibilities, Afghan-led sustained efforts to address, in cooperation with relevant international and regional actors, the threat posed by the illicit production of and trafficking in drugs,

Expressing its concern over the harmful consequences of violent and terrorist activities by the Taliban, Al-Qaida and other extremist groups on the capacity of the Government of Afghanistan to guarantee the rule of law, to provide security and basic services to the Afghan people and to ensure the full enjoyment of their human rights and fundamental freedoms,

Reiterating its support for the continuing endeavours of the Government of Afghanistan, with the assistance of the international community, including the Force and the Operation Enduring Freedom coalition, to improve the security situation and to continue to address the threat posed by the Taliban, Al-Qaida and other extremist groups, and stressing in this context the need for sustained international efforts, including those of the Force and the coalition,

Condemning in the strongest terms all attacks, including improvised explosive device attacks, suicide attacks and abductions, targeting civilians and Afghan and international forces and their deleterious effect on the stabilization, reconstruction and development efforts in Afghanistan, and condemning further the use by the Taliban and other extremist groups of civilians as human shields,

Recognizing the increased threats posed by the Taliban, Al-Qaida and other extremist groups as well as the challenges related to the efforts to address such threats, expressing its serious concern about the high number of civilian casualties in this context, noting relevant statements of Afghan authorities and high-ranking United Nations officials, as well as statements to the press by the President of the Security Council in this regard, and calling for compliance with international humanitarian and human rights law and for all appropriate measures to be taken to ensure the protection of civilians,

Recognizing also the efforts made by the Force and other international forces to minimize the risk of civilian casualties, and calling upon them to make additional robust efforts in this regard, notably by the continuous review of tactics and procedures and the conduct of after-action reviews and investigations in cooperation with the Government of Afghanistan in cases where civilian casualties have occurred and when the Government finds these joint investigations appropriate,

Stressing the need for further progress in security sector reform, including further strengthening of the Afghan National Army and, in particular, of the Afghan National Police, disbandment of illegal armed groups, justice sector reform and counter-narcotics,

Stressing also, in this context, the importance of further progress in the reconstruction and reform of the prison sector in Afghanistan, in order to improve respect for the rule of law and human rights therein,

Reiterating its call upon all Afghan parties and groups to engage constructively in peaceful political dialogue within the framework of the Afghan Constitution and in the socio-economic development of the country and to avoid resorting to violence, including through the use of illegal armed groups, and encouraging the implementation of Afghan-led reconciliation programmes within the framework of the Afghan Constitution and with full respect for the implementation of measures introduced by the Security Council in its resolution 1267(1999) and other relevant resolutions of the Council,

Recalling the leading role that the Afghan authorities will play in the organization of the next presidential elections, with the assistance of the United Nations, and stressing the importance of the assistance to be provided to the Afghan authorities by the Force in ensuring a secure environment conducive to the elections,

Recognizing the importance of the contribution of neighbouring and regional partners for the stabilization of Afghanistan, and stressing the crucial importance of advancing regional cooperation as an effective means to promote security, governance and development in Afghanistan,

Welcoming the continued coordination between the Force and the coalition, and the cooperation established between the Force and the European Union presence in Afghanistan, in particular the European Union Police Mission in Afghanistan,

Expressing its appreciation for the leadership provided by the North Atlantic Treaty Organization and for the contributions of many nations to the Force and to the coalition, including its maritime interdiction component, which operates within the framework of the counter-terrorism operations in Afghanistan and in accordance with the applicable rules of international law,

Determining that the situation in Afghanistan still constitutes a threat to international peace and security,

Determined to ensure the full implementation of the mandate of the Force, in coordination with the Government of Afghanistan,

Acting, for these reasons, under Chapter VII of the Charter,

1. *Decides* to extend the authorization of the International Security Assistance Force, as defined in resolutions 1386(2001) and 1510(2003), for a period of twelve months beyond 13 October 2008;

2. *Authorizes* the Member States participating in the Force to take all necessary measures to fulfil its mandate;

3. *Recognizes* the need to further strengthen the Force to meet all its operational requirements, and in this regard calls upon Member States to contribute personnel, equipment and other resources to the Force and to make contributions to the trust fund established pursuant to resolution 1386(2001);

4. *Stresses* the importance of increasing, within a comprehensive framework, the functionality, professionalism and accountability of the Afghan security sector, encourages the Force and other partners to sustain their efforts, as resources permit, to train, mentor and empower the Afghan national security forces in order to accelerate progress towards the goal of self-sufficient and ethnically balanced Afghan security forces providing security and ensuring the rule of law throughout the country, welcomes in this context the progress achieved by the Afghan authorities in assuming lead security responsibility for Kabul, and stresses the importance of supporting the planned expansion of the Afghan National Army;

5. *Calls upon* the Force to continue to work in close consultation with the Government of Afghanistan and the Special Representative of the Secretary-General for Afghanistan as well as with the coalition in the implementation of the mandate of the Force;

6. *Requests* the leadership of the Force to keep the Security Council regularly informed, through the Secretary-General, on the implementation of its mandate, including through the provision of quarterly reports;

7. *Decides* to remain actively seized of the matter.

Sanctions

United Nations sanctions-related activities were guided by the measures adopted by Security Council resolutions 1617(2005) [YUN 2005, p. 410] and 1735(2006) [YUN 2006, p. 384] against Osama bin Laden, Al-Qaida, the Taliban, their associates and associated entities, which further refined the financial measures, travel ban and arms embargo imposed on those persons identified in the consolidated list created pursuant to resolution 1267(1999) [YUN 1999, p. 265]. The Al-Qaida and Taliban Sanctions Committee, established pursuant to resolution 1267(1999), oversaw the implementation of those measures. The Committee was assisted by an Analytical Support and Sanctions Monitoring Team.

Following the Security Council's adoption of resolution 1822(2008) (see p. 377), in which it extended the Monitoring Team's mandate for a further 18 months, the Secretary-General informed the Council on 7 July [S/2008/441] that he had reappointed six experts for a period ending 31 December 2009. On 2 October [S/2008/632], he informed the Council that he had identified replacements for the two experts who resigned from the Team on 22 and 30 June, respectively, to serve on the Team through 31 December 2009.

Sanctions Committee activities

On 31 December, the Al-Qaida and Taliban Sanctions Committee submitted a report [S/2008/848] covering its activities in 2008. During the year, the Committee held 3 formal meetings and 32 informal meetings. Following consultations among Security Council members, the Council elected the Bureau of the Committee, which consisted of Belgium as Chairman, with the delegations of Burkina Faso and the Russian Federation providing the two Vice-Chairmen. On 4 June, Jan Grauls (Belgium) succeeded Johan Verbeke (Belgium) as Chairman.

A central objective of the Committee was keeping the consolidated list of individuals and entities subject to sanctions measures as up to date and accurate as possible. The list was updated 25 times in 2008; by the end of the year, 507 individuals and entities were included.

The Committee conducted a last round of reviews on 38 names that had not been updated in four or more years. Within one week after a name was added to or removed from the list, the Committee notified the country or countries where the individual or entity was believed to be located and, in the case of individuals, the country of which the person was a national.

During 2008, the Committee responded to four requests from States seeking its assistance in confirming the identity of 44 individuals for the purpose of implementing the sanctions measures, in particular with regard to the assets freeze. Mindful that the Council provided for exemptions to the freeze, including for humanitarian purposes, the Committee continued to consider notifications and requests for exemptions submitted pursuant to resolution 1452(2002) [YUN 2002, p. 280], receiving 21 such communications from States in 2008.

Briefing the Council on 6 May [meeting 5886], the Chairman said that during the previous six months the Committee had discussed issues relating to the three sanctions measures—the assets freeze, travel ban and arms embargo. The Committee also focused on identifying possible cases of non-compliance with the sanctions and considered the criminal misuse of the Internet for terrorist purposes.

Briefing the Council on 12 November [meeting 6015], the Sanctions Committee Chairman said that the Committee, together with the Monitoring Team, had given attention to implementing two new mechanisms introduced by resolution 1822(2008): the review, by 30 June 2010, of all the names on the consolidated list at the time of the adoption of the resolution; and posting on the Committee's website the narrative summary of reasons for the listings.

On 8 January [S/2008/16], the Chairman transmitted to the Security Council a report containing the Committee's position on the recommendations contained in the seventh report of the Monitoring Team [YUN 2007, p. 341].

Monitoring Team

The Analytical Support and Sanctions Monitoring Team (the Monitoring Team), established by Security Council resolution 1526(2004) [YUN 2004, p. 332] and extended by resolutions 1617(2005) [YUN 2005, p. 410], 1735(2006) [YUN 2006, p. 384] and 1822(2008), had the mandate of collating, assessing, monitoring, and reporting and making recommendations on the implementation of measures imposed by that resolution.

The Monitoring Team visited 26 States. At the request of the Council, it continued to organize regional meetings with the heads and deputy heads of intelligence and security services to discuss how the sanctions could be adapted to address changes in the threat posed by Al-Qaida-related terrorism.

Report of Monitoring Team (May). In accordance with resolution 1735(2006), the Sanctions Committee Chairman on 13 May transmitted to the Security Council the Monitoring Team's eighth report [S/2008/324]. According to the report, the Al-Qaida and Taliban leadership continued to try to exert control over a movement that it inspired but did not direct. The report noted the growing problem in Afghanistan and the Afghanistan/Pakistan border area, and a continuing threat in North Africa, with no reduction in activity elsewhere. It saw the failure of many plots and attacks as confirmation of the need to prevent Al-Qaida and the Taliban from passing their skills and experience to a new generation of supporters.

The report examined the continuing problems associated with the consolidated list and concluded that they undermined its implementation; at the same time, it noted the many improvements that had been made. The report also drew attention to legal challenges by Member States to the implementation of the measures, and the likely consequences should they be successful. It examined the three sanctions measures and how they might become more effective.

The Security Council sanctions regime was at the forefront of the international operational effort, but Member States were responsible for the security of their citizens. The sanctions regime had to retain their confidence and support. The Sanctions Committee had done much to provide Member States with opportunities to express their views, and it was only through such dialogue that the Committee could develop the regime to respond to the changing threat, improve implementation of the measures, and reassure international opinion that the sanctions were appropriate to the challenge.

The Team recommended, among other things, that the arms embargo should also be enforced by prohibiting activities over the Internet that included technical advice, assistance or military training for the benefit of those on the list; that the Committee approach each of the 39 non-reporting States—7 in Asia, 23 in Africa and 9 in Latin America and the Caribbean; and that banks allow incoming payments in favour of listed parties to be credited to their frozen accounts.

An annex to the report contained litigation by or relating to individuals on the consolidated list.

On 18 June, the Sanctions Committee Chairman submitted a report [S/2008/408] containing the Committee's position on the recommendations made in the Monitoring Team's eighth report.

Communications. On 29 February [S/AC.37/2008/(1455)/1], the Comoros submitted a report on its compliance with the sanctions regime. Madagascar submitted a similar report [S/AC.37/2008/(1455)/2] on 12 May.

SECURITY COUNCIL ACTION

On 30 June [meeting 5928], the Security Council unanimously adopted **resolution 1822(2008)**. The draft [S/2008/424] was submitted by Belgium, Burkina Faso, Croatia, France, Italy, the Russian Federation, the United Kingdom and the United States.

The Security Council,

Recalling its resolutions 1267(1999) of 15 October 1999, 1333(2000) of 19 December 2000, 1363(2001) of 30 July 2001, 1373(2001) of 28 September 2001, 1390(2002) of 16 January 2002, 1452(2002) of 20 December 2002, 1455(2003) of 17 January 2003, 1526(2004) of 30 January 2004, 1566(2004) of 8 October 2004, 1617(2005) of 29 July 2005, 1624(2005) of 14 September 2005, 1699(2006) of 8 August 2006, 1730(2006) of 19 December 2006 and 1735(2006) of 22 December 2006, and the relevant statements by its President,

Reaffirming that terrorism in all its forms and manifestations constitutes one of the most serious threats to peace and security and that any acts of terrorism are criminal and unjustifiable regardless of their motivation, whenever and by whomsoever committed, and reiterating its unequivocal condemnation of Al-Qaida, Osama bin Laden and the Taliban, and other individuals, groups, undertakings and entities associated with them, for ongoing and multiple criminal terrorist acts aimed at causing the death of innocent civilians and other victims, destruction of property and greatly undermining stability,

Reaffirming also the need to combat by all means, in accordance with the Charter of the United Nations and international law, including applicable international human rights, refugee and humanitarian law, threats to international peace and security caused by terrorist acts, stressing in this regard the important role that the United Nations plays in leading and coordinating this effort,

Welcoming the adoption by the General Assembly of the United Nations Global Counter-Terrorism Strategy on 8 September 2006 and the creation of the Counter-Terrorism Implementation Task Force to ensure overall coordination and coherence in the counter-terrorism efforts of the United Nations system,

Reiterating its deep concern about the increased violent and terrorist activities in Afghanistan of the Taliban and Al-Qaida, and other individuals, groups, undertakings and entities associated with them,

Recalling its resolution 1817(2008) of 11 June 2008, and reiterating its support for the fight against the illicit production of and trafficking in drugs from, and chemical precursors to, Afghanistan, in neighbouring countries, countries on trafficking routes, drug destination countries and precursor-producing countries,

Expressing its deep concern about the criminal misuse of the Internet by Al-Qaida, Osama bin Laden and the Taliban, and other individuals, groups, undertakings and entities associated with them, in furtherance of terrorist acts,

Stressing that terrorism can only be defeated by a sustained and comprehensive approach involving the active participation and collaboration of all States and international and regional organizations to impede, impair, isolate and incapacitate the terrorist threat,

Emphasizing that sanctions are an important tool under the Charter in the maintenance and restoration of international peace and security, and stressing in this regard the need for robust implementation of the measures in paragraph 1 of the present resolution as a significant tool in combating terrorist activity,

Urging all Member States, international bodies and regional organizations to allocate sufficient resources to meet the ongoing and direct threat posed by Al-Qaida, Osama bin Laden and the Taliban, and other individuals, groups, undertakings and entities associated with them, including by participating actively in identifying which individuals, groups, undertakings and entities should be subject to the measures referred to in paragraph 1 of the present resolution,

Reiterating that dialogue between the Security Council Committee established pursuant to resolution 1267(1999) ("the Committee") and Member States is vital to the full implementation of measures,

Taking note of challenges to measures implemented by Member States in accordance with the measures referred to in paragraph 1 of the present resolution, and recognizing continuing efforts of Member States and the Committee to ensure that fair and clear procedures exist for placing individuals, groups, undertakings and entities on the list created pursuant to resolutions 1267(1999) and 1333(2000) ("the Consolidated List") and for removing them, as well as for granting humanitarian exemptions,

Reiterating that the measures referred to in paragraph 1 of the present resolution are preventative in nature and are not reliant upon criminal standards set out under national law,

Emphasizing the obligation placed upon all Member States to implement, in full, resolution 1373(2001), including with regard to the Taliban or Al-Qaida, and any individuals, groups, undertakings or entities associated with Al-Qaida, Osama bin Laden or the Taliban, who have participated in financing, planning, facilitating, recruiting for, preparing, perpetrating or otherwise supporting terrorist activities or acts, as well as to facilitate the implementation of counter-terrorism obligations in accordance with relevant Council resolutions,

Welcoming the establishment by the Secretary-General, pursuant to resolution 1730(2006), of the Focal Point within the Secretariat to receive de-listing requests, and taking note with appreciation of the ongoing cooperation between the Focal Point and the Committee,

Welcoming also the continuing cooperation of the Committee and the International Criminal Police Organization (INTERPOL), in particular on the development of Special Notices, which assists Member States in their implementation of the measures, and recognizing the role of the Analytical Support and Sanctions Monitoring Team ("the Monitoring Team") in this regard,

Welcoming further the continuing cooperation of the Committee with the United Nations Office on Drugs and Crime, in particular on technical assistance and capacity-building, to assist Member States in implementing their obligations under the present resolution and other relevant resolutions and international instruments,

Noting with concern the continued threat posed to international peace and security by Al-Qaida, Osama bin Laden and the Taliban, and other individuals, groups, undertakings and entities associated with them, and reaffirming its resolve to address all aspects of that threat,

Acting under Chapter VII of the Charter,

Measures

1. *Decides* that all States shall take the following measures as previously imposed by paragraph 4 *(b)* of resolution 1267(1999), paragraph 8 *(c)* of resolution 1333(2000), and paragraphs 1 and 2 of resolution 1390(2002), with respect to Al-Qaida, Osama bin Laden and the Taliban, and other individuals, groups, undertakings and entities associated with them, as referred to in the list created pursuant to resolutions 1267(1999) and 1333(2000) ("the Consolidated List"):

(a) Freeze without delay the funds and other financial assets or economic resources of those individuals, groups, undertakings and entities, including funds derived from property owned or controlled directly or indirectly, by them or by persons acting on their behalf or at their direction, and ensure that neither these nor any other funds, financial assets or economic resources are made available, directly or indirectly, for the benefit of such persons by their nationals or by persons within their territory;

(b) Prevent the entry into or transit through their territories of those individuals, provided that nothing in the present paragraph shall oblige any State to deny entry into or require the departure from its territories of its own nationals and that the present paragraph shall not apply where entry or transit is necessary for the fulfilment of a judicial

process, or the Committee determines on a case-by-case basis only that entry or transit is justified;

(c) Prevent the direct or indirect supply, sale or transfer to those individuals, groups, undertakings and entities, from their territories or by their nationals outside their territories, or using their flag vessels or aircraft, of arms and related materiel of all types, including weapons and ammunition, military vehicles and equipment, paramilitary equipment, and spare parts for the aforementioned, and technical advice, assistance or training related to military activities;

2. *Reaffirms* that acts or activities indicating that an individual, group, undertaking or entity is "associated with" Al-Qaida, Osama bin Laden or the Taliban include:

(a) Participating in the financing, planning, facilitating, preparing or perpetrating of acts or activities by, in conjunction with, under the name of, on behalf of, or in support of;

(b) Supplying, selling or transferring arms and related materiel to;

(c) Recruiting for; or

(d) Otherwise supporting acts or activities of;

Al-Qaida, Osama bin Laden or the Taliban, or any cell, affiliate, splinter group or derivative thereof;

3. *Further reaffirms* that any undertaking or entity owned or controlled, directly or indirectly, by, or otherwise supporting, such an individual, group, undertaking or entity associated with Al-Qaida, Osama bin Laden or the Taliban shall be eligible for designation;

4. *Confirms* that the requirements in paragraph 1 *(a)* above apply to financial and economic resources of every kind, including but not limited to those used for the provision of Internet hosting or related services, used for the support of Al-Qaida, Osama bin Laden and the Taliban, and other individuals, groups, undertakings or entities associated with them;

5. *Encourages* Member States to continue their efforts to act vigorously and decisively to cut the flow of funds and other financial assets and economic resources to Al-Qaida, Osama bin Laden and the Taliban, and other individuals, groups, undertakings and entities associated with them;

6. *Decides* that Member States may permit the addition to accounts frozen pursuant to the provisions of paragraph 1 above of any payment in favour of listed individuals, groups, undertakings or entities, provided that any such payments continue to be subject to the provisions in paragraph 1 above and are frozen;

7. *Reaffirms* the provisions regarding available exemptions to the measures in paragraph 1 *(a)* above, set out in paragraphs 1 and 2 of resolution 1452(2002), as amended by resolution 1735(2006), and reminds Member States to use the procedures for exemptions as set out in the Committee guidelines;

8. *Reiterates* the obligation of all Member States to implement and enforce the measures set out in paragraph 1 above, and urges all States to redouble their efforts in this regard;

Listing

9. *Encourages* all Member States to submit to the Committee for inclusion on the Consolidated List names of individuals, groups, undertakings and entities participating, by any means, in the financing or support of acts or activities of Al-Qaida, Osama bin Laden and the Taliban, and other individuals, groups, undertakings and entities associated with them, as described in paragraph 2 of resolution 1617(2005) and reaffirmed in paragraph 2 above;

10. *Notes* that such means of financing or support include but are not limited to the use of proceeds derived from illicit cultivation and production of and trafficking in narcotic drugs originating in Afghanistan and their precursors;

11. *Reiterates its call for* continued cooperation between the Committee and the Government of Afghanistan and the United Nations Assistance Mission in Afghanistan, including by identifying individuals and entities participating in the financing or support of acts or activities of Al-Qaida and the Taliban as described in paragraph 30 of resolution 1806(2008) of 20 March 2008;

12. *Reaffirms* that, when proposing names to the Committee for inclusion on the Consolidated List, Member States shall act in accordance with paragraph 5 of resolution 1735(2006) and provide a detailed statement of case, and decides further that for each such proposal Member States shall identify those parts of the statement of case that may be publicly released, including for use by the Committee for the development of the summary described in paragraph 13 below or for the purpose of notifying or informing the listed individual or entity, and those parts which may be released, upon request, to interested States;

13. *Directs* the Committee, with the assistance of the Monitoring Team and in coordination with the relevant designating States, after a name is added to the Consolidated List, to make accessible on the Committee website a narrative summary of reasons for listing for the corresponding entry or entries on the Consolidated List, and further directs the Committee, with the assistance of the Monitoring Team and in coordination with the relevant designating States, to make accessible on the Committee website narrative summaries of reasons for listing for entries that were added to the Consolidated List before the date of adoption of the present resolution;

14. *Calls upon* Member States, when proposing names to the Committee for inclusion on the Consolidated List, to use the cover sheet in annex I to resolution 1735(2006), and requests that they provide the Committee with as much relevant information as possible on the proposed name, in particular sufficient identifying information to allow for the positive identification of individuals, groups, undertakings and entities by Member States, and directs the Committee to update the cover sheet in line with the provisions outlined in paragraphs 12 and 13 above;

15. *Decides* that the Secretariat shall, after publication but within one week after a name is added to the Consolidated List, notify the permanent mission of the country or countries where the individual or entity is believed to be located and, in the case of individuals, the country of which the person is a national (to the extent this information is known) in accordance with paragraph 10 of resolution 1735(2006);

16. *Underlines* the need for the prompt update of the Consolidated List on the Committee website;

17. *Demands* that Member States receiving notification as in paragraph 15 above take, in accordance with their

domestic laws and practices, all possible measures to notify or inform in a timely manner the listed individual or entity of the designation and to include with this notification a copy of the publicly releasable portion of the statement of case, any information on reasons for listing available on the Committee website, a description of the effects of designation, as provided in the relevant resolutions, the procedures of the Committee for considering de-listing requests, and the provisions of resolution 1452(2002) regarding available exemptions;

18. *Encourages* Member States receiving notification as in paragraph 15 above to inform the Committee on steps they have taken to implement the measures set out in paragraph 1 above, and on the measures taken in accordance with paragraph 17 above, and further encourages Member States to use the tools provided on the Committee website to provide this information;

De-listing

19. *Welcomes* the establishment within the Secretariat of the Focal Point, pursuant to resolution 1730(2006), that provides listed individuals, groups, undertakings or entities with the option to submit a petition for de-listing directly to the Focal Point;

20. *Urges* designating States and States of citizenship and residence to review de-listing petitions received through the Focal Point, in accordance with the procedures outlined in the annex to resolution 1730(2006), in a timely manner and to indicate whether they support or oppose the request in order to facilitate review by the Committee;

21. *Directs* the Committee to continue to work, in accordance with its guidelines, to consider petitions for the removal from the Consolidated List of members and/or associates of Al-Qaida, Osama bin Laden or the Taliban who no longer meet the criteria established in the relevant resolutions;

22. *Also directs* the Committee to consider an annual review of the names on the Consolidated List of individuals reported to be deceased, in which the names are circulated to the relevant States pursuant to the procedures set forth in the Committee guidelines, in order to ensure that the Consolidated List is as updated and accurate as possible and to confirm that listing remains appropriate;

23. *Decides* that the Secretariat shall, within one week after a name is removed from the Consolidated List, notify the permanent mission of the country or countries where the individual or entity is believed to be located and, in the case of individuals, the country of which the person is a national (to the extent this information is known), and demands that States receiving such notification take measures, in accordance with their domestic laws and practices, to notify or inform the concerned individual or entity of the de-listing in a timely manner;

Review and maintenance of the Consolidated List

24. *Encourages* all Member States, in particular designating States and States of residence or nationality, to submit to the Committee additional identifying and other information, along with supporting documentation, on listed individuals, groups, undertakings and entities, including updates on the operating status of listed entities, groups and undertakings, the movement, incarceration or death of listed individuals and other significant events, as such information becomes available;

25. *Directs* the Committee to conduct a review of all names on the Consolidated List at the date of adoption of the present resolution by 30 June 2010, in which the relevant names are circulated to the designating States and States of residence and/or citizenship, where known, pursuant to the procedures set forth in the Committee guidelines, in order to ensure that the Consolidated List is as updated and accurate as possible and to confirm that listing remains appropriate;

26. *Also directs* the Committee, upon completion of the review described in paragraph 25 above, to conduct an annual review of all names on the Consolidated List that have not been reviewed in three or more years, in which the relevant names are circulated to the designating States and States of residence and/or citizenship, where known, pursuant to the procedures set forth in the Committee guidelines, in order to ensure that the Consolidated List is as updated and accurate as possible and to confirm that listing remains appropriate;

Measures-implementation

27. *Reiterates* the importance of all States identifying, and if necessary introducing, adequate procedures to implement fully all aspects of the measures described in paragraph 1 above;

28. *Encourages* the Committee to continue to ensure that fair and clear procedures exist for placing individuals and entities on the Consolidated List and for removing them as well as for granting humanitarian exemptions, and directs the Committee to keep its guidelines under active review in support of these objectives;

29. *Directs* the Committee, as a matter of priority, to review its guidelines with respect to the provisions of the present resolution, in particular paragraphs 6, 12, 13, 17, 22 and 26 above;

30. *Encourages* Member States to send representatives to meet the Committee for more in-depth discussion of relevant issues, and welcomes voluntary briefings from interested Member States on their efforts to implement the measures referred to in paragraph 1 above, including particular challenges that hinder full implementation of the measures;

31. *Requests* the Committee to report to the Security Council on its findings regarding implementation efforts by Member States, and identify and recommend steps necessary to improve implementation;

32. *Directs* the Committee to identify possible cases of non-compliance with the measures pursuant to paragraph 1 above and to determine the appropriate course of action on each case, and requests the Chairman of the Committee, in periodic reports to the Council pursuant to paragraph 38 below, to provide progress reports on the work of the Committee on this issue;

33. *Urges* all Member States, in their implementation of the measures set out in paragraph 1 above, to ensure that fraudulent, counterfeit, stolen and lost passports and other travel documents are invalidated and removed from circulation, in accordance with domestic laws and practices, as soon as possible, and to share information on those docu-

ments with other Member States through the INTERPOL database;

34. *Encourages* Member States to share with the private sector, in accordance with their domestic laws and practices, information in their national databases related to fraudulent, counterfeit, stolen and lost identity or travel documents pertaining to their own jurisdictions, and if a listed party is found to be using a false identity, including to secure credit or fraudulent travel documents, to provide the Committee with information in this regard;

Coordination and outreach

35. *Reiterates* the need to enhance ongoing cooperation among the Committee, the Security Council Committee established pursuant to resolution 1373(2001) concerning counter-terrorism ("the Counter-Terrorism Committee"), and the Security Council Committee established pursuant to resolution 1540(2004), as well as their respective groups of experts, including through, as appropriate, enhanced information-sharing, coordination on visits to countries within their respective mandates, on technical assistance, on relations with international and regional organizations and agencies and on other issues of relevance to all three Committees, and expresses its intention to provide guidance to the Committees on areas of common interest in order better to coordinate their efforts;

36. *Encourages* the Monitoring Team and the United Nations Office on Drugs and Crime to continue their joint activities, in cooperation with the Counter-Terrorism Committee Executive Directorate and experts of the Committee established pursuant to resolution 1540(2004), to assist Member States in their efforts to comply with their obligations under the relevant resolutions, including by organizing subregional workshops;

37. *Requests* the Committee to consider, where and when appropriate, visits to selected countries by the Chairman and/or Committee members to enhance the full and effective implementation of the measures referred to in paragraph 1 above, with a view to encouraging States to comply fully with the present resolution and resolutions 1267(1999), 1333(2000), 1390(2002), 1455(2003), 1526(2004), 1617(2005) and 1735(2006);

38. *Also requests* the Committee to report orally, through its Chairman, at least every one hundred and eighty days to the Council on the overall work of the Committee and the Monitoring Team and, as appropriate, in conjunction with the reports of the Chairmen of the Counter-Terrorism Committee and the Committee established pursuant to resolution 1540(2004), including briefings for all interested Member States;

Monitoring Team

39. *Decides*, in order to assist the Committee in the fulfillment of its mandate, to extend the mandate of the current New York-based Monitoring Team, appointed by the Secretary-General pursuant to paragraph 20 of resolution 1617(2005), for a further period of eighteen months, under the direction of the Committee, with the responsibilities outlined in the annex to the present resolution, and requests the Secretary-General to make the necessary arrangements to this effect;

Reviews

40. *Decides* to review the measures described in paragraph 1 above with a view to their possible further strengthening in eighteen months, or sooner if necessary;

41. *Decides also* to remain actively seized of the matter.

ANNEX

In accordance with paragraph 39 of this resolution, the Monitoring Team shall operate under the direction of the Security Council Committee established pursuant to resolution 1267(1999) and shall have the following responsibilities:

(a) To submit, in writing, two comprehensive, independent reports to the Committee, the first by 28 February 2009 and the second by 31 July 2009, on implementation by States of the measures referred to in paragraph 1 of this resolution, including specific recommendations for improved implementation of the measures and possible new measures;

(b) To analyse reports submitted pursuant to paragraph 6 of resolution 1455(2003), the checklists submitted pursuant to paragraph 10 of resolution 1617(2005) and other information submitted by Member States to the Committee as instructed by the Committee;

(c) To assist the Committee in following up on requests to Member States for information, including with respect to implementation of the measures referred to in paragraph 1 of this resolution;

(d) To submit a comprehensive programme of work to the Committee for its review and approval, as necessary, in which the Monitoring Team should detail the activities envisaged in order to fulfill its responsibilities, including proposed travel, based on close coordination with the Counter-Terrorism Committee Executive Directorate and the group of experts of the Committee established pursuant to resolution 1540(2004) to avoid duplication and reinforce synergies;

(e) To work closely and share information with the Counter-Terrorism Committee Executive Directorate and the group of experts of the Committee established pursuant to resolution 1540(2004) to identify areas of convergence and overlap and to help to facilitate concrete coordination, including in the area of reporting, among the three Committees;

(f) To participate actively in and support all relevant activities under the United Nations Global Counter-Terrorism Strategy, including within the Counter-Terrorism Implementation Task Force established to ensure overall coordination and coherence in the counter-terrorism efforts of the United Nations system;

(g) To assist the Committee with its analysis of non-compliance with the measures referred to in paragraph 1 of this resolution by collating information collected from Member States and submitting case studies, both on its own initiative and upon the Committee's request, to the Committee for its review;

(h) To present to the Committee recommendations which could be used by Member States to assist them with the implementation of the measures referred to in paragraph 1 of this resolution and in preparing proposed additions to the Consolidated List;

(*i*) To assist the Committee in compiling publicly releasable information referred to in paragraph 13 of this resolution;

(*j*) To consult with Member States in advance of travel to selected Member States, based on its programme of work as approved by the Committee;

(*k*) To encourage Member States to submit names and additional identifying information for inclusion on the Consolidated List, as instructed by the Committee;

(*l*) To present to the Committee additional identifying and other information to assist the Committee in its efforts to keep the Consolidated List as updated and accurate as possible;

(*m*) To study and report to the Committee on the changing nature of the threat of Al-Qaida and the Taliban and the best measures to confront it, including by developing a dialogue with relevant scholars and academic bodies, in consultation with the Committee;

(*n*) To collate, assess, monitor and report on and make recommendations regarding implementation of the measures, including implementation of the measure in paragraph 1 (*a*) of this resolution as it pertains to preventing the criminal misuse of the Internet by Al-Qaida, Osama bin Laden and the Taliban, and other individuals, groups, undertakings and entities associated with them; to pursue case studies, as appropriate; and to explore in depth any other relevant issues as directed by the Committee;

(*o*) To consult with Member States and other relevant organizations, including regular dialogue with representatives in New York and in capitals, taking into account their comments, especially regarding any issues that might be contained in the reports of the Monitoring Team referred to in paragraph (*a*) of this annex;

(*p*) To consult with Member States' intelligence and security services, including through regional forums, in order to facilitate the sharing of information and to strengthen enforcement of the measures;

(*q*) To consult with relevant representatives of the private sector, including financial institutions, to learn about the practical implementation of the assets freeze and to develop recommendations for the strengthening of that measure;

(*r*) To work with relevant international and regional organizations in order to promote awareness of, and compliance with, the measures;

(*s*) To work with INTERPOL and Member States to obtain photographs of listed individuals for possible inclusion in INTERPOL Special Notices;

(*t*) To assist other subsidiary bodies of the Security Council, and their expert panels, upon request, with enhancing their cooperation with INTERPOL, referred to in resolution 1699(2006);

(*u*) To report to the Committee, on a regular basis or when the Committee so requests, through oral and/or written briefings on the work of the Monitoring Team, including its visits to Member States and its activities;

(*v*) Any other responsibility identified by the Committee.

Iraq

Political and security situation

In 2008, the United Nations, through the Secretary-General's Special Representative for Iraq and the United Nations Assistance Mission for Iraq (UNAMI), continued to assist Iraq in its transition to democratic governance and in promoting reconstruction and reconciliation. On 7 August, by resolution 1830(2008), the Security Council extended the UNAMI mandate until 7 August 2009. On 22 December, by resolution 1859(2008), the Council took note of the agreed expiration of the mandate of the multinational force in Iraq on 31 December 2008. It also extended until 31 December 2009 the arrangements for the deposit of oil revenues into the Development Fund for Iraq, and for its monitoring by the International Advisory and Monitoring Board.

UN Assistance Mission for Iraq

UNAMI, established by Security Council resolution 1500(2003) [YUN 2003, p. 346], continued to support the Secretary-General in fulfilling his mandate under Council resolution 1483(2003) [ibid., p. 338], as extended by resolution 1546(2004) [YUN 2004, p. 348]. The Secretary-General's Special Representative and Head of UNAMI, Staffan de Mistura (Sweden) and his staff were based in Baghdad, with regional offices in Basra and Arbil.

During the year, the Secretary-General submitted four reports on UNAMI activities [S/2008/19, S/2008/266, S/2008/495, S/2008/688].

Report of Secretary-General (January). In his second report on UNAMI activities [S/2008/19], submitted in response to resolution 1770(2007) [YUN 2007, p. 346], the Secretary-General summarized developments since his October 2007 report [ibid., p. 347]. There was a welcome reduction in the overall number of attacks across Iraq in 2007, but mass casualty attacks on civilians were a reminder that those using terrorism in pursuit of political aims had no regard for human rights or human life.

The Iraqi Government had continued to move forward on issues related to national security and the administration of Government, but progress had been slow. Reasons included the refusal of ministers belonging to Tawafoq, the largest Sunni bloc in the Parliament, to resume their places in the Cabinet. The continuing stalemate over the filling of vacant Cabinet posts was symptomatic of an ongoing uncertainty about the political process.

"Awakening Councils" of concerned local citizens were still being established. As key components of the strategy of the multinational force, those units served as a proxy civil defence corps in predominantly Sunni areas. In Anbar, the Awakening Council was active in combating Al-Qaida violence and appeared to enjoy broad support. But the Government had serious long-term concerns about the implications of armed territorial Sunni tribal forces operating outside its control.

Overall violence across Iraq had declined steadily, due to the deployment of additional multinational force troops, the ceasefire declared by the Shiite Muslim cleric Moqtada al-Sadr, the role of the Awakening Councils and increased cooperation between the Government and some regional neighbours on security-related issues. The Mahdi Army ceasefire had been instrumental in reducing the level of violence in Baghdad.

Following the withdrawal of British forces from the city of Basra, Basra Province was transferred to provincial Iraqi control in December. Nevertheless, the situation on the ground was still dominated by rivalry among key parties—mainly groups affiliated with Sadrists, the Supreme Iraqi Islamic Council and Fadhila. The Governor of Basra survived a number of attacks, and the newly appointed police commander, sent by the Prime Minister to contain local violence, reportedly survived several attempts on his life.

The status of Kirkuk and of disputed internal boundaries continued to be subject to discussion, as it became clear that the timetable for a referendum could not be met for technical and logistical reasons. UNAMI was planning to re-engage in Basra, and it was considered timely for the United Nations to re-establish a small presence at Basra International Airport until the security and political situation allowed the establishment of a formal United Nations office inside the city.

UNAMI continued to work with the Independent High Electoral Commission to help ensure that it reached the appropriate state of preparedness for future electoral events. Electoral legislation needed to be revised, particularly that relating to the complex issue of the inclusion of internally displaced persons and refugees. Substantial progress had been made in developing a reliable approach for voter registration.

As at 31 December 2007, contributions to the United Nations Development Group Iraq Trust Fund, one of the two funds of the International Reconstruction Fund Facility for Iraq, totalled $1.28 billion; 134 projects and joint programmes valued at $1.08 billion were approved by the end of 2007 for financing under the Trust Fund.

Indiscriminate and targeted violence continued to claim civilian victims in 2008, even though the overall number of reported attacks and casualties had declined. The UNAMI Human Rights Office visited detention facilities and prisons in Baghdad and in the Kurdistan region at the invitation of the Ministries of Justice, Defence, Interior, and Labour and Social Affairs. UNAMI organized specialized meetings and workshops for staff of the Ministries of Human Rights and Justice, Members of Parliament, and the national non-governmental sector, focused on the rule of law and human rights. They included a seminar in the Kurdistan region aimed at integrating human rights protection into counter-terrorism strategies and practices.

Member States had not responded to a request to provide an aircraft equipped with appropriate countermeasures for the movement of UN staff into, out of and within Iraq, so UNAMI initiated a process to procure such an aircraft from a commercial provider. UNAMI had also been negotiating with coalition forces to provide an aircraft with self-defence systems for use by the Mission until such an aircraft was procured.

Security Council consideration (January). On 21 January [meeting 5823], the Security Council was briefed by the Secretary-General's Special Representative for Iraq, Staffan de Mistura, and by the representative of the United States, Zalmay Khalilzad, on behalf of the multinational force in Iraq (MNF-I). Mr. de Mistura said that the new and enlarged team would give UNAMI the opportunity to help fulfil the agenda set by the Iraqis. Mr. Khalilzad said that continued implementation of the New Way Forward strategy, combined with the surge in force levels, had improved security considerably. Civilian casualties were below the levels of February 2006, and December 2007 had seen the second lowest coalition death toll since May 2003.

Iraq said that its Government was determined to continue its efforts to achieve national reconciliation. It was keen to reform its economy, which had been damaged as a result of wars launched by the previous regime. Iraq looked forward to the international community's continued support for its economic and development processes through the International Compact with Iraq [YUN 2006, p. 391].

Report of Secretary-General (April). In his third report on UNAMI activities [S/2008/266], the Secretary-General summarized developments since his January report. Despite some improvements in the security situation, the Government faced formidable challenges in reaching a national consensus on the sharing of power and resources. Efforts were being made at reconciliation through legislation, effecting compromise among the interests of three parliamentary blocks—the Kurdistan Alliance, the United Iraqi Alliance and Tawafuq. Efforts to persuade Tawafuq to rejoin the

Cabinet were continuing as part of a wider attempt to restructure the Government.

Following a period of improvements in security, the first quarter of 2008 witnessed a slow but steady increase in violent incidents. From over 200 recorded incidents of violence per day in the summer of 2007, the figure had dropped to averages below 80 during the last quarter of the year, but that figure now averaged around 130. More disturbing was the renewed propensity for mass-casualty attacks using suicide vests and vehicle bombs, particularly in Baghdad—believed to be the result of re-engagement by specialized insurgent groups such as the Islamic State of Iraq, which claimed affiliation with Al-Qaida in Iraq.

The growing Sahwa movement—local alliances of tribal sheikhs that were instrumental in providing neighbourhood-level security in Anbar province and other formerly restive areas—established the "Awakening Conference" at a meeting in Ramadi on 13 February. It announced its transformation from a tribal grouping to a political bloc with aspirations for participating in Governorate Councils and the next general legislative elections. Sahwa Council forces numbered over 90,000 nationwide, and slightly more than 10,000 Sahwas had been transferred into the regular security forces.

On 22 February, Moqtada al-Sadr extended the freeze on military activities by the Mahdi Army. However, on 24 March the Government announced an operation to pursue criminal elements in Basra. That led to six days of intense fighting with armed groups, including elements of the Mahdi Army, in many parts of the country until agreement was reached to stop the violence. The security situation in Basra and Baghdad subsequently eased.

Nevertheless, the March spiral of violence in southern Iraqi towns and cities, as well as in areas of Baghdad dominated by Shia, resulted in more than 700 people reported dead and 1,500 injured, many of them civilians. The United Nations Children's Fund (UNICEF) and MercyCorps distributed tankered water in Basra and Sadr City, while UNICEF and the International Committee of the Red Cross delivered surgical and medical supplies in the conflict-affected areas. The International Organization for Migration, the United Nations High Commissioner for Refugees (UNHCR) and MercyCorps also delivered food and non-food items in Basra and other locations.

UNICEF continued to deliver humanitarian assistance in the wake of attacks in Mosul and Karbala that had caused numerous casualties, dispatching emergency medical supplies for 500 people and supporting school recovery. Humanitarian water-tankering operations continued to reach 125,000 people during the crisis, mostly in Baghdad. UNICEF also distributed 745 emergency Early Childhood Development kits to kindergartens and nurseries in 15 governorates to help young children cope with psychosocial distress.

In March, the World Health Organization (WHO) and UNICEF supported the Ministry of Health in containing a measles outbreak in Anbar with a 10-day immunization drive, executed through house-to-house visits, which reached 198,075 children from 9 to 59 months of age, representing 96 per cent of the target of 206,549. The United Nations Human Settlements Programme, for its part, completed the rehabilitation of two schools in Missan, and work was ongoing in 12 schools in Missan, Samawa, Najaf, Sulaymaniyah and Kirkuk.

Meanwhile, the Government continued to strengthen ties with neighbouring countries. On 28 February, a delegation from the League of Arab States concluded a three-day visit to Baghdad to discuss national reconciliation with Iraqi officials, as well as political and tribal leaders. On 2 and 3 March, for the first time in the modern political history of Iraq and Iran, the Iranian President, Mahmoud Ahmadinejad, visited Baghdad, meeting with President Jalal Talabani, Prime Minister Nuri Kamel al-Maliki and others—primarily to discuss economic and development cooperation. On 7 March, President Talabani became the first democratically elected Iraqi Head of State to visit Turkey. On 30 March, Iraq participated in the Arab League Summit in Damascus.

The Special Representative and other senior UNAMI officials continued to engage with a wide range of Iraqi political figures in Government, as well as diplomatic and military officials based in Baghdad. The Special Representative travelled to Turkey in March for discussions with senior officials on the United Nations role in facilitating national reconciliation and regional dialogue, including in the context of northern Iraq. He visited the city of Najaf and held extensive meetings with Grand Ayatollah Ali al-Sistani, Grand Ayatollah al-Hakim, Ayatollah Muhammad al-Yacoubi, the Governor of Najaf and other religious leaders and political figures, including representatives of the Sadrist Trend. The meetings focused on provincial elections, national reconciliation, Government performance, and assistance to Iraq's vulnerable communities, especially internally displaced persons. The Special Representative also chaired the first comprehensive anti-corruption conference for Iraq (17–18 March).

UNAMI continued working closely with the Independent High Electoral Commission to ensure that it would be able to conduct elections that would be seen as credible and be accepted by the Iraqi people. UNAMI assisted the Commission and Government in developing an election system that would better reflect the wishes of the Iraqi people and better accommodate women, internally displaced persons and minority groups.

The Iraq 2008 consolidated appeal was launched on 12 February in Baghdad and was also presented to the Kurdistan regional government Council of Ministers in Arbil on 13 February. It included appeals from 14 UN agencies and 10 NGOs for $265 million in support of targeted relief operations to deliver emergency aid in the areas of health and nutrition, education, water and sanitation, housing and shelter, food and protection. By the end of the first quarter of 2008, $43 million of the consolidated appeal process (16 per cent) had been funded and an additional $62 million had been pledged.

Although violence against women in the Kurdistan region remained a concern, the regional government had initiated protection procedures for women and was working closely with UNAMI to improve the human rights situation. In March, the Special Representative opened a conference organized by UNAMI in Baghdad on the protection of human rights in the context of counter-terrorism measures, with the participation of the Ministers of Human Rights and Interior.

Meanwhile, the UNAMI Human Rights Office continued to visit detention facilities and prisons at the invitation of the authorities in Baghdad and Arbil. It documented cases involving the denial of due process, including the deprivation of access to defence counsel and prolonged pretrial detention, as well as instances of torture and ill-treatment of detainees, including juveniles.

Security Council consideration (April). On 28 April [meeting 5878], the Council was briefed by the Under-Secretary-General for Political Affairs and by the representative of the United States on behalf of MNF-I.

The former said that Iraq had taken important steps in January, including passage of the Justice and Accountability Law replacing earlier de-Ba'athification policies, and a package of laws that included the Law on Governorates not Organized into a Region, the General Amnesty Law and the 2008 budget.

The latter observed that the overall security environment continued to improve, and there were gains on the political, economic and diplomatic fronts as well. Although many challenges remained, the Iraqi security forces were developing increased capability and proficiency; and the Ministries of Defence and Interior were improving their ability to execute their budgets.

Iraq said that the Government was determined to limit weapons to the hands of the Government, disband militias and ensure there was no army but the Iraqi army. At the political level, it was determined to bring into being a Government of national unity on a nationally agreed basis.

Communications. On 23 April [S/2008/296], the Secretary-General of the League of Arab States forwarded to the Council President the resolutions adopted by the Arab summit (Damascus, Syria, 29–30 March), including resolutions on the situation in Iraq, on the situation of Iraqi émigrés in host Arab States and on the transfer of Palestinian refugees from the Iraqi borders to the Sudan.

On 12 May [A/62/842-S/2008/320], Iraq and Kuwait transmitted the final communiqué of the third expanded meeting of the Foreign Ministers of the countries neighbouring Iraq (Kuwait, 22 April) and the recommendations of its three working groups. The communiqué said that the meeting was convened to provide "ongoing strong and effective support" to Iraq's Government and people. In a letter dated 10 June [S/2008/380], Iraq's Foreign Minister, Hoshyar Zebari, welcomed the continued support of the multinational force and arrangements affecting the Development Fund for Iraq and its International Advisory and Monitoring Board.

Security Council consideration (June). On 13 June [meeting 5910], the Council was briefed by Ibrahim Gambari, Special Adviser on the International Compact with Iraq and Other Political Issues, and the representative of the United States, Mr. Khalilzad, on behalf of the MNF-I.

Mr. Khalilzad said that the security environment had continued to improve, thanks to the efforts of the Iraqi security forces and MNF-I. Security incidents had fallen to their lowest level in over four years, notwithstanding a temporary increase in violence associated with recent Iraqi military operations in Basra, Sadr City and Mosul.

Mr. Gambari said that the first annual Review Conference of the International Compact with Iraq (Stockholm, Sweden, 29 May) had met with a feeling of new hope that the people and the Government of Iraq had started to overcome daunting challenges and to work together at rebuilding their country.

Iraqi Foreign Minister Zebari said that his country had recently passed the five-year milestone in its democratic transition. Iraq had stepped back from the brink of civil war, the volume of oil output was at its highest level since 2004 and annual core inflation had been reduced from 36 per cent at the end of 2006 to 16 per cent. Iraq was negotiating bilateral strategic agreements with the United States to provide the framework for security arrangements that would address Iraq's security needs covered at present by the multinational force.

Security Council statement. Following the briefing, Security Council members, in a press statement [SC/9358], expressed their agreement with the continuation of the MNF-I mandate and other arrangements, as discussed by the Iraqi Government in its 10 June letter.

Report of Secretary-General (July). In his fourth report on UNAMI operations [S/2008/495], the Secretary-General said that a combination of political and military efforts had contributed to improvements in security across Iraq. Nevertheless, Diyala Province in north-central Iraq continued to experience daily attacks against Government, security and international elements, and in Kirkuk, targeted assassinations occurred against law enforcement and other officials. Ansar al-Sunnah and numerous affiliates were still capable of carrying out deadly attacks, and Al-Qaida maintained a presence in Anbar, where it appeared intent on attacking tribal groups that were cooperating with local or international security forces.

The Iraqi security forces commenced several major operations concurrently: Operation Peace, against renegade groups in the Sadr City area of Baghdad; Operation Promise of Peace, in the southern town of Amarah in Missan Province; and Operation Lion's Roar, against insurgent groups in Mosul and other parts of Ninawa Province. The ceasefire declared by Moqtada al-Sadr on 11 May for Sadr City remained in effect, and State authority and basic services were being restored in coordination with Sadr movement leaders.

On 19 July, Tawafuq ended a year-long boycott and rejoined Prime Minister al-Maliki's Cabinet when Parliament approved six Sunni officials. Four members of the Shiite Unified Iraqi Alliance also joined the Cabinet in the place of Sadrist and Iraqi National List members of Parliament, who had initiated a boycott in April and August 2007, respectively. On 29 April, more than 30 representatives from the main political and ethnic groups held a reconciliation meeting in Helsinki, Finland, under the auspices of a Finnish NGO, and formulated principles for joint national action, agreeing on a set of principles at a second meeting in Baghdad on 5 July.

On 5 June, UNAMI, which had been working to establish a process for addressing disputed internal boundaries, presented to the Government its initial analysis on the first four of several disputed areas in northern Iraq. Reactions reflected the sensitive nature of the issue, but the Mission was committed to promoting a political and constitutional process acceptable to the major stakeholders to resolve disputed internal boundaries—including the status of Kirkuk.

Regionally, Bahrain, Jordan, Kuwait and the United Arab Emirates announced the resumption of full diplomatic representation in Iraq. Following the high-level International Compact with Iraq Annual Review Conference (Stockholm, 29 May), the United Arab Emirates announced on 6 July that it would forgive Iraqi debt. Turkey's Prime Minister visited Baghdad on 10 July—the first such visit in 18 years—and a border security pact was signed. The Special Representative continued outreach to prepare for the provincial elections and held bilateral meetings in Amman, Jordan, Baghdad and Kuwait on Iraq's further stabilization and development.

Iraq began its voter registration update as scheduled on 15 July, opening all but one of the 564 voter registration centres on the first day. The update would run for 30 days, giving some 15 million eligible Iraqis the opportunity to verify their details, and adding new eligible voters to the provisional list. On other matters, the constitutional review process remained deadlocked over the powers of the presidency, the powers of regions and governorates, and oil and gas provisions.

Despite improved security conditions in Baghdad, Amarah and Mosul after the operations against armed militias, UNAMI remained concerned about the safety and legal protection of hundreds of arrested suspects, as well as detention conditions and lack of due process. Those apparently rounded up as suspects included a number of children.

Many abductions were reported, followed by ransom demands or killings, as were assassinations of targeted individuals, including public officials. Journalists, educators, medical doctors, judges and lawyers remained prime targets for armed militias and criminal gangs. Gender-based violence, murders, suicides, so-called accidents and other suspected "honour crimes" continued to be documented in the Kurdistan region.

Violations against children were being committed on a large scale and included child recruitment, attacks on schools and hospitals, killing and maiming by indiscriminate attacks, and lack of humanitarian access due to insecure conditions. Some 1,500 children were known to be held in detention facilities for alleged association with armed groups. The Secretary-General's Special Representative on Children and Armed Conflict visited Iraq from 20 to 25 April and reported that children lacked access to education, health care and clean water. She expressed concern about the use of children by armed groups as spies or messengers; even more troubling was their use as soldiers and bomb planters or carriers.

UNAMI continued to conduct field visits in the Kurdistan region, including to detention facilities. Its frequent and intensive contacts with governmental and civil society counterparts on a range of human rights issues had resulted in positive changes, including measures by the regional authorities aimed at improving the conduct of their law-enforcement officials.

During the first half of 2008, the Expanded Humanitarian Response Fund for Iraq funded 23 Iraqi and international NGO projects, with grants of up to $400,000 to deliver emergency relief assistance to the most vulnerable or most seriously affected Iraqis. The UN country team developed an assistance strategy for Iraq for 2008–2010, which was approved by an interministerial committee within the Government in June.

Major security operations in Sadr City, Mosul and Amarah prompted the UN country team to work closely on contingency plans for humanitarian response. In the most acute of the three crises, the United Nations delivered water and sanitation assistance for an estimated 120,000 families in Sadr City. Sanitation agencies supplied 10 million litres of safe water to residents and hospitals, as well as water hygiene/purification kits. UNHCR provided non-food items to internally displaced persons and supported the repair of some 300 conflict-affected houses and shops in the Sadr City and Shula districts of Baghdad. The World Food Programme (WFP) delivered 296 tons of emergency food to 38,500 residents of Sadr City, and the International Organization for Migration delivered 2,000 food baskets to hospitals in Sadr City and Shula. In addition, 1,500 food baskets were delivered to hospitals in Basra, Wassit, Babylon and Qadisiyah.

Refugees and internally displaced persons continued to return to their places of origin at a steady rate of some 10,000 persons a month, and there had been no major incidence of displacement during the quarter. WHO and UNICEF supported a vaccination drive for 239,000 children, which contained a measles outbreak. UNHCR, with its partners, rehabilitated 311 housing units in Baghdad, including in Sadr City, and another 300 were being completed or under way in Basra and Mosul. Advocacy by the United Nations Human Settlements Programme (UN-Habitat) resulted in the establishment of an emergency shelter committee and the allocation of $12 million by the Ministry of Construction and Housing for house rehabilitation in Sadr City.

In addition to 17 ongoing education projects funded by the International Reconstruction Fund Facility for Iraq, UN country team agencies started repairs on 14 of 22 damaged schools in Sadr City. UN-Habitat was also working on schools in Najaf and Samawa, while UNICEF had projects in Sadr City, Babylon, Karbala, Missan and Kirkuk. UNICEF continued to focus on accelerated learning programmes for students whose education had been interrupted.

Security Council consideration (August). The Security Council met on 6 August [meeting 5949] to consider the Secretary-General's report. It was briefed by the Under-Secretary-General for Political Affairs, B. Lynn Pascoe, and by the representative of the United States, Alejandro Wolff, on behalf of MNF-I.

Mr. Pascoe said that political and military efforts had contributed to improved security in most parts of Iraq, but civilian casualties remained high. The Independent High Electoral Commission had reached a number of milestones; it was now crucial to come to agreement on new electoral legislation.

Mr. Wolff said that security incidents were at their lowest level in over four years, even as MNF-I had drawn down its forces from surge levels. The increase in the capacity of the Iraqi security forces, with more than 580,000 personnel, had contributed substantially to the improved environment. Out of 161 Iraqi army combat battalions, 93 were rated as able to fully plan, execute and sustain operations with minimal or no assistance from coalition forces beyond enablers and adviser teams.

Iraq said that its Government's success in building its armed forces on a national, professional and neutral basis led to their determination to strike at Al-Qaida and other militias. The decline in violence led to a return to normal life in all parts of the country, and encouraged internally displaced families and Iraqi refugees to return home. Adoption of a general amnesty law had enhanced the national reconciliation efforts. The Government's top priorities were to improve economic conditions and revive trade.

Extension of UNAMI mandate

By a 4 August letter to the Council President [S/2008/523], the Iraqi Foreign Minister conveyed his Government's wish that the UNAMI mandate be extended for a 12-month period. The Government looked forward to a more effective role for UNAMI with the return to Iraq of the UN specialized agencies, funds and programmes and their valuable contribution to its reconstruction.

SECURITY COUNCIL ACTION

On 7 August [meeting 5950], the Security Council unanimously adopted **resolution 1830(2008)**. The draft [S/2008/529] was submitted by Italy, the United Kingdom and the United States.

The Security Council,

Recalling all its previous relevant resolutions on Iraq, in particular resolutions 1500(2003) of 14 August 2003, 1546(2004) of 8 June 2004, 1557(2004) of 12 August 2004, 1619(2005) of 11 August 2005, 1700(2006) of 10 August 2006 and 1770(2007) of 10 August 2007,

Reaffirming the independence, sovereignty, unity and territorial integrity of Iraq,

Emphasizing the importance of the stability and security of Iraq for the people of Iraq, the region and the international community,

Acknowledging that a democratically elected and constitutionally based Government of Iraq is now in place,

Welcoming improvements in the security situation in Iraq achieved through concerted political and security efforts, and stressing that challenges to security in Iraq still exist and improvements need to be sustained through meaningful political dialogue and national reconciliation,

Underscoring the need for all communities in Iraq to reject sectarianism, participate in the political process and an inclusive political dialogue, reach a comprehensive solution on the distribution of resources and work towards national reconciliation for the sake of Iraq's political stability and unity,

Reaffirming the importance of the United Nations, in particular the United Nations Assistance Mission for Iraq, in supporting the efforts of the people and Government of Iraq to strengthen institutions for representative government, promote political dialogue and national reconciliation, engage neighbouring countries, assist vulnerable groups, including refugees and internally displaced persons, and promote the protection of human rights and judicial and legal reform,

Expressing concern about human rights challenges in Iraq, and stressing the importance of addressing these challenges,

Expressing concern also about the humanitarian issues confronting the Iraqi people, and stressing the need for a coordinated response and adequate resources to address these issues,

Underscoring the sovereignty of the Government of Iraq, reaffirming that all parties should continue to take all feasible steps and develop modalities to ensure the protection of affected civilians, including children, and should create conditions conducive to the voluntary, safe, dignified and sustainable return of refugees and internally displaced persons, welcoming new commitments of the Government for the relief of internally displaced persons, encouraging continued efforts for internally displaced persons and refugees, and noting the important role of the Office of the United Nations High Commissioner for Refugees, based on its mandate, in providing advice and support to the Government, in coordination with the Mission,

Urging all those concerned, as set forth in international humanitarian law, including the Geneva Conventions of 1949 and the Regulations annexed to the Hague Convention IV of 1907, to allow full, unimpeded access by humanitarian personnel to all people in need of assistance and to make available, as far as possible, all facilities necessary for their operations, and to promote the safety, security and freedom of movement of humanitarian personnel and United Nations and associated personnel and their assets,

Welcoming the appointment by the Secretary-General on 11 September 2007 of a new Special Representative for Iraq, and recognizing the expanded role given to him and the Mission, as established in resolution 1770(2007),

Acknowledging the important roles played by the United Nations and the Government of Iraq in the first annual ministerial review of the International Compact with Iraq, held in Stockholm on 29 May 2008, as well as in the expanded neighbours conference held in Kuwait City on 22 April 2008, its working groups and its ad hoc support mechanism, and underscoring the importance of continued regional and international support for Iraq's development,

Welcoming the decision of the Government of Iraq to allocate a parcel of land in Baghdad to the United Nations for its new integrated headquarters, and urging the Government to fulfill its commitment to contribute financially to this project,

Welcoming also the letter dated 4 August 2008 from the Minister for Foreign Affairs of Iraq to the Secretary-General setting forth the request of the Government of Iraq that the Mission continue to assist Iraqi efforts to build a productive and prosperous nation at peace with itself and its neighbours,

1. *Decides* to extend the mandate of the United Nations Assistance Mission for Iraq for a period of twelve months from the date of the present resolution;

2. *Decides also* that the Special Representative of the Secretary-General for Iraq and the Mission, at the request of the Government of Iraq and taking into account the letter dated 4 August 2008 from the Minister for Foreign Affairs of Iraq to the Secretary-General, shall continue to pursue their expanded mandate as stipulated in resolution 1770(2007);

3. *Recognizes* that the security of United Nations personnel is essential for the Mission to carry out its work for the benefit of the people of Iraq, and calls upon the Government of Iraq and other Member States to continue to provide security and logistical support to the United Nations presence in Iraq;

4. *Welcomes* the contributions of Member States in providing the Mission with the financial, logistical and security resources and support that it needs to fulfill its mission, and calls upon Member States to continue to provide the Mission with these resources and support;

5. *Expresses its intention* to review the mandate of the Mission in twelve months or sooner, if requested by the Government of Iraq;

6. *Requests* the Secretary-General to report to the Security Council on a quarterly basis on the progress made towards the fulfilment of all the responsibilities of the Mission;

7. *Decides* to remain seized of the matter.

Report of Secretary-General (November). In his report on UNAMI activities [S/2008/688], submitted in response to resolution 1830(2008), the Secretary-General said that the decrease in security incidents and relative stability had continued, even though United States troops deployed for the military surge had been withdrawn. The Government had taken control of the Sons of Iraq forces, and Moqtada al-Sadr's ceasefire instruction to the Jaysh al-Mahdi militia remained in force.

The multinational force formally transferred security responsibilities to the Iraqi army in Al-Anbar Governorate in September, in Babil Governorate on 23 October, and in Wassit Governorate on 27 October, bringing the number of provinces under Iraqi control to 13. The integration of some 100,000 members of the Sons of Iraq into Government structures began on 1 October, when 54,000 fighters in the Baghdad area came under Iraqi supervision.

Armed opposition groups continued targeting Iraqi security forces and prominent individuals, and security remained particularly challenging in Mosul (Ninawa) and Khanaqin (Diyala). On 5 September, agreement was reached on a separation of forces in and around Khanaqin town, where the situation was tense but stable.

The Council of Representatives adopted the provincial election law on 24 September, and the Presidency Council ratified it on 7 October. It was amended on 3 November to include provisions for minority representation in Baghdad, Basra and Ninawa. Provincial council elections were to take place in early 2009 in 14 of Iraq's 18 governorates. UNAMI launched a nationwide project aimed at providing Iraqi citizens with balanced and reliable information on the elections.

On 26 October, United States forces in Iraq attacked a house in the village of Sukkariyah in the Syrian Arab Republic (see below). The Secretary-General expressed regret over the loss of civilian lives and called for regional cooperation to solve issues of common concern, including border security.

UNAMI continued its work on disputed internal boundaries, conducting multiple field visits to meet with provincial, district and subdistrict officials, party representatives, religious leaders, tribal elders, minority groups and members of civil society. Bahrain, Jordan, Kuwait, Syria and the United Arab Emirates resumed the functioning of their embassies in Baghdad, and Egypt indicated that it would reopen its embassy in the near future.

The United Nations Assistance Strategy for Iraq 2008–2010 was signed on 13 August. It included three $30 million cross-sectoral initiatives on private sector development, to reform Iraq's investment laws; on public sector reform, to strengthen anti-corruption and transparency initiatives; and on decentralization, to enable local governments to plan, fund and manage the delivery of social services.

With fewer children attending school and dropout rates rising, the United Nations developed a $13 million programme for the education sector. Humanitarian assistance increased during the quarter, as new funds were pledged in response to the $267 million 2008 consolidated appeal—of which 55 per cent was funded. In September, UNDP and the United Nations Office on Drugs and Crime launched a five-year anti-corruption programme.

In September, Parliament approved the public census bill, and United Nations Population Fund was implementing a support programme for the census. National survey data being finalized by WFP suggested that access to social services, including electricity, had improved from its lowest levels in 2005 and 2006. However, access to safe drinking water had fallen to as low as 31 per cent in the poorest subdistricts, and access to sanitation services to 35 per cent.

Communications. On 28 October [S/2008/676], the Syrian Arab Republic said that on 26 October, four United States helicopters had violated Syrian airspace from Iraq, attacking a civilian building in Sukkariyah and killing eight persons, including four children. Condemning the act as a grave infraction of its sovereignty and a violation of the UN Charter, Syria demanded that Iraq prevent any further use of its territory to launch such attacks. On 5 November [S/2008/687], Cuba, in its capacity as Chair of the Coordinating Bureau of the Non-Alignment Movement and the Movement's 118 members, also condemned that attack and deplored the loss of civilian lives.

Security Council consideration (November). On 14 November [meeting 6016], the Council was briefed by the Special Representative, Mr. de Mistura, and by the representative of the United States, Mr. Khalilzad, on behalf of MNF-I.

Mr. de Mistura said that the forthcoming provincial elections of 31 January 2009 were rightly viewed as an opportunity to establish a more inclusive sectarian balance and shape a new political landscape. The Electoral Commission, supported by UNAMI, had trained 42,785 local observers and was working with the Minister of Education to employ some 270,000 teachers, clerks and headmasters to assist on polling day.

Mr. Khalilzad said that there had been an 81 per cent decrease in improvised explosive device explosions and a 72 per cent decrease in suicide explosions. Nevertheless, Al-Qaida remained a significant threat, as did Iranian surrogate militants and Jaysh al-Mahdi militia forces. Countering that threat were 165 Iraqi army combat battalions conducting operations; the air force was flying more than 300 sorties a week; the navy was conducting three times as many patrols as in 2007; and the national police had over 41,000 personnel.

Iraq said that the number of officers in the Iraqi army had increased from 9,800 to 13,911 and the number of soldiers from 116,135 to 217,176. Following terrorist attacks on the Christian community in Mosul Province, the Government sent security forces to protect those civilians. More than 300 Christian families returned to their homes after security and stability were restored in their neighbourhoods.

Report of Secretary-General. In a later report [S/2009/102], the Secretary-General reviewed developments through the end of 2008. He said that on 27 November, the Iraqi Council of Representatives had approved the final draft of a bilateral security agreement which placed United States forces under the authority and jurisdiction of the Government of Iraq, and included a timeline for their withdrawal from Iraq by December 2011. The Council of Representatives also voted on 23 December to authorize the Government to allow non-United States forces to remain in Iraq until 31 July 2009.

The activities of the Special Representative and UNAMI had focused on supporting the Independent High

Electoral Commission in preparing for the elections on 31 January 2009. Preparation of UNAMI's analytical report on disputed internal boundaries for presentation to the Government continued, and UNAMI provided support to the Government in its relations with neighbouring countries.

Following the report of the Constitutional Review Committee in July, UNAMI's Office of Constitutional Support identified federalism and hydrocarbon regulation as priority issues for resolution and for the country's long-term stability. To build on the impetus generated by the report, UNAMI hosted a round-table discussion in November in Baghdad to discuss hydrocarbon management in the context of a federal system.

In advance of the elections, UNAMI led efforts to address the issue of minority representation in the form of an amendment to the 2008 electoral law. The Independent High Electoral Commission, assisted by UNAMI, developed polling and counting procedures; formulated public and civil society outreach strategies; and procured materials, including the final voter's lists and ballots. The public outreach unit of the Independent High Electoral Commission, backed by electoral assistance and public information officers from UNAMI and the United Nations Office for Project Services, held dozens of civil and voter education events for opinion leaders throughout the country to address key election topics, including anti-fraud measures, campaign rules and regulations, and voting procedures.

Iraq's efforts to meet internationally agreed development targets, as set forth in the International Compact for Iraq, received recognition through cancellation of Iraq's debt in December by the Paris Club, an informal group of rich lender nations. As at 31 December, commitments to the United Nations Development Group Iraq Trust Fund amounted to $1.36 billion, with total deposits of $1.33 billion; 159 projects and joint programmes valued at $1.22 billion had been approved for funding as at 31 December, including $15 million for humanitarian relief through the Expanded Humanitarian Response Fund.

Despite progress on humanitarian issues throughout 2008, conditions for vulnerable and displaced Iraqis were still a concern. Security improvements had increased opportunities for UN relief programmes, but implementation had been constrained due to limited funding, with only 67 per cent of those programmes funded as at December. The 2009 consolidated appeal for Iraq and the subregion, launched on 19 November, sought to address that issue. It aimed to provide relief for the most vulnerable, including returnee families; support Iraqi refugees in safety and dignity until return was possible; and offer a platform for dialogue between Iraq and its neighbours on issues of common concern. The final appeal requested $192 million for activities inside Iraq and $355 million for activities outside Iraq—the latter to be coordinated by UNHCR. Efforts to restore essential services continued, with education and environmental issues a priority.

Although Iraq, in recent months, had witnessed gradual stabilization and further improvements in security conditions—with a decrease in violent, high-visibility, mass-casualty attacks by militias, insurgents and criminal gangs—indiscriminate attacks by roadside, car or suicide bombs were almost a daily occurrence. A troubling aspect was the frequent use of women, and occasionally even children, as suicide bombers.

The Council of Representatives, on 16 November, enacted a law establishing an Independent High Commission for Human Rights—marking the culmination of two years of advocacy work by UNAMI and its international partners. A role for UNAMI during the establishment and start-up phase of the Commission was enshrined in the law.

The General Assembly approved $5 million for work on the design of the UNAMI integrated headquarters in Baghdad, the construction of which remained essential for the continued delivery of its mandate. Further to his letter of 12 December to the Security Council President and the President's reply (see p. 391), the Secretary-General proceeded to negotiate a new agreement with the United States, setting out arrangements concerning the continued provision by the United States forces of security support for the UN presence in Iraq. Those negotiations were concluded on 31 December. The Iraqi Government was kept informed of the negotiations and was provided with the text of the signed agreement.

UNAMI financing

On 10 October [A/63/346/Add.5], the Secretary-General submitted the proposed resource requirements for UNAMI for the period from 1 January to 31 December 2009, totalling $161,760,800 net ($168,972,900 gross).

In December [A/63/593], ACABQ recommended that the General Assembly approve the resources requested by the Secretary-General, subject to its observations and recommendations.

On 24 December, the General Assembly, by **resolution 63/263,** section XI (see p. 1548), approved that amount as part of the $429,497,600 budget for the 27 special political missions authorized by the General Assembly and/or the Security Council.

UN integrated compound

In response to the General Assembly's request, in resolution 62/238, section V [YUN 2007, p. 1452], for a new, detailed proposal on the construction of the UN integrated compound in Baghdad, the Secretary-General, in May [A/62/828], reported that a site formerly known as the Al-Sijud Palace had been identified as more suitable. He requested that the Assembly approve in principle the proposal to build the headquarters there; note the preliminary cost estimate of $98.6 million; approve $5 million for preparatory work; and ask for a new, complete and detailed proposal to be considered by the Assembly in March 2009.

In a report on the proposed UNAMI headquarters dated 11 December [A/63/601], ACABQ noted that the Secretary-General's cost estimate of $98.6 million for the project was based on preliminary assumptions. It recommended that the Assembly await his new, detailed proposal before pronouncing itself on the cost requirements.

On 24 December, by **resolution 63/263,** section X (see p. 1548), the Assembly approved commitment authority for 2009 for UNAMI in the amount of $5 million to undertake design work in connection with the construction of the compound. The Secretary-General was requested to submit a new, complete and detailed proposal, with detailed financial requirements and clear timelines, to be considered by the Assembly during its resumed sixty-third (2009) session.

Multinational force

In December 2007, Iraq had requested the extension of the mandate multinational force in Iraq (MNF-I) until 31 December 2008, and considered that request to be the final one [YUN 2007, p. 349].

In a letter to the Security Council dated 10 June [S/2008/380], Iraq's Foreign Minister Zebari welcomed the support of MNF-I and noted that Iraq was negotiating bilateral security arrangements with the United States and other friendly nations that should address its security needs currently covered by MNF-I.

In a 7 December letter to the Security Council President (see p. 393), Prime Minister al-Maliki said that in view of the fact that Iraq had signed the Agreement between the United States and Iraq on the Withdrawal of United States Forces from Iraq and the Organization of Their Activities during Their Temporary Presence in Iraq, his country looked forward to the end of the MNF-I mandate on 31 December. Iraq expressed its gratitude to the Governments of the States that had contributed to those forces, and to the forces themselves, for the services rendered during their presence.

On 12 December [S/2008/783], the Secretary-General informed the Security Council that MNF-I's authorization was to expire on 31 December. With the new Iraq-United States agreement, the United States forces were expected to remain beyond that date. He would therefore seek to negotiate an agreement for the continued provision by United States forces of security support for the UN presence in Iraq. On 16 December [S/2008/784], the Council welcomed the proposed arrangements for the establishment of an integrated UN security structure for UNAMI.

On 16 July, Poland transferred to the Iraqi authorities control of the province of Al-Qadisiyah, for whose security and stabilization it had been responsible in the framework of the multinational force. The process of withdrawing Polish military personnel was concluded by the end of October. On 19 November [S/2008/722], Poland transmitted to the Security Council a letter on its decision to withdraw its military contingent from Iraq.

International Advisory and Monitoring Board

The International Advisory and Monitoring Board for Iraq (IAMB), established by Security Council resolution 1483(2003) [YUN 2003, p. 338] to ensure that the Development Fund for Iraq was used in a transparent manner for the benefit of the Iraqi people and that Iraqi export sales of petroleum products were consistent with international market best practices, continued to oversee the auditing of the Fund.

Security Council consideration (June). On 13 June [meeting 5910], the Council was briefed by the United Nations Controller, Warren Sach, speaking as the Secretary-General's designated representative on IAMB. He said that from its inception in December 2003 to 31 December 2007, IAMB had been informed that approximately $106.3 billion had been deposited in the Development Fund for Iraq from the sale of oil and oil products. The sum of $10.4 billion had also been deposited with the Fund from the balance of the oil-for-food funds held under escrow by the United Nations, and a further $1.5 billion had been deposited as proceeds from frozen assets.

Since his previous briefing to the Council [YUN 2007, p. 353], IAMB had met twice, making a total of 23 meetings since its inception. It approved the appointment by the Government of Iraq of independent public accountants as external auditors, reviewed the periodic audit results, and requested and approved special audits. The results of its work were available on its website.

In 2007 and 2008, IAMB oversaw two audits of the Fund, covering 2006 and 2007. Those audits were conducted by the international accounting firm Ernst & Young, and covered oil export sales, the accounting for the proceeds from oil export sales, the Fund's financial statements and disbursement procedures for its resources. In a draft report covering 2007, the auditors, while highlighting some improvements, especially in access to spending ministries, also underscored weaknesses in internal controls. Those weaknesses included incomplete record-keeping at the Ministry of Finance, the lack of a comprehensive oil metering system, the sale of oil and oil products outside of the Fund, incomplete contract information associated with the United States agencies' contracts, and bartering.

IAMB welcomed the progress made in 2007 to strengthen the financial and administrative controls over the use of Fund resources in the spending ministries. However, there continued to be insufficient progress in internal control matters in Iraq. IAMB found that further measures to strengthen the internal control framework were necessary.

IAMB had recommended in 2004 the installation of a comprehensive oil metering system in Iraq in accordance with standard oil industry practices, as oil metering was a key factor in achieving financial transparency and accountability. While the Government supported oil metering, progress had been slow. Some metering had been installed at some oil terminals, but there continued to be no metering in the oil fields. A metering system would help improve overall controls and curtail smuggling. Steps were being taken to address the problem, but the matter was urgent, especially in the light of the auditors' report that showed unreconciled differences related to production, export sales and internal consumption.

IAMB was concerned that barter transactions were not accounted for in the Fund. The use of barter transactions made it difficult to determine whether fair value had been received for Iraq's oil export revenues. Moreover, as no revenues were generated from such barter or other in-kind deals and the notional value of such transactions was not recorded against the Fund, IAMB felt that they could be inconsistent with resolution 1483(2003), which required that all Iraqi oil export sales be deposited into the Development Fund and the United Nations Compensation Fund.

The results of the audits in 2007 indicated that the overall financial system of controls in place in the spending ministries, in the United States agencies' handling of outstanding commitments using Fund resources and in the Iraqi administration of Fund resources remained deficient, and financial management reforms needed to be pursued further.

The Foreign Minister of Iraq, Hoshyar Zebari, said that his country welcomed the continuation of the arrangements regarding the Development Fund and IAMB, as extended in resolution 1790(2007) [YUN 2007, p. 349].

Following the briefing, Security Council members, in a press statement [SC/9358], agreed upon the continuation of the arrangements for the Development Fund and IAMB, as requested by the Iraqi Government in its 10 June letter [S/2008/380].

On 22 December, by resolution 1859(2008) (see below), the Security Council extended the mandate of IAMB until 31 December 2009.

SECURITY COUNCIL ACTION

On 22 December [meeting 6059], the Security Council unanimously adopted **resolution 1859(2008)**. The draft [S/2008/805] was submitted by the United Kingdom and the United States.

The Security Council,

Welcoming the efforts of the democratically elected, constitutionally based national unity Government of Iraq in fulfilling its detailed political, economic and security programme and national reconciliation agenda, and encouraging in that regard the holding of inclusive and peaceful provincial elections,

Recalling all of its previous relevant resolutions on Iraq,

Reaffirming the independence, sovereignty, unity and territorial integrity of Iraq, and reaffirming further the importance of the principle of non-interference in the internal affairs of Iraq,

Noting the progress that is taking place in Iraq, particularly in achieving security and stability and in strengthening the armed forces and other Iraqi security forces, and noting likewise Iraq's progress in the political and economic fields,

Welcoming the continuing work of the Government of Iraq towards a federal, democratic, pluralistic and unified Iraq, in which there is full respect for human rights,

Noting the Government of Iraq's progress in pursuing an atmosphere in which sectarianism is totally rejected, and underscoring the importance of inclusive political dialogue and national reconciliation,

Recognizing that international support for security and stability is essential to the well-being of the people of Iraq as well as the ability of all concerned, including the United Nations, to carry out their work for the benefit of the people of Iraq, and expressing appreciation for contributions by Member States in this regard under resolutions 1483(2003) of 22 May 2003, 1511(2003) of 16 October 2003, 1546(2004) of 8 June 2004, 1637(2005) of 8 November 2005, 1723(2006) of 28 November 2006 and 1790(2007) of 18 December 2007,

Recognizing also that Iraq is still in need of regional and international support so that it can continue to make progress so its people can flourish and prosper in peace,

Welcoming continuing progress under the International Compact with Iraq, an initiative of the Government of Iraq that has created a new partnership with the international community and is building a strong framework for Iraq's continued political, economic and security transformation and integration into the regional and global economy, as confirmed in the Stockholm Declaration of 29 May 2008, and welcoming also the important role that the United Nations is playing by jointly chairing the Compact with the Government of Iraq,

Recalling the establishment of the United Nations Assistance Mission for Iraq, and affirming that the United Nations should continue to play a leading role in supporting the efforts of the Government of Iraq to strengthen institutions for representative government, promote political dialogue and national reconciliation, engage neighbouring countries, assist vulnerable groups, including refugees and internally displaced persons, and promote the protection of human rights and judicial and legal reform in accordance with resolutions 1770(2007) of 10 August 2007 and 1830(2008) of 7 August 2008,

Calling upon the international community, particularly countries in the region and Iraq's neighbours, to support the Iraqi people in their pursuit of peace, stability, security, democracy and prosperity, welcoming the expanded neighbours conferences held in Sharm el-Sheikh, Egypt, in Istanbul, Turkey, and in Kuwait City and their role in supporting the efforts of the Government of Iraq to achieve security and stability in Iraq, and the positive results thereof on regional and international peace and security, welcoming also the fact that the expanded neighbours conference held in Kuwait City on 22 April 2008 approved the terms of reference of the support mechanism, and noting that the successful implementation of the present resolution will contribute to regional stability,

Taking note of the letter dated 7 December 2008 from the Prime Minister of Iraq to the President of the Security Council, which is annexed to the present resolution, welcoming the affirmation by the Prime Minister of Iraq's commitment to living in peace with its neighbours in a manner that contributes to the security and stability of the region, and recognizing the expiration of the mandate of the multinational force on 31 December 2008,

Recognizing the positive developments in Iraq and that the situation now existing in Iraq is significantly different from that which existed at the time of the adoption of resolution 661(1990) on 6 August 1990, and further recognizing the importance of Iraq achieving international standing equal to that which it held prior to the adoption of resolution 661(1990),

Recognizing also that the letter from the Prime Minister of Iraq also reaffirms the commitment by the Government of Iraq to resolve the debts and settle the claims inherited from the previous regime, and to continue to address those debts and claims until they are resolved or settled, and requests the continued assistance of the international community, as the Government of Iraq works to complete this process,

Recognizing further the significant role of the Development Fund for Iraq and the International Advisory and Monitoring Board and the provisions of paragraph 22 of resolution 1483(2003) in helping the Government of Iraq to ensure that Iraq's resources are being used transparently and accountably for the benefit of the Iraqi people, and recognizing also the need for Iraq to transition during 2009 to successor arrangements for the Development Fund and the Board, to include the Committee of Financial Experts,

Reaffirming that acts of terrorism must not be allowed to disrupt Iraq's political and economic transition, and further reaffirming the obligations of Member States under resolution 1618(2005) of 4 August 2005 and other relevant resolutions and international conventions with respect, inter alia, to terrorist activities in and from Iraq or against its citizens,

Recognizing that the Government of Iraq will continue to have the leading role in coordinating international assistance to Iraq, and reaffirming the importance of international assistance and the development of the Iraqi economy and the importance of coordinated donor assistance,

Acting under Chapter VII of the Charter of the United Nations,

1. *Decides* to extend until 31 December 2009 the arrangements established in paragraph 20 of resolution 1483(2003) for the deposit into the Development Fund for Iraq of proceeds from export sales of petroleum, petroleum products and natural gas and the arrangements referred to in paragraph 12 of resolution 1483(2003) and paragraph 24 of resolution 1546(2004) for the monitoring of the Development Fund by the International Advisory and Monitoring Board, and further decides that, subject to the exception provided for in paragraph 27 of resolution 1546(2004), the provisions of paragraph 22 of resolution 1483(2003) shall continue to apply until that date, including with respect to funds, financial assets and economic resources described in paragraph 23 of that resolution;

2. *Decides also* that the provisions in paragraph 1 above for the deposit of proceeds into the Development Fund for Iraq and for the role of the International Advisory and Monitoring Board and the provisions of paragraph 22 of resolution 1483(2003) shall be reviewed at the request of the Government of Iraq or no later than 15 June 2009;

3. *Requests* the Secretary-General to report to the Security Council on a quarterly basis, with the first briefing to be no later than 31 March 2009 and with a written report on a semi-annual basis, on the activities of the Development Fund for Iraq and the International Advisory and Monitoring Board, including on progress made in strengthening the financial and administrative oversight of the Development Fund;

4. *Encourages* the International Monetary Fund and the World Bank, as members of the International Advisory and Monitoring Board, to brief the Council in January 2009;

5. *Decides* to review the resolutions pertaining specifically to Iraq, beginning with resolution 661(1990), and in that regard requests the Secretary-General to report, after consultations with Iraq, on facts relevant to consideration by the Council of actions necessary for Iraq to achieve international standing equal to that which it held prior to the adoption of such resolutions;

6. *Decides also* to remain actively seized of the matter.

ANNEX

Letter dated 7 December 2008 from Mr. Nuri Kamel al-Maliki, Prime Minister of Iraq, to the President of the Security Council

Further to our letter dated 31 December 2007 addressed to you, in which we indicated that the extension of the mandate of the Multinational Forces in Iraq (MNF-I) would be for one final time, with appreciation for the important role and efforts of those forces in assisting Iraq to achieve security and stability, and in view of the fact that Iraq has signed the Agreement between the United States of America and the Republic of Iraq on the Withdrawal of United States Forces from Iraq and the Organization of Their Activities during Their Temporary Presence in Iraq, we look forward to the ending of the mandate of MNF-I on 31 December 2008. On behalf of the Government and people of Iraq, I express my gratitude to the Governments of the States that have contributed to those forces and to the forces themselves for the services rendered during their presence in the territory, waters and airspace of Iraq.

Iraq has inherited debts and claims from the previous regime and has made great progress in settling them. However, much remains to be done, and our efforts to settle those claims and debts will require some time. Temporary support from the international community will continue to be required during the coming phase. Therefore, we hope that the international community will continue current protections and arrangements for petroleum, petroleum products and natural gas from Iraq and the proceeds thereof until such time as the Government of Iraq is able to take the measures necessary to settle those debts and claims inherited from the previous regime. Oil revenues constitute 95 per cent of Government resources, and these claims have an impact on reconstruction and the economic transformations taking place in Iraq, and consequently pose a grave threat to Iraq's stability and security and by extension to international peace and security.

The Government of Iraq recognizes the importance of the provisions of paragraph 22 of Security Council resolution 1483(2003) ensuring that Iraq's petroleum and natural gas resources and proceeds and obligations arising from sales thereof, as well as funds deposited in the Development Fund for Iraq, shall be used for reconstruction projects and other purposes benefiting the people of Iraq. Therefore, bearing in mind the exception provided for in paragraph 27 of Security Council resolution 1546(2004), Iraq requests that the Security Council continue to implement the provisions of paragraph 22 of Security Council resolution 1483(2003) until 31 December 2009, including those relating to funds or other financial assets or economic resources mentioned in paragraph 23 of that resolution.

The Government of Iraq believes that the provisions of Security Council resolution 1546(2004) relating to the deposit of proceeds into the Development Fund for Iraq will help to ensure that proceeds from Iraq's natural resources will be used for the benefit of the Iraqi people, as will the role played by the International Advisory and Monitoring Board. The Government of Iraq recognizes that the Development Fund for Iraq plays an important role in helping Iraq to reassure donors and creditors that Iraq is administering its resources and debts in a responsible manner in the service of the Iraqi people. It should be noted that Iraq is attempting, after years of isolation under the previous regime, to form a new partnership with the international community with a view to integrating its economy into those of the region and the world through the International Compact with Iraq, and its efforts were endorsed by more than 90 countries and international organizations in the Stockholm Declaration of 29 May 2008. In view of this, Iraq requests the Security Council to extend the mandates of the Development Fund for Iraq and the International Advisory and Monitoring Board for a period of 12 months, with a review of the extension to be conducted before 15 June 2009 at the request of the Government of Iraq.

The Government of Iraq affirms that it honours its obligations under Security Council resolutions and follows policies of peaceful coexistence with its neighbours conducive to the security and stability of the region. The Government of Iraq looks forward to recognition by the Security Council that major positive developments have taken place in Iraq, that the situation in Iraq is fundamentally different from that prevailing at the time of the adoption of Security Council resolution 661(1990), and that the time has come for Iraq to regain its legal and international status prevailing prior to the adoption by the Security Council of that resolution and the subsequent sanctions imposed on it under Chapter VII of the Charter of the United Nations.

The Government of Iraq requests that the Security Council include this letter as an annex to the resolution currently being drafted on Iraq, and should be grateful if the President of the Security Council would circulate it to the members of the Security Council as soon as possible.

Following the adoption of the resolution, Iraqi Foreign Minister Zebari told the Security Council that the situation in Iraq was fundamentally different from that prevailing when resolution 661(1990) [YUN 1990, p. 192] was adopted. Iraq was no longer a rogue State flouting international law and posing a threat to international peace and regional security. His Government therefore requested a review of all Security Council resolutions pertaining to Iraq to be undertaken jointly by the Secretary-General and Iraq and reported to the Security Council as the final arbiter, to take stock of its remaining obligations and to assess the relevance and validity of all such resolutions to Iraq's current situation. Iraq looked forward to recognition by the United Nations of its positive development, so Iraq could resume its legal and international status that prevailed before the adoption of resolution 661(1990).

Security Council Committee established pursuant to resolution 1518(2003)

On 14 February [S/2008/109], the Chairman of the Security Council Committee established pursuant to resolution 1518(2003) [YUN 2003, p. 362] submitted to the Council President the Committee's annual report for 2007. The Committee was established to continue to identify, in accordance with paragraphs 19 and 23 of resolution 1483(2003) [ibid., p. 338], individuals and entities associated with the former Iraqi regime whose funds, other financial assets and economic resources should be frozen and transferred to the Development Fund for Iraq. During the reporting period, the Committee considered communications from countries requesting to list five individuals in its asset-freeze list and delist three, without arriving at a decision on those requests, which remained under consideration.

Subsequently, the Committee Chairman submitted to the Council President the annual report for 2008 [S/2009/79]. During that period, the Committee received requests for delisting from an individual and an entity included on the Committee's asset-freeze and transfer lists. The Committee decided to keep the individual and the entity on the lists. A number of issues brought to the Committee's attention in 2007 remained before it in 2008. By year's end, the Committee had not arrived at a decision regarding those issues, which remained under its consideration. The asset-freeze and transfer lists of individuals and entities were available on the Committee's website.

UN Monitoring, Verification and Inspection Commission and IAEA activities

In 2007, by resolution 1762(2007) [YUN 2007, p. 356], the Security Council terminated the mandate of the United Nations Monitoring, Verification and Inspection Commission (UNMOVIC), as well as the related Nuclear Verification Office of the International Atomic Energy Agency (IAEA) in Iraq. The Council had established UNMOVIC in 1999 [YUN 1999, p. 230] to verify Iraq's compliance with its obligation to be rid of its weapons of mass destruction and to operate a monitoring and verification system to ascertain that Iraq did not reacquire those weapons.

Final report of UNMOVIC. As called for in Security Council resolution 1762(2007), UNMOVIC submitted its final report to the Council on 9 June [S/2008/372]. The report provided a final account of UNMOVIC activities since the Secretary-General's report of September 2007 [YUN 2007, p. 358], and described the work undertaken to appropriately dispose of its archives and other property. Work relating to the disposition of its archives containing paper documents and multimedia material had been completed, with more than 1,200 boxes containing some 8,500 folders transferred to the United Nations Archives and Records Management Section. Over the years, the Special Commission and UNMOVIC had developed a unique UN verification and monitoring mechanism in the area of weapons of mass destruction and long-range delivery systems that had been recognized as a valuable contribution to international efforts to eliminate and counter threats of weapons of mass destruction. The Special Commission and UNMOVIC had put into practice many innovative verification and monitoring procedures, and established a roster of inspectors comprising more than 350 experts in the biological, chemical and missile areas drawn from more than 50 countries.

On 27 June [S/2008/423], the Security Council informed the Secretary-General that its members supported the actions and recommendations contained in the report regarding the disposition and safeguarding of the records and archives, strictly controlling access to archives provided by Member States in confidence or with proliferation potential, and the disposition of non-expendable and other property.

Communication. Pursuant to resolution 1762(2007), Iraq on 29 May [S/2008/350] reported to the Council on progress made in adhering to all applicable disarmament and non-proliferation treaties and international agreements—notably the 1992 Convention on the Prohibition of the Development, Production, Stockpiling and Use of Chemical Weapons [YUN 1992, p. 65], an Additional Protocol to its Safeguards Agreement, and progress made by the National Monitoring Directorate and the Government with regard to dual-use controls and the harmonization of Iraq's export legislation with international standards. Iraq had declared its support for the international non-proliferation regime and its adherence to all disarmament and non-proliferation treaties. It had made arrangements for joining the Organisation for the Prohibition of Chemical Weapons, had approved accession to the Chemical Weapons Convention, and was making preparations for signing the model Additional Protocol to the IAEA Comprehensive Safeguards Agreement [YUN 1997, p. 486]. It was making preparations for accession to the Comprehensive Nuclear-Test-Ban Treaty and the Convention on the Physical Protection of Nuclear Material, in addition to preparing mechanisms for dealing with the illicit trade in nuclear material. Iraq believed in the necessity of making the Middle East a region free from weapons of mass destruction, particularly nuclear weapons.

On 27 June [S/2008/423], the Security Council welcomed Iraq's May report.

Oil-for-food programme

Under the oil-for-food programme, established by Security Council resolution 986(1995) [YUN 1995, p. 475], Iraq had been authorized to sell petroleum and petroleum products to finance humanitarian assistance, thereby alleviating the adverse consequences of the sanctions imposed by the Council. The programme was phased out in November 2003 [YUN 2003, p. 362].

United Nations Iraq Account

Following the termination of all activities under the oil-for-food programme [ibid., p. 366], the United Nations retained responsibility for the administration and execution of letters of credit issued under the programme by the bank holding the United Nations Iraq Account, Banque Nationale de Paris (BNP) Paribas, for purchasing humanitarian supplies for the south/centre of Iraq, until such letters were executed or expired, in accordance with Security Council resolution 1483(2003) [ibid., p. 338].

On 23 January [S/2008/41], the Secretary-General informed the Council of progress made with respect to the Working Group set up to minimize the number of unpaid letters of credit [YUN 2007, p. 361].

The Group, composed of representatives of the Iraqi Ministry of Foreign Affairs, the Iraqi Central Bank and the UN Secretariat, met in Amman, Jordan, from 7 to 17 January. On 27 December 2007, the Secretary-General had transferred some $161 million of unencumbered funds to the Development Fund for Iraq. It was his intention to continue transferring unencumbered funds consistent with Council resolution 1483(2003), as the termination process continued. At the same time, the reserve of $187 million and the balance of $225 million referred to in his December 2007 note [ibid.] would be retained until all remaining issues had been resolved.

On 29 February [S/2008/140], the Council took note of the $161 million transfer to the Development Fund for Iraq. It called upon the Government of Iraq and its Central Bank to transmit by 31 March the necessary confirmations of arrival of goods for which there were no commercial disputes or for which there were commercial disputes that could be resolved in the meantime. It also requested a comprehensive report from the Secretary-General by 15 March on progress achieved in reducing the number of outstanding letters of credit and any other outstanding issues.

On 11 March [S/2008/175], the Secretary-General informed the Council that the number of outstanding letters of credit had decreased from 210 at the end of 2007 to 167, which was still high. In addition, the processing of the authentication documents by the Government of Iraq remained slow. He recommended that the Working Group meet in May to review results achieved as at 30 April. He also recommended that $100 million of the $225 million held pending resolution of certain issues be released and transferred to the Development Fund for Iraq pursuant to resolution 1483(2003), subject to no objection by the Council, while the $187 million of unencumbered funds in the United Nations Iraq Account should continue to be held as a financial reserve.

On 9 May [S/2008/318], the Secretary-General provided the Council with the Working Group's report on its meeting (Amman, 1–5 May). He said that as at 30 April, the number of outstanding letters of credit had decreased to 151, but the provision of authentication documents was slow or non-existent. The Secretary-General said that he would report to the Council following the Group's final meeting in July, when the Council might decide how to resolve outstanding issues, including the establishment of a dispute resolution mechanism. He also sought the Council's guidance on the timing of any possible release and transfer of unencumbered funds to the Development Fund for Iraq.

On 13 May [S/2008/369], Iraq suggested that the deadline for providing the confirmations of arrival and resolving the disputes between Iraq's concerned ministries and the sellers be extended to 30 June, and that the Working Group should review the situation early in July.

On 23 May [S/2008/341], the Security Council requested that the Working Group reconvene in June, so that the Council might receive an updated report in July. It would then take the necessary decisions in order to conclude all outstanding issues and end the oil-for-food programme without the possibility of any further extensions. It encouraged the Iraqi Government to do its utmost to expedite the processing of the remaining letters of credit. While recognizing that unencumbered funds were available, in principle, for transfer to the Development Fund for Iraq, the Council recommended that all such funds associated with the oil-for-food programme remain in the Iraq escrow account until such time as all outstanding issues were resolved.

On 25 July [S/2008/492], the Secretary-General informed the Council about the Working Group's meeting (Amman, 27–30 June). As at 30 June, 132 letters of credit with an approximate value of claims of $273 million remained outstanding. The Working Group held that any commercial disputes in connection with the letters of credit should be addressed through the dispute resolution mechanism established in the underlying commercial contract between the Government of Iraq and the relevant suppliers or, in the absence of such a mechanism, by a competent court.

The Working Group indicated a series of alternatives that the Security Council could consider in order to conclude all outstanding issues. Following the current approach, the Council might instruct the Working Group to continue its work. Alternatively, a dispute resolution mechanism might be used to resolve all outstanding issues relating to the unpaid letters of credit—either as proposed by the Secretary-General [YUN 2007, p. 361] or in a simplified version. Finally, responsibility for the administration of remaining activity under the programme might be transferred to the Government of Iraq. In that case, the disposition of funds in the escrow account would be determined by the Security Council and be kept until all issues were resolved. Alternatively, they could be released without delay to the Development Fund for Iraq.

In addition, the Government of Iraq would be required to indemnify the United Nations with regard to all activities of the Organization, its representatives and agents in connection with the programme since its inception and with regard to funds transferred to the Development Fund. The Government would waive the right to any and all actions against the United Nations, its representatives and agents with regard to all activities of the Organization in connection with the programme since its inception.

On 25 July [S/2008/521], Costa Rica requested that the Security Council coordinate with the Secretary-

General to ensure that closure of the oil-for-food programme not expose the United Nations to questions regarding its financial management. Costa Rica suggested measures to prevent conflicts of interest, surcharges and other irregularities.

On 26 August [S/2008/588], Costa Rica's Foreign Minister requested the Secretary-General, as a matter of urgency, to provide the list of all natural and legal persons with outstanding invoices from the oil-for-food programme. He noted that the reports of the International Advisory and Monitoring Board in 2004, 2006 and 2008 revealed shortcomings in the administration of the Development Fund. In view of that, he considered the proposal by the Working Group on the possibility of transferring funds corresponding to outstanding claims from the escrow account to the Development Fund to be a matter of concern.

On 15 September (**decision 62/555**), the General Assembly deferred consideration of the item entitled "Follow-up to the recommendations on administrative management and internal oversight of the Independent Inquiry Committee into the United Nations Oil-for-Food Programme" to its sixty-third (2008) session. On 24 December (**decision 63/552**), the General Assembly decided that the agenda item would remain for consideration during its sixty-third (2009) session.

Report of Board of Auditors

On 4 August, the Secretary-General transmitted to the Security Council the report [S/2008/510] of the Board of Auditors on the financial statements of the United Nations escrow (Iraq) accounts for the biennium ended 31 December 2007. Those financial statements reflected the transactions covering the fourth year of the phase-down operations following the termination of the oil-for-food programme in November 2003 pursuant to Council resolution 1483(2003).

Total income was $162.6 million in 2006–2007 compared with $255.8 million for the previous biennium. The 36 per cent decrease was primarily attributable to the transfers made to the Development Fund for Iraq, amounting to $371.1 million. Total expenditure amounted to $118 million, compared with $421.5 million for the previous biennium, a decrease of 72 per cent. That resulted in an excess of income over expenditure of $44.6 million, compared with a deficit of $165.7 million in the preceding biennium.

As the programme was under liquidation, 62 per cent or $100.6 million of the total income was derived from interest on cash and term deposits and the cash pool. The cash pool was maintained to cover claims for outstanding obligations and other liquidation expenses.

The total cash resources of $1 billion adequately covered the $657.5 million in current and prior period unliquidated obligations arising from approved contracts for humanitarian supplies and oil spares. Total reserves and fund balances increased by 40 per cent, or $111 million, from $277 million in 2005 to $388 million in 2007. The increase was principally brought about by the excess of income over expenditure of $44.6 million and the increase in operating reserves of $60 million.

The Board made one recommendation arising out of its audit, relating to the release of cash collaterals associated with the expired letters of credit with no claims of delivery.

Iraq–Kuwait

POWs, Kuwaiti property and missing persons

Reports of Secretary-General. In response to Security Council resolution 1284(1999) [YUN 1999, p. 230], the Secretary-General submitted reports in June [S/2008/405] and December [S/2008/761] on Iraq's compliance with its obligations regarding the repatriation or return of all Kuwaiti and third-country nationals or their remains, and on the return of all Kuwaiti property, including archives, seized by Iraq during its occupation of Kuwait, which began in August 1990 [YUN 1990, p. 189].

In June, the Secretary-General reported that Kuwait had added two new names to the list of those whose remains had been identified, bringing their total number to 235. The Kuwaiti national archives had not been found. There was guarded hope of progress owing to improvements in Iraq's security situation.

In December, the Secretary-General reported that Kuwait had added one new name to the list, bringing their number to 236. No visits to burial sites in Iraq were conducted, and no credible facts or possible leads had emerged regarding the missing Kuwaiti national archives.

High-level Coordinator. On 11 March [S/2008/205], the Secretary-General drew the Council's attention to its resolution 1284(1999) [YUN 1999, p. 230], which established the mandate of the High-level Coordinator for missing Kuwaitis and third-country citizens and missing Kuwaiti property, and suggested that the Council earmark $900,000 from the Iraq escrow account to support the Coordinator's activities for a four-year period, beginning on 1 January 2008.

On 26 March [S/2008/206], the Council earmarked $225,000 from the escrow account to finance those activities for a 12-month period from the date of the appointment of the new Coordinator.

On 8 April [S/2008/238], the Secretary-General informed the Council President that he had appointed

Gennady P. Tarasov (Russian Federation) as the High-level Coordinator, replacing Yuli M. Vorontsov, who had passed away in December 2007. On 11 April [S/2008/239], the Council took note of that appointment.

Mr. Tarasov briefed the Council regularly throughout the year. Following his 25 June briefing, Council members, in a press statement [SC/9375], noted that the number of positive identifications of human remains by the Kuwaiti authorities had increased since the last report and said that they were hopeful about the possibility of further progress in the repatriation of remains. Council members noted that there had been no further progress on the fate of the Kuwaiti national archive, and called on Governments and individuals who might know what had happened to those documents, or possessed information on their whereabouts, to help clarify their fate. They noted the Iraqi Government's intention to assist in resolving the outstanding cases, and expressed their confidence that all parties, in particular Iraq and Kuwait, would enable a satisfactory solution. Council members requested the Secretary-General to report, 12 months after Mr. Tarasov's appointment, on any further progress and assess the progress that might be achieved, including the conditions that would be necessary and a time frame for completing the mandate.

On 12 May [A/62/842-S/2008/320], Iraq and Kuwait transmitted to the Secretary-General the final communiqué of the third expanded meeting of the Foreign Ministers of the countries neighbouring Iraq (Kuwait, 22 April), which invited all concerned parties to continue their cooperation with the International Committee of the Red Cross to uncover the fate of the rest of the missing Kuwaiti citizens and others.

Following Mr. Tarasov's briefings of 10 December, Security Council members, in a press statement [SC/9529], noted that a positive identification of human remains had been made, regretted the lack of progress on exhumation activities and expressed their appreciation for the support offered by UNAMI to the Iraqi Ministry for Human Rights to accelerate progress. Council members expressed their concern at the absence of progress on clarifying the fate of the national archives. They noted the positive stance taken by the Iraqi authorities, welcomed the first visit by the High-level Coordinator to Baghdad since 2003 to pursue dialogue on the outstanding issues, and urged collaboration among all parties to bring those long-standing issues to a resolution.

UN Compensation Commission and Fund

The United Nations Compensation Commission, established in 1991 [YUN 1991, p. 195] for the resolution and payment of claims against Iraq for losses and damages resulting from its 1990 invasion and occupation of Kuwait, continued in 2008 to expedite the settlement of claims through the United Nations Compensation Fund, which was established at the same time as the Commission. Under Council resolution 1483(2003) [YUN 2003, p. 338], the Fund received 5 per cent of the proceeds generated by export sales of Iraqi petroleum and petroleum products.

On 29 April, the Commission paid out $972.4 million to four Governments for distribution to 26 claimants; $982.3 million on 29 July to three Governments for distribution to 18 claimants; and $888.6 million on 29 October to three Governments for distribution to 16 claimants; bringing the overall amount of compensation made available by the Commission to $26.3 billion.

Governing Council. The Commission's Governing Council held two sessions in Geneva during the year—the sixty-fifth (8–9 April) [S/2008/265] and the sixty-sixth (21–22 October) [S/2008/658]—at which it considered reports on the activities of the Commission, the distribution by Governments and international organizations of payments to claimants, its follow-up programme for environmental awards, and the return of undistributed funds. The Governing Council took note of the report of the Board of Auditors on the financial statements of the Commission for the biennium ended 31 December 2007 [S/2008/509], as well as of the report of the Office of Internal Oversight Services to the General Assembly [A/63/302 (Part I)] (see below).

Oversight activities

The Office of Internal Oversight Services (OIOS), in an August report on its activities for the period 1 July 2007–30 June 2008 [A/63/302 (Part I)], stated that the Compensation Commission continued to disburse award payments and monitor environmental projects being undertaken by claimant Governments with funds awarded for environmental damages, while also winding down its operations. As at May, $24 billion of the total $52 billion awarded by the Commission had been disbursed, leaving a balance of unpaid awards of $28 billion, which comprised 18 large awards that would continue to be paid out of the Compensation Fund. Payments of claims from July 2007 to May 2008 amounted to some $2 billion.

For 2008, the Commission had made available $50,000 for internal audit resources. OIOS was using that sum to continue the audit of award payments, assessing the Commission's compliance with Governing Council decisions, and Governments' compliance with Governing Council reporting requirements.

The Commission had implemented all audit recommendations issued by OIOS, including: requiring audit certificates for payment reports submitted to the Commission; obtaining full accounting from Governments on the distribution of funds received; updating its financial records; and following up on the recovery of long-outstanding receivables from Governments. The Commission also reported that Governments and other paying entities had remitted some $2.4 million as at May 2008 for overpayments to claimants.

In August, the Secretary-General transmitted to the Security Council the report of the Board of Auditors on the financial statements of the United Nations Compensation Commission for the biennium ended 31 December 2007 [S/2008/509]. According to the report, from its inception until the completion of processing in early 2005, the Commission had received more than 2.6 million claims. The Commission had now resolved all of the claims submitted, consisting of the claims of individuals for departure from Kuwait or Iraq, for serious personal injury or death, for losses up to $100,000 and for losses over $100,000; as well as the claims of corporations, other private legal entities and public sector enterprises, and the claims of Governments and international organizations. Expenses during the 2006–2007 period amounted to $3,511.9 million, comprising compensation awards of $3,497.2 million as well as administrative expenses of the Commission of $13.8 million and of the Follow-up Programme for Environmental Awards of $0.9 million. Total income was $3.450 billion.

On 24 December, the General Assembly decided that the item on the "Consequences of the Iraqi occupation of and aggression against Kuwait" would remain for consideration during its resumed sixty-third (2009) session (**decision 63/552**).

Timor-Leste

The United Nations Integrated Mission in Timor-Leste (UNMIT), established by Security Council resolution 1704(2006) [YUN 2006, p. 422], continued to carry out its mandate to assist the Government in consolidating stability, enhancing democratic governance and facilitating political dialogue. It also cooperated closely with the Government in its response to the attempted assassination of Timor-Leste's President and Prime Minister on 11 February; provided support to the national police; helped strengthen the country's human rights capacity; and cooperated with UN bodies and their partners in peacebuilding and capacity-building. The Mission was headed by Atul Khare (India), who also served as the Secretary-General's Special Representative for Timor-Leste.

United Nations Integrated Mission in Timor-Leste

Report of Secretary-General (January). Pursuant to Security Council resolution 1745(2007) [YUN 2007, p. 364], the Secretary-General, on 17 January, submitted a report [S/2008/26] on major developments in Timor-Leste and on the activities of UNMIT since his previous report [ibid., p. 366]. As at 7 January, UNMIT consisted of a civilian component comprising 341 international staff (123 women), 806 national staff (135 women), 1,480 police officers (77 women) and 33 military liaison and staff officers (all men).

Prime Minister Kay Rala Xanana Gusmão continued to lead the Government formed by the Alliance for a Parliamentary Majority (AMP). However, the 21 parliamentarians from the Frente Revolucionária de Timor-Leste (Fretilin), the party with the largest number of seats, continued to consider the AMP-led Government as unconstitutional, referring to it as a "de facto Government". Among the short-term priorities identified in the Government's programme were improving security, addressing the internally displaced persons (IDP) situation, and resolving the cases of the nearly 600 "petitioners"—dismissed members of the Timorese armed forces whose grievances triggered the 2006 security and political crisis [YUN 2006, p. 416]—as well as prison escapee and deserted military police commander of the armed forces Alfredo Reinado.

Parliamentary discussions were generally marked by lively and constructive debate among all political parties, including Fretilin. Dialogue initiatives to bring opposing stakeholders together were assisted by the Fretilin leadership's public rejection of violence as an expression of political discontent. With respect to Mr. Reinado, the Government's ultimate goal continued to be his voluntary surrender and submission to judicial proceedings. Still, the political situation remained fragile, with Fretilin's leaders calling for the Government to step down and for early elections to be held in 2009. Since the formation of the new Government, the Secretary-General's Special Representative had held weekly meetings with the Secretary-General of Fretilin, former Prime Minister Mari Alkatiri, and monthly meetings with representatives of civil society.

Following the 2007 elections, UNMIT police strength decreased from 1,641 in July of that year to 1,480 (77 women) by 7 January 2008. The overall security situation had improved, helped by the good offices and dialogue efforts of the national leadership and UNMIT, as well as Fretilin's rejection of violence. The need for a strong UNMIT police presence to maintain stability until the national police developed adequate capacities was evident both in the positive impact of police efforts in reducing serious crimes, and the daily occurrence of public disturbances.

Under the registration, screening and certification programme for the national police, all 3,108 registered officers (570 women) had completed the screening process as at 7 January. Of those, 186 (42 women) successfully completed both the provisional certification course and the six-month mentoring process and became fully certified officers. Another 1,503 (271 women) were provisionally certified and in the mentoring stage. However, 296 (22 women) required further investigation due to allegations of criminal acts or human rights violations, which would be adjudicated by a Timorese-led police evaluation panel. The remaining 1,123 screened officers were either undertaking, or waiting to take, the provisional certification course.

Despite resource constraints of the judicial system, notable progress was made in establishing accountability for serious criminal offences committed during the 2006 crisis. The trials held were important signals to the population that Timor-Leste was committed to applying the law in an impartial manner and to combating impunity. The new Government had accelerated the permanent deployment of judiciary staff to the districts and focused its attention on strengthening the prison system, with the support of UNMIT and UNDP.

UNMIT, the UN country team and development partners continued to foster a culture of democratic governance by supporting the four organs of sovereignty (presidency, parliament, executive and judiciary), civil society and the media. UNMIT worked closely with UNDP to promote responsible citizen involvement and understanding of governance processes through training-of-trainers sessions with 13 civic education groups throughout the country.

The Government's longer-term socio-economic priorities were: economic growth; reforming State management; qualifying youth and developing national human resources; solidarity, health and social protection; infrastructure and improving the quality of life; promoting equality and tolerance, internal security and strengthening democracy; and national defence and foreign policy. Its 2008 budget of about $348 million reflected those priorities. Meanwhile, about one tenth of the population (100,000 persons) remained displaced—30,000 in the capital, Dili, and 70,000 in the districts—living in poor conditions in camps or with host families.

By resolution 61/249 C [YUN 2007, p. 371], the General Assembly had appropriated $160.6 million for UNMIT for the period from 1 July 2007 to 30 June 2008. Should the Security Council approve the Secretary-General's recommendation for a one-year extension, the cost would be limited to resources approved by the Assembly.

Attacks against President and Prime Minister. On 11 February, the armed group led by the fugitive Alfredo Reinado carried out separate armed attacks against the President, José Ramos-Horta, and the Prime Minister, Kay Rala Xanana Gusmão. Rapid medical intervention in Dili and subsequently in Australia saved the life of the President. Mr. Reinado was killed during the attacks.

SECURITY COUNCIL ACTION

On 11 February [meeting 5833], following consultations among Security Council members, the President made statement **S/PRST/2008/5** on behalf of the Council:

> The Security Council condemns in the strongest possible terms the attempt on the life of the President of Timor-Leste, Mr. José Ramos-Horta, during an attack at his residence on 11 February 2008, and wishes him a speedy recovery. The Council also condemns the attack on the convoy of the Prime Minister of Timor-Leste, Mr. Kay Rala Xanana Gusmão. These represent an attack on the legitimate institutions of Timor-Leste.
>
> The Council calls upon the Government of Timor-Leste to bring to justice those responsible for these heinous acts, and urges all parties in Timor-Leste to cooperate actively with the authorities in this regard.
>
> The Council further calls upon all people in Timor-Leste to remain calm, exercise restraint and maintain stability in the country. The Council urges all parties in Timor-Leste to resolve any disputes through political and peaceful means within the framework of its democratic institutions.
>
> The Council reaffirms its full support to the Government and people of Timor-Leste in their continued efforts to strengthen democracy and ensure public security and maintain stability in their country.
>
> The Council expresses its full support for the work of the United Nations Integrated Mission in Timor-Leste and for the continued deployment of the international security forces in response to the requests of the Government of Timor-Leste.
>
> The Council requests the Secretary-General to report on developments in Timor-Leste, as necessary. The Council will continue to monitor closely the situation in Timor-Leste and will act, as appropriate.

Security Council consideration (February). On 21 February [meeting 5843], the Security Council was briefed by Jean-Marie Guéhenno, Under-Secretary-General for Peacekeeping Operations. He said that the Special Representative, Mr. Khare, had come to brief the Council but had returned to Timor-Leste in the wake of the tragic events of 11 February. President Ramos-Horta, though still hospitalized, was in stable condition and his doctors were hopeful of a full recovery.

A state of siege was declared on 11 February. In close cooperation with UNMIT, the Government had shown leadership in carrying out and coordinating subsequent security operations. Immediately following the attacks, Timorese leaders from all parties came together to urge calm, and the country remained peaceful—including throughout the funeral ceremonies for the fugitive Alfredo Reinado and one of his accomplices. The destabilizing crisis some feared had not happened, and the Government was intensifying outreach efforts to his followers to join discussions on resolving their grievances.

Prior to that incident, on 17 January, the President and Prime Minister engaged in constructive discussions with Fretilin President Lu-Olo Guterres and Secretary-General Alkatiri on mechanisms to promote more inclusive approaches to the country's problems. On 7 February, the President convened a meeting between the leaders of the four parties comprising the Government coalition and Fretilin to discuss mechanisms to jointly address such pressing issues as the IDPs, the petitioners and Mr. Reinado—as well as critical longer-term issues of security sector review and reform, and strengthening the justice sector and public administration—in what was seen as another step forward.

A durable solution to the IDP situation through voluntary return or relocation would require an improved security environment, a strengthened legal framework to resolve land and property disputes, and economic regeneration and livelihood activities. The President's efforts to bring Fretilin and the Government coalition together to solve pressing issues should continue, as the solution of those issues would allow the country to give its full attention to the underlying socio-economic challenges which posed a continuing threat to its political stability.

Timor-Leste expressed the country's gratitude for the convening of an emergency meeting of the Security Council immediately following the attempted assassination of its President and Prime Minister. A continued UN presence in Timor-Leste remained crucial for consolidating peace and security.

SECURITY COUNCIL ACTION

On 25 February [meeting 5844], the Security Council unanimously adopted **resolution 1802(2008)**. The draft [S/2008/124] was submitted by Australia, New Zealand, Portugal and South Africa.

The Security Council,

Reaffirming all its previous resolutions and the statements by its President on the situation in Timor-Leste, in particular resolutions 1599(2005) of 28 April 2005, 1677(2006) of 12 May 2006, 1690(2006) of 20 June 2006, 1703(2006) of 18 August 2006, 1704(2006) of 25 August 2006 and 1745(2007) of 22 February 2007, and the statement of 11 February 2008,

Welcoming the report of the Secretary-General of 17 January 2008, and recalling the report of the Security Council mission to Timor-Leste which took place from 24 to 30 November 2007,

Reaffirming its full commitment to the sovereignty, independence, territorial integrity and national unity of Timor-Leste and the promotion of long-term stability in the country,

Welcoming the successful conclusion of the presidential and parliamentary elections in 2007 and the formation of a democratically elected Government and institutions in Timor-Leste,

Urging the Government and people of Timor-Leste to continue their efforts to resolve their political challenges, taking note with appreciation the determination of the Government to restore stability and normalcy while reaffirming their commitment to democracy and the rule of law, and further taking note with appreciation of the commitment of the opposition to support peace and national stability,

Noting that the political, security, social and humanitarian situation in Timor-Leste remains fragile,

Reiterating its call upon the leadership and other stakeholders in Timor-Leste to pursue peaceful dialogue and to avoid violent means to resolve differences,

Reaffirming the need for respect for the independence of the judiciary and its responsibility, welcoming the conviction of the leaders of Timor-Leste on the need for justice and their determination to act against impunity, and in this regard acknowledging the serious resource constraints of the judicial system, and encouraging the leadership of Timor-Leste to continue efforts to establish accountability for serious criminal offences committed during the 2006 crisis as recommended by the Independent Special Commission of Inquiry for Timor-Leste,

Recalling its previous statements on the need to implement fully the "Arrangement on the Restoration and Maintenance of Public Security in Timor-Leste and Assistance to the Reform, Restructuring and Rebuilding of the Timorese National Police (PNTL) and the Ministry of the Interior", concluded between the Government of Timor-Leste and the United Nations Integrated Mission in Timor-Leste on 1 December 2006, and in this regard stressing the need for constructive engagement between Mission police and the national police in view of developing the capacity and capability of the national police,

Expressing its full support for the role of the international security forces in assisting the Government of Timor-Leste and the Mission in the restoration and maintenance of law and stability, in response to the requests of the Government,

Recalling that, while the manifestations of the current challenges in Timor-Leste are political and institutional in nature, poverty and its associated deprivations also contributed to these challenges, paying tribute to Timor-Leste's bilateral and multilateral partners for their invaluable assistance, particularly with regard to institutional capacity-building and social and economic development, and recognizing the progress being made in the development of many aspects of governance in Timor-Leste,

Reaffirming its resolution 1325(2000) of 31 October 2000 on women and peace and security and its resolution 1502(2003) of 26 August 2003 on the protection of humanitarian and United Nations personnel,

Recognizing the important role that the Mission continues to play in promoting peace, stability and development in Timor-Leste, and expressing its appreciation for the efforts of the Mission and the United Nations country team, under the leadership of the Special Representative of the Secretary-General for Timor-Leste,

1. *Decides* to extend the mandate of the United Nations Integrated Mission in Timor-Leste until 26 February 2009 at the current authorized levels;

2. *Condemns in the strongest possible terms* the attacks on the President and Prime Minister of Timor-Leste on 11 February 2008 and all attempts to destabilize the country, noting that these heinous acts represent an attack on the legitimate institutions of Timor-Leste, and welcomes the swift and constructive reaction by the neighbouring countries;

3. *Calls upon* the Government of Timor-Leste to bring to justice those responsible for these heinous acts, and urges all parties to cooperate actively with the authorities in this regard;

4. *Calls upon* the people of Timor-Leste to remain calm, exercise restraint and maintain stability in the country;

5. *Urges* all parties in Timor-Leste, in particular political leaders, to continue to work together and engage in political dialogue and consolidate peace, democracy, the rule of law, sustainable social and economic development and national reconciliation in the country, and expresses its full support for the continued efforts of the Special Representative of the Secretary-General for Timor-Leste aimed at addressing critical political and security-related issues facing the country through inclusive and collaborative processes, including the High-level Coordination Committee and the Trilateral Coordination Forum;

6. *Reaffirms* the importance of ongoing efforts to reach accountability and justice, and underlines the importance of the implementation by the Government of Timor-Leste of the recommendations contained in the report of the Independent Special Commission of Inquiry for Timor-Leste of 2 October 2006;

7. *Emphasizes* the need for sustained support of the international community to Timor-Leste to develop and strengthen its institutions and further build capacities in the justice sector;

8. *Requests* the Mission to continue its efforts, adjusting them as necessary, to enhance the effectiveness of the judiciary system and assist the Government of Timor-Leste in carrying out the proceedings recommended by the Commission of Inquiry;

9. *Calls upon* the Mission to support the Government of Timor-Leste in its efforts to coordinate donor cooperation in areas of institutional capacity-building;

10. *Further calls upon* the Government of Timor-Leste, assisted by the Mission, to continue working on a comprehensive review of the future role and needs of the security sector, including the Ministry of the Interior, the National Police of Timor-Leste, the Ministry of Defence and the Falintil-Forças Armadas de Defesa de Timor-Leste; given the sector's importance to long-term stability, requests the Mission to intensify its efforts in support of the review in close coordination with the Government and relevant donors, and welcomes the establishment in August 2007 of a three-tier coordination mechanism to address the broader challenges in the security sector;

11. *Requests* the Mission, working with partners, to intensify its efforts to assist with further training, mentoring, institutional development and strengthening of the National Police of Timor-Leste with a view to enhancing its effectiveness, including with respect to addressing the special needs of women, while continuing to ensure, through the presence of the police component of the Mission, the restoration and maintenance of public security in Timor-Leste through the provision of support to the National Police, which includes interim law enforcement and public security until the National Police is reconstituted;

12. *Welcomes* the intention of the Secretary-General to send an expert mission to the Mission in the first quarter of 2008 to conduct a thorough assessment of the requirements of the National Police of Timor-Leste as well as possible adjustments needed to the Mission's police skill sets, and requests him to inform the Security Council of the finding of the expert mission;

13. *Takes note* of the establishment of the Timor-Leste National Recovery Strategy aimed at addressing the socio-economic challenges facing the country, including the issue of internally displaced persons and the promotion of sustainable livelihoods, and in this regard calls upon the Mission to continue to cooperate and coordinate with the United Nations agencies, funds and programmes as well as all relevant partners to support the Government of Timor-Leste and relevant institutions in designing poverty reduction and economic growth policies;

14. *Requests* the Mission fully to take into account gender considerations, as set out in resolution 1325(2000) as a cross-cutting issue throughout its mandate, and further requests the Secretary-General to include in his reporting to the Council progress on gender mainstreaming throughout the Mission and all other aspects relating to the situation of women and girls, especially in relation to the need to protect them from gender-based violence, detailing special measures proposed and taken to protect women and girls from such violence;

15. *Requests* the Secretary-General to continue to take the necessary measures to ensure full compliance in the Mission with the United Nations zero-tolerance policy on sexual exploitation and abuse and to keep the Council informed, and urges those countries contributing troops and police to take appropriate preventive action and to ensure full accountability in cases of such conduct involving their personnel;

16. *Also requests* the Secretary-General to keep the Council regularly informed of the developments on the ground and on the implementation of the present resolution, including, in particular, progress on the efforts of his Special Representative in support of dialogue and reconciliation, and to submit to the Council, no later than 1 August 2008, a report which includes possible adjustments in the mandate and strength of the Mission, and further requests the Secretary-General, in consultation with the Government of Timor-Leste, to develop a medium-term strategy with appropriate benchmarks to measure and track progress, and to submit further reports as and when he considers appropriate;

17. *Decides* to remain seized of the matter.

Expert mission to UNMIT

Report of expert mission (March). By a 16 May letter to the Security Council President [S/2008/329], the Secretary-General forwarded the report of the expert mission he had sent to UNMIT from 17 to 27 March, submitted by its Team Leader and UN Police Adviser, Andrew Hughes. The aim of the mission was to assess the requirements of the national police, as well as possible adjustments to UNMIT police skill sets.

The report said that to strengthen the fragile achievements made towards restoring and maintaining public security since the events of April/May 2006, the Security Council should call upon Member States to contribute human and financial resources to develop the national police, including through UNMIT. The General Assembly should approve additional civilian professional posts for UNMIT police, as submitted by the Secretary-General in UNMIT's 2009–2010 budget.

The mission recommended that the Timor-Leste authorities ensure that national police officers found responsible for acts of serious misconduct were immediately removed, and that they facilitate the processing of complaints from the public. It also made recommendations relating to UNMIT's police, including its support to the national police, as well as to UN agencies, funds and programmes, police-contributing countries, bilateral donors and civil society.

Report of Secretary-General (July). Pursuant to Security Council resolution 1802(2008), the Secretary-General, on 29 July, submitted a report [S/2008/501] on major developments in Timor-Leste and UNMIT's activities since 17 January. As at 8 July, UNMIT consisted of a civilian component comprising 319 international staff (117 women); 846 national staff (147 women); 1,542 police officers (76 women); and 33 military liaison and staff officers (all men).

The events of 11 February and the response to them dominated the political and security environment. The incidents presented an unexpected and serious challenge to State institutions, but they had responded in an appropriate and responsible manner, with the Prime Minister demonstrating firm and reasoned leadership, the Parliament functioning effectively, the leaders of all political parties urging their supporters to remain calm, and the population demonstrating faith in the State's ability to deal with the situation. On 17 February, the Council of Ministers approved a resolution mandating the Commander of the Falintil-Forças de Defesa de Timor-Leste (F-FDTL) to create a Joint Command integrating F-FDTL members and the national police for security operations conducted during the siege. As the security situation improved, the state of siege was gradually reduced in geographic scope and degree.

The death of Mr. Reinado, who had played a significant role in the intractability of the issues of the F-FDTL petitioners and IDPs, opened new possibilities to address those two remaining consequences of the 2006 crisis. On 4 June, the Government adopted a legislative decree offering financial compensation packages for petitioners who decided to return to civilian life—the great majority. While the underlying grievances that had sparked their original desertion, culminating in the 2006 crisis, were yet to be addressed, their agreement to the packages was a positive development. By the beginning of March, returns of IDPs had also markedly accelerated.

On 23 April, in his first major address after returning to Timor-Leste, the President called on the Government to work together with Fretilin as "the party with the most votes". Encouragingly, Fretilin continued to play an important role as an active opposition within the Parliament, whose legitimacy it acknowledged—although it continued to describe the AMP-formed Government as an unconstitutional "de facto Government".

The Special Representative, Mr. Khare, had used his good offices role to promote a more conciliatory atmosphere among the political leaders and to stress the value of a strong opposition and an effective Parliament.

Considerable progress was made in the registration, screening and certification programme for the national police. In June, when provisional certification ended, 3,114 officers (570 women) had been assessed as suitable to be provisionally certified. Of those, 599 (126 women) became fully certified officers. All remaining officers were in different stages of the mentoring programme, except the 242 (11 women) found with integrity issues requiring adjudication by the Timorese-led Evaluation Panel, and 117 officers (10 women) who were recruits during the crisis of 2006 and needed to return to the Academy for basic training.

Some progress was made towards holding accountable those responsible for criminal acts and human rights violations during the 2006 crisis. However, a presidential decree of 20 May providing pardons and commutations of sentence to 94 sentenced individuals, while legal, was considered by many as undermining efforts to promote accountability and justice and combat impunity. The former Minister of the Interior, Rogério Lobato, who had been sentenced to seven and a half years' imprisonment for his role in the 2006 crisis, and who in August 2007 was permitted to travel to Malaysia to receive medical treatment and had yet to return, was granted conditional release early in June after his sentence was commuted. Nine inmates serving sentences for crimes against humanity committed in 1999 also received commutations of their sentence, and four of them were released in June.

The Government continued to focus on key pieces of legislation, including the criminal code and the law against domestic violence, and on developing the capacity of judiciary personnel. However, despite the best efforts of the Government and its partners, Timor-Leste had not experienced significant progress in poverty alleviation or achievement of the Millennium Development Goals since its restoration of independence in 2002.

With respect to the medium-term strategy and appropriate benchmarks, as requested by the Security Council in its resolution 1802(2008), it was envisaged that they would cover four mandated UNMIT priority areas: review and reform of the security sector; strengthening the rule of law; economic and social development; and promotion of a culture of democratic governance, together with efforts to enhance dialogue and reconciliation.

Security Council consideration (August). On 19 August [meeting 5958], the Council was briefed by the Special Representative, who said that public confidence in the national police was essential for its long-term success. As it took on greater responsibilities, newer cases of corruption and abuse of authority would have to be pursued. Noting that long-term strategies to preclude the establishment of a culture of impunity depended on an effective judiciary, he said that the third training course for 18 additional judicial officers—judges, public prosecutors and public defenders—had begun on 29 July.

Timor-Leste's Foreign Minister, Zacarias Albano da Costa, said that his Government had established a Joint Command led by the national police and the defence force for the conduct of security operations during the state of siege. The efforts of the Joint Command, together with political mediation initiatives, resulted in the eventual surrender of the President's attackers and their associates without notable violence. The cooperation between the political authorities, defence force and police services illustrated the progress made in rebuilding the latter two institutions. With respect to the more than 14,450 internally displaced families that had expressed their desire for return or resettlement, he said that with the assistance of UNMIT, UN agencies and other international partners, the Government had facilitated the return of large numbers of IDPs. Twenty IDP camps had been closed and more than 3,650 internally displaced families had received recovery packages. The Government had concluded a dialogue with the F-FDTL petitioners and was committed to rebuilding the national police as a long-term undertaking. It was also working to strengthen the civil service, and the National Parliament had become a credible and dynamic forum for debate. The economic stabilization fund, with capital of $240 million, was an important tool the Government was using to counter the rising global cost of food and other commodities.

SECURITY COUNCIL ACTION

On 19 August [meeting 5959], following consultations among Security Council members, the President made statement **S/PRST/2008/29** on behalf of the Council:

The Security Council welcomes the report of the Secretary-General on the United Nations Integrated Mission in Timor-Leste, as well as the briefing by the Special Representative of the Secretary-General for Timor-Leste, Mr. Atul Khare, on 19 August 2008.

The Council commends the political leadership and State institutions of Timor-Leste for the rapid, firm and responsible manner, that respected constitutional procedures of the country, in which they responded to the deplorable events of 11 February 2008. The Council acknowledges that, while progress has been made in the overall security situation in Timor-Leste since the events of May and June 2006, the political, security, social and humanitarian situation in the country remains fragile.

The Council welcomes the continued efforts to foster dialogue and national reconciliation in Timor-Leste through various mechanisms, in particular the expanded meetings of the High-level Coordination Committee, the Trilateral Coordination Forum and the continued good offices of the Special Representative. The Council also welcomes recent progress in addressing the situation of internally displaced persons.

The Council reaffirms the continued importance of the review and reform of the security sector in Timor-Leste, in particular the need to ensure clear separation of internal and external security roles and responsibilities between the National Police of Timor-Leste and the military, Falintil-Forças de Defesa de Timor-Leste, to strengthen legal frameworks and to enhance civilian oversight and accountability mechanisms. The Council recognizes efforts made by the national authorities and the Mission for the reconstitution of the National Police and welcomes the report of the expert mission to Timor-Leste on policing of 16 May 2008 and the necessary steps taken to implement the recommendations contained in the report. The Council underlines that the building of an independent, professional and impartial national police service in Timor-Leste is a long-term process, that national ownership is a central element in this regard and that the Mission has a key role in helping to ensure that the National Police is ready and able to resume its policing responsibilities.

The Council recalls the need for sustained support of the international community to Timor-Leste to develop and strengthen its institutions and further build capacities in the justice sector.

The Council further reaffirms the importance of ongoing efforts to reach accountability and justice, and underlines the importance of the implementation by the Government of Timor-Leste of the recommendations contained in the report of the Independent Special Commission of Inquiry for Timor-Leste of 2 October 2006. It welcomes the conviction of the leaders of Timor-Leste of the need for justice and their determination to act against impunity. The Council underscores the importance of the promotion and protection of human rights.

The Council recognizes the need to address socio-economic challenges in Timor-Leste. In this regard, the Council welcomes the launching by the Government of Timor-Leste of the National Priorities for 2008, including public safety and security, social protection and solidarity, addressing the needs of youth, employment and income generation, improving social service delivery, and greater transparency and effective government. It also welcomes the signing on 8 August 2008 by Timor-Leste and the United Nations of the United Nations Development Assistance Framework 2009–2013, which can provide the country with an important instrument on its path to development.

The Council reaffirms its full support for the Mission in its work and appreciates the continued efforts of the Secretary-General and his Special Representative to ensure the full implementation of the mandate of the Mission. It encourages the Mission, in accordance with its mandate, to continue to cooperate with the United Nations agencies, funds and programmes as well as all relevant partners to support the Government of Timor-Leste. The Council recalls its requests to the Secretary-General, in consultation with the Government of Timor-Leste, to develop a medium-term strategy with appropriate benchmarks to measure and track progress, and to submit further reports as and when he considers appropriate.

Later developments

Report of Secretary-General. In a later report [S/2009/72], which included developments through the end of 2008, the Secretary-General said that the period had marked an important stage in the recovery from the 2006 crisis and a return to normalcy following the events of 11 February. The security situation remained calm and security arrangements had generally followed constitutional and legal parameters since the lifting of the states of exception. The Government made remarkable progress in addressing the issues relating to the F-FDTL petitioners and IDPs. Nevertheless, further efforts were needed.

Fretilin continued to play an important role within Parliament, but still refused to recognize the legitimacy of the AMP Government. UNMIT and the UN country team continued to promote a culture of democratic governance, including improved accountability mechanisms, increased citizen participation, and support for the development of important legislative frameworks. UNMIT also continued to assist in capacity-building for local journalists through radio internships, technical and on-the-job training, and the facilitation of regular press trips.

The generally calm security situation was attributable in part to proactive policing strategies adopted by the police, but also to UNMIT's engagement with key political stakeholders. The Government sponsored a six-week nationwide weapons collection campaign that ended on 31 August—a police-led effort that collected 864 homemade and other light firearms; 48 explosive devices; 7,930 homemade weapons; 9,116 rounds of ammunition; and 164 weapons of other types.

There had been further progress in the registration, screening and certification programme for the national police. Of the 3,108 provisionally certified national police officers, 2,644 officers (538 women), or 85 per cent of the force, had become fully certified. The remaining officers were in different stages of the mentoring programme, except 171 (5 women) who were found to have integrity issues. Of those cases, 99 (1 woman) required adjudication by the Timorese-led Evaluation Panel, and the balance were in other stages of investigation and inquiry.

Following the end of the states of exception and disbandment of the Joint Command, the number of allegations of ill-treatment and excessive use of force and intimidation during arrests decreased. During that period, UNMIT documented 50 alleged incidents of human rights violations and ill-treatment during arrests by the national police.

Some progress was made towards holding accountable those responsible for criminal acts and human rights violations during the crisis of 2006. Of the 11 ongoing investigations, one trial involving 16 defendants began in October. UNMIT investigations into cases of serious human rights violations in 1999 continued under the supervision of and in close collaboration with the Office of the Prosecutor-General. In addition, coordination between the police and the prosecution had improved under the auspices of a joint Prosecutor-General/UN working group.

Financing of UN operations

In 2008, the General Assembly considered the financing of the United Nations Mission in East Timor (UNAMET), the United Nations Mission of Support in East Timor (UNMISET) and the United Nations Integrated Mission in Timor-Leste (UNMIT). UNAMET was established by Security Council resolution 1246(1999) [YUN 1999, p. 283] to conduct the 1999 popular consultation on East Timor's autonomy [ibid., p. 288]. UNMISET was established by Council resolution 1410(2002) [YUN 2002, p. 321] to assist the administrative, law enforcement and public security structures critical to Timor-Leste's viability and political stability. UNMIT was established by Council resolution 1704(2006) [YUN 2006, p. 422] to support the Government in consolidating stability, enhancing a culture of democratic governance and facilitating political dialogue; support the country in all aspects of the 2007 presidential and parliamentary elections; ensure the maintenance of public security; assist the Government in reviewing the role and needs of the security sector; strengthen capacity for promoting human rights, justice and reconciliation; and assist in implementing the Secretary-General's recommendations on justice and reconciliation.

UNAMET

On 15 September [meeting 122], by **decision 62/556**, the General Assembly decided to defer consideration of the item entitled "Financing of the United Nations Mission in East Timor" and to include it in the draft agenda of its sixty-third (2008) session. On 24 December, by **decision 63/552**, the Assembly decided that the item would remain for consideration during its resumed sixty-third (2009) session.

UNMISET

GENERAL ASSEMBLY ACTION

On 20 June [meeting 109], the General Assembly, having considered the report of the Secretary-General on the final performance of UNMISET [A/62/555] and the related report of ACABQ [A/62/574], on the recommendation of the Fifth (Administrative and Budgetary) Committee [A/62/870], adopted **resolution 62/257** without vote [agenda item 146].

Financing of the United Nations Mission of Support in East Timor

The General Assembly,

Recalling its decision 62/545 A of 22 December 2007,

Having considered the report of the Secretary-General on the final performance of the United Nations Mission of Support in East Timor and the related report of the Advisory Committee on Administrative and Budgetary Questions,

1. *Takes note* of the status of contributions to the United Nations Transitional Administration in East Timor and the United Nations Mission of Support in East Timor as at 31 March 2008, including the contributions outstanding in the amount of 10 million United States dollars, representing some 1 per cent of the total assessed contributions, notes with concern that only one hundred and forty-three Member States have paid their assessed contributions in full, and urges all other Member States, in particular those in arrears, to ensure payment of their outstanding assessed contributions;

2. *Endorses* the conclusions and recommendations contained in the report of the Advisory Committee on Administrative and Budgetary Questions, subject to the provisions of the present resolution;

3. *Takes note* of the report of the Secretary-General on the final performance of the United Nations Mission of Support in East Timor;

4. *Decides* that Member States that have fulfilled their financial obligations to the Mission shall be credited with their respective share of the net cash available in the Special Account for the United Nations Mission of Support in East Timor in the amount of 3,853,000 dollars as at 30 April 2008 from the unencumbered balance and other income in the amount of 31,835,900 dollars in respect of the financial period ended 30 June 2006, in accordance with the levels updated in General Assembly resolution 58/256 of 23 December 2003, and taking into account the scale of assessments for 2006, as set out in its resolution 58/1 B of 23 December 2003;

5. *Encourages* Member States that are owed credits referred to in paragraph 4 above to apply those credits to any accounts where the Member State concerned has outstanding assessed contributions;

6. *Decides* that, for Member States that have not fulfilled their financial obligations to the Mission, there shall be set off against their outstanding obligations their respective share of the net cash available in the Special Account for the Mission in the amount of 3,853,000 dollars as at 30 April 2008 from the unencumbered balance and other income in the amount of 31,835,900 dollars in respect of the financial period ended 30 June 2006, in accordance with the scheme set out in paragraph 4 above;

7. *Also decides* that updated information on the financial position of the Mission shall be included in the report to be considered by the General Assembly at its sixty-third session on the updated position of closed peacekeeping missions under the item entitled "Administrative and budgetary aspects of the financing of the United Nations peacekeeping operations";

8. *Further decides* that the item entitled "Financing of the United Nations Mission of Support in East Timor" shall be deleted from its agenda.

UNMIT

A performance report by the Secretary-General on UNMIT for the period from 25 August 2006 to 30 June 2007 [A/62/645] was submitted to the General Assembly on 15 January. It was followed by a report of 18 March on UNMIT's proposed budget for the period from 1 July 2008 to 30 June 2009 [A/62/753], amounting to $173,439,800, and a note of 9 April on financing arrangements for UNMIT for the period from 1 July 2007 to 30 June 2008 [A/62/796].

On 16 May, ACABQ issued its report [A/62/781/Add.11] on UNMIT's financial performance report for the period from 25 August 2006 to 30 June 2007, and its proposed budget for the period from 1 July 2008 to 30 June 2009. With respect to the financing of UNMIT for the period from 1 July 2006 to 30 June 2007, ACABQ recommended that the unencumbered balance of $37,971,100, as well as other income and adjustments in the amount of $1,106,900, be credited to Member States in a manner to be determined by the Assembly. It further recommended that the Assembly authorize the appropriation and assessment of $16,436,500 for the maintenance of the Mission for the period from 1 July 2007 to 30 June 2008, in addition to the $160,589,900 already appropriated for the same period under the provisions of General Assembly resolution 61/249 C [YUN 2007, p. 371]. With respect to the period from 1 July 2008 to 30 June 2009, it recommended that the estimated budget requirement of $173,439,800 be reduced by $597,800. Accordingly, ACABQ recommended that the Assembly appropriate $172,842,000 for the maintenance of the Mission from 1 July 2008 to 30 June 2009.

GENERAL ASSEMBLY ACTION

On 20 June [meeting 109], on the recommendation of the Fifth Committee [A/62/871], the Assembly adopted **resolution 62/258** without vote [agenda item 147].

Financing of the United Nations Integrated Mission in Timor-Leste

The General Assembly,

Having considered the reports of the Secretary-General on the financing of the United Nations Integrated Mission in Timor-Leste, the note by the Secretary-General on the financing arrangements for the Mission and the related report of the Advisory Committee on Administrative and Budgetary Questions,

Recalling Security Council resolution 1704(2006) of 25 August 2006, by which the Council decided to establish a follow-on mission in Timor-Leste, the United Nations Integrated Mission in Timor-Leste, for an initial period of six months, with the intention to renew it for further periods, and the subsequent resolutions by which the Council extended the mandate of the Mission, the latest of which was resolution 1802(2008) of 25 February 2008, by which the Council extended the mandate of the Mission until 26 February 2009,

Recalling also its resolutions 61/249 A of 22 December 2006 and 61/249 B of 2 April 2007, as well as resolution 61/249 C of 29 June 2007 on the financing of the Mission,

Reaffirming the general principles underlying the financing of United Nations peacekeeping operations, as stated in General Assembly resolutions 1874(S-IV) of 27 June 1963, 3101(XXVIII) of 11 December 1973 and 55/235 of 23 December 2000,

Mindful of the fact that it is essential to provide the Mission with the financial resources necessary to enable it to fulfill its responsibilities under the relevant resolutions of the Security Council,

1. *Requests* the Secretary-General to entrust the Head of Mission with the task of formulating future budget proposals in full accordance with the provisions of General Assembly resolutions 59/296 of 22 June 2005, 60/266 of 30 June 2006 and 61/276 of 29 June 2007, as well as other relevant resolutions;

2. *Takes note* of the status of contributions to the United Nations Integrated Mission in Timor-Leste as at 31 March 2008, including the contributions outstanding in the amount of 61.3 million United States dollars, representing some 18 per cent of the total assessed contributions, notes with concern that only seventy-six Member States have paid their assessed contributions in full, and urges all other Member States, in particular those in arrears, to ensure payment of their outstanding assessed contributions;

3. *Expresses its appreciation* to those Member States which have paid their assessed contributions in full, and urges all other Member States to make every possible effort to ensure payment of their assessed contributions to the Mission in full;

4. *Expresses concern* at the financial situation with regard to peacekeeping activities, in particular as regards the reimbursements to troop contributors that bear additional burdens owing to overdue payments by Member States of their assessments;

5. *Also expresses concern* at the delay experienced by the Secretary-General in deploying and providing adequate resources to some recent peacekeeping missions, in particular those in Africa;

6. *Emphasizes* that all future and existing peacekeeping missions shall be given equal and non-discriminatory treatment in respect of financial and administrative arrangements;

7. *Also emphasizes* that all peacekeeping missions shall be provided with adequate resources for the effective and efficient discharge of their respective mandates;

8. *Reiterates its request* to the Secretary-General to make the fullest possible use of facilities and equipment at the United Nations Logistics Base at Brindisi, Italy, in order to minimize the costs of procurement for the Mission;

9. *Endorses* the conclusions and recommendations contained in the report of the Advisory Committee on Administrative and Budgetary Questions, subject to the provisions of the present resolution, and requests the Secretary-General to ensure their full implementation;

10. *Decides* to establish one P-4 general temporary assistance position for a Legal Officer and one P-3 post for a Legal Officer;

11. *Also decides* to establish one P-3 general temporary assistance position for a Coordination Officer;

12. *Further decides* not to approve the upgrading of the two Security Officers;

13. *Requests* the Secretary-General to review the staffing structure, including the senior management level, of the Mission on an ongoing basis, bearing in mind, in particular, the mandate and concept of operations of the Mission, and to report thereon in his budget proposals;

14. *Also requests* the Secretary-General to take the necessary steps to facilitate the acceleration of the recruitment process and improve incumbency levels in the Mission and to report on the results achieved in the context of the budget for the Mission for the period from 1 July 2009 to 30 June 2010;

15. *Further requests* the Secretary-General to ensure the full implementation of the relevant provisions of its resolutions 59/296, 60/266 and 61/276;

16. *Requests* the Secretary-General to take all necessary action to ensure that the Mission is administered with a maximum of efficiency and economy;

17. *Also requests* the Secretary-General, in order to reduce the cost of employing General Service staff, to continue efforts to recruit local staff for the Mission against General Service posts, commensurate with the requirements of the Mission;

Financial performance report for the period from 1 July 2006 to 30 June 2007

18. *Takes note* of the report of the Secretary-General on the financial performance of the Mission for the period from 25 August 2006 to 30 June 2007;

Financing arrangements for the period from 1 July 2007 to 30 June 2008

19. *Also takes note* of the note by the Secretary-General on the financing arrangements for the Mission for the period from 1 July 2007 to 30 June 2008;

20. *Decides* to appropriate to the Special Account for the United Nations Integrated Mission in Timor-Leste the amount of 16,436,500 dollars for the maintenance of the Mission for the period from 1 July 2007 to 30 June 2008, in addition to the amount of 160,589,900 dollars already appropriated for the Mission for the same period under the terms of its resolution 61/249 C;

Financing of the additional appropriation for the period from 1 July 2007 to 30 June 2008

21. *Also decides,* taking into account the amount of 160,589,900 dollars already apportioned under the terms of its resolution 61/249 C, to apportion among Member States the additional amount of 16,436,500 dollars for the maintenance of the Mission for the period from 1 July 2007 to 30 June 2008, in accordance with the levels updated in General Assembly resolution 61/243 of 22 December 2006, and taking into account the scale of assessments for 2007 and 2008, as set out in its resolution 61/237 of 22 December 2006;

22. *Further decides* that, in accordance with the provisions of its resolution 973(X) of 15 December 1955, there shall be set off against the apportionment among Member States, as provided for in paragraph 21 above, their respective share in the Tax Equalization Fund of the amount of 1,439,800 dollars, representing the additional staff assessment income approved for the Mission for the period from 1 July 2007 to 30 June 2008;

Budget estimates for the period from 1 July 2008 to 30 June 2009

23. *Decides* to appropriate to the Special Account for the Mission the amount of 180,841,100 dollars for the period from 1 July 2008 to 30 June 2009, inclusive of 172,842,000 dollars for the maintenance of the Mission, 6,973,100 dollars for the support account for peacekeeping operations and 1,026,000 dollars for the United Nations Logistics Base;

Financing of the appropriation for the period from 1 July 2008 to 30 June 2009

24. *Also decides* to apportion among Member States the amount of 119,484,292 dollars for the period from 1 July 2008 to 26 February 2009, in accordance with the levels updated in resolution 61/243, and taking into account the scale of assessments for 2008 and 2009, as set out in resolution 61/237;

25. *Further decides* that, in accordance with the provisions of its resolution 973(X), there shall be set off against the apportionment among Member States, as provided for in paragraph 24 above, their respective share in the Tax Equalization Fund of 4,982,574 dollars, comprising the estimated staff assessment income of 4,486,382 dollars approved for the Mission, the prorated share of 442,675 dollars of the estimated staff assessment income approved for the support account and the prorated share of 53,517 dollars of the estimated staff assessment income approved for the United Nations Logistics Base;

26. *Decides* to apportion among Member States the amount of 61,356,808 dollars for the period from 27 February to 30 June 2009 at a monthly rate of 15,070,091 dollars, in accordance with the levels updated in resolution 61/243, and taking into account the scale of assessments for 2009, as set out in resolution 61/237, subject to a decision of the Security Council to extend the mandate of the Mission;

27. *Also decides* that, in accordance with the provisions of its resolution 973(X), there shall be set off against the apportionment among Member States, as provided for in paragraph 26 above, their respective share in the Tax Equalization Fund of 2,558,626 dollars, comprising the estimated staff assessment income of 2,303,818 dollars approved for the Mission, the prorated share of 227,325 dollars of the estimated staff assessment income approved for the support account and the prorated share of 27,483 dollars of the estimated staff assessment income approved for the United Nations Logistics Base;

28. *Further decides* that, for Member States that have fulfilled their financial obligations to the Mission, there shall be set off against their apportionment, as provided for in paragraph 24 above, their respective share of the unencumbered balance and other income in the total amount of 39,078,000 dollars in respect of the financial period ended 30 June 2007, in accordance with the levels updated in resolution 61/243, and taking into account the scale of assessments for 2007, as set out in resolution 61/237;

29. *Decides* that, for Member States that have not fulfilled their financial obligations to the Mission, there shall be set off against their outstanding obligations their respective share of the unencumbered balance and other income in the total amount of 39,078,000 dollars in respect of the financial period ended 30 June 2007, in accordance with the scheme set out in paragraph 28 above;

30. *Also decides* that the decrease of 827,600 dollars in the estimated staff assessment income in respect of the financial period ended 30 June 2007 shall be set off against the credits from the amount of 39,078,000 dollars referred to in paragraphs 28 and 29 above;

31. *Emphasizes* that no peacekeeping mission shall be financed by borrowing funds from other active peacekeeping missions;

32. *Encourages* the Secretary-General to continue to take additional measures to ensure the safety and security of all personnel participating in the Mission under the auspices of the United Nations, bearing in mind paragraphs 5 and 6 of Security Council resolution 1502(2003) of 26 August 2003;

33. *Invites* voluntary contributions to the Mission in cash and in the form of services and supplies acceptable to

the Secretary-General, to be administered, as appropriate, in accordance with the procedure and practices established by the General Assembly;

34. *Decides* to include in the provisional agenda of its sixty-third session the item entitled "Financing of the United Nations Integrated Mission in Timor-Leste".

On 24 December, by **decision 63/552**, the General Assembly decided that the item on UNMIT financing would remain for consideration during its sixty-third (2009) session.

Iran

In 2008, the United Nations continued to address Iran's nuclear programme. On 3 March, the Security Council, by resolution 1803(2008) (see below), strengthened the sanctions it had imposed by resolutions 1737(2006) [YUN 2006, p. 436] and 1747(2007) [YUN 2007, p. 374]. On 27 September, by resolution 1835(2008) (see p. 414), the Council called on Iran to comply with its previous resolutions, requesting the country to stop uranium enrichment and reprocessing activities. Iran stated once again that its nuclear programme was and would remain absolutely peaceful. Meanwhile, the Security Council Committee established pursuant to resolution 1737(2006) continued overseeing implementation of the sanctions regime.

The International Atomic Energy Agency (IAEA) reported that during 2008, Iran had not implemented the Additional Protocol to Iran's Safeguards Agreement. It had also failed to provide access to additional locations related to the manufacture of centrifuges, uranium enrichment, mining and milling, as required by the Council—giving rise to concerns about possible military dimensions of its nuclear programme.

IAEA reports

During 2008, the Council had before it a number of reports by the IAEA Board of Governors on Iran's implementation of the Non-Proliferation Treaty Safeguards Agreement and relevant provisions of Security Council resolutions. Each one stated that the Agency had been able to continue its activities to verify the non-diversion of declared nuclear material in Iran, while elaborating on that process and the difficulties encountered.

IAEA report (February). IAEA's report of 22 February [GOV/2008/4] on developments since 15 November 2007 stated that answers provided by Iran were in some cases consistent with the Agency's findings, and in other cases were not inconsistent with those findings. The major remaining issue relevant to the nature of Iran's nuclear programme concerned alleged studies on the conversion of uranium dioxide into uranium tetrafluoride (the green salt project)—which could have a military nuclear dimension. In addition, Iran had not suspended its enrichment-related activities, having continued the operation of its pilot fuel enrichment plant (PFEP) and its fuel enrichment plant. It had also begun the development of new-generation centrifuges, and continued construction of its IR-40 reactor and operation of its heavy water production plant.

Communication. By a 27 February letter [A/62/712-S/2008/138], Iran's Foreign Minister, Manouchehr Mottaki, said that Iran had answered all the questions presented by IAEA concerning outstanding issues according to the work plan, and that those answers had been consistent with the Agency's findings. Consequently, all the justifications and foundations for the Security Council's action on the issue had vanished.

SECURITY COUNCIL ACTION

On 3 March [meeting 5848], the Security Council adopted **resolution 1803(2008)** by vote (14-0-1). The draft [S/2008/141] was submitted by France, Germany and the United Kingdom.

The Security Council,

Recalling the statement by its President of 29 March 2006 and its resolutions 1696(2006) of 31 July 2006, 1737(2006) of 23 December 2006 and 1747(2007) of 24 March 2007, and reaffirming their provisions,

Reaffirming its commitment to the Treaty on the Non-Proliferation of Nuclear Weapons and the need for all States parties to the Treaty to comply fully with all their obligations, and recalling the right of States parties, in conformity with articles I and II of the Treaty, to develop research, production and use of nuclear energy for peaceful purposes without discrimination,

Recalling resolution GOV/2006/14 adopted by the Board of Governors of the International Atomic Energy Agency on 4 February 2006, which states that a solution to the Iranian nuclear issue would contribute to global non-proliferation efforts and to realizing the objective of a Middle East free of weapons of mass destruction, including their means of delivery,

Noting with serious concern that, as confirmed in the reports of the Director General of the Agency of 23 May, 30 August and 15 November 2007 and 22 February 2008, the Islamic Republic of Iran has not established full and sustained suspension of all enrichment-related and reprocessing activities and heavy water-related projects as set out in Security Council resolutions 1696(2006), 1737(2006) and 1747(2007), nor resumed its cooperation with the Agency under the Additional Protocol, nor taken the other steps required by the Board of Governors, nor complied with the provisions of resolutions 1696(2006), 1737(2006) and 1747(2007), which are essential to build confidence, and deploring the Islamic Republic of Iran's refusal to take these steps,

Noting with concern that the Islamic Republic of Iran has taken issue with the right of the Agency to verify design information which had been provided by the Islamic Republic of Iran pursuant to the modified Code 3.1, emphasizing that, in accordance with article 39 of the safeguards agreement between the Islamic Republic of Iran and the Agency, Code 3.1 cannot be modified nor suspended unilaterally and that the Agency's right to verify design information provided to it is a continuing right which is not dependent on the stage of construction of, or the presence of nuclear material at, a facility,

Reiterating its determination to reinforce the authority of the Agency, strongly supporting the role of the Board of Governors, commending the Agency for its efforts to resolve outstanding issues relating to the Islamic Republic of Iran's nuclear programme in the work plan between the secretariat of the Agency and the Islamic Republic of Iran, welcoming the progress in the implementation of the work plan, as reflected in the reports of the Director General of 15 November 2007 and 22 February 2008, underlining the importance of the Islamic Republic of Iran producing tangible results rapidly and effectively by completing implementation of the work plan, including by providing answers to all the questions the Agency asks so that the Agency, through the implementation of the required transparency measures, can assess the completeness and correctness of the Islamic Republic of Iran's declaration,

Expressing the conviction that the suspension set out in paragraph 2 of resolution 1737(2006) as well as full, verified Iranian compliance with the requirements set out by the Board of Governors would contribute to a diplomatic, negotiated solution that guarantees that the Islamic Republic of Iran's nuclear programme is for exclusively peaceful purposes,

Stressing that China, France, Germany, the Russian Federation, the United Kingdom of Great Britain and Northern Ireland and the United States of America are willing to take further concrete measures on exploring an overall strategy of resolving the Iranian nuclear issue through negotiation on the basis of their proposals of June 2006, and noting the confirmation by those countries that, once the confidence of the international community in the exclusively peaceful nature of the Islamic Republic of Iran's nuclear programme is restored, it will be treated in the same manner as any non-nuclear-weapon State party to the Treaty on the Non-Proliferation of Nuclear Weapons,

Having regard to the rights and obligations of States relating to international trade,

Welcoming the guidance issued by the Financial Action Task Force to assist States in implementing their financial obligations under resolution 1737(2006),

Determined to give effect to its decisions by adopting appropriate measures to persuade the Islamic Republic of Iran to comply with resolutions 1696(2006), 1737(2006) and 1747(2007) and with the requirements of the Agency, and also to constrain the Islamic Republic of Iran's development of sensitive technologies in support of its nuclear and missile programmes, until such time as the Council determines that the objectives of those resolutions have been met,

Concerned by the proliferation risks presented by the Iranian nuclear programme and, in this context, by the Islamic Republic of Iran's continuing failure to meet the requirements of the Board of Governors and to comply with the provisions of resolutions 1696(2006), 1737(2006) and 1747(2007), and mindful of its primary responsibility under the Charter of the United Nations for the maintenance of international peace and security,

Acting under Article 41 of Chapter VII of the Charter,

1. *Reaffirms* that the Islamic Republic of Iran shall without further delay take the steps required by the Board of Governors of the International Atomic Energy Agency in its resolution GOV/2006/14, which are essential to build confidence in the exclusively peaceful purpose of its nuclear programme and to resolve outstanding questions, and in this context affirms its decision that the Islamic Republic of Iran shall without delay take the steps required in paragraph 2 of resolution 1737(2006), and underlines that the Agency has sought confirmation that the Islamic Republic of Iran will apply the modified Code 3.1;

2. *Welcomes* the agreement between the Islamic Republic of Iran and the Agency to resolve all outstanding issues concerning the Islamic Republic of Iran's nuclear programme and progress made in this regard, as set out in the report of 22 February 2008 of the Director General of the Agency, encourages the Agency to continue its work to clarify all outstanding issues, stresses that this would help to re-establish international confidence in the exclusively peaceful nature of the Islamic Republic of Iran's nuclear programme, and supports the Agency in strengthening its safeguards on the Islamic Republic of Iran's nuclear activities in accordance with the safeguards agreement between the Islamic Republic of Iran and the Agency;

3. *Calls upon* all States to exercise vigilance and restraint regarding the entry into or transit through their territories of individuals who are engaged in, directly associated with or providing support for the Islamic Republic of Iran's proliferation-sensitive nuclear activities or for the development of nuclear weapon delivery systems, and decides in this regard that all States shall notify the Security Council Committee established pursuant to paragraph 18 of resolution 1737(2006) (hereinafter "the Committee") of the entry into or transit through their territories of the persons designated in the annex to resolution 1737(2006), annex I to resolution 1747(2007) or annex I to the present resolution, as well as of additional persons designated by the Council or the Committee as being engaged in, directly associated with or providing support for the Islamic Republic of Iran's proliferation-sensitive nuclear activities or for the development of nuclear weapon delivery systems, including through the involvement in procurement of the prohibited items, goods, equipment, materials and technology specified by and under the measures in paragraphs 3 and 4 of resolution 1737(2006), except where such entry or transit is for activities directly related to the items in paragraphs 3 *(b)* (i) and (ii) of resolution 1737(2006);

4. *Underlines* that nothing in paragraph 3 above requires a State to refuse its own nationals entry into its territory, and that all States shall, in the implementation of paragraph 3 above, take into account humanitarian considerations, including religious obligations, as well as the necessity to meet the objectives of the present resolution and resolutions 1737(2006) and 1747(2007), including where article XV of the statute of the Agency is engaged;

5. *Decides* that all States shall take the necessary measures to prevent the entry into or transit through their territories of individuals designated in annex II to

the present resolution as well as of additional persons designated by the Council or the Committee as being engaged in, directly associated with or providing support for the Islamic Republic of Iran's proliferation-sensitive nuclear activities or for the development of nuclear weapon delivery systems, including through the involvement in procurement of the prohibited items, goods, equipment, materials and technology specified by and under the measures in paragraphs 3 and 4 of resolution 1737(2006), except where such entry or transit is for activities directly related to the items in paragraphs 3 *(b)* (i) and (ii) of resolution 1737(2006) and provided that nothing in the present paragraph shall oblige a State to refuse its own nationals entry into its territory;

6. *Decides also* that the measures imposed by paragraph 5 above shall not apply where the Committee determines on a case-by-case basis that such travel is justified on the grounds of humanitarian need, including religious obligations, or where the Committee concludes that an exemption would otherwise further the objectives of the present resolution;

7. *Decides further* that the measures specified in paragraphs 12 to 15 of resolution 1737(2006) shall apply also to the persons and entities listed in annexes I and III to the present resolution, and any persons or entities acting on their behalf or at their direction, and to entities owned or controlled by them and to persons and entities determined by the Council or the Committee to have assisted designated persons or entities in evading sanctions of, or in violating the provisions of, the present resolution, resolution 1737(2006) or resolution 1747(2007);

8. *Decides* that all States shall take the necessary measures to prevent the supply, sale or transfer directly or indirectly from their territories or by their nationals or using their flag vessels or aircraft to, or for use in or the benefit of, the Islamic Republic of Iran, and whether or not originating in their territories, of:

(a) All items, materials, equipment, goods and technology set out in INFCIRC/254/Rev.7/Part 2 in document S/2006/814, except the supply, sale or transfer, in accordance with the requirements of paragraph 5 of resolution 1737(2006), of items, materials, equipment, goods and technology set out in sections 1 and 2 of the annex to that document, and sections 3 to 6 as notified in advance to the Committee, only when for exclusive use in light water reactors, and where such supply, sale or transfer is necessary for technical cooperation provided to the Islamic Republic of Iran by the Agency or under its auspices as provided for in paragraph 16 of resolution 1737(2006);

(b) All items, materials, equipment, goods and technology set out in 19.A.3 of Category II in document S/2006/815;

9. *Calls upon* all States to exercise vigilance in entering into new commitments for public-provided financial support for trade with the Islamic Republic of Iran, including the granting of export credits, guarantees or insurance, to their nationals or entities involved in such trade, in order to avoid such financial support contributing to the proliferation-sensitive nuclear activities, or to the development of nuclear weapon delivery systems, as referred to in resolution 1737(2006);

10. *Also calls upon* all States to exercise vigilance over the activities of financial institutions in their territories with all banks domiciled in the Islamic Republic of Iran, in particular with Bank Melli and Bank Saderat, and their branches and subsidiaries abroad, in order to avoid such activities contributing to the proliferation-sensitive nuclear activities, or to the development of nuclear weapon delivery systems, as referred to in resolution 1737(2006);

11. *Further calls upon* all States, in accordance with their national legal authorities and legislation and consistent with international law, in particular the law of the sea and relevant international civil aviation agreements, to inspect the cargoes to and from the Islamic Republic of Iran of aircraft and vessels, at their airports and seaports, owned or operated by Iran Air Cargo and Islamic Republic of Iran Shipping Line, provided that there are reasonable grounds to believe that the aircraft or vessel is transporting goods prohibited under the present resolution or resolution 1737(2006) or resolution 1747(2007);

12. *Requires* all States, in cases when inspection mentioned in paragraph 11 above is undertaken, to submit to the Council within five working days a written report on the inspection containing, in particular, an explanation of the grounds for the inspection, as well as information on its time, place, circumstances, results and other relevant details;

13. *Calls upon* all States to report to the Committee within sixty days of the adoption of the present resolution on the steps they have taken with a view to implementing effectively paragraphs 3, 5 and 7 to 11 above;

14. *Decides* that the mandate of the Committee as set out in paragraph 18 of resolution 1737(2006) shall also apply to the measures imposed in resolution 1747(2007) and the present resolution;

15. *Stresses* the willingness of China, France, Germany, the Russian Federation, the United Kingdom of Great Britain and Northern Ireland and the United States of America to further enhance diplomatic efforts to promote resumption of dialogue, and consultations on the basis of their offer to the Islamic Republic of Iran, with a view to seeking a comprehensive, long-term and proper solution of this issue which would allow for the development of all-round relations and wider cooperation with the Islamic Republic of Iran based on mutual respect and the establishment of international confidence in the exclusively peaceful nature of the Islamic Republic of Iran's nuclear programme, and inter alia, starting direct talks and negotiation with the Islamic Republic of Iran as long as the Islamic Republic of Iran suspends all enrichment-related and reprocessing activities, including research and development, as verified by the Agency;

16. *Encourages* the High Representative for the Common Foreign and Security Policy of the European Union to continue communication with the Islamic Republic of Iran in support of political and diplomatic efforts to find a negotiated solution, including relevant proposals by China, France, Germany, the Russian Federation, the United Kingdom and the United States, with a view to creating the necessary conditions for resuming talks;

17. *Emphasizes* the importance of all States, including the Islamic Republic of Iran, taking the necessary measures to ensure that no claim shall lie at the instance of the Government of the Islamic Republic of Iran, or of any person or entity in the Islamic Republic of Iran, or of persons

or entities designated pursuant to resolution 1737(2006) and related resolutions, or any person claiming through or for the benefit of any such person or entity, in connection with any contract or other transaction where its performance was prevented by reason of the measures imposed by the present resolution, resolution 1737(2006) or resolution 1747(2007);

18. *Requests* within ninety days a further report from the Director General of the Agency on whether the Islamic Republic of Iran has established full and sustained suspension of all activities mentioned in resolution 1737(2006), as well as on the process of Iranian compliance with all the steps required by the Board of Governors of the Agency and with the other provisions of resolutions 1737(2006) and 1747(2007) and the present resolution, to the Board and, in parallel, to the Council for its consideration;

19. *Reaffirms* that it shall review the actions of the Islamic Republic of Iran in the light of the report referred to in paragraph 18 above, and:

(a) That it shall suspend the implementation of measures if and for so long as the Islamic Republic of Iran suspends all enrichment-related and reprocessing activities, including research and development, as verified by the Agency, to allow for negotiations in good faith in order to reach an early and mutually acceptable outcome;

(b) That it shall terminate the measures specified in paragraphs 3 to 7 and 12 of resolution 1737(2006), as well as in paragraphs 2 and 4 to 7 of resolution 1747(2007) and in paragraphs 3, 5 and 7 to 11 above as soon as it determines, following receipt of the report referred to in paragraph 18 above, that the Islamic Republic of Iran has fully complied with its obligations under the relevant resolutions of the Council and met the requirements of the Board of Governors, as confirmed by the Board;

(c) That it shall, in the event that the report shows that the Islamic Republic of Iran has not complied with resolutions 1696(2006), 1737(2006) and 1747(2007) and the present resolution, adopt further appropriate measures under Article 41 of Chapter VII of the Charter of the United Nations to persuade the Islamic Republic of Iran to comply with these resolutions and the requirements of the Agency, and underlines that further decisions will be required should such additional measures be necessary;

20. *Decides* to remain seized of the matter.

ANNEX I

1. Amir Moayyed Alai (involved in managing the assembly and engineering of centrifuges)

2. Mohammad Fedai Ashiani (involved in the production of ammonium uranyl carbonate and management of the Natanz enrichment complex)

3. Abbas Rezaee Ashtiani (a senior official at the AEOI Office of Exploration and Mining Affairs)

4. Haleh Bakhtiar (involved in the production of magnesium at a concentration of 99.9 per cent)

5. Morteza Behzad (involved in making centrifuge components)

6. Dr. Mohammad Eslami (Head of Defence Industries Training and Research Institute)

7. Seyyed Hussein Hosseini (AEOI official involved in the heavy water research reactor project at Arak)

8. M. Javad Karimi Sabet (Head of Novin Energy Company, which is designated under resolution 1747(2007))

9. Hamid-Reza Mohajerani (involved in production management at the Uranium Conversion Facility (UCF) at Esfahan)

10. Brigadier-General Mohammad Reza Naqdi (former Deputy Chief of Armed Forces General Staff for Logistics and Industrial Research/Head of State Anti-Smuggling Headquarters, engaged in efforts to get round the sanctions imposed by resolutions 1737(2006) and 1747(2007))

11. Houshang Nobari (involved in the management of the Natanz enrichment complex)

12. Abbas Rashidi (involved in enrichment work at Natanz)

13. Ghasem Soleymani (Director of Uranium Mining Operations at the Saghand Uranium Mine)

ANNEX II

A. Individuals listed in resolution 1737(2006)

1. Mohammad Qannadi, AEOI Vice President for Research & Development

2. Dawood Agha-Jani, Head of the PFEP (Natanz)

3. Behman Asgarpour, Operational Manager (Arak)

B. Individuals listed in resolution 1747(2007)

1. Seyed Jaber Safdari (Manager of the Natanz Enrichment Facilities)

2. Amir Rahimi (Head of Esfahan Nuclear Fuel Research and Production Center, which is part of the AEOI's Nuclear Fuel Production and Procurement Company, which is involved in enrichment-related activities)

ANNEX III

1. Abzar Boresh Kaveh Co. (BK Co.) (involved in the production of centrifuge components)

2. Barzagani Tejarat Tavanmad Saccal companies (subsidiary of Saccal System companies) (this company tried to purchase sensitive goods for an entity listed in resolution 1737(2006))

3. Electro Sanam Company (E.S. Co./E.X. Co.) (AIO front company, involved in the ballistic missile programme)

4. Ettehad Technical Group (AIO front company, involved in the ballistic missile programme)

5. Industrial Factories of Precision (IFP) Machinery (AKA Instrumentation Factories Plant) (used by AIO for some acquisition attempts)

6. Jabber Ibn Hayan (AEOI laboratory involved in fuel-cycle activities)

7. Joza Industrial Co. (AIO front company, involved in the ballistic missile programme)

8. Khorasan Metallurgy Industries (subsidiary of the Ammunition Industries Group (AMIG) which depends on DIO. Involved in the production of centrifuge components)

9. Niru Battery Manufacturing Company (subsidiary of the DIO. Its role is to manufacture power units for the Iranian military, including missile systems)

10. Pishgam (Pioneer) Energy Industries (has participated in construction of the Uranium Conversion Facility at Esfahan)

11. Safety Equipment Procurement (SEP) (AIO front company, involved in the ballistic missile programme)

12. Tamas Company (involved in enrichment-related activities. Tamas is the overarching body, under which four subsidiaries have been established, including one for uranium extraction to concentration and another in charge of uranium processing, enrichment and waste)

RECORDED VOTE ON RESOLUTION 1803(2008):

In favour: Belgium, Burkina Faso, China, Costa Rica, Croatia, France, Italy, Lybian Arab Jamahiriya, Panama, Russian Federation, South Africa, United Kingdom, United States, Viet Nam.

Against: None.

Abstaining: Indonesia.

Speaking before the vote, Iran said that the draft resolution did not meet the minimum standards of legitimacy and legality, and emphasized that Iran's nuclear programme was entirely peaceful and did not fall within the purview of the Council. Indonesia said that the IAEA report of 22 February had recognized the important progress made in Iran's cooperation with the Agency, as well as its lack of compliance with Council resolutions. Indonesia had expected the draft to reflect those complex dynamics and mixed findings. Indonesia was not convinced of the efficacy of additional sanctions at present.

Communication. A 3 March statement [S/2008/147] by the Foreign Ministers of China, France, Germany, Russia, the United Kingdom and the United States, with the support of the High Representative of the European Union (EU), deplored Iran's continued failure to comply with Security Council and IAEA requirements, but remained committed to a negotiated solution. It said that the Ministers were prepared to further develop the proposals they presented to Iran in June 2006 [YUN 2006, p. 432], which offered substantial opportunities for benefits to Iran and the region.

Security Council consideration. On 17 March [meeting 5853], Johan Verbeke (Belgium), the Chairman of the Security Council Committee established pursuant to Council resolution 1737(2006) [ibid., p. 436] (Iran Sanctions Committee), briefed the Council on its activities from 19 December 2007 to 17 March 2008. He noted that by resolution 1803(2008) (see p. 409), the Council had called upon all States to exercise vigilance in the areas of financial support for trade with Iran and of banking with Iran, and to inspect the cargoes to and from Iran of aircraft and vessels, at their airports and seaports, owned or operated by two Iranian companies, when there were reasonable grounds to believe that they were transporting goods prohibited under resolutions 1737(2006), 1747(2007) or 1803(2008).

Communications. By a 17 March letter [S/2008/190], Iran commented on the discussions in the Security Council at its 3 and 17 March meetings, stating that the Council had once again been "downgraded to a mere tool of the national foreign policy of just a few countries". Iran's nuclear programme was and would remain absolutely peaceful. A statement of 24 March [A/62/767-S/2008/203] from Iranian Foreign Minister Mottaki also referred to the Council's "unlawful engagement" with respect to Iran's nuclear activities.

IAEA report (May). Pursuant to resolution 1803(2008), the IAEA Director General on 26 May [S/2008/338] reported that Iran's alleged studies on the green salt project, high explosives testing and missile re-entry vehicle project were of concern. Their clarification was critical to an assessment of the nature of Iran's past and present nuclear programme. Further, Iran had continued the operation of PFEP and the fuel enrichment plant, as well as the installation of new cascades and new generation centrifuges for test purposes. It had also continued with construction of its IR-40 reactor.

Security Council consideration (June). On 13 June [meeting 5909], Jan Grauls (Belgium), Chairman of the Security Council Committee established pursuant to resolution 1737(2006), briefed the Council on its activities since 18 March. The Committee had granted two requests for exemption to the assets freeze for meeting extraordinary expenses. The Committee had also received one notification of one State regarding its intention to make or receive payments, or to authorize the unfreezing of funds, in connection with contracts entered into prior to the listing of persons and entities.

Communications. By a 16 June letter [S/2008/393], the Council received a set of proposals by the Foreign Ministers of China, France, Germany, the Russian Federation, the United Kingdom and the United States, with the support of the High Representative of the EU, which had been passed to Iran on 14 June. A 17 June letter from Iran [S/2008/397] transmitted a proposed package for constructive negotiations, together with a letter of 13 May from its Foreign Minister, calling for wide-ranging negotiations, to the countries of the "five plus one" group (the five permanent members of the Security Council plus Germany).

On 1 August [S/2008/520], France, the United Kingdom and the United States, in support of the Council's call in resolution 1803(2008) for States to be vigilant over the activities of financial institutions in their territories with Iranian banks, in particular with Bank Melli and Bank Saderat, provided information on the branches and subsidiaries of those banks. In a reply dated 15 August [S/2008/554], Iran stated that those Iranian banks had never been involved in any illicit activities, including non-peaceful nuclear activities, simply because there were no such non-peaceful nuclear activities in Iran.

During the year, Iran transmitted to the Security Council letters referring to what it described as baseless allegations made against it during Council meetings, mainly attributed to the United States [S/2008/280, S/2008/391, S/2008/530, S/2008/706]. Another letter, dated 30 April [S/2008/288], cited a televised interview with United States Senator Hilary Rodham Clinton, stating that she had threatened the use of force against Iran. Other letters [S/2008/377, S/2008/599] referred to threats from the "Israeli regime".

Security Council consideration (September). On 11 September [meeting 5973], Security Council Committee Chairman Grauls briefed the Council on its activities since 14 June. He said that the Committee had recently focused on ensuring greater vigilance from Member States over the activities of financial institutions that dealt with banks domiciled in Iran. The Committee also probed reports that one State might have contravened an export ban on arms and related materiel from Iran, and received assurances from the country involved that it would continue to fully implement the sanctions.

IAEA report (September). IAEA's report of 15 September [GOV/2008/38] said that Iran had provided the Agency with access to declared nuclear material and had provided the required nuclear material accounting reports in connection with declared nuclear material and activities. Regrettably, the Agency had not been able to make any substantive progress on the alleged green salt studies and other key issues. Iran needed to provide the Agency with substantive information to support its statements and provide access to relevant documentation and individuals.

SECURITY COUNCIL ACTION

On 27 September [meeting 5984], the Security Council unanimously adopted **resolution 1835(2008)**. The draft [S/2008/624] was submitted by Belgium, China, Croatia, France, Germany, Italy, the Russian Federation, the United Kingdom and the United States.

The Security Council,

Taking note of the report of the Director General of the International Atomic Energy Agency of 15 September 2008 on the implementation of the Treaty on the Non-Proliferation of Nuclear Weapons safeguards agreement and relevant provisions of Security Council resolutions 1737(2006), 1747(2007) and 1803(2008) in the Islamic Republic of Iran,

Reaffirming its commitment to the Treaty on the Non-Proliferation of Nuclear Weapons,

1. *Reaffirms* the statement by its President of 29 March 2006, and its resolutions 1696(2006) of 31 July 2006, 1737(2006) of 23 December 2006, 1747(2007) of 24 March 2007 and 1803(2008) of 3 March 2008;

2. *Takes note* of the statement of 3 March 2008 by the Ministers for Foreign Affairs of China, France, Germany, the Russian Federation, the United Kingdom of Great Britain and Northern Ireland and the United States of America, with the support of the High Representative for the Common Foreign and Security Policy of the European Union, describing the dual-track approach to the Iranian nuclear issue;

3. *Reaffirms its commitment*, within this framework, to an early negotiated solution to the Iranian nuclear issue, and welcomes the continuing efforts in this regard;

4. *Calls upon* the Islamic Republic of Iran to comply fully and without delay with its obligations under the above-mentioned resolutions of the Security Council, and to meet the requirements of the Board of Governors of the International Atomic Energy Agency;

5. *Decides* to remain seized of the matter.

Communications. By a 10 October letter [S/2008/643], Iran forwarded a 6 October letter from the Secretary of its Supreme National Security Council to the EU High Representative, as well as to the Foreign Ministers of the "five plus one" group of countries. In the letter, Iran regretted that its package of proposals for paving the way to talks had not yet been accepted.

A 23 October letter from Iran [A/63/507-S/2008/675] protested the United Kingdom's removal of "the so-called 'People's Mojahedin Organization of Iran', a notorious terrorist group", from its list of proscribed groups.

IAEA report (November). In its report of 19 November [GOV/2008/59], the Agency came to essentially the same conclusions as in its previous report.

Security Council consideration (December). On 10 December [meeting 6036], Security Council Committee Chairman Grauls briefed the Council on its activities since 12 September. He said that the Council, by its resolution 1835(2008), had reaffirmed its commitment to an early negotiated solution through a dual-track approach to the Iranian nuclear issue that included both targeted sanctions and generous incentives.

Communication. On the same day, the Council President received a letter from Iran [S/2008/776] responding to allegations against its peaceful nuclear programme by certain Council members, particularly the United States, the United Kingdom and France, made at that day's Security Council meeting.

IAEA report. A later IAEA report [GOV/2009/8], covering developments from 19 November to the end of 2008, stated that Iran had neither implemented the Additional Protocol nor agreed to IAEA's request for access to the additional locations mentioned in its previous reports. IAEA was not in a position to provide assurance about the absence of undeclared nuclear material and activities in Iran. The IAEA

Director General urged Iran to implement all measures required to build confidence in the exclusively peaceful nature of its nuclear programme.

Sanctions Committee report. On 31 December, the Committee Chairman transmitted to the Security Council a report [S/2008/839] on its activities in 2008. During the year, the Committee held five informal consultations. It decided to consolidate into a single document the lists of names of persons and entities subject to the travel ban, travel notification requirement and assets freeze. The Committee granted two requests for exemptions to the assets freeze and received four notifications of exemptions to the freeze for transactions made prior to the sanctions. In a 27 March note, the Committee Chairman reminded Member States that, as requested by various Council resolutions, they should report to the Committee about the steps they had taken to implement the sanctions outlined in those resolutions. By year's end, the Committee had received 90 reports pursuant to resolution 1737(2006), 77 reports pursuant to resolution 1747(2007) and 63 reports pursuant to resolution 1803(2008). The list of those reports was appended to the Committee's report.

Democratic People's Republic of Korea

Statements by Secretary-General. On 26 June [SG/SM/11659], the Secretary-General welcomed progress in the six-party talks—China, Democratic People's Republic of Korea (DPRK), Japan, Republic of Korea, Russian Federation, United States—towards the verifiable denuclearization of the Korean peninsula. That day's submission by the DPRK of the declaration of its nuclear programmes to China as chair of the talks, followed by the reciprocal actions of the United States, were important steps forward. The Secretary-General called on all six participants to take that opportunity to expedite movement towards the full implementation of the 2005 Joint Statement [YUN 2005, p. 450].

On 16 July [SG/SM/11704], the Secretary-General welcomed the progress at the sixth round of the six-party talks in Beijing, which included an agreement to establish mechanisms to verify the denuclearization of the Korean peninsula and to monitor the implementation of related commitments. He urged participants to further advance that multilateral process and to contribute to resolving bilateral issues.

Communications. On 3 July [S/2008/435], the DPRK forwarded to the Security Council a statement from its Foreign Ministry saying that the United States, on 26 June, had begun the process of taking the DPRK off the list of state sponsors of terrorism and exempting it from the "Trading with the Enemy Act," as a practical measure for lifting economic sanctions against it under a 2007 agreement [YUN 2007, p. 380] reached at the six-party talks. Expressing appreciation for that move, the statement said that it should lead the United States to totally withdrawing its hostile policy towards the DPRK in all fields, adding that only then could the denuclearization process make smooth progress.

On 11 August [S/2008/547], the DPRK transmitted a report entitled "The United States should not abuse the Armistice Agreement Supervisory Mechanism she scrapped", issued by the Panmunjom Mission of the Korean People's Army on 8 August. The report concluded that the only valid choice to promote lasting peace and secure stability on the Korean peninsula was to replace the 1953 Armistice Agreement [YUN 1953, p. 121] with a peace agreement and establish a new system to ensure peace.

Statements by Secretary-General. On 13 October [SG/SM/11862], the Secretary-General welcomed the agreement between the United States and the DPRK on denuclearization verification measures, allowing for the resumption of the six-party process and related activities. He urged all participants of the talks to meet their respective obligations and to complete the "disablement phase" as soon as possible.

On 12 December [SG/SM/12001], the Secretary-General noted that at the six-party talks, held in Beijing from 8 to 11 December, despite serious discussions, differences remained unresolved, including on terms of verification of the nuclear activities by the DPRK. He strongly supported the goal of verifiable denuclearization of the Korean Peninsula in a peaceful manner, and appreciated that the parties had reaffirmed that goal and unanimously agreed to advance the talks. He expressed his hope that the parties would overcome their remaining differences and complete the implementation of the second-phase actions, and stood ready to assist in any way possible.

Security Council consideration. On 15 December [meeting 6043], Giulio Terzi di Sant'Agata (Italy), the Chairman of the Security Council Committee established pursuant to resolution 1718(2006) [YUN 2006, p. 444] to oversee sanctions measures, briefed the Council on the Committee's activities since 1 January 2007. Resolution 1718(2006) required Member States to prevent the supply, sale or transfer to the DPRK of specific listed items, materials, equipment, goods and technology that could contribute to developing weapons of mass destruction. States were required to freeze the assets and ban the travel of designated persons involved in such efforts. They were also to report to the Council within 30 days of the adoption of the resolution on the steps they had taken to implement it. The tasks of the Committee included seeking from States—in particular those producing or possessing the items, materials, equipment, goods and technology listed in the resolution—information on the actions they had taken to implement the measures imposed by the resolution; to examine and take action on information regarding alleged violations of those measures; and to consider and decide upon requests for exemptions.

Security Council resolution 1718(2006) Committee report. On 31 December [S/2008/830], the Committee Chairman transmitted to the Council President a report on the Committee's activities during 2008. As at 31 December, the Committee had received replies from 73 countries and the European Union concerning the implementation of that resolution. Those replies were accessible on the Committee website, unless a State requested that its reply be kept confidential. The list of replies was annexed to the report.

Nepal

The United Nations Mission in Nepal (UNMIN), established in 2007 [YUN 2007, p. 385], continued to assist the country in its transition to peace following a decade of armed conflict. Headed by Ian Martin (United Kingdom), the Secretary-General's Personal Representative in Nepal, the Mission helped build confidence in the peace process, including through arms monitoring. Unarmed UN arms monitors were deployed in the Maoist cantonment and satellite sites around the country, as well as at the Nepal Army arms storage depot in Kathmandu. The Security Council extended the Mission's mandate on 23 January and 23 July, the last time until 23 January 2009.

Report of Secretary-General (January). By his 3 January report [S/2008/5] on the peace process in Nepal and UNMIN's activities since his previous report [YUN 2007, p. 386], the Secretary-General said that the period had been characterized by stalemate and crisis. Nevertheless, the seven political parties had remained in dialogue and increasingly turned their attention to an array of critical issues—including review of past agreements and their implementation, security sector reform and the need for setting up commissions on land reform and investigating disappearances.

UNMIN continued to monitor the arms and armies of the two sides (Maoist army and Nepal Army). The Arms Monitoring Office remained at its full strength of 186 monitors, and all five sectors were fully operational under senior sector commanders. The two Joint Monitoring Teams in each sector—each comprising one UN monitor, one Nepal Army monitor and one Maoist army monitor—had proven effective for the early resolution of potential local violations and for enabling a rapid response to incidents requiring investigation. UNMIN continued its focus on election security issues, and one police adviser had been deployed to each of the five operational regions.

SECURITY COUNCIL ACTION

On 23 January [meeting 5825], the Security Council unanimously adopted **resolution 1796(2008)**. The draft [S/2008/34] was submitted by the United Kingdom.

The Security Council,

Recalling its resolution 1740(2007) of 23 January 2007,

Recalling also the signing on 21 November 2006 by the Government of Nepal and the Communist Party of Nepal (Maoist) of the Comprehensive Peace Agreement, and the stated commitment of both parties to transforming the existing ceasefire into a permanent and sustainable peace, and commending the steps taken to date to implement the Agreement,

Reaffirming the sovereignty, territorial integrity and political independence of Nepal and its ownership of the implementation of the Comprehensive Peace Agreement and subsequent agreements,

Expressing its continued readiness to support the peace process in Nepal in the timely and effective implementation of the Comprehensive Peace Agreement and subsequent agreements,

Recognizing the strong desire of the Nepalese people for peace and the restoration of democracy and the importance in this respect of the implementation of the Comprehensive Peace Agreement and subsequent agreements,

Recognizing also that civil society can play an important role in conflict prevention,

Welcoming the report of the Secretary-General of 3 January 2008 on the United Nations Mission in Nepal, in accordance with his mandate,

Welcoming also the 23-point agreement reached by the Seven-Party Alliance on 23 December 2007 with a view to holding Constituent Assembly elections on 10 April 2008, and recognizing that the challenging timelines set out in the agreement will require efforts among all the parties to build mutual confidence,

Recognizing the need to pay special attention to the needs of women, children and traditionally marginalized groups in the peace process, as mentioned in the Comprehensive Peace Agreement and Security Council resolution 1325(2000) of 31 October 2000,

Echoing the call by the Secretary-General for all parties in Nepal to move forward swiftly in the implementation of the agreements reached,

Noting that the Government of Nepal, in its letter dated 18 December 2007 to the Secretary-General, recognizes the contribution of the Mission and requests an extension of the mandate for six months,

Welcoming the completion of the two phases of the verification process and continuing assistance with the management of arms and armed personnel of both sides in accordance with resolution 1740(2007) and in line with the provisions of the Comprehensive Peace Agreement, noting the importance of a durable long-term solution in helping to create the conditions for the completion of the activities of the Mission, and noting too in this regard the need to address outstanding issues, including those relating to minors,

Expressing its appreciation for the efforts of the Special Representative of the Secretary-General in Nepal and his team in the Mission, and the United Nations country team, including the Office of the United Nations High Commissioner for Human Rights, which is monitoring human rights at the request of the Government of Nepal, and stressing the need for coordination and complementarity of efforts between the Mission and all the United Nations actors in the Mission area,

1. *Decides*, following the request of the Government of Nepal and based on the recommendation of the Secretary-General, to renew the mandate of the United Nations Mission in Nepal, as set out in resolution 1740(2007), until 23 July 2008;
2. *Expresses its full support* for the Comprehensive Peace Agreement, and calls upon all parties to maintain momentum in the implementation of the Agreement, to continue constructive engagement with the United Nations, including reaching an early status-of-mission agreement, and to work together to progress to Constituent Assembly elections;
3. *Encourages* all parties to take full advantage of the expertise and readiness of the Mission, within its existing mandate, to support the peace process;
4. *Requests* the Secretary-General to keep the Security Council regularly informed of progress towards the implementation of the present resolution and, in particular, to review the activities of the Mission in the light of the elections scheduled for 10 April 2008, taking into account the views of the Government of Nepal and the developments on the ground;
5. *Requests* the parties in Nepal to take the necessary steps to promote the safety, security and freedom of movement of Mission and associated personnel in executing the tasks defined in the mandate;
6. *Decides* to remain seized of the matter.

Report of Secretary-General (May). By his report of 12 May [S/2008/313] on the peace process and UNMIN's activities since 3 January, the Secretary-General said that the twice-postponed election for a Constituent Assembly—the centrepiece of the political transition charted in the 12-point understanding of 22 November 2005 between the then Seven-Party Alliance and the Communist Party of Nepal (Maoist) (CPN(M)) and in the Comprehensive Peace Agreement of 21 November 2006—was held on 10 April in a generally orderly and peaceful atmosphere. More than 63 per cent of the 17.6 million eligible voters participated, with a high turnout of women and young people. The election was the most observed in Nepal's history, with more than 60,000 national and nearly 800 international observers deployed across the country; despite reservations, the major parties accepted the results. Final official results were announced on 8 May, and the 601-member Constituent Assembly would comprise people representing all of the major social groups, with a greatly increased proportion of women and younger members.

Nevertheless, significant challenges remained. First and foremost was the formation of a new Government. A second challenge was the building of sufficient agreement on how to fulfil the commitment in the interim Constitution that the republic be implemented at the first meeting of the Constituent Assembly, and interim arrangements made for the functions of Head of State during the drafting of the new Constitution. A third challenge was completion of the peace process, for although the 23-point agreement of the Seven-Party Alliance and CPN(M) provided the basis for moving forward to the election [YUN 2007, p. 386], many of its commitments and those of the Comprehensive Peace Agreement remained unfulfilled.

As at 24 April, 968 of the authorized 1,048 UNMIN personnel had been recruited. Of 795 civilian personnel on board, 233 (29.3 per cent) were female. UNMIN's efforts to recruit national staff from traditionally marginalized communities had yielded positive results: 46 per cent of staff (169 out of 367) was from those groups.

Report of Secretary-General (July). By his report of 10 July [S/2008/454], the Secretary-General said that the convening on 28 May of the Constituent Assembly was a milestone in the peace process. The Assembly was to draft a new Constitution within two years, and would act as the legislature during that transitional period. At its first session, the Assembly voted by 560 votes to 4 to end the 239-year-old monarchy and to implement a federal democratic republic. A constitutional amendment was also adopted creating the posts of President and Vice-President.

The former king, Gyanendra Shah, was afforded all the rights and responsibilities of any Nepali citizen and given 15 days to vacate the Narayanhiti Palace in central Kathmandu, which he did on 11 June. The republic was established peacefully amid public celebrations, apart from some minor incidents involving improvised explosive devices detonated at the venue of the Assembly and at other locations in Kathmandu, allegedly by Hindu fundamentalist groups, in the week when the Assembly's inaugural session was held.

Some impediments to forming a new Government were removed on 25 June when the Seven-Party Alliance signed an agreement providing for the time-bound resolution of key issues in the peace process. It required termination within 15 days of the paramilitary functioning and activities of the Maoist Young Communist League, which CPN(M) had indicated would fully comply with the laws of the land.

The Maoists were also required to return all seized property within the same time frame, after which legal action would be taken.

The negotiation of the agreement and the consequent amendments to the Interim Constitution had involved significant, difficult compromises among the three largest parties. The Nepali Congress had insisted that, as the second-largest party, it should be able to nominate its candidate to the presidency, and that it might otherwise remain in opposition.

At the following Assembly meeting, on 26 June, Prime Minister Girija Prasad Koirala announced his resignation and called on the Maoists to form a government. Nevertheless, newly elected members of the Assembly, in which 25 political parties were represented, had begun to question their relevancy, as the negotiations had been conducted principally among the three largest parties and other members of the Seven-Party Alliance.

Many of the commitments in the Comprehensive Peace Agreement, the 23-point agreement of 2007 and other agreements remained unfulfilled. Of particular concern was the fact that no progress had been made regarding the discharge from the Maoist cantonments of minors and others found ineligible by UNMIN. The Maoist leadership said that it remained committed to their discharge as soon as a new government was in office.

Following the completion of the election on 10 April, the number of UNMIN arms monitors declined. As at 30 June, there were 155 monitors remaining out of the authorized strength of 186. Overall UNMIN staffing stood at 802, out of the authorized 1,045 personnel. In preparation for the end of the UNMIN mandate on 23 July, an end-of-mission task force was established for transferring the residual tasks to the UN system in Nepal, and to assist national and international staff in applying for alternative employment.

Communication. On 22 July [S/2008/476], the Secretary-General transmitted to the Security Council a letter of 8 July from Nepal requesting a six-month extension of UNMIN's mandate from 23 July, the date of the expiration of its previous mandate.

Security Council consideration (July). Briefing the Security Council on 18 July [meeting 5938], the Special Representative, Mr. Martin, said that on 19 July the Constituent Assembly was scheduled to elect Nepal's first president and then name a prime minister, who would form a new government. Although the Secretary-General had not anticipated a further extension of UNMIN's mandate, the Council had before it a request based on a consensus among the main parties for such an extension.

The most contentious issue concerned the sharing of posts and power among the parties. The Maoists were acknowledged by the other parties as having the right, as the largest party in the Assembly, to name the prime minister. But both the Nepali Congress and the Communist Party of Nepal (Unified Marxist-Leninist (UML)) laid claim to the presidency, with the Nepali Congress stating that otherwise it would not participate in a new coalition government. The Maoists continued to appeal to all major parties to participate in a Maoist-led Government, but had not accepted the preferred presidential nominees of either the Nepali Congress or UML. Instead, they had nominated a Madhesi, who was not from any of the major parties.

Nepalis agreed that the peace process would not be complete while there were still two armies—a dangerous situation. All main political actors believed that a limited further UNMIN presence was necessary—a view that the Secretary-General supported.

SECURITY COUNCIL ACTION

On 23 July [meeting 5941], the Security Council unanimously adopted **resolution 1825(2008)**. The draft [S/2008/472] was submitted by the United Kingdom.

The Security Council,

Recalling its resolutions 1740(2007) of 23 January 2007 and 1796(2008) of 23 January 2008,

Reaffirming the sovereignty, territorial integrity and political independence of Nepal and its ownership of the implementation of the Comprehensive Peace Agreement and subsequent agreements,

Recalling the signing on 21 November 2006 by the Government of Nepal and the Communist Party of Nepal (Maoist) of the Comprehensive Peace Agreement, and the stated commitment of both parties to find a permanent and sustainable peace, and commending the steps taken to date to implement the Agreement,

Acknowledging the strong desire of the Nepalese people for peace and the restoration of democracy and the importance in this respect of the implementation of the Comprehensive Peace Agreement and subsequent agreements by the relevant parties,

Expressing its continued readiness to support the peace process in Nepal in the timely and effective implementation of the Comprehensive Peace Agreement and subsequent agreements, in particular the agreement of 25 June 2008, as requested by the Government of Nepal,

Welcoming the successful conclusion of the Constituent Assembly elections on 10 April 2008, and the progress made by the parties since the formation of the Assembly in working towards a democratic government, including the decision made at the first session of the Assembly to establish Nepal as a federal democratic republic,

Welcoming also the prospect of the formation of a democratically elected government and institutions in Nepal,

Echoing the call by the Secretary-General for all parties in Nepal to move forward swiftly in the implementation of the agreements reached, noting the assessment of the Secretary-General that the United Nations Mission in Nepal will be well placed to assist in the management of arms and armed personnel in accordance with the agreement of 25 June 2008 between the political parties, and recognizing the willingness of the Mission to assist the parties in this, as requested, in order to achieve a durable solution,

Welcoming the report of the Secretary-General of 10 July 2008 on the Mission, in accordance with his mandate,

Welcoming also the completion of the two phases of the verification process and continuing assistance with the management of arms and armed personnel of both sides in accordance with resolution 1740(2007) and in line with the provisions of the Comprehensive Peace Agreement, noting the importance of a durable long-term solution in helping to create the conditions for the completion of the activities of the Mission, and noting also in this regard the need to address outstanding issues, including the release of minors in cantonment sites and continued reporting on this issue as required under resolution 1612(2005) of 26 July 2005,

Noting with appreciation that, with the successful holding of the Constituent Assembly elections, some of the elements of the mandate relating to the Mission as set out in resolution 1740(2007) have already been accomplished,

Taking note of the letter dated 8 July 2008 from the Government of Nepal to the Secretary-General, in which it recognizes the contribution of the Mission and requests an extension of the Mission at a smaller scale to carry out the remainder of the mandate for six months,

Recognizing the need to pay special attention to the needs of women, children and traditionally marginalized groups in the peace process, as mentioned in the Comprehensive Peace Agreement and in resolution 1325(2000) of 31 October 2000,

Recognizing also that civil society can play an important role in democratic transition and conflict prevention,

Expressing its appreciation for the efforts of the Special Representative of the Secretary-General in Nepal and his team in the Mission, and the United Nations country team, including the Office of the United Nations High Commissioner for Human Rights, which is monitoring human rights at the request of the Government of Nepal, and stressing the need for coordination and complementarity of efforts between the Mission and all the United Nations actors in the Mission area, particularly in order to ensure continuity, as the mandate comes to an end,

1. *Decides*, in line with the request of the Government of Nepal and the recommendations of the Secretary-General, to renew the mandate of the United Nations Mission in Nepal, as established under resolution 1740(2007), until 23 January 2009, taking into account the completion of some elements of the mandate, and the ongoing work on the monitoring of the management of arms and armed personnel in line with the agreement of 25 June 2008 among the political parties, which will support the completion of the peace process;

2. *Calls upon* all parties to take full advantage of the expertise and readiness of the Mission, within its mandate, to support the peace process to facilitate the completion of outstanding aspects of the mandate of the Mission;

3. *Concurs* with the view of the Secretary-General that the current monitoring arrangements should not be necessary for a substantial further period, and expects to see them concluded within the period of this mandate;

4. *Endorses* the recommendations of the Secretary-General for a phased, gradual drawdown and withdrawal of Mission staff, including arms monitors;

5. *Requests* the Secretary-General to keep the Security Council informed of progress towards implementation of the present resolution and to submit a report on this and the implications for the Mission no later than 31 October 2008;

6. *Calls upon* the Government of Nepal to continue to take the necessary decisions to create conditions conducive to the completion of the activities of the Mission by the end of the current mandate, including through implementation of the agreement of 25 June 2008, in order to facilitate the withdrawal of the Mission from Nepal;

7. *Calls upon* all parties in Nepal to work together in a spirit of cooperation, consensus and compromise in order to continue the transition to a durable long-term solution to enable the country to move to a peaceful, democratic and more prosperous future;

8. *Requests* the parties in Nepal to take the necessary steps to promote the safety, security and freedom of movement of Mission and associated personnel in executing the tasks defined in the mandate;

9. *Decides* to remain seized of the matter.

Report of Secretary-General (October). In a 24 October report [S/2008/670], the Secretary-General said that developments had included the election by the Constituent Assembly of the first President, Vice-President and Prime Minister of the Federal Democratic Republic of Nepal, and the formation of a Council of Ministers, bringing to an end a period of political uncertainty. On the other hand, there had been little progress by the Constituent Assembly towards its main task of drafting a new Constitution. Despite some improvements, problems had persisted at the Maoist army cantonment sites, with combatants frequently complaining about the lack of Government support in meeting their food requirements, the availability of clean drinking water and the provision of adequate health facilities.

Continuing challenges at the local level included weak rule of law in the Tarai, where abductions and killings continued, and the distinction between politically motivated incidents by illegal armed groups and criminal actions was becoming increasingly blurred. Moreover, a series of strikes and other protests over a range of issues had caused disruption and economic loss.

As for UNMIN, its staffing level had been substantially reduced. As at 10 October, the staffing level was 283 out of the authorized 306 civilian personnel, together with 85 arms monitors out of the authorized strength of 90.

Security Council consideration (November). Briefing the Council on 7 November [meeting 6013], the Special Representative said that on 31 October and 1 November, the Secretary-General had paid a two-day visit to Nepal, where he had addressed the

Constituent Assembly, congratulating it on the country's historic transformation.

The new Government's three priorities were completing the peace process, drafting the new Constitution and achieving rapid economic progress, each of which faced major challenges. The extension of UNMIN's mandate in July related only to an aspect of the first challenge—dealing with the management of arms and armies.

Nepal said that UNMIN, among other things, was mandated to monitor the cantonments and assist in the peace process through arms management. If the process extended beyond the end of the Mission's mandate on 23 January 2009, the Government might request a six-month extension.

Report of Secretary-General. In a later report [S/2009/1], the Secretary-General reviewed the situation since 24 October. He said there had been slow progress on key issues relating to the peace process since the swearing-in of the CPN(M)-led coalition Government in August—particularly with respect to the special committee to supervise, integrate and rehabilitate the Maoist army personnel, which had yet to convene. On 28 October, just prior to the Secretary-General's visit to Nepal, the Government announced the formation of the special committee.

Noting that the Seven-Party Alliance agreement of 25 June provided that the committee would comprise members from "major parties"—whether or not they were represented in the Government—he said that the Government decision provided for one representative each from CPN(M), UML, the Madhesi People's Rights Forum and the Nepali Congress, with the UML Deputy Prime Minister and Home Minister acting as coordinator, and the CPN(M) Minister for Peace and Reconstruction as an additional ex officio member.

The formation of the special committee immediately met with controversy. The Nepali Congress objected that the terms of reference decided upon by the Government were at variance with the 25 June agreement. Other smaller opposition parties expressed disappointment at not being consulted. Negotiations among the largest parties subsequently appeared to resolve their differences regarding the terms of reference. However, the Nepali Congress also objected to the composition of the committee, calling for equal representation of parties, and no agreement had yet been reached on that point.

With respect to UNMIN, as at 1 December, 355 of the authorized 396 personnel were in the Mission.

Communication. By a 30 December letter to the Council [S/2008/837], the Secretary-General transmitted a 12 December letter from Nepal requesting a six-month extension of UNMIN's mandate, from 23 January 2009.

Children and armed conflict

By an 18 April report [S/2008/259] prepared pursuant to Council resolution 1612(2005) [YUN 2005, p. 863], the Secretary-General reviewed the situation of children and armed conflict in Nepal from 1 October 2006 to 31 December 2007. He said that while grave violations of children's rights had decreased significantly since the signing of the Comprehensive Peace Agreement in 2006, violations against children had not ceased.

Prior to the signing of the ceasefire agreement, substantial numbers of children had been recruited by CPN(M) and moved into cantonments. While no progress had been made in securing their formal discharge, many had been released informally. Meanwhile, social unrest in the Terai region had contributed to a pattern of protests and the emergence of political and armed groups, creating new risks for children. Those included not only recruitment, but also their increasing use by all major political parties in political demonstrations, strikes and blockades.

The Secretary-General recommended that CPN(M) agree to a concrete, time-bound action plan to implement its commitment to release children in its army, and end obstacles to the reintegration of informally released children. He also recommended that the Government clearly commit to reintegrating children associated with armed forces and armed groups, to criminalizing child recruitment, and to prosecuting violators of their rights. He called on armed groups in the Terai to end such violations, and on political parties to end the use of children in demonstrations, strikes and blockades.

Financing of UNMIN

In October [A/63/346/Add.3], the Secretary-General estimated UNMIN's resource requirements for 2009 at $6,932,600. In a report of 10 December [A/63/593], ACABQ said that those requirements covered operations through January 2009 and the planned liquidation of the Mission in the period from February to May 2009. It noted, however, from the Security Council's meeting on 7 November [meeting 6013], that UNMIN's presence might be required for another six months, with further adjustments. If the Council were to extend the Mission's mandate, the liquidation activities would be postponed accordingly.

On 24 December, the General Assembly, in **resolution 63/263** section XI (see p. 1548), approved the amount submitted by the Secretary-General as part of the $429,497,600 budget for the 27 special political missions authorized by the General Assembly and/or Security Council.

Myanmar

Statement by Secretary-General. On 11 February, the Secretary-General, in a statement [SG/SM/11409], said that the announcement by the Myanmar Government that it planned to hold a constitutional referendum in May and multiparty democratic elections by 2010 marked the first establishment of a time frame for implementing its political road map process. The Secretary-General called on the authorities to make the process inclusive, participatory and transparent in order to ensure that any draft Constitution was representative of the views of all the Myanmar people. It was important for the leadership to engage in a substantive dialogue with the General Secretary of the National League for Democracy (NLD), Daw Aung San Suu Kyi and other parties to the national reconciliation process. The United Nations remained ready to support that process. This latest development also made it essential that a visit to Myanmar by his Special Adviser be allowed to proceed.

Security Council consideration (March). On 18 March [meeting 5854], the Special Adviser, Ibrahim Gambari, briefed the Security Council on his visit to Myanmar (6–10 March). The authorities had granted most of the meetings he requested. Mr. Gambari met with various Government ministers, and met twice with Daw Aung San Suu Kyi. He also met with the political parties, including NLD, the National Unity Party and the PaO National Organization—which represented ethnic and nationality groups—as well as the Union Solidarity and Development Association. Regrettably, he had been unable to meet with the senior Government leadership or with other political parties, or with representatives of ethnic minority groups.

The visit provided an opportunity to exchange views on the preparations for the planned constitutional referendum in May and for multiparty democratic elections by 2010.

Mr. Gambari regarded the fact that he had been granted a second meeting with Daw Aung San Suu Kyi as an indication that the Government remained interested in maintaining that channel of communication. The Government had appointed a minister for liaison with Daw Aung San Suu Kyi who, on her part, had signalled her willingness to cooperate with the Government in the interest of the nation. She expected the United Nations, through its good offices mission, to help facilitate a substantive and time-bound dialogue to that end.

Meanwhile, the United Nations remained the only international actor maintaining face-to-face dialogue with Myanmar's leaders on the need for further efforts towards national reconciliation, democracy and human rights. It was also the only outsider with access to both the Government and Daw Aung San Suu Kyi and acting as a go-between between the two.

SECURITY COUNCIL ACTION

On 2 May [meeting 5885], following consultations among Security Council members, the President made statement **S/PRST/2008/13** on behalf of the Council:

The Security Council reaffirms the statement made by its President on 11 October 2007 and the statement made by its President to the press on 14 November 2007, and all the expectations expressed in those statements.

The Council takes note of the announcement by the Government of Myanmar of a referendum on a draft constitution in May 2008 and elections in 2010. It further notes the commitment by the Government to ensure that the referendum process will be free and fair. The Council underlines the need for the Government to establish the conditions and create an atmosphere conducive to an inclusive and credible process, including the full participation of all political actors and respect for fundamental political freedoms.

The Council reaffirms its unwavering support for the Secretary-General's good offices mission and expresses its appreciation for the work of his Special Adviser on Myanmar, Mr. Ibrahim Gambari. The Council encourages the Government of Myanmar and all parties concerned to cooperate fully with the United Nations.

The Council welcomes the important role that the countries of the Association of Southeast Asian Nations continue to play in supporting the United Nations good offices mission.

The Council affirms its commitment to the sovereignty and territorial integrity of Myanmar and, in that context, reiterates that the future of Myanmar lies in the hands of all of its people.

The Council remains seized of the matter.

Communication. A 2 May letter [S/2008/289] from Myanmar to the Council President stated that pressure exerted by members of the Security Council on other members had resulted in the issuance of the presidential statement of the same day. Myanmar not being a threat to international or regional peace and security, the statement delved into domestic matters, and that appeared highly objectionable.

Cyclone Nargis. In a statement of 4 May [SG/SM/11545], the Secretary-General expressed his sadness by the loss of life and the destruction suffered by the people of Myanmar after Cyclone Nargis struck the country on 2 May. As a first step, a UN Disaster Assessment and Coordination had been organized and was on stand-by to assist the Government in responding to humanitarian needs. The United Nations was prepared to extend other assistance and to mobilize international aid in support of the Government.

On 7 May [SG/SM/11552], the Secretary-General expressed his concern about the continuing tragedy in Myanmar, where the Government had confirmed that over 22,000 people had died and more than 41,000 people were missing following the impact of the cyclone on 2–3 May. He urged the Government to respond to the outpouring of international support and solidarity by facilitating the arrival of aid workers and the clearance of relief supplies in every way possible.

On 8 May [SG/SM/11556], the Secretary-General took note of the Government's decision to proceed with the constitutional referendum on 10 May, while postponing it in some of the areas most affected by the cyclone. Due to the scope of the disaster, he believed that it might be prudent to focus instead on mobilizing all available resources and capacity for the emergency response efforts.

By a joint statement of 19 May [SG/2138-IHA/1260], the Secretary-General and the Chair of the Association of South-East Asian Nations (ASEAN), citing the devastating impact of Cyclone Nargis, announced the convening of an ASEAN-United Nations International Pledging Conference, to be held on 25 May in Yangon, Myanmar.

On 23 May [SG/T/2605], the Secretary-General met with the Head of State, Senior General Than Shwe. Following the meeting, he said that the Senior General had agreed to allow international aid workers into the affected areas, regardless of nationality.

Addressing the Pledging Conference on 25 May [SG/SM/11597], the Secretary-General said that he had visited Myanmar's Irrawaddy Delta a few days earlier. The Government had put in place a functioning relief programme, but much more needed to be done. Experienced international relief workers should have unhindered access to the areas hardest hit, and extra helicopters and boats were urgently required. The Secretary-General's discussions with Myanmar's leadership had been encouraging: they agreed on the need to act urgently, and any hesitation the Government might have had about allowing international humanitarian groups to operate freely in the affected areas had passed. The United Nations Flash Appeal sought $201 million to assist roughly 1.5 million survivors for the next three months; contributions amounting to some 20 per cent of that amount had been received, with a further 20 per cent pledged.

Statements by Secretary-General. By a statement of 27 May [SG/SM/11598], the Secretary-General regretted the Government's decision to extend for a sixth consecutive year the detention under house arrest of Daw Aung San Suu Kyi. The sooner restrictions on her and other political figures were lifted, the sooner Myanmar would be able to move towards inclusive national reconciliation, the restoration of democracy and full respect for human rights.

On 23 July [SG/SM/11716], the Secretary-General said that on that day he had convened a meeting of the Group of Friends of the Secretary-General on Myanmar (Australia, China, the EU, France, India, Indonesia, Japan, Norway, Russian Federation, Singapore, Republic of Korea, Thailand, United Kingdom, United States, Viet Nam) to discuss the upcoming visit of his Special Adviser to the country. The Group expressed its expectation that Mr. Gambari's next visit would yield tangible progress on the issues of concern to the international community, particularly on the resumption of dialogue between Daw Aung San Suu Kyi and the Government, the credibility of the electoral process and the regularization of engagement with the good offices of the Secretary-General.

On 24 September [SG/SM/11810], the Secretary-General welcomed the release by the Government on 23 September of several political prisoners as part of an amnesty procedure, including Myanmar's longest-serving political prisoner, U Win Tin, and six other senior NLD members. The release of political prisoners had been one focus of discussion between the Special Adviser and the Government during his latest visit to Myanmar (18–23 August). The Secretary-General reiterated that all political prisoners should be released and that all Myanmar citizens should be able to enjoy political freedoms—necessary steps towards the process of national reconciliation and dialogue.

On 27 September [SG/SM/11835], the Secretary-General chaired the first high-level meeting of the Group of Friends—the sixth meeting of the Group since it was established in December 2007. While noting the recent actions taken by the Government, the Group encouraged it to work more closely with the UN good offices to address key issues of international concern, especially the release of political prisoners and the initiation of an all-inclusive dialogue with the opposition. The Group encouraged all parties to seize the opportunity of the UN good offices, while stressing the Government's responsibility to demonstrate its commitment through further tangible results.

On 12 November [SG/SM/11922], the Secretary-General expressed his concern at the reports of sentences and severe prison terms imposed in connection with the 2007 peaceful demonstrations [YUN 2007, p. 383]. He called for all political prisoners to be released and for all citizens to be allowed to freely participate in their country's political future as part of an inclusive national reconciliation process.

General Assembly action (December). On 24 December, the General Assembly adopted **resolution 63/245** (see p. 886), by which it called on the Government to release political prisoners; to resume a dialogue with all political actors, including NLD and representatives of ethnic nationalities; to pursue, through dialogue and peaceful means, the suspension and end of conflict with all ethnic nationalities; and to allow the full participation of representatives of all political parties and representatives of ethnic nationalities in a process of national reconciliation, democratization and the establishment of the rule of law.

Children and armed conflict

On 25 July [S/AC.51/2008/9], in a statement addressed to the non-State armed groups in Myanmar, the Chairman of the Security Council Working Group on Children and Armed Conflict urged the leaders of the United Wa State Army, the Karen National Union/Karen National Liberation Army (KNU-KNLA), the Karenni National Progressive Party, the Kachin Independence Organization, the Karenni National People's Liberation Front, the Democratic Karen Buddhist Army, the Shan State Army-South, the Myanmar National Democratic Alliance Army and the KNU-KNLA Peace Council to end the recruitment and use of child soldiers; to allow and facilitate unhindered access to the UN country task force on monitoring and reporting established pursuant to Security Council resolution 1612 (2005) [YUN 2005, p. 863]; to release the children associated with their forces and facilitate their follow-up by UNICEF, with a view to their reintegration; and to enter into dialogue with the UN country task force on monitoring and reporting to devise a time-bound action plan.

Other matters

Cambodia–Thailand border dispute

Communications. During 2008, the Security Council was kept informed of developments in a border dispute between Cambodia and Thailand, through a series of letters from those countries to the Council President.

On 18 July [S/2008/470], Cambodia described what it called Thailand's violation of its sovereignty and territorial integrity. It noted that the Temple of Preah Vihear in Cambodia was inscribed into the World Heritage List on 7 July by UNESCO's World Heritage Committee. On 15 July, some 50 Thai soldiers crossed into Keo Sikha Kiri Svara pagoda, located inside Cambodian territory, about 300 metres from the Temple. By 16 and 17 July, the number of Thai soldiers on the grounds of the pagoda had increased to 480. According to Cambodia, the Thai side used its unilaterally designed map to indicate that the pagoda was in a so-called "overlapping area." In adjudicating the conflict between Cambodia and Thailand over the Temple in 1962 [YUN 1962, p. 467], however, the International Court of Justice (ICJ) had pronounced in favour of the map that situated Preah Vihear in Cambodian territory, stating that both parties, by their conduct, had recognized the line and thereby in effect agreed to regard it as being the frontier line. Cambodia concluded that it could not ignore that the Thai military provocation was aimed at creating a de facto "overlapping area" that legally did not exist on Cambodian soil. On 19 July, Cambodia addressed a similar letter [A/62/917] to the President of the General Assembly.

On 21 July [S/2008/474], Thailand replied that the area adjacent to the Temple of Preah Vihear, where the pagoda was situated, was part of Thailand's territory, and that Thailand's position was fully consistent with the 1962 ICJ judgment. Cambodia's territorial claim was based on its unilateral understanding of that judgement.

Also on 21 July [S/2008/475], Cambodia stated that subsequent negotiations with Thailand had been inconclusive and that Thailand, in the meantime, had built up its military presence with artillery and tanks along the border. Cambodia asked for the convening of an urgent meeting of the Security Council, describing the issue as a grave threat to peace and security in the region.

Statement by Secretary-General. On 21 July [SG/SM/11710], the Secretary-General called for restraint on both sides and expressed his hope that the matter could be resolved peacefully and by diplomatic means in the context of the traditionally excellent relations between the two countries.

Communications. On 22 July [S/2008/478], Thailand, commenting on Cambodia's request for an urgent Security Council meeting, said that the matter could be resolved amicably. The first step had already been taken on 21 July in Thailand's Sa Kaeo Province under the General Border Committee, headed by high-level representatives from both countries.

On 25 July [S/2008/490], following up on that letter, Thailand said that bilateral consultations between the two countries' Foreign Ministers would take place on 28 July in Cambodia. Within that context, it welcomed the Security Council's decision to postpone consideration of Cambodia's request for an urgent meeting.

Foreign Ministers meetings. On 28 July, Cambodia [S/2008/498] and Thailand [S/2008/494] informed the Security Council that their Foreign Ministers, meeting on 28 July, had agreed on a common recommendation to their Governments, calling on both countries to exercise the utmost restraint so that the problem could be settled through peaceful means, using bilateral mechanisms. They also outlined their agreement on provisional arrangements pending survey and demarcation by a joint boundary commission. Thailand also sent an account of the meeting to the General Assembly President on 30 July [A/62/919].

On 19 August, Thailand [S/2008/565], and on 20 August, Cambodia [S/2008/569], provided accounts of a second meeting of their Foreign Ministers (Cha-Am, Thailand, 18–19 August). Both sides welcomed the first-phase redeployment of their respective troops out of the pagoda, the area surrounding the pagoda and the Temple; agreed to hold a second meeting in Cambodia on 29 August to discuss the second phase of troop redeployment; and agreed that the next meeting of the Joint Commission on Demarcation for Land Boundary be convened in early October. Both sides agreed to consider the issue of the Ta Muen/Tamone Temples (also located in the border area) at the next Foreign Ministers' meeting.

Communications. On 15 September [S/2008/606], Cambodia forwarded a letter dated 14 August from its Deputy Foreign Minister to Thailand's Foreign Minister, stating that, on 26 July, the Thai armed forces had moved troops into the Tamone Temple Complex and begun to occupy the temples by constructing a fence and other structures, in violation of Cambodia's sovereignty and territorial integrity and of international law. Thailand should immediately remove the fence and other structures in the area, withdraw its troops, pull down the military camp from the Tamone Thom Temple, and restore the Tamone Temple complex and nearby area to their condition prior to the Thai occupation.

In response, Thailand, on 19 September [S/2008/611], forwarded a letter dated 18 August from its Foreign Minister to Cambodia's Foreign Minister asserting Thailand's ownership of the Prasat Ta Muen Temple complex. It also contained an aide-memoire of 16 September from the Foreign Ministry to the Cambodian Government protesting Cambodia's violation of Thailand's sovereignty over the Temple of Ta Kwai, an archeological site in Thailand.

Statement by Secretary-General. On 15 October [SG/SM/11865], the Secretary-General expressed concern about the exchange of gunfire on that day along the Cambodia–Thailand border and the reported casualties. He called on both parties to exercise utmost restraint and urged them to expedite bilateral talks so that their differences could be resolved peacefully.

Communications. Also on 15 October [S/2008/653], Cambodia stated that Thai troops crossed into Cambodian territory at three locations in the area of the Temple of Preah Vihear and fired on Cambodian soldiers stationed there. Those locations were the Keo Sikha Kiri Svara Pagoda (approximately 300 metres from the Temple of Preah Vihear and 700 metres from the border), Veal Intry (approximately 1,120 metres from the border) and Phnom Trap (approximately 1,600 metres from the border).

In response, Thailand, on 16 October [S/2008/657], said that on the previous day, while conducting a routine patrol near the area called Phu Ma Khua in Thai territory, Thai soldiers came under attack by Cambodian soldiers using rocket-propelled grenades and submachine guns. At the same time, around the area near Pha Mor I Dang in Thai territory, another group of Cambodian soldiers opened fire, using recoilless guns, rocket-propelled grenades, mortars and rifles, on Thai soldiers—acts which Thailand considered a serious violation of its sovereignty and territorial integrity.

On 17 October [S/2008/660], Cambodia informed the Security Council that unilateral demining activity by Thai soldiers in Cambodia's territory in the area adjacent to the Temple of Preah Vihear contravened the agreements made by both sides. That letter was also sent to the General Assembly [A/63/495].

Also on 17 October [S/2008/661], referring to that letter, Thailand said that the urgency of demining in the area adjacent to the Temple of Phra Viharn came after two Thai rangers, who were on routine patrol inside Thailand's territory on 6 October, stepped on landmines and lost their legs. Thailand was alarmed by the incident because Thai rangers had been using this patrol route for a long time without any incident, since that route was known to have been cleared of landmines. The NGO Thai Mine Action Centre found a number of newly planted mines in a nearby area. The landmines were of a type known to be in the possession of Cambodian authorities. Despite that incident, Thailand had chosen the path of dialogue, transparency and goodwill in solving the problem.

Cambodia

Statement by Secretary-General. On 15 April [SG/SM/11514], on the tenth anniversary of the death of the Khmer Rouge leader Pol Pot, the Secretary-General reminded the international community of the importance of bringing to closure one of history's darkest chapters. The United Nations and the Government of Cambodia remained engaged in efforts to hold the Khmer Rouge senior leaders and those most responsible accountable for their horrific crimes. The Secretary-General expressed his hope that, with the support of the international community, the Extraordinary Chambers in the Courts of Cambodia would soon deliver justice for the Cambodian people.

India–Pakistan

The UN Military Observer Group in India and Pakistan (UNMOGIP) continued in 2008 to monitor the situation in Jammu and Kashmir. By a letter of 16 October [S/2008/663], the Secretary-General conveyed to the Security Council his intention to appoint Major General Kim Moon Hwa (Republic of Korea) as Chief Military Observer of UNMOGIP, replacing

Major General Dragutin Repinc (Croatia), who had relinquished his post on 28 December 2007. By a reply of 20 October [S/2008/664], the Council took note of that intention.

Statement by OHCHR. On 27 August, the Office of the High Commissioner for Human Rights (OHCHR) expressed concern about the violent protests in Indian-administered Kashmir that reportedly led to civilian casualties as well as restrictions on the right to freedom of assembly and expression. The Office called on the Indian authorities—and in particular the security forces—to respect the right to freedom of assembly and expression and comply with international human rights principles in controlling the demonstrators. The Office called for a thorough and independent investigation into all killings, and called on the demonstrators to protest using peaceful means only.

Mongolia

Statement by Secretary-General. On 2 July [SG/SM/11673], the Secretary-General expressed concern at the violence resulting from the demonstrations in Mongolia and regretted the consequent loss of life. He deplored the resort to violence to protest the conduct of the parliamentary elections on 29 June. He urged all parties to exercise restraint and engage in dialogue, and appealed to all demonstrators to refrain from any further acts of violence. Mongolia had made a peaceful transition to democracy, and all parties should respect that achievement and find ways to settle the crisis.

Also on 2 July [A/62/894], Mongolia transmitted to the Secretary-General a presidential decree of 1 July and a recommendation of 2 July of Mongolia's National Security Council on the state of emergency declared in the capital, Ulaanbaatar. The President of Mongolia, Nambaryn Enkhbayar, drew attention to the property destruction, fire-setting, threats against law-enforcement officers and disorder caused by violent actions of a group of persons in Ulaanbaatar's Sukhbaatar District on 1 July. To normalize social life, a four-day state of emergency had been declared in Ulaanbaatar. The National Security Council called on political parties to refrain from inciting the population to carry out illegal actions and to refrain from disturbing the social order. It also called on the media to report accurately and to refrain from distributing information that justified or encouraged illegal acts.

Statement by OHCHR. On 3 July, OHCHR expressed concerns about developments in Mongolia. There had been reports of at least five deaths, numerous injuries and around 700 protestors detained. The Office called upon the authorities to exercise utmost restraint, to ensure that due process was followed in the case of any detentions, and to properly investigate the incidents leading to deaths and injuries.

The Philippines

Children and armed conflict

In April, pursuant to Security Council resolution 1612(2005) [YUN 2005, p. 863], the Secretary-General submitted a report [S/2008/272] on children and armed conflict in the Philippines. The report, which covered the period from 1 July 2005 to 30 November 2007, focused on grave violations perpetrated against children in the country, including the recruitment and use of children, killing and maiming of children, sexual violence against children, attacks on schools and hospitals, denial of humanitarian access and abductions of children. The report identified parties to the conflict, both State and non-State actors, who committed grave abuses against children, including Government security forces, the Moro Islamic Liberation Front, the New People's Army and the Abu Sayyaf Group/Jemaah Islamiya.

Acknowledging the challenges in addressing such violations, the report recommended that State and non-State actors enter into dialogue with the United Nations for preparing action plans to end the recruitment and use of children by armed forces and groups, as well as other violations of children's rights. All parties to the conflict should facilitate access to their areas of operation and ensure the safety of staff carrying out monitoring and reporting. The Government should investigate and prosecute those responsible for grave violations against children.

Tajikistan

UN Regional Centre for Preventive Diplomacy

Communication. On 28 April [S/2008/285], the Secretary-General informed the Security Council President of his intention to appoint Miroslav Jenča (Slovakia) as his Special Representative and Head of the United Nations Regional Centre for Preventive Diplomacy for Central Asia in Ashgabat, Turkmenistan [YUN 2007, p. 387]. On 30 April [S/2008/286], the Council took note of that intention.

Security Council statement. By a press statement of 10 December [SC/9528], Security Council members welcomed the engagement by the Centre with the Governments of the region and regional organizations on issues of preventive diplomacy, in accordance with its mandate.

United Arab Emirates–Iran

Greater Tunb, Lesser Tunb and Abu Musa

On 21 January [S/2008/33], the United Arab Emirates requested that the Security Council retain on its agenda for 2008 the item entitled "Letter dated 3 December 1971 from the Permanent Representatives of Algeria, Iraq, the Libyan Arab Republic and the People's Democratic Republic of Yemen to the United Nations addressed to the President of the Security Council" [YUN 1971, p. 209] concerning Iran's occupation of "the Greater Tunb, the Lesser Tunb and Abu Musa, three islands belonging to the United Arab Emirates", until such time as the dispute was resolved by peaceful means through direct negotiations or through the International Court of Justice.

The League of Arab States (LAS), in communications transmitted on 10 March [S/2008/179], 19 May [S/2008/344] and 17 September [S/2008/609], informed the Security Council of the adoption of three resolutions denouncing the Iranian Government's consolidation of its occupation of the three islands, and affirming the sovereignty of the United Arab Emirates over them. The League also resolved to inform the Secretary-General and the Security Council of the importance that the Council remain seized of the issue until Iran ended its occupation of the islands and the United Arab Emirates regained its full sovereignty over them.

In a 31 March letter [S/2008/220] referring to the LAS letters, Iran said that the islands were an integral and eternal part of the Iranian territory and rejected any claims to the contrary. By a letter of 21 August [S/2008/577], the United Arab Emirates protested Iran's establishment of a maritime rescue office and an office for registering ships and sailors on Abu Musa as a blatant violation of the Memorandum of Understanding concluded in November 1971 concerning the island. By a letter of 3 September [S/2008/593], Iran said that those actions had been in accordance with its sovereign rights and with the ongoing arrangements emanating from the documents exchanged in 1971.

Regional meetings

On 30 May [A/62/853-S/2008/358], the Russian Federation transmitted a joint communiqué by the Foreign Ministers of China, India and Russia on the outcome of their meeting in Yekaterinburg, Russia, on 14 and 15 May. With respect to the Asia-Pacific region, it included comments on expanding cooperation with Central Asian countries, as well as on the situation in Afghanistan, the Iranian nuclear programme and the six-party talks for resolving the nuclear problem in the Korean Peninsula.

Chapter V

Europe and the Mediterranean

The restoration of peace and stability in the post-conflict countries of the European and Mediterranean region advanced in 2008, as efforts to re-establish their institutions and social and economic infrastructure continued. However, a number of issues remained unresolved, and in some countries the peace process was seriously challenged.

The international community, led by the European Union (EU), continued to assist Bosnia and Herzegovina in moving towards full integration into Europe through the EU Stabilization and Association Process. The country in June signed the Stabilization and Association Agreement with the EU and was provided with a road map for visa liberalization. Nevertheless, nationalist rhetoric prevailed in the political scene as a result of a municipal election campaign and other developments in the region.

The United Nations Interim Administration Mission in Kosovo continued to assist in building a modern, multiethnic society. In February, Kosovo declared independence, an act followed by boycotts by Kosovo Serbs and protests in many areas in Kosovo and Serbia. In light of developments, the United Nations Mission in June launched a reconfiguration process. In October, acting on a Serbian proposal, the General Assembly requested the International Court of Justice for an advisory opinion on whether Kosovo's unilateral declaration of independence was in accordance with international law.

Renewed efforts to end the stalemate in the Georgian-Abkhaz peace process were threatened in August by the war in South Ossetia and by the Georgian-Russian conflict. The recognition of Abkhazia and South Ossetia by the Russian Federation further increased tensions. Georgia withdrew from the 1994 Agreement on a Ceasefire and Separation of Forces (Moscow Agreement), and the Collective Peacekeeping Force of the Commonwealth of Independent States was officially terminated, substantially changing the context in which the United Nations Observer Mission in Georgia operated.

No progress was made towards settling the conflict between Armenia and Azerbaijan over the occupied Nagorny Karabakh region in Azerbaijan. In March, acting on a proposal by Azerbaijan, the General Assembly called for the withdrawal of Armenian forces from Azerbaijan.

The situation in Cyprus appeared to improve, and UN efforts focused on assisting the two sides in implementing the 8 July 2006 Agreement. Full-fledged negotiations between the Greek Cypriot and Turkish Cypriot sides were launched in September under UN auspices. The United Nations Peacekeeping Force in Cyprus continued to cooperate with the two communities, facilitating projects benefiting Greek and Turkish Cypriots in the buffer zone and advancing the goal of restoring normal conditions and humanitarian functions on the island.

Bosnia and Herzegovina

During 2008, the European Union (EU) continued to lead the international community's efforts in assisting the two entities comprising the Republic of Bosnia and Herzegovina—the Federation of Bosnia and Herzegovina (where mainly Bosnian Muslims (Bosniacs) and Bosnian Croats resided) and the Republika Srpska (where mostly Bosnian Serbs resided)—in implementing the 1995 General Framework Agreement for Peace in Bosnia and Herzegovina and the annexes thereto (the Peace Agreement) [YUN 1995, pp. 544 & 551]. The Office of the High Representative for the Implementation of the Peace Agreement on Bosnia and Herzegovina (OHR) was responsible for the Agreement's civilian aspects [YUN 1996, p. 293], while the European Union Police Mission in Bosnia and Herzegovina (EUPM) was responsible for helping develop sustainable policing arrangements. The EU Force (EUFOR) mission was responsible for the Agreement's military aspects, which were transferred to it by the North Atlantic Treaty Organization (NATO) in 2004 [YUN 2004, p. 401]. The Peace Implementation Council (PIC) and its Steering Board continued to monitor and facilitate the Agreement's implementation.

The High Representative reported on progress made in the Agreement's implementation and related political developments during the year in the context of his mission implementation plan, which set out a number of core tasks to be accomplished [YUN 2003, p. 401]. Bosnia and Herzegovina made progress on its European integration path when two police reform laws were adopted in April, opening the way for the signature of the Stabilization and Association Agreement in June. In addition, the European Commission released a road map for visa liberalization. Several processes dominated the political landscape, such as the run-up to the municipal elections held in October and the transition from OHR to a reinforced EU engagement. In November, leaders of three political parties signed the Prud Agreement addressing key issues in the country. The police services improved their capacity to maintain public peace and order, including in complex situations such as the commemoration ceremonies in Srebrenica and eastern Bosnia and the aftermath of the arrest of Radovan Karadžić, a fugitive from the International Criminal Tribunal for the former Yugoslavia (ICTY).

In November, the Security Council extended by one year the mandate of EUFOR. The Council welcomed the decision of NATO to continue to maintain the headquarters in Bosnia and Herzegovina so that it could work with EUFOR to help implement the 1995 Peace Agreement. In addition, the Council reiterated that the primary responsibility for implementing the Peace Agreement lay with the authorities in Bosnia and Herzegovina, and underlined the need for their full cooperation with ICTY and for strengthening joint institutions.

Implementation of Peace Agreement

Civilian aspects

The civilian aspects of the 1995 Peace Agreement entailed a broad range of activities, including the provision of humanitarian aid and resources for infrastructure rehabilitation, the establishment of political and constitutional institutions, the promotion of respect for human rights and the holding of free and fair elections. The High Representative, who chaired the PIC Steering Board and other key implementation bodies, was the final authority with regard to implementing the civilian aspects of the Peace Agreement [YUN 1995, p. 547]. The reports on EUPM activities were submitted by the High Representative to the Security Council through the Secretary-General.

Office of High Representative

Reports of High Representative. The High Representative, Miroslav Lajčák (Slovakia), reported to the Security Council, through the Secretary-General, on the peace implementation process for the periods 1 October 2007 to 31 March 2008 [S/2008/300], 1 April to 31 October 2008 [S/2008/705], and 1 November to 30 April 2009.

The Council considered the High Representative's reports on 19 May and 5 December.

On 20 November, the Council adopted resolution 1845(2008) (see p. 431), authorizing the extension of EUFOR until 20 November 2009.

In 2008, the PIC Steering Board determined that OHR should remain in place until the authorities fulfilled five objectives and two general conditions.

Mission implementation plan

The High Representative, briefing the Security Council on 19 May [meeting 5894] when it considered his report covering the latter half of 2007 [YUN 2007, p. 390] and the first quarter of 2008, said that the situation had improved considerably as Bosnia and Herzegovina had taken a significant step towards stabilizing the political situation by adopting two police reform laws. The country was on the verge of signing a Stabilization and Association Agreement with the EU and moving towards membership in NATO. The PIC Steering Board in February had reached a consensus on a set of five objectives and two conditions, the fulfilment of which would end the High Representative's tenure and trigger a transition to an EU Special Representative.

However, following Kosovo's unilateral declaration of independence in February (see p. 436), the leadership of the Republika Srpska had linked its future status with that of Kosovo. The entity's ruling Alliance of Independent Social Democrats (SNSD) had called for the transformation of Bosnia and Herzegovina into an asymmetric federation or confederation, claiming the right to self-determination for the Republika Srpska. The High Representative had responded by stressing that Bosnia and Herzegovina was an internationally recognized State whose sovereignty and territorial integrity were guaranteed by the Dayton Peace Agreement [YUN 1995, p. 544 & 551] and from which there was no right to secede.

During the year, Bosnia and Herzegovina made important progress on the reforms required for it to integrate into Euro-Atlantic institutions. An agreement in March among the State and entity governments on moveable defence property resulted in securing intensified dialogue towards a membership action plan at the NATO summit in Bucharest in April. Two long-awaited police reform laws were adopted in April and came into force on 14 May, opening the way for signing a Stabilization and Association Agreement and an Interim Agreement with the EU on 16 June. As part of an overall programme for Western Balkan countries, the European Commission provided Bosnia and Herzegovina with a road map for visa liberalization that contained requirements in the fields of document security, illegal migration, public order and security, and external relations.

The conjunction of continuing domestic political stalemate with mounting regional uncertainty in the run-up to and immediate aftermath of Kosovo's declaration of independence made it impossible for the PIC Steering Board to confirm the closure of OHR in June. At a meeting of 26–27 February, the Steering Board determined that the Office should remain in place and continue to carry out its mandate under the Dayton Peace Agreement until such time as the domestic authorities fulfilled five objectives (resolution of State property, resolution of defence property, completion of the Brcko Final Award, fiscal sustainability, entrenchment of the rule of law) and two general conditions (signing of the Stabilization and Association Agreement and a positive assessment of the situation by the Steering Board). The Steering Board recognized the progress made by the authorities in delivering the objectives and conditions at its meetings of 24–25 June and 19–20 November. However, concerns remained regarding the prevailing political situation, including challenges to the country's sovereignty, territorial integrity and constitutional order.

The arrest of ICTY fugitive Radovan Karadžić in July resulted in a worsening political climate following statements and actions of both Serb and Bosniak political leaders, although reactions to the arrest did not affect the security situation.

On 8 November, the leader of SNSD, Milorad Dodik, that of the Party of Democratic Action (SDA), Sulejman Tihić, and that of the Croatian Democratic Union of Bosnia and Herzegovina (HDZ BiH), Dragan Čović, signed the Prud Agreement, which addressed constitutional reform; resolution of the State property objective for the transition from OHR to the EU Special Representative; implementation of annex 7 of the Dayton Peace Agreement in connection with the organizing of a census; a constitutional solution for Brčko's access to the Bosnia and Herzegovina Constitutional Court; and Bosnia and Herzegovina Fiscal Council and budget issues. The agreement reflected an apparent willingness to make progress on important political issues.

Briefing the Council on 5 December [meeting 6033], the High Representative cautioned that negative and nationalist rhetoric threatened to dampen fresh momentum in Bosnia and Herzegovina's journey towards the EU, just months after its milestone signing of the Stabilization and Association Agreement. Despite signs of progress, notably an 8 November agreement among three major Bosnian parties on key issues, nationalist and ethnic agendas prevailed over the Euro-Atlantic agenda. Hence, the 16 June signing of the Agreement, progress towards visa liberalization with the EU and a decision by NATO to begin membership dialogue had not delivered the change in approach needed. Challenges had come from all sides. The negative political climate hindered progress on delivering the five objectives and two conditions set out by PIC to allow for the closure of OHR and transition to a stronger EU engagement. Stressing the need for continued international attention to Bosnia and Herzegovina, the High Representative said that it would be important to recognize the recent, more positive atmosphere and build on the emerging readiness to compromise.

Civil affairs

The High Representative, in his November report [S/2008/705], noted that the October municipal election campaign had provided for a further hardening of positions on all sides and that nationalist rhetoric continued to dominate politics at all levels. The Republika Srpska National Assembly on 21 February adopted a resolution condemning Kosovo's unilateral declaration of independence and demanding that Bosnia and Herzegovina not recognize it. It went on to state that the Republika Srpska "would consider that it too possessed the right to establish its future legal status by means of a referendum". The High Representative reacted immediately and stressed that entities of Bosnia and Herzegovina had no right to secede.

In that political environment, the six parties in the coalition at the State level met on 23 August and were unable to make any headway on the reform agenda. A Serbian Democratic Party initiative on an ethnically based census was defeated in the House of Peoples of Bosnia and Herzegovina on 27 October. In September, President Haris Silajdžić gave speeches to the UN General Assembly and to the Parliamentary Assembly of the Council of Europe—which had not been cleared with the other two members of the Bosnia and Herzegovina Presidency—which caused controversy in the Republika Srpska, as they emphasized the genocide committed in Srebrenica in 1995 [YUN 1995, p. 530].

Despite the negative political atmosphere, amendments to the Election Law of Bosnia and Herzegovina were adopted in May, which allowed all who were residents in Srebrenica in 1991 to have the option of casting votes in its 2008 municipal elections only, irrespective of their displaced person status.

Little progress was made towards reaching an agreement on immovable defence property that would continue to serve defence purposes. To invigorate the process, the NATO Headquarters in Sarajevo in July developed a concept paper outlining the key issues that should be regulated by a transfer agreement on immovable property. Overall, Bosnia and Herzegovina worked hard to achieve progress within the NATO Partnership for Peace Programme. However, the lack of staff capacity in ministries had begun to impose friction on the country's hitherto rapid progress through the various stages of the Programme.

Successful implementation of the Mostar Statute hinged on a delicate balance of power between the main national parties, SDA and HDZ Bosnia and Herzegovina. The issue of financing the Croat-dominated Herzegovina Radio-Television, which the city of Mostar wrote off its own books in 2007, and the appointment of a Bosniak candidate as Police Commissioner were resolved. A Police Commissioner was appointed immediately after the local elections on 9 October, and on 29 October the Federation government passed a decision allocating €150,000 (€75,000 each) to Hercegovačka Radio-Television and Radio Herceg Bosna. While developments within the Brčko District, with the exception of implementation of the 2008 elections results, were nearing the point where closure of Supervision was possible, a key issue remained unresolved. The provision of guarantees for the status of the District after Supervision through modest additions to the Constitution of Bosnia and Herzegovina reached a stalemate when the Party for Bosnia and Herzegovina, SNSD, the Party of Democratic Progress and HDZ 1990 decided to support a law to the exclusion of the constitutional additions required by the Supervisor.

The combined efforts of OHR, NATO, EUFOR, ICTY, the Bosnia and Herzegovina Intelligence and Security Agency and the Republika Srpska police, all of which contributed to locating fugitives Stojan Župlijanin and Radovan Karadžić, were critically facilitated by the various sanctions of OHR, the EU and the United States, as well as the sanctions of Bosnia and Herzegovina against members of the Persons Indicted for War Crimes support network. ICTY fugitives Goran Hadžić and Ratko Mladić remained a priority for OHR.

Judicial reform

The main development in 2008 was the decision in February of the PIC Steering Board's Political Directors to single out "entrenchment of the rule of law" as one of the objectives to be delivered before the transition from OHR to the EU Special Representative could be effected. PIC underscored the need to demonstrate this entrenchment through the adoption of a national war crimes strategy, the law on aliens and asylum, and a national justice sector reform strategy. Progress on that objective was achieved despite attempts by political leaders elsewhere to undermine the independence of the judiciary and the mandate of State law-enforcement agencies. Positive outcomes were achieved with the adoption of the Law on Stay and Movement of Aliens and Asylum in April and of the National Justice Sector Reform Strategy in June, which addressed the key elements of a functional justice sector. The National War Crimes Strategy was adopted on 29 December and the implementation action plans of the National Justice Sector Reform Strategy were endorsed in December. The Strategy set criteria for distributing cases between the Bosnia and Herzegovina and entity judiciaries; reflected work done on cataloguing crime events; recognized the need for resources and legislative amendments; stressed the importance of regional cooperation in war crimes investigations; and called upon the authorities to improve that cooperation.

Economic reforms

The Bosnia and Herzegovina Fiscal Council—aimed at facilitating better coordination between the State and the entities on fiscal policies—was established on 23 July, and held its first meeting on 11 September. A major step towards creating a single pharmaceutical market was taken in June with the adoption of the Law on Pharmaceuticals and Medical Devices. The energy sector faced a challenge when the Republika Srpska Government on 11 September announced its unilateral withdrawal from the Electricity Transmission Company—the cornerstone of Bosnia and Herzegovina's energy sector reform. The Federation enacted a Law on Profit Tax, which was in harmony with its Republika Srpska equivalent and would prevent double taxation, and a new Law on Income Tax.

Public administration reform

Progress in public administration reform was limited and uneven, and dogged by persistent political disagreements and lack of progress on constitutional reform. The Federation and the Republika Srpska Governments proposed amendments to the law on the civil service that would change the status of civil servants and run contrary to the public administration reform strategy in Bosnia and Herzegovina, which was adopted by all levels of government in 2006 [YUN 2006, p. 456]. In effect, those proposed changes would make civil servants political appointees, opening the door to nepotism and political influence in both entities. OHR and the European Commission reacted to those draft laws.

Media development

The reform of the public broadcasting system was achieved with the adoption on 26 July of the Federation's public broadcasting framework law. It followed a ruling on 10 June by the Federation Constitutional Court that the law did not violate the vital national interest of the Croat people [YUN 2006, p. 456]. Croat political representatives continued to press for a channel that would broadcast exclusively in Croat, and the Croat caucus in the Bosnia and Herzegovina House of Peoples succeeded in having an initiative adopted that tasked the Council of Ministers to look into the matter.

The independence of the Communications Regulatory Agency continued to be challenged. On 15 October, the Republika Srpska National Assembly adopted a declaration claiming that the Agency was, for the second year in a row, being run by an illegal body. The appointment of a new director of the Agency continued to be blocked by the ruling coalition, which, through its representatives in the Council of Ministers, continued to fail to appoint a new Director. This encouraged political actors to challenge the legality of the decisions of the Agency.

Relations with other countries

The issue of Kosovo's future status featured prominently in the country's political discourse. The countdown to a unilateral declaration of independence in February exacerbated rhetoric and concern on the part of Bosnia and Herzegovina's Serbs, who shared the general Serb identification of Kosovo with their faith, culture and nationhood, albeit to a lesser degree than in Serbia proper. The Prime Minister of the Republika Srpska, Milorad Dodik, took part in many manifestations of Serb solidarity over Kosovo, but argued that its fate should not cause disturbances in Bosnia and Herzegovina; he did not support the more extreme manifestations of Serb anger over Kosovo's declaration of independence and its recognition by many countries. Demonstrations against Kosovo's independence in the Republika Srpska were relatively small.

The border-definition issues with Croatia and Serbia remained unresolved, as well as the problem of Croatia's plan to build a bridge, bypassing the small slice of Adriatic coastline of Bosnia and Herzegovina, between the mainland and the Pelješac peninsula, possibly impairing Bosnia and Herzegovina's access to the sea. Inadequacies in judicial cooperation among Bosnia and Herzegovina, Croatia, Montenegro and Serbia, particularly over war crime prosecutions, also remained.

SECURITY COUNCIL ACTION

On 20 November [meeting 6021], the Security Council unanimously adopted **resolution 1845(2008)**. The draft [S/2008/720] was submitted by Belgium, Croatia, France, Italy, the Russian Federation, the United Kingdom and the United States.

The Security Council,

Recalling all its previous relevant resolutions concerning the conflicts in the former Yugoslavia and relevant statements by its President, including resolutions 1031(1995) of 15 December 1995, 1088(1996) of 12 December 1996, 1423(2002) of 12 July 2002, 1491(2003) of 11 July 2003, 1551(2004) of 9 July 2004, 1575(2004) of 22 November 2004, 1639(2005) of 21 November 2005, 1722(2006) of 21 November 2006, 1764(2007) of 29 June 2007 and 1785(2007) of 21 November 2007,

Reaffirming its commitment to the political settlement of the conflicts in the former Yugoslavia, preserving the sovereignty and territorial integrity of all States there within their internationally recognized borders,

Emphasizing its full support for the continued role in Bosnia and Herzegovina of the High Representative for Bosnia and Herzegovina,

Underlining its commitment to support the implementation of the General Framework Agreement for Peace in Bosnia and Herzegovina and the annexes thereto (collectively the "Peace Agreement"), as well as the relevant decisions of the Peace Implementation Council,

Recalling all the agreements concerning the status of forces referred to in appendix B to annex 1-A of the Peace Agreement, and reminding the parties of their obligation to continue to comply therewith,

Recalling also the provisions of its resolution 1551(2004) concerning the provisional application of the status-of-forces agreements contained in appendix B to annex 1-A of the Peace Agreement,

Emphasizing its appreciation to the High Representative, the Commander and personnel of the multinational stabilization force (the European Union Force), the Senior Military Representative and personnel of the North Atlantic Treaty Organization Headquarters Sarajevo, the Organization for Security and Cooperation in Europe, the European Union and the personnel of other international organizations and agencies in Bosnia and Herzegovina for their contributions to the implementation of the Peace Agreement,

Emphasizing that a comprehensive and coordinated return of refugees and displaced persons throughout the region continues to be crucial to lasting peace,

Recalling the declarations of the ministerial meetings of the Peace Implementation Council,

Recognizing that full implementation of the Peace Agreement is not yet complete, while paying tribute to the achievements of the authorities at State and entity level in Bosnia and Herzegovina and of the international community in the thirteen years since the signing of the Peace Agreement,

Emphasizing the importance of Bosnia and Herzegovina's progress towards Euro-Atlantic integration on the basis of the Peace Agreement, while recognizing the importance of Bosnia and Herzegovina's transition to a functional, reform-oriented, modern and democratic European country,

Taking note of the reports of the High Representative, including his latest report of 10 November 2008,

Determined to promote the peaceful resolution of the conflicts in accordance with the purposes and principles of the Charter of the United Nations,

Recalling the relevant principles contained in the Convention on the Safety of United Nations and Associated Personnel of 9 December 1994 and the statement by its President of 9 February 2000,

Welcoming and encouraging efforts by the United Nations to sensitize peacekeeping personnel in the prevention and control of HIV/AIDS and other communicable diseases in all its peacekeeping operations,

Taking note of the conclusions of the Ministers for Foreign Affairs and Ministers of Defence of the European Union at their joint meeting, held on 14 May 2007, in which they reiterate that the European Union would retain a military presence in the country as long as necessary, in order to continue contributing to the maintenance of a safe and secure environment, and the conclusions of the Ministers for Foreign Affairs and Ministers of Defence of the European Union at their joint meeting, held on 10 November 2008,

Recalling the letters between the European Union and the North Atlantic Treaty Organization sent to the Security Council on 19 November 2004 on how those organizations will cooperate together in Bosnia and Herzegovina, in which both organizations recognize that the European Union Force will have the main peace stabilization role under the military aspects of the Peace Agreement,

Recalling also the confirmation by the Presidency of Bosnia and Herzegovina, on behalf of Bosnia and Herzegovina, including its constituent entities, of the arrangements for the European Union Force and the North Atlantic Treaty Organization Headquarters presence,

Welcoming the increased engagement of the European Union in Bosnia and Herzegovina and the continued engagement of the North Atlantic Treaty Organization,

Reiterating once again its calls upon the authorities in Bosnia and Herzegovina to implement in full their undertakings, as also confirmed in the declaration by the Steering Board of the Peace Implementation Council of 27 February 2008,

Noting that the signing of the Stabilization and Association Agreement marked a fundamental step forward in the relationship between Bosnia and Herzegovina and the European Union, and calling upon the authorities in Bosnia and Herzegovina to shoulder their responsibilities and renew their efforts in this regard,

Noting with satisfaction the agreement between the leaders of three of the main parties in Bosnia and Herzegovina reached on 8 November 2008, calling for these proposals to be rapidly put into concrete form in close cooperation with the High Representative and the Steering Board of the Peace Implementation Council, and inviting Bosnian political forces to unite around this project,

Determining that the situation in the region continues to constitute a threat to international peace and security,

Acting under Chapter VII of the Charter,

1. *Reaffirms once again its support* for the General Framework Agreement for Peace in Bosnia and Herzegovina and the annexes thereto (collectively the "Peace Agreement"), as well as for the Dayton Agreement on Implementing the Federation of Bosnia and Herzegovina of 10 November 1995, and calls upon the parties to comply strictly with their obligations under those Agreements;

2. *Reiterates* that the primary responsibility for the further successful implementation of the Peace Agreement lies with the authorities in Bosnia and Herzegovina themselves and that the continued willingness of the international community and major donors to assume the political, military and economic burden of implementation and reconstruction efforts will be determined by the compliance and active participation by all the authorities in Bosnia and Herzegovina in implementing the Peace Agreement and rebuilding a civil society, in particular in full cooperation with the International Tribunal for the Prosecution of Persons Responsible for Serious Violations of International Humanitarian Law Committed in the Territory of the Former Yugoslavia since 1991, in strengthening joint institutions, which foster the building of a fully functioning self-sustaining State able to integrate itself into the European structures, and in facilitating returns of refugees and displaced persons;

3. *Reminds* the parties once again that, in accordance with the Peace Agreement, they have committed themselves to cooperate fully with all entities involved in the implementation of this peace settlement, as described in the Peace Agreement, or which are otherwise authorized by the Security Council, including the International Tribunal for the Former Yugoslavia, as it carries out its responsibilities for dispensing justice impartially, and underlines that full cooperation by States and entities with the Tribunal includes, inter alia, the surrender for trial or apprehension of all persons indicted by the Tribunal and the provision of information to assist in Tribunal investigations;

4. *Emphasizes its full support* for the continued role of the High Representative for Bosnia and Herzegovina in monitoring the implementation of the Peace Agreement and giving guidance to and coordinating the activities of the civilian organizations and agencies involved in assisting the parties to implement the Peace Agreement, and reaffirms that, under annex 10 of the Peace Agreement, the High Representative is the final authority in theatre regarding the interpretation of civilian implementation of the Peace Agreement and that, in case of dispute, he may give his interpretation and make recommendations, and make binding decisions as he judges necessary on issues as elaborated by the Peace Implementation Council in Bonn, Germany, on 9 and 10 December 1997;

5. *Expresses its support* for the declarations of the ministerial meetings of the Peace Implementation Council;

6. *Reaffirms* its intention to keep implementation of the Peace Agreement and the situation in Bosnia and Herzegovina under close review, taking into account the reports submitted pursuant to paragraphs 18 and 21 below, and any recommendations those reports might include, and its readiness to consider the imposition of measures if any party fails significantly to meet its obligations under the Peace Agreement;

7. *Recalls* the support of the authorities of Bosnia and Herzegovina for the European Union Force and the continued North Atlantic Treaty Organization presence and their confirmation that both are the legal successors to the Stabilization Force for the fulfilment of their missions for the purposes of the Peace Agreement, its annexes and appendices and relevant Security Council resolutions and can take such actions as are required, including the use of force, to ensure compliance with annexes 1-A and 2 of the Peace Agreement and relevant Council resolutions;

8. *Pays tribute* to those Member States which participated in the multinational stabilization force (the European Union Force), and in the continued North Atlantic Treaty Organization presence, established in accordance with its resolution 1575(2004) and extended by its resolutions 1639(2005), 1722(2006) and 1785(2007), and welcomes their willingness to assist the parties to the Peace Agreement by continuing to deploy a multinational stabilization force (the European Union Force) and by maintaining a continued North Atlantic Treaty Organization presence;

9. *Welcomes* the intention of the European Union to maintain a European Union military operation to Bosnia and Herzegovina from November 2008;

10. *Authorizes* the Member States acting through or in cooperation with the European Union to establish for a further period of twelve months, starting from the date of the adoption of the present resolution, a multinational stabilization force (the European Union Force) as a legal successor to the Stabilization Force under unified command and control, which will fulfil its missions in relation to the implementation of annexes 1-A and 2 of the Peace Agreement in cooperation with the North Atlantic Treaty Organization Headquarters presence in accordance with the arrangements agreed between the North Atlantic Treaty Organization and the European Union as communicated to the Security Council in their letters of 19 November 2004, which recognize that the European Union Force will have the main peace stabilization role under the military aspects of the Peace Agreement;

11. *Welcomes* the decision of the North Atlantic Treaty Organization to continue to maintain a presence in Bosnia and Herzegovina in the form of a North Atlantic Treaty Organization Headquarters in order to continue to assist in implementing the Peace Agreement in conjunction with the European Union Force, and authorizes the Member States acting through or in cooperation with the North Atlantic Treaty Organization to continue to maintain a North Atlantic Treaty Organization Headquarters as a legal successor to the Stabilization Force under unified command and control, which will fulfil its missions in relation to the implementation of annexes 1-A and 2 of the Peace Agreement in cooperation with the European Union Force in accordance with the arrangements agreed between the North Atlantic Treaty Organization and the European Union as communicated to the Security Council in their letters of 19 November 2004, which recognize that the European Union Force will have the main peace stabilization role under the military aspects of the Peace Agreement;

12. *Reaffirms* that the Peace Agreement and the provisions of its previous relevant resolutions shall apply to and in respect of both the European Union Force and the North Atlantic Treaty Organization presence as they have applied to and in respect of the Stabilization Force and that, therefore, references in the Peace Agreement, in particular in annex 1-A and the appendices thereto, and in relevant resolutions to the Implementation Force and/or the Stabilization Force, the North Atlantic Treaty Organization and the North Atlantic Council shall be read as applying, as appropriate, to the North Atlantic Treaty Organization presence, the European Union Force, the European Union and the Political and Security Committee and Council of the European Union respectively;

13. *Expresses its intention* to consider the terms of further authorization as necessary in the light of developments in the implementation of the Peace Agreement and the situation in Bosnia and Herzegovina;

14. *Authorizes* the Member States acting under paragraphs 10 and 11 above to take all necessary measures to effect the implementation of and to ensure compliance with annexes 1-A and 2 of the Peace Agreement, stresses that the parties shall continue to be held equally responsible for compliance with those annexes and shall be equally subject to such enforcement action by the European Union Force and the North Atlantic Treaty Organization presence as may be necessary to ensure the implementation of those annexes and the protection of the European Union Force and the North Atlantic Treaty Organization presence;

15. *Authorizes* Member States to take all necessary measures, at the request of either the European Union Force or the North Atlantic Treaty Organization Headquarters, in defence of the European Union Force or the North Atlantic Treaty Organization presence respectively, and to assist both organizations in carrying out their missions, and recognizes the right of both the European Union Force and the North Atlantic Treaty Organization presence to take all necessary measures to defend themselves from attack or threat of attack;

16. *Authorizes* the Member States acting under paragraphs 10 and 11 above, in accordance with annex 1-A of the Peace Agreement, to take all necessary measures to ensure compliance with the rules and procedures governing command and control of airspace over Bosnia and Herzegovina with respect to all civilian and military air traffic;

17. *Demands* that the parties respect the security and freedom of movement of the European Union Force, the North Atlantic Treaty Organization presence and other international personnel;

18. *Requests* the Member States acting through or in cooperation with the European Union and the Member States acting through or in cooperation with the North Atlantic Treaty Organization to report to the Security Council on the activity of the European Union Force and the North Atlantic Treaty Organization Headquarters presence respectively, through the appropriate channels and at least at three-monthly intervals;

19. *Invites* all States, in particular those in the region, to continue to provide appropriate support and facilities, including transit facilities, for the Member States acting under paragraphs 10 and 11 above;

20. *Reiterates its appreciation* for the deployment by the European Union of its Police Mission to Bosnia and Herzegovina since 1 January 2003;

21. *Requests* the Secretary-General to continue to submit to the Council reports from the High Representative, in accordance with annex 10 of the Peace Agreement and the conclusions of the Peace Implementation Conference held in London on 4 and 5 December 1996, and later Peace Implementation Conferences, on the implementation of the Peace Agreement and, in particular, on compliance by the parties with their commitments under that Agreement;

22. *Decides* to remain seized of the matter.

European Union missions in Bosnia and Herzegovina

EUPM

Report of EU Secretary-General. As requested by the Security Council in presidential statement S/PRST/2002/33 [YUN 2002, p. 363], the EU High Representative for the Common Foreign and Security Policy and Secretary-General of the EU Council, Javier Solana, reported to the Security Council through the UN Secretary-General on the activities of the European Union Police Mission (EUPM).

The report [S/2008/732], covering the period from April to September, stated that the Mission's progress in support of police restructuring and police reform had been consistent. The Mission continued to advise the harmonization and development of the legislation to reform the police bodies in the entities, cantons and Brčko District.

Although considerable achievements had been made since the launch of EUPM in 2003 [YUN 2003, p. 399], effective results in the fight against organized crime and in the establishment of key State law-enforcement agencies such as the Border Police or the State Investigation and Protection Agency (SIPA) were a long-term endeavour. The recent arrests of prominent figures allegedly involved in organized crime represented, however, a significant breakthrough.

The report stressed the need for implementing the two police reform laws. EUPM was advising and monitoring implementation and was acting as a facilitator to overcome technical difficulties and different views among local stakeholders about the scope of the reform. The Mission would continue to focus on a concrete operational approach, and continue to reach out to the judiciary and, in particular, to prosecutors to improve cooperation between police forces and the prosecutors' offices. It would also assist the authorities in harmonizing the police legislation and in implementing the integrated border management strategy.

At the end of September, the Mission numbered 418 staff (167 international police officers, 30 international civilian experts and 221 national staff). All 27 EU Member States as well as six non-EU countries contributed to EUPM. On 1 November, Brigadier General Stefan Feller (Germany) succeeded Brigadier General Vincenzo Coppola (Italy) as Head of Mission/Police Commissioner.

Police restructuring

Police restructuring efforts included the implementation of two police reform laws (the Law on the Directorate for Coordination of Police Bodies and Agencies for Support of Police Structure, and the Law on Independent and Supervisory Bodies of Police Structure), which came into force on 14 May. With their adoption, four new coordination and support institutions and three supervisory and oversight bodies would be established at the State level. The Ministry of Security had established the Selection Commission in charge of choosing the Directors and the Deputy Directors of the Agency for Police Support, the Agency for Education and the Agency for Forensic Examinations and Expertise. The Ministry in July also established the Commission for Harmonization to align relevant laws with the two new police reform laws. EUPM participated in its work and followed related developments. The Parliamentary Assembly appointed the ad hoc Joint Commission for conducting the procedure for appointing the Independent Board and the Public Complaints Board. However, the Commission failed to complete its task by the set deadline of 14 August and asked for EUPM assistance in drafting the necessary decisions and fulfilling its task.

The police reform laws were of crucial importance in prompting a review of the SIPA structure and functioning, which led to amending the SIPA Law and establishing a commission to streamline the structure. EUPM provided assistance in building up the Border Police by advising it on implementing the integrated border management strategy. EUPM also provided technical assistance to the Ministries of Security and Finance in harmonizing the Law on Salaries with police-related legislation. EUPM was assisting in drafting the Law on Police Officials and the Law on Internal Affairs of the Republika Srpska; in the Brčko District it assisted local authorities in drafting the District Law on Police. It also assisted cantonal authorities in finalizing the cantonal Law on Internal Affairs. In support of the fight against organized crime, EUPM advised on specific cases and provided advice on institution building.

In April, an agreement to enhance mechanisms of cooperation between the police and prosecutors' offices was signed. From May to July, the Mission organized media workshops for prosecutors, helping them enhance their skills in communicating with the public on organized crime.

EUFOR

The EU FORCE (EUFOR) mission in Bosnia and Herzegovina executed the military aspects of the Peace Agreement specified in annexes 1-A and 2, which were transferred to it by NATO in 2004 [YUN 2004, p. 401]. Its 2008 activities were described in five reports, covering the periods from 1 December 2007 to 29 February 2008 [S/2008/242], 1 March to 31 May [S/2008/413], 1 June to 31 August [S/2008/838], 1 September to 30 November [S/2009/44] and 1 December 2008 to 28 February 2009 [S/2009/418], submitted by the EU High Representative for the Common Foreign and Security Policy and Secretary-General of the EU Council, in accordance with various UN Security Council resolutions.

As at 30 November, the force of some 2,200 EUFOR troops was concentrated in Sarajevo, with liaison and observation teams deployed throughout Bosnia and Herzegovina. EUFOR continued to provide deterrence, ensure compliance in relation to the responsibilities specified in the Peace Agreement, and contribute to maintaining a safe and secure environment. It provided support to law-enforcement agencies in fighting organized crime, in close cooperation with the EU Police Mission, and to ICTY in the search for persons indicted for war crimes.

In July, EUFOR and Bosnia and Herzegovina's Ministry of Defence signed a memorandum of understanding covering the participation of the Armed Forces of Bosnia and Herzegovina (AFBiH) in EUFOR exercises. EUFOR continued to assist and support AFBiH with planning for the disposal of surplus arms and ammunition.

The EU Council reviewed the operation on 10 November and highlighted the decisive progress made towards accomplishing its mandate. The Council considered that the preparatory work for a possible development of the operation should be continued, taking into account the future role of the EU Special Representative and political developments.

Serbia

The Kosovo province of Serbia continued to receive UN assistance in 2008 in building a multi-ethnic society. The United Nations Interim Administration Mission in Kosovo (UNMIK), together with the Kosovo leadership, led efforts to strengthen the Provisional Institutions of Self-Government, mainly the Kosovo Assembly and the Kosovo Government, and to transfere authority to those institutions, in line with the 2001 Constitutional Framework for Provisional Self-Government [YUN 2001, p. 352]. UNMIK also monitored progress in achieving the standards set out in the 2003 "standards for Kosovo" document [YUN 2003, p. 420], by which Kosovo was expected to develop stable democratic institutions under UNMIK administration before any decision could be made on its future status. However, on 17 February the Assembly of Kosovo adopted a "declaration of independence" declaring Kosovo an independent and sovereign state. This led to condemnation by the Serbian authorities, boycott of Kosovo institutions by Kosovo Serbs and protests in several areas in Kosovo and in Serbia. Some of the protests turned violent, but the overall security situation in Kosovo remained calm.

On 12 June the Secretary-General, in letters addressed to Boris Tadić, President of Serbia, and Fatmir Sejdiu, President of Kosovo, outlined plans to reconfigure UNMIK and the broader international civil presence in Kosovo. The letters also confirmed that the position of the United Nations on Kosovo status was of status neutrality, and detailed the commitment to a dialogue with Serbia in six areas: police, courts, boundary management, Serbian patrimony, transport and infrastructure, and customs. Kosovo's Constitution, which did not envisage a real role for UNMIK and did not contain a reference to resolution 1244(1999) [YUN 1999, p. 353], came into force in June and was rejected by Kosovo Serbs.

In June, Lamberto Zannier was appointed as Special Representative for Kosovo and Head of UNMIK, succeeding Joachim Rücker, and a few days later the start of UNMIK's reconfiguration was formally announced. The Special Representative facilitated preparations for the EU to undertake an operational role in Kosovo in the rule-of-law area, under the framework of resolution 1244(1999) and the overall authority of the United Nations.

In October, the General Assembly, by **resolution 63/3** (see p. 1404), requested an advisory opinion from the International Court of Justice on whether the unilateral declaration of independence of Kosovo was in accordance with international law.

Situation in Kosovo

Security Council consideration (January). On 16 January [meeting 5821], the President of Serbia, Boris Tadić, told the Security Council that despite enormous efforts by the Serbian negotiating team to reach a compromise, four months of negotiations led by the international mediating troika—the EU, the Russian Federation and the United States—had failed to yield results. Serbia and its people had suffered from the tragic mistakes of the past regime: they should not be punished again because of a flawed policy of a bad regime almost a decade ago. The parties should make every effort to resolve the misunderstandings and conflicts peacefully and by agreement alone, not by making unilateral moves. Unilateral recognition of Kosovo's independence would no doubt be a precedent. No one had the right to destabilize Serbia and the Balkans through hasty decisions, which would have unforeseeable consequences for other regions fraught with problems of ethnic separatism. The UN Charter guaranteed the principle of respect for the sovereignty and territorial integrity of internationally recognized States, and Serbia was such a State.

Following his statement, Council members continued their discussion in a private meeting [meeting 5822], during which President Tadić, the Secretary-General's Special Representative for Kosovo, Joachim Rücker, and the Kosovo Prime Minister, Hashim Thaçi, had an exchange of views.

Communication. In January [S/2008/7], Serbia forwarded to the Security Council its comments on the Secretary-General's report on UNMIK [YUN 2007, p. 403] covering the period from 1 September to 15 December 2007.

Security Council consideration (February). On 12 February [S/2008/92], Serbia requested an urgent meeting of the Security Council to consider an extremely grave situation in the Serbian province of Kosovo and Metohija, where the final preparations were taking place for a unilateral declaration of independence by the Provisional Institutions of Self-Government, which would constitute a violation of Security Council resolution 1244(1999) and Serbia's territorial integrity, and would endanger the maintenance of international peace and security. Also on 12 February [S/2008/93], the Russian Federation supported Serbia's request.

On 14 February [meeting 5835], the Council held a closed meeting, during which Council Members and Serbia's Minister for Foreign Affairs, Vuk Jeremić, had an exchange of views.

On 17 February [A/62/703-S/2008/111], Serbia informed the Secretary-General that on that day the Provisional Institutions of Self-Government of its southern province of Kosovo and Metohija had unilaterally declared independence, in violation of Security Council resolution 1244(1999). In the wake of that attempt to establish a fait accompli, Serbia had adopted a Decision to abrogate the unilateral secessionist acts and activities of the Provisional Institutions. Serbia demanded that the Special Representative take all necessary measures, in accordance with resolution 1244(1999) and other Council decisions, as he had on previous occasions, to abrogate all acts and actions by which unilateral independence had been declared. Serbia called upon the Secretary-General to ensure that his Special Representative exercised his powers and responsibilities by declaring that act null and void and dissolve the Assembly of Kosovo, since its "declaration of independence" was not in conformity with the resolution. By its Decision, Serbia had also requested that the Security Council declare that unilateral act legally invalid. It demanded that the Council call for the continuation of the political process leading towards a solution. Finally, Serbia demanded that all Members States respect Serbia's sovereignty and territorial integrity and thereby reject the so-called independence of Kosovo and Metohija.

Also on 17 February [S/2008/103], Serbia requested an emergency meeting of the Security Council to consider the unilateral declaration of independence. Supporting that request [S/2008/104], the Russian Federation on the same day requested that a meeting be convened on 18 February, in view of the dangerous situation with grave, damaging consequences for peace and security in the Balkans.

Addressing the Council on 18 February [meeting 5839], the Secretary-General stressed the need to ensure the stability of Kosovo and the safety and security of its population, in particular the minority communities. He urged all to refrain from any actions or statements that could endanger peace, incite violence or jeopardize security in Kosovo and the region, adding that his efforts, and those of his Special Representative, were aimed at ensuring that the situation in Kosovo and in the wider region remained stable, and that the population of Kosovo was protected. Pending guidance from the Security Council, UNMIK would continue to carry out its mandate under Council resolution 1244(1999).

Serbian President Tadić requested the Secretary-General to instruct his Special Representative to declare Kosovo's "unilateral and illegal" declaration of independence "null and void". The action by the Kosovo Provisional Institutions violated resolution 1244(1999), which reaffirmed Serbia's sovereignty and territorial integrity, including Kosovo and Metohija. He requested the Security Council to ensure that the provisions of that resolution were fully respected. Serbia would never recognize the independence of Kosovo, would never renounce Kosovo and would not give up the struggle for its legitimate interests. For the citizens of Serbia and its institutions, Kosovo would forever remain a part of Serbia.

Supporting Serbia's call, Russia emphasized that the actions by the Kosovo Albanian leadership and those who supported them set a dangerous precedent and might lead to an escalation of tensions and inter-ethnic violence in the province. A durable solution to the Kosovo status issue could be achieved only on the basis of a decision to be worked out with the Security Council taking the leading role, a decision in line with the norms of international law and based on agreements between Belgrade and Pristina.

China expressed concern over the unilateral declaration of independence and hoped that the EU would take into account not only the interests of Serbia and Kosovo, but also the concerns of other countries in the region. More important, it needed to pay attention to and uphold the role of the Security Council in resolving the issue. The Council should encourage Serbia and Kosovo to continue their pursuit of a mutually acceptable solution through political and diplomatic means.

Meanwhile, several Council members indicated their support for the "new state", including Belgium, France, Italy, the United Kingdom and the United States. The United Kingdom noted that it was not ideal for Kosovo to become independent without the consent of Serbia and without consensus in the Council. However, the unique circumstances of the violent break-up of the former Yugoslavia and the unprecedented UN administration of Kosovo made that a sui generis case, which created no wider precedent. The United States noted that Kosovo's independence was a culmination of a long and unique process. Intensive efforts to settle the final status of Kosovo had left no stone unturned, but the parties had been unable to reach agreement. Kosovo's declaration of independence was a logical, legitimate and legal response to the situation at hand, and fully consistent with resolution 1244(1999). The people of Kosovo had decided to bring the issue to a close, and had done so in a mature, non-violent and responsible manner.

Communication. On 18 February [S/2008/106], the Secretary-General transmitted to the Security Council a letter from Javier Solana, EU High Representative for the Common Foreign and Security Policy, informing him that on 4 February the EU Council had decided to deploy a rule-of-law mission in Kosovo. The mission sought to maintain an international civilian presence, within the framework of resolution 1244(1999), and to contribute to the maintenance of regional peace and security. At the same time, the EU had appointed Pieter Feith (the Netherlands) as its Special Representative in Kosovo to coordinate EU activities on the ground.

Press statement. On 21 February, the Security Council condemned that day's mob attacks against embassies in Belgrade, which—amid protests over the decision by the Assembly of Kosovo to declare independence from Serbia—had resulted in damage to embassy premises and had endangered diplomatic personnel. In a press statement [SC/9260], the Council recalled the fundamental principle of the inviolability of diplomatic missions and the obligations on host Governments, including under the 1961 Vienna Convention on Diplomatic Relations, to protect embassy premises. It welcomed the steps taken by the Serbian authorities to restore order and protect diplomatic property and personnel.

Security Council consideration (March). On 6 March [S/2008/162], Serbia requested an urgent meeting of the Security Council to consider the aggravation of the situation concerning the Serbian province of Kosovo and Metohija owing to the unilateral declaration of independence by the Provisional Institutions of Self-Government and the subsequent recognition of that act by some Member States in alleged violation of Serbia's sovereignty and territorial integrity, as well as of the provisions of resolution 1244(1999).

At the Council meeting of 11 March [meeting 5850], Serbia's Foreign Affairs Minister Jeremić said that the situation on the ground had deteriorated since 17 February. Those 20 or so countries that had furthered the secessionist cause of the Kosovo Albanians had made the international system more unstable, more insecure and more unpredictable. Recognizing the unilateral declaration of Kosovo's independence legitimized the act of unilateral secession by a provincial non-State actor, transformed the right to self-determination into an avowed right to independence and legitimized the forced partition of sovereign States. Stressing that Serbia would never recognize Kosovo's unilateral secession, he called for resolution 1244(1999) to be observed in full. There must be no erosion of the mandate of UNMIK, and no further transfers of competencies from UNMIK to any other body. Serbia wished no ill to the ethnic Albanians in its southern province and took seriously their right to obtain substantial self-governance while remaining under a common sovereign roof. Serbia was committed to open dialogue and good-faith negotiations. It was in Serbia's vital interest that all of Kosovo's communities prosper together in peace, security and reconciliation.

Council members subsequently went into informal consultations on the issue.

Report of Secretary-General (March). Reporting in March [S/2008/211], the Secretary-General said that following mayoral and municipal elections in 2007 [YUN 2007, p. 404], the Assembly of Kosovo on 9 January elected its President and members of its Presidency, and re-elected Fatmir Sejdiu as President of Kosovo. A new coalition government was formed by the Democratic Party of Kosovo and the Democratic League of Kosovo, led by Prime Minister Thaçi. Six out of 10 Kosovo Serb members of the Assembly took the oath of office.

The Assembly on 17 February adopted a "declaration of independence", declaring Kosovo an independent and sovereign State. The declaration received the support of 109 of the 120 members of the Assembly; the 10 Kosovo Serb members did not attend. The declaration stated that Kosovo fully accepted the obligations of the Comprehensive Proposal for the Kosovo Status Settlement [YUN 2007, p. 399], and pledged that Kosovo would adhere to resolution 1244(1999) and would work constructively with the United Nations. The Secretary-General immediately drew that development to the attention of the Security Council and reaffirmed that, pending guidance from the Council, the United Nations would continue to operate on the understanding that resolution 1244(1999) remained in force, and that UNMIK would continue to implement its mandate in the light of the evolving circumstances.

Serbian President Tadić informed the Secretary-General that Serbia had adopted a decision that Kosovo's declaration of independence represented a forceful and unilateral secession of a part of the territory of Serbia, and did not produce any legal effect either in Serbia or in the international legal order.

Kosovo Serbs protested peacefully in several areas in Kosovo, including northern Mitrovicë/Mitrovica, Graçanicë/Gračanica, Kamenicë/Kamenica and Shtërpcë/Štrpce. However, some protests turned violent, particularly in northern Kosovo. The Kosovo Albanian community's reaction had been restrained. Following the declaration of independence, Kosovo Serbs, with the support of the Serbian authorities, expanded their boycott of the institutions of Kosovo to include UNMIK Customs, the Kosovo Police Service, the judicial system, municipal administration and UNMIK Railways, but they continued to work in municipalities where they remained a small minority. Meanwhile, leaders of Kosovo Serb political parties continued to have informal contacts with UNMIK and the Government of Kosovo.

Despite a number of serious security incidents, the overall security situation remained calm; the majority of incidents occurred in the days immediately before and after the declaration of independence. An explosion between the UNMIK-run Court and a police station in northern Mitrovicë/Mitrovica on 29 February damaged four UN vehicles. The Kosovo Serb protests against Kosovo institutions had been generally peaceful, with the exception of the burning down of UNMIK police and customs facilities at the two crossing points with Serbia on the Administrative Boundary Line in northern Kosovo.

In several Kosovo Serb areas in southern Kosovo, where operational police competencies had been transferred to the Kosovo Ministry of the Interior, Kosovo Serb police officers no longer recognized the Kosovo police chain of command and demanded to be placed under the direct command of UNMIK police officers. In northern Kosovo, where competencies had not been transferred, the situation remained unchanged.

The Secretary-General stated that the declaration of independence and subsequent events had posed significant challenges to the ability of UNMIK to exercise its administrative authority. To address those challenges, UNMIK would continue to act in a realistic and practical manner and in the light of the evolving circumstances to ensure peace and security. Pending Security Council guidance, there might be a need for UNMIK to adjust its operational deployment to developments and changes on the ground, in a manner consistent with the operational framework established under resolution 1244(1999).

Communication. On 17 April [S/2008/260], Serbia transmitted to the Security Council its comments on the Secretary-General's report, together with comments on the technical assessment of progress in implementing the standard for Kosovo and the resolution of Serbia's National Assembly confirming the Government's decision on the annulment of allegedly illegitimate acts concerning the proclamation of Kosovo's unilateral independence.

Security Council consideration (April). On 21 April [meeting 5871], the Security Council held a closed meeting on the situation in Kosovo, during which Council members, Special Representative Rücker, Serbian President Tadić and Kosovo Prime Minister Thaçi had an exchange of views.

Report of Secretary-General (June). In a special 12 June report [S/2008/354], the Secretary-General noted that the Security Council had taken no position following the 17 February declaration, and that 42 Member States had recognized the independence of Kosovo. In addition, a new reality and challenges to UNMIK authority had emerged on the ground in Kosovo Albanian majority areas. The Assembly of Kosovo on 9 April had passed a "Constitution of the Republic of Kosovo" that was scheduled to come into force on 15 June. The Constitution would effectively remove from UNMIK its powers as an interim civil administration. In that regard, the government of Kosovo had indicated that it would welcome a continued UN presence in Kosovo provided that it carried out only limited residual tasks.

The Secretary-General said that, following the entry into force of the Kosovo Constitution, UNMIK would no longer be able to perform effectively the vast majority of its tasks as an interim administration and expressed his intention to reconfigure UNMIK in order to allow the EU to enhance its operational role in Kosovo in the area of the rule of law under the framework of resolution 1244(1999) and the overall authority of the United Nations. The UN presence would carry out monitoring and reporting, facilitate arrangements for Kosovo's engagement in international agreements and facilitate dialogue between Pristina and Belgrade on issues of practical concern.

In letters dated 12 June addressed to Presidents Tadić and Sejdiu [S/2008/354, annex I & II], the Secretary-General said that the position of the United Nations on Kosovo's status was of a strict neutrality, and that he intended to exercise the authority vested in him by resolution 1244(1999) to reconfigure the international civil presence as set out in the report. In the letter to President Tadić, the Secretary-General said that UN engagement in dialogue with Belgrade would be in six key areas of practical mutual concern: police, the courts, customs, transportation and infrastructure, boundaries, and the Serbian patrimony.

Security Council consideration (June). On 17 June [S/2008/401], Serbia requested a meeting of the Security Council to consider the report of the Secretary-General.

Addressing the Council on 20 June [meeting 5917], the Secretary-General said that his proposal to reconfigure the UN presence in Kosovo was a practical and workable solution to a complex and difficult situation. In almost 40 years of diplomatic life, he had never encountered an issue as divisive, as delicate and as intractable. The declaration of independence, the ensuing violence, the elections organized by the Serbs and the promulgation of a new Constitution had profoundly changed the environment. Those developments had created a profoundly new reality in which UNMIK was no longer able to perform as effectively as in the past, the vast majority of its tasks as an interim administration. The EU had expressed its readiness to perform an enhanced role in the area of the rule of law, and had put in place measures to do so. Such an enhanced role would be in the interest of the international community. His reconfiguration package was an effort in the light of new developments to try to find an operational modus vivendi to help move Kosovo a few steps back from the brink of further conflict. The package was founded on the imperative to maintain peace, security and stability in Kosovo and the region, while responding and adapting to changing circumstances on the ground.

Serbian President Tadić said that Kosovo's unilateral declaration of independence directly contravened the UN Charter, the Helsinki Final Act and other cornerstone documents upon which the international system had been built. That was why Serbia's National Assembly had declared Kosovo's action—and all subsequent decisions stemming from it—null and void. The Secretary-General's report referred to a "so-called Constitution" intended to implement the Ahtisaari Proposal [YUN 2007, pp. 398 & 399], which the UN Security Council had not endorsed and, therefore, carried no legal weight whatsoever. The report said that the "Constitution" was designed to effectively remove from UNMIK its powers of civil administration. That usurpation by the Pristina authorities of UNMIK's mandate was deeply troubling, as was the impression the report gave of acquiescing to an unjustifiable violation of resolution 1244(1999).

Kosovo President Sejdiu said that Kosovo's independence was declared in line with the Ahtisaari plan, and the transition to the new status had gone well. The country had since been recognized by 43 Member States, and more nations were recognizing it every month. The Ahtisaari plan, overwhelmingly endorsed by the Assembly of Kosovo, was the guiding framework for Kosovo's efforts. The Assembly had since adopted more than 40 pieces of legislation. Those changes had created a new situation requiring the United Nations, once again, to adapt its presence. The people of Kosovo, therefore, appreciated the Secretary-General's initiative to reconfigure the UN presence. The United Nations would continue to perform rule-of-law functions in accordance with resolution 1244(1999), until the EU was able to perform fully its operational role—all steps that Kosovo would support.

Several Council members, including France, Italy, the United Kingdom and the United States, expressed support for the package, but others, notably the Russian Federation, had serious objections to the reconfiguration and the enhanced EU role in Kosovo. China acknowledged the many changes in Kosovo since 1999, but said that the basis for implementing resolution 1244(1999) had not changed.

New Head of UNMIK. On 20 June [S/2008/411], the Secretary-General informed the Security Council of his intention to appoint Lamberto Zannier (Italy) as his Special Representative for Kosovo and Head of UNMIK. On 23 June [S/2008/412], the President of the Council informed the Secretary-General that Council members had taken note of that intention.

Report of Secretary-General (July). The Secretary-General reported in July [S/2008/458] that the Kosovo Constitution had come into force on 15 June, along with a package of laws covering decentralization and borders, and authorizing the creation of a Kosovo Foreign Ministry and Intelligence Service. On 10 June, the Kosovo Assembly adopted a national anthem, and on 17 June, the Kosovo Government authorized the establishment of nine "embassies" in Member States that had recognized the declaration of independence. The Kosovo authorities committed themselves to implementing in full the Comprehensive Proposal for the Kosovo Status Settlement prepared by the Secretary-General's Special Envoy for the future status process for Kosovo, Martti Ahtisaari, which was presented to the Council in March 2007 [YUN 2007, p. 399].

Kosovo Serbs had rejected the Constitution. Following Serbian parliamentary and local municipal elections on 11 May, organized by the Serbian Electoral Commission in 23 of Kosovo's 30 municipalities, Serbian officials and Kosovo Serb leaders started to establish parallel municipal government structures in Serb-majority municipalities in accordance with Serbian law. Kosovo Serbs had continued to strongly oppose the declaration of independence. They had carried out continued protests, some of which had turned violent, like the one on 17 March, when an UNMIK police operation, supported by the international security presence in Kosovo (KFOR), re-established UNMIK control over the UNMIK courthouse in northern Mitrovicë/Mitrovica, which had been forcefully seized on 14 March by Kosovo Serb judicial employees protesting and asking to be reinstated in their positions. During the operation, the UNMIK police and KFOR came under attack by the protesters. The confrontation resulted in the death of Kynal Ihor, an international police officer from Ukraine, and in the wounding of 64 UNMIK police officers, 24 KFOR soldiers and several Kosovo Serb protesters. The incident led to a 36-hour withdrawal of UNMIK police from northern Mitrovicë/Mitrovica, leaving KFOR as the first responder during the interim period.

The Secretary-General said that the ability of UNMIK to operate as before had been fundamentally challenged owing to actions taken by both the authorities in Pristina and the Kosovo Serbs. In Pristina, Kosovo's authorities had instituted measures that sought to effectively assume the Mission's powers. The Constitution made no mention of any role or function of the United Nations and did not contain a reference to resolution 1244(1999), although Kosovo's authorities had welcomed the continued UN presence. Kosovo had also passed legislation whose purpose was to assume legal control and responsibility over areas that were previously reserved to the Secretary-General's Special Representative. Kosovo Serbs, on their part, had rejected the Constitution and connected legislation and, with the support of Belgrade, had expanded their boycott of Kosovo's institutions and widened their parallel structures, particularly in northern Kosovo. Following the meeting of the Security Council on 20 June (see p. 438), and in light of the fact that the Council was unable to provide guidance, the Secretary-General decided to move forward with the reconfiguration and instructed UNMIK to cooperate with the EU in order for it to assume an enhanced operational role in Kosovo in the area of the rule of law, in accordance with resolution 1244(1999) and under a "United Nations umbrella" headed by the Special Representative.

UNMIK would continue to support Kosovo in its effort to consolidate democratic governance institutions, advance economic growth and move towards a future in Europe. Building a society in which all communities could coexist in peace remained a difficult and long-term challenge. The Secretary-General called upon the authorities in Pristina and Belgrade, and representatives of all of Kosovo's communities, to continue to work together with UNMIK.

Security Council consideration (July). Addressing the Council on 25 July [meeting 5944], the new Special Representative for Kosovo, Mr. Zannier, said that events on the ground had contributed to creating a profoundly new operating reality for UNMIK. The ability of UNMIK to perform the vast majority of its tasks as an interim administration had been fundamentally challenged, owing to actions taken by the authorities in Pristina and the Kosovo Serbs. The Kosovo authorities continued to seek to assume the powers and responsibilities of a sovereign State. Those included the approval by the Kosovo Assembly of funds for establishing a Ministry of Foreign Affairs; a Minister had been appointed and was present in the Security Council. The Assembly of Kosovo continued to pass legislation, which was now promulgated by the President of Kosovo without reference to the Special Representative's powers under resolution 1244(1999) or the constitutional framework. Meanwhile, the Kosovo Serbs continued to oppose cooperation with the authorities in Pristina, stressing that they would only cooperate with UNMIK. As a result of the Serbian local elections of 11 May, new parallel municipal authorities were operating in all Serb-majority municipalities. As a consequence of the stark divergence of paths taken by the Serbian and Albanian communities, the space in which UNMIK could operate had changed. While he and his staff continued to monitor the work of the authorities and to mediate disputes between communities, his power to impose solutions had in practice disappeared throughout much of the territory. The EU decision to end funding for UNMIK's economic reconstruction pillar had left UNMIK as from 30 June without the technical capacity or budget to operate in most economic areas. As a result, UNMIK had been engaged in planning for a reconfiguration of its presence which took into account those circumstances. An initial reconfiguration plan had been developed, outlining measures which would reduce the Mission's capacity in areas where it could no longer effectively function, for example, in civil administration, and enhance it in others, with particular attention to minorities. Mr. Zannier remained optimistic that UNMIK could continue to facilitate dialogue on matters affecting the lives of all communities.

While maintaining that Serbia could not accept its own forcible partition, Serbian Foreign Minister Jeremić called the way in which the reconfiguration had started "an inglorious episode", but stressed that it was now essential to proceed in the right way—with the full engagement of Serbia. The reconfiguration must be completed with Serbia's acceptance and the Council's explicit approval. That was the only way to ensure legitimacy and sustainability. The voice of Serbia, on the reconfiguration and much else, could no longer be disregarded. Serbia would spare no effort in honestly engaging with the United Nations in forging an acceptable, forward-looking reconfiguration arrangement that would uphold the overall authority of the United Nations, while opening up space for the institutional inclusion of regional organizations.

Skënder Hyseni, Minister for Foreign Affairs of Kosovo, said that Pristina was ready to engage in discussions with Belgrade, as two independent States, on a wide range of practical issues of mutual interest. Such dialogue was indispensable because of the ties of the past. It was in the very best interests of both Belgrade and Pristina to talk, as they aspired to join the western community of nations as represented in the EU.

The Russian Federation said that UNMIK's reconfiguration was inadmissible without the Security Council's authorization. The Secretary-General had exceeded his authority and intruded on the Council's prerogative in taking that decision. There seemed to be an attempt to legalize a structure for implementing the Ahtisaari Proposal, which had not been approved by the Council but which would abet the unilateral establishment of an unlawfully proclaimed construct. The EU's aspiration to play a more robust role in Kosovo was understandable, but should be met on the basis of resolution 1244(1999) and with respect for the prerogatives of the Council.

General Assembly action. On 8 October [A/63/PV.22], Serbia's Foreign Minister Jeremić introduced in the General Assembly a draft resolution [A/63/L.2] requesting an advisory opinion of the International Court of Justice (ICJ) on whether the unilateral declaration of independence of Kosovo was in accordance with international law. Sending the question to the Court, he said, would prevent the Kosovo crisis from serving as a deeply problematic precedent in any part of the globe where secessionist ambitions were harboured. An advisory opinion would provide politically neutral, yet judicially authoritative, guidance to many countries still deliberating how to approach such unilateral declarations. The question posed refrained from taking political positions on the Kosovo issue.

On the same day, the General Assembly adopted **resolution 63/3** by a recorded vote of 77 to 6, with 74 abstentions (see p. 1404). By that action, the Assembly requested the ICJ to render a non-binding advisory opinion on whether the unilateral declaration of independence by the Provisional Institutions of Self-Government of Kosovo was in accordance with international law.

Report of Secretary-General (November). In a report [S/2008/692] issued in November, the Secretary-General said that Kosovo had been recognized as an independent state by 52 countries and had applied for membership in the International Monetary Fund and the World Bank Group. Kosovo also decided to undertake a census of the population, established a Ministry for Security Forces and appointed an 11-member Central Election Commission.

The Kosovo authorities underlined that independence was irreversible and the review by the ICJ of the legality of the declaration of independence would not prevent other countries from recognizing Kosovo as an independent State. The Kosovo Serb political leadership in northern Kosovo continued to oppose the deployment to the north of the International Civilian Office, foreseen in the Comprehensive Proposal for the Kosovo Status Settlement—which was not endorsed by the Security Council—and the deployment of the EU Rule of Law Mission in Kosovo (EULEX).

KFOR launched the recruitment process for a future Kosovo security force. During the first stage, the selection would be made from the Kosovo Protection Corps (KPC). Non-recruited KPC members would be resettled, reintegrated or retired with dignity. A resettlement programme would be funded by a NATO trust fund and implemented by the United Nations Development Programme.

UNMIK announced the start of the reconfiguration process on 26 June and had begun to adapt its structure within the framework of resolution 1244(1999). The reconfiguration of UNMIK was being accelerated, was taking place in a transparent manner and was consistent with the UN position of strict neutrality on the question of Kosovo's status. The Special Representative was facilitating the EU's preparations to undertake an enhanced operational role in the rule-of-law area, focusing on policing, justice and customs. EULEX would fully respect resolution 1244(1999), operate under the overall authority and within the status-neutral framework of the United Nations and submit reports to it on a regular basis. UNMIK had been working closely with EULEX on technical arrangements designed to facilitate its deployment under resolution 1244(1999). The Pristina authorities had welcomed the beginning of the reconfiguration, but had expressed reservations about a perceived lack of clarity on the timing of the process and about the competencies to be retained by UNMIK. The Organization for Security and Cooperation in Europe (OSCE) would remain a central element of a reconfigured UNMIK through the OSCE mission in Kosovo.

Serbia had accepted the results of the dialogue with the Special Representative on the six key areas and the arrangements set out in the report, while the Pristina authorities had stated that they did not accept those arrangements: they favoured the quick deployment of EULEX and would cooperate with it on its deployment throughout the territory of Kosovo.

Security Council consideration (November). Briefing the Council on 26 November [meeting 6025], the Special Representative said that UNMIK was reorienting its field presence to concentrate on areas occupied by non-Albanian communities, monitoring the interests of those communities and retaining a supporting and mediation role. UNMIK needed to concentrate on the areas where it could still make a difference for good, rather than attempt to continue functions that were neither relevant nor needed. EULEX was deploying at an increasingly accelerated rate, but UNMIK remained the principal international guarantor of the rule of law in Kosovo. Its role was becoming much more political, for example, in providing an interface for the dialogue between Belgrade and Pristina. Since it had not yet been possible to establish conditions for the two sides to talk to each other, UNMIK had a role as an interlocutor of both, although each side interpreted that role in a different way.

Stressing that Serbia's voice must be respected, Foreign Minister Jeremić said that a dialogue between Serbia and the United Nations had begun, focusing on the six topics of mutual concern proposed by the Secretary-General. That dialogue created the conditions to protect the well-being of Serbs and other gravely endangered communities in Kosovo. It cemented the fact that Serbia remained indispensable to the self-governance of its southern province.

While underscoring Kosovo's full support for the deployment of EULEX, Kosovo Foreign Minister Hyseni said that, in a declaration of 18 November, Kosovo had made very clear its rejection of the six-point proposal made by the Secretary-General. Kosovo could not permit any action that infringed upon its sovereignty and territorial integrity. Kosovo would cooperate with EULEX for its deployment throughout Kosovo on the basis of Kosovo's declaration of independence, Constitution and laws, as well as the Ahtisaari package, the EU joint action plan of 4 February and the initiatives for EULEX deployment, as its mandate fully respected Kosovo's sovereignty, territorial integrity and unity.

SECURITY COUNCIL ACTION

On 26 November [meeting 6025], following consultations among Security Council members, the President made statement **S/PRST/2008/44** on behalf of the Council:

> The Security Council welcomes the report of the Secretary-General of 24 November 2008 on the United Nations Interim Administration Mission in Kosovo and, taking into account the positions of Belgrade and Pristina on the report, which were reflected in their respective statements, welcomes their intentions to cooperate with the international community.
>
> The Council welcomes the cooperation between the United Nations and other international actors, within the framework of Council resolution 1244(1999), and also welcomes the continuing efforts of the European Union to advance the European perspective of the whole of the Western Balkans, thereby making a decisive contribution to regional stability and prosperity.

Communication. On 12 December [S/2008/803], Serbia clarified its position on the reconfiguration of the international civilian presence in Kosovo and Metohija. Serbia had indicated its support for EULEX on the assumption that, in addition to being status-neutral, EULEX fully respected resolution 1244(1999) and operated under UN authority, serving as the implementing arm of the United Nations. EULEX's mandate did not include the implementation of any portion of the Ahtisaari Comprehensive Proposal for a Kosovo Status Settlement, which was not endorsed by the Security Council and therefore had no standing in international law. In a letter to Serbia received on 6 December, the Special Representative had indicated his intention to reconfigure UNMIK operations in the rule-of-law area following the deployment of EULEX. The letter did not specify how the Special Representative intended to implement the provisions agreed to in the "dialogue with Belgrade" outlined in the Secretary-General's November report, especially those relating to the rule of law. Serbia viewed UNMIK as its primary interlocutor on implementation and all other issues related to the interim administration of Kosovo. It was therefore essential that the executive and reserved powers accorded to it by the Constitutional Framework for Provisional Self-Government [YUN 2001, p. 352] continued to be exercised. Moreover, the UN field presence through regional and subregional offices remained vital, as did its presence in Belgrade. Accordingly, the Special Representative was expected to propose a schedule of meetings on implementation. Sustaining the engagement of the United Nations and the Special Representative remained a crucial component in achieving success on the ground and contributing to stability. The Representative's continuing activities served as a guarantee of the status-neutrality of the international presence.

Further report of Secretary-General. In a later report [S/2009/149], the Secretary-General said that EULEX deployed Kosovo-wide without incident on 9 December, assuming full operational responsibility in the area of the rule of law. Serbia and a majority of Kosovo Serbs accepted that deployment on condition that it would fully respect resolution 1244(1999) and that it would operate under the overall authority of the United Nations and within its status-neutral framework.

As a result, after almost 10 years of service in Kosovo, UNMIK police successfully completed their operations, including in the Mitrovicë/Mitrovica region. By 9 December, EULEX had deployed 1,045 police officers throughout Kosovo. Over a three-day period, UNMIK police throughout Kosovo reported to their former posts in civilian clothes and introduced the EULEX police monitors/advisers to their Kosovo police counterparts. On 12 December, an agreement was signed between UNMIK police and EULEX on the transfer of crime investigation files.

Progress on standards implementation

The Secretary-General transmitted to the Security Council the technical assessments of progress in implementing the standards for Kosovo (functioning democratic institutions, rule of law, freedom of movement, returns and reintegration, economy, property rights, cultural heritage, dialogue with Belgrade and the Kosovo Protection Corps), which it had to meet to comply with resolution 1244(1999) [YUN 1999, p. 353]; the Constitutional Framework for Provisional Self-Government [YUN 2001, p. 352]; the original standards/benchmarks statement endorsed by the Council in presidential statement S/PRST/2002/11 [YUN 2002, p. 369]; and the 2004 Kosovo Standards Implementation Plan [YUN 2004, p. 408]. The assessments, prepared by the Special Representative, were annexed to the Secretary-General's three reports to the Council on UNMIK covering 2008 [S/2008/211, S/2008/458, S/2008/692].

Functioning democratic institutions. Following the November 2007 elections [YUN 2007, p. 404], the new Assembly of Kosovo was inaugurated on 4

January. On 9 January, it elected its President and six members of its Presidency, while the election of the Kosovo Serb representative and the other non-Albanian representative was completed in February. The Assembly on 9 January re-elected the President of Kosovo and elected the Prime Minister and Government. The new Government included two female Ministers and two female deputy Ministers, compared with one female Minister and one female Deputy Minister in the previous Government. In April, the Government approved the Kosovo programme on gender equality, which focused on education of women, integration of women into the economy, labour and social welfare, culture and the media, health, gender relations and decision-making processes.

Many Kosovo Serbs started to report back to work, after an initial boycott following the declaration of independence, but the situation varied in different areas of Kosovo. Some Kosovo Serb leaders announced the formation of parallel municipal assemblies based on the local elections organized by Belgrade in Kosovo Serb areas in May. The Anti-Corruption Agency [YUN 2007, p. 405] in March submitted its first annual report to the President of the Assembly. The implementation of the Law on the Use of Languages continued to suffer from insufficient allocation of human and financial resources, and only one municipality had adopted a municipal regulation on the use of languages. A new 11-member Central Election Commission was appointed by presidential decree in August. The newly formed Election Complaints and Appeals Commission, a five-member body of Supreme Court judges, provided for redress of grievances relating to electoral issues. Kosovo's new legal framework envisaged an increase in the number of municipalities from 33 to 38, but the non-participation of the Kosovo Serb community was paralysing the process of creating the new Kosovo Serb majority municipalities foreseen in the new Law on Municipal Boundaries.

Most of the municipalities had not met their fair-share financing obligations. As a result of the new Law on Local Government Finance, municipalities were expected to integrate fair-share financing into their regular budget from 2009 onwards: that would make it challenging to follow up on the use of funds targeted for minority communities.

Rule of law. Five District Legal Aid Bureaux were opened in January and three new Special Prosecutors were recruited for the Special Prosecutors Office. The multi-ethnic character of the police had been challenged since the declaration of independence, because Kosovo Serb police officers in many southern Kosovo municipalities were suspended following their statement that they would no longer recognize the police chain of command and their demand to be placed under the direct command of UNMIK police. In May, the Government decided to continue to pay the suspended police officers to encourage them to return to their posts, and an operational plan to assist those who wished to return was put in place. Despite progress in the relationship between the Ministry of Internal Affairs and the police, sustained efforts were needed to get the police to accept the Ministry's oversight. Kosovo Serb judges and prosecutors continued their protests in northern Mitrovicë/Mitrovica. The Judicial Council and the Ministry of Justice continued to pay salaries to all court staff and prosecutors' office staff pending their return to work. In the north, the courthouse in Mitrovicë/Mitrovica reopened on 3 October, on the basis of the dialogue of the Special Representative with the Government of Serbia and his consultations with other stakeholders, and following approximately six months of legal vacuum.

In July, a suspect was arrested in an outstanding case related to the March 2004 riots [YUN 2004, p. 405] and charged with participation, as a leader, in a crowd that committed criminal offences against Kosovo Serb residents, Serbian Orthodox religious sites and the UNMIK headquarters in Prizren. The first Kosovo passports were issued in July. However, the authorities had not placed any restrictions on the use by Kosovo Serbs of Serbian passports, and had begun issuing new Kosovo identity cards, while UNMIK and Serbian identity documents continued to be valid.

Freedom of movement. In 2008, regular surveys showed that more than 96 per cent of minority community members continued to travel outside their areas of residence. Freedom of movement was not a concern of the minority communities, except for the Kosovo Albanian minorities in northern Kosovo, according to the Office of the United Nations High Commissioner for Refugees (UNHCR). Nevertheless, efforts were needed from the Ministry of Transport and Communications to develop the humanitarian transport service. The humanitarian bus line from a Kosovo Albanian neighbourhood in northern Mitrovicë/Mitrovica to the southern part of the city was restored on 7 April after being temporarily halted following the declaration of independence. The railway service between Zveçan/Zvečan and Fushë Kosovë/Kosovo Polje had not resumed after it was stopped in early March, when Serbian Railways began illegally operating train service in the north of Kosovo and Kosovo Serb staff ceased to report to work. A replacement footbridge built across the Ibar River connecting south Mitrovicë/Mitrovica to the Three Towers mixed area in the north was inaugurated in July, facilitating freedom of movement for all communities.

Returns and reintegration. The number of minority returns declined sharply in comparison with previous years, which could be attributed to political developments, including the declaration of independence, as well as to the non-transparent allocation of returns funding and the non-consultative approach to returns-related issues adopted by the Ministry of Communities and Returns. UNHCR estimated that only 582 minority community members returned to Kosovo in 2008, compared with 1,816 in 2007 and 1,669 in 2006. UNHCR reported a very high percentage (84.45 per cent) of sustainable returns to Kosovo between March 2005 and June 2008. The boycott by Kosovo Serb representatives of various decision-making forums on returns had affected the work and quality of decisions on communities and returns-related issues. With the signing of a memorandum of understanding on 23 May between the Ministry of Communities and Returns and an internally displaced persons association, the Ministry expected to enhance its relations with such associations in many communities and improve returns-related projects. The allocated funding for the Ministry increased to €7.1 million for 2008, with a funding gap of €18 million for 23 approved organized returns projects. The Ministry faced a wide range of irregularities in administration, management, and budget and finance-related issues. The arrival of the new Minister for Communities and Returns coincided with the suspension and subsequent dismissal of five directors in the Ministry on charges of corruption and misuse of funds. The Ministry had proposed a revision of the beneficiary selection criteria for individual returns so as to include Kosovo residents who were not displaced as a result of the 1999 conflict.

Economy. On 15 February, the Assembly of Kosovo approved the budget for 2008, as previously endorsed by the Economic and Fiscal Council. The budget amounted to €1.1 billion, a substantial increase over the €718 million budget for 2007, and was promulgated by the Special Representative on 29 February. An International Monetary Fund (IMF) mission visited Kosovo in April to assess the macroeconomic framework and fiscal policies. The IMF had revised upwards the Kosovo GDP figures, which were estimated at €3,343 million (€1,573 per capita) in 2007, and forecast a real GDP growth of about 5 per cent per annum over a five-year period. As at 30 April, the Kosovo Trust Agency (KTA) had launched 30 waves of privatization, with 551 new companies derived from the assets of 313 socially owned enterprises tendered for sale. In June, UNMIK and the Ministry of Transport and Communications participated in the launch of a treaty establishing a transport community of the western Balkans, opening the way for the inclusion of Kosovo in the treaty. In July, UNMIK and the Ministry participated in the steering committee meeting of the South-East Europe Transport Observatory.

In August, UNMIK, in cooperation with Kosovo authorities, completed the signing of an agreement on privileges and immunities of the secretariat of the Central European Free Trade Agreement, thereby clearing the way for the implementation of the agreement. The European Commission adopted the 2008 progress report for Kosovo, and would present a feasibility study that would assess further means for Kosovo's progress towards integration with the EU. The situation along the Administrative Boundary Line had not changed since the destruction of customs facilities in northern Kosovo on 19 February. UNMIK Customs continued to have no presence there, leading to an estimated loss of €2 million a week in customs and value added tax revenue in both the Kosovo and Serbian budgets. UNMIK's economic reconstruction pillar (pillar IV) ceased all substantive operations on 30 June, pursuant to a decision by the European Commission. As a consequence, UNMIK no longer possessed any technical capacity or budgetary allocation to perform functions formerly carried out by that pillar. In that context, on 24 August, former KTA officials, appointed by the Kosovo authorities to official positions in the newly established Privatization Agency of Kosovo, took over the KTA compound in the presence of police officers. Following the takeover of the compound, the Privatization Agency was expected to attempt to restart the privatization process.

Property rights. The Kosovo Cadastral Agency had completed a pilot project on the registration of apartments in seven municipalities, which would be used as a model for the registration of apartments throughout Kosovo. The draft law on the treatment of illegal construction was adopted by the Assembly and was pending promulgation, as well as the draft law on the sale of apartments where tenure rights existed. The draft law on the organization of cadastral institutions was included in the Government's legislative strategy for 2008. The number of cases adjudicated by the Property Claims Commission stood at 14,105, or 39 per cent of all claims received. The Kosovo Property Agency (KPA) had kept up the momentum in the adjudication process, and continued to administer abandoned properties and the voluntary rental scheme. There were 4,325 abandoned properties under KPA administration, of which 2,258 participated in the rental scheme with the consent of their owners.

Cultural heritage. The private security company contracted by the Ministry of Culture, Youth and Sports to implement additional security measures for 15 Orthodox sites under the €50,000 grant from the Government [YUN 2007, p. 406] began its work following approval of its plan by the Serbian Orthodox Church in February. Also in February, the Assembly adopted a Law on the Establishment of Special Protective Zones. The Special Representative issued two executive decisions regarding a property dispute involving the Visoki Dečani Monastery. Works on the Hadum Mosque in Gjakovë/Djakovica under the auspices of the United Nations Educational, Scientific and Cultural Organization, with a United States donation, commenced in April.

In 2008, the Kosovo police recorded 51 incidents targeting religious and cultural heritage sites, including vandalism and theft. Security for cultural and religious heritage sites continued to be a priority. The police continued to maintain a round-the-clock presence at the Church of Saint Nicholas in Prishtinë/Priština, as well as routine patrolling of cultural and religious sites across Kosovo. The Reconstruction Implementation Committee would require the support of all stakeholders, particularly the Serbian Orthodox Church, to conclude its undertaking.

Dialogue with Belgrade. Discussions were conducted on the Secretary-General's proposals as set out in his June report (see p. 438). The Special Representative stated that dialogue and consultations with all parties had been conducted in Belgrade and Pristina, without prejudice to their positions on the status issue. All parties had accepted the reconfiguration of the structure and profile of the international presence and had sought pragmatic progress in the discussions with the Special Representative on the six provisions—police, courts, customs, transportation and infrastructure, boundaries and Serbian patrimony.

Kosovo Protection Corps. KPC remained focused on developing its operational capability. From 22 March to 12 April, a detachment of KPC deminers, accompanied by an UNMIK representative took part in rescue operations in the village of Gërdec near Tirana, Albania, to help deal with the consequences of the explosion of an ammunition depot on 15 March. Following the declaration of independence in February, eight Kosovo Serb members of the KPC stopped working. No disciplinary action had been taken against them and efforts continued to persuade them to return to work. Minority representation in the KPC, which had 2,865 active members at the end of 2008, remained at 6.1 per cent, including the representation of Kosovo Serbs, which had decreased slightly from 1 per cent to 0.98 per cent since May. Women were represented at all levels, although total numbers were relatively small, at 3 per cent.

UN Interim Administration Mission in Kosovo

THE United Nations Interim Administration Mission in Kosovo (UNMIK), established in 1999 [YUN 1999, p. 357] to facilitate a political process to determine Kosovo's political future, comprised five components: interim administration (led by the United Nations); institution-building (led by OSCE); economic reconstruction (led by the EU); humanitarian affairs (led by UNHCR); and police and justice (led by the United Nations). UNMIK was headed by the Special Representative of the Secretary-General Joachim Rücker (Germany), who was succeeded by Lamberto Zannier (Italy) on 20 June.

The Secretary-General reported to the Security Council on UNMIK activities and developments in Kosovo for the periods from 16 December 2007 to 1 March 2008 [S/2008/211], 1 March to 25 June [S/2008/458], 26 June to 31 October [S/2008/692], 1 November to 9 March 2009 [S/2009/149] and in a special report submitted on 12 June [S/2008/354].

OIOS report. In April, the Office of Internal Oversight Services (OIOS) issued a report on the comprehensive audit of UNMIK's mandate implementation [A/62/807], which focused on establishing the police and an independent and multi-ethnic judiciary and reforming the correctional system; performing basic civil administrative functions, promoting the establishment of self-government, promoting human rights and ensuring the return of refugees and displaced persons; and developing the legal, institutional and policy framework for economic reconstruction and development. The audit identified a number of failures and deficiencies in implementing the mandates. OIOS had concerns about the management of the transfer of responsibilities to the central government ministries and local municipalities. It also noted deficiencies in the governance mechanisms and internal control processes at the KTA. Furthermore, the continued weaknesses and backlog of court cases in the judiciary system were of concern.

UNMIK had transferred more than 80 per cent of the competencies for law enforcement to the Kosovo police and had established judicial systems that had been "Kosovorized" to a large extent. However, a lack of leadership and managerial skills had limited UNMIK's ability to accomplish the mandated goals in an effective manner, and the continued weaknesses in the judiciary system were of concern. The staff strengths of the police and the Kosovo Correctional Service were built up on an ad hoc basis. The UNMIK Regulation was not promptly amended to provide clear goals for the required multi-ethnic composition of the judiciary. Moreover, the number of pending court cases, which stood at 160,238 as at March 2007, was alarming.

Turning to civil administration, OIOS said that UNMIK had not established minimum criteria for assessing the preparedness of central government ministries and local government municipalities before the transfer of civil administration competencies, and failed to put effective mechanisms in place to monitor and determine whether the ministries and municipalities had adequately assumed those competencies. Significant deficiencies were also identified in the governance mechanisms and internal control processes at KTA. OIOS maintained that UNMIK and the KTA

Board of Directors operated the Agency in a way that did not adhere to the KTA Regulation, corporate governance principles, financial fiduciary responsibilities and public accountability requirements. For example, the KTA Board contravened the KTA Regulation and the Agency's governance principles and guidelines when it approved the appointment of politically active members to the Board of Directors of the Kosovo Energy Corporation. That has resulted in a weak corporate governance framework that could jeopardize the effective performance and financial sustainability of the Agency.

OIOS issued a series of recommendations, and suggested that the Secretary-General bring the report to the attention of the Security Council.

Report of Secretary-General. In his July report on UNMIK [S/2008/458], the Secretary-General said that the OIOS report identified a number of failures and deficiencies. His Special Representative had raised concerns that the report did not reflect a balanced assessment of the UNMIK performance throughout the course of its nine years in Kosovo. Taking into account the evolving circumstances on the ground, the Special Representative would monitor gaps in the standards implementation and assist the local authorities in implementing the standards in order to fulfil the UNMIK mandate.

Financing

On 20 June [meeting 109], the General Assembly, having considered the Secretary-General's reports on the UNMIK budget for the periods from 1 July 2006 to 30 June 2007 [A/62/610] and from 1 July 2008 to 30 June 2009 [A/62/687]; the Secretary-General's note on the financing arrangements for the Mission for the period from 1 July 2007 to 30 June 2008 [A/62/801] and the related report of the Advisory Committee on Administrative and Budgetary Questions (ACABQ) [A/62/781/Add.18]; the OIOS report on the comprehensive audit of the Mission mandate implementation [A/62/807]; and the statement by the representative of the Secretary-General transmitting his comments thereon [A/C.5/62/SR.49], adopted, on the recommendation of the Fifth (Administrative and Budgetary) Committee [A/62/875], **resolution 62/262** without vote [agenda item 151].

Financing of the United Nations Interim Administration Mission in Kosovo

The General Assembly,

Having considered the reports of the Secretary-General on the financing of the United Nations Interim Administration Mission in Kosovo, the note by the Secretary-General on the financing arrangements for the Mission and the related report of the Advisory Committee on Administrative and Budgetary Questions, the report of the Office of Internal Oversight Services on the comprehensive audit of the Mission mandate implementation and the oral statement by the representative of the Secretary-General transmitting his comments thereon,

Recalling Security Council resolution 1244(1999) of 10 June 1999 regarding the establishment of the United Nations Interim Administration Mission in Kosovo,

Recalling also its resolution 53/241 of 28 July 1999 on the financing of the Mission and its subsequent resolutions thereon, the latest of which was resolution 61/285 of 29 June 2007,

Acknowledging the complexity of the Mission,

Reaffirming the general principles underlying the financing of United Nations peacekeeping operations, as stated in General Assembly resolutions 1874(S-IV) of 27 June 1963, 3101(XXVIII) of 11 December 1973 and 55/235 of 23 December 2000,

Mindful of the fact that it is essential to provide the Mission with the financial resources necessary to enable it to fulfil its responsibilities under the relevant resolution of the Security Council,

1. *Requests* the Secretary-General to entrust the Head of Mission with the task of formulating future budget proposals in full accordance with the provisions of General Assembly resolutions 59/296 of 22 June 2005, 60/266 of 30 June 2006 and 61/276 of 29 June 2007, as well as other relevant resolutions;

2. *Takes note* of the status of contributions to the United Nations Interim Administration Mission in Kosovo as at 30 April 2008, including the contributions outstanding in the amount of 48.9 million United States dollars, representing some 2 per cent of the total assessed contributions, notes with concern that only ninety-six Member States have paid their assessed contributions in full, and urges all other Member States, in particular those in arrears, to ensure payment of their outstanding assessed contributions;

3. *Expresses its appreciation* to those Member States which have paid their assessed contributions in full, and urges all other Member States to make every possible effort to ensure payment of their assessed contributions to the Mission in full;

4. *Expresses concern* at the financial situation with regard to peacekeeping activities, in particular as regards the reimbursements to troop contributors that bear additional burdens owing to overdue payments by Member States of their assessments;

5. *Also expresses concern* at the delay experienced by the Secretary-General in deploying and providing adequate resources to some recent peacekeeping missions, in particular those in Africa;

6. *Emphasizes* that all future and existing peacekeeping missions shall be given equal and non-discriminatory treatment in respect of financial and administrative arrangements;

7. *Also emphasizes* that all peacekeeping missions shall be provided with adequate resources for the effective and efficient discharge of their respective mandates;

8. *Reiterates its request* to the Secretary-General to make the fullest possible use of facilities and equipment at

the United Nations Logistics Base at Brindisi, Italy, in order to minimize the costs of procurement for the Mission;

9. *Endorses* the conclusions and recommendations contained in the report of the Advisory Committee on Administrative and Budgetary Questions, and requests the Secretary-General to ensure their full implementation;

10. *Requests* the Secretary-General to ensure the full implementation of the relevant provisions of its resolutions 59/296, 60/266 and 61/276;

11. *Also requests* the Secretary-General to take all necessary action to ensure that the Mission is administered with a maximum of efficiency and economy;

12. *Further requests* the Secretary-General, in order to reduce the cost of employing General Service staff, to continue efforts to recruit local staff for the Mission against General Service posts, commensurate with the requirements of the Mission;

13. *Takes note* of the report of the Office of Internal Oversight Services on the comprehensive audit of the Mission mandate implementation and the oral statement by the representative of the Secretary-General transmitting his comments thereon;

Financial performance report for the period from 1 July 2006 to 30 June 2007

14. *Also takes note* of the report of the Secretary-General on the financial performance of the Mission for the period from 1 July 2006 to 30 June 2007;

Financing arrangements for the period from 1 July 2007 to 30 June 2008

15. *Further takes note* of the note by the Secretary-General on the financing arrangements for the Mission for the period from 1 July 2007 to 30 June 2008;

16. *Decides* to appropriate to the Special Account for the United Nations Interim Administration Mission in Kosovo the additional amount of 9,799,600 dollars for the maintenance of the Mission for the period from 1 July 2007 to 30 June 2008, taking into account the amount of 220,897,200 dollars already appropriated for the Mission for the same period under the provisions of resolution 61/285;

Financing of the additional appropriation for the period from 1 July 2007 to 30 June 2008

17. *Also decides* to apportion among Member States the amount of 9,799,600 dollars, taking into account the amount of 220,897,200 dollars already apportioned by the General Assembly for the maintenance of the Mission in its resolution 61/285 for the period from 1 July 2007 to 30 June 2008, in accordance with the levels updated in General Assembly resolution 61/243 of 22 December 2006, and taking into account the scale of assessments for 2007 and 2008, as set out in its resolution 61/237 of 22 December 2006;

18. *Further decides* that, in accordance with the provisions of its resolution 973(X) of 15 December 1955, the decrease of 823,800 dollars in estimated staff assessment income in respect of the financial period from 1 July 2007 to 30 June 2008 shall be added to the apportionment among Member States as provided for in paragraph 17 above;

Budget estimates for the period from 1 July 2008 to 30 June 2009

19. *Decides* to appropriate to the Special Account for the Mission the amount of 207,203,100 dollars for the period from 1 July 2008 to 30 June 2009, inclusive of 198,012,000 dollars for the maintenance of the Mission, 8,012,200 dollars for the support account for peacekeeping operations and 1,178,900 dollars for the United Nations Logistics Base;

Financing of the appropriation

20. *Also decides* to apportion among Member States the amount of 207,203,100 dollars, in accordance with the levels updated in resolution 61/243, and taking into account the scale of assessments for 2008 and 2009, as set out in resolution 61/237;

21. *Further decides* that, in accordance with the provisions of its resolution 973(X), there shall be set off against the apportionment among Member States, as provided for in paragraph 20 above, their respective share in the Tax Equalization Fund of the amount of 16,141,400 dollars, comprising the estimated staff assessment income of 15,278,400 dollars approved for the Mission, the prorated share of 769,900 dollars of the estimated staff assessment income approved for the support account and the prorated share of 93,100 dollars of the estimated staff assessment income approved for the United Nations Logistics Base;

22. *Decides* that, for Member States that have fulfilled their financial obligations to the Mission, there shall be set off against their apportionment, as provided for in paragraph 20 above, their respective share of the unencumbered balance and other income in the total amount of 13,465,200 dollars in respect of the financial period ended 30 June 2007, in accordance with the levels updated in resolution 61/243, and taking into account the scale of assessments for 2007, as set out in resolution 61/237;

23. *Also decides* that, for Member States that have not fulfilled their financial obligations to the Mission, there shall be set off against their outstanding obligations their respective share of the unencumbered balance and other income in the total amount of 13,465,200 dollars in respect of the financial period ended 30 June 2007, in accordance with the scheme set out in paragraph 22 above;

24. *Further decides* that the decrease of 171,300 dollars in the estimated staff assessment income in respect of the financial period ended 30 June 2007 shall be set off against the credits from the amount of 13,465,200 dollars referred to in paragraphs 22 and 23 above;

25. *Emphasizes* that no peacekeeping mission shall be financed by borrowing funds from other active peacekeeping missions;

26. *Encourages* the Secretary-General to continue to take additional measures to ensure the safety and security of all personnel participating in the Mission under the auspices of the United Nations, bearing in mind paragraphs 5 and 6 of Security Council resolution 1502(2003) of 26 August 2003;

27. *Invites* voluntary contributions to the Mission in cash and in the form of services and supplies acceptable to the Secretary-General, to be administered, as appropriate, in accordance with the procedure and practices established by the General Assembly;

28. *Decides* to include in the provisional agenda of its sixty-third session the item entitled "Financing of the United Nations Interim Administration Mission in Kosovo".

By **decision 63/552** of 24 December, the Assembly decided that the agenda item on the financing of UNMIK would remain for consideration during its resumed sixty-third (2009) session.

International security presence (KFOR)

In accordance with resolution 1244(1999) [YUN 1999, p. 353], the Secretary-General transmitted to the Security Council reports on the activities during 2008 of the international security presence in Kosovo (KFOR), also known as Operation Joint Guard, covering the periods 1 to 31 January [S/2008/204], 1 to 29 February [S/2008/331], 1 to 31 March [S/2008/362], 1 to 30 April [S/2008/477], 1 to 31 May [S/2008/549], 1 to 30 June [S/2008/600] and 1 to 31 July [S/2008/638]. As at 31 July, the force, which operated under NATO leadership, comprised 14,409 troops, including 2,173 troops from non-NATO countries.

As before, KFOR handled incidents related to unexploded ordnance, counterfeit currency, illegal weapons possession, drugs, human trafficking and smuggling. KFOR units continued to focus on maintaining a safe and secure environment and freedom of movement throughout Kosovo, as well as on preventing non-compliant-group activities. They conducted high-visibility operations throughout Kosovo to deter any possible attempt at destabilization.

Georgia

In 2008, efforts continued to advance the Georgian-Abkhaz peace process, based on the 2001 Basic Principles for the Distribution of Competences between Tbilisi (Georgia's Government) and Sukhumi (the Abkhaz leadership) [YUN 2001, p. 386]. That document was intended to serve as a framework for substantive negotiations on the status of Abkhazia as a sovereign entity within the State of Georgia.

The escalation of hostilities and war in South Ossetia in August, as well as the subsequent Georgian-Russian conflict, deeply affected the situation in the Georgian-Abkhaz zone of conflict and the overall conflict-settlement process. In the aftermath of the conflict, the Russian Federation recognized Abkhazia's and South Ossetia's independence, while Georgia declared them territories occupied by the Russian Federation. Following Russia's recognition of Abkhazia, Georgia withdrew from the 1994 Moscow Agreement on a Ceasefire and Separation of Forces [YUN 1994, p. 583]. Subsequently, the Commonwealth of Independent States decided to suspend its peacekeeping operation in the conflict zone, which had been in place for 14 years [ibid.], monitored by the United Nations Observer Mission in Georgia.

In the EU-mediated agreement signed in Moscow on 8 September, it was agreed that the UN Mission would continue to carry out its mandate as before the August hostilities. In October, the Council extended the mandate of the Mission until 15 February 2009.

UN Observer Mission in Georgia

The United Nations Observer Mission in Georgia (UNOMIG), established by Security Council resolution 858(1993) [YUN 1993, p. 509], continued to monitor compliance with the 1994 Moscow Agreement and to fulfil other tasks, as mandated by Council resolution 937(1994) [YUN 1994, p. 584]. The Mission operated in close collaboration with the collective peacekeeping forces of the Commonwealth of Independent States (CIS), located since 1994 in the zone of conflict [ibid., p. 583]. The Council extended the Mission's mandate twice during the year, the first time until 15 October, and the second until 15 February 2009.

UNOMIG main headquarters was located in Sukhumi (Abkhazia, Georgia), with a liaison office in the Georgian capital of Tbilisi, and team bases and sector headquarters in the Gali and Zugdidi sectors. A team base in the Kodori Valley was manned by observers operating from Sukhumi. As at December 2008, UNOMIG strength stood at 136 military observers and 20 police advisers.

In September [S/2008/631], Johan Verbeke (Belgium) succeeded Jean Arnault (France) as the Secretary-General's Special Representative for Georgia and Head of UNOMIG. He was assisted by the UNOMIG Chief Military Observer, Major General Anwar Hussain (Bangladesh), who succeeded Major General Niaz Muhammad Khan Khattak (Pakistan).

Political aspects of the conflict

Report of Secretary-General (January). In a January report on the situation in Abkhazia [S/2008/38], the Secretary-General stated that UNOMIG continued its efforts to prevent the escalation of tensions in the zone of conflict and to facilitate dialogue between the Georgian and Abkhaz sides. The Secretary-General noted that no incident had occurred between those sides and that no further confrontation had taken place between Georgian security forces and CIS peacekeeping forces since their tense stand-off on 30 October 2007 [YUN 2007, p. 417]. A string of allegations concerning either the deployment of forces on both sides of the ceasefire line or incidents involving the Abkhaz forces or the CIS peacekeeping force, however, generated tensions and, occasionally, alarm in the zone of conflict and beyond.

While some work had been done following up on the Bonn meeting [YUN 2007, p. 413], differences between the sides persisted on the formal political dialogue. Concerned that internal problems in Georgia could set the stage for military action in the zone of conflict, the Abkhaz side announced a strengthening of security measures along the ceasefire line until mid-January. The Government of Georgia denied any aggressive intentions and, in turn, interpreted Abkhaz security measures as the introduction of a state of emergency in the Gali district, possibly aimed against the Georgian population in the district. The two electoral campaigns that had taken place in 2007 [ibid., p. 412], for the Georgian presidency and the de facto Abkhaz parliament, illustrated the rift between the political aspirations of the sides and their constituencies, with reunification and independence seen as top, non-negotiable priorities in Tbilisi and Sukhumi, respectively, and promoted with an equal sense of urgency. The Security Council had repeatedly called upon the sides to exercise restraint. A successful dialogue on security, economic rehabilitation and the return of internally displaced persons and refugees would help bring about a comprehensive political settlement.

Following a statement by a Russian ruling party official about possible deliberations in the Russian Duma in January on a request by the Abkhaz de facto parliament for Russian recognition of Abkhaz independence, Georgian officials stated that the Government would take all necessary measures under the Constitution to protect Georgia's territorial integrity.

Meeting of Group of Friends (February). On 18 and 19 February, senior representatives of the Group of Friends of the Secretary-General (France, Germany, Russian Federation, United Kingdom and United States) met in Geneva under the chairmanship of the Assistant Secretary-General for Peacekeeping Operations, Edmond Mulet. The meeting was attended by Georgian and Abkhaz delegations.

The Georgian side stressed the importance of the international community's commitment to Georgia's territorial integrity and sovereignty, as reflected in Council resolutions, and noted progress in implementing measures discussed in Geneva and Bonn. It stated that its commitments regarding the upper Kodori Valley were fulfilled and verifiable, thanks to transparency measures such as the establishment of a UNOMIG team base there, and therefore believed that the issue should be removed from the agenda. It underscored its readiness to elaborate and implement jointly with the Abkhaz side proposals aimed at increasing confidence, people-to-people contacts and the development of strong ties between civil societies. The Georgian delegation emphasized the establishment of economic links and the lifting of economic sanctions, and stressed that joint economic activities could be the best mechanism to ensure confidence-building. It expressed its readiness to revisit the package of documents prepared in 2005 on the non-use of force and the return of internally displaced persons and refugees.

The Abkhaz side said that international intermediaries should take into account in a more balanced way the international principles of self-determination and territorial integrity, particularly in light of recent decisions on Kosovo, and proposed that comprehensive settlement negotiations use as a basis the Abkhaz position paper "Key to the Future", submitted in 2006. It reaffirmed its commitment to the implementation of the confidence-building measures proposed by the Friends. It stressed the main issues apt to improve confidence and, to a large extent, the credibility of the negotiation itself, such as the full implementation of the Moscow Agreement with regard to the Kodori Valley, the non-use of force and the lifting of the CIS embargo against Abkhazia. The Abkhaz side stressed its flexibility in finding compromises on those issues, including the gradual establishment of a local police force in the upper Kodori Valley with international assistance, and the adoption of the already negotiated package of documents on non-use of force and the return of internally displaced persons.

The Group of Friends stressed the importance of cooperation by the two sides in enhancing the security situation. The Group reiterated its call for the resumption of the security meetings between the sides, UNOMIG and the CIS peacekeeping force. It also expressed disappointment at the lack of progress made since the Bonn meeting and underscored the importance of implementing the proposals for confidence-building measures made by the Group in February 2007 and endorsed by the Security Council [YUN 2007, p. 412]. The Group reaffirmed the importance of the right of return for all the refugees and internally displaced persons to Abkhazia, Georgia, and encouraged the sides to focus on practical steps to improve conditions for returns.

Communications. In letters dated 7 March [A/62/732, S/2008/167], Georgia expressed concern about the Russian Federation's withdrawal from the 1996 decision of the CIS Council of Heads of State on measures aimed at settling the conflict in Abkhazia [YUN 1996, p. 352]. By that withdrawal, Russia considered itself no longer bound by the obligation to prevent the sale and supply of armaments to the Abkhaz side, or to prevent the enrolment of its own citizens in armed groups in the conflict zone. By withdrawing unilaterally, Russia created the basis for providing the separatist government with military assistance and for establishing its military presence in Abkhazia.

On 10 March [S/2008/168], the Russian Federation said that on 6 March it had informed the CIS Executive Committee that the Russian Federation, due to a change in the circumstances, no longer considered itself bound by the 1996 decision of the CIS Council that had established sanctions against Abkhazia to induce it to take a more flexible position on the return of refugees and temporarily displaced persons. The situation had cardinally changed. Most of the Georgian refugees that lived in Abkhazia's Gali District had returned there. Further progress was impeded by Georgia's rejection of the system for their registration proposed by UNHCR. The Abkhaz side had been fulfilling its obligations under the agreements of the conflict settlement process. The Georgian side had not displayed a similar constructive approach and was actually undermining negotiations, having placed its administrative structure in the upper Kodori Valley. Against that background, the sanctions had lost their meaning: they were hindering the implementation of economic and social programmes and were causing unjustified hardship for the Abkhaz people. Russia had therefore decided to lift the sanctions.

Report of Secretary-General (April). In an April report [S/2008/219], the Secretary-General said that, despite the efforts of his Special Representative, the negotiation process remained suspended, as the Abkhaz side continued to insist on the withdrawal of Georgian armed personnel from the upper Kodori Valley as a precondition for resuming negotiations. He welcomed the dialogue between the Georgian Ministry of Internal Affairs, the CIS peacekeeping force and UNOMIG, which had been taking place regularly on the Zugdidi side of the ceasefire line.

In March, the de facto Abkhaz Parliament adopted a statement that supported the suspension of negotiations with the Georgian side until the withdrawal of Georgian forces from the upper Kodori Valley. It also called upon the de facto leadership to take measures to re-establish Abkhaz "jurisdiction" over the upper Kodori Valley and appealed to the United Nations, international organizations and States to consider recognition of Abkhazia's independence. On 6 March, the Russian Federation announced that it no longer considered itself bound by the restrictions introduced by the 1996 decision of the CIS Council of Heads of State. Georgia considered the decision as an overt attempt to infringe upon its sovereignty and territorial integrity, declared a "policy of zero tolerance towards the militarization of Abkhazia, Georgia" and pledged to work with the international community to prevent complications. In March, the Russian State Duma held three hearings on Abkhaz and South Ossetian appeals for recognition of their independence, and on 21 March adopted a statement that, while expressing support for the sovereignty and territorial integrity of Georgia, deemed necessary an adjustment in Russian policy in the light of Kosovo's unilateral declaration of independence. The Duma called on the executive branch to strengthen protection of Russian citizens living in Abkhazia and proposed that the executive branch consider recognizing Abkhazia's independence. Georgia's Ministry of Foreign Affairs viewed the statement of the Duma as an attempt to interfere in Georgia's internal affairs and warned that any modification in the deployment of the CIS peacekeeping force without the consent of the Georgian authorities in Abkhazia would constitute an act of aggression against Georgia.

On 28 March, President Mikheil Saakashvili outlined Georgia's proposals for resolving the conflict, which included: unlimited autonomy and wide federalism, supported by international guarantees; broad Abkhaz political representation in the official structures of Georgia, including a new post of Vice-President to be occupied by an Abkhaz; the right to veto legislation and decisions related to the constitutional status of Abkhazia and to issues related to Abkhaz culture, language and ethnicity; the establishment of jointly controlled free economic zones in the Gali and Ochamchira districts; and the gradual merger of law-enforcement and customs services. He also suggested that the Russian Federation become, together with other members of the international community, a mediator to the conflict. The de facto Abkhaz leadership stated that those proposals were not acceptable and confirmed its position that building good-neighbourly relations with Georgia on an equal basis was the only subject it was prepared to consider.

In light of the situation and the role UNOMIG played in promoting stability, cooperation and the restoration of dialogue, the Secretary-General recommended that its mandate be extended for another six months, until 15 October.

Security Council consideration (April). At a closed meeting on 14 April [meeting 5865], Mr. Mulet briefed Security Council members and representatives of UNOMIG troop-contributing countries. The briefing was followed by an exchange of views.

SECURITY COUNCIL ACTION

On 15 April [meeting 5866], the Security Council unanimously adopted **resolution 1808(2008)**. The draft [S/2008/248] was submitted by Croatia, France, Germany, the Russian Federation, the United Kingdom and the United States.

The Security Council,

Recalling all its relevant resolutions, including resolution 1781(2007) of 15 October 2007,

Welcoming the reports of the Secretary-General of 23 January and 2 April 2008 on the activities of the United Nations Observer Mission in Georgia,

Reiterating the importance of maintaining the separation of forces and the preservation of the ceasefire,

Supporting the sustained efforts of the Secretary-General and of his Special Representative for Georgia, with the assistance of the Group of Friends of the Secretary-General on Georgia, as well as the Russian Federation in its capacity as facilitator, and of the Organization for Security and Cooperation in Europe, underlining the increased importance of the meetings in the Geneva format as the forum for meaningful political dialogue, and welcoming the Georgian and Abkhaz renewed commitment to this process,

Noting that, whereas the United Nations and the Group of Friends of the Secretary-General will continue to support the process of conflict resolution between the Georgian and Abkhaz sides, the primary responsibility to make use of this support and to implement measures to advance the process, in particular measures to build confidence, remains with both sides,

Regretting the continued lack of progress in implementing confidence-building measures, and underlining the importance of constructive goodwill between the sides and respect for each other's concerns,

Stressing the importance of close and effective cooperation between the Mission and the peacekeeping force of the Commonwealth of Independent States, as they currently play an important stabilizing role in the conflict zone, and recalling that a lasting and comprehensive settlement of the conflict will require appropriate security guarantees,

Stressing also that economic development is urgently required in Abkhazia, Georgia, to improve the livelihoods of the communities affected by the conflict, in particular refugees and internally displaced persons,

1. *Reaffirms* the commitment of all Member States to the sovereignty, independence and territorial integrity of Georgia within its internationally recognized borders, and supports all efforts by the United Nations and the Group of Friends of the Secretary-General on Georgia, which are guided by their determination to promote a settlement of the Georgian-Abkhaz conflict only by peaceful means and within the framework of the resolutions of the Security Council;

2. *Reaffirms its strong support* for the United Nations Observer Mission in Georgia, again urges the parties to cooperate fully with the Mission and to actively and sustainably engage in the political process led by the Special Representative of the Secretary-General for Georgia, and welcomes the Mission's continued consultations with the parties on strengthening its observation capacity;

3. *Welcomes* the recent improvements in the overall security situation, calls upon both sides to consolidate and broaden those improvements, underlines the need for a period of sustained stability along the ceasefire line and in the Kodori Valley, and stresses the necessity to keep under close observation the situation in the upper Kodori Valley, which has to be in line with the Agreement on a Ceasefire and Separation of Forces signed at Moscow on 14 May 1994;

4. *Also welcomes* the renewed commitment given by both sides during the meeting chaired by the United Nations in Geneva on 18 and 19 February 2008 to resume regular consultations within the quadripartite meetings on security issues without delay, and once more urges both sides to finally fulfil this commitment;

5. *Expresses its concern* at any violation of the ceasefire and separation of forces regime in the zone of conflict;

6. *Strongly urges* all parties to consider and address seriously each other's legitimate security concerns, to refrain from any acts of violence or provocation, including political action or rhetoric, to comply fully with previous agreements regarding ceasefire and non-use of violence, and to maintain the security zone and the restricted weapons zone free of any unauthorized military activities, and in this regard recalls the recommendations of the Secretary-General contained in his report of 18 July 2007 and his subsequent reports;

7. *Calls upon* both sides to finalize without delay the document on the non-use of violence, and also calls upon both sides to finalize without delay the document on the return of refugees and internally displaced persons;

8. *Stresses anew* the urgent need to alleviate the plight of refugees and internally displaced persons and the need for a perspective of life in security and dignity, in particular for a new generation growing up outside Abkhazia, Georgia;

9. *Reiterates and reaffirms* as fundamentally important the right of return for all refugees and internally displaced persons to Abkhazia, Georgia, reaffirms the importance of such people's return to their homes and property, that individual property rights have not been affected by the fact that owners had to flee during the conflict and that the residency rights and the identity of those owners will be respected, and calls upon both sides to implement the Office of the United Nations High Commissioner for Refugees' "Strategic Directions" for their return in the first instance to the Gali region;

10. *Calls upon* the parties to increase their bilateral contacts by making full use of all existing mechanisms as described in the relevant Council resolutions in order to come to a peaceful settlement, and to commit themselves to fulfil within a reliable time frame the conditions necessary for the safe, dignified and swift return of refugees and internally displaced persons;

11. *Firmly convinced* that the confidence-building measures proposed by the Group of Friends of the Secretary-General and endorsed through resolution 1752(2007) of 13 April 2007, will serve the development of broader and unbiased contacts between the communities of the divided country, regrets the lack of progress made with regard to confidence-building measures, and again urges the Georgian and Abkhaz sides to implement those measures without conditions;

12. *Recalls*, with a view to achieving a lasting and comprehensive settlement, its support for the principles contained in the paper on "Basic Principles for the Distribution of Competences between Tbilisi and Sukhumi", and welcomes additional ideas that the sides would be willing to offer with a view to conducting creatively and constructively a political dialogue under the aegis of the United Nations;

13. *Welcomes* existing contacts and encourages further contacts between representatives of civil society, and ap-

peals to both sides to continue to promote without reservation the active engagement of citizens and officials in such contacts;

14. *Underlines* that it is the primary responsibility of both sides to provide appropriate security and to ensure the freedom of movement throughout the zone of conflict of the Mission, the peacekeeping force of the Commonwealth of Independent States and other international personnel, and calls upon both sides to fulfil their obligations in this regard and to extend full cooperation to the Mission and the peacekeeping force;

15. *Welcomes* the efforts being undertaken by the Mission to implement the Secretary-General's zero-tolerance policy on sexual exploitation and abuse and to ensure full compliance of its personnel with the United Nations code of conduct, requests the Secretary-General to continue to take all necessary action in this regard and to keep the Council informed, and urges troop-contributing countries to take appropriate preventive action, including conducting predeployment awareness training, and to take disciplinary action and other action to ensure full accountability in cases of such conduct involving their personnel;

16. *Decides* to extend the mandate of the Mission for a new period terminating on 15 October 2008;

17. *Requests* the Secretary-General to make use of this mandate in order to encourage and support the parties in implementing measures to build confidence and to establish an intensive and meaningful dialogue, with a view to achieving a lasting and comprehensive settlement, including the facilitation of a meeting at the highest level, and to inform the Council in his next report on the situation in Abkhazia, Georgia, on progress made in this respect;

18. *Strongly supports* the efforts of the Special Representative of the Secretary-General, and encourages the Group of Friends of the Secretary-General to continue giving him their steadfast and unified support;

19. *Decides* to remain actively seized of the matter.

Communications. On 15 April [A/62/802], Georgia transmitted the new proposals of President Saakashvili on the peaceful resolution of the conflicts in Georgia.

On 17 April [S/2008/257], Georgia informed the Security Council that on 16 April, Russian President Vladimir Putin had instructed the Russian Government to launch formal cooperation with the de facto authorities of Abkhazia and the Tskhinvali region/South Ossetia. That action was designed for annexing parts of Georgian territory and threatened Georgia's sovereignty and territorial integrity. Georgia therefore requested a meeting of the Security Council. On the same day [A/62/810], Georgia informed the Secretary-General that Russia's "very dangerous step" aimed to legalize factual annexation of Abkhazia and the Tskhinvali region/South Ossetia.

Georgia transmitted further communications on 25 March [A/62/765-S/2008/197], 9 April [S/2008/234], 28 April [A/62/824], 5 May [A/62/830-S/2008/299], 2 June [A/62/852-S/2008/357], 8 July [A/62/904-S/2008/450], 10 July [A/62/909-S/2008/464], 16 July [S/2008/469] and 25 July [S/2008/497]. The Russian Federation transmitted a further communication on 4 June [S/2008/363].

Security Council consideration (April). Meeting in closed session on 23 April [meeting 5874], Council members and David Bakradze, Minister for Foreign Affairs of Georgia, had an exchange of views.

Communication. On 1 May [A/62/827-S/2008/298], Georgia transmitted a 30 April joint statement of the Presidents of Ukraine and Georgia expressing concern over Russia's attempt to call into question Georgia's territorial integrity by elevating the status of relations with Abkhazia and South Ossetia, thereby encouraging the self-recognized republics to secede from Georgia.

General Assembly action. On 12 May, Georgia submitted to the General Assembly a draft resolution [A/62/L.45] on the status of internally displaced persons and refugees from Abkhazia, Georgia. The draft recognized the right of return of all refugees and internally displaced persons, regardless of their ethnicity, to Abkhazia, Georgia. The Assembly adopted the draft by a recorded vote of 14 to 11, with 105 abstentions, as **resolution 62/249** (see p. 891).

Communication. On 27 May [S/2008/342], Georgia informed the Security Council that the UNOMIG report regarding the downing on 20 April of a Georgian unmanned aerial vehicle by a Russian military aircraft over Abkhazia was released on 26 May. Georgia requested a meeting of the Council to address the issue.

Security Council consideration (May). On 30 May [meeting 5900], at a closed session, Council members and the representatives of Georgia and Germany had an exchange of views on the situation in Georgia.

Report of Secretary-General (July). In July, the Secretary-General reported [S/2008/480] that UNOMIG continued to seek to prevent an escalation of tensions in the zone of conflict and facilitate a resumption of dialogue. However, the situation on the ground had severely deteriorated in both political and security terms.

The Abkhaz side continued to insist on the withdrawal of Georgian forces from the upper Kodori Valley and the signing of a document on non-resumption of hostilities as a precondition for re-engaging in negotiations. The Georgian side focused on President Saakashvili's peace initiative and developed its various components. Georgia emphasized the need to change the negotiating formats, including by granting a prominent role to the EU, as a condition for progress, while the Abkhaz side remained opposed to any modification.

On 16 April, Russian Federation President Putin issued an instruction authorizing direct relations with the Abkhaz and South Ossetian de facto authorities in a number of fields. Russia stated that the decision was aimed at supporting Russian citizens and the local population and responded to what it called Georgia's aggressive intentions. The Georgian side protested what it considered a blatant violation of Georgia's sovereignty and territorial integrity, amounting to legalizing a factual annexation of Abkhazia and South Ossetia. In late April, the Russian Federation reinforced the Russian-manned CIS peacekeeping force stationed in the restricted weapons zone, and in May it introduced a military railways unit to rehabilitate the railways south of Sukhumi, outside the area of responsibility of UNOMIG and the CIS peacekeeping force. Differences between the two countries rose to a new level, with Georgia blaming Russia for "accelerated annexation" of Abkhazia, and Russia accusing Georgia of preparing for the imminent implementation of a military option in Abkhazia.

Concerned over those developments, senior representatives of the Group of Friends met in Berlin on 30 June, together with the Special Representative, to discuss ways to prevent further deterioration. However, the subsequent period saw a dramatic increase in violence, including indiscriminate bombings of public places in Gagra, Sukhumi and Gali on the Abkhaz-controlled side of the ceasefire line, as well as roadside explosions on the Georgian-controlled side. The bombings resulted in four fatalities, including one UNOMIG staff member.

The Secretary-General called upon every stakeholder to preserve the integrity of the ceasefire regime. He appealed to the Abkhaz side to observe the freedom of movement of UNOMIG and to the Georgian side to observe the freedom of movement of the CIS peacekeeping force.

Communication. On 10 July [S/2008/453], Georgia informed the Security Council that on 8 July Russian military aircraft had intruded into Georgian airspace, and requested a meeting of the Council.

Security Council consideration (July). On 21 July [meeting 5939], at a closed Security Council meeting, Council members and the representative of Georgia had an exchange of views.

New Special Representative. On 30 July [S/2008/518], the Secretary-General informed the Security Council of his intention to appoint Johan Verbeke (Belgium) as the Special Representative for Georgia and Head of UNOMIG. On 1 August [S/2008/519], the Council took note of that intention.

Georgian-Russian conflict

Escalation of hostilities

On 9 July, in the lower Kodori Valley, a clash between the Abkhaz and Georgian sides on the Achamkhara heights was reported. The Abkhaz side claimed that an Abkhaz de facto security post had been raided by the Georgian side, resulting in two Abkhaz reservists being injured, while the Georgian side stated that one of its patrols had been attacked while securing the Achamkhara heights in anticipation of a UNOMIG visit to the Kvabchara Valley. It reported that three Georgian Ministry of Internal Affairs personnel had been injured. Tensions rose further after allegations by the Georgian side of mortar firing by the Abkhaz side into the Kvabchara valley on 26 July. UNOMIG began investigations of both incidents, but had to suspend them because of ensuing events the following month.

In the Zugdidi sector, existing tensions between the CIS peacekeeping force and Georgian law enforcement representatives led to the suspension in July of the sector-level tripartite meetings which—by bringing together the Georgian side, the CIS peacekeeping force and UNOMIG—had served as a forum for resolving operational issues. Following a series of bomb blasts in public places in Gagra and Sukhumi on 29 and 30 June, in which 12 people were injured, the Abkhaz de facto authorities ordered the closure of the ceasefire line as at 1 July. The most serious incident in years in the UNOMIG area of responsibility occurred on 6 July, when four people were killed and six injured following an explosion in a cafe in the town of Gali, near the Mission's sector headquarters. Among the fatalities were a UNOMIG language assistant and the head of the Gali de facto Abkhaz security service.

During this period, UNOMIG was assisting the efforts of Germany, as the Coordinator of the Group of Friends, to advance a plan for the settlement of the Georgian-Abkhaz conflict that had been proposed by the German Minister for Foreign Affairs, Frank-Walter Steinmeier, and presented to the sides during his visit to the region in mid-July. The plan contemplated a three-phase process: agreements on security measures, including a declaration on the non-use of force and modalities for the return of internally displaced persons and refugees; economic rehabilitation and confidence-building measures; and discussions on the political status of Abkhazia. The Georgian and Abkhaz sides stated their readiness to participate in a meeting in Berlin, but predicated their support for the proposed plan on a number of conditions.

At the same time, tensions between Georgia and Russia were rising. Russian officials were increasingly insisting that the Georgian side sign non-use of force agreements with the Abkhaz and South Ossetian sides to defuse tensions and restore confidence as a basis for negotiation. Georgian officials accused the Russian Federation of attempting to annex Georgian territories and demanded again that both the negotiations and peacekeeping formats be further internationalized.

On 4 August, as exchanges of fire between the Georgian and South Ossetian sides intensified, the Abkhaz side announced the postponement of its participation in the Berlin meeting and warned that "if Georgia starts fighting against South Ossetia, Abkhazia will open a second front".

Communications. On 7 August [S/2008/533], the Russian Federation requested an emergency meeting of the Security Council to consider the aggressive actions of Georgia against South Ossetia. That same day [A/62/924-S/2008/535], Georgia transmitted a statement by the President of Georgia on the latest developments in the Tskhinvali region, Georgia.

Security Council consideration. The Russian Federation told the Security Council, which met on 8 August [meeting 5951], that just hours after reaching agreement on holding negotiations to resolve the escalating South Ossetia conflict, Georgian military divisions had begun a massive attack against Tskhinvali, South Ossetia's capital. The Georgian authorities had pursued the military option despite diplomatic efforts by Moscow, Tbilisi, Tskhinvali, Washington, D.C., and other capitals. The situation in the conflict zone was critical, with massive artillery fire directed against a peaceful civilian population. Georgian tanks and infantry had reportedly begun to attack the southern parts of Tskhinvali. The Council had to play its role by immediately calling for an end to the hostilities and a rejection of the use of force.

Georgia maintained that following attacks by South Ossetian separatists, it had announced a unilateral ceasefire on 7 August as a sign of its willingness to defuse tensions. President Saakashvili had explained in a televised address of that evening that he had ordered the ceasefire specifically to give the South Ossetian secessionist regime the chance to resume talks. Military action had been taken in self-defence after repeated armed provocations, and with the sole goal of protecting civilians. Additional illegal forces and military equipment were entering Georgia from Russia through the Roki tunnel. The separatists were continuing to threaten attacks outside South Ossetia, and Russian peacekeepers had told Georgia that they were unable to control the separatists, who were ignoring appeals for direct talks. The illegal separatist authorities and armed formations were under the control and direction of Russian security and defence agencies. Numerous high-ranking Russian officers among the peacekeepers, as well as other officials from the Russian military, intelligence and law-enforcement services, were serving in senior roles—a clear violation of Russia's obligation to remain neutral. Georgia was seeking a negotiated solution to the conflict, with international engagement: Georgia's offer of autonomy stood, with international guarantees including an elected regional parliament, an elected regional president, shared sovereignty and protections for South Ossetian identity, culture and language. Georgia had sought Russia's constructive engagement in the region's economic rehabilitation and agreed security arrangements. Instead, Russia had become a party to the conflict. Georgia called on the international community to condemn Russia's continuing infringement of Georgian sovereignty and territorial integrity. Georgia was ready to immediately begin peace talks aimed at resolving the conflict. The United States called on the parties to respect the territorial integrity and sovereignty of Georgia, and called on Russia to pull its troops back and not inflame the situation by sending its forces into Georgia. France called for an immediate cessation of hostilities and a resumption of dialogue, with a view to a ceasefire.

On 8 August [S/2008/536], however, Georgia informed the Security Council that on that same day, Russian military aircraft had intruded into Georgian airspace and bombed civilians and military infrastructure. Russian army units had invaded Georgia, in the Tskhinvali region. Georgia requested a meeting of the Security Council to address the threat to Georgia's independence, sovereignty and territorial integrity.

Georgia told the Security Council's second meeting of 8 August [meeting 5952] that Russia had started a full-scale military invasion of Georgia, with troops entering the country and jets bombing airfields, military bases and villages. Georgia called on Russia to stop the bombing campaign, withdraw its forces and negotiate a ceasefire, adding that Georgian President Saakashvili was offering direct dialogue with Moscow.

The Russian Federation said that Georgia had carried out an attack on South Ossetia despite Russian appeals for a ceasefire, an end to that fratricidal conflict and resumption of negotiations. Georgian forces were bombarding towns, including those outside the immediate conflict zones, and had created panic among the civilian population, many of whom were trying to flee to safety. Many of the people living in South Ossetia were Russian citizens. Georgia's actions had caused casualties among Russian peacekeepers. Russia was present on the territory of Georgia on an absolutely legal basis, pursuant to its peacekeeping mission in accordance with international agreements.

Heightened conflict and ceasefire

The escalating hostilities in South Ossetia on 7 and 8 August and the ensuing Georgian-Russian conflict profoundly affected the situation in the Georgian-Abkhaz zone of conflict and the overall conflict-settlement process. On 8 August, the Abkhaz side began introducing heavy weapons into the restricted weapons zone in violation of the 1994 Moscow Agreement [YUN 1994, p. 583]; and on 9 August, a series of bombardments was carried out in the upper Kodori Valley. The same day, Russian forces reportedly carried out aerial attacks in western Georgia, including on the railway station and military base in Senaki and the seaport of Poti—all located outside the zone of conflict—as well as around the town of Zugdidil. Georgia [S/2008/537] requested another meeting of the Security Council on the military aggression launched by Russia against Georgia.

Meanwhile, Abkhaz de facto authorities requested UNOMIG on 9 August to leave immediately its team base in Adjara in the upper Kodori Valley. When exiting through the lower Kodori Valley, the patrol heard sounds of an aerial attack from the direction of the upper Kodori Valley and saw a convoy of Abkhaz tanks and military personnel in the lower Kodori Valley. On the same day, the Abkhaz de facto Ministry of Defence declared that aerial strikes had been carried out on the military infrastructure in the upper Kodori Valley. After entering the Kodori Valley, the Abkhaz side claimed to have found heavy weapons and found evidence of the presence of personnel of the Georgian Ministry of Defence and accommodation facilities suitable for some thousands of personnel. UNOMIG indicated that the infrastructure in the upper Kodori Valley was suitable for the accommodation of personnel in numbers exceeding those provided by the Georgian side. UNOMIG was not able to resume its regular patrolling of the Kodori Valley since its team withdrew on 9 August, however, as the CIS peacekeeping force indicated that the safety of UNOMIG staff could not be guaranteed.

On 10 August, an air attack was reported on the Georgian signals unit south of the village of Urta; and on the same and following day, Russia introduced large numbers of troops into the zone of conflict. Although the troops were initially deployed on the Gali side of the ceasefire line, they were later moved into the Zugdidi side of the zone of conflict and adjacent areas in Senaki and Poti.

The United States requested an emergency meeting of the Council on 10 August [S/2008/538] to address the escalation of violence in Georgia. On that day [meeting 5953], Georgia told the Council that all Georgian troops had withdrawn from the conflict zone in South Ossetia and a humanitarian corridor had been established for civilians south of Tskhinvali. During the ceasefire, however, Georgian forces had been bombed many times and prevented from a full withdrawal. Russia said that the crisis was due to the aggression by Georgia against South Ossetia, and that Russia had reacted appropriately to defend civilians and its peacekeepers. Russia was ready to put an end to the war, was withdrawing from South Ossetia and was ready to sign an agreement on the non-use of force. The United States said that Russia had claimed that its military operations were intended to protect its peacekeepers and civilians in South Ossetia, yet its actions went far beyond that, and its expansion of the conflict to another separatist area of Georgia suggested other motives. The Council should condemn Russia's military assault on Georgia. Russia should carefully consider the implications of its aggression against a sovereign and democratic State.

The Secretary-General reported [S/2008/631] that from 8 to 11 August, UNOMIG issued three violation reports to the Abkhaz side for the presence of heavy military equipment in the restricted weapons zone, which the Abkhaz side refused to sign. On 10 August, the Abkhaz de facto authorities proclaimed martial law in the districts of Gali, Ochamchira and Tkvarcheli and announced partial mobilization. On several occasions, Abkhaz servicemen denied freedom of movement to UNOMIG patrols, threatening them with weapons. Seven violation reports involving nine cases of restriction of movement were issued to the Abkhaz side. A senior Georgian representative in Zugdidi informed UNOMIG on 11 August that the CIS peacekeeping force had issued an ultimatum to all Georgian law-enforcement agencies in the Zugdidi area to surrender all weapons. At the request of UNOMIG, the leadership of the CIS peacekeeping force agreed to allow law-enforcement personnel to carry side arms while on duty. Later that day, UNOMIG patrols observed that Georgian security posts at the ceasefire line that had been manned by special police forces had been abandoned, although Georgian criminal police and others remained on duty in the Zugdidi sector with side arms. Also on 11 August, the CIS peacekeeping force occupied five buildings, most of them belonging to the Georgian Ministry of Internal Affairs.

That same day [S/2008/540], Georgia requested a public emergency meeting of the Security Council on the military occupation of Georgia by the Russian Federation.

Meeting in closed session on that date [meeting 5954], the Security Council was briefed by the Under-Secretary-General for Political Affairs, B. Lynn Pascoe, and Mr. Mulet. Council members, the representative of Georgia, Mr. Pascoe and Mr. Mulet had an exchange of views.

Also on 11 August [S/2008/545], the Russian Federation again stated its position on the conflict. On 7 August, Georgian forces, in violation of the ceasefire agreements in the zone of Georgian-Ossetian conflict, had launched a military operation in South Ossetia. In the city of Tshinval, about 1,500 peaceful civilians—most of them Russian citizens—had lost their lives. A targeted massive assault had been launched on the Russian peacekeeping contingent which was part of the Joint Peacekeeping Forces, leading to casualties. In those circumstances, Russia had no choice but to use its right to self-defence. The use of force by Russia pursued no other goal but to protect the Russian peacekeeping contingent and Russian citizens.

Ukraine expressed concern that same day [A/62/928-S/2008/546] over the deterioration of the situation in South Ossetia (Georgia) and reaffirmed its position on Georgia's territorial integrity and sovereignty.

On 12 August, the Abkhaz side launched a ground attack and established control over the upper Kodori Valley.

Ceasefire plan. On 12 August, the French presidency of the EU visited Moscow and Tbilisi, and discussions led to a six-point ceasefire plan whose provisions also affected the situation in the UNOMIG area of responsibility. The Secretary-General, in a statement of 13 August [SG/SM/11743], welcomed the acceptance by Georgia and Russia of a peace plan proposed by French President Nicolas Sarkozy, and urged the parties to move quickly to halt the fighting. He called for immediate follow-through in implementing the agreed principles, including the end to hostilities and the withdrawal of forces to previous positions. He reiterated his support for a solution based on the respect of Georgia's territorial integrity and sovereignty, and offered his good offices.

The Parliament of Georgia [A/62/935-S/2008/557] issued an appeal three days later to the international community.

On 19 August [S/2008/561], France requested an emergency Security Council meeting on the situation in Georgia. On that day [meeting 5961], the Council was briefed by Mr. Pascoe, who said that agreement to six principles sponsored by the French Presidency of the EU had ended the military hostilities. Those principles were: commitment by all parties to renounce the use of force; immediate and definitive cessation of hostilities; free access to humanitarian aid; withdrawal of Georgian forces to their places of permanent deployment; withdrawal of Russian forces to their lines of deployment prior to 7 August 2008; and convening of international discussions on lasting security and stability arrangements for Abkhazia, Georgia, and South Ossetia, Georgia. The implementation of those principles would allow for the provision of international assistance, defuse the situation and offer hope for a political solution. As a result of the hostilities, 158,600 people had been displaced: 98,600 within Georgia, about 30,000 within South Ossetia and another 30,000 in other parts of the area. The United Nations was ready to facilitate international discussions to implement the accord and to take part in concrete arrangements for a settlement.

Post-ceasefire events

On 26 August, the Russian President stated that the attack by Georgia on South Ossetia had left Russia with no choice but to recognize Abkhazia and South Ossetia as independent States. In response to strong international criticism and support expressed for Georgia's territorial integrity, Russia stated that any return to status quo ante was no longer possible in the light of the genocide in South Ossetia.

The next day [S/2008/587], Georgia requested a Security Council meeting to consider the illegal unilateral actions of the Russian Federation with regard to two Georgian provinces, Abkhazia and South Ossetia. On 28 August, the Parliament of Georgia declared Abkhazia and South Ossetia territories occupied by the Russian Federation, and the Russian peacekeepers an occupying force. Georgia subsequently severed diplomatic relations with Russia.

Also on 28 August [meeting 5969], the Security Council was briefed by Elizabeth Spehar, Officer-in-Charge of the Department of Political Affairs, who reported that 18 checkpoints of the Russian forces remained north of Gori, Georgia, as well as in other areas. Wolfgang Weisbrod-Weber, Officer-in-Charge of the Department of Peacekeeping Operations, told the Council that UNOMIG had observed large-scale Russian troop and military hardware withdrawal from Georgia to the Abkhaz-controlled side of the ceasefire line. Nonetheless, Abkhaz forces continued to control pockets north of the Inguri River, on the Georgian side of the ceasefire line, and the situation in and around the Georgian-Abkhaz conflict zone remained tense.

On 29 August, Georgia declared that the 1994 Moscow Agreement was null and void and reiterated its commitment to the six-point ceasefire plan as the only valid basis for conflict resolution. Following those decisions, the Abkhaz side announced its intention to reinforce the "State border".

Moldova transmitted to the Secretary-General that same day [A/62/950] a statement on the events in South Ossetia and Abkhazia. Moldova did not consider that the international recognition of Abkhazia and South Ossetia would stabilize the situation. At the same time, it deemed it inappropriate to compare the situation in Georgia with the one in Transnistria, and believed that speculations on how the situation in Abkhazia and South Ossetia might affect the Transnistrian settlement process [YUN 2007, p. 423] were counterproductive. Moldova had created very favourable prerequisites for its settlement, and there was political will on all sides participating in the settlement to the conflict.

On 1 September, Georgia decided to terminate the CIS peacekeeping operation in Abkhazia, Georgia.

On 7 September, UNOMIG, accompanied by the CIS peacekeeping force, conducted a special patrol to the Kodori Valley. Abkhaz forces were occupying the entire Valley, and a battalion of CIS peacekeepers was stationed there. It found that the UNOMIG Kodori team base in Adjara was occupied by Abkhaz personnel. All the movable assets that had been left at the base on 9 August were missing.

On 8 September, the French presidency of the EU and the Russian President elaborated provisions for implementing the six-point ceasefire plan, which were agreed upon on the same day by the President of Georgia. Among those provisions, it was reaffirmed that UNOMIG observers would continue to carry out their mandate as had existed on 7 August, subject to possible future adjustments decided on by the Security Council.

Meanwhile, the next day, the Russian Minister for Foreign Affairs and the Abkhaz de facto Foreign Minister signed a document establishing formal diplomatic relations, followed by the signing of an agreement on friendship, cooperation and mutual assistance in Moscow on 17 September.

Communications. Georgia transmitted further communications on 7 August [A/62/923-S/2008/534], 9 August [A/62/926-S/2008/542, A/62/925-S/2008/543, A/62/953-S/2008/544], 13 August [A/62/931-S/2008/551], 16 August [A/62/936-S/2008/562], 20 August [A/62/941-S/2008/573], 21 August [A/62/942-S/2008/574] and 20 November [S/2008/725, A/63/561-S/2008/727].

Report of Secretary-General (October). In a 3 October report [S/2008/631], the Secretary-General stated that following the outbreak of hostilities in South Ossetia in August, the context in which UNOMIG had operated during the past 14 years had changed considerably. It was not yet known which features, if any, of the Moscow Agreement—the basis of the Mission's observation mandate—would be retained when the security discussions concluded. As long as international involvement in the Georgian-Abkhaz conflict was seen as helping to prevent future conflict, however, UNOMIG might be called upon to make a contribution, and both the Georgian and Abkhaz sides supported its continuation. In that context, the Secretary-General recommended extending the Mission for a four-month period.

Communications. On 6 October [S/2008/637], the Russian Federation informed the Council that the deployment of the mission of EU observers in the security zones along the borders of Abkhazia and South Ossetia was proceeding smoothly. They were beginning to interact with the Russian peacekeepers, who were being withdrawn from those zones. At the same time, the situation remained tense and dangerous incidents persistently occurred. Nevertheless, Russia intended to complete the withdrawal of its military from Georgia on time, by 10 October.

On 24 October [A/63/508-S/2008/674], Georgia transmitted a statement of its Parliament on facts concerning violations of the ceasefire agreement by the Russian Federation.

Security Council consideration (October). At a closed meeting on 9 October [meeting 5991], Mr. Mulet briefed Security Council members and representatives of UNOMIG troop-contributing countries. The briefing was followed by an exchange of views.

SECURITY COUNCIL ACTION

On 9 October [meeting 5992], the Security Council unanimously adopted **resolution 1839(2008)**. The draft [S/2008/639] was prepared in consultations among Council members.

The Security Council,

Recalling all its relevant resolutions, including resolution 1808(2008) of 15 April 2008,

Taking note of the reports of the Secretary-General of 23 July and 3 October 2008,

1. *Decides* to extend the mandate of the United Nations mission for a new period terminating on 15 February 2009;
2. *Decides* also to remain actively seized of the matter.

Year-end developments. In a later report [S/2009/69 & Corr.1], the Secretary-General proposed measures that could be a basis for an effective security regime, and that the Council endorse the continued presence of a UN mission retaining the existing configuration and deployment. He also noted that as a result of recent events, the position of the Mission, whose operation and security depended largely on the goodwill of the sides, and which had continued its activities of patrolling, observation and liaison in its area of responsibility, had become precarious and could rapidly become unsustainable.

The security regime based on the Moscow Agreement had seen further erosion. The Collective CIS Peacekeeping Force, which had been in place in the conflict zone for the previous 14 years, was officially terminated by the decision adopted at the meeting of the Council of the Heads of State of CIS, held in Bishkek on 10 October. Russian armed forces remained deployed on the Abkhaz-controlled side of the zone of conflict. Georgian and Abkhaz forces were deployed on their respective sides of the ceasefire line, facing each other in a potentially dangerous stand-off. The Special Representative and the Mission maintained regular contacts with the Georgian and Abkhaz sides, urging them to comply with the spirit of the Moscow Agreement and inviting their views on a possible future UN mission. The Special Representative also held consultations with senior representatives of the Russian Federation, the United States, the EU and its members, as well as the OSCE.

In October, the Abkhaz side destroyed several improvised pedestrian bridges in the Gali Sector to prevent "illegal" crossing of the ceasefire line. Afterwards, the Abkhaz de facto authorities announced that there were three "official" crossing points: at the Inguri River bridge and at the villages of Saberio and Meore Otobaya.

Subsequently, on 23 October, the Parliament of Georgia adopted a law declaring Abkhazia and South Ossetia "occupied territories" and the Russian Federation a "military occupier". The law, signed on 31 October by President Saakashvili of Georgia, declared null and void all legislative and administrative acts issued by the de facto authorities in Abkhazia and South Ossetia. It also restricted access to these territories and prohibited economic and financial activities that did not comply with Georgian law.

The Russian Parliament ratified on 4 November the Russian-Abkhaz and Russian-South Ossetian treaties on friendship, cooperation and mutual assistance. Russian officials stated that the presence of Russian armed forces in Abkhazia and South Ossetia would be based on those documents and announced plans for the establishment of military bases and the deployment of 3,700 troops in Abkhazia and South Ossetia each.

A Georgian serviceman was killed on 15 November during an exchange of fire close to Kalagali village. While the UN police and personnel of the EU monitoring mission were inspecting the scene of the incident, a second round of shooting came from the Abkhaz-controlled side. Following another exchange of fire in Ganmukhuri on 20 November, at the same time as a UN police patrol was examining the scene, another round of shootings occurred. In both incidents, the Abkhaz side claimed that it opened fire to prevent an armed group from crossing the ceasefire line; however, the Mission could not find evidence substantiating that claim.

In October, November and December, UNOMIG conducted three patrols to the upper Kodori Valley to assess the security and humanitarian conditions, including the situation regarding the return of the population displaced as a result of the August events. The patrols spoke with several inhabitants and members of the new de facto local administration, and the Abkhaz de facto authorities announced that all the local population, estimated in 2002 at up to 2,000, could return if the displaced persons obtained Abkhaz "passports" and gave up their Georgian citizenship. In December, UNOMIG observed a convoy of Russian forces composed of heavy military equipment entering the security zone. According to information provided by the Russian forces, their deployment in the security zone was concentrated in five areas along the ceasefire line, stretching from the upper Gali district to the Black Sea coast. The Mission also reported the introduction of heavy weapons and military personnel by the Abkhaz side into the zone of conflict. The Special Representative and the Chief Military Observer urged the Abkhaz side to comply with the spirit of the Moscow Agreement and to withdraw their military materiel from the zone of conflict.

Pursuant to the six-point ceasefire agreement (see p. 456) and subsequent implementing measures, the Special Representative co-chaired, together with representatives of the EU and OSCE, three rounds of international discussions in Geneva, in which delegations from Georgia, the Russian Federation and the United States, as well as Abkhaz and South Ossetian representatives participated. In the second round (18–19 November) two working groups—on security and stability and on refugees and internally displaced persons—agreed to focus on practical issues; and at the third round (17–18 December) the working group on security and stability discussed a proposal for joint incident prevention and response mechanisms. Although all participants agreed on most elements of the proposed mechanisms, differences prevented an agreement. The working group on refugees and internally displaced persons discussed concrete steps to improve the living conditions of the displaced population. Participants agreed in principle to hold the next round of discussions in Geneva in February 2009.

On 23 December, the Russian Minister for Foreign Affairs and the de facto Minister for Foreign Affairs of Abkhazia signed a memorandum of understanding on cooperation in international affairs. The Russian Minister for Foreign Affairs announced that additional agreements, including an agreement on military cooperation and joint protection of "Abkhazia's borders", would be signed at the beginning of 2009.

Humanitarian situation and human rights

The UNOMIG Human Rights Office in Abkhazia continued to promote human rights protection and to provide support to local non-governmental organizations (NGOs), except when its activities in the zone of conflict were restricted due to the events in August. It continued to facilitate the Assisting Communities Together project, which promoted small grants to local NGOs to carry out human rights education and training projects. The Office conducted regular monitoring visits to detention facilities, monitored court trials and provided legal advisory services to the local population. It also gathered first-hand information from victims, witnesses and other reliable sources; it monitored and followed up on individual cases related to due process and the right to a fair trial, the treatment of detainees, the illegal occupation of property, the right to adequate housing, and housing and property rights.

From 4 to 7 February, the Office, the Mission gender focal point and the UN police held a seminar in Pitsunda on the protection of women and minors against domestic violence. From 12 to 18 August, UNHCR and its implementing partners assisted approximately 1,000 internally displaced persons from the upper Kodori Valley, who were transported to Kutaisi where the Government of Georgia provided them with temporary accommodation.

UNHCR, together with its partners, completed its planned activities including community-based protection and confidence-building, education-related projects, basic shelter repair, income generation, agricultural support and training.

Financing

On 20 June [meeting 109], the General Assembly, having considered the Secretary-General's reports on the UNOMIG budget for the periods from 1 July 2006 to 30 June 2007 [A/62/633] and from 1 July 2008 to 30 June 2009 [A/62/680] and ACABQ comments and recommendations [A/62/781/Add.1.], adopted, on the recommendation of the Fifth Committee [A/62/873], **resolution 62/260** without vote [agenda item 149].

Financing of the United Nations Observer Mission in Georgia

The General Assembly,

Having considered the reports of the Secretary-General on the financing of the United Nations Observer Mission in Georgia and the related report of the Advisory Committee on Administrative and Budgetary Questions,

Recalling Security Council resolution 854(1993) of 6 August 1993, by which the Council approved the deployment of an advance team of up to ten United Nations military observers for a period of three months and the incorporation of the advance team into a United Nations observer mission if such a mission was formally established by the Council,

Recalling also Security Council resolution 858(1993) of 24 August 1993, by which the Council established the United Nations Observer Mission in Georgia, and the subsequent resolutions by which the Council extended the mandate of the Observer Mission, the latest of which was resolution 1808(2008) of 15 April 2008,

Recalling further its decision 48/475 A of 23 December 1993 on the financing of the Observer Mission and its subsequent resolutions and decisions thereon, the latest of which was resolution 61/283 of 29 June 2007,

Reaffirming the general principles underlying the financing of United Nations peacekeeping operations, as stated in General Assembly resolutions 1874(S-IV) of 27 June 1963, 3101(XXVIII) of 11 December 1973 and 55/235 of 23 December 2000,

Mindful of the fact that it is essential to provide the Observer Mission with the financial resources necessary to enable it to fulfill its responsibilities under the relevant resolutions of the Security Council,

1. *Requests* the Secretary-General to entrust the Head of Mission with the task of formulating future budget proposals in full accordance with the provisions of General Assembly resolutions 59/296 of 22 June 2005, 60/266 of 30 June 2006 and 61/276 of 29 June 2007, as well as other relevant resolutions;

2. *Takes note* of the status of contributions to the United Nations Observer Mission in Georgia as at 31 March 2008, including the contributions outstanding in the amount of 9.3 million United States dollars, representing some 3 per cent of the total assessed contributions, notes with concern that only sixty-nine Member States have paid their assessed contributions in full, and urges all other Member States, in particular those in arrears, to ensure payment of their outstanding assessed contributions;

3. *Expresses its appreciation* to those Member States which have paid their assessed contributions in full, and urges all other Member States to make every possible effort to ensure payment of their assessed contributions to the Observer Mission in full;

4. *Expresses concern* at the delay experienced by the Secretary-General in deploying and providing adequate resources to some recent peacekeeping missions, in particular those in Africa;

5. *Emphasizes* that all future and existing peacekeeping missions shall be given equal and non-discriminatory treatment in respect of financial and administrative arrangements;

6. *Also emphasizes* that all peacekeeping missions shall be provided with adequate resources for the effective and efficient discharge of their respective mandates;

7. *Reiterates its request* to the Secretary-General to make the fullest possible use of facilities and equipment at the United Nations Logistics Base at Brindisi, Italy, in order to minimize the costs of procurement for the Observer Mission;

8. *Endorses* the conclusions and recommendations contained in the report of the Advisory Committee on Administrative and Budgetary Questions, subject to the provisions of the present resolution, and requests the Secretary-General to ensure their full implementation;

9. *Decides* to maintain the staffing for the General Services Office for the Observer Mission at the level currently funded under the provisions of its resolution 61/283;

10. *Requests* the Secretary-General to ensure the full implementation of the relevant provisions of its resolutions 59/296, 60/266 and 61/276;

11. *Also requests* the Secretary-General to take all action necessary to ensure that the Observer Mission is administered with a maximum of efficiency and economy;

12. *Further requests* the Secretary-General, in order to reduce the cost of employing General Service staff, to continue efforts to recruit local staff for the Observer Mission against General Service posts, commensurate with the requirements of the Mission;

Financial performance report for the period from 1 July 2006 to 30 June 2007

13. *Takes note* of the report of the Secretary-General on the financial performance of the Observer Mission for the period from 1 July 2006 to 30 June 2007;

Budget estimates for the period from 1 July 2008 to 30 June 2009

14. *Decides* to appropriate to the Special Account for the United Nations Observer Mission in Georgia the amount of 36,084,000 dollars for the period from 1 July 2008 to 30 June 2009, inclusive of 34,484,200 dollars for the maintenance of the Observer Mission, 1,394,600 dollars for the support account for peacekeeping operations and 205,200 dollars for the United Nations Logistics Base;

Financing of the appropriation

15. *Also decides* to apportion among Member States the amount of 10,524,500 dollars for the period from 1 July to 15 October 2008, in accordance with the levels updated in General Assembly resolution 61/243 of 22 December 2006, and taking into account the scale of assessments for 2008, as set out in its resolution 61/237 of 22 December 2006;

16. *Further decides* that, in accordance with the provisions of its resolution 973(X) of 15 December 1955, there shall be set off against the apportionment among Member States, as provided for in paragraph 15 above, their respective share in the Tax Equalization Fund of 747,804 dollars, comprising the estimated staff assessment income of 703,996 dollars approved for the Observer Mission, the prorated share of 39,083 dollars of the estimated staff assessment income approved for the support account and the prorated share of 4,725 dollars of the estimated staff assessment income approved for the United Nations Logistics Base;

17. *Decides* to apportion among Member States the amount of 25,559,500 dollars for the period from 16 October 2008 to 30 June 2009 at a monthly rate of 3,007,000 dollars, in accordance with the levels updated in resolution 61/243, and taking into account the scale of assessments for 2008 and 2009, as set out in resolution 61/237, subject to a decision of the Security Council to extend the mandate of the Observer Mission;

18. *Also decides* that, in accordance with the provisions of its resolution 973(X), there shall be set off against the apportionment among Member States, as provided for in paragraph 17 above, their respective share in the Tax Equalization Fund of 1,816,096 dollars, comprising the estimated staff assessment income of 1,709,704 dollars approved for the Observer Mission, the prorated share of 94,917 dollars of the estimated staff assessment income approved for the support account and the prorated share of 11,475 dollars of the estimated staff assessment income approved for the United Nations Logistics Base;

19. *Further decides* that, for Member States that have fulfilled their financial obligations to the Observer Mission, there shall be set off against their apportionment, as provided for in paragraph 15 above, their respective share of the unencumbered balance and other income in the amount of 1,906,700 dollars in respect of the financial period ended 30 June 2007, in accordance with the levels updated in resolution 61/243, and taking into account the scale of assessments for 2007, as set out in resolution 61/237;

20. *Decides* that, for Member States that have not fulfilled their financial obligations to the Observer Mission, there shall be set off against their outstanding obligations their respective share of the unencumbered balance and other income in the total amount of 1,906,700 dollars in respect of the financial period ended 30 June 2007, in accordance with the scheme set out in paragraph 19 above;

21. *Also decides* that the decrease of 85,100 dollars in the estimated staff assessment income in respect of the financial period ended 30 June 2007 shall be set off against the credits from the amount of 1,906,700 dollars referred to in paragraphs 19 and 20 above;

22. *Emphasizes* that no peacekeeping mission shall be financed by borrowing funds from other active peacekeeping missions;

23. *Encourages* the Secretary-General to continue to take additional measures to ensure the safety and security of all personnel participating in the Observer Mission under the auspices of the United Nations, bearing in mind paragraphs 5 and 6 of Security Council resolution 1502(2003) of 26 August 2003;

24. *Invites* voluntary contributions to the Observer Mission in cash and in the form of services and supplies acceptable to the Secretary-General, to be administered, as appropriate, in accordance with the procedure and practices established by the General Assembly;

25. *Decides* to include in the provisional agenda of its sixty-third session the item entitled "Financing of the United Nations Observer Mission in Georgia".

By **decision 63/552** of 24 December, the Assembly decided that the agenda item on the financing of UNOMIG would remain for consideration during its resumed sixty-third (2009) session.

Armenia and Azerbaijan

In 2008, Armenia and Azerbaijan maintained their positions with regard to the Nagorno-Karabakh region of Azerbaijan, which had erupted in conflict in 1992 [YUN 1992, p. 388], followed by a ceasefire agreement in May 1994 [YUN 1994, p. 577]. Both sides addressed communications regarding the conflict to the Secretary-General. The Organization for Security and Cooperation in Europe (OSCE) Minsk Group (France, Russian Federation, United States) continued to mediate the dispute between Armenia and Azerbaijan.

Communication. On 5 March [A/62/724-S/2008/163], Azerbaijan informed the Secretary-General that since early morning on 4 March, the Armenian occupying forces had violated the ceasefire regime, which led to escalation. The Azerbaijani Army had repulsed the attacks. Four Azerbaijani military personnel were killed and the Armenian forces lost 12 military personnel. The violation of the ceasefire regime by Armenia was directed to divert the attention of its citizens and the international community from the country's internal difficulties.

General Assembly consideration. On 14 March, Azerbaijan submitted to the General Assembly a draft resolution [A/62/L.42] on the situation in the occupied territories of Azerbaijan.

Introducing the draft resolution, Azerbaijan said that it did not accept the argument that the text was unilateral and untimely. It had been prepared in accordance with international law and was impartial. It had been prompted by unfolding circumstances, both regionally and internationally, which had heightened concerns over the status of the settlement process. It was, therefore, apropos and timely. Azerbaijan was concerned and alarmed at the lack of clear proposals from the Co-Chairs of the OSCE Minsk Group with regard to the resolution of issues regarding the liberation of all of the occupied territories and the return of the Azerbaijani population to Nagorno-Karabakh. The Co-Chairs had no right to deviate from the principle of territorial integrity for the sake of their "notorious neutrality". Such neutrality was not a position, but a lack of one. There could be no neutrality when the norms of international law were violated. Four Security Council resolutions adopted in 1993 demanded the withdrawal of the occupying forces from Azerbaijan and the creation of the conditions for the return of internally displaced persons, while the General Assembly's dispatch of a fact-finding mission to the occupied territories in 2005 had confirmed the Armenian settlement of the territories.

Calling the resolution a wasted attempt to predetermine the outcome of the peace talks, Armenia said that was not how responsible members of the international community conducted the difficult but rewarding mission of bringing peace and stability to peoples and regions. The three Minsk Group Co-Chairs had found that the draft resolution did not help the peace talks, and the Assembly should follow their lead. Refugees and territories were a problem created by Azerbaijan, which had unleashed war against people it claimed as its sovereign citizens. Only when the initial cause was resolved would the fate of all the territories and refugees concerned be put right.

The United States noted that the Minsk Group Co-Chairs had proposed a set of basic principles for the peaceful settlement of the conflict to the two sides in November 2007 on the margins of the OSCE Ministerial Council in Madrid. The proposal comprised a balanced package of principles currently under negotiation. The draft resolution did not consider the proposal in its balanced entirety. Because of that selective approach, the Co-Chairs opposed that unilateral text, which threatened to undermine the peace process. However, the negotiators reaffirmed their support for Azerbaijan's territorial integrity, and thus did not recognize the independence of Nagorny Karabakh. In light of the clashes along the line of contact, which had occasioned loss of life, both sides must refrain from unilateral actions, either at the negotiations table or in the field.

GENERAL ASSEMBLY ACTION

On 14 March [meeting 86], the Assembly adopted **resolution 62/243** [draft: A/62/L.42] by recorded vote (39-7-100) [agenda item 20].

The situation in the occupied territories of Azerbaijan

The General Assembly,

Guided by the purposes, principles and provisions of the Charter of the United Nations,

Recalling Security Council resolutions 822(1993) of 30 April 1993, 853(1993) of 29 July 1993, 874(1993) of 14 October 1993 and 884(1993) of 12 November 1993, as well as General Assembly resolutions 48/114 of 20 December 1993, entitled "Emergency international assistance to refugees and displaced persons in Azerbaijan", and 60/285 of 7 September 2006, entitled "The situation in the occupied territories of Azerbaijan",

Recalling also the report of the fact-finding mission of the Minsk Group of the Organization for Security and Cooperation in Europe to the occupied territories of Azerbaijan surrounding Nagorno-Karabakh and the letter on the fact-finding mission from the Co-Chairmen of the Minsk Group addressed to the Permanent Council of the Organization for Security and Cooperation in Europe,

Taking note of the report of the environmental assessment mission led by the Organization for Security and Cooperation in Europe to the fire-affected territories in and around the Nagorno-Karabakh region,

Reaffirming the commitments of the parties to the conflict to abide scrupulously by the rules of international humanitarian law,

Seriously concerned that the armed conflict in and around the Nagorno-Karabakh region of the Republic of Azerbaijan continues to endanger international peace and security, and mindful of its adverse implications for the humanitarian situation and development of the countries of the South Caucasus,

1. *Reaffirms* continued respect and support for the sovereignty and territorial integrity of the Republic of Azerbaijan within its internationally recognized borders;

2. *Demands* the immediate, complete and unconditional withdrawal of all Armenian forces from all the occupied territories of the Republic of Azerbaijan;

3. *Reaffirms* the inalienable right of the population expelled from the occupied territories of the Republic of Azerbaijan to return to their homes, and stresses the necessity of creating appropriate conditions for this return, including the comprehensive rehabilitation of the conflict-affected territories;

4. *Recognizes* the necessity of providing normal, secure and equal conditions of life for Armenian and Azerbaijani communities in the Nagorno-Karabakh region of the Republic of Azerbaijan, which will allow an effective democratic system of self-governance to be built up in this region within the Republic of Azerbaijan;

5. *Reaffirms* that no State shall recognize as lawful the situation resulting from the occupation of the territories of the Republic of Azerbaijan, nor render aid or assistance in maintaining this situation;

6. *Expresses its support* to the international mediation efforts, in particular those of the Co-Chairmen of the Minsk Group of the Organization for Security and Cooperation in Europe, aimed at peaceful settlement of the conflict in accordance with the norms and principles of international law, and recognizes the necessity of intensifying these efforts with a view to achieving a lasting and durable peace in compliance with the provisions stipulated above;

7. *Calls upon* Member States and international and regional organizations and arrangements to effectively contribute, within their competence, to the process of settlement of the conflict;

8. *Requests* the Secretary-General to submit to the General Assembly at its sixty-third session a comprehensive report on the implementation of the present resolution;

9. *Decides* to include in the provisional agenda of its sixty-third session the item entitled "The situation in the occupied territories of Azerbaijan".

RECORDED VOTE ON RESOLUTION 62/243:

In favour: Afghanistan, Azerbaijan, Bahrain, Bangladesh, Brunei Darussalam, Cambodia, Colombia, Comoros, Djibouti, Gambia, Georgia, Indonesia, Iraq, Jordan, Kuwait, Libyan Arab Jamahiriya, Malaysia, Maldives, Moldova, Morocco, Myanmar, Niger, Nigeria, Oman, Pakistan, Qatar, Saudi Arabia, Senegal, Serbia, Sierra Leone, Somalia, Sudan, Turkey, Tuvalu, Uganda, Ukraine, United Arab Emirates, Uzbekistan, Yemen.

Against: Angola, Armenia, France, India, Russian Federation, United States, Vanuatu.

Abstaining: Albania, Algeria, Andorra, Antigua and Barbuda, Argentina, Australia, Austria, Bahamas, Barbados, Belgium, Bolivia, Bosnia and Herzegovina, Botswana, Brazil, Bulgaria, Cameroon, Canada, Chile, China, Congo, Costa Rica, Croatia, Cyprus, Czech Republic, Democratic People's Republic of Korea, Denmark, Dominican Republic, Ecuador, Egypt, El Salvador, Equatorial Guinea, Estonia, Finland, Germany, Ghana, Greece, Grenada, Guatemala, Guyana, Haiti, Honduras, Hungary, Iceland, Ireland, Israel, Italy, Jamaica, Japan, Kazakhstan, Kenya, Latvia, Liberia, Liechtenstein, Lithuania, Luxembourg, Madagascar, Malta, Mauritius, Mexico, Monaco, Mongolia, Montenegro, Mozambique, Namibia, Nepal, Netherlands, New Zealand, Nicaragua, Norway, Panama, Papua New Guinea, Peru, Philippines, Poland, Portugal, Republic of Korea, Romania, Saint Lucia, Samoa, San Marino, Singapore, Slovakia, Slovenia, Solomon Islands, South Africa, Spain, Sri Lanka, Suriname, Swaziland, Sweden, Switzerland, Thailand, the former Yugoslav Republic of Macedonia, Timor-Leste, Togo, Trinidad and Tobago, United Kingdom, Uruguay, Venezuela, Zambia.

Communications. On 7 April [A/62/789-S/2008/227], Azerbaijan transmitted to the Secretary-General a resolution entitled "The Aggression of the Republic of Armenia against the Republic of Azerbaijan", adopted by the eleventh session of the Islamic Summit Conference (Dakar, Senegal, 13–14 March), as well as paragraph 43 of the Bucharest Summit Declaration, issued by the heads of State and Government participating in the meeting of the North Atlantic Council (Bucharest, Romania, 3 April). Azerbaijan noted that, following the General Assembly, the Organization of the Islamic Conference and NATO also reaffirmed the sovereignty and territorial integrity of Azerbaijan, calling for the peaceful settlement of the conflict on the basis of those principles.

Moscow Declaration. On 6 November [A/63/527], Armenia transmitted to the Secretary-General the text of the declaration adopted by the Presidents of Armenia, Azerbaijan and the Russian Federation at their meeting in Moscow on 2 November. The Presidents pledged to work to improve the situation in the South Caucasus and establish stability and security through a political settlement of the Nagorny Karabakh conflict; affirmed the importance of the mediation efforts of the OSCE Minsk Group Co-Chairs, taking into account the meeting of the parties in Madrid on 29 November 2007 and subsequent discussions; agreed that a settlement should be accompanied by legally binding international guarantees; and noted that the Presidents of Armenia and Azerbaijan had agreed to continue their work to reach a political settlement of the conflict and had instructed their Foreign Ministers to take further action in the negotiations in liaison with the OSCE Minsk Group Co-Chairs.

On 10 December [A/63/596], Armenia transmitted to the Secretary-General a joint declaration of the Foreign Ministers and Deputy Ministers of France, the Russian Federation and the United States on Nagorno-Karabakh, adopted at the OSCE ministerial meeting held in Helsinki on 4 December. The Ministers called on the parties to build on the momentum established during the Moscow meeting of 2 November. The Moscow Declaration signed that day opened a promising phase in the endeavour to expand peace in the South Caucasus. In that declaration, the Presidents reaffirmed their commitment to advancing a peaceful settlement in the framework of the Basic Principles developed by the Minsk Group Co-Chairs in collaboration with the leaders of Armenia and Azerbaijan on the basis of the proposals advanced in Madrid. The Ministers called on the parties to: work with the Co-Chairs to finalize the Basic Principles and begin drafting a comprehensive peace settlement, and to develop confidence-building measures, beginning with pulling back snipers from the Line of Contact; and work with each other, the Co-Chairs and the Personal Representative of the Chairman-in-Office to stabilize the ceasefire.

Other communications were submitted by Azerbaijan to the General Assembly and the Security Council on 14 January [A/62/651-S/2008/27], 7 February [A/62/682-S/2008/82], 12 February [A/62/691-S/2008/95], 3 March [A/62/713-S/2008/151], 19 March [A/62/759-S/2008/191], 6 May [A/62/835-S/2008/303], 20 October [A/63/497-S/2008/668], 31 October [A/63/516-S/2008/683], 22 December [A/63/662-S/2008/812] and 26 December [A/63/664-S/2008/823].

The General Assembly, by **decision 63/552** of 24 December, decided that the agenda item on the situation in the occupied territories of Azerbaijan would remain for consideration during its resumed sixty-third (2009) session.

Organization for Democracy and Economic Development

Communication. On 17 July [A/62/916], Azerbaijan, as chair of the Organization for Democracy and Economic Development-GUAM (Azerbaijan, Georgia, Moldova, Ukraine) [YUN 2006, p. 486], transmitted to the Secretary-General the summary report of the International Conference on Basic Principles for the Settlement of the Conflicts on the Territories of the GUAM States (Baku, Azerbaijan, 15–16 April). At the Conference, the GUAM States, together with officials from Latvia, Lithuania, Poland, Romania, Slovenia and Switzerland and representatives of leading academic institutions, addressed issues of international law, including those relating to correlation between the principles of the territorial integrity of States and the right of people to self-determination; consequences of the illegal use of force and territorial acquisitions; and the responsibility for internationally wrongful acts and perspectives of making use of mechanisms of the international judicial institutions to that end.

The General Assembly, by **decision 63/552** of 24 December, decided that the agenda item "Protracted conflicts in the GUAM area and their implications for international peace, security and development" would remain for consideration during its resumed sixty-third (2009) session.

Cyprus

During 2008, progress was made in resolving the Cyprus problem. The Secretary-General's Special Representative in Cyprus continued to assist the two sides in implementing the 8 July 2006 Set of Principles and Decision [YUN 2006, p. 487], which included commitment to the unification of Cyprus based on a bizonal, bicommunal federation and political equality, and an agreement to meet regularly on issues affecting day-to-day life of the Cypriot people. The Greek and Turkish Cypriot leaders agreed to establish working groups and technical committees, and in September launched full-fledged negotiations under UN auspices, aimed at finding a mutually acceptable solution.

The United Nations Peacekeeping Force in Cyprus (UNFICYP) continued to cooperate with its UN partners and local actors to facilitate projects benefiting both Greek and Turkish Cypriots in and outside the buffer zone and to promote confidence-building measures between them. The Security-Council extended the UNFICYP mandate twice during the year, the second time until 15 June 2009.

Incidents and position statements

Communications. Throughout 2008, the Secretary-General received letters from the Government of Cyprus and from Turkish Cypriot authorities containing charges and counter-charges, protests and accusations, and explanations of positions regarding the question of Cyprus. Letters from the "Turkish Republic of Northern Cyprus" were transmitted by Turkey. In communications dated between 7 February and 16 December, Cyprus reported violations of the international air traffic regulations and the national airspace by Turkish military aircraft [A/62/683-S/2008/83, A/62/803-S/2008/253, A/62/882-S/2008/389, A/62/920-S/2008/524, A/63/543 & Corr.1-S/2008/704 & Corr.1, A/63/599-S/2008/788]. The "Turkish Republic of Northern Cyprus" refuted those allegations, stating that the flights mentioned took place within the sovereign airspace of the "Turkish Republic of Northern Cyprus", over which the Cypriot administration in South Cyprus had no jurisdiction or right of say [A/62/699-S/2008/101, A/62/819-S/2008/276, A/62/892-S/2008/429, A/62/932-S/2008/552, A/63/566-S/2008/731].

On 14 November [A/63/554-S/2008/719], Cyprus informed the Secretary-General that, on 13 November, vessels legitimately conducting exploratory surveys within the exclusive economic zone of Cyprus received threats by a Turkish warship and were forced to withdraw within the territorial waters of Cyprus. On 26 November [A/63/574-S/2008/741], Turkey transmitted a letter from the "Turkish Republic of Northern Cyprus" stating that the Greek Cypriot side's unilateral activities regarding the delimitation of maritime jurisdiction before a comprehensive settlement violated the rights and interests of the Turkish Cypriot people, who had equal rights and say over the natural resources in and around the island. Also on 26 November [A/63/575-S/2008/742], Cyprus reported that the harassment of vessels by Turkish warships within the exclusive economic zone of Cyprus had continued unabated, in complete disregard of Cyprus's sovereign rights.

Other communications were transmitted by Turkey from the "Turkish Republic of Northern Cyprus" on 25 January [A/62/666-S/2008/56] and 28 November [A/63/578-S/2008/749, A/63/579-S/2008/750], and by Cyprus on 25 September [A/63/378].

Good offices mission

On 21 March, Demetris Christofias, who became President following elections in Cyprus in February, met with Mehmet Ali Talat, the Turkish Cypriot leader, in the presence of the Special Representative, and agreed on a path towards a comprehensive settlement. The agreement entailed the establishment of a number of working groups to consider the core issues pertaining to an eventual settlement plan, and of technical committees to seek immediate solutions to everyday problems. Moreover, the leaders decided to open a crossing at Ledra Street in the centre of old town Nicosia, which had for many years been a symbol of the division of Cyprus.

On 26 March, representatives of the leaders agreed to establish six working groups on governance and power-sharing, EU matters, security and guarantees, territory, property and economic matters, as well as seven technical committees on crime and criminal matters, economic and commercial matters, cultural heritage, crisis management, humanitarian matters, health and the environment. The groups and committees began to meet regularly on 22 April, as foreseen by the leaders, facilitated by the United Nations. From late March, the Under-Secretary-General for Political Affairs, Lynn Pascoe, met five times with President Christofias and Mr. Talat, and both confirmed their commitment to reaching a comprehensive settlement under the auspices of the Secretary-General.

Following the meeting on 23 May hosted by the Special Representative, the leaders issued a joint statement [S/2008/353, annex III] reaffirming their commitment to a bizonal, bicommunal federation with political equality, as defined in relevant Security Council resolutions. The partnership would comprise a federal Government with a single international personality, as well as a Turkish Cypriot Constituent State and a Greek Cypriot Constituent State, which would be of equal status.

Since his appointment as the Special Adviser on Cyprus as from 14 July [S/2008/456, S/2008/457], Alexander Downer (Australia) conducted four visits to facilitate meetings between the leaders and their representatives and officials.

On 1 July, the leaders issued a joint statement stating that they had discussed the issues of single sovereignty and citizenship. On 25 July the leaders undertook a final review of the progress made by the working groups and technical committees, which had held more than 270 meetings, and agreed to launch full-fledged negotiations, which began as scheduled on 3 September. The aim of the negotiations was to find a mutually acceptable solution to the Cyprus problem that would safeguard the fundamental and legitimate rights and interests of all Cypriots. Any agreed solution would be put to separate, simultaneous referendums. Subsequently, the leaders met on nine occasions under UN auspices. In the first phase of negotiations the focus was on the key issues of governance and power-sharing.

On 22 December, the leaders, in a joint statement, reaffirmed their commitment and resolve to finding a comprehensive settlement of the Cyprus problem. They also recognized that although some progress had been made, it had been insufficient.

The Secretary-General noted [S/2008/744] that efforts to solve the Cyprus problem had entered a new phase and that the decision to resume fully fledged negotiations was encouraging. Differences along the way would naturally appear, considering that the issues to be addressed were difficult. Nonetheless, he expressed optimism about the process, and underscored that the parties should not neglect the political aspects of the process, explaining to their communities the benefits of a solution. To support the efforts of the parties throughout the process, the United Nations had adopted an integrated approach that maximized synergies among the good-offices mission and UNFICYP.

UNFICYP

In 2008, the United Nations Peacekeeping Force in Cyprus (UNFICYP), established in 1964 [YUN 1964, p. 165], continued to monitor the ceasefire lines between the Turkish and Turkish Cypriot forces on the northern side and the Cypriot National Guard on the southern side of the island; to maintain the military status quo and prevent a recurrence of fighting; and to undertake humanitarian and economic activities.

On 9 April [S/2008/244], the Secretary-General informed the Security Council of his intention to appoint Tayé-Brook Zerihoun (Ethiopia) as his Special Representative in Cyprus and Head of UNFICYP, replacing Michael Møller (Denmark), who completed his assignment on 31 March. Also on 9 April [S/2008/246], the Secretary-General informed the Council of his intention to appoint Rear Admiral Mario Sánchez Debernardi (Peru) as UNFICYP Force Commander, replacing Major General Rafael José Barni (Argentina). The Council took note of those intentions on 14 April [S/2008/245, S/2008/247].

As at 31 October, UNFICYP comprised 858 troops and 69 civilian police.

The Secretary-General submitted two reports covering UNFICYP activities for the periods from 16 November 2007 to 23 May 2008 [S/2008/353] and from 24 May to 23 November [S/2008/744].

Activities

Report of Secretary-General (June). In a June report [S/2008/353], the Secretary-General noted that the situation in Cyprus remained calm and stable, with no major incidents along the ceasefire lines.

UNFICYP liaised extensively with senior commanders of the opposing forces to agree on the military-technical terms in order to implement the 21 March decision of the leaders and prepare for the opening of the crossing point at Ledra Street. On 3 April, UNFICYP conducted a major security operation to support the opening of the crossing point on that day. An incident on the evening of 3 April resulted in a brief closing of the crossing point, which was reopened later that night and since then had been functioning without problems. However, the incident showed that both sides needed to demonstrate cooperation and restraint while managing the crossing point.

The Turkish Forces provided minefield records and maps of 16 suspected mined areas after an agreement on the guidelines for clearing those areas was reached after a protracted series of meetings. In March, a deminer from Mozambique lost a limb in a mine explosion.

The requests for facilitation from Cypriots to UNFICYP ranged from religious and educational issues, the conduct of commemorative and sociocultural events, the evacuation of patients and the transfer of the deceased, to law enforcement matters. During the reporting period, the Force facilitated 77 bicommunal events, which brought together more than 4,117 persons from both communities. In addition, UNFICYP carried out 62 humanitarian convoys and visits in support of 375 Greek Cypriots and 136 Maronites living in the northern part of the island. It also continued to assist Turkish Cypriots in the southern part in obtaining identity documents, housing, welfare services, medical care, employment and education. The Force continued to receive with concern reports about the demolition of Greek Cypriot houses in the north.

UNFICYP continued to develop working relations with police forces on both sides of the buffer zone. Its relations with the Cyprus police had been positive and constructive, while relations with the Turkish Cypriot police were developing at a slower pace.

The Secretary-General expressed commitment to helping the parties in moving forward to the formal talks as expeditiously and smoothly as possible. He also recommended that the Council extend the UNFICYP mandate until 15 December.

SECURITY COUNCIL ACTION

On 17 April [meeting 5869], following consultations among Security Council members, the President made **statement S/PRST/2008/9** on behalf of the Council:

The Security Council warmly welcomes the agreement reached on 21 March 2008 by the Greek Cypriot and Turkish Cypriot leaders and commends them for the political leadership they have shown.

The Council is encouraged by the launch of the working groups and technical committees that will prepare the ground for the start of fully fledged negotiations, in a spirit of good faith, on a comprehensive and durable settlement under the auspices of the Secretary-General's good offices mission. The Council looks forward to the results of this preparatory process within the three-month timeline agreed by the two leaders, which, it is hoped, will build trust, momentum and a sense of common interest in the search for a just and lasting solution.

The Council further welcomes the opening of the Ledra Street crossing as an indication of political will to tackle issues that have obstructed progress and an important signal that both sides seek to improve the lives of all Cypriots. The Council looks forward to further such confidence-building measures.

The Council reaffirms its commitment to the reunification of Cyprus based on a bicommunal, bizonal federation and political equality, as set out in the relevant Council resolutions, and its willingness to support the efforts of the Secretary-General to this end. In this context, the Council welcomes the readiness of the Secretary-General to assist the parties in Cyprus, and further welcomes the prospect of the appointment, after the completion of the preparatory period and based on progress, of a Special Adviser to facilitate movement towards a comprehensive settlement.

The Council welcomes the appointment of Mr. Tayé-Brook Zerihoun as the new Special Representative of the Secretary-General in Cyprus, and expresses its appreciation for the work of the previous Special Representative, Mr. Michael Møller.

Security Council consideration. On 9 June [meeting 5906], in a closed meeting, the Special Representative briefed the Security Council and countries contributing troops to UNFICYP. The briefing was followed by an exchange of views.

SECURITY COUNCIL ACTION

On 13 June [meeting 5911] the Council unanimously adopted **resolution 1818(2008)**. The draft [S/2008/384] was prepared in consultations among Council members.

The Security Council,

Welcoming the report of the Secretary-General of 2 June 2008 on the United Nations operation in Cyprus,

Noting that the Government of Cyprus has agreed that, in view of the prevailing conditions on the island, it is necessary to keep the United Nations Peacekeeping Force in Cyprus beyond 15 June 2008,

Echoing the Secretary-General's firm belief that the responsibility of finding a solution lies first and foremost with the Cypriots themselves, and that there now exists an important window of opportunity to make decisive progress, which must be fully utilized by all parties in the search for a comprehensive solution, and noting the primary role of the United Nations in assisting the parties to bring the Cyprus conflict and division of the island to a comprehensive and durable settlement,

Welcoming the agreement of 21 March 2008 and the joint statement of 23 May 2008, which, inter alia, have demonstrated a renewed political willingness to support and engage fully and in good faith with the United Nations efforts, reaffirmed the commitment of the leaders to a bicommunal, bizonal federation with political equality, as set out in the relevant Security Council resolutions, and to consider further civilian and military confidence-building measures,

Welcoming also the opening of the Ledra Street crossing, which has helped to foster greater trust and interaction between the two communities, reaffirming the importance of continued crossings of the Green Line by Cypriots, and encouraging the opening of other crossing points,

Welcoming further the intention of the Secretary-General to appoint a Special Adviser at the appropriate time and to keep the Council informed of further developments and progress,

Taking note of the assessment of the Secretary-General that the security situation on the island and along the Green Line remains generally stable, welcoming the decrease in the overall number of incidents involving the two sides, and urging both sides to avoid any action, including restrictions on the movements of the Force, which could lead to an increase in tension,

Welcoming the coordination arrangements agreed with the United Nations to address unauthorized construction within the buffer zone, including large-scale commercial projects, and echoing the Secretary-General's firm belief that the situation in the buffer zone would be improved if both sides accepted the 1989 aide-memoire used by the United Nations,

Welcoming also the agreement with the Turkish forces to proceed with demining activities, but urging that further guidelines be agreed to permit such activities to take place in all outstanding minefields, and noting with concern that funding for the Mine Action Centre beyond 2008 has not yet been secured but that this work will need to continue beyond that period,

Welcoming also the progress and continuation of the important activities of the Committee on Missing Persons in Cyprus, and expressing the hope that this process will promote reconciliation between the communities,

Agreeing that an active and flourishing civil society is essential to the political process, and welcoming all efforts to promote bicommunal contacts and events, including on the part of all United Nations bodies on the island, and urging the two sides to promote the active engagement of civil society and the encouragement of cooperation between economic and commercial bodies and to remove all obstacles to such contacts,

Reaffirming the importance of the Secretary-General continuing to keep the operations of the Force under close review while continuing to take into account developments on the ground and the views of the parties, and reverting to the Council with recommendations, as appropriate, for further adjustments to the mandate, force levels and concept of operation of the Force as soon as warranted,

Welcoming the appointment of Mr. Tayé-Brook Zerihoun as the new Special Representative of the Secretary-General in Cyprus, and echoing the Secretary-General's appreciation for the work of the previous Special Representative, Mr. Michael Møller,

Echoing the Secretary-General's gratitude to the Government of Cyprus and the Government of Greece for their voluntary contributions to the funding of the Force, and his request for further voluntary contributions from other countries and organizations,

Welcoming and encouraging efforts by the United Nations to sensitize peacekeeping personnel in the prevention and control of HIV/AIDS and other communicable diseases in all its peacekeeping operations,

1. *Welcomes* the analysis of developments on the ground over the last six months in the report of the Secretary-General;

2. *Urges* the parties to build on the present momentum and continue their efforts to identify to the greatest possible extent areas of convergence and disagreement, while preparing options, where feasible, on the more sensitive elements, and to work to ensure that fully fledged negotiations can begin expeditiously and smoothly, in line with the agreement of 21 March 2008 and the joint statement of 23 May 2008;

3. *Reaffirms* all its relevant resolutions on Cyprus, in particular resolution 1251(1999) of 29 June 1999 and subsequent resolutions;

4. *Expresses its full support* for the United Nations Peacekeeping Force in Cyprus, and decides to extend its mandate for a further period ending 15 December 2008;

5. *Calls upon* both sides to continue to engage, as a matter of urgency and while respecting the mandate of the Force, in consultations with the Force on the demarcation of the buffer zone and on the United Nations 1989 aide-memoire, with a view to reaching early agreement on outstanding issues;

6. *Calls upon* the Turkish Cypriot side and Turkish forces to restore in Strovilia the military status quo which existed there prior to 30 June 2000;

7. *Requests* the Secretary-General to submit a report on the implementation of the present resolution by 1 December 2008 and to keep the Security Council updated on events as necessary;

8. *Welcomes* the efforts being undertaken by the Force to implement the Secretary-General's zero-tolerance policy on sexual exploitation and abuse and to ensure full compliance of its personnel with the United Nations code of conduct, requests the Secretary-General to continue to take all necessary action in this regard and to keep the Council informed, and urges troop-contributing countries to take appropriate preventive action, including conducting pre-deployment awareness training, and to take disciplinary action and other action to ensure full accountability in cases of such conduct involving their personnel;

9. *Decides* to remain seized of the matter.

On 4 September [meeting 5971], following consultations among Security Council members, the President made statement **S/PRST/2008/34** on behalf of the Council:

The Security Council warmly welcomes the launch of fully fledged negotiations between the two leaders, under the good offices mission of the Secretary-General, aimed at the reunification of Cyprus.

The Council commends the two leaders for the progress made since their first meeting on 21 March 2008 and supports their common approach. The Council calls upon both sides to continue to work together in a constructive and positive manner in order to reach a comprehensive and durable settlement approved in separate and simultaneous referendums. The Council looks forward to progress in the negotiations and reiterates its readiness to support the process.

The Council welcomes the appointment of Mr. Alexander Downer as the Special Adviser to the Secretary-General on Cyprus and looks forward to being briefed on the progress of the good offices process.

Report of Secretary-General (November). In November [S/2008/744], the Secretary-General noted that the situation in the buffer zone remained stable and that only minor incidents were recorded.

UNFICYP no longer maintained an overt military presence at the Ledra Street crossing, and crossings had continued without incident. The Secretary-General commended both sides for their decision to cancel their main annual military exercises. In a significant confidence-building measure, the National Guard cancelled the "Exercise Nikiforos" and the Turkish Forces responded by cancelling its "Exercise Toros". However, the Turkish Forces continued to impose restrictions on the movement of UNFICYP on the Karpas peninsula and at the walled area of Varosha. Regarding the clearance of 26 Turkish Forces minefields, 17 minefields would be completed by the end of December, leaving 9 to be cleared.

Cypriots from both sides continued to seek the resolution of day-to-day issues that affected their lives, with the assistance of UNFICYP, which also continued to facilitate the normalization of conditions in the buffer zone and humanitarian assistance to both communities. Regular monthly meetings between Greek Cypriot and Turkish Cypriot political party leaders continued at the Ledra Palace Hotel under the auspices of the Embassy of Slovakia. The 54 requests made by Greek Cypriot and Maronite internally displaced and refugee families that wished to return and permanently reside in the north were still pending. Following a review of its activities in facilitating humanitarian assistance to Turkish Cypriots in the south, UNFICYP began discussions with local authorities and community representatives to further improve the humanitarian and welfare action directed to them. During the reporting period, UNFICYP, in cooperation with international and local partners, facilitated 56 bicommunal events, with the participation of nearly 5,300 persons from both communities. The Force authorized six projects in the buffer zone, outside of civil-use areas, including telecommunications infrastructure, sewage system, housing and road construction. Relations between UNFICYP and the police forces on both sides remained cooperative and constructive.

The Secretary-General recommended that the Council extend the UNFICYP mandate until 15 June 2009.

Security Council consideration. On 5 December [meeting 6032], in a closed meeting, the Special Representative briefed the Security Council and countries contributing troops to UNFICYP. The briefing was followed by an exchange of views.

SECURITY COUNCIL ACTION

On 12 December [meeting 6038] the Council unanimously adopted **resolution 1847(2008)**. The draft [S/2008/779] was submitted by China, France, the Russian Federation, the United Kingdom and the United States.

The Security Council,

Welcoming the report of the Secretary-General of 28 November 2008 on the United Nations operation in Cyprus,

Noting that the Government of Cyprus has agreed that, in view of the prevailing conditions on the island, it is necessary to keep the United Nations Peacekeeping Force in Cyprus beyond 15 December 2008,

Echoing the Secretary-General's firm belief that the responsibility for finding a solution lies first and foremost with the Cypriots themselves, stressing that there now exists an unprecedented opportunity to make decisive progress, and reaffirming the primary role of the United Nations in assisting the parties to bring the Cyprus conflict and division of the island to a comprehensive and durable settlement,

Welcoming the launch of fully fledged negotiations on 3 September 2008, the progress made so far and the leaders' joint statements,

Emphasizing the importance of all parties engaging fully, flexibly and constructively in those negotiations in order to make decisive progress towards a comprehensive settlement based on a bicommunal, bizonal federation with political equality, as set out in the relevant Security Council resolutions,

Encouraging continued momentum in the negotiations and the maintenance of goodwill and trust, looking forward to substantive progress and the full exploitation of the current opportunity, commending the Greek Cypriot and Turkish Cypriot leaders for the political leadership they have shown so far, and welcoming the intention of the Secretary-General to keep the Council informed of further development and progress,

Welcoming the announcement of confidence-building measures and the cancellation of military exercises, and looking forward to the implementation of these measures and agreement on and implementation of further steps to build trust between the communities,

Reaffirming the importance of continued crossings of the Green Line by Cypriots, reiterating its welcome of the opening of the Ledra Street crossing, encouraging the opening by mutual agreement of other crossing points, and noting in this context the commitment in the leaders' joint statements to pursue the opening of the Limnitis/Yeşilirmak crossing point,

Convinced of the many important benefits for all Cypriots that would flow from a comprehensive and durable Cyprus settlement, and encouraging both sides clearly to explain these benefits, as well as the need for flexibility in order to secure them, to both communities well in advance of any eventual referendums,

Highlighting the supportive role that the international community will continue to play in helping the Greek Cypriot and Turkish Cypriot leaders to exploit fully the current opportunity,

Taking note of the assessment of the Secretary-General that the security situation on the island and along the Green Line remains generally stable, welcoming the decrease in the overall number of incidents involving the two sides, and urging both sides to avoid any action, including restrictions on the movements of the Force, which could lead to an increase in tension, undermine the good progress achieved so far or damage the goodwill on the island,

Recalling the Secretary-General's firm belief that the situation in the buffer zone would be improved if both sides accepted the 1989 aide-memoire used by the United Nations,

Welcoming the progress made in proceeding with demining activities, echoing the Secretary-General's call for the remaining minefields to be cleared, and noting with concern that funding is urgently required by the Mine Action Centre beyond 2008 to allow this work to continue beyond that period,

Welcoming also the progress and continuation of the important activities of the Committee on Missing Persons in Cyprus, and trusting that this process will promote reconciliation between the communities,

Agreeing that an active and flourishing civil society is essential to the political process, welcoming all efforts to promote bicommunal contacts and events, including on the part of all United Nations bodies on the island, and urging the two sides to promote the active engagement of civil society and the encouragement of cooperation between economic and commercial bodies and to remove all obstacles to such contacts,

Reaffirming the importance of the Secretary-General continuing to keep the operations of the Force under close review while continuing to take into account developments on the ground and the views of the parties, and reverting to the Council with recommendations, as appropriate, for further adjustments to the mandate, force levels and concept of operations of the Force as soon as warranted,

Welcoming the appointment of Mr. Alexander Downer as the Special Adviser to the Secretary-General on Cyprus with a mandate to assist the parties in the conduct of fully fledged negotiations aimed at reaching a comprehensive settlement,

Echoing the Secretary-General's gratitude to the Government of Cyprus and the Government of Greece for their voluntary contributions to the funding of the Force, and his request for further voluntary contributions from other countries and organizations,

Welcoming and encouraging efforts by the United Nations to sensitize peacekeeping personnel in the prevention and control of HIV/AIDS and other communicable diseases in all its peacekeeping operations,

1. *Welcomes* the analysis of developments on the ground over the last six months in the report of the Secretary-General in accordance with his mandate;

2. *Welcomes also* the launch of fully fledged negotiations on 3 September 2008, and the prospect of a comprehensive and durable settlement that this has created;

3. *Urges* full exploitation of this opportunity, including by intensifying the momentum of the negotiations, preserving the current atmosphere of trust and goodwill and engaging in the process in a constructive and open manner;

4. *Welcomes* the announcement on confidence-building measures and the cancellation of military exercises, and looks forward to these measures being fully implemented as well as to agreement on further such steps, including the possible opening of other crossing points, as mentioned in the leaders' joint statements;

5. *Reaffirms* all its relevant resolutions on Cyprus, in particular resolution 1251(1999) of 29 June 1999 and subsequent resolutions;

6. *Expresses its full support* for the United Nations Peacekeeping Force in Cyprus, and decides to extend its mandate for a further period ending 15 June 2009;

7. *Calls upon* both sides to continue to engage, as a matter of urgency and while respecting the mandate of the Force, in consultations with the Force on the demarcation of the buffer zone, and on the United Nations 1989 aide-memoire, with a view to reaching early agreement on outstanding issues;

8. *Calls upon* the Turkish Cypriot side and Turkish forces to restore in Strovilia the military status quo which existed there prior to 30 June 2000;

9. *Requests* the Secretary-General to submit a report on the implementation of the present resolution by 1 June 2009 and to keep the Security Council updated on events as necessary;

10. *Welcomes* the efforts being undertaken by the Force to implement the Secretary-General's zero-tolerance policy on sexual exploitation and abuse and to ensure full compliance of its personnel with the United Nations code of conduct, requests the Secretary-General to continue to take all necessary action in this regard and to keep the Council informed, and urges troop-contributing countries to take appropriate preventive action, including conducting predeployment awareness training, and to take disciplinary action and other action to ensure full accountability in cases of such conduct involving their personnel;

11. *Decides* to remain seized of the matter.

By **decision 63/552** of 24 December, the Assembly decided that the agenda item on the question of Cyprus would remain for consideration during its resumed sixty-third (2009) session.

Financing

On 20 June [meeting 109], the General Assembly, having considered the Secretary-General's report on UNFICYP's financial performance for the period from 1 July 2006 to 30 June 2007 [A/62/649], the report on its budget for the period from 1 July 2008 to 30 June 2009 [A/62/718 & Corr.1.], the note of the Secretary-General [A/62/779] and ACABQ related comments and recommendations [A/62/781/Add.9], adopted, on the recommendation of the Fifth Committee [A/62/868], **resolution 62/255** without vote [agenda item 143].

Financing of the United Nations Peacekeeping Force in Cyprus

The General Assembly,

Having considered the reports of the Secretary-General on the financing of the United Nations Peacekeeping Force in Cyprus, the note by the Secretary-General on the financing arrangements for the Force and the related report of the Advisory Committee on Administrative and Budgetary Questions,

Recalling Security Council resolution 186(1964) of 4 March 1964, regarding the establishment of the United Nations Peacekeeping Force in Cyprus and the subsequent resolutions by which the Council extended the mandate of the Force, the latest of which was resolution 1789(2007) of 14 December 2007, by which the Council extended the mandate of the Force until 15 June 2008,

Recalling also its resolution 47/236 of 14 September 1993 on the financing of the Force and its subsequent resolutions and decisions thereon, the latest of which was resolution 61/280 of 29 June 2007,

Reaffirming the general principles underlying the financing of United Nations peacekeeping operations, as stated in General Assembly resolutions 1874(S-IV) of 27 June 1963, 3101(XXVIII) of 11 December 1973 and 55/235 of 23 December 2000,

Noting with appreciation that voluntary contributions have been made to the Force by certain Governments,

Noting that voluntary contributions were insufficient to cover all the costs of the Force, including those incurred by troop-contributing Governments prior to 16 June 1993, and regretting the absence of an adequate response to appeals for voluntary contributions, including that contained in the letter dated 17 May 1994 from the Secretary-General to all Member States,

Mindful of the fact that it is essential to provide the Force with the financial resources necessary to enable it to fulfil its responsibilities under the relevant resolutions of the Security Council,

1. *Requests* the Secretary-General to entrust the Head of Mission with the task of formulating future budget proposals in full accordance with the provisions of General Assembly resolutions 59/296 of 22 June 2005, 60/266 of 30 June 2006 and 61/276 of 29 June 2007, as well as other relevant resolutions;

2. *Takes note* of the status of contributions to the United Nations Peacekeeping Force in Cyprus as at 31 March 2008, including the contributions outstanding in the amount of 19.1 million United States dollars, representing some 6 per cent of the total assessed contributions, notes with concern that only forty-one Member States have paid their assessed contributions in full, and urges all other Member States, in particular those in arrears, to ensure payment of their outstanding assessed contributions;

3. *Expresses its appreciation* to those Member States which have paid their assessed contributions in full, and urges all other Member States to make every possible effort to ensure payment of their assessed contributions to the Force in full;

4. *Expresses concern* at the financial situation with regard to peacekeeping activities, in particular as regards the reimbursements to troop contributors that bear additional burdens owing to overdue payments by Member States of their assessments;

5. *Also expresses concern* at the delay experienced by the Secretary-General in deploying and providing adequate resources to some recent peacekeeping missions, in particular those in Africa;

6. *Emphasizes* that all future and existing peacekeeping missions shall be given equal and non-discriminatory treatment in respect of financial and administrative arrangements;

7. *Also emphasizes* that all peacekeeping missions shall be provided with adequate resources for the effective and efficient discharge of their respective mandates;

8. *Reiterates its request* to the Secretary-General to make the fullest possible use of facilities and equipment at the United Nations Logistics Base at Brindisi, Italy, in order to minimize the costs of procurement for the Force;

9. *Endorses* the conclusions and recommendations contained in the report of the Advisory Committee on Administrative and Budgetary Questions, subject to the provisions of the present resolution, and requests the Secretary-General to ensure their full implementation;

10. *Decides* to reclassify the posts of Associate Public Information Officer, Chief Security Officer and Chief of Integrated Support Services to the P-3, P-4 and P-5 levels, respectively;

11. *Welcomes* the steps taken so far by the host Government and the Force regarding the renovation of the accommodation of military contingent personnel and of other personnel of the Force, and requests the Secretary-General to continue making every effort, in coordination with the host Government, to ensure that the renovations are completed as scheduled and to report thereon in the context of his next budget submission;

12. *Requests* the Secretary-General to ensure the full implementation of the relevant provisions of its resolutions 59/296, 60/266 and 61/276;

13. *Also requests* the Secretary-General to take all necessary action to ensure that the Force is administered with a maximum of efficiency and economy;

14. *Further requests* the Secretary-General, in order to reduce the cost of employing General Service staff, to continue efforts to recruit local staff for the Force against General Service posts, commensurate with the requirements of the Force;

Financial performance report for the period from 1 July 2006 to 30 June 2007

15. *Takes note* of the report of the Secretary-General on the financial performance of the Force for the period from 1 July 2006 to 30 June 2007;

16. *Decides* to appropriate to the Special Account for the United Nations Peacekeeping Force in Cyprus the amount of 2,516,500 dollars for the maintenance of the Force for the period from 1 July 2006 to 30 June 2007, in addition to the amount of 46,770,000 dollars already appropriated for the Force for the same period under the terms of its resolution 60/270 of 30 June 2006;

Financing of the additional appropriation for the period from 1 July 2006 to 30 June 2007

17. *Notes with appreciation* that a one-third share of the net additional appropriation, equivalent to 741,433 dollars, will be funded through voluntary contributions from the Government of Cyprus;

18. *Decides*, taking into account the amount of 25,354,700 dollars already apportioned under the terms of its resolution 60/270, to apportion among Member States the additional amount of 1,775,067 dollars for the maintenance of the Force for the period from 1 July 2006 to 30 June 2007, in accordance with the levels updated in its resolutions 58/256 of 23 December 2003 and 61/243 of 22 December 2006, and taking into account the scale of assessments for 2006, as set out in its resolution 58/1 B of 23 December 2003, and the scale of assessments for 2007, as set out in its resolution 61/237 of 22 December 2006;

19. *Also decides* that, in accordance with the provisions of its resolution 973(X) of 15 December 1955, there shall be set off against the apportionment among Member States, as provided for in paragraph 18 above, their respective share in the Tax Equalization Fund of the amount of 292,200 dollars, representing the additional staff assessment income for the Force for the period from 1 July 2006 to 30 June 2007;

20. *Further decides* that, for Member States that have fulfilled their financial obligations to the Force, there shall be set off against their apportionment, as provided for in paragraph 18 above, their respective share of other income in the amount of 641,518 dollars in respect of the financial period ended 30 June 2007, in accordance with the scheme set out in paragraph 18 above;

21. *Decides* that, for Member States that have not fulfilled their financial obligations to the Force, there shall be set off against their outstanding obligations their respective share of other income in the amount of 641,518 dollars in respect of the financial period ended 30 June 2007, in accordance with the scheme set out in paragraph 18 above;

22. *Also decides*, taking into account its voluntary contribution for the financial period ended 30 June 2007, that one third of other income in the amount of 403,829 dollars in respect of the financial period ended 30 June 2007 shall be returned to the Government of Cyprus;

23. *Further decides*, taking into account its voluntary contribution for the financial period ended 30 June 2007, that the prorated share of other income in the amount of 167,353 dollars in respect of the financial period ended 30 June 2007 shall be returned to the Government of Greece;

Financing arrangements for the period from 1 July 2007 to 30 June 2008

24. *Takes note* of the note by the Secretary-General on the financing arrangements for the Force for the period from 1 July 2007 to 30 June 2008;

25. *Decides* to appropriate to the Special Account for the Force the amount of 3,646,500 dollars for the maintenance of the Force for the period from 1 July 2007 to 30 June 2008, in addition to the amount of 48,847,500 dollars already appropriated for the Force for the same period under the terms of its resolution 61/280;

Financing of the additional appropriation for the period from 1 July 2007 to 30 June 2008

26. *Notes with appreciation* that a one-third share of the net additional appropriation, equivalent to 1,166,700 dollars, will be funded through voluntary contributions from the Government of Cyprus;

27. *Decides*, taking into account the amount of 26,804,234 dollars already apportioned under the terms of its resolution 61/280, to apportion among Member States the additional amount of 2,376,475 dollars for the maintenance of the Force for the period from 1 July 2007 to 15 June 2008, in accordance with the levels updated in resolution 61/243, and taking into account the scale of assessments for 2007 and 2008, as set out in resolution 61/237;

28. *Also decides* that, in accordance with the provisions of its resolution 973(X), there shall be set off against the apportionment among Member States, as provided for in paragraph 27 above, their respective share in the Tax Equalization Fund of the amount of 140,204 dollars, representing the additional staff assessment income approved for the Force for the period from 1 July 2007 to 15 June 2008;

29. *Further decides* to apportion among Member States the additional amount of 103,325 dollars for the maintenance of the Force for the period from 16 to 30 June 2008, in accordance with the levels updated in resolution 61/243, and taking into account the scale of assessments for 2008, as set out in resolution 61/237, subject to a decision by the Security Council to extend the mandate of the Force;

30. *Decides* that, in accordance with the provisions of its resolution 973(X), there shall be set off against the apportionment among Member States, as provided for in paragraph 29 above, their respective share in the Tax Equalization Fund of the amount of 6,096 dollars, representing the additional estimated staff assessment income approved for the Force for the period from 16 to 30 June 2008;

Budget estimates for the period from 1 July 2008 to 30 June 2009

31. *Also decides* to appropriate to the Special Account for the Force the amount of 57,392,000 dollars for the period from 1 July 2008 to 30 June 2009, inclusive of 54,851,100 dollars for the maintenance of the Force, 2,215,000 dollars for the support account for peacekeeping operations and 325,900 dollars for the United Nations Logistics Base;

Financing of the appropriation for the period from 1 July 2008 to 30 June 2009

32. *Notes with appreciation* that a one-third share of the net appropriation, equivalent to 18,264,450 dollars,

will be funded through voluntary contributions from the Government of Cyprus and the amount of 6.5 million dollars from the Government of Greece;

33. *Decides* to apportion among Member States the amount of 32,627,550 dollars at a monthly rate of 2,718,962 dollars, in accordance with the levels updated in resolution 61/243, and taking into account the scale of assessments for 2008 and 2009, as set out in resolution 61/237, subject to a decision of the Security Council to extend the mandate of the Force;

34. *Also decides* that, in accordance with the provisions of its resolution 973(X), there shall be set off against the apportionment among Member States, as provided for in paragraph 33 above, their respective share in the Tax Equalization Fund of 2,543,800 dollars, comprising the estimated staff assessment income of 2,305,200 dollars approved for the Force, the prorated share of 212,900 dollars of the estimated staff assessment income approved for the support account and the prorated share of 25,700 dollars of the estimated staff assessment income approved for the United Nations Logistics Base;

35. *Further decides* to continue to maintain as separate the account established for the Force for the period prior to 16 June 1993, invites Member States to make voluntary contributions to that account, and requests the Secretary-General to continue his efforts in appealing for voluntary contributions to the account;

36. *Emphasizes* that no peacekeeping mission shall be financed by borrowing funds from other active peacekeeping missions;

37. *Encourages* the Secretary-General to continue to take additional measures to ensure the safety and security of all personnel participating in the Force under the auspices of the United Nations, bearing in mind paragraphs 5 and 6 of Security Council resolution 1502(2003) of 26 August 2003;

38. *Invites* voluntary contributions to the Force in cash and in the form of services and supplies acceptable to the Secretary-General, to be administered, as appropriate, in accordance with the procedure and practices established by the General Assembly;

39. *Decides* to include in the provisional agenda of its sixty-third session the item entitled "Financing of the United Nations Peacekeeping Force in Cyprus".

By **decision 63/552** of 24 December, the Assembly decided that the agenda item on the financing of UNFICYP would remain for consideration during its resumed sixty-third (2009) session.

Other issues

Strengthening of security and cooperation in the Mediterranean

In response to General Assembly resolution 62/58 [YUN 2007, p. 432], the Secretary-General in July submitted a report [A/63/138] containing replies received from Bosnia and Herzegovina, the Netherlands, Poland, Qatar and Ukraine to his 19 February note verbale requesting the views of all Member States on ways to strengthen security and cooperation in the Mediterranean region.

GENERAL ASSEMBLY ACTION

On 2 December [meeting 61], the General Assembly, on the recommendation of the First (Disarmament and International Security) Committee [A/63/394], adopted **resolution 63/86** without vote [agenda item 94].

Strengthening of security and cooperation in the Mediterranean region

The General Assembly,

Recalling its previous resolutions on the subject, including resolution 62/58 of 5 December 2007,

Reaffirming the primary role of the Mediterranean countries in strengthening and promoting peace, security and cooperation in the Mediterranean region,

Welcoming the efforts deployed by the Euro-Mediterranean countries to strengthen their cooperation in combating terrorism, in particular by the adoption of the Euro-Mediterranean Code of Conduct on Countering Terrorism by the Euro Mediterranean Summit, held in Barcelona, Spain, on 27 and 28 November 2005,

Bearing in mind all the previous declarations and commitments, as well as all the initiatives taken by the riparian countries at the recent summits, ministerial meetings and various forums concerning the question of the Mediterranean region,

Welcoming, in this regard, the adoption on 13 July 2008 of the joint Declaration of the Paris Summit, which launched a reinforced partnership, "the Barcelona Process: Union for the Mediterranean", and the common political will to revive efforts to transform the Mediterranean into an area of peace, democracy, cooperation and prosperity,

Recognizing the indivisible character of security in the Mediterranean and that the enhancement of cooperation among Mediterranean countries with a view to promoting the economic and social development of all peoples of the region will contribute significantly to stability, peace and security in the region,

Recognizing also the efforts made so far and the determination of the Mediterranean countries to intensify the process of dialogue and consultations with a view to resolving the problems existing in the Mediterranean region and to eliminating the causes of tension and the consequent threat to peace and security, and their growing awareness of the need for further joint efforts to strengthen economic, social, cultural and environmental cooperation in the region,

Recognizing further that prospects for closer Euro-Mediterranean cooperation in all spheres can be enhanced by positive developments worldwide, in particular in Europe, in the Maghreb and in the Middle East,

Reaffirming the responsibility of all States to contribute to the stability and prosperity of the Mediterranean region and their commitment to respecting the purposes and principles of the Charter of the United Nations as well as the provisions of the Declaration on Principles of International Law concerning Friendly Relations and Cooperation among States in accordance with the Charter of the United Nations,

Noting the peace negotiations in the Middle East, which should be of a comprehensive nature and represent an appropriate framework for the peaceful settlement of contentious issues in the region,

Expressing its concern at the persistent tension and continuing military activities in parts of the Mediterranean that hinder efforts to strengthen security and cooperation in the region,

Taking note of the report of the Secretary-General,

1. *Reaffirms* that security in the Mediterranean is closely linked to European security as well as to international peace and security;

2. *Expresses its satisfaction* at the continuing efforts by Mediterranean countries to contribute actively to the elimination of all causes of tension in the region and to the promotion of just and lasting solutions to the persistent problems of the region through peaceful means, thus ensuring the withdrawal of foreign forces of occupation and respecting the sovereignty, independence and territorial integrity of all countries of the Mediterranean and the right of peoples to self-determination, and therefore calls for full adherence to the principles of non-interference, non-intervention, non-use of force or threat of use of force and the inadmissibility of the acquisition of territory by force, in accordance with the Charter and the relevant resolutions of the United Nations;

3. *Commends* the Mediterranean countries for their efforts in meeting common challenges through coordinated overall responses, based on a spirit of multilateral partnership, towards the general objective of turning the Mediterranean basin into an area of dialogue, exchanges and cooperation, guaranteeing peace, stability and prosperity, encourages them to strengthen such efforts through, inter alia, a lasting multilateral and action-oriented cooperative dialogue among States of the region, and recognizes the role of the United Nations in promoting regional and international peace and security;

4. *Recognizes* that the elimination of the economic and social disparities in levels of development and other obstacles as well as respect and greater understanding among cultures in the Mediterranean area will contribute to enhancing peace, security and cooperation among Mediterranean countries through the existing forums;

5. *Calls upon* all States of the Mediterranean region that have not yet done so to adhere to all the multilaterally negotiated legal instruments related to the field of disarmament and non-proliferation, thus creating the necessary conditions for strengthening peace and cooperation in the region;

6. *Encourages* all States of the region to favour the necessary conditions for strengthening the confidence-building measures among them by promoting genuine openness and transparency on all military matters, by participating, inter alia, in the United Nations system for the standardized reporting of military expenditures and by providing accurate data and information to the United Nations Register of Conventional Arms;

7. *Encourages* the Mediterranean countries to strengthen further their cooperation in combating terrorism in all its forms and manifestations, including the possible resort by terrorists to weapons of mass destruction, taking into account the relevant resolutions of the United Nations, and in combating international crime and illicit arms transfers and illicit drug production, consumption and trafficking, which pose a serious threat to peace, security and stability in the region and therefore to the improvement of the current political, economic and social situation and which jeopardize friendly relations among States, hinder the development of international cooperation and result in the destruction of human rights, fundamental freedoms and the democratic basis of pluralistic society;

8. *Requests* the Secretary-General to submit a report on means to strengthen security and cooperation in the Mediterranean region;

9. *Decides* to include in the provisional agenda of its sixty-fourth session the item entitled "Strengthening of security and cooperation in the Mediterranean region".

Stability and development in South-Eastern Europe

On 2 December **(decision 63/517)**, the General Assembly decided to include in the provisional agenda of its sixty-fifth (2010) session the item entitled "Maintenance of international security–good-neighbourliness, stability and development in South-Eastern Europe".

Cooperation with the Council of Europe

In a consolidated report on cooperation between the United Nations and regional and other organizations [A/63/228 & Corr.1-S/2008/531 & Corr.1], submitted in response to General Assembly resolution 63/13 [YUN 2006, p. 496], the Secretary-General described strengthened cooperation with the Council of Europe.

GENERAL ASSEMBLY ACTION

On 3 November [meeting 37], the General Assembly adopted **resolution 63/14** [draft: A/63/L.12 & Add.1] without vote [agenda item 114 *(g)*].

Cooperation between the United Nations and the Council of Europe

The General Assembly,

Recalling the Agreement between the Council of Europe and the Secretariat of the United Nations signed on 15 December 1951 and the Arrangement on Cooperation and Liaison between the Secretariats of the United Nations and the Council of Europe of 19 November 1971,

Recalling also its previous resolutions on cooperation between the United Nations and the Council of Europe,

Recalling further the sixtieth anniversary of the Universal Declaration of Human Rights, in 2008, and noting the sixtieth anniversary of the European Convention for the Protection of Human Rights and Fundamental Freedoms, in 2010,

Acknowledging the contribution of the Council of Europe, at the European level, to the protection and strengthening of human rights and fundamental freedoms, democracy and the rule of law through its standards, principles and monitoring mechanisms, as well as to the effective implementation of all relevant international legal instruments of the United Nations,

Taking note of the contribution of the Council of Europe to the universal periodic review by the Human Rights Council of the situation of human rights in States members of the Council of Europe,

Welcoming the declaration of the Council of Europe to improve the protection of human rights defenders and promote their activities within the European sphere,

Acknowledging the contribution of the Council of Europe to the development of international law, and noting that a number of legal instruments of the Council are open to the participation of States of other regions,

Acknowledging also the continued interest of the Parliamentary Assembly of the Council of Europe in the ongoing reform process of the United Nations,

Welcoming the increasingly close relations between the United Nations and the Council of Europe,

Noting with appreciation the report of the Secretary-General,

1. *Calls for* the reinforcement of cooperation and synergies with the Council of Europe regarding the protection of human rights and fundamental freedoms, inter alia, the promotion of democracy and the rule of law, the prevention of torture, the fight against trafficking in human beings, the fight against racism, discrimination, xenophobia and intolerance, the promotion of gender equality and the protection of the rights of persons belonging to minorities;

2. *Recognizes* the important role of the European Court of Human Rights in protecting human rights as the guardian of the implementation of the European Convention on Human Rights, which applies to the eight hundred million individuals in the forty-seven States members of the Council of Europe, and invites the Human Rights Council and the Office of the United Nations High Commissioner for Human Rights to strengthen their cooperation with the Council of Europe, including its Commissioner for Human Rights, in promoting respect for human rights, while encouraging close cooperation with the Special Representative of the Secretary-General on human rights defenders;

3. *Encourages* further cooperation, where appropriate, between the United Nations and the Council of Europe through their mechanisms regarding the prevention of torture and inhuman or degrading treatment or punishment;

4. *Supports* the development of cooperation, where appropriate, between the United Nations Peacebuilding Commission and the Council of Europe, with a view to promoting post-conflict reconstruction and development and the consolidation of peace, with full respect for human rights and the rule of law;

5. *Takes note with appreciation* of the entry into force on 1 February 2008 of the Council of Europe Convention on Action against Trafficking in Human Beings, to which any non-member State of the Council of Europe may accede after having obtained unanimous consent of the parties to the Convention, commends the enhanced cooperation between the United Nations and the Council of Europe in this regard, and expresses its appreciation for the preparation of a joint study on trafficking in organs and tissues, including trafficking in persons for the purpose of the removal of organs;

6. *Encourages* further cooperation between the Office of the United Nations High Commissioner for Refugees and the Council of Europe in the field of nationality, in particular in the prevention and reduction of statelessness, and in the protection and promotion of the rights of refugees, asylum-seekers and internally displaced persons;

7. *Also encourages* further cooperation between the United Nations and the Council of Europe in the area of democracy and good governance, and in particular with regard to the International Day of Democracy, inter alia, through the Venice Commission and the Forum for the Future of Democracy, and through the strengthening of links between the United Nations Decade of Education for Sustainable Development and the Council of Europe Project on Education for Democratic Citizenship and Human Rights;

8. *Welcomes* the signing of a joint declaration between the United Nations Children's Fund and the Council of Europe to further cooperation on the protection and promotion of the rights of the child;

9. *Notes with appreciation* the Council of Europe Campaign to Combat Violence against Women, including Domestic Violence, and calls for increased cooperation regarding all forms of violence against women, in the framework of the Secretary-General's campaign to end violence against women;

10. *Recognizes* the fruitful cooperation between the United Nations missions and the field offices of the Council of Europe;

11. *Takes note* of the contribution of the Council of Europe to the implementation of Security Council resolutions 1373(2001) of 28 September 2001 and 1624(2005) of 14 September 2005, and welcomes the entry into force on 1 June 2007 of the Council of Europe Convention on the Prevention of Terrorism and on 1 May 2008 of the Council of Europe Convention on Laundering, Search, Seizure and Confiscation of the Proceeds from Crime and on the Financing of Terrorism, and encourages the Council of Europe to promote the implementation of the United Nations Global Counter-Terrorism Strategy while protecting human rights;

12. *Encourages* further cooperation between the two organizations regarding the fight against transnational organized crime, cybercrime, corruption and money-laundering, as well as regarding the protection of the rights of victims of crime and the promotion of human rights and the rule of law in the information society, and takes note of the contribution of the Council of Europe to the Internet Governance Forum and the Council of Europe Convention on Cybercrime and the Additional Protocol thereto;

13. *Notes* the interaction between the Council of Europe and the Sixth Committee of the General Assembly and with the International Law Commission, and encourages cooperation between the Council of Europe and the Rule of Law Coordination and Resource Group with the purpose of strengthening the rule of law;

14. *Encourages* further cooperation between the United Nations and its specialized agencies, the United Nations

Educational, Scientific and Cultural Organization and the World Health Organization and the Council of Europe;

15. *Reiterates its support* for cooperation between the two organizations in the social field, in particular concerning the protection and promotion of the rights of persons with disabilities, combating poverty and social exclusion and ensuring equal access to economic, social and cultural rights for all;

16. *Encourages* joint action between the United Nations Educational, Scientific and Cultural Organization and the Council of Europe in the context of the follow-up to the Faro Platform, takes note of the intention of the Council of Europe to work in close cooperation with the Alliance of Civilizations, a forum for intercultural dialogue created under the auspices of the United Nations, on the basis of a memorandum of understanding, and welcomes the role of the North-South Centre;

17. *Requests* the Secretaries-General of the United Nations and the Council of Europe to combine their efforts in seeking answers to global challenges, within their respective mandates, and calls upon all relevant United Nations bodies to support the enhancement of cooperation with the Council of Europe in the areas mentioned above;

18. *Decides* to include in the provisional agenda of its sixty-fifth session the sub-item entitled "Cooperation between the United Nations and the Council of Europe", and requests the Secretary-General to submit to the General Assembly at its sixty-fifth session a report on cooperation between the United Nations and the Council of Europe in implementation of the present resolution.

Cooperation with the Organization for Security and Cooperation in Europe

On 26 September [meeting 5982], the Chairman-in-Office of the Organization for Security and Cooperation in Europe (OSCE), Alexander Stubb, briefed the Security Council about the work and priorities of OSCE. He noted that recent crises, such as the situation in Georgia, had underlined the critical importance of cooperation between OSCE and the United Nations. The 56-member organization intended to promote the implementation of all UN principles, conventions and other global instruments. The OSCE early warning, crisis management and post-conflict activities were crucial components of the UN-based international order. In many ways, both the United Nations and OSCE were in the business of preventing and resolving conflicts. The challenges the two organizations currently shared were Afghanistan, Georgia and Kosovo. The work of international security structures should be redirected in the spirit of effective multilateralism, so that they provide genuine security and stability to member countries and their inhabitants. Both OSCE and the United Nations should be a part of such long-term efforts.

By **decision 63/552** of 24 December, the General Assembly decided that the agenda item on cooperation between the United Nations and OSCE would remain for consideration during its resumed sixty-third (2009) session.

Chapter VI

Middle East

The year 2008 was marked by a number of encouraging developments in the Middle East. Bilateral and multilateral efforts intensified to find a comprehensive, just and lasting settlement of the Israeli-Palestinian conflict within the framework set out at the 2007 Annapolis Conference. Nonetheless, the goal of a peaceful settlement of the conflict by the end of the year remained elusive, and the situation on the ground in Israel and the Occupied Palestinian Territory, including East Jerusalem, remained difficult, hampering political efforts to achieve the vision of two States existing side by side in peace and security. In the Gaza Strip, in particular, prolonged violence and a deepening humanitarian crisis prevailed, complicated by the widening rift between the Palestinian factions in the Fatah-controlled West Bank and the Hamas-controlled Gaza Strip. As part of the recently intensified diplomatic efforts in the Middle East peace process, the good offices of the Secretary-General continued, as well as those of the Middle East Quartet (European Union, Russian Federation, United Nations, United States) to promote the road map initiative endorsed by the Security Council in 2003 and confirmed at Annapolis in 2007.

The year 2008 also marked 60 years of Palestinian dispossession. At a special meeting to commemorate that event, the Committee on the Exercise of the Inalienable Rights of the Palestinian People (Committee on Palestinian Rights) reiterated the permanent responsibility of the United Nations towards the question of Palestine until it was resolved in all its aspects in accordance with international law, and urged the international community to continue its support for the Middle East peace process.

The Special Committee to Investigate Israeli Practices Affecting the Human Rights of the Palestinian People and Other Arabs in the Occupied Territories reported to the General Assembly on the situation in the West Bank, including East Jerusalem, and in the Gaza Strip and the Golan Heights. The United Nations Relief and Works Agency for Palestine Refugees in the Near East, working under increasingly difficult circumstances, continued to provide education, health and social services to over 4 million Palestinians living in and outside camps in the West Bank and Gaza Strip, as well as in Jordan, Lebanon and the Syrian Arab Republic.

In Lebanon, marked progress was made in returning the country to stability and reconciliation. An agreement among Lebanese political leaders was reached on 21 May that led to the election of General Michel Sleiman as President of Lebanon, the formation of a Government of national unity and the launching of a national dialogue. Despite the improved political climate, however, the country's stability remained fragile and was threatened by a number of serious security incidents involving Lebanese and non-Lebanese militias. Progress towards a permanent ceasefire and long-term solution between Israel and Lebanon remained elusive.

The United Nations International Independent Investigation Commission continued to investigate the 14 February 2005 assassination of former Lebanese Prime Minister Rafik Hariri and 22 others. The Security Council extended the Commission's mandate until February 2009 to allow for a smooth transition and handover to the Special Tribunal for Lebanon, which was to begin its work in March 2009.

The United Nations Interim Force in Lebanon (UNIFIL) continued to cooperate closely with the Lebanese Armed Forces in consolidating the strategic military and security environment in southern Lebanon. UNIFIL's mandate was extended in August for another 12 months. Also during the year, the Security Council twice extended the mandate of the United Nations Disengagement Observer Force (UNDOF) in the Golan Heights. The United Nations Truce Supervision Organization continued to assist UNIFIL and UNDOF in their tasks.

Peace process

Political developments

In 2008, the Middle East peace process, revived in November 2007 [YUN 2007, p. 445] at the Annapolis Conference in Maryland, United States, took centre stage as bilateral and multilateral efforts continued to find a comprehensive, just and lasting settlement of the Israeli-Palestinian conflict. Both the General Assembly and the Security Council reaffirmed their support for the peace process, and called on the parties to fulfil their obligations under the road map, as stated in the Annapolis Joint Understanding [ibid., p. 446].

Israeli Prime Minister Ehud Olmert and Palestinian Authority (PA) President Mahmoud Abbas met for bilateral negotiations on 8 and 27 January, 7 and 13 April, 5 May, 2 June, 13 July, 6 and 31 August, and 16 September. In addition, negotiations within the Annapolis framework were held by a joint steering committee headed by Israel's Minister for Foreign Affairs, Tzipi Livni, and the Palestinian Chief Negotiator, Ahmed Qurei. Despite intensive efforts, the goal of a peace settlement by the end of the year was not reached, but the parties remained committed to continuing their confidential bilateral negotiations, to which the international community pledged its ongoing support.

Representatives of the Middle East Quartet (European Union, Russian Federation, United Nations, United States), who continued to monitor the political and economic situation in the Middle East and the bilateral Israeli-Palestinian negotiations, met several times throughout the year, joined by Quartet Representative Tony Blair, former Prime Minister of the United Kingdom.

The Security Council discussed the situation in the Middle East, including the Palestine question, at meetings held on 22 January [meeting 5824 & Res.1], 30 January [meeting 5827], 26 February [meeting 5846], 1 March [meeting 5847], 25 March [meeting 5859 & Res.1], 23 April [meeting 5873], 28 May [meeting 5899], 27 June [meeting 5927], 22 July [meeting 5940 & Res.1], 20 August [meeting 5963], 18 September [meeting 5974], 26 September [meeting 5983], 22 October [meeting 5999], 25 November [meeting 6022], 3 December [meeting 6030], 16 December [meeting 6045], 18 December [meeting 6049 & Res.1] and 31 December [meeting 6060]. During those meetings, the Council was briefed by Secretariat officials on the peace process and developments in the Occupied Palestinian Territory, especially the precarious situation in the Gaza Strip. On 18 December, the Council adopted a resolution declaring its support for the negotiations initiated at Annapolis.

Occupied Palestinian Territory

Although Israeli-Palestinian negotiations within the framework of the Annapolis peace process gathered momentum in 2008, the situation in the Occupied Palestinian Territory of the West Bank, including East Jerusalem, and the Gaza Strip remained volatile. Israel and Palestine brought to the attention of the Secretary-General and the Security Council President information on attacks committed by both sides throughout the year [A/ES-10/409-S/2008/8 & Corr.1; A/ES-10/410-S/2008/23; A/62/647-S/2008/24; A/ES-10/411-S/2008/35; A/62/667-S/2008/55; A/62/673-S/2008/72; A/62/674-S/2008/73; A/ES-10/412-S/2008/81; A/62/685-S/2008/86; A/62/688-S/2008/90; S/2008/131; A/62/710-S/2008/132; A/ES-10/413-S/2008/144; A/ES-10/414-S/2008/149; A/ES-10/415-S/2008/150; A/62/735-S/2008/169; S/2008/189; A/62/770-S/2008/209; A/62/797-S/2008/233; A/ES-10/417-S/2008/256; S/2008/261; A/62/812-S/2008/269; A/62/820-S/2008/277; A/ES-10/418-S/2008/282; A/62/839-S/2008/311; A/62/840-S/2008/316; A62/843-S/2008/328; A/ES-10/419-S/2008/365; A/62/857-S/2008/367; S/2008/420; S/2008/430; A/ES-10/420-S/2008/404; A/ES-10/421-S/2008/421; A/ES-10/425-S/2008/689; A/ES-10/426-S/2008/717; A/ES-10/427-S/2008/768; S/2008/807; S/2008/814; S/2008/816; A/ES-10/428-S/2008/819; A/ES-10/429-S/2008/828; A/ES-10/430-S/2008/835; A/ES-10/429-S/2008/828].

The deteriorating humanitarian and security situation in the Occupied Palestinian Territory, particularly the escalation of violence in the Gaza Strip, was discussed by the Security Council throughout the year. A number of third parties, among them Cuba on behalf of the Non-Aligned Movement (NAM) [A/62/652-S/2008/28, A/62/665-S/2008/47, S/2008/57, A/62/672-S/2008/70, A/62/715-S/2008/152, A/63/571-S/2008/735, A/63/673-S/2009/13], the European Union [S/2008/841], Iran [S/2008/790, S/2008/817, S/2008/845], Jordan [S/2008/818], Malaysia [S/2008/37], and Pakistan on behalf of the Organization of the Islamic Conference [A/62/693-S/2008/96, A/62/731, S/2008/153], also expressed concern about the situation in the Occupied Territory and the events in Gaza.

Political and security situation

The beginning of 2008 was marked by a serious and rapid deterioration in the security situation in the Occupied Palestinian Territory, especially in the Gaza Strip. On 4 [A/ES-10/409-S/2008/8], 15 [A/ES-10/410-S/2008/23] and 21 January [A/ES-10/411-S/2008/35], Palestine complained to the Security Council President that the Occupied Palestinian Territory had begun the year under increasing assault by Israel, with lethal raids and attacks against towns in the Gaza Strip, and air missile attacks on 2 and 3 January, killing some 23 Palestinians and wounding many others. Ten days later another 37 Palestinians were killed, including children. Palestine said that, even as they engaged in direct bilateral negotiations in the fragile peace process, Israel intensified its military campaign, spreading more death, destruction and terror among the civilian population, particularly in the Gaza Strip. In addition, Israel intensified its closure of the Occupied Palestinian Territory by sealing all border crossings, preventing the delivery of food supplies since 18 January, and persisted with the reduction of fuel supplies to the Gaza Strip, cutting off fuel to the main power plant. Such collective punishment threatened to exacerbate the humanitarian crisis and was hastening the deterioration of the situation on the ground. In response, Israel, on 15 January

[A/62/647-S/2008/24], said that it would not stand by when its citizens were under attack, and reserved the right to defend itself from armed attacks. Since June 2007 [YUN 2007, p. 441], when Hamas took control of Gaza, more than 1,000 Qassam rockets and mortar shells had been fired and Hamas and other Palestinian groups continued their quest to murder Israelis and destroy Israel. Those acts were indicative of the daily dangers facing Israeli civilians, particularly those living near the Gaza Strip, and the two acts of terrorism that took place on the same day reminded that Palestinian terrorism remained the greatest obstacle to peace and security in the region. The Palestinian leadership had to stop the violence, dismantle the terrorist infrastructure and the cycle of impunity, and bring terrorists to justice.

Replying to a 17 January 2008 letter [A/62/652-S/2008/28] from Cuba on behalf of the NAM Coordinating Bureau condemning Israel's recent military assaults against Palestinian civilians in the Gaza Strip, Israel stated, on 28 January [A/62/667-S/2008/55], that putting blame on Israel demonstrated a failure to understand the realities on the ground. Palestinian terrorism, stewarded by Hamas, made security measures a necessity. Hamas fired at border-crossings, forcing closures and hampering Israeli and international efforts to deliver humanitarian aid and relief. Recently, Hamas allegedly attempted to smuggle explosives and weapons material into Gaza, using humanitarian convoys, and diverted fuel from domestic generators to produce Qassam rockets. Israel believed that responsible members of the international community could play a constructive role by supporting the bilateral process between Israel and the PA. That meant taking a balanced approach rather than a one-sided stance as the NAM statement reflected.

On 21 January [A/62/655], Israel charged that negotiations with the Palestinians had been met with an escalation of Palestinian violence and terrorist activity, specifically by Hamas terrorists who controlled the Gaza Strip. While Israel worked to facilitate humanitarian assistance, Palestinian terrorists did everything to thwart those efforts and provoke Israeli reactions. Since June 2007, Israel had permitted more than 9,000 Palestinians to enter Israel to seek medical treatment, while Hamas had fired over 1,500 rockets and mortars.

Security Council consideration (January). Speaking at an emergency meeting of the Security Council on 22 January [meeting 5824], convened in response to a request by Saudi Arabia on behalf of the Group of Arab States [S/2008/31], the Under-Secretary-General for Political Affairs, B. Lynn Pascoe, reported that the crisis in the Gaza Strip and southern Israel had escalated dramatically since 15 January, when the Israeli Defence Force (IDF) entered the Gaza Strip and engaged Hamas militants in a heavy battle. The precursor to that escalation lay in daily rocket and mortar attacks on Israeli civilian residential areas by several militant groups from Gaza and regular IDF military attacks on and into Gaza. During that week, over 150 rockets and mortar attacks were launched at Israel, injuring 11 Israelis, while IDF launched 8 ground incursions, 15 air strikes and 10 surface-to-surface missiles, killing 42 Palestinians and injuring 117, among them civilians. This revealed the ever-present potential for the Annapolis process to be undermined by the deterioration of the situation on the ground. Less than two weeks earlier, the parties began negotiations on core issues, and United States President George W. Bush had visited the region to underline his commitment to assisting them in reaching a peace treaty in 2008 and implementing the first phase of the road map presented to the parties by the Quartet in 2003 [YUN 2003, p. 464] and endorsed by the Security Council [ibid., p. 472].

The Secretary-General had appealed for an immediate end to the violence and stressed the responsibility of all parties to adhere to their obligations under international humanitarian law and not to endanger civilians. Indiscriminate rocket and mortar firing towards civilian population centres and crossing points was unacceptable, Mr. Pascoe said; such attacks terrorized Israeli communities near Gaza, particularly in the town of Sderot, endangered humanitarian workers at crossing points, a regular occurrence well before Israel's disengagement, and caused civilian casualties, damage, school closures and high levels of post-traumatic stress disorders. Over 100,000 Israelis lived within range of standard Qassam rocket fire.

The Gaza crossings remained largely closed since the Hamas takeover. To bring about a cessation of rocket fire, Israelis had tightened restrictions on crossings into Gaza, except for imports to meet minimal humanitarian needs. Compared with the first half of 2007, Gaza's imports had dropped 77 per cent, and exports by 98 per cent. Most Palestinians could not exit Gaza, and large UN construction projects were frozen because of the unavailability of building materials. On 18 January 2008, as rocket fire intensified, Israel imposed a comprehensive closure of the Gaza Strip, halting the import of fuel, food and medical and relief items. The shut-down of the Gaza power plant left every area in Gaza, except Rafah, with power cuts of 8 to 12 hours a day, and approximately 40 per cent of the population without access to running water. Thirty million litres of raw sewage were pumped into the Mediterranean Sea owing to the breakdown of equipment.

The United Nations was actively involved, through interventions of the Secretary-General, the United Nations Special Coordinator for the Middle East Peace

Process, Robert H. Serry, and the UNRWA Commissioner-General, Karen Koning AbuZayd, in seeking an urgent easing of the blanket closure of Gaza. Israel reopened two crossings for fuel and the delivery of humanitarian supplies by international organizations, but the humanitarian situation was still extremely fragile as the entry of commercial humanitarian supplies was still not permitted. Mr. Pascoe reiterated the United Nations' commitment to the welfare of the civilian population affected by the conflict. The work being performed in Gaza by UN agencies and non-governmental organizations (NGOs) was one of the few things that stood between the existing crisis conditions and an even more dramatic deterioration of the situation. The United Nations would continue to ensure that civilians were protected and assisted, whatever the political environment.

At the Council's 30 January meeting [meeting 5827], Mr. Pascoe said that the past month underscored the gap between the aspirations of the political process and the grim realities of the ground. Continued efforts to progress along the Annapolis track were overshadowed by an intensification of violence in Gaza and southern Israel, combined with periods of total closure of the Gaza Strip and increased humanitarian suffering and violations of human rights. Mr. Pascoe noted that President Bush had stressed that the point of departure for permanent status negotiations was an end to the occupation that began in 1967 [YUN 1967, p. 177], and that he had made a number of public observations regarding borders, refugees, Jerusalem and security. He had also issued calls for both sides to fulfil their commitments under the road map, including removal of outposts and a settlement freeze, and action against violence and terrorism.

Since his 22 January briefing, Mr. Pascoe added, there had been significant developments in the crisis in Gaza. On 23 January, Palestinian militants destroyed entire sections of the border fence at the Rafah crossing with Egypt, and hundreds of thousands of Gazans crossed the border. Following efforts by Egyptian security forces to close the border on 25 January, Hamas had toppled additional sections of the border fence. A number of Egyptian security personnel sustained injuries when fired upon by Palestinian militants, but they exercised restraint and the situation remained calm. By 29 January, shops in the border area in Egypt had largely run out of goods, and Egyptian forces resealed the border.

From 18 January, when Israel imposed a comprehensive closure, to 29 January, only 32 truckloads of goods had entered Gaza, compared to a daily average of 93 trucks during the first two weeks of 2008 and 250 trucks before June 2007. There was a backlog of some 224 trucks of UNRWA, the World Health Organization (WHO) and the World Food Programme (WFP). Fuel imports from Israel resumed on 22 January, although due to the level of supply, electricity cuts would continue. Some water wells were functioning again, but according to the United Nations Children's Fund (UNICEF), 40 per cent of Gazans still had limited access to safe water.

The crisis added new urgency to the PA proposal to operate the Gaza crossings. The Secretary-General supported that proposal and welcomed the recent Arab League and European Council resolutions in that respect, as well as the diplomatic efforts under way. Mr. Pascoe called on all parties to work urgently towards the controlled reopening of the crossings for both humanitarian reasons and commercial flows, which should include materials and equipment to enable UN re-housing and rubble removal projects to resume. The United Nations stood ready to assist efforts to implement the PA's proposals in any way it could.

Mr. Pascoe said that 108 Palestinians had been killed and 229 injured in January. There were also a number of violent incidents in the West Bank, including in occupied East Jerusalem, where Palestinian militants attacked Israeli border police and religious seminary students. Three Israelis were killed and 24 injured by Palestinian militants. IDF incursions into West Bank cities and towns continued on a regular basis. In early January, the entire city of Nablus was placed under a three-day curfew.

On 30 January, Israel's Supreme Court declared legal the reductions of fuel and electricity supplies to Gaza, effectively approving the Government's 19 September 2007 decision [YUN 2007, p. 444] to impose sanctions on the Gaza Strip in response to continued rocket and mortar fire on Israel. Mr. Pascoe noted that the level of violence had reduced significantly during the past week, but he remained concerned that 77 rockets and mortars had been fired by Palestinian militants in that time and that IDF had carried out four incursions and air strikes on Gaza.

Communications. On 2 January [A/62/629-S/2008/3], Israel called the international community's attention to the fate of Israeli soldier, Corporal Gilad Shalit. Since his capture by Palestinian militants on 25 June 2006 [YUN 2006, p. 510], there had been no verification of his health or condition.

On 24 January [A/62/661-S/2008/42], Iran requested relevant UN agencies to take immediate measures to provide the Palestinian people in the Gaza Strip with basic goods and services. On 30 January [S/2008/57], Cuba protested the Security Council's rejection of NAM's request to participate in its deliberations. On 31 January [S/2008/62], Cuba responded to what it called fallacious remarks against NAM made by Israel during the Council debate.

Security Council consideration (February). On 26 February [meeting 5846], Mr. Serry, the Special Coordinator for the Middle East Peace Process and the Secretary-General's Personal Representative to the Palestine Liberation Organization (PLO) and the Palestinian Authority, reported to the Council that Israeli Foreign Minister Livni and Palestinian lead negotiator Qurei met on a continuous basis, while President Abbas and Prime Minister Olmert continued their fortnightly meetings. Mr. Serry also met United States General William Fraser—appointed to lead United States efforts to monitor implementation of phase I of the road map in accordance with the Annapolis Joint Understanding—during his first visit to the region, offered full UN support to the United States-led monitoring process and looked forward to regular Quartet consultation on it.

John Holmes, the Under-Secretary-General for Humanitarian Affairs and Emergency Relief Coordinator, briefed the Council on his visit to the Occupied Palestinian Territory and Israel from 14 to 18 February. Mr. Holmes said he found the conditions for the people of Gaza grim and miserable, as eight months of severe restrictions on the movement of goods and people had taken a heavy economic and social toll, in addition to years of difficulty and economic decline. The consequences were increasingly severe. Almost 80 per cent of the population was receiving food aid as most industry and agriculture had collapsed, raising unemployment and poverty to new heights. Vulnerability to disease was rising, notably among children who made up more than half of the Gaza population.

The effective Israeli isolation of Gaza was not justified, Mr. Holmes stated, in spite of the provocation and illegality of the continuing firing of rockets by Hamas, whose physical and psychological damage to the population in Sderot he had witnessed during his mission. The isolation of Gaza amounted to collective punishment and did not appear to have the desired effect, either in halting the rockets or in weakening Hamas' position among the Gaza people. Meanwhile, the consequences for civilians on both sides were dramatic. The fundamental principles of distinction between combatants and non-combatants and of proportionality in attacks during the conduct of hostilities had to be respected by all sides.

The situation in Gaza was not sustainable and was extremely damaging to the prospects for the peace process, and only political efforts could change that dynamic. Meanwhile, Mr. Holmes said he had pressed the Israeli Government and the PA to ensure that more humanitarian and other goods were allowed into Gaza on a more predictable and systematic basis. He had also made the same message clear to Hamas. That meant reopening the crossings and establishing better mechanisms to identify and address the fundamental needs of the population. There were some indications that the Israeli authorities were willing to respond positively to his requests that the materials necessary for the resumption of $213 million worth of frozen humanitarian projects in sanitation, housing, education and health be allowed into Gaza and that spares and equipment for medical and sanitation services be given priority. The Palestinian Prime Minister's proposals for the reopening of the key Karni crossing—the only one with adequate infrastructure for processing large quantities of goods—deserved support, and a properly negotiated role was necessary for the Rafah crossing; one that did not give credence to the idea that Israel could hand over its responsibilities for Gaza to Egypt or any other State or authority. Arrangements to ensure proper screening for goods passing in both directions through the crossings, in order to meet Israel's security concerns, should be possible, with appropriate international support.

Conditions of life in the West Bank were better than those in Gaza, Mr. Holmes observed, but the situation there was of no less concern. The construction of the barrier, the steady expansion of settlements and the 580 separate checkpoints and blockages within the West Bank fragmented communities and seriously impaired the access of tens of thousands of people to their lands and to essential services, especially medical services. Severe movement restrictions affected economic growth, increased poverty and food insecurity and reduced health standards, thus further threatening the viability of a future Palestinian State.

In Mr. Holmes' view, the disconnect between the deteriorating realities on the ground in Gaza and the West Bank, as well as in Sderot, and the hopes and aims of the continuing peace talks, seemed almost total and risked making a mockery of the readiness of the international community to invest $7.7 billion in the economic development of the Occupied Palestinian Territory. As the Special Coordinator had stressed, unless that chasm was bridged quickly and the humanitarian indicators began to rise, the chances of success in the peace talks might be fatally undermined. Notwithstanding all the difficulties, Mr. Holmes concluded, the humanitarian community would continue to respond to the moral imperative of saving and improving lives and preserving human dignity. UNRWA and other agencies, as well as NGOs working in Gaza, were doing a heroic job under difficult and dangerous circumstances.

Security Council consideration (March). Opening the Council's emergency session on 1 March [meeting 5847], convened on the request by the Libyan Arab Jamahiriya [S/2008/142], the Secretary-General reported an alarming escalation of violence in Gaza and southern Israel during the preceding week, and a terrible civilian death toll. Some 117 rockets had been fired from Gaza at civilian centres in southern Israel, as far north as the city of Ashkelon. According to press reports and Israeli Government sources, those rockets were not home-made Qassams, but of advanced Katyusha-like design, allegedly smuggled into Gaza when the border with Egypt was breached. During the same period, IDF attacked Gaza from air and by land, killing an estimated 90 Palestinians and causing heavy property damage. All UNRWA schools were closed and many families were trapped inside their houses by the violence, unable to obtain medical aid or reach safety.

The Secretary-General condemned Palestinian rocket attacks as acts of terrorism and called for their immediate cessation. While recognizing Israel's right to defend itself, he condemned the disproportionate and excessive use of force that had killed and injured so many civilians, including children, and called on Israel to cease such attacks, comply with international humanitarian law and exercise the utmost restraint. Incidents in which civilians were killed or injured should be investigated and accountability ensured.

Concerned at the possibility of escalating violence, the Secretary-General offered UN support for all efforts to end it and bring about a period of calm, and called on all parties to step back from the brink of even deeper and more deadly clashes. He was also concerned at the impact of those developments on the negotiation process, and called on the international community, important stakeholders and Security Council members to exercise their influence on the parties to stop the violence and allow humanitarian relief.

Addressing the Council again on 25 March [meeting 5859], the Secretary-General said that the process was too important to be allowed to lose momentum through inaction or indifference, or to be overwhelmed by violence.

Under-Secretary-General for Political Affairs Pascoe regretted that the reporting period had seen major escalations of violence: heavy Israeli air and land military assault in Gaza; the firing of over 390 rockets and mortars at Israel, including longer-range rockets; an attack on a Jewish school in West Jerusalem; IDF operations targeting alleged militants throughout the West Bank; and clashes between the IDF and protesting Palestinians in West Bank cities, including East Jerusalem. In total, 124 Palestinians, among them 36 children, were killed in IDF operations, and 359 injured, while Palestinian militants killed 13 Israelis, including 4 children, and injured 55. Tensions remained high, and although there was an observable reduction of violence in and around Gaza, violence had spread to Jerusalem and the West Bank. The United Nations supported Egyptian efforts to bring about a cessation of violence, particularly in Gaza, and to facilitate a gradual reopening of crossings into Gaza in coordination with the parties. All parties were urged to cooperate with those efforts and ensure that legitimate traffic into and out of Gaza at all crossing points took place and concerns about alleged smuggling were addressed.

Although the volume of goods entering the Gaza Strip had improved, the humanitarian situation remained grave. Shortages continued in the health sector, and sanitation authorities had dumped 60,000 cubic metres of raw and partially treated sewage into the sea. Fuel shortages prevented 63 per cent of Gaza's regular fishing trips, further exacerbating the dire socio-economic scenario. Food insecurity increased as salaries dried up, and at least 50,000 additional beneficiaries were added to food assistance distribution lists.

In the West Bank, 580 IDF-imposed obstacles continued to block Palestinian movement. Restrictions, which were at the root of Palestinian economic decline, continued despite PA security efforts. Action to ease closure inside the West Bank was essential if the Palestinian economy was to develop as the basis for a viable Palestinian State.

Israeli settlement activity continued, including in East Jerusalem. The PLO raised concerns about Israeli archeological excavations bordering the Haram Al-Sharif/Temple Mount, and about alleged plans to bring more Israeli settlers to East Jerusalem. Israel's failure to cease its settlement activity—including natural growth—or to dismantle the outposts erected after March 2001 was contrary to the road map. The Secretary-General made public his concerns that urgent action had to be taken on that issue. Construction work on the barrier continued within occupied Palestinian territory, and the number of house demolitions in the West Bank had noticeably increased. Since the beginning of the year, over 100 structures—at least half of them residential—had been demolished, displacing nearly 400 Palestinians.

Mr. Pascoe said that there was little to report about the state of the bilateral negotiations, reflecting the confidentiality being maintained, which enabled Israeli and Palestinian leaders to be candid in their discussions. While those negotiations had been suspended for a period by Palestinian President Abbas due to the significant Palestinian casualties in Gaza, meetings between the heads of the two negotiating teams had resumed and the work of the technical groups formed between the parties was being pursued. Palestinian Prime Minister Salam Fayyad and a senior Israeli Ministry of Defence official attended the first trilateral meeting on monitoring the implementation of phase I road map commitments, hosted by General Fraser.

The United Nations supported the reform efforts of Prime Minister Fayyad's Government. A recent International Monetary Fund (IMF) mission confirmed that, despite the difficult environment, impressive financial reform measures had been taken. The Palestinian Development Plan was being finalized and would be shared with the international community to enlist support. Efforts to reform, train and equip the Palestinian security forces in the West Bank continued, and Palestinian security forces had undertaken operations to disarm and arrest militants. However, more work had to be done by the PA to reassert law and order across the West Bank and meet its road map obligations to combat terrorism effectively; if those obligations were to be met, greater Israeli-PA security cooperation was essential.

The Quartet continued to be in close contact at the principal and envoy levels. The United Nations supported ongoing discussions over the idea of a renewed international meeting to be held in Moscow, and continued to stress the vital role of Arab States in support of the peace process, the central importance of the 2002 Arab Peace Initiative [YUN 2002, p. 415], and the ultimate need for a comprehensive regional peace.

Security Council consideration (April). At the Security Council's 23 April meeting [meeting 5873], Angela Kane, Assistant Secretary-General for Political Affairs, reported that there had been major episodes of violence, especially in and around Gaza, which had also witnessed heightened humanitarian distress, while conditions in the West Bank, including East Jerusalem, had not significantly improved. During the reporting period, 69 Palestinians, including 15 children, were killed in IDF operations and 95 were injured. Six Israelis were killed by Palestinian militants and 27 injured. Some 70 rockets and mortars were fired at Israel or at crossing points. Hamas and other militant organizations also staged attacks against crossing points between Gaza and Israel, which were the only outlets for international humanitarian assistance. Alarmed at the prospects of a further intensification of violence, with its implications for civilians and the security of all parties, the United Nations supported and encouraged Egyptian efforts to achieve calm in Gaza leading to a reopening of crossings, as well as to ensure security along the border. It also urged all parties to work with Egypt, and regional States with influence to work for calm.

Following a trilateral meeting between United States Secretary of State Condoleezza Rice, Palestinian Prime Minister Fayyad and Israeli Defence Minister Ehud Barak on 30 March, Israel announced measures to ease conditions in the West Bank, among them the opening of additional PA police stations, approval of delivery of equipment to Palestinian security forces, an additional 5,000 permits for Palestinian construction workers in Israel, and the passage of regional and international business figures to a planned investment conference to be convened by Prime Minister Fayyad in Bethlehem from 21 to 23 May. Israel also announced its intention to remove obstacles in the West Bank, and subsequently reported that it had removed 61 of them. UN staff on the ground confirmed that 44 had been removed. The United Nations urged further and more substantive progress to ease restrictions, as envisaged in the 2005 Agreement on Movement and Access [YUN 2005, p. 519], as that was vital to Palestinian economic revival.

Tenders and construction permits for hundreds of housing units in Israeli settlements in the Occupied Palestinian Territory were announced, and construction work on the barrier continued, in deviation from the 1949 Armistice Demarcation Line (Green Line) [YUN 1948–49, p. 184] and contrary to the 2004 Advisory Opinion of the International Court of Justice (ICJ) [YUN 2004, p. 452]. Restrictions on UN operations increased in the West Bank, with the installation of Israeli civilian police checkpoints, causing significant delays and security concerns. Twenty incidents of violence between settlers and Palestinians during March were reported in the southern West Bank alone. Palestinian security forces in the West Bank pursued militants and criminal elements during the reporting period. Some militants were granted amnesty, pursuant to PA-Israel understandings. A newly trained battalion of Palestinian security forces was expected to be deployed and efforts to increase national security planning, reform and train security services, and strengthen all aspects of the rule of law needed to continue, with support by international partners.

Efforts to advance the political process continued through direct bilateral negotiations. The Quartet principals were to meet in London on 2 May, on the margins of the Ad Hoc Liaison Committee meeting assessing progress in Palestinian institutional and economic development, to review all aspects of the Annapolis process and the situation on the ground. In the meantime, the Secretary-General and Special Coordinator Serry were working with the parties, regional partners and the Quartet to support the political process, encourage action to meet commitments and improve conditions on the ground, and address the grave humanitarian, political and security situation in and around Gaza.

Quartet meeting (May). Meeting in London on 2 May [SG/2137], the Quartet encouraged the parties in the Israeli-Palestinian negotiations to make every effort to realize the shared goal of an agreement by the end of the year on the establishment of a Palestinian State, and called on the international community to remain constructively engaged in support of that goal and an end to the conflict. It emphasized the importance of visible progress on the ground to build confidence and create an atmosphere supportive of negotiations. The Quartet welcomed the steps taken by both sides in the wake of the trilateral meeting between United States Secretary of State Rice, Palestinian Prime Minister Fayyad and Israeli Defence Minister Barak, and stressed the urgent need for rapid and continued implementation of those and previous commitments to improve conditions on the ground. While noting some positive steps taken, including the removal of roadblocks and an outpost by Israel, as well as improved security performance by the PA, the Quartet stressed that much more remained to be done to improve the situation on the ground, change the conditions of life in the West Bank and keep the political process on track. In that context, it supported Quartet Representative Tony Blair, and underscored the need for donor coordination. The Quartet backed the planned Bethlehem Conference on Private Sector Investment (21–23 May), as well as the parties' agreement to improve security and economic conditions in Jenin, which it felt could be a model for progress. Noting the importance of justice sector reform, it looked forward to the upcoming June meeting in Berlin to promote and coordinate donor assistance in that area.

The Quartet called on both sides to fulfil their obligations under the road map and refrain from any steps that could undermine confidence, or prejudice the outcome of negotiations. In that context, it called on Israel to freeze its settlement activity, including natural growth, and to dismantle outposts erected since March 2001. The PA should also fight terrorism and accelerate steps to rebuild and refocus its security apparatus; both sides should increase cooperation in that respect and facilitate the delivery of security assistance to the PA.

Looking forward to a productive meeting of the Ad Hoc Liaison Committee, the Quartet encouraged all parties to support Palestinian institutional capacity-building and economic development, and called on donors to follow through on pledges made at the December 2007 Paris Donors' Conference [YUN 2007, p. 446]. Emphasizing the crucial role of Arab States in support of the peace process, and the importance of the 2002 Arab League peace initiative [YUN 2002, p. 415], the Quartet encouraged Arab States to fulfil their political and financial roles in support of the process begun at the Annapolis Conference.

The Quartet also discussed the proposed international meeting in Moscow to lend support to the parties in their negotiations and efforts on the ground. It authorized its envoys to continue to facilitate the achievement of those goals, and reaffirmed its commitment to a just, lasting and comprehensive peace in the Middle East based on Security Council resolutions 242(1967) [YUN 1967, p. 257], 338(1973) [YUN 1973, p. 213], 1397(2002) [YUN 2002, p. 418] and 1515(2003) [YUN 2003, p. 483].

Communications. Underscoring its commitment to the bilateral negotiations, Israel, on 24 March [S/2008/189], stressed that Palestinian terrorism remained the greatest obstacle to peace and security and called on the Palestinian leadership to stop the violence, dismantle the terrorist infrastructure, end the cycle of impunity and bring the terrorists to justice. Israel remained committed to the bilateral process, and despite the escalation of rocket attacks, its leaders continued to meet with their Palestinian counterparts and move forward with negotiations. The first trilateral meeting with General Fraser, the PA and Israel took place the previous week, and the IDF Civil Administration hosted a one-day symposium with its Palestinian counterparts, bringing together, for the first time since 1998, all officials coordinating civilian and defence issues between Israel and the PA. On 18 April [S/2008/261], Israel reiterated its commitment to the bilateral process.

Security Council consideration (May). Addressing the Security Council on 28 May [meeting 5899], Mr. Serry noted that during the past month, the complex political, security, human rights and humanitarian crisis in Gaza and southern Israel had deepened. Four Israeli civilians were killed by Palestinian militants and at least 30 injured, while IDF operations killed at least 50 Palestinians, among them 11 children, and injured 207, including at least 22 children. Humanitarian conditions for the 1.5 million people in the Gaza Strip were increasingly grave. Approximately 5 per cent of the weekly average supply of petrol and 16 per cent of the weekly average of diesel entering Gaza prior to June 2007 were delivered during the reporting period, leading to a virtual cessation of vehicular traffic and of some UNRWA operations, including food distribution, for four working days. The Gaza power plant shut down entirely for two days due to the sporadic nature of import and delivery.

Gazans faced significant interruptions in their access to water, due to a lack of fuel and spare parts. Up to 80 million litres of raw and partially treated sewage continued to be discarded into the Mediterranean Sea every day, and an estimated 600 tons of rubbish accumulated in the streets daily, with attendant health risks. In May, the catch by fishermen was 50 per cent less than that of the same month the previous year, and meat shortages were compounded by the destruction of two chicken farms on 17 May during IDF operations. No exports had left Gaza for five months, and only 77 trucks during the six months before that.

The Rafah crossing to Egypt opened on an exceptional basis between 10 and 12 May, to allow 140 of the 1,700 patients seeking medical treatment and about 750 students and others to cross into Egypt. Some 550 Gaza residents also crossed back from Egypt.

Meanwhile Palestinian institutions in Gaza were more and more separated from the PA itself, and Hamas-Fatah tensions were increasingly evident. In addition, Salafist elements were suspected of attacks on cafes and other institutions associated with Christians in Gaza. The United Nations repeatedly made clear its concern that the situation in and around Gaza was unsustainable, and called for a different and more positive strategy for Gaza. In London, the Quartet threw its weight behind a new strategy to provide security for all Gazans, end all acts of terror, provide for the controlled and sustained opening of the Gaza crossings for humanitarian reasons and commercial flows, support the legitimate PA Government and work towards conditions that would permit implementation of the 2005 Agreement on Movement and Access. The United Nations also commended and supported the Egyptian effort to calm the violence and ease the situation on the ground, through contacts with representatives of Hamas and other groups in Gaza, and with the Israeli and Palestinian Governments.

Mr. Serry reported that a number of important political developments in the Middle East had taken place during the previous month, with the potential for lasting change, but they all remained fragile, as underlying sources of tension had to be addressed through further political progress and action on the ground. While comprehensive discussions were under way and the parties remained committed to the process, important gaps had to be overcome. United States Secretary of State Rice visited the region immediately after the 2 May Quartet meeting to push the Annapolis process forward, and President Bush underlined his support for the process during a subsequent trip. In the economic sphere, the Ad Hoc Liaison Committee, also meeting on 2 May, stressed that Israel had to enable Palestinian reform and economic revival, while the Palestinians had to continue their reform efforts, and regional and international players needed to continue providing concrete support. On 13 May, Quartet Representative Blair announced a package of measures coordinated with the parties to stimulate economic development, ease movement and access restrictions, develop 60 per cent of the West Bank in Area C and build Palestinian security capability and performance. The package also included measures to establish an economic and security zone around Jenin, which, if successful, could be replicated elsewhere.

Those measures held promise, Mr. Serry said, but much more remained to be done to improve conditions, implement recent commitments and fulfil road map obligations. Steps taken—such as continued efforts by Palestinian security forces to disarm and arrest militants—needed encouragement and support from all parties. He noted that Israel had approved the reopening of 20 Palestinian police stations, but IDF incursions continued in the West Bank, including in areas where Palestinian security forces were deployed. Additionally, Israel had not consented to the delivery of certain equipment to those forces. Construction in a majority of Israeli settlements continued, as did the building of settlement infrastructure in East Jerusalem and throughout the West Bank. Palestinian institutions in East Jerusalem remained closed by Israeli order, despite road map commitments, and hundreds of demolition orders remained pending against Palestinian structures, along with some 3,000 further orders in the remainder of the West Bank. The Israeli Government had undertaken to review them as part of Quartet Representative Blair's package for stimulating economic development.

Quartet meeting (June). At a 24 June meeting in Berlin [SG/2140], the Quartet, stressing the urgent need for tangible progress towards an agreement by the end of 2008 on the establishment of an independent and viable Palestinian State, and an end to the conflict, committed to supporting the parties in implementing the difficult decisions required to achieve those outcomes. It underscored the need for more visible progress on the ground to build confidence and support progress in the negotiations. Israel's removal of some significant West Bank checkpoints and the opening of a number of Palestinian police stations in Area B (which was under full Palestinian civil control and joint Israeli-Palestinian security control) represented a good step, but greater efforts were required to project a new reality, including through further steps improving access and movement. The Quartet noted the improvement in Palestinian security performance, including in Jenin, but stressed that continued efforts to fight terrorism and implement a more comprehensive security strategy were necessary for sustainable long-term improvement. It urged the parties to build on those efforts, fulfil all their obligations under the road map and refrain from any steps that could undermine confidence or prejudice the outcome of negotiations. The Quartet reiterated its concern at continuing settlement activity and called on Israel to freeze all such activity.

The Quartet endorsed the outcome of the Berlin Conference in Support of Palestinian Civil Security and the Rule of Law, which took place on 24 June on the invitation of Germany, and with the participation Prime Minister Fayyad, foreign ministers and representatives of over 40 countries and international organizations. With its focus on the Palestinian police and justice sector, the Quartet stated that the Conference provided a timely forum to refocus and direct international support efforts towards two key sectors of Palestinian state-building. It called for speedy implementation of projects agreed and robust donor support, and emphasized the importance of unobstructed delivery of security assistance to the PA.

Noting the dire budget situation facing the PA, the Quartet urged all donors to fulfil their pledges from the December 2007 Paris donors conference [YUN 2007, p. 446] and looked to the next Ad Hoc Liaison Committee meeting on 22 September to take stock of progress. It reaffirmed its support for the Quartet Representative and congratulated the PA on the success of the Palestine Investment Conference (Bethlehem, 21–23 May). It commended the close cooperation between Israel and the PA on that initiative and encouraged similar cooperation on short- and medium-term projects and private sector activities.

The Quartet expressed its continuing support for the Egyptian-brokered calm that came into effect on 19 June, urged that it be respected and extended, and expressed the hope that it would lead to improved security and humanitarian conditions for Israelis and Palestinians alike, and the restoration of normal civilian life in Gaza. As a matter of urgency, it tasked the Quartet Representative to develop and promote measures to improve conditions in Gaza.

The Quartet welcomed the 21 May announcement that indirect talks between Israel and the Syrian Arab Republic had been launched with Turkey's facilitation, aimed at achieving peace in accordance with the 1991 Madrid terms of reference [YUN 1991, p. 221].

Security Council consideration (June). On 27 June [meeting 5927], the Director of the Asia and the Pacific Division in the Department of Political Affairs reported to the Security Council that, owing to Egypt's efforts over the past several months, a cessation of all acts of violence began on 19 June. The calm, which prevailed for several days, was broken on 24 June, when Palestinian militants fired one mortar and three rockets at Israel, injuring two Israeli civilians. Another rocket was fired from Gaza at Israel on 25 June, and two mortar shells on 27 June. In response, Israel closed the border crossings for three days. In the reporting period before the ceasefire, Palestinian militants launched 125 rockets and 149 mortars at Israel and Gaza crossings. Those attacks, as well as clashes with IDF soldiers operating in Gaza, resulted in the death of one Israeli civilian and the injury of 12 civilians and four IDF soldiers. On 12 June, direct mortar hits on the Erez crossing terminal caused significant damage and led to its closure for a number of days. The attack followed an explosion in Gaza caused by Palestinian militants, killing eight Palestinians, and injuring 40 others, including 21 children. Also prior to the ceasefire, IDF conducted 25 air strikes and a number of land incursions into the Gaza Strip. Thirty Palestinians, including at least six civilians, two of them children, were killed; 53 others, among them at least 25 civilians, five of them children, were injured. Conditions in Gaza were still grave, despite a 30 per cent increase in the number of truckloads of supplies into Gaza between 22 and 24 June and slightly increased fuel imports since mid-May.

The United Nations encouraged the parties to pursue discussions under Egypt's auspices to secure the release of Gilad Shalit [YUN 2006, p. 510]. A letter from Mr. Shalit to his parents was forwarded by Hamas to representatives of former United States President Jimmy Carter on 9 June, but the International Committee of the Red Cross (ICRC) had still not been granted access to him after two years in captivity. The United Nations also hoped that the issue of Palestinian prisoners would be addressed. Measures to support the PA and the Palestinian economy in the West Bank should be intensified, including by donors fulfilling pledges for budgetary support and by Israel easing closures, and road map obligations should be acted upon, particularly an Israeli settlement freeze. Palestinian efforts on security performance and reform should continue and be supported.

Security Council consideration (July). On 22 July [meeting 5940], Mr. Pascoe reported to the Security Council that the security situation in Gaza and Israel had improved, as the Egyptian-mediated ceasefire had generally been upheld. During the reporting period, one Palestinian civilian was killed by IDF near the Gaza-Israel border, and two others were injured. Palestinian militants fired 7 rockets and 10 mortars at Israel, which did not result in casualties; no IDF air strikes or incursions were reported. Hamas communicated to the Gaza public its support for the calm, and detained individuals involved in firing mortars. However, 9 Palestinians were killed and 29 injured by internal violence, reckless handling of weaponry and tunnel collapses along the Gaza-Egyptian border.

The number of truckloads of supplies entering the Gaza Strip through the Sufa and Karni crossings increased by 54 per cent during the four weeks following the ceasefire, compared to the previous month. Imports of cement increased substantially, but the import of non-food commodities increased only slightly. The continued lack of raw materials and prohibition against exports precluded any significant economic recovery. Approximately 95 per cent of local industrial establishments remained closed.

On 17 July, Israeli officials informed their PA counterparts that they would increase the amount of fuel allowed into Gaza. However, between 27 June and 20 July, only 17 per cent of daily needs of petrol, 57 per cent of diesel, 40 per cent of cooking gas and 81 per cent of industrial gas requirements were met. The Gaza Electricity Company continued to operate at less than 70 per cent of its full capacity.

According to Mr. Pascoe, UN Special Coordinator Serry visited the Gaza Strip on 10 July to explore ways to resume stalled projects, including UN projects, as requested by the Quartet. The United Nations asked Israel to facilitate the resumption of priority projects as a matter of urgency. Prime Minister Olmert, in his discussions with the Secretary-General, undertook to consider that matter.

President Abbas continued wide-ranging consultations on a national dialogue to implement the Yemeni initiative for Palestinian reunification. Both the Secretary-General and the Special Coordinator supported President Abbas' initiative for progress towards the reunification of the Gaza Strip and the West Bank within the framework of the legitimate PA. The League of Arab States (LAS) would have a leading role to play in facilitating such efforts.

As efforts continued to solidify the ceasefire in Gaza, it was critical to accelerate progress in the West Bank. In that connection, it was noted with concern that Israeli forces had stepped up their military operations throughout the West Bank since 19 June. IDF closed down and seized equipment of alleged Hamas-affiliated institutions in Nablus, including schools, medical centres, media outlets and civic associations. Israel outlawed 36 international NGOs, charging them with fundraising for Hamas. Israeli troops raided the Nablus municipality, arrested elected PA officials and ordered the closure of the Nablus main shopping mall. PA officials, including Prime Minister Abbas, criticized those operations as undermining the economy and the Authority's efforts to improve security in the West Bank. Palestinian security forces continued to impose law and order and disarm and arrest militants. The United Nations was concerned about the effects of Israeli raids on the efforts of Palestinian security forces to operate effectively in areas under their control.

On 2 July, three Israeli civilians, including two women, were killed and 30 others injured when a Palestinian from East Jerusalem using a bulldozer attacked vehicles in West Jerusalem. In the West Bank, three Palestinians were killed by IDF, and 136 others injured, including at least 22 children. Most of the injuries occurred during anti-barrier demonstrations. On three occasions since mid-June, Israeli settlers reportedly fired rockets towards the Palestinian villages of Burin, southwest of Nablus. On 12 July, Israeli police arrested a settler suspected of that attack. On 21 July, another rocket was fired from the settlement.

Construction activity in settlements across the West Bank, including East Jerusalem, continued. On 3 July it was reported that Defense Minister Ehud Barak approved the construction of a new building in the Beit Romano settlement in Hebron's old city. Across the West Bank, movement and access deteriorated slightly. Four significant obstacles removed during June were reinstalled by IDF in July, bringing the number of closure obstacles to 609. Meanwhile, Israel renovated the Wadi Nar, or Container, checkpoint controlling movement from the north to the southern part of the West Bank, rather than honouring its prior commitment to remove it.

Within the context of the Annapolis political process, Israeli Prime Minister Olmert and PA President Abbas met on 13 July on the margins of the Paris Summit for the Mediterranean, underscoring their determination to reach an agreement. However, significant gaps remained, and in discussions with both parties, the Secretary-General emphasized the need to press ahead with bilateral talks, with the goal of overcoming all outstanding differences. It was nevertheless encouraging that on 22 July, for the first time, Israeli President Shimon Peres hosted President Abbas in his residence in Jerusalem.

Communication. On 22 July, [S/2008/482], Israel submitted to the Security Council a written statement in addition to its remarks made before the Council. In the statement, Israel charged that the Council meetings on the Question of Palestine were detached from daily reality and served to feed the rhetoric that fuelled a business-as-usual mentality. If the vision of peace had not yet been turned into reality, it was not for lack of meetings in the Council, or lack of agreements or UN resolutions or international conferences. It was because there was still daily terrorism and violence and hatred. Israel was not asking for special treatment. Like any other country, it should be subject to criticism and debate on a fair and impartial basis. Israel had tried to engage the international community with openness and transparency. The Council held periodical briefings for Council members to hear updates from intelligence and military experts on the ground. However, even those briefings, which were vital and necessary to understand the real situation in the region, were not attended by all Council members for political reasons. All too often the finger was pointed at Israel without any consideration as to the whole picture.

Security Council consideration (August). Briefing the Security Council on 20 August [meeting 5963], Mr. Pascoe stated that Palestinian internal violence had increased considerably. One Israeli soldier died of injuries sustained on 11 July in East Jerusalem, and nine Israelis were reported injured. The Egyptian-mediated ceasefire in Gaza had largely held but remained fragile. Ten rockets and one mortar had been fired from Gaza into Israel without causing casualties, and there had been no IDF air strikes or incursions, although one Palestinian child had been injured by IDF shooting near the border. Due to the collapse of tunnels along the Gaza-Egypt border, 12 Palestinians had been killed and 34 injured. Over 25 tunnels had been closed as a result of Egyptian efforts against smuggling. The United Nations welcomed Israel's decision to release approximately 200 Palestinian prisoners as a goodwill gesture to President Abbas. However, Mr. Pascoe noted, the benefits of the ceasefire had not yet translated into any significant improvement in the living conditions of the people of Gaza. Further to the Secretary-General's discussions with Prime Minister Olmert in Paris in July on stalled UN projects in Gaza, Israeli authorities were considering allowing the import of additional quantities of construction materials for UN priority projects for housing, school construction and water and sanitation. The United Nations hoped for the early resumption of all its suspended projects in Gaza.

In the West Bank, three Palestinians, among them two children, had been killed and 185 injured, including 47 children. There had also been a rise in settler violence. Settlement activity continued across the West Bank, particularly in East Jerusalem, and tenders were announced for over 400 new settlements. On 10 August, two major checkpoints in the West Bank had been partially reopened to Palestinian traffic, leading to significant access improvements. However, the overall number of closures remained unchanged at 608, as some previously removed obstacles had been reinstalled.

The implementation of Quartet Representative Blair's May economic stimulation package advanced, as selected obstacles to movement had been eased, and a telecommunications contract was signed between Israel and the PA on 28 July, enabling a second mobile phone operator to launch in the Occupied Palestinian Territory. To achieve significant economic impact, all outstanding measures needed to be implemented rapidly and as originally negotiated.

Mr. Pascoe noted that Israeli-Palestinian negotiations were ongoing at both political and technical levels. On 6 August, Prime Minister Olmert met again with President Abbas, but it appeared that the gaps between the parties' positions remained. Mr. Pascoe reiterated the Secretary-General's call for them to make real progress in overcoming differences to reach the goal of an agreement by the end of the year, despite the political constraints. Those discussions took place against the background of the 30 July announcement by Prime Minister Olmert that he would not be seeking re-election as leader of the Kadima party and would therefore be stepping down as Prime Minister, but would remain in office until either a new Government was formed by the new party leader or after general elections were held.

Security Council consideration (September). Appearing before the Security Council on 18 September [meeting 5974], Mr. Serry said that the ceasefire in Gaza continued to hold, as Hamas made efforts to prevent the launching of rockets and mortars into Israel and there was no reported IDF incursion or air strike. However, Israel responded to isolated rocket fire by closing crossings for a period. The humanitarian situation remained grim, given the continued closure and restricted movement into and out of the Gaza Strip. Imports decreased by 21 per cent compared with the preceding four weeks, and the import of all types of fuel remained below previous levels. UN priority projects remained stalled and the shortage of raw materials, combined with the total ban on exports, had kept more than 95 per cent of Gaza's industry closed. Hamas' actions compounded the problems facing Gazans, increasingly divorcing Palestinian institutions from the PA itself and interrupting basic service delivery. Palestinian interfactional violence during the reporting period resulted in the death of 14 people, including two children, and another 52 injured. Most of the casualties occurred on 15 and 16 September in Gaza City during armed clashes between security forces and militants affiliated with Hamas and members of one armed clan.

The only way to begin addressing the overall crisis and lay the basis for a two-State solution was for Gaza to be peacefully reunited with the West Bank, within the framework of the legitimate PA and in a manner that allowed the peace process to advance. In that context, Egypt started consultations with each Palestinian faction to formulate a proposal that could serve as a common national platform. Egypt's efforts were strongly supported at the LAS Foreign Ministers' meeting (Cairo, 9 September) and welcomed by the United Nations.

Mr. Serry told the Council that although bilateral negotiations between Israel and the PLO continued, no agreement had been reached on the core issues. The potential of those substantive discussions had to be built upon through the continuation of intensive negotiations. Notwithstanding the prevailing uncertainties surrounding the political process, there had been a gradual but systematic process of Palestinian self-empowerment in the West Bank, under the leadership of President Abbas and Prime Minister Fayyad. Although those efforts were imperfect and faced many obstacles, they reflected a determination to build the institutions of a future Palestinian State.

The PA continued to make real strides in implementing its security plan, which included action against militants in accordance with obligations under phase 1 of the road map. Further improvement of the security conditions in Hebron was a priority for the Palestinian Government. In pursuing its reform and development plan [YUN 2007, p. 446], the PA also made notable gains in other areas, including public finance and the initiation of microfinance projects.

As to Israeli settlement activity, the Secretary-General had repeatedly stated that it was contrary to the Fourth Geneva Convention as well as Israel's commitments under the road map and the Annapolis process. His repeated calls and those of the Quartet as a whole had not brought about significant action; rectifying that unacceptable situation should be the urgent priority of any new Israeli Government. Contrary to the road map, Palestinian institutions in East Jerusalem remained closed by Israeli order, and barrier construction continued around East Jerusalem and within the West Bank, in deviation from the Green Line, and contrary to the 2004 advisory opinion of the ICJ.

On 26 September [meeting 5983], the Council held an urgent meeting, in response to a request by Saudi Arabia on behalf of LAS [S/2008/615], to discuss the continued Israeli settlement activity which, Saudi Arabia said, in its opening statement, was clearly violating international law, UN resolutions and Israel's obligations under the road map and the Annapolis process.

Communication. On 26 September [S/2008/625], Cuba expressed regret over the Security Council's refusal to allow NAM to participate in its deliberations, calling the Council's decision an example of its customary lack of transparency.

Quartet statement (September). In a statement issued following its meeting in New York, on 26 September [SG/2143], the Quartet reaffirmed its support for the Israeli-Palestinian negotiations and commended the parties for their efforts. Recognizing that a meaningful and results-oriented process was under way, the Quartet called on the parties to make every effort to conclude an agreement before the end of 2008. It noted the significance of the Annapolis process and the importance of confidentiality for preserving its integrity, and underlined its commitment to the negotiations' irreversibility, as well as to the creation of an independent, democratic and viable Palestinian State in the West Bank and Gaza, living in peace and security alongside Israel, and an end to the conflict. The Quartet expressed its desire to see the continuation of negotiations, involving substantive discussions on all issues, including core issues without exception, in order to ensure the fulfilment of the Annapolis goals. It reiterated its call on all Palestinians to commit themselves to non-violence, recognition of Israel and acceptance of previous agreements and obligations, noting that restoring Palestinian unity based on PLO commitments would be an important factor in that process.

The Quartet emphasized the need for a renewed focus on improvements in the situation on the ground and stated that visible and tangible progress should accompany the negotiations. The Quartet commended the PA for the encouraging results of its efforts to reform the security sector, confront militias and terrorism, and enforce the rule of law in areas under its control, as well as Israeli measures to lift restrictions to access and movement. It encouraged further steps to ease conditions for Palestinian civilian life and economy. The parties should redouble their cooperative efforts on security, and expand the success in Jenin to other major centres in the West Bank. The international community, including regional partners, should support those efforts with targeted and coordinated assistance and through the continued efforts of the Quartet Representative. The Quartet called for speedy implementation of the outcome of the Berlin Conference and invited donors to fulfil the pledges made at the Paris Donor Conference [YUN 2007, p. 446], in line with the Palestinian Reform and Development Plan 2008–2010. It welcomed the 22 September statement of the Ad Hoc Liaison Committee reaffirming that economic progress in the Occupied Palestinian Territory was an essential part of bringing the Israeli-Palestinian conflict to an end, and recalling the importance of equitable burden-sharing.

The Quartet discussed the status of the parties' obligations under the road map as an integral part of the Annapolis follow-up. Concerned about the increasing settlement activity, it called on Israel to freeze such activity as it had a damaging impact on the negotiating environment and was an impediment to economic recovery, and to dismantle outposts erected since March 2001. It reiterated that the parties should avoid actions that undermined confidence and could prejudice the outcome of negotiations. Quartet principals condemned the rise in settler violence against Palestinian civilians, urging the enforcement of the rule of law without discrimination or exception. Likewise, it condemned acts of terrorism against Israelis, including rocket attacks from the Palestinian territories, and stressed the need for further Palestinian efforts to fight terrorism and dismantle the terror infrastructure, as well as foster an atmosphere of tolerance.

The Quartet commended Egypt for its effort to overcome Palestinian divisions and to reunite the West Bank and Gaza under the legitimate PA. It welcomed the continuing calm between Gaza and southern Israel, and hoped that it would result in further relief for the civilian population of Gaza, including the regular opening of the crossings for both humanitarian and commercial flows, and sustained peace on Israel's southern border. The Quartet expected the movement of persons and goods to be normalized in the coming months, as foreseen in the 2005 Agreement on Movement and Access [YUN 2005, p. 519], and supported the immediate resumption of stalled United Nations and other donor projects in Gaza to facilitate economic activity, reduce dependence on humanitarian assistance and restore links between Gaza and the West Bank.

Security Council consideration (October). The Egypt-brokered calm was by and large holding between Gaza and southern Israel, Mr. Pascoe noted in his statement before the Security Council on 22 October [meeting 5999], although incidents had taken place, including the firing of a rocket into the Negev on 21 October and the subsequent closure of border crossings. The movement of goods and people in and out of Gaza had not improved and construction projects, including those of the United Nations, remained on hold. The split between the West Bank and Gaza was having increasingly adverse effects. The strike of teachers continued to affect some 250,000 pupils, and the strike of health workers caused concern over the quality and timely provision of services.

The Egyptian-mediated process aimed at the reunification of Gaza and the West Bank within the framework of the legitimate PA was ongoing. Earlier in the month, Egyptian mediators completed a round of meetings with Palestinian factions, which had since received a draft proposal for consideration. President Abbas also continued regional consultations. The United Nations looked forward to all regional States lending their support to Egypt's efforts under the auspices of LAS, which was to meet at the Foreign Ministers' level in Cairo in November.

Bilateral contacts between Israel and the Palestinians continued, with meetings held between Israeli negotiators and Foreign Minister Livni and lead Palestinian negotiator Qurei on 23 September; between Presidents Abbas and Peres on 26 September in New York; and between advisers. In Israel, the process of political transition was ongoing, with President Peres commissioning newly elected Kadima Party leader Livni, on 21 September, to form a new Government. On 26 September, the Secretary-General convened a meeting of the Quartet principals at UN Headquarters, and on the same date, Quartet members and Arab League representatives discussed how to work together in the crucial period ahead in support of the Israeli-Palestinian process, Palestinian reunification and regional peace. They also reaffirmed the central importance of the Arab Peace Initiative [YUN 2002, p. 495].

The Ad Hoc Liaison Committee comprising the parties and key donors, as well as Quartet Representative Blair, who met (22 September) on the margins of the General Assembly, commended the efforts of Prime Minister Fayyad's Government to implement its reform and development agenda, and encouraged the continuation of ongoing security and institution-building efforts.

PA security efforts, in accordance with the road map, focused on deepening progress in the Jenin governorate, which Special Coordinator Serry visited on 22 October. Efforts were being extended to Hebron, where Palestinian security forces discovered a tunnel allegedly used by militants. The PA also made considerable progress in defining a strategy for developing the judicial sector, including the doubling of the number of judges and prosecutors.

Despite those efforts, the situation on the ground did not improve, as Israeli-Palestinian violence claimed the lives of seven Palestinians, two of them children, while injuring 116 Palestinians and 34 Israelis. No progress was made in the reporting period on Israel's key road map and Annapolis commitments. Settlement construction continued across the West Bank, including in East Jerusalem, and a majority of Palestinian Muslims had not been able to pray at the Al-Aqsa mosque during the month of Ramadan due to permit and access restrictions. The Secretary-General continued to call for an end to unilateral action in Jerusalem and reminded all parties that the status of the city remained an issue for permanent status negotiations.

Quartet meeting (November). In Sharm el-Sheikh, Egypt, on 9 November [SG/2145], the Quartet was briefed in a first-ever joint meeting with the parties by PA President Abbas and Israeli Foreign Minister Livni on the negotiating efforts since the Annapolis Conference. Over the past year they had engaged in direct, sustained and intensive bilateral negotiations, based on a joint work plan that included the establishment of more than 10 committees, not only on core issues, but on an array of other topics necessary to turn the two-State solution into a reality. The parties reached a number of mutual understandings on the principles governing the negotiating process, including the need for continuous, uninterrupted, direct, bilateral negotiations; the principle that nothing would be considered agreed until everything was agreed; and the need to reach a comprehensive agreement addressing all issues, rather than just announcing agreement on selected items in isolation. The parties remained committed to implementing their respective obligations under the road map, and to the agreed mechanisms for monitoring and judging its implementation, as well as to implementation of the future peace treaty being subject to implementation of the road map. President Abbas and Foreign Minister Livni asked that the international community continue to support the parties' efforts in the framework of the Annapolis process and that all States promote an environment conducive to peace, non-violence and the two-State solution. They urged political and economic assistance, especially in relation to institutional and security reform, capacity-building, economic development and the fulfilment of pledges to the legitimate Palestinian Government, which had accepted the Quartet principles and respected the PLO commitments. They asked the international community to redouble efforts to confront extremism, incitement, terrorism and intolerance, and stressed that, absent the joint request of the parties, third parties should not intervene in the bilateral negotiations.

The Quartet endorsed the goals set out by the parties and called upon all States to lend their diplomatic and political support. It renewed its call on relevant States and international organizations to assist in developing the Palestinian economy, maximizing resources available to the PA and contributing to Palestinian institution-building in preparation for statehood. The Quartet welcomed the deployment of Palestinian security services in the Hebron governorate as a sign of the progress resulting from increased security cooperation. It emphasized its determination to continue working with Israel and the Palestinian Government to facilitate access and movement, and an improvement in conditions on the ground in order to address urgent humanitarian needs, foster economic activity and improve the atmosphere of negotiations. The Quartet reiterated its call to the parties to fully implement their obligations under phase I of the road map, including the freezing of settlement activity and the dismantlement of the terrorism infrastructure.

Security Council consideration (November). At the 25 November Security Council meeting [meeting 6022], Mr. Pascoe noted that recent developments underscored the fact that the gap between the political tracks and the situation on the ground remained large. Israeli-Palestinian violence during the reporting period resulted in the deaths of 16 Palestinians, while injuring 122 others, mainly civilians. One Israeli was killed in a stabbing attack in Jerusalem, and 25 Israeli soldiers and civilians were injured during the period. The *tahdiya*, or period of calm, in Gaza and southern Israel, in effect since 19 June, was threatened by a number of violent incidents. Israel conducted a military incursion into Gaza on 4 November to destroy a tunnel allegedly used to abduct Israeli soldiers, and a number of smaller incursions followed. More than 123 rockets and 118 mortars were fired by Palestinian militants into Israel or at the crossings between Israel and Gaza. Between 4 and 23 November, Israel severely restricted the access of humanitarian workers and commercial and humanitarian goods to Gaza, causing UNRWA and WFP to suspend food aid. Fuel shortages, causing the Gaza power plant to shut down for more than 12 days, led to water rationing throughout the Gaza Strip, affecting approximately 600,000 people. Despite fuel deliveries, the Gaza power plant was still not working due to a technical malfunction and lack of spare parts.

Rocket fire decreased dramatically on 23 November and the following day, Israel reopened the Kerem Shalom crossing. After rocket-firing towards Ashkelon on the evening of 24 November, however, all crossings were closed again. Major news agencies and organizations protested to the Israeli Government that foreign and Israeli media had not been allowed entry for more than 14 days.

Mr. Pascoe stated that the joint meeting of the parties with the Quartet in Sharm el-Sheikh on 9 November was an important marker of the ongoing political process pursuant to the Annapolis Conference. Following their bilateral meeting at Sharm el-Sheikh, Prime Minister Olmert and President Abbas met in Jerusalem on 17 November, the same date of the announcement by Prime Minister Olmert of Israel's intention to release some 250 Palestinian prisoners as a gesture to President Abbas prior to the upcoming Muslim festival of Eid al-Adha.

Mr. Pascoe expressed regret that Israel and the Palestinians would likely fall short of their commitment made at Annapolis to reach an agreement by the end of the year. The parties stated that negotiations would continue uninterrupted, and their goal remained a comprehensive peace agreement addressing all issues, without exception. Furthermore, they recommitted to the implementation of their road map commitments, on which more urgent action was vital to ensure the credibility of the process.

Recent developments in the Occupied Palestinian Territory and in Israel underscored the large gap remaining between the political tracks and the situation on the ground, posing considerable obstacles to the path that lay ahead. Palestinians remained divided, and the rhetoric between Hamas and Fatah had intensified. The PLO Central Committee announced the election of Mahmoud Abbas as the President of the State of Palestine, but the Hamas leadership rejected that move. Developments on the ground remained the biggest challenge to building lasting peace.

The importance of the Arab Peace Initiative was widely discussed as a vital platform for reaching the goal of a comprehensive regional peace. The United Nations commended the efforts of King Abdullah of Saudi Arabia, which led to the convening of a high-level General Assembly meeting under the agenda item "Culture of Peace" on 13 November, attended by numerous leaders from the Middle East. In addition, the Secretary-General urged United States President-elect Barack Obama to engage early in the Middle East.

The Secretary-General expressed his concern over the deteriorating humanitarian situation in Gaza to Prime Minister Olmert and Foreign Minister Livni on 18 and 20 November, respectively. He restated his condemnation of rocket fire, but stressed that Israel had to uphold humanitarian principles. In public statements of 14 and 21 November, the Secretary-General urged Israel to facilitate freer movement of urgently needed humanitarian supplies and of UN personnel into Gaza, and emphasized that measures which increased the hardship and suffering of the civilians of Gaza were unacceptable and should cease immediately. He was pleased that some humanitarian supplies and fuel had been allowed into Gaza and expected Israel to resume facilitating regular deliveries of both. The United Nations was concerned about reports of human rights abuses in Gaza under the de facto Hamas regime, which had apparently strengthened its control, divorcing Gaza institutions from those of the PA.

Communications. On 25 November [A/63/572-S/2008/736], the Syrian Arab Republic transmitted a request by the Syrian President, as Chairman of the Arab Summit, that the United Nations prevail on Israel "to desist immediately from its immoral and inhuman practices in the Gaza Strip".

Quartet statement (December). In a 15 December statement [SG/2147], the Quartet affirmed that a final treaty and lasting peace would be reached through simultaneous and mutually re-enforcing efforts on three tracks: negotiations; building the institutions of a Palestinian State, including facilitating economic development through an improvement of conditions on the ground; and implementation of the parties' obligations under the road map, as stated in the Annapolis Joint Understanding [YUN 2007, p. 446].

The Quartet urged that the calm that came into effect on 19 June be respected and extended. It condemned the indiscriminate attacks on Israel and called for an immediate cessation of violence. The Quartet reiterated its call for Israel to allow into Gaza sufficient materials to facilitate the resumption of stalled UN and other donor projects and supported the efforts of the Secretary-General and Quartet Representative Blair in that regard.

The Quartet called on all States to demonstrate their support for the Annapolis process and their commitment to the two-State solution by contributing to an environment conducive to an end to the conflict. It noted that at the Paris Donor Conference [YUN 2007, p. 446], international donors had pledged unprecedented levels of support for the success of the Annapolis process, providing an essential element of stability as the process unfolded. The Quartet called on all States and international organizations to continue to provide economic assistance to the legitimate Palestinian Government in security reform, institution- and capacity-building, and economic development, and to fulfil their pledges. The Quartet welcomed the robust Israeli-Palestinian cooperation for the expansion of security and law and order in the West Bank, most notably in Jenin and Hebron, the successful deployment of the Palestinian security services to Hebron being the most recent demonstration of substantial progress. The Quartet urged the Palestinians to continue reforming the security services and dismantling terrorism infrastructure, and Israel to freeze all settlement activities and address the growing threat of settler extremism.

The Quartet offered its support for an intensification of diplomatic efforts towards a peaceful coexistence among all States in the region and a just, lasting and comprehensive Middle East peace, based on UN Security Council resolutions. In that context, it welcomed efforts to invigorate the Arab Peace Initiative as part of a comprehensive approach to resolving the Arab-Israeli conflict, and looked forward to the intensification of the Israeli-Syrian negotiations. In consultation with the parties, the Quartet supported the convening of an international meeting in Moscow in 2009.

Security Council consideration (December). Addressing the Council on 16 December [meeting 6045], the Secretary-General regretted that the peace agreement had not been concluded as originally envisioned and that there were still many hurdles to face, but noted that a serious process was under way. The Secretary-General reiterated his commitments to the goal of a just, lasting and comprehensive peace in the region, based on Council resolutions, the principle of land for peace, the 1991 Madrid Conference terms of reference [YUN 1991, p. 221] and the 2002 Arab Peace Initiative [YUN 2002, p. 415].

United States Secretary of State Rice stated that the resolution before the Council built on the work of the international community through the Quartet. Firstly, the resolution confirmed the irreversibility of the bilateral negotiations and endorsed the parties' brave efforts. There was no substitute for the Annapolis process, and stagnation was not an option. The Annapolis process had advanced under the leadership of President Abbas, Prime Minister Olmert and Foreign Minister Livni, and those advances had to be preserved and built upon. Secondly, the resolution reiterated the importance of fulfilling obligations under the road map. Neither party should undertake any activity that contravened road map obligations or prejudiced the final status negotiations. The United States' view had been made very clear in that regard, especially in connection with settlement activity. At the same time, the PA had an absolute obligation to dismantle the infrastructure of terror in the territories, reform its security services and end incitement. Thirdly, the resolution underscored that peace would be built on mutual recognition, freedom from violence and terror, the two-State solution and previous agreements and obligations. The threat of extremism and terrorism posed by Hamas was a threat to the Annapolis process and to the fulfilment of legitimate Palestinian aspirations. Fourthly, the resolution emphasized that the solution to the Israeli-Palestinian conflict should be aligned with efforts towards broader regional peace. The Arab Peace Initiative was a historic proposal in that regard. Just as Arab States should reach out to Israel, so should Israel reach out to Arab States.

The Annapolis negotiations gave confidence that the goal of two independent and democratic States, Israel and Palestine, living in peace and security was not just a vision but a commitment of the parties and of the international community. The chosen path would finally bring Israel the peace and security that could only come from living side-by-side in reconciliation with its democratic neighbour, Palestine, and that path forward would finally give to the people of Palestine the dignity and humanity that could only come from living in an independent and sovereign State.

Foreign Minister Sergey Lavrov of the Russian Federation, which co-sponsored the resolution, considered it essential to continue the negotiations while building on what had been achieved. Of particular importance were the resolution's provisions calling for the full implementation by both parties of their obligations under the road map. The text also underscored the crucial need to allow the Arab Peace Initiative to work effectively. Under the current circumstances, it was especially important to restore the territorial and political unity of the Palestinian national administration as quickly as possible, which was essential for strengthening the Israeli-Palestinian dialogue and ensuring the viability of future final arrangements in the framework of that dialogue. The Israeli and Palestinian parties faced a very complex problem that required political will and courage, qualities which the negotiators had shown, but progress was impossible without the active support of the international community. Russia, along with its partners, would take every step necessary to ensure that the international meeting on the Middle East, scheduled for 2009 in Moscow, would mark an important step forward and would serve to accelerate the process to reach an agreement, which was the goal of the Council's resolution.

SECURITY COUNCIL ACTION

On 16 December [meeting 6045], the Security Council adopted **resolution 1850(2008)** by vote (14-0-1). The draft [S/2008/787] was submitted by the Russian Federation and the United States.

The Security Council,

Recalling all its previous relevant resolutions, in particular resolutions 242(1967) of 22 November 1967, 338(1973) of 22 October 1973, 1397(2002) of 12 March 2002 and 1515(2003) of 19 November 2003, and the Madrid principles,

Reiterating its vision of a region where two democratic States, Israel and Palestine, live side by side in peace within secure and recognized borders,

Welcoming the statement by the Quartet of 9 November 2008 and the Israeli-Palestinian Joint Understanding announced at the conference held in Annapolis, United States of America, on 27 November 2007, including in relation to the implementation of the performance-based road map to a permanent two-State solution to the Israeli-Palestinian conflict,

Noting that lasting peace can only be based on an enduring commitment to mutual recognition, freedom from violence, incitement and terror, and the two-State solution, building upon previous agreements and obligations,

Noting also the importance of the 2002 Arab Peace Initiative,

Encouraging the ongoing work of the Quartet to support the parties in their efforts to achieve a comprehensive, just and lasting peace in the Middle East,

1. *Declares* its support for the negotiations initiated at Annapolis, United States of America, on 27 November 2007 and its commitment to the irreversibility of the bilateral negotiations;

2. *Supports* the parties' agreed principles for the bilateral negotiating process and their determined efforts to reach their goal of concluding a peace treaty resolving all outstanding issues, including all core issues, without exception, which confirm the seriousness of the Annapolis process;

3. *Calls upon* both parties to fulfil their obligations under the performance-based road map to a permanent two-State solution to the Israeli-Palestinian conflict, as stated in their Annapolis Joint Understanding, and to refrain from any steps that could undermine confidence or prejudice the outcome of negotiations;

4. *Calls upon* all States and international organizations to contribute to an atmosphere conducive to negotiations and to support the Palestinian government that is committed to the Quartet principles and the Arab Peace Initiative and respects the commitments of the Palestine Liberation Organization, to assist in the development of the Palestinian economy, to maximize the resources available to the Palestinian Authority, and to contribute to the Palestinian institution-building programme in preparation for statehood;

5. *Urges* an intensification of diplomatic efforts to foster, in parallel with progress in the bilateral process, mutual recognition and peaceful coexistence between all States in the region in the context of achieving a comprehensive, just and lasting peace in the Middle East;

6. *Welcomes* the Quartet's consideration, in consultation with the parties, of an international meeting in Moscow in 2009;

7. *Decides* to remain seized of the matter.

VOTE ON RESOLUTION 1850(2008):

In favour: Belgium, Burkina Faso, China, Costa Rica, Croatia, France, Indonesia, Italy, Panama, Russian Federation, South Africa, United Kingdom, United States, Viet Nam.

Against: None.

Abstaining: Libyan Arab Jamahiriya.

Speaking before the Security Council on 18 December [meeting 6049], Mr. Serry observed that for the previous six weeks, the calm in Gaza had been gravely challenged, with heightened rhetoric and continued violence in recent days, an increase in rocket-firing and a resumption of Israeli air strikes. Expressing concern about Hamas' statements questioning the renewal of the calm, which expired that day, Mr. Serry appealed for the calm to be respected and extended. He also appealed for respect of basic humanitarian principles. The unprecedented level of closure of crossing points caused unacceptable hardship. UNRWA again had to suspend all food distribution. Price increases resulted in Gazans spending approximately two thirds of their income on food. Limitations on cash allowed into Gaza left beneficiaries of humanitarian organizations, PA employees and pensioners unable to collect salaries, pensions and welfare payments, and forced UNRWA to suspend cash assistance to 94,000 beneficiaries. A one-time transfer of 100 million new Israeli shekels had alleviated the crisis for the time being, but a predictable mechanism for the transfer of cash was required. UN projects worth over $150 million, including six priority projects identified by the Secretary-General in May, remained suspended due to a lack of materials.

The Secretary-General outlined his concerns about conditions in Gaza in a letter delivered to his Quartet colleagues the previous week, Mr. Serry said. The United Nations welcomed the Quartet's call for the provision of humanitarian supplies to the people in Gaza to be assured continuously, and noted its call for Israel to allow into Gaza sufficient materials to facilitate the resumption of stalled UN and other donor projects. The United Nations sought more effective communication and cooperation with Israel to ensure that it was able to execute its mandated programmes to the civilian population.

Preparations for the Israeli general election scheduled for 10 February 2009 continued, Mr. Serry said, and a new United States administration would take office on 20 January. There were also internal challenges on the Palestinian side. The immediate priority was to sustain the process during the transition period by building a solid bridge to carry through the fragile period ahead. Ensuring calm in and around Gaza and improving humanitarian conditions had to be a priority. The decision of the Arab League to ensure that there was no vacuum on the Palestinian side, to support the legitimate Palestinian Government and pursue Palestinian unity demanded support. It was important to pursue specific action to improve conditions on the ground in the West Bank. The three tracks of the Annapolis process—negotiations, institution-building and phase I road map implementation—had to be protected, preserved and, where possible, advanced to set the stage for a decisive push for peace in 2009.

Security Council meeting on crisis in Gaza (31 December). On 31 December, the Council convened [meeting 6060] in response to requests by Egypt [S/2008/842] and the Libyan Arab Jamahiriya [S/2008/815, S/2008/843]. In his address to the Council, the Secretary-General stated that a dramatic crisis in Gaza and southern Israel had reached its fifth day. The civilian population, the fabric of Gaza, the future of the peace process, stability in the region and goodwill among people throughout the world were trapped between the irresponsibility displayed in the indiscriminate rocket attacks by Hamas militants and the disproportionality of the continuing Israeli military operation. As a result of the crisis and violence, conditions for the 1.5 million people in Gaza were nothing short of terrifying, as they were living under heavy bombardment targeted at the infrastructure of Hamas, as well as the former PA security structure, government buildings, residential homes, mosques and businesses. More than 300 people were dead—among them at least 60 women and children—and over 800 were wounded. In southern Israel, a continuous stream of rockets was being fired from Gaza, hitting major cities with hundreds of thousands of people. Four Israelis died during the preceding four days, and over 30 more were injured. Schools were closed and daily life was extremely difficult, as Israelis were in constant fear of rockets hitting homes and schools.

Condemning the ongoing rocket and mortar attacks by Hamas and other Palestinian militants, the Secretary-General also condemned Israel's excessive use of force, and reminded all parties that they had to fully uphold international humanitarian law. It was the civilian population that bore the brunt of the escalation, and the international community had to act swiftly and decisively to end their suffering. All parties should address the humanitarian and economic needs in Gaza and take measures to ensure the provision of humanitarian supplies. The Secretary-General paid tribute to UN staff in the area, working under adverse conditions to address the humanitarian situation of Gaza, and was pained at the death, injury and damage that UN personnel and premises, as well as others associated with UN programmes, had sustained. He urged the international community, in particular those in the region, to exert what influence they had on the parties to end the violence. There was need for decisive action. He welcomed the efforts under way, including by Arab and European leaders, but stressed that not enough had been done and more was urgently required. There had to be an immediate ceasefire fully respected by all parties to create new conditions on the ground that ensured that crossings into Gaza would be reopened, rocket and weapons smuggling ended, political dialogue pursued to reunite Gaza with the West Bank, and that the root cause of the suffering—the absence of Israeli-Palestinian peace—also ended.

Nineteen other speakers addressed the Council in the ensuing debate.

Committee on Palestinian Rights. The Committee on the Exercise of the Inalienable Rights of the Palestinian People, in its annual report to the General Assembly [A/63/35], noted that the reporting period from 5 October 2007 to 6 October 2008 was characterized by a dichotomy between the resumption of the Israeli-Palestinian negotiations and intensified international engagement, on one hand, and on the other, a deteriorating situation on the ground. The lack of tangible progress in the situation on the ground had a negative effect on the ongoing negotiations between the parties. The Committee stressed the need for a complete cessation of all acts of violence, including military attacks, destruction and acts of terror. It called on Israel to end its illegal policies and oppressive practices in the Occupied Palestinian Territory, including East Jerusalem, such as settlement activities, the construction of the wall and numerous measures of collective punishment. The Committee was of the view that the Israeli occupation of the Palestinian territory had to end without conditions, allowing the Palestinian people to establish an independent State on all territories occupied in 1967, including East Jerusalem, and to exercise their inalienable rights, including the right to self-determination. The Committee firmly supported the two-State solution in accordance with Security Council resolutions 242(1967) [YUN 1967, p. 257], 338(1973) [YUN 1973, p. 213], 1397(2002) [YUN 2002, p. 418] and 1515(2003) [YUN 2003, p. 483].

Peaceful settlement of question of Palestine

Report of Secretary-General. In a 23 September report [A/63/368-S/2008/612], submitted in response to General Assembly resolution 62/83 [YUN 2007, p. 462] and covering the period from September 2007 through August 2008, the Secretary-General put forward his observations on the state of the Israeli-Palestinian conflict and on international efforts to move the peace process forward, as well as the views of the Security Council and the concerned parties on the question of Palestine.

For the Council, the goal of achieving a peaceful settlement remained one of the major challenges facing the international community. It considered the situation in Palestine every month under the agenda item "The situation in the Middle East, including the question of Palestine", with briefings by either the Under-Secretary-General for Political Affairs or the Special Coordinator for the Middle East Peace Process, followed by an open Council meeting or consultations among the Council members.

In a 30 July note verbale, Israel declared that it remained committed to the bilateral process with the moderate, legitimate PA leadership that embraced its responsibility and the vision of two States living side by side in peace and security. In the past months, meetings had taken place to set in motion the building blocks for a political horizon and to maintain a dialogue between Israel and the PA. Israel hoped to work with its moderate counterparts in the region to advance mutual understanding and the bilateral process. Rather than promoting a vision that recognized both sides' rights and responsibilities, however, General Assembly resolution 62/83 [YUN 2007, p. 462] obscured the parties' efforts to achieve a negotiated outcome.

Also on the same date in a note verbale, the Permanent Observer of Palestine to the United Nations stated that 2008 marked the passage of 60 years since the Palestinians had lost their homeland. The situation in the Occupied Palestinian Territory, including East Jerusalem, remained critical, with little progress towards the realization by the Palestinians of their inalienable rights and the achievement of a peaceful settlement of the Palestine question. While the Annapolis Conference had set the end of 2008 as the timeline for establishing an independent Palestinian State and a comprehensive settlement to the Israeli-Palestinian conflict, bilateral negotiations and several high-level meetings had been held between Israeli and Palestinian leadership, and the Middle East peace process remained high on the international agenda, progress had been minimal. Moreover, negative developments on the ground continued to impede the process and complicate efforts to address the core, final status issues of Jerusalem, settlements, borders, refugees, water and security. The peace process was in a state of serious disrepair, as it was constantly being undermined by Israel's illegal actions that precluded the full implementation of resolution 62/83. Since the adoption of that resolution, Israel had not ceased its collective punishment, reprisals and military operations against the Palestinian civilian population, but instead pursued its settlement activities, particularly around East Jerusalem and the Jordan Valley. Continuation of that situation would make the establishment of a sovereign, contiguous, viable and independent Palestinian State, with East Jerusalem as its capital, and the realization of the two-State solution impossible.

The situation in the Gaza Strip remained critical, as Israel continued to close border crossings and the Gaza Strip was separated from the West Bank with no functional territorial link. Consequently, poverty had increased, and health conditions had deteriorated. The majority of the more than 1.4 million Palestinians in Gaza lived in poverty and depended on food aid for survival.

The Secretary-General regretted the continued violence between Israelis and Palestinians, as well as among Palestinians, but noted that road map implementation saw some arguable progress. He welcomed the parties' diplomatic efforts, as well as those of the League of Arab States and several Arab countries to advance regional efforts for peace, and affirmed that the United Nations would continue to work towards the creation of an independent, democratic, contiguous and viable Palestinian State living side by side in peace with a secure Israel, within the framework of a comprehensive regional settlement, consistent with Security Council resolutions and in accordance with the road map, the Arab Peace Initiative and the principle of land for peace.

The situation on the ground, both in Gaza and the West Bank, including East Jerusalem, had deteriorated in many instances, the Secretary-General observed, and much more needed to be done to build the necessary foundations for a successful political process and for eventual and sustainable implementation of any agreement reached. Settlement activity had to stop completely and restrictions on movement and access lifted, while the PA needed to make further progress in imposing law and order.

GENERAL ASSEMBLY ACTION

On 26 November [meeting 60], the General Assembly adopted **resolution 63/29** [draft: A/63/L.35 & Add.1] by recorded vote (164-7-3) [agenda item 16].

Peaceful settlement of the question of Palestine

The General Assembly,

Recalling its relevant resolutions, including those adopted at its tenth emergency special session,

Recalling also its resolution 58/292 of 6 May 2004,

Recalling further relevant Security Council resolutions, including resolutions 242(1967) of 22 November 1967, 338(1973) of 22 October 1973, 1397(2002) of 12 March 2002, 1515(2003) of 19 November 2003 and 1544(2004) of 19 May 2004,

Welcoming the affirmation by the Security Council of the vision of a region where two States, Israel and Palestine, live side by side within secure and recognized borders,

Noting with concern that it has been more than sixty years since the adoption of resolution 181(II) of 29 November 1947 and forty-one years since the occupation of Palestinian territory, including East Jerusalem, in 1967,

Having considered the report of the Secretary-General submitted pursuant to the request made in its resolution 62/83 of 10 December 2007,

Reaffirming the permanent responsibility of the United Nations with regard to the question of Palestine until the question is resolved in all its aspects in accordance with international law,

Recalling the advisory opinion rendered on 9 July 2004 by the International Court of Justice on the *Legal Consequences of the Construction of a Wall in the Occupied Palestinian Territory*, and recalling also its resolutions ES-10/15 of 20 July 2004 and ES-10/17 of 15 December 2006,

Convinced that achieving a just, lasting and comprehensive settlement of the question of Palestine, the core of the Arab-Israeli conflict, is imperative for the attainment of comprehensive and lasting peace and stability in the Middle East,

Aware that the principle of equal rights and self-determination of peoples is among the purposes and principles enshrined in the Charter of the United Nations,

Affirming the principle of the inadmissibility of the acquisition of territory by war,

Recalling its resolution 2625(XXV) of 24 October 1970,

Reaffirming the illegality of the Israeli settlements in the Palestinian territory occupied since 1967, including East Jerusalem,

Reaffirming also the illegality of Israeli actions aimed at changing the status of Jerusalem, including measures such as the so-called E-l plan and all other unilateral measures aimed at altering the character, status and demographic composition of the city and the territory as a whole,

Reaffirming further that the construction by Israel, the occupying Power, of a wall in the Occupied Palestinian Territory, including in and around East Jerusalem, and its associated regime, are contrary to international law,

Expressing deep concern about the continuing Israeli policy of closures and severe restrictions on the movement of persons and goods, including medical and humanitarian personnel and goods, via the imposition of crossing closures as well as the continued establishment of checkpoints and the imposition of a permit regime throughout the Occupied Palestinian Territory, including East Jerusalem, and the consequent negative impact on the socio-economic situation of the Palestinian people, which remains that of a dire humanitarian crisis, as well as on efforts aimed at rehabilitating and developing the damaged Palestinian economy, and on the contiguity of the Territory,

Recalling the mutual recognition between the Government of the State of Israel and the Palestine Liberation Organization, the representative of the Palestinian people, and the need for full compliance with the agreements concluded between the two sides,

Recalling also the endorsement by the Security Council, in resolution 1515(2003), of the Quartet road map to a permanent two-State solution to the Israeli-Palestinian conflict, and stressing the urgent need for its implementation and compliance with its provisions,

Recalling further the Arab Peace Initiative adopted by the Council of the League of Arab States at its fourteenth session, held in Beirut on 27 and 28 March 2002,

Recalling the convening of the international conference held at Annapolis, United States of America, on 27 November 2007, in particular the decision by the parties to launch meaningful, direct negotiations towards the achievement of a just, lasting and peaceful settlement of the Israeli-Palestinian conflict and ultimately the Arab-Israeli conflict as a whole for the realization of a comprehensive peace in the Middle East,

Noting the important contribution to the peace process of the United Nations Special Coordinator for the Middle East Peace Process and Personal Representative of the Secretary-General to the Palestine Liberation Organization and the Palestinian Authority, including in the framework of the activities of the Quartet,

Welcoming the reconvening of the Ad Hoc Liaison Committee for the Coordination of the International Assistance to Palestinians, under the chairmanship of Norway, at United Nations Headquarters on 22 September 2008, and affirming the importance of continued follow-up and fulfilment of pledges made at the Paris donors' conference of 17 December 2007 to mobilize donors to provide financial support to the Palestinian Authority to enable it to build a prosperous and viable Palestinian State and, in the meantime, to also provide assistance to alleviate the socio-economic and humanitarian crisis being faced by the Palestinian people, and acknowledging the contribution of the Palestinian-European Mechanism for the Management of Socio-Economic Aid of the European Commission in this regard,

Welcoming also the convening of the Bethlehem Conference on Private-Sector Investment from 21 to 23 May 2008, aimed at promoting an enabling environment for Palestinian private-sector growth and development,

Recognizing the efforts being undertaken by the Palestinian Authority, with international support, to rebuild, reform and strengthen its damaged institutions, and emphasizing the need to preserve the Palestinian institutions and infrastructure,

Welcoming the outcome of the Berlin Conference in Support of Palestinian Civil Security and the Rule of Law, held on 24 June 2008, and calling for its speedy implementation,

Welcoming also the progress observed in Jenin, and calling upon the parties to continue cooperation benefiting both Palestinians and Israelis, in particular for promoting security and building confidence, and expressing the hope that such progress will be extended to other major population centres,

Expressing its concern over the negative developments that have continued to occur in the Occupied Palestinian Territory, including East Jerusalem, including the large number of deaths and injuries, mostly among Palestinian civilians, the acts of violence and brutality committed against Palestinian civilians by Israeli settlers in the West Bank, the widespread destruction of public and private Palestinian property and infrastructure, the internal displacement of civilians and the serious deterioration of the socio-economic and humanitarian conditions of the Palestinian people,

Expressing its grave concern over continuing military actions in the Occupied Palestinian Territory and the reoccupation of Palestinian population centres by the Israeli occupying forces, and emphasizing in this regard the need for the implementation by both sides of the Sharm el-Sheikh understandings,

Taking note of the calm prevailing between the Gaza Strip and southern Israel since June 2008, and calling for its continued respect by both sides,

Emphasizing the importance of the safety and well-being of all civilians in the whole Middle East region, and condemning all acts of violence and terror against civilians on both sides,

Expressing concern over the unlawful takeover of Palestinian Authority institutions in the Gaza Strip in June 2007, and calling for the restoration of the situation to that which existed prior to June 2007 and for the continuation of serious efforts for the resumption of dialogue and the restoration of Palestinian national unity,

Stressing the urgent need for sustained and active international involvement, including by the Quartet, to support both parties in advancing and accelerating the peace process negotiations between the parties for the achievement of a just, lasting and comprehensive peace settlement, on the basis of United Nations resolutions, the road map and the Arab Peace Initiative,

Acknowledging the efforts being undertaken by civil society to promote a peaceful settlement of the question of Palestine,

Taking note of the findings by the International Court of Justice, in its advisory opinion, including on the urgent necessity for the United Nations as a whole to redouble its efforts to bring the Israeli-Palestinian conflict, which continues to pose a threat to international peace and security, to a speedy conclusion, thereby establishing a just and lasting peace in the region,

Affirming once again the right of all States in the region to live in peace within secure and internationally recognized borders,

1. *Reaffirms* the necessity of achieving a peaceful settlement of the question of Palestine, the core of the Arab-Israeli conflict, in all its aspects, and of intensifying all efforts towards that end;

2. *Also reaffirms* its full support for the Middle East peace process, which began in Madrid, and the existing agreements between the Israeli and Palestinian sides, stresses the necessity for the establishment of a comprehensive, just and lasting peace in the Middle East, and welcomes in this regard the ongoing efforts of the Quartet and of the League of Arab States;

3. *Further reaffirms* the importance of the Arab Peace Initiative, adopted by the Council of the League of Arab States at its fourteenth session, and encourages continued serious efforts to follow up and promote the Initiative, including by the Ministerial Committee formed at the Riyadh summit in March 2007;

4. *Reaffirms* the importance of the international conference convened at Annapolis, and urges the parties to undertake, with the support of the Quartet and the international community, immediate and concrete steps in follow-up to their joint understanding, including through active and serious resumed bilateral negotiations;

5. *Calls upon* both parties to fulfil their obligations in respect of the implementation of the road map by taking immediate parallel and reciprocal steps in this regard;

6. *Calls upon* the parties themselves, with the support of the Quartet and other interested parties, to exert all efforts necessary to halt the deterioration of the situation and

to reverse all measures taken on the ground since 28 September 2000;

7. *Underscores* the need for the parties to take confidence-building measures aimed at improving the situation on the ground, promoting stability and fostering the peace process, including the need for the further release of prisoners;

8. *Stresses* the need for a speedy end to the reoccupation of Palestinian population centres, inter alia, by easing movement and access, including by the removal of checkpoints and other obstructions to movement, and the need for respect and preservation of the territorial unity, contiguity and integrity of all of the Occupied Palestinian Territory, including East Jerusalem;

9. *Also stresses* the need for an immediate and complete cessation of all acts of violence, including military attacks, destruction and acts of terror;

10. *Notes* the Israeli withdrawal in 2005 from within the Gaza Strip and parts of the northern West Bank and the dismantlement of the settlements therein as a step towards the implementation of the road map, and the need for the parties to resolve all remaining issues in the Gaza Strip;

11. *Reiterates* the need for the full implementation by both parties of the Agreement on Movement and Access and the Agreed Principles for the Rafah Crossing, of 15 November 2005, and the need, in specific, to allow for the opening of all crossings into and out of the Gaza Strip for humanitarian supplies, movement and access as well as for commercial flows, which are essential for improving the living conditions of the Palestinian people and ensuring the viability of the Palestinian economy;

12. *Calls upon* Israel, the occupying Power, to comply strictly with its obligations under international law, including international humanitarian law, and to cease all of its measures that are contrary to international law and unilateral actions in the Occupied Palestinian Territory, including East Jerusalem, that are aimed at altering the character, status and demographic composition of the Territory, including via the de facto annexation of land, and thus at prejudging the final outcome of peace negotiations;

13. *Demands*, accordingly, that Israel, the occupying Power, comply with its legal obligations under international law, as mentioned in the advisory opinion and as demanded in resolutions ES-10/13 of 21 October 2003 and ES-10/15 and, inter alia, that it immediately cease its construction of the wall in the Occupied Palestinian Territory, including East Jerusalem, and calls upon all States Members of the United Nations to comply with their legal obligations, as mentioned in the advisory opinion;

14. *Reiterates its demand* for the complete cessation of all Israeli settlement activities in the Occupied Palestinian Territory, including East Jerusalem, and in the occupied Syrian Golan, and calls for the full implementation of the relevant Security Council resolutions;

15. *Reaffirms its commitment*, in accordance with international law, to the two-State solution of Israel and Palestine, living side by side in peace and security within recognized borders, based on the pre-1967 borders;

16. *Stresses* the need for:

(a) The withdrawal of Israel from the Palestinian territory occupied since 1967, including East Jerusalem;

(b) The realization of the inalienable rights of the Palestinian people, primarily the right to self-determination and the right to their independent State;

17. *Also stresses* the need for justly resolving the problem of Palestine refugees in conformity with its resolution 194(III) of 11 December 1948;

18. *Calls upon* the parties to accelerate direct peace negotiations towards the conclusion of a final peaceful settlement on the basis of relevant United Nations resolutions, especially of the Security Council, the terms of reference of the Madrid Conference, the road map and the Arab Peace Initiative;

19. *Urges* Member States to expedite the provision of economic, humanitarian and technical assistance to the Palestinian people and the Palestinian Authority during this critical period to help to alleviate the humanitarian crisis being faced by the Palestinian people, particularly in the Gaza Strip, to rehabilitate the Palestinian economy and infrastructure and to support the rebuilding, restructuring and reform of Palestinian institutions;

20. *Welcomes*, in this regard, the continuing efforts of the Quartet's Special Representative, Tony Blair, to strengthen Palestinian institutions, promote Palestinian economic development and mobilize international donor support;

21. *Requests* the Secretary-General to continue his efforts with the parties concerned, and in consultation with the Security Council, towards the attainment of a peaceful settlement of the question of Palestine and the promotion of peace in the region and to submit to the General Assembly at its sixty-fourth session a report on these efforts and on developments on this matter.

RECORDED VOTE ON RESOLUTION 63/29:

In favour: Afghanistan, Albania, Algeria, Andorra, Angola, Antigua and Barbuda, Argentina, Armenia, Austria, Azerbaijan, Bahamas, Bahrain, Bangladesh, Barbados, Belarus, Belgium, Benin, Bhutan, Bolivia, Bosnia and Herzegovina, Botswana, Brazil, Brunei Darussalam, Bulgaria, Burundi, Cambodia, Cape Verde, Central African Republic, Chile, China, Colombia, Comoros, Congo, Costa Rica, Côte d'Ivoire, Croatia, Cuba, Cyprus, Czech Republic, Democratic People's Republic of Korea, Denmark, Djibouti, Dominica, Dominican Republic, Ecuador, Egypt, El Salvador, Eritrea, Estonia, Ethiopia, Fiji, Finland, France, Gabon, Gambia, Georgia, Germany, Ghana, Greece, Grenada, Guatemala, Guinea, Guinea-Bissau, Guyana, Haiti, Honduras, Hungary, Iceland, India, Indonesia, Iran, Iraq, Ireland, Italy, Jamaica, Japan, Jordan, Kazakhstan, Kenya, Kuwait, Kyrgyzstan, Lao People's Democratic Republic, Latvia, Lebanon, Lesotho, Liberia, Libyan Arab Jamahiriya, Liechtenstein, Lithuania, Luxembourg, Malaysia, Maldives, Mali, Malta, Mauritania, Mauritius, Mexico, Moldova, Monaco, Mongolia, Montenegro, Morocco, Mozambique, Myanmar, Namibia, Nepal, Netherlands, New Zealand, Nicaragua, Nigeria, Norway, Oman, Pakistan, Panama, Papua New Guinea, Paraguay, Peru, Philippines, Poland, Portugal, Qatar, Republic of Korea, Romania, Russian Federation, Saint Lucia, Saint Vincent and the Grenadines, Samoa, San Marino, Saudi Arabia, Senegal, Serbia, Singapore, Slovakia, Slovenia, Solomon Islands, Somalia, South Africa, Spain, Sri Lanka, Sudan, Suriname, Swaziland, Sweden, Switzerland, Syrian Arab Republic, Tajikistan, Thailand, The former Yugoslav Republic of Macedonia, Timor-Leste, Togo, Trinidad and Tobago, Tunisia, Turkey, Uganda, Ukraine,

United Arab Emirates, United Kingdom, Uruguay, Uzbekistan, Venezuela, Viet Nam, Yemen, Zambia, Zimbabwe.

Against: Australia, Israel, Marshall Islands, Micronesia, Nauru, Palau, United States.

Abstaining: Cameroon, Canada, Tonga.

In resolution 63/26 (see p. 516) adopted on the same day, the Assembly requested the Committee on Palestinian Rights to support the Middle East peace process, and in **resolution 63/165** (see p. 790), the Assembly reaffirmed the right of the Palestinian people to self-determination, including the right to their independent State of Palestine. By **decision 63/552** of 24 December, the Assembly decided that the agenda items on the situation in the Middle East and on the Question of Palestine would remain for consideration during its resumed (2009) sixty-third session.

Fatah-Hamas relations

Communication. On 25 March [S/2008/201], Yemen informed the Security Council of its initiative regarding the resumption of dialogue between the two Palestinian movements, Fatah and Hamas, which had signed, on 23 March, the Sana'a Declaration to restart negotiations, in affirmation of the unity of the territory and the people of the Palestinian homeland and of a single authority. Yemen's initiative, the elements of which were annexed to its letter, foresaw a restoration of the status quo ante of 13 June 2007 in Gaza, adherence to commitments made by the PLO, and the holding of early presidential and parliamentary elections. The resumption of dialogue should be founded on the 2005 Cairo Agreement and the Agreement on Palestinian National Reconciliation (Mecca, Saudi Arabia, February 2007) [YUN 2007, p. 437]; on the basis that the Palestinian people were an indivisible whole, and that the PA was composed of an elected President and Parliament and an executive authority in the form of a Government of national unity; and on a commitment to Palestinian legitimacy in all its elements. All parties were to affirm respect for and commitment to the Palestinian constitution and law, and national security services loyal to the Government. A coalition Government of national unity would be formed, in which all factions were represented according to the number of seats each held in Parliament. Palestinian institutions should include all factions without distinction and be under the control of the supreme authority and of the national unity Government. LAS would form a committee composed of Egypt, Jordan, Saudi Arabia and the Syrian Arab Republic, whose task would be to implement those points; Yemen was ready to participate in that committee should it be asked.

Security Council consideration. On 27 June [meeting 5927], the Director of the Asia and Pacific Division in the Department of Political Affairs brought the Security Council's attention to President Abbas' 5 June statement, made after extensive internal consultations, calling for a comprehensive national dialogue in order to implement the proposed initiative by the President of Yemen on Palestinian reunification (see above). It was hoped that such dialogue could support the calm in Gaza and the sustained reopening of the crossings, and make progress towards the goal of reunifying Gaza and the West Bank within the framework of the legitimate PA.

Briefing the Council on 20 August [meeting 5963], the Under-Secretary-General for Political Affairs, Mr. Pascoe, stated that there had been a major increase in Palestinian internal violence, contributing to a total of 43 Palestinians killed and 366 injured. The rise in internal Palestinian violence stemmed from an incident on 25 July in which five Hamas members and a child were killed in a beachside bombing in Gaza. Hamas claimed that the Fatah-affiliated Hillis clan was sheltering the perpetrators and attacked the clan's stronghold in eastern Gaza City, the last bastion of the Fatah military presence in the Gaza Strip. The ensuing violence left 10 members of the Hillis family dead, with dozens of clan members fleeing to the West Bank through Israel. Members of the Hillis family were detained by Hamas along with dozens of Fatah and other activists, and there had been allegations of torture committed by Hamas.

Following the 25 July bombing, Hamas initiated a campaign for total control of the Gaza Strip. It raided and closed down over 200 community-based organizations in Gaza, which disrupted activities involving thousands of beneficiaries. Eighty organizations reopened following Hamas's review of their operations. Hamas also seized control of the last remaining PA institutions within the Gaza Strip, notably the Governorates, which continued to report to President Abbas and which Hamas had previously recognized as legitimate PA structures. Three Governors had been detained by Hamas, and two of them were still in prison. Those actions, Mr. Pascoe said, severely prejudiced the prospects for Palestinian reunification within the framework of the legitimate PA and raised concern at the potential consequences for UN operations in Gaza.

In reaction to Hamas' actions in Gaza, Palestinian security forces in the West Bank arrested dozens of Hamas activists, most of whom were later freed on President Abbas' orders. They also closed a number of Hamas-linked institutions in the West Bank. Mr. Pascoe called on both Hamas and the PA to release detainees seized as a result of the recent violence, as a first step in a process leading to reconciliation and the reunification of Gaza and the West Bank under the PA.

Hamas' actions compounded the problems facing Gazans, divorcing Palestinian institutions from the PA itself and interrupting basic service delivery, Mr. Serry, Special Coordinator for the Middle East Peace Process reported to the Council on 18 September [meeting 5974]. Following Hamas' decision to replace head and deputy head teachers with Hamas-affiliated staff and to reallocate thousands of teachers to new schools, a teachers' strike led to major disruptions in the education sector since the start of the new academic year on 24 August. On 30 August, health workers joined the strike after the dismissal of a number of employees, forcing hospitals to postpone elective surgery and many health centres to close or suspend services. There were reports of Hamas marching doctors to their hospitals at gunpoint to ensure continuity of critical services. Despite the efforts of Mr. Serry's office to resolve the crisis for the sake of the welfare of the population, Hamas' unwillingness to restore the status ante quo was blocking a resolution of the conflict.

On 25 November [meeting 6022], Mr. Pascoe told the Security Council that Palestinians remained divided. Further to its reconciliation proposal to the Palestinian factions, Egypt had invited them to a meeting in Cairo on 9 November, but Hamas did not attend. The Secretary-General called on Hamas and all Palestinian factions to work urgently to reunify the Gaza Strip and West Bank within the PA framework and in a manner that allowed the peace process to move forward. However, rhetoric between Hamas and Fatah intensified. The PLO Central Committee announced its election of Mahmoud Abbas as President of the State of Palestine, but the Hamas leadership rejected that move.

On 18 December [meeting 6049], Mr. Serry reported to the Council that Hamas leader Ismail Haniyeh continued to challenge the continuation in office of President Abbas pending a resolution of the internal divide. While calling for Palestinian reunification, he rejected agreements signed and commitments undertaken by the PLO. President Abbas publicly raised the possibility of calling elections if reconciliation was not achieved. Foreign Ministers of LAS, meeting in Cairo on 26 November, called on President Abbas to continue his mandate until such time as Palestinian reconciliation was possible and presidential and legislative elections could be held simultaneously in both the Gaza Strip and the West Bank. They affirmed basic terms for such reunification and their continued support for efforts to achieve it, so as to reunite Gaza and the West Bank. The Quartet noted that position, stressing that restoring Palestinian unity would be an important step forward. Mr. Serry urged Hamas to respond positively to those exhortations, as it could not be in the interests of the Palestinian people for essential cornerstones of Palestinian legitimacy and national aspirations to be challenged.

Aid shipment to Gaza

Communication. On 2 December [S/2008/754], the Libyan Arab Jamahiriya requested a Security Council emergency meeting to consider an incident on 1 December involving the Libyan ship *Al-Marwa*, which it said had been heading for Gaza to deliver humanitarian aid, when two Israeli gunboats forced it to turn back. Libya requested the Council to act urgently to allow the ship to enter the port of Gaza and unload its cargo. In a letter on the same date [S/2008/753], Libya provided details on its cargo which, it affirmed, contained only foodstuffs and medicines, and invited the United Nations and the International Red Cross to inspect the ship to verify that it was on a humanitarian mission.

Security Council consideration. In response to Libya's request, the Security Council met on 3 December [meeting 6030]. Opening the Council debate, Libya claimed that Israel's action amounted to piracy under article 101 of the 1982 United Nations Convention on the Law of the Sea [YUN 1982, p. 178], and called on the Council to ensure Israel's compliance with the Convention.

Israel, on the other hand, charged that Libya, since its election to the Council, had prevented any initiative on Middle East issues that contradicted its own narrow agenda. If Libya were genuinely interested in supporting peace and security in the Middle East, it would have condemned Hamas when it brutally took control of the Gaza Strip in a violent coup against the moderate PA, as well as the constant barrage of thousands of rockets and mortars on Israeli towns and villages by terrorists, Iran and the Syrian Arab Republic for harbouring, supporting and training terrorists, and the ongoing transfer of sophisticated weapons and financial resources to terrorist groups.

The United States said that those seeking to provide assistance to the people of Gaza could work through existing institutions and UN programmes and non-provocative and non-confrontational mechanisms. Direct delivery by sea was neither appropriate nor responsible under the circumstances.

The Council did not take any action on Libya's request.

Israeli settlements

The issue of Israeli settlements in the West Bank, including East Jerusalem, remained central to the question of the Occupied Palestinian Territory, as it did to the peace negotiations. The road map and the Annapolis joint statement committed Israel to dismantle all settlement outposts erected since 2001 and to freeze—in a manner consistent with the 2001 report of the Sharm el-Sheikh Fact-Finding Committee (Mitchell Report) [YUN 2001, p. 409]—all settlement activity including natural growth.

Communications. Throughout the year, Palestine brought to the attention of the Secretary-General and the Security Council President the ongoing construction and expansion of Israeli settlements in the Occupied Palestinian Territory, especially in and around East Jerusalem [A/ES-10/416-S/2008/170, A/ES-10/419-S/2008/365, A/ES-10/422-S/2008/513, A/ES-10/423-S/2008/629, A/ES-10/424-S/2008/667, A/ES-10/427-S/2008/768]. Cuba, on behalf of NAM [S/2008/396], and Pakistan [S/2008/440], on behalf of the Organization of the Islamic Conference, called on the Security Council to address the critical settlements issue. The Special Rapporteur on the situation of human rights in the Palestinian territory [A/63/326] also dealt with the issue of Israeli settlements in the Palestinian territory and their impact on the enjoyment of human rights by the Palestinians.

Report of Secretary-General. In response to General Assembly resolution 62/108 [YUN 2007, p. 458], the Secretary-General submitted a November report [A/63/519], prepared by the Office of the United Nations High Commissioner for Human Rights (OHCHR), on the implementation of that resolution, especially the continuation of Israeli settlements activities in the occupied territories, covering the period from January to August 2008.

According to the Israeli Ministry of the Interior, the settler population in the West Bank, excluding East Jerusalem, had increased by 5.1 per cent from 268,163 in January 2007 to 282,362 in January 2008. According to UN sources, almost 40 per cent of the West Bank was taken up by Israeli infrastructure associated with the settlements, including roads, barriers, buffer zones and military bases.

Construction in the settlements had increased in 2008 by a factor of 1.8, in comparison with the same period in 2007; from January to May 2008, 433 new housing units were initiated, compared to just 240 units from January to May 2007. As at August 2008, more than 1,000 new buildings with approximately 2,600 housing units were being constructed in the settlements, about 55 per cent of which were located to the east of the separation wall. The number of tenders for construction in the settlements increased by 540 per cent in 2008 (417 housing units, compared with 65 in 2007), and in East Jerusalem for the construction of 1,761 housing units, up from 46 in 2007. Furthermore, 125 new structures were added to existing outputs, including 30 permanent houses.

Settlements, including their municipal boundaries, took up some 9 per cent of the total West Bank territory. Additional areas for agricultural and industrial use, as well as for future settlement expansion and military purposes, were included within the settlement regional jurisdiction, all of which were prohibited to Palestinians. Despite Israel's claim that the internal closure system within the West Bank was imposed on Palestinian residents for security purposes, most of those restrictions on movement were largely for the protection of Israeli settlers and settlements and to provide settlers with unobstructed travel between settlements and Israel itself; none of the restrictions on freedom of movement applied to Israeli settlers or Israeli citizens.

The Palestinians' right to an adequate standard of living were negatively affected by the settlements and the associated security regime and repeated instances of settler violence, as was their right to own property, since the building of settlements entailed expropriation and destruction of private Palestinian lands. It was estimated that 33 per cent of settlement areas was private Palestinian land.

In view of the worsening human rights situation in the occupied territory, the protection of both Palestinian and Israeli civilians required action by all parties and the international community, according to the Secretary-General. Israel should abide by its commitments, as stated in the road map and reiterated in the Annapolis Joint Statement, to immediately dismantle settlement outposts erected since March 2001 and to freeze all settlement activity, including natural growth. It should also halt attacks by settlers and ensure proper investigation and redress for the victims of such violence. The General Assembly and the international community should promote implementation of its decisions, resolutions and recommendations and those of the Security Council, the ICJ and UN human rights mechanisms.

GENERAL ASSEMBLY ACTION

On 5 December [meeting 64], the General Assembly, on the recommendation of the Fourth (Special Political and Decolonization) Committee [A/63/401], adopted **resolution 63/97** by recorded vote (171-6-2) [agenda item 30].

Israeli settlements in the Occupied Palestinian Territory, including East Jerusalem, and the occupied Syrian Golan

The General Assembly,

Guided by the principles of the Charter of the United Nations, and affirming the inadmissibility of the acquisition of territory by force,

Recalling its relevant resolutions, including resolution 62/108 of 17 December 2007, as well as those resolutions adopted at its tenth emergency special session,

Recalling also relevant Security Council resolutions, including resolutions 242(1967) of 22 November 1967, 446(1979) of 22 March 1979, 465(1980) of 1 March 1980, 476(1980) of 30 June 1980, 478(1980) of 20 August 1980, 497(1981) of 17 December 1981 and 904(1994) of 18 March 1994,

Reaffirming the applicability of the Geneva Convention relative to the Protection of Civilian Persons in Time of War, of 12 August 1949, to the Occupied Palestinian Territory, including East Jerusalem, and to the occupied Syrian Golan,

Considering that the transfer by the occupying Power of parts of its own civilian population into the territory it occupies constitutes a breach of the Fourth Geneva Convention and relevant provisions of customary law, including those codified in Additional Protocol I to the four Geneva Conventions,

Recalling the advisory opinion rendered on 9 July 2004 by the International Court of Justice on the *Legal Consequences of the Construction of a Wall in the Occupied Palestinian Territory*, and recalling also General Assembly resolutions ES-10/15 of 20 July 2004 and ES-10/17 of 15 December 2006,

Noting that the International Court of Justice concluded that "the Israeli settlements in the Occupied Palestinian Territory (including East Jerusalem) have been established in breach of international law",

Taking note of the recent report of the Special Rapporteur of the Human Rights Council on the situation of human rights in the Palestinian territories occupied by Israel since 1967,

Recalling the Declaration of Principles on Interim Self-Government Arrangements of 13 September 1993 and the subsequent implementation agreements between the Palestinian and Israeli sides,

Recalling also the Quartet road map to a permanent two-State solution to the Israeli-Palestinian conflict, and noting specifically its call for a freeze on all settlement activity,

Aware that Israeli settlement activities involve, inter alia, the transfer of nationals of the occupying Power into the occupied territories, the confiscation of land, the exploitation of natural resources and other actions against the Palestinian civilian population that are contrary to international law,

Bearing in mind the detrimental impact of Israeli settlement policies, decisions and activities on efforts to achieve peace in the Middle East,

Expressing grave concern about the continuation by Israel, the occupying Power, of settlement activities in the Occupied Palestinian Territory, in violation of international humanitarian law, relevant United Nations resolutions and the agreements reached between the parties, and concerned particularly about Israel's construction and expansion of settlements in and around Occupied East Jerusalem, including its so-called E-1 plan that aims to connect its illegal settlements around and further isolate Occupied East Jerusalem, and in the Jordan Valley,

Expressing grave concern also about the continuing unlawful construction by Israel of the wall inside the Occupied Palestinian Territory, including in and around East Jerusalem, and expressing its concern in particular about the route of the wall in departure from the Armistice Line of 1949, which is causing humanitarian hardship and a serious decline of socio-economic conditions for the Palestinian people, is fragmenting the territorial contiguity of the Territory, and could prejudge future negotiations and make the two-State solution physically impossible to implement,

Deeply concerned that the wall's route has been traced in such a way as to include the great majority of the Israeli settlements in the Occupied Palestinian Territory, including East Jerusalem,

Deploring settlement activities in the Occupied Palestinian Territory, including East Jerusalem, and in the occupied Syrian Golan and any activities involving the confiscation of land, the disruption of the livelihood of protected persons and the de facto annexation of land,

Recalling the need to end all acts of violence, including acts of terror, provocation, incitement and destruction,

Gravely concerned about the rising incidents of violence by illegal armed Israeli settlers in the Occupied Palestinian Territory against Palestinian civilians and their properties and agricultural lands,

Noting the Israeli withdrawal from within the Gaza Strip and parts of the northern West Bank and the importance of the dismantlement of the settlements therein as a step towards the implementation of the road map,

Taking note of the relevant reports of the Secretary-General,

Taking note also of the special meeting of the Security Council convened on 26 September 2008,

1. *Reaffirms* that the Israeli settlements in the Palestinian territory, including East Jerusalem, and in the occupied Syrian Golan are illegal and an obstacle to peace and economic and social development;

2. *Calls upon* Israel to accept the de jure applicability of the Geneva Convention relative to the Protection of Civilian Persons in Time of War, of 12 August 1949, to the Occupied Palestinian Territory, including East Jerusalem, and to the occupied Syrian Golan and to abide scrupulously by the provisions of the Convention, in particular article 49;

3. *Notes* the Israeli withdrawal from within the Gaza Strip and parts of the northern West Bank and the importance of the dismantlement of the settlements therein as a step towards the implementation of the road map and the need for the parties to speedily resolve all remaining issues in the Gaza Strip;

4. *Calls upon* Israel, the occupying Power, to comply strictly with its obligations under international law, including international humanitarian law, with respect to the alteration of the character, status and demographic composition of the Occupied Palestinian Territory, including East Jerusalem;

5. *Reiterates its demand* for the immediate and complete cessation of all Israeli settlement activities in all of the Occupied Palestinian Territory, including East Jerusalem, and in the occupied Syrian Golan, and calls in this regard for the full implementation of the relevant Security Council resolutions, including resolution 465(1980);

6. *Demands* that Israel, the occupying Power, comply with its legal obligations, as mentioned in the advisory opinion rendered on 9 July 2004 by the International Court of Justice;

7. *Reiterates its calls for* the prevention of all acts of violence and harassment by Israeli settlers, especially against

Palestinian civilians and their properties and agricultural lands, and stresses the need for the implementation of Security Council resolution 904(1994), in which the Council called upon Israel, the occupying Power, to continue to take and implement measures, including confiscation of arms, aimed at preventing illegal acts of violence by Israeli settlers, and called for measures to be taken to guarantee the safety and protection of the Palestinian civilians in the occupied territory;

8. *Requests* the Secretary-General to report to the General Assembly at its sixty-fourth session on the implementation of the present resolution.

RECORDED VOTE ON RESOLUTION 63/97:

In favour: Afghanistan, Albania, Algeria, Andorra, Angola, Antigua and Barbuda, Argentina, Armenia, Australia, Austria, Azerbaijan, Bahamas, Bahrain, Bangladesh, Barbados, Belarus, Belgium, Belize, Benin, Bhutan, Bolivia, Bosnia and Herzegovina, Botswana, Brazil, Brunei Darussalam, Bulgaria, Burkina Faso, Burundi, Cambodia, Canada, Cape Verde, Central African Republic, Chile, China, Colombia, Comoros, Congo, Costa Rica, Croatia, Cuba, Cyprus, Czech Republic, Democratic People's Republic of Korea, Denmark, Djibouti, Dominica, Dominican Republic, Ecuador, Egypt, El Salvador, Eritrea, Estonia, Ethiopia, Finland, France, Gabon, Georgia, Germany, Ghana, Greece, Grenada, Guatemala, Guinea, Guinea-Bissau, Guyana, Haiti, Honduras, Hungary, Iceland, India, Indonesia, Iran, Iraq, Ireland, Italy, Jamaica, Japan, Jordan, Kazakhstan, Kenya, Kuwait, Kyrgyzstan, Lao People's Democratic Republic, Latvia, Lebanon, Lesotho, Liberia, Libyan Arab Jamahiriya, Liechtenstein, Lithuania, Luxembourg, Malawi, Malaysia, Maldives, Mali, Malta, Mauritania, Mauritius, Mexico, Monaco, Mongolia, Montenegro, Morocco, Mozambique, Myanmar, Namibia, Nepal, Netherlands, New Zealand, Nicaragua, Niger, Nigeria, Norway, Oman, Pakistan, Panama, Papua New Guinea, Paraguay, Peru, Philippines, Poland, Portugal, Qatar, Republic of Korea, Moldova, Romania, Russian Federation, Saint Lucia, Saint Vincent and the Grenadines, Samoa, San Marino, Sao Tome and Principe, Saudi Arabia, Senegal, Serbia, Singapore, Slovakia, Slovenia, Solomon Islands, South Africa, Spain, Sri Lanka, Sudan, Suriname, Swaziland, Sweden, Switzerland, Syrian Arab Republic, Tajikistan, Thailand, The former Yugoslav Republic of Macedonia, Timor-Leste, Togo, Trinidad and Tobago, Tunisia, Turkey, Turkmenistan, Tuvalu, Uganda, Ukraine, United Arab Emirates, United Kingdom, United Republic of Tanzania, Uruguay, Uzbekistan, Vanuatu, Venezuela, Viet Nam, Yemen, Zambia, Zimbabwe.

Against: Israel, Marshall Islands, Micronesia, Nauru, Palau, United States.

Abstaining: Cameroon, Côte d'Ivoire.

Communications. On 5 December [S/2008/765], Egypt, as Chair of the Arab Group, requested an urgent meeting of the Security Council to address the recent escalation of Israeli settler violence, harassment, intimidation and provocation against Palestinian civilians, their properties and agricultural lands. Of particular concern was the rise of tensions in Al-Khalil (Hebron). On the same date [A/ES-10/427-S/2008/768], Palestine reported that Israeli settler terrorism against Palestinian civilians had intensified during recent weeks, especially in Hebron.

Jerusalem

East Jerusalem, where most of the city's Arab population lived, remained one of the most sensitive issues in the Middle East peace process and a focal point for the United Nations. Continued settlement activities in East Jerusalem, like those throughout the West Bank, raised the concern of the Secretary-General and the Human Rights Council, as well as others. The Human Rights Council, by resolution 7/18 of 27 March [A/HRC/7/78] (see p. 894), deplored Israel's announcement of the construction of new housing units in East Jerusalem, as they undermined the peace process and the creation of a contiguous, sovereign and independent Palestinian State, and violated international law and pledges made by Israel at the Annapolis Conference. The Special Committee on Israeli Practices reported [A/63/273] (see p. 502) that it had heard detailed testimony, supported by maps and photographs, on an excavation project in the Arab neighbourhood of Silwan in East Jerusalem, a few hundred metres from Al-Haram Al-Sharif/Temple Mount, which troubled the Palestinian population and archaeological experts. The Special Rapporteur on the situation of human rights in the occupied Palestinian territories, in an August report [A/63/326] (see p. 896), stated that the expansion of settlements had been particularly notable in East Jerusalem, where 1,800 new housing units had been approved. That expansion, accompanied by expulsions of Palestinians, furthered the Israeli policy of making East Jerusalem into a place of majority Jewish residence. In addition, he said, the presence of 250,000 Jews living illegally in East Jerusalem was being overlooked.

Report of Secretary-General. On 29 October [A/63/361], the Secretary-General reported that four Member States (Colombia, Ecuador, Mexico, Syria) had replied to his request for information on steps taken or envisaged to implement General Assembly resolution 62/84 [YUN 2007, p. 447], which addressed the transfer by some States of their diplomatic missions to Jerusalem, in violation of Security Council resolution 478(1980) [YUN 1980, p. 426].

GENERAL ASSEMBLY ACTION

On 26 November [meeting 60], the General Assembly adopted **resolution 63/30** [draft: A/63/L.36 & Add.1] by recorded vote (163-6-6) [agenda item 15].

Jerusalem

The General Assembly,

Recalling its resolution 181(II) of 29 November 1947, in particular its provisions regarding the City of Jerusalem,

Recalling also its resolution 36/120 E of 10 December 1981 and all subsequent resolutions, including resolution 56/31 of 3 December 2001, in which it, inter alia, determined that all legislative and administrative measures and actions taken by Israel, the occupying Power, which have altered or purported to alter the character and status of the Holy City of Jerusalem, in particular the so-called "Basic Law" on Jerusalem and the proclamation of Jerusalem as the capital of Israel, were null and void and must be rescinded forthwith,

Recalling further the Security Council resolutions relevant to Jerusalem, including resolution 478(1980) of 20 August 1980, in which the Council, inter alia, decided not to recognize the "Basic Law" on Jerusalem,

Recalling the advisory opinion rendered on 9 July 2004 by the International Court of Justice on the *Legal Consequences of the Construction of a Wall in the Occupied Palestinian Territory*, and recalling resolution ES-10/15 of 20 July 2004,

Expressing its grave concern about any action taken by anybody, governmental or non-governmental, in violation of the above-mentioned resolutions,

Expressing its grave concern in particular about the continuation by Israel, the occupying Power, of illegal settlement activities, including the so-called E-1 plan, its construction of the wall in and around East Jerusalem, its restrictions on access to and residence in East Jerusalem, and the further isolation of the city from the rest of the Occupied Palestinian Territory, which is having a detrimental effect on the lives of Palestinians and could prejudge a final status agreement on Jerusalem,

Reaffirming that the international community, through the United Nations, has a legitimate interest in the question of the City of Jerusalem and the protection of the unique spiritual, religious and cultural dimensions of the city, as foreseen in relevant United Nations resolutions on this matter,

Having considered the report of the Secretary-General,

1. *Reiterates its determination* that any actions taken by Israel, the occupying Power, to impose its laws, jurisdiction and administration on the Holy City of Jerusalem are illegal and therefore null and void and have no validity whatsoever, and calls upon Israel to cease all such illegal and unilateral measures;

2. *Stresses* that a comprehensive, just and lasting solution to the question of the City of Jerusalem should take into account the legitimate concerns of both the Palestinian and Israeli sides and should include internationally guaranteed provisions to ensure the freedom of religion and of conscience of its inhabitants, as well as permanent, free and unhindered access to the holy places by the people of all religions and nationalities;

3. *Requests* the Secretary-General to report to the General Assembly at its sixty-fourth session on the implementation of the present resolution.

RECORDED VOTE ON RESOLUTION 63/30:

In favour: Afghanistan, Albania, Algeria, Andorra, Angola, Antigua and Barbuda, Argentina, Armenia, Austria, Azerbaijan, Bahamas, Bahrain, Bangladesh, Barbados, Belarus, Belgium, Belize, Benin, Bhutan, Bolivia, Bosnia and Herzegovina, Botswana, Brazil, Brunei Darussalam, Bulgaria, Burundi, Cambodia, Canada, Cape Verde, Central African Republic, Chile, China, Colombia, Comoros, Congo, Costa Rica, Croatia, Cuba, Cyprus, Czech Republic, Democratic People's Republic of Korea, Denmark, Djibouti, Dominica, Dominican Republic, Ecuador, Egypt, El Salvador, Eritrea, Estonia, Ethiopia, Finland, France, Gabon, Gambia, Georgia, Germany, Ghana, Greece, Grenada, Guatemala, Guinea, Guinea-Bissau, Guyana, Honduras, Hungary, Iceland, India, Indonesia, Iran, Iraq, Ireland, Italy, Jamaica, Japan, Jordan, Kazakhstan, Kenya, Kuwait, Kyrgyzstan, Lao People's Democratic Republic, Latvia, Lebanon, Lesotho, Liberia, Libyan Arab Jamahiriya, Liechtenstein, Lithuania, Luxembourg, Malaysia, Maldives, Mali, Malta, Mauritania, Mauritius, Mexico, Moldova, Monaco, Mongolia, Montenegro, Morocco, Mozambique, Myanmar, Namibia, Nepal, Netherlands, New Zealand, Nicaragua, Nigeria, Norway, Oman, Pakistan, Panama, Papua New Guinea, Paraguay, Peru, Philippines, Poland, Portugal, Qatar, Republic of Korea, Romania, Russian Federation, Saint Lucia, Saint Vincent and the Grenadines, Samoa, San Marino, Saudi Arabia, Senegal, Serbia, Singapore, Slovakia, Slovenia, Solomon Islands, Somalia, South Africa, Spain, Sri Lanka, Sudan, Suriname, Swaziland, Sweden, Switzerland, Syrian Arab Republic, Tajikistan, Thailand, The former Yugoslav Republic of Macedonia, Timor-Leste, Togo, Trinidad and Tobago, Tunisia, Turkey, Uganda, Ukraine, United Arab Emirates, United Kingdom, Uruguay, Uzbekistan, Venezuela, Viet Nam, Yemen, Zambia, Zimbabwe.

Against: Israel, Marshall Islands, Micronesia, Nauru, Palau, United States.

Abstaining: Australia, Cameroon, Côte d'Ivoire, Fiji, Haiti, Tonga.

Other aspects

Special Committee to Investigate Israeli Practices Affecting Human Rights

In response to General Assembly resolution 62/106 [YUN 2007, p. 455], the Special Committee to Investigate Israeli Practices Affecting the Human Rights of the Palestinian People and Other Arabs of the Occupied Territories (Special Committee on Israeli Practices), established by Assembly resolution 2443(XXIII) [YUN 1968, p. 555], reported for the fortieth time on the human rights situation in the territories it considered occupied by Israel—the Syrian Arab Golan, and the occupied Palestinian territory of the West Bank, East Jerusalem and the Gaza Strip [A/63/273].

The report was based on information gathered during the Special Committee's mission to the Middle East (23 June–5 July), visiting Egypt, Jordan and the Syrian Arab Republic, where it heard the testimony of 33 witnesses. As in previous years, the Committee was not authorized by Israel to visit the occupied territories, as had been the case since 1968.

The Special Committee noted once again the serious deterioration of the human rights situation in the occupied territories due to the Israeli occupation and the population's despondency in view of the violations of their basic human rights. Palestinians continued to suffer from Israeli military action that resulted in considerable loss of life and injuries and damage to property and infrastructure. They were subjected to collective punishment and had seen their rights violated with an ever-decreasing possibility to seek effective redress. The construction of the separation wall in the West Bank and East Jerusalem was ongoing in defiance of the 2004 ICJ Advisory Opinion [YUN 2004, p. 452]. Settlements and bypass roads continued to expand, while restrictions on the freedom of movement intensified, severely affecting the enjoyment of virtually all human rights by the Palestinian population. The situation in the Gaza Strip was particularly serious, despite the hope resulting from the 19 June ceasefire (see p. 484). The Committee also noted that the shift from development to humanitarian assistance had increased even further.

The deterioration of the human rights situation could be largely attributed to Israeli practices, the Committee concluded. Israel and the international community had an obligation to ensure the realization of the human rights of the Palestinian people—including the population of Gaza—not as a matter of humanitarian charity, but as an obligation.

The Special Committee reiterated some of its recommendations made in 2007 [YU 2007, p. 452], calling on the Assembly to urgently consider all means to fulfil its responsibilities regarding all aspects of the Palestine question until it was resolved in conformity with UN resolutions and norms of international law and until the inalienable rights of the Palestinians were fully realized. The Assembly should urge the Security Council to ensure implementation of the 2004 ICJ Advisory Opinion and Assembly resolution ES-10/15, adopted at the tenth emergency special session on Palestine [YUN 2004, p. 465], requesting Israel to dismantle the segments of the separation wall and make reparations for the damage arising from its construction. The Council should consider sanctions against Israel if it persisted in neglecting its international legal obligations, ensure that States were not assisting in the construction of the wall, and encourage Quartet members to fully implement the road map to achieve a comprehensive, just and lasting settlement.

Israel should recognize the applicability of the Fourth Geneva Convention in the Occupied Palestinian Territory, respect international law, cease its excessive use of force and the destruction of land, property, houses and infrastructure, and stop confiscating Palestinian land and expanding Jewish settlements. It should restore freedom of movement throughout the territory, end the closure and collective punishment of the people of Gaza, stop mass arrests and arbitrary detention, and guarantee those arrested a fair trial and detention conditions in keeping with international conventions. Israel should urgently implement its obligations set forth in the road map [YUN 2003, p. 464] and withdraw its military presence from the Occupied Palestinian Territory and its occupation of the Syrian Golan. Israel should also implement the recommendations of UN treaty bodies, the Special Representative of the Secretary-General for Children and Armed Conflict, and the High Commissioner for Human Rights. Furthermore, it should establish an independent and transparent system of accountability, ensuring prompt and impartial investigations.

For its part, the PA should abide by human rights law and international humanitarian law, aim to resolve the urgent human rights and humanitarian crisis in the territory, and fully restore the rule of law in areas under its control, as well as comply with the road map requirements.

The Special Committee urged civil society groups, and diplomatic, academic and research institutions to use their influence to make widely known the serious human rights and humanitarian situation of the Palestinians, as well as the human rights situation in the occupied Syrian Golan. It commended the efforts of Israeli NGOs made on behalf of Palestinian rights, and encouraged international and national media to provide broad and accurate coverage of the situation in the occupied territory, with a view to mobilizing international public opinion in favour of a just and lasting settlement.

Report of Secretary-General. On 5 November [A/63/518], the Secretary-General submitted a report by the Office of the United Nations High Commissioner for Human Rights (OHCHR) on the implementation of resolution 62/109 [YUN 2007, p. 453] on Israeli practices affecting the human rights of the Palestinian people in the Occupied Palestinian Territory, including East Jerusalem, covering the period from January to August 2008. The report addressed the policy of Israeli closures and severe restrictions, including their impact on the socio-economic situation in the Occupied Palestinian Territory, the separation wall and the destruction of property, and the conditions affecting Palestinian prisoners in Israel.

Claiming that it was necessary for its security, Israel continued to impose a comprehensive closure system, which consisted of a complex array of physical and administrative obstacles that had a severe and detrimental impact on the rights of the Palestinians, specifically the right to freedom of movement, to choose a residence, and to leave and re-enter the Occupied Territory. The restrictions also had serious economic consequences, impeded access to health care, education and employment and caused significant financial hardship and the interruption of essential social networks and communities. The permit system imposed on all Palestinian identification card holders remained active; permits for Palestinians to enter Israel, and hence travel to East Jerusalem and the West Bank were still difficult to obtain, and the rules as to whether a permit was required or would be granted were fluid and could change daily. The permit system was enforced by a web of checkpoints along the Green Line and in the West Bank and Jerusalem. In April, the United Nations Office for the Coordination of Humanitarian Affairs estimated that there were 88 manned obstacles out of a total of 607 closure obstacles in the West Bank. During the first half of 2008, 41 days of general closure were enforced in the West Bank, compared to 19 in 2007.

Israel had not met the conditions established under article 4 of the International Covenant on Civil and Political Rights [YUN 1996, p. 423] for derogation from the right to freedom of movement, requiring that, when imposed, a derogation had to be temporary, existing only during an officially proclaimed state of emergency that threatened the life of the nation. The restrictions imposed by Israel on the Palestinian population also infringed on its duties under international humanitarian law.

The construction of the wall, which fragmented the West Bank into non-contiguous enclaves, brought new restrictions on movement and access. In July, after years of deliberations by the Israeli High Court, Israel declared that it would demolish sections of the wall around the village of Bil'in, west of Ramallah, and near Qalqilia in the northern West Bank, moving the wall's location in those two areas by 2.4 kilometres to allow Palestinian farmers access to 2,600 dunums of land. In areas where the wall had already been built, extensive rights violations of Palestinians living nearby were frequently reported. In areas located between the barrier and the 1949 Armistice Demarcation Line (Green Line) [YUN 1948–49, p. 184], representing 9.8 per cent of the West Bank, access by Palestinian farmers to their lands and water resources was severely limited and could be achieved only through restrictive permit and gate regimes.

A 168-kilometre-long section of the wall separated East Jerusalem from the rest of the West Bank, which, in conjunction with the identification card and permit system and the series of checkpoints, had weakened the social and economic connection between residents of East Jerusalem and the West Bank. By contrast, the wall encircled settlements around Jerusalem and within the West Bank and connected them to Israel, ensuring that Israeli settlers had unimpeded access to Jerusalem. IDF security measures had an impact on access to religious sites in East Jerusalem, and traders and consumers no longer had access to its markets.

Since the 1993 Declaration of Principles on Interim Self-Government Arrangements (Oslo Agreement) [YUN 1993, p. 521], land in the West Bank had been divided into three areas. Area C, which accounted for around 61 per cent of West Bank territory, remained under Israeli military authority, including building and planning. During the first quarter of 2008, Israeli authorities demolished 124 structures for lack of permit; 61 of those were residential buildings that caused the displacement of 435 Palestinians, including 135 children.

On Palestinians in Israeli prisons, the report noted that more than 650,000 Palestinians had been detained since the beginning of Israeli occupation in 1967. As at 31 August 2008, there were 8,403 prisoners in Israeli jails and detention centres, 649 of whom were administrative detainees held without charge or trial. Serious concerns existed regarding the conditions of Palestinians during detention. Torture and other forms of ill treatment continued to be prevalent in the context of arrest and interrogation of persons suspected of being a security threat. Palestinian prisoners faced inadequate access to health care and food. Female prisoners were reportedly subjected to sexual harassment, frequent body searches and physical intimidation, and minors were not treated in accordance with international standards. Following the Hamas takeover of the Gaza Strip in June 2007 [YUN 2007, p. 441], Israel suspended visits from family members travelling from Gaza to Palestinian detainees in Israel, thus depriving more than 900 detainees of direct contact with their relatives for over one year.

The report recommended that, in view of the worsening human rights situation in the Territory, the United Nations should reiterate its commitment to ensuring strong advocacy for the needs and rights of civilians and remind the parties of their primary responsibility for protecting civilians.

Report of Special Rapporteur. By a 25 August note [A/63/326], the Secretary-General transmitted the report of the Special Rapporteur (Richard Falk) on the situation of human rights in the Palestinian territories occupied since 1967, covering the period from 1 January to 31 July 2008 (see p. 896).

UN Register of Damage. The UN Register of Damage Caused by the Construction of the Wall in the Occupied Palestinian Territory, established in Vienna in accordance with General Assembly resolution ES-10/17 [YUN 2006, p. 529], became operational in June, with a small team of 18 substantive and technical staff, following the appointment of a three-member Board in 2007 [YUN 2007, p. 461] and of the Executive Director in January 2008. The Board adopted provisional rules of procedure for claims registration and a claim form for registration of damage, and began the work of collecting claim forms and considering them for inclusion in the Register.

The Board reviewed the first 30 claim forms translated from Arabic into English, processed through the Register's electronic database and reviewed by staff of the Office. It decided to include in the Register losses set out in each of those forms, signifying the beginning of the existence of the Register.

The Special Committee on Palestinian Rights [A/63/273] stated that the establishment of the Register had been a lengthy and—as considered by many—disappointing process owing to its lack of presence in the Occupied Palestinian Territory and narrow mandate.

GENERAL ASSEMBLY ACTION

On 5 December [meeting 64], on the recommendation of the Fourth Committee [A/63/401], the General Assembly adopted **resolution 63/98** by recorded vote (165-8-4) [agenda item 30].

Israeli practices affecting the human rights of the Palestinian people in the Occupied Palestinian Territory, including East Jerusalem

The General Assembly,

Recalling the Universal Declaration of Human Rights,

Recalling also the International Covenant on Civil and Political Rights, the International Covenant on Economic, Social and Cultural Rights and the Convention on the Rights of the Child, and affirming that these human rights instruments must be respected in the Occupied Palestinian Territory, including East Jerusalem,

Reaffirming its relevant resolutions, including resolution 62/109 of 17 December 2007, as well as those adopted at its tenth emergency special session,

Recalling the relevant resolutions of the Commission on Human Rights and the Human Rights Council,

Recalling also the relevant resolutions of the Security Council, and stressing the need for their implementation,

Having considered the report of the Special Committee to Investigate Israeli Practices Affecting the Human Rights of the Palestinian People and Other Arabs of the Occupied Territories and the report of the Secretary-General,

Taking note of the recent reports of the Special Rapporteur of the Human Rights Council on the situation of human rights in the Palestinian territories occupied since 1967,

Recalling the advisory opinion rendered on 9 July 2004 by the International Court of Justice, and recalling also General Assembly resolutions ES-10/15 of 20 July 2004 and ES-10/17 of 15 December 2006,

Noting in particular the Court's reply, including that the construction of the wall being built by Israel, the occupying Power, in the Occupied Palestinian Territory, including in and around East Jerusalem, and its associated regime are contrary to international law,

Aware of the responsibility of the international community to promote human rights and ensure respect for international law, and recalling in this regard its resolution 2625(XXV) of 24 October 1970,

Reaffirming the principle of the inadmissibility of the acquisition of territory by force,

Reaffirming also the applicability of the Geneva Convention relative to the Protection of Civilian Persons in Time of War, of 12 August 1949, to the Occupied Palestinian Territory, including East Jerusalem, and other Arab territories occupied by Israel since 1967,

Reaffirming further the obligation of the States parties to the Fourth Geneva Convention under articles 146, 147 and 148 with regard to penal sanctions, grave breaches and responsibilities of the High Contracting Parties,

Reaffirming that all States have the right and the duty to take actions in conformity with international law and international humanitarian law to counter deadly acts of violence against their civilian population in order to protect the lives of their citizens,

Stressing the need for full compliance with the Israeli-Palestinian agreements reached within the context of the Middle East peace process, including the Sharm el-Sheikh understandings, and the implementation of the Quartet road map to a permanent two-State solution to the Israeli-Palestinian conflict,

Stressing also the need for the full implementation of the Agreement on Movement and Access and the Agreed Principles for the Rafah Crossing, both of 15 November 2005, to allow for the freedom of movement of the Palestinian civilian population within and into and out of the Gaza Strip,

Expressing grave concern about the continuing systematic violation of the human rights of the Palestinian people by Israel, the occupying Power, including that arising from the excessive use of force, the use of collective punishment, the reoccupation and closure of areas, the confiscation of land, the establishment and expansion of settlements, the construction of a wall in the Occupied Palestinian Territory in departure from the Armistice Line of 1949, the destruction of property and infrastructure, and all other actions by it designed to change the legal status, geographical nature and demographic composition of the Occupied Palestinian Territory, including East Jerusalem,

Gravely concerned about the military actions that have been carried out since 28 September 2000 and that have led to thousands of deaths among Palestinian civilians, including hundreds of children, and tens of thousands of injuries,

Expressing deep concern about the continuing deterioration in the humanitarian and security situation in the Gaza Strip, including that resulting from the Israeli military actions against civilian areas, and the prolonged closure of crossings into and out of the Gaza Strip, as well as from the firing of rockets into Israel and the negative impact of the events of June 2007 leading to the unlawful takeover of Palestinian Authority institutions in the Gaza Strip,

Expressing deep concern also about the vast destruction caused by the Israeli occupying forces to Palestinian homes, properties, vital infrastructure, agricultural lands and institutions of the Palestinian Authority, and expressing deep concern about the short- and long-term detrimental impact of such destruction on the socio-economic and humanitarian conditions and human rights of the Palestinian civilian population,

Expressing deep concern further about the Israeli policy of closures, severe restrictions, and a permit regime that obstruct the freedom of movement of persons and goods, including medical and humanitarian personnel and goods, throughout the Occupied Palestinian Territory, including East Jerusalem, and about the consequent violation of the human rights of the Palestinian people and the negative impact on their socioeconomic situation, which remains that of a dire humanitarian crisis, particularly in the Gaza Strip,

Concerned in particular about the continued establishment of Israeli checkpoints in the Occupied Palestinian Territory, including East Jerusalem, and the transformation of several of these checkpoints into structures akin to permanent border crossings inside the Occupied Palestinian Territory, which are severely impairing the territorial contiguity of the Territory and undermining efforts and aid aimed at rehabilitating and developing the Palestinian economy, adversely affecting other aspects of the socio-economic conditions of the Palestinian people,

Expressing deep concern that thousands of Palestinians, including hundreds of children and women, continue to be held in Israeli prisons or detention centres under harsh conditions that impair their well-being, and expressing concern about the ill treatment and harassment of any Palestinian prisoners and all reports of torture,

Convinced of the need for an international presence to monitor the situation, to contribute to ending the violence and protecting the Palestinian civilian population and to help the parties implement the agreements reached, and, in this regard, recalling the positive contribution of the Temporary International Presence in Hebron,

Emphasizing the right of all people in the region to the enjoyment of human rights as enshrined in the international human rights covenants,

1. *Reiterates* that all measures and actions taken by Israel, the occupying Power, in the Occupied Palestinian Territory, including East Jerusalem, in violation of the relevant provisions of the Geneva Convention relative to the Protection of Civilian Persons in Time of War, of 12 August 1949, and contrary to the relevant resolutions of the Security Council, are illegal and have no validity;

2. *Demands* that Israel, the occupying Power, cease all practices and actions that violate the human rights of the Palestinian people, including extrajudicial executions, and that it respect human rights law and comply with its legal obligations in this regard;

3. *Also demands* that Israel, the occupying Power, comply fully with the provisions of the Fourth Geneva Convention of 1949 and cease immediately all measures and actions taken in violation and in breach of the Convention, including all of its settlement activities and the construction of the wall in the Occupied Palestinian Territory, including in and around East Jerusalem, which, inter alia, gravely and detrimentally impact the human rights of the Palestinian people;

4. *Condemns* all acts of violence, including all acts of terror, provocation, incitement and destruction, especially the excessive use of force by the Israeli occupying forces against Palestinian civilians, which have caused extensive loss of life and vast numbers of injuries, including among children, massive destruction of homes, properties, agricultural lands and vital infrastructure, and internal displacement of civilians;

5. *Expresses grave concern* at the firing of rockets against Israeli civilian areas resulting in loss of life and injury;

6. *Notes* the Israeli withdrawal in 2005 from within the Gaza Strip and parts of the northern West Bank and the dismantlement of the settlements therein as a step towards the implementation of the road map;

7. *Calls upon* Israel, the occupying Power, to comply strictly with its obligations under international law, including international humanitarian law, with respect to the alteration of the character, status and demographic composition of the Occupied Palestinian Territory, including East Jerusalem;

8. *Demands* that Israel, the occupying Power, comply with its legal obligations under international law, as mentioned in the advisory opinion rendered on 9 July 2004 by the International Court of Justice and as demanded in resolutions ES-10/15 of 20 July 2004 and ES-10/13 of 21 October 2003, and that it immediately cease the construction of the wall in the Occupied Palestinian Territory, including in and around East Jerusalem, dismantle forthwith the structure situated therein, repeal or render ineffective all legislative and regulatory acts relating thereto, and make reparation for all damage caused by the construction of the wall, which has gravely impacted the human rights and the socio-economic living conditions of the Palestinian people;

9. *Reiterates* the need for respect for the unity and territorial contiguity and integrity of all of the Occupied Palestinian Territory and for guarantees of the freedom of movement of persons and goods within the Palestinian territory, including movement into and from East Jerusalem, into and from the Gaza Strip, and to and from the outside world;

10. *Calls upon* Israel, the occupying Power, to cease its imposition of closures and restrictions on movement, and, in this regard, to implement the Agreement on Movement and Access and the Agreed Principles for the Rafah Crossing, both of 15 November 2005;

11. *Urges* Member States to continue to provide emergency assistance to the Palestinian people to alleviate the financial crisis and the dire socio-economic and humanitarian situation, particularly in the Gaza Strip;

12. *Emphasizes* the need to preserve the Palestinian institutions and infrastructure for the provision of vital public services to the Palestinian civilian population and the promotion of human rights, including civil, political, economic, social and cultural rights;

13. *Requests* the Secretary-General to report to the General Assembly at its sixty-fourth session on the implementation of the present resolution.

RECORDED VOTE ON RESOLUTION 63/98:

In favour: Afghanistan, Albania, Algeria, Andorra, Angola, Antigua and Barbuda, Argentina, Armenia, Austria, Azerbaijan, Bahamas, Bahrain, Bangladesh, Barbados, Belarus, Belgium, Belize, Benin, Bhutan, Bolivia, Bosnia and Herzegovina, Botswana, Brazil, Brunei Darussalam, Bulgaria, Burundi, Cambodia, Cape Verde, Central African Republic, Chile, China, Colombia, Comoros, Congo, Costa Rica, Croatia, Cuba, Cyprus, Czech Republic, Democratic People's Republic of Korea, Denmark, Djibouti, Dominica, Dominican Republic, Ecuador, Egypt, Eritrea, Estonia, Ethiopia, Fiji, Finland, France, Gabon, Georgia, Germany, Ghana, Greece, Grenada, Guatemala, Guinea, Guinea-Bissau, Guyana, Haiti, Hungary, Iceland, India, Indonesia, Iran, Iraq, Ireland, Italy, Jamaica, Japan, Jordan, Kazakhstan, Kenya, Kuwait, Kyrgyzstan, Lao People's Democratic Republic, Latvia, Lebanon, Lesotho, Liberia, Libyan Arab Jamahiriya, Liechtenstein, Lithuania, Luxembourg, Malawi, Malaysia, Maldives, Mali, Malta, Mauritania, Mauritius, Mexico, Moldova, Monaco, Mongolia, Montenegro, Morocco,

Mozambique, Myanmar, Namibia, Nepal, Netherlands, New Zealand, Nicaragua, Niger, Nigeria, Norway, Oman, Pakistan, Panama, Papua New Guinea, Paraguay, Peru, Philippines, Poland, Portugal, Qatar, Republic of Korea, Romania, Russian Federation, Saint Lucia, Saint Vincent and the Grenadines, San Marino, Sao Tome and Principe, Saudi Arabia, Senegal, Serbia, Singapore, Slovakia, Slovenia, Solomon Islands, South Africa, Spain, Sri Lanka, Sudan, Suriname, Swaziland, Sweden, Switzerland, Syrian Arab Republic, Tajikistan, Thailand, The former Yugoslav Republic of Macedonia, Timor-Leste, Togo, Trinidad and Tobago, Tunisia, Turkey, Turkmenistan, Tuvalu, Uganda, Ukraine, United Arab Emirates, United Kingdom, United Republic of Tanzania, Uruguay, Uzbekistan, Venezuela, Viet Nam, Yemen, Zambia, Zimbabwe.

Against: Australia, Canada, Israel, Marshall Islands, Micronesia, Nauru, Palau, United States.

Abstaining: Cameroon, Côte d'Ivoire, El Salvador, Honduras.

Work of Special Committee

Report of Secretary-General. On 15 October [A/63/483], the Secretary-General reported to the General Assembly on the implementation of resolution 62/106 [YUN 2007, p. 455] as it concerned the work of the Special Committee and that of the UN Department of Public Information (DPI) in support of the Committee's efforts during the period from August 2007 to July 2008.

The Special Committee was supported by various UN agencies in the implementation of its mandate, specifically OHCHR and the offices of the United Nations Resident Coordinators in Egypt, Jordan and the Syrian Arab Republic in the organization of a mission and by offering in situ support. DPI continued to disseminate information on the Special Committee's work through various means, ensuring that such information was available to global audiences in the six official UN languages. The Department held its annual training programme for Palestinian journalists, published a new version of the booklet *The United Nations and the Question of Palestine* and displayed a new exhibit on Palestine at UN Headquarters on the issue of human rights in the Occupied Palestinian Territory.

GENERAL ASSEMBLY ACTION

On 5 December [meeting 64], the General Assembly, on the recommendation of the Fourth Committee [A/63/401], adopted **resolution 63/95** by recorded vote (94-8-73) [agenda item 30].

Work of the Special Committee to Investigate Israeli Practices Affecting the Human Rights of the Palestinian People and Other Arabs of the Occupied Territories

The General Assembly,

Guided by the purposes and principles of the Charter of the United Nations,

Guided also by international humanitarian law, in particular the Geneva Convention relative to the Protection of Civilian Persons in Time of War of 12 August 1949, as well as international standards of human rights, in particular the Universal Declaration of Human Rights and the International Covenants on Human Rights,

Recalling its relevant resolutions, including resolutions 2443(XXIII) of 19 December 1968 and 62/106 of 17 December 2007, and the relevant resolutions of the Commission on Human Rights and the Human Rights Council,

Recalling also the relevant resolutions of the Security Council,

Taking into account the advisory opinion rendered on 9 July 2004 by the International Court of Justice on the *Legal Consequences of the Construction of a Wall in the Occupied Palestinian Territory*, and recalling in this regard General Assembly resolution ES-10/15 of 20 July 2004,

Convinced that occupation itself represents a gross and grave violation of human rights,

Gravely concerned about the continuing detrimental impact of the events that have taken place since 28 September 2000, including the excessive use of force by the Israeli occupying forces against Palestinian civilians, resulting in thousands of deaths and injuries, the widespread destruction of property and vital infrastructure and the internal displacement of civilians,

Having considered the report of the Special Committee to Investigate Israeli Practices Affecting the Human Rights of the Palestinian People and Other Arabs of the Occupied Territories and the relevant reports of the Secretary-General,

Recalling the Declaration of Principles on Interim Self-Government Arrangements of 13 September 1993 and the subsequent implementation agreements between the Palestinian and Israeli sides,

Expressing the hope that the Israeli occupation will be brought to an early and complete end and that therefore the violation of the human rights of the Palestinian people will cease, and recalling in this regard its resolution 58/292 of 6 May 2004,

1. *Commends* the Special Committee to Investigate Israeli Practices Affecting the Human Rights of the Palestinian People and Other Arabs of the Occupied Territories for its efforts in performing the tasks assigned to it by the General Assembly and for its impartiality;

2. *Reiterates its demand* that Israel, the occupying Power, cooperate, in accordance with its obligations as a State Member of the United Nations, with the Special Committee in implementing its mandate;

3. *Deplores* those policies and practices of Israel that violate the human rights of the Palestinian people and other Arabs of the occupied territories, as reflected in the report of the Special Committee covering the reporting period;

4. *Expresses grave concern* about the critical situation in the Occupied Palestinian Territory, including East Jerusalem, since 28 September 2000, as a result of unlawful Israeli practices and measures, and especially condemns all illegal Israeli settlement activities and the construction of the wall, as well as the excessive and indiscriminate use of force against the civilian population, including extrajudicial executions;

5. *Requests* the Special Committee, pending complete termination of the Israeli occupation, to continue to investigate Israeli policies and practices in the Occupied Palestinian Territory, including East Jerusalem, and other Arab territories occupied by Israel since 1967, especially Israeli violations of the Geneva Convention relative to the Protection of Civilian Persons in Time of War of 12 August 1949, and to consult, as appropriate, with the International Committee of the Red Cross according to its regulations in order to ensure that the welfare and human rights of the peoples of the occupied territories are safeguarded and to report to the Secretary-General as soon as possible and whenever the need arises thereafter;

6. *Also requests* the Special Committee to submit regularly to the Secretary-General periodic reports on the current situation in the Occupied Palestinian Territory, including East Jerusalem;

7. *Further requests* the Special Committee to continue to investigate the treatment of the thousands of prisoners and detainees in the Occupied Palestinian Territory, including East Jerusalem, and other Arab territories occupied by Israel since 1967;

8. *Requests* the Secretary-General:

(*a*) To provide the Special Committee with all necessary facilities, including those required for its visits to the occupied territories, so that it may investigate the Israeli policies and practices referred to in the present resolution;

(*b*) To continue to make available such staff as may be necessary to assist the Special Committee in the performance of its tasks;

(*c*) To circulate regularly to Member States the periodic reports mentioned in paragraph 6 above;

(*d*) To ensure the widest circulation of the reports of the Special Committee and of information regarding its activities and findings, by all means available, through the Department of Public Information of the Secretariat and, where necessary, to reprint those reports of the Special Committee that are no longer available;

(*e*) To report to the General Assembly at its sixty-fourth session on the tasks entrusted to him in the present resolution;

9. *Decides* to include in the provisional agenda of its sixty-fourth session the item entitled "Report of the Special Committee to Investigate Israeli Practices Affecting the Human Rights of the Palestinian People and Other Arabs of the Occupied Territories".

RECORDED VOTE ON RESOLUTION 63/95:

In favour: Afghanistan, Algeria, Angola, Antigua and Barbuda, Armenia, Azerbaijan, Bahrain, Bangladesh, Barbados, Belarus, Belize, Benin, Bhutan, Bolivia, Brazil, Brunei Darussalam, Cambodia, Central African Republic, Chile, China, Comoros, Congo, Cuba, Democratic People's Republic of Korea, Djibouti, Dominica, Dominican Republic, Ecuador, Egypt, Eritrea, Gabon, Ghana, Grenada, Guinea, Guinea-Bissau, Guyana, Haiti, India, Indonesia, Iran, Iraq, Jamaica, Jordan, Kenya, Kuwait, Kyrgyzstan, Lao People's Democratic Republic, Lebanon, Lesotho, Libyan Arab Jamahiriya, Malawi, Malaysia, Maldives, Mali, Mauritania, Mauritius, Morocco, Mozambique, Myanmar, Namibia, Nepal, Nicaragua, Niger, Oman, Pakistan, Qatar, Saint Lucia, Saint Vincent and the Grenadines, Sao Tome and Principe, Saudi Arabia, Senegal, Singapore, South Africa, Sri Lanka, Sudan, Suriname, Swaziland, Syrian Arab Republic, Tajikistan, Togo, Trinidad and Tobago, Tunisia, Turkey, Turkmenistan, Tuvalu, Uganda, United Arab Emirates, United Republic of Tanzania, Uzbekistan, Venezuela, Viet Nam, Yemen, Zambia, Zimbabwe.

Against: Australia, Canada, Israel, Marshall Islands, Micronesia, Nauru, Palau, United States.

Abstaining: Albania, Andorra, Argentina, Austria, Bahamas, Belgium, Bosnia and Herzegovina, Botswana, Bulgaria, Burundi, Cameroon, Colombia, Costa Rica, Côte d'Ivoire, Croatia, Cyprus, Czech Republic, Denmark, El Salvador, Estonia, Ethiopia, Fiji, Finland, France, Georgia, Germany, Greece, Guatemala, Honduras, Hungary, Iceland, Ireland, Italy, Japan, Kazakhstan, Latvia, Liberia, Liechtenstein, Lithuania, Luxembourg, Malta, Mexico, Moldova, Monaco, Mongolia, Montenegro, Netherlands, New Zealand, Norway, Panama, Paraguay, Peru, Philippines, Poland, Portugal, Republic of Korea, Romania, Russian Federation, Samoa, San Marino, Serbia, Slovakia, Slovenia, Spain, Sweden, Switzerland, Thailand, The former Yugoslav Republic of Macedonia, Timor-Leste, Tonga, Ukraine, United Kingdom, Uruguay.

Economic and social situation

ESCWA report. By a 6 May note [A/63/74-E/2008/13], the Secretary-General submitted a report on the economic and social repercussions of the Israeli occupation on the living conditions of the Palestinian people in the Occupied Palestinian Territory, including East Jerusalem, and of the Arab population in the occupied Syrian Golan, prepared by the Economic and Social Commission for Western Asia (ESCWA), in accordance with Economic and Social Council resolution 2007/26 [YUN 2007, p. 449] and General Assembly resolution 62/181 [ibid., p. 450].

The report concluded that a combination of intensified closures and sanctions imposed by Israel, as well as heightened Palestinian internal conflict, had led to a measurable deepening of the socio-economic crisis in the Occupied Palestinian Territory. Living conditions were declining and social and spatial dismemberment was occurring, as residents of the Gaza Strip had become almost completely isolated, with access only to basic commodities and humanitarian items.

The situation in the Occupied Territory prompted the UN country team to launch the 2008 consolidated appeal which, at $452.2 million, represented about an 8 per cent increase over 2007 (see p. 1005). The appeal focused on humanitarian aid; the protection of civilians and the implementation of international humanitarian law; humanitarian monitoring and reporting; and the strengthening of UN humanitarian coordination. While those measures were aimed at stabilizing socio-economic conditions, they were not expected to contribute to their long-term improvement.

The Secretary-General observed that the water supply and sanitation services for Palestinians were insufficient and unreliable in terms of quality. The daily average of per capita water consumption was below the minimum recommended standard. In 2007, on average, 35.2 per cent in the West Bank and 36.3 per cent of households in the Gaza Strip had piped water. In the Gaza Strip, 15 per cent of the population was receiving water for only one or two hours per day, owing to the lack of electrical power due to fuel supply cuts and the ban on the importation of spare parts, water wells and pumping stations. As at 23 January 2008, about 30 per cent of Gazans had limited access to running water, and about 35 million litres of sewage daily were entering the sea.

Special Committee on Israeli Practices. The Special Committee on Israeli Practices, in its annual report [A/63/273], noted that one of the major issues in the Occupied Palestinian Territory was competition for resources, most significantly the control of water resources. According to testimony received, Palestinians suffered from acute water scarcity, resulting from the continuous expansion of settlements, with Israeli consumption reaching 4.3 times that of the average of the Occupied Territory and Israeli settlers' consumption 5.3 times that of the West Bank average. Of available groundwater resources in the West Bank, 18 per cent was used by Palestinians, while 82 per cent was controlled and used by Israelis.

ECONOMIC AND SOCIAL COUNCIL ACTION

On 25 July [meeting 44], the Economic and Social Council adopted **resolution 2008/31** [draft: E/2008/L.26] as orally revised by roll-call vote (49-2-2) [agenda item 11].

Economic and social repercussions of the Israeli occupation on the living conditions of the Palestinian people in the Occupied Palestinian Territory, including East Jerusalem, and of the Arab population in the occupied Syrian Golan

The Economic and Social Council,

Recalling General Assembly resolution 62/181 of 19 December 2007,

Recalling also its resolution 2007/26 of 26 July 2007,

Guided by the principles of the Charter of the United Nations affirming the inadmissibility of the acquisition of territory by force, and recalling relevant Security Council resolutions, including resolutions 242(1967) of 22 November 1967, 252(1968) of 21 May 1968, 338(1973) of 22 October 1973, 465(1980) of 1 March 1980 and 497(1981) of 17 December 1981,

Recalling the resolutions of the tenth emergency special session of the General Assembly, including resolutions ES-10/13 of 21 October 2003, ES-10/14 of 8 December 2003, ES-10/15 of 20 July 2004 and ES-10/17 of 15 December 2006,

Reaffirming the applicability of the Geneva Convention relative to the Protection of Civilian Persons in Time of War, of 12 August 1949, to the Occupied Palestinian Territory, including East Jerusalem, and other Arab territories occupied by Israel since 1967,

Recalling the International Covenant on Civil and Political Rights, the International Covenant on Economic, Social and Cultural Rights and the Convention on the Rights of the Child, and affirming that these human rights instruments must be respected in the Occupied Palestinian Territory, including East Jerusalem, as well as in the occupied Syrian Golan,

Stressing the importance of the revival of the Middle East peace process on the basis of Security Council resolutions 242(1967), 338(1973), 425(1978) of 19 March 1978, 1397(2002) of 12 March 2002, 1515(2003) of 19 November 2003 and 1544(2004) of 19 May 2004 and the principle of land for peace as well as compliance with the agreements reached between the Government of Israel and the Palestine Liberation Organization, the representative of the Palestinian people,

Reaffirming the principle of the permanent sovereignty of peoples under foreign occupation over their natural resources, and expressing concern in this regard about the exploitation of natural resources by Israel, the occupying Power, in the Occupied Palestinian Territory, including East Jerusalem, and in the occupied Syrian Golan,

Convinced that the Israeli occupation has gravely impeded the efforts to achieve sustainable development and a sound economic environment in the Occupied Palestinian Territory, including East Jerusalem, and in the occupied Syrian Golan, and expressing grave concern about the consequent deterioration of economic and living conditions,

Gravely concerned, in this regard, about the continuation of settlement activities by Israel and other related measures in the Occupied Palestinian Territory, particularly in and around occupied East Jerusalem, as well as in the occupied Syrian Golan in violation of international humanitarian law and relevant United Nations resolutions,

Gravely concerned also by the serious repercussions on the economic and social conditions of the Palestinian people caused by Israel's construction of the wall and its associated regime inside the Occupied Palestinian Territory, including in and around East Jerusalem, and the resulting violation of their economic and social rights, including the right to work, to health, to education and to an adequate standard of living,

Recalling, in this regard, the advisory opinion rendered on 9 July 2004 by the International Court of Justice on the *Legal Consequences of the Construction of a Wall in the Occupied Palestinian Territory*, recalling also Assembly resolution ES-10/15, and stressing the need to comply with the obligations mentioned therein,

Expressing grave concern at the extensive destruction by Israel, the occupying Power, of properties, agricultural land and orchards in the Occupied Palestinian Territory, including East Jerusalem, including, in particular, in connection with its construction of the wall, contrary to international law, in the Occupied Palestinian Territory, including in and around East Jerusalem,

Expressing deep concern about continuing Israeli military operations and the continuing Israeli policy of closures and severe restrictions on the movement of persons and goods, including humanitarian personnel and food, medical, fuel and other essential supplies, via the imposition of crossing closures, checkpoints and a permit regime throughout the Occupied Palestinian Territory, including East Jerusalem, and the consequent negative impact on the socio-economic situation of the Palestinian people, which remains that of dire humanitarian crisis, in particular in the Gaza Strip,

Gravely concerned by various reports of the United Nations and the specialized agencies regarding the inordinate rates of unemployment, widespread poverty and severe humanitarian hardships, including food insecurity and rising health-related problems, including high levels of malnutrition, among the Palestinian people, especially children, in the Occupied Palestinian Territory, including East Jerusalem,

Expressing grave concern at the increasing number of deaths and injuries of civilians, including children and women,

Emphasizing the importance of the safety and well-being of all civilians, and calling for the cessation of all acts of violence, including all acts of terror, provocation, incitement and destruction, and all firing of rockets,

Conscious of the urgent need for the reconstruction and development of the economic and social infrastructure of the Occupied Palestinian Territory, including East Jerusalem, as well as the urgent need to address the dire humanitarian crisis facing the Palestinian people,

Commending the important work being done by the United Nations, the specialized agencies and the donor community in support of the economic and social development of the Palestinian people, as well as the assistance being provided in the humanitarian field,

Recognizing the efforts being undertaken by the Palestinian Authority, with international support, to rebuild, reform and strengthen its damaged institutions and promote good governance, and emphasizing the need to preserve the Palestinian institutions and infrastructure and to ameliorate economic and social conditions,

Stressing the importance of national unity among the Palestinian people, and emphasizing the need for the respect and preservation of the territorial integrity and unity of the Occupied Palestinian Territory, including East Jerusalem,

Calling upon both parties to fulfil their obligations under the road map in cooperation with the Quartet,

1. *Calls for* the lifting of the severe restrictions imposed on the Palestinian people, including those arising from ongoing Israeli military operations, and for other urgent measures to be taken to alleviate the desperate humanitarian situation in the Occupied Palestinian Territory, especially in the Gaza Strip;

2. *Stresses* the need to preserve the national unity and the territorial integrity of the Occupied Palestinian Territory, including East Jerusalem, and to guarantee the freedom of movement of persons and goods throughout the Occupied Palestinian Territory, including East Jerusalem, as well as to and from the outside world;

3. *Demands* that Israel comply with the Protocol on Economic Relations between the Government of Israel and the Palestine Liberation Organization signed in Paris on 29 April 1994;

4. *Calls upon* Israel to restore and replace civilian properties, vital infrastructure, agricultural lands and governmental institutions that have been damaged or destroyed as a result of its military operations in the Occupied Palestinian Territory;

5. *Reiterates* the call for the full implementation of the Agreement on Movement and Access of 15 November 2005, particularly the urgent and uninterrupted reopening of Rafah and Karni crossings, which is crucial to ensuring the passage of foodstuffs and essential supplies, including fuel, as well as the unhindered access of the United Nations agencies to and within the Occupied Palestinian Territory, and expresses deep concern at any actions that threaten the integrity of the border crossings and the distribution of fuel;

6. *Calls upon* all parties to respect the rules of international humanitarian law and to refrain from violence against the civilian population in accordance with the Geneva Convention relative to the Protection of Civilian Persons in Time of War, of 12 August 1949;

7. *Reaffirms* the inalienable right of the Palestinian people and the Arab population of the occupied Syrian Golan to all their natural and economic resources, and calls upon Israel, the occupying Power, not to exploit, endanger or cause loss or depletion of those resources;

8. *Calls upon* Israel, the occupying Power, to cease its destruction of homes and properties, economic institutions and agricultural lands and orchards in the Occupied Palestinian Territory, including East Jerusalem, as well as in the occupied Syrian Golan;

9. *Also calls upon* Israel, the occupying Power, to cease the dumping of all kinds of waste materials in the Occupied Palestinian Territory, including East Jerusalem, and in the occupied Syrian Golan, which gravely threaten their natural resources, namely, the water and land resources, and pose an environmental hazard and health threat to the civilian populations, and calls for the further implementation of critical environmental projects, including the sewage treatment plant in the Gaza Strip;

10. *Reaffirms* that Israeli settlements in the Occupied Palestinian Territory, including East Jerusalem, and the occupied Syrian Golan, are illegal and constitute a major obstacle to economic and social development, and calls for the full implementation of the relevant Security Council resolutions and compliance by Israel, the occupying Power, with international law, including the Fourth Geneva Convention;

11. *Also reaffirms* that Israel's ongoing construction of the wall in the Occupied Palestinian Territory, including in and around East Jerusalem, is contrary to international law and is isolating East Jerusalem, fragmenting the West Bank and seriously debilitating the economic and social development of the Palestinian people, and calls in this regard for full compliance with the legal obligations mentioned in the advisory opinion rendered on 9 July 2004 by the International Court of Justice and in Assembly resolution ES-10/15;

12. *Calls upon* Israel to comply with the provisions of the Fourth Geneva Convention, and to facilitate the visits of Syrian citizens of the occupied Syrian Golan whose family members reside in their mother homeland, the Syrian Arab Republic, via the Qunaitra entrance;

13. *Emphasizes* the importance of the work of the organizations and agencies of the United Nations system and of the United Nations Special Coordinator for the Mid-

dle East Peace Process and Personal Representative of the Secretary-General to the Palestine Liberation Organization and the Palestinian Authority;

14. *Expresses its hope* that the resumed peace process will speedily advance to pave the way for the establishment of the independent Palestinian State and the achievement of a just, lasting and comprehensive peace settlement in accordance with relevant United Nations resolutions, and stressing in this regard the importance of the Madrid Conference, the Arab Peace Initiative and the principle of land for peace;

15. *Requests* the Secretary-General to submit to the General Assembly at its sixty-third session, through the Economic and Social Council, a report on the implementation of the present resolution and to continue to include in the report of the United Nations Special Coordinator an update on the living conditions of the Palestinian people, in collaboration with relevant United Nations agencies;

16. *Decides* to include the item entitled "Economic and social repercussions of the Israeli occupation on the living conditions of the Palestinian people in the Occupied Palestinian Territory, including East Jerusalem, and the Arab population in the occupied Syrian Golan" in the agenda of its substantive session of 2009.

ROLL-CALL VOTE ON RESOLUTION 2008/31:

In favour: Algeria, Angola, Austria, Barbados, Belarus, Benin, Bolivia, Brazil, Cape Verde, China, Congo, Cuba, Czech Republic, El Salvador, France, Greece, Guinea-Bissau, Guyana, Haiti, Iceland, Indonesia, Iraq, Kazakhstan, Liechtenstein, Luxembourg, Malawi, Malaysia, Mauritania, Moldova, Mozambique, Netherlands, New Zealand, Niger, Pakistan, Paraguay, Philippines, Poland, Portugal, Republic of Korea, Romania, Russian Federation, Saint Lucia, Saudi Arabia, Somalia, Sri Lanka, Sudan, Sweden, United Kingdom, Uruguay.

Against: Canada, United States.

Abstaining: Cameroon, Japan.

On 25 July **(decision 2008/253)**, the Council took note of the ESCWA report.

GENERAL ASSEMBLY ACTION

On 19 December [meeting 72], the General Assembly, on the recommendation of the Second Committee [A/63/410], adopted **resolution 63/201** by recorded vote (164-8-5) [agenda item 38].

Permanent sovereignty of the Palestinian people in the Occupied Palestinian Territory, including East Jerusalem, and of the Arab population in the occupied Syrian Golan over their natural resources

The General Assembly,

Recalling its resolution 62/181 of 19 December 2007, and taking note of Economic and Social Council resolution 2008/31 of 25 July 2008,

Recalling also its resolutions 58/292 of 6 May 2004 and 59/251 of 22 December 2004,

Reaffirming the principle of the permanent sovereignty of peoples under foreign occupation over their natural resources,

Guided by the principles of the Charter of the United Nations, affirming the inadmissibility of the acquisition of territory by force, and recalling relevant Security Council resolutions, including resolutions 242(1967) of 22 November 1967, 465(1980) of 1 March 1980 and 497(1981) of 17 December 1981,

Recalling its resolution 2625(XXV) of 24 October 1970,

Reaffirming the applicability of the Geneva Convention relative to the Protection of Civilian Persons in Time of War, of 12 August 1949, to the Occupied Palestinian Territory, including East Jerusalem, and other Arab territories occupied by Israel since 1967,

Recalling, in this regard, the International Covenant on Civil and Political Rights and the International Covenant on Economic, Social and Cultural Rights, and affirming that these human rights instruments must be respected in the Occupied Palestinian Territory, including East Jerusalem, as well as in the occupied Syrian Golan,

Recalling also the advisory opinion rendered on 9 July 2004 by the International Court of Justice on the *Legal Consequences of the Construction of a Wall in the Occupied Palestinian Territory,* and recalling further its resolutions ES-10/15 of 20 July 2004 and ES-10/17 of 15 December 2006,

Expressing its concern at the exploitation by Israel, the occupying Power, of the natural resources of the Occupied Palestinian Territory, including East Jerusalem, and other Arab territories occupied by Israel since 1967,

Expressing its grave concern at the extensive destruction by Israel, the occupying Power, of agricultural land and orchards in the Occupied Palestinian Territory, including the uprooting of a vast number of fruit-bearing trees,

Expressing its concern at the widespread destruction caused by Israel, the occupying Power, to vital infrastructure, including water pipelines and sewage networks, in the Occupied Palestinian Territory, which, inter alia, pollutes the environment and negatively affects the natural resources of the Palestinian people,

Aware of the detrimental impact of the Israeli settlements on Palestinian and other Arab natural resources, especially as a result of the confiscation of land and the forced diversion of water resources, and of the dire socio-economic consequences in this regard,

Aware also of the detrimental impact on Palestinian natural resources being caused by the unlawful construction of the wall by Israel, the occupying Power, in the Occupied Palestinian Territory, including in and around East Jerusalem, and of its grave effect as well on the economic and social conditions of the Palestinian people,

Reaffirming the need for the advancement of negotiations within the Middle East peace process, on the basis of Security Council resolutions 242(1967), 338(1973) of 22 October 1973, 425(1978) of 19 March 1978 and 1397(2002) of 12 March 2002, the principle of land for peace, the Arab Peace Initiative, and the Quartet performance-based road map to a permanent two-State solution to the Israeli-Palestinian conflict, as endorsed by the Security Council in its resolution 1515(2003) of 19 November 2003, for the achievement of a final settlement on all tracks,

Noting the Israeli withdrawal from within the Gaza Strip and parts of the northern West Bank and the importance of the dismantlement of settlements therein as a step towards the implementation of the road map,

Stressing the need for respect and preservation of the territorial unity, contiguity and integrity of all of the Occupied Palestinian Territory, including East Jerusalem,

Recalling the need to end all acts of violence, including acts of terror, provocation, incitement and destruction,

Taking note with appreciation of the note by the Secretary-General transmitting the report prepared by the Economic and Social Commission for Western Asia on the economic and social repercussions of the Israeli occupation on the living conditions of the Palestinian people in the Occupied Palestinian Territory, including East Jerusalem, and of the Arab population in the occupied Syrian Golan,

1. *Reaffirms* the inalienable rights of the Palestinian people and the population of the occupied Syrian Golan over their natural resources, including land and water;

2. *Calls upon* Israel, the occupying Power, not to exploit, damage, cause loss or depletion of, or endanger the natural resources in the Occupied Palestinian Territory, including East Jerusalem, and in the occupied Syrian Golan;

3. *Recognizes* the right of the Palestinian people to claim restitution as a result of any exploitation, damage, loss or depletion, or endangerment of their natural resources resulting from illegal measures taken by Israel, the occupying Power, in the Occupied Palestinian Territory, including East Jerusalem, and expresses the hope that this issue will be dealt with in the framework of the final status negotiations between the Palestinian and Israeli sides;

4. *Stresses* that the wall being constructed by Israel in the Occupied Palestinian Territory, including in and around East Jerusalem, is contrary to international law and is seriously depriving the Palestinian people of their natural resources, and calls in this regard for full compliance with the legal obligations mentioned in the 9 July 2004 advisory opinion of the International Court of Justice and in resolution ES-10/15;

5. *Calls upon* Israel, the occupying Power, to comply strictly with its obligations under international law, including international humanitarian law, with respect to the alteration of the character and status of the Occupied Palestinian Territory, including East Jerusalem;

6. *Also calls upon* Israel, the occupying Power, to cease the dumping of all kinds of waste materials in the Occupied Palestinian Territory, including East Jerusalem, and in the occupied Syrian Golan, which gravely threaten their natural resources, namely water and land resources, and pose an environmental hazard and health threat to the civilian populations;

7. *Further calls upon* Israel to cease its destruction of vital infrastructure, including water pipelines and sewage networks, which, inter alia, has a negative impact on the natural resources of the Palestinian people;

8. *Requests* the Secretary-General to report to it at its sixty-fourth session on the implementation of the present resolution, and decides to include in the provisional agenda of its sixty-fourth session the item entitled "Permanent sovereignty of the Palestinian people in the Occupied Palestinian Territory, including East Jerusalem, and of the Arab population in the occupied Syrian Golan over their natural resources".

RECORDED VOTE ON RESOLUTION 63/201:

In favour: Afghanistan, Albania, Algeria, Andorra, Angola, Antigua and Barbuda, Argentina, Armenia, Austria, Azerbaijan, Bahamas, Bahrain, Bangladesh, Barbados, Belarus, Belgium, Belize, Benin, Bhutan, Bolivia, Bosnia and Herzegovina, Brazil, Brunei Darussalam, Bulgaria, Burkina Faso, Burundi, Cambodia, Cape Verde, Chile, China, Colombia, Comoros, Congo, Costa Rica, Croatia, Cuba, Cyprus, Czech Republic, Democratic People's Republic of Korea, Denmark, Djibouti, Dominica, Dominican Republic, Ecuador, Egypt, El Salvador, Eritrea, Estonia, Ethiopia, Finland, France, Georgia, Germany, Ghana, Greece, Grenada, Guatemala, Guinea, Guyana, Haiti, Honduras, Hungary, Iceland, India, Indonesia, Iran, Iraq, Ireland, Italy, Jamaica, Japan, Jordan, Kazakhstan, Kenya, Kuwait, Kyrgyzstan, Lao People's Democratic Republic, Latvia, Lebanon, Liberia, Libyan Arab Jamahiriya, Liechtenstein, Lithuania, Luxembourg, Madagascar, Malawi, Malaysia, Maldives, Mali, Malta, Mauritania, Mauritius, Mexico, Moldova, Monaco, Mongolia, Montenegro, Morocco, Mozambique, Myanmar, Namibia, Nepal, Netherlands, New Zealand, Nicaragua, Niger, Nigeria, Norway, Oman, Pakistan, Panama, Papua New Guinea, Paraguay, Peru, Philippines, Poland, Portugal, Qatar, Republic of Korea, Romania, Russian Federation, Rwanda, Saint Lucia, Saint Vincent and the Grenadines, Samoa, San Marino, Sao Tome and Principe, Saudi Arabia, Senegal, Serbia, Singapore, Slovakia, Slovenia, Solomon Islands, South Africa, Spain, Sri Lanka, Sudan, Swaziland, Sweden, Switzerland, Syrian Arab Republic, Tajikistan, Thailand, The former Yugoslav Republic of Macedonia, Timor-Leste, Togo, Trinidad and Tobago, Tunisia, Turkey, Turkmenistan, Tuvalu, Uganda, Ukraine, United Arab Emirates, United Kingdom, United Republic of Tanzania, Uruguay, Uzbekistan, Venezuela, Viet Nam, Yemen, Zambia, Zimbabwe.

Against: Australia, Canada, Israel, Marshall Islands, Micronesia, Nauru, Palau, United States.

Abstaining: Cameroon, Côte d'Ivoire, Fiji, Tonga, Vanuatu.

Fourth Geneva Convention

The applicability of the 1949 Geneva Convention relative to the Protection of Civilian Persons in Time of War (Fourth Geneva Convention) to the Israeli-occupied territories was reaffirmed during the year by the General Assembly and several other UN bodies, including the Special Committee on Israeli Practices.

Report of Secretary-General. In a 15 October report [A/63/484], the Secretary-General informed the General Assembly that Israel had not replied to his September request for information on steps taken or envisaged to implement resolution 62/107 [YUN 2007, p. 457] demanding that Israel accept the de jure applicability of the Fourth Geneva Convention to the Occupied Palestinian Territory, including East Jerusalem, and other Arab territories occupied since 1967, and that it comply scrupulously with its provisions. The Secretary-General said that had drawn the attention of all High Contracting Parties to paragraph 3 of resolution 62/107, calling on them to ensure Israel's respect for the Convention's provisions, and to paragraph 6 of Assembly resolution 62/110 [ibid., p. 518] calling on Member States not to recognize Israeli actions to change the physical character, demographic composition, institutional structure and legal status of the Syrian Golan. Two Member States had replied to his request for information on steps taken to implement the resolution.

GENERAL ASSEMBLY ACTION

On 5 December [meeting 64], on the recommendation of the Fourth Committee [A/63/401], the General Assembly adopted **resolution 63/96** by recorded vote (173-6-1) [agenda item 30].

Applicability of the Geneva Convention relative to the Protection of Civilian Persons in Time of War, of 12 August 1949, to the Occupied Palestinian Territory, including East Jerusalem, and the other occupied Arab territories

The General Assembly,

Recalling its relevant resolutions, including its resolution 62/107 of 17 December 2007,

Bearing in mind the relevant resolutions of the Security Council,

Recalling the Regulations annexed to the Hague Convention IV of 1907, the Geneva Convention relative to the Protection of Civilian Persons in Time of War, of 12 August 1949, and relevant provisions of customary law, including those codified in Additional Protocol I, to the four Geneva Conventions,

Having considered the report of the Special Committee to Investigate Israeli Practices Affecting the Human Rights of the Palestinian People and Other Arabs of the Occupied Territories and the relevant reports of the Secretary-General,

Considering that the promotion of respect for the obligations arising from the Charter of the United Nations and other instruments and rules of international law is among the basic purposes and principles of the United Nations,

Recalling the advisory opinion rendered on 9 July 2004 by the International Court of Justice, and also recalling General Assembly resolution ES-10/15 of 20 July 2004,

Noting in particular the Court's reply, including that the Fourth Geneva Convention is applicable in the Occupied Palestinian Territory, including East Jerusalem, and that Israel is in breach of several of the provisions of the Convention,

Recalling the Conference of High Contracting Parties to the Fourth Geneva Convention on measures to enforce the Convention in the Occupied Palestinian Territory, including East Jerusalem, held on 15 July 1999, as well as the Declaration adopted by the reconvened Conference on 5 December 2001 and the need for the parties to follow up the implementation of the Declaration,

Welcoming and encouraging the initiatives by States parties to the Convention, both individually and collectively, according to article 1 common to the four Geneva Conventions, aimed at ensuring respect for the Convention,

Stressing that Israel, the occupying Power, should comply strictly with its obligations under international law, including international humanitarian law,

1. *Reaffirms* that the Geneva Convention relative to the Protection of Civilian Persons in Time of War, of 12 August 1949, is applicable to the Occupied Palestinian Territory, including East Jerusalem, and other Arab territories occupied by Israel since 1967;

2. *Demands* that Israel accept the de jure applicability of the Convention in the Occupied Palestinian Territory, including East Jerusalem, and other Arab territories occupied by Israel since 1967, and that it comply scrupulously with the provisions of the Convention;

3. *Calls upon* all High Contracting Parties to the Convention, in accordance with article 1 common to the four Geneva Conventions and as mentioned in the advisory opinion of the International Court of Justice of 9 July 2004, to continue to exert all efforts to ensure respect for its provisions by Israel, the occupying Power, in the Occupied Palestinian Territory, including East Jerusalem, and other Arab territories occupied by Israel since 1967;

4. *Reiterates* the need for speedy implementation of the relevant recommendations contained in the resolutions adopted by the General Assembly at its tenth emergency special session, including resolution ES-10/15, with regard to ensuring respect by Israel, the occupying Power, for the provisions of the Convention;

5. *Requests* the Secretary-General to report to the General Assembly at its sixty-fourth session on the implementation of the present resolution.

RECORDED VOTE ON RESOLUTION 63/96:

In favour: Afghanistan, Albania, Algeria, Andorra, Angola, Antigua and Barbuda, Argentina, Armenia, Australia, Austria, Azerbaijan, Bahamas, Bahrain, Bangladesh, Barbados, Belarus, Belgium, Belize, Benin, Bhutan, Bolivia, Bosnia and Herzegovina, Botswana, Brazil, Brunei Darussalam, Bulgaria, Burkina Faso, Burundi, Cambodia, Canada, Cape Verde, Central African Republic, Chile, China, Colombia, Comoros, Congo, Costa Rica, Côte d'Ivoire, Croatia, Cuba, Cyprus, Czech Republic, Democratic People's Republic of Korea, Denmark, Djibouti, Dominica, Dominican Republic, Ecuador, Egypt, El Salvador, Eritrea, Estonia, Ethiopia, Fiji, Finland, France, Gabon, Georgia, Germany, Ghana, Greece, Grenada, Guatemala, Guinea, Guinea-Bissau, Guyana, Haiti, Honduras, Hungary, Iceland, India, Indonesia, Iran, Iraq, Ireland, Italy, Jamaica, Japan, Jordan, Kazakhstan, Kenya, Kuwait, Kyrgyzstan, Lao People's Democratic Republic, Latvia, Lebanon, Lesotho, Liberia, Libyan Arab Jamahiriya, Liechtenstein, Lithuania, Luxembourg, Malawi, Malaysia, Maldives, Mali, Malta, Mauritania, Mauritius, Mexico, Moldova, Monaco, Mongolia, Montenegro, Morocco, Mozambique, Myanmar, Namibia, Nepal, Netherlands, New Zealand, Nicaragua, Niger, Norway, Oman, Pakistan, Panama, Papua New Guinea, Paraguay, Peru, Philippines, Poland, Portugal, Qatar, Republic of Korea, Romania, Russian Federation, Saint Lucia, Saint Vincent and the Grenadines, Samoa, San Marino, Sao Tome and Principe, Saudi Arabia, Senegal, Serbia, Singapore, Slovakia, Slovenia, Solomon Islands, South Africa, Spain, Sri Lanka, Sudan, Suriname, Swaziland, Sweden, Switzerland, Syrian Arab Republic, Tajikistan, Thailand, The former Yugoslav Republic of Macedonia, Timor-Leste, Togo, Tonga, Trinidad and Tobago, Tunisia, Turkey, Turkmenistan, Tuvalu, Uganda,

Ukraine, United Arab Emirates, United Kingdom, United Republic of Tanzania, Uruguay, Uzbekistan, Vanuatu, Venezuela, Viet Nam, Yemen, Zambia, Zimbabwe.

Against: Israel, Marshall Islands, Micronesia, Nauru, Palau, United States.

Abstaining: Cameroon.

Palestinian women

Report of Secretary-General. In a report submitted to the Commission on the Status of Women [E/CN.6/2008/6], in accordance with Economic and Social Council resolution 2007/7 [YUN 2007, p. 460], the Secretary-General summarized the situation of Palestinian women and reviewed UN assistance to them during the period between October 2006 and September 2007, with particular reference to humanitarian assistance, economic activities, education and training, health and human rights.

As the crisis in the Occupied Palestinian Territory deepened, Palestinian women and girls experienced increased poverty and unemployment and a decline in living standards and food security, the Secretary-General said. Their movement and access to health care, employment and schools were further restricted by closures, checkpoints and roadblocks. Close to 30 per cent of pregnant women in the West Bank had difficulties accessing antenatal care and safe delivery. Declines in the education system led to high dropout and low graduation rates. Violence against women, especially domestic violence, remained widespread.

Women should be fully involved in conflict resolution and peacebuilding initiatives in the region. UN assistance focusing on the empowerment of women should be strengthened and women's full participation in decision-making increased. A gender perspective should be fully integrated into international assistance programmes. UN studies and reports on the situation of the Palestinian people should incorporate gender perspectives, research on the situation of Palestinian women and girls should be encouraged, and assistance to them intensified.

ECONOMIC AND SOCIAL COUNCIL ACTION

On 23 July [meeting 40], the Economic and Social Council, on the recommendation of the Commission on the Status of Women [E/2008/27], adopted **resolution 2008/11** by roll-call vote (25-2-17) [agenda item 14 *(a)*].

Situation of and assistance to Palestinian women

The Economic and Social Council,

Having considered with appreciation the report of the Secretary-General on the situation of and assistance to Palestinian women,

Recalling the Nairobi Forward-looking Strategies for the Advancement of Women, in particular paragraph 260 concerning Palestinian women and children, the Beijing Platform for Action adopted at the Fourth World Conference on Women, and the outcome of the twenty-third special session of the General Assembly, entitled "Women 2000: gender equality, development and peace for the twenty-first century",

Recalling also its resolution 2007/7 of 24 July 2007 and other relevant United Nations resolutions,

Recalling further the Declaration on the Elimination of Violence against Women as it concerns the protection of civilian populations,

Recalling the importance of the implementation of General Assembly resolution 57/337 of 3 July 2003 on the prevention of armed conflict, and Security Council resolution 1325(2000) of 31 October 2000 on women and peace and security,

Noting the resumption of bilateral negotiations within the Middle East peace process on its agreed basis, and expressing the need for the speedy achievement of a final and comprehensive peace settlement between the Palestinian and Israeli sides,

Reaffirming the important role of women in the prevention and resolution of conflicts and in peacebuilding, and stressing the importance of their equal participation and involvement in all efforts for the maintenance and promotion of peace and security and the need to increase their role in decision-making with regard to conflict prevention and resolution,

Concerned about the grave situation of Palestinian women resulting from the severe impact of ongoing illegal Israeli practices, including settlement activities and the unlawful construction of the wall in the Occupied Palestinian Territory, including in and around East Jerusalem, the continued imposition of closures and restrictions on the movement of persons and goods and the many severe consequences arising from Israeli military operations in and sieges of civilian areas, in particular in the Gaza Strip, which have impacted detrimentally their social and economic conditions and deepened the humanitarian crisis faced by Palestinian women and their families,

Stressing the importance of providing assistance, especially emergency assistance, to alleviate the dire socio-economic and humanitarian situation being faced by Palestinian women and their families,

Taking note of the report of the United Nations High Commissioner for Human Rights of 31 August 2005 regarding the issue of Palestinian women giving birth at checkpoints, and expressing grave concern at the increasing difficulties faced by pregnant Palestinian women owing to a lack of appropriate and timely antenatal, delivery and post-natal care due to the obstruction of access to proper medical care,

Recalling the advisory opinion rendered on 9 July 2004 by the International Court of Justice on the *Legal Consequences of the Construction of a Wall in the Occupied Palestinian Territory*, and recalling also General Assembly resolution ES-10/15 of 20 July 2004,

Recalling also the International Covenant on Civil and Political Rights, the International Covenant on Economic, Social and Cultural Rights and the Convention on the

Rights of the Child, and affirming that these human rights instruments must be respected in the Occupied Palestinian Territory, including East Jerusalem,

Expressing its condemnation of all acts of violence, including all acts of terror, provocation, incitement and destruction, especially the excessive use of force against Palestinian civilians, many of them women and children, resulting in injury and loss of human life,

Expressing grave concern over the increased difficulties faced by Palestinian women, including the sharp increase in poverty, soaring unemployment, incidents of domestic violence, and declining health and education standards as a result of the deterioration in the economic and social conditions on the ground in the Occupied Palestinian Territory,

Emphasizing the importance of increasing the role of women in decision-making with regard to conflict prevention and the peaceful resolution of conflicts as part of efforts to ensure the safety and well-being of all women in the region,

1 *Calls upon* the concerned parties, as well as the international community, to exert all the efforts necessary to support the resumption of the peace process on its agreed basis, taking into account the common ground already gained, and calls for intensified measures to be taken for the tangible improvement of the difficult situation on the ground and the living conditions faced by Palestinian women and their families;

2. *Reaffirms* that the Israeli occupation remains a major obstacle for Palestinian women with regard to their advancement, self-reliance and integration in the development of their society, and encourages all women in the region to take an active role in supporting the peace process;

3. *Demands* that Israel, the occupying Power, comply fully with the provisions and principles of the Universal Declaration of Human Rights, the Regulations annexed to the Hague Convention IV of 18 October 1907 and the Geneva Convention relative to the Protection of Civilian Persons in Time of War, of 12 August 1949, in order to protect the rights of Palestinian women and their families;

4. *Calls upon* Israel to facilitate the return of all refugees and displaced Palestinian women and children to their homes and properties, in compliance with the relevant United Nations resolutions;

5. *Calls upon* the international community to continue to provide urgently needed assistance and services in an effort to alleviate the dire humanitarian crisis being faced by Palestinian women and their families, to promote their development in various fields and to help in the reconstruction of relevant Palestinian institutions;

6. *Requests* the Commission on the Status of Women to continue to monitor and take action with regard to the implementation of the Nairobi Forward-looking Strategies for the Advancement of Women, in particular paragraph 260 concerning Palestinian women and children, the Beijing Platform for Action and the outcome of the twenty-third special session of the General Assembly, entitled "Women 2000: gender equality, development and peace for the twenty-first century";

7. *Requests* the Secretary-General to continue to review the situation, to assist Palestinian women by all available means, including those set out in his report, and to submit to the Commission on the Status of Women, at its fifty-third session, a report, including information provided by the Economic and Social Commission for Western Asia, on the progress made in the implementation of the present resolution.

ROLL-CALL VOTE ON RESOLUTION 2008/11:

In favour: Algeria, Angola, Barbados, Belarus, Benin, Brazil, Cape Verde, China, Congo, Cuba, El Salvador, Haiti, Iceland, Indonesia, Iraq, Kazakhstan, Malaysia, Mozambique, New Zealand, Pakistan, Paraguay, Russian Federation, Saudi Arabia, Sri Lanka, Sudan.

Against: Canada, United States.

Abstaining: Austria, Czech Republic, France, Greece, Japan, Liechtenstein, Luxembourg, Madagascar, Moldova, Netherlands, Poland, Portugal, Republic of Korea, Romania, Saint Lucia, Sweden, United Kingdom.

Other issues related to Palestine

General aspects

The General Assembly again considered the question of Palestine in 2008, which took centre stage within the framework of the Annapolis process. Following its discussion of the annual report of the Committee on the Exercise of the Inalienable Rights of the Palestinian People (Committee on Palestinian Rights) [A/63/35], the Assembly adopted a resolution requesting the Committee to continue promoting the realization of the rights of the Palestinians, including their right to self-determination, to support the Middle East peace process, and to mobilize international support for and assistance to the Palestinians. In observance of the International Day of Solidarity with the Palestinian People, celebrated annually on 29 November in accordance with Assembly resolution 32/40 B [YUN 1977, p. 304], the Committee held a solemn meeting. At a special meeting at UN Headquarters on 20 June, it marked 60 years of dispossession of Palestine refugees.

Communications. On 10 April [S/2008/243], the Chairman of the Committee on Palestinian Rights, referring to the Secretary-General's summary statement [S/2008/10] concerning the list of items of which the Security Council was seized, reiterated the Committee's continuing objection to deleting from that list the items relating to the exercise of the rights of the Palestinian people, the Palestine question and the situation in the Middle East. Those items, the Chairman stressed, should remain on the list since they continued to engage the Council's primary responsibility with regard to the maintenance of international peace and security. Any decisions to delete them, especially at that critical point, would go well beyond procedural exercise and would have far-reaching political implications.

On 22 August [A/62/946-S/2008/584], Indonesia and South Africa submitted the statement of the co-chairs of the New Asian-African Strategic Partnership Ministerial Conference on Capacity-Building for Palestine (Jakarta, Indonesia, 14 July).

Communications. Iran, in a series of letters [A/62/705-S/2008/117, S/2008/198, A/62/792-S/2008/228, A/62/798-S/2008/246, A/62/815-S/2008/275, S/2008/377, S/2008/599], voiced its support for the peoples of Palestine, condemned Israel's treatment of Palestinians and accused Israeli officials of making threats against Iran and its officials.

In a letter of 19 February [S/2008/110], Israel informed the Secretary-General and the Security Council of remarks made by two senior members of the Iranian leadership allegedly threatening Israel.

Committee on Palestinian Rights

As mandated by General Assembly resolution 62/80 [YUN 2007, p. 466], the Committee on the Exercise of the Inalienable Rights of the Palestinian People (Committee on Palestinian Rights) reviewed and reported on the Palestine question and made suggestions to the Assembly and the Security Council. By **decision 62/553** of 11 September, the Assembly, on the Committee's request [A/62/951], increased its membership to 23, following the appointment of Nicaragua to the Committee.

In pursuance of its mandate, the Committee continued to mobilize the international community in support of the Palestinian people, in cooperation with UN bodies, Governments, intergovernmental and civil society organizations.

Through international meetings and conferences, the Committee raised awareness of the various aspects of the Palestine question and garnered international support for the rights of the Palestinians and for a peaceful settlement. During the period under review, the following international events were held under the Committee's auspices: UN Seminar on Assistance to the Palestinian People (Amman, Jordan, 19–20 February); UN International Conference on Palestine Refugees (Paris, 29–30 April); and UN International Meeting on the Question of Palestine (Qawra, Malta, 3–4 June).

The Committee's annual report to the Assembly [A/63/35] covered the period from 5 October 2007 to 6 October 2008. The Committee noted that the year 2008 marked 60 years of Palestinian dispossession. It reiterated the permanent responsibility of the United Nations towards the Palestine question until it was resolved, and urged the international community to continue its support for the Middle East process.

The Committee considered that its programme of international meetings and conferences contributed to focusing attention on the need for advancing a peaceful settlement and mobilizing much-needed assistance to the Palestinians. Wishing to make its contribution to achieving a comprehensive, just and lasting settlement, and in view of the many difficulties facing the Palestinians and besetting the peace process, the Committee called on all States to join it in that endeavour and to extend their cooperation and support to the Committee. It invited the Assembly again to recognize the importance of its role and to reconfirm its mandate.

At a special meeting on 20 June marking 60 years since the dispossession of the Palestinian people, the Committee Chairman urged the international community to live up to its responsibility to bring about a just solution to the Palestine question, give support to advancing the political process and bolster it through real changes on the ground, thereby enabling the parties to make progress in negotiations on all the permanent status issues.

GENERAL ASSEMBLY ACTION

On 26 November [meeting 60], the General Assembly adopted **resolution 63/26** [draft: A/63/L.32 & Add.1] by recorded vote (107-8-57) [agenda item 16].

Committee on the Exercise of the Inalienable Rights of the Palestinian People

The General Assembly,

Recalling its resolutions 181(II) of 29 November 1947, 194(III) of 11 December 1948, 3236(XXIX) of 22 November 1974, 3375(XXX) and 3376(XXX) of 10 November 1975, 31/20 of 24 November 1976 and all subsequent relevant resolutions, including those adopted by the General Assembly at its emergency special sessions and resolution 62/80 of 10 December 2007,

Recalling also its resolution 58/292 of 6 May 2004,

Having considered the report of the Committee on the Exercise of the Inalienable Rights of the Palestinian People,

Recalling the mutual recognition between the Government of the State of Israel and the Palestine Liberation Organization, the representative of the Palestinian people, as well as the existing agreements between the two sides and the need for full compliance with those agreements,

Recalling also the Quartet road map to a permanent two-State solution to the Israeli-Palestinian conflict, endorsed by the Security Council in its resolution 1515(2003) of 19 November 2003,

Recalling further the Arab Peace Initiative adopted by the Council of the League of Arab States at its fourteenth session, held in Beirut on 27 and 28 March 2002,

Recalling the advisory opinion rendered on 9 July 2004 by the International Court of Justice on the *Legal Consequences of the Construction of a Wall in the Occupied Palestinian Territory*, and recalling also its resolutions ES-10/15 of 20 July 2004 and ES-10/17 of 15 December 2006,

Reaffirming that the United Nations has a permanent responsibility towards the question of Palestine until the question is resolved in all its aspects in a satisfactory manner in accordance with international legitimacy,

1. *Expresses its appreciation* to the Committee on the Exercise of the Inalienable Rights of the Palestinian People for its efforts in performing the tasks assigned to it by the General Assembly, and takes note of its annual report, including the conclusions and valuable recommendations contained in chapter VII thereof;

2. *Requests* the Committee to continue to exert all efforts to promote the realization of the inalienable rights of the Palestinian people, including their right to self-determination, to support the Middle East peace process and to mobilize international support for and assistance to the Palestinian people, and authorizes the Committee to make such adjustments in its approved programme of work as it may consider appropriate and necessary in the light of developments and to report thereon to the General Assembly at its sixty-fourth session and thereafter;

3. *Also requests* the Committee to continue to keep under review the situation relating to the question of Palestine and to report and make suggestions to the General Assembly, the Security Council or the Secretary-General, as appropriate;

4. *Further requests* the Committee to continue to extend its cooperation and support to Palestinian and other civil society organizations and to continue to involve additional civil society organizations in its work in order to mobilize international solidarity and support for the Palestinian people, particularly during this critical period of humanitarian hardship and financial crisis, with the overall aim of promoting the achievement by the Palestinian people of its inalienable rights and a peaceful settlement of the question of Palestine;

5. *Requests* the United Nations Conciliation Commission for Palestine, established under General Assembly resolution 194(III), and other United Nations bodies associated with the question of Palestine to continue to cooperate fully with the Committee and to make available to it, at its request, the relevant information and documentation which they have at their disposal;

6. *Invites* all Governments and organizations to extend their cooperation to the Committee in the performance of its tasks;

7. *Requests* the Secretary-General to circulate the report of the Committee to all the competent bodies of the United Nations, and urges them to take the necessary action, as appropriate;

8. *Also requests* the Secretary-General to continue to provide the Committee with all the necessary facilities for the performance of its tasks.

RECORDED VOTE ON RESOLUTION 63/26:

In favour: Afghanistan, Algeria, Angola, Antigua and Barbuda, Argentina, Armenia, Azerbaijan, Bahamas, Bahrain, Bangladesh, Barbados, Belarus, Benin, Bhutan, Bolivia, Botswana, Brazil, Brunei Darussalam, Burkina Faso, Cambodia, Cape Verde, Central African Republic, Chile, China, Comoros, Congo, Costa Rica, Côte d'Ivoire, Cuba, Cyprus, Democratic People's Republic of Korea, Djibouti, Dominica, Dominican Republic, Ecuador, Egypt, Eritrea, Ethiopia, Gabon, Ghana, Grenada, Guinea, Guinea-Bissau, Guyana, Haiti, Honduras, India, Indonesia, Iran, Iraq, Jamaica, Jordan, Kazakhstan, Kenya, Kuwait, Kyrgyzstan, Lao People's Democratic Republic, Lebanon, Lesotho, Liberia, Libyan Arab Jamahiriya, Malaysia, Maldives, Mali, Malta, Mauritania, Mauritius, Mexico, Morocco, Mozambique, Myanmar, Namibia, Nepal, Nicaragua, Nigeria, Oman, Pakistan, Paraguay, Philippines, Qatar, Saint Lucia, Saint Vincent and the Grenadines, Saudi Arabia, Senegal, Singapore, Solomon Islands, Somalia, South Africa, Sri Lanka, Sudan, Suriname, Swaziland, Syrian Arab Republic, Tajikistan, Timor-Leste, Togo, Trinidad and Tobago, Tunisia, Turkey, Uganda, United Arab Emirates, Uzbekistan, Venezuela, Viet Nam, Yemen, Zambia, Zimbabwe.

Against: Australia, Canada, Israel, Marshall Islands, Micronesia, Nauru, Palau, United States.

Abstaining: Albania, Andorra, Austria, Belgium, Bosnia and Herzegovina, Bulgaria, Cameroon, Colombia, Croatia, Czech Republic, Denmark, El Salvador, Estonia, Fiji, Finland, France, Georgia, Germany, Greece, Guatemala, Hungary, Iceland, Ireland, Italy, Japan, Latvia, Liechtenstein, Lithuania, Luxembourg, Moldova, Monaco, Montenegro, Netherlands, New Zealand, Norway, Panama, Papua New Guinea, Peru, Poland, Portugal, Republic of Korea, Romania, Russian Federation, Samoa, San Marino, Serbia, Slovakia, Slovenia, Spain, Sweden, Switzerland, Thailand, The former Yugoslav Republic of Macedonia, Tonga, Ukraine, United Kingdom, Uruguay.

Division for Palestinian Rights

Under the guidance of the Committee on Palestinian Rights, the Division for Palestinian Rights of the UN Secretariat continued to prepare studies and research, and monitor, collect and disseminate information related to the Palestine question. The Division responded to requests for information and issued a number of publications, such as reports of international meetings and conferences organized under the Committee's auspices. It continued to administer, maintain and expand the United Nations Information System on the Question of Palestine (UNISPAL) and the "Question of Palestine" website on the UN home page. The Division also conducted the annual training programme for PA staff and organized the observance of the International Day of Solidarity with the Palestinian People (29 November).

The Committee, in its annual report [A/63/35], requested the Division to continue its work.

GENERAL ASSEMBLY ACTION

On 26 November [meeting 60], the General Assembly adopted **resolution 63/27** [draft: A/63/L.33 & Add.1] by recorded vote (106-8-57) [agenda item 16].

Division for Palestinian Rights of the Secretariat

The General Assembly,

Having considered the report of the Committee on the Exercise of the Inalienable Rights of the Palestinian People,

Taking note in particular of the relevant information contained in chapter V.B of that report,

Recalling its resolution 32/40 B of 2 December 1977 and all subsequent relevant resolutions, including resolution 62/81 of 10 December 2007,

1. *Notes with appreciation* the action taken by the Secretary-General in compliance with its resolution 62/81;

2. *Considers* that, by assisting the Committee on the Exercise of the Inalienable Rights of the Palestinian People in the implementation of its mandate, the Division for Palestinian Rights of the Secretariat continues to make a useful and constructive contribution to raising international awareness of the question of Palestine and generating international support for the rights of the Palestinian people and a peaceful settlement of the question of Palestine;

3. *Requests* the Secretary-General to continue to provide the Division with the necessary resources and to ensure that it continues to carry out its programme of work as detailed in relevant earlier resolutions, in consultation with the Committee on the Exercise of the Inalienable Rights of the Palestinian People and under its guidance, including, in particular, the monitoring of developments relevant to the question of Palestine, the organization of international meetings and conferences in various regions with the participation of all sectors of the international community, liaison and cooperation with civil society, the further development and expansion of the documents collection of the United Nations Information System on the Question of Palestine, the preparation and widest possible dissemination of publications and information materials on various aspects of the question of Palestine, and the conduct of the annual training programme for staff of the Palestinian Authority;

4. *Also requests* the Secretary-General to ensure the continued cooperation of the Department of Public Information and other units of the Secretariat in enabling the Division to perform its tasks and in covering adequately the various aspects of the question of Palestine;

5. *Invites* all Governments and organizations to extend their cooperation to the Division in the performance of its tasks;

6. *Requests* the Division, as part of the observance of the International Day of Solidarity with the Palestinian People on 29 November, to continue to organize, under the guidance of the Committee on the Exercise of the Inalienable Rights of the Palestinian People, an annual exhibit on Palestinian rights or a cultural event in cooperation with the Permanent Observer Mission of Palestine to the United Nations, and encourages Member States to continue to give the widest support and publicity to the observance of the Day of Solidarity.

RECORDED VOTE ON RESOLUTION 63/27:

In favour: Afghanistan, Algeria, Angola, Antigua and Barbuda, Argentina, Azerbaijan, Bahamas, Bahrain, Bangladesh, Barbados, Belarus, Benin, Bhutan, Bolivia, Botswana, Brazil, Brunei Darussalam, Burkina Faso, Cambodia, Cape Verde, Central African Republic, Chile, China, Comoros, Congo, Costa Rica, Côte d'Ivoire, Cuba, Cyprus, Democratic People's Republic of Korea, Djibouti, Dominica, Dominican Republic, Ecuador, Egypt, Eritrea, Ethiopia, Gabon, Ghana, Grenada, Guinea, Guinea-Bissau, Guyana, Haiti, India, Indonesia, Iran, Iraq, Jamaica, Jordan, Kazakhstan, Kenya, Kuwait, Kyrgyzstan, Lao People's Democratic Republic, Lebanon, Lesotho, Liberia, Libyan Arab Jamahiriya, Malaysia, Maldives, Mali, Malta, Mauritania, Mauritius, Mexico, Morocco, Mozambique, Myanmar, Namibia, Nepal, Nicaragua, Nigeria, Oman, Pakistan, Panama, Paraguay, Philippines, Qatar, Saint Lucia, Saint Vincent and the Grenadines, Saudi Arabia, Senegal, Singapore, Solomon Islands, South Africa, Sri Lanka, Sudan, Suriname, Swaziland, Syrian Arab Republic, Tajikistan, Timor-Leste, Togo, Trinidad and Tobago, Tunisia, Turkey, Uganda, United Arab Emirates, Uruguay, Uzbekistan, Venezuela, Viet Nam, Yemen, Zambia, Zimbabwe.

Against: Australia, Canada, Israel, Marshall Islands, Micronesia, Nauru, Palau, United States.

Abstaining: Albania, Andorra, Armenia, Austria, Belgium, Bosnia and Herzegovina, Bulgaria, Cameroon, Colombia, Croatia, Czech Republic, Denmark, El Salvador, Estonia, Fiji, Finland, France, Georgia, Germany, Greece, Guatemala, Honduras, Hungary, Iceland, Ireland, Italy, Japan, Latvia, Liechtenstein, Lithuania, Luxembourg, Moldova, Monaco, Montenegro, Netherlands, New Zealand, Norway, Papua New Guinea, Peru, Poland, Portugal, Republic of Korea, Romania, Russian Federation, Samoa, San Marino, Serbia, Slovakia, Slovenia, Spain, Sweden, Switzerland, Thailand, The former Yugoslav Republic of Macedonia, Tonga, Ukraine, United Kingdom.

Special information programme

As requested by General Assembly resolution 62/82 [YUN 2007, p. 468], the UN Department of Public Information (DPI) continued its special information programme on the question of Palestine, which included the issuing of press releases and the preparation for the annual training programme for Palestinian journalists. The video news service UNifeed produced and distributed 11 packages on the Palestine question, and the *UN News Centre* Internet portal highlighted stories related to the question of Palestine in all six official UN languages.

As in previous years, the network of the United Nations Information Centres (UNICs) and other UN offices carried out activities in connection with the International Day of Solidarity with the Palestinian People on 29 November.

GENERAL ASSEMBLY ACTION

On 26 November [meeting 60], the General Assembly adopted **resolution 63/28** [draft: A/63/L.34 & Add.1] by recorded vote (162-8-4) [agenda item 16].

Special information programme on the question of Palestine of the Department of Public Information of the Secretariat

The General Assembly,

Having considered the report of the Committee on the Exercise of the Inalienable Rights of the Palestinian People,

Taking note in particular of the information contained in chapter VI of that report,

Recalling its resolution 62/82 of 10 December 2007,

Convinced that the worldwide dissemination of accurate and comprehensive information and the role of civil society organizations and institutions remain of vital importance in heightening awareness of and support for the inalienable rights of the Palestinian people,

Recalling the mutual recognition between the Government of the State of Israel and the Palestine Liberation Organization, the representative of the Palestinian people, as well as the existing agreements between the two sides,

Recalling also the Quartet road map to a permanent two-State solution to the Israeli-Palestinian conflict,

Recalling further the Arab Peace Initiative adopted by the Council of the League of Arab States at its fourteenth session, held in Beirut on 27 and 28 March 2002,

Recalling the advisory opinion rendered on 9 July 2004 by the International Court of Justice on the *Legal Consequences of the Construction of a Wall in the Occupied Palestinian Territory*,

Reaffirming that the United Nations has a permanent responsibility towards the question of Palestine until the question is resolved in all its aspects in a satisfactory manner in accordance with international legitimacy,

Expressing the hope that the Department of Public Information of the Secretariat, in its upcoming programme for 2009–2010, will continue to examine ways to foster and encourage the contribution of media in support of the peace process between the Palestinian and Israeli sides,

1. *Notes with appreciation* the action taken by the Department of Public Information in compliance with resolution 62/82;

2. *Considers* that the special information programme on the question of Palestine of the Department is very useful in raising the awareness of the international community concerning the question of Palestine and the situation in the Middle East and that the programme is contributing effectively to an atmosphere conducive to dialogue and supportive of the peace process;

3. *Requests* the Department, in full cooperation and coordination with the Committee on the Exercise of the Inalienable Rights of the Palestinian People, to continue, with the necessary flexibility as may be required by developments affecting the question of Palestine, its special information programme for the biennium 2009–2010, in particular:

(a) To disseminate information on all the activities of the United Nations system relating to the question of Palestine and the peace process, including reports on the work carried out by the relevant United Nations organizations, as well as on the efforts of the Secretary-General and his Special Envoy vis-à-vis the peace process;

(b) To continue to issue and update publications on the various aspects of the question of Palestine in all fields, including materials concerning the relevant recent developments in that regard, in particular the efforts to achieve a peaceful settlement of the question of Palestine;

(c) To expand its collection of audio-visual material on the question of Palestine, to continue the production and preservation of such material and to update, on a periodic basis, the public exhibit on the question of Palestine displayed in the General Assembly building;

(d) To organize and promote fact-finding news missions for journalists to the Occupied Palestinian Territory, including East Jerusalem, and Israel;

(e) To organize international, regional and national seminars or encounters for journalists, aiming in particular at sensitizing public opinion to the question of Palestine and the peace process and at enhancing dialogue and understanding between Palestinians and Israelis for the promotion of a peaceful settlement to the Israeli-Palestinian conflict;

(f) To continue to provide assistance to the Palestinian people in the field of media development, in particular to strengthen the annual training programme for Palestinian broadcasters and journalists;

4. *Encourages* the Department to formulate ways for the media and representatives of civil society to engage in an open and positive discussion on means for encouraging people-to-people dialogue and promoting peace and mutual understanding in the region.

RECORDED VOTE ON RESOLUTION 63/28:

In favour: Afghanistan, Albania, Algeria, Andorra, Angola, Antigua and Barbuda, Argentina, Armenia, Austria, Azerbaijan, Bahamas, Bahrain, Bangladesh, Barbados, Belarus, Belgium, Benin, Bhutan, Bolivia, Bosnia and Herzegovina, Botswana, Brazil, Brunei Darussalam, Bulgaria, Burkina Faso, Cambodia, Cape Verde, Central African Republic, Chile, China, Colombia, Comoros, Congo, Costa Rica, Côte d'Ivoire, Croatia, Cuba, Cyprus, Czech Republic, Democratic People's Republic of Korea, Denmark, Djibouti, Dominica, Dominican Republic, Ecuador, Egypt, El Salvador, Eritrea, Estonia, Ethiopia, Finland, France, Gabon, Gambia, Georgia, Germany, Ghana, Greece, Grenada, Guatemala, Guinea, Guinea-Bissau, Guyana, Haiti, Honduras, Hungary, Iceland, India, Indonesia, Iran, Iraq, Ireland, Italy, Jamaica, Japan, Jordan, Kazakhstan, Kenya, Kuwait, Kyrgyzstan, Lao People's Democratic Republic, Latvia, Lebanon, Lesotho, Liberia, Libyan Arab Jamahiriya, Liechtenstein, Lithuania, Luxembourg, Malaysia, Maldives, Mali, Malta, Mauritania, Mauritius, Mexico, Moldova, Monaco, Mongolia, Montenegro, Morocco, Mozambique, Myanmar, Namibia, Nepal, Netherlands, New Zealand, Nicaragua, Nigeria, Norway, Oman, Pakistan, Panama, Paraguay, Peru, Philippines, Poland, Portugal, Qatar, Republic of Korea, Romania, Russian Federation, Saint Lucia, Saint Vincent and the Grenadines, Samoa, San Marino, Saudi Arabia, Senegal, Serbia, Singapore, Slovakia, Slovenia, Solomon Islands, Somalia, South Africa, Spain, Sri Lanka, Sudan, Suriname, Swaziland, Sweden, Switzerland, Syrian Arab Republic, Tajikistan, Thailand, The former Yugoslav Republic of Macedonia, Timor-Leste, Togo, Trinidad and Tobago, Tunisia, Turkey, Uganda, Ukraine, United Arab Emirates, United Kingdom, Uruguay, Uzbekistan, Venezuela, Viet Nam, Yemen, Zambia, Zimbabwe.

Against: Australia, Canada, Israel, Marshall Islands, Micronesia, Nauru, Palau, United States.

Abstaining: Cameroon, Fiji, Papua New Guinea, Tonga.

Assistance to Palestinians

UN activities

In response to General Assembly resolution 62/93 [YUN 2007, p. 470], the Secretary-General, in a May report [A/63/75-E/2008/52], described UN and other assistance to the Palestinian people from May 2007 to April 2008. The report provided an overview of the work of UN agencies, in cooperation with Palestinian and donor counterparts, to assist the Palestinian people and institutions with regard to economic and fiscal development, humanitarian and socio-economic development, human and social development, UN system support, private sector development, emergency assistance, and donor response and coordination.

UN agencies and programmes had to adjust to a situation in which priorities and activities with respect to the Gaza Strip and the West Bank diverged significantly under the impact of the de facto political split between the two constituent parts of the Occupied Palestinian Territory. In Gaza, UN entities faced severe restrictions and obstacles, which made the delivery of assistance more urgent, and more difficult.

The Palestinian economy continued to decline, especially in the Gaza Strip, where the private sector collapsed in the aftermath of Hamas' takeover in 2007 and the near-complete closure by Israel. The West Bank, however, witnessed some modest economic recovery under the new PA Government. There was significant progress in reform [YUN 2007, p. 441], including pledges from international donors of $7.7 billion for a three-year period to enable the implementation of the new Palestinian Reform and Development Plan. By April, half of the pledges targeting recurrent expenditures had been disbursed, in addition to $500 million towards budgetary support. The United Nations Relief and Works Agency for Palestine Refugees in the Near East (UNRWA) continued to ensure free education for over 250,000 pupils in 306 schools in the West Bank and Gaza through its network of vocational, technical and teacher training. In Gaza, a recovery plan was introduced to provide support to 50,000 pupils in UNRWA schools. Under the Palestinian Education programme, implemented in cooperation with the United Nations Development Programme (UNDP), five new schools were constructed in the West Bank and Gaza and 10 buildings rehabilitated, creating 1,880 new seats for students. The Programme also provided equipment, computer labs, libraries and other teaching aids to 190 schools, benefiting over 5,000 students. UNESCO provided technical assistance for the Ministry of Education and Higher Education in sectoral policy and planning efforts, supporting the preparation of the five-year Education Development Strategic Plan (2008-2012). The United Nations Children's Fund (UNICEF) provided technical and financial assistance for building capacity and establishing teacher-training centres in disadvantaged districts. It also provided equipment for the National Institute for Teacher Education in Ramallah and Gaza, supported informal learning and recreational activities for adolescents to improve literacy and vocational skills, and implemented short-term training for teachers and school administrators. The United Nations Population Fund (UNFPA) developed a national referral system for youth-friendly services, and continued to build the capacity of teachers, counsellors, health staff and school health committee coordinators for in-school information and counselling activities.

The World Health Organization (WHO) provided technical expertise to the Ministry of Health, training staff in child nutrition, safe water, hygiene, outbreaks and epidemics, and control and prevention of non-communicable diseases. It also supported the Ministry in procuring and delivering essential pharmaceutical supplies, substantially improving drug availability in the West Bank and Gaza. The Food and Agriculture Organization of the United Nations (FAO), together with the Ministry of Agriculture and other partners, implemented 19 projects focusing on the recovery of crop and animal production, the introduction of aquaculture, support for backyard farming, gardening and cottage industries for women, and emergency assistance for preparedness and response to avian influenza outbreaks. FAO also assisted in technical training in agricultural production and marketing, irrigation and greenhouse rehabilitation, land reclamation, water resource management and the improvement of livestock production, crops and orchards.

The Office of the United Nations Special Coordinator continued to coordinate UN assistance to the Palestinian people and to represent the UN system at donor forums, while OCHA continued humanitarian coordination through the 2008 consolidated appeal (see p. 1005) and its ongoing collection of data and reporting on closures, violence and other issues. With field offices throughout the Occupied Palestinian Territory, OCHA identified programming gaps, published monthly reports monitoring humanitarian indicators and facilitated NGO projects through the Humanitarian and Emergency Response Fund.

Those developments occurred against the backdrop of an escalation of conflict, which remained the single greatest challenge to economic revival and viability in the Occupied Palestinian Territory and compelled agencies to deliver increasing emergency and humanitarian assistance instead of longer-term development programming. The new Palestinian Reform and Development Plan challenged the United Nations and the international community to increase the predictability of funding and programming and to ensure that their programming met the objectives identified in the Plan. The process of establishing shared strategic objectives for UN programming, initiated in early 2008, would need to translate into a common UN programmatic response to the Plan.

The Economic and Social Council, by **decision 2008/243** of 24 July, took note of the Secretary-General's report.

UNCTAD assistance to Palestinians

At its fifty-fifth session (Geneva, 15 September–26 October), the Trade and Development Board of the United Nations Conference on Trade and Development (UNCTAD) considered its report on assistance to the Palestinian people [TD/B/55/2]. The report stated that the economy of the Occupied Palestinian Territory stagnated in 2007, as a result of which gross domestic product (GDP) per capita continued its downward trend and poverty deepened. If it were not for the resumption of foreign aid in the second half of 2007, the GDP would have contracted for the second year in a row. The construction of the separation barrier, the Israeli closure policy and the erosion of productive capacity continued to prevent recovery and entrenched "de-development". The economic gap between the West Bank and Gaza widened as a result of political developments and the tight closure imposed on the Gaza Strip.

The report noted that the PA had announced significant reforms for achieving fiscal sustainability, but to put the economy on a path of sustainable development and self-sufficiency, those reforms needed to be complemented by empowering the PA with appropriate policy instruments. In addition, there was an urgent need to strengthen PA capacity to formulate and implement development policies and to provide sound economic management for their implementation.

UNCTAD responded to the emerging needs of the Palestinian economy through a programme of assistance designed to achieve specific national development objectives in four clusters: trade policies and strategies; trade facilitation and logistics; finance and development; and enterprise, investment and competition policy. In line with the UN Strategic Framework for 2008–2009 [YUN 2006, p. 1635], assistance to the Palestinian people had intensified in the past year, involving new research areas and technical assistance activities to mitigate the adverse economic and social conditions and to contribute to building the economic capacities of a sovereign and viable Palestinian State. However, progress towards those objectives continued to be affected by adverse conditions, especially the restrictions on the mobility of national project staff and access of UNCTAD experts to the Occupied Palestinian Territory. Political instability compelled the secretariat to suspend planned activities in the Gaza Strip, and several projects remained unfunded, despite the secretariat's appeals to donors. Nonetheless, UNCTAD was able, through a selective and flexible mode of operation, to make significant progress.

GENERAL ASSEMBLY ACTION

On 11 December [meeting 68], the General Assembly adopted **resolution 63/140** [draft: A/63/L.50 & Add.1] without vote [agenda item 65 *(c)*].

Assistance to the Palestinian people

The General Assembly,

Recalling its resolution 62/93 of 17 December 2007, as well as previous resolutions on the question,

Recalling also the signing of the Declaration of Principles on Interim Self-Government Arrangements in Washington, D.C., on 13 September 1993, by the Government of the State of Israel and the Palestine Liberation Organization, the representative of the Palestinian people, and the subsequent implementation agreements concluded by the two sides,

Recalling further all relevant international law, including humanitarian and human rights law, and, in particular, the International Covenant on Civil and Political Rights, the International Covenant on Economic, Social and Cultural Rights, the Convention on the Rights of the Child, and the Convention on the Elimination of All Forms of Discrimination against Women,

Gravely concerned at the deterioration in the living conditions of the Palestinian people, in particular women and children, throughout the occupied Palestinian territory, which constitutes a mounting humanitarian crisis,

Conscious of the urgent need for improvement in the economic and social infrastructure of the occupied territory,

Welcoming, in this context, the development of projects, notably on infrastructure, to revive the Palestinian economy and improve the living conditions of the Palestinian people, stressing the need to create the appropriate conditions to facilitate the implementation of these projects, and noting the contribution of partners in the region and the international community,

Aware that development is difficult under occupation and is best promoted in circumstances of peace and stability,

Noting the great economic and social challenges facing the Palestinian people and their leadership,

Emphasizing the importance of the safety and well-being of all people, in particular women and children, in the whole Middle East region,

Deeply concerned about the negative impact, including the health and psychological consequences, of violence on the present and future well-being of children in the region,

Conscious of the urgent necessity for international assistance to the Palestinian people, taking into account the Palestinian priorities,

Expressing grave concern about the humanitarian situation in Gaza, and underlining the importance of emergency and humanitarian assistance,

Welcoming the results of the Conference to Support Middle East Peace, convened in Washington, D.C., on 1 October 1993, the establishment of the Ad Hoc Liaison Committee for the Coordination of the International Assistance to Palestinians and the work being done by the World Bank as its secretariat and the establishment of the Consultative Group, as well as all follow-up meetings and international mechanisms established to provide assistance to the Palestinian people,

Underlining the importance of the International Donors' Conference for the Palestinian State, held in Paris on 17 December 2007, in mobilizing donors to provide financial and political support for the Palestinian Authority and, in the meantime, also to provide assistance to alleviate the socio-economic and humanitarian situation being faced by the Palestinian people, and welcoming the meetings of the Ad Hoc Liaison Committee for the Coordination of the International Assistance to Palestinians, held in London on 2 May 2008 and in New York on 22 September 2008,

Welcoming the plan to resume the activities of the Joint Liaison Committee, which provides a forum in which economic policy and practical matters related to donor assistance are discussed with the Palestinian Authority,

Stressing the need for the full engagement of the United Nations in the process of building Palestinian institutions and in providing broad assistance to the Palestinian people, and welcoming in this regard the support provided to the Palestinian Authority by the Task Force on Palestinian Reform, established by the Quartet in 2002,

Welcoming the outcome of the Berlin Conference in Support of Palestinian Civil Security and the Rule of Law, held on 24 June 2008, and calling for its speedy implementation,

Welcoming also the convening of the Palestine Investment Conference, held in Bethlehem from 21 to 23 May 2008, aimed at promoting an enabling environment for Palestinian private sector growth and development,

Welcoming further the action of the Special Representative of the Quartet, Tony Blair, charged with developing, with the Government of the Palestinian Authority, a multi-year agenda to strengthen institutions, promote economic development and mobilize international funds,

Welcoming the continuing calm between Gaza and southern Israel, and expressing hope that this calm will persist and result in further relief for the civilian population of Gaza, including the regular opening of the crossings for the movement of persons and goods, for both humanitarian and commercial flows,

Noting the active participation of the United Nations Special Coordinator for the Middle East Peace Process and Personal Representative of the Secretary-General to the Palestine Liberation Organization and the Palestinian Authority in the activities of the Special Envoys of the Quartet,

Welcoming the endorsement by the Security Council, in its resolution 1515(2003) of 19 November 2003, of the performance-based road map to a permanent two-State solution to the Israeli-Palestinian conflict, and stressing the need for its implementation and compliance with its provisions,

Noting the Israeli withdrawal from the Gaza Strip in 2005 and parts of the northern West Bank as a step towards implementation of the road map,

Commending the continuous efforts made by both parties since the convening of the international conference in Annapolis, United States of America, on 27 November 2007, in order to reach an agreement as soon as possible, so as to ensure the establishment of an independent, democratic and viable Palestinian state, living in peace and security alongside Israel,

Having considered the report of the Secretary-General,

Expressing grave concern about the continuation of the tragic and violent events that have led to many deaths and injuries, including among children and women,

1. *Takes note* of the report of the Secretary-General;

2. *Expresses its appreciation* to the Secretary-General for his rapid response and efforts regarding assistance to the Palestinian people;

3. *Also expresses its appreciation* to the Member States, United Nations bodies and intergovernmental, regional and non-governmental organizations that have provided and continue to provide assistance to the Palestinian people;

4. *Stresses* the importance of the work of the United Nations Special Coordinator for the Middle East Peace Process and Personal Representative of the Secretary-General to the Palestine Liberation Organization and the Palestinian Authority and of the steps taken under the auspices of the Secretary-General to ensure the achievement of a coordinated mechanism for United Nations activities throughout the occupied territories;

5. *Urges* Member States, international financial institutions of the United Nations system, intergovernmental and non-governmental organizations and regional and interregional organizations to extend, as rapidly and as generously as possible, economic and social assistance to the Palestinian people, in close cooperation with the Palestine Liberation Organization and through official Palestinian institutions;

6. *Welcomes*, in this regard, the meeting of the Ad Hoc Liaison Committee for the Coordination of the International Assistance to Palestinians and the significant results of the Paris International Donors' Conference for the Palestinian State which succeeded in mobilizing the international community and led to the disbursement of 1.36 billion United States dollars in budgetary support as of 22 September 2008;

7. *Stresses* the importance of following up on the results of the Paris Conference, including calls upon donors that have not yet converted their budget support pledges into disbursements to transfer funds as soon as possible, encourages all donors to increase their direct assistance to the Palestinian Authority in accordance with its government programme in order to enable it to build a viable and prosperous Palestinian state, underlines the need for equitable burden-sharing by donors in this effort, and encourages donors to consider aligning funding cycles with the Palestinian Authority's national budget cycle;

8. *Calls upon* relevant organizations and agencies of the United Nations system to intensify their assistance in response to the urgent needs of the Palestinian people in accordance with priorities set forth by the Palestinian side;

9. *Calls upon* the international community to provide urgently needed assistance and services in an effort to alleviate the dire humanitarian situation being faced by Palestinian women, children and their families and to help in the reconstruction of relevant Palestinian institutions;

10. *Stresses* the role that all funding instruments, including the European Commission's Palestinian-European Mechanism for the Management of Socio-Economic Aid

and the World Bank trust fund, have been playing in directly assisting the Palestinian people;

11. *Urges* Member States to open their markets to exports of Palestinian products on the most favourable terms, consistent with appropriate trading rules, and to implement fully existing trade and cooperation agreements;

12. *Calls upon* the international donor community to expedite the delivery of pledged assistance to the Palestinian people to meet their urgent needs;

13. *Stresses*, in this context, the importance of ensuring free humanitarian access to the Palestinian people and the free movement of persons and goods;

14. *Also stresses* the need for the full implementation by both parties of the Agreement on Movement and Access and of the Agreed Principles for the Rafah Crossing, of 15 November 2005, to allow for the freedom of movement of the Palestinian civilian population, as well as for imports and exports, within and into and out of the Gaza Strip;

15. *Urges* the international donor community, United Nations agencies and organizations and non-governmental organizations to extend to the Palestinian people, as rapidly as possible, emergency economic assistance and humanitarian assistance, particularly in the Gaza Strip, to counter the impact of the current crisis;

16. *Stresses* the need for the continued implementation of the Paris Protocol on Economic Relations of 29 April 1994, fifth annex to the Israeli-Palestinian Interim Agreement on the West Bank and the Gaza Strip, signed in Washington, D.C., on 28 September 1995, including with regard to the full, prompt and regular transfer of Palestinian indirect tax revenues;

17. *Requests* the Secretary-General to submit a report to the General Assembly at its sixty-fourth session, through the Economic and Social Council, on the implementation of the present resolution, containing:

(a) An assessment of the assistance actually received by the Palestinian people;

(b) An assessment of the needs still unmet and specific proposals for responding effectively to them;

18. *Decides* to include in the provisional agenda of its sixty-fourth session the sub-item entitled "Assistance to the Palestinian people".

UNRWA

The United Nations Relief and Works Agency for Palestine Refugees in the Near East (UNRWA) continued to provide vital education, health, relief and social services, and micro-finance to an ever-growing refugee population in the Gaza Strip, the West Bank, Jordan, Lebanon and the Syrian Arab Republic.

Report of Commissioner-General. In his report on the work of the Agency in 2008 [A/64/13], the UNRWA Commissioner-General said that the Occupied Palestinian Territory continued to experience the most dramatic developments. In the Gaza Strip, the year began and ended with major conflicts. The blockade imposed by Israel in June 2007 after the Hamas takeover [YUN 2007, p. 441] and the dissolution of the Palestinian National Unity Government by President Abbas [ibid.] seriously affected all aspects of Palestinian life, even though it allowed for the exceptional importation of some essential humanitarian supplies, urgent medical evacuations and the passage of a small number of Palestinians. Unemployment rose as more private enterprises closed, depleting further the capacity of Palestinian society to support itself.

The Agency provided emergency food assistance to 190,000 refugee families and introduced a feeding programme for all 200,000 pupils in its schools in the Gaza Strip. Around $12 million was disbursed as cash grants to 30,000 poor refugee families and $6 million to cover back-to-school costs. In addition, UNRWA created 3 million job days for 56,000 refugees.

A lack of currency notes, due to the Gaza blockade, forced the Agency to suspend, effective 19 November, social welfare payments to 19,000 destitute families in the Gaza Strip. By December, UNRWA warehouses were almost empty and the Agency was unable to consolidate strategic reserves, despite the ceasefire, and was forced to delay emergency food aid to 135,000 families towards the end of the year.

During the Israeli offensive in December (see p. 492), UNRWA provided temporary shelter to over 50,000 Palestinians seeking refuge in 50 Agency installations. Critical operations, including food distributions, continued where possible.

In the West Bank, UNRWA faced increased difficulties in accessing refugee communities to meet their humanitarian needs. A total of 918 access incidents were reported, compared with 231 the previous year. In Lebanon, despite the tense political and security situation, UNRWA was able to operate with little interruption. However, tensions between Palestinian factions mounted during the second half of the year, leading to an unstable situation in the Ein el-Hilweh refugee camp, in particular. In Jordan and the Syrian Arab Republic, UNRWA and the refugees enjoyed a secure and stable environment, but the continued presence of Iraqi refugees in both countries contributed to inflation and strained services provided by the Government and by UNRWA.

The security of UNRWA staff remained a concern, especially in the Gaza Strip, as did obstructions to the Agency's services and damage to its premises. An action plan was developed for mainstreaming security at all levels, as a step towards the adoption of an UNRWA security policy. Under its management reform programme, initiated in 2006 [YUN 2006, p. 557], UNRWA made significant progress in achieving best practice standards in programme cycle management. The basis for a medium-term strategy for 2010–2015 was developed. A needs assessment was undertaken and results-based planning commenced for the 2010–2011 biennium; the Agency's performance indicator framework was revised accordingly.

Advisory Commission. In its comments on the Agency's 2008 report, transmitted by its Chairman [A/64/13], the UNRWA Advisory Commission commended the Agency for continuing to deliver its programmes and services to all Palestinian refugees and its vital role in contributing to regional stability. The Commission was concerned about the loss of life and hardships endured by the majority of Palestinian refugees in the West Bank and Gaza, and that the separation barrier, closures, curfews and other movement restrictions were hindering economic development, as well as UNRWA's ability to carry out its mandated tasks. The Commission reiterated the urgent need to remove restrictions regarding the movement of UNRWA staff and goods.

The Commission was also concerned about obstructions to the Agency's services and damage to its premises. It called on the General Assembly to examine the direct taxation level and additional restrictions imposed by Israel on Agency containers passing through Gaza crossings and to consider calling for reimbursement of those charges by Israel. It called on all parties to fully respect international law and urged UNRWA to continue to report on the impact of international humanitarian law violations on its operations. It remained concerned about the lack of Agency access to, and information on, its staff held by both Israeli and Palestinian authorities.

The Commission restated its view that the enduring hardships of Palestine refugees underscored UNRWA's critical role. It noted the difficulties the Agency faced in reaching a funding level sufficient to maintain adequate service delivery, and urged the international donor community to mobilize the resources needed. Noting that UNRWA's emergency appeal for $262 million in 2008 for the Occupied Palestinian Territory was its largest to date, the Commission expressed concern that only $176 million had been received.

The Commission emphasized its ongoing support for the Agency's continuing reform to improve its effectiveness in service delivery, develop the medium-term strategy for 2010–2015 and establish a clearer link between the strategy and the three corresponding biennial budgets.

The Commission called for full support for the rebuilding of the Nahr El-Bared camp in Lebanon and for relief assistance to some 30,000 refugees displaced following its destruction in 2007 [YUN 2007, p. 472] .

Report of Conciliation Commission. The United Nations Conciliation Commission for Palestine, established by General Assembly resolution 194(III) [YUN 1948–49, p. 203] to facilitate the repatriation, resettlement and economic and social rehabilitation of the refugees and the payment of compensation, in its sixty-second report, covering the period from 1 September 2007 to 31 August 2008 [A/63/317], submitted in accordance with General Assembly resolution 62/102 [YUN 2007, p. 473], noted the submission of its August 2007 report [ibid.] and observed that it had nothing further to report.

GENERAL ASSEMBLY ACTION

On 5 December [meeting 64], the General Assembly, having considered the UNRWA Commissioner-General's report covering the period from 1 January to 31 December 2007 [YUN 2007, p. 471], on the recommendation of the Fourth Committee [A/63/400], adopted **resolution 63/91** by recorded vote (173-1-6) [agenda item 29].

Assistance to Palestine refugees

The General Assembly,

Recalling its resolution 194(III) of 11 December 1948 and all its subsequent resolutions on the question, including resolution 62/102 of 17 December 2007,

Recalling also its resolution 302(IV) of 8 December 1949, by which, inter alia, it established the United Nations Relief and Works Agency for Palestine Refugees in the Near East,

Recalling further relevant Security Council resolutions,

Aware of the fact that, for six decades, the Palestine refugees have suffered from the loss of their homes, lands and means of livelihood,

Affirming the imperative of resolving the problem of the Palestine refugees for the achievement of justice and for the achievement of lasting peace in the region,

Acknowledging the essential role that the United Nations Relief and Works Agency for Palestine Refugees in the Near East has played for fifty-nine years since its establishment in ameliorating the plight of the Palestine refugees through its provision of education, health, relief and social services and emergency assistance,

Taking note of the report of the Commissioner-General of the United Nations Relief and Works Agency for Palestine Refugees in the Near East covering the period from 1 January to 31 December 2007,

Aware of the continuing needs of the Palestine refugees throughout all the fields of operation, namely, Jordan, Lebanon, the Syrian Arab Republic and the Occupied Palestinian Territory,

Expressing grave concern at the especially difficult situation of the Palestine refugees under occupation, including with regard to their safety, well-being and socio-economic living conditions,

Expressing grave concern in particular at the humanitarian situation in the Gaza Strip, and underlining the importance of emergency and humanitarian assistance,

Noting the signing of the Declaration of Principles on Interim Self-Government Arrangements on 13 September 1993 by the Government of Israel and the Palestine Liberation Organization and the subsequent implementation agreements,

Aware of the role to be played by the Multilateral Working Group on Refugees of the Middle East peace process,

1. *Notes with regret* that repatriation or compensation of the refugees, as provided for in paragraph 11 of General Assembly resolution 194(III), has not yet been effected, and that, therefore, the situation of the Palestine refugees continues to be a matter of grave concern and the Palestine refugees continue to require assistance to meet basic health, education and living needs;

2. *Also notes with regret* that the United Nations Conciliation Commission for Palestine has been unable to find a means of achieving progress in the implementation of paragraph 11 of General Assembly resolution 194(III), and reiterates its request to the Conciliation Commission to continue exerting efforts towards the implementation of that paragraph and to report to the Assembly as appropriate, but no later than 1 September 2009;

3. *Affirms* the necessity for the continuation of the work of the United Nations Relief and Works Agency for Palestine Refugees in the Near East and the importance of its unimpeded operation and its provision of services for the well-being and human development of the Palestine refugees and for the stability of the region, pending the just resolution of the question of the Palestine refugees;

4. *Calls upon* all donors to continue to make the most generous efforts possible to meet the anticipated needs of the United Nations Relief and Works Agency for Palestine Refugees in the Near East, including with regard to increased expenditures arising from the continuing deterioration of the socio-economic and humanitarian situation in the region, particularly in the Occupied Palestinian Territory, and those mentioned in recent emergency appeals;

5. *Decides* to commemorate the work of the United Nations Relief and Works Agency for Palestine Refugees in the Near East on the occasion of the sixtieth anniversary of its establishment at a high-level meeting to be convened on 1 October 2009, during the sixty-fourth session of the General Assembly, and encourages the participation of Member States at the ministerial level;

6. *Decides also* to invite Finland and Ireland, in accordance with the criterion set forth in General Assembly decision 60/522 of 8 December 2005, to become members of the Advisory Commission of the United Nations Relief and Works Agency for Palestine Refugees in the Near East.

RECORDED VOTE ON RESOLUTION 63/91:

In favour: Afghanistan, Albania, Algeria, Andorra, Angola, Antigua and Barbuda, Argentina, Armenia, Australia, Austria, Azerbaijan, Bahamas, Bahrain, Bangladesh, Barbados, Belarus, Belgium, Belize, Benin, Bhutan, Bolivia, Bosnia and Herzegovina, Botswana, Brazil, Brunei Darussalam, Bulgaria, Burkina Faso, Burundi, Cambodia, Canada, Cape Verde, Central African Republic, Chile, China, Colombia, Comoros, Congo, Costa Rica, Côte d'Ivoire, Croatia, Cuba, Cyprus, Czech Republic, Democratic People's Republic of Korea, Denmark, Djibouti, Dominica, Dominican Republic, Ecuador, Egypt, El Salvador, Eritrea, Estonia, Ethiopia, Fiji, Finland, France, Gabon, Georgia, Germany, Ghana, Greece, Grenada, Guatemala, Guinea, Guinea-Bissau, Guyana, Haiti, Honduras, Hungary, Iceland, India, Indonesia, Iran, Iraq, Ireland, Italy, Jamaica, Japan, Jordan, Kazakhstan, Kenya, Kuwait, Kyrgyzstan, Lao People's Democratic Republic, Latvia, Lebanon, Lesotho, Liberia, Libyan Arab Jamahiriya, Liechtenstein, Lithuania, Luxembourg, Madagascar, Malawi, Malaysia, Maldives, Mali, Malta, Mauritania, Mauritius, Mexico, Moldova, Monaco, Mongolia, Montenegro, Morocco, Mozambique, Myanmar, Namibia, Nepal, Netherlands, New Zealand, Nicaragua, Niger, Norway, Oman, Pakistan, Panama, Papua New Guinea, Paraguay, Peru, Philippines, Poland, Portugal, Qatar, Republic of Korea, Romania, Russian Federation, Saint Lucia, Saint Vincent and the Grenadines, Samoa, San Marino, Sao Tome and Principe, Saudi Arabia, Senegal, Serbia, Singapore, Slovakia, Slovenia, Solomon Islands, South Africa, Spain, Sri Lanka, Sudan, Suriname, Swaziland, Sweden, Switzerland, Syrian Arab Republic, Tajikistan, Thailand, The former Yugoslav Republic of Macedonia, Timor-Leste, Togo, Tonga, Trinidad and Tobago, Tunisia, Turkey, Turkmenistan, Tuvalu, Uganda, Ukraine, United Arab Emirates, United Kingdom, United Republic of Tanzania, Uruguay, Uzbekistan, Venezuela, Viet Nam, Yemen, Zambia, Zimbabwe.

Against: Israel.

Abstaining: Cameroon, Marshall Islands, Micronesia, Nauru, Palau, United States.

The Assembly, also on 5 December [meeting 64], on the recommendation of the Fourth Committee [A/63/400], adopted **resolution 63/93** by recorded vote (172-6-1) [agenda item 29].

Operations of the United Nations Relief and Works Agency for Palestine Refugees in the Near East

The General Assembly,

Recalling its resolutions 194(III) of 11 December 1948, 212(III) of 19 November 1948, 302(IV) of 8 December 1949 and all subsequent related resolutions, including its resolution 62/104 of 17 December 2007,

Recalling also the relevant Security Council resolutions,

Having considered the report of the Commissioner-General of the United Nations Relief and Works Agency for Palestine Refugees in the Near East covering the period from 1 January to 31 December 2007,

Taking note of the letter dated 11 June 2008 from the Chairman of the Advisory Commission of the United Nations Relief and Works Agency for Palestine Refugees in the Near East addressed to the Commissioner-General,

Deeply concerned about the critical financial situation of the Agency, as well as about its rising expenditures resulting from the deterioration of the socio-economic and humanitarian conditions in the region and their significant negative impact on the provision of necessary Agency services to the Palestine refugees, including its emergency-related and development programmes,

Recalling Articles 100, 104 and 105 of the Charter of the United Nations and the Convention on the Privileges and Immunities of the United Nations,

Recalling also the Convention on the Safety of United Nations and Associated Personnel,

Affirming the applicability of the Geneva Convention relative to the Protection of Civilian Persons in Time of War, of 12 August 1949, to the Palestinian territory occupied since 1967, including East Jerusalem,

Aware of the continuing needs of the Palestine refugees throughout the Occupied Palestinian Territory and in the other fields of operation, namely Jordan, Lebanon and the Syrian Arab Republic,

Gravely concerned about the extremely difficult living conditions being faced by the Palestine refugees in the Occupied Palestinian Territory, including East Jerusalem, particularly in the refugee camps in the Gaza Strip, resulting, inter alia, from the loss of life and injury, the extensive destruction of their shelters, properties and vital infrastructure, the displacement of the Palestine refugees, the prolonged closures and socio-economic decline,

Aware of the extraordinary efforts being undertaken by the Agency for the repair or rebuilding of thousands of damaged or destroyed refugee shelters and for the provision of shelter and emergency aid for those refugee families internally displaced as a result of Israeli military actions, as well as for those refugees affected and displaced by the crisis in the Nahr el-Bared refugee camp in northern Lebanon, and welcoming the efforts of the Government of Lebanon and the international community to support the rebuilding by the Agency of the Nahr el-Bared camp,

Welcoming, in this regard, the pledges made at the International Donor Conference for the Recovery and Reconstruction of the Nahr el-Bared Palestine Refugee Camp and Conflict-affected Areas of Northern Lebanon, held in Vienna on 23 June 2008, and urging the early fulfilment of pledges as well as a rapid response by donors to the additional relief and recovery appeal for the Nahr el-Bared camp launched by the Agency on 11 September 2008,

Aware of the valuable work done by the Agency in providing protection to the Palestinian people, in particular Palestine refugees,

Gravely concerned about the endangerment of the safety of the Agency's staff and about the damage caused to the facilities of the Agency, in particular as a result of Israeli military operations during the reporting period,

Deploring the killing of nineteen Agency staff members by the Israeli occupying forces in the Occupied Palestinian Territory since September 2000,

Also deploring the killing and wounding of refugee children, including in the Agency's schools, by the Israeli occupying forces,

Expressing deep concern about the gravely negative impact of the continuing closures, the imposition of severe restrictions on the movement of persons and goods, and the construction of the wall, contrary to international law, in the Occupied Palestinian Territory, including in and around East Jerusalem, on the socio-economic situation of the Palestine refugees,

Deeply concerned about the continuing imposition of restrictions on the freedom of movement and access of the Agency's staff, vehicles and goods, and the injury, harassment and intimidation of the Agency's staff, which undermine and obstruct the work of the Agency, including its ability to provide essential basic and emergency services,

Aware of the agreement between the Agency and the Government of Israel,

Taking note of the agreement reached on 24 June 1994, embodied in an exchange of letters between the Agency and the Palestine Liberation Organization,

1. *Reaffirms* that the functioning of the United Nations Relief and Works Agency for Palestine Refugees in the Near East remains essential in all fields of operation;

2. *Expresses its appreciation* to the Commissioner-General of the United Nations Relief and Works Agency for Palestine Refugees in the Near East, as well as to all of the staff of the Agency, for their tireless efforts and valuable work, particularly in the light of the difficult conditions during the past year;

3. *Expresses its appreciation also* to the Advisory Commission of the United Nations Relief and Works Agency for Palestine Refugees in the Near East of the Agency, and requests it to continue its efforts and to keep the General Assembly informed of its activities;

4. *Takes note with appreciation* of the report of the Working Group on the Financing of the United Nations Relief and Works Agency for Palestine Refugees in the Near East and the efforts of the Working Group to assist in ensuring the financial security of the Agency, and requests the Secretary-General to provide the necessary services and assistance to the Working Group for the conduct of its work;

5. *Commends* the continuing efforts of the Commissioner-General to increase the budgetary transparency and efficiency of the Agency, as reflected in the Agency's programme budget for the biennium 2008–2009 and in its comprehensive, three-year organizational development plan;

6. *Requests* the Secretary-General to support the institutional strengthening of the Agency through the provision of sufficient financial resources from the regular budget of the United Nations;

7. *Endorses*, meanwhile, the efforts of the Commissioner-General to continue to provide humanitarian assistance, as far as practicable, on an emergency basis, and as a temporary measure, to persons in the area who are internally displaced and in serious need of continued assistance as a result of recent crises in the Occupied Palestinian Territory and Lebanon;

8. *Acknowledges* the important support provided by the host Governments to the Agency in the discharge of its duties;

9. *Encourages* the Agency, in close cooperation with other relevant United Nations entities, to continue making progress in addressing the needs and rights of children and women in its operations in accordance with the Convention on the Rights of the Child and the Convention on the Elimination of All Forms of Discrimination against Women, respectively;

10. *Expresses concern* about the continuing relocation of the international staff of the Agency from its headquarters in Gaza City and the disruption of operations at the headquarters due to the deterioration and instability of the situation on the ground;

11. *Calls upon* Israel, the occupying Power, to comply fully with the provisions of the Geneva Convention relative to the Protection of Civilian Persons in Time of War, of 12 August 1949;

12. *Also calls upon* Israel to abide by Articles 100, 104 and 105 of the Charter of the United Nations and the Convention on the Privileges and Immunities of the United Nations in order to ensure the safety of the personnel of the Agency, the protection of its institutions and the safeguarding of the security of its facilities in the Occupied Palestinian Territory, including East Jerusalem;

13. *Urges* the Government of Israel to speedily compensate the Agency for damage to its property and facili-

ties resulting from actions by the Israeli side and to expeditiously reimburse the Agency for all transit charges incurred and other financial losses sustained by the Agency as a result of delays and restrictions on movement and access imposed by Israel;

14. *Calls upon* Israel particularly to cease obstructing the movement and access of the staff, vehicles and supplies of the Agency and to cease the levying of extra fees and charges, which affect the Agency's operations detrimentally;

15. *Requests* the Commissioner-General to proceed with the issuance of identification cards for Palestine refugees and their descendants in the Occupied Palestinian Territory;

16. *Reiterates its request* to the Commissioner-General to proceed with the modernization of the archives of the Agency through the Palestine Refugee Records Project, and to indicate progress in her report to the General Assembly at its sixty-fourth session;

17. *Notes* the success of the Agency's microfinance and microenterprise programmes, and calls upon the Agency, in close cooperation with the relevant agencies, to continue to contribute to the development of the economic and social stability of the Palestine refugees in all fields of operation;

18. *Reiterates its appeals* to all States, specialized agencies and non-governmental organizations to continue and to augment the special allocations for grants and scholarships for higher education to Palestine refugees in addition to their contributions to the regular budget of the Agency and to contribute to the establishment of vocational training centres for Palestine refugees, and requests the Agency to act as the recipient and trustee for the special allocations for grants and scholarships;

19. *Urges* all States, specialized agencies and non-governmental organizations to continue and to increase their contributions to the Agency so as to ease the ongoing financial constraints, exacerbated by the current humanitarian situation on the ground that has resulted in rising expenditures, in particular with regard to emergency services, and to support the Agency's valuable and necessary work in assisting the Palestine refugees in all fields of operation.

RECORDED VOTE ON RESOLUTION 63/93:

In favour: Afghanistan, Albania, Algeria, Andorra, Angola, Antigua and Barbuda, Argentina, Armenia, Australia, Austria, Azerbaijan, Bahamas, Bahrain, Bangladesh, Barbados, Belarus, Belgium, Belize, Benin, Bhutan, Bolivia, Bosnia and Herzegovina, Botswana, Brazil, Brunei Darussalam, Bulgaria, Burkina Faso, Burundi, Cambodia, Canada, Cape Verde, Central African Republic, Chile, China, Colombia, Comoros, Congo, Costa Rica, Côte d'Ivoire, Croatia, Cuba, Cyprus, Czech Republic, Democratic People's Republic of Korea, Denmark, Djibouti, Dominica, Dominican Republic, Ecuador, Egypt, El Salvador, Eritrea, Estonia, Ethiopia, Fiji, Finland, France, Gabon, Georgia, Germany, Ghana, Greece, Grenada, Guatemala, Guinea, Guinea-Bissau, Guyana, Haiti, Honduras, Hungary, Iceland, India, Indonesia, Iran, Iraq, Ireland, Italy, Jamaica, Japan, Jordan, Kazakhstan, Kenya, Kuwait, Kyrgyzstan, Lao People's Democratic Republic, Latvia, Lebanon, Lesotho, Liberia, Libyan Arab Jamahiriya, Liechtenstein, Lithuania, Luxembourg, Malawi, Malaysia, Maldives, Mali, Malta, Mauritania, Mauritius, Mexico, Moldova, Monaco, Mongolia, Montenegro, Morocco, Mozambique, Myanmar, Namibia, Nepal, Netherlands, New Zealand, Nicaragua, Niger, Norway, Oman, Pakistan, Panama, Papua New Guinea, Paraguay, Peru, Philippines, Poland, Portugal, Qatar, Republic of Korea, Romania, Russian Federation, Saint Lucia, Saint Vincent and the Grenadines, Samoa, San Marino, Sao Tome and Principe, Saudi Arabia, Senegal, Serbia, Singapore, Slovakia, Slovenia, Solomon Islands, South Africa, Spain, Sri Lanka, Sudan, Suriname, Swaziland, Sweden, Switzerland, Syrian Arab Republic, Tajikistan, Thailand, The former Yugoslav Republic of Macedonia, Timor-Leste, Togo, Tonga, Trinidad and Tobago, Tunisia, Turkey, Turkmenistan, Tuvalu, Uganda, Ukraine, United Arab Emirates, United Kingdom, United Republic of Tanzania, Uruguay, Uzbekistan, Venezuela, Viet Nam, Yemen, Zambia, Zimbabwe.

Against: Israel, Marshall Islands, Micronesia, Nauru, Palau, United States.

Abstaining: Cameroon.

UNRWA financing

In 2008, UNRWA expended $807.1 million—against a budget of $897.1 million—on its regular budget, projects and emergency appeal activities. The largest component was an expenditure of $496 million under the regular budget, accounting for 61.5 per cent of total expenditure. Emergency activities and projects accounted for 23 per cent and 15.4 per cent, respectively. The self-supporting microfinance department made up less than 1 per cent of total expenditure. Education remained the largest programme, accounting for 60 per cent of the regular budget, followed by health (18 per cent) and relief and social services (11 per cent). The unfunded portion of $48.4 million resulted from a difference between a needs-based budget and the donor contributions. The shortfall necessitated the adoption of stringent austerity measures throughout the Agency.

Working Group. The Working Group on the Financing of UNRWA held two meetings in 2008, on 12 and 19 September. In its report to the General Assembly [A/63/375], the Working Group noted that the deficit against the 2008 project budget of $56.8 million was expected to reach $38.1 million. The Working Group was particularly concerned that, in light of the constraints on the Agency's ability to deliver quality services imposed by inadequate physical facilities, large recurrent project budget deficits could adversely affect the regular services for refugees.

The Working Group was informed by UNRWA that its $1,093 million budget for the 2008–2009 biennium, excluding projects, had been endorsed by the Advisory Committee on Administrative and Budgetary Questions (ACABQ) and subsequently approved by the Fifth Committee. Overall pledges to UNRWA's 2008 regular budget were anticipated to fall significantly short of adjusted budget expenditure.

The Working Group noted with regret that the 2006–2007 budget had been seriously underfunded and was concerned at the large funding gap anticipated for the Agency's 2008 regular budget. It reiterated that it was the responsibility of the international community to ensure that UNRWA services were maintained at an acceptable level and that funding kept pace with the changing needs of the refugee population. It urged donors to fully fund the emergency appeal, since 70 per cent of registered refugees in the Gaza Strip were dependent on UNRWA for essential sustenance. The Working Group urged Governments to fully fund the 2008–2009 UNRWA budget and ensure that the real value of contributions to the Agency was maintained, as well as that donor support of emergency-related and special programmes did not decrease or divert contributions to its regular programme.

Displaced persons

In an August report [A/63/315], submitted in compliance with General Assembly resolution 62/103 [YUN 2007, p. 477], which called for the accelerated return of all persons displaced as a result of the June 1967 and subsequent hostilities to their homes in the territories occupied by Israel since then, the Secretary-General said that, based on information obtained from the UNRWA Commissioner-General during the period from 1 July 2007 to 30 June 2008, 1,171 refugees registered with the Agency had returned to the West Bank and 389 to the Gaza Strip from places outside the Occupied Palestinian Territory. The number of displaced registered refugees known by the Agency to have returned since June 1967 was about 30,563. The Agency was unable to estimate the total number of displaced inhabitants who had returned as it kept records only of registered refugees, and even those might be incomplete. It was not involved in any arrangements for the return of refugees or displaced persons who were not registered.

On 28 April, the Secretary-General sought information from Member States on action taken or envisaged to implement the relevant provisions of resolution 62/103. In a 7 August note verbate, Israel replied that it supported UNRWA's humanitarian mission and its contribution to the welfare of Palestinians, but remained concerned about the political motivation of resolutions 62/102 to 62/105 on UNRWA [ibid, pp. 473 & 478], as they did not reflect the reality on the ground. Israel favoured consolidating UNRWA resolutions and removing extraneous political language. It looked forward to continuing its working relationship with UNRWA, and urged the Secretary-General and the Agency to consider ways in which the fulfilment of its mandate could be enhanced in an accountable and responsible manner.

GENERAL ASSEMBLY ACTION

On 5 December [meeting 64], the General Assembly, on the recommendation of the Fourth Committee [A/63/400], adopted **resolution 63/92** by recorded vote (172-6-2) [agenda item 29].

Persons displaced as a result of the June 1967 and subsequent hostilities

The General Assembly,

Recalling its resolutions 2252(ES-V) of 4 July 1967, 2341 B(XXII) of 19 December 1967 and all subsequent related resolutions,

Recalling also Security Council resolutions 237(1967) of 14 June 1967 and 259(1968) of 27 September 1968,

Taking note of the report of the Secretary-General submitted in pursuance of its resolution 62/103 of 17 December 2007,

Taking note also of the report of the Commissioner-General of the United Nations Relief and Works Agency for Palestine Refugees in the Near East covering the period from 1 January to 31 December 2007,

Concerned about the continuing human suffering resulting from the June 1967 and subsequent hostilities,

Taking note of the relevant provisions of the Declaration of Principles on Interim Self-Government Arrangements of 13 September 1993 with regard to the modalities for the admission of persons displaced in 1967, and concerned that the process agreed upon has not yet been effected,

1. *Reaffirms* the right of all persons displaced as a result of the June 1967 and subsequent hostilities to return to their homes or former places of residence in the territories occupied by Israel since 1967;

2. *Expresses deep concern* that the mechanism agreed upon by the parties in article XII of the Declaration of Principles on Interim Self-Government Arrangements of 13 September 1993 on the return of displaced persons has not been complied with, and stresses the necessity for an accelerated return of displaced persons;

3. *Endorses*, in the meanwhile, the efforts of the Commissioner-General of the United Nations Relief and Works Agency for Palestine Refugees in the Near East to continue to provide humanitarian assistance, as far as practicable, on an emergency basis, and as a temporary measure, to persons in the area who are currently displaced and in serious need of continued assistance as a result of the June 1967 and subsequent hostilities;

4. *Strongly appeals* to all Governments and to organizations and individuals to contribute generously to the Agency and to the other intergovernmental and non-governmental organizations concerned for the above-mentioned purposes;

5. *Requests* the Secretary-General, after consulting with the Commissioner-General, to report to the General Assembly before its sixty-fourth session on the progress made with regard to the implementation of the present resolution.

RECORDED VOTE ON RESOLUTION 63/92:

In favour: Afghanistan, Albania, Algeria, Andorra, Angola, Antigua and Barbuda, Argentina, Armenia, Australia, Austria, Azerbaijan, Bahamas, Bahrain, Bangladesh, Barbados, Belarus, Belgium, Belize, Benin, Bhutan, Bolivia, Bosnia and Herzegovina, Botswana, Brazil, Brunei Darussalam, Bulgaria, Burkina Faso, Burundi, Cambodia, Cape Verde, Central African Republic, Chile, China, Colombia, Comoros, Congo, Costa Rica, Côte d'Ivoire, Croatia, Cuba, Cyprus, Czech Republic, Democratic People's Republic of Korea, Denmark, Djibouti, Dominica, Dominican Republic, Ecuador, Egypt, El Salvador, Eritrea, Estonia, Ethiopia, Fiji, Finland, France, Gabon, Georgia, Germany, Ghana, Greece, Grenada, Guatemala, Guinea, Guinea-Bissau, Guyana, Haiti, Honduras, Hungary, Iceland, India, Indonesia, Iran, Iraq, Ireland, Italy, Jamaica, Japan, Jordan, Kazakhstan, Kenya, Kuwait, Kyrgyzstan, Lao People's Democratic Republic, Latvia, Lebanon, Lesotho, Liberia, Libyan Arab Jamahiriya, Liechtenstein, Lithuania, Luxembourg, Madagascar, Malawi, Malaysia, Maldives, Mali, Malta, Mauritania, Mauritius, Mexico, Moldova, Monaco, Mongolia, Montenegro, Morocco, Mozambique, Myanmar, Namibia, Nepal, Netherlands, New Zealand, Nicaragua, Niger, Norway, Oman, Pakistan, Panama, Papua New Guinea, Paraguay, Peru, Philippines, Poland, Portugal, Qatar, Republic of Korea, Romania, Russian Federation, Saint Lucia, Saint Vincent and the Grenadines, Samoa, San Marino, Sao Tome and Principe, Saudi Arabia, Senegal, Serbia, Singapore, Slovakia, Slovenia, Solomon Islands, South Africa, Spain, Sri Lanka, Sudan, Suriname, Swaziland, Sweden, Switzerland, Syrian Arab Republic, Tajikistan, Thailand, The former Yugoslav Republic of Macedonia, Timor-Leste, Togo, Tonga, Trinidad and Tobago, Tunisia, Turkey, Turkmenistan, Tuvalu, Uganda, Ukraine, United Arab Emirates, United Kingdom, United Republic of Tanzania, Uruguay, Uzbekistan, Venezuela, Viet Nam, Yemen, Zambia, Zimbabwe.

Against: Israel, Marshall Islands, Micronesia, Nauru, Palau, United States.

Abstaining: Cameroon, Canada.

Property rights

In response to General Assembly resolution 62/105 [YUN 2007, p. 478], the Secretary-General submitted an August report [A/63/269] on Palestine refugees' properties and their revenues. Only one Member State (Mexico) had replied to his note requesting information from Israel and Member States on action taken or envisaged in relation to the implementation of the resolution.

GENERAL ASSEMBLY ACTION

On 5 December [meeting 64], the General Assembly, on the recommendation of the Fourth Committee [A/63/400], adopted **resolution 63/94** by recorded vote (173-6-2) [agenda item 29].

Palestine refugees' properties and their revenues

The General Assembly,

Recalling its resolutions 194(III) of 11 December 1948 and 36/146 C of 16 December 1981 and all its subsequent resolutions on the question,

Taking note of the report of the Secretary-General submitted pursuant to its resolution 62/105 of 17 December 2007, as well as that of the United Nations Conciliation Commission for Palestine for the period from 1 September 2007 to 31 August 2008,

Recalling that the Universal Declaration of Human Rights and the principles of international law uphold the principle that no one shall be arbitrarily deprived of his or her property,

Recalling in particular its resolution 394(V) of 14 December 1950, in which it directed the Conciliation Commission, in consultation with the parties concerned, to prescribe measures for the protection of the rights, property and interests of the Palestine refugees,

Noting the completion of the programme of identification and evaluation of Arab property, as announced by the Conciliation Commission in its twenty-second progress report, and the fact that the Land Office had a schedule of Arab owners and a file of documents defining the location, area and other particulars of Arab property,

Expressing its appreciation for the preservation and modernization of the existing records, including the land records, of the Conciliation Commission and the importance of such records for a just resolution of the plight of the Palestine refugees in conformity with resolution 194(III),

Recalling that, in the framework of the Middle East peace process, the Palestine Liberation Organization and the Government of Israel agreed, in the Declaration of Principles on Interim Self-Government Arrangements of 13 September 1993, to commence negotiations on permanent status issues, including the important issue of the refugees,

1. *Reaffirms* that the Palestine refugees are entitled to their property and to the income derived therefrom, in conformity with the principles of equity and justice;

2. *Requests* the Secretary-General to take all appropriate steps, in consultation with the United Nations Conciliation Commission for Palestine, for the protection of Arab property, assets and property rights in Israel;

3. *Calls once again upon* Israel to render all facilities and assistance to the Secretary-General in the implementation of the present resolution;

4. *Calls upon* all the parties concerned to provide the Secretary-General with any pertinent information in their possession concerning Arab property, assets and property rights in Israel that would assist him in the implementation of the present resolution;

5. *Urges* the Palestinian and Israeli sides, as agreed between them, to deal with the important issue of Palestine refugees' properties and their revenues within the framework of the final status negotiations of the Middle East peace process;

6. *Requests* the Secretary-General to report to the General Assembly at its sixty-fourth session on the implementation of the present resolution.

RECORDED VOTE ON RESOLUTION 63/94:

In favour: Afghanistan, Albania, Algeria, Andorra, Angola, Antigua and Barbuda, Argentina, Armenia, Australia, Austria, Azerbaijan, Bahamas, Bahrain, Bangladesh, Barbados, Belarus, Belgium, Belize, Benin, Bhutan, Bolivia, Bosnia and Herzegovina, Botswana, Brazil, Brunei Darussalam, Bulgaria,

Burkina Faso, Burundi, Cambodia, Canada, Cape Verde, Central African Republic, Chile, China, Colombia, Comoros, Congo, Costa Rica, Côte d'Ivoire, Croatia, Cuba, Cyprus, Czech Republic, Democratic People's Republic of Korea, Denmark, Djibouti, Dominica, Dominican Republic, Ecuador, Egypt, El Salvador, Eritrea, Estonia, Ethiopia, Fiji, Finland, France, Gabon, Georgia, Germany, Ghana, Greece, Grenada, Guatemala, Guinea, Guinea-Bissau, Guyana, Haiti, Honduras, Hungary, Iceland, India, Indonesia, Iran, Iraq, Ireland, Italy, Jamaica, Japan, Jordan, Kazakhstan, Kenya, Kuwait, Kyrgyzstan, Lao People's Democratic Republic, Latvia, Lebanon, Lesotho, Liberia, Libyan Arab Jamahiriya, Liechtenstein, Lithuania, Luxembourg, Madagascar, Malawi, Malaysia, Maldives, Mali, Malta, Mauritania, Mauritius, Mexico, Moldova, Monaco, Mongolia, Montenegro, Morocco, Mozambique, Myanmar, Namibia, Nepal, Netherlands, New Zealand, Nicaragua, Niger, Norway, Oman, Pakistan, Panama, Papua New Guinea, Paraguay, Peru, Philippines, Poland, Portugal, Qatar, Republic of Korea, Romania, Russian Federation, Saint Lucia, Saint Vincent and the Grenadines, Samoa, San Marino, Sao Tome and Principe, Saudi Arabia, Senegal, Serbia, Singapore, Slovakia, Slovenia, Solomon Islands, South Africa, Spain, Sri Lanka, Sudan, Suriname, Swaziland, Sweden, Switzerland, Syrian Arab Republic, Tajikistan, Thailand, The former Yugoslav Republic of Macedonia, Timor-Leste, Togo, Tonga, Trinidad and Tobago, Tunisia, Turkey, Turkmenistan, Tuvalu, Uganda, Ukraine, United Arab Emirates, United Kingdom, United Republic of Tanzania, Uruguay, Uzbekistan, Venezuela, Viet Nam, Yemen, Zambia, Zimbabwe.

Against: Israel, Marshall Islands, Micronesia, Nauru, Palau, United States.

Abstaining: Cameroon, Vanuatu.

Peacekeeping operations

In 2008, the United Nations Truce Supervision Organization (UNTSO), originally set up to monitor the ceasefire called for by Security Council resolution S/801 of 29 May 1948 [YUN 1947–48, p. 427] in the newly partitioned Palestine, continued its work. UNTSO unarmed military observers fulfilled evolving mandates—from supervising the four armistice agreements between Israel and its neighbours (Egypt, Jordan, Lebanon and the Syrian Arab Republic) to observing and monitoring other ceasefires, as well as performing a number of additional tasks. During the year, UNTSO personnel worked with two remaining UN peacekeeping forces in the Middle East—the United Nations Disengagement Observer Force (UNDOF) in the Golan Heights and the United Nations Interim Force in Lebanon (UNIFIL).

Lebanon

Lebanon remained in the focus of international attention and concern throughout 2008, as the country was taken to the brink of civil war. Terrorist attacks and assassinations targeting symbols of Lebanese sovereignty continued unabated until a reconciliation agreement among Lebanese political leaders was reached on 21 May, which led to the election of General Michel Sleiman as President of Lebanon, the formation of a Government of national unity and the launching of a national dialogue. The Secretary-General extended his good offices with a view to sustaining the relative calm that prevailed in the post-election period. However, despite the improved political climate, the country's stability remained fragile and was threatened by a number of serious security incidents involving Lebanese and non-Lebanese militias.

The paramilitary group Hizbullah maintained a major armed component separate from the State, while Palestinian militias kept up significant paramilitary structures inside and outside refugee camps, and along the Lebanese-Syrian border. Hizbullah carried out further attacks against positions of the Israeli Defence Forces (IDF) inside Israel, while IDF continued attacks within Lebanon.

The Secretary-General reported during the year on the implementation of Security Council resolutions 1559(2004) [YUN 2004, p. 506] and 1701(2006) [YUN 2006, p. 583]. The election of President Sleiman and the establishment of diplomatic relations between Lebanon and the Syrian Arab Republic represented significant steps forward in the implementation of the former. Some progress was made with regard to the implementation of resolution 1701(2006) as well, most notably the signing of a humanitarian agreement between Hizbullah and Israel in July. On 16 July, Israel swapped the bodies of some 200 Lebanese and Palestinian fighters and five Lebanese prisoners for the bodies of two Israeli soldiers captured in 2006—Ehud Goldwasser and Eldad Regev. Major challenges remained, however, including the activities of Lebanese and non-Lebanese militias, alleged breaches of the arms embargo, border violations and Israeli overflights of Lebanese territory, all of which hindered the establishment of a permanent ceasefire and a long-term solution between Israel and Lebanon as called for by the resolution.

In order to assist in enhancing border security between Lebanon and Syria, the Secretary-General dispatched the Lebanon Independent Border Assessment Team II to undertake a thorough follow-up assessment of the implementation of the recommendations of the first team of border security experts, which had conducted an initial assessment in 2007 [YUN 2007, p. 484].

The United Nations International Independent Investigation Commission (UNIIIC) continued to investigate the 14 February 2005 assassination of former Lebanese Prime Minister Rafik Hariri and 22 others [YUN 2005, p. 550].

The United Nations Interim Force in Lebanon (UNIFIL), whose mandate the Security Council renewed in August for another 12 months, continued to play a crucial role in ensuring peace and stability in southern Lebanon, as well as full respect for the Blue Line, the provisional border drawn by the United Nations following the withdrawal of Israeli troops from southern Lebanon in 2000 [YUN 2000, p. 465].

On 19 December, by **resolution 63/211**, the General Assembly, noting the environmental disaster caused by the destruction by the Israeli Air Force on 15 July 2006 of oil storage tanks near the el Jiyeh electric power plant in Lebanon, resulting in an oil slick that covered the entire Lebanese coastline [YUN 2006, p. 1215], requested Israel to compensate Lebanon and other affected countries for the costs of repairing the environmental damage (see p. 1150).

Appointment of Special Coordinator. On 8 April [S/2008/236], the Secretary-General informed the Security Council of his intention to appoint Johan Verbeke (Belgium) as his Special Coordinator for Lebanon, replacing Geir Pedersen, who had been appointed in 2007 [YUN 2007, p. 479]. The Council took note of the Secretary-General's intention on 11 April [S/2008/237]. On 30 July [S/2008/516], the Secretary-General informed the Council of his intention to appoint Michael C. Williams (United Kingdom) as Special Coordinator to succeed Mr. Verbeke. The Council, on 1 August [S/2008/517], took note of the Secretary-General's intention.

Communications. In communications received throughout the year [A/62/630-S/2008/4, A/62/634-S/2008/9, A/62/635-S/2008/11, A/62/637-S/2008/13, A/62/646-S/2008/22, A/62/656-S/2008/30, A/62/664-S/2008/46, A/62/675-S/2008/74, A/62/677-S/2008/79, A/62/678-S/2008/78, A/62/690-S/2008/94, A/62/702-S/2008/112, A/62/709-S/2008/129, A/62/716-S/2008/154, A/62/717-S/2008/155, A/62/738-S/2008/174, A/62/786-S/2008/224, A/62/787-S/2008/225, A/62/832-S/2008/301, A/62/833-S/2008/302, A/62/844-S/2008/333, A/62/861-S/2008/374, A/62/862-S/2008/375, A/62/886-S/2008/406, A/62/907-S/2008/461, A/62/908-S/2008/462, A/62/911-S/2008/484, A/62/937-S/2008/563, A/62/938-S/2008/564, A/62/944-S/2008/576, A62/954-S/2008/604, A/63/357-S/2008/607, A/63/358-S/2008/608, A/63/380-S/2008/627, A/63/480-S/2008/650, A/63/481-S/2008/651, A/63/502-S/2008/669, A/63/533-S/2008/698, A/63/534-S/2008/699, A/63/557-S/2008/721, A/63/577-S/2008/747, A/63/585-S/2008/759, A/63/586-S/2008/758, A/63/661-S/2008/810] Lebanon reported on Israeli acts of aggression by air, land and sea, along with violations of the Blue Line, and consequently, of Lebanese sovereignty and territorial integrity.

In a series of letters [A/62/636-S/2008/12, A/62/655, S/2008/131, S/2008/189, S/2008/730], Israel called the attention of the Secretary-General and the Security Council to alleged violations of resolution 1701(2006). In other letters [A/62/725-S/2008/164, S/2008/232], Syria responded to Israeli allegations of weapon smuggling across the Syrian-Lebanese border and its alleged support of terrorist organizations in the region.

Political situation

Lebanon continued to experience a severe political crisis due to its failure to elect a President, an office vacant since 24 November 2007 [YUN 2007, p. 501], when the extended term of President Émile Lahoud ended, as the Secretary-General reported in his semi-annual April report [S/2008/264] on the implementation of resolution 1559(2004) [YUN 2004, p. 506]. Despite the efforts of Lebanese, regional and international players, all attempts to elect a new President were fruitless. The electoral void fuelled political polarization and impeded the functioning of the country's legitimate constitutional institutions, in particular the Government and the Parliament, and contributed to violent confrontations between the opposing parties. The absence of an agreement on the presidential elections threatened the very foundations of the Lebanese State and the sovereignty, independence and stability of the country.

Following a ministerial meeting convened by the Secretary-General in December 2007 on the sidelines of the Paris donor conference [YUN 2007, p. 446], the Foreign Ministers of LAS convened in 2008 (Cairo, Egypt, 6 January) and agreed unanimously on a three-point plan to end the constitutional crisis in Lebanon. At a further meeting on 27 January in Cairo, the Foreign Ministers noted the continuing impasse, as the majority and the opposition disagreed on the interpretation of the portion of the plan related to the composition of the Government of national unity. On 6 March, the Foreign Ministers added to their original plan a provision calling for the improvement of Syria-Lebanon relations. At the twentieth ordinary Arab League summit (Damascus, Syria, 29–30 March) [S/2008/296], several Arab delegations reduced the level of their representation in protest at the non-implementation of the plan, while Lebanon did not attend. In the final summit communiqué, the Arab leaders called for adherence to the Arab League initiative to settle the Lebanese crisis, and urged Lebanon's leaders to elect consensus candidate Sleiman and agree on the basis for the formation of a national unity Government. They also stressed placing Lebanese-Syrian relations on the proper track and emphasized the importance of the formation of the international tribunal on the assassination of former Prime Minister Hariri [YUN 2005, p. 551].

In his observations, the Secretary-General stressed that the Lebanese people had a unique opportunity to open a new chapter in their difficult history. They and their political representatives had to rise to the occasion and elect a President without any conditions beyond those prescribed by the constitution. Such an election would signify a major milestone on the road towards full reassertion of Lebanon's sovereignty, territorial integrity, unity and political independence. The Secretary-General regretted that despite the numerous calls of the Lebanese people and the international community, such an election had still not been held. He firmly believed that the Lebanese leaders first and foremost had to think about the future of their country and transcend sectarian and individual interests. Parliament, which had not met in more than a year, had to be allowed to convene urgently to fulfil its constitutional duties, without foreign interference or influence. The Secretary-General was concerned that further delay in electing a President would complicate the adoption of an electoral law and the holding of parliamentary elections on time, in the first quarter of 2009.

Security Council consideration. On 8 May [meeting 5888], Terje Roed-Larsen, Special Envoy for the implementation of Security Council resolution 1599(2004), told the Council that in the context of the prolonged electoral void in Lebanon, representatives of Egypt, France, Germany, Italy, Jordan, Kuwait, Qatar, Saudi Arabia, the United Arab Emirates, the United Kingdom and the United States; the Secretaries-General of the Council of the European Union, the United Nations and the Arab League; and Lebanon's acting Foreign Minister met in Kuwait on 22 April. They expressed support to the legitimate Lebanese Government and called for the immediate election of the consensus candidate, General Sleiman, as president without prior conditions, the establishment of a national unity Government, and the holding of general elections in conformity with an electoral law agreed by all parties, in accordance with the Arab League Plan (see p. 531). Noting that the election of a president had been postponed for the eighteenth time, to 13 May, the Secretary-General urged the Parliament to convene on that date to fulfil its constitutional duties.

Doha Agreement. At a meeting in Doha, Qatar (16–21 May), rival Lebanese factions reached an agreement ending the 18-month political crisis and opening the way for the election of a President of the Republic. The Doha Agreement on the outcome of the meeting of the Lebanese National Dialogue (the Doha Agreement), signed on 21 May by all participating political leaders, was transmitted to the Security Council by LAS on 22 May [S/2008/392] and by Qatar on 22 August [S/2008/578]. The Agreement provided for the election of the consensus candidate General Michel Sleiman as President of the Republic; the formation of a national unity Government, comprising 30 ministers—16 of whom would be allocated to the majority, 11 to the opposition, and 3 to the President; the submission of the reform clauses of the draft electoral law, drafted by the National Electoral Law Drafting Commission, to Parliament for consideration; and the initiation of dialogue on the reinforcement of the authority of the State in accordance with paragraph 5 of the 15 May 2008 Beirut agreement.

All parties pledged by virtue of the Agreement not to resign or obstruct the Government's work, to refrain from using weapons or violence to achieve political gains, as well as from using mutual recrimination or political and sectarian propaganda, and to commit themselves to security and military authority being the sole province of the State.

SECURITY COUNCIL ACTION

On 22 May [meeting 5896], following consultations among Security Council members, the President made statement **S/PRST/2008/17** on behalf of the Council:

> The Security Council congratulates the leaders and people of Lebanon and welcomes and strongly supports the agreement reached in Doha on May 21 under the auspices of the Arab League, which constitutes an essential step towards the resolution of the current crisis, the return to the normal functioning of Lebanese democratic institutions and the complete restoration of Lebanon's unity and stability.
>
> The Council commends the efforts of the League of Arab States, in particular of the committee of Ministers for Foreign Affairs, under the leadership of the Emir of the State of Qatar, Sheikh Hamad bin Khalifa Al-Thani, the Prime Minister and Minister for Foreign Affairs of Qatar, Sheikh Hamad bin Jassim bin Jabr Al-Thani, and the Secretary-General of the League of Arab States, Mr. Amre Moussa, in helping Lebanese leaders to reach an agreement.
>
> The Security Council welcomes the agreement to elect a President of the Republic, to establish a national unity cabinet and to address Lebanon's electoral law, in accordance with the League of Arab States initiative, as well as the decision to continue the national dialogue on ways to reinforce the authority of the State over all its territory, in such a way to guarantee the sovereignty and the safety of the State and the people of Lebanon. It welcomes the agreement to ban the use of weapons and violence as a means to settle disputes, irrespective of their nature and under any circumstances.
>
> The Council calls for the implementation of this agreement in its entirety, in accordance with the League of Arab States initiative, and in conformity with the Taef agreement and all relevant Council resolutions and statements of its President on the situation in Lebanon.
>
> The Council reaffirms its strong support for the territorial integrity, sovereignty, unity and political independence of Lebanon within its internationally recognized borders and under the sole and exclusive authority of the Government of Lebanon over all Lebanese territory.

New President and unity Government. In his eighth semi-annual report [S/2008/654] on the implementation of Security Council resolution 1559(2004), the Secretary-General reported in October that due to the tireless efforts of the Emir of Qatar, his Prime Minister and the LAS Secretary-General, the Lebanese Parliament convened on 25 May to elect a new President as part of the Doha Agreement. General Michel Sleiman, who received 118 out of 127 votes, was the first president to take office in Lebanon since the withdrawal of Syrian troops in 2005. On 11 July, following intense negotiations, President Sleiman issued a decree forming a national unity Government, headed by Fouad Siniora as Prime Minister. In accordance with the Doha Agreement, the 30-member cabinet included 16 seats allocated to the Parliamentary majority, 11 to the opposition and 3 to the President. On 12 August, by an overwhelming majority, the Parliament expressed confidence in the new cabinet and its policy. On 30 September, the Parliament adopted a new electoral law paving the way for parliamentary elections in 2009.

The Secretary-General said that the Lebanese had taken a step further towards strengthening their country's sovereignty, stability, unity and political independence. It was important that the parties implement in full the provisions of the Doha Agreement, including their commitment to refrain from the use of weapons to settle internal political disputes. He welcomed the first session of the National Dialogue, held on 16 September to address the question of a national defence strategy and the status of armed groups. If Lebanon was to accomplish the process of consolidating its sovereignty and national unity, all parties had to fully engage in that national process in a spirit of genuine cooperation.

Security Council consideration. Reporting to the Security Council on 30 October [meeting 6008], Special Envoy Roed-Larsen said that the Secretary-General was concerned that the scars left by the clashes in spring might have prompted, if not accelerated, a process of rearmament in Lebanon. That activity and the continued presence of groups with military and paramilitary capacities threatened the holding of the free and fair parliamentary elections in 2009. The United Nations supported the Government's efforts to ensure a stable security environment in which those elections could be held. The United Nations welcomed attempts by Lebanese leaders to normalize their relations in the interests of Lebanon's security and political stability.

Implementation of resolution 1559(2004)

The Secretary-General submitted his seventh and eighth semi-annual reports on the implementation of Security Council resolution 1559(2004) [YUN 2004, p. 506], which called for strict respect of the sovereignty, territorial integrity, unity and political independence of Lebanon under the sole and exclusive authority of the Government, the withdrawal of all remaining foreign forces and the disbanding and disarmament of all Lebanese and non-Lebanese militias. He also declared the Council's support for the extension of the Government's control over all Lebanese territory, and for a free and fair electoral process in the presidential election.

Report of Secretary-General (April). In his seventh semi-annual report on the implementation of resolution 1559(2004) [S/2008/264], the Secretary-General stated that in the six months since his last report [YUN 2007, p. 499], Lebanon continued to experience a severe political crisis, centred on the failure to elect a President. It had also contributed, at times, to violent confrontations between the opposing parties, leading to casualties. The absence of an agreement on the presidential elections threatened the very foundations of the State, which confronted challenges of a magnitude unseen since the end of the civil war, with possible regional repercussions. The series of terrorist attacks and assassinations that had shaken Lebanon since October 2004, targeting symbols of its sovereignty, continued unabated. On 25 January, Major Wissam Eid, head of the technical section of the Information Branch of the Internal Security Forces, was killed along with five others, and 20 people were injured.

On 8 January, UNIFIL troops were attacked for the third time since the July/August 2006 war [YUN 2006, p. 574] outside the area of operations. On 15 January, in the first attack on a diplomatic target in Beirut since the civil war, an explosion apparently targeted a vehicle of the United States Embassy, leaving three people dead and dozens wounded. The climate of insecurity induced several countries to issue travel warnings to Lebanon and to reduce their Embassy staff.

Since the withdrawal of Syrian troops, military assets and the military intelligence apparatus from Lebanon in 2005 [YUN 2005, p. 560], the Secretary-General had encouraged the initiation by Lebanon and the Syrian Arab Republic of a process that would eventually lead to the establishment of full diplomatic relations, which would significantly contribute to the stability of the region. Regrettably, there had been no progress towards that goal. The delineation of the border between the two countries remained an element of crucial importance. The mandate in resolution 1559(2004) for Lebanon to extend its governmental authority over all of its territory could only be realized if the entirety of that territory was known by the Government and all other parties, with its exact boundaries determined and delineated. The implementation of measures towards that end would be an important step towards the extension of the Government's control over all of its territory and to stability in the region. Preventing breaches of the arms embargo was also critical to achieving that objective. Lebanon continued to be concerned about smuggling activities along its eastern and northern land borders. A number of Member States had provided the Secretary-General with information that appeared to corroborate the allegation of the flow of weapons and fighters across the Syrian-Lebanese border. Syria continued to deny any involvement in those breaches and pointed to contacts between itself and Lebanon regarding the control of their common borders. It affirmed that it had increased the presence of its border guards.

Due to the ongoing political crisis, in particular the impasse in electing a President and the deteriorating security situation, the Government's ability to extend its authority over all of Lebanese territory remained restricted and the opposition continued to question the Government's legitimacy. The Government reiterated its interest in improving the monitoring of its land borders to prevent the unauthorized flow of weapons, munitions and personnel into the country. The armed forces helped to improve peace and stability in southern Lebanon, despite being overstretched as a result of competing security challenges. The existence of Lebanese and non-Lebanese militias and allegations of widespread rearming and paramilitary training across the spectrum constituted a challenge for the Government's authority throughout its territory. The most significant militia was the armed component of Hizbullah. In addition, several Palestinian militias operated inside and outside of refugee camps. The existence of armed groups challenged the control of the legitimate Government. The Secretary-General regretted that in recent months, there had been no discussion among Lebanese leaders about a political process leading to the disbanding and disarming of the militias, as called for by the 1989 Taif Agreement [YUN 1989, p. 203] and resolution 1559(2004).

On 7 January, at the initiative of PA President Mahmoud Abbas, in cooperation with Lebanese Prime Minister Fouad Siniora, the PLO representative in Lebanon, Abbas Zaki, launched the Palestine Declaration for Lebanon, setting out for the first time since the end of the civil war in 1991 the PLO policy towards Lebanon. The Declaration addressed the two main concerns of resettlement and arms. It rejected any resettlement plan and emphasized Palestinian respect for Lebanon's independence and sovereignty, and stipulated that all arms carried by various Palestinian factions, be they inside or outside refugee camps, had to be subject to Lebanese laws and not used in any inter-Lebanese conflict. The PLO offered an unconditional apology for any damage caused by the Palestinians to Lebanon, whether intentionally or not, since 1948. In the same spirit, the document urged the Lebanese to improve the living conditions of the refugees.

Palestinian refugee camps continued to pose a major challenge to Lebanon's stability and security, owing in particular to the presence of a range of non-State actors. The Secretary-General was concerned over the threats from Al-Qaida-inspired militias in the camps and the emergence of new militant groups. On 21 March, clashes between Fatah and the extremist militant group Jund al-Sham, known to espouse Al-Qaida-oriented ideology, erupted in the Ain al-Hilweh camp, leading to one fatality. While the situation in most of the 12 Palestinian camps remained relatively stable, the threat of internal violence spilling over into surrounding areas existed in a number of them, particularly in southern Lebanon. Given the detrimental effects of living conditions in the camps on the wider security situation in Lebanon, it was imperative that progress be made towards disbanding and disarming Palestinian militias, as well as improving the living conditions of the refugees.

The Secretary-General was concerned also over the activities of the Popular Front for the Liberation of Palestine-General Command and Fatah al-Intifada, which maintained significant paramilitary infrastructures outside refugee camps and along the Lebanese-Syrian border. As both groups had their headquarters in Damascus, the Secretary-General reminded Syria that it bore responsibility for urging them to abide by Security Council resolutions and the decisions of the Lebanese Government. He took note of the public call on Syria by Prime Minister Siniora, on the eve of the Arab League summit on 28 March, to cooperate with Lebanon on disarming Palestinian militias headquartered in Damascus.

Hizbullah's maintenance of an armed component and a paramilitary structure separate from the State had an adverse effect on the Government's efforts to assert its exclusive control over the entire territory of Lebanon and constituted a threat to regional peace and security. In several public announcements, the leaders of Hizbullah claimed that it had rebuilt and increased its military capacity since the July/August 2006 war [YUN 2006, p. 574]. Hizbullah also reportedly continued to develop throughout the country a secure communication network separate from the State's system. Those developments gave rise to a growing impression that parallel institutional structures were being built up.

The Secretary-General called on all Lebanese leaders to initiate discussions on the status of Hizbullah's paramilitary arsenal. Mindful of the regional ramifications, the Secretary-General called on those parties with close ties to Hizbullah, in particular Iran and Syria, to support its transformation in the best interest of regional peace and stability.

The Secretary-General was alarmed by the consistent allegations that militias on all sides of the political spectrum were reappearing, in contravention of the Taif Agreement [YUN 1989, p. 203] and resolution 1559(2004). He called on the Lebanese parties to halt immediately all efforts to rearm and engage in weapons training, and to return instead to dialogue through the legitimate political institutions, in particular the Parliament, as the only viable method of settling issues and resolving the ongoing political crisis.

The disarming and disbanding of Lebanese and non-Lebanese militias was necessary to complete Lebanon's consolidation as a sovereign and democratic State, and should be carried out through an inclusive political dialogue that addressed the political and economic interests of all Lebanese. The Secretary-General urged renewed political dialogue to affirm the commitment of all parties to the disarmament of the militias, including Hizbullah, in fulfilment of resolution 1559(2004). In that context, he emphasized, Syria and Iran, which maintained close ties with the party, bore a significant responsibility in supporting such a process, for the sake of the security, stability and welfare of both Lebanon and the wider region.

Three years after Syria's military withdrawal from Lebanon, the Secretary-General said that the time had come for a redefinition and formalization of ties between the two historically close neighbours, in mutual respect for their sovereignty, territorial integrity and independence.

Conscious of the conditions in the Palestinian refugee camps in Lebanon and the challenges arising from them, the Secretary-General commended the Lebanese Government, working in close cooperation with the PLO and UNRWA, for its commitment to improving those conditions. The UN system stood ready to work with its Lebanese and Palestinian partners towards that goal, while helping to bring about an Israeli-Palestinian peace agreement. He called on Member States to contribute generously to the forthcoming appeal by Lebanon and UNRWA for the reconstruction of the Nahr al-Bared camp and the rehabilitation of the surrounding area affected by the previous year's violence, at a donor conference to be held under World Bank auspices.

Communications. On 2 May [S/2008/293], Iran brought to the Security Council President's attention allegedly unwarranted references against Iran contained in the Secretary-General's April report (see p. 533).

On 4 May [S/2008/295], Syria said that the Secretary-General's report went well beyond the mandate of the Special Envoy for the Implementation of Security Council resolution 1559(2004) and addressed issues unrelated to the resolution.

Report of Secretary-General (October). On 16 October, the Secretary-General, in his eighth semi-annual report [S/2008/654] on the implementation of Security Council resolution 1559(2004), stated that over the previous six months, Lebanon had experienced both the ruinous effects of sectarian violence, as well as hope and optimism. On 6 May, the Lebanese Cabinet declared Hizbullah's secure communication network separate from the State's system illegal and unconstitutional, and announced the dismissal of the chief of security of Beirut International Airport. In protest, Hizbullah closed all roads leading to and from the airport and other principal roads in parts of the capital, and threatened to continue its action until the Government rescinded both decisions. Later that day, there were exchanges of fire throughout several districts of Beirut between members of the opposition and pro-Government forces, which also closed the main border crossing between Lebanon and Syria. The violence, which included the use of heavy weaponry, escalated and spread to other parts of the country, bringing it to an effective standstill. Hostilities continued until 14 May, resulting in 69 fatalities and more than 180 wounded. During the clashes, many alleged human rights violations were registered, including illegal detention and ill-treatment, civilian deaths, instances of summary execution, destruction of private property, and attacks on the media and freedom of expression.

On 11 May, LAS condemned the use of armed violence to achieve political objectives, and at an emergency meeting, decided to dispatch a delegation to Beirut. On 14 May, a Ministerial Committee of Arab Foreign Ministers, headed by the Prime Minister of Qatar, Sheikh Hamad bin Jasseim Al-Thani, and by the Secretary-General of LAS, Amre Moussa, held discussions in Lebanon with the parties aimed at ending the crisis. The following day, the Cabinet rescinded its 6 May decision, and shortly afterwards, the Arab Committee announced an inter-Lebanese understanding that called for calm on the streets and the withdrawal of all armed elements. The agreement also called for a Lebanese national dialogue to begin the following day in Doha, Qatar, where Lebanese leaders reached a comprehensive political understanding on 21 May, leading to the election of General Sleiman as President of Lebanon on 25 May (see p. 533). On the eve of the election, the long-standing protests outside the Prime Minister's Office were brought to an end. On 13 and 14 August, at the invitation of President Bashar Al-Assad, President Sleiman visited the Syrian Arab Republic, where a series of agreements were reached of significant relevance to the implementation of resolution 1559(2004).

Despite the reconciliation agreement reached in Doha, there were violent clashes leading to fatalities, especially in and around the northern city of

Tripoli. In a particularly serious incident of 13 August, an improvised explosive device was detonated at a bus stop frequently used by Lebanese soldiers in Tripoli, killing 15 people, among them 10 soldiers. On 10 September, Saleh Aridi, a senior member of the Lebanese Democratic Party, was killed in a car bomb in Baysur. On 29 September, a new terrorist attack targeted the Lebanese Armed Forces (LAF) in Tripoli, killing six people, including four soldiers, and injuring 32, among them 18 soldiers. The clashes in May and the several security incidents emphasized the threats posed by the presence of militias to the stability of the country, and the need for the Government and LAF to exercise the monopoly on the use of force throughout Lebanon.

The Secretary-General encouraged the early initiation of a process for the establishment of full diplomatic relations between Lebanon and Syria. Following a meeting in Paris on 12 July, convened by French President Nicolas Sarkozy, and talks on 13 and 14 August, between the Presidents of Lebanon and Syria, the Foreign Ministers of both countries, on 15 October, signed in Damascus a memorandum announcing the establishment of diplomatic relations effective the same day. In that document, the two countries reaffirmed their determination to reinforce and consolidate their relations on the basis of mutual respect for their sovereignty and independence. They informed the Secretary-General that embassies would be established in both capitals by the end of the year.

No significant progress was made towards the full delineation of the common border between the two countries. However, noting that the parties on 14 August had announced the revival of the work of the joint committee for delineating the common borders, the Secretary-General welcomed their renewed intention to make progress on the matter.

Over the reporting period, there was no tangible progress towards the disbanding and disarming of militias, as called for in the Taif Agreement and resolution 1559(2004). Hizbullah's parallel structures prevented exclusive government control over the entire Lebanese territory and threatened international peace and security. The Secretary-General called on Hizbullah to comply with all relevant Security Council resolutions and urged all parties with close ties to that organization, in particular Syria and Iran, to support its transformation into a political party.

At the conclusion of the national dialogue held in Doha (16–21 May), Lebanese leaders reaffirmed their commitment to the principles of the Lebanese Constitution and the Taif Agreement. They also committed themselves to prohibiting the use of weapons or violence in any internal conflict and pledged to pursue the national dialogue under the auspices of the Lebanese President, and to promote the Government's authority throughout its territory and its relations with different groups in a way that would guarantee the security of the State and its citizens. No progress was made in disarming Palestinian militias.

While rejecting the permanent resettlement of Palestinians in Lebanon, the Government acknowledged their right to a dignified life and pledged to continue efforts to resolve their humanitarian and social concerns inside and outside the camps. It intended to work with Palestinians to implement the decisions of the 2006 national dialogue [YUN 2006, pp. 569–73], while assuming the responsibility of protecting the camps from any attack. During an historic visit to Lebanon on 28 and 29 August, PA President Abbas reiterated his support for the decisions of the national dialogue and the need for Palestinians in Lebanon to respect the country's sovereignty and political independence.

The Secretary-General urged Syria to ensure that the two Palestinian groups headquartered in Damascus, the Popular Front for the Liberation of Palestine-General Command and Fatah al-Intifada, abided by Lebanese Government's decisions and Lebanese law, in line with relevant Security Council resolutions. Continuing security incidents in the Ain al-Hilweh camp and the precarious situation of the Al-Beddawi camp indicated that the restoration of law and order in the camps would be key to ensuring stability and security in Lebanon. The Secretary-General welcomed the Government's commitment—negotiated with the Palestinian authorities and announced at the international donor conference held in Vienna on 23 June—to rebuild the Nahr al-Bared camp and to take joint responsibility for security therein. He hoped that it would serve as a model for Lebanon's other Palestinian camps.

The Secretary-General called on Lebanese parties to halt immediately all efforts to acquire and build paramilitary capacities. He also welcomed the outcome of the Syrian-Lebanese summit held in Damascus in August, at which both Presidents announced important steps their countries would take to normalize their relations.

Communication. Commenting on the Secretary-General's report, the Syrian Arab Republic, on 29 October [S/2008/680], stated that the resolutions adopted by the LAS Ministerial Council in March underlined support for Lebanon's national reconciliation process and the sovereignty and integrity of its territory. Syria reaffirmed its denial of claims in the Secretary-General's report that weapons and fighters continued to flow across the border. Syria reaffirmed that the delineation of the border with Lebanon was a bilateral issue, the real impediment to which was Israel's continued occupation of the Syrian Golan, the Shab'a Farms and the northern part of the village of

Ghajar, and its refusal to comply with international resolutions.

Security Council consideration. On 30 October [meeting 6008], the Security Council considered the Secretary-General's eighth semi-annual report on the implementation of resolution 1559(2004), which was introduced by his Special Envoy. The Council did not take any action on the report.

Further developments. In accordance with the 15 October memorandum establishing diplomatic relations between Lebanon and the Syrian Arab Republic, the Secretary-General indicated, in a later report [S/2009/218], that on 23 December, the Lebanese President issued a presidential decree naming the Lebanese members of the Lebanese-Syrian border committee tasked with delineating their common border, which was reactivated pursuant to the agreement reached in Damascus in August.

Implementation of resolution 1701(2006) and UNIFIL activities

In three periodic reports submitted to the Security Council during the year, the Secretary-General updated the Security Council on the implementation of resolution 1701(2006) [YUN 2006, p. 583], highlighting progress made, as well as areas that continued to impede the establishment of a permanent ceasefire and a long-term solution between Israel and Lebanon. By the same resolution, the Council had expanded the mandate of the United Nations Interim Force in Lebanon (UNIFIL) to undertake substantial new tasks, in addition to those mandated under resolutions 425(1978) and 426(1978) [YUN 1978, p. 312], and authorized an increase in the Force strength from 2,000 to a maximum of 15,000 troops. In August, the Council extended UNIFIL's mandate for another year.

Communication. On 15 February [A/62/698-S/2008/102], Lebanon transmitted to the Secretary-General and the Security Council a position paper, prepared in anticipation of the Secretary-General's periodic report on the implementation of resolution 1701(2006). Lebanon declared its commitment to the resolution's full implementation, and abided by its obligations thereunder. It looked forward to serious progress on the resolution's remaining elements and to the full abiding by Israel.

Report of Secretary-General (February). On 28 February, the Secretary-General submitted his sixth report [S/2008/135] on the implementation of resolution 1701(2006). He noted that both Lebanon and Israel expressed continued commitment to implementing the resolution, and cooperation between UNIFIL and LAF had increased through the augmentation of coordinated operations, which contributed significantly to the general calm prevailing in the UNIFIL area.

In the UNIFIL area of operations, the military and security situation was generally stable. The deployment and activities of UNIFIL and LAF contributed to the longest period of relative stability in southern Lebanon in many years and helped to establish a new strategic environment south of the Litani River. Those efforts were also felt in northern Israel, as acknowledged by the Israeli authorities. However, a number of serious incidents raised tension, particularly along known points of friction along the Blue Line.

On 8 January, IDF informed UNIFIL that two rockets had hit the northern Israeli town of Shelomi, causing minor damage, but no injuries. No trace of the launching site was discovered, and no one had claimed responsibility. Lebanese civilians from around Ghajar village were involved in smuggling illegal substances and commercial goods into Israel. On 3 February, an IDF patrol opened fire and wounded two Lebanese civilians suspected of smuggling in the Israeli-occupied area around Ghajar village, north of the Blue Line. One of them subsequently died, and the other was in LAF custody. UNIFIL was investigating the incident.

During the reporting period, there were three instances of IDF soldiers pointing their weapons, including lasers, in the direction of UNIFIL patrols. UNIFIL, as well as IDF, were investigating an incident on 13 February, when small arms fire from the Israeli side hit a minefield warning sign in the vicinity of a UN mine clearance team operating close to the Blue Line. On 24 February, a UNIFIL vehicle patrol in the area of operations was blocked for a few hours by a group of Lebanese civilians. On two occasions in January, in the Shab'a Farms area and in the vicinity of Ghajar, IDF apprehended a Lebanese shepherd crossing the Blue Line. UNIFIL also reported a number of minor ground violations by local shepherds, which might be inadvertent, but could lead to incidents and unintended escalation of tension along the Blue Line. A pilot project was initiated by UNIFIL, with LAF and IDF, to visibly mark a six-kilometre stretch of the Blue Line in the western sector of the area of operations.

UNIFIL observed a significant number of Israeli violations of Lebanese airspace on an almost daily basis, particularly on 7 and 11 February, involving large numbers of fighter aircraft and unmanned aerial vehicles. Some of the aircraft flew at low altitude, including over UNIFIL headquarters in Naquora. On 17 February, UNIFIL recorded 36 air violations, mainly by unmanned aerial vehicles. Israeli overflights of Lebanese territory violated Lebanese sovereignty and resolution 1701(2006), escalated tensions and significantly increased the possibility of security incidents—as demonstrated on 21 January, when LAF opened fire on Israeli aircraft violating Lebanese airspace. Air violations caused unnecessary apprehension among the local population, particularly when conducted at low altitude and in a provocative manner, and impeded UNIFIL's ability to further stabilize the situation. Lebanon continued to protest those violations of its sovereignty and of resolution 1701(2006), while Israel maintained that overflights were a necessary security measure that would continue until its two soldiers, Ehud Goldwasser and Eldad Regev, abducted in 2006, were released and the measures set out in paragraphs 14 and 15 of resolution 1701(2006) concerning the arms embargo were implemented in full.

Concerning security and liaison arrangements, the UNIFIL Force Commander and senior representatives of LAF and IDF held regular tripartite meetings as a confidence-building mechanism, and addressed key security and military operational issues to help prevent incidents and violations, and enhance liaison and coordination. Despite intensive efforts, the impasse over the temporary security arrangements for the northern part of Ghajar village had not been overcome.

In the area of operations controlled by the combined presence of UNIFIL and LAF troops, UNIFIL maintained 61 permanent positions, 136 observation posts and six temporary checkpoints and observation posts. The Force conducted an average of 400 vehicle, foot and air patrols, day and night, in any 24-hour period throughout its area of operations in both rural and urban areas. LAF deployed four brigades of different sizes, operated more than 100 checkpoints and observation posts, and patrolled critical locations south of the Litani River. In maintaining that significant commitment of resources, LAF contributed to the improvement of peace and stability in southern Lebanon, despite being overstretched as a result of additional responsibilities, such as manning the border areas and providing security in main Lebanese urban centres, particularly Beirut. On occasion, LAF had to temporarily redeploy some troops from the UNIFIL area of operations to address such specific security requirements.

Coordination and liaison between UNIFIL and LAF strengthened during the reporting period to ensure that the area between the Blue Line and the Litani River was free of unauthorized armed personnel, assets and weapons. Coordinated operations, including temporary observation posts, co-located checkpoints and coordinated vehicle and foot patrols increased, resulting in enhanced monitoring and control over the UNIFIL area. Those operations resulted in 96 findings of abandoned arms, ammunition and explosive devices, and the discovery of rocket launchers, rockets, mortar bombs, explosive devices, and caves or bunkers. LAF destroyed or confiscated arms and ammunition found south of the Litani River. UNIFIL and LAF ensured that the area south of the Litani River was free of unauthorized armed personnel, assets and weapons. Rocket firings and attacks against UNIFIL indicated that there were still hostile elements and unauthorized arms, including in the area of operations, undermining joint efforts to implement resolution 1701(2006) and posing a direct threat to peace and security. It was therefore necessary for UNIFIL and LAF to intensify their coordinated efforts, through increased controls on the Litani River, to counter any movement of weapons and prevent hostile activities.

The UNIFIL Maritime Task Force continued to perform maritime interdiction operations along the Lebanese coast to prevent the entry into Lebanon of unauthorized arms and related materiel. Since the Task Force assumed its mission in 2006 [YUN 2006, p. 589], more than 12,500 ships had been hailed and queried, with close to 70 vessels identified as suspicious.

Overall coordination between UNIFIL and IDF was good, the Secretary-General stated, with UNIFIL maintaining a liaison office with two officers at the IDF Northern Command headquarters in Zefat. Progress was also made towards the establishment of a UNIFIL office in Tel Aviv.

The Secretary-General was concerned about the smuggling of weapons into Lebanon across the Lebanese-Syrian border. Also of concern were the heavily armed military positions of the Popular Front for the Liberation of Palestine-General Command and Fatah al-Intifada along the same border, whose existence challenged Lebanon's sovereignty, owing to their de facto control of that stretch of the border. LAF maintained a defensive line around both of those military camps.

Lebanon continued to enhance its capacity to secure its borders. The Lebanese Common Border Force, which brought together about 800 personnel from the four main Lebanese security agencies (Army, Internal Security, General Security and Customs Authorities), began ground operations between December 2007 and January 2008, in an area of operations some 130 kilometres along Lebanon's northern border with the Syrian Arab Republic and 20 kilometres into Lebanese territory. The Lebanese authorities also relocated the key northern border crossing of Aboudieh to a location along the Nahr al-Kabir river to reduce the possibility for diversionary routes and illicit cross-border activity. The customs authorities updated and enhanced the computerization of their tracking and control mechanisms with support from the international community.

Key aspects of the recommendations of the Lebanon Independent Border Assessment Team for enhancing security arrangements along the border remained to be implemented. As requested by the Security Council in statement S/PRST/2007/29 [YUN 2007, p. 487], the Secretary-General intended to dispatch a second team to Lebanon to carry out an assessment, in coordination with the Lebanese Government.

UNIFIL's total strength amounted to 12,707 military personnel as at 25 February. It was supported by 51 United Nations Truce Supervision Organization (UNTSO) military observers of the Observer Group Lebanon. In addition, 313 international and 612 national staff served with UNIFIL. The Maritime Task Force comprised four out of five required frigates and seven out of ten required corvettes/patrol boats. A ship-to-task analysis to ensure that the UNIFIL naval assets were optimally equipped to carry out their tasks was being finalized. At the end of February, Germany would hand over leadership of the Task Force to the European Maritime Force, a southern European naval initiative supported by France, Italy, Portugal and Spain. A comprehensive review of UNIFIL's Strategic Military Cell was finalized, as requested by General Assembly resolution 61/250 B [ibid., p. 492].

The Secretary-General noted that since the adoption of resolution 1701(2006), the deployment and activities of both UNIFIL and LAF had contributed to the longest period of stability in southern Lebanon for many years and helped to establish a new strategic environment in the area south of the Litani River. Those effects were also felt in northern Israel and acknowledged by the Israeli authorities. However, a number of incidents occurring over the reporting period had raised tensions in the UNIFIL area of operations. The Secretary-General was concerned about the threats of open war against Israel uttered by the Secretary-General of Hizbullah on 14 and 22 February, following the funeral of Imad Mughniyeh, assassinated on 13 February in Damascus; such rhetoric was against the spirit and intentions of resolution 1701(2006), which aimed to achieve a permanent ceasefire.

SECURITY COUNCIL ACTION

On 15 April [meeting 5867], following consultations among Security Council members, the President made statement **S/PRST/2008/8** on behalf of the Council:

> The Security Council recalls its resolution 1773(2007) as well as the statements by its President on Lebanon and welcomes the reports of the Secretary-General of 30 October 2007 and of 28 February 2008.
>
> It reiterates its commitment to the full implementation of all provisions of its resolution 1701(2006) and reaffirms its strong support for the efforts of the Secretary-General in this regard.
>
> The Council takes note of the progress as well as of the concerns expressed by the Secretary-General regarding the implementation of resolution 1701(2006) and emphasizes the need for greater progress on all the key issues required for a permanent ceasefire and long-term solution, as referred to in the reports of the Secretary-General.
>
> It also calls upon all concerned parties, in particular in the region, to intensify their efforts in implementing resolution 1701(2006), including by fully cooperating with the Secretary-General in this regard.
>
> The Council reiterates its full support for the United Nations Interim Force in Lebanon and calls upon all parties to abide by their obligations to respect the safety of United Nations personnel. It welcomes the further enhancement of the cooperation between the Force and the Lebanese Armed Forces.
>
> It stresses the importance of, and the need to achieve, a comprehensive, just and lasting peace in the Middle East, based on all its relevant resolutions including resolutions 242(1967) of 22 November 1967 and 338(1973) of 22 October 1973.

Communications. In a 4 April letter [S/2008/223], Iran rejected allegations in the Secretary-General's February report (see p. 537) concerning the transfer of sophisticated weaponry to Lebanon, which it claimed were based on false and misleading information provided by Israel.

On 18 April [S/2008/261], Israel welcomed the Council President's statement, but stated it would have preferred specific reference made to the major aspects of the arms embargo, the rearming of Hizbullah and the abducted Israeli soldiers. A detailed list of Blue Line violations was annexed to Israel's letter.

On 17 June [A/62/883-S/2008/399], Lebanon forwarded a position paper on the implementation of resolution 1701(2006), as well as lists of 633 air, 13 maritime and 143 land violations by Israel during the period from 11 February to 29 March. Lebanon declared that it looked forward to achieving serious progress on the outstanding elements of the resolution and to Israel's full implementation of its articles.

Report of Secretary-General (June). On 27 June, the Secretary-General submitted his seventh report [S/2008/425] on the implementation of resolution 1701(2006). Following the efforts of LAS and the mediation by Qatar, Lebanon started to emerge from the crisis that had paralyzed the normal functioning of State institutions for the past year and a half. The Doha Agreement reached on 21 May (see p. 532) established the basis for resolving many long-standing issues.

There were no breaches of the cessation of hostilities, and UNIFIL continued, with the parties, to ensure full respect for the Blue Line. UNIFIL and LAF also continued to ensure that the area between the Blue Line and the Litani River was not utilized for hostile activities and was free of any unauthorized armed personnel, assets and weapons. Cooperation between UNIFIL and LAF continued to be good. The military and security situation in the UNIFIL area was generally quiet, although a number of incidents on occasion raised tensions. The Blue Line continued to be respected by the parties, although there were allegations of violations that could, however, not be corroborated by UNIFIL. Some progress was made with respect to the pilot project for visibly marking a 6-kilometre stretch of the Blue Line, although the process seemed to have slowed down. The pumping by Israel of accumulated flood water to Lebanese territory in the vicinity of Kafr Kila prompted demonstrations by affected Lebanese farmers; UNIFIL defused tension by pumping the water into trucks for dispersal elsewhere and submitted a proposal to the parties to prevent a recurrence of the problem.

During the reporting period, UNIFIL recorded and protested unprecedented violations by Israel of Lebanese airspace, at an average of more than 20 per day, in March and April. Israel had not completed its withdrawal from southern Lebanon in accordance with its obligations under resolution 1701(2006), which, according to the Secretary-General, was a continuous source of tension. To break the impasse and facilitate IDF withdrawal, UNIFIL submitted a new proposal and was awaiting the parties' response. Following shooting incidents the previous year and in February in the vicinity of Ghajar, UNIFIL implemented security measures to prevent violations of the Blue Line and smuggling activities, in accordance with an agreement reached with the parties during an April tripartite meeting. UNIFIL and LAF also intensified patrolling in the area.

In April, UNIFIL and LAF conducted the first session of a strategic review of their military tasks and reached agreement on measures to strengthen coordination and liaison; increasing the number of daily counter-rocket launching operations and expanding coverage from areas adjacent to the Blue Line to other parts of the area of operations; enhancing efforts to deter and prevent hunting in the area of operations; intensifying of surveillance in areas near the Blue Line; and operating co-located checkpoints and increasing the number of vehicle checks. They also agreed to improve liaison and interaction at the operational and tactical levels. As a result, coordinated operations increased in frequency and complexity. During coordinated operations, 92 items, including abandoned arms, ammunitions and explosive devices from the 2006 conflict or before were discovered in the area south of the Litani River.

To date, UNIFIL, working in cooperation with LAF, had found no evidence of new military infrastructure in the UNIFIL area of operations. However, UNIFIL did encounter unauthorized armed personnel on one occasion, and past attacks on UNIFIL and rocket attacks against Israel demonstrated that there were unauthorized arms and hostile groups prepared to use them. Several incidents during the reporting period highlighted the challenges that UNIFIL faced in fulfilling its mandated activities.

The UNIFIL Maritime Task Force continued to perform maritime interdiction operations along the Lebanese coast to prevent the entry of unauthorized arms and related material. On 17 March, the Task Force electronically detected a vessel entering the UNIFIL area of maritime operations from Israeli waters without following proper procedure, and on 22 and 23 May, LAF protested the alleged hailing by IDF navy of two ships in Lebanese territorial waters.

During the reporting period, there were several incidents in or around the camps, in particular the Ein el-Hilweh camp in Sidon and the Nahr al-Bared camp in northern Lebanon, as well as near the city of Tripoli. Seven people were killed and 26 injured as a result. In one of those incidents, which occurred on 31 May near the entrance of Nahr al-Bared, a LAF outpost was targeted by an explosion that killed one soldier. Due to the deterioration of the security situation early in May and the resignation of the Government later that month, it was not possible to dispatch a team of experts to carry out a detailed assessment of the implementation of the recommendations of the 2007 Lebanon Independent Border Assessment Team [YUN 2007, p. 484].

There was no significant change in the border security arrangements along the eastern frontier of Lebanon with the Syrian Arab Republic. The Lebanese Common Border Force, deployed along the northern border with the Syrian Arab Republic, in the context of a German-led pilot project, uncovered numerous cases of smuggling, mostly involving fuel and other consumer products, but no incidents of weapons smuggling were observed. Measures were taken to close the illegal smuggling routes and enhance procedures at official crossing points.

The Lebanese authorities, with international donor support, worked to improve Lebanon's capacity to control its borders in other areas, such as the Beirut International Airport, and Lebanese Customs and General Security. Lebanon emphasized the need for cooperation on border management with Syrian counterparts.

During the period from the end of the 2006 conflict through 19 June 2008, incidents involving unexploded ordnance, including cluster munitions, led to 27 civilian fatalities and 231 civilian injuries, while mine-clearance incidents resulted in 13 fatalities and 38 injuries. The UN Mine Action Coordination Centre-South Lebanon coordinated the clearance and reduction of approximately 36.6 million square metres of contaminated land, comprising 49 per cent of the surface and 29 per cent of the sub-surface areas, through a joint effort including LAF, the United Nations, bilaterally funded clearance organizations and UNIFIL. In total, 145,580 cluster munitions were located and destroyed. The size of the affected area, originally estimated at 32 million square metres, had increased to 39.4 million. The Mine Action Coordination Centre identified 21 additional cluster-bomb strike locations, bringing the total to 984 locations recorded.

On the issue of Shab'a Farms, the Secretary-General had received a letter from Prime Minister Siniora, dated 2 April, welcoming the completion of the cartographic work on the definition of the area. The Prime Minister considered that the provisional definition in the Secretary-General's 30 October 2007 report [YUN 2007, p. 490] provided a reasonable and practical basis for removing one of the obstacles standing in the way of establishing a permanent ceasefire. The Secretary-General had not received any official responses from Israel or the Syrian Arab Republic to his provisional definition, nor to his repeated requests for documents from the Syrian Arab Republic.

UNIFIL continued to focus on mitigating risks to its personnel, assets and installations through infrastructure enhancement projects, information-gathering and analysis, as well as the ongoing acquisition of electronic countermeasures to jam explosive devices and micro-unmanned aerial vehicles. In accordance with the plans outlined in his previous report to increase the Force's intelligence capabilities, a Joint Mission Analysis Centre was established. In addition, UNIFIL continued to implement security enhancements throughout its area of operations through the construction of reinforced perimeter structures, permanent observation towers and underground reinforced shelters, as well as the replacement of temporary water and sanitation infrastructure in military positions.

On 16 May, an armoured personnel carrier with Malaysian UNIFIL soldiers overturned near the town of Srifa in the western sector of the UNIFIL area of operation; one peacekeeper died and five others were wounded, four of them seriously. On 15 June, one Spanish peacekeeper died and two others were injured after an armoured personnel carrier overturned near the UNIFIL Sector East headquarters in Marjayoun. UNIFIL was supported by 52 UNTSO military observers of the Observer Group Lebanon.

In line with the second comprehensive review of the Strategic Military Cell, and taking into consideration the decision in General Assembly resolution 62/265 on the financing of UNIFIL (see p. 546), the Strategic Military Cell would undergo a phased downsizing aimed at full integration of its functions within the reinforced Office of Military Affairs of the UN Department of Peacekeeping Operations.

Communication. On 7 July [A/62/899-S/2008/448], Iran called on the Security Council and the Secretary-General to address the issue of the 1982 abduction of three members of the Iranian Embassy staff in Beirut and an Iranian journalist, for which it held Israel responsible, and to help secure their release.

Report of Secretary-General (November). In his eighth report on the implementation of resolution 1701(2006), of 18 November [S/2008/715], the Secretary-General said that he was pleased to report that all parties continued to express their commitment to resolution 1701(2006). The political climate in Lebanon had improved in the past months, due to the implementation of the elements of the Doha Agreement, the election of President Sleiman, the formation of a national unity Government and the launching of a National Dialogue (see p. 533).

The cessation of hostilities between Israel and Lebanon continued to hold and the military and security situation in the UNIFIL area of operations remained generally quiet. The parties generally maintained respect for the Blue Line, apart from the Ghajar area, where IDF still occupied part of the village and an adjacent area north of the Blue Line, in violation of resolution 1701(2006). Incursions into Lebanese airspace by Israeli aircraft and unmanned aerial vehicles continued in high numbers, which UNIFIL and Lebanon protested. Control by IDF of northern Ghajar continued to be a source of tension. On 22 August, Lebanon informed the Force Commander of its readiness to accept the UNIFIL proposal (see p. 540) to facilitate the withdrawal of IDF from the area, on the condition that Israel agreed to the proposal within three months, and that a date for Israel's eventual withdrawal be established. UNIFIL invested considerable efforts in mediating the proposal between the parties and the Secretary-General hoped that Israel would endorse it.

Progress on the pilot project to visibly mark a 6-kilometre stretch of the Blue Line was slow. After extensive field work and discussions at both the bilateral level and in the tripartite forum, the parties reached agreement on a further seven points to be marked, which brought the total number of points to 16. The parties also agreed on an additional 4-kilometre stretch to extend the pilot project. UNIFIL proposed a new plan to accelerate the process, which was accepted by both parties.

UNIFIL and the LAF Senior Command continued their strategic review sessions of military tasks carried out by the two Forces in implementing resolution 1701(2006) in order to intensify cooperation in operational activities and expand coordination and liaison procedures. At their 21 October meeting, the Senior Commands assessed the level of cooperation achieved and agreed, in an effort to mitigate potential effects of the reduced LAF presence due to temporary redeployment to the north, to conduct a joint review to enhance the effectiveness of the coordinated checkpoints. They also agreed to increase regular vehicle checks, intensify efforts to curtail hunters, expand liaison arrangements, and review operating procedures between the UNIFIL Maritime Task Force and the Lebanese navy. The Maritime Task Force would assist in further institutionalizing naval training programmes at the Lebanese naval training institute. Continued material and technical support over the medium- to long-term to enable the Lebanese navy to gradually assume responsibilities currently undertaken by the Maritime Task Force was a high priority.

Coordination and liaison with IDF remained good and efficient. The UNIFIL Force Commander met with the Israeli Minister of Defense and the IDF Chief of Staff to discuss issues related to UNIFIL mandate. In late August, owing to the deterioration of the security situation elsewhere in the country, the Lebanese authorities temporarily redeployed troops from southern Lebanon to strengthen LAF presence in the north of the country. To ensure that the reduction did not negatively affect implementation of resolution 1701(2006), they assured the UNIFIL Force Commander that the redeployment would be limited in scope, of short duration and balanced by further enhancements of the coordinated activities.

LAF and UNIFIL continued to discover abandoned armed-element facilities, arms and ammunitions dating back to the 2006 conflict or before in the area between the Litani River and the Blue Line.

During the reporting period, a series of grave security incidents highlighted the threat posed by armed groups operating inside Lebanon but outside State control. President Suleiman conveyed to the Secretary-General his concern over the presence and activities of extremist groups. The continued risk that Hizbullah's separate military capacity posed to Lebanon's sovereignty was evidenced on 28 August, when armed elements opened fire on a LAF helicopter patrolling north of the Litani. The pilot died in the attack, for which Hizbullah later admitted responsibility, and one person was arrested. Palestinian arms inside and outside of the 12 registered refugee camps remained a serious threat to Lebanon's stability and sovereignty, the Secretary-General stated. He welcomed the initiatives between the Lebanese Government and Palestinian authorities to take joint responsibility for security inside the Nahr al-Bared camp.

The Secretary-General, on 16 July, dispatched for the second time a team of independent border security experts to assess implementation by the Government of the 2007 recommendations of the Lebanon Independent Border Assessment Team (LIBAT I) [YUN 2007, p. 486] and gauge the impact of those measures on progress on the ground for Lebanon's overall border management capacity. On 26 August, the Secretary-General conveyed the expert's report, known as LIBAT II, to the Security Council, indicating his full support for its conclusions and recommendations, including the proposal that the Government develop a strategic plan for border security.

The deployment of Syrian troops along Lebanon's northern border started in late September and continued. Syrian authorities stated, on 29 October, that the deployment, one of the outcomes of the August summit meeting between the Presidents, aimed to halt and prevent smuggling and sabotage. Both Lebanese and Syrian senior officials confirmed that the extension of the Syrian deployment to the eastern border in late October was conducted in close coordination.

The UN Mine Action Coordination Centre-South Lebanon conducted an operational reassessment to review new and existing data on the contaminated area in southern Lebanon. The review established that some previously known and recorded strikes might be bigger than originally estimated. Some 74 additional cluster bomb strike locations were identified, making a total of 1,058 locations recorded thus far. As a result, the estimated contaminated area increased to 48.1 million square metres. To date, the Centre had coordinated the clearance and reduction of 40.2 million square metres of the contaminated area and located and destroyed 150,255 cluster munitions.

On 3 September, one UNIFIL explosive ordnance disposal expert with the Belgian contingent was killed. In addition, three mine-clearance personnel were injured in separate incidents, bringing the totals to 14 killed and 41 injured.

The Mine Action Coordination Centre carried out a minefield clearance project in the Addaisseh area in Sector East. More than 70,000 square metres were cleared and 4,569 mines located and destroyed in areas adjacent to the Blue Line. That was the first such clearance project of minefields by the Centre in the sensitive areas near the Blue Line. The transfer of primary responsibility for managing humanitarian clearance operations to LAF, as at 1 January 2009, was under way. The remaining Mine Action Coordination Centre staff would work exclusively in support of UNIFIL clearance and explosive ordnance disposal assets.

Negotiations on the release of the abducted Israeli soldiers Ehud Goldwasser and Eldad Regev, and Lebanese prisoners detained in Israel, including Samir Quntar and Nassim Nisr, as well as the five Hizbullah combatants captured by Israel during the 2006 conflict, resumed in earnest in March. The Secretary-General's facilitator submitted a modified draft formula to the sides, culminating in the development of a humanitarian agreement by late April. On 1 June, one of the Lebanese prisoners, Nassim Nisr, was released, having completed a six-year jail sentence, and was repatriated to Lebanon. At the same time, Hizbullah returned the remains of some Israeli soldiers killed in action.

Following further negotiations, the humanitarian agreement was signed by Hizbullah and Israel on 2 July, providing for an exchange of reports on humanitarian cases of particular sensitivity, including the case of Ron Arad, an Israeli airman missing in Lebanon since 1986, as well as on the fate of four Iranians abducted in Lebanon in 1982. The second phase of the agreement called for the two Israeli soldiers to be repatriated in exchange for the five Lebanese prisoners remaining in Israeli custody, the remains of eight Lebanese killed in action during the 2006 war, information on two Lebanese citizens, Yahya Skaff and Muhammad Farran, the remains of four members of the Dallal Mughrabi group, as well as up to 199 other Lebanese citizens, mostly of Palestinian origin. In a final phase, Israel would release Palestinian detainees in appreciation of successful UN facilitation and in anticipation of further UN-sponsored support for its endeavours to uncover the fate of Ron Arad and other persons missing in action.

Implementation of the agreement started shortly after it was signed, with the exchange of the bodies of the two Israeli soldiers for the bodies of some 200 Lebanese and Palestinian fighters and five Lebanese prisoners. After 18 months of intense efforts, the Secretary-General remarked, the humanitarian aspect of resolution 1701(2006) had been met. On 6 August, Israel freed five Palestinian prisoners in a move directly related to the agreement with Hizbullah, and Prime Minister Olmert announced that a large number of Palestinian prisoners would be released later in the month in a move designed to support the Annapolis peace process [YUN 2007, p. 445]. On 25 August, 198 Palestinian detainees were released.

Following their summit meeting in Damascus on 13 and 14 August, the Presidents of Lebanon and the Syrian Arab Republic announced the reactivation of the Lebanese-Syrian committee tasked with delineating their common border.

Concerning the key question of Shab'a Farms, in a meeting in Damascus on 6 November, the Syrian Foreign Minister categorically reiterated to the Special Coordinator for Lebanon that Shab'a Farms fell under Lebanon's sovereignty. The Secretary-General still had not received any response from either Israel or the Syrian Arab Republic to the provisional geographical definition of the area.

The period under review was one of relative calm in the UNIFIL area of operations, albeit punctuated by specific threat warnings emanating from militant and extremist groups, including Al-Qaida. Joint efforts and cooperation with the Lebanese authorities and LAF continued to ensure that such threats were addressed appropriately. As at 11 November, UNIFIL total military strength was 12,770 personnel, with a civilian strength of 318 international and 656 national staff. The Force was supported by 51 UNTSO military observers of the Observer Group Lebanon.

In his concluding observations, the Secretary-General stated that, although there were no breaches of the cessation of hostilities between Lebanon and Israel and relative calm continued to prevail, greater progress should have been achieved since the adoption of resolution 1701(2006). The general improvement of the situation, together with the continued stability in the area of operations and encouraging prospects in the region, created a momentum that both Lebanon and Israel should seize to make bold strides towards a permanent ceasefire and long-term solution.

Further developments. According to the Secretary-General's ninth report on the implementation of resolution 1701(2006) [S/2009/119], tension in the UNIFIL area of operations rose in late December, with the outbreak of the crisis in Gaza (see p. 492). On 25 December, LAF discovered, and with UNIFIL's assistance, defused and dismantled eight rockets that were armed and ready to be launched in the direction of Israel. Several violations of the Blue Line by IDF, as well as Lebanese civilians, were registered. Regarding Israel's claim that Hizbullah had held manoeuvres both north and south of the Litani River on 22 November, UNIFIL did not observe any activity that would substantiate that allegation.

Lebanon Independent Border Assessment Team

On 25 August [S/2008/582], the Secretary-General transmitted to the Security Council the report of the Lebanon Independent Border Assessment Team II (LIBAT II), dispatched, in coordination with the Lebanese Government, to undertake a thorough follow-up assessment of the implementation of the recommendations of the Lebanon Independent Border Assessment Team I, which, in accordance with resolution 1701(2006), had conducted a first assessment in 2007 [YUN 2007, p. 484].

Led by Lasse Christensen (Denmark), LIBAT II visited Lebanon from 15 to 31 July. It held talks with the Prime Minister, the Minister of Defence, the directors of the four border security agencies and regional military commanders, stakeholders in the German-led Northern Border Pilot Project and donor representatives. The Team visited all four operational border crossing points and one not yet open, as well as locations along the Green Border in the north and east of Lebanon, including locations of Lebanese-Syrian territorial dispute and cross-border areas under Palestinian control. It also visited the Beirut airport and the Beirut and Tripoli seaports.

Although the Northern Border Pilot Project was deemed to be in a consolidation phase, the Team believed that it had not yet reached the stage of full implementation. Equipment for essential operations had yet to arrive, there were cases of incompatibility of equipment and power, vehicles were not being used as intended, and there did not appear to be any output, coordination or sharing of intelligence among agencies. Moreover, the level of operational integration between the four border security agencies was less than optimal. There was also concern over the manner in which the Project was planned and executed.

To a certain degree, the Northern Border Project incorporated a number of Team I recommendations. At the border crossing points, in particular along the Green Border in the east, little progress was observed, despite the fact that a number of recommendations could easily have been implemented without political, structural or financial implications. At the airport and seaports, some minor progress could be observed, but there still remained considerable room for improvement. It was the opinion of Team II that the lack of a strategic master plan was a primary cause for the inactivity, in particular along the eastern border. The lack of strategic planning and desired end state for border security had a negative impact on the Lebanese potential to uphold and enforce control of its borders.

Among the positive steps taken was the relocation of the Aboudieh border crossing point to the actual border, the installation of additional border security equipment such as scanners, and the computerization of passport control. However, the overall situation rendered Lebanon's borders as penetrable as they had been during the first assessment in 2007. LIBAT II, therefore, reiterated the 2007 recommendations, especially those regarding the establishment of a multi-agency mobile force focusing on arms smugglings; the establishment of an intelligence and analysis component within that force; the deployment of international border security experts to it; the establishment of a dedicated border guard agency to streamline border security procedures and gather all expertise and intelligence in one agency; full and absolute control over border crossing points by creating standard operating procedures; measures to separate legal and illegal near-border or border-crossing activities; training programmes and the provision of border-specific equipment; and the establishment of cooperation with Syrian counterparts.

LIBAT II further suggested that the Lebanese Government instigate the formation of a strategic plan, which should include its desired end state and objectives, as well as ways of achieving them, and that donors enhance cooperation and coordination of their activities. The expansion of the Northern Border Pilot Project to include responsibility for the border crossing points should be considered, and the issue of delineation of the Lebanon's border with the Syrian Arab Republic should be addressed vigorously.

In transmitting the report, the Secretary-General stated that he fully supported the conclusions and recommendations of the Team II.

The Secretary-General, in his November report on the implementation of resolution 1701(2006) [S/2008/715], said that the LIBAT II report was widely distributed among Lebanese and international officials and was well received by all key stakeholders. Following the recommendations in the report, the Government formed a steering committee to begin preparing a border strategy, through a process designed to include the views and expertise of the four security agencies, as well as key government ministries. A group of donor countries working on border management was also assembled to assist in the process. The steering committee, which held its first meeting on 31 October, under the chairmanship of Prime Minister Siniora, reaffirmed its commitment to improve border management along Lebanon's northern and eastern borders and agreed on a mechanism and timeline to develop the strategy.

UNIFIL

The United Nations Interim Force in Lebanon (UNIFIL) continued to discharge its mandate by observing, monitoring and reporting on developments in its area of operation. Established by Security Council resolution 425(1978), following Israel's invasion of Lebanon [YUN 1978, p. 312], UNIFIL was mandated to confirm the withdrawal of Israeli forces, restore international peace and security, and assist Lebanon in regaining authority in southern Lebanon. In 1982, the Council, by resolution 511(1982) [YUN 1982, p. 450], authorized the Force to provide protection and humanitarian assistance to the local population. Following the withdrawal of Israeli forces in June 2000 [YUN 2000, p. 465], UNIFIL was reinforced to monitor the territories previously occupied by Israeli forces, prevent the recurrence of fighting and create conditions for the restoration of Lebanese authority.

On 21 August [S/2008/568], the Secretary-General recommended that the Council renew the UNIFIL mandate for a further 12 months.

SECURITY COUNCIL ACTION

On 27 August [meeting 5967], the Security Council unanimously adopted **resolution 1832(2008)**. The draft [S/2008/583] was prepared in consultations among Council members.

The Security Council,

Recalling all its previous resolutions on Lebanon, in particular resolutions 425(1978) and 426(1978) of 19 March 1978, 1559(2004) of 2 September 2004, 1680(2006) of 17 May 2006, 1701(2006) of 11 August 2006 and 1773(2007) of 24 August 2007, as well as the statements by its President on the situation in Lebanon,

Responding to the request of the Government of Lebanon to extend the mandate of the United Nations Interim Force in Lebanon for a new period of one year, without amendment, presented in a letter dated 18 August 2008 from the Prime Minister of Lebanon to the Secretary-General, and welcoming the letter dated 21 August 2008 from the Secretary-General to the President of the Security Council recommending this extension,

Reaffirming its commitment to the full implementation of all provisions of resolution 1701(2006), and aware of its responsibilities to help to secure a permanent ceasefire and a long-term solution as envisioned in the resolution,

Recalling the relevant principles contained in the Convention on the Safety of United Nations and Associated Personnel,

Commending the active role and dedication of the personnel of the Force, notably of its Commander, expressing its strong appreciation to Member States that contribute to the Force, and underlining the necessity that the Force have at its disposal all necessary means and equipment to carry out its mandate,

Determining that the situation in Lebanon continues to constitute a threat to international peace and security,

1. *Decides* to extend the present mandate of the United Nations Interim Force in Lebanon until 31 August 2009;

2. *Commends* the positive role of the Force, whose deployment together with the Lebanese Armed Forces has helped to establish a new strategic environment in southern Lebanon, welcomes the expansion of coordinated activities between the Force and the Lebanese Armed Forces, and encourages further enhancement of this cooperation;

3. *Calls upon* all parties concerned to respect the cessation of hostilities and the Blue Line in its entirety, to cooperate fully with the United Nations and the Force and to abide scrupulously by their obligation to respect the safety of the Force and other United Nations personnel, including by avoiding any course of action which endangers United Nations personnel and by ensuring that the Force is accorded full freedom of movement within its area of operation;

4. *Calls upon* all parties to cooperate fully with the Security Council and the Secretary-General to achieve a permanent ceasefire and a long-term solution as envisioned in resolution 1701(2006), and emphasizes the need for greater progress in this regard;

5. *Welcomes* the efforts being undertaken by the Force to implement the Secretary-General's zero-tolerance policy on sexual exploitation and abuse and to ensure full compliance of its personnel with the United Nations code of conduct, requests the Secretary-General to continue to take all necessary action in this regard and to keep the Council informed, and urges troop-contributing countries to take preventive and disciplinary action to ensure that such acts are properly investigated and punished in cases involving their personnel;

6. *Requests* the Secretary-General to continue to report to the Council on the implementation of resolution 1701(2006) every four months, or at any time as he deems appropriate;

7. *Stresses* the importance of, and the need to achieve, a comprehensive, just and lasting peace in the Middle East, based on all its relevant resolutions, including resolutions 242(1967) of 22 November 1967, 338(1973) of 22 October 1973 and 1515(2003) of 19 November 2003;

8. *Decides* to remain actively seized of the matter.

Lebanon, speaking after the adoption of Security Council resolution 1832(2008), extending UNIFIL's mandate until 31 August 2009, expressed appreciation for the technical support provided by the two Lebanon Independent Border Assessment Team (LIBAT) missions and assured the Council that it would give due consideration to the LIBAT reports.

Review of UNIFIL Strategic Military Cell

Report of Secretary-General. In response to the General Assembly request in resolution 61/250 B [YUN 2007, p. 492] for a comprehensive review of the Strategic Military Cell, created to ensure that UNIFIL's expansion, deployment and additional mandated responsibilities were conducted with and supported by sufficiently dedicated capabilities, the Secretary-General, on 14 March, submitted a report [A/62/744] outlining its role, structure and functions, as well as options for its future phased reduction.

The General Assembly, by resolution 62/265 of 20 June (see p. 546), decided that the target date for the termination of the Strategic Military Cell should be no later than 30 June 2010.

UNIFIL financing

Reports of Secretary-General. In January [A/62/632], the Secretary-General submitted a performance report on the UNIFIL budget for the period from 1 July 2006 to 30 June 2007. Expenditures amounted to $495,735,600, out of an appropriation of $496,615,500, leaving an unencumbered balance of $879,900. In March [A/62/751], the Secretary-General submitted the budget for UNIFIL for the period from 1 July 2008 to 30 June 2009, totalling $688,813,300 and providing for the deployment of 15,000 military personnel, and 415 international and 842 national staff, including temporary positions.

Report of ACABQ. The Advisory Committee on Administrative and Budgetary Questions (ACABQ), in its April report [A/62/781/Add.5], recommended that the unencumbered balance of $879,900, as well as other income and adjustments in the amount of $7,372,800 for the period ended 30 June 2007, be credited to Member States in a manner to be determined by the General Assembly, and that the proposed UNIFIL budget for the period from 1 July 2008 to 30 June 2009, be reduced to $668,370,300, largely in view of a projected delayed deployment of troops, downsizing of the Strategic Military Cell and rationalization of expenditures for communication.

GENERAL ASSEMBLY ACTION

On 20 June [meeting 109], the General Assembly, on the recommendation of the Fifth (Administrative and Budgetary) Committee [A/62/878], adopted **resolution 62/265** by recorded vote (142-2-1) [agenda item 153 (*b*)].

Financing of the United Nations Interim Force in Lebanon

The General Assembly,

Having considered the reports of the Secretary-General on the financing of the United Nations Interim Force in Lebanon, the report of the Secretary-General on the comprehensive review of the Strategic Military Cell and the related report of the Advisory Committee on Administrative and Budgetary Questions,

Recalling Security Council resolution 425(1978) of 19 March 1978 regarding the establishment of the United Nations Interim Force in Lebanon and the subsequent resolutions by which the Council extended the mandate of the Force, the latest of which was resolution 1773(2007) of 24 August 2007, by which the Council extended the mandate of the Force until 31 August 2008,

Recalling also its resolution S-8/2 of 21 April 1978 on the financing of the Force and its subsequent resolutions thereon, the latest of which was resolution 61/250 C of 29 June 2007,

Reaffirming its resolutions 51/233 of 13 June 1997, 52/237 of 26 June 1998, 53/227 of 8 June 1999, 54/267 of 15 June 2000, 55/180 A of 19 December 2000, 55/180 B of 14 June 2001, 56/214 A of 21 December 2001, 56/214 B of 27 June 2002, 57/325 of 18 June 2003, 58/307 of 18 June 2004, 59/307 of 22 June 2005, 60/278 of 30 June 2006, 61/250 A of 22 December 2006, 61/250 B of 2 April 2007 and 61/250 C,

Reaffirming also the general principles underlying the financing of United Nations peacekeeping operations, as stated in General Assembly resolutions 1874(S-IV) of 27 June 1963, 3101(XXVIII) of 11 December 1973 and 55/235 of 23 December 2000,

Noting with appreciation that voluntary contributions have been made to the Force,

Mindful of the fact that it is essential to provide the Force with the financial resources necessary to enable it to fulfil its responsibilities under the relevant resolutions of the Security Council,

1. *Requests* the Secretary-General to entrust the Head of the United Nations Interim Force in Lebanon with the task of formulating future budget proposals in full accordance with the provisions of General Assembly resolutions 59/296 of 22 June 2005, 60/266 of 30 June 2006 and 61/276 of 29 June 2007, as well as other relevant resolutions;

2. *Takes note* of the status of contributions to the Force as at 31 March 2008, including the contributions outstanding in the amount of 144.9 million United States dollars, representing some 3 per cent of the total assessed contributions, notes with concern that only seventy-four Member States have paid their assessed contributions in full, and urges all other Member States, in particular those in arrears, to ensure payment of their outstanding assessed contributions;

3. *Expresses its appreciation* to those Member States which have paid their assessed contributions in full, and urges all other Member States to make every possible effort to ensure payment of their assessed contributions to the Force in full;

4. *Expresses deep concern* that Israel did not comply with General Assembly resolutions 51/233, 52/237, 53/227, 54/267, 55/180 A, 55/180 B, 56/214 A, 56/214 B, 57/325, 58/307, 59/307, 60/278, 61/250 A, 61/250 B and 61/250 C;

5. *Stresses once again* that Israel should strictly abide by General Assembly resolutions 51/233, 52/237, 53/227, 54/267, 55/180 A, 55/180 B, 56/214 A, 56/214 B, 57/325, 58/307, 59/307, 60/278, 61/250 A, 61/250 B and 61/25 C;

6. *Expresses concern* at the financial situation with regard to peacekeeping activities, in particular as regards the reimbursements to troop contributors that bear additional burdens owing to overdue payments by Member States of their assessments;

7. *Also expresses concern* at the delay experienced by the Secretary-General in deploying and providing adequate resources to some recent peacekeeping missions, in particular those in Africa;

8. *Emphasizes* that all future and existing peacekeeping missions shall be given equal and non-discriminatory treatment in respect of financial and administrative arrangements;

9. *Also emphasizes* that all peacekeeping missions shall be provided with adequate resources for the effective and efficient discharge of their respective mandates;

10. *Reiterates its request* to the Secretary-General to make the fullest possible use of facilities and equipment at the United Nations Logistics Base at Brindisi, Italy, in order to minimize the costs of procurement for the Force;

11. *Endorses* the conclusions and recommendations contained in the report of the Advisory Committee on Administrative and Budgetary Questions, subject to the provisions of the present resolution, and requests the Secretary-General to ensure their full implementation;

12. *Takes note* of paragraph 38 of the report of the Advisory Committee;

13. *Requests* the Secretary-General to ensure the full implementation of the relevant provisions of its resolutions 59/296, 60/266 and 61/276;

14. *Also requests* the Secretary-General to take all necessary action to ensure that the Force is administered with a maximum of efficiency and economy;

15. *Further requests* the Secretary-General, in order to reduce the cost of employing General Service staff, to continue efforts to recruit local staff for the Force against General Service posts, commensurate with the requirements of the Force;

16. *Notes* the significant projected underexpenditure for the period from 1 July 2007 to 30 June 2008, as in-

dicated in the report of the Advisory Committee, and requests the Secretary-General, to the extent possible, to take measures to improve budget forecasting with respect to the Force, bearing in mind the unpredictable nature of peacekeeping operations;

17. *Recalls* paragraph 1, section XXI, of resolution 61/276, and welcomes the cooperation among the missions in the region and the efforts of the Secretary-General in this regard;

18. *Notes with concern* the high vacancy rate among international and national staff of the Force, and decides to apply a vacancy factor of 14 per cent for international staff and 15 per cent for national staff;

19. *Notes* paragraphs 16 and 17 of the report of the Advisory Committee, and decides to apply a delayed deployment factor of 8 per cent to the cost estimates for military contingents;

20. *Requests* the Secretary General to keep the requirements for the Force under constant review and to report thereon in the context of his future budget proposals;

21. *Reiterates its request* to the Secretary-General to take the necessary measures to ensure the full implementation of paragraph 8 of its resolution 51/233, paragraph 5 of its resolution 52/237, paragraph 11 of its resolution 53/227, paragraph 14 of its resolution 54/267, paragraph 14 of its resolution 55/180 A, paragraph 15 of its resolution 55/180 B, paragraph 13 of its resolution 56/214, paragraph 13 of its resolution 56/214 B, paragraph 14 of its resolution 57/325, paragraph 13 of its resolution 58/307, paragraph 13 of its resolution 59/307, paragraph 17 of its resolution 60/278, paragraph 21 of its resolution 61/250 A, paragraph 20 of its resolution 61/250 B and paragraph 20 of its resolution 61/250 C, stresses once again that Israel shall pay the amount of 1,117,005 dollars resulting from the incident at Qana on 18 April 1996, and requests the Secretary-General to report on this matter to the General Assembly at its sixty-third session;

22. *Decides* to approve the post of Chief of the Joint Mission Analysis Cell (P-5) and the post of Associate Political Affairs Officer (P-2) in the Office of Political and Civil Affairs;

23. *Also decides* to maintain a D-2 post for the leadership of the Strategic Military Cell and a General Service post;

24. *Further decides* that the target date of the termination of the Strategic Military Cell shall be no later than 30 June 2010;

25. *Requests* the Secretary-General to assess whether the strengthening of the Office of Military Affairs approved in its resolution 62/250 of 20 June 2008 has provided sufficient capacity and capability to meet the target date referred to above for the termination of the Strategic Military Cell and to report thereon in the context of the comprehensive report requested in resolution 62/250;

Financial performance report for the period from 1 July 2006 to 30 June 2007

26. *Takes note* of the report of the Secretary-General on the financial performance of the Force for the period from 1 July 2006 to 30 June 2007;

Budget estimates for the period from 1 July 2008 to 30 June 2009

27. *Decides* to appropriate to the Special Account for the United Nations Interim Force in Lebanon the amount of 680,932,600 dollars for the period from 1 July 2008 to 30 June 2009, inclusive of 650,755,600 dollars for the maintenance of the Force, 26,306,200 dollars for the support account for peacekeeping operations and 3,870,800 dollars for the United Nations Logistics Base;

Financing of the appropriation

28. *Also decides* to apportion among Member States the amount of 113,488,767 dollars for the period from 1 July to 31 August 2008, in accordance with the levels updated in General Assembly resolution 61/243 of 22 December 2006, and taking into account the scale of assessments for 2008, as set out in its resolution 61/237 of 22 December 2006;

29. *Further decides* that, in accordance with the provisions of its resolution 973(X) of 15 December 1955, there shall be set off against the apportionment among Member States, as provided for in paragraph 28 above, their respective share in the Tax Equalization Fund of the amount of 2,312,883 dollars, comprising the estimated staff assessment income of 1,840,633 dollars approved for the Force, the prorated share of 421,267 dollars of the estimated staff assessment income approved for the support account and the prorated share of 50,983 dollars of the estimated staff assessment income approved for the United Nations Logistics Base;

30. *Decides* to apportion among Member States the amount of 567,443,833 dollars for the period from 1 September 2008 to 30 June 2009 at a monthly rate of 56,744,383 dollars, in accordance with the levels updated in resolution 61/243, and taking into account the scale of assessments for 2008 and 2009, as set out in resolution 61/237, subject to a decision of the Security Council to extend the mandate of the Force;

31. *Also decides* that, in accordance with the provisions of its resolution 973(X), there shall be set off against the apportionment among Member States, as provided for in paragraph 30 above, their respective share in the Tax Equalization Fund of 11,564,417 dollars, comprising the estimated staff assessment income of 9,203,167 dollars approved for the Force, the prorated share of 2,106,333 dollars of the estimated staff assessment income approved for the support account and the prorated share of 254,917 dollars of the estimated staff assessment income approved for the United Nations Logistics Base;

32. *Further decides* that, for Member States that have fulfilled their financial obligations to the Force, there shall be set off against their apportionment, as provided for in paragraph 28 above, their respective share of the unencumbered balance and other income in the total amount of 8,252,700 dollars in respect of the financial period ended 30 June 2007, in accordance with the levels updated in resolution 61/243, and taking into account the scale of assessments for 2007, as set out in resolution 61/237;

33. *Decides* that, for Member States that have not fulfilled their financial obligations to the Force, there

shall be set off against their outstanding obligations their respective share of the unencumbered balance and other income in the total amount of 8,252,700 dollars in respect of the financial period ended 30 June 2007, in accordance with the scheme set out in paragraph 32 above;

34. *Also decides* that the decrease of 370,300 dollars in the estimated staff assessment income in respect of the financial period ended 30 June 2007 shall be set off against the credits from the amount of 8,252,700 dollars referred to in paragraphs 32 and 33 above;

35. *Emphasizes* that no peacekeeping mission shall be financed by borrowing funds from other active peacekeeping missions;

36. *Encourages* the Secretary-General to continue to take additional measures to ensure the safety and security of all personnel participating in the Force under the auspices of the United Nations, bearing in mind paragraphs 5 and 6 of Security Council resolution 1502(2003) of 26 August 2003;

37. *Invites* voluntary contributions to the Force in cash and in the form of services and supplies acceptable to the Secretary-General, to be administered, as appropriate, in accordance with the procedure and practices established by the General Assembly;

38. *Decides* to include in the provisional agenda of its sixty-third session, under the item entitled "Financing of the United Nations peacekeeping forces in the Middle East", the sub-item entitled "United Nations Interim Force in Lebanon".

RECORDED VOTE ON RESOLUTION 62/265:

In favour: Afghanistan, Albania, Algeria, Andorra, Angola, Antigua and Barbuda, Argentina, Armenia, Austria, Bahamas, Bahrain, Bangladesh, Barbados, Belarus, Belgium, Benin, Bolivia, Bosnia and Herzegovina, Brazil, Brunei Darussalam, Bulgaria, Burkina Faso, Cambodia, Canada, Chile, China, Colombia, Comoros, Congo, Costa Rica, Croatia, Cuba, Cyprus, Czech Republic, Democratic People's Republic of Korea, Denmark, Djibouti, Dominican Republic, Ecuador, Egypt, El Salvador, Estonia, Fiji, Finland, France, Gabon, Germany, Ghana, Greece, Guatemala, Guyana, Haiti, Honduras, Hungary, Iceland, India, Indonesia, Iran, Iraq, Ireland, Italy, Jamaica, Japan, Jordan, Kazakhstan, Kenya, Kuwait, Kyrgyzstan, Lao People's Democratic Republic, Latvia, Lebanon, Lesotho, Libyan Arab Jamahiriya, Liechtenstein, Lithuania, Luxembourg, Malawi, Malaysia, Maldives, Mali, Mauritania, Mauritius, Mexico, Moldova, Monaco, Mongolia, Morocco, Mozambique, Myanmar, Namibia, Nepal, Netherlands, New Zealand, Nicaragua, Niger, Nigeria, Norway, Oman, Pakistan, Panama, Paraguay, Peru, Philippines, Poland, Portugal, Qatar, Republic of Korea, Romania, Russian Federation, Rwanda, San Marino, Saudi Arabia, Senegal, Serbia, Singapore, Slovakia, Slovenia, South Africa, Spain, Sri Lanka, Sudan, Suriname, Sweden, Switzerland, Syrian Arab Republic, Tajikistan, Thailand, The former Yugoslav Republic of Macedonia, Togo, Tunisia, Turkey, Uganda, Ukraine, United Arab Emirates, United Kingdom, United Republic of Tanzania, Uruguay, Venezuela, Viet Nam, Yemen, Zambia, Zimbabwe.

Against: Israel, United States.

Abstaining: Australia.

Other security issues

Investigation of assassination of former Prime Minister Rafik Hariri

UN International Independent Investigation Commission

The United Nations International Independent Investigation Commission (UNIIIC), established by Security Council resolution 1595(2005) [YUN 2005, p. 553], continued to assist Lebanese authorities in their investigation of the assassination of former Prime Minister Rafik Hariri and 22 others on 14 February 2005 [ibid., p. 551]. The Commission was headed by Judge Daniel A. Bellemare (Canada), who was appointed Commissioner by the Secretary-General in November 2007 [YUN 2007, p. 502], succeeding Serge Brammertz (Belgium).

Communications. On 30 January [S/2008/60], the Secretary-General transmitted to the Security Council a letter from the Lebanese Prime Minister requesting technical assistance for his Government's efforts to investigate the murder, in a 25 January terrorist act, of Major Wissam Eid, head of the technical department in the Intelligence Service of the Internal Security Forces, and Adjutant Oussama Merheb and other innocent civilians. Major Eid had played a central role in uncovering the perpetrators of several of the terrorist assassinations and attacks that Lebanon had recently witnessed. The Prime Minister requested that UNIIIC contact the Lebanese authorities for that purpose. Replying on 31 January [S/2008/61], the Council invited the Commission to extend appropriate technical assistance to the Lebanese authorities in the investigation.

Report of UNIIIC (March). The tenth UNIIIC report on progress in implementing the Commission's mandate, covering the period since its last report [YUN 2007, p. 505], was transmitted by the Secretary-General to the Security Council on 28 March [S/2008/210]. The Commission reported that it had evidence that a network of individuals acted in concert to carry out the assassination of former Prime Minister Hariri, and that criminal network, or parts thereof, were linked to some of the other cases within the Commission's mandate. The report also provided details of UNIIIC's assistance to the Lebanese authorities in their investigation of 20 other bombings and assassinations in Lebanon since October 2004, including recent attacks targeting members of Lebanon's security forces. In carrying out its mandate, UNIIIC continued to work closely with the Lebanese authorities. Its cooperation with the Syrian Arab Republic was generally satisfactory. The Commission implemented new working practices to foster additional assistance from Member States, as well as encourage the cooperation of witnesses and other sources. Out of the 256 requests for assistance, 28 had been sent to 11 Member States other than Lebanon and the Syrian Arab Republic.

UNIIIC was also preparing for the transition to the Special Tribunal in Lebanon [YUN 2007, p. 505], scheduled for 1 March 2009.

Security Council consideration. Introducing UNIIIC's tenth report to the Security Council on 8 April [meeting 5863], Commissioner Bellemare noted that not only was the investigation very complex, but it was conducted in an extremely volatile environment. Unfortunately, UNIIIC's establishment did not have an immediate deterrent effect on terrorists as bombings continued, with two more deadly attacks added to the Commission's mandate since its November 2007 report [ibid.].

In order to give UNIIIC the time to continue its investigation, Mr. Bellemare requested the Council to consider extending its mandate beyond 15 June. The Council did not take any action on the report at that meeting.

Communication. By a letter of 8 May, transmitted to the Council by the Secretary-General [S/2008/334], the Lebanese Prime Minister expressed the hope that the Council would respond favourably to Commissioner Bellemare's 8 April request to extend UNIIIC's mandate to 31 December.

SECURITY COUNCIL ACTION

On 2 June [meeting 5901], the Security Council unanimously adopted **resolution 1815(2008)**. The draft [S/2008/349] was submitted by France.

The Security Council,

Recalling all its previous relevant resolutions, in particular resolutions 1595(2005) of 7 April 2005, 1636(2005) of 31 October 2005, 1644(2005) of 15 December 2005, 1664(2006) of 29 March 2006, 1686(2006) of 15 June 2006, 1748(2007) of 27 March 2007, 1757(2007) of 30 May 2007, 1373(2001) of 28 September 2001 and 1566(2004) of 8 October 2004,

Reaffirming its strongest condemnation of the terrorist bombing of 14 February 2005, as well as of all other attacks in Lebanon since October 2004, and reaffirming also that those involved in these attacks must be held accountable for their crimes,

Having examined the report of the International Independent Investigation Commission ("the Commission"), submitted pursuant to resolutions 1595(2005), 1636(2005), 1644(2005), 1686(2006) and 1748(2007),

Commending the Commission for its outstanding professional work and the progress it continues to achieve under difficult circumstances in assisting the Lebanese authorities in their investigation into all aspects of this terrorist act,

Taking note of the request to extend the mandate of the Commission, expressed by the Commissioner in his briefing to the Security Council on 8 April 2008, in order to ensure stability and continuity in the investigative process,

Taking note also of the letter dated 8 May 2008 from the Prime Minister of Lebanon to the Secretary-General expressing the hope that the Council will respond favourably to the request of the Commissioner by extending the mandate of the Commission until 31 December 2008, and noting the concurrent recommendation of the Secretary-General in this regard,

Willing to continue to assist Lebanon in the search for the truth and in holding all those involved in this terrorist attack accountable,

1. *Welcomes* the report of the Commission;
2. *Decides* to extend the mandate of the Commission until 31 December 2008, and declares its readiness to terminate the mandate earlier if the Commission reports that it has completed the implementation of its mandate;
3. *Requests* the Commission to report to the Security Council on the progress of the investigation in six months at the latest, and at any other earlier time if it deems it appropriate;
4. *Decides* to remain seized of the matter.

Report of UNIIIC (December). On 2 December [S/2008/752], the Secretary-General transmitted to the Security Council UNIIIC's eleventh report, which gave an overview of progress made since the Commission's March report. The Commission reported that it had acquired new information that might allow it to link additional individuals to the network that had carried out the assassination of former Prime Minister Hariri. It provided details of its assistance to the Lebanese authorities in their investigation of 20 other bombings and assassinations in Lebanon since October 2004, as well as an update on the links between those attacks and the Hariri case.

As to progress achieved, the Commission found that members of the Hariri network were also associated with other attacks. A review of financial transactions revealed other leads that were being pursued. The inventory of exhibits, which consisted of over 10,000 forensic items, including more than 7,000 related to the Hariri case, had been completed and reviewed. The results of recently conducted forensic examinations revealed information regarding the explosives used in certain of the targeted attacks and their placements in the vehicles used during the attacks. Moreover, forensic examinations in five of the targeted attacks revealed new DNA profiles and fingerprints from the vehicles and other items used in the attacks. The Commission had also been provided with a weapon allegedly used in the attack on former Minister Pierre Gemayel [YUN 2006, p. 596]; reports of a ballistics analysis to determine whether it had indeed been used were expected in the coming weeks.

Since March, 29 persons had been indicted in connection with the 13 February 2007 twin bus bombing in Ain Alaq, which left three people dead and 20 others injured [YUN 2007, p. 502]. UNIIIC provided technical assistance in analysing the explosive devices used and DNA profiles.

A significant amount of investigative work related to all the cases within UNIIIC's mandate remained to be done and the Prosecutor would need to continue investigating them to establish which ones were connected with the Hariri case in the manner required under the statute of the Tribunal.

Since its March report, UNIIIC had submitted 24 assistance requests to the Syrian Arab Republic, which provided responses within the specified deadlines. The Syrian authorities had also facilitated nine missions to the country. Out of the 619 assistance requests issued by the Commission during the reporting period, 96 were sent to 40 Member States other than Lebanon and Syria.

Following the Secretary-General's announcement that the Special Tribunal for Lebanon was on track to commence functioning on 1 March 2009, the Commission requested an extension of its mandate to 28 February 2009, to enable it to continue its investigation without interruption and gradually transfer its operations, staff and assets to The Hague. Once the Office of the Prosecutor of the Tribunal was operational, it would need to continue investigating all the cases within the Commission's current mandate in order to establish which of them were connected to the Hariri case in the manner required under the Tribunal's statute. The Office would require the full cooperation and support of the Lebanese authorities, as well as other Member States, in order to conduct effective investigations and prosecutions.

Communication. On 4 December [S/2008/764], Lebanon submitted to the Secretary-General a letter from its Prime Minister supporting the Commissioner's request for an extension of UNIIIC's mandate until 28 February 2009.

SECURITY COUNCIL ACTION

On 17 December [meeting 6048], the Security Council unanimously adopted **resolution 1852(2008)**. The draft [S/2008/792] was submitted by France.

The Security Council,

Recalling all its previous relevant resolutions, in particular resolutions 1595(2005) of 7 April 2005, 1636(2005) of 31 October 2005, 1644(2005) of 15 December 2005, 1664(2006) of 29 March 2006, 1686(2006) of 15 June 2006, 1748(2007) of 27 March 2007, 1757(2007) of 30 May 2007, 1815(2008) of 2 June 2008, 1373(2001) of 28 September 2001 and 1566(2004) of 8 October 2004,

Reaffirming its strongest condemnation of the terrorist bombing of 14 February 2005, as well as of all other attacks in Lebanon since October 2004, and reaffirming also that those involved in these attacks must be held accountable for their crimes,

Having examined the report of the International Independent Investigation Commission ("the Commission"), submitted pursuant to resolutions 1595(2005), 1636(2005), 1644(2005), 1686(2006), 1748(2007) and 1815(2008),

Taking note of the announcement by the Secretary-General that the Special Tribunal for Lebanon ("the Tribunal") is fully on track to commence functioning on 1 March 2009,

Taking note also of the request of the Commission to extend its mandate until 28 February 2009 so that it can continue its investigation without interruption and gradually transfer operations, staff and assets to The Hague with a view to completing the transition by the time the Tribunal starts functioning,

Taking note further of the letter dated 4 December 2008 from the Prime Minister of Lebanon to the Secretary-General expressing the hope that the Council will respond favourably to the request of the Commission,

Commending the Commission for its extensive work and the progress it continues to achieve in the investigation of all cases within its mandate, and looking forward to further progress in this regard by the Commission as well as by the Office of the Prosecutor, once it begins to operate and takes over the continuation of the investigation into the death of former Prime Minister Rafiq Hariri and other cases which may be connected with the attack of 14 February 2005, in conformity with the statute of the Tribunal,

Recognizing the commitment of Member States to the work of the Commission, and underlining the importance of the continuation of their full cooperation with the Commission and, once it begins to operate, with the Office of the Prosecutor, in accordance with resolution 1757(2007), in order to enable effective investigations and prosecutions,

1. *Welcomes* the report of the Commission;

2. *Decides* to extend the mandate of the Commission until 28 February 2009;

3. *Decides also* to remain seized of the matter.

Special Tribunal for Lebanon

During the year, progress was made in establishing the Special Tribunal for Lebanon which, pursuant to Security Council resolution 1757(2007) [YUN 2007, p. 506], was created with a dual mandate to investigate and prosecute the perpetrators of the Hariri assassination and related attacks.

On 30 November, the Secretary-General announced that the Special Tribunal was on track to commence functioning on 1 March 2009. To ensure continuity of the investigations and a smooth and coordinated transition from UNIIIC to the Tribunal, the Council extended the Commission's mandate until 28 February 2009. Judge Daniel A. Bellemare, the UNIIIC Commissioner since 1 January 2008, was appointed Prosecutor of the Tribunal and was to take up his office on 1 March 2009.

Reports of Secretary-General. On 12 March [S/2008/173], the Secretary-General submitted his second report, pursuant to resolution 1757(2007), under which he had been mandated to establish the Special Tribunal for Lebanon, in coordination with the Government of Lebanon.

Since his first progress report [YUN 2007, p. 515], substantial progress had been made in a number of areas. All actions relating to the preparatory phase had been undertaken, if not completed. The United Nations and the Netherlands had signed the agreement concerning the Tribunal headquarters [YUN 2007, p. 516], and premises for the Tribunal had been identified. The judges, Prosecutor and Registrar had been selected, the Management Committee established and the recruitment process for the Head of the Defence Office had begun. A draft budget, including a staffing table, would be submitted to the Management Committee, and communication and outreach policies had been prepared.

The start-up phase had commenced, as work on the preparation of the premises and on a coordinated transition between UNIIIC and the Tribunal was being conducted. Once the Registrar started operating, a core unit of Registry personnel would be established in The Hague to assist the Registrar in his functions.

The Tribunal would commence functioning in successive phases. It was anticipated that early informal consultations among the judges would facilitate the drafting of the rules of procedure and evidence and other necessary documents. In addition to the Registrar, the Prosecutor, followed by the pre-trial judge, would start their duties earlier than the other senior officials. The Tribunal President would also take up duties on a full-time basis at an earlier date to ensure the Tribunal's efficient management and functioning, and the judges of the Trial and Appeals Chambers would do so on a date to be determined.

The Secretary-General assured the Council that the Secretariat was dedicated to establishing the Tribunal in a timely manner, with the generosity and support of Member States.

In his third report [S/2008/734] pursuant to resolution 1757(2007), submitted on 26 November, the Secretary-General said that on the basis of the progress reported so far, and following consultations by the UN Legal Counsel with the Lebanese Prime Minister and the UNIIIC Commissioner, it was envisaged that the Tribunal would commence functioning on 1 March 2009. The transition period should begin on 1 January and extend to 28 February 2009. All practical arrangements would be in place for the Prosecutor to arrive on 1 March and continue the investigation with minimum disruption. The Trust Fund created for the Tribunal's establishment and activities had received approximately $55.1 million in contributions. In November, the Legal Counsel invited Member States to make further pledges and called for assurances of the donors' continuing commitment to the Tribunal's financial viability. Given the current budget proposal totalling $51 million, the contributions received were sufficient for the commencement and first year of operation. The Legal Counsel was engaged in efforts to increase the pledges of financing for the subsequent two years. Against that background, the Secretary-General would be taking a decision regarding the commencement of the Tribunal on 1 March 2009, after a transition period starting on 1 January.

The Secretary-General believed that the impending start of the Tribunal would send a strong signal that the Lebanese Government and the United Nations remained committed to ending impunity in Lebanon.

In a later report [S/2009/106], the Secretary-General stated that on 12 December, the Management Committee approved the Special Tribunal's budget of $51.4 million for its first year of operation starting on 1 January 2009. The budget was adopted on the understanding that the Registrar could propose a supplementary budget if activities not anticipated in the budget arose. Arrangements between the United Nations and the Special Tribunal were being made to close the United Nations Trust Fund and to transfer the amount remaining in the Fund to the Special Tribunal before its commencement date. On 30 December, the first transfer of $10 million was made from the Trust Fund to the Special Tribunal.

Communications. On 18 December [S/2008/824], the Secretary-General informed the Security Council that following adoption of resolution 1852(2008) extending UNIIIC's mandate to the end of February 2009, he had decided that the Special Tribunal should commence on 1 March 2009. The Council took note of that decision on 29 December [S/2008/825].

Syrian Arab Republic

The Golan Heights in the Syrian Arab Republic, occupied since 1967, was effectively annexed when Israel extended its laws, jurisdiction and administration to the territory at the end of 1981 [YUN 1981, p. 309]. The General Assembly again demanded that Israel withdraw from all the occupied Syrian Golan to the line of 4 June 1967, in implementation of the relevant Security Council resolutions, and called upon the two countries to resume talks. The United Nations Disengagement Observer Force (UNDOF) continued to supervise the ceasefire between Israel and Syria in the Golan Heights and to ensure the separation of forces. The Mission's mandate was extended twice during the year. In May 2008, indirect talks were launched between Israel and Syria, facilitated by Turkey.

Communications. In a 3 March letter [A/62/723-S/2008/161], Syria charged Israel with uprooting tree seedlings on 23 February belonging to a Syrian citizen and resident of the village of Buq'ata in the occupied Golan, in an attempt to alter the demographic character of the Golan.

In a 31 December letter [A/63/669] to the Secretary-General and the General Assembly President, Syria requested that the international community prevent Israel from continuing any behaviour that exploited, damaged, caused loss or depletion of or endangered the Golan's natural resources.

Special Committee on Israeli Practices. In its annual report [A/63/273], the Special Committee to Investigate Israeli Practices Affecting the Human Rights of the Palestinian People and other Arabs of the Occupied Territories (Special Committee on Israeli Practices) summarized the views contained in the fortieth annual report of the Syrian Arab Republic on Israeli practices affecting the human rights of Syrian citizens in the occupied Golan Heights, covering the period from 31 July 2007 to 1 July 2008. The report noted a deteriorating human rights situation in the occupied Golan, with an increasing number of Israeli settlers and expansion of settlements, which numbered 45. Syrian citizens were denied access to water resources and permission to dig artesian wells or build cisterns, whereas numerous wells had been dug for the nearby settlements, lowering the groundwater level in the Arab villages. The waters of Mas'adah Lake had been diverted to the settlements, whereas the inhabitants of the occupied villages were prevented from using them. In general, Syrian citizens in the Golan received only 20 per cent of their annual needs, while settlers in the same area received 120 per cent.

According to Syria's report, prisoners from the Golan were subjected to the harshest forms of physical and mental torture and denied their most basic rights. Israeli authorities repeatedly refused requests from international institutions, including the ICRC, to visit Syrian prisoners. Women were subjected to repeated arrest. There were an estimated 2 million landmines and 76 minefields in the occupied Golan, posing a constant threat to the local people and their livestock. The five occupied Arab villages in the Golan suffered from a chronic shortage of health centres and clinics, and schools were overcrowded and unsanitary. Discrimination existed also with regard to wages and taxes. Syria reiterated its demand for the resumption of family visits through the Quneitra crossing point, under ICRC supervision. President Bashar al-Assad had issued instructions that Syrian citizens in the occupied Golan had to be issued a national identity number and identity card, to make it clear that they belonged to the Syrian homeland.

Human Rights Council action. By resolution 7/30 of 28 March [A/HRC/7/78] (see p. 895) on human rights in the occupied Syrian Golan, the Human Rights Council reaffirmed the illegality of Israel's decision to impose its laws, jurisdiction and administration on the Golan, and called on Israel to comply with General Assembly and Security Council resolutions declaring that decision null and void.

Reports of Secretary-General. On 15 October [A/63/482], responding to General Assembly resolution 62/110 [YUN 2007, p. 518], the Secretary-General reported that no reply had been received in response to his request for information from Israel on its implementation of that resolution. Two Member States had responded.

In his 29 October report on the situation in the Middle East [A/63/361], the Secretary-General stated that four Member States had replied to his request for information on steps taken or envisaged to implement Assembly resolution 62/85 [YUN 2007, p. 518], which dealt with Israeli policies in the occupied Syrian territory.

A 5 November report [A/63/519] of the Secretary-General, prepared by OHCHR, described the continued Israeli settlements activities in the occupied territories, including the Syrian Golan Heights, covering the period from January to August 2008. At the end of June, some 18,000 Israelis were estimated to be living in 32 settlements in the occupied Syrian Golan. Construction of infrastructure and housing was pursued actively in early 2008, notwithstanding calls by the international community to halt construction in the occupied territories and despite the fact that the Golan Height were on the agenda of recent peace talks between Syria and Israel. The detrimental impact of the Israeli occupation on the livelihood of the population of the Golan related to the restrictions on land cultivation and farming. Such practices were contrary to the standards and principles set out by the International Labour Organization concerning equality of opportunity and treatment in employment and occupation, which included the right to equal access to water and other resources.

GENERAL ASSEMBLY ACTION

On 26 November [meeting 60], the General Assembly adopted **resolution 63/31**[draft: A/63/L.37 & Add.1] by recorded vote (116-6-52) [agenda item 15].

The Syrian Golan

The General Assembly,

Having considered the item entitled "The situation in the Middle East",

Taking note of the report of the Secretary-General,

Recalling Security Council resolution 497(1981) of 17 December 1981,

Reaffirming the fundamental principle of the inadmissibility of the acquisition of territory by force, in accordance with international law and the Charter of the United Nations,

Reaffirming once more the applicability of the Geneva Convention relative to the Protection of Civilian Persons in Time of War, of 12 August 1949, to the occupied Syrian Golan,

Deeply concerned that Israel has not withdrawn from the Syrian Golan, which has been under occupation since 1967, contrary to the relevant Security Council and General Assembly resolutions,

Stressing the illegality of the Israeli settlement construction and other activities in the occupied Syrian Golan since 1967,

Noting with satisfaction the convening in Madrid on 30 October 1991 of the Peace Conference on the Middle East, on the basis of Security Council resolutions 242(1967) of 22 November 1967, 338(1973) of 22 October 1973 and 425(1978) of 19 March 1978 and the formula of land for peace,

Expressing grave concern over the halt in the peace process on the Syrian track, and expressing the hope that peace talks will soon resume from the point they had reached,

1. *Declares* that Israel has failed so far to comply with Security Council resolution 497(1981);

2. *Also declares* that the Israeli decision of 14 December 1981 to impose its laws, jurisdiction and administration on the occupied Syrian Golan is null and void and has no validity whatsoever, as confirmed by the Security Council in its resolution 497(1981), and calls upon Israel to rescind it;

3. *Reaffirms its determination* that all relevant provisions of the Regulations annexed to the Hague Convention of 1907, and the Geneva Convention relative to the Protection of Civilian Persons in Time of War, continue to apply to the Syrian territory occupied by Israel since 1967, and calls upon the parties thereto to respect and ensure respect for their obligations under those instruments in all circumstances;

4. *Determines once more* that the continued occupation of the Syrian Golan and its de facto annexation constitute a stumbling block in the way of achieving a just, comprehensive and lasting peace in the region;

5. *Calls upon* Israel to resume the talks on the Syrian and Lebanese tracks and to respect the commitments and undertakings reached during the previous talks;

6. *Demands once more* that Israel withdraw from all the occupied Syrian Golan to the line of 4 June 1967 in implementation of the relevant Security Council resolutions;

7. *Calls upon* all the parties concerned, the co-sponsors of the peace process and the entire international community to exert all the necessary efforts to ensure the resumption of the peace process and its success by implementing Security Council resolutions 242(1967) and 338(1973);

8. *Requests* the Secretary-General to report to the General Assembly at its sixty-fourth session on the implementation of the present resolution.

RECORDED VOTE ON RESOLUTION 63/31:

In favour: Afghanistan, Algeria, Angola, Antigua and Barbuda, Argentina, Armenia, Azerbaijan, Bahamas, Bahrain, Bangladesh, Barbados, Belarus, Belize, Benin, Bhutan, Bolivia, Botswana, Brazil, Brunei Darussalam, Burkina Faso, Cambodia, Cape Verde, Central African Republic, Chile, China, Colombia, Comoros, Congo, Costa Rica, Cuba, Cyprus, Democratic People's Republic of Korea, Djibouti, Dominica, Dominican Republic, Ecuador, Egypt, El Salvador, Eritrea, Ethiopia, Gabon, Gambia, Ghana, Grenada, Guatemala, Guinea, Guinea-Bissau, Guyana, Honduras, India, Indonesia, Iran, Iraq, Jamaica, Jordan, Kazakhstan, Kenya, Kuwait, Kyrgyzstan, Lao People's Democratic Republic, Lebanon, Lesotho, Liberia, Libyan Arab Jamahiriya, Malaysia, Maldives, Mali, Mauritania, Mauritius, Mexico, Mongolia, Morocco, Mozambique, Myanmar, Namibia, Nepal, Nicaragua, Nigeria, Oman, Pakistan, Panama, Papua New Guinea, Paraguay, Peru, Philippines, Qatar, Russian Federation, Saint Lucia, Saint Vincent and the Grenadines, Saudi Arabia, Senegal, Singapore, Solomon Islands, Somalia, South Africa, Sri Lanka, Sudan, Suriname, Swaziland, Syrian Arab Republic, Tajikistan, Thailand, Timor-Leste, Togo, Trinidad and Tobago, Tunisia, Turkey, Uganda, United Arab Emirates, Uruguay, Uzbekistan, Venezuela, Viet Nam, Yemen, Zambia, Zimbabwe.

Against: Canada, Israel, Marshall Islands, Micronesia, Palau, United States.

Abstaining: Albania, Andorra, Australia, Austria, Belgium, Bulgaria, Cameroon, Côte d'Ivoire, Croatia, Czech Republic, Denmark, Estonia, Fiji, Finland, France, Georgia, Germany, Greece, Haiti, Hungary, Iceland, Ireland, Italy, Japan, Latvia, Liechtenstein, Lithuania, Luxembourg, Malta, Moldova, Monaco, Montenegro, Nauru, Netherlands, New Zealand, Norway, Poland, Portugal, Republic of Korea, Romania, Samoa, San Marino, Serbia, Slovakia, Slovenia, Spain, Sweden, Switzerland, The former Yugoslav Republic of Macedonia, Tonga, Ukraine, United Kingdom.

On 5 December [meeting 64], the Assembly, on the recommendation of the Fourth Committee [A/63/401], adopted **resolution 63/99** by recorded vote (171-1-7) [agenda item 30].

The occupied Syrian Golan

The General Assembly,

Having considered the report of the Special Committee to Investigate Israeli Practices Affecting the Human Rights of the Palestinian People and Other Arabs of the Occupied Territories,

Deeply concerned that the Syrian Golan, occupied since 1967, has been under continued Israeli military occupation,

Recalling Security Council resolution 497(1981) of 17 December 1981,

Recalling also its previous relevant resolutions, the most recent of which was resolution 62/110 of 17 December 2007,

Having considered the report of the Secretary-General submitted in pursuance of resolution 62/110,

Recalling its previous relevant resolutions in which, inter alia, it called upon Israel to put an end to its occupation of the Arab territories,

Reaffirming once more the illegality of the decision of 14 December 1981 taken by Israel to impose its laws, jurisdiction and administration on the occupied Syrian Golan, which has resulted in the effective annexation of that territory,

Reaffirming that the acquisition of territory by force is inadmissible under international law, including the Charter of the United Nations,

Reaffirming also the applicability of the Geneva Convention relative to the Protection of Civilian Persons in Time of War, of 12 August 1949, to the occupied Syrian Golan,

Bearing in mind Security Council resolution 237(1967) of 14 June 1967,

Welcoming the convening at Madrid of the Peace Conference on the Middle East on the basis of Security Council resolutions 242(1967) of 22 November 1967 and 338(1973) of 22 October 1973 aimed at the realization of a just, comprehensive and lasting peace, and expressing grave concern about the stalling of the peace process on all tracks,

1. *Calls upon* Israel, the occupying Power, to comply with the relevant resolutions on the occupied Syrian Golan, in particular Security Council resolution 497(1981), in which the Council, inter alia, decided that the Israeli decision to impose its laws, jurisdiction and administration on the occupied Syrian Golan was null and void and without international legal effect and demanded that Israel, the occupying Power, rescind forthwith its decision;

2. *Also calls upon* Israel to desist from changing the physical character, demographic composition, institutional structure and legal status of the occupied Syrian Golan and in particular to desist from the establishment of settlements;

3. *Determines* that all legislative and administrative measures and actions taken or to be taken by Israel, the occupying Power, that purport to alter the character and legal status of the occupied Syrian Golan are null and void, constitute a flagrant violation of international law and of the Geneva Convention relative to the Protection of Civilian Persons in Time of War, of 12 August 1949, and have no legal effect;

4. *Calls upon* Israel to desist from imposing Israeli citizenship and Israeli identity cards on the Syrian citizens in the occupied Syrian Golan, and from its repressive measures against the population of the occupied Syrian Golan;

5. *Deplores* the violations by Israel of the Geneva Convention relative to the Protection of Civilian Persons in Time of War, of 12 August 1949;

6. *Calls once again upon* Member States not to recognize any of the legislative or administrative measures and actions referred to above;

7. *Requests* the Secretary-General to report to the General Assembly at its sixty-fourth session on the implementation of the present resolution.

RECORDED VOTE ON RESOLUTION 63/99:

In favour: Afghanistan, Albania, Algeria, Andorra, Angola, Antigua and Barbuda, Argentina, Armenia, Australia, Austria, Azerbaijan, Bahamas, Bahrain, Bangladesh, Barbados, Belarus, Belgium, Belize, Benin, Bhutan, Bolivia, Bosnia and Herzegovina, Botswana, Brazil, Brunei Darussalam, Bulgaria, Burkina Faso, Burundi, Cambodia, Canada, Cape Verde, Central African Republic, Chile, China, Colombia, Comoros, Congo, Costa Rica, Croatia, Cuba, Cyprus, Czech Republic, Democratic People's Republic of Korea, Denmark, Djibouti, Dominica, Dominican Republic, Ecuador, Egypt, El Salvador, Eritrea, Estonia, Ethiopia, Fiji, Finland, France, Gabon, Georgia, Germany, Ghana, Greece, Grenada, Guatemala, Guinea, Guinea-Bissau, Guyana, Haiti, Honduras, Hungary, Iceland, India, Indonesia, Iran, Iraq, Ireland, Italy, Jamaica, Japan, Jordan, Kazakhstan, Kenya, Kuwait, Kyrgyzstan, Lao People's Democratic Republic, Latvia, Lebanon, Lesotho, Liberia, Libyan Arab Jamahiriya, Liechtenstein, Lithuania, Luxembourg, Malawi, Malaysia, Maldives, Mali, Malta, Mauritania, Mauritius, Mexico, Moldova, Monaco, Mongolia, Montenegro, Morocco, Mozambique, Myanmar, Namibia, Nepal, Netherlands, New Zealand, Nicaragua, Niger, Nigeria, Norway, Oman, Pakistan, Panama, Papua New Guinea, Paraguay, Peru, Philippines, Poland, Portugal, Qatar, Republic of Korea, Romania, Russian Federation, Saint Lucia, Saint Vincent and the Grenadines, San Marino, Sao Tome and Principe, Saudi Arabia, Senegal, Serbia, Singapore, Slovakia, Slovenia, Solomon Islands, South Africa, Spain, Sri Lanka, Sudan, Suriname, Swaziland, Sweden, Switzerland, Syrian Arab Republic, Tajikistan, Thailand, The former Yugoslav Republic of Macedonia, Timor-Leste, Togo, Trinidad and Tobago, Tunisia, Turkey, Turkmenistan, Tuvalu, Uganda, Ukraine, United Arab Emirates, United Kingdom, United Republic of Tanzania, Uruguay, Uzbekistan, Vanuatu, Venezuela, Viet Nam, Yemen, Zambia, Zimbabwe.

Against: Israel.

Abstaining: Cameroon, Côte d'Ivoire, Marshall Islands, Micronesia, Nauru, Palau, United States.

UNDOF

The mandate of the United Nations Disengagement Observer Force (UNDOF), established by Security Council resolution 350(1974) [YUN 1974, p. 205] to supervise the observance of the ceasefire between Israel and the Syrian Arab Republic in the Golan Heights and ensure the separation of their forces, was renewed twice in 2008: in June and December, each time for a six-month period.

UNDOF maintained an area of separation, some 75 kilometres long and varying in width between 12.5 kilometres in the centre to less than 200 metres in the extreme south. The area of separation was inhabited and policed by the Syrian authorities, and no military forces other than UNDOF were permitted within it.

As at 15 November, UNDOF comprised 1,039 troops from six member States. It was assisted by 75 UNTSO military observers.

Reports of Secretary-General. The Secretary-General reported to the Security Council on UNDOF activities between 1 January and 30 June [S/2008/390] and 1 July and 31 December 2008 [S/2008/737]. Both reports noted that the UNDOF area of operations remained generally quiet. The Force supervised the area of separation by means of fixed positions and patrols and carried out inspections of equipment and force levels in the areas of limitation. As in the past, both sides denied inspection teams access to some of their positions and imposed restrictions on the Force's freedom of movement. UNDOF continued to adapt its operation posture to the ongoing IDF training in the area of limitation on the Alpha side and Syrian civilian settlement growth in the proximity to the ceasefire line in the area of separation. Both sides continued to construct new and renovate existing defensive positions in the respective areas of limitations, and the security forces of both sides undertook anti-smuggling actions. Israeli national customs officials continued to operate periodically at the IDF post at the UNDOF crossing gate between the Israeli-occupied Golan and the Syrian Arab Republic. Both parties took steps to ease limitations on the movement of UNDOF supplies. The Force also assisted the ICRC with the passage of persons through the area of separation and carried out operational mine clearance. The Force Commander and his staff maintained close contact with the military authorities of both sides, and both parties generally cooperated with UNDOF in the execution of its tasks.

The Secretary-General observed that the situation in the Middle East was tense and likely to remain so, unless and until a comprehensive settlement could be reached. Stating that he considered UNDOF's continued presence in the area to be essential, the Secretary-General, with the agreement of both Israel and Syria, recommended in June that its mandate be extended until 31 December 2008, and in December, until 30 June 2009.

SECURITY COUNCIL ACTION

On 27 June [meeting 5926], the Security Council unanimously adopted **resolution 1821(2008)**. The draft [S/2008/415] was prepared in consultations among Council members.

The Security Council,

Having considered the report of the Secretary-General of 16 June 2008 on the United Nations Disengagement Observer Force, and reaffirming its resolution 1308(2000) of 17 July 2000,

1. *Calls upon* the parties concerned to implement immediately its resolution 338(1973) of 22 October 1973;

2. *Welcomes* the efforts being undertaken by the United Nations Disengagement Observer Force to implement the Secretary-General's zero-tolerance policy on sexual exploitation and abuse and to ensure full compliance of its personnel with the United Nations code of conduct, requests the Secretary-General to continue to take all necessary action in this regard and to keep the Security Council informed, and urges troop-contributing countries to take preventive and disciplinary action to ensure that such acts are properly investigated and punished in cases involving their personnel;

3. *Decides* to renew the mandate of the Force for a period of six months, that is, until 31 December 2008;

4. *Requests* the Secretary-General to submit, at the end of this period, a report on developments in the situation and the measures taken to implement resolution 338(1973).

On 12 December [meeting 6039], the Council unanimously adopted **resolution 1848(2008)**. The draft [S/2008/771] was prepared in consultations among Council members.

The Security Council,

Having considered the report of the Secretary-General of 26 November 2008 on the United Nations Disengagement Observer Force, and reaffirming its resolution 1308(2000) of 17 July 2000,

1. *Calls upon* the parties concerned to implement immediately its resolution 338(1973) of 22 October 1973;

2. *Welcomes* the efforts being undertaken by the United Nations Disengagement Observer Force to implement the Secretary-General's zero-tolerance policy on sexual exploitation and abuse and to ensure full compliance of its personnel with the United Nations code of conduct, requests the Secretary-General to continue to take all necessary action in this regard and to keep the Security Council informed, and urges troop-contributing countries to take preventive and disciplinary action to ensure that such acts are properly investigated and punished in cases involving their personnel;

3. *Decides* to renew the mandate of the Force for a period of six months, that is, until 30 June 2009;

4. *Requests* the Secretary-General to submit, at the end of this period, a report on developments in the situation and the measures taken to implement resolution 338(1973).

After the adoption of each resolution, the President made identical statements, **S/PRST/2008/25** on 27 June, and **S/PRST/2008/46** on 12 December, on behalf of the Council:

In connection with the resolution just adopted on the renewal of the mandate of the United Nations Disengagement Observer Force, I have been authorized to make the following complementary statement on behalf of the Security Council:

As is known, the report of the Secretary-General on the United Nations Disengagement Observer Force states in paragraph 11: "... the situation in the Middle East is tense and is likely to remain so, unless and until a comprehensive settlement covering all aspects of the Middle East problem can be reached". That statement of the Secretary-General reflects the view of the Security Council.

UNDOF financing

Reports of Secretary-General. The General Assembly had before it the performance report on the UNDOF budget for the period from 1 July 2006 to 30 June 2007 [A/62/562], which showed expenditures totalling $39,549,000 against an apportionment of $39,865,200.

It also had the UNDOF budget for the period from 1 July 2008 to 30 June 2009 [A/62/719 & Corr.1] in the amount of $45,726,000, which provided for the deployment of 1,047 military contingent personnel, and 45 international and 108 national staff. The comments of ACABQ on both reports were contained in its April report [A/62/781/Add.7 & Corr.1].

GENERAL ASSEMBLY ACTION

On 20 June [meeting 109], the General Assembly, on the recommendation of the Fifth Committee [A/62/877], adopted **resolution 62/264** without vote [agenda item 153 (*a*)].

Financing of the United Nations Disengagement Observer Force

The General Assembly,

Having considered the reports of the Secretary-General on the financing of the United Nations Disengagement Observer Force and the related report of the Advisory Committee on Administrative and Budgetary Questions,

Recalling Security Council resolution 350(1974) of 31 May 1974 regarding the establishment of the United Nations Disengagement Observer Force and the subsequent resolutions by which the Council extended the mandate of the Force, the latest of which was resolution 1788(2007) of 14 December 2007,

Recalling also its resolution 3211 B(XXIX) of 29 November 1974 on the financing of the United Nations Emergency Force and of the United Nations Disengagement Observer Force and its subsequent resolutions thereon, the latest of which was resolution 61/287 of 29 June 2007,

Reaffirming the general principles underlying the financing of United Nations peacekeeping operations, as stated in General Assembly resolutions 1874(S-IV) of 27 June 1963, 3101(XXVIII) of 11 December 1973 and 55/235 of 23 December 2000,

Mindful of the fact that it is essential to provide the Force with the financial resources necessary to enable it to fulfil its responsibilities under the relevant resolutions of the Security Council,

1. *Requests* the Secretary-General to entrust the Head of Mission with the task of formulating future budget proposals in full accordance with the provisions of General Assembly resolutions 59/296 of 22 June 2005, 60/266 of 30 June 2006 and 61/276 of 29 June 2007, as well as other relevant resolutions;

2. *Takes note* of the status of contributions to the United Nations Disengagement Observer Force as at 31 March 2008, including the contributions outstanding in the amount of 15 million United States dollars, representing some 1 per cent of the total assessed contributions, notes with concern that only forty-nine Member States have paid their assessed contributions in full, and urges all other Member States, in particular those in arrears, to ensure payment of their outstanding assessed contributions;

3. *Expresses its appreciation* to those Member States which have paid their assessed contributions in full, and urges all other Member States to make every possible effort to ensure payment of their assessed contributions to the Force in full;

4. *Expresses concern* at the financial situation with regard to peacekeeping activities, in particular as regards the reimbursements to troop contributors that bear additional burdens owing to overdue payments by Member States of their assessments;

5. *Also expresses concern* at the delay experienced by the Secretary-General in deploying and providing adequate resources to some recent peacekeeping missions, in particular those in Africa;

6. *Emphasizes* that all future and existing peacekeeping missions shall be given equal and non-discriminatory treatment in respect of financial and administrative arrangements;

7. *Also emphasizes* that all peacekeeping missions shall be provided with adequate resources for the effective and efficient discharge of their respective mandates;

8. *Reiterates its request* to the Secretary-General to make the fullest possible use of facilities and equipment at the United Nations Logistics Base at Brindisi, Italy, in order to minimize the costs of procurement for the Force;

9. *Endorses* the conclusions and recommendations contained in the report of the Advisory Committee on Administrative and Budgetary Questions, subject to the provisions of the present resolution, and requests the Secretary-General to ensure their full implementation;

10. *Takes note* of paragraph 30 of the report of the Advisory Committee;

11. *Requests* the Secretary-General to ensure the full implementation of the relevant provisions of its resolutions 59/296, 60/266 and 61/276;

12. *Also requests* the Secretary-General to take all necessary action to ensure that the Force is administered with a maximum of efficiency and economy;

13. *Further requests* the Secretary-General, in order to reduce the cost of employing General Service staff, to continue efforts to recruit local staff for the Force against General Service posts, commensurate with the requirements of the Force;

Financial performance report for the period from 1 July 2006 to 30 June 2007

14. *Takes note* of the report of the Secretary-General on the financial performance of the Force for the period from 1 July 2006 to 30 June 2007;

Budget estimates for the period from 1 July 2008 to 30 June 2009

15. *Decides* to appropriate to the Special Account for the United Nations Disengagement Observer Force the amount of 47,859,100 dollars for the period from 1 July 2008 to 30 June 2009, inclusive of 45,726,000 dollars for the maintenance of the Force, 1,859,500 dollars for the support account for peacekeeping operations and 273,600 dollars for the United Nations Logistics Base;

Financing of the appropriation

16. *Also decides* to apportion among Member States the amount of 47,859,100 dollars at a monthly rate of 3,988,258 dollars, in accordance with the levels updated in General Assembly resolution 61/243 of 22 December 2006, and taking into account the scale of assessments for 2008 and 2009, as set out in its resolution 61/237 of 22 December 2006, subject to a decision of the Security Council to extend the mandate of the Force;

17. *Further decides* that, in accordance with the provisions of its resolution 973(X) of 15 December 1955, there shall be set off against the apportionment among Member States, as provided for in paragraph 16 above, their respective share in the Tax Equalization Fund of 1,448,000 dollars, comprising the estimated staff assess-

ment income of 1,247,700 dollars approved for the Force for the period from 1 July 2008 to 30 June 2009, the prorated share of 178,700 dollars of the estimated staff assessment income approved for the support account and the prorated share of 21,600 dollars of the estimated staff assessment income approved for the United Nations Logistics Base;

18. *Decides* that, for Member States that have fulfilled their financial obligations to the Force, there shall be set off against their apportionment, as provided for in paragraph 16 above, their respective share of the unencumbered balance and other income in the total amount of 2,728,700 dollars in respect of the financial period ended 30 June 2007, in accordance with the levels updated in resolution 61/243, and taking into account the scale of assessments for 2007, as set out in resolution 61/237;

19. *Also decides* that, for Member States that have not fulfilled their financial obligations to the Force, there shall be set off against their outstanding obligations their respective share of the unencumbered balance and other income in the total amount of 2,728,700 dollars in respect of the financial period ended 30 June 2007, in accordance with the scheme set out in paragraph 18 above;

20. *Further decides* that the increase of 72,600 dollars in the estimated staff assessment income in respect of the financial period ended 30 June 2007 shall be added to the credits from the amount of 2,728,700 dollars referred to in paragraphs 18 and 19 above;

21. *Emphasizes* that no peacekeeping mission shall be financed by borrowing funds from other active peacekeeping missions;

22. *Encourages* the Secretary-General to continue to take additional measures to ensure the safety and security of all personnel participating in the Force under the auspices of the United Nations, bearing in mind paragraphs 5 and 6 of Security Council resolution 1502(2003) of 26 August 2003;

23. *Invites* voluntary contributions to the Force in cash and in the form of services and supplies acceptable to the Secretary-General, to be administered, as appropriate, in accordance with the procedure and practices established by the General Assembly;

24. *Decides* to include in the provisional agenda of its sixty-third session, under the item entitled "Financing of the United Nations peacekeeping forces in the Middle East", the sub-item entitled "United Nations Disengagement Observer Force".

Chapter VII

Disarmament

Nuclear disarmament and non-proliferation issues remained in 2008 at the forefront of the international agenda, with the objective of moving towards a nuclear-weapons-free world. Advances towards that goal, however, were modest, as both the Conference on Disarmament and the United Nations Disarmament Commission remained in deadlock. The Conference was unable to reach a consensus on a substantive programme of work, while the Commission concluded its three-year cycle without any consensus on recommendations concerning nuclear disarmament and non-proliferation, as well as practical confidence-building measures in the field of conventional weapons. Meanwhile, the chronic pattern of deeply divided voting on nuclear resolutions in the General Assembly continued.

In other developments, the second session of the Preparatory Committee for the 2010 Review Conference of the Parties to the Treaty on the Non-Proliferation of Nuclear Weapons (NPT) concluded in May, although it was unable to agree to attach the Chairman's factual summary to its report. The United Nations Panel of Governmental Experts on the Issue of Missiles in All Its Aspects could not reach a consensus on measures to deal with that issue. Several States ratified and signed the Comprehensive Nuclear-Test-Ban Treaty, and a Joint Ministerial Statement was adopted at the Ministerial Meeting held in September, urging the Treaty's early entry into force.

Throughout the year, regional organizations continued to address disarmament and non-proliferation issues. With respect to nuclear-weapon-free zones, a significant advance came with the ratification of the Central Asian Nuclear-Weapon-Free-Zone Treaty, paving the way for its entry into force in 2009. The verification programme of the International Atomic Energy Agency remained at the core of multilateral efforts to curb the proliferation of nuclear weapons and move towards nuclear disarmament. Comprehensive safeguards agreements, concluded pursuant to NPT, and the Model Additional Protocols to those agreements, which granted the Agency complementary inspection authority, remained the principal legal instruments upholding the Agency's safeguards regime. In 2008, safeguards were applied for 163 States with safeguards agreements in force. However, there was little progress on safeguard issues in Iran and the Syrian Arab Republic, or on proliferation issues in the Democratic People's Republic of Korea, as the Agency and concerned States worked to resolve remaining issues.

Other gains included the issuance by the Russian Federation and the United States of a Strategic Framework Declaration covering several areas of cooperation, including the intention to pursue legally binding arrangements to replace the expiring Treaty on the Reduction and Limitation of Strategic Offensive Arms (START I). Australia and Japan established the International Commission on Nuclear Non-Proliferation and Disarmament, and nuclear disarmament proposals were put forward by the European Union and the United Kingdom. In October, the UN Secretary-General launched his five-point proposal for a world free of nuclear weapons.

A major highlight in the field of conventional arms was the adoption of the Convention on Cluster Munitions, a milestone in global efforts to ban such weapons, although member States of the Convention on Certain Conventional Weapons were unable to reach a consensus in addressing issues relating to the humanitarian impact of cluster munitions. Parties to that Convention held their ninth annual meeting in November. Also in November, the Ninth Meeting of the States Parties to the Anti-Personnel Mine-Ban Treaty took place in Geneva, which resulted in the approval of requests by 15 States to extend the 10-year deadline for clearance and destruction of such mines.

Progress towards establishing an arms trade treaty gained momentum, with the convening of a Group of Governmental Experts to examine the feasibility and scope of a comprehensive, legally binding instrument establishing international standards for the import, export and transfer of conventional arms. The Group recommended further consideration of efforts within the United Nations to address the issue on a step-by-step basis. The General Assembly established an open-ended working group to implement that recommendation in 2009.

With respect to transparency measures, the number of States using the Standardized Instrument for Reporting Military Expenditures remained stable. While the number of States reporting data to the UN Register of Conventional Arms had dropped sharply in recent years, there was an increase in the number of States reporting on transfer of small arms and light weapons.

In April, the Security Council held a debate on small arms and light weapons, and in July, the General Assembly convened its third biennial meeting of States on the implementation of the programme of action to combat their illicit trade. For the first time, such a biennial meeting was able to adopt a substantive outcome document, one that identified a way forward for international cooperation; assistance and capacity-building to combat illicit brokering; management and surplus disposal; and marking and tracing. The Assembly agreed to convene another conference to review the implementation of the programme of action in 2012.

The Security Council in November held a high-level debate on the relationship between disarmament and development—another issue of long-standing interest at the United Nations.

UN role in disarmament

UN machinery

Disarmament issues before the United Nations were considered mainly through the Security Council, the General Assembly and its First (Disarmament and International Security) Committee, the Disarmament Commission (a deliberative body) and the Conference on Disarmament (a multilateral negotiating forum, which met in Geneva). The Organization also maintained efforts to engage civil society organizations concerned with disarmament issues.

The Office of Disarmament Affairs continued to advance the disarmament agenda (see below).

The Assembly, by **decision 63/503** of 19 September, included in its agenda, under items 81 to 96, issues related to disarmament, allocating them to the First Committee. Agenda item 80, on the report of the International Atomic Energy Agency, would be considered directly in plenary. By **decision 63/552**, of 24 December, the Assembly decided that the agenda item on general and complete disarmament would remain for consideration during its resumed sixty-third (2009) session.

Advancing the disarmament agenda

UN Office for Disarmament Affairs

The UN Office for Disarmament Affairs (UNODA), established in 2007 [YUN 2007, p. 524], on the proposal of the Secretary-General and confirmed by the General Assembly in resolution 61/257 [ibid., p. 525], assumed the functions of the Department for Disarmament Affairs in supporting the work of Member States and treaty bodies, servicing the Advisory Board on Disarmament Matters and administering the UN disarmament fellowship programme.

It reinforced the advocacy potential of the Organization in the field of disarmament and non-proliferation. Under the leadership of the High Representative for Disarmament Affairs, the Office enhanced its engagement and cooperation with Member States, intergovernmental organizations and civil society.

Report of Secretary-General. In response to the Assembly's request in resolution 61/257, the Secretary-General submitted in July a report [A/63/125] summarizing the activities of UNODA and the High Representative since their establishment. The report outlined the Secretary-General's vision for 2008 and beyond as it related to disarmament and non-proliferation. The Secretary-General highlighted the need to reinvigorate the collective response to disarmament and non-proliferation by addressing long-standing deadlocks in nuclear disarmament, and stepping up efforts to combat the scourge of proliferation of small arms and light weapons that undermined the security of individuals, countries and regions that could least afford it, as well as addressing the threats that were growing fastest—those facilitated by the revolution in life sciences. The Secretary-General stressed the need to promote biotechnology benefits to developing countries while mitigating the risks of misuse.

As noted in the report, the High Representative participated in and/or represented the Secretary-General at increased number of conferences, meetings and seminars. During the 12 months since his appointment in July 2007, he delivered 33 addresses and five statements and/or messages on behalf of the Secretary-General, focusing on nuclear disarmament and non-proliferation issues in response to the interest manifested by the organizers of pertinent events. The High Representative called for full compliance with existing treaty obligations, greater reductions in the stockpiles of nuclear weapons, greater transparency, diminished reliance on nuclear weapons in security policies and universalization of existing norms. He pressed the need for early entry into force of the Comprehensive Nuclear-Test-Ban Treaty and the negotiation and early conclusion of a treaty banning the production of fissile material for nuclear weapons and nuclear explosive devices. He supported the existing nuclear-weapon-free zones and encouraged the establishment of new ones. Furthermore, he highlighted the efforts to promote multilateral norms in such fields as illicit trade in small arms and light weapons; the transparency of conventional arms transfers, holdings and production; transfers of conventional arms; and the regulation of missiles. Those efforts complemented initiatives at governmental and non-governmental levels which showed a resurgence of interest in and commitment to achieving a world free of nuclear weapons.

An important area of UNODA activities involved information dissemination, including raising public awareness of disarmament and non-proliferation issues, and maintaining close liaison with the United Nations Institute for Disarmament Research, other research and educational institutions outside the United Nations, and non-governmental organizations (NGOs). The Office continued to implement the United Nations Disarmament Fellowship, Training and Advisory Services Programme. To heighten public awareness on disarmament issues, the Office disseminated to Member States and the international community comprehensive, objective and factual information on disarmament through its website, publications and other activities.

In accordance with General Assembly resolution 61/95 [YUN 2006, p. 679], UNODA released electronic Disarmament Updates to all Permanent Missions in New York and Geneva and to civil society at large. The Office published three *Occasional Papers,* as well as *The United Nations Disarmament Yearbook* in hard copy and on UNODA's website. The Disarmament Studies Series No. 32, *Verification in all its Aspects, including the Role of the United Nations in the Field of Verification,* was released. Between April 2007 and April 2008, the Office briefed more than a thousand students from all over the world on disarmament issues.

As stipulated in General Assembly resolutions 59/93 [YUN 2004, p. 582] and 61/73 [YUN 2006, p. 678], UNODA, in cooperation with the UN Department of Public Information, launched educational disarmament and non-proliferation pages on the UN *CyberSchoolBus* website focusing on nuclear disarmament and small arms. Video messages by the High Representative addressing specific issues—such as the Third Biennial Meeting of States to Consider the Implementation of the Programme of Action to Prevent, Combat and Eradicate the Illicit Trade in Small Arms and Light Weapons in All Its Aspects; the fortieth anniversary of the opening for signature of the landmark Treaty on the Non-Proliferation of Nuclear Weapons; the Global Week of Action Against Gun Violence; and the World Federation of United Nations Associations initiative devoted to a nuclear-weapon-free world—were posted on the UNODA website.

UNODA carried out a number of activities in support of multilateral efforts on disarmament and the non-proliferation of weapons of mass destruction, in particular nuclear weapons, as well as in support of conventional disarmament, especially with regard to major weapons systems, small arms and light weapons, landmines and cluster munitions. Through its regional centres for Africa, Asia and the Pacific, and Latin America and the Caribbean, the Office contributed to generating a more active involvement in disarmament and non-proliferation issues of regional and subregional stakeholders.

The Secretary-General concluded that the reorganization of the former Department for Disarmament Affairs into UNODA and the appointment of the High Representative did not have financial, administrative or budgetary implications and did not affect the Office's objectives for the biennium.

The Secretary-General pointed out that the activities described in his report demonstrated the growing tasks asked of the newly established Office. The implementation of resolution 61/257 did not result in any net increase in UNODA's regular budget, and additional responsibilities resulting from new mandates and activities requested by Member States required additional human and financial resources. In light of the limited resources available through the regular budget, the Office intensified its resource mobilization efforts.

The financial stability and sustainability of UNODA, which relied on extrabudgetary funds, particularly with regard to its three regional centres, remained a challenge to the operational capacity of the Office. Strengthening the Office to better support a proactive United Nations in the area of disarmament and non-proliferation would require additional resources. Such resources would enable comprehensive monitoring and in-depth analysis of salient and emerging issues and trends, effective policy formulation, timely expert advice and assistance to the Secretary-General, and support to Member States to facilitate negotiations and deliberations in multilateral bodies, including the Conference on Disarmament. It would also strengthen the ability of the United Nations to implement relevant elements of the UN Global Counter-Terrorism Strategy. Securing regular budget funding for the biennium 2010–2011 was therefore essential.

The Secretary-General considered the establishment of UNODA and the appointment of the High Representative vital steps in his efforts to revitalize the disarmament agenda and to meet the increasingly complex responsibilities assigned to the Organization by Member States in the area of disarmament and non-proliferation, both regarding weapons of mass destruction and conventional weapons.

The General Assembly on 17 November [A/63/PV.51] had before it the Secretary-General's report, but did not take any action.

Fourth special session devoted to disarmament

During the year, no progress was made towards the convening of a fourth special session devoted to disarmament. Previously, the General Assembly had held three Special Sessions devoted to Disarmament—

in 1978, 1982 and 1988. Only the first special session succeeded in producing a final document. Since 1996 [YUN 1996, p. 447], the Assembly had called for a fourth special session. It then established in 2002 a Working Group [YUN 2002, p. 487] to discuss the agenda and the possibility of establishing a preparatory committee for a fourth session. In 2006 [YUN 2006, p. 611], the Assembly established an Open-Ended Working Group to consider objectives and agenda, including the possible establishment of a preparatory committee.

By resolution 62/29 [YUN 2007, p. 526], the General Assembly mandated the reconvening of the Open-ended Working Group and requested the Working Group to submit a report, including possible substantive recommendations, to the Assembly's sixty-second session. However, as the Group did not convene its organizational or substantive sessions during the year, the Assembly decided on 11 September (**decision 62/552**) to continue work on convening those sessions. As no related resolution was adopted during its sixty-third session, the Assembly took **decision 63/519,** by which it included the item in the provisional agenda of its sixty-fourth (2009) session.

Disarmament Commission

The Disarmament Commission, comprising all UN Member States, held seven plenary meetings of the final session (New York, 7–24 April) of its three-year cycle of deliberations. Prior to its substantive session, an organizational session was convened on 18 March, at which the Commission took note of the provisional agenda and approved the general programme of work. The two main agenda items under consideration were recommendations for achieving disarmament and non-proliferation of nuclear weapons (see p. 572), and practical confidence-building measures (CBMs) in the field of conventional weapons (see p. 611). As in previous years, two Workings Groups were set up to deal with the substantive agenda items.

In his address to the opening session, the Secretary-General renewed his call for States to move forward in a spirit of compromise and accommodation. He underscored the Commission's importance and stressed that incremental progress could have positive spillover effects not only across the UN disarmament machinery, but also to other multilateral forums, including those dealing with treaty regimes. He urged Member States to make an extra effort to reach consensus, thereby bringing the Commission's work during the past three years to a successful conclusion.

However, Member States were unable to bridge the gap in their positions and failed to reach consensus on the Working Groups' recommendations. Notwithstanding the lack of concrete results, the Commission, at its final meeting on 24 April, adopted its 2008 report [A/63/42] to the General Assembly.

In introducing his report to the Committee of the Whole, the Chair of Working Group I commended the Group's efforts in seeking to reconcile the concerns of nuclear-weapon States and non-nuclear-weapon States. While no State questioned that the three pillars of nuclear consensus—disarmament, non-proliferation and the peaceful use of nuclear energy—were inextricably linked, States prioritized them differently. Despite a lack of consensus, the Chair stressed that the well-founded discussions of the Group allowed the Commission to maintain its unique framework for deliberations within the UN disarmament machinery.

The Chair of Working Group II stated that despite extensive discussions and constructive engagement, the Group was unable to overcome outstanding issues in the Chair's revised paper.

In his concluding statement, the Chairman of the Commission stressed that although final consensus eluded the Commission's work, the meetings allowed for valuable exchanges of views and deliberations on the most crucial topics, which in itself served as a CBM.

GENERAL ASSEMBLY ACTION

On 2 December [meeting 61], the General Assembly, on the recommendation of the First Committee [A/63/391], adopted **resolution 63/83** without vote [agenda item 91 *(a)*].

Report of the Disarmament Commission

The General Assembly,

Having considered the report of the Disarmament Commission,

Recalling its resolutions 47/54 A of 9 December 1992, 47/54 G of 8 April 1993, 48/77 A of 16 December 1993, 49/77 A of 15 December 1994, 50/72 D of 12 December 1995, 51/47 B of 10 December 1996, 52/40 B of 9 December 1997, 53/79 A of 4 December 1998, 54/56 A of 1 December 1999, 55/35 C of 20 November 2000, 56/26 A of 29 November 2001, 57/95 of 22 November 2002, 58/67 of 8 December 2003, 59/105 of 3 December 2004, 60/91 of 8 December 2005, 61/98 of 6 December 2006 and 62/54 of 5 December 2007,

Considering the role that the Disarmament Commission has been called upon to play and the contribution that it should make in examining and submitting recommendations on various problems in the field of disarmament and in the promotion of the implementation of the relevant decisions adopted by the General Assembly at its tenth special session,

1. *Takes note* of the report of the Disarmament Commission;

2. *Reaffirms* the validity of its decision 52/492 of 8 September 1998, concerning the efficient functioning of the Disarmament Commission;

3. *Recalls* its resolution 61/98, by which it adopted additional measures for improving the effectiveness of the Commission's methods of work;

4. *Reaffirms* the mandate of the Disarmament Commission as the specialized, deliberative body within the United Nations multilateral disarmament machinery that allows for in-depth deliberations on specific disarmament issues leading to the submission of concrete recommendations on those issues;

5. *Also reaffirms* the importance of further enhancing the dialogue and cooperation among the First Committee, the Disarmament Commission and the Conference on Disarmament;

6. *Requests* the Disarmament Commission to continue its work in accordance with its mandate, as set forth in paragraph 118 of the Final Document of the Tenth Special Session of the General Assembly, and with paragraph 3 of Assembly resolution 37/78 H of 9 December 1982, and to that end to make every effort to achieve specific recommendations on the items on its agenda, taking into account the adopted "Ways and means to enhance the functioning of the Disarmament Commission";

7. *Recommends* that the Disarmament Commission include in the agenda of its 2009 substantive session an item entitled "Elements of a draft declaration of the 2010s as the fourth disarmament decade", in accordance with resolution 61/67;

8. *Also recommends* that the Disarmament Commission intensify consultations with a view to reaching agreement on the remaining agenda items, in accordance with decision 52/492, before the start of its substantive session of 2009;

9. *Requests* the Disarmament Commission to meet for a period not exceeding three weeks during 2009, namely from 13 April to 1 May, and to submit a substantive report to the General Assembly at its sixty-fourth session;

10. *Requests* the Secretary-General to transmit to the Disarmament Commission the annual report of the Conference on Disarmament, together with all the official records of the sixty-third session of the General Assembly relating to disarmament matters, and to render all assistance that the Commission may require for implementing the present resolution;

11. *Also requests* the Secretary-General to ensure full provision to the Disarmament Commission and its subsidiary bodies of interpretation and translation facilities in the official languages and to assign, as a matter of priority, all the necessary resources and services, including verbatim records, to that end;

12. *Decides* to include in the provisional agenda of its sixty-fourth session the item entitled "Report of the Disarmament Commission".

Conference on Disarmament

The Conference on Disarmament, a multilateral negotiating body, held a three-part session in Geneva in 2008 (23 January–28 March, 12 May–27 June and 28 July–12 September) [A/63/27]. The Conference held 35 formal and 33 informal plenary meetings, at which it continued to consider the cessation of the nuclear arms race and nuclear disarmament; prevention of nuclear war; prevention of an arms race in outer space; effective international arrangements to assure non-nuclear-weapon States against the use or threat of use of nuclear weapons; new types of weapons of mass destruction and new systems of such weapons; a comprehensive programme of disarmament; and transparency in armaments.

To facilitate the work of the Conference, the six 2008 Presidents appointed seven Coordinators to oversee two rounds of deliberations on each of the items on the Conference agenda, under the authority of the Presidents. At the inaugural meeting on 23 January, the UN Secretary-General urged the Conference to rekindle the ambition and sense of common purpose that had produced its past accomplishments, move forward in a spirit of compromise and return to productive work.

The Presidents of the Conference tabled a draft decision, which was initially challenged by China, to bridge the long-standing differences that had prevented members from reaching a substantive agreement. Inter alia, it was decided to appoint a coordinator to preside over negotiations on a treaty banning the production of fissile materials for nuclear weapons. While there had been no opposition to securing a fissile materials treaty per se, a number of countries insisted that its mandate specifically encompassed existing stocks and a verification mechanism. Despite a wide range of delegations supporting the Presidential proposal, the Conference was not able to secure a consensus.

One noteworthy development was the tabling on 12 February of a draft Treaty on Prevention of the Placement of Weapons in Outer Space and of the Threat or Use of Force Against Outer Space Objects by China and the Russian Federation.

GENERAL ASSEMBLY ACTION

On 2 December [meeting 61], the General Assembly, on the recommendation of the First Committee [A/63/391], adopted **resolution 63/82** without vote [agenda item 91 *(b)*].

Report of the Conference on Disarmament

The General Assembly,

Having considered the report of the Conference on Disarmament,

Convinced that the Conference on Disarmament, as the sole multilateral disarmament negotiating forum of the international community, has the primary role in substantive negotiations on priority questions of disarmament,

Recognizing the need to conduct multilateral negotiations with the aim of reaching agreement on concrete issues,

Recalling, in this respect, that the Conference has a number of urgent and important issues for negotiation,

Taking note of active discussions held on the programme of work during the 2008 session of the Conference, as duly reflected in the report and the records of the plenary meetings,

Taking note also of the increased deliberations of the Conference due to the constructive contribution of its member States, the work done under the authority of the 2008 Presidents of the Conference, including focused structured debates on all substantive agenda items and with the participation of experts from capitals, and the cooperation among the Presidents of the Conference,

Taking note further of significant contributions made during the 2008 session to promote substantive discussions on issues on the agenda, as well as of discussions held on other issues that could also be relevant to the current international security environment,

Stressing the urgent need for the Conference to commence its substantive work at the beginning of its 2009 session,

Recognizing the address by the Secretary-General of the United Nations, as well as the addresses by Ministers for Foreign Affairs and other high-level officials, as expressions of support for the endeavours of the Conference and its role as the sole multilateral disarmament negotiating forum,

Bearing in mind the importance of efforts towards revitalization of the disarmament machinery, including the Conference,

Recognizing the importance of continuing consultations on the question of the expansion of the Conference membership,

1. *Reaffirms* the role of the Conference on Disarmament as the sole multilateral disarmament negotiating forum of the international community;

2. *Calls upon* the Conference to further intensify consultations and explore possibilities with a view to reaching an agreement on a programme of work;

3. *Takes note* of the strong collective interest of the Conference to build on the increased level and focus of its activities through 2008 and to commence substantive work as soon as possible during its 2009 session;

4. *Welcomes* the decision of the Conference to request its current President and the incoming President to conduct consultations during the intersessional period and, if possible, to make recommendations, taking into account all relevant proposals, past, present and future, including those submitted as documents of the Conference, views presented and discussions held, and to endeavour to keep the membership of the Conference informed, as appropriate, of their consultations, as contained in paragraph 53 of its report;

5. *Requests* all States members of the Conference to cooperate with the current President and successive Presidents in their efforts to guide the Conference to the early commencement of substantive work in its 2009 session;

6. *Requests* the Secretary-General to continue to ensure the provision to the Conference of adequate administrative, substantive and conference support services;

7. *Requests* the Conference to submit a report on its work to the General Assembly at its sixty-fourth session;

8. *Decides* to include in the provisional agenda of its sixty-fourth session the item entitled "Report of the Conference on Disarmament".

Multilateral disarmament agreements

As at 31 December 2008, the following number of States had become parties to the multilateral arms regulation and disarmament agreements listed below (in chronological order, with the years in which they were initially signed or opened for signature):

(Geneva) Protocol for the Prohibition of the Use in War of Asphyxiating, Poisonous or Other Gases, and of Bacteriological Methods of Warfare (1925): 135 parties

The Antarctic Treaty (1959): 47 parties

Treaty Banning Nuclear Weapons Tests in the Atmosphere, in Outer Space and under Water (1963): 125 parties

Treaty on Principles Governing the Activities of States in the Exploration and Use of Outer Space, including the Moon and Other Celestial Bodies (1967) [YUN 1966, p. 41, GA res. 2222(XXI), annex]: 105 parties

Treaty for the Prohibition of Nuclear Weapons in Latin America and the Caribbean (Treaty of Tlatelolco) (1967): 39 parties

Treaty on the Non-Proliferation of Nuclear Weapons (1968) [YUN 1968, p. 17, GA res. 2373(XXII), annex]: 190 parties

Treaty on the Prohibition of the Emplacement of Nuclear Weapons and Other Weapons of Mass Destruction on the Sea-Bed and the Ocean Floor and in the Subsoil Thereof (1971) [YUN 1970, p. 18, GA res. 2660(XXV), annex]: 97 parties

Convention on the Prohibition of the Development, Production and Stockpiling of Bacteriological (Biological) and Toxin Weapons and on Their Destruction (1972) [YUN 1971, p. 19, GA res. 2826(XXV), annex]: 163 parties

Convention on the Prohibition of Military or Any Other Hostile Use of Environmental Modification Techniques (1977) [YUN 1976, p. 45, GA res. 31/72, annex]: 73 parties

Agreement Governing the Activities of States on the Moon and Other Celestial Bodies (1979) [YUN 1979, p. 111, GA res. 34/68, annex]: 13 parties

Convention on Prohibitions or Restrictions on the Use of Certain Conventional Weapons Which May Be Deemed to Be Excessively Injurious or to Have Indiscriminate Effects (1981): 108 parties

South Pacific Nuclear Free Zone Treaty (Treaty of Rarotonga) (1985): 17 parties

Treaty on Conventional Armed Forces in Europe (CFE Treaty) (1990): 30 parties

Treaty on Open Skies (1992): 33 parties

Convention on the Prohibition of the Development, Production, Stockpiling and Use of Chemical Weapons and on Their Destruction (1993): 185 parties

Treaty on the South-East Asia Nuclear-Weapon-Free Zone (Bangkok Treaty) (1995): 10 parties

African Nuclear-Weapon-Free-Zone Treaty (Pelindaba Treaty) (1996): 26 parties

Comprehensive Nuclear-Test-Ban Treaty (1996): 148 parties

Inter-American Convention against the Illicit Manufacturing of and Trafficking in Firearms, Ammunition, Explosives, and Other Related Materials (1997): 29 parties

Convention on the Prohibition of the Use, Stockpiling, Production and Transfer of Anti-personnel Mines and on Their Destruction (Mine-Ban Convention, formerly known as Ottawa Convention) (1997): 156 parties

Inter-American Convention on Transparency in Conventional Weapons Acquisitions (1999): 12 parties

Agreement on Adaptation of the CFE Treaty (1999): 4 parties

Treaty on a Nuclear-Weapon-Free Zone in Central Asia (2006): 2 parties

Convention on Cluster Munitions (2008): 4 parties

[*United Nations Disarmament Yearbook*, vol. 33 (Part II): *2008*, Sales No. E.09.IX.1]

Nuclear disarmament

Report of Secretary-General. In response to General Assembly resolutions 62/32 [YUN 2007, p. 535], 62/39 [ibid., p. 545] and 62/42 [ibid., p. 538], the Secretary-General submitted a July report on nuclear disarmament [A/63/135], describing international efforts to address the threats posed by nuclear weapons through disarmament initiatives aimed at eliminating those weapons, as well as arms control and non-proliferation and risk reduction measures. Each of the three resolutions, the Secretary-General noted, dealt with specific aspects of nuclear disarmament. In resolution 62/32, the Assembly had called for a review of nuclear doctrines and requested the five nuclear-weapon States to take measures towards implementing immediate steps to reduce the risks of unintentional and accidental use of nuclear weapons. In resolution 62/39, the Assembly had underlined the unanimous conclusion of the International Court of Justice (ICJ) [YUN 1996, p. 461] that there existed an obligation to pursue in good faith and bring to a conclusion negotiations leading to nuclear disarmament in all its aspects under international control. In resolution 62/42, the Assembly had reaffirmed that nuclear disarmament and non-proliferation were substantively interrelated and mutually reinforcing, and outlined specific steps to achieve nuclear disarmament.

Some nuclear-weapon States had announced reductions in the number of nuclear weapons in their stockpiles, the Secretary-General reported, while other unilateral declarations by some nuclear-weapon States included efforts to accelerate the dismantlement of nuclear warheads, the closing of nuclear test sites, and reductions in deployed weapons and the number of their delivery systems.

On 6 April, agreement was reached between the United States and the Russian Federation to develop a legally binding arrangement as a follow-up to the Treaty on the Reduction and Limitation of Strategic Offensive Arms (START I). The Intermediate Range Nuclear Forces Treaty had also been opened to multilateralization, and several new initiatives by Governments and civil society promoted proposals aimed at achieving the vision of a world free of nuclear weapons, including a call from four statesmen from the United States and an international conference (Oslo, Norway, 26–27 February).

Yet many concerns and challenges remained, according to the Secretary-General. Reductions in the number of nuclear weapons fell short of expectations and had not been internationally verified. Irreversibility was not guaranteed and precise numbers regarding the size and composition of the world's nuclear weapons arsenals remained undisclosed. While the total number of nuclear weapons had fallen significantly from the heights of the cold war, reportedly 26,000 nuclear weapons were left in stockpiles. Concerns remained over nuclear doctrines, particularly the reaffirmation by some nuclear-weapon States of the vital role of a nuclear deterrent in their security policies, and about extending the life of and modernizing warheads and weapon systems.

The Comprehensive Nuclear-Test-Ban Treaty (CTBT) had yet to enter into force (see p. 579), and efforts to achieve universalization over the previous year had resulted in the addition of one signatory State, bringing the total to 178 States. Six States had also ratified the Treaty, bringing the total number of ratifications to 144; that included a ratification by an "annex 2" State, so that 35 of the 44 nuclear-capable States whose ratification was needed for CTBT's entry into force had ratified it.

The Secretary-General also noted that the Disarmament Commission in April held constructive deliberations on recommendations for achieving nuclear disarmament and non-proliferation of nuclear weapons at the last session of its three-year cycle, but substantive differences remained and the Commission ended without reaching an agreement.

Proliferation threats. In the previous decade, three States had announced their acquisition of nuclear weapons. The 1968 Treaty on the Non-Proliferation of Nuclear Weapons (NPT) [YUN 1968, p. 17, GA res. 2373(XXII), annex] still fell short of universal membership, and while 88 States had adopted the Additional Protocol, 30 States parties had not yet concluded their comprehensive safeguard agreements with the International Atomic Energy Agency (IAEA), as required under the Treaty. Diplomatic efforts continued with a view to achieving the full compliance of Iran with Security Council resolutions 1737(2006) [YUN 2006, p. 436], 1747(2007) [YUN 2007, p. 374] and **1803(2008)** (see p. 409). Efforts in the six-party talks regarding implementation by the Democratic People's Republic of Korea (DPRK) of the 2005 joint statement [YUN 2005, p. 450] and the agreement of 13 February 2007 [YUN 2007, p. 380] continued. Work on disabling nuclear facilities was progressing and in June the DPRK submitted a declaration on its nuclear programme activities.

States parties to NPT concluded the second session of the Preparatory Committee for the 2010 Review Conference (Geneva, 28 April–9 May). The Committee held substantive discussions on principles, objectives and ways to promote the implementation of the Treaty and its universality. Non-nuclear-weapon States recognized the recent announcements by nuclear-weapon States regarding reductions to their stockpiles, but expressed concern over the slow pace of implementation of their disarmament obligations. The need to address proliferation issues effectively was discussed, as was the need for States parties to fulfil their compliance and safeguard commitments, including maximum efforts to bring about diplomatic solutions to compliance concerns and to strengthen confidence among all States parties. The importance of achieving universality of the Treaty was underlined and the contribution of nuclear-weapon-free zones to global and regional security was emphasized. States parties reaffirmed the importance of the resolution on the Middle East adopted at the 1995 Review and Extension Conference [YUN 1995, p. 189] and stressed its validity until its goals and objectives were achieved. States parties also reaffirmed that nothing in the Treaty should be interpreted as affecting their inalienable right to use nuclear energy for peaceful purposes and that the exercise of that right must be consistent with the Treaty's non-proliferation obligations.

Several new proposals for the development of a multilateral approach to the nuclear fuel cycle had been put forward as a means of coping with an expected expansion in nuclear energy and dealing with the possible associated risks. Various initiatives were acknowledged as contributing to cooperation in reducing threats from weapons of mass destruction (WMDs), including the Global Initiative to Combat Nuclear Terrorism, the Global Partnership against the Spread of Weapons and Materials of Mass Destruction, and the Global Threat Reduction Initiative. The entry into force of the International Convention for the Suppression of Acts of Nuclear Terrorism in July 2007 [YUN 2007, p. 550] had strengthened efforts to combat nuclear terrorism and the Security Council, by resolution 1810(2008) (see p. 585), responded to the threat posed by the proliferation of WMDs and related materials to non-State actors. By that resolution, the Council extended by three years the mandate of the Committee established pursuant to resolution 1540(2004) [YUN 2004, p. 544] and decided that the Committee should promote the resolution's implementation.

The Secretary-General concluded that despite progress in some areas, greater collaborative efforts were required to reduce nuclear danger and address disarmament and non-proliferation challenges. The revitalization of the disarmament and non-proliferation agenda remained a priority for the United Nations. The Secretary-General and his High Representative for Disarmament Affairs, through advocacy and direct interaction with States, international and regional organizations and civil society, continued to highlight the need for further advancement in reducing the threat of nuclear weapons and the importance of achieving progress in the pursuit of a world free of nuclear weapons.

Included in the report were replies from four Member States—Canada, Cuba, Japan and Qatar—to the Secretary-General's invitation of February 2008 to inform him of measures they had taken with regard to the implementation of resolution 62/39 [YUN 2007, p. 545] concerning the follow-up to the ICJ advisory opinion on the *Legality of the Threat or Use of Nuclear Weapons* (see p. 583).

Five-point proposal. In an address to the East-West Institute (New York, 24 October), the Secretary-General put forward a five-point proposal on nuclear disarmament. He urged all NPT parties, in particular the nuclear-weapon States, to fulfil their Treaty obligations and undertake negotiations on effective measures leading to nuclear disarmament. Permanent members of the Security Council should commence discussions on security issues in the nuclear disarmament process. New efforts were needed: to bring CTBT and the Central Asian and African nuclear-weapon-free-zone treaties into force; for the Conference on Disarmament to begin immediately and without preconditions negotiations on a fissile material treaty; to establish a nuclear-weapon-free zone in the Middle East (see p. 601); and for all NPT parties to conclude safeguards agreements with the IAEA and voluntarily adopt the safeguards under the Additional Protocol. Nuclear-weapon States were invited to send descriptions of their work regarding accountability and transparency in nuclear disarmament to the United Nations for wider dissemination. Finally, a number of complementary measures were needed, including the elimination of other types of WMDs; new efforts against WMD terrorism; limits on production and trade in conventional arms; and new weapons bans, including of missiles and space weapons.

GENERAL ASSEMBLY ACTION

On 2 December [meeting 61], on the recommendation of the First Committee [A/63/389], the General Assembly adopted **resolution 63/47** by recorded vote (118-50-14) [agenda item 89 *(q)*].

Reducing nuclear danger

The General Assembly,

Bearing in mind that the use of nuclear weapons poses the most serious threat to mankind and to the survival of civilization,

Reaffirming that any use or threat of use of nuclear weapons would constitute a violation of the Charter of the United Nations,

Convinced that the proliferation of nuclear weapons in all its aspects would seriously enhance the danger of nuclear war,

Convinced also that nuclear disarmament and the complete elimination of nuclear weapons are essential to remove the danger of nuclear war,

Considering that, until nuclear weapons cease to exist, it is imperative on the part of the nuclear-weapon States to adopt measures that assure non-nuclear-weapon States against the use or threat of use of nuclear weapons,

Considering also that the hair-trigger alert of nuclear weapons carries unacceptable risks of unintentional or accidental use of nuclear weapons, which would have catastrophic consequences for all mankind,

Emphasizing the need to adopt measures to avoid accidental, unauthorized or unexplained incidents arising from computer anomaly or other technical malfunctions,

Conscious that limited steps relating to de-alerting and de-targeting have been taken by the nuclear-weapon States and that further practical, realistic and mutually reinforcing steps are necessary to contribute to the improvement in the international climate for negotiations leading to the elimination of nuclear weapons,

Mindful that a diminishing role for nuclear weapons in the security policies of nuclear-weapon States would positively impact on international peace and security and improve the conditions for the further reduction and the elimination of nuclear weapons,

Reiterating the highest priority accorded to nuclear disarmament in the Final Document of the Tenth Special Session of the General Assembly and by the international community,

Recalling the advisory opinion of the International Court of Justice on the *Legality of the Threat or Use of Nuclear Weapons* that there exists an obligation for all States to pursue in good faith and bring to a conclusion negotiations leading to nuclear disarmament in all its aspects under strict and effective international control,

Recalling also the call in the United Nations Millennium Declaration to seek to eliminate the dangers posed by weapons of mass destruction and the resolve to strive for the elimination of weapons of mass destruction, particularly nuclear weapons, including the possibility of convening an international conference to identify ways of eliminating nuclear dangers,

1. *Calls for* a review of nuclear doctrines and, in this context, immediate and urgent steps to reduce the risks of unintentional and accidental use of nuclear weapons, including through the de-alerting and de-targeting of nuclear weapons;

2. *Requests* the five nuclear-weapon States to take measures towards the implementation of paragraph 1 above;

3. *Calls upon* Member States to take the necessary measures to prevent the proliferation of nuclear weapons in all its aspects and to promote nuclear disarmament, with the objective of eliminating nuclear weapons;

4. *Takes note* of the report of the Secretary-General submitted pursuant to paragraph 5 of General Assembly resolution 62/32 of 5 December 2007;

5. *Requests* the Secretary-General to intensify efforts and support initiatives that would contribute towards the full implementation of the seven recommendations identified in the report of the Advisory Board on Disarmament Matters that would significantly reduce the risk of nuclear war, and also to continue to encourage Member States to consider the convening of an international conference, as proposed in the United Nations Millennium Declaration, to identify ways of eliminating nuclear dangers, and to report thereon to the General Assembly at its sixty-fourth session;

6. *Decides* to include in the provisional agenda of its sixty-fourth session the item entitled "Reducing nuclear danger".

RECORDED VOTE ON RESOLUTION 63/47:

In favour: Afghanistan, Algeria, Angola, Antigua and Barbuda, Bahamas, Bahrain, Bangladesh, Barbados, Belize, Benin, Bhutan, Bolivia, Botswana, Brazil, Brunei Darussalam, Burkina Faso, Burundi, Cambodia, Cameroon, Cape Verde, Chile, Colombia, Comoros, Congo, Costa Rica, Côte d'Ivoire, Cuba, Democratic People's Republic of Korea, Democratic Republic of the Congo, Djibouti, Dominica, Dominican Republic, Ecuador, Egypt, El Salvador, Equatorial Guinea, Eritrea, Ethiopia, Ghana, Grenada, Guatemala, Guinea, Guinea-Bissau, Guyana, Haiti, Honduras, India, Indonesia, Iran, Iraq, Jamaica, Jordan, Kenya, Kuwait, Lao People's Democratic Republic, Lebanon, Lesotho, Liberia, Libyan Arab Jamahiriya, Madagascar, Malawi, Malaysia, Maldives, Mali, Mauritania, Mauritius, Mexico, Mongolia, Morocco, Mozambique, Myanmar, Namibia, Nauru, Nepal, Nicaragua, Niger, Nigeria, Oman, Pakistan, Panama, Papua New Guinea, Paraguay, Peru, Philippines, Qatar, Rwanda, Saint Lucia, Saint Vincent and the Grenadines, Samoa, Sao Tome and Principe, Saudi Arabia, Senegal, Singapore, Solomon Islands, South Africa, Sri Lanka, Sudan, Suriname, Swaziland, Syrian Arab Republic, Thailand, Timor-Leste, Togo, Tonga, Trinidad and Tobago, Tunisia, Turkmenistan, Tuvalu, Uganda, United Arab Emirates, United Republic of Tanzania, Uruguay, Vanuatu, Venezuela, Viet Nam, Yemen, Zambia, Zimbabwe.

Against: Albania, Andorra, Australia, Austria, Belgium, Bosnia and Herzegovina, Bulgaria, Canada, Croatia, Cyprus, Czech Republic, Denmark, Estonia, Finland, France, Georgia, Germany, Greece, Hungary, Iceland, Ireland, Israel, Italy, Latvia, Liechtenstein, Lithuania, Luxembourg, Malta, Micronesia, Moldova, Monaco, Montenegro, Netherlands, New Zealand, Norway, Palau, Poland, Portugal, Romania, San Marino, Slovakia, Slovenia, Spain, Sweden, Switzerland, the former Yugoslav Republic of Macedonia, Turkey, Ukraine, United Kingdom, United States.

Abstaining: Argentina, Armenia, Azerbaijan, Belarus, China, Japan, Kazakhstan, Kyrgyzstan, Marshall Islands, Republic of Korea, Russian Federation, Serbia, Tajikistan, Uzbekistan.

Also on 2 December [meeting 61], the General Assembly, on the recommendation of the First Committee [A/63/389], adopted **decision 63/520** by recorded vote (130-3-46) [agenda item 89 *(bb)*].

United Nations conference to identify appropriate ways of eliminating nuclear dangers in the context of nuclear disarmament

At its 61st plenary meeting, on 2 December 2008, the General Assembly, on the recommendation of the First

Committee, decided, by a recorded vote of 130 to 3, with 46 abstentions, to include in the provisional agenda of its sixty-fourth session the item entitled "United Nations conference to identify appropriate ways of eliminating nuclear dangers in the context of nuclear disarmament".

RECORDED VOTE ON DECISION 63/520:

In favour: Afghanistan, Algeria, Angola, Antigua and Barbuda, Argentina, Bahamas, Bahrain, Bangladesh, Barbados, Belarus, Belize, Benin, Bhutan, Bolivia, Botswana, Brazil, Brunei Darussalam, Burkina Faso, Burundi, Cambodia, Cameroon, Cape Verde, Chad, Chile, China, Colombia, Comoros, Congo, Costa Rica, Côte d'Ivoire, Cuba, Cyprus, Democratic People's Republic of Korea, Democratic Republic of the Congo, Djibouti, Dominica, Dominican Republic, Ecuador, Egypt, El Salvador, Ethiopia, Fiji, Ghana, Grenada, Guatemala, Guinea, Guinea-Bissau, Guyana, Haiti, Honduras, India, Indonesia, Iran, Iraq, Ireland, Jamaica, Jordan, Kazakhstan, Kenya, Kuwait, Kyrgyzstan, Lao People's Democratic Republic, Lebanon, Lesotho, Liberia, Libyan Arab Jamahiriya, Madagascar, Malawi, Malaysia, Maldives, Mali, Malta, Mauritania, Mauritius, Mexico, Mongolia, Morocco, Mozambique, Myanmar, Namibia, Nauru, Nepal, New Zealand, Nicaragua, Niger, Nigeria, Oman, Pakistan, Panama, Papua New Guinea, Paraguay, Peru, Philippines, Qatar, Russian Federation, Rwanda, Saint Lucia, Saint Vincent and the Grenadines, Samoa, Sao Tome and Principe, Saudi Arabia, Senegal, Singapore, Solomon Islands, South Africa, Sri Lanka, Sudan, Suriname, Swaziland, Sweden, Syrian Arab Republic, Tajikistan, Thailand, Timor-Leste, Togo, Trinidad and Tobago, Tunisia, Tuvalu, Uganda, Ukraine, United Arab Emirates, United Republic of Tanzania, Uruguay, Uzbekistan, Vanuatu, Venezuela, Viet Nam, Yemen, Zambia, Zimbabwe.

Against: France, United Kingdom, United States.

Abstaining: Albania, Andorra, Armenia, Australia, Austria, Azerbaijan, Belgium, Bosnia and Herzegovina, Bulgaria, Canada, Croatia, Czech Republic, Denmark, Estonia, Finland, Georgia, Germany, Greece, Hungary, Iceland, Israel, Italy, Japan, Latvia, Liechtenstein, Lithuania, Luxembourg, Marshall Islands, Moldova, Monaco, Montenegro, Netherlands, Norway, Palau, Poland, Portugal, Republic of Korea, Romania, San Marino, Serbia, Slovakia, Slovenia, Spain, Switzerland, The former Yugoslav Republic of Macedonia, Turkey.

Conference on Disarmament

In 2008, the Conference on Disarmament was unable to arrive at a consensus on the establishment of a subsidiary body to address nuclear disarmament or on a substantive programme of work. As a result, the item was considered only during general debates and informal meetings. The Conference had before it a proposal for the programme of work [CD/1840] and letters submitted by Pakistan on the proposal [CD/1843 & 1851]. It held two informal meetings on 5 and 19 February, followed by a session on nuclear disarmament on 31 July. During those discussions, Canada underlined NPT's pivotal role in nuclear disarmament, non-proliferation and peaceful use of nuclear energy, and reiterated that a fissile material agreement would be a step forward in meeting the Article VI obligations of the nuclear-weapon States. To enhance transparency, it made proposals for: regular updates by nuclear-weapon States on policies and doctrines; numbers and status of nuclear weapons and delivery systems; reduction of operational readiness of nuclear weapons systems; nuclear reduction to be transparent; and a multilateral agreement to reduce nuclear weapons. China noted that peace and international security and a healthy international environment were the basis of nuclear disarmament, and added that the United States and the Russian Federation had a special responsibility in that regard. It reiterated its pledge not to use nuclear weapons against non-nuclear-weapon States and urged other nuclear powers to follow its example. The United States, on 7 February, organized a presentation by the Administrator of its National Nuclear Security Administration, at which time some concern about certain elements were introduced. Concerns were also expressed on 5 February, when a statement was made by the Defence Minister of the United Kingdom to shift and shape the interpretation of NPT commitments, particularly those under Article VI. Some States said that greater emphasis was placed on nuclear non-proliferation at the expense of nuclear disarmament. The Group of 21's (G-21) position on the subject was reiterated by the Syrian Arab Republic, the Regional Group Coordinator, and supported by Algeria, Egypt, Iran and Pakistan.

Other developments included the establishment of the International Commission on Nuclear Non-Proliferation and Disarmament, which sought to shape a global consensus for the 2010 NPT Review Conference and beyond. The 15-member panel was led by former Australian and Japanese Foreign Ministers and was comprised of former heads of State, ministers, military strategists and disarmament experts.

On 25 March, France transmitted President Nicolas Sarkozy's 21 March statement setting out his country's non-proliferation and disarmament policies, announcing new reductions in nuclear weapons and delivery systems, and outlining a disarmament "action plan", primarily aimed at the eight States that had declared they had conducted nuclear tests [CD/1842].

Presidential reports [CD/1841, 1845 & 1848] were submitted for Parts I–III of the Conference.

GENERAL ASSEMBLY ACTION

On 2 December [meeting 61], the General Assembly, on the recommendation of the First Committee [A/63/389], adopted **resolution 63/73** by recorded vote (173-4-6) [agenda item 89].

Renewed determination towards the total elimination of nuclear weapons

The General Assembly,

Recalling the need for all States to take further practical steps and effective measures towards the total elimination of nuclear weapons, with a view to achieving a peaceful and safe world free of nuclear weapons, and renewing the determination to do so,

Noting that the ultimate objective of the efforts of States in the disarmament process is general and complete disarmament under strict and effective international control,

Recalling its resolution 62/37 of 5 December 2007,

Convinced that every effort should be made to avoid nuclear war and nuclear terrorism,

Reaffirming the crucial importance of the Treaty on the Non-Proliferation of Nuclear Weapons as the cornerstone of the international nuclear disarmament and non-proliferation regime, and expressing regret over the lack of agreement on substantive issues at the Review Conference of the Parties to the Treaty on the Non-Proliferation of Nuclear Weapons, as well as over the elimination of references to nuclear disarmament and non-proliferation in the World Summit Outcome in 2005, the year of the sixtieth anniversary of the atomic bombings in Hiroshima and Nagasaki, Japan,

Recalling the decisions and the resolution of the 1995 Review and Extension Conference of the Parties to the Treaty on the Non-Proliferation of Nuclear Weapons and the Final Document of the 2000 Review Conference of the Parties to the Treaty,

Recognizing that the enhancement of international peace and security and the promotion of nuclear disarmament are mutually reinforcing,

Reaffirming that further advancement in nuclear disarmament will contribute to consolidating the international regime for nuclear non-proliferation, which is, inter alia, essential to international peace and security,

Taking note of concrete proposals and initiatives on nuclear disarmament, including those put forward or undertaken by nuclear-weapon States, including recently by France and the United Kingdom of Great Britain and Northern Ireland,

Expressing deep concern regarding the growing dangers posed by the proliferation of weapons of mass destruction, inter alia, nuclear weapons, including that caused by proliferation networks,

Recognizing the importance of implementing Security Council resolution 1718(2006) of 14 October 2006 with regard to the nuclear test proclaimed by the Democratic People's Republic of Korea on 9 October 2006, while taking note of the progress achieved by the Six-Party Talks,

1. *Reaffirms* the importance of all States parties to the Treaty on the Non-Proliferation of Nuclear Weapons complying with their obligations under all the articles of the Treaty;

2. *Stresses* the importance of an effective Treaty review process, welcoming the substantive discussions held at the second session of the Preparatory Committee in 2008, and calls upon all States parties to the Treaty to work together to ensure that the third session of the Preparatory Committee, in 2009, is held constructively, in order to facilitate the successful outcome of the 2010 Review Conference of the Parties to the Treaty on the Non-Proliferation of Nuclear Weapons;

3. *Reaffirms* the importance of the universality of the Treaty, and calls upon States not parties to the Treaty to accede to it as non-nuclear-weapon States without delay and without conditions, and pending their accession to refrain from acts that would defeat the objective and purpose of the Treaty as well as to take practical steps in support of the Treaty;

4. *Encourages* further steps leading to nuclear disarmament, to which all States parties to the Treaty are committed under article VI of the Treaty, including deeper reductions in all types of nuclear weapons, and emphasizes the importance of applying irreversibility and verifiability, as well as increased transparency in a way that promotes international stability and undiminished security for all, in the process of working towards the elimination of nuclear weapons;

5. *Calls upon* all nuclear-weapon States to undertake reductions of nuclear weapons in a transparent manner, and invites all nuclear-weapon States to agree on transparency and confidence-building measures, while noting in this regard the increased transparency recently demonstrated by nuclear-weapon States on their nuclear arsenals, including the current number of their nuclear warheads;

6. *Encourages* the Russian Federation and the United States of America to implement fully the Treaty on Strategic Offensive Reductions, which should serve as a step for further nuclear disarmament, and to undertake nuclear arms reductions beyond those provided for by the Treaty, including through the conclusion of a legally binding successor to the Treaty on the Reduction and Limitation of Strategic Offensive Arms (START I), which is due to expire in 2009, while welcoming the progress made by nuclear-weapon States, including the Russian Federation and the United States of America, on nuclear arms reductions;

7. *Encourages* States to continue to pursue efforts, within the framework of international cooperation, contributing to the reduction of nuclear-weapons-related materials;

8. *Calls for* the nuclear-weapon States to further reduce the operational status of nuclear weapons systems in ways that promote international stability and security;

9. *Stresses* the necessity of a diminishing role for nuclear weapons in security policies to minimize the risk that these weapons will ever be used and to facilitate the process of their total elimination, in a way that promotes international stability and based on the principle of undiminished security for all;

10. *Urges* all States that have not yet done so to sign and ratify the Comprehensive Nuclear-Test-Ban Treaty at the earliest opportunity with a view to its early entry into force, stresses the importance of maintaining existing moratoriums on nuclear-weapon test explosions pending the entry into force of the Treaty, and reaffirms the importance of the continued development of the Treaty verification regime, including the international monitoring system, which will be required to provide assurance of compliance with the Treaty;

11. *Calls upon* the Conference on Disarmament to immediately resume its substantive work to its fullest, considering the developments of this year in the Conference;

12. *Emphasizes* the importance of the immediate commencement of negotiations on a fissile material cut-off treaty in the Conference on Disarmament and its early conclusion, and calls upon all nuclear-weapon States and States not parties to the Treaty on the Non-Proliferation of Nuclear Weapons to declare moratoriums on the production of fissile

material for any nuclear weapons or other nuclear explosive devices pending the entry into force of the Treaty;

13. *Calls upon* all States to redouble their efforts to prevent and curb the proliferation of nuclear and other weapons of mass destruction and their means of delivery;

14. *Stresses* the importance of further efforts for non-proliferation, including the universalization of the International Atomic Energy Agency comprehensive safeguards agreements, while also strongly encouraging further works for achieving the universalization of the Model Protocol Additional to the Agreement(s) between State(s) and the International Atomic Energy Agency for the Application of Safeguards approved by the Board of Governors of the International Atomic Energy Agency on 15 May 1997, and the full implementation of relevant Security Council resolutions, including resolution 1540(2004) of 28 April 2004;

15. *Encourages* all States to undertake concrete activities to implement, as appropriate, the recommendations contained in the report of the Secretary-General on the United Nations study on disarmament and non-proliferation education, submitted to the General Assembly at its fifty-seventh session, and to voluntarily share information on efforts they have been undertaking to that end;

16. *Encourages* the constructive role played by civil society in promoting nuclear non-proliferation and nuclear disarmament;

17. *Decides* to include in the provisional agenda of its sixty-fourth session an item entitled "Renewed determination towards the total elimination of nuclear weapons".

RECORDED VOTE ON RESOLUTION 63/73:

In favour: Afghanistan, Albania, Algeria, Andorra, Angola, Antigua and Barbuda, Argentina, Armenia, Australia, Austria, Azerbaijan, Bahamas, Bahrain, Bangladesh, Barbados, Belarus, Belgium, Belize, Benin, Bolivia, Bosnia and Herzegovina, Botswana, Brazil, Brunei Darussalam, Bulgaria, Burkina Faso, Burundi, Cambodia, Cameroon, Canada, Cape Verde, Chad, Chile, Colombia, Comoros, Congo, Costa Rica, Côte d'Ivoire, Croatia, Cyprus, Czech Republic, Democratic Republic of the Congo, Denmark, Djibouti, Dominica, Dominican Republic, Ecuador, Egypt, El Salvador, Eritrea, Estonia, Ethiopia, Fiji, Finland, France, Georgia, Germany, Ghana, Greece, Grenada, Guatemala, Guinea, Guinea-Bissau, Guyana, Haiti, Honduras, Hungary, Iceland, Indonesia, Iraq, Ireland, Italy, Jamaica, Japan, Jordan, Kazakhstan, Kenya, Kuwait, Kyrgyzstan, Lao People's Democratic Republic, Latvia, Lebanon, Lesotho, Liberia, Libyan Arab Jamahiriya, Liechtenstein, Lithuania, Luxembourg, Madagascar, Malawi, Malaysia, Maldives, Mali, Malta, Marshall Islands, Mauritania, Mauritius, Mexico, Micronesia, Moldova, Monaco, Mongolia, Montenegro, Morocco, Mozambique, Namibia, Nauru, Nepal, Netherlands, New Zealand, Nicaragua, Niger, Nigeria, Norway, Oman, Palau, Panama, Papua New Guinea, Paraguay, Peru, Philippines, Poland, Portugal, Qatar, Republic of Korea, Romania, Russian Federation, Rwanda, Saint Lucia, Saint Vincent and the Grenadines, Samoa, San Marino, Sao Tome and Principe, Saudi Arabia, Senegal, Serbia, Singapore, Slovakia, Slovenia, Solomon Islands, South Africa, Spain, Sri Lanka, Sudan, Suriname, Swaziland, Sweden, Switzerland, Syrian Arab Republic, Tajikistan, Thailand, The former Yugoslav Republic of Macedonia, Timor-Leste, Togo, Tonga, Trinidad and Tobago, Tunisia, Turkey, Turkmenistan, Tuvalu, Uganda, Ukraine, United Arab Emirates, United Kingdom, United Republic of Tanzania, Uruguay, Uzbekistan, Vanuatu, Venezuela, Viet Nam, Yemen, Zambia, Zimbabwe.

Against: Democratic People's Republic of Korea, India, Israel, United States.

Abstaining: Bhutan, China, Cuba, Iran, Myanmar, Pakistan.

Fissile material

Throughout the 2008 session of the Conference on Disarmament, most of its members, particularly from the Western Group, supported negotiations on a treaty to ban the production of fissile material for nuclear weapons and other nuclear explosive devices. However, as a programme of work was not accepted, the Conference was unable to begin negotiating such a treaty. Notwithstanding, the Conference on 6 and 20 February held two rounds of informal deliberations on the prohibition of production of fissile material for nuclear weapons and explosive devices, under the chairmanship of the Coordinators for that issue. Another round of informal deliberations was held on 31 July.

During plenary meetings and informal deliberations, many delegations reiterated the need to commence negotiations on a fissile material cut-off treaty (FMCT). They urged Conference members to agree to the 2008 President's proposal on a programme of work (see p. 567) and immediately begin those negotiations without precondition. The Secretary-General, at the Conference's inaugural meeting, remarked that the negotiations would advance nuclear disarmament and non-proliferation. The United Kingdom called on the three countries that had not taken part in the previous year's negotiations to do so in 2008. The United States stood by the draft it had tabled in 2006 [YUN 2006, p. 617]. France outlined an "action plan" that included immediate negotiations on a treaty and a moratorium on the production of fissile material. China, stressing that a balanced and acceptable work programme must first be agreed upon, considered the Conference the only venue for negotiating an FMCT, whereas for the Russian Federation, a treaty on the prevention of an arms race in outer space was a priority, although it noted that it would not object to negotiations within the agreed work programme.

During the high-level segment of the 2008 session from 3 to 5 March, Foreign Ministers from Argentina, Iran, Kazakhstan, the Netherlands, Norway, Romania and Slovakia underlined the importance of negotiating an FMCT. Similarly, Japan, Sweden, Turkey and Ukraine highlighted the need for the Conference to start negotiations.

Broad support for starting negotiations came also from regional groups, including the European Union (EU), members of the Western Group and the Eastern European Group. On behalf of the G-21, Sri Lanka stated that while the Group reiterated its position that total nuclear disarmament remained a priority, it was mindful of the need to address issues pertaining to fissile material, the prevention of an arms race in outer space, and negative security assurances. A number of G-21 countries, such as Brazil, Colombia and South Africa, were in favour of commencing, without precondition, FMCT negotiations. India also expressed support for establishing an FMCT ad hoc committee as part of the Conference's programme of work. On behalf of the Latin American countries, Chile supported the proposal on a programme of work.

Despite the overwhelming support for the proposed programme of work, which would allow the Conference to begin negotiations, no consensus was reached during the year. However, substantive discussions continued through all three rounds of informal deliberations. In his assessment of the February deliberations, the Coordinator noted that no delegation had expressed opposition to FMCT negotiations, with many stressing the need to commence such a treaty without delay.

The Coordinator also reported that no new positions were put forward on sub-issues, including: definition; scope; production of fissile material for non-explosive purposes; transparency; stocks; and compliance and verification. The 2008 deliberations contained no new elements, but helped reaffirm the need for FMCT negotiations and revalidated the outcome of previous agenda item discussions, which was the goal of the 2008 Presidents.

During the final part of the session, the Conference President (United States) held the third round of informal meetings under the Coordinators on all seven agenda items (see p. 562). At the end of its Presidency, the United States noted with regret that the meetings had failed to reach consensus on a programme of work, which was perplexing as the discussions had underscored the common understanding of the Conference's purpose and the importance of substantive work on its core issues—including the prompt commencement of negotiations on an FMCT.

While the Conference was unable to agree on a mandate to negotiate an FMCT, France, the Russian Federation, the United Kingdom and the United States recommitted themselves to the current moratoria for the production of weapon-usable fissile material. A number of countries called on all nuclear weapon States to declare such a moratorium.

The General Assembly, in resolution 63/73 of 2 December, called for the immediate commencement of negotiations on an FMCT (see p. 567).

Security assurances

The Conference on Disarmament, based on its organizational framework and under the guidance of Senegal, held two informal meetings on 12 and 21 February, followed by an additional session on 7 August, to discuss international arrangements to assure non-nuclear-weapon States against the use or threat of use of nuclear weapons. The Coordinator, in an effort to build on areas of consensus, drew on the previous year's work [YUN 2007, p. 532]; however, the deliberations revealed that most positions remained unchanged. Some delegations believed that the existing frameworks, such as Security Council resolutions and nuclear-weapon-free zones, sufficiently addressed the objective, while others, arguing that the existing guarantees were inadequate, supported the development of a new legally binding instrument.

GENERAL ASSEMBLY ACTION

On 2 December [meeting 61], the General Assembly, on the recommendation of the First Committee [A/63/387], adopted **resolution 63/39** by recorded vote (122-1-58) [agenda item 87].

Conclusion of effective international arrangements to assure non-nuclear-weapon States against the use or threat of use of nuclear weapons

The General Assembly,

Bearing in mind the need to allay the legitimate concern of the States of the world with regard to ensuring lasting security for their peoples,

Convinced that nuclear weapons pose the greatest threat to mankind and to the survival of civilization,

Welcoming the progress achieved in recent years in both nuclear and conventional disarmament,

Noting that, despite recent progress in the field of nuclear disarmament, further efforts are necessary towards the achievement of general and complete disarmament under effective international control,

Convinced that nuclear disarmament and the complete elimination of nuclear weapons are essential to remove the danger of nuclear war,

Determined to abide strictly by the relevant provisions of the Charter of the United Nations on the non-use of force or threat of force,

Recognizing that the independence, territorial integrity and sovereignty of non-nuclear-weapon States need to be safeguarded against the use or threat of use of force, including the use or threat of use of nuclear weapons,

Considering that, until nuclear disarmament is achieved on a universal basis, it is imperative for the international community to develop effective measures and arrangements to ensure the security of non-nuclear-weapon States against the use or threat of use of nuclear weapons from any quarter,

Recognizing that effective measures and arrangements to assure non-nuclear-weapon States against the use or threat of use of nuclear weapons can contribute positively to the prevention of the spread of nuclear weapons,

Bearing in mind paragraph 59 of the Final Document of the Tenth Special Session of the General Assembly, the first special session devoted to disarmament, in which it urged the nuclear-weapon States to pursue efforts to conclude, as appropriate, effective arrangements to assure non-nuclear-weapon States against the use or threat of use of nuclear weapons, and desirous of promoting the implementation of the relevant provisions of the Final Document,

Recalling the relevant parts of the special report of the Committee on Disarmament submitted to the General Assembly at its twelfth special session, the second special session devoted to disarmament, and of the special report of the Conference on Disarmament submitted to the Assembly at its fifteenth special session, the third special session devoted to disarmament, as well as the report of the Conference on its 1992 session,

Recalling also paragraph 12 of the Declaration of the 1980s as the Second Disarmament Decade, contained in the annex to its resolution 35/46 of 3 December 1980, which states, inter alia, that all efforts should be exerted by the Committee on Disarmament urgently to negotiate with a view to reaching agreement on effective international arrangements to assure non-nuclear-weapon States against the use or threat of use of nuclear weapons,

Noting the in-depth negotiations undertaken in the Conference on Disarmament and its Ad Hoc Committee on Effective International Arrangements to Assure Non-Nuclear-Weapon States against the Use or Threat of Use of Nuclear Weapons, with a view to reaching agreement on this question,

Taking note of the proposals submitted under the item in the Conference on Disarmament, including the drafts of an international convention,

Taking note also of the relevant decision of the Thirteenth Conference of Heads of State or Government of Non-Aligned Countries, held at Kuala Lumpur on 24 and 25 February 2003, which was reiterated at the Fourteenth Conference of Heads of State or Government of Non-Aligned Countries, held at Havana on 15 and 16 September 2006, as well as the relevant recommendations of the Organization of the Islamic Conference,

Taking note further of the unilateral declarations made by all the nuclear-weapon States on their policies of non-use or non-threat of use of nuclear weapons against the non-nuclear-weapon States,

Noting the support expressed in the Conference on Disarmament and in the General Assembly for the elaboration of an international convention to assure non-nuclear-weapon States against the use or threat of use of nuclear weapons, as well as the difficulties pointed out in evolving a common approach acceptable to all,

Taking note of Security Council resolution 984(1995) of 11 April 1995 and the views expressed on it,

Recalling its relevant resolutions adopted in previous years, in particular resolutions 45/54 of 4 December 1990, 46/32 of 6 December 1991, 47/50 of 9 December 1992, 48/73 of 16 December 1993, 49/73 of 15 December 1994, 50/68 of 12 December 1995, 51/43 of 10 December 1996, 52/36 of 9 December 1997, 53/75 of 4 December 1998, 54/52 of 1 December 1999, 55/31 of 20 November 2000, 56/22 of 22 November 2002, 58/35 of 8 December 2003, 59/64 of 3 December 2004, 60/53 of 8 December 2005, 61/57 of 6 December 2006 and 62/19 of 5 December 2007,

1. *Reaffirms* the urgent need to reach an early agreement on effective international arrangements to assure non-nuclear-weapon States against the use or threat of use of nuclear weapons;

2. *Notes with satisfaction* that in the Conference on Disarmament there is no objection, in principle, to the idea of an international convention to assure non-nuclear-weapon States against the use or threat of use of nuclear weapons, although the difficulties with regard to evolving a common approach acceptable to all have also been pointed out;

3. *Appeals* to all States, especially the nuclear-weapon States, to work actively towards an early agreement on a common approach and, in particular, on a common formula that could be included in an international instrument of a legally binding character;

4. *Recommends* that further intensive efforts be devoted to the search for such a common approach or common formula and that the various alternative approaches, including, in particular, those considered in the Conference on Disarmament, be explored further in order to overcome the difficulties;

5. *Also recommends* that the Conference on Disarmament actively continue intensive negotiations with a view to reaching early agreement and concluding effective international agreements to assure the non-nuclear-weapon States against the use or threat of use of nuclear weapons, taking into account the widespread support for the conclusion of an international convention and giving consideration to any other proposals designed to secure the same objective;

6. *Decides* to include in the provisional agenda of its sixty-fourth session the item entitled "Conclusion of effective international arrangements to assure non-nuclear-weapon States against the use or threat of use of nuclear weapons".

RECORDED VOTE ON RESOLUTION 63/39:

In favour: Afghanistan, Algeria, Angola, Antigua and Barbuda, Azerbaijan, Bahamas, Bahrain, Bangladesh, Barbados, Belarus, Belize, Benin, Bhutan, Bolivia, Botswana, Brazil, Brunei Darussalam, Burkina Faso, Burundi, Cambodia, Cameroon, Cape Verde, Chile, China, Colombia, Comoros, Congo, Costa Rica, Côte d'Ivoire, Cuba, Democratic People's Republic of Korea, Democratic Republic of the Congo, Djibouti, Dominica, Dominican Republic, Ecuador, Egypt, El Salvador, Equatorial Guinea, Eritrea, Ethiopia, Gabon, Ghana, Grenada, Guatemala, Guinea, Guinea-Bissau, Guyana, Haiti, Honduras, India, Indonesia, Iran, Iraq, Jamaica, Japan, Jordan, Kazakhstan, Kenya, Kuwait, Kyrgyzstan, Lao People's Democratic Republic, Lebanon, Lesotho, Liberia, Libyan Arab Jamahiriya, Madagascar, Malawi, Malaysia, Maldives, Mali, Mauritania, Mauritius, Mexico, Mongolia, Morocco, Mozambique, Myanmar, Namibia, Nepal, Nicaragua, Niger, Nigeria, Oman, Pakistan, Panama, Papua New Guinea, Paraguay, Peru, Philippines, Qatar, Rwanda, Saint Lucia, Saint Vincent and the Grenadines, Samoa, Sao Tome and Principe, Saudi Arabia, Senegal, Singapore, Solomon Islands, Sri Lanka, Sudan, Suriname, Swaziland, Syrian Arab Republic, Tajikistan, Thailand, Timor-Leste, Togo, Trinidad and Tobago, Tunisia, Turkmenistan, Uganda, United Arab Emirates, United Republic of Tanzania, Uruguay, Uzbekistan, Venezuela, Viet Nam, Yemen, Zambia, Zimbabwe.

Against: United States.

Abstaining: Albania, Andorra, Argentina, Armenia, Australia, Austria, Belgium, Bosnia and Herzegovina, Bulgaria, Canada, Croatia, Cyprus, Czech Republic, Denmark, Estonia, Finland, France, Georgia, Germany, Greece, Hungary,

Iceland, Ireland, Israel, Italy, Latvia, Liechtenstein, Lithuania, Luxembourg, Malta, Marshall Islands, Micronesia, Moldova, Monaco, Montenegro, Nauru, Netherlands, New Zealand, Norway, Palau, Poland, Portugal, Republic of Korea, Romania, Russian Federation, San Marino, Serbia, Slovakia, Slovenia, South Africa, Spain, Sweden, Switzerland, Tthe former Yugoslav Republic of Macedonia, Turkey, Tuvalu, Ukraine, United Kingdom.

Disarmament Commission

Working Group I of the Disarmament Commission [A/63/42] continued to consider recommendations for achieving the objective of disarmament and non-proliferation of nuclear weapons, on which it held pre-session informal consultations on 18 March, as well as a number of informal and formal meetings during the session. Despite extensive deliberations, Member States could not reach consensus on the Working Group's recommendations.

During the discussions, most States acknowledged NPT as the cornerstone of the international non-proliferation and disarmament regime and urged its full implementation. In that respect, numerous States endorsed the outcomes of the 1995 [YUN 1995, p. 189] and 2000 NPT Review Conferences [YUN 2000, p. 487]. Many States expressed support for the entry into force of CTBT, the establishment of nuclear-weapon-free zones and negotiations on a fissile material treaty.

Slovenia, on behalf of the EU, emphasized that all disarmament and non-proliferation agreements should be effectively resourced, fully implemented and complied with. In addition, the EU stressed that a multilateral approach to non-proliferation provided the best way of countering the threat of WMD proliferation and their means of delivery.

Repeated calls were made for the complete, verifiable and irreversible elimination of nuclear weapons. Indonesia, on behalf of the Movement of Non-Aligned Countries (NAM), underscored the need for nuclear-weapon States to implement the unequivocal undertaking of totally eliminating nuclear weapons. In that regard, NAM called for an international conference to establish a phased programme for their complete elimination, as well as their development, production, acquisition, testing, stockpiling, transfer, use and threat of use, and to provide for their destruction. Mexico, for the Rio Group, expressed concern about the lack of substantive agreement on nuclear disarmament. Many States stressed that reducing the role of nuclear weapons in strategic and security doctrines was essential to realize the goal of nuclear disarmament. Kazakhstan, for its part, lamented the absence of political will to promote the disarmament agenda, and reiterated its proposal to draft an international legally binding instrument banning the use of nuclear weapons against non-nuclear weapon States.

Some States expressed concern over the prospect of an arms race in outer space. The Russian Federation reiterated its view that devising measures to keep outer space free from any weapons and prevent it from turning into a new arena of confrontation was of vital importance for ensuring the development of science and maintaining international peace and security.

Bilateral agreements and unilateral measures

Russian Federation–United States framework for strategic cooperation

The United States–Russia Strategic Framework Declaration was signed by both States on 6 April to set forth a foundation for strategic cooperation between the two countries. Areas identified in the Declaration included steps to: promote security in the face of new and emerging threats; prevent the spread of WMDS; combat global terrorism; and advance economic cooperation. The two countries agreed to develop a legally binding arrangement following the expiration of the 1991 landmark Treaty on the Reduction and Limitation of Strategic Offensive Arms (START I) [YUN 1991, p. 34] that was due to expire in December 2009. Both States aimed to engage in a high-level dialogue to analyse and address intermediate and shorter-range missile threats and inventory options. Furthermore, they agreed to intensify dialogue on issues concerning bilateral and multilateral missile defence cooperation, and to continue cooperation on preventing the spread of WMDS and on combating global terrorism.

United States–India Agreement for Peaceful Nuclear Cooperation

On 1 October, the United States Congress approved the Agreement for Peaceful Nuclear Cooperation with India, which was subsequently signed by both States on 10 October. That was made possible through the IAEA Board of Governors' approval of the India-specific Safeguards Agreement given on 1 August and the exception the Nuclear Suppliers Group (NSG) granted to its full-scope safeguard requirements on 6 September.

The IAEA Board of Governors approved by consensus the "Agreement between the Government of India and the IAEA for the Application of Safeguards to Civilian Nuclear Facilities", which required IAEA to verify that certain nuclear material and facilities declared by India were used only for peaceful purposes. Under the agreement, India could add facilities over time to come under IAEA safeguards.

After addressing a series of questions concerning the United States' draft proposal, NSG also reached a consensus agreement to adopt the "Statement on Civil Nuclear Cooperation with India", thus enabling the necessary exception to its full-scope safeguards requirements that would allow civil nuclear trade with India.

In the NSG statement, the Participating Governments declared their desire to contribute to the effectiveness, integrity and widest possible implementation of the provisions of NPT. They further noted that India had: decided to separate its civilian nuclear facilities; concluded negotiations with IAEA for the application of safeguards to civilian nuclear facilities; committed to the Additional Protocol to the safeguards agreement, which would harmonize its export control guidelines with those of NSG; and continued its unilateral moratorium on nuclear testing. On that basis, NSG agreed to adopt and implement a policy on civil nuclear cooperation by the Participating Governments with the IAEA-safeguarded Indian nuclear programme. That would allow the Participating Governments to transfer trigger-list items and/or related technology, nuclear-related dual-use equipment, materials, software and related technology to India for peaceful purposes and for use in IAEA-safeguarded facilities, provided that the transfer satisfied all other provisions of the NSG revised guidelines.

Democratic People's Republic of Korea

Work continued in 2008 under the Six-Party Talks (China, Democratic People's Republic of Korea (DPRK), Japan, Republic of Korea, Russian Federation, United States) to achieve the verifiable denuclearization of the Korean Peninsula. As part of the denuclearization process, the DPRK submitted to the United States for review documentation on its nuclear programmes and, in July, demolished the cooling tower of its experimental nuclear power plant. However, on 18 August, IAEA was informed that the DPRK had decided to suspend disabling activities at its reactor site and, by month's end, commented that it would consider restoring its plutonium-producing facility over the perceived failure of the United States to fulfil its side of the October 2007 agreement on "Second-Phase Actions for the Implementation of the Joint Statement". On 23 September, the DPRK informed IAEA that its inspectors would have no further access to its reprocessing plant, from which agency seals had already been removed, and stated its intent to introduce nuclear material back into the plant (see p. 595).

In early October, intense negotiations between the United States and the DPRK led to an agreement on verification measures, which would serve as a baseline for a Verification Protocol to be finalized and adopted by the Six Parties. That led to the removal of the DPRK from the United States list of State Sponsors of Terrorism, while the DPRK restored the access of IAEA inspectors to its nuclear facilities and confirmed that it would resume its disablement. However, new complications arose towards the end of year, as the DPRK claimed that it had not agreed to sampling as one of the verification measures, since that would be a breach of its sovereignty. Consequently, the last round of the Six-Party Talks ended in early December in Beijing without agreement.

GENERAL ASSEMBLY ACTION

On 2 December [meeting 61], the General Assembly, on the recommendation of the First Committee [A/63/389], adopted **resolution 63/41** by recorded vote (141-3-34) [agenda item 89].

Decreasing the operational readiness of nuclear weapons systems

The General Assembly,

Recalling its resolution 62/36 of 5 December 2007,

Recalling also that the maintenance of nuclear weapons on high alert was a feature of cold war nuclear postures, and welcoming the increased confidence and transparency since the cessation of the cold war,

Concerned that, notwithstanding the end of the cold war, several thousand nuclear weapons remain on high alert, ready to be launched within minutes,

Noting the increased engagement in multilateral disarmament forums in support of further reductions to the operational status of nuclear weapons systems,

Recognizing that the maintenance of nuclear weapons systems at a high level of readiness increases the risk of the use of such weapons, including the unintentional or accidental use, which would have catastrophic consequences,

Recognizing also that reductions in deployments and the lowering of operational status contribute to the maintenance of international peace and security, as well as to the process of nuclear disarmament, through the enhancement of confidence-building and transparency measures and a diminishing role for nuclear weapons in security policies,

Welcoming bilateral initiatives, such as the proposed United States/Russian Federation Joint Centre for the Exchange of Data from Early Warning Systems and Notification of Missile Launches, which can play a central role in operational status reduction processes,

Welcoming also the steps taken by some States to reduce the operational status of their nuclear weapons systems, including de-targeting initiatives and increasing the amount of preparation time required for deployment,

1. *Calls for* further practical steps to be taken to decrease the operational readiness of nuclear weapons systems, with a view to ensuring that all nuclear weapons are removed from high alert status;

2. *Urges* States to update the General Assembly on progress made in the implementation of the present resolution;

3. *Decides* to remain seized of the matter.

RECORDED VOTE ON RESOLUTION 63/41:

In favour: Afghanistan, Algeria, Angola, Antigua and Barbuda, Argentina, Armenia, Australia, Austria, Azerbaijan, Bahamas, Bahrain, Bangladesh, Barbados, Belgium, Belize, Benin, Bhutan, Bolivia, Botswana, Brazil, Brunei Darussalam, Burkina Faso, Burundi, Cambodia, Cameroon, Cape Verde, Chile, Colombia, Comoros, Congo, Costa Rica, Côte d'Ivoire, Cuba, Cyprus, Democratic Republic of the Congo, Djibouti, Dominica, Dominican Republic, Ecuador, Egypt, El Salvador, Equatorial Guinea, Eritrea, Ethiopia, Finland, Gabon, Germany, Ghana, Grenada, Guatemala, Guinea, Guinea-Bissau, Guyana, Haiti, Honduras, Iceland, India, Indonesia, Iran, Iraq, Ireland, Italy, Jamaica, Japan, Jordan, Kazakhstan, Kenya, Kuwait, Kyrgyzstan, Lao People's Democratic Republic, Lebanon, Lesotho, Liberia, Libyan Arab Jamahiriya, Liechtenstein, Madagascar, Malawi, Malaysia, Maldives, Mali, Malta, Mauritania, Mauritius, Mexico, Mongolia, Morocco, Mozambique, Myanmar, Namibia, Nepal, New Zealand, Nicaragua, Niger, Nigeria, Norway, Oman, Pakistan, Panama, Papua New Guinea, Paraguay, Peru, Philippines, Portugal, Qatar, Rwanda, Saint Lucia, Saint Vincent and the Grenadines, Samoa, San Marino, Sao Tome and Principe, Saudi Arabia, Senegal, Singapore, Solomon Islands, South Africa, Spain, Sri Lanka, Sudan, Suriname, Swaziland, Sweden, Switzerland, Syrian Arab Republic, Tajikistan, Thailand, Timor-Leste, Togo, Trinidad and Tobago, Tunisia, Turkmenistan, Tuvalu, Uganda, United Arab Emirates, United Republic of Tanzania, Uruguay, Uzbekistan, Venezuela, Viet Nam, Yemen, Zambia, Zimbabwe.

Against: France, United Kingdom, United States.

Abstaining: Albania, Andorra, Belarus, Bosnia and Herzegovina, Bulgaria, Canada, China, Croatia, Czech Republic, Denmark, Estonia, Georgia, Greece, Hungary, Israel, Latvia, Lithuania, Luxembourg, Marshall Islands, Micronesia, Moldova, Montenegro, Netherlands, Palau, Poland, Republic of Korea, Romania, Russian Federation, Serbia, Slovakia, Slovenia, The former Yugoslav Republic of Macedonia, Turkey, Ukraine.

Also on 2 December [meeting 61], the General Assembly, on the recommendation of the First Committee [A/63/389], adopted **resolution 63/46** by recorded vote (117-45-19) [agenda item 89 *(v)*].

Nuclear disarmament

The General Assembly,

Recalling its resolution 49/75 E of 15 December 1994 on a step-by-step reduction of the nuclear threat, and its resolutions 50/70 P of 12 December 1995, 51/45 O of 10 December 1996, 52/38 L of 9 December 1997, 53/77 X of 4 December 1998, 54/54 P of 1 December 1999, 55/33 T of 20 November 2000, 56/24 R of 29 November 2001, 57/79 of 22 November 2002, 58/56 of 8 December 2003, 59/77 of 3 December 2004, 60/70 of 8 December 2005, 61/78 of 6 December 2006 and 62/42 of 5 December 2007 on nuclear disarmament,

Reaffirming the commitment of the international community to the goal of the total elimination of nuclear weapons and the establishment of a nuclear-weapon-free world,

Bearing in mind that the Convention on the Prohibition of the Development, Production and Stockpiling of Bacteriological (Biological) and Toxin Weapons and on Their Destruction of 1972 and the Convention on the Prohibition of the Development, Production, Stockpiling and Use of Chemical Weapons and on Their Destruction of 1993 have already established legal regimes on the complete prohibition of biological and chemical weapons, respectively, and determined to achieve a nuclear weapons convention on the prohibition of the development, testing, production, stockpiling, loan, transfer, use and threat of use of nuclear weapons and on their destruction, and to conclude such an international convention at an early date,

Recognizing that there now exist conditions for the establishment of a world free of nuclear weapons, and stressing the need to take concrete practical steps towards achieving this goal,

Bearing in mind paragraph 50 of the Final Document of the Tenth Special Session of the General Assembly, the first special session devoted to disarmament, calling for the urgent negotiation of agreements for the cessation of the qualitative improvement and development of nuclear-weapon systems, and for a comprehensive and phased programme with agreed time frames, wherever feasible, for the progressive and balanced reduction of nuclear weapons and their means of delivery, leading to their ultimate and complete elimination at the earliest possible time,

Reaffirming the conviction of the States parties to the Treaty on the Non-Proliferation of Nuclear Weapons that the Treaty is a cornerstone of nuclear non-proliferation and nuclear disarmament and the importance of the decision on strengthening the review process for the Treaty, the decision on principles and objectives for nuclear non-proliferation and disarmament, the decision on the extension of the Treaty and the resolution on the Middle East, adopted by the 1995 Review and Extension Conference of the Parties to the Treaty on the Non-Proliferation of Nuclear Weapons,

Stressing the importance of the thirteen steps for the systematic and progressive efforts to achieve the objective of nuclear disarmament leading to the total elimination of nuclear weapons, as agreed to by the States parties in the Final Document of the 2000 Review Conference of the Parties to the Treaty on the Non-Proliferation of Nuclear Weapons,

Reiterating the highest priority accorded to nuclear disarmament in the Final Document of the Tenth Special Session of the General Assembly and by the international community,

Reiterating its call for an early entry into force of the Comprehensive Nuclear-Test-Ban Treaty,

Noting with appreciation the entry into force of the Treaty on the Reduction and Limitation of Strategic Offensive Arms (START I), to which Belarus, Kazakhstan, the Russian Federation, Ukraine and the United States of America are States parties,

Recalling the entry into force of the Treaty on Strategic Offensive Reductions ("the Moscow Treaty") between the United States of America and the Russian Federation as a significant step towards reducing their deployed strategic nuclear weapons, while calling for further irreversible deep cuts in their nuclear arsenals,

Noting with appreciation the unilateral measures taken by the nuclear-weapon States for nuclear arms limitation, and encouraging them to take further such measures, while reiterating deep concern over the slow pace of progress towards nuclear disarmament and the lack of progress by the nuclear-weapon States towards accomplishing the total elimination of their nuclear arsenals,

Recognizing the complementarity of bilateral, plurilateral and multilateral negotiations on nuclear disarmament, and that bilateral negotiations can never replace multilateral negotiations in this respect,

Noting the support expressed in the Conference on Disarmament and in the General Assembly for the elaboration of an international convention to assure non-nuclear-weapon States against the use or threat of use of nuclear weapons, and the multilateral efforts in the Conference on Disarmament to reach agreement on such an international convention at an early date,

Recalling the advisory opinion of the International Court of Justice on the *Legality of the Threat or Use of Nuclear Weapons*, issued on 8 July 1996, and welcoming the unanimous reaffirmation by all Judges of the Court that there exists an obligation for all States to pursue in good faith and bring to a conclusion negotiations leading to nuclear disarmament in all its aspects under strict and effective international control,

Mindful of paragraph 98 of the Final Document of the Fifteenth Ministerial Conference of the Movement of Non-Aligned Countries, held in Tehran on 29 and 30 July 2008,

Recalling paragraph 70 and other relevant recommendations in the Final Document of the Fourteenth Conference of Heads of State or Government of Non-Aligned Countries, held in Havana on 15 and 16 September 2006, calling upon the Conference on Disarmament to establish, as soon as possible and as the highest priority, an ad hoc committee on nuclear disarmament and to commence negotiations on a phased programme for the complete elimination of nuclear weapons with a specified time framework,

Reaffirming the specific mandate conferred upon the Disarmament Commission by the General Assembly, in its decision 52/492 of 8 September 1998, to discuss the subject of nuclear disarmament as one of its main substantive agenda items,

Recalling the United Nations Millennium Declaration, in which Heads of State and Government resolved to strive for the elimination of weapons of mass destruction, in particular nuclear weapons, and to keep all options open for achieving this aim, including the possibility of convening an international conference to identify ways of eliminating nuclear dangers,

Reaffirming that, in accordance with the Charter of the United Nations, States should refrain from the use or threat of use of nuclear weapons in settling their disputes in international relations,

Seized of the danger of the use of weapons of mass destruction, particularly nuclear weapons, in terrorist acts and the urgent need for concerted international efforts to control and overcome it,

1. *Recognizes* that the time is now opportune for all the nuclear-weapon States to take effective disarmament measures to achieve the total elimination of these weapons at the earliest possible time;

2. *Reaffirms* that nuclear disarmament and nuclear non-proliferation are substantively interrelated and mutually reinforcing, that the two processes must go hand in hand and that there is a genuine need for a systematic and progressive process of nuclear disarmament;

3. *Welcomes and encourages* the efforts to establish new nuclear-weapon-free zones in different parts of the world on the basis of agreements or arrangements freely arrived at among the States of the regions concerned, which is an effective measure for limiting the further spread of nuclear weapons geographically and contributes to the cause of nuclear disarmament;

4. *Recognizes* that there is a genuine need to diminish the role of nuclear weapons in strategic doctrines and security policies to minimize the risk that these weapons will ever be used and to facilitate the process of their total elimination;

5. *Urges* the nuclear-weapon States to stop immediately the qualitative improvement, development, production and stockpiling of nuclear warheads and their delivery systems;

6. *Also urges* the nuclear-weapon States, as an interim measure, to de-alert and deactivate immediately their nuclear weapons and to take other concrete measures to reduce further the operational status of their nuclear-weapon systems, while stressing that reductions in deployments and in operational status cannot substitute for irreversible cuts in, and the total elimination of, nuclear weapons;

7. *Reiterates its call upon* the nuclear-weapon States to undertake the step-by-step reduction of the nuclear threat and to carry out effective nuclear disarmament measures with a view to achieving the total elimination of these weapons with a specified framework of time;

8. *Calls upon* the nuclear-weapon States, pending the achievement of the total elimination of nuclear weapons, to agree on an internationally and legally binding instrument on a joint undertaking not to be the first to use nuclear weapons, and calls upon all States to conclude an internationally and legally binding instrument on security assurances of non-use and non-threat of use of nuclear weapons against non-nuclear-weapon States;

9. *Urges* the nuclear-weapon States to commence plurilateral negotiations among themselves at an appropriate stage on further deep reductions of nuclear weapons as an effective measure of nuclear disarmament;

10. *Underlines* the importance of applying the principles of transparency, irreversibility and verifiability to the process of nuclear disarmament, and nuclear and other related arms control and reduction measures;

11. *Underscores* the importance of the unequivocal undertaking by the nuclear-weapon States, in the Final Document of the 2000 Review Conference of the Parties to the Treaty on the Non-Proliferation of Nuclear Weapons, to accomplish the total elimination of their nuclear arsenals leading to nuclear disarmament, to which all States parties are committed under article VI of the Treaty, and the reaffirmation by the States parties that the total elimination of nuclear weapons is the only absolute guarantee against the use or threat of use of nuclear weapons;

12. *Calls for* the full and effective implementation of the thirteen practical steps for nuclear disarmament contained in the Final Document of the 2000 Review Conference;

13. *Urges* the nuclear-weapon States to carry out further reductions of non-strategic nuclear weapons, based on unilateral initiatives and as an integral part of the nuclear arms reduction and disarmament process;

14. *Calls for* the immediate commencement of negotiations in the Conference on Disarmament on a non-discriminatory, multilateral and internationally and effectively verifiable treaty banning the production of fissile material for nuclear weapons or other nuclear explosive devices on the basis of the report of the Special Coordinator and the mandate contained therein;

15. *Urges* the Conference on Disarmament to agree on a programme of work that includes the immediate commencement of negotiations on such a treaty with a view to their conclusion within five years;

16. *Calls for* the conclusion of an international legal instrument or instruments on adequate security assurances to non-nuclear-weapon States;

17. *Also calls for* the early entry into force and strict observance of the Comprehensive Nuclear-Test-Ban Treaty;

18. *Expresses its regret* that the 2005 Review Conference of the Parties to the Treaty on the Non-Proliferation of Nuclear Weapons was unable to achieve any substantive result and that the 2005 World Summit Outcome adopted by the General Assembly failed to make any reference to nuclear disarmament and nuclear non-proliferation;

19. *Also expresses its regret* that the Conference on Disarmament was unable to establish an ad hoc committee to deal with nuclear disarmament early in 2008, as called for by the General Assembly in its resolution 62/42;

20. *Reiterates its call upon* the Conference on Disarmament to establish, as soon as possible and as the highest priority, an ad hoc committee on nuclear disarmament early in 2009 and to commence negotiations on a phased programme of nuclear disarmament leading to the total elimination of nuclear weapons with a specified framework of time;

21. *Calls for* the convening of an international conference on nuclear disarmament in all its aspects at an early date to identify and deal with concrete measures of nuclear disarmament;

22. *Requests* the Secretary-General to submit to the General Assembly at its sixty-fourth session a report on the implementation of the present resolution;

23. *Decides* to include in the provisional agenda of its sixty-fourth session the item entitled "Nuclear disarmament".

RECORDED VOTE ON RESOLUTION 63/46:

In favour: Afghanistan, Algeria, Angola, Antigua and Barbuda, Argentina, Bahamas, Bahrain, Bangladesh, Barbados, Belize, Benin, Bhutan, Bolivia, Botswana, Brazil, Brunei Darussalam, Burkina Faso, Burundi, Cambodia, Cameroon, Cape Verde, Chile, China, Colombia, Comoros, Congo, Costa Rica, Côte d'Ivoire, Cuba, Democratic People's Republic of Korea, Democratic Republic of the Congo, Djibouti, Dominica, Dominican Republic, Ecuador, Egypt, El Salvador, Equatorial Guinea, Eritrea, Ethiopia, Ghana, Grenada, Guatemala, Guinea, Guinea-Bissau, Guyana, Haiti, Honduras, Indonesia, Iran, Iraq, Jamaica, Jordan, Kenya, Kuwait, Lao People's Democratic Republic, Lebanon, Lesotho, Liberia, Libyan Arab Jamahiriya, Madagascar, Malawi, Malaysia, Maldives, Mali, Mauritania, Mexico, Mongolia, Morocco, Mozambique, Myanmar, Namibia, Nauru, Nepal, New Zealand, Nicaragua, Niger, Nigeria, Oman, Panama, Papua New Guinea, Paraguay, Peru, Philippines, Qatar, Rwanda, Saint Lucia, Saint Vincent and the Grenadines, Samoa, Sao Tome and Principe, Saudi Arabia, Senegal, Singapore, Solomon Islands, South Africa, Sri Lanka, Sudan, Suriname, Swaziland, Syrian Arab Republic, Thailand, Timor-Leste, Togo, Tonga, Trinidad and Tobago, Tunisia, Tuvalu, Uganda, United Arab Emirates, United Republic of Tanzania, Uruguay, Vanuatu, Venezuela, Viet Nam, Yemen, Zambia, Zimbabwe.

Against: Albania, Andorra, Australia, Belgium, Bosnia and Herzegovina, Bulgaria, Canada, Croatia, Cyprus, Czech Republic, Denmark, Estonia, Finland, France, Georgia, Germany, Greece, Hungary, Iceland, Israel, Italy, Latvia, Liechtenstein, Lithuania, Luxembourg, Micronesia, Moldova, Monaco, Montenegro, Netherlands, Norway, Palau, Poland, Portugal, Romania, San Marino, Slovakia, Slovenia, Spain, Switzerland, The former Yugoslav Republic of Macedonia, Turkey, Ukraine, United Kingdom, United States.

Abstaining: Armenia, Austria, Azerbaijan, Belarus, India, Ireland, Japan, Kazakhstan, Kyrgyzstan, Malta, Marshall Islands, Mauritius, Pakistan, Republic of Korea, Russian Federation, Serbia, Sweden, Tajikistan, Uzbekistan.

Missiles

Panel of Governmental Experts

Report of Secretary-General. In July [A/63/176], the Secretary-General transmitted to the General Assembly a report of the Panel of Governmental Experts on the issue of missiles in all its aspects, established in 2007 [YUN 2007, p. 541] pursuant to Assembly resolution 59/67 [YUN 2004, p. 537]. The Panel held its second and third sessions from 25 to 29 February and 2 to 6 June, respectively. During those sessions, it conducted in-depth discussions on all aspects of the subject, including the peaceful uses of missile technology, export control, missile defence, global and regional security implications of missiles, missile-relevant confidence-building measures, and a possible UN role for addressing the issue. At the end of its third and final session in June, the Panel adopted a consensus report concluding, among other things, that in the interest of international peace and security, continued international efforts were important to deal with the increasingly complex subject of missiles. The Panel noted that it would be useful to try to develop understandings on how to categorize and describe missiles, how their different aspects interrelated, and how they impacted on global and regional security scenarios. It emphasized the value of further deliberations, focusing on areas of existing and emerging consensus as well as the important role of the United Nations in building such a consensus.

GENERAL ASSEMBLY ACTION

On 2 December [meeting 61], the General Assembly, on the recommendation of the First Committee [A/63/389], adopted **resolution 63/55** by recorded vote (120-10-50) [agenda item 89 *(b)*].

Missiles

The General Assembly,

Recalling its resolutions 54/54 F of 1 December 1999, 55/33 A of 20 November 2000, 56/24 B of 29 November 2001, 57/71 of 22 November 2002, 58/37 of 8 December 2003, 59/67 of 3 December 2004 and 61/59 of 6 December 2006, and its decisions 60/515 of 8 December 2005 and 62/514 of 5 December 2007,

Reaffirming the role of the United Nations in the field of arms regulation and disarmament and the commitment of Member States to take concrete steps to strengthen that role,

Realizing the need to promote regional and international peace and security in a world free from the scourge of war and the burden of armaments,

Convinced of the need for a comprehensive approach towards missiles, in a balanced and non-discriminatory manner, as a contribution to international peace and security,

Bearing in mind that the security concerns of Member States at the international and regional levels should be taken into consideration in addressing the issue of missiles,

Underlining the complexities involved in considering the issue of missiles in the conventional context,

Expressing its support for the international efforts against the development and proliferation of all weapons of mass destruction,

Considering that the Secretary-General, in response to resolution 59/67, established a Panel of Governmental Experts to assist him in preparing a report for consideration by the General Assembly at its sixty-third session on the issue of missiles in all its aspects,

1. *Welcomes* the report of the Secretary-General on the issue of missiles in all its aspects, submitted pursuant to resolution 59/67;

2. *Requests* the Secretary-General to seek the views of Member States on the report on the issue of missiles in all its aspects, and to submit them to the General Assembly at its sixty-fifth session;

3. *Decides* to include in the provisional agenda of its sixty-fifth session the item entitled "Missiles".

RECORDED VOTE ON RESOLUTION 63/55:

In favour: Afghanistan, Algeria, Angola, Antigua and Barbuda, Argentina, Armenia, Bahamas, Bahrain, Bangladesh, Barbados, Belarus, Belize, Benin, Bhutan, Bolivia, Botswana, Brazil, Brunei Darussalam, Burkina Faso, Burundi, Cambodia, Cameroon, Cape Verde, Chile, China, Colombia, Comoros, Congo, Costa Rica, Côte d'Ivoire, Cuba, Democratic People's Republic of Korea, Djibouti, Dominica, Dominican Republic, Ecuador, Egypt, El Salvador, Equatorial Guinea, Eritrea, Ethiopia, Ghana, Grenada, Guatemala, Guinea, Guinea-Bissau, Guyana, Haiti, Honduras, India, Indonesia, Iran, Iraq, Jamaica, Jordan, Kazakhstan, Kenya, Kuwait, Kyrgyzstan, Lao People's Democratic Republic, Lebanon, Lesotho, Libyan Arab Jamahiriya, Madagascar, Malawi, Malaysia, Maldives, Mali, Mauritania, Mauritius, Mexico, Mongolia, Morocco, Mozambique, Myanmar, Namibia, Nepal, Nicaragua, Niger, Nigeria, Oman, Pakistan, Panama, Paraguay, Peru, Philippines, Qatar, Russian Federation, Rwanda, Saint Lucia, Saint Vincent and the Grenadines, Sao Tome and Principe, Saudi Arabia, Senegal, Solomon Islands, South Africa, Sri Lanka, Sudan, Suriname, Swaziland, Syrian Arab Republic, Tajikistan, Thailand, Timor-Leste, Togo, Trinidad and Tobago, Tunisia, Turkmenistan, Tuvalu, Uganda, United Arab Emirates, United Republic of Tanzania, Uruguay, Uzbekistan, Vanuatu, Venezuela, Viet Nam, Yemen, Zambia, Zimbabwe.

Against: Denmark, France, Israel, Lithuania, Marshall Islands, Micronesia, Netherlands, Palau, United Kingdom, United States.

Abstaining: Albania, Andorra, Australia, Austria, Azerbaijan, Belgium, Bosnia and Herzegovina, Bulgaria, Canada, Croatia, Cyprus, Czech Republic, Estonia, Finland, Georgia, Germany, Greece, Hungary, Iceland, Ireland, Italy, Japan, Latvia, Liberia, Liechtenstein, Luxembourg, Malta, Moldova, Monaco, Montenegro, New Zealand, Norway, Papua New Guinea, Poland, Portugal, Republic of Korea, Romania, Samoa, San Marino, Serbia, Singapore, Slovakia, Slovenia, Spain, Sweden, Switzerland, The former Yugoslav Republic of Macedonia, Tonga, Turkey, Ukraine.

Hague Code of Conduct

At the Seventh Regular Meeting of the Hague Code of Conduct (Vienna, 29–30 May), the subscribing States to the 2002 Hague Code of Conduct against Ballistic Missile Proliferation [YUN 2002, p. 504] discussed, inter alia, the strengthening of confidence-building measures such as pre-launch notifications and annual declarations of ballistic missiles, space-launch vehicles, and the importance of outreach activities to increase the number of subscribing States and foster universalization of the Code. As at year's end, subscribing States numbered 130.

GENERAL ASSEMBLY ACTION

On 2 December [meeting 61], the General Assembly, on the recommendation of the First Committee [A/63/389], adopted **resolution 63/64** by recorded vote (159-1-18) [agenda item 89].

The Hague Code of Conduct against Ballistic Missile Proliferation

The General Assembly,

Concerned about the increasing regional and global security challenges caused, inter alia, by the ongoing proliferation of ballistic missiles capable of delivering weapons of mass destruction,

Bearing in mind the purposes and principles of the United Nations and its role and responsibility in the field of international peace and security in accordance with the Charter of the United Nations,

Emphasizing the significance of regional and international efforts to prevent and curb comprehensively the proliferation of ballistic missile systems capable of delivering weapons of mass destruction, as a contribution to international peace and security,

Welcoming the adoption of the Hague Code of Conduct against Ballistic Missile Proliferation on 25 November 2002 at The Hague, and convinced that the Code of Conduct will contribute to enhancing transparency and confidence among States,

Recalling its resolution 60/62 of 8 December 2005 entitled "The Hague Code of Conduct against Ballistic Missile Proliferation",

Confirming its commitment to the Declaration on International Cooperation in the Exploration and Use of Outer Space for the Benefit and in the Interest of All States, Taking into Particular Account the Needs of Developing Countries, as contained in the annex to its resolution 51/122 of 13 December 1996,

Recognizing that States should not be excluded from utilizing the benefits of space for peaceful purposes, but that in reaping such benefits and in conducting related cooperation they must not contribute to the proliferation of ballistic missiles capable of carrying weapons of mass destruction,

Mindful of the need to combat the proliferation of weapons of mass destruction and their means of delivery,

1. *Notes with satisfaction* that one hundred and thirty States have already subscribed to the Hague Code of Conduct against Ballistic Missile Proliferation as a practical step against the proliferation of weapons of mass destruction and their means of delivery;

2. *Invites* all States that have not yet subscribed to the Code of Conduct to do so;

3. *Encourages* the exploration of further ways and means to deal effectively with the problem of the proliferation of ballistic missiles capable of delivering weapons of mass destruction;

4. *Decides* to include in the provisional agenda of its sixty-fourth session the item entitled "The Hague Code of Conduct against Ballistic Missile Proliferation".

RECORDED VOTE ON RESOLUTION 63/64:

In favour: Afghanistan, Albania, Andorra, Angola, Antigua and Barbuda, Argentina, Armenia, Australia, Austria, Azerbaijan, Bahamas, Bangladesh, Barbados, Belarus, Belgium, Belize, Benin, Bhutan, Bolivia, Bosnia and Herzegovina, Botswana, Brazil, Brunei Darussalam, Bulgaria, Burkina Faso, Burundi, Cambodia, Cameroon, Canada, Cape Verde, Chile, China, Colombia, Comoros, Congo, Costa Rica, Côte d'Ivoire, Croatia, Cyprus, Czech Republic, Denmark, Djibouti, Dominica, Dominican Republic, Ecuador, El Salvador, Equatorial Guinea, Eritrea, Estonia, Ethiopia, Fiji, Finland, France, Georgia, Germany, Ghana, Greece, Grenada, Guatemala, Guinea, Guinea-Bissau, Guyana, Haiti, Honduras, Hungary, Iceland, Iraq, Ireland, Israel, Italy, Jamaica, Japan, Jordan, Kazakhstan, Kenya, Kuwait, Kyrgyzstan, Latvia, Lesotho, Liberia, Libyan Arab Jamahiriya, Liechtenstein, Lithuania, Luxembourg, Madagascar, Malawi, Maldives, Mali, Malta, Marshall Islands, Mauritania, Micronesia, Moldova, Monaco, Mongolia, Montenegro, Morocco, Mozambique, Myanmar, Namibia, Nauru, Nepal, Netherlands, New Zealand, Nicaragua, Niger, Nigeria, Norway, Palau, Panama, Papua New Guinea, Paraguay, Peru, Philippines, Poland, Portugal, Republic of Korea, Romania, Russian Federation, Rwanda, Saint Lucia, Saint Vincent and the Grenadines, Samoa, San Marino, Sao Tome and Principe, Senegal, Serbia, Singapore, Slovakia, Slovenia, Solomon Islands, South Africa, Spain, Sri Lanka, Sudan, Suriname, Swaziland, Sweden, Switzerland, Tajikistan, Thailand, The former Yugoslav Republic of Macedonia, Timor-Leste, Togo, Tonga, Trinidad and Tobago, Tunisia, Turkey, Turkmenistan, Tuvalu, Uganda, Ukraine, United Kingdom, United Republic of Tanzania, United States, Uruguay, Uzbekistan, Vanuatu, Zambia.

Against: Iran.

Abstaining: Algeria, Bahrain, Chad, Cuba, Egypt, India, Indonesia, Lebanon, Malaysia, Mauritius, Mexico, Oman, Pakistan, Qatar, Syrian Arab Republic, United Arab Emirates, Venezuela, Yemen.

Missile Technology Control Regime

The Missile Technology Control Regime (MTCR)—an informal and voluntary association of countries sharing the goal of non-proliferation of unmanned systems capable of delivering WMDs—at its twenty-third plenary meeting (Canberra, Australia, 5–7 November) recognized that more must be done to discourage WMD means-of-delivery programmes and proliferation activities, and acknowledged that particular challenges were posed by missile proliferation in Northeast Asia, South Asia and the Middle East. At the meeting, the partners discussed export control challenges and confirmed their determination to strengthen MTCR controls to meet proliferation threats, including those posed by rapid technological change. The partners discussed a number of proposals to maintain the accuracy and comprehensiveness of MTCR controls, and agreed on changes to the list of controlled goods, as well as on nationally implemented measures to improve the effectiveness of controls. The partners expressed their determination to implement the Security Council resolutions relevant to MTCR export controls and to prevent the transfer of any items, materials, goods and technology that could contribute to WMD missile proliferation. More broadly, the partners reiterated their support for implementation of Council resolution 1540(2004) [YUN 2004, p. 544], which called on all States to establish effective national export controls to prevent WMD proliferation.

Missile defence system in Europe

Plans for stationing a missile defence system in Europe were further consolidated when the United States and the Czech Republic issued a Joint Statement on 3 April announcing the completion of negotiations on a missile defence agreement that called for the stationing of a ballistic missile-tracking radar in the Czech Republic, and on 20 August when the United States and Poland signed the legally binding "Agreement between the Government of the United States of America and the Government of the Republic of Poland Concerning the Deployment of Ground-Based Ballistic Missile Defense Interceptors in the Territory of the Republic of Poland". Those plans were criticized by the Russian Federation, which declared its intention to deploy countermeasures should the missile defence system become reality.

Comprehensive Nuclear-Test-Ban Treaty

Status

As at 31 December, 179 States had signed the 1996 Comprehensive Nuclear-Test-Ban Treaty (CTBT) adopted by General Assembly resolution 50/245 [YUN 1996, p. 454], and 148 had ratified it. In accordance with article XIV, CTBT would enter into force 180 days after the 44 States possessing nuclear reactors, listed in annex 2 of the Treaty, had deposited their instruments of ratification. At year's end, 35 of those States had ratified the Treaty. During the year, instruments of ratification were deposited by Barbados, Burundi, Colombia, Lebanon, Malawi, Malaysia and Mozambique.

Report of Secretary General. In July [A/63/124], pursuant to General Assembly resolution 62/59 [YUN 2007, p. 543], the Secretary-General reported, in consultation with the Preparatory Commission for CTBT, on efforts of States that had ratified the Treaty towards its universalization and possibilities for providing assistance on ratification procedures to States that so requested it.

Ministerial Meeting in support of CTBT entry into force

The Fourth Ministerial Meeting in support of CTBT's entry into force (New York, 24 September) was convened by the Ministers for Foreign Affairs of Australia, Austria, Canada, Costa Rica, Finland, Japan and the Netherlands. In his opening address, the Secretary-General reiterated his appeal to those States whose ratification was needed for the entry into force—China, the DPRK, Egypt, India, Indonesia, Iran, Israel, Pakistan and the United States—to sign and ratify the Treaty, underlining that it would be a major step in the efforts to build a safer, more peaceful world. Approximately 40 Foreign Ministers participated in the Meeting and issued a Joint Ministerial Statement that was subsequently endorsed by 96 countries. In the Statement, which was annexed to a letter of 19 December [A/63/634] to the Secretary-General, the Ministers called on all States that had not yet done so to sign and ratify the Treaty without delay, in particular those whose ratification was needed for its entry into force, and committed themselves individually and together to make the Treaty a focus of attention at the highest political levels.

GENERAL ASSEMBLY ACTION

On 2 December [meeting 61], the General Assembly, on the recommendation of the First Committee [A/63/395], adopted **resolution 63/87** by recorded vote (175-1-3) [agenda item 95].

Comprehensive Nuclear-Test-Ban Treaty

The General Assembly,

Reiterating that the cessation of nuclear-weapon test explosions or any other nuclear explosions constitutes an effective nuclear disarmament and non-proliferation measure, and convinced that this is a meaningful step in the realization of a systematic process to achieve nuclear disarmament,

Recalling that the Comprehensive Nuclear-Test-Ban Treaty, adopted by its resolution 50/245 of 10 September 1996, was opened for signature on 24 September 1996,

Stressing that a universal and effectively verifiable Treaty constitutes a fundamental instrument in the field of nuclear disarmament and non-proliferation and that after more than ten years, its entry into force is more urgent than ever before,

Encouraged by the signing of the Treaty by one hundred and eighty States, including forty-one of the forty-four needed for its entry into force, and welcoming the ratification of one hundred and forty-five States, including thirty-five of the forty-four needed for its entry into force, among which there are three nuclear-weapon States,

Recalling its resolution 62/59 of 5 December 2007,

Welcoming the Joint Ministerial Statement on the Comprehensive Nuclear-Test-Ban Treaty, adopted at the Ministerial Meeting held in New York on 24 September 2008,

1. *Stresses* the vital importance and urgency of signature and ratification, without delay and without conditions, to achieve the earliest entry into force of the Comprehensive Nuclear-Test-Ban Treaty;

2. *Welcomes* the contributions by the States signatories to the work of the Preparatory Commission for the Comprehensive Nuclear-Test-Ban Treaty Organization, in particular its efforts to ensure that the Treaty's verification regime will be capable of meeting the verification requirements of the Treaty upon its entry into force, in accordance with article IV of the Treaty;

3. *Underlines* the need to maintain momentum towards completion of all elements of the verification regime;

4. *Urges* all States not to carry out nuclear-weapon test explosions or any other nuclear explosions, to maintain their moratoriums in this regard and to refrain from acts that would defeat the object and purpose of the Treaty, while stressing that these measures do not have the same permanent and legally binding effect as the entry into force of the Treaty;

5. *Calls for* the verifiable denuclearization of the Korean Peninsula in a peaceful manner through the successful implementation of the Joint Statement of 19 September 2005, and the initial and second-phase actions to implement it, agreed upon in the framework of the Six-Party Talks;

6. *Urges* all States that have not yet signed the Treaty to sign and ratify it as soon as possible;

7. *Urges* all States that have signed but not yet ratified the Treaty, in particular those whose ratification is needed for its entry into force, to accelerate their ratification processes with a view to ensuring their earliest successful conclusion;

8. *Welcomes* the ratification of the Treaty in 2008 by Colombia, Barbados, Malaysia and Burundi, as well as the signature in 2008 by Iraq and Timor-Leste, as significant steps towards the early entry into force of the Treaty;

9. *Urges* all States to remain seized of the issue at the highest political level and, where in a position to do so, to promote adherence to the Treaty through bilateral and joint outreach, seminars and other means;

10. *Requests* the Secretary-General, in consultation with the Preparatory Commission for the Comprehensive Nuclear-Test-Ban Treaty Organization, to prepare a report on the efforts of States that have ratified the Treaty towards its universalization and possibilities for providing assistance on ratification procedures to States that so request it, and to submit such a report to the General Assembly at its sixty-fourth session;

11. *Decides* to include in the provisional agenda of its sixty-fourth session the item entitled "Comprehensive Nuclear-Test-Ban Treaty".

RECORDED VOTE ON RESOLUTION 63/87:

In favour: Afghanistan, Albania, Algeria, Andorra, Antigua and Barbuda, Argentina, Armenia, Australia, Austria, Azerbaijan, Bahamas, Bahrain, Bangladesh, Barbados, Belarus, Belgium, Belize, Benin, Bhutan, Bolivia, Bosnia and Herzegovina, Botswana, Brazil, Brunei Darussalam, Bulgaria, Burkina Faso, Burundi, Cambodia, Cameroon, Canada, Cape Verde, Chad, Chile, China, Colombia, Congo, Costa Rica, Côte d'Ivoire, Croatia, Cuba, Cyprus, Czech Republic, Democratic Republic of the Congo, Denmark, Djibouti, Dominica, Dominican Republic, Ecuador, Egypt, El Salvador, Equatorial Guinea, Eritrea, Estonia, Ethiopia, Fiji, Finland, France, Gabon, Georgia, Germany, Ghana, Greece, Grenada, Guatemala, Guinea, Guinea-Bissau, Guyana, Honduras, Hungary, Iceland, Indonesia, Iran, Iraq, Ireland, Israel, Italy, Jamaica, Japan, Jordan, Kazakhstan, Kenya, Kuwait, Kyrgyzstan, Lao People's Democratic Republic, Latvia, Lebanon, Lesotho, Liberia, Libyan Arab Jamahiriya, Liechtenstein, Lithuania, Luxembourg, Madagascar, Malawi, Malaysia, Maldives, Mali, Malta, Marshall Islands, Mauritania, Mexico, Micronesia, Moldova, Monaco, Mongolia, Montenegro, Morocco, Mozambique, Myanmar, Namibia, Nauru, Nepal, Netherlands, New Zealand, Nicaragua, Niger, Nigeria, Norway, Oman, Pakistan, Palau, Panama, Papua New Guinea, Paraguay, Peru, Philippines, Poland, Portugal, Qatar, Republic of Korea, Romania, Russian Federation, Rwanda, Saint Lucia, Saint Vincent and the Grenadines, Samoa, San Marino, Sao Tome and Principe, Saudi Arabia, Serbia, Singapore, Slovakia, Slovenia, Solomon Islands, South Africa, Spain, Sri Lanka, Sudan, Suriname, Swaziland, Sweden, Switzerland, Tajikistan, Thailand, The former Yugoslav Republic of Macedonia, Timor-Leste, Togo, Tonga, Trinidad and Tobago, Tunisia, Turkey, Turkmenistan, Uganda, Ukraine, United Arab Emirates, United Kingdom, United Republic of Tanzania, Uruguay, Uzbekistan, Vanuatu, Venezuela, Viet Nam, Yemen, Zambia, Zimbabwe.

Against: United States.

Abstaining: India, Mauritius, Syrian Arab Republic.

Also on 2 December [meeting 61], the Assembly, on the recommendation of the First Committee's [A/63/389], adopted **resolution 63/58** by recorded vote (166-5-7) [agenda item 89 *(l)*].

Towards a nuclear-weapon-free world: accelerating the implementation of nuclear disarmament commitments

The General Assembly,

Recalling its resolution 62/25 of 5 December 2007,

Continuing to express its grave concern at the danger to humanity posed by the possibility that nuclear weapons could be used,

Reaffirming that nuclear disarmament and nuclear non-proliferation are mutually reinforcing processes requiring urgent irreversible progress on both fronts,

Recognizing the continued vital importance of the early entry into force of the Comprehensive Nuclear-Test-Ban Treaty to the advancement of nuclear disarmament and nuclear non-proliferation objectives, and welcoming the recent ratifications of the Treaty by Barbados, Burundi, Colombia and Malaysia,

Recalling the decisions entitled "Strengthening the review process for the Treaty", "Principles and objectives for nuclear non-proliferation and disarmament" and "Extension of the Treaty on the Non-Proliferation of Nuclear Weapons" and the resolution on the Middle East, adopted at the 1995 Review and Extension Conference of the Parties to the Treaty on the Non-Proliferation of Nuclear Weapons and the Final Document of the 2000 Review Conference of the Parties to the Treaty on the Non-Proliferation of Nuclear Weapons,

Recalling also the unequivocal undertaking by the nuclear-weapon States to accomplish the total elimination of their nuclear arsenals, leading to nuclear disarmament, in accordance with commitments made under article VI of the Treaty on the Non-Proliferation of Nuclear Weapons,

Mindful of the approaching 2010 Review Conference of the Parties to the Treaty on the Non-Proliferation of Nuclear Weapons, and in this regard urging States parties to intensify their constructive engagement in the work of the Preparatory Committee for the 2010 Review Conference at its third session, in 2009,

1. *Continues to emphasize* the central role of the Treaty on the Non-Proliferation of Nuclear Weapons and its universality in achieving nuclear disarmament and nuclear non-proliferation, and calls upon all States parties to respect their obligations;

2. *Calls upon* all States to comply fully with all commitments made regarding nuclear disarmament and nuclear non-proliferation and not to act in any way that may compromise either cause or that may lead to a new nuclear arms race;

3. *Reaffirms* that the outcome of the 2000 Review Conference of the Parties to the Treaty on the Non-Proliferation of Nuclear Weapons sets out the agreed process for systematic and progressive efforts towards nuclear disarmament, and in this regard renews its call upon the nuclear-weapon States to accelerate the implementation of the practical steps towards nuclear disarmament that were agreed upon at the 2000 Review Conference, thereby contributing to a safer world for all;

4. *Reiterates its call upon* all States parties to spare no effort to achieve the universality of the Treaty on the Non-Proliferation of Nuclear Weapons, and in this regard urges India, Israel and Pakistan to accede to the Treaty as non-nuclear-weapon States promptly and without conditions;

5. *Urges* the Democratic People's Republic of Korea to rescind its announced withdrawal from the Treaty on the Non-Proliferation of Nuclear Weapons, while recognizing the efforts undertaken during 2008 within the framework of the Six-Party Talks to achieve the denuclearization of the Korean Peninsula in a peaceful manner;

6. *Stresses* the need for a constructive and successful preparatory process leading to the 2010 Review Conference, which should contribute to strengthening the Treaty on the Non-Proliferation of Nuclear Weapons in all its aspects and achieving its full implementation and universality;

7. *Welcomes* the second session of the Preparatory Committee for the 2010 Review Conference, held in Geneva from 28 April to 9 May 2008, and calls upon the Preparatory Committee at its third session, in 2009, to identify and address specific aspects where urgent progress is required in order to advance the objective of a nuclear-weapon-free world, building on the outcomes of the 1995 and 2000 Conferences;

8. *Decides* to include in the provisional agenda of its sixty-fourth session the item entitled "Towards a nuclear-weapon-free world: accelerating the implementation of nuclear disarmament commitments" and to review the implementation of the present resolution at that session.

RECORDED VOTE ON RESOLUTION 63/58:

In favour: Afghanistan, Albania, Algeria, Andorra, Angola, Antigua and Barbuda, Argentina, Armenia, Australia, Austria, Azerbaijan, Bahamas, Bahrain, Bangladesh, Barbados, Belarus, Belgium, Belize, Benin, Bolivia, Bosnia and Herzegovina, Botswana, Brazil, Brunei Darussalam, Bulgaria, Burkina Faso, Burundi, Cambodia, Cameroon, Canada, Cape Verde, Chile, China, Colombia, Comoros, Congo, Costa Rica, Côte d'Ivoire, Croatia, Cuba, Cyprus, Czech Republic, Denmark, Djibouti, Dominica, Dominican Republic, Ecuador, Egypt, El Salvador, Equatorial Guinea, Eritrea, Estonia, Ethiopia, Finland, Georgia, Germany, Ghana, Greece, Grenada, Guatemala, Guinea, Guinea-Bissau, Guyana, Haiti, Honduras, Hungary, Iceland, Indonesia, Iran, Iraq, Ireland, Italy, Jamaica, Japan, Jordan, Kazakhstan, Kenya, Kuwait, Kyrgyzstan, Lao People's Democratic Republic, Lebanon, Lesotho, Liberia, Libyan Arab Jamahiriya, Liechtenstein, Lithuania, Luxembourg, Madagascar, Malawi, Malaysia, Maldives, Mali, Malta, Marshall Islands, Mauritania, Mauritius, Mexico, Moldova, Mongolia, Montenegro, Morocco, Mozambique, Myanmar, Namibia, Nauru, Nepal, Netherlands, New Zealand, Nicaragua, Niger, Nigeria, Norway, Oman, Panama, Paraguay, Peru, Philippines, Poland, Portugal, Qatar, Republic of Korea, Romania, Rwanda, Saint Lucia, Saint Vincent and the Grenadines, Samoa, San Marino, Sao Tome and Principe, Saudi Arabia, Senegal, Serbia, Singapore, Slovakia, Slovenia, Solomon Islands, South Africa, Spain, Sri Lanka, Sudan, Suriname, Swaziland, Sweden, Switzerland, Syrian Arab Republic, Tajikistan, Thailand, The former Yugoslav Republic of Macedonia, Timor-Leste, Togo, Tonga, Trinidad and Tobago, Tunisia, Turkey, Tuvalu, Uganda, Ukraine, United Arab Emirates, United Republic of Tanzania, Uruguay, Uzbekistan, Vanuatu, Venezuela, Viet Nam, Yemen, Zambia, Zimbabwe.

Against: Democratic People's Republic of Korea, France, India, Israel, United States.

Abstaining: Bhutan, Latvia, Micronesia, Pakistan, Palau, Russian Federation, United Kingdom.

Preparatory Commission for the CTBT Organization

The Preparatory Commission for the Comprehensive Nuclear-Test-Ban Treaty Organization (CTBTO), established in 1996 [YUN 1996, p. 452], continued to develop the Treaty's verification regime. Further progress was made in setting up the International Monitoring System (IMS) [YUN 1999, p. 472], the global network of 337 facilities to be built in 90 countries and designed to detect nuclear explosions prohibited by CTBT. By the end of 2008, approximately 250 IMS stations, representing 70 per cent of the entire network, had been verified and were transmitting information to the International Data Centre in Vienna. The migration of the Global Communications Infrastructure had been completed, with the data volume transmitted through the system. The number of IMS data users increased further, crossing the threshold of 1,000 authorized individual users in 100 countries. In September, a major on-site inspection in Kazakhstan was carried out successfully—the first comprehensive inspection ever conducted, involving all major elements of the on-site inspection regime. Additionally, equipment weighing 50 tons was deployed in Semipalatinsk, a former Soviet nuclear test site in Kazakhstan. Speaking before the First Committee on 15 October, the CTBTO Executive Secretary informed members that the International Scientific Studies project was launched in March, whereby participating scientific institutions independently assessed the verification regime and explored future opportunities for cooperation between CTBTO and the scientific community. The project was to culminate in a conference in Vienna in June 2009.

The Preparatory Commission held its thirtieth (23–24 June) [CTBT/PC-30/1] and thirty-first (17–18 November) [CTBT/PC-31/1] sessions, both in Vienna, to consider the reports of its working groups and to discuss organizational, budgetary and other matters. The Commision adopted its 2009 programme budget in the amounts of $52,614,400 and €18,543,600.

Note and report of Secretary-General. By a July note [A/63/156], the Secretary-General submitted to the General Assembly the report of the Commision's Executive Committee for 2007. In an August report [A/63/228-S/2008/531], the Secretary-General noted that the report of the Executive Secretary for 2006 [YUN 2007, p. 542] had been submitted to the Assembly pursuant to article IV, paragraph 1, of the Agreement to Regulate the Relationship between the United Nations and the Preparatory Commission, annexed to Assembly resolution 54/280 [YUN 2000, p. 501].

GENERAL ASSEMBLY ACTION

On 3 November [meeting 37], the General Assembly adopted **resolution 63/13** [draft: A/63/L.11] by recorded vote (64-1-0) [agenda item 114 *(t)*].

Cooperation between the United Nations and the Preparatory Commission for the Comprehensive Nuclear-Test-Ban Treaty Organization

The General Assembly,

Taking note of the report of the Secretary-General,

Taking note also of the report of the Executive Secretary of the Preparatory Commission for the Comprehensive Nuclear-Test-Ban Treaty Organization,

Decides to include in the provisional agenda of its sixty-fifth session the sub-item entitled "Cooperation between the United Nations and the Preparatory Commission for the Comprehensive Nuclear-Test-Ban Treaty Organization".

RECORDED VOTE ON RESOLUTION 63/13:

In favour: Albania, Argentina, Australia, Austria, Bahrain, Belarus, Belgium, Bosnia and Herzegovina, Brazil, Brunei Darussalam, Burundi, Cambodia, China, Congo, Croatia, Cuba, Cyprus, Czech Republic, Djibouti, Dominican Republic, Egypt, Estonia, Finland, France, Germany, Greece, Guatemala, Guinea, Hungary, Indonesia, Iran, Iraq, Ireland, Israel, Italy, Libyan Arab Jamahiriya, Liechtenstein, Lithuania, Mexico, Moldova, Mongolia, Montenegro, Myanmar, New Zealand, Peru, Poland, Portugal, Romania, Russian Federation, Rwanda, San Marino, Singapore, Slovakia, South Africa, Spain, Sri Lanka, Sweden, Switzerland, Thailand, Togo, United Arab Emirates, United Republic of Tanzania, Yemen, Zambia.

Against: United States.

Abstaining: None.

Prohibition of the use of nuclear weapons

In 2008, the Conference on Disarmament did not hold negotiations on a convention on the prohibition of the use of nuclear weapons, as called for in General Assembly resolution 62/51 [YUN 2007, p. 545]. The Assembly, in resolution 63/75 (see below), reiterated its request to the Conference on Disarmament to commence negotiations.

GENERAL ASSEMBLY ACTION

On 2 December [meeting 61], the General Assembly, on the recommendation of the First Committee [A/63/390], adopted **resolution 63/75** by recorded vote (121-50-10) [agenda item 90 *(e)*].

Convention on the Prohibition of the Use of Nuclear Weapons

The General Assembly,

Convinced that the use of nuclear weapons poses the most serious threat to the survival of mankind,

Bearing in mind the advisory opinion of the International Court of Justice of 8 July 1996 on the *Legality of the Threat or Use of Nuclear Weapons,*

Convinced that a multilateral, universal and binding agreement prohibiting the use or threat of use of nuclear weapons would contribute to the elimination of the nuclear threat and to the climate for negotiations leading to the ultimate elimination of nuclear weapons, thereby strengthening international peace and security,

Conscious that some steps taken by the Russian Federation and the United States of America towards a reduction of their nuclear weapons and the improvement in the international climate can contribute towards the goal of the complete elimination of nuclear weapons,

Recalling that paragraph 58 of the Final Document of the Tenth Special Session of the General Assembly states that all States should actively participate in efforts to bring about conditions in international relations among States in which a code of peaceful conduct of nations in international affairs could be agreed upon and that would preclude the use or threat of use of nuclear weapons,

Reaffirming that any use of nuclear weapons would be a violation of the Charter of the United Nations and a crime against humanity, as declared in its resolutions 1653(XVI) of 24 November 1961, 33/71 B of 14 December 1978, 34/83 G of 11 December 1979, 35/152 D of 12 December 1980 and 36/92 I of 9 December 1981,

Determined to achieve an international convention prohibiting the development, production, stockpiling and use of nuclear weapons, leading to their ultimate destruction,

Stressing that an international convention on the prohibition of the use of nuclear weapons would be an important step in a phased programme towards the complete elimination of nuclear weapons, with a specified framework of time,

Noting with regret that the Conference on Disarmament, during its 2008 session, was unable to undertake negotiations on this subject as called for in General Assembly resolution 62/51 of 5 December 2007,

1. Reiterates its request to the Conference on Disarmament to commence negotiations in order to reach agreement on an international convention prohibiting the use or threat of use of nuclear weapons under any circumstances;

2. Requests the Conference on Disarmament to report to the General Assembly on the results of those negotiations.

RECORDED VOTE ON RESOLUTION 63/75:

In favour: Afghanistan, Algeria, Antigua and Barbuda, Argentina, Bahamas, Bahrain, Bangladesh, Barbados, Belarus, Belize, Bhutan, Bolivia, Botswana, Brazil, Brunei Darussalam, Burkina Faso, Burundi, Cambodia, Cameroon, Cape Verde, Chad, Chile, China, Colombia, Congo, Costa Rica, Côte d'Ivoire, Cuba, Democratic People's Republic of Korea, Democratic Republic of the Congo, Djibouti, Dominica, Dominican Republic, Ecuador, Egypt, El Salvador, Equatorial Guinea, Eritrea, Ethiopia, Fiji, Ghana, Grenada, Guatemala, Guinea, Guinea-Bissau, Guyana, Haiti, Honduras, India, Indonesia, Iran, Iraq, Jamaica, Jordan, Kenya, Kuwait, Lao People's Democratic Republic, Lebanon, Lesotho, Liberia, Libyan Arab Jamahiriya, Madagascar, Malawi, Malaysia, Maldives, Mali, Mauritania, Mauritius, Mexico, Mongolia, Morocco, Mozambique, Myanmar, Namibia, Nauru, Nepal, Nicaragua, Niger,

Nigeria, Oman, Pakistan, Panama, Papua New Guinea, Paraguay, Peru, Philippines, Qatar, Rwanda, Saint Lucia, Saint Vincent and the Grenadines, Samoa, Sao Tome and Principe, Saudi Arabia, Senegal, Singapore, Solomon Islands, South Africa, Sri Lanka, Sudan, Suriname, Swaziland, Syrian Arab Republic, Tajikistan, Thailand, Timor-Leste, Togo, Tonga, Trinidad and Tobago, Tunisia, Turkmenistan, Tuvalu, Uganda, United Arab Emirates, United Republic of Tanzania, Uruguay, Vanuatu, Venezuela, Viet Nam, Yemen, Zambia, Zimbabwe.

Against: Albania, Andorra, Australia, Austria, Belgium, Bosnia and Herzegovina, Bulgaria, Canada, Croatia, Cyprus, Czech Republic, Denmark, Estonia, Finland, France, Georgia, Germany, Greece, Hungary, Iceland, Ireland, Israel, Italy, Latvia, Liechtenstein, Lithuania, Luxembourg, Malta, Micronesia, Moldova, Monaco, Montenegro, Netherlands, New Zealand, Norway, Palau, Poland, Portugal, Romania, San Marino, Slovakia, Slovenia, Spain, Sweden, Switzerland, The former Yugoslav Republic of Macedonia, Turkey, Ukraine, United Kingdom, United States.

Abstaining: Armenia, Azerbaijan, Japan, Kazakhstan, Kyrgyzstan, Marshall Islands, Republic of Korea, Russian Federation, Serbia, Uzbekistan.

Advisory opinion of the International Court of Justice

Pursuant to General Assembly resolutions 62/32 [YUN 2007, p. 535], 62/39 [ibid., p. 545] and 62/42 [ibid., p. 538], on the advisory opinion of the International Court of Justice that the threat or use of nuclear weapons was contrary to the UN Charter [YUN 1999, p. 461], the Secretary-General in July presented information from four States (Canada, Cuba, Japan, Qatar) on measures they had taken to implement resolution 62/39 and towards nuclear disarmament [A/63/135].

GENERAL ASSEMBLY ACTION

On 2 December [meeting 61], on the recommendation of the First Committee [A/63/389], the General Assembly adopted **resolution 63/49** by recorded vote (127-30-23) [agenda item 89 *(u)*].

Follow-up to the advisory opinion of the International Court of Justice on the *Legality of the Threat or Use of Nuclear Weapons*

The General Assembly,

Recalling its resolutions 49/75 K of 15 December 1994, 51/45 M of 10 December 1996, 52/38 O of 9 December 1997, 53/77 W of 4 December 1998, 54/54 Q of 1 December 1999, 55/33 X of 20 November 2000, 56/24 S of 29 November 2001, 57/85 of 22 November 2002, 58/46 of 8 December 2003, 59/83 of 3 December 2004, 60/76 of 8 December 2005, 61/83 of 6 December 2006 and 62/39 of 5 December 2007,

Convinced that the continuing existence of nuclear weapons poses a threat to all humanity and that their use would have catastrophic consequences for all life on Earth, and recognizing that the only defence against a nuclear catastrophe is the total elimination of nuclear weapons and the certainty that they will never be produced again,

Reaffirming the commitment of the international community to the goal of the total elimination of nuclear weapons and the creation of a nuclear-weapon-free world,

Mindful of the solemn obligations of States parties, undertaken in article VI of the Treaty on the Non-Proliferation of Nuclear Weapons, particularly to pursue negotiations in good faith on effective measures relating to cessation of the nuclear arms race at an early date and to nuclear disarmament,

Recalling the principles and objectives for nuclear non-proliferation and disarmament adopted at the 1995 Review and Extension Conference of the Parties to the Treaty on the Non-Proliferation of Nuclear Weapons,

Emphasizing the unequivocal undertaking by the nuclear-weapon States to accomplish the total elimination of their nuclear arsenals leading to nuclear disarmament, adopted at the 2000 Review Conference of the Parties to the Treaty on the Non-Proliferation of Nuclear Weapons,

Recalling the adoption of the Comprehensive Nuclear-Test-Ban Treaty in its resolution 50/245 of 10 September 1996, and expressing its satisfaction at the increasing number of States that have signed and ratified the Treaty,

Recognizing with satisfaction that the Antarctic Treaty and the treaties of Tlatelolco, Rarotonga, Bangkok, Pelindaba and Semipalatinsk, as well as Mongolia's nuclear-weapon-free status, are gradually freeing the entire southern hemisphere and adjacent areas covered by those treaties from nuclear weapons,

Stressing the importance of strengthening all existing nuclear-related disarmament and arms control and reduction measures,

Recognizing the need for a multilaterally negotiated and legally binding instrument to assure non-nuclear-weapon States against the threat or use of nuclear weapons,

Reaffirming the central role of the Conference on Disarmament as the sole multilateral disarmament negotiating forum, and regretting the lack of progress in disarmament negotiations, particularly nuclear disarmament, in the Conference during its 2008 session,

Emphasizing the need for the Conference on Disarmament to commence negotiations on a phased programme for the complete elimination of nuclear weapons with a specified framework of time,

Expressing its regret over the failure of the 2005 Review Conference of the Parties to the Treaty on the Non-Proliferation of Nuclear Weapons to reach agreement on any substantive issues,

Expressing its deep concern at the lack of progress in the implementation of the thirteen steps to implement article VI of the Treaty on the Non-Proliferation of Nuclear Weapons agreed to at the 2000 Review Conference of the Parties to the Treaty,

Desiring to achieve the objective of a legally binding prohibition of the development, production, testing, deployment, stockpiling, threat or use of nuclear weapons and their destruction under effective international control,

Recalling the advisory opinion of the International Court of Justice on the *Legality of the Threat or Use of Nuclear Weapons*, issued on 8 July 1996,

Taking note of the relevant portions of the report of the Secretary-General relating to the implementation of resolution 62/39,

1. *Underlines once again* the unanimous conclusion of the International Court of Justice that there exists an obligation to pursue in good faith and bring to a conclusion negotiations leading to nuclear disarmament in all its aspects under strict and effective international control;

2. *Calls once again upon* all States immediately to fulfil that obligation by commencing multilateral negotiations leading to an early conclusion of a nuclear weapons convention prohibiting the development, production, testing, deployment, stockpiling, transfer, threat or use of nuclear weapons and providing for their elimination;

3. *Requests* all States to inform the Secretary-General of the efforts and measures they have taken on the implementation of the present resolution and nuclear disarmament, and requests the Secretary-General to apprise the General Assembly of that information at its sixty-fourth session;

4. *Decides* to include in the provisional agenda of its sixty-fourth session the item entitled "Follow-up to the advisory opinion of the International Court of Justice on the *Legality of the Threat or Use of Nuclear Weapons*".

RECORDED VOTE ON RESOLUTION 63/49:

In favour: Afghanistan, Algeria, Angola, Antigua and Barbuda, Argentina, Austria, Bahamas, Bahrain, Bangladesh, Barbados, Belize, Benin, Bhutan, Bolivia, Botswana, Brazil, Brunei Darussalam, Burkina Faso, Burundi, Cambodia, Cameroon, Cape Verde, Chile, China, Colombia, Comoros, Congo, Costa Rica, Côte d'Ivoire, Cuba, Democratic People's Republic of Korea, Democratic Republic of the Congo, Djibouti, Dominica, Dominican Republic, Ecuador, Egypt, El Salvador, Equatorial Guinea, Eritrea, Ethiopia, Ghana, Grenada, Guatemala, Guinea, Guinea-Bissau, Guyana, Haiti, Honduras, India, Indonesia, Iran, Iraq, Ireland, Jamaica, Jordan, Kenya, Kuwait, Lao People's Democratic Republic, Lebanon, Lesotho, Liberia, Libyan Arab Jamahiriya, Madagascar, Malawi, Malaysia, Maldives, Mali, Malta, Mauritania, Mauritius, Mexico, Mongolia, Morocco, Mozambique, Myanmar, Namibia, Nepal, New Zealand, Nicaragua, Niger, Nigeria, Oman, Pakistan, Panama, Papua New Guinea, Paraguay, Peru, Philippines, Qatar, Rwanda, Saint Lucia, Saint Vincent and the Grenadines, Samoa, San Marino, Sao Tome and Principe, Saudi Arabia, Senegal, Serbia, Singapore, Solomon Islands, South Africa, Sri Lanka, Sudan, Suriname, Swaziland, Sweden, Switzerland, Syrian Arab Republic, Thailand, Timor-Leste, Togo, Tonga, Trinidad and Tobago, Tunisia, Turkmenistan, Tuvalu, Uganda, United Arab Emirates, United Republic of Tanzania, Uruguay, Vanuatu, Venezuela, Viet Nam, Yemen, Zambia, Zimbabwe.

Against: Albania, Belgium, Bulgaria, Czech Republic, Denmark, Estonia, France, Georgia, Germany, Greece, Hungary, Iceland, Israel, Italy, Latvia, Lithuania, Luxembourg, Netherlands, Norway, Palau, Poland, Portugal, Russian Federation, Slovakia, Slovenia, Spain, The former Yugoslav Republic of Macedonia, Turkey, United Kingdom, United States.

Abstaining: Andorra, Armenia, Australia, Azerbaijan, Belarus, Bosnia and Herzegovina, Canada, Croatia, Cyprus, Finland, Japan, Kazakhstan, Kyrgyzstan, Liechtenstein, Marshall Islands, Micronesia, Moldova, Montenegro, Republic of Korea, Romania, Tajikistan, Ukraine, Uzbekistan.

Non-proliferation issues

Non-proliferation treaty

Status

In 2008, the number of States party to the 1968 Treaty on the Non-Proliferation of Nuclear Weapons (NPT) adopted by the General Assembly in resolution 2373(XXII) [YUN 1968, p. 17], remained at 190. NPT entered into force on 5 March 1970. It was extended indefinitely by Assembly resolution 50/70 in 1995 [YUN 1995, p. 189].

2010 review conference

Following the entry into force of NPT, quinquennial review conferences, as called for under article VIII, paragraph 3, of the Treaty, were held, the first one in 1975 [YUN 1975, p. 27], and the most recent in 2005 [YUN 2005, p. 597].

As decided by the NPT parties in 2007 [YUN 2007, p. 547], the Preparatory Committee for the 2010 Review Conference held its second session in 2008 (Geneva, 28 April–9 May) [NPT/CONF.2010/PC.II/13]. Participants included 106 States parties, one specialized agency, the IAEA, five intergovernmental organizations and 63 NGOs.

The Committee held 14 meetings, nine of which were devoted to a substantive discussion on three main clusters and three specific blocks of issues. The clusters dealt with implementation of the Treaty provisions related to: non-proliferation of nuclear weapons, disarmament and international peace and security; non-proliferation of nuclear weapons, safeguards and nuclear-weapon-free zones; and the inalienable right of all NPT parties to develop research, produce and use nuclear energy for peaceful purposes, without discrimination and in conformity with articles I and II. The specific blocks of issues addressed: nuclear disarmament and security assurances; regional issues, including with respect to the Middle East and the implementation of the resolution on the Middle East adopted by the 1995 Review Conference [YUN 1995, p. 189]; and other Treaty provisions, including article X. The Committee also held an interactive debate on each topic.

The Committee invited the UN Secretary-General, in consultation with the members of the Preparatory Committee, to nominate a provisional Secretary-General for the Review Conference, who would later be confirmed by the Conference itself. To promote greater financial transparency and accountability, it requested the Secretary-General to provide a financial report to the Conference as well as to each session of the Preparatory Committee.

The Committee decided to meet for its third session in New York from 4 to 15 May 2009, and that the Review Conference would be held from 26 April to 21 May 2010, also in New York.

The General Assembly, in resolution 63/58 (see p. 580), welcomed the second session of the Preparatory Committee for the 2010 Review Conference and called on the Committee, at its third session in 2009, to identify and address specific aspects where progress was required, in order to advance the objective of a nuclear-weapon-free world, building on the outcomes of the 1995 [ibid.] and 2005 [YUN 2005, p. 597] Conferences.

Non-proliferation of weapons of mass destruction

Security Council Committee on WMDs

In April, the Security Council, by resolution 1810(2008) (see below), extended until 2011 the mandate of the 1540 Committee, established in 2004 for a period of no longer than two years, with a mandate to report to the Council on the implementation of resolution 1540(2004) [YUN 2004, p. 544] concerning the non-proliferation of weapons of mass destruction (WMDS). The Committee's mandate had been extended until 2008 by resolution 1673(2006) [YUN 2006, p. 635].

In July, the Committee presented its second report (see p. 587), identifying implementation measures that States had put in place, especially since the adoption of resolution 1673(2006). New reports and information submitted by States and governmental sources since 2006 demonstrated a qualitative improvement in progress towards full implementation of resolution 1540(2004). As at November, 159 States had submitted their first national reports, and 102 States had also provided additional or updated information.

The key activities undertaken by the Committee in 2008 included examining measures taken to implement resolution 1540(2004); conducting outreach activities; developing deeper and mutually beneficial cooperation with other Security Council counter-terrorism bodies, as well as with global, regional and subregional intergovernmental organizations; and creating new tools to facilitate assistance.

The Committee Chair, members and experts participated in numerous international, regional and national workshops, conferences and seminars to advance the full implementation of Security Council resolutions 1540(2004), 1673(2006) and 1810(2008). The events addressed topics ranging from the broad challenge of preventing WMD proliferation to specific aspects of resolution 1540(2004) and included issues concerning chemical and biological weapons-related materials; the prevention of nuclear terrorism; trafficking in nuclear materials; border and export controls; brokering and financial control; and criminal law aspects of countering nuclear, chemical and biological terrorism, in light of relevant universal instruments. Some workshops addressed capacity-building and assistance as priority areas.

On 6 May [meeting 5886] and 12 November [meeting 6015], the Committee, jointly with the Counter-Terrorism Committe and the Al-Qaida and Taliban Sanctions Committee, briefed the Council on progress achieved in fulfilling their respective mandates.

SECURITY COUNCIL ACTION

On 25 April [meeting 5877] the Security Council unanimously adopted **resolution 1810(2008)**. The draft [S/2008/273] was prepared in consultations among Council members.

The Security Council,

Reaffirming its resolutions 1540(2004) of 28 April 2004 and 1673(2006) of 27 April 2006,

Reaffirming also that the proliferation of nuclear, chemical and biological weapons, as well as their means of delivery, constitutes a threat to international peace and security,

Reaffirming further the statement made by the President of the Security Council at the meeting of the Council held at the level of Heads of State and Government on 31 January 1992, including the need for all Member States to fulfil their obligations in relation to arms control and disarmament and to prevent the proliferation in all its aspects of all weapons of mass destruction,

Reaffirming that prevention of the proliferation of nuclear, chemical and biological weapons should not hamper international cooperation in materials, equipment and technology for peaceful purposes, while goals of peaceful utilization should not be used as a cover for proliferation,

Affirming its resolve to take appropriate and effective actions against any threat to international peace and security caused by the proliferation of nuclear, chemical and biological weapons and their means of delivery, in conformity with its primary responsibilities, as provided for in the Charter of the United Nations,

Reaffirming its decision that none of the obligations in resolution 1540(2004) shall be interpreted so as to conflict with or alter the rights and obligations of State parties to the Treaty on the Non-Proliferation of Nuclear Weapons, the Convention on the Prohibition of the Development, Production, Stockpiling and Use of Chemical Weapons and on Their Destruction and the Convention on the Prohibition of the Development, Production and Stockpiling of Bacteriological (Biological) and Toxin Weapons and on Their Destruction or alter the responsibilities of the International Atomic Energy Agency or the Organization for the Prohibition of Chemical Weapons,

Noting that international cooperation between States, in accordance with international law, is required to counter the illicit trafficking by non-State actors in nuclear, chemical and biological weapons, their means of delivery, and related materials,

Endorsing the work already carried out by the Security Council Committee established pursuant to resolution 1540(2004) (hereinafter "the 1540 Committee"), in accordance with its fifth programme of work,

Bearing in mind the importance of the report requested in paragraph 6 of resolution 1673(2006),

Noting that not all States have presented to the 1540 Committee their national reports on implementation of resolution 1540(2004), and that the full implementation of resolution 1540(2004) by all States, including the adoption of national laws and measures to ensure implementation of these laws, is a long-term task that will require continuous efforts at the national, regional and international levels,

Recognizing, in that regard, the importance of dialogue between the 1540 Committee and Member States, and stressing that direct contact is an effective means of such dialogue,

Recognizing also the need to enhance the coordination of efforts at the national, subregional, regional and international levels, as appropriate, in order to strengthen a global response to this serious challenge and threat to international security,

Emphasizing, in that regard, the importance of providing States, in response to their requests, with effective assistance that meets their needs, and stressing the importance of ensuring that the clearing-house function for assistance is efficient and accessible,

Taking note of international efforts towards full implementation of resolution 1540(2004), including on preventing the financing of proliferation-related activities, taking into consideration the guidance of the framework of the Financial Action Task Force,

Acting under Chapter VII of the Charter,

1. *Reiterates* its decisions taken in, and the requirements of, resolution 1540(2004), and emphasizes the importance for all States to implement fully that resolution;

2. *Again calls upon* all States that have not yet presented a first report on steps they have taken or intend to take to implement resolution 1540(2004) to submit such a report to the 1540 Committee without delay;

3. *Encourages* all States that have submitted such reports to provide, at any time or upon the request of the 1540 Committee, additional information on their implementation of resolution 1540(2004);

4. *Encourages* all States to prepare on a voluntary basis summary action plans, with the assistance of the 1540 Committee as appropriate, mapping out their priorities and plans for implementing the key provisions of resolution 1540(2004), and to submit those plans to the 1540 Committee;

5. *Encourages* States that have requests for assistance to convey them to the 1540 Committee, and encourages them to make use of the 1540 Committee's assistance template to that effect; urges States and international, regional and subregional organizations to inform the 1540 Committee, as appropriate, by 25 June 2008 of areas in which they are able to provide assistance; and calls upon States and such organizations, if they have not done so previously, to provide the 1540 Committee with a point of contact for assistance by 25 June 2008;

6. *Decides* to extend the mandate of the 1540 Committee for a period of three years, with the continued assistance of experts, until 25 April 2011;

7. *Requests* the 1540 Committee to complete its report, as set out in paragraph 6 of resolution 1673(2006), and to submit it to the Security Council as soon as possible but no later than 31 July 2008;

8. *Also requests* the 1540 Committee to consider a comprehensive review of the status of implementation of resolution 1540(2004) and to report to the Council on its consideration of the matter no later than 31 January 2009;

9. *Decides* that the 1540 Committee shall submit an annual programme of work to the Council before the end of January of each year;

10. *Also decides* that the 1540 Committee shall continue to intensify its efforts to promote the full implementation by all States of resolution 1540(2004), through its programme of work, which includes the compilation of information on the status of implementation by States of all aspects of resolution 1540(2004), outreach, dialogue, assistance and cooperation, and which addresses, in particular, all aspects of paragraphs 1 and 2 of that resolution, as well as of paragraph 3, which encompasses *(a)* accountability, *(b)* physical protection, *(c)* border controls and law enforcement efforts, and *(d)* national export and trans-shipment controls, including controls on providing funds and services, such as financing, to such export and trans-shipment;

11. *Further decides*, in that regard:

(a) To encourage the pursuit of the ongoing dialogue between the 1540 Committee and States on their further actions to implement fully resolution 1540(2004) and on technical assistance needed and offered;

(b) To request the 1540 Committee to continue to organize and participate in outreach events at the regional, subregional and, as appropriate, national levels promoting the implementation by States of resolution 1540(2004);

(c) To urge the 1540 Committee to continue strengthening its role in facilitating technical assistance for the implementation of resolution 1540(2004), including by engaging actively in matching offers and requests for assistance through such means as assistance templates, action plans or other information submitted to the 1540 Committee;

(d) To encourage the 1540 Committee to engage actively with States and relevant international, regional and subregional organizations to promote the sharing of experience and lessons learned in the areas covered by resolution 1540(2004), and to liaise on the availability of programmes which might facilitate the implementation of resolution 1540(2004);

(e) To request the 1540 Committee to provide opportunities for interaction with interested States and relevant international, regional and subregional organizations to promote the implementation of resolution 1540(2004);

12. *Reiterates* the need to enhance ongoing cooperation between the 1540 Committee, the Security Council Committee established pursuant to resolution 1267(1999) concerning Al-Qaida and the Taliban and associated individuals and entities, and the Security Council Committee established pursuant to resolution 1373(2001) concerning counter-terrorism, including through, as appropriate, en-

hanced information-sharing, coordination on visits to countries, within their respective mandates, technical assistance and other issues of relevance to all three Committees, and expresses its intention to provide guidance to the Committees on areas of common interest in order better to coordinate their efforts;

13. *Urges* the 1540 Committee to encourage and take full advantage of voluntary financial contributions to assist States in identifying and addressing their needs for the implementation of resolution 1540(2004), and requests the 1540 Committee to consider options for developing and making more effective existing funding mechanisms and to report to the Council on its consideration of the matter no later than 31 December 2008;

14. *Decides* that the 1540 Committee shall submit to the Council no later than 24 April 2011 a report on compliance with resolution 1540(2004) through the achievement of the implementation of its requirements;

15. *Also decides* to remain seized of the matter.

Implementation report. In July [S/2008/493], the Committee on WMDS reported on its work to promote full implementation of Council resolution 1540(2004) by Member States.

Since the extension of its mandate in 2006, the Committee had held formal and informal meetings, as well as informal consultations. Its three sub-committees, established in 2004 [YUN 2004, p. 545], held meetings to consider national reports and additional information submitted by States. The Committee continued to be assisted by experts who received substantive and logistical support from UNODA.

In September 2007, the Committee had adopted its sixth programme of work, for the period from 1 October 2007 to 27 April 2008, which represented a continuation of the fifth programme with the addition of the preparation of the Committee's report on the second biennium of its work. In October and November 2007, the Committee had sent letters to all 192 Member States, each of them accompanied by a matrix prepared by the Committee's experts, reminding them to submit reports or provide up-to-date information on further steps they had taken or planned to take to achieve full implementation of resolution 1540(2004). As at 1 July 2008, 103 States had responded and the total number of States having submitted at least one report since 2004 stood at 155, with one organization also having reported. Of those States that had submitted first reports, 102 provided additional information.

The Committee believed that it had made considerable progress with regard to implementation of resolution 1540(2004), assisting the Council in implementation monitoring through: the examination of relevant measures taken by Member States; the organization of intensive outreach activities; the development of deeper and mutually beneficial cooperation with other Council counter-terrorism bodies, as well as with global, regional and subregional intergovernmental organizations; the creation of new tools to facilitate assistance and transparency; and the enhancement of dialogue with individual States. The Committee futher believed that those activities had substantially raised the awareness of the international community about the dangers associated with the potential nexus between the proliferation of WMDS, their means of delivery and related materials, and non-State actors. Since the adoption of Council resolution 1673(2006), the Committee had sought to facilitate Member States' efforts to prepare to address that nexus.

The Committee identified specific measures that States had in place to implement resolution 1540(2004), including steps they had taken since April 2006. Those measures ranged from developing new institutional means to incorporate the obligations from the resolution into national practices to adopting new legislation and enforcement measures, executing new policies and creating new assistance programmes geared towards resolution implementation.

Notwithstanding the progress made, the Committee concluded that Member States needed to do far more. Consequently, achieving the resolution goals required further attention by the Council and more intensive action, particularly on capacity-building and sharing lessons learned. Among other recommendations, the Committee believed that, consistent with resolution 1810(2008), it should strengthen its clearing-house role for channelling assistance to States in need; increase tailored dialogue with and among States to identify assistance needs and projects to meet them; and promote awareness of, make better use of and consider options for developing funding mechanisms in order to build capacity for implementation. To those ends, it should work more closely with global and regional intergovernmental organizations and arrangements, within and outside the UN system, to foster experience-sharing, create discussion forums and develop innovative mechanisms to achieve implementation.

The Committee Chair presented the Committee's report to the Security Council on 18 August [meeting 5955].

Communications. By a letter of 26 December [S/2008/821], the Chair of the Committee on WMDS informed the Security Council President that the Committee had initiated a discussion on options for developing and making more effective the existing funding mechanisms for the implementation of resolution 1540(2004).

By a communication of the same date [S/2008/820], the Secretary-General informed the Council President that on 19 December, the Committee had approved the recruitment of three new experts to the group of experts assisting the Committee, effective 1 April 2009.

By a letter of 24 October to the First Committee Chairperson [A/C.1/63/9], Ecuador expressed concern at a publication sponsored by the United Nations Institute for Disarmament Research, entitled *Implementing Resolution 1540: the Role of Regional Organizations*, which had been presented to Member States during an event on 22 October. The chapter referring to the resolution's implementation in Latin America and the role of the Organization of American States allegedly contained errors, outdated information and a baseless statement about the status of implementation by certain regional States. Such occurrences in no way contributed to the efforts being made by all countries of Latin America and the Caribbean to ensure the full implementation. Similar sentiments were voiced by Cuba [A/C.1/63/7].

New types of WMDs

The issue of radiological weapons had been on the Conference on Disarmament agenda since 1979. In accordance with the joint initiative by the 2008 Presidents, and under the guidance of the Coordinator (Bulgaria), the Conference [A/63/27] held three informal meetings on 13 and 29 February and on 7 August on "New types of WMDs and new systems of such weapons; radiological weapons".

During the discussions, delegations validated the outcome of the 2007 Conference meetings on the subject [YUN 2007, p. 550]. While a number of delegations underscored the continued relevance of that agenda item, particularly considering the threat of dirty bombs by non-State actors, most agreed that it was not a key issue and that priority should be given to the core issues on the agenda. Consequently, no specific issues or new proposals were raised during the proceedings in 2008.

GENERAL ASSEMBLY ACTION

On 2 December [meeting 61], the General Assembly, on the recommendation of the First Committee [A/63/382], adopted **resolution 63/36** by recorded vote (175-1-1) [agenda item 82].

Prohibition of the development and manufacture of new types of weapons of mass destruction and new systems of such weapons: report of the Conference on Disarmament

The General Assembly,

Recalling its previous resolutions on the prohibition of the development and manufacture of new types of weapons of mass destruction and new systems of such weapons,

Recalling also its resolutions 51/37 of 10 December 1996, 54/44 of 1 December 1999, 57/50 of 22 November 2002 and 60/46 of 8 December 2005 relating to the prohibition of the development and manufacture of new types of weapons of mass destruction and new systems of such weapons,

Recalling further paragraph 77 of the Final Document of the Tenth Special Session of the General Assembly,

Determined to prevent the emergence of new types of weapons of mass destruction that have characteristics comparable in destructive effect to those of weapons of mass destruction identified in the definition of weapons of mass destruction adopted by the United Nations in 1948,

Noting the desirability of keeping the matter under review, as appropriate,

1. *Reaffirms* that effective measures should be taken to prevent the emergence of new types of weapons of mass destruction;

2. *Requests* the Conference on Disarmament, without prejudice to further overview of its agenda, to keep the matter under review, as appropriate, with a view to making, when necessary, recommendations on undertaking specific negotiations on identified types of such weapons;

3. *Calls upon* all States, immediately following any recommendations of the Conference on Disarmament, to give favourable consideration to those recommendations;

4. *Requests* the Secretary-General to transmit to the Conference on Disarmament all documents relating to the consideration of this item by the General Assembly at its sixty-third session;

5. *Requests* the Conference on Disarmament to report the results of any consideration of the matter in its annual reports to the General Assembly;

6. *Decides* to include in the provisional agenda of its sixty-sixth session the item entitled "Prohibition of the development and manufacture of new types of weapons of mass destruction and new systems of such weapons: report of the Conference on Disarmament".

RECORDED VOTE ON RESOLUTION 63/36:

In favour: Afghanistan, Albania, Algeria, Andorra, Angola, Antigua and Barbuda, Argentina, Armenia, Australia, Austria, Azerbaijan, Bahamas, Bahrain, Bangladesh, Barbados, Belarus, Belgium, Belize, Benin, Bhutan, Bolivia, Bosnia and Herzegovina, Botswana, Brazil, Brunei Darussalam, Bulgaria, Burkina Faso, Burundi, Cambodia, Cameroon, Canada, Cape Verde, Chile, China, Colombia, Comoros, Congo, Costa Rica, Côte d'Ivoire, Croatia, Cuba, Cyprus, Czech Republic, Democratic People's Republic of Korea, Democratic Republic of the Congo, Denmark, Djibouti, Dominican Republic, Ecuador, Egypt, El Salvador, Equatorial Guinea, Eritrea, Estonia, Ethiopia, Finland, France, Gabon, Georgia, Germany, Ghana, Greece, Grenada, Guatemala, Guinea, Guinea-Bissau, Guyana, Haiti, Honduras, Hungary, Iceland, India, Indonesia, Iran, Iraq, Ireland, Italy, Jamaica, Japan, Jordan, Kazakhstan, Kenya, Kuwait, Kyrgyzstan, Lao People's Democratic Republic, Latvia, Lebanon, Lesotho, Liberia, Libyan Arab Jamahiriya, Liechtenstein, Lithuania, Luxembourg, Madagascar, Malawi, Malaysia, Maldives, Mali, Malta, Marshall Islands, Mauritania, Mauritius, Mexico, Micronesia, Moldova, Monaco, Mongolia, Montenegro, Morocco, Mozambique, Myanmar, Namibia, Nepal, Netherlands, New Zealand, Nicaragua, Niger, Nigeria, Norway, Oman, Pakistan, Palau, Panama, Papua New Guinea, Paraguay, Peru, Philippines, Poland, Portugal, Qatar, Republic of Korea, Romania, Russian Federation, Rwanda, Saint Lucia, Samoa, San Marino, Sao Tome and

Principe, Saudi Arabia, Senegal, Serbia, Singapore, Slovakia, Slovenia, Solomon Islands, South Africa, Spain, Sri Lanka, Sudan, Suriname, Swaziland, Sweden, Switzerland, Syrian Arab Republic, Tajikistan, Thailand, The former Yugoslav Republic of Macedonia, Timor-Leste, Togo, Trinidad and Tobago, Tunisia, Turkey, Turkmenistan, Tuvalu, Ukraine, United Arab Emirates, United Kingdom, United Republic of Tanzania, Uruguay, Uzbekistan, Venezuela, Viet Nam, Yemen, Zambia, Zimbabwe.

Against: United States.

Abstaining: Israel.

Terrorism and WMDs

During the year, the United Nations continued to promote international action against terrorism through collaborative efforts with Member States and regional and international organizations, and through the work of the Counter-Terrorism Committee (see p. 70) and the Al-Qaida and Taliban Sanctions Committee (see p. 376). In combating terrorism, the Committee on WMDS worked with those bodies, and on 6 May [meeting 5886] and 12 November [meeting 6015], the three Committees jointly briefed the Security Council on progress achieved in fulfilling their mandates. The Council, in **resolution 1805(2008)** of 20 March (see p. 71), reiterated the need to enhance ongoing cooperation among the three bodies regarding non-proliferation of nuclear, chemical and biological weapons and their means of delivery, as well as their respective groups of experts, through information-sharing, coordinated visits to countries, technical assistance and other relevant issues.

Report of Secretary-General. Pursuant to General Assembly resolution 62/33 [YUN 2007, p. 551], the Secretary-General, in a July report [A/63/153], presented the views of 10 Member States and 11 international organizations, including UN agencies, on measures they reported on preventing terrorists from acquiring WMDS, their means of delivery, and related materials and technologies.

IAEA action. During the year, IAEA continued to emphasize the need to advance Member States' capacity to tackle potential threats associated with nuclear terrorism. On 4 October [GC/52/RES/10], the IAEA General Conference, in a resolution on measures to protect against nuclear terrorism, invited all States to consider the potential danger of illicit trafficking of nuclear and other radioactive material across their borders and within their countries, and welcomed the Agency's activities in support of States' efforts to enhance nuclear security worldwide.

GENERAL ASSEMBLY ACTION

On 2 December [meeting 61], on the recommendation of the First Committee [A/63/389], the General Assembly adopted **resolution 63/60** without vote [agenda item 89 *(r)*].

Measures to prevent terrorists from acquiring weapons of mass destruction

The General Assembly,

Recalling its resolution 62/33 of 5 December 2007,

Recognizing the determination of the international community to combat terrorism, as evidenced in relevant General Assembly and Security Council resolutions,

Deeply concerned by the growing risk of linkages between terrorism and weapons of mass destruction, and in particular by the fact that terrorists may seek to acquire weapons of mass destruction,

Cognizant of the steps taken by States to implement Security Council resolution 1540(2004) on the non-proliferation of weapons of mass destruction, adopted on 28 April 2004,

Welcoming the entry into force on 7 July 2007 of the International Convention for the Suppression of Acts of Nuclear Terrorism,

Welcoming also the adoption, by consensus, of amendments to strengthen the Convention on the Physical Protection of Nuclear Material by the International Atomic Energy Agency on 8 July 2005,

Noting the support expressed in the Final Document of the Fourteenth Conference of Heads of State or Government of Non-Aligned Countries, which was held in Havana on 15 and 16 September 2006 for measures to prevent terrorists from acquiring weapons of mass destruction,

Noting also that the Group of Eight, the European Union, the Regional Forum of the Association of Southeast Asian Nations and others have taken into account in their deliberations the dangers posed by the likely acquisition by terrorists of weapons of mass destruction, and the need for international cooperation in combating it,

Noting further the Global Initiative to Combat Nuclear Terrorism, launched jointly by the Russian Federation and the United States of America,

Acknowledging the consideration of issues relating to terrorism and weapons of mass destruction by the Advisory Board on Disarmament Matters,

Taking note of the relevant resolutions adopted by the General Conference of the International Atomic Energy Agency at its fifty-second regular session,

Taking note also of the 2005 World Summit Outcome adopted on 16 September 2005 at the High-level Plenary Meeting of the sixtieth session of the General Assembly and the adoption on 8 September 2006 of the United Nations Global Counter-Terrorism Strategy,

Taking note further of the report of the Secretary-General submitted pursuant to paragraphs 3 and 5 of resolution 62/33,

Mindful of the urgent need for addressing, within the United Nations framework and through international cooperation, this threat to humanity,

Emphasizing that progress is urgently needed in the area of disarmament and non-proliferation in order to maintain international peace and security and to contribute to global efforts against terrorism,

1. *Calls upon* all Member States to support international efforts to prevent terrorists from acquiring weapons of mass destruction and their means of delivery;

2. *Appeals* to all Member States to consider early accession to and ratification of the International Convention for the Suppression of Acts of Nuclear Terrorism;

3. *Urges* all Member States to take and strengthen national measures, as appropriate, to prevent terrorists from acquiring weapons of mass destruction, their means of delivery and materials and technologies related to their manufacture;

4. *Encourages* cooperation among and between Member States and relevant regional and international organizations for strengthening national capacities in this regard;

5. *Requests* the Secretary-General to compile a report on measures already taken by international organizations on issues relating to the linkage between the fight against terrorism and the proliferation of weapons of mass destruction and to seek the views of Member States on additional relevant measures, including national measures, for tackling the global threat posed by the acquisition by terrorists of weapons of mass destruction and to report to the General Assembly at its sixty-fourth session;

6. *Decides* to include in the provisional agenda of its sixty-fourth session the item entitled "Measures to prevent terrorists from acquiring weapons of mass destruction".

Multilateralism in disarmament and non-proliferation

Given the multifaceted challenges confronting international disarmament and non-proliferation, the United Nations continued in 2008 to reinforce and strengthen multilateralism as the core principle in addressing those issues.

The Secretary-General, with the support of the High Representative on Disarmament and UNODA, remained committed to revitalizing the international disarmament agenda, as well as the effectiveness of the United Nations in that area. He continued to play a large role in promoting and supporting multilateral efforts to strengthen the implementation of existing multilateral disarmament, non-proliferation and arms limitation agreements, and encouraged new inclusive, complementary and mutually reinforcing initiatives. Under the leadership of the High Representative for Disarmament, UNODA enhanced its engagement and cooperation with Member States, intergovernmental organizations and civil society.

At its Fifteenth Ministerial Conference (Tehran, Iran, 27–30 July), the Non-Aligned Movement (NAM) underlined multilateralism and multilaterally agreed solutions, in accordance with the UN Charter, as the only sustainable method of addressing disarmament and international security issues.

Reports of Secretary-General. In his annual report to the General Assembly on the work of the Organization [A/63/1], the Secretary-General noted that the risks inherent in the existence of WMDs, especially nuclear weapons, were universally recognized. Though welcoming recent initiatives aimed at achieving a world free of nuclear weapons, as well as reductions of nuclear arsenals and reduced reliance on nuclear weapons, he stressed that further reductions in strategic and non-strategic stockpiles, greater transparency, de-alerting and a diminished role for nuclear weapons in security policies were needed.

Noting that the year 2008 marked the fortieth anniversary of the opening for signature of the NPT, the Secretary-General said that the Treaty must be strengthened and trust in it be rebuilt, as part of a broader process of reaffirming the rule of law as well as the importance of multilateralism.

The Secretary-General was encouraged by the continued determination and efforts by States to bring the CTBT into force as soon as possible and was pleased to report progress in the implementation of the Convention on the Prohibition of the Development, Production and Stockpiling of Bacteriological (Biological) and Toxin Weapons and on Their Destruction (see p. 604). The Secretary-General noted that efforts continued in the Conference on Disarmament to overcome the long-standing deadlock over its priorities. In January, he had urged Members to forestall arms races, reduce tensions and free resources for achieving the Millennium Development Goals. Successful negotiations on a fissile material ban and substantive discussions on preventing the placement of weapons in outer space, nuclear disarmament and security assurances depended on high-level leadership and political support. Controlling conventional weapons remained central to UN disarmament efforts, the Secretary-General asserted, and strong calls to address the humanitarian impact of cluster munitions had been answered with the adoption in May of the Convention on Cluster Munitions (see p. 623).

According to the Secretary-General, the revitalization of multilateral disarmament efforts was within reach. Full implementation of multilateral disarmament and non-proliferation arrangements and the achievement of their universality remained a major challenge. Strengthening regional mechanisms and developing effective partnerships, in accordance with Chapter VIII of the UN Charter, would help bolster progress and unlock the disarmament stalemate.

Pursuant to General Assembly resolution 62/27 [YUN 2007, p. 553], the Secretary-General, in a July report [A/63/126], presented replies received from five Member States (Cuba, the Netherlands, Panama, Qatar, Spain) on the promotion of multilateralism in the area of disarmament and non-proliferation.

The Security Council, in presidential statement S/PRST/2008/43, of 19 November (see p. 592), stressed the importance of a multilateral system to better address, in accordance with international law, the multifaceted and interconnected challenges and threats confronting the world. It expressed its support for multilateralism as one of the most important means for resolving security concerns in accordance with international law.

GENERAL ASSEMBLY ACTION

On 2 December [meeting 61], the General Assembly, on the recommendation of the First Committee [A/63/389], adopted **resolution 63/50** by recorded vote (126-5-50) [agenda item 89 *(m)*].

Promotion of multilateralism in the area of disarmament and non-proliferation

The General Assembly,

Determined to foster strict respect for the purposes and principles enshrined in the Charter of the United Nations,

Recalling its resolution 56/24 T of 29 November 2001 on multilateral cooperation in the area of disarmament and non-proliferation and global efforts against terrorism and other relevant resolutions, as well as its resolutions 57/63 of 22 November 2002, 58/44 of 8 December 2003, 59/69 of 3 December 2004, 60/59 of 8 December 2005, 61/62 of 6 December 2006 and 62/27 of 5 December 2007 on the promotion of multilateralism in the area of disarmament and non-proliferation,

Recalling also the purpose of the United Nations to maintain international peace and security and, to that end, to take effective collective measures for the prevention and removal of threats to the peace and for the suppression of acts of aggression or other breaches of the peace, and to bring about by peaceful means, and in conformity with the principles of justice and international law, adjustment or settlement of international disputes or situations which might lead to a breach of the peace, as enshrined in the Charter,

Recalling further the United Nations Millennium Declaration, which states, inter alia, that the responsibility for managing worldwide economic and social development, as well as threats to international peace and security, must be shared among the nations of the world and should be exercised multilaterally and that, as the most universal and most representative organization in the world, the United Nations must play the central role,

Convinced that, in the globalization era and with the information revolution, arms regulation, non-proliferation and disarmament problems are more than ever the concern of all countries in the world, which are affected in one way or another by these problems and, therefore, should have the possibility to participate in the negotiations that arise to tackle them,

Bearing in mind the existence of a broad structure of disarmament and arms regulation agreements resulting from non-discriminatory and transparent multilateral negotiations with the participation of a large number of countries, regardless of their size and power,

Aware of the need to advance further in the field of arms regulation, non-proliferation and disarmament on the basis of universal, multilateral, non-discriminatory and transparent negotiations with the goal of reaching general and complete disarmament under strict international control,

Recognizing the complementarity of bilateral, plurilateral and multilateral negotiations on disarmament,

Recognizing also that the proliferation and development of weapons of mass destruction, including nuclear weapons, are among the most immediate threats to international peace and security which need to be dealt with, with the highest priority,

Considering that the multilateral disarmament agreements provide the mechanism for States parties to consult one another and to cooperate in solving any problems which may arise in relation to the objective of, or in the application of, the provisions of the agreements and that such consultations and cooperation may also be undertaken through appropriate international procedures within the framework of the United Nations and in accordance with the Charter,

Stressing that international cooperation, the peaceful settlement of disputes, dialogue and confidence-building measures would contribute essentially to the creation of multilateral and bilateral friendly relations among peoples and nations,

Being concerned at the continuous erosion of multilateralism in the field of arms regulation, non-proliferation and disarmament, and recognizing that a resort to unilateral actions by Member States in resolving their security concerns would jeopardize international peace and security and undermine confidence in the international security system as well as the foundations of the United Nations itself,

Noting that the Fourteenth Conference of Heads of State or Government of Non-Aligned Countries, held in Havana on 15 and 16 September 2006, and the Fifteenth Ministerial Conference of the Movement of Non-Aligned Countries, held in Tehran on 29 and 30 July 2008, welcomed, respectively, the adoption of General Assembly resolutions 60/59 and 62/27 on the promotion of multilateralism in the area of disarmament and non-proliferation, and underlined the fact that multilateralism and multilaterally agreed solutions, in accordance with the Charter, provide the only sustainable method of addressing disarmament and international security issues,

Reaffirming the absolute validity of multilateral diplomacy in the field of disarmament and non-proliferation, and determined to promote multilateralism as an essential way to develop arms regulation and disarmament negotiations,

1. *Reaffirms* multilateralism as the core principle in negotiations in the area of disarmament and non-proliferation with a view to maintaining and strengthening universal norms and enlarging their scope;

2. *Also reaffirms* multilateralism as the core principle in resolving disarmament and non-proliferation concerns;

3. *Urges* the participation of all interested States in multilateral negotiations on arms regulation, non-proliferation and disarmament in a non-discriminatory and transparent manner;

4. *Underlines* the importance of preserving the existing agreements on arms regulation and disarmament, which constitute an expression of the results of international cooperation and multilateral negotiations in response to the challenges facing mankind;

5. *Calls once again upon* all Member States to renew and fulfil their individual and collective commitments to multilateral cooperation as an important means of pursuing and achieving their common objectives in the area of disarmament and non-proliferation;

6. *Requests* the States parties to the relevant instruments on weapons of mass destruction to consult and cooperate among themselves in resolving their concerns with regard to cases of non-compliance as well as on implementation, in accordance with the procedures defined in those instruments, and to refrain from resorting or threatening to resort to unilateral actions or directing unverified non-compliance accusations against one another to resolve their concerns;

7. *Takes note* of the report of the Secretary-General containing the replies of Member States on the promotion of multilateralism in the area of disarmament and non-proliferation, submitted pursuant to resolution 62/27;

8. *Requests* the Secretary-General to seek the views of Member States on the issue of the promotion of multilateralism in the area of disarmament and non-proliferation and to submit a report thereon to the General Assembly at its sixty-fourth session;

9. *Decides* to include in the provisional agenda of its sixty-fourth session the item entitled "Promotion of multilateralism in the area of disarmament and non-proliferation".

RECORDED VOTE ON RESOLUTION 63/50:

In favour: Afghanistan, Algeria, Angola, Antigua and Barbuda, Argentina, Azerbaijan, Bahamas, Bahrain, Bangladesh, Barbados, Belarus, Belize, Benin, Bhutan, Bolivia, Botswana, Brazil, Brunei Darussalam, Burkina Faso, Burundi, Cambodia, Cameroon, Cape Verde, Chile, China, Colombia, Comoros, Congo, Costa Rica, Côte d'Ivoire, Cuba, Democratic People's Republic of Korea, Democratic Republic of the Congo, Djibouti, Dominica, Dominican Republic, Ecuador, Egypt, El Salvador, Equatorial Guinea, Eritrea, Ethiopia, Ghana, Grenada, Guatemala, Guinea, Guinea-Bissau, Guyana, Haiti, Honduras, India, Indonesia, Iran, Iraq, Jamaica, Jordan, Kazakhstan, Kenya, Kuwait, Kyrgyzstan, Lao People's Democratic Republic, Lebanon, Lesotho, Liberia, Libyan Arab Jamahiriya, Madagascar, Malawi, Malaysia, Maldives, Mali, Marshall Islands, Mauritania, Mauritius, Mexico, Mongolia, Morocco, Mozambique, Myanmar, Namibia, Nepal, Nicaragua, Niger, Nigeria, Oman, Pakistan, Panama, Papua New Guinea, Paraguay, Peru, Philippines, Qatar, Russian Federation, Rwanda, Saint Lucia, Saint Vincent and the Grenadines, Sao Tome and Principe, Saudi Arabia, Senegal, Singapore, Solomon Islands, South Africa, Sri Lanka, Sudan, Suriname, Swaziland, Syrian Arab Republic, Tajikistan, Thailand, Timor-Leste, Togo, Tonga, Trinidad and Tobago, Tunisia, Turkmenistan, Tuvalu, Uganda, United Arab Emirates, United Republic of Tanzania, Uruguay, Uzbekistan, Vanuatu, Venezuela, Viet Nam, Yemen, Zambia, Zimbabwe.

Against: Israel, Micronesia, Palau, United Kingdom, United States.

Abstaining: Albania, Andorra, Armenia, Australia, Austria, Belgium, Bosnia and Herzegovina, Bulgaria, Canada, Croatia, Cyprus, Czech Republic, Denmark, Estonia, Finland, France, Georgia, Germany, Greece, Hungary, Iceland, Ireland, Italy, Japan, Latvia, Liechtenstein, Lithuania, Luxembourg, Malta, Moldova, Monaco, Montenegro, Netherlands, New Zealand, Norway, Poland, Portugal, Republic of Korea, Romania, Samoa, San Marino, Serbia, Slovakia, Slovenia, Spain, Sweden, Switzerland, The former Yugoslav Republic of Macedonia, Turkey, Ukraine.

Collective security through regulation and reduction of armaments

Communication. In a concept paper on strengthening collective security through general regulation and reduction of armaments [S/2008/697], submitted to the Security Council on 10 November, Costa Rica said that in the context of the challenges and opportunities of the twenty-first century, the regulation and limitation of armaments should be understood as one element of the broader and more comprehensive design for the maintenance of peace and security, and should be seen as part of the toolkit the United Nations had at its disposal to enhance the stability of international relations, development and the peaceful settlement of disputes. Another means to help prevent conflict was an enhanced system of regional arrangements, duly coordinated and supported by the United Nations.

Security Council consideration. On 19 November [meeting 6017], the Security Council held an open debate on the item "Maintenance of international peace and security: strengthening collective security through general regulation and reduction of armaments", based on Costa Rica's proposal. The meeting was presided over by the President of Costa Rica, Óscar Arias Sánchez, who noted that it would focus on Article 26 of the UN Charter, which gave the Council the responsibility to promote peace and security with the least diversion of resources for armaments by formulating plans for a system for the regulation of armaments. He underlined that the time had come to recognize the link between the waste of resources devoted to arms and the need for resources for development.

Addressing the Council, the High Representative for Disarmament Affairs read a statement by the Secretary-General stressing that the strengthening of collective security could build trust between States and pave the way for agreements and cooperation in other fields.

SECURITY COUNCIL ACTION

On 19 November [meeting 6017], following consultations among Security Council members, the President made statement **S/PRST/2008/43** on behalf of the Council:

The Security Council recalls its primary responsibility under the Charter of the United Nations for the maintenance of international peace and security.

The Council remains convinced of the necessity to strengthen international peace and security through, inter alia, disarmament, non-proliferation and arms control. It considers that the regulation and reduction of armaments and armed forces, as appropriate, constitutes one of the most important measures to promote international peace and security with the least diversion of the world's human and economic resources.

The Council notes the importance of collective security and its impact on disarmament and development, and stresses its concern at increasing global military expenditure.

The Council stresses the importance of appropriate levels of military expenditure, in order to achieve undiminished security for all at the lowest appropriate level of armaments. It urges all States to devote as many resources as possible to economic and social development, in particular in the fight against poverty and the achievement of the Millennium Development Goals.

The Council affirms the 2005 World Summit Outcome, in which Heads of State and Government recognized that development, peace and security and human rights are interlinked and mutually reinforcing.

The Council stresses the vital importance of an effective multilateral system to better address, in accordance with international law, the multifaceted and interconnected challenges and threats confronting our world and to achieve progress in the areas of peace and security, development and human rights, which are the pillars of the United Nations system and the foundations for collective security and well-being. It also expresses its support for multilateralism as one of the most important means for resolving security concerns in accordance with international law.

The Council expresses its support for national, bilateral, regional and multilateral measures adopted by Governments aimed at reducing military expenditure, where appropriate, thereby contributing to strengthening regional and international peace and security.

The Council underlines the importance of promoting norm-setting in accordance with international law, as part of the efforts to strengthen non-proliferation, disarmament and arms control measures, as well as the importance of compliance with and reinforcing of the existing agreements, conventions and treaties which relate to these matters and international peace and security.

The Council reiterates that cooperation with regional and subregional organizations in matters relating to the maintenance of peace and security and consistent with Chapter VIII of the Charter can improve collective security and therefore should be continuously strengthened. In this regard, it underlines the importance of strengthening the capacity of such organizations in conflict prevention, crisis management, armaments control and in supporting States recovering from conflict and laying the foundation for sustainable peace and development.

The Council recalls the obligation of all States to accept and carry out its decisions in accordance with Article 25 of the Charter and affirms its commitment to continue monitoring and promoting the effective implementation of its decisions, in order to avoid conflict, promote and maintain international peace and security and further confidence in collective security.

The Council calls upon Member States, regional and subregional organizations, the Secretariat and the competent United Nations funds and programmes, as appropriate, to make further efforts to preserve, facilitate, develop and strengthen international and regional cooperation in the areas of arms control, non-proliferation and disarmament, through, inter alia, further implementation, development and strengthening of relevant agreements and instruments.

The Council intends to continue following this issue.

International Atomic Energy Agency

The International Atomic Energy Agency (IAEA) continued to serve as the focal point for worldwide cooperation in the peaceful uses of nuclear technology; for promoting global nuclear safety and security; and, through its verification activities, for assuring compliance with international obligations to use nuclear material and facilities for peaceful purposes. Accordingly, the fifty-second session of the IAEA General Conference (Vienna, 29 September–4 October) adopted resolutions on measures to strengthen international cooperation in nuclear, radiation, transport and waste safety; nuclear security; strengthening the Agency's technical cooperation activities; strengthening activities related to nuclear science, technology and application; strengthening the effectiveness and improving the efficiency of the safeguards system and application of the Model Additional Protocol; and implementation of the NPT safeguards agreement between the Agency and the Democratic People's Republic of Korea (DPRK) and of IAEA safeguards in the Middle East.

The General Assembly, in **resolution 63/6** (see p. 1138), took note of the IAEA's 2007 annual report.

IAEA activities

In its 2008 annual report [GC(53)/7], the Agency detailed its activities during the year. With projections of future growth of nuclear power revised upward, the Agency continued to facilitate coordination and information-sharing in the area of technology innovation and development. Specifically, it compiled the expectations of developing countries in the form of "common user considerations" for appropriate designs to be developed in the near future. Six countries completed assessments of innovative nuclear systems using the evaluation methodology developed by the Agency's International Project on Innovative Nuclear Reactors and Fuel Cycles, and a group of eight countries completed a similar joint study, the results of which would be used to update the methodology.

There were a number of positive responses to the Director General's proposal to establish a nuclear fuel reserve of last resort, under Agency auspices, in the event of supply disruptions. Also, progress was made on other proposals related to assurances of fuel supply by Member States.

The growing interest among Member States in starting nuclear power programmes was reflected in a larger number of requests for IAEA assistance in analysing energy options and in preparing for the introduction of nuclear power. With more than 50 Member States expressing interest in considering the introduction of nuclear power, the number of approved technical cooperation projects on analysing energy options went up from 29 in 2006–2007 to 41 in 2008, while the number of projects on considering the introduction of nuclear power increased from 13 to 44 during the same period. The Agency conducted four missions in 2008—to the Cooperation Council for the Arab States of the Gulf, Nigeria, the Philippines and the Sudan—to advise on their consideration of nuclear power. In December, the Agency introduced a new Integrated Nuclear Infrastructure Review service to assist States in adopting a comprehensive and integrated approach to the introduction of nuclear power. In addition, the Agency published *Evaluation of the Status of National Nuclear Infrastructure Development* and held a workshop to discuss the evaluation guidance.

There was an increased demand for IAEA assistance in assessing national and regional energy systems and energy strategies; its analytical tools were being used by 115 Member States and six international organizations. During the year, the Agency trained 402 energy analysts and planners from 58 countries in the use of the analytical tools. To meet the increased demand for training, the Agency introduced "technology supported learning" and used the cyber platforms of the Asian Network for Education in Nuclear Technology and the Latin American Energy Organization.

The Agency provided training, assistance missions and guidance to support both the planning for and development of human resources needed for the introduction or expansion of nuclear power. It reviewed countries' human resource needs for that purpose, and completed two reports, entitled *Commissioning of Nuclear Power Plants: Training and Human Resource Consideration* and *Managing Human Resources in the Field of Nuclear Energy*.

The twenty-second edition of the "Red Book", *Uranium 2007: Resources, Production and Demand*, published in 2008, reported an increase in uranium resources due to recent growth in worldwide exploration. The study predicted that the resources would last another 83 years at the current rate of consumption.

To facilitate greater international cooperation in the utilization of research reactors, the Agency began establishing a number of regional networks. It also increased the number of technical cooperation projects supporting research reactors from four to ten. A training course to help build up the necessary human resources was developed for Member States with little or no nuclear infrastructure.

Responding to the world's food, environmental and cancer crises, the Agency strengthened its partnerships to enhance State and regional capacities in the use of nuclear technologies for sustainable solutions in such areas as food security, disease prevention and control, water resources and environmental management.

In the area of nuclear safety and security, IAEA continued to play an important role, supporting the development and implementation of international conventions and codes of conduct, helping to establish international standards and guidelines, and assisting Member States through peer review missions in enhancing their national safety and security infrastructures, as well as supporting regional and global knowledge networks. In 2008, the Agency celebrated the fiftieth anniversary of its safety standards programme, through which it supported States in meeting their national safety and security objectives; since 1958, over 200 safety standards had been published. In more than 150 safety reviews, security reviews and experts' missions and over 170 workshops, seminars and training courses during the year, the Agency helped Member States appraise national application of safety standards and security guidelines and provided advice and assistance.

Missions of the Integrated Regulatory Review Service (IRRS), an international mechanism for sharing regulatory knowledge and experience among senior regulators, visited Botswana, Côte d'Ivoire, Germany, Guatemala, Madagascar, Namibia, Sierra Leone, Spain and Ukraine. In order to promote high quality self-assessments—one of the major goals of IRRS—the Agency developed a methodology that could also be used for other self-assessment activities. The Agency assisted Iran, Lebanon, Peru, Ukraine and Viet Nam with their self-assessments in preparation for IRRS missions to those countries. A network for sharing information among countries' regulatory bodies was being developed.

By the end of the year, 14 Member States had registered their expert capabilities with the Agency's Response Assistance Network. In July, an emergency exercise tested the international response to a simulated accident at a nuclear power plant. Also during the year, IAEA established the International Seismic Safety Centre as a focal point for seismic safety at nuclear installations worldwide.

Dealing with other nuclear safety matters, the Agency completed an updated safety standard on the classification of radioactive waste. Its International Steering Committee on Denials of Shipment of Radioactive Material, set up in 2006 [YUN 2006, p. 644], organized four workshops on establishing regional networks to deal with the issue, and oversaw the establishment of a database for denials of shipment, receiving more than 100 denial reports by the end of the year.

The deposit by the United States in May of its instrument of ratification of the Convention on Supplementary Compensation for Nuclear Damage marked an important milestone in the Agency's efforts to strengthen the global nuclear liability regime.

IAEA provided training to more than 1,700 people from approximately 90 States in all aspects of nuclear security, and assisted in recovering more than 1,500 disused radioactive sources and moving them to national storage facilities. Nearly 600 pieces of radiation detection equipment were delivered to 24 States, in some cases with Agency training on the use of the equipment.

Assisting States by establishing nuclear security information tools continued to be a high priority. During the year, ten States approved Integrated Nuclear Security Support Plans, developed by the Agency as a blueprint for nuclear security work to be implemented over time.

The Agency worked with the Chinese authorities to ensure nuclear security at the Beijing Olympic Games in August—the largest security project it had ever been involved in—and provided security support to Peru for the Latin American and Caribbean-European Union Summit and the Asia-Pacific Economic Cooperation CEO Summit.

Through its technical cooperation projects, the Agency supported the use of appropriate nuclear science and technology to address major sustainable priorities at the national, regional and interregional levels. Support was delivered principally in the areas of human health; agricultural productivity and food security; water resources management; environmental protection; physical and chemical applications; and sustainable energy development, with safety and security a cross-cutting area.

The main focus of technical cooperation activities in the Asia and Pacific region was on strengthening the technical capacity of national and regional institutions and resource centres for applications in health, agriculture, environmental protection and energy. In Africa, IAEA supported 37 Member States in developing technical, managerial and institutional capacities in nuclear science and technology and applications. In Latin America, support was given to 22 Member States in the areas of human health, food and agriculture, and radiation and transport safety, while in Europe, fuel repatriation, core conversion and related research reactor upgrades and activities continued. The Agency also supported countries interested in starting a nuclear power programme.

IAEA safeguards

IAEA's verification programme remained at the core of multilateral efforts to curb the proliferation of nuclear weapons and move towards nuclear disarmament. The purpose of its safeguards system was to provide credible assurance to the international community that nuclear material and other specified items were not diverted from peaceful nuclear uses. Under the system, the Agency established and administered safeguards, and the rights and obligations assumed in safeguards agreements, thus enabling it to independently verify the declarations made by States about their nuclear material and activities. The nature and scope of such declarations—and of the measures implemented to verify them—stemmed from the type of safeguards agreement that a State had with the Agency.

Comprehensive safeguards agreements, concluded pursuant to NPT, and the Model Additional Protocols to those agreements, which granted the Agency complementary verification authority, had been approved by the IAEA Board of Governors in 1997 [YUN 1997, p. 486]; they remained the principal legal instruments strengthening the Agency's safeguards regime. In 2008, safeguards were applied for 163 States with agreements in force. Additional protocols entered into force for two States during the year, bringing the number of States in force to 88. States for which both the safeguards and Additional Protocols were in force numbered 84.

In a 4 October resolution [GC(52)/RES/13], the IAEA General Conference stressed the need for effective safeguards to prevent the use of nuclear material for prohibited purposes, and requested all concerned States and other parties to safeguards agreements, including nuclear-weapon States, that had not yet done so to promptly sign additional protocols and bring them into force as soon as possible, in conformity with their national legislation. The Conference noted that as at 4 October, IAEA was implementing State-level integrated safeguards approaches for 29 States and acknowledged that Agency safeguards could achieve further effectiveness and efficiency when a State-level perspective was used in safeguards activities planning, implementation and evaluation. The Conference encouraged increased cooperation between the IAEA secretariat and State and regional systems of accounting for and control of nuclear material, and commended Member States, notably Japan, which had implemented elements of a plan of action outlined in a 2000 Conference resolution [YUN 2000, p. 505] and updated in September; it recommended that other States consider doing so to facilitate the entry into force of comprehensive safeguards agreements and additional protocols.

Democratic People's Republic of Korea

In the DPRK, the Agency had not implemented safeguards for a number of years and therefore could not draw any safeguard conclusions regarding the country. It continued, however, to monitor and verify the shutdown-status of the Yongbyon nuclear facilities and one facility at Taechon as agreed on in the Six-Party Talks. Those activities were partially discontinued from 22 September to 13 October at the request of the DPRK, resulting in a lack of access for Agency inspectors to the Yongbyon facilities and in the removal of Agency seals and surveillance equipment at the Radiochemical Laboratory. Resuming its activities on 14 October, the Agency found no indication of operation during that period.

Reporting to the General Conference on 2 September [GOV/2008/40-GC(52)/14], the Director General stated that the Agency was continuing to implement the ad hoc monitoring and verification arrangement with the cooperation of the DPRK. While it had not been able to take part in the disablement activities, IAEA had been able to observe and document those activities, which had started in November 2007.

In a 4 October resolution [GC(52)/RES/14] on the implementation of the NPT safeguards agreement between the Agency and the DPRK, the General Conference supported the continuation of IAEA's monitoring and verification activities at the Yongbyon facilities as agreed in the Six-Party Talks, and acknowledged the Agency's activities in relation to the disablement process. It stressed the essential verification role of the Agency and called on the DPRK to come into full compliance with NPT.

Iran

International concern over Iran's nuclear programme persisted during the year. The IAEA Director General submitted four reports [GOV/2008/4, GOV/2008/15, GOV/2008/38, GOV/2008/59] to the Board of Governors on the implementation of Iran's NPT safeguards agreement and relevant Security Council resolutions. The Agency was able to verify the non-diversion of the declared nuclear material in Iran, but remained unable to draw a conclusion regarding the absence of undeclared nuclear material and activities. Contrary to Security Council decisions, Iran did not suspend its uranium enrichment-related activities and continued its heavy water-related projects.

In a 27 February letter [A/62/712-S/2008/138], Iran stated that the IAEA Director General's report of 22 February [GOV/2008/4] had clearly and evidently declared that all six remaining issues regarding its peaceful nuclear programme had been resolved and that all current nuclear activities in Iran were under Agency monitoring, and thus all the justifications and foundations for the Security Council's actions on the issue had vanished.

On 3 March, the Security Council adopted **resolution 1803(2008)** (see p. 409), noting with concern that, as confirmed by the Director General's reports, Iran had not established full and sustained suspension of all enrichment-related and reprocessing activities and heavy water-related projects, nor resumed cooperation with IAEA under the Additional Protocol, nor taken the other steps required by the Board of Governors, nor complied with Council resolutions 1696(2006) [YUN 2006, p. 433], 1737(2006) [ibid., p. 436] and 1747(2007) [YUN 2007, p. 374]. The Council, welcoming the agreement between Iran and IAEA to resolve all outstanding issues concerning Iran's nuclear programme and progress made in that regard, encouraged IAEA to continue its work to clarify all outstanding issues, stressing that this would help re-establish international confidence in the exclusively peaceful nature of Iran's nuclear programme. The Council supported the Agency in strengthening its safeguards on Iran's nuclear activities and requested within 90 days a further report from the Director General. The Director General transmitted [S/2008/338] on 26 May to the Council a report [GOV/2008/15] stating that contrary to its decisions, Iran had not suspended its enrichment-related activities and had continued with the construction of an IR-40 reactor.

In a September report [GOV/2008/38], the Director General noted that the Agency had not been able to make any substantive progress on the alleged studies and issues relating to the green salt project, high explosives testing and missile re-entry vehicle project and other key remaining issues of concern. Unless Iran provided substantive information and implemented the Additional Protocol, the Agency would not be able to provide credible assurance about the absence of undeclared nuclear material and activities in the country. Reaffirming its commitment to an early negotiated solution to the Iranian nuclear issue, the Security Council, in **resolution 1835(2008)** of 27 September (see p. 414), called on Iran to comply fully and without delay with its obligations.

On 19 November, the Director General reported [GOV/2008/59] that due to a lack of cooperation by Iran, the Agency had not been able to make substantive progress on key remaining issues and had not been able to verify the current status of the construction of the IR-40 reactor. It affirmed that Iran had not suspended its enrichment-related activities.

Syrian Arab Republic

The Director-General in November presented a report to the Board of Governors on the implementation of the Syrian Arab Republic's safeguards agreement [GC(53)/7]. In April, the Agency was provided with information alleging that an installation at Dair Alzour, destroyed by Israel in September 2007, had been a nuclear reactor, while Syria stated that it had been a military site not involved in any nuclear activities. From environmental samples, the Agency found that a significant number of natural uranium particles had been produced as a result of chemical processing. The issues related to the Dair Alzour site and some other locations remained unresolved and as a consequence, the Agency was not able to make progress towards resolving those issues. At the end of 2008, the Agency's verification work in the country was continuing. For 2008, IAEA found no indication of the diversion of declared nuclear material and was able to conclude that all such material in Syria remained in peaceful activities.

Middle East

In a September report on application of IAEA safeguards in the Middle East [GOV/2008/29/Rev.1-GC(52)/10/Rev.1], the IAEA Director General noted that all States of the Middle East region, except Israel, were parties to NPT. There continued to be a fundamental difference between Israel and other States of the region with regard to the application of comprehensive Agency safeguards. Israel took the view that safeguards as well as all other regional security issues should be addressed in the framework of a regional security and arms control dialogue in the context of a multilateral peace process, whereas the other States of the region emphasized that they were all parties to NPT and that there was no automatic sequence that linked the application of comprehensive safeguards to all nuclear activities in the Middle East. The Director General stated that he would continue with his consultations regarding the early application of comprehensive safeguards to all nuclear activities in the region.

In a 4 October resolution [GC(52)/RES/15], the IAEA General Conference affirmed the need for States in the region to accept the application of full-scope safeguards to all their nuclear activities as an important confidence-building measure, and requested the Director General to continue consultations with the States of the region to facilitate the early application of full-scope safeguards as relevant to the preparation of model agreements and as necessary steps towards the establishment of a nuclear-weapon-free zone.

Pursuant to General Assembly resolution 62/56 [YUN 2007, p. 557], the Secretary-General reported in October [A/63/115 (Part II)] that apart from the IAEA resolution on the application of Agency safeguards in the Middle East, which was annexed to his report, he had not received any additional information since his 2007 report [YUN 2007, p. 557].

GENERAL ASSEMBLY ACTION

On 2 December [meeting 61], the General Assembly, on the recommendation of the First Committee [A/63/392], adopted **resolution 63/84** by recorded vote (169-5-6) [agenda item 92].

The risk of nuclear proliferation in the Middle East

The General Assembly,

Bearing in mind its relevant resolutions,

Taking note of the relevant resolutions adopted by the General Conference of the International Atomic Energy Agency, the latest of which is resolution GC(52)/RES/15, adopted on 4 October 2008,

Cognizant that the proliferation of nuclear weapons in the region of the Middle East would pose a serious threat to international peace and security,

Mindful of the immediate need for placing all nuclear facilities in the region of the Middle East under full-scope safeguards of the Agency,

Recalling the decision on principles and objectives for nuclear non-proliferation and disarmament adopted by the 1995 Review and Extension Conference of the Parties to the Treaty on the Non-Proliferation of Nuclear Weapons on 11 May 1995, in which the Conference urged universal adherence to the Treaty as an urgent priority and called upon all States not yet parties to the Treaty to accede to it at the earliest date, particularly those States that operate unsafeguarded nuclear facilities,

Recognizing with satisfaction that, in the Final Document of the 2000 Review Conference of the Parties to the Treaty on the Non-Proliferation of Nuclear Weapons, the Conference undertook to make determined efforts towards the achievement of the goal of universality of the Treaty, called upon those remaining States not parties to the Treaty to accede to it, thereby accepting an international legally binding commitment not to acquire nuclear weapons or nuclear explosive devices and to accept Agency safeguards on all their nuclear activities, and underlined the necessity of universal adherence to the Treaty and of strict compliance by all parties with their obligations under the Treaty,

Recalling the resolution on the Middle East adopted by the 1995 Review and Extension Conference on 11 May 1995, in which the Conference noted with concern the continued existence in the Middle East of unsafeguarded nuclear facilities, reaffirmed the importance of the early realization of universal adherence to the Treaty and called upon all States in the Middle East that had not yet done so, without exception, to accede to the Treaty as soon as possible and to place all their nuclear facilities under full-scope Agency safeguards,

Noting that Israel remains the only State in the Middle East that has not yet become party to the Treaty,

Concerned about the threats posed by the proliferation of nuclear weapons to the security and stability of the Middle East region,

Stressing the importance of taking confidence-building measures, in particular the establishment of a nuclear-weapon-free zone in the Middle East, in order to enhance peace and security in the region and to consolidate the global non-proliferation regime,

Emphasizing the need for all parties directly concerned to seriously consider taking the practical and urgent steps required for the implementation of the proposal to establish a nuclear-weapon-free zone in the region of the Middle East in accordance with the relevant resolutions of the General Assembly and, as a means of promoting this objective, inviting the countries concerned to adhere to the Treaty and, pending the establishment of the zone, to agree to place all their nuclear activities under Agency safeguards,

Noting that one hundred and eighty States have signed the Comprehensive Nuclear-Test-Ban Treaty, including a number of States in the region,

1. *Welcomes* the conclusions on the Middle East of the 2000 Review Conference of the Parties to the Treaty on the Non-Proliferation of Nuclear Weapons;

2. *Reaffirms* the importance of Israel's accession to the Treaty on the Non-Proliferation of Nuclear Weapons and placement of all its nuclear facilities under comprehensive International Atomic Energy Agency safeguards, in realizing the goal of universal adherence to the Treaty in the Middle East;

3. *Calls upon* that State to accede to the Treaty without further delay and not to develop, produce, test or otherwise acquire nuclear weapons, and to renounce possession of nuclear weapons, and to place all its unsafeguarded nuclear facilities under full-scope Agency safeguards as an important confidence-building measure among all States of the region and as a step towards enhancing peace and security;

4. *Requests* the Secretary-General to report to the General Assembly at its sixty-fourth session on the implementation of the present resolution;

5. *Decides* to include in the provisional agenda of its sixty-fourth session the item entitled "The risk of nuclear proliferation in the Middle East".

RECORDED VOTE ON RESOLUTION 63/84:

In favour: Afghanistan, Albania, Algeria, Andorra, Antigua and Barbuda, Argentina, Armenia, Austria, Azerbaijan, Bahamas, Bahrain, Bangladesh, Barbados, Belarus, Belgium, Belize, Benin, Bhutan, Bolivia, Bosnia and Herzegovina, Botswana, Brazil, Brunei Darussalam, Bulgaria, Burkina Faso, Burundi, Cambodia, Chad, Chile, China, Colombia, Congo, Costa Rica, Côte d'Ivoire, Croatia, Cuba, Cyprus, Czech Republic, Democratic People's Republic of Korea, Democratic Republic of the Congo, Denmark, Djibouti, Dominica, Dominican Republic, Ecuador, Egypt, El Salvador, Equatorial Guinea, Eritrea, Estonia, Fiji, Finland, France, Georgia, Germany, Ghana, Greece, Grenada, Guatemala, Guinea, Guinea-Bissau, Guyana, Haiti, Honduras, Hungary, Iceland, Indonesia, Iran, Iraq, Ireland, Italy, Jamaica, Japan, Jordan, Kazakhstan, Kenya, Kuwait, Kyrgyzstan, Lao People's Democratic Republic, Latvia, Lebanon, Lesotho, Liberia, Libyan Arab Jamahiriya, Liechtenstein, Lithuania, Luxembourg, Madagascar, Malawi, Malaysia, Maldives, Mali, Malta, Mauritania, Mauritius, Mexico, Moldova, Monaco, Mongolia, Montenegro, Morocco, Mozambique, Myanmar, Namibia, Nepal, Netherlands, New Zealand, Nicaragua, Niger, Nigeria, Norway, Oman, Pakistan, Panama, Papua New Guinea, Paraguay, Peru, Philippines, Poland, Portugal, Qatar, Republic of Korea, Romania, Russian Federation, Rwanda, Saint Lucia, Saint Vincent and the Grenadines, Samoa, San Marino, Sao Tome and Principe, Saudi Arabia, Senegal, Serbia, Singapore, Slovakia, Slovenia, Solomon Islands, South Africa, Spain, Sri Lanka, Sudan, Suriname, Swaziland, Sweden, Switzerland, Syrian Arab Republic, Tajikistan, Thailand, The former Yugoslav Republic of Macedonia, Timor-Leste, Togo, Trinidad and Tobago, Tunisia, Turkey, Turkmenistan, Tuvalu, Uganda, Ukraine, United Arab Emirates, United Kingdom, United Republic of Tanzania, Uruguay, Uzbekistan, Vanuatu, Venezuela, Viet Nam, Yemen, Zambia, Zimbabwe.

Against: Israel, Marshall Islands, Micronesia, Palau, United States.

Abstaining: Australia, Cameroon, Canada, Ethiopia, India, Tonga.

Radioactive waste

IAEA's safety standards provided the global reference for the high safety level required for the use of nuclear power and other applications. In April, the Contracting Parties to the Convention on Nuclear Safety held their fourth review meeting. Efforts were made to increase the number of Contracting Parties to the Joint Convention on the Safety of Spent Fuel Management and on the Safety of Radioactive Waste Management. With the addition of Senegal and Tajikistan, the Joint Convention had 46 Contracting Parties at the end of 2008. During the year, the Agency updated a safety standard on the classification of radioactive waste, covering all radioactive waste types and recognizing the clearance concept for identifying the boundary between waste that needed to be managed as radioactive and that which could be removed from regulatory control for management as conventional waste. The Agency organized a series of regional workshops to explain to decision makers and technical experts the importance of having a national policy and related strategies in place for the management of radioactive waste and spent fuel. It also organized appraisals of policies and strategies in Bolivia, Costa Rica, Cuba, Namibia, Spain, Ukraine and Venezuela.

At an inaugural meeting that took place in Paris in June, IAEA launched the International Project on Demonstrating the Safety of Geological Disposal to provide a forum for the exchange of experience and opinions in demonstrations of the safety of geological disposal and aimed at providing a platform for knowledge transfer.

At the request of the Nuclear Agency of Romania, IAEA reviewed the radiological situation of workers, the population and the environment surrounding the Cernavoda nuclear power plant, and concluded that the plant had a radiation protection programme in place for workers, the public and the environment consistent with the recommendations of international safety standards. The Agency conducted a peer review of the Technical Programme for the Development of the Slovenian National Repository for Low and Intermediate Level Radioactive Waste, at the request of Slovenia's national radioactive waste management agency. Focusing on the Bradwell nuclear power plant in the United Kingdom, it conducted an International Peer Review of the Magnox Decommissioning Programme in that country; the achievements and issues from that review were examined at an international meeting in November.

The Agency project to assist Iraq in the evaluation and decommissioning of the former facilities that used radioactive waste continued, with the support of France, Germany, Italy, Ukraine, the United Kingdom and the United States. Following its launch in 2007, the International Decommissioning Network expanded its activities in 2008, including by acting as focal point for integrating complementary efforts in decommissioning. The Contact Expert Group, with 13 participating Member States, made substantial progress in solving nuclear legacy issues in the Russian Federation.

In a 3 October resolution [GC(52)/RES/9], the IAEA General Conference urged Member States to continue increasing regulatory effectiveness in the field of nuclear, radiation, transport and waste safety, and encouraged them to become party to the Joint Convention. Those already parties to the Joint Convention were encouraged to continue pursuing efforts to enhance transparency, efficiency and effectiveness of the review process, in preparation for the third Review Meeting to be held in May 2009.

Nuclear-weapon-free zones

Africa

As at 31 December, 26 States had ratified the African Nuclear-Weapon-Free Zone (Treaty of Pelindaba) [YUN 1995, p. 203], which was opened for signature in 1996 [YUN 1996, p. 486]. The Treaty had 56 signatories. China, France, and the United Kingdom had ratified Protocols I and II thereto, and France had also ratified Protocol III. The Russian Federation and the United States had signed Protocols I and II. By the terms of the Treaty, ratification by 28 States was required for its entry into force.

In resolution 63/65 (see p. 603) on a nuclear-weapon-free southern hemisphere and adjacent areas, the General Assembly welcomed the efforts towards the completion of the ratification process of the Pelindaba Treaty and called on the States of the region that had not yet done so to sign and ratify the Treaty.

Asia

Central Asia

In 2008, three of the five Central Asian States—Kazakhstan, Tajikistan and Turkmenistan—ratified the Treaty on a Nuclear-Weapon-Free Zone in Central Asia, paving the way for its entry into force, after Kyrgyzstan and Uzbekistan had ratified it in 2007 [YUN 2007, p. 561]. Having been opened for signature in 2006 [YUN 2006, p. 644], the Treaty was signed that same year by all five Central Asian States. The Protocol to the Treaty was open for signature by the five nuclear-weapon States, none of which had signed it by the end of 2008, partly owing to their concern over some of the Treaty terms.

The Treaty was the first nuclear-weapon-free zone located entirely in the northern hemisphere. Under its terms, the Central Asian States were the first countries in the world legally bound to adhere to enhanced IAEA safeguards on their civilian nuclear assets. The Treaty required them to meet international standards for the physical protection of nuclear material, and not to research, develop, manufacture, test, stockpile, acquire, possess, or have any control over any nuclear weapon.

GENERAL ASSEMBLY ACTION

On 2 December [meeting 61], the General Assembly, on the recommendation of the First Committee [A/63/389], adopted **resolution 63/63** by recorded vote (141-3-36) [agenda item 89 *(i)*].

Establishment of a nuclear-weapon-free zone in Central Asia

The General Assembly,

Recalling its resolutions 52/38 S of 9 December 1997, 53/77 A of 4 December 1998, 55/33 W of 20 November 2000, 57/69 of 22 November 2002 and 61/88 of 6 December 2006, and its decisions 54/417 of 1 December 1999, 56/412 of 29 November 2001, 58/518 of 8 December 2003, 59/513 of 3 December 2004 and 60/516 of 8 December 2005,

Convinced that the establishment of nuclear-weapon-free zones contributes to the achievement of general and complete disarmament, and emphasizing the importance of internationally recognized treaties on the establishment of such zones in different regions of the world in the strengthening of the non-proliferation regime,

Considering that the establishment of a nuclear-weapon-free zone in Central Asia on the basis of arrangements freely arrived at among the States of the region constitutes an important step towards strengthening the nuclear non-proliferation regime and ensuring regional and international peace and security,

Considering also the establishment of a nuclear-weapon-free zone in Central Asia as an effective contribution to combating international terrorism and preventing nuclear materials and technologies from falling into the hands of non-State actors, primarily terrorists,

Reaffirming the universally recognized role of the United Nations in the establishment of nuclear-weapon-free zones,

Emphasizing the role of a nuclear-weapon-free zone in Central Asia in promoting cooperation in the peaceful uses of nuclear energy and in the environmental rehabilitation of territories affected by radioactive contamination, and the importance of stepping up efforts to ensure the safe and reliable storage of radioactive waste in the Central Asian States,

Recognizing the importance of the Treaty on a Nuclear-Weapon-Free Zone in Central Asia, signed in Semipalatinsk, Kazakhstan, on 8 September 2006, and emphasizing its significance in the attainment of peace and security,

1. *Welcomes* the ratification of the Treaty on a Nuclear-Weapon-Free Zone in Central Asia by Kyrgyzstan, Turkmenistan and Uzbekistan;

2. *Notes* the readiness of the Central Asian countries to continue consultations with the nuclear-weapon States on a number of provisions of the Treaty;

3. *Welcomes* the convening of an international conference on the problem of uranium tailings, to be held in Bishkek in 2009, and calls upon the specialized agencies of the United Nations and other stakeholders to participate in that conference;

4. *Decides* to include in the provisional agenda of its sixty-fifth session the item entitled "Establishment of a nuclear-weapon-free zone in Central Asia".

RECORDED VOTE ON RESOLUTION 63/63:

In favour: Afghanistan, Algeria, Angola, Antigua and Barbuda, Argentina, Armenia, Austria, Azerbaijan, Bahamas, Bahrain, Bangladesh, Barbados, Belarus, Belize, Benin, Bhutan, Bolivia, Botswana, Brazil, Brunei Darussalam, Burkina Faso, Burundi, Cambodia, Cameroon, Cape Verde, Chile, China, Colombia, Comoros, Congo, Costa Rica, Côte d'Ivoire, Cuba, Cyprus, Democratic People's Republic of Korea, Djibouti, Dominica, Dominican Republic, Ecuador, Egypt, El Salvador, Equatorial Guinea, Eritrea, Ethiopia, Fiji, Georgia, Ghana, Grenada, Guatemala, Guinea, Guinea-Bissau, Guyana, Haiti, Honduras, India, Indonesia, Iran, Iraq, Ireland, Jamaica, Japan, Jordan, Kazakhstan, Kenya, Kuwait, Kyrgyzstan, Lao People's Democratic Republic, Lebanon, Lesotho, Liberia, Libyan Arab Jamahiriya, Liechtenstein, Madagascar, Malawi, Malaysia, Maldives, Mali, Malta, Marshall Islands, Mauritania, Mauritius, Mexico, Moldova, Mongolia, Morocco, Mozambique, Myanmar, Namibia, Nauru, Nepal, New Zealand, Nicaragua, Niger, Nigeria, Oman, Pakistan, Panama, Papua New Guinea, Paraguay, Peru, Philippines, Qatar, Republic of Korea, Russian Federation, Rwanda, Saint Lucia, Saint Vincent and the Grenadines, Samoa, Sao Tome and Principe, Saudi Arabia, Senegal, Singapore, Solomon Islands, South Africa, Sri Lanka, Sudan, Suriname, Swaziland, Sweden, Switzerland, Syrian Arab Republic, Tajikistan, Thailand, Timor-Leste, Togo, Trinidad and Tobago, Tunisia, Turkmenistan, Tuvalu, Uganda, Ukraine, United Arab Emirates, United Republic of Tanzania, Uruguay, Uzbekistan, Vanuatu, Venezuela, Viet Nam, Yemen, Zambia, Zimbabwe.

Against: France, United Kingdom, United States.

Abstaining: Albania, Andorra, Australia, Belgium, Bosnia and Herzegovina, Bulgaria, Canada, Croatia, Czech Republic, Denmark, Estonia, Finland, Germany, Greece, Hungary, Iceland, Israel, Italy, Latvia, Lithuania, Luxembourg, Monaco, Montenegro, Netherlands, Norway, Palau, Poland, Portugal, Romania, San Marino, Serbia, Slovakia, Slovenia, Spain, The former Yugoslav Republic of Macedonia, Turkey.

Mongolia

Communication. On 30 April [A/63/73-S/2008/297], Mongolia transmitted a memorandum on activities for promoting its nuclear-weapon-free status since its earlier memorandum on the issue in 1999 [YUN 1999, p. 477].

Report of Secretary-General. In response to General Assembly resolution 61/87 [YUN 2006, p. 646], the Secretary-General submitted a July report [A/63/122] reviewing new developments and UN assistance to Mongolia to consolidate and strengthen its nuclear-weapon-free status. The range of activities described in the report related both to Mongolia's nuclear-weapon-free status and the non-nuclear aspects of its international security. The Secretary-General noted that during the ten years since the General Assembly had adopted resolution 53/77 D on the topic [YUN 1998, p. 515], the country's nuclear-weapon-free status was being institutionalized and gaining wider recognition. In September 2007, Mongolia had presented a draft trilateral treaty on its nuclear-weapon-free status to China and the Russian Federation. The Secretary-General hoped that UN assistance, geared to helping the country cope with its economic and ecological vulnerabilities, would further contribute to consolidating Mongolia's nuclear-weapon-free status and to achieving sustainable development and balanced growth, as well as reinforcing its efforts to achieve the Millennium Development Goals.

GENERAL ASSEMBLY ACTION

On 2 December [meeting 61], the General Assembly, on the recommendation of the First Committee [A/63/389], adopted **resolution 63/56** without vote [agenda item 89 *(h)*].

Mongolia's international security and nuclear-weapon-free status

The General Assembly,

Recalling its resolutions 53/77 D of 4 December 1998, 55/33 S of 20 November 2000, 57/67 of 22 November 2002, 59/73 of 3 December 2004 and 61/87 of 6 December 2006,

Recalling also the purposes and principles of the Charter of the United Nations, as well as the Declaration on Principles of International Law concerning Friendly Relations and Cooperation among States in accordance with the Charter of the United Nations,

Bearing in mind its resolution 49/31 of 9 December 1994 on the protection and security of small States,

Proceeding from the fact that nuclear-weapon-free status is one of the means of ensuring the national security of States,

Convinced that the internationally recognized status of Mongolia contributes to enhancing stability and confidence-building in the region and promotes Mongolia's security by strengthening its independence, sovereignty and territorial integrity, the inviolability of its borders and the preservation of its ecological balance,

Taking note of the adoption by the Mongolian parliament of legislation defining and regulating Mongolia's nuclear-weapon-free status as a concrete step towards promoting the aims of nuclear non-proliferation,

Bearing in mind the joint statement of the five nuclear-weapon States on security assurances to Mongolia in connection with its nuclear-weapon-free status as a contribution to implementing resolution 53/77 D as well as their commitment to Mongolia to cooperate in the implementation of the resolution, in accordance with the principles of the Charter,

Noting that the joint statement was transmitted to the Security Council by the five nuclear-weapon States,

Mindful of the support expressed for Mongolia's nuclear-weapon-free status by the Heads of State and Government of Non-Aligned Countries at the Thirteenth Conference of Heads of State or Government of Non-Aligned Countries, held in Kuala Lumpur on 24 and 25 February 2003, and the Fourteenth Conference, held in Havana on 15 and 16 September 2006, as well as by Ministers at the Fifteenth Ministerial Conference of the Movement of Non-Aligned Countries, held in Tehran on 29 and 30 July 2008,

Noting that the States parties and signatories to the Treaties of Tlatelolco, Rarotonga, Bangkok and Pelindaba and the State of Mongolia expressed their recognition and full support of Mongolia's international nuclear-weapon-free status at the first Conference of States Parties and Signatories to Treaties that Establish Nuclear-Weapon-Free Zones, held in Tlatelolco, Mexico, from 26 to 28 April 2005,

Noting also other measures taken to implement resolution 61/87 at the national and international levels,

Welcoming Mongolia's active and positive role in developing peaceful, friendly and mutually beneficial relations with the States of the region and other States,

Having considered the report of the Secretary-General on Mongolia's international security and nuclear-weapon-free status,

1. *Takes note* of the report of the Secretary-General on the implementation of resolution 61/87;

2. *Expresses its appreciation* to the Secretary-General for the efforts to implement resolution 61/87;

3. *Endorses and supports* Mongolia's good-neighbourly and balanced relationship with its neighbours as an important element of strengthening regional peace, security and stability;

4. *Welcomes* the efforts made by Member States to cooperate with Mongolia in implementing resolution 61/87, as well as the progress made in consolidating Mongolia's international security;

5. *Invites* Member States to continue to cooperate with Mongolia in taking the necessary measures to consolidate and strengthen Mongolia's independence, sovereignty and territorial integrity, the inviolability of its borders, its independent foreign policy, its economic security and its ecological balance, as well as its nuclear-weapon-free status;

6. *Appeals* to the Member States of the Asia and Pacific region to support Mongolia's efforts to join the relevant regional security and economic arrangements;

7. *Requests* the Secretary-General and relevant United Nations bodies to continue to provide assistance to Mongolia in taking the necessary measures mentioned in paragraph 5 above;

8. *Requests* the Secretary-General to report to the General Assembly at its sixty-fifth session on the implementation of the present resolution;

9. *Decides* to include in the provisional agenda of its sixty-fifth session the item entitled "Mongolia's international security and nuclear-weapon-free status".

South-East Asia

The ten States parties to the Treaty on the South-East Asia Nuclear-Weapon-Free Zone (Bangkok Treaty), which had opened for signature in 1995 [YUN 1995, p. 207] and entered into force in 1997 [YUN 1997, p. 495], continued to establish an institutional framework to implement the Treaty. At the forty-first Ministerial Meeting of the Association of Southeast Asian Nations (Singapore, 20–21 July), the Ministers reaffirmed the importance of persevering in strengthening cooperation to implement the Treaty and instructed their officials to continue engaging nuclear-weapon States to secure their accession to the Treaty Protocol as soon as possible.

Latin America and the Caribbean

States parties to the Treaty for the Prohibition of Nuclear Weapons in Latin America and the Caribbean (Treaty of Tlatelolco) [YUN 1967, p. 13] continued to consolidate the Treaty regime. In a resolution [AG/RES.2377(XXXVIII-O/08)] adopted at its thirty-eighth session (Medellin, Colombia, 1–3 June), the General Assembly of the Organization of American States (OAS), reaffirming that the consolidation of the nuclear-weapon-free zone set forth in the Treaty constituted a demonstration of the commitment to complete and verifiable disarmament and the non-proliferation of nuclear weapons, called on regional States that had not yet done so to sign or ratify the amendments to the Treaty. It reaffirmed the importance of strengthening the Agency for the Prohibition of Nuclear Weapons in Latin America and the Caribbean (OPANAL), recognized its work in ensuring compliance with the Treaty obligations, and supported OPANAL's cooperation and coordination mechanisms with the other nuclear-weapon-free-zone Treaties, in order to expedite the achievement of common objectives.

In February, the OAS Permanent Council's Committee on Hemispheric Security convened a special session to consider OAS progress with respect to initiatives on CTBT and related instruments. The session reaffirmed OAS's commitment to the Western Hemisphere as a nuclear-weapon-free zone and stressed its support for CTBT. Also in February, OPANAL organized a seminar on the other nuclear-weapon-free-zone-treaty: the Treaty of Tlatelolco, on the occasion of the forty-first anniversary of its opening for signature.

Middle East

In response to General Assembly resolution 62/18 [YUN 2007, p. 563], the Secretary-General, in July [A/63/115 (Part I) & Add.1] reported on the establishment of a nuclear-weapon-free zone in the Middle East. He had continued consultations with concerned parties and observed that the issue of establishing a zone remained important. At the second session of the Preparatory Committee for the 2010 Review Conference of NPT Parties (see p. 584), States parties reiterated their support for the establishment of such a zone and reaffirmed the importance of implementing the resolution on the Middle East adopted by the 1995 NPT Review and Extension Conference [YUN 1995, p. 205]. The League of Arab States had reiterated its call on the international community to take effective practical steps to that end.

The Secretary-General called on all concerned parties to resume dialogue with a view to creating stable security conditions and establishing a nuclear-weapon-free zone, and reiterated the readiness of the United Nations to provide assistance. His report included the views of 11 Governments—Cuba, Iran, Iraq, Israel, Jamaica, Japan, Kuwait, the Netherlands, Qatar, Spain and the Syrian Arab Republic.

In October, the IAEA General Conference adopted a resolution [GC(52)/RES/15] calling on all parties directly concerned to take the steps required, including confidence-building and verification measures, for the establishment of a mutually and effectively verifiable nuclear-weapon-free zone in the region. The resolution was transmitted to the General Assembly annexed to a report of the Secretary-General [A/63/115 (Part II)].

GENERAL ASSEMBLY ACTION

On 2 December [meeting 61], the General Assembly, on the recommendation of the First Committee [A/63/386], adopted **resolution 63/38** without vote [agenda item 86].

Establishment of a nuclear-weapon-free zone in the region of the Middle East

The General Assembly,

Recalling its resolutions 3263(XXIX) of 9 December 1974, 3474(XXX) of 11 December 1975, 31/71 of 10 December 1976, 32/82 of 12 December 1977, 33/64 of 14 December 1978, 34/77 of 11 December 1979, 35/147 of 12 December 1980, 36/87 A and B of 9 December 1981, 37/75 of 9 December 1982, 38/64 of 15 December 1983, 39/54 of 12 December 1984, 40/82 of 12 December 1985, 41/48 of 3 December 1986, 42/28 of 30 November 1987, 43/65 of 7 December 1988, 44/108 of 15 December 1989, 45/52 of 4 December 1990, 46/30 of 6 December 1991, 47/48 of 9 December 1992, 48/71 of 16 December 1993, 49/71 of 15 December 1994, 50/66 of 12 December 1995, 51/41 of 10 December 1996, 52/34 of 9 December 1997, 53/74 of 4 December 1998, 54/51 of 1 December 1999, 55/30 of 20 November 2000, 56/21 of 29 November 2001, 57/55 of 22 November 2002, 58/34 of 8 December 2003, 59/63 of 3 December 2004, 60/52 of 8 December 2005, 61/56 of 6 December 2006 and 62/18 of 5 December 2007 on the establishment of a nuclear-weapon-free zone in the region of the Middle East,

Recalling also the recommendations for the establishment of such a zone in the Middle East consistent with paragraphs 60 to 63, and in particular paragraph 63 *(d)*, of the Final Document of the Tenth Special Session of the General Assembly,

Emphasizing the basic provisions of the above-mentioned resolutions, which call upon all parties directly concerned to consider taking the practical and urgent steps required for the implementation of the proposal to establish a nuclear-weapon-free zone in the region of the Middle East and, pending and during the establishment of such a zone, to declare solemnly that they will refrain, on a reciprocal basis, from producing, acquiring or in any other way possessing nuclear weapons and nuclear explosive devices and from permitting the stationing of nuclear weapons on their territory by any third party, to agree to place their nuclear facilities under International Atomic Energy Agency safeguards and to declare their support for the establishment of the zone and to deposit such declarations with the Security Council for consideration, as appropriate,

Reaffirming the inalienable right of all States to acquire and develop nuclear energy for peaceful purposes,

Emphasizing the need for appropriate measures on the question of the prohibition of military attacks on nuclear facilities,

Bearing in mind the consensus reached by the General Assembly since its thirty-fifth session that the establishment of a nuclear-weapon-free zone in the Middle East would greatly enhance international peace and security,

Desirous of building on that consensus so that substantial progress can be made towards establishing a nuclear-weapon-free zone in the Middle East,

Welcoming all initiatives leading to general and complete disarmament, including in the region of the Middle East, and in particular on the establishment therein of a zone free of weapons of mass destruction, including nuclear weapons,

Noting the peace negotiations in the Middle East, which should be of a comprehensive nature and represent an appropriate framework for the peaceful settlement of contentious issues in the region,

Recognizing the importance of credible regional security, including the establishment of a mutually verifiable nuclear-weapon-free zone,

Emphasizing the essential role of the United Nations in the establishment of a mutually verifiable nuclear-weapon-free zone,

Having examined the report of the Secretary-General on the implementation of resolution 62/18,

1. *Urges* all parties directly concerned seriously to consider taking the practical and urgent steps required for the implementation of the proposal to establish a nuclear-weapon-free zone in the region of the Middle East in accordance with the relevant resolutions of the General Assembly, and, as a means of promoting this objective, invites the countries concerned to adhere to the Treaty on the Non-Proliferation of Nuclear Weapons;

2. *Calls upon* all countries of the region that have not done so, pending the establishment of the zone, to agree to place all their nuclear activities under International Atomic Energy Agency safeguards;

3. *Takes note* of resolution GC(52)/RES/15, adopted on 4 October 2008 by the General Conference of the International Atomic Energy Agency at its fifty-second regular session, concerning the application of Agency safeguards in the Middle East;

4. *Notes* the importance of the ongoing bilateral Middle East peace negotiations and the activities of the multilateral Working Group on Arms Control and Regional Security in promoting mutual confidence and security in the Middle East, including the establishment of a nuclear-weapon-free zone;

5. *Invites* all countries of the region, pending the establishment of a nuclear-weapon-free zone in the region of the Middle East, to declare their support for establishing such a zone, consistent with paragraph 63 (*d*) of the Final Document of the Tenth Special Session of the General Assembly, and to deposit those declarations with the Security Council;

6. *Also invites* those countries, pending the establishment of the zone, not to develop, produce, test or otherwise acquire nuclear weapons or permit the stationing on their territories, or territories under their control, of nuclear weapons or nuclear explosive devices;

7. *Invites* the nuclear-weapon States and all other States to render their assistance in the establishment of the zone and at the same time to refrain from any action that runs counter to both the letter and the spirit of the present resolution;

8. *Takes note* of the report of the Secretary-General;

9. *Invites* all parties to consider the appropriate means that may contribute towards the goal of general and complete disarmament and the establishment of a zone free of weapons of mass destruction in the region of the Middle East;

10. *Requests* the Secretary-General to continue to pursue consultations with the States of the region and other concerned States, in accordance with paragraph 7 of resolution 46/30 and taking into account the evolving situation in the region, and to seek from those States their views on the measures outlined in chapters III and IV of the study annexed to the report of the Secretary-General of 10 October 1990 or other relevant measures, in order to move towards the establishment of a nuclear-weapon-free zone in the Middle East;

11. *Also requests* the Secretary-General to submit to the General Assembly at its sixty-fourth session a report on the implementation of the present resolution;

12. *Decides* to include in the provisional agenda of its sixty-fourth session the item entitled "Establishment of a nuclear-weapon-free zone in the region of the Middle East".

South Pacific

In 2008, the number of States that had ratified the 1985 South Pacific Nuclear-Free Zone Treaty (Treaty of Rarotonga) [YUN 1985, p. 58] remained at 17. China and the Russian Federation had ratified Protocols 2 and 3, and France and the United Kingdom had ratified all three Protocols.

Under Protocol 1, the States internationally responsible for territories situated within the zone would undertake to apply the relevant prohibitions of the Treaty to those territories; under Protocol 2, the five nuclear-weapon States would provide security assurances to parties or territories within the same zone; and under Protocol 3, the five would not carry out any nuclear tests in the zone.

Southern hemisphere and adjacent areas

On 2 December [meeting 61], the General Assembly, on the recommendation of the First Committee [A/63/389], adopted **resolution 63/65** by recorded vote (171-3-7) [agenda item 89 (*s*)].

Nuclear-weapon-free southern hemisphere and adjacent areas

The General Assembly,

Recalling its resolutions 51/45 B of 10 December 1996, 52/38 N of 9 December 1997, 53/77 Q of 4 December 1998, 54/54 L of 1 December 1999, 55/33 I of 20 November 2000, 56/24 G of 29 November 2001, 57/73 of 22 November 2002, 58/49 of 8 December 2003, 59/85 of 3 December 2004, 60/58 of 8 December 2005, 61/69 of 6 December 2006 and 62/35 of 5 December 2007,

Recalling also the adoption by the Disarmament Commission at its 1999 substantive session of a text entitled "Establishment of nuclear-weapon-free zones on the basis of arrangements freely arrived at among the States of the region concerned",

Determined to pursue the total elimination of nuclear weapons,

Determined also to continue to contribute to the prevention of the proliferation of nuclear weapons in all its aspects and to the process of general and complete disarmament under strict and effective international control, in particular in the field of nuclear weapons and other weapons of mass destruction, with a view to strengthening international peace and security, in accordance with the purposes and principles of the Charter of the United Nations,

Recalling the provisions on nuclear-weapon-free zones of the Final Document of the Tenth Special Session of the General Assembly, the first special session devoted to disarmament,

Stressing the importance of the treaties of Tlatelolco, Rarotonga, Bangkok and Pelindaba establishing nuclear-weapon-free zones, as well as the Antarctic Treaty, to, inter alia, achieve a world entirely free of nuclear weapons,

Underlining the value of enhancing cooperation among the nuclear-weapon-free-zone treaty members by means of mechanisms such as joint meetings of States parties, signatories and observers to those treaties,

Noting the adoption of the Declaration of Santiago de Chile by the Governments of the States members of the Agency for the Prohibition of Nuclear Weapons in Latin America and the Caribbean and the States parties to the Treaty of Tlatelolco, during the nineteenth regular session of the General Conference of the Agency, held in Santiago on 7 and 8 November 2005,

Recalling the applicable principles and rules of international law relating to the freedom of the high seas and the rights of passage through maritime space, including those of the United Nations Convention on the Law of the Sea,

1. *Welcomes* the continued contribution that the Antarctic Treaty and the treaties of Tlatelolco, Rarotonga, Bangkok and Pelindaba are making towards freeing the southern hemisphere and adjacent areas covered by those treaties from nuclear weapons;

2. *Also welcomes* the ratification by all original parties of the Treaty of Rarotonga, and calls upon eligible States to adhere to the Treaty and the protocols thereto;

3. *Further welcomes* the efforts towards the completion of the ratification process of the Treaty of Pelindaba, and calls upon the States of the region that have not yet done so to sign and ratify the Treaty, with the aim of its early entry into force;

4. *Welcomes* the signing of the Semipalatinsk Treaty on 8 September 2006, and urges all relevant States to cooperate in resolving outstanding issues with a view to the full implementation of the Treaty;

5. *Calls upon* all concerned States to continue to work together in order to facilitate adherence to the protocols to nuclear-weapon-free-zone treaties by all relevant States that have not yet adhered to them;

6. *Welcomes* the steps taken to conclude further nuclear-weapon-free-zone treaties on the basis of arrangements freely arrived at among the States of the region concerned, and calls upon all States to consider all relevant proposals, including those reflected in its resolutions on the establishment of nuclear-weapon-free zones in the Middle East and South Asia;

7. *Affirms its conviction* of the important role of nuclear-weapon-free zones in strengthening the nuclear non-proliferation regime and in extending the areas of the world that are nuclear-weapon-free, and, with particular reference to the responsibilities of the nuclear-weapon States, calls upon all States to support the process of nuclear disarmament and to work for the total elimination of all nuclear weapons;

8. *Welcomes* the progress made on increased collaboration within and between zones at the first Conference of States Parties and Signatories to Treaties that Establish Nuclear-Weapon-Free Zones, held in Tlatelolco, Mexico, from 26 to 28 April 2005, at which States reaffirmed their need to cooperate in order to achieve their common objectives;

9. *Congratulates* the States parties and signatories to the treaties of Tlatelolco, Rarotonga, Bangkok and Pelindaba, as well as Mongolia, for their efforts to pursue the common goals envisaged in those treaties and to promote the nuclear-weapon-free status of the southern hemisphere and adjacent areas, and calls upon them to explore and implement further ways and means of cooperation among themselves and their treaty agencies;

10. *Encourages* the competent authorities of the nuclear-weapon-free-zone treaties to provide assistance to the States parties and signatories to those treaties so as to facilitate the accomplishment of the goals;

11. *Decides* to include in the provisional agenda of its sixty-fourth session the item entitled "Nuclear-weapon-free southern hemisphere and adjacent areas".

RECORDED VOTE ON RESOLUTION 63/65:

In favour: Afghanistan, Albania, Andorra, Angola, Antigua and Barbuda, Argentina, Armenia, Australia, Austria, Azerbaijan, Bahamas, Bahrain, Bangladesh, Barbados, Belarus, Belgium, Belize, Benin, Bhutan, Bolivia, Bosnia and Herzegovina, Botswana, Brazil, Brunei Darussalam, Bulgaria, Burkina Faso, Burundi, Cambodia, Cameroon, Canada, Cape Verde, Chad, Chile, China, Colombia, Comoros, Congo, Costa Rica, Côte d'Ivoire, Croatia, Cuba, Cyprus, Czech Republic, Democratic People's Republic of Korea, Denmark, Djibouti, Dominica, Dominican Republic, Ecuador, Egypt, El Salvador, Equatorial Guinea, Eritrea, Estonia, Ethiopia, Fiji, Finland, Georgia, Germany, Ghana, Greece, Grenada, Guatemala, Guinea, Guinea-Bissau, Guyana, Haiti, Honduras, Hungary, Iceland, Indonesia, Iran, Iraq, Ireland, Italy, Jamaica, Japan, Jordan, Kazakhstan, Kenya, Kuwait, Kyrgyzstan, Lao People's Democratic Republic, Latvia, Lebanon, Lesotho, Liberia, Libyan Arab Jamahiriya, Liechtenstein, Lithuania, Luxembourg, Madagascar, Malawi, Malaysia, Maldives, Mali, Malta, Mauritania, Mauritius, Mexico, Moldova, Mongolia, Montenegro, Morocco, Mozambique, Myanmar, Namibia, Nauru, Nepal, Netherlands, New Zealand, Nicaragua, Niger, Nigeria, Norway, Oman, Panama, Papua New Guinea, Paraguay, Peru, Philippines, Poland, Portugal, Qatar, Republic of Korea, Romania, Rwanda, Saint Lucia, Saint Vincent and the Grenadines, Samoa, San Marino, Sao Tome and Principe, Saudi Arabia, Senegal, Serbia, Singapore, Slovakia, Slovenia, Solomon Islands, South Africa, Spain, Sri Lanka, Sudan, Suriname, Swaziland, Sweden, Switzerland, Syrian Arab Republic, Tajikistan, Thailand, The former Yugoslav Republic of Macedonia, Timor-Leste, Togo, Tonga, Trinidad and Tobago, Tunisia, Turkey, Turkmenistan, Tuvalu, Uganda, Ukraine, United Arab Emirates, United Republic of Tanzania, Uruguay, Uzbekistan, Vanuatu, Venezuela, Viet Nam, Yemen, Zambia, Zimbabwe.

Against: France, United Kingdom, United States.

Abstaining: India, Israel, Marshall Islands, Micronesia, Pakistan, Palau, Russian Federation.

Bacteriological (biological) and chemical weapons

The threat of biological and chemical weapons as well as related materials and technology remained of concern to the international community. In accordance with the decisions and recommendations adopted at the 2006 Sixth Review Conference [YUN 2006, p. 650], the States parties to the 1972 Convention on the Prohibition of the Development, Production and Stockpiling of Bacteriological (Biological) and Toxin Weapons and on Their Destruction (BWC) [YUN 1972, p. 5] continued the intersessional process leading to the 2011 Seventh Review Conference. The Second Review Conference of the 1993 Convention on the Prohibition of the Development, Production, Stockpiling and Use of Chemical Weapons and on Their Destruction (CWC) [YUN 1993, p. 111], in April, examined the operation of the Convention since the First Review Conference in 2003 [YUN 2003, p. 560] and provided recommendations for its future implementation. Significant advances were also made pursuant to the Action Plan on national implementation of CWC, as nearly all States parties had either established or designated a National Authority as required by the Convention.

Other activities. Pursuant to a request of the 2006 Global Counter-Terrorism Strategy [YUN 2006, p. 65], UNODA started in April to develop the software platform for the Biological Incident Data Base for reporting incidents categorized as unusual but natural, accidental or deliberate outbreak of diseases. Also in 2008, UNODA continued to update the roster of experts and laboratories whose services were available to the Secretary-General for the investigation of reports of the possible use of chemical and bacteriological (biological) and toxin weapons. The Office also worked on technical guidelines and procedures for investigations of cases of alleged use of biological and chemical weapons.

Bacteriological (biological) weapons

As the international community continued to focus on the increasingly important issue of biological weapons, by the end of the year, States parties to BWC were halfway through their intersessional programme of annual meetings to discuss effective action on issues critical to implementing the Convention. While other disarmament and non-proliferation areas were characterized by setbacks and stalemates, the States parties to BWC were working towards cementing their gains at the next Review Conference, the seventh, scheduled for 2011. The 2008 meetings—made up of sessions at both the expert and the State party levels—considered two specific topics as mandated by the Sixth Review Conference in 2006 [YUN 2006, p. 650]: national, regional and international measures to improve biosafety and biosecurity, including laboratory safety and security of pathogens and toxins; and oversight, education, awareness-raising and adopting and/or developing codes of conduct to prevent misuse in the context of advances in bio-science and bio-technology research.

Meeting of States parties

As decided by the Sixth Review Conference of the States parties to BWC [YUN 2006, p. 650], the meeting of those States was convened in 2008 (Geneva, 1–5 December) [BWC/MSP/2008/5]. It was attended by 97 States parties, five signatory States and one State currently not party, as well as four international organizations and 17 NGOs and research institutes. The Meeting succeeded in delivering a comprehensive range of common understandings. Participants agreed that biosafety referred to principles, technologies, practices and measures implemented to prevent the accidental release of, or unintentional exposure to, biological agents and toxins, and that biosecurity meant the protection, control and accountability measures implemented to prevent the loss, theft, misuse, diversion or intentional release of biological agents and toxins and related resources, as well as unauthorized access to, retention or transfer of such material. It was established that the aims of dealing with bio-safety and biosecurity were to contribute to: preventing the development, acquisition or use of biological and toxin weapons; implementing BWC; and fulfilling other international obligations and agreements, such as the revised International Health Regulations of the World Health Organization and the provisions of Security Council resolution 1540(2004) [YUN 2004, p. 544]. The report also recorded common understandings on how to realize those aims. Tools on biosafety and biosecurity would support accreditation, certification, audit or licensing of facilities, organizations or individuals, as well as training requirements, mechanisms to check qualifications and expertise, national criteria for relevant activities and national lists of agents, equipment and other resources. It was determined that States parties needed assistance in the following areas: to enact and improve relevant legislation; to strengthen laboratory infrastructure, technology, security and management; to provide training; and to help incorporate biosafety and biosecurity into existing efforts to address disease. The report affirmed the importance of balancing "top-down" government and institutional controls with "bottom-up" scientific oversight. The Meeting reviewed a report by the Chairman on efforts to expand BWC membership. The Meeting recognized that progress had been made during the year as the Cook Islands, Madagascar, the United Arab Emirates and Zambia had joined the Convention. The Meeting also had before it the second annual report by the Implementation Support Unit.

Experts' meeting. In accordance with the outcome of the Sixth Review Conference [YUN 2006, p. 650], the 2008 meeting of States parties was preceded by a preparatory expert meeting (Geneva, 18–22 August) [BWC/MSP/2008/MX/3]. A total of 103 States took part in the meeting. Also represented were four UN institutions and seven specialized agencies or other international organizations, and representatives from science, academia and industry. The two topics of biosafety (improvement through national, regional and international measures) and biosecurity (oversight of science, education, awareness-raising and codes of conduct) were addressed in seven working sessions which, in a departure from past practices, were open to the public. Three panel discussions focused on specific aspects of the two main topics, the role of industry and the private sector in biosafety and biosecurity; risk assessment, management and communication concepts and techniques; and oversight of science and engagement of stakeholders. During the meeting, 35 working papers were circulated and several Compendiums of National Approaches were introduced.

GENERAL ASSEMBLY ACTION

On 2 December [meeting 61], the General Assembly, on the recommendation of the First Committee [A/63/396], adopted **resolution 63/88** without vote [agenda item 96].

Convention on the Prohibition of the Development, Production and Stockpiling of Bacteriological (Biological) and Toxin Weapons and on Their Destruction

The General Assembly,

Recalling its previous resolutions relating to the complete and effective prohibition of bacteriological (biological) and toxin weapons and to their destruction,

Noting with satisfaction that there are one hundred and sixty-two States parties to the Convention on the Prohibition of the Development, Production and Stockpiling of Bacteriological (Biological) and Toxin Weapons and on Their Destruction, including all of the permanent members of the Security Council,

Bearing in mind its call upon all States parties to the Convention to participate in the implementation of the recommendations of the Review Conferences, including the exchange of information and data agreed to in the Final Declaration of the Third Review Conference of the Parties to the Convention, and to provide such information and data in conformity with standardized procedure to the Secretary-General on an annual basis and no later than 15 April,

Welcoming the reaffirmation made in the Final Declaration of the Fourth Review Conference that under all circumstances the use of bacteriological (biological) and toxin weapons and their development, production and stockpiling are effectively prohibited under article I of the Convention,

Recalling the decision reached at the Sixth Review Conference to hold four annual meetings of the States parties of one week's duration each year commencing in 2007, prior to the Seventh Review Conference, which is to be held no later than the end of 2011, and to hold a one-week meeting of experts to prepare for each meeting of the States parties,

1. *Notes with satisfaction* the increase in the number of States parties to the Convention on the Prohibition of the Development, Production and Stockpiling of Bacteriological (Biological) and Toxin Weapons and on Their Destruction, reaffirms the call upon all signatory States that have not yet ratified the Convention to do so without delay, and calls upon those States that have not signed the Convention to become parties thereto at an early date, thus contributing to the achievement of universal adherence to the Convention;

2. *Welcomes* the information and data provided to date, and reiterates its call upon all States parties to the Convention to participate in the exchange of information and data agreed to in the Final Declaration of the Third Review Conference of the Parties to the Convention;

3. *Also welcomes* the successful launching of the 2007–2010 intersessional process, and in this context further welcomes the discussion aimed at the promotion of common understanding and effective action on topics agreed on at the Sixth Review Conference, and urges States parties to continue to participate actively in the intersessional process;

4. *Notes with satisfaction* that the Sixth Review Conference agreed on several measures to update the mechanism for the transmission of information in the framework of the confidence-building measures;

5. *Recalls* the decisions reached at the Sixth Review Conference, and calls upon States parties to the Convention to participate in their implementation;

6. *Urges* States parties to continue to work closely with the Implementation Support Unit of the Conference on Disarmament Secretariat and Conference Support Branch of the Office for Disarmament Affairs in fulfilling its mandate, in accordance with the decision of the Sixth Review Conference;

7. *Requests* the Secretary-General to continue to render the necessary assistance to the depositary Governments of the Convention and to provide such services as may be required for the implementation of the decisions and recommendations of the Review Conferences, including all assistance to the annual meetings of the States parties and the meetings of experts;

8. *Decides* to include in the provisional agenda of its sixty-fourth session the item entitled "Convention on the Prohibition of the Development, Production and Stockpiling of Bacteriological (Biological) and Toxin Weapons and on Their Destruction".

Chemical weapons

Chemical weapons convention

Guinea-Bissau and Lebanon ratified or acceded to the Convention on the Prohibition of the Development, Production, Stockpiling and Use of Chemical Weapons and on Their Destruction (CWC), bringing the number of States parties to 185 by the end of 2008. The Convention was adopted by the Conference on Disarmament in 1992 [YUN 1992, p. 65] and entered into force in 1997 [YUN 1997, p. 499] with 165 signatories.

Second Review Conference

The Second Review Conference of the States Parties to the Convention (The Hague, 7–18 April), with the participation of 114 States parties, reviewed the operation of the Convention since the First Review Conference in 2003 [YUN 2003, p. 560]. The Conference adopted a final report [RC-2/4] containing an in-depth review of the Convention's implementation and future guidance.

In his message to the Conference, the Secretary-General stressed that CWC was one of the world's most successful disarmament treaties, with near-universal membership. He noted that the Action Plan on universality and national implementation, recommended by the First Review Conference, had been effective both in promoting adherence to the Convention and in implementation assistance. In his capacity as depositary, the Secretary-General urged Governments that had not yet done so to ratify or accede to it without delay. He further stressed that all States parties had the obligation to destroy their chemical weapons and production facilities, noting that the possessor States must destroy their stockpiles completely before the final 29 April 2012 deadline established pursuant to the Convention.

In his opening statement, the Director-General of the Organization for the Prohibition of Chemical Weapons (OPCW) recalled its core objectives, including complete chemical disarmament. He reported that 26,538 metric tons of Category 1 chemical weapons, which represented over 38 per cent of the total declared stockpiles, had been destroyed under OPCW verification, while 52 per cent of Category 2 chemical weapons, had been completely eliminated. The 65 chemical weapons production facilities declared to OPCW by 12 States parties had all been inactivated, with 94 per cent of them either having been destroyed or converted for peaceful purposes. Noting that the non-proliferation of chemical weapons was a long-term fundamental goal of the Convention and OPCW's second core objective, he highlighted the substantial progress made by its industry verification regime through data monitoring and on-site inspection, as envisaged in the Convention's article VI.

The report adopted by the Second Review Conference reaffirmed that complete destruction of chemical weapons was essential for the realization of the objectives and purposes of the Convention. It reaffirmed the importance of the possessor States parties' obligation to complete the destruction of their stockpiles within the final extended deadline of April 2012, as set by the Conference at its eleventh session [YUN 2006, p. 653], and welcomed the statements of possessor States reiterating their commitment to doing so. Noting that OPCW had established an effective verification system to achieve CWC's non-proliferation and confidence-building aims, it highlighted that after more than 3,000 inspections were carried out at over 1,080 sites in 80 States, not one case of non-compliance was reported. The Conference re-emphasized the continuing relevance and importance of article X on assistance and protection against chemical weapons for States parties. That was recognized as being a motivating factor for States not party to the Convention to join it. Similarly, States parties emphasized the importance of article XI on international cooperation to promote peaceful uses of chemistry as fundamental tools for the objectives and purposes of CWC.

The Conference again stressed the importance of achieving CWC universality and full and effective national implementation. It urged the remaining 12 States not party to the Convention to ratify or accede to it as a matter of urgency and without preconditions.

Thirteenth Session of the Conference of States Parties

At the thirteenth session of the Conference of States Parties (The Hague, 2–5 December), the Director-General of OPCW noted that in follow-up to the Second Review Conference (see p. 606), the OPCW Secretariat had prepared a number of documents, one of which referred to the long-term strategy to address the relationship with the various stakeholders, and that the Secretariat would submit to the Executive Council its views on options to enhance the interaction among the Scientific Advisory Board, States parties and the policymaking organs.

GENERAL ASSEMBLY ACTION

On 2 December [meeting 61], the General Assembly, on the recommendation of the First Committee [A/63/389], adopted **resolution 63/48** without vote [agenda item 89 *(k)*].

Implementation of the Convention on the Prohibition of the Development, Production, Stockpiling and Use of Chemical Weapons and on Their Destruction

The General Assembly,

Recalling its previous resolutions on the subject of chemical weapons, in particular resolution 62/23 of 5 December 2007, adopted without a vote, in which it noted with appreciation the ongoing work to achieve the objective and purpose of the Convention on the Prohibition of the Development, Production, Stockpiling and Use of Chemical Weapons and on Their Destruction,

Determined to achieve the effective prohibition of the development, production, acquisition, transfer, stockpiling and use of chemical weapons and their destruction,

Noting with satisfaction that, since the adoption of resolution 62/23, two additional States have acceded to the Convention, bringing the total number of States parties to the Convention to one hundred and eighty-four,

Reaffirming the importance of the outcome of the Second Special Session of the Conference of the States Parties to Review the Operation of the Chemical Weapons Convention (hereinafter "the Second Review Conference"), including the consensus final report, which addressed all aspects of the Convention and made important recommendations on its continued implementation,

Emphasizing that the Second Review Conference welcomed the fact that, eleven years after its entry into force, the Convention remains a unique multilateral agreement banning an entire category of weapons of mass destruction in a non-discriminatory and verifiable manner under strict and effective international control,

1. *Emphasizes* that the universality of the Convention on the Prohibition of the Development, Production, Stockpiling and Use of Chemical Weapons and on Their Destruction is fundamental to the achievement of its objective and purpose, acknowledges progress made in the implementation of the action plan for the universality of the Convention, and calls upon all States that have not yet done so to become parties to the Convention without delay;

2. *Underlines* that implementation of the Convention makes a major contribution to international peace and security through the elimination of existing stockpiles of chemical weapons, the prohibition of the acquisition or use of chemical weapons, and provides for assistance and protection in the event of use, or threat of use, of chemical weapons and for international cooperation for peaceful purposes in the field of chemical activities;

3. *Stresses* the importance to the Convention that all possessors of chemical weapons, chemical weapons production facilities or chemical weapons development facilities, including previously declared possessor States, should be among the States parties to the Convention, and welcomes progress to that end;

4. *Reaffirms* the obligation of the States parties to the Convention to destroy chemical weapons and to destroy or convert chemical weapons production facilities within the time limits provided for by the Convention;

5. *Stresses* that the full and effective implementation of all provisions of the Convention, including those on national implementation (article VII) and assistance and protection (article X), constitutes an important contribution to the efforts of the United Nations in the global fight against terrorism in all its forms and manifestations;

6. *Notes* that the effective application of the verification system builds confidence in compliance with the Convention by States parties;

7. *Stresses* the importance of the Organization for the Prohibition of Chemical Weapons in verifying compliance with the provisions of the Convention as well as in promoting the timely and efficient accomplishment of all its objectives;

8. *Urges* all States parties to the Convention to meet in full and on time their obligations under the Convention and to support the Organization for the Prohibition of Chemical Weapons in its implementation activities;

9. *Welcomes* progress made in the national implementation of article VII obligations, commends the States parties and the Technical Secretariat for assisting other States parties, on request, with the implementation of the follow-up to the plan of action regarding article VII obligations, and urges States parties that have not fulfilled their obligations under article VII to do so without further delay, in accordance with their constitutional processes;

10. *Emphasizes* the continuing relevance and importance of the provisions of article X of the Convention, and welcomes the activities of the Organization for the Prohibition of Chemical Weapons in relation to assistance and protection against chemical weapons;

11. *Reaffirms* that the provisions of the Convention shall be implemented in a manner that avoids hampering the economic or technological development of States parties and international cooperation in the field of chemical activities for purposes not prohibited under the Convention, including the international exchange of scientific and technical information, and chemicals and equipment for the production, processing or use of chemicals for purposes not prohibited under the Convention;

12. *Emphasizes* the importance of article XI provisions relating to the economic and technological development of States parties, recalls that the full, effective and non-discriminatory implementation of those provisions contributes to universality, and also reaffirms the undertaking of the States parties to foster international cooperation for peaceful purposes in the field of chemical activities of the States parties and the importance of that cooperation and its contribution to the promotion of the Convention as a whole;

13. *Notes with appreciation* the ongoing work of the Organization for the Prohibition of Chemical Weapons to achieve the objective and purpose of the Convention, to ensure the full implementation of its provisions, including those for international verification of compliance with it, and to provide a forum for consultation and cooperation among States parties, and also notes with appreciation the substantial contribution of the Technical Secretariat and the Director-General to the continued development and success of the Organization;

14. *Welcomes* the cooperation between the United Nations and the Organization for the Prohibition of Chemical Weapons within the framework of the Relationship Agreement between the United Nations and the Organization, in accordance with the provisions of the Convention;

15. *Decides* to include in the provisional agenda of its sixty-fourth session the item entitled "Implementation of the Convention on the Prohibition of the Development, Production, Stockpiling and Use of Chemical Weapons and on Their Destruction".

Organization for the Prohibition of Chemical Weapons

OPCW, mandated to oversee CWC implementation and to provide a forum for consultations and cooperation among States parties, continued to make progress in the three areas of work under the Convention: chemical disarmament; non-proliferation, assistance and protection; and international cooperation, as detailed in a December report [C-14/4] on its activities during the year.

In 2008, OPCW verified the destruction of 4,137 metric tonnes of chemical weapons, with more than 30,000 metric tonnes of chemical weapons having been verified as destroyed by 31 December. One State party completed the destruction of all its chemical weapons, leaving four remaining possessor States at the end of the year. By 31 December, India had destroyed 99 per cent, the Libyan Arab Jamahiriya 2 per cent, the Russian Federation 30 per cent, and the United States 57 per cent of their declared stockpiles. Nine of the 12 States parties that had declared chemical weapons production facilities had either destroyed or converted all of them. Out of 65 declared facilities, four remained to be fully destroyed or converted.

Under article VI of the Convention, the OPCW secretariat inspected 200 chemical-industry facilities. Measures undertaken to further optimize the chemical-industry inspection regime included a greater use of sequential inspections (that is, conducting several inspections during a single mission), a reduction in the size of inspection teams, increased electronic processing of declarations through the Verification Information System, and the release of the software for creating electronic declarations. The start-up phase of sampling and analysis was completed in March.

OPCW continued to coordinate and deliver protection against chemical weapons under article X of the Convention and provided training to strengthen national capacities. It organized seminars, workshops, and a regional exercise with a view to establishing regional coordination. The Secretariat continued to develop its capacity to coordinate and mobilize the international-response mechanism. As part of that effort, exercise TRIPLEX 2008 focused on the development of capacities for a humanitarian response to complex emergencies.

OPCW also continued to promote the peaceful use of chemistry, and to facilitate fulfilment by Member States of their national obligations. It assisted them in developing capabilities to deal with any situation arising from the use or threat of use of chemical weapons, and continued to provide support to the African States parties to enable them to meet their requirements under the Convention, holding a number of training and capacity-building courses.

OPCW further pursued the implementation of its mandate under article XI, relating to economic and technological development, through a number of programmes. It assisted States parties, in the form of workshops, courses, and visits, to meet their obligations under article VII of the Convention. At the Tenth Annual Meeting of National Authorities (The Hague, 28–30 November), 92 States parties were represented. The Meeting included a thematic segment devoted to the role of industry in CWC implementation. The Director-General noted that 177 out of 184 States parties had established national authorities, a requirement under the Convention and a key element in its implementation. A European Union-sponsored day for national authorities of OPCW Member States was held at OPCW headquarters on 1 December, focusing in two separate sessions on the import and export of scheduled chemicals, article X submissions and legal aspects related to CWC implementation, and on preparing and handling industry inspections.

The OPCW Executive Council, at its fifty-second (4–7 March), fifty-third (24–27 June) and fifty-fourth (14–17 October) sessions, addressed issues relating to deadlines for the destruction of chemical weapons stockpiles; the agreed detailed plans for verification of the destruction of chemical weapons at a number of facilities and approved amendments to various facility agreements regarding on-site inspections; revisions to the specifications for three items of inspection equipment; the guidelines regarding declaration of import and export data for chemicals; and the obligation of possessor States parties to destroy their chemical weapons within the extended deadlines. It welcomed the positive steps the Secretariat was undertaking on the implementation of the programme for Africa.

The Secretary-General, by a 22 July note [A/63/155], transmitted to the General Assembly the 2006 OPCW report and the 2007 draft report, in accordance with the Agreement concerning the Relationship between the United Nations and OPCW, signed in 2000 [YUN 2000, p. 516], as outlined in Assembly resolution 55/283 [YUN 2001, p. 495], and which entered into force in 2001.

GENERAL ASSEMBLY ACTION

On 5 December [meeting 64], the General Assembly adopted **resolution 63/115** [draft A/63/L.46 & Add.1] without vote [agenda item 114 *(o)*].

Cooperation between the United Nations and the Organization for the Prohibition of Chemical Weapons

The General Assembly,

Recalling its resolution 61/224 of 20 December 2006 on cooperation between the United Nations and the Organization for the Prohibition of Chemical Weapons,

Having received the annual report for 2006 and the draft report for 2007 of the Organization for the Prohibition of Chemical Weapons on the implementation of the Convention on the Prohibition of the Development, Production, Stockpiling and Use of Chemical Weapons and on Their Destruction,

1. *Takes note* of the annual report for 2006 and the draft report for 2007 of the Organization for the Prohibition of Chemical Weapons submitted on its behalf by its Director-General;

2. *Welcomes* the successful conclusion of the Second Special Session of the Conference of the States Parties to Review the Operation of the Chemical Weapons Convention, held in The Hague from 7 to 18 April 2008, and its important outcome, including the consensus final report, which addressed all aspects of the Convention and made important recommendations on its continued implementation;

3. *Decides* to include in the provisional agenda of its sixty-fifth session the sub-item entitled "Cooperation

between the United Nations and the Organization for the Prohibition of Chemical Weapons".

1925 Geneva Protocol

On 8 February, the Protocol for the Prohibition of the Use in War of Asphyxiating, Poisonous or Other Gases, and of Bacteriological Methods of Warfare (the 1925 Geneva Protocol) attained the 80th anniversary of its entry into force.

In response to General Assembly resolution 61/61 [YUN 2006, p. 652], the Secretary-General reported in a June note [A/63/91] that the depositary of the 1925 Geneva Protocol had received no notice of withdrawals of reservations since the adoption of that resolution.

GENERAL ASSEMBLY ACTION

On 2 December [meeting 61], the General Assembly, on the recommendation of the First Committee [A/63/389], adopted **resolution 63/53** by recorded vote (174-0-4) [agenda item 89].

Measures to uphold the authority of the 1925 Geneva Protocol

The General Assembly,

Recalling its previous resolutions on the subject, in particular resolution 61/61 of 6 December 2006,

Determined to act with a view to achieving effective progress towards general and complete disarmament under strict and effective international control,

Recalling the long-standing determination of the international community to achieve the effective prohibition of the development, production, stockpiling and use of chemical and biological weapons as well as the continuing support for measures to uphold the authority of the Protocol for the Prohibition of the Use in War of Asphyxiating, Poisonous or Other Gases, and of Bacteriological Methods of Warfare, signed at Geneva on 17 June 1925, as expressed by consensus in many previous resolutions,

Emphasizing the necessity of easing international tension and strengthening trust and confidence between States,

1. *Takes note* of the note by the Secretary-General;

2. *Renews its previous call* to all States to observe strictly the principles and objectives of the Protocol for the Prohibition of the Use in War of Asphyxiating, Poisonous or Other Gases, and of Bacteriological Methods of Warfare, and reaffirms the vital necessity of upholding its provisions;

3. *Calls upon* those States that continue to maintain reservations to the 1925 Geneva Protocol to withdraw them;

4. *Requests* the Secretary-General to submit to the General Assembly at its sixty-fifth session a report on the implementation of the present resolution.

RECORDED VOTE ON RESOLUTION 63/53:

In favour: Afghanistan, Albania, Algeria, Andorra, Angola, Antigua-Barbuda, Argentina, Armenia, Australia, Austria, Azerbaijan, Bahamas, Bahrain, Bangladesh, Barbados, Belarus, Belgium, Belize, Benin, Bhutan, Bolivia, Bosnia and Herzegovina, Botswana, Brazil, Brunei Darussalam, Bulgaria, Burkina Faso, Burundi, Cambodia, Cameroon, Canada, Cape Verde, Chile, China, Colombia, Comoros, Congo, Costa Rica, Côte d'Ivoire, Croatia, Cuba, Cyprus, Czech Republic, Democratic People's Republic of Korea, Denmark, Djibouti, Dominica, Dominican Republic, Ecuador, Egypt, El Salvador, Equatorial Guinea, Eritrea, Estonia, Ethiopia, Finland, France, Georgia, Germany, Ghana, Greece, Grenada, Guatemala, Guinea, Guinea-Bissau, Guyana, Haiti, Honduras, Hungary, Iceland, India, Indonesia, Iran, Iraq, Ireland, Italy, Jamaica, Japan, Jordan, Kazakhstan, Kenya, Kuwait, Kyrgyzstan, Lao People's Democratic Republic, Latvia, Lebanon, Lesotho, Liberia, Libyan Arab Jamahiriya, Liechtenstein, Lithuania, Luxembourg, Madagascar, Malawi, Malaysia, Maldives, Mali, Malta, Mauritania, Mauritius, Mexico, Moldova, Monaco, Mongolia, Montenegro, Morocco, Mozambique, Myanmar, Namibia, Nauru, Nepal, Netherlands, New Zealand, Nicaragua, Niger, Nigeria, Norway, Oman, Pakistan, Panama, Papua New Guinea, Paraguay, Peru, Philippines, Poland, Portugal, Qatar, Republic of Korea, Romania, Russian Federation, Rwanda, Saint Lucia, Saint Vincent and the Grenadines, Samoa, San Marino, Sao Tome and Principe, Saudi Arabia, Senegal, Serbia, Singapore, Slovakia, Slovenia, Solomon Islands, South Africa, Spain, Sri Lanka, Sudan, Suriname, Swaziland, Sweden, Switzerland, Syrian Arab Republic, Tajikistan, The former Yugoslav Republic of Macedonia, Timor-Leste, Togo, Trinidad and Tobago, Tunisia, Turkey, Turkmenistan, Tuvalu, Uganda, Ukraine, United Arab Emirates, United Kingdom, United Republic of Tanzania, Uruguay, Uzbekistan, Vanuatu, Venezuela, Viet Nam, Yemen, Zambia, Zimbabwe.

Against: None.

Abstaining: Israel, Marshall Islands, Palau, United States.

Conventional weapons

Member States accorded considerable attention to conventional weapons, including small arms and light weapons, anti-personnel mines and cluster munitions. The Security Council in April held an open debate on issues related to the topic, and for the first time, the debate was broadened beyond merely the illicit trade. In July, the General Assembly convened its Third Biennial Meeting of States on the implementation of the UN Programme of Action to Prevent, Combat and Eradicate the Illicit Trade in Small Arms and Light Weapons in All Its Aspects, which produced a substantive outcome document with recommendations on its implementation. The Assembly decided to convene, no later than 2012, a conference to review progress made in implementing the Programme of Action. Sustained efforts resulted in the conclusion on 30 May of the Convention on Cluster Munitions in Dublin, Ireland. The process of examining the feasibility, scope and parameters of a possible arms trade treaty to provide international standards for the import, export and transfer of conventional arms continued, with emphasis on strengthening conventional arms control initiatives at the regional and subregional levels. Progress was made in the area of conventional ammunition with the conclusion of the work of the Group of Governmental Experts on enhancing cooperation on surplus ammunition stockpiles.

Meetings of States parties to the Convention on the Prohibition of the Use, Stockpiling, Production and Transfer of Anti-Personnel Mines and on Their Destruction (Mine-Ban Convention) and to the Convention on Prohibitions or Restrictions on the Use of Certain Conventional Weapons Which May Be Deemed to Be Excessively Injurious or to Have Indiscriminate Effects took place in November.

Disarmament Commission action. Working Group II of the Commission on Disarmament [A/63/42] continued its consideration of practical confidence-building measures in the field of conventional weapons, on which it held 10 meetings between 9 and 22 April. Despite extensive discussions and constructive engagement, the Working Group was unable to overcome outstanding issues in the Chairman's revised paper which constituted the basis of its deliberations.

GENERAL ASSEMBLY ACTION

On 2 December [meeting 61], on the recommendation of the First Committee [A/63/389], the General Assembly adopted **resolution 63/57** without vote [agenda item 89 *(g)*].

Information on confidence-building measures in the field of conventional arms

The General Assembly,

Guided by the purposes and principles enshrined in the Charter of the United Nations,

Bearing in mind the contribution of confidence-building measures in the field of conventional arms, adopted on the initiative and with the agreement of the States concerned, to the improvement of the overall international peace and security situation,

Convinced that the relationship between the development of confidence-building measures in the field of conventional arms and the international security environment can also be mutually reinforcing,

Considering the important role that confidence-building measures in the field of conventional arms can also play in creating favourable conditions for progress in the field of disarmament,

Recognizing that the exchange of information on confidence-building measures in the field of conventional arms contributes to mutual understanding and confidence among Member States,

Recalling its resolutions 59/92 of 3 December 2004, 60/82 of 8 December 2005 and 61/79 of 6 December 2006,

1. *Welcomes* all confidence-building measures in the field of conventional arms already undertaken by Member States as well as the information on such measures voluntarily provided;

2. *Encourages* Member States to continue to adopt confidence-building measures in the field of conventional arms and to provide information in that regard;

3. *Also encourages* Member States to continue the dialogue on confidence-building measures in the field of conventional arms;

4. *Welcomes* the establishment of the electronic database containing information provided by Member States, and requests the Secretary-General to keep the database updated and to assist Member States, at their request, in the organization of seminars, courses and workshops aimed at enhancing the knowledge of new developments in this field;

5. *Decides* to include in the provisional agenda of its sixty-fifth session the item entitled "Information on confidence-building measures in the field of conventional arms".

Towards an arms trade treaty

Pursuant to General Assembly resolution 61/89 [YUN 2006, p. 655], the Secretary-General established a Group of Governmental Experts to examine the feasibility, scope and draft parameters for a comprehensive, legally binding instrument establishing international standards for the import, export and transfer of conventional arms.

The Group, comprised of experts from 28 countries, met for three sessions (New York, 11–15 February, 12–16 May, 28 July–8 August), and noted that the question of feasibility had both political and technical dimensions, which impacted the security concerns of all States. Treaty feasibility would be dependent on establishing: collectively agreed- upon objectives; practical applicability; resistance to political abuse; and potential for universality. On the issue of scope, the Group noted that no single existing instrument contained an all-encompassing list of options raised by Member States. The Group considered the seven categories of the UN Register of Conventional Arms, small arms and light weapons, and if categories such as ammunition, explosives, components, defence services, technology related to the manufacture of weapons and ammunition should be included. On types of activities, the Experts looked at exports, imports, transfers, re-exports, transit, trans-shipment, licensing, transportation, technology transfer and manufacturing, and foreign licensing production, as well as countering illegal re-exports, unlicensed production and transfers, illicit arms brokering, and transfer of arms to non-State actors. Also mentioned were stockpiles and conventional weapons production.

On the issue of draft parameters, the Group agreed that UN Charter principles would be central to any potential treaty and would have to take into account General Assembly resolutions and the Guidelines for international arms transfers adopted by the Disarmament Commission in 1996 [YUN 1996, p. 448]. Terrorism and organized crime, regional stability, socio-economic development, end-use and end-user assurances, diversion, and compliance with Security Council arms embargoes and other international obligations were among the aspects that needed to be addressed.

Noting the complexity of the issues related to conventional arms, the Group concluded that further consideration was required, within the UN framework and in an open and transparent manner, to achieve, on the basis of consensus, a balance that would benefit all.

The Secretary-General, in August, presented the Group's report to the General Assembly [A/63/334]. Earlier, in a February addendum [A/62/278/Add.4], to a 2007 report [YUN 2007, p. 570], he had submitted the view of a Member State on an arms trade treaty.

GENERAL ASSEMBLY ACTION

On 24 December [meeting 74], the General Assembly, on the recommendation of the First Committee [A/63/389], adopted **resolution 63/240** by recorded vote (133-1-19) [agenda item 89].

Towards an arms trade treaty: establishing common international standards for the import, export and transfer of conventional arms

The General Assembly,

Guided by the purposes and principles enshrined in the Charter of the United Nations, and reaffirming its respect for and commitment to international law,

Recalling its resolutions 46/36 L of 9 December 1991, 51/45 N of 10 December 1996, 51/47 B of 10 December 1996, 56/24 V of 24 December 2001, 60/69 and 60/82 of 8 December 2005, and 61/89 of 6 December 2006,

Recognizing that arms control, disarmament and non-proliferation are essential for the maintenance of international peace and security,

Reaffirming the inherent right of all States to individual or collective self-defence in accordance with Article 51 of the Charter,

Acknowledging the right of all States to manufacture, import, export, transfer and retain conventional arms for self-defence and security needs, and in order to participate in peace support operations,

Recalling the obligations of all States to fully comply with arms embargoes decided by the Security Council in accordance with the Charter,

Reaffirming its respect for international law, including international human rights law and international humanitarian law, and the Charter,

Taking note of and encouraging relevant initiatives, undertaken at the international, regional and subregional levels between States, including those of the United Nations, and of the role played by non-governmental organizations and civil society, to enhance cooperation, improve information exchange and transparency and implement confidence-building measures in the field of responsible arms trade,

Recognizing that the absence of common international standards for the import, export and transfer of conventional arms is one of the contributory factors to conflict, the displacement of people, crime and terrorism, thereby undermining peace, reconciliation, safety, security, stability and sustainable social and economic development,

Acknowledging the growing support across many regions for concluding a legally binding instrument negotiated on a non-discriminatory, transparent and multilateral basis, to establish common international standards for the import, export and transfer of conventional arms, including through regional and subregional workshops and seminars held in order to discuss the initiative launched by the General Assembly in its resolution 61/89,

Taking due note of the views expressed by Member States on the feasibility, scope and draft parameters for a comprehensive, legally binding instrument establishing common international standards for the import, export and transfer of conventional arms, submitted to the Secretary-General at his request,

Welcoming the report of the Secretary-General, prepared with the assistance of the Group of Governmental Experts, which states that, in view of the complexity of the issues of conventional arms transfers, further consideration of efforts within the United Nations to address the international trade in conventional arms is required on a step-by-step basis in an open and transparent manner to achieve, on the basis of consensus, a balance that will provide benefit to all, with the principles of the Charter of the United Nations at the centre of such efforts,

Determined to prevent the diversion of conventional arms, including small arms and light weapons, from the legal to the illicit market,

1. *Endorses* the report of the Secretary-General prepared with the assistance of the Group of Governmental Experts, taking into account the views of Member States;

2. *Encourages* all States to implement and address, on a national basis, the relevant recommendations contained in paragraphs 28 and 29 of the report of the Secretary-General, and commends all States to carefully consider how to achieve such implementation in order to ensure that their national systems and internal controls are at the highest possible standards to prevent the diversion of conventional arms from the legal to the illicit market, where they can be used for terrorist acts, organized crime and other criminal activities, and further calls upon those States in a position to do so to render assistance in this regard upon request;

3. *Decides*, in order to facilitate further consideration on the implementation of the relevant recommendation contained in paragraph 27 of the report of the Secretary-General on a step-by-step basis among all States Members of the United Nations, in an open and transparent manner, to establish an open-ended working group, to meet for up to six one-week sessions starting in 2009, of which the two sessions foreseen in 2009 will be held in New York, from 2 to 6 March and 13 to 17 July, respectively;

4. *Decides also* that the open-ended working group will hold a one-day organizational session in New York by 27 February 2009 in order to agree on the organiza-

tional arrangements connected with the working group, including the dates and venues for its future substantive sessions;

5. *Decides further* that the open-ended working group will, during 2009, further consider those elements in the report of the Group of Governmental Experts where consensus could be developed for their inclusion in an eventual legally binding treaty on the import, export and transfer of conventional arms which provides a balance giving benefit to all, with the principles of the Charter of the United Nations and other existing international obligations at the centre of such considerations, and transmit an initial report from the working group to the General Assembly for consideration at its sixty-fourth session;

6. *Requests* the Secretary-General to transmit the replies of Member States and the report of the Group of Governmental Experts to the open-ended working group and to render the working group all necessary assistance, including the provision of essential background information and relevant documents;

7. *Decides* to include in the provisional agenda of its sixty-fourth session an item entitled "Towards an arms trade treaty: establishing common international standards for the import, export and transfer of conventional arms".

RECORDED VOTE ON RESOLUTION 63/240:

In favour: Afghanistan, Albania, Algeria, Angola, Antigua and Barbuda, Argentina, Armenia, Australia, Austria, Azerbaijan, Bangladesh, Barbados, Belgium, Bolivia, Bosnia and Herzegovina, Botswana, Brazil, Brunei Darussalam, Bulgaria, Burkina Faso, Burundi, Cambodia, Cameroon, Canada, Chile, Colombia, Congo, Costa Rica, Côte d'Ivoire, Croatia, Cuba, Cyprus, Czech Republic, Denmark, Djibouti, Dominican Republic, Ecuador, Eritrea, Estonia, Ethiopia, Finland, France, Gambia, Georgia, Germany, Ghana, Greece, Grenada, Guatemala, Honduras, Hungary, Iceland, Indonesia, Ireland, Italy, Jamaica, Japan, Jordan, Kazakhstan, Kenya, Kyrgyzstan, Latvia, Lebanon, Lesotho, Liechtenstein, Lithuania, Luxembourg, Madagascar, Malawi, Malaysia, Maldives, Mali, Malta, Marshall Islands, Mauritania, Mauritius, Mexico, Micronesia, Moldova, Monaco, Mongolia, Montenegro, Morocco, Mozambique, Myanmar, Namibia, Nauru, Nepal, Netherlands, New Zealand, Nicaragua, Niger, Nigeria, Norway, Oman, Palau, Panama, Paraguay, Peru, Philippines, Poland, Portugal, Republic of Korea, Romania, Samoa, San Marino, Senegal, Serbia, Singapore, Slovakia, Slovenia, Solomon Islands, South Africa, Spain, Sri Lanka, Swaziland, Sweden, Switzerland, Tajikistan, Thailand, The former Yugoslav Republic of Macedonia, Timor-Leste, Togo, Trinidad and Tobago, Tunisia, Turkey, Uganda, Ukraine, United Kingdom, United Republic of Tanzania, Uruguay, Zambia, Zimbabwe.

Against: United States.

Abstaining: Bahrain, Belarus, China, Egypt, India, Iran, Iraq, Israel, Kuwait, Libyan Arab Jamahiriya, Pakistan, Qatar, Russian Federation, Saudi Arabia, Sudan, Syrian Arab Republic, United Arab Emirates, Venezuela, Yemen.

Small arms

Report of Secretary-General. In an April report [S/2008/258] submitted pursuant to a 2007 Security Council request [YUN 2007, p. 570], the Secretary-General discussed various aspects of small arms, with an emphasis on the negative impact illicit small arms had on security, human rights and social and economic development, in particular in areas of crisis and post-conflict situations. The report analysed global instruments of relevance in stemming uncontrolled proliferation of small arms. The Secretary-General made 13 recommendations geared to strengthening coordination on the issue, especially within the UN system.

Security Council consideration. Having the Secretary-General's report before it, the Security Council met on 30 April [meeting 5881] in an open debate to discuss small arms and light weapons-related issues. For the first time, the debate was broadened beyond the illicit trade of such weapons, reflecting the increased recognition that effective policy measures should be comprehensive and cross-cutting. UNODA introduced the report, and speakers from almost 50 countries joined in the discussion.

Report of Secretary-General. In an August report [A/63/261], the Secretary-General described activities to consolidate peace through practical disarmament measures, and summarized national, regional and subregional assistance to States in their efforts to curb the illicit trade of small arms and light weapons. The report also provided an overview of the implementation by the UN system, intergovernmental organizations and States of General Assembly resolution 62/47 [YUN 2007, p. 574]. Pursuant to that resolution, 109 reports from States had been received on the implementation of the Programme of Action to curb illicit trade in small arms, 104 of which also included information on the implementation of the International Tracing Instrument, while 84 also provided information on activities related to curbing illicit brokering.

The Secretary-General reported that under the auspices of the UN Coordinating Action on Small Arms (CASA), two important initiatives had been launched: the Programme of Action Implementation Support System, which succeeded the CASA database and served as an electronic "one-stop shop" for information on the implementation of the Programme of Action and as a clearing house for international cooperation and assistance; and the development of international small arms control standards aimed at responding to the challenges posed by the uncontrolled proliferation of small arms.

In conclusion, the Secretary-General stated that the unprecedented adoption of an outcome document at the Third Biennial Meeting of States (see p. 614) constituted a reaffirmation of Member States' commitment to the full implementation of the Programme of Action and the adoption of a more results-oriented approach. The discussion at the Meeting emphasized the critical importance of international cooperation and assistance and highlighted the need for States to implement the 2007 Group of Governmental Experts recommendations on illicit arms brokering [ibid., p. 571].

During the reporting period, the implementation of the International Tracing Instrument was one of the priorities of States, and the regional workshops organized by UNODA underscored the need for continued efforts to promote the Instrument and to develop concrete projects aimed at building States' capacity in marking, record-keeping and tracing. The workshops were useful in enhancing the understanding of the Instrument's provisions, familiarizing participants with the tracing tools available through the International Criminal Police Organization (Interpol) and preparing for consideration of the Instrument at the Third Biennial Meeting of States.

Other action. In an effort to publicize linkages between gender and small arms issues, UNODA organized during the year a number of public events in partnership with civil society.

Programme of Action on illicit trade in small arms

Third Biennial Meeting of States. Pursuant to General Assembly resolution 62/47 [YUN 2007, p. 574], the Third Biennial Meeting of States to Consider the Implementation of the Programme of Action to Prevent, Combat and Eradicate the Illicit Trade in Small Arms and Light Weapons in All Its Aspects [YUN 2001, p. 499] was held (New York, 14–18 July) [A/CONF.192/BMS/2008/3]. During ten plenary sessions, Member States considered four main themes: international cooperation, assistance and national capacity-building; illicit brokering; stockpile management; and small arms and light weapons tracing. The outcome of the first Meeting of States to consider the implementation of the International Instrument to Enable States to Identify and Trace, in a Timely and Reliable Manner, Illicit Small Arms and Light Weapons (International Tracing Instrument or ITI) was annexed to the report of the Third Biennial Meeting .

The national reports on implementation of the Programme of Action submitted by 109 States were analysed by the United Nations Institute for Disarmament Research in a draft report entitled *Implementing the United Nations Programme of Action on Small Arms and Light Weapons.*

The Meeting was able to adopt, for the first time, a report that contained a substantive outcome for each theme considered, including recommendations for the "way forward". Despite the efforts of the Chair and the facilitators to achieve consensus on the recommendations, the report was adopted by recorded vote (134-0-2).

As a contribution to the Meeting, UNODA, together with the Office of the Special Representative for Children and Armed Conflict and the International Action Network on Small Arms of Belgium, on 15 June, sponsored a high-profile panel discussion on the impact of small arms on children, which was aimed at raising global awareness and exploring solutions for better protection of children.

Illicit arms brokering

The United Nations continued to pay attention to the threat posed by black-market weapons-related activities, including through illicit brokering and intermediation services. The Organization remained engaged in efforts to prevent and combat illicit arms brokering, particularly with respect to small arms and light weapons. The report of the Group of Governmental Experts, established by General Assembly resolution 60/81 [YUN 2005, p. 625] to consider further steps for enhancing international cooperation in preventing, combating and eradicating illicit brokering, emphasized that the globalized environment in which arms brokering took place necessitated the development of a holistic approach to address the issue.

At the Third Biennial Meeting, States noted the negative impact of illicit brokering on security, stability, conflict resolution, development, the prevention of crime and drug trafficking, humanitarian assistance, international humanitarian law and the implementation of arms embargoes. They reaffirmed that illicit brokering was a global problem requiring a comprehensive approach, and noted that the 2007 Group of Governmental Experts [YUN 2007, p. 571] had provided a set of key recommendations to address the challenges posed by illicit brokering. The importance of end-user certification was noted, as was the importance of regional and international initiatives and of subregional, regional and international cooperation. The UN role in enhancing information-sharing on illicit brokering was also recognized. In addition, States exchanged views on the possibility of negotiating an international legally binding instrument on illicit brokering.

Recognizing that addressing illicit brokering was essential to the full and effective implementation of the Programme of Action, States reaffirmed their commitment to develop regulatory national legislation or administrative procedures; acknowledged the importance of implementing the recommendations by the Group of Governmental Experts; underlined the importance of international cooperation, including among national law enforcement agencies; and declared that they would consider working to advance the process in order to reach agreements and establish mechanisms to find solutions.

GENERAL ASSEMBLY ACTION

On 2 December [meeting 61], the General Assembly, on the recommendation of the First Committee [A/63/389], adopted **resolution 63/67** without vote [agenda item 89].

Preventing and combating illicit brokering activities

The General Assembly,

Noting the threat to international peace and security posed by illicit brokering activities circumventing the international arms control and non-proliferation framework,

Concerned that, if proper measures are not taken, the illicit brokering of arms in all its aspects will adversely affect the maintenance of international peace and security and prolong conflicts, thereby impeding sustainable economic and social development, and result in the threat of illicit transfers of conventional arms and the acquisition of weapons of mass destruction by non-State actors,

Recognizing the need for Member States to prevent and combat illicit brokering activities, which covers not only conventional arms but also materials, equipment and technology that could contribute to the proliferation of weapons of mass destruction and their means of delivery,

Reaffirming that efforts to prevent and combat illicit brokering activities should not hamper the legitimate arms trade and international cooperation with respect to materials, equipment and technology for peaceful purposes,

Recalling Security Council resolution 1540(2004) of 28 April 2004, in particular paragraph 3, which determined that all States should develop and maintain appropriate effective border controls and law enforcement efforts to detect, deter, prevent and combat, including through international cooperation when necessary, illicit trafficking and brokering in accordance with their national legal authorities and legislation and consistent with international law,

Recalling also relevant resolutions adopted in previous years, including resolutions 62/40 and 62/47 of 5 December 2007, which include calls for the control of brokering activities, as well as resolution 62/26 of 5 December 2007, by which the General Assembly invited Member States to enact or improve national legislation on the transfer of arms, military equipment and dual-use goods and technology,

Taking note of international efforts to prevent and combat illicit arms brokering, in particular in small arms and light weapons, as demonstrated by the adoption in 2001 of the Programme of Action to Prevent, Combat and Eradicate the Illicit Trade in Small Arms and Light Weapons in All Its Aspects, and the entry into force in 2005 of the Protocol against the Illicit Manufacturing of and Trafficking in Firearms, Their Parts and Components and Ammunition, supplementing the United Nations Convention against Transnational Organized Crime,

Noting the report of the Group of Governmental Experts established pursuant to resolution 60/81 of 8 December 2005 to consider further steps to enhance international cooperation in preventing, combating and eradicating illicit brokering in small arms and light weapons as an international initiative within the framework of the United Nations,

Recalling the report of the Third Biennial Meeting of States to Consider the Implementation of the Programme of Action to Prevent, Combat and Eradicate the Illicit Trade in Small Arms and Light Weapons in All Its Aspects, which acknowledges the importance of implementing the recommendations contained in the report of the Group of Governmental Experts on illicit brokering, and of developing national legislation and administrative procedures in this area,

Underlining the inherent right of Member States to determine the specific scope and content of domestic regulations in accordance with their legislative frameworks and export control systems, consistent with international laws,

Welcoming the efforts made by Member States to implement laws and/or administrative measures to regulate arms brokering within their legal systems,

Acknowledging the constructive role civil society can play in raising awareness and providing practical expertise on the prevention of illicit brokering activities,

1. *Underlines* the commitment of Member States to address the threat posed by illicit brokering activities;

2. *Encourages* Member States to fully implement relevant international treaties, instruments and resolutions to prevent and combat illicit brokering activities;

3. *Calls upon* Member States to establish appropriate national laws and/or measures to prevent and combat the illicit brokering of conventional arms and of materials, equipment and technology that could contribute to the proliferation of weapons of mass destruction and their means of delivery, in a manner consistent with international law;

4. *Acknowledges* that national efforts to prevent and combat illicit brokering activities can be reinforced by such efforts at the regional and subregional levels;

5. *Emphasizes* the importance of international cooperation and assistance, capacity-building and information-sharing in preventing and combating illicit brokering activities;

6. *Encourages* Member States to draw, where appropriate, on the relevant expertise of civil society in developing effective measures to prevent and combat illicit brokering activities;

7. *Decides* to include in the provisional agenda of its sixty-fifth session an item entitled "Preventing and combating illicit brokering activities".

Stockpile management

In accordance with General Assembly resolution 61/72 [YUN 2006, p. 661], the Secretary-General established a Group of Governmental Experts to consider further steps to enhance cooperation with regard to the issue of conventional ammunition stockpiles in surplus. In three one-week sessions (Geneva, 14–18 January; New York, 30 March–4 April and 7–11 July), the Group examined a wide range of issues relating to conventional ammunition stockpiles and adopted a report [A/63/182] with a set of recommendations on measures that could be undertaken to address the problem at the national, regional and global levels.

The Group stressed that the problem was largely a result of inadequate stockpile management, which posed an excessive risk for two main reasons: stockpiles could become unstable and threaten public safety with explosions or contamination, and unsecured stockpiles could easily be diverted for illicit use. The Group's recommendations emphasized the need for greater international cooperation and assistance to address the problem. It proposed that: national stockpile management staff be educated and trained; technical guidelines be developed to assist States in improving their management capacities; and knowledge resource management on ammunition and technical issues within the UN system be improved to ensure that States had ready access to technical expertise and guidance for the safe and secure storage of ammunition and the disposal of surplus stockpiles.

Acting on the Group's recommendations, UNODA formulated a project for the development of technical guidelines for the stockpile management of conventional ammunition, which was expected to commence in 2009. The guidelines would be available for States to use on a voluntary basis.

Recognizing that effective stockpile management and responsible surplus disposal were essential to full and effective implementation of the Programme of Action and that poorly managed and inadequately secured stockpiles posed a security threat, States at the Third Biennial Meeting stressed the need for raising awareness among national authorities of the critical importance of putting in place adequate systems and procedures for national stockpile management. Among those procedures were revising policies and developing practical guidelines, as well as enhancing cooperation and exchange of information on national experiences and providing technical and financial support for capacity-building.

GENERAL ASSEMBLY ACTION

On 2 December [meeting 61], the General Assembly, on the recommendation of the First Committee [A/63/389], adopted **resolution 63/61** without vote [agenda item 89 *(c)*].

Problems arising from the accumulation of conventional ammunition stockpiles in surplus

The General Assembly,

Mindful of contributing to the process initiated within the framework of the United Nations reform to make the Organization more effective in maintaining peace and security by giving it the resources and tools it needs for conflict prevention, peaceful resolution of disputes, peacekeeping, post-conflict peacebuilding and reconstruction,

Underlining the importance of a comprehensive and integrated approach to disarmament through the development of practical measures,

Taking note of the report of the Group of Experts on the problem of ammunition and explosives,

Recalling the recommendation contained in paragraph 27 of the report submitted by the Chairman of the Open-ended Working Group to Negotiate an International Instrument to Enable States to Identify and Trace, in a Timely and Reliable Manner, Illicit Small Arms and Light Weapons, namely, to address the issue of small arms and light weapons ammunition in a comprehensive manner as part of a separate process conducted within the framework of the United Nations,

Noting with satisfaction the work and measures pursued at the regional and subregional levels with regard to the issue of conventional ammunition,

Recalling its decision 59/515 of 3 December 2004 and its resolution 60/74 of 8 December 2005, as well as its resolution 61/72 of 6 December 2006, by which it decided to include the issue of conventional ammunition stockpiles in surplus in the agenda of its sixty-third session,

1. *Encourages* all interested States to assess, on a voluntary basis, whether, in conformity with their legitimate security needs, parts of their stockpiles of conventional ammunition should be considered to be in surplus, and recognizes that the security of such stockpiles must be taken into consideration and that appropriate controls with regard to the security and safety of stockpiles of conventional ammunition are indispensable at the national level in order to eliminate the risk of explosion, pollution or diversion;

2. *Appeals* to all interested States to determine the size and nature of their surplus stockpiles of conventional ammunition, whether they represent a security risk, if appropriate, their means of destruction, and whether external assistance is needed to eliminate this risk;

3. *Encourages* States in a position to do so to assist interested States within a bilateral framework or through international or regional organizations, on a voluntary and transparent basis, in elaborating and implementing programmes to eliminate surplus stockpiles or to improve their management;

4. *Encourages* all Member States to examine the possibility of developing and implementing, within a national, regional or subregional framework, measures to address accordingly the illicit trafficking related to the accumulation of such stockpiles;

5. *Takes note* of the replies submitted by Member States in response to the Secretary-General's request for views regarding the risks arising from the accumulation of conventional ammunition stockpiles in surplus and regarding national ways of strengthening controls on conventional ammunition;

6. *Welcomes* the report by the Group of Governmental Experts established pursuant to resolution 61/72 to consider further steps to enhance cooperation with regard to the issue of conventional ammunition stockpiles in surplus, and strongly encourages States to implement its recommendations;

7. *Encourages* States in a position to do so to contribute, on a voluntary and transparent basis, to the development within the United Nations of technical guidelines for the stockpile management of conventional ammunition, which would be available for States to use on a voluntary basis, in order to assist States in improving their national stockpile management capacity, preventing the growth of conventional ammunition surpluses and addressing wider risk mitigation;

8. *Reiterates* its decision to address the issue of conventional ammunition stockpiles in surplus in a comprehensive manner;

9. *Decides* to include this issue in the provisional agenda of its sixty-fourth session.

International Tracing Instrument

The International Instrument to Enable States to Identify and Trace, in a Timely and Reliable Manner, Illicit Small Arms and Light Weapons (International Tracing Instrument or ITI) was adopted by General Assembly decision 60/519 [YUN 2005, p. 621]. The first Meeting of States to consider the implementation of ITI constituted a segment of the Third Meeting of States. In four regional workshops (Nairobi, 10–11 December 2007; Lome, Togo, 17–18 April 2008; Seoul, Republic of Korea, 27–28 May; Rio de Janeiro, Brazil, 11–12 June), UNODA, in collaboration with Interpol, raised awareness and helped States build capacity to implement the Instrument.

The Secretary-General, in his April report on small arms [S/2008/258] to the Security Council, stated that the Instrument could be of high practical value to counter illicit small arms trade, but its ultimate success depended on its actual implementation, for which a framework for assistance and cooperation was essential; it needed to be promoted and its implications understood by policymakers and practitioners.

With a view to ensuring full and effective implementation of the Instrument, States at the Third Meeting of States agreed to a number of measures, including: bringing national laws, regulations and administrative procedures in line with the Instrument; including in national reports information on experiences in tracing illicit small arms and light weapons; supporting the role of the United Nations in building national capacity; supporting the role of Interpol, including further development and promotion of the Interpol Weapons Electronic Tracing System and other mechanisms facilitating tracing; making use of and supporting the web-based Programme of Action Implementation Support System; and cooperating with civil society to advance implementation of the Instrument.

GENERAL ASSEMBLY ACTION

On 2 December [meeting 61], the General Assembly, on the recommendation of the First Committee [A/63/389], adopted **resolution 63/72** by recorded vote (181-1-0) [agenda item 89 *(z)*].

The illicit trade in small arms and light weapons in all its aspects

The General Assembly,

Recalling its resolution 62/47 of 5 December 2007 as well as all previous resolutions entitled "The illicit trade in small arms and light weapons in all its aspects", including resolution 56/24 V of 24 December 2001,

Emphasizing the importance of the continued and full implementation of the Programme of Action to Prevent, Combat and Eradicate the Illicit Trade in Small Arms and Light Weapons in All Its Aspects, adopted by the United Nations Conference on the Illicit Trade in Small Arms and Light Weapons in All Its Aspects,

Emphasizing also the importance of the continued and full implementation of the International Instrument to Enable States to Identify and Trace, in a Timely and Reliable Manner, Illicit Small Arms and Light Weapons (the International Tracing Instrument),

Recalling the commitment of States to the Programme of Action as the main framework for measures within the activities of the international community to prevent, combat and eradicate the illicit trade in small arms and light weapons in all its aspects,

Underlining the need for States to enhance their efforts to build national capacity for the effective implementation of the Programme of Action and the International Tracing Instrument,

Welcoming the efforts by Member States to submit, on a voluntary basis, national reports on their implementation of the Programme of Action,

Bearing in mind the importance of regular national reporting, which could greatly facilitate the rendering of international cooperation and assistance to affected States,

Noting the analysis of national reports prepared for the biennial meetings of States to consider the implementation of the Programme of Action by the United Nations Institute for Disarmament Research,

Taking into account the importance of regional approaches to the implementation of the Programme of Action,

Noting with satisfaction regional and subregional efforts being undertaken in support of the implementation of the Programme of Action, and commending the progress that has already been made in this regard, including tackling both supply and demand factors that are relevant to addressing the illicit trade in small arms and light weapons,

Recognizing that illicit brokering in small arms and light weapons is a serious problem that the international community should address urgently,

Recognizing also the efforts undertaken by non-governmental organizations in the provision of assistance to States for the implementation of the Programme of Action,

Welcoming the holding of the third biennial meeting of States to consider the implementation of the Programme of Action in New York, from 14 to 18 July 2008,

Welcoming also the establishment by the United Nations of the Programme of Action Implementation Support System, as well as the initiative by the United Nations Institute for Disarmament Research to develop the database for matching needs and resources,

Taking note of the report of the Secretary-General on the implementation of resolution 62/47,

1. *Underlines* the fact that the issue of the illicit trade in small arms and light weapons in all its aspects requires concerted efforts at the national, regional and international levels to prevent, combat and eradicate the illicit manufacture, transfer and circulation of small arms and light weapons and that their uncontrolled spread in many regions of the world has a wide range of humanitarian and

socio-economic consequences and poses a serious threat to peace, reconciliation, safety, security, stability and sustainable development at the individual, local, national, regional and international levels;

2. *Encourages* all initiatives, including those of the United Nations, other international organizations, regional and subregional organizations, non-governmental organizations and civil society, for the successful implementation of the Programme of Action to Prevent, Combat and Eradicate the Illicit Trade in Small Arms and Light Weapons in All Its Aspects, and calls upon all Member States to contribute towards the continued implementation of the Programme of Action at the national, regional and global levels;

3. *Encourages* States to implement the recommendations contained in the report of the Group of Governmental Experts established pursuant to resolution 60/81 to consider further steps to enhance international cooperation in preventing, combating and eradicating illicit brokering in small arms and light weapons;

4. *Endorses* the report adopted at the third biennial meeting of States to consider the implementation of the Programme of Action, and encourages all States to implement the measures highlighted in the section of the report entitled "The way forward";

5. *Encourages* all efforts to build national capacity for the effective implementation of the Programme of Action, including those highlighted in the report of the third biennial meeting of States;

6. *Decides* that, in conformity with the follow-up to the Programme of Action, the next biennial meeting of States to consider the national, regional and global implementation of the Programme of Action shall be held in New York for a period of one week, no later than in 2010;

7. *Also decides* that the meeting of States to consider the implementation of the International Tracing Instrument shall be held within the framework of the biennial meeting of States;

8. *Encourages* States to submit their national reports, to the extent possible, by the end of 2009, and for those in a position to do so to use the reporting template prepared by the United Nations Development Programme, and to include therein information on progress made in the implementation of the measures highlighted in the report of the third biennial meeting of States;

9. *Calls upon* all States to implement the International Tracing Instrument by, inter alia, including in their national reports information on the name and contact information of the national points of contact and on national marking practices related to markings used to indicate country of manufacture and/or country of import, as applicable;

10. *Encourages* States, on a voluntary basis, to make increasing use of their national reports as another tool for communicating assistance needs and information on the resources and mechanisms available to address such needs, and encourages States in a position to render such assistance to make use of these national reports;

11. *Stresses* the importance of the early designation of the Chair, and encourages the regional group which will designate the Chair of the fourth biennial meeting of States to nominate the Chair-designate by October 2009;

12. *Encourages* States to identify, in cooperation with the Chair-designate, well in advance of the fourth biennial meeting of States, priority issues or topics of relevance in the illicit trade in small arms and light weapons in all its aspects, including their implementation challenges and opportunities, as well as any follow-up to the third biennial meeting of States;

13. *Decides* to convene an open-ended meeting of governmental experts for a period of one week, no later than in 2011, to address key implementation challenges and opportunities relating to particular issues and themes, including international cooperation and assistance;

14. *Also decides* to convene a conference to review progress made in implementation of the Programme of Action, for a period of two weeks in New York, no later than in 2012;

15. *Encourages* interested States and international, regional and other relevant organizations in a position to do so, to convene regional meetings to consider and advance the implementation of the Programme of Action as well as the International Tracing Instrument;

16. *Emphasizes* the need to facilitate the implementation at the national level of the Programme of Action through the strengthening of national coordination agencies or bodies and institutional infrastructure;

17. *Also emphasizes* the fact that initiatives by the international community with respect to international cooperation and assistance remain essential and complementary to national implementation efforts, as well as to those at the regional and global levels;

18. *Recognizes* the necessity for interested States to develop effective coordination mechanisms, where they do not exist, in order to match the needs of States with existing resources to enhance the implementation of the Programme of Action and to make international cooperation and assistance more effective;

19. *Encourages* States to consider, among other mechanisms, the coherent identification of needs, priorities, national plans and programmes that may require international cooperation and assistance from States and regional and international organizations in a position to do so;

20. *Encourages* civil society and relevant organizations to strengthen their cooperation and work with States at the respective national and regional levels to achieve the implementation of the Programme of Action;

21. *Requests* the Secretary-General to report to the General Assembly at its sixty-fourth session on the implementation of the present resolution;

22. *Decides* to include in the provisional agenda of its sixty-fourth session the item entitled "The illicit trade in small arms and light weapons in all its aspects".

RECORDED VOTE ON RESOLUTION 63/72:

In favour: Afghanistan, Albania, Algeria, Andorra, Angola, Antigua and Barbuda, Argentina, Armenia, Australia, Austria, Azerbaijan, Bahamas, Bahrain, Bangladesh, Barbados, Belarus, Belgium, Belize, Benin, Bhutan, Bolivia, Bosnia and Herzegovina, Botswana, Brazil, Brunei Darussalam, Bulgaria, Burkina Faso, Burundi, Cambodia, Cameroon, Canada, Cape Verde, Chad, Chile, China, Colombia, Comoros, Congo, Costa Rica, Côte d'Ivoire, Croatia, Cuba, Cyprus, Czech Republic, Democratic Republic of the Congo, Denmark, Djibouti, Dominica, Dominican Republic, Ecuador, Egypt, El Salvador, Eritrea, Estonia, Ethiopia, Fiji, Finland, France, Georgia, Germany, Ghana, Greece, Grenada, Guatemala, Guinea, Guinea-Bissau, Guyana, Haiti, Honduras, Hungary, Iceland, India, Indonesia,

Iran, Iraq, Ireland, Israel, Italy, Jamaica, Japan, Jordan, Kazakhstan, Kenya, Kuwait, Kyrgyzstan, Lao People's Democratic Republic, Latvia, Lebanon, Lesotho, Liberia, Libyan Arab Jamahiriya, Liechtenstein, Lithuania, Luxembourg, Madagascar, Malawi, Malaysia, Maldives, Mali, Malta, Marshall Islands, Mauritania, Mauritius, Mexico, Micronesia, Moldova, Monaco, Mongolia, Montenegro, Morocco, Mozambique, Myanmar, Namibia, Nauru, Nepal, Netherlands, New Zealand, Nicaragua, Niger, Nigeria, Norway, Oman, Pakistan, Palau, Panama, Papua New Guinea, Paraguay, Peru, Philippines, Poland, Portugal, Qatar, Republic of Korea, Romania, Russian Federation, Rwanda, Saint Lucia, Saint Vincent and the Grenadines, Samoa, San Marino, Sao Tome and Principe, Saudi Arabia, Senegal, Serbia, Singapore, Slovakia, Slovenia, Solomon Islands, South Africa, Spain, Sri Lanka, Sudan, Suriname, Swaziland, Sweden, Switzerland, Syrian Arab Republic, Tajikistan, Thailand, The former Yugoslav Republic of Macedonia, Timor-Leste, Togo, Tonga, Trinidad and Tobago, Tunisia, Turkey, Turkmenistan, Tuvalu, Uganda, Ukraine, United Arab Emirates, United Kingdom, United Republic of Tanzania, Uruguay, Uzbekistan, Vanuatu, Venezuela, Viet Nam, Yemen, Zambia, Zimbabwe.

Against: United States.

Abstaining: None.

Assistance to States for curbing illicit small arms traffic

The Secretary-General, in his August report [A/63/261] on consolidation of peace through practical disarmament measures, discussed assistance to States for curbing illicit traffic in small arms, including activities undertaken at the regional and subregional levels.

The Economic Community of West African States (ECOWAS), in partnership with the West African Action Network on Smalls Arms and the national commissions on small arms and light weapons, conducted campaigns in its member States to raise awareness of the negative impact of illicit traffic and to advocate for the ratification of the 2006 ECOWAS Convention on Small Arms and Light Weapons. Through its Smalls Arms Control Programme, ECOWAS strengthened its efforts to institutionalize the national commissions and build their capacity, and convened the Second Annual Consultative Meeting of National Commissions on Small Arms and Light Weapons (Cotonou, Banin, 3–4 July). The Regional Centre on Small Arms and Light Weapons in the Great Lakes Region, the Horn of Africa and Borderning States [YUN 2007, p. 1430], to assist its 12 member States in implementing their commitments, organized a regional workshop on marking and record-keeping (Mombasa, Kenya, 31 March–4 April) and a seminar on man-portable air defence systems (Nairobi, 1–2 July).

The Organization of American States had approved three pieces of model legislation covering: marking and tracing of firearms; legislative measures to establish criminal offences for illicit manufacturing of and trafficking in firearms and related materials; and strengthening controls at export points. The models were designed to promote the adoption of legislative and other measures as part of the implementation of the Inter-American Convention against the Illicit Manufacturing of and Trafficking in Firearms, Ammunition, Explosives, and Other Related Materials.

The European Union (EU) reported that its Council adopted, on 17 March, a Joint Action to support EU activities to promote, among developing countries, the control of arms exports and the principles of the EU Code of Conduct on Arms Exports. Its members agreed to exchange information on a confidential basis on brokering licences granted. The Organization for Security and Cooperation in Europe promoted information-sharing among its members through annual and one-off confidential information exchanges, and NATO continued to support projects for the destruction of small arms and light weapons stockpiles.

GENERAL ASSEMBLY ACTION

On 2 December [meeting 61], the General Assembly, on the recommendation of the First Committee [A/63/389], adopted **resolution 63/66** without vote [agenda item 89 *(j)*].

Assistance to States for curbing the illicit traffic in small arms and light weapons and collecting them

The General Assembly,

Recalling its resolution 62/22 of 5 December 2007 on assistance to States for curbing the illicit traffic in small arms and collecting them,

Deeply concerned by the magnitude of human casualty and suffering, especially among children, caused by the illicit proliferation and use of small arms and light weapons,

Concerned by the negative impact that the illicit proliferation and use of those weapons continue to have on the efforts of States in the Sahelo-Saharan subregion in the areas of poverty eradication, sustainable development and the maintenance of peace, security and stability,

Bearing in mind the Bamako Declaration on an African Common Position on the Illicit Proliferation, Circulation and Trafficking of Small Arms and Light Weapons, adopted at Bamako on 1 December 2000,

Recalling the report of the Secretary-General entitled "In larger freedom: towards development, security and human rights for all", in which he emphasized that States must strive just as hard to eliminate the threat of illicit small arms and light weapons as they do to eliminate the threat of weapons of mass destruction,

Taking note of the International Instrument to Enable States to Identify and Trace, in a Timely and Reliable Manner, Illicit Small Arms and Light Weapons, adopted on 8 December 2005,

Welcoming the expression of support in the 2005 World Summit Outcome for the implementation of the Programme of Action to Prevent, Combat and Eradicate the Illicit Trade in Small Arms and Light Weapons in All Its Aspects,

Welcoming also the adoption, at the thirtieth ordinary summit of the Economic Community of West African States, held in Abuja in June 2006, of the Convention on Small Arms and Light Weapons, Their Ammunition and Other Related Materials, in replacement of the moratorium on the importation, exportation and manufacture of small arms and light weapons in West Africa,

Welcoming further the decision taken by the Economic Community to establish a Small Arms Unit responsible for advocating appropriate policies and developing and implementing programmes, as well as the establishment of the Economic Community's Small Arms Control Programme, launched on 6 June 2006 in Bamako, in replacement of the Programme for Coordination and Assistance for Security and Development,

Taking note of the latest report of the Secretary-General on assistance to States for curbing the illicit traffic in small arms and light weapons and collecting them and the illicit trade in small arms and light weapons in all its aspects,

Welcoming, in that regard, the decision of the European Union to significantly support the Economic Community in its efforts to combat the illicit proliferation of small arms and light weapons,

Recognizing the important role that civil society organizations play, by raising public awareness, in efforts to curb the illicit traffic in small arms and light weapons,

Taking note of the report of the United Nations Conference to Review Progress Made in the Implementation of the Programme of Action to Prevent, Combat and Eradicate the Illicit Trade in Small Arms and Light Weapons in All Its Aspects, held in New York from 26 June to 7 July 2006,

1. *Commends* the United Nations and international, regional and other organizations for their assistance to States for curbing the illicit traffic in small arms and light weapons and collecting them;

2. *Encourages* the Secretary-General to pursue his efforts in the context of the implementation of General Assembly resolution 49/75 G of 15 December 1994 and the recommendations of the United Nations advisory missions aimed at curbing the illicit circulation of small arms and light weapons and collecting them in the affected States that so request, with the support of the United Nations Regional Centre for Peace and Disarmament in Africa and in close cooperation with the African Union;

3. *Encourages* the international community to support the implementation of the Economic Community of West African States Convention on Small Arms and Light Weapons, Their Ammunition and Other Related Materials;

4. *Encourages* the countries of the Sahelo-Saharan subregion to facilitate the effective functioning of national commissions to combat the illicit proliferation of small arms and light weapons, and, in that regard, invites the international community to lend its support wherever possible;

5. *Encourages* the collaboration of civil society organizations and associations in the efforts of the national commissions to combat the illicit traffic in small arms and light weapons and in the implementation of the Programme of Action to Prevent, Combat and Eradicate the Illicit Trade in Small Arms and Light Weapons in All Its Aspects;

6. *Also encourages* cooperation among State organs, international organizations and civil society in supporting programmes and projects aimed at combating the illicit traffic in small arms and light weapons and collecting them;

7. *Calls upon* the international community to provide technical and financial support to strengthen the capacity of civil society organizations to take action to help to combat the illicit trade in small arms and light weapons;

8. *Invites* the Secretary-General and those States and organizations that are in a position to do so to continue to provide assistance to States for curbing the illicit traffic in small arms and light weapons and collecting them;

9. *Requests* the Secretary-General to continue to consider the matter and to report to the General Assembly at its sixty-fourth session on the implementation of the present resolution;

10. *Decides* to include in the provisional agenda of its sixty-fourth session the item entitled "Assistance to States for curbing the illicit traffic in small arms and light weapons and collecting them".

Convention on excessively injurious conventional weapons and Protocols

Status

As at 31 December, the accession of Guinea-Bissau, Iceland, Jamaica and Madagascar brought to 108 the number of States parties to the 1980 Convention on Prohibitions or Restrictions on the Use of Certain Conventional Weapons Which May Be Deemed to Be Excessively Injurious or to Have Indiscriminate Effects (CCW) and its annexed Protocols [YUN 1980, p. 76] on Non-Detectable Fragments (Protocol I); on Prohibitions or Restrictions on the Use of Mines, Booby Traps and Other Devices, as amended on 3 May 1996 (Protocol II) [YUN 1996, p. 484]; and on Prohibitions or Restrictions on the Use of Incendiary Weapons (Protocol III). Amended Protocol II, which had entered into force on 3 December 1998 [YUN 1998, p. 844], had 92 acceptances as at the end of 2008. The 1995 Protocol on Blinding Laser Weapons (Protocol IV) [YUN 1995, p. 530], which took effect on 30 July 1998 [YUN 1998, p. 530], had 93 parties, following the consent to be bound by five States. The Protocol on Explosive Remnants of War (Protocol V), which was adopted in 2003 [YUN 2003, p. 566] and entered into force in 2006 [YUN 2006, p. 663], had 51 acceptances. The number of parties to the amendment to Article I of the Convention, which entered into force on 18 May 2004 [YUN 2004, p. 563], stood at 72.

Group of Governmental Experts

The Group of Governmental Experts, established by the Second Review Conference of the States Parties to the Convention [YUN 2001, p. 504], held five sessions (14–18 January, 7–11 April, 7–11 July, 1–5 September, 3–7 November). In December 2007 [YUN 2007, p. 576], the States parties had mandated the Group to negotiate a proposal urgently addressing the humanitarian impact of cluster munitions, while striking a balance between military and humanitarian considerations, and to report to the November 2008 Meeting of the High Contracting Parties. The mandate proved to be a difficult challenge. It became clear that minimizing the hazards caused by cluster munitions required a comprehensive approach. The negotiations also revealed the technical complexity and political sensitivity of the process, and were under pressure from and dependent on the development of the Oslo Process [YUN 2007, p. 576], which resulted in the Convention on Cluster Munitions (see p. 623), with a strong humanitarian focus. Building on the political momentum and substantive foundation set by the 2007 Group of Governmental Experts [ibid., p. 575], the Chair submitted a paper that listed the elements identified by the States as those most essential for the draft protocol on cluster munitions.

It appeared possible for the Group to make progress on some less controversial and divisive issues, such as most definitions, victim assistance, international cooperation and assistance, and stockpile management. However, discussions on other elements, among them the definition of cluster munitions, the core provisions of international humanitarian law, the scope of prohibitions and restrictions, and the issue of transfers, revealed a divergence of views. By the fifth session, the Group encountered much difficulty in striking a balance between military and humanitarian considerations. On 3 November, the Chair produced a text before the opening of the final plenary meeting. The Convention on Cluster Munitions adherents felt that humanitarian considerations were inadequately reflected. The International Committee of the Red Cross, the UN Mine Action Service and civil society expressed concerns over deficiencies in the protection of civilians. In a statement, some 25 delegations stressed that the text did not meet humanitarian standards and would only serve to justify the continued use of those weapons. A number of delegations also tabled amendments and proposals, including the text of a draft protocol prohibiting the transfer of cluster munitions.

The Group adopted its procedural report [CCW/GGE/2008-V/2], which stated that at its final plenary meeting on 12 November, the Group had not concluded its negotiations on the Chair's text and recommended to the Meeting of the High Contracting Parties that possible further negotiations take place in 2009, without prejudice to any present or future proposals.

Meeting of High Contracting Parties to the Convention

The Meeting of the High Contracting Parties to the Convention (Geneva, 13–14 November) ended on a positive note due to the number of solid decisions taken by the Conferences of the High Contracting Parties to Amended Protocol II and Protocol V, and to a compromise solution for continuation in 2009 of the Group of Governmental Experts' work on cluster munitions. The Meeting adopted a report [CCW/MSP/2008/4] that included all decisions for 2009 activities.

The most tangible action was that surrounding the Convention Parties' work on cluster munitions. The Chair renewed a mandate for the Group of Governmental Experts: to address urgently the humanitarian impact of cluster munitions, while striking a balance between military and humanitarian considerations, and to report to the next Meeting of the High Contracting Parties. The Group would meet for up to two weeks in early 2009.

Other issues considered by the Meeting were impacted by the fate of the new protocol on cluster munitions that shifted the focus on negotiating a new mandate for the Group of Governmental Experts. Nonetheless, the following were included: the report on implementation of the Plan of Action; the report on the activities of the Sponsorship Programme; the compliance mechanism whereby States parties were requested to submit annually national compliance reports and to nominate experts for inclusion in the Pool of Experts the issue of mines other than anti-personnel mines, which was to be considered under the overall responsibility of the future Chair-designate; and the proposal to establish an Implementation Support Unit. The Meeting further decided on 2009 dates and the duration of the Convention's activities.

Protocol V on explosive remnants of war

The year marked the commencement of implementing the relevant decisions by the First Conference of the High Contracting Parties to Protocol V held in 2007 [YUN 2007, p. 576]. At the first Meeting of Experts (see below) several substantive aspects of implementing Protocol V provisions at the national level were considered, and tools were developed to assist States parties in complying with the Protocol as well as with some of the decisions of the First Conference. Subsequently, the tools were approved by the Second Conference of the High Contracting Parties.

Meeting of Experts

Pursuant to a 2007 decision of the First Conference of the High Contracting Parties to Protocol V, the first Protocol V Meeting of Experts took place (Geneva, 2–4 July). The substantive discussions addressed each of the five main topics identified by the First Conference: clearance of explosive remnants of war; cooperation and assistance and requests for assistance; Article 4 generic electronic template for recording information; generic preventive measures; and victim assistance.

Second Conference of the High Contracting Parties to Protocol V

The Second Conference of the High Contracting Parties to Protocol V met (Geneva, 10–11 November) on ways to enhance the implementation mechanism of the Protocol.

Based on the Coordinators' reports of the discussions held during the July Meeting of Experts and the recommendations contained therein, the Second Conference decided to adopt the Plan of Action of Victim Assistance; continue consideration of victim assistance and of clearance, removal or destruction of explosive remnants of war; change the reporting format of form "G" to conform with the Technical Annex to Protocol V; adopt the revised Article 4 Generic Electronic Template and keep under review its usefulness as a tool for recording and retaining information; approve the formats for request for assistance to the database submissions; further develop the concept for a web-based information system for Protocol V, in order that the 2009 Meeting of Experts could develop a proposal for consideration and adoption by the Third Conference of the High Contracting Parties; and link the available materials on generic preventive measures to the Protocol V website. The Coordinator was invited to undertake open-ended consultations to identify how best to use existing theory and practice, and to develop recommendations for progress in the field of preventive technical measures; a proposal by France [CCW/P.V/CONF/2008/7] would be used as a starting point.

The Second Conference adopted its report [CCW/P.V/CONF./2008/12], containing the mandate for the Third Conference in 2009, including the Meeting of Experts, to be held in Geneva in April 2009.

Annual Conference of States Parties to Amended Protocol II

The Tenth Annual Conference of High Contracting Parties to Amended Protocol II on Mines, Booby-traps and Other Devices (Geneva, 12 November) successfully revitalized the activities under that Protocol. The most important outcome of the Conference was the decision to establish an informal open-ended group of experts to be overseen by the President of the Eleventh Annual Conference, which would meet from 20 to 21 April 2009 to review the operation and status of the Protocol; consider matters arising from States parties' reports and the development of technologies to protect civilians against indiscriminate effects of mines; and address the issue of improvised explosive devices.

The Conference also considered matters arising from reports of the parties, and noted that only 45 of the 92 States parties had submitted annual reports or updates. An appeal for universality was adopted on the occasion of the Protocol's tenth anniversary of entering into force on 3 December. The Conference adopted its final report [CCW/AP.II/CONF.10/2], and nominated the office holders of the 2009 Eleventh Annual Conference.

In an effort to encourage more accessions to the Convention and its Protocols and continue the 2006 Plan of Action to Promote Universality [YUN 2006, p. 664], six regional seminars were organized during 2008.

GENERAL ASSEMBLY ACTION

On 2 December [meeting 61], the General Assembly, on the recommendation of the First Committee [A/63/393], adopted **resolution 63/85** without vote [agenda item 93].

Convention on Prohibitions or Restrictions on the Use of Certain Conventional Weapons Which May Be Deemed to Be Excessively Injurious or to Have Indiscriminate Effects

The General Assembly,

Recalling its resolution 62/57 of 5 December 2007,

Recalling with satisfaction the adoption and the entry into force of the Convention on Prohibitions or Restrictions on the Use of Certain Conventional Weapons Which May Be Deemed to Be Excessively Injurious or to Have Indiscriminate Effects, and its amended article 1, and the Protocol on Non-Detectable Fragments (Protocol I), the Protocol on Prohibitions or Restrictions on the Use of Mines, Booby Traps and Other Devices (Protocol II) and its amended version, the Protocol on Prohibitions or Restrictions on the Use of Incendiary Weapons (Protocol III), the Protocol on Blinding Laser Weapons (Protocol IV) and the Protocol on Explosive Remnants of War (Protocol V),

Welcoming the results of the Third Review Conference of the States Parties to the Convention on Prohibitions or Restrictions on the Use of Certain Conventional Weapons Which May Be Deemed to Be Excessively Injurious or to Have Indiscriminate Effects,

Welcoming also the results of the 2007 Meeting of the High Contracting Parties to the Convention, held from 7 to 13 November 2007 in Geneva,

Welcoming further the results of the Ninth Annual Conference of the High Contracting Parties to Amended Protocol II, held on 6 November 2007 in Geneva,

Welcoming the results of the First Conference of the High Contracting Parties to Protocol V, held on 5 November 2007 in Geneva,

Recalling the role played by the International Committee of the Red Cross in the elaboration of the Convention and the Protocols thereto, and welcoming the particular efforts of various international, non-governmental and other organizations in raising awareness of the humanitarian consequences of explosive remnants of war,

1. *Calls upon* all States that have not yet done so to take all measures to become parties, as soon as possible, to the Convention on Prohibitions or Restrictions on the Use of Certain Conventional Weapons Which May Be Deemed to Be Excessively Injurious or to Have Indiscriminate Effects and the Protocols thereto, as amended, with a view to achieving the widest possible adherence to these instruments at an early date, and so as to ultimately achieve their universality;

2. *Calls upon* all States parties to the Convention that have not yet done so to express their consent to be bound by the Protocols to the Convention and the amendment extending the scope of the Convention and the Protocols thereto to include armed conflicts of a non-international character;

3. *Emphasizes* the importance of the universalization of the Protocol on Explosive Remnants of War (Protocol V);

4. *Welcomes* the additional ratifications and acceptances of or accessions to the Convention, as well as the consents to be bound by the Protocols thereto;

5. *Also welcomes* the adoption by the Third Review Conference of a Plan of Action to promote universality of the Convention and its annexed Protocols, and expresses appreciation for the continued efforts of the Secretary-General, as depositary of the Convention and its annexed Protocols, the Chairperson of the Meeting of the High Contracting Parties to the Convention, the President of the First Conference of the High Contracting Parties to Protocol V and the President of the Ninth Annual Conference of the High Contracting Parties to Amended Protocol II, on behalf of the High Contracting Parties, to achieve the goal of universality;

6. *Further welcomes* the commitment by States parties to continue to address the humanitarian problems caused by certain specific types of munitions in all their aspects, including cluster munitions, with a view to minimizing the humanitarian impact of these munitions;

7. *Expresses support* for the work conducted by the Group of Governmental Experts to negotiate a proposal to address urgently the humanitarian impact of cluster munitions, while striking a balance between military and humanitarian considerations, and to make every effort to negotiate this proposal as rapidly as possible and report on the progress made to the next Meeting of the High Contracting Parties, in November 2008;

8. *Welcomes* the commitment of States parties to the Protocol on Explosive Remnants of War (Protocol V) to the effective and efficient implementation of the Protocol and the decisions by the First Conference of the High Contracting Parties establishing a comprehensive framework for exchange of information and cooperation, and also welcomes the holding of the first Meeting of Experts as a mechanism for consultation and cooperation among the States parties;

9. *Notes with appreciation* that 2008 marks the twenty-fifth anniversary of the entry into force of the Convention, as well as the tenth anniversary of the entry into force of the Amended Protocol II;

10. *Notes* that, in conformity with article 8 of the Convention, conferences may be convened to examine amendments to the Convention or to any of the Protocols thereto, to examine additional protocols concerning other categories of conventional weapons not covered by existing Protocols or to review the scope and application of the Convention and the Protocols thereto and to examine any proposed amendments or additional protocols;

11. *Requests* the Secretary-General to render the necessary assistance and to provide such services, including summary records, as may be required for the Second Conference of the High Contracting Parties to Protocol V, to be held on 10 and 11 November 2008, for the Tenth Annual Conference of the High Contracting Parties to Amended Protocol II, to be held on 12 November 2008, and for the Meeting of the High Contracting Parties to the Convention, to be held on 13 and 14 November 2008, as well as for any continuation of work after the meetings;

12. *Also requests* the Secretary-General, in his capacity as depositary of the Convention and the Protocols thereto, to continue to inform the General Assembly periodically, by electronic means, of ratifications and acceptances of and accessions to the Convention, its amended article 1 and the Protocols thereto;

13. *Decides* to include in the provisional agenda of its sixty-fourth session the item entitled "Convention on Prohibitions or Restrictions on the Use of Certain Conventional Weapons Which May Be Deemed to Be Excessively Injurious or to Have Indiscriminate Effects".

Cluster munitions

The Convention on Cluster Munitions (CCM), which prohibits all use, stockpiling, production and transfer of cluster munitions causing unacceptable harm to civilians and provides for support to victims and affected communities, was adopted in Dublin, Ireland, on 30 May by 107 States, and signed in Oslo, Norway, on 3 December by 94 States and simultaneously ratified by four.

The cluster munitions ban process, also known as the Oslo Process, was launched in February 2007 [YUN 2007, p. 576]. At that time, 46 nations issued the "Oslo Declaration", committing themselves to conclude by 2008 a legally binding international instrument. The Oslo Process held meetings in Lima, Peru, in May 2007 and in Vienna in December 2007. In February 2008, 79 countries adopted the "Wellington Declaration" at a conference in Wellington, New Zealand, setting forth the principles to be included in the Convention.

During the year, the United Nations Development Programme (UNDP) supported seven regional meetings on cluster munitions (Livingstone, Zambia, 31 March–1 April; Mexico City, 16–17 April; Sofia, Bulgaria, 18–19 September; Kampala, Uganda, 29–30 September; Xiengkhuang, Lao People's Democratic Republic, 20–22 October; Quito, Ecuador, 6–7 November; Beirut, Lebanon, 11–12 November).

On 13 October, Ireland transmitted to the General Assembly's First Committee the Final Document of the Diplomatic Conference for the Adoption of a Convention on Cluster Munitions (Dublin, 19–30 May) [A/C.1/63/5], adding that the President of the Conference would report to the Committee on 21 October.

GENERAL ASSEMBLY ACTION

On 2 December [meeting 61], the General Assembly, on the recommendation of the First Committee [A/63/389], adopted **resolution 63/71** without vote [agenda item 89].

Convention on Cluster Munitions

The General Assembly,

Recalling the conclusion of negotiations on the Convention on Cluster Munitions at Dublin on 30 May 2008,

Noting that the Convention will be opened for signature at Oslo on 3 December 2008, and will remain open for signature thereafter at United Nations Headquarters in New York until its entry into force,

Bearing in mind, in particular, the tasks entrusted to the Secretary-General pursuant to the terms of the Convention,

Requests the Secretary-General to render the necessary assistance and to provide such services as may be necessary to fulfil the tasks entrusted to him by the Convention on Cluster Munitions.

Anti-personnel mines

1997 Convention

The number of States parties to the Convention on the Prohibition of the Use, Stockpiling, Production and Transfer of Anti-personnel Mines and on Their Destruction (Mine-Ban Convention), which was adopted in 1997 [YUN 1997, p. 503] and entered into force in 1999 [YUN 1999, p. 498], remained at 156.

Meeting of States parties

The Ninth Meeting of the States Parties to the Mine-Ban Convention (Geneva, 24–28 November) [APLC/MSP.9/2008/4] was held in accordance with General Assembly resolution 62/41 [YUN 2007, p. 582] . A total of 95 States parties, 2 signatories and 20 States not parties, together with international organizations and institutions, as well as NGOs, participated in the meeting. Intersessional preparatory work was conducted in Standing Committees (Geneva, 2–6 June).

The most significant challenge confronting the Meeting was in relation to implementing Article 5. For the first time, States parties had to decide whether or not to grant requests for extension to 15 States parties that were unable to meet their mine-clearance deadline. Consequently, all requests submitted earlier in 2008 were examined by a group of States parties under the authority of the President of the Eighth Meeting of States Parties to the Convention [YUN 2007, p. 581]. The report of the former President and the requests by 15 States were considered by the States parties at an informal session. While most of the cases did not pose any significant problem, it was possible to avoid a vote and grant the extensions.

The implementation of Article 4 proved to be another pointed issue. The Meeting focused on three cases of failure to comply with obligations to destroy or ensure the destruction of stockpiled anti-personnel mines. Non-compliance represented a serious challenge as stockpile destruction was essential for implementing the Convention's comprehensive ban. To prevent future non-compliance, the Meeting welcomed a proposal by the Co-Chairs of the Standing Committee on Stockpile Destruction on steps to ensure full Article 4 implementation [APLC/MSP.9/2008/WP.36].

The Meeting agreed to hold the Convention's Second Review Conference in Cartagena, Colombia (30 November–4 December 2009).

GENERAL ASSEMBLY ACTION

On 2 December [meeting 61], the General Assembly, on the recommendation of the First Committee [A/63/389], adopted **resolution 63/42** by recorded vote (163-0-18) [agenda item 89].

Implementation of the Convention on the Prohibition of the Use, Stockpiling, Production and Transfer of Anti-personnel Mines and on Their Destruction

The General Assembly,

Recalling its resolutions 54/54 B of 1 December 1999, 55/33 V of 20 November 2000, 56/24 M of 29 November 2001, 57/74 of 22 November 2002, 58/53 of 8 December 2003, 59/84 of 3 December 2004, 60/80 of 8 December 2005, 61/84 of 6 December 2006 and 62/41 of 5 December 2007,

Reaffirming its determination to put an end to the suffering and casualties caused by anti-personnel mines, which kill or maim hundreds of people every week, mostly innocent and defenceless civilians, including children, obstruct economic development and reconstruction, inhibit the repatriation of refugees and internally displaced persons and have other severe consequences for years after emplacement,

Believing it necessary to do the utmost to contribute in an efficient and coordinated manner to facing the challenge of removing anti-personnel mines placed throughout the world and to assure their destruction,

Wishing to do the utmost in ensuring assistance for the care and rehabilitation, including the social and economic reintegration, of mine victims,

Welcoming the entry into force, on 1 March 1999, of the Convention on the Prohibition of the Use, Stockpiling, Production and Transfer of Anti-personnel Mines and on Their Destruction, and noting with satisfaction the work undertaken to implement the Convention and the substantial progress made towards addressing the global anti-personnel landmine problem,

Recalling the first to eighth meetings of the States parties to the Convention, held in Maputo (1999), Geneva (2000), Managua (2001), Geneva (2002), Bangkok (2003), Zagreb (2005), Geneva (2006), and the Dead Sea (2007) and the First Review Conference of the States Parties to the Convention, held in Nairobi (2004),

Recalling also that at the eighth meeting of the States parties to the Convention, held at the Dead Sea from 18 to 22 November 2007, the international community monitored progress on implementation of the Convention and supported continued application of the Nairobi Action Plan 2005–2009, and established priorities to achieve further progress towards ending, for all people and for all time, the suffering caused by anti-personnel mines,

Noting with satisfaction that additional States have ratified or acceded to the Convention, bringing the total number of States that have formally accepted the obligations of the Convention to one hundred and fifty-six,

Emphasizing the desirability of attracting the adherence of all States to the Convention, and determined to work strenuously towards the promotion of its universalization,

Noting with regret that anti-personnel mines continue to be used in conflicts around the world, causing human suffering and impeding post-conflict development,

1. *Invites* all States that have not signed the Convention on the Prohibition of the Use, Stockpiling, Production and Transfer of Anti-personnel Mines and on Their Destruction to accede to it without delay;

2. *Urges* all States that have signed but have not ratified the Convention to ratify it without delay;

3. *Stresses* the importance of the full and effective implementation of and compliance with the Convention, including through the continued implementation of the Nairobi Action Plan 2005–2009;

4. *Urges* all States parties to provide the Secretary-General with complete and timely information as required under article 7 of the Convention in order to promote transparency and compliance with the Convention;

5. *Invites* all States that have not ratified the Convention or acceded to it to provide, on a voluntary basis, information to make global mine action efforts more effective;

6. *Renews its call upon* all States and other relevant parties to work together to promote, support and advance the care, rehabilitation and social and economic reintegration of mine victims, mine risk education programmes and the removal and destruction of anti-personnel mines placed or stockpiled throughout the world;

7. *Urges* all States to remain seized of the issue at the highest political level and, where in a position to do so, to promote adherence to the Convention through bilateral, subregional, regional and multilateral contacts, outreach, seminars and other means;

8. *Reiterates its invitation and encouragement* to all interested States, the United Nations, other relevant international organizations or institutions, regional organizations, the International Committee of the Red Cross and relevant non-governmental organizations to participate in the ninth meeting of the States parties to the Convention, to be held in Geneva from 24 to 28 November 2008 and in the intersessional work programme established at the first meeting of the States parties and further developed at subsequent meetings of the States parties;

9. *Requests* the Secretary-General, in accordance with article 12, paragraph 1, of the Convention, to undertake the preparations necessary to convene the next Review Conference of the States parties to the Convention and, pending a decision to be taken at the ninth meeting of the States parties, and on behalf of the States parties and in accordance with article 11, paragraph 4, of the Convention, to invite States not parties to the Convention, as well as the United Nations, other relevant international organizations or institutions, regional organizations, the International Committee of the Red Cross and relevant non-governmental organizations to attend the Review Conference as observers;

10. *Decides* to remain seized of the matter.

RECORDED VOTE ON RESOLUTION 63/42:

In favour: Afghanistan, Albania, Algeria, Andorra, Angola, Antigua and Barbuda, Argentina, Armenia, Australia, Austria, Azerbaijan, Bahamas, Bahrain, Bangladesh, Barbados, Belarus, Belgium, Belize, Benin, Bhutan, Bolivia, Bosnia and Herzegovina, Botswana, Brazil, Brunei Darussalam, Bulgaria, Burkina Faso, Burundi, Cambodia, Cameroon, Canada, Cape Verde, Chile, China, Colombia, Comoros, Congo, Costa Rica, Côte d'Ivoire, Croatia, Cyprus, Czech Republic, Democratic Republic of the Congo, Denmark, Djibouti, Dominica, Dominican Republic, Ecuador, El Salvador, Equatorial Guinea, Eritrea, Estonia, Ethiopia, Finland, France, Gabon, Georgia, Germany, Ghana, Greece, Grenada, Guatemala, Guinea, Guinea-Bissau, Guyana, Haiti, Honduras, Hungary, Iceland, Indonesia, Iraq, Ireland, Italy, Jamaica, Japan, Jordan, Kazakhstan, Kenya, Kuwait, Lao People's Democratic Republic, Latvia, Lesotho, Liberia, Liechtenstein, Lithuania, Luxembourg, Madagascar, Malawi, Malaysia, Maldives, Mali, Malta, Marshall Islands, Mauritania, Mauritius, Mexico, Micronesia, Moldova, Monaco, Mongolia, Montenegro, Morocco, Mozambique, Namibia, Nauru, Netherlands, New Zealand, Nicaragua, Niger, Nigeria, Norway, Oman, Palau, Panama, Papua New Guinea, Paraguay, Peru, Philippines, Poland, Portugal, Qatar, Romania, Rwanda, Saint Lucia, Saint Vincent and the Grenadines, Samoa, San Marino, Sao Tome and Principe, Senegal, Serbia, Singapore, Slovakia, Slovenia, Solomon Islands, South Africa, Spain, Sri Lanka, Sudan, Suriname, Swaziland, Sweden, Switzerland, Tajikistan, Thailand, The former Yugoslav Republic of Macedonia, Timor-Leste, Togo, Trinidad and Tobago, Tunisia, Turkey, Turkmenistan, Tuvalu, Uganda, Ukraine, United Arab Emirates, United Kingdom, United Republic of Tanzania, Uruguay, Vanuatu, Venezuela, Yemen, Zambia, Zimbabwe.

Against: None.

Abstaining: Cuba, Democratic People's Republic of Korea, Egypt, India, Iran, Israel, Kyrgyzstan, Lebanon, Libyan Arab Jamahiriya, Myanmar, Nepal, Pakistan, Republic of Korea, Russian Federation, Syrian Arab Republic, United States, Uzbekistan, Viet Nam.

Practical disarmament

Disarmament Commission action. The Disarmament Commission [A/63/42] allocated to Working Group II the item "Practical confidence-building measures in the field of conventional weapons". The Group discussed the item between 9 and 22 April, based on a paper by its Chairman, and decided to continue consideration of the issue in the future.

Report of Secretary-General. Pursuant to General Assembly resolution 61/76 [YUN 2006, p. 666], the Secretary-General, in August [A/63/261], presented an overview of action taken by States and regional and subregional organizations regarding practical disarmament measures, especially those by the Group of Interested States in Practical Disarmament Measures. He reported that following a review of its mandate in light of the overlap with some of the activities included in the Programme of Action, the Group resolved to refocus on its original activities, which included examination and provision of joint support for concrete projects in disarmament, demobilization and reintegration, weapons collection programmes, demining, conversion and public awareness campaigns. The Group engaged in exchanging information on lessons learned and their dissemination to interested States. At its March meeting, the Group considered a funding proposal by the Nairobi-based Regional Centre on Small Arms [YUN 2007, p. 1430] to support practical disarmament projects in Burundi, the Democratic Republic of the Congo, Somalia and the Sudan.

In addition to the assistance by some of the Group's members, UNDP provided support to over 15 States and led several joint missions with other UN agencies and departments in the fields of disarmament, demobilization and reintegration, security sector reform, gender and early recovery. In the Sudan, UNDP, the UN Department of Peacekeeping Operations and the United Nations Children's Fund coordinated their efforts in supporting a national strategy for disarmament, demobilization and reintegration programmes, complemented by community security and small arms control initiatives.

The Secretary-General noted that 12 States had submitted information in the areas of capacity-building of national institutions dealing with small arms and light weapons; collection and destruction of surplus and illicit arms; destruction and demilitarization of ammunition; support to civil society with a view to enhancing capacity to assist in combating illicit arms; support for disarmament, demobilization and reintegration in countries emerging from conflict; and disarmament of illegal armed groups in countries not in conflict.

GENERAL ASSEMBLY ACTION

On 2 December [meeting 61], the General Assembly, on the recommendation of the First Committee [A/63/389], adopted **resolution 63/62** by recorded vote (182-0-0) [agenda item 89 *(e)*].

Consolidation of peace through practical disarmament measures

The General Assembly,

Recalling its resolutions 51/45 N of 10 December 1996, 52/38 G of 9 December 1997, 53/77 M of 4 December 1998, 54/54 H of 1 December 1999, 55/33 G of 20 November 2000, 56/24 P of 29 November 2001 and 57/81 of 22 November 2002, its decision 58/519 of 8 December 2003, as well as its resolutions 59/82 of 3 December 2004 and 61/76 of 6 December 2006 entitled "Consolidation of peace through practical disarmament measures",

Convinced that a comprehensive and integrated approach towards certain practical disarmament measures often is a prerequisite to maintaining and consolidating peace and security and thus provides a basis for effective post-conflict peacebuilding; such measures include collection and responsible disposal, preferably through destruction, of weapons obtained through illicit trafficking or illicit manufacture as well as of weapons and ammunition declared by competent national authorities to be surplus to requirements, particularly with regard to small arms and light weapons, unless another form of disposition or use has been officially authorized and provided that such weapons have been duly marked and registered; confidence-building measures; disarmament, demobilization and reintegration of former combatants; demining; and conversion,

Noting with satisfaction that the international community is more than ever aware of the importance of such practical disarmament measures, especially with regard to the growing problems arising from the excessive accumulation and uncontrolled spread of small arms and light weapons, including their ammunition, which pose a threat to peace and security and reduce the prospects for economic development in many regions, particularly in post-conflict situations,

Stressing that further efforts are needed in order to develop and effectively implement programmes of practical disarmament in affected areas as part of disarmament, demobilization and reintegration measures so as to complement, on a case-by-case basis, peacekeeping and peacebuilding efforts,

Taking note with appreciation of the report of the Secretary-General on prevention of armed conflict, which, inter alia, refers to the role which the proliferation and the illicit transfer of small arms and light weapons play in the context of the build-up and sustaining of conflicts,

Taking note of the statement by the President of the Security Council of 31 August 2001 underlining the importance of practical disarmament measures in the context of armed conflicts, and, with regard to disarmament, demobilization and reintegration programmes, emphasizing the importance of measures to contain the security risks stemming from the use of illicit small arms and light weapons,

Taking note also of the report of the Secretary-General prepared with the assistance of the Group of Governmental Experts on Small Arms and, in particular, the recommendations contained therein, as an important contribution to the consolidation of the peace process through practical disarmament measures,

Welcoming the work of the United Nations Coordinating Action on Small Arms mechanism, which was established by the Secretary-General to bring about a holistic and multidisciplinary approach to this complex and multifaceted global problem,

Welcoming also the establishment, within the United Nations system, of the Programme of Action Implementation Support System, which provides a comprehensive tool to facilitate international cooperation and assistance for the implementation of practical disarmament measures, including the matching of assistance needs with available resources,

Welcoming further the reports of the first, second and third biennial meetings of States to consider the implementation of the Programme of Action to Prevent, Combat and Eradicate the Illicit Trade in Small Arms and Light Weapons in All Its Aspects, held in New York from 7 to 11 July 2003, from 11 to 15 July 2005 and from 14 to 18 July 2008,

1. *Stresses* the particular relevance of the "Guidelines on conventional arms control/limitation and disarmament, with particular emphasis on consolidation of peace in the context of General Assembly resolution 51/45 N", adopted by the Disarmament Commission by consensus at its 1999 substantive session;

2. *Takes note* of the report of the Secretary-General on the consolidation of peace through practical disarmament measures, submitted pursuant to resolution 61/76, and once again encourages Member States as well as regional arrangements and agencies to lend their support to the implementation of recommendations contained therein;

3. *Emphasizes* the importance of including in United Nations-mandated peacekeeping missions, as appropriate and with the consent of the host State, practical disarmament measures aimed at addressing the problem of the illicit trade in small arms and light weapons in conjunction with disarmament, demobilization and reintegration programmes aimed at former combatants, with a view to promoting an integrated comprehensive and effective weapons management strategy that would contribute to a sustainable peacebuilding process;

4. *Welcomes* the activities undertaken by the Group of Interested States, and invites the Group to continue to promote, on the basis of lessons learned from previous disarmament and peacebuilding projects, new practical disarmament measures to consolidate peace, especially as undertaken or designed by affected States themselves, regional and subregional organizations as well as United Nations agencies;

5. *Encourages* Member States, also in the framework of the Group of Interested States, to continue to lend their support to the Secretary-General, relevant international, regional and subregional organizations, in accordance with Chapter VIII of the Charter of the United Nations, and non-governmental organizations in responding to requests by Member States to collect and destroy small arms and light weapons, including their ammunition, in post-conflict situations;

6. *Welcomes* the synergies within the multi-stakeholder process, including Governments, the United Nations system, regional and subregional organizations and institutions as well as non-governmental organizations in support of practical disarmament measures and the Programme of Action to Prevent, Combat and Eradicate the Illicit Trade in Small Arms and Light Weapons in All Its Aspects;

7. *Requests* the Secretary-General to submit to the General Assembly at its sixty-fifth session a report on the implementation of practical disarmament measures, taking into consideration the activities of the Group of Interested States in this regard;

8. *Decides* to include in the provisional agenda of its sixty-fifth session the item entitled "Consolidation of peace through practical disarmament measures".

RECORDED VOTE ON RESOLUTION 63/62:

In favour: Afghanistan, Albania, Algeria, Andorra, Angola, Antigua and Barbuda, Argentina, Armenia, Australia, Austria, Azerbaijan, Bahamas, Bahrain, Bangladesh, Barbados, Belarus, Belgium, Belize, Benin, Bhutan, Bolivia, Bosnia and Herzegovina, Botswana, Brazil, Brunei Darussalam, Bulgaria, Burkina Faso, Burundi, Cambodia, Cameroon, Canada, Cape Verde, Chile, China, Colombia, Comoros, Congo, Costa Rica, Côte d'Ivoire, Croatia, Cuba, Cyprus, Czech Republic, Democratic People's Republic of Korea, Denmark, Djibouti, Dominica, Dominican Republic, Ecuador, Egypt, El Salvador, Equatorial Guinea, Eritrea, Estonia, Ethiopia, Fiji, Finland, France, Georgia, Germany, Ghana, Greece, Grenada, Guatemala, Guinea, Guinea-Bissau, Guyana, Haiti, Honduras, Hungary, Iceland, India, Indonesia, Iran, Iraq, Ireland, Israel, Italy, Jamaica, Japan, Jordan, Kazakhstan, Kenya, Kuwait, Kyrgyzstan, Lao People's Democratic Republic, Latvia, Lebanon, Lesotho, Liberia, Libyan Arab Jamahiriya, Liechtenstein, Lithuania, Luxembourg, Madagascar, Malawi, Malaysia, Maldives, Mali, Malta, Marshall Islands, Mauritania, Mauritius, Mexico, Micronesia, Moldova, Monaco, Mongolia, Montenegro, Morocco, Mozambique, Myanmar, Namibia, Nauru, Nepal, Netherlands, New Zealand, Nicaragua, Niger, Nigeria, Norway, Oman, Pakistan, Palau, Panama, Papua New Guinea, Paraguay, Peru, Philippines, Poland, Portugal, Qatar, Republic of Korea, Romania, Russian Federation, Rwanda, Saint Lucia, Saint Vincent and the Grenadines, Samoa, San Marino, Sao Tome and Principe, Saudi Arabia, Senegal, Serbia, Singapore, Slovakia, Slovenia, Solomon Islands, South Africa, Spain, Sri Lanka, Sudan, Suriname, Swaziland, Sweden, Switzerland, Syrian Arab Republic, Tajikistan, Thailand, The former Yugoslav Republic of Macedonia, Timor-Leste, Togo, Tonga, Trinidad and Tobago, Tunisia, Turkey, Turkmenistan, Tuvalu, Uganda, Ukraine, United Arab Emirates, United Kingdom, United Republic of Tanzania, United States, Uruguay, Uzbekistan, Vanuatu, Venezuela, Viet Nam, Yemen, Zambia, Zimbabwe.

Against: None.

Abstaining: None.

Transparency

Conference on Disarmament. The Conference on Disarmament [A/63/27] held two informal meetings, on 15 and 28 February, followed by a 12 August session on "Transparency in Armaments".

Israel's initiative to ban arms transfers to terrorists remained the most sensitive issue. The discussions revealed considerable divergences of views, particularly with Algeria and the Syrian Arab Republic warning of potentially politicizing the issue.

A number of delegations were of the view that transparency in armaments remained important, and while there was no opposition to the idea of appointing a Special Coordinator or establishing an Ad Hoc Committee, it was deemed essential to remain focused on an agreed programme of work, based primarily on the four core issues of nuclear disarmament, a Fissile Material Cut-off Treaty, prevention of an arms race in outer space, and negative security assurances.

UN Register of Conventional Arms

In response to General Assembly resolution 61/77 [YUN 2006, p. 668], the Secretary-General in July submitted the sixteenth annual report on the United Nations Register of Conventional Arms [A/63/120 & Add.1–3], established in 1992 [YUN 1992, p. 75] to promote transparency on arms transfers.

The report presented information provided by 91 Governments on imports and exports in 2007 in the seven categories of conventional arms (battle tanks, armoured combat vehicles, large-calibre artillery systems, attack helicopters, combat aircraft, warships and missiles, and missile launchers). Governments also provided information on military holdings, procurement through national production, and international transfers of small arms and light weapons. The number of States complementing their reports with data on international small arms and light weapons transfers increased from 37 in 2006 to 48 in 2007.

The report also highlighted numerous activities undertaken by the Secretariat during the year, through UNODA, in collaboration with Governments and regional organizations, to enhance awareness of the Register and encourage greater participation in it.

GENERAL ASSEMBLY ACTION

On 2 December [meeting 61], the General Assembly, on the recommendation of the First Committee [A/63/389], adopted **resolution 63/69** by recorded vote (160-0-22) [agenda item 89 *(f)*].

Transparency in armaments

The General Assembly,

Recalling its resolutions 46/36 L of 9 December 1991, 47/52 L of 15 December 1992, 48/75 E of 16 December 1993, 49/75 C of 15 December 1994, 50/70 D of 12 December 1995, 51/45 H of 10 December 1996, 52/38 R of 9 December 1997, 53/77 V of 4 December 1998, 54/54 O of 1 December 1999, 55/33 U of 20 November 2000, 56/24 Q of 29 November 2001, 57/75 of 22 November 2002, 58/54 of 8 December 2003, 60/226 of 23 December 2005 and 61/77 of 6 December 2006 entitled "Transparency in armaments",

Continuing to take the view that an enhanced level of transparency in armaments contributes greatly to confidence-building and security among States and that the establishment of the United Nations Register of Conventional Arms constitutes an important step forward in the promotion of transparency in military matters,

Welcoming the consolidated reports of the Secretary-General on the Register, which includes the returns of Member States for 2006 and 2007,

Welcoming also the response of Member States to the request contained in paragraphs 9 and 10 of resolution 46/36 L to provide data on their imports and exports of arms, as well as available background information regarding their military holdings, procurement through national production and relevant policies,

Welcoming further the inclusion by some Member States of their transfers of small arms and light weapons in their annual report to the Register as part of their additional background information,

Noting the focused discussion on transparency in armaments that took place in the Conference on Disarmament in 2007 and 2008,

Stressing that the continuing operation of the Register and its further development should be reviewed in order to secure a Register that is capable of attracting the widest possible participation,

1. *Reaffirms its determination* to ensure the effective operation of the United Nations Register of Conventional Arms, as provided for in paragraphs 7 to 10 of resolution 46/36 L;

2. *Calls upon* Member States, with a view to achieving universal participation, to provide the Secretary-General, by 31 May annually, with the requested data and information for the Register, including nil reports if appropriate, on the basis of resolutions 46/36 L and 47/52 L, the recommendations contained in paragraph 64 of the 1997 report of the Secretary-General on the continuing operation of the Register and its further development, the recommendations contained in paragraph 94 of the 2000 report of the Secretary-General and the appendices and annexes thereto, the recommendations contained in paragraphs 112 to 114 of the 2003 report of the Secretary-General and the recommendations contained in paragraphs 123 to 127 of the 2006 report of the Secretary-General;

3. *Invites* Member States in a position to do so, pending further development of the Register, to provide additional information on procurement through national production and military holdings and to make use of the "Remarks" column in the standardized reporting form to provide additional information such as types or models;

4. *Also invites* Member States in a position to do so to provide additional background information on transfers of small arms and light weapons on the basis of the optional standardized reporting form, as adopted by the 2006 group of governmental experts, or by any other methods they deem appropriate;

5. *Reaffirms* its decision, with a view to further development of the Register, to keep the scope of and participation in the Register under review and, to that end:

(a) Recalls its request to Member States to provide the Secretary-General with their views on the continuing operation of the Register and its further development and on transparency measures related to weapons of mass destruction;

(b) Requests the Secretary-General, with the assistance of a group of governmental experts to be convened in 2009, within available resources, on the basis of equitable geographical representation, to prepare a report on the continuing operation of the Register and its further development, taking into account the work of the Conference on Disarmament, the views expressed by Member States and the reports of the Secretary-General on the continuing operation of the Register and its further development, with a view to taking a decision at its sixty-fourth session;

6. *Requests* the Secretary-General to implement the recommendations contained in his 2000, 2003 and 2006 reports on the continuing operation of the Register and its further development and to ensure that sufficient resources are made available for the Secretariat to operate and maintain the Register;

7. *Invites* the Conference on Disarmament to consider continuing its work undertaken in the field of transparency in armaments;

8. *Reiterates its call upon* all Member States to cooperate at the regional and subregional levels, taking fully into account the specific conditions prevailing in the region or subregion, with a view to enhancing and coordinating international efforts aimed at increased openness and transparency in armaments;

9. *Requests* the Secretary-General to report to the General Assembly at its sixty-fourth session on progress made in implementing the present resolution;

10. *Decides* to include in the provisional agenda of its sixty-fourth session the item entitled "Transparency in armaments".

RECORDED VOTE ON RESOLUTION 63/69:

In favour: Afghanistan, Albania, Andorra, Angola, Antigua and Barbuda, Argentina, Armenia, Australia, Austria, Azerbaijan, Bahamas, Bangladesh, Barbados, Belarus, Belgium, Belize, Benin, Bhutan, Bolivia, Bosnia and Herzegovina, Botswana, Brazil, Brunei Darussalam, Bulgaria, Burkina Faso, Burundi, Cambodia, Cameroon, Canada, Cape Verde, Chad, Chile, China, Colombia, Congo, Costa Rica, Côte d'Ivoire, Croatia, Cuba, Cyprus, Czech Republic, Democratic Republic of the Congo, Denmark, Dominica, Dominican Republic, Ecuador, El Salvador, Equatorial Guinea, Eritrea, Estonia, Ethiopia, Fiji, Finland, France, Georgia, Germany, Ghana, Greece, Grenada, Guatemala, Guinea, Guinea-Bissau, Guyana, Haiti, Honduras, Hungary, Iceland, India, Indonesia, Ireland, Israel, Italy, Jamaica, Japan, Kazakhstan, Kenya, Kyrgyzstan, Lao People's Democratic Republic, Latvia, Lesotho, Liberia, Liechtenstein, Lithuania, Luxembourg, Madagascar, Malawi, Malaysia, Maldives, Mali, Malta, Marshall Islands, Mauritius, Mexico, Micronesia, Moldova, Monaco, Mongolia, Montenegro, Mozambique, Namibia, Nauru, Nepal, Netherlands, New Zealand, Nicaragua, Niger, Nigeria, Norway, Pakistan, Palau, Panama, Papua New Guinea, Paraguay, Peru, Philippines, Poland, Portugal, Republic of Korea, Romania, Russian Federation, Rwanda, Saint Lucia, Saint Vincent and the Grenadines, Samoa, San Marino, Sao Tome and Principe, Senegal, Serbia, Singapore, Slovakia, Slovenia, Solomon Islands, South Africa, Spain, Sri Lanka, Suriname, Swaziland, Sweden, Switzerland, Tajikistan, Thailand, The former Yugoslav Republic of Macedonia, Timor-Leste, Togo, Tonga, Trinidad and Tobago, Turkey, Turkmenistan, Tuvalu, Uganda, Ukraine, United Kingdom, United Republic of Tanzania, United States, Uruguay, Uzbekistan, Vanuatu, Venezuela, Zambia, Zimbabwe.

Against: None.

Abstaining: Algeria, Bahrain, Comoros, Djibouti, Egypt, Iran, Iraq, Jordan, Kuwait, Lebanon, Libyan Arab Jamahiriya, Mauritania, Morocco, Myanmar, Oman, Qatar, Saudi Arabia, Sudan, Syrian Arab Republic, Tunisia, United Arab Emirates, Yemen.

Transparency of military expenditures

UNODA continued its efforts to raise awareness of and promote transparency in military matters. During the First Committee session, it prepared and distributed among delegations a fact sheet on the Standardized Instrument for Reporting Military Expenditures, recommended by the General Assembly in resolution 35/142 B [YUN 1980, p. 88]. In view of the forthcoming governmental review of the operation and further development of the Instrument in 2010, efforts were made to start preparations for the review, as mandated by General Assembly resolution 62/13 [YUN 2007, p. 579].

Report of Secretary-General. In response to Assembly resolution 62/13, the Secretary-General, in a July report with later addenda [A/63/97 & Add.1–3], presented reports from 77 Member States on their national military expenditures for the latest fiscal year for which data were available. The reporting instrument was that recommended by the Assembly in resolution 35/142 B [YUN 1980, p. 88].

The report was presented to the First Committee under agenda item 81, "Reduction of military budgets". In the Committee, no proposal was submitted and no action was taken under that item.

On 2 December, the General Assembly took note of the First Committee's report [A/63/381] on the item "Reduction of military budgets" (**decision 63/516**).

Verification

The United Nations continued to consider the issue of verification of arms agreements and the work of the Panel of Governmental Experts in 2006 [YUN 2006, p. 670]. The Panel's report including recommendations was presented to the General Assembly in 2007 [YUN 2007, p. 580].

Report of Secretary-General. Pursuant to General Assembly resolution 62/21 [ibid., p. 581], the

Secretary-General submitted a report on the issue of verification of arms agreements, treaties and other commitments [A/63/114 & Add.1], including the views of five Governments (Canada, Cuba, Spain, Sweden, United States) and one international treaty organization (OPCW).

GENERAL ASSEMBLY ACTION

On 2 December [meeting 61], the General Assembly, on the recommendation of the First Committee [A/63/389], adopted **resolution 63/59** by recorded vote (158-0-18) [agenda item 89].

Compliance with non-proliferation, arms limitation and disarmament agreements and commitments

The General Assembly,

Recalling its resolution 60/55 of 8 December 2005 and other relevant resolutions on the question, and noting the report of the Panel of Government Experts on verification in all its aspects, including the role of the United Nations in the field of verification,

Recognizing the abiding concern of all Member States for ensuring respect for the rights and obligations arising from treaties to which they are parties and from other sources of international law,

Convinced that observance by Member States of the Charter of the United Nations and compliance with non-proliferation, arms limitation and disarmament agreements to which they are parties and with other agreed obligations are essential for regional and global peace, security and stability,

Stressing that failure by States parties to comply with such agreements and with other agreed obligations not only adversely affects the security of States parties but also can create security risks for other States relying on the constraints and commitments stipulated in those agreements,

Stressing also that the viability and effectiveness of non-proliferation, arms limitation and disarmament agreements and of other agreed obligations require that those agreements be fully complied with and enforced,

Concerned by non-compliance by some States with their respective obligations,

Noting that verification and compliance, and enforcement in a manner consistent with the Charter, are integrally related,

Recognizing the importance of and support for effective national, regional, and international capacities for such verification, compliance, and enforcement,

Recognizing also that full compliance by States with all their respective non-proliferation, arms limitation and disarmament agreements and with other agreed obligations they have undertaken contributes to efforts to prevent the development and proliferation, contrary to international obligations, of weapons of mass destruction, related technologies and means of delivery, as well as to efforts to deny non-State actors access to such capabilities,

1. *Underscores* the contribution that compliance with non-proliferation, arms limitation and disarmament agreements and with other agreed obligations makes to enhancing confidence and to strengthening international security and stability;

2. *Urges* all States to implement and to comply fully with their respective obligations;

3. *Calls upon* all Member States to encourage and, for those States in a position to do so, to appropriately assist States which request assistance to increase their capacity to implement fully their obligations;

4. *Calls upon* all concerned States to take concerted action, in a manner consistent with relevant international law, to encourage, through bilateral and multilateral means, the compliance by all States with their respective non-proliferation, arms limitation and disarmament agreements and with other agreed obligations, and to hold those not in compliance with such agreements accountable for their non-compliance in a manner consistent with the Charter of the United Nations;

5. *Urges* those States not currently in compliance with their respective obligations and commitments to make the strategic decision to come back into compliance;

6. *Encourages* efforts by all States, the United Nations and other international organizations, pursuant to their respective mandates, to take action, consistent with the Charter, to prevent serious damage to international security and stability arising from non-compliance by States with their existing non-proliferation, arms limitation and disarmament obligations.

RECORDED VOTE ON RESOLUTION 63/59:

In favour: Afghanistan, Albania, Algeria, Andorra, Angola, Antigua and Barbuda, Argentina, Armenia, Australia, Austria, Azerbaijan, Bahamas, Bangladesh, Barbados, Belgium, Belize, Benin, Bhutan, Bolivia, Bosnia and Herzegovina, Botswana, Brazil, Brunei Darussalam, Bulgaria, Burkina Faso, Burundi, Cambodia, Cameroon, Canada, Cape Verde, Chile, Colombia, Comoros, Congo, Costa Rica, Côte d'Ivoire, Croatia, Cyprus, Czech Republic, Denmark, Djibouti, Dominica, Dominican Republic, Ecuador, El Salvador, Equatorial Guinea, Eritrea, Estonia, Ethiopia, Finland, France, Georgia, Germany, Ghana, Greece, Grenada, Guatemala, Guinea, Guinea-Bissau, Guyana, Haiti, Honduras, Hungary, Iceland, India, Indonesia, Iraq, Ireland, Israel, Italy, Jamaica, Japan, Jordan, Kazakhstan, Kenya, Kyrgyzstan, Latvia, Lebanon, Lesotho, Liberia, Liechtenstein, Lithuania, Luxembourg, Madagascar, Malawi, Malaysia, Maldives, Mali, Malta, Marshall Islands, Mauritania, Mauritius, Mexico, Micronesia, Moldova, Monaco, Mongolia, Montenegro, Morocco, Mozambique, Myanmar, Namibia, Nauru, Nepal, Netherlands, New Zealand, Niger, Nigeria, Norway, Palau, Panama, Papua New Guinea, Paraguay, Peru, Philippines, Poland, Portugal, Republic of Korea, Romania, Rwanda, Saint Lucia, Saint Vincent and the Grenadines, Samoa, San Marino, Sao Tome and Principe, Senegal, Serbia, Singapore, Slovakia, Slovenia, Solomon Islands, South Africa, Spain, Sri Lanka, Suriname, Swaziland, Sweden, Switzerland, Tajikistan, Thailand, The former Yugoslav Republic of Macedonia, Timor-Leste, Togo, Tonga, Trinidad and Tobago, Tunisia, Turkey, Turkmenistan, Tuvalu, Uganda, Ukraine, United Kingdom, United Republic of Tanzania, United States, Uruguay, Vanuatu, Viet Nam, Zambia.

Against: None.

Abstaining: Bahrain, Belarus, Cuba, Egypt, Iran, Kuwait, Libyan Arab Jamahiriya, Nicaragua, Pakistan, Qatar, Russian Federation, Saudi Arabia, Sudan, Syrian Arab Republic, United Arab Emirates, Venezuela, Yemen, Zimbabwe.

Other disarmament issues

Prevention of an arms race in outer space

Conference on Disarmament. The issue of the prevention of an arms race in outer space was again addressed by the Conference on Disarmament [A/63/27]. In the absence of a programme of work, the Conference was unable to establish a formal framework for dealing with the issue, but in accordance with the agreed organizational procedure, it held three rounds of informal deliberations, on 7 and 21 February and 5 August. In February, China and the Russian Federation presented a draft "Treaty on Prevention of the Placement of Weapons in Outer Space and of the Threat or Use of Force Against Outer Space Objects", which was welcomed by a number of countries, including the 21 members of the Non-Aligned Movement, as well as the EU. During the high-level segment in March, a number of dignitaries underlined the importance of the issue and welcomed the draft treaty, whereas the United States, in a paper submitted in August, informed the Conference that the draft provided no grounds for it to change its long-standing principle that arms control constraints or limitations on space-based systems and activities, beyond the existing regimes in force, were not in its national security interests, and that it was not possible to develop an effectively verifiable agreement for banning either space-based weapons or a terrestrial-based anti-satellite system.

A number of Conference members stressed the importance of transparency and confidence-building measures (TCBMS) in outer space activities. In particular, the EU referred to its code of conduct on outer space activities and announced that it was working on a set of TCBMS for presentation to the Conference. Several countries supported the establishment of a code of conduct for outer space activities. At the informal meeting on 21 February, the Chairman of the United Nations Committee on the Peaceful Uses of Outer Space made a presentation to the Conference, clarifying the Committee's mandate, roles and responsibilities in relation to the Conference.

Summarizing the discussion, the Coordinator observed that there was broad consensus on the existence of deficiencies in the current outer space architecture; TCBMS could either be complementary to a future legal instrument, be sufficient on their own, or taken up in the context of the draft Treaty that was welcomed by many delegations, with several expressing interest in continuing more substantive discussions thereon and one opposing new binding space control agreements. The Coordinator reported that interest was shown in continuing work in two areas: TCBMS, with the work of the EU serving as a basis for further discussions, and the Chinese-Russian draft treaty.

Report of Secretary-General. In accordance with General Assembly resolution 62/43 [YUN 2007, p. 585], the Secretary-General submitted a July report [A/63/136 & Add.1] containing proposals from six States (Bangladesh, Chile, Cuba, France (on behalf of the EU), Qatar, Ukraine) on transparency and confidence-building measures in outer space activities in the interest of maintaining international peace and security and promoting international cooperation and the prevention of an arms race in outer space.

GENERAL ASSEMBLY ACTION

On 2 December [meeting 61], the General Assembly, on the recommendation of the First Committee [A/63/388], adopted **resolution 63/40** by recorded vote (177-1-1) [agenda item 88].

Prevention of an arms race in outer space

The General Assembly,

Recognizing the common interest of all mankind in the exploration and use of outer space for peaceful purposes,

Reaffirming the will of all States that the exploration and use of outer space, including the Moon and other celestial bodies, shall be for peaceful purposes and shall be carried out for the benefit and in the interest of all countries, irrespective of their degree of economic or scientific development,

Reaffirming also the provisions of articles III and IV of the Treaty on Principles Governing the Activities of States in the Exploration and Use of Outer Space, including the Moon and Other Celestial Bodies,

Recalling the obligation of all States to observe the provisions of the Charter of the United Nations regarding the use or threat of use of force in their international relations, including in their space activities,

Reaffirming paragraph 80 of the Final Document of the Tenth Special Session of the General Assembly, in which it is stated that in order to prevent an arms race in outer space, further measures should be taken and appropriate international negotiations held in accordance with the spirit of the Treaty,

Recalling its previous resolutions on this issue, and taking note of the proposals submitted to the General Assembly at its tenth special session and at its regular sessions, and of the recommendations made to the competent organs of the United Nations and to the Conference on Disarmament,

Recognizing that prevention of an arms race in outer space would avert a grave danger for international peace and security,

Emphasizing the paramount importance of strict compliance with existing arms limitation and disarmament agreements relevant to outer space, including bilateral agreements, and with the existing legal regime concerning the use of outer space,

Considering that wide participation in the legal regime applicable to outer space could contribute to enhancing its effectiveness,

Noting that the Ad Hoc Committee on the Prevention of an Arms Race in Outer Space, taking into account its previous efforts since its establishment in 1985 and seeking to enhance its functioning in qualitative terms, continued the examination and identification of various issues, existing agreements and existing proposals, as well as future initiatives relevant to the prevention of an arms race in outer space, and that this contributed to a better understanding of a number of problems and to a clearer perception of the various positions,

Noting also that there were no objections in principle in the Conference on Disarmament to the re-establishment of the Ad Hoc Committee, subject to re-examination of the mandate contained in the decision of the Conference on Disarmament of 13 February 1992,

Emphasizing the mutually complementary nature of bilateral and multilateral efforts in the field of preventing an arms race in outer space, and hoping that concrete results will emerge from those efforts as soon as possible,

Convinced that further measures should be examined in the search for effective and verifiable bilateral and multilateral agreements in order to prevent an arms race in outer space, including the weaponization of outer space,

Stressing that the growing use of outer space increases the need for greater transparency and better information on the part of the international community,

Recalling, in this context, its previous resolutions, in particular resolutions 45/55 B of 4 December 1990, 47/51 of 9 December 1992 and 48/74 A of 16 December 1993, in which, inter alia, it reaffirmed the importance of confidence-building measures as a means conducive to ensuring the attainment of the objective of the prevention of an arms race in outer space,

Conscious of the benefits of confidence- and security-building measures in the military field,

Recognizing that negotiations for the conclusion of an international agreement or agreements to prevent an arms race in outer space remain a priority task of the Ad Hoc Committee and that the concrete proposals on confidence-building measures could form an integral part of such agreements,

Noting with satisfaction the constructive, structured and focused debate on the prevention of an arms race in outer space at the Conference on Disarmament in 2008,

1. *Reaffirms* the importance and urgency of preventing an arms race in outer space and the readiness of all States to contribute to that common objective, in conformity with the provisions of the Treaty on Principles Governing the Activities of States in the Exploration and Use of Outer Space, including the Moon and Other Celestial Bodies;

2. *Reaffirms its recognition*, as stated in the report of the Ad Hoc Committee on the Prevention of an Arms Race in Outer Space, that the legal regime applicable to outer space does not in and of itself guarantee the prevention of an arms race in outer space, that the regime plays a significant role in the prevention of an arms race in that environment, that there is a need to consolidate and reinforce that regime and enhance its effectiveness and that it is important to comply strictly with existing agreements, both bilateral and multilateral;

3. *Emphasizes* the necessity of further measures with appropriate and effective provisions for verification to prevent an arms race in outer space;

4. *Calls upon* all States, in particular those with major space capabilities, to contribute actively to the objective of the peaceful use of outer space and of the prevention of an arms race in outer space and to refrain from actions contrary to that objective and to the relevant existing treaties in the interest of maintaining international peace and security and promoting international cooperation;

5. *Reiterates* that the Conference on Disarmament, as the sole multilateral disarmament negotiating forum, has the primary role in the negotiation of a multilateral agreement or agreements, as appropriate, on the prevention of an arms race in outer space in all its aspects;

6. *Invites* the Conference on Disarmament to complete the examination and updating of the mandate contained in its decision of 13 February 1992 and to establish an ad hoc committee as early as possible during its 2009 session;

7. *Recognizes*, in this respect, the growing convergence of views on the elaboration of measures designed to strengthen transparency, confidence and security in the peaceful uses of outer space;

8. *Urges* States conducting activities in outer space, as well as States interested in conducting such activities, to keep the Conference on Disarmament informed of the progress of bilateral and multilateral negotiations on the matter, if any, so as to facilitate its work;

9. *Decides* to include in the provisional agenda of its sixty-fourth session the item entitled "Prevention of an arms race in outer space".

RECORDED VOTE ON RESOLUTION 63/40:

In favour: Afghanistan, Albania, Algeria, Andorra, Angola, Antigua and Barbuda, Argentina, Armenia, Australia, Austria, Azerbaijan, Bahamas, Bahrain, Bangladesh, Barbados, Belarus, Belgium, Belize, Benin, Bhutan, Bolivia, Bosnia and Herzegovina, Botswana, Brazil, Brunei Darussalam, Bulgaria, Burkina Faso, Burundi, Cambodia, Cameroon, Canada, Cape Verde, Chile, China, Colombia, Comoros, Congo, Costa Rica, Côte d'Ivoire, Croatia, Cuba, Cyprus, Czech Republic, Democratic People's Republic of Korea, Democratic Republic of the Congo, Denmark, Djibouti, Dominican Republic, Ecuador, Egypt, El Salvador, Equatorial Guinea, Eritrea, Estonia, Ethiopia, Finland, France, Gabon, Georgia, Germany, Ghana, Greece, Grenada, Guatemala, Guinea, Guinea-Bissau, Guyana, Haiti, Honduras, Hungary, Iceland, India, Indonesia, Iran, Iraq, Ireland, Italy, Jamaica, Japan, Jordan, Kazakhstan, Kenya, Kuwait, Kyrgyzstan, Lao People's Democratic Republic, Latvia, Lebanon, Lesotho, Liberia, Libyan Arab Jamahiriya, Liechtenstein, Lithuania, Luxembourg, Madagascar, Malawi, Malaysia, Maldives, Mali, Malta, Marshall Islands, Mauritania, Mauritius, Mexico, Micronesia, Moldova, Monaco, Mongolia, Montenegro, Morocco, Mozambique, Myanmar, Namibia, Nepal, Netherlands, New Zealand, Nicaragua, Niger, Nigeria, Norway, Oman, Pakistan, Palau, Panama, Papua New Guinea, Paraguay, Peru, Philippines, Poland, Portugal, Qatar, Republic of Korea, Romania, Russian Federation, Rwanda, Saint Lucia, Saint Vincent and the Grenadines, Samoa, San Marino, Sao Tome and Principe, Saudi Arabia, Senegal, Serbia, Singapore, Slovakia, Slovenia, Solomon Islands, South Africa,

Spain, Sri Lanka, Sudan, Suriname, Swaziland, Sweden, Switzerland, Syrian Arab Republic, Tajikistan, Thailand, The former Yugoslav Republic of Macedonia, Timor-Leste, Togo, Trinidad and Tobago, Tunisia, Turkey, Turkmenistan, Tuvalu, Uganda, Ukraine, United Arab Emirates, United Kingdom, United Republic of Tanzania, Uruguay, Uzbekistan, Venezuela, Viet Nam, Yemen, Zambia, Zimbabwe.

Against: United States.

Abstaining: Israel.

Also on 2 December [meeting 61], the General Assembly, on the recommendation of the First Committee [A/63/389], adopted **resolution 63/68** by recorded vote (180-1-1) [agenda item 89 *(w)*].

Transparency and confidence-building measures in outer space activities

The General Assembly,

Recalling its resolutions 60/66 of 8 December 2005, 61/75 of 6 December 2006 and 62/43 of 5 December 2007,

Reaffirming that the prevention of an arms race in outer space would avert a grave danger to international peace and security,

Conscious that further measures should be examined in the search for agreements to prevent an arms race in outer space, including the weaponization of outer space,

Recalling, in this context, its previous resolutions, including resolutions 45/55 B of 4 December 1990 and 48/74 B of 16 December 1993, which, inter alia, emphasize the need for increased transparency and confirm the importance of confidence-building measures as a means conducive to ensuring the attainment of the objective of the prevention of an arms race in outer space,

Recalling also the report of the Secretary-General of 15 October 1993 to the General Assembly at its forty-eighth session, the annex to which contains the study by governmental experts on the application of confidence-building measures in outer space,

Noting the constructive debate which the Conference on Disarmament held on this subject in 2008, including the views and ideas expressed by the European Union and other States,

Noting also the introduction by the Russian Federation and China at the Conference on Disarmament of the draft treaty on the prevention of the placement of weapons in outer space and of the threat or use of force against outer space objects,

Noting further the contribution of Member States which have submitted to the Secretary-General concrete proposals on international outer space transparency and confidence-building measures pursuant to paragraph 1 of resolution 61/75 and paragraph 2 of resolution 62/43,

1. *Takes note* of the reports of the Secretary-General containing concrete proposals from Member States on international outer space transparency and confidence-building measures;

2. *Invites* all Member States to continue to submit to the Secretary-General concrete proposals on international outer space transparency and confidence-building measures in the interest of maintaining international peace and security and promoting international cooperation and the prevention of an arms race in outer space;

3. *Requests* the Secretary-General to submit to the General Assembly at its sixty-fourth session a report with an annex containing concrete proposals from Member States on international outer space transparency and confidence-building measures;

4. *Decides* to include in the provisional agenda of its sixty-fourth session the item entitled "Transparency and confidence-building measures in outer space activities".

RECORDED VOTE ON RESOLUTION 63/68:

In favour: Afghanistan, Albania, Algeria, Andorra, Angola, Antigua and Barbuda, Argentina, Armenia, Australia, Austria, Azerbaijan, Bahamas, Bahrain, Bangladesh, Barbados, Belarus, Belgium, Belize, Benin, Bhutan, Bolivia, Bosnia and Herzegovina, Botswana, Brazil, Brunei Darussalam, Bulgaria, Burkina Faso, Burundi, Cambodia, Cameroon, Canada, Cape Verde, Chad, Chile, China, Colombia, Comoros, Congo, Costa Rica, Côte d'Ivoire, Croatia, Cuba, Cyprus, Czech Republic, Democratic People's Republic of Korea, Denmark, Djibouti, Dominica, Dominican Republic, Ecuador, Egypt, El Salvador, Equatorial Guinea, Eritrea, Estonia, Ethiopia, Fiji, Finland, France, Georgia, Germany, Ghana, Greece, Grenada, Guatemala, Guinea, Guinea-Bissau, Guyana, Haiti, Honduras, Hungary, Iceland, India, Indonesia, Iran, Iraq, Ireland, Italy, Jamaica, Japan, Jordan, Kazakhstan, Kenya, Kuwait, Kyrgyzstan, Lao People's Democratic Republic, Latvia, Lebanon, Lesotho, Liberia, Libyan Arab Jamahiriya, Liechtenstein, Lithuania, Luxembourg, Madagascar, Malawi, Malaysia, Maldives, Mali, Malta, Marshall Islands, Mauritania, Mauritius, Mexico, Micronesia, Moldova, Monaco, Mongolia, Montenegro, Morocco, Mozambique, Myanmar, Namibia, Nepal, Netherlands, New Zealand, Nicaragua, Niger, Nigeria, Norway, Oman, Pakistan, Palau, Panama, Papua New Guinea, Paraguay, Peru, Philippines, Poland, Portugal, Qatar, Republic of Korea, Romania, Russian Federation, Rwanda, Saint Lucia, Saint Vincent and the Grenadines, Samoa, San Marino, Sao Tome and Principe, Saudi Arabia, Senegal, Serbia, Singapore, Slovakia, Slovenia, Solomon Islands, South Africa, Spain, Sri Lanka, Sudan, Suriname, Swaziland, Sweden, Switzerland, Syrian Arab Republic, Tajikistan, Thailand, The former Yugoslav Republic of Macedonia, Timor-Leste, Togo, Tonga, Trinidad and Tobago, Tunisia, Turkey, Turkmenistan, Tuvalu, Uganda, Ukraine, United Arab Emirates, United Kingdom, United Republic of Tanzania, Uruguay, Uzbekistan, Vanuatu, Venezuela, Viet Nam, Yemen, Zambia, Zimbabwe.

Against: United States.

Abstaining: Israel.

Maritime security and safety

At the ninth meeting [A/63/174] of the Consultative Process on Oceans and the Law of the Sea (New York, 23–27 June) (see p. 1497), delegations underscored the danger posed to maritime security by illicit trafficking of small arms and weapons of mass destruction. It was recognized that the legal regimes governing maritime security and safety might have common and mutually reinforcing objectives that could benefit from synergies with non-proliferation measures and instruments such as the Treaty on the

Prohibition of the Emplacement of Nuclear Weapons and Other Weapons of Mass Destruction on the Sea-Bed and the Ocean Floor and the Subsoil Thereof (Seabed Treaty), adopted by the General Assembly in resolution 2660(XXV) [YUN 1970, p. 17].

Disarmament and development

The issue of the relationship between disarmament and development remained controversial in 2008.

In accordance with General Assembly resolution 62/48 [YUN 2007, p. 586] the Secretary-General submitted a July report [A/63/134], summarizing activities to implement the action programme adopted by the 1987 International Conference on the Relationship between Disarmament and Development [YUN 1987, p. 82] and the recommendations of the Group of Governmental Experts on the relationship [YUN 2004, p. 579]. It also detailed information received from five Governments (Cuba, Dominican Republic, Lebanon, Qatar, Serbia). To strengthen the UN role in disarmament and development, a high-level Steering Group had designated focal points at the working level to discuss the issue, but a significant divergence of views between States had resulted in a limited response from Member States, which impacted the Steering Group's ability to take decisive action and to commit the necessary resources.

GENERAL ASSEMBLY ACTION

On 2 December [meeting 61], the General Assembly, on the recommendation of the First Committee [A/63/389], adopted **resolution 63/52** without vote [agenda item 89 *(aa)*].

Relationship between disarmament and development

The General Assembly,

Recalling that the Charter of the United Nations envisages the establishment and maintenance of international peace and security with the least diversion for armaments of the world's human and economic resources,

Recalling also the provisions of the Final Document of the Tenth Special Session of the General Assembly concerning the relationship between disarmament and development, as well as the adoption on 11 September 1987 of the Final Document of the International Conference on the Relationship between Disarmament and Development,

Recalling further its resolutions 49/75 J of 15 December 1994, 50/70 G of 12 December 1995, 51/45 D of 10 December 1996, 52/38 D of 9 December 1997, 53/77 K of 4 December 1998, 54/54 T of 1 December 1999, 55/33 L of 20 November 2000, 56/24 E of 29 November 2001, 57/65 of 22 November 2002, 59/78 of 3 December 2004, 60/61 of 8 December 2005, 61/64 of 6 December 2006 and 62/48 of 5 December 2007, and its decision 58/520 of 8 December 2003,

Bearing in mind the Final Document of the Twelfth Conference of Heads of State or Government of Non-Aligned Countries, held in Durban, South Africa, from 29 August to 3 September 1998, and the Final Document of the Thirteenth Ministerial Conference of the Movement of Non-Aligned Countries, held in Cartagena, Colombia, on 8 and 9 April 2000,

Mindful of the changes in international relations that have taken place since the adoption on 11 September 1987 of the Final Document of the International Conference on the Relationship between Disarmament and Development, including the development agenda that has emerged over the past decade,

Bearing in mind the new challenges for the international community in the field of development, poverty eradication and the elimination of the diseases that afflict humanity,

Stressing the importance of the symbiotic relationship between disarmament and development and the important role of security in this connection, and concerned at increasing global military expenditure, which could otherwise be spent on development needs,

Recalling the report of the Group of Governmental Experts on the relationship between disarmament and development and its reappraisal of this significant issue in the current international context,

Bearing in mind the importance of following up on the implementation of the action programme adopted at the 1987 International Conference on the Relationship between Disarmament and Development,

1. *Stresses* the central role of the United Nations in the disarmament-development relationship, and requests the Secretary-General to strengthen further the role of the Organization in this field, in particular the high-level Steering Group on Disarmament and Development, in order to ensure continued and effective coordination and close cooperation between the relevant United Nations departments, agencies and sub-agencies;

2. *Requests* the Secretary-General to continue to take action, through appropriate organs and within available resources, for the implementation of the action programme adopted at the 1987 International Conference on the Relationship between Disarmament and Development;

3. *Urges* the international community to devote part of the resources made available by the implementation of disarmament and arms limitation agreements to economic and social development, with a view to reducing the ever-widening gap between developed and developing countries;

4. *Encourages* the international community to achieve the Millennium Development Goals and to make reference to the contribution that disarmament could provide in meeting them when it reviews its progress towards this purpose in 2008, as well as to make greater efforts to integrate disarmament, humanitarian and development activities;

5. *Encourages* the relevant regional and subregional organizations and institutions, non-governmental organizations and research institutes to incorporate issues related to the relationship between disarmament and development in their agendas and, in this regard, to take into account

the report of the Group of Governmental Experts on the relationship between disarmament and development;

6. *Reiterates the invitation* to Member States to provide the Secretary-General with information regarding measures and efforts to devote part of the resources made available by the implementation of disarmament and arms limitation agreements to economic and social development, with a view to reducing the ever-widening gap between developed and developing countries;

7. *Requests* the Secretary-General to report to the General Assembly at its sixty-fourth session on the implementation of the present resolution, including the information provided by Member States pursuant to paragraph 6 above;

8. *Decides* to include in the provisional agenda of its sixty-fourth session the item entitled "Relationship between disarmament and development".

Promoting development through reduction of armed violence

In September, 85 States met in Geneva for a Review Summit of the 2006 Geneva Declaration on Armed Violence and Development, hosted by Switzerland and UNDP. On 16 October [A/63/494], Switzerland, on behalf of the Geneva Declaration core group of States (Brazil, Finland, Guatemala, Indonesia, Kenya, Morocco, the Netherlands, Norway, Philippines, Spain, Switzerland, Thailand, United Kingdom) forwarded to the General Assembly the Geneva Declaration and the statement adopted by the Review Summit.

By the Declaration, 42 countries acknowledged that armed violence and conflict impeded realization of the Millennium Development Goals (MDGS), and that conflict prevention and resolution, violence reduction, human rights, good governance and peacebuilding were key steps towards reducing poverty, promoting economic growth and improving people's lives. The participants agreed to work individually and together, at national, regional and multilateral levels, on practical measures that: promoted conflict prevention, resolution and reconciliation and supported post-conflict peacebuilding; stemmed the proliferation and illegal trafficking of small arms and light weapons; upheld respect for human rights and promoted the peaceful settlement of conflicts based on justice and the rule of law; fostered public security institutions; and ensured that armed violence prevention and reduction initiatives targeted specific risk factors and groups, and were linked to providing alternative livelihoods. They supported initiatives to measure the human, social and economic costs of armed violence, to assess risks, and to disseminate best practices. They set the goal of achieving, by 2015, measurable reductions in armed violence and tangible improvements in human security worldwide.

At the conclusion of the Review Summit, a statement was adopted reaffirming the goals of the Geneva Declaration, to which meanwhile 94 States had subscribed. The participating States recognized that development, peace and security and human rights were interlinked and mutually reinforcing, and that armed violence might hinder the achievement of the MDGS. They commended the efforts made to promote sustainable security and a culture of peace by taking action to reduce armed violence and its negative impact on socio-economic and human development. They further commended Guatemala, Kenya and Thailand for having hosted regional conferences on armed violence and development, which had resulted in regional declarations, and encouraged States and organizations to implement those declarations. They acknowledged that States bore the primary responsibility for preventing, reducing and ending armed violence through practical measures, reaffirmed the commitments in the Millennium Declaration and the 2005 World Summit Outcome, as expressed in Assembly resolution 60/1 [YUN 2005, p. 48], and reaffirmed their support for UN efforts to promote implementation of the Programme of Action to Prevent, Combat and Eradicate the Illicit Trade in Small Arms and Light Weapons in All Its Aspects. They agreed to meet again no later than 2011 to assess progress in achieving those goals.

GENERAL ASSEMBLY ACTION

On 17 November [meeting 51], the General Assembly adopted **resolution 63/23** [draft A/63/L.27 & Add.1, as orally revised] without vote [agenda item 107].

Promoting development through the reduction and prevention of armed violence

The General Assembly,

Reaffirming the commitments made by the international community in the United Nations Millennium Declaration, in particular its goal to create an environment conducive to development and the elimination of poverty,

Recalling the 2005 World Summit Outcome,

Recalling also the 2001 Programme of Action to Prevent, Combat and Eradicate the Illicit Trade in Small Arms and Light Weapons in All Its Aspects, reflecting, inter alia, the concern with the implications that poverty and underdevelopment may have for the illicit trade in small arms and light weapons in all its aspects,

Taking note of the Geneva Declaration on Armed Violence and Development of 7 June 2006, and the regional declarations adopted by regional conferences hosted by the Governments of Guatemala, Kenya and Thailand, having the aim of raising awareness among Member States of the relationship between armed violence and development,

Reaffirming that development, peace and security, and human rights are interlinked and mutually reinforcing,

Stressing the importance of the symbiotic relationship between disarmament and development and the important role of security in this connection,

Recognizing that sustained socio-economic development and the reduction of inequalities, including measures aimed at improving social inclusion, employment and education, constitute essential requirements for reducing levels of armed violence,

Taking note of the resolve expressed in the Summit statement, adopted at the conclusion of the Review Summit of the Geneva Declaration on Armed Violence and Development, to develop goals, targets and measurable indicators on armed violence and development as a complement to the Millennium Development Goals,

Cognizant of past and ongoing efforts, including within the United Nations system, to achieve the Millennium Development Goals through the prevention and reduction of armed violence at national, regional and international levels,

Mindful of the primary responsibility of national Governments for curbing armed violence and for fostering the Millennium Development Goals,

1. *Stresses* the need for a coherent and integrated approach to the prevention of armed violence, with a view to achieving sustainable peace and development;

2. *Requests* the Secretary-General to seek the views of Member States on the interrelation between armed violence and development and, in close consultation with the relevant agencies, funds and programmes of the United Nations system, and with the three United Nations regional centres for peace and disarmament, to submit a report to the General Assembly at its sixty-fourth session.

Observance of environmental norms

Pursuant to General Assembly resolution 62/28 [YUN 2007, p. 587], the Secretary-General submitted a July report [A/63/116 & Add.1] containing information from 10 Member States (Canada, Cuba, Finland, Greece, Lebanon, Panama, Qatar, Serbia, Spain, Ukraine) on measures they had adopted to promote the observance of environmental norms in the drafting and implementation of agreements on disarmament and arms control.

GENERAL ASSEMBLY ACTION

On 2 December [meeting 61], the General Assembly, on the recommendation of the First Committee [A/63/389], adopted **resolution 63/51** without vote [agenda item 89 *(n)*].

Observance of environmental norms in the drafting and implementation of agreements on disarmament and arms control

The General Assembly,

Recalling its resolutions 50/70 M of 12 December 1995, 51/45 E of 10 December 1996, 52/38 E of 9 December 1997, 53/77 J of 4 December 1998, 54/54 S of 1 December 1999, 55/33 K of 20 November 2000, 56/24 F of 29 November 2001, 57/64 of 22 November 2002, 58/45 of 8 December 2003, 59/68 of 3 December 2004, 60/60 of 8 December 2005, 61/63 of 6 December 2006 and 62/28 of 5 December 2007,

Emphasizing the importance of the observance of environmental norms in the preparation and implementation of disarmament and arms limitation agreements,

Recognizing that it is necessary to take duly into account the agreements adopted at the United Nations Conference on Environment and Development, as well as prior relevant agreements, in the drafting and implementation of agreements on disarmament and arms limitation,

Taking note of the report of the Secretary-General submitted pursuant to resolution 62/28,

Mindful of the detrimental environmental effects of the use of nuclear weapons,

1. *Reaffirms* that international disarmament forums should take fully into account the relevant environmental norms in negotiating treaties and agreements on disarmament and arms limitation and that all States, through their actions, should contribute fully to ensuring compliance with the aforementioned norms in the implementation of treaties and conventions to which they are parties;

2. *Calls upon* States to adopt unilateral, bilateral, regional and multilateral measures so as to contribute to ensuring the application of scientific and technological progress within the framework of international security, disarmament and other related spheres, without detriment to the environment or to its effective contribution to attaining sustainable development;

3. *Welcomes* the information provided by Member States on the implementation of the measures they have adopted to promote the objectives envisaged in the present resolution;

4. *Invites* all Member States to communicate to the Secretary-General information on the measures they have adopted to promote the objectives envisaged in the present resolution, and requests the Secretary-General to submit a report containing that information to the General Assembly at its sixty-fourth session;

5. *Decides* to include in the provisional agenda of its sixty-fourth session the item entitled "Observance of environmental norms in the drafting and implementation of agreements on disarmament and arms control".

Effects of depleted uranium

In accordance with General Assembly resolution 62/30 [YUN 2007, p. 588], the Secretary-General, in a July report with a later addendum [A/63/170 & Add.1], submitted the views of 19 Member States (Andorra, Argentina, Austria, Bangladesh, Belgium, Bolivia, Bosnia and Herzegovina, Canada, Cuba, Finland, Germany, Italy, Jamaica, Japan, Mali, the Netherlands, Qatar, Serbia, Spain) and three international organizations (IAEA, United Nations Environment Programme, World Health Organization) on the effects of the use of armaments and ammunitions containing depleted uranium on human health and the environment.

GENERAL ASSEMBLY ACTION

On 2 December [meeting 61], the General Assembly, on the recommendation of the First Committee [A/63/389], adopted **resolution 63/54** by recorded vote (141-4-34) [agenda item 89 *(p)*].

Effects of the use of armaments and ammunitions containing depleted uranium

The General Assembly,

Guided by the purposes and principles enshrined in the Charter of the United Nations and the rules of humanitarian international law,

Recalling its resolution 62/30 of 5 December 2007,

Determined to promote multilateralism as an essential means to carry forward negotiations on arms regulation and disarmament,

Taking note of the opinions expressed by Member States and relevant international organizations on the effects of the use of armaments and ammunitions containing depleted uranium, as reflected in the report submitted by the Secretary-General pursuant to resolution 62/30,

Convinced that as humankind is more aware of the need to take immediate measures to protect the environment, any event that could jeopardize such efforts requires urgent attention to implement the required measures,

Taking into consideration the potential harmful effects of the use of armaments and ammunitions containing depleted uranium on human health and the environment,

1. *Expresses its appreciation* to the Member States and international organizations that submitted their views to the Secretary-General pursuant to resolution 62/30;

2. *Invites* Member States and relevant international organizations, particularly those that have not yet done so, to communicate to the Secretary-General their views on the effects of the use of armaments and ammunitions containing depleted uranium;

3. *Requests* the Secretary-General to request relevant international organizations to update and complete, as appropriate, their studies and research on the effects of the use of armaments and ammunitions containing depleted uranium on human health and the environment;

4. *Encourages* Member States, particularly the affected States, as necessary, to facilitate the studies and research referred to in paragraph 3 above;

5. *Requests* the Secretary-General to submit an updated report on this subject to the General Assembly at its sixty-fifth session, reflecting the information presented by Member States and relevant international organizations, including that submitted pursuant to paragraphs 2 and 3 above;

6. *Decides* to include in the provisional agenda of its sixty-fifth session the item entitled "Effects of the use of armaments and ammunitions containing depleted uranium".

RECORDED VOTE ON RESOLUTION 63/54:

In favour: Afghanistan, Algeria, Angola, Antigua and Barbuda, Argentina, Armenia, Austria, Azerbaijan, Bahamas, Bahrain, Bangladesh, Barbados, Belarus, Belize, Benin, Bhutan, Bolivia, Botswana, Brazil, Brunei Darussalam, Burkina Faso, Burundi, Cambodia, Cameroon, Cape Verde, Chile, Colombia, Comoros, Congo, Costa Rica, Côte d'Ivoire, Cuba, Cyprus, Democratic People's Republic of Korea, Djibouti, Dominica, Dominican Republic, Ecuador, Egypt, El Salvador, Equatorial Guinea, Eritrea, Ethiopia, Finland, Germany, Ghana, Grenada, Guatemala, Guinea, Guinea-Bissau, Guyana, Haiti, Honduras, Iceland, India, Indonesia, Iran, Iraq, Ireland, Italy, Jamaica, Japan, Jordan, Kenya, Kuwait, Lao People's Democratic Republic, Lebanon, Lesotho, Liberia, Libyan Arab Jamahiriya, Liechtenstein, Madagascar, Malawi, Malaysia, Maldives, Mali, Malta, Marshall Islands, Mauritania, Mauritius, Mexico, Mongolia, Montenegro, Morocco, Mozambique, Myanmar, Namibia, Nauru, Nepal, Netherlands, New Zealand, Nicaragua, Niger, Nigeria, Norway, Oman, Pakistan, Panama, Papua New Guinea, Paraguay, Peru, Philippines, Qatar, Rwanda, Saint Lucia, Saint Vincent and the Grenadines, Samoa, San Marino, Sao Tome and Principe, Saudi Arabia, Senegal, Serbia, Singapore, Solomon Islands, South Africa, Sri Lanka, Sudan, Suriname, Swaziland, Switzerland, Syrian Arab Republic, Tajikistan, Thailand, Timor-Leste, Togo, Tonga, Trinidad and Tobago, Tunisia, Turkmenistan, Tuvalu, Uganda, United Arab Emirates, United Republic of Tanzania, Uruguay, Uzbekistan, Vanuatu, Venezuela, Viet Nam, Yemen, Zambia, Zimbabwe.

Against: France, Israel, United Kingdom, United States.

Abstaining: Albania, Andorra, Australia, Belgium, Bosnia and Herzegovina, Bulgaria, Canada, Croatia, Czech Republic, Denmark, Estonia, Georgia, Greece, Hungary, Kazakhstan, Kyrgyzstan, Latvia, Lithuania, Luxembourg, Micronesia, Moldova, Palau, Poland, Portugal, Republic of Korea, Romania, Russian Federation, Slovakia, Slovenia, Spain, Sweden, The former Yugoslav Republic of Macedonia, Turkey, Ukraine.

Science and technology and disarmament

Discussions on science and technology in the context of international security had featured regularly at the United Nations during the past decade. The agenda item "Role of science and technology in the context of international security and disarmament" was included in the sixty-third session of the General Assembly in accordance with Assembly resolution 61/55 [YUN 2006, p. 740].

By **decision 63/518** of 2 December, the General Assembly, on the recommendation of the First Committee [A/63/384], included the item in the provisional agenda of its sixty-fourth (2009) session.

The Assembly took related action on the same day in **resolution 63/37** (see p. 696) on developments in the field of information and telecommunications in the context of international security, calling on Member States to promote the consideration of existing and potential threats in the field of information security, as well as possible measures to limit them. It requested the Secretary-General to study those threats as well as cooperative measures to address them, with the assistance of a governmental group of experts.

Studies, information and training

Disarmament studies

During the year, the following expert groups on disarmament issues, established by the General Assembly, completed their work: the Group of Governmental Experts towards an arms trade treaty, establishing common international standards for the import, export and transfer of conventional arms, mandated by General Assembly resolution 61/89 [YUN 2006, p. 655]; the Group of Governmental Experts on problems arising from the accumulation of conventional ammunition stockpiles in surplus, established in accordance with resolution 61/72 [ibid., p. 661]; and the Group of Governmental Experts on missiles in all its aspects, established pursuant to resolution 59/67 [YUN 2004, p. 537]. Preparations started for a governmental review of the operation and further development of the Standardized Instrument for Reporting Military Expenditures, mandated by resolution 62/13 [YUN 2007, p. 579]. In December, the Assembly, by **resolutions 63/37** (see p. 696) and **63/89** (see p. 695), called for further studies on developments in the field of information and telecommunications in the context of international security, and on the UN Register of Conventional Arms, respectively.

The United Nations Institute for Disarmament Research (UNIDIR) was involved in a number of studies. Among others, it began work on a study of the political and legal aspects of multinational approaches to the nuclear fuel cycle and was continuing research on the role of regional bodies in implementing global treaties. Its ongoing multi-year research project entitled "Disarmament as humanitarian action: making multilateral negotiations work" was aimed at rethinking and reframing the ways and means of international arms control and disarmament. The project "Creating a new dynamic for public-private partnerships for peaceful and sustainable development: human security and equitable access to resources" was completed in May. A draft security needs assessment protocol, for use by UN agencies in post-conflict environments, was nearing completion and a report outlining the purposes of the protocol was published in April. Under the project "International assistance for implementing the Programme of Action to Prevent, Combat and Eradicate the Illicit Trade in Small Arms and Light Weapons in All Its Aspects", a mechanism was being developed to assist in matching needs and resources with respect to implementing the Programme of Action. UNIDIR continued to explore the possibilities for a weapons-of-mass-destruction-free zone in the Middle East.

The Comprehensive Nuclear-Test-Ban Treaty Organization (CTBTO) in February launched an International Scientific Studies Project with the participation of over 100 scientists from 33 countries, to evaluate through independent studies and assessments the capabilities and level of readiness of the Treaty verification system; findings were to be presented at an international scientific conference in Vienna in June 2009.

Disarmament education

In accordance with General Assembly resolution 61/73 [YUN 2006, p. 678], the Secretary-General, in a July report [A/63/158 & Add.1], reviewed the results of the implementation of the 34 recommendations of a 2002 UN study [YUN 2002, p. 544] on disarmament and non-proliferation education and possible new opportunities for promoting such education. Seven Member States (Burundi, Cambodia, Italy, Mauritius, the Netherlands, Qatar, Spain) had submitted information, as well as nine UN entities and international organizations and 16 civil society and non-governmental organizations.

The Secretary-General in his conclusions noted that the 34 recommendations were aimed at Governments and international and regional organizations, as well as civil society, encouraging actors to recognize the contribution such education could make to a well-informed citizenry and thus a more secure world. For the two-year review of the implementation of those recommendations, a large quantity of information was received. Several Governments had used the framework of the 2010 Review Conference of the States Parties to the Treaty on the Non-Proliferation of Nuclear Weapons to promote education and training in nuclear non-proliferation. As in previous reports, most initiatives had been carried out by civil society, which remained the creative and driving force. In order to take advantage of the renewed global interest in the possibilities offered by a world free of nuclear weapons, much work remained to be done. Some of the most effective efforts involved partnerships among Governments and international, regional and civil society organizations that could serve as a model for future activities. The United Nations would continue to seek opportunities to promote and participate in such collaborative work.

Among UN entities, UNODA, in cooperation with the UN Department of Public Information (DPI), had launched an educational disarmament and non-proliferation website that was expanded with additional interactive capacities. UNODA also co-sponsored the World Federation of United Nations Associations educational programme entitled "Students for a nuclear-weapons-free world", in preparation for the 2010 Treaty on the Non-Proliferation of Nuclear Weapons Review Conference. UNIDIR held a seminar on disarmament and non-proliferation education, continued to issue its quarterly journal, and expanded distribution of its material through online social networking. An electronic newsletter was launched in June by CTBTO, whose education activities increasingly focused on electronic dissemination of information to targeted audiences.

GENERAL ASSEMBLY ACTION

On 2 December [meeting 61], the General Assembly, on the recommendation of the First Committee [A/63/389], adopted **resolution 63/70** without vote [agenda item 89 *(d)*].

United Nations study on disarmament and non-proliferation education

The General Assembly,

Recalling its resolutions 55/33 E of 20 November 2000, 57/60 of 22 November 2002, 59/93 of 3 December 2004 and 61/73 of 6 December 2006,

Welcoming the report of the Secretary-General on disarmament and non-proliferation education, in which the Secretary-General reported on the implementation of the recommendations contained in the United Nations study on disarmament and non-proliferation education,

Also welcoming the launch of the disarmament and non-proliferation education website, "Disarmament Education: Resources for Learning", by the Office for Disarmament Affairs of the Secretariat, and the educational disarmament and non-proliferation website on the United Nations CyberSchoolBus site, launched by the Department of Public Information of the Secretariat and the Office for Disarmament Affairs,

Emphasizing that the Secretary-General concludes in his report that efforts need to be continued to implement the recommendations of the study and follow the good examples of how they are being implemented to stimulate even further long-term results,

Desirous of stressing the urgency of promoting concerted international efforts at disarmament and non-proliferation, in particular in the field of nuclear disarmament and non-proliferation, with a view to strengthening international security and enhancing sustainable economic and social development,

Conscious of the need to combat the negative effects of cultures of violence and complacency in the face of current dangers in this field through long-term programmes of education and training,

Remaining convinced that the need for disarmament and non-proliferation education has never been greater, not only on the subject of weapons of mass destruction but also in the field of small arms and light weapons, terrorism and other challenges to international security and the process of disarmament, as well as on the relevance of implementing the recommendations contained in the United Nations study,

Recognizing the importance of the role of civil society, including non-governmental organizations, in the promotion of disarmament and non-proliferation education,

1. *Expresses its appreciation* to the Member States, the United Nations and other international and regional organizations, civil society and non-governmental organizations, which, within their purview, implemented the recommendations made in the United Nations study, as discussed in the report of the Secretary-General reviewing the implementation of the recommendations, and encourages them once again to continue applying those recommendations and reporting to the Secretary-General on steps taken to implement them;

2. *Requests* the Secretary-General to prepare a report reviewing the results of the implementation of the recommendations and possible new opportunities for promoting disarmament and non-proliferation education, and to submit it to the General Assembly at its sixty-fifth session;

3. *Reiterates the request* to the Secretary-General to utilize electronic means to the fullest extent possible in the dissemination, in as many official languages as feasible, of information related to that report and any other information that the Office for Disarmament Affairs gathers on an ongoing basis in regard to the implementation of the recommendations of the United Nations study;

4. *Decides* to include in the provisional agenda of its sixty-fifth session the item entitled "Disarmament and non-proliferation education".

Disarmament Information Programme

During the year, UNODA continued to raise awareness and understanding of the work of the United Nations on disarmament and related issues. *The United Nations Disarmament Yearbook* was distributed worldwide and was also accessible electronically. The quarterly e-publication *UNODA Update* continued to highlight events and activities of the Office and other disarmament forums. On the subject of verification in all its aspects, *Study Series 32* was released in 2008, and two booklets were published, entitled *Small Arms and Light Weapons: Selected United Nations Documents* and *Disarmament 2007: Critical Disarmament Issues.*

Dedicated websites were designed for major disarmament-related conferences, including the first and second sessions of the Preparatory Committee for the 2010 NPT Review Conference and the Third Biennial Meeting of States, as well as in connection with issues such as efforts to achieve an arms trade treaty.

During the four-week session of the General Assembly's First Committee in October, two exhibits were displayed: one, organized by Mayors for Peace, showing photographs of the Hiroshima-Nagasaki Atomic Bomb project, and another, entitled "The World is Watching", sponsored by UNODA and organized by Control Arms, highlighting the dangers of the spread of illicit small arms and UN efforts towards an international arms trade treaty.

UNODA also facilitated the participation of civil society organizations in disarmament-related meetings and conferences and collaborated closely with coalitions of NGOs that spearheaded such participation.

Messenger of Peace Michael Douglas, continuing to use his celebrity status to promote disarmament and advocate for peace, conducted radio and television interviews, participated in round-table discussions with policy-makers and journalists and held discussions with senior members of the United States Senate and the House of Representatives.

Report of Secretary-General. In the Secretary-General's July report [A/63/162], priority issues for UNODA's Disarmament Information Programme included WMDs; conventional weapons, particularly small arms and light weapons; and the dissemination of information on disarmament.

In conclusion, the Secretary-General stated that the Disarmament Information Programme was orienting its publications to electronic formats. DPI had highlighted disarmament and arms control issues of topical interest, especially nuclear weapons and small arms and light weapons, using its network of information centres around the world and its outreach capacity.

The Secretary-General appealed for continued support, and expressed appreciation to Governments and private donors for their contributions to the Voluntary Trust Fund for the Programme. As at the end of 2007, the Fund balance stood at $328,216. During the per-iod from 1 January through 30 June 2008, additional contributions totalling $51,000 were received.

GENERAL ASSEMBLY ACTION

On 2 December [meeting 61], the General Assembly, on the recommendation of the First Committee [A/63/390], adopted **resolution 63/81** without vote [agenda item 90 *(b)*].

United Nations Disarmament Information Programme

The General Assembly,

Recalling its decision taken in 1982 at its twelfth special session, the second special session devoted to disarmament, by which the World Disarmament Campaign was launched,

Bearing in mind its resolution 47/53 D of 9 December 1992, in which it decided, inter alia, that the World Disarmament Campaign should be known thereafter as the "United Nations Disarmament Information Programme" and the World Disarmament Campaign Voluntary Trust Fund as the "Voluntary Trust Fund for the United Nations Disarmament Information Programme",

Recalling its resolutions 51/46 A of 10 December 1996, 53/78 E of 4 December 1998, 55/34 A of 20 November 2000, 57/90 of 22 November 2002, 59/103 of 3 December 2004 and 61/95 of 6 December 2006,

Welcoming the report of the Secretary-General,

1. *Welcomes* the launch of the new United Nations Office for Disarmament Affairs website, and invites Member States and other users to make use of its expanded content and specialization;

2. *Commends* the Secretary-General for his efforts to make effective use of the limited resources available to him in disseminating as widely as possible, including by electronic means, information on arms control and disarmament to Governments, the media, non-governmental organizations, educational communities and research institutes, and in carrying out a seminar and conference programme;

3. *Stresses* the importance of the United Nations Disarmament Information Programme as a significant instrument in enabling all Member States to participate fully in the deliberations and negotiations on disarmament in the various United Nations bodies, in assisting them in complying with treaties, as required, and in contributing to agreed mechanisms for transparency;

4. *Commends with satisfaction* the launch of *The United Nations Disarmament Yearbook* for 2007, with new format and content, as well as its online edition, by the United Nations Office for Disarmament Affairs;

5. *Notes with appreciation* the cooperation of the Department of Public Information of the Secretariat and its information centres in pursuit of the objectives of the Programme;

6. *Recommends* that the Programme continue to inform, educate and generate public understanding of the importance of multilateral action and support for it, including action by the United Nations and the Conference on Disarmament, in the field of arms control and disarmament, in a factual, balanced and objective manner, and that it focus its efforts:

(a) To continue to publish in all official languages *The United Nations Disarmament Yearbook*, the flagship publication of the United Nations Office for Disarmament Affairs;

(b) To continue to maintain the disarmament website as a part of the United Nations website and to produce versions of the site in as many official languages as feasible;

(c) To continue to intensify United Nations interaction with the public, principally non-governmental organizations and research institutes, to help further an informed debate on topical issues of arms limitation, disarmament and security;

(d) To continue to organize discussions on topics of interest in the field of arms limitation and disarmament with a view to broadening understanding and facilitating an exchange of views and information among Member States and civil society;

7. *Recognizes* the importance of all support extended to the Voluntary Trust Fund for the United Nations Disarmament Information Programme, and invites once again all Member States to make further contributions to the Fund with a view to sustaining a strong outreach programme;

8. *Takes note* of the recommendations contained in the report of the Secretary-General, which reviews the implementation of the recommendations made in the 2002 study on disarmament and non-proliferation education;

9. *Requests* the Secretary-General to submit to the General Assembly at its sixty-fifth session a report covering both the implementation of the activities of the Programme by the United Nations system during the previous two years and the activities of the Programme contemplated by the system for the following two years;

10. *Decides* to include in the provisional agenda of its sixty-fifth session the item entitled "United Nations Disarmament Information Programme".

Advisory Board on Disarmament Matters

The Advisory Board on Disarmament Matters, which advised the Secretary-General and also served as the Board of Trustees of UNIDIR, held its forty-ninth (New York, 20–22 February) and fiftieth (Geneva, 9–11 July) sessions, discussing energy security and the environment in the field of disarmament and non-proliferation; multilateralism and the UN dimension; and, in continuation of discussions from its 2007 session [YUN 2007, p. 590], emerging weapons technologies, including outer space aspects. The Board's deliberations and recommendations were summarized in an August report of the Secretary-General [A/63/279].

The Board encouraged a broader dialogue on the peaceful use of nuclear energy, including the various proposals for establishing national and multilateral nuclear fuel supply arrangements under a multilateral framework. Following an exchange of views on the Nuclear Security Project, or "Hoover Plan", a proposal launched in 2007 by former high-ranking United States officials, the Board recommended that the Secretary-General continue to strengthen his personal role in generating political will in the field of nuclear disarmament and non-proliferation, seizing the momentum created by the Plan and encouraging wider discussions on its objective, with the United Nations possibly acting as a multilateral forum. With regard to emerging weapons technologies, including outer space issues, the Board suggested that the Secretary-General continue raising awareness of the risks related to those technologies and initiate a dialogue between Governments and the scientific community on emerging technologies with military applications. It also proposed that he consider creating a high-level panel, including eminent scientists, on the issue of emerging weapons technologies, including outer space aspects, and their possible implications for international peace and security.

In its capacity as UNIDIR Board of Trustees (see below), the Board adopted the Institute's 2008 programme of work and budget.

UN Institute for Disarmament Research

The Secretary-General transmitted to the General Assembly the report of the UNIDIR Director [A/63/177] covering the period from August 2007 to July 2008 and the proposed 2008–2009 programme of work and budget, as approved by the Advisory Board in its capacity as UNIDIR's Board of Trustees.

The Institute's work programme remained centred on the three main areas of global security and disarmament, regional security and disarmament, and human security and disarmament, thus addressing the full range of substantive disarmament issues from small arms to weapons in outer space. The period under review was characterized by increased outreach and relations with the UN system, in particular through two research projects on security needs assessment and disarmament as humanitarian action. The Institute engaged in a range of consultations, discussions and seminars pertaining to the work of the Conference on Disarmament. It also increased the number of institutes with which it collaborated on research projects and meetings and organized a range of research meetings, both in Geneva and in different regions. UNIDIR held a series of meetings on creative approaches to the entry into force of CTBT, and in April, it was involved in a seminar on CTBT and the fissile material cut-off treaty. In May, it co-organized a seminar during the 2008 Preparatory Committee for the 2010 Review Conference of the NPT. Under the umbrella project "Working our way to nuclear disarmament", it produced a paper on the role of regional organizations in implementing Security Council resolution 1540(2004) [YUN 2004, p. 544].

The Institute was engaged in a UNODA-executed project on promoting the universalization of the Convention on Certain Conventional Weapons through regional seminars. UNIDIR was also involved in organizing a series of discussions on cluster munitions and controlling the spread of small arms and light weapons. In preparation for an arms trade treaty, it co-organized seminars and analysed the elements required for such a treaty. It presented to the Third Biennial Meeting of States a draft report assessing implementation of the UN Programme of Action to Prevent, Combat and Eradicate the Illicit Trade in Small Arms and Light Weapons in All Its Aspects and developed needs assessments and an inventory of expertise as part of the Coordinating Action on Small Arms mechanism for disseminating information.

UNIDIR continued to update the *Disarmament Insight* website, launched in April 2007, and to publish its bilingual quarterly journal *Disarmament Forum*. In early 2008, it launched a project entitled "The road from Oslo: analysis of negotiations to address the humanitarian effects of cluster munitions" and issued a publication, *The Humanitarian Impact of Cluster Munitions*.

Disarmament fellowship, training and advisory services

In June 2008, 25 fellows participated in the UN disarmament fellowship, training and advisory services programme, which began in Geneva on 25 August and concluded in New York on 24 October. The programme continued to be structured in three segments: a study session in Geneva; study visits to disarmament-related intergovernmental organizations and to Member States; and a study session at UN Headquarters in New York.

Report of Secretary-General. In response to General Assembly resolution 61/91 [YUN 2006, p. 680], the Secretary-General reported in July [A/63/129] on the UN disarmament fellowship, training and advisory services programme, which, since being launched in 1979 [YUN 1979, p. 92], had trained 759 officials from 159 States. He observed that the programme continued to enhance disarmament expertise, particularly in developing countries, and contributed to better understanding Member States' and the international community's concerns in the fields of disarmament and security and to fostering progress in disarmament, arms limitation and non-proliferation.

GENERAL ASSEMBLY ACTION

On 2 December [meeting 61], the General Assembly, on the recommendation of the First Committee [A/63/390], adopted **resolution 63/79** without vote [agenda item 90 *(a)*].

United Nations disarmament fellowship, training and advisory services

The General Assembly,

Having considered the report of the Secretary-General,

Recalling its decision, contained in paragraph 108 of the Final Document of the Tenth Special Session of the General Assembly, the first special session devoted to disarmament, to establish a programme of fellowships on disarmament, as well as its decisions contained in annex IV to the Concluding Document of the Twelfth Special Session of the General Assembly, the second special session devoted to disarmament, in which it decided, inter alia, to continue the programme,

Noting that the programme continues to contribute significantly to developing greater awareness of the importance and benefits of disarmament and a better understanding of the concerns of the international community in the field of disarmament and security, as well as to enhancing the knowledge and skills of fellows, allowing them to participate more effectively in efforts in the field of disarmament at all levels,

Noting with satisfaction that the programme has trained a large number of officials from Member States throughout its thirty years of existence, many of whom hold positions of responsibility in the field of disarmament within their own Governments,

Recognizing the need for Member States to take into account gender equality when nominating candidates to the programme,

Recalling all the annual resolutions on the matter since the thirty-seventh session of the General Assembly, in 1982, including resolution 50/71 A of 12 December 1995,

Believing that the forms of assistance available to Member States, in particular to developing countries, under the programme will enhance the capabilities of their officials to follow ongoing deliberations and negotiations on disarmament, both bilateral and multilateral,

1. *Reaffirms* its decisions contained in annex IV to the Concluding Document of the Twelfth Special Session of the General Assembly and the report of the Secretary-General approved by the Assembly in its resolution 33/71 E of 14 December 1978;

2. *Expresses its appreciation* to all Member States and organizations that have consistently supported the programme throughout the years, thereby contributing to its success, in particular to the Governments of Germany and Japan for the continuation of extensive and highly educative study visits for the participants in the programme, to the Government of the People's Republic of China for organizing a study visit for the fellows in the area of disarmament in 2007 and to the Government of Switzerland for organizing a study visit in 2008;

3. *Expresses its appreciation* to the International Atomic Energy Agency, the Organization for the Prohibition of Chemical Weapons, the Preparatory Commission for the Comprehensive Nuclear-Test-Ban Treaty Organization and the James Martin Center for Nonproliferation Studies of the Monterey Institute of International Studies for having organized specific study programmes in the field of disarmament in their respective areas of competence, thereby contributing to the objectives of the programme;

4. *Commends* the Secretary-General for the diligence with which the programme has continued to be carried out;

5. *Requests* the Secretary-General to continue to implement annually the Geneva-based programme within existing resources and to report thereon to the General Assembly at its sixty-fifth session;

6. *Decides* to include in the provisional agenda of its sixty-fifth session the item entitled "United Nations disarmament fellowship, training and advisory services".

Regional disarmament

The added value of a regional approach to UN disarmament efforts having been acknowledged for almost three decades, the United Nations over the years sought to enhance, in tangible terms, the role of regional approaches to disarmament and security, including as a complement to global efforts.

In April, the Secretary-General transmitted to the Security Council a report on the relationship between the United Nations and regional organizations in the maintenance of international peace and security [S/2008/186], and noted the growing significance of regional organizations for maintaining international peace and security. Efforts continued to address regional disarmament and non-proliferation issues, such as curbing the spread of WMDs, tackling the illicit trade in small arms and light weapons, establishing confidence- and security-building measures, and promoting nuclear-weapon-free zones at the regional and subregional level.

In accordance with the Security Council President's request in his statement S/PRST/2007/7 [YUN 2007, p. 109], the Secretary-General's report included specific proposals on how the United Nations could support arrangements on cooperation and coordination with regional organizations. To support endeavours in non-proliferation and disarmament, the report recommended that cooperation be increased in three areas: counter-terrorism; Security Council resolutions 1540(2004) [YUN 2004, p. 544] and 1673(2006) [YUN 2006, p. 635]; and illicit trafficking in small arms and light weapons.

GENERAL ASSEMBLY ACTION

On 2 December [meeting 61], the General Assembly, on the recommendation of the First Committee [A/63/389], adopted **resolution 63/43** without vote [agenda item 89 *(t)*].

Regional disarmament

The General Assembly,

Recalling its resolutions 45/58 P of 4 December 1990, 46/36 I of 6 December 1991, 47/52 J of 9 December 1992, 48/75 I of 16 December 1993, 49/75 N of 15 December 1994, 50/70 K of 12 December 1995, 51/45 K of 10 December 1996, 52/38 P of 9 December 1997, 53/77 O of 4 December 1998, 54/54 N of 1 December 1999, 55/33 O of 20 November 2000, 56/24 H of 29 November 2001, 57/76 of 22 November 2002, 58/38 of 8 December 2003, 59/89 of 3 December 2004, 60/63 of 8 December 2005, 61/80 of 6 December 2006 and 62/38 of 5 December 2007 on regional disarmament,

Believing that the efforts of the international community to move towards the ideal of general and complete disarmament are guided by the inherent human desire for genuine peace and security, the elimination of the danger of war and the release of economic, intellectual and other resources for peaceful pursuits,

Affirming the abiding commitment of all States to the purposes and principles enshrined in the Charter of the United Nations in the conduct of their international relations,

Noting that essential guidelines for progress towards general and complete disarmament were adopted at the tenth special session of the General Assembly,

Taking note of the guidelines and recommendations for regional approaches to disarmament within the context of global security adopted by the Disarmament Commission at its 1993 substantive session,

Welcoming the prospects of genuine progress in the field of disarmament engendered in recent years as a result of negotiations between the two super-Powers,

Taking note of the recent proposals for disarmament at the regional and subregional levels,

Recognizing the importance of confidence-building measures for regional and international peace and security,

Convinced that endeavours by countries to promote regional disarmament, taking into account the specific characteristics of each region and in accordance with the principle of undiminished security at the lowest level of armaments, would enhance the security of all States and would thus contribute to international peace and security by reducing the risk of regional conflicts,

1. *Stresses* that sustained efforts are needed, within the framework of the Conference on Disarmament and under the umbrella of the United Nations, to make progress on the entire range of disarmament issues;

2. *Affirms* that global and regional approaches to disarmament complement each other and should therefore be pursued simultaneously to promote regional and international peace and security;

3. *Calls upon* States to conclude agreements, wherever possible, for nuclear non-proliferation, disarmament and confidence-building measures at the regional and subregional levels;

4. *Welcomes* the initiatives towards disarmament, nuclear non-proliferation and security undertaken by some countries at the regional and subregional levels;

5. *Supports and encourages* efforts aimed at promoting confidence-building measures at the regional and subregional levels to ease regional tensions and to further disarmament and nuclear non-proliferation measures at the regional and subregional levels;

6. *Decides* to include in the provisional agenda of its sixty-fourth session the item entitled "Regional disarmament".

Conventional arms control at regional and subregional levels

The Secretary-General, in response to General Assembly resolution 62/44 [YUN 2007, p. 591], submitted a July report [A/63/117 & Add.1] containing the views of nine Member States—Cambodia, Lebanon, Mauritius, Mexico, Panama, Qatar, Serbia, Spain, Ukraine—on conventional arms control at the regional and subregional levels. By its 2007 action, the Assembly decided to give urgent consideration to conventional arms control at the regional and subregional levels, since threats to peace and security in the post-cold-war era arose mainly among States in the same region or subregion.

Among its activities, UNODA, through regional workshops, helped States build capacity in implementing the International Tracing Instrument. In partnership with the EU, UNODA organized six regional seminars to promote the universality of the Convention on Certain Conventional Weapons Which May Be Deemed Inhuman or to Have Indiscriminate Effects and its annexed Protocols.

GENERAL ASSEMBLY ACTION

On 2 December [meeting 61], the General Assembly, on the recommendation of the First Committee [A/63/389], adopted **resolution 63/44** by recorded vote (175-1-2) [agenda item 89 *(x)*].

Conventional arms control at the regional and subregional levels

The General Assembly,

Recalling its resolutions 48/75 J of 16 December 1993, 49/75 O of 15 December 1994, 50/70 L of 12 December 1995, 51/45 Q of 10 December 1996, 52/38 Q of 9 December 1997, 53/77 P of 4 December 1998, 54/54 M of 1 December 1999, 55/33 P of 20 November 2000, 56/24 I of 29 November 2001, 57/77 of 22 November 2002, 58/39 of 8 December 2003, 59/88 of 3 December 2004, 60/75 of 8 December 2005, 61/82 of 6 December 2006 and 62/44 of 5 December 2007,

Recognizing the crucial role of conventional arms control in promoting regional and international peace and security,

Convinced that conventional arms control needs to be pursued primarily in the regional and subregional contexts since most threats to peace and security in the post-cold-war era arise mainly among States located in the same region or subregion,

Aware that the preservation of a balance in the defence capabilities of States at the lowest level of armaments would contribute to peace and stability and should be a prime objective of conventional arms control,

Desirous of promoting agreements to strengthen regional peace and security at the lowest possible level of armaments and military forces,

Noting with particular interest the initiatives taken in this regard in different regions of the world, in particular the commencement of consultations among a number of Latin American countries and the proposals for conventional arms control made in the context of South Asia, and recognizing, in the context of this subject, the relevance and value of the Treaty on Conventional Armed Forces in Europe, which is a cornerstone of European security,

Believing that militarily significant States and States with larger military capabilities have a special responsibility in promoting such agreements for regional security,

Believing also that an important objective of conventional arms control in regions of tension should be to prevent the possibility of military attack launched by surprise and to avoid aggression,

1. *Decides* to give urgent consideration to the issues involved in conventional arms control at the regional and subregional levels;

2. *Requests* the Conference on Disarmament to consider the formulation of principles that can serve as a framework for regional agreements on conventional arms control, and looks forward to a report of the Conference on this subject;

3. *Requests* the Secretary-General, in the meantime, to seek the views of Member States on the subject and to submit a report to the General Assembly at its sixty-fourth session;

4. *Decides* to include in the provisional agenda of its sixty-fourth session the item entitled "Conventional arms control at the regional and subregional levels".

RECORDED VOTE ON RESOLUTION 63/44:

In favour: Afghanistan, Albania, Algeria, Andorra, Angola, Antigua and Barbuda, Argentina, Armenia, Australia, Austria, Azerbaijan, Bahamas, Bahrain, Bangladesh, Barbados, Belarus, Belgium, Belize, Benin, Bolivia, Botswana, Brazil, Brunei Darussalam, Bulgaria, Burkina Faso, Burundi, Cambodia, Cameroon, Canada, Cape Verde, Chile, China, Colombia, Comoros, Congo, Costa Rica, Côte d'Ivoire, Croatia, Cyprus, Czech Republic, Democratic People's Republic of Korea, Democratic Republic of the Congo, Denmark, Djibouti, Dominica, Dominican Republic, Ecuador, Egypt, El Salvador, Equatorial Guinea, Eritrea, Estonia, Ethiopia, Finland, France, Gabon, Georgia, Germany, Ghana, Greece, Grenada, Guatemala, Guinea, Guinea-Bissau, Guyana, Haiti, Honduras, Hungary, Iceland, Indonesia, Iran, Iraq, Ireland, Israel, Italy, Jamaica, Japan, Jordan, Kazakhstan, Kenya, Kuwait, Kyrgyzstan, Latvia, Lebanon, Lesotho, Liberia, Libyan Arab Jamahiriya, Liechtenstein, Lithuania, Luxembourg, Madagascar, Malawi, Malaysia, Maldives, Mali, Malta, Marshall Islands, Mauritania, Mauritius, Mexico, Micronesia, Moldova, Monaco, Mongolia, Montenegro, Morocco, Mozambique, Myanmar, Namibia, Nepal, Netherlands, New Zealand, Nicaragua, Niger, Nigeria, Norway, Oman, Pakistan, Palau, Panama, Papua New Guinea, Paraguay, Peru, Philippines, Poland, Portugal, Qatar, Republic of Korea, Romania, Rwanda, Saint Lucia, Saint Vincent and the Grenadines, Samoa, San Marino, Sao Tome and Principe, Saudi Arabia, Senegal, Serbia, Singapore, Slovakia, Slovenia, Solomon Islands, South Africa, Spain, Sri Lanka, Sudan, Suriname, Swaziland, Sweden, Switzerland, Syrian Arab Republic, Tajikistan, Thailand, The former Yugoslav Republic of Macedonia, Timor-Leste, Togo, Tonga, Trinidad and Tobago, Tunisia, Turkey, Turkmenistan, Tuvalu, Uganda, Ukraine, United Arab Emirates, United Kingdom, United Republic of Tanzania, United States, Uruguay, Uzbekistan, Vanuatu, Venezuela, Yemen, Zambia, Zimbabwe.

Against: India.

Abstaining: Bhutan, Russian Federation.

Regional and subregional confidence-building measures

In accordance with the General Assembly's request in resolution 62/45 [YUN 2007, p. 592], the Secretary-General presented a July report [A/63/171 & Add.1] containing the views of 10 Member States—Bangladesh, Bosnia and Herzegovina, Chile, Cuba, Mexico, Panama, Qatar, Republic of Korea, Spain, Ukraine—on confidence-building measures in the regional and subregional context.

GENERAL ASSEMBLY ACTION

On 2 December [meeting 61], the General Assembly, on the recommendation of the First Committee [A/63/389], adopted **resolution 63/45** without vote [agenda item 89 *(y)*].

Confidence-building measures in the regional and subregional context

The General Assembly,

Guided by the purposes and principles enshrined in the Charter of the United Nations,

Recalling its resolutions 58/43 of 8 December 2003, 59/87 of 3 December 2004, 60/64 of 8 December 2005, 61/81 of 6 December 2006 and 62/45 of 5 December 2007,

Recalling also its resolution 57/337 of 3 July 2003 entitled "Prevention of armed conflict", in which it calls upon Member States to settle their disputes by peaceful means, as set out in Chapter VI of the Charter, inter alia, by any procedures adopted by the parties,

Recalling further the resolutions and guidelines adopted by consensus by the General Assembly and the Disarmament Commission relating to confidence-building measures and their implantation at the global, regional and subregional levels,

Considering the importance and effectiveness of confidence-building measures taken at the initiative and with the agreement of all States concerned and taking into account the specific characteristics of each region, since such measures can contribute to regional stability,

Convinced that resources released by disarmament, including regional disarmament, can be devoted to economic and social development and to the protection of the environment for the benefit of all peoples, in particular those of the developing countries,

Recognizing the need for meaningful dialogue among States concerned to avert conflict,

Welcoming the peace processes already initiated by States concerned to resolve their disputes through peaceful means bilaterally or through mediation, inter alia, by third parties, regional organizations or the United Nations,

Recognizing that States in some regions have already taken steps towards confidence-building measures at the bilateral, subregional and regional levels in the political and military fields, including arms control and disarmament, and noting that such confidence-building measures have improved peace and security in those regions and contributed to progress in the socio-economic conditions of their people,

Concerned that the continuation of disputes among States, particularly in the absence of an effective mechanism to resolve them through peaceful means, may contribute to the arms race and endanger the maintenance of international peace and security and the efforts of the international community to promote arms control and disarmament,

1. *Calls upon* Member States to refrain from the use or threat of use of force in accordance with the purposes and principles of the Charter of the United Nations;

2. *Reaffirms its commitment* to the peaceful settlement of disputes under Chapter VI of the Charter, in particular Article 33, which provides for a solution by negotiation, enquiry, mediation, conciliation, arbitration, judicial settlement, resort to regional agencies or arrangements or other peaceful means chosen by the parties;

3. *Reaffirms* the ways and means regarding confidence- and security-building measures set out in the report of the Disarmament Commission on its 1993 session;

4. *Calls upon* Member States to pursue these ways and means through sustained consultations and dialogue, while at the same time avoiding actions that may hinder or impair such a dialogue;

5. *Urges* States to comply strictly with all bilateral, regional and international agreements, including arms control and disarmament agreements, to which they are party;

6. *Emphasizes* that the objective of confidence-building measures should be to help to strengthen international peace and security and to be consistent with the principle of undiminished security at the lowest level of armaments;

7. *Encourages* the promotion of bilateral and regional confidence-building measures, with the consent and participation of the parties concerned, to avoid conflict and prevent the unintended and accidental outbreak of hostilities;

8. *Requests* the Secretary-General to submit a report to the General Assembly at its sixty-fourth session containing the views of Member States on confidence-building measures in the regional and subregional context;

9. *Decides* to include in the provisional agenda of its sixty-fourth session the item entitled "Confidence-building measures in the regional and subregional context".

On 2 December [meeting 61], the General Assembly, on the recommendation of the First Committee [A/63/390], adopted **resolution 63/76** without vote [agenda item 90 *(d)*].

United Nations regional centres for peace and disarmament

The General Assembly,

Recalling its resolutions 60/83 of 8 December 2005, 61/90 of 6 December 2006, and 62/50 of 5 December 2007 regarding the maintenance and revitalization of the three United Nations regional centres for peace and disarmament,

Recalling also the reports of the Secretary-General on the United Nations Regional Centre for Peace and Disarmament in Africa, the United Nations Regional Centre for Peace and Disarmament in Asia and the Pacific and the United Nations Regional Centre for Peace, Disarmament and Development in Latin America and the Caribbean,

Reaffirming its decision, taken in 1982 at its twelfth special session, to establish the United Nations Disarmament Information Programme, the purpose of which is to inform, educate and generate public understanding and support for the objectives of the United Nations in the field of arms control and disarmament,

Bearing in mind its resolutions 40/151 G of 16 December 1985, 41/60 J of 3 December 1986, 42/39 D of 30 November 1987 and 44/117 F of 15 December 1989 on the regional centres for peace and disarmament in Nepal, Peru and Togo,

Recognizing that the changes that have taken place in the world have created new opportunities as well as posed new challenges for the pursuit of disarmament, and, in this regard, bearing in mind that the regional centres for peace and disarmament can contribute substantially to understanding and cooperation among States in each particular region in the areas of peace, disarmament and development,

Noting that in paragraph 91 of the Final Document of the Fourteenth Conference of Heads of State or Government of Non-Aligned Countries, held in Havana, on 15 and 16 September 2006, the Heads of State or Government emphasized the importance of the United Nations activities at the regional level to increase the stability and security of its Member States, which could be promoted in a substantive manner by the maintenance and revitalization of the three regional centres for peace and disarmament,

1. *Reiterates* the importance of the United Nations activities at the regional level to advancement in disarmament and to increase the stability and security of its Member States, which could be promoted in a substantive manner by the maintenance and revitalization of the three regional centres for peace and disarmament;

2. *Reaffirms* that, in order to achieve positive results, it is useful for the three regional centres to carry out dissemination and educational programmes that promote regional peace and security that are aimed at changing basic attitudes with respect to peace and security and disarmament so as to support the achievement of the purposes and principles of the United Nations;

3. *Appeals* to Member States in each region and those that are able to do so, as well as to international governmental and non-governmental organizations and foundations, to make voluntary contributions to the regional centres in their respective regions to strengthen their activities and initiatives;

4. *Emphasizes* the importance of the activities of the regional disarmament branch of the Office for Disarmament Affairs of the Secretariat;

5. *Requests* the Secretary-General to provide all necessary support, within existing resources, to the regional centres in carrying out their programmes of activities;

6. *Decides* to include in the provisional agenda of its sixty-fourth session the item entitled "United Nations regional centres for peace and disarmament".

Africa

The year was characterized by an increased involvement of the African Union (AU) and other subregional organizations in small arms and light weapons-related matters. The results were noticeable in efforts to coordinate the continent's response to the proliferation and misuse of small arms and light weapons. In particular, following a meeting of regional bodies (Mombasa, Kenya, 9–10 June) the AU set up a Steering Committee comprising all regional and subregional organizations engaged in the issue.

At the subregional level, the members of the Economic Community of West African States (ECOWAS) moved towards the entry into force of ECOWAS's small arms and light weapons Convention, as seven of the nine States required for its entry into force had ratified the Convention. The ECOWAS Small Arms Control Programme [YUN 2006, p. 685] continued to assist West African States in practical disarmament, specifically in building the capacity of national small arms commissions and civil society to control illicit flow.

Focusing on States not party to the Chemical Weapons Convention (CWC), UNODA, in partnership with the EU, conducted two regional seminars, one for West and East Africa, and the other for the Horn of Africa, Great Lakes region and Southern Africa, (Lome, Togo, 21–22 April, 24–25 April), to promote CWC's universality.

State members of the Nairobi Protocol for the Prevention, Control and Reduction of Small Arms and Light Weapons in the Great Lakes Region and the Horn of Africa, adopted in 2004 [YUN 2004, p. 571] and in force since 2006 [YUN 2006, p. 684], worked to implement the Protocol.

In Central Africa, members of the Economic Community of Central African States (ECCAS), with the support of the United Nations and the EU, began drafting a legal instrument to control small arms and light weapons in the region. The members also began drafting a programme to promote cross-border cooperation and enhance the management of border security and trafficking issues. Disarmament programmes were carried out in the member States of the Regional Centre on Small Arms and Light Weapons in the Great Lakes Region, the Horn of Africa and Bordering States (RECSA). The Centre supported the destruction of surplus weapons and commissioned national studies to help develop a regional strategy for a 2009 launch. It conducted regional training courses for police and the military (Mombasa, Kenya, 31 March–4 April; Nairobi, 3 July).

UNDP supported the ECOWAS and RECSA small arms control programmes in strengthening their capacities through training, research and awareness-raising. UNDP also supported countries having obligations under article 4 of the Mine-Ban Convention (calling for the destruction of stockpiled anti-personnel mines), due to be fulfilled in 2008.

Standing Advisory Committee

At its twenty-seventh ministerial meeting (Luanda, Angola, 13–15 May) [A/63/82-S/2008/360], the Standing Advisory Committee on Security Questions in Central Africa reviewed the geopolitical and security situation in some of its States members, specifically Burundi, Cameroon, Central African Republic, Chad and the Democratic Republic of the Congo. It discussed promotion of disarmament and arms limitation in Central Africa, focusing on a draft code of conduct for armed and security forces known as the "Sao Tome Initiative", and a legally binding instrument, prepared by the United Nations Regional Centre for Peace and Disarmament in Africa, as well as implementation of the UN Programme of Action on small arms and light weapons and related issues, and on the implementation of Security Council resolution 1540(2004) [YUN 2004, p. 544]. The Committee endorsed the principal recommendations of the ECCAS report, which included proceeding with the draft for adoption in 2010, and developing a Small Arms Unit within the ECCAS secretariat that would campaign for ratification of the instrument and focus on small arms and light weapons trade-related issues in the subregion.

In response to General Assembly resolution 62/53 [YUN 2007, p. 594], the Secretary-General, in a July report [A/63/164], described the activities of the Advisory Committee from July 2007 to June 2008, during which period the Committee's twenty-sixth and twenty-seventh ministerial meetings took place. The Memorandum of Understanding between the ECCAS secretariat and UNODA had contributed to strengthening their cooperation, the Secretary-General concluded, particularly with regard to the joint implementation of the Sao Tome Initiative. The ongoing efforts to revitalize the Committee's work illustrated its relevance and adaptability. States members were committed to working together, with the support of the United Nations and its partners, to implement the decisions taken. In that connection, the Committee called on interested States to help it finance the implementation of specific projects through the Committee's Trust Fund.

GENERAL ASSEMBLY ACTION

On 2 December [meeting 61], the General Assembly, on the recommendation of the First Committee [A/63/390], adopted **resolution 63/78** without vote [agenda item 90 *(g)*].

Regional confidence-building measures: activities of the United Nations Standing Advisory Committee on Security Questions in Central Africa

The General Assembly,

Recalling its previous relevant resolutions, in particular resolution 62/53 of 5 December 2007,

Recalling also the guidelines for general and complete disarmament adopted at its tenth special session, the first special session devoted to disarmament,

Bearing in mind the establishment by the Secretary-General on 28 May 1992 of the United Nations Standing Advisory Committee on Security Questions in Central Africa, the purpose of which is to encourage arms limitation, disarmament, non-proliferation and development in the subregion,

Convinced that the resources released by disarmament, including regional disarmament, can be devoted to economic and social development and to the protection of the environment for the benefit of all peoples, in particular those of the developing countries,

Considering the importance and effectiveness of confidence-building measures taken on the initiative and with the participation of all States concerned and taking into account the specific characteristics of each region, since such measures can contribute to regional stability and to international peace and security,

Convinced that development can be achieved only in a climate of peace, security and mutual confidence both within and among States,

Recalling the Brazzaville Declaration on Cooperation for Peace and Security in Central Africa, the Bata Declaration for the Promotion of Lasting Democracy, Peace and Development in Central Africa and the Yaoundé Declaration on Peace, Security and Stability in Central Africa,

Bearing in mind resolutions 1196(1998) and 1197(1998), adopted by the Security Council on 16 and 18 September 1998 respectively, following its consideration of the report of the Secretary-General on the causes of conflict and the promotion of durable peace and sustainable development in Africa,

Emphasizing the need to strengthen the capacity for conflict prevention and peacekeeping in Africa, and welcoming the partnership established between the United Nations and the Economic Community of Central African States for that purpose,

1. *Reaffirms its support* for efforts aimed at promoting confidence-building measures at the regional and subregional levels in order to ease tensions and conflicts in Central Africa and to further peace, stability and sustainable development in the subregion;

2. *Reaffirms* the importance of disarmament, demobilization and reintegration programmes, and encourages the United Nations Peacebuilding Commission to support efforts for the political stabilization and reconstruction of post-conflict countries;

3. *Welcomes* the significant progress made by the States members of the United Nations Standing Advisory Committee on Security Questions in Central Africa, under the "Sao Tome Initiative", with respect to the drafting of a legal instrument on the control of small arms and light weapons in Central Africa and of a code of conduct for defence and security forces in Central Africa, in particular the decision by the twenty-seventh ministerial meeting of the Standing Advisory Committee, held in Luanda from 13 to 15 May 2008, to complete the process of drafting the code of conduct with a view to its possible adoption during the twenty-eighth ministerial meeting and the decision to examine during the same meeting a draft text containing elements drawn from relevant legal instruments on small arms and light weapons, and encourages interested countries to provide their financial support for the implementation of these two projects;

4. *Encourages* the States members of the Standing Advisory Committee to continue their efforts to promote peace and security in their subregion;

5. *Also encourages* the States members of the Standing Advisory Committee to continue their efforts to render the early-warning mechanism for Central Africa fully operational as an instrument for analysing and monitoring the political situation in the subregion within the framework of the prevention of crises and armed conflicts, and requests the Secretary-General to provide the necessary assistance for its smooth functioning;

6. *Emphasizes* the importance of providing the States members of the Standing Advisory Committee with the essential support they need to carry out the full programme of activities which they adopted at their ministerial meetings;

7. *Appeals* to the international community to support the efforts undertaken by the States concerned to implement disarmament, demobilization and reintegration programmes;

8. *Requests* the Secretary-General and the Office of the United Nations High Commissioner for Refugees to continue their assistance to the countries of Central Africa in tackling the problems of refugees and displaced persons in their territories;

9. *Requests* the Secretary-General and the United Nations High Commissioner for Human Rights to continue to provide their full assistance for the proper functioning of the Subregional Centre for Human Rights and Democracy in Central Africa;

10. *Urges* Member States and intergovernmental and non-governmental organizations to support the activities of the Standing Advisory Committee effectively through voluntary contributions to the Trust Fund for the United Nations Standing Advisory Committee on Security Questions in Central Africa;

11. *Requests* the Secretary-General to continue to support the ongoing efforts of the States members of the Standing Advisory Committee, including through provision of the assistance needed to ensure the success of their regular biannual meetings;

12. *Calls upon* the Secretary-General to submit to the General Assembly at its sixty-fourth session a report on the implementation of the present resolution;

13. *Decides* to include in the provisional agenda of its sixty-fourth session the item entitled "Regional confidence-building measures: activities of the United Nations Standing Advisory Committee on Security Questions in Central Africa".

Regional Centre for Peace and Disarmament in Africa

In accordance with the priorities expressed by Member States during the 2007 Consultative Mechanism for the Reorganization of the United Nations Regional Centre for Peace and Disarmament in Africa [YUN 2007, p. 596], the Centre, established in Lome, Togo, in 1986 [YUN 1986, p. 85], focused on conventional arms, broadening its scope of activities while strengthening relationships with regional and civil sector organizations, as well as on security sector reform. It continued to assist and advise the Standing Advisory Committee on Security Questions in Central Africa, and provided technical support for regional and subregional workshops and seminars, among them a workshop on the International Tracing Instrument (Lome, 17–18 April 2008) and two regional seminars (Lome, 21–22 April, 24–25 April).

The Centre participated in the subregional meeting on the implementation of the Nairobi Protocol (Uganda, 17–22 August), organized by the African Centre for Securities Studies, and in the first AU Region's Steering Committee for regional and subregional entities (United Republic of Tanzania, 24–26 November). The Centre organized a seminar on a legal framework for interventions of armed forces within a democratic context (Togo, 11–13 March) and in collaboration with the African Security Sector Network, a subregional workshop entitled "Parliamentary oversight of security: an interactive needs assessment of the defence and security commissions of Benin and Togo". A workshop conducted by the United Nations Office for West Africa on linkages between security and elections resulted in a recommendation that the Office develop, in partnership with the Centre and ECOWAS, a regional code of conduct on the use of security and armed forces during an electoral period.

The Centre continued to maintain a small arms register for Africa to promote confidence-building and transparency in arms transfers between the countries participating in the Small Arms Transparency and Control Regime in Africa project [YUN 2003, p. 587].

The Centre's capacity-building programme for civil society was aimed at supporting mostly West African organizations. It published a training manual to assist in delivering courses and conducted training sessions in the region. The first phase of a proposed programme in East Africa was discussed by the Regional Centre on Small Arms and the East African Action Network on Small Arms.

Focusing its outreach and information efforts on its Internet portal, the Centre's new key component was a freely accessible database on peace, security and disarmament in Africa. The Centre organized youth forums with graduate and undergraduate students to discuss the challenges of disarmament in Africa, armed conflict and international human rights law, and the problem of child soldiers.

Report of Secretary-General. The Centre's activities from July 2007 to June 2008 were described in a report of the Secretary-General [A/63/163], submitted pursuant to General Assembly resolution 62/216 [YUN 2007, p. 596]. In the report, the Secretary-General expressed gratitude to the Assembly for its decision to fund the Centre's operating costs and three new posts from the regular UN budget, and called on all countries, especially the States of the region, to contribute more actively to the Centre's disarmament projects through voluntary contributions.

The Secretary-General reported that during the period under review, the Trust Fund for the Centre had received by 31 December 2007 voluntary contributions totalling $1,123,990 for the 2006–2007 biennium for the execution of new projects, and the Fund's balance stood at $1,124,973 at that date.

GENERAL ASSEMBLY ACTION

On 2 December [meeting 61], the General Assembly, on the recommendation of the First Committee [A/63/390], adopted **resolution 63/80** without vote [agenda item 90 *(h)*].

United Nations Regional Centre for Peace and Disarmament in Africa

The General Assembly,

Mindful of the provisions of Article 11, paragraph 1, of the Charter of the United Nations stipulating that a function of the General Assembly is to consider the general principles of cooperation in the maintenance of international peace and security, including the principles governing disarmament and arms limitation,

Recalling its resolutions 40/151 G of 16 December 1985, 41/60 D of 3 December 1986, 42/39 J of 30 November 1987 and 43/76 D of 7 December 1988 on the United Nations Regional Centre for Peace and Disarmament in Africa, and its resolutions 46/36 F of 6 December 1991 and 47/52 G of 9 December 1992 on regional disarmament, including confidence-building measures,

Recalling also its resolutions 48/76 E of 16 December 1993, 49/76 D of 15 December 1994, 50/71 C of 12 December 1995, 51/46 E of 10 December 1996, 52/220 of 22 December 1997, 53/78 C of 4 December 1998, 54/55 B of 1 December 1999, 55/34 D of 20 November 2000, 56/25 D of 29 November 2001, 57/91 of 22 November 2002, 58/61 of 8 December 2003, 59/101 of 3 December 2004, 60/86 of 8 December 2005, 61/93 of 6 December 2006 and 62/216 of 22 December 2007,

Aware of the role of the Regional Centre in promoting confidence-building and arms-limitation measures at the regional level,

Taking into account the need to establish close cooperation between the Regional Centre and the Peace and Security Council of the African Union, in particular its institutions in the field of peace, disarmament and security, as well as with relevant United Nations bodies and programmes in Africa for greater effectiveness,

Taking note of the report of the Secretary-General, in which he stated that an increase in the Regional Centre's human and operational capacity would enable it to discharge its mandate in full and to respond more effectively to requests for assistance from African States,

Deeply concerned that, as noted in the report of the Secretary-General, despite the decision taken in Khartoum in January 2006 by the Executive Council of the African Union, in which the Council called upon member States to make voluntary contributions to the Regional Centre to maintain its operations, no such funds have been received to ensure its operations,

Recalling that, in its resolution 60/86, it requested the Secretary-General to establish, within existing resources, a consultative mechanism of interested States, in particular African States, for the reorganization of the Regional Centre,

Taking note of the concrete recommendations on the Regional Centre's future work programme, as well as on its staffing and funding, made by the Consultative Mechanism for the Reorganization of the United Nations Regional Centre for Peace and Disarmament in Africa upon the conclusion of its work,

1. *Notes* the implementation of the recommendations of the Consultative Mechanism for the Reorganization of the United Nations Regional Centre for Peace and Disarmament in Africa to fund the Centre's operating costs and three new posts from the regular budget of the Organization;

2. *Notes with appreciation* the efforts of the Regional Centre to align its actions with the priorities identified in the recommendations of the Consultative Mechanism;

3. *Welcomes* the undertaking by the Regional Centre of new initiatives and projects in the fields of security sector reform and practical disarmament measures, as detailed in the report of the Secretary-General;

4. *Urges* all States, as well as international governmental and non-governmental organizations and foundations, to make voluntary contributions to strengthen the programmes and activities of the Regional Centre and facilitate their implementation;

5. *Urges*, in particular, States members of the African Union to make voluntary contributions to the Regional Centre's trust funds in conformity with the decision taken by the Executive Council of the African Union, in Khartoum in January 2006;

6. *Requests* the Secretary-General to facilitate closer cooperation between the Regional Centre and the African Union, in particular in the areas of peace, security and development;

7. *Also requests* the Secretary-General to continue to provide the necessary support to the Regional Centre for greater achievements and results;

8. *Further requests* the Secretary-General to report to the General Assembly at its sixty-fourth session on the implementation of the present resolution;

9. *Decides* to include in the provisional agenda of its sixty-fourth session the item entitled "United Nations Regional Centre for Peace and Disarmament in Africa".

Asia and the Pacific

Three nuclear-related developments were significant for the region in 2008. The ratification of the Central Asian Nuclear-Weapon-Free-Zone Treaty by Turkmenistan on 19 April, Tajikistan on 12 November and Kazakhstan on 11 December, paved the way for the Treaty to enter into force. As part of the process of the Six-Party Talks to denuclearize the Korean Peninsula, the first informal meeting of the relevant Foreign Ministers was held (Beijing, 8–11 December), with the parties discussing nuclear verification activities and reaffirming the goal of verifiable denuclearization of the Peninsula. Australia and Japan co-chaired the first session of the International Commission on Nuclear Non-proliferation and Disarmament (Sydney, Australia, 9 July), a global initiative co-sponsored by the two countries with the aim of reinvigorating the global effort against nuclear proliferation and strengthening

NPT during the lead-up to the 2010 Review Conference and beyond.

During the forty-first Ministerial Meeting of the Association of Southeast Asian Nations (ASEAN) (Singapore, 20–21 July), the Ministers in a joint communiqué welcomed the progress made in implementing the 2007 Plan of Action by the Treaty on the South-East Asia Nuclear-Weapon-Free Zone. They noted that States parties should resume direct consultations with nuclear-weapon States to resolve outstanding issues regarding the Treaty on the Zone and Protocol. Reaffirming that the denuclearization of the Korean Peninsula was necessary for regional peace and security, the Ministers expressed support for the Six-Party Talks. They agreed that the ASEAN Regional Forum (ARF) should initiate concrete measures on regional security challenges, particularly through cooperation in non-proliferation and disarmament.

At the Fifteenth Meeting of ARF (Singapore, 24 July), the Singapore Declaration was adopted to promote and maintain regional peace and security through strengthening dialogue and cooperation. At the meeting, the Ministers endorsed the establishment of a new working group, the ARF Inter-Sessional Meeting on Non-Proliferation and Disarmament, to provide a discussion platform and concentrate on Security Council resolution 1540(2004) implementation in the region.

The Council of Heads of the Shanghai Cooperation Organization, at its eighth meeting (Dushanbe, Tajikistan, 28 August), adopted the Dushanbe Declaration stating that the Central Asian Nuclear-Weapon-Free Zone was an important step in consolidating the NPT regime and would help strengthen regional security and contribute to the fight against international nuclear terrorism. During the meeting, member States (China, Kazakhstan, Kyrgyzstan, Russian Federation, Tajikistan, Uzbekistan) signed an agreement on cooperation in combating illegal circulation of weapons, ammunition and explosives.

The Pacific Islands Forum Secretariat worked with its 16 member countries on a range of security and disarmament issues and continued to support the South Pacific Nuclear-Weapons-Free Zone. It engaged France, Japan and the United Kingdom on the safety and security of civil nuclear shipments through the Pacific Ocean. In cooperation with the Secretariat, the CTBTO Preparatory Commission provided practical assistance for a regional workshop for Pacific Island States (Apia, Samoa, 8–9 May) on CTBT ratification and implementation. The Secretariat consulted with its members on a new small arms and light weapons project, to be launched in 2009, focusing on police control of ammunition, registration of weapons and holders, weapons safety, and educational material for weapons users. The Secretariat began drafting a "Regional Model Law Governing the Control of Weapons". It supported members' compliance with international counter-terrorism obligations, and in cooperation with New Zealand convened a regional counter-terrorism working group. It worked with members and international partners on other regional priorities, such as enhancing border security capacity and strengthening maritime security.

UNDP, together with Switzerland and Thailand, hosted a regional meeting on armed violence and development (Bangkok, 8–9 May), during which 24 Governments adopted a declaration on armed violence and development.

Regional Centre for Peace and Disarmament in Asia and the Pacific

The new office for the United Nations Regional Centre for Peace and Disarmament in Asia and the Pacific opened in Kathmandu, Nepal, on 18 August, following its relocation from New York, in accordance with General Assembly resolution 62/52 [YUN 2007, p. 598].

The Centre organized several annual conferences. The twentieth UN Conference on Disarmament Issues (Saitama City, Japan, 27–29 August) focused on reinforcing the three pillars of the NPT (safety, security and safeguards), the nuclear renaissance and non-proliferation, arms control and security in East Asia, and cooperation with civil society. The Centre and the Republic of Korea organized the seventh Joint Conference entitled "Nuclear Renaissance and the NPT: Reinforcing the Three Pillars of the NPT" (Jeju Island, Republic of Korea, 24–26 November). With EU support and in collaboration with Kazakhstan, the Centre organized two seminars to promote the universality of the CCW and its Protocols in the region (Almaty, 24–25 September; Kathmandu, 17–18 December).

Report of Secretary-General. In a July report [A/63/178], the Secretary-General gave an account of the activities of the Centre from July 2007 to June 2008. He noted that positive developments had paved the way for its relocation to the region and marked a turning point for its operation and activities. The Centre continued to promote disarmament and security dialogue and cooperation in the region through organizing conferences.

The Secretary-General reiterated his appeal to Member States, in particular those of the region, to increase their financial support of the Centre, in particular its core funding in support of the Centre's programme and activities. As at 31 December 2007, he noted that the Centre's trust fund balance stood at $299,736.

GENERAL ASSEMBLY ACTION

On 2 December [meeting 61], the General Assembly, on the recommendation of the First Committee [A/63/390], adopted **resolution 63/77** without vote [agenda item 90 *(f)*].

United Nations Regional Centre for Peace and Disarmament in Asia and the Pacific

The General Assembly,

Recalling its resolutions 42/39 D of 30 November 1987 and 44/117 F of 15 December 1989, by which it established the United Nations Regional Centre for Peace and Disarmament in Asia and renamed it the United Nations Regional Centre for Peace and Disarmament in Asia and the Pacific, with headquarters in Kathmandu and with the mandate of providing, on request, substantive support for the initiatives and other activities mutually agreed upon by the Member States of the Asia-Pacific region for the implementation of measures for peace and disarmament, through appropriate utilization of available resources,

Welcoming the relocation of the Regional Centre from New York to Kathmandu in accordance with General Assembly resolution 62/52 of 5 December 2007,

Taking note of the report of the Secretary-General, in which he expresses his belief that in cementing its partnership with States in the Asia-Pacific region and other stakeholders, the Centre will be the primary United Nations regional entity advocating the disarmament and non-proliferation agenda,

Expressing its appreciation to the Regional Centre for its important work in promoting confidence-building measures through the organization of meetings, conferences and workshops in the region, including conferences held in Sapporo, Japan, from 27 to 29 August 2007 and in Seoul from 5 to 7 December 2007,

Concerned with the report of the Secretary-General, in which he indicates that the Regional Centre urgently needs more core funding for its staffing and operations to allow it to sustain its work and be in a position to respond to the requests for technical assistance from countries of the region,

Appreciating the timely execution by Nepal of its financial commitments for the relocation of the Regional Centre,

1. *Welcomes* the relocation of the Regional Centre for Peace and Disarmament in Asia and the Pacific from New York to Kathmandu and its coming into operation on 18 August 2008;

2. *Expresses its gratitude* to the Government of Nepal for its cooperation and financial support, which allowed the new office of the Regional Centre to be opened in Kathmandu;

3. *Expresses its appreciation* to the Secretary-General and the Office for Disarmament Affairs of the Secretariat for making the necessary preparations with a view to ensuring the physical operation of the Regional Centre from Kathmandu to enable the Centre to function effectively;

4. *Appeals* to Member States, in particular those within the Asia-Pacific region, as well as to international governmental and non-governmental organizations and foundations, to make voluntary contributions, the only resources of the Regional Centre, to strengthen the programme of activities of the Centre and the implementation thereof;

5. *Requests* the Secretary-General to provide from the regular budget, starting in the biennium 2010–2011, the necessary support to ensure the sustainability of the core activities and operations of the Regional Centre, in order to enable it to carry out its programme of activities in accordance with its mandate;

6. *Also requests* the Secretary-General to continue to provide the necessary support to the Regional Centre for greater achievements and results, within existing resources, until the regular budget is approved;

7. *Reaffirms its strong support* for the role of the Regional Centre in the promotion of United Nations activities at the regional level to strengthen peace, stability and security among its Member States;

8. *Underlines* the importance of the Kathmandu process for the development of the practice of region-wide security and disarmament dialogues;

9. *Requests* the Secretary-General to report to the General Assembly at its sixty-fourth session on the implementation of the present resolution;

10. *Decides* to include in the provisional agenda of its sixty-fourth session the item entitled "United Nations Regional Centre for Peace and Disarmament in Asia and the Pacific".

Europe

During 2008, European intergovernmental organizations continued to promote the implementation of international disarmament instruments and to fund disarmament initiatives throughout Europe and other regions.

Disarmament activities of the EU further expanded within the framework of the European Security Strategy, as well as within the EU strategy on the non-proliferation of WMDs and on combating the illicit accumulation and trafficking of small arms and light weapons and their ammunition. The EU supported the implementation of Security Council resolutions 1540(2004) [YUN 2004, p. 544], 1673(2006) [YUN 2006, p. 635] and 1810(2008) (see p. 585), and sponsored workshops to strengthen the capacity of States involved in the export control process. On 14 May, the EU adopted a second Joint Action aimed at strengthening the capacities of non-EU States involved in export control, and on 8 December, the EU Council adopted a Council Common Position defining rules for the control of exports of military technology and equipment that replaced the Code of Conduct. The EU adopted a model article, to be inserted in relevant agreements with non-EU countries, that would constitute the legal basis for enhanced cooperation in combating illicit trade, and co-financed three regional seminars (Lome, Togo; Rio de Janeiro, Brazil; Seoul, Republic of Korea). Projects in the Western Balkans were carried out in Albania, Bosnia and Herzegovina, Croatia, Kosovo, Montenegro, Serbia and the former Yugoslav Republic of Macedonia to aid those States in establishing legal and institutional control frameworks harmonized with EU policies and practices. The EU provided financial assistance to the UN Regional Centre for Latin America and the Caribbean for activities in that field, ensuring training courses for law enforcement authorities and Members of Parliament.

As part of a Joint Action to promote universalization of the CCW, the EU sponsored regional seminars in the Dominican Republic, Kazakhstan, Morocco, Nepal and Togo on issues concerning anti-personnel landmines and explosive remnants of war. On 23 June, the EU Council adopted a Joint Action in support of the universalization of the Mine-Ban Convention, to enable regional accession seminars. Mine action continued to be part of wider assistance and development programmes in third countries. On 24 November, a set of guidelines on European Community mine action for 2008–2013 was endorsed to steer mine-affected countries towards effective mine action programming. Additionally, European Commission support to mine action continued to be carried out in nine countries, where activities encompassed mine clearance (including cluster bombs), mine risk education, stockpile destruction, and assistance in the safe return, resettlement and establishment of livelihoods of internally displaced persons and refugees. On 8 December, the EU Council adopted new lines of action in combating the proliferation of WMDs and their delivery systems. As a major IAEA donor, the EU continued to support IAEA nuclear terrorism prevention activities and assisted in securing nuclear materials throughout the world. Also in December, the EU adopted a draft international Code of Conduct for outer space activities.

The EU assisted African countries in developing national infrastructures for CTBT monitoring and verification and supported the International Science and Technology Centre and the Science and Technology Centre of Ukraine in mitigating the risk of WMD proliferation in the Commonwealth of Independent States.

The Organization for Security and Cooperation in Europe (OSCE) supported work identifying illicit transfers of small arms and light weapons and implementing the UN Programme of Action to Prevent, Combat and Eradicate the Illicit Trade in Small Arms and Light Weapons in All Its Aspects.

In the South-East European region, OSCE, the Regional Cooperation Council (RCC), the Regional Arms Control Verification and Implementation Assistance Centre (RACVIAC) and the South Eastern and Eastern Europe Clearinghouse for the Control of Small Arms and Light Weapons promoted and funded disarmament projects. OSCE States participating in the Forum for Security Cooperation continued to exchange views on WMD proliferation. They also continued developing a handbook of best practice guides for implementing resolution 1540(2004).

In the field of conventional weapons, OSCE updated its 2004 commitments on small arms export control and initiated a comprehensive review of controls. An initiative was launched that led to best practices to prevent destabilizing transfers through air transport, as well as the adoption of an information-exchange questionnaire on the topic.

Following the signing of a Memorandum of Understanding between UNDP and the OSCE Secretariat, two joint projects were initiated in Belarus and Montenegro, on joint implementation projects and on conventional ammunition, respectively.

According to their own reports, OSCE participating States destroyed a total of 7,685,424 units of small arms and light weapons from 2001 to 2007. The destruction of approximately 120 tons of mélange (a rocket fuel component) was completed, and in Albania, an OSCE project to destroy 30 tons of mélange was initiated.

On 3 April, the Heads of State and Government of the North Atlantic Treaty Organization (NATO) reaffirmed in the Bucharest Summit Declaration that arms control, disarmament and non-proliferation would make an important contribution to peace, security and stability and to preventing the spread and use of WMDs and their means of delivery. NATO's main non-proliferation activity in 2008 was the convening of a seminar on proliferation issues (Germany, 13–14 November), with the participation of representatives from the Euro-Atlantic Partnership Council, the Mediterranean Dialogue, the Istanbul Cooperation Initiative, Asian and Pacific nations (Australia, China, India, Japan, Pakistan), international organizations, academic institutions and think tanks. NATO also organized a regional workshop on the practical implementation of Security Council resolution 1540(2004) (Croatia, 5–6 June), where participants from South-Eastern Europe, allies and international organizations discussed lessons learned and best practices in export controls, including national action plans, information-sharing and cooperation among different agencies and with the private sector and academia.

On 28 March, the North Atlantic Council issued a statement on the Treaty on Conventional Armed Forces in Europe urging the Russian Federation to end the suspension of its legal obligations and work together to reach agreement on the basis of the parallel action package and preserve the benefits of the regime. Moreover, NATO continued to coordinate conventional arms control through the Verification Coordinating Committee, which held 17 meetings for national delegates and experts in 2008.

On 27 February, RCC was launched as the successor to the Stability Pact for South-Eastern Europe and focused on developing a strategic and operational framework on security issues for increased regional cooperation and ownership. A Memorandum of Understanding was signed between RCC and UNDP, key promoters of regional security cooperation.

RACVIAC fostered cooperation and broader security dialogue among the South-East European countries by enhancing openness, predictability and transparency in the field of military security. Thirty-eight seminars, conferences, workshops and training courses, with a total of 980 participants, were carried out in cooperation with a wide range of partners, such as OPCW, the Stockholm International Peace Research Institute, NATO, UNDP, UNODA and the International Action Network on Small Arms. The Centre also assisted South-East European countries in fulfilling their arms control commitments and in preparing them for accession to other arms control agreements.

UNDP, Bosnia and Herzegovina and Switzerland hosted a regional meeting (Sarajevo, 13–14 November) on armed violence and development, bringing together Governments from the Caucasus and Eastern and South-Eastern Europe. Fourteen countries subsequently adopted the Sarajevo Declaration on Armed Violence and Development.

Latin America and the Caribbean

Member States of the Organization of American States (OAS) approved on 21 February the Tlatelolco Commitment as the first joint initiative to strengthen border controls, adopt best practices at customs facilities and implement model regulations. In harmony with the 1997 Inter-American Convention Against the Illicit Manufacturing of and Trafficking in Firearms, Ammunition, Explosives, and Other Related Materials (CIFTA) [YUN 1997, p. 519], the Commitment aimed at improving controls of firearms imports and exports. The Banff Declaration, adopted on 5 September, called for ratification of CIFTA and the Inter-American Convention on Transparency in Conventional Weapons Acquisition and emphasized States' commitment to reduce WMD proliferation and their delivery vehicles. As at 31 December, 29 OAS members had ratified CIFTA, and during the year, member States approved two new model legislations. An OAS programme was initiated in Central America to strengthen national capacities to prevent and eliminate illicit firearms trafficking by training national authorities in stockpile management techniques, modernizing stockpile facilities and destroying obsolete or surplus firearms and ammunitions.

The Commitment to Public Security in the Americas, adopted on 8 October in Mexico City by the OAS Public Security Ministers, constituted the first joint policy coordination effort in the hemisphere at the ministerial level. Building on the Tlatelolco Commitment and the Banff Declaration, it further engaged States to strengthen their border security, conduct public security training and create observatories of crime and violence, thereby setting the direction to combat collectively armed violence.

On 23 May, the South American Community of Nations was created as a regional forum to foster dialogue on a number of issues, including peace and security. On 16 December, it formed an additional coordination entity, the South American Defense Council, to promote a common vision of defence, reinforce confidence-building and cooperation, preserve South America as a nuclear and other WMD-free zone, as well as to promote disarmament and a culture of peace.

Throughout the year, members of the Caribbean Community and Common Market accelerated small arms and light weapons initiatives and tasked its Implementation Agency for Crime and Security to coordinate a more effective regional approach. Two main initiatives were undertaken, encouraging member States to sign and ratify all relevant conventions and protocols, and targeting increased compliance with the UN Programme of Action. In that connection, a capacity-building project was developed to share information through a "Regional Integrated Ballistic Information Network", and expanding a ballistics database.

UNODA, in partnership with the EU, organized a regional seminar promoting national accession to CCW and its Protocols (Santo Domingo, Dominican Republic, 11–12 March). UNDP, the UN Regional Centre for Peace, Disarmament and Development in Latin America and the Caribbean and the Spanish Government co-hosted a meeting on armed violence prevention and small arms control in Latin America (Antigua, Guatemala, 28–30 April). UNDP also supported the Central America Small Arms control initiative to strengthen subregional cooperation in preventing proliferation.

Regional Centre for Peace, Disarmament and Development

Throughout 2008, the United Nations Regional Centre for Peace, Disarmament and Development in Latin America and the Caribbean, in Lima, Peru [YUN 1987, p. 88], conducted major multi-year projects in assisting States to address illicit firearm trafficking, while fostering national ownership of disarmament activities. Specifically, it helped train law-enforcement officials in both populated and border areas, as well as to consolidate capacity-building in Brazil, Colombia, the Dominican Republic, Jamaica and Paraguay.

The Centre continued to collaborate with the Brazilian Ministry of the Interior and UNDP-Brazil to maintain a network of relevant entities in the field, such as the International Criminal Police Organization (Interpol), the World Customs Organization and UN agencies. In 2008, that network was reinforced by the participation of the newly created American Police Community and the Latin American and Caribbean Community for Police Intelligence. Supported by the Centre's online resource platform, it boosted networking and exchanges between representatives from several countries in the region, as well as from Australia, Belgium, Canada, China, the Dutch Antilles, France, Italy, Spain, the United Kingdom and the United States.

In cooperation with UNDP and the United Nations Office on Drugs and Crime (UNODC), the Centre worked with parliamentary representatives, NGOs, community groups and the media to make recommendations on harmonizing national firearms legislations with international firearms instruments. In cooperation with UNDP, the Centre facilitated a regional debate on armed violence and appropriate public responses.

In the context of peacekeeping operations, the Centre engaged in greater coordination with NGOs, research institutions and the media on disarmament and weapons destruction training of Brazilian and Peruvian peacekeepers.

The Centre also worked with the Provisional Technical Secretariat of the CTBTO Preparatory Commission to promote Treaty adhesion. Further to the ratifications by Barbados and Colombia in January, the Centre and the Preparatory Commission, with the support of the CTBT Article XIV Conference Co-Chairs Austria and Costa Rica, undertook coordinated missions to Dominica, Guatemala, St. Vincent and the Grenadines, and Trinidad and Tobago for consultations. Those dialogues led to advances in the national adhesion process of the four States.

Report of Secretary-General. In a July report [A/63/157] submitted pursuant to General Assembly resolution 62/49 [YUN 2007, p. 601], the Secretary-General described the Centre's activities from July 2007 to June 2008. The Centre celebrated its twentieth anniversary in 2007.

During the reporting period, it undertook an extensive review of its past and current programme of activities with a view to reaffirming its identity as a specialized regional centre for the promotion and execution of disarmament activities, in accordance with its mandate and in compliance with requests from Member States throughout the region. To meet the priorities of the United Nations and address the requirements of both donors and regional Member States, the Centre adjusted its organizational structure and operational approach. In that connection, it organized its practical disarmament activities and the promotion of disarmament and confidence-building measures under four thematic programmes: disarmament instruments and policy-making; public security; regional security and confidence-building measures; and disarmament advocacy.

The Secretary-General reported that the Centre concluded three of its most significant donor agreements to date and delivered technical assistance on issues related to illicit firearms trafficking, which was identified by regional Member States as their most pressing security concern. The Centre strengthened cooperation within the regional law enforcement community, as evidenced by the increase in information-sharing activities, the adoption of standardized best practices and the establishment of permanent coordination entities.

The Secretary-General stressed that, in the absence of assessed contributions from the UN regular budget, voluntary financial contributions, in particular for core funding, were of crucial importance for Centre operation and activities; that situation continued to have an impact on the sustainability and quality of services provided. As at 31 December 2007, the balance of the Trust Fund for the Centre stood at $1,250,946.

GENERAL ASSEMBLY ACTION

On 2 December [meeting 61, the General Assembly, on the recommendation of the First Committee [A/63/390], adopted **resolution 63/74** without vote [agenda item 90 *(c)*].

United Nations Regional Centre for Peace, Disarmament and Development in Latin America and the Caribbean

The General Assembly,

Recalling its resolutions 41/60 J of 3 December 1986, 42/39 K of 30 November 1987 and 43/76 H of 7 December 1988 on the United Nations Regional Centre for Peace, Disarmament and Development in Latin America and the Caribbean, with headquarters in Lima,

Recalling also its resolutions 46/37 F of 9 December 1991, 48/76 E of 16 December 1993, 49/76 D of 15 December 1994, 50/71 C of 12 December 1995, 52/220 of 22 December 1997, 53/78 F of 4 December 1998, 54/55 F of 1 December 1999, 55/34 E of 20 November 2000, 56/25 E of 29 November 2001, 57/89 of 22 November 2002, 58/60 of 8 December 2003, 59/99 of 3 December 2004, 60/84 of 8 December 2005, 61/92 of 6 December 2006 and 62/49 of 5 December 2007,

Recognizing that the Regional Centre has continued to provide substantive support for the implementation of regional and subregional initiatives and has intensified its contribution to the coordination of United Nations efforts towards peace and disarmament and for the promotion of economic and social development,

Welcoming the report of the Secretary-General, which states, inter alia, that during the period under consideration, the Regional Centre undertook an extensive review of its past and present programme of activities which reaffirmed its identity as a specialized regional centre for the promotion and execution of peace, disarmament and development activities, in accordance with its mandate and in compliance with requests from Member States throughout the Latin American and Caribbean region,

Deeply concerned that, as mentioned in the report of the Secretary-General, in the absence of assessed contributions from the United Nations regular budget, the provision of voluntary financial contributions is of crucial importance for the operation and activities of the Regional Centre, in particular core funding, the lack of which could seriously hinder the Centre's ability to efficiently carry out its mandate and respond to the increasingly diversified and numerous requests from States,

Taking note with interest of the suggestion of the Secretary-General that Member States may wish to consider alternative means of ensuring stable core funding for the Centre,

Recalling the report of the Group of Governmental Experts on the relationship between disarmament and development, referred to in General Assembly resolution 59/78 of 3 December 2004, which is of utmost interest with regard to the role that the Regional Centre plays in promoting the issue in the region in pursuit of its mandate to promote economic and social development related to peace and disarmament,

Noting that security and disarmament issues have always been recognized as significant topics in Latin America and the Caribbean, the first inhabited region in the world to be declared a nuclear-weapon-free zone,

Welcoming the support provided by the Regional Centre to strengthening the nuclear-weapon-free zone established by the Treaty for the Prohibition of Nuclear Weapons in Latin America and the Caribbean (Treaty of Tlatelolco), as well as to promoting and assisting the ratification and implementation of existing multilateral agreements related to weapons of mass destruction and to promoting peace and disarmament education projects during the period under review,

Bearing in mind the important role of the Regional Centre in promoting confidence-building measures, arms control and limitation, disarmament and development at the regional level,

Bearing in mind also the importance of information, research, education and training for peace, disarmament and development in order to achieve understanding and cooperation among States,

Recognizing the need to provide the three United Nations regional centres for peace and disarmament with sufficient financial resources and cooperation for the planning and implementation of their programmes of activities,

1. *Reiterates its strong support* for the role of the United Nations Regional Centre for Peace, Disarmament and Development in Latin America and the Caribbean in the promotion of United Nations activities at the regional level to strengthen peace, stability, security and development among its member States;

2. *Expresses its satisfaction* for the activities carried out in the last year by the Regional Centre in the areas of peace, disarmament and development, and requests the Centre to take into account the proposals to be submitted by the countries of the region in promoting confidence-building measures, arms control and limitation, transparency, disarmament and development at the regional level;

3. *Requests* the Secretary-General to provide from the regular budget, starting in the biennium 2010–2011, the necessary support to ensure the sustainability of the core activities and operations of the Regional Centre, in order to enable it to carry out its programme of activities in accordance with its mandate;

4. *Expresses its appreciation* for the political support and financial contributions to the Regional Centre, which are essential for its continued operation;

5. *Appeals* to Member States, in particular those within the Latin American and Caribbean region, and to international governmental and non-governmental organizations and foundations to make and to increase voluntary contributions to strengthen the Regional Centre, its programme of activities and the implementation thereof;

6. *Invites* all States of the region to continue to take part in the activities of the Regional Centre, proposing items for inclusion in its programme of activities and making greater and better use of the potential of the Centre to meet the current challenges facing the international community with a view to fulfilling the aims of the Charter of the United Nations in the areas of peace, disarmament and development;

7. *Recognizes* that the Regional Centre has an important role in the promotion and development of regional initiatives agreed upon by the countries of Latin America and the Caribbean in the field of weapons of mass destruction, in particular nuclear weapons, and conventional arms, including small arms and light weapons, as well as in the relationship between disarmament and development;

8. *Encourages* the Regional Centre to further develop activities in all countries of the region in the important area of disarmament and development;

9. *Highlights* the conclusion contained in the report of the Secretary-General to the sixty-first session of the General Assembly, that, through its activities, the Regional Centre has demonstrated its role as a viable regional actor in assisting States in the region to advance the cause of peace, disarmament and development in Latin America and the Caribbean;

10. *Requests* the Secretary-General to report to the General Assembly at its sixty-fourth session on the implementation of the present resolution;

11. *Decides* to include in the provisional agenda of its sixty-fourth session the item entitled "United Nations Regional Centre for Peace, Disarmament and Development in Latin America and the Caribbean".

Middle East

In the Middle East, the League of Arab States (LAS) continued to promote a nuclear-weapon-free zone in the region, as well as proceed with work on disarmament issues. Disarmament and international humanitarian law were also examined in relation to the UN-facilitated Convention on Certain Conventional Weapons and to cluster munitions.

A LAS Council resolution to draft a treaty for a WMDs free-zone in the Middle East continued to be suspended until further assessment. The League hosted the twenty-fifth and twenty-sixth meetings of the "Follow-up Committee on Israeli nuclear activities", which coordinated Arab positions on various nuclear disarmament issues. Also, the LAS Summit Council adopted two new resolutions on peaceful uses of nuclear energy.

In connection with conventional arms activities, the Second Annual Meeting of Arab National Points of Contact was held in Cairo, Egypt, from 20 to 21 May.

Supported by the EU and in collaboration with Morocco, UNODA organized a seminar on promoting the universality of CCW and its annexed Protocols in the Middle East and the Mediterranean (19–20 November). The seminar succeeded in fulfilling a need for clarification about the Convention among non-State parties from the region, many of which were affected by regulated weapons, particularly landmines and explosive remnants of war.

The General Assembly, in resolution 63/84 (see p. 597), dealt with the risk of nuclear proliferation in the Middle East, and in resolution 63/38 (see p. 602), it urged all concerned parties to take steps for the establishment of a nuclear-weapon-free Zone in that region.

Chapter VIII

Other political and security questions

In 2008, the United Nations continued to address political and security questions relating to its support for democratization worldwide, the promotion of decolonization, and the peaceful uses of outer space, as well as the Organization's public information activities.

In February, the General Assembly received the text of the Bamako Consensus on "Democracy, Development and Poverty Reduction", adopted by the Fourth Ministerial Conference of the Community of Democracies in November 2007. Conference participants committed to the enhancement of democratic governance in all regions and to upholding the conclusions of previous Ministerial Conferences. They also decided to establish a permanent secretariat in Warsaw, Poland.

The Special Committee on the Situation with regard to the Implementation of the Declaration on the Granting of Independence to Colonial Countries and Peoples continued to review progress in implementing the 1960 Declaration, particularly the exercise of self-determination by the remaining Non-Self-Governing Territories. During the year, the Special Committee organized a Pacific regional seminar in Bandung, Indonesia, as part of its efforts to implement the plan of action for the Second International Decade for the Eradication of Colonialism (2001–2010). Territories under review by the Special Committee included the Falkland Islands (Malvinas), Gibraltar, New Caledonia, Tokelau and Western Sahara.

The Committee on the Peaceful Uses of Outer Space considered the implementation of the recommendations of the Third (1999) United Nations Conference on the Exploration and Peaceful Uses of Outer Space (UNISPACE III) and welcomed the link between the work on UNISPACE III and that of the Commission on Sustainable Development. There was progress in the implementation of the United Nations Platform for Space-based Information for Disaster Management and Emergency Response (UN-SPIDER). The Committee set forth guidelines for selecting and setting up regional UN-SPIDER offices. In December, the Assembly endorsed the recommendations of the Committee.

The United Nations Scientific Committee on the Effects of Atomic Radiation held its fifty-sixth session in Vienna in July. It considered reports on sources of radiation exposure, the 1986 Chernobyl accident and effects on non-human biota.

In a December resolution on developments in information and telecommunications in the context of international security, the Assembly called on Member States to promote consideration of existing and potential threats in the field of information security, as well as possible measures to limit emerging threats.

The Committee on Information considered UN information policies and activities and reviewed the management and operation of the UN Department of Public Information (DPI). During the year, DPI highlighted UN priority issues in the areas of peace and security, development and human rights, and promoted the sixtieth anniversaries of United Nations peacekeeping and of the adoption of the Universal Declaration of Human Rights.

General aspects of international security

Support for democracies

Bamako Consensus

By a January letter [A/62/662], Mali transmitted to the Secretary-General the Bamako Consensus on "Democracy, Development and Poverty Reduction", adopted by the Fourth Ministerial Conference of the Community of Democracies (Bamako, Mali, 14–17 November 2007). In the Consensus, participants committed to promote democracy in all regions, support the integrity of democratic processes in societies pursuing democracy and coordinate policies to enhance democratic governance. They reaffirmed their commitment to promote human rights and fundamental freedoms and to uphold the principles agreed to in previous Ministerial Conferences. They resolved to take action on issues related to democracy, development and poverty reduction, and emphasized the role of State institutions, non-State actors and international institutions, and the functioning and outreach activities of the Community of Democracies.

Regional aspects of international peace and security

South Atlantic

In response to General Assembly resolution 61/294 [YUN 2007, p. 606], the Secretary-General submitted a

7 November report on the zone of peace and cooperation of the South Atlantic [A/63/525] declared in 1986 to promote cooperation among States of the region [YUN 1986, p. 369]. The Secretary-General stated that, as at 3 November, two States and five UN organizations and bodies had replied to his September request for contributions to the report.

On 24 December (**decision 63/552**), the Assembly decided that the item on the zone of peace and cooperation of the South Atlantic would remain for consideration during its resumed sixty-third (2009) session.

Decolonization

The General Assembly's Special Committee on the Situation with regard to the Implementation of the Declaration on the Granting of Independence to Colonial Countries and Peoples (Special Committee on decolonization) held its annual session in New York in two parts—28 February and 15 April (first part); and 27 May and 9, 11–12, 18–19 and 23 June (second part). Various aspects of the implementation of the 1960 Declaration, adopted by the Assembly in resolution 1514(XV) [YUN 1960, p. 49], were considered by the Special Committee, including general decolonization issues and the situation in the individual Non-Self-Governing Territories (NSGTs). The Special Committee adopted three resolutions and recommended eight resolutions for adoption by the General Assembly. In accordance with Assembly resolution 62/120 [YUN 2007, p. 609], the Special Committee transmitted to the Assembly the report on its 2008 activities [A/63/23].

By **decision 63/526** of 5 December, the General Assembly increased the Special Committee's membership from twenty-seven to twenty-eight. On the same date (**decision 63/413**), the Assembly appointed Ecuador as a member of the Special Committee.

Decade for the Eradication of Colonialism

Pacific regional seminar

The Special Committee on decolonization organized a Pacific regional seminar (Bandung, Indonesia, 14–16 May) [A/63/23] to review implementation of the plan of action for the Second International Decade for the Eradication of Colonialism (2001–2010) [YUN 2001, p. 530] and define priority action for the remaining years of the Decade, as declared by General Assembly resolution 55/146 [YUN 2000, p. 548]. The seminar recommended that the Special Committee, as the primary vehicle for fostering the decolonization process, continue to monitor the evolution of NSGTs towards self-determination and include the participation of NSGT representatives, on a case-by-case basis, in consultations between the Special Committee and the administering Powers. The Special Committee should also continue to develop a mechanism to systematically review, on an annual basis, the implementation of Assembly recommendations on decolonization and to explore the array of legitimate transitions to self-determination—provided that the people of a Territory had the opportunity to make a fully informed choice, in accordance with relevant UN resolutions. Participants noted with concern the military installations and activities of the administering Powers in NSGTs, which created health and environmental hazards and ran counter to the rights and interests of the people concerned.

The importance of education, awareness-raising and continued dialogue on decolonization issues was underscored, and participants reaffirmed the need for the Special Committee, in collaboration with DPI, to embark on a public-awareness campaign aimed at fostering an understanding among the people of the Territories about self-determination options. DPI should continue to disseminate relevant information, using its communication tools and making use of such opportunities as regional seminars and visiting missions.

The role of the United Nations Development Programme (UNDP) in providing assistance to NSGTs was reiterated by participants, who encouraged the Programme to further explore ways to help identify financial resources for the development of self-government structures and prepare for self-determination. NSGTs should be given access to relevant UN programmes in the economic and social sphere in furtherance of capacity-building for the attainment of full self-government. The wider UN system should continue to strengthen support measures and formulate programmes of assistance to NSGTs, and seek proposals for the implementation of relevant resolutions by specialized agencies, as detailed in Assembly resolution 62/114 [YUN 2007, p. 613], and the Special Committee should encourage NSGTs to develop closer contacts with relevant regional organizations.

Participants welcomed the presence of representatives of France, New Zealand and the United States at the seminar, but expressed disappointment that the United Kingdom was not present. They considered cooperation from the administering Powers to be imperative, and recommended that the Special Committee, the administering Powers and NSGTs engage in constructive discussions and ways to expedite the implementation of the goals of the Second International Decade and its plan of action.

GENERAL ASSEMBLY ACTION

On 5 December [meeting 64], the General Assembly, on the recommendation of the Fourth (Special Political and Decolonization) Committee [A/63/408], adopted **resolution 63/110** by recorded vote (177-3-1) [agenda item 37].

Implementation of the Declaration on the Granting of Independence to Colonial Countries and Peoples

The General Assembly,

Having examined the report of the Special Committee on the Situation with regard to the Implementation of the Declaration on the Granting of Independence to Colonial Countries and Peoples,

Recalling its resolution 1514(XV) of 14 December 1960, containing the Declaration on the Granting of Independence to Colonial Countries and Peoples, and all its subsequent resolutions concerning the implementation of the Declaration, the most recent of which was resolution 62/120 of 17 December 2007, as well as the relevant resolutions of the Security Council,

Bearing in mind its resolution 55/146 of 8 December 2000, by which it declared the period 2001–2010 the Second International Decade for the Eradication of Colonialism, and the need to examine ways to ascertain the wishes of the peoples of the Non-Self-Governing Territories on the basis of resolution 1514(XV) and other relevant resolutions on decolonization,

Recognizing that the eradication of colonialism has been one of the priorities of the United Nations and continues to be one of its priorities for the decade that began in 2001,

Reconfirming the need to take measures to eliminate colonialism by 2010, as called for in its resolution 55/146,

Reiterating its conviction of the need for the eradication of colonialism, as well as racial discrimination and violations of basic human rights,

Noting with satisfaction the achievements of the Special Committee in contributing to the effective and complete implementation of the Declaration and other relevant resolutions of the United Nations on decolonization,

Stressing the importance of the formal participation of the administering Powers in the work of the Special Committee,

Noting with interest the cooperation and active participation of some administering Powers in the work of the Special Committee, and encouraging the others also to do so,

Taking note that the Pacific regional seminar was held in Bandung, Indonesia, from 14 to 16 May 2008,

1. *Reaffirms* its resolution 1514(XV) and all other resolutions and decisions on decolonization, including its resolution 55/146, by which it declared the period 2001–2010 the Second International Decade for the Eradication of Colonialism, and calls upon the administering Powers, in accordance with those resolutions, to take all steps necessary to enable the peoples of the Non-Self-Governing Territories concerned to exercise fully as soon as possible their right to self-determination, including independence;

2. *Reaffirms once again* that the existence of colonialism in any form or manifestation, including economic exploitation, is incompatible with the Charter of the United Nations, the Declaration on the Granting of Independence to Colonial Countries and Peoples and the Universal Declaration of Human Rights;

3. *Reaffirms its determination* to continue to take all steps necessary to bring about the complete and speedy eradication of colonialism and the faithful observance by all States of the relevant provisions of the Charter, the Declaration on the Granting of Independence to Colonial Countries and Peoples and the Universal Declaration of Human Rights;

4. *Affirms once again its support* for the aspirations of the peoples under colonial rule to exercise their right to self-determination, including independence, in accordance with the relevant resolutions of the United Nations on decolonization;

5. *Calls upon* the administering Powers to cooperate fully with the Special Committee on the Situation with regard to the Implementation of the Declaration on the Granting of Independence to Colonial Countries and Peoples to develop and finalize, before the end of the Second International Decade for the Eradication of Colonialism, a constructive programme of work on a case-by-case basis for the Non-Self-Governing Territories to facilitate the implementation of the mandate of the Special Committee and the relevant resolutions on decolonization, including resolutions on specific Territories;

6. *Recalls with satisfaction* the professional, open and transparent conduct of both the February 2006 and the October 2007 referendums to determine the future status of Tokelau, monitored by the United Nations;

7. *Requests* the Special Committee to continue to seek suitable means for the immediate and full implementation of the Declaration and to carry out the actions approved by the General Assembly regarding the International Decade for the Eradication of Colonialism and the Second International Decade for the Eradication of Colonialism in all Territories that have not yet exercised their right to self-determination, including independence, and in particular:

(*a*) To formulate specific proposals to bring about an end to colonialism and to report thereon to the General Assembly at its sixty-fourth session;

(*b*) To continue to examine the implementation by Member States of resolution 1514(XV) and other relevant resolutions on decolonization;

(*c*) To continue to examine the political, economic and social situation in the Non-Self-Governing Territories, and to recommend, as appropriate, to the General Assembly the most suitable steps to be taken to enable the populations of those Territories to exercise their right to self-determination, including independence, in accordance with the relevant resolutions on decolonization, including resolutions on specific Territories;

(*d*) To develop and finalize, before the end of the Second International Decade for the Eradication of Colonialism and in cooperation with the administering Power and the Territory in question, a constructive programme of work on a case-by-case basis for the Non-Self-Governing Territories to facilitate the implementation of the mandate of the Special Committee and the relevant resolutions on decolonization, including resolutions on specific Territories;

(*e*) To continue to dispatch visiting and special missions to the Non-Self-Governing Territories in accordance with the relevant resolutions on decolonization, including resolutions on specific Territories;

(*f*) To conduct seminars, as appropriate, for the purpose of receiving and disseminating information on the work of the Special Committee, and to facilitate participation by the peoples of the Non-Self-Governing Territories in those seminars;

(*g*) To take all steps necessary to enlist worldwide support among Governments, as well as national and international organizations, for the achievement of the objectives of the Declaration and the implementation of the relevant resolutions of the United Nations;

(*h*) To observe annually the Week of Solidarity with the Peoples of Non-Self-Governing Territories;

8. *Recognizes* that the plan of action for the Second International Decade for the Eradication of Colonialism represents an important legislative authority for the attainment of self-government by the Non-Self-Governing Territories, and that the case-by-case assessment of the attainment of self-government in each Territory can make an important contribution to this process;

9. *Calls upon* all States, in particular the administering Powers, as well as the specialized agencies and other organizations of the United Nations system, to give effect within their respective spheres of competence to the recommendations of the Special Committee for the implementation of the Declaration and other relevant resolutions of the United Nations;

10. *Calls upon* the administering Powers to ensure that economic and other activities in the Non-Self-Governing Territories under their administration do not adversely affect the interests of the peoples but instead promote development, and to assist them in the exercise of their right to self-determination;

11. *Urges* the administering Powers concerned to take effective measures to safeguard and guarantee the inalienable rights of the peoples of the Non-Self-Governing Territories to their natural resources, and to establish and maintain control over the future development of those resources, and requests the administering Powers to take all steps necessary to protect the property rights of the peoples of those Territories;

12. *Urges* all States, directly and through their action in the specialized agencies and other organizations of the United Nations system, to provide moral and material assistance as needed to the peoples of the Non-Self-Governing Territories, and requests the administering Powers to take steps to enlist and make effective use of all possible assistance, on both a bilateral and a multilateral basis, in the strengthening of the economies of those Territories;

13. *Reaffirms* that the United Nations visiting missions to the Territories are an effective means of ascertaining the situation in the Territories, as well as the wishes and aspirations of their inhabitants, and calls upon the administering Powers to continue to cooperate with the Special Committee in the discharge of its mandate and to facilitate visiting missions to the Territories;

14. *Calls upon* all the administering Powers to cooperate fully in the work of the Special Committee and to participate formally in its future sessions;

15. *Requests* the Secretary-General, the specialized agencies and other organizations of the United Nations system to provide economic, social and other assistance to the Non-Self-Governing Territories and to continue to do so, as appropriate, after they exercise their right to self-determination, including independence;

16. *Approves* the report of the Special Committee on the Situation with regard to the Implementation of the Declaration on the Granting of Independence to Colonial Countries and Peoples covering its work during 2008, including the programme of work envisaged for 2009;

17. *Requests* the Secretary-General to provide the Special Committee with the facilities and services required for the implementation of the present resolution, as well as the other resolutions and decisions on decolonization adopted by the General Assembly and the Special Committee.

RECORDED VOTE ON RESOLUTION 63/110:

In favour: Afghanistan, Albania, Algeria, Andorra, Angola, Antigua and Barbuda, Argentina, Armenia, Australia, Austria, Azerbaijan, Bahamas, Bahrain, Bangladesh, Barbados, Belarus, Belgium, Belize, Benin, Bhutan, Bolivia, Bosnia and Herzegovina, Botswana, Brazil, Brunei Darussalam, Bulgaria, Burkina Faso, Burundi, Cambodia, Cameroon, Canada, Cape Verde, Central African Republic, Chile, China, Colombia, Comoros, Congo, Costa Rica, Côte d'Ivoire, Croatia, Cuba, Cyprus, Czech Republic, Democratic People's Republic of Korea, Denmark, Djibouti, Dominica, Dominican Republic, Ecuador, Egypt, El Salvador, Eritrea, Estonia, Ethiopia, Fiji, Finland, Gabon, Georgia, Germany, Ghana, Greece, Grenada, Guatemala, Guinea, Guinea-Bissau, Guyana, Haiti, Honduras, Hungary, Iceland, India, Indonesia, Iran, Iraq, Ireland, Italy, Jamaica, Japan, Jordan, Kazakhstan, Kenya, Kuwait, Kyrgyzstan, Lao People's Democratic Republic, Latvia, Lebanon, Lesotho, Liberia, Libyan Arab Jamahiriya, Liechtenstein, Lithuania, Luxembourg, Madagascar, Malawi, Malaysia, Maldives, Mali, Malta, Marshall Islands, Mauritania, Mauritius, Mexico, Monaco, Moldova, Mongolia, Montenegro, Morocco, Mozambique, Myanmar, Namibia, Nauru, Nepal, Netherlands, New Zealand, Nicaragua, Niger, Nigeria, Norway, Oman, Pakistan, Panama, Papua New Guinea, Paraguay, Peru, Philippines, Poland, Portugal, Qatar, Republic of Korea, Romania, Russian Federation, Rwanda, Saint Lucia, Saint Vincent and the Grenadines, Samoa, San Marino, Sao Tome and Principe, Saudi Arabia, Senegal, Serbia, Singapore, Slovakia, Slovenia, Solomon Islands, Somalia, South Africa, Spain, Sri Lanka, Sudan, Suriname, Swaziland, Sweden, Switzerland, Syrian Arab Republic, Tajikistan, Thailand, The former Yugoslav Republic of Macedonia, Timor-Leste, Togo, Tonga, Trinidad and Tobago, Tunisia, Turkey, Tuvalu, Uganda, Ukraine, United Arab Emirates, United Republic of Tanzania, Uruguay, Uzbekistan, Vanuatu, Venezuela, Viet Nam, Yemen, Zambia, Zimbabwe.

Against: Israel, United Kingdom, United States.

Abstaining: France.

Implementation by international organizations

In a February report [A/63/61] the Secretary-General stated that he had brought General Assembly resolution 62/114 [YUN 2007, p. 613] to the attention of the specialized agencies and other international institutions associated with the United Nations and invited them to submit information regarding their implementation activities in support of NSGTs. Replies received from six agencies or institutions were summarized in a May report of the Economic and Social Council President on his consultations with the Special Committee on decolonization [E/2008/47]. According to the information provided, a number of specialized agencies and organizations continued to provide support to NSGTs from their own budgetary resources, in addition to their respective contributions as executing agencies of projects funded by UNDP, the primary provider of support. Three agencies and one regional association indicated that they were not currently conducting any assistance programmes in NSGTs.

ECONOMIC AND SOCIAL COUNCIL ACTION

On 24 July [meeting 42], the Economic and Social Council adopted **resolution 2008/15** [draft: E/2008/L.17] by roll-call vote (27-0-20) [agenda item 9].

Support to Non-Self-Governing Territories by the specialized agencies and international institutions associated with the United Nations

The Economic and Social Council,

Having examined the report of the Secretary-General and the report of the President of the Economic and Social Council containing the information submitted by the specialized agencies and other organizations of the United Nations system on their activities with regard to the implementation of the Declaration on the Granting of Independence to Colonial Countries and Peoples,

Having heard the statement by the representative of the Special Committee on the Situation with regard to the Implementation of the Declaration on the Granting of Independence to Colonial Countries and Peoples,

Recalling General Assembly resolutions 1514(XV) of 14 December 1960 and 1541(XV) of 15 December 1960, the resolutions of the Special Committee and other relevant resolutions and decisions, including, in particular, Economic and Social Council resolution 2007/25 of 26 July 2007,

Bearing in mind the relevant provisions of the final documents of the successive Conferences of Heads of State or Government of Non-Aligned Countries and of the resolutions adopted by the Assembly of Heads of State and Government of the African Union, the Pacific Islands Forum and the Caribbean Community,

Conscious of the need to facilitate the implementation of the Declaration on the Granting of Independence to Colonial Countries and Peoples,

Welcoming the current participation, in their capacity as observers, of those Non-Self-Governing Territories that are associate members of the regional commissions in the world conferences in the economic and social sphere, subject to the rules of procedure of the General Assembly and in accordance with relevant United Nations resolutions and decisions, including resolutions and decisions of the Assembly and the Special Committee on specific Non-Self-Governing Territories,

Noting that only some specialized agencies and organizations of the United Nations system have been involved in providing assistance to Non-Self-Governing Territories,

Welcoming the assistance extended to Non-Self-Governing Territories by certain specialized agencies and other organizations of the United Nations system, in particular the United Nations Development Programme,

Stressing that, because the development options of the small island Non-Self-Governing Territories are limited, they face special challenges in planning for and implementing sustainable development, and that they will be constrained in meeting those challenges without the continuing cooperation and assistance of the specialized agencies and other organizations of the United Nations system,

Stressing also the importance of securing the resources necessary for funding expanded programmes of assistance for the peoples concerned and the need to enlist the support of all the major funding institutions within the United Nations system in that regard,

Reaffirming the mandates of the specialized agencies and other organizations of the United Nations system to take all appropriate measures, within their respective spheres of competence, to ensure the full implementation of Assembly resolution 1514(XV) and other relevant resolutions,

Expressing its appreciation to the African Union, the Pacific Islands Forum, the Caribbean Community and other regional organizations for the continued cooperation and assistance they have extended to the specialized agencies and other organizations of the United Nations system in this regard,

Expressing its conviction that closer contacts and consultations between and among the specialized agencies and other organizations of the United Nations system and regional organizations help to facilitate the effective formulation of programmes of assistance for the peoples concerned,

Mindful of the imperative need to keep under continuous review the activities of the specialized agencies and other organizations of the United Nations system in the implementation of the various United Nations decisions relating to decolonization,

Bearing in mind the extremely fragile economies of the small island Non-Self-Governing Territories and their vulnerability to natural disasters, such as hurricanes, cyclones and sea-level rise, and recalling the relevant resolutions of the General Assembly,

Recalling General Assembly resolution 62/114 of 17 December 2007 entitled "Implementation of the Declaration on the Granting of Independence to Colonial Countries and Peoples by the specialized agencies and the international institutions associated with the United Nations",

1. *Takes note* of the report of the President of the Economic and Social Council, and endorses the observations and suggestions arising therefrom;

2. *Also takes note* of the report of the Secretary-General;

3. *Recommends* that all States intensify their efforts within the specialized agencies and other organizations of the United Nations system of which they are members to

ensure the full and effective implementation of the Declaration on the Granting of Independence to Colonial Countries and Peoples, contained in General Assembly resolution 1514(XV), and other relevant resolutions of the United Nations;

4. *Reaffirms* that the specialized agencies and other organizations and institutions of the United Nations system should continue to be guided by the relevant resolutions of the United Nations in their efforts to contribute to the implementation of the Declaration and all other relevant General Assembly resolutions;

5. *Also reaffirms* that the recognition by the General Assembly, the Security Council and other United Nations organs of the legitimacy of the aspirations of the peoples of the Non-Self-Governing Territories to exercise their right to self-determination entails, as a corollary, the extension of all appropriate assistance to those peoples;

6. *Expresses its appreciation* to those specialized agencies and other organizations of the United Nations system that have continued to cooperate with the United Nations and the regional and subregional organizations in the implementation of Assembly resolution 1514(XV) and other relevant resolutions of the United Nations, and requests all of the specialized agencies and other organizations of the United Nations system to implement the relevant provisions of those resolutions;

7. *Requests* the specialized agencies and other organizations of the United Nations system and international and regional organizations to examine and review conditions in each Non-Self-Governing Territory so that they may take appropriate measures to accelerate progress in the economic and social sectors of those Territories;

8. *Urges* those specialized agencies and organizations of the United Nations system that have not yet provided assistance to Non-Self-Governing Territories to do so as soon as possible;

9. *Requests* the specialized agencies and other organizations and bodies of the United Nations system and regional organizations to strengthen existing measures of support and to formulate appropriate programmes of assistance to the remaining Non-Self-Governing Territories, within the framework of their respective mandates, in order to accelerate progress in the economic and social sectors of those Territories;

10. *Recommends* that the executive heads of the specialized agencies and other organizations of the United Nations system formulate, with the active cooperation of the regional organizations concerned, concrete proposals for the full implementation of the relevant resolutions of the United Nations and submit those proposals to their governing and legislative organs;

11. *Also recommends* that the specialized agencies and other organizations of the United Nations system continue to review, at the regular meetings of their governing bodies, the implementation of Assembly resolution 1514(XV) and other relevant resolutions of the United Nations;

12. *Welcomes* the preparation by the Department of Public Information and the Department of Political Affairs of the Secretariat, in consultation with the United Nations Development Programme, the specialized agencies and the Special Committee on the Situation with regard to the Implementation of the Declaration on the Granting of Independence to Colonial Countries and Peoples, of an informational leaflet on assistance programmes available to the Non-Self-Governing Territories, and requests that it be disseminated as widely as possible;

13. *Also welcomes* the continuing efforts made by the United Nations Development Programme in maintaining a close liaison between the specialized agencies and other organizations of the United Nations system, including the Economic Commission for Latin America and the Caribbean and the Economic and Social Commission for Asia and the Pacific, and in providing assistance to the peoples of the Non-Self-Governing Territories;

14. *Encourages* the Non-Self-Governing Territories to take steps to establish and/or strengthen disaster preparedness and management institutions and policies;

15. *Requests* the administering Powers concerned to facilitate, when appropriate, the participation of appointed and elected representatives of Non-Self-Governing Territories in the relevant meetings and conferences of the specialized agencies and other organizations of the United Nations system, in accordance with relevant United Nations resolutions and decisions, including the resolutions and decisions of the General Assembly and the Special Committee, on specific Territories, so that they may benefit from the related activities of those agencies and organizations;

16. *Recommends* that all Governments intensify their efforts within the specialized agencies and other organizations of the United Nations system of which they are members to accord priority to the question of providing assistance to the peoples of the Non-Self-Governing Territories;

17. *Draws the attention* of the Special Committee to the present resolution and to the discussion held on the subject at the substantive session of 2008 of the Economic and Social Council;

18. *Recalls* the adoption on 16 May 1998 by the Economic Commission for Latin America and the Caribbean of resolution 574(XXVII), in which the Commission called for the mechanisms necessary for its associate members, including the Non-Self-Governing Territories, to participate, subject to the rules of procedure of the General Assembly, in the special sessions of the Assembly convened to review and assess the implementation of the plans of action of those United Nations world conferences in which the Territories had originally participated in their capacity as observers, and in the work of the Economic and Social Council and its subsidiary bodies;

19. *Requests* the President of the Economic and Social Council to continue to maintain close contact on these matters with the Chairman of the Special Committee and to report thereon to the Council;

20. *Requests* the Secretary-General to follow up on the implementation of the present resolution, paying particular attention to cooperation and integration arrangements for maximizing the efficiency of the assistance activities undertaken by various organizations of the United Nations system, and to report thereon to the Economic and Social Council at its substantive session of 2009;

21. *Decides* to keep the above questions under continuous review.

ROLL-CALL VOTE ON RESOLUTION 2008/15:

In favour: Algeria, Angola, Barbados, Benin, Bolivia, Brazil, Cameroon, Cape Verde, China, Congo, Cuba, El Salvador, Haiti, Indonesia, Iraq, Madagascar, Malaysia, Mozambique, New Zealand, Niger, Pakistan, Paraguay, Philippines, Saudi Arabia, Sri Lanka, Sudan, Uruguay.

Against: None.

Abstaining: Austria, Canada, Czech Republic, France, Greece, Iceland, Japan, Kazakhstan, Liechtenstein, Luxembourg, Moldova, Netherlands, Poland, Portugal, Republic of Korea, Romania, Russian Federation, Sweden, United Kingdom, United States.

GENERAL ASSEMBLY ACTION

On 5 December [meeting 64], the General Assembly, on the recommendation of the Fourth Committee [A/63/406], adopted **resolution 63/103** by recorded vote (125-0-55) [agenda item 35].

Implementation of the Declaration on the Granting of Independence to Colonial Countries and Peoples by the specialized agencies and the international institutions associated with the United Nations

The General Assembly,

Having considered the item entitled "Implementation of the Declaration on the Granting of Independence to Colonial Countries and Peoples by the specialized agencies and the international institutions associated with the United Nations",

Having also considered the report of the Secretary-General and the report of the Economic and Social Council on the item,

Having examined the chapter of the report of the Special Committee on the Situation with regard to the Implementation of the Declaration on the Granting of Independence to Colonial Countries and Peoples relating to the item,

Recalling its resolutions 1514(XV) of 14 December 1960 and 1541(XV) of 15 December 1960 and the resolutions of the Special Committee, as well as other relevant resolutions and decisions, including in particular Economic and Social Council resolution 2007/25 of 26 July 2007,

Bearing in mind the relevant provisions of the final documents of the successive Conferences of Heads of State or Government of Non-Aligned Countries and of the resolutions adopted by the Assembly of Heads of State and Government of the African Union, the Pacific Islands Forum and the Caribbean Community,

Conscious of the need to facilitate the implementation of the Declaration on the Granting of Independence to Colonial Countries and Peoples, contained in resolution 1514(XV),

Noting that the large majority of the remaining Non-Self-Governing Territories are small island Territories,

Welcoming the assistance extended to Non-Self-Governing Territories by certain specialized agencies and other organizations of the United Nations system, in particular the United Nations Development Programme,

Also welcoming the participation in the capacity of observers of those Non-Self-Governing Territories that are associate members of regional commissions in the world conferences in the economic and social sphere, subject to the rules of procedure of the General Assembly and in accordance with relevant United Nations resolutions and decisions, including resolutions and decisions of the Assembly and the Special Committee on specific Territories,

Noting that only some specialized agencies and other organizations of the United Nations system have been involved in providing assistance to Non-Self-Governing Territories,

Stressing that, because the development options of the small island Non-Self-Governing Territories are limited, there are special challenges to planning for and implementing sustainable development and that those Territories will be constrained in meeting the challenges without the continuing cooperation and assistance of the specialized agencies and other organizations of the United Nations system,

Stressing also the importance of securing the necessary resources for funding expanded programmes of assistance for the peoples concerned and the need to enlist the support of all major funding institutions within the United Nations system in that regard,

Reaffirming the mandates of the specialized agencies and other organizations of the United Nations system to take all appropriate measures, within their respective spheres of competence, to ensure the full implementation of General Assembly resolution 1514(XV) and other relevant resolutions,

Expressing its appreciation to the African Union, the Pacific Islands Forum, the Caribbean Community and other regional organizations for the continued cooperation and assistance they have extended to the specialized agencies and other organizations of the United Nations system in this regard,

Expressing its conviction that closer contacts and consultations between and among the specialized agencies and other organizations of the United Nations system and regional organizations help to facilitate the effective formulation of programmes of assistance to the peoples concerned,

Mindful of the imperative need to keep under continuous review the activities of the specialized agencies and other organizations of the United Nations system in the implementation of the various United Nations resolutions and decisions relating to decolonization,

Bearing in mind the extremely fragile economies of the small island Non-Self-Governing Territories and their vulnerability to natural disasters, such as hurricanes, cyclones and sea-level rise, and recalling the relevant resolutions of the General Assembly,

Recalling its resolution 62/114 of 17 December 2007 on the implementation of the Declaration by the specialized agencies and the international institutions associated with the United Nations,

1. *Takes note* of the report of the Secretary-General;

2. *Recommends* that all States intensify their efforts in the specialized agencies and other organizations of the United Nations system in which they are members to ensure the full and effective implementation of the Declaration on the Granting of Independence to Colonial Countries and Peoples, contained in General Assembly resolution 1514(XV), and other relevant resolutions of the United Nations;

3. *Reaffirms* that the specialized agencies and other organizations and institutions of the United Nations system should continue to be guided by the relevant resolutions of the United Nations in their efforts to contribute to the implementation of the Declaration and all other relevant resolutions of the General Assembly;

4. *Reaffirms also* that the recognition by the General Assembly, the Security Council and other United Nations organs of the legitimacy of the aspirations of the peoples of the Non-Self-Governing Territories to exercise their right to self-determination entails, as a corollary, the extension of all appropriate assistance to those peoples;

5. *Expresses its appreciation* to those specialized agencies and other organizations of the United Nations system that have continued to cooperate with the United Nations and the regional and subregional organizations in the implementation of General Assembly resolution 1514(XV) and other relevant resolutions of the United Nations, and requests all the specialized agencies and other organizations of the United Nations system to implement the relevant provisions of those resolutions;

6. *Requests* the specialized agencies and other organizations of the United Nations system and international and regional organizations to examine and review conditions in each Territory so as to take appropriate measures to accelerate progress in the economic and social sectors of the Territories;

7. *Urges* those specialized agencies and other organizations of the United Nations system that have not yet provided assistance to Non-Self-Governing Territories to do so as soon as possible;

8. *Requests* the specialized agencies and other organizations and institutions of the United Nations system and regional organizations to strengthen existing measures of support and formulate appropriate programmes of assistance to the remaining Non-Self-Governing Territories, within the framework of their respective mandates, in order to accelerate progress in the economic and social sectors of those Territories;

9. *Requests* the specialized agencies and other organizations of the United Nations system concerned to provide information on:

(a) Environmental problems facing the Non-Self-Governing Territories;

(b) The impact of natural disasters, such as hurricanes and volcanic eruptions, and other environmental problems, such as beach and coastal erosion and droughts, on those Territories;

(c) Ways and means to assist the Territories to fight drug trafficking, money-laundering and other illegal and criminal activities;

(d) Illegal exploitation of the marine and other natural resources of the Territories and the need to utilize those resources for the benefit of the peoples of the Territories;

10. *Recommends* that the executive heads of the specialized agencies and other organizations of the United Nations system formulate, with the active cooperation of the regional organizations concerned, concrete proposals for the full implementation of the relevant resolutions of the United Nations and submit the proposals to their governing and legislative organs;

11. *Also recommends* that the specialized agencies and other organizations of the United Nations system continue to review at the regular meetings of their governing bodies the implementation of General Assembly resolution 1514(XV) and other relevant resolutions of the United Nations;

12. *Recalls* the adoption by the Economic Commission for Latin America and the Caribbean of its resolution 574(XXVII) of 16 May 1998, calling for the necessary mechanisms for its associate members, including Non-Self-Governing Territories, to participate in the special sessions of the General Assembly, subject to the rules of procedure of the Assembly, to review and assess the implementation of the plans of action of those United Nations world conferences in which the Territories originally participated in the capacity of observer, and in the work of the Economic and Social Council and its subsidiary bodies;

13. *Requests* the Chairperson of the Special Committee on the Situation with regard to the Implementation of the Declaration on the Granting of Independence to Colonial Countries and Peoples to continue to maintain close contact on these matters with the President of the Economic and Social Council;

14. *Welcomes* the publication by the Department of Public Information and the Department of Political Affairs of the Secretariat, in consultation with the United Nations Development Programme, the specialized agencies and the Special Committee, of an information leaflet on assistance programmes available to the Non-Self-Governing Territories, and requests that it be disseminated widely;

15. *Welcomes also* the continuing efforts made by the United Nations Development Programme in maintaining close liaison among the specialized agencies and other organizations of the United Nations system, including the Economic Commission for Latin America and the Caribbean and the Economic and Social Commission for Asia and the Pacific, and in providing assistance to the peoples of the Non-Self-Governing Territories;

16. *Encourages* the Non-Self-Governing Territories to take steps to establish and/or strengthen disaster preparedness and management institutions and policies, inter alia, with the assistance of the relevant specialized agencies;

17. *Requests* the administering Powers concerned to facilitate, when appropriate, the participation of appointed and elected representatives of Non-Self-Governing Territories in the relevant meetings and conferences of the specialized agencies and other organizations of the United Nations system, in accordance with relevant resolutions and decisions of the United Nations, including resolutions and decisions of the General Assembly and the Special Committee on specific Territories, so that the Territories may benefit from the related activities of those agencies and organizations;

18. *Recommends* that all Governments intensify their efforts in the specialized agencies and other organizations of the United Nations system of which they are members to accord priority to the question of providing assistance to the peoples of the Non-Self-Governing Territories;

19. *Requests* the Secretary-General to continue to assist the specialized agencies and other organizations of the United Nations system in working out appropriate measures for implementing the relevant resolutions of the United Na-

tions and to prepare for submission to the relevant bodies, with the assistance of those agencies and organizations, a report on the action taken in implementation of the relevant resolutions, including the present resolution, since the circulation of his previous report;

20. *Commends* the Economic and Social Council for its debate and resolution on this question, and requests it to continue to consider, in consultation with the Special Committee, appropriate measures for the coordination of the policies and activities of the specialized agencies and other organizations of the United Nations system in implementing the relevant resolutions of the General Assembly;

21. *Requests* the specialized agencies to report periodically to the Secretary-General on the implementation of the present resolution;

22. *Requests* the Secretary-General to transmit the present resolution to the governing bodies of the appropriate specialized agencies and international institutions associated with the United Nations so that those bodies may take the measures necessary to implement the resolution, and also requests the Secretary-General to report to the General Assembly at its sixty-fourth session on the implementation of the present resolution;

23. *Requests* the Special Committee to continue to examine the question and to report thereon to the General Assembly at its sixty-fourth session.

RECORDED VOTE ON RESOLUTION 63/103:

In favour: Afghanistan, Algeria, Angola, Antigua and Barbuda, Australia, Azerbaijan, Bahamas, Bahrain, Bangladesh, Barbados, Belarus, Belize, Benin, Bhutan, Bolivia, Botswana, Brazil, Brunei Darussalam, Burkina Faso, Burundi, Cambodia, Cameroon, Cape Verde, Central African Republic, Chile, China, Colombia, Comoros, Congo, Costa Rica, Cuba, Democratic People's Republic of Korea, Djibouti, Dominica, Dominican Republic, Ecuador, Egypt, El Salvador, Eritrea, Ethiopia, Fiji, Gabon, Ghana, Grenada, Guinea, Guinea-Bissau, Guyana, Haiti, Honduras, India, Indonesia, Iran, Iraq, Jamaica, Japan, Jordan, Kenya, Kuwait, Kyrgyzstan, Lao People's Democratic Republic, Lebanon, Lesotho, Liberia, Libyan Arab Jamahiriya, Madagascar, Malawi, Malaysia, Maldives, Mali, Marshall Islands, Mauritania, Mauritius, Mexico, Mongolia, Morocco, Mozambique, Myanmar, Namibia, Nauru, Nepal, New Zealand, Nicaragua, Niger, Nigeria, Oman, Pakistan, Panama, Papua New Guinea, Paraguay, Peru, Philippines, Qatar, Rwanda, Saint Lucia, Saint Vincent and the Grenadines, Samoa, Sao Tome and Principe, Saudi Arabia, Senegal, Singapore, Solomon Islands, Somalia, South Africa, Sri Lanka, Sudan, Swaziland, Syrian Arab Republic, Tajikistan, Thailand, Timor-Leste, Togo, Tonga, Trinidad and Tobago, Tunisia, Tuvalu, Uganda, United Arab Emirates, United Republic of Tanzania, Uruguay, Vanuatu, Venezuela, Viet Nam, Yemen, Zambia, Zimbabwe.

Against: None.

Abstaining: Albania, Andorra, Argentina, Armenia, Austria, Belgium, Bosnia and Herzegovina, Bulgaria, Canada, Côte d'Ivoire, Croatia, Cyprus, Czech Republic, Denmark, Estonia, Finland, France, Georgia, Germany, Greece, Hungary, Iceland, Ireland, Israel, Italy, Kazakhstan, Latvia, Liechtenstein, Lithuania, Luxembourg, Malta, Micronesia, Moldova, Monaco, Montenegro, Netherlands, Norway, Poland, Portugal, Republic of Korea, Romania, Russian Federation, San Marino, Serbia, Slovakia, Slovenia, Spain, Suriname, Sweden, Switzerland, The former Yugoslav Republic of Macedonia, Turkey, Ukraine, United Kingdom, United States.

Military activities and arrangements in colonial countries

In accordance with General Assembly decision 57/525 [YUN 2002, p. 564], Secretariat working papers on Bermuda [A/AC.109/2008/10 & Corr.1], Guam [A/AC.109/2008/15] and the United States Virgin Islands [A/AC.109/2008/17] contained information on, among other things, military activities and arrangements by the administering Powers in those Territories.

Economic and other activities affecting the interests of NSGTs

The Special Committee on decolonization, in June [A/63/23], continued consideration of economic and other activities affecting the interests of the peoples of NSGTs. It had before it Secretariat working papers containing information on, among other things, economic conditions in American Samoa [A/AC.109/2008/3], Anguilla [A/AC.109/2008/7], Bermuda [A/AC.109/2008/10 & Corr.1], the British Virgin Islands [A/AC.109/2008/2], the Cayman Islands [A/AC.109/2008/11], the Falkland Islands (Malvinas) [A/AC.109/2008/13], Gibraltar [A/AC.109/2008/8 & Corr.1], Guam [A/AC.109/2008/15], Montserrat [A/AC.109/2008/16], New Caledonia [A/AC.109/2008/9], Pitcairn [A/AC.109/2008/4], St. Helena [A/AC.109/2008/6], Tokelau [A/AC.109/2008/1], the Turks and Caicos Islands [A/AC.109/2008/12] and the United States Virgin Islands [A/AC.109/2008/17].

GENERAL ASSEMBLY ACTION

On 5 December [meeting 64], the General Assembly, on the recommendation of the Fourth Committee [A/63/405], adopted **resolution 63/102** by recorded vote (179-2-2) [agenda item 34].

Economic and other activities which affect the interests of the peoples of the Non-Self-Governing Territories

The General Assembly,

Having considered the item entitled "Economic and other activities which affect the interests of the peoples of the Non-Self-Governing Territories",

Having examined the chapter of the report of the Special Committee on the Situation with regard to the Implementation of the Declaration on the Granting of Independence to Colonial Countries and Peoples relating to the item,

Recalling General Assembly resolution 1514(XV) of 14 December 1960, as well as all other relevant resolutions of the Assembly, including, in particular, resolutions 46/181 of 19 December 1991 and 55/146 of 8 December 2000,

Reaffirming the solemn obligation of the administering Powers under the Charter of the United Nations to promote the political, economic, social and educational advancement of the inhabitants of the Territories under their administration and to protect the human and natural resources of those Territories against abuses,

Reaffirming also that any economic or other activity that has a negative impact on the interests of the peoples of the Non-Self-Governing Territories and on the exercise of their right to self-determination in conformity with the Charter and resolution 1514(XV) is contrary to the purposes and principles of the Charter,

Reaffirming further that the natural resources are the heritage of the peoples of the Non-Self-Governing Territories, including the indigenous populations,

Aware of the special circumstances of the geographical location, size and economic conditions of each Territory, and bearing in mind the need to promote the economic stability, diversification and strengthening of the economy of each Territory,

Conscious of the particular vulnerability of the small Territories to natural disasters and environmental degradation,

Conscious also that foreign economic investment, when undertaken in collaboration with the peoples of the Non-Self-Governing Territories and in accordance with their wishes, could make a valid contribution to the socio-economic development of the Territories and also to the exercise of their right to self-determination,

Concerned about any activities aimed at exploiting the natural and human resources of the Non-Self-Governing Territories to the detriment of the interests of the inhabitants of those Territories,

Bearing in mind the relevant provisions of the final documents of the successive Conferences of Heads of State or Government of Non-Aligned Countries and of the resolutions adopted by the Assembly of Heads of State and Government of the African Union, the Pacific Islands Forum and the Caribbean Community,

1. *Reaffirms* the right of peoples of Non-Self-Governing Territories to self-determination in conformity with the Charter of the United Nations and with General Assembly resolution 1514(XV), containing the Declaration on the Granting of Independence to Colonial Countries and Peoples, as well as their right to the enjoyment of their natural resources and their right to dispose of those resources in their best interest;

2. *Affirms* the value of foreign economic investment undertaken in collaboration with the peoples of the Non-Self-Governing Territories and in accordance with their wishes in order to make a valid contribution to the socio-economic development of the Territories;

3. *Reaffirms* the responsibility of the administering Powers under the Charter to promote the political, economic, social and educational advancement of the Non-Self-Governing Territories, and reaffirms the legitimate rights of their peoples over their natural resources;

4. *Reaffirms its concern* about any activities aimed at the exploitation of the natural resources that are the heritage of the peoples of the Non-Self-Governing Territories, including the indigenous populations, in the Caribbean, the Pacific and other regions, and of their human resources, to the detriment of their interests, and in such a way as to deprive them of their right to dispose of those resources;

5. *Reaffirms* the need to avoid any economic and other activities that adversely affect the interests of the peoples of the Non-Self-Governing Territories;

6. *Calls once again upon* all Governments that have not yet done so to take, in accordance with the relevant provisions of General Assembly resolution 2621(XXV) of 12 October 1970, legislative, administrative or other measures in respect of their nationals and the bodies corporate under their jurisdiction that own and operate enterprises in the Non-Self-Governing Territories that are detrimental to the interests of the inhabitants of those Territories, in order to put an end to such enterprises;

7. *Calls upon* the administering Powers to ensure that the exploitation of the marine and other natural resources in the Non-Self-Governing Territories under their administration is not in violation of the relevant resolutions of the United Nations, and does not adversely affect the interests of the peoples of those Territories;

8. *Invites* all Governments and organizations of the United Nations system to take all possible measures to ensure that the permanent sovereignty of the peoples of the Non-Self-Governing Territories over their natural resources is fully respected and safeguarded in accordance with the relevant resolutions of the United Nations on decolonization;

9. *Urges* the administering Powers concerned to take effective measures to safeguard and guarantee the inalienable right of the peoples of the Non-Self-Governing Territories to their natural resources and to establish and maintain control over the future development of those resources, and requests the administering Powers to take all necessary steps to protect the property rights of the peoples of those Territories in accordance with the relevant resolutions of the United Nations on decolonization;

10. *Calls upon* the administering Powers concerned to ensure that no discriminatory working conditions prevail in the Territories under their administration and to promote in each Territory a fair system of wages applicable to all the inhabitants without any discrimination;

11. *Requests* the Secretary-General to continue, through all means at his disposal, to inform world public opinion of any activity that affects the exercise of the right of the peoples of the Non-Self-Governing Territories to self-determination in conformity with the Charter and resolution 1514(XV);

12. *Appeals* to trade unions and non-governmental organizations, as well as individuals, to continue their efforts to promote the economic well-being of the peoples of the Non-Self-Governing Territories, and also appeals to the media to disseminate information about the developments in this regard;

13. *Decides* to follow the situation in the Non-Self-Governing Territories so as to ensure that all economic activities in those Territories are aimed at strengthening and diversifying their economies in the interest of their peoples, including the indigenous populations, and at promoting the economic and financial viability of those Territories;

14. *Requests* the Special Committee on the Situation with regard to the Implementation of the Declaration on the Granting of Independence to Colonial Countries and Peoples to continue to examine this question and to report thereon to the General Assembly at its sixty-fourth session.

RECORDED VOTE ON RESOLUTION 63/102:

In favour: Afghanistan, Albania, Algeria, Andorra, Angola, Antigua and Barbuda, Argentina, Armenia, Australia, Austria, Azerbaijan, Bahamas, Bahrain, Bangladesh, Barbados, Belarus, Belgium, Belize, Benin, Bhutan, Bolivia, Bosnia and Herzegovina, Botswana, Brazil, Brunei Darussalam, Bulgaria, Burkina Faso, Burundi, Cambodia, Cameroon, Canada, Cape Verde, Central African Republic, Chile, China, Colombia, Comoros, Congo, Costa Rica, Côte d'Ivoire, Croatia, Cuba, Cyprus, Czech Republic, Democratic People's Republic of Korea, Denmark, Djibouti, Dominica, Dominican Republic, Ecuador, Egypt, El Salvador, Eritrea, Estonia, Ethiopia, Fiji, Finland, Gabon, Georgia, Germany, Ghana, Greece, Grenada, Guatemala, Guinea, Guinea-Bissau, Guyana, Haiti, Honduras, Hungary, Iceland, India, Indonesia, Iran, Iraq, Ireland, Italy, Jamaica, Japan, Jordan, Kazakhstan, Kenya, Kuwait, Kyrgyzstan, Lao People's Democratic Republic, Latvia, Lebanon, Lesotho, Liberia, Libyan Arab Jamahiriya, Liechtenstein, Lithuania, Luxembourg, Madagascar, Malawi, Malaysia, Maldives, Mali, Malta, Marshall Islands, Mauritania, Mauritius, Mexico, Micronesia, Moldova, Mongolia, Montenegro, Morocco, Mozambique, Myanmar, Namibia, Nauru, Nepal, Netherlands, New Zealand, Nicaragua, Niger, Nigeria, Norway, Oman, Pakistan, Palau, Panama, Papua New Guinea, Paraguay, Peru, Philippines, Poland, Portugal, Qatar, Republic of Korea, Romania, Russian Federation, Rwanda, Saint Lucia, Saint Vincent and the Grenadines, Samoa, San Marino, Sao Tome and Principe, Saudi Arabia, Senegal, Serbia, Singapore, Slovakia, Slovenia, Solomon Islands, Somalia, South Africa, Spain, Sri Lanka, Sudan, Suriname, Swaziland, Sweden, Switzerland, Syrian Arab Republic, Tajikistan, Thailand, The former Yugoslav Republic of Macedonia, Timor-Leste, Togo, Tonga, Trinidad and Tobago, Tunisia, Turkey, Turkmenistan, Tuvalu, Uganda, Ukraine, United Arab Emirates, United Republic of Tanzania, Uruguay, Uzbekistan, Vanuatu, Venezuela, Viet Nam, Yemen, Zambia, Zimbabwe.

Against: Israel, United States.

Abstaining: France, United Kingdom.

Dissemination of information

In May [A/63/23], the Special Committee on decolonization held consultations with representatives of the UN Department of Political Affairs and DPI on the dissemination of information on decolonization. It also considered a report of the Secretary-General on the subject covering the period from April 2007 to March 2008 [A/AC.109/2008/18].

GENERAL ASSEMBLY ACTION

On 5 December [meeting 64], the General Assembly, on the recommendation of the Fourth Committee [A/63/408], adopted **resolution 63/109** by recorded vote (177-3-1) [agenda item 37].

Dissemination of information on decolonization

The General Assembly,

Having examined the chapter of the report of the Special Committee on the Situation with regard to the Implementation of the Declaration on the Granting of Independence to Colonial Countries and Peoples relating to the dissemination of information on decolonization and publicity for the work of the United Nations in the field of decolonization,

Recalling General Assembly resolution 1514(XV) of 14 December 1960, containing the Declaration on the Granting of Independence to Colonial Countries and Peoples, and other resolutions and decisions of the United Nations concerning the dissemination of information on decolonization, in particular Assembly resolution 62/119 of 17 December 2007,

Recognizing the need for flexible, practical and innovative approaches towards reviewing the options of self-determination for the peoples of Non-Self-Governing Territories with a view to implementing the plan of action for the Second International Decade for the Eradication of Colonialism,

Reiterating the importance of dissemination of information as an instrument for furthering the aims of the Declaration, and mindful of the role of world public opinion in effectively assisting the peoples of Non-Self-Governing Territories to achieve self-determination,

Recognizing the role played by the administering Powers in transmitting information to the Secretary-General in accordance with the terms of Article 73 *e* of the Charter of the United Nations,

Recognizing also the role of the Department of Public Information of the Secretariat, through the United Nations information centres, in the dissemination of information at the regional level on the activities of the United Nations,

Welcoming the issuance by the Department of Public Information, in consultation with the United Nations Development Programme, the specialized agencies and the Special Committee, of an information leaflet on assistance programmes available to the Non-Self-Governing Territories,

Aware of the role of non-governmental organizations in the dissemination of information on decolonization,

1. *Approves* the activities in the field of dissemination of information on decolonization undertaken by the Department of Public Information and the Department of Political Affairs of the Secretariat, in accordance with the relevant resolutions of the United Nations on decolonization, in particular the preparation, in accordance with General Assembly resolution 61/129 of 14 December 2006, of the information leaflet entitled "What the UN Can Do to Assist Non-Self-Governing Territories", issued in March 2007, and encourages wide dissemination of the information leaflet;

2. *Considers it important* to continue and expand its efforts to ensure the widest possible dissemination of information on decolonization, with particular emphasis on the options of self-determination available for the peoples of Non-Self-Governing Territories, and to this end, requests the Department of Public Information to empower the United Nations information centres in the relevant regions to disseminate material to the Non-Self-Governing Territories;

3. *Requests* the Secretary-General to further enhance the information provided on the United Nations decolonization website by including the full series of reports of the regional seminars on decolonization, the statements and scholarly papers presented at those seminars and links to the full series of reports of the Special Committee on the Situation with regard to the Implementation of the Dec-

laration on the Granting of Independence to Colonial Countries and Peoples;

4. *Requests* the Department of Public Information to continue its efforts to update web-based information on the assistance programmes available to the Non-Self-Governing Territories;

5. *Requests* the Department of Political Affairs and the Department of Public Information to implement the recommendations of the Special Committee and to continue their efforts to take measures through all the media available, including publications, radio and television, as well as the Internet, to give publicity to the work of the United Nations in the field of decolonization and, inter alia:

(a) To develop procedures to collect, prepare and disseminate, particularly to the Territories, basic material on the issue of self-determination of the peoples of the Non-Self-Governing Territories;

(b) To seek the full cooperation of the administering Powers in the discharge of the tasks referred to above;

(c) To explore the idea of a programme of collaboration with the decolonization focal points of territorial Governments, particularly in the Pacific and Caribbean regions, to help improve the exchange of information;

(d) To encourage the involvement of non-governmental organizations in the dissemination of information on decolonization;

(e) To encourage the involvement of Non-Self-Governing Territories in the dissemination of information on decolonization;

(f) To report to the Special Committee on measures taken in the implementation of the present resolution;

6. *Requests* all States, including the administering Powers, to accelerate the dissemination of information referred to in paragraph 2 above;

7. *Requests* the Special Committee to continue to examine this question and to report to the General Assembly at its sixty-fourth session on the implementation of the present resolution.

RECORDED VOTE ON RESOLUTION 63/109:

In favour: Afghanistan, Albania, Algeria, Andorra, Angola, Antigua and Barbuda, Argentina, Armenia, Australia, Austria, Azerbaijan, Bahamas, Bahrain, Bangladesh, Barbados, Belarus, Belgium, Belize, Benin, Bhutan, Bolivia, Bosnia and Herzegovina, Botswana, Brazil, Brunei Darussalam, Bulgaria, Burkina Faso, Burundi, Cambodia, Cameroon, Canada, Cape Verde, Central African Republic, Chile, China, Colombia, Comoros, Congo, Costa Rica, Côte d'Ivoire, Croatia, Cuba, Cyprus, Czech Republic, Democratic People's Republic of Korea, Denmark, Djibouti, Dominica, Dominican Republic, Ecuador, Egypt, El Salvador, Eritrea, Estonia, Ethiopia, Fiji, Finland, Gabon, Georgia, Germany, Ghana, Greece, Grenada, Guatemala, Guinea, Guinea-Bissau, Guyana, Haiti, Honduras, Hungary, Iceland, India, Indonesia, Iran, Iraq, Ireland, Italy, Jamaica, Japan, Jordan, Kazakhstan, Kenya, Kuwait, Kyrgyzstan, Lao People's Democratic Republic, Latvia, Lebanon, Lesotho, Liberia, Libyan Arab Jamahiriya, Liechtenstein, Lithuania, Luxembourg, Madagascar, Malawi, Malaysia, Maldives, Mali, Malta, Marshall Islands, Mauritania, Mauritius, Mexico, Moldova, Monaco, Mongolia, Montenegro, Morocco, Mozambique, Myanmar, Namibia, Nauru, Nepal, Netherlands, New Zealand, Nicaragua, Niger, Nigeria, Norway, Oman, Pakistan, Panama, Papua New Guinea, Paraguay, Peru, Philippines, Poland, Portugal, Qatar, Republic of Korea, Romania, Russian Federation, Rwanda, Saint Lucia, Saint Vincent and the Grenadines, Samoa, San Marino, Sao Tome and Principe, Saudi Arabia, Senegal, Serbia, Singapore, Slovakia, Slovenia, Solomon Islands, Somalia, South Africa, Spain, Sri Lanka, Sudan, Suriname, Swaziland, Sweden, Switzerland, Syrian Arab Republic, Tajikistan, Thailand, The former Yugoslav Republic of Macedonia, Timor-Leste, Togo, Tonga, Trinidad and Tobago, Tunisia, Turkey, Tuvalu, Uganda, Ukraine, United Arab Emirates, United Republic of Tanzania, Uruguay, Uzbekistan, Vanuatu, Venezuela, Viet Nam, Yemen, Zambia, Zimbabwe.

Against: Israel, United Kingdom, United States.

Abstaining: France.

Information on Territories

In response to General Assembly resolution 62/112 [YUN 2007, p. 618], the Secretary-General submitted a March report [A/63/65] indicating the dates of transmittal of information on economic, social and educational conditions in NSGTs for 2007, under Article 73 *e* of the Charter of the United Nations.

GENERAL ASSEMBLY ACTION

On 5 December [meeting 64], the General Assembly, on the recommendation of the Fourth Committee [A/63/404], adopted **resolution 63/101** by recorded vote (177-0-4) [agenda item 33].

Information from Non-Self-Governing Territories transmitted under Article 73 *e* of the Charter of the United Nations

The General Assembly,

Recalling its resolution 1970(XVIII) of 16 December 1963, in which it requested the Special Committee on the Situation with regard to the Implementation of the Declaration on the Granting of Independence to Colonial Countries and Peoples to study the information transmitted to the Secretary-General in accordance with Article 73 *e* of the Charter of the United Nations and to take such information fully into account in examining the situation with regard to the implementation of the Declaration, contained in General Assembly resolution 1514(XV) of 14 December 1960,

Recalling also its resolution 62/112 of 17 December 2007, in which it requested the Special Committee to continue to discharge the functions entrusted to it under resolution 1970(XVIII),

Stressing the importance of timely transmission by the administering Powers of adequate information under Article 73 *e* of the Charter, in particular in relation to the preparation by the Secretariat of the working papers on the Territories concerned,

Having examined the report of the Secretary-General,

1. *Reaffirms* that, in the absence of a decision by the General Assembly itself that a Non-Self-Governing Territory has attained a full measure of self-government in terms of Chapter XI of the Charter of the United Nations, the administering Power concerned should continue to transmit information under Article 73 *e* of the Charter with respect to that Territory;

2. *Requests* the administering Powers concerned, in accordance with their Charter obligations, to transmit or continue to transmit regularly to the Secretary-General for information purposes, subject to such limitation as security and constitutional considerations may require, statistical and other information of a technical nature relating to economic, social and educational conditions in the Territories for which they are respectively responsible, as well as the fullest possible information on political and constitutional developments in the Territories concerned, including the constitution, legislative act or executive order providing for the government of the Territory and the constitutional relationship of the Territory to the administering Power, within a maximum period of six months following the expiration of the administrative year in those Territories;

3. *Requests* the Secretary-General to continue to ensure that adequate information is drawn from all available published sources in connection with the preparation of the working papers relating to the Territories concerned;

4. *Requests* the Special Committee on the Situation with regard to the Implementation of the Declaration on the Granting of Independence to Colonial Countries and Peoples to continue to discharge the functions entrusted to it under General Assembly resolution 1970(XVIII), in accordance with established procedures.

RECORDED VOTE ON RESOLUTION 63/101:

In favour: Afghanistan, Algeria, Andorra, Angola, Antigua and Barbuda, Argentina, Armenia, Australia, Austria, Azerbaijan, Bahamas, Bahrain, Bangladesh, Barbados, Belarus, Belgium, Belize, Benin, Bhutan, Bolivia, Bosnia and Herzegovina, Botswana, Brazil, Brunei Darussalam, Bulgaria, Burkina Faso, Burundi, Cambodia, Cameroon, Canada, Cape Verde, Central African Republic, Chile, China, Colombia, Comoros, Congo, Costa Rica, Côte d'Ivoire, Croatia, Cuba, Cyprus, Czech Republic, Democratic People's Republic of Korea, Denmark, Djibouti, Dominica, Dominican Republic, Ecuador, Egypt, El Salvador, Eritrea, Estonia, Ethiopia, Fiji, Finland, Gabon, Georgia, Germany, Ghana, Greece, Grenada, Guatemala, Guinea, Guinea-Bissau, Guyana, Haiti, Honduras, Hungary, Iceland, India, Indonesia, Iran, Iraq, Ireland, Italy, Jamaica, Japan, Jordan, Kazakhstan, Kenya, Kuwait, Kyrgyzstan, Lao People's Democratic Republic, Latvia, Lebanon, Lesotho, Liberia, Libyan Arab Jamahiriya, Liechtenstein, Lithuania, Luxembourg, Madagascar, Malawi, Malaysia, Maldives, Mali, Malta, Marshall Islands, Mauritania, Mauritius, Mexico, Micronesia, Moldova, Mongolia, Montenegro, Morocco, Mozambique, Myanmar, Namibia, Nauru, Nepal, Netherlands, New Zealand, Nicaragua, Niger, Nigeria, Norway, Oman, Pakistan, Palau, Panama, Papua New Guinea, Paraguay, Peru, Philippines, Poland, Portugal, Qatar, Republic of Korea, Romania, Russian Federation, Saint Lucia, Saint Vincent and the Grenadines, Samoa, San Marino, Sao Tome and Principe, Saudi Arabia, Senegal, Serbia, Singapore, Slovakia, Slovenia, Solomon Islands, Somalia, South Africa, Spain, Sri Lanka, Sudan, Suriname, Swaziland, Sweden, Switzerland, Syrian Arab Republic, Tajikistan, Thailand, The former Yugoslav Republic of Macedonia, Timor-Leste, Togo, Tonga, Trinidad and Tobago, Tunisia, Turkey, Turkmenistan, Tuvalu, Uganda, Ukraine, United Arab Emirates, United Republic of Tanzania, Uruguay, Uzbekistan, Venezuela, Viet Nam, Yemen, Zambia, Zimbabwe.

Against: None.

Abstaining: France, Israel, United Kingdom, United States.

Study and training

In response to General Assembly resolution 62/115 [YUN 2007, p. 619], the Secretary-General submitted a March report [A/63/67] on offers of study scholarships and training facilities for inhabitants of NSGTs during the period from 29 March 2007 to 20 March 2008 by the following Member States: Argentina, Australia, Cuba, Japan, Malaysia, the United Kingdom and the United States; and one non-member: the Holy See. Over the years, a total of 59 Member States and one non-member State had made such offers.

GENERAL ASSEMBLY ACTION

On 5 December [meeting 64], the General Assembly, on the recommendation of the Fourth Committee [A/63/407], adopted **resolution 63/104** without vote [agenda item 36].

Offers by Member States of study and training facilities for inhabitants of Non-Self-Governing Territories

The General Assembly,

Recalling its resolution 62/115 of 17 December 2007,

Having examined the report of the Secretary-General on offers by Member States of study and training facilities for inhabitants of Non-Self-Governing Territories, prepared pursuant to its resolution 845(IX) of 22 November 1954,

Conscious of the importance of promoting the educational advancement of the inhabitants of Non-Self-Governing Territories,

Strongly convinced that the continuation and expansion of offers of scholarships is essential in order to meet the increasing need of students from Non-Self-Governing Territories for educational and training assistance, and considering that students in those Territories should be encouraged to avail themselves of such offers,

1. *Takes note* of the report of the Secretary-General;

2. *Expresses its appreciation* to those Member States that have made scholarships available to the inhabitants of Non-Self-Governing Territories;

3. *Invites* all States to make or continue to make generous offers of study and training facilities to the inhabitants of those Territories that have not yet attained self-government or independence and, wherever possible, to provide travel funds to prospective students;

4. *Urges* the administering Powers to take effective measures to ensure the widespread and continuous dissemination in the Territories under their administration of information relating to offers of study and training facilities made by States and to provide all the necessary facilities to enable students to avail themselves of such offers;

5. *Requests* the Secretary-General to report to the General Assembly at its sixty-fourth session on the implementation of the present resolution;

6. *Draws the attention* of the Special Committee on the Situation with regard to the Implementation of the Declaration on the Granting of Independence to Colonial Countries and Peoples to the present resolution.

Visiting Missions

In May [A/63/23], the Special Committee on decolonization considered the question of sending visiting missions to NSGTs. It adopted a resolution in which it stressed the need to dispatch periodic visiting missions to facilitate the full implementation of the 1960 Declaration on decolonization, and called on administering Powers to receive those missions in the Territories under their administration. It also requested the administering Powers to cooperate with the Special Committee in exploring the possibility of undertaking visiting or special missions in furtherance of the decolonization mandate of the General Assembly. The Committee Chair was asked to consult with the administering Powers concerned and report on the results.

In June, the Special Committee recommended to the General Assembly for adoption draft resolutions on 11 small NSGTs (see p. 677) and on Tokelau (see p. 675), endorsing a number of conclusions and recommendations concerning the sending of visiting and special missions to those Territories.

Puerto Rico

In accordance with the Special Committee's 2007 resolution concerning the self-determination and independence of Puerto Rico [YUN 2007, p. 620], the Committee's Rapporteur, in March [A/AC.109/2008/L.3], provided information on Puerto Rico, including recent political, military and economic developments and UN action.

Following its usual practice, the Committee [A/63/23] acceded to requests for hearings from representatives of a number of organizations, which presented their views on 9 June [A/AC.109/2008/SR.4,5]. The Committee adopted a resolution by which it reaffirmed the inalienable right of the people of Puerto Rico to self-determination and independence; urged the United States to return the occupied land and installations on Vieques Island and in Ceiba to the people of Puerto Rico and to respect fundamental human rights, such as the right to health and economic development; and requested the General Assembly to consider the question of Puerto Rico. The Rapporteur was requested to report in 2009 on the resolution's implementation.

Territories under review

Falkland Islands (Malvinas)

The Special Committee on decolonization, in considering the question of the Falkland Islands (Malvinas) on 12 June [A/63/23], had before it a Secretariat working paper on the Territory [A/AC.109/2008/13] that addressed constitutional and political developments, mine clearance, economic and social conditions and participation in international organizations and arrangements. The Committee heard two representatives of the Territory and two petitioners [A/AC.109/2008/SR.7], and adopted a resolution requesting Argentina and the United Kingdom to consolidate the process of dialogue and cooperation by resuming negotiations to find a peaceful solution to the sovereignty dispute relating to the Territory as soon as possible.

Argentina, in a 3 January letter to the Secretary-General [A/62/639], recalled its objective of recovering full sovereignty over the Malvinas Islands, South Georgia and the South Sandwich Islands and surrounding maritime areas in accordance with the principles of international law. On the understanding that cooperation on practical aspects of the dispute would help create a climate favourable to the resumption of negotiations, Argentina had reached bilateral understandings with the United Kingdom. However, Argentina considered the United Kingdom's readiness to take unilateral actions concerning the Territory, and its refusal to address the question of sovereignty, to be unjustified and contrary to bilateral cooperation. It suggested that both countries jointly analyse all the bilateral understandings in light of their goals, and reiterated its permanent willingness to resume bilateral negotiations with a view to settling the sovereignty dispute.

In a 16 January response [A/62/660], the United Kingdom stated that it had no doubt about its sovereignty over the Falkland Islands, South Georgia and the South Sandwich Islands and their surrounding maritime areas, and rejected Argentina's claim to sovereignty. It said that its position was underlined by the principle of self-determination enshrined in the Charter of the United Nations, and no negotiation on the sovereignty of the Falkland Islands was warranted unless and until such time as the Territory's inhabitants so wished. Additionally, the United Kingdom believed that there were opportunities for cooperation in the South Atlantic under the sovereignty formula established in the United Kingdom-Argentina Joint Statement of 19 October 1989 [YUN 1989, p. 766], which would benefit both parties. A number of proposals had been made, and the United Kingdom remained interested in fostering a constructive relationship with Argentina.

On 10 April [A/HRC/8/G/1], Argentina transmitted to the President of the Human Rights Council a letter in which it rejected sections of a national report of the United Kingdom [A/HRC/WG.6/1/GBR/1], because the Falkland Islands, South Georgia and the South Sandwich Islands were designated therein as "Overseas Territories". It reiterated the fact that, as an integral part of Argentine national territory, the Malvinas Islands, South Georgia and the South Sandwich Islands were illegally occupied by the United Kingdom and formed the subject of a recognized sovereignty dispute between the two countries. Argentina's aforementioned rejection extended to the United Kingdom's efforts to apply its human rights obligations and instruments to the Islands in question, noting that the illegal occupation of those Territories prevented Argentina from reporting on the application of the human rights instruments to which it was party throughout its national territory.

In a 1 July letter [A/62/900] to the Secretary-General, Argentina referred to the agenda item of the ninth meeting of the United Nations Open-ended Informal Consultative Process on Oceans and the Law of the Sea concerning progress made on the state of the marine environment. An analysis of that progress, as called for in General Assembly resolution 60/30 [YUN 2005, p. 1436], was conducted on 26 June. The result was a progress report containing a table of ocean regions, which included the "South West Atlantic Ocean" region. Argentina pointed out that the United Kingdom was listed among the coastal States for that region, inferring a reference to the Malvinas Islands, and rejected the contents of the document, particularly the authors' attempt to consider the Malvinas Islands as a possession of the United Kingdom.

In a 13 October [A/63/485] response to the Secretary-General, the United Kingdom rejected the contents of Argentina's letter and the claim that the Falkland Islands, South Georgia and the South Sandwich Islands were an integral part of Argentina's national territory.

Addressing the General Assembly on 23 September [A/63/PV.5], Argentina's President Cristina Fernández de Kirchner raised the Malvinas Islands question in the context of the need to face the twenty-first century without colonial enclaves. Despite the resolutions and measures taken by the Assembly to encourage negotiations between the two parties, the President stated that the United Kingdom refused to discuss it with Argentina and asked the Assembly to cooperate in urging the United Kingdom to comply with international law and demonstrate its seriousness in wishing to build a different world. In reply, the United Kingdom, in a 29 September letter [A/63/462] to the president of the Assembly, said that the Falkland Islands were not a colonial enclave and the overseas territories of the United Kingdom were British for as long as they wanted to remain British. Accordingly, the people of the Falkland Islands had chosen to retain their link with the United Kingdom and did not wish for any change in their status, as expressed by the democratically elected representatives of the Islands when they visited the United Nations for the Special Committee on decolonization's consideration of the question in 2008.

A 10 November letter [A/63/542] from Argentina to the Secretary-General contained a note to the United Kingdom and a press release, both dated 6 November. The contents referred to a unilateral act performed by the United Kingdom whereby it claimed to have adopted a new constitution for the Malvinas Islands. Argentina protested against that act in relation to what it called an integral part of its national territory that was subject to a sovereignty dispute. For Argentina, the act constituted an expression of disregard for the resolutions adopted by the General Assembly and the Special Committee on decolonization calling for resumed negotiations to reach a solution to the dispute. In particular, it constituted a new violation of Assembly resolution 31/49 [YUN 1976, p. 747], which called on parties to refrain from unilateral modifications while the Islands were going through processes recommended by the Assembly resolutions. Argentina also reaffirmed its sovereignty rights over the Malvinas Islands, South Georgia and the South Sandwich Islands.

On 3 December [A/63/589], the United Kingdom rejected Argentina's assertion that its Falkland Islands Constitution Order 2008 was contrary to any aspect of the Joint Statements agreed between the two parties to the dispute [YUN 1989, p. 766; YUN 1990, p. 918]. The formula on sovereignty agreed to by both States was designed to enable the re-establishment of diplomatic relations between the United Kingdom and Argentina, while protecting both countries' positions on the sovereignty of the Falkland Islands. The formula, as understood by the United Kingdom, would enable practical cooperation in the South Atlantic, but neither of the Joint Statements made reference to negotiations on sovereignty. Also rejected by the United Kingdom was Argentina's assertion that the Constitution Order contravened any General Assembly resolutions.

On 24 December, the General Assembly decided that the agenda item on the question of the Falkland Islands (Malvinas) would remain for consideration during its resumed sixty-third (2009) session (**decision 63/552**).

Gibraltar

The Special Committee on decolonization considered the question of Gibraltar on 18 June [A/63/23]. Before it was a Secretariat working paper describing political developments and economic and social conditions in the Territory, and presenting the positions of the United Kingdom (the administering Power), Gibraltar and Spain concerning Gibraltar's future status [A/AC.109/2008/8 & Corr.1].

Central to the territorial dispute in 2008 was the entry into force, on 2 January 2007, of a new constitution—the Gibraltar Constitution Order 2006—approved by the people of the Territory in a 2006 referendum [YUN 2006, p. 714]. The Constitution gave Gibraltar power of self-governance, except in relation to external affairs, defence and certain aspects of policing and civil service. For nationality purposes, Gibraltar remained listed as a British Overseas Territory in the British Nationality Act of 1981, as amended by the British Overseas Territory Act 2002 [YUN 2002, p. 569]. Gibraltar and the United Kingdom, on one hand, and, on the other, Spain differed as to the significance of the new constitution for the decolonization process [YUN 2007, p. 622].

Addressing the Special Committee on decolonization on 18 June [A/AC.109/2008/SR.9], Spain reaffirmed that the question of Gibraltar involved both a sovereignty dispute and a dispute over the Territory's geographical boundaries, and that, in the case of Gibraltar, the decolonization and sovereignty disputes were inextricably linked. Spain remained committed to the Trilateral Forum for Dialogue on Gibraltar [YUN 2004, p. 606], but noted that the Forum was not for discussing sovereignty issues and that the Constitution Order 2006 could not be recognized by the United Nations as the final resolution of Gibraltar's decolonization process.

At the same meeting, Gibraltar's Chief Minister said that, according to UN doctrine and international law, decolonization could be brought about only through application of the principle of self-determination. Furthermore, and despite the statement made by Spain, no rule existed which enabled decolonization to be carried out other than by self-determination in the case of a sovereignty dispute. An appeal was made to the Special Committee to clarify whether its mandate was to promote and defend the sovereignty claim of the territorial claimant, or the rights and aspirations of its people. In that regard, the Chief Minister questioned how the Special Committee viewed Gibraltar's status in light of the dispute: if it considered Gibraltar to be pending decolonization, then it should apply the principle of self-determination; if, on the other hand, it considered it to be an occupied territory subject to a sovereignty dispute, it should delist Gibraltar, as it had no mandate to deal with such disputes. Under those circumstances, Gibraltar no longer looked to the Committee to help bring about its decolonization, and it was left with no choice than to claim its own self-determination, demonstrated by its acceptance of the new constitutional relationship with the United Kingdom. Gibraltar, too, remained committed to the Forum for Dialogue.

A Secretariat working paper [A/AC.109/2009/15] reported that on 2 July, a ministerial meeting of the Forum for Dialogue on Gibraltar took place in London. The parties reviewed progress in the implementation of the Cordoba Statements [YUN 2006, p. 714] and endorsed future objectives, encompassing cooperation on the environment; maritime communications; judicial, customs and police cooperation; financial services and taxation; and visa-related issues and education. The Forum met again in Gibraltar from 29 to 31 October at the non-ministerial level and worked on drafting documents with objectives for cooperation in the areas mentioned above.

Speaking before the Fourth Committee on 7 October [A/C.4/63/SR.3], Spain reiterated that, as recognized by UN resolutions, the colonial status of Gibraltar violated the UN Charter because it undermined Spain's territorial integrity. In the case of Gibraltar, it was also General Assembly doctrine that decolonization could occur only after the sovereignty issues were resolved. With reference to the Brussels Process [YUN 1984, p. 1075], Spain said that it had repeatedly expressed its willingness to resume negotiations, but no bilateral meeting had taken place since 2002. It did not accept the United Kingdom's claims that its 2006 constitutional decree towards Gibraltar had made the fulfilment of earlier UN resolutions moot, and that it was justified in not resuming negotiations because it had committed to the people of Gibraltar not to reach understandings on sovereignty without their consent. In view of the sovereignty dispute, the related issue of Spain's territorial integrity and the UN position that Gibraltar's decolonization could only result from bilateral negotiations between Spain and the United Kingdom, the principle of self-determination did not apply in the case of Gibraltar.

At the same meeting, Gibraltar's Chief Minister asserted that the question of Gibraltar was no longer a question of decolonization, as that was settled by means of the new constitution approved in a referendum of self-determination. Gibraltar's decolonization model was different from that chosen by most colonial territories in the past, namely sovereign independence. It had opted for the best model for itself. Gibraltar considered itself a victim of the Special Committee's application of the "invented doctrine" that in case of a sovereignty dispute affecting a Territory, the principle of self-determination did not apply to the decolonization process, and that the supposed national integrity of a claimant country was an acceptable decolonization consideration, regardless of the wishes of the colonial people. The Special Committee was not mandated to deal with sovereignty disputes, so Gibraltar had broken ties with the Committee and acted alone to achieve decolonization. The Assembly was therefore urged to remove Gibraltar from its list of NSGTs.

At the same meeting, the United Kingdom regretted that the Special Committee's outdated approach did not allow for the acceptance of the 2006 Constitution by Gibraltar to be recognized. The criteria used by the Committee to determine whether an NSGT should be delisted failed to take into account the modernized relationship between the United Kingdom and Gibraltar, non-colonial in nature. The Constitution confirmed the right to self-determination of the Gibraltarian people, and the United Kingdom retained its international responsibility for Gibraltar, in accord with the wishes of its people. The United Kingdom did not accept that the principle of territorial integrity had ever been applicable to Gibraltar's decolonization, or that the existence of a sovereignty dispute implied that its people did not have the right to self-determination. It reaffirmed its commitment to never enter into arrangements under which Gibraltar would pass under the sovereignty of another State against its wishes, and welcomed the continued progress of the trilateral process of dialogue.

By **decision 63/525** of 5 December, the General Assembly urged Spain and the United Kingdom to reach, in the spirit of the 27 November 1984 statement on Gibraltar [YUN 1984, p. 1075], a definitive solution to the question of Gibraltar, in the light of the relevant Assembly resolutions and applicable principles, and in the spirit of the UN Charter. It also welcomed the successful implementation of the first package of measures concluded at the Forum for Dialogue on Gibraltar [YUN 2006, p. 714] and the will to reach new agreements by July 2009.

New Caledonia

The Special Committee on decolonization considered the question of New Caledonia on 23 June [A/63/23]. Before it was a Secretariat working paper [A/AC.109/2008/9] describing the political and socio-economic conditions and developments in the Territory.

The working paper noted that New Caledonia's political and administrative structures had been fundamentally altered by the 1998 Nouméa Accord on the future status of the Territory, signed in 1998 by France (the administering Power), the pro-independence coalition Front de libération national kanak socialiste (FLNKS) and the integrationist Rassemblement pour la Calédonie dans la République (RPCR) [YUN 1998, p. 574]. For 25 years, the party system of the Territory was dominated by the anti-independence RPCR, since renamed Rassemblement-Union progressiste mélanesienne (UMP). That dominance ended prior to the Caledonian elections of May 2004 with the emergence of a new party, l'Avenir Ensemble (AE), seen as more supportive of the Nouméa Accord. An addition to the political scene came with the 2007 launch, by the Union for Kanak and Exploited Workers, of a new Labour Party [YUN 2007, p. 623], a pro-independence party focusing on the complete application of the Nouméa Accord, particularly regarding the rights of the indigenous people.

As noted in a later Secretariat working paper [A/AC.109/2009/9], all those parties experienced tensions and internal divisions, heightened in advance or as a result of Territorial elections. The AE candidates' failure to win seats in the June 2007 elections for the French National Assembly [YUN 2007, p. 623] was a divisive factor for that party, which consequently split in two in October 2008.

Following a meeting of the signatories to the Nouméa Accord in December 2007, a statement was issued by the French Prime Minister indicating that the transfer to New Caledonia of the next set of powers was foreseen for 2009. In preparation, 13 working groups were established, one for each power to be transferred. A task force to help New Caledonia's working groups prepare for the transfer was established on 20 February 2008 under the auspices of the High Commissioner, representing France in the Territory. At the seventh meeting of the Committee of Signatories in Paris on 15 December, an agreement was reached on the 2009 transfer of powers.

While on official travel to New Caledonia in May and November 2008, the new French Secretary of State for Overseas, Yves Jégo, appointed in March, reaffirmed France's commitment to implementation of the Nouméa Accord; however, his message and the State's impartial action in the Territory did not reassure the New Caledonian political parties. At a 9 October meeting of the Fourth Committee, representatives of the Kanak people and of FLNKS [A/C.4/63/SR.5] indicated that despite French promises in conjunction with both the Matignon [YUN 1988, p. 742] and Nouméa Accords, the administering Power was not upholding its commitments, and Kanaks remained economically and professionally marginalized, especially in key sectors of society. Attention was drawn to the increasing immigration to the Territory from France and the need for a bill to restrict the right of immigrants to work; the continuing pillage of New Caledonian natural resources; the decision by the French President to regroup military forces in the Pacific in New Caledonia; and the insufficient support for a land tenure agency enabling Kanaks to buy property in suburban areas. As a result, the decolonization process was stalled and France was preventing New Caledonia from achieving sovereignty.

GENERAL ASSEMBLY ACTION

On 5 December [meeting 64], the General Assembly, on the recommendation of the Fourth Committee [A/63/408], adopted **resolution 63/106** without vote [agenda item 37].

Question of New Caledonia

The General Assembly,

Having considered the question of New Caledonia,

Having examined the chapter of the report of the Special Committee on the Situation with regard to the Implementation of the Declaration on the Granting of Independence to Colonial Countries and Peoples relating to New Caledonia,

Reaffirming the right of peoples to self-determination as enshrined in the Charter of the United Nations,

Recalling General Assembly resolutions 1514(XV) of 14 December 1960 and 1541(XV) of 15 December 1960,

Noting the importance of the positive measures being pursued in New Caledonia by the French authorities, in cooperation with all sectors of the population, to promote political, economic and social development in the Territory, including measures in the area of environmental protection and action with respect to drug abuse and trafficking, in order to provide a framework for its peaceful progress to self-determination,

Noting also, in this context, the importance of equitable economic and social development, as well as continued dialogue among the parties involved in New Caledonia in the preparation of the act of self-determination of New Caledonia,

Noting with satisfaction the intensification of contacts between New Caledonia and neighbouring countries of the South Pacific region,

1. *Welcomes* the significant developments that have taken place in New Caledonia since the signing of the Nouméa Accord of 5 May 1998 by the representatives of New Caledonia and the Government of France;

2. *Urges* all the parties involved, in the interest of all the people of New Caledonia, to maintain, in the framework of the Nouméa Accord, their dialogue in a spirit of harmony;

3. *Notes* the relevant provisions of the Nouméa Accord aimed at taking more broadly into account the Kanak identity in the political and social organization of New Caledonia, and welcomes, in this context, efforts under way towards jointly devising identity symbols for the Territory, such as name, flag, anthem, motto and banknotes, as required under the Nouméa Accord;

4. *Acknowledges* those provisions of the Nouméa Accord relating to control of immigration and protection of local employment, and notes that unemployment remains high among Kanaks and that recruitment of foreign mine workers continues;

5. *Notes* the concerns expressed by a group of indigenous people in New Caledonia regarding their under-representation in the Territory's governmental and social structures;

6. *Takes note* of the relevant provisions of the Nouméa Accord to the effect that New Caledonia may become a member or associate member of certain international organizations, such as international organizations in the Pacific region, the United Nations, the United Nations Educational, Scientific and Cultural Organization and the International Labour Organization, according to their regulations;

7. *Notes* the agreement between the signatories to the Nouméa Accord that the progress made in the emancipation process shall be brought to the attention of the United Nations;

8. *Recalls* the fact that the administering Power invited to New Caledonia, at the time the new institutions were established, a mission of information which comprised representatives of countries of the Pacific region;

9. *Notes* the continuing strengthening of ties between New Caledonia and both the European Union and the European Development Fund in such areas as economic and trade cooperation, the environment, climate change and financial services;

10. *Calls upon* the administering Power to continue to transmit to the Secretary-General information as required under Article 73 *e* of the Charter of the United Nations;

11. *Invites* all the parties involved to continue promoting a framework for the peaceful progress of the Territory towards an act of self-determination in which all options are open and which would safeguard the rights of all sectors of the population, according to the letter and the spirit of the Nouméa Accord, which is based on the principle that it is for the populations of New Caledonia to choose how to control their destiny;

12. *Recalls with satisfaction* the efforts of the French authorities to resolve the question of voter registration by adopting, in the French Congress of Parliament, on 19 February 2007, amendments to the French Constitution allowing New Caledonia to restrict eligibility to vote in local polls to those voters registered on the 1998 electoral rolls when the Nouméa Accord was signed, thus ensuring strong representation of the Kanak population;

13. *Welcomes* all measures taken to strengthen and diversify the New Caledonian economy in all fields, and encourages further such measures in accordance with the spirit of the Matignon and Nouméa Accords;

14. *Also welcomes* the importance attached by the parties to the Matignon and Nouméa Accords to greater progress in housing, employment, training, education and health care in New Caledonia;

15. *Notes* the financial assistance rendered by the Government of France to the Territory in areas such as health, education, payment of public-service salaries and funding development schemes;

16. *Acknowledges* the contribution of the Melanesian Cultural Centre to the protection of the indigenous Kanak culture of New Caledonia;

17. *Notes* the positive initiatives aimed at protecting the natural environment of New Caledonia, including the "Zonéco" operation designed to map and evaluate marine resources within the economic zone of New Caledonia;

18. *Welcomes* the cooperation among Australia, France and New Zealand in terms of surveillance of fishing zones, in accordance with the wishes expressed by France during the France-Oceania Summits in July 2003 and June 2006;

19. *Acknowledges* the close links between New Caledonia and the peoples of the South Pacific and the positive actions being taken by the French and territorial authorities to facilitate the further development of those links, including the development of closer relations with the countries members of the Pacific Islands Forum;

20. *Welcomes*, in this regard, the participation of New Caledonia in the Pacific Islands Forum, following its accession to the Forum as associate member in October 2006, at the 37th Summit of the Forum;

21. *Also welcomes* the continuing high-level visits to New Caledonia by delegations from countries of the Pacific region and high-level visits by delegations from New Caledonia to countries members of the Pacific Islands Forum;

22. *Further welcomes* the cooperative attitude of other States and Territories in the region towards New Caledonia, its economic and political aspirations and its increasing participation in regional and international affairs;

23. *Recalls* the endorsement of the report of the Forum Ministerial Committee on New Caledonia by leaders of the Pacific Islands Forum at its 36th Summit, held in Papua New Guinea in October 2005, and the continuing role of the Forum Ministerial Committee in monitoring developments in the Territory and encouraging closer regional engagements;

24. *Decides* to keep under continuous review the process unfolding in New Caledonia as a result of the signing of the Nouméa Accord;

25. *Requests* the Special Committee on the Situation with regard to the Implementation of the Declaration on the Granting of Independence to Colonial Countries and Peoples to continue the examination of the question of the Non-Self-Governing Territory of New Caledonia and to report thereon to the General Assembly at its sixty-fourth session.

Tokelau

On 23 June, the Special Committee on decolonization considered the question of Tokelau (the three small atolls of Nukunonu, Fakaofo and Atafu in the South Pacific), administered by New Zealand [A/63/23]. Before it was a Secretariat working paper [A/AC.109/2008/1] covering constitutional and political developments, external relations and economic and social conditions in the Territory, and presenting the positions of New Zealand and Tokelau on the Territory's future status.

A later Secretariat working paper [A/AC.109/2009/2] reported on progress in Tokelau's decolonization process in light of referendums on self-determination in 2006 [YUN 2006, p. 717] and 2007 [YUN 2007, p. 625]. The so-called referendum package, or self-determination package, which consisted of the draft treaty and constitution approved by the General Fono (Tokelau's national representative body) in 2005 [YUN 2005, p. 675], formed the basis for the referendums, which took place, in the presence of UN monitoring missions, on the three atolls and in Samoa (the nearest sizeable neighbour to Tokelau) for eligible Tokelauans based there. However, neither referendum produced enough votes in favour to reach the legal threshold for acceptance of the package, and the status of Tokelau as an NSGT remained unchanged. Following the 2007 referendum, the General Fono referred the question on Tokelau's way forward to the Taupulega (the Council of Elders), requested New Zealand to leave the self-determination package on the table and decided that there would be a report, taking into account the views of New Zealand, from the Council of Ongoing Government, which met in the margins of the General Fono and was composed of three Faipule and three Pulenuku (representatives and mayors of each village/atoll, respectively). New Zealand recognized that, on the matter of decolonization, it was Tokelau's decision about how to proceed, and suggested that it might be helpful if several years were allowed to elapse before holding another referendum. The Council of Ongoing Government noted that Tokelau could change the two-thirds majority threshold for the referendum, but should implement measures to ensure that a threshold was supported by a clear majority in each of Tokelau's three villages to guarantee unity. It also noted Tokelau's commitment to self-determination and wish to have a constitution not encompassing the free association self-government provisions, and it therefore directed its legal advisors to make the required amendments.

Addressing the Special Committee on 23 June [A/AC.109/2008/SR.11], Pio Tuia, the Ulu-o-Tokelau (titular head of the Territory, a position rotated annually among the three Faipule), indicated that the General Fono had agreed that a period of reflection was needed. Tokelau remained committed to achieving self-government and, with the assistance of New Zealand, it was directing resources towards the priority areas it had identified. He said that Tokelau, being extremely vulnerable to the effects of climate change, was working on an energy policy that would allow the small atolls to operate on renewable energy, and appealed to the Committee to consider global warming, climate change and rising sea levels as important development concerns regarding Tokelau, and to convey that concern to the General Assembly's sixty-third (2008) session.

Speaking before the Fourth Committee on 10 October [A/C.4/63/SR.6], New Zealand confirmed that it understood the approach of Tokelau in deciding to focus on enhancing core services on the atolls rather than moving to a third referendum. The right to self-determination was fundamental and deserved full support, but needed to be accompanied by opportunities for the development of the full needs of the peoples who sought to exercise that right, and New Zealand was committed to providing those opportunities for the people of Tokelau.

GENERAL ASSEMBLY ACTION

On 5 December [meeting 64], the General Assembly, on the recommendation of the Fourth Committee [A/63/408], adopted **resolution 63/107** [agenda item 37].

Question of Tokelau

The General Assembly,

Having considered the question of Tokelau,

Having examined the chapter of the report of the Special Committee on the Situation with regard to the Implementation of the Declaration on the Granting of Independence to Colonial Countries and Peoples relating to Tokelau,

Recalling its resolution 1514(XV) of 14 December 1960, containing the Declaration on the Granting of Independence to Colonial Countries and Peoples, and all resolutions and decisions of the United Nations relating to Non-Self-Governing Territories, in particular General Assembly resolution 62/121 of 17 December 2007,

Noting with appreciation the continuing exemplary cooperation of New Zealand as the administering Power with regard to the work of the Special Committee relating to Tokelau and its readiness to permit access by United Nations visiting missions to the Territory,

Also noting with appreciation the collaborative contribution to the development of Tokelau by New Zealand and the specialized agencies and other organizations of the United Nations system, in particular the United Nations Development Programme,

Recalling the inauguration in 1996 of a national legislative body, the General Fono, based on village elections by universal adult suffrage and the assumption by that body in June 2003 of full responsibility for the Tokelau budget,

Noting that, as a small island Territory, Tokelau exemplifies the situation of most remaining Non-Self-Governing Territories and that, as a case study pointing to successful cooperation for decolonization, Tokelau has wider significance for the United Nations as it seeks to complete its work in decolonization,

Recalling that New Zealand and Tokelau signed in November 2003 a document entitled "Joint statement of the principles of partnership", which sets out in writing, for the first time, the rights and obligations of the two partner countries,

Bearing in mind the decision of the General Fono at its meeting in November 2003, following extensive consultations undertaken in all three villages, to explore formally with New Zealand the option of self-government in free association and its decision in August 2005 to hold a referendum on self-government on the basis of a draft constitution for Tokelau and a treaty of free association with New Zealand,

1. *Notes* that Tokelau and New Zealand remain firmly committed to the ongoing development of Tokelau for the long-term benefit of the people of Tokelau, with particular emphasis on the further development of facilities on each atoll that meet their current requirements;

2. *Notes also* the ongoing recognition by New Zealand of the complete right of the people of Tokelau to undertake the act of self-determination when this is considered by the people of Tokelau to be appropriate;

3. *Welcomes* the substantial progress made towards the devolution of power to the three taupulega (village councils), in particular the delegation of the Administrator's powers to the three taupulega with effect from 1 July 2004 and the assumption by each taupulega from that date of full responsibility for the management of all its public services;

4. *Recalls* the decision of the General Fono in November 2003, following extensive consultations in all three villages and a meeting of the Special Committee on the Constitution of Tokelau, to explore formally with New Zealand the option of self-government in free association, and the discussions subsequently held between Tokelau and New Zealand pursuant to the decision of the General Fono;

5. *Recalls also* the decision of the General Fono in August 2005 to hold a referendum on self-government on the basis of a draft constitution for Tokelau and a treaty of free association with New Zealand, and notes the enactment by the General Fono of rules for the referendum;

6. *Acknowledges* Tokelau's initiative in devising a strategic economic development plan for the period 2007–2010;

7. *Also acknowledges* the ongoing and consistent commitment of New Zealand to meeting the social and economic requirements of the people of Tokelau, as well as the support and cooperation of the United Nations Development Programme;

8. *Further acknowledges* Tokelau's need for continued support from the international community;

9. *Recalls with satisfaction* the establishment and operation of the Tokelau International Trust Fund to support the future development needs of Tokelau, and calls upon Member States and international and regional agencies to contribute to the Fund and thereby lend practical support to assist this emerging country in overcoming the problems of smallness, isolation and lack of resources;

10. *Welcomes* the assurance of the Government of New Zealand that it will meet its obligations to the United Nations with respect to Tokelau and abide by the freely expressed wishes of the people of Tokelau with regard to their future status;

11. *Also welcomes* the cooperative attitude of the other States and territories in the region towards Tokelau, and their support for its economic and political aspirations and its increasing participation in regional and international affairs;

12. *Calls upon* the administering Power and United Nations agencies to continue to provide assistance to Tokelau as it further develops;

13. *Welcomes* the actions taken by the administering Power to transmit information regarding the political, economic and social situation of Tokelau to the Secretary-General;

14. *Notes with appreciation* the considerable progress made in the negotiation of a draft constitution by New Zealand and Tokelau, as well as the decisions on proposed national symbols by Tokelau, and the steps taken by Tokelau and New Zealand to agree to a draft treaty of free association as a basis for an act of self-determination;

15. *Notes* that a referendum to determine the future status of Tokelau held in February 2006 failed to produce the two-thirds majority of the valid votes cast required by the General Fono to change Tokelau's status from that of a Non-Self-Governing Territory under the administration of New Zealand;

16. *Also notes* the subsequent decision of the General Fono to conduct a further referendum to determine the future status of Tokelau from 20 to 24 October 2007;

17. *Commends* the professional and transparent conduct of both the February 2006 and the October 2007 referendums, monitored by the United Nations;

18. *Notes* that the October 2007 referendum also did not produce the two-thirds majority of the valid votes cast required by the General Fono to change the status of Tokelau from that of a Non-Self-Governing Territory under the administration of New Zealand to that of self-government in free association with New Zealand;

19. *Acknowledges* the decision of the General Fono that consideration of any future act of self-determination by Tokelau will be deferred and that New Zealand and Tokelau will devote renewed effort and attention to ensuring that essential services and infrastructure on the atolls of Tokelau are enhanced and strengthened, thereby ensuring an enhanced quality of life for the people of Tokelau;

20. *Welcomes* the commitment of both Tokelau and New Zealand to continue to work together in the interests of Tokelau and its people, taking into account the principle of the right to self-determination;

21. *Requests* the Special Committee on the Situation with regard to the Implementation of the Declaration on the Granting of Independence to Colonial Countries and Peoples to continue to examine the question of the Non-Self-Governing Territory of Tokelau and to report thereon to the General Assembly at its sixty-fourth session.

Western Sahara

The Special Committee on decolonization considered the question of Western Sahara on 11 June [A/63/23]. A Secretariat working paper [A/AC.109/2008/14] described the Secretary-General's good offices with the parties concerned and actions taken by the General Assembly and the Security Council (see p. 319). The Committee granted a request for hearing to Ahmed Boukhari of the Frente Popular para la Liberación de Saguía el-Hamra y de Río de Oro (Frente POLISARIO), who made a statement at the same meeting [A/AC.109/2008/SR.6].

The Special Committee transmitted the relevant documentation to the Assembly's sixty-third (2008) session to facilitate the Fourth Committee's consideration of the question. The Secretary-General's report [A/63/131] was submitted to the Assembly in July.

By **resolution 63/105** of 5 December (see p. 322), the Assembly supported the process of negotiations initiated by the Council in 2007, with a view to achieving a political solution which would provide for the self-determination of the people of Western Sahara; commended the efforts by the Secretary-General and his Personal Envoy in that respect; and requested the Special Committee to continue to consider the situation in Western Sahara.

Island Territories

On 11 June, the Special Committee on decolonization [A/63/23] considered working papers on American Samoa [A/AC.109/2008/3], Anguilla [A/AC.109/2008/7], Bermuda [A/AC.109/2008/10 & Corr.1], the British Virgin Islands [A/AC.109/2008/2], the Cayman Islands [A/AC.109/2008/11], Guam [A/AC.109/2008/15], Montserrat [A/AC.109/2008/16], Pitcairn [A/AC.109/2008/4], Saint Helena [A/AC.109/2008/6], the Turks and Caicos Islands [A/AC.109/2008/12] and the United States Virgin Islands [A/AC.109/2008/17] that described political developments and economic and social conditions in each of those 11 island Territories. It also heard statements from two petitioners, one addressing the question of Guam and the other the question of the United States Virgin Islands [A/AC.109/2008/SR.6]. The Committee approved a two-part consolidated draft resolution for adoption by the General Assembly (see below).

At its 7 October meeting [A/C.4/63/SR.3] the Fourth Committee heard statements from four petitioners on the question of Guam and one petitioner on the question of the United States Virgin Islands.

GENERAL ASSEMBLY ACTION

On 5 December [meeting 64], the General Assembly, on the recommendation of the Fourth Committee [A/63/408], adopted **resolutions 63/108 A** and **B** without vote [agenda item 37].

Question of American Samoa, Anguilla, Bermuda, the British Virgin Islands, the Cayman Islands, Guam, Montserrat, Pitcairn, Saint Helena, the Turks and Caicos Islands and the United States Virgin Islands

A

General

The General Assembly,

Having considered the questions of the Non-Self-Governing Territories of American Samoa, Anguilla, Bermuda, the British Virgin Islands, the Cayman Islands, Guam, Montserrat, Pitcairn, Saint Helena, the Turks and Caicos Islands and the United States Virgin Islands, hereinafter referred to as "the Territories",

Having examined the relevant chapter of the report of the Special Committee on the Situation with regard to the Implementation of the Declaration on the Granting of Independence to Colonial Countries and Peoples,

Recalling all resolutions and decisions of the United Nations relating to those Territories, including, in particular, the resolutions adopted by the General Assembly at its sixty-second session on the individual Territories covered by the present resolution,

Recognizing that all available options for self-determination of the Territories are valid as long as they are in accordance with the freely expressed wishes of the peoples concerned and in conformity with the clearly defined principles contained in General Assembly resolutions 1514(XV) of 14 December 1960, 1541(XV) of 15 December 1960 and other resolutions of the Assembly,

Recalling its resolution 1541(XV), containing the principles that should guide Member States in determining whether or not an obligation exists to transmit the information called for under Article 73 *e* of the Charter of the United Nations,

Expressing concern that more than forty-seven years after the adoption of the Declaration on the Granting of Independence to Colonial Countries and Peoples, there still remain a number of Non-Self-Governing Territories,

Conscious of the importance of continuing effective implementation of the Declaration, taking into account the target set by the United Nations to eradicate colonialism by 2010 and the plan of action for the Second International Decade for the Eradication of Colonialism,

Recognizing that the specific characteristics and the aspirations of the peoples of the Territories require flexible, practical and innovative approaches to the options of self-determination, without any prejudice to territorial size, geographical location, size of population or natural resources,

Noting the stated position of the Government of the United Kingdom of Great Britain and Northern Ireland, and the stated position of the Government of the United States of America on the Non-Self-Governing Territories under their administration,

Noting also the stated positions of the representatives of the Non-Self-Governing Territories before the Special Committee and in its regional seminars,

Noting further the constitutional developments in some Non-Self-Governing Territories affecting the internal structure of governance about which the Special Committee has received information,

Aware of the importance both to the Territories and to the Special Committee of the participation of elected and appointed representatives of the Territories in the work of the Special Committee,

Convinced that the wishes and aspirations of the peoples of the Territories should continue to guide the development of their future political status and that referendums, free and fair elections and other forms of popular consultation play an important role in ascertaining the wishes and aspirations of the people,

Convinced also that any negotiations to determine the status of a Territory must take place with the active involvement and participation of the people of that Territory, under the aegis of the United Nations, on a case-by-case basis, and that the views of the peoples of the Non-Self-Governing Territories in respect of their right to self-determination should be ascertained,

Noting that a number of Non-Self-Governing Territories have expressed concern at the procedure followed by some administering Powers, contrary to the wishes of the Territories themselves, of amending or enacting legislation for application to the Territories, either through Orders in Council, in order to apply to the Territories the international treaty obligations of the administering Power, or through the unilateral application of laws and regulations,

Aware of the importance of the international financial services sector for the economies of some of the Non-Self-Governing Territories,

Noting the continued cooperation of the Non-Self-Governing Territories at the local and regional levels, including participation in the work of regional organizations,

Mindful that United Nations visiting and special missions provide an effective means of ascertaining the situation in the Territories, that some Territories have not received a United Nations visiting mission for a long time and that no visiting missions have been sent to some of the Territories, and considering the possibility of sending further visiting missions to the Territories at an appropriate time and in consultation with the administering Powers,

Mindful also that, in order for the Special Committee to enhance its understanding of the political status of the peoples of the Territories and to fulfil its mandate effectively, it is important for it to be apprised by the administering Powers and to receive information from other appropriate sources, including the representatives of the Territories, concerning the wishes and aspirations of the peoples of the Territories,

Recognizing the need for the Special Committee to ensure that the appropriate bodies of the United Nations actively pursue a public awareness campaign aimed at assisting the peoples of the Territories in gaining a better understanding of the options of self-determination,

Mindful, in this connection, that the holding of regional seminars in the Caribbean and Pacific regions and at Headquarters, with the active participation of representatives of the Non-Self-Governing Territories, provides a helpful means for the Special Committee to fulfil its mandate, and that the regional nature of the seminars, which alternate between the Caribbean and the Pacific, is a crucial element in the context of a United Nations programme for ascertaining the political status of the Territories,

Mindful also that the 2008 Pacific regional seminar was held in Bandung, Indonesia, from 14 to 16 May,

Conscious of the particular vulnerability of the Territories to natural disasters and environmental degradation, and, in this connection, bearing in mind the applicability to the Territories of the programmes of action of all United Nations world conferences and special sessions of the General Assembly in the economic and social sphere,

Noting with appreciation the contribution to the development of some Territories by the specialized agencies and other organizations of the United Nations system, in particular the United Nations Development Programme, the Economic Commission for Latin America and the Caribbean and the Economic and Social Commission for Asia and the Pacific, as well as regional institutions such as the Caribbean Development Bank, the Caribbean Community, the Organization of Eastern Caribbean States, the Pacific Islands Forum and the agencies of the Council of Regional Organizations in the Pacific,

Aware that the Human Rights Committee, as part of its mandate under the International Covenant on Civil and Political Rights, reviews the status of the self-determination process, including in small island Territories under examination by the Special Committee,

Recalling the ongoing efforts of the Special Committee in carrying out a critical review of its work with the aim of making appropriate and constructive recommendations and decisions to attain its objectives in accordance with its mandate,

Recognizing that the annual background working papers prepared by the Secretariat on developments in each of the small Territories, as well as the substantive documentation and information furnished by experts, scholars, non-governmental organizations and other sources, have provided important inputs to update the present resolution,

1. *Reaffirms* the inalienable right of the peoples of the Territories to self-determination, in conformity with the Charter of the United Nations and with General Assembly resolution 1514(XV), containing the Declaration on the Granting of Independence to Colonial Countries and Peoples;

2. *Also reaffirms* that, in the process of decolonization, there is no alternative to the principle of self-determination, which is also a fundamental human right, as recognized under the relevant human rights conventions;

3. *Further reaffirms* that it is ultimately for the peoples of the Territories themselves to determine freely their future political status in accordance with the relevant provisions of the Charter, the Declaration and the relevant resolutions of the General Assembly, and in that connection reiterates its long-standing call for the administering Powers, in cooperation with the territorial Governments and appropriate bodies of the United Nations system, to develop political education programmes for the Territories in order to foster an awareness among the people of their right to self-determination in conformity with the legitimate political status options, based on the principles clearly defined in General Assembly resolution 1541(XV) and other relevant resolutions and decisions;

4. *Requests* the administering Powers to transmit regularly to the Secretary-General information called for under Article 73 *e* of the Charter;

5. *Stresses* the importance of the Special Committee being apprised of the views and wishes of the peoples of the Territories and enhancing its understanding of their conditions, including the nature and scope of the existing political and constitutional arrangements between the Non-Self-Governing Territories and their respective administering Powers;

6. *Reaffirms* the responsibility of the administering Powers under the Charter to promote the economic and social development and to preserve the cultural identity of the Territories, and recommends that priority continue to be given, in consultation with the territorial Governments concerned, to the strengthening and diversification of their respective economies;

7. *Requests* the Territories and the administering Powers to take all measures necessary to protect and conserve the environment of the Territories against any degradation, and once again requests the specialized agencies concerned to continue to monitor environmental conditions in the Territories and to provide assistance to those Territories, consistent with their prevailing rules of procedure;

8. *Welcomes* the participation of the Non-Self-Governing Territories in regional activities, including the work of regional organizations;

9. *Stresses* the importance of implementing the plan of action for the Second International Decade for the Eradication of Colonialism, in particular by expediting the application of the work programme for the decolonization of each Non-Self-Governing Territory, on a case-by-case basis, as well as by ensuring that periodic analyses are undertaken of the progress and extent of the implementation of the Declaration in each Territory, and that the working papers prepared by the Secretariat on each Territory should fully reflect developments in those Territories;

10. *Calls upon* the administering Powers to participate in and cooperate fully with the work of the Special Committee in order to implement the provisions of Article 73 *e* of the Charter and the Declaration, and in order to advise the Special Committee on the implementation of provisions under Article 73 *b* of the Charter on efforts to promote self-government in the Territories, and encourages the administering Powers to facilitate visiting and special missions to the Territories;

11. *Urges* Member States to contribute to the efforts of the United Nations to usher in a world free of colonialism within the Second International Decade for the Eradication of Colonialism, and calls upon them to continue to give their full support to the Special Committee in its endeavours towards that noble goal;

12. *Stresses* the importance of the constitutional reviews in the respective Territories administered by the United Kingdom of Great Britain and Northern Ireland and the United States of America, and led by the territorial Governments, designed to address internal constitutional structures within the present territorial arrangements, and decides to follow closely the developments concerning the future political status of those Territories;

13. *Requests* the Secretary-General to report to the General Assembly at its sixty-fourth session on the implementation of decolonization resolutions adopted since the declaration of the First and Second International Decades for the Eradication of Colonialism;

14. *Reiterates its request* that the Human Rights Committee collaborate with the Special Committee, within the framework of its mandate on the right to self-determination as contained in the International Covenant on Civil and Political Rights, with the aim of exchanging information, given that the Human Rights Committee is mandated to review the situation, including political and constitutional developments, in many of the Non-Self-Governing Territories that are within the purview of the Special Committee;

15. *Requests* the Special Committee to collaborate with the Economic and Social Council and its relevant subsidiary intergovernmental bodies, within the framework of their respective mandates, with the aim of exchanging information on developments in those Non-Self-Governing Territories which are reviewed by those bodies;

16. *Also requests* the Special Committee to continue to examine the question of the Non-Self-Governing Territories and to report thereon to the General Assembly at its sixty-fourth session and on the implementation of the present resolution.

B

Individual Territories

The General Assembly,

Referring to resolution A above,

I

American Samoa

Taking note of the working paper prepared by the Secretariat on American Samoa and other relevant information,

Aware that under United States law the Secretary of the Interior has administrative jurisdiction over American Samoa,

Noting the position of the administering Power and the statements made by representatives of American Samoa in regional seminars expressing satisfaction with the Territory's present relationship with the United States of America,

Aware of the work of the Future Political Status Study Commission, completed in 2006, and the release of its report, with recommendations, in January 2007, to help the Territory study alternative forms of future political status open to American Samoa and to assess the advantages and disadvantages of each,

Noting, in that regard, the information contained in the paper provided by the Chairman of the Future Political Status Study Commission and distributed at the 2008 Pacific regional seminar requesting the Special Committee to review the Territory's status as a Non-Self-Governing Territory, with a view to accepting the Territory's future political status once chosen by its people,

Aware that American Samoa continues to be the only United States Territory to receive financial assistance from the administering Power for the operations of the territorial Government, and calling upon the administering Power to assist the territorial Government in the diversification of its economy,

1. *Welcomes* the work of the territorial Government and legislature with regard to the recommendations made by the Future Political Status Study Commission in preparation for a constitutional convention addressing issues related to the future status of American Samoa;

2. *Stresses* the importance of the invitation previously extended to the Special Committee by the Governor of American Samoa to send a visiting mission to the Territory, calls upon the administering Power to facilitate such a mission if the territorial Government so desires, and requests the Chairperson of the Special Committee to take all the necessary steps to that end;

3. *Requests* the administering Power to assist the Territory by facilitating its work concerning a public awareness programme recommended by the Future Political Status Study Commission in its 2007 report, consistent with Article 73 *b* of the Charter of the United Nations and, in that regard, calls upon the relevant United Nations organizations to provide assistance to the Territory, if requested;

II

Anguilla

Taking note of the working paper prepared by the Secretariat on Anguilla and other relevant information,

Recalling the holding of the 2003 Caribbean regional seminar in Anguilla, hosted by the territorial Government and made possible by the administering Power, the first time that the seminar had been held in a Non-Self-Governing Territory,

Taking note of the internal constitutional review process resumed by the territorial Government in 2006, the work of the Constitutional and Electoral Reform Commission, which prepared its report in August 2006, and the holding of public and other consultative meetings in 2007 on proposed constitutional amendments to be presented to the administering Power, as well as of the territorial Government's recent decision to revisit the recommendations of the Commission, in order to move the process forward, with the aim of seeking full internal self-government,

Aware that the Government intends to continue its commitment to high-end tourism and the implementation of various regulations in the financial services sector,

Noting the participation of the Territory as an associate member in the Caribbean Community, the Organization of Eastern Caribbean States and the Economic Commission for Latin America and the Caribbean,

1. *Welcomes* the work of the Constitutional and Electoral Reform Commission and its report of 2006, the holding of public and other consultative meetings in 2007, with the aim of making recommendations to the administering Power on proposed changes to the Constitution of the Territory and the subsequent efforts of the territorial Government to advance the internal constitutional review exercise;

2. *Stresses* the importance of the previously expressed desire of the territorial Government for a visiting mission by the Special Committee, calls upon the administering Power to facilitate such a mission, if the territorial Government so desires, and requests the Chairperson of the Special Committee to take all the necessary steps to that end;

3. *Requests* the administering Power to assist the Territory by facilitating its work concerning public consultative outreach efforts, consistent with Article 73 *b* of the Charter of the United Nations and, in that regard, calls upon the relevant United Nations organizations to provide assistance to the Territory, if requested;

III

Bermuda

Taking note of the working paper prepared by the Secretariat on Bermuda and other relevant information,

Conscious of the different viewpoints of the political parties on the future status of the Territory, and noting a recent survey by local media on the matter,

Recalling the dispatch of the United Nations special mission to Bermuda in 2005 at the request of the territorial Government and with the concurrence of the administering Power, which provided information to the people of the Territory on the role of the United Nations in the process of self-determination, on the legitimate political status options as clearly defined in General Assembly resolution 1541(XV) and on the experiences of other small States that have achieved a full measure of self-government,

1. *Stresses* the importance of the 2005 report of the Bermuda Independence Commission, which provides a thorough examination of the facts surrounding independence, and regrets that the plans for public meetings and the presentation of a Green Paper to the House of Assembly followed by a White Paper outlining the policy proposals for an independent Bermuda have so far not materialized;

2. *Requests* the administering Power to assist the Territory by facilitating its work concerning public educational outreach efforts, consistent with Article 73 *b* of the Charter of the United Nations and, in that regard, calls upon the relevant United Nations organizations to provide assistance to the Territory, if requested;

IV

British Virgin Islands

Taking note of the working paper prepared by the Secretariat on the British Virgin Islands and other relevant information,

Recalling the 1993 report of the Constitutional Commissioners, the 1996 debate on the report in the Legislative Council of the Territory, the establishment of the Constitutional Review Commission in 2004, the completion in 2005 of its report providing recommendations on internal constitutional modernization and the debate held in 2005 on the report in the Legislative Council, as well as the negotiations between the administering Power and the territorial Government, which resulted in the adoption of the new Constitution of the Territory in 2007,

Noting that the 2007 Constitution of the British Virgin Islands provides for a Governor, who maintains reserved powers in the Territory, to be appointed by the administering Power,

Noting also the statement made by an expert from the Territory at the 2008 Pacific regional seminar, who presented an analysis of the recently concluded constitutional review process,

Noting further that the Territory continues to emerge as a leading offshore financial centre, with unprecedented growth in its financial and tourism services sectors,

Cognizant of the potential usefulness of regional ties for the development of a small island Territory,

1. *Welcomes* the new Constitution of the British Virgin Islands, which took effect in June 2007, and notes the need expressed by the territorial Government for minor constitutional amendments in the years to come;

2. *Requests* the administering Power to assist the Territory by facilitating its work concerning public outreach efforts, consistent with Article 73 *b* of the Charter of the United Nations and, in that regard, calls upon the relevant United Nations organizations to provide assistance to the Territory, if requested;

3. *Welcomes* the efforts made by the Territory to focus its economic base more on local ownership and on professional service industries other than financial services;

4. *Appreciates* the efforts made to continue the work of the Inter-Virgin Islands Council between the elected Governments of the British Virgin Islands and the United States Virgin Islands to advance cooperation between the two neighbouring Territories;

V

Cayman Islands

Taking note of the working paper prepared by the Secretariat on the Cayman Islands and other relevant information,

Aware of the 2002 report of the Constitutional Modernization Review Commission, which contained a draft constitution for the consideration of the people of the Territory, the 2003 draft constitution offered by the administering Power and the subsequent discussions between the Territory and the administering Power in 2003, and the reopening of discussions between the administering Power and the territorial Government on internal constitutional modernization in 2006, with the aim of ascertaining the views of the people by way of referendum,

Noting with interest the establishment of the Cayman Islands Constitutional Review Secretariat, which began its work in March 2007 in support of the Territory's constitution modernization initiative, which comprises four phases with regard to constitutional reform, including research and publicity, consultation and public education, a referendum on reform proposals, and negotiations between the administering Power and the territorial Government,

Acknowledging the indication by the territorial Government that certain cost-of-living issues, such as inflation, continue to be a cause for concern,

1. *Welcomes* the publication by the territorial Government of a consultation paper in January 2008 setting out a number of proposals for constitutional reform, with a view to holding a referendum on those proposals, or revised proposals, later in the year;

2. *Requests* the administering Power to assist the Territory by facilitating its work concerning public awareness outreach efforts, consistent with Article 73 *b* of the Charter of the United Nations and, in that regard, calls upon the relevant United Nations organizations to provide assistance to the Territory, if requested;

3. *Welcomes* the efforts made by the territorial Government to address cost-of-living issues in various economic sectors;

VI

Guam

Taking note of the working paper prepared by the Secretariat on Guam and other relevant information,

Aware that under United States law the relations between the territorial Government and the federal Government in all matters that are not the programme responsibility of another federal department or agency are under the general administrative supervision of the Secretary of the Interior,

Recalling that, in a referendum held in 1987, the registered and eligible voters of Guam endorsed a draft Guam Commonwealth Act that would establish a new framework for relations between the Territory and the administering Power, providing for a greater measure of internal self-government for Guam and recognition of the right of the Chamorro people of Guam to self-determination for the Territory,

Recalling also the previously expressed requests by the elected representatives and non-governmental organizations of the Territory that Guam not be removed from the list of the Non-Self-Governing Territories with which the Special Committee is concerned, pending the self-determination of the Chamorro people and taking into account their legitimate rights and interests,

Aware that negotiations between the administering Power and the territorial Government on the draft Guam Commonwealth Act ended in 1997 and that Guam has subsequently established a non-binding plebiscite process for a self-determination vote by the eligible Chamorro voters,

Cognizant that the administering Power continues to implement its programme of transferring surplus federal land to the Government of Guam,

Noting that the people of the Territory have called for reform in the programme of the administering Power with respect to the thorough, unconditional and expeditious transfer of land property to the people of Guam,

Aware of deep concerns expressed by civil society and others, including at the 2008 Pacific regional seminar, regarding the potential social and other impacts of the impending transfer of additional military personnel of the administering Power to the Territory,

Aware also of the austerity and fiscal measures undertaken by the territorial Government since 2007, when the Governor declared a financial "state of emergency",

Conscious that immigration into Guam has resulted in the indigenous Chamorros becoming a minority in their homeland,

1. *Calls once again upon* the administering Power to take into consideration the expressed will of the Chamorro people as supported by Guam voters in the referendum of 1987 and as subsequently provided for in Guam law regarding Chamorro self-determination efforts, and encourages the administering Power and the territorial Government to enter into negotiations on the matter;

2. *Requests* the administering Power, in cooperation with the territorial Government, to continue to transfer land to the original landowners of the Territory, to continue to recognize and to respect the political rights and the cultural and ethnic identity of the Chamorro people of Guam and to take all measures necessary to address the concerns of the territorial Government with regard to the question of immigration;

3. *Also requests* the administering Power to cooperate in establishing programmes for the sustainable development of the economic activities and enterprises of the Territory, noting the special role of the Chamorro people in the development of Guam;

4. *Recalls* the previously made request by the elected Governor to the administering Power to lift restrictions to allow for foreign airlines to transport passengers between Guam and the United States of America to provide for a more competitive market and increased visitor arrivals;

5. *Requests* the administering Power to assist the Territory by facilitating public outreach efforts, consistent with Article 73 *b* of the Charter of the United Nations and, in that regard, calls upon the relevant United Nations organizations to provide assistance to the Territory, if requested;

VII

Montserrat

Taking note of the working paper prepared by the Secretariat on Montserrat and other relevant information,

Recalling the 2002 report of the Constitutional Review Commission, the convening of a committee of the House of Assembly in 2005 to review the report and the subsequent discussions between the administering Power and the territorial Government on internal constitutional advancement and devolution of power,

Noting that the negotiating process with the administering Power on a draft constitution, expected to be finalized in the first quarter of 2007, is in progress and that talks, postponed at the request of the territorial Government since more time was needed, are expected to resume in the course of 2008,

Aware that Montserrat continues to receive budgetary aid from the administering Power for the operation of the territorial Government,

Recalling the statements made by participants at the 2007 Caribbean regional seminar encouraging the administering Power to commit sufficient resources to meet the Territory's special needs,

Noting with concern the continued consequences of the volcanic eruption, which led to the evacuation of three quarters of the Territory's population to safe areas of the island and to areas outside the Territory, which continues to have enduring consequences for the economy of the island,

Acknowledging the continued assistance provided to the Territory by States members of the Caribbean Community, in particular Antigua and Barbuda, which has offered safe refuge and access to educational and health facilities, as well as employment for thousands who have left the Territory,

Noting the continuing efforts of the administering Power and the territorial Government to deal with the consequences of the volcanic eruption,

1. *Welcomes* the efforts of the territorial Government to continue to negotiate improvements to the Constitution of the Territory so as to preserve its ability to move towards greater self-determination at a later stage;

2. *Requests* the administering Power to assist the Territory by facilitating its work concerning public outreach efforts, consistent with Article 73 *b* of the Charter of the United Nations and, in that regard, calls upon the relevant United Nations organizations to provide assistance to the Territory, if requested;

3. *Calls upon* the administering Power, the specialized agencies and other organizations of the United Nations system, as well as regional and other organizations, to continue to provide assistance to the Territory in alleviating the consequences of the volcanic eruption;

VIII

Pitcairn

Taking note of the working paper prepared by the Secretariat on Pitcairn and other relevant information,

Taking into account the unique character of Pitcairn in terms of population and area,

Noting that the internal review of the Constitution of the Territory is still deferred,

Aware that the administering Power and the territorial Government are in the process of restructuring the relationship between the Governor's Office and the territorial Government, based on consultations with the people of the Territory, and that Pitcairn continues to receive budgetary aid from the administering Power for the operation of the territorial Government,

1. *Welcomes* all efforts by the administering Power that would devolve operational responsibilities to the territorial Government, with a view to expanding self-government;

2. *Requests* the administering Power to assist the Territory by facilitating its work concerning public outreach efforts, consistent with Article 73 *b* of the Charter of the United Nations and, in that regard, calls upon the relevant United Nations organizations to provide assistance to the Territory, if requested;

3. *Also requests* the administering Power to continue its assistance for the improvement of the economic, social, educational and other conditions of the population of the Territory and to continue its discussions with the territorial Government on how best to support economic security in Pitcairn;

IX

Saint Helena

Taking note of the working paper prepared by the Secretariat on Saint Helena and other relevant information,

Taking into account the unique character of Saint Helena in terms of its population, geography and natural resources,

Noting the internal constitutional review process led by the territorial Government since 2001, the completion of a draft constitution following negotiations between the administering Power and the territorial Government in 2003 and 2004, the consultative poll with regard to a new constitution, held in Saint Helena in May 2005, the subsequent preparation of a revised draft constitution as a basis for discussion and the efforts of the territorial Government to keep the constitutional review exercise high on its agenda, including through public meetings,

Noting in that regard the importance of the right to nationality for Saint Helenians and their previously expressed request that the right, in principle, be included in a new constitution,

Aware that Saint Helena continues to receive budgetary aid from the administering Power for the operation of the territorial Government,

Aware also of the efforts of the administering Power and the territorial Government to improve the socio-economic conditions of the population of Saint Helena, in particular in the areas of employment and transport and communications infrastructure,

Noting the efforts of the Territory to address the problem of unemployment on the island and the joint action of the administering Power and the territorial Government in dealing with it,

Noting also the importance of improving the infrastructure and accessibility of Saint Helena,

1. *Welcomes* the Territory's continuing constitutional review process, including the related public meetings, and calls upon the administering Power to take into account the previously expressed concerns of Saint Helenians with regard to the right to nationality;

2. *Requests* the administering Power to assist the Territory by facilitating its work concerning public outreach efforts, consistent with Article 73 *b* of the Charter of the United Nations and, in that regard, calls upon the relevant United Nations organizations to provide assistance to the Territory, if requested;

3. *Requests* the administering Power and relevant international organizations to continue to support the efforts of the territorial Government to address the Territory's socio-economic development challenges, including unemployment, and limited transport and communications infrastructure;

4. *Welcomes* the decision by the administering Power to provide funding for the construction of an international airport on Saint Helena, which is to become operational in 2011–2012, including all required infrastructure;

X

Turks and Caicos Islands

Taking note of the working paper prepared by the Secretariat on the Turks and Caicos Islands and other relevant information,

Recalling the dispatch of the United Nations special mission to the Turks and Caicos Islands in 2006, at the request of the territorial Government and with the concurrence of the administering Power,

Recalling also the 2002 report of the Constitutional Modernization Review Body, and acknowledging the Constitution agreed between the administering Power and the territorial Government, which entered into force in 2006,

Noting that the 2006 Constitution of the Turks and Caicos Islands provides for a Governor, who maintains reserved powers in the Territory, to be appointed by the administering Power,

Acknowledging the significant and steady period of economic expansion fuelled by the continuing growth of high-end tourism and related real estate development,

1. *Recalls* the Constitution of the Territory, which took effect in 2006, and notes the view of the territorial Government that there remains scope for a degree of delegation of the Governor's power to the Territory so as to secure greater autonomy;

2. *Requests* the administering Power to assist the Territory by facilitating its work concerning public outreach efforts, consistent with Article 73 *b* of the Charter of the United Nations and, in that regard, calls upon the relevant United Nations organizations to provide assistance to the Territory, if requested;

3. *Welcomes* the continuing efforts made by the Government addressing the need for attention to be paid to the enhancement of social cohesion across the Territory;

XI

United States Virgin Islands

Taking note of the working paper prepared by the Secretariat on the United States Virgin Islands and other relevant information,

Aware that under United States law the relations between the territorial Government and the federal Government in all matters that are not the programme responsibility of another federal department or agency are under the general administrative supervision of the Secretary of the Interior,

Aware also of the ongoing Constitutional Convention, the fifth attempt of the Territory to review the existing Revised Organic Act, which organizes its internal governance arrangements, as well as the various related efforts in implementing a public education programme on the Constitution, as outlined in a statement by a participant from the Territory presented to the 2008 Pacific regional seminar,

Cognizant of the potential usefulness of regional ties for the development of a small island Territory,

1. *Welcomes* the establishment of the Constitutional Convention in 2007, and requests the administering Power to assist the territorial Government in achieving its political, economic and social goals, in particular the successful conclusion of the ongoing internal Constitutional Convention exercise;

2. *Requests* the administering Power to assist the Territory by facilitating its work concerning a public education programme, consistent with Article 73 *b* of the Charter of the United Nations and, in that regard, calls upon the relevant United Nations organizations to provide assistance to the Territory, if requested;

3. *Reiterates its call* for the inclusion of the Territory in regional programmes of the United Nations Development Programme, consistent with the participation of other Non-Self-Governing Territories;

4. *Appreciates* the efforts made to continue the work of the Inter-Virgin Islands Council between the elected Governments of the United States Virgin Islands and the British Virgin Islands to advance cooperation between the two neighbouring Territories.

Other territorial issues

Province of West Papua (Indonesia)

On 29 September, Indonesia transmitted to the General Assembly a note verbale [A/63/491] that contained a statement in reply to remarks made by the President of Vanuatu, Kalkot Matas Kelekele, to the Assembly on 26 September [A/63/PV.11].

In his remarks, the President of Vanuatu recalled the UN Millennium Summit address of the then-Prime Minister of Vanuatu, who, speaking as Chairman of the Melanesian Spearhead Group of countries, called on the United Nations to review the legality of its 1962 action to endorse the New York Agreement between Indonesia and the Netherlands that allowed for administration of the Act of Free Choice [YUN 1962, p. 124] regarding West Papua—then called West New Guinea (West Irian). The President noted that the UN Charter espoused the principles that guided UN efforts in the process of self-determination, and stated that democracy could not be championed if the United Nations continued to hang a blanket of silence over the case of West Papua.

In its reply, Indonesia said it was disturbed by the suggestion that the legality of Indonesia's sovereignty over Papua was questionable. The reintegration of West Papua into Indonesia took place when the 1969 Act of Free Choice was carried out as part of the 1962 New York Agreement, which was a solution to the conflict between Indonesia and the Netherlands because of the latter's recalcitrance to return West Papua to the former. In 1969, with the adoption of resolution 2504(XXIV) [YUN 1969, p. 179], the Assembly endorsed that solution, which was therefore valid, legal and final. The attempt to reopen the question of the legality of Indonesia's sovereignty over Papua was an irrelevant initiative that would serve the interests of secessionists and ran counter to the purposes and principles of the UN Charter.

Peaceful uses of outer space

The Committee on the Peaceful Uses of Outer Space (Committee on Outer Space), at its fifty-first session (Vienna, 11–20 June) [A/63/20], discussed ways and means to maintain outer space for peaceful purposes; the spin-off benefits of space technology; space and society; and space and water. It also considered the implementation of the recommendations of the Third (1999) United Nations Conference on the Exploration and Peaceful Uses of Outer Space (UNISPACE III) [YUN 1999, p. 556] and reviewed the work of its two subcommittees, one dealing with scientific and technical issues and the other with legal questions. In accordance with General Assembly resolution 62/217 [YUN 2007, p. 634], the Committee also considered international cooperation in promoting the use of space-derived geospatial data for sustainable development, and heard expert presentations on experiences in establishing infrastructure for data collection, processing and application.

GENERAL ASSEMBLY ACTION

On 5 December [meeting 64], the General Assembly, on the recommendation of the Fourth Committee [A/63/399], adopted **resolution 63/90** without vote [agenda item 28].

International cooperation in the peaceful uses of outer space

The General Assembly,

Recalling its resolutions 51/122 of 13 December 1996, 54/68 of 6 December 1999, 59/2 of 20 October 2004, 61/110 and 61/111 of 14 December 2006, 62/101 of 17 December 2007 and 62/217 of 22 December 2007,

Deeply convinced of the common interest of mankind in promoting and expanding the exploration and use of outer space, as the province of all mankind, for peaceful purposes and in continuing efforts to extend to all States the benefits derived therefrom, and also of the importance of international cooperation in this field, for which the United Nations should continue to provide a focal point,

Reaffirming the importance of international cooperation in developing the rule of law, including the relevant norms of space law and their important role in international cooperation for the exploration and use of outer space for peaceful purposes, and of the widest possible adherence to international treaties that promote the peaceful uses of outer space in order to meet emerging new challenges, especially for developing countries,

Seriously concerned about the possibility of an arms race in outer space, and bearing in mind the importance of article IV of the Treaty on Principles Governing the Activities of States in the Exploration and Use of Outer Space, including the Moon and Other Celestial Bodies (Outer Space Treaty),

Recognizing that all States, in particular those with major space capabilities, should contribute actively to the goal of preventing an arms race in outer space as an essential condition for the promotion and strengthening of international cooperation in the exploration and use of outer space for peaceful purposes,

Considering that space debris is an issue of concern to all nations,

Noting the progress achieved in the further development of peaceful space exploration and applications as well as in various national and cooperative space projects, which contributes to international cooperation, and the importance of further developing the legal framework to strengthen international cooperation in this field,

Convinced of the importance of the recommendations in the resolution entitled "The Space Millennium: Vienna Declaration on Space and Human Development", adopted by the Third United Nations Conference on the Exploration and Peaceful Uses of Outer Space (UNISPACE III), held at Vienna from 19 to 30 July 1999, and the need to promote the use of space technology towards implementing the United Nations Millennium Declaration,

Seriously concerned about the devastating impact of disasters,

Desirous of enhancing international coordination and cooperation at the global level in disaster management and emergency response through greater access to and use of space-based services for all countries and facilitating capacity-building and institutional strengthening for disaster management, in particular in developing countries,

Deeply convinced that the use of space science and technology and their applications in such areas as telemedicine, and tele-education, disaster management, environmental protection and other Earth observation applications contribute to achieving the objectives of the global conferences of the United Nations that address various aspects of economic, social and cultural development, particularly poverty eradication,

Taking note, in that regard, of the fact that the 2005 World Summit recognized the important role that science and technology play in promoting sustainable development,

Having considered the report of the Committee on the Peaceful Uses of Outer Space on the work of its fifty-first session,

1. *Endorses* the report of the Committee on the Peaceful Uses of Outer Space on the work of its fifty-first session;

2. *Urges* States that have not yet become parties to the international treaties governing the uses of outer space to give consideration to ratifying or acceding to those treaties in accordance with their domestic law, as well as incorporating them in their national legislation;

3. *Notes* that, at its forty-seventh session, the Legal Subcommittee of the Committee on the Peaceful Uses of Outer Space continued its work, as mandated by the General Assembly in its resolution 62/217;

4. *Endorses* the recommendation of the Committee that the Legal Subcommittee, at its forty-eighth session, taking into account the concerns of all countries, in particular those of developing countries:

(a) Consider the following as regular agenda items:

- (i) General exchange of views;
- (ii) Status and application of the five United Nations treaties on outer space;
- (iii) Information on the activities of international intergovernmental and non-governmental organizations relating to space law;
- (iv) Matters relating to:
  - *a.* The definition and delimitation of outer space;
  - *b.* The character and utilization of the geostationary orbit, including consideration of ways and means to ensure the rational and equitable use of the geostationary orbit without prejudice to the role of the International Telecommunication Union;

(b) Consider the following single issues/items for discussion:

- (i) Review and possible revision of the Principles Relevant to the Use of Nuclear Power Sources in Outer Space;
- (ii) Examination and review of the developments concerning the draft protocol on matters specific to space assets to the Convention on International Interests in Mobile Equipment;
- (iii) Capacity-building in space law;
- (iv) General exchange of information on national mechanisms relating to space debris mitigation measures;

(c) Consider the general exchange of information on national legislation relevant to the peaceful exploration and use of outer space in accordance with the workplan adopted by the Committee;

5. *Notes* that the Legal Subcommittee, at its forty-eighth session, will submit its proposals to the Committee for new items to be considered by the Subcommittee at its forty-ninth session, in 2010;

6. *Also notes* that, in the context of paragraph 4 *(a)* (ii) above, the Legal Subcommittee, at its forty-eighth session, will reconvene its Working Group on the Status and Application of the Five United Nations Treaties on Outer Space;

7. *Further notes* that, in the context of paragraph 4 *(a)* (iv) *a.* above, the Legal Subcommittee will reconvene its Working Group on Matters Relating to the Definition and Delimitation of Outer Space;

8. *Notes* that, in the context of paragraph 4 *(c)* above, the Legal Subcommittee will establish a working group to consider this item in accordance with the multi-year workplan agreed by the Subcommittee at its forty-sixth session and endorsed by the Committee at its fiftieth session;

9. *Also notes* that the Scientific and Technical Subcommittee, at its forty-fifth session, continued its work as mandated by the General Assembly in its resolution 62/217;

10. *Endorses* the recommendation of the Committee that the Scientific and Technical Subcommittee, at its forty-sixth session, taking into account the concerns of all countries, in particular those of developing countries:

(a) Consider the following items:

(i) General exchange of views and introduction to reports submitted on national activities;

(ii) United Nations Programme on Space Applications;

(iii) Implementation of the recommendations of the Third United Nations Conference on the Exploration and Peaceful Uses of Outer Space (UNISPACE III);

(iv) Matters relating to remote sensing of the Earth by satellite, including applications for developing countries and monitoring of the Earth's environment;

(v) Space debris;

(vi) Space-system-based disaster management support;

(vii) Recent developments in global navigation satellite systems;

(b) Consider the following items in accordance with the workplans adopted by the Committee:

(i) Use of nuclear power sources in outer space;

(ii) Near-Earth objects;

(c) Consider the following single issues/items for discussion:

(i) Examination of the physical nature and technical attributes of the geostationary orbit and its utilization and applications, including in the field of space communications, as well as other questions relating to developments in space communications, taking particular account of the needs and interests of developing countries;

(ii) International Heliophysical Year 2007;

11. *Notes* that the Scientific and Technical Subcommittee, at its forty-sixth session, will submit its proposal to the Committee for a draft provisional agenda for the forty-seventh session of the Subcommittee, in 2010;

12. *Endorses* the agreement of the Committee, at its fifty-first session, that the topic for the 2009 symposium, to be organized by the International Astronautical Federation, would be "The role of Earth observation satellites in promoting understanding of and addressing climate change concerns" and that the symposium should be held during the first week of the forty-sixth session of the Subcommittee;

13. *Agrees* that, in the context of paragraphs 10 *(a)* (ii), (iii), (vi) and 11 above, the Scientific and Technical Subcommittee, at its forty-sixth session, should reconvene the Working Group of the Whole;

14. *Also agrees* that, in the context of paragraph 10 *(b)* (i) above, the Scientific and Technical Subcommittee, at its forty-sixth session, should reconvene its Working Group on the Use of Nuclear Power Sources in Outer Space and that the Working Group should continue its work on the topics described in the multi-year workplan as agreed by the Subcommittee at its forty-fourth session and the Committee at its fiftieth session;

15. *Further agrees* that, in the context of paragraph 10 *(b)* (ii) above, the Scientific and Technical Subcommittee, at its forty-sixth session, should reconvene its Working Group on Near-Earth Objects, in accordance with the workplan under this item;

16. *Endorses* the United Nations Programme on Space Applications for 2009, as proposed to the Committee by the Expert on Space Applications and endorsed by the Committee;

17. *Recognizes* that, in accordance with paragraph 30 of its resolution 50/27 of 6 December 1995, the African regional centres for space science and technology education, in the French language and in the English language, located in Morocco and Nigeria, respectively, as well as the Centre for Space Science and Technology Education in Asia and the Pacific and the Regional Centre for Space Science and Technology Education for Latin America and the Caribbean, entered into an affiliation agreement with the Office for Outer Space Affairs of the Secretariat and have continued their education programmes in 2008;

18. *Agrees* that the regional centres referred to in paragraph 17 above should continue to report to the Committee on their activities on an annual basis;

19. *Notes with satisfaction* the contribution being made by the Scientific and Technical Subcommittee and the efforts of Member States and the Office for Outer Space Affairs to promote and support the activities being organized within the framework of the International Heliophysical Year 2007;

20. *Recognizes* that the second African Leadership Conference on Space Science and Technology for Sustainable Development was held in Pretoria from 2 to 5 October 2007, with a focus on capacity-building, knowledge-sharing and the joint participation of African countries in mutually beneficial projects in the area of space science and technology for sustainable development, and that the third African Leadership Conference will be held in Algeria in 2009;

21. *Also recognizes* the preparations being undertaken for the Sixth Space Conference of the Americas, and that in this regard the pro tempore secretariat of the Fifth Space Conference of the Americas, established by the Government of Ecuador, organized a meeting in Quito, on 13 and 14 December 2007, with representatives of the Governments of Colombia, Ecuador and Guatemala, the International Group of Experts of the Space Conferences of the Americas and the Office for Outer Space Affairs, which resulted in a set of recommendations for the preparation of the Sixth Conference, and that a second meeting with representatives of the pro tempore secretariat, the International Group of Experts and the Office for Outer Space Affairs was held in the Galapagos Islands, Ecuador, on 28 and 29 August 2008, following a regional seminar on space law, held in Quito on 26 and 27 August 2008;

22. *Further recognizes* the important role played by these conferences and other initiatives in building regional and international partnerships among States, such as the International Air and Space Fair, held in Santiago from 31 March to 6 April 2008, during which a conference was organized on space technology and climate change in relation to achieving the Millennium Development Goals,

and the ongoing preparations for the fifteenth session of the Asia-Pacific Regional Space Agency Forum, to be held in Hanoi and Ha Long Bay, Viet Nam, from 10 to 12 December 2008;

23. *Welcomes* the collaboration between the Government of Thailand, the Office for Outer Space Affairs, the European Space Agency and the Asian Society of International Law, in organizing the United Nations workshop on space law, to be held in Bangkok in 2009, on the theme "Activities of States in outer space in the light of new developments: meeting international responsibilities and establishing national legal and policy frameworks", which will serve as a forum for representatives, experts and other stakeholders from various countries to share expertise and experiences in space law;

24. *Emphasizes* that regional and interregional cooperation in the field of space activities is essential to strengthen the peaceful uses of outer space, assist States in the development of their space capabilities and contribute to the achievement of the goals of the United Nations Millennium Declaration;

25. *Notes with appreciation* that some States are already implementing space debris mitigation measures on a voluntary basis, through national mechanisms and consistent with the Space Debris Mitigation Guidelines of the Inter-Agency Space Debris Coordination Committee and with the Space Debris Mitigation Guidelines of the Committee on the Peaceful Uses of Outer Space, endorsed by the General Assembly in its resolution 62/217;

26. *Invites* other Member States to implement, through relevant national mechanisms, the Space Debris Mitigation Guidelines of the Committee on the Peaceful Uses of Outer Space;

27. *Considers* that it is essential that Member States pay more attention to the problem of collisions of space objects, including those with nuclear power sources, with space debris, and other aspects of space debris, calls for the continuation of national research on this question, for the development of improved technology for the monitoring of space debris and for the compilation and dissemination of data on space debris, also considers that, to the extent possible, information thereon should be provided to the Scientific and Technical Subcommittee, and agrees that international cooperation is needed to expand appropriate and affordable strategies to minimize the impact of space debris on future space missions;

28. *Urges* all States, in particular those with major space capabilities, to contribute actively to the goal of preventing an arms race in outer space as an essential condition for the promotion of international cooperation in the exploration and use of outer space for peaceful purposes;

29. *Emphasizes* the need to increase the benefits of space technology and its applications and to contribute to an orderly growth of space activities favourable to sustained economic growth and sustainable development in all countries, including mitigation of the consequences of disasters, in particular in the developing countries;

30. *Notes* that space science and technology and their applications could make important contributions to economic, social and cultural development and welfare, as indicated in the resolution entitled "The Space Millennium: Vienna Declaration on Space and Human Development", its resolution 59/2 of 20 October 2004 and the Plan of Action of the Committee on the Peaceful Uses of Outer Space on the implementation of the recommendations of UNISPACE III;

31. *Notes with appreciation* that a number of the recommendations, as set out in the Plan of Action on the implementation of the recommendations of UNISPACE III, have been implemented and that satisfactory progress is being made in implementing the outstanding recommendations;

32. *Reiterates* that the benefits of space technology and its applications should continue to be brought to the attention, in particular, of the major United Nations conferences and summits for economic, social and cultural development and related fields and that the use of space technology should be promoted towards achieving the objectives of those conferences and summits and for implementing the United Nations Millennium Declaration;

33. *Notes with satisfaction* that the panel on space applications and food security, comprising the Chairman of the Committee on the Peaceful Uses of Outer Space and representatives of the Division for Sustainable Development of the Department of Economic and Social Affairs of the Secretariat, the International Institute for Applied Systems Analysis and the Food and Agriculture Organization of the United Nations, held a discussion at United Nations Headquarters on 13 October 2008;

34. *Welcomes* the increased efforts to strengthen further the Inter-Agency Meeting on Outer Space Activities as the central United Nations mechanism for building partnerships and coordinating space-related activities within the framework of the ongoing reforms in the United Nations system to work in unison and deliver as one, and encourages entities of the United Nations system to participate fully in the work of the Inter-Agency Meeting;

35. *Urges* entities of the United Nations system, particularly those participating in the Inter-Agency Meeting on Outer Space Activities, to continue to examine, in cooperation with the Committee, how space science and technology and their applications could contribute to implementing the United Nations Millennium Declaration on the development agenda, particularly in the areas relating to, inter alia, food security and increasing opportunities for education;

36. *Invites* the Inter-Agency Meeting on Outer Space Activities to continue to contribute to the work of the Committee and to report to the Committee on the work conducted at its annual sessions;

37. *Notes with satisfaction* that the open informal meetings, held in conjunction with the annual sessions of the Inter-Agency Meeting on Outer Space Activities and in which representatives of member States and observers in the Committee participate, provide a constructive mechanism for an active dialogue between the entities of the United Nations system and member States and observers in the Committee;

38. *Encourages* the United Nations University and other scientific institutions to explore the possibilities of providing training and policy research at the crossroads of international law, climate change and outer space;

39. *Notes with satisfaction* the progress made within the framework of the United Nations Platform for Space-based

Information for Disaster Management and Emergency Response (UN-SPIDER) in the implementation of the platform programme for the period 2007–2009, including inaugurating and making fully operational the UN-SPIDER office in Bonn, Germany;

40. *Notes* that, in accordance with paragraph 11 of its resolution 61/110, the UN-SPIDER programme should work closely with regional and national centres of expertise in the use of space technology in disaster management to form a network of regional support offices for implementing the activities of the programme in their respective regions in a coordinated manner, and agrees with the guidelines proposed by the Committee for selecting and setting up the proposed UN-SPIDER regional support offices;

41. *Requests* the Committee to continue to consider, as a matter of priority, ways and means of maintaining outer space for peaceful purposes and to report thereon to the General Assembly at its sixty-fourth session, and agrees that during its consideration of the matter the Committee could continue to consider ways to promote regional and interregional cooperation based on experiences stemming from the Space Conferences of the Americas, the African Leadership Conferences on Space Science and Technology for Sustainable Development and the role space technology could play in the implementation of recommendations of the World Summit on Sustainable Development;

42. *Notes with satisfaction* that the Committee established a closer link between its work to implement the recommendations of UNISPACE III and the work of the Commission on Sustainable Development by contributing to the thematic areas that are addressed by the Commission, and agrees that the Director of the Division for Sustainable Development of the Department of Economic and Social Affairs should continue to be invited to participate in the sessions of the Committee to inform it how it could best contribute to the work of the Commission and that the Director of the Office for Outer Space Affairs should continue to participate in the sessions of the Commission to raise awareness and promote the benefits of space science and technology for sustainable development;

43. *Notes with appreciation* that the International Committee on Global Navigation Satellite Systems was established on a voluntary basis as a forum to promote cooperation, as appropriate, on matters of mutual interest to its members related to civil satellite-based positioning, navigation, timing and value-added services, as well as cooperation on the compatibility and interoperability of global navigation satellite systems, and to promote their use to support sustainable development, particularly in developing countries; that it held its first meeting in Vienna on 1 and 2 November 2006 and its second meeting in Bangalore, India, from 4 to 7 September 2007; that it will hold its third meeting in Pasadena, United States of America, from 8 to 12 December 2008; and that its fourth meeting will be held in the Russian Federation in 2009;

44. *Notes* the fact that the Office for Outer Space Affairs could integrate into its programme of work a number of actions identified for implementation by the Office contained in the Plan of Action of the Committee on the Peaceful Uses of Outer Space for the implementation of the recommendations of UNISPACE III and that some of those actions could be integrated into its programme of work only if additional staff and financial resources were to be provided;

45. *Urges* all Member States to contribute to the Trust Fund for the United Nations Programme on Space Applications to enhance the capacity of the Office for Outer Space Affairs to provide technical and legal advisory service and initiate pilot projects in accordance with the Plan of Action of the Committee, while maintaining the priority thematic areas agreed by the Committee;

46. *Agrees* that the Committee should continue to consider a report on the activities of the International Satellite System for Search and Rescue as a part of its consideration of the United Nations Programme on Space Applications under the agenda item entitled "Report of the Scientific and Technical Subcommittee", and invites Member States to report on their activities regarding the system;

47. *Requests* the Committee to continue to consider, at its fifty-second session, its agenda item entitled "Spin-off benefits of space technology: review of current status";

48. *Also requests* the Committee, in view of the importance of space and education, to continue to consider, at its fifty-second session, under its agenda item entitled "Space and society", the special theme for the focus of discussions "Space and education", in accordance with the workplan adopted by the Committee;

49. *Agrees* that the Committee should continue to consider, at its fifty-second session, its agenda item entitled "Space and water";

50. *Also agrees* that the Committee should continue to consider, at its fifty-second session, its agenda item entitled "International cooperation in promoting the use of space-derived geospatial data for sustainable development", in accordance with the multi-year workplan adopted by the Committee;

51. *Further agrees* that two new items entitled "Space and climate change" and "Use of space technology in the United Nations system" should be included in the agenda of the Committee at its fifty-second session;

52. *Agrees* that the Committee should continue to consider, at its fifty-second session, under its agenda item entitled "Other matters", the issue of its future role and activities;

53. *Notes* that in accordance with the agreement reached by the Committee at its forty-sixth session on the measures relating to the future composition of the bureaux of the Committee and its subsidiary bodies, on the basis of the measures relating to the working methods of the Committee and its subsidiary bodies, the Group of Asian States, the Group of Latin American and Caribbean States and the Group of Western European and Other States have nominated their candidates for the offices of Chair of the Legal Subcommittee, Second Vice-Chairman/Rapporteur of the Committee and Chair of the Scientific and Technical Subcommittee, respectively, for the period 2010–2011;

54. *Urges* the Group of African States and the Group of Eastern European States to nominate their candidates for the office of First Vice Chair of the Committee and Chair of the Committee, respectively, for the period 2010–2011;

55. *Endorses* the decision of the Committee to grant permanent observer status to the European Organisation for Astronomical Research in the Southern Hemisphere, the European Telecommunications Satellite Organization, the International Institute of Space Law, the Prince Sultan

Bin Abdulaziz International Prize for Water and the Secure World Foundation;

56. *Notes* that each of the regional groups has the responsibility for actively promoting the participation in the work of the Committee and its subsidiary bodies of the member States of the Committee that are also members of the respective regional groups, and agrees that the regional groups should consider this Committee-related matter among their members;

57. *Requests* entities of the United Nations system and other international organizations to continue and, where appropriate, to enhance their cooperation with the Committee and to provide it with reports on the issues dealt with in the work of the Committee and its subsidiary bodies.

Implementation of UNISPACE III recommendations

In response to General Assembly resolution 62/217 [YUN 2007, p. 634], the Committee on Outer Space considered the implementation of the recommendations of UNISPACE III [YUN 1999, p. 556]. It agreed that they were being implemented effectively through the use of multi-year workplans, the establishment of actions teams and task forces, and reports from ad hoc and other groups. Member States were contributing to the implementation through regional and national activities, including by supporting and participating in work related to the 10-Year Implementation Plan of the Global Earth Observation System of Systems (GEOSS).

The Committee welcomed the established link between its work on UNISPACE III and the work conducted by the Commission on Sustainable Development, and noted that a report [A/AC.105/892] on the Committee's contribution to the Commission's work for the thematic cluster 2008–2009 circulated at the Commission's sixteenth (2008) session. It also noted that the important role of space technology applications in sustainable development was mentioned by the Secretary-General in his report on the review of implementation of Agenda 21 and the Johannesburg Plan of Implementation: drought [E/CN.17/2008/6]. The Committee agreed upon the plan for its contribution to the Commission's work for the thematic cluster 2010–2011 [A/AC.105/2008/CRP.3]. Its contribution should examine the areas in which space technology and its applications played an important role; pay attention to the cross-cutting issues identified by the Commission; and identify areas where space-based systems could complement terrestrial systems. It also agreed that the Director of the Division for Sustainable Development of the Department of Economic and Social Affairs should continue to be invited to participate in the Committee's sessions to advise on how it could best contribute to the work of the Commission. Likewise, the Director of the United Nations Office for Outer Space Affairs should attend the Commission's sessions to raise awareness and promote the benefits of space science and technology, particularly in the areas addressed by the Commission. The Committee requested the Secretariat to organize a panel discussion on space applications and food security, to be held in the Fourth Committee of the General Assembly at its sixty-third (2008) session, when it considered international cooperation in the peaceful uses of outer space.

The Committee noted that, in accordance with Assembly resolution 62/217, the Scientific and Technical Subcommittee convened the Working Group of the Whole to consider the implementation of the UNISPACE III recommendations; and it agreed that the Working Group should focus on implementation of three actions called for in the Plan of Action: maximizing the benefits of space for disaster management; maximizing the benefits of the use and applications of Global Navigation Satellite Systems (GNSS) to support sustainable development; and enhancing capacity-building in space-related activities.

Scientific and Technical Subcommittee

The Scientific and Technical Subcommittee of the Committee on Outer Space, at its forty-fifth session (Vienna, 11–22 February) [A/AC.105/911], considered the United Nations Programme on Space Applications and the implementation of the UNISPACE III recommendations. It also dealt with matters relating to remote sensing of the Earth by satellite, including applications for developing countries and monitoring of the Earth's environment; space debris; the use of nuclear power sources in outer space; near-Earth objects; recent developments in GNSS; space-system-based disaster management support; the examination of the physical nature and technical attributes of the geostationary orbit and its utilization and applications; and the International Heliophysical Year 2007.

UN Programme on Space Applications

The United Nations Programme on Space Applications, as mandated by General Assembly resolution 37/90 [YUN 1982, p. 163], continued to promote the use of space technologies and data for sustainable economic and social development in developing countries by providing long-term training fellowships, training programmes and seminars, and technical advisory services in capacity-building and regional cooperation. The Programme increased the awareness of knowledge-based themes in space science, law and exploration through multi-year workplans and projects, and by convening outreach events and workshops.

The United Nations Expert on Space Applications [A/AC.105/925] said that the Programme continued to provide support for education and training for capacity-building in developing countries through regional centres for space science and technology education, which were affiliated with the United Nations Office for Outer Space Affairs. The goal of the regional centres—located in Morocco and Nigeria for the African region, India for Asia and the Pacific, and Brazil and Mexico for Latin America and the Caribbean—remained to develop an indigenous capability for research and applications in remote sensing and geographic information systems; satellite communications; satellite meteorology and global climate; and space and atmospheric science. Education curricula for those disciplines had been developed through expert meetings held under the Programme, and two further model curricula were being developed in the areas of GNSS and space law. At its third meeting (Pasadena, United States, 8–12 December), the International Committee on GNSS (ICG) decided that the centres would act as ICG information centres. The Office for Outer Space Affairs was carrying out preparatory work to hold the fourth UN expert meeting on the regional centres in 2010. Activities conducted by the Office within the frame of the ICG workplan included: session on ionospheric storms and space weather effects during the twelfth International Symposium on Equatorial Aeronomy (Heraklion, Greece, 18–24 May); International Training Course on Satellite Navigation and Location-Based Services (Ahmedabad, India, 18 June–18 July); and ICG expert meeting on GNSS and services (Montreal, Canada, 15 July). The United Nations/Colombia/United States of America Workshop on Applications of GNSS (Medellin, Colombia, 23–27 June) addressed the use of GNSS applications for precision farming, food security, climate change, land use, forestry, agriculture, tele-health and e-learning.

Several other meetings promoting the use of and access to space-based technologies and information were convened throughout the year. With regard to integrated space technology applications, the United Nations/Saudi Arabia/United Nations Educational, Scientific and Cultural Organization International Conference on the Use of Space Technology for Water Management (Riyadh, Saudi Arabia, 12–16 April) explored space technology applications providing solutions for water resources management and mitigating water-related emergencies; the United Nations/Indonesia Regional Workshop on Applications of Integrated Space Technology in Water Resources Management, Environmental Protection and Disaster Vulnerability Mitigation (Jakarta, Indonesia, 7–11 July) addressed initiatives in the areas of water resources management, use of space technologies in environmental-related emergencies, natural hazards and climate change; and the United Nations/Kenya/European Space Agency (ESA) Regional Workshop on the Use of Integrated Space Technology Applications in Monitoring the Impact of Climate Change on Agricultural Development and Food Security (Nairobi, Kenya, 1–5 December) addressed monitoring of climate-related disasters and environmental hazards, and improvement of regional food security.

As to tele-health and tele-education, the United Nations/Burkina Faso/World Health Organization/ESA/Centre national d'études spatiales Workshop on the Use of Space Technology in Tele-health to Benefit Africa (Ouagadougou, Burkina Faso, 5–9 May) examined tele-health practices and development in Africa; and the United Nations/India/ESA Regional Workshop on the Use of Space Technology in Tele-epidemiology to Benefit Asia and the Pacific (Lucknow, India, 21–24 October) focused on the use of space technology for public health surveillance and tropical diseases health care. Meetings on space application for sustainable development included the United Nations/Austria/ESA Symposium on Space Tools and Solutions for Monitoring the Atmosphere and Land Cover (Graz, Austria, 9–12 September); and the United Nations/International Astronautical Federation Workshop on Space Technology Support for an Integrated Approach to Address Potential Environmental Hazards (Glasgow, United Kingdom, 26–27 September). Other meetings included the Fourth United Nations/ESA/National Aeronautics and Space Administration/Japan Aerospace Exploration Agency Workshop on the International Heliophysical Year 2007 and Basic Space Science (Sozopol, Bulgaria, 2–6 June); and the United Nations/International Academy of Astronautics Workshop on Small Satellites in the Service of Developing Countries (Glasgow, 30 September).

Following consideration of the report of the Expert on Space Applications [A/AC.105/900] describing 2007 activities, those scheduled for 2008 and activities of UN-affiliated regional centres for space science and technology education scheduled for 2007–2009, the Subcommittee expressed concern over the Programme's limited financial resources and appealed to Member States for voluntary contributions.

The General Assembly, in resolution 63/90 (see p. 684), endorsed the Programme on Space Applications for 2009 as proposed by the Expert.

Cooperation

The Inter-Agency Meeting on Outer Space Activities, at its twenty-eighth session (Geneva, 16–18 January) [A/AC.105/909], discussed the coordination of plans and programmes in the practical application of space technology and related areas; space-related outcomes of the 2002 World Summit on Sustainable Development [YUN 2002, p. 821]; implementation of UNISPACE III recommendations; use by the UN system of the International Charter on Space and Major Disasters, to which the Office for Outer Space Affairs became a cooperating body in 2003 [YUN 2003, p. 643], and methods to increase operational collaboration in the use of space technology in emergency response; lessons learned and good practices in the use of space technologies for relief efforts and disaster reduction; participation of UN system entities in the process of the Group on Earth Observations; public-private partnerships and innovative funding approaches in the UN system to promote the use of space technology and its applications; and public outreach and information exchange to promote inter-agency cooperation.

The Meeting agreed on the importance of enhancing inter-agency cooperation and coordination and identified the following key issues: strengthening the Meeting as the UN central mechanism for coordination of space-related activities; enhancing the use of space-based assets in support of disaster management; and reinforcing the contributions made by UN entities to the UN spatial data infrastructure and to GEOSS. Representatives of participating UN entities reported on their activities and plans for 2008–2009, the details of which were included in the Secretary-General's draft report on the coordination of space-related activities within the UN system: directions and anticipated results for the 2008–2009 period [A/AC.105/910]. The report was reviewed and amended by the Meeting.

Pursuant to discussions at its 2007 session [YUN 2007, p. 639], the Meeting agreed that a report on initiatives and applications for space-related inter-agency cooperation should be prepared by the Office for Outer Space Affairs in cooperation with the Economic Commission for Africa and in consultation with other UN entities for endorsement at its 2009 session. The report should consider the use of space technology for sustainable development in Africa and should be presented to the third African Leadership Conference on Space Science and Technology for Sustainable Development in 2009.

The Office for Outer Space Affairs presented the list of space-related initiatives and programmes carried out by member States of the Committee on the Peaceful Uses of Outer Space and within the UN system in response to recommendations contained in the Johannesburg Plan of Implementation [YUN 2002, p. 821]. The usefulness of the list was reviewed by the Meeting, which noted that the Commission on Sustainable Development was the General Assembly's established mechanism for providing policy guidelines to follow up on the implementation of recommendations on sustainable development. In that context, the Meeting agreed that updating the list was a duplication of effort and should be phased out.

The Meeting noted that the International Charter on Space and Major Disasters invited UN bodies that had accessed the Charter to participate in the next meeting of its secretariat, to be hosted by the Canadian Space Agency from 15 to 17 April. The Office for Outer Space Affairs would organize the Fifth UN-wide meeting on the use of space technologies for emergency response and humanitarian assistance (Bonn, Germany, 14 October) to bring together representatives from the field.

The Office for Outer Space Affairs made a presentation on the development of the United Nations Platform for Space-based Information for Disaster Management and Emergency Response (UN-SPIDER) programme. The Meeting took note of the programme for 2007–2009 and the workplan for 2008–2009 [YUN 2007, p. 641]. The implementation of UN-SPIDER would be supported by a network of regional support offices and national focal points, and the Office would coordinate with other UN entities in implementation of the planned activities, cooperating in particular with the secretariat of the International Strategy for Disaster Reduction within the Hyogo Framework for Action 2005–2015 [YUN 2005, p. 1016] and with UNDP in the definition of national risk reduction and disaster management plans and policies.

The Office for Outer Space Affairs briefed the Inter-Agency Meeting on the continued improvements to the website of the United Nations Coordination of Outer Space Activities and noted that the brochure "Space solutions for the world's problems: how the United Nations family uses space technology for achieving development goals", prepared by the Office, was produced in four languages and was available on that website. The Meeting decided to review the brochure at its thirtieth (2010) session.

Scientific and technical issues

In 2008, the Scientific and Technical Subcommittee [A/AC.105/911] continued to emphasize the importance of Earth observation satellite data to support activities in a number of key development areas. It also noted the importance of providing, for peaceful purposes, non-discriminatory access to remote sensing data and to derived information at reasonable cost and in a timely manner, and of building capacity for the adoption and use of remote sensing technology, particularly to meet the needs of developing countries. The Subcommittee encouraged further international cooperation in the use of remote sensing satellites, in particular by sharing experiences and technologies through bilateral, regional and international collaborative projects.

For its consideration of space debris, the Subcommittee had before it a Secretariat note on national research on space debris, containing replies on the issue from five Member States and one international organization [A/AC.105/918 & Add. 1]. The Subcommittee agreed that States, in particular space-faring countries, should pay more attention to the problem of collisions of space objects, including those with nuclear power sources (NPS) on board, with space debris and to other aspects of space debris, including its re-entry into the atmosphere. Research on space debris should continue, and States should make available the results of that research, including information on practices that proved effective in minimizing space debris creation. The Subcommittee noted that some States were implementing mitigation measures consistent with the Space Debris Mitigation Guidelines of the Committee on the Peaceful Uses of Outer Space, adopted in 2007 [YUN 2007, p. 640], and/or the Space Debris Mitigation Guidelines of the Inter-Agency Space Debris Coordination Committee, or that they had developed their own mitigation standards based on those guidelines. The view was expressed that those States most responsible for the creation of space debris and those having the capability to take action on its mitigation should make a greater contribution to mitigation efforts.

The Subcommittee considered the use of nuclear power sources in outer space under the multi-year workplan for the 2007–2010 period, adopted at its 2007 session [YUN 2007, p. 640]. It discussed progress of the Joint Expert Group of the Subcommittee and of the International Atomic Energy Agency (IAEA) in the development of an international technically-based framework of goals and recommendations for the safety of NPS applications in outer space. The Subcommittee reconvened its Working Group on the Use of NPS in Outer Space and noted that the Working Group updated the draft safety framework prepared by the Joint Expert Group on the basis of comments received from States [A/AC.105/C.1/L.292 & Rev.1]. The Subcommittee endorsed the report of the Working Group, which was annexed to its report.

The Subcommittee agreed that national and international efforts to detect and track near-Earth objects should be continued and expanded. Pursuant to Assembly resolution 62/217 [YUN 2007, p. 636], it reconvened its Working Group on Near-Earth Objects. The Subcommittee endorsed the Working Group's report, which included the amended multi-year work-plan proposed for 2009–2011 and was annexed to the Subcommittee's report. The Secretariat submitted to the Subcommittee a note on research in the field of near-Earth objects carried out by Member States, international organizations and other entities, containing replies from two States and four international organizations [A/AC.105/926].

Also submitted to the Subcommittee were Secretariat notes on international cooperation in the peaceful uses of outer space [A/AC.105/907/Add.2 & Add.3 & A/AC.105/923], containing replies from 11 Member States on their space activities.

Space-based disaster management and emergency response

The Scientific and Technical Subcommittee, at its forty-fifth session in February [A/AC.105/911], considered the January report on activities carried out in 2007 in the framework of UN-SPIDER [A/AC.105/899], established by Assembly resolution 61/110 [YUN 2006, p. 748], and heard a statement made by the UN-SPIDER Programme Coordinator on the 2007 activities and on activities to be conducted in 2008–2009. The Subcommittee noted the progress made in the implementation of the activities for 2007, including the inauguration of the UN-SPIDER office in Bonn, Germany, and agreed that UN-SPIDER should continue coordinating its activities with other institutions and initiatives promoting the use of space-based solutions for disaster risk management and with UN specialized agencies and programmes. It also noted the significant extrabudgetary resources provided by various Member States. The Subcommittee reconvened its Working Group of the Whole and endorsed its report, which was annexed to the Subcommittee's report. The Working Group noted that the Office for Outer Space Affairs was working with China and Switzerland to ensure the openings of UN-SPIDER offices in Beijing and Geneva, respectively, and was following up on commitments from various countries and institutions towards the establishment of a network of regional support offices. It agreed that the UN-SPIDER programme should work to raise the level of extrabudgetary resources.

The Committee on Outer Space [A/63/20] acknowledged the progress made within the UN-SPIDER framework and the significant extra-budgetary resources provided by various States to support UN-SPIDER activities in 2008 and 2009, and noted the increase in the availability of space-based information and in the provision of expertise to support emergency relief efforts. The Committee agreed that UN-SPIDER should work closely with national and regional centres of expertise in the use of disaster management space technology to form a network of regional support offices for implementing the programme, and proposed guidelines for selecting and setting up the support offices.

An April report [A/AC.105/916] to the Committee considered outreach activities carried out in 2007 in the framework of UN-SPIDER.

International Heliophysical Year 2007

The Scientific and Technical Subcommittee [A/AC.105/911] considered the activities conducted in conjunction with the International Heliophysical Year 2007 [YUN 2007, p. 641], in accordance with the three-year workplan adopted by the Subcommittee in 2005 [YUN 2005, p. 702]. The Subcommittee welcomed the progress made by States and national and international institutions in conducting outreach, educational and research campaigns, and noted that the United Nations Basic Space Science Initiative of the Office for Outer Space Affairs continued to support the deployment in countries throughout the world, in particular in developing countries, of small instruments to provide global measurements of heliospheric phenomena.

The Committee on the Peaceful Uses of Outer Space [A/63/20] noted that the three-year workplan had been extended to cover four years, and recognized that the International Heliophysical Year 2007 was an international endeavour that engaged States from every region to host instrument arrays, provide scientific investigators or offer supporting space missions.

Legal Subcommittee

The Legal Subcommittee, at its forty-seventh session (Vienna, 31 March–11 April) [A/AC.105/917] considered: the status and application of the five UN treaties on outer space; information on the activities of international organizations relating to space law; matters related to the definition and delimitation of outer space and the character and utilization of the geostationary orbit; review and possible revision of the Principles Relevant to the Use of Nuclear Power Soarces in Outer Space; review of developments concerning the draft protocol on matters specific to space assets to the Convention on International Interests in Mobile Equipment; capacity building in space law; and exchange of information on national legislation relevant to the peaceful exploration and use of outer space.

The Subcommittee welcomed the General Assembly's adoption of resolution 62/101 [YUN 2007, p. 642] and its endorsement, in resolution 62/217 [ibid., p. 634], of the Space Debris Mitigation Guidelines of the Committee on the Peaceful Uses of Outer Space. It expressed the view that arrangements for space debris mitigation should consider the principle of common but differentiated responsibilities, and that the Committee should develop guidelines for space traffic management.

The Subcommittee appreciated the distribution by the Secretariat of a revised version of the United Nations Treaties and Principles on Outer Space and Related General Assembly Resolutions [ST/SPACE/11/Rev.2], and the distribution of an updated document containing information, as at 1 January 2008, on States parties and additional signatories to the UN treaties and other international agreements relating to outer space [ST/SPACE/11/Rev.2/Add.1]. It noted that in 2007, a number of States had concluded agreements promoting international cooperation in space activities and a number of States were developing national mechanisms for registration of space objects. The Subcommittee reconvened its Working Group on the Status and Application of the Five United Nations Treaties on Outer Space [YUN 2001, p. 570], which continued its consideration of a questionnaire on the possible options for future development of international space law and agreed that, at the Subcommittee's 2009 session, it would not discuss the list of questions in the questionnaire, but the state of international space law and possible options for its development. The Working Group had before it two Secretariat notes: one on activities carried out on the Moon and other celestial bodies, international and national rules governing those activities, and information from States parties to the 1979 Agreement Governing the Activities of States on the Moon and Other Celestial Bodies [YUN 1979, p. 111] about the benefits of adherence to that Agreement [A/AC.105/C.2/L.271 & Corr.1]; the other on a joint statement on the benefits of adherence to the Agreement by its States parties [A/AC.105/C.2/L.272]. The Working Group requested the Secretariat to prepare a more detailed background paper on activities on the Moon either planned or being conducted by States, and agreed that the Subcommittee, in 2009, should continue its discussion on the low rate of participation of States in the Agreement. The Subcommittee endorsed the report of the Working Group and the recommendation that its mandate be extended for one additional year.

The Subcommittee reconvened its Working Group on the Definition and Delimitation of Outer Space, which considered three Secretariat notes on: replies from Member States to the questionnaire on possible legal issues with regard to aerospace objects [A/AC.105/635/Add.16]; national legislation and practice relating to the definition and delimitation of outer space [A/AC.105/865/Add.3]; and replies from Member States to questions on the definition and delimitation of outer space [A/AC.105/889/Add.1]. It also had before it several conference room papers. The Working Group agreed to suspend the invitation to the Committee's member States to submit their preferences with regard to the replies of Member States to the questionnaire and to submit proposals on criteria for analysing the replies. It also agreed to suspend the invitation to Member States to reply to the questionnaire, and to suspend consideration of aerospace objects until new events warranted its reconsideration. The Committee's member States should still submit information on national legislation or practices in relation to the definition and/or delimitation of outer space and air space. The Subcommittee endorsed the report of the Working Group.

For its consideration of capacity-building in space law, the Subcommittee had before it a report on the 2007 United Nations Expert Meeting on Promoting Education in Space Law [A/AC.105/908] and a Secretariat note containing the updated directory of education opportunities in space law [A/AC.105/C.2/2008/CRP.3]. It agreed that capacity-building, training and education in space law were of paramount importance to international, regional and national efforts to develop space activities and increase knowledge of their legal framework, noted efforts undertaken by governmental and non-governmental organizations and UN entities, and highlighted the continued role of the Office for Outer Space Affairs in providing legal advisory services and strengthening cooperation with space law entities and organizations. The Subcommittee outlined initiatives to strengthen capacity in space law, particularly in developing countries, and recommended that member States, permanent observers of the Committee on Outer Space and the Office for Outer Space Affairs consider the initiatives and inform the Subcommittee on actions taken or planned.

For its discussion on exchange of information on national legislation relevant to the peaceful exploration and use of outer space, the Subcommittee considered a Secretariat note [A/AC.105/912] and two conference room papers [A/AC.105/C.2/2008/CRP.9 & A/AC.105/C.2/2008/CRP.14] containing information on national legislation governing space activities of Member States. The Subcommittee noted that an exchange of information would allow it to examine the main developments at the national level in order to identify common principles, norms and procedures, encouraged States to continue to submit to the Office for Outer Space Affairs the texts of laws and regulations related to space activities, and noted the important role played by regional coordination mechanisms in promoting cooperation among States. It agreed that a working group would be established at the Subcommittee's 2009 session.

The Committee on Outer Space [A/63/20] approved the Subcommittee's endorsement of the report of the Working Group on the Status and Application of the Five United Nations Treaties on Outer Space, including the recommendation that its mandate be extended by an additional year. The Committee noted the progress of the Working Group on the Definition and Delimitation of Outer Space and welcomed its decision to suspend consideration of the issue of aerospace objects until new events warranted its resumption. It also welcomed the Subcommittee's agreement to include the item of capacity-building in space law on the agenda at its 2009 session, noted its consideration of specific measures to strengthen capacity in space law and encouraged response to those initiatives by member States, permanent observers, intergovernmental organizations and the Office for Outer Space Affairs.

Effects of atomic radiation

At its fifty-sixth session (Vienna, 10–18 July) [A/63/46], the United Nations Scientific Committee on the Effects of Atomic Radiation approved for publication five scientific annexes that had last been considered at its 2007 session [YUN 2007, p. 644]. With regard to the report with scientific annexes, approved in 2006 [YUN 2006, p. 751], the Committee was disappointed that volume I had not been published until July and that volume II would not likely be published before December, and observed that such delays were traceable in part to inadequate staffing and lack of funding. On that issue, the Committee noted that the General Assembly, in resolution 62/100 [YUN 2007, p. 645], had requested the Secretary-General to take measures so that its professional secretariat could service the Committee in a sustainable manner, and to provide a report to the Assembly's 2008 session addressing the issues of financial and administrative implications of increased Committee membership, staffing of its professional secretariat and methods to ensure sufficient, assured and predictable funding.

In an October report [A/63/478], the Secretary-General considered those issues and noted that six States had declared their interest in becoming members of the Committee, which comprised scientists from 21 States. The Committee had noted that the current critical financial and resource issues should be addressed prior to reaching a decision on the membership question and had suggested flexible arrangements whereby, for reasons of efficiency, the maximum number of members would remain at about the present level. The report concluded that, in order to provide up-to-date, timely and high-quality assessments, improve dissemination of findings and ensure the technical infrastructure to support the Committee, the staffing of its secretariat should be strengthened with an additional professional post, at an estimated cost to the programme budget of $169,600 per biennium. It also estimated that, should the Committee membership be increased by six members, the additional biennial requirements would amount to $90,000.

At its July session [A/63/46], the Committee also considered reports on sources of radiation exposure, the 1986 Chernobyl accident [YUN 1986, p. 584] and effects on non-human biota. In its discussion of the strategic plan for the period 2009–2013, it identified the strategic objective of increasing awareness and deepening understanding among authorities, the scientific community and civil society on the levels of ionizing radiation and its health and environmental effects. It also established the thematic priorities of medical exposures of patients, radiation levels and effects of energy production, exposure to natural sources of radiation and improved understanding of the effects from low-dose-rate radiation exposure. For its future programme of work, the Committee decided to work on assessments of levels of radiation from energy production and the effects on human health and the environment; uncertainty in radiation risk estimation; health effects that may be attributable to radiation exposure; updating methodology for estimating exposures due to discharges from nuclear installations; a summary of radiation effects; and improving data collection, analysis and dissemination. It decided to hold its fifty-seventh session in Vienna from 25 to 29 May 2009.

GENERAL ASSEMBLY ACTION

On 5 December [meeting 64], the General Assembly, on the recommendation of the Fourth Committee [A/63/398], adopted **resolution 63/89** without vote [agenda item 27].

Effects of atomic radiation

The General Assembly,

Recalling its resolution 913(X) of 3 December 1955, by which it established the United Nations Scientific Committee on the Effects of Atomic Radiation, and its subsequent resolutions on the subject, including resolution 62/100 of 17 December 2007, in which, inter alia, it requested the Scientific Committee to continue its work,

Taking note with appreciation of the work of the Scientific Committee, and of the release of its report on its fifty-sixth session,

Reaffirming the desirability of the Scientific Committee continuing its work,

Concerned about the potentially harmful effects on present and future generations resulting from the levels of radiation to which mankind and the environment are exposed,

Conscious of the continuing need to examine and compile information about atomic and ionizing radiation and to analyse its effects on mankind and the environment, and conscious also of the increased volume, complexity and diversity of that information,

Noting the views expressed by Member States at its sixty-third session with regard to the work of the Scientific Committee,

Recalling the deep concern of the Scientific Committee expressed in the report on its fifty-sixth session that reliance on a single post at the Professional level in its secretariat had left the Committee seriously vulnerable and had hampered the efficient implementation of its approved programme of work, and noting that a solution to this concern has not yet been achieved,

Recalling also its request at its sixty-second session that the Secretary-General provide a comprehensive and consolidated report, to be prepared in consultation with the Scientific Committee as appropriate, addressing the financial and administrative implications of increased Committee membership, staffing of the professional secretariat and methods to ensure sufficient, assured and predictable funding,

1. *Commends* the United Nations Scientific Committee on the Effects of Atomic Radiation for the valuable contribution it has been making in the course of the past fifty-three years, since its inception, to wider knowledge and understanding of the levels, effects and risks of ionizing radiation, and for fulfilling its original mandate with scientific authority and independence of judgement;

2. *Reaffirms* the decision to maintain the present functions and independent role of the Scientific Committee;

3. *Takes note with appreciation* of the work of the Scientific Committee and of the release of its extensive report to the General Assembly, with scientific annexes, which provide the scientific and world community with the Committee's latest evaluations;

4. *Requests* the Scientific Committee to continue its work, including its important activities to increase knowledge of the levels, effects and risks of ionizing radiation from all sources;

5. *Endorses* the future programme of work of scientific review and assessment of the Scientific Committee on behalf of the General Assembly on assessments of levels of radiation from energy production and the effects on human health and the environment, uncertainty in radiation risk estimation, attributability of health effects due to radiation exposure, updating its methodology for estimating exposures due to discharges from nuclear installations, a summary of radiation effects and improving data collection, analysis and dissemination, notes with concern that the Committee cannot initiate work immediately on topics which make up half of the entire programme due to the lack of resources within the professional secretariat, and endorses the longer-term strategic plan of the Committee for its work, as reported to the Assembly at its sixty-third session;

6. *Requests* the Scientific Committee to continue at its next session the review of the important questions in the field of ionizing radiation and to report thereon to the General Assembly at its sixty-fourth session;

7. *Emphasizes* the need for the Scientific Committee to hold regular sessions on an annual basis so that its report can reflect the latest developments and findings in the field of ionizing radiation and thereby provide updated information for dissemination among all States;

8. *Expresses its appreciation* for the assistance rendered to the Scientific Committee by Member States, the specialized agencies, the International Atomic Energy Agency and non-governmental organizations, and invites them to increase their cooperation in this field;

9. *Invites* the Scientific Committee to continue its consultations with scientists and experts from interested Member States in the process of preparing its future scien-

tific reports, and requests the Secretariat to facilitate such consultations;

10. *Welcomes*, in this context, the readiness of Member States to provide the Scientific Committee with relevant information on the effects of ionizing radiation in affected areas, and invites the Committee to analyse and give due consideration to such information, particularly in the light of its own findings;

11. *Invites* Member States, the organizations of the United Nations system and non-governmental organizations concerned to provide further relevant data about doses, effects and risks from various sources of radiation, which would greatly help in the preparation of future reports of the Scientific Committee to the General Assembly;

12. *Requests* the United Nations Environment Programme to continue providing support for the effective conduct of the work of the Scientific Committee and for the dissemination of its findings to the General Assembly, the scientific community and the public;

13. *Urges* the United Nations Environment Programme to review and strengthen the present funding of the Scientific Committee, pursuant to paragraph 14 of resolution 62/100, and to continue to seek out and consider temporary funding mechanisms to complement existing ones, and, in that context, takes note of the establishment by the Executive Director of the United Nations Environment Programme of a general trust fund to receive and manage voluntary contributions to support the work of the Committee, and encourages Member States to consider making voluntary contributions to the trust fund;

14. *Takes note* of the comprehensive report of the Secretary-General, prepared in consultation with the Scientific Committee as appropriate, on the financial and administrative implications of increased membership of the Committee, staffing of its professional secretariat and methods to ensure sufficient, assured and predictable funding;

15. *Recognizes* the conclusion, outlined in paragraph 48 of the report of the Secretary-General, on the need for strengthened human resources for the professional, scientific secretariat in order to support the Scientific Committee in a more predictable and sustainable manner with a longer-term perspective, to effectively facilitate the use of the invaluable expertise offered to the Committee by its members, and to enable the Committee to discharge the responsibilities and mandate entrusted to it by the General Assembly, and emphasizes in this context that these resources are needed in any case and before Member States can agree to a change in Committee membership;

16. *Requests* the Secretary-General, in formulating his proposed programme budget for the biennium 2010–2011, to consider all options, including the possibility of internal reallocation, to provide the Scientific Committee with the resources outlined in paragraphs 48 and 50 of the report of the Secretary-General;

17. *Directs* the Scientific Committee to continue its reflection on how the current, as well as a potentially revised, membership for the Scientific Committee could best support the essential work of the Committee, including by developing detailed, objective and transparent criteria to be applied equitably to present and future members alike, and to report on these efforts before the end of the sixty-third session of the General Assembly;

18. *Welcomes* the attendance of Belarus, Finland, Pakistan, the Republic of Korea, Spain and Ukraine as observers at the fifty-sixth session of the Scientific Committee, invites each of those States to designate one scientist to attend, as observers, the fifty-seventh session of the Committee, and resolves to take a decision on full membership for these countries once a decision on resource allocation has been made, pursuant to paragraph 16 above, but no later than the end of the sixty-fourth session of the General Assembly.

Information and telecommunications in international security

In response to General Assembly resolution 62/17 [YUN 2007, p. 646], the Secretary-General, in a July report [A/63/139], transmitted the views of six Member States on the general appreciation of the issues of information security; national efforts to strengthen information security and promote international cooperation in that area; the content of relevant international concepts aimed at strengthening the security of global information and telecommunications systems; and possible measures that the international community could take to strengthen global information security.

GENERAL ASSEMBLY ACTION

On 2 December [meeting 61], the General Assembly, on the recommendation of the First (Disarmament and International Security) Committee [A/63/385], adopted **resolution 63/37** by recorded vote (178-1) [agenda item 85].

Developments in the field of information and telecommunications in the context of international security

The General Assembly,

Recalling its resolutions 53/70 of 4 December 1998, 54/49 of 1 December 1999, 55/28 of 20 November 2000, 56/19 of 29 November 2001, 57/53 of 22 November 2002, 58/32 of 8 December 2003, 59/61 of 3 December 2004, 60/45 of 8 December 2005, 61/54 of 6 December 2006 and 62/17 of 5 December 2007,

Recalling also its resolutions on the role of science and technology in the context of international security, in which, inter alia, it recognized that scientific and technological developments could have both civilian and military applications and that progress in science and technology for civilian applications needed to be maintained and encouraged,

Noting that considerable progress has been achieved in developing and applying the latest information technologies and means of telecommunication,

Affirming that it sees in this process the broadest positive opportunities for the further development of civilization, the expansion of opportunities for cooperation for the common good of all States, the enhancement of the creative potential of humankind and additional improvements in the circulation of information in the global community,

Recalling, in this connection, the approaches and principles outlined at the Information Society and Development Conference, held in Midrand, South Africa, from 13 to 15 May 1996,

Bearing in mind the results of the Ministerial Conference on Terrorism, held in Paris on 30 July 1996, and the recommendations that it made,

Bearing in mind also the results of the World Summit on the Information Society, held in Geneva from 10 to 12 December 2003 (first phase) and in Tunis from 16 to 18 November 2005 (second phase),

Noting that the dissemination and use of information technologies and means affect the interests of the entire international community and that optimum effectiveness is enhanced by broad international cooperation,

Expressing its concern that these technologies and means can potentially be used for purposes that are inconsistent with the objectives of maintaining international stability and security and may adversely affect the integrity of the infrastructure of States to the detriment of their security in both civil and military fields,

Considering that it is necessary to prevent the use of information resources or technologies for criminal or terrorist purposes,

Noting the contribution of those Member States that have submitted their assessments on issues of information security to the Secretary-General pursuant to paragraphs 1 to 3 of resolutions 53/70, 54/49, 55/28, 56/19, 57/53, 58/32, 59/61, 60/45, 61/54 and 62/17,

Taking note of the reports of the Secretary-General containing those assessments,

Welcoming the initiative taken by the Secretariat and the United Nations Institute for Disarmament Research in convening international meetings of experts in Geneva in August 1999 and April 2008 on developments in the field of information and telecommunications in the context of international security, as well as the results of those meetings,

Considering that the assessments of the Member States contained in the reports of the Secretary-General and the international meetings of experts have contributed to a better understanding of the substance of issues of international information security and related notions,

Bearing in mind that the Secretary-General, in fulfilment of resolution 58/32, established in 2004 a group of governmental experts, which, in accordance with its mandate, considered existing and potential threats in the sphere of information security and possible cooperative measures to address them and conducted a study on relevant international concepts aimed at strengthening the security of global information and telecommunications systems,

Taking note of the report of the Secretary-General on the Group of Governmental Experts on Developments in the Field of Information and Telecommunications in the Context of International Security, prepared on the basis of the results of the Group's work,

1. *Calls upon* Member States to promote further at multilateral levels the consideration of existing and potential threats in the field of information security, as well as possible measures to limit the threats emerging in this field, consistent with the need to preserve the free flow of information;

2. *Considers* that the purpose of such measures could be served through the examination of relevant international concepts aimed at strengthening the security of global information and telecommunications systems;

3. *Invites* all Member States to continue to inform the Secretary-General of their views and assessments on the following questions:

(a) General appreciation of the issues of information security;

(b) Efforts taken at the national level to strengthen information security and promote international cooperation in this field;

(c) The content of the concepts mentioned in paragraph 2 above;

(d) Possible measures that could be taken by the international community to strengthen information security at the global level;

4. *Requests* the Secretary-General, with the assistance of a group of governmental experts, to be established in 2009 on the basis of equitable geographical distribution, to continue to study existing and potential threats in the sphere of information security and possible cooperative measures to address them, as well as the concepts referred to in paragraph 2 above, and to submit a report on the results of this study to the General Assembly at its sixty-fifth session;

5. *Decides* to include in the provisional agenda of its sixty-fourth session the item entitled "Developments in the field of information and telecommunications in the context of international security".

RECORDED VOTE ON RESOLUTION 63/37:

In favour: Afghanistan, Albania, Algeria, Andorra, Angola, Antigua and Barbuda, Argentina, Armenia, Australia, Austria, Azerbaijan, Bahamas, Bahrain, Bangladesh, Barbados, Belarus, Belgium, Belize, Benin, Bhutan, Bolivia, Bosnia and Herzegovina, Botswana, Brazil, Brunei Darussalam, Bulgaria, Burkina Faso, Burundi, Cambodia, Cameroon, Canada, Cape Verde, Chile, China, Colombia, Comoros, Congo, Costa Rica, Côte d'Ivoire, Croatia, Cuba, Cyprus, Czech Republic, Democratic People's Republic of the Congo, Denmark, Djibouti, Dominica, Dominican Republic, Ecuador, Egypt, El Salvador, Equatorial Guinea, Eritrea, Estonia, Ethiopia, Finland, France, Gabon, Georgia, Germany, Ghana, Greece, Grenada, Guatemala, Guinea, Guinea-Bissau, Guyana, Haiti, Honduras, Hungary, Iceland, India, Indonesia, Iran, Iraq, Ireland, Israel, Italy, Jamaica, Japan, Jordan, Kazakhstan, Kenya, Kuwait, Kyrgyzstan, Lao People's Democratic Republic, Latvia, Lebanon, Lesotho, Liberia, Libyan Arab Jamahiriya, Liechtenstein, Lithuania, Luxembourg, Madagascar, Malawi, Malaysia, Maldives, Mali, Malta, Marshall Islands, Mauritania, Mauritius, Mexico, Micronesia, Moldova, Monaco, Mongolia, Montenegro, Morocco, Mozambique, Myanmar, Namibia, Nepal, Netherlands, New Zealand, Nicaragua, Niger, Nigeria, Norway, Oman, Pakistan, Palau, Panama, Papua New Guinea, Paraguay, Peru, Philippines, Poland, Portugal, Qatar, Republic of Korea, Romania, Russian Federation, Rwanda, Saint Lucia, Samoa, San Marino, Sao Tome and Principe, Saudi Arabia, Senegal, Serbia, Singapore, Slovakia, Slovenia, Solomon Islands, South Africa, Spain, Sri Lanka, Sudan, Suriname, Swaziland, Sweden, Switzerland, Syrian Arab Republic, Tajikistan, Thailand, The former Yugoslav Republic of Macedonia, Timor-Leste, Togo, Trinidad and Tobago, Tunisia, Turkey, Turkmenistan, Tuvalu, Uganda, Ukraine, United Arab Emirates, United Kingdom, United Republic of Tanzania, Uruguay, Uzbekistan, Venezuela, Viet Nam, Yemen, Zambia, Zimbabwe.

Against: United States.

On 2 December, the General Assembly, on the recommendation of the First Committee [A/63/384], included in the provisional agenda of its sixty-fourth (2009) session the item entitled "Role of science and technology in the context of international security and disarmament" (**decision 63/518**).

UN public information

The General Assembly's Committee on Information, at its thirtieth session (New York, 28 April–9 May) [A/63/21], continued to consider UN information policies and activities, and to evaluate and follow up on efforts made and progress achieved in information and communications.

The Committee had before it two February reports of the Secretary-General on activities of the UN Department of Public Information (DPI) for the period from July 2007 to February 2008. Part one [A/AC.198/2008/2] addressed advancements in DPI's thematic areas; strategic directions; public information and UN peacekeeping; news services; knowledge-sharing and library services; outreach and public relations; building partnerships with civil society; sales and marketing services; publications board; and capital master plan and its impact. Part two [A/AC.198/2008/3] covered the activities of the network of UN information centres (UNICs) and the UN website with particular focus on progress towards parity among official languages, accessibility and content management.

The Committee deferred its consideration of the document containing DPI's proposed strategic framework for 2010–2011 [A/63/6] until its thirty-first (2009) session.

By **decision 63/524** of 5 December, the General Assembly increased the Committee's membership from 110 to 112. On the same date, by **decision 63/412**, the Assembly appointed Antigua and Barbuda and Zambia as members of the Committee.

GENERAL ASSEMBLY ACTION

On 5 December [meeting 64], the General Assembly, on the recommendation of the Fourth Committee [A/63/403], adopted **resolutions 63/100 A** and **B** without vote [agenda item 32].

Questions relating to information

A

Information in the service of humanity

The General Assembly,

Taking note of the comprehensive and important report of the Committee on Information,

Also taking note of the report of the Secretary-General on questions relating to information,

Urges all countries, organizations of the United Nations system as a whole and all others concerned, reaffirming their commitment to the principles of the Charter of the United Nations and to the principles of freedom of the press and freedom of information, as well as to those of the independence, pluralism and diversity of the media, deeply concerned by the disparities existing between developed and developing countries and the consequences of every kind arising from those disparities that affect the capability of the public, private or other media and individuals in developing countries to disseminate information and communicate their views and their cultural and ethical values through endogenous cultural production, as well as to ensure the diversity of sources and their free access to information, and recognizing the call in this context for what in the United Nations and at various international forums has been termed "a new world information and communication order, seen as an evolving and continuous process":

(*a*) To cooperate and interact with a view to reducing existing disparities in information flows at all levels by increasing assistance for the development of communications infrastructures and capabilities in developing countries, with due regard for their needs and the priorities attached to such areas by those countries, and in order to enable them and the public, private or other media in developing countries to develop their own information and communications policies freely and independently and increase the participation of media and individuals in the communication process, and to ensure a free flow of information at all levels;

(*b*) To ensure for journalists the free and effective performance of their professional tasks and condemn resolutely all attacks against them;

(*c*) To provide support for the continuation and strengthening of practical training programmes for broadcasters and journalists from public, private and other media in developing countries;

(*d*) To enhance regional efforts and cooperation among developing countries, as well as cooperation between developed and developing countries, to strengthen communications capacities and to improve the media infrastructure and communications technology in the developing countries, especially in the areas of training and dissemination of information;

(*e*) To aim at, in addition to bilateral cooperation, providing all possible support and assistance to the developing countries and their media, public, private or other, with due regard to their interests and needs in the field of information and to action already adopted within the United Nations system, including:

(i) The development of the human and technical resources that are indispensable for the improvement of information and communications systems in developing countries and support for the continuation and strengthening of practical training programmes, such as those already operating under both public and private auspices throughout the developing world;

(ii) The creation of conditions that will enable developing countries and their media, public, private or other, to have, by using their national and regional resources, the communications technology suited to their national needs, as well as the necessary programme material, especially for radio and television broadcasting;

(iii) Assistance in establishing and promoting telecommunication links at the subregional, regional and interregional levels, especially among developing countries;

(iv) The facilitation, as appropriate, of access by the developing countries to advanced communications technology available on the open market;

(f) To provide full support for the International Programme for the Development of Communication of the United Nations Educational, Scientific and Cultural Organization, which should support both public and private media.

B

United Nations public information policies and activities

The General Assembly,

Emphasizing the role of the Committee on Information as its main subsidiary body mandated to make recommendations to it relating to the work of the Department of Public Information of the Secretariat,

Reaffirming its resolution 13(I) of 13 February 1946, establishing the Department of Public Information, which states in paragraph 2 of annex I that "the activities of the Department should be so organized and directed as to promote to the greatest possible extent an informed understanding of the work and purposes of the United Nations among the peoples of the world",

Emphasizing that the contents of public information and communications should be placed at the heart of the strategic management of the United Nations and that a culture of communications and transparency should permeate all levels of the Organization, as a means of fully informing the peoples of the world of the aims and activities of the United Nations, in accordance with the purposes and principles enshrined in the Charter of the United Nations, in order to create broad-based global support for the United Nations,

Stressing that the primary mission of the Department of Public Information is to provide, through its outreach activities, accurate, impartial, comprehensive, timely and relevant information to the public on the tasks and responsibilities of the United Nations in order to strengthen international support for the activities of the Organization with the greatest transparency,

Recalling the comprehensive review of the work of the Department of Public Information, requested by the General Assembly in its resolution 56/253 of 24 December 2001, as well as the report of the Secretary-General entitled "Strengthening of the United Nations: an agenda for further change" and Assembly resolutions 57/300 of 20 December 2002 and 60/109 B of 8 December 2005, which provided an opportunity to take due steps to enhance the efficiency and effectiveness of the Department and to maximize the use of its resources,

Expressing its concern that the gap in information and communications technology between the developed and the developing countries has continued to widen and that vast segments of the population in developing countries are not benefiting from the present information and communications technologies, and, in this regard, underlining the necessity of rectifying the imbalances in the present development of information and communications technologies in order to make it more just, equitable and effective,

Recognizing that developments in information and communications technologies open vast new opportunities for economic growth and social development and can play an important role in the eradication of poverty in developing countries, and, at the same time, emphasizing that the development of these technologies poses challenges and risks and could lead to the further widening of disparities between and within countries,

Recalling its resolution 61/266 of 16 May 2007 on multilingualism, and emphasizing the importance of making appropriate use of the official languages of the United Nations in the activities of the Department of Public Information, with the aim of eliminating the disparity between the use of English and the five other official languages,

Welcoming Antigua and Barbuda and Zambia to membership in the Committee on Information,

I

Introduction

1. *Reaffirms* its resolution 13(I), in which it established the Department of Public Information, and all other relevant resolutions of the General Assembly related to the activities of the Department, and requests the Secretary-General, in respect of the public information policies and activities of the United Nations, to continue to implement fully the recommendations contained in paragraph 2 of its resolution 48/44 B of 10 December 1993 and other mandates as established by the General Assembly;

2. *Also reaffirms* that the United Nations remains the indispensable foundation of a peaceful and just world and that its voice must be heard in a clear and effective manner, and emphasizes the essential role of the Department of Public Information in this context;

3. *Stresses* the importance of the clear, timely, accurate and comprehensive provision of information by the Secretariat to Member States, upon their request, within the framework of existing mandates and procedures;

4. *Reaffirms* the central role of the Committee on Information in United Nations public information policies and activities, including the prioritization of those

activities, and decides that recommendations relating to the programme of the Department of Public Information shall originate, to the extent possible, in the Committee and shall be considered by the Committee;

5. *Requests* the Department of Public Information, following the priorities laid down by the General Assembly in its resolution 61/235 of 22 December 2006, and guided by the United Nations Millennium Declaration and reaffirming the 2005 World Summit Outcome, to pay particular attention to peace and security, development and human rights and to major issues such as the eradication of poverty, including the global food crisis, conflict prevention, sustainable development, the HIV/AIDS epidemic, combating terrorism in all its forms and manifestations and the needs of the African continent;

6. *Also requests* the Department of Public Information to pay particular attention to progress in implementing the internationally agreed development goals, including those contained in the Millennium Declaration, and the outcomes of the major related United Nations summits and conferences in carrying out its activities;

7. *Further requests* the Department of Public Information and its network of United Nations information centres to play an active role in raising public awareness of the global challenge of climate change, and encourages the Department to pay particular attention to the actions taken in the framework of the United Nations Framework Convention on Climate Change, in accordance with the principles of common but differentiated responsibilities, especially in the context of the forthcoming sessions of the Conference of the Parties and of the Meetings of the Parties to the Kyoto Protocol to be held in Poznan, Poland, from 1 to 12 December 2008 and in Copenhagen from 30 November to 11 December 2009;

8. *Reaffirms* the need to enhance the technological infrastructure of the Department of Public Information on a continuous basis in order to widen its outreach and to continue to improve the United Nations website;

II

General activities of the Department of Public Information

9. *Takes note* of the reports of the Secretary-General on the activities of the Department of Public Information;

10. *Requests* the Department of Public Information to maintain its commitment to a culture of evaluation and to continue to evaluate its products and activities with the objective of improving their effectiveness, and to continue to cooperate and coordinate with Member States and the Office of Internal Oversight Services of the Secretariat;

11. *Reaffirms* the importance of more effective coordination between the Department of Public Information and the Office of the Spokesperson for the Secretary-General, and requests the Secretary-General to ensure consistency in the messages of the Organization;

12. *Encourages* continued collaboration between the Department of Public Information and the United Nations Educational, Scientific and Cultural Organization in the promotion of culture and in the fields of education and communication, bridging the existing gap between the developed and the developing countries;

13. *Reaffirms* that the Department of Public Information must prioritize its work programme, while respecting existing mandates and in line with regulation 5.6 of the Regulations and Rules Governing Programme Planning, the Programme Aspects of the Budget, the Monitoring of Implementation and the Methods of Evaluation, to focus its message and better concentrate its efforts and to match its programmes with the needs of its target audiences, on the basis of improved feedback and evaluation mechanisms;

14. *Notes* the efforts of the Department of Public Information to continue to publicize the work and decisions of the General Assembly, and requests the Department to continue to enhance its working relationship with the Office of the President of the General Assembly;

15. *Requests* the Secretary-General to continue to exert all efforts to ensure that publications and other information services of the Secretariat, including the United Nations website and the United Nations News Service, contain comprehensive, objective and equitable information in all official languages about the issues before the Organization and that they maintain editorial independence, impartiality, accuracy and full consistency with resolutions and decisions of the General Assembly;

16. *Requests* the Department of Public Information and content-providing offices of the Secretariat to ensure that United Nations publications are produced in a cost-effective manner and to continue to coordinate closely with all other entities, including all other departments of the Secretariat and funds and programmes of the United Nations system, in order to avoid duplication, within their respective mandates, in the issuance of United Nations publications;

17. *Emphasizes* that the Department of Public Information should maintain and improve its activities in the areas of special interest to developing countries and where appropriate, other countries with special needs, and that the activities of the Department should contribute to bridging the existing gap between the developing and the developed countries in the crucial field of public information and communications;

18. *Notes* the issuance of daily press releases, and requests the Department of Public Information to continue to improve their production process and streamline their format, structure and length, keeping in mind the views of Member States, including their views on expanding them to the other official languages;

19. *Notes with appreciation* the efforts of the Department of Public Information to work at the local level with other organizations and bodies of the United Nations system to enhance the coordination of their communications activities, and requests the Secretary-General to report to the Committee on Information at its thirty-first session on progress achieved in this regard and on the activities of the United Nations Communications Group;

20. *Calls upon* the Department of Public Information, recognizing the importance of audio-visual archives in preserving our common heritage, to continue to examine its policies and activities regarding the durable preservation of its radio, television and photographic archives and to take action within existing resources in ensuring that such archives are preserved and are accessible, and encourages the

Department to work further with all interested partners in order to reach that objective;

Multilingualism and public information

21. *Emphasizes* the importance of making appropriate use and ensuring equitable treatment of all the official languages of the United Nations in all the activities of the Department of Public Information, including in presentations to the Committee on Information, with the aim of eliminating the disparity between the use of English and the five other official languages;

22. *Reiterates its request* to the Secretary-General to ensure that the Department of Public Information has appropriate staffing capacity in all the official languages of the United Nations to undertake all its activities and to include this aspect in future programme budget proposals for the Department, bearing in mind the principle of parity of all six official languages, while respecting the workload of each official language;

23. *Welcomes* the ongoing efforts of the Department of Public Information to enhance multilingualism in all its activities, and stresses the importance of fully implementing its resolution 61/266 by ensuring that the texts of all new public documents in all six official languages and information materials of the United Nations are made available daily through the United Nations website and are accessible to Member States without delay;

24. *Requests* the Secretary-General to continue towards completion of the task of uploading all important older United Nations documents on the United Nations website in all six official languages on a priority basis, so that these archives are also available to Member States through that medium;

Bridging the digital divide

25. *Recalls with satisfaction* its resolution 60/252 of 27 March 2006, in which it endorsed the Tunis Commitment and the Tunis Agenda for the Information Society, as adopted at the second phase of the World Summit on the Information Society, held in Tunis from 16 to 18 November 2005, and proclaimed 17 May annual World Information Society Day, recalls the adoption of the Declaration of Principles and the Plan of Action at the first phase of the World Summit on the Information Society, held in Geneva from 10 to 12 December 2003, and in this regard requests the Department of Public Information to contribute to the celebration of this event and to play a role in raising awareness of the possibilities that the use of the Internet and other information and communications technologies can bring to societies and economies, as well as of ways to bridge the digital divide;

26. *Calls upon* the Department of Public Information to contribute to raising the awareness of the international community of the importance of the implementation of the outcome documents of the World Summit on the Information Society;

Network of United Nations information centres

27. *Emphasizes* the importance of the network of United Nations information centres in enhancing the public image of the United Nations and in disseminating messages on the United Nations to local populations, especially in developing countries;

28. *Welcomes* the work done by the network of United Nations information centres in favour of the publication of United Nations information materials and the translation of important documents in languages other than the official languages of the United Nations, with a view to reaching the widest possible spectrum of audiences and extending the United Nations message to all the corners of the world in order to strengthen international support for the activities of the Organization, and encourages the continuation of efforts in this regard;

29. *Stresses* the importance of rationalizing the network of United Nations information centres, and, in this regard, requests the Secretary-General to continue to make proposals in this direction, including through the redeployment of resources where necessary, and to report to the Committee on Information at its successive sessions;

30. *Reaffirms* that the rationalization of United Nations information centres must be carried out on a case-by-case basis in consultation with all concerned Member States in which existing information centres are located, the countries served by those information centres and other interested countries in the region, taking into consideration the distinctive characteristics of each region;

31. *Recognizes* that the network of United Nations information centres, especially in developing countries, should continue to enhance its impact and activities, including through strategic communications support, and calls upon the Secretary-General to report on the implementation of this approach to the Committee on Information at its successive sessions;

32. *Encourages* the Department of Public Information, through the information centres, to strengthen its cooperation with all other United Nations entities at the country level, in order to enhance coherence in communications and to avoid duplication of work;

33. *Stresses* the importance of taking into account the special needs and requirements of developing countries in the field of information and communications technology for the effective flow of information in those countries;

34. *Also stresses* that the Department of Public Information, through the network of United Nations information centres, should continue to promote public awareness of and mobilize support for the work of the United Nations at the local level, bearing in mind that information in local languages has the strongest impact on local populations;

35. *Further stresses* the importance of efforts to strengthen the outreach activities of the United Nations to those Member States remaining outside the network of United Nations information centres, and encourages the Secretary-General, within the context of rationalization, to extend the services of the network of United Nations information centres to those Member States;

36. *Stresses* that the Department of Public Information should continue to review the allocation of both staff and financial resources to the United Nations information centres in developing countries, emphasizing the needs of the least developed countries;

37. *Encourages* the network of United Nations information centres to continue to develop web pages in local languages, encourages the Department of Public Information to provide necessary resources and technical facilities,

and encourages host countries to respond to the needs of the information centres;

38. *Takes note* of the proposal by the Secretary-General to work closely with the Governments concerned to explore the possibility of identifying rent-free premises, while taking into account the economic condition of the host countries and bearing in mind that such support should not be a substitute for the full allocation of financial resources for the information centres in the context of the programme budget of the United Nations;

39. *Also takes note* of the strengthening of the information centres in Cairo, Mexico City and Pretoria, and encourages the Secretary-General to explore the strengthening of other centres, especially in Africa, in cooperation with the Member States concerned and within existing resources;

40. *Recalls* the offer made by the Government of Angola to host a United Nations information centre in Luanda to address the special needs of Portuguese-speaking African countries, through the provision of rent-free premises, and regrets the lack of progress in this regard, and requests the Secretary-General to report to the Committee on Information at its thirty-first session on the measures necessary, including the budgetary requirements, to accommodate those needs, as well as any proposal to move this process forward;

III

Strategic communications services

41. *Reaffirms* the role of the strategic communications services in devising and disseminating United Nations messages by developing communications strategies, in close collaboration with the substantive departments, United Nations funds and programmes and the specialized agencies, in full compliance with their legislative mandates;

Promotional campaigns

42. *Appreciates* the work of the Department of Public Information in promoting, through its campaigns, issues of importance to the international community, such as the United Nations Millennium Declaration and the progress made in implementing the internationally agreed development goals, United Nations reform, the eradication of poverty, conflict prevention, sustainable development, disarmament, decolonization, human rights, including the rights of women and children and of persons with disabilities, strategic coordination in humanitarian relief, especially in natural disasters and other crises, HIV/AIDS, malaria, tuberculosis and other diseases, the needs of the African continent and combating terrorism in all its forms and manifestations, as well as dialogue among civilizations, the culture of peace and tolerance and the consequences of the Chernobyl disaster;

43. *Commends* the role of the Department of Public Information in observing the first International Day of Remembrance of the Victims of Slavery and the Transatlantic Slave Trade, and looks forward to its further work in promoting the establishment of the permanent memorial to the victims of slavery and the transatlantic slave trade;

44. *Requests* the Department, in this regard, in cooperation with the countries concerned and with the relevant organizations and bodies of the United Nations system, to continue to take appropriate measures to enhance world public awareness of these and other important global issues;

45. *Stresses* the need to continue the renewed emphasis in support of Africa's development, in particular by the Department of Public Information, in order to promote awareness in the international community of the nature of the critical economic and social situation in Africa and of the priorities of the New Partnership for Africa's Development;

46. *Recognizes* the role of the Department of Public Information and its network of United Nations information centres in commemorating the sixtieth anniversary of the Universal Declaration of Human Rights;

Role of the Department of Public Information in United Nations peacekeeping operations

47. *Commends* the role of the Department of Public Information and its network of United Nations information centres in commemorating the sixtieth anniversary of United Nations peacekeeping;

48. *Requests* the Secretariat to continue to ensure the involvement of the Department of Public Information from the planning stage of future peacekeeping operations through interdepartmental consultations and coordination with other departments of the Secretariat, in particular with the Department of Peacekeeping Operations and the Department of Field Support;

49. *Stresses* the importance of enhancing the public information capacity of the Department of Public Information in the field of peacekeeping operations and its role, in close cooperation with the Department of Peacekeeping Operations and the Department of Field Support, in the process of selecting public information staff for United Nations peacekeeping operations or missions, and, in this regard, invites the Department of Public Information to second public information staff who have the necessary skills to fulfil the tasks of the operations or missions, taking into account the principle of equitable geographical distribution in accordance with Chapter XV, Article 101, paragraph 3, of the Charter of the United Nations, and to consider views expressed, especially by host countries, when appropriate, in this regard;

50. *Emphasizes* the importance of the peacekeeping gateway on the United Nations website, and requests the Department of Public Information to continue its efforts in supporting the peacekeeping missions to further develop their websites;

51. *Requests* the Department of Public Information, the Department of Peacekeeping Operations and the Department of Field Support to continue their cooperation in raising awareness of the new realities, far-reaching successes and challenges faced by peacekeeping operations, especially multidimensional and complex ones, and the recent surge in United Nations peacekeeping activities, and welcomes efforts by the three Departments to develop and implement a comprehensive communications strategy on current challenges facing United Nations peacekeeping;

52. *Requests* the Department of Public Information and the Department of Peacekeeping Operations to continue to cooperate in implementing an effective outreach programme to explain the zero-tolerance policy of the Organization regarding sexual exploitation and abuse and to

inform the public of the outcome of all such cases involving peacekeeping personnel, including cases where allegations are ultimately found to be legally unproven, and also to inform the public of the adoption by the General Assembly of the United Nations Comprehensive Strategy on Assistance and Support to Victims of Sexual Exploitation and Abuse by United Nations Staff and Related Personnel;

Role of the Department of Public Information in strengthening dialogue among civilizations and the culture of peace as means of enhancing understanding among nations

53. *Recalls* its resolutions on dialogue among civilizations and the culture of peace, requests the Department of Public Information, while ensuring the pertinence and relevance of subjects for promotional campaigns under this issue, to continue to provide the necessary support for the dissemination of information pertaining to dialogue among civilizations and the culture of peace, as well as the initiative on the Alliance of Civilizations, and to take due steps in fostering the culture of dialogue among civilizations and promoting cultural understanding, tolerance, respect for and freedom of religion or belief and effective enjoyment by all of all human rights and civil, political, economic, social and cultural rights, including the right to development, recognizes the efforts made by the High Representative of the Secretary-General for the Alliance of Civilizations, and takes note of the initiatives launched at the first Alliance of Civilizations Forum, held in Madrid on 15 and 16 January 2008;

IV

News services

54. *Stresses* that the central objective of the news services implemented by the Department of Public Information is the timely delivery of accurate, objective and balanced news and information emanating from the United Nations system in all four mass media, namely, print, radio, television and the Internet, to the media and other audiences worldwide, with the overall emphasis on multilingualism, and reiterates its request to the Department to ensure that all news-breaking stories and news alerts are accurate, impartial and free of bias;

55. *Emphasizes* the importance of the Department of Public Information continuing to draw the attention of world media to stories that do not obtain prominent coverage, through the initiative entitled "10 Stories the World Should Hear More About" and through video and audio coverage by United Nations Television and United Nations Radio;

Traditional means of communication

56. *Welcomes* the initiative of United Nations Radio, which remains one of the most effective and far-reaching traditional media available to the Department of Public Information and an important instrument in United Nations activities, to enhance its live radio broadcasting service by making more frequently updated reports in all six official languages and features available to broadcasters on a daily basis on all United Nations activities, and requests the Secretary-General to continue to make every effort to achieve parity in the six official languages in United Nations Radio productions;

57. *Notes* the efforts being made by the Department of Public Information to disseminate programmes directly to broadcasting stations all over the world in the six official languages, with the addition of Portuguese and Kiswahili, as well as in other languages where possible;

58. *Requests* the Department of Public Information to continue building partnerships with local, national and regional broadcasters to extend the United Nations message to all the corners of the world in an accurate and impartial way, and requests the Radio and Television Service of the Department to continue to take full advantage of the technological infrastructure made available in recent years;

United Nations website

59. *Reaffirms* that the United Nations website is an essential tool for the media, non-governmental organizations, educational institutions, Member States and the general public, and, in this regard, reiterates the continued need for efforts by the Department of Public Information to maintain and improve it;

60. *Recognizes* the efforts made by the Department of Public Information to implement the basic accessibility requirements for persons with disabilities to access the United Nations website, and calls upon the Department to continue to work towards compliance with accessibility requirements on all new and updated pages of the website, with the aim of ensuring its accessibility for persons with different kinds of disabilities;

61. *Takes note* of the fact that the multilingual development and enrichment of the United Nations website has improved, and, in this regard, requests the Department of Public Information, in coordination with content-providing offices, to further improve the actions taken to achieve full parity among the six official languages on the United Nations website, and especially reiterates its request to ensure the adequate distribution of financial and human resources within the Department of Public Information allocated to the United Nations website among all official languages, taking into consideration the specificity of each official language;

62. *Welcomes* the cooperative arrangements undertaken by the Department of Public Information with academic institutions to increase the number of web pages available in some official languages, and requests the Secretary-General to extend those arrangements to all the official languages of the United Nations;

63. *Recalls* paragraph 74 of its resolution 60/109 B, and in this regard reiterates that all content-providing offices in the Secretariat should continue their efforts to translate into all official languages all English-language materials and databases posted on the United Nations website and to make them available on the respective language websites in the most practical, efficient and cost-effective manner;

64. *Requests* the Secretary-General to continue to take full advantage of new developments in information technology in order to improve, in a cost-effective manner, the expeditious dissemination of information on the United Nations, in accordance with the priorities established by the General Assembly in its resolutions and taking into account the linguistic diversity of the Organization;

65. *Recognizes* that some official languages use non-Latin and bidirectional scripts and that technological in-

frastructures and supportive applications in the United Nations are based on Latin script, which leads to difficulties in processing non-Latin and bidirectional scripts, and urges the Information Technology Services Division of the Department of Management to further collaborate with the Department of Public Information and to continue its efforts to ensure that technological infrastructures and supportive applications in the United Nations fully support Latin, non-Latin and bidirectional scripts in order to enhance the equality of all official languages on the United Nations website;

66. *Welcomes* the continuing growth in the popularity of the e-mail news alerts service provided by the Department of Public Information on the United Nations News Centre portal in English and French, and encourages the Department to consult with the Information Technology Services Division of the Department of Management and to explore, as a matter of priority, ways of upgrading the technical capabilities of the service and providing it in all official languages;

V

Library services

67. *Calls upon* the Department of Public Information to continue to lead the Steering Committee for the Modernization and Integrated Management of United Nations Libraries and further commends the steps taken by the Dag Hammarskjöld Library and the other member libraries of the Steering Committee to align their activities, services and outputs more closely with the goals, objectives and operational priorities of the Organization;

68. *Reiterates* the need to maintain a multilingual collection of books, periodicals and other materials in hard copy, accessible to Member States, ensuring that the Library continues to be a broadly accessible resource for information about the United Nations and its activities;

69. *Takes note* of the initiative taken by the Dag Hammarskjöld Library, in its capacity as the focal point, to expand the scope of the regional training and knowledge-sharing workshops organized for the depository libraries in developing countries to include outreach in their activities;

70. *Acknowledges* the role of the Dag Hammarskjöld Library, in enhancing knowledge-sharing and networking activities to ensure access to the vast store of United Nations knowledge for delegates, permanent missions of Member States, the Secretariat, researchers and depository libraries worldwide, takes note of the proposal to rename the library the Dag Hammarskjöld Library and Knowledge-Sharing Centre, reflecting its new direction, and also takes note of the proposal to change the designation of the depository libraries to partner libraries;

71. *Notes with appreciation* the Personal Knowledge Management initiative to assist representatives of Member States and Secretariat staff in the use of information products and tools as a complement to the traditional training programmes;

72. *Encourages* the Secretariat to develop and implement cost-neutral measures to provide Member States with secure access to the information currently accessible only on the Intranet of the Secretariat (iSeek), taking note that Member States have access to iSeek only through the facilities of the Dag Hammarskjöld Library;

VI

Outreach services

73. *Acknowledges* that the outreach services provided by the Department of Public Information continue to work towards promoting awareness of the role and work of the United Nations;

74. *Welcomes* the educational outreach activities of the Department of Public Information, through the United Nations Works programme and the Global Teaching and Learning Project, to reach educators and young people worldwide via a range of multimedia platforms, and encourages the United Nations Works programme to continue to develop further its partnerships with global media networks and celebrity advocates and the Global Teaching and Learning Project to further expand its activities to teachers and students in primary, intermediate and secondary schools;

75. *Notes* the importance of the continued implementation by the Department of Public Information of the ongoing programme for broadcasters and journalists from developing countries and countries with economies in transition, as mandated by the General Assembly, and requests the Department to consider how best to maximize the benefits derived from the programme by extending, inter alia, its duration and the number of its participants;

76. *Welcomes* the movement towards educational outreach and the orientation of the *UN Chronicle*, both print and online editions, and, to this end, encourages the *UN Chronicle* to continue to develop co-publishing partnerships, collaborative educational activities and events, including the "Unlearning Intolerance" seminar series, with civil society organizations and institutions of higher learning;

77. *Takes note* of the intention of the Department of Public Information to have the *UN Chronicle* magazine evolve into a journal called "UN Affairs", and requests, for further consideration, a comprehensive and detailed report on the progress of the project in due course;

78. *Considers it necessary* for the Department of Public Information to clearly identify practical improvements intended by the change from the *UN Chronicle* to "UN Affairs", taking into account parity of languages, editorial policy, potential qualitative gains and other improvements and urges that the Department, while considering these aspects, place emphasis on cost-effective measures and the present budgetary constraints, and welcomes any other alternative in line with the mandate of the Department for the consideration of Member States;

79. *Requests* the Department of Public Information to continue the *UN Chronicle* until a decision is taken on "UN Affairs" or any other alternative in line with the mandate of the Department;

80. *Reaffirms* the important role that guided tours play as a means of reaching out to the general public, and takes note of the efforts undertaken by the Department of Public Information in organizing exhibitions on important United Nations-related issues within existing mandates at United

Nations Headquarters and at other United Nations offices as a useful tool for reaching out to the general public;

81. *Requests* the Department of Public Information to strengthen its role as a focal point for two-way interaction with civil society relating to those priorities and concerns of the Organization identified by Member States;

82. *Commends*, in a spirit of cooperation, the United Nations Correspondents Association for its ongoing activities and for its Dag Hammarskjöld Memorial Scholarship Fund, which sponsors journalists from developing countries to come to the United Nations Headquarters and report on the activities during the General Assembly, and further encourages the international community to continue its financial support for the Fund;

83. *Expresses its appreciation* for the efforts and contribution of United Nations Messengers of Peace, Goodwill Ambassadors and other advocates to promote the work of the United Nations and to enhance international public awareness of its priorities and concerns, and calls upon the Department of Public Information to continue to involve them in its communications and media strategies and outreach activities;

VII

Final remarks

84. *Requests* the Secretary-General to report to the Committee on Information at its thirty-first session and to the General Assembly at its sixty-fourth session on the activities of the Department of Public Information and on the implementation of all recommendations and requests contained in the present resolution;

85. *Also requests* the Secretary-General to make every effort to ensure that the level of services provided by the Department of Public Information is maintained throughout the period of the implementation of the capital master plan;

86. *Strongly urges* the Secretary-General to accede to the request by Member States to provide additional passes to press officers of Member States to gain access to areas that are deemed restricted, in order to effectively and comprehensively report on high-level meetings that include officials of delegations of Member States;

87. *Requests* the Committee on Information to report to the General Assembly at its sixty-fourth session;

88. *Decides* to include in the provisional agenda of its sixty-fourth session the item entitled "Questions relating to information".

DPI activities

In response to General Assembly resolution 62/111 B [YUN 2007, p. 648], the Secretary-General submitted an August report [A/63/258] on questions relating to information, covering DPI's activities since his February reports to the Committee on Information.

DPI continued to address the Organization's key thematic priorities, including issues related to peace and security, development and human rights. It paid particular attention to promoting the sixtieth anniversary of the adoption of the Universal Declaration of Human Rights and the sixtieth anniversary of United Nations peacekeeping. The network of UN information centres, services and components played a key role in that effort and was increasingly integrated with UN country teams. The Department further expanded its media services, widening the daily delivery of news and information products via radio, television and print media. A marked increase in the use of the UN website over the previous six months was reported, and the Department worked in close cooperation with non-governmental organizations (NGOs) and civil society to expand its outreach and promotional activities, and utilized the Internet and videoconferencing to connect with an increasing number of young people.

Regarding its strategic communication services, DPI cooperated with the Department of Peacekeeping Operations (DPKO) and the Department of Field Support on activities to mark the sixtieth anniversary of UN peacekeeping. The global year-long observance was launched on 29 May, the International Day of United Nations Peacekeepers. The Departments created policy and best practices for UN radio stations in peacekeeping operations—of which there were five—and helped 12 peace operations create content management system websites. They also produced and disseminated around the world coordinated products, exhibitions and events on historical and contemporary issues in peacekeeping, highlighting the role of major troop-contributing countries. DPI and DPKO continued to raise awareness on progress in ending sexual exploitation and abuse by UN personnel by means of public information materials and press briefings. To mark the sixtieth anniversary of the Universal Declaration of Human Rights, DPI co-sponsored, with the Office of the United Nations High Commissioner for Human Rights, the New Human Rights Dialogue Series, a monthly series of discussions at UN Headquarters on human rights issues. Many UN national and regional information centres organized events in support of the year-long campaign.

DPI-supported projects included the display of multilingual versions of the exhibition "Lessons from Rwanda", which focused on the history of the Rwandan genocide and its impact on survivors, at two universities in Rwanda and several other national and international locations. DPI also prepared and launched the "Lessons from Rwanda" website in all six official languages. With DPI's assistance, the Secretary-General launched his system-wide campaign to end violence against women on 25 February. Information materials were developed in six languages, a logo and website were created, and several information centres mobilized public awareness through country-specific seminars and events.

As for climate change issues, DPI convened a communication task force of 17 UN entities working on climate change with a view to implementing a system-wide strategy, and maintained a website detailing the UN system's work. DPI's efforts to raise public awareness of the New Partnership for Africa's Development resulted in broader dissemination of information on its goals, challenges and achievements. In that regard, particularly notable was the role played by its quarterly magazine *Africa Renewal*. DPI also sought to raise awareness on Africa's special needs in relation to climate change. The focus of the Department's communication work for the Millennium Development Goals (MDGs) was the planning for the High-level Event of 25 September (see p. 926), which was coordinated by DPI through a UN Communications Group Task Force.

The Department increased its promotion of the work of the General Assembly and the Economic and Social Council. Through its outreach services and programmes, DPI continued to expand its association with journalists, schools, the general public, advocacy groups, UN entities, NGOs and cultural organizations. The number of NGOs associated with the Department as at July 2008 was 1,664. Programme subjects for which communications activities took place included the International Day of Commemoration in memory of the victims of the Holocaust, World Environment Day and the Programme of Remembrance of the Victims of Slavery and the Transatlantic Slave Trade.

In sales and marketing, DPI introduced a new pricing policy for UN publications. The three-tier policy retained the current level of pricing in developed countries, but featured more affordable pricing in developing and least developed countries, where sales prices were reduced by 50 and 75 per cent, respectively. DPI also completed a major renovation of the bookshop in the Palais des Nations in Geneva, and the new store reopened on schedule in May. In an initiative to increase dissemination of the Organization's legal publications, the Department established a co-publishing venture with a major international legal publisher.

To maintain a culture of evaluation, DPI increased the number of evaluation projects it would complete each year, improved its data-collection tools and continued to provide staff training on survey research, polling data and media analysis. It also strengthened its partnership with an international polling organization to ensure that it regularly received global polling data on a pro bono basis. The Department used its annual programme impact review to evaluate specific programmes and, from that evaluation, derived lessons and action points for application by managers.

UN website

In response to General Assembly resolution 62/111 B [YUN 2007, p. 648], the Secretary-General included in his February report to the Committee on Information [A/AC.198/2008/3] a section on the developments and progress made by DPI towards parity among the official languages on the UN website, as well as its accessibility and content management.

The report acknowledged the Department's continued efforts in addressing the challenge of language parity and the progress in adding new pages to the website. However, it noted that the number of new pages added in English continued to exceed that in other languages, and progress towards parity remained a difficult challenge. DPI, through its Web Services Section, handled the bulk of the languages other than English and French. Agreements with universities for pro bono translations resulted in the addition of 2,552 new pages to the website in Chinese, Russian and Spanish, and DPI continued to enlist the support of an institution of higher learning for pro bono translations into Arabic. The Department also enhanced the multilingual nature of the UN website. Websites created by the network of UNICs provided information in 28 non-official languages.

Regarding accessibility, all new web projects were designed to meet accessibility requirements and comply with the World Wide Web Consortium standards, which were the only standards with global recognition and acceptance. As to content management, DPI faced challenges involved with establishing a governance scheme for management of the public website that allowed author offices the flexibility to meet the needs of their respective audiences and ensured a unified technical infrastructure. To that end, it worked with the Chief Information Technology Officer and the Information Technology Services Division (ITSD) to link the implementation of a content management system with the gradual adoption of a more robust governance system.

In his August report [A/63/258] on questions relating to information, the Secretary-General described a marked increase in the use of the UN website during the first half of the year, with a growing number of visitors viewing it as a resource for news and information in various languages and forms. He also highlighted an upsurge in the use of video materials: an average of over 32,000 video clips were viewed every 24 hours, representing a 116 per cent increase in the number of video clips viewed per day. Between January and June, 23 multilingual websites were created or redesigned in response to an array of new developments or special events. There was a related growth of interest in the live and archived videos produced by UN webcast (www.un.org/webcast), the alert system for which gained 1,000 new subscribers who had access to coverage of several major UN conferences.

The report noted that DPI continued efforts to ensure accessibility of the UN website in the six official languages by persons with disabilities. In order to assist other departments and offices in producing accessible web content, the Department created a special website (www.un.org/webaccessibility) that contained a set of guidelines aimed at promoting compliance with accessibility requirements, monitoring progress and serving as a teaching aid for webmasters and related staff. In another effort to enhance website performance in all official languages, the Department launched a redesigned French version of the UN News Centre website in April, while work continued on the development of similar redesigns in other official languages. There was steady growth in the number of visitors to the site, as well as in the number of users of the UN News Centre Really Simple Syndication feeds and the number of subscribers to the associated e-mail news alerts service.

Radio, television, video and photo services

In his August report on questions relating to information [A/63/258], the Secretary-General considered DPI's activities in providing radio, television and photo services. To make use of advances in communications and Internet technologies, DPI continued to pursue a two-pronged approach aimed at delivering its radio programming to the broadest possible range of audiences. It expanded partnerships with international broadcasters in the six official languages, as well as in Portuguese and Kiswahili, while also relying on the Internet as a means of bringing audio content to its listeners in the six official languages and Portuguese.

In June, the Department launched the UNifeed service on the Web, enabling television broadcasters to download video for immediate use. The initiative opened up a new means to distribute UN television clips from Headquarters, agencies and peacekeeping missions with suggested story lines and shot lists. Feedback from major broadcasters and press agencies since deployment of UNifeed confirmed the growing interest in the service. To capitalize on trends in online distribution of video content, the Department formed a partnership with You Tube/Google, leading to the creation of a UN Television channel.

The Department installed high-definition electronic photo and video displays in several high-traffic areas of the Secretariat building. The electronic boards included UNifeed programmes, themed slideshows, wrap-ups of the latest news developments and public service announcements.

Library and knowledge services

DPI, through its Personal Knowledge Management programme and the research support services of the Dag Hammarskjöld Library, continued to address the information needs of Secretariat and mission staff in a way that aimed to be user-customized. The Personal Knowledge Management initiative helped individuals understand how to better create, manage and access information and improve their utilization of technological tools. The training programmes of the Library were revised in 2008 to address the changing needs of clients. To prepare for implementation of the capital master plan, DPI provided consultations with Secretariat offices needing assistance in organizing their UN document collections. Providing access to important historic UN documentation remained a priority, including the objective of completing the digitization of all major Security Council documents by the end of March 2009.

Further progress was made in implementing the One United Nations initiative through the promotion of internal communications designed for the Secretariat. The Secretariat intranet, iSeek, was launched as the default homepage at most major duty stations, including Addis Ababa, Bangkok, Geneva, Nairobi, New York, Santiago and Vienna.

The depository library programme continued to coordinate a series of regional workshops, focusing on information-sharing, outreach and new roles for libraries as UN partners. One such programme (Saint Petersburg, Russian Federation, June) brought together national and depository library directors from 11 countries in the Commonwealth of Independent States and staff of the UN Information Centre, Moscow and the UN Office, Minsk to encourage the promotion and sharing of information on and knowledge of the United Nations.

UN information centres

In response to General Assembly resolution 62/111 B [YUN 2007, p. 648], the Secretary-General included in his February report to the Committee on Information [A/AC.198/2008/3] a section on the network of UN information centres (UNICs). The report summarized its activities in the areas of communications campaigns, media outreach, partnership building with civil society, multilingualism, library services, regional interaction, consultations with Member States and capacity-building, particularly through staff development and training, expansion of Internet services and the provision of new equipment.

The UNICs network included 63 information centres, services and information components around the world. They served as DPI field offices, providing a public information presence for the Organization in countries around the world, enhancing the UN public image and disseminating messages on the United Nations to local populations, especially in developing countries. Guided by the decisions of the Committee on Information, DPI further strengthened the work of UNICs by expanding partnerships with UN system organizations, Governments, civil society and the private sector, making better use of new information and communications technologies, bolstering their presence in key locations by reallocating resources, and strengthening professional staffing. The overall objective was to provide a structure and support base that made possible more efficient service to a larger audience. UNICs supported UN country teams through the United Nations Communications Group (UNCG), which contributed to higher visibility for the work of the country teams and increased coherence in communications work at the country level.

Discussion on improvements in the information and communications technology infrastructure of UNICs led to the introduction of an e-mail hosting solution that produced coherent e-mail addresses for the UNIC network, thereby alleviating problems associated with the use of multiple and varied e-mail systems. In December 2007, the UNIC in Lagos, Nigeria, became the first to use the new system, which expanded in 2008 with the establishment of unic.org e-mail accounts for information centre staff worldwide.

In his August report to the General Assembly on questions relating to information [A/63/258], the Secretary-General said that nine librarians and seven webmasters from information centres attended workshops on project management in New York, conducted by the Dag Hammarskjöld Library and under the UN external training programme, respectively. By including staff from information centres that had been given a greater regional role, namely those at Brussels, Cairo, Mexico City and Pretoria, DPI sought to "train the trainers" and enhance their ability to provide guidance to other centres in their regions. To strengthen communication infrastructure and enhance the use of information and communications technology, DPI, in cooperation with ITSD, provided 152 computers and related equipment to 26 information centres in developing countries. Internet corners were set up at information centres in 20 countries to provide journalists, researchers, students and the public with Internet access and information on the United Nations.

UN Communications Group

The Secretary-General's report on DPI activities [A/AC.198/2008/2] included information on UNCG, which, since its establishment in 2002 [YUN 2002, p. 589], had evolved into a communication platform for the entire UN system. The Group was widely considered to be an effective means for ensuring coordinated communications on key issues, and its membership and number of annual meetings continued to grow. The Group created several communications task forces on specific issues, including climate change, the MDGs, the Arab region, human and avian influenza and public opinion polling. Additionally, the establishment of over 80 country-level communications groups enabled national communicators to pool their resources and combine efforts to achieve common goals.

The Secretary-General, in his August report on questions relating to information [A/63/258], summarized the outcomes of the Group's seventh annual meeting (Paris, 16–17 June). Discussions and points of agreement focused on UNCG collaboration in the implementation of a climate change communications work programme for 2008–2009; transmission to the UN country teams of a standard operating procedure on cooperative communication in times of crisis; establishment of a working group on communications aspects of "Delivering as one" UN pilots, with a view to increasing internal and inter-agency communications in that area; and continued support for the United Nations Human Settlements Programme as the lead organizing agency for the United Nations Pavilion at Expo 2010 in Shanghai, China.

PART TWO

Human rights

Chapter I

Promotion of human rights

Efforts to promote human rights were boosted in 2008 by several notable developments. The new machinery of the Human Rights Council, created in 2006, began working in earnest with the launch of the Universal Periodic Review mechanism (UPR). Under UPR, the Council examined the human rights record of 48 countries—the first step in reviewing the record of all Member States every four years. Several countries under review undertook firm commitments to better implement human rights, ratify human rights instruments and strengthen their cooperation with the Council's special procedures. Moreover, the Advisory Committee, established to provide expertise to the Council, held its first session and submitted 13 recommendations, while the Council's new complaint procedure, made up of the Working Group on Communications and the Working Group on Situations, addressed consistent patterns of gross and reliably attested violations of human rights and fundamental freedoms throughout the world. Human rights were also promoted through the work of the committees of experts (treaty bodies) monitoring compliance with the legally binding human rights instruments, as well as by the network of human rights defenders in individual countries operating within the framework of the 1998 Declaration on Human Rights Defenders. During the year, the Council held three regular sessions (seventh, eighth and ninth) and three special sessions (sixth, seventh and eighth).

On 10 December, the General Assembly held a plenary meeting to mark the sixtieth anniversary of the adoption of the Universal Declaration of Human Rights. On the same day, it adopted the Optional Protocol to the International Covenant on Economic, Social and Cultural Rights, which established a procedure of individual communications for cases of alleged violations of economic, social and cultural rights. Also in December, the Assembly stressed the role of the Ombudsman, the mediator and other human rights institutions in promoting and protecting human rights. The year also marked the sixtieth anniversary of the 1948 Convention on the Prevention and Punishment of the Crime of Genocide.

The Convention on the Rights of Persons with Disabilities and its Optional Protocol entered into force in May. In November, the Conference of States Parties to the Convention, at its first session, elected the 12 members of the Committee on the Rights of Persons with Disabilities—the body of independent experts to help monitor implementation of the Convention.

The Office of the High Commissioner for Human Rights strengthened its country engagement and expanded its presence at the country and regional levels. It continued to support the work of the Council and its mechanisms, including the special procedures. In July, the Assembly approved the appointment by the Secretary-General of Navanethem Pillay (South Africa) to replace Louise Arbour (Canada) as United Nations High Commissioner for Human Rights for a four-year term of office beginning on 1 September.

UN machinery

Human Rights Council

Council sessions

During the year, the Human Rights Council held its seventh (3–28 March and 1 April) [A/HRC/7/78], eighth (2–18 June) [A/HRC/8/52] and ninth (8–24 September) [A/HRC/9/28] regular sessions. Its second organizational meeting was held on 19 and 20 June.

The Council also held three special sessions: its sixth (23–24 January) [A/HRC/S-6/2] on human rights violations emanating from Israeli military attacks and incursions in the Occupied Palestinian Territory, particularly in the Gaza Strip (see p. 893); its seventh (22 May) [A/HRC/S-7/2] on the negative impact of the worsening world food crisis on the realization of the right to food for all (see p. 835); and its eighth (28 November and 1 December) [A/HRC/S-8/2] on the human rights situation in the eastern Democratic Republic of the Congo (DRC) (see p. 863). All sessions were held in Geneva. The Council held a commemorative session on 12 December to mark the sixtieth anniversary of the Universal Declaration of Human Rights (see p. 726).

The Council adopted 71 resolutions, 35 decisions and six president's statements. It recommended one draft resolution [A/63/53 (res. 8/2)] on the Optional Protocol to the International Covenant on Economic, Social and Cultural Rights for adoption by the General Assembly. The resolutions, decisions and president's statements adopted at those sessions were contained in the Council's report to the Assembly [A/63/53 & Add.1].

The General Assembly addressed revised estimates resulting from resolutions and decisions adopted by the Council in section I of **resolution 62/245** of

3 April (see p. 1550) and in section V of **resolution 63/263** of 24 December (see p. 1547).

GENERAL ASSEMBLY ACTION

On 18 December [meeting 70], the General Assembly, on the recommendation of the Third (Social, Humanitarian and Cultural) Committee [A/63/435/Add.1], adopted **resolution 63/160** by recorded vote (121-7-58) [agenda item 58].

Report of the Human Rights Council

The General Assembly,

Having considered the recommendations contained in the report of the Human Rights Council,

Takes note of the report of the Human Rights Council, and acknowledges the recommendations contained therein.

RECORDED VOTE ON RESOLUTION 63/160:

In favour: Afghanistan, Algeria, Angola, Antigua and Barbuda, Armenia, Azerbaijan, Bahamas, Bahrain, Bangladesh, Barbados, Belarus, Belize, Benin, Bhutan, Botswana, Brunei Darussalam, Burkina Faso, Burundi, Cambodia, Cameroon, Cape Verde, Central African Republic, Chile, China, Colombia, Comoros, Congo, Côte d'Ivoire, Cuba, Democratic People's Republic of Korea, Djibouti, Dominica, Dominican Republic, Ecuador, Egypt, Eritrea, Ethiopia, Gabon, Gambia, Ghana, Grenada, Guatemala, Guinea, Guinea-Bissau, Guyana, Haiti, Honduras, India, Indonesia, Iran, Iraq, Jamaica, Jordan, Kazakhstan, Kenya, Kuwait, Kyrgyzstan, Lao People's Democratic Republic, Lebanon, Lesotho, Liberia, Libyan Arab Jamahiriya, Madagascar, Malawi, Malaysia, Maldives, Mali, Mauritania, Mauritius, Mongolia, Morocco, Mozambique, Myanmar, Namibia, Nepal, Nicaragua, Niger, Nigeria, Oman, Pakistan, Panama, Papua New Guinea, Paraguay, Peru, Philippines, Qatar, Russian Federation, Rwanda, Saint Kitts and Nevis, Saint Lucia, Saint Vincent and the Grenadines, Sao Tome and Principe, Saudi Arabia, Senegal, Sierra Leone, Singapore, Solomon Islands, Somalia, South Africa, Sri Lanka, Sudan, Suriname, Swaziland, Syrian Arab Republic, Tajikistan, Thailand, Timor-Leste, Togo, Trinidad and Tobago, Tunisia, Turkey, Turkmenistan, Uganda, United Arab Emirates, United Republic of Tanzania, Uzbekistan, Venezuela, Viet Nam, Yemen, Zambia, Zimbabwe.

Against: Australia, Canada, Israel, Marshall Islands, Micronesia, Palau, United States.

Abstaining: Albania, Andorra, Argentina, Austria, Belgium, Bolivia, Bosnia and Herzegovina, Brazil, Bulgaria, Costa Rica, Croatia, Cyprus, Czech Republic, Denmark, El Salvador, Estonia, Fiji, Finland, France, Georgia, Germany, Greece, Hungary, Iceland, Ireland, Italy, Japan, Latvia, Liechtenstein, Lithuania, Luxembourg, Malta, Mexico, Moldova, Monaco, Montenegro, Nauru, Netherlands, New Zealand, Norway, Poland, Portugal, Republic of Korea, Romania, Samoa, San Marino, Serbia, Slovakia, Slovenia, Spain, Sweden, Switzerland, The former Yugoslav Republic of Macedonia, Tonga, Ukraine, United Kingdom, Uruguay, Vanuatu.

Election of Council members

On 21 May, by **decision 62/415**, the General Assembly, in accordance with resolution 60/251 [YUN 2006, p. 757], elected Argentina, Bahrain, Brazil, Burkina Faso, Chile, France, Gabon, Ghana, Japan, Pakistan, the Republic of Korea, Slovakia, Ukraine, the United Kingdom and Zambia as members of the Human Rights Council for a three-year term of office beginning on 19 June. They would fill the vacancies occurring on the expiration of the terms of office of Brazil, France, Gabon, Ghana, Guatemala, Japan, Mali, Pakistan, Peru, the Republic of Korea, Romania, Sri Lanka, Ukraine, the United Kingdom and Zambia.

On 24 December, the Assembly decided that the item on the election of 18 members of the Human Rights Council would remain for consideration during its resumed sixty-third (2009) session (**decision 63/552**).

Conference facilities and financial support

Human Rights Council action (June). On 18 June [A/63/53 (res. 8/1)], the Human Rights Council reaffirmed the need to ensure the provision of financial resources to the Council and its working groups for it to discharge its mandate fully, as stipulated in General Assembly resolution 60/251 [YUN 2006, p. 757] and implemented by Council resolution 5/1 [YUN 2007, p. 662].

The Council, concerned at the delays in the submission of documents, in particular their translation into the six official UN languages, requested the Office of the UN High Commissioner for Human Rights (OHCHR) and the Conference Services Division (later the Division of Conference Management) of the United Nations Office at Geneva to propose measures for addressing the situation at the Council's ninth (September) session. It also requested the Department of Public Information (DPI) in Geneva to establish a permanent capacity for webcasting all public proceedings of the Council and its working groups.

OHCHR report. In September [A/HRC/9/18], in response to the Council's request, OHCHR reported that, to meet the increased documentation requirements of the Council and its subsidiary machinery, especially urgent and unforeseen requests for meetings, the Division of Conference Management would require an estimated $7,500,000 annually in additional staff resources. The establishment of editor posts in OHCHR would also provide for the editing of documents. DPI would need an additional $2,500,000 for infrastructure and $1,700,000 in related staffing and other recurring costs for information work.

Human Rights Council action (September). On 24 September [A/63/53/Add.1 (dec. 9/103)], the Human Rights Council took note of the OHCHR report (see above) and requested the Secretary-General to submit to the General Assembly during the main segment of its sixty-third (2008) session a report detailing the resources required to ensure the provision of the services indicated in that report. It recommended that the Assembly establish an Office of the President of the Human Rights Council, with adequate staffing resources and equipment.

The Secretary-General, in response to that request, reported on those requirements [A/63/541/Add.1] to the Assembly, which took action on them in section V of **resolution 63/263** of 24 December (see p. 1547).

Institutional mechanisms

Universal Periodic Review

The Universal Periodic Review mechanism (UPR) was established by the Human Rights Council in 2007 [YUN 2007, p. 663], as an instrument for assessing every four years the human rights records of all Member States. Each review, to be conducted by the Working Group on the Universal Periodic Review, would be facilitated by groups of three States, or "troikas", acting as rapporteurs.

Modalities and practices

Human Rights Council action. In a 9 April president's statement [A/63/53 (PRST/8/1)], the Council President outlined the modalities and practices of the review process. States wishing to raise issues with the State under review might do so through the troika, which would relay them to the Secretariat for submission to that State before consideration by the Working Group on UPR, made up of the 47 Council members. The State under review was sovereign in addressing the questions and/or issues it chose to answer of those transmitted to it by the troika members or raised during the Working Group sessions.

During an interactive dialogue in the Working Group, the State under review would present its national report, reply to written questions and those raised during the dialogue, and make concluding comments. The Working Group's report of its proceedings, to be drafted by the troika, with the involvement of the State under review, would summarize the dialogue and reflect the recommendations and conclusions made by delegations. The State under review would examine the recommendations and identify those it supported. Other recommendations, together with the comments of the State under review, would be noted. Both would be included in the Working Group's report, to be adopted by the Council in plenary through a standardized decision. The State under review was expected to follow up on the recommendations it supported, as well as on voluntary commitments and pledges, and inform the Council about its views concerning the recommendations, conclusions and voluntary commitments.

The review process would end with the Council's adoption of the outcome of the review, consisting of the Working Group's report; the views of the State under review on the recommendations and/or conclusions; its voluntary commitments; and its replies to questions or issues not sufficiently addressed during the interactive dialogue. The Council's report would also include the views of all parties on the review's outcome.

In a follow-up president's statement [A/63/53/Add.1 (PRST/9/2)] of 24 September, the Council President said that, to ensure the smooth adoption of future review reports, the Council's report on its sessions would comprise a summary of the views expressed by the State under review in plenary before the adoption of the outcome, its replies to questions and issues not sufficiently addressed during the interactive dialogue, its views on conclusions and recommendations, its voluntary commitments and concluding remarks, the summary of the views expressed by Council Member and observer States, and a summary of comments made by other stakeholders.

Working Group activities and UPR results

Working Group sessions. The Working Group on UPR held its first (7–18 April), second (5–19 May) and third (1–15 December) sessions in Geneva. It reviewed 48 countries in the order of consideration determined by the Council in 2007 [YUN 2007, p. 663]. As provided for in Council resolution 5/1 [ibid.], the review was based on a national report prepared by the State under review; a compilation by OHCHR of information relating to the human rights situation in the concerned State, as reported by treaty bodies and special procedures; and a summary by OHCHR of credible information from other stakeholders.

The Working Group submitted reports on the States reviewed during its first session: Bahrain [A/HRC/8/19 & Corr.1], Ecuador [A/HRC/8/20 & Corr.1], Tunisia [A/HRC/8/21 & Corr.1], Morocco [A/HRC/8/22 & Corr.1], Indonesia [A/HRC/8/23 & Add.1 & Corr.1], Finland [A/HRC/8/24 & Add.1], the United Kingdom [A/HRC/8/25 & Add.1], India [A/HRC/8/26 & Add.1], Brazil [A/HRC/8/27], the Philippines [A/HRC/8/28 & Corr.1 & Add.1,2], Algeria [A/HRC/8/29], Poland [A/HRC/8/30 & Add.1], the Netherlands [A/HRC/8/31 & Add.1], South Africa [A/HRC/8/32], the Czech Republic [A/HRC/8/33 & Add.1] and Argentina [A/HRC/8/34]. The reports summarized the proceedings, presentation, interactive dialogue and responses by the State under review, as well as its conclusions and/or recommendations, and voluntary commitments. Each review consisted of the views expressed by the State under review on the recommendations and conclusions, as well as on its voluntary commitments; views expressed by member and observer States of the Council on the review outcome; general comments made by other stakeholders, including human rights non-governmental organizations (NGOs); and views expressed by the State under review on the outcome and concluding remarks.

Views on conclusions and/or recommendations, voluntary commitments and replies were submitted by Bahrain [A/HRC/8/19/Add.1 & Corr.1], Indonesia [A/HRC/8/23/Add.1 & Corr.1], the United Kingdom [A/HRC/8/25/Add.1] and Brazil [A/HRC/8/27/Add.1 & Corr.1]. Responses to the recommendations received during the interactive dialogue were submitted by the Philippines [A/HRC/8/28/Add.1,2 & Add.2/Corr.1] and the Netherlands [A/HRC/8/31/Add.1,2 & Add.2/Corr.1].

Responses to the recommendations and conclusions included in the Working Group's report were submitted by the Czech Republic [A/HRC/8/33/Add.1,2 & Add.2/Corr.1], Finland [A/HRC/8/24/Add.1,2 & Add.2/Corr.1], India [A/HRC/8/26/Add.1,2 & Add.2/Corr.1] and Poland [A/HRC/8/30/Add.1,2 & Add.2/Corr.1].

At its second session, the Working Group reviewed the reports of Gabon [A/HRC/8/35], Ghana [A/HRC/8/36], Peru [A/HRC/8/37], Guatemala [A/HRC/8/38], Benin [A/HRC/8/39], the Republic of Korea [A/HRC/8/40], Switzerland [A/HRC/8/41], Pakistan [A/HRC/8/42], Zambia [A/HRC/8/43], Japan [A/HRC/8/44], Ukraine [A/HRC/8/45 & Corr.1], Sri Lanka [A/HRC/8/46], France [A/HRC/8/47], Tonga [A/HRC/8/48], Romania [A/HRC/8/49] and Mali [A/HRC/8/50].

Views on conclusions and/or recommendations, voluntary commitments and replies were presented by Peru [A/HRC/8/36/Add.1 & Corr.1], Ghana [A/HRC/8/37/Add.1 & Corr.1], Guatemala [A/HRC/8/38/Add.1 & Corr.1] and Japan [A/HRC/8/44/Add.1,2 & Corr.1]. Responses to the recommendations made during the review were submitted by the Republic of Korea [A/HRC/8/40/Add.1], Switzerland [A/HRC/8/41/Add.1], Zambia [A/HRC/8/43/Add.1,2 & Add.2/Corr.1], Sri Lanka [A/HRC/8/46/Add.1], France [A/HRC/8/47/Add.1] and Mali [A/HRC/8/50/Add.1]. Pakistan submitted a statement [A/HRC/8/42/Add.1] on the outcome report and Romania provided additional information [A/HRC/8/49/Add.1].

The States reviewed during the Working Group's third session were: Botswana [A/HRC/10/69], the Bahamas [A/HRC/10/70 & Corr.1], Burundi [A/HRC/10/71], Luxembourg [A/HRC/10/72], Barbados [A/HRC/10/73], Montenegro [A/HRC/10/74], the United Arab Emirates [A/HRC/10/75], Israel [A/HRC/10/76], Liechtenstein [A/HRC/10/77], Serbia [A/HRC/10/78], Turkmenistan [A/HRC/10/79], Burkina Faso [A/HRC/10/80 & Corr.1], Cape Verde [A/HRC/10/81], Colombia [A/HRC/10/82], Uzbekistan [A/HRC/10/83] and Tuvalu [A/HRC/10/84].

Views on conclusions and/or recommendations, voluntary commitments and replies were presented by Botswana [A/HRC/10/69/Add.1], the Bahamas [A/HRC/10/70/Add.1], Luxembourg [A/HRC/10/72/Add.1], Barbados [A/HRC/10/73/Add.1], Montenegro [A/HRC/10/74/Add.1], Liechtenstein [A/HRC/10/77/Add.1], Serbia [A/HRC/10/78/Add.1], Turkmenistan [A/HRC/10/79/Add.1], Colombia [A/HRC/10/82/Add.1] and Uzbekistan [A/HRC/10/83/Add.1].

Human Rights Council action. The Human Rights Council [A/63/53], through standardized decisions, adopted the outcomes of UPR.

On 9 June, the Council adopted the outcomes on Bahrain [dec. 8/101], Ecuador [dec. 8/102], Tunisia [dec. 8/103], Morocco [dec. 8/104] and Finland [dec. 8/105]. On 10 June, it adopted the outcomes on Indonesia [dec. 8/106], the United Kingdom [dec. 8/107], India [dec. 8/108], Brazil [dec. 8/109], the Philippines [dec. 8/110], Algeria [dec. 8/111] and Poland [dec. 8/112]. On 11 June, it adopted the outcomes on the Netherlands [dec. 8/113], South Africa [dec. 8/114], the Czech Republic [dec. 8/115], Argentina [dec. 8/116], Gabon [dec. 8/117], Ghana [dec. 8/118] and Guatemala [dec. 8/119]. On 12 June, it adopted the outcomes on Peru [dec. 8/120], Benin [dec. 8/121], Switzerland [dec. 8/122], the Republic of Korea [dec. 8/123], Pakistan [dec. 8/124], Zambia [dec. 8/125], Japan [dec. 8/126] and Ukraine [dec. 8/127]. On 13 June, it adopted the outcomes on Sri Lanka [dec. 8/128], France [dec. 8/129], Tonga [dec. 8/130], Romania [dec. 8/131] and Mali [dec. 8/132].

Reports of High Commissioner. In her annual report [A/63/36], the High Commissioner noted that the launch of UPR was a major achievement of the Council in ensuring the universality of all human rights and their equal and impartial application to all States. The Review was aimed at overcoming criticisms of the former Commission on Human Rights—that held its final session in 2006 [YUN 2006, p. 755]—in terms of politicization and narrow focus, and at enhancing universality, impartiality, objectivity and non-selectivity. The experience in reviewing the first group of countries was largely successful. OHCHR support of UPR was appreciated by Member States and other stakeholders, and the involvement of civil society and other stakeholders was welcome. Although a final review was not due until the end of the four-year cycle, OHCHR anticipated some fine-tuning, in particular some form of independent expertise for the process so that it could evolve into an implementation-oriented mechanism, with targeted and prioritized recommendations addressed to the States under review.

In a later report [A/HRC/10/31], the High Commissioner stated that UPR had reinforced the cooperation between States, the Council and UN human rights mechanisms. The review of the first 48 States showed that States had assumed their responsibility seriously, engaging in the preparation of national reports through broad consultation, and participating in the Review at all levels. Some countries reviewed had made firm commitments to strengthen their cooperation with the special procedures, ratify human rights instruments and take initiatives to better implement human rights. The Review permitted the assessment of the human rights situation in all States, including those that had not come under the scrutiny of the former Commission, and revealed that all States faced challenges in implementing their human rights obligations and commitments. Good practices were emerging in various States. The mechanism might also serve as a tool for strengthening human rights protection on the ground.

Human Rights Council Advisory Committee

The Human Rights Council Advisory Committee, established in 2007 [YUN 2007, p. 664] as a think-tank for the Council and composed of 18 experts serving in their personal capacity, held its first session in Geneva (4–15 August) [A/HRC/10/2]. The Committee, which replaced the Subcommission on the Promotion and Protection of Human Rights [YUN 2006, p. 762], adopted 13 recommendations for submission to the Council. It recommended that the Council authorize that all reports and working papers completed by OHCHR, pursuant to the resolutions and decisions of the Subcommission at its fifty-eighth session [ibid.], should be sent to the Council [rec. 1/10]. The Council should also decide on follow-up to all pending studies commissioned by the Subcommission, including those on discrimination in the criminal justice system, corruption and its impact on the full enjoyment of human rights, discrimination based on work and descent, and the role of States in the guarantee of human rights with reference to the activities of transnational corporations and other business enterprises [rec. 1/13].

The Committee recommended that the Council and the Secretary-General make available their good offices to extend the right to non-refoulement to hunger refugees fleeing famine-hit countries [rec. 1/6]. Noting the large numbers of underfed refugees and displaced persons in many camps run by the Office of the United Nations High Commissioner for Refugees due to the shortfall in voluntary contributions, constituting a violation of the right to food, the Committee suggested that the Council launch an appeal to Member States to increase their voluntary contributions substantially so as to enable the Office to discharge its mandate [rec. 1/7]. The Committee also recommended that the Council approve the preparation by the drafting group on the right to food of studies on hunger refugees and the rights of peasants [rec. 1/8]. The Committee decided to consider the matter of the right of all peoples, including indigenous peoples, to self-determination, only if requested by the Council [rec. 1/12]. It recommended entrusting a drafting group with the preparation of a draft declaration on human rights education and training [rec. 1/1]. The Committee asked one of its members to formulate draft principles and guidelines for eliminating discrimination against persons affected by leprosy and their families [rec. 1/5], and two other members to participate in the Council's panel discussion on missing persons and to report to the Committee at its next session [rec. 1/3]. Five Committee members were asked to prepare for its next session draft guidelines for operationalizing gender mainstreaming, and to identify proposals for action in specific areas, special procedures or further measures to enhance gender equality throughout the UN system [rec. 1/4]. Two Committee members were designated to follow the work of the Social Forum [YUN 1999, p. 657] and to brief the Committee at its next session on issues of relevance to its work [rec. 1/11]. The Council should request OHCHR to provide official summary records of all Committee plenary meetings, and webcasting should be made available to enhance public access to its proceedings [rec. 1/9].

Complaint Procedure

The new Complaint Procedure of the Human Rights Council, established in 2007 by Council resolution 5/1 [YUN 2007, p. 664] on the basis of Economic and Social Council resolution 1503(XLVIII) (1503 procedure) [YUN 1970, p. 530] and revised in resolution 2000/3 [YUN 2000, p. 595], comprised the Working Group on Communications to decide on the admissibility of communications of alleged violations, and assess their merits, and the Working Group on Situations, which, on the recommendation of the Working Group on Communications, would report to the Council on consistent patterns of gross violations and recommend a course of action. During the year, 13,404 communications were examined under the Complaint Procedure.

Working Group on Communications. The five-member Working Group on Communications held its first session (Geneva, 19–23 November 2007) [A/HRC/7/WG.5/R.2 & Add.1–9], in accordance with Human Rights Council resolution 5/1 [YUN 2007, p. 664] and decision 6/101 [ibid., p. 665]. It considered 80 files concerning 37 countries. A total of 90 responses relating to those files were received from Governments. The Working Group also examined 55 files relating to pending communications concerning 29 countries, for which 127 responses had been received from Governments. It referred to the Working Group on Situations communications concerning Botswana, Maldives, Nepal, Peru, Spain and Syria, and decided to keep under review until its next session communications relating to Colombia and

Greece. It also decided to keep communications processed between June 2006 and May 2007, in compliance with Council decision 1/102 [YUN 2007, p. 663], from Cameroon, Colombia, the DRC, Egypt, Eritrea, Guinea, India, Iran, Nigeria, Peru, the Philippines, and Sri Lanka under review until its next session and to request further information. The Working Group dismissed consideration of communications that were left pending by the former working group under the 1503 procedure [YUN 1970, p. 530] relating to Ecuador, Guatemala, Indonesia, Iran, Japan, Kyrgyzstan, Mexico, Nepal, Togo and the United States. It also dismissed consideration of communications concerning Cameroon, Ethiopia, Greece, India, Indonesia, Malaysia, the Philippines and Viet Nam.

In light of the establishment of the new Complaint Procedure and the transitional nature of its mandate, the Working Group agreed that its Chairperson should provide members at the Group's second session with a list of all communications rejected after an initial screening. It noted that communications and responses by Governments submitted to the working group of the 1503 procedure were not translated in other languages, posing difficulties for the Working Group and creating inequality among the languages. It requested the High Commissioner to take measures to remedy the situation. It also decided to continue during the period of transition, and until the end of its second session, the same working methods followed in recent years; to keep available for consideration and decision of the Working Group communications in the roster submitted by the Secretariat for the current session and on which no decision had been taken, as well as communications kept under review at the current session and those received and considered admissible on 14 December 2007; and to conclude consideration of all those communications at its April 2008 session (see below).

At its second session (Geneva, 14–18 April) [A/HRC/WG.5/2/R.2], the Working Group had before it 23 new files containing communications and Government replies thereto relating to 15 countries. A total of 17 replies relating to 16 files were received from Governments. The Working Group also had 17 files relating to pending communications concerning 13 countries, and 89 files relating to 38 countries, which the Working Group had decided to keep available for possible further consideration. A total of 193 replies were received from concerned Governments in relation to those communications. The Working Group adopted 44 decisions. It referred to the Working Group on Situations communications in relation to human rights situations in the DRC, Greece, Guinea, Nigeria and Peru, and decided to keep under review until its next session communications relating to Argentina, Cambodia, Cameroon, Colombia, the Gambia, India, the Libyan Arab Jamahiriya, the Philippines, Portugal, the Sudan and the United States. The Working Group discontinued consideration of communications relating to Bangladesh, Bhutan, Chile, Colombia, Iran, Mexico, Pakistan and Sri Lanka.

At its third session (Geneva, 20–24 October) [A/HRC/WG.5/3/R.2], the Working Group had before it 44 files of communications relating to 25 countries, comprising 28 new files relating to 20 countries, and 16 files relating to 11 countries that the Working Group had decided previously to keep under review. A total of 24 replies were received from concerned Governments in relation to those communications. The Working Group decided to refer to the Working Group on Situations (see below) communications concerning Cambodia, Cameroon, Colombia and the Gambia and to keep under review until its next session communications concerning Bulgaria, Colombia, India, Iraq, Japan, Libya, the Philippines, the Republic of Korea, Romania, the Sudan, Tajikistan, Thailand, Tunisia and the United States. It discontinued consideration of communications from Argentina, Bangladesh, India, Malaysia, the Philippines, Portugal, Sri Lanka, the Sudan, the United States and Viet Nam.

The Working Group expressed its appreciation to Governments that had replied to communications examined under the Complaint Procedure, especially those that had provided detailed and comprehensive replies. It encouraged Governments to provide not only procedural arguments in their replies, but to address the allegations raised on their merits. The Secretary-General would inform the Governments of Cambodia, Cameroon, Colombia and the Gambia, as well as the authors of the respective communications, of the relevant decisions of the Working Group. The Working Group noted with concern the number of communications received relating to alleged forced displacement and evictions, often affecting large numbers of persons, as well as communications with respect to alleged human rights violations committed by transnational corporations.

Members expressed concern over the unavailability on many occasions of translations of communications and Government replies into UN working languages, and requested that effective measures be taken to ensure their timely translation.

Working Group on Situations. The Working Group on Situations, established by the Human Rights Council in 2007 [YUN 2007, p. 664] and composed of five members serving in their personal capacity, held its first (28–31 January) [A/HRC/WG.1/1/R.1] and second (23–24 June and 2 July) [AHRC/WG.1/2/R.3] sessions in Geneva.

At its first session, the Working Group had before it dossiers relating to human rights situations in Botswana, Iran, Maldives, Nepal, Nigeria, Peru, Spain,

Syria and Turkmenistan. The Working Group decided, by a vote of 4 to 1, to refer the human rights situation in Turkmenistan to the Human Rights Council at its seventh session, based on the unsatisfactory nature and reliability of the replies provided by that Government. It also decided to dismiss the cases of Nepal, Nigeria, Peru and Spain, and to keep under review until its next session the cases of Botswana, Iran, Maldives, Nigeria, Peru and Syria.

At its second session, the Working Group had before it the dossiers relating to the human rights situation in Botswana, the DRC, Greece, Guinea, Iran, Maldives, Nigeria, Peru and Syria. Regretting that no reply had been received from the Government of Maldives, despite repeated communications by both Working Groups, it decided to refer the matter to the Council with a recommendation that the Council keep the matter under review and request the Government to provide further information, and requested the Secretary-General to communicate that decision to the Government. The Working Group also decided to dismiss the cases of Greece, Iran and Peru, and to keep under review until its next session the cases of Botswana, the DRC, Guinea, Nigeria and Syria.

Human Rights Council action. On 25 March, by a recorded vote of 46 to 1, the Human Rights Council decided to keep the human rights situation in Turkmenistan under review and to request the Government to provide further information. It decided to further consider the situation at its ninth (September 2008) session in light of the new information received, and requested the Secretary-General to communicate that decision to the Government. On 23 September, the Council decided to keep the situation under review and requested Turkmenistan to provide further information at the Council's tenth (2009) session.

Also on 23 September, the Council decided to discontinue consideration of the human rights situation in Maldives following the replies received from the Government and Government efforts to respond to the complaints.

Special procedures

Report of Secretary-General. In response to Human Rights Council decision 2/102 [YUN 2006, p. 760], the Secretary-General submitted, in March [A/HRC/7/49], a report listing references to the conclusions and recommendations of special procedures in their annual reports submitted to the Council's sixth and seventh sessions. The reports were available on the OHCHR website.

In her annual report [A/63/36], the High Commissioner noted that, as a result of the exercise (review, rationalization and improvement) launched in June 2006 [YUN 2006, p. 761], all thematic mandates had been extended, one country mandate terminated and two new thematic mandates established—those of the Special Rapporteur on contemporary forms of slavery [YUN 2007, p. 784] and the Special Rapporteur on the right to access to safe drinking water and sanitation (see p. 844). The exercise reaffirmed the standing of the special procedures before the Human Rights Council, and the new selection procedure was designed to uphold the highest standards of competence and integrity among mandate holders.

Human Rights Council action. In an 18 June president's statement [A/63/53 (PRST/8/2)] on the terms of office of special procedures mandate holders, the Human Rights Council President said that, in accordance with General Assembly resolution 60/251 [YUN 2006, p. 757] and Council resolution 5/1 [YUN 2007, p. 662], a special procedures mandate holder's tenure would not exceed six years in a particular position (two terms of three years for thematic procedures). The Council guaranteed the integrity and independence of the system of special procedures, and would follow up on the implementation of the Code of Conduct for special procedures mandate holders, as contained in Council resolution 5/2 [ibid., p. 666]. In that regard, the President would convey to the Council any information brought to his or her attention, including by States and/or by the coordination committee of special procedures, concerning cases of persistent non-compliance by a mandate holder with the Code of Conduct, especially prior to the renewal of mandate holders' terms of office. In the absence of such information, the Council would extend the terms of office for a second three-year term.

Office of the High Commissioner for Human Rights

Appointment of High Commissioner. On 28 July, the General Assembly approved the appointment by the Secretary-General [A/62/913] of Navanethem Pillay (South Africa) as United Nations High Commissioner for Human Rights for a four-year term of office beginning on 1 September and expiring on 31 August 2012 (**decision 62/420**).

Reports of High Commissioner. In her annual report to the Human Rights Council [A/HRC/7/38 & Add.1,2], the United Nations High Commissioner for Human Rights, Louise Arbour (Canada), outlined the efforts of her Office to implement its mandate. She detailed the support given to the Council, reviewed efforts to strengthen country engagement and proposed activities to mark the sixtieth anniversary of the Universal Declaration of Human Rights (see p. 726). The report also focused on the commitment to the fight against racism, in particular through the Durban Review process, and highlighted the support for human rights instruments and the role of UPR in promoting their universal application. Obstacles to the full realization of human rights included impunity, poverty, discrimination, armed conflict, democratic deficits and weak institutions. The report described OHCHR activities to address those problems, including technical cooperation, advisory services and support.

The annual report of the High Commissioner to the Economic and Social Council [E/2008/76] considered the principles of equality between men and women and non-discrimination against women in promoting and implementing economic, social and cultural rights under international human rights law. The report also focused on efforts to clarify the scope of States parties' obligations to eliminate discrimination and ensure equality between women and men in relation to those rights. It also illustrated the relevance of women's economic, social and cultural rights in the context of post-conflict reconstruction and democratization policies.

According to the High Commissioner, women suffered disproportionally from inequality and discrimination in the protection and enjoyment of their economic, social and cultural rights, and the gap between de jure and de facto discrimination against them was pervasive and often concealed. The private sector continued to impose norms, rules and practices that prevented the enjoyment by women of their rights, in developed and developing societies alike. Direct and indirect discrimination was widespread, despite the adoption of international human rights norms prohibiting discrimination against women. In post-conflict transition, ensuring meaningful participation by women and women's organizations and the inclusion of specific concerns in relation to women's economic, social and cultural rights were paramount. In the design of legislation, programmes and policies at all levels, a human rights approach increased the likelihood that women's rights would be best served by any measure adopted. Post-conflict societies had to make an effort to incorporate measures founded on equality between women and men and non-discrimination against women in the realm of economic, social and cultural rights in order to redress conflict-related violations, build sustainable peace and rectify prior inequalities.

On 25 July, the Economic and Social Council took note of the High Commissioner's report (**decision 2008/256**).

In her annual report to the General Assembly [A/63/36], covering activities since the previous report [YUN 2007, p. 667], the High Commissioner said that OHCHR continued to support Member States in meeting their human rights obligations, while empowering rights-holders, in particular through country engagement and work with national partners, civil society and UN country teams. Priorities included supporting the Human Rights Council, treaty bodies and special procedures, as well as national protection systems. OHCHR capacity to support country engagement had increased significantly, particularly its rapid response capacity, allowing the Office to initiate and support emergency and technical missions. Support for national human rights institutions was also reinforced. As at August, OHCHR was operating and supporting 53 field presences, including nine regional presences, seven country offices, human rights components in 17 UN peace missions and human rights advisers in 16 UN country teams. The Regional Office for West Africa was established in January in Senegal and, in May, an agreement was signed with Kyrgyzstan for the opening of a Regional Office for Central Asia.

OHCHR capacity to react promptly to critical human rights situations continued to develop through its Peace Missions Support and Rapid Response Unit. The Office deployed a fact-finding mission to Kenya in February to look into allegations of grave human rights violations following the December 2007 elections, and a rapid-response mission in March to Armenia to advise the UN resident coordinator in the wake of violent clashes following presidential elections. In June, it supported the OHCHR country office in Bolivia in monitoring the human rights situation in the context of regional referendums.

OHCHR support of national human rights institutions had a significant impact. It advised some 100 such institutions worldwide on a continuing basis, in collaboration with its field offices, as well as peace missions and the United Nations Development Programme. It also provided technical advice on the establishment and responsibilities of such institutions to Azerbaijan, Bangladesh, Burundi, Cambodia, Chile, Côte d'Ivoire, the DRC, Ethiopia, France, Indonesia, Italy, Japan, Lesotho, Madagascar, Mauritania, Mauritius, Palau, Sierra Leone, the Sudan, Swaziland, Tajikistan, Timor-Leste and Uganda.

The Office supported the activities of human rights special procedures through over 50 country visits, and provided more than 1,000 communications to Governments concerning alleged violations and more than 100 reports to the Human Rights Council or the General Assembly. In the area of partnerships, OHCHR, the Department of Peacekeeping Operations and the Department of Political Affairs issued in July a joint policy directive for public reporting by human rights components of peace operations to improve that key aspect of human rights work. The report also highlighted OHCHR efforts in addressing issues in strategic thematic areas, such as equality and non-discrimination; development, poverty and the Millennium Development Goals [YUN 2000, p. 51]; economic, social and cultural rights; indigenous peoples; minorities; migration and trafficking; the rule of law and democracy; the Global Compact and the human rights responsibilities of businesses; human rights education and training; climate change and human rights and women's rights and gender work.

The General Assembly took note of the High Commissioner's report on 18 December (**decision 63/534**).

Composition of staff

Report of High Commissioner. Pursuant to Human Rights Council decision 2/102 [YUN 2006, p. 760], the High Commissioner submitted a February report [A/HRC/7/57] updating information on the composition of OHCHR staff, including data on staff members in posts subject to geographical distribution, as well as on staff members in temporary posts funded from extrabudgetary resources or in technical cooperation project posts. The report described measures taken by the High Commissioner to address the geographical imbalances identified by the Commission on Human Rights in resolution 2005/72 [YUN 2005, p. 716], and efforts to achieve equitable geographical representation. It concluded that the success of such efforts was apparent in the improved geographical diversity of OHCHR staff, and that the additional measures developed in consultation with the Office of Human Resources Management would further strengthen those efforts.

Human Rights Council action. On 27 March [A/63/53 (res. 7/2)], the Human Rights Council, by a recorded vote of 34 to 10, with 3 abstentions, requested the High Commissioner to undertake all measures needed to redress the imbalance in geographical distribution of OHCHR staff.

General Assembly action. As requested by the General Assembly in resolution 61/159 [YUN 2006, p. 764], the Secretary-General transmitted, by a September note [A/63/290], the High Commissioner's report to the Assembly, which took note of it on 18 December (**decision 63/534**).

Report of Secretary-General. In response to General Assembly resolution 62/236 [YUN 2007, p. 1441], the Secretary-General submitted a July report on measures to improve the imbalance in the geographical distribution of OHCHR staff [A/63/204].

The Secretary-General reported a substantial improvement in the overall geographic diversity of OHCHR during the previous 18 months. OHCHR continued to vigorously implement the measures identified in the Secretary-General's 2007 report [YUN 2007, p. 668], including the High Commissioner's procedures and framework for improving geographical diversity. Another round of the national competitive recruitment examinations was held at the beginning of the year, especially for Member States that were unrepresented or underrepresented in the Secretariat. Forty-one of the 49 Member States invited to participate attracted 845 applicants. Of the 326 candidates selected to participate, 236 or 72.4 per cent sat for the examination in February. The examinations were expected to result in a larger pool of successful candidates on the roster for selection against vacant, regular-budget P-2 and P-3 positions from Member States requiring geographical improvement in OHCHR. In addition to advertising vacancies through established procedures, OHCHR continued to ensure the widest possible circulation of vacancy notices, using the mailing list of over 1,200 governmental institutions, non-governmental human rights organizations, national human rights institutions and academic institutions. It also shared vacancy notices with its offices in the field. Those efforts were yielding positive results. Of the 122 selection decisions for Professional posts taken since the introduction of the High Commissioner's procedures and framework for improving geographical diversity, 72 (59 per cent) were made in favour of candidates from regions requiring improved representation in OHCHR. On the other hand, of the 50 selections from the regions well represented in OHCHR, 32 (64 per cent) were in respect of internal staff transferred or promoted, thus having no net impact on the geographical balance of the Office. Similar progress was made with regard to senior posts at the P-5 and higher levels. Some 28 selection decisions were made for senior posts since the procedures were introduced, 16 (57 per cent) of which were in favour of candidates from regions requiring improved representation.

On 24 December, the Assembly, in section XIII of **resolution 63/250** (see p. 1616), took note of the Secretary-General's 2007 report [YUN 2007, p. 668] on the subject.

OHCHR funding and staffing

JIU report. In May [A/62/845], the Secretary-General transmitted to the General Assembly a report of the Joint Inspection Unit (JIU) on OHCHR funding and staffing. The report said that OHCHR had taken action to improve its management and organization in response to recommendations by oversight bodies. However, the Office should link the budget and planning process to results and managerial performance, in line with a results-based management approach. The Trust Fund for the Support to the Activities of OHCHR, one of the eight funds managed by the Office, represented 78 per cent of its total extrabudgetary resources. However, the Fund did not have a board of trustees to review and approve projects and activities, and approval was granted solely by an internal body consisting of senior managers and chaired by the Deputy High Commissioner. OHCHR total resource requirements for the 2006–2007 biennium were estimated at $265.3 million, 35.3 per cent of which would be funded from the UN regular budget and 64.7 per cent from extrabudgetary resources. Although Member States at the 2005 World Summit had called for a doubling of the regular budget resources over the ensuing five years, that target might not be reached. Additionally, OHCHR depended heavily on voluntary contributions to fund core and mandated activities, which were often subject to conditionalities imposed by Member States. The dependency on voluntary contributions was compounded by the reliance on a relatively small number of donors. In 2006, 97.6 per cent of pledged voluntary contributions came from 20 donors, 80.8 per cent of which came from just 10 countries. The donor base should be broadened by encouraging non-traditional donor countries to make contributions. Moreover, donors earmarked a large percentage of the funding for specific purposes: 63 per cent of the total funds from the top 20 donors in 2006 had been earmarked. There was no mechanism for Member States to review or approve individual voluntary contributions made to OHCHR, nor were they informed of the conditions imposed when individual contributions were being made. The Human Rights Council should be informed of such contributions above a significant level, as well as the conditionalities that might be attached to them.

The issue of the imbalance in the geographical distribution of the OHCHR staff had been repeatedly raised by the former Commission on Human Rights and the Human Rights Council (see p. 719). However, the situation had not significantly improved, as evidenced from the figures for Professional staff: staff from the Group of Western European and Other States accounted for 61.7 per cent, the highest representation. Although figures as at 30 June 2007 showed a slight improvement, the serious and continuing imbalance in the geographical distribution of the Professional and higher staff could diminish the effectiveness and credibility of OHCHR work if it was perceived to be culturally biased and unrepresentative of the United Nations.

The report recommended, among other things, that the Assembly: instruct the High Commissioner to seek the advice and the views of the Human Rights Council in preparing the proposed strategic framework and the associated budget requirements prior to finalizing those documents; establish a reasonable balance between the OHCHR regular budget and voluntary contributions; and instruct OHCHR to convince donors to reduce earmarked funding or enhance the flexibility of funds, applying principles such as the Good Humanitarian Donorship principles [YUN 2003, p. 916]. The Assembly should also introduce a temporary maximum level on the recruitment of new Professional staff from overrepresented regions.

Note by Secretary-General. Also in May [A/62/845/Add.1], the Secretary-General transmitted to the Assembly his comments on the JIU recommendations. He concluded that OHCHR had policies and procedures in place to ensure the effective management of its resources, using results-based management principles, as well as the effective management of its trust funds. The High Commissioner fully recognized the role of the Human Rights Council in accordance with UN regulations and rules, policies and procedures. In that regard, submission of the biennial strategic framework to the Council prior to its submission to the Committee for Programme and Coordination for review and subsequent approval by the Assembly should be considered. In respect of human resources management, every effort would be made to build on the improvements already achieved and to attain geographic diversity of the OHCHR staff in line with the system of desirable ranges mandated by the Assembly.

Human rights defenders

Reports of Special Representative. In her annual report to the Human Rights Council [A/HRC/7/28], the Secretary-General's Special Representative on human rights defenders, Hina Jilani (Pakistan), focused on follow-up activities in the implementation of her recommendations and highlighted her work in the three main areas of activities: communications, country visits and thematic reports. The Special Representative showed that the follow-up on cases included not only individual situations, but the identification of general trends. The quantitative and thematic analysis of communications made it possible to identify challenges and achievements in the implementation of the 1998 Declaration on the Right and Responsibility of Individuals, Groups and Organs of Society to Promote and Protect Universally Recognized Human Rights and Fundamental Freedoms (Declaration on Human Rights Defenders) [YUN 1998, p. 608] and to formulate recommendations addressing implementation gaps. The Representative proposed methodological tools to facilitate follow-up activities, in particular to assess the situation of human rights defenders on the ground and a matrix for undertaking follow-up visits.

The Special Representative recommended that States respond in a timely, systematic and comprehensive manner to her communications, and invited them to consider the communications procedure as an opportunity to redress situations and correct structural gaps. The role of regional and international networks and organizations, which often acted as interfaces between the Special Representative and sources on the ground, should be strengthened. The situation of human rights defenders should be one of the elements to be reviewed in the Universal Periodic Review, while stronger collaboration and joint initiatives among international and regional mechanisms for the protection of human rights defenders would reinforce the system overall.

The Special Representative visited Guatemala (18–22 February) [A/HRC/10/12/Add.3] to evaluate the implementation of the recommendations issued following her visit in 2002 [YUN 2002, p. 620]. While acknowledging some progress, particularly in the establishment of institutions and the self-protection initiatives of defenders, the Representative was concerned at the deteriorating environment in which human rights defenders operated, characterized by endemic impunity for crimes and violations committed against them. Guatemala was the third most unequal country in Latin America in terms of wealth distribution, and the worst in the region's human development index. The level of violence and killings was extremely high, and journalists who reported on organized crime, drug trafficking, corruption and other criminal activities faced death threats, physical and verbal attacks, and even murder. Trade unionists were the target of many attacks. While impunity remained pervasive, steps had been taken to increase police performance and protection, including the establishment in January of the new Unit on Human Rights of the Criminal Investigation Division of the National Civil Police.

Stressing that the human rights situation was unlikely to improve without a clear turning point on impunity, the Special Representative recommended that the Government: turn the commitment to human rights into a political agenda permeating Government action; adopt a policy on the protection of human rights defenders and report on its implementation; and condemn attacks against defenders and acknowledge the importance of their work. The Government should also ensure coordination among institutions responsible for the investigation of cases, reform measures for witness protection, and tackle the flaws and weaknesses of the police, including the need to gain the trust of the population.

Human Rights Council action. On 26 March, the Human Rights Council appointed Margaret Sekaggya (Uganda) as Special Rapporteur on the situation of human rights defenders. Ms. Sekaggya assumed her functions on 1 May.

On 27 March [A/63/53 (res. 7/8)], the Council extended the special procedure on the situation of human rights defenders as a Special Rapporteur for a three-year period. The Rapporteur was requested to report regularly to the Council and the General Assembly.

Reports of Special Rapporteur. In accordance with Assembly resolution 62/152 [YUN 2007, p. 670], the Secretary-General, in an August note [A/63/288], transmitted to the Assembly the report of the Special Rapporteur on human rights defenders, which focused on her vision and priorities with regard to her mandate. Priority areas for future action included the analysis of trends and challenges concerning defenders; attention to defenders most exposed to attacks and violations; analysis of the obstacles and challenges to defenders' exercise of their rights; the development of enhanced protection measures for defenders; enhancing collaboration with stakeholders; and formulating recommendations to make UPR an effective mechanism for assessing the situation of defenders. The establishment and strengthening of regional mechanisms for the protection of defenders—including the African Commission on Human and Peoples' Rights, the Inter-American Commission on Human Rights, the Council of Europe and the Organization for Security and Cooperation in Europe—were fundamental to improving their situation. The Special Rapporteur intended to place greater emphasis on the promotion aspect of her role by focusing on good practices for protecting defenders and popularizing the Declaration on Human Rights Defenders.

On 18 December, the Assembly took note of the Special Rapporteur's report on human rights defenders (**decision 63/534**).

Following her visit to Togo (28 July–4 August) [A/HRC/10/12/Add.2], the Special Rapporteur said that, since 2005, the country had been engaged in a political transition, and the prospects for human rights promotion and protection had improved. The Rapporteur welcomed initiatives for ensuring an environment conducive to the work of human rights defenders, but regretted that insufficient funds had been allocated to the institutions undertaking such initiatives. Human rights defenders continued to face several challenges, including the achievement of unity and coordination within the defenders' community; the stigmatization of defenders by the authorities, who associated them with the political opposition; the plight of women defenders and the difficulties inherent in their work; unjustified delays in delivering registration certificates to NGOs; restrictions on the exercise of the rights to freedom of peaceful assembly and freedom of opinion and expression; and impunity for abuses against defenders.

The Special Rapporteur recommended that the Government and relevant State actors take steps to give legitimacy to human rights defenders by removing the stigmatization of being accused of affiliation to political parties; speed up the delivery of registration certificates to NGOs so as to facilitate their activities; recognize the legitimate work of women human rights defenders, remove obstacles impeding their work and take proactive measures to support such work; sensitize the police, gendarmerie and military officers, as well as judicial and prosecution officials, on the role and activities of defenders; and make the fight against impunity for violations against defenders a priority. The Special Rapporteur recommended that human rights defenders end the fragmentation of their community, improve coordination networks to strengthen the protection of defenders and expand the capacity among defenders to make full use of national, regional and international human rights mechanisms and institutions.

Other aspects

Sexual orientation and gender identity

Communications. By an 18 December letter [A/63/635] to the General Assembly President, Argentina, Brazil, Croatia, France, Gabon, Japan, the Netherlands and Norway transmitted a statement on human rights, sexual orientation and gender identity, signed by 66 countries. The signatories expressed concern at human rights violations based on sexual orientation or gender identity, and at violence, harassment, discrimination, exclusion, stigmatization and prejudice directed against them in all countries. The signatories urged States to take measures, in particular legislative or administrative, to ensure that sexual orientation or gender identity might under no circumstances be the basis for criminal penalties, in particular executions, arrests or detention; and that violations based on sexual orientation or gender identity were investigated and perpetrators brought to justice.

On 19 December [A/63/663], Syria transmitted to the Secretary-General a declaration in relation to the above statement on "the so-called notions" of sexual orientation and gender identity, on behalf of 59 Member States. The signatory States expressed concern at the attempt to introduce in the United Nations notions that had no legal foundation in international human rights instruments, and to focus on certain persons on the grounds of sexual interests and behaviours, while ignoring intolerance and discrimination on the basis of colour, race, gender or religion. They deplored all forms of stereotyping, exclusion, stigmatization, prejudice, intolerance, discrimination and violence directed against peoples, communities and individuals on any grounds whatsoever. They also reaffirmed article 29 of the Universal Declaration of Human Rights, establishing the right of Member States to enact laws that met "just requirements of morality, public order and the general welfare in a democratic society", and expressed concern at attempts to create "new rights" or "new standards" by misinterpreting the Declaration and international treaties to include notions that were never articulated or agreed by the general membership. Those attempts jeopardized the entire international human rights framework.

The signatories called on States to refrain from attempting to give priority to the rights of certain individuals, which could result in positive discrimination at the expense of others' rights, in contradiction with the principles of non-discrimination and equality.

Good governance

Human Rights Council action. On 27 March [A/63/53 (res. 7/11)], the Human Rights Council, by a recorded vote of 41 to none, with 6 abstentions, welcomed the High Commissioner's note transmitting the report on the 2006 United Nations conference on anti-corruption, good governance and human rights [YUN 2006, p. 767]. The Council invited States to consider ratifying or acceding to the United Nations Convention against Corruption [YUN 2003, p. 1128], and to promote transparency, accountability, prevention and enforcement as key principles of anti-corruption efforts. It requested OHCHR to prepare a publication on anti-corruption, good governance and human rights, and decided to continue its consideration of the role of good governance, including the issue of the fight against corruption in the promotion and protection of human rights, at a future session.

Human rights instruments

General aspects

In 2008, eight UN human rights instruments were in force, with expert bodies monitoring their implementation. Those instruments and their treaty bodies were: the 1965 International Convention on the Elimination of All Forms of Racial Discrimination [YUN 1965, p. 440, GA res. 2106 A (XX)] (Committee on the Elimination of Racial Discrimination); the 1966 International Covenant on Civil and Political Rights and the Optional Protocol thereto [YUN 1966, p. 423, GA res. 2200 A (XXI)] and the Second Optional Protocol aiming at the abolition of the death penalty [YUN 1989, p. 484, GA res. 44/128] (Human Rights Committee); the 1966 International Covenant on Economic, Social and Cultural Rights [YUN 1966, p. 419, GA res. 2200 A (XXI)] and the Optional Protocol thereto, adopted by General Assembly resolution 63/117 of 10 December (see p. 729) (Committee on Economic, Social and Cultural Rights); the 1979 Convention on the Elimination of All Forms of Discrimination against Women [YUN 1979, p. 895, GA res. 34/180] and Optional Protocol [YUN 1999, p. 1100, GA res. 54/4] (Committee on the Elimination of Discrimination against Women); the 1984 Convention against Torture and Other Cruel, Inhuman or Degrading Treatment or Punishment [YUN 1984, p. 813, GA res. 39/46] and 2002 Optional Protocol [YUN 2002, p. 631, GA res. 57/199] (Committee against Torture and Subcommittee on Prevention); the 1989 Convention on the Rights of the Child [YUN 1989, p. 560, GA res. 44/25] and Optional Protocols on the involvement of children in armed conflict and on the sale of children, child prostitution and child pornography [YUN 2000, pp. 616 & 618, GA res. 54/263] (Committee on the Rights of the Child); the 1990 International Convention on the Protection of the Rights of All Migrant Workers and Members of Their Families [YUN 1990, p. 594, GA res. 45/158] (Committee on the Protection of the Rights of All Migrant Workers and Members of Their Families); and the Convention on the Rights of Persons with Disabilities and its Optional Protocol [YUN 2006, p. 785, GA res. 61/106] (Committee on the Rights of Persons with Disabilities).

Note by Secretariat. To facilitate access to information relating to the status of the International Covenants on Civil and Political Rights and on Economic, Social and Cultural Rights, and on the Conventions against Torture, on the Rights of the Child and on the Protection of the Rights of Migrant Workers, the Secretariat, in January [A/HRC/7/60], informed the Human Rights Council that such information was available on the OHCHR website and was updated regularly.

Report of Secretary-General. Pursuant to Assembly resolutions 52/118 [YUN 1997, p. 594] and 53/138 [YUN 1998, p. 612], the Secretary-General, in May, submitted a report [HRI/GEN/2/Rev.5] containing a compilation in a single volume of guidelines regarding the form and content of reports to be submitted by States parties to the Human Rights Committee, the Committee on Economic, Social and Cultural Rights, the Committee on the Elimination of Discrimination against Women, the Committee on the Elimination of Racial Discrimination, the Committee on the Rights of the Child and the Committee against Torture. In addition, the updated compilation contained guidelines for reports to be submitted to the Committee on Migrant Workers, and harmonized guidelines on reporting under international human rights treaties.

Human rights treaty body system

Meeting of chairpersons. In an August note [A/63/280], the Secretary-General submitted the report on the twentieth meeting of chairpersons of human rights treaty bodies (Geneva, 26–27 June), which considered follow-up to the recommendations of the nineteenth meeting [YUN 2007, p. 673] and reviewed developments relating to the work of the treaty bodies. Participants also discussed the reform of the treaty body system, including the harmonization of working methods and the UPR mechanism, as well as the work of the Human Rights Council. They met with representatives of States parties and the Council President.

The meeting had before it reports on: the implementation of recommendations of the sixth inter-committee meeting and the nineteenth meeting of chairpersons [HRI/MC/2008/2]; indicators for promoting and monitoring the implementation of human rights [HRI/MC/2008/3]; working methods of the human rights treaty bodies relating to the State party reporting process [HRI/MC/2008/4]; and States' parties reservations to human rights treaties [HRI/MC/2008/5].

The meeting endorsed the points of agreement concluded at the seventh inter-committee meeting of human rights treaty bodies (see below) and called on those bodies to follow up on those recommendations and report on their implementation in 2009. Concerning the relationship with special procedure mandate holders, the chairpersons and the special procedures agreed to organize future joint meetings in a more structured fashion and requested the Secretariat to prepare a list of common procedural and thematic issues to be discussed at their eleventh joint meeting. The meeting also recommended that a one-day meeting be allocated for informal consultations with States parties at its twenty-first (2009) meeting. It recognized the need for developing effective cooperation between treaty bodies and the Council and for strengthening the institutional links between them. The meeting recommended that treaty body secretaries prioritize documents to ensure their timely translation.

Annexed to the Secretary-General's note was the report of the seventh inter-committee meeting of human rights treaty bodies (Geneva, 23–25 June), which decided on points of an agreement on the revised harmonized reporting guidelines [HRI/GEN/2/Rev.5]; follow-up to concluding observations; and decisions on individual complaints, consideration of a State party in the absence of a report, the independence of treaty-body experts, cooperation with NGOs, and business and human rights, among other issues.

The General Assembly took note of the meeting's report on 18 December (**decision 63/534**).

The tenth joint meeting of treaty body chairpersons with mandate holders of the Council's special procedures was held on 26 June. Participants discussed follow-up to the recommendations of special procedures and treaty bodies, and agreed on the need for stronger cooperation between the two groups. They underlined the importance of building on each other's recommendations.

Meeting of special rapporteurs, independent experts and chairpersons. In November [A/HRC/10/24], the High Commissioner transmitted to the Council the report on the fifteenth meeting of special rapporteurs/representatives, independent experts and chairpersons of working groups of the Council's special procedures (Geneva, 23–27 June). Participants adopted the draft revised Manual of special procedures mandate holders, presented by the task force appointed in 2007 [YUN 2007, p. 674]. Substantive changes related to the appointment of mandate holders, the criteria for taking action on communications and the transmission of urgent appeals to Governments, Government responses appended to mission reports, and the sharing of public statements with concerned Governments in advance of their release. The meeting agreed that the Manual should be updated as necessary. It also adopted the internal advisory procedure, annexed to the High Commissioner's note, for facilitating implementation of the Code of Conduct for Special Procedures Mandate Holders, adopted by the Council in 2007 [ibid., p. 666], and the Manual of the human rights special procedures. It was noted that, even though the system of communication had evolved over the years, some issues needed further reflection, such as the low rate of responses by Governments, the protection of witnesses, feedback to sources and the issuance of a common report on communications. The proposal that a common report on communications collated on a country-by-country basis should be issued was widely supported. Participants also discussed the development of a common approach to crisis situations, and stressed that the special procedures were uniquely placed to act as an early warning system in situations involving serious human rights violations. General comments or guidelines by mandate holders on human rights requirements in humanitarian crises should be elaborated. Participants further discussed cooperation with regional human rights mechanisms and with the UN system, integrating human rights approaches and mechanisms into the work of the special procedures, cooperation with human rights treaty bodies, and consultations with NGOs and national human rights organizations.

Membership of human rights treaty bodies

On 18 December [meeting 70], the General Assembly, on the recommendation of the Third Committee [A/63/430/Add.1], adopted **resolution 63/167** by recorded vote (128-55-2) [agenda items 64 *(a)* & *(b)*].

Equitable geographical distribution in the membership of the human rights treaty bodies

The General Assembly,

Recalling its previous resolutions on this question,

Reaffirming the importance of the goal of universal ratification of the United Nations human rights instruments,

Welcoming the significant increase in the number of ratifications of United Nations human rights instruments, which has especially contributed to their universality,

Reiterating the importance of the effective functioning of treaty bodies established pursuant to United Nations human rights instruments for the full and effective implementation of those instruments,

Recalling that, with regard to the election of the members of the human rights treaty bodies, the General Assembly as well as the Commission on Human Rights recognized the importance of giving consideration in their membership to equitable geographical distribution, gender balance and representation of the principal legal systems and of bearing in mind that the members shall be elected and shall serve in their personal capacity, and shall be of high moral character, acknowledged impartiality and recognized competence in the field of human rights,

Reaffirming the significance of national and regional particularities and various historical, cultural and religious backgrounds, as well as of different political, economic and legal systems,

Recognizing that the United Nations pursues multilingualism as a means of promoting, protecting and preserving diversity of languages and cultures globally and that genuine multilingualism promotes unity in diversity and international understanding,

Recalling that the General Assembly as well as the Commission on Human Rights encouraged States parties to United Nations human rights treaties, individually and through meetings of States parties, to consider how to give better effect, inter alia, to the principle of equitable geographical distribution in the membership of treaty bodies,

Expressing concern at the regional imbalance in the current composition of the membership of some of the human rights treaty bodies,

Noting in particular that the status quo tends to be particularly detrimental to the election of experts from some regional groups,

Convinced that the goal of equitable geographical distribution in the membership of human rights treaty bodies is perfectly compatible and can be fully realized and achieved in harmony with the need to ensure gender balance and the representation of the principal legal systems in those bodies and the high moral character, acknowledged impartiality and recognized competence in the field of human rights of their members,

1. *Encourages* the States parties to the United Nations human rights instruments to consider and adopt concrete actions, inter alia, the possible establishment of quota distribution systems by geographical region for the election of the members of the treaty bodies, thereby ensuring the paramount objective of equitable geographical distribution in the membership of those human rights bodies;

2. *Calls upon* the States parties to the United Nations human rights instruments to include in their work a debate on ways and means to ensure equitable geographical distribution in the membership of the human rights treaty bodies, based on previous recommendations of the Commission on Human Rights and the Economic and Social Council and the provisions of the present resolution;

3. *Recommends*, when considering the possible establishment of a quota by region for the election of the membership of each treaty body, the introduction of flexible procedures that encompass the following criteria:

(a) Each of the five regional groups established by the General Assembly must be assigned a quota of the membership of each treaty body in equivalent proportion to the number of States parties to the instrument that it represents;

(b) There must be provision for periodic revisions that reflect the relative changes in the geographical distribution of States parties;

(c) Automatic periodic revisions should be envisaged in order to avoid amending the text of the instrument when the quotas are revised;

4. *Stresses* that the process needed to achieve the goal of equitable geographical distribution in the membership of human rights treaty bodies can contribute to raising awareness of the importance of gender balance, the representation of the principal legal systems and the principle that the members of the treaty bodies shall be elected and shall serve in their personal capacity, and shall be of high moral character, acknowledged impartiality and recognized competence in the field of human rights;

5. *Requests* the chairpersons of the human rights treaty bodies to consider at their next meeting the content of the present resolution and to submit, through the United Nations High Commissioner for Human Rights, specific recommendations for the achievement of the goal of equitable geographical distribution in the membership of the human rights treaty bodies;

6. *Requests* the High Commissioner to submit concrete recommendations on the implementation of the present resolution to the General Assembly at its sixty-fourth session;

7. *Decides* to continue its consideration of the question at its sixty-fourth session under the item entitled "Promotion and protection of human rights".

RECORDED VOTE ON RESOLUTION 63/167:

In favour: Afghanistan, Algeria, Angola, Antigua and Barbuda, Argentina, Azerbaijan, Bahamas, Bahrain, Bangladesh, Barbados, Belarus, Belize, Benin, Bhutan, Bolivia, Botswana, Brunei Darussalam, Burkina Faso, Burundi, Cambodia, Cameroon, Central African Republic, China, Colombia, Comoros, Congo, Costa Rica, Côte d'Ivoire, Cuba, Democratic People's Republic of Korea, Djibouti, Dominica, Dominican Republic, Ecuador, Egypt, Eritrea, Ethiopia, Fiji, Gabon, Gambia, Ghana, Grenada, Guatemala, Guinea, Guinea-Bissau, Guyana, Haiti, Honduras, India, Indonesia, Iran, Iraq, Jamaica, Jordan, Kazakhstan, Kenya, Kuwait, Kyrgyzstan, Lao People's Democratic Republic, Lebanon, Lesotho, Liberia, Libyan Arab Jamahiriya, Madagascar, Malawi, Malaysia, Maldives, Mali, Marshall Islands, Mauritania, Mauritius, Mexico, Mongolia, Morocco, Mozambique, Myanmar, Namibia, Nauru, Nepal, Nicaragua, Niger, Nigeria, Oman, Pakistan, Papua New Guinea, Paraguay, Peru, Philippines, Qatar, Russian Federation, Rwanda, Saint Kitts and Nevis, Saint Lucia, Saint Vincent and the Grenadines, Samoa, Sao Tome and Principe, Saudi Arabia, Senegal, Sierra Leone, Singapore, Solomon Islands, Somalia, South Africa, Sri Lanka, Sudan, Suriname, Swaziland, Syrian Arab Republic, Tajikistan, Thailand, Timor-Leste, Togo, Tonga, Trinidad and Tobago, Tunisia, Turkmenistan, Tuvalu, Uganda, United Arab Emirates, United Republic of Tanzania, Uruguay, Uzbekistan, Vanuatu, Venezuela, Viet Nam, Yemen, Zambia, Zimbabwe.

Against: Albania, Andorra, Armenia, Australia, Austria, Belgium, Bosnia and Herzegovina, Bulgaria, Canada, Chile, Croatia, Cyprus, Czech Republic, Denmark, Estonia, Finland, France, Georgia, Germany, Greece, Hungary, Iceland, Ireland, Israel, Italy, Japan, Latvia, Liechtenstein, Lithuania, Luxembourg, Malta, Moldova, Monaco, Montenegro, Netherlands, New Zealand, Norway, Palau, Panama, Poland, Portugal, Republic of Korea, Romania, San Marino, Serbia, Slovakia, Slovenia, Spain, Sweden, Switzerland, The former Yugoslav Republic of Macedonia, Turkey, Ukraine, United Kingdom, United States.

Abstaining: Brazil, Cape Verde.

Effective implementation of international human rights instruments

Human Rights Council action. On 24 September [A/63/53/Add.1 (res. 9/8)], the Human Rights Council took note of the Secretary-General's 2007 report on the effective implementation of international human rights instruments [YUN 2007, p. 674]. It welcomed the measures taken by the human rights treaty bodies to improve their functioning and encouraged continuing efforts to further improve their effectiveness by reducing duplication of reporting required under the different instruments, harmonizing general guidelines on the form and content of reports across all treaty bodies, coordinating the schedule for the consideration of reports, limiting the length of reports, providing practical concluding observations addressed to States parties, and harmonizing practices for the publication and reporting of responses and practices for inviting comments from States and other stakeholders.

The Council urged States to consider signing and ratifying or acceding to international human rights instruments and accepting the individual communications procedures under applicable instruments; meet their reporting obligations, in particular by submitting initial and overdue reports; submit common-core documents and take into consideration reporting guidelines; provide effective follow-up to concluding observations of the treaty bodies on their reports and disseminate their full text; consider carefully the views of the treaty bodies on individual communications relating to them and provide adequate follow-up; encourage the involvement of civil society in the report preparation process; avail themselves of technical assistance; and when nominating their candidates to treaty bodies, consider the principle of non-accumulation of UN human rights mandates. The Council encouraged OHCHR to enhance its use of modern technologies, such as webcasts, with a view to strengthening the treaty body system. It emphasized the need to ensure financing and adequate staff and information resources for the operation of human rights bodies. The Secretary-General was requested to report to the Council annually on the implementation of the resolution, including recommendations for further improving the effectiveness of, harmonizing and reforming the treaty body system, and seek the views of States and other stakeholders.

Reservations to human rights treaties

A May report on reservations to human rights treaties [HRI/MC/2008/5] recalled that the International Law Commission, during its fifty-ninth session [YUN 2007, p. 1356], had convened a meeting with UN human rights experts, including representatives from human rights treaty bodies, to discuss issues relating to reservations [ibid., p. 674]. A report on the outcome of the meeting was prepared by the Special Rapporteur on reservations to treaties [ILC(LIX)/RT/CRP.1]. The Commission had revised the wording of several guidelines (3.1.8 to 3.1.10) relating to reservations and provisionally adopted them in 2007 [YUN 2007, p. 1356]. At the request of the General Assembly, the Secretary-General, in January, issued a summary of the debate on the report of the Commission during the Assembly's sixty-second session [A/CN.4/588], which included discussion related to reservations.

During the first session of the Working Group on UPR (see p. 713), the issue of reservations was raised with States under review, with several being urged to withdraw their reservations to international human rights treaties. Annexed to the report was a summary of the practice of human rights treaty bodies with respect to reservations—concluding observations/comments relating to the Committee on the Rights of the Child, the Human Rights Committee, the Committee on Economic, Social and Cultural Rights, the Committee on the Elimination of Racial Discrimination, the Committee on the Elimination of Discrimination against Women and the Committee on Migrant Workers. Also annexed to the report was a table of reservations, interpretative declarations, objections and withdrawals.

The Special Rapporteur also issued his twelfth report on the formulation and withdrawal of acceptances and objections to treaties [YUN 2007, p. 1371].

Universal Declaration of Human Rights

Human rights voluntary goals

The Human Rights Council initiated in 2007 [YUN 2007, p. 673] an open-ended intergovernmental process to elaborate a set of human rights voluntary goals to promote the realization of the Universal Declaration of Human Rights [YUN 1948–49, p. 535], to be launched on 10 December 2008 in celebration of the Declaration's sixtieth anniversary. A high-level panel discussion on human rights voluntary goals was held on 5 March, during the Council's seventh session [A/HRC/7/78].

Human Rights Council action. On 24 September [A/63/53/Add.1 (res. 9/12)], the Human Rights Council encouraged States to accomplish progressively a set of human rights voluntary goals, namely: universal ratification of the core international human rights instruments and universalization of the international human rights obligations of States; strengthening of national legal, institutional and policy frameworks to ensure the promotion and protection of human rights; establishment of national human rights institutions; elaboration of national human rights programmes and plans of action to strengthen States' capacity to promote and protect human rights; definition and implementation of national programmes of action promoting the realization of the rights and goals set forth in the Universal Declaration to eliminate discrimination of any kind and all forms of violence; adoption and implementation of programmes of human rights education in all learning institutions, including capacity-building programmes for law enforcement professionals; increased cooperation with all mechanisms of the UN human rights system; strengthening of mechanisms to facilitate human rights international cooperation; creation of favourable conditions at all levels to ensure the full and effective enjoyment of all human rights, including the right to development; and strengthening the capacity to fight hunger and poverty through additional forms of international cooperation.

States were invited to report on the progressive implementation of the voluntary goals, including in the context of UPR, and on the occasion of the seventieth (2018) anniversary of the Declaration. The Council welcomed the convening of a commemorative session on the sixtieth anniversary of the Declaration (see below) and the launch of the human rights voluntary goals.

Sixtieth anniversary of Universal Declaration

Human Rights Council action. On 24 September [A/63/53/Add.1 (dec. 9/102)], the Human Rights Council decided to convene a one-day session to commemorate the sixtieth anniversary of the Universal Declaration of Human Rights, to be held during the week of 8 December, for the presentation of national, regional and international initiatives launched on the occasion of the anniversary. The Council invited the Secretary-General and the High Commissioner to address the Council.

GENERAL ASSEMBLY ACTION

On 24 November [meeting 57], the General Assembly adopted **resolution 63/25** [draft: A/63/L.31] without vote [agenda item 64].

Commemoration of the sixtieth anniversary of the Universal Declaration of Human Rights

The General Assembly,

Guided by the purposes, principles and provisions of the Charter of the United Nations, which include the promotion of, and respect for, human rights and fundamental freedoms for all,

Recalling its resolution 62/171 of 18 December 2007 entitled "International Year of Human Rights Learning", in which it decided to commemorate the sixtieth anniversary of the Universal Declaration of Human Rights at a plenary meeting to be held on 10 December 2008,

Recalling also its resolution 2217 A (XXI) of 19 December 1966, in which it decided to award at five-year intervals the United Nations award for outstanding achievements in the field of human rights,

1. *Reaffirms* its decision to commemorate the sixtieth anniversary of the Universal Declaration of Human Rights on 10 December 2008;

2. *Decides* that the commemorative event will comprise a plenary meeting, including the award ceremony for the United Nations prize in the field of human rights, and two consecutive informal interactive panel discussions;

3. *Encourages* all Member States and observers to participate at the highest level possible;

4. *Decides* that the President of the General Assembly, the President of the Human Rights Council, the Secretary-General and the United Nations High Commissioner for Human Rights will address the commemorative plenary meeting;

5. *Invites* intergovernmental organizations and entities that have observer status with the General Assembly, relevant entities of the United Nations system and non-governmental organizations in consultative status with the Economic and Social Council to be represented at the commemorative event;

6. *Requests* the President of the General Assembly, in consultation with Member States and with the technical support of the Office of the United Nations High Commissioner for Human Rights, to draw up, no later than 30 November 2008, a list of two representatives of pertinent non-governmental organizations for each of the informal interactive panel discussions who will speak on behalf of civil society, and to circulate the list to Member States to be considered on a no-objection basis;

7. *Also requests* the President of the General Assembly, in consultation with Member States and with the technical support of the Office of the United Nations High Commissioner for Human Rights, to finalize the organizational arrangements for the commemorative event, including the identification of themes and the assignment of panellists for the informal interactive panel discussions;

8. *Further requests* the President of the General Assembly to hold open consultations with Member States and observers in order to prepare a brief declaration reaffirming the Universal Declaration of Human Rights and the commitment for its full implementation, to be adopted by consensus at the commemorative plenary meeting.

Commemorative meetings. On 10 December [A/63/PV.65], the General Assembly marked the sixtieth anniversary of the adoption of the Universal Declaration with a half-day plenary meeting. Assembly President Miguel d'Escoto Brockmann, Human Rights Council President Martin Ihoeghian Uhomoibhi, High Commissioner for Human Rights Navanethem Pillay and 15 other speakers addressed the meeting. The Secretary-General, who was attending the United Nations Climate Change Conference in Poznań, Poland (see p. 1155), addressed the meeting by video. A ceremony for the award of the United Nations Prizes in the Field of Human Rights for 2008 recognized individuals and organizations that had made outstanding contributions to the promotion and protection of human rights. The prizes were awarded to former High Commissioner Louise Arbour; veteran human rights defender Ramsey Clark; Dr. Carolyn Gomes, co-founder of Jamaicans for Justice; Dr. Denis Mukwege, co-founder of the General Referral Hospital of Panzi, DRC; and Human Rights Watch. Two special posthumous awards recognized former Pakistani Prime Minister Benazir Bhutto and Sister Dorothy Stang, human rights defender of the indigenous population of the Anapu region of Brazil, who was murdered in 2005.

The Human Rights Council held a commemorative session on 12 December, which was addressed by the Human Rights Council President, the Secretary-General, the High Commissioner and speakers representing States, international organizations and civil society.

GENERAL ASSEMBLY ACTION

On 10 December [meeting 65], the General Assembly adopted **resolution 63/116** [draft: A/63/L.54] without vote [agenda item 64].

Sixtieth anniversary of the Universal Declaration of Human Rights

The General Assembly

Adopts the following Declaration:

Declaration on the sixtieth anniversary of the Universal Declaration of Human Rights

We, the States Members of the United Nations, celebrate today the sixtieth anniversary of the adoption of the Universal Declaration of Human Rights, which is a common standard of achievement for all peoples and all nations in the field of human rights. Since its adoption, it has inspired the world and empowered women and men around the globe to assert their inherent dignity and rights without discrimination on any grounds. It is and will remain a source of progressive development of all human rights.

The Universal Declaration of Human Rights calls upon us to recognize and respect the dignity, freedom and equality of all human beings. We applaud the efforts undertaken by States to promote and protect all human rights for all. We must strive to enhance international cooperation and the dialogue among peoples and nations on the basis of mutual respect and understanding towards this goal.

In an ever-changing world, the Universal Declaration of Human Rights remains a relevant ethical compass that guides us in addressing the challenges we face today. The living, driving force of all human rights unites us in our common goal to eradicate the manifold ills that plague our world. We remain committed to development and to the internationally agreed development goals, and are convinced that their fulfilment will be instrumental to the enjoyment of human rights.

We deplore that human rights and fundamental freedoms are not yet fully and universally respected in all parts of the world. In no country or territory can it be claimed that all human rights have been fully realized at all times for all. Human beings continue to suffer from the neglect and violation of their human rights and fundamental freedoms. We laud the courage and commitment of all women and men around the world who have devoted their lives to promoting and protecting human rights.

We all have the duty to step up our efforts to promote and protect all human rights and to prevent, stop and redress all human rights violations. We must give everybody a chance to learn about and better understand all human rights and fundamental freedoms. We must continue to strengthen the human rights pillar of the United Nations, as we undertook with the creation of the Human Rights Council.

Today, we, the States Members of the United Nations, reiterate that we will not shy away from the magnitude of this challenge. We reaffirm our commitment towards the full realization of all human rights for all, which are universal, indivisible, interrelated, interdependent and mutually reinforcing.

Communications. On 3 June [A/62/858], Australia, Honduras, Mali, Slovenia, Ukraine and the United States, on behalf of 63 countries, transmitted to the Secretary-General a Declaration of Prisoners of Conscience on the occasion of the sixtieth anniversary of the Universal Declaration.

On 10 December [A/63/627], Cuba, as Chair of the Coordinating Bureau, transmitted to the Secretary-General the Declaration of the Coordinating Bureau of the Non-Aligned Movement on the commemoration of the sixtieth anniversary of the Universal Declaration.

Covenant on Civil and Political Rights and Optional Protocols

Accessions and ratifications

As at 31 December, parties to the International Covenant on Civil and Political Rights and the Optional Protocol thereto, adopted by the General Assembly in resolution 2200 A (XXI) [YUN 1966, p. 423], numbered 164 and 111, respectively. During the year, the Bahamas, Papua New Guinea, Samoa and Vanuatu became parties to the treaty, and Moldova became party to the Optional Protocol.

The Second Optional Protocol, aimed at the abolition of the death penalty, adopted by the Assembly in resolution 44/128 [YUN 1989, p. 484], was ratified or acceded to by Argentina, Chile, Honduras, Rwanda and Uzbekistan, bringing the number of States parties to 70 as at 31 December.

Implementation

Monitoring body. The Human Rights Committee, established under article 28 of the Covenant, held three sessions in 2008: its ninety-second (New York, 17 March–4 April); ninety-third (Geneva, 7–25 July) [A/63/40, vol. I]; and ninety-fourth (Geneva, 13–31 October) [A/64/40, vol. I]. Under article 40, it considered reports from 13 States—Botswana, Denmark, France, Ireland, Japan, Monaco, Nicaragua, Panama, San Marino, Spain, the former Yugoslav Republic of Macedonia, Tunisia and the United Kingdom—and adopted concluding observations on them. The Committee adopted views on communications from individuals alleging violations of their rights under the Covenant, and decided that other such communications were inadmissible. Those views and decisions were annexed to the Committee's reports [A/63/40, vol. II; A/64/40, vol. II].

Within the framework of article 14 of the Covenant, aimed at ensuring the effective administration of justice, the Committee adopted, on 28 October, General Comment No. 33 on the obligations of States parties under the Optional Protocol.

By notifications of 2 January, 21 February, 7 and 29 August, 17 September, 12 November and 12 December, Peru stated that it had declared a state of emergency in certain provinces, during which certain rights covered by the Covenant would be suspended. On 2 September, Peru notified other States parties, through the Secretary-General, that the state of emergency in certain districts and several provinces had been declared null and void.

On 9 May, Guatemala notified other States parties, through the Secretary-General, that it had declared a state of emergency throughout the country, and specified the restriction placed on certain rights and freedoms. On 9 October, Guatemala notified other States parties, through the Secretary-General, of the declaration of a state of emergency for a 15-day period in part of the country, specifying the restriction placed on certain rights and freedoms. On 24 October, Guatemala notified other States of the prorogation of the state of emergency for 15 days.

On 18 October, Colombia notified other States, through the Secretary-General, of the declaration of a 90-day nationwide state of internal disturbance.

(For the Organization's efforts to protect civil and political rights, within the framework established by the Covenant, see p. 772.)

Covenant on Economic, Social and Cultural Rights

Accessions and ratifications

As at 31 December, there were 160 parties to the International Covenant on Economic, Social and Cultural Rights, adopted by the General Assembly in resolution 2200 A (XXI) [YUN 1966, p. 419]. During the year, the Bahamas, Pakistan and Papua New Guinea became parties to the Covenant.

Implementation

Monitoring body. The Committee on Economic, Social and Cultural Rights held its fortieth (28 April–16 May) and forty-first (3–21 November) sessions in Geneva [E/2009/22]. Its pre-sessional working group met in Geneva from 19 to 23 May and from 24 to 28 November to identify issues to be discussed with reporting States. The Committee examined reports submitted under articles 16 and 17 of the Covenant by Angola, Benin, Bolivia, France, India, Kenya, Nicaragua, the Philippines, Sweden and the United Nations Interim Administration Mission in Kosovo, and adopted concluding observations on them. On 17 November, the Committee discussed draft General Comment No. 20 on non-discrimination and economic, social and cultural rights.

In a statement on the world food crisis, adopted on 16 May [E/C.12/2008/1], the Committee urged States to: ensure freedom from hunger through the provision of emergency humanitarian aid without discrimination; limit the rapid rise in food prices by encouraging production of local staple food products for local consumption instead of diverting prime arable land for the production of agrofuels; introduce measures to combat speculation in food commodities; and establish an international coordination mechanism to oversee responses to the food crisis and to ensure that the policy measures adopted would fulfil the realization of the right to adequate food. The Committee also urged States to: revise the global trade regime to ensure that global agricultural trade rules promoted, rather than undermined, the right to adequate food; implement strategies to combat climate change; invest in small-scale agriculture, small-scale irrigation and other appropriate technologies; and apply human rights principles, especially those relating to the right to adequate food, by assessing the impact of their financial, trade and development policies.

The Economic and Social Council, on 5 February, took note of the Committee's report on its thirty-sixth and thirty-seventh sessions [YUN 2006, p. 772] (**decision 2008/202**), and on 25 July, it took note of the reports on its thirty-eighth and thirty-ninth sessions [YUN 2007, p. 677] (**decision 2008/256**).

Optional Protocol

The Open-ended Working Group to consider options for elaborating an optional protocol to the Covenant, at its fifth session (Geneva, 4–8 February and 31 March–4 April) [A/HRC/8/7 & Corr.1,2], finalized the text of the protocol and transmitted it to the Human Rights Council for consideration. The Protocol established a procedure of individual communications for cases of alleged violations of economic, social and cultural rights.

Human Rights Council action. On 18 June [A/63/53 (res. 8/2)], the Human Rights Council adopted the Optional Protocol to the International Covenant on Economic, Social and Cultural Rights, annexed to the resolution, and recommended its adoption by the General Assembly (see below).

GENERAL ASSEMBLY ACTION

On 10 December [meeting 66], the General Assembly, on the recommendation of the Third Committee [A/63/435], adopted **resolution 63/117** without vote [agenda item 58].

Optional Protocol to the International Covenant on Economic, Social and Cultural Rights

The General Assembly,

Taking note of the adoption by the Human Rights Council, by its resolution 8/2 of 18 June 2008, of the Optional Protocol to the International Covenant on Economic, Social and Cultural Rights,

1. *Adopts* the Optional Protocol to the International Covenant on Economic, Social and Cultural Rights, the text of which is annexed to the present resolution;

2. *Recommends* that the Optional Protocol be opened for signature at a signing ceremony to be held in 2009, and requests the Secretary-General and the United Nations High Commissioner for Human Rights to provide the necessary assistance.

ANNEX

Optional Protocol to the International Covenant on Economic, Social and Cultural Rights

Preamble

The States Parties to the present Protocol,

Considering that, in accordance with the principles proclaimed in the Charter of the United Nations, recognition of the inherent dignity and of the equal and inalienable rights of all members of the human family is the foundation of freedom, justice and peace in the world,

Noting that the Universal Declaration of Human Rights proclaims that all human beings are born free and equal in dignity and rights and that everyone is entitled to all the rights and freedoms set forth therein, without distinction of any kind, such as race, colour, sex, language, religion, political or other opinion, national or social origin, property, birth or other status,

Recalling that the Universal Declaration of Human Rights and the International Covenants on Human Rights recognize that the ideal of free human beings enjoying freedom from fear and want can only be achieved if conditions are created whereby everyone may enjoy civil, cultural, economic, political and social rights,

Reaffirming the universality, indivisibility, interdependence and interrelatedness of all human rights and fundamental freedoms,

Recalling that each State Party to the International Covenant on Economic, Social and Cultural Rights (hereinafter referred to as "the Covenant") undertakes to take steps, individually and through international assistance and cooperation, especially economic and technical, to the maximum of its available resources, with a view to achieving progressively the full realization of the rights recognized in the Covenant by all appropriate means, including particularly the adoption of legislative measures,

Considering that, in order further to achieve the purposes of the Covenant and the implementation of its provisions, it would be appropriate to enable the Committee on Economic, Social and Cultural Rights (hereinafter referred to as "the Committee") to carry out the functions provided for in the present Protocol,

Have agreed as follows:

Article 1

Competence of the Committee to receive and consider communications

1. A State Party to the Covenant that becomes a Party to the present Protocol recognizes the competence of the Committee to receive and consider communications as provided for by the provisions of the present Protocol.

2. No communication shall be received by the Committee if it concerns a State Party to the Covenant which is not a Party to the present Protocol.

Article 2

Communications

Communications may be submitted by or on behalf of individuals or groups of individuals, under the jurisdiction of a State Party, claiming to be victims of a violation of any of the economic, social and cultural rights set forth in the Covenant by that State Party. Where a communication is submitted on behalf of individuals or groups of individuals, this shall be with their consent unless the author can justify acting on their behalf without such consent.

Article 3

Admissibility

1. The Committee shall not consider a communication unless it has ascertained that all available domestic remedies have been exhausted. This shall not be the rule where the application of such remedies is unreasonably prolonged.

2. The Committee shall declare a communication inadmissible when:

(a) It is not submitted within one year after the exhaustion of domestic remedies, except in cases where the author can demonstrate that it had not been possible to submit the communication within that time limit;

(b) The facts that are the subject of the communication occurred prior to the entry into force of the present Protocol for the State Party concerned unless those facts continued after that date;

(c) The same matter has already been examined by the Committee or has been or is being examined under another procedure of international investigation or settlement;

(d) It is incompatible with the provisions of the Covenant;

(e) It is manifestly ill-founded, not sufficiently substantiated or exclusively based on reports disseminated by mass media;

(f) It is an abuse of the right to submit a communication; or when

(g) It is anonymous or not in writing.

Article 4

Communications not revealing a clear disadvantage

The Committee may, if necessary, decline to consider a communication where it does not reveal that the author has suffered a clear disadvantage, unless the Committee considers that the communication raises a serious issue of general importance.

Article 5

Interim measures

1. At any time after the receipt of a communication and before a determination on the merits has been reached, the Committee may transmit to the State Party concerned for its urgent consideration a request that the State Party take such interim measures as may be necessary in exceptional circumstances to avoid possible irreparable damage to the victim or victims of the alleged violations.

2. Where the Committee exercises its discretion under paragraph 1 of the present article, this does not imply a determination on admissibility or on the merits of the communication.

Article 6

Transmission of the communication

1. Unless the Committee considers a communication inadmissible without reference to the State Party concerned, the Committee shall bring any communication submitted to it under the present Protocol confidentially to the attention of the State Party concerned.

2. Within six months, the receiving State Party shall submit to the Committee written explanations or statements clarifying the matter and the remedy, if any, that may have been provided by that State Party.

Article 7

Friendly settlement

1. The Committee shall make available its good offices to the parties concerned with a view to reaching a friendly settlement of the matter on the basis of the respect for the obligations set forth in the Covenant.

2. An agreement on a friendly settlement closes consideration of the communication under the present Protocol.

Article 8

Examination of communications

1. The Committee shall examine communications received under article 2 of the present Protocol in the light of all documentation submitted to it, provided that this documentation is transmitted to the parties concerned.

2. The Committee shall hold closed meetings when examining communications under the present Protocol.

3. When examining a communication under the present Protocol, the Committee may consult, as appropriate, relevant documentation emanating from other United Nations bodies, specialized agencies, funds, programmes and mechanisms, and other international organizations, including from regional human rights systems, and any observations or comments by the State Party concerned.

4. When examining communications under the present Protocol, the Committee shall consider the reasonableness of the steps taken by the State Party in accordance with part II of the Covenant. In doing so, the Committee shall bear in mind that the State Party may adopt a range of possible policy measures for the implementation of the rights set forth in the Covenant.

Article 9
Follow-up to the views of the Committee

1. After examining a communication, the Committee shall transmit its views on the communication, together with its recommendations, if any, to the parties concerned.

2. The State Party shall give due consideration to the views of the Committee, together with its recommendations, if any, and shall submit to the Committee, within six months, a written response, including information on any action taken in the light of the views and recommendations of the Committee.

3. The Committee may invite the State Party to submit further information about any measures the State Party has taken in response to its views or recommendations, if any, including as deemed appropriate by the Committee, in the State Party's subsequent reports under articles 16 and 17 of the Covenant.

Article 10
Inter-State communications

1. A State Party to the present Protocol may at any time declare under the present article that it recognizes the competence of the Committee to receive and consider communications to the effect that a State Party claims that another State Party is not fulfilling its obligations under the Covenant. Communications under the present article may be received and considered only if submitted by a State Party that has made a declaration recognizing in regard to itself the competence of the Committee. No communication shall be received by the Committee if it concerns a State Party which has not made such a declaration. Communications received under the present article shall be dealt with in accordance with the following procedure:

(a) If a State Party to the present Protocol considers that another State Party is not fulfilling its obligations under the Covenant, it may, by written communication, bring the matter to the attention of that State Party. The State Party may also inform the Committee of the matter. Within three months after the receipt of the communication, the receiving State shall afford the State that sent the communication an explanation, or any other statement in writing clarifying the matter, which should include, to the extent possible and pertinent, reference to domestic procedures and remedies taken, pending or available in the matter;

(b) If the matter is not settled to the satisfaction of both States Parties concerned within six months after the receipt by the receiving State of the initial communication, either State shall have the right to refer the matter to the Committee, by notice given to the Committee and to the other State;

(c) The Committee shall deal with a matter referred to it only after it has ascertained that all available domestic remedies have been invoked and exhausted in the matter. This shall not be the rule where the application of the remedies is unreasonably prolonged;

(d) Subject to the provisions of subparagraph *(c)* of the present paragraph, the Committee shall make available its good offices to the States Parties concerned with a view to a friendly solution of the matter on the basis of the respect for the obligations set forth in the Covenant;

(e) The Committee shall hold closed meetings when examining communications under the present article;

(f) In any matter referred to it in accordance with subparagraph *(b)* of the present paragraph, the Committee may call upon the States Parties concerned, referred to in subparagraph *(b)*, to supply any relevant information;

(g) The States Parties concerned, referred to in subparagraph *(b)* of the present paragraph, shall have the right to be represented when the matter is being considered by the Committee and to make submissions orally and/or in writing;

(h) The Committee shall, with all due expediency after the date of receipt of notice under subparagraph *(b)* of the present paragraph, submit a report, as follows:

(i) If a solution within the terms of subparagraph *(d)* of the present paragraph is reached, the Committee shall confine its report to a brief statement of the facts and of the solution reached;

(ii) If a solution within the terms of subparagraph *(d)* is not reached, the Committee shall, in its report, set forth the relevant facts concerning the issue between the States Parties concerned. The written submissions and record of the oral submissions made by the States Parties concerned shall be attached to the report. The Committee may also communicate only to the States Parties concerned any views that it may consider relevant to the issue between them.

In every matter, the report shall be communicated to the States Parties concerned.

2. A declaration under paragraph 1 of the present article shall be deposited by the States Parties with the Secretary-General of the United Nations, who shall transmit copies thereof to the other States Parties. A declaration may be withdrawn at any time by notification to the Secretary-General. Such a withdrawal shall not prejudice the consideration of any matter that is the subject of a communication already transmitted under the present article; no further communication by any State Party shall be received under the present article after the notification of withdrawal of the declaration has been received by the

Secretary-General, unless the State Party concerned has made a new declaration.

Article 11

Inquiry procedure

1. A State Party to the present Protocol may at any time declare that it recognizes the competence of the Committee provided for under the present article.

2. If the Committee receives reliable information indicating grave or systematic violations by a State Party of any of the economic, social and cultural rights set forth in the Covenant, the Committee shall invite that State Party to cooperate in the examination of the information and to this end to submit observations with regard to the information concerned.

3. Taking into account any observations that may have been submitted by the State Party concerned as well as any other reliable information available to it, the Committee may designate one or more of its members to conduct an inquiry and to report urgently to the Committee. Where warranted and with the consent of the State Party, the inquiry may include a visit to its territory.

4. Such an inquiry shall be conducted confidentially and the cooperation of the State Party shall be sought at all stages of the proceedings.

5. After examining the findings of such an inquiry, the Committee shall transmit these findings to the State Party concerned together with any comments and recommendations.

6. The State Party concerned shall, within six months of receiving the findings, comments and recommendations transmitted by the Committee, submit its observations to the Committee.

7. After such proceedings have been completed with regard to an inquiry made in accordance with paragraph 2 of the present article, the Committee may, after consultations with the State Party concerned, decide to include a summary account of the results of the proceedings in its annual report provided for in article 15 of the present Protocol.

8. Any State Party having made a declaration in accordance with paragraph 1 of the present article may, at any time, withdraw this declaration by notification to the Secretary-General.

Article 12

Follow-up to the inquiry procedure

1. The Committee may invite the State Party concerned to include in its report under articles 16 and 17 of the Covenant details of any measures taken in response to an inquiry conducted under article 11 of the present Protocol.

2. The Committee may, if necessary, after the end of the period of six months referred to in article 11, paragraph 6, invite the State Party concerned to inform it of the measures taken in response to such an inquiry.

Article 13

Protection measures

A State Party shall take all appropriate measures to ensure that individuals under its jurisdiction are not subjected to any form of ill-treatment or intimidation as a consequence of communicating with the Committee pursuant to the present Protocol.

Article 14

International assistance and cooperation

1. The Committee shall transmit, as it may consider appropriate, and with the consent of the State Party concerned, to United Nations specialized agencies, funds and programmes and other competent bodies, its views or recommendations concerning communications and inquiries that indicate a need for technical advice or assistance, along with the State Party's observations and suggestions, if any, on these views or recommendations.

2. The Committee may also bring to the attention of such bodies, with the consent of the State Party concerned, any matter arising out of communications considered under the present Protocol which may assist them in deciding, each within its field of competence, on the advisability of international measures likely to contribute to assisting States Parties in achieving progress in implementation of the rights recognized in the Covenant.

3. A trust fund shall be established in accordance with the relevant procedures of the General Assembly, to be administered in accordance with the Financial Regulations and Rules of the United Nations, with a view to providing expert and technical assistance to States Parties, with the consent of the State Party concerned, for the enhanced implementation of the rights contained in the Covenant, thus contributing to building national capacities in the area of economic, social and cultural rights in the context of the present Protocol.

4. The provisions of the present article are without prejudice to the obligations of each State Party to fulfil its obligations under the Covenant.

Article 15

Annual report

The Committee shall include in its annual report a summary of its activities under the present Protocol.

Article 16

Dissemination and information

Each State Party undertakes to make widely known and to disseminate the Covenant and the present Protocol and to facilitate access to information about the views and recommendations of the Committee, in particular, on matters involving that State Party, and to do so in accessible formats for persons with disabilities.

Article 17

Signature, ratification and accession

1. The present Protocol is open for signature by any State that has signed, ratified or acceded to the Covenant.

2. The present Protocol is subject to ratification by any State that has ratified or acceded to the Covenant. Instruments of ratification shall be deposited with the Secretary-General of the United Nations.

3. The present Protocol shall be open to accession by any State that has ratified or acceded to the Covenant.

4. Accession shall be effected by the deposit of an instrument of accession with the Secretary-General of the United Nations.

Article 18

Entry into force

1. The present Protocol shall enter into force three months after the date of the deposit with the Secretary-General of the United Nations of the tenth instrument of ratification or accession.

2. For each State ratifying or acceding to the present Protocol after the deposit of the tenth instrument of ratification or accession, the Protocol shall enter into force three months after the date of the deposit of its instrument of ratification or accession.

Article 19

Amendments

1. Any State Party may propose an amendment to the present Protocol and submit it to the Secretary-General of the United Nations. The Secretary-General shall communicate any proposed amendments to States Parties, with a request to be notified whether they favour a meeting of States Parties for the purpose of considering and deciding upon the proposals. In the event that, within four months from the date of such communication, at least one third of the States Parties favour such a meeting, the Secretary-General shall convene the meeting under the auspices of the United Nations. Any amendment adopted by a majority of two thirds of the States Parties present and voting shall be submitted by the Secretary-General to the General Assembly for approval and thereafter to all States Parties for acceptance.

2. An amendment adopted and approved in accordance with paragraph 1 of the present article shall enter into force on the thirtieth day after the number of instruments of acceptance deposited reaches two thirds of the number of States Parties at the date of adoption of the amendment. Thereafter, the amendment shall enter into force for any State Party on the thirtieth day following the deposit of its own instrument of acceptance. An amendment shall be binding only on those States Parties which have accepted it.

Article 20

Denunciation

1. Any State Party may denounce the present Protocol at any time by written notification addressed to the Secretary-General of the United Nations. Denunciation shall take effect six months after the date of receipt of the notification by the Secretary-General.

2. Denunciation shall be without prejudice to the continued application of the provisions of the present Protocol to any communication submitted under articles 2 and 10 or to any procedure initiated under article 11 before the effective date of denunciation.

Article 21

Notification by the Secretary-General

The Secretary-General of the United Nations shall notify all States referred to in article 26, paragraph 1, of the Covenant of the following particulars:

(a) Signatures, ratifications and accessions under the present Protocol;

(b) The date of entry into force of the present Protocol and of any amendment under article 19;

(c) Any denunciation under article 20.

Article 22

Official languages

1. The present Protocol, of which the Arabic, Chinese, English, French, Russian and Spanish texts are equally authentic, shall be deposited in the archives of the United Nations.

2. The Secretary-General of the United Nations shall transmit certified copies of the present Protocol to all States referred to in article 26 of the Covenant.

Convention against racial discrimination

Accessions and ratifications

As at 31 December, the number of parties to the International Convention on the Elimination of All Forms of Racial Discrimination, adopted by the General Assembly in resolution 2106 A (XX) [YUN 1965, p. 440], stood at 173.

The Secretary-General reported on the status of the Convention as at 15 August [A/63/473].

A Secretariat note [A/HRC/8/15], submitted in April in response to a Human Rights Council request [YUN 2006, p. 760], described OHCHR efforts towards universal ratification of the Convention and listed six States that had signed but not ratified the instrument, and 16 others that had neither signed nor ratified it. OHCHR wrote to the 22 States that had yet to become parties, encouraging them to take the necessary action.

Complementary standards

Pursuant to Human Rights Council resolution 6/21 [YUN 2007, p. 678], the Ad Hoc Committee on the Elaboration of Complementary Standards held the first (11–21 February) and second (15–19 December) parts of its first session in Geneva [A/HRC/10/88]. The Committee was established in 2006 [YUN 2006, p. 774] to elaborate complementary standards to the International Convention, in the form of either a convention or an additional protocol, filling gaps in the Convention and providing new normative standards.

In February, the Committee recommended that the Human Rights Council refer to the Committee on the Elimination of Racial Discrimination proposals regarding the elaboration of an optional protocol as contained in its "Study of the Committee on the Elimination of Racial Discrimination on possible measures to strengthen implementation through optional recommendations or the update of its monitoring procedures" [A/HRC/4/WG.3/7]. The Ad Hoc Committee expressed its readiness to further review the proposals included in the suggested protocol, and acknowledged that disagreements remained on whether substantial protection gaps needed to be addressed through complementary standards.

In conclusions and recommendations adopted in December, the Committee agreed on a road map for its future work, including the preparation of complementary international standards in the field of racism, racial discrimination, xenophobia and related intolerance, the scope, form and nature of which could vary according to the gap to be filled. The Committee Chairperson would solicit contributions from Member States; compile, integrate and structure them; and consult Member States on the outcome, which should be submitted to Member States by 31 July 2009, as the basis for the work of the Committee in October 2009.

Implementation

Monitoring body. The Committee on the Elimination of Racial Discrimination (CERD), established under article 8 of the Convention, held its seventy-second (18 February–7 March) and seventy-third (28 July–15 August) sessions in Geneva [A/63/18]. The Committee considered reports submitted by 15 countries—Austria, Belgium, the Dominican Republic, Ecuador, Fiji, Germany, Italy, Moldova, Namibia, Nicaragua, the Russian Federation, Sweden, Switzerland, Togo and the United States—and adopted concluding observations on them.

With regard to the Convention's implementation by States parties whose reports were seriously overdue, the Committee noted that 20 of them were at least 10 years late in submitting their reports, and 30 were at least five years late. The review of the Convention's implementation continued for those States parties on the basis of the last reports submitted, in addition to information prepared by UN organs and other sources, including NGOs. Of those States with seriously overdue reports scheduled for review at the Committee's seventy-third session, Peru reconfirmed its intention to submit its report by the end of 2008 and requested that the review be postponed. The Committee postponed the review of the situation in Belize, in light of that country's request for technical assistance in the reporting process.

Under article 14 of the Convention, CERD considered communications from individuals or groups claiming violation by a State party of their rights as enumerated in the Convention. Fifty-three States parties had recognized CERD competence to do so (Algeria, Andorra, Argentina, Australia, Austria, Azerbaijan, Belgium, Bolivia, Brazil, Bulgaria, Chile, Costa Rica, Cyprus, Czech Republic, Denmark, Ecuador, Finland, France, Georgia, Germany, Hungary, Iceland, Ireland, Italy, Kazakhstan, Liechtenstein, Luxembourg, Malta, Mexico, Monaco, Montenegro, Morocco, Netherlands, Norway, Peru, Poland, Portugal, Republic of Korea, Romania, Russian Federation, San Marino, Senegal, Serbia, Slovakia, Slovenia, South Africa, Spain, Sweden, Switzerland, the former Yugoslav Republic of Macedonia, Ukraine, Uruguay, Venezuela).

Pursuant to article 15 of the Convention, which empowered the Committee to consider petitions, reports and other information relating to Trust and Non-Self-Governing Territories, CERD noted, as it had in the past, the difficulty in fulfilling its functions in that regard, owing to the lack of copies of relevant petitions and the scant information relating directly to the Convention's principles and objectives in the reports received.

The Committee considered a number of situations under its early warning and urgent action procedure, including situations in Belize, Brazil, Canada, Chile, China, the Czech Republic, Ethiopia, India, Italy, Kenya, Panama, Peru and the Philippines. It decided to hold at its next session a thematic discussion on special measures within the meaning of articles 1 (4) and 2 (2) of the Convention, with a view to elaborating a general comment on the subject.

Financial situation. In August [A/63/306], the Secretary-General reported that outstanding arrears by States parties for the functioning of the Committee totalled $141,810 as at 30 June. As at 31 December, 43 States parties had accepted an amendment to article 8 of the Convention regarding the financing of CERD [YUN 1992, p. 714]. The amendment was to enter into force when accepted by a two-thirds majority of States parties, comprising approximately 115 of the 173 States parties to the Convention.

(For information on the Organization's activities to combat racial discrimination, including contemporary forms of racism, in accordance with the Convention and under the Programme of Action of the 2001 World Conference against Racism, Racial Discrimination, Xenophobia and Related Intolerance, see p. 761.)

GENERAL ASSEMBLY ACTION

On 24 December [meeting 74], the General Assembly, on the recommendation of the Third Committee [A/63/428], adopted **resolution 63/243** without vote [agenda item 62 *(a)*].

International Convention on the Elimination of All Forms of Racial Discrimination

The General Assembly,

Recalling its previous resolutions on the International Convention on the Elimination of All Forms of Racial Discrimination, most recently resolution 61/148 of 19 December 2006,

Bearing in mind the Vienna Declaration and Programme of Action adopted by the World Conference on Human Rights on 25 June 1993, in particular section II.B of the Declaration, relating to equality, dignity and tolerance,

Reiterating the need to intensify the struggle to eliminate all forms of racism, racial discrimination, xenophobia and related intolerance throughout the world,

Reiterating also the importance of the Convention, which is one of the most widely accepted human rights instruments adopted under the auspices of the United Nations,

Reaffirming that universal adherence to and full implementation of the Convention are of paramount importance for promoting equality and non-discrimination in the world, as stated in the Durban Declaration and Programme of Action adopted by the World Conference against Racism, Racial Discrimination, Xenophobia and Related Intolerance on 8 September 2001,

Mindful of the importance of the contributions of the Committee on the Elimination of Racial Discrimination to the effective implementation of the Convention and to the efforts of the United Nations to combat racism, racial discrimination, xenophobia and related intolerance,

Emphasizing the obligation of all States parties to the Convention to take legislative, judicial and other measures to secure full implementation of the provisions of the Convention,

Recalling its resolution 47/111 of 16 December 1992, in which it welcomed the decision, taken on 15 January 1992 by the Fourteenth Meeting of States Parties to the International Convention on the Elimination of All Forms of Racial Discrimination, to amend paragraph 6 of article 8 of the Convention and to add a new paragraph, as paragraph 7 of article 8, with a view to providing for the financing of the Committee from the regular budget of the United Nations, and reiterating its deep concern that the amendment to the Convention has not yet entered into force,

Stressing the importance of enabling the Committee to function smoothly and to have all necessary facilities for the effective performance of its functions under the Convention,

I

Reports of the Committee on the Elimination of Racial Discrimination

1. *Takes note* of the reports of the Committee on the Elimination of Racial Discrimination on its seventieth and seventy-first and its seventy-second and seventy-third sessions;

2. *Commends* the Committee for its contributions to the effective implementation of the International Convention on the Elimination of All Forms of Racial Discrimination, especially through the examination of reports under article 9 of the Convention, action on communications under article 14 of the Convention and thematic discussions, which contribute to the prevention and elimination of racism, racial discrimination, xenophobia and related intolerance;

3. *Calls upon* States parties to fulfil their obligation, under article 9, paragraph 1, of the Convention, to submit their periodic reports on measures taken to implement the Convention in due time;

4. *Expresses its concern* at the fact that a great number of reports are overdue and continue to be overdue, in particular initial reports, which constitutes an obstacle to the full implementation of the Convention;

5. *Encourages* States parties to the Convention whose reports are seriously overdue to avail themselves of the advisory services and technical assistance that the Office of the United Nations High Commissioner for Human Rights can provide, upon their request, for the preparation of the reports;

6. *Encourages* the Committee to continue to cooperate and exchange information with United Nations bodies and mechanisms, in particular with the Human Rights Council, its Advisory Committee and the Special Rapporteur on contemporary forms of racism, racial discrimination, xenophobia and related intolerance, and with intergovernmental organizations, as well as with non-governmental organizations;

7. *Encourages* States parties to the Convention to continue to include a gender perspective in their reports to the Committee on the Elimination of Racial Discrimination, and invites the Committee to take into account a gender perspective in the implementation of its mandate;

8. *Notes with appreciation* the engagement of the Committee in the follow-up to the Durban Declaration and Programme of Action;

9. *Expresses its appreciation* for the efforts made so far by the Committee to improve the efficiency of its working methods, including with a view to further harmonizing the working methods of the treaty bodies, and encourages the Committee to continue its activities in this regard;

10. *Welcomes*, in this regard, measures taken by the Committee to follow up on its concluding observations and recommendations, such as the appointment of a follow-up coordinator and the adoption of the guidelines on follow-up;

11. *Encourages* the continued participation of members of the Committee in the annual inter-committee meetings and meetings of chairpersons of the human rights treaty bodies, especially with a view to a more coordinated approach to the activities of the treaty body system and standardized reporting as well as to solving the problem of the backlog of reports of States parties in an effective manner, including by identifying efficiencies and maximizing the use of their resources as well as learning and sharing best practices and experiences in this regard;

12. *Notes* the persistent backlog of reports of States parties awaiting consideration, which prevents the Committee from considering the periodic reports of States parties in a timely manner and without undue delay, as well as the request of the Committee that the General Assembly authorize an extension of its meeting time, which is currently only six weeks per year;

13. *Decides* to authorize the Committee to meet for an additional week per session, as a temporary measure, with effect from August 2009, until 2011;

14. *Also decides* to assess the situation regarding the meeting time of the Committee at its sixty-fifth session on the basis of an evaluation made by the Office of the High Commissioner, taking into account a more comprehensive approach to the backlog of human rights treaty bodies and the increasing number of reports of States parties to the human rights conventions;

II

Financial situation of the Committee on the Elimination of Racial Discrimination

15. *Takes note* of the report of the Secretary-General on the financial situation of the Committee on the Elimination of Racial Discrimination;

16. *Expresses its profound concern* at the fact that a number of States parties to the International Convention on the Elimination of All Forms of Racial Discrimination have still not fulfilled their financial obligations, as shown in the report of the Secretary-General, and strongly appeals to all States parties that are in arrears to fulfil their outstanding financial obligations under article 8, paragraph 6, of the Convention;

17. *Strongly urges* States parties to the Convention to accelerate their domestic ratification procedures with regard to the amendment to the Convention concerning the financing of the Committee and to notify the Secretary-General expeditiously in writing of their agreement to the amendment, as decided upon at the Fourteenth Meeting of States Parties to the International Convention on the Elimination of All Forms of Racial Discrimination on 15 January 1992, endorsed by the General Assembly in its resolution 47/111 and further reiterated at the Sixteenth Meeting of States Parties on 16 January 1996;

18. *Requests* the Secretary-General to continue to ensure adequate financial arrangements and to provide the necessary support, including an adequate level of Secretariat assistance, in order to ensure the functioning of the Committee and to enable it to cope with its increasing amount of work;

19. *Also requests* the Secretary-General to invite those States parties to the Convention that are in arrears to pay the amounts in arrears, and to report thereon to the General Assembly at its sixty-fifth session;

III

Status of the International Convention on the Elimination of All Forms of Racial Discrimination

20. *Takes note* of the report of the Secretary-General on the status of the International Convention on the Elimination of All Forms of Racial Discrimination;

21. *Expresses its satisfaction* at the number of States that have ratified or acceded to the Convention, which now stands at one hundred and seventy-three;

22. *Urges* States parties to comply fully with their obligations under the Convention and to take into consideration the concluding observations and general recommendations of the Committee on the Elimination of Racial Discrimination;

23. *Reaffirms its conviction* that ratification of or accession to the Convention on a universal basis and the implementation of its provisions are necessary for the effectiveness of the fight against racism, racial discrimination, xenophobia and related intolerance and for the implementation of the commitments undertaken under the Durban Declaration and Programme of Action, and expresses its disappointment that universal ratification of the Convention was not achieved by the targeted date of 2005;

24. *Urges* all States that have not yet become parties to the Convention to ratify or accede to it as a matter of urgency;

25. *Urges* States to limit the extent of any reservation they lodge to the Convention and to formulate any reservation as precisely and as narrowly as possible in order to ensure that no reservation is incompatible with the object and purpose of the Convention, to review their reservations on a regular basis with a view to withdrawing them, and to withdraw reservations that are contrary to the object and purpose of the Convention;

26. *Notes* that the number of States parties to the Convention that have made the declaration provided for in article 14 of the Convention now stands at fifty-three, and requests States parties that have not yet done so to consider making that declaration;

27. *Invites* the Chairperson of the Committee on the Elimination of Racial Discrimination to present an oral report on the work of the Committee and to engage in an interactive dialogue with the General Assembly at its sixty-fifth session under the item entitled "Elimination of racism, racial discrimination, xenophobia and related intolerance";

28. *Decides* to consider, at its sixty-fifth session, under the item entitled "Elimination of racism, racial discrimination, xenophobia and related intolerance", the reports of the Committee on its seventy-fourth and seventy-fifth and its seventy-sixth and seventy-seventh sessions, the report of the Secretary-General on the financial situation of the Committee and the report of the Secretary-General on the status of the Convention.

Convention against torture

Accessions and ratifications

As at 31 December, 146 States were parties to the 1984 Convention against Torture and Other Cruel, Inhuman or Degrading Treatment or Punishment, adopted by the General Assembly in resolution 39/46 [YUN 1984, p. 813]. Rwanda became a party to the Convention in 2008.

During the year, Bosnia and Herzegovina, Chile, France, Germany, Guatemala, Kazakhstan, Kyrgyzstan and Lebanon became parties to the Optional Protocol to the Convention, bringing the total number of parties to 42. The Protocol, which established an international inspection system for places of detention, was adopted in Assembly resolution 57/199 [YUN 2002, p. 631] and entered into force in 2006 [YUN 2006, p. 776]. As at 16 May, 56 parties had made the required declarations under articles 21 and 22, in which a party recognized the competence of the Committee against Torture to receive and consider communications by which a State party claimed that another party was not fulfilling its obligations under the Convention, and from or on behalf of individuals who claimed to be victims of a violation of the Convention's provisions by a State party. Four parties had made the declaration under article 21, concerning inter-State communications, bringing the total number of declarations under that article to 60, while five had done so under article 22, concerning individual communications, bringing the total under that article to 61. Amendments to articles 17 and 18, adopted in 1992 [YUN 1992, p. 735], had been accepted by 27 States parties as at year's end.

Implementation

Monitoring body. During the year, the Committee against Torture, established as a monitoring body under the Convention, held its fortieth (28 April–16 May) [A/63/44] and forty-first (3–21 November) [A/64/44] sessions in Geneva. Under article 19 of the Convention, it considered reports submitted by 15 countries—Algeria, Australia, Belgium, China (including the Hong Kong and Macao Special Administrative Regions), Costa Rica, Kazakhstan, Kenya, Iceland, Indonesia, Lithuania, Montenegro, Serbia, Sweden, the former Yugoslav Republic of Macedonia and Zambia—and adopted concluding observations on them.

The Committee continued, in accordance with article 20, to study reliable information that appeared to contain well-founded indications that torture was systematically practised by a State party. In the framework of its follow-up activities, the Rapporteur on article 20 continued to encourage those States parties on which enquiries had been conducted to implement the Committee's related recommendations. Under article 22, the Committee considered communications submitted by individuals claiming that their rights under the Convention had been violated by a State party and who had exhausted all available domestic remedies.

Subcommittee on Prevention. The 10-member Subcommittee on Prevention of Torture and Other Cruel, Inhuman or Degrading Treatment or Punishment (Subcommittee on Prevention), established in 2006 [YUN 2006, p. 776] to carry out the functions laid down in the Optional Protocol adopted by resolution 57/199 [YUN 2002, p. 631], held its fourth (11–15 February) [A/63/44, annex VII], fifth (23–28 June) and sixth (17–21 November) sessions [CAT/C/42/2 & Corr.1] in Geneva. In 2008, the Subcommittee visited Benin [CAT/OP/BEN/1], Mexico [CAT/OP/MEX/1] and Sweden [CAT/OP/SWE/1 & Add.1], focusing on the development of national preventive mechanisms and the protection of people held in places of deprivation of liberty. The Subcommittee had various contacts with national preventive mechanisms and with organizations, including national human rights institutions and NGOs involved in the development of such mechanisms. It also maintained contact with the International Committee of the Red Cross, the Inter-American Commission on Human Rights, the European Committee for the Prevention of Torture and Inhuman or Degrading Treatment or Punishment, the Organization for Security and Cooperation in Europe, and international and national NGOs engaged in strengthening protection against torture.

The Subcommittee's first annual report [CAT/C/40/2], covering the period from February 2007 to March 2008, was submitted to the Committee against Torture at its fortieth session. The report noted that the full mandate envisaged in the Optional Protocol had not yet been realized owing to limited budgetary resources. It looked to the United Nations to provide the financial and human resources necessary for the fulfilment of its mandate.

(For the protection of the right not to be subjected to torture and other cruel, inhuman or degrading treatment or punishment, see the work of the Special Rapporteur on the question of torture on p. 808.)

Convention on elimination of discrimination against women and Optional Protocol

(For details on the status of the Convention and on the Optional Protocol, see p. 1277. For insight on the activities designed to protect the rights of women and girls worldwide, in accordance with the provisions of the Convention, see the work of the Special Rapporteur on Violence against Women, Its Causes and Consequences on p. 846.)

Convention on the Rights of the Child

Accessions and ratifications

As at 31 December, the number of States parties to the 1989 Convention on the Rights of the Child, adopted by the General Assembly in resolution 44/25 [YUN 1989, p. 560], stood at 193. States parties to the Optional Protocol to the Convention on the involvement of children in armed conflict, adopted in Assembly resolution 54/263 [YUN 2000, p. 615], rose to 126, with Albania, Burundi, China, Iraq, the Russian Federation, Singapore and Uzbekistan becoming parties in 2008. The Optional Protocol on the sale of children, child prostitution and child pornography, also adopted by resolution 54/263, had 130 States parties, with Albania, Greece, Iraq, Israel, Monaco and Uzbekistan becoming parties in 2008.

The Secretary-General reported on the status of the Convention and its Optional Protocols as at 1 July [A/63/160].

Implementation

Monitoring body. The Committee on the Rights of the Child (CRC) held its forty-seventh (14 January–1 February) [CRC/C/47/3], forty-eighth (19 May–6 June) [CRC/C/48/3] and forty-ninth (15 September–3 October) [CRC/C/49/3] sessions in Geneva. Each session was preceded by a working group meeting to review State party reports and identify the main questions to be discussed with representatives of the reporting States.

Under article 44 of the Convention, CRC considered initial or periodic reports submitted by Austria, Bhutan, Bulgaria, Chile, Djibouti, the Dominican Republic, Eritrea, Georgia, Germany, Ireland, Kuwait, Lithuania, the Philippines, Republic of Korea, Serbia, Sierra Leone, the Timor-Leste, Uganda, the United Kingdom, the United Republic of Tanzania and the United States, and adopted concluding observations on them.

On 19 September, the Committee held its annual day of general discussion on "The right to education in situations of emergency". It also discussed the drafts of its two forthcoming general comments, on the right of the child to express views and be heard, and on the rights of indigenous children.

The Committee submitted to the General Assembly its biennial report covering activities from its forty-second to forty-seventh sessions [A/63/41].

On 25 July, the Economic and Social Council took note of the Committee's report (**decision 2008/256**).

Human Rights Council action. On 28 March [A/63/53 (res. 7/29)], the Human Rights Council addressed implementation of the Convention and other instruments. The Council called on States parties to implement the Convention and its Optional Protocols fully by putting in place effective national legislation, policies and action plans, complying with their reporting obligations in a timely manner, and taking into account the Committee's recommendations. They should designate, establish or strengthen governmental structures for children and ensure adequate training in the rights of the child for professional groups working with and for children; and develop and assess social programmes so that economic and social resources were sufficiently developed for the full realization of the rights of the child.

The Council reaffirmed the findings in General Assembly resolution 62/141 [YUN 2007, p. 681] and the importance of promoting appropriate parental care and family preservation where possible. It encouraged States to adopt laws to protect children growing up without parents or caregivers; where alternative care was necessary, decision-making should be in the best interests of the child. It also encouraged the advancement of the draft UN guidelines for the appropriate use and conditions of alternative care for children, to which further attention should be given at the Council's future sessions.

On 24 September [A/63/53/Add.1 (res. 9/13)], the Council took note of the draft UN guidelines for the appropriate use and conditions of alternative care for children, requested the High Commissioner to circulate them, and invited States to work towards taking action on the guidelines at the Council's tenth (2009) session. The initial draft guidelines for the protection of children without parental care were reviewed at an intergovernmental meeting of experts in Brasilia, Brazil, in August 2006.

(For information on the Organization's efforts to protect the rights of the child everywhere in the world, in accordance with the provisions outlined in the Convention, see the work of the Special Rapporteur on the Sale of Children, Child Prostitution and Child Pornography on p. 849. See also the activities of the Special Representative of the Secretary-General for Children and Armed Conflict on p. 851.)

GENERAL ASSEMBLY ACTION

On 24 December [meeting 74], the General Assembly, on the recommendation of the Third Committee [A/63/430/Add.2], adopted **resolution 63/244** without vote [agenda item 64 *(b)*].

Committee on the Rights of the Child

The General Assembly,

Reaffirming the Convention on the Rights of the Child and the Optional Protocols thereto,

Noting the report of the Secretary-General on the status of the Convention and the report of the Committee on the Rights of the Child,

1. *Notes,* while welcoming the entry into force of the Optional Protocols to the Convention on the Rights of the Child, that a backlog of more than eighty reports exists related to the submission by States parties of their initial reports under the Optional Protocols in conformity with their obligations, and notes with concern that if this backlog is not addressed, it will impede the ability of the Committee on the Rights of the Child to consider reports in a timely manner, and in this regard takes note of the request of the Committee to meet in parallel chambers to address this backlog in an effective and timely manner;

2. *Decides,* as an exceptional and temporary measure, to authorize the Committee to meet in parallel chambers, of nine members each, for ten working days of each of its three regular sessions and the five working days of each of its three presessional working group meetings between October 2009 and October 2010, for the purposes of considering the reports of the States parties submitted under article 44 of the Convention, article 8 of the Optional Protocol thereto on the involvement of children in armed conflict and article 12 of the Optional Protocol thereto on the sale

of children, child prostitution and child pornography, taking due account of equitable geographical distribution and the principal legal systems;

3. *Also decides* to assess the situation regarding the meeting time of the Committee at its sixty-fifth session on the basis of an evaluation made by the Office of the United Nations High Commissioner for Human Rights, taking into account a more comprehensive approach towards the backlog of human rights treaty bodies and the increasing number of reports of States parties to the human rights conventions;

4. *Requests* the Committee to intensify its review of its working methods in order to enhance the efficiency and quality of its proceedings, with the aim of achieving timely consideration of reports submitted by States parties, and also requests the Committee to review and assess its progress in order to provide an update on this question in its report to the General Assembly at its sixty-fourth session and inputs to the evaluation to be made by the Office of the High Commissioner, taking into account the wider context of treaty body reform.

Also on 24 December [meeting 74], the General Assembly, on the recommendation of the Third Committee [A/63/426], adopted **resolution 63/241** by recorded vote (159-1-0) [agenda item 60 *(a)*].

Rights of the child

The General Assembly,

Recalling its previous resolutions on the rights of the child, the most recent of which is resolution 62/141 of 18 December 2007, and its resolution 62/140 of 18 December 2007, as well as Human Rights Council resolution 7/29 of 28 March 2008,

Emphasizing that the Convention on the Rights of the Child must constitute the standard in the promotion and protection of the rights of the child, and bearing in mind the importance of the Optional Protocols to the Convention, as well as other human rights instruments,

Reaffirming the Vienna Declaration and Programme of Action, the United Nations Millennium Declaration and the outcome document of the twenty-seventh special session of the General Assembly on children, entitled "A world fit for children", and recalling the Copenhagen Declaration on Social Development and the Programme of Action, the Dakar Framework for Action adopted at the World Education Forum, the Declaration on Social Progress and Development, the Universal Declaration on the Eradication of Hunger and Malnutrition, the Declaration on the Right to Development and the Declaration of the commemorative high-level plenary meeting devoted to the follow-up to the outcome of the special session on children, held in New York from 11 to 13 December 2007,

Recognizing the link between an improved situation for children and achieving the internationally agreed development goals, including the Millennium Development Goals, in particular those related to education, poverty eradication, gender equality, reduction of child mortality and global partnership for development, and welcoming in this context the outcomes of the high-level event on the Millennium Development Goals, held in New York on 25 September 2008,

Recognizing also the importance of the integration of child rights issues into the follow-up of the outcome documents of all major United Nations conferences, special sessions and summits,

Taking note with appreciation of the reports of the Secretary-General on progress made towards achieving the commitments set out in the outcome document of the twenty-seventh special session of the General Assembly and on the status of the Convention on the Rights of the Child and the issues raised in Assembly resolution 62/141, as well as the report of the Committee on the Rights of the Child,

Recognizing the importance of incorporating a child-protection perspective across the human rights agenda, as highlighted in the 2005 World Summit Outcome,

Welcoming the entry into force of the Convention on the Rights of Persons with Disabilities, and the attention paid to children in this international instrument,

Noting with appreciation the attention paid to children in the International Convention for the Protection of All Persons from Enforced Disappearance, and stressing the importance of its entry into force,

Noting with appreciation also the attention paid to children in the United Nations Declaration on the Rights of Indigenous Peoples,

Profoundly concerned that the situation of children in many parts of the world remains critical, in an increasingly globalized environment, as a result of the persistence of poverty, social inequality, inadequate social and economic conditions, pandemics, in particular HIV/AIDS, malaria and tuberculosis, environmental damage, natural disasters, armed conflict, foreign occupation, displacement, violence, terrorism, abuse, trafficking in children and their organs, all forms of exploitation, commercial sexual exploitation of children, child prostitution, child pornography and child sex tourism, neglect, illiteracy, hunger, intolerance, discrimination, racism, xenophobia, gender inequality, disability and inadequate legal protection, and convinced that urgent and effective national and international action is called for,

Reiterating that eradicating poverty is the greatest global challenge facing the world today and an indispensable requirement for sustainable development, in particular for developing countries, and recognizing that chronic poverty remains the single biggest obstacle to meeting the needs of and promoting and protecting the rights of children, and that urgent national and international action is therefore required to eliminate it,

Reaffirming that democracy, development, peace and security, and the full and effective enjoyment of all human rights and fundamental freedoms are interdependent and mutually reinforcing and contribute to the eradication of extreme poverty,

Reaffirming also the need for mainstreaming a gender perspective in all policies and programmes relating to children, and recognizing the child as a rights holder in all policies and programmes relating to children,

Bearing in mind that 2009 marks the twentieth anniversary of the adoption of the Convention on the Rights of the Child and the fiftieth anniversary of the adoption of the Declaration of the Rights of the Child, which provided a foundation for the Convention, and considering that these anniversaries are suitable occasions for strengthening the efforts of Member States to promote the rights of the child,

I

Implementation of the Convention on the Rights of the Child and the Optional Protocols thereto

1. *Reaffirms* that the general principles of, inter alia, the best interests of the child, non-discrimination, participation and survival and development provide the framework for all actions concerning children, including adolescents;

2. *Urges* States that have not yet done so to become parties to the Convention on the Rights of the Child and the Optional Protocols thereto as a matter of priority and to implement them fully by, inter alia, putting in place effective national legislation, policies and action plans, strengthening relevant governmental structures for children and ensuring adequate and systematic training in the rights of the child for all those working with and for children, as well as ensuring child rights education for children themselves;

3. *Urges* States parties to withdraw reservations that are incompatible with the object and purpose of the Convention or the Optional Protocols thereto and to consider reviewing regularly other reservations with a view to withdrawing them in accordance with the Vienna Declaration and Programme of Action;

4. *Calls upon* States to designate, establish or strengthen governmental structures for children, including, where appropriate, ministers in charge of child and youth issues and independent ombudspersons for children or other institutions for the promotion and protection of the rights of the child;

5. *Welcomes* the work of the Committee on the Rights of the Child, and calls upon all States to strengthen their cooperation with the Committee, to comply in a timely manner with their reporting obligations under the Convention and the Optional Protocols thereto, in accordance with the guidelines elaborated by the Committee, and to take into account its recommendations on the implementation of the Convention;

6. *Takes note with appreciation* of the initiatives undertaken by the Committee aimed at promoting a better understanding of and fuller compliance with the rights enshrined in the Convention, namely, through the organization of days of general discussion and the adoption of general comments;

7. *Requests* all relevant organs and mechanisms of the United Nations system regularly and systematically to incorporate a strong child rights perspective throughout all activities in the fulfilment of their mandates, as well as to ensure that their staff are trained in child rights matters, and calls upon States to continue to cooperate closely with all those organs and mechanisms, in particular the special rapporteurs and special representatives of the United Nations system;

8. *Encourages* States to strengthen their national statistical capacities and to use statistics disaggregated, inter alia, by age, gender and other relevant factors that may lead to disparities and other statistical indicators at the national, subregional, regional and international levels to develop and assess social policies and programmes so that economic and social resources are used efficiently and effectively for the full realization of the rights of the child;

II

Promotion and protection of the rights of the child and non-discrimination against children

Non-discrimination

9. *Calls upon* all States:

(a) To ensure the enjoyment by children of all their civil, cultural, economic, political and social rights without discrimination of any kind;

(b) To provide special support and ensure equal access to services for all children, noting with concern the large number of children who are among the victims of racism, racial discrimination, xenophobia and related intolerance, and stressing the need to incorporate special measures, in accordance with the principles of the best interests of the child and respect for his or her views and the child's gender-specific needs, in education programmes and programmes to combat such practices;

(c) To take all necessary and effective measures, including legal reforms where appropriate, to eliminate all forms of discrimination against girls and all forms of violence, including female infanticide and prenatal sex selection, rape, sexual abuse and harmful traditional or customary practices, including female genital mutilation, early marriage, marriage without the free and full consent of the intending spouses and forced sterilization, by enacting and enforcing legislation and, where appropriate, by formulating comprehensive, multidisciplinary and coordinated national plans, programmes or strategies to protect girls;

(d) To ensure the full and equal enjoyment of all human rights and fundamental freedoms by children with disabilities, in both the public and the private spheres, including by ensuring that the principle of the best interests of the child and the rights of children with disabilities are integrated into policies and programmes for children, including their rights to education, to the highest attainable standard of physical and mental health and to protection from violence, abuse and neglect, and to develop and, where it already exists, enforce legislation to prohibit discrimination against them in order to ensure their inherent dignity, to promote their self-reliance and to facilitate their full and active participation and inclusion in their communities, taking into account the particular situation of children with disabilities who may be subject to multiple or aggravated forms of discrimination, including girls with disabilities and children with disabilities living in poverty;

10. *Urges* all States to respect and promote the right of girls and boys to express themselves freely, to ensure that their views are given due weight, in accordance with their age and maturity, in all matters affecting them and to involve children, including children with special needs, in decision-making processes, taking into account the evolving capacities of children and the importance of involving children's organizations and child-led initiatives;

11. *Also urges* all States in particular to strengthen the participation of children and adolescents in planning and implementation relating to matters that affect them, such as health, environment, education, social and economic welfare and protection against violence, abuse and exploitation;

Registration, family relations and adoption or other forms of alternative care

12. *Once again urges* all States parties to intensify their efforts to comply with their obligations under the Convention on the Rights of the Child to preserve the child's identity, including nationality, name and family relations, as recognized by law, to allow for the registration of the child immediately after birth, to ensure that registration procedures are simple, expeditious and effective and provided at minimal or no cost and to raise awareness of the importance of birth registration at the national, regional and local levels;

13. *Encourages* States to adopt and enforce laws and improve the implementation of policies and programmes to protect children growing up without parents or caregivers, recognizing that, where alternative care is necessary, family- and community-based care should be promoted over placement in institutions, and in this context invites States to dedicate all their efforts, in a transparent process, with a view to possible action on the draft United Nations guidelines for the appropriate use and conditions of alternative care for children at the tenth session of the Human Rights Council;

14. *Calls upon* States to guarantee, to the extent consistent with the obligations of each State, the right of a child whose parents reside in different States to maintain, on a regular basis, save in exceptional circumstances, personal relations and direct contact with both parents by providing enforceable means of access and visitation in both States and by respecting the principle that both parents have common responsibilities for the upbringing and development of their children;

15. *Also calls upon* States to address and pay particular attention to cases of international parental or familial child abduction, and encourages States to engage in multilateral and bilateral cooperation to resolve those cases, preferably by accession to or ratification of the Hague Convention on the Civil Aspects of International Child Abduction, and to comply fully with the Convention, and to facilitate, inter alia, the return of the child to the country in which he or she resided immediately before the removal or retention;

16. *Further calls upon* States to take all necessary measures to prevent and combat illegal adoptions and all adoptions that are not in the best interests of the child;

Economic and social well-being of children

17. *Calls upon* States and the international community to create an environment in which the well-being of the child is ensured, including by strengthening international cooperation in this field;

Eradication of poverty

18. *Calls upon* States to cooperate, support and participate in the global efforts for poverty eradication at the global, regional and country levels, recognizing that strengthened availability and effective allocation of resources are required at all these levels, in order to ensure that all the internationally agreed development and poverty eradication goals, including those set out in the United Nations Millennium Declaration, are realized within their time framework, and reaffirms that investments in children and the realization of their rights are among the most effective ways to eradicate poverty;

19. *Reaffirms* that the primary responsibility for ensuring an enabling environment for securing the well-being of children, in which the rights of each and every child are promoted and respected, rests with each individual State;

20. *Calls upon* all States and the international community to mobilize all necessary resources, support and efforts to eradicate poverty, according to national plans and strategies and in consultation with national Governments, including through an integrated and multifaceted approach based on the rights and well-being of children, and to continue their efforts to realize the internationally agreed development and poverty eradication goals, including the Millennium Development Goals;

Right to education

21. *Recognizes* the right to education on the basis of equal opportunity and non-discrimination by making primary education compulsory and available free to all children, ensuring that all children have access to education of good quality, as well as making secondary education generally available and accessible to all, in particular through the progressive introduction of free education, bearing in mind that special measures to ensure equal access, including affirmative action, contribute to achieving equal opportunity and combating exclusion, and ensuring school attendance, in particular for girls and children from low-income families in order to achieve the objectives of Education for All, with the aim of realizing the millennium development goal aimed at achieving universal primary education;

22. *Welcomes* the work of the Special Rapporteur on the right to education, takes note of his report on the right to education in emergency situations, recognizes that the right to education is to be respected at all times, and calls upon Member States to adopt legal and other measures to ensure that education is included in emergency preparedness plans;

23. *Urges* Member States to implement strategies for the realization of the right to education as an integral element in the context of humanitarian assistance, with the support of the international community, the United Nations system, donors, multilateral agencies, the private sector, civil society and non-governmental organizations;

Right to the enjoyment of the highest attainable standard of health

24. *Calls upon* States:

(a) To take all necessary measures to ensure the right of the child to the enjoyment of the highest attainable standard of health and to develop sustainable health systems and social services, ensuring access to such systems and services without discrimination, paying special attention to adequate food and nutrition and combating disease and malnutrition, to access to safe drinking water and sanitation, to the special needs of male and female adolescents and to reproductive and sexual health, and securing appropriate prenatal and post-natal care for mothers, including measures to prevent mother-to-child transmission of HIV, and in this context to realize the millennium development goals aimed at reducing child mortality, improving maternal health and combating HIV/AIDS, malaria and other diseases;

(*b*) To assign priority to developing and implementing activities and programmes aimed at treating and preventing addictions, in particular addiction to alcohol and tobacco, and the abuse of narcotic drugs, psychotropic substances and inhalants;

(*c*) To support adolescents to be able to deal positively and responsibly with their sexuality in order to protect themselves from HIV/AIDS infection and to implement measures to increase their capacity to protect themselves from HIV/AIDS through, inter alia, the provision of health care, including for sexual and reproductive health, and through preventive education that promotes gender equality;

(*d*) To develop and implement strategies, policies and programmes that identify and address those factors that make individuals particularly vulnerable to HIV infection in order to complement prevention programmes that address activities that place individuals at risk for HIV infection, such as risky and unsafe behaviour and injecting drug use;

(*e*) To promote initiatives aimed at reducing the prices of antiretroviral drugs, especially second-line drugs, available to boys and girls, including bilateral and private sector initiatives, as well as initiatives on a voluntary basis taken by groups of States, including those based on innovative financing mechanisms that contribute to the mobilization of resources for social development, especially those that aim to provide further access to drugs at affordable prices to children in developing countries on a sustainable and predictable basis, and in this regard takes note of the International Drug Purchase Facility, UNITAID;

(*f*) To design and implement programmes to provide social services and support to pregnant adolescents and adolescent mothers, in particular by enabling them and also the adolescent fathers to continue and complete their education;

Right to food

25. *Expresses grave concern* at the worsening of the world food crisis, which seriously undermines the realization of the right to food for all, including mothers and children, and also expresses grave concern that this crisis threatens to further undermine the achievement of the Millennium Development Goals and stresses that solutions need a comprehensive and multifaceted approach requiring short-, medium- and long-term and sustained actions;

26. *Calls upon* all States to take immediate steps to eliminate child hunger, including through the adoption or strengthening of national programmes to address food security and adequate livelihoods, as well as nutritional security, especially regarding vitamin A, iron and iodine deficiencies, the promotion of breastfeeding, as well as programmes, for example, school meal programmes, that should ensure adequate nutrition for all children;

Elimination of violence against children

27. *Condemns* all forms of violence against children, and urges all States:

(*a*) To take effective and appropriate legislative and other measures or, where it exists, to strengthen legislation to prohibit and eliminate all forms of violence against children in all settings;

(*b*) To respect fully the rights, human dignity and physical integrity of children and to prohibit and eliminate any emotional or physical violence or any other humiliating or degrading treatment;

(*c*) To give priority attention to the prevention of all forms of violence against children and to addressing its underlying causes and its gender dimension through a systematic, comprehensive and multifaceted approach, recognizing that witnessing violence, including domestic violence, also causes harm to children;

(*d*) To protect children from all forms of violence or abuse by all those who work with and for children, including in educational settings, as well as by Government officials, such as the police, law enforcement authorities and employees and officials in detention centres or welfare institutions;

(*e*) To establish complaint mechanisms that are confidential, age-appropriate, gender-sensitive and accessible to all children and to undertake thorough and prompt investigations of all acts of violence and discrimination;

(*f*) To take measures to ensure that all those who work with and for children protect children from bullying and implement preventive and anti-bullying policies in order to ensure a safe and supportive environment free from harassment and violence;

(*g*) To strive to change attitudes that condone or normalize any form of violence against children, including cruel, inhuman or degrading forms of discipline, harmful traditional practices and all forms of sexual violence;

(*h*) To take measures to promote constructive and positive forms of discipline and child development approaches in all settings, including the home, schools and other educational settings, and throughout care and justice systems;

(*i*) To end impunity for perpetrators of crimes against children and to investigate and prosecute such acts of violence and impose appropriate penalties, recognizing that persons convicted of violent offences against children, including sexual abuse, who continue to pose a risk of harm to children should be prevented from working with children;

(*j*) To establish and develop safe, well-publicized, confidential and accessible mechanisms to enable children, their representatives and others to report violence against children as well as to file complaints in cases of violence against children, and to ensure that all victims of violence have access to appropriate confidential, child-sensitive health and social services, paying special attention to the gender-specific needs of girls and boys who are victims of violence;

(*k*) To address the gender dimension of all forms of violence against children and incorporate a gender perspective in all policies adopted and actions taken to protect children against all forms of violence, acknowledging that girls and boys face varying risks from different forms of violence at different ages and in different situations, and in this context recalls the agreed conclusions on the elimination of all forms of discrimination and violence against the girl child adopted by the Commission on the Status of Women at its fifty-first session;

28. *Expresses deep concern* about the impact of all forms of sexual violence in situations of armed conflict and about

the harm caused by witnessing sexual violence, reaffirms in this regard relevant resolutions of the General Assembly, the Economic and Social Council and the Human Rights Council, and notes with appreciation the attention paid to this issue in Security Council resolution 1820(2008) of 19 June 2008;

29. *Condemns* all kinds of abduction of children, in particular extortive abduction and abduction of children in situations of armed conflict, including for their recruitment and use in armed conflict, and urges States to take all appropriate measures to secure their unconditional release, rehabilitation and reintegration and their reunification with their families;

30. *Urges* all States to strengthen international cooperation and mutual assistance to prevent and protect children from all forms of violence and to end impunity for crimes against children;

31. *Recognizes* the contribution of the International Criminal Court in ending impunity for the most serious crimes against children, including genocide, crimes against humanity and war crimes, and calls upon States not to grant amnesties for such crimes;

32. *Encourages* all States and requests United Nations entities, regional organizations and civil society, including non-governmental organizations, to continue to widely disseminate and follow up on the study on violence against children by the independent expert appointed by the Secretary-General and to cooperate with the Special Representative of the Secretary-General on violence against children, once appointed, in promoting the implementation of the recommendations of the study, while promoting and ensuring country ownership and national plans and programmes in this regard;

33. *Expresses deep concern* about the delay in the appointment of the new mandate-holder as requested by the General Assembly in its resolution 62/141, and requests the Secretary-General to comply fully with the request and to take urgent action to appoint, in accordance with the above-mentioned resolution, at the highest possible level and without delay, a Special Representative on violence against children;

Promoting and protecting the rights of children, including children in particularly difficult situations

34. *Calls upon* all States to prevent violations of the rights of children working and/or living on the street, including discrimination, arbitrary detention and extrajudicial, arbitrary or summary executions, torture and all kinds of violence and exploitation, and to bring the perpetrators to justice, to adopt and implement policies for the protection, social and psychosocial rehabilitation and reintegration of those children and to adopt economic, social and educational strategies to address the problems of children working and/or living on the street;

35. *Also calls upon* all States to protect refugee, asylum-seeking and internally displaced children, taking into account their gender-specific needs, in particular those who are unaccompanied, who are particularly exposed to violence and risks in connection with armed conflict, such as recruitment, killing, maiming, sexual violence and exploitation, as well as trafficking, stressing the need for States as well as the international community to continue to pay more systematic and in-depth attention to the special assistance, protection and development needs of those children through, inter alia, programmes aimed at rehabilitation and physical and psychological recovery, and to programmes for voluntary repatriation and, where appropriate and feasible, local integration and resettlement, to give priority to family tracing and family reunification and, where appropriate, to cooperate with international humanitarian and refugee organizations, including by facilitating their work;

36. *Further calls upon* all States to ensure, for children belonging to minorities and vulnerable groups, including migrant children and indigenous children, the enjoyment of all human rights as well as access to health care, social services and education on an equal basis with others and to ensure that all such children, in particular victims of violence and exploitation, receive special protection and assistance;

37. *Calls upon* all States to ensure that any migration policies, including repatriation mechanisms, are in accordance with the best interests of the child and to take all necessary actions to ensure that unaccompanied migrant children and those who are victims of violence and exploitation receive special protection and assistance in accordance with international law;

38. *Also calls upon* all States to address, as a matter of priority, the vulnerabilities faced by children affected by and living with HIV, by providing support and rehabilitation to those children and their families, women and the elderly, particularly in their role as caregivers, promoting child-oriented HIV/AIDS policies and programmes and increased protection for children orphaned and affected by HIV/AIDS, pursuing all necessary efforts towards the goal of universal access to comprehensive prevention programmes, treatment, care and support by 2010 and intensifying efforts to develop new treatments for children, and building, where needed, and supporting the social security systems that protect them;

39. *Further calls upon* all States to protect, in law and in practice, the inheritance and property rights of orphans, with particular attention to underlying gender-based discrimination, which may interfere with the fulfilment of these rights;

40. *Encourages* States to promote actions, including through bilateral and multilateral technical cooperation and financial assistance, for the social reintegration of children in difficult situations, considering, inter alia, views, skills and capacities that those children have developed in the conditions in which they lived and, where appropriate, with their meaningful participation;

41. *Calls upon* States to protect all human rights of children in particularly difficult situations and to ensure that the best interests of the child are accorded primary consideration, and encourages the Committee on the Rights of the Child, the United Nations Children's Fund, other relevant United Nations bodies and mandate-holders, within their respective mandates, to pay particular attention to the conditions of these children in all States and, as appropriate, to make recommendations to strengthen their protection;

42. *Recognizes* that the mass media and their organizations have a key role to play in raising awareness about the

situation of children and the challenges facing them and that they should also play a more active role in informing children, parents, families and the general public about initiatives that promote and protect the rights of children and should also contribute to educational programmes for children;

Children alleged to have infringed or recognized as having infringed penal law

43. *Calls upon* all States:

(*a*) To abolish by law and in practice the death penalty and life imprisonment without possibility of release for those under the age of 18 years at the time of the commission of the offence, including by taking all necessary measures to comply with their obligations assumed under relevant provisions of international human rights instruments, including the Convention on the Rights of the Child and the International Covenant on Civil and Political Rights; and

(*b*) To keep in mind the safeguards guaranteeing protection of the rights of those facing the death penalty and the guarantees set out in United Nations safeguards adopted by the Economic and Social Council;

44. *Encourages* all States to develop and implement a comprehensive juvenile justice policy that includes, where appropriate, the introduction of alternative measures allowing for responses to juvenile delinquency without resorting to judicial procedures;

45. *Urges* States to take special measures to protect juvenile offenders, including the provision of adequate legal assistance, the training in juvenile justice of judges, police officers and prosecutors, as well as specialized defenders or other representatives who provide legal or other appropriate assistance, such as social workers, the establishment of specialized courts, the promotion of universal birth registration and age documentation and the protection of the right of juvenile offenders to maintain contact with their families through correspondence and visits, save in exceptional circumstances;

46. *Calls upon* all States to ensure that no child in detention is sentenced to forced labour or any form of cruel or degrading punishment or is deprived of access to and provision of health-care services, hygiene and environmental sanitation, education, basic instruction and vocational training;

Children of persons alleged to have infringed or recognized as having infringed penal law

47. *Also calls upon* all States to give attention to the impact of parental detention and imprisonment on children and, in particular:

(*a*) To give priority consideration to non-custodial measures when sentencing or deciding on pre-trial measures for a child's sole or primary caretaker, subject to the need to protect the public and the child, and bearing in mind the gravity of the offence;

(*b*) To identify and promote good practices in relation to the needs and physical, emotional, social and psychological development of babies and children affected by parental detention and imprisonment;

Prevention and eradication of the sale of children, child prostitution and child pornography

48. *Welcomes* the extension of the mandate of the Special Rapporteur on the sale of children, child prostitution and child pornography by the Human Rights Council;

49. *Also welcomes* the convening of the World Congresses against Sexual Exploitation of Children and Adolescents, including the Third World Congress, held from 25 to 28 November 2008 in Rio de Janeiro, Brazil, aimed at stimulating debate and mobilizing the efforts of the international community to eradicate the sexual exploitation of children and adolescents;

50. *Expresses deep concern* about the persistence of the practices of the sale of children, child slavery, commercial sexual exploitation of children, child prostitution and child pornography in many parts of the world, and calls upon all States:

(*a*) To criminalize and penalize effectively all forms of sexual exploitation and sexual abuse of children, including all acts of paedophilia, including within the family or for commercial purposes, child pornography and child prostitution, child sex tourism, trafficking in children, the sale of children and the use of the Internet and other information and communications technologies for these purposes, and to take effective measures against the criminalization of children who are victims of exploitation;

(*b*) To ensure the prosecution and punishment of offenders, whether local or foreign, by the competent national authorities, either in the country in which the crime was committed, in the country of which the offender is a national or resident, in the country of which the victim is a national, or on any other basis permitted under domestic law, and for these purposes to afford one another the greatest measure of assistance and the necessary collaboration for prevention, detection, investigations or criminal or extradition proceedings;

(*c*) To criminalize and penalize effectively the sale of children, including for the purposes of transfer of organs of the child for profit, to increase cooperation at all levels to prevent and dismantle networks trafficking in or selling children and their organs and, for those States that have not yet done so, to consider signing and ratifying or acceding to the Protocol to Prevent, Suppress and Punish Trafficking in Persons, Especially Women and Children, supplementing the United Nations Convention against Transnational Organized Crime;

(*d*) To give due consideration to the recommendations made by the Special Rapporteur on the human rights aspects of the victims of trafficking in persons, especially women and children, in her report, devoted to the subject of forced marriage in the context of trafficking in persons;

(*e*) In cases of trafficking in children, the sale of children, child prostitution, child pornography and child sex tourism, to address effectively the needs of victims, including their safety, legal assistance and protection, physical and psychological recovery and full reintegration into society, paying particular attention to their gender-specific needs, including through bilateral and multilateral technical cooperation and financial assistance;

(*f*) To combat the existence of a market that encourages such criminal practices against children, including through the adoption, effective application and enforcement of preventive, rehabilitative and punitive measures targeting customers or individuals who sexually exploit or sexually abuse children, as well as by ensuring public awareness;

(*g*) To give priority to the identification of norms and standards on the responsibilities of transnational corporations and other business enterprises, particularly those involved in information and communications technologies, related to respect for the rights of children, including the right to be protected from sexual abuse and exploitation, particularly in the virtual realm, as set out in the relevant legal instruments, and to outline basic measures to be taken for implementation;

(*h*) To mobilize public awareness, involving families and communities, with the participation of children, concerning the protection of children against all forms of sexual exploitation and abuse;

(*i*) To contribute to the prevention and elimination of the sale of children, child prostitution and child pornography by adopting a holistic approach, addressing the contributing factors, including underdevelopment, poverty, economic disparities, inequitable socio-economic structures, dysfunctional families, lack of education, urban-rural migration, gender discrimination, criminal or irresponsible adult sexual behaviour, child sex tourism, organized crime, harmful traditional practices, armed conflicts and trafficking in children;

(*j*) To take measures to eliminate the demand that fosters all forms of exploitation that leads to trafficking, including sexual exploitation and the sex tourism demand;

Children affected by armed conflict

51. *Strongly condemns* any recruitment or use of children in armed conflict contrary to international law, as well as other violations and abuses committed against children affected by armed conflict, and urges all States and other parties to armed conflict that are engaged in such practices to end them;

52. *Recalls*, in accordance with international humanitarian law, that indiscriminate attacks against civilians, including children, are prohibited and that they shall not be the object of attack, including by way of reprisal or excessive use of force, condemns such practices resulting in the killing and maiming of children, and demands that an end be immediately put to them;

53. *Urges* States, United Nations agencies, funds and programmes, other relevant international and regional organizations and civil society to give serious attention to all violations and abuses committed against children in situations of armed conflict;

54. *Calls upon* all States, relevant United Nations bodies and agencies and regional organizations to mainstream the rights of the child into all activities in conflict and post-conflict situations, to ensure adequate child protection training of their staff and personnel, including through the drafting and dissemination of codes of conduct, and to facilitate the participation of children in the development of strategies in this regard, inter alia, by ensuring that there are opportunities for children's voices to be heard and given due weight in accordance with the age and maturity of the child;

55. *Calls upon* States:

(*a*) To enhance complementarity and coordination of national policies and strategies related to security, development, human rights and humanitarian issues with a view to addressing the short-, medium- and long-term impacts of armed conflict on children in an effective, sustainable and comprehensive manner;

(*b*) When ratifying the Optional Protocol to the Convention on the Rights of the Child on the involvement of children in armed conflict, to raise the minimum age for voluntary recruitment of persons into the national armed forces from that set out in article 38, paragraph 3, of the Convention, bearing in mind that under the Convention persons under 18 years of age are entitled to special protection, and to adopt safeguards to ensure that such recruitment is not forced or coerced;

(*c*) To take all feasible measures to ensure the demobilization and effective disarmament of children used in armed conflicts and to implement effective measures for their rehabilitation, physical and psychological recovery and reintegration into society, in particular through educational measures, taking into account the rights and the specific needs and capacities of girls;

(*d*) To ensure timely and adequate funding for national disarmament, demobilization and reintegration programmes for children and for settlement, rehabilitation and reintegration efforts for all children associated with armed forces and groups, including detained children, particularly in support of national initiatives, to secure the long-term sustainability of such efforts, including through the use of a multisectoral and community-based approach that is inclusive of all children, family-based care arrangements, as also highlighted in the Principles and Guidelines on Children Associated with Armed Forces or Armed Groups (the Paris Principles), and the mobilization of financial resources and technical assistance from international cooperation for rehabilitation and reintegration programmes for children, including by making use of all international forums and conferences related to this matter, including the meetings in follow-up to the "Free Children from War" conference, held in Paris on 5 and 6 February 2007;

(*e*) To undertake measures to ensure that children in situations of armed conflict enjoy all the rights enshrined in relevant international instruments, and that national authorities, with the support of the international community, as appropriate, take steps to ensure the delivery of basic services necessary for the survival of children in different areas, including health, education, nutrition, water, sanitation and psychosocial recovery;

(*f*) To encourage the involvement of young people in activities concerning the protection of children affected by armed conflict, including programmes for reconciliation, peace consolidation, peacebuilding and children-to-children networks;

(*g*) To protect children affected by armed conflict, in particular from violations of international humanitarian law and human rights law, and to ensure that they receive timely, effective humanitarian assistance, in accordance with international humanitarian law, including the Geneva Conventions of 12 August 1949, and calls upon the international community to hold those responsible for violations accountable, inter alia, through the International Criminal Court;

(*h*) To take all feasible measures, in accordance with international humanitarian law and human rights law, as a matter of priority, to prevent the recruitment and use of children by armed groups, as distinct from the armed forces of a State, including the adoption of policies that do not tolerate such practices and legal measures necessary to prohibit and criminalize them;

(*i*) To support relevant existing internationally agreed mechanisms established to address the issue of children in armed conflict that contribute to the roles, responsibilities and capacities of national Governments in this field;

56. *Takes note* of the updating of the Cape Town Principles on child soldiers, which led to the Paris Principles, encourages Member States to consider using the Paris Principles to inform their work in protecting children from the effects of armed conflicts, and requests the relevant entities of the United Nations system, within their mandates, and invites civil society to assist Member States in this field;

57. *Calls upon* all States and relevant United Nations bodies to continue to support, as appropriate, national and international mine action efforts, including with regard to cluster munitions and other unexploded ordnance;

58. *Condemns in the strongest terms* rape and sexual violence committed against children in armed conflict, expresses deep concern at mass and systematic rape and sexual violence committed against children in armed conflict, in some instances calculated to humiliate, dominate, instil fear and disperse and/or forcibly relocate a population, calls upon all States and relevant United Nations bodies and agencies and regional organizations to address this issue, as well as the issue of sexual exploitation and abuse of children in United Nations peacekeeping operations, and urges States to adopt appropriate national legislation and to ensure rigorous investigation and prosecution of such crimes;

59. *Reaffirms* the essential roles of the General Assembly, the Economic and Social Council and the Human Rights Council for the promotion and protection of the rights and welfare of children, including children affected by armed conflict, and notes the increasing role played by the Security Council in ensuring protection for children affected by armed conflict;

60. *Notes with appreciation* the steps taken regarding Security Council resolution 1612(2005) of 26 July 2005 and the efforts of the Secretary-General to implement the monitoring and reporting mechanism on children and armed conflict in accordance with that resolution, with the participation of and in cooperation with national Governments and relevant United Nations and civil society actors, including at the country level, as well as the work carried out by United Nations child protection advisers in peacekeeping operations;

61. *Takes note with appreciation* of the work of the Special Representative of the Secretary-General for Children and Armed Conflict, recognizes the increased level of activity of her office and the progress achieved since the establishment of the mandate of the Special Representative, and, bearing in mind its resolution 60/231 of 23 December 2005, recommends that the Secretary-General extend the mandate of the Special Representative for a further period of three years;

62. *Also takes note with appreciation* of the report of the Special Representative and of the significant developments and achievements in the protection of children in armed conflict at the national and international levels, and emphasizes the contribution of her field visits conducted with the consent of the State concerned in situations of armed conflict as an important element in the implementation of her mandate;

63. *Recognizes* the need for discussion on the issues raised in the report of the Special Representative, calls upon Member States and observers and invites relevant entities of the United Nations system as well as civil society, as appropriate, to carefully study the recommendations contained therein, and stresses the need for the views of Member States to be fully taken into account in this regard;

III

Child labour

64. *Expresses deep concern* about the fact that about 218 million children in the world today are involved in child labour, and that more than half of those children are involved in hazardous work that is damaging to their safety, mental and physical health or moral development, including in hazardous activities in agriculture, mining and domestic labour, or in the worst forms of child labour, such as child pornography and sexual exploitation, sale and trafficking in children, forced or compulsory labour, including forced or compulsory recruitment of children for use in armed conflict, and different forms of slavery or practices similar to slavery;

65. *Recognizes* that a comprehensive and coherent approach to preventing and eradicating child labour must aim at poverty eradication, sustainable development and the provision of quality education and social protection measures, including protection against economic exploitation; special attention should be given to preventing any work that is likely to be hazardous, to interfere with the child's education or to be harmful to the child's health or physical, mental, spiritual, moral or social development so as to respond to the multidimensional reality of child labour;

66. *Also recognizes* that the prevention and eradication of child labour and action towards the achievement of the Millennium Development Goals, in particular those related to education, poverty eradication, gender equality and global partnership for development, mutually reinforce each other;

67. *Further recognizes* that, given the role of the family environment in the full and harmonious development of the child and in preventing and eradicating child labour, children and their families should be entitled to receive comprehensive protection and support;

68. *Recognizes* that child labour contributes to the perpetuation of poverty and remains a central obstacle to realizing the right of all children to education and to protection from violence, abuse and exploitation and that education, at the same time, including literacy and adult education initiatives within the framework of international and regional cooperation, is a key element in preventing and eradicating poverty and child labour;

69. *Takes note with appreciation* of the establishment of the Global Task Force on Child Labour and Education for All by a number of relevant organizations of the United Nations system and civil society representatives and of the effort to integrate more closely work on tackling child labour and promoting education for all children;

70. *Urges* all States that have not yet ratified the Convention concerning Minimum Age for Admission to Employment, 1973 (Convention No. 138) and the Convention concerning the Prohibition and Immediate Action for the Elimination of the Worst Forms of Child Labour, 1999 (Convention No. 182) of the International Labour Organization to consider doing so as a matter of priority;

71. *Recognizes* the decisive role of employers' and workers' organizations in the prevention and eradication of child labour and that their continuous commitment and engagement remain essential;

72. *Also recognizes* the prevalence of violence against children in many work settings, including physical punishment, humiliation and sexual harassment, including in the context of unregulated domestic work, and encourages the International Labour Organization to pay particular attention to violence against children in work settings, including the issue of domestic work;

73. *Calls upon* all States to translate into concrete action their commitment to the progressive and effective elimination of child labour that is likely to be hazardous or to interfere with the child's education or to be harmful to the child's health or physical, mental, spiritual, moral or social development, to eliminate immediately the worst forms of child labour, to promote education as a key strategy in this regard, including the creation of vocational training and apprenticeship programmes and the integration of working children into the formal education system, and to examine and devise economic policies, where necessary, in cooperation with the international community, that address factors contributing to these forms of child labour;

74. *Also calls upon* all States:

(*a*) To elaborate and implement strategies for the prevention and elimination of child labour contrary to accepted international standards, including time-bound strategies for the immediate elimination of the worst forms of child labour, and for the protection of children from all forms of economic exploitation, giving special attention to specific dangers faced by girls and by boys;

(*b*) To increase the focus on access to quality education as a way to help attract and keep children in school, including by emphasizing the goal of a well-trained teaching force with appropriate salaries and working and living conditions and ongoing professional support for children in educational settings, as well as increasing access to information and communications technologies for schools, and calls upon the international community to provide cooperation in these fields;

(*c*) To assess and systematically examine the magnitude, nature and causes of child labour and to strengthen the collection and analysis of data on child labour, giving special attention to specific dangers faced by girls;

(*d*) To take concrete measures for the rehabilitation and social integration of children removed from situations involving the worst forms of child labour by, inter alia, ensuring access to education and social services;

(*e*) To take appropriate steps to assist one another in the elimination of the worst forms of child labour through enhanced international cooperation and/or assistance, including support for social and economic development, poverty eradication programmes and universal education;

(*f*) To promote policies and legislation aimed at addressing national priorities relating to the prevention and eradication of child labour through family-centred components of policies and programmes as part of an integrated comprehensive approach to development, bearing in mind equality between women and men;

(*g*) To ensure that the applicable requirements of the International Labour Organization for the employment of girls and boys are respected and effectively enforced, to ensure also that girls who are employed have equal access to decent work and equal pay and remuneration, and are protected from economic exploitation, discrimination, sexual harassment, violence and abuse in the workplace, are aware of their rights and have access to formal and non-formal education, skills development and vocational training, and to raise government and public awareness as to the nature and scope of the special needs of girls, including migrant girls, employed as domestic workers and of those performing excessive domestic chores in their own households;

(*h*) To put in place programmes and social protection systems, guided by the principle of the best interests of the child, to support and protect migrant children, especially the girl child, who are vulnerable to child labour, including the worst forms of child labour;

(*i*) To develop gender-sensitive measures, including national action plans, where appropriate, to eliminate child labour, including the worst forms of child labour, including commercial sexual exploitation, slavery-like practices, forced and bonded labour, trafficking and hazardous forms of child labour, and to ensure that children have access to education and vocational training, health services, food, shelter and recreation;

75. *Urges* all States to pursue a national policy designed to ensure the effective eradication of child labour, and encourages those States that have not yet done so to raise progressively the minimum age for admission to employment or work to a level consistent with the fullest physical and mental development of young persons;

76. *Calls upon* all States and the United Nations system to strengthen international cooperation as a means of assisting Governments in ensuring the realization of the rights of the child and in attaining the objective of eradicating child labour contrary to accepted international standards;

77. *Calls upon* all States to protect children from all forms of economic exploitation by mobilizing national partnerships and international cooperation, to improve the conditions of children by, inter alia, providing working children with free basic education and vocational training and integrating them into the education system in every way possible, and to encourage support for social and economic policies aimed at poverty eradication and at providing families, particularly women, with employment and income-generating opportunities;

78. *Calls upon* the international community to promote international cooperation to assist developing countries, upon request, in addressing child labour and its root

causes, inter alia, through social and economic policies aimed at poverty eradication, while stressing that labour standards should not be used for protectionist trade purposes;

79. *Calls upon* States and the international community to mainstream action relating to child labour into national poverty eradication and development efforts, especially in policies and programmes in the areas of health, education, employment and social protection;

80. *Welcomes* the efforts of the Committee on the Rights of the Child in the area of child labour, and encourages the Committee, as well as other relevant human rights treaty bodies, within their respective mandates, to continue to monitor this growing problem when examining the reports of States parties;

IV

Follow-up

81. *Decides:*

(a) To request the Secretary-General to submit to the General Assembly at its sixty-fourth session a report on the rights of the child containing information on the status of the Convention on the Rights of the Child and the issues addressed in the present resolution, with a focus on international efforts and national progress in tackling child labour and progress towards meeting the target of eliminating the worst forms of child labour by 2016, as agreed in the context of the International Labour Organization;

(b) To request the Special Representative of the Secretary-General for Children and Armed Conflict to continue to submit reports to the General Assembly and the Human Rights Council on the activities undertaken in discharging her mandate, including information on her field visits, and on the progress achieved and the challenges remaining on the children and armed conflict agenda;

(c) To invite the Chairperson of the Committee on the Rights of the Child to present an oral report on the work of the Committee to the General Assembly at its sixty-fourth session as a way to enhance communication between the Assembly and the Committee;

(d) To invite all Member States, organizations of the United Nations system, non-governmental organizations and individuals to observe the twentieth anniversary of the adoption of the Convention and to request the Secretary-General to take the measures necessary, within existing resources, for the observance of this anniversary by the United Nations;

(e) To continue its consideration of the question at its sixty-fourth session under the item entitled "Promotion and protection of the rights of children", focusing section III of the resolution on the rights of the child on "The right of the child to express his or her views freely in all matters affecting him or her".

RECORDED VOTE ON RESOLUTION 63/241:

In favour: Afghanistan, Albania, Algeria, Angola, Antigua and Barbuda, Argentina, Armenia, Australia, Austria, Azerbaijan, Bahrain, Bangladesh, Barbados, Belarus, Belgium, Benin, Bolivia, Bosnia and Herzegovina, Botswana, Brazil, Brunei Darussalam, Bulgaria, Burkina Faso, Burundi, Cambodia, Cameroon, Canada, Chile, China, Colombia, Congo, Costa Rica, Côte d'Ivoire, Croatia, Cuba, Cyprus, Czech Republic, Democratic People's Republic of Korea, Denmark, Djibouti, Dominican Republic, Ecuador, Egypt, Eritrea, Estonia, Ethiopia, Finland, France, Gabon, Gambia, Georgia, Germany, Ghana, Greece, Grenada, Guatemala, Guinea-Bissau, Honduras, Hungary, Iceland, India, Indonesia, Iran, Iraq, Ireland, Israel, Italy, Jamaica, Japan, Jordan, Kazakhstan, Kenya, Kuwait, Kyrgyzstan, Lao People's Democratic Republic, Latvia, Lebanon, Lesotho, Libyan Arab Jamahiriya, Liechtenstein, Lithuania, Luxembourg, Madagascar, Malawi, Malaysia, Maldives, Mali, Malta, Marshall Islands, Mauritania, Mauritius, Mexico, Micronesia, Moldova, Monaco, Mongolia, Montenegro, Morocco, Mozambique, Myanmar, Namibia, Nauru, Nepal, Netherlands, New Zealand, Nicaragua, Niger, Nigeria, Norway, Oman, Pakistan, Palau, Panama, Paraguay, Peru, Philippines, Poland, Portugal, Qatar, Republic of Korea, Romania, Russian Federation, Samoa, San Marino, Saudi Arabia, Senegal, Serbia, Singapore, Slovakia, Slovenia, Solomon Islands, South Africa, Spain, Sri Lanka, Sudan, Swaziland, Sweden, Switzerland, Syrian Arab Republic, Tajikistan, Thailand, The former Yugoslav Republic of Macedonia, Timor-Leste, Togo, Trinidad and Tobago, Tunisia, Turkey, Uganda, Ukraine, United Arab Emirates, United Kingdom, United Republic of Tanzania, Uruguay, Uzbekistan, Venezuela, Viet Nam, Yemen, Zambia, Zimbabwe.

Against: United States.

Abstaining: None.

Convention on migrant workers

Accessions and ratifications

As at 31 December, the number of parties to the International Convention on the Protection of the Rights of All Migrant Workers and Members of Their Families, adopted by the General Assembly in resolution 45/158 [YUN 1990, p. 594] and which entered into force in 2003 [YUN 2003, p. 676], rose to 40, with Jamaica, Paraguay and Rwanda becoming parties in 2008.

Implementation

Monitoring body. The Committee on the Protection of the Rights of All Migrant Workers and Members of Their Families held its eighth (14–25 April) [A/63/48] and ninth (24–28 November) [A/64/48] sessions in Geneva. Under article 74 of the Convention, the Committee considered the reports of Bolivia, El Salvador and Syria, and adopted concluding observations on them. The Committee noted with concern that many initial reports from States parties under article 73 of the Convention requiring them to report on the measures they had taken to give effect to the provisions of the Convention, had not yet been received. It decided to send reminders to those States whose reports were overdue. The Committee adopted its guidelines for the submission of periodic reports by States parties, which were annexed to its report. It also adopted a proposal on the topic of migration, development and human rights in preparation for the Global Forum on Migration and Development 2008 (see p. 1185).

(Regarding efforts to protect the rights of migrants beyond national borders, in accordance with the Convention, see p. 772.)

Convention on genocide

As at 31 December, 140 States were parties to the 1948 Convention on the Prevention and Punishment of the Crime of Genocide, adopted by the General Assembly in resolution 260 A (III) [YUN 1948–49, p. 959].

Report of Secretary-General. Pursuant to a Human Rights Council request [YUN 2007, p. 689], the Secretary-General submitted in March an updated report [A/HRC/7/37] on the implementation of the Five-Point Action Plan to prevent genocide [YUN 2006, p. 784] and on the activities of the Special Adviser on the Prevention of Genocide. In terms of the implementation of the Action Plan, some progress was made in developing a culture of prevention within the UN system, including improved coordination in the response of different UN entities. However, UN system capacity for effective and timely prevention needed further strengthening. The report also covered the responsibility to protect populations from genocide, war crimes, ethnic cleansing and crimes against humanity, as embodied in the 2005 World Summit Outcome [YUN 2005, p. 48]. In February, the Secretary-General appointed as Special Adviser Edward Luck (United States) to develop ideas contained in the Outcome that would assist the Assembly in its consideration of the responsibility to protect.

Within the context of his mandate, the activities of the Special Adviser on the Prevention of Genocide focused on the importance of adapting his work to the challenges of prevention on the ground, including the interrelated areas of protecting populations at risk, accountability, humanitarian assistance and addressing the underlying causes of conflict. In that regard, the Special Adviser was developing a strategy and methodology to identify and address gaps between those responsibilities and responses to conditions on the ground, and to utilize opportunities in the UN response to specific country situations. The Special Adviser's activities also related to individual countries. Activities with regard to post-electoral violence in Kenya included dispatching staff to the country and making recommendations to the Secretary-General following the missions to that country. He also engaged with governmental, intergovernmental and non-governmental actors to strengthen collaboration. Concerning challenges and opportunities for the prevention of genocide, the report noted the difficulty experienced by the United Nations in recognizing the risks of large-scale violence and in acting early enough to ensure timely and effective prevention. It was suggested that the Special Adviser could contribute to improving that situation by ensuring that risks of large-scale violence were promptly recognized and opportunities provided for UN agencies, departments and programmes to play a preventive role.

Human Rights Council action. On 28 March [A/63/53 (res. 7/25)], the Human Rights Council, considering the sixtieth anniversary of the Convention, reiterated the responsibility of each State to protect its population from genocide, and called on States that had not become parties to the Convention to do so as a matter of priority. States should cooperate in strengthening collaboration among mechanisms that contributed to the early detection and prevention of massive, serious and systematic violations of human rights that led to genocide. The Council welcomed the decisions of the Secretary-General and of the Assembly in resolution 62/238 [YUN 2007, p. 1451] to retain the mandate of the Special Adviser, to upgrade the position to the level of Under-Secretary-General and to strengthen the office. The Council requested the High Commissioner to circulate the Secretary-General's reports to obtain views, and to report to the Council at its tenth (2009) session. The High Commissioner should elaborate and implement commemorative events to mark the sixtieth anniversary of the Convention, including a seminar on the prevention of genocide. The Secretary-General should submit to the Council's tenth session an updated report on UN system efforts to prevent genocide and on the activities of the Special Adviser.

Convention on rights of persons with disabilities

Accessions and ratifications

As at 31 December, the number of States parties to the Convention on the Rights of Persons with Disabilities, adopted by the General Assembly in resolution 61/106 [YUN 2006, p. 785], stood at 46. During the year the Convention was ratified or acceded to by Argentina, Australia, Austria, Brazil, Chile, China, Costa Rica, Ecuador, Egypt, Guinea, Honduras, Jordan, Kenya, Lesotho, Mali, New Zealand, the Niger, Paraguay, Peru, the Philippines, Qatar, the Republic of Korea, Rwanda, San Marino, Saudi Arabia, Slovenia, Sweden, Thailand, Tunisia, Turkmenistan, Uganda and Vanuatu. The Optional Protocol, which established an individual complaints mechanism, was ratified during the year by Argentina, Austria, Bangladesh, Brazil, Chile, Costa Rica, Ecuador, Guinea, Mali, the Niger, Paraguay, Peru, Rwanda, San Marino, Saudi Arabia, Slovenia, Sweden, Tunisia and Uganda, bringing the number of States parties to 27 as at 31 December. The Convention and its Optional Protocol entered into force on 3 May.

In August, the Secretary-General reported on the status of the Convention and its Optional Protocol [A/63/264 & Corr.1].

Conference of States Parties. The Conference of States Parties to the Convention, at its first session (New York, 31 October and 3 November) [CRPD/CSP/2008/4], elected, in accordance with article 34 of the Convention, the 12 members of the Committee on the Rights of Persons with Disabilities—the body of independent experts that would monitor implementation of the Convention by States parties. Six experts were selected to serve a two-year term, beginning on 1 January 2009, while the other six experts would serve for four years, beginning on 1 January 2009. In accordance with article 40 of the Convention, an interactive panel discussion focused on "The Convention of the Rights of Persons with Disabilities as a human rights instrument and a tool for achieving the Millennium Development Goals".

UN Inter-Agency Support Group. The United Nations Inter-Agency Support Group for the Convention on the Rights of Persons with Disabilities, formed to coordinate UN system support to the Convention, issued a statement articulating UN system commitment to promote, protect and ensure the full and equal enjoyment of all human rights and fundamental freedoms by all persons with disabilities and to promote respect for their dignity as laid out in the Convention.

Human Rights Council action. On 27 March [A/63/53 (res. 7/9)], the Human Rights Council called upon Governments to prevent and prohibit all forms of discrimination against persons with disabilities, and to ensure their full and effective participation and inclusion, as well as respect for their autonomy, independence and equality of opportunity. It encouraged States to raise awareness about the rights of persons with disabilities and promote positive perceptions and greater social awareness. It requested OHCHR to prepare a study to enhance awareness and understanding of the Convention, to be made available on the OHCHR website in an accessible format prior to the Council's tenth (2009) session. It decided to hold an annual interactive debate on the rights of persons with disabilities; the first debate, to be held at its tenth session, would focus on key legal measures for ratification and effective implementation of the Convention.

(For information on the Organization's efforts to protect the rights of persons with disabilities, see p. 856.)

GENERAL ASSEMBLY ACTION

On 18 December [meeting 71], the General Assembly, on the recommendation of the Third Committee [A/63/430/Add.5], adopted **resolution 63/192** without vote [agenda item 64 *(e)*].

Convention on the Rights of Persons with Disabilities and the Optional Protocol thereto

The General Assembly,

Recalling its previous relevant resolutions, the most recent of which was resolution 62/170 of 18 December 2007, as well as relevant resolutions of the Human Rights Council, the Commission for Social Development and the Commission on Human Rights,

1. *Welcomes* the entry into force of the Convention on the Rights of Persons with Disabilities and the Optional Protocol thereto on 3 May 2008;

2. *Also welcomes* the fact that, since the opening for signature of the Convention and the Optional Protocol on 30 March 2007, one hundred and thirty-seven States have already signed and forty-five States have ratified the Convention and eighty States have signed and twenty-seven States have ratified the Optional Protocol, and that one regional integration organization has signed the Convention;

3. *Calls upon* those States that have not yet done so to consider signing and ratifying the Convention and the Optional Protocol as a matter of priority;

4. *Welcomes* the holding of the first session of the Conference of States Parties to the Convention on 31 October and 3 November 2008, and the establishment of the Committee on the Rights of Persons with Disabilities;

5. *Also welcomes* the report of the Secretary-General;

6. *Further welcomes* the Joint Statement of Commitment to the Convention of the Inter-Agency Support Group on the Convention;

7. *Invites* the Secretary-General to intensify efforts to assist States to become parties to the Convention and the Optional Protocol, including by providing assistance with a view to achieving universal adherence;

8. *Requests* the Secretary-General to provide the staff and facilities necessary to support the effective performance of the functions of the Conference of States Parties and of the Committee established under the Convention and the Optional Protocol, as well as for the dissemination of information on the Convention and the Optional Protocol, taking into account the provisions of the Convention, in particular on accessibility;

9. *Also requests* the Secretary-General to continue the progressive implementation of standards and guidelines for the accessibility of facilities and services of the United Nations system, taking into account relevant provisions of the Convention, in particular when undertaking renovations, including interim arrangements;

10. *Further requests* the Secretary-General to take further actions to promote the rights of persons with disabilities in the United Nations system in accordance with the Convention, including the retention and recruitment of persons with disabilities;

11. *Requests* United Nations agencies and organizations, and invites intergovernmental and non-governmental organizations, to continue to strengthen efforts undertaken to disseminate accessible information on the Convention and the Optional Protocol, including to children and young people to promote their understanding, and to assist States parties in implementing their obligations under those instruments;

12. *Requests* the Secretary-General to submit to the General Assembly at its sixty-fourth session a report on the status of the Convention and the Optional Protocol and the implementation of the present resolution.

International Convention for protection from enforced disappearance

Accessions and ratifications

As at 31 December, the International Convention for the Protection of All Persons from Enforced Disappearance, adopted by the General Assembly in resolution 61/177 [YUN 2006, p. 800], had seven States parties. In 2008, Bolivia, France, Honduras, Mexico and Senegal became parties to the Convention, which would enter into force when ratified or acceded to by 20 States.

Human Rights Council action. On 28 March [A/63/53 (res. 7/26)], the Human Rights Council encouraged States that were in the process of becoming parties to the Convention to complete their internal procedures towards that end as expeditiously as possible; and those States that had not done so to become parties. It invited States to join the campaign for the sharing of information on best practices and to work towards the early coming into force of the Convention.

(For insight on the operation of the Organization's mechanism to protect all persons from enforced disappearances, see the work of the Working Group on Enforced or Involuntary Disappearances on p. 807.)

GENERAL ASSEMBLY ACTION

On 18 December [meeting 70], the General Assembly, on the recommendation of the Third Committee [A/63/430/Add.2], adopted **resolution 63/186** without vote [agenda item 64 *(b)*].

International Convention for the Protection of All Persons from Enforced Disappearance

The General Assembly,

Reaffirming its resolution 61/177 of 20 December 2006, by which it adopted and opened for signature, ratification and accession the International Convention for the Protection of All Persons from Enforced Disappearance,

Recalling its resolution 47/133 of 18 December 1992, by which it adopted the Declaration on the Protection of All Persons from Enforced Disappearances as a body of principles for all States,

Recalling also Human Rights Council resolution 7/12 of 27 March 2008, by which the Council extended the mandate of the Working Group on Enforced or Involuntary Disappearances for a further period of three years,

Deeply concerned, in particular, by the increase in enforced or involuntary disappearances in various regions of the world, including arrest, detention and abduction, when these are part of or amount to enforced disappearances, and by the growing number of reports concerning harassment, ill-treatment and intimidation of witnesses of disappearances or relatives of persons who have disappeared,

Acknowledging that acts of enforced disappearance are recognized in the Convention as crimes against humanity, in certain circumstances,

Recognizing that the entry into force of the Convention, as soon as possible, through its ratification by twenty States, will be a significant event,

1. *Welcomes* the adoption on 20 December 2006 of the International Convention for the Protection of All Persons from Enforced Disappearance, and looks forward to its entry into force at an early date;

2. *Also welcomes* the fact that since the signing ceremony for the Convention, on 6 February 2007, eighty States have signed the Convention and seven have ratified it, and calls upon States which have not yet done so to consider signing and ratifying the Convention as a matter of priority, as well as to consider the option provided for in articles 31 and 32 of the Convention regarding the Committee on Enforced Disappearances;

3. *Requests* the Secretary-General and the United Nations High Commissioner for Human Rights to intensify efforts to assist States to become parties to the Convention, with a view to achieving universal adherence;

4. *Requests* United Nations agencies and organizations, and invites intergovernmental and non-governmental organizations and the Working Group on Enforced or Involuntary Disappearances, to continue undertaking efforts to disseminate information on the Convention, to promote understanding of it, to prepare for its entry into force and to assist States parties in implementing their obligations under this instrument;

5. *Requests* the Secretary-General to submit to the General Assembly at its sixty-fourth session a report on the status of the Convention and the implementation of the present resolution.

Other activities

Follow-up to 1993 World Conference

Report of High Commissioner. In February, the High Commissioner issued a report [A/HRC/7/38 & Add.1,2] on follow-up to the World Conference on Human Rights [YUN 1993, p. 908], which created the basis for the establishment of OHCHR. The report elaborated on the themes identified in the Strategic Management Plan for 2006–2007 [YUN 2006, p. 766] and their implementation. It reviewed efforts to strengthen country engagement, as well as activities for the sixtieth anniversary of the Universal Declaration of Human Rights (see p. 726). The report focused on the commitment to fight racism, particularly within the Durban Review process (see p. 762); the preparation of the OHCHR Strategic Management Plan for 2008–2009; support for human rights instruments; and the potential role of the Universal Periodic Review in promoting their universal application.

On 18 December, the General Assembly took note of the Third Committee's report [A/63/430/Add.4] on the implementation of and follow-up to the Vienna Declaration and Programme of Action, adopted at the 1993 World Conference (**decision 63/535**).

Human rights education

Public information

Progress report. A joint progress report of the Secretary-General and OHCHR, submitted in February [A/HRC/7/34], covered public information activities in human rights and global activities carried out for the sixtieth anniversary of the Universal Declaration of Human Rights, carried out by OHCHR and DPI, including the UN information services in Geneva and Vienna, and other UN information centres. It described a variety of information products, services and activities, with an emphasis on the use of modern communication tools.

World programme for human rights education

Report of High Commissioner. In July [A/HRC/9/4 & Corr.1], the High Commissioner reported on OHCHR activities from January 2007 to June 2008 to implement the World Programme for Human Rights Education, proclaimed by the General Assembly in 2004 [YUN 2004, p. 678]. In 2005, the Assembly had adopted the plan of action for the World Programme's first phase (2005–2007) [YUN 2005, p. 745], which focused on primary and secondary school systems. Activities centred on promoting and assisting national implementation of the plan of action, as well as on coordinating related international efforts. OHCHR devoted a section of its website to the World Programme, supported the collection and documentation of good practices on human rights education in regional school systems, and was developing a compendium of good practices for Central Asia, Europe and North America. OHCHR contributed to the implementation of the World Programme and its plan of action by facilitating information-sharing and networking among all actors; supporting national capacities for human rights education and training, as well as grass-roots human rights education initiatives; developing and disseminating human rights training and education materials; and globally disseminating the Universal Declaration of Human Rights.

Human Rights Council action. On 24 September [A/63/53/Add.1 (res. 9/12)], the Human Rights Council encouraged States to adopt and implement programmes of human rights education, such as the World Programme for Human Rights Education, in all learning institutions, including capacity-building programmes for law enforcement professionals, in order to advance a culture of respect for human rights.

GENERAL ASSEMBLY ACTION

On 18 December [meeting 70], the General Assembly, on the recommendation of the Third Committee [A/63/430/Add.2], adopted **resolution 63/173** without vote [agenda item 64 *(b)*].

International Year of Human Rights Learning

The General Assembly,

Recalling that the purposes and principles contained in the Charter of the United Nations include promoting and encouraging respect for human rights and fundamental freedoms for all,

Recalling also its resolution 60/251 of 15 March 2006, in which it decided that the Human Rights Council should, inter alia, promote human rights education and learning as well as advisory services, technical assistance and capacity-building,

Recalling further the 2005 World Summit Outcome, in which Heads of State and Government expressed their support for the promotion of human rights education and learning at all levels, including through the implementation of the World Programme for Human Rights Education, as appropriate, and encouraged all States to develop initiatives in that regard,

Recalling its resolution 62/171 of 18 December 2007, by which it proclaimed the year commencing on 10 December 2008 the International Year of Human Rights Learning,

Considering that the sixtieth anniversary of the Universal Declaration of Human Rights in 2008 is a suitable occasion for the United Nations to increase its efforts to promote a human rights culture worldwide through human rights learning as a way of life, at all levels,

Reaffirming the complementarities between the World Programme for Human Rights Education and the International Year of Human Rights Learning,

Recognizing human rights learning as encompassing the acquisition and internalization of knowledge and understanding of one's own and others' human dignity,

Reaffirming that activities undertaken during the International Year of Human Rights Learning should broaden and deepen human rights learning on the basis of the principles of universality, indivisibility, interdependency, impartiality and objectivity, and on non-selectivity, constructive dialogue and cooperation, with a view to enhancing the promotion and protection of all human rights and fundamental freedoms, bearing in mind the duty of the State, regardless of its political, economic or cultural system, to promote and protect all human rights and fundamental freedoms, and the significance of national and regional particularities and various historical, cultural and religious backgrounds,

Acknowledging that civil society, academia, the private sector, where appropriate, and parliamentarians can play an important role at the national, regional and international levels in the promotion and protection of human rights, including in the development of ways and means to promote and implement learning about human rights as a way of life at the community level,

1. *Reaffirms its conviction* that every woman, man, youth and child can realize his or her full human potential through learning about all human rights and fundamental

freedoms, including the ability to act on that knowledge in order to ensure the effective realization of human rights and fundamental freedoms for all;

2. *Urges* Member States to develop throughout the International Year of Human Rights Learning and beyond, in coordination with civil society, the private sector, academia and parliamentarians and regional organizations, including the appropriate specialized agencies, funds and programmes of the United Nations system, international strategies and/or regional, national and local programmes of action aimed at broad-based and sustained human rights learning at all levels, bearing in mind the complementary efforts undertaken within the framework of the World Programme for Human Rights Education;

3. *Calls upon* the United Nations High Commissioner for Human Rights and the Human Rights Council to support, cooperate and collaborate with civil society, the private sector, academia, regional organizations and other relevant stakeholders, as well as with organizations, programmes and funds of the United Nations system, in efforts to develop, in particular, the design of international strategies and/or regional, national and local programmes of action aimed at broad-based and sustained human rights learning for all, including seminars and workshops for community leaders, keeping in mind a long-term multi-year process involving several countries in all regions;

4. *Requests* the Secretary-General to include the implementation of the present resolution in the report to the General Assembly at its sixty-fourth session, in accordance with its resolution 62/171.

National institutions

Reports of Secretary-General. In a January report [A/HRC/7/69], the Secretary-General reviewed OHCHR activities in 2007 to establish and strengthen national human rights institutions; measures taken by Governments and such institutions in that regard; and cooperation between such institutions and international human rights mechanisms. Information was also provided on the work of specific national human rights institutions in respect of thematic issues.

The Secretary-General concluded that national human rights institutions compliant with the principles relating to the status of national institutions for the promotion and protection of human rights (Paris Principles), adopted by the General Assembly in 1993 [YUN 1993, p. 898], were key elements of strong and effective national human rights protection systems. They could support Governments in ensuring that international human rights norms were applied at the national level. Ensuring their independence and autonomy was a priority. The accreditation process of the International Coordinating Committee of National Institutions for the Promotion and Protection of Human Rights (ICC) had become more rigorous and thorough to ensure the independence and effectiveness of those institutions. OHCHR enhanced its support to ICC and its newly established Bureau, as well as its accreditation procedure, so that national human rights institutions could ensure that international human rights norms were translated into consistent national laws and practices. OHCHR would provide secretariat support to ICC in upholding the Paris Principles and ensure the review of compliance by those institutions. The process had resulted in an increase in applications for accreditation and the rise in the number of institutions with "A status" (compliance with the Paris Principles), as well as in the access recognized for such institutions by international human rights mechanisms.

Also in January [A/HRC/7/70], the Secretary-General reported on the ICC process for accrediting national human rights institutions, and on ways of enhancing the participation of those institutions in the work of the Human Rights Council. An annex to the report listed 60 national institutions that were in compliance with the Paris Principles ("A status"); 3 institutions accredited that status with reserve, as the documentation submitted was insufficient to confer "A status"; 12 institutions not fully in compliance or which had provided insufficient information ("B status"); 9 institutions that were non-compliant ("C Status"); and 1 institution that had been suspended.

GENERAL ASSEMBLY ACTION

On 18 December [meeting 70], the General Assembly, on the recommendation of the Third Committee [A/63/430/Add.2], adopted **resolution 63/172** without vote [agenda item 64 *(b)*].

National institutions for the promotion and protection of human rights

The General Assembly,

Recalling its resolutions and those of the Commission on Human Rights concerning national institutions for the promotion and protection of human rights,

Welcoming the rapidly growing interest throughout the world in the creation and strengthening of independent, pluralistic national institutions for the promotion and protection of human rights,

Recalling the principles relating to the status of national institutions for the promotion and protection of human rights ("the Paris Principles"),

Reaffirming the important role that such national institutions play and will continue to play in promoting and protecting human rights and fundamental freedoms and in developing and enhancing public awareness of those rights and freedoms,

Recognizing the important role of the United Nations in assisting the development of independent and effective national human rights institutions, guided by the Paris Principles, and recognizing also in this regard the potential for strengthened and complementary cooperation between the United Nations and those national institutions in the promotion and protection of human rights,

Recalling the Vienna Declaration and Programme of Action adopted by the World Conference on Human Rights on 25 June 1993, which reaffirmed the important and constructive role played by national human rights institutions, in particular in their advisory capacity to the competent authorities and their role in remedying human rights violations, in disseminating information on human rights and in education in human rights,

Recalling also the Beijing Declaration and Platform for Action, in which Governments were urged to create or strengthen independent national institutions for the promotion and protection of human rights, including the human rights of women,

Reaffirming that all human rights are universal, indivisible, interrelated, interdependent and mutually reinforcing, and that all human rights must be treated in a fair and equal manner, on the same footing and with the same emphasis,

Bearing in mind the significance of national and regional particularities and various historical, cultural and religious backgrounds, and that all States, regardless of their political, economic and cultural systems, have the duty to promote and protect all human rights and fundamental freedoms,

Recalling the programme of action adopted by national institutions, at their meeting held in Vienna in June 1993 during the World Conference on Human Rights, for the promotion and protection of human rights, in which it was recommended that United Nations activities and programmes should be reinforced to meet the requests for assistance from States wishing to establish or strengthen their national institutions for the promotion and protection of human rights,

Noting the valuable role played and contributions made by national institutions in United Nations meetings dealing with human rights and the importance of their continued appropriate participation,

Welcoming the strengthening in all regions of regional cooperation among national human rights institutions and between national human rights institutions and other regional human rights forums,

Taking note with appreciation of the reports of the Secretary-General to the Human Rights Council on national institutions for the promotion and protection of human rights and on the accreditation process of the International Coordinating Committee of National Institutions for the Promotion and Protection of Human Rights,

Noting with satisfaction the strengthening of the accreditation procedure of the International Coordinating Committee of National Institutions,

Noting with appreciation the continuing work of the regional human rights networks in Europe, the Network of National Institutions for the Promotion and Protection of Human Rights in the Americas, the Asia Pacific Forum of National Human Rights Institutions and the Network of African National Human Rights Institutions,

Welcoming the strengthening of international cooperation among national human rights institutions, including through the International Coordinating Committee of National Institutions,

1. *Takes note with appreciation* of the report of the Secretary-General;

2. *Reaffirms* the importance of the development of effective, independent and pluralistic national institutions for the promotion and protection of human rights, in accordance with the principles relating to the status of national institutions for the promotion and protection of human rights ("the Paris Principles");

3. *Recognizes* the role of independent national institutions for the promotion and protection of human rights in working together with Governments to ensure full respect for human rights at the national level, including by contributing to follow-up actions, as appropriate, to the recommendations resulting from the international human rights mechanisms;

4. *Welcomes* the increasingly important role of national institutions for the promotion and protection of human rights in supporting cooperation between their Governments and the United Nations for the promotion and protection of human rights;

5. *Recognizes* that, in accordance with the Vienna Declaration and Programme of Action, it is the right of each State to choose the framework for national institutions that is best suited to its particular needs at the national level in order to promote human rights in accordance with international human rights standards;

6. *Also recognizes* that national institutions have a crucial role to play in promoting and ensuring the indivisibility and interdependence of all human rights, and calls upon States to ensure that all human rights are appropriately reflected in the mandate of their national human rights institutions when established;

7. *Encourages* Member States to establish effective, independent and pluralistic national institutions or, where they already exist, to strengthen them for the promotion and protection of human rights, as outlined in the Vienna Declaration and Programme of Action;

8. *Welcomes* the growing number of States establishing or considering the establishment of national institutions for the promotion and protection of human rights;

9. *Encourages* national institutions for the promotion and protection of human rights established by Member States to continue to play an active role in preventing and combating all violations of human rights as enumerated in the Vienna Declaration and Programme of Action and relevant international instruments;

10. *Recognizes* the role played by national institutions for the promotion and protection of human rights in the Human Rights Council, including its universal periodic review mechanism and the special procedures, as well as in the human rights treaty bodies, in accordance with Human Rights Council resolutions 5/1 and 5/2 of 18 June 2007 and Commission on Human Rights resolution 2005/74 of 20 April 2005;

11. *Notes with satisfaction* the efforts of those States that have provided their national institutions with more autonomy and independence, including by giving them an investigative role or enhancing such a role, and encourages other Governments to consider taking similar steps;

12. *Acknowledges* the role of national institutions in the strengthening of the rule of law and the promotion and protection of human rights in all sectors, and encourages cooperation, where appropriate, with the United Nations

system, international financial institutions, and non-governmental organizations;

13. *Urges* the Secretary-General to continue to give high priority to requests from Member States for assistance in the establishment and strengthening of national human rights institutions;

14. *Commends* the high priority given by the Office of the United Nations High Commissioner for Human Rights to work on national institutions, encourages the High Commissioner, in view of the expanded activities relating to national institutions, to ensure that appropriate arrangements are made and budgetary resources provided to continue and further extend activities in support of national human rights institutions, and invites Governments to contribute additional voluntary funds to that end;

15. *Welcomes* the national institutions website as an important vehicle for the delivery of information to national institutions and also the launch of a database of comparative analysis of procedures and methods of complaint-handling by national human rights institutions;

16. *Notes with appreciation* the increasingly active and important role of the International Coordinating Committee of National Institutions for the Promotion and Protection of Human Rights, in close cooperation with the Office of the High Commissioner, in assisting Governments and national institutions, when requested, to follow up on relevant resolutions and recommendations concerning the strengthening of national institutions;

17. *Also notes with appreciation* the holding of regular meetings of the International Coordinating Committee of National Institutions and the arrangements for the participation of national human rights institutions in the sessions of the Human Rights Council;

18. *Requests* the Secretary-General to continue to provide the necessary assistance for holding meetings of the International Coordinating Committee of National Institutions during the sessions of the Human Rights Council, in cooperation with the Office of the High Commissioner;

19. *Encourages* national institutions to seek accreditation status through the International Coordinating Committee of National Institutions, and notes with satisfaction the strengthening of the accreditation procedure and the continued assistance of the Office of the High Commissioner in this regard, as well as the assistance of the Office to the conferences of the International Coordinating Committee;

20. *Welcomes* the continuation of the practice of national institutions convening regional meetings in some regions, and its initiation in others, and encourages national institutions, in cooperation with the High Commissioner, to organize similar events with Governments and non-governmental organizations in their own regions;

21. *Requests* the Secretary-General to continue to provide the necessary assistance for holding international and regional meetings of national institutions;

22. *Recognizes* the important and constructive role that the judiciary, parliament and civil society can play, in cooperation with national institutions, for better promotion and protection of human rights;

23. *Encourages* all Member States to take appropriate steps to promote the exchange of information and experience concerning the establishment and effective operation of national institutions;

24. *Encourages* all United Nations human rights mechanisms as well as agencies, funds and programmes to work within their respective mandates with Member States and national institutions in the promotion and protection of human rights with respect to, inter alia, projects in the area of good governance and rule of law, and in this regard welcomes the efforts made by the Office of the High Commissioner to develop partnerships in support of national institutions;

25. *Requests* the Secretary-General to report to the General Assembly at its sixty-fourth session on the implementation of the present resolution.

Also on 18 December [meeting 70], the Assembly, on the recommendation of the Third Committee [A/63/430/Add.2], adopted **resolution 63/169** without vote [agenda item 64 *(b)*].

The role of the Ombudsman, mediator and other national human rights institutions in the promotion and protection of human rights

The General Assembly,

Reaffirming its commitment to the principles and purposes of the Charter of the United Nations and the Universal Declaration of Human Rights,

Reaffirming the commitment of Member States, in accordance with the Charter, to promote and ensure the respect of human rights and fundamental freedoms, without distinction of any kind, such as race, colour, sex, language, religion, political or other opinion, national or social origin, property, birth or other status,

Recalling the principles relating to the status of national institutions for the promotion and protection of human rights, welcomed by the General Assembly in its resolution 48/134 of 20 December 1993 and annexed thereto,

Recognizing the role of the existing Ombudsman, whether a male or female, mediator and other national human rights institutions in the promotion and protection of human rights and fundamental freedoms,

Underlining the importance of the autonomy and independence of the Ombudsman, mediator and other national human rights institutions, where they exist, in order to enable them to consider all issues related to the field of their competences,

Considering the role of the Ombudsman, mediator and other national human rights institutions in promoting good governance in public administrations, as well as improving their relations with citizens, and in strengthening the delivery of public services,

Considering also the important role of the existing Ombudsman, mediator and other national human rights institutions in contributing to the effective realization of the rule of law and respect for the principles of justice and equality,

Stressing that these institutions, where they exist, can have an important role in advising the Government with respect to bringing national legislation and national practices in line with their international human rights obligations,

Stressing also the importance of international cooperation in the field of human rights, and recalling the role played by regional and international associations of the Ombudsman, mediator and other national human rights institutions in promoting cooperation and sharing best practices,

1. *Encourages* Member States:

(a) To consider the creation or the strengthening of independent and autonomous Ombudsman, mediator and other national human rights institutions;

(b) To develop, where appropriate, mechanisms of cooperation between these institutions, where they exist, in order to coordinate their action, strengthen their achievements and enable the exchange of lessons learned;

2. *Also encourages* Member States:

(a) To consider conducting communication campaigns, with other relevant actors, in order to enhance public awareness on the importance of the role of the Ombudsman, mediator and other national human rights institutions;

(b) To give serious consideration to implementing the recommendations and proposals of their Ombudsman, mediator and other national human rights institutions, with the aim of addressing claims of the complainants, consistent with the principles of justice, equality and rule of law;

3. *Requests* the Secretary-General to report to the General Assembly at its sixty-fifth session on the implementation of the present resolution;

4. *Decides* to consider this issue at its sixty-fifth session.

Regional arrangements

Workshop on regional arrangements. As requested by the Human Rights Council in 2007 [YUN 2007, p. 699], a workshop (Geneva, 24–25 November) [A/HRC/11/3], attended by 28 representatives of regional and subregional mechanisms, national human rights institutions and NGOs, as well as diplomats, addressed regional arrangements for human rights promotion and protection. The workshop examined human rights commissions and similar mechanisms, including emerging mechanisms; human rights courts; and the relationship of regional human rights mechanisms with the UN human rights system. Participants concluded that regional human rights commissions and courts played an invaluable role in promoting and protecting international human rights standards. The High Commissioner should appoint a focal point to facilitate networking and information-sharing among the Human Rights Council, regional and subregional human rights mechanisms and OHCHR. The focal point should act as a clearing house of best practices and lessons learned in the experience of regional and subregional human rights mechanisms, including in the implementation of human rights standards at the regional level, and facilitate the provision of training to emerging regional and subregional mechanisms. The workshop should be held on a regular basis to promote the sharing of information and proposals for strengthening cooperation between the United Nations and human rights regional arrangements, and the identification of strategies for overcoming obstacles to human rights promotion and protection at the regional and international levels.

GENERAL ASSEMBLY ACTION

On 18 December [meeting 70], the General Assembly, on the recommendation of the Third Committee [A/63/430/Add.2], adopted **resolution 63/170** without vote [agenda item 64 *(b)*].

Regional arrangements for the promotion and protection of human rights

The General Assembly,

Recalling its resolution 32/127 of 16 December 1977 and its subsequent resolutions concerning regional arrangements for the promotion and protection of human rights,

Recalling also Commission on Human Rights resolution 1993/51 of 9 March 1993 and its subsequent resolutions in this regard, and Human Rights Council resolution 6/20 of 28 September 2007,

Bearing in mind the Vienna Declaration and Programme of Action adopted by the World Conference on Human Rights on 25 June 1993, which reiterates, inter alia, the need to consider the possibility of establishing regional and subregional arrangements for the promotion and protection of human rights where they do not already exist,

Recalling that the World Conference recommended that more resources should be made available for the strengthening of regional arrangements for the promotion and protection of human rights under the programme of technical cooperation in the field of human rights of the Office of the United Nations High Commissioner for Human Rights,

Reaffirming that regional arrangements play an important role in promoting and protecting human rights and should reinforce universal human rights standards, as contained in international human rights instruments,

Welcoming the fact that the Office of the High Commissioner has been systematically pursuing a regional and subregional approach through a variety of complementary means and methods, in order to maximize the impact of the activities of the United Nations at the national level, and that the Office intends to establish new regional offices,

1. *Welcomes* the continuing cooperation and assistance of the Office of the United Nations High Commissioner for Human Rights in the further strengthening of the existing regional arrangements and regional machinery for the promotion and protection of human rights, in particular through technical cooperation aimed at national capacity-building, public information and education, with a view to exchanging information and experience in the field of human rights;

2. *Also welcomes*, in that respect, the close cooperation of the Office of the High Commissioner in the organization of regional and subregional training courses and workshops in the field of human rights, high-level governmental expert meetings and regional conferences of national human rights institutions;

3. *Recognizes*, therefore, that progress in promoting and protecting all human rights depends primarily on efforts made at the national and local levels, and that the regional approach should imply intensive cooperation and coordination with all partners involved, while bearing in mind the importance of international cooperation;

4. *Welcomes* the growing exchanges between the United Nations and the United Nations human rights treaty bodies, on the one hand, and regional organizations and institutions, such as the African Commission on Human and Peoples' Rights, the Community of Portuguese-speaking Countries, the Council of Europe, the Inter-American Commission on Human Rights, the International Organization of la Francophonie, the League of Arab States, the Organization for Security and Cooperation in Europe and other regional institutions, on the other;

5. *Also welcomes* the placement by the Office of the High Commissioner of regional representatives in subregions and in regional commissions;

6. *Further welcomes* the progress achieved in the establishment of regional and subregional arrangements for the promotion and protection of human rights, and, in this regard, notes with interest:

(*a*) The increasing cooperation between the Office of the High Commissioner and African organizations and suborganizations, in particular the African Union, the Economic Community of Central African States, the Economic Community of West African States and the Southern African Development Community;

(*b*) The support provided by the Office of the High Commissioner to the African Union for the strengthening of the promotion and protection of human rights in Africa, and welcomes in this regard the establishment of the African Court on Human and Peoples' Rights;

(*c*) The convening of the fourteenth annual Workshop on Regional Cooperation for the Promotion and Protection of Human Rights in the Asia-Pacific Region, held in Bali, Indonesia, from 10 to 12 July 2007, which, inter alia, included a discussion on future challenges for the Regional Framework for the Promotion and Protection of Human Rights in the Asia-Pacific Region and adopted a comprehensive set of points for follow-up action entitled the "Bali Action Points";

(*d*) The ongoing consultations among Governments aimed at the possible establishment of regional human rights arrangements held in the context of the Regional Framework, with the support and advice of national human rights institutions and civil society organizations of the Asia-Pacific region;

(*e*) The recent decision by the Association of the Southeast Asian Nations (ASEAN) to develop a mechanism for the promotion and protection of human rights;

(*f*) Activities undertaken within the framework of the regional project of the Office of the High Commissioner for the promotion and protection of human rights in the Latin American and Caribbean region and the strengthening of the cooperation between the Office of the High Commissioner, the Inter-American Commission on Human Rights and the Organization of American States;

(*g*) Ongoing initiatives to further develop arrangements for the promotion and protection of human rights by the Common Market of the South (MERCOSUR);

(*h*) Activities undertaken within the framework of cooperation between the Office of the High Commissioner and the League of Arab States;

(*i*) The continued cooperation towards the realization of universal standards between the Office of the High Commissioner and regional organizations in Europe and Central Asia, namely, the Council of Europe, and its various human rights bodies and mechanisms, the European Union and the Organization for Security and Cooperation in Europe, in particular for activities at the country level;

7. *Invites* States in areas in which regional arrangements in the field of human rights do not yet exist to consider, with the support and advice of national human rights institutions and civil society organizations, concluding agreements with a view to establishing, within their respective regions, suitable regional machinery for the promotion and protection of human rights;

8. *Requests* the Secretary-General to continue to strengthen exchanges between the United Nations and regional intergovernmental organizations dealing with human rights and to make available adequate resources from within the regular budget of technical cooperation to the activities of the Office of the High Commissioner to promote regional arrangements;

9. *Requests* the Office of the High Commissioner to continue to pay special attention to the most appropriate ways of assisting countries of the various regions, at their request, under the programme of technical cooperation and to make, where necessary, relevant recommendations, and in this regard welcomes the decision of the Office to strengthen national protection systems in accordance with action 2 of the reform programme of the Secretary-General;

10. *Requests* the Secretary-General to submit to the General Assembly at its sixty-fifth session a report on the state of regional arrangements for the promotion and protection of human rights, formulating concrete proposals and recommendations on ways and means to strengthen cooperation between the United Nations and regional arrangements in the field of human rights, and to include therein the results of action taken in pursuance of the present resolution;

11. *Decides* to consider the question further at its sixty-fifth session.

Africa

Report of Secretary-General. In response to General Assembly resolution 62/221 [YUN 2007, p. 699], the Secretary-General submitted, in September [A/63/367], a report reviewing the activities of the Yaoundé-based Subregional Centre for Human Rights and Democracy in Central Africa from September 2007 to August 2008. The report detailed activities in capacity-building carried out by Governments and civil society organizations; technical cooperation and advisory activities; democracy, peace and security support; public information and dissemination of documentation; commemorative activities, including those relating to the sixtieth anniversary of the Universal Declaration of Human Rights; and the strengthening of partnerships with Governments, subregional organizations, civil society organizations and UN agencies.

The Secretary-General said that the strategy undertaken by the Centre in 2006 [YUN 2006, p. 699] had started to bear fruit. The Centre had become very visible and was trusted by national and regional organizations to provide input, advice and expertise. Relationships with Governments had been enhanced, and counterparts in relevant ministries had been identified. The Centre did not have the capacity to respond to all the requests it received for technical cooperation, training and legal advice. In 2008, four Governments and one subregional network expressed interest in technical cooperation with the Centre. The Centre advanced implementation of the memorandum of understanding with the Economic Community of Central African States, in particular regarding child rights, peace and security and general human rights training. It planned to further develop its democracy and transitional justice programmes to make them useful tools in political peacebuilding processes and transitions in Central Africa, and continued to broaden its impact on gender-based discrimination and violence.

GENERAL ASSEMBLY ACTION

On 18 December [meeting 70], the General Assembly, on the recommendation of the Third Committee [A/63/430/Add.2], adopted **resolution 63/177** without vote [agenda item 64 *(b)*].

Subregional Centre for Human Rights and Democracy in Central Africa

The General Assembly,

Recalling its resolution 55/105 of 4 December 2000 concerning regional arrangements for the promotion and protection of human rights,

Recalling also its resolutions 55/34 B of 20 November 2000 and 55/233 of 23 December 2000, section III of its resolution 55/234 of 23 December 2000, its resolution 56/253 of 24 December 2001, and its resolutions 58/176 of 22 December 2003, 59/183 of 20 December 2004, 60/151 of 16 December 2005, 61/158 of 19 December 2006 and 62/221 of 22 December 2007 on the Subregional Centre for Human Rights and Democracy in Central Africa,

Recalling further that the World Conference on Human Rights recommended that more resources be made available for the strengthening of regional arrangements for the promotion and protection of human rights under the programme of technical cooperation in the field of human rights of the Office of the United Nations High Commissioner for Human Rights,

Recalling the report of the High Commissioner,

Taking note of the holding of the twenty-seventh ministerial meeting of the United Nations Standing Advisory Committee on Security Questions in Central Africa, in Luanda from 13 to 15 May 2008,

Taking note also of the report of the Secretary-General,

Welcoming the 2005 World Summit Outcome, in particular the decision confirmed therein to double the regular budget of the Office of the High Commissioner over the next five years,

1. *Welcomes* the activities of the Subregional Centre for Human Rights and Democracy in Central Africa at Yaoundé;

2. *Notes with satisfaction* the support provided for the establishment of the Centre by the host country;

3. *Takes note* of the implementation of the new three-year strategy for the Centre, which aims to reinforce its activities;

4. *Notes* the efforts of the Secretary-General and the United Nations High Commissioner for Human Rights to ensure the full implementation of the relevant resolutions of the General Assembly in order to provide sufficient funds and human resources for the missions of the Centre;

5. *Requests* the Secretary-General and the High Commissioner to continue to provide additional funds and human resources within the existing resources of the Office of the United Nations High Commissioner for Human Rights to enable the Centre to respond positively and effectively to the growing needs in the promotion and protection of human rights and in developing a culture of democracy and the rule of law in the Central African subregion;

6. *Requests* the Secretary-General to submit to the General Assembly at its sixty-fourth session a report on the implementation of the present resolution.

Asia and the Pacific

Report of High Commissioner. In January [A/HRC/7/35], the High Commissioner submitted to the Human Rights Council the conclusion of the Fourteenth Annual Workshop on Regional Cooperation for the Promotion and Protection of Human Rights in the Asia-Pacific Region, held in Bali, Indonesia, in July 2007 [YUN 2007, p. 700]. The Workshop reviewed progress under the Tehran Framework of Regional Technical Cooperation Programme for Asia and the Pacific and discussed the theme of human rights and extreme poverty, as well as future challenges for the Asia-Pacific Regional Framework. The Workshop adopted the Bali Action Points for follow-up action.

Strengthening action to promote human rights

International cooperation in the field of human rights

Report of High Commissioner. Pursuant to a Human Rights Council request [YUN 2007, p. 700], the High Commissioner, in February, submitted a report [A/HRC/7/31] on the enhancement of international cooperation in the field of human rights, which summarized replies received, in response to a request for information, from Belarus, Bosnia and Herzegovina, Cuba, Guatemala, Iran, Japan, Oman, the Russian Federation and Switzerland, as well as from two human rights organizations—the Asia Pacific Forum of National Human Rights Institutions and the Commonwealth Human Rights Initiative.

Human Rights Council action. On 27 March [A/63/53 (res. 7/3)], the Human Rights Council reaffirmed the importance of enhancing international cooperation for the promotion and protection of human rights and for the achievement of the objectives of the fight against racism, racial discrimination, xenophobia and related intolerance. Considering that international human rights cooperation should contribute to preventing human rights violations, it requested the High Commissioner to consult States, intergovernmental organizations and NGOs on ways to enhance international cooperation and dialogue within the UN human rights machinery, and to report to the Council in 2009.

GENERAL ASSEMBLY ACTION

On 18 December [meeting 70], the General Assembly, on the recommendation of the Third Committee [A/63/430/Add.2], adopted **resolution 63/180** without vote [agenda item 64 *(b)*].

Enhancement of international cooperation in the field of human rights

The General Assembly,

Reaffirming its commitment to promoting international cooperation, as set forth in the Charter of the United Nations, in particular Article 1, paragraph 3, as well as relevant provisions of the Vienna Declaration and Programme of Action adopted by the World Conference on Human Rights on 25 June 1993, for enhancing genuine cooperation among Member States in the field of human rights,

Recalling its adoption of the United Nations Millennium Declaration on 8 September 2000 and of its resolution 62/160 of 18 December 2007, Human Rights Council resolution 7/3 of 27 March 2008 and the resolutions of the Commission on Human Rights on the enhancement of international cooperation in the field of human rights,

Recalling also the World Conference against Racism, Racial Discrimination, Xenophobia and Related Intolerance, held at Durban, South Africa, from 31 August to 8 September 2001, and its role in the enhancement of international cooperation in the field of human rights,

Recognizing that the enhancement of international cooperation in the field of human rights is essential for the full achievement of the purposes of the United Nations, including the effective promotion and protection of all human rights,

Recognizing also that the promotion and protection of human rights should be based on the principle of cooperation and genuine dialogue and aimed at strengthening the capacity of Member States to comply with their human rights obligations for the benefit of all human beings,

Reaffirming that dialogue among religions, cultures and civilizations in the field of human rights could contribute greatly to the enhancement of international cooperation in this field,

Emphasizing the need for further progress in the promotion and encouragement of respect for human rights and fundamental freedoms through, inter alia, international cooperation,

Underlining the fact that mutual understanding, dialogue, cooperation, transparency and confidence-building are important elements in all activities for the promotion and protection of human rights,

Recalling the adoption of resolution 2000/22 of 18 August 2000, on the promotion of dialogue on human rights issues, by the Subcommission on the Promotion and Protection of Human Rights at its fifty-second session,

1. *Reaffirms* that it is one of the purposes of the United Nations and the responsibility of all Member States to promote, protect and encourage respect for human rights and fundamental freedoms through, inter alia, international cooperation;

2. *Recognizes* that, in addition to their separate responsibilities to their individual societies, States have a collective responsibility to uphold the principles of human dignity, equality and equity at the global level;

3. *Reaffirms* that dialogue among cultures and civilizations facilitates the promotion of a culture of tolerance and respect for diversity, and welcomes in this regard the holding of conferences and meetings at the national, regional and international levels on dialogue among civilizations;

4. *Urges* all actors on the international scene to build an international order based on inclusion, justice, equality and equity, human dignity, mutual understanding and promotion of and respect for cultural diversity and universal human rights, and to reject all doctrines of exclusion based on racism, racial discrimination, xenophobia and related intolerance;

5. *Reaffirms* the importance of the enhancement of international cooperation for the promotion and protection of human rights and for the achievement of the objectives of the fight against racism, racial discrimination, xenophobia and related intolerance;

6. *Considers* that international cooperation in the field of human rights, in conformity with the purposes and principles set out in the Charter of the United Nations and international law, should make an effective and practical contribution to the urgent task of preventing violations of human rights and fundamental freedoms;

7. *Reaffirms* that the promotion, protection and full realization of all human rights and fundamental freedoms should be guided by the principles of universality, nonselectivity, objectivity and transparency, in a manner consistent with the purposes and principles set out in the Charter;

8. *Calls upon* Member States, the specialized agencies and intergovernmental organizations to continue to carry out a constructive dialogue and consultations for the enhancement of understanding and the promotion and protection of all human rights and fundamental freedoms, and encourages non-governmental organizations to contribute actively to this endeavour;

9. *Invites* States and relevant United Nations human rights mechanisms and procedures to continue to pay attention to the importance of mutual cooperation, understanding and dialogue in ensuring the promotion and protection of all human rights;

10. *Requests* the Secretary-General, in collaboration with the United Nations High Commissioner for Human Rights, to consult States and intergovernmental and nongovernmental organizations on ways and means to enhance

international cooperation and dialogue in the United Nations human rights machinery, including the Human Rights Council;

11. *Decides* to continue its consideration of the question at its sixty-fourth session.

Advisory services and technical cooperation

Report of Secretary-General. A report of the Secretary-General [A/HRC/10/57 & Corr.1] provided information on human rights advisory services and technical cooperation. In Africa, most activities were carried out by the 22 OHCHR entities in the region, including support to 11 UN peace operations. The OHCHR Africa programme helped Governments, institutions and civil society organizations to incorporate human rights principles into their efforts to respond to the human rights needs of their people, reduce poverty, fight impunity and address discrimination, especially against women.

In Asia, the Office's capacity to implement technical cooperation was facilitated by the expansion of field presences, including the deployment of four human rights advisers in Indonesia, Maldives, Papua New Guinea and Sri Lanka. OHCHR also maintained two country offices in Cambodia and Nepal, two components of peacekeeping missions in Afghanistan and Timor-Leste and two regional offices in Bangkok, Thailand and Suva, Fiji. The Office worked with Member States, UN country teams and regional partners, including the Association of Southeast Asian Nations, the Pacific Islands Forum and the Asia Pacific Forum of National Human Rights Institutions.

In the Europe, North America and Central Asia region, the Office was increasingly engaged in Central Asia, where a regional office was established in Kyrgyzstan. The Office was also represented by human rights advisers to the UN country teams in the Russian Federation and the south Caucasus. Technical assistance and policy advocacy work in the region focused on impunity, weak institutions, women's rights, restrictions on freedom of expression and association, human rights in the fight against terrorism, racism and xenophobia, the treatment of asylum-seekers, irregular migrants and Roma, as well as poverty and the right to housing.

Technical cooperation activities in Latin America were mainly implemented through the regional office for Latin America in Panama; the four country offices in Bolivia, Colombia, Guatemala and Mexico; two human rights advisers in Ecuador and Nicaragua; and the human rights component in the United Nations Stabilization Mission in Haiti. Priorities included addressing impunity and weak institutions; discrimination, particularly against Afro-descendants and indigenous persons; poverty and inequality; and violence, mainly against women and children.

In the Middle East and North Africa, the Office had a regional office in Beirut, Lebanon, and a country office in the Occupied Palestinian Territory. It also supported the Human Rights Office of the United Nations Assistance Mission for Iraq. Thematic priorities included freedom of expression, association and assembly; the fight against impunity; attending to the needs of countries in conflict; and the human rights of non-citizens, namely refugees, stateless persons and migrant workers.

Voluntary Fund

During the year, the Board of Trustees of the UN Voluntary Fund for Technical Cooperation in the Field of Human Rights held its twenty-eighth (May) and twenty-ninth (November) sessions in Geneva [A/HRC/10/57 & Corr.1]. At the sessions, the Board examined various components of the United Nations Human Rights Programme on Technical Cooperation funded by the Voluntary Fund. In November, the annual OHCHR consultation with heads of field presences gave the Board the opportunity to learn first-hand from field representatives about the implementation of technical cooperation activities on the ground. Activities were implemented by OHCHR advisers in UN country teams in 12 countries; by Human Rights Units of peace missions in eight such missions; and by OHCHR field presences in six countries and territories.

As at 31 December, the estimated balance of the Fund was $12,108,096. Income in 2008 was $14,674,741 and total expenditures $13,573,336.

Cooperation with human rights bodies

Report of Secretary-General. In a February report [A/HRC/7/45 & Corr.1], submitted in accordance with a 2006 Human Rights Council request [YUN 2006, p. 760], the Secretary-General described situations in which individuals or members of NGOs had allegedly suffered intimidation or reprisal for having cooperated with UN human rights bodies regarding human rights violations. The report summarized related cases in Fiji, Indonesia, the Philippines and the Russian Federation, and underlined the seriousness of the alleged reprisals. Many other cases had not been recorded in the report due to security concerns or because the victims had requested that their cases not be publicized. Victims suffered violations of the most fundamental human rights, including the right to liberty and security of person and the right to freedom from torture and cruel, inhuman or degrading treatment. The report observed that the gravity of those reprisals reinforced the need for all representatives of UN human rights bodies, in cooperation with States, to continue to take urgent steps to help prevent the occurrence of such acts.

Chapter II

Protection of human rights

In 2008, the United Nations continued to protect human rights worldwide through several mechanisms. Its main organs—the Economic and Social Council, the General Assembly and the Security Council—remained actively engaged in protecting those rights. The Assembly's Human Rights Council carried out its task as the central United Nations intergovernmental body responsible for promoting and protecting all human rights and fundamental freedoms. It addressed human rights violations, worked to prevent abuses, provided overall policy guidance, monitored the observance of human rights around the world and assisted States in fulfilling their human rights obligations.

The special procedures mandate-holders—special rapporteurs, working groups, independent experts and special representatives—monitored, examined, advised and publicly reported on human rights situations in specific countries or on major human rights violations worldwide. In 2008, 30 thematic mandate-holders reported on adequate housing, people of African descent, arbitrary detention, children and armed conflict, the sale of children, education, enforced or involuntary disappearances, extralegal executions, effects of foreign debt on human rights, extreme poverty, the right to food, freedom of opinion and expression, freedom of religion or belief, physical and mental health, human rights defenders, independence of the judiciary, indigenous peoples, internally displaced persons, human rights and international solidarity, mercenaries, migrants, minority issues, racism and racial discrimination, slavery, human rights protection while countering terrorism, torture, the illicit movement and dumping of toxic and dangerous products and wastes, trafficking in persons, transnational corporations, and violence against women. During the year, mandate-holders sent 911 communications to 118 countries regarding 2,206 individuals; two thirds were joint communications sent by two or more mandates. They also conducted 53 fact-finding missions to 48 countries, issued 177 statements and press releases, and submitted 135 reports to the Human Rights Council (120 by thematic mandate-holders), including 79 annual reports and 56 country visit reports, and 19 reports to the General Assembly. In June, the Council created the mandate of the independent expert on the issue of human rights obligations related to access to safe drinking water and sanitation.

In May, the Council held a special session to take action on the negative impact on the realization of the right to food of the worsening world food crisis, caused by soaring food prices, among other things.

The rights of minorities continued to be a major focus. The Forum on Minority Issues, created by the Council in 2007, met for the first time in December under the guidance of the independent expert on minority issues. The Permanent Forum on Indigenous Issues addressed indigenous concerns relating to economic and social development, culture, education, the environment, health and human rights, and helped to coordinate related UN activities. The Expert Mechanism on the Rights of Indigenous Peoples, at its first session, discussed participation of indigenous peoples in its work, as well as issues related to discrimination and the rights of indigenous peoples to education.

Preparations continued for the Durban Review Conference, scheduled for 2009, whose objectives included a review of the progress made in implementing the 2001 Durban Programme of Action and an assessment of the effectiveness of mechanisms and instruments for tackling racial discrimination.

Racism and racial discrimination

Follow-up to 2001 World Conference

Intergovernmental Working Group. The Intergovernmental Working Group on the effective implementation of the Durban Declaration and Programme of Action (DDPA), adopted by the 2001 World Conference against Racism, Racial Discrimination, Xenophobia and Related Intolerance [YUN 2001, p. 615], held its sixth session in two parts (Geneva, 21 January–1 February and 18 December) [A/HRC/10/87].

The Working Group discussed its contribution to the work of the Preparatory Committee for the Durban Review Conference (see p. 762) and its future work. The Working Group adopted a compilation of conclusions and recommendations adopted at its five previous sessions [A/CONF.211/PC.2/7], which was submitted to the Preparatory Committee as part of the Working Group's contribution. The recommendations covered, among other issues, education, poverty, racism and health, racism and the Internet, globalization and racism and the migration dimension. A Secretariat note [A/HRC/10/WG.3/2] provided updated information on the Working Group's sixth session.

In September [A/HRC/9/5], the Office of the United Nations High Commissioner for Human Rights (OHCHR) reported on actions it had taken to implement the recommendations made by the Working Group at its fifth session [YUN 2007, p. 706].

Report of Secretary-General. Pursuant to General Assembly resolution 62/220 [ibid., p. 708], the Secretary-General, in October, submitted a report [A/63/366] on activities undertaken between August 2006 and July 2007 by States, human rights mechanisms and OHCHR to implement DDPA. The report, which built on the Secretary-General's 2006 report on the topic [YUN 2007, p. 707], concluded that, since the adoption of DDPA, many countries had demonstrated commitment to combating racism and related phenomena. Nearly all constitutions guaranteed the principle of equality, and many countries had reformed their laws to eliminate those that were discriminatory. At the regional level, harmonization of national laws with European Union (EU) human rights principles, including the prohibition of racism and discrimination, had indirectly benefited the implementation of DDPA.

Working Group on people of African descent. At its seventh session (Geneva, 14–18 January) [A/HRC/7/36], the Working Group of Experts on People of African Descent, established by the defunct Commission on Human Rights in 2002 [YUN 2002, p. 661] to consider problems of racial discrimination affecting people of African descent, in accordance with DDPA, reviewed the recommendations made at previous sessions in order to distil its contribution to the Review Conference. After reviewing those recommendations, the Working Group, as part of its contribution to the Preparatory Committee, called upon States that had not yet elaborated national plans of action to combat racism to do so, preferably before the Conference, and those that had should implement them fully and report thereon at the Conference. States should identify factors resulting in the over-representation in arrests, sentencing and incarceration of people of African descent, particularly young men, and take measures to eliminate those factors and adopt crime-prevention strategies and programmes that included alternatives to incarceration. They should also address the disproportionately low levels of representation of people of African descent in the judiciary and other areas of the justice system. States should implement mechanisms for effectively collecting disaggregated information on health, education, access to housing, employment, treatment in the criminal justice system and political participation and representation as regards people of African descent, which should be the basis for creating and monitoring policies and practices that addressed any discrimination found. OHCHR should provide guidelines on the collection of disaggregated information to States requesting them. A code of conduct for the media should be drawn up that, taking into account such issues as the right to freedom of expression, combated racial discrimination against people of African descent by elaborating compulsory standards. The aim would be to eliminate the projection and perpetuation, through the media and new technologies, of negative images and stereotypes of Africa and people of African descent. The code should also include provisions to address and combat incitement to racial hatred. States and international and regional organizations should establish independent bodies, where they did not already exist, to receive complaints by people of African descent of discrimination in accessing housing, education, health, employment and other fundamental rights. The Human Rights Council should request OHCHR to produce best practices in areas such as access to housing, education, health, employment and institutional and legal frameworks pertaining to people of African descent, as well as in combating stereotyping against that group in the media.

The Working Group recommended that the issue of reparations for people of African descent should be considered at the Durban Review Conference. The United Nations should also create a UN fellowship programme for people of African descent.

Human Rights Council action. On 28 March [A/63/53 (res. 7/33)], the Council, by a recorded vote of 34-0-13, saluted the positive developments in the fight against racism, racial discrimination, xenophobia and related intolerance, and urged all Governments to summon the political will to take decisive steps to combat racism in all its forms and manifestations. It acknowledged the report of the Working Group of Experts on People of African Descent on its seventh session (above) and decided to invite the Group to address the Council at its tenth (2010) session.

On 24 September [A/63/53/Add.1 (res. 9/14)], the Council extended the mandate of the Working Group for three years and requested it to report on progress in elaborating its mandate. It recommended that States ensure adequate representation of people of African descent in the judiciary and other areas of the justice system, identify factors that had resulted in their disproportionate arrest, sentencing and incarceration, and take measures to eliminate those factors and adopt crime-prevention strategies and programmes that included alternatives to incarceration.

Preparations for Durban Review Conference

Preparatory Committee session (April–May). The Preparatory Committee for the Durban Review Conference held its first substantive session (Geneva, 21 April–2 May and 26 May) [A/63/112], in accordance with General Assembly resolution 61/149 [YUN

2006, p. 824] and Human Rights Council resolutions 3/2 [ibid.] and 6/23 [YUN 2007, p. 706]. Among the documents before the Committee were the OHCHR questionnaire to Member States [A/CONF.211/PC.2/2], in accordance with a decision adopted at its first session [YUN 2007, p. 706], to facilitate the Durban Review process. The questionnaire consisted of six core questions drafted on the basis of the objectives of the Durban Review Conference [YUN 2007, p. 706], and replies to the questionnaire by States [A/CONF.211/PC.2/CRP.6], the Special Rapporteur on the right to education [A/CONF.211/PC.2/CRP.3], and the Committee on the Elimination of Racial Discrimination [A/CONF.211/PC.2/CRP.5]; proposals by the Committee's Bureau and Chairperson [A/CONF.211/PC.2/4 & Add.1]; a compilation of contributions submitted by UN system specialized agencies and bodies, other intergovernmental organizations, and non-governmental organizations (NGOs) [A/CONF.211/PC.2/CRP.2]; and a compilation of the conclusions and recommendations adopted by the Intergovernmental Working Group on the Effective Implementation of the Durban Declaration and Programme of Action [A/CONF.211/PC.2/CRP.4].

The Committee decided that the Durban Review Conference, which would include a high-level segment, would be convened in Geneva from 20 to 24 April 2009 [A/63/112 (dec. PC.2/13)] under the theme "United against Racism: Dignity and Justice for All" [dec. PC.2/14]. It adopted the provisional agenda of the Conference [dec. PC.2/11], and decided [dec. PC.2/8] on the structure of the draft outcome document, which would be based on the review of progress and assessment on implementation of DDPA [YUN 2001, p. 615] by all stakeholders at all levels, including the assessment of contemporary manifestations of racism, racial discrimination, xenophobia and related intolerance; assessment of the effectiveness of Durban follow-up mechanisms and other UN mechanisms in order to enhance them; promotion of the universal ratification and implementation of the International Convention on the Elimination of All Forms of Racial Discrimination [YUN 1965, p. 433] and consideration of the recommendations on the Committee on the Elimination of Racial Discrimination; identification and sharing of best practices achieved at national, regional and international levels in the fight against racism, racial discrimination, xenophobia and related intolerance; and identification of further measures and initiatives for fostering the implementation of DDPA and addressing challenges and impediments thereto, including in light of developments since its adoption. The Committee also took decisions on the accreditation of NGOs, the participation of observers, an information strategy for the Conference and its logo.

It established an intersessional open-ended intergovernmental working group to follow up on its work, including through reviewing contributions and starting negotiations on the draft outcome document [dec. PC.2/4].

Intersessional working group. The intersessional open-ended working group to follow up the work of the Preparatory Committee held two sessions in Geneva: the first from 26 to 28 May, and the second on 5 and 29 September [A/CONF.211/PC.3/2]. At its first session, the working group had before it a "non-paper" submitted by the Chairperson-Rapporteur, containing an inventory of issues corresponding to the structure of the draft outcome document. The working group established an informal "Group of friends of the Chair" to meet during the intersessional period to facilitate work at the second session. At its second session, the working group considered a working document submitted by the Chairperson-Rapporteur entitled "Certain indicative elements in relation to the outcome document", and a set of draft recommendations on the modalities of the organization of work and negotiations on the draft outcome document at the second session of the Preparatory Committee. On 29 September, the working group adopted recommendations on the organization of work and negotiations on the draft outcome document at the second session of the Preparatory Committee.

Preparatory Committee session (October). At its second substantive session (Geneva, 6–17 October) [A/CONF.211/PC.3/11 & Corr.1], the Preparatory Committee considered the report of the intersessional open-ended working group (above), the draft outcome document of the Durban Review Conference, and the organization of work of the Conference. The Preparatory Committee adopted one resolution and nine decisions. It decided to commence negotiation on and the drafting of the outcome document on the basis of the working document entitled "Certain indicative elements in relation to the outcome document" [A/63/112/Add.1 (res. PC.3/1)]. It invited the High Commissioner for Human Rights to report on the implementation of DDPA [YUN 2001, p. 615] and make proposals for enhancing its implementation, as well as for implementation of relevant decisions and resolutions of the Assembly and the Council [dec. PC.3/103]. The Preparatory Committee established an intersessional open-ended intergovernmental working group to finalize the drafting of the outcome document. The working group would meet on 27 November, and 19–23 January and 6–9 April 2009 [dec. PC.3/108]. It requested the Assembly to allocate resources for the participation of relevant human rights treaty bodies, and thematic special procedures and mechanisms in the Review Conference [dec. PC.3/109]. It also adopted decisions on the accreditation of NGOs.

Intersessional working group. At its first meeting (27 November) [A/CONF.211/PC.4/2], the reconvened intersessional working group reviewed the compilation of proposals submitted by delegations at the Preparatory Committee's second substantive session corresponding to the structure of the draft outcome document [A/CONF.211/PC/WG.2/CRP.1]. The working group agreed that its Chairperson should be entrusted with undertaking a technical review of the proposals with a view to shortening and streamlining the document.

Regional preparatory meetings. Regional preparatory meetings for the Durban Review Conference were held for Latin America and the Caribbean (Brasilia, Brazil, 17–19 June) [A/CONF/211/PC.3/3] and Africa (Abuja, Nigeria, 24–26 August) [A/CONF.211/PC.3/4].

Communications. On 13 September [A/CONF.211/PC.3/10], Pakistan submitted to the High Commissioner for Human Rights the contribution of the Organization of the Islamic Conference to the Review Conference. On 8 October [A/CONF.211/PC.3/5], Sri Lanka submitted the contribution of the Asian region. On 7 October [A/CONF.211/PC.3/6], France submitted the contribution of the EU.

GENERAL ASSEMBLY ACTION

On 24 December [meeting 74], the General Assembly, on the recommendation of the Third (Social, Humanitarian and Cultural) Committee [A/63/428], adopted **resolution 63/242** by recorded vote (109-13-35) [agenda item 62 *(b)*].

Global efforts for the total elimination of racism, racial discrimination, xenophobia and related intolerance and the comprehensive implementation of and follow-up to the Durban Declaration and Programme of Action

The General Assembly,

Recalling its resolution 52/111 of 12 December 1997, in which it decided to convene the World Conference against Racism, Racial Discrimination, Xenophobia and Related Intolerance, and its resolutions 56/266 of 27 March 2002, 57/195 of 18 December 2002, 58/160 of 22 December 2003, 59/177 of 20 December 2004 and 60/144 of 16 December 2005, which guided the comprehensive follow-up to and effective implementation of the World Conference, and in this regard underlining the importance of their full and effective implementation,

Noting its resolution 61/149 of 19 December 2006, in which it decided to convene in 2009 a review conference on the implementation of the Durban Declaration and Programme of Action, hereinafter referred to as the Durban Review Conference, to be conducted within the framework of the General Assembly, and its resolution 62/220 of 22 December 2007,

Noting also, in the above context, the decisions adopted by the Preparatory Committee for the Durban Review Conference at its organizational session and its first and second substantive sessions, including decision PC.1/13 on the objectives of the Durban Review Conference and decision PC.2/8 on the structure of the outcome document,

Noting further all the relevant resolutions and decisions of the Commission on Human Rights and of the Human Rights Council on this subject, and calling for their implementation,

Noting Human Rights Council decision 3/103 of 8 December 2006, by which, heeding the decision and instruction of the 2001 World Conference, the Council established the Ad Hoc Committee of the Human Rights Council on the Elaboration of Complementary Standards,

Reiterating that all human beings are born free and equal in dignity and rights and have the potential to contribute constructively to the development and well-being of their societies, and that any doctrine of racial superiority is scientifically false, morally condemnable, socially unjust and dangerous and must be rejected, together with theories that attempt to determine the existence of separate human races,

Convinced that racism, racial discrimination, xenophobia and related intolerance manifest themselves in a differentiated manner for women and girls and may be among the factors leading to a deterioration in their living conditions, poverty, violence, multiple forms of discrimination and the limitation or denial of their human rights, and recognizing the need to integrate a gender perspective into relevant policies, strategies and programmes of action against racism, racial discrimination, xenophobia and related intolerance in order to address multiple forms of discrimination,

Underlining the primacy of political will, international cooperation and adequate funding at the national, regional and international levels for the successful implementation of the Durban Programme of Action,

Alarmed at the increase in racist violence and xenophobic ideas in many parts of the world, in political circles, in the sphere of public opinion and in society at large, inter alia, as a result of the resurgent activities of associations established on the basis of racist and xenophobic platforms and charters, and the persistent use of those platforms and charters to promote or incite racist ideologies,

Underlining the importance of urgently eliminating continuing and violent trends involving racism and racial discrimination, and conscious that any form of impunity for crimes motivated by racist and xenophobic attitudes plays a role in weakening the rule of law and democracy, tends to encourage the recurrence of such crimes and requires resolute action and cooperation for its eradication,

Welcoming the continued determination of the former United Nations High Commissioner for Human Rights to profile and increase the visibility of the struggle against racism, racial discrimination, xenophobia and related intolerance and the intention of the High Commissioner to make this a cross-cutting issue in the activities and programmes of her Office,

I
General principles

1. *Acknowledges* that no derogation from the prohibition of racial discrimination, genocide, the crime of apartheid or slavery is permitted, as defined in the obligations under the relevant human rights instruments;

2. *Expresses its profound concern about and its unequivocal condemnation* of all forms of racism and racial discrimination, including related acts of racially motivated violence, xenophobia and intolerance, as well as propaganda activities and organizations that attempt to justify or promote racism, racial discrimination, xenophobia and related intolerance in any form;

3. *Expresses deep concern* at the attempts to establish hierarchies among emerging and resurgent forms of racism, racial discrimination, xenophobia and related intolerance, and urges States to adopt measures to address these scourges with the same emphasis and vigour with a view to preventing this practice and protecting victims;

4. *Stresses* that States and international organizations have a responsibility to ensure that measures taken in the struggle against terrorism do not discriminate in purpose or effect on grounds of race, colour, descent or national or ethnic origin, and urges all States to rescind or refrain from all forms of racial profiling;

5. *Recognizes* that States should implement and enforce appropriate and effective legislative, judicial, regulatory and administrative measures to prevent and protect against acts of racism, racial discrimination, xenophobia and related intolerance, thereby contributing to the prevention of human rights violations;

6. *Also recognizes* that racism, racial discrimination, xenophobia and related intolerance occur on the grounds of race, colour, descent or national or ethnic origin and that victims can suffer multiple or aggravated forms of discrimination based on other related grounds, such as sex, language, religion, political or other opinion, social origin, property, birth or other status;

7. *Reaffirms* that any advocacy of national, racial or religious hatred that constitutes incitement to discrimination, hostility or violence shall be prohibited by law;

8. *Emphasizes* that it is the responsibility of States to adopt effective measures to combat criminal acts motivated by racism, racial discrimination, xenophobia and related intolerance, including measures to ensure that such motivations are considered an aggravating factor for the purposes of sentencing, to prevent those crimes from going unpunished and to ensure the rule of law;

9. *Urges* all States to review and, where necessary, revise their immigration laws, policies and practices so that they are free of racial discrimination and compatible with their obligations under international human rights instruments;

10. *Calls upon* all States, in accordance with the commitments undertaken in paragraph 147 of the Durban Programme of Action, to take all necessary measures to combat incitement to violence motivated by racial hatred, including through the misuse of print, audio-visual and electronic media and new communication technologies, and, in collaboration with service providers, to promote the use of such technologies, including the Internet, to contribute to the fight against racism, in conformity with international standards of freedom of expression and taking all necessary measures to guarantee that right;

11. *Encourages* all States to include in their educational curricula and social programmes at all levels, as appropriate, knowledge of and tolerance and respect for all cultures, civilizations, religions, peoples and countries, as well as information on the follow-up to and implementation of the Durban Declaration and Programme of Action;

12. *Stresses* the responsibility of States to mainstream a gender perspective in the design and development of prevention, education and protection measures aimed at the eradication of racism, racial discrimination, xenophobia and related intolerance at all levels, to ensure that they effectively target the distinct situations of women and men;

II

International Convention on the Elimination of All Forms of Racial Discrimination

13. *Reaffirms* that universal adherence to and full implementation of the International Convention on the Elimination of All Forms of Racial Discrimination are of paramount importance for the fight against racism, racial discrimination, xenophobia and related intolerance, including contemporary forms of racism and racial discrimination, and for the promotion of equality and non-discrimination in the world;

14. *Expresses grave concern* at the fact that universal ratification of the Convention was not attained by 2005 in accordance with commitments under the Durban Declaration and Programme of Action, and calls upon those States that have not yet done so to accede to the Convention as a matter of urgency;

15. *Urges*, in the above context, the Office of the United Nations High Commissioner for Human Rights to maintain on its website and issue regular updates on a list of countries that have not yet ratified the Convention and to encourage such countries to ratify it at the earliest;

16. *Expresses its concern* at the serious delays in the submission of overdue reports to the Committee on the Elimination of Racial Discrimination, which impedes the effectiveness of the Committee, makes a strong appeal to all States parties to the Convention to comply with their treaty obligations, and reaffirms the importance of the provision of technical assistance to the requesting countries in the preparation of their reports to the Committee;

17. *Invites* States parties to the Convention to ratify the amendment to article 8 of the Convention on the financing of the Committee, and calls for adequate additional resources from the regular budget of the United Nations to enable the Committee to discharge its mandate fully;

18. *Urges* all States parties to the Convention to intensify their efforts to implement the obligations that they have accepted under article 4 of the Convention, with due regard to the principles of the Universal Declaration of Human Rights and article 5 of the Convention;

19. *Recalls* that the Committee holds that the prohibition of the dissemination of ideas based on racial superiority or racial hatred is compatible with the right to freedom of opinion and expression as outlined in article 19 of the Universal Declaration of Human Rights and in article 5 of the Convention;

20. *Welcomes* the emphasis placed by the Committee on the importance of follow-up to the World Conference and the measures recommended to strengthen the implementation of the Convention as well as the functioning of the Committee;

III

Comprehensive implementation of and follow-up to the Durban Declaration and Programme of Action

21. *Expresses its appreciation* for the commitment of the United Nations High Commissioner for Human Rights to contribute to the successful outcome of the Durban Review Conference, including her appeal to all Member States and other stakeholders to participate in the Durban Review Conference;

22. *Acknowledges* that the outcome of the World Conference against Racism, Racial Discrimination, Xenophobia and Related Intolerance is on an equal footing with the outcomes of all the major United Nations conferences, summits and special sessions in the human rights and social fields;

23. *Also acknowledges* that the World Conference, which was the third world conference against racism, was significantly different from the previous two conferences, as evidenced by the inclusion in its title of two important components relating to contemporary forms of racism, namely, xenophobia and related intolerance;

24. *Emphasizes* that the basic responsibility for effectively combating racism, racial discrimination, xenophobia and related intolerance lies with States, and to this end stresses that States have the primary responsibility to ensure full and effective implementation of all commitments and recommendations contained in the Durban Declaration and Programme of Action;

25. *Reaffirms its commitment* to eliminating all forms of racism, racial discrimination, xenophobia and other forms of related intolerance against indigenous peoples, and in this regard notes the attention paid to the objectives of combating prejudice and eliminating discrimination and promoting tolerance, understanding and good relations among indigenous peoples and all other segments of society in the United Nations Declaration on the Rights of Indigenous Peoples;

26. *Emphasizes* the fundamental and complementary role of national human rights institutions, regional bodies or centres and civil society, working jointly with States towards the achievement of the objectives of the Durban Declaration and Programme of Action;

27. *Welcomes* the steps taken by numerous Governments, in particular the elaboration and implementation of national action plans to combat racism, racial discrimination, xenophobia and related intolerance, and steps taken by national human rights institutions and non-governmental organizations, towards the full implementation of the Durban Declaration and Programme of Action, and affirms this trend as a demonstration of commitment to the elimination of all scourges of racism at the national level;

28. *Calls upon* all States that have not yet elaborated their national action plans on combating racism, racial discrimination, xenophobia and related intolerance to comply with their commitments undertaken at the World Conference;

29. *Calls upon* all States to formulate and implement without delay, at the national, regional and international levels, policies and plans of action to combat racism, racial discrimination, xenophobia and related intolerance, including their gender-based manifestations;

30. *Welcomes* the adoption of the laudable initiative led by the States members of the Caribbean Community and other Member States for the establishment of a permanent memorial at the United Nations to the victims of slavery and the transatlantic slave trade as a contribution towards the fulfilment of paragraph 101 of the Durban Declaration, expresses its appreciation for contributions made to the voluntary fund established in this regard, and urges other countries to contribute to the fund;

31. *Urges* States to support the activities of existing regional bodies or centres that combat racism, racial discrimination, xenophobia and related intolerance in their respective regions, and recommends the establishment of such bodies in all regions where they do not exist;

32. *Recognizes* the fundamental role of civil society in the fight against racism, racial discrimination, xenophobia and related intolerance, in particular in assisting States to develop regulations and strategies, in taking measures and action against such forms of discrimination and through follow-up implementation;

33. *Reaffirms* that the General Assembly is the highest intergovernmental mechanism for the formulation and appraisal of policy on matters relating to the economic, social and related fields, in accordance with Assembly resolution 50/227 of 24 May 1996, and that, together with the Human Rights Council, it shall constitute an intergovernmental process for the comprehensive implementation of and follow-up to the Durban Declaration and Programme of Action, and further reaffirms that the Council shall continue to have a central role in the follow-up to the implementation of the Declaration and Programme of Action within the United Nations system;

34. *Expresses its appreciation* for the continuing work of the mechanisms mandated to follow up the World Conference, bearing in mind the assessment of the effectiveness of those mechanisms to be undertaken at the Durban Review Conference;

35. *Acknowledges* Human Rights Council resolution 9/14 of 24 September 2008, by which the Council decided to extend for three years the mandate of the Working Group of Experts on People of African Descent;

36. *Takes note* of the convening of the first part of the first session of the Ad Hoc Committee on the Elaboration of Complementary Standards from 11 to 21 February 2008, and requests the Ad Hoc Committee to comply with the mandate contained in Human Rights Council decision 3/103;

37. *Acknowledges* the centrality of resource mobilization, effective global partnership and international cooperation in the context of paragraphs 157 and 158 of the Durban Programme of Action for the successful realization of commitments undertaken at the World Conference, and to this end emphasizes the importance of the mandate of the group of independent eminent experts on the implementation of the Durban Declaration and Programme of Action, especially in mobilizing the necessary political will for the successful implementation of the Declaration and Programme of Action;

38. *Requests* the Secretary-General to provide the necessary resources for the effective fulfilment of the mandates of the Intergovernmental Working Group on the Effective Implementation of the Durban Declaration and Pro-

gramme of Action, the Working Group of Experts on People of African Descent, the group of independent eminent experts on the implementation of the Durban Declaration and Programme of Action and the Ad Hoc Committee on the Elaboration of Complementary Standards;

39. *Expresses its concern* at the increasing incidence of racism in various sporting events, while noting with appreciation the efforts made by some governing bodies of the various sporting codes to combat racism, and in this regard invites all international sporting bodies to promote, through their national, regional and international federations, a world of sport free from racism and racial discrimination;

40. *Welcomes*, in this context, the initiative of the Fédération internationale de football association to introduce a visible theme on non-racism in football, and invites the Fédération to continue with this initiative at the 2010 soccer World Cup tournament to be held in South Africa;

41. *Calls upon* those States that have not yet done so to consider signing and ratifying or acceding to the instruments enumerated in paragraph 78 of the Durban Programme of Action, including the International Convention on the Protection of the Rights of All Migrant Workers and Members of Their Families of 1990;

IV

Special Rapporteur on contemporary forms of racism, racial discrimination, xenophobia and related intolerance and follow-up to his visits

42. *Expresses its appreciation* for the work done by the former Special Rapporteur on contemporary forms of racism, racial discrimination, xenophobia and related intolerance, and welcomes Human Rights Council resolution 7/34 of 28 March 2008, by which the Council decided to extend the mandate of the Special Rapporteur for a period of three years;

43. *Takes note with appreciation* of the report of the Special Rapporteur, and encourages Member States and other relevant stakeholders to consider implementing the recommendations contained in his report;

44. *Reiterates its call* to all Member States, intergovernmental organizations, relevant organizations of the United Nations system and non-governmental organizations to cooperate fully with the Special Rapporteur, and calls upon States to consider responding favourably to his requests for visits so as to enable him to fulfil his mandate fully and effectively;

45. *Recognizes with deep concern* the increase in anti-Semitism, Christianophobia and Islamophobia in various parts of the world, as well as the emergence of racial and violent movements based on racism and discriminatory ideas directed against Arab, Christian, Jewish and Muslim communities, as well as all religious communities, communities of people of African descent, communities of people of Asian descent, communities of indigenous people and other communities;

46. *Encourages* closer collaboration between the Special Rapporteur and the Office of the United Nations High Commissioner for Human Rights, in particular the Anti-Discrimination Unit;

47. *Urges* the High Commissioner to provide States, at their request, with advisory services and technical assistance to enable them to implement fully the recommendations of the Special Rapporteur;

48. *Requests* the Secretary-General to provide the Special Rapporteur with all the human and financial assistance necessary to carry out his mandate efficiently, effectively and expeditiously and to enable him to submit a report to the General Assembly at its sixty-fourth session;

49. *Requests* the Special Rapporteur to continue giving particular attention to the negative impact of racism, racial discrimination, xenophobia and related intolerance on the full enjoyment of civil, cultural, economic, political and social rights by national or ethnic, religious and linguistic minorities, immigrant populations, asylum-seekers and refugees;

50. *Invites* Member States to demonstrate greater commitment to fighting racism in sport by conducting educational and awareness-raising activities and by strongly condemning the perpetrators of racist incidents, in cooperation with national and international sports organizations;

V

Convening of the Durban Review Conference

51. *Welcomes* the reports of the Preparatory Committee for the Durban Review Conference on its organizational session and its first and second substantive sessions, and endorses the decisions contained therein;

52. *Calls upon* all Member States to participate in the Durban Review Conference;

53. *Expresses its appreciation* for the convening of the regional preparatory meeting for the Durban Review Conference for Latin America and the Caribbean in Brasilia from 17 to 19 June 2008 and the regional preparatory meeting for Africa in Abuja from 24 to 26 August 2008;

54. *Takes note* of the contributions by Member States, regional groups and all other relevant stakeholders consistent with the objectives of the Durban Review Conference, in accordance with decision PC.1/10 of the Preparatory Committee;

55. *Reaffirms* that the Durban Review Conference will be undertaken on the basis of and with full respect for the Durban Declaration and Programme of Action and that there will be no renegotiation of the existing agreements therein, and that the issues raised will be in conformity with the contents of the Declaration and Programme of Action;

56. *Requests* the Secretary-General and the United Nations High Commissioner for Human Rights to undertake initiatives to encourage contributions to the voluntary fund established pursuant to decision PC.1/12 of the Preparatory Committee, including the decision to appeal for contributions from extrabudgetary resources to cover the costs of participation of representatives of the least developed countries in the Durban Review Conference;

VI

General

57. *Recommends* that the meetings of the Human Rights Council focusing on the follow-up to the World Conference and the implementation of the Durban Declaration and Programme of Action be scheduled in a manner that allows broad participation and that avoids overlap with the meetings devoted to the consideration of this item in the General Assembly;

58. *Requests* the Secretary-General to submit a report with recommendations on the implementation of the present resolution to the General Assembly at its sixty-fourth session;

59. *Decides* to remain seized of this important matter at its sixty-fourth session under the item entitled "Elimination of racism, racial discrimination, xenophobia and related intolerance".

RECORDED VOTE ON RESOLUTION 63/242:

In favour: Afghanistan, Algeria, Angola, Antigua and Barbuda, Argentina, Azerbaijan, Bahrain, Bangladesh, Barbados, Belarus, Benin, Bolivia, Botswana, Brazil, Brunei Darussalam, Burkina Faso, Burundi, Cambodia, Cameroon, Chile, China, Colombia, Congo, Costa Rica, Côte d'Ivoire, Cuba, Democratic People's Republic of Korea, Djibouti, Dominican Republic, Ecuador, Egypt, Eritrea, Ethiopia, Gambia, Ghana, Grenada, Guatemala, Guinea-Bissau, Honduras, Iceland, India, Indonesia, Iran, Iraq, Jamaica, Jordan, Kazakhstan, Kenya, Kuwait, Kyrgyzstan, Lao People's Democratic Republic, Lebanon, Lesotho, Libyan Arab Jamahiriya, Liechtenstein, Madagascar, Malawi, Malaysia, Maldives, Mali, Mauritania, Mauritius, Mexico, Mongolia, Morocco, Mozambique, Myanmar, Namibia, Nepal, Nicaragua, Niger, Nigeria, Norway, Oman, Pakistan, Panama, Paraguay, Peru, Philippines, Qatar, Russian Federation, Samoa, Saudi Arabia, Senegal, Singapore, Solomon Islands, South Africa, Sri Lanka, Sudan, Swaziland, Switzerland, Syrian Arab Republic, Tajikistan, Thailand, Timor-Leste, Togo, Trinidad and Tobago, Tunisia, Turkey, Uganda, United Arab Emirates, United Republic of Tanzania, Uruguay, Uzbekistan, Venezuela, Viet Nam, Yemen, Zambia, Zimbabwe.

Against: Australia, Canada, Czech Republic, Denmark, Israel, Marshall Islands, Netherlands, New Zealand, Palau, Poland, Romania, United Kingdom, United States.

Abstaining: Albania, Armenia, Austria, Belgium, Bosnia and Herzegovina, Bulgaria, Croatia, Cyprus, Estonia, Finland, France, Georgia, Germany, Greece, Hungary, Ireland, Italy, Japan, Latvia, Lithuania, Luxembourg, Malta, Moldova, Monaco, Montenegro, Portugal, Republic of Korea, San Marino, Serbia, Slovakia, Slovenia, Spain, Sweden, The former Yugoslav Republic of Macedonia, Ukraine.

Contemporary forms of racism

In a February report [A/HRC/7/19], submitted pursuant to a Human Rights Council request [YUN 2007, p. 662], the Special Rapporteur on contemporary forms of racism, racial discrimination, xenophobia and related intolerance stated that efforts to combat those phenomena were encountering major challenges, such as the erosion of the political will, as shown by the non-implementation of the Durban Programme of Action; the resurgence of racist and xenophobic violence; the political trivialization of racism and xenophobia, demonstrated by the spread of racist and xenophobic political platforms and their implementation through government alliances with democratic parties; the legitimization of racist and xenophobic discourse through ethnic or racial interpretation of social and political problems and immigration issues; the increase in racial and religious hatred and intolerance, reflected in anti-Semitism and Christianophobia and, more especially, Islamophobia; and the increasing importance in identity constructs of a rejection of diversity and resistance to multiculturalism. To reverse those trends, the Special Rapporteur promoted the development of a dual strategy: political and legal, aimed at strengthening the political will of Governments to combat racism and xenophobia and acquire the legal and administrative instruments for that purpose; and cultural, intellectual and ethical, targeting the root causes of those trends, in particular the value systems which legitimized them, the identity constructs supporting them, and the rejection of diversity and multiculturalism which sustained them. The report also dealt with discrimination on the grounds of caste in Asia and Africa.

The Special Rapporteur called on the Council to encourage Member States to adopt legislation against racism, racial discrimination and xenophobia; promote the fight against the defamation of religion, anti-Semitism, Christianophobia and Islamophobia; fight racial and religious hatred by maintaining a careful balance between the defence of secularism and respect for religious freedom; and adopt an approach to questions relating to immigration, asylum and the situation of foreigners and minorities on the basis of international law. He recommended the establishment within OHCHR of a permanent centre for monitoring racist phenomena that would report to the Council and the General Assembly. The Rapporteur's reports and recommendations should be submitted to all bodies involved in the Durban Review Conference and to regional meetings held as part of that process.

An addendum to the report [A/HRC/7/19/Add.1] summarized communications sent to 12 Governments between 1 May and 31 December 2007 on cases of racism and related phenomena and replies received thereto.

As requested by the Human Rights Council in March (see p. 782), the Special Rapporteur in September submitted a report [A/HRC/9/12] on the manifestations of defamation of religions and, in particular, on the serious implications of Islamophobia for the enjoyment of all rights. The Rapporteur stressed that the report did not imply the establishment of any hierarchy in the forms of discrimination to which different religions were subject, and strategies to combat anti-Semitism, Christianophobia and Islamophobia should treat those phobias in the same way and avoid establishing any priorities in combating discrimination. The Rapporteur stressed that political and ideological polarization on the question of the defamation of religions was artificial. Analysis of international, regional and national human rights instruments showed that provisions against inducement to racial or religious hatred were almost universal. However, shifting the debate away from the sociological concepts of defamation of religions towards the legal concept of incitement to national, racial or religious hatred was not only a way of refocusing on human rights but also a strategy for depolarizing and depoliticizing the discussion. He drew attention to recommendations made in previous reports to the Council for promoting measures to combat racism, racial discrimination and xenophobia.

The Special Rapporteur recommended that the Council invite Member States to accord equal treatment to combating the defamation of religions, having particular regard to: the need to avoid establishing any hierarchy in the different manifestations of discrimination, even if they varied in nature and degree depending on the context; the deep historical and cultural roots of all forms of defamation of religions and the corresponding need to combine legal measures with an intellectual, cultural and ethical approach that took account of the processes, mechanisms and representations at the origin of those manifestations of discrimination over time; the link between the different spiritual, historical and cultural forms of religious discrimination and the universal nature of their underlying causes; the need to create conditions conducive to social harmony, peace, respect for human rights and development, and to combat all forms of racism, xenophobia and discrimination relating to religious and spiritual traditions; and the need to renew the approach to defamation of religions by focusing on the principles embodied in international human rights instruments.

The Special Rapporteur visited Mauritania (20–24 January) [A/HRC/11/36/Add.2] to contribute to the elimination—in the context of the drive towards democracy—of the historical legacy of ethnic discrimination that had long characterized that society.

He concluded that while there were no manifestations of legally endorsed or State-approved racism in the country, the society had been marked by continuing ethnic and racial discriminatory practices rooted in cultural traditions and pervasively present in attitudes, social structures and State institutions, in particular the armed forces and the justice system. Some features of Mauritanian society had given substance and depth to such discrimination over time, including the central role of traditional slavery, the entrenchment of the caste system, and the use of ethnicity as a political tool, such as language policies that had contributed to the polarization of various communities. The pervasiveness of a culture of racism and discrimination was the greatest obstacle to the establishment of democracy and respect for human rights. Mauritania faced three major challenges: construction of a democratic, egalitarian and participatory society; eradication of discriminatory cultural traditions; and the correction of political, economic and social inequalities caused by discrimination.

The Special Rapporteur's recommendations to the authorities included: consistent communication to the public of a clear political will to combat all forms of racism and discrimination and to foster a democratic, egalitarian and participatory multiculturalism; recognition that the eradication of racism and discrimination was the key to the establishment of sustainable democracy; the adoption of comprehensive legislation against all forms of discrimination and recognition in the Constitution of the multicultural and multi-ethnic character of the society and of its main ethnic groups and communities, as well as their languages and cultures; the insertion of provisions on racial and ethnic discrimination in the criminal code; the creation of an independent special commission tasked with reporting on the status, root causes, manifestations and consequences of discrimination and with establishing an independent national institution responsible for upholding human rights, combating discrimination and promoting multiculturalism; and the adoption of a strategy aimed at eradicating the underlying causes of the culture of discrimination and building a spirit of partnership.

The Special Rapporteur visited the United States (19 May–6 June) [A/HRC/11/36/Add.3], where he had extensive meetings with State institutions, including the Supreme Court, civil society organizations, minority communities and victims of racism. He visited Washington, D.C., New York, Chicago, Omaha, Los Angeles, New Orleans, the Louisiana and Mississippi Gulf Coast, Miami and San Juan (Puerto Rico). He formulated several recommendations, including that: Congress establish a bipartisan commission to evaluate progress and failures in the fight against racism and the ongoing process of resegregation, particularly in housing and education, and to find responses for checking those trends; the Federal Government reassess legislation on racism and related phenomena in view of the main guidelines for addressing the overlapping nature of poverty and race or ethnicity, and linking the fight against racism to the construction of a democratic, egalitarian and interactive multiculturalism; and the Government intensify efforts to enforce federal civil rights laws, and clarify to law enforcement officials the obligation of equal treatment and the prohibition of racial profiling. To monitor trends regarding racial profiling and treatment of minorities by law enforcement officials, federal, state and local governments should collect data about police stops and searches, as well as instances of police abuse. Independent oversight bodies should be established within police agencies, with real authority to investigate complaints of racism. Mandatory minimum sentences should be reviewed to assess disproportionate impact on racial or ethnic minorities. The Government should increase funding for programmes and investigations to assess discrimination, particularly in the areas of housing and employment.

Human Rights Council action. On 28 March [A/63/53 (res. 7/34)], the Human Rights Council extended the mandate of the Special Rapporteur for a three-year period, and requested the Rapporteur to report regularly to the Council and the General Assembly.

On 18 June, the Council appointed Githu Muigai (Kenya) as Special Rapporteur.

Report by new Special Rapporteur. Pursuant to General Assembly resolution 62/220 [YUN 2007, p. 708], the Secretary-General, in August, transmitted to the Assembly the interim report [A/63/339] of the new Special Rapporteur, who outlined the main objectives for fulfilling his mandate. The International Convention on the Elimination of All Forms of Racial Discrimination, DDPA and other international instruments would remain the central framework for implementing the mandate. In light of the emphasis in DDPA on victim-orientation in anti-racism policies, that approach would be further strengthened in the discharge of the mandate, in cooperation with civil society organizations. The Rapporteur attached central importance to cooperation and engagement with Member States, including engaging with Governments to share expertise and advocate the implementation of anti-racism policies, while continuing to monitor and report on human rights violations. In planning and undertaking country visits, the Rapporteur would take into account the underlying principle that racism was a universal problem, and would strive to achieve geographical balance and address a wide range of situations. The Rapporteur noted the Council's request for Member States to cooperate fully with him in the discharge of his mandate, including by responding promptly to communications and providing information. He urged Governments to respond favourably to his requests to visit their countries.

Communication. On 13 March [A/HRC/7/G/10], the Dominican Republic transmitted to OHCHR its comments on the joint report of the Special Rapporteur on contemporary forms of racism, racial discrimination, xenophobia and related intolerance and the independent expert on minority issues on their 2007 mission to the country [YUN 2007, p. 715].

GENERAL ASSEMBLY ACTION

On 18 December [meeting 70], the General Assembly, on the recommendation of the Third Committee [A/63/428], adopted **resolution 63/162** by recorded vote (129-2-54) [agenda item 62 *(a)*].

Inadmissibility of certain practices that contribute to fuelling contemporary forms of racism, racial discrimination, xenophobia and related intolerance

The General Assembly,

Guided by the Charter of the United Nations, the Universal Declaration of Human Rights, the International Covenant on Civil and Political Rights, the International Convention on the Elimination of All Forms of Racial Discrimination and other relevant human rights instruments,

Recalling the provisions of Commission on Human Rights resolutions 2004/16 of 16 April 2004 and 2005/5 of 14 April 2005, and relevant Human Rights Council resolutions, in particular resolution 7/34 of 28 March 2008,as well as General Assembly resolutions 60/143 of 16 December 2005, 61/147 of 19 December 2006 and 62/142 of 18 December 2007 on this issue and resolutions 61/149 of 19 December 2006 and 62/220 of 22 December 2007, both entitled "Global efforts for the total elimination of racism, racial discrimination, xenophobia and related intolerance and the comprehensive implementation of and follow-up to the Durban Declaration and Programme of Action",

Recalling also the Charter of the Nuremberg Tribunal and the Judgement of the Tribunal, which recognized, inter alia, the SS organization and all its integral parts, including the Waffen SS, as criminal and declared it responsible for many war crimes and crimes against humanity,

Recalling further the relevant provisions of the Durban Declaration and Programme of Action adopted by the World Conference against Racism, Racial Discrimination, Xenophobia and Related Intolerance on 8 September 2001, in particular paragraph 2 of the Declaration and paragraph 86 of the Programme of Action,

Recalling equally the study undertaken by the Special Rapporteur on contemporary forms of racism, racial discrimination, xenophobia and related intolerance, and taking note of his report,

Alarmed, in this regard, at the spread in many parts of the world of various extremist political parties, movements and groups, including neo-Nazis and skinhead groups,

1. *Reaffirms* the provision of the Durban Declaration in which States condemned the persistence and resurgence of neo-Nazism, neo-Fascism and violent nationalist ideologies based on racial and national prejudice and stated that those phenomena could never be justified in any instance or in any circumstances;

2. *Expresses deep concern* about the glorification of the Nazi movement and former members of the Waffen SS organization, including by erecting monuments and memorials and holding public demonstrations in the name of the glorification of the Nazi past, the Nazi movement and neo-Nazism, as well as by declaring or attempting to declare such members and those who fought against the anti-Hitler coalition and collaborated with the Nazi movement as participants in national liberation movements;

3. *Expresses concern* at recurring attempts to desecrate or demolish monuments erected in remembrance of those who fought against Nazism during the Second World War, as well as to unlawfully exhume or remove the remains of such persons, and urges States in this regard to fully comply with their relevant obligations, inter alia, under article 34 of Additional Protocol I to the Geneva Conventions of 1949;

4. *Notes with concern* the increase in the number of racist incidents in several countries and the rise of skinhead groups, which have been responsible for many of these incidents, as well as the resurgence of racist and xenophobic violence targeting members of ethnic, religious or cultural communities and national minorities, as observed by the

Special Rapporteur on contemporary forms of racism, racial discrimination, xenophobia and related intolerance in his latest report;

5. *Reaffirms* that such acts may be qualified to fall within the scope of activities described in article 4 of the International Convention on the Elimination of All Forms of Racial Discrimination, and that they may represent a clear and manifest abuse of the rights to freedom of peaceful assembly and of association as well as the rights to freedom of opinion and expression within the meaning of those rights as guaranteed by the Universal Declaration of Human Rights, the International Covenant on Civil and Political Rights and the International Convention on the Elimination of All Forms of Racial Discrimination;

6. *Stresses* that the practices described above do injustice to the memory of the countless victims of crimes against humanity committed in the Second World War, in particular those committed by the SS organization and those who fought against the anti-Hitler coalition or collaborated with the Nazi movement, and poison the minds of young people, and that those practices are incompatible with the obligations of States Members of the United Nations under its Charter and are incompatible with the goals and principles of the Organization;

7. *Also stresses* that such practices fuel contemporary forms of racism, racial discrimination, xenophobia and related intolerance and contribute to the spread and multiplication of various extremist political parties, movements and groups, including neo-Nazis and skinhead groups;

8. *Emphasizes* the need to take the necessary measures to put an end to the practices described above, and calls upon States to take more effective measures in accordance with international human rights law to combat those phenomena and the extremist movements, which pose a real threat to democratic values;

9. *Reaffirms* that, according to article 4 of the International Convention on the Elimination of All Forms of Racial Discrimination, States parties to that instrument are, inter alia, under the obligation:

(*a*) To condemn all propaganda and all organizations that are based on ideas of racial superiority or that attempt to justify or promote racial hatred and discrimination in any form;

(*b*) To undertake to adopt immediate and positive measures designed to eradicate all incitement to, or acts of, such discrimination with due regard to the principles embodied in the Universal Declaration of Human Rights and the rights expressly set forth in article 5 of the Convention;

(*c*) To declare as an offence punishable by law all dissemination of ideas based on racial superiority or hatred, and incitement to racial discrimination, as well as all acts of violence or incitement to such acts against any race or group of persons of another colour or ethnic origin, and also the provision of any assistance to racist activities, including the financing thereof;

(*d*) To declare illegal and prohibit organizations and organized and all other propaganda activities that promote and incite racial discrimination and to recognize participation in such organizations or activities as an offence punishable by law;

(*e*) To prohibit public authorities or public institutions, national or local, from promoting or inciting racial discrimination;

10. *Encourages* those States that have made reservations to article 4 of the International Convention on the Elimination of All Forms of Racial Discrimination to give serious consideration to withdrawing such reservations as a matter of priority;

11. *Recalls* the request of the Commission on Human Rights in its resolution 2005/5 that the Special Rapporteur continue to reflect on this issue, make relevant recommendations in his future reports and seek and take into account in this regard the views of Governments and non-governmental organizations;

12. *Requests* the Special Rapporteur to prepare, within existing resources, for submission to the General Assembly at its sixty-fourth session and the Human Rights Council, reports on the implementation of the present resolution based on the views collected in accordance with the request of the Commission on Human Rights, as recalled by the Assembly in paragraph 11 above;

13. *Urges* Governments and non-governmental organizations to cooperate fully with the Special Rapporteur in the exercise of the aforementioned tasks;

14. *Decides* to remain seized of the issue.

RECORDED VOTE ON RESOLUTION 63/162:

In favour: Afghanistan, Algeria, Angola, Antigua and Barbuda, Argentina, Armenia, Azerbaijan, Bahamas, Bahrain, Bangladesh, Barbados, Belarus, Belize, Benin, Bhutan, Bolivia, Botswana, Brazil, Brunei Darussalam, Burkina Faso, Burundi, Cambodia, Cameroon, Cape Verde, Central African Republic, Chile, China, Colombia, Comoros, Congo, Costa Rica, Côte d'Ivoire, Cuba, Democratic People's Republic of Korea, Djibouti, Dominica, Dominican Republic, Ecuador, Egypt, El Salvador, Eritrea, Ethiopia, Gabon, Gambia, Ghana, Grenada, Guatemala, Guinea, Guyana, Haiti, Honduras, India, Indonesia, Iran, Iraq, Israel, Jamaica, Jordan, Kazakhstan, Kenya, Kuwait, Kyrgyzstan, Lao People's Democratic Republic, Lebanon, Lesotho, Liberia, Libyan Arab Jamahiriya, Madagascar, Malawi, Malaysia, Maldives, Mali, Mauritania, Mauritius, Mexico, Mongolia, Morocco, Mozambique, Myanmar, Namibia, Nepal, Nicaragua, Niger, Nigeria, Oman, Pakistan, Paraguay, Peru, Philippines, Qatar, Russian Federation, Rwanda, Saint Kitts and Nevis, Saint Lucia, Saint Vincent and the Grenadines, Sao Tome and Principe, Saudi Arabia, Senegal, Serbia, Sierra Leone, Singapore, Solomon Islands, Somalia, South Africa, Sri Lanka, Sudan, Suriname, Swaziland, Syrian Arab Republic, Tajikistan, Thailand, Timor-Leste, Togo, Trinidad and Tobago, Tunisia, Turkey, Turkmenistan, Tuvalu, Uganda, United Arab Emirates, United Republic of Tanzania, Uruguay, Uzbekistan, Vanuatu, Venezuela, Viet Nam, Yemen, Zambia, Zimbabwe.

Against: Marshall Islands, United States.

Abstaining: Albania, Andorra, Australia, Austria, Belgium, Bosnia and Herzegovina, Bulgaria, Canada, Croatia, Cyprus, Czech Republic, Denmark, Estonia, Fiji, Finland, France, Georgia, Germany, Greece, Guinea-Bissau, Hungary, Iceland, Ireland, Italy, Japan, Latvia, Liechtenstein, Lithuania, Luxembourg, Malta, Monaco, Moldova, Montenegro, Netherlands, New Zealand, Norway, Palau, Panama, Papua New Guinea, Poland, Portugal, Republic of Korea, Romania, Samoa, San Marino, Slovakia, Slovenia, Spain, Sweden, Switzerland, The former Yugoslav Republic of Macedonia, Tonga, Ukraine, United Kingdom.

Civil and political rights

Right to nationality

Human Rights Council action. On 27 March [A/63/53 (res. 7/10)], the Human Rights Council called on States to refrain from enacting or maintaining legislation that would arbitrarily deprive persons of their nationality on grounds of race, colour, gender, religion, political opinion or national or ethnic origin. It urged States to adopt and implement nationality legislation with a view to avoiding statelessness, in particular by preventing arbitrary deprivation of nationality and statelessness as a result of State succession. States were also urged to ensure that an effective remedy was available to persons who had been arbitrarily deprived of their nationality. The Secretary-General was requested to collect information on human rights and arbitrary deprivation of nationality from all relevant sources and to make it available to the Council at its tenth (2009) session.

Protection of migrants

Reports of Special Rapporteur. In a February report to the Human Rights Council [A/HRC/7/12], the Special Rapporteur on the human rights of migrants, Jorge Bustamante (Mexico), summarized his activities, including visits requested and undertaken, and communications and replies received. The report highlighted some key challenges with regard to the criminalization of irregular migration, and outlined elements for State responsibility with regard to the protection of irregular migrants. The Special Rapporteur drew attention to the increasing criminalization of irregular migration and the abuses committed as a result of persistent anti-immigration sentiments, often reflected in restrictive policies and institutional frameworks for managing migratory flows. He had received reports of the criminal justice practices used by States to combat irregular migration, including greater criminalization of migration offences and cross-national collaboration by police and other authorities resulting in violations against migrants. Within the two broad categories of the externalization of migration control policies and the criminalization of labour migration, he identified three sub-issues for examination: violations against irregular migrants pertaining to interception and rescue at sea, detention and expulsion and smuggling and trafficking. The Special Rapporteur emphasized that the report was not an excuse for irregular migration but underscored the importance of States to adhere to international human rights standards during engagement with all migrants.

The Special Rapporteur encouraged States to view irregular migration as an administrative offence, reversing the trend toward greater criminalization, and to incorporate the applicable human rights framework into their bilateral and regional arrangements for managing migration flows and protecting national security interests, as well as to harmonize their laws and policies with international human rights norms. At the core of immigration policies should be the protection of migrants, regardless of their status or mode of entry. He proposed a number of recommendations for the formation or reform of regional and bilateral cooperation mechanisms and agreements, as well as the enhancement of national training and analysis programmes and policy measures.

An addendum to the report [A/HRC/7/12/Add.1] summarized 25 communications the Special Rapporteur had sent to 22 Governments during 2007 and responses thereto. Fourteen of those communications were urgent appeals. Only 12 communications received a response.

After visiting Mexico (9–15 March) [A/HRC/11/7/Add.2], the Special Rapporteur highlighted the legal framework pertaining to the human rights of migrants at the federal level, underscoring gaps in implementation of laws and noting problematic policies. He examined groups of the Mexican migrant phenomenon and drew attention to challenges such as the detention of migrants, assistance to migrants, organized crime networks and impunity among governmental and law enforcement officials and assistance to migrants. He concluded that Mexico's progress in implementing programmes to protect the rights of migrants was evident, in terms of both the Government's capacity and willingness. The authorities had made notable efforts to improve detention centres, especially overcrowding, training of border officials, return, and protection of children. Nevertheless, many issues still warranted attention and resources. The Rapporteur recommended that Mexico: review its law regarding expulsion and formulate policies in line with international human rights standards; classify illegal entry as an administrative rather than a criminal offence; take measures against migrant child labour practices; and continue efforts to professionalize and train the police and border control officials. Mexico should improve bilateral arrangements with countries of origin regarding the return of undocumented migrants, and notify the consular or diplomatic authorities of the State of origin without delay whenever a migrant was arrested or detained. The UN Resident Coordinator, the International Organization for Migration, OHCHR and specialized agencies should review UN system programmes for the protection of migrants and integrate them for a more comprehensive approach.

During his visit to Guatemala (24–28 March) [A/HRC/11/7/Add.3], a country of origin, destination and especially transit, the Special Rapporteur noted the Government's interest in addressing some of the problems related to the human rights of migrants, but expressed concern about gaps and ambiguities in the legislative framework on migration. Those gaps led to abuses and violations of the rights of the migrant population, most of which went unreported. He noted information about cases in which, during the interception and deportation of migrants from the United States to Guatemala, various abuses were committed, including ill-treatment, and lack of medical assistance in detention centres, of information on the deportation and of communication with consular representatives. He also noted procedures for deporting undocumented migrants, which lasted longer than necessary, particularly for migrants from countries outside Central America, as their countries of origin had no diplomatic representation in Guatemala.

In his recommendations, the Special Rapporteur invited the Government to conclude regional multilateral agreements among countries of origin and destination, strengthening protection of the rights of migrants. He called upon Guatemala to bring legislation in line with international standards, step up the struggle against corruption and impunity, bring proceedings against those responsible and ensure the execution of sentences, in cooperation with the International Commission against Impunity in Guatemala.

Report of Secretary-General. In response to General Assembly resolution 62/156 [YUN 2007, p. 719], the Secretary-General submitted an August report [A/63/287] summarizing information received from 12 Governments on the implementation of resolutions 62/156 and 61/165 [YUN 2006, p. 837] on the protection of migrants. The Secretary-General also reported on the status of the International Convention on the Protection of the Rights of All Migrant Workers and Members of Their Families [YUN 1990, p. 594], the activities of the Special Rapporteur on the human rights of migrants and the Committee on the Protection of the Rights of All Migrant Workers and Members of Their Families. Regretting the lack of precise statistics on migration flows and other migration-related issues, he encouraged States to create a comprehensive database on labour demand in host countries. He also encouraged States to undertake information campaigns addressed to migrants aimed at clarifying their rights and opportunities and stressing the dangers of undocumented migration.

The General Assembly took note of the Secretary-General's report on 18 December **(decision 63/534)**.

Human Rights Council action. On 18 June [A/63/53 (res. 8/10)], the Human Rights Council extended the mandate of the Special Rapporteur for a three-year period. The Council encouraged Governments to invite the Rapporteur to visit their countries and encouraged them to cooperate fully with the Rapporteur.

On 24 September [A/63/53/Add.1 (res. 9/5)], the Council reaffirmed the duty of States to promote and protect the human rights of all migrants, regardless of their immigration status; urged that they adopt effective measures to put an end to arbitrary arrest and detention of migrants and prevent and punish illegal deprivation of the liberty of migrants; emphasized the importance of protecting vulnerable groups, especially migrant children; and stressed the importance of international, regional and bilateral cooperation in the protection of the rights of migrants.

GENERAL ASSEMBLY ACTION

On 18 December [meeting 70], the General Assembly, on the recommendation of the Third Committee [A/63/430], adopted **resolution 63/184** without vote [agenda item 64 *(b)*].

Protection of migrants

The General Assembly,

Recalling all its previous resolutions on the protection of migrants, the most recent of which is resolution 62/156 of 18 December 2007, and recalling also Human Rights Council resolution 9/5 of 24 September 2008,

Reaffirming, in the year of its sixtieth anniversary, the Universal Declaration of Human Rights, which proclaims that all human beings are born free and equal in dignity and rights and that everyone is entitled to all the rights and freedoms set out therein, without distinction of any kind, in particular as to race, colour or national origin,

Reaffirming also that everyone has the right to freedom of movement and residence within the borders of each State, and to leave any country, including his own, and return to his country,

Recalling the International Covenant on Civil and Political Rights and the International Covenant on Economic, Social and Cultural Rights, the Convention against Torture and Other Cruel, Inhuman or Degrading Treatment or Punishment, the Convention on the Elimination of All Forms of Discrimination against Women, the Convention on the Rights of the Child, the International Convention on the Elimination of All Forms of Racial Discrimination, the Vienna Convention on Consular Relations and the International Convention on the Protection of the Rights of All Migrant Workers and Members of Their Families,

Recalling also the provisions concerning migrants contained in the outcomes of all major United Nations conferences and summits,

Underlining the importance of the Human Rights Council in promoting respect for the protection of the human rights and fundamental freedoms of all, including migrants,

Taking note of advisory opinion OC-16/99 of 1 October 1999 on the Right to Information on Consular Assistance in the Framework of the Guarantees of the Due Process of Law and advisory opinion OC-18/03 of 17 September 2003

on the Juridical Condition and Rights of Undocumented Migrants, issued by the Inter-American Court of Human Rights,

Taking note also of the Judgment of the International Court of Justice of 31 March 2004 in the case concerning *Avena and Other Mexican Nationals*, and recalling the obligations of States reaffirmed therein,

Recalling the High-level Dialogue on International Migration and Development, held in New York on 14 and 15 September 2006 for the purpose of discussing the multidimensional aspects of international migration and development, which recognized the relationship between international migration, development and human rights,

Noting the second meeting of the Global Forum on Migration and Development, organized and hosted by the Government of the Philippines from 27 to 30 October 2008, and recognizing the inclusion of a discussion on migration, development and human rights as one of the steps to address the multidimensional nature of international migration,

Recalling its resolution 62/270 of 20 June 2008 on the Global Forum on Migration and Development, as adopted, in which, inter alia, it recognized that exchanges of information and expertise, consultation and closer cooperation between the Global Forum and the United Nations could have a positive impact,

Noting the International Meeting on the Protection of the Rights of Children in the Context of International Migration, held in Mexico City on 30 September and 1 October 2008, and co-organized by the Office of the United Nations High Commissioner for Human Rights,

Emphasizing the global character of the migratory phenomenon, the importance of international, regional and bilateral cooperation and dialogue in this regard, as appropriate, and the need to protect the human rights of migrants, particularly at a time in which migration flows have increased in the globalized economy and take place in a context of new security concerns,

Bearing in mind that policies and initiatives on the issue of migration, including those that refer to the orderly management of migration, should promote holistic approaches that take into account the causes and consequences of the phenomenon, as well as full respect for the human rights and fundamental freedoms of migrants,

Noting that many migrant women are employed in the informal economy and in less skilled work compared with that of men, which puts those women at greater risk of abuse and exploitation,

Concerned about the large and growing number of migrants, especially women and children, who place themselves in a vulnerable situation by attempting to cross international borders without the required travel documents, and recognizing the obligation of States to respect the human rights of those migrants,

Stressing the importance of regulations and laws regarding irregular migration being in accordance with the obligations of States under international law, including international human rights law,

Stressing also that penalties and the treatment given to irregular migrants should be commensurate with their infraction,

Recognizing the importance of having a comprehensive and balanced approach to international migration, and bearing in mind that migration enriches the economical, political, social and cultural fabric of States and the historical and cultural ties that exist among some regions,

Underlining the importance for States, in cooperation with non-governmental organizations, to undertake information campaigns aimed at clarifying opportunities, limitations and rights in the event of migration, so as to enable everyone to make informed decisions and to prevent them from utilizing dangerous means to cross international borders,

1. *Calls upon* States to promote and protect effectively the human rights and fundamental freedoms of all migrants, regardless of their migration status, especially those of women and children, and to address international migration through international, regional or bilateral cooperation and dialogue and through a comprehensive and balanced approach, recognizing the roles and responsibilities of countries of origin, transit and destination in promoting and protecting the human rights of all migrants, and avoiding approaches that might aggravate their vulnerability;

2. *Also calls upon* States to ensure that their laws and policies, including in the areas of counter-terrorism and combating transnational organized crime such as trafficking in persons and smuggling of migrants, fully respect the human rights of migrants;

3. *Calls upon* States that have not done so to consider signing and ratifying or acceding to the International Convention on the Protection of the Rights of All Migrant Workers and Members of Their Families as a matter of priority, and requests the Secretary-General to continue his efforts to raise awareness of and promote the Convention;

4. *Urges* States parties to the United Nations Convention against Transnational Organized Crime and supplementing protocols thereto, namely, the Protocol against the Smuggling of Migrants by Land, Sea and Air and the Protocol to Prevent, Suppress and Punish Trafficking in Persons, Especially Women and Children, to implement them fully, and calls upon States that have not done so to consider ratifying or acceding to them as a matter of priority;

5. *Takes note* of the report of the Committee on the Protection of the Rights of All Migrant Workers and Members of Their Families on its seventh and eighth sessions;

6. *Requests* all States, international organizations and relevant stakeholders to take into account in their policies and initiatives on migration issues the global character of the migratory phenomenon and to give due consideration to international, regional and bilateral cooperation in this field, including by undertaking dialogues on migration that include countries of origin, destination and transit, as well as civil society, including migrants, with a view to addressing, in a comprehensive manner, inter alia, its causes and consequences and the challenge of undocumented or irregular migration, granting priority to the protection of the human rights of migrants;

7. *Expresses concern* about legislation and measures adopted by some States that may restrict the human rights and fundamental freedoms of migrants, and reaffirms that, when exercising their sovereign right to enact and implement migratory and border security measures, States have

the duty to comply with their obligations under international law, including international human rights law, in order to ensure full respect for the human rights of migrants;

8. *Takes note with appreciation* of the measures adopted by some States to reduce detention periods for irregular migrants in the application of domestic regulations and laws regarding irregular migration;

9. *Calls upon* all States to respect the human rights and the inherent dignity of migrants and to put an end to arbitrary arrest and detention and, where necessary, to review detention periods in order to avoid excessive detention of irregular migrants, and to adopt, where applicable, alternative measures to detention;

10. *Urges* all States to adopt effective measures to prevent and punish any form of illegal deprivation of liberty of migrants by individuals or groups;

11. *Requests* States to adopt concrete measures to prevent the violation of the human rights of migrants while in transit, including in ports and airports and at borders and migration checkpoints, to train public officials who work in those facilities and in border areas to treat migrants respectfully and in accordance with the law, and to prosecute, in conformity with applicable law, any act of violation of the human rights of migrants, inter alia, arbitrary detention, torture and violations of the right to life, including extrajudicial executions, during their transit from their country of origin to the country of destination and vice versa, including their transit through national borders;

12. *Recalls* that the Universal Declaration of Human Rights recognizes that everyone has the right to an effective remedy by the competent national tribunals for acts violating the fundamental rights granted to him or her;

13. *Takes note with appreciation* of the successful implementation by some States of alternative measures to detention in cases of undocumented migration as a practice that deserves consideration by all States;

14. *Urges* States to ensure that repatriation mechanisms allow for the identification and special protection of persons in vulnerable situations and take into account, in conformity with their international obligations and commitments, the principle of the best interest of the child and family reunification;

15. *Underlines* the right of migrants to return to their country of citizenship, and recalls that States must ensure that their returning nationals are duly received;

16. *Reaffirms emphatically* the duty of States parties to ensure full respect for and observance of the Vienna Convention on Consular Relations, in particular with regard to the right of all foreign nationals, regardless of their immigration status, to communicate with a consular official of the sending State in case of arrest, imprisonment, custody or detention, and the obligation of the receiving State to inform the foreign national without delay of his or her rights under the Convention;

17. *Strongly condemns* the manifestations and acts of racism, racial discrimination, xenophobia and related intolerance against migrants and the stereotypes often applied to them, including on the basis of religion or belief, and urges States to apply and, where needed, reinforce the existing laws when xenophobic or intolerant acts, manifestations or expressions against migrants occur, in order to eradicate impunity for those who commit xenophobic and racist acts;

18. *Requests* all States, in conformity with national legislation and applicable international legal instruments to which they are party, to enforce labour law effectively, including by addressing violations of such law, with regard to migrant workers' labour relations and working conditions, inter alia, those related to their remuneration and conditions of health, safety at work and the right to freedom of association;

19. *Encourages* all States to remove obstacles that may prevent the safe, unrestricted and expeditious transfer of remittances of migrants to their country of origin or to any other countries, in conformity with applicable legislation, and to consider, as appropriate, measures to solve other problems that may impede such transfers;

20. *Welcomes* immigration programmes, adopted by some countries, that allow migrants to integrate fully into the host countries, facilitate family reunification and promote a harmonious, tolerant and respectful environment, and encourages States to consider the possibility of adopting these types of programmes;

21. *Requests* Member States, the United Nations system, international organizations, civil society and all relevant stakeholders, especially the United Nations High Commissioner for Human Rights and the Special Rapporteur on the human rights of migrants, to ensure that the perspective of the human rights of migrants is included among the priority issues in the ongoing discussions on international migration and development within the United Nations system, bearing in mind the discussions of the High-level Dialogue on International Migration and Development held pursuant to General Assembly resolution 58/208 of 23 December 2003;

22. *Invites* the Chairperson of the Committee to address the General Assembly at its future sessions under the item entitled "Promotion and protection of human rights";

23. *Invites* the Special Rapporteur to present his reports to the General Assembly at its future sessions under the item entitled "Promotion and protection of human rights";

24. *Invites* Member States to strengthen their efforts to raise awareness of the important contribution of migrants to all spheres of society and to consider the development of appropriate tools to highlight the contribution of migrants to recipient countries, including through the collection of data and the development of statistics;

25. *Requests* the Secretary-General to provide the resources necessary, from within existing resources of the United Nations, for the Committee to meet for two separate sessions in 2009, the first session to be of two consecutive weeks' duration and the second session to be of one week's duration, for the purpose of meeting the demands of the workload arising from the increasing number of reports of States parties that have been submitted to the Committee, and invites the Committee to consider ways of further improving the effectiveness of its working sessions;

26. *Also requests* the Secretary-General to report on the implementation of the present resolution at its sixty-fourth session and to include in that report an analysis of the ways and means to promote the human rights of

migrants, taking into account the views of the Special Rapporteur, and decides to examine the question further under the item entitled "Promotion and protection of human rights".

Also on 18 December [meeting 70], the Assembly, on the recommendation of the Third Committee [A/63/430/Add.2], adopted **resolution 63/188** by recorded vote (121-4-60) [agenda item 64 *(b)*].

Respect for the right to universal freedom of travel and the vital importance of family reunification

The General Assembly,

Recalling its resolution 61/162 of 19 December 2006,

Reaffirming that all human rights and fundamental freedoms are universal, indivisible, interdependent and interrelated,

Recalling the provisions of the Universal Declaration of Human Rights, as well as article 12 of the International Covenant on Civil and Political Rights,

Stressing that, as stated in the Programme of Action of the International Conference on Population and Development, family reunification of documented migrants is an important factor in international migration and that remittances by documented migrants to their countries of origin often constitute a very important source of foreign exchange and are instrumental in improving the well-being of relatives left behind,

Noting with great concern that, while some positive developments have occurred during the past few years in the accomplishment of the objectives highlighted in previous resolutions adopted by the General Assembly on this matter, in particular relating to facilitating the flow of remittances across international borders to help families, in certain cases it has been reported that measures have been adopted that increased the restrictions imposed on documented migrants in relation to family reunification and the possibility of sending remittances to their relatives in the country of origin,

Recalling that the family is the basic unit of society and, as such, should be strengthened, and that it is entitled to receive comprehensive protection and support,

1. *Once again calls upon* all States to guarantee the universally recognized freedom of travel to all foreign nationals legally residing in their territory;

2. *Reaffirms* that all Governments, in particular those of receiving countries, must recognize the vital importance of family reunification and promote its incorporation into national legislation in order to ensure protection of the unity of families of documented migrants;

3. *Calls upon* all States to allow, in conformity with international legislation, the free flow of financial remittances by foreign nationals residing in their territory to relatives in the country of origin;

4. *Also calls upon* all States to refrain from enacting, and to repeal if it already exists, legislation intended as a coercive measure that discriminates against individuals or groups of legal migrants by adversely affecting family reunification and the right to send financial remittances to relatives in the country of origin;

5. *Decides* to continue its consideration of the question at its sixty-fifth session under the item entitled "Promotion and protection of human rights".

RECORDED VOTE ON RESOLUTION 63/188:

In favour: Afghanistan, Algeria, Angola, Antigua and Barbuda, Argentina, Azerbaijan, Bahamas, Bahrain, Bangladesh, Barbados, Belarus, Belize, Bhutan, Bolivia, Brazil, Burkina Faso, Burundi, Cambodia, Cameroon, Cape Verde, Central African Republic, Chad, Chile, China, Colombia, Comoros, Congo, Costa Rica, Cuba, Democratic People's Republic of Korea, Djibouti, Dominica, Dominican Republic, Ecuador, Egypt, El Salvador, Eritrea, Ethiopia, Fiji, Gabon, Gambia, Ghana, Grenada, Guatemala, Guinea, Guinea-Bissau, Guyana, Haiti, Honduras, India, Indonesia, Iran, Iraq, Jamaica, Jordan, Kazakhstan, Kenya, Kuwait, Kyrgyzstan, Lao People's Democratic Republic, Lebanon, Lesotho, Liberia, Libyan Arab Jamahiriya, Madagascar, Malawi, Maldives, Mali, Mauritania, Mauritius, Mexico, Mongolia, Morocco, Mozambique, Myanmar, Namibia, Nauru, Nepal, Nicaragua, Niger, Nigeria, Oman, Pakistan, Panama, Papua New Guinea, Paraguay, Peru, Philippines, Qatar, Russian Federation, Rwanda, Saint Lucia, Saint Vincent and the Grenadines, Sao Tome and Principe, Saudi Arabia, Senegal, Sierra Leone, Solomon Islands, Somalia, South Africa, Sri Lanka, Sudan, Suriname, Swaziland, Syrian Arab Republic, Tajikistan, Timor-Leste, Togo, Tunisia, Turkmenistan, Tuvalu, Uganda, United Arab Emirates, United Republic of Tanzania, Uruguay, Uzbekistan, Venezuela, Viet Nam, Yemen, Zambia, Zimbabwe.

Against: Israel, Marshall Islands, Palau, United States.

Abstaining: Albania, Andorra, Armenia, Australia, Austria, Belgium, Bosnia and Herzegovina, Botswana, Brunei Darussalam, Bulgaria, Canada, Côte d'Ivoire, Croatia, Cyprus, Czech Republic, Denmark, Estonia, Finland, France, Georgia, Germany, Greece, Hungary, Iceland, Ireland, Italy, Japan, Latvia, Liechtenstein, Lithuania, Luxembourg, Malaysia, Malta, Micronesia, Moldova, Monaco, Montenegro, Netherlands, New Zealand, Norway, Poland, Portugal, Republic of Korea, Romania, Samoa, San Marino, Serbia, Singapore, Slovakia, Slovenia, Spain, Sweden, Switzerland, Thailand, The former Yugoslav Republic of Macedonia, Tonga, Turkey, Ukraine, United Kingdom, Vanuatu.

Discrimination against minorities

Forum on minority issues. The Forum on Minority Issues, established by the Human Rights Council in 2007 [YUN 2007, p. 723] as a platform for promoting dialogue and cooperation on issues pertaining to persons belonging to national or ethnic, religious and linguistic minorities, held its inaugural session (Geneva, 15–16 December) with a thematic focus on minorities and the right to education. Discussions centred on the identification of challenges and problems facing minorities and States; identification of good practices in relation to minorities and education; and consideration of opportunities, initiatives and solutions. The Forum's recommendations, contained in the report of the independent expert on minority issues [A/HRC/10/11/Add.1], addressed core principles, essential requirements for an effective education strategy, equal access to quality education for minorities, the learning environment and the content and delivery of the curriculum. Among the recommendations were that States should take measures to implement education rights actively to the maximum of their available resources, individually and through international assistance programmes. They should review, enact and amend legislation to affirm the right to education for all; eliminate discrimination and guarantee quality education for minorities; and create conditions for institutions representing minorities to participate meaningfully in the development and implementation of policies and programmes relating to education for minorities. In drafting education budgets, clear criteria tailored to the special needs of the minority group were required. Education services should reach minority communities throughout the national territory, be adequate to address their needs, and be comparable with national standards.

Reports of Independent Expert. In her annual report [A/HRC/7/23], the Independent Expert on minority issues, Gay McDougall (United States), focused on the discriminatory denial or deprivation of citizenship as a tool for exclusion of national, ethnic, religious and linguistic minorities. Minorities often faced discrimination and exclusion as they struggled to gain access to their human rights even under conditions of full citizenship. Denying or stripping them of citizenship could be an effective method of compounding their vulnerability, and could even lead to mass expulsion. Once denied or deprived of citizenship, minorities were inevitably denied protection of their basic rights and freedoms, including minority rights. According to the United Nations High Commissioner for Refugees, close to 15 million people in more than 49 countries were stateless, and numbers appeared to be increasing. Many minorities lived in a precarious legal situation. Even though entitled under law to citizenship in their State of residence, they were often denied or deprived of that right and in a situation of statelessness. While many conditions gave rise to statelessness, including protracted refugee situations and State succession, most stateless persons were members of minority groups.

In her recommendations, the Independent Expert said that while States had a prerogative to establish laws governing the acquisition or loss of nationality, they should do so within the framework of international human rights law. In situations relating to constitutional amendments or changes to legislation on the conferral of citizenship, States should not revoke citizenship retroactively. They should not arbitrarily deny or deprive minorities of citizenship on the basis of colour, descent, national or ethnic origin, language, race or religion; and should not consider citizenship a condition for the enjoyment of human rights, including those belonging to minorities. States should grant nationality to children born on their territory if the child would otherwise be stateless, and in that case the immigration status of parents should be irrelevant. States should facilitate the acquisition of citizenship through naturalization or permanent residency to persons lawfully resident in the country for a period commensurate with their having created established ties in the State, and that period should not be longer than 10 years. State requirements for the granting of citizenship should be reasonable and not overly burdensome, and States should conduct information campaigns on the right to citizenship and procedures for obtaining recognition of that right, in a language and form accessible to all.

An addendum to the report [A/HRC/7/23/Add.1] summarized 26 communications the Independent Expert had sent to 19 countries and the United Nations Interim Administration Mission in Kosovo from 29 July 2005 to 25 December 2007, and to which she had received nine replies.

The Independent Expert visited Guyana (28 July–1 August) [A/HRC/10/11/Add.2], where she witnessed a societal malaise that in some instances had deepened into despair, anger and resistance. That was particularly evident among Afro-Guyanese individuals and communities that reported feeling excluded, discriminated against and criminalized. Ethnically divided political and administrative structures and failed political processes had created frustrations and distrust in the institution of government. Violent incidents in 2008 had fuelled a climate of suspicion, rumour and conspiracy theory. Two separate and conflicting narratives and perceptions of reality among Afro- and Indo-Guyanese people threatened to undermine shared values and common goals. The Government had taken steps to address issues of ethnic tensions, criminal activities and economic underdevelopment, but further action was required to restore confidence in good governance and the rule of law among all communities. Afro-Guyanese people felt excluded from having a full voice and stake in the national polity and equal enjoyment of rights in many areas, including employment and economic participation. They reported stigmatization of young males and entire African communities, with derogatory stereotypes of criminality colouring societal perceptions of Afro-Guyanese. Particular challenges affected women from minority communities, including a scarcity of employment opportunities for Afro-Guyanese women, the heavy burden of care shouldered by single mothers and a culture of domestic violence. Women felt that the criminal justice system did not treat seriously cases of domestic violence.

Anti-discrimination legislation and policies were insufficient to address discrimination, exclusion and ethnically based bias. A robust anti-discrimination and equality plan of action should be applied across all sectors of society to break down ingrained barriers.

Reforms had to be far-reaching and highly consultative, and should lead to concrete outputs ensuring non-discrimination and equality. Promises should be delivered upon, including the creation of credible human rights commissions to deliver change and build new foundations. An open, constructive dialogue on inclusive governance was an essential component of such process. The Government, political parties and religious, cultural and civil society groups should reach out beyond the ethnic divide and build bridges between communities. The Government and both political parties should take full responsibility for ensuring that decisions taken to resolve conflict were fully implemented. Decisions taken at the National Stakeholder Forum (February/March) should be implemented, including the establishment of a new Parliamentary Standing Committee on National Security with ministerial representation; the appointment of the constitutional commissions expedited; and the Parliamentary Constitutional Reform Committee convened. The Government should support and fund educational and cultural projects established by institutions and organizations within the Afro-Guyanese community. Affirmative action programmes should address the economic, educational and social inequalities comparable to those in the Indo-Guyanese communities that existed in the Afro-Guyanese communities.

The independent expert visited Greece (8–16 September) [A/HRC/10/11/Add.3] to promote the implementation of the Declaration on the Rights of Persons Belonging to National, Ethnic, Religious and Linguistic Minorities (the 1992 Declaration on Minorities) [YUN 1992, p. 722]. Greece recognized only the Muslim religious minority in Western Thrace, protected under the 1923 Treaty of Lausanne, and no other minority communities. The Government was convinced that the claims of the existence of other minorities were unsubstantiated and politically motivated. However, whether a State officially recognized a minority was not conclusive with respect to its obligations. The expert visited Roma communities, which lacked basic facilities and faced the constant threat of eviction. Many Roma children were either in segregated schools or did not have access to education owing to their identity. While commending Government efforts to develop policies through the Integrated Action Programme on Roma, the expert noted problems of implementation at the local level, particularly regarding living conditions and segregation in public schools.

The expert urged the Government to ensure that national policies were not subverted by local authorities responsive to local prejudices. It should comply with European Court judgements with respect to the segregation of Roma children. The Government should refrain from disputing whether there was a Macedonian or a Turkish minority and focus on protecting the rights to self-identification, freedom of expression and freedom of association of those communities. Their rights to minority protections should be honoured in accordance with the 1992 Declaration on Minorities and international human rights treaties. Greece should comply fully with the judgements of the European Court of Human Rights, specifically those decisions recommending that associations should be allowed to use the words "Macedonian" and "Turkish" in their names and to express their ethnic identities.

Report of Secretary-General. An August report of the Secretary-General [A/HRC/9/8], submitted in accordance with a Human Rights Council request [YUN 2006, p. 760], outlined interventions undertaken by OHCHR to promote the rights of minorities. Those activities included capacity-building, inter-agency cooperation, building thematic expertise and preparations for the Forum on Minority Issues (see above). The Council was invited to consider whether a final report and a review of relevant developments should be submitted at the Council's tenth (2009) session. The Council might also consider grouping all reports on minorities, including that of the independent experts on minority issues, the forum on minority issues and the High Commissioner at one time of the year.

Communications. On 13 March [A/HRC/7/G/10], the Dominican Republic transmitted to OHCHR its comments on the joint report of the independent expert on minority issues and the Special Rapporteur on contemporary forms of racism, racial discrimination, xenophobia and related intolerance on their 2007 mission to the country [YUN 2007, p. 715].

On 19 March [A/HRC/7/G/14], Turkey informed the Human Rights Council secretariat that, according to the Turkish constitutional system, the word "minorities" encompassed only groups of persons defined and recognized as such on the basis of multilateral or bilateral instruments to which Turkey was party. The country's cooperation with the independent expert concerning Turkey would continue in relation to the minorities recognized in line with the aforementioned understanding.

Human Rights Council action. On 27 March [A/63/53 (res. 7/6)], the Human Rights Council extended the mandate of the independent expert for a three-year period and called on States to cooperate with the expert in the performance of her tasks and duties.

GENERAL ASSEMBLY ACTION

On 18 December [meeting 70], the General Assembly, on the recommendation of the Third Committee [A/63/430/Add.2], adopted **resolution 63/174** without vote [agenda item 64 *(b)*].

Effective promotion of the Declaration on the Rights of Persons Belonging to National or Ethnic, Religious and Linguistic Minorities

The General Assembly,

Recalling its resolution 47/135 of 18 December 1992, by which it adopted the Declaration on the Rights of Persons Belonging to National or Ethnic, Religious and Linguistic Minorities annexed to that resolution, and bearing in mind article 27 of the International Covenant on Civil and Political Rights as well as other relevant existing international standards and national legislation,

Recalling also its subsequent resolutions on the effective promotion of the Declaration, as well as Human Rights Council resolutions 6/15 of 28 September 2007, by which the Council established the Forum on Minority Issues, and 7/6 of 27 March 2008 on the mandate of the independent expert on minority issues,

Noting that the promotion and protection of the rights of persons belonging to national or ethnic, religious and linguistic minorities contributes to political and social stability and peace and enriches the cultural diversity and heritage of society, as reaffirmed in the 2005 World Summit Outcome,

Affirming that effective measures and the creation of favourable conditions for the promotion and protection of the rights of persons belonging to national or ethnic, religious and linguistic minorities, ensuring effective non-discrimination and equality for all, as well as full and effective participation in matters affecting them, contribute to the prevention and peaceful solution of human rights problems and situations involving them,

Expressing concern at the frequency and severity of disputes and conflicts involving persons belonging to national or ethnic, religious and linguistic minorities in many countries and their often tragic consequences, and that they often suffer disproportionately from the effects of conflict resulting in the violation of their human rights and are particularly vulnerable to displacement through, inter alia, population transfers, refugee flows and forced relocation,

Emphasizing the need for reinforced efforts to meet the goal of the full realization of the rights of persons belonging to national or ethnic, religious and linguistic minorities, including by addressing economic and social conditions and marginalization, as well as to end any type of discrimination against them,

Emphasizing also the importance of human rights education, training and learning as well as of dialogue and interaction among all relevant stakeholders and members of society on the promotion and protection of the rights of persons belonging to national or ethnic, religious and linguistic minorities as an integral part of the development of society as a whole, including the sharing of best practices such as for the promotion of mutual understanding of minority issues, managing diversity by recognizing plural identities and promoting inclusive and stable societies as well as social cohesion therein,

Emphasizing further the important role that national institutions can play in the promotion and protection of rights of persons belonging to national or ethnic, religious and linguistic minorities as well as in early warning and awareness raising for problems regarding minority situations,

Acknowledging that the United Nations has an important role to play regarding the protection of the rights of persons belonging to national or ethnic, religious and linguistic minorities by, inter alia, taking due account of, and giving effect to, the Declaration,

1. *Reaffirms* the obligation of States to ensure that persons belonging to national or ethnic, religious and linguistic minorities may exercise fully and effectively all human rights and fundamental freedoms without any discrimination and in full equality before the law, as proclaimed in the Declaration on the Rights of Persons Belonging to National or Ethnic, Religious and Linguistic Minorities, and draws attention to the relevant provisions of the Durban Declaration and Programme of Action, including the provisions on forms of multiple discrimination;

2. *Urges* States and the international community to promote and protect the rights of persons belonging to national or ethnic, religious and linguistic minorities, as set out in the Declaration, including through the encouragement of conditions for the promotion of their identity, the provision of adequate education and the facilitation of their participation in all aspects of the political, economic, social, religious and cultural life of society and in the economic progress and development of their country, without discrimination, and to apply a gender perspective while doing so;

3. *Urges* States to take, as appropriate, all necessary constitutional, legislative, administrative and other measures to promote and give effect to the Declaration, and appeals to States to cooperate bilaterally and multilaterally, in particular on the exchange of best practices and lessons learned, in accordance with the Declaration, in order to promote and protect the rights of persons belonging to national or ethnic, religious and linguistic minorities;

4. *Welcomes* in this regard the initiative of the Office of the United Nations High Commissioner for Human Rights to organize, in cooperation with the International Labour Organization and the United Nations Office on Drugs and Crime, the expert meeting on integration with diversity in policing, held in Vienna on 15 and 16 January 2008, bringing together police service professionals of different regions and countries of the world in order to share good experiences and lessons learned in relation to the inclusion of persons belonging to national or ethnic, religious and linguistic minorities in law enforcement systems, and takes note of the ongoing work on the elaboration of the Office of the United Nations High Commissioner for Human Rights guidelines on integration with diversity in policing;

5. *Encourages* States, in their follow-up to the World Conference against Racism, Racial Discrimination, Xenophobia and Related Intolerance, to include aspects relating to persons belonging to national or ethnic, religious and linguistic minorities in their national plans of action and, in this context, to take forms of multiple discrimination fully into account;

6. *Commends* the independent expert on minority issues for the work that she has undertaken so far, for the important role that she has played in raising the level of awareness of, and in giving added visibility to the rights of persons belonging to national or ethnic, religious and linguistic minorities and for her ongoing efforts to promote and protect their rights in order to ensure equitable development and peaceful and stable societies, including through

close cooperation with Governments, the relevant United Nations bodies and mechanisms and non-governmental organizations, as provided for in Human Rights Council resolution 7/6;

7. *Calls upon* all States to cooperate with the independent expert in the performance of the tasks and duties mandated to her, and encourages the specialized agencies, regional organizations, national human rights institutions and non-governmental organizations to develop regular dialogue and cooperation with the mandate-holder;

8. *Takes note with appreciation* of the decision of the Human Rights Council to establish the Forum on Minority Issues, which shall provide a platform for promoting dialogue and cooperation on issues pertaining to persons belonging to national or ethnic, religious and linguistic minorities as well as thematic contributions and expertise to the work of the independent expert on minority issues and identify and analyse best practices, challenges, opportunities and initiatives for the further implementation of the Declaration;

9. *Invites* States, United Nations mechanisms, bodies, the specialized agencies, funds and programmes, regional, intergovernmental and non-governmental organizations and national human rights institutions as well as academics and experts on minority issues to participate actively in the inaugural session of the Forum on Minority Issues, to be held in Geneva in December 2008, which will be dedicated to the subject of the rights of persons belonging to minorities and the right to education;

10. *Calls upon* the United Nations High Commissioner for Human Rights to promote, within her mandate, the implementation of the Declaration, to continue to engage in a dialogue with Governments for that purpose and to regularly update and disseminate widely the United Nations Guide for Minorities;

11. *Welcomes* the inter-agency consultation of the High Commissioner with United Nations agencies, funds and programmes on minority issues, and calls upon those agencies, funds and programmes to contribute actively to this process;

12. *Also welcomes* the cooperation of the independent expert on minority issues with United Nations agencies, funds and programmes, such as the United Nations Children's Fund, the United Nations Development Programme and the United Nations Educational, Scientific and Cultural Organization, in continuing their engagement with persons belonging to national or ethnic, religious and linguistic minorities in their work in all parts of the world;

13. *Requests* the High Commissioner to continue her efforts to improve coordination and cooperation among United Nations agencies, funds and programmes on activities related to the promotion and protection of the rights of persons belonging to national or ethnic, religious and linguistic minorities and to take the work of relevant regional organizations active in the field of human rights into account in her endeavours;

14. *Invites* the human rights treaty bodies, when considering reports submitted by States parties as well as special procedures of the Human Rights Council, to continue to give attention, within their respective mandates, to situations and rights of persons belonging to national or ethnic, religious and linguistic minorities;

15. *Invites* the High Commissioner to continue to seek voluntary contributions to facilitate the effective participation of representatives of non-governmental organizations and persons belonging to national or ethnic, religious and linguistic minorities, in particular those from developing countries, in minority-related activities organized by the United Nations, particularly its human rights bodies, and in doing so to give particular attention to ensuring the participation of young people and women;

16. *Invites* the independent expert on minority issues to report to the General Assembly at its sixty-fifth session on the implementation of the present resolution;

17. *Decides* to continue consideration of the question at its sixty-fifth session under the item entitled "Human rights questions".

Leprosy victims

Human Rights Council action. On 18 June [A/63/53 (res. 8/13)], the Human Rights Council called upon Governments to take measures to eliminate discrimination against persons affected by leprosy and their family members, including awareness-raising. OHCHR was requested to include the issue in its human rights and awareness-raising activities, and collect information on measures taken by Governments to eliminate such discrimination and to report to the Council and the Human Rights Council Advisory Committee. The Committee was requested to examine the OHCHR report and formulate draft principles and guidelines for eliminating such discrimination for submission to the Council in 2009.

Religious intolerance

Note by OHCHR. A January Secretariat note [A/HRC/7/10] recalled that the Human Rights Council, in 2007 [YUN 2007, p. 726], had requested the Special Rapporteur on freedom of religion or belief, Asma Jahangir (Pakistan), to submit the next annual report, as well as outstanding reports, to the Council in 2009 in accordance with its annual work programme. The annual report (see below) would summarize communications sent by the Special Rapporteur from 1 December 2006 to 30 November 2007 and replies received from Governments by January 2008.

Reports of Special Rapporteur. The Special Rapporteur's report, submitted in February [A/HRC/7/10/Add.1], summarized cases transmitted to 31 Governments and replies received thereto during that period.

In July, the Secretary-General transmitted to the General Assembly the Special Rapporteur's interim report [A/63/161], submitted in accordance with Assembly resolution 62/157 [YUN 2007, p. 728], which addressed citizenship issues and religious discrimination in administrative procedures, as well as applicable legal standards and case law. The Rapporteur noted that while most States did not openly discriminate on the basis of religion with respect to citizenship issues and administrative procedures, there were instances where State practice or legislation was inconsistent with human rights standards. Of concern were: the denial or deprivation of citizenship based on a person's religious affiliation; compulsory mentioning of selected religions on official identity cards or passports; requirements to denounce a particular faith when applying for official documents; and restricted eligibility for State functions for persons of certain faiths.

In her conclusions and recommendations, the Special Rapporteur emphasized that the legitimate interests of the State had to be balanced on a case-by-case basis with the individual's freedom of religion or belief. She highlighted some aspects that might help determine whether certain restrictions on the right to freedom of religion or belief were in contravention of human rights law.

The Special Rapporteur carried out a mission to Israel and the Occupied Palestinian Territory (20–27 January) [A/HRC/10/8/Add.2], where she focused on restricted access to places of worship; the preservation and protection of religious sites; the indication of religious affiliation on official identity cards; matters of personal status; the preferential treatment of Orthodox Judaism; the religious rights of persons deprived of their liberty; advocacy of religious hatred that constituted incitement to discrimination, hostility or violence; conversions and missionary activities; and further concerns within the Occupied Palestinian Territory. She noted that liberty of movement, including access to places of worship, was restricted, in particular for Palestinian Muslims and Christians, through the system of permits, visas, checkpoints and the Barrier. While Israel informed the Special Rapporteur that those restrictions were necessary for security reasons, any measure taken to combat terrorism should comply with States' obligations under international law.

The Rapporteur recommended, among other things, that all parties bind themselves legally to protect the rights of religious minorities and include comprehensive guarantees for equality and non-discrimination on grounds of religion or belief. Israel should issue non-selective regulations to protect and preserve religious sites on a non-discriminatory basis. Additional recommendations referred to official documents, matters of personal status and training for police, military and prison personnel. Lastly, in both the State of Israel and in the Occupied Palestinian Territory, any advocacy of religious hatred that constituted incitement to discrimination, hostility or violence should be investigated, prosecuted and punished.

The Special Rapporteur visited India (3–20 March) [A/HRC/10/8/Add.3], where she focused on the situation of religious or belief minorities; justice for victims and survivors of communal violence; freedom of religion or belief in Jammu and Kashmir; the negative impact of laws on religious conversion in several states; and implications of religion-based personal laws. The Special Rapporteur noted the religious diversity of society and the positive impact of secularism as embodied in the Constitution, as well as the high degree of human rights activism in the country. However, even though a comprehensive legal framework to protect freedom of religion or belief did exist, many interlocutors, especially from religious minorities, were dissatisfied with its implementation. Owing to the federal nature of the political system, states had wide powers, including in the field of law and order. While recognizing the efforts and achievements of the central Government, the Special Rapporteur expressed concern about intolerance and discrimination based on religion or belief, especially in certain states. Organized groups claiming adherence to religious ideologies had unleashed an all-pervasive fear of mob violence in many parts of the country. Law enforcement officials were often reluctant to take any action against individuals or groups that perpetrated violence in the name of religion or belief. She stressed the need to prevent political exploitation of communal distinctions and to address advocacy of religious hatred that constituted incitement to discrimination, hostility or violence.

In her recommendations, the Rapporteur appealed to the authorities to protect members of religious minorities from attacks and to step up efforts to prevent communal violence. Legislation on communal violence should take into account the concerns of religious minorities and should not reinforce impunity of communalized police forces at the state level. Inquiries into large-scale communal violence should be accorded the highest priority by investigation teams, the judiciary and any commission appointed to study the situation. Laws and bills on religious conversion in several states should be reconsidered since they raised human rights concerns, in particular the use of vague or extremely broad terminology and discriminatory provisions. The eligibility for affirmative action benefits should be restored to those members of scheduled castes and scheduled tribes who had converted to another religion. Religion-based personal laws should be reviewed to prevent discrimination based on religion or belief and to ensure gender equality.

The Special Rapporteur, during her mission to Turkmenistan (4–10 September) [A/HRC/10/8/Add.4], was impressed by the high level of tolerance and the climate of religious harmony. However, there was still mistrust of religious organizations and collective manifestation of religion. Over the past eight years, reports had been received of arrests, intimidation, harassment and restrictions on the religious activities of individuals and groups allegedly perpetrated by the authorities. Although the situation had much improved since 2007, individuals and religious communities remained under scrutiny and faced difficulties when manifesting their freedom of religion or belief. The Special Rapporteur was concerned about the imposition of legal or policy restrictions on registration, places of worship, religious material, religious education and proselytism. Those laws and their implementation amounted in some instances to undue limitations on freedom to manifest one's religion or belief, as well as on other rights, such as freedom of association and freedom of expression.

In her conclusions and recommendations, the Special Rapporteur emphasized that the enactment and implementation of laws unduly restricting freedom of religion or belief could not provide a long-term solution to concerns of the Turkmenistan authorities that external extremist groups might disrupt the climate of religious harmony. Law-making in the area of religion or belief was sensitive. Vague or excessive legislative provisions could create tensions and give rise to multiple problems rather than solving them. In addition, they might be subject to arbitrary interpretation by law enforcement agencies and local administration. Consequently, the Rapporteur urged the Government to review the amended law on freedom of conscience and religious organizations so that it no longer infringed on the rights of individuals and groups in their exercise of freedom of religion or belief. In particular, the prohibition on unregistered religious activities and undue restrictions on religious material, education and attire should be removed from the law. Similarly, the Government should ensure that religious communities did not encounter obstructions with regard to the building, opening, renting or use of places of worship. The Council on Religious Affairs should include representatives of religious minorities and become a facilitating rather than a monitoring mechanism. On conscientious objection, the Government should offer an alternative civilian service for those who refused to perform military service owing to their religious beliefs. It should also reform the judiciary, offering legal redress and compensation for denial of freedom of religion or belief. Law enforcement officials and local representatives should receive adequate training about international human rights standards, including on freedom of religion or belief.

Communication. On 29 February [A/62/714-S/2008/157], Pakistan, as Chair of the Organization of the Islamic Conference (OIC) Group at New York, transmitted to the Secretary-General a statement by the OIC Group expressing concern about the increasing manifestations of Islamophobia that encouraged incitement to hatred against Islam and Muslims around the world and posed a threat to peace and security within and among States. Those acts called for redoubling efforts to promote understanding and respect for religions, cultures and civilizations.

Human Rights Council action. On 27 March [A/63/53 (res. 7/19)], by a recorded vote of 21 to 10, with 14 abstentions, the Human Rights Council deplored attacks and assaults on businesses, cultural centres and places of worship of all religions and targeting of religious symbols. It urged States to prohibit the dissemination of racist and xenophobic ideas and material aimed at any religion or its followers that constituted incitement to racial and religious hatred, hostility or violence. They should provide adequate protection against acts of hatred, discrimination, intimidation and coercion resulting from the defamation of any religion, and take all possible measures to promote tolerance and respect for all religions and their value systems. The High Commissioner should report on the implementation of the resolution and submit a study compiling legislation and jurisprudence on defamation of and contempt for religions to the Council's ninth (2008) session.

Reports of High Commissioner. In response to that request, the High Commissioner, in September, submitted a report [A/HRC/9/7] on the implementation of Council resolution 7/19 on combating defamation of religion. The report summarized replies received from nine States, the Council of Europe and five NGOs.

Also pursuant to the Council's request, the High Commissioner submitted a study [A/HRC/9/25] compiling legislation and jurisprudence concerning defamation and contempt of religion. The study presented preliminary findings on international, regional and national legislation and relevant jurisprudence; summarized relevant provisions of international instruments and jurisprudence; highlighted the conclusions and recommendations of Special Rapporteurs and former mandate holders; and reviewed regional norms and jurisprudence on freedom of thought, conscience and religion and freedom of expression. The study concluded that further clarity was needed with regard to the demarcation line between freedom of expression and incitement to religious hatred. To protect individuals and groups, a better understanding of the permissible limitations to freedom of expression in accordance with international human rights law should be developed. OHCHR would organize, in October, an expert seminar entitled "Links between articles 19 and 20 of the International Covenant on Civil and Political Rights: Freedom of expression and advocacy of religious hatred that constitutes incitement to discrimination, hostility or violence".

Expert seminar. The expert seminar (Geneva, 2–3 October) [A/HRC/10/31/Add.3] discussed: analogies and parallels with other types of "incitement"; analysis of the notion of advocacy of religious hatred that constituted incitement to discrimination, hostility or violence; limits to the restrictions to freedom of expression: criteria and application; and the international legal framework and the interrelatedness between States' obligations and articles 19 and 20 of the International Covenant on Civil and Political Rights.

Report of Secretary-General. In accordance with General Assembly resolution 62/154 [YUN 2007, p. 726], the Secretary-General in October submitted a report [A/63/365] on measures and activities undertaken by Member States, UN bodies, regional organizations, national human rights institutions and NGOs to implement that resolution. The Assembly had requested that the report address the possible correlation between defamation of religions and the upsurge in incitement, intolerance and hatred in many parts of the world. The report concluded that a comprehensive review of trends and patterns would be required to establish how and where incidence of religious defamation and incitement to racial and religious hatred were manifested and thereby establish such a correlation. The results of such a review would help in evaluating the effectiveness of the international legal framework, as well as in determining conditions that would facilitate dialogue and joint action for combating racism, discrimination and xenophobia.

Communication. On 26 June [A/HRC/9/G/2], OIC forwarded to the High Commissioner an updated version of the OIC Observatory Report on Islamophobia as its contribution to the implementation of General Assembly resolution 62/154.

GENERAL ASSEMBLY ACTION

On 18 December [meeting 70], the General Assembly, on the recommendation of the Third Committee [A/63/430/Add.2], adopted **resolution 63/171** by recorded vote (86-53-42) [agenda item 64 *(b)*].

Combating defamation of religions

The General Assembly,

Reaffirming the pledge made by all States, under the Charter of the United Nations, to promote and encourage universal respect for and observance of all human rights and fundamental freedoms without distinction as to race, sex, language or religion,

Recalling the relevant international instruments on the elimination of discrimination, in particular the International Convention on the Elimination of All Forms of Racial Discrimination, the International Covenant on Civil and Political Rights, the Declaration on the Elimination of All Forms of Intolerance and of Discrimination Based on Religion or Belief, the Declaration on the Human Rights of Individuals Who are not Nationals of the Country in which They Live and the Declaration on the Rights of Persons Belonging to National or Ethnic, Religious and Linguistic Minorities,

Reaffirming that all human rights are universal, indivisible, interdependent and interrelated,

Recalling the relevant resolutions of the Commission on Human Rights and the Human Rights Council in this regard,

Welcoming the resolve expressed in the United Nations Millennium Declaration adopted by the General Assembly on 8 September 2000 to take measures to eliminate the increasing acts of racism and xenophobia in many societies and to promote greater harmony and tolerance in all societies, and looking forward to its effective implementation at all levels,

Underlining in this regard the importance of the Durban Declaration and Programme of Action adopted by the World Conference against Racism, Racial Discrimination, Xenophobia and Related Intolerance, held in Durban, South Africa, in 2001, welcoming the progress achieved in implementing them, and emphasizing that they constitute a solid foundation for the elimination of all scourges and manifestations of racism, racial discrimination, xenophobia and related intolerance,

Expressing concern at the increase in racist violence and xenophobic ideas in many parts of the world, in political circles, in the sphere of public opinion and in society at large, as a result, inter alia, of the resurgence of activities of political parties and associations established on the basis of racist, xenophobic and ideological superiority platforms and charters, and the persistent use of those platforms and charters to promote or incite racist ideologies,

Deeply alarmed at the rising trends towards discrimination based on religion or belief, including in some national policies, laws and administrative measures that stigmatize groups of people belonging to certain religions and beliefs under a variety of pretexts relating to security and irregular immigration, thereby legitimizing discrimination against them, and consequently impairing their enjoyment of the right to freedom of thought, conscience and religion, and impeding their ability to observe, practise and manifest their religion freely and without fear of coercion, violence or reprisal,

Noting with deep concern the serious instances of intolerance, discrimination and acts of violence based on religion or belief, intimidation and coercion motivated by extremism, religious or otherwise, occurring in many parts of the world, in addition to the negative projection of certain religions in the media and the introduction and enforcement of laws and administrative measures that specifically discriminate against and target persons with certain ethnic and religious backgrounds, particularly Muslim minorities following the events of 11 September 2001, and that threaten to impede their full enjoyment of human rights and fundamental freedoms,

Stressing that defamation of religions is a serious affront to human dignity leading to the illicit restriction of the freedom of religion of their adherents and incitement to religious hatred and violence,

Stressing also the need to effectively combat defamation of all religions, and incitement to religious hatred in general,

Reaffirming that discrimination on the grounds of religion or belief constitutes a violation of human rights and a disavowal of the principles of the Charter,

Noting with concern that defamation of religions, and incitement to religious hatred in general, could lead to social disharmony and violations of human rights, and alarmed at the inaction of some States to combat this burgeoning trend and the resulting discriminatory practices against adherents of certain religions,

Taking note of the reports of the Special Rapporteur on contemporary forms of racism, racial discrimination, xenophobia and related intolerance submitted to the Human Rights Council at its fourth and sixth sessions, which draw attention to the serious nature of the defamation of all religions, and reiterating the call of the Special Rapporteur to all States to wage a systematic campaign against incitement to racial and religious hatred by maintaining a careful balance between the defence of secularism and respect for freedom of religion and by acknowledging and respecting the complementarity of all the freedoms embodied in internationally agreed human rights instruments, including the International Covenant on Civil and Political Rights,

Recalling the proclamation of the Global Agenda for Dialogue among Civilizations, and inviting States, the organizations and bodies of the United Nations system, within existing resources, other international and regional organizations and civil society to contribute to the implementation of the Programme of Action contained in the Global Agenda,

Welcoming the efforts of the Alliance of Civilizations initiative in promoting mutual respect and understanding among different cultures and societies, as well as the forthcoming second forum of the Alliance, to be held in Istanbul, Turkey, on 6 and 7 April 2009,

Convinced that respect for cultural, ethnic, religious and linguistic diversity, as well as dialogue among and within civilizations, is essential for peace, understanding and friendship among individuals and people of the different cultures and nations of the world, while manifestations of cultural prejudice, intolerance and xenophobia towards people belonging to different cultures, religions and beliefs generate hatred and violence among peoples and nations throughout the world,

Recognizing the valuable contributions of all religions and beliefs to modern civilization and the contribution that dialogue among civilizations can make to an improved awareness and understanding of common values,

Underlining the important role of education in the promotion of tolerance, which involves acceptance by the public of, and its respect for, diversity, including with regard to religious expressions, and underlining also the fact that education should contribute in a meaningful way to promoting tolerance and the elimination of discrimination based on religion or belief,

Reaffirming the need for all States to continue their national and international efforts to enhance dialogue and broaden understanding among civilizations, cultures, religions and beliefs, and emphasizing that States, regional organizations, non-governmental organizations, religious bodies and the media have an important role to play in promoting tolerance, respect for and freedom of religion and belief,

Welcoming all international and regional initiatives aimed at promoting cross-cultural and interfaith harmony, including the international dialogue on interfaith cooperation, and the World Conference on Dialogue, held in Madrid from 16 to 18 July 2008, and their valuable efforts towards the promotion of a culture of peace and dialogue at all levels, and taking note with appreciation of the programmes led by the United Nations Educational, Scientific and Cultural Organization in this regard,

Underlining the importance of increasing contacts at all levels in order to deepen dialogue and reinforce understanding among different cultures, religions, beliefs and civilizations, and in this regard taking note with appreciation of the Declaration and Programme of Action adopted by the Ministerial Meeting on Human Rights and Cultural Diversity of the Movement of Non-Aligned Countries, held in Tehran on 3 and 4 September 2007,

Recalling its resolution 62/154 of 18 December 2007,

1. *Takes note* of the report of the Secretary-General and the conclusions contained therein;

2. *Expresses deep concern* at the negative stereotyping of religions and manifestations of intolerance and discrimination in matters of religion or belief still evident in the world;

3. *Strongly deplores* all acts of psychological and physical violence and assaults, and incitement thereto, against persons on the basis of their religion or belief, and such acts directed against their businesses, properties, cultural centres and places of worship, as well as targeting of holy sites and religious symbols of all religions;

4. *Expresses deep concern* at the programmes and agendas pursued by extremist organizations and groups aimed at creating and perpetuating stereotypes about certain religions, in particular when condoned by Governments;

5. *Notes with deep concern* the intensification of the overall campaign of defamation of religions, and incitement to religious hatred in general, including the ethnic and religious profiling of Muslim minorities in the aftermath of the tragic events of 11 September 2001;

6. *Recognizes* that, in the context of the fight against terrorism, defamation of religions and incitement to religious hatred in general become aggravating factors that contribute to the denial of fundamental rights and freedoms of members of target groups, as well as their economic and social exclusion;

7. *Expresses deep concern* in this respect that Islam is frequently and wrongly associated with human rights violations and terrorism;

8. *Reiterates* the commitment of all States to the implementation, in an integrated manner, of the United Nations Global Counter-Terrorism Strategy, which was adopted without a vote by the General Assembly on 8 September 2006 and reaffirmed by the Assembly in its resolution 62/272 of 5 September 2008, and which clearly confirms, inter alia, that terrorism cannot and should not be associated with any religion, nationality, civilization or ethnic group, stressing the need to reinforce the international community's commitment to promote a culture of peace, justice and human development, ethnic, national and religious tolerance, and respect for all religions, religious values, beliefs or cultures and prevent the defamation of religions;

9. *Deplores* the use of the print, audio-visual and electronic media, including the Internet, and any other means to incite acts of violence, xenophobia or related intolerance and discrimination against any religion, as well as targeting of religious symbols;

10. *Emphasizes* that, as stipulated in international human rights law, everyone has the right to hold opinions without interference, and has the right to freedom of expression, the exercise of which carries with it special duties and responsibilities and may therefore be subject to limitations as are provided for by law and are necessary for respect of the rights or reputations of others, protection of national security or of public order, public health or morals;

11. *Reaffirms* that general recommendation XV(42) of the Committee on the Elimination of Racial Discrimination, in which the Committee stipulated that the prohibition of the dissemination of all ideas based upon racial superiority or hatred is compatible with freedom of opinion and expression, is equally applicable to the question of incitement to religious hatred;

12. *Welcomes* the work undertaken by the Special Rapporteur on contemporary forms of racism, racial discrimination, xenophobia and related intolerance and the Special Rapporteur on the promotion and protection of the right to freedom of opinion and expression in accordance with their mandates defined by the Human Rights Council in its resolutions 7/34 and 7/36 of 28 March 2008;

13. *Strongly condemns* all manifestations and acts of racism, racial discrimination, xenophobia and related intolerance against national or ethnic, religious and linguistic minorities and migrants and the stereotypes often applied to them, including on the basis of religion or belief, and urges all States to apply and, where applicable, reinforce existing laws when such xenophobic or intolerant acts, manifestations or expressions occur, in order to eradicate impunity for those who commit xenophobic and racist acts;

14. *Reaffirms* the obligation of all States to enact the necessary legislation to prohibit the advocacy of national, racial or religious hatred that constitutes incitement to discrimination, hostility or violence, and encourages States, in their follow-up to the World Conference against Racism, Racial Discrimination, Xenophobia and Related Intolerance, to include aspects relating to national or ethnic, religious and linguistic minorities in their national plans of action and, in this context, to take forms of multiple discrimination against minorities fully into account;

15. *Invites* all States to put into practice the provisions of the Declaration on the Elimination of All Forms of Intolerance and of Discrimination Based on Religion or Belief;

16. *Urges* all States to provide, within their respective legal and constitutional systems, adequate protection against acts of hatred, discrimination, intimidation and coercion resulting from defamation of religions, and incitement to religious hatred in general, to take all possible measures to promote tolerance and respect for all religions and beliefs and the understanding of their value systems and to complement legal systems with intellectual and moral strategies to combat religious hatred and intolerance;

17. *Also urges* all States to ensure that all public officials, including members of law enforcement bodies, the military, civil servants and educators, in the course of their official duties, respect people regardless of their different religions and beliefs and do not discriminate against persons on the grounds of their religion or belief, and that any necessary and appropriate education or training is provided;

18. *Underscores* the need to combat defamation of religions, and incitement to religious hatred in general, by strategizing and harmonizing actions at the local, national, regional and international levels through education and awareness-raising, and urges all States to ensure equal access to education for all, in law and in practice, including access to free primary education for all children, both girls and boys, and access for adults to lifelong learning and education based on respect for human rights, diversity and tolerance, without discrimination of any kind, and to refrain from any legal or other measures leading to racial segregation in access to schooling;

19. *Calls upon* all States to exert the utmost efforts, in accordance with their national legislation and in conformity with international human rights and humanitarian law, to ensure that religious places, sites, shrines and symbols are fully respected and protected, and to take additional measures in cases where they are vulnerable to desecration or destruction;

20. *Calls upon* the international community to foster a global dialogue to promote a culture of tolerance and peace at all levels, based on respect for human rights and diversity of religion and belief, and urges States, non-governmental organizations, religious leaders and bodies and the print and electronic media to support and foster such a dialogue;

21. *Affirms* that the Human Rights Council shall promote universal respect for all religious and cultural values and address instances of intolerance, discrimination and incitement of hatred against members of any community or adherents of any religion, as well as the means to consolidate international efforts in order to combat impunity for such deplorable acts;

22. *Welcomes* the initiative by the United Nations High Commissioner for Human Rights on the recently held expert seminar on freedom of expression and advocacy of religious hatred that constitutes incitement to discrimination, hostility or violence, on 2 and 3 October 2008, and requests the High Commissioner to continue to build on this initiative, with a view to concretely contributing to the prevention and elimination of all such forms of incitement and the consequences of negative stereotyping of religions or beliefs, and their adherents, on the human rights of those individuals and their communities;

23. *Takes note* of the efforts of the High Commissioner to promote and include human rights aspects in educational programmes, particularly the World Programme for Human Rights Education proclaimed by the General Assembly on 10 December 2004, and calls upon the High Commissioner to continue those efforts, with particular focus on:

(a) The contributions of cultures, as well as religious and cultural diversity;

(b) Collaboration with other relevant bodies of the United Nations system and regional and international organizations in holding joint conferences designed to encourage dialogue among civilizations and promote understanding of the universality of human rights and their implementation at various levels, in particular the Office of the United Nations High Representative for the Alliance of

Civilizations and the unit within the Secretariat mandated to interact with various entities within the United Nations system and coordinate their contribution to the intergovernmental process;

24. *Requests* the Secretary-General to submit a report on the implementation of the present resolution, including on the possible correlation between defamation of religions and the upsurge in incitement, intolerance and hatred in many parts of the world, to the General Assembly at its sixty-fourth session.

RECORDED VOTE ON RESOLUTION 63/171:

In favour: Afghanistan, Algeria, Angola, Antigua and Barbuda, Azerbaijan, Bahamas, Bahrain, Bangladesh, Barbados, Belarus, Bhutan, Bolivia, Brunei Darussalam, Cambodia, China, Comoros, Côte d'Ivoire, Cuba, Democratic People's Republic of Korea, Djibouti, Dominica, Egypt, El Salvador, Eritrea, Ethiopia, Fiji, Gabon, Gambia, Guinea, Guinea-Bissau, Guyana, Honduras, Indonesia, Iran, Iraq, Jamaica, Jordan, Kazakhstan, Kuwait, Kyrgyzstan, Lao People's Democratic Republic, Lebanon, Lesotho, Libyan Arab Jamahiriya, Malaysia, Maldives, Mali, Mauritania, Morocco, Mozambique, Myanmar, Namibia, Nicaragua, Niger, Nigeria, Oman, Pakistan, Philippines, Qatar, Russian Federation, Saint Vincent and the Grenadines, Sao Tome and Principe, Saudi Arabia, Senegal, Sierra Leone, Singapore, Somalia, South Africa, Sri Lanka, Sudan, Suriname, Swaziland, Syrian Arab Republic, Tajikistan, Thailand, Togo, Tunisia, Turkey, Turkmenistan, Uganda, United Arab Emirates, Uzbekistan, Venezuela, Viet Nam, Yemen, Zimbabwe.

Against: Andorra, Australia, Austria, Belgium, Belize, Bulgaria, Canada, Cape Verde, Croatia, Cyprus, Czech Republic, Denmark, Estonia, Finland, France, Georgia, Germany, Greece, Hungary, Iceland, Ireland, Israel, Italy, Latvia, Liberia, Liechtenstein, Lithuania, Luxembourg, Malta, Marshall Islands, Micronesia, Moldova, Monaco, Montenegro, Netherlands, Norway, Palau, Poland, Portugal, Republic of Korea, Romania, Samoa, San Marino, Serbia, Slovakia, Slovenia, Spain, Sweden, Switzerland, The former Yugoslav Republic of Macedonia, Ukraine, United Kingdom, United States.

Abstaining: Argentina, Armenia, Benin, Botswana, Brazil, Burkina Faso, Burundi, Central African Republic, Chile, Colombia, Congo, Costa Rica, Dominican Republic, Ecuador, Ghana, Grenada, Guatemala, Haiti, India, Japan, Kenya, Madagascar, Malawi, Mauritius, Mexico, Mongolia, Nauru, Nepal, Panama, Papua New Guinea, Paraguay, Peru, Rwanda, Saint Lucia, Timor-Leste, Tonga, Trinidad and Tobago, Tuvalu, United Republic of Tanzania, Uruguay, Vanuatu, Zambia.

Also on 18 December [meeting 70], the Assembly, on the recommendation of the Third Committee [A/63/430/Add.2], adopted **resolution 63/181** without vote [agenda item 64 *(b)*].

Elimination of all forms of intolerance and of discrimination based on religion or belief

The General Assembly,

Recalling its resolution 36/55 of 25 November 1981, by which it proclaimed the Declaration on the Elimination of All Forms of Intolerance and of Discrimination Based on Religion or Belief,

Recalling also article 18 of the International Covenant on Civil and Political Rights, article 18 of the Universal Declaration of Human Rights and other relevant human rights provisions,

Recalling further its previous resolutions on the elimination of all forms of intolerance and of discrimination based on religion or belief, including resolution 62/157 of 18 December 2007, as well as Human Rights Council resolution 6/37 of 14 December 2007, in which the Council, inter alia, extended the mandate of the Special Rapporteur on freedom of religion or belief,

Reaffirming the recognition by the 1993 World Conference on Human Rights that all human rights are universal, indivisible, interdependent and interrelated, and its call upon all Governments to take all appropriate measures in compliance with their international obligations and with due regard to their respective legal systems to counter intolerance and related violence based on religion or belief, including practices of discrimination against women and the desecration of religious sites, recognizing that every individual has the right to freedom of thought, conscience, expression and religion,

Considering that religion or belief, for those who profess either, is one of the fundamental elements in their conception of life and that freedom of religion or belief should be fully respected and guaranteed,

Considering also that the disregard for and infringement of human rights and fundamental freedoms, in particular the right to freedom of thought, conscience and religion or belief, have brought, directly or indirectly, wars and great suffering to humankind,

Recognizing the important work carried out by the Human Rights Committee in providing guidance with respect to the scope of the freedom of religion or belief,

Resolved to speed up the implementation of the Declaration on the Elimination of All Forms of Intolerance and of Discrimination Based on Religion or Belief,

Believing that further intensified efforts are therefore required to promote and protect the right to freedom of thought, conscience and religion or belief and to eliminate all forms of hatred, intolerance and discrimination based on religion or belief, as also noted at the World Conference against Racism, Racial Discrimination, Xenophobia and Related Intolerance,

Reaffirming that everyone has the right to freedom of thought, conscience and religion or belief, which includes the freedom to have or to adopt a religion or belief of one's choice and the freedom, either alone or in community with others and in public or private, to manifest one's religion or belief in teaching, practice, worship and observance,

Seriously concerned at all attacks on religious places, sites and shrines in violation of international law, in particular human rights and humanitarian law, including any deliberate destruction of relics and monuments,

Seriously concerned also at any misuse of registration procedures and at the resort to discriminatory registration procedures as a means to limit the right to freedom of religion or belief of members of certain religious communities, at the limitations placed on religious materials and at the obstacles placed in the way of construction of places of worship, inconsistent with the exercise of the right to freedom of religion or belief,

Noting that a formal or legal distinction at the national level between different kinds of religions or beliefs may, in some cases, constitute discrimination and may impinge on the enjoyment of the freedom of religion or belief,

Expressing deep concern at all forms of discrimination and intolerance, including prejudices against persons and derogatory stereotyping of persons, based on religion or belief,

Recognizing the importance of enhanced interreligious and intrareligious dialogue in promoting tolerance in matters relating to religion or belief, and welcoming different initiatives in this regard, including the Alliance of Civilizations and the programmes led by the United Nations Educational, Scientific and Cultural Organization,

Emphasizing that States, regional organizations, non-governmental organizations, religious bodies and the media have an important role to play in promoting tolerance and respect for religious and cultural diversity and in the universal promotion and protection of human rights, including freedom of religion or belief,

Convinced of the need to address the rise in various parts of the world of religious extremism that affects the rights of individuals, the situations of violence and discrimination that affect many women as well as other individuals on the grounds or in the name of religion or belief or in accordance with cultural and traditional practices, and the misuse of religion or belief for ends inconsistent with the Charter of the United Nations, as well as other relevant instruments of the United Nations,

Underlining the importance of education in the promotion of tolerance, which involves the acceptance by the public of, and its respect for, diversity, including with regard to religious expression, and underlining also the fact that education, in particular at school, should contribute in a meaningful way to promoting tolerance and the elimination of discrimination based on religion or belief,

Reaffirming, in this regard, that education shall be directed to the full development of the human personality and to the strengthening of respect for human rights and fundamental freedoms and shall promote understanding, tolerance and friendship among all nations and racial or religious groups and further the activities of the United Nations for the maintenance of peace,

1. *Condemns* all forms of intolerance and of discrimination based on religion or belief, as well as violations of freedom of thought, conscience and religion or belief;

2. *Stresses* that the right to freedom of thought, conscience and religion applies equally to all people, regardless of their religions or beliefs, and without any discrimination as to their equal protection by the law;

3. *Emphasizes* that, as underlined by the Human Rights Committee, restrictions on the freedom to manifest one's religion or belief are permitted only if limitations are prescribed by law, are necessary to protect public safety, order, health or morals, or the fundamental rights and freedoms of others, are non-discriminatory and are applied in a manner that does not vitiate the right to freedom of thought, conscience and religion;

4. *Recognizes with deep concern* the overall rise in instances of intolerance and violence directed against members of many religious and other communities in various parts of the world, including cases motivated by Islamophobia, anti-Semitism and Christianophobia;

5. *Expresses concern* over the persistence of institutionalized social intolerance and discrimination practised against many in the name of religion or belief;

6. *Recalls* that legal procedures pertaining to religious or belief-based groups and places of worship are not a prerequisite for the exercise of the right to manifest one's religion or belief;

7. *Emphasizes* that such procedures, as described in paragraph 6 above, at the national or local level, as and when legally required, should be non-discriminatory in order to contribute to the effective protection of the right of all persons to practise their religion or belief either individually or in community with others and in public or private;

8. *Recognizes with concern* the situation of persons in vulnerable situations, including persons deprived of their liberty, refugees, asylum-seekers and internally displaced persons, children, persons belonging to national or ethnic, religious and linguistic minorities and migrants, as regards their ability to freely exercise their right to freedom of religion or belief;

9. *Urges* States to step up their efforts to protect and promote freedom of thought, conscience and religion or belief, and to this end:

(a) To ensure that their constitutional and legislative systems provide adequate and effective guarantees of freedom of thought, conscience, religion and belief to all without distinction, inter alia, by the provision of effective remedies in cases where the right to freedom of thought, conscience, religion or belief, or the right to practise freely one's religion, including the right to change one's religion or belief, is violated;

(b) To ensure that no one within their jurisdiction is deprived of the right to life, liberty or security of person because of religion or belief and that no one is subjected to torture or other cruel, inhuman or degrading treatment or punishment, or arbitrary arrest or detention on that account and to bring to justice all perpetrators of violations of these rights;

(c) To ensure that no one is discriminated against on the basis of his or her religion or belief when accessing, inter alia, education, medical care, employment, humanitarian assistance or social benefits;

(d) To review, whenever relevant, existing registration practices in order to ensure that such practices do not limit the right of all persons to manifest their religion or belief, alone or in community with others and in public or private;

(e) To ensure that no official documents are withheld from the individual on the grounds of religion or belief and that everyone has the right to refrain from disclosing information concerning one's religious affiliation on such documents against one's will;

(f) To ensure that everyone has the right and the opportunity to have access, on general terms of equality, to public service in one's country, without any discrimination on the basis of religion or belief;

(g) To ensure, in particular, the right of all persons to worship or assemble in connection with a religion or belief and their right to establish and maintain places for these purposes and the right of all persons to write, issue and disseminate relevant publications in these areas;

(h) To ensure that, in accordance with appropriate national legislation and in conformity with international human rights law, the freedom of all persons and members

of groups to establish and maintain religious, charitable or humanitarian institutions is fully respected and protected;

(i) To exert the utmost efforts, in accordance with their national legislation and in conformity with international human rights law, to ensure that religious places, sites, shrines and symbols are fully respected and protected and to take additional measures in cases where they are vulnerable to desecration and destruction;

(j) To ensure that all public officials and civil servants, including members of law enforcement bodies, the military and educators, in the course of fulfilling their official duties, respect all religions or beliefs and do not discriminate for reasons based on religion or belief, and that all necessary and appropriate education or training is provided;

10. *Condemns* any advocacy of religious hatred that constitutes incitement to discrimination, hostility or violence, whether it involves the use of print, audio-visual or electronic media or any other means;

11. *Emphasizes* that freedom of religion or belief and freedom of expression are interdependent, interrelated and mutually reinforcing;

12. *Urges* States to step up their efforts to eliminate intolerance and discrimination based on religion or belief, notably by:

(a) Taking all necessary and appropriate action, in conformity with international standards of human rights, to combat hatred, discrimination, intolerance and acts of violence, intimidation and coercion motivated by intolerance based on religion or belief, as well as incitement to hostility and violence, with particular regard to members of religious minorities in all parts of the world, and devoting particular attention to practices that violate the human rights of women and discriminate against women, including in the exercise of their right to freedom of thought, conscience and religion or belief;

(b) Promoting and encouraging, through education and other means, understanding, tolerance and respect in all matters relating to freedom of religion or belief and undertaking all appropriate efforts to encourage those engaged in teaching to promote mutual understanding, tolerance and respect;

13. *Emphasizes* that no religion should be equated with terrorism, as this may have adverse consequences on the enjoyment of the right to freedom of religion or belief of all members of the religious communities concerned;

14. *Stresses* the need to strengthen dialogue, inter alia, through the Alliance of Civilizations and its High Representative and the focal point within the Secretariat designated by the General Assembly, in its resolution 62/90 of 17 December 2007, to interact with various entities in the United Nations system and coordinate their contribution to dialogue;

15. *Emphasizes* the importance of a continued and strengthened dialogue among and within religions or beliefs, at all levels and with broader participation, including of women, to promote greater tolerance, respect and mutual understanding;

16. *Invites* all actors to address, in the context of interreligious and intercultural dialogue, inter alia, the following issues within the framework of international human rights:

(a) The rise of religious extremism affecting religions in all parts of the world;

(b) The situations of violence and discrimination that affect many women as well as other individuals on the grounds or in the name of religion or belief or in accordance with cultural and traditional practices;

(c) The misuse of religion or belief for ends inconsistent with the Charter of the United Nations, as well as other relevant instruments of the United Nations;

17. *Welcomes and encourages* the continuing efforts of all actors in society, including non-governmental organizations and bodies and groups based on religion or belief, to promote the implementation of the Declaration on the Elimination of All Forms of Intolerance and of Discrimination Based on Religion or Belief, and further encourages their work in promoting freedom of religion or belief and in highlighting cases of religious intolerance, discrimination and persecution;

18. *Recommends* that States, the United Nations and other actors, including non-governmental organizations and bodies and groups based on religion or belief, in their efforts to promote freedom of religion or belief, ensure the widest possible dissemination of the text of the Declaration on the Elimination of All Forms of Intolerance and of Discrimination Based on Religion or Belief, in as many different languages as possible, and promote its implementation;

19. *Welcomes* the work and the interim report of the Special Rapporteur on freedom of religion or belief;

20. *Urges* all Governments to cooperate fully with the Special Rapporteur, to respond favourably to her requests to visit their countries and to provide all necessary information for the effective fulfilment of her mandate;

21. *Requests* the Secretary-General to ensure that the Special Rapporteur receives the resources necessary to fully discharge her mandate;

22. *Requests* the Special Rapporteur to submit an interim report to the General Assembly at its sixty-fourth session;

23. *Decides* to consider the question of the elimination of all forms of religious intolerance at its sixty-fourth session under the item entitled "Promotion and protection of human rights".

Conscientious objection

OHCHR report. In an August report [A/HRC/9/24] submitted in accordance with a Human Rights Council request [YUN 2006, p. 760], OHCHR addressed recent developments on conscientious objection to military service. An important development was a 2006 decision by the Human Rights Committee regarding two Jehovah's Witnesses in the Republic of Korea who had refused to be drafted on account of their religious beliefs and conscience. The Committee concluded that the International Covenant on Civil and Political Rights provided certain protection against being forced to act against genuinely held religious belief. It was in practice common to conceive alternatives to compulsory military service that provided equivalent social good and made equivalent demands on the individual. In other developments, the Ibero-American Convention on Young People's Rights, which entered into force on 1 March, recognized the right to conscientious objection. OHCHR was preparing a publication on conscientious objection to military service and alternative service programmes for persons determined to be conscientious objectors, so as to consolidate in a single source applicable law and jurisprudence. The publication would also take note of resolutions and recommendations adopted by intergovernmental bodies, and contain examples of national practice. It would provide guidance to States, organizations and academics on applicable law and practice on the subject.

Right to self-determination

Report of Secretary-General. In response to General Assembly resolution 62/144 [YUN 2007, p. 730], the Secretary-General, in an August report [A/63/254], summarized the Human Rights Council's consideration of the implementation of the right of peoples to self-determination. It also outlined the jurisprudence of the Human Rights Committee on the treaty-based human rights norms relating to the realization of that right.

GENERAL ASSEMBLY ACTION

On 18 December [meeting 70], the General Assembly, on the recommendation of the Third Committee [A/63/429], adopted **resolution 63/163** without vote [agenda item 63].

Universal realization of the right of peoples to self-determination

The General Assembly,

Reaffirming the importance, for the effective guarantee and observance of human rights, of the universal realization of the right of peoples to self-determination enshrined in the Charter of the United Nations and embodied in the International Covenants on Human Rights, as well as in the Declaration on the Granting of Independence to Colonial Countries and Peoples contained in General Assembly resolution 1514(XV) of 14 December 1960,

Welcoming the progressive exercise of the right to self-determination by peoples under colonial, foreign or alien occupation and their emergence into sovereign statehood and independence,

Deeply concerned at the continuation of acts or threats of foreign military intervention and occupation that are threatening to suppress, or have already suppressed, the right to self-determination of peoples and nations,

Expressing grave concern that, as a consequence of the persistence of such actions, millions of people have been and are being uprooted from their homes as refugees and displaced persons, and emphasizing the urgent need for concerted international action to alleviate their condition,

Recalling the relevant resolutions regarding the violation of the right of peoples to self-determination and other human rights as a result of foreign military intervention, aggression and occupation, adopted by the Commission on Human Rights at its sixty-first and previous sessions,

Reaffirming its previous resolutions on the universal realization of the right of peoples to self-determination, including resolution 62/144 of 18 December 2007,

Reaffirming also its resolution 55/2 of 8 September 2000, containing the United Nations Millennium Declaration, and recalling its resolution 60/1 of 16 September 2005, containing the 2005 World Summit Outcome, which, inter alia, upheld the right to self-determination of peoples under colonial domination and foreign occupation,

Taking note of the report of the Secretary-General,

1. *Reaffirms* that the universal realization of the right of all peoples, including those under colonial, foreign and alien domination, to self-determination is a fundamental condition for the effective guarantee and observance of human rights and for the preservation and promotion of such rights;

2. *Declares its firm opposition* to acts of foreign military intervention, aggression and occupation, since these have resulted in the suppression of the right of peoples to self-determination and other human rights in certain parts of the world;

3. *Calls upon* those States responsible to cease immediately their military intervention in and occupation of foreign countries and territories and all acts of repression, discrimination, exploitation and maltreatment, in particular the brutal and inhuman methods reportedly employed for the execution of those acts against the peoples concerned;

4. *Deplores* the plight of millions of refugees and displaced persons who have been uprooted as a result of the aforementioned acts, and reaffirms their right to return to their homes voluntarily in safety and honour;

5. *Requests* the Human Rights Council to continue to give special attention to the violation of human rights, especially the right to self-determination, resulting from foreign military intervention, aggression or occupation;

6. *Requests* the Secretary-General to report on the question to the General Assembly at its sixty-fourth session under the item entitled "Right of peoples to self-determination".

Rights of Palestinians

During the year, the General Assembly reaffirmed the right of the Palestinian people to self-determination, including the right to their independent State of Palestine, as well as the right of all States in the region to live in peace within secure and internationally recognized borders. States and UN system specialized agencies were urged to assist Palestinians in the early realization of the right.

Human Rights Council action. On 27 March [A/63/53 (res. 7/17)], the Human Rights Council reaffirmed the inalienable right of the Palestinian people to self-determination, including their right to establish their sovereign, independent, democratic and viable contiguous State; reaffirmed its support for the solution of two States—Israel and Palestine—living side by side in peace and security; and stressed the need for respect for and preservation of the territorial unity, contiguity and integrity of all of the Occupied Palestinian Territory, including East Jerusalem.

GENERAL ASSEMBLY ACTION

On 18 December [meeting 70], the General Assembly, on the recommendation of the Third Committee [A/63/429], adopted **resolution 63/165** by recorded vote (173-5-7) [agenda item 63].

The right of the Palestinian people to self-determination

The General Assembly,

Aware that the development of friendly relations among nations, based on respect for the principle of equal rights and self-determination of peoples, is among the purposes and principles of the United Nations, as defined in the Charter,

Recalling, in this regard, its resolution 2625(XXV) of 24 October 1970 entitled "Declaration on Principles of International Law concerning Friendly Relations and Cooperation among States in accordance with the Charter of the United Nations",

Bearing in mind the International Covenants on Human Rights, the Universal Declaration of Human Rights, the Declaration on the Granting of Independence to Colonial Countries and Peoples and the Vienna Declaration and Programme of Action adopted at the World Conference on Human Rights on 25 June 1993,

Recalling the Declaration on the Occasion of the Fiftieth Anniversary of the United Nations,

Recalling also the United Nations Millennium Declaration,

Recalling further the advisory opinion rendered on 9 July 2004 by the International Court of Justice on the *Legal Consequences of the Construction of a Wall in the Occupied Palestinian Territory*, and noting in particular the reply of the Court, including on the right of peoples to self-determination, which is a right *erga omnes*,

Recalling the conclusion of the Court, in its advisory opinion of 9 July 2004, that the construction of the wall by Israel, the occupying Power, in the Occupied Palestinian Territory, including East Jerusalem, along with measures previously taken, severely impedes the right of the Palestinian people to self-determination,

Expressing the urgent need for the resumption of negotiations within the Middle East peace process on its agreed basis and for the speedy achievement of a just, lasting and comprehensive peace settlement between the Palestinian and Israeli sides,

Stressing the need for respect for and preservation of the territorial unity, contiguity and integrity of all of the Occupied Palestinian Territory, including East Jerusalem,

Recalling its resolution 62/146 of 18 December 2007,

Affirming the right of all States in the region to live in peace within secure and internationally recognized borders,

1. *Reaffirms* the right of the Palestinian people to self-determination, including the right to their independent State of Palestine;

2. *Urges* all States and the specialized agencies and organizations of the United Nations system to continue to support and assist the Palestinian people in the early realization of their right to self-determination.

RECORDED VOTE ON RESOLUTION 63/165:

In favour: Afghanistan, Albania, Algeria, Andorra, Angola, Antigua and Barbuda, Argentina, Armenia, Austria, Azerbaijan, Bahamas, Bahrain, Bangladesh, Barbados, Belarus, Belgium, Belize, Benin, Bhutan, Bolivia, Bosnia and Herzegovina, Botswana, Brazil, Brunei Darussalam, Bulgaria, Burkina Faso, Burundi, Cambodia, Cape Verde, Central African Republic, Chile, China, Colombia, Comoros, Congo, Costa Rica, Côte d'Ivoire, Croatia, Cuba, Cyprus, Czech Republic, Democratic People's Republic of Korea, Denmark, Djibouti, Dominica, Dominican Republic, Ecuador, Egypt, El Salvador, Eritrea, Estonia, Ethiopia, Finland, France, Gabon, Gambia, Georgia, Germany, Ghana, Greece, Grenada, Guatemala, Guinea, Guinea-Bissau, Guyana, Haiti, Honduras, Hungary, Iceland, India, Indonesia, Iran, Iraq, Ireland, Italy, Jamaica, Japan, Jordan, Kazakhstan, Kenya, Kuwait, Kyrgyzstan, Lao People's Democratic Republic, Latvia, Lebanon, Lesotho, Liberia, Libyan Arab Jamahiriya, Liechtenstein, Lithuania, Luxembourg, Madagascar, Malawi, Malaysia, Maldives, Mali, Malta, Mauritania, Mauritius, Mexico, Moldova, Monaco, Mongolia, Montenegro, Morocco, Mozambique, Myanmar, Namibia, Nepal, Netherlands, New Zealand, Nicaragua, Niger, Nigeria, Norway, Oman, Pakistan, Panama, Papua New Guinea, Paraguay, Philippines, Poland, Portugal, Qatar, Republic of Korea, Romania, Russian Federation, Rwanda, Saint Lucia, Saint Vincent and the Grenadines, Samoa, San Marino, Sao Tome and Principe, Saudi Arabia, Senegal, Serbia, Sierra Leone, Singapore, Slovakia, Slovenia, Solomon Islands, Somalia, South Africa, Spain, Sri Lanka, Sudan, Suriname, Swaziland, Sweden, Switzerland, Syrian Arab Republic, Tajikistan, Thailand, The former Yugoslav Republic of Macedonia, Timor-Leste, Togo, Trinidad and Tobago, Tunisia, Turkey, Turkmenistan, Tuvalu, Uganda, Ukraine, United Arab Emirates, United Kingdom, United Republic of Tanzania, Uruguay, Uzbekistan, Venezuela, Viet Nam, Yemen, Zambia, Zimbabwe.

Against: Israel, Marshall Islands, Micronesia, Palau, United States.

Abstaining: Australia, Cameroon, Canada, Fiji, Nauru, Tonga, Vanuatu.

Mercenaries

In its annual report [A/HRC/7/7], issued in January, the Working Group on the use of mercenaries as a means of violating human rights and impeding the exercise of the right of peoples to self-determination presented an overview of activities undertaken during the reporting period and discussed transnational issues, including the privatization of warfare, the activities of private military and private security companies, and extraterritorial and accountability issues. The Group concluded that the proliferation of private military and security companies worldwide was a direct consequence of the outsourcing and privatization of many military and security functions. Many of those companies were the supply side for contracts granted by the United States Department of Defence or Department of State in connection with low-intensity armed conflicts or post-conflict situations, such as in Afghanistan, Colombia and Iraq. To implement their contracts and make the most profits, some of those transnational companies, through subsidiaries or hiring companies, created and fuelled demand in developing countries. Former military personnel and ex-policemen were recruited as "security guards", but became private soldiers in low-intensity armed conflicts or post-conflict situations. Provisions in national legislation granting immunity to such personnel could easily lead to de facto impunity, with those private soldiers being accountable only to the company employing them. Those individuals were the new modalities of "mercenarism". They often encountered contractual irregularities, poor working conditions, failures in obtaining basic needs and problems in obtaining financial compensation for injuries.

The Working Group recommended that regional and intergovernmental organizations, in particular the European Union and the Organization of American States, elaborate a common system to regulate private military and security companies exporting their services. It urged Governments of States from which private military and security companies exported military assistance, consultancy and security services to avoid granting immunity to those companies and their personnel. Governments of States from which those private companies exported such services should adopt legislation and set up regulatory mechanisms to control their activities, including a registering and licensing system for authorizing those companies to operate and to be sanctioned when norms were not respected. States outsourcing such activities should demand the authorization of States from which the security personnel were recruited before the recruitment took place.

An addendum to the report [A/HRC/7/7/Add.1] summarized communications concerning allegations transmitted to eight Governments between 1 January and 30 September 2007 and responses thereto.

In August [A/63/325], the Secretary-General transmitted to the General Assembly, in accordance with Assembly resolution 62/145 [YUN 2007, p. 734], the Working Group's report. The Group had three sessions: its third session (Geneva, 7–11 April), fourth (New York, 2–5 September) and fifth (Geneva, 15–19 December). During the period under review, transnational private military and security companies, mainly from the United States and the United Kingdom, but also from Australia, Canada, Israel and other countries, continued to export their services to over 50 countries, including Afghanistan, Iraq, the Democratic Republic of the Congo, Somalia and the Sudan. The industry was estimated to earn between $100 and $120 billion annually. The Working Group had started to establish a framework of principles and criteria for the elaboration of national and international regulation mechanisms to address the activities of those companies, and would continue consultations with Governments, international and regional organizations, civil society and the private military and security industry on possible complementary and new standards. The Group would focus its work on the study and legal codification of the comprehensive system of oversight and regulation of such companies, including legal and procedural means at the international, regional and national levels. The Group concluded that the activities of those companies could not be regulated only on the basis of the 1989 International Convention against the Recruitment, Use, Financing and Training of Mercenaries [YUN 1989, p. 825], even if modernized and amended. A new international legal instrument, possibly in the format of a new UN convention, might be required, supplemented by a model law that would assist Governments in elaborating their legislation.

Human Rights Council action. On 28 March [A/63/53 (res. 7/21)], the Human Rights Council, by a recorded vote of 32 to 11, with 2 abstentions, extended the Working Group's mandate for a three-year period. States were urged to cooperate with the Working Group in fulfilment of its mandate. The Working Group was requested to report to the Council in 2009.

Mission report. The Working Group visited the United Kingdom (26–30 May) [A/HRC/10/14/Add.2], and noted that although the Government did not have any register for private military and security companies, general industry estimates indicated that there were some 40 such companies based in the country operating internationally. Their revenues were estimated to have risen from $320 million before the war in Iraq to over $1.6 billion by 2004. The Group recognized that a positive step towards better oversight was the elaboration of the United Kingdom Green Paper, which outlined six options for regulating companies operating outside of the country. However, the Government had failed to take those options forward.

The Working Group recommended making public the results of the 2005 review of the United Kingdom Green Paper or undertaking a new review, as well as conducting a comprehensive discussion among concerned bodies on the options for regulation, including the potential sharing of responsibilities and functions between national and international levels of regulation and sanctions. It also recommended that the United Kingdom consider initiating and sponsoring, within the UN system, the elaboration of an international instrument on private military and security companies to complement national regulations, and assure clear criteria and permitted limits for normal operation, as well as full compliance with international law.

Regional consultation. In accordance with General Assembly resolution 62/145 [YUN 2007, p. 734] and Human Rights Council resolution 7/21 (above), the Working Group held a regional consultation for the Eastern European Group and Central Asian Region (Moscow, 17–18 October) [A/HRC/10/14/Add.3] to gain a regional perspective about current practices related to mercenaries and private military and security companies registered, operating or recruiting personnel in the region. It discussed the role of the State as holder of the monopoly on the use of force, and shared information on steps taken by regional States to introduce legislation and other measures to regulate and monitor the activities of such companies on the international market. The Group discussed also general guidelines, norms and basic principles for the regulation and oversight of the activities of those companies to encourage human rights protection

The Working Group elaborated principles for the legal codification of the comprehensive system of oversight and regulation for private military and security companies. In accordance with those principles, the Working Group believed that an effective vetting system for selecting employees of such companies should be developed to prevent persons posing a higher risk of human rights violations from performing those duties. A draft international convention on the regulation of private military and security companies and a draft model law were introduced.

1989 International Convention

As at 31 December, 32 States had become parties to the 1989 International Convention against the Recruitment, Use, Financing and Training of Mercenaries, adopted by the General Assembly in resolution 44/34 [YUN 1989, p. 825], with Honduras and the Syrian Arab Republic acceding in 2008. The Convention entered into force in 2001 [YUN 2001, p. 632].

GENERAL ASSEMBLY ACTION

On 18 December [meeting 70], the General Assembly, on the recommendation of the Third Committee [A/63/429], adopted **resolution 63/164** by recorded vote (125-52-5) [agenda item 63].

Use of mercenaries as a means of violating human rights and impeding the exercise of the right of peoples to self-determination

The General Assembly,

Recalling all of its previous resolutions on the subject, including resolution 62/145 of 18 December 2007, and Human Rights Council resolution 7/21 of 28 March 2008, as well as all resolutions adopted by the Commission on Human Rights in this regard,

Recalling also all of its relevant resolutions in which, inter alia, it condemned any State that permitted or tolerated the recruitment, financing, training, assembly, transit and use of mercenaries with the objective of overthrowing the Governments of States Members of the United Nations, especially those of developing countries, or of fighting against national liberation movements, and recalling further the relevant resolutions and international instruments adopted by the General Assembly, the Security Council, the Economic and Social Council and the Organization of African Unity, inter alia, the Organization of African Unity Convention for the elimination of mercenarism in Africa, as well as by the African Union,

Reaffirming the purposes and principles enshrined in the Charter of the United Nations concerning the strict observance of the principles of sovereign equality, political independence, the territorial integrity of States, the self-determination of peoples, the non-use of force or of the threat of use of force in international relations and non-interference in affairs within the domestic jurisdiction of States,

Reaffirming also that, by virtue of the principle of self-determination, all peoples have the right freely to determine their political status and to pursue their economic, social and cultural development, and that every State has the duty to respect this right in accordance with the provisions of the Charter,

Reaffirming further the Declaration on Principles of International Law concerning Friendly Relations and Cooperation among States in accordance with the Charter of the United Nations,

Alarmed and concerned at the danger that the activities of mercenaries constitute to peace and security in developing countries, in particular in Africa and in small States,

Deeply concerned at the loss of life, the substantial damage to property and the negative effects on the policy and economies of affected countries resulting from criminal mercenary activities,

Extremely alarmed and concerned about recent mercenary activities in Africa and other places and the threat they pose to the integrity of and respect for the constitutional order of those countries,

Concerned by the new modalities of mercenarism, and noting that the recruitment of former military personnel and ex-policemen by private military and private security companies to serve in their employ as "security guards" in zones of armed conflict seems to be continuing,

Convinced that, notwithstanding the way in which they are used or the form that they take to acquire some semblance of legitimacy, mercenaries or mercenary-related activities are a threat to peace, security and the self-determination of peoples and an obstacle to the enjoyment of all human rights by peoples,

1. *Takes note with appreciation* of the report of the Working Group on the use of mercenaries as a means of violating human rights and impeding the exercise of the right of peoples to self-determination, and expresses its appreciation for the work of the experts of the Working Group;

2. *Reaffirms* that the use of mercenaries and their recruitment, financing and training are causes for grave concern to all States and violate the purposes and principles enshrined in the Charter of the United Nations;

3. *Recognizes* that armed conflict, terrorism, arms trafficking and covert operations by third Powers, inter alia, encourage the demand for mercenaries on the global market;

4. *Urges once again* all States to take the necessary steps and to exercise the utmost vigilance against the menace posed by the activities of mercenaries and to take legislative measures to ensure that their territories and other territories under their control, as well as their nationals, are not used for the recruitment, assembly, financing, training and transit of mercenaries for the planning of activities designed to impede the right of peoples to self-determination, to destabilize or overthrow the Government of any State or to dismember or impair, totally or in part, the territorial integrity or political unity of sovereign and independent States conducting themselves in compliance with the right of peoples to self-determination;

5. *Requests* all States to exercise the utmost vigilance against any kind of recruitment, training, hiring or financing of mercenaries, including nationals, by private companies offering international military consultancy and security services, as well as to impose a specific ban on such companies intervening in armed conflicts or actions to destabilize constitutional regimes;

6. *Encourages* States that import the military assistance, consultancy and security services provided by private companies to establish regulatory national mechanisms for the registering and licensing of those companies in order to ensure that imported services provided by those private companies neither impede the enjoyment of human rights nor violate human rights in the recipient country;

7. *Calls upon* all States that have not yet done so to consider taking the necessary action to accede to or ratify the International Convention against the Recruitment, Use, Financing and Training of Mercenaries;

8. *Welcomes* the adoption by some States of national legislation that restricts the recruitment, assembly, financing, training and transit of mercenaries;

9. *Condemns* mercenary activities in Africa and commends the Governments of Africa on their collaboration in thwarting those illegal actions, which have posed a threat to the integrity of and respect for the constitutional order of those countries and the exercise of the right of their peoples to self-determination, and stresses the importance for the Working Group of looking into sources and root causes, as well as the political motivations of mercenaries and for mercenary-related activities;

10. *Calls upon* States to investigate the possibility of mercenary involvement whenever and wherever criminal acts of a terrorist nature occur and to bring to trial those found responsible or to consider their extradition, if so requested, in accordance with domestic law and applicable bilateral or international treaties;

11. *Condemns* any form of impunity granted to perpetrators of mercenary activities and to those responsible for the use, recruitment, financing and training of mercenaries, and urges all States, in accordance with their obligations under international law, to bring them, without distinction, to justice;

12. *Calls upon* Member States, in accordance with their obligations under international law, to cooperate with and assist the judicial prosecution of those accused of mercenary activities in transparent, open and fair trials;

13. *Requests* the Working Group to continue the work already done by the previous Special Rapporteurs on the strengthening of the international legal framework for the prevention and sanction of the recruitment, use, financing and training of mercenaries, taking into account the proposal for a new legal definition of a mercenary drafted by the Special Rapporteur in his report to the Commission on Human Rights at its sixtieth session, including the elaboration and presentation of concrete proposals on possible complementary and new standards aimed at filling existing gaps, as well as general guidelines or basic principles encouraging the further protection of human rights, in particular the right of peoples to self-determination, while facing current and emergent threats posed by mercenaries or mercenary-related activities;

14. *Requests* the Office of the United Nations High Commissioner for Human Rights, as a matter of priority, to publicize the adverse effects of the activities of mercenaries on the right of peoples to self-determination and, when requested and where necessary, to render advisory services to States that are affected by those activities;

15. *Welcomes* the convening in Panama on 17 and 18 December 2007 of the regional governmental consultation for Latin American and Caribbean States on traditional and new forms of mercenary activities as a means of violating human rights and impeding the exercise of the right of peoples to self-determination, in particular regarding the effects of the activities of private military and security companies on the enjoyment of human rights;

16. *Requests* the Office of the High Commissioner to inform the Human Rights Council, in a timely manner, of the dates and places for the convening of the other regional governmental consultations on this matter, bearing in mind that this process may lead to the holding of a high-level round table of States, under the auspices of the United Nations, to discuss the fundamental question of the role of the State as holder of the monopoly of the use of force, with the objective of facilitating a critical understanding of the responsibilities of the different actors, including private military and security companies, in the current context, and their respective obligations for the promotion and protection of human rights and in reaching a common understanding as to which additional regulations and controls are needed at the international level;

17. *Requests* the Working Group to continue to take into account, in the discharge of its mandate, the fact that mercenary activities continue to occur in many parts of the world and are taking on new forms, manifestations and modalities, and in this regard requests its members to continue to pay particular attention to the impact of the activities of private companies offering military assistance, consultancy and security services on the international market on the enjoyment of human rights and the exercise of the right of peoples to self-determination;

18. *Urges* all States to cooperate fully with the Working Group in the fulfilment of its mandate;

19. *Requests* the Secretary-General and the United Nations High Commissioner for Human Rights to provide the Working Group with all the necessary assistance and support for the fulfilment of its mandate, both professional and financial, including through the promotion of cooperation between the Working Group and other components

of the United Nations system that deal with countering mercenary-related activities, in order to meet the demands of its current and future activities;

20. *Requests* the Working Group to consult States and intergovernmental and non-governmental organizations in the implementation of the present resolution and to report, with specific recommendations, to the General Assembly at its sixty-fourth session its findings on the use of mercenaries to undermine the enjoyment of all human rights and to impede the exercise of the right of peoples to self-determination;

21. *Decides* to consider at its sixty-fourth session the question of the use of mercenaries as a means of violating human rights and impeding the exercise of the right of peoples to self-determination under the item entitled "Right of peoples to self-determination".

RECORDED VOTE ON RESOLUTION 63/164:

In favour: Afghanistan, Algeria, Angola, Antigua and Barbuda, Argentina, Armenia, Azerbaijan, Bahamas, Bahrain, Bangladesh, Barbados, Belarus, Belize, Benin, Bhutan, Bolivia, Botswana, Brazil, Brunei Darussalam, Burkina Faso, Burundi, Cambodia, Cameroon, Cape Verde, Central African Republic, China, Colombia, Comoros, Congo, Costa Rica, Côte d'Ivoire, Cuba, Democratic People's Republic of Korea, Djibouti, Dominica, Dominican Republic, Ecuador, Egypt, El Salvador, Eritrea, Ethiopia, Gabon, Gambia, Ghana, Grenada, Guatemala, Guinea, Guinea-Bissau, Guyana, Haiti, Honduras, India, Indonesia, Iran, Iraq, Jamaica, Jordan, Kazakhstan, Kenya, Kuwait, Kyrgyzstan, Lao People's Democratic Republic, Lebanon, Lesotho, Liberia, Libyan Arab Jamahiriya, Madagascar, Malawi, Malaysia, Maldives, Mali, Mauritania, Mauritius, Mexico, Mongolia, Morocco, Mozambique, Myanmar, Namibia, Nepal, Nicaragua, Niger, Nigeria, Oman, Pakistan, Panama, Papua New Guinea, Paraguay, Philippines, Qatar, Russian Federation, Rwanda, Saint Lucia, Saint Vincent and the Grenadines, Samoa, Sao Tome and Principe, Saudi Arabia, Senegal, Sierra Leone, Singapore, Solomon Islands, Somalia, South Africa, Sri Lanka, Sudan, Suriname, Swaziland, Syrian Arab Republic, Tajikistan, Thailand, Timor-Leste, Togo, Trinidad and Tobago, Tunisia, Tuvalu, Uganda, United Arab Emirates, United Republic of Tanzania, Uruguay, Uzbekistan, Venezuela, Viet Nam, Yemen, Zambia, Zimbabwe.

Against: Albania, Andorra, Australia, Austria, Belgium, Bosnia and Herzegovina, Bulgaria, Canada, Croatia, Cyprus, Czech Republic, Denmark, Estonia, Finland, France, Georgia, Germany, Greece, Hungary, Iceland, Ireland, Israel, Italy, Japan, Latvia, Liechtenstein, Lithuania, Luxembourg, Malta, Marshall Islands, Micronesia, Moldova, Monaco, Montenegro, Netherlands, Norway, Palau, Poland, Portugal, Republic of Korea, Romania, San Marino, Serbia, Slovakia, Slovenia, Spain, Sweden, The former Yugoslav Republic of Macedonia, Turkey, Ukraine, United Kingdom, United States.

Abstaining: Chile, Fiji, New Zealand, Switzerland, Tonga.

Administration of justice

Transitional justice

Human Rights Council action. On 24 September [A/63/53/Add.1 (res. 9/10)], the Human Rights Council underlined the urgency of national and international efforts to restore justice and the rule of law in conflict and post-conflict situations and in the context of transitional processes; and emphasized the importance of a comprehensive approach to transitional justice, incorporating judicial and non-judicial measures, including individual prosecutions, reparations, truth-seeking, institutional reform and vetting of public employees and officials to ensure accountability, serve justice, provide remedies to victims, promote healing and reconciliation, establish independent oversight of the security system, restore confidence in State institutions and promote the rule of law. OHCHR was requested to assist States to establish and implement transitional justice mechanisms from a human rights perspective, and to submit an analytical study on human rights and transitional justice.

Fundamental standards of humanity

Report of Secretary-General. A June report by the Secretary-General [A/HRC/8/14], submitted pursuant to a Human Rights Council request [YUN 2006, p. 760], outlined progress in fundamental standards of humanity and issues related to securing the practical protection of all individuals in all circumstances and by all actors. A number of developments had contributed to securing the respect for international human rights and humanitarian law standards. The General Assembly adopted the Basic Principles and Guidelines on the Right to a Remedy and Reparation for Victims of Gross Violations of International Human Rights Law and Serious Violations of International Humanitarian Law [YUN 2005, p. 793], as well as the International Convention for the Protection of All Persons from Enforced Disappearance [YUN 2006, p. 800]. The work of the International Criminal Tribunals for the Former Yugoslavia and for Rwanda had elaborated on the nature and elements of certain war crimes, genocide and crimes against humanity. The work of the Special Court for Sierra Leone and the Extraordinary Chambers in the Courts of Cambodia represented a further step into incorporating standards of humanity into the work of hybrid courts. The International Court of Justice, in its 2007 decision in the case of the *Application of the Convention on the Prevention and Punishment of the Crime of Genocide (Bosnia and Herzegovina v. Serbia and Montenegro)* [YUN 2007, p. 1325], provided further clarification as to the interpretation of the scope and certain key notions of the Convention on the Prevention and Punishment of the Crime of Genocide [YUN 1948–49, p. 959]. That decision further clarified the interpretation of the term "ethnic cleansing" and its significance in international law within the scope of crimes against humanity, genocide and war crimes in the context of the responsibility to protect. Finally, the commencement of operations of the International Criminal Court contributed to securing the protection of victims and achieving accountability for serious violations of international humanitarian and human rights law. To build on that progress, the Council might wish to keep itself informed of relevant developments, including further international and regional case law, which contributed to the interpretation of existing standards.

Civilians in armed conflict

Security Council consideration (May). On 27 May [meeting 5898], the Security Council considered the protection of civilians in armed conflict, during which it was briefed by John Holmes, Under-Secretary-General for Humanitarian Affairs and Emergency Relief Coordinator. Mr. Holmes observed that millions of people were still trapped in the horror of war and conflict, hoping desperately to rise from the chaos surrounding them. While in Kenya, Côte d'Ivoire, Nepal, Timor-Leste and, in a more fragile way, Uganda, violence had subsided, recent upsurges in recovering areas like Burundi and Southern Sudan were of concern. The full deployment of peacekeepers in Chad, the Central African Republic and the Darfur region of the Sudan had the potential to augment efforts to protect and assist those caught in the turmoil in the region, but those missions should be given the requisite support and resources to fulfil their mandates. Despite that progress, countless civilians in conflicts throughout the world continued to see their hopes shattered by violence and displacement, as well as by physical violence, deprivation and neglect. In the first five months of the year, more than half a million people had been displaced by conflict. In Burundi, the Central African Republic, Chad, Somalia and the Sudan, over 337,000 civilians had been forced to flee violence. In the Democratic Republic of the Congo (DRC), 175,000 people were newly displaced. Continued havoc was occurring in Colombia, Somalia, southern Israel, and Sri Lanka, as well as in the Darfur region of the Sudan and Gaza. In Afghanistan and Iraq, civilians remained victims of suicide attacks, aerial bombardments and search operations against anti-Government elements. There were difficulties in conducting those operations but, nonetheless, any military response to insurgent attacks should comply with international humanitarian law. Robust action was needed against sexual violence, which continued to ravage the women of the DRC, Côte d'Ivoire and the Sudan. Humanitarian access was crucial for protecting civilians, yet millions of people in need of assistance remained beyond reach. Progress had been made in the nine years since the Council first considered the item. There was an increased awareness among Member States of the issues involved, and four resolutions on civilian protection had established an ambitious framework for action. The challenge was to realize that ambition and ensure the systematic consideration of the issue. The establishment of an informal expert group, attached to the Council, would allow for transparent, systematic and timely consultation on the protection of civilians concerns.

SECURITY COUNCIL ACTION

On 27 May [meeting 5898], following consultations among Security Council members, the President made statement **S/PRST/2008/18** on behalf of the Council:

> The Security Council reaffirms its commitment to the full and effective implementation of its resolutions on the protection of civilians in armed conflict and recalls previous statements on the issue made by its President.
>
> The Council remains committed to addressing the impact of armed conflict on civilians. The Council expresses its deepest concern that civilians continue to account for the majority of victims of acts of violence committed by parties to armed conflict, including as a result of deliberate targeting, of indiscriminate and excessive use of force and of sexual and gender-based violence. The Council condemns all violations of international law, including international humanitarian law, human rights law and refugee law committed against civilians in situations of armed conflict. The Council demands that all relevant parties immediately put an end to such practices. The Council reaffirms in this regard that parties to armed conflict bear the primary responsibility to take all feasible steps to ensure the protection of affected civilians, in particular giving attention to the specific needs of women and children.
>
> The Council re-emphasizes the responsibility of States to comply with their relevant obligations to end impunity and to prosecute those responsible for war crimes, genocide, crimes against humanity and serious violations of international humanitarian law.
>
> The Council underlines the importance of safe and unhindered access of humanitarian personnel to provide assistance to civilians in armed conflict in accordance with international law, and stresses the importance, within the framework of humanitarian assistance, of upholding and respecting the humanitarian principles of humanity, neutrality, impartiality and independence.
>
> The Council recognizes the increasingly valuable role that regional organizations and other intergovernmental institutions play in the protection of civilians, and encourages the Secretary-General and the heads of regional and other intergovernmental organizations to continue their efforts to strengthen their partnership in this regard.
>
> The Council takes note of the report of the Secretary-General of 28 October 2007 on the protection of civilians in armed conflict, and requests the Secretary-General to submit his next report on this subject by May 2009. The Council invites the Secretary-General to provide an update in that report on the implementation of protection mandates in United Nations missions as mandated by the Council. The Council encourages the Secretary-General to continue to include such updates on the protection of civilians in his regular reporting on United Nations missions.

Human Rights Council action. On 24 September [A/63/53/Add.1 (res. 9/9)], the Human Rights Council resolved to address systematic and gross violations of the human rights of civilians in conflicts in order to facilitate the work of any mechanism that the Council might decide to establish in response to such violations. It called upon States to respect the human rights of civilians in armed conflicts; stressed the importance of combating impunity; and urged States to bring perpetrators to justice. OHCHR was invited to convene an expert consultation on the issue and to report at the Council's eleventh (2009) session.

Missing persons

Human Rights Council action. On 28 March [A/63/53 (res. 7/28)], the Human Rights Council called upon States parties to an armed conflict to take all appropriate measures to prevent persons from going missing, account for persons reported missing as a result of such a situation, take all necessary measures to determine the identity and fate of persons reported missing and provide their family members with all relevant information on their fate. It decided to hold a panel discussion on the subject at its ninth (2008) session and asked the High Commissioner to prepare a report on those deliberations, with a view to charging the Council's Advisory Committee with the preparation of a study on best practices in the matter. It requested the Secretary-General to bring the resolution to the attention of Governments, UN bodies, specialized agencies, regional intergovernmental organizations and international human rights organizations, and to submit a report on its implementation at the Council's tenth (2009) session.

On 22 September [A/HRC/9/28], the Council held a panel discussion on missing persons. On 24 September [A/63/53/Add.1 (dec. 9/101)], it adopted a text welcoming that discussion and looked forward to receiving the High Commissioner's summary of the panel's deliberations. The Council requested the Advisory Committee to prepare a study on best practices in the matter of missing persons and submit it to the Council's twelfth (2009) session.

Report of Secretary-General. In response to General Assembly resolution 61/155 [YUN 2006, p. 861], the Secretary-General, in August [A/63/299], summarized replies received from 10 Governments, two international humanitarian organizations and the Argentine Forensic Anthropology Team on the implementation of that resolution. The Secretary-General recommended that measures be taken to minimize the problem of missing persons in the context of armed conflict by establishing adequate identification processes and addressing it as part of peacebuilding processes. The right of families to know the fate of missing persons should be respected at all times. Forensic work should be supported as a component of the investigation of human rights violations. Access to independent forensic investigations of such violations should be improved, and mechanisms created to continue the recovery and identification process beyond the mandate of judicial and non-judicial mechanisms. Contacts should be enhanced between independent forensic experts and local judiciaries, prosecutors, judges and lawyers, and accountability for enforced disappearances ensured. States should ratify the International Convention for the Protection of All Persons from Enforced Disappearance [YUN 2006, p. 800], and bring their laws and practices into conformity with the Convention.

GENERAL ASSEMBLY ACTION

On 18 December [meeting 70], the General Assembly, on the recommendation of the Third Committee [A/63/430/Add.2], adopted **resolution 63/183** without vote [agenda item 64 *(b)*].

Missing persons

The General Assembly,

Guided by the purposes, principles and provisions of the Charter of the United Nations,

Guided also by the principles and norms of international humanitarian law, in particular the Geneva Conventions of 12 August 1949 and the Additional Protocols thereto, of 1977, as well as international standards of human rights, in particular the Universal Declaration of Human Rights, the International Covenant on Economic, Social and Cultural Rights, the International Covenant on Civil and Political Rights, the Convention on the Elimination of All Forms of Discrimination against Women, the Convention on the Rights of the Child and the Vienna Declaration and Programme of Action adopted by the World Conference on Human Rights on 25 June 1993,

Acknowledging the adoption of the International Convention for the Protection of All Persons from Enforced Disappearance, and looking forward to its entry into force,

Recalling all previous relevant resolutions on missing persons adopted by the General Assembly, as well as the resolutions adopted by the Commission on Human Rights and the Human Rights Council,

Noting with deep concern that armed conflicts are continuing in various parts of the world, often resulting in serious violations of international humanitarian law and human rights law,

Noting that the issue of persons reported missing in connection with international or non-international armed conflicts, in particular those who are victims of serious violations of international humanitarian law and human rights law, continues to have a negative impact on efforts to put an end to those conflicts and causes suffering to the families of missing persons, and stressing in this regard the need to address the issue from a humanitarian perspective, among others,

Considering that the problem of missing persons may raise questions of international humanitarian law and international human rights law, as appropriate,

Being cognizant that States that are parties to an armed conflict have a responsibility for countering the phenomenon of missing persons and determining the fate of missing persons and for recognizing their accountability as regards implementing the relevant mechanisms, policies and laws,

Bearing in mind the effective search for and identification of missing persons through traditional forensic methods, and recognizing that great technological progress has been achieved in the field of DNA forensic sciences, which could significantly assist efforts to identify missing persons,

Recalling the Agenda for Humanitarian Action, in particular its general objective 1, to "respect and restore the dignity of persons missing as a result of armed conflicts or other situations of armed violence and of their families", adopted at the Twenty-eighth International Conference of the Red Cross and Red Crescent, held in Geneva from 2 to 6 December 2003, and resolution 3 entitled "Reaffirmation and implementation of international humanitarian law: preserving human life and dignity in armed conflict", adopted at the Thirtieth International Conference of the Red Cross and Red Crescent, held in Geneva from 26 to 30 November 2007,

Taking note with appreciation of the report of the Secretary-General of 18 August 2008 on missing persons, prepared pursuant to General Assembly resolution 61/155 of 19 December 2006,

Taking note with appreciation also of the ongoing international and regional efforts to address the question of missing persons and of the initiatives undertaken by international and regional organizations in this field,

1. *Urges* States strictly to observe and respect and ensure respect for the rules of international humanitarian law, as set out in the Geneva Conventions of 12 August 1949 and, where applicable, in the Additional Protocols thereto, of 1977;

2. *Calls upon* States that are parties to an armed conflict to take all appropriate measures to prevent persons from going missing in connection with armed conflict and account for persons reported missing as a result of such a situation;

3. *Reaffirms* the right of families to know the fate of their relatives reported missing in connection with armed conflicts;

4. *Also reaffirms* that each party to an armed conflict, as soon as circumstances permit and, at the latest, from the end of active hostilities, shall search for the persons who have been reported missing by an adverse party;

5. *Calls upon* States that are parties to an armed conflict to take all necessary measures, in a timely manner, to determine the identity and fate of persons reported missing in connection with the armed conflict and, to the greatest possible extent, to provide their family members, through appropriate channels, with all relevant information they have on their fate;

6. *Recognizes*, in this regard, the need for the collection, protection and management of data on missing persons according to international and national legal norms and standards, and urges States to cooperate with each other and with other concerned actors working in this area, inter alia, by providing all relevant and appropriate information related to missing persons;

7. *Requests* States to pay the utmost attention to cases of children reported missing in connection with armed conflicts and to take appropriate measures to search for and identify those children and to reunite them with their families;

8. *Invites* States that are parties to an armed conflict to cooperate fully with the International Committee of the Red Cross in establishing the fate of missing persons and to adopt a comprehensive approach to this issue, including all such legal and practical measures and coordination mechanisms as may be necessary, based on humanitarian considerations only;

9. *Urges* States and encourages intergovernmental and non-governmental organizations to take all necessary measures at the national, regional and international levels to address the problem of persons reported missing in connection with armed conflicts and to provide appropriate assistance as requested by the concerned States, and welcomes in this regard the establishment and efforts of commissions and working groups on missing persons;

10. *Calls upon* States, without prejudice to their efforts to determine the fate of persons missing in connection with armed conflicts, to take appropriate steps with regard to the legal situation of the missing persons and the need of their family members, in fields such as social welfare, financial matters, family law and property rights;

11. *Stresses* the need for addressing the issue of missing persons as a part of peacebuilding processes, with reference to all justice and rule of law mechanisms, on the basis of transparency, accountability and public involvement and participation;

12. *Welcomes* the panel discussion on the question of missing persons held at the ninth session of the Human Rights Council, and takes note of the request of the Council to the United Nations High Commissioner for Human Rights to prepare a summary of the panel's deliberations;

13. *Takes note* of the request of the Human Rights Council to its Advisory Committee to prepare a study on the best practices in the matter of missing persons and to submit that study to the Council at its twelfth session;

14. *Invites* relevant human rights mechanisms and procedures, as appropriate, to address the problem of persons reported missing in connection with armed conflicts in their forthcoming reports to the General Assembly;

15. *Requests* the Secretary-General to submit a comprehensive report on the implementation of the present resolution, including relevant recommendations, to the Human Rights Council at its relevant session and to the General Assembly at its sixty-fifth session;

16. *Also requests* the Secretary-General to bring the present resolution to the attention of all Governments, the competent United Nations bodies, the specialized agencies, regional intergovernmental organizations and international humanitarian organizations;

17. *Decides* to consider the question at its sixty-fifth session.

Arbitrary detention

Working Group activities. The five-member Working Group on Arbitrary Detention held its fifty-first (5–9 May), fifty-second (8–12 September) and fifty-third (19–28 November) sessions, all in Geneva [A/HRC/10/21]. During the year, the Group adopted 46 opinions concerning 183 persons in 22 countries; the texts of those opinions were contained in a separate report [A/HRC/10/21/Add.1]. The Group transmitted 130 urgent appeals to 44 Governments concerning 1,256 individuals, including 57 women, 4 boys and 3 girls. Governments informed the Group that they had taken measures to remedy the situation of the detainees: in some cases, the detainees were released; in other cases, the Group was assured that the detainees concerned would enjoy fair trial guarantees. The Group engaged in a continuous dialogue with the countries it had visited, in respect of which it had recommended changes to legislation governing detention or the adoption of other measures. Information about the implementation of those recommendations was received from Belarus, Canada, China, Ecuador and Turkey.

Several issues had given rise to concern during 2008. In particular, the Working Group denounced the fact that an important proportion of the 9 million persons deprived of their liberty worldwide were unable to benefit from the legal resources and guarantees to which they were entitled for the conduct of their defence. Most did not have the means to afford expensive and complex legal procedures, and had difficulties in verifying the lawfulness of their detention and no effective control of their other rights. Detained persons suspected of terrorist activities should be immediately informed of such charges, brought before a competent judicial authority and enjoy the right to habeas corpus.

The Working Group therefore proposed that the Human Rights Council extend its mandate to include the monitoring of State compliance with their obligations concerning all human rights of detained and imprisoned persons.

The Working Group elaborated a list of principles concerning deprivation of liberty of persons accused of acts of terrorism, which it included in its report, and proposed holding a special forum on the respect of the right not to be arbitrarily deprived of liberty in the counter-terrorism context, especially in emergency situations. It noted that the corruption it had observed in some countries made the whole system of guarantees devoid of any content and reduced the credibility of the entire administration of justice system. The Group called upon States to become a party to the United Nations Convention against Corruption [YUN 2003, p. 1127]. It reiterated that immigrants in irregular situations should not be qualified or treated as criminals nor viewed only from the perspective of national security. Detention should be of the last resort, permissible only for the shortest period of time.

A Working Group delegation visited Mauritania (19 February–3 March) [A/HRC/10/21/Add.2], which was undergoing a transitional period. A number of institutional and legislative reforms had been carried out, including the establishment of a National Human Rights Commission and a general inspectorate of the judicial and penitentiary administration. The Government sought to improve the working conditions of the judiciary and to strengthen its power, reform the system of legal assistance and build new prisons. However, the legacy of the authoritarian system was still making itself felt. There were shortcomings in its legislation, but above all a gap between the legal instruments in force and actual practice. The cases of arbitrary detention that were observed stemmed mainly from dysfunction in the administration of justice, as reflected in a failure to respect the time limit for police custody; violations of the right to a fair trial; ineffective judicial oversight of the police and gendarmerie; corruption; and inconsistent interpretations of sharia.

In its conclusions and recommendations, the Working Group placed priority on guaranteeing the rights of the defence, strengthening oversight of police custody and places of detention, and training programmes for all those involved in the criminal justice system, including judges and prosecutors. The international community and OHCHR should provide technical and financial support to strengthen Mauritania's national capacity for the protection of human rights and to support the Government's reform process.

The Working Group visited Colombia (1–10 October) [A/HRC/10/21/Add.3], noting progress and setbacks in applying the new accusatorial criminal procedure for ensuring that national police officers respected the time limits on police detention, and in keeping up-to-date records. It highlighted the work of the Office of the Procurator-General within the Public Prosecutor's Office, which acted, in judicial proceedings, as guarantor of respect for due process and the right to defence. It also drew attention to the work of the judges responsible for procedural safeguards. The Group expressed satisfaction at the existence of judicial services centres and the work done in prisons by the human rights committees, which were elected by the prisoners by secret ballot.

The Working Group noted the gap between the Constitution, the law and reality. It criticized the practice of administrative pretrial detention; mass or multiple arrests by the military in rural areas; detentions in the poor areas of large cities, especially of beggars, the destitute and members of ethnic and sexual minorities; military round-ups and forced conscription; and the absence of criminal enforcement judges in prisons; prison overcrowding; and the practice of citizen's arrests. It expressed concern at the problem of "false positives", whereby, to obtain privileges, soldiers would detain innocent, vulnerable people without any valid reason, execute them and later identify such persons as guerrillas killed in combat.

The Working Group highlighted Government efforts to guarantee legislatively the protection of basic rights through such measures as the new code of criminal procedure, but criticized lapses in legislation and case law since its adoption. It noted the practice of mass detentions, as well as the lack of solid evidence required to carry out an arrest, particularly when the only evidence was the accusation of former guerrillas. The Group recommended that the Government eradicate the practice of mass arrests and administrative pretrial detention; eliminate detentions by military personnel and agents of private companies; appoint expedited procedure judges to clear cases under the old code of criminal procedure; and strengthen human rights institutions.

The Working Group visited Ukraine (22 October–5 November) [A/HRC/10/21/Add.4] and noted the reforms implemented with respect to the administration of justice since the country's independence in 1991. While commending the existence of several monitoring mechanisms, such as the Ombudsperson, mobile monitoring clinics and public councils, which worked to combat arbitrary detention, the Working Group recognized the need for strengthening them. It expressed concern about allegations of confessions obtained under torture from detainees of the *Militsia* (police force), which abused its arresting powers under the laws on administrative offences and on vagrants. Allegations of torture were not properly addressed by the Office of the Prosecutor General, nor were extracted confessions excluded as evidence in trials. Impunity for perpetrators of ill-treatment largely prevailed. Arbitrary detention resulted from the accumulation of powers in the Office of the Prosecutor General, which had both criminal prosecution and oversight powers, answered extradition requests and could, at the same time, challenge in court the refugee status of the person for whom extradition was sought. It also resulted from the perceived lack of an independent judiciary and an ineffective system of criminal defence and legal aid. The situation was aggravated by corruption throughout the law enforcement system. Also of concern was the high number of arrests, many of them not registered, which some sources estimated at approximately 1 million each year. Moreover, pre-trial detention and restrictions applied during detention on remand were too frequent, with courts not exercising genuine control when authorizing such detention.

The Working Group addressed 24 recommendations to the Government concerning, among other issues, allegations of torture to extract confessions; the various law enforcement institutions governing deprivation of liberty; pre-trial detention and legal aid; imprisonment, administrative offences and immigration detention; detention pending extradition; and juvenile justice and monitoring mechanisms.

The Working Group visited Italy (3–14 November) [A/HRC/10/21/Add.5] and reported numerous safeguards against illegal detention in the criminal justice system. However, the excessive duration of criminal proceedings could lead to situations of arbitrary detention, when defendants were in remand custody or when, though not detained pending trial, they were ordered to serve a prison sentence after an unreasonable amount of time had lapsed since the offence. The percentage of prisoners awaiting final judgement—and thus not serving a final sentence—was far in excess of that of other Western European countries. Immigrants were seriously over-represented in the prison population and did not benefit from access to alternatives to imprisonment to the same extent as Italian citizens.

The Government declared mafia-type organized crime, the threat of international terrorism, and crime by irregular migrants to be public security emergencies and responded by adopting extraordinary measures. The Group expressed concern about the safeguards regarding repeated extensions of detention under the law on the penitentiary system; the deportation of foreigners suspected of terrorist activities to countries where they could face arbitrary detention and torture; and norms that would increase the already disproportionate incarceration of foreigners. Limitations on the liberty of asylum-seekers in first reception centres did not have a sound legal basis. Also of concern was the detention of irregular migrants in identification and expulsion centres, including persons already having served a criminal sentence, asylum-seekers, and persons who were unlikely to be deported.

The Working Group called on the Government to take legislative and other measures to decrease the duration of criminal trials, and to reduce the share of the prison population held on remand. Judicial oversight regarding repeated extensions of detention should be strengthened. Legislation making non-compliance with immigration laws punishable by imprisonment, or as an aggravating circumstance, should be reconsidered. Limitations on the liberty of asylum-seekers should be applied on a sound legal basis and unnecessary or unreasonable detention in identification and expulsion centres of irregular migrants to be deported should be reduced.

Right to the truth

Human Rights Council action. On 24 September [A/63/53/Add.1 (res. 9/11)], the Human Rights

Council, recognizing the importance of respecting and ensuring the right to the truth in order to end impunity and promote and protect human rights, welcomed the establishment in several States of judicial and non-judicial mechanisms, such as truth and reconciliation commissions, to investigate human rights violations; encouraged those States to implement the recommendations of those mechanisms; and encouraged other States to establish such mechanisms to investigate violations of international humanitarian law. OHCHR was requested to prepare a study, to be presented to the Council's twelfth (2009) session, on best practices for the effective implementation of the right to the truth, and to prepare a report, to be presented to the Council's fifteenth (2010) session, on the use of forensic experts in cases of gross human rights violations.

Independence of the judicial system

Reports of Special Rapporteur. In a May report [A/HRC/8/4], the Special Rapporteur on the independence of judges and lawyers, Leandro Despouy (Argentina), addressed the impact of states of emergency on the right to a fair trial and access to justice, and discussed recent developments in international justice. The report analysed the two most important aspects of access to justice: access to justice as a fundamental right and the conditions for its effective implementation. It examined in particular the content and scope of the right of access to justice and the different economic, social, cultural and operational barriers to the exercise of that right; how access was affected by the type and characteristics of the various courts dispensing justice and the conditions in which judicial actors carried out their work; and the impact of corruption and judicial delay. The report also indicated the main consequences of the shortcomings in access to justice and recommended, in particular, that a database of best practice be developed to help States bridge that gap.

It also warned of the consequences, for the relatives of Sergio Vieira de Mello, former Special Representative for Iraq, and 21 other staff members who lost their lives in the 19 August 2003 attack on the UN headquarters in Baghdad [YUN 2003, p. 346], of the execution of a witness who could have helped to shed light on the incident, in blatant violation of the right to the truth. The Special Rapporteur urged that a commission of eminent persons be created to establish the facts. He proposed examining more closely the impact of states of emergency on human rights and asked the Council to give the subject the attention it deserved.

An addendum to the report [A/HRC/8/4/Add.1] summarized the 138 communications sent by the Special Rapporteur to 64 Governments between 16 January 2007 and 15 March 2008, and the 59 replies received.

In an August note [A/63/271], the Secretary-General transmitted to the General Assembly the Special Rapporteur's fourth report on the subject. The report stressed the central role of the judiciary in guaranteeing due process and safeguards against arbitrary detention, and warned of the consequences that attempts to deprive judges of that responsibility might have on the exercise of human rights. Judges had an important role in protecting human rights during states of emergency, and States should not interfere with the operation of the justice system in times of national emergency. The role of the judiciary was crucial for guaranteeing that states of emergency were declared and implemented in accordance with the principles governing them and that the measures taken in emergency situations did not interfere with the exercise of human rights, especially with rights considered non-derogable under international law. The Special Rapporteur urged States not to limit the operation of the judicial system in such circumstances and invited the Assembly to pay special attention to the issue. He recommended that a permanent list of countries in such circumstances should be maintained and continuously updated, as well as a list of the rights suspended and the starting and ending dates of the measures. An international instrument on principles for the protection of human rights during emergencies should also be drafted. In addition to states of emergency, there was a trend towards the restriction of rights in the name of defending national security, combating terrorism and controlling immigration. In such cases, the judiciary should clarify the limits of executive power where human rights were concerned. The Rapporteur undertook to explore how the underpayment of judges or linking their pay levels to the decisions they made compromised their independence and impartiality. He urged that every effort should be made to investigate the criminal attack on the UN headquarters in Baghdad in 2003, and reiterated his proposal that a panel of high-level experts should be established for that purpose.

The General Assembly took note of the report on 18 December **(decision 63/534)**.

The Special Rapporteur visited the Russian Federation (19–29 May) [A/HRC/11/41/Add.2], where important reforms had been implemented since 1993, particularly the adoption of new legislation governing judicial proceedings and the significant improvement of working conditions of the judiciary. However, concerns remained about the practical implementation of equal access to the courts and the fact that many judicial decisions were not implemented. There was insufficient transparency in the selection process of judges and the implementation of disciplinary measures. Political and other interference had damaged the image of the justice system in the eyes of the population. The role of defence lawyers had not yet been fully recognized. However, the reform aimed at separating the functions of investigation and prosecution had the potential to give judges a stronger guiding role and to achieve a more effective and balanced system in judicial proceedings. A solid legal framework was needed to achieve a judicial system with independent courts and guaranteeing adversarial proceedings, as well as a change in attitude. Recent initiatives, in particular the setting-up of a special working group on judicial reform, were encouraging. The Government's 2007–2011 reform programme, focusing on increased transparency, accessibility and effectiveness of the courts, should be refined and expanded.

The Rapporteur recommended, among other things, establishing a mechanism for rapid and comprehensive execution of domestic and international judicial decisions; monitoring closely courts' adherence to jurisprudence established at the highest domestic instances; institutionalizing closer cooperation between bailiffs and courts; and establishing an administrative court system to fight corruption and ensure liability of state officials. Other recommendations sought to strengthen procedural legislation and practice, enhance the independent role of judges and strengthen the role of the bar.

Human Rights Council action. On 18 June [A/63/53 (res. 8/6)], the Human Rights Council extended the mandate of the Special Rapporteur for a three-year period. It called upon Governments to respond favourably to the Rapporteur's requests to visit their countries and urged them to enter into a constructive dialogue with the Rapporteur.

Capital punishment

Communications. By a January note [A/62/658] to the Secretary-General, 58 Member States referred to General Assembly resolution 62/149 [YUN 2007, p. 744], entitled "Moratorium on the use of the death penalty", which was adopted by a recorded vote. Those States wished to place on record their persistent objection to any attempt to impose a moratorium on the use of the death penalty or its abolition, in contravention to existing stipulations under international law. There was no international consensus that the death penalty should be abolished, and the issue had proven to be a divisive one. Capital punishment had been characterized as a human rights issue in the context of the right of the convicted prisoner to life. However, it was first and foremost a criminal justice issue and an important deterrent vis-à-vis the most serious crimes. It should therefore be viewed from a broader perspective and weighed against the rights of the victims and the right of the community to live in peace and security. Every State had an inalienable right to choose its political, economic, social, cultural and legal justice systems, without interference by another State. Some States had decided to abolish the death penalty, others had chosen to apply a moratorium on executions, and many others had retained the death penalty in their legislation. All sides were acting in compliance with their international obligations. Each State had decided freely to determine the path that corresponded to its own social, cultural and legal needs, in order to maintain security, order and peace. No side had the right to impose its standpoint on the other.

By a 19 March letter [A/62/761], Uzbekistan informed the Secretary-General that it had abolished the death penalty as at 1 January.

Reports of Secretary-General. Pursuant to a Human Rights Council request [YUN 2006, p. 760], the Secretary-General, in a May report [A/HRC/8/11] on the question of the death penalty, covering the period from January 2006 to May 2008, found that the trend towards abolition had continued. The number of countries that were completely abolitionist had risen from 85 to 93, and the number of retentionist countries had decreased from 65 to 60. The number of countries that had ratified international instruments providing for the abolition of the death penalty had also increased significantly.

Pursuant to General Assembly resolution 62/149, the Secretary-General, in an August report [A/63/293 & Corr.1] on moratoriums on the use of the death penalty, surveyed respect for the rights of those sentenced to death as set out in the international human rights treaties and the guidelines established by the Economic and Social Council in 1984 [YUN 1984, p. 709]. Drawing on contributions of Member States, the report examined the motivations for establishing a moratorium on or abolishing the death penalty, as well as those for retaining it. The report confirmed the global trend towards abolition; suggested that the establishment of a moratorium was a key step towards eventual abolition; and observed that for States maintaining the death penalty, the standards to safeguard the rights of those sentenced to death were crucial for ensuring that the punishment was carried out in a manner consistent with States' international legal obligations. Further work could usefully be carried out on specific restrictions on the use of capital punishment, such as the prohibition of the execution of certain groups of individuals; the prohibition of torture and other cruel, inhuman or degrading treatment; or punishment in the application of the death penalty, including the conditions of detention on death row.

GENERAL ASSEMBLY ACTION

On 18 December [meeting 70], the General Assembly, on the recommendation of the Third Committee [A/63/430/Add.2], adopted **resolution 63/168** by recorded vote (106-46-34) [agenda item 64 *(b)*].

Moratorium on the use of the death penalty

The General Assembly,

Reaffirming its resolution 62/149 of 18 December 2007 on a moratorium on the use of the death penalty,

Welcoming the decisions taken by an increasing number of States to apply a moratorium on executions and the global trend towards the abolition of the death penalty,

1. *Welcomes* the report of the Secretary-General on the implementation of resolution 62/149, and the conclusions and recommendations contained therein;

2. *Requests* the Secretary-General to provide a report on progress made in the implementation of resolution 62/149 and the present resolution, for consideration during its sixty-fifth session, and calls upon Member States to provide the Secretary-General with information in this regard;

3. *Decides* to continue consideration of the matter at its sixty-fifth session under the item entitled "Promotion and protection of human rights".

RECORDED VOTE ON RESOLUTION 63/168:

In favour: Albania, Algeria, Andorra, Angola, Argentina, Armenia, Australia, Austria, Azerbaijan, Belgium, Benin, Bolivia, Bosnia and Herzegovina, Brazil, Bulgaria, Burkina Faso, Burundi, Cambodia, Canada, Cape Verde, Chile, Colombia, Congo, Costa Rica, Côte d'Ivoire, Croatia, Cyprus, Czech Republic, Denmark, Dominican Republic, Ecuador, El Salvador, Estonia, Ethiopia, Finland, France, Gabon, Georgia, Germany, Greece, Guinea-Bissau, Haiti, Honduras, Hungary, Iceland, Ireland, Israel, Italy, Kazakhstan, Kyrgyzstan, Latvia, Liechtenstein, Lithuania, Luxembourg, Madagascar, Mali, Malta, Marshall Islands, Mauritius, Mexico, Micronesia, Moldova, Monaco, Montenegro, Mozambique, Namibia, Nauru, Nepal, Netherlands, New Zealand, Nicaragua, Norway, Palau, Panama, Paraguay, Peru, Philippines, Poland, Portugal, Romania, Russian Federation, Rwanda, Samoa, San Marino, Sao Tome and Principe, Serbia, Slovakia, Slovenia, Somalia, South Africa, Spain, Sri Lanka, Sweden, Switzerland, Tajikistan, The former Yugoslav Republic of Macedonia, Timor-Leste, Turkey, Turkmenistan, Tuvalu, Ukraine, United Kingdom, Uruguay, Uzbekistan, Vanuatu, Venezuela.

Against: Afghanistan, Antigua and Barbuda, Bahamas, Bangladesh, Barbados, Belize, Botswana, Brunei Darussalam, China, Comoros, Democratic People's Republic of Korea, Dominica, Egypt, Grenada, Guyana, India, Indonesia, Iran, Iraq, Jamaica, Japan, Kuwait, Libyan Arab Jamahiriya, Malaysia, Maldives, Mongolia, Myanmar, Nigeria, Pakistan, Qatar, Saint Kitts and Nevis, Saint Lucia, Saint Vincent and the Grenadines, Saudi Arabia, Singapore, Solomon Islands, Sudan, Swaziland, Syrian Arab Republic, Thailand, Tonga, Trinidad and Tobago, Uganda, United States, Yemen, Zimbabwe.

Abstaining: Bahrain, Belarus, Bhutan, Cameroon, Central African Republic, Cuba, Djibouti, Eritrea, Fiji, Gambia, Ghana, Guatemala, Guinea, Jordan, Kenya, Lao People's Democratic Republic, Lebanon, Lesotho, Liberia, Malawi, Mauritania, Morocco, Niger, Oman, Papua New Guinea, Republic of Korea, Senegal, Sierra Leone, Suriname, Togo, United Arab Emirates, United Republic of Tanzania, Viet Nam, Zambia.

Other issues

Extralegal executions

Reports of Special Rapporteur. The Special Rapporteur on extrajudicial, summary or arbitrary executions, Philip Alston (Australia), in a May report [A/HRC/8/3 & Corr.1], submitted pursuant to a Human Rights Council request [YUN 2006, p. 759], reviewed activities undertaken in 2007 to address extralegal executions worldwide. The report highlighted the Special Rapporteur's communications to and replies received from Governments [A/HRC/8/3/Add.1]. Between 1 December 2006 and 15 March 2008, the Rapporteur sent 127 communications to 46 countries, including 58 urgent appeals and 69 letters of allegation. The main issues covered in the communications were the death penalty, deaths in custody, the death penalty for minors, excessive use of force, impunity, attacks or killings, armed conflict and death threats. As in previous years, the proportion of Government replies was problematically low. In addition, 22 countries had so far not responded affirmatively to requests for a visit.

The Special Rapporteur highlighted three issues of particular importance: the role of national commissions of inquiry in impunity for extrajudicial executions; the right to seek pardon or commutation of a death sentence; and prisoners running prisons. According to the Rapporteur, Governments were obligated to hold an independent inquiry into deaths where extrajudicial execution might have taken place. Commissions of inquiry were often established as a result of concerted demands by civil society or the international community, and usually in the aftermath of major incidents in which the authorities normally relied on to investigate were feared to be reluctant or unlikely to do so adequately. However, the mere setting up of a commission of inquiry and its formal completion were often not adequate to satisfy the obligation to undertake an independent inquiry. Evidence had shown that such inquiries were frequently used to avoid meaningful accountability. The international community should scrutinize such initiatives more carefully and develop a mechanism for monitoring and evaluating their adequacy. Concerning the right to seek pardon or commutation of a death sentence, the Special Rapporteur concluded that both law and practice demanded that the right be accompanied by guarantees, if it were not to be a meaningless formality. Those procedural guarantees included the right of the condemned person to affirmatively request pardon or commutation; to make representation in support of that request; to be informed in advance of when the request would be considered; and be informed promptly thereafter of whatever decision was reached. The issue of prisoners running prisons demanded the attention of the Council. The temptation to rely on prisoners to carry out basic functions of maintaining order and imposing discipline was appealing to administrators grappling with shrinking budgets, staff shortages, overcrowded facilities, demanding gang-based populations and little public or Government support. However, there were major problems in opting for that choice. States should develop plans to reassert responsible control over prison populations and effectively protect prisoners from each other.

The Special Rapporteur recommended that the Council appoint a Special Rapporteur on the rights of detainees and address the failure of States where there were serious concerns over extrajudicial executions to respond to requests to visit by the Special Rapporteur. The Council should reconsider its action in not renewing the mandate of the Group of Experts on Darfur in December 2007, despite its conclusion that the Sudan had failed to meet many of the benchmarks that had been set, as it represented the triumph of politics over human rights.

Human Rights Council action. On 18 June [A/63/53 (res. 8/3)], the Human Rights Council noted the Special Rapporteur's report and extended the Rapporteur's mandate for a three-year period. It urged States to consider responding favourably to the Rapporteur's requests to visit their countries, and urged Governments that had not yet responded to his communications to answer without further delay.

By an August note [A/63/313], the Secretary-General transmitted the Special Rapporteur's report to the General Assembly, in response to resolution 61/173 [YUN 2006, p. 870]. The report focused on outstanding country visit requests and on visits undertaken since the previous report [YUN 2007, p. 746]. It also addressed two neglected but vital dimensions of the struggle to combat impunity for extrajudicial executions: the provision of effective witness protection arrangements; and the importance of ensuring that military justice systems were compatible with human rights standards. In many States, witness protection programmes were wholly inadequate, and military justice systems were structured in ways that promoted impunity for killings. The report surveyed best practices in both areas. The Special Rapporteur recommended that OHCHR develop policy tools to encourage and facilitate greater attention to witness protection in national level programmes to combat impunity for killings and other crimes; and that the Assembly call upon States to report on the extent to which their military justice systems complied with human rights standards.

The Assembly took note of the Secretary-General's note on 18 December (**decision 63/534**).

Reports on country visits. A further addendum to the Special Rapporteur's May report [A/HRC/8/3/Add.3] tracked the implementation of recommendations made by visits to Nigeria [YUN 2005, p. 808] and Sri Lanka [ibid., p. 809]. The Rapporteur stated that recommendations made with respect to Sri Lanka had not been implemented. Those directed to the Government were all but completely disregarded, and in most areas there was significant backward movement. The same was true of recommendations directed to the Liberation Tigers of Tamil Eelam. As to Nigeria, the Government had enacted some reforms in partial fulfilment of the Special Rapporteur's recommendations, but for the majority of them, Nigeria had failed to make sufficient progress, or any progress at all. Moreover, on some issues, the situation appeared to be worse. The high level of extrajudicial executions reported by the Special Rapporteur continued. However, the positive initiatives implemented by the Government over the past two and a half years were encouraging, and Nigeria should continue to promote their effective follow-through. With respect to the measures upon which there had been no progress, the Government should take action to ensure their implementation.

The Special Rapporteur visited the Central African Republic (31 January–7 February) [A/HRC/11/2/Add.3], where a low-intensity conflict continued in the north-west. Large-scale abuses had declined significantly by mid-2007 due to positive steps taken by President François Bozizé and the waning of conflict in the north-east. Since the Rapporteur's visit, there had been encouraging moves towards securing a durable peace in the north. Those steps were, however, interrupted during 2008 by sporadic fighting in the north-west and renewed rebel activity in the north-east. Overall progress in resolving that conflict had not been matched with progress in securing human rights. Killings continued, accountability for past abuses was non-existent, and a general lack of security in the north prevailed. The most pressing human rights issues remained securing the population from banditry, remedying general lawlessness, countering impunity and reforming the security forces. As fighting between the Government and the rebels ebbed, banditry took its place as the prime threat to civilians. The security forces were largely unwilling and unable to protect villagers, and were responsible for killings of suspected criminals and killings motivated by personal or corrupt ends. Killings in police custody and in detention centres were common, as were killings of persons alleged to be "witches", which were often carried out with the participation of the security forces. Investigations and prosecutions rarely occurred due to the unwillingness to tackle abuses by State actors and a lack of resources in the justice sector.

The Special Rapporteur proposed a number of recommendations for implementation so as to reduce extrajudicial executions and provide for accountability when they occurred. He recommended that the security forces should be reformed so that they could protect the people from cross-border raids and threats by rebel groups and bandits, and obey human rights norms in carrying out military and law enforcement operations. Although those reforms were extensive, the country was at an unusually favourable juncture for change. In June, the Government pledged wide-ranging security sector reform, and the President showed a willingness to take steps to reduce killings by his troops. Former rebel groups were brought into a multiparty Government. International financial institutions had re-engaged in the country, and international aid and the presence of humanitarian organizations had increased substantially. If the Government's willingness to reform was supported internationally, the country could break its long pattern of abuse and impunity.

The Special Rapporteur visited Afghanistan (4–15 May) [A/HRC/11/2/Add.4], a country engulfed in a conflict in which large numbers of civilians were killed every day. An estimated 2,118 civilians were killed in 2008, nearly 40 per cent more than in 2007. The Rapporteur's concern was to understand how and why those killings were happening, and to formulate recommendations for reducing them. The Taliban, Afghan forces and international military forces all bore responsibility, and therefore responsibility for reducing the killings. The Taliban leadership should order its fighters to respect human rights and humanitarian law, particularly by ending the use of human shields, the assassination of civilians and the use of suicide attacks. Human rights proponents should engage in dialogue with the leadership to promote those objectives. Afghan and international forces should review procedures for conducting air strikes and raids. More effective procedures for vetting targets should be developed, and the forces should ensure that their methods of attack did not result in civilian casualties that were excessive in relation to the military advantage. The international forces should pay significantly more attention to promoting transparency and accountability in their operations and investigations. Estimates of civilian casualties should be made public. International forces should ensure that Afghans could readily obtain information on the progress of investigations and prosecutions of killings. Military operations by unaccountable foreign intelligence personnel should not be permitted.

The Rapporteur also addressed other unlawful killings in a law enforcement or private context, such as by police and other armed personnel acting under the authority of Government officials, which were rarely investigated seriously. Also, a significant number of Afghans, especially women, were the victims of "honour killings". The State largely failed to investigate and prosecute those murders. Moreover, the criminal justice system was deeply flawed, and corruption and incompetence were widespread. Powerful or wealthy perpetrators were set free, while the likelihood of innocent people being sentenced to death was high. The Special Rapporteur recommended that action should be taken against serious cases of corruption by Government officials as a first step in reducing systemic corruption. The focus of police reform efforts should be on creating a truly national police force, and on breaking the links between police, militias and particular tribes and politicians. A moratorium on the death penalty should be imposed.

The Special Rapporteur visited the United States (16–30 June) [A/HRC/11/2/Add.5] and commended the country's record on extrajudicial killings: there was no lack of laws or procedures for addressing potentially unlawful killings and data were generally gathered systematically and responsibly. However, improvement was necessary in three areas to bring the Government's actions into line with its stated commitment to human rights and the rule of law. The imposition of the death penalty should comply with fundamental due process requirements: the current system's flaws increased the likelihood that innocent people would be executed. The Government should provide greater transparency in law enforcement, military and intelligence operations that resulted in potentially unlawful deaths. It should also ensure greater accountability for potentially unlawful deaths in its international operations: political expediency was never a permissible basis for any State to deviate from its obligation to investigate and punish violations of the right to life. Deficiencies that should be remedied included the lack of adequate counsel for indigent defendants and racial disparities in sentencing. Given the inadequacies of state criminal justice systems, Congress should enact legislation permitting federal court review of state and federal death penalty cases. Transparency should also be promoted in the case of potentially unlawful killings. Although the Government did well in collecting data, it failed to provide timely and meaningful information about deaths in immigration detention or arising out of law-enforcement activities. Transparency failures were far more acute in the Government's international military and intelligence operations. The Government did not track and make public the number of civilian casualties or the conditions under which deaths occurred. The military justice system did not provide ordinary people, including United States citizens and the families of Iraqi or Afghan victims, with basic information on the status of investigations and prosecutions related to civilian casualties. The Government had also refused to disclose the legal basis for targeted killings conducted in other States through drone attacks or to identify any safeguards in place to reduce collateral civilian casualties and ensure that the Government had targeted the correct person. Those transparency failures contributed to the lack of accountability for wrongful deaths.

All States had an obligation to investigate, prosecute and punish violations of the right to life, including in situations of armed conflict. While some aspects of the rule of law had been taken seriously during United States military operations, there were chronic accountability failures with respect to policies, practices and conduct that had resulted in alleged unlawful killings. The Government had failed to investigate and punish those responsible and had created a zone of impunity for private contractors and intelligence agents by failing to investigate and prosecute them. In addition to prosecuting violations of the right to life, the Government should create a national commission of inquiry to conduct an independent investigation of policies and practices that led to deaths and abuses. It should also appoint a special prosecutor independent of the pressures on the political branches of Government.

Communication. On 30 May [A/HRC/8/G/6], the Philippines replied to the Special Rapporteur's report on his 2007 visit to the country [YUN 2007, p. 746].

GENERAL ASSEMBLY ACTION

On 18 December [meeting 70], the General Assembly, on the recommendation of the Third Committee [A/63/430/Add.2], adopted **resolution 63/182** by recorded vote (127-0-58) [agenda item 64 *(b)*].

Extrajudicial, summary or arbitrary executions

The General Assembly,

Recalling the Universal Declaration of Human Rights, which guarantees the right to life, liberty and security of person, the relevant provisions of the International Covenant on Civil and Political Rights and other relevant human rights conventions,

Reaffirming the mandate of the Special Rapporteur of the Human Rights Council on extrajudicial, summary or arbitrary executions, as set out in Council resolution 8/3 of 18 June 2008,

Welcoming the universal ratification of the Geneva Conventions of 12 August 1949, which alongside human rights law provide an important framework of accountability in relation to extrajudicial, summary or arbitrary executions during armed conflict,

Mindful of all its resolutions on the subject of extrajudicial, summary or arbitrary executions and the resolutions of the Commission on Human Rights and of the Human Rights Council on the subject,

Noting with deep concern that impunity continues to be a major cause of the perpetuation of violations of human rights, including extrajudicial, summary or arbitrary executions,

Acknowledging that international human rights law and international humanitarian law are complementary and mutually reinforcing,

Noting with deep concern the growing number of civilians and persons *hors de combat* killed in situations of armed conflict and internal strife,

Acknowledging that extrajudicial, summary or arbitrary executions may under certain circumstances amount to genocide, crimes against humanity or war crimes, as defined in international law, including in the Rome Statute of the International Criminal Court, and recalling in this regard that each individual State has the responsibility to protect its populations from such crimes as set out in General Assembly resolution 60/1 of 16 September 2005,

Convinced of the need for effective action to prevent, combat and eliminate the abhorrent practice of extrajudicial, summary or arbitrary executions, which represent flagrant violations of human rights, particularly the right to life,

1. *Strongly condemns once again* all the extrajudicial, summary or arbitrary executions that continue to occur throughout the world;

2. *Demands* that all States ensure that the practice of extrajudicial, summary or arbitrary executions is brought to an end and that they take effective action to prevent, combat and eliminate the phenomenon in all its forms and manifestations;

3. *Reiterates* the obligation of all States to conduct exhaustive and impartial investigations into all suspected cases of extrajudicial, summary or arbitrary executions, to identify and bring to justice those responsible, while ensuring the right of every person to a fair and public hearing by a competent, independent and impartial tribunal established by law, to grant adequate compensation within a reasonable time to the victims or their families, and to adopt all necessary measures, including legal and judicial measures, to put an end to impunity and to prevent the further occurrence of such executions, as recommended in the Principles on the Effective Prevention and Investigation of Extralegal, Arbitrary and Summary Executions;

4. *Calls upon* Governments and invites intergovernmental and non-governmental organizations to pay greater attention to the work of national-level commissions of inquiry into extrajudicial, summary or arbitrary executions with a view to ensuring the effective contribution of these commissions to accountability and to combating impunity;

5. *Calls upon* all States, in order to prevent extrajudicial, summary and arbitrary executions, to comply with their obligations under relevant provisions of international human rights instruments, and further calls upon those States which have not abolished the death penalty to pay particular regard to the provisions contained in articles 6, 14 and 15 of the International Covenant on Civil and Political Rights and articles 37 and 40 of the Convention on the Rights of the Child, bearing in mind the safeguards and guarantees set out in Economic and Social Council resolutions 1984/50 of 25 May 1984 and 1989/64 of 24 May 1989, and taking into account the recommendations of the Special Rapporteur of the Human Rights Council on extrajudicial, summary or arbitrary executions regarding the need to respect essential procedural guarantees, including the right to seek pardon or commutation of sentence;

6. *Urges* all States:

(a) To take all necessary and possible measures, in conformity with international human rights law and international humanitarian law, to prevent loss of life, in particular that of children, during public demonstrations, internal and communal violence, civil unrest, public emergencies or armed conflicts, and to ensure that the police, law enforcement agents, armed forces and other agents acting on behalf of or with the consent or acquiescence of the State act with restraint and in conformity with international human rights law and international humanitarian law, including the principles of proportionality and necessity, and in this regard to ensure that police and law enforcement officials are guided by the Code of Conduct for Law Enforcement Officials and the Basic Principles on the Use of Force and Firearms by Law Enforcement Officials;

(b) To ensure the effective protection of the right to life of all persons under their jurisdiction and to investigate promptly and thoroughly all killings, including those targeted at specific groups of persons, such as racially motivated violence leading to the death of the victim, killings of persons belonging to national or ethnic, religious and linguistic minorities, killings of persons affected by terrorism, hostage-taking or foreign occupation, killings of refugees, internally displaced persons, migrants, street children or members of indigenous communities, killings of persons for reasons related to their activities as human rights defenders, lawyers, journalists or demonstrators, killings committed in the name of passion or in the name of honour, all killings committed for any discriminatory reason, including sexual orientation, as well as all other cases where a person's right to life has been violated, and to bring those responsible to justice before a competent, independent and impartial judiciary at the national or, where appropriate, international level, and to ensure that such killings, including those committed by security forces, police and law enforcement agents, paramilitary groups or private forces, are neither condoned nor sanctioned by State officials or personnel;

7. *Affirms* the obligation of States, in order to prevent extrajudicial, summary or arbitrary executions, to protect the lives of all persons deprived of their liberty in all circumstances and to investigate and respond to deaths in custody;

8. *Urges* all States to ensure that persons deprived of their liberty are treated humanely and with full respect for their human rights and to ensure that their treatment, including judicial guarantees, and conditions conform to the Standard Minimum Rules for the Treatment of Prisoners and, where applicable, to the Geneva Conventions of 12 August 1949 and the Additional Protocols thereto, of 8 June 1977 in relation to all persons detained in armed conflict, as well as to other pertinent international instruments;

9. *Welcomes* the International Criminal Court as an important contribution to ending impunity concerning extrajudicial, summary or arbitrary executions, and, taking note of the growing awareness of the Court worldwide, calls upon those States that are under an obligation to cooperate with the Court to provide such cooperation and assistance in the future, in particular with regard to arrest and surrender, the provision of evidence, the protection and relocation of victims and witnesses and the enforcement of sentences, and further welcomes the fact that one hundred and eight States have already ratified or acceded to and one hundred and thirty-nine States have signed the Rome Statute of the Court, and calls upon all those States that have not ratified or acceded to the Rome Statute to give serious consideration to doing so;

10. *Acknowledges* the importance of ensuring the protection of witnesses for the prosecution of those suspected of extrajudicial, summary or arbitrary executions, and urges States to intensify efforts to establish and implement effective witness protection programmes or other measures, and in this regard encourages the Office of the United Nations High Commissioner for Human Rights to develop practical tools designed to encourage and facilitate greater attention to the protection of witnesses;

11. *Encourages* Governments and intergovernmental and non-governmental organizations to organize training programmes and to support projects with a view to training or educating military forces, law enforcement officers and government officials in human rights and humanitarian law issues connected with their work and to include a gender and child rights perspective in such training, and appeals to the international community and requests the Office of the High Commissioner to support endeavours to that end;

12. *Takes note with appreciation* of the report of the Special Rapporteur to the General Assembly;

13. *Commends* the important role that the Special Rapporteur plays towards the elimination of extrajudicial, summary or arbitrary executions, and encourages the Special Rapporteur to continue, within his mandate, to collect information from all concerned, to respond effectively to reliable information that comes before him, to follow up on communications and country visits and to seek the views and comments of Governments and to reflect them, as appropriate, in his reports;

14. *Acknowledges* the important role of the Special Rapporteur in identifying cases where extrajudicial, summary and arbitrary executions could amount to genocide and crimes against humanity or war crimes, and urges him to collaborate with the United Nations High Commissioner for Human Rights and, as appropriate, the Special Adviser to the Secretary-General on the Prevention of Genocide, in addressing situations of extrajudicial, summary or arbitrary executions that are of particularly serious concern or in which early action might prevent further deterioration;

15. *Welcomes* the cooperation established between the Special Rapporteur and other United Nations mechanisms and procedures in the field of human rights, and encourages the Special Rapporteur to continue efforts in that regard;

16. *Urges* all States, in particular those that have not done so, to cooperate with the Special Rapporteur so that his mandate can be carried out effectively, including by favourably and rapidly responding to requests for visits, mindful that country visits are one of the essential tools for the fulfilment of the mandate of the Special Rapporteur, and by responding in a timely manner to communications and other requests transmitted to them by the Special Rapporteur;

17. *Expresses its appreciation* to those States that have received the Special Rapporteur and asks them to examine his recommendations carefully, invites them to inform him of the actions taken on those recommendations, and requests other States to cooperate in a similar way;

18. *Again requests* the Secretary-General to continue to use his best endeavours in cases where the minimum standards of legal safeguards provided for in articles 6, 9, 14 and 15 of the International Covenant on Civil and Political Rights appear not to have been respected;

19. *Requests* the Secretary-General to provide the Special Rapporteur with adequate human, financial and material resources to enable him to carry out his mandate effectively, including through country visits;

20. *Also requests* the Secretary-General to continue, in close collaboration with the High Commissioner, in conformity with the mandate of the High Commissioner established by the General Assembly in its resolution 48/141 of 20 December 1993, to ensure that personnel specialized in human rights and humanitarian law issues form part of United Nations missions, where appropriate, in order to deal with serious violations of human rights, such as extrajudicial, summary or arbitrary executions;

21. *Requests* the Special Rapporteur to submit to the General Assembly at its sixty-fourth and sixty-fifth sessions a report on the situation worldwide in regard to extrajudicial, summary or arbitrary executions and his recommendations for more effective action to combat this phenomenon;

22. *Decides* to continue its consideration of the question at its sixty-fifth session.

RECORDED VOTE ON RESOLUTION 63/182:

In favour: Afghanistan, Albania, Algeria, Andorra, Angola, Antigua and Barbuda, Argentina, Armenia, Australia, Austria, Azerbaijan, Barbados, Belarus, Belgium, Belize, Bhutan, Bolivia, Bosnia and Herzegovina, Botswana, Brazil, Bulgaria, Burundi, Cambodia, Cameroon, Canada, Cape Verde, Chad, Chile, Colombia, Comoros, Congo, Costa Rica, Croatia, Cuba, Cyprus, Czech Republic, Denmark, Dominica, Dominican Republic, Ecuador, El Salvador, Eritrea, Estonia, Ethiopia, Fiji, Finland, France, Gabon, Georgia, Germany, Ghana, Greece, Grenada, Guatemala, Guinea, Guinea-Bissau, Guyana, Haiti, Honduras, Hungary, Iceland, India, Ireland, Italy, Jamaica, Japan, Jordan, Kazakhstan, Kyrgyzstan, Latvia, Lesotho, Liechtenstein, Lithuania, Luxembourg, Maldives, Mali, Malta, Mauritania, Mauritius, Mexico, Micronesia, Moldova, Monaco, Mongolia, Montenegro, Morocco, Mozambique, Nepal, Netherlands, New Zealand, Nicaragua, Norway, Panama, Papua New Guinea, Paraguay, Peru, Philippines, Poland, Portugal, Republic of Korea, Romania, Samoa, San Marino, Sao Tome and Principe, Serbia, Singapore, Slovakia, Slovenia, Somalia, South Africa, Spain, Suriname, Sweden, Switzerland, Tajikistan, Thailand, The former Yugoslav Republic of Macedonia, Timor-Leste, Togo, Tonga, Tunisia, Ukraine, United Kingdom, Uruguay, Uzbekistan, Vanuatu, Venezuela.

Against: None.

Abstaining: Bahamas, Bahrain, Bangladesh, Benin, Brunei Darussalam, Burkina Faso, Central African Republic, China, Côte d'Ivoire, Democratic People's Republic of Korea, Djibouti, Egypt, Gambia, Indonesia, Iran, Iraq, Israel, Kenya, Kuwait, Lao People's Democratic Republic, Lebanon, Liberia, Libyan Arab Jamahiriya, Madagascar, Malawi, Malaysia, Marshall Islands, Myanmar, Namibia, Niger, Nigeria, Oman, Pakistan, Palau, Qatar, Russian Federation, Rwanda, Saint Lucia, Saint Vincent and the Grenadines, Saudi Arabia, Senegal, Sierra Leone, Solomon Islands, Sri Lanka, Sudan, Swaziland, Syrian Arab Republic, Trinidad and Tobago, Turkey, Tuvalu, Uganda, United Arab Emirates, United Republic of Tanzania, United States, Viet Nam, Yemen, Zambia, Zimbabwe.

Disappearance of persons

Working Group activities. The five-member Working Group on Enforced or Involuntary Disappearances held three sessions in 2008: its eighty-fourth (Geneva, 10–14 March), eighty-fifth (Buenos Aires, Argentina, 24–26 July) and eighty-sixth (Geneva, 26 November–4 December) [A/HRC/10/9]. In addition to its core mandate to act as a communication channel between families of disappeared persons and the Governments concerned, with a view to ensuring that sufficiently documented individual cases were investigated, the Working Group monitored compliance with the 1992 Declaration on the Protection of All Persons from Enforced Disappearance [YUN 1992, p. 744]. Cases under active consideration by the Group totalled 42,393, concerning 79 countries. The Working Group had clarified 1,763 cases over the past five years. Between 1 December 2007 and 30 November 2008, the Working Group transmitted 1,203 new cases of enforced disappearance to 28 Governments, 83 of which allegedly occurred during the same period. Of those, 69 were urgent action appeals sent to 14 countries. The Group also clarified 54 cases in 12 countries. The Group's report summarized information on disappearances relating to 81 countries and the Palestinian Authority.

The Working Group remained concerned that of the 79 States with outstanding cases, some Governments (Burundi, Guinea, Israel, Mozambique, Namibia, Seychelles and Timor-Leste, as well as the Palestinian Authority) had never replied to the Group's communications. Some Governments provided responses that did not contain relevant information. The Working Group urged those Governments to fulfil their obligations under international law. The Group also noted that 79 countries had signed and five had ratified the International Convention for the Protection of All Persons from Enforced Disappearance, adopted in 2006 [YUN 2006, p. 800].

Following its visit to Argentina (21–24 July) [A/HRC/10/9/Add.1], the Working Group recommended that the Government define enforced disappearance as an autonomous crime and adopt a comprehensive protection programme for witnesses, families, lawyers, prosecutors, judges and civil society organizations involved in the investigation of cases of enforced disappearance. Efforts to locate disappeared persons should be strengthened by establishing a public body with operational and financial autonomy. Government policies launched in 2007, which created the Programme of Truth and Justice, should be consolidated through legislation into State policies unaffected by Government changes. An Integral Reparation Plan should be established for the families of victims, carried out through a body established by the National Congress.

Human Rights Council action. On 27 March [A/63/53 (res. 7/12)], the Human Rights Council noted the Working Group's 2007 report [YUN 2007, p. 747], and extended its mandate for a further three-year period. It urged Governments to make provision in their legal systems for victims of enforced or involuntary disappearances, or their families, to seek fair, prompt and adequate reparation, and consider symbolic measures recognizing the suffering of victims and restoring their dignity and reputation. The Council called on Governments that had not recently provided substantive replies concerning claims of enforced disappearances to do so.

Holocaust remembrance

Report of Secretary-General. In accordance with General Assembly resolution 60/7 [YUN 2005, p. 811], the Secretary-General reported, in August [A/63/316], on the programme of outreach on the Holocaust and the United Nations, carried out by the UN Department of Public Information. Since its establishment in 2006, the outreach programme had developed an international network of civil society groups, collaborated with world-renowned institutions and garnered the support of experts in Holocaust and genocide studies to develop a multifaceted programme that included seminars for UN information officers, exhibitions, discussion papers drafted by distinguished scholars, panel discussions, a film series, innovative online information products for educators, a permanent exhibition at UN Headquarters, and the annual observance in January of the International Day of Commemoration in memory of the victims of the Holocaust. The outreach programme worked closely with survivors to ensure that their stories were heard and heeded as a warning of the consequences of anti-Semitism and other forms of discrimination. It also provided civil society with communications tools to combat Holocaust denial.

By **decision 63/552** of 24 December, the General Assembly decided that the agenda item on Holocaust remembrance remained for consideration during its resumed sixty-third (2009) session.

Torture and cruel treatment

Reports of Special Rapporteur. In a 15 January report [A/HRC/7/3], the Special Rapporteur on the question of torture, Manfred Nowak (Austria), summarized his activities and focused on the protection of women from torture. With regard to a gender-sensitive definition of torture, the Special Rapporteur noted the element of discrimination contained in the definition of the 1984 Convention against Torture and Other Cruel, Inhuman or Degrading Treatment or Punishment [YUN 1984, p. 813]. He proposed to introduce an additional element: "powerlessness", of which detention contexts were classic situations. Powerlessness could also pertain, however, to situations outside of detention or direct State control. De facto deprivation of liberty might occur in private settings, especially where fear created a situation of total control, as was the case with battered wives, victims of trafficking, and abused women prisoners. The Special Rapporteur considered that the State had a duty to prevent acts of torture in the private sphere, and recalled that the concept of due diligence should be applied to examine whether States had lived up to their obligations. To ensure a gender-inclusive approach to torture, the Special Rapporteur underlined the need to understand that stigma was an element at all stages of sexual violence. It was crucial to interpret the torture protection framework in light of a wide range of human rights guarantees, in particular the rules developed to combat violence against women. In many contexts, the criminal law system, court rules of procedure and evidence, as well as reparation and rehabilitation programmes, were not sufficiently gender-sensitive. He called upon States to ensure that women victims of torture and of ill-treatment by officials enjoyed full protection under the law and that special measures be taken to prevent sexual violence in detention. States should address stigma as an obstacle hindering women victims from seeking justice. Special measures should be taken to ensure that women reported torture and ill-treatment, and that those who received those reports secured the evidence in a gender-sensitive manner. Court rules needed to be adapted to the needs of victims of sexual violence.

An addendum [A/HRC/7/3/Add.1] summarized communications transmitted to Governments by the Special Rapporteur and the replies received thereto between 16 December 2006 and 14 December 2007. He had sent 79 letters of allegations of torture to 51 Governments and 187 urgent appeals to 59 Governments on behalf of persons who might be at risk of torture or ill-treatment.

A further addendum [A/HRC/7/3/Add.2] summarized information provided by Governments and NGOs on the implementation of the Special Rapporteur's recommendations following country visits to Azerbaijan [YUN 2000, p. 682], Brazil [ibid., p. 681], Cameroon [YUN 1999, p. 636], Chile [YUN 1995, p. 756], China [YUN 2006, p. 875], Colombia [YUN 1994, p. 1022], Georgia [YUN 2005, p. 813], Jordan [YUN 2006, p. 875], Kenya [YUN 1999, p. 636], Mexico [YUN 1997, p. 666], Mongolia [YUN 2005, p. 813], Nepal [ibid., p. 814], Pakistan [YUN 1996, p. 639], Romania [YUN 1999, p. 636], Russian Federation [YUN 1994, p. 1016], Spain [YUN 2003, p. 742], Turkey [YUN 1998, p. 681], Uzbekistan [YUN 2002, p. 712] and Venezuela [YUN 1996, p. 640].

In accordance with General Assembly resolution 62/148 [YUN 2007, p. 750], the Secretary-General, in July [A/63/175], transmitted the Special Rapporteur's interim report, which drew the Assembly's attention to the situation of persons with disabilities, who were frequently subjected to neglect, severe forms of restraint and seclusion, as well as physical, mental and sexual violence. Such practices, perpetrated in public institutions, as well as in the private sphere, remained invisible and were not recognized as torture or other cruel, inhuman or degrading treatment or punishment. The anti-torture framework should be reviewed in relation to persons with disabilities. By reframing violence and abuse perpetrated against them as torture or ill-treatment, victims and advocates could be afforded stronger legal protection and redress for human rights violations.

The Special Rapporteur also examined the use of solitary confinement for detainees, with its negative impact on mental health, and accordingly should be used only in exceptional circumstances or when absolutely necessary for criminal investigations, and for the shortest period of time only. The Special Rapporteur recommended that States should adopt legislation recognizing the legal capacity of persons with disabilities; ensure that they were provided with the support needed to make informed decisions; issue clear guidelines on what constituted "free and informed consent"; and make available accessible procedures. Attention was drawn also to the Istanbul Statement on the Use and Effects of Solitary Confinement, adopted at the International Psychological Trauma Symposium (Istanbul, Turkey, 9 December 2007), as a useful tool for promoting respect for and protection of the rights of detainees.

Following his mission to Denmark (2–9 May) [A/HRC/10/44/Add.2], the Special Rapporteur noted the country's long-standing leadership in anti-torture efforts worldwide and its history of support to civil society in the rehabilitation for torture victims. While no allegations of torture and very few complaints of ill-treatment from detainees were received, he cautioned against complacency, encouraging the Government to ensure that all allegations and suspicions of torture and ill-treatment were investigated, and the perpetrators punished. Noting legislative initiatives to add torture as an aggravating circumstance of various criminal offences, he regretted that a specific crime of torture was still missing in criminal law. The Special Rapporteur noted the high standard of conditions of detention, both in terms of infrastructure and day-to-day living standards. However, the extensive recourse to the use of solitary confinement remained a concern, particularly with respect to pretrial detainees. The establishment of an inter-ministerial working group to investigate alleged Central Intelligence Agency rendition flights operating through Denmark and Greenland was encouraging.

The Special Rapporteur, together with the Special Rapporteur on violence against women, its causes and consequences, Yakin Ertürk (Turkey), visited Moldova, including the Transnistrian region (4–11 July) [A/HRC/10/44/Add.3]. The Rapporteur noted the Government's commitment to promoting human rights, the progress made since independence in 1991, and the initiatives to prevent torture, in particular the creation of a national preventive mechanism. However, ill-treatment during the initial period of police custody was widespread, and allegations were received of torture in some police stations and reports of ill-treatment in other institutions. While some torture cases had reached the courts, most complaints mechanisms were ineffective. Conditions in police cells did not conform to international standards and were not suited to holding people for long periods. Detention in such conditions for up to several months amounted to inhuman treatment. Within the legal framework, torture had been criminalized and legislation provided for safeguards. However, for these to be effective, the various players in the criminal law cycle should live up to their responsibilities and denounce cases of torture.

The Rapporteur recommended that the Government implement fully its obligations under international human rights law; equip the recently created national preventive mechanism with the necessary human and other resources; and ensure that the penitentiary system was truly aimed at the rehabilitation and reintegration of offenders. Accessible and confidential complaints mechanisms, as well as effective and independent criminal investigation and prosecution mechanisms against alleged perpetrators of torture, should be established. The time limits for police custody should be reduced to 48 hours. The prosecution should be required to prove beyond reasonable doubt that no unlawful means had been used to obtain evidence, rather than leave the burden of proof on the victim. The Rapporteur expressed concern about the lack of a complaints and monitoring mechanism in the Transnistrian region, and recommended extending the activities of the national preventive mechanism to the region, criminalizing torture and abolishing the death penalty. The practice of solitary confinement for persons sentenced to death or to life imprisonment should be stopped immediately. The international community should assist the Government in its fight against torture by providing financial and technical support.

Following his visit to Equatorial Guinea (9–18 November) [A/HRC/13/39/Add.4], the Special Rapporteur noted the adoption in 2006 of a comprehensive law prohibiting torture and providing for its prosecution, but found torture by the police to be systematic in the initial period after arrest and during interrogation. Neither safeguards against ill-treatment nor complaints mechanisms were effective, and perpetrators of torture and ill-treatment were not prosecuted. On the contrary, in many cases, victims of torture experienced a total lack of justice, which, combined with the physical and psychological consequences of ill-treatment and the absence of any rehabilitation or compensation mechanism, caused suffering that might amount to inhuman treatment. Conditions of detention in many prisons and police custody facilities were in need of refurbishment to fulfil international minimum standards. In one prison, persons suspected of political crimes had been held in solitary confinement for up to four years. Women and children in police and gendarmerie custody were not separated from male adults and were therefore vulnerable to sexual violence and other forms of abuse. Immigrants detained pending deportation were frequently held in police detention in poor conditions for long periods, with little access to food and water. A comprehensive institutional and legal overhaul establishing law enforcement bodies based on the rule of law, an independent judiciary, and effective monitoring and accountability mechanisms were necessary to combat torture, and comply with the country's Constitution and its obligations under international law. The international community, including transnational corporations, should ensure that, in their development cooperation and business practices, they were not complicit in violations of human rights by State authorities.

Human Rights Council action. On 18 June [A/63/53 (res. 8/8)], the Human Rights Council welcomed the report of the Special Rapporteur and extended the mandate for a further three years. It urged States to implement effective measures to prevent torture and other cruel, inhuman or degrading treatment, particularly in places of detention and other places where persons were deprived of their liberty, and to adopt a gender-sensitive approach in the fight against torture, paying special attention to violence against women. States should respond favourably to the Special Rapporteur's requests for visits to their countries and ensure follow-up to his recommendations and conclusions.

Voluntary fund for torture victims

Report of Board of Trustees (February). At its twenty-eighth session (Geneva, 6–8 February), the Board of Trustees of the United Nations Voluntary Fund for Victims of Torture allocated grants amounting to $1,219,100 to 43 projects carried out by NGOs, and recommended setting aside $665,400 for intersessional grants for 2008. It issued revised guidelines for use during 2008, including new decisions on admissibility criteria for projects. It decided that grantees should identify in-kind contributions in order to enable the secretariat to determine future policy in that regard. The Board also discussed a number of policy issues. It approved the principle of multi-year funding for a three-year period, and endorsed a secretariat suggestion on strengthening the capacity of grantees and to resume the practice of meeting with them.

Report of Secretary-General. In his annual report [A/63/220] to the General Assembly on the status of the Fund, the Secretary-General provided information on the recommendations of the Fund's Board of Trustees at its twenty-seventh [YUN 2007, p. 750] and twenty-eighth (see above) sessions. Contributions from 11 countries and three individuals from 3 October 2007 to 30 June 2008 amounted to $1,731,668, while pledges from eight countries totalled $1,116,543. The High Commissioner approved those recommendations on behalf of the Secretary-General.

Human Rights Council action. On 18 June [A/63/53 (res. 8/8)], the Human Rights Council took note of the Secretary-General's report and called on the Board of the Fund to report to the Council in accordance with the annual programme of work. It appealed to Governments, organizations and individuals to increase contributions to the Fund and encouraged contributions to the Special Fund established by the Optional Protocol to the Convention, as well as education programmes of national preventive mechanisms.

Report of Board of Trustees (October). At its twenty-ninth session (Geneva, 13–17 October) [A/HRC/10/40], the Board recommended allocating grants amounting $10,200,950 to 195 projects in more than 65 countries, which the High Commissioner approved on behalf of the Secretary-General on 27 October. Between 1 January and 3 December, the Fund received $11,397,548 from 34 countries and the Holy See. The Board also maintained its practice of financing requests for training and seminars, and recommended allocating $136,400 to nine organizations in seven countries for that purpose.

GENERAL ASSEMBLY ACTION

On 18 December [meeting 70], the General Assembly, on the recommendation of the Third Committee [A/63/430/Add.1], adopted **resolution 63/166** without vote [agenda item 64 *(a)*].

Torture and other cruel, inhuman or degrading treatment or punishment

The General Assembly,

Reaffirming that no one shall be subjected to torture or to other cruel, inhuman or degrading treatment or punishment,

Recalling that freedom from torture and other cruel, inhuman or degrading treatment or punishment is a non-derogable right that must be protected under all circumstances, including in times of international or internal armed conflict or disturbance, and that the absolute prohibition of torture and other cruel, inhuman or degrading treatment or punishment is affirmed in relevant international instruments,

Recalling also that the prohibition of torture is a peremptory norm of international law and that international, regional and domestic courts have held the prohibition of cruel, inhuman or degrading treatment or punishment to be customary international law,

Recalling further the definition of torture contained in article 1 of the Convention against Torture and Other Cruel, Inhuman or Degrading Treatment or Punishment, without prejudice to any international instrument or national legislation which contains or may contain provisions of wider application,

Emphasizing the importance of properly interpreting and implementing the obligations of States with respect to torture and other cruel, inhuman or degrading treatment or punishment, and of abiding strictly by the definition of torture contained in article 1 of the Convention,

Noting that under the Geneva Conventions of 1949 torture and inhuman treatment are a grave breach and that under the statute of the International Tribunal for the Prosecution of Persons Responsible for Serious Violations of International Humanitarian Law Committed in the Territory of the Former Yugoslavia since 1991, the statute of the International Criminal Tribunal for the Prosecution of Persons Responsible for Genocide and Other Serious Violations of International Humanitarian Law Committed in the Territory of Rwanda and Rwandan Citizens Responsible for Genocide and Other Such Violations Committed in the Territory of Neighbouring States between 1 January and 31 December 1994 and the Rome Statute of the International Criminal Court acts of torture can constitute crimes against humanity and, when committed in a situation of armed conflict, constitute war crimes,

Acknowledging the adoption of the International Convention for the Protection of All Persons from Enforced Disappearance in its resolution 61/177 of 20 December 2006, and recognizing that its entry into force as soon as possible and its implementation will make a significant contribution to the prevention of torture, including by prohibiting places of secret detention,

Commending the persistent efforts of civil society organizations, including non-governmental organizations, national human rights institutions and the considerable network of centres for the rehabilitation of victims of torture, to combat torture and to alleviate the suffering of victims of torture,

Welcoming the entry into force of the Convention on the Rights of Persons with Disabilities, which reaffirms that no one shall be subjected to torture or to cruel, inhuman or degrading treatment or punishment,

1. *Condemns* all forms of torture and other cruel, inhuman or degrading treatment or punishment, including through intimidation, which are and shall remain prohibited at any time and in any place whatsoever and can thus never be justified, and calls upon all States to implement fully the absolute prohibition of torture and other cruel, inhuman or degrading treatment or punishment;

2. *Emphasizes* that States must take persistent, determined and effective measures to prevent and combat torture and other cruel, inhuman or degrading treatment or punishment, and stresses that all acts of torture must be made offences under domestic criminal law;

3. *Welcomes* the establishment of national preventive mechanisms to prevent torture and encourages all States that have not yet done so to establish such mechanisms, and calls upon States parties to the Optional Protocol to the Convention against Torture and Other Cruel, Inhuman or Degrading Treatment or Punishment to fulfil their obligation to designate or establish truly independent and effective national preventive mechanisms for the prevention of torture;

4. *Emphasizes* the importance of States' ensuring proper follow-up to the recommendations and conclusions of the relevant treaty bodies and mechanisms, including the Committee against Torture, the Subcommittee on Prevention of Torture and Other Cruel, Inhuman or Degrading Treatment or Punishment and the Special Rapporteur of the Human Rights Council on torture and other cruel, inhuman or degrading treatment or punishment;

5. *Condemns* any action or attempt by States or public officials to legalize, authorize or acquiesce in torture and other cruel, inhuman or degrading treatment or punishment under any circumstances, including on grounds of national security or through judicial decisions;

6. *Stresses* that all allegations of torture or other cruel, inhuman or degrading treatment or punishment must be promptly and impartially examined by the competent domestic authority, and that those who encourage, order, tolerate or perpetrate such acts must be held responsible, brought to justice and punished in a manner commensurate with the severity of the offence, including the officials in charge of the place of detention where the prohibited act is found to have been committed;

7. *Takes note* in this respect of the Principles on the Effective Investigation and Documentation of Torture and Other Cruel, Inhuman or Degrading Treatment or Punishment (the Istanbul Principles) as a useful tool in efforts to prevent and combat torture and of the updated set of principles for the protection of human rights through action to combat impunity;

8. *Calls upon* all States to implement effective measures to prevent torture and other cruel, inhuman or degrading treatment or punishment, particularly in places of detention and other places where persons are deprived of their liberty, including education and training of personnel who may be involved in the custody, interrogation or treatment of any individual subjected to any form of arrest, detention or imprisonment;

9. *Also calls upon* all States to adopt a gender-sensitive approach in the fight against torture and other cruel, inhuman or degrading treatment or punishment, paying special attention to violence against women and girls;

10. *Calls upon* States to ensure that the rights of persons with disabilities, bearing in mind the Convention on the Rights of Persons with Disabilities, are fully integrated into torture prevention and protection, and welcomes the efforts of the Special Rapporteur in this regard;

11. *Encourages* all States to ensure that persons convicted of torture or other cruel, inhuman or degrading treatment or punishment have no subsequent involvement in the custody, interrogation or treatment of any person under arrest, detention, imprisonment or other deprivation of liberty;

12. *Emphasizes* that acts of torture in armed conflict are serious violations of international humanitarian law and in this regard constitute war crimes, that acts of torture can constitute crimes against humanity and that the perpetrators of all acts of torture must be prosecuted and punished;

13. *Strongly urges* States to ensure that no statement that is established to have been made as a result of torture is invoked as evidence in any proceedings, except against a person accused of torture as evidence that the statement was made;

14. *Stresses* that States must not punish personnel for not obeying orders to commit or conceal acts amounting to torture or other cruel, inhuman or degrading treatment or punishment;

15. *Urges* States not to expel, return ("refouler"), extradite or in any other way transfer a person to another State where there are substantial grounds for believing that the person would be in danger of being subjected to torture, and recognizes that diplomatic assurances, where used, do not release States from their obligations under international human rights, humanitarian and refugee law, in particular the principle of non-refoulement;

16. *Recalls* that, for the purpose of determining whether there are such grounds, the competent authorities shall take into account all relevant considerations, including, where applicable, the existence in the State concerned of a consistent pattern of gross, flagrant or mass violations of human rights;

17. *Calls upon* States parties to the Convention against Torture and Other Cruel, Inhuman or Degrading Treatment or Punishment to fulfil their obligation to submit for prosecution or extradite those alleged to have committed acts of torture, and encourages other States to do likewise, bearing in mind the need to fight impunity;

18. *Stresses* that national legal systems must ensure that victims of torture and other cruel, inhuman or degrading treatment or punishment obtain redress, are awarded fair and adequate compensation and receive appropriate social and medical rehabilitation, urges States to take effective measures to this end, and in this regard encourages the development of rehabilitation centres;

19. *Recalls* its resolution 43/173 of 9 December 1988 on the Body of Principles for the Protection of All Persons under Any Form of Detention or Imprisonment, and in this context stresses that ensuring that any individual arrested or detained is promptly brought before a judge or other independent judicial officer in person and permitting prompt and regular medical care and legal counsel as well as visits by family members and independent monitoring mechanisms are effective measures for the prevention of torture and other cruel, inhuman or degrading treatment or punishment;

20. *Reminds* all States that prolonged incommunicado detention or detention in secret places can facilitate the perpetration of torture and other cruel, inhuman or degrading treatment or punishment and can in itself constitute a form of such treatment, and urges all States to respect the safeguards concerning the liberty, security and dignity of the person;

21. *Notes* the concerns about solitary confinement expressed in the interim report of the Special Rapporteur, and highlights the importance of reflecting on this in efforts to promote respect for and protection of the rights of detainees;

22. *Calls upon* all States to take appropriate effective legislative, administrative, judicial and other measures to prevent and prohibit the production, trade, export and use of equipment that is specifically designed to inflict torture or other cruel, inhuman or degrading treatment or punishment;

23. *Urges* all States that have not yet done so to become parties to the Convention as a matter of priority, and calls upon States parties to give early consideration to signing and ratifying the Optional Protocol to the Convention;

24. *Invites* all States parties to the Convention that have not yet done so to make the declarations provided for in articles 21 and 22 of the Convention concerning inter-State and individual communications, to consider the possibility of withdrawing their reservations to article 20 of the Convention and to notify the Secretary-General of their acceptance of the amendments to articles 17 and 18 of the Convention with a view to enhancing the effectiveness of the Committee against Torture as soon as possible;

25. *Urges* States parties to comply strictly with their obligations under the Convention, including, in view of the high number of reports not submitted in time, their obligation to submit reports in accordance with article 19 of the Convention, and invites States parties to incorporate a gender perspective and information concerning children and juveniles and persons with disabilities when submitting reports to the Committee;

26. *Welcomes* the work of the Committee and its report submitted in accordance with article 24 of the Convention, recommends that the Committee continue to include information on the follow-up by States to its recommendations, and supports the Committee in its intention to further improve the effectiveness of its working methods;

27. *Invites* the Chairpersons of the Committee and the Subcommittee to present oral reports on the work of the committees and to engage in an interactive dialogue with the General Assembly at its sixty-fourth session under the sub-item entitled "Implementation of human rights instruments";

28. *Calls upon* the United Nations High Commissioner for Human Rights, in conformity with her mandate established by the General Assembly in its resolution 48/141 of 20 December 1993, to continue to provide, at the request of States, advisory services for the prevention of torture and other cruel, inhuman or degrading treatment or punishment, including for the preparation of national reports to the Committee and for the establishment and operation of national preventive mechanisms, as well as technical assistance for the development, production and distribution of teaching material for this purpose;

29. *Notes with appreciation* the interim report of the Special Rapporteur, and encourages the Special Rapporteur to continue to include in his recommendations proposals

on the prevention and investigation of torture and other cruel, inhuman or degrading treatment or punishment, including its gender-based manifestations;

30. *Requests* the Special Rapporteur to continue to consider including in his report information on the follow-up by States to his recommendations, visits and communications, including progress made and problems encountered, and on other official contacts;

31. *Calls upon* all States to cooperate with and assist the Special Rapporteur in the performance of his task, to supply all necessary information requested by the Special Rapporteur, to fully and expeditiously respond to and follow up his urgent appeals, to give serious consideration to responding favourably to requests by the Special Rapporteur to visit their countries and to enter into a constructive dialogue with the Special Rapporteur on requested visits to their countries as well as with respect to the follow-up to his recommendations;

32. *Stresses* the need for the continued regular exchange of views among the Committee, the Subcommittee, the Special Rapporteur and other relevant United Nations mechanisms and bodies, as well as for the pursuance of cooperation with relevant United Nations programmes, notably the United Nations Crime Prevention and Criminal Justice Programme, with regional organizations and mechanisms, as appropriate, and civil society organizations, including non-governmental organizations, with a view to enhancing further their effectiveness and cooperation on issues relating to the prevention and eradication of torture, inter alia, by improving their coordination;

33. *Recognizes* the global need for international assistance to victims of torture, stresses the importance of the work of the Board of Trustees of the United Nations Voluntary Fund for Victims of Torture, appeals to all States and organizations to contribute annually to the Fund, preferably with a substantial increase in the level of contributions, and encourages contributions to the Special Fund established by the Optional Protocol to help finance the implementation of the recommendations made by the Subcommittee as well as education programmes of the national preventive mechanisms;

34. *Requests* the Secretary-General to continue to transmit to all States the appeals of the General Assembly for contributions to the Funds and to include the Funds on an annual basis among the programmes for which funds are pledged at the United Nations Pledging Conference for Development Activities;

35. *Also requests* the Secretary-General to submit to the Human Rights Council and to the General Assembly at its sixty-fourth session a report on the operations of the Funds;

36. *Further requests* the Secretary-General to ensure, within the overall budgetary framework of the United Nations, the provision of adequate staff and facilities for the bodies and mechanisms involved in preventing and combating torture and assisting victims of torture or other cruel, inhuman or degrading treatment or punishment commensurate with the strong support expressed by Member States for preventing and combating torture and assisting victims of torture;

37. *Calls upon* all States, the Office of the United Nations High Commissioner for Human Rights and other United Nations bodies and agencies, as well as relevant intergovernmental and civil society organizations, including non-governmental organizations, to commemorate, on 26 June, the United Nations International Day in Support of Victims of Torture;

38. *Decides* to consider at its sixty-fourth session the reports of the Secretary-General, including the report on the United Nations Voluntary Fund for Victims of Torture and the Special Fund established by the Optional Protocol, the report of the Committee against Torture and the interim report of the Special Rapporteur on torture and other cruel, inhuman or degrading treatment or punishment.

Freedom of expression

Report of Special Rapporteur. In a February report [A/HRC/7/14], the Special Rapporteur on the promotion and protection of the right to freedom of opinion and expression, Ambeyi Ligabo (Kenya), reviewed the main trends and issues addressed during his tenure expiring in August. He had focused on the right of access to information, safety and protection of media professionals, legal restrictions on freedom of opinion and expression, as well as the impact of freedom of expression on the realization of other human rights. The Rapporteur urged Governments to assess legislation and judicial practices related to freedom of opinion and expression and to reform processes to guarantee conformity with international human rights standards. Governments should focus on the protection and promotion of media independence as a priority, and adopt legislation prohibiting all forms of censorship in media outlets. Defamation, libel and insult charges, particularly when stemming from public figures and State authorities, did not justify any form of prior censorship. Governments should extend the measures to protect freedom of opinion and expression to the Internet, in particular to web site contributors and bloggers, who should be granted the same level of protection as any other type of media. The Human Rights Council should focus on the safety and protection of journalists, in particular in situations of armed conflict, and request the Special Rapporteur to prepare a study on the causes of violence against media professionals, including draft guidelines for their protection. Media professionals should be conscious of the potential impact their expressed ideas might have in raising cultural and religious sensitivities. The Special Rapporteur emphasized that although international instruments foresaw limitations to the right to freedom of opinion and expression to prevent incitement of hatred, those limitations were designed to protect individuals against violations of their rights, and were not intended to suppress the expression of critical views, controversial opinions or politically incorrect statements.

An addendum to the report [A/HRC/7/14/Add.1] summarized 241 communications on behalf of 623 persons sent by the Special Rapporteur in 2007 to 81 Governments and the Palestinian Authority, and replies received thereto by 15 January 2008.

Human Rights Council action. On 28 March [A/63/53 (res. 7/36)], the Human Rights Council, by a recorded vote of 32 to none, with 15 abstentions, took note of the Special Rapporteur's report, extended the mandate for three years, and requested the Rapporteur to report to the Council annually.

On 18 June, the Human Rights Council appointed Frank William La Rue (Guatemala) as Special Rapporteur.

Terrorism

Human Rights Council action. On 27 March [A/63/53 (res. 7/7)], the Human Rights Council reaffirmed that counter-terrorism measures should be implemented in full consideration of the human rights of minorities and should not be discriminatory. It called on States not to resort to profiling based on stereotypes founded on grounds of discrimination, and to comply with their obligations in respect of torture and other cruel, inhuman or degrading treatment or punishment. States should, while encountering terrorism, ensure due-process guarantees. It requested the High Commissioner to continue efforts regarding the protection of human rights and fundamental freedoms while countering terrorism and to report regularly to the Council.

Report of High Commissioner. In response to that request, the High Commissioner submitted a report in June [A/HRC/8/13] highlighting the need to protect and promote all human rights and effective counter-terrorism measures. Those two complementary and mutually reinforcing objectives should be pursued together as part of States' duty to protect. Human rights should be placed at the core of international cooperation in counter-terrorism, and States had an obligation to ensure that measures taken to combat terrorism crimes complied with their obligations under international human rights law—in particular the right to recognition as a person before the law, due process and non-refoulement. Compliance with international human rights standards was essential, especially where counter-terrorism measures involved the deprivation of individual liberty. The High Commissioner expressed concern about the obstacles to truly effective international and judicial cooperation in counter-terrorism, such as unlawful interferences with privacy, search, seizure and surveillance; the insufficient remedies for human rights violations in the context of evidence-gathering and information-sharing; the transfer and admissibility of evidence gathered by unlawful means; insufficient respect for the principle of legality in relation to the definition of terrorist offences; the protection of witnesses; and inappropriate redistribution of burdens of proof in legal proceedings. Failure by States to safeguard human rights in countering terrorism would lead to increased instability and decreased legitimacy of Governments, polarization in and between societies, and increased radicalization.

Reports of Special Rapporteur. In an August note [A/63/223], the Secretary-General transmitted to the General Assembly the report of Special Rapporteur Martin Scheinin (Finland) on the protection and promotion of human rights while countering terrorism, submitted in accordance with Assembly resolution 62/159 [YUN 2007, p. 757]. The report focused on the fundamental right to a fair trial in the context of prosecuting terrorist suspects. It reviewed the applicable legal framework as reflected in international human rights treaties, treaty and customary international law, and conventions to counter terrorism, and analysed the role of the judiciary as a legal recourse to ensure that all terrorist suspects had effective access to the courts. Also addressed were the independence and impartiality of a judicial institution, and key areas of concern regarding access to justice in the context of the listing and de-listing of individuals and groups as terrorist or associated entities. The Special Rapporteur emphasized that fundamental principles of the right to a fair trial might not be subject to derogation, and any derogation should not circumvent the protection of non-derogable rights. All aspects of counter-terrorism law and practice had to be in compliance with international human rights law, including the right to a fair trial. Having regard to emerging practices in the fight against terrorism, the Special Rapporteur emphasized a number of basic principles as elements of best practice in securing the right to a fair trial in terrorism cases.

On 18 December, the Assembly took note of the Special Rapporteur's report (**decision 63/534**).

The Special Rapporteur visited Spain (7–14 May) [A/HRC/10/3/Add.2] and welcomed national and international efforts promote human rights in the fight against terrorism and to foster tolerance and solidarity so as to avoid conditions conducive to terrorism. However, certain legal definitions of terrorist crimes did not ensure full respect for the principle of legality. The Special Rapporteur highlighted the positive aspects in the trial of those accused of the 11 March 2004 bombings in Madrid [YUN 2004, p. 72] carried out by members of an international terrorist cell, but expressed concerns regarding the pretrial phase and the right to review by a higher court. A successful and legitimate fight against terrorism required that provisions on terrorist offences strictly adhered to the principle of legality, so that all elements of the crime were explicitly and precisely encapsulated in the legal definitions of the crimes. The Government should therefore initiate a review of the penal code to improve the current definition.

The Special Rapporteur recommended that any proscription of illicit organizations be carried out in accordance with the law and the principles of necessity and proportionality. Spain should bring vague formulations of Organic Law on Political Parties in line with international standards on the limitation of freedom of expression to avoid the risk of applying it to non-violent political parties sharing the political orientation of a terrorist organization. The country should also revise mechanisms of appeal in terrorist cases, reduce the duration of pretrial detention for cases linked to the notion of terrorism but did not entail the intention of deadly or serious violence and eradicate the institution of incommunicado detention—an exceptional regime that entailed a risk of prohibited treatment against the detainee.

Report of Secretary-General. In response to General Assembly resolution 62/159 [YUN 2007, p. 757], the Secretary-General, in August, submitted a report [A/63/337] on the protection of human rights and fundamental freedoms while countering terrorism. The report examined States' practice in protecting non-derogable rights, in particular the right to life and the absolute prohibition of torture and ill-treatment, as well as obligations concerning the transfer of persons suspected of engagement in terrorist activities or deemed to be a threat to national security. It also examined States' practice to protect human rights and the limitations placed on the exercise of fundamental freedoms and human rights in the context of counter-terrorism, particularly freedom of expression, and considered the impact on the right to a fair trial. The Secretary-General noted in his conclusions that the High Commissioner, human rights treaty bodies and special procedures mandate-holders had expressed concerns regarding extrajudicial killings and summary executions, the alleged use of secret detention centres, the practice of irregular transfers of terrorism suspects and the use of diplomatic assurances to justify the transfer of suspects to countries where they might face a risk of torture. States should ensure respect for all rights—in particular non-derogable rights, such as the right to life and the prohibition of torture. Derogation measures should be allowed only in exceptional circumstances, and should be proportional and necessary. Member States should prohibit torture and cruel, inhuman or degrading treatment in national law; prosecute those responsible for torture and ill-treatment; and prohibit the use of statements extracted under torture. Measures should be taken to ensure the access of monitoring bodies to all prisoners in all places of detention, and to abolish places of secret detention. Member States should abide by the principle of non-refoulement and refrain from returning persons to countries where they might face torture. States resorting to military or specialized courts or tribunals in countering terrorism should accord due attention to the basic standards of fair trial and the right of equality before the courts.

GENERAL ASSEMBLY ACTION

On 18 December [meeting 70], the General Assembly, on the recommendation of the Third Committee [A/63/430/Add.2], adopted **resolution 63/185** without vote [agenda item 64 *(b)*].

Protection of human rights and fundamental freedoms while countering terrorism

The General Assembly,

Reaffirming the purposes and principles of the Charter of the United Nations,

Reaffirming also the fundamental importance, including in response to terrorism and the fear of terrorism, of respecting all human rights and fundamental freedoms and the rule of law,

Reaffirming further the Universal Declaration of Human Rights,

Reaffirming that States are under the obligation to protect all human rights and fundamental freedoms of all persons,

Reiterating the important contribution of measures taken at all levels against terrorism, consistent with international law, in particular international human rights, refugee and humanitarian law, to the functioning of democratic institutions and the maintenance of peace and security and thereby to the full enjoyment of human rights, as well as the need to continue this fight, including through international cooperation and the strengthening of the role of the United Nations in this respect,

Deeply deploring the occurrence of violations of human rights and fundamental freedoms in the context of the fight against terrorism, as well as violations of international refugee law and international humanitarian law,

Recognizing that respect for all human rights, respect for democracy and respect for the rule of law are interrelated and mutually reinforcing,

Noting with concern measures that can undermine human rights and the rule of law, such as the detention of persons suspected of acts of terrorism in the absence of a legal basis for detention and due process guarantees, the deprivation of liberty that amounts to placing a detained person outside the protection of the law, the trial of suspects without fundamental judicial guarantees, the illegal deprivation of liberty and transfer of individuals suspected of terrorist activities, and the return of suspects to countries without individual assessment of the risk of there being substantial grounds for believing that they would be in danger of subjection to torture, and limitations to effective scrutiny of counter-terrorism measures,

Stressing that measures used in the fight against terrorism, including the profiling of individuals and the use of diplomatic assurances, memorandums of understanding and other transfer agreements or arrangements, must be in compliance with the obligations of States under international law, including international human rights law, international refugee law and international humanitarian law,

Recalling article 30 of the Universal Declaration of Human Rights, and reaffirming that acts, methods and practices of terrorism in all its forms and manifestations are activities aimed at the destruction of human rights, fundamental freedoms and democracy, threatening the territorial integrity and security of States and destabilizing legitimately constituted Governments, and that the international community should take the necessary steps to enhance cooperation to prevent and combat terrorism,

Reaffirming its unequivocal condemnation of all acts, methods and practices of terrorism in all its forms and manifestations, wherever and by whomsoever committed, regardless of their motivation, as criminal and unjustifiable, and renewing its commitment to strengthen international cooperation to prevent and combat terrorism,

Reaffirming that terrorism cannot and should not be associated with any religion, nationality, civilization or ethnic group,

Noting the declarations, statements and recommendations of a number of human rights treaty monitoring bodies and special procedures on the question of the compatibility of counter-terrorism measures with human rights obligations,

Emphasizing the importance of properly interpreting and implementing the obligations of States with respect to torture and other cruel, inhuman or degrading treatment or punishment, and of abiding strictly by the definition of torture contained in article 1 of the Convention against Torture and Other Cruel, Inhuman or Degrading Treatment or Punishment, in the fight against terrorism,

Recalling its resolutions 57/219 of 18 December 2002, 58/187 of 22 December 2003, 59/191 of 20 December 2004, 60/158 of 16 December 2005, 61/171 of 19 December 2006 and 62/159 of 18 December 2007, Commission on Human Rights resolutions 2003/68 of 25 April 2003, 2004/87 of 21 April 2004 and 2005/80 of 21 April 2005, and other relevant resolutions of the General Assembly, the Commission on Human Rights and the Human Rights Council, including Council resolution 7/7 of 27 March 2008, and Council decision 2/112 of 27 November 2006,

Recalling also Human Rights Council resolution 6/28 of 14 December 2007, by which the Council decided to extend the mandate of the Special Rapporteur on the promotion and protection of human rights and fundamental freedoms while countering terrorism for a period of three years,

Recalling further its resolution 48/141 of 20 December 1993 and, inter alia, the responsibility of the United Nations High Commissioner for Human Rights to promote and protect the effective enjoyment of all human rights,

Acknowledging the work of the Human Rights Council in promoting respect for the protection of human rights and fundamental freedoms in the fight against terrorism,

Recognizing the importance of the United Nations Global Counter-Terrorism Strategy, adopted on 8 September 2006, and reaffirming its relevant clauses on measures to ensure respect for human rights for all, international humanitarian law and the rule of law as the fundamental basis for the fight against terrorism,

Recalling its resolution 62/272 of 5 September 2008, in which it called upon the United Nations entities involved in supporting counter-terrorism efforts to continue to facilitate the promotion and protection of human rights and fundamental freedoms while countering terrorism,

1. *Reaffirms* that States must ensure that any measure taken to combat terrorism complies with their obligations under international law, in particular international human rights, refugee and humanitarian law;

2. *Deeply deplores* the suffering caused by terrorism to the victims and their families, expresses its profound solidarity with them, and stresses the importance of providing them with assistance;

3. *Expresses serious concern* at the occurrence of violations of human rights and fundamental freedoms in the context of countering terrorism;

4. *Reaffirms* the obligation of States, in accordance with article 4 of the International Covenant on Civil and Political Rights, to respect certain rights as non-derogable in any circumstances, recalls, in regard to all other Covenant rights, that any measures derogating from the provisions of the Covenant must be in accordance with that article in all cases, and underlines the exceptional and temporary nature of any such derogations;

5. *Calls upon* States to raise awareness about the importance of these obligations among national authorities involved in combating terrorism;

6. *Reaffirms* that counter-terrorism measures should be implemented in full consideration of the human rights of all, including persons belonging to national or ethnic, religious and linguistic minorities, and must not be discriminatory on grounds such as race, colour, sex, language, religion or social origin;

7. *Calls upon* States not to resort to profiling based on stereotypes founded on grounds of discrimination prohibited by international law, including discrimination on racial, ethnic and/or religious grounds;

8. *Urges* States, while countering terrorism, to fully comply with their obligations with regard to the absolute prohibition of torture and other cruel, inhuman or degrading treatment or punishment;

9. *Also urges* States to fully respect non-refoulement obligations under international refugee and human rights law and, at the same time, to review, with full respect for these obligations and other legal safeguards, the validity of a refugee status decision in an individual case if credible and relevant evidence comes to light that indicates that the person in question has committed any criminal acts, including terrorist acts, falling under the exclusion clauses under international refugee law;

10. *Calls upon* States to refrain from returning persons, including in cases related to terrorism, to their countries of origin or to a third State whenever such transfer would be contrary to their obligations under international law, in particular international human rights law, international humanitarian law and international refugee law, including in cases where there are substantial grounds for believing that they would be in danger of subjection to torture, or where their life or freedom would be threatened in violation of international refugee law on account of their race, reli-

gion, nationality, membership of a particular social group or political opinion, bearing in mind obligations that States may have to prosecute individuals not returned;

11. *Also calls upon* States to ensure that guidelines and practices in all border control operations and other pre-entry mechanisms are clear and fully respect their obligations under international law, particularly refugee law and human rights law, towards persons seeking international protection;

12. *Urges* States, while countering terrorism, to ensure due process guarantees, consistent with all relevant provisions of the Universal Declaration of Human Rights, and their obligations under the International Covenant on Civil and Political Rights, the Geneva Conventions of 1949 and the Additional Protocols thereto, of 1977, and the 1951 Convention relating to the Status of Refugees and the 1967 Protocol thereto in their respective fields of applicability;

13. *Urges* all States to take all steps necessary to ensure that persons deprived of liberty, regardless of the place of arrest or detention, benefit from the guarantees to which they are entitled under international law, including the review of the detention and, if they are subjected to trial, fundamental judicial guarantees;

14. *Opposes* any form of deprivation of liberty that amounts to placing a detained person outside the protection of the law, and urges States to respect the safeguards concerning the liberty, security and dignity of the person and to treat all prisoners in all places of detention in accordance with international law, including international human rights law and international humanitarian law;

15. *Acknowledges* the adoption of the International Convention for the Protection of All Persons from Enforced Disappearance in its resolution 61/177 of 20 December 2006, and recognizes that the entry into force of the Convention will be an important step in support of the rule of law in countering terrorism;

16. *Reaffirms* that it is imperative that all States work to uphold and protect the dignity of individuals and their fundamental freedoms, as well as democratic practices and the rule of law, while countering terrorism;

17. *Encourages* States, while countering terrorism, to take into account relevant United Nations resolutions and decisions on human rights, and encourages them to give due consideration to the recommendations of the special procedures and mechanisms of the Human Rights Council and the relevant comments and views of United Nations human rights treaty bodies;

18. *Calls upon* States to ensure that their laws criminalizing acts of terrorism are accessible, formulated with precision, non-discriminatory, non-retroactive and in accordance with international law, including human rights law;

19. *Recognizes* the need to continue ensuring that fair and clear procedures under the United Nations terrorism-related sanctions regime are strengthened in order to enhance their efficiency and transparency, and welcomes and encourages the Security Council's continued enhancement of efforts in support of these objectives, while emphasizing the importance of these sanctions in countering terrorism;

20. *Urges* States, while ensuring full compliance with their international obligations, to include adequate human rights guarantees in their national procedures for the listing of individuals and entities with a view to combating terrorism;

21. *Takes note with appreciation* of the report of the Secretary-General and the report of the Special Rapporteur of the Human Rights Council on the promotion and protection of human rights and fundamental freedoms while countering terrorism submitted pursuant to resolution 62/159, and takes note of the recommendations and conclusions contained therein;

22. *Welcomes* the ongoing dialogue established in the context of the fight against terrorism between the Security Council and its Counter-Terrorism Committee and the relevant bodies for the promotion and protection of human rights, and encourages the Security Council and its Counter-Terrorism Committee to strengthen the links and to continue to develop cooperation with relevant human rights bodies, in particular with the Office of the United Nations High Commissioner for Human Rights, the Special Rapporteur on the promotion and protection of human rights and fundamental freedoms while countering terrorism and other relevant special procedures and mechanisms of the Human Rights Council, giving due regard to the promotion and protection of human rights in the ongoing work pursuant to relevant Security Council resolutions relating to terrorism;

23. *Calls upon* States and other relevant actors, as appropriate, to continue to implement the United Nations Global Counter-Terrorism Strategy, which, inter alia, reaffirms respect for human rights for all and the rule of law as the fundamental basis of the fight against terrorism;

24. *Requests* the Office of the High Commissioner and the Special Rapporteur to continue to contribute to the work of the Counter-Terrorism Implementation Task Force, including by raising awareness about the need to respect human rights while countering terrorism;

25. *Requests* the Counter-Terrorism Implementation Task Force to continue its efforts to ensure that the United Nations can better coordinate and enhance support to Member States in their efforts to implement their obligations under international law, including international human rights law, international refugee law and international humanitarian law, while countering terrorism;

26. *Calls upon* international, regional and subregional organizations to strengthen information-sharing, coordination and cooperation in promoting the protection of human rights and fundamental freedoms while countering terrorism;

27. *Acknowledges with appreciation* the cooperation between the Special Rapporteur and all other relevant procedures and mechanisms of the Human Rights Council as well as the United Nations human rights treaty bodies, and urges them to continue their cooperation, in accordance with their mandates, and to coordinate their efforts, where appropriate, in order to promote a consistent approach on this subject;

28. *Requests* the Special Rapporteur, in the context of his mandate, to continue to make recommendations with regard to preventing, combating and redressing violations of human rights and fundamental freedoms in the context of countering terrorism;

29. *Requests* all Governments to cooperate fully with the Special Rapporteur in the performance of the tasks and

duties mandated, including by reacting promptly to the urgent appeals of the Special Rapporteur and providing the information requested, as well as to cooperate with other relevant procedures and mechanisms of the Human Rights Council dealing with the promotion and protection of human rights and fundamental freedoms while countering terrorism;

30. *Calls upon* States to give serious consideration to responding favourably to requests by the Special Rapporteur to visit their countries;

31. *Welcomes* the work of the United Nations High Commissioner for Human Rights to implement the mandate given to her in 2005, in resolution 60/158, and requests the High Commissioner to continue her efforts in this regard;

32. *Requests* the Secretary-General to submit a report on the implementation of the present resolution to the Human Rights Council and to the General Assembly at its sixty-fourth session;

33. *Decides* to consider at its sixty-fourth session the report of the Special Rapporteur on the promotion and protection of human rights and fundamental freedoms while countering terrorism.

Peace and security

Human Rights Council action. On 18 June [A/63/53 (res. 8/9)], the Human Rights Council, by a recorded vote of 32 to 13, with 2 abstentions, reaffirmed that all peoples had a sacred right to peace, and the preservation of that right and promotion of its implementation constituted a fundamental obligation of each State. It requested the High Commissioner to convene a workshop on the right of peoples to peace to clarify its content and scope, propose measures to raise awareness of its importance and suggest actions to mobilize States, intergovernmental and non-governmental organizations in the promotion of the right. The High Commissioner should select 10 experts for the workshop and report on its outcome at the Council's eleventh (2009) session.

Economic, social and cultural rights

Report of Secretary-General. In a 15 February report [A/HRC/7/58] on the question of the realization in all countries of economic, social and cultural rights, submitted in accordance with a 2007 Human Rights Council request [YUN 2007, p. 761], the Secretary-General reviewed the activities of UN human rights mechanisms and OHCHR relating to those rights during 2007. The report also covered OHCHR assistance and technical cooperation to States, UN agencies, civil society and others. In line with the Strategic Management Plan for 2006–2007 [YUN 2006, p. 766], the report reflected a significant increase in the work on those rights, highlighting major areas of enhanced capacity and engagement. Those activities included the monitoring of violations; providing technical assistance to States to promote such rights, including the drafting of legislation; strengthening the legal protection of those rights; undertaking research into new and challenging issues, such as the right to water, climate change and human rights; following up the recommendations of treaty bodies and special procedures; and building and strengthening partnerships with UN bodies, intergovernmental organizations and NGOs.

Right to development

Working Group activities. The high-level task force of the Working Group on the Right to Development, established by the Commission on Human Rights in 2004 [YUN 2004, p. 746] to assist the Working Group in making recommendations on the implementation of that right, held its fourth session in Geneva (7–15 January) [A/HRC/4/WG.2/TF/2]. The task force considered progress made towards application to selected partnerships of the criteria for the evaluation of global partnerships for development, adopted by the Working Group in 2006 [YUN 2006, p. 886]. It revised the criteria in light of lessons learned from their application and recommended their approval. The task force recommended continued dialogue and follow-up activities with institutional partners on previously selected global development partnerships [YUN 2007, p. 762]; and, in the context of assessing additional partnerships, that priority be given to Latin America and the Caribbean in terms of geographical expansion and to access to affordable essential drugs, debt relief, and trading and financial systems in terms of thematic expansion.

The Working Group on the Right to Development, at its ninth session (Geneva, 18–22 August) [A/HRC/9/17], considered the report of the task force on its fourth session (above). The Working Group recommended that the task force improve the right-to-development criteria in light of lessons learned from their application in, and with a view to, submitting a revised list of criteria. The criteria should be analytically and methodologically rigorous, empirically oriented and cover all aspects of the Millennium Development Goal to develop a global partnership for development and other aspects not yet covered. The Group recommended a workplan for the task force covering phase II (2008) and phase III (2009). The Group recommended that the Human Rights Council extend the task force's mandate until 2010, or until it completed the tasks entrusted to it by the Council.

In September [A/63/340], the Secretary-General reported to the Assembly on the outcome of the ninth session of the Working Group.

Reports of Secretary-General. In an April report [A/HRC/8/9], submitted in accordance with General Assembly resolution 62/161 [YUN 2007, p. 763], the Secretary-General summarized OHCHR activities to implement the right to development, in particular those in support of the Working Group and its task force, as well as other activities that contributed to the implementation of that right.

Also in response to that resolution, the Secretary-General, in a 22 August note [A/63/318], reported on the work on the right to development undertaken by the former Subcommission on the Promotion and Protection of Human Rights, and the Human Rights Council Advisory Committee at its first session (4–15 August) (see p. 715).

The General Assembly took note of the Secretary-General's note on 18 December (**decision 63/534**).

Human Rights Council action. On 24 September [A/63/53/Add.1 (res. 9/3)], the Human Rights Council welcomed the Working Group's report (see p. 818) and endorsed the task force's work plan for 2008–2010 outlined in the report. It decided that the criteria for the periodic evaluation of global partnerships, once endorsed by the Working Group, should be used in elaborating a comprehensive set of standards for the implementation of the right to development, which could include guidelines on the implementation of the right to development and evolve into a binding international legal standard. The Council also decided to renew the mandate of the Working Group until it completed the tasks entrusted to it, as well as that of the task force until the Working Group's eleventh (2010) session.

GENERAL ASSEMBLY ACTION

On 18 December [meeting 70], the General Assembly, on the recommendation of the Third Committee [A/63/430/Add.2], adopted **resolution 63/178** by recorded vote (182-4-2) [agenda item 64 *(b)*].

The right to development

The General Assembly,

Guided by the Charter of the United Nations, which expresses, in particular, the determination to promote social progress and better standards of life in larger freedom, as well as to employ international mechanisms for the promotion of the economic and social advancement of all peoples,

Recalling the Universal Declaration of Human Rights, as well as the International Covenant on Civil and Political Rights and the International Covenant on Economic, Social and Cultural Rights,

Recalling also the outcomes of all the major United Nations conferences and summits in the economic and social fields,

Recalling further that the Declaration on the Right to Development, adopted by the General Assembly in its resolution 41/128 of 4 December 1986, confirmed that the right to development is an inalienable human right and that equality of opportunity for development is a prerogative both of nations and of individuals who make up nations, and that the individual is the central subject and beneficiary of development,

Stressing that the Vienna Declaration and Programme of Action reaffirmed the right to development as a universal and inalienable right and an integral part of fundamental human rights, and the individual as the central subject and beneficiary of development,

Reaffirming the objective of making the right to development a reality for everyone, as set out in the United Nations Millennium Declaration, adopted by the General Assembly on 8 September 2000,

Deeply concerned that the majority of indigenous peoples in the world live in conditions of poverty, and recognizing the critical need to address the negative impact of poverty and inequity on indigenous peoples by ensuring their full and effective inclusion in development and poverty eradication programmes,

Reaffirming the universality, indivisibility, interrelatedness, interdependence and mutually reinforcing nature of all civil, cultural, economic, political and social rights, including the right to development,

Expressing deep concern over the lack of progress in the trade negotiations of the World Trade Organization, and reaffirming the need for a successful outcome of the Doha Development Round in key areas such as agriculture, market access for non-agricultural products, trade facilitation, development and services,

Recalling the outcome of the twelfth session of the United Nations Conference on Trade and Development, held in Accra from 20 to 25 April 2008, on the theme "Addressing the opportunities and challenges of globalization for development",

Recalling also all its previous resolutions, Human Rights Council resolution 9/3 of 24 September 2008, previous resolutions of the Council and those of the Commission on Human Rights on the right to development, in particular Commission resolution 1998/72 of 22 April 1998, on the urgent need to make further progress towards the realization of the right to development as set out in the Declaration on the Right to Development,

Welcoming the outcome of the ninth session of the Working Group on the Right to Development of the Human Rights Council, held in Geneva from 18 to 22 August 2008, as contained in the report of the Working Group and as referred to in the report of the Secretary-General on the right to development,

Recalling the Fourteenth Conference of Heads of State or Government of Non-Aligned Countries, held in Havana on 15 and 16 September 2006, the Fifteenth Ministerial Conference of the Movement of Non-Aligned Countries, held in Tehran on 29 and 30 July 2008, and the Ministerial Meeting of the Coordinating Bureau of the Movement of Non-Aligned Countries, held in Putrajaya, Malaysia, on 29 and 30 May 2006,

Reiterating its continuing support for the New Partnership for Africa's Development as a development framework for Africa,

Recognizing that poverty is an affront to human dignity,

Recognizing also that extreme poverty and hunger are the greatest global threat that requires the collective commitment of the international community for its eradication, pursuant to millennium development goal 1, and therefore calling upon the international community, including the Human Rights Council, to contribute towards achieving that goal,

Recognizing further that historical injustices have undeniably contributed to the poverty, underdevelopment, marginalization, social exclusion, economic disparity, instability and insecurity that affect many people in different parts of the world, in particular in developing countries,

Stressing that poverty eradication is one of the critical elements in the promotion and realization of the right to development and that poverty is a multifaceted problem that requires a multifaceted and integrated approach in addressing economic, political, social, environmental and institutional dimensions at all levels, especially in the context of the millennium development goal of halving, by 2015, the proportion of the world's people whose income is less than one dollar a day and the proportion of people who suffer from hunger,

1. *Endorses* the conclusions and recommendations adopted by consensus by the Working Group on the Right to Development of the Human Rights Council at its ninth session, and calls for their immediate, full and effective implementation by the Office of the United Nations High Commissioner for Human Rights and other relevant actors;

2. *Supports* the realization of the mandate of the Working Group as renewed by the Human Rights Council in its resolution 9/3, with the recognition that the Working Group will convene annual sessions of five working days and submit its reports to the Council;

3. *Also supports* the realization of the mandate of the high-level task force on the implementation of the right to development, established within the framework of the Working Group, as renewed by the Human Rights Council in its resolution 9/3, with the further recognition that the task force will convene annual sessions of seven working days and submit its reports to the Working Group;

4. *Emphasizes* the relevant provisions of General Assembly resolution 60/251 of 15 March 2006 establishing the Human Rights Council, and in this regard calls upon the Council to implement the agreement to continue to act to ensure that its agenda promotes and advances sustainable development and the achievement of the Millennium Development Goals, and also in this regard, to lead to raising the right to development, as set out in paragraphs 5 and 10 of the Vienna Declaration and Programme of Action, to the same level and on a par with all other human rights and fundamental freedoms;

5. *Notes with appreciation* that the high-level task force, at its second meeting, examined millennium development goal 8, on developing a global partnership for development, and suggested criteria for its periodic evaluation with the aim of improving the effectiveness of global partnership with regard to the realization of the right to development;

6. *Stresses* the importance of endorsement of the workplan for the task force for the period 2008–2010, outlined in paragraph 43 of the report of the Working Group, which requires that the criteria for the periodic evaluation of global partnerships, as identified in millennium development goal 8, to be submitted by the task force to the Working Group at its eleventh session in 2010, be extended to other components of millennium development goal 8;

7. *Also stresses* that the above criteria, once considered, revised and endorsed by the Working Group, should be used, as appropriate, in the elaboration of a comprehensive and coherent set of standards for the implementation of the right to development;

8. *Emphasizes* the importance that, upon completion of the three phases of the road map, the Working Group take appropriate steps to ensure respect for and practical application of these standards, which could take various forms, including guidelines on the implementation of the right to development, and evolve into a basis for consideration of an international legal standard of a binding nature, through a collaborative process of engagement;

9. *Stresses* the importance of the core principles contained in the conclusions of the Working Group at its third session, congruent with the purpose of international human rights instruments, such as equality, non-discrimination, accountability, participation and international cooperation, as critical to mainstreaming the right to development at the national and international levels, and underlines the importance of the principles of equity and transparency;

10. *Also stresses* that it is important that the high-level task force and the Working Group, in the discharge of their mandates, take into account the need:

(*a*) To promote the democratization of the system of international governance in order to increase the effective participation of developing countries in international decision-making;

(*b*) To also promote effective partnerships such as the New Partnership for Africa's Development and other similar initiatives with the developing countries, particularly the least developed countries, for the purpose of the realization of their right to development, including the achievement of the Millennium Development Goals;

(*c*) To strive for greater acceptance, operationalization and realization of the right to development at the international level, while urging all States to undertake at the national level the necessary policy formulation and to institute the measures required for the implementation of the right to development as an integral part of fundamental human rights, and also urging all States to expand and deepen mutually beneficial cooperation in ensuring development and eliminating obstacles to development in the context of promoting effective international cooperation for the realization of the right to development, bearing in mind that lasting progress towards the implementation of the right to development requires effective development policies at the national level and a favourable economic environment at the international level;

(*d*) To consider ways and means to continue to ensure the operationalization of the right to development as a priority;

(*e*) To mainstream the right to development in the policies and operational activities of the United Nations and the specialized agencies, programmes and funds, as well as in policies and strategies of the international financial and multilateral trading systems, taking into account in this regard that the core principles of the international economic, commercial and financial spheres, such as equity, non-discrimination, transparency, accountability, participation and international cooperation, including effective partnerships for development, are indispensable in achieving the right to development and preventing discriminatory treatment arising out of political or other non-economic considerations, in addressing the issues of concern to the developing countries;

11. *Encourages* the Human Rights Council to consider how to ensure follow-up to the ongoing work of the former Subcommission on the Promotion and Protection of Human Rights on the right to development, in accordance with the relevant provisions of the resolutions General Assembly and the Commission on Human Rights, and in compliance with decisions to be taken by the Human Rights Council;

12. *Invites* Member States and all other stakeholders to participate actively in future sessions of the Social Forum, while recognizing the strong support extended to the Forum at its previous four sessions by the Subcommission on the Promotion and Protection of Human Rights;

13. *Reaffirms* the commitment to implement the goals and targets set out in all the outcome documents of the major United Nations conferences and summits and their review processes, in particular those relating to the realization of the right to development, recognizing that the realization of the right to development is critical to achieving the objectives, goals and targets set in those outcome documents;

14. *Also reaffirms* that the realization of the right to development is essential to the implementation of the Vienna Declaration and Programme of Action, which regards all human rights as universal, indivisible, interdependent and interrelated, places the human person at the centre of development and recognizes that, while development facilitates the enjoyment of all human rights, the lack of development may not be invoked to justify the abridgement of internationally recognized human rights;

15. *Stresses* that the primary responsibility for the promotion and protection of all human rights lies with the State, and reaffirms that States have the primary responsibility for their own economic and social development and that the role of national policies and development strategies cannot be overemphasized;

16. *Reaffirms* the primary responsibility of States to create national and international conditions favourable to the realization of the right to development, as well as their commitment to cooperate with each other to that end;

17. *Also reaffirms* the need for an international environment that is conducive to the realization of the right to development;

18. *Stresses* the need to strive for greater acceptance, operationalization and realization of the right to development at the international and national levels, and calls upon States to institute the measures required for the implementation of the right to development as an integral part of fundamental human rights;

19. *Emphasizes* the critical importance of identifying and analysing obstacles impeding the full realization of the right to development at both the national and the international levels;

20. *Affirms* that, while globalization offers both opportunities and challenges, the process of globalization remains deficient in achieving the objectives of integrating all countries into a globalized world, and stresses the need for policies and measures at the national and global levels to respond to the challenges and opportunities of globalization if this process is to be made fully inclusive and equitable;

21. *Recognizes* that, despite continuous efforts on the part of the international community, the gap between developed and developing countries remains unacceptably wide, that most of the developing countries continue to face difficulties in participating in the globalization process and that many risk being marginalized and effectively excluded from its benefits;

22. *Expresses its deep concern* in this regard at the negative impact on the realization of the right to development owing to the further aggravation of the economic and social situation, in particular of developing countries, as the result of the ongoing international energy, food and financial crises;

23. *Underlines* the fact that the international community is far from meeting the target set in the United Nations Millennium Declaration of halving the number of people living in poverty by 2015, reaffirms the commitment made to meet that target, and emphasizes the principle of international cooperation, including partnership and commitment, between developed and developing countries towards achieving the goal;

24. *Urges* developed countries that have not yet done so to make concrete efforts towards meeting the targets of 0.7 per cent of their gross national product for official development assistance to developing countries and 0.15 to 0.2 per cent of their gross national product to least developed countries, and encourages developing countries to build on the progress achieved in ensuring that official development assistance is used effectively to help to meet development goals and targets;

25. *Recognizes* the need to address market access for developing countries, including in agriculture, services and non-agricultural products, in particular those of interest to developing countries;

26. *Calls for* the implementation of a desirable pace of meaningful trade liberalization, including in areas under negotiation in the World Trade Organization; implementation of commitments on implementation-related issues and concerns; review of special and differential treatment provisions, with a view to strengthening them and making them more precise, effective and operational; avoidance of new forms of protectionism; and capacity-building and technical assistance for developing countries as important issues in making progress towards the effective implementation of the right to development;

27. *Recognizes* the important link between the international economic, commercial and financial spheres and the realization of the right to development, stresses, in this regard, the need for good governance and broadening the base of decision-making at the international level on issues of development concern and the need to fill organizational gaps, as well as to strengthen the United Nations system and other multilateral institutions, and also stresses the need to broaden and strengthen the participation of developing countries and countries with economies in transition in international economic decision-making and norm-setting;

28. *Also recognizes* that good governance and the rule of law at the national level assist all States in the promotion and protection of human rights, including the right to development, and agrees on the value of the ongoing efforts being made by States to identify and strengthen good governance practices, including transparent, responsible, accountable and participatory government, that are responsive and appropriate to their needs and aspirations, including in the context of agreed partnership approaches to development, capacity-building and technical assistance;

29. *Further recognizes* the important role and the rights of women and the application of a gender perspective as a cross-cutting issue in the process of realizing the right to development, and notes in particular the positive relationship between women's education and their equal participation in the civil, cultural, economic, political and social activities of the community and the promotion of the right to development;

30. *Stresses* the need for the integration of the rights of children, girls and boys alike, in all policies and programmes, and for ensuring the promotion and protection of those rights, especially in areas relating to health, education and the full development of their capacities;

31. *Welcomes* the Political Declaration on HIV/AIDS adopted at the High-level Meeting of the General Assembly on 2 June 2006, stresses that further and additional measures must be taken at the national and international levels to fight HIV/AIDS and other communicable diseases, taking into account ongoing efforts and programmes, and reiterates the need for international assistance in this regard;

32. *Also welcomes* the entry into force of the Convention on the Rights of Persons with Disabilities on 3 May 2008;

33. *Stresses its commitment* to indigenous peoples in the process of the realization of the right to development, and reaffirms the commitment to promote their rights in the areas of education, employment, vocational training and retraining, housing, sanitation, health and social security in accordance with recognized international human rights obligations and taking into account, as appropriate, the United Nations Declaration on the Rights of Indigenous Peoples, adopted by the General Assembly in its resolution 61/295 of 13 September 2007;

34. *Recognizes* the need for strong partnerships with civil society organizations and the private sector in pursuit of poverty eradication and development, as well as for corporate social responsibility;

35. *Emphasizes* the urgent need for taking concrete and effective measures to prevent, combat and criminalize all forms of corruption at all levels, to prevent, detect and deter in a more effective manner international transfers of illicitly acquired assets and to strengthen international cooperation in asset recovery consistent with the principles of the United Nations Convention against Corruption, particularly chapter V thereof, stresses the importance of a genuine political commitment on the part of all Governments through a firm legal framework, and in this context urges States to sign and ratify the Convention as soon as possible, and States parties to implement it effectively;

36. *Also emphasizes* the need to strengthen further the activities of the Office of the United Nations High Commissioner for Human Rights in the promotion and realization of the right to development, including ensuring effective use of the financial and human resources necessary to fulfil its mandate, and calls upon the Secretary-General to provide the Office of the High Commissioner with the necessary resources;

37. *Reaffirms* the request to the United Nations High Commissioner for Human Rights, in mainstreaming the right to development, to undertake effectively activities aimed at strengthening the global partnership for development between Member States, development agencies and the international development, financial and trade institutions, and to reflect those activities in detail in her next report to the Human Rights Council;

38. *Calls upon* the United Nations agencies, funds and programmes, as well as the specialized agencies, to mainstream the right to development in their operational programmes and objectives, and stresses the need for the international financial and multilateral trading systems to mainstream the right to development in their policies and objectives;

39. *Requests* the Secretary-General to bring the present resolution to the attention of Member States, United Nations organs and bodies, specialized agencies, funds and programmes, international development and financial institutions, in particular the Bretton Woods institutions, and non-governmental organizations;

40. *Also requests* the Secretary-General to submit a report to the General Assembly at its sixty-fourth session and an interim report to the Human Rights Council on the implementation of the present resolution, including efforts undertaken at the national, regional and international levels in the promotion and realization of the right to development, and invites the Chairperson of the Working Group on the Right to Development to present a verbal update to the Assembly at its sixty-fourth session.

RECORDED VOTE ON RESOLUTION 63/178:

In favour: Afghanistan, Albania, Algeria, Andorra, Angola, Antigua and Barbuda, Argentina, Armenia, Australia, Austria, Azerbaijan, Bahamas, Bahrain, Bangladesh, Barbados, Belarus, Belgium, Belize, Benin, Bhutan, Bolivia, Bosnia and Herzegovina, Botswana, Brazil, Brunei Darussalam, Bulgaria, Burkina Faso, Burundi, Cambodia, Cameroon, Cape Verde, Central African Republic, Chad, Chile, China, Colombia, Comoros, Congo, Costa Rica, Côte d'Ivoire, Croatia, Cuba, Cyprus, Czech Republic, Democratic People's Republic of Korea, Denmark, Djibouti, Dominica, Dominican Republic, Ecuador, Egypt, El Salvador, Eritrea, Estonia, Ethiopia, Fiji, Finland, France, Gabon, Gambia, Georgia, Germany, Ghana, Greece, Grenada, Guatemala, Guinea, Guinea-Bissau, Guyana, Haiti, Honduras, Hungary, Iceland, India, Indonesia, Iran, Iraq, Ireland, Italy, Jamaica, Japan, Jordan, Kazakhstan, Kenya, Kuwait, Kyrgyzstan, Lao People's Democratic Republic, Latvia, Lebanon, Lesotho, Liberia, Libyan Arab Jamahiriya, Liechtenstein, Lithuania, Luxembourg, Madagascar, Malawi, Malaysia, Maldives, Mali, Malta, Mauritania, Mauritius, Mexico, Micronesia, Moldova, Monaco, Mongolia, Montenegro, Morocco, Mozambique, Myanmar, Namibia, Nauru, Nepal, Netherlands, New Zealand, Nicaragua, Niger, Nigeria, Norway, Oman, Pakistan, Panama, Papua New Guinea, Paraguay, Peru, Philippines, Poland, Portugal, Qatar, Republic of Korea, Romania, Russian Federation, Rwanda, Saint Kitts and Nevis, Saint Lucia, Saint Vincent and the Grenadines, Samoa, San Marino, Sao Tome and Principe, Saudi Arabia, Senegal, Serbia, Sierra Leone, Singapore, Slovakia, Slovenia, Solomon Islands, Somalia, South Africa, Spain, Sri Lanka, Sudan, Suriname, Swaziland, Sweden, Switzerland, Syrian Arab Republic, Tajikistan, Thailand, The former Yugoslav Republic of Macedonia, Timor-Leste, Togo, Tonga, Trinidad and Tobago, Tunisia, Turkey, Turkmenistan, Tuvalu, Uganda, United Arab Emirates, United Kingdom, United Republic of Tanzania, Uruguay, Uzbekistan, Vanuatu, Venezuela, Viet Nam, Yemen, Zambia, Zimbabwe.

Against: Marshall Islands, Palau, Ukraine, United States.

Abstaining: Canada, Israel.

Human rights and international solidarity

Human Rights Council action (March). On 27 March [A/63/53 (res. 7/5)], the Human Rights Council, by a recorded vote of 34 to 13, extended the mandate of the independent expert on human rights and international solidarity for a three-year period. The independent expert would continue to prepare a draft declaration on the right of peoples and individuals to international solidarity and submit a report to the Council.

Report by independent expert. By a 15 August note [A/HRC/9/10], the High Commissioner transmitted the report of the Independent Expert on human rights and international solidarity, Rudi Muhammad Rizki (Indonesia), pursuant to a 2007 Human Rights Council request [YUN 2007, p. 767]. The report focused on international cooperation and outlined steps for preparing the draft declaration on the rights of peoples and individuals to international solidarity. In that regard, the independent expert intended to seek, through a questionnaire, the views and contributions from Governments, UN agencies, other relevant international organizations and NGOs on the content, scope and nature of obligations for the promotion and protection of that right.

Human Rights Council action (September). On 24 September [A/63/53/Add.1 (res. 9/2)], the Council, by a recorded vote of 33 to 13, requested the independent expert to continue his work in the preparation of the draft declaration, and in developing guidelines, standards, norms and principles to promote and protect the right to international solidarity. It also requested the Human Rights Council Advisory Committee to prepare inputs to the draft declaration and to the development of guidelines, standards, norms and principles. The independent expert was requested to submit a report to the Council's twelfth (2009) session.

Democratic and equitable international order

Human Rights Council action. On 18 June [A/63/53 (res. 8/5)], the Human Rights Council, by a recorded vote of 33 to 13 with 1 abstention, affirmed that everyone and every people had the right to a democratic and equitable international order. Such an international order required the realization of the right of all peoples to self-determination; the right of peoples and nations to permanent sovereignty over their natural wealth and resources; the right of every individual and all peoples to development; the right of all peoples to peace; and the right to an international economic order based on equal participation in decision-making, interdependence, mutual interest, international solidarity and cooperation.

GENERAL ASSEMBLY ACTION

On 18 December [meeting 70], the General Assembly, on the recommendation of the Third Committee [A/63/430/Add.2], adopted **resolution 63/189** by recorded vote (124-55-7) [agenda item 64 *(b)*].

Promotion of a democratic and equitable international order

The General Assembly,

Recalling its previous resolutions on the promotion of a democratic and equitable international order, including resolution 61/160 of 19 December 2006, and taking note of Human Rights Council resolution 8/5 of 18 June 2008,

Reaffirming the commitment of all States to fulfil their obligations to promote universal respect for, and observance and protection of, all human rights and fundamental freedoms for all, in accordance with the Charter of the United Nations, other instruments relating to human rights and international law,

Affirming that the enhancement of international cooperation for the promotion and protection of all human rights should continue to be carried out in full conformity with the purposes and principles of the Charter and international law as set forth in Articles 1 and 2 of the Charter and, inter alia, with full respect for sovereignty, territorial integrity, political independence, the non-use of force or the threat of force in international relations and non-intervention in matters that are essentially within the domestic jurisdiction of any State,

Recalling the Preamble to the Charter, in particular the determination to reaffirm faith in fundamental human rights, in the dignity and worth of the human person and in the equal rights of men and women and of nations large and small,

Reaffirming that everyone is entitled to a social and international order in which the rights and freedoms set forth in the Universal Declaration of Human Rights can be fully realized,

Reaffirming also the determination expressed in the Preamble to the Charter to save succeeding generations from the scourge of war, to establish conditions under which justice and respect for the obligations arising from treaties and other sources of international law can be maintained, to promote social progress and better standards of life in larger freedom, to practise tolerance and good-neighbourliness, and to employ international machinery for the promotion of the economic and social advancement of all peoples,

Stressing that the responsibility for managing worldwide economic and social issues, as well as threats to international peace and security, must be shared among the nations of the world and should be exercised multilaterally, and that in this regard the central role must be played by the United Nations, as the most universal and representative organization in the world,

Considering the major changes taking place on the international scene and the aspirations of all peoples for an international order based on the principles enshrined in the Charter, including promoting and encouraging respect for human rights and fundamental freedoms for all and respect for the principle of equal rights and self-determination of peoples, peace, democracy, justice, equality, the rule of law, pluralism, development, better standards of living and solidarity,

Considering also that the Universal Declaration of Human Rights proclaims that all human beings are born free and equal in dignity and rights and that everyone is entitled to all the rights and freedoms set out therein, without distinction of any kind, such as race, colour, sex, language, religion, political or other opinion, national or social origin, property, birth or other status,

Reaffirming that democracy, development and respect for human rights and fundamental freedoms are interdependent and mutually reinforcing, and that democracy is based on the freely expressed will of the people to determine their own political, economic, social and cultural systems and their full participation in all aspects of their lives,

Emphasizing that democracy is not only a political concept but that it also has economic and social dimensions,

Recognizing that democracy, respect for all human rights, including the right to development, transparent and accountable governance and administration in all sectors of society, and effective participation by civil society are an essential part of the necessary foundations for the realization of social and people-centred sustainable development,

Noting with concern that racism, racial discrimination, xenophobia and related intolerance may be aggravated by, inter alia, inequitable distribution of wealth, marginalization and social exclusion,

Underlining the fact that it is imperative for the international community to ensure that globalization becomes a positive force for all the world's people, and that only through broad and sustained efforts, based on common humanity in all its diversity, can globalization be made fully inclusive and equitable,

Recognizing the complex character of the current global food, fuel and financial crises, in which the adequate enjoyment of all human rights is threatened to be violated, as a combination of several major factors, including macroeconomic and other factors, such as environmental degradation, desertification and global climate change, natural disasters and the lack of the technology necessary to confront their impact, particularly in developing countries and least developed countries,

Stressing that efforts to make globalization fully inclusive and equitable must include policies and measures, at the global level, that correspond to the needs of developing countries and countries with economies in transition and are formulated and implemented with their effective participation,

Stressing also the need for adequate financing of and technology transfer to developing countries, in particular the landlocked developing countries and small island developing States, including to support their efforts to adapt to climate change,

Having listened to the peoples of the world, and recognizing their aspirations to justice, to equality of opportunity for all, to the enjoyment of their human rights, including the right to development, to live in peace and freedom and to equal participation without discrimination in economic, social, cultural, civil and political life,

Resolved to take all measures within its power to secure a democratic and equitable international order,

1. *Affirms* that everyone is entitled to a democratic and equitable international order;

2. *Also affirms* that a democratic and equitable international order fosters the full realization of all human rights for all;

3. *Calls upon* all Member States to fulfil their commitment expressed in Durban, South Africa, during the World Conference against Racism, Racial Discrimination, Xenophobia and Related Intolerance to maximize the benefits of globalization through, inter alia, the strengthening and enhancement of international cooperation to increase equality of opportunities for trade, economic growth and sustainable development, global communications through the use of new technologies, and increased intercultural exchange through the preservation and promotion of cultural diversity, and reiterates that only through broad and sustained efforts to create a shared future based upon our common humanity and all its diversity can globalization be made fully inclusive and equitable;

4. *Affirms* that a democratic and equitable international order requires, inter alia, the realization of the following:

(a) The right of all peoples to self-determination, by virtue of which they can freely determine their political status and freely pursue their economic, social and cultural development;

(b) The right of peoples and nations to permanent sovereignty over their natural wealth and resources;

(c) The right of every human person and all peoples to development;

(d) The right of all peoples to peace;

(e) The right to an international economic order based on equal participation in the decision-making process, interdependence, mutual interest, solidarity and cooperation among all States;

(f) International solidarity, as a right of peoples and individuals;

(g) The promotion and consolidation of transparent, democratic, just and accountable international institutions in all areas of cooperation, in particular through the implementation of the principles of full and equal participation in their respective decision-making mechanisms;

(h) The right to equitable participation of all, without any discrimination, in domestic and global decision-making;

(i) The principle of equitable regional and gender-balanced representation in the composition of the staff of the United Nations system;

(j) The promotion of a free, just, effective and balanced international information and communications order, based on international cooperation for the establishment of a new equilibrium and greater reciprocity in the inter-

national flow of information, in particular correcting the inequalities in the flow of information to and from developing countries;

(k) Respect for cultural diversity and the cultural rights of all, since this enhances cultural pluralism, contributes to a wider exchange of knowledge and understanding of cultural backgrounds, advances the application and enjoyment of universally accepted human rights across the world and fosters stable, friendly relations among peoples and nations worldwide;

(l) The right of every person and all peoples to a healthy environment and to enhanced international cooperation that responds effectively to the needs for assistance of national efforts to adapt to climate change, particularly in developing countries, and that promotes the fulfilment of international agreements in the field of mitigation;

(m) The promotion of equitable access to benefits from the international distribution of wealth through enhanced international cooperation, in particular in economic, commercial and financial international relations;

(n) The enjoyment by everyone of ownership of the common heritage of mankind in connection to the public right of access to culture;

(o) The shared responsibility of the nations of the world for managing worldwide economic and social development as well as threats to international peace and security that should be exercised multilaterally;

5. *Stresses* the importance of preserving the rich and diverse nature of the international community of nations and peoples, as well as respect for national and regional particularities and various historical, cultural and religious backgrounds in the enhancement of international cooperation in the field of human rights;

6. *Also stresses* that all human rights are universal, indivisible, interdependent and interrelated and that the international community must treat human rights globally in a fair and equal manner, on the same footing and with the same emphasis, and reaffirms that, while the significance of national and regional particularities and various historical, cultural and religious backgrounds must be borne in mind, it is the duty of States, regardless of their political, economic and cultural systems, to promote and protect all human rights and fundamental freedoms;

7. *Urges* all actors on the international scene to build an international order based on inclusion, justice, equality and equity, human dignity, mutual understanding and promotion of and respect for cultural diversity and universal human rights, and to reject all doctrines of exclusion based on racism, racial discrimination, xenophobia and related intolerance;

8. *Reaffirms* that all States should promote the establishment, maintenance and strengthening of international peace and security and, to that end, should do their utmost to achieve general and complete disarmament under effective international control, as well as to ensure that the resources released by effective disarmament measures are used for comprehensive development, in particular that of the developing countries;

9. *Recalls* the proclamation by the General Assembly of its determination to work urgently for the establishment of an international economic order based on equity, sovereign equality, interdependence, common interest and cooperation among all States, irrespective of their economic and social systems, which shall correct inequalities and redress existing injustices, make it possible to eliminate the widening gap between the developed and the developing countries, and ensure steadily accelerating economic and social development and peace and justice for present and future generations;

10. *Reaffirms* that the international community should devise ways and means to remove the current obstacles and meet the challenges to the full realization of all human rights and to prevent the continuation of human rights violations resulting there from throughout the world;

11. *Urges* States to continue their efforts, through enhanced international cooperation, towards the promotion of a democratic and equitable international order;

12. *Requests* the Human Rights Council, the human rights treaty bodies, the Office of the United Nations High Commissioner for Human Rights, the special mechanisms extended by the Council and the Human Rights Council Advisory Committee to pay due attention, within their respective mandates, to the present resolution and to make contributions towards its implementation;

13. *Calls upon* the Office of the High Commissioner to build upon the issue of the promotion of a democratic and equitable international order;

14. *Requests* the Secretary-General to bring the present resolution to the attention of Member States, United Nations organs, bodies and components, intergovernmental organizations, in particular the Bretton Woods institutions, and non-governmental organizations, and to disseminate it on the widest possible basis;

15. *Decides* to continue consideration of the matter at its sixty-fifth session under the item entitled "Promotion and protection of human rights".

RECORDED VOTE ON RESOLUTION 63/189:

In favour: Algeria, Angola, Antigua and Barbuda, Azerbaijan, Bahamas, Bahrain, Bangladesh, Barbados, Belarus, Belize, Benin, Bhutan, Bolivia, Botswana, Brazil, Brunei Darussalam, Burkina Faso, Burundi, Cambodia, Cameroon, Cape Verde, Central African Republic, Chad, China, Colombia, Comoros, Congo, Costa Rica, Côte d'Ivoire, Cuba, Democratic People's Republic of Korea, Djibouti, Dominica, Dominican Republic, Ecuador, Egypt, El Salvador, Eritrea, Ethiopia, Fiji, Gabon, Gambia, Ghana, Grenada, Guatemala, Guinea, Guinea-Bissau, Guyana, Haiti, Honduras, India, Indonesia, Iran, Iraq, Jamaica, Jordan, Kazakhstan, Kenya, Kuwait, Kyrgyzstan, Lao People's Democratic Republic, Lebanon, Lesotho, Liberia, Libyan Arab Jamahiriya, Madagascar, Malawi, Malaysia, Maldives, Mali, Mauritania, Mauritius, Mongolia, Morocco, Mozambique, Myanmar, Namibia, Nepal, Nicaragua, Niger, Nigeria, Oman, Pakistan, Panama, Papua New Guinea, Paraguay, Philippines, Qatar, Russian Federation, Rwanda, Saint Kitts and Nevis, Saint Lucia, Saint Vincent and the Grenadines, Sao Tome and Principe, Saudi Arabia, Senegal, Sierra Leone, Singapore, Solomon Islands, Somalia, South Africa, Sri Lanka, Sudan, Suriname, Swaziland, Syrian Arab Republic, Tajikistan, Thailand, Togo, Tonga, Trinidad and Tobago, Tunisia, Turkmenistan, Tuvalu, Uganda, United Arab Emirates, United Republic of Tanzania, Uruguay, Uzbekistan, Venezuela, Viet Nam, Yemen, Zambia, Zimbabwe.

Against: Albania, Andorra, Australia, Austria, Belgium, Bosnia and Herzegovina, Bulgaria, Canada, Croatia, Cyprus, Czech Republic, Denmark, Estonia, Finland, France, Georgia, Germany, Greece, Hungary, Iceland, Ireland, Israel, Italy,

Japan, Latvia, Liechtenstein, Lithuania, Luxembourg, Malta, Marshall Islands, Micronesia, Moldova, Monaco, Montenegro, Netherlands, New Zealand, Norway, Palau, Poland, Portugal, Republic of Korea, Romania, Samoa, San Marino, Serbia, Slovakia, Slovenia, Spain, Sweden, Switzerland, The former Yugoslav Republic of Macedonia, Turkey, Ukraine, United Kingdom, United States.

Abstaining: Argentina, Armenia, Chile, Mexico, Peru, Timor-Leste, Vanuatu.

Globalization

Report of Secretary-General. In response to General Assembly resolution 62/151 [YUN 2007, p. 767], the Secretary-General, in an August report [A/63/259], summarized the replies received from 10 Governments and the UN Department of Economic and Social Affairs containing their views on the issue of globalization and its impact on the full enjoyment of all human rights.

The General Assembly took note of the report on 18 December (**decision 63/534**).

GENERAL ASSEMBLY ACTION

On 18 December [meeting 70], the General Assembly, on the recommendation of the Third Committee [A/63/430/Add.2], adopted **resolution 63/176** by recorded vote (129-54-4) [agenda item 64 *(b)*].

Globalization and its impact on the full enjoyment of all human rights

The General Assembly,

Guided by the purposes and principles of the Charter of the United Nations, and expressing, in particular, the need to achieve international cooperation in promoting and encouraging respect for human rights and fundamental freedoms for all without distinction,

Recalling the Universal Declaration of Human Rights, as well as the Vienna Declaration and Programme of Action adopted by the World Conference on Human Rights on 25 June 1993,

Recalling also the International Covenant on Civil and Political Rights and the International Covenant on Economic, Social and Cultural Rights,

Recalling further the Declaration on the Right to Development adopted by the General Assembly in its resolution 41/128 of 4 December 1986,

Recalling the United Nations Millennium Declaration and the outcome documents of the twenty-third and twenty-fourth special sessions of the General Assembly, held in New York from 5 to 10 June 2000 and in Geneva from 26 June to 1 July 2000, respectively,

Recalling also its resolution 62/151 of 18 December 2007,

Recalling further Commission on Human Rights resolution 2005/17 of 14 April 2005 on globalization and its impact on the full enjoyment of all human rights,

Recognizing that all human rights are universal, indivisible, interdependent and interrelated and that the international community must treat human rights globally in a fair and equal manner, on the same footing and with the same emphasis,

Realizing that globalization affects all countries differently and makes them more exposed to external developments, positive as well as negative, inter alia, in the field of human rights,

Realizing also that globalization is not merely an economic process, but that it also has social, political, environmental, cultural and legal dimensions, which have an impact on the full enjoyment of all human rights,

Emphasizing the need to fully implement the global partnership for development and enhance the momentum generated by the 2005 World Summit in order to operationalize and implement the commitments made in the outcomes of the major United Nations conferences and summits, including the 2005 World Summit, in the economic, social and related fields, and reaffirming in particular the commitment contained in paragraphs 19 and 47 of the 2005 World Summit Outcome to promote fair globalization and the development of the productive sectors in developing countries to enable them to participate more effectively in and benefit from the process of globalization,

Realizing the need to undertake a thorough, independent and comprehensive assessment of the social, environmental and cultural impact of globalization on societies,

Recognizing in each culture a dignity and value that deserve recognition, respect and preservation, convinced that, in their rich variety and diversity and in the reciprocal influences that they exert on one another, all cultures form part of the common heritage belonging to all humankind, and aware that the risk of a global monoculture poses more of a threat if the developing world remains poor and marginalized,

Recognizing also that multilateral mechanisms have a unique role to play in meeting the challenges and opportunities presented by globalization,

Emphasizing the global character of the migratory phenomenon, the importance of international, regional and bilateral cooperation and the need to protect the human rights of migrants, particularly at a time in which migration flows have increased in the globalized economy,

Expressing concern at the negative impact of international financial turbulence on social and economic development and on the full enjoyment of all human rights, particularly in the light of the current international financial challenges,

Expressing deep concern at the negative impact of the rising global food and energy challenges on social and economic development and on the full enjoyment of all human rights,

Recognizing that globalization should be guided by the fundamental principles that underpin the corpus of human rights, such as equity, participation, accountability, non-discrimination at both the national and the international levels, respect for diversity, tolerance and international cooperation and solidarity,

Emphasizing that the existence of widespread extreme poverty inhibits the full and effective enjoyment of human rights, and that its immediate alleviation and eventual elimination must remain a high priority for the international community,

Strongly reiterating the determination to ensure the timely and full realization of the development goals and objectives agreed at the major United Nations conferences and summits, including those agreed at the Millennium Summit that are described as the Millennium Development Goals, which have helped to galvanize efforts towards poverty eradication,

Deeply concerned at the inadequacy of measures to narrow the widening gap between the developed and the developing countries, and within countries, which has contributed, inter alia, to deepening poverty and has adversely affected the full enjoyment of all human rights, in particular in developing countries,

Noting that human beings strive for a world that is respectful of human rights and cultural diversity and that, in this regard, they work to ensure that all activities, including those affected by globalization, are consistent with those aims,

1. *Recognizes* that, while globalization, by its impact on, inter alia, the role of the State, may affect human rights, the promotion and protection of all human rights is first and foremost the responsibility of the State;

2. *Emphasizes* that development should be at the centre of the international economic agenda and that coherence between national development strategies and international obligations and commitments is imperative for an enabling environment for development and an inclusive and equitable globalization;

3. *Reaffirms* that narrowing the gap between rich and poor, both within and between countries, is an explicit goal at the national and international levels, as part of the effort to create an enabling environment for the full enjoyment of all human rights;

4. *Also reaffirms* the commitment to create an environment at both the national and the global levels that is conducive to development and to the elimination of poverty through, inter alia, good governance within each country and at the international level, transparency in the financial, monetary and trading systems and commitment to an open, equitable, rule-based, predictable and non-discriminatory multilateral trading and financial system;

5. *Recognizes* that, while globalization offers great opportunities, the fact that its benefits are very unevenly shared and its costs unevenly distributed represents an aspect of the process that affects the full enjoyment of all human rights, in particular in developing countries;

6. *Welcomes* the report of the United Nations High Commissioner for Human Rights on globalization and its impact on the full enjoyment of human rights, which focuses on the liberalization of agricultural trade and its impact on the realization of the right to development, including the right to food, and takes note of the conclusions and recommendations contained therein;

7. *Calls upon* Member States, relevant agencies of the United Nations system, intergovernmental organizations and civil society to promote equitable and environmentally sustainable economic growth for managing globalization so that poverty is systematically reduced and the international development targets are achieved;

8. *Recognizes* that only through broad and sustained efforts, including policies and measures at the global level to create a shared future based upon our common humanity in all its diversity, can globalization be made fully inclusive and equitable and have a human face, thus contributing to the full enjoyment of all human rights;

9. *Underlines* the urgent need to establish an equitable, transparent and democratic international system to strengthen and broaden the participation of developing countries in international economic decision-making and norm-setting;

10. *Affirms* that globalization is a complex process of structural transformation, with numerous interdisciplinary aspects, which has an impact on the enjoyment of civil, political, economic, social and cultural rights, including the right to development;

11. *Also affirms* that the international community should strive to respond to the challenges and opportunities posed by globalization in a manner that ensures respect for the cultural diversity of all;

12. *Underlines*, therefore, the need to continue to analyse the consequences of globalization for the full enjoyment of all human rights;

13. *Takes note* of the report of the Secretary-General, and requests him to seek further the views of Member States and relevant agencies of the United Nations system and to submit a substantive report on the subject to the General Assembly at its sixty-fourth session.

RECORDED VOTE ON RESOLUTION 63/176:

In favour: Afghanistan, Algeria, Angola, Antigua and Barbuda, Argentina, Armenia, Azerbaijan, Bahamas, Bahrain, Bangladesh, Barbados, Belarus, Belize, Benin, Bhutan, Bolivia, Botswana, Brunei Darussalam, Burkina Faso, Burundi, Cambodia, Cameroon, Cape Verde, Central African Republic, Chad, China, Colombia, Comoros, Congo, Costa Rica, Côte d'Ivoire, Cuba, Democratic People's Republic of Korea, Djibouti, Dominica, Dominican Republic, Ecuador, Egypt, El Salvador, Eritrea, Ethiopia, Fiji, Gabon, Gambia, Ghana, Grenada, Guatemala, Guinea, Guinea-Bissau, Guyana, Haiti, Honduras, India, Indonesia, Iran, Iraq, Jamaica, Jordan, Kazakhstan, Kenya, Kuwait, Kyrgyzstan, Lao People's Democratic Republic, Lebanon, Lesotho, Liberia, Libyan Arab Jamahiriya, Madagascar, Malawi, Malaysia, Maldives, Mali, Mauritania, Mauritius, Mexico, Mongolia, Morocco, Mozambique, Myanmar, Namibia, Nepal, Nicaragua, Niger, Nigeria, Oman, Pakistan, Panama, Papua New Guinea, Paraguay, Peru, Philippines, Qatar, Russian Federation, Rwanda, Saint Kitts and Nevis, Saint Lucia, Saint Vincent and the Grenadines, Samoa, Sao Tome and Principe, Saudi Arabia, Senegal, Sierra Leone, Solomon Islands, Somalia, South Africa, Sri Lanka, Sudan, Suriname, Swaziland, Syrian Arab Republic, Tajikistan, Thailand, Togo, Tonga, Trinidad and Tobago, Tunisia, Turkmenistan, Tuvalu, Uganda, United Arab Emirates, United Republic of Tanzania, Uruguay, Uzbekistan, Vanuatu, Venezuela, Viet Nam, Yemen, Zambia, Zimbabwe.

Against: Albania, Andorra, Australia, Austria, Belgium, Bosnia and Herzegovina, Bulgaria, Canada, Croatia, Cyprus, Czech Republic, Denmark, Estonia, Finland, France, Georgia, Germany, Greece, Hungary, Iceland, Ireland, Israel, Italy, Japan, Latvia, Liechtenstein, Lithuania, Luxembourg, Malta, Marshall Islands, Micronesia, Moldova, Monaco, Montenegro, Netherlands, New Zealand, Norway, Palau, Poland, Portugal, Republic of Korea, Romania, San Marino, Serbia, Slovakia, Slovenia, Spain, Sweden, Switzerland, The former Yugoslav Republic of Macedonia, Turkey, Ukraine, United Kingdom, United States.

Abstaining: Brazil, Chile, Singapore, Timor-Leste.

Economic reform policies

Reports of independent expert. In a report [A/HRC/7/9] issued in February, the independent expert on the effects of economic reform policies and foreign debt on the full enjoyment of all human rights, particularly economic, social and cultural rights, Bernards Mudho (Kenya), focused on the draft general guidelines on and execution of debt payments and economic reform policies requested by the Commission on Human Rights in 2004 [YUN 2004, p. 755] and in 2005 [YUN 2005, p. 832], to be eventually implemented by States and private and financial institutions. The guidelines would guarantee that compliance with the commitments arising from foreign debt did not undermine the capacity of States to fulfil their human rights obligations, particularly those relating to economic, social and cultural rights. Among the key principles of the draft guidelines were that they should be designed to encourage countries to elaborate flexible context-specific standards, benchmarks and indicators based on the core content or minimum human rights standards. The concept and definition of debt sustainability played a major role in the discussions on the effects of foreign debt on human rights. A main challenge was to define the responsibility and obligations of national and international stakeholders in the design of analytical tools, which should combine financial parameters, measurable human rights needs and poverty reduction objectives. In his conclusions and recommendation, the independent expert noted that economic reform and foreign debt measures had gradually become components of poverty reduction strategies, raising a need for a new approach to economic management. He recommended refocusing the mandate on the impact of public finance management on the achievement of human rights. The central issue would be how to secure a sufficient fiscal space to respect human rights standards while receiving financial assistance with non-disabling repayment obligations. The new mandate-holder should collaborate with the Working Group on the Right to Development and its high-level task force to ensure synergy of their action.

An annex to the report [A/HRC/7/9/Add.1] covered the independent expert's mission to Burkina Faso (23–27 April 2007), where debt relief initiatives had substantially reduced the foreign debt burden. Debt sustainability indicators were well below the thresholds defined by international financial institutions, and foreign debt did not appear to threaten the country's capacity to comply with its human rights obligations. Burkina Faso allocated debt service savings obtained through debt relief to a special anti-poverty account. Although the expenditure priorities of that account were not explicitly human rights-based, resources had generally been used in areas such as education and health. The expert encouraged the Government to continue its prudent debt policy and called on the donor community to help by ensuring that the national development strategy was financed to the largest possible extent with grants. The accountability and participation elements within the debt planning and decision process should be strengthened, particularly through a more systematic recourse to parliamentary and civil society advice. The poverty reduction strategy paper preparation process should be strengthened through a human rights-based approach, stipulating more clearly State obligations under international human rights law and elaborating the means to implement them.

Human Rights Council action. On 27 March [A/63/53 (res. 7/4)], the Human Rights Council, by a recorded vote of 34 to 13, extended the mandate for a three-year period, and redefined the mandate, renaming it the "independent expert on the effects of foreign debt and other related international financial obligations of States on the full enjoyment of all human rights, particularly economic, social and cultural rights". The expert was requested to seek the views of States, international organizations, UN agencies, funds and programmes, regional economic commissions, international and regional financial institutions and NGOs on the draft general guidelines [A/HRC/7/CRP.2], with a view to improving them and presenting an updated text to the Council in 2010. He should also explore further the interlinkages with trade and other issues, including HIV/AIDS, when examining the effects of foreign debt and other related international obligations of States.

On 26 March, the Council appointed Cephas Lumina (Zambia) as independent expert.

Report of independent expert. Pursuant to Human Rights Council resolution 7/4 (see above), the Secretary-General, in August, transmitted to the General Assembly the report [A/63/289] of the new independent expert, who outlined his vision and plan of implementation for the mandate. His work would be guided by the principles of the primacy of human rights, international cooperation, participation, and the responsibilities of all actors. The mandate's broad objectives were to: raise awareness of the need to consider foreign debt as a human rights issue; broaden support for the mandate through regular dialogue with all stakeholders, including States that had not traditionally supported the mandate; clarify some conceptual issues, including the linkages between foreign debt and human rights; and review, revise and develop the draft general guidelines.

The General Assembly took note of the independent expert's report on 18 December (**decision 63/534**).

Social Forum

Social Forum session. In accordance with a Human Rights Council request [YUN 2007, p. 769], the 2008 Social Forum (Geneva, 1–3 September) [A/HRC/10/65] brought together representatives of Member States and civil society, including grass-roots and intergovernmental organizations, to address the rising awareness and international concern regarding the problem of poverty and extreme poverty; implementable practical initiatives; technical support and capacity-building for countries and agencies in need; and the need for a more structured UN role in developing and coordinating international efforts to tackle poverty. The Forum had before it a background report of the High Commissioner [A/HRC/SF/2008/2], requested by the Human Rights Council [YUN 2007, p. 769], which addressed poverty and human rights and the work of international human rights mechanisms in the field of economic, social and cultural rights and the right to development in relation to poverty, and the social dimension of globalization.

The Forum heard expert presentations and held interactive debates on the normative framework of human rights and extreme poverty; foreign debt; international trade policies; the role and responsibility of the State, civil society and transnational corporations in poverty eradication; international assistance and cooperation in poverty reduction and eradication; decent and favourable work conditions; good governance; corruption; access to affordable essential drugs and health care; climate change; and food security, the food crisis and the right to food.

Participants recommended that the Council should ensure greater participation of grass-roots organizations, as well as of people living in poverty, particularly women, in future Forum sessions, and set up a voluntary UN fund for that purpose. The Forum should function as an instrument for dialogue and as a think-tank on a human rights-based approach to poverty reduction, and promote better interaction between developed and developing countries, particularly through concerted efforts to achieve poverty reduction. Its themes should be better defined, narrower in scope and focus on discrimination as cause and consequence of poverty. The universal periodic review mechanism should monitor national poverty reduction policies. The Council should urge States to increase their official development assistance and establish mechanisms to ensure that assistance reached the poorest. Governance indicators should be developed for the next Social Forum to serve as a point of reference for dialogue. The Council should also advance a human rights-based approach to the global fight against corruption, which was one of the main causes of poverty and human rights violations.

Transnational corporations

Reports of Special Representative. In a 7 April report [A/HRC/8/5], the Special Representative of the Secretary-General on the issue of human rights and transnational corporations (TNCs) and other business enterprises, John Ruggie (United States), presented a conceptual and policy framework to anchor the business and human rights debate and to help guide all relevant actors. The framework comprised three core principles: the State duty to protect against human rights abuses by third parties, including business; the corporate responsibility to respect human rights; and the need for more effective access to remedies. The three principles formed a complementary whole in that each supported the others in achieving sustainable progress.

The Special Representative noted that rapid market expansion had created governance gaps in numerous policy domains, including business and human rights. Those gaps were between the scope of economic activities and actors, and the capacity of political institutions to manage their adverse consequences. Progress had been made, at least in some industries and by growing numbers of firms. There had been novel initiatives, public-private hybrids combining mandatory and voluntary measures, and industry and company self-regulation. Likewise, there was an expanding web of potential corporate liability for international crimes, reflecting international standards but imposed through national courts. Governments had adopted a variety of measures to promote a corporate culture respectful of human rights. Fragments of international institutional provisions existed with similar aims. The fundamental problem was that there were too few such steps. None had reached a scale commensurate with the challenges at hand, there was little cross-learning, and they did not cohere into a systemic response. The framework of "protect, respect and remedy" was intended to address the problem. The United Nations should lead intellectually and by setting expectations and aspirations. The Human Rights Council could help close the governance gaps in business and human rights by supporting the framework, inviting its elaboration, and fostering its uptake by relevant social actors.

In an addendum to the report [A/HRC/8/5/Add.1], the Special Representative summarized the outcome of five international multi-stakeholder consultations held in 2007 concerning the conceptual and policy framework: the role of States vis-à-vis business and human rights (Copenhagen, Denmark, 8–9 November); business and human rights in conflict zones (Berlin, Germany, 5 November 2007); multi-stakeholder initiatives (The Hague, 6–7 November); accountability mechanisms for resolving complaints and disputes (Cambridge, Massachusetts, United States, 19–20

November); and corporate responsibility to respect human rights (Geneva, 4–5 December).

In a further addendum, [A/HRC/8/5/Add.2], the Special Representative summarized the scope and patterns of alleged corporate-related human rights abuse found in a sample of 320 cases posted on the Business and Human Rights Resource Centre web page from February 2005 to December 2007. An initial coding of cases showed that all industry sectors in all regions were alleged to impact human rights. Allegations of abuse were reviewed for the rights impacted. Environmental harms were also noted, as they were often connected to claims of negative impacts on human rights, and allegations of corruption recorded. Persons affected by the alleged abuses included workers, communities and end-users, such as consumers of goods or users of services.

The Special Representative, in a 15 May report [A/HRC/8/16], clarified the concepts of "sphere of influence" and "complicity" and explained how both concepts fit into the corporate responsibility to respect human rights—one of the three principles composing the strategic policy framework. As the concept of sphere of influence was considered too broad and ambiguous to define the scope of due diligence required to fulfil the responsibility to respect, the Representative set out an alternative approach to defining that scope that would depend on the potential and actual human rights impacts resulting from a company's business activities and the relationships connected to those activities. In contrast, avoiding complicity was viewed as an essential ingredient in the due diligence carried out to respect rights because it described a subset of the indirect ways in which companies could have an adverse effect on rights through their relationships.

Human Rights Council action. On 18 June [A/63/53 (res. 8/7)], the Human Rights Council welcomed the framework contained in the Special Representative's report (above) and recognized the need to operationalize it with a view to providing more effective protection against human rights abuses by or involving TNCs and other business enterprises, and to contribute to the consolidation of norms and standards and any future initiatives, such as a comprehensive international framework. It extended the Special Representative's mandate for a three-year period to include promoting the framework and reporting annually to the Council and to the General Assembly. It requested OHCHR to organize a two-day consultation to discuss ways to operationalize the framework, and to submit a report on the meeting to the Council.

Report of Special Representative. Pursuant to that resolution, the Secretary-General, by a 12 August note [A/63/270], transmitted the Special Representative's report to the Assembly, which outlined the main components of the policy framework, the anticipated work streams to be undertaken in implementing the Special Representative's extended mandate and summarized some of his main activities. In his conclusion, the Special Representative stated that the business and human rights agenda was enormously complex, and much hung in the balance, including the rights of individuals to enjoy lives of dignity, the role of business in achieving economic development and the social sustainability of globalization itself. The Representative believed that progress would be achieved only if actions were based on careful analysis and broad social and political support. Accordingly, in planning the next phase of his work, he intended to continue employing the methodology that had served the mandate so well: objective research, inclusive consultations and the engagement of a wide range of actors whose expertise and influence could turn principles into practice.

The General Assembly took note of that report on 18 December (**decision 63/534**).

Coercive economic measures

Reports of Secretary-General. Pursuant to a 2007 Human Rights Council request [YUN 2007, p. 771], the Secretary-General, in a July report [A/HRC/9/2], summarized information received from seven States (Albania, Algeria, Belarus, Cuba, Ecuador, Iraq and Venezuela) on the implications and negative effects of unilateral coercive measures on their populations.

In an August report [A/63/272] submitted in accordance with General Assembly resolution 62/162 [YUN 2007, p. 772], which also requested him to collect the same information, the Secretary-General summarized responses from Belarus and the Syrian Arab Republic.

Human Rights Council action. On 24 September [A/63/53/Add.1 (res. 9/4)], the Human Rights Council, by a recorded vote of 33 to 11, with 2 abstentions, urged all States to stop adopting or implementing unilateral coercive measures not in accordance with international law and international humanitarian law, in particular those with extraterritorial effects, which hampered trade relations among States, thus impeding the full realization of human rights, in particular the right of individuals and peoples to development. The Secretary-General was requested to seek from Member States their views and information on the implications of those measures on their populations, and to report to the Council's twelfth (2009) session.

Communication. On 8 August [A/62/929], Cuba transmitted to the General Assembly the outcome document of the fifteenth Ministerial Conference of the Non-Aligned Movement (Tehran, Iran, 27–30 July), in which Ministers urged States to refrain from recognizing, adopting or implementing extraterritorial or unilateral coercive measures or laws, including unilateral economic sanctions, other intimidating measures, and arbitrary travel restrictions, that sought to exert pressure on Non-Aligned Countries, threatening their sovereignty and independence, and their freedom of trade and investment, and preventing them from exercising their right to decide their own political, economic and social systems. They agreed to oppose and condemn those measures or laws, and urged other States to do likewise, as called for by the Assembly and other UN organs. They called on States applying those measures or laws to revoke them.

GENERAL ASSEMBLY ACTION

On 18 December [meeting 70], the General Assembly, on the recommendation of the Third Committee [A/63/430/Add.2], adopted **resolution 63/179** by recorded vote (132-54) [agenda item 64 *(b)*].

Human rights and unilateral coercive measures

The General Assembly,

Recalling all its previous resolutions on this subject, the most recent of which was resolution 62/162 of 18 December 2007, Human Rights Council resolution 9/4 of 24 September 2008, and previous resolutions of the Council and the Commission on Human Rights,

Reaffirming the pertinent principles and provisions contained in the Charter of Economic Rights and Duties of States proclaimed by the General Assembly in its resolution 3281(XXIX) of 12 December 1974, in particular article 32 thereof, in which it declared that no State may use or encourage the use of economic, political or any other type of measures to coerce another State in order to obtain from it the subordination of the exercise of its sovereign rights,

Taking note of the report of the Secretary-General submitted pursuant to Commission on Human Rights resolution 1999/21 of 23 April 1999, and the reports of the Secretary-General on the implementation of General Assembly resolutions 52/120 of 12 December 1997 and 55/110 of 4 December 2000,

Stressing that unilateral coercive measures and legislation are contrary to international law, international humanitarian law, the Charter of the United Nations and the norms and principles governing peaceful relations among States,

Recognizing the universal, indivisible, interdependent and interrelated character of all human rights, and in this regard reaffirming the right to development as an integral part of all human rights,

Recalling the final document of the Fourteenth Conference of Heads of State or Government of Non-Aligned Countries, held in Havana on 15 and 16 September 2006, and the final document of the Fifteenth Ministerial Conference of the Movement of Non-Aligned Countries, held in Teheran on 29 and 30 July 2008, in which the Ministers of the Movement of Non-Aligned Countries agreed to oppose and condemn those measures or laws and their continued application, persevere with efforts to effectively reverse them and urge other States to do likewise, as called for by the General Assembly and other United Nations organs, and to request States applying those measures or laws to revoke them fully and immediately,

Recalling also that at the World Conference on Human Rights, held in Vienna from 14 to 25 June 1993, States were called upon to refrain from any unilateral coercive measure not in accordance with international law and the Charter that creates obstacles to trade relations among States and impedes the full realization of all human rights, and also severely threatens the freedom of trade,

Bearing in mind all the references to this question in the Copenhagen Declaration on Social Development adopted by the World Summit for Social Development on 12 March 1995, the Beijing Declaration and Platform for Action adopted by the Fourth World Conference on Women on 15 September 1995, the Istanbul Declaration on Human Settlements and the Habitat Agenda adopted by the second United Nations Conference on Human Settlements (Habitat II) on 14 June 1996, and their five-year reviews,

Expressing concern about the negative impact of unilateral coercive measures on international relations, trade, investment and cooperation,

Expressing its grave concern that, in some countries, the situation of children is adversely affected by unilateral coercive measures not in accordance with international law and the Charter that create obstacles to trade relations among States, impede the full realization of social and economic development and hinder the well-being of the population in the affected countries, with particular consequences for women and children, including adolescents,

Deeply concerned that, despite the recommendations adopted on this question by the General Assembly, the Human Rights Council, the Commission on Human Rights and recent major United Nations conferences, and contrary to general international law and the Charter, unilateral coercive measures continue to be promulgated and implemented with all their negative implications for the social humanitarian activities and economic and social development of developing countries, including their extraterritorial effects, thereby creating additional obstacles to the full enjoyment of all human rights by peoples and individuals under the jurisdiction of other States,

Bearing in mind all the extraterritorial effects of any unilateral legislative, administrative and economic measures, policies and practices of a coercive nature against the development process and the enhancement of human rights in developing countries, which create obstacles to the full realization of all human rights,

Reaffirming that unilateral coercive measures are a major obstacle to the implementation of the Declaration on the Right to Development,

Recalling article 1, paragraph 2, common to the International Covenant on Civil and Political Rights and the International Covenant on Economic, Social and Cultural Rights, which provides, inter alia, that in no case may a people be deprived of its own means of subsistence,

Noting the continuing efforts of the open-ended Working Group on the Right to Development of the Human Rights Council, and reaffirming in particular its criteria, according to which unilateral coercive measures are one of the obstacles to the implementation of the Declaration on the Right to Development,

1. *Urges* all States to cease adopting or implementing any unilateral measures not in accordance with international law, the Charter of the United Nations and the norms and principles governing peaceful relations among States, in particular those of a coercive nature with all their extraterritorial effects, which create obstacles to trade relations among States, thus impeding the full realization of the rights set forth in the Universal Declaration of Human Rights and other international human rights instruments, in particular the right of individuals and peoples to development;

2. *Also urges* all States not to adopt any unilateral measures not in accordance with international law and the Charter that impede the full achievement of economic and social development by the population of the affected countries, in particular children and women, that hinder their well-being and that create obstacles to the full enjoyment of their human rights, including the right of everyone to a standard of living adequate for his or her health and well-being and his or her right to food, medical care and the necessary social services, as well as to ensure that food and medicine are not used as tools for political pressure;

3. *Strongly objects* to the extraterritorial nature of those measures which, in addition, threaten the sovereignty of States, and in this context calls upon all Member States to neither recognize those measures nor to apply them, as well as to take administrative or legislative measures, as appropriate, to counteract the extraterritorial applications or effects of unilateral coercive measures;

4. *Condemns* the continued unilateral application and enforcement by certain Powers of unilateral coercive measures, and rejects those measures with all their extraterritorial effects as being tools for political or economic pressure against any country, in particular against developing countries, adopted with a view to preventing those countries from exercising their right to decide, of their own free will, their own political, economic and social systems, and because of the negative effects of those measures on the realization of all the human rights of vast sectors of their populations, in particular children, women and the elderly;

5. *Reaffirms* that essential goods such as food and medicines should not be used as tools for political coercion and that under no circumstances should people be deprived of their own means of subsistence and development;

6. *Calls upon* Member States that have initiated such measures to abide by the principles of international law, the Charter, the declarations of the United Nations and world conferences and relevant resolutions and to commit themselves to their obligations and responsibilities arising from the international human rights instruments to which they are party by revoking such measures at the earliest possible time;

7. *Reaffirms*, in this context, the right of all peoples to self-determination, by virtue of which they freely determine their political status and freely pursue their economic, social and cultural development;

8. *Recalls* that, according to the Declaration on Principles of International Law concerning Friendly Relations and Cooperation among States in accordance with the Charter of the United Nations, contained in the annex to General Assembly resolution 2625(XXV) of 24 October 1970, and the relevant principles and provisions contained in the Charter of Economic Rights and Duties of States proclaimed by the Assembly in its resolution 3281(XXIX), in particular article 32 thereof, no State may use or encourage the use of economic, political or any other type of measures to coerce another State in order to obtain from it the subordination of the exercise of its sovereign rights and to secure from it advantages of any kind;

9. *Rejects* all attempts to introduce unilateral coercive measures, and urges the Human Rights Council to take fully into account the negative impact of those measures, including through the enactment of national laws and their extraterritorial application which are not in conformity with international law, in its task concerning the implementation of the right to development;

10. *Requests* the United Nations High Commissioner for Human Rights, in discharging her functions relating to the promotion, realization and protection of the right to development and bearing in mind the continuing impact of unilateral coercive measures on the population of developing countries, to give priority to the present resolution in her annual report to the General Assembly;

11. *Underlines* that unilateral coercive measures are one of the major obstacles to the implementation of the Declaration on the Right to Development, and in this regard calls upon all States to avoid the unilateral imposition of economic coercive measures and the extraterritorial application of domestic laws which run counter to the principles of free trade and hamper the development of developing countries, as recognized by the Intergovernmental Group of Experts on the Right to Development;

12. *Recognizes* that in the Declaration of Principles adopted at the first phase of the World Summit on the Information Society, held in Geneva from 10 to 12 December 2003, States were strongly urged to avoid and refrain from any unilateral measure in building the information society;

13. *Supports* the invitation of the Human Rights Council to all special rapporteurs and existing thematic mechanisms of the Council in the field of economic, social and cultural rights to pay due attention, within the scope of their respective mandates, to the negative impact and consequences of unilateral coercive measures;

14. *Requests* the Secretary-General to bring the present resolution to the attention of all Member States, to continue to collect their views and information on the implications and negative effects of unilateral coercive measures on their populations and to submit an analytical report thereon to the General Assembly at its sixty-fourth session, while reiterating once again the need to highlight the practical and preventive measures in this respect;

15. *Decides* to examine the question on a priority basis at its sixty-fourth session under the sub-item entitled "Human rights questions, including alternative approaches for improving the effective enjoyment of human rights and fundamental freedoms".

RECORDED VOTE ON RESOLUTION 63/179:

In favour: Afghanistan, Algeria, Angola, Antigua and Barbuda, Argentina, Armenia, Azerbaijan, Bahamas, Bahrain, Bangladesh, Barbados, Belarus, Belize, Benin, Bhutan, Bolivia, Botswana, Brazil, Brunei Darussalam, Burkina Faso, Burundi, Cambodia, Cameroon, Cape Verde, Central African Republic,

Chad, Chile, China, Colombia, Comoros, Congo, Costa Rica, Côte d'Ivoire, Cuba, Democratic People's Republic of Korea, Djibouti, Dominica, Dominican Republic, Ecuador, Egypt, El Salvador, Eritrea, Ethiopia, Fiji, Gabon, Gambia, Ghana, Grenada, Guatemala, Guinea, Guinea-Bissau, Guyana, Haiti, Honduras, India, Indonesia, Iran, Iraq, Jamaica, Jordan, Kazakhstan, Kenya, Kuwait, Kyrgyzstan, Lao People's Democratic Republic, Lebanon, Lesotho, Liberia, Libyan Arab Jamahiriya, Madagascar, Malawi, Malaysia, Maldives, Mali, Mauritania, Mauritius, Mexico, Mongolia, Morocco, Mozambique, Myanmar, Namibia, Nepal, Nicaragua, Niger, Nigeria, Oman, Pakistan, Panama, Papua New Guinea, Paraguay, Peru, Philippines, Qatar, Russian Federation, Rwanda, Saint Lucia, Saint Vincent and the Grenadines, Samoa, Sao Tome and Principe, Saudi Arabia, Senegal, Sierra Leone, Singapore, Solomon Islands, Somalia, South Africa, Sri Lanka, Sudan, Suriname, Swaziland, Syrian Arab Republic, Tajikistan, Thailand, Timor-Leste, Togo, Tonga, Trinidad and Tobago, Tunisia, Turkmenistan, Tuvalu, Uganda, United Arab Emirates, United Republic of Tanzania, Uruguay, Uzbekistan, Vanuatu, Venezuela, Viet Nam, Yemen, Zambia, Zimbabwe.

Against: Albania, Andorra, Australia, Austria, Belgium, Bosnia and Herzegovina, Bulgaria, Canada, Croatia, Cyprus, Czech Republic, Denmark, Estonia, Finland, France, Georgia, Germany, Greece, Hungary, Iceland, Ireland, Israel, Italy, Japan, Latvia, Liechtenstein, Lithuania, Luxembourg, Malta, Marshall Islands, Micronesia, Moldova, Monaco, Montenegro, Netherlands, New Zealand, Norway, Palau, Poland, Portugal, Republic of Korea, Romania, San Marino, Serbia, Slovakia, Slovenia, Spain, Sweden, Switzerland, The former Yugoslav Republic of Macedonia, Turkey, Ukraine, United Kingdom, United States.

Extreme poverty

Report of High Commissioner. As requested by the Human Rights Council in 2006 [YUN 2006, p. 900], the High Commissioner in February submitted a report [A/HRC/7/32] summarizing replies and contributions received from 18 Governments, as well as UN agencies, intergovernmental organizations, national human rights institutions and civil society organizations concerning the draft guiding principles on extreme poverty and human rights: the rights of the poor [YUN 2006, p. 900].

Human Rights Council action. On 28 March [A/63/53 (res. 7/27)], the Human Rights Council noted the High Commissioner's report on the draft guiding principles on the rights of persons living in extreme poverty. It invited OHCHR to consult with relevant stakeholders, including by organizing a seminar on the draft guiding principles; and to submit a report to the Council, no later than its last session of 2009, that would allow it to decide how to move forward, with a view to possibly adopting the guiding principles.

Report of independent expert. The independent expert on the question of human rights and extreme poverty, Arjun Sengupta (India), in February [A/HRC/7/15], submitted a report that took stock of the key issues raised during his tenure. He reiterated that extreme poverty should be regarded as the combination of income poverty, human development poverty and social exclusion. Attention should be focused on the intersection of those three components when formulating poverty reduction strategies. Equally important was the importance of international cooperation, which was enshrined in international human rights law. In examining the effectiveness of such cooperation, the independent expert made observations on past experiences with poverty reduction strategy papers in Africa. He emphasized the need to recognize extreme poverty as a denial of human rights, and suggested that the guiding principles on extreme poverty should become legally binding.

Human Rights Council action. On 26 March, the Human Rights Council appointed Magdalena Sepúlveda Carmona (Chile) as independent expert.

On 18 June [A/63/53 (res. 8/11)], the Council noted the independent expert proposal to define extreme poverty as a combination of income poverty, human development poverty and social exclusion. It extended the independent expert's mandate for three years and requested that the expert report to the General Assembly and to the Council annually.

Reports of independent expert. As requested by that resolution, the Secretary-General submitted to the Assembly in August [A/63/274] the interim report of the new independent expert outlining the main concerns that would guide her activities. Those included the impact of discrimination and social exclusion, the challenges faced by women, children and persons with disabilities, the lack of meaningful participation of people living in poverty, the impact of public policies on people living in extreme poverty, and the lack of awareness of poverty as a human rights issue. Eliminating extreme poverty was not a question of charity but a pressing human rights issue. States had legal obligations towards people living in extreme poverty that were linked to a whole range of civil, economic, political, cultural and social rights. Through the exercise of her mandate, the independent expert would formulate pragmatic, action-orientated guidance and recommendations on how the human rights framework could strengthen efforts to eradicate extreme poverty.

The General Assembly took note of that report on 18 December (**decision 63/534**).

The independent expert visited Ecuador (10–15 November) [A/HRC/11/9/Add.1], where major advances had been made in terms of a rights-based approach to public policy planning and increases in social spending. However, political and institutional instability, the global economic crisis and economic and social inequities, further deepened by the persistence of inequities between different geographical areas and ethnic groups and between men and women, were cause for concern. The State should make certain that protection and social integration programmes were accessible to groups living in extreme poverty, take steps to increase opportunities for social participation, and strengthen mechanisms for distributing information and ensuring accountability. The Bono de Desarrollo Humano ("human development voucher") cash transfer programme had had an impact on the status of communities living in extreme poverty, but should take into account the need for full observance of human rights standards. In that connection, social protection policies should aim at the universal enjoyment of the right to social security.

GENERAL ASSEMBLY ACTION

On 18 December [meeting 70], the General Assembly, on the recommendation of the Third Committee [A/63/430/Add.2], adopted **resolution 63/175** without vote [agenda item 64 *(b)*].

Human rights and extreme poverty

The General Assembly,

Reaffirming the Universal Declaration of Human Rights, the International Covenant on Civil and Political Rights, the International Covenant on Economic, Social and Cultural Rights, the Convention on the Elimination of All Forms of Discrimination against Women, the Convention on the Rights of the Child, the International Convention on the Elimination of All Forms of Racial Discrimination, the Convention on the Rights of Persons with Disabilities and other human rights instruments adopted by the United Nations,

Recalling its resolution 47/196 of 22 December 1992, by which it declared 17 October the International Day for the Eradication of Poverty, and its resolution 62/205 of 19 December 2007, by which it proclaimed the Second United Nations Decade for the Eradication of Poverty (2008–2017), as well as its resolution 61/157 of 19 December 2006 and its previous resolutions on human rights and extreme poverty, in which it reaffirmed that extreme poverty and exclusion from society constitute a violation of human dignity and that urgent national and international action is therefore required to eliminate them,

Recalling also its resolution 52/134 of 12 December 1997, in which it recognized that the enhancement of international cooperation in the field of human rights was essential for the effective understanding, promotion and protection of all human rights,

Reaffirming the internationally agreed development goals, including the Millennium Development Goals,

Deeply concerned that extreme poverty persists in all countries of the world, regardless of their economic, social and cultural situation, and that its extent and manifestations, such as hunger, trafficking in human beings, disease, lack of adequate shelter, illiteracy and hopelessness, are particularly severe in developing countries, while acknowledging the significant progress made in several parts of the world in combating extreme poverty,

Deeply concerned also that gender inequality, violence and discrimination exacerbate extreme poverty, disproportionally impacting women and girls,

Stressing that special attention should be given to children, persons with disabilities and indigenous peoples who are living in extreme poverty,

Concerned by the challenges faced today, including those derived from the food crisis, the energy crisis and the financial crisis, and by their impact on the increase in the number of people living in extreme poverty and their negative effect on the capacity of all States, especially developing countries, to fight extreme poverty,

Recalling Human Rights Council resolutions 2/2 of 27 November 2006, 7/27 of 28 March 2008 and 8/11 of 18 June 2008, as well as resolution 2006/9 of 24 August 2006 of the Subcommission on the Promotion and Protection of Human Rights, and taking note of the annex thereto, containing the draft guiding principles on extreme poverty and human rights: the rights of the poor,

Welcoming the Summit of World Leaders for Action against Hunger and Poverty of 20 September 2004, convened in New York by the Presidents of Brazil, Chile and France and the Prime Minister of Spain with the support of the Secretary-General,

Recognizing that the eradication of extreme poverty is a major challenge within the process of globalization and requires coordinated and continued policies through decisive national action and international cooperation,

Stressing the necessity of better understanding the causes and consequences of extreme poverty,

Reaffirming that, since the existence of widespread extreme poverty inhibits the full and effective enjoyment of human rights and might, in some situations, constitute a threat to the right to life, its immediate alleviation and eventual eradication must remain a high priority for the international community,

Stressing that respect for all human rights, which are universal, indivisible, interdependent and interrelated, is of crucial importance for all policies and programmes to fight extreme poverty,

Reaffirming that democracy, development and the full and effective enjoyment of human rights and fundamental freedoms are interdependent and mutually reinforcing and contribute to the eradication of extreme poverty,

1. *Reaffirms* that extreme poverty and exclusion from society constitute a violation of human dignity and that urgent national and international action is therefore required to eliminate them;

2. *Reaffirms also* that it is essential for States to foster participation by the poorest people in the decision-making process in the societies in which they live, in the promotion of human rights and in efforts to combat extreme poverty, and that it is essential for people living in poverty and vulnerable groups to be empowered to organize themselves and to participate in all aspects of political, economic and social life, in particular the planning and implementation of policies that affect them, thus enabling them to become genuine partners in development;

3. *Emphasizes* that extreme poverty is a major issue to be addressed by Governments, civil society and the United Nations system, including international financial institutions, and in this context reaffirms that political commitment is a prerequisite for the eradication of poverty;

4. *Reaffirms* that the existence of widespread absolute poverty inhibits the full and effective enjoyment of human

rights and renders democracy and popular participation fragile;

5. *Recognizes* the need to promote respect for human rights and fundamental freedoms in order to address the most pressing social needs of people living in poverty, including through the design and development of appropriate mechanisms to strengthen and consolidate democratic institutions and governance;

6. *Reaffirms* the commitments contained in the United Nations Millennium Declaration, in particular the commitments to spare no effort to fight against extreme poverty and to achieve development and poverty eradication, including the commitment to halve, by 2015, the proportion of the world's people whose income is less than one United States dollar a day and the proportion of people who suffer from hunger;

7. *Reaffirms also* the commitment made at the 2005 World Summit to eradicate poverty and promote sustained economic growth, sustainable development and global prosperity for all, including women and girls;

8. *Encourages* the international community to strengthen its efforts to address challenges that are contributing to extreme poverty, including those posed by the current food, energy and financial crises in all parts of the world, especially in developing countries, by enhancing its cooperation to help build national capacities;

9. *Reaffirms* the critical role of both formal and informal education in the achievement of poverty eradication and other development goals as envisaged in the Millennium Declaration, in particular basic education and training for eradicating illiteracy, and efforts towards expanded secondary and higher education as well as vocational education and technical training, especially for girls and women, the creation of human resources and infrastructure capabilities and the empowerment of those living in poverty, and in this context reaffirms the Dakar Framework for Action adopted at the World Education Forum in 2000, and recognizes the importance of the United Nations Educational, Scientific and Cultural Organization strategy for the eradication of poverty, especially extreme poverty, in supporting the Education for All programmes as a tool to achieve the millennium development goal of universal primary education by 2015;

10. *Invites* the United Nations High Commissioner for Human Rights to continue to give high priority to the question of the relationship between extreme poverty and human rights, and also invites her to further pursue the work in this area;

11. *Calls upon* States, United Nations bodies, in particular the Office of the United Nations High Commissioner for Human Rights and the United Nations Development Programme, intergovernmental organizations and non-governmental organizations to continue to give appropriate attention to the links between human rights and extreme poverty, and encourages the private sector and the international financial institutions to proceed likewise;

12. *Invites* States, as well as relevant United Nations agencies, the specialized agencies, programmes and funds, intergovernmental organizations, United Nations treaty bodies, special procedures, including the independent expert on the question of human rights and extreme poverty, national human rights institutions, within their respective mandates, and also non-governmental organizations, especially those in which people in situations of extreme poverty express their views, to contribute further to the consultations led by the High Commissioner on the draft guiding principles on extreme poverty and human rights: the rights of the poor;

13. *Welcomes* the efforts of entities throughout the United Nations system to incorporate the Millennium Declaration and the internationally agreed development goals set out therein into their work;

14. *Also welcomes* the appointment of the new independent expert on the question of human rights and extreme poverty and the renewed mandate that she has received, and takes note with appreciation of her report to the General Assembly;

15. *Decides* to consider the question further at its sixty-fifth session under the sub-item entitled "Human rights questions, including alternative approaches for improving the effective enjoyment of human rights and fundamental freedoms".

Right to food

Human Rights Council special session

At the request of Cuba [A/HRC/S-7/1], on behalf of 30 other States and groups of States, the Human Rights Council held its seventh special session (Geneva, 22 May) [A/HRC/S-7/2] to consider and take action on the negative impact on the realization of the right to food of the worsening of the world food crisis, caused, inter alia, by soaring food prices. During its consideration of the issue, the Council heard statements from its members, observer States, the Special Rapporteur on the right to food, UN entities, intergovernmental organizations and NGOs.

On the same day, the Council adopted a resolution [A/63/53 (res. S-7/1)], by which it expressed concern at the worsening of the world food crisis, which undermined the realization of the right to food for all. The Council called on States, multilateral institutions and other parties to ensure the realization of that right as an essential human rights objective, and to review any policy or measure which could have a negative impact on its realization. The Council stressed that States had a primary obligation to meet the food needs of their own populations, while the international community should provide assistance for increasing food production. It called upon UN members and other stakeholders to participate in the High-level Conference on World Food Security: the Challenges of Climate Change and Bioenergy (see p. 1343). The Special Rapporteur on the right to food was requested to make a presentation to the Council's eighth (2008) session on his participation in the Conference and on his initial recommendations regarding action to promote, respect and protect the right to food and freedom from hunger. The Rapporteur should also report to the

Council's ninth (2009) session, inviting comments from States and other relevant actors on the crisis and remedies from a human rights perspective.

In response to the Council's request, Special Rapporteur on the right to food Olivier de Schutter gave a presentation to the Council on 6 June, during its eighth session [A/HRC/8/52], on the High-level Conference on World Food Security.

Also in response to that resolution, the Special Rapporteur submitted in September [A/HRC/9/23] a report putting forward a human rights framework for world food and nutrition security. According to the Rapporteur, the marked increase in the price of food commodities on international markets had a severe negative impact on the right to food of the poorest households. The increase would not benefit many small producers facing steep rises in costs and lacking the infrastructure and support to increase food supply. What mattered in human rights terms was who would produce food, and for the benefit of whom. If a new global partnership for agriculture and food was to emerge from the crisis, such a partnership should not simply seek to boost supply by promoting technology-driven recipes, but also empower those who were hungry and malnourished and whose livelihoods might be threatened by a renewed interest in agricultural production. A human rights framework would contribute to keeping the search for solutions on track, because it would improve accountability and ensure that the most vulnerable would be given priority. However, such a framework was absent from current discussions.

The Special Rapporteur encouraged States to build national strategies for realizing the right to adequate food, taking into account the need to strengthen the protection of the human rights of the most vulnerable groups; to develop an international consensus on agrofuels, based on the need to ensure that agrofuel production respected human rights and did not result in distorted development in producer countries; to clarify how the private sector could contribute to a more just food production and distribution system; to request further studies on the role of international cooperation; and to examine the contribution the establishment of a global reinsurance fund could make to the realization of the right to food.

In a follow-up resolution of 24 September [A/63/53/Add.1 (res. 9/6)], the Council took note of the Special Rapporteur's recommendations. It encouraged States to incorporate the human rights perspective in their national strategies for the realization of the right to adequate food for all, which could include mapping the food insecure, adopting legislation and policies with a right to food framework, and establishing mechanisms for ensuring the participation of rights-holders in the design and monitoring of such legislation. States should promote investment in agriculture and rural infrastructure and take all necessary measures to ensure the realization of that right. The Special Rapporteur on the right to food was requested to report on the implementation of the resolution at the Council's twelfth (2009) session.

Other activities

Reports of Special Rapporteur. In a January report [A/HRC/7/5], the Special Rapporteur on the right to food, Jean Ziegler (Switzerland), said that, despite advances in various countries such as China, India, South Africa and several Latin American and Caribbean countries, there had been little progress overall in reducing the number of victims of hunger and malnutrition. The number of people suffering from hunger had increased every year since 1996, despite Government commitments to halve hunger. Yet hunger and famine were not inevitable. One of the key problems was the lack of coherence within the UN system between the positive developments in some sectors of the system, as evidenced by the right to food guidelines [YUN 2004, p. 1226] of the Food and Agriculture Organization of the United Nations, and the way in which the policies and practices of other agencies, such as the International Monetary Fund and the World Bank, as well as the World Trade Organization, undermined protection of the right to food. State policies showed similar patterns of inconsistency. While States had recognized the right to food in the World Food Summit Declaration [YUN 1996, p. 1129] and more than 150 States were parties to the International Covenant on Economic, Social and Cultural Rights, at the same time they engaged in trade policies that were detrimental to the enjoyment of human rights in other countries. Also affecting the right were transnational corporations, which were not subject to mechanisms to guard against the right-to-food violations that some of them were sometimes committing. An issue to be addressed was the exclusion and discrimination of the most vulnerable; attention should be given to the protection of the right to food for disadvantaged groups, especially women and indigenous people. Other issues requiring work in the future were desertification, biofuels and refugees from hunger.

The Rapporteur recommended that States take action to realize the right to food of all their people; ensure that their international trade agreements did not have any negative impact on the right to food in other countries; improve the international supervisory mechanisms for transnational corporations, especially those controlling the food and water system; give priority to investments in long-term development projects that reduced vulnerability to drought and desertification; establish a moratorium on initiatives to develop biofuels that aimed to convert food into fuel; and strengthen protection mechanisms for people forced to leave their homes and lands because of hunger and violations of their right to food.

In a later addendum [A/HRC/7/5/Add.1], the Special Rapporteur summarized 61 communications sent to 31 Governments and eight other actors between 2 December 2006 and 4 December 2007. Thirty-three Governments and six actors had replied.

Human Rights Council action. On 26 March, the Human Rights Council appointed Olivier de Schutter (Belgium) as Special Rapporteur.

On 27 March [A/63/53 (res. 7/14)], the Council took note of the Special Rapporteur's report on the right to food. It requested the Advisory Committee to consider recommendations for approval by the Council on further measures to enhance realization of the right to food, bearing in mind the importance of promoting the implementation of existing standards. The Council decided to convene a panel discussion on the realization of the right to food during its main session in 2009.

Reports of Special Rapporteur. In his interim report [A/63/278], transmitted by the Secretary-General to the General Assembly in accordance with resolution 62/164 [YUN 2007, p. 776], the new Special Rapporteur highlighted some of the challenges facing the realization of the right to adequate food and presented his priorities. He undertook to work with all interested parties towards developing sustainable solutions for eradicating hunger and implementing the right to food, and to devote equal attention to establishing an international environment enabling States to develop strategies for the fulfilment of that right and to developing such strategies at the domestic level. During the first year of the mandate, the focus would be on the future of food aid; the impact of trade in agricultural commodities on the right to food; the impact of the protection of intellectual property rights on agriculture; and the impact of the activities of the agribusiness sector on the right to food. As regards national strategies for fulfilling the right to food, the Rapporteur would explore the institutional tools that could best contribute to that objective, focusing on human rights relating to the use of land and on women's rights.

Communication. In February, Cuba transmitted its observations [A/HRC/7/G/5] on the Special Rapporteur's report on his 2007 visit to the country [YUN 2007, p. 775].

GENERAL ASSEMBLY ACTION

On 18 December [meeting 70], the General Assembly, on the recommendation of the Third Committee [A/63/430/Add.2], adopted **resolution 63/187** by recorded vote (184-1) [agenda item 64 *(b)*].

The right to food

The General Assembly,

Reaffirming all previous resolutions and decisions on the right to food adopted within the framework of the United Nations,

Recalling the Universal Declaration of Human Rights, which provides that everyone has the right to a standard of living adequate for her or his health and well-being, including food, the Universal Declaration on the Eradication of Hunger and Malnutrition and the United Nations Millennium Declaration, in particular millennium development goal 1 on eradicating extreme poverty and hunger by 2015,

Recalling also the provisions of the International Covenant on Economic, Social and Cultural Rights, in which the fundamental right of every person to be free from hunger is recognized,

Bearing in mind the Rome Declaration on World Food Security and the World Food Summit Plan of Action and the Declaration of the World Food Summit: five years later, adopted in Rome on 13 June 2002,

Reaffirming the concrete recommendations contained in the Voluntary Guidelines to Support the Progressive Realization of the Right to Adequate Food in the Context of National Food Security, adopted by the Council of the Food and Agriculture Organization of the United Nations in November 2004,

Bearing in mind paragraph 6 of its resolution 60/251 of 15 March 2006,

Reaffirming that all human rights are universal, indivisible, interdependent and interrelated, and that they must be treated globally, in a fair and equal manner, on the same footing and with the same emphasis,

Reaffirming also that a peaceful, stable and enabling political, social and economic environment, at both the national and the international levels, is the essential foundation that will enable States to give adequate priority to food security and poverty eradication,

Reiterating, as in the Rome Declaration on World Food Security and the Declaration of the World Food Summit: five years later, that food should not be used as an instrument of political or economic pressure, and reaffirming in this regard the importance of international cooperation and solidarity, as well as the necessity of refraining from unilateral measures that are not in accordance with international law and the Charter of the United Nations and that endanger food security,

Convinced that each State must adopt a strategy consistent with its resources and capacities to achieve its individual goals in implementing the recommendations contained in the Rome Declaration on World Food Security and the World Food Summit Plan of Action and, at the same time, cooperate regionally and internationally in order to organize collective solutions to global issues of food security in a world of increasingly interlinked institutions, societies and economies where coordinated efforts and shared responsibilities are essential,

Recognizing the complex character of the worsening of the current global food crisis, in which the right to adequate food is threatened to be violated on a massive scale, as a combination of several major factors, including macroeconomic factors, exacerbated by environmental degradation, desertification and global climate change, natural disasters and the lack of the technology necessary to confront its impact, particularly in developing countries, least developed countries and small island developing States,

Resolved to act to ensure that the human rights perspective is taken into account at the national, regional and international levels in measures to address the current global food crisis,

Expressing its deep concern at the number and scale of natural disasters, diseases and pests and their increasing impact in recent years, which have resulted in massive loss of life and livelihood and threatened agricultural production and food security, in particular in developing countries,

Stressing the importance of reversing the continuing decline of official development assistance devoted to agriculture, both in real terms and as a share of total official development assistance,

Recognizing the role of the Food and Agriculture Organization of the United Nations as the key United Nations agency for rural and agricultural development and its work in supporting the efforts of Member States to achieve the full realization of the right to food, including through its provision of technical assistance to developing countries in support of the implementation of national priority frameworks,

Taking note of the final Declaration adopted at the International Conference on Agrarian Reform and Rural Development of the Food and Agriculture Organization of the United Nations in Porto Alegre, Brazil, on 10 March 2006,

Acknowledging the High-level Task Force on the Global Food Security Crisis established by the Secretary-General, and supporting the Secretary-General in his continuing efforts in this regard, including continued engagement with Member States and the Special Rapporteur of the Human Rights Council on the right to food,

1. *Reaffirms* that hunger constitutes an outrage and a violation of human dignity and therefore requires the adoption of urgent measures at the national, regional and international levels for its elimination;

2. *Also reaffirms* the right of everyone to have access to safe, sufficient and nutritious food, consistent with the right to adequate food and the fundamental right of everyone to be free from hunger, so as to be able to fully develop and maintain his or her physical and mental capacities;

3. *Considers it intolerable* that more than 6 million children still die every year from hunger-related illness before their fifth birthday and that the number of people who are undernourished has grown to about 923 million worldwide, including as a result of the global food crisis, while, according to the Food and Agriculture Organization of the United Nations, the planet could produce enough food to feed 12 billion people, twice the world's present population;

4. *Expresses its concern* that women and girls are disproportionately affected by hunger, food insecurity and poverty, in part as a result of gender inequality and discrimination, that in many countries, girls are twice as likely as boys to die from malnutrition and preventable childhood diseases and that it is estimated that almost twice as many women as men suffer from malnutrition;

5. *Encourages* all States to take action to address gender inequality and discrimination against women, in particular where it contributes to the malnutrition of women and girls, including measures to ensure the full and equal realization of the right to food and ensuring that women have equal access to resources, including income, land and water and their ownership, as well as full and equal access to education, science and technology, to enable them to feed themselves and their families;

6. *Encourages* the Special Rapporteur of the Human Rights Council on the right to food to continue mainstreaming a gender perspective in the fulfilment of his mandate, and encourages the Food and Agriculture Organization of the United Nations and all other United Nations bodies and mechanisms addressing the right to food and food insecurity to integrate a gender perspective into their relevant policies, programmes and activities;

7. *Reaffirms* the need to ensure that programmes delivering safe and nutritious food are inclusive of and accessible to persons with disabilities;

8. *Encourages* all States to take steps with a view to achieving progressively the full realization of the right to food, including steps to promote the conditions for everyone to be free from hunger and, as soon as possible, to enjoy fully the right to food, and to create and adopt national plans to combat hunger;

9. *Recognizes* the advances reached through South-South cooperation in developing countries and regions in connection with food security and the development of agricultural production for the full realization of the right to food;

10. *Stresses* that improving access to productive resources and public investment in rural development are essential for eradicating hunger and poverty, in particular in developing countries, including through the promotion of investments in appropriate small-scale irrigation and water management technologies in order to reduce vulnerability to droughts;

11. *Recognizes* that 80 per cent of hungry people live in rural areas and 50 per cent are small-scale farm-holders, and that these people are especially vulnerable to food insecurity, given the increasing cost of inputs and the fall in farm incomes; that access to land, water, seeds and other natural resources is an increasing challenge for poor producers; that sustainable and gender-sensitive agricultural policies are important tools for promoting land and agrarian reform, rural credit and insurance, technical assistance and other associated measures to achieve food security and rural development; and that support by States for small farmers, fishing communities and local enterprises is a key element for food security and the provision of the right to food;

12. *Stresses* the importance of fighting hunger in rural areas, including through national efforts supported by international partnerships to stop desertification and land degradation and through investments and public policies that are specifically appropriate to the risk of drylands, and in this regard calls for the full implementation of the United Nations Convention to Combat Desertification in Those Countries Experiencing Serious Drought and/or Desertification, Particularly in Africa;

13. *Also stresses* its commitments to promote and protect, without discrimination, the economic, social and cultural rights of indigenous peoples in accordance with international human rights obligations and, taking into account, as appropriate, the United Nations Declaration on the Rights of Indigenous Peoples, acknowledges that many indigenous organizations and representatives of indigenous communities have expressed in different forums their deep concerns over the obstacles and challenges they face for the full enjoyment of the right to food, and calls upon States to take special actions to combat the root causes of the disproportionately high level of hunger and malnutrition among indigenous peoples and the continuous discrimination against them;

14. *Notes* the need to further examine various concepts such as, inter alia, "food sovereignty" and their relation with food security and the right to food, bearing in mind the need to avoid any negative impact on the enjoyment of the right to food for all people at all times;

15. *Requests* all States and private actors, as well as international organizations within their respective mandates, to take fully into account the need to promote the effective realization of the right to food for all, including in the ongoing negotiations in different fields;

16. *Recognizes* the need to strengthen national commitment as well as international assistance, upon the request of and in cooperation with the affected countries, towards the full realization and protection of the right to food, and in particular to develop national protection mechanisms for people forced to leave their homes and land because of hunger or humanitarian emergencies affecting the enjoyment of the right to food;

17. *Stresses* the need to make efforts to mobilize and optimize the allocation and utilization of technical and financial resources from all sources, including external debt relief for developing countries, and to reinforce national actions to implement sustainable food security policies;

18. *Calls for* the early conclusion and a successful, development-oriented outcome of the Doha Round of trade negotiations of the World Trade Organization as a contribution to creating international conditions that permit the full realization of the right to food;

19. *Stresses* that all States should make all efforts to ensure that their international policies of a political and economic nature, including international trade agreements, do not have a negative impact on the right to food in other countries;

20. *Recalls* the importance of the New York Declaration on Action against Hunger and Poverty, and recommends the continuation of efforts aimed at identifying additional sources of financing for the fight against hunger and poverty;

21. *Recognizes* that the promises made at the World Food Summit in 1996 to halve the number of persons who are undernourished are not being fulfilled, and invites once again all international financial and development institutions, as well as the relevant United Nations agencies and funds, to give priority to and provide the necessary funding to realize the aim of halving by 2015 the proportion of people who suffer from hunger, as well as the right to food as set out in the Rome Declaration on World Food Security and the United Nations Millennium Declaration;

22. *Reaffirms* that integrating food and nutritional support, with the goal that all people at all times will have access to sufficient, safe and nutritious food to meet their dietary needs and food preferences for an active and healthy life, is part of a comprehensive response to the spread of HIV/AIDS, tuberculosis, malaria and other communicable diseases;

23. *Urges* States to give adequate priority in their development strategies and expenditures to the realization of the right to food;

24. *Stresses* the importance of international development cooperation and assistance, both as an effective contribution to the expansion of agriculture and food production and, in particular in activities related to emergency situations, for the realization of the right to food and the achievement of sustainable food security, while recognizing that each country has the primary responsibility for ensuring the implementation of national programmes and strategies in this regard;

25. *Also stresses* that States parties to the World Trade Organization Agreement on Trade-Related Aspects of Intellectual Property Rights should consider implementing that agreement in a manner supportive of food security, while mindful of the obligation of Member States to promote and protect the right to food;

26. *Calls upon* Member States, the United Nations system and other relevant stakeholders to support national efforts aimed at responding rapidly to the food crises currently occurring across Africa, and expresses its deep concern that funding shortfalls are forcing the World Food Programme to cut operations across different regions, including Southern Africa;

27. *Invites* all relevant international organizations, including the World Bank and the International Monetary Fund, to continue to promote policies and projects that have a positive impact on the right to food, to ensure that partners respect the right to food in the implementation of common projects, to support strategies of Member States aimed at the fulfilment of the right to food and to avoid any actions that could have a negative impact on the realization of the right to food;

28. *Takes note with appreciation* of the interim report of the Special Rapporteur and the work and commitment of the first mandate holder to achieving the realization of the right to food;

29. *Supports* the realization of the mandate of the Special Rapporteur, as extended by the Human Rights Council in its resolution 6/2 of 27 September 2007;

30. *Requests* the Secretary-General and the United Nations High Commissioner for Human Rights to provide all the necessary human and financial resources for the effective fulfilment of the mandate of the Special Rapporteur;

31. *Welcomes* the work already done by the Committee on Economic, Social and Cultural Rights in promoting the right to adequate food, in particular its General Comment No. 12 (1999) on the right to adequate food (article 11 of the International Covenant on Economic, Social and Cultural Rights), in which the Committee affirmed, inter alia, that the right to adequate food is indivisibly linked to the inherent dignity of the human person and is indispensable for the fulfilment of other human rights enshrined in the International Bill of Human Rights, and is also inseparable

from social justice, requiring the adoption of appropriate economic, environmental and social policies, at both the national and the international levels, oriented to the eradication of poverty and the fulfilment of all human rights for all;

32. *Recalls* General Comment No. 15 (2002) of the Committee on Economic, Social and Cultural Rights on the right to water (articles 11 and 12 of the Covenant), in which the Committee noted, inter alia, the importance of ensuring sustainable water resources for human consumption and agriculture in realization of the right to adequate food;

33. *Reaffirms* that the Voluntary Guidelines to Support the Progressive Realization of the Right to Adequate Food in the Context of National Food Security, adopted by the Council of the Food and Agriculture Organization of the United Nations in November 2004, represent a practical tool to promote the realization of the right to food for all, contribute to the achievement of food security and thus provide an additional instrument in the attainment of internationally agreed development goals, including those contained in the Millennium Declaration;

34. *Welcomes* the continued cooperation of the High Commissioner, the Committee and the Special Rapporteur, and encourages them to continue their cooperation in this regard;

35. *Calls upon* all Governments to cooperate with and assist the Special Rapporteur in his task, to supply all necessary information requested by him and to give serious consideration to responding favourably to the requests of the Special Rapporteur to visit their countries to enable him to fulfil his mandate more effectively;

36. *Requests* the Special Rapporteur to submit an interim report to the General Assembly at its sixty-fourth session on the implementation of the present resolution and to continue his work, including by examining the emerging issues with regard to the realization of the right to food within his existing mandate;

37. *Invites* Governments, relevant United Nations agencies, funds and programmes, treaty bodies, civil society actors and non-governmental organizations, as well as the private sector, to cooperate fully with the Special Rapporteur in the fulfilment of his mandate, inter alia, through the submission of comments and suggestions on ways and means of realizing the right to food;

38. *Decides* to continue the consideration of the question at its sixty-fourth session under the item entitled "Promotion and protection of human rights".

RECORDED VOTE ON RESOLUTION 63/187:

In favour: Afghanistan, Albania, Algeria, Andorra, Angola, Antigua and Barbuda, Argentina, Armenia, Australia, Austria, Azerbaijan, Bahamas, Bahrain, Bangladesh, Barbados, Belarus, Belgium, Belize, Benin, Bhutan, Bolivia, Bosnia and Herzegovina, Botswana, Brazil, Brunei Darussalam, Bulgaria, Burkina Faso, Burundi, Cambodia, Cameroon, Canada, Central African Republic, Chad, Chile, China, Colombia, Comoros, Congo, Costa Rica, Côte d'Ivoire, Croatia, Cuba, Cyprus, Czech Republic, Democratic People's Republic of Korea, Denmark, Djibouti, Dominica, Dominican Republic, Ecuador, Egypt, El Salvador, Eritrea, Estonia, Ethiopia, Fiji, Finland, France, Gabon, Gambia, Georgia, Germany, Ghana, Greece, Grenada, Guatemala, Guinea, Guinea-Bissau, Guyana, Haiti, Honduras, Hungary, Iceland, India, Indonesia, Iran, Iraq, Ireland, Israel, Italy, Jamaica, Japan, Jordan, Kazakhstan, Kenya, Kuwait, Kyrgyzstan, Lao People's Democratic Republic, Latvia, Lebanon, Lesotho, Liberia, Libyan Arab Jamahiriya, Liechtenstein, Lithuania, Luxembourg, Madagascar, Malawi, Malaysia, Maldives, Mali, Malta, Marshall Islands, Mauritania, Mauritius, Mexico, Micronesia, Moldova, Monaco, Mongolia, Montenegro, Morocco, Mozambique, Myanmar, Namibia, Nauru, Nepal, Netherlands, New Zealand, Nicaragua, Niger, Nigeria, Norway, Oman, Pakistan, Palau, Panama, Paraguay, Peru, Philippines, Poland, Portugal, Qatar, Republic of Korea, Romania, Russian Federation, Rwanda, Saint Kitts and Nevis, Saint Lucia, Saint Vincent and the Grenadines, Samoa, San Marino, Sao Tome and Principe, Saudi Arabia, Senegal, Serbia, Sierra Leone, Singapore, Slovakia, Slovenia, Solomon Islands, Somalia, South Africa, Spain, Sri Lanka, Sudan, Suriname, Swaziland, Sweden, Switzerland, Syrian Arab Republic, Tajikistan, Thailand, The former Yugoslav Republic of Macedonia, Timor-Leste, Togo, Tonga, Trinidad and Tobago, Tunisia, Turkey, Turkmenistan, Tuvalu, Ukraine, United Arab Emirates, United Kingdom, United Republic of Tanzania, Uruguay, Uzbekistan, Vanuatu, Venezuela, Viet Nam, Yemen, Zambia, Zimbabwe.

Against: United States.

Right to adequate housing

Reports of Special Rapporteur. In a February report [A/HRC/7/16], the Special Rapporteur on adequate housing as a component of the right to an adequate standard of living, and on the right to non-discrimination in this context, Miloon Kothari (India), reviewed his work and activities since his appointment in 2000. He provided recommendations to the Human Rights Council and the next mandate holder concerning the obstacles to the realization of that right: lack of legislation and implementation, homelessness, forced evictions, discrimination, lack of access to water and basic services, and affordability.

The Special Rapporteur stated that after the seven years of his mandate, there was a severe and growing global housing and land rights crisis that needed to be given priority on the global agenda and accorded greater attention. He asserted that the right to adequate housing should be interpreted on the basis of the indivisibility and universality of human rights, and the struggle against discrimination was of utmost importance in realizing that right. Various tools had been elaborated during his term: the basic principles and guidelines on development-based evictions and displacement, the questionnaires on women and adequate housing and on the right to adequate housing, and the development of indicators to monitor the progressive realization of the right. The Special Rapporteur encouraged relevant actors to employ such tools, and develop and adapt them to national and local situations. A combination of a humanitarian and human rights-based approach should be employed to address the situation of millions of people living in grossly inadequate housing conditions or facing homelessness and landlessness. Stronger support and response from

States were needed to develop the mandate. Issues for further consideration included the recognition of the link between access to land and the human right to adequate housing; rural areas; natural disasters and humanitarian emergencies; climate change; and the role of civil society.

An addendum to the report [A/HRC/7/16/Add.1] summarized 50 communications sent to 25 Governments and the United Nations Interim Administration Mission in Kosovo between 1 December 2006 and 4 December 2007, and replies received thereto. The Special Rapporteur regretted that most Governments had not responded, or had done so in a selective manner.

Communication. On 13 March, Spain submitted its reply [A/HRC/7/G/13] to the Special Rapporteur's 2006 report [YUN 2006, p. 906] on his mission to the country.

Human Rights Council action. On 26 March, the Human Rights Council appointed Raquel Rolnik (Brazil) as Special Rapporteur.

Report of Special Rapporteur. In August [A/63/275], the Secretary-General transmitted to the General Assembly the report of the new Special Rapporteur, in accordance with a 2007 Human Rights Council request [YUN 2007, p. 780]. The report reviewed the issues addressed under the mandate, including homelessness, affordability, forced evictions, discrimination in accessing adequate housing and the gender perspective. The Rapporteur urged States to include provisions on the protection, fulfilment and justiciability of that right in their national and constitutional law; to integrate the right in local and national urban planning and housing policies; to adopt and ratify the Optional Protocol to the International Covenant on Economic, Social and Cultural Rights; and to address the plight of the homeless and stop their criminalization.

The General Assembly took note of that report on 18 December (**decision 63/534**).

Cultural rights

Human Rights Council action. On 28 March [A/63/53 (res. 7/34)], the Human Rights Council reaffirmed that the establishment of a thematic procedure in cultural rights should not mean a new monitoring mechanism. It acknowledged that the process of review, rationalization and improvement of mandates represented momentum towards the establishment of an independent expert in the field of cultural rights, and requested the High Commissioner to consult States, intergovernmental organizations and NGOs on the content and scope of such a mandate. The Council underlined the importance of avoiding overlapping with the activities of the United Nations Educational, Scientific and Cultural Organization and other bodies and organizations of the UN system when establishing the mandate of the independent expert.

Right to education

Reports of Special Rapporteur. The Special Rapporteur on the right to education, Vernor Muñoz (Costa Rica), in a May report [A/HRC/8/10] focused on the right to education in emergency situations. Emergencies, whether arising out of armed conflict or natural disaster, were a source of violations of the right to education, affecting a large number of people. He urged States, donors, multilateral agencies and organizations to commit to the implementation of that right in emergencies and recommended that the right be recognized as an integral part of the humanitarian response. Action should be taken to put an end to impunity for persons and armed groups who attacked schools, students and teachers. Measures should be developed to give physical and emotional protection to girls and female adolescents to ensure that they went to school. States should develop plans for education in emergencies to include measures for continuity of education at all levels and during all phases of an emergency. They should draw up a programme of studies that was adaptable, non-discriminatory, gender-sensitive and of high quality that met the needs of children and young people throughout an emergency, and design and implement specific plans to avoid the exploitation of girls and young women in the wake of emergencies.

In an addendum [A/HRC/8/10/Add.1], the Rapporteur summarized 14 communications sent to 12 countries between 12 January 2007 and 29 February 2008, and the replies received thereto.

During his mission to Guatemala (20–28 July) [A/HRC/11/8/Add.3], the Special Rapporteur observed challenges facing the education system, including the low level of investment in education—which, at approximately 2 per cent of gross domestic product, was the lowest in the region. Indigenous peoples' right to education was confined to the issue of bilingualism, with the teaching of indigenous languages provided solely in the first three years of primary schooling in a very small number of State schools and only in some languages. The trend towards the privatization of education undermined the established principle of free education. With 80 per cent of secondary education in the hands of private schools, it was impossible to ensure education for all at the lower and upper secondary levels. Legislation, including constitutional provisions, revealed a gulf between the law and its application. Constitutional principles on education should cease to be a dead letter and become everyday practice guiding concrete actions.

The Rapporteur recommended that the Government increase investment in education and secure national political consensus on granting an adequate budget to fulfil its obligation in that regard. It should also increase the budget for intercultural bilingual education in proportion to the population served, ensure a stronger participation by the Office of the Deputy Minister for Intercultural Bilingual Education and establish criteria for multiculturalism, interculturalism and multilingualism to address the specificities of indigenous communities.

Human Rights Council action. On 18 June [A/63/53 (res. 8/4)], the Human Rights Council urged States to take measures to eliminate obstacles limiting effective access to education, notably by girls; support implementation of plans and programmes of action to ensure quality education and improved enrolment, and the elimination of gender discrimination and stereotypes in educational curricula and materials; and ensure that the right to education was respected in emergency situations. It extended the mandate of the Special Rapporteur for three years and requested him to report yearly to the Council, and to the General Assembly on an interim basis.

Report of Special Rapporteur. In accordance with that resolution, the Secretary-General, in August, transmitted the Special Rapporteur's interim report [A/63/292] to the General Assembly. Expanding on his May report on education in emergency situations, he recommended that the international community intensify its search for best practices in such situations. He called on donors to include education in all their humanitarian assistance plans, and increase their education allocation to at least 4.2 per cent of total humanitarian assistance.

The General Assembly took note of that report on 18 December (**decision 63/534**).

Communication. In a 20 September letter [A/C.3/63/5] to the General Assembly President, Benin, Bosnia and Herzegovina, Costa Rica, Nicaragua, Norway and Qatar conveyed their interest to convene a thematic debate during the Assembly's sixty-third session on the issue of access to education in emergency, post-crisis and transition situations caused by man-made conflicts or natural disasters.

Environmental and scientific concerns

Human rights and climate change

Human Rights Council action. On 28 March [A/63/53 (res. 7/23)], the Human Rights Council, concerned that climate change posed an immediate and far-reaching threat to people and communities around the word and had implications for the full enjoyment of human rights, requested OHCHR, in consultation with States and other stakeholders, to prepare a study on the relationship between climate change and human rights, to be submitted to the Council prior to its tenth (2009) session. It decided to consider the issue at its tenth session and to make the study available to the Conference of the Parties to the 1992 United Nations Framework Convention on Climate Change [YUN 1992, p. 681].

Toxic wastes

Reports of Special Rapporteur. In a February report [A/HRC/7/21], the Special Rapporteur on the adverse effects of the illicit movement and dumping of toxic and dangerous products and wastes on the enjoyment of human rights, Okechukwu Ibeanu (Nigeria), highlighted the importance of the right to information and to participation. Those rights were both rights in themselves and essential tools for the exercise of other rights, such as the right to life and to health.

The main obligation in dealing with toxic wastes and dangerous products lay mainly with States, which should not abuse that responsibility by withholding information, given the potential risks and dangers to the health and well-being of the population and the potential impact on the environment. While developing countries were sometimes left with little choice owing to developmental needs and situations of poverty, both developing and developed States needed to find alternative solutions to the trade of toxic wastes and dangerous products. Although the income generated by such trade was attractive, States needed to take into account the future costs and long-term consequences of environmental degradation and health problems, especially those affecting women and young persons. He appealed to States to put in place adequate means for their protection.

An addendum to the report [A/HRC/7/21/Add.1] summarized communications sent by the Special Rapporteur to eight countries and the United Nations Interim Administration Mission in Kosovo between 1 January 2006 and 4 December 2007 and replies thereto.

In August [A/HRC/9/22], the Special Rapporteur summarized his activities since his February report and challenges faced in discharging his mandate. He remained discouraged by the lack of attention to the mandate and arguments by States that issues of toxic wastes management were more appropriately discussed in environmental forums that at the Human Rights Council. Implementation of the mandate was also hampered by the lack of adequate financial resources. He also proposed requesting the Council to consider enhancing the mandate by broadening it to include all types of movement and dumping of toxic and dangerous products and wastes.

An addendum [A/HRC/9/22/Add.1] summarized communications sent to France and Niger, and replies received thereto, between 15 October 2007 and 28 July 2008.

During his mission to the United Republic of Tanzania (21–30 January) [A/HRC/9/22/Add.2], the Special Rapporteur noted that there was an adequate legal framework to deal with the transboundary movement of toxic and dangerous products and wastes. However, there was a lack of regulation for both small-scale and large-scale mining activities, while as much as 1 million people where engaged in artisanal and small-scale mining.

He recommended that the Government: step up its efforts in educating the public as to the effects that artisanal and small-scale mining could have on health and livelihood; provide more resources to step up inspection of artisanal and small-scale mining areas; be mindful of the specific concerns of indigenous communities and land rights when allocating land for artisanal and small-scale or large-scale mining; pay extra attention to the situation of vulnerable groups, including women and children, due to the exposure to highly toxic substances while engaging in artisanal and small-scale mining; and set up a database of mining-related illnesses to monitor environmental and human rights impacts of mining activities. The Government should also monitor the operations of large-scale mining corporations, particularly in regard to occupational health, safety standards and compliance with environmental and other legislation.

The Special Rapporteur visited Côte d'Ivoire (4–8 August) and the Netherlands (26–28 November) [A/HRC/12/26/Add.2] to examine the effects of the movement and dumping of toxic and dangerous products and wastes from the vessel *Probo Koala*, in Abidjan, on and around 19 August 2006 [YUN 2006, p. 1080]. The vessel, chartered by the commodity trading company Trafigura, had docked in Amsterdam before heading to Côte d'Ivoire, where the waste from the ship was dumped in various sites in the district of Abidjan.

The visit to the Netherlands focused on events surrounding the aborted offloading of the waste from the vessel in the port of Amsterdam, the reloading of the waste and the departure of the ship. The Rapporteur assessed the actions taken by the Dutch authorities after the dumping in Côte d'Ivoire, and concluded that improved measures had been taken to avoid the recurrence of similar incidents. He encouraged public authorities to ensure the rigorous inspection and, where necessary, detention of ships. The Netherlands should also continue to support Côte d'Ivoire in monitoring and addressing possible long-term health and environmental effects of the incident.

The scope of the visit to Côte d'Ivoire included a review of procedures followed prior to and during the offloading and dumping of the waste, and an assessment of remedial action taken by the Government. There was a need to tackle outstanding issues, in particular decontamination, health care and compensation. The Ivorian authorities should take further action to protect the right to life, to health and to a healthy environment of all victims and their families.

Regarding the role of Trafigura and its responsibility to respect human rights, the Rapporteur recommended that the company should continue to fund and support outstanding remedial work in Côte d'Ivoire, ensure that timely and reliable information was disclosed regarding its activities and on their potential environment, health and safety impact. It should also balance commercial interests with human rights and environmental requirements.

Human Rights Council action. On 24 September [A/63/53/Add.1 (res. 9/1)], the Human Rights Council extended the mandate of the Special Rapporteur for a three-year period. His next report to the Council should include information on persons killed, maimed or injured in developing countries by the movement and dumping of toxic and dangerous products and wastes; human rights standards applicable to transnational corporations and other business enterprises that dumped such products and wastes; rehabilitation of and assistance to victims; the scope of related national legislation; the question of waste-recycling programmes and the transfer of polluting industries, industrial activities and technologies from developed to developing countries; and the ambiguities in international instruments.

Right to health

Reports of Special Rapporteur. In a January report [A/HRC/7/11 & Corr.1], the Special Rapporteur on the right of everyone to the enjoyment of the highest attainable standard of physical and mental health, Paul Hunt (New Zealand), said that at the heart of that right lay an effective and integrated health system, responsive to national and local priorities, and accessible to all. Such a system was an essential element of a healthy and equitable society, a core social institution, no less than a fair justice system or democratic political system. However, health systems in many countries were failing and collapsing. The report identified a general approach to strengthening health systems that should be applied consistently and systematically. As the right to a fair trial had helped to strengthen court systems, in a similar way, the right to health could help to strengthen health systems.

In an addendum [A/HRC/7/11/Add.1], the Special Rapporteur summarized cases transmitted to Governments and replies received thereto. Between 2 December 2006 and 1 December 2007, he had sent 27 communications to 22 Governments and one to the United Nations Interim Administration Mission in Kosovo (UNMIK). Replies were received from 17 Governments and from UNMIK.

In June [A/HRC/11/12/Add.2], the Special Rapporteur visited the headquarters of GlaxoSmithKline, one of the world's leading research-based pharmaceutical companies, to interview the company's senior management. Enhancing access to medicines was a shared responsibility, and the Millennium Development Goals [YUN 2000, p. 51] recognized that pharmaceutical companies had a responsibility to improve such access. A company that developed a life-saving medicine had performed a critically important social, medical, public health and right-to-health function. While the company's "reward" was the grant of a limited monopoly over the medicine, enabling it to enhance shareholder value and invest in further research and development, the company also had a right-to-health responsibility to take all reasonable steps to make the life-saving medicine accessible to all those in need. Companies should grasp their social function and right-to-health responsibilities, and do everything possible, within a viable business model, to fulfil their social function and human rights responsibilities. That would not only enhance companies' status but also pressure States, generic manufacturers and others to provide the environment that companies needed if they were to enter into arrangements, such as commercial voluntary licences, that enhanced access to medicines for all.

In accordance with a Human Rights Council request [YUN 2007, p. 783], the Secretary-General in August transmitted to the General Assembly the Special Rapporteur's interim report [A/63/263]. The annex to the report contained the Human Rights Guidelines for Pharmaceutical Companies in relation to Access to Medicines, which set out the human rights responsibilities of pharmaceutical companies. The Guidelines, prepared by the Special Rapporteur on the basis of wide-ranging discussions over five years with a stakeholders, considered issues such as transparency, management, accountability, patents, licensing and pricing. They provided detailed guidance for pharmaceutical companies on their right-to-health responsibilities, as well as on society's legitimate expectations of the pharmaceutical sector. The report also discussed the importance of effective, transparent, accessible and independent accountability mechanisms in relation to the right to health.

The General Assembly took note of the report on 18 December (**decision 63/534**).

Human Rights Council action. On 18 June, the Human Rights Council appointed Anand Grover (India) as Special Rapporteur.

Human rights and HIV/AIDS

In March [A/HRC/7/59], OHCHR recalled that the Secretary-General's report on the protection of human rights in the context of human immunodeficiency virus and acquired immunodeficiency syndrome (HIV/AIDS) was submitted on a biennial basis. The latest report was submitted in 2007 [YUN 2007, p. 783], and the next report would be submitted in 2009, unless otherwise decided by the Council.

Access to medication

Report of Secretary-General. In March, in accordance with a 2006 Human Rights Council request [YUN 2006, p. 911], the Secretary-General submitted a report [A/HRC/7/30] summarizing information received from 15 Governments, three UN system bodies and three NGOs on the steps they had taken to improve access to medication in the context of pandemics such as HIV/AIDS, tuberculosis and malaria. The number of people receiving treatment for those diseases had increased due to national and international efforts. In some countries, the spread of those diseases had been significantly reduced, customs duties and taxes had been revised to facilitate access to medicines, and progress towards universal access had been made. However, the large number of people that continued to live with, were affected by, and died from those diseases meant that renewed efforts were required to ensure better access to medicines, especially among vulnerable groups. Moreover, the need to overcome legal and regulatory, trade and other barriers that blocked access to prevention, treatment, care and support was critically important to the enjoyment of the right of access to medicines. The continued lack of affordable drugs, together with the unequal geographical spread of health services, continued to impede access to medicines.

Water and sanitation services

Human Rights Council action. On 28 March [A/63/53 (res. 7/22)], the Human Rights Council, concerned that over one billion people lacked access to safe drinking water and 2.6 billion lacked access to basic sanitation, appointed for a three-year period an independent expert on the issue of human rights obligations related to access to safe drinking water and sanitation. The expert's mandate would include developing dialogue with concerned stakeholders to identify, promote and exchange views on and prepare a compendium of best practices related to access to safe drinking water and sanitation. The expert would also undertake a study on the further clarification of the content of human rights obligations, including non-discrimination obligations, in relation to access to safe drinking water and sanitation, and to submit a report to the Council's tenth (2009) session.

On 24 September, the Council appointed Catarina de Albuquerque (Portugal) as independent expert.

Bioethics

Report of Secretary-General. Pursuant to Economic and Social Council decision 2007/269 [YUN 2007, p. 784], the Secretary-General, in May, submitted a report [E/2008/51] presenting the views of two Member States and three UN entities on the most appropriate forums for considering the issue of genetic privacy and non-discrimination within the UN system. The Secretary-General recommended that the Council invite the Director-General of the United Nations Educational, Scientific and Cultural Organization (UNESCO) to consult with other UN entities on the implementation of and follow-up to Economic and Social Council resolutions 2001/39 [YUN 2001, p. 675] and 2004/9 [YUN 2004, p. 771] and related UNESCO Declarations; and to constitute an inter-agency coordination mechanism, such as an ad hoc inter-agency task force on genetic privacy and non-discrimination, which should report to the Council in 2010 and on a triennial basis thereafter.

By **decision 2008/233** of 22 July, the Economic and Social Council took note of the Secretary-General's report and invited the UNESCO Director-General to consult with UN entities on the implementation of and follow-up to those resolutions and Declarations and other norms and instruments adopted by the UN system that were relevant to genetic privacy and non-discrimination, and on a possible interagency coordination mechanism. The Director-General was invited to report to the Council on relevant developments at its 2010 substantive session and on a possible inter-agency mechanism, in consultation with and taking into account the views of Member States.

Slavery and related issues

Human Rights Council action. Further to its resolution 6/14 [YUN 2007, p. 784], the Human Rights Council, on 26 March, appointed Gulnara Shahinian (Armenia) Special Rapporteur on contemporary forms of slavery, including its causes and consequences.

Report of Special Rapporteur. In her first report [A/HRC/9/20], submitted in accordance with a 2007 Human Rights Council request [YUN 2007, p. 784], the new Special Rapporteur said that contemporary forms of slavery affected the lives of millions of people around the world. Based on the 1926 Slavery Convention definition, there were an estimated 27 million enslaved people throughout the world. No country was immune to its proliferation. Of special concern was the situation of children. No other UN special procedures mandate provided an opportunity to apply a holistic approach to issues such as forced labour, which were related to slavery. The Rapporteur would focus on the causes and consequences of forced labour and its impact on men, women and children; on domestic labour and child labour as it pertained to the economic exploitation of children, as well as traditional forms of slavery, such as bonded labour and serfdom; and address the protection, prevention and restoration of human rights and dignity of victims.

Report of Secretary-General. In August [A/63/213], the Secretary-General reported to the General Assembly on the programme of educational outreach on the transatlantic slave trade and slavery, as requested by General Assembly resolution 62/122 [YUN 2007, p. 784]. Through that programme, the UN Department of Public Information (DPI) had sought to address the lack of knowledge about the slave trade and encourage study and discussion of the topic. To that end, DPI developed a diverse educational outreach strategy about the causes, consequences, lessons and legacy of the 400-year slave trade and about the dangers of racism and prejudice. The strategy comprised a series of activities that began on the International Day of Remembrance of the Victims of Slavery and the Transatlantic Slave Trade, included follow-up activities throughout the year and had, as its core, an educational programme for intermediate and high school students that built on the UNESCO Slave Route Project.

GENERAL ASSEMBLY ACTION

On 20 October [meeting 29], the General Assembly adopted **resolution 63/5** [draft: A/63/L.5 & Add.1] without vote [agenda item 108].

Permanent memorial to and remembrance of the victims of slavery and the transatlantic slave trade

The General Assembly,

Recalling its resolution 61/19 of 28 November 2006, entitled "Commemoration of the two-hundredth anniversary of the abolition of the transatlantic slave trade", and its resolution 62/122 of 17 December 2007, entitled "Permanent memorial to and remembrance of the victims of slavery and the transatlantic slave trade",

Recalling also the designation of 25 March as the annual International Day of Remembrance of the Victims of Slavery and the Transatlantic Slave Trade, beginning in 2008, as a complement to the existing International Day for the Remembrance of the Slave Trade and its Abolition of the United Nations Educational, Scientific and Cultural Organization,

Noting the initiatives undertaken by States in reaffirming their commitment to implement paragraphs 101 and 102 of the Durban Declaration of the World Conference against Racism, Racial Discrimination, Xenophobia and Related Intolerance aimed at countering the legacy of slavery and contributing to the restoration of the dignity of the victims of slavery and the slave trade,

Stressing the importance of educating and informing future generations about the causes, consequences and lessons of slavery and the transatlantic slave trade,

Recognizing how little is known about the four-hundred-year-long transatlantic slave trade and its lasting consequences, felt throughout the world, and welcoming the increased attention that the General Assembly commemoration brought to the issue, including the raising of its profile in many States,

Recalling, in particular, paragraph 101 of the Durban Declaration which, inter alia, invited the international community and its members to honour the memory of the victims,

1. *Welcomes* the initiative of the States members of the Caribbean Community to erect, at a place of prominence at United Nations Headquarters that is easily accessible to delegates, United Nations staff and visitors, a permanent memorial in acknowledgement of the tragedy and in consideration of the legacy of slavery and the transatlantic slave trade;

2. *Also welcomes* the establishment of a committee of interested States to oversee the permanent memorial project, drawn from all geographical regions of the world, with Member States from the Caribbean Community and the African Union playing a primary role, in collaboration with the United Nations Educational, Scientific and Cultural Organization, representatives of the Secretariat, the Schomburg Center for Research in Black Culture of the New York Public Library and civil society;

3. *Notes* that the committee will oversee the voluntary fund established for the erection of the permanent memorial to the victims of slavery and the transatlantic slave trade;

4. *Expresses sincere appreciation* to those Member States that have already made contributions to the fund, and invites Member States and other interested parties that have not done so to do likewise;

5. *Expresses appreciation* to the Secretary-General, the Secretariat and members of the committee for their invaluable support, technical advice and assistance towards implementation of the project;

6. *Reiterates its request* contained in resolution 61/19 for Member States that have not already done so to develop educational programmes, including through school curricula, designed to educate and inculcate in future generations an understanding of the lessons, history and consequences of slavery and the slave trade;

7. *Takes note with appreciation* of the report of the Secretary-General on the programme of outreach on the transatlantic slave trade and slavery, which highlights developments relating to a diverse educational outreach strategy to increase awareness of and to educate future generations about the causes, consequences, lessons and legacy of the four-hundred-year-long slave trade and to communicate the dangers of racism and prejudice, and encourages continued action in this regard;

8. *Requests* the Secretary-General to report to the General Assembly at its sixty-fourth session on continued action to implement the programme of educational outreach, including action by Member States;

9. *Decides* to include in the provisional agenda of its sixty-fourth session the item entitled "Follow-up to the commemoration of the two-hundredth anniversary of the abolition of the transatlantic slave trade".

Fund on slavery

Report of Secretary-General. The Secretary-General reported [A/HRC/10/49] on the financial status of the United Nations Voluntary Trust Fund on Contemporary Forms of Slavery. At its thirteenth session (Geneva, 8–12 September), the Fund's Board of Trustees recommended 71 new project grants amounting to $733,109 to assist 71 NGO projects in 45 countries in Africa, the Americas, Asia and Europe. It also recommended a contingency list of 15 project grants amounting to $108,000 to assist 15 NGOs in India. The Board estimated that the Fund would need an additional $1,376,000 before its fourteenth session, scheduled for September 2009. The High Commissioner, on behalf of the Secretary-General, approved the Board's recommendations.

Vulnerable groups

Women

Violence against women

Note by Secretary-General. In accordance with General Assembly resolution 50/166 [YUN 1995, p. 1188], the Secretary-General submitted to the Human Rights Council and the Commission on to the Status of Women the report of the United Nations Development Fund for Women regarding the Fund's activities to eliminate violence against women [A/HRC/10/43-E/CN.6/2009/10] (see p. 1259).

Reports of Special Rapporteur. In January [A/HRC/7/6], the Special Rapporteur on violence against women, its causes and consequences, Yakin Ertürk (Turkey), proposed indicators on violence against women and State response towards ending such violence. She suggested that moving the indicators from proposal to implementation should be undertaken by an expert working group with the aim of creating a technical manual. A concurrent process should build support for the management of national data systems. An addendum to the report [A/HRC/7/6/Add.5] discussed the development of the indicators on violence against women upon which the Special Rapporteur's report was built.

Another addendum [A/HRC/7/6/Add.1] summarized 59 communications which the Special Rapporteur had sent to 38 Governments in 2007, and responses thereto. Thirty-one communications were urgent appeals, and 52 had been sent jointly with other Human Rights Council mandate holders. Sixteen countries had not responded to any of the communications. The communications concerned arbitrary detention, torture or cruel, inhuman or degrading treatment or punishment, summary and extrajudicial executions; rape, sexual abuse and sexual exploitation; trafficking; and other forms of violence grounded in discrimination against women.

The Rapporteur visited Saudi Arabia (4–13 February) [A/HRC/11/6/Add.3], where pressures for change had resulted in modest reforms that nonetheless had significant implications for women's rights. Positive developments, particularly in access to education, had resulted in improvements in women's literacy rates within a relatively short period, but that progress had not been accompanied by a comparable increase in women's participation in the labour force, and they remained largely excluded from decision-making processes. Sex segregation and the practice of male guardianship posed obstacles to women's autonomy, legal capacity as adults, and ability to participate in society and in the workplace. While violence against women had been recognized as a public policy issue, judicial practices pertaining to divorce and child custody, as well as women's lack of autonomy and economic independence, continued to limit their ability to escape from abusive marriages. Issues related to early or forced marriage and divorce were gaining public attention, although there were few opportunities for redress due to lack of legal clarity and the discretionary power of judges on those matters. Violence against female domestic workers was not sufficiently recognized.

The Rapporteur made recommendations concerning measures necessary to women's empowerment and increased participation in the public sphere; the elimination of violence against women and girls; judicial and legal reforms; and measures to combat abuse of migrant workers.

The Special Rapporteur visited Tajikistan (15–23 May) [A/HRC/11/6/Add.2], where, although the country had achieved political stability and entered a phase of economic growth, the situation remained fragile due to the country's transition to a market-led economy, the erosion of sources of livelihood and social services and massive poverty. Women had been especially affected by the consequences of the transition. While formal equality was guaranteed in law, socio-economic and political achievements during the Soviet era had faded away, and patriarchal practices perpetuating women's subordinate position had resurfaced, leading to their increased vulnerability to violence and exploitation. Violence against women and girls was accepted by men and women alike as part of everyday behaviour. Violence by husbands and other family members was widespread. Women and girls were also victims of sexual violence and exploitation on the streets and to trafficking inside and outside Tajikistan. Women's lack of awareness of their rights, and issues pertaining to residency registration and the rise of early, polygamous and unregistered marriages aggravated their vulnerability. While some encouraging steps had been taken, responses by State bodies to protect and support victims of violence and prosecute perpetrators were insufficient. As a result, some women perceived suicide or murder of the abuser as the only way out.

The Rapporteur called on the Government to take measures in the priority areas of women's empowerment and gender equality; elimination of violence against women and girls; statistics and data collection; marriage practices; and residency registration and housing.

The Special Rapporteur visited Moldova (4–11 July) [A/HRC/11/6/Add.4] together with the Special Rapporteur on torture and other cruel, inhuman and degrading treatment or punishment, Manfred Nowak. The country's transformation to a political democracy and market economy, following the break-up of the Soviet Union, resulted in economic and social difficulties that placed a heavy burden on women. Although gender equality was ensured by law, in practice women's subordination was exacerbated by high levels of unemployment and low-paid jobs. In addition, patriarchal and discriminatory attitudes increased women's vulnerability to violence and abuse. Domestic violence was widespread, largely condoned by society, and did not receive appropriate recognition among officials, society and women themselves, thus resulting in insufficient protective infrastructure for victims. The need to escape an abusive environment, including domestic violence, prejudice and economic deprivation, motivated women to seek work abroad. As a result, many of them fell victim to slave-like work conditions and to trafficking networks in situations that amounted to torture and ill-treatment. Moldova had come a long way in terms of institution building and human rights protection since independence. The entry into force of the law on preventing and combating family violence was promising. That law, along with the law on ensuring equal opportunities for women and men, would contribute to improved prevention, protection against and prosecution of incidents of violence. However, many gaps remained between the normative framework and practice.

The Rapporteur made recommendations concerning the elimination of violence; empowerment and equality of women; the set-up of gender sensitive database systems; institutional and public sector reforms; and international cooperation. States shared the responsibility for developing bilateral and international solutions to the problem of trafficking in women and girls.

Human Rights Council action. On 28 March [A/63/53 (res. 7/24)], the Human Rights Council, welcoming the launch by the Secretary-General in February of the campaign to end violence against women, took note of the Special Rapporteur's reports, and extended the mandate for three years. The Rapporteur was requested to report to the Council in accordance with its annual programme of work.

Integrating women's rights

Note by OHCHR. In August [A/HRC/9/6], OHCHR informed the Human Rights Council that the report on integrating the human rights of women throughout the UN system, requested by the Council in 2007 [YUN 2007, p. 787], would not be submitted to the Council's ninth (2008) session, but to the tenth (2009) session, after the annual discussion on the integration of a gender perspective in the work of the Council. That would allow all interested parties to benefit from the discussion before submitting their views.

Trafficking in women and girls

Report of Secretary-General. In response to General Assembly resolution 61/144 [YUN 2006, p. 1342], the Secretary-General submitted an August report [A/63/215] on measures taken by 40 Member States and activities undertaken within the UN system to combat and eliminate trafficking in women and girls. The report concluded that despite the many actions taken at the national, regional and international levels to prevent and combat trafficking in persons, trafficking persisted. A comprehensive, coordinated, cohesive and gender-sensitive approach was required to address the root causes and risk factors, and to ensure prosecution of the perpetrators and protection of the victims. States should put in place comprehensive and multidisciplinary anti-trafficking action plans and strategies; implement bilateral and multilateral agreements and cooperation programmes; focus on prevention and address the conditions that made women and girls vulnerable to trafficking, including poverty, unemployment, limited education and discrimination; improve data collection and analysis; and strengthen support systems for victims.

Communication. On 29 July [A/62/933], Uzbekistan transmitted to the Secretary-General information on measures it had taken since December 2006 to combat trafficking in women.

Human Rights Council action. On 18 June, the Council appointed Joy Ngozi Ezeilo (Nigeria) as Special Rapporteur on trafficking in persons, especially women and children.

On the same day, [A/63/53 (res. 8/12)], the Human Rights Council extended the mandate of the Special Rapporteur for a three-year period. The Rapporteur was requested to report annually, starting in 2009, to the Council and the General Assembly. OHCHR was requested to submit to the Council's ninth (2008) session a report on the latest developments in the United Nations relating to combating trafficking in persons, as well as on its activities on that issue, including by presenting the recommended Principles and Guidelines on Human Rights and Human Trafficking developed by OHCHR [YUN 2002, p. 748].

Note by OHCHR. In response to that request, OHCHR in August [A/HRC/9/27] informed the Council that it would submit the requested report at the Council's tenth (2009) session, to ensure that a comprehensive overview of the developments on trafficking in the UN system was provided and distributed well in advance of that session.

On 18 December, the General Assembly, in **resolution 63/156** on trafficking in women and girls, took note of the renewal of the Special Rapporteur's mandate (see above).

Children

Violence against children

Note by OHCHR. In January [A/HRC/7/54], OHCHR provided information on activities undertaken in 2007 as follow-up to the final report on the study on violence against children conducted by the independent expert for the UN study on violence against children [YUN 2006, p. 918].

Human Rights Council action. On 28 March [A/63/53 (res. 7/29)], the Human Rights Council welcomed that report, as well as the establishment by the General Assembly, by resolution 62/141 [YUN 2007, p. 681], of the mandate of the Special Representative of the Secretary-General on violence against children. The Council requested the Secretary-General to take action to appoint a Special Representative and to report to the Council's eighth (2008) session.

Note by OHCHR. In response to that request, OHCHR in May [A/HRC/8/51] informed the Council that the Secretary-General had undertaken broad consultations with relevant UN actors, including through the Inter-Agency Working Group on Violence against Children, regarding the establishment of the Office of the Special Representative of the Secretary-General on Violence against Children. The terms of reference of the Special Representative had been approved. The Representative would be appointed at the Assistant Secretary-General level, reporting directly to the

Secretary-General. The Office, to be located in New York, would be supported administratively by the United Nations Children's Fund. The position would be established for a three-year period and would be funded from voluntary contributions.

Note by Secretariat. In September [A/63/203], the Secretariat informed the General Assembly that a number of well-qualified candidates had applied for the position and a shortlist had been established. In addition, the chairpersons of the five regional groups had been solicited to recommend further qualified candidates. The Secretary-General had set up an interview panel to provide him with a final shortlist of recommended candidates. The interview panel had commenced its work and welcomed further recommendations of qualified candidates, even as the interview process was under way.

The General Assembly took note of Secretariat's note on 18 December (**decision 63/532**).

Sale of children, child prostitution and child pornography

Reports of Special Rapporteur. In his annual report [A/HRC/7/8], the Special Rapporteur on the sale of children, child prostitution and child pornography, Juan Miguel Petit (Uruguay), in reviewing his mandates, stated that most States had put in place programmes and facilities for children who were victims of commercial sexual exploitation and trafficking. However, they encompassed either adult victims of commercial sexual exploitation and trafficking, or child victims of domestic abuse and violence. The Special Rapporteur was of the view that child victims of commercial sexual exploitation were in need of special, separate programmes and facilities, the absence of which made them more vulnerable to exploitation by organized criminal groups. He put forward guidelines and options to better assist child victims of trafficking and sexual commercial exploitation.

The Special Rapporteur called upon States, NGOs and civil society actors to set up rehabilitation and assistance programmes for children and minors. Such programmes and facilities might take different forms and should be adapted to the local and cultural contexts, be it a closed shelter, rehabilitation activities in the form of outpatient assistance or educational programmes. States should incorporate in their legislation and budget provisions for funding such programmes and activities, and carry out educational programmes and awareness-raising activities.

An addendum to the report [A/HRC/7/8/Add.1] summarized 12 communications which the Special Rapporteur had sent to 11 Governments between 1 January and 30 November 2007, and the replies thereto.

Human Rights Council action. On 26 March, the Human Rights Council appointed Najat M'jid Maalla (Morocco) as Special Rapporteur.

On 27 March [A/63/53 (res. 7/13)], the Council extended the mandate of the Special Rapporteur for a three-year period, and requested the Rapporteur to submit a report to the Council in accordance with its annual programme of work.

Reports of Special Rapporteur. In response to that resolution, the new Special Rapporteur outlined, in July [A/HRC/9/21], her view of the mandate and the methods by which she would discharge it. She also set out the strategic directions to be undertaken during her mandate. She stressed the many dimensions of the phenomenon, which called for cooperation from all those involved with children's issues, and the importance of implementing a comprehensive child protection system ensuring the best interest of the child and encompassing prevention and care as well as medical, psychological, social and legal support for child victims. That would require concerted national, regional and international coordination and cooperation.

The Special Rapporteur visited Estonia (20–24 October) [A/HRC/12/23/Add.2], where she noted a significant political commitment to prioritize the rights of the child. While the number of reported cases of child prostitution and child pornography was low, vigilance was required and efforts should be directed towards prevention. Actions to be implemented included adopting legislative amendments; training of the police, particularly in detecting cases of sexual exploitation of children and online child pornography; ensuring that programmes and policies were sustainable and accessible throughout the country; and strengthening of the NGO sector. The Special Rapporteur recalled the importance of a holistic approach to the fundamental rights of children, paving the way for the implementation of social policies that favoured children, youth and the family.

The Rapporteur recommended amending legislation on the rights of the child, training the police in detecting cases of sexual exploitation of children and online child pornography and training judges on the rights of the child. Child victims of offences should not be criminalized or penalized, and all possible measures should be taken to avoid their stigmatization and social marginalization. Internet service providers and telecommunications companies should become involved in initiatives to combat and prevent online child pornography. International and regional cooperation should be strengthened to combat and prevent child sex tourism and online child pornography. Sexual education programmes should also be strengthened.

The Special Rapporteur visited Latvia (25–31 October) [A/HRC/12/23/Add.1], where significant legislative and policy efforts had been made in protecting the rights of the child. The number of reported cases of child prostitution and trafficking of children for sexual purposes was low. However, child pornography, mainly via the Internet, was on the rise. Because of the proliferation of tourism, easy accessibility of new methods of information technology by children, increasing demand in the sex industry and the establishment of increasingly structured trafficking networks, children were increasingly vulnerable to risk of abuse, violence and exploitation. Vigilance was required, and efforts should be concentrated on prevention, including the provision of training and human and financial resources. The Rapporteur called for the implementation of social policies favouring children, youth and the family. Legislation should clearly stipulate that a child under 18 years of age was unable to consent to any form of sexual exploitation, including child pornography and child prostitution. Training should be provided to the authorities for combating cybercrime, particularly online child pornography. Internet service providers and telecommunications companies should be involved in initiatives to combat and prevent online child pornography. Complaints mechanisms should be strengthened for children placed in alternative care institutions, or who were victims of violence or abuse, while ensuring their protection and privacy.

Children and armed conflict

Security Council consideration (February). On 12 February [meeting 5834], the Security Council considered the Secretary-General's 2007 report on children and armed conflict [YUN 2007, p. 790]. Opening the meeting, the Secretary-General's Special Representative for Children and Armed Conflict, Radhika Coomaraswamy, outlined the main areas of concern, recalling that 58 offending parties in 13 situations of concern had been listed in the annex to the Secretary-General's report. In spite of impressive progress, the overall situation of children affected by conflict remained grave and unacceptable. The Security Council should move from words toward effective action against the 16 persistent violators who had been on the lists of violators for five consecutive years. Targeted measures could include the imposition of travel restrictions on leaders and their exclusion from any governance structures and amnesty provisions; the imposition of arms embargoes; a ban on military assistance; and restrictions on the flow of financial resources.

SECURITY COUNCIL ACTION

On 12 February [meeting 5834], following consultations among Security Council members, the President made statement **S/PRST/2008/6** on behalf of the Council:

The Security Council takes note with appreciation of the seventh report of the Secretary-General on children and armed conflict, and the positive developments, as well as outstanding challenges in the implementation of its resolution 1612(2005) reflected therein.

The Council, reiterating its primary responsibility for the maintenance of international peace and security, reaffirms its commitment to address the widespread impact of armed conflict on children, its determination to ensure respect for and the implementation of resolution 1612(2005) and all of its previous resolutions on children and armed conflict, as well as respect for other international norms and standards for the protection of children affected by armed conflict.

The Council stresses in this regard the need to adopt a broad strategy of conflict prevention which addresses the root causes of armed conflict in a comprehensive manner in order to enhance the protection of children on a long-term basis, including by promoting sustainable development, poverty eradication, national reconciliation, good governance, democracy, the rule of law and respect for and protection of human rights.

The Council reiterates the primary responsibility of national Governments in providing effective protection and relief to all children affected by armed conflict, and encourages further cooperation and coordination between Member States, the United Nations system and the international community, in a spirit of partnership.

The Council reiterates the importance of the full, safe and unhindered access of humanitarian personnel and goods and the delivery of humanitarian assistance to all children affected by armed conflict, and stresses the importance for all, within the framework of humanitarian assistance, of upholding and respecting the humanitarian principles of humanity, neutrality, impartiality and independence.

The Council calls for the full implementation of the monitoring and reporting mechanism on children and armed conflict as called for in paragraph 3 of resolution 1612(2005) in all situations of armed conflict listed in the annexes to the report of the Secretary-General.

In this regard the Council reiterates that the mechanism should continue to collect and provide timely, objective, accurate and reliable information on violations and abuses committed against children affected by armed conflict and to operate with the participation of and in cooperation with national Governments and relevant United Nations and civil society actors, including at the country level.

The Council commends the work carried out by the Special Representative of the Secretary-General for Children and Armed Conflict, Ms. Radhika Coomaraswamy, including her field activities in situations of armed conflict.

The Council also commends the work carried out by the United Nations Children's Fund and the child protection advisers of peacekeeping operations and political missions in cooperation with other relevant United Nations entities.

The Council welcomes the sustained activity of its Working Group on Children and Armed Conflict, as outlined, inter alia, in the latest report of its Chairman, and invites it to continue adopting conclusions and proposing effective recommendations for consideration and, where appropriate, implementation by the Council, including through mandates of United Nations peacekeeping operations and political missions.

The Council will continue to consider including or enhancing the presence of child protection advisers in the mandates of all relevant United Nations peacekeeping operations and political missions.

The Council strongly emphasizes the need to end impunity for violations and abuses perpetrated against children in armed conflict, and in this regard welcomes the fact that several individuals who are alleged to have committed such crimes have been brought to justice by national, international and 'mixed' criminal courts and tribunals.

The Council acknowledges that the implementation of resolution 1612(2005) has already generated progress, resulting in the release and reintegration of children in their families and communities, and in a more systematic dialogue between the United Nations country task forces on monitoring and reporting and parties to armed conflict on the implementation of time-bound action plans.

Nonetheless, the Council strongly condemns the continuing recruitment and use of children in armed conflict in violation of applicable international law, the killing and maiming of children, rape and other sexual violence, abductions, the denial of humanitarian access to children and attacks against schools and hospitals by parties to armed conflict.

The Council is concerned by the widespread and systematic use of rape and other forms of sexual violence against children, in particular girls, in situations of armed conflict, and calls upon all parties to armed conflict to take special measures to protect girls and boys from sexual and gender-based violence, particularly rape, in situations of armed conflict.

The Council expresses its concern that civilians, particularly children, continue to account for the vast majority of victims of acts of violence committed by parties to armed conflict, including killing and maiming as a result of deliberate targeting, and indiscriminate and excessive use of force in violation of applicable international law. The Council condemns these acts and demands that those parties immediately put an end to such practices.

The Council is gravely concerned by the persistent disregard of its resolutions on children and armed conflict by parties to armed conflict identified in the reports of the monitoring and reporting mechanism, including parties to whom precise, immediate and unequivocal requests have been addressed. Recalling the statement made by its President on 28 November 2006, the Council reaffirms its intention to make use of all the tools provided in resolution 1612(2005).

The Council reiterates its call upon the parties to armed conflict listed in the annexes to the report of the Secretary-General that have not already done so to prepare and implement, without further delay, concrete time-bound action plans to halt the recruitment and use of children in violation of applicable international law and to address all violations and abuses against children in close cooperation with the Special Representative of the Secretary-General, as well as with the United Nations Children's Fund and the United Nations country task forces on monitoring and reporting.

The Council expresses concern over the casualties inflicted on children in armed conflict by the indiscriminate use of landmines and cluster munitions, and in this regard calls upon all parties to armed conflict to desist from such practice.

In order to further strengthen the comprehensive framework of the protection of children in armed conflict, considering the changing nature of armed conflict and the issues raised by the Secretary-General in his report, the Council expresses its readiness to review the relevant provisions of its resolutions on children and armed conflict, building on the provisions of resolution 1612(2005), with a view to further increasing the efficiency of its actions.

The Council recognizes that a stronger focus is required on the reintegration and rehabilitation of children associated with armed forces and armed groups, and in this regard invites all parties concerned, including Member States, regional organizations, the Secretariat and other relevant United Nations entities, including the United Nations Children's Fund, the United Nations Population Fund, the United Nations Development Fund for Women, the World Health Organization, the United Nations Development Programme, the Office of the United Nations High Commissioner for Refugees, the Office of the United Nations High Commissioner for Human Rights, the International Labour Organization and the United Nations Educational, Scientific and Cultural Organization, international financial institutions, including the World Bank, as well as civil society, to enhance their exchange of information about programmes and best practices, bearing in mind the relevant provisions of international law, Council resolutions on children and armed conflict, as well as the Paris principles to protect children from unlawful recruitment by armed forces or groups, and to ensure that adequate resources and funding are available to support national strategies or action plans in the area of child protection and welfare, and community-based programmes, with a view to ensuring the long-term sustainability and success of their programmatic response to the release, rehabilitation and reintegration of all children associated with armed forces and armed groups.

The Council requests the Secretary-General to submit his next report on the implementation of its resolutions on children and armed conflict by May 2009.

Reports of Special Representative. In June, the Special Representative, in her annual report [A/HRC/9/3], submitted in response to General Assembly resolution 62/141 [YUN 2007, p. 681], noted that new developments in the field of children and armed conflict had given rise to several issues of concern. The changing nature of conflicts, the recruitment of children across borders, forced displacements, an increase in sexual violence and a greater number of children being held in detention had created new dilemmas for the protection of children. Terrorism and counter-terrorism measures also posed their own special problems. Suicide bombing sometimes resulted in child victims on both ends: children were being used as suicide bombers in certain instances, and many children were killed in those bombings.

Since the Special Representative's last report [ibid., p. 789], several significant developments had taken place in the fight to end impunity through the application of international norms and standards for the protection of children. Trials had been held and convictions rendered before national courts in the Democratic Republic of the Congo (DRC), and internationally by the International Criminal Court and the Special Court for Sierra Leone for the crime of recruitment and use of child soldiers. The application of international norms to such cases, combined with the political process in the context of Security Council resolution 1612(2005) [YUN 2005, p. 863], had strengthened the work of child protection advocates by opening dialogue on protection with parties to conflict, with significant results in Cote d'Ivoire. There had also been progress on plans of action with armed forces and groups in the Central African Republic, Myanmar, the Sudan, Sri Lanka and Uganda. Country visits by the Special Representative had also provided the opportunity for high-level advocacy; opened doors for follow-up dialogue with military and political authorities by UN country task forces on monitoring and reporting; and elicited commitments by the relevant parties to address the recruitment and use of children and their protection from other grave violations during armed conflict.

The Special Representative called on the Human Rights Council and the human rights community to make systematic use of Security Council resolution 1612(2005) as an advocacy tool, in particular the monitoring and reporting mechanism on grave violations against children in armed conflict. Since the vast majority of parties to conflict using children were non-State actors, Member States should help facilitate dialogue between the UN country task forces on monitoring and reporting and those groups, for the purposes of developing plans of action to halt the recruitment and use of children. Member States should comply with international norms and standards for the protection of children in armed conflict, and take all measures to mitigate the impact of conflict on children.

Annexed to the report was a list of parties that recruited or used children in conflict situations on the agenda of the Security Council.

In August, in response to Assembly resolution 62/141, the Special Representative submitted to the Assembly a report [A/63/227] highlighting progress made on the children and armed conflict agenda, in particular in the fight against impunity for grave child rights violations and in the incorporation of children's concerns into the mandates, policies and priorities of key UN organs, entities, processes and activities. The report recognized the changing nature and characteristics of armed conflict and the impact on children; identified priority areas for action; and outlined recommendations, including strengthening the international normative structure, strengthening monitoring and reporting, consolidating the role of UN peacekeeping in child protection, and focusing on prevention.

Working group activities. In July [S/2008/455], the Chairman of the Working Group of the Security Council on Children and Armed Conflict, established pursuant to Council resolution 1612(2005), reported on the Group's activities since the submission of its last report [YUN 2007, p. 790]. The report noted that contacts between the Secretariat, the Working Group Chairman and the countries concerned had made it possible to prepare for or establish the monitoring and reporting mechanism provided for in resolution 1612(2005) in all the conflict situations referred to in the annexes to the Secretary-General's most recent report on children and armed conflict [ibid.] and to include those situations in the Group's work programme for the May 2008 to April 2009 period. The Group sought to engage in dialogue with the countries concerned, all of which participated in the Group's consideration of their situation and made comments upon the adoption of conclusions concerning them. Varying degrees of progress had been made in a number of situations, including in the implementation of action plans, the initiation or resumption of discussions on such plans between certain armed groups and UN task forces, the release of children, the decrease in their recruitment, the establishment of focal points in Government administrations and the provision of services to children in disarmament, demobilization and reintegration programmes. The Group agreed on the need to provide it with more logistical support, particularly Secretariat services.

During the year, the Group held eight meetings (5 and 21 February, 8 May, 20 June, 25 July, 5 September, 14 November, 19 December), during which it adopted conclusions on Côte d'Ivoire [S/AC.51/2008/5 & Corr.1], Burundi [S/AC.51/2008/6], the Sudan [S/AC.51/2008/7], Myanmar [S/AC.51/2008/8], the Philippines [S/AC.51/2008/10], Sri Lanka [S/AC.51/2008/11], Nepal [S/AC.51/2008/12], Uganda [S/AC.51/2008/13], Somalia [S/AC.51/2008/14], Chad [S/AC.51/2008/15], Afghanistan [S/AC.51/2009/1] and the DRC [S/AC.51/2009/3].

On 14 January, the Security Council President sent letters to the DRC [S/AC.51/2008/2], Rwanda [S/AC.51/2008/3] and the Security Council Committee established pursuant to resolution 1533(2004) concerning the DRC [S/AC.51/2008/4] in follow-up to the Working Group's 2007 conclusions [YUN 2007, p. 131]. On 12 September, the Working Group Chairman addressed a statement [S/AC.51/2008/9] to the non-State armed groups in Myanmar.

Security Council consideration (July). On 17 July [meeting 5936], the Security Council considered the report of the Working Group on Children and Armed Conflict (above) and a concept paper prepared by Viet Nam [S/2008/442].

Addressing the meeting, the Secretary-General described the progress made in standard-setting over the past 12 years. He said that the international community was shifting its focus from standard-setting to an era of application. Council resolutions had focused on six grave violations: abduction, sexual violence, child soldiers, killing and maiming, attacks on schools and hospitals, and denial of humanitarian access. A monitoring and reporting mechanism was operational in 15 situations of concern. Action plans had been secured from several parties to conflict, with those parties agreeing to release children from their ranks. Once children were released, they should be fully reintegrated into society, and the international community should strengthen its support for Governments, development partners and others involved in reintegration efforts. He called on the international community to strengthen its support to Governments, development partners and others involved in such efforts. Only concerted international action involving all UN partners would be capable of meeting the needs of children living in situations of armed conflict.

The Special Representative for Children and Armed Conflict requested the Council to expand the scope of the Working Group to cover all situations of concern and all grave violations against children, especially sexual violence. As requested by Member States, her office was initiating a research project on the root causes of children being associated with armed groups, and would convene a meeting of child protection experts to identify messages and gaps to reintegrating children affected by conflict. A seminal study by the Harvard School of Public Health had shown that the impact of conflict continued even after 10 years. The younger the child recruited and the longer the association with the armed group, the more difficult the adjustment. With the United Nations Educational, Scientific and Cultural Organization, her office would compile a manual of best practices in line with the "Paris Principles and Guidelines on Children Associated with Armed Forces or Groups", an initiative by the Government of France setting out the standards for reintegration programmes.

SECURITY COUNCIL ACTION

On 17 July [meeting 5936], following consultations among Security Council members, the President made statement **S/PRST/2008/28** on behalf of the Council:

> The Security Council reiterates its commitment to address the widespread impact of armed conflict on children and its determination to ensure respect for and implementation of its resolution 1612(2005) and all its previous resolutions on children and armed conflict, and the statements by its President of 24 July and 28 November 2006 and 12 February 2008, which provide a comprehensive framework for addressing the protection of children affected by armed conflict, as well as the provisions on children contained in other resolutions, including resolutions 1325(2000), 1674(2006) and 1820(2008).
>
> The Council reiterates its strong and equal condemnation of the continuing recruitment and use of children in armed conflict in violation of applicable international law, killing and maiming of children, rape and other sexual violence, abductions, denial of humanitarian access to children and attacks against schools and hospitals by parties to armed conflict, while acknowledging that the implementation of resolution 1612(2005) has already generated progress, resulting in the release and reintegration of children into their families and communities, through, inter alia, a more systematic dialogue between the United Nations country task forces on monitoring and reporting and parties to armed conflict on the implementation of time-bound action plans.
>
> The Council reaffirms the need for States parties to comply with their obligations under the Convention on the Rights of the Child and the Optional Protocols thereto for armed groups distinct from the State to refrain from recruiting or using children in hostilities, and urges States that have not yet done so to consider ratifying or acceding to those instruments.
>
> The Council welcomes the ongoing implementation of the monitoring and reporting mechanism on children and armed conflict, in particular the efforts that have made possible the implementation of the mechanism in all situations listed in the annexes to the latest report of the Secretary-General, and invites the Secretary-General, where applicable, to bring the mechanism to its full efficiency, in accordance with resolution 1612(2005).
>
> The Council welcomes the sustained activity of its Working Group on Children and Armed Conflict, as outlined, inter alia, in the latest report of its Chairman, and as the monitoring and reporting mechanism is being implemented in a growing number of situations of armed conflict, requests the Secretary-General to provide additional administrative support in order for the Working Group to continue to fully carry out its mandate in an effective manner.
>
> The Council invites the Working Group to continue adopting conclusions providing clear guidance to the parties to armed conflict and relevant international actors on the concrete steps that need to be taken in order to respect their obligations under international law, in particular Council resolutions on children and armed conflict, and proposing to the Council effective recom-

mendations based on timely, objective, accurate and reliable information, with a view to promoting the protection of children affected by armed conflict, including through appropriate mandates of United Nations peacekeeping operations and political missions. The Council welcomes the efforts of the Working Group to improve its working methods and encourages it to continue to do so with a view to further improving its transparency and efficiency.

The Council commends the work carried out by the Special Representative of the Secretary-General for Children and Armed Conflict, Ms. Radhika Coomaraswamy, and underlines the importance of her country visits in facilitating better coordination among United Nations partners at the field level, promoting collaboration between the United Nations and Governments, enhancing dialogue with parties to conflicts in implementing applicable international law, including their obligations under resolution 1612(2005), and thereby securing concrete child protection commitments.

The Council also commends the work carried out by the United Nations Children's Fund, as well as other relevant United Nations agencies, funds and programmes, within their respective mandates, the child protection advisers of peacekeeping operations and political missions in cooperation with national Governments and relevant civil society actors, in enhancing the activities of the United Nations country task forces on monitoring and reporting and promoting child protection at the field level, including through implementation of resolution 1612(2005) and following up on the relevant conclusions of the Working Group.

The Council recognizes the important role of education in armed conflict areas as a means to achieve the goal of halting and preventing recruitment and re-recruitment of children and calls upon all parties concerned to continue to ensure that all children associated with armed forces and groups, as well as issues related to children, are systematically included in every disarmament, demobilization and reintegration process, with a particular emphasis on education.

The Council reiterates the need for stronger focus by all parties concerned, including Governments and the donor community, on the long-term effects of armed conflict on children and the impediments to their full rehabilitation and reintegration into their families and communities, by, inter alia, addressing the need for providing appropriate health care, enhancing their exchange of information about programmes and best practices, and ensuring the availability of adequate resources, funding and technical assistance to support national strategies or action plans in the area of child protection and welfare, and community-based programmes, bearing in mind the Paris principles to protect children from unlawful recruitment by armed forces or groups, with a view to ensuring the long-term sustainability and success of their programmatic response to the release, rehabilitation and reintegration of all children associated with armed forces and armed groups.

The Council looks forward to the next report of the Secretary-General on children and armed conflict, and reiterates its readiness to continue to review the relevant provisions of its resolutions on children and armed conflict, building on the provisions of resolution 1612(2005), with a view to further enhancing the comprehensive framework of the protection of children in armed conflict.

Internally displaced persons

Reports of Secretary-General's Representative. As requested by the Human Rights Council [YUN 2007, p. 793], the Secretary-General's Representative on the human rights of internally displaced persons (IDPs), Walter Kälin (Switzerland), submitted an April report [A/HRC/8/6] reviewing the background to the mandate, major achievements and an outline of future work. He acknowledged the greater recognition of the phenomenon of internal displacement, progress in developing a normative framework, and the coordinated response. However, millions of people were still displaced, living in distress and in need of assistance and protection. Governments had the primary duty and responsibility for providing that protection and assistance at all stages of displacement. On the occasion of the tenth anniversary of the 1998 Guiding Principles on Internal Displacement [YUN 1998, p. 675], the Representative welcomed the fact that the Principles were widely accepted. In that context, Governments and regional organizations should develop national legislation and policies in keeping with the Principles and ensure that they were implemented; bring legislation into line with the Principles; and develop regional legal instruments based on the Principles and ensure that they were implemented. He expressed concern at the difficulties encountered by humanitarian personnel in gaining access to displaced persons, and called on Governments and others concerned to facilitate speedy, unhindered access. Noting that the way in which durable solutions to displacement were implemented had a considerable impact on the sustainability of peace, the Representative recommended that Governments should guarantee the safety of returnees; create an independent mechanism to monitor returns; set up machinery for the restitution of property; give returnees back their documents; and guarantee returnees access to public services, livelihoods and income-generating activities. The international community should give further thought to the machinery for financing early recovery programmes to ensure a smooth transition between the emergency phase and the development phase.

In his report to the Assembly [A/63/286], transmitted in August by the Secretary-General, in accordance with Human Rights Council resolution 6/32 and General Assembly resolution 62/153 [YUN 2007, p. 793], the Representative described activities undertaken from August 2007 to July 2008. He welcomed progress made by Governments and the international community in strengthening protection and assistance for displaced persons, particularly the drafting of national legislation and policies in countries affected by internal displacement and the entry into force of the Protocol on the Protection and Assistance to Internally Displaced Persons, adopted at the Second International Conference on the Great Lakes Region [YUN 2006, p. 124]. Non-State actors had an obligation to respect and protect the rights of displaced persons in accordance with international criminal law and international humanitarian law. Returns should be the result of an individual decision taken freely, without coercion and on the basis of adequate information. He noted the high-level international conference (16 October), organized by Norway to mark the tenth anniversary of the Guiding Principles, which would pay particular attention to incorporating those into national law and policy, and their relevance in situations in which displacement was caused by natural disaster and other environmental factors, and the prospects for elaborating legally binding instruments on the protection of and assistance to displaced persons at regional and subregional levels. The Representative would also present the legislators' handbook, intended to provide guidance on ways of incorporating the human rights of internally displaced persons into internal displacement laws and policies.

The General Assembly took note of the report on 18 December (**decision 63/534**).

Following his visit to the Democratic Republic of the Congo (12–22 February) [A/HRC/8/6/Add.3], the Representative concluded that the eastern part of the country was experiencing a protection and humanitarian crisis, highlighted by the very large numbers of displaced persons, estimated at over 1 million in the four eastern regions, including about 800,000 in North Kivu and over 300,000 in South Kivu. More than 500,000 persons were reported to have been displaced in 2007, the highest number since the end of the civil war in 2003. In most cases, people had been forced to leave their homes owing to clashes between the Congolese armed forces and armed groups, or between different armed groups, as well as due to the widespread insecurity, violence and human rights abuses committed by armed groups and by members of armed forces. The situation of displaced persons was cause for concern: most were living with host families and in informal camps, in situations of absolute poverty. Many had lost their voters' cards, which served as identity cards, and that increased their vulnerability. Women suffered from near-systematic sexual violence, while children were forcibly recruited into the ranks of rebel factions. The statements of commitment signed at the Conference for Peace, Security and Development in North and South Kivu (Goma, 6–23 January) offered genuine opportunities for stabilization and for a possible return home (see p. 120). Returns had occurred in some regions. Nevertheless, the situation remained unstable and displacements continued following localized clashes.

The Representative asked all those involved to implement the statements of commitment without delay. He called for political dialogue between the Government, the various armed groups and other groups concerned, as well as the boosting of assistance and protection activities for the displaced population. He also recommended the implementation of early recovery measures where returns were under way or being contemplated. To achieve durable solutions, the Government should pursue reconciliation between ethnic communities; transitional justice and efforts to combat impunity; and settlement of land-related disputes. The armed groups were under an obligation to respect international humanitarian law, in particular the distinction between combatants and civilians, and refrain from any act prohibited by international humanitarian law. The international community should provide assistance to displaced persons programmes, and embark on activities for development, economic reintegration and the relaunching of basic services.

Having visited Georgia (1–4 October) [A/HRC/10/13/Add.2], the Representative said that as a result of the hostilities in northern Georgia in August (see p. 453), some 133,000 persons were displaced within the country. The Representative welcomed the Government's prompt response to the displacement crisis and its plans to find durable solutions for all IDPs, including those in protracted displacement since the early 1990s. The Representative urged the Government to create the conditions for sustainable return, allowing IDPs to return voluntarily, in safety and with dignity. According to Government estimates, about 37,605 IDPs would not return in the foreseeable future, and the Representative commended the Government for its decision to provide durable solutions for them. However, he was concerned about the almost exclusive emphasis on infrastructure, and recommended that the Government develop a comprehensive integration policy encompassing education, health care and economic opportunities. The biggest challenge was to integrate the approximately 220,000 IDPs living in protracted displacement for more than a decade. He welcomed the adoption of the action plan aimed at integrating IDPs into mainstream society. While welcoming the policy shift away from considering local reintegration and return to be mutually exclusive, the Representative remained concerned about the lack of integration of the "old" IDPs, the rights of whom needed to be ensured in tandem with responding to the new group of IDPs on a non-discriminatory basis. Unimpeded humanitarian access to the Tskhinvali region/South Ossetia and Abkhazia continued to be a concern. He urged the Government to ensure human rights protection for all internally displaced populations.

Persons with disabilities

Report of High Commissioner. In response to a 2005 Commission on Human Rights request [YUN 2005, p. 873], the High Commissioner, in January, submitted a report [A/HRC/7/61] on progress made in implementing the recommendations of the 2002 study on the human rights of persons with disabilities [YUN 2002, p. 771] and on the related OHCHR activities in 2007. The year had seen a continuation of the strengthening of OHCHR work on the issue. The opening for signature of the Convention on the Rights of Persons with Disabilities [YUN 2006, p. 785] and its Optional Protocol had shifted focus from support for standard-setting to promotion of ratification and implementation of standards. OHCHR strengthened technical assistance and promoted partnerships with UN bodies in preparation for the entry into force of both instruments (see p. 749). The formation of a joint secretariat for the Convention with the UN Department of Economic and Social Affairs would help maximize strengths across UN departments. The first session of the Inter-Agency Support Group on the Convention had provided an opportunity to ensure that the United Nations and the World Bank would work jointly on implementation. Partnerships with civil society organizations were enhanced, and work in the area of country engagement had significantly increased. While establishing specific projects on human rights and disability, the Office also aimed to incorporate disability rights in the work of human rights bodies. In addition, OHCHR improved the accessibility of its own premises, facilities and technologies.

Human Rights Council action. On 27 March [A/63/53 (res. 7/9)], the Human Rights Council welcomed the report and invited the High Commissioner to provide support for the integration of the perspective of persons with disabilities in the Council's work, and to continue the activities of her Office that contributed to raising awareness of the Convention on the Rights of Persons with Disabilities.

Communication. On 11 January [A/62/654], Spain transmitted to the General Assembly the Declaration of Madrid, the outcome of the expert group meeting on "Making it work: civil society participation in the implementation of the Convention on the Rights of Persons with Disabilities" (Madrid, 27–29 November 2007).

Indigenous peoples

Human Rights Council action. On 26 March, the Human Rights Council appointed S. James Anaya (United States) as Special Rapporteur on the situation of human rights and fundamental freedoms of indigenous people.

On 28 March [A/63/53 (res. 7/33)], the Council, by a recorded vote of 34 votes to none, with 13 abstentions, welcomed the landmark and historic formal apology by the Government of Australia for the past laws and policies that inflicted profound grief, suffering and loss on its indigenous peoples. It urged Governments that had not done so to issue formal apologies to the victims of past and historic injustices and take all necessary measures to achieve the healing and reconciliation of, and the restoration of dignity to, those victims.

Reports of Special Rapporteur. In accordance with a 2007 Human Rights Council request [YUN 2007, p. 798], the new Special Rapporteur submitted his first report [A/HRC/9/9], which analysed the United Nations Declaration on the Rights of Indigenous Peoples, [YUN 2007, p. 691] in the context of other international instruments regarding indigenous peoples and human rights instruments; the different measures required to implement and make operative the rights affirmed in the Declaration; and joint efforts by States, the UN system, indigenous peoples and civil society actors.

According to the Special Rapporteur, the Declaration did not attempt to bestow indigenous peoples with a set of special or new human rights, but elaborated general human rights principles and rights as they related to the specific circumstances of indigenous peoples. The standards affirmed in the Declaration shared a remedial character, seeking to redress the obstacles and discrimination that indigenous peoples faced in their enjoyment of basic human rights. From that perspective, the standards connected to State obligations under other human rights instruments. For the Declaration to be fully operative, States should pursue a range of affirmative, special measures in lawmaking and public administration, including legal and institutional reform, judicial action, specific policies and special reparations procedures. UN human rights bodies and mechanisms, specialized agencies and mechanisms with indigenous-specific mandates were central in promoting the Declaration's implementation at the local level, including with regard to development cooperation benefiting indigenous peoples. Implementing the Declaration depended also on the establishment of strong partnerships between States and indigenous peoples. Civil society organizations had a role in supporting the societal changes required to make the Declaration a living reality.

An addendum [A/HRC/9/9/Add.1 & Corr.1] summarized 39 communications on alleged human rights violations sent to 25 States between 2 September 2007 and 9 June 2008, and 19 responses thereto. Most communications had been sent jointly with other special procedures mandate-holders. An annex provided observations by the Special Rapporteur on the process of constitutional revision in Ecuador.

Report of High Commissioner. A September report of the High Commissioner [A/HRC/9/11] provided information on OHCHR activities related to indigenous peoples in the previous 18 months. To promote dissemination, understanding and implementation of the Declaration, OHCHR, in cooperation with the International Labour Office, convened a meeting of the Inter-Agency Support Group on Indigenous Peoples' Issues (26–27 September) to discuss integration of the Declaration in UN programmes and policies. A communications strategy was developed to promote the Declaration. The High Commissioner recommended that the Council consider grouping all reports on indigenous peoples, including that of the Special Rapporteur, the Expert Mechanism and the High Commissioner, at one time of the year to facilitate the work of governmental delegations and permit greater participation by indigenous peoples' organizations in the Council's work.

On 24 September [A/63/53/Add.1 (res. 9/7)], the Council welcomed the reports of the High Commissioner and the Special Rapporteur.

Expert Mechanism on the rights of indigenous peoples

Human Rights Council action. On 24 September [A/63/53/Add.1 (res. 9/7)], the Human Rights Council requested the Expert Mechanism on the Rights of Indigenous Peoples, established in 2007 [YUN 2007, p. 798], to identify proposals for the Council's consideration in 2009. It should also prepare a study on lessons learned and challenges to achieve the implementation of the right of indigenous peoples to education and conclude it in 2009.

Meeting of Expert Mechanism. The five-member Expert Mechanism on the Rights of Indigenous Peoples, at its first session (Geneva, 1–3 October) [A/HRC/10/56], discussed implementation of Human Rights Council resolution 6/36 [YUN 2007, p. 798], by which it established the mechanism, including thematic expertise. It also addressed issues related to the study on lessons learned and challenges to achieve the implementation of the rights of indigenous peoples to education, as requested by the Council (above). The Mechanism reviewed the Durban Declaration and Programme of Action [YUN 2001, p. 615] for the purpose of submitting recommendations as contributions to the outcome of the Durban Review Conference (see p. 762). The Expert Mechanism adopted five proposals for consideration and approval by the Council that related to the organization of work; the Durban Review Conference; the right of indigenous peoples to education; participation of indigenous peoples in the work of the Mechanism; and coordination with other UN bodies and mandates. In particular, it proposed that the Human Rights Council suggest to the General Assembly the broadening of the mandate of the United Nations Voluntary Fund for Indigenous Populations (below) to help indigenous peoples participate in the sessions of the Council and its treaty bodies. The Mechanism encouraged the Fund's Board of Trustees to identify beneficiaries of the Fund who could effectively contribute to the thematic agenda of the Expert Mechanism.

Voluntary Fund for Indigenous Populations

The Board of Trustees of the Voluntary Fund for Indigenous Populations, at its twenty-first session (Geneva, 4–8 February) [A/63/166], recommended 78 travel grants worth to some $209,066 to enable indigenous representatives to attend the first session of the Expert Mechanism (see above), and another 78 travel grants totalling $357,199 to enable representatives to attend the seventh session of the Permanent Forum on Indigenous Issues (see p. 858). On 15 February, the High Commissioner approved the Board's recommendations on behalf of the Secretary-General.

The General Assembly took note of that report on 18 December (**decision 63/533**).

Human Rights Council Action. On 24 September [A/63/53/Add.1 (res. 9/7)], the Human Rights Council suggested that the General Assembly adjust the mandate of the Voluntary Fund to take into account the creation of the expert mechanism on the rights of indigenous peoples.

Voluntary Fund for International Decade

The Voluntary Fund for the Second International Decade of the World's Indigenous People, 2005–2014, established in General Assembly resolution 59/174 [YUN 2004, p. 799] to succeed the pre-existing Fund for the First Decade, continued to promote, support and implement the goals of the Second Decade in terms of promoting indigenous peoples' culture, education, health, human rights, environment and economic development. In April, the Bureau of the United Nations Permanent Forum on Indigenous Issues (see p. 858), serving as the Advisory Group for the Fund, considered project proposals for funding received by the Secretariat, in accordance with resolution 59/174. It proposed to award grants totalling $137,779 to 14 projects being implemented by indigenous organizations and related NGOs in Africa; Asia; Central and South America and the Caribbean; Eastern Europe, the Russian Federation, Central Asia and Transcaucasia; North America; and the Pacific.

GENERAL ASSEMBLY ACTION

On 18 December [meeting 70], the General Assembly, on the recommendation of the Third Committee [A/63/427], adopted **resolution 63/161** without vote [agenda item 61].

Indigenous issues

The General Assembly,

Recalling all relevant resolutions of the General Assembly, the Human Rights Council and the Economic and Social Council relating to indigenous issues,

Recalling also that the Assembly proclaimed, in its resolution 59/174 of 20 December 2004, the Second International Decade of the World's Indigenous People,

Bearing in mind that the Assembly adopted, by its resolution 61/295 of 13 September 2007, the United Nations Declaration on the Rights of Indigenous Peoples,

Recalling that, at previous sessions of the Assembly, constructive dialogues were held with the Special Rapporteur on the situation of human rights and fundamental freedoms of indigenous people,

1. *Requests* the Special Rapporteur on the situation of human rights and fundamental freedoms of indigenous people to report on the implementation of his mandate to the General Assembly at its sixty-fourth session;

2. *Requests* the Secretary-General, in consultation with Member States, relevant United Nations organizations and mechanisms and other stakeholders, including indigenous organizations, to submit to the Assembly at its sixty-fifth session a midterm assessment report that evaluates progress made in the achievement of the goal and objectives of the Second International Decade of the World's Indigenous People;

3. *Decides* to adjust the mandate of the United Nations Voluntary Fund for Indigenous Populations so as to facilitate the participation of representatives of indigenous peoples' organizations in the expert mechanism established in accordance with Human Rights Council resolution 6/36 of 14 December 2007.

Permanent Forum on Indigenous Issues

Report of Permanent Forum. The 16-member Permanent Forum on Indigenous Issues, established by Economic and Social Council resolution 2000/22 [YUN 2000, p. 731] to address indigenous issues relating to economic and social development, the environment, health, education and culture, and human rights, at its seventh session (New York, 21 April–2 May) [E/2008/43], considered as its theme "Climate change, biocultural diversity and livelihoods: the stewardship role of indigenous peoples and new challenges". It had before it background reports relating to its work submitted by its secretariat and subsidiary mechanisms, UN system bodies and other intergovernmental organizations, Governments, NGOs and regional organizations [E/C.19/2008/INF/1/Rev.1]. The Forum recommended three draft decisions for adoption by the Economic and Social Council on: an international expert group meeting on the implementation of article 42 of the United Nations Declaration on the Rights of Indigenous Peoples; the venue and dates for the Forum's eight session; and the provisional agenda and documentation for that session. Matters brought to the Council's attention related to the session's theme; economic and social development; the environment, health, education and human rights; indigenous children and youth; the Second International Decade of the World's Indigenous People; urban indigenous peoples and migration; future work; implementation of the United Nations Declaration on the Rights of Indigenous Peoples; and dialogue with the Special Rapporteur on the situation of human rights and fundamental freedoms of indigenous people. The Forum held half-day discussions on indigenous languages and the situation of indigenous peoples in the Pacific.

On 25 July, the Economic and Social Council took note of the report of the Permanent Forum on its seventh session (**decision 2008/256**). On 24 July, it authorized a three-day expert group meeting on the implementation of article 42 of the United Nations Declaration on the Rights of Indigenous Peoples, and requested that the results of the meeting be reported to the Permanent Forum at its eighth session (**decision 2008/249**), which would be held at UN Headquarters from 18 to 29 May 2009 (**decision 2008/250**). The Council also approved the provisional agenda and documentation for that session (**decision 2008/251**).

Expert meetings and conferences

In response to Economic and Social Council decision 2007/244 [YUN 2007, p. 799], an international expert group meeting on indigenous languages (New York, 8–10 January) [E/C.19/2008/3] discussed linguistic diversity, the connection between language rights and other rights, the lack of urgency in the face of the threatened extinction of most indigenous languages, and proposals for revitalizing, promoting and protecting indigenous languages.

A conference (Copenhagen, 21–22 February) [E/C.19/2008/CRP.3] organized by the International Work Group for Indigenous Affairs discussed the impact of climate change on indigenous peoples and how global agreements, political processes and restrictive regulations hindered indigenous peoples in responding and adapting to climate change. The conference looked at how to secure indigenous peoples' contributions to discussions on those issues.

An international expert group meeting (Darwin, Australia, 2–4 April) [E/C.19/2008/CRP.9] also focused on indigenous people and climate change. It recognized that indigenous peoples—particularly those living in small island developing States, the Arctic region, high-altitude areas, tropical forests and coastal and desert regions—were already dealing with the impacts of climate change in their daily lives. States and other actors should therefore include indigenous peoples in decision-making to address the issue.

Chapter III

Human rights country situations

In 2008, human rights situations of concern in Member States, particularly regarding alleged violations and how best to assist and guide Governments and national institutions in combating them, were addressed by the General Assembly and the Human Rights Council, and by special rapporteurs, the Secretary-General's special representatives and independent experts appointed to examine those situations.

In Myanmar, the human rights situation remained grave despite some improvements as a result of political developments, according to the Special Rapporteur. In February, a draft Constitution was finalized—the fourth step in the Government's seven-step road map to democracy—and a referendum on its adoption was held on 10 May. The lack of participation in the drafting process, the small degree of transparency, the limited public knowledge about its contents, and the conditions under which the referendum was held all raised concerns from a human rights perspective. In addition, a large number of opposition leaders remained in detention. The situation of the National League for Democracy General Secretary, Daw Aung San Suu Kyi, was a matter of concern as the Government, in May, extended her house arrest with no new evidence against her. In the wake of Cyclone Nargis, the Secretary-General visited Myanmar on 22 and 23 May. Following his discussions with Government officials, some access for international aid workers was granted. In June, the Human Rights Council called on the Government to implement commitments it had made to the Secretary-General on granting access by relief workers to those in need.

The protection of human rights in the Sudan remained challenging. There were continued violations of the freedoms of expression and association that were of particular concern as the country prepared for elections in 2009. Gross violations of human rights continued to be perpetrated in the Darfur region. The Special Rapporteur said that in general, the human rights situation remained grim and violations continued to be committed by all parties. Some progress had been made in implementing the 2005 Comprehensive Peace Agreement, and by July, the National Assembly had passed 59 new bills, including acts on the armed forces, criminal procedure, elections, the police and political parties. Overall, the human rights legal and institutional framework remained weak. In September, the Council acknowledged the progress made in the implementation of the Comprehensive Peace Agreement and the steps taken by the Government to strengthen the human rights legal and institutional framework, principally in law reform. It expressed concern at the overall human rights situation and called on the Government to accelerate implementation of the Agreement, to establish the remaining commissions, in particular the national human rights commission, and to intensify efforts for promoting and protecting human rights.

The Special Rapporteur reported that the human rights situation in the Democratic People's Republic of Korea remained grave in 2008. In addition to systematic human rights violations, the country was enduring an economic crisis characterized by rampant and chronic shortages of food. Civil and political rights were severely constrained due to the repression imposed by the regime, coupled with intimidation and an extensive informant system, creating insecurity among the population. A new development during the year was the resumption of talks between the Democratic People's Republic of Korea and Japan on abducted Japanese nationals, aimed at reopening investigations on unresolved cases. The food shortages became more evident as the year progressed, with reports that millions of people were facing severe deprivations. A new agreement was reached between the authorities and the World Food Programme to assist 6.5 million people, whereby the Programme was granted access to households and warehouses that had previously been inaccessible.

The Human Rights Council held its sixth special session (23–24 January) on the human rights violations emanating from Israeli military attacks and incursions in the Occupied Palestinian Territory, and its eighth special session (28 November and 1 December) on the human rights situation in the east of the Democratic Republic of the Congo.

Also during the year, the High Commissioner for Human Rights reported on the efforts of her Office to strengthen country engagements, especially through increased activities of field representatives as the main means for promoting human rights and reducing violations. The Council, its special procedures and the Office of the High Commissioner for Human Rights strengthened country engagements through advisory services, technical cooperation and monitoring activities as a means of advancing international human rights principles and preventing violations in several countries, including Afghanistan, Burundi, Cambodia, Colombia, Cyprus, the Democratic People's Republic of Korea, the Democratic Republic of the Congo, Guatemala, Haiti, Iran, Liberia, Myanmar, Nepal, the Occupied Palestinian Territory, Sierra Leone, Somalia and the Sudan. For its part, the General Assembly took action on the human rights situation in the Democratic People's Republic of Korea, Georgia, Iran and Myanmar.

General aspects

In accordance with a procedure established by Human Rights Council resolution 5/1 [YUN 2007, p. 664] to deal with communications alleging denial or violation of human rights, the Secretary-General during the year forwarded communications to the Council, giving each an indication of the article or articles of the Universal Declaration of Human Rights to which the communication related. Copies of communications were sent to the Governments concerned, so as to obtain their views on the allegations of violations.

Strengthening country engagements

Report of High Commissioner. In an 11 February report [A/HRC/7/38], the High Commissioner outlined the efforts of the Office of the United Nations High Commissioner for Human Rights (OHCHR) to strengthen country engagement through increased field presences and enhanced dialogue with and capacity-building of national counterparts, as well as interaction with regional organizations. At the beginning of 2008, the Office had 47 field presences, including regional offices, country offices, human rights components in peace missions and human rights advisers in country teams. There were 11 country offices (Angola, Bolivia, Cambodia, Colombia, Guatemala, Mexico, Nepal, Togo and Uganda, and presences in Kosovo and Palestine), including the new office established in La Paz, Bolivia, in early 2007. As envisaged in the 2006–2007 Strategic Management Plan [YUN 2006, p. 766], the offices in Bosnia and Herzegovina and Serbia (Belgrade) were closed in June 2007, while the office in Kosovo was strengthened in the light of remaining human rights concerns and future challenges. In 2007, OHCHR renewed memorandums of understanding with Nepal, Colombia and Cambodia. The agreement with Cambodia, extending the OHCHR mandate for 18 months, was reached on the understanding that negotiations aimed at concluding a standard agreement for future operations of the Office would resume in 2008. At the time of the report, OHCHR was running nine regional human rights presences: those for Southern Africa (Pretoria); East Africa (Addis Ababa); South-East Asia (Bangkok); the Middle East (Beirut); the Pacific (Suva); Central America (Panama City); the liaison office for Latin America and the Caribbean (Santiago); the regional representative for Central Asia (Bishkek); and the United Nations Centre for Human Rights and Democracy in Central Africa (Yaoundé). The regional office for Central America was established early in 2007, and in November 2007, a memorandum of understanding was signed with Senegal for a regional office for West Africa in Dakar. It was expected that three new regional offices would be operational in 2008—in Central Asia (Bishkek), South-West Asia and North Africa—together with a human rights training and documentation centre for South-West Asia and the Arab region. Those offices were foreseen in the 2006–2007 Strategic Plan (except South-West Asia), but significant delays had been faced, essentially due to the complexity of the negotiations, including host country agreements and consultations on selection of the seat. Important achievements of cooperation were reached with two countries where OHCHR did not have offices—China and the Russian Federation. A framework agreement for cooperation was reached with the former, and several technical cooperation activities were completed with the latter.

The OHCHR Peace Missions Support and Rapid Response Unit, established in 2006, increased the Office's capacity to react promptly to critical human rights situations, particularly by deploying missions and mobilizing capacity in support of country or regional offices, as well as UN country teams or peace operations. For example, in response to the declaration of a state of emergency in Guinea in early 2007, OHCHR supported the UN country team and assisted a civil society initiative on documenting allegations of human rights violations committed in January 2007 to repress peaceful protests. Other activities included support for a forensic investigation in Afghanistan, assistance to the UN country team in Somalia, and surge capacity to support OHCHR offices in their response to critical situations, such as violence in the Terai region of Nepal in January 2007; the deteriorating situation in the Occupied Palestinian territories; and monitoring human rights in the context of parliamentary elections in Togo. The Unit also provided secretariat support to the high-level Fact-finding Mission to Beit Hanoun, which was reactivated in 2007 [YUN 2007, p. 826], and to the high-level mission/group of experts mandated by the Human Rights Council to assess human rights in Darfur, Sudan [ibid., p. 805]. It also assisted the Special Rapporteur on human rights in Myanmar (see p. 881).

The High Commissioner conducted visits to 18 countries in 2007, and in most countries emphasized the need to end impunity for human rights violations as well as the need for independence of the judiciary.

OHCHR also continued to assist peacekeeping missions and was involved with humanitarian organizations.

Africa

Burundi

Report of independent expert. In a 15 August report [A/HRC/9/14], the independent expert on the situation of human rights in Burundi, Akich Okola (Kenya), provided information on his ninth (2–8 December 2007) and tenth (29 June–12 July 2008) visits to the country, during which he noted that the overall human rights situation there had deteriorated. More than 4,000 cases of human right violations were committed in the first half of 2008 by law enforcement personnel and administrators of provinces, most of them relating to ill-treatment, rape, torture of suspects and violations of due process. Those issues were taken to Government officials by the Human Rights and Justice Section of the United Nations Integrated Office in Burundi (BINUB) in the context of its monitoring activities. During the reporting period, several cases of violations of the right to life were committed by law enforcement agencies and the rebel movement. The expert described the political crisis which deepened in early 2008, when opposition representatives were removed from Parliament. He felt that the executive had enlisted the Constitutional Court to serve a political objective, thereby bringing into question its independence and credibility. The expert called on the Government to open a dialogue with all political parties in order to avoid any institutional and political crisis, which would have a negative impact on the human rights and stability of the country, and he urged the international community to support the Government in reforming the justice system.

The expert noted that the situation had improved in late 2007 when the President and opposition parties had reached an agreement to form a new Government to reflect the composition of society, providing for the allocation of ministries on the basis of the number of seats in Parliament won in the 2005 elections. However, in February 2008, the situation worsened when a political crisis erupted, resulting in gridlock in Parliament. A decision by the Constitutional Court forced 22 members to leave Parliament, and the President appointed party loyalists to replace them, thus allowing the ruling party (Conseil national pour la défense de la démocratie-Forces pour la défense de la démocratie) to regain its majority. The decision, widely condemned by jurists and others as a use of the judiciary for political objectives, exacerbated the precarious political situation. The expert met representatives of all major political parties. Opposition parties complained that they faced harassment by security organs whenever they held meetings and that the Government refused to register any political party from the opposition. Freedom of expression and the right to assembly were of great concern to opposition parties. The Government appeared determined to muzzle any political party that might challenge the ruling party during the elections in 2010. The situation was further complicated by the return of the rebel movement Palipehutu-Forces nationales de libération (Palipehutu-FNL) leadership to the capital without official status. Palipehutu-FNL demanded to be registered as a political party and that their forces be integrated in the security apparatus of the country, which the Government rejected. Opposition politicians appealed to the international community for intervention to help Burundi find a solution. As the result of hostilities between Palipehutu-FNL and the national defence forces, the Government arrested more than 1,000 alleged FNL members.

Some progress had been made towards establishing the mechanisms of transitional justice since the Government and the United Nations signed an agreement on 2 November 2007 for creating a tripartite steering committee, composed of the Government, civil society and the United Nations, to organize national consultations on transitional justice mechanisms. Questions remained relating to the special tribunal and its relationship with the truth and reconciliation commission; further discussions between the United Nations and the national authorities should ensure that the most serious crimes committed during the Burundian conflicts were investigated and perpetrators brought to justice. Progress was also made towards establishing an independent national human rights commission. The workplan and budget of the proposed commission were approved in February by a technical committee composed of members of the Government and civil society, but the budget was not included in the national budget because of the absence of an enabling law. The expert was informed in June that the law on the mandate, composition and functioning of the commission was under consideration by the Government, and the expert urged the Government to send the draft law to Parliament without delay.

In regard to human rights violations, the expert noted that respect for the right to physical integrity improved slightly in late 2007, which might be the result of advocacy and training sessions organized by human rights non-governmental organizations (NGOs) and BINUB. Training sessions targeted law enforcement personnel and administrators who had allegedly been involved in physical abuse of suspects. However, in early 2008 there were allegations of ill treatment committed by the security forces and combatants of Palipehutu-FNL and cases of violation of the right to physical integrity committed by the police during operations to combat banditry. Denial of the rights to assembly and freedom of expression were reported. The expert received copies of letters from administrators of various provinces in which the authorities denied opposition parties the right to organize meetings, and the ruling party controlled all administration in the country. He called on the international community to provide technical assistance to Burundi in order to better prepare for the forthcoming elections. Sexual violence had increased since late 2007. A significant increase in gang rape had been recorded in the first half of 2008. Most cases did not reach court because the perpetrators were released during investigations or escaped; some cases occurred on police premises. The Government had made no progress in addressing the 2004 Gatumba massacre or the 2006 Muyinga massacre; in the case of the latter event, there appeared to be an attempt by the Government to use legal and administrative technicalities to prevent full disclosure of the relevant facts, and in general, the Government displayed a lack of transparency and commitment to fight impunity. Similarly, the administration of justice and judicial reform remained weak, contributing to an increase in cases of mob justice, which was prevalent in Burundi. From January to June, more than 23 cases of mob justice were reported. Lack of confidence in the police and the judiciary was a major explanation for the trend, and allegations of interference by political and executive organs in judicial functions to shield the perpetrators contributed to the judiciary's weakness. Prisons remained overcrowded and the majority of detainees had been awaiting trial for more than a year. Detention beyond the legal limit, illegal detention and detention for minor offences were among the irregularities noticed. Violations of economic, social and cultural rights remained a concern. On a positive note, a programme of free medical care for pregnant women and children under 5 years of age was launched. Many promotion and capacity-building activities were carried out by the Human Rights and Justice Section of BINUB, human rights NGOs and the Burundi Ministry for Human Rights. OHCHR organized a workshop (18–19 February) on the follow-up to the recommendations of the Committee against Torture. Participants made recommendations to the Government on legal reform, the independence of judges and lawyers, sexual violence and conditions of detention.

Among his recommendations, the expert urged the Government to allow the registration of all political parties in compliance with the Constitution, and called on the Government and Palipehutu-FNL to work in all mechanisms foreseen by the 2006 Comprehensive Ceasefire Agreement. He commended the Government for supporting the establishment of a national human rights commission. The international community was urged to help the country achieve an impartial justice system, and to ensure that the process leading to the 2010 elections and the elections themselves were free and fair. The expert encouraged the Peacebuilding Commission to continue to support the Government in disbursing funds to implement the 2007–2008 development plan.

Human Rights Council action. On 24 September [A/63/53/Add.1 (res. 9/19)], the Council called on the Government and Palipehutu-FNL to work through all mechanisms established to ensure implementation of the Comprehensive Ceasefire Agreement and welcomed the project to support national consultations on transitional justice mechanisms in the context of the peacebuilding process. It also called for the early establishment of a national human rights commission. The Council called on the international community to increase its technical and financial assistance to the Government in support of its human rights efforts, in particular in the areas of economic and social rights and justice system reform, and to assist in preparing elections. OHCHR was requested to continue its activities through its presence in Burundi and to report on its activities and the human rights situation. The Council extended the mandate of the independent expert until an independent national human rights commission was established, and invited him to report to the Council following the establishment of such a commission.

Democratic Republic of the Congo

Report of independent expert. In a 29 February report [A/HRC/7/25], the independent expert on the situation of human rights in the Democratic Republic of the Congo (DRC), Titinga Frédéric Pacéré (Burkina Faso), remarked that the human rights situation remained serious. In particular, the lack of security was worrying, especially in the east, where militias and armed groups, as well as the DRC armed forces, had committed human rights violations with impunity, and in Bas-Congo. Little progress had been made and a climate of generalized impunity seemed to persist. Several important investigations and trials had shown little progress towards resolution and remained stalled. An exception was that the convictions handed down in the trials for the 2006 Bavi massacre and the murder of two UN military observers were upheld. Many cases of human rights violations had not been investigated, despite the information sent to the judicial authorities by the United Nations Organization Mission in the Democratic Republic of the Congo (MONUC) and local NGOs, particularly in North Kivu, where no trials had been held for cases of serious human rights violations. The expert described two well-known cases—the Kilwa massacre and the murder of journalist Serge Maheshe—as sham trials that had provoked international condemnation. The weakness of the judiciary and its lack of independence vis-à-vis the executive, which had control over judicial decisions, were deplorable. Frequent obstructions of justice were linked to political and military interference, the judiciary was subject to corruption, and its independence and capacity were undermined by insufficient financial resources and the use of the Constitution to reassert the executive's control over the judiciary. In order to combat impunity, the expert recommended the creation of a special international tribunal for the DRC or, failing that, joint criminal chambers in the appeal courts to try crimes committed since 1993, the year when serious violations of humanitarian law were first taken up in UN resolutions.

The expert reported that the incidence of sexual violence continued to increase at an alarming rate, with almost total impunity. In the absence of a functioning judicial system, many out-of-court settlements were concluded under the authority of traditional chiefs or local administrative officials, in breach of legislation and to the detriment of the victims' basic rights. Between 2005 and 2007, 14,200 rapes were recorded by health institutions, but less than 1 per cent were reported to local authorities. Of those complaints, 56 per cent were still at the preliminary investigation stage after a year. To handle cases of sexual violence, the expert proposed that an investigating judge be appointed to specialize in such cases in each prosecutor's office in the country. Child soldiers remained a problem, and minors continued to be forcibly recruited. Civil and political rights, as well as economic, social and cultural rights, continued to be violated. On 23 January, all the armed groups operating in North and South Kivu signed a peace agreement in Goma in the presence of the Head of State (see p. 120), providing for, among other things, cessation of hostilities, observance of the rules of international human rights and the return of refugees and internally displaced persons. The expert recommended that the Goma peace agreement be implemented. Other recommendations were made to the Government concerning steps to fight against impunity, improve the administration of justice and bring to the courts complaints of sexual violence. The international community was called on to support DRC institutions to permit the establishment of the rule of law, reform of the army and security forces, and economic recovery.

Human Rights Council action. On 27 March [A/63/53 (res. 7/20)], the Human Rights Council requested OHCHR to increase its technical assistance to the country, in consultation with the authorities. It called on the international community to support the implementation of the local mechanism of cooperation between the Government, OHCHR and the human rights section of MONUC, called "Entité de liaison des droits de l'homme", and to provide the DRC with the assistance it requested for improving the human rights situation. The High Commissioner was requested to report to the Council in March 2009 on the human rights situation in the country and the activities of her Office there.

Human Rights Council special session

At the request of France on behalf of 15 other countries [A/HRC/S-8/1], the Council held its eighth special session (Geneva, 28 November and 1 December) [A/HRC/S-8/2] on the situation of human rights in the eastern DRC. During its consideration of the issue, the Council heard statements from its members, the representative of the DRC as a concerned country, non-member countries, intergovernmental organizations and NGOs.

At the conclusion of the session, the Council adopted a resolution [ibid., (res. S-8/1)] expressing concern at the deteriorating human rights and humanitarian situation in North Kivu since the resumption of hostilities on 28 August, and calling on all parties to comply with international law to ensure the protection of the civilian population and to facilitate the work of humanitarian agencies. It called for the immediate end to human rights violations, urged parties to facilitate humanitarian assistance through corridors in the area so as to allow access and free movement of people and goods, and condemned the acts of violence and human rights violations in Kivu, in particular sexual violence and the recruitment by the militia of child soldiers. Expressing support for international efforts to restore long-term peace and stability, the Council urged all parties to cooperate with the Special Envoy of the Secretary-General for the conflict in the eastern DRC, Olusegun Obasanjo. It suggested strengthening the MONUC mandate to increase its capacity to protect civilians and to restore peace and security in Kivu. The international community was called on to address the root causes of the conflict, including the illicit exploitation of natural resources and the establishment of militias, and to provide the DRC with the assistance it requested for improving the humanitarian and human rights situation. The Council invited the High Commissioner to report at its tenth (2009) session on the human rights situation in the eastern DRC and on OHCHR activities in the region.

Kenya

At the end of December 2007, widespread violence broke out in Kenya following the announcement of the results of the 27 December presidential elections. In the ensuing days, official figures stated that over 1,200 people were killed. There was massive destruction of property, and several hundred thousand people were internally displaced. In light of that situation,

OHCHR deployed a fact-finding mission to Kenya from 6 to 28 February.

The report of the mission said that, in most parts of Kenya, the population had voted in a peaceful and orderly manner. However, procedural irregularities in the vote counting and tallying cast doubts on the legality of the election results. Voters who did not support the incumbent President, Mwai Kibaki, and who felt they had been deprived of their democratic rights, unleashed a wave of protests and violence that engulfed the country for weeks.

The mission observed that patterns of violence varied from one region to the next, greatly depending on region-specific dynamics. The first observed pattern of violence—the burning and looting of shops, houses and commercial outlets in the slums of Nairobi and Kisumu by youth groups—seemed spontaneous to most observers. It stemmed from the frustrations generated by poor living conditions and historical disenfranchisement, and was triggered by the anger of opposition supporters at what they saw as the theft of the election. In a second pattern of violence, perpetrators mainly targeted communities of small farmers and land-holders perceived to be Government supporters in the Rift Valley and aimed at driving them away from the region. Credible evidence suggested that the violence was partially organized by local political or traditional leaders seeking to settle long-held grievances over land issues and other real and perceived discrimination. The third pattern of violence was retaliatory: Government supporters and militias reportedly carried out reprisals targeting communities of migrant workers perceived to be opposition supporters.

The mission could not substantiate allegations of a steep increase in cases of sexual violence. OHCHR was nevertheless concerned that some 322 women and girls sought hospital treatment for sexual assaults and rape.

While the violations of democratic rights provided the trigger for the bulk of the street violence and human rights violations, underlying causes contributed to the outburst, such as lack of access to water, food, health and decent housing, together with high rates of youth unemployment and gross inequalities. The colonial legacy and mismanagement of land distribution had generated conflict over what was perceived as the most important source of wealth and power: arable land. Actual and perceived discrimination in the distribution of economic and political power among various communities, together with the absence of effective remedy, had fed serious grievances within the population. The failure to embrace constitutional, judicial, police and civil service reform had left the State with a diminished ability to tackle the root causes of violence and little credibility that it would do so.

During the crisis, the State appeared to have failed to prevent or stop the violence and the human rights violations. The mission acknowledged that the State faced limitations, including inadequate resources, and that it did provide last-resort protection to the fleeing population. However, the State had failed to take measures to protect its citizens. During the attacks, the police were often present, but were either overwhelmed or passive. In some instances, the policing of demonstrations and crowds was conducted with excessive use of force, resulting in death and injuries. According to the Government's own figures, 10 per cent of the killings were carried out by the police.

The Government and the opposition had agreed on a framework to address the violence: the Kenya National Dialogue and Reconciliation. According to the agreement, the goal of the dialogue was to achieve peace, stability and justice through the rule of law and respect for human rights. The parties had made commitments to address land reform, police and judicial reform, socio-economic inequalities, corruption, accountability and the disarmament of militias.

The mission recommended that the Government take independent prosecutorial measures to bring the perpetrators, including planners and organizers, to justice. The new Truth, Justice and Reconciliation Commission should have a clear mandate to feed into criminal prosecution of individual perpetrators. The Government should ensure the protection of all the victims and witnesses of human rights violations. Perpetrators of gross violations should under no circumstances be recommended for amnesty. Other recommendations dealt with passing a hate speech bill; securing the rights of internally displaced people to return or resettle; and carrying out the review and reform of the Constitution, the Parliament, the police and the legal and judicial system. (See also p. 326.)

Liberia

Reports of independent expert. The independent expert on technical cooperation and advisory services in Liberia, Charlotte Abaka (Ghana), reported to the Council on 14 February [A/HRC/7/67] and 15 August [A/HRC/9/15]. The latter report covered her mission to Liberia from 6 to 20 July, during which she noted that the Government, led by President Ellen Johnson Sirleaf, had brought governance to the people by periodically holding cabinet meetings in the counties. Many ministries were planning programmes taking into account the need for greater control at the county level. The Truth and Reconciliation Commission was nearing completion of its core activities, with public hearings coming to a close and an extension of its mandate to December. Draft legislation to establish the Independent National Commission on Human Rights was before the legislature, as was that for establishing the law reform commission, which would review the Constitution and the compatibility of domestic legislation with international human rights standards. Liberia needed to establish the rule of law and the administration of justice throughout the country. An increase in armed robbery constituted a threat to internal security, as did the resort to violence to resolve land and property disputes. Reform of the justice system needed attention, and the launching of the Judicial Training Institute was a step in that direction. Currently, however, the dysfunctional judiciary was resulting in many trials being conducted in violation of fair trial standards, and courts remained non-operational. Much work had been done in police reform, and the United Nations Mission in Liberia (UNMIL) had assisted with training 3,700 new police officers. Rape and sexual violence remained the most frequently committed serious crimes. The Government and UNMIL had launched an awareness campaign which had led to an increase in the reported incidents of rape. The national action plan on gender-based violence would be supported by a four-year joint United Nations/Government programme. In May, the decision was made to dedicate a court to hearing cases of gender and sexual violence. Harmful and discriminatory traditional and customary practices, such as trial by ordeal, female genital mutilation and early child marriage, continued to exist. The Government faced serious challenges in rebuilding the economy and in meeting its obligations to respect and fulfil human rights guarantees. Some progress had been made: for example, in June, the Government launched the Poverty Reduction Strategy, and indicators for key economic and social growth improved, with economic growth at nearly 10 per cent. The expert called on the Government to formulate a national policy on decentralization and to increase political participation at the local level. She urged Liberia to convene a national conference on the rule of law and establish the Law Reform Commission. She also recommended that the Government domesticate international and regional human rights instruments that were already ratified and eliminate harmful and discriminatory traditional practices. The expert invited donor countries to support the Government in poverty reduction and to assist it in establishing safe havens for victims of rape and domestic violence in all 15 counties. UNMIL was called on to support capacity-building in the Government and civil society.

Human Rights Council action. On 24 September [A/63/53/Add.1 (res. 9/16)], the Human Rights Council encouraged Liberia to continue its work to improve human rights promotion and protection, including in the areas highlighted by the expert, and to reinforce its commitment to establish a national human rights protection system. The Council requested OHCHR, through its presence in Liberia, to pursue its technical assistance activities in consultation with the authorities, and to report to the Council at its twelfth (2009) session on progress made in the human rights situation and relevant activities. The international community was urged to provide Liberia with assistance to enable it to consolidate human rights, peace and security.

Sierra Leone

Report of High Commissioner. In a 26 February report [A/HRC/7/66] on assistance to Sierra Leone in the field of human rights, the High Commissioner addressed related developments in 2007. Political, legislative and administrative developments had a positive impact on the human rights situation in the country. The National Human Rights Commission was established and was being operationalized. The Constitutional Review Commission to review the 1991 Constitution was established and work was in progress. Parliament passed legislation on protection of human rights, in particular women's and children's rights. The devolution of powers from the central Government to local district councils continued to increase political participation in governance and the promotion of human rights in local districts and at the community level. United Nations support for Sierra Leone under the Peacebuilding Fund was beginning to facilitate peace by addressing the root causes of the conflict. Projects to strengthen the National Human Rights Commission and the justice institutions, and to increase youth employment and empowerment were being implemented. Presidential and parliamentary elections had been successful, resulting in a change in Government and a new political leadership that appeared to be committed to respect for human rights and the rule of law. A number of challenges remained, including political tensions since the change in ruling parties, delays in judicial hearings, mismanagement of public resources, prolonged pretrial detention, poor prison conditions and increasing incidents of gender-based violence, including rape, domestic violence and female genital mutilation. No significant progress was noted in social and economic rights. Other issues included widespread corruption, environmental degradation, lawlessness among students, and the abuse of human rights by mining companies operating in the country. The law reform and the constitutional review process needed greater attention to ensure that the reforms proposed by the Truth and Reconciliation Commission were implemented. The United Nations Integrated Office in Sierra Leone continued to assist the Government in promoting and protecting human rights, particularly in supporting the National Human Rights Commission, developing a national plan of action for human rights, and strengthening the rule of law. In 2007, it assisted in monitoring the elections and found the process to be free, fair and generally peaceful.

The High Commissioner urged the Government to implement the recommendations of the Truth and Reconciliation Commission, in particular the reparations programme, and encouraged the Constitutional Review Commission to incorporate the recommendations of the Truth and Reconciliation Commission concerning constitutional reform. The Government was encouraged to provide adequate and timely funding for its Human Rights Commission, to strengthen the capacity of the courts and the Ministry of Justice, and to establish a legal aid programme in order to address the delay in trials, prolonged pretrial detentions and excessive remand and adjournment of cases. A comprehensive review of all customary laws, with a view to harmonizing practices that were inconsistent with the Constitution and international human rights standards, was also recommended. The High Commissioner encouraged the Government to take legal action to eliminate discrimination against women, implement the three gender bills passed by Parliament in 2007, reform the rape laws and embark upon national awareness-raising of women's rights and gender-based violence. Also recommended was the establishment of a ministry to coordinate human rights activities within the Government.

Somalia

Reports of independent experts. On 17 March, the independent expert on the situation of human rights in Somalia, Ghanim Alnajjar (Kuwait) submitted his last report to the Human Rights Council [YUN 2007, p. 804], covering events in 2007 and containing his recommendations. On 1 May, Shamsul Bari (Bangladesh) took up his mandate as the newly appointed independent expert and issued a preliminary report on 15 September [A/HRC/9/CRP.2], following a curtailed and restricted visit to Somalia, due to the ongoing violence there, and to the region (28 June–12 July). He stated that since 1991 there had been no central Government in Somalia and a state of lawlessness had engulfed most of the country as a result of the ongoing civil war. Hope for improvement had resulted from the signing on 18 August in Djibouti of a Peace Agreement between the Transitional Federal Government (TFG) of Somalia and the Alliance for the Re-liberation of Somalia, calling for a ceasefire, for the United Nations to deploy an international stabilization force and for the withdrawal of Ethiopian troops. Over the previous months, the human rights situation appeared to have further worsened and was characterized by indiscriminate violence and frequent attacks against civilians, including attacks against large civilian groups, arbitrary detention of human rights defenders, arbitrary arrests and extrajudicial killings of journalists, death threats against human rights defenders, and sexual and gender-based violence. The expert called on the TFG to develop laws and mechanisms for good governance and to take measures to end human rights violations, at least those caused by authorities under its control. In particular, it should safeguard the lives and property of people; end harassment and torture of innocent civilians; ensure that the TFG and Ethiopian forces avoided undue use of force against opposition forces that affected civilian populations; eliminate extortion; ensure there was no intimidation of the media; and ensure protection of human rights defenders, proper distribution of humanitarian aid and respect for humane treatment of all. Educational institutions needed to be reopened, as did medical services. The TFG should work with UN bodies to establish an independent human rights commission. Civil society should be involved in bringing about peace and reconciliation as well as social, political and economic change, including in developing a mechanism for the establishment of accountability, ending the prevailing culture of impunity, and reviewing the Somali Transitional Federal Charter and other laws. The expert recommended that the Security Council decide to deploy UN peacekeepers in Somalia as stipulated in the Djibouti Agreement, give that mission a mandate for protecting civilian populations and include a human rights component for monitoring and investigating violations. The Council should also consider establishing a commission of inquiry to investigate violations of human rights and humanitarian law in Somalia in the last two years by all parties and identify the perpetrators. The expert recommended that OHCHR reinforce the human rights capacity within the United Nations Political Office for Somalia to improve human rights monitoring and to address accountability issues. The expert made further recommendations for other UN bodies, Somali political parties, Ethiopia, the African Union, the international community and NGOs.

Human Rights Council action. On 28 March [A/63/53 (res. 7/35)], the Human Rights Council demanded that all parties reject and stop all acts of violence, abstain from engaging in hostilities and respect their obligations under international human rights law and humanitarian law. The parties were urged to work towards national reconciliation within the framework of the Transitional Federal Charter, including by holding fair, national multiparty elections in 2009. The international community was called on to support the legitimate Somali institutions and to provide development and humanitarian assistance to Somalia. The Council renewed the mandate of the independent expert for one year, and requested him/her to report to the Council in September 2008 and March 2009. The Council requested OHCHR to strengthen its presence in Somalia with a view to providing technical assistance and advisory services to the relevant institutions.

Sudan

Report of Special Rapporteur. In a 3 March report [A/HRC/7/22], the Special Rapporteur on the situation of human rights in the Sudan, Sima Samar (Afghanistan), updated her report submitted to the General Assembly in September 2007 [YUN 2007, p. 805] and covered events from September to December 2007. Some slow progress had been made in the enormous challenge of protecting human rights in the Sudan, including the drafting of new bills, issuance of orders and new policies, but they had not yet had an effect on the situation. One year later, many of the concerns mentioned in the previous report remained the same. Despite the potential for democratic transition and optimism created by the Interim National Constitution and the Bill of Rights, violations of civil and political rights remained widespread. Delays in the implementation of the Comprehensive Peace Agreement [YUN 2005, p. 301] continued to hamper the protection and promotion of human rights, particularly economic, social and cultural rights. The Rapporteur was particularly concerned by the situation of women's rights. Early and forced marriages, violence against women and female genital mutilation were still widely practiced. Women were frequently placed in detention for non-payment of dowry. Concern was expressed at the repression of fundamental rights and freedoms, the excessive use of force, arbitrary arrest and detention, torture and ill-treatment of human rights defenders and political opponents. The measures taken by the Government of Southern Sudan to strengthen the administration of justice remained inadequate in light of the thousands of cases of people in pretrial detention. A considerable number of them were held for long periods without their cases being reviewed and without receiving legal assistance.

As Chairperson of the group of experts on Darfur, the Special Rapporteur participated in a dialogue with the Government of the Sudan to foster implementation of the group's recommendations for the protection of human rights in Darfur [YUN 2007, p. 807]. The group noted that the Government's preparation of laws and instructions could be instrumental in improving human rights; however, those efforts had not led to any actual improvement. Concerns about Darfur remained regarding the Government's use of disproportionate and indiscriminate warfare in violation of international humanitarian law. Government forces carried out aerial bombardments against dissident Arab groups and others. Civilians continued to be exposed to violence and abuses either from Government-supported militias or some of the rebel groups, or as a result of being caught between warring factions. The proliferation of weapons, the presence of armed elements inside camps and the widening divisions along tribal affiliations added to the insecurity felt by internally displaced persons. People also continued to be arbitrarily arrested and held for prolonged periods. The female population of Darfur, in particular internally displaced persons, continued to be victims of rape and sexual violence. Most incidents of sexual violence went unreported because of lack of confidence that the police would take action. Widespread impunity continued to prevail. Despite the obstacles, humanitarian services continued to be provided to the majority of the conflict-affected civilians; however, access to parts of Darfur was limited owing to increasing insecurity.

In northern Sudan, despite the potential for democratic transition, violations of civil and political rights remained widespread. There was a pattern of arbitrary arrests and prosecutions in an apparent effort to stifle community protests against the Kajbar dam project. Khartoum media were subject to restrictions on freedom of expression through censorship, imposition of public information bans and use of criminal legislation. Justice and accountability continued to be a challenge. In Southern Sudan, key laws still needed to be passed or amended so as to comply with the Comprehensive Peace Agreement, the Constitution of Southern Sudan and international human rights treaties. Mechanisms needed to be put in place for the protection of basic human rights. The Southern Sudan Human Rights Commission had not been fully operational, as the enabling law had not been passed. The demobilization and integration of opposition forces had proceeded with difficulty, and the administration of justice was challenged by interference by military and civil officials. Tribal clashes in Southern Sudan over water points, land and cattle continued.

The protection of human rights in the Sudan remained challenging, and there were continued violations of the freedoms of expression and association, which were of particular concern as the country prepared for elections in 2009. Gross human rights violations continued to be perpetrated in the Darfur region. The Special Rapporteur hoped that the deployment of the African Union-United Nations Hybrid Operation in Darfur (UNAMID) would increase security and the protection of civilians, but at the time of the report, UNAMID was still facing difficulties, including shortages in troops and assets, and the Sudanese Government was not facilitating its deployment. The Special Rapporteur called on the Government of National Unity to: intensify efforts to implement the recommendations compiled by the group of experts on Darfur [ibid., p. 806]; accelerate the implementation of the Comprehensive Peace Agreement and establish the remaining commissions, in particular the national human rights commission; revise national laws to conform with the Comprehensive Peace Agreement, the Interim National Constitution and international human rights standards; address impunity and ensure that allegations of human rights violations were investigated and perpetrators brought to justice; and facilitate the deployment of UNAMID. UNAMID was called on to provide support and technical assistance to the Government of the Sudan for implementation of its obligations under international human rights law, provide technical assistance in the area of justice and encourage the Government to ensure that there was no amnesty for war crimes and crimes against humanity. Other recommendations were addressed to the warring factions and the Government of Southern Sudan.

Human Rights Council action. On 27 March [A/63/53 (res. 7/16)], the Council, while acknowledging the Government's measures to address the human rights situation, expressed concern that their implementation had not yet led to the desired impact. It expressed concern at the seriousness of the violations in some parts of Darfur, and reiterated its call to all parties to end violence against civilians, with special focus on vulnerable groups, including women, children and internally displaced persons, as well as human rights defenders and humanitarian workers. The Council stressed the primary responsibility of the Government to protect all its citizens, including vulnerable groups. The signatories of the Darfur Peace Agreement were called upon to comply with their obligations under the Agreement, and the Government was urged to implement the recommendations of the group of experts, within the specified time frames and indicators. UN bodies and donors were invited to continue providing support and technical assistance to the Sudan for the improvement of human rights and implementation of the Comprehensive Peace Agreement. The Council called on the Government to accelerate the implementation of the Agreement and to establish the remaining commissions, in particular the national human rights commission. It also urged the Government to address the impunity issue relating to the perpetrators of past and ongoing violations of human rights and international humanitarian law in Darfur.

Communication. On 13 June [A/HRC/8/G/11], the Sudan requested OHCHR to distribute its note quoting the High Commissioner's remarks on the armed attack by the Justice and Equality Movement on the Sudanese capital on 10 May. In those remarks, the High Commissioner condemned the use of child combatants by all parties and welcomed attempts to enforce the prohibition on the recruitment of children into armed groups.

Report of Special Rapporteur. The Special Rapporteur, in a 2 September report [A/HRC/9/13], covered the January to July 2008 period, including her visits to the Sudan from 28 February to 10 March and from 29 June to 11 July. In general, the human rights situation remained grim and violations continued to be committed by all parties. Some progress had been made in implementing the Comprehensive Peace Agreement, and by July, the National Assembly had passed 59 new bills, including acts on the armed forces, criminal procedure, elections, the police forces and political parties. Among laws not passed were those on the National Intelligence and Security Services (NISS) and on establishing the national human rights commission. An amended Child Act, finalized but not yet endorsed, would prohibit female genital mutilation, raise the age of criminal responsibility to 18 years of age, and dedicate a section for juvenile trials. On 8 June, President Omar Al-Bashir issued a decree on internally displaced persons dealing with their return and security arrangements. Overall, the human rights legal and institutional framework remained weak, and some even reported a deterioration in the country. On 10 May, members of the Darfurian Justice and Equality Movement (JEM), using child soldiers, launched an attack on Khartoum, and 34 civilians were reportedly killed. Afterwards, the Government granted access to captured children to international agencies, including the Special Rapporteur. The Government responded to the attack by making numerous arrests. According to reports, hundreds of detainees, mostly of Darfurian origin, were held incommunicado. In July, anti-terrorism courts in Khartoum pronounced 30 death sentences for alleged participation in the attacks. The verdicts were reached chiefly on the basis of confessions that the defendants said were made under torture and which they retracted in court. Many arrests were reportedly carried out arbitrarily. Freedom of expression was further restricted, most likely as the result of the 10 May incident, and media organizations, NGOs and human rights defenders reported increasing harassment and censorship by the Government and NISS, which visited newspaper premises on a daily basis and demanded changes to articles about to be published. As the Sudan was preparing for a general election scheduled for 2009, it was essential that freedoms of expression, association, assembly and movement be guaranteed and respected. The lack of justice and accountability for serious crimes remained one of the most important challenges to human rights protection in the Sudan. In Darfur, despite increasing insecurity, the Government had taken some steps to implement the recommendations of the group of experts on Darfur and address human rights concerns. For example, the number of police deployed there had been increased, State committees had undertaken activities against sexual and gender-based violence, and several military personnel had been indicted, tried and found guilty of rape. More fighting by many parties, including air attacks by Government forces, had resulted in civilian casualties, widespread destruction of property and mass displacement. Many communities in Darfur described the inability of UNAMID, which suffered seven deaths when attacked on 8 July, to protect the civilian population from the conflict. Humanitarian personnel were also victims of killings, armed assaults, abductions and carjackings, thus forcing agencies to reduce activities in dangerous areas. In the transitional area of Abyei, heavy fighting broke out between 14 and 20 May between the Sudanese Armed Forces (SAF) and the Sudan People's Liberation Army (SPLA), both supported by groups of armed civilians. The battle left large areas of the town completely destroyed and looted, and an estimated 50,000 people were displaced. A political agreement was reached on 8 July to de-escalate the crisis. The United Nations Mission in the Sudan (UNMIS), without the mandate or means to halt the fighting, was limited to sheltering civilians seeking refuge and evacuating them. The transitional areas faced serious problems in the administration of justice. Frequently, local armed groups set up areas of control, and SAF and SPLA were involved in arrests and detention falling outside their legal mandates. In Southern Sudan, major human rights concerns were linked to prevailing insecurity and the proliferation of firearms, as well as the role of SPLA in law enforcement. The recently established Southern Sudan Human Rights Commission had made progress towards carrying out its role as an independent oversight mechanism, promoting human rights and raising concerns with the authorities. Numerous people in Southern Sudan were killed as a result of localized armed clashes and general insecurity. A particular security concern was the continuing presence of the Lord's Resistance Army and other armed groups across a wide area of Southern Sudan, where armed clashes between tribes commonly occurred over land, cattle and family affairs. There were continued reports of SPLA personnel enjoying impunity for their crimes, including assault, rape and arbitrary arrest.

The Special Rapporteur repeated her recommendations outlined in her earlier report for the Government of National Unity, the United Nations and the international community. The Government was also urged to cooperate fully with UNMIS and UNAMID to remove any obstacles that might hinder humanitarian efforts and to engage with civil society to develop strategies to improve human rights. The Government of Southern Sudan was called on to ensure that adequate means and resources were provided to the institutions responsible for the administration of justice and rule of law, and to ensure that its budget covered key sectors such as education, health, social services, law enforcement and the rule of law, as well as human rights.

Follow-up to report of expert group. In an addendum to her 2 September report [A/HRC/9/13/Add.1 & Corr.1], the Special Rapporteur, as requested by the Council, reported on the status of implementation of the recommendations on Darfur compiled by the group of experts mandated by the Human Rights Council in 2007 [YUN 2007, p. 806]. The Rapporteur, through dialogue with the Government of the Sudan, had worked to ensure follow-up and to foster implementation of the recommendations. She described national efforts to bring accountability and justice measures to combat impunity, as well as to monitor the implementation of the expert group's recommendations. The Rapporteur concluded that while certain recommendations were implemented, certain others were partially implemented, while others remained without implementation. Several recommendations that were prioritized as short-term and could have been implemented within a short-term time frame had not been implemented. The Government needed to engage fully in an open and constructive dialogue and take concrete steps to improve the human rights situation. Only in a few areas were necessary steps taken fully or to a significant degree to have a tangible impact. In more cases, activities were undertaken but little or no impact was reported, or only initial steps were taken towards implementation. With very few exceptions, those efforts had not led to an improvement of the human rights situation. In certain specific instances, the feasibility of full implementation could have been affected by a lack of resources and technical assistance. However, the lack of resources could not justify any acts of violence against the civilian population or the lack of action to prevent such acts.

The Rapporteur recommended that the Human Rights Council continue the process of review, in accordance with the indicators for assessing implementation developed by the group of experts, until there was full implementation, or at least significant activities, and tangible impact had been reported. Noting that the time frame for implementing the short- and medium-term recommendations had elapsed on 20 June, she suggested that the Council consider what further action was required to concretely protect the human rights of people in Darfur.

Human Rights Council action. On 24 September [A/63/53/Add.1 (res. 9/17)], the Council, taking note of the Special Rapporteur's reports on Darfur, acknowledged the progress made in the implementation of the Comprehensive Peace Agreement and the steps taken by the Government to strengthen the human rights legal and institutional framework, principally in law reform. It expressed concern at the overall human rights situation and called on the Government to accelerate implementation of the Agreement, to establish the remaining commissions, in particular the national human rights commission, and to intensify efforts for promoting and protecting human rights. Noting its initial steps, the Council urged the Government to strengthen efforts to implement the recommendations compiled by the group of experts, in accordance with the specified indicators. Calling on all parties to respect their obligations under international human rights law and humanitarian law, it stressed the primary responsibility of the Government to protect all vulnerable groups. The Council urged all parties to cooperate with UNMIS and UNAMID, and to allow humanitarian agencies to move freely throughout the Sudan. The Government was urged to cooperate with the Special Rapporteur and respond favourably to her requests to visit the Sudan. The Council extended until June 2009 the Special Rapporteur's mandate, and requested her to assess the human rights needs of the Sudan and to mobilize the necessary international technical and financial support. The Rapporteur was also requested to ensure follow-up to the implementation of the remaining recommendations of the group of experts through dialogue with the Government, and to include the information in her next report to the Council's eleventh (2009) session.

Communication. In a 29 October letter [A/HRC/10/G/1] to the Human Rights Council, the Sudan said that JEM forces in Darfur had killed four civilian Chinese nationals working on development projects in Western Kurdufan State, and it condemned four other armed attacks allegedly committed by JEM and other groups active in Darfur as acts of terrorism. The Sudan called on UN Member States to condemn the crimes.

Americas

Colombia

Report of High Commissioner. In a report on the situation of human rights in Colombia during 2008 [A/HRC/10/32], the High Commissioner described the main developments in the country within the framework of the agreement between the Government and OHCHR, which was extended in 2007 and was to remain in force until 2010. Violations of human rights and international humanitarian law by the guerrilla groups and the armed forces, as well as the activities of illegal armed groups and drug traffickers, coupled with underlying problems such as inequitable distribution of wealth, discrimination and stigmatization of vulnerable groups, impunity and difficulties in accessing justice, continued to limit full enjoyment of human rights. The Government had sought to strengthen the rule of law, mainly through increasing regional State presence in locations previously under the control of illegal armed groups. However, human rights violations continued to take place. Stigmatization of human rights defenders, opposition leaders and social activists by some Government officials continued. The Government had striven to address extrajudicial executions and those efforts should continue: the number of complaints and victims recorded showed that institutional policies adopted by the Ministry of Defence and the army High Command to combat such practices had not managed to curb violations. Recent extraordinary measures, including separating some senior military commanders from service, had reinforced the "zero tolerance" policy for human rights violations. Those measures should be accompanied by greater operational control over military units and thorough investigations of allegations of extrajudicial execution. All parties to the conflict continued to breach international humanitarian law; moreover, the Revolutionary Armed Forces of Colombia-People's Army and the National Liberation Army refused to be bound by international humanitarian law. Besides continuing to recruit children and to commit crimes of sexual violence against women and girls, guerrilla groups continued planting anti-personnel mines, taking hostages and holding kidnapped persons for long periods under inhuman conditions. The illegal armed groups that had emerged since the paramilitary demobilization presented a major challenge to the rule of law. Those groups continued to endanger the civilian population, and a comprehensive response from the authorities was required. The rights to truth, justice and reparations had been given more prominence in the political and public agendas in 2008. However, few of the victims had effectively enjoyed those rights, especially the victims of actions or omissions by State agents. The economic growth of previous years had not resulted in sufficient progress in achieving the Millennium Development Goals, and the gap had not narrowed between those who had opportunities to generate income and those who did not.

In her recommendations, the High Commissioner called on all parties to the conflict to abide by international humanitarian law, respecting the life, integrity and property of the civilian population; required members of illegal armed groups to release all kidnapped persons; and urged the Government to implement the measures announced to eliminate the practice of extrajudicial execution and to step up its cooperation with the Attorney-General's Office for the investigation, trial and punishment of those crimes. The Government should also carry out measures to protect the civilian population in the face of actions by the illegal armed groups that had emerged since the paramilitary demobilization. The High Commissioner called on the judicial authorities and supervisory bodies to strengthen investigations and oversight, with a view to increasing protection of human rights defenders and trade unionists.

Annexed to the report were several examples of human rights violations and breaches of international humanitarian law.

Communication. On 26 February [A/HRC/7/G/4], Colombia transmitted to the Human Rights Council its observations on the 2007 report of the

High Commissioner [YUN 2007, p. 808]. Colombia said that recent visits to the country by the High Commissioner and high-level officials and ongoing dialogue had resulted in a clearer picture of the situation and the efforts that the State was making to promote the full enjoyment of human rights. A more extensive dialogue with civil society was achieved in 2007, during which agreements were reached on methodology, the scope of the consultation process and the ground rules for the joint elaboration of a National Human Rights Plan of Action. Colombia stated its intention to promote the implementation of the High Commissioner's recommendations; a mechanism for evaluating the implementation of those recommendations was put into operation.

Regarding allegations that human rights defenders had been tortured, Colombia said that such cases were of concern and were isolated exceptions. The Government enumerated steps it had taken to protect the human rights of the indigenous and Afro-Colombian population and to overcome racial discrimination. It had expanded human rights guarantees for victims of any type of violence, including a budget for a protection programme for victims and witnesses. A legal framework had been created for the disarmament, demobilization and reintegration process to guarantee the rights of victims to truth, justice and reparation. The Justice and Peace Act imposed conditions on anyone seeking to benefit from its provisions. These included: genuine demobilization; the renunciation of all criminal activity; confession of any incidents in which the individual might have taken part in an illegal armed group; and contribution to the reparation of victims. The claims of 126,000 victims had been registered. As at 31 December 2007, 46,127 persons had been demobilized. Colombia reiterated its commitment to combating impunity, and to that end the executive power had guaranteed conditions of security throughout the country, the presence of institutions and the weakening of illegal armed groups and their interference in the economic, social and political life of the country. To deal with such cases, the Attorney-General's Office and the judiciary had been given additional staff and resources. To tackle the problem of alleged killings of protected persons, additional prosecutors and investigators had been appointed in 2007. Regarding economic, social and cultural rights, Colombia had adopted a strategy for coordinating activities of State agencies under the Social Protection Network for Overcoming Extreme Poverty.

Guatemala

Report of High Commissioner. Reporting on the work of the OHCHR office in Guatemala during the year [A/HRC/10/31/Add.1] within the framework of the 2005 joint agreement between the Government and OHCHR [YUN 2005, p. 374], which was extended for three years in September 2008, the High Commissioner said that the office had continued to monitor the human rights situation and to provide advisory and technical assistance services to national institutions, geared towards the implementation of the recommendations contained in the previous report [YUN 2007, p. 809]. The national context was characterized by persistent and increasing violence and public insecurity. The office observed with concern the difficult situation hindering full enjoyment of the right to life, which required that the State strengthen the prevention, investigation and punishment of violations of that right. Other issues of concern included violence against women; attacks against human rights defenders; the rule of law and impunity; combating racism and discrimination; transitional justice; and economic, social and cultural rights. The office provided technical advice to various national institutions such as Congress, the Presidential Human Rights Commission, the Ministry of the Interior, the Public Prosecutor's Office, the Presidential Commission on Discrimination and Racism, the Office for the Defence of Indigenous Women, the National Reparations Programme and the Office of the Human Rights Procurator. The office carried out 50 monitoring missions in the 22 departments of Guatemala: 135 complaints were received, of which 47 were selected for follow-up as they referred to human rights violations. In addition, the office carried out 595 meetings and interviews with authorities and representatives of civil society to supplement its assessment of the human rights situation. This enabled the office to gather the information needed to analyse the human rights situation, adjust its advisory and technical cooperation services, and provide support to victims and witnesses, facilitating their cooperation with authorities.

In her recommendations, the High Commissioner urged Congress and the Government to continue to refine the legislative framework for human rights protection. The Government should improve criminal investigations carried out by the police, on the basis of an appropriate organizational structure, trained personnel, an adequate territorial deployment, and the availability of technical and scientific resources. The General Directorate of the Prisons System and the Public Prosecutor's Office should investigate the deaths of persons deprived of their liberty, prevent the recurrence of violent incidents within detention centres and protect the life and integrity of all persons. The Government and Congress should establish a national mechanism for the prevention of torture. Special measures should be adopted to overcome the conditions of inequality which impeded indigenous peoples' access to economic, social and cultural rights. Other recommendations addressed the rule of law, impunity and women's rights.

Haiti

Note by OHCHR. On 13 June [A/HRC/8/2], the Human Rights Council was informed that for personal reasons beyond his control, the independent expert on the situation of human rights in Haiti, Louis Joinet (France), had been unable to carry out his last mission to Haiti, initially planned for late 2007, and would not be able to present his report to the Council's eighth session in June 2008.

Human Rights Council action. In a 24 September president's statement [A/63/53/Add.1 (PRST/9/1)], the Council welcomed recent political developments in Haiti, marked by the installation of a new Government, and commended the reaffirmation by the authorities of their commitments and determination to improve living conditions for Haitians, with a special emphasis on human rights. The Council noted the cooperation between the police and the United Nations Stabilization Mission in Haiti in curbing violence, crime and banditry. It welcomed the adoption of regulations on the judiciary and the new Act on the High Council of the Judiciary, as well as the reopening of the Judicial Training College. It encouraged authorities to continue efforts to eliminate prolonged pretrial detention, introduce a legal aid scheme and strengthen the Office of Citizen Protection. The Council was concerned at the deterioration of living standards in recent months, partly as a result of the economic crisis and food shortage, and deplored the loss of life and material damage caused by four recent hurricanes. Aware of the many obstacles to development in Haiti and difficulties encountered by its leaders in daily governance, the Council recognized that full enjoyment of human rights was a factor of peace, stability and progress in the country. The Council encouraged the international community to step up its cooperation with the authorities for the full realization of human rights.

The Council thanked the outgoing independent expert for his contribution to consolidating the rule of law, welcomed the appointment of Michel Forst (France) as his successor and supported the Haitian authorities' request to extend the mission of the independent expert to September 2010. He was invited to continue the work undertaken and bring his experience and expertise to bear in contributing to the cause of human rights in Haiti, with a particular emphasis on economic, social and cultural rights. The Council invited him to undertake a mission to Haiti in the near future and report to it each year.

Asia

Afghanistan

Report of High Commissioner. In a 21 February report [A/HRC/7/27] on the situation of human rights in Afghanistan and on technical assistance in human rights, submitted pursuant to a Human Rights Council decision [YUN 2006, p. 948], the High Commissioner made recommendations to address ongoing human rights concerns raised in previous reports. With the intensification of armed conflict, protection of civilians had become a major human rights concern. Insurgency-related violence had cost hundreds of civilian lives and created new groups of displaced persons. Coupled with increased criminality, it had hindered aid delivery and humanitarian access. Poverty and lack of access to food, medical care and education persisted, and national institutions remained unable to deliver essential services, including security and justice. Despite some advances, women still faced social, economic and political discrimination. Efforts had been made to improve the rule of law, but the necessary institutions for protecting human rights were still lacking. Arbitrary detention remained commonplace. Impunity remained entrenched and there was little progress in transitional justice. Journalists faced increased levels of threats and intimidation.

The High Commissioner recommended that the international community ensure that international human rights and humanitarian law informed an integrated governance strategy, with Afghans in the lead. That would require promoting civil, political, economic, social and cultural rights as interdependent foundations for progress, and ensuring participation of civil society and disadvantaged groups. All parties to the conflict should take measures to ensure respect for human rights and international humanitarian law. The international military forces should be more responsive and accessible to families in ensuring redress. The international community should nurture and defend civil society and freedom of expression. The Government, with international support, should strengthen the delivery of services necessary for the enjoyment of social, economic and cultural rights, including human rights reporting mechanisms. The Government and the international community should provide the necessary political, technical and financial support for the Ministry of Justice to monitor and report on State implementation of human rights benchmarks in the Afghanistan Compact [ibid., p. 363]. They should reinstate women's rights at the top of policy and donor agendas, providing financial and policy support, in order to reverse marginalization and combat violence against women. They should act to build the rule-of-law sector, including a commitment to truth-seeking, compensation and rehabilitation. The Government was called on to provide a clear mandate for forensic experts to investigate mass graves related to past abuses. With international support, the authorities should develop initiatives to prevent arbitrary arrests and detentions, promote the role of defence counsels, and develop judicial capacity to deal with cases in a timely manner. The Government was urged to reinstate its moratorium on the death penalty. With the support of the international community, it was urged to address deficiencies in the system of administration and protection of property rights, and in particular to build on traditional mechanisms where they could be used to ensure that individuals' property rights were protected in a fair and just manner.

Azerbaijan

In a 26 February communication [A/HRC/7/NI/7] to the Human Rights Council, Azerbaijan described the steps it had taken over the previous six years to promote and protect human rights, particularly through the newly established Office of the Commissioner for Human Rights (Ombudsman), which focused on restoring human rights and liberties violated by governmental bodies and officials. The Commissioner paid close attention to the problems of human rights of women and children, the elderly, persons with disabilities, refugees and internally displaced persons, detainees and prison inmates, and military personnel. As part of its activities, the Office received and analysed complaints and defined the areas of human rights concern. A new National Action Plan for human rights protection was adopted in 2006 that outlined a strategy to strengthen human rights protection with both short- and long-term objectives.

Subsequent communications from Azerbaijan covered the protection of internally displaced persons [A/HRC/8/NI/1], persons with disabilities [A/HRC/8/NI/2] and the right to development [A/HRC/8/NI/3].

Cambodia

Reports of Secretary-General. In a February report [A/HRC/7/56] on the role of OHCHR in assisting the Government and people of Cambodia to promote and protect human rights during 2007, submitted pursuant to Human Rights Council decision 2/102 [YUN 2006, p. 760], the Secretary-General said that the OHCHR programme was structured around three areas: fundamental rights and freedoms and civil society; rule of law; and land and livelihoods. OHCHR monitored developments, conducted legal analysis relevant to the exercise of those rights, provided technical assistance to Government institutions, drew the attention of the authorities to violations or matters of concern, and worked with civil society actors involved in economic, social and legal fields, helping to protect their ability to operate.

In a later report [A/HRC/12/41], the Secretary-General covered OHCHR activities in 2008 to assist human rights in Cambodia. The Office had stepped up efforts to engage in dialogue and cooperation with the Government. It developed initiatives with Government institutions whereby human rights issues were jointly assessed and discussed with relevant authorities, solutions were explored, and support offered in the form of technical and other assistance. That approach, based on direct dialogue with Government interlocutors, aimed to build working relationships with them, while OHCHR continued to draw public attention to certain issues when avenues of dialogue were exhausted. Several Government institutions had shown willingness to cooperate, while others had demonstrated little or no interest. Meanwhile, OHCHR developed its cooperation with community-based organizations, NGOs and other civil society actors. It provided support to correctional reform through such activities as working with the Ministry of Interior to improve prison conditions and the treatment of prisoners and to strengthen prison management. It conducted seven visits to provincial prisons to provide the authorities with an independent assessment of prison conditions. The rule of law programme sought to promote adherence to international human rights standards, in particular by building an institutional framework allowing Cambodians to obtain a remedy for violations of their rights. The Office continued to advise on the establishment of a national human rights institution, but there was little progress in that regard in 2008. Technical advice was provided to strengthen national torture prevention measures, but impunity remained a major challenge to the rule of law. In the context of the implementation in early 2008 of a new anti-trafficking law, sex workers were arbitrarily arrested by the police during night-time "sweeps" in Phnom Penh. OHCHR continued its work of promoting adherence to international trial standards in domestic courts. In the effort to support the general election on 27 July, the Office monitored instances of violence. The elections were held without significant violence, a welcome change from previous elections. During the months preceding the election, OHCHR observed an organized attempt by the ruling party to pressure, intimidate and offer rewards to persuade opposition leaders to switch allegiance, as well as the use of threats and intimidation, particularly with the media. The Office also observed a growing recourse of officials to criminal defamation. A number of NGOs and community organizations, particularly those involved in the protection of land rights of the poor, natural resources management, and human rights advocacy, had come under increasing official pressure. The draft law on peaceful assembly was submitted to Parliament in early 2008, and revisions were made at the request of OHCHR and others. Land conflicts and forced evictions affected large numbers of people, and a reported 150,000 people had been evicted over the previous few years. OHCHR worked with communities and NGOs to protect their rights and seek redress, and it worked on improving legal protections pertaining to resettlement.

Report of Special Representative. In a 29 February report [A/HRC/7/42], the Secretary-General's Special Representative for human rights in Cambodia, Yash Ghai (Kenya), stated that his fourth mission to that country [YUN 2007, p. 811] had centred on the theme of the rule of law, including access to justice. The report examined how to maximize the impact of the jurisprudence and practice of the Extraordinary Chambers in the Courts of Cambodia (ECCC), which were trying those most responsible for the atrocities of the Khmer Rouge regime, on the Cambodian legal system.

The report concluded that laws, institutions and procedures critical to the rule of law were very little respected in Cambodia—especially by the State. For the most part, the Government had not attempted to deny, much less refute, those findings or to take action to address the issue. Special Representatives and others had repeatedly addressed the problems of the legal and judicial system and made numerous recommendations, to no avail. The Government had no incentives for reform, as the international community continued to make large financial contributions regardless of widespread violations of human rights.

Resignation of Special Representative. On 10 September, the Special Representative announced his resignation. On 15 September, in a statement read to the Council by the Special Rapporteur on the human rights situation in the Sudan, Sima Samar, Mr. Ghai said that he had to cancel his visit to Cambodia due to difficulties in obtaining a visa. With the help of the OHCHR Office in Cambodia and NGO reports, however, he was able to apprise himself of the situation. There were serious deficiencies in the general elections in July, and little progress had been made in other areas in which human rights continued to be violated. Allegations of irregularities in the management of ECCC continued to undermine the work of the prosecutors and judges. The Special Representative's successor should have the full support of the Human Rights Council, the United Nations and the international community.

Cambodia replied that it had made great efforts to face major challenges by engaging itself in the promotion and protection of human rights. The recent national elections were qualified by international observers as smoothly conducted in a democratic atmosphere. The new mandate holder should focus his or her work on more relevant areas, namely advisory services and technical cooperation, which reflected a genuine need for Cambodia.

Human Rights Council action. On 24 September [A/63/53/Add.1 (res. 9/15)], the Human Rights Council extended by one year the mandate on the situation of human rights in Cambodia through the appointment of a Special Rapporteur to carry out the former functions of the Special Representative, and requested the Special Rapporteur to report on implementation of his/her mandate at its twelfth (2009) session.

Taking note of the new developments, especially those associated with recent progress by the Government in promoting and protecting human rights, the Council reaffirmed the importance of ECCC, which could contribute to eradicating impunity and establishing the rule of law. It welcomed the progress of ECCC, including the detention in 2007 of five suspects and the submission of the first closing order on 8 August, and supported proceeding with the tribunal in a fair and expeditious manner, given the advanced age of those charged and the long-overdue justice for the people of Cambodia. The Council encouraged Cambodia to work with the United Nations and States providing assistance to ensure high standards of administration of ECCC. The Council welcomed: the Government's efforts in promoting legal and judicial reform under the leadership of the Council of Legal and Judicial Reform, including adopting and/or enforcing basic laws, such as the civil procedure code, the criminal procedure code and the civil code; the Government's efforts in combating corruption, including the drafting of an anti-corruption law; the Government's efforts in combating trafficking in persons, including the creation of a national anti-trafficking task force in 2007, increased law enforcement action against traffickers and complicit officials, and the promulgation of a new law on the suppression of human trafficking in 2008; the Government's efforts to resolve land issues through such measures as land demarcation and titling programmes; the Government's commitment to adhere to and implement the international human rights conventions; efforts by the Cambodian Human Rights Committee in resolving complaints from people, improving prisons and intervening in prolonged pretrial detentions; the renewal in 2007 of the memorandum of understanding between Cambodia and OHCHR on implementing a technical cooperation programme on human rights; the good administration and generally peaceful conclusion of the general elections held in July, which demonstrated the continued development of the democratic process in Cambodia. The Council noted remaining shortcomings about the conduct of the election process and the need to strengthen the enforcement capacity of the national election committee; and the Government's progress in promoting decentralization by strengthening subnational and grassroots institutions, including the local elections planned for 2009.

The Council expressed concern about some areas of human rights practices and urged the Government to: strengthen its efforts to establish the rule of law, especially to ensure the independence, impartiality, transparency and effectiveness of the judicial system; enhance efforts to combat corruption, particularly by enacting and implementing a relevant law; address the problem of impunity and prosecute all those who had perpetrated serious crimes; enhance efforts to resolve land ownership issues by strengthening the capacity of institutions such as the National Authority for Land Dispute Resolution and Cadastral Committees at national, provincial and district levels; continue to improve human rights, especially those of women and children, and to combat key problems such as human trafficking, poverty, sexual violence, domestic violence and sexual exploitation; and promote the rights of all Cambodians by providing political, economic and social freedom. The Council invited the Secretary-General, UN agencies and the international community to provide assistance to Cambodia in drafting laws, strengthening legal institutions, strengthening national institutions for criminal investigation and law enforcement, and assisting assessment of progress in human rights issues. The Council took note of the work of the Special Representative and of the re-engagement of OHCHR with the Government.

Democratic People's Republic of Korea

Communications. In a 30 January letter to the Human Rights Council President [A/HRC/7/G/3], the Democratic People's Republic of Korea (DPRK) reiterated that it opposed and rejected the mandate of the Special Rapporteur on the situation of human rights in the DPRK. It affirmed that the mandate was a product of political confrontation, unjust manipulations, and the politicization of human rights. The DPRK called for the Council to terminate that politicized procedure.

In a 22 February note [A/HRC/7/47] to the Human Rights Council, the High Commissioner said that she had proposed to the DPRK discussions on a future technical assistance programme in the areas of treaty body reporting and ratification of core human rights treaties, and that an OHCHR mission visit the DPRK to explore such possibilities. The DPRK responded that it did not recognize the resolutions adopted by the Council and the General Assembly on the human rights situation in the DPRK, which it found to be selective, politicized and reflecting double standards. The Government was therefore unable to accept the High Commissioner's offer.

Report of Special Rapporteur. In a 15 February report [A/HRC/7/20], the Special Rapporteur on the situation of human rights in the DPRK, Vitit Muntarbhorn (Thailand), said that the country had been in the news during the previous year due to the nuclear issue, which was being dealt with under the umbrella of the six-party talks involving China, the DPRK, Japan, the Republic of Korea, the Russian Federation and the United States. Those talks, at which agreement was reached in February and October 2007 on disabling a nuclear plant in the DPRK, provided an avenue to address some human rights issues. The human rights situation remained grave in a number of areas. The Rapporteur regretted that the authorities had declined his invitation to cooperate with him. On a positive note, the Government was party to four human rights treaties. In addition, following floods in the country in August 2007, it had allowed humanitarian agencies to have greater access to the counties affected by flooding. There was a paucity of data on economic development in the country, but the estimated per capita national income in 2004 was $914, and the growth rate of gross domestic product was estimated at 1 per cent per annum in 2006. Military expenditure was 15.6 per cent. The lack of equity was due to the highly stratified political structure, with a ruling elite who did well and the rest left at the margins in the development process. The economic crisis was illustrated by the rampant shortages of food, which had been a factor since the mid-1990s. The social safety nets that the State had offered in the past were no longer reliable. Civil and political rights were severely constrained due to the repression imposed by the regime, coupled with intimidation and an extensive informant system, creating insecurity among the general population. There was rigid control over the media, and people were not allowed to own mobile phones or computers without permission from the authorities. Access to television and radio programmes was limited. Public executions continued, despite various law reforms in 2004 and 2005. Harsh conditions were imposed by the criminal justice system and torture was committed against people in detention. The authorities had been engaged in abducting nationals of other countries, as Japanese officials had reported to the Rapporteur. The impunity factor had enabled human rights violations to exist for a long time. During the reporting period, the Rapporteur visited Mongolia (15–21 December 2007), Japan (15–19 January) and the Republic of Korea (19–24 January) to assess the impact of the human rights situation in the DPRK on those countries. In Mongolia, there had been an influx of DPRK nationals in search of asylum, and improvements had been made in the facilities sheltering asylum-seekers. Most of them were women and some ended up in exploitative situations, such as forced marriage, before reaching Mongolia, and some had been subjected to human trafficking. In Japan, the Rapporteur discussed the two key challenges facing Japan in relation to the DPRK. In regard to the denuclearization of nuclear facilities, progress had been made in disabling core nuclear facilities at Yongbyon, but not all commitments made at the six-party talks had been met. The abductions issue was also of concern, and 17 Japanese were officially listed as abducted by the DPRK. The Rapporteur called on the DPRK to show a sense of responsibility in addressing the issue of abductions, and he called on the international community to ensure accountability and to influence the country to settle the issue expeditiously. On 4 October 2007, the Republic of Korea and the DPRK adopted the Declaration on the Advancement of South-North Korean Relations, Peace and Prosperity, under which they pledged to cooperate on a variety of issues. Since the Korean war of 1950–1953, the two countries had come together periodically to facilitate the reunion of families separated by the war. There remained the issue of nationals of the Republic of Korea taken as prisoners of war and missing persons taken by the DPRK during and after the war. The Republic of Korea had provided various forms of emergency and humanitarian aid to the DPRK and accepted over 10,000 DPRK nationals for settlement in their search for refuge. The Rapporteur suggested a more comprehensive support system for those who sought refuge.

In his recommendations, the Special Rapporteur called on the DPRK to ensure a more equitable development process; overcome the disparities in access to food and other necessities; modernize its administration of the justice and prison system; help solve the issue of abductions/disappearances; abide by the rule of law; address the root causes leading to refugee outflows; address the problems which gave rise to impunity; and invite the Rapporteur to visit the country to assess the human rights situation. He invited the international community to emphasize the need for participatory and sustainable development in the DPRK while continuing to provide humanitarian aid on the basis that aid had to reach the target groups; respect the rights of refugees, particularly the principle of non-refoulement; maximize dialogue with the DPRK to promote dispute resolution; and ensure a calibrated approach within the United Nations so as to influence the DPRK to respect human rights.

Human Rights Council action. On 27 March [A/63/53 (res. 7/15)], the Human Rights Council, by a recorded vote of 22 to 7, with 18 abstentions, extended the mandate of the Special Rapporteur for one year and invited the Rapporteur to submit regular reports to the Council and the General Assembly. The Council urged the DPRK Government to cooperate fully with the Rapporteur and to respond favourably to his requests to visit the country and to provide him with all necessary information. The Government was urged to ensure safe and unhindered access of humanitarian assistance, delivered impartially on the basis of need.

Further report by Special Rapporteur. The Special Rapporteur, in a 22 August report [A/63/322] transmitted by the Secretary-General to the General Assembly, underlined the systematic nature of human rights transgressions in the country, which were highly visible and substantial. Further progress was made at the six-party talks in July, when the Government agreed to disable its principal nuclear facilities by the end of October and allow on-site inspections as part of the verification process. A cooling tower related to the nuclear reactor at Yongbyon was subsequently demolished. Another development was the resumption of talks between the DPRK and Japan on abducted Japanese nationals, aimed at reopening investigations on unresolved cases. In July, the DPRK acceded to a non-aggression pact with the Association of Southeast Asian Nations. The serious food shortage became more evident in 2008, with reports that millions of people were facing severe deprivations. A new agreement was reached between the authorities and the World Food Programme (WFP) to assist 6.5 million people. WFP reported access to a number of households and county warehouses that had previously been inaccessible, adding that it would need an estimated $500 million in food aid for the next two years to respond to the critical food situation. Following a widespread food security assessment in June, WFP reported that close to three quarters of DPRK households had reduced food intake. In delivering food, the agency was hindered by the Government's requirements of advance notice for planned food monitoring visits, limited access to field operations, and the presence of Government officials during WFP interviews in the field. In the long term, foreign food aid could not replace national food security. In a joint communication of 20 March to the DPRK, the Rapporteur on the human rights situation in the DPRK and other Special Rapporteurs expressed concern about alleged public executions of 15 nationals who were reportedly accused of planning to leave the country to receive economic assistance with the help of relatives living abroad. The DPRK did not reply to a communication of 7 April from the Rapporteur seeking clarification on the whereabouts of 22 DPRK nationals after they reportedly drifted to southern waters in the Western Sea near Yongpyong Island by accident.

The Special Rapporteur reiterated past recommendations to the DPRK and recommended that the country: ensure provision of food and cooperate with UN agencies and others on the issue; end punishment of asylum-seekers returned from abroad; terminate public executions; adopt a policy not to punish those leaving the country without permission; become a party to the conventions of the International Labour Organization and implement them; protect the rights of women, children and other groups; request technical assistance from OHCHR on human rights protection and promotion; and engage with the treaty bodies to which the DPRK was party, with follow-up and access to the country.

Report of Secretary-General. In a 26 August report [A/63/332] on the human rights situation in the DPRK, submitted pursuant to General Assembly resolution 62/167 [YUN 2007, p. 813], the Secretary-General discussed the country's cooperation and status of engagement with international human rights mechanisms such as the treaty bodies, special procedures and the Universal Periodic Review of the Human Rights Council. It outlined the role of OHCHR in assisting the Government in promoting and protecting human rights, and assistance extended by the UN system for promoting and protecting human rights there. The Secretary-General expressed concern at the lack of tangible progress by the Government in addressing the human rights issues raised in the 2007 resolution, and noted that OHCHR had not yet succeeded in engaging the Government in a substantive dialogue on the human rights situation. Regarding the food situation and its impact on the population, the Secretary-General welcomed the Government's efforts to facilitate food aid and promote food sustainability. He advocated the need for it to allocate budget resources and adopt policy measures to alleviate the impact of the food situation, and highlighted the need to prevent discrimination in the distribution of food and health services. The DPRK was urged to sustain cooperation with UN agencies and the international community to support humanitarian efforts. The Secretary-General urged the Government to safeguard fundamental rights and freedoms, fulfil its treaty obligations, comply with international standards, engage in a constructive dialogue with OHCHR, and grant access to the Special Rapporteur. He welcomed the positive developments under the six-party talks and expressed the hope that the United Nations, through gradual cooperation and incremental confidence-building measures, would be able to take on a greater role in helping promote and protect human rights in the country.

GENERAL ASSEMBLY ACTION

On 18 December [meeting 71], the General Assembly, on the recommendation of the Third (Social, Humanitarian and Cultural) Committee [A/63/430/Add.3 & Corr.1], adopted **resolution 63/190** by recorded vote (94-22-63) [agenda item 64 *(c)*].

Situation of human rights in the Democratic People's Republic of Korea

The General Assembly,

Reaffirming that States Members of the United Nations have an obligation to promote and protect human rights and fundamental freedoms and to fulfil the obligations that they have undertaken under the various international instruments,

Mindful that the Democratic People's Republic of Korea is a party to the International Covenant on Civil and Political Rights, the International Covenant on Economic, Social and Cultural Rights, the Convention on the Rights of the Child and the Convention on the Elimination of All Forms of Discrimination against Women,

Noting the submission by the Democratic People's Republic of Korea of its combined third and fourth periodic reports on the implementation of the Convention on the Rights of the Child as a sign of engagement in international cooperative efforts in the field of human rights,

Taking note of the concluding observations of the treaty monitoring bodies under the four treaties to which the Democratic People's Republic of Korea is a party, the most recent of which were given by the Committee on the Elimination of Discrimination against Women in July 2005,

Noting with appreciation the collaboration established between the Government of the Democratic People's Republic of Korea and the United Nations Children's Fund and the World Health Organization in order to improve the health situation in the country, and the collaboration established with the United Nations Children's Fund in order to improve the quality of education for children, as well as the recent request by the Government of the Democratic People's Republic of Korea to the World Food Programme for increased food assistance and the expanded access and improved working conditions granted,

Noting that the Democratic People's Republic of Korea and the United Nations Development Programme have started consultations regarding possible resumption of the activities of the Programme in the country,

Recalling its resolutions 60/173 of 16 December 2005, 61/174 of 19 December 2006 and 62/167 of 18 December 2007, Commission on Human Rights resolutions 2003/10 of 16 April 2003, 2004/13 of 15 April 2004 and 2005/11 of 14 April 2005, Human Rights Council decision 1/102 of 30 June 2006 and Council resolution 7/15 of 27 March 2008, and mindful of the need for the international community to strengthen its coordinated efforts aimed at achieving the implementation of those resolutions,

Taking note of the report of the Special Rapporteur on the situation of human rights in the Democratic People's Republic of Korea, regretting that he was not allowed to visit the country and that he received no cooperation from the authorities of the Democratic People's Republic of Korea, and taking note also of the comprehensive report of the Secretary-General on the situation of human rights in the Democratic People's Republic of Korea submitted in accordance with resolution 62/167,

Noting the importance of the inter-Korean dialogue, which could contribute to the improvement of the human rights and humanitarian situation in the Democratic People's Republic of Korea, including by means of securing access,

1. *Expresses its very serious concern* at:

(a) The persistence of continuing reports of systematic, widespread and grave violations of civil, political, economic, social and cultural rights in the Democratic People's Republic of Korea, including:

(i) Torture and other cruel, inhuman or degrading treatment or punishment, including inhuman conditions of detention, public executions, extrajudicial and arbitrary detention; the absence of due process and the rule of law, including fair trial guarantees and an independent judiciary; the imposition of the death penalty for political and religious reasons; and the existence of a large number of prison camps and the extensive use of forced labour;

(ii) The situation of refugees and asylum-seekers expelled or returned to the Democratic People's Republic of Korea and sanctions imposed on citizens of the Democratic People's Republic of Korea who have been repatriated from abroad, leading to punishments of internment, torture, cruel, inhuman or degrading treatment or the death penalty, and in this regard urges all States to respect the fundamental principle of non-refoulement, to treat those who seek refuge humanely and to ensure unhindered access to the United Nations High Commissioner for Refugees and his Office, with a view to improving the situation of those who seek refuge;

(iii) All-pervasive and severe restrictions on the freedoms of thought, conscience, religion, opinion and expression, peaceful assembly and association, and on equal access to information, by such means as the persecution of individuals exercising their freedom of opinion and expression, and their families;

(iv) Limitations imposed on every person who wishes to move freely within the country and travel abroad, including the punishment of those who leave or try to leave the country without permission, or their families, as well as punishment of persons who are returned by other countries;

(v) The violations of economic, social and cultural rights, which have led to severe malnutrition, widespread health problems and other hardship for the population in the Democratic People's Republic of Korea, in particular for persons belonging to vulnerable groups, inter alia, women, children and the elderly;

(vi) Continuing violation of the human rights and fundamental freedoms of women, in particular the trafficking of women for the purpose of prostitution or forced marriage and the subjection of women to human smuggling, forced abortions, gender-based discrimination and violence;

(vii) Continuing reports of violations of the human rights and fundamental freedoms of persons with disabilities, especially on the use of collective camps and of coercive measures that target the rights of persons with disabilities to decide freely and responsibly on the number and spacing of their children;

(viii) Violations of workers' rights, including the right to freedom of association and collective bargaining, the right to strike as defined by the obligations of the Democratic People's Republic of Korea under the International Covenant on Economic, Social and Cultural Rights, and the prohibition of the economic exploitation of children and of any harmful or hazardous work of children as defined by the obligations of the Democratic People's Republic of Korea under the Convention on the Rights of the Child;

(b) The continued refusal of the Government of the Democratic People's Republic of Korea to recognize the mandate of the Special Rapporteur on the situation of human rights in the Democratic People's Republic of Korea or to extend cooperation to him, despite the renewal of the mandate by the Human Rights Council in its resolution 7/15;

2. *Reiterates its very serious concern* at unresolved questions of international concern relating to the abduction of foreigners in the form of enforced disappearance, which violates the human rights of the nationals of other sovereign countries, and in this regard strongly calls upon the Government of the Democratic People's Republic of Korea urgently to resolve these questions, including through existing channels, in a transparent manner, including by ensuring the immediate return of abductees;

3. *Expresses its very deep concern*, while noting the willingness to seek humanitarian assistance, at the precarious humanitarian situation in the country, compounded by the misallocation of resources away from the satisfaction of basic needs and by frequent natural disasters, in particular the prevalence of maternal malnutrition and of infant malnutrition, which, despite recent progress, continues to affect the physical and mental development of a significant proportion of children, and urges the Government of the Democratic People's Republic of Korea, in this regard, to take preventive and remedial action;

4. *Commends* the Special Rapporteur for the activities undertaken so far and for his continued efforts in the conduct of his mandate despite the limited access to information;

5. *Strongly urges* the Government of the Democratic People's Republic of Korea to respect fully all human rights and fundamental freedoms and, in this regard:

(a) To immediately put an end to the systematic, widespread and grave violations of human rights mentioned above, inter alia, by implementing fully the measures set out in the above-mentioned resolutions of the General Assembly, the Commission on Human Rights and the Human Rights Council, and the recommendations addressed to the Democratic People's Republic of Korea by the United Nations special procedures and treaty bodies;

(b) To protect its inhabitants, address the issue of impunity and ensure that those responsible for violations of human rights are brought to justice before an independent judiciary;

(c) To tackle the root causes leading to refugee outflows and prosecute those who exploit refugees by human smuggling, trafficking and extortion, while not criminalizing the victims, and to ensure that citizens of the Democratic People's Republic of Korea expelled or returned to the Democratic People's Republic of Korea are able to return in safety and dignity, are humanely treated and are not subjected to any kind of punishment;

(d) To extend its full cooperation to the Special Rapporteur, including by granting him full, free and unimpeded access to the Democratic People's Republic of Korea, and to other United Nations human rights mechanisms;

(e) To engage in technical cooperation activities in the field of human rights with the United Nations High Commissioner for Human Rights and her Office, as pursued by the High Commissioner in recent years, with a view to improving the situation of human rights in the country, and to

prepare for the universal periodic review of the Democratic People's Republic of Korea by the Human Rights Council, which will be conducted in 2009;

(f) To engage in cooperation with the International Labour Organization with a view to significantly improving workers' rights;

(g) To continue and reinforce its cooperation with United Nations humanitarian agencies;

(h) To ensure full, safe and unhindered access to humanitarian aid and take measures to allow humanitarian agencies to secure its impartial delivery to all parts of the country on the basis of need in accordance with humanitarian principles, as it pledged to do, and to ensure access to adequate food and implement food security policies, including through sustainable agriculture;

6. *Decides* to continue its examination of the situation of human rights in the Democratic People's Republic of Korea at its sixty-fourth session, and to this end requests the Secretary-General to submit a comprehensive report on the situation in the Democratic People's Republic of Korea and the Special Rapporteur to continue to report his findings and recommendations.

RECORDED VOTE ON RESOLUTION 63/190:

In favour: Afghanistan, Albania, Andorra, Argentina, Australia, Austria, Bahamas, Bahrain, Bangladesh, Belgium, Belize, Bhutan, Bosnia and Herzegovina, Botswana, Bulgaria, Burundi, Canada, Chile, Comoros, Costa Rica, Croatia, Cyprus, Czech Republic, Denmark, El Salvador, Eritrea, Estonia, Fiji, Finland, France, Georgia, Germany, Ghana, Greece, Guinea-Bissau, Honduras, Hungary, Iceland, Iraq, Ireland, Israel, Italy, Japan, Kazakhstan, Kiribati, Latvia, Lebanon, Liberia, Liechtenstein, Lithuania, Luxembourg, Madagascar, Malawi, Maldives, Malta, Marshall Islands, Mexico, Micronesia, Moldova, Monaco, Montenegro, Morocco, Nauru, Netherlands, New Zealand, Norway, Palau, Panama, Papua New Guinea, Paraguay, Peru, Poland, Portugal, Republic of Korea, Romania, Saint Lucia, Samoa, San Marino, Saudi Arabia, Slovakia, Slovenia, Spain, Sweden, Switzerland, The former Yugoslav Republic of Macedonia, Timor-Leste, Togo, Turkey, Ukraine, United Kingdom, United Republic of Tanzania, United States, Uruguay, Vanuatu.

Against: Algeria, Belarus, China, Cuba, Democratic People's Republic of Korea, Egypt, Guinea, Indonesia, Iran, Libyan Arab Jamahiriya, Malaysia, Myanmar, Oman, Russian Federation, Somalia, Sri Lanka, Sudan, Syrian Arab Republic, Uzbekistan, Venezuela, Viet Nam, Zimbabwe.

Abstaining: Angola, Antigua and Barbuda, Azerbaijan, Barbados, Benin, Bolivia, Brazil, Brunei Darussalam, Burkina Faso, Cambodia, Cameroon, Cape Verde, Central African Republic, Chad, Colombia, Congo, Côte d'Ivoire, Dominica, Dominican Republic, Ecuador, Ethiopia, Gambia, Grenada, Guatemala, Guyana, Haiti, India, Jamaica, Jordan, Kenya, Kuwait, Kyrgyzstan, Lao People's Democratic Republic, Lesotho, Mali, Mauritania, Mauritius, Mozambique, Namibia, Nepal, Nicaragua, Niger, Nigeria, Pakistan, Philippines, Qatar, Rwanda, Saint Kitts and Nevis, Saint Vincent and the Grenadines, Sao Tome and Principe, Senegal, Singapore, Solomon Islands, South Africa, Suriname, Swaziland, Tajikistan, Thailand, Turkmenistan, Uganda, United Arab Emirates, Yemen, Zambia.

Iran

Report of Secretary-General. In a 1 October report [A/63/459] submitted to the General Assembly pursuant to resolution 62/168 [YUN 2007, p. 815], the Secretary-General described the situation of human rights in Iran. The report was intended to reflect the broader patterns and trends in the human rights situation in Iran on the basis of that country's international treaty obligations and the observations made by treaty monitoring bodies and the special procedures of the Human Rights Council. It reviewed the legal and institutional framework; positive developments as well as protection gaps in economic, social and cultural rights; thematic issues in civil and political rights identified in the Assembly resolution, in particular concerns raised by the international human rights mechanisms; and an overview of the country's cooperation with OHCHR and international human rights mechanisms, including in the areas of treaty ratification and reporting and interaction with the special procedures, including in-country missions. While the 1979 Constitution guaranteed a wide range of human rights and fundamental freedoms, in practice there were a number of impediments to the full protection of human rights and the independent functioning of the different institutions of the State. Iran had made gains over the previous decade or more in economic, social and cultural rights, although significant disparities remained between urban centres and less developed regions. Its per capita income had increased, improvements had been made in education, and health care had been expanded. Human rights activists had increased their activities. The authorities had taken some steps to address discriminatory laws and restrict aspects of the death penalty. Among negative trends was an increase in rights violations targeting women, university students, teachers, workers and activist groups. The independent media had experienced tightened restrictions. The death penalty continued to be widely applied, and there were some cases of stoning and public execution despite moves by the authorities to curb such practices. Cases of flogging and amputation and suspicious deaths and suicides of prisoners in custody were also reported.

The Secretary-General encouraged the Government to address the concerns highlighted in the report and to continue to revise national laws, particularly the new Penal Code and juvenile justice laws, to ensure compliance with international human rights standards and prevent discriminatory practices against women, ethnic and religious minorities and other minority groups. The Secretary-General noted the positive achievements of Iran against many economic and social indicators and encouraged the Government to address regional disparities in the enjoyment of rights. He welcomed the Government's steps to explore cooperation on human rights and justice reform with the United Nations, including OHCHR. He encouraged Iran to ratify major international human rights treaties and to withdraw the general reservations it had made on the signature and ratification of various treaties. The Secretary-General hoped that Iran would finalize its long-outstanding periodic reports under human rights treaties to allow a systematic review of progress in implementing the related obligations. He welcomed the Government's standing invitation to the Human Rights Council special procedures mandate holders and encouraged the Government to facilitate their visits to the country in order that they might conduct more comprehensive assessments.

Communication. In a 3 November letter to the Secretary-General [A/C.3/63/6], Iran transmitted an account of its policies and practices on promoting and protecting human rights. Outlining the human rights enshrined in its Constitution, Iran stated that the rules and principles of its judicial system were equally applicable to all individuals irrespective of gender, religion or ethnicity. Those principles included the rule of law; independence of the judiciary; presumption of innocence unless guilt had been established by a competent court; the right to open trials unless the trial would be detrimental to public morality; the right to a jury trial for political and press offences; and the right to defence counsel. In addition, Iran had many laws promoting political and civil rights and had taken practical steps to implement them. It also provided for the economic, social and cultural rights of the people. In addition to having its own national human rights institutions, Iran cooperated with international human rights mechanisms and with UN treaty bodies. Iran was making unprecedented strides into the new historical stage of democracy, prosperity and the rule of law. The Government had accorded priority to human rights promotion and protection and had undertaken all necessary measures to ensure the enjoyment of all human rights.

GENERAL ASSEMBLY ACTION

On 18 December [meeting 71], the General Assembly, on the recommendation of the Third Committee [A/63/430/Add.3 & Corr.1], adopted **resolution 63/191** by recorded vote (69-54-57) [agenda item 64 *(c)*].

Situation of human rights in the Islamic Republic of Iran

The General Assembly,

Guided by the Charter of the United Nations, as well as the Universal Declaration of Human Rights, the International Covenants on Human Rights and other international human rights instruments,

Recalling its previous resolutions on the situation of human rights in the Islamic Republic of Iran, the most recent of which is resolution 62/168 of 18 December 2007,

1. *Takes note* of the report of the Secretary-General submitted pursuant to its resolution 62/168, which highlights a broad range of serious human rights violations, legal and institutional gaps and impediments to the protection of human rights and which discusses some positive developments in a few areas;

2. *Expresses its deep concern* at serious human rights violations in the Islamic Republic of Iran relating to, inter alia:

(a) Torture and cruel, inhuman or degrading treatment or punishment, including flogging and amputations;

(b) The continuing high incidence of executions carried out in the absence of internationally recognized safeguards, including public executions and executions of juveniles;

(c) Persons in prison who continue to face sentences of execution by stoning;

(d) Arrests, violent repression and sentencing of women exercising their right to peaceful assembly, a campaign of intimidation against women's human rights defenders, and continuing discrimination against women and girls in law and in practice;

(e) Increasing discrimination and other human rights violations against persons belonging to religious, ethnic, linguistic or other minorities, recognized or otherwise, including, inter alia, Arabs, Azeris, Baluchis, Kurds, Christians, Jews, Sufis and Sunni Muslims and their defenders, and, in particular, attacks on Baha'is and their faith in State-sponsored media, increasing evidence of efforts by the State to identify and monitor Baha'is, preventing members of the Baha'i faith from attending university and from sustaining themselves economically, and the arrest and detention of seven Baha'i leaders without charge or access to legal representation;

(f) Ongoing, systemic and serious restrictions of freedom of peaceful assembly and association and freedom of opinion and expression, including those imposed on the media, Internet users and trade unions, and increasing harassment, intimidation and persecution of political opponents and human rights defenders from all sectors of Iranian society, including arrests and violent repression of labour leaders, labour members peacefully assembling and students, in particular with regard to the 2008 Majles electoral process;

(g) Severe limitations and restrictions on freedom of religion and belief, including the provision in the proposed draft penal code that sets out a mandatory death sentence for apostasy;

(h) Persistent failure to uphold due process of law rights, and violation of the rights of detainees, including the systematic and arbitrary use of prolonged solitary confinement;

3. *Calls upon* the Government of the Islamic Republic of Iran to address the substantive concerns highlighted in the report of the Secretary-General and the specific calls to action found in previous resolutions of the General Assembly, and to respect fully its human rights obligations, in law and in practice, in particular:

(a) To eliminate, in law and in practice, amputations, flogging and other forms of torture and other cruel, inhuman or degrading treatment or punishment;

(b) To abolish, in law and in practice, public executions and other executions carried out in the absence of respect for internationally recognized safeguards;

(c) To abolish, pursuant to its obligations under article 37 of the Convention on the Rights of the Child and article 6 of the International Covenant on Civil and Political Rights, executions of persons who at the time of their offence were under the age of 18;

(d) To abolish the use of stoning as a method of execution;

(e) To eliminate, in law and in practice, all forms of discrimination and other human rights violations against women and girls;

(f) To eliminate, in law and in practice, all forms of discrimination and other human rights violations against persons belonging to religious, ethnic, linguistic or other minorities, recognized or otherwise, to refrain from monitoring individuals on the basis of their religious beliefs, and to ensure that access of minorities to education and employment is on par with that of all Iranians;

(g) To implement, inter alia, the 1996 report of the Special Rapporteur on religious intolerance, which recommended ways in which the Islamic Republic of Iran could emancipate the Baha'i community;

(h) To end the harassment, intimidation and persecution of political opponents and human rights defenders, including by releasing persons imprisoned arbitrarily or on the basis of their political views;

(i) To uphold due process of law rights and to end impunity for human rights violations;

4. *Notes* the positive, though limited, gains, developments and steps discussed in the report of the Secretary-General, but remains concerned that many such steps have yet to be implemented in law or in practice;

5. *Further calls upon* the Government of the Islamic Republic of Iran to redress its inadequate record of cooperation with international human rights mechanisms by, inter alia, reporting pursuant to its obligations to the treaty bodies of the instruments to which it is a party and cooperating fully with all international human rights mechanisms, including facilitating visits to its territory of special procedures mandate holders, and encourages the Government of the Islamic Republic of Iran to continue exploring cooperation on human rights and justice reform with the United Nations, including the Office of the United Nations High Commissioner for Human Rights;

6. *Requests* an update from the Secretary-General on the situation of human rights in the Islamic Republic of Iran, including its cooperation with international human rights mechanisms, at its sixty-fourth session;

7. *Decides* to continue its examination of the situation of human rights in the Islamic Republic of Iran at its sixty-fourth session under the item entitled "Promotion and protection of human rights".

RECORDED VOTE ON RESOLUTION 63/191:

In favour: Albania, Andorra, Argentina, Australia, Austria, Bahamas, Belgium, Bosnia and Herzegovina, Botswana, Bulgaria, Canada, Chile, Costa Rica, Croatia, Cyprus, Czech Republic, Denmark, El Salvador, Estonia, Fiji, Finland, France, Germany, Greece, Honduras, Hungary, Iceland, Ireland, Israel, Italy, Japan, Kiribati, Latvia, Liberia, Liechtenstein, Lithuania, Luxembourg, Malta, Marshall Islands, Mexico, Micronesia, Moldova, Monaco, Montenegro, Nauru, Netherlands, New Zealand, Norway, Palau, Panama, Peru, Poland, Portugal, Romania, Saint Lucia, Samoa, San Marino, Slovakia, Slovenia, Spain, Sweden, Switzerland, The former Yugoslav Republic of Macedonia, Timor-Leste, Tuvalu, Ukraine, United Kingdom, United States, Vanuatu.

Against: Afghanistan, Algeria, Armenia, Azerbaijan, Bahrain, Bangladesh, Belarus, Belize, China, Comoros, Congo, Cuba, Democratic People's Republic of Korea, Ecuador, Egypt, Eritrea, Gambia, Guinea, India, Indonesia, Iran, Kazakhstan, Kuwait, Kyrgyzstan, Lebanon, Libyan Arab Jamahiriya, Malawi, Malaysia, Mauritania, Morocco, Myanmar, Nicaragua, Niger, Oman, Pakistan, Qatar, Russian Federation, Saudi Arabia, Senegal, Serbia, Somalia, South Africa, Sri Lanka, Sudan, Syrian Arab Republic, Tajikistan, Togo, Tunisia, Turkmenistan, Uzbekistan, Venezuela, Viet Nam, Yemen, Zimbabwe.

Abstaining: Angola, Antigua and Barbuda, Barbados, Benin, Bhutan, Bolivia, Brazil, Brunei Darussalam, Burkina Faso, Burundi, Cameroon, Cape Verde, Central African Republic, Chad, Colombia, Côte d'Ivoire, Dominica, Dominican Republic, Ethiopia, Georgia, Ghana, Grenada, Guatemala, Guinea-Bissau, Guyana, Haiti, Jamaica, Jordan, Kenya, Lao People's Democratic Republic, Lesotho, Mali, Mauritius, Mongolia, Mozambique, Namibia, Nepal, Nigeria, Papua New Guinea, Paraguay, Philippines, Republic of Korea, Rwanda, Saint Kitts and Nevis, Saint Vincent and the Grenadines, Sao Tome and Principe, Sierra Leone, Singapore, Solomon Islands, Suriname, Swaziland, Thailand, Uganda, United Arab Emirates, United Republic of Tanzania, Uruguay, Zambia.

Myanmar

Reports of Special Rapporteur. The Special Rapporteur on the situation of human rights in Myanmar, Paulo Sérgio Pinheiro (Brazil), issued two reports on 7 March. In the first report [A/HRC/7/18], submitted in accordance with Human Rights Council resolution S-5/1 [YUN 2007, p. 663], the Rapporteur focused on the main patterns of human rights violations committed from February 2007 to February 2008. Having been denied permission by the Government to visit the country between November 2003 and November 2007, the Rapporteur was invited to conduct a five-day mission in November 2007 [ibid., p. 818], after which he reported to the Council; however, he was not permitted to return for a follow-up mission as the Council had requested. On the basis of independent and reliable sources, he reported that changes were taking place in the country as a result of political and economic developments, including the planned adoption of a new Constitution that would redefine the political structures. The Government announced on 9 February that it would hold a referendum on the new Constitution in May 2008 and multi-party democratic elections in 2010. The Special Rapporteur joined the Secretary-General in his call to the authorities to engage in a dialogue with the General Secretary of the National League for Democracy (NLD), Daw Aung San Suu Kyi, and other relevant parties to the national reconciliation process. Despite the declaration of good intentions, the detention of political opposition leaders continued. In October 2007, there were allegations of the use of force on citizens to participate in pro-Government rallies in support of the constitutional process. In November 2007, the authorities informed the Rapporteur that a 20-member human rights group had been established. According to reports, there were marked signs of deterioration in the economic and social sector in such areas as food supply, health services and education. There continued to be some reports of forced labour, mostly by local authorities for public infrastructure work. The authorities continued to impose restrictions on the freedoms of movement, expression, association and assembly. A culture of non-accountability in human rights violations obstructed the rule of law and the administration of justice, and the judiciary provided a legal basis for abuses of power and exoneration for those responsible for violations. Under vaguely worded security laws, the authorities for years had justified the imprisonment of hundreds on the basis that they were causing "unrest". Access to and control over land and natural resources had been central to the political economy, and in many areas populated by ethnic minorities, forced displacement had been a fact of life for generations. The majority of new incidents of internal displacement and forced migration were concentrated in north-east Karen State and adjacent areas of Pegu Division, which were still subject to armed conflict. In October 2007, sources estimated the number of internally displaced persons in eastern Myanmar to be 503,000, including 295,000 people in ceasefire zones, 99,000 hiding in the jungle and 109,000 elsewhere in Myanmar. The Rapporteur was concerned about the intensified military campaigns in ethnic areas and their impact on the humanitarian and human rights situation. That situation was connected with the widespread practice of land confiscation throughout the country, seemingly aimed at anchoring military control, especially in ethnic areas. It had led to forced evictions, relocations and resettlements, forced migration and internal displacement. Many ethnic minorities living along areas bordering Thailand were vulnerable; most armed ethnic groups had either agreed to ceasefires with the Government or been reduced to exhausted remnants in the jungle. As at 15 February, the Office of the United Nations High Commissioner for Refugees estimated the population of refugees from Myanmar in Thailand at 130,241. In Karen State, over 40,000 villagers had reportedly been internally displaced and thousands rendered homeless due to an increased army presence. In the northern Rakhine State (Arakan), Sunni Muslim returnees were subjected to political, economic, religious and social repression. The estimated 728,000 Muslim residents had been denied citizenship under the 1982 citizenship law, effectively rendering them stateless. The Government had included Muslim residents as part of its national documentation programme, initially providing 35,000 persons in northern Arakan State with identity documents (temporary registration certificates). While noting the importance of that process, the Rapporteur expressed concern that the certificates could not be used to claim citizenship, nor could they be seen as a long-term solution. He encouraged the Government to change its citizenship law. Concern was also expressed at recent reports of human rights violations in Kayin State, including killings, attacks on civilians and forced displacement.

In his recommendations, the Special Rapporteur called on the Government to: release all political prisoners at risk; resume dialogue with all political actors, with a view to including their contribution to drafting a new Constitution; secure the rights of freedom of opinion and expression, and peaceful association; end the prosecution of political and human rights activists; eliminate discriminatory practices against ethnic groups; seek international technical assistance in establishing an independent judiciary; improve prison conditions; authorize access to conflict-affected areas by the United Nations and associated personnel; put an end to the recruitment of child soldiers; and end impunity of officials who committed human rights abuses. The international community was called on to provide humanitarian assistance and support for health, education and human rights, and to engage in dialogue with the Government on an adequate response to the conflict situation in eastern Myanmar.

In his second report of 7 March [A/HRC/7/24], submitted in response to a Human Rights Council request in 2007 [ibid., p. 819], the Special Rapporteur, following up on his report on the human rights implications of the crackdown on the peaceful demonstrations in Myanmar in September 2007 [ibid., p. 818], covered the period from December 2007 to March 2008. Following the demonstrations, thousands of people were arrested in September and October, and between 500 and 1,000 were still being detained by the end of the year. There were reports of an ongoing trend to arrest individuals who had any relation with the organization of the demonstrations, and of State surveillance of monasteries and monks, many of whom had participated in the demonstrations. On 4 December, the Rapporteur transmitted to the Government a letter containing three lists—of those believed to be detained (653), killed (16 in addition to the names of 15 dead provided by the authorities) or disappeared (75), and requested information on their cases. No information was received. Some 70 individuals were reportedly arrested between 15 November 2007 and 18 February 2008 in connection with their involvement with the demonstrations, and 62 were reportedly still detained at the time of the report. Freedom of expression had been further curtailed, as seen by the arrest of journalists and the banning of media. The Rapporteur received information regarding the arrests and searching of activists. He had received the names of 718 individuals arrested between August 2007 and February 2008 who were still being detained, including the 93 individuals confirmed by the Government during the Rapporteur's mission in November 2007. The arrests ongoing since September 2007 had reportedly not been carried out in accordance with the criminal procedure. A number of people had reportedly been arrested without warrant and detained in unknown locations. After interrogation, some had been released and some sent to prison in Yangon and charged. At the time of the report, 145 detainees had been charged under various laws, while others were being unlawfully detained. The Rapporteur took note of 75 persons who were reported missing by a number of sources and were still unaccounted for. Detention conditions in Yangon's Insein prison remained appalling. The International Committee of the Red Cross (ICRC) had been denied access to detention centres.

Among his recommendations, the Special Rapporteur called on the Government to secure the physical and psychological integrity of all persons in custody; reveal the whereabouts of those detained or missing; provide information to the families of the deceased; bring the perpetrators of human rights violations to justice; ensure access by ICRC and other humanitarian personnel to all detainees; release all persons taken into custody for peaceful assembly or peaceful expression of political beliefs; grant amnesty to people sentenced for such charges; conduct an independent investigation into cases of killings, beatings, hostage-taking, torture and disappearance; ban militias as illegal groups; engage in a constructive dialogue with the Human Rights Council and its special procedures, especially the Rapporteur; and ensure a follow-up mission of the Rapporteur to further investigate the September events. Other recommendations concerned transitional measures for the Government: opening a channel for follow-up communications and cooperation with the Rapporteur and provision for regular access to Myanmar; the release of all political prisoners under a plan of action; pursuit of dialogue with Daw Aung San Suu Kyi through Government officials; repeal or amendment of laws in relation to the rights of peaceful assembly, freedom of expression, freedom of movement, and prison regulations; and seeking technical assistance to repeal or amend the Penal Code and Code of Criminal Procedure, and to review the rules governing the policing of demonstrations.

Communication. In a 10 March note [A/HRC/7/G/8] to the Human Rights Council, Myanmar commented on the Rapporteur's two latest reports on the country's human rights situation (see above), both of which it viewed as intrusive, highly politicized and strident. The Government found the reports neither balanced nor objective; they contained many unfounded allegations originating from insurgents and anti-Government groups. Myanmar had adopted a seven-step road map to democracy in 2003, which had been initiated in 2004 with the holding of the National Convention, an all-inclusive forum. As at 30 January, the Minister for Relations had held five meetings with Daw Aung San Suu Kyi. Thus, Myanmar was moving towards a new democratic society. Despite those achievements, the Rapporteur had been critical of the road map and political progress, thus acting beyond his mandate. Myanmar described its recent efforts in economic and social development, health, education, and reducing forced labour, and claimed that many of the allegations concerning denial of freedom of association and expression, lack of independence in the judicial system, sexual violence against women, repression of displaced persons, and forced evictions and migrations were untrue.

Human Rights Council action. On 28 March [A/63/53 (res. 7/31)], the Council, deploring the ongoing systematic violations of human rights and fundamental freedoms of the people of Myanmar, urged the Government to receive a follow-up mission by the Rapporteur, to cooperate with him, and to implement his recommendations. It called on the authorities to: make the constitutional process fully inclusive, participatory and transparent; engage in a national dialogue with all parties with a view to achieving national reconciliation, democratization and the establishment of the rule of law; ensure basic freedoms and desist from further denial of freedoms such as expression, assembly and religion; cooperate with humanitarian organizations and ensure their access to persons in need; end violations of human rights and humanitarian law, including forced displacement and arbitrary detention; and release all political prisoners. The Council also requested the Rapporteur to report on the implementation of its 2007 resolutions [YUN 2007, pp. 818 & 819] at its next session.

Also on 28 March [A/63/53 (res. 7/32)], the Council extended the Special Rapporteur's mandate for one year and requested the Rapporteur to report to the Council and the General Assembly.

Report of Special Rapporteur. On 26 March, Tomás Ojea Quintana (Argentina) was appointed as the new Special Rapporteur on the situation of human rights in Myanmar; he assumed the function on 1 May. As requested by the Council, he issued a 3 June report [A/HRC/8/12], which focused on the human rights issues pertinent to the constitutional process, developments with regard to the crackdown on the 2007 demonstrations, and the human rights impact of Cyclone Nargis, which struck Myanmar on 2 and 3 May, killing more than 77,000 people. On 19 February, the finalization of the draft Constitution, the fourth step in the Government's seven-step road map to democracy, was announced; a referendum on its adoption was scheduled for 10 May, and multi-party democratic elections for 2010. The people of Myanmar had not voted since 1990. Copies of the 457-article draft Constitution were made public on 9 April and put on sale in bookshops for $1 a copy, a price that was reportedly unaffordable for a significant proportion of the population. Rejecting the recommendation of the Special Adviser, Ibrahim Gambari, Myanmar declined to invite international observers for the referendum. The Government decided to go ahead as scheduled, except in 40 towns in Yangon Division and 7 towns in Irrawaddy Division, devastated by the cyclone, where the referendum would be held on 24 May. Before those 47 towns voted, the Government announced that the draft Constitution had been approved by 92.4 per cent of the 22 million eligible voters. The NLD, under the leadership of General Secretary Daw Aung San Suu Kyi, dismissed the referendum, stating that it was not inclusive and was unclear. The lack of participation in the drafting process, the small degree of transparency, the limited public knowledge about its contents, and the conditions under which the referendum was held all raised concerns. The Rapporteur received allegations regarding the arrest, detention and charges against individuals who had expressed opposition to the referendum and draft Constitution, particularly in Yangon and Mandalay. The reported number of political prisoners as at 20 May was 1,900. Detention conditions in prisons were appalling. Daw Aung San Suu Kyi, having been charged in 2003 with acts against peace and order and making speeches against the Government, remained under house arrest.

The Special Rapporteur concluded that no improvement had been made and critical issues still had to be addressed. In addition to recommendations made by the previous Rapporteur, he called on Myanmar to: set up a mechanism to establish the whereabouts of those reportedly subjected to forced disappearance during and after the crackdown of September 2007; prepare a public report on how the referendum was conducted and the lessons learned; continue to uphold the agreements made by the Secretary-General to allow international humanitarian workers and supplies unhindered access to the country and particularly to the areas affected by Cyclone Nargis; and cooperate with the Rapporteur, accepting his requests for visits.

Human Rights Council action. On 18 June [A/63/53 (res. 8/14)], the Council, condemning the systematic violations of human rights of the people of Myanmar, urged the Government to desist from further politically motivated arrests and release all political prisoners. It called on the Government to implement commitments it had made to the Secretary-General on granting access by relief workers to all those in need; to cooperate with humanitarian organizations, in particular in the Irrawaddy Delta; to refrain from sending people back to areas where they could not have access to emergency relief; and to ensure that return was voluntary. The Government was urged to end discrimination and protect civil, political, economic, social and cultural rights, and, in particular, to comply with its human rights obligations under international conventions in regard to women and children. The Council condemned the recruitment of child soldiers into Government armed forces and armed groups, and it called for an independent investigation into all reports of human rights violations. It called on the Government to engage in a real process of dialogue and national reconciliation with the participation of representatives of all parties and ethnic groups who had been excluded from the political process. The Council urged the Government to receive the Rapporteur and to cooperate fully with him, and requested the Rapporteur to report on the fulfilment of his mandate.

Report of Special Rapporteur. By a 5 September note [A/63/341], the Secretary-General transmitted to the General Assembly the report of the Rapporteur, in accordance with resolution 62/222 [YUN 2007, p. 819]. Having requested a visit to Myanmar from 3 to 13 August, the Rapporteur received a response from the Government that he was invited to undertake a mission from 3 to 7 August. He considered the visit to be fruitful, since the objective was to establish positive working relations with the authorities and meet with civil society and with those who did not enjoy fundamental rights. Since Myanmar had conducted the referendum on the new Constitution, the next step in the road map for national reconciliation and democratic transition was the election in 2010. During his visit, the Rapporteur was informed by the Commission for Holding the Referendum that free campaigning either in favour or against the approval of the Constitution was not permitted. When he asked about the possibility of the Government issuing a report on how the referendum had been held, as recommended in his report to the Human Rights Council, the response was that all relevant information had already been released. The prospect of the country becoming a democratic State would depend on each of the remaining steps of the road map being conducted in a democratic and inclusive manner. The Rapporteur, noting that a number of domestic laws did not comply with constitutional provisions, called for the revision of such laws. The Rapporteur received reliable reports of new arrests of political and civil rights activists. As at 10 August, some 2,000 such activists were in detention. Provisions of the law on the referendum had called into question the openness of the environment in which the referendum was held, given the fact that opposition to the referendum was proscribed. In the lead-up to the 2010 election, a number of legal reforms were required for a genuine democratic election, such as ways to guarantee respect for the anonymity of voters, free campaigning by candidates and free access by voters to information. The situation of NLD General Secretary Daw Aung San Suu Kyi was a matter of concern, as the Government in May extended her house arrest beyond the five-year limit provided for by law, with no new evidence against her. In his meetings with relevant authorities, the Rapporteur reiterated the right to legal counsel. He noted that thereafter, she met with her lawyer after five years, and reportedly met her lawyer again to discuss a lawsuit against her continuing detention. During his mission, the Rapporteur met with a number of activists, and he received allegations that proceedings against prisoners of conscience did not respect basic guarantees such as the right to counsel, and that courts lacked independence and impartiality. There were still 700 individuals detained as a consequence of the crackdown on the September 2007 demonstrations. Accountability for those human rights violations was still pending, demonstrating the vulnerability of the freedoms of opinion, expression and peaceful assembly. The protection of civilians and ethnic minorities remained a concern. Information was received concerning a large number of internally displaced persons in northern Kayin State, as well as allegations about civilians being forcibly used by the military as porters, and violence against unarmed civilians. As at July, the population of refugees from Myanmar in Thailand was estimated at 131,000. Concern was also expressed about the situation of a Muslim community in the border area of Northern Rakhine State that had been deprived of citizenship. As a result of Cyclone Nargis in May, human rights problems arose related to internally displaced persons and their access to food, shelter, health care, water and sanitation facilities. Malnutrition remained a problem and the rate for children was 32 per cent. The Rapporteur continued to receive allegations of arbitrary land confiscation throughout the country.

In his recommendations to the Government, the Special Rapporteur proposed four core human rights elements to pave the road to democracy: a review of national legislation in accordance with the new Constitution and international obligations; a progressive release of prisoners of conscience; a transition from a rule by armed forces to governance by a multiparty democratic and civil government; and an independent and impartial judiciary.

Report of Secretary-General. The Secretary-General, having designated his Special Adviser, Ibrahim Gambari, to continue his good offices in promoting national reconciliation in Myanmar on his behalf (see p. 421), reported on 17 September [A/63/356] on the human rights situation, pursuant to General Assembly resolution 62/222 [YUN 2007, p. 819]. The Special Adviser visited Myanmar three times—in November 2007 and in March and August 2008—and engaged with representatives of the Government and the opposition on reconciliation, restoration of democracy and respect for human rights. His efforts focused on five key areas: the release of all political prisoners, including Daw Aung San Suu Kyi; the need for a substantive and time-bound dialogue; an inclusive political transition to civilian and democratic government; avenues for improving socio-economic conditions; and ways to regularize mutual engagement and cooperation through the good offices process. The Secretary-General described the good offices as a process that required sustained engagement through regular visits and consultations with all concerned on political, human rights, humanitarian and socio-economic issues. The international community needed to work together in support of the goals of the good offices. The report mentioned the five meetings of Daw Aung San Suu Kyi with the Minister for Relations between November 2007 and January 2008—the first attempt at a dialogue between her and the Government since 2003. In addition, for the first time in four years, she was allowed to meet twice with the Central Executive Committee of NLD. However, by March those meetings had been discontinued. In the wake of Cyclone Nargis, following which an estimated 140,000 people were believed to be dead or missing, the Secretary-General visited Myanmar on 22 and 23 May. Following his discussions with Government officials, access for international aid workers was facilitated after Myanmar's initial reluctance to grant access. The Secretary-General and the Special Adviser had emphasized that only a credible and inclusive political process could advance the prospects of durable peace, national reconciliation, democracy and respect for human rights. In that regard, the Secretary-General welcomed the support of neighbouring countries and the Association of Southeast Asian Nations for his good offices and the work of his Special Adviser. While the spirit of cooperation between Myanmar and the United Nations had been marked by improvement in recent months, it remained a source of frustration that meaningful steps with tangible results had yet to be taken by the authorities in response to the concerns and expectations of the United Nations and the international community in the context of the good offices process. In particular, concern was expressed that the international community had not been involved in monitoring the referendum vote, nor had the Government considered the proposal to establish a broad-based national economic forum. The fact that Daw Aung San Suu Kyi did not meet with the Special Adviser during his August visit, as arranged by the Government, was a source of disappointment, although the Special Adviser did meet with the NLD Central Executive Committee. On 23 September, the Government announced the amnesty release of a number of prisoners, including several political prisoners, notably Myanmar's longest-serving prisoner of conscience, U Win Tin, and other senior NLD members. Although the Government had reached ceasefire agreements with most armed ethnic groups, those agreements had not yet been finalized to meet political and socio-economic aspirations, including formalizing disarmament plans and ensuring the full participation of ethnic nationality representatives in the national political process. Ultimately, the future of Myanmar rested with the Government and people, while the UN role was to ascertain the positions of all parties and facilitate their efforts to work together towards a mutually acceptable process of national reconciliation and democratization, in full respect of Myanmar's sovereignty. It was time for the Government and opposition alike to find ways to talk to each other and work together in the interest of the nation.

Communication. On 17 October [A/C.3/63/4], Myanmar transmitted to the Secretary-General a memorandum on the human rights situation. Outlining some political background and recent developments, Myanmar presented statistics on the relief efforts in the aftermath of Cyclone Nargis, as well as the results of the referendum on the Constitution. It listed recent visits by senior UN officials and stressed that it had consistently cooperated with the United Nations in various fields, including human rights. Myanmar asserted that although it had attempted to arrange a meeting between the Special Adviser and Daw Aung San Suu Kyi, she had refused to meet him. Myanmar continued to promote human rights, and it accorded priority to the right to development. It had long been a victim of a systematic disinformation campaign launched by anti-Government elements, funded by their foreign supporters. Myanmar described its efforts to combat and refute allegations regarding internally displaced persons, child soldiers, trafficking in persons, violence against women, forced labour and religious intolerance. It protested sanctions imposed against the country, which it said were unwarranted, unfair and immoral, as well as counter-productive. Myanmar, home to over 100 national races, felt that national unity was of paramount importance and therefore it was pursuing a policy of national reconciliation. Its efforts had resulted in the return to the legal fold of 17 armed groups, and peace and stability prevailed in almost all parts of the country. Those conditions had led to economic and social progress, and the country was proceeding on its chosen path towards democracy.

GENERAL ASSEMBLY ACTION

On 24 December [meeting 74], the General Assembly, on the recommendation of the Third Committee [A/63/430/Add.3 & Corr.1], adopted **resolution 63/245** by recorded vote (80-25-45) [agenda item 64 *(c)*].

Situation of human rights in Myanmar

The General Assembly,

Guided by the Charter of the United Nations and the Universal Declaration of Human Rights, and recalling the International Covenants on Human Rights and other relevant human rights instruments,

Reaffirming that all Member States have an obligation to promote and protect human rights and fundamental freedoms and the duty to fulfil the obligations they have undertaken under the various international instruments in this field,

Reaffirming also its previous resolutions on the situation of human rights in Myanmar, the most recent of which is resolution 62/222 of 22 December 2007, those of the Commission on Human Rights, and Human Rights Council resolutions S-5/1 of 2 October 2007, 6/33 of 14 December 2007, 7/31 of 28 March 2008 and 8/14 of 18 June 2008,

Welcoming the statements made by the President of the Security Council on 11 October 2007 and 2 May 2008,

Welcoming also the reports of the Special Rapporteur on the situation of human rights in Myanmar and his oral presentations, as well as the agreement by the Government of Myanmar to the visit of the Special Rapporteur, for the first time in four years, in November 2007 and then again in August 2008 soon after the appointment of the new Special Rapporteur, and encouraging the continuation of such visits, welcoming further the report of the Secretary-General and his designation of a Special Adviser on Myanmar to continue to pursue the mandate of good offices, and affirming its full support for this mission,

Taking note of the cooperation of the Government of Myanmar with the international community, including the United Nations, in delivering humanitarian assistance to the people affected by Cyclone Nargis despite its initial denial of access, which resulted in widespread suffering and increased the risk of loss of lives, and calling upon the Government of Myanmar, in the interest of the people of Myanmar, to cooperate on humanitarian access in all other areas of the country where the United Nations, other international humanitarian organizations and their partners continue to experience difficulties in delivering assistance to persons in need,

Calling upon the Government of Myanmar to cooperate with the international community in order to achieve concrete progress in areas such as human rights and political processes leading to a genuine democratic transition through concrete measures,

Deeply concerned that the urgent calls contained in the above-mentioned resolutions, as well as the statements of other United Nations bodies concerning the situation of human rights in Myanmar, have not been met, and emphasizing that, without significant progress towards meeting these calls of the international community, the situation of human rights in Myanmar will continue to deteriorate,

1. *Strongly condemns* the ongoing systematic violations of civil, political, economic, social and cultural rights of the people of Myanmar, as described in resolution 62/222 and the previous resolutions of the General Assembly, the Commission on Human Rights and the Human Rights Council;

2. *Expresses grave concern*, in particular, at:

(a) The continuing practice of enforced disappearances, use of violence against peaceful demonstrators, rape and other forms of sexual violence, torture and cruel, inhuman or degrading treatment, arbitrary detentions, including those that resulted from the repression of peaceful protests in 2007, the extension, once again, of the house arrest of the General Secretary of the National League for Democracy, Daw Aung San Suu Kyi, as well as the high and increasing number of political prisoners, including other political leaders, persons belonging to ethnic nationalities and human rights defenders, despite the recent release of a small number of them, including U Win Tin;

(b) The continuing imposition of severe restrictions on the exercise of fundamental freedoms such as the freedom of movement, expression, association and assembly, in particular the lack of an independent judiciary and the use of censorship;

(c) The major and repeated violations of international humanitarian law committed against civilians;

(d) The continuing discrimination and violations suffered by persons belonging to ethnic nationalities of Myanmar, and attacks by military forces and non-State armed groups on villages in Karen State and other ethnic States in Myanmar, leading to extensive forced displacements and serious violations and other abuses of the human rights of the affected populations;

(e) The absence of effective and genuine participation of the representatives of the National League for Democracy and other political parties and some ethnic groups in a genuine process of dialogue, national reconciliation and transition to democracy; the fact that the country's political processes are not transparent, inclusive, free and fair, and that the procedures established for the drafting of the constitution resulted in the de facto exclusion of the opposition from the process; and the decision of the Government of Myanmar to proceed with the constitutional referendum in an atmosphere of intimidation and without regard to international standards of free and fair elections at a time of dire humanitarian need;

(f) Forced labour and forced displacement, as well as the continuous deterioration of the living conditions and the increase of poverty affecting a significant part of the population throughout the country, with serious consequences for the enjoyment of their economic, social and cultural rights;

(g) The climate of impunity due to the fact that perpetrators of human rights violations and abuses are not brought to justice, thereby denying the victims any effective remedy;

3. *Welcomes:*

(a) The visits to Myanmar of the Special Adviser to the Secretary-General on Myanmar, and expresses appreciation for the work of the good offices mission of the Secretary-General but notes only limited cooperation by the Government of Myanmar with this mission in 2008;

(b) The progress report presented by the Government of Myanmar and the steps taken so far, though limited, in implementing the supplementary understanding between the International Labour Organization and the Government of Myanmar signed in 2007 and designed to provide a mechanism to enable victims of forced labour to seek redress;

(c) The submission by the Government of Myanmar of its third periodic report on the implementation of the Convention on the Elimination of All Forms of Discrimination against Women;

(d) The progress reported on the work conducted by the Government of Myanmar and international humanitarian entities on HIV/AIDS and avian influenza;

(e) The establishment of the Group of Friends of the Secretary-General on Myanmar, calls upon the Group to facilitate the work of the good offices mission of the Secretary-General, including by assisting with the preparation of his visits and by urging the Government of Myanmar to cooperate fully with the mission, and encourages the Group to do its utmost to encourage the Government to respect human rights and allow a peaceful transition to democracy;

(f) The role played by countries neighbouring Myanmar and members of the Association of Southeast Asian Nations in support of the good offices mission of the Secretary-General, and encourages the continuation and intensification of efforts in this regard;

(g) The constructive role played by the Association of Southeast Asian Nations and the United Nations in working with the Government of Myanmar to respond to the humanitarian crisis caused by Cyclone Nargis;

4. *Strongly calls upon* the Government of Myanmar:

(a) To ensure full respect for all human rights and fundamental freedoms, including by ending restrictions on these freedoms that are incompatible with the obligations of the Government of Myanmar under international human rights law, and to protect the inhabitants of the country;

(b) To allow a full, transparent, effective, impartial and independent investigation, primarily by the Special Rapporteur on the situation of human rights in Myanmar, into all reports of human rights violations, including enforced disappearances, use of violence against peaceful demonstrators, arbitrary detentions, torture and cruel, inhuman or degrading treatment, rape and other forms of sexual violence, forced labour and forced displacement, and to bring those responsible to justice in order to end impunity for violations of human rights;

(c) To reveal the whereabouts of persons who are detained or missing or who have been subjected to enforced disappearance;

(d) To seize the opportunity of the good offices of the Secretary-General and to cooperate fully with the good offices mission in the fulfilment of its responsibilities as mandated by the General Assembly, namely, the release of political prisoners and the commencement of a substantive dialogue on democratic transition; such cooperation shall include facilitating the visits of the Special Adviser to the

country, allowing him unrestricted access to all relevant parties, including the highest level of leadership within the regime, human rights defenders, representatives of ethnic minorities, student leaders and other opposition groups, and engaging in a genuine and fruitful process aimed at achieving tangible progress towards democratic reform and full respect for human rights;

(e) To fully implement previous recommendations of the Special Rapporteur, the General Assembly, the Human Rights Council, the Commission on Human Rights, the International Labour Organization and other United Nations bodies;

(f) To desist from further politically motivated arrests and to release without delay and without conditions those who have been arbitrarily arrested and detained, as well as all political prisoners, including Daw Aung San Suu Kyi, other leaders of the National League for Democracy, "88 Generation" group leaders, ethnic group leaders and all those detained as the result of the protests which took place in September 2007;

(g) To lift all restraints on the peaceful political activity of all persons by, inter alia, guaranteeing freedom of peaceful assembly and association and freedom of opinion and expression, including for free and independent media, and to ensure unhindered access to media information for the people of Myanmar;

(h) To cooperate fully with the Special Rapporteur, including by granting him full, free and unhindered access in his upcoming visits to Myanmar to monitor the implementation of Human Rights Council and General Assembly resolutions, and to ensure that no person cooperating with the Special Rapporteur or any international organization is subjected to any form of intimidation, harassment or punishment;

(i) To ensure timely, safe, full and unhindered access to all parts of Myanmar, including conflict and border areas, for the United Nations, international humanitarian organizations and their partners and to cooperate fully with those actors to ensure that humanitarian assistance is delivered to all persons in need throughout the country;

(j) To put an immediate end to the continuing recruitment and use of child soldiers in violation of international law, by all parties, to intensify measures to ensure the protection of children from armed conflict and to pursue its collaboration with the Special Representative of the Secretary-General for Children and Armed Conflict;

(k) To take urgent measures to put an end to violations of international human rights and humanitarian law, including the targeting of civilians by military operations, rape and other forms of sexual violence persistently carried out by members of the armed forces, and the targeting of persons belonging to particular ethnic groups;

(l) To end the systematic forced displacement of large numbers of persons within their country and the violence contributing to refugee flows into neighbouring countries, and to respect ceasefire agreements;

5. *Calls upon* the Government of Myanmar:

(a) To permit all political representatives and representatives of ethnic nationalities to participate fully in the political transition process without restrictions and, to that end, to resume without further delay a dialogue with all political actors, including the National League for Democracy and representatives of ethnic nationalities;

(b) To pursue, through dialogue and peaceful means, the immediate suspension and permanent end of conflict with all ethnic nationalities in Myanmar and to allow the full participation of representatives of all political parties and representatives of ethnic nationalities in an inclusive and credible process of national reconciliation, democratization and the establishment of the rule of law;

(c) To allow human rights defenders to pursue their activities unhindered and to ensure their safety, security and freedom of movement in that pursuit;

(d) To refrain from imposing restrictions on access to and flow of information from the people of Myanmar, including through the openly available and accessible use of Internet and mobile telephone services;

(e) To fulfil its obligations to restore the independence of the judiciary and due process of law, the current state of which is not in compliance with international human rights law, as well as to ensure that discipline in prisons does not amount to torture or cruel, inhuman or degrading treatment or punishment and that conditions of detention otherwise meet international standards;

(f) To engage in a dialogue with the Office of the United Nations High Commissioner for Human Rights with a view to ensuring full respect for all human rights and fundamental freedoms;

(g) To engage more actively to eliminate the use of forced labour and to increase its efforts with the International Labour Organization towards the effective implementation of the national mechanism established to receive complaints of forced labour, including allowing the International Labour Organization to distribute informational material in Myanmar on that mechanism;

(h) To resume its humanitarian dialogue with the International Committee of the Red Cross and allow it to carry out its activities according to its mandate, in particular by granting access to persons detained and to areas of internal armed conflict;

6. *Requests* the Secretary-General:

(a) To continue to provide his good offices and to pursue his discussions on the situation of human rights, the transition to democracy and the national reconciliation process with the Government and the people of Myanmar, including democracy and human rights groups and all relevant parties, and to offer technical assistance to the Government in this regard;

(b) To give all necessary assistance to enable the Special Adviser and the Special Rapporteur to discharge their mandates fully and effectively and in a coordinated manner;

(c) To report to the General Assembly at its sixty-fourth session as well as to the Human Rights Council on the progress made in the implementation of the present resolution;

7. *Decides* to continue the consideration of the question at its sixty-fourth session, on the basis of the report of the Secretary-General and the interim report of the Special Rapporteur.

RECORDED VOTE ON RESOLUTION 63/245:

In favour: Afghanistan, Albania, Argentina, Armenia, Australia, Austria, Belgium, Bosnia and Herzegovina, Botswana, Brazil, Bulgaria, Burundi, Canada, Chile, Costa Rica, Croatia, Cyprus, Czech Republic, Denmark, Dominican Republic, Eritrea, Estonia, Finland, France, Georgia, Germany, Greece, Guatemala, Honduras, Hungary, Iceland, Iraq, Ireland, Israel, Italy, Japan, Kazakhstan, Latvia, Lebanon, Liechtenstein, Lithuania, Luxembourg, Maldives, Malta, Marshall Islands, Mauritius, Mexico, Micronesia, Moldova, Monaco, Mongolia, Montenegro, Morocco, Nauru, Netherlands, New Zealand, Norway, Palau, Panama, Paraguay, Peru, Poland, Portugal, Republic of Korea, Romania, Samoa, San Marino, Slovakia, Slovenia, Spain, Sweden, Switzerland, The former Yugoslav Republic of Macedonia, Timor-Leste, Togo, Turkey, Ukraine, United Kingdom, United States, Uruguay.

Against: Algeria, Azerbaijan, Bangladesh, Belarus, Brunei Darussalam, China, Cuba, Democratic People's Republic of Korea, Egypt, India, Iran, Lao People's Democratic Republic, Libyan Arab Jamahiriya, Malaysia, Myanmar, Nicaragua, Oman, Russian Federation, Sri Lanka, Sudan, Syrian Arab Republic, Uzbekistan, Venezuela, Viet Nam, Zimbabwe.

Abstaining: Angola, Antigua and Barbuda, Bahrain, Barbados, Bolivia, Burkina Faso, Cameroon, Colombia, Congo, Côte d'Ivoire, Ecuador, Ethiopia, Gambia, Ghana, Grenada, Guinea-Bissau, Indonesia, Jamaica, Jordan, Kenya, Kuwait, Kyrgyzstan, Lesotho, Malawi, Mali, Mauritania, Mozambique, Namibia, Nepal, Niger, Pakistan, Philippines, Qatar, Saudi Arabia, Singapore, Solomon Islands, South Africa, Swaziland, Tajikistan, Thailand, Trinidad and Tobago, United Arab Emirates, United Republic of Tanzania, Yemen, Zambia.

Nepal

Reports of High Commissioner. In an 18 February report [A/HRC/7/68] on the human rights situation and the activities of OHCHR in Nepal, the High Commissioner said that although there had been significant political developments since her previous report [YUN 2007, p. 821], including the establishment of an interim Government and Parliament, and legislative and institutional reforms aimed at strengthening human rights protection, respect for and protection of human rights had diminished. In particular, there were concerns about the lack of political will to end impunity for past and ongoing human rights abuses by the State and the Communist Party of Nepal (Maoist) (CPN(M)), and about insufficient action to address discrimination and—against a backdrop of increased violence by armed groups in the plains—the State's obligation to protect the rights of the population to life, liberty and security. There continued to be a lack of implementation of many provisions of the 2006 Comprehensive Peace Agreement and of new and existing legislation that could strengthen human rights protection. Frustration arose from long delays in resolving the question of participation of marginalized groups in the Constituent Assembly and in State institutions, and in addressing economic, social and cultural rights violations. A programme to strengthen and reform the security forces and the administration of justice was urgently needed.

In a later report [A/HRC/10/53] covering developments in 2008, the High Commissioner said that there had been significant political developments during the year, including the election of the Constituent Assembly, the declaration of a Republic and the formation of a new Government, as well as legislative and institutional reforms aimed at strengthening human rights protection. The human rights situation had improved significantly since the conflict ended. Challenges remained with regard to addressing the root causes of the conflict, which included impunity and deep-seated inequalities and discrimination. Other needs were improving public security and the protection of the population's rights to life, liberty and security, which were threatened by the proliferation of armed groups operating in the Terai (plains). OHCHR-Nepal, whose mandate had been renewed in 2007 for another two years, adjusted its monitoring and capacity-building activities to developments in the peace process. Technical assistance was extended to the Government through analysis of legislation and policies, training, consultations and reports on cases or thematic issues. In 2008, OHCHR-Nepal increasingly focused on three areas: strengthening national human rights institutions and civil society; impunity, rule of law and accountability; and discrimination and economic, social and cultural rights. It continued investigations into human rights violations in collaboration with national partners, and supported victims in their search for justice and remedial action. OHCHR-Nepal worked closely with, among others, the United Nations Mission in Nepal since its establishment in January 2007. Following national elections on 10 April, the Assembly, at its first session on 28 May, voted to end the 239-year-old monarchy and establish a republic. In August, a new Government, led by CPN(M), was formed, and it made commitments to respect human rights. The Constituent Assembly was much more reflective of Nepal's diverse society than any previous representative body: one third of its members were women, and it had a significant representation of historically marginalized groups, including Madhesis, indigenous peoples and "lower" castes. The new Government took steps to end traditional discriminatory practices, such as banning the use of bonded labour, and committed itself to eliminating "untouchability". However, long-standing discrimination based on class, caste, gender, ethnicity, geography and other considerations remained deeply rooted, and rampant inequalities persisted. Many people faced barriers to access to justice as a result of poverty and discrimination. Women in particular suffered from many forms of discrimination. Marginalized and disadvantaged groups, internally displaced persons and populations in remote areas continued to be the most affected by inequalities in land, food, health and justice. Despite efforts to end impunity and to enforce the rule of law, no visible steps were taken in 2008 to hold accountable any individual responsible for human rights violations committed during or after the conflict. Most of the estimated 1,500 cases of conflict-related disappearances remained unresolved. The OHCHR-Nepal Office received reports of frequent political interference in criminal justice processes, especially in Terai districts. The security situation remained difficult due to the presence of armed groups, resulting in a growing sense of lawlessness and a security vacuum in many areas. Some of the armed groups were connected to political parties, and there were daily reports of abductions, killings, explosion of improvised explosive devices and acts of extortion. OHCHR-Nepal documented cases of excessive use of force by the police and of torture and ill-treatment of detainees. It received reports of abuses by members of CPN(M), although the number of such incidents diminished after April. The April elections constituted an important advance in the peace process, with a voter turnout of 63 per cent, broad representation of previously marginalized groups, and the largely peaceful environment in which the election was held. Nevertheless, there were some reports of voter intimidation and violence, including 21 deaths in the month prior to the voting. The Assembly, which also functioned as the Legislature-Parliament during the transitional period, focused almost exclusively on drafting the Constitution, albeit at a slow pace. OHCHR-Nepal collaborated with the National Human Rights Commission on capacity-building activities, and provided support on the conduct of investigations into allegations of human rights violations. It provided training to Commission staff on indicators to monitor the implementation of economic, social and cultural rights. In 2008, 2,158 civil society and youth representatives participated in 60 activities organized by OHCHR-Nepal to strengthen national capacity to protect and promote human rights. Those activities focused on issues critical to advancing human rights aspects of the peace process, including the rule of law, transitional justice and addressing impunity, as well as monitoring of the Assembly election and participation of civil society in drafting the Constitution. OHCHR-Nepal offered support to the Assembly related to protection of human rights through the Constitution. It continued training and awareness-raising activities with the police, focusing on human rights standards pertaining to law enforcement and the rule of law. Many provisions of the Comprehensive Peace Agreement had yet to be implemented, including mechanisms for monitoring the peace process.

OHCHR-Nepal urged the Government to put in place mechanisms to protect human rights defenders and allow them to undertake vital human rights work free from intimidation. It also called on the Government to prosecute the perpetrators of serious human rights violations that occurred both during and after the conflict, which would require strong and independent rule-of-law institutions. Conflict over land was one of the causes of the conflict, and the establishment of a land commission was an important step forward. The Government was encouraged to ensure that the Commission was able to function in a transparent, inclusive and impartial manner.

Communications. In a 6 March note [A/HRC/7/G/7 & Rev.1] addressed to the High Commissioner, Nepal submitted its observations on her February report. Nepal rejected some of the High Commissioner's criticisms of the situation in Nepal and of the new Government's activities since it came to power. The Government was fully occupied by the overarching national objective of establishing peace in the country. It was aware of its duty to maintain law and order in all of its territory. Many more of the decisions of the Government, which were of far-reaching importance to the people of Nepal, should have found recognition in the report.

Europe and the Mediterranean

Cyprus

Note by Secretary-General. In accordance with Human Rights Council decision 2/102 [YUN 2006, p. 760] requesting the Secretary-General and the High Commissioner to update relevant reports, the Secretary-General transmitted the OHCHR report on human rights in Cyprus [A/HRC/10/37], covering the year up to 20 December. Without a field presence in Cyprus, OHCHR relied on a variety of sources for information. The persisting division of the country had consequences for human rights issues, including freedom of movement, property rights, missing persons, discrimination, freedom of religion, the right to education, human trafficking and economic rights. With regard to freedom of movement, the United Nations Peacekeeping Force in Cyprus (UNFICYP) had recorded approximately 16.5 million crossings since the opening of the four crossing points in 2003. The highly symbolic opening on 3 April of the Ledra Street crossing point in Nicosia had translated into a confidence-building factor with a positive impact on contacts between the Turkish Cypriot and Greek Cypriot communities, including a proposal at a meeting of the two sides for opening the Limnitis/Yeşilirmak crossing point. Restrictions on freedom of movement persisted, in particular with regard to villages in the military zones in the northern part of the island. Since the last report [YUN 2007, p. 824], there had been no positive change in relation to increased access to two Maronite villages. Restrictions of movement imposed upon UNFICYP by the Turkish forces had a negative impact on the delivery of its humanitarian tasks in the northern part of the island. In the context of law enforcement, particularly in relation to trafficking in human beings, organized criminals were able to benefit from the lack of contact and cooperation between the law enforcement agencies from both sides. There was concern about trafficking of women for sexual exploitation. With regard to complaints of discrimination made by the Turkish Cypriot community in Limassol, principally related to the lack of social services, adequate housing and the difficulty in obtaining identity documents, a committee comprising representatives from different local authorities had been established to improve the coordination of welfare action directed to Turkish Cypriots in the south. The bicommunal social centre established by the municipality of Limassol to address some of those concerns continued to function. Members of the Turkish Cypriot community living in the south, among them Roma, had continued to seek UNFICYP facilitation in obtaining identity documents, housing, welfare services, medical care and employment. Property rights remained a concern, and property disputes continued to be brought before the European Court of Human Rights. Meanwhile, the Committee of Ministers of the Council of Europe continued to supervise execution of the judgements of the landmark property cases brought before the Court. Respect for ownership rights remained a problem, and there were reports regarding demolition of Greek Cypriot houses in the north. Concerns continued to be received from the Government of Cyprus regarding increased construction on the Turkish Cypriot side. The Committee on Missing Persons continued its work of exhumation, identification and return of remains of missing persons. As at November, the Committee's bicommunal team of scientists had exhumed the remains of 455 individuals from sites on both sides of the buffer zone. The remains of more than 292 missing persons had undergone examination, and, following DNA analysis, the remains of 105 individuals were returned to their families. There continued to be issues between the two communities on economic rights. Although the European Union aid programme for the Turkish Cypriot community, which sought to encourage economic development in the northern part of the island, had continued, its implementation faced challenges, including the state of cooperation between the two communities. Despite the problems, the report expressed the hope that the new momentum to achieve a comprehensive settlement of the Cyprus problem would provide avenues to improve the human rights situation.

Communications. In a 28 March note [A/HRC/7/G/16] to OHCHR, Turkey transmitted a letter reflecting the Turkish Cypriot views on the Secretary-General's report [YUN 2007, p. 824] on the human rights situation in Cyprus. On 16 May [A/HRC/8/G/5], Cyprus, in a letter to the Human Rights Council, referred to Turkey's communication, rejected the reference to the "Turkish Republic of Northern Cyprus" and criticized Turkey for trying to undermine the relations between the two communities in Cyprus through such documents.

Georgia

On 15 May [A/62/PV.97], Georgia presented to the General Assembly a draft resolution [A/62/L.45] on the status of internally displaced persons and refugees from Abkhazia, Georgia. Introducing the draft, Georgia emphasized the right of those refugees and displaced persons to return to their homes, despite the lack of developments in the political settlement process. For more than 14 years, people who had fled their homes had been denied the right to live in dignity and not to be subject to arbitrary exile. More than 500,000 people of various ethnic origins were suffering a humanitarian disaster as a consequence of the conflict in Abkhazia, Georgia. There had been "complete ethnic cleansing" of the Georgian population from Abkhazia, and the people who had fled their homes were forced to live with a growing sense of hopelessness. By challenging the status quo, Georgia was striving to create new ways to bring about a lasting resolution to the conflict.

The Russian Federation said that the draft, while purporting to address a humanitarian problem, took a political approach to the conflict. It provided a distorted impression of the conflict and was silent on its background. It considered only certain consequences, neglecting the root causes of the situation. If adopted, the text would destabilize UN conflict resolution activities, because the problem of return, while important, was not the only one in achieving a comprehensive settlement of the conflict. The draft had separated the issue of return from related tasks for achieving peace in the region and made the resolution of the problem more difficult. The adoption of such a selective draft would lead to a worsening of Georgian-Abkhaz relations.

GENERAL ASSEMBLY ACTION

On the same day [meeting 97], the General Assembly adopted **resolution 62/249** [draft: A/62/L.45] by recorded vote (14-11-105) [agenda item 16].

Status of internally displaced persons and refugees from Abkhazia, Georgia

The General Assembly,

Recalling its relevant resolutions on the protection of and assistance to internally displaced persons, including its resolution 62/153 of 18 December 2007,

Recognizing the Guiding Principles on Internal Displacement as an important international framework for the protection of internally displaced persons,

Deeply concerned about violations of human rights and international humanitarian law in Abkhazia, Georgia, particularly ethnicity-based violence,

Recalling all relevant Security Council resolutions, and noting the conclusions of the Budapest (1994), Lisbon (1996) and Istanbul (1999) summits of the Organization for Security and Cooperation in Europe, in particular the reports of "ethnic cleansing" and other serious violations of international humanitarian law in Abkhazia, Georgia,

Deploring practices of arbitrary forced displacement and their negative impact on the enjoyment of human rights and fundamental freedoms by large groups of people, and deeply concerned by the humanitarian situation created by the expulsion of hundreds of thousands of persons from Abkhazia, Georgia,

Deeply concerned by the demographic changes resulting from the conflict in Abkhazia, Georgia, and regretting any attempt to alter the pre-conflict demographic composition in Abkhazia, Georgia,

Emphasizing that the rights of the Abkhaz population living in Abkhazia, Georgia, have to be protected and guaranteed,

1. *Recognizes* the right of return of all refugees and internally displaced persons and their descendants, regardless of ethnicity, to Abkhazia, Georgia;

2. *Emphasizes* the importance of preserving the property rights of refugees and internally displaced persons from Abkhazia, Georgia, including victims of reported "ethnic cleansing", and calls upon all Member States to deter persons under their jurisdiction from obtaining property within the territory of Abkhazia, Georgia, in violation of the rights of returnees;

3. *Underlines* the urgent need for the rapid development of a timetable to ensure the prompt voluntary return of all refugees and internally displaced persons to their homes in Abkhazia, Georgia;

4. *Requests* the Secretary-General to submit to the General Assembly at its sixty-third session a comprehensive report on the implementation of the present resolution;

5. *Decides* to include in the provisional agenda of its sixty-third session the item entitled "Protracted conflicts in the GUAM area and their implications for international peace, security and development".

RECORDED VOTE ON RESOLUTION 62/249:

In favour: Albania, Azerbaijan, Czech Republic, Estonia, Georgia, Hungary, Latvia, Lithuania, Poland, Romania, Slovakia, Sweden, Ukraine, United States.

Against: Armenia, Belarus, Democratic People's Republic of Korea, India, Iran, Myanmar, Russian Federation, Serbia, Sudan, Syrian Arab Republic, Venezuela.

Abstaining: Algeria, Andorra, Argentina, Australia, Austria, Bahamas, Bahrain, Bangladesh, Belgium, Bhutan, Bolivia, Bosnia and Herzegovina, Botswana, Brunei Darussalam, Bulgaria, Burkina Faso, Canada, Chile, China, Colombia, Comoros, Congo, Costa Rica, Cyprus, Denmark, Djibouti, Dominican Republic, Ecuador, Egypt, El Salvador, Finland, France, Germany, Ghana, Greece, Guatemala, Guinea, Guyana, Haiti, Honduras, Iceland, Indonesia, Ireland, Israel, Italy, Jamaica, Japan, Jordan, Kazakhstan, Kenya, Kuwait, Kyrgyzstan, Lesotho, Liberia, Libyan Arab Jamahiriya, Liechtenstein, Luxembourg, Madagascar, Malaysia, Maldives, Malta, Mauritius, Mexico, Moldova, Monaco, Mongolia, Montenegro, Morocco, Mozambique, Namibia, Nepal, Netherlands, New Zealand, Nicaragua, Nigeria, Norway, Pakistan, Panama, Peru, Philippines, Portugal, Qatar, Republic of Korea, San Marino, Saudi Arabia, Senegal, Singapore, Slovenia, South Africa, Spain, Sri Lanka, Swaziland, Switzerland, Thailand, The former Yugoslav Republic of Macedonia, Togo, Tunisia, Turkey, United Arab Emirates, United Kingdom, Uruguay, Uzbekistan, Viet Nam, Yemen, Zambia.

Communications. In a 9 September note [A/HRC/9/G/4] to the Human Rights Council, the Russian Federation said that on 8 August, the Georgian leadership had commenced an armed conflict in an attempt to annex South Ossetia through the annihilation of a whole people. Reviewing the recent history and conflict of the region, the Russian Federation said that difficulties had arisen since Mikhail Saakashvili had become leader, as his rule was marked by his inability to negotiate, continuous provocations and staged incidents in the conflict areas, attacks against Russian peacekeepers, and a disparaging attitude towards democratically elected leaders of Abkhazia and South Ossetia. Having considered the appeals of South Ossetian and Abkhaz people, of the Parliaments and Presidents of both Republics, the Russian Federation decided to recognize the independence of both and to conclude treaties of friendship, cooperation and mutual assistance with them. Due to the relief efforts of Russia, refugees had started returning to their homes in South Ossetia following the outbreak of hostilities, and 29,108 refugees had returned there from Russia since 12 August.

In a 12 September note [A/HRC/9/G/5] to OHCHR, the Russian Federation transmitted information on what it called crimes against children committed by Georgian troops in South Ossetia during the Georgian-South Ossetian conflict.

(See also PART ONE, Chapter V. On the mission to Georgia of the Representative on the human rights of internally displaced persons, see p. 855).

Middle East

Territories occupied by Israel

In 2008, human rights questions, including cases of violations in the territories occupied by Israel following the 1967 hostilities in the Middle East, were addressed by the Human Rights Council. Political and other aspects were considered by the General Assembly, its Special Committee to Investigate Israeli Practices Affecting the Human Rights of the Palestinian People and Other Arabs of the Occupied Territories (Committee on Israeli Practices) and other bodies (see PART ONE, Chapter VI).

Human Rights Council special session

At the request of the Syrian Arab Republic and Pakistan [A/HRC/S-6/1], backed by 21 Human Rights Council members, the Council held its sixth special session (Geneva, 23–24 January) [A/HRC/S-6/2] to consider human rights violations emanating from Israeli military attacks and incursions in the Occupied Palestinian Territory, particularly in the occupied Gaza Strip. During its consideration of the issue, the Council heard statements from its members, the representative of Palestine as a concerned country, non-member countries, intergovernmental organizations and NGOs.

On 24 January [A/HRC/S-6/2 (res. S-6/1)], by a recorded vote of 30 to 1, with 15 abstentions, the Council expressed grave concern at the repeated Israeli military attacks carried out in the Occupied Palestinian Territory, particularly in the occupied Gaza Strip, which had resulted in loss of life and injuries among Palestinian civilians, including women and children. The Council called for international action to put an immediate end to the violations committed by the occupying Power, Israel, in the Occupied Palestinian Territory, including the incessant and repeated Israeli military attacks and incursions therein and the siege of the occupied Gaza Strip. It demanded that Israel lift the siege it had imposed on the Gaza Strip, restore supply of fuel, food and medicine and reopen the border crossings. Calling for protection of the Palestinian civilians in the Territory, in compliance with human rights law and international humanitarian law, the Council urged all parties to respect the rules of those laws, as well as to refrain from violence against civilians. The High Commissioner for Human Rights was requested to report to the Council, at its next session, on the progress made in implementing the resolution.

Other developments

Report of High Commissioner. In response to the 24 January resolution of the Human Rights Council (see above), the High Commissioner, in a report of 14 March [A/HRC/7/76], assessed implementation of the resolution for a one-month period from the day it was adopted. She provided the general context of the situation and focused on Gaza, particularly its closure and violence against the civilian population there, from 24 January to 24 February. As background, she outlined developments since the 2006 elections for the Palestinian Legislative Council in the West Bank and Gaza and the win of the Hamas movement over the Fatah movement, followed by Israel's imposing economic sanctions, including its withholding tax revenues collected on imports, and its introducing additional restrictions on the movement of goods to, from and within the Palestinian territory. Through international efforts, the Palestinian Government and Israel, in late 2007, agreed to work on reaching a two-State solution by the end of 2008, a commitment that was repeated on the occasion of United States President George Bush's visit to Jerusalem on 9 January 2008. The High Commissioner examined violations committed by three actors: Israel as the occupying Power; the Palestinian Authority; and the de facto authorities of the Gaza Strip under the effective control of Hamas. As a result of restrictions on the movement of goods and reduction of fuel supply and electricity to Gaza, all six crossings into Gaza had been opened only sporadically since June 2007 and, with few exceptions, all legitimate trade with Gaza had come to a halt. As a result of shortages of food and medical and relief items, the Gaza Strip was on the brink of a humanitarian disaster. According to the Israeli Ministry of Defense, electricity cuts to Gaza were made in response to rocket firings from Gaza into Israel. The electricity shortages had a significant effect on the Gazans' right to an adequate standard of living. As concerned the right to water, during the second half of January, almost half of the Gaza population of 1.4 million had no access to running water. An estimated 80 per cent of the population lived beneath the poverty line and depended on food aid from international organizations. Israeli security forces continued military incursions into Gaza and the West Bank throughout 2007, and the situation escalated in January 2008 with more Israeli incursions and air strikes, while Palestinian militants fired hundreds of mortar shells and around 210 rockets (mostly Qassam type) into western Negev, including the cities of Sderot and Ashkelon. During the reporting period, 1 Israeli and 41 Palestinians were reported killed, a decrease from the first three weeks of the year. Most of the rocket and mortar attacks carried out by Palestinian militants were indiscriminate and against civilian targets, a violation of international humanitarian law. During the reporting period, Israeli security forces conducted at least nine military incursions into Gaza and 106 into various locations of the West Bank. Over 560 blockages of various sorts prevented ordinary Palestinians from enjoying their right to freedom of movement within the West Bank. With regard to Israeli military operations, the report said that while Israel had a right to defend itself, disproportionate use of force was prohibited under international humanitarian law. Israel, as the occupying Power, bore a special responsibility under international human rights and humanitarian law to protect the civilian population. The violence of the conflict had led to the breakdown of law and order in Gaza, especially between Hamas and Fatah supporters. In view of the worsening human rights situation in the Occupied Palestinian Territory, the protection of both Palestinian and Israeli civilians required immediate action by all parties and the international community.

The High Commissioner recommended that all parties to the conflict cease actions violating international human rights and humanitarian law. Israel, the Palestinian Authority and the de facto Government of the Gaza Strip under the control of Hamas should establish accountability mechanisms providing for law-based, independent, transparent and accessible investigations of alleged breaches of such law. Such investigations must hold perpetrators to account and provide redress to victims where violations of law were found. Mechanisms that lacked impartiality or accessibility should be replaced by accountability mechanisms that met international standards. Investigations should address such allegations as indiscriminate attacks and incursions, indiscriminate firing of rockets or mortars, suicide bombings, targeted killings and torture. The international community should promote the implementation of the decisions, resolutions and recommendations of international accountability mechanisms. Urgent action was needed to end the closure of Gaza. Israel should cease all action violating international human rights and humanitarian law. The de facto Government in Gaza should take all possible measures to minimize the negative effects of the siege on the enjoyment of human rights by Gazans, and ensure that action against both Palestinian and Israeli civilians ceased, notably the indiscriminate firing of rockets into Israel. The Palestinian Authority should take all measures in its power to alleviate the situation.

Note by High Commissioner. By a 14 March note [A/HRC/7/77], the High Commissioner, pursuant to Human Rights Council resolution 6/19 [YUN 2007, p. 828] requesting her to report on the access of Palestinians to their holy sites, informed the Council that the issue had been covered briefly in her report of 14 March. She would report in greater detail to the Council's eighth session on any policies or measures taken by Israel which limited access of Palestinian residents in the Occupied Palestinian Territory (both Christians and Muslims) to their religious sites located in the Territory, including East Jerusalem.

Human Rights Council action. On 6 March [A/63/53 (res. 7/1)], the Human Rights Council, by a recorded vote of 33 to 1, with 13 abstentions, condemned the persistent Israeli military attacks and incursions in the Occupied Palestinian Territory, particularly the recent ones in Gaza, which resulted in the loss of more than 125 lives and hundreds of injuries among Palestinian civilians. It expressed shock at the Israeli bombardment of Palestinian homes and the Israeli policy of inflicting collective punishment against the civilian population, and called for bringing the perpetrators to justice. It called for the immediate cessation of all Israeli military attacks in the Territory as well as the firing of rockets, which had taken two civilian lives in southern Israel. Calling for international action to put an end to the Israeli violations, the Council reiterated its calls for immediate protection of the Palestinian people in the Territory in compliance with international human rights law and international humanitarian law. It urged all parties to respect the rule of such law and to refrain from violence against civilian populations. The Council requested the High Commissioner to report, at its next session, on progress made in implementing the resolution.

On 27 March [A/63/53 (res. 7/17)], the Council reaffirmed the inalienable, permanent and unqualified right of the Palestinian people to self-determination, including their right to live in freedom, justice and dignity and to establish their sovereign, independent, democratic and viable contiguous State. It reaffirmed its support for the solution of two States—Palestine and Israel—living side by side in peace and security. It stressed the need for respect and preservation of the territorial unity, contiguity and integrity of all of the Occupied Palestinian Territory, including East Jerusalem, and urged Member States and UN bodies to support the Palestinian people in realizing their right to self-determination.

On the same day [A/63/53 (res. 7/18)], the Council, by a recorded vote of 46 to 1, deplored the recent Israeli announcements of housing construction for Israeli settlers in and around East Jerusalem, as they undermined the peace process and the creation of a contiguous Palestinian State. The Council expressed concern at: the continuing Israeli settlement, including the expansion of settlements, the expropriation of land, the demolition of houses, the expulsion of Palestinians, and the construction of bypass roads; the Israeli plan (E-1) to expand the settlement of Maale Adumim and build a wall around it, thereby further disconnecting East Jerusalem from the West Bank; Israel's announcement that it would retain major blocks in the Occupied Palestinian Territory, including settlements in the Jordan Valley; the expansion of Israeli settlements and the construction of new ones in the Territory, which would be tantamount to de facto annexation; the Israeli decision to establish a tramway between West Jerusalem and the Israeli settlement of Pisgat Zeev; the continued closures of the Territory and the restriction of movement of people and goods, impairing the economic and social rights of the Palestinians; and the continued construction, contrary to international law, of the wall inside the Occupied Palestinian Territory. The Council urged Israel to reverse the settlement policy in the occupied territories, including East Jerusalem and the Syrian Golan, and to prevent any new installation of settlers in the territories. It urged implementation of the

2005 Access and Movement Agreement, particularly the reopening of the Rafah and Karni crossings, and the access of UN agencies to and within the Occupied Palestinian Territory. The Council called on Israel to implement measures, including confiscation of arms, to prevent violence by Israeli settlers, in order to guarantee the safety of the Palestinian civilians in Territory. The Council demanded that Israel comply with its legal obligations as mentioned in the 2004 advisory opinion by the International Court of Justice [YUN 2004, p. 1272]. It urged the parties to give impetus to the peace process in line with earlier agreements and Security Council resolutions.

On 28 March [A/63/53 (res. 7/30)], by a recorded vote of 32 to 1, with 14 abstentions, the Council called on Israel, the occupying Power, to comply with relevant resolutions of UN bodies, and determined that Israel's decision to impose its laws, jurisdiction and administration on the occupied Syrian Golan was null and void. It called on Israel to desist from changing the physical character, demographic composition, institutional structure and legal status of the Golan, and emphasized that the displaced persons must be allowed to return to their homes and to recover their property. Israel was called on to desist from imposing Israeli citizenship and identity cards on the Syrian citizens in the Golan; to desist from its repressive measures against them; to allow the Syrian population of the Golan to visit their families in the Syrian motherland; and to rescind its decision to prohibit those visits, as it was in violation of the Fourth Geneva Convention and the International Covenant on Civil and Political Rights. The Council further called on Israel to release the Syrian detainees in Israeli prisons, and to allow the International Committee of the Red Cross (ICRC) to visit those prisoners to assess their physical and mental health. The Council determined that all legislative and administrative measures taken by Israel that purported to alter the character and legal status of the occupied Syrian Golan were null and void, constituted a violation of international law and had no legal effect.

Communications. The Syrian Arab Republic, in a 13 May note [A/HRC/8/G/4] to OHCHR, brought to the Office's attention the poor state of health of the Syrian citizen Beshir Almeket, who had been detained in Israeli prisons for more than 23 years. Mr. Almeket had suffered a heart attack on 24 March and his health was deteriorating. Syria called on the Council to urge Israel to allow ICRC to intervene with specialized doctors in order to save his life, which was in jeopardy as a result of the inhumane conditions in the Israeli prison where he was detained. In a response of 5 June [A/HRC/8/G/8], Israel said that the allegations were baseless and that Mr. Almeket, who was arrested in 1985, was serving a 27-year sentence for his attack on an Israeli army base. Israel denied the allegations that he was gravely ill and had been denied medical treatment. ICRC enjoyed access to all Syrian detainees and visited them regularly. In an 11 June note [A/HRC/8/G/10], Syria reiterated the information concerning Mr. Almeket and said that the state of health of Syrian prisoners was deteriorating daily, due to the inhumane conditions to which they were subjected. Syrian prisoner Saytan al-Wali, imprisoned for more than 23 years, was suffering from a tumour and a number of diseases, and Israeli procrastination and delays had led to that critical situation. Syria held the Israeli occupation authorities responsible for the deterioration in the health of all Syrian prisoners, and for all the consequences which might follow. Pressure should be brought to bear on Israel to comply with the norms of international humanitarian law and the Geneva Conventions.

Reports of High Commissioner. In response to Human Rights Council resolution 7/1 (see p. 894), the High Commissioner, on 6 June [A/HRC/8/17], reported on human rights violations emanating from Israeli military attacks and incursions in the Occupied Palestinian Territory, particularly the recent ones in the occupied Gaza Strip. The report assessed the progress made in the implementation of the resolution for a two-month period (25 February–25 April), from the end of the previous reporting period (see p. 893), and focused on the closure of Gaza and violence against the civilian populations. The Gaza Strip remained closed to the outside world during the reporting period, with the exception of limited humanitarian imports and movements of a few international visitors, patients requiring emergency care and Palestinians who received exit permits from Israel. Fuel shortages were having a profound effect on all aspects of life in Gaza, and electricity was reduced to around two thirds of its normal capacity, causing daily power outages. The activities of UN agencies working in the Gaza Strip were hampered by the fuel shortage. Fuel shortages and the absence of spare parts and equipment continued to paralyze the water, sewage and garbage networks. Food prices were rising rapidly and essential goods were increasingly hard to find, while the quality of health care was declining. It was reported that 50 per cent of the Gaza educational sector was not functioning, as students and teachers could not reach schools. The closure of Gaza also impacted on the residents' freedom of religion by preventing them from worshipping at some of the most sacred Muslim and Christian sites. During the reporting period, 221 Palestinians were killed as a result of the armed Israeli-Palestinian conflict (19 in the West Bank, 202 in Gaza) and about 460 Palestinians were injured; 10 Israeli civilians were killed and around 25 injured. The Israeli air force conducted at least 75 air strikes on the Gaza Strip during that period. Israeli security forces conducted at least 30 military incursions into Gaza and 348 into the West Bank. It was estimated that during the reporting period, Palestinian militants fired around 640 mortar shells and 450 rockets from Gaza into southern Israel, most of which were indiscriminate firings. On 6 March, eight Israeli civilians were killed when a Palestinian gunman opened fire inside a Jewish religious school in West Jerusalem. During the reporting period, around 30 Palestinians, of whom nine were allegedly civilians, were killed in intra-Palestinian violence, according to Palestinian human rights organizations. Several incidents were reported involving unidentified armed groups in Gaza, while law and order continued to deteriorate. The human rights situation in the Occupied Palestinian Territory remained grave, particularly in Gaza. The High Commissioner's previous recommendations, notably concerning the establishment of accountability mechanisms and the closure of Gaza, had not been implemented, and the actions taken by the parties continued to violate international human rights and humanitarian law. Accordingly, all previous recommendations by the High Commissioner remained valid and the parties should urgently implement them.

The High Commissioner, as requested by the Human Rights Council in resolution 6/19 [YUN 2007, p. 828], reported on 10 June [A/HRC/8/18] on religious and cultural rights in the Occupied Palestinian Territory, including East Jerusalem. In accordance with the resolution, the report assessed legislative and policy measures taken by Israel that had an adverse impact on the enjoyment of religious and cultural rights, focusing in particular on those measures that had limited the access of Palestinian residents in the Occupied Palestinian Territory to religious sites located in the Territory, including East Jerusalem. The report outlined the international legal framework applicable to the exercise of religious and cultural rights, under four international conventions, and it described developments related to the implementation of resolution 6/19. Limited access of Palestinians to religious sites was the result of physical obstacles such as the wall under construction in the Territory, checkpoints, closed areas, road barriers and trenches, as well as curfews and the permit system for Palestinians entering East Jerusalem and Israel. The justification for the closure regime cited by the Israeli authorities was the need to provide security and protection to all people within its jurisdiction. In February, the Israeli Defense Forces raided buildings and schools run by the Hebron Islamic Charity. Restrictions on freedom of movement limited the possibilities for Palestinians to enjoy the right to participate freely in the cultural life of the community and to enjoy the arts. As a consequence, all forms of cultural and educational contacts and exchange, such as theatre, cinema, fine arts and music, were limited inside the Territory. The importation of Arabic language books was subject to restrictions. International humanitarian law required that the occupying Power permit ministers of religion to give spiritual assistance to their religious communities. In that regard, Israel should ease restrictions on clergy and allow movement and access for spiritual leaders to communicate with members of their faith. Israel should consider revisiting its rules governing the importation of Arabic books to the Territory. The freedom to establish seminaries or religious schools and religious, charitable or humanitarian institutions should be respected and protected. While restrictions on such institutions might be necessary to protect public safety, any such restrictions had to be prescribed by law. As the occupying Power, Israel bore responsibility under international law for preserving the cultural and religious heritage in the Territory, and should take measures to preserve that heritage and refrain from action that could negatively affect the sites.

Report of Special Rapporteur. On 26 March, the Human Rights Council appointed Richard Falk (United States) as the Special Rapporteur on the situation of human rights in the Palestinian territories occupied by Israel since 1967. On 25 August [A/63/326], the Secretary-General transmitted the Rapporteur's report to the General Assembly. The report, covering the period from 1 January to 31 July, examined the observance of international humanitarian and international human rights standards in the Palestinian territories, focusing on the consequences of a prolonged occupation that had ignored the directives of the United Nations with respect to upholding the legal rights of an occupied people. Recalling the undertaking associated with the revival of the peace process at the Annapolis summit of December 2007, in particular the expectation that Israel would freeze settlement expansion and ease restrictions on movement in the West Bank, the Rapporteur noted the discouraging settlement growth and the further restrictions on West Bank movement. On a positive note, secret negotiations under Egyptian auspices in Cairo between Israel and Hamas, with the objective of establishing a ceasefire agreement that would end the firing of rockets into Israel from Gaza and military incursions, and targeted assassinations by Israel in Gaza, were fruitful. On 20 June, a ceasefire was declared, and despite some infractions on both sides, it had generally held. Israel eased some restrictions on the Gazans by increasing the supply of food and medicine; nevertheless, humanitarian conditions remained dire. The report noted the abuse of international humanitarian law associated with the separation wall, and Palestinian fatalities, including children, owing to Israeli use of excessive force to quell non-violent demonstrations. Abuses by Israel at border crossings were reported, and special concern was expressed with regard to the harassment and assault of Palestinian journalists. A persistent health crisis existed in Gaza and the West Bank, and there was a risk of a collapse of the basic health system.

Among his recommendations, the Special Rapporteur emphasized that the General Assembly should ask the International Court of Justice for a legal assessment of the Israeli occupation of Palestinian territory from the perspective of the Palestinian right of self-determination. The assistance of the Security Council should be sought in implementing the Court's 2004 advisory opinion on the legal consequences of the construction of a wall in the Occupied Palestinian Territory. In view of the health crisis in Gaza, the international community should resume economic assistance as a matter of priority.

The General Assembly took note of the report on 18 December **(decision 63/534)**.

Report of fact-finding mission. The high-level fact-finding mission to Beit Hanoun, established by the Human Rights Council in resolution S-3/1 [YUN 2006, p. 969] following an Israeli military operation in the Gaza town, issued its third and final report on 1 September [A/HRC/9/26]. Led by Archbishop Desmond Tutu of South Africa, and with Professor Christine Chinkin (United Kingdom) as its other member, the mission visited the town from 27 to 29 May to inspect the site and speak to victims, travelling through Egypt after having been denied access through Israel. Its mandate was to assess the situation of victims, address the needs of survivors, and make recommendations on ways and means to protect Palestinian civilians against any further Israeli assaults. Beit Hanoun, a town in the Gaza Strip with a population of 35,000, of which 70 per cent were registered refugees, was attacked on 8 November 2006 during a period of increased military activity. Since the Palestinian Legislative Council elections in early 2006, the Israeli military had fired approximately 15,000 artillery shells and conducted more than 550 air strikes into the Gaza Strip, killing approximately 525 Gazans and injuring 1,527. According to Israel, most of its military operations in Gaza were aimed at stopping rocket-launching activity. Over the same period, at least 1,700 Qassam rockets were fired into Israel by Palestinian militants, injuring 41 Israelis. On 8 November, the heavy Israeli shelling of Beit Hanoun killed 19 civilians, including seven children and six women, and wounded 50 others. Some of the injured tried to reach Israeli hospitals for treatment but could not obtain permission to cross into Israel for some hours, and in some cases were not allowed to be accompanied by family members. Following the attack, Israel enforced a curfew and hundreds of male residents aged between 16 and 40 were taken to an Israeli holding centre north of the town for questioning. Most electricity, water and telephone services were cut, movement was restricted, and scores of homes and other buildings were destroyed. Primary health care effectively ceased to function. Following the shelling, the Israeli Prime Minister and Defense Minister expressed regret over the deaths of Palestinian civilians and offered humanitarian assistance and medical care for the wounded. The Israeli military also expressed regret, but stressed that the responsibility rested with terror organizations, which used civilians as human shields while carrying out terror attacks and firing rockets at Israel. On the same day as the attack, Israel announced an inquiry into the incident, intimating that the shells were not fired on civilians intentionally but as the result of technical error. Use of artillery in Gaza was halted after 8 November 2006. The Israeli military conducted an internal investigation which, according to a press communiqué, determined that a rare and severe failure in the firing control system caused a mistake in targeting the weapons. The report was never made public, which the mission found disturbing, and no individual was charged. The mission maintained that the use of artillery in urban areas was inappropriate and likely contrary to international humanitarian and human rights law, and it agreed with the Secretary-General and others that the blockade amounted to collective punishment contrary to international humanitarian law. The mission recognized a nation's right to self-defence, but also that self-defence was subject to the requirements of necessity and proportionality, which required careful examination of the facts. However, the mission saw no evidence of any necessity for the shelling. The mission, while recognizing that the use of force with an impact on civilians was permissible if it was directed at a legitimate military target and was proportionate to the overall threat faced, said that it had received no evidence that the shelled area was a legitimate military target and noted that it had been occupied by Israeli military earlier in the week. The firing of artillery towards Beit Hanoun was a deliberate act in the context of the long-term occupation of Gaza and the deaths of civilians and destruction of property. Taken together with further facts—such as the reduction of the safety zone for artillery use—and the obligation under international humanitarian law to protect civilian life, the mission considered that there was evidence of a disproportionate and reckless disregard for Palestinian civilian life, raising concerns about the possibility of a war crime having been committed. Human rights law was applicable in armed conflict and occupation, and the mission considered that the reckless disregard for civilian life constituted a violation of the right to life. Expressing sympathy to the victims, the mission noted that the attack took lives, inflicted horrendous physical and mental injuries, tore families apart, destroyed homes, took away livelihoods and traumatized a population, which faced incursions after the shelling. The mission also expressed sympathy to all affected by the rocket attacks in southern Israel. It regretted that Israel had withheld cooperation with the mission.

The mission concluded that the violence in Gaza and southern Israel had led to countless violations of international human rights and international humanitarian law. The lack of respect on both sides for the rules of conflict not only led to incidents such as Beit Hanoun, but also undermined respect for the laws of war and human rights in other conflicts. The people of Gaza had to be afforded protection in compliance with international law and, above all, the Fourth Geneva Convention. Without input from the Israeli military, the mission had to conclude that the shelling might constitute a war crime as defined in the Rome Statute of the International Criminal Court. Similarly, the firing of rockets on the civilian population in Israel had to stop. The Israeli response of a largely secret internal investigation of the shelling was unacceptable from both legal and moral points of view, and those responsible had to be held accountable. Those firing rockets on Israeli civilians were no less accountable than the Israeli military for their actions. Accountability involved redress for victims, but none had been provided so far. Meanwhile, the situation of victims and survivors remained grim. A major barrier to the enjoyment of human rights was the blockade, which limited individuals' ability to provide an adequate standard of living for themselves and their families and the capacity of local authorities to provide essential services for the population. As for recommendations on ways to protect Palestinian civilians against any further Israeli assaults, the mission reiterated the recommendations made in its previous report [YUN 2007, p. 826], and it reaffirmed that one of the most effective ways was to insist on respect for the rule of law and accountability.

Human Rights Council action. On 24 September [A/63/53/Add.1 (res. 9/18)], by a recorded vote of 32 to 9, with 5 abstentions, the Human Rights Council welcomed the report of the high-level fact-finding mission and called on all parties to ensure implementation of its recommendations. It recommended that the General Assembly consider the report with the participation of the mission's members. The Council regretted the delay in the fulfilment of the mission owing to the non-cooperation of Israel, the occupying Power, and called on Israel to abide by its obligations under international law, international humanitarian law and international human rights law. The Council requested the Secretary-General to report on the implementation of the recommendations at its next session (2009).

PART THREE

Economic and social questions

Chapter I

Development policy and international economic cooperation

In 2008, the global economy was on the brink of recession, due to the fallout from the financial crisis in the United States, the bursting of the housing bubbles there and in other large economies, soaring commodity prices, increasingly restrictive monetary policies in a number of countries, and stock market volatility. In December, the General Assembly called on countries to manage their macroeconomic and financial policies in ways that contributed to global stability, sustained economic growth and sustainable development, and recognized that greater coherence was required among the macroeconomic, trade, aid, financial, environmental and gender-equality policies to ensure that globalization worked as a positive force for all. The Assembly also reaffirmed the need to continue working towards a new international economic order based on the principles of equity, sovereign equality, interdependence, common interest, cooperation and solidarity among all States.

During the year, the United Nations continued consideration of a number of development issues. The Economic and Social Council, at its high-level segment (30 June–3 July), discussed the promotion of an integrated approach to rural development in developing countries for poverty eradication and sustainable development. As part of that segment, the Council held the first biennial Development Cooperation Forum, which discussed a new vision for development cooperation in the twenty-first century and its changing landscape and dynamics, and a high-level policy dialogue with the representatives of international financial and trade institutions on developments in the world economy. It also held its annual ministerial review on "Implementing the internationally agreed goals and commitments in regard to sustainable development", and adopted a Ministerial Declaration on the theme. In August, the development needs of middle-income countries were considered at the third Ministerial Conference on Development Cooperation with Middle-Income Countries (MICs), held in Windhoek, Namibia. The Conference adopted the Windhoek Ministerial Declaration, which recognized the importance of reflecting the development needs of MICs in the outcomes of the international economic development processes.

The Commission on Sustainable Development reviewed progress in the follow-up to the 2002 World Summit on Sustainable Development and implementation of Agenda 21, the action plan on sustainable development adopted by the 1992 United Nations Conference on Environment and Development. The Commission's high-level segment discussed the theme "The way forward", which focused on investing in Africa to achieve the Millennium Development Goals (MDGs) and sustainable development, and interlinkages among the issues of agriculture, rural development, land, drought, desertification and Africa, including adaptation to climate change in the context of sustainable development.

The eradication of poverty and the achievement of the MDGs continued to be a major focus of attention. The Economic and Social Council reviewed implementation of its 2007 Ministerial Declaration on strengthening efforts to eradicate poverty and hunger, and requested the UN system to adopt more comprehensive, coherent and multidimensional approaches in formulating its eradication policies, programmes and operations. During the year, the General Assembly decided that the theme for the Second United Nations Decade for the Eradication of Poverty, proclaimed in 2007, would be "Full employment and decent work for all", and requested the Secretary-General to appoint a focal point to coordinate implementation of the Decade. The Assembly also considered the legal empowerment of the poor on the basis of the final report of the Commission on Legal Empowerment of the Poor, entitled "Making the law work for everyone". It reaffirmed that the rule of law was essential for sustained economic growth, sustainable development and the eradication of poverty and hunger, and stressed the importance of sharing best national practices. The Assembly held a high-level event on the MDGs, the theme of which was "End poverty 2015: make it happen". The objective was to review progress and take stock of gaps at the midway point in the global effort to achieve the MDGs by 2015, identify actions and help ensure that the goals and international targets remained on track, and that the momentum was maintained beyond 2008. In that regard, the Secretary-General and the Assembly President proposed to hold an MDG Summit in 2010 to galvanize efforts and actions in the final five years before the 2015 deadline, and to convene an informal thematic debate on "Strengthening global health: the health MDGs and beyond".

The Commission on Science and Technology for Development considered as its priority themes development-oriented policies for a socio-economically inclusive information society; and science, technology and engineering for innovation and capacity-building in education and research. It also considered progress made in the implementation of and follow-up to the outcomes of the first (2003) and second (2005) phases of the World Summit on the Information Society at the regional and international levels.

The UN system continued to address the development problems of groups of countries in special situations. The Assembly decided to convene, in 2011, the Fourth United Nations Conference on the Least Developed Countries to undertake a comprehensive appraisal of the implementation of the 2001 Brussels Programme of Action and identify obstacles and constraints encountered, as well as actions and initiatives needed. It also reviewed progress in the implementation of the 1994 Programme of Action for the Sustainable Development of Small Island Developing States and the 2005 Mauritius Strategy for the Further Implementation of the Programme of Action. The Assembly requested UN system agencies to intensify efforts for mainstreaming the Mauritius Strategy in their work programmes. It conducted its midterm review of the Almaty Programme of Action, adopted in 2003 by the International Ministerial Conference of Landlocked and Transit Developing Countries and Donor Countries and International Financial and Development Institutions on Transit Transport Cooperation, and called on donors and the multilateral, regional, financial and development institutions to provide landlocked and transit developing countries with technical and financial assistance for its implementation.

International economic relations

Development and international economic cooperation

International economic cooperation issues were considered in 2008 by a number of UN bodies, including the General Assembly and the Economic and Social Council.

On 19 December, the Assembly took note of the report of the Second (Economic and Financial) Committee [A/63/412] on its discussion of macroeconomic policy questions (**decision 63/539**).

High-level meeting of Economic and Social Council, Bretton Woods institutions and WTO. On 14 April, the Economic and Social Council held in New York its eleventh special high-level meeting with the Bretton Woods institutions (the World Bank Group and the International Monetary Fund (IMF)), the World Trade Organization (WTO) and the United Nations Conference on Trade and Development (UNCTAD), in accordance with its **decision 2008/203** of 5 February. The meeting discussed the theme of coherence, coordination and cooperation in the context of the implementation of the Monterrey Consensus, adopted by the International Conference on Financing for Development [YUN 2002, p. 953], including new challenges and emerging issues, and had before it a March note by the Secretary-General on the subject [E/2008/7]. A summary of the meeting by the Council President [A/63/80-E/2008/67] outlined the five subthemes that served as the focus of the substantive discussions: new initiatives on financing for development; supporting development efforts and enhancing the role of middle-income countries, including in the area of trade; supporting development efforts of the least developed countries (LDCs), including through trade capacity-building; building and sustaining solid financial markets: challenges for international cooperation; and financing of climate change mitigation and adaptation.

High-level segment of Economic and Social Council

The Economic and Social Council, at the high-level segment of its 2008 substantive session (30 June–3 July) [A/63/3/Rev.1], discussed the theme of promoting an integrated approach to rural development in developing countries for poverty eradication and sustainable development, taking into account current challenges, in accordance with its **decision 2008/208** of 8 February. It held two panel discussions on: bioenergy, sustainable livelihoods and rural poor; and harnessing the current boom in agricultural commodities for poverty eradication and sustainable development: the case of small-scale farmers. The Council had before it a May report by the Secretary-General on the subject [E/2008/68], which reviewed implementation of the Council's 2003 Ministerial Declaration [YUN 2003, p. 853] on promoting an integrated approach to rural development, discussed current challenges and proposed as a way forward the adoption by the Council of a programme on rural development (see p. 919).

Development Cooperation Forum. As part of the high-level segment, the Council held its first biennial Development Cooperation Forum on 30 June and 1 July. In preparation for the Forum, Egypt submitted the report of the second High-level Symposium (Cairo, 19–20 January) [E/2008/56], which had as its theme "Trends in development cooperation: South-South and triangular cooperation and aid effectiveness".

The Forum discussed a new vision for international development cooperation in the twenty-first century and its changing landscape and dynamics. It considered a May report [E/2008/69] of the Secretary-General on trends and progress in international cooperation, as requested by General Assembly resolution 61/16 [YUN 2006, p. 1589]. The main findings of the report were that, despite progress in some areas of the global partnership for development, agreements on trade and investment, as well as on the participation of developing countries in international economic decision-making, were not meeting expectations. Progress was insufficient to ensure realization of the internationally agreed development goals, including the Millennium Development Goals (MDGs). Official development assistance (ODA), excluding debt relief, had grown at less than half the rate needed. Most donors were not on track and were not planning sufficiently far ahead to meet their targets. Although increased flows from sources other than the Development Assistance Committee of the Organization for Economic Co-operation and Development were helping diversify financing, aid allocation was not conducive to the achievement of internationally agreed development goals. While a higher proportion of aid was going to the poorest countries, allocations were often not adequately based on needs, results or the vulnerability of countries to exogenous shocks. Particularly significant was the decline in agricultural aid. Development cooperation in the form of budget and sector support was growing slowly. The adoption of the Paris Declaration on Aid Effectiveness [YUN 2005, p. 957] marked a change in the articulation of benchmarks for progress, yet negotiations did not engage the full range of stakeholders nor deal with issues of key concern to programme country Governments and those of other stakeholders. Primarily preoccupied with monitoring aid delivery, the Paris process had not demonstrated ability to change donor behaviour or to link the aid effectiveness agenda with sustainable development results. While the capacities of programme countries to coordinate and manage aid were growing, major gaps remained in terms of analytical, policy, strategic and evaluation capacities. The Secretary-General made a number of action-oriented recommendations, including on the possible future of the Development Cooperation Forum.

The Forum held round tables on: identifying gaps and obstacles; reviewing trends and progress; and exchanging lessons learned. Following a special presentation on key policy messages and recommendations of the Rome Stakeholder Forum, it also held a round table on aid effectiveness.

Annual ministerial review. On 2 July, the Council held its annual ministerial review on the theme "Implementing the internationally agreed goals and commitments in regard to sustainable development". In preparation for the review, a number of countries submitted national reports: Belgium [E/2008/81], Brazil [E/2008/87], Chile [E/2008/75], Colombia [E/2008/74], Finland [E/2008/86], Kazakhstan [E/2008/79], the Lao People's Democratic Republic [E/2008/78], Luxembourg [E/2008/70], the United Kingdom [E/2008/85] and the United Republic of Tanzania [E/2008/89]. On 25 June [E/2008/88], Bahrain submitted the report of the Western Asia regional preparatory meeting (Manama, 1–2 June) on sustainable urbanization.

The Council held a round table on the role of ecosystem services in sustainable development. It had before it the Secretary-General's report [E/2008/12] on the theme of the review, which stated that the three pillars of sustainable development—integrating economic growth, social development and protection of the environment—had been adopted in principle but not in practice. Although some approaches offered benefits in all three areas, costs and trade-offs were often involved. Striking an optimal balance among the three areas remained a central challenge of sustainable development. Moreover, while some progress had been achieved in building the economic and social pillars of sustainable development, greater efforts were still required. The long-term sustainability issues of climate change, deforestation, biodiversity and marine resources were in particular need of attention. There was also an urgent need to implement the global consensus on sustainable development, particularly Agenda 21, adopted at the 1992 United Nations Conference on Environment and Development [YUN 1992, p. 672], the Johannesburg Plan of Implementation adopted at the 2002 World Summit on Sustainable Development [YUN 2002, p. 821] and the MDG on ensuring environmental sustainability [YUN 2000, p. 51]. To that end, the Secretary-General made recommendations on, among other issues, strengthening governance and global cooperation, creating markets for sustainable development, increasing financial assistance and promoting the transfer of technology.

Policy dialogue. On 30 June, the Council held a high-level policy dialogue on developments in the world economy with the representatives of international financial and trade institutions.

Ministerial Declaration. On 3 July, the Council adopted the draft Ministerial Declaration entitled "Implementing the internationally agreed goals and commitments in regard to sustainable development" [E/2008/L.10].

Globalization and interdependence

In response to General Assembly resolution 62/199 [YUN 2007, p. 835], the Secretary-General submitted an August report [A/63/333] on the impact of globalization on the achievement of the internationally agreed development goals, including the MDGs. The report examined the new threats to the achievement of those goals, including the current economic outlook and the food crisis (see p. 1343), and the social and environmental impact of globalization, particularly on the eradication of poverty, hunger and education, gender equality, health and sustainable development.

According to the report, the relationship between globalization and development outcomes was complex. Each of the forces powering globalization—finance, trade, investment, technology and migration—had economic, social and environmental impacts that affected the formulation and implementation of policies at the national, regional and global levels. Among significant impacts were the reduction in national autonomy in policymaking and the need to harmonize national policy formulation with international obligations, commitments and compulsions. The realization of the MDGs was dependent on the strengthening of the global partnership for development. Buffeted by economic forces outside their control, smaller economies could not succeed by themselves in realizing the goals. The gloomy economic outlook and inflationary pressures, driven by rising food and fuel prices, pointed to a less supportive environment for meeting the internationally agreed development goals than had been the case since the Millennium Summit [YUN 2000, p. 48]. The dilemma facing policymakers in the poorest countries was particularly stark, given that the surge in fuel and food prices would likely lead to a deterioration of household incomes, reversing many of the gains made by countries in poverty reduction. While emergency support could ease the threat in the short run, the only lasting solution was to raise investment and stimulate productivity in the food-producing sector. Public spending on research and development and investment in rural infrastructure should be increased, and access to credit improved. That, in turn, would require that macroeconomic policies gave as much priority to investment, employment and economic security as to fighting inflation.

The report concluded that global forces, such as trade and cross-border flows of capital and labour, had important consequences for the achievement of internationally agreed development goals. Development, therefore, should be central to consideration of how globalization was managed, rather than viewed as a by-product of globalization. Given the nature of linkages and interdependence in driving globalization and its cumulative impact on growth and development, greater consistency should be achieved among the macroeconomic, trade, aid, financial, environmental and gender equality policies of all countries, so that they supported the common aim of making globalization work for all. More international efforts were needed to establish fair and equitable trade, investment, technology and knowledge regimes. Multilateral institutions and global governance should be reformed. Ensuring greater participation of developing countries was essential in the decision-making processes of international institutions so that their needs in managing globalization were fairly represented and addressed. Domestic resources and institutions should be strengthened and mobilized to ensure that a development strategy advanced the objectives and priorities of national development agendas and enabled country-specific responses to global trends and impacts. Safety nets and social protection schemes that sheltered the poor during crises should be given priority; statistics, including data disaggregated by sex and gender-sensitive indicators, should be improved; and monitoring and evaluation capacity should be strengthened.

Communications. On 3 October [A/63/464], Antigua and Barbuda, as the Chairman of the Group of 77, transmitted to the Secretary-General the Ministerial Declaration adopted at the thirty-second annual meeting of the Ministers for Foreign Affairs of the Group of 77 and China (New York, 26 September), which reviewed progress of the world economy and challenges in the economic development and social progress of developing countries. The Declaration recognized that the global food, financial and energy crises constituted a major multidimensional challenge for development and the achievement of the internationally agreed development goals, and emphasized the need for a strengthened global partnership for development, based on the recognition of national leadership and ownership of development strategies.

GENERAL ASSEMBLY ACTION

On 19 December [meeting 72], the General Assembly, on the recommendation of the Second Committee [A/63/416/Add.1], adopted **resolution 63/222** without vote [agenda item 54 *(a)*].

Role of the United Nations in promoting development in the context of globalization and interdependence

The General Assembly,

Recalling its resolutions 53/169 of 15 December 1998, 54/231 of 22 December 1999, 55/212 of 20 December 2000, 56/209 of 21 December 2001, 57/274 of 20 December 2002, 58/225 of 23 December 2003, 59/240 of 22 December 2004, 60/204 of 22 December 2005, 61/207 of 20 December 2006 and 62/199 of 19 December 2007 on the role of the United Nations in promoting development in the context of globalization and interdependence,

Recalling also the 2005 World Summit Outcome and all relevant General Assembly resolutions, in particular those that have built upon the 2005 World Summit Outcome, in the economic, social and related fields, including resolution 60/265 of 30 June 2006 on follow-up to the development outcome of the 2005 World Summit, including the Millennium Development Goals and the other internationally agreed development goals,

Reaffirming that the United Nations has a central role in promoting international cooperation for development and in promoting policy coherence on global development issues, including in the context of globalization and interdependence,

Reaffirming also the resolve expressed in the United Nations Millennium Declaration to ensure that globalization works as a positive force for all,

Recognizing that all human rights are universal, indivisible, interdependent and interrelated,

Recognizing also that globalization, driven largely by economic liberalization and technology, implies that the economic performance of a country is increasingly affected by factors outside its geographical borders and that maximizing in an equitable manner the benefits of globalization requires developing responses to globalization through a strengthened global partnership for development to achieve the internationally agreed development goals, including the Millennium Development Goals,

Expressing concern that the number of people living in poverty is higher than previously estimated, despite significant progress, and that the current financial and food insecurity crises and unpredictable energy prices may pose significant challenges for the achievement of the internationally agreed development goals, including the Millennium Development Goals,

Recognizing that domestic economies are now interwoven with the global economy and that globalization affects all countries in different ways, and that countries on the one hand have trade and investment opportunities to, inter alia, fight poverty, while on the other hand they face constraints in the degree of flexibility they have in pursuing their national development strategies,

Reaffirming its strong support for fair and inclusive globalization and the need to translate growth into reduction of poverty and, in this regard, its resolve to make the goals of full and productive employment and decent work for all, including for women and young people, a central objective of relevant national and international policies as well as national development strategies, including poverty reduction strategies, as part of efforts to achieve the Millennium Development Goals,

Noting that particular attention must be given, in the context of globalization, to the objective of protecting, promoting and enhancing the rights and welfare of women and girls, as stated in the Beijing Declaration and Platform for Action,

Reaffirming its commitment to governance, equity and transparency in the financial, monetary and trading systems and its commitment to open, equitable, rule-based, predictable and non-discriminatory multilateral trading and financial systems,

1. *Takes note* of the report of the Secretary-General;

2. *Expresses deep concern* at the impact of the current financial crisis and global economic slowdown on the ability of developing countries to gain access to the financing necessary for their development objectives, and underlines the fact that developing countries and countries with economies in transition risk suffering very serious setbacks to their development objectives, in particular the achievement of the internationally agreed development goals, including the Millennium Development Goals;

3. *Recognizes* the measures adopted by Governments to address the present financial crisis, and, in that regard, calls upon all countries to manage their macroeconomic and financial policies in ways that contribute to global stability and sustained economic growth and sustainable development;

4. *Also recognizes* that greater coherence is required among the macroeconomic, trade, aid, financial, environmental and gender-equality policies to support the common aim of ensuring that globalization works as a positive force for all;

5. *Further recognizes* that new and highly globalized financial instruments continue to change the nature of risks in the world economy, requiring continuing enhancement of market oversight and regulation, and underlines the fact that, to strengthen the resilience of the international financial system, reforms will need to be implemented that will strengthen the regulatory and supervisory frameworks of financial markets;

6. *Underlines* the fact that economies exist in a globalizing world where the emergence of rule-based regimes for international economic relations has meant that the space for national economic policy, that is to say the scope for domestic policies, especially in the areas of trade, investment and industrial development, is now often framed by international disciplines, commitments and global market considerations, that it is for each Government to evaluate the trade-off between the benefits of accepting international rules and commitments and the constraints posed by the loss of policy space, and that it is particularly important for developing countries, bearing in mind development goals and objectives, that all countries take into account the need for appropriate balance between national policy space and international disciplines and commitments, and, in this regard, notes with appreciation the outcome of the twelfth session of the United Nations Conference on Trade and Development, held in Accra from 20 to 25 April 2008;

7. *Reaffirms* that good governance is essential for sustainable development, that sound economic policies, solid democratic institutions responsive to the needs of the people and improved infrastructure are the basis for sustained economic growth, poverty eradication and employment creation, and that freedom, peace and security, domestic stability, respect for human rights, including the right to development, and the rule of law, gender equality, market-oriented policies and an overall commitment to just and democratic societies are also essential and mutually reinforcing;

8. *Also reaffirms* that good governance at the international level is fundamental for achieving sustainable development, that, in order to ensure a dynamic and enabling international economic environment, it is important to promote global economic governance by addressing the international finance, trade, technology and investment patterns that have an impact on the development prospects of developing countries and that, to this end, the international community should take all necessary and appropriate measures, including ensuring support for structural and macroeconomic reform, a comprehensive solution to

the external debt problem and increasing the market access of developing countries;

9. *Further reaffirms* that each country has primary responsibility for its own development, that the role of national policies and development strategies cannot be overemphasized in the achievement of sustainable development, and that national efforts should be complemented by supportive global programmes, measures and policies aimed at expanding the development opportunities of developing countries, while taking into account national conditions and ensuring respect for national ownership, strategies and sovereignty;

10. *Reaffirms* the commitment to broaden and strengthen the participation of developing countries and countries with economies in transition in international economic decision-making and norm-setting, stresses, to that end, the importance of continuing efforts to reform the international financial architecture, noting that enhancing the voice and participation of developing countries and countries with economies in transition in the Bretton Woods institutions remains a continuous concern, and calls in this regard for further and effective progress;

11. *Stresses* the need for increased support for investment in agricultural productivity, particularly in developing countries, in order to achieve the internationally agreed development goals, including the Millennium Development Goals;

12. *Encourages* all development partners to help to strengthen and support the national health and education policies and plans of developing countries by providing assistance and funding in accordance with their development needs and priorities;

13. *Calls upon* Governments to assign a high priority to education, including by establishing institutions, in particular for basic education and vocational training, and improving access to and the quality of primary, secondary and tertiary education, including by developing a clear vision for the long-term development of a comprehensive, diversified and well-articulated tertiary education system;

14. *Calls upon* countries to increase public expenditure and encourage greater private and community investment to achieve international goals and targets in the areas of health, nutrition and sanitation consistent with public policy objectives related to equitable access as well as meeting the specific health goals of reducing child and maternal mortality and reducing the spread of diseases such as HIV/AIDS, tuberculosis and malaria;

15. *Calls upon* all countries to promote sustainable consumption and production patterns, with the developed countries taking the lead and all countries benefiting from the process, taking into account the Rio principles, including, inter alia, the principle of common but differentiated responsibilities as set out in principle 7 of the Rio Declaration on Environment and Development;

16. *Stresses* the need for all countries to harness knowledge and technology and stimulate innovation if they are to improve their competitiveness and benefit from trade and investment, and in this regard underlines the importance of concrete actions to facilitate technology transfer under fair, transparent and mutually agreed terms to developing countries in support of the implementation of their sustainable development strategies;

17. *Requests* the Secretary-General to submit to the General Assembly at its sixty-fourth session a report on the theme "Globalization and interdependence: the role of the United Nations in poverty reduction and sustainable development" under the item entitled "Globalization and interdependence";

18. *Decides* to include in the provisional agenda of its sixty-fourth session, under the item entitled "Globalization and interdependence", the sub-item entitled "Role of the United Nations in promoting development in the context of globalization and interdependence".

Also on 19 December, the Assembly, by **decision 63/540**, took note of the report of the Second Committee on its consideration of globalization and interdependence [A/63/416].

Development cooperation with middle-income countries

The third Ministerial Conference on Development Cooperation with Middle-Income Countries (MICs) was held in Windhoek, Namibia, from 4 to 6 August [A/C.2/63/3]. Previous conferences were held in Madrid, Spain [A/62/71-E/2007/46], and El Salvador [A/62/483-E/2007/90] in 2007. The Conference adopted the Windhoek Ministerial Declaration on Development Cooperation with Middle-Income Countries, which recognized the importance of reflecting the development needs of MICs, including those contained in its Declaration and in the outcomes of the international economic development processes. It invited the UN development system to enhance support to MICs and strengthen its coordination and exchange of experiences with other regional and international organizations and financial institutions. The Conference decided to present for the General Assembly's consideration, at its sixty-third (2008) session, a draft resolution mandating a comprehensive review of the practices of the international cooperation system, particularly international financial institutions associated with the UN system, its cooperation and development agencies and other international organizations regarding the development of MICs, with a view to achieving more effective cooperation and fostering international support. The Conference would continue to hold yearly follow-up conferences and other meetings on development cooperation with MICs. It also asked the UN system and other international organizations to support those endeavours and agreed to carry forward the work related to MIC issues, including the possibility of convening the next Conference at UN Headquarters in New York.

GENERAL ASSEMBLY ACTION

On 19 December [meeting 72], the General Assembly, on the recommendation of the Second Committee [A/63/416/Add.1], adopted **resolution 63/223** without vote [agenda item 51 *(a)*].

Development cooperation with middle-income countries

The General Assembly,

Recalling the outcomes of the United Nations major international conferences and summits, including the United Nations Millennium Declaration and the 2005 World Summit Outcome, as well as the relevant provisions of General Assembly resolutions,

Reaffirming its resolution 62/208 of 19 December 2007, entitled "Triennial comprehensive policy review of operational activities for development of the United Nations system", in which it recognized that middle-income developing countries still face significant challenges in the area of poverty eradication and that efforts to address those challenges should be supported in order to ensure that achievements made to date are sustained, including through support to the effective development of comprehensive cooperation policies,

Emphasizing that middle-income countries must take primary responsibility for their own development, and that their national efforts should be complemented by supportive global programmes, measures and policies aimed at expanding the development opportunities of middle-income countries, while taking into account their specific national conditions,

Noting that national averages based on criteria such as per capita income do not always reflect the actual particularities and development needs of the middle-income countries, and recognizing the significant diversity of middle-income countries,

Taking note of the outcomes of the international conferences on development cooperation with middle-income countries held in Madrid, El Salvador and Windhoek, and the regional conference on the theme "Increasing the competitiveness of African middle-income countries", held in Cairo,

1. *Recognizes* that middle-income countries still face significant challenges in their efforts to achieve the internationally agreed development goals, including the Millennium Development Goals, and, in that regard, underlines the importance of international support, through various forms, that is well aligned with national priorities, to address the development needs of middle-income countries;

2. *Acknowledges* the efforts made and successes achieved by many middle-income countries to eradicate poverty and achieve the internationally agreed development goals, including the Millennium Development Goals, as well as their significant contribution to global and regional development and economic stability;

3. *Recognizes* the solidarity of middle-income countries with other developing countries with a view to supporting their development efforts, including in the context of South-South and triangular cooperation;

4. *Invites* the United Nations development system to support middle-income countries, as appropriate, and to improve its coordination and exchange of experiences with other international organizations, international financial institutions and regional organizations in this field;

5. *Acknowledges* the initiative of middle-income countries to hold follow-up conferences and other meetings regarding their development on a yearly basis, and, in this regard, requests the United Nations system to continue supporting these endeavours in collaboration with other relevant international organizations;

6. *Requests* the Secretary-General to submit a comprehensive report on the implementation of all the elements of the present resolution to the General Assembly at its sixty-fourth session under the item entitled "Globalization and interdependence", with a focus on existing strategies and actions of the United Nations development system on development cooperation with middle-income countries, and taking into account the work of other relevant international organizations, including international financial institutions.

Industrial development

In response to General Assembly resolution 61/215 [YUN 2006, p. 980], the Secretary-General transmitted an August report [A/63/309] by the Director-General of the United Nations Industrial Development Organization (UNIDO) on industrial development cooperation that highlighted trends and developments in the industrial performance of developing countries, explored the challenges of industrialization and examined the response of the multilateral development system to them. The report also highlighted UNIDO's role in meeting the challenges of industrial development in partnership with UN and non-UN entities, particularly in LDCs, and outlined its contributions to the African Union New Partnership for Africa's Development [YUN 2001, p. 900].

According to the report, trends in industrial development showed that the manufacturing industry was shifting from developed to a number of developing countries, creating disparities in the industrial performance of various regions and within regions in the developing world. East Asia, and China in particular, far surpassed others in growth in manufactures. Other developing country regions showed a decline in growth, particularly Latin America, or continued to stagnate, as in sub-Saharan Africa. With support from international development partners, the green shoots of economic development could, as in many parts of Asia, transform Africa and the poorest countries of the world. However, the chief obstacles to doing so were: ongoing poverty in the face of an underdeveloped private sector, especially where small and medium-sized enterprises (SMEs) were concerned; barriers to international trade, which limited exports from developing countries; energy access; and climate change effects and the need for environmental protection to be built into industrial development, as well as access to information and technology.

The report concluded that, to narrow the disparities and fight poverty, private sector-led growth should be encouraged in those regions and countries left behind, particularly in LDCs. Industrial strategy should remove regulatory obstacles to economic activity and focus on building the "missing middle" by supporting the development of innovative and dynamic SMEs capable of competing locally and internationally. At the international level, equitable globalization required a multilateral trading agreement that reflected the development intentions of the Doha Round of trade negotiations (see p. 1050). Trade-related challenges facing developing-country enterprises, such as non-tariff barriers, growth in regionalism and over-reliance on primary commodity exports, should be addressed. Climate change should also be addressed, inter alia, through an international mechanism for the development and dissemination of technologies, with the aim of removing barriers and providing predictable financial resources and other incentives for scaling up investment in environmentally sound technologies, especially in developing countries. The multilateral development system, including international financial institutions and the UN system, should respond to those challenges and adapt to sudden changes or emerging needs. UNIDO should continue, in partnership with other relevant actors, to promote sustainable, private sector-led industrial development in order to help developing countries, especially LDCs, build up human and institutional capacities, enhance their international competitiveness, promote investment and technology transfer, promote small and medium-sized entrepreneurship development, develop agro-industries and strengthen its activities in energy for industry and in combating climate change.

GENERAL ASSEMBLY ACTION

On 19 December [meeting 72], the General Assembly, on the recommendation of the Second Committee [A/63/418/Add.2], adopted **resolution 63/231** without vote [agenda item 53 *(b)*].

Industrial development cooperation

The General Assembly,

Recalling its resolutions 46/151 of 18 December 1991, 49/108 of 19 December 1994, 51/170 of 16 December 1996, 53/177 of 15 December 1998, 55/187 of 20 December 2000, 57/243 of 20 December 2002, 59/249 of 22 December 2004 and 61/215 of 20 December 2006 on industrial development cooperation,

Recalling also the United Nations Millennium Declaration, the Monterrey Consensus of the International Conference on Financing for Development and the Plan of Implementation of the World Summit on Sustainable Development ("Johannesburg Plan of Implementation"),

Recalling further the 2005 World Summit Outcome and resolution 60/265 of 30 June 2006 on the follow-up to the development outcome of the 2005 World Summit, including the Millennium Development Goals and the other internationally agreed development goals,

Recognizing that industrialization is an essential driver of sustained economic growth, sustainable development and poverty eradication in developing countries and countries with economies in transition, including through the creation of productive employment, income generation and the facilitation of social integration, including the integration of women into the development process,

Stressing the importance of international cooperation to promote equitable and sustainable patterns of industrial development,

Recognizing the role of the business community, including the private sector, in enhancing the dynamic process of the development of the industrial sector, underlining the importance of the benefits of foreign direct investment in that process, and recognizing also, in this regard, that an enabling domestic environment is vital for mobilizing domestic resources, increasing productivity, reducing capital flight, encouraging the private sector and attracting and making effective use of international investment and assistance and that efforts to create such an environment should be supported by the international community,

Recognizing also the importance of the transfer of technology on mutually agreed terms to the developing countries as well as countries with economies in transition as an effective means of international cooperation in the pursuit of poverty eradication and sustainable development,

Noting that the United Nations Industrial Development Organization was awarded the Africa Investor Award for 2007 in the category "best initiative in support of small and medium-sized enterprise development",

Taking note of the important role played by the United Nations Industrial Development Organization in the development of the public and private sectors, productivity growth, trade capacity-building, corporate social responsibility, environmental protection, energy efficiency and the promotion of renewable energies,

1. *Takes note* of the note by the Secretary-General transmitting the report of the Director-General of the United Nations Industrial Development Organization;

2. *Reaffirms* that each country must take primary responsibility for its own industrial development and that national efforts should be complemented by supportive global programmes, measures and policies aimed at expanding the development opportunities of developing countries;

3. *Also reaffirms* the essential contribution of industrial development to sustained economic growth and social development and the achievement of the internationally agreed development goals, including the Millennium Development Goals;

4. *Emphasizes* the importance of the creation of wealth for poverty reduction and for pro-poor growth, especially with regard to women, through the development and strengthening of productive capacities in developing countries and countries with economies in transition, including through the development of the public and private sectors and entrepreneurship and through small and medium-sized enterprises, enterprise upgrading, training, education and skills enhancement and an enabling environment for the

transfer of technology on mutually agreed terms, the flow of investments and participation in global supply chains;

5. *Underlines* the necessity of favourable national and international measures for industrialization in developing countries and countries with economies in transition, and urges all Governments to develop and implement policies that will lead to the development of a dynamic industrial sector through, inter alia, public- and private-sector development, the diffusion of environmentally sound and emerging technologies, investment promotion and enhanced access to markets;

6. *Calls for* the continuing use of official development assistance for sustainable industrial development, the achievement of greater efficiency and effectiveness of official development assistance resources and industrial development cooperation between developing countries and with countries with economies in transition;

7. *Underlines* the importance of mobilizing resources for sustainable industrial development at the country level;

8. *Calls for* the continuing use of all other resources, including private and public, foreign and domestic resources, for industrial development in the developing countries as well as countries with economies in transition;

9. *Recognizes* the key role of the United Nations Industrial Development Organization in promoting sustainable industrial development and in industrial development cooperation, and welcomes its increased programmatic focus on three thematic priorities, namely, poverty reduction through productive activities, trade capacity-building and environment and energy;

10. *Calls upon* the United Nations Industrial Development Organization to take appropriate actions for the full implementation of General Assembly resolution 62/208 of 19 December 2007;

11. *Recognizes* that the current food crisis represents a serious and complex challenge affecting the world's poor, and looks forward to discussions and a report on how the United Nations Industrial Development Organization might best contribute to a system-wide solution to the crisis;

12. *Stresses* the importance of the development of agro-industries and the reduction of post-harvest losses, including through the introduction of improved technologies and the increased processing of agricultural products in developing countries and countries with economies in transition, and encourages the parties in the ongoing discussions being held in Vienna to consider how the United Nations Industrial Development Organization could best contribute to those objectives, including discussions aimed at helping to achieve global food security;

13. *Notes* the emphasis placed by the United Nations Industrial Development Organization on assisting developing countries and countries with economies in transition to strengthen their capacity to engage in international trade through small and medium-sized enterprise development and by helping them to meet international product and process standards;

14. *Welcomes* the increased cooperation of the United Nations Industrial Development Organization with the United Nations Conference on Trade and Development, the International Trade Centre UNCTAD/WTO, the World Trade Organization, the United Nations Development Programme, the United Nations Environment Programme, the World Health Organization, the Food and Agriculture Organization of the United Nations and the regional commissions, and invites the United Nations Industrial Development Organization to continue to build and strengthen its partnership with other United Nations organizations having complementary mandates and activities with a view to achieving greater effectiveness and development impact and promoting increased coherence within the United Nations system;

15. *Encourages* the United Nations Industrial Development Organization to continue to promote environmentally sound and sustainable production through, inter alia, its programmes on cleaner production, industrial water management and industrial energy efficiency and the utilization of renewable energy for productive uses, especially in rural areas;

16. *Takes note* of the increased emphasis given by the United Nations Industrial Development Organization to South-South cooperation, including triangular cooperation, and encourages it to pay particular attention to promoting industrial cooperation among developing countries, including through its centres for South-South industrial cooperation and through the promotion of various forms of public/private-sector partnerships and the exchange of experiences in public- and private-sector development, including at the regional, subregional and country levels, with regard to industrial development;

17. *Welcomes* the support of the United Nations Industrial Development Organization for the New Partnership for Africa's Development and other programmes of the African Union, including the Pharmaceutical Manufacturing Plan for Africa, aimed at further strengthening the industrialization process in Africa, inter alia, through its role as the convener of the industry, trade and market access cluster of the regional consultation meetings led by the Economic Commission for Africa;

18. *Recognizes* the importance of industrial development in post-conflict countries, particularly through employment-generating activities and energy supply, and encourages the United Nations Industrial Development Organization to assist in these efforts within its mandate, including, where applicable, by providing assistance in the implementation of the integrated peacebuilding strategies of the Peacebuilding Commission;

19. *Encourages* the United Nations Industrial Development Organization to develop further its global forum capacity according to its mandate, with the aim of enhancing, in the context of the globalization process, a common understanding of global and regional industrial sector issues and their impact on poverty eradication and sustainable development;

20. *Requests* the Secretary-General to submit to the General Assembly at its sixty-fifth session a report on the implementation of the present resolution.

Towards a New International Economic Order

On 19 December [meeting 72], the General Assembly, on the recommendation of the Second Committee [A/63/416/Add.1], adopted **resolution 63/224** by recorded vote (123-1-52) [agenda item 51 *(a)*].

Towards a New International Economic Order

The General Assembly,

Bearing in mind the purposes and principles of the Charter of the United Nations to promote the economic advancement and social progress of all peoples,

Recalling the principles of the Declaration on the Establishment of a New International Economic Order and the Programme of Action on the Establishment of a New International Economic Order, as set out in resolutions 3201(S-VI) and 3202(S-VI), respectively, adopted by the General Assembly at its sixth special session, on 1 May 1974,

Taking into account the fact that the year 2009 marks the thirty-fifth anniversary of the adoption of the Declaration and the Programme of Action,

Reaffirming the United Nations Millennium Declaration,

Recalling the outcomes of the major United Nations conferences and summits in the economic, social and related fields, including the development goals and objectives contained therein, and recognizing the vital role played by those conferences and summits in shaping a broad development vision and in identifying commonly agreed objectives,

Concerned that the current international economic, financial, energy and food crises, as well as the challenges posed by climate change, aggravate the existing international situation and have a negative impact on the development prospects of developing countries, while threatening to further widen the gap between developed and developing countries, including the technological and income gap,

1. *Reaffirms* the need to continue working towards a new international economic order based on the principles of equity, sovereign equality, interdependence, common interest, cooperation and solidarity among all States;

2. *Decides* to consider in depth the international economic situation and its impact on development during the sixty-fourth session of the General Assembly, and in that regard requests the Secretary-General to include in his next report, under the item entitled "Globalization and interdependence", an overview of the major international economic and policy challenges for equitable and inclusive sustained economic growth and sustainable development, and of the role of the United Nations in addressing these issues, in the light of the relevant principles contained in the Declaration on the Establishment of a New International Economic Order and the Programme of Action on the Establishment of a New International Economic Order.

RECORDED VOTE ON RESOLUTION 63/224:

In favour: Afghanistan, Algeria, Angola, Antigua and Barbuda, Argentina, Armenia, Azerbaijan, Bahamas, Bahrain, Bangladesh, Barbados, Belize, Benin, Bhutan, Bolivia, Brazil, Brunei Darussalam, Burkina Faso, Burundi, Cambodia, Cameroon, Cape Verde, Chad, Chile, China, Colombia, Comoros, Congo, Costa Rica, Côte d'Ivoire, Cuba, Democratic People's Republic of Korea, Djibouti, Dominica, Dominican Republic, Ecuador, Egypt, El Salvador, Eritrea, Ethiopia, Fiji, Ghana, Grenada, Guatemala, Guinea, Guyana, Haiti, Honduras, India, Indonesia, Iran, Iraq, Jamaica, Jordan, Kazakhstan, Kenya, Kuwait, Kyrgyzstan, Lao People's Democratic Republic, Lebanon, Liberia, Libyan Arab Jamahiriya, Madagascar, Malawi, Malaysia, Maldives, Mali, Marshall Islands, Mauritania, Mauritius, Mexico, Micronesia, Mongolia, Morocco, Mozambique, Myanmar, Namibia, Nepal, Nicaragua, Niger, Nigeria, Oman, Pakistan, Panama, Papua New Guinea, Paraguay, Peru, Philippines, Qatar, Russian Federation, Rwanda, Saint Lucia, Saint Vincent and the Grenadines, Samoa, Sao Tome and Principe, Saudi Arabia, Senegal, Singapore, Solomon Islands, South Africa, Sri Lanka, Sudan, Suriname, Swaziland, Syrian Arab Republic, Tajikistan, Thailand, Timor-Leste, Togo, Tonga, Trinidad and Tobago, Tunisia, Uganda, United Arab Emirates, United Republic of Tanzania, Uruguay, Uzbekistan, Vanuatu, Venezuela, Viet Nam, Yemen, Zambia, Zimbabwe.

Against: United States.

Abstaining: Albania, Andorra, Australia, Austria, Belgium, Bosnia and Herzegovina, Bulgaria, Canada, Croatia, Cyprus, Czech Republic, Denmark, Estonia, Finland, France, Georgia, Germany, Greece, Hungary, Iceland, Ireland, Israel, Italy, Japan, Latvia, Liechtenstein, Lithuania, Luxembourg, Malta, Moldova, Monaco, Montenegro, Netherlands, New Zealand, Norway, Palau, Poland, Portugal, Republic of Korea, Romania, San Marino, Serbia, Slovakia, Slovenia, Spain, Sweden, Switzerland, The Former Yugoslav Republic of Macedonia, Turkey, Tuvalu, Ukraine, United Kingdom.

Sustainable development

Implementation of Agenda 21, Programme for Further Implementation of Agenda 21 and Johannesburg Plan of Implementation

In 2008, several UN bodies, including the General Assembly, the Economic and Social Council and the Commission on Sustainable Development, considered the implementation of outcomes of the 2002 World Summit on Sustainable Development [YUN 2002, p. 821], particularly the Johannesburg Declaration and Plan of Implementation, which outlined actions and targets for stepping up implementation of Agenda 21—a programme of action for sustainable development worldwide, adopted at the 1992 United Nations Conference on Environment and Development [YUN 1992, p. 672]—and of the Programme for the Further Implementation of Agenda 21, adopted by the Assembly at its nineteenth special session in 1997 [YUN 1997, p. 792].

Commission on Sustainable Development consideration. As the body responsible for coordinating and monitoring implementation of the Summit outcomes, the Commission on Sustainable Development, at its sixteenth session (New York, 11 May 2007, 5–16 May 2008) [E/2008/29], discussed, in line with the multi-year programme adopted by the Council in resolution 2003/61 [YUN 2003, p. 842], the thematic cluster for the 2008–2009 implementation cycle: agriculture; rural development; land; drought; desertification; and Africa.

Intersessional events. The following intersessional events took place in preparation for the sixteenth session: Water Technologies and Environmental Control Conference (Tel Aviv, Israel, 30–31 October

2007); Seventh Global Forum on Sustainable Energy (Vienna, 21–23 November 2007); International Conference on Combating Desertification (Beijing, 22–24 January 2008); Oslo Policy Forum on Changing the Way We Develop: Dealing with Disasters and Climate Change (Oslo, Norway, 27–29 February); and High-level Round Table on International Cooperation for Sustainable Development in Caribbean Small Island Developing States (Bridgetown, Barbados, 25–27 March).

Thematic issues. For its consideration of the thematic cluster for the 2008–2009 implementation cycle, the Commission considered the Secretary-General's reports on: agriculture [E/CN.17/2008/3]; rural development [E/CN.17/2008/4]; Africa [E/CN.17/2008/8]; review of implementation on land [E/CN.17/2008/5]; review of implementation of Agenda 21 and the Johannesburg Plan of Implementation: drought [E/CN.17/2008/6] and desertification [E/CN.17/2008/7]; integrated review of the thematic cluster in small island developing States [E/CN.17/2008/9]; overview of progress towards sustainable development: a review of the implementation of Agenda 21, the Programme for the Further Implementation of Agenda 21 and the Johannesburg Plan of Implementation [E/CN.17/2008/2]; partnerships for sustainable development [E/CN.17/2008/10]; and review of progress in implementing the decision of the thirteenth session of the Commission on water and sanitation [E/CN.17/2008/11]. It also considered a note by the Secretariat on the outcomes of the regional implementation meetings [E/CN.17/2008/12]; reports on the five regional discussions [E/CN.17/2008/12/Add.1-5]; and discussion papers by major groups [E/CN.17/2008/13 & Add.1–9].

Implementation activities

In response to General Assembly resolution 62/189 [YUN 2007, p. 842], the Secretary-General submitted an August report [A/63/304] on the implementation of Agenda 21, the Programme for the Further Implementation of Agenda 21 and the outcomes of the World Summit on Sustainable Development that provided an update on actions taken by Governments, UN system organizations and major groups of civil society in advancing the implementation of sustainable development goals and targets, including through partnerships. The report reviewed new and emerging challenges, actions undertaken at the intergovernmental level, implementation by the UN system, activities undertaken by regions and special groups and the creation of partnerships to foster sustainable development. According to the report, the international community was tackling multiple interlinked challenges arising from the food and energy crises and climate change, which adversely affected the most vulnerable populations and impeded progress towards the achievement of the internationally agreed development goals. Integrated and coordinated action was therefore necessary to alleviate their impact and create global partnerships for their short- and long-term solutions. Meeting those challenges would require a more integrated and balanced approach to economic, social and environmental policies tailored to each country's needs, more space for implementing counter-cyclical macroeconomic policies, international support for broader social protection schemes, and more investment in environmental policies, multi-stakeholder dialogues, decision-making, monitoring and evaluation. It also required incorporating the three pillars of sustainable development into national strategies. As at February, 82 countries had implemented development strategies, while an additional 16 had formulated, and would soon start implementing, them. Many countries had applied the principles of sustainable development to the formulation of sector strategies, as the current crises showed the need for more investment in agriculture and rural development, together with the prevention of land degradation, the development of land tenure systems and the sustainable management of natural resources.

At the intergovernmental level, the Economic and Social Council focused on sustainable development challenges, including the state of the world economy and its implications for the achievement of UN development goals. The sixteenth session of the Commission on Sustainable Development, during its review session, focused on the thematic cluster of agriculture, rural development, land, drought, desertification and Africa. At the inter-agency level, UN-Water—the official UN mechanism for follow-up to the water-related decisions of the 2002 World Summit and the MDGs—continued its work in all aspects related to water and sanitation, including the preparation of a status report on integrated water resources management and a water efficiency plan for the Commission's sixteenth session. UN-Water also launched a status report on integrated water resources management and plans for efficient, equitable and sustainable development and management of the world's limited water resources and for coping with conflicting demands. It also continued working on the decade's central themes: scarcity, access to sanitation and health, water and gender, capacity-building, financing, valuation, integrated water resources management, environment and biodiversity, disaster prevention, food and agriculture, and coordinated activities for the International Year of Sanitation 2008. The Division for Sustainable Development of the Department of Economic and Social Affairs (DESA) organized a Caribbean workshop on sanitation, entitled "Integration of sanitation policies into national development plans in the Caribbean region" (Kingston, Jamaica, 28–29 April).

At the regional level, the UN regional commissions and offices, regional development banks and other organizations expedited the implementation of sustainable development goals and targets. The five regional commissions—for Africa, Western Asia, Asia and the Pacific, Latin America and the Caribbean, and Europe—organized ministerial-level implementation meetings and continued to integrate sustainable development into their work. The Economic Commission for Africa and the secretariat of the United Nations Convention to Combat Desertification signed a memorandum of understanding in March aimed at enhancing collaboration in implementing the Convention, notably in those countries experiencing serious drought and/or desertification. Major groups implemented innovative policies and programmes and made progress in carrying out projects related to the thematic issues addressed in the Commission's multi-year programme of work and in addressing cross-cutting issues such as poverty eradication, education, health and gender equality.

Voluntary multi-stakeholder partnerships proved to be an important complementary outcome of the World Summit and a viable implementation mechanism. They continued to develop and grow, and their wide acceptance was embedded in the international dialogue and had become an integral part of the work of the UN system. By collaborating across all levels, pooling skills and resources, and developing innovative policy and technical and financing solutions to overcome barriers to sustainable development, partnerships contributed to the implementation of internationally agreed sustainable development goals and commitments. They were also useful as a vehicle for effecting change by catalysing Government action, engaging a wide range of stakeholders and creating new, innovative models for the implementation of goals and commitments. As at July, 344 partnerships were registered with the Commission secretariat, 102 of which had identified agriculture, drought, desertification, land, rural development and Africa as the primary focus of their activities.

The Secretary-General recommended that the Assembly call on Governments, UN system organizations and major groups to deepen their commitments to sustainable development by redoubling their efforts to implement Agenda 21, the Programme for the Further Implementation of Agenda 21 and the Johannesburg Plan of Implementation, expediting progress in implementation through the exchange of lessons learned and best practices. Governments should support the Commission and organize intersessional activities, taking into account the Commission's 2008–2009 thematic cluster of issues, and emphasize the importance of a consensus outcome and action-oriented policy sessions; and contribute to the Commission's trust fund in support of enhanced participation of representatives of developing countries and of major groups in the Commission's work. The Assembly should invite the United Nations System Chief Executives Board for Coordination (CEB) to continue monitoring, through its High-level Committee on Programmes, the operational efficiency and effectiveness of inter-agency collaborative mechanisms, including UN-Energy, UN-Water and UN-Oceans. Donors should target funding support to help developing countries overcome constraints identified during the review year in the thematic cluster.

GENERAL ASSEMBLY ACTION

On 19 December [meeting 72], the General Assembly, on the recommendation of the Second Committee [A/63/414/Add.1], adopted **resolution 63/212** without vote [agenda item 49 *(a)*].

Implementation of Agenda 21, the Programme for the Further Implementation of Agenda 21 and the outcomes of the World Summit on Sustainable Development

The General Assembly,

Recalling its resolutions 55/199 of 20 December 2000, 56/226 of 24 December 2001, 57/253 of 20 December 2002, 57/270 A and B of 20 December 2002 and 23 June 2003, respectively, 61/195 of 20 December 2006 and 62/189 of 19 December 2007, and all other previous resolutions on the implementation of Agenda 21, the Programme for the Further Implementation of Agenda 21 and the outcomes of the World Summit on Sustainable Development,

Recalling also the Rio Declaration on Environment and Development, Agenda 21, the Programme for the Further Implementation of Agenda 21, the Johannesburg Declaration on Sustainable Development and the Plan of Implementation of the World Summit on Sustainable Development ("Johannesburg Plan of Implementation"), as well as the Monterrey Consensus of the International Conference on Financing for Development,

Reaffirming the commitment to implement Agenda 21, the Programme for the Further Implementation of Agenda 21, the Johannesburg Plan of Implementation, including the time-bound goals and targets, and the other internationally agreed development goals, including the Millennium Development Goals,

Recalling the 2005 World Summit Outcome,

Reaffirming the decisions taken at the eleventh session of the Commission on Sustainable Development,

Reiterating that sustainable development in its economic, social and environmental aspects is a key element of the overarching framework for United Nations activities, and reaffirming the continuing need to ensure a balance among economic development, social development and environmental protection as interdependent and mutually reinforcing pillars of sustainable development,

Noting that challenges remain in achieving the goals of the three pillars of sustainable development, particularly in the context of the current global crises,

Taking note of the proposal to convene a world summit on sustainable development in 2012,

Bearing in mind the need for further consultations on this matter, in the light of the variety of views expressed by Member States, recognizing that the preparatory process, content, modalities and timing for such a possible high-level event on sustainable development would need to be determined taking into account the work of the Commission, particularly as established in its multi-year programme of work, with a view to avoiding duplication of work,

Recalling the adoption of the Commission multi-year programme of work designed to contribute to advancing the implementation of Agenda 21, the Programme for the Further Implementation of Agenda 21 and the Johannesburg Plan of Implementation at all levels,

Reaffirming that eradicating poverty, changing unsustainable patterns of production and consumption and protecting and managing the natural resource base of economic and social development are overarching objectives of and essential requirements for sustainable development,

Recognizing that good governance within each country and at the international level is essential for sustainable development,

Recalling that the Johannesburg Plan of Implementation designated the Commission to serve as the focal point for discussion on partnerships that promote sustainable development and contribute to the implementation of intergovernmental commitments in Agenda 21, the Programme for the Further Implementation of Agenda 21 and the Johannesburg Plan of Implementation,

Recognizing that eradicating poverty is the greatest global challenge facing the world today and an indispensable requirement for sustainable development, in particular for developing countries, and that although each country has the primary responsibility for its own sustainable development and poverty eradication and the role of national policies and development strategies cannot be overemphasized, concerted and concrete measures are required at all levels to enable developing countries to achieve their sustainable development goals as related to the internationally agreed poverty-related targets and goals, including those contained in Agenda 21, the relevant outcomes of other United Nations conferences and the United Nations Millennium Declaration,

Recalling that the Economic and Social Council should increase its role in overseeing system-wide coordination and the balanced integration of economic, social and environmental aspects of United Nations policies and programmes aimed at promoting sustainable development, and reaffirming that the Commission should continue to be the high-level commission on sustainable development within the United Nations system and serve as a forum for consideration of issues related to integration of the three dimensions of sustainable development,

Recalling also that agriculture, rural development, land, drought and desertification are interlinked and should be addressed in an integrated manner, taking into account economic, social and environmental dimensions of sustainable development, related sectoral policies and cross-cutting issues including means of implementation, as identified at the eleventh session of the Commission,

Recognizing the problems and constraints that African countries are facing in the areas of agriculture, rural development, land, drought and desertification, and emphasizing that those problems and constraints should be adequately addressed during the seventeenth session of the Commission, which will be a policy session,

Recalling the decision of the Commission at its eleventh session, endorsed by the Economic and Social Council in its resolution 2003/61 of 25 July 2003, that the Commission, at its policy sessions, to be held in April/May of the second year of the cycle of the Commission's work programme, would take policy decisions on practical measures and options to expedite implementation in the selected thematic cluster of issues, taking account of the discussions of the Intergovernmental Preparatory Meeting, the reports of the Secretary-General and other relevant inputs,

Recalling also the decision of the Commission at its eleventh session that the discussions of the Intergovernmental Preparatory Meeting would be based on the outcome of the review session and reports of the Secretary-General, as well as other relevant inputs, and that, on the basis of those discussions, the Chair would prepare a draft negotiating document for consideration at the policy session,

Recognizing the importance of the Intergovernmental Preparatory Meeting in respect of discussing policy options and possible actions to address the constraints and obstacles in the process of implementation identified during the review year,

Noting with satisfaction that the Commission at its sixteenth session undertook an in-depth evaluation of progress in implementing Agenda 21, the Programme for the Further Implementation of Agenda 21 and the Johannesburg Plan of Implementation, focusing on the thematic cluster of issues on agriculture, rural development, land, drought, desertification and Africa, taking into account the interlinkages as well as addressing the cross-cutting issues, and identified best practices, constraints and obstacles in the process of implementation,

Noting with satisfaction also the review of the implementation of the Commission's decisions on water, held by the Commission at its sixteenth session,

1. *Takes note* of the report of the Secretary-General;

2. *Reiterates* that sustainable development is a key element of the overarching framework for United Nations activities, in particular for achieving the internationally agreed development goals, including the Millennium Development Goals, and those contained in the Johannesburg Plan of Implementation;

3. *Calls upon* Governments, all relevant international and regional organizations, the Economic and Social Council, the United Nations funds and programmes, the regional commissions and the specialized agencies, the international financial institutions, the Global Environment Facility and other intergovernmental organizations, in accordance with their respective mandates, as well as major groups, to take action to ensure the effective implementation of and follow-up to the commitments, programmes and time-bound targets adopted at the World Summit on Sustainable Development, and encourages them to report on concrete progress in that regard;

4. *Calls for* the effective implementation of the commitments, programmes and time-bound targets adopted at the World Summit on Sustainable Development and for the fulfilment of the provisions relating to the means of implementation, as contained in the Johannesburg Plan of Implementation;

5. *Invites* Member States to express their views on the possibility of convening a high-level event on sustainable development, and requests the Secretary-General, in his report on the implementation of Agenda 21, the Programme for the Further Implementation of Agenda 21 and the outcomes of the World Summit on Sustainable Development, to include the views expressed, and decides to consider this matter further at the sixty-fourth session of the General Assembly;

6. *Reiterates* that the Commission on Sustainable Development is the high-level body responsible for sustainable development within the United Nations system and serves as a forum for the consideration of issues related to the integration of the three dimensions of sustainable development;

7. *Emphasizes* the importance of a consensus outcome and action-oriented policy sessions;

8. *Encourages* Governments to participate at the appropriate level with representatives, including ministers, from the relevant departments and organizations working in the areas of agriculture, rural development, land, drought, desertification and Africa, as well as finance, in the seventeenth session of the Commission and its Intergovernmental Preparatory Meeting;

9. *Recalls* the decision of the Commission at its eleventh session that activities during Commission meetings should provide for the balanced involvement of participants from all regions, as well as for gender balance;

10. *Invites* donor countries to consider supporting the participation of representatives from the developing countries in the seventeenth session of the Commission and its Intergovernmental Preparatory Meeting, inter alia, through contributions to the Commission's trust fund;

11. *Reaffirms* the objective of strengthening the implementation of Agenda 21, including through the mobilization of financial and technological resources, as well as capacity-building programmes, in particular for developing countries;

12. *Invites* donor Governments and international financial institutions to support the efforts of developing countries to overcome barriers and constraints identified during the review year in the thematic cluster of issues of agriculture, rural development, land, drought, desertification and Africa;

13. *Reaffirms* the objective of enhancing the participation and effective involvement of civil society and other relevant stakeholders, as well as promoting transparency and broad public participation, in the implementation of Agenda 21;

14. *Requests* the secretariat of the Commission to coordinate the participation of the relevant major groups in the thematic discussions at the seventeenth session of the Commission and its Intergovernmental Preparatory Meeting and the reporting on the fulfilment of corporate accountability and responsibility with respect to the thematic cluster of issues, in accordance with the provisions of the Johannesburg Plan of Implementation;

15. *Reaffirms* the need to promote corporate responsibility and accountability as envisaged by the Johannesburg Plan of Implementation;

16. *Also reaffirms* the need to promote the development of microenterprises and small and medium-sized enterprises, including by means of training, education and skill enhancement, with a special focus on agro-industry as a provider of livelihoods for rural communities;

17. *Requests* the secretariat of the Commission to make arrangements to facilitate the balanced representation of major groups from developed and developing countries in the sessions of the Commission, and in this regard invites donor countries to consider supporting the participation of major groups from developing countries, inter alia, through contributions to the Commission's trust fund;

18. *Reiterates the invitation* to the relevant specialized agencies, including the Food and Agriculture Organization of the United Nations and the International Fund for Agricultural Development, United Nations funds and programmes, the Global Environment Facility and international and regional financial and trade institutions, as well as the secretariat of the United Nations Convention to Combat Desertification in Those Countries Experiencing Serious Drought and/or Desertification, Particularly in Africa, and other relevant bodies, to actively participate, within their mandates, in the work of the Commission and its Intergovernmental Preparatory Meeting at its seventeenth session;

19. *Encourages* Governments and organizations at all levels, as well as major groups, to undertake results-oriented initiatives and activities to support the work of the Commission and to promote and facilitate the implementation of Agenda 21, the Programme for the Further Implementation of Agenda 21 and the Johannesburg Plan of Implementation, including through voluntary multi-stakeholder partnership initiatives;

20. *Requests* the Secretary-General, in reporting to the Commission at its seventeenth session, on the basis of appropriate inputs from all levels, to submit thematic reports on each of the six issues contained in the thematic cluster of issues on agriculture, rural development, land, drought, desertification and Africa, taking into account their interlinkages, while addressing the cross-cutting issues, including means of implementation identified by the Commission at its eleventh session, and also takes into account the relevant provisions of paragraphs 10, 14 and 15 of draft resolution I of the eleventh session of the Commission;

21. *Underlines* the importance of setting aside adequate time for all envisaged activities in the policy session, including for negotiations on policy options and possible actions, at the seventeenth session of the Commission, and in this regard notes the importance of having all required documents, including the Chair's draft negotiating document, made available for consideration prior to the beginning of the session;

22. *Decides* to include in the provisional agenda of its sixty-fourth session the sub-item entitled "Implementation of Agenda 21, the Programme for the Further Implementation of Agenda 21 and the outcomes of the World Summit on Sustainable Development", and requests the Secretary-General, at that session, to submit a report on the implementation of the present resolution.

Sustainable development goals and climate change

CDP consideration. At its tenth session (New York, 17–20 March) [E/2008/33], the Committee for Development Policy (CDP) considered the theme "Achieving sustainable development goals in the context of climate change". CDP addressed the key channels through which climate change could affect development and ways of protecting against those impacts, namely through adaptation and mitigation policies, international cooperation (especially in finance and technology) and policy coherence.

The Committee was of the view that, for developing countries, sustainable development confronted a three-dimensional threat from climate change: its implications for human development and prosperity, which were at the heart of the MDGs; the spillover of climate-related policies in the industrialized world; and the implications of actions by developing countries to adapt to and mitigate it, even as they avoided the previous damaging pattern to the environment of developed countries. The challenge was to ensure that a coherent approach at the national and international levels protected the momentum of development against the possible adverse impacts of the three sources of threat. Those threats would particularly affect the development prospects of LDCs and small island developing States, which had contributed the least to the emission of greenhouse gases but were the most vulnerable and had the least capacity to adapt. Over time, one likely outcome of climate change was the disappearance of some small island developing States as a result of a rise in the sea level. African countries were among the most vulnerable, owing to a low adaptive capacity caused by widespread, extreme poverty and projected changes in precipitation coming on top of an already stressed situation. Achieving the internationally agreed goals on sustainable development would not be possible without deep overall reductions in carbon emissions. The developed countries should take the lead in cutting their emissions and assisting developing countries to take action. However, reductions in developed countries alone could not be globally effective without slowing down the growth of emissions in the developing countries as well. A critical issue was whether and how developing countries could achieve such emission reductions while maintaining the economic growth needed to support their developmental efforts. To do so would require significant financial support from developed countries, and technology transfer and capacity-building in taking mitigation measures.

CDP concluded that, as adapting to climate change was critical for sustainable development, the adaptive capacity of developing countries, especially LDCs, should be strengthened. Progress in that regard would also require mainstreaming adaptation into sectoral and national planning processes, including poverty reduction strategies. Mitigation actions by both developed and developing countries to achieve sustainable development should take place in accordance with the principle of common but differentiated responsibilities. The most promising mitigation strategy for developing countries would be an investment-based approach that encouraged greater energy efficiency and renewable energy alternatives, with technological support, regulatory and fiscal instruments, and research and education, thereby fostering sustainable development. Achieving the MDGs while dealing with climate change would require access by developing countries to sufficient funds and knowledge and the development of new technologies. CDP recommended that the Economic and Social Council review the adequacy of international commitments on financing for development, particularly the resources required for achieving sustainable development. Urgent consideration should be given to the creation of large-scale global funds to finance the transfer of technology for mitigation and meeting adaptation costs.

Commission on Sustainable Development

The Commission on Sustainable Development held its sixteenth session (policy session) in New York on 11 May 2007 and from 5 to 16 May 2008 [E/2008/29]. On 16 May, it held the first part of its seventeenth session, at which it elected the members of the Bureau [E/2009/29]. The Commission's high-level segment (14–16 May) considered the topic "The way forward". On 14 May, the Commission held parallel high-level round-table meetings on investing in Africa to achieve the MDGs and sustainable development, and interlinkages among the thematic issues, including adaptation to climate change in the context of sustainable development. On 15 May, it held an interactive discussion with UN organizations, regional commissions, specialized agencies and the Bretton Woods institutions (the World Bank Group and IMF), as well as an interactive discussion with representatives of major groups.

The Commission recommended to the Economic and Social Council for adoption one draft decision on its report on its sixteenth session and provisional agenda for its seventeenth session. It also adopted three decisions on: participation of intergovernmental organizations in the work of its sixteenth session [dec. 16/1]; the review of the Mauritius Strategy for the Further Implementation of the Programme of Action for the Sustainable Development of Small Island Developing States [dec. 16/2] (see p. 946); and the proposed strategic framework for the period 2010–2011: subprogramme 4, Sustainable development [E/CN.17/2008/14] [dec. 16/3].

Ministers and delegations undertook negotiations on the interlinked issues of the thematic cluster: agriculture, rural development; land; drought, desertification and Africa. The Commission devoted a meeting, on 12 May, to the review of the implementation of the Programme of Action for the Sustainable Development of Small Island Developing States, focusing on the thematic cluster for the 2008–2009 implementation cycle (see p. 945).

On 13 and 14 May, the Commission discussed implementation of the decisions on water and sanitation and their interlinkages taken at its thirteenth session [YUN 2005, p. 917]. Various aspects were addressed, including: the importance of global and national monitoring of the sector at all levels; the need for reliable data supported by improved knowledge and research; transfer of technology and capacity-building; the importance of water governance and a participatory approach to water and sanitation; the role of partnerships, including the public-private partnership; and the importance of strengthening water utilities to extend the provision of services.

The partnerships fair (5–13 May) showcased activities focusing on agriculture, drought, desertification, land, rural development and Africa, small island developing States, and water and sanitation. The fair provided a venue for registered Partnerships for Sustainable Development to showcase progress, network with existing and potential partners, create synergies and learn from each other's experiences. It also allowed participants to gather information and discuss the contribution of innovative initiatives to supporting the implementation of internationally agreed sustainable development goals and objectives. A learning centre offered 20 courses on topics related to the themes and cross-cutting issues under review, including education, gender, decision-making tools, financing and national sustainable development strategies. Some 88 side events and related activities were organized by major groups, Governments, UN agencies and other international organizations, focusing on issues related to the thematic cluster.

The Economic and Social Council, on 23 July, took note of the Commission's report at its sixteenth session [E/2008/29] and approved the provisional agenda for its seventeenth (2009) session (**decision 2008/237**).

Eradication of poverty

UN Decade for the Eradication of Poverty

In response to General Assembly resolution 62/205 [YUN 2007, p. 847], the Secretary-General, in July [A/63/190], submitted a report on the implementation of the Second United Nations Decade for the Eradication of Poverty (2008–2017), proclaimed by the Assembly in 2007, which provided recommendations on how to make the Second Decade effective in support of poverty eradication-related internationally agreed development goals. The report summarized the conclusions of the review of the First United Nations Decade for the Eradication of Poverty (1997–2006); highlighted lessons learned from other current international decades proclaimed by the Assembly; summarized inputs received from Governments and civil society on how to make the Second Decade effective; and examined the UN system's role in scaling up poverty eradication efforts in support of the Second Decade. It concluded with a number of recommendations for consideration by the Assembly.

The Secretary-General considered the Second Decade as a framework for reflection and action to achieve the poverty eradication-related internationally agreed development goals, and an opportunity for strengthening social institutions and implementing public policies to generate development. Based on a review of practical examples and the experience of the First Decade, the implementation of the Second Decade would depend on national ownership of activities and should be encouraged and supported by the international community. Achievements and failures in fighting poverty during the First Decade pointed to the critical importance of productive employment and decent work. Striving to ensure basic economic security for all in the face of growing job insecurity should be part of collective efforts to make the Second Decade a success. At the dawn of the Second Decade, the theme for the First Decade had become reality: eradicating poverty was universally perceived as an ethical, social, political and economic imperative of humankind, and the onus was on Governments, civil society, including the private sector, and international organizations to respond effectively.

The Secretary-General recommended that the Assembly adopt an overall action theme for the Second Decade that would convey a sense of urgency towards implementing the commitments made to eradicate poverty and to halve poverty by 2015; and integrate the observance of the International Day for the Eradication of Poverty into the plan of action for the Second Decade to enhance the role the observance could play in raising public awareness and mobilizing stakeholders. A pragmatic plan of action in support of the Second Decade, critical to ensuring its implementation, should focus on the complementarities of efforts to support national poverty eradication strategies and programmes, and make maximum use of inter-agency mechanisms to support those activities. The plan of action would include a programme of substantive work in poverty eradication spanning the work of the United Nations in the area, and would highlight opportunities for collaboration between various other stakeholders, non-governmental organizations (NGOs) and civil society organizations engaged in poverty eradication at the national and community levels. Using as its starting point the follow-up activities to the 2005 World Summit, which recognized the need to accelerate progress in countries where current trends made the achievement of the internationally agreed development goals—especially poverty eradication—unlikely, the Second Decade should build on the implementation, support for and monitoring of such initiatives to generate greater momentum for global action. The Assembly should request the Secretary-General, in consultation with Member States, UN system organizations, NGOs, the private sector and civil society, to prepare the plan of action and submit it to the Assembly at its resumed sixty-third (2009) session.

Communication. On 6 November, the Secretary-General transmitted to the Assembly President the outcome of the Third High-level Forum on Aid Effectiveness (Accra, Ghana, 2–4 September) [A/63/539], including the Accra Agenda for Action.

GENERAL ASSEMBLY ACTION

On 19 December [meeting 72], the General Assembly, on the recommendation of the Second Committee [A/63/418/Add.1], adopted **resolution 63/230** without vote [agenda item 53 *(a)*].

Second United Nations Decade for the Eradication of Poverty (2008–2017)

The General Assembly,

Recalling its resolutions 47/196 of 22 December 1992, 48/183 of 21 December 1993, 50/107 of 20 December 1995, 56/207 of 21 December 2001, 57/265 and 57/266 of 20 December 2002, 58/222 of 23 December 2003, 59/247 of 22 December 2004, 60/209 of 22 December 2005, 61/213 of 20 December 2006 and 62/205 of 19 December 2007,

Recalling also the United Nations Millennium Declaration, adopted by Heads of State and Government on the occasion of the Millennium Summit, as well as the international commitment to eradicate extreme poverty and to halve, by 2015, the proportion of the world's people whose income is less than one dollar a day and the proportion of people who suffer from hunger,

Recalling further the 2005 World Summit Outcome,

Recalling its resolution 60/265 of 30 June 2006 on the follow-up to the development outcome of the 2005 World Summit, including the Millennium Development Goals and the other internationally agreed development goals,

Recalling also its resolution 61/16 of 20 November 2006 on the strengthening of the Economic and Social Council,

Welcoming the poverty-related discussions in the annual ministerial reviews held by the Economic and Social Council, which play an important supporting role in the implementation of the Second United Nations Decade for the Eradication of Poverty (2008–2017),

Recalling the outcomes of the World Summit for Social Development and the twenty-fourth special session of the General Assembly,

Expressing concern that, after the First United Nations Decade for the Eradication of Poverty (1997–2006) and midway to the 2015 Millennium Development Goals target date, while there has been progress in reducing poverty in some regions, this progress has been uneven and the number of people living in poverty in some countries continues to increase, with women and children constituting the majority of the most affected groups, especially in the least developed countries and particularly in sub-Saharan Africa,

Recognizing that rates of economic growth vary between countries and that these differences must be addressed by, among other actions, promoting pro-poor growth and social protection,

Concerned by the global nature of poverty and inequality, and underlining that the eradication of poverty and hunger is an ethical, social, political and economic imperative of humankind,

Reaffirming that eradicating poverty is one of the greatest global challenges facing the world today, particularly in Africa and in least developed countries, and underlining the importance of accelerating sustainable broad-based and inclusive economic growth, including full, productive employment-generation and decent work,

Expressing concern that the number of people living in poverty is higher than previously estimated, despite significant progress, and that the current financial and food insecurity crises and unpredictable energy prices may pose significant challenges for the achievement of the internationally agreed development goals, including the Millennium Development Goals,

Recognizing that mobilizing financial resources for development at the national and international levels and the effective use of those resources are central to a global partnership for development in support of the achievement of the internationally agreed development goals, including the Millennium Development Goals,

Recognizing also the contributions of South-South and triangular cooperation to the efforts of developing countries to eradicate poverty and to pursue sustainable development,

Acknowledging that good governance at national and international levels and sustained and inclusive economic growth, supported by full employment and decent work, rising productivity, and a favourable environment, including public and private investment and entrepreneurship, are necessary to eradicate poverty, achieve the internationally agreed development goals, including the Millennium Development Goals, and realize a rise in living standards, and that corporate social responsibility initiatives play an important role in maximizing the impact of public and private investment,

Underlining the priority and urgency given by the Heads of State and Government to the eradication of poverty, as expressed in the outcomes of the major United Nations conferences and summits in the economic and social fields,

1. *Takes note* of the report of the Secretary-General on the implementation of the Second United Nations Decade for the Eradication of Poverty (2008–2017);

2. *Reaffirms* that the objective of the Second United Nations Decade is to support, in an efficient and coordinated manner, the follow-up to the implementation of the internationally agreed development goals, including the Millennium Development Goals, related to the eradication of poverty and to coordinate international support to that end;

3. *Also reaffirms* that each country must take primary responsibility for its own development and that the role of national policies and strategies cannot be overemphasized in the achievement of sustainable development and poverty eradication, and recognizes that increased effective national efforts should be complemented by concrete, effective and supportive international programmes, measures and policies aimed at expanding the development opportunities of developing countries, while taking into account national conditions and ensuring respect for national ownership, strategies and sovereignty;

4. *Emphasizes* the need to accord the highest priority to poverty eradication within the United Nations development agenda, while stressing the importance of addressing the causes and challenges of poverty through integrated, coordinated and coherent strategies at the national, intergovernmental and inter-agency levels;

5. *Reiterates* the need to strengthen the leadership role of the United Nations in promoting international cooperation for development, critical for the eradication of poverty;

6. *Stresses* the importance of ensuring, at the national, intergovernmental and inter-agency levels, coherent, comprehensive and integrated activities for the eradication of poverty in accordance with the outcomes of the major United Nations conferences and summits in the economic, social and related fields;

7. *Emphasizes* that education and training are among the critical factors in empowering those living in poverty, while recognizing the complexity of the challenge of poverty eradication;

8. *Calls upon* the international community to continue to give priority to the eradication of poverty and on donor countries in a position to do so to support the effective national efforts of developing countries in this regard, through adequate predictable financial resources on either a bilateral or a multilateral basis;

9. *Acknowledges* efforts of developed countries to increase their assistance for development, including commitments by some developed countries to increase official development assistance; notes with concern, however, the overall decline in official development assistance in 2006 and 2007, and calls for the fulfilment of all official development assistance-related commitments, including the commitments made by many developed countries to achieve the target of 0.7 per cent of gross national product for official development assistance by 2015 and to reach the target of at least 0.5 per cent of gross national product for official development assistance by 2010, as well as to achieve the target of 0.15 to 0.20 per cent of gross national product for official development assistance to least developed countries; and urges those developed countries that have not yet done so to make concrete efforts in this regard in accordance with their commitments;

10. *Welcomes* recent efforts and initiatives to enhance the quality of aid and to increase its impact, including the Paris Declaration on Aid Effectiveness and the Accra Agenda for Action, and the resolve to take concrete, effective and timely action in implementing all agreed commitments on aid effectiveness, with clear monitoring and deadlines, including through further aligning assistance with countries' strategies, building institutional capacities, reducing transaction costs and eliminating bureaucratic procedures, making progress on untying aid, enhancing the absorptive capacity and financial management of recipient countries and strengthening the focus on development results;

11. *Recognizes* that sustained and inclusive economic growth is essential for eradicating poverty and hunger, in particular in developing countries, and stresses that national efforts in this regard should be complemented by an enabling international environment;

12. *Also recognizes* that, for developing countries to reach the targets set in the context of national development strategies for the achievement of the internationally agreed development goals, including the Millennium Development Goals, in particular the goal on the eradication of extreme poverty, and for such poverty eradication strategies to be effective, it is imperative that developing countries increase their efforts to be integrated into the world economy in order to share the benefits of globalization;

13. *Requests* the Secretary-General to appoint a focal point from within the United Nations system to coordinate the implementation of the Second United Nations Decade in close consultation with Member States;

14. *Considers* that a theme for the Second United Nations Decade, to be reviewed at the sixty-fifth session of the General Assembly, shall be "Full employment and decent work for all", and requests the Secretary-General to submit to the Assembly at that session a report that details the current response of the United Nations system to the theme;

15. *Recognizes* the need to give the highest priority to its consideration of the item on poverty eradication in its agenda, and in that regard, as a contribution to the Second United Nations Decade, decides to convene, during its sixty-eighth session, a meeting of the General Assembly at the highest appropriate political level centred on the review process devoted to the theme for the issue of poverty eradication, and stresses that the meeting and the preparatory activities should be carried out within the budget level proposed by the Secretary-General for the biennium 2012–2013 and should be organized in the most effective and efficient manner;

16. *Decides* to include in the provisional agenda of its sixty-fourth session an item entitled "Implementation of the Second United Nations Decade for the Eradication of Poverty (2008–2017)", and requests the Secretary-General to brief Member States orally on progress in the implementation of efforts related to the theme for the Second Decade.

On 19 December, the Assembly, by **decision 63/544**, took note of the report of the Second Committee [A/63/418] on its consideration of the eradication of poverty and other development issues.

Rural development

Commission on Sustainable Development consideration. The Commission on Sustainable Development, at its sixteenth session [E/2008/29], discussed rural development as one of the subjects of its thematic cluster for the 2008–2009 implementation cycle. The Commission had before it a February report of the Secretary-General on the subject [E/CN.17/2008/4], which presented an updated analysis of the state of implementation of the internationally agreed framework for rural development as contained in chapter 14, "Promoting sustainable agriculture and rural development", of Agenda 21 [YUN 1992, p. 672], the Programme for the Further Implementation of Agenda 21 [YUN 1997, p. 792], the Plan of Implementation of the World Summit on Sustainable Development ("Johannesburg Plan of Implementation") [YUN 2002, p. 821], and various sessions of the Commission.

According to the report, overall progress in reducing rural poverty was slow, but several successful experiences showed what could work. While the main thrust of efforts remained in agriculture, reducing rural poverty through agricultural development alone would be difficult, and the challenge was to foster development in rural areas that benefited entire rural communities. The lack of broad-based investments in the rural sector for enhancing agricultural efficiency and rural infrastructure, tapping the potential of the non-farm sector and improving the management of natural resources, was a barrier to growth promotion and poverty reduction in rural areas. Further challenges included strengthening partnerships and providing technical assistance on market-oriented farming and small- and medium-scale agro-enterprise development to promote competitive rural agro-industries. Other major barriers included limited access to rural finance, improved agricultural inputs, modern energy services, local markets and market information, storage facilities, transportation, technology, education and other social services. The overexploitation of natural resources in many countries was creating a devastating impact on the living conditions of the rural poor. It was therefore crucial to secure a balance between maximizing the productivity of natural resources and ensuring their conservation. While rural development was essential to achieving sustainable development, it could not be realized without adequate community empowerment and participation. One key obstacle was the lack of education and literacy in rural communities, as investment in rural education in developing countries was often inadequate. In addition to increasing public spending on education and the participation of civil society organizations and other stakeholders, it was important to bridge the education gaps in remote rural areas and to address the social and cultural constraints to the full participation of marginalized and disadvantaged groups in the development and implementation of rural development programmes.

During the Commission's high-level segment on rural development, Commission members were of the view that investment in infrastructure was critical to boosting agriculture and rural development. While priorities would differ according to local, national and regional circumstances, adequate rural roads and other means of transport, irrigation and water storage, electrification and telecommunications were all important, as was infrastructure for social development, including rural health-care facilities and schools. Domestic public investment would be a vital source of finance, and although many Governments had increased those investments, further resources were needed and ODA for agricultural and rural development should be substantially increased. New and innovative sources and methods of finance, including public-private partnerships, could contribute to meeting financing needs. Diversification of rural economies was a priority, including through the strengthening of productive capacity, the development of value-added agro-processing, the promotion of small- and medium-sized enterprises (SMEs) and other rural industries, rural cooperatives and the expansion of social, financial, infrastructural and tourism services in rural areas. Enhanced access to global markets, technology transfer and sharing of experiences, know-how and best practices were all important, and increased rural finance on favourable terms should be made available to small-scale entrepreneurs through a variety of means, including loan guarantees, microcredit and venture capital. Local authorities and communities played a vital role in the management of land, water and other natural resources in rural areas, and their capacities should be strengthened.

Economic and Social Council consideration. In accordance with **decision 2008/208** of 8 February, the Economic and Social Council, on 3 July, held a thematic discussion for its 2008 high-level segment on promoting an integrated approach to rural development in developing countries for poverty eradication and sustainable development, taking into account current challenges. For consideration of the theme, it held two parallel panel discussions on: bioenergy, sustainable livelihoods and rural poor; and harnessing the current boom in agricultural commodities for poverty eradication and sustainable development: the case of small-scale farmers.

In a May report on the theme [E/2008/68], the Secretary-General noted that the Ministerial Declaration on promoting an integrated approach to rural development in developing countries for poverty eradication and sustainable development, adopted by the Council in 2003 [YUN 2003, p. 853], outlined essential elements for pursuing rural development in developing countries. Since the adoption of the declaration, many developments had taken place, including greater awareness of the importance of agriculture and rural development in achieving the MDGs, in particular with respect to attacking poverty and hunger. At the regional level, notably in Africa, countries had committed themselves to strengthening agriculture and, at the national level, to eliminating poverty and hunger. The challenge of rural poverty reduction was, however, even greater than in 2003: old challenges persisted and new ones threatened to push the rural poor ever deeper into poverty. The impact of the increase in global food prices on the poorest in rural areas signalled the urgency of improving agricultural productivity and increasing food production. At the same time, the effects of climate change were undermining agricultural production. An integrated approach to rural development should be pursued, linking environmental sustainability, agricultural productivity and rural poverty, and the Council should adopt a programme on rural development in the short run, as well as in the medium-to-long term.

In the short run, the international community should protect the most vulnerable against the rapid increase in food prices, sufficient support should be given to humanitarian agencies to cover budget shortfalls and additional resources should be provided. Support should also be extended to Governments of net food-importing developing countries to ensure that social protection programmes were not cut back, but still reached those affected. The international community and Governments should ensure access by poor farmers to production inputs, to help them maintain or expand food production. In the medium-to-long term, development partners should: improve the coordination of activities for the integration of rural development initiatives into national strategies and increase investment in rural areas; improve assistance for productivity growth through the application of innovation, research and development, with more efforts directed towards bringing about the green revolution in Africa; increase assistance for improving infrastructure, and assistance to programmes enhancing the status of women and other vulnerable groups. Stakeholders should: improve the understanding of the impacts of increased biofuels on food prices, livelihoods of the poor and the environment; address the impact of climate change on the rural poor, design and develop cost-effective adaptation programmes, mobilize financial support for their implementation and improve early warning systems and vulnerability analysis to assess the risks associated with climate change; and launch actions designed to manage and use biodiversity. Governments could integrate rural development policies into national strategies; increase public funding on research and development; support policies and institutions that linked public and private research centres to farmers; improve policy and regulatory frameworks for the management of growing biofuel demand and its potential impact on food security; and intensify the application of science, technology and innovation to traditional agricultural practices.

In their Ministerial Declaration adopted on 3 July, Council members reaffirmed the importance of investing in infrastructure for rural development and agriculture and recognized the importance of non-farming economic activities in eradicating poverty in rural areas. In that regard, they recognized the discussion at the sixteenth session of the Commission on Sustainable Development (see p. 919) and looked forward to the Commission's recommendations at its seventeenth (2009) session that would advance rural development. Council members further recognized that agriculture played a crucial role in addressing the needs of a growing global population and was inextricably linked to poverty eradication, especially in developing countries. Integrated and sustainable agriculture and rural development approaches were therefore essential to achieving enhanced food security and safety in an environmentally sustainable way. They also recognized the importance of enhanced access of the rural poor to productive assets, in particular land and water, and stressed that priority attention should be given to the adoption of policies and the implementation of laws that guaranteed well-defined and enforceable land- and water-use rights and promoted legal security of tenure, while recognizing the existence of different national laws and/or systems of land access and tenure.

Microcredit and microfinance in the eradication of poverty

In July, the Secretary-General, in response to General Assembly resolution 61/214 [YUN 2006, p. 996], submitted a report [A/63/159] on the role of microcredit and microfinance in the eradication of poverty. The report reassessed their role based on recent studies and described the latest developments in microfinance, including the emergence of new providers. It examined in particular microfinance penetration and client demand, including population penetration, understanding the demand for microfinance, and emerging clients; the impact of microcredit and microfinance on the welfare of the poor, especially in income and employment, consumption smoothing and microinsurance, the impact on poor women and empowerment, and social performance audits; and developments among microfinance providers, such as the growth and transformation of microfinance and its commercialization, increased competition, innovations in microfinance, the impact of technology, the challenges faced by microfinance providers, policymakers and regulatory authorities.

According to the report, in recent years, microfinance had experienced tremendous growth and gained wide acclaim in helping the poor, especially women, through increased incomes, self-employment and empowerment. Although there was greater awareness of its positive impact, the challenge of scaling it up remained. Its success was due in part to a growing recognition that the poor were viable customers, as well as to the entry of mainstream financial institutions into the microfinance business, which provided alternative sources of funds. By adapting new technologies, microfinance had broadened its outreach and reduced costs to both clients and providers. There was growing concern, however, about increasing commercialization and profit orientation in microfinance, which had led to the promotion of a paradigm shift from microfinance to a vision of inclusive finance.

The Secretary-General concluded that, while microfinance had contributed to alleviating the conditions of over 100 million people living in poverty, the breadth of its outreach continued to be limited and the need to broaden the institutional capacity, focus and approach of its institutions remained. Its current contribution lay in improving the lives of the poor rather than as a pathway out of poverty. Self-employment activities generated by microloans were low-productive in nature and rarely led to the development of small enterprises, because the poor, in particular the rural poor, lived in areas that typically lacked economic opportunities. Moreover, most microfinance institutions could not provide the financial services that SMEs, as opposed to microenterprises, needed. SME development was critical to the generation of productive employment, which was of central importance to poverty eradication. Catering to their financial needs should be an extension of the traditional lending rationale, and successful microfinance providers should therefore forge alliances with other financial service providers to build sound, sustainable and inclusive national financial sectors that could cater to the needs of all, from the poorest households to enterprises, and promote business opportunities and productive employment on a significant scale. Governments also played an important role in providing an enabling environment conducive to the achievement of an inclusive financial sector encompassing the poor.

The Secretary-General recommended that Member States: establish a framework for promoting the development of inclusive financial institutions that offered appropriate financial products and services to all segments of the population; adopt a coherent financial regulatory framework, in consultation with microfinance providers, that would protect the stability of the financial system and increase access of the poor and micro- and small enterprises to financial services; adopt regulatory standards that protected consumers, in particular the poor, given their limited financial literacy, against predatory and abusive lending practices; integrate financial and consumer education for the poor as part of the framework to promote awareness of microfinance programmes; and support the expansion and reach of microfinance through the promotion of entrepreneurship development programmes.

GENERAL ASSEMBLY ACTION

On 19 December [meeting 72], the General Assembly, on the recommendation of the Second Committee [A/63/418/Add.1], adopted **resolution 63/229** without vote [agenda item 53 *(a)*].

Role of microcredit and microfinance in the eradication of poverty

The General Assembly,

Recalling its resolutions 52/193 and 52/194 of 18 December 1997, 53/197 of 15 December 1998, 58/221 of 23 December 2003, 59/246 of 22 December 2004 and 61/214 of 20 December 2006,

Recognizing the need for access to financial services, in particular for the poor, including access to microfinance and microcredit,

Recognizing also that microfinance, in particular microcredit programmes, has succeeded in generating productive self-employment and proved to be an effective tool in overcoming poverty and reducing the vulnerability of poor people to crisis and has led to their growing participation, in particular the participation of women, in the mainstream socioeconomic and political processes of society, and bearing in mind that microfinance, in particular microcredit, has especially benefited women and has resulted in the achievement of their empowerment,

Recognizing further that the majority of the world's poor still do not have access to financial services and that microcredit and microfinance are the subject of significant demand worldwide,

Bearing in mind the importance of providing access to microfinance instruments and services, such as credit, savings, insurance, money transfers and other financial products and services, for poor people,

Recognizing that inclusive financial sectors can offer appropriate financial services and products to poor people,

Noting with appreciation the efforts of the United Nations Advisers Group on Inclusive Financial Sectors to promote the building of inclusive financial sectors to meet the needs and demands of poor people, and noting also the recommendations containing key messages to build inclusive financial sectors put forward in June 2008,

Noting events organized for the promotion of inclusive financial sectors, including the convening of the Global Microcredit Summit in Halifax, Canada, from 12 to 15 November 2006,

Welcoming the efforts made in the field of property rights, and noting that an enabling environment at all levels, including transparent regulatory systems and competitive markets, fosters the mobilization of resources and access to finance for people living in poverty,

Noting with appreciation the contribution of awards and prizes to increasing the visibility and awareness of the role of microfinance, including microcredit, in the eradication of poverty, most notably the awarding of the 2006 Nobel Peace Prize,

1. *Takes note* of the report of the Secretary-General;

2. *Welcomes* the successful observance of the International Year of Microcredit, 2005, which constituted a special occasion to raise awareness and share best practices and lessons learned on microcredit and microfinance;

3. *Recognizes* that access to microfinance and microcredit can contribute to the achievement of the goals and targets of major United Nations conferences and summits in the economic and social fields, including those contained in the United Nations Millennium Declaration, in particular the goals relating to poverty eradication, gender equality and the empowerment of women;

4. *Underlines* the need for greater access to microfinance, including microcredit, in developing countries, in particular for small farmers, which can contribute to increased agricultural productivity and rural development;

5. *Also underlines* the importance of strengthening domestic financial sectors as a source of capital by making them inclusive, thus expanding access to financial services;

6. *Recognizes* that microfinance has experienced tremendous growth in the number of people served and the diversity of financial services offered, and that, along with the growth in numbers served as well as products and services offered, there has also been a large increase in the number of public and private microfinance providers, all of which share the common characteristic of providing financial services to poor and socio-economically vulnerable people, as well as micro-entrepreneurs who would not normally be served, or are underserved, by traditional financial institutions;

7. *Notes* that, despite progress, there is still lack of relevant statistical data on inclusive financial sectors, in particular microcredit and microfinance programmes, in particular at the national and regional levels, and in this regard invites the international community, in particular the donor community, to support developing countries in collecting and preserving necessary statistical data and information on this issue, specifically on defining and measuring access to financial services and products at the country level and measuring the type, quality and usage of such services and products over time;

8. *Calls upon* Member States, the United Nations system and other relevant stakeholders to fully maximize the role of microfinance instruments, including microcredit, for poverty eradication and especially for the empowerment of women and rural populations, and to ensure that best practices in the microfinance sector are widely disseminated;

9. *Invites* Member States, the United Nations system, the Bretton Woods institutions, regional development banks and other relevant stakeholders to support, financially and technically, in a coordinated manner, the efforts of developing countries in capacity-building for microcredit and microfinance institutions to expand their products and services, including by improving their policy and regulatory framework;

10. *Invites* Member States to consider adopting policies to facilitate the expansion of microcredit and microfinance institutions in order to service the large unmet demand among poor people for financial services, including the identification and development of mechanisms to promote access to sustainable financial services, the removal of institutional and regulatory obstacles, the promotion of financial literacy and the provision of incentives to microfinance institutions that meet national standards for delivering sound financial services to the poor;

11. *Encourages* Member States to adopt coherent financial regulatory frameworks, including in consultation with microfinance providers, that can effectively protect the stability of their national financial systems and increase access of the poor and microenterprises and small enterprises to financial services, and also to protect consumers, in particular the poor, and in this regard invites the development partners to support the efforts of developing countries in the promotion of entrepreneurship development programmes, including for microenterprises and small and medium-sized enterprises;

12. *Recognizes* that the current financial crisis can adversely impact financial flows to microcredit and microfinance institutions as well as the services that they provide to the poor, and emphasizes that such instruments should be protected, as appropriate, from potential credit deficiency;

13. *Decides* to devote one plenary meeting at its sixty-fifth session to the consideration of the outcome of and follow-up to the International Year of Microcredit, with a view to broadening and deepening the discussion about microcredit and microfinance and inclusive financial sectors;

14. *Requests* the Secretary-General to submit to the General Assembly at its sixty-fifth session a report on the implementation of the present resolution, under the item entitled "Eradication of poverty and other development issues".

Evaluation

CPC consideration. The Committee for Programme and Coordination (CPC), at its forty-eighth session (9 June–3 July) [A/63/16], considered the triennial review on the evaluation of linkages between Headquarters and field activities: a review of best practices for poverty eradication in the framework of the United Nations Millennium Declaration. It had before it an Office of Internal Oversight Services (OIOS) report on the triennial review of the implementation of recommendations made by the Committee at its forty-fifth session on the evaluation of linkages between Headquarters and field activities [E/AC.51/2008/4] and the comments of the Secretary-General thereon [E/AC.51/2008/4/Add.1].

According to the OIOS report, progress had been made on enhancing collaboration among inter-agency coordinating bodies, and according to CEB, the United Nations Development Group was working within the context of CEB in support of operational activities. OIOS noted, however, that the Secretary-General had not established a working group to review the roles and responsibilities of the inter-agency coordinating bodies on common policy issues on the eradication of poverty and hunger, and that a structured, facilitated and strategic approach to system-wide knowledge management networks around issues of poverty eradication had not yet been introduced. Progress was made in establishing institutional mechanisms for informing country offices about the poverty-related work of non-resident agencies, and DESA and the regional economic commissions were working with UN country teams in their respective regions. In addition, regional commissions had agreed to a cooperation framework with the United Nations Development Programme (UNDP) to enable them to participate and contribute more actively in the work of country offices.

CPC recommended that the General Assembly request the Secretary-General, as CEB Chairman, to ensure enhanced collaboration among inter-agency coordinating bodies, in respect of poverty eradication within the framework of the United Nations Millennium Declaration, in light of the results already achieved by the Board, and continue implementing the remaining recommendations.

Implementation of Ministerial Declaration on eradication of poverty and hunger

Coordination segment of Economic and Social Council. At its 2008 coordination segment (7–9 and 24 July) [A/63/3/Rev.1], the Economic and Social Council considered the UN role in implementing the Ministerial Declaration on strengthening efforts to eradicate poverty and hunger, including through the global partnership for development, adopted at the Council's 2007 high-level segment [YUN 2007, p. 833]. It had before it a report of the Secretary-General on the subject [E/2008/21], submitted in response to Council decision 2007/261 [YUN 2007, p. 1425].

According to the report, the eradication of poverty and hunger had always been a central objective of UN development work, and all system organizations pursued that goal within their respective mandates. They had made progress in integrating the framework into policies, programmes and operations, with a number of initiatives under way to promote system-wide approaches, ranging from joint efforts to evaluate progress towards the achievement of the MDGs to joint studies to advance understanding of the complementarities between relevant policy areas and activities to build national capacity to formulate comprehensive development strategies and mobilize resources. Some of those initiatives were beginning to promote more integrated UN responses in line with the thrust of the 2007 Ministerial Declaration. In response to the Declaration's emphasis on the importance of the MDG framework to assess progress towards the realization of the MDG on the eradication of poverty and hunger, the Secretary-General launched a major communications and advocacy initiative to renew political momentum around the MDGs and scale up their implementation in 2007 and 2008 at the midpoint towards the target year 2015. To support that process, he established a United Nations Millennium Development Goal Gap Task Force to track international commitments made under the MDG on a global partnership for development to support the achievement of the MDGs, determine the extent to which they had been fulfilled at the international and country levels; identify gaps preventing faster progress; and suggest ways to addressed them. The Task Force would develop a common methodology for tracking progress and gaps and provide a common framework for monitoring the commitments. Its first report would be submitted to the intergovernmental process in mid-2008. The Secretary-General also set up the Millennium Development Goal Africa Steering Group to scale up progress to achieve the MDGs in the region and implement existing commitments.

The Secretary-General concluded that, while the UN system had made progress in developing and pursuing more comprehensive approaches for the eradication of poverty and hunger, especially in employment generation, trade and rural and agricultural development, more needed to be done to integrate sustainable development and science and technology dimensions in UN system programmes and activities in support of national efforts. Country-level experience offered lessons on how UN system support could be strengthened; harnessing its potential would require increasing UN system collaboration at the analytical, programmatic and operational levels, especially in the areas of statistics, labour, trade and information and communication technologies (ICTs). At the operational level, the UN system should make more effective use of frameworks and instruments for country-level support, such as the United Nations Development Assistance Framework (UNDAF), the poverty reduction strategy paper and the poverty and social impact analysis, to ensure that the various dimensions of poverty and hunger were taken into account in those frameworks.

The Secretary-General made the following recommendations: strengthen national capacity to analyse the social impact of rural and agricultural development, especially on employment, in order to facilitate the integration of social dimensions in such development; build national capacity to analyse the impact of natural resource management, including water, land and forestry, on the livelihoods of those depending on those resources; promote the integration of an "urban pillar", focused on the poor of populated slums, in the common country assessment and the UNDAF processes to facilitate the inclusion of sustainable urbanization and urban poverty reduction in national strategies, as well as the integration of sustainable development and science and technology in the policies, programmes and operations of all UN system organizations; promote a system-wide programme of work on science and technology, including ICTs, for poverty reduction, and joint inter-agency efforts to support the UNCTAD sixth tranche programme for strengthening implementation of internationally agreed development goals, including the MDGs, through innovation, networking and knowledge management; encourage the development of analytical tools for identifying sector imbalances in resource and investment allocations and addressing new resource needs to deal with emerging challenges, such as climate change and urban poverty; and further promote the joint assessment of aid flows and their impact on rural development social indicators. The UN system should continue to support national development strategies to ensure that all relevant dimensions of poverty and hunger were taken into account; and promote national participation in and ownership of poverty reduction strategies through its system-wide coordination mechanism and by promoting multi-stakeholder approaches to enhance the participation of local authorities, civil society organizations and the private sector.

ECONOMIC AND SOCIAL COUNCIL ACTION

On 24 July [meeting 42], the Economic and Social Council adopted **resolution 2008/28** [draft: E/2008/L.22] without vote [agenda item 4].

The role of the United Nations system in implementing the Ministerial Declaration on strengthening efforts to eradicate poverty and hunger, including through the global partnership for development, adopted at the high-level segment of the substantive session of 2007 of the Economic and Social Council

The Economic and Social Council,

Recalling the United Nations Millennium Declaration and the 2005 World Summit Outcome,

Recalling also the Ministerial Declaration adopted at the high-level segment of its substantive session of 2007,

Recalling further its decision 2007/261 of 27 July 2007 on the theme of the 2008 coordination segment,

Recognizing that the challenge of eradicating poverty and hunger requires a comprehensive and multidimensional response by the United Nations system, including the funds, programmes and agencies, as appropriate within their respective mandates,

Reaffirming the commitments to the global partnership for development set out in the United Nations Millennium Declaration, the Monterrey Consensus of the International Conference on Financing for Development and the Plan of Implementation of the World Summit on Sustainable Development ("Johannesburg Plan of Implementation"),

1. *Requests* the funds, programmes and agencies of the United Nations system, as appropriate within their mandates, to make further progress towards more comprehensive, coherent and multidimensional approaches in the formulation of their policies, programmes and operations supporting the eradication of poverty and hunger;

2. *Also requests* the funds, programmes and agencies of the United Nations system, as appropriate within their mandates, to strengthen their efforts to provide policy support to developing countries and assist them upon request in building their capacity to analyse the impact of a broad range of policy areas on the eradication of poverty and hunger, including through the promotion of interdisciplinary research and studies;

3. *Invites* all member organizations of the United Nations System Chief Executives Board for Coordination to enhance policy coherence and cooperation in areas vital to achieving the eradication of poverty and hunger;

4. *Requests* all member organizations of the United Nations System Chief Executives Board for Coordination to approach rural and urban development in an integrated manner and to consider ways to support countries' strategies for reducing urban poverty, as appropriate;

5. *Encourages* the funds, programmes and agencies of the United Nations system to promote policy coherence and cooperation on science and technology, where relevant, including information and communications technology where appropriate, for poverty reduction that should promote both the formulation of science and technology programmes and the development of national institutional capacities in science and technology in support of the eradication of poverty and hunger;

6. *Also encourages* the funds, programmes and agencies of the United Nations system, as appropriate within their mandates, to coordinate their assessments of the impact of development cooperation on the eradication of poverty and hunger;

7. *Requests* the funds, programmes and agencies of the United Nations system, as appropriate within their mandates and in consultation with Member States, to continue to promote multi-stakeholder approaches involving local authorities, civil society and the private sector, inter alia, through its system-wide coordination mechanisms for the eradication of poverty and hunger, as appropriate;

8. *Encourages* the United Nations system, especially its funds, programmes and agencies, to continue to accord the highest priority to the eradication of poverty and hunger, as appropriate, in developing the common country assessment and the United Nations Development Assistance Framework, or other frameworks and instruments guiding country-level operational activities, in consultation with Governments;

9. *Encourages* the funds, programmes and agencies of the United Nations system, as appropriate within their mandates, to continue to strengthen efforts to eradicate poverty and hunger, including through the promotion of the global partnership for development, and supporting countries in that regard.

By **decision 2008/252** of the same date, the Economic and Social Council took note of the Secretary-General's report on the role of the UN system in implementing the Ministerial Declaration of the high-level segment of the 2007 substantive session of the Council.

Legal empowerment of the poor and eradication of poverty

The Commission on Legal Empowerment of the Poor held its fifth meeting (New York, 6–8 February) to finalize its report, agree on modalities for its launch and propose guidelines for implementing its recommendations. The outcome of the meeting included agreement on a plan of action to bring the legal empowerment agenda to the world's attention. The Commission comprised 21 commissioners, including former Heads of State and Government, cabinet ministers, jurists, economic researchers, and other senior policymakers. During the previous three years, it conducted 22 national consultation processes with representatives from local governments, academia, civil society and grassroots movements; launched five technical working groups, which submitted specialized reports; and debated with national and international policymakers.

In its 2008 report "Making the Law Work for Everyone" (Vol. I), the Commission argued that at least 4 billion people were robbed of the chance to better their lives and climb out of poverty because they were excluded from the rule of law. In many countries, the laws, institutions and policies governing economic, social and political affairs denied a large part of society the chance to participate on equal terms, and the outcomes of governance—the cumulative effect of policies and institutions on people—would only change if the processes of governance were fundamentally changed. As the poor lacked recognized rights, they were vulnerable to discrimination by the authorities, which had massive consequences.

The Commission emphasized that legal empowerment was a process of systemic change through which the poor and excluded were empowered to use the law and the legal system and services to protect and advance their rights as citizens and economic actors. It was not a substitute for other development initiatives—such as investing more in education, public services and infrastructure, enhancing participation in trade and adapting to climate change—but complemented such initiatives, multiplying their impact. The Commission developed a comprehensive agenda for achieving legal empowerment, encompassing four pillars that reinforced each other: access to justice and the rule of law; property rights; labour rights; and business rights. To succeed, legal empowerment had to lead to systemic change, including institutional reform. While Governments were the responsible actors in human rights terms, in a process of legal empowerment of the poor, the United Nations and the broader multilateral system could help by lending their support. More specifically, the legal empowerment agenda should be integrated as a core concern of global multilateral agencies, such as the World Bank, UNDP, the International Labour Organization, the Food and Agriculture Organization of the United Nations and the United Nations Human Settlements Programme. It should also become a core mission for regional political organizations, banks and UN institutions. Civil society and community-based organizations could contribute by connecting the poor to political institutions at every level, and the business community could smooth the way for legal empowerment through the United Nations Global Compact and by supporting local and national reform efforts. Religious communities and indigenous spiritual traditions could translate the moral imperatives of legal empowerment into action, and professional associations could gather and disseminate information and offer political support for legal empowerment and access to justice reform, as well as increased funding for legal aid and other services. Those initiatives should support efforts in individual countries; foster a regional and global political consensus; and create new instruments for supporting legal empowerment, such as a "Global Legal Empowerment Compact" as a first step in codifying core rights and spelling out a framework for their realization; mechanisms for tracking progress; a clearing-house for recording, storing and disseminating experiences and lessons learned; public-private partnerships; and a global initiative to promote grass-roots knowledge and innovation.

GENERAL ASSEMBLY ACTION

On 11 December [meeting 68], the General Assembly adopted **resolution 63/142** [draft: A/63/L.25/Rev.1 & Add.1] without vote [agenda item 107].

Legal empowerment of the poor and eradication of poverty

The General Assembly,

Recalling the 2005 World Summit Outcome,

Recalling also the United Nations Millennium Declaration, the Monterrey Consensus of the International Conference on Financing for Development and the Plan of Implementation of the World Summit on Sustainable Development ("Johannesburg Plan of Implementation"),

Reaffirming the importance of the timely and full realization of the development goals and objectives agreed at the major United Nations conferences and summits, including the Millennium Development Goals,

Recognizing that empowerment of the poor is essential for the effective eradication of poverty and hunger,

Reaffirming that the rule of law at the national and international levels is essential for sustained economic growth, sustainable development and the eradication of poverty and hunger,

Reaffirming also that each country must take primary responsibility for its own development and that the role of national policies and development strategies cannot be overemphasized in the achievement of sustainable development, and recognizing that national efforts should be complemented by supportive global programmes, measures and policies aimed at expanding the development opportunities of developing countries, while taking into account national conditions and ensuring respect for national ownership, strategies and sovereignty,

1. *Takes note* of the final report of the Commission on Legal Empowerment of the Poor, entitled "Making the Law Work for Everyone";

2. *Stresses* the importance of sharing best national practices in the area of legal empowerment of the poor;

3. *Requests* the Secretary-General to submit a report to the General Assembly at its sixty-fourth session on the legal empowerment of the poor, under the item entitled "Eradication of poverty and other development issues", taking into account national experiences in this regard.

Millennium Development Goals

The Millennium Development Goals Report 2008, published by DESA [Sales No. E.08.I.18], summarized progress towards the goals in each region. The single most important success had been the unprecedented breadth and depth of the commitment to the MDGs. Governments of developing countries and the international community adopted the MDGs as their framework for international development cooperation, as did the private sector and civil society in both developed and developing countries. Private foundations in developed countries had become an important source of funding for a wide range of activities intended to achieve the MDGs, and NGOs in developing countries were increasingly engaged in those activities. That global collective effort was yielding results. There had been sound progress in some MDG areas, even in some of the more challenging regions, and a number of targets were expected to be reached by their target dates. Some of those successes had been achieved by means of targeted interventions or programmes, but achieving some other goals would depend on country-wide systems of qualified and equipped personnel and an effective institutional infrastructure. Building those capacities would require strong political commitment and adequate funding over a longer period and the delivery of additional ODA.

Most developing countries' efforts to achieve the MDGs had benefited from improved economic growth and relatively low inflation since 2000. However, the immediate prospects of reduced global growth and higher inflation threatened success in reducing poverty and making progress towards other MDGs unless there was a response from all stakeholders. A first component of that response was to ensure that action was accelerated and expanded. All stakeholders should renew their commitment to the wide range of interrelated activities. Successful policies, programmes and projects should be expanded, and Governments and the international community should respond to the lessons of experience and adjust to changing circumstances. Additional resources should be mobilized by both developed and developing countries to address long-term challenges in agriculture, rural development, infrastructure and environmental sustainability, including climate change. The current food crisis (see p. 1343) called for special attention to the potential escalation in hunger and malnutrition.

That agenda would require a sustained and wide-ranging effort beyond 2015. The task was broad and complex, but the progress achieved demonstrated that success was feasible with sound strategies and political will, which should include a greater financial commitment. Despite the potentially less favourable economic conditions, developed countries should provide substantial increases in ODA and foster an international environment more conducive to development.

General Assembly high-level event on MDGs

The General Assembly held a high-level event on the MDGs at UN Headquarters on 25 September, the theme of which was "End poverty 2015: make it happen". Its objectives were to review progress and take stock of gaps at the midway point in the global effort to achieve the MDGs by 2015; identify actions to scale up efforts; and help ensure that the goals and international targets remained on track and that the momentum was maintained beyond 2008. Three parallel round tables on poverty and hunger, education and health, and environmental sustainability were held, with gender equality and global partnership for development as cross-cutting themes. A 25 July background note by the Secretary-General addressed each of the round-table topics, as well as the cross-cutting themes. The meeting also had before it supporting background documentation, including the report of the Millennium Development Goal Africa Steering Group, the *MDG Gap Task Force Report 2008: Delivering on the Global Partnership for Achieving the Millennium Development Goals* [Sales No. E.08.I.17] and *The Millennium Development Goals Report 2008* (see above).

Partnership events sponsored by a variety of constituencies took place during the week of the high-level event (22–26 September), which shared success stories and lessons learned and provided opportunities to forge new partnerships and generate commitments. UN Member States, groups of States and civil society partners, including the private sector and philanthropists, made commitments and announced initiatives on concrete next steps for achieving the MDGs by 2015.

The Secretary-General, in his address to the gathering, recalled the ambitious goals set eight years before to free humankind from hunger, illiteracy, disease, disempowerment and environmental degradation, and noted the successes achieved: measles vaccinations that had prevented 7.5 million deaths; inroads made against AIDS; surging school enrolment in several African countries following the abolition of school fees; and millions of poor households risen out of extreme poverty. He declared that the world was on the way to cutting extreme poverty and hunger in half by 2015, but while things were moving in the right direction, they were not moving quickly enough. Sub-Saharan Africa had actually seen the number of poor increase between 1990 and 2005. Women and girls continued to suffer persistent bias and neglect, evidenced by gender gaps in health, education, employment and empowerment. The financial crisis threatened the well-being of billions of people, none more so than the poorest of the poor, compounding the damage being caused by much higher food and fuel prices. The Secretary-General urged States to rise to those challenges and inject new energy into the global partnership for development. He also asked participants to be bold and generous in their commitments and to agree to his proposal to hold a formal Summit in 2010 to take stock of MDG achievements.

The Assembly President, in his closing statement, said that he supported the Secretary-General's proposal to hold an MDG Summit in 2010 to galvanize efforts and actions in the final five years before the 2015 deadline, and would launch consultations to develop a resolution on its objectives and modalities. Noting that health was an area still lagging far behind, he announced that global health would be made a priority and that he would convene an informal thematic debate on "Strengthening Global Health: The Health MDGs and Beyond". The process would be advanced through a high-level debate in June 2009 and would complement the work the Economic and Social Council on global public health.

The Secretary-General announced that commitments made by participants had generated an estimated $16 billion, including some $1.6 billion to bolster food security, more than $4.5 billion for education and $3 billion to combat malaria.

Science and technology for development

Commission on Science and Technology for Development

The Commission on Science and Technology for Development held its eleventh session in Geneva from 26 to 30 May [E/2008/31] and an intersessional meeting in Santiago, Chile, from 12 to 14 November. It considered as its priority themes: development-oriented policies for a socio-economically inclusive information society, including access, infrastructure and an enabling environment; and science, technology and engineering for innovation and capacity-building in education and research. It also considered progress made in the implementation of and follow-up to the World Summit on the Information Society (WSIS) outcomes [YUN 2003, p. 857 & YUN 2005, p. 933] at the regional and international levels. The Commission had before it reports of the Secretary-General on the WSIS outcomes [A/63/72-E/2008/48] (see p. 930) and on the priority themes [E/CN.16/2008/3 & E/CN.16/2008/4], a summary report by the UNCTAD secretariat on the meeting of the Commission's intersessional panel (Kuala Lumpur, Malaysia, 28–30 November 2007) [E/CN.16/2008/CRP.1], and an UNCTAD background paper on its follow-up report on WSIS.

The Commission recommended a draft resolution and four draft decisions for adoption by the Economic and Social Council, and brought to the Council's attention a decision by which the Commission took note of the Secretary-General's reports on the priority themes.

On 18 July, the Council took note of the Commission's report on its eleventh session and approved the provisional agenda and documentation for its twelfth (2009) session (**decision 2008/220**). It also requested the Secretary-General to report to the Commission at its twelfth session on science, technology and innovation priority themes addressed during its eleventh session (**decision 2008/219**).

Participation in Commission work

By **decision 2008/217** of 18 July, the Economic and Social Council decided, on an exceptional basis and without prejudice to the rules of procedure of its functional commissions, to invite NGOs and civil society entities that were not in consultative status with the Council but had received accreditation to WSIS to participate in the Commission's work at its twelfth and thirteenth sessions. It pleaded for voluntary contributions to facilitate the participation of developing country NGOs and civil society entities and to ensure their balanced representation, including in the Commission's panels, and invited the Committee on Non-Governmental Organizations to consider the applications of such entities as expeditiously as possible.

By **decision 2008/218** of the same date, the Economic and Social Council decided that academic entities accredited to WSIS might participate in the work of the Commission, in accordance with the Council's rules of procedure. It requested the secretariat of the Commission to submit for the Council's consideration and approval the names of those entities, including academies of science and engineering, that had not been accredited to WSIS and wished to participate in the Commission's work. The Council emphasized that its decision was taken on an exceptional basis, without prejudice to the Council's rules of procedure, in particular resolution 1996/31 [YUN 1996, p. 1360] concerning the accreditation and participation of NGOs and other major groups in the work of the Council and its subsidiary bodies, and should not be construed as creating a precedent. The Council decided to review in 2010 the list of academic entities, as well as the modalities for their participation in the Commission's work.

Information and communication technologies

During 2008, the United Nations continued to consider how the benefits of new technologies, especially information and communication technologies (ICTs), could be made available to all, in keeping with recommendations contained in the Ministerial Declaration adopted by the Economic and Social Council at its 2000 high-level segment [YUN 2000, p. 799], the Millennium Declaration [ibid., p. 49], the Geneva Declaration of Principles and Plan of Action adopted at the first phase of WSIS [YUN 2003, p. 857], and the Tunis Commitment and Tunis Agenda adopted at its second phase [YUN 2005, p. 933].

In April, the Secretary-General submitted a report on progress made in the implementation of and follow-up to the WSIS outcomes at the regional and international levels [A/63/72-E/2008/48] (see p. 930) and a note transmitting the report of the Director-General of the United Nations Educational, Scientific and Cultural Organization (UNESCO) on the implementation of Assembly resolution 50/130 [YUN 1995, p. 1438], including the recommendations of the tenth United Nations Inter-Agency Round Table on Communication for Development (Addis Ababa, Ethiopia, 12–14 February 2007) [A/63/180].

The Inter-Agency Round Table reviewed communication for development coordination arrangements around the theme "Towards a common system approach for harnessing communication for development to achieve the MDGs". It focused on interventions around which UN system organizations could develop a common approach, strategy and action plan for the implementation of communication for development practice. The objectives of the meeting were to increase inter-agency collaboration at Headquarters and UN country team levels, strengthen awareness among UN system organizations on ways to measure the impact and effectiveness of communication for development, and introduce mechanisms to harmonize UN system approaches. The Round Table reiterated that communication for development was critical for the success of the MDGs, acknowledged the vital role of the media in the process, and emphasized that higher priority allocation was essential for coherent and harmonized country-level actions. It took stock of relevant UN system initiatives and activities in a number of areas.

Participants observed that the methodology of communication for development needs assessments was missing from the UN approach, particularly at the country level. UN system communication was often viewed mainly in relation to channelling information downstream to promote specific mandates, methods and policy-related agendas, and to build public image and visibility and support for fund-raising. Its public information strategies, which were consolidated through the United Nations Department of Public Information, did not necessarily equal communication for development practice. Systematic and operational linkages between the United Nations Inter-Agency Round Table and the United Nations Communications Group might improve awareness and capacity-building needs concerning communication for development practice, and help harmonize United Nations programming priorities and communication activities. Similar linkages with the United Nations Development Group might underscore the added value of communication in development planning, and integrating it in upstream policy-setting would guarantee its consideration throughout UN priorities and responses.

The general recommendations of the Round Table were to: impress upon UN specialized agencies, programmes and funds the importance of prioritizing communication for development principles and methodologies in all programmatic areas, and the need to allocate human, technical and financial resources for that effort; advise the heads of those bodies to integrate communication for development principles and methodologies into programme and project planning, execution, monitoring and evaluation; ensure incorporation of its principles and methodologies, including needs assessments, into the common country assessment/UNDAF guidelines, or equivalent exercises, so as to improve development results; call upon the UN resident coordinator system to ensure coherence and coordination of communication for development at the country level; and establish an inter-agency mechanism for promoting and enhancing communication for development within the UN system.

GENERAL ASSEMBLY ACTION

On 19 December [meeting 72], the General Assembly, on the recommendation of the Second Committee [A/63/411], adopted **resolution 63/202** without vote [agenda item 46].

Information and communication technologies for development

The General Assembly,

Recalling its resolution 55/2 of 8 September 2000, by which it adopted the United Nations Millennium Declaration,

Recalling also its resolutions 56/183 of 21 December 2001, 57/238 of 20 December 2002, 57/270 B of 23 June 2003, 59/220 of 22 December 2004 and 62/182 of 19 December 2007, Economic and Social Council resolution 2008/3 of 18 July 2008 and other relevant resolutions,

Noting that cultural diversity is the common heritage of humankind and that the information society should be founded on and stimulate respect for cultural identity, cultural and linguistic diversity, traditions and religions, and foster dialogue among cultures and civilizations, and noting also that the promotion, affirmation and preservation of diverse cultural identities and languages as reflected in relevant agreed United Nations documents, including the Universal Declaration on Cultural Diversity of the United Nations Educational, Scientific and Cultural Organization, will further enrich the information society,

Recalling the Declaration of Principles and the Plan of Action adopted by the World Summit on the Information Society at its first phase, held in Geneva from 10 to 12 December 2003, as endorsed by the General Assembly, and the Tunis Commitment and the Tunis Agenda for the Information Society adopted by the Summit at its second phase, held in Tunis from 16 to 18 November 2005, and endorsed by the General Assembly,

Recalling also the 2005 World Summit Outcome,

Stressing the need to reduce the digital divide and to ensure that the benefits of new technologies, especially information and communication technologies, are available to all,

Recalling the first and second meetings of the Internet Governance Forum, held in Athens from 30 October to 2 November 2006 and in Rio de Janeiro, Brazil, from 12 to 15 November 2007, respectively, and welcoming the convening of the third meeting of the Forum in Hyderabad, India, from 3 to 6 December 2008,

Welcoming, in view of the existing gaps in information and communication technologies infrastructure across Africa, the launching in Kigali, in October 2007, of Connect Africa, an initiative aimed at mobilizing human, financial and technical resources to accelerate the implementation of the connectivity goals of the World Summit on the Information Society,

Recognizing the role of the Commission on Science and Technology for Development in assisting the Economic and Social Council as the focal point in the system-wide follow-up, in particular the review and assessment, of progress made in implementing the outcomes of the World Summit on the Information Society, while at the same time maintaining its original mandate on science and technology for development,

Recalling Economic and Social Council resolution 2007/8 of 25 July 2007, in which, inter alia, the Council requested various entities, including the Global Alliance for Information and Communication Technologies and Development, to submit reports to the Commission on the implications of the outcomes of the World Summit on the Information Society,

Taking note of the report of the Secretary-General to the Commission on the implementation of the outcomes of the World Summit on the Information Society,

Noting the intersessional meeting of the Commission, held in Santiago from 12 to 14 November 2008,

Stressing that, for the majority of the poor, the developmental promise of science and technology, including information and communication technologies, remains unfulfilled, and emphasizing the need to effectively harness technology, including information and communication technologies, to bridge the digital divide,

Recognizing the pivotal role of the United Nations system in promoting development, including with respect to enhancing access to information and communication technologies, inter alia, through partnerships with all relevant stakeholders,

1. *Recognizes* that information and communication technologies have the potential to provide new solutions to development challenges, particularly in the context of globalization, and can foster economic growth, competitiveness, access to information and knowledge, poverty eradication and social inclusion that will help to expedite the integration of all countries, particularly developing countries, into the global economy;

2. *Stresses* the important role of Governments in the design of public policies and in the provision of public services responsive to national needs and priorities through, inter alia, making effective use of information and communication technologies, on the basis of a multi-stakeholder approach, to support national development efforts;

3. *Recognizes* that, in addition to financing by the public sector, financing of information and communication technologies infrastructure by the private sector has come to play an important role in many countries and that domestic financing is being augmented by North-South flows and South-South cooperation;

4. *Also recognizes* that information and communication technologies present new opportunities and challenges, and that there is a pressing need to address the major impediments that developing countries face in accessing the new technologies, such as insufficient resources, infrastructure, education, capacity, investment and connectivity and issues related to technology ownership, standards and flows, and in this regard calls upon all stakeholders to provide adequate resources, enhanced capacity-building and technology transfer, on mutually agreed terms, to developing countries, particularly the least developed countries;

5. *Further recognizes* the immense potential that information and communication technologies have in promoting the transfer of technologies in a wide spectrum of socio-economic activity;

6. *Acknowledges* that a gender divide exists as part of the digital divide, and encourages all stakeholders to ensure the full participation of women in the information society and women's access to the new technologies, especially information and communication technologies for development;

7. *Recalls* the improvements and innovations in financial mechanisms, including the creation of a voluntary Digital Solidarity Fund, as mentioned in the Geneva Dec-

laration of Principles, and, in this regard, invites voluntary contributions to its financing;

8. *Recognizes* that South-South cooperation, particularly through triangular cooperation, can be a useful tool to promote the development of information and communication technologies;

9. *Encourages* strengthened and continuing cooperation between and among stakeholders to ensure effective implementation of the outcomes of the Geneva and Tunis phases of the World Summit on the Information Society, through, inter alia, the promotion of national, regional and international multi-stakeholder partnerships, including public-private partnerships, and the promotion of national and regional multi-stakeholder thematic platforms, in a joint effort and dialogue with developing and least developed countries, development partners and actors in the information and communication technologies sector;

10. *Encourages* the United Nations funds and programmes and the specialized agencies, within their respective mandates, to contribute to the implementation of the outcomes of the World Summit on the Information Society, and emphasizes the need for resources in this regard;

11. *Recognizes* the urgent need to harness the potential of knowledge and technology, and in that regard encourages the United Nations development system to continue its effort to promote the use of information and communication technologies as a critical enabler of development and a catalyst for the achievement of the internationally agreed development goals, including the Millennium Development Goals;

12. *Requests* the Secretary-General to submit to the Economic and Social Council at its substantive session of 2009, on the basis of his consultations with all relevant organizations, including international organizations, a report which may contain recommendations on how the process towards enhanced cooperation should be pursued;

13. *Invites* Member States to support the meaningful participation of stakeholders from developing countries in the preparatory meetings of the Internet Governance Forum and in the Forum itself in 2009 and 2010, and to consider contributing to the multi-stakeholder trust fund created for the Forum, as appropriate;

14. *Requests* the Secretary-General to submit to the General Assembly at its sixty-fourth session, through the Economic and Social Council, a report on the status of the implementation of and follow-up to the present resolution.

Follow-up to World Summit on the Information Society

In response to Economic and Social Council resolution 2007/8 [YUN 2007, p. 853], the Secretary-General submitted an April report [A/63/72-E/2008/48] on progress made in the implementation of and follow-up to the WSIS outcomes at the regional and international levels. The report reviewed progress made, incorporating analyses of responses provided by 14 international and regional organizations on trends, achievements and obstacles to WSIS implementation. It also highlighted major initiatives undertaken since February 2007, as reported by international and regional organizations.

At the regional level, UN regional commissions supported WSIS implementation through regional action plans. They highlighted the importance of collaborating with other development partners and of bridging the digital divide between and within their regions. The Economic and Social Commission for Western Asia led an initiative involving all the regional commissions in creating knowledge networks through ICT access points for disadvantaged communities. Those networks provided a platform for developing and sharing knowledge pertinent to those communities in key areas of sustainable development, such as employment, education, gender and health.

At the international level, UN system entities reported a wide range of programme activities, and several entities reported on institutional mechanisms to facilitate implementation. To strengthen the secretariat of the Commission on Science and Technology for Development, UNCTAD formed the Science, Technology and ICTs branch, while the Secretary-General entrusted DESA to oversee and manage the secretariats of the Internet Governance Forum (IGF) and the UN Global Alliance for ICT and Development. The International Telecommunication Union (ITU), as outlined in its Strategic Plan (2008–2011), established a WSIS Task Force to coordinate ITU strategies and activities in relation to WSIS. WSIS outcomes were also integrated into the UNESCO 2008–2013 Medium-term Strategy and its 2008–2009 programme and budget.

The Secretary-General concluded that progress towards the implementation of WSIS outcomes seemed to be on track. UN system activities to implement those outcomes were carried out in multi-stakeholder partnerships with other organizations at the international, regional, national and local levels. However, while some entities reported on successful mobilization of relevant stakeholders through electronic networks and face-to-face consultations and meetings, others encountered difficulty in securing the participation of all stakeholders, and reported low involvement of new stakeholders in the facilitation process. The high cost associated with face-to-face facilitation meetings in Geneva deterred participation by developing country stakeholders. Entities called for greater coordination among the leading facilitator agencies, with a view to providing coherent measuring tools to monitor and assess the status of implementation of the main themes. However, progress towards the attainment of the targets and goals set out in the Geneva Plan of Action and the Tunis Agenda for the Information Society needed to be benchmarked. In that regard, the Commission, through the UNCTAD secretariat, should collaborate with the United Nations Group on the Information Society, the lead moderators and facilitators to group the 11 action lines into thematic clusters. In addition, the UNCTAD secretariat should consult with action line facilitators during the 2008–2009 intersessional period to define roles and explore ways of streamlining the reporting process. The Commission should also explore ways of maximizing the participation of—and contribution by—civil society and business entities in its work.

By **decision 2008/216** of 18 July, the Economic and Social Council took note of the Secretary-General's report.

ECONOMIC AND SOCIAL COUNCIL ACTION

On 18 July, the Economic and Social Council, on the recommendation of the Commission on Science and Technology for Development [E/2008/31], adopted **resolution 2008/3** without vote [agenda item 13 *(b)*].

Assessment of the progress made in the implementation of and follow-up to the outcomes of the World Summit on the Information Society

The Economic and Social Council,

Recalling the outcome documents of the World Summit on the Information Society,

Recalling also that access to information and the sharing and creation of knowledge contribute significantly to strengthening economic, social and cultural development, thus helping all countries to reach the internationally agreed development goals and objectives, including the Millennium Development Goals, considering that this process can be enhanced by removing barriers to universal, ubiquitous, equitable and affordable access to information, and underlining the importance of removing barriers to bridging the digital divide, particularly those that hinder the full achievement of the economic, social and cultural development of countries and the welfare of their people, in particular in developing countries,

Recognizing the efforts by all stakeholders to implement the outcomes of the two phases of the Summit,

Recognizing also the efforts of the United Nations organizations and programmes and of all the regional commissions in implementing the goals, commitments and recommendations of the Summit,

Recalling its resolution 2006/46 of 28 July 2006 on the follow-up to the Summit and review of the Commission on Science and Technology for Development and the mandate that it gave to the Commission,

Recalling also General Assembly resolution 57/270 B of 23 June 2003 and Economic and Social Council resolution 2007/29 of 27 July 2007,

Taking note of the report of the Secretary-General on the progress made in the implementation of and follow-up to the outcomes of the Summit at the regional and international levels,

Evolving challenges and opportunities

1. *Notes* that the digital divide is changing in some respects and that while in general the divide may be shrinking, a new form of digital divide is emerging in terms of difference in quality and speed of access to information and communications technologies;

2. *Also notes* the continuing relevance of assisting developing countries in their efforts to overcome the digital divide, particularly with regard to both access and capacity;

3. *Further notes* that the disparity continues between developed and developing countries in respect of the cost and quality of access and that in developed, high-income economies, the average cost of a broadband connection is significantly less than in developing countries, both in nominal terms and as a percentage of the average monthly income;

4. *Notes* that the gender divide still persists in respect of the quality and variety of means of access to the Internet and information and communications technologies in the building of the information society in both developed and developing countries;

5. *Also notes* the strong growth of mobile telephony subscriptions, especially in developing countries;

6. *Notes with concern* the growing number of incidents affecting global network safety and security and provoking service outages in large regions of the world;

7. *Notes* that in many countries there is inadequate coherence and complementarity between national information and communications technology policies and national development and poverty reduction strategies and that, especially in the poorer rural areas, the potential of the Internet and information and communications technologies in general for promoting development has not yet been fully utilized;

8. *Calls upon* all stakeholders to increase efforts towards funding of and investment in information and communications technologies in order to advance broadband access, including wireless access, in areas and countries in which it is still limited or non-existent;

9. *Calls upon* all States, in building the information society, to take steps with a view to avoiding, and to refrain from taking, any unilateral measure not in accordance with international law and the Charter of the United Nations that impedes the full achievement of economic and social development by the population of the affected countries and that hinders their well-being;

10. *Reaffirms* that the protection of intellectual property is important for encouraging innovation and creativity in the information society, that, similarly, the wide dissemination, diffusion and sharing of knowledge is important for encouraging innovation and creativity, and that facilitating meaningful participation by all in intellectual property issues and knowledge-sharing through full awareness and capacity-building is a fundamental function of an inclusive information society;

11. *Calls upon* all stakeholders to increase their efforts to reduce the disparity in cost of access, through, for example, the establishment of Internet exchange points and the creation of a competitive environment, at both the backbone network and local levels;

12. *Recommends* that all States strive for gender equality in access to the Internet and in building the information society in both developed and developing countries, by ensuring the inclusion of the gender approach in information and communications technology policies in national strategies;

13. *Calls upon* all stakeholders to continue the development and spread of easy-to-use applications and services for mobile phones and related devices, especially those that are useful in rural areas and work with low bandwidth and high latency;

14. *Also calls upon* all stakeholders to cooperate more closely in making global networks more stable, resilient and secure and in overcoming outages of, incidents affecting and attacks on those networks;

15. *Calls upon* international and regional organizations to assess and report on a regular basis on the universal accessibility of nations to information and communications technologies, with the aim of creating equitable opportunities for the growth of the information and communications technology sectors of developing countries;

16. *Recommends* the mainstreaming of information and communications technology policies into national development or poverty reduction strategies, in accordance with the priorities of countries;

17. *Also recommends* increased international cooperation at all levels and among all stakeholders to help rural areas to access and benefit from the Internet and information and communications technologies in general;

Successes and shortcomings to date in respect of the implementation of the outcomes of the World Summit on the Information Society

18. *Takes note with appreciation* of the ongoing work of the Internet Governance Forum, its multi-stakeholder approach and its innovative platform, and expresses its thanks to host Governments for their contributions;

19. *Acknowledges* the progress made towards developing multilingual capabilities on the Internet;

20. *Also acknowledges* the work of the Partnership on Measuring Information and Communications Technologies for Development on developing indicators for further consideration and decision by the Statistical Commission;

21. *Notes* the lack of indicators needed to measure progress towards achieving the targets as set out in section B of the Plan of Action adopted by the World Summit on the Information Society at its first phase, held in Geneva from 10 to 12 December 2003, and endorsed by the General Assembly;

22. *Takes note* of the efforts undertaken by the regional commissions in respect of the coordination of the implementation of the outcomes of the Summit, including in developing e-strategies, capacity-building and measuring of information and communications technologies;

23. *Acknowledges* the efforts of all action line facilitators, especially the International Telecommunication Union and the United Nations Educational, Scientific and Cultural Organization in their role as lead facilitators;

24. *Notes* that the architecture for the implementation of the outcomes of the Summit, as defined in the Tunis Agenda for the Information Society, is rather complex and has also imposed limitations in respect of the participation of all stakeholders, in particular those from developing countries;

25. *Takes note* of the letter from the Secretary-General addressed to relevant organizations responsible for essential tasks associated with the Internet in which he requested them to report on the steps they had taken towards achieving enhanced cooperation in accordance with paragraph 71 of the Tunis Agenda, looks forward to the report to be prepared by the Secretary-General, which may contain recommendations on how the process should be pursued, and notes that all stakeholders, in their respective roles, will be included in this process;

26. *Reaffirms* the relevance of decisions on Internet governance in their entirety, as outlined in the Tunis Agenda;

27. *Recommends* that the Internet Governance Forum, as a multi-stakeholder discussion forum, retain its focus on public policy issues related to Internet governance;

28. *Encourages* collaboration among all stakeholders, including international organizations, consistent with their mandate and existing budgetary resources, in regard to the multilingualization of the Internet;

29. *Recommends* that the Partnership on Measuring Information and Communication Technologies for Development consider the creation of benchmarks and indicators, including impact indicators, for further consideration and decision by the Statistical Commission, in order to track progress towards the attainment of the specific goals and targets set out in the outcome documents of the Summit, particularly section B of the Plan of Action adopted in Geneva;

30. *Also recommends* that action line facilitators, in cooperation with all stakeholders, establish milestones, deadlines and calendars for their action lines, taking into account the outcome documents of the Summit;

31. *Further recommends* that lead facilitators conduct open-ended multi-stakeholder consultations with a view to improving the effectiveness and coherence of the annual clustering of activities related to the Summit;

32. *Recommends* that the United Nations Group on the Information Society organize focused, open-ended multi-stakeholder consultations on the implementation of paragraphs 3 to 28 of the Tunis Agenda, concerning financial mechanisms for meeting the challenges of information and communications technologies for development;

33. *Also recommends* the introduction in the facilitation process of electronic collaboration tools such as mailing lists, Web 2.0 applications, observatories and clearing-house models in order to enhance multi-stakeholder participation, in particular from developing countries;

34. *Further recommends* that in submitting their reports to the secretariat of the Commission on Science and Technology for Development, in accordance with Economic and Social Council resolution 2007/8 of 25 July 2007, action line facilitators bring to the attention of the Commission obstacles and difficulties encountered by all stakeholders in regard to the commitments and recommendations pertaining to their respective action lines at the regional and international levels and make proposals to the Commission for possible actions, whenever deemed necessary;

35. *Invites* all actors and institutions involved in the implementation of and follow-up to the outcomes of the Summit to clarify further their respective roles, improve coordination and information-sharing and build synergies to make the most effective use of available resources;

36. *Invites* the international community to make voluntary contributions to the special trust fund established by the United Nations Conference on Trade and Development to support the review and assessment work of the Commission in regard to the follow-up to the Summit;

37. *Recommends* that all stakeholders redouble their efforts to implement the vision of the Summit of a people-centred, inclusive and development-oriented information society, so as to enhance digital opportunities for all people and help to bridge the digital divide.

UN role in ICT development

CEB consideration. At its fifteenth session (Rome, 17–18 March) [CEB/2008/3], the CEB High-level Committee on Management was briefed by the Chairperson of the ICT Network on the three major areas of activity and discussion within that Network: the plan of action for harmonization and reform of business practices, data communications study, and collaboration with the United Nations Development Group. Regarding the business practices proposals, much of the recent work of the Network focused on that subject, with the lead agencies working to refine the proposals and commence planning activities, pending the availability of funding. The Network had not commenced its study on common data communications services, owing to the delay in obtaining funding from agencies. The final contributions had been confirmed, leaving only the finalization of the memorandum of understanding between the CEB secretariat and the United Nations Children's Fund, the procuring agency, to be completed.

At its sixteenth session (New York, 18–19 September) [CEB/2008/5], the CEB High-level Committee on Management encouraged all agencies that had not done so to closely examine their ICT services, with a view to utilizing the services of the International Computer Centre more fully.

Internet Governance Forum meeting. The IGF, established in 2006 [YUN 2006, p. 1001] to support the Secretary-General in carrying out the WSIS mandate to convene a multi-stakeholder policy dialogue on Internet governance issues, held its third meeting in Hyderabad, India, from 3 to 6 December. The overall theme was "Internet for All", which looked at the question of the adequacy of the way the Internet was managed, for the day when several billion users with varying cultural and ethical predilections and language competencies became users.

Economic and social trends

The *World Economic Situation and Prospects 2008* [Sales No. E.08.II.C.2], jointly issued by the United Nations Conference on Trade and Development (UNCTAD) and the United Nations Department of Economic and Social Affairs, stated that, in 2007, except for the United States, the growth of the world economy was broad-based. The majority of countries (102 out of 106 for which data were available) increased per capita output by 3 per cent or more. At the same time, the number of countries registering a decline in gross domestic product (GDP) per capita fell to nine, less than the previous year. Nevertheless, the divergence in economic performance remained across countries, particularly the least developed countries, where per capita income growth ranged from close to zero to well over 10 per cent. Africa as a whole showed further strong performance, but still accounted for many of the countries with sub-par performance. Among the developed economies, a continued slump in the housing sector and the associated credit tightening were expected to lead the United States into another year of below-trend growth, expected to reach only 2 per cent in 2008. Private consumption was expected to weaken with the housing downturn, while corporate investment spending and hiring were also likely to decelerate. Growth in Western Europe was also expected to slow in 2008, with GDP growing by 2.3 per cent for the euro area, down from 2.7 per cent in 2007. The economies of the newer European Union member States were expected to grow to about 5.4 per cent in 2008, compared to 6 per cent in 2007. Vibrant economic activity in the region was, however, accompanied by weakening indicators of macroeconomic stability. Economic growth in Japan was expected to reach 1.7 per cent in 2008, representing a slowdown from the 2 per cent expansion in 2007. In other developed economies, growth in Canada moderated in the second half of 2007 and was expected to remain subdued in 2008. Growth in Australia was strong during 2007, driven by domestic demand. Among the economies in transition, growth in the Commonwealth of Independent States maintained a strong pace of 8.2 per cent for 2007, and strengthened further in the South-Eastern European economies to 6 per cent. Robust domestic demand, particularly private consumption and fixed investment, remained the key driver.

Among the developing economies, growth in Africa strengthened in 2007, driven largely by buoyant domestic demand, booming mining and gas production and broad-based recovery in those countries recovering from economic decline. However, in some countries, it continued to be hampered by political and social tensions. East Asian economies maintained a solid pace of 8.4 per cent in 2007, with exports being the main driver of growth, followed by domestic demand. China continued to lead that growth, expanding at a pace of 11.4 per cent. In South Asia, growth decelerated to 6.9 per cent, while Western Asia benefited from the favourable effects of high oil prices, propelling growth to 5.7 per cent. In Latin America and the Caribbean, growth seemed to have peaked after the robust performance of the previous four years. The 5 per cent growth rate in 2007 was attributed to an improved economic performance in Brazil, led by domestic demand and strong business and public infrastructure investments. Further slowdown in the United States would pose risks for the region, affecting not only Mexico and Central America, but also some countries in South America.

According to the *Trade and Development Report, 2008* [Sales No. E.08.II.D.21], published by UNCTAD, in mid-2008 the global economy was teetering on the brink of recession. The downturn, after four years of relatively fast growth, was due to the global fallout from the financial crisis in the United States, the bursting of the housing bubble there and in other large economies, soaring commodity prices, increasingly restrictive monetary policies in a number of countries and stock market volatility. In that uncertain environment, the world economy was expected to grow by around 3 per cent in 2008, almost one percentage point less than the previous year, with GDP in developed countries expected to fall to about half that rate. By contrast, GDP growth in developing countries was expected to remain robust at around 6.4 per cent. Despite a slowdown, output growth in China in 2008 was expected to expand close to 10 per cent. West Asia (6.7 per cent) and both North Africa (6 per cent) and sub-Saharan Africa (excluding South Africa) (7.1 per cent) were the only regions where average rates of output growth were likely to rise compared to the previous two years. The growth in sub-Saharan Africa was the highest annual rate in more than three decades, largely due to higher income from primary commodity exports, particularly oil.

Overall, the financial turmoil, commodity price hikes and huge exchange-rate swings were having an enormous impact on the global economy, casting a shadow on the outlook for 2009. The fallout from the collapse of the United States mortgage market and the reversal of the housing boom in a number of countries were more profound and persistent than expected, and the shock waves spread beyond the countries directly involved, triggering widespread uncertainty in the financial markets. A year after the outbreak of the crisis, it remained unclear how long it would last. For a large number of developing countries, the outlook depended primarily on future trends in the prices of their primary commodity exports. Some developing and transition economies with substantial external debt and large current-account deficits, mainly in Eastern Europe and Central Asia, could face an increase in their financing costs and a reversal of their currency valuations.

One of the reasons for the fragile state of the world economy was the weakness in the system of global economic governance, in particular a lack of coherence between the international trading system, which was governed by internationally agreed rules and regulations, and the international monetary and financial system, which was not. The financial turbulence, the speculative forces affecting food and oil prices, and the apparent failure of foreign exchange markets to bring about changes in exchange rates that reflected shifts in the international competitiveness of countries suggested that there was an urgent need for redesigning the system of global economic governance. The meltdown of the sub-prime mortgage market had once again exposed the fragility of the global financial sector, and the complex financial instruments developed in recent years had served to spread the impact of risky investments across continents, institutions and markets. The recurrent episodes of financial volatility seemed to be driven by a mix of opaque instruments and massive leverage with which financial firms attempted to extract double-digit returns out of a real economy that was growing at a much slower rate. Since the outbreak of the sub-prime crisis, the risks of securitization had become more evident, and there were concerns over the financial industry's ability to generate large temporary profits by applying unsustainable refinancing schemes, while passing part of the losses that arose from inevitable market corrections to the public sector and the taxpayer. Indeed, since financial crises could have enormous negative effects on the real economy, policymakers had to bail out parts of the financial sector when systemic threats loomed. Just as with deposit-taking commercial banks, recent actions of the United States Federal Reserve had shown that investment banks and mortgage lenders, too, could be deemed "too big to fail" and that their liabilities were protected by implicit insurance. Given the risks to financial stability, the Federal Reserve was right to provide such insurance and prevent the bankruptcy of a large investment bank and the two largest mortgage lenders in the United States; but insurance should not come without cost. If the Government decided that different types of financial institutions needed to be bailed out because their failure could lead to a systemic crisis, those institutions should be subject to tighter prudential regulation similar to that imposed on deposit-taking banks. The recent crisis had shown once again that market discipline alone was ineffective in preventing recurrent episodes of "irrational exuberance" and that the market mechanism could not cope with massive drops in financial asset prices.

The *World Economic and Social Survey 2008* [Sales No. E.08.II.C.1], entitled "Overcoming Economic Insecurity", stated that, in 2008, rising food prices and a growing incidence of hunger demonstrated the mismatch between market forces and socio-economic well-being. For many of the countries facing severe food insecurity, the problem was often one of multiple threats from poverty, natural disasters and civil violence; but the outbreak of food riots in rapidly urbanizing middle-income countries, some with a solid growth record, suggested more serious structural deficiencies. Since early 2008, a growing mismatch between the supply of—and demand for—agricultural products had also triggered political unrest in a number of countries and put the issue of food security back in the international agenda. The problem was compounded by energy insecurity, as fuel prices hit new highs and future supplies became entangled in geopolitical calculations, and by increasingly flexible labour markets, which also undermined employment security. Instead of providing shelter against the upsurge of that turbulent economy, money markets added greatly to the sense of expanding insecurity. Volatile international financial flows, boom-bust cycles, collapsing currencies and speculative panics had put jobs, homes and pensions at risk. Still, heightened insecurity could not be put down simply to the destructive impulses of markets. Rather, it had much to do with the eagerness with which policymakers ceded economic responsibility to central bankers, corporations and managers of unregulated hedge funds on the promise that they would deliver a healthy investment climate and help secure large economic gains. While the macroeconomic climate had become less volatile, productive investment had not picked up. At the same time, more households, communities and countries were exposed to adverse shocks and downside risks, while their ability to recover from the consequences was sharply diminished. Despite greater price stability and increased openness, the growth record was uneven and the macroeconomic environment unbalanced. Food, fuel and financial markets were not delivering economic security.

Those concerns were compounded by new global threats, such as climate change. Several increasingly destructive natural disasters provided evidence of the threat posed to economic livelihoods in rich and poor countries alike. The attention brought to the presence of those heightened economic risks and compounded threats was often met with the response that the forces behind them were autonomous and irresistible, and beyond collective political control. The call invariably had been to cast aside old institutions and loyalties and embrace the new and efficient market practices of a borderless world. The *Survey* argued that it was the wrong response to increasing levels of economic insecurity, and that the deepening sense of insecurity had just as much to do with the lack of effective policy responses. It associated that failure, in part, with a policy bias built around the misguided idea of a self-regulating market economy, and stressed the need for a new balance between the market and the public interest along with a more integrated social and economic policy framework, which could provide and preserve a secure and stable economic future.

Human development

The Executive Board of the United Nations Development Programme/United Nations Population Fund, at its 2008 annual session (Geneva, 16–27 June) [E/2008/35], considered an April update on *Human Development Report* consultations [DP/2008/30], which revealed that 2008 was an exceptional year for the *Report* and the Human Development Report Office. Given the importance of the topic of climate change, the 2007 *Report* [YUN 2007 p. 857] covered 2008 also. That decision was taken in order to allow for a more sustained follow-up to the messages and policy implications presented in the climate change report. Moreover, the Director of the Office ceased his functions as at 31 December 2007. Those two facts affected the content and frequency of the informal consultations, and the research and writing of the 2009 Report started later than usual. The update described the consultations held during the transition period. The Executive Board took note of the update[E/2008/35 (dec. 25)].

Development policy and public administration

Committee for Development Policy

The Committee for Development Policy (CDP), at its tenth session (New York, 17–20 March) [E/2008/33], addressed three major themes: achieving sustainable development goals in the context of climate change; the worsening of global economic prospects and implications for developing countries; and matters related to the identification and graduation from the list of least developed countries (LDCs). Regarding the first theme, CDP stressed that achieving and sustaining the goals of the international sustainable development agenda required deep reductions in carbon emissions and adaptation policies to address current and future consequences of global warming. Key issues for developing countries were: creating less carbon-intensive incentives for economic growth; and enhancing adaptive capacities, particularly in the most vulnerable and poorest countries. An effective sustainable development strategy should be based on investment, innovation and institutional capacity, and international cooperation was fundamental, as the strategy would require appropriate funds, as well as technology development, transfer and dissemination. Greater coherence and integration between climate and development policies at national and international levels were necessary.

As to the second theme, the Committee examined the worsening global economic outlook at the beginning of 2008, and its possible impact on economic growth in developing countries through trade and external account shocks, with a potential to further delay the achievement of internationally agreed development goals. That outlook was set against the accumulation of large foreign-exchange reserves by many developing countries, which had been judged costly in terms of the opportunity costs of forgoing consumption and investment, and direct financial costs and implications for macroeconomic indicators. The Committee outlined the features of a reformed contingency finance architecture, based on a robust and flexible compensatory financing mechanism that, in the face of shocks, would provide sufficient resources in a timely manner, thereby obviating the need for developing countries to maintain large balances of foreign-exchange reserves.

With regard to the third theme, CDP continued developing criteria to be applied to all recommendations regarding the inclusion in and graduation from the list of LDCs. It reconfirmed the reliability of the current approach and recognized that the criteria should not be used mechanically, particularly in situations where country indicators were very close to inclusion or graduation thresholds. It proposed that the vulnerability profile take due account of aspects of countries' economic vulnerability not currently covered by the criteria used in the identification of LDCs, and that the impact assessments address the anticipated implications of the loss of LDC status. It also considered practical measures concerning the smooth transition of graduating countries and recommended that the United Nations give concrete leadership in the implementation of such measures.

ECONOMIC AND SOCIAL COUNCIL ACTION

On 23 July [meeting 42], the Economic and Social Council, on the recommendation of CDP [E/2008/33], adopted **resolution 2008/12** without vote [agenda item 13 *(a)*].

Report of the Committee for Development Policy on its tenth session

The Economic and Social Council,

Recalling General Assembly resolution 59/209 of 20 December 2004 on a smooth transition strategy for countries graduating from the list of least developed countries,

Recalling also its resolutions 2007/34 and 2007/35 of 27 July 2007,

1. *Takes note* of the report of the Committee for Development Policy on its tenth session;

2. *Requests* the Committee, at its eleventh session, to examine and make recommendations on the themes chosen by the Economic and Social Council for the high-level segment of its substantive session of 2009;

3. *Takes note* of the proposals made by the Committee regarding its future work programme, in particular regarding the monitoring of the development progress of Cape Verde;

4. *Requests* the Committee to monitor the development progress of countries graduating from the list of least developed countries and to include its findings in its annual report to the Economic and Social Council;

5. *Invites* the Chairperson and, as necessary, other members of the Committee to continue the practice of reporting orally on the work of the Committee.

Public administration

Committee of Experts. The Committee of Experts on Public Administration, at its seventh session (New York, 14–18 April) [E/2008/44], had before it Secretariat notes on: strengthening governance and public administration capacities for development [E/C.16/2008/2]; the review of the United Nations Programme in Public Administration and Finance [E/C.16/2008/4]; and the public administration perspective on implementing the internationally agreed goals and commitments in regard to sustainable development [E/C.16/2008/5]. It also considered a compendium of basic UN terminology in governance and public administration [E/C.16/2008/3]. The Committee concluded that there should be a much stronger awareness of the importance of capacity-building by the United Nations and Member States. The United Nations, particularly the Economic and Social Council, should prioritize capacity-building for countries in transition for achieving the Millennium Development Goals (MDGs), post-conflict reconstruction and disaster management and preparedness.

Regarding capacity-building for achieving the MDGs, the Committee recommended that the Council reiterate the need to monitor progress towards the Goals, including time-bound targets and national/subnational action plans. It also recommended national evidence-based reporting, with sets of data disaggregated by socially relevant categories, such as gender, income levels, age groups and subnational factors. The Council should also urge Member States to prepare an inventory of good administrative policies and practices to support the MDGs, which would include the capacities, institutional preparedness aspects and a strategic vision for a modern civil service; the UN system, particularly the Department of Economic and Social Affairs (DESA) and other concerned bodies, should support such efforts.

As to capacity-building in post-conflict reconstruction, public administration reconstruction in a post-conflict environment should be done at the systemic, societal, organizational and individual levels, and start before the end of a conflict. The Secretariat should compile the lessons learned in post-conflict recovery and reconstruction in the next *World Public Sector Report*. At the systemic level, capacity-building involved the basic elements of State-building, including legitimacy, social cohesion, the value of citizenship, coherence between traditional and modern systems, consultations with stakeholders—such as eminent members of the diaspora community—and reconciliation. At the organizational level, public administration reconstruction should aim for continuity of administration services, coherence of the public sector and the inclusion of different groups. At the individual level, political leadership was required to guide the processes for participation in all aspects of State reconstruction to build a shared understanding, develop an awareness of the rights and responsibilities of citizens, create an environment conducive to reconciliation, and develop decision-making processes that reformulated the citizen/State relationship. Training individuals in a new, common and shared understanding of political and social institutions, economic development and reconstruction was of the utmost importance, and the international community should strengthen public institutions and leaders. Early warning systems for future conflicts should be identified and mechanisms put into place to eliminate sources of conflict.

Concerning capacity-building in disaster management and prevention, Member States should conduct post-crisis evaluations and research and make them publicly available so as to enhance transparency and accountability in the management of the resources allocated to disaster management. Such evaluations could be carried out on a country-by-country basis or through peer review or other means, which would allow States to exchange information on best practices and learn from one another. States should also develop capacities at the individual level through the training of public servants in disaster management; DESA should expand its disaster management activities; and the UN Secretariat should create a working group or task force jointly with other international organizations to raise global awareness within public administrations and create a trans-administrative response.

ECONOMIC AND SOCIAL COUNCIL ACTION

On 25 July [meeting 44], the Economic and Social Council, on the recommendation of the Committee of Experts on Public Administration [E/2008/44], adopted **resolution 2008/32** without vote [agenda item 13 *(g)*].

Report of the Committee of Experts on Public Administration on its seventh session

The Economic and Social Council,

Recalling its resolutions 2002/40 of 19 December 2002, 2003/60 of 25 July 2003, 2005/3 of 31 March 2005, 2005/55 of 21 October 2005, 2006/47 of 28 July 2006 and 2007/38 of 4 October 2007 on public administration and development,

Recalling also General Assembly resolutions 50/225 of 19 April 1996, 56/213 of 21 December 2001, 57/277 of 20 December 2002, 58/231 of 23 December 2003, 59/55 of 2 December 2004 and 60/34 of 30 November 2005 on public administration and development,

Recalling further paragraph 11 of General Assembly resolution 60/1 of 16 September 2005,

Taking note with appreciation of the pioneering work of the United Nations Programme on Public Administration, Finance and Development in supporting Member States with administrative reforms, public institution-building, civil service training and post-conflict reconstruction of public administrations during the past sixty years, since its inception in 1948,

Recognizing that although the conditions and context of development and governance have changed, public administration priorities, including capacity-building for development and ownership of national development, still remain critical cross-cutting issues for the achievement of the internationally agreed development goals, including the Millennium Development Goals,

1. *Takes note* of the conclusions on the topic of capacity-building for development in the report of the Committee of Experts on Public Administration on its seventh session;

2. *Encourages* Member States to continue to strengthen their capacities to better utilize the various aid modalities and to disseminate the understanding and implementation of capacity-building as a judicious combination of institution-building and human resource development, whereby people, organizations, States and society as a whole develop and maintain their ability to manage their public affairs successfully, among other means, by fostering public participation in governance and development processes, harnessing the potential of information and communications technology to promote people-centred development, effectively combining decentralization and centralization policies, and forging regional and national partnerships with institutions of public administration to provide needed training;

3. *Emphasizes* that capacity-building is essential and needed in administrative restructuring, civil service reform, human resources development and public administration training, improving performance in the public sector, financial management, public-private interaction, social development, developing infrastructure and protecting the environment, governmental legal and regulatory capacity, and the management and implementation of development programmes;

4. *Invites* Member States to continue to monitor the progress made towards the achievement of the internationally agreed development goals, including the Millennium Development Goals, and to prepare an inventory of good administrative policies implemented to support the Goals, including the necessary capacities, institutional development aspects and strategic visions concerning a modern civil service, and emphasizes that the United Nations system, particularly the Department of Economic and Social Affairs of the Secretariat and other concerned United Nations bodies, should support such efforts and the sharing of best practices and lessons learned;

5. *Stresses* that capacity-building for public administration is of utmost importance for all transitioning economies, the achievement of the internationally agreed development goals, including the Millennium Development Goals, post-conflict rehabilitation and reconstruction, and disaster/crisis management and preparedness, that capacity-building processes in those areas share a number of important common features and experiences concerning the interaction of societal, systemic, organizational and individual levels of action, and that Member States should share those experiences in a more systematic and comprehensive way;

6. *Emphasizes* that in capacity-building for post-conflict recovery and reconstruction, the continuity of administration and public services, the coherence of the public sector and a multi-stakeholder approach are important prerequisites, and that in capacity-building for post-disaster and crisis situations, the United Nations system, particularly the Department of Economic and Social Affairs and other United Nations bodies, should support efforts to distil and share lessons learned and best practices;

7. *Requests* the Secretariat to enhance its support for capacity-building, including in the public sector, ensuring that available resources are adequate and existing resource levels are maintained;

8. *Also requests* the Secretariat to continually focus on the United Nations Public Service Awards, the United Nations Online Network in Public Administration and Finance, the Network of Innovators, the *World Public Sector Reports* and the Global Forum on Reinventing Government, and further requests the Secretariat to continue its useful role in facilitating the implementation of the action lines contained in the Tunis Agenda for the Information Society;

9. *Notes* the latest phase of the work done by the Committee of Experts on basic United Nations terminology in governance and public administration through a review of proposed definitions;

10. *Also notes* the input by the Committee of Experts to the theme of the 2008 annual ministerial review: Implementing the internationally agreed goals and commitments in regard to sustainable development.

On the same date, by **decision 2008/254**, the Council approved the convening of the eighth session of the Committee of Experts on Public Administration from 30 March to 3 April 2009 on the main theme "The human factor in capacity-building and development", and the provisional agenda for that session.

Groups of countries in special situations

On 19 September, the General Assembly, on the recommendation of the General Committee, included in the agenda of its sixth-third session the item entitled "Groups of countries in special situations", covering least developed countries and landlocked and transit developing countries, and allocated it to the Second Committee.

By **decision 63/543** of 19 December, the Assembly took note of the report of the Second Committee on the subject [A/63/417].

Least developed countries

The special problems of the least developed countries (LDCs) were considered in several UN forums in 2008, particularly in connection with the implementation of the Brussels Declaration and Programme of Action for the Least Developed Countries for the Decade 2001–2010, adopted at the Third United Nations Conference on the Least Developed Countries in 2001 [YUN 2001, p. 770] and endorsed by the General Assembly in resolution 55/279 in July of that year [ibid., p. 771]; and the reaffirmation by world leaders, in the 2005 World Summit Outcome document [YUN 2005, p. 48], of their commitment to addressing the special needs of LDCs and the urgency of meeting the goals and targets of the Brussels Programme, particularly the official development assistance (ODA) target. The Committee for Development Policy (CDP) and UNCTAD also considered LDC-related issues.

LDC list

In 2008, the number of countries officially designated as LDCs stood at 49, following the graduation of Cape Verde in December 2007 [YUN 2007, p. 861]. Maldives had been recommended for graduation from the list of LDCs in resolution 59/209 [YUN 2004, p. 854], however, the General Assembly, in resolution 60/33 [YUN 2005, p. 942], deferred until January 2008 the start of the three-year transition period for its graduation, in the wake of the destruction and damage caused by the December 2004 Indian Ocean tsunami to the country's social and economic infrastructure and disruption of its development plans. Also in 2007, the Assembly, in resolution 62/97 [YUN 2007, p. 863], noted the Economic and Social Council's decision to endorse the CDP recommendation that Samoa be graduated from the list.

The full list of LDCs comprised the following countries: Afghanistan, Angola, Bangladesh, Benin, Bhutan, Burkina Faso, Burundi, Cambodia, Central African Republic, Chad, Comoros, Democratic Republic of the Congo, Djibouti, Equatorial Guinea, Eritrea, Ethiopia, the Gambia, Guinea, Guinea-Bissau, Haiti, Kiribati, the Lao People's Democratic Republic, Lesotho, Liberia, Madagascar, Malawi, Maldives, Mali, Mauritania, Mozambique, Myanmar, Nepal, the Niger, Rwanda, Samoa, Sao Tome and Principe, Senegal, Sierra Leone, Solomon Islands, Somalia, Sudan, Timor-Leste, Togo, Tuvalu, Uganda, United Republic of Tanzania, Vanuatu, Yemen and Zambia.

Smooth transition strategy

CDP consideration. At its tenth session (New York, 17–20 March) [E/2008/33], CDP, which was responsible for adding countries to—or graduating them from—the LDC list, re-examined, in preparation for the 2009 triennial review of that list, the methodology for the identification of such countries, pursuant to Economic and Social Council resolution 2007/35 [YUN 2007, p. 858]. It also deliberated on the graduation process, and the contents of future vulnerability profiles and of impact assessments. Also reviewed were the question of a smooth transition, guidelines for monitoring the progress of graduated countries and a handbook on the LDC category.

In terms of the graduation procedures, including vulnerability profiles and impact assessment, CDP stated that, for countries found eligible for the first time, a vulnerability profile would be prepared by UNCTAD and an impact assessment by the UN Department of Economic and Social Affairs (DESA), in cooperation with UNCTAD, in the year prior to the next triennial review. The vulnerability profile and the impact assessment would provide the Committee with information to help it decide whether a country found eligible at the previous triennial review should be recommended for graduation. The vulnerability profile should give the overall background of a country's economy and development situation, compare the values of the indicators used in the criteria with national statistics, and further assess other vulnerabilities, such as instability of remittances, dependency on tourism, high infrastructure cost due to geographical conditions and the impact of climate change. The Committee also requested UNCTAD to provide comparative data for other low-income countries in similar situations; in view of the increased number of countries under review for graduation and the increased demand on the substantive content of the vulnerability profiles, it stressed the need for the availability of sufficient resources for that purpose. CDP agreed that the impact assessment should address the expected implications of the loss of LDC status, in particular with regard to development financing, international trade and technical assistance. The effective implementation of the impact assessments would require that DESA be able to draw on the cooperation of donor countries, international cooperation agencies, trading partners and the country concerned.

The Committee addressed the question of a smooth transition for graduating countries, as set out in Assembly resolution 59/209, and reiterated the need to effectively implement the measures contained therein. In that regard, the United Nations should give concrete leadership in the implementation of smooth transition measures by maintaining the travel-related benefits to delegates from graduated countries over a period appropriate to the development situation of the country. CDP stated that an expert group should be convened to consider the phasing out of LDC benefits, with a view to identifying those that could be maintained for a period, and proposing specific phasing-out periods. Case studies could be conducted assessing the situation of Cape Verde and countries that had qualified for graduation.

CDP examined a report submitted by Cape Verde and noted the country's continued rate of growth and achievements on the MDG indicators, despite continuing economic vulnerability. It encouraged Cape Verde and its development partners to make full use of future meetings of the consultative mechanism (Grupo de Apoio à Transição) to obtain support for its economic transformation agenda.

The Economic and Social Council, in resolution 2008/12 of 23 July (see ES/1/38), requested CDP to monitor the development progress of countries graduating from the LDC list and to include its findings in its annual report to the Council. It also took note of the proposals regarding its future work in relation to the monitoring of Cape Verde's development progress.

Programme of Action (2001–2010)

UNCTAD consideration. LDC Ministers, meeting on 19 April in the context of the twelfth session of the United Nations Conference on Trade and Development (UNCTAD XII) (Accra, Ghana, 20–25 April) [TD/442], issued the Declaration of the Least Developed Countries Ministerial Meeting at UNCTAD XII, in which they accorded high priority to national ownership of the Enhanced Integrated Framework for Trade-Related Technical Assistance to Least Developed Countries (EIF) as an effective tool for enhancing economic development, and urged UNCTAD, as an EIF-participating agency, to work towards its operationalization so that LDCs could start benefiting from it by mid-2008. They welcomed the graduation of a number of LDCs to developing-country status as a sign of economic progress within the group, but recognized the accompanying challenges and opportunities that needed to be addressed effectively in order for progress in graduating countries to be broad-based and sustainable. They urged the international community to put in place a smooth transition strategy for those countries, and UNCTAD to continue to play a lead role through its policy research and analysis in support of recently graduated countries and those in the transition phase for graduation. Concerned by soaring food prices, against the backdrop of the global financial crisis and economic slowdown, the Ministers proposed that the UN Secretary-General establish a mechanism to address the food crisis in LDCs, including the establishment of a panel of eminent persons to address the issue and long-term food security issues and the convening of an international meeting. They encouraged UNCTAD to strengthen its policy research and analysis, consensus-building and technical cooperation functions in favour of LDCs and to make a substantive contribution to the Fourth United Nations Conference on the Least Developed Countries (see ES/1/45). Donors that had not done so were invited to make financial contributions to the UNCTAD trust fund for LDCs, which needed urgent replenishment on a more predictable and secure basis.

Report of Secretary-General. In accordance with General Assembly resolution 62/203 [YUN 2007, p. 866] and Economic and Social Council resolution 2007/31 [ibid., p. 863], the Secretary-General submitted, in May [A/63/77-E/2008/61], his annual report on the implementation of the Programme of Action for the Least Developed Countries for the Decade 2001–2010. The Secretary-General stated that most LDCs, except those in the Pacific, had met or were on track to achieve the Brussels Programme growth and investment targets by 2010. Progress made in human development targets was noticeable in the areas of health and education, but further advances would depend on improved access to water and sanitation, where less progress had been made. Less progress than previously thought had also been made in gender parity in education, and none in maternal mortality. Data on extreme poverty suggested that almost 50 per cent of the population in one half of the LDCs for which data were available lived in extreme poverty, while malnutrition seemed to be worsening, particularly among children and women. The rising costs of basic food exacerbated malnutrition; jeopardized efforts to achieve the objective of the Brussels Programme; and risked destabilizing the political situation and triggering social unrest in many countries—including 26 of the LDCs—experiencing political instability.

The Secretary-General concluded that, on the demand side, energy consumption could be significantly decreased by adopting cost-effective, energy-efficient technologies, as well as carbon-saving strategies to tackle climate change and secure the provision of sustainable energy. On the supply side, the short-term strategy should include immediate humanitarian assistance to countries in food crisis, which required scaling up international assistance and closing a $750 million shortfall in the World Food Programme's budget caused by high food prices; social protection programmes, such as cash support, food-for-work programmes and school feeding programmes; and financial lending and crop insurance schemes.

In the medium term, the prospects for supply relied on an increase in agricultural productivity by improving farmers' access to finance and markets, enabling them to purchase agricultural inputs, machinery and tools and other innovations for obtaining higher yields, as well as better irrigation, transport infrastructure, electricity, investment in research and development and improvement of market information systems. A medium-term solution to the food crisis also required rethinking the use of biofuel, which accounted for between 10 and 30 per cent of the increase in global food prices. In the long term, the State-led green revolution should facilitate the transition to a high-value agricultural revolution led by the private sector. The agriculture-for-development agenda called for full trade liberalization, which could increase agricultural commodity prices and welfare gains for LDCs. Reduction of deforestation, control of wildfires, management of livestock waste and adoption of conservation agriculture could reduce the environmental footprint, while sustainable land cultivation, livestock and forest management, and irrigation and watershed management, along with the development of crop varieties resistant to pests and drought, could increase the resilience of agricultural production in LDCs to climate change. Carbon trading schemes also could reduce emissions from agriculture.

The global food crisis provided an opportunity to address the issue of high fertility, especially in the African LDCs, as slower population growth would reduce the pressures faced by LDCs in regard to food security, land tenure, environmental degradation and water supply, and strengthen the human capital critical for sustained growth and sustainable development.

ECONOMIC AND SOCIAL COUNCIL ACTION

On 25 July [meeting 45], the Economic and Social Council adopted **resolution 2008/37** [draft: E/2008/L.38] without vote [agenda item 6 *(b)*].

Implementation of the Programme of Action for the Least Developed Countries for the Decade 2001–2010

The Economic and Social Council,

Recalling the Brussels Declaration and the Programme of Action for the Least Developed Countries for the Decade 2001–2010,

Recalling also its decision 2001/320 of 24 October 2001, in which it decided to establish, under the regular agenda item entitled "Integrated and coordinated implementation of and follow-up to major United Nations conferences and summits", a regular sub-item entitled "Review and coordination of the implementation of the Programme of Action for the Least Developed Countries for the Decade 2001–2010",

Affirming the Ministerial Declaration of the high-level segment of its substantive session of 2008, and recognizing the impacts of the financial, economic, social and environmental challenges identified therein on the implementation of the Programme of Action,

Recalling the Ministerial Declaration of the high-level segment of its substantive session of 2004 on the theme "Resources mobilization and enabling environment for poverty eradication in the context of the implementation of the Programme of Action for the Least Developed Countries for the Decade 2001–2010",

Taking note of the Istanbul Declaration on the Least Developed Countries: Time for Action, adopted at the Ministerial Conference of the Least Developed Countries, held in Istanbul on 9 and 10 July 2007 on the theme "Making globalization work for the least developed countries",

Recalling its resolution 2007/31 of 27 July 2007,

Recalling also General Assembly resolutions 61/1 of 19 September 2006 and 62/203 of 19 December 2007,

1. *Takes note* of the annual progress report of the Secretary-General on the implementation of the Programme of Action for the Least Developed Countries for the Decade 2001–2010;

2. *Reaffirms* that the Programme of Action constitutes a fundamental framework for a strong global partnership aimed at accelerating sustained economic growth, sustainable development and poverty eradication in the least developed countries;

3. *Welcomes* the Declaration adopted by Heads of State and Government and heads of delegations participating in the high-level meeting of the sixty-first session of the General Assembly on the midterm comprehensive global review of the implementation of the Programme of Action, in which they recommitted themselves to addressing the special needs of the least developed countries by making progress towards the goals of poverty eradication, peace and development;

4. *Also welcomes* the contributions made in the lead-up to the midterm comprehensive global review of the implementation of the Programme of Action, and notes the Cotonou Strategy for the Further Implementation of the Programme of Action for the Least Developed Countries for the Decade 2001–2010 as an initiative owned and led by the least developed countries;

5. *Further welcomes* the continued economic and social progress of many least developed countries, which has led to the fact that a number of countries are proceeding towards graduation from the list of least developed countries and that some of them are on track to achieving the growth and investment targets of the Programme of Action by 2010;

6. *Remains concerned*, however, about the insufficient and uneven progress achieved in the implementation of the Programme of Action, and stresses the need to address, within the time frame set by the Programme of Action, areas of weakness in its implementation and the continued precarious socio-economic situation in some least developed countries, through a strong commitment to the objectives, goals and targets of the Programme of Action;

7. *Expresses its deep concern* that the number of people living in extreme poverty remains significantly high in the least developed countries, while an increasing number of people are at risk of malnutrition, in particular children and women, and recognizes that there are important linkages between development, poverty eradication and gender equality;

8. *Stresses* that the internationally agreed development goals, including the Millennium Development Goals, can be effectively achieved in the least developed countries through, in particular, the timely fulfilment of the seven commitments of the Programme of Action;

9. *Underlines* the fact that, for the further implementation of the Programme of Action, the least developed countries and their development partners must be guided by an integral approach, a broader genuine partnership, country ownership, market considerations and results-oriented actions encompassing:

(*a*) Fostering a people-centred policy framework;

(*b*) Ensuring good governance at both the national and the international levels as essential for the implementation of the commitments embodied in the Programme of Action;

(*c*) Building human and institutional capacities;

(*d*) Building productive capacities to make globalization work for the least developed countries;

(*e*) Enhancing the role of trade in development;

(*f*) Reducing vulnerability and protecting the environment;

(*g*) Mobilizing financial resources;

10. *Reaffirms* that progress in the implementation of the Programme of Action will require effective implementation of national policies and priorities for the sustained economic growth and sustainable development of the least developed countries, as well as strong and committed partnership between those countries and their development partners;

11. *Urges* the least developed countries to strengthen country ownership in the implementation of the Programme of Action by, inter alia, translating its goals and targets into specific measures within their national development frameworks and poverty eradication strategies, including, where they exist, poverty reduction strategy papers, promoting broad-based and inclusive dialogue on development with relevant stakeholders, including civil society and the private sector, and enhancing domestic resource mobilization and aid management;

12. *Urges* development partners to fully implement, in a timely manner, commitments in the Programme of Action and to exercise individual best efforts to continue to increase their financial and technical support for its implementation;

13. *Welcomes* the graduation of Cape Verde from the list of least developed countries;

14. *Reiterates its invitation* to all development and trading partners to support the implementation of the transition strategy of countries graduating from the list of least developed countries, to avoid any abrupt reductions in either official development assistance or technical assistance provided to the graduated country and to consider extending to the graduated country trade preferences previously made available as a result of least developed country status, or reducing them in a phased manner;

15. *Encourages* the United Nations resident coordinator system, the Bretton Woods institutions, bilateral and multilateral donors and other development partners to assist the least developed countries in translating goals and targets of the Programme of Action into concrete actions in the light of their national development priorities and to collaborate with and provide support to, as appropriate,

the relevant national development forums and follow-up mechanisms;

16. *Stresses* the crucial importance of integrated and coordinated follow-up, monitoring and reporting for the effective implementation of the Programme of Action at the national, subregional, regional and global levels;

17. *Also stresses*, within the context of the annual global reviews, as envisaged in the Programme of Action, the need to assess the implementation of the Programme of Action sector by sector, and in this regard invites the United Nations system and all relevant international organizations, consistent with their respective mandates, to report on the progress made in its implementation using quantifiable criteria and indicators to be measured against the goals and targets of the Programme of Action and to participate fully in reviews of the Programme of Action at the national, subregional, regional and global levels;

18. *Reiterates its invitation* to the organs, organizations and bodies of the United Nations system and other relevant multilateral organizations to provide full support to and cooperation with the Office of the High Representative for the Least Developed Countries, Landlocked Developing Countries and Small Island Developing States;

19. *Requests* the Secretary-General to ensure, at the Secretariat level, the full mobilization and coordination of all parts of the United Nations system to facilitate coordinated implementation and coherence in the follow-up to and monitoring and review of the Programme of Action at the national, subregional, regional and global levels, including through such coordination mechanisms as the United Nations System Chief Executives Board for Coordination, the United Nations Development Group, the Executive Committee on Economic and Social Affairs and the Inter-Agency Expert Group on the Millennium Development Goals Indicators;

20. *Expresses its concern* about the insufficiency of resources in the trust fund established for the participation of the least developed countries in the annual review of the implementation of the Programme of Action by the Economic and Social Council, and expresses its appreciation to those countries that have made voluntary contributions;

21. *Reiterates* the critical importance of the participation of Government representatives from the least developed countries in the annual review of the Programme of Action by the Economic and Social Council, expresses, in this regard, its deep appreciation to those countries that have made voluntary contributions to the special trust fund established for this purpose by the Secretary-General, invites donor countries to continue to support the participation of two representatives from each least developed country in the annual review of the implementation of the Programme of Action, including by contributing in an adequate and timely manner to the special trust fund, and requests the Secretary-General to intensify his efforts to mobilize the resources necessary in order to ensure that the trust fund is adequately resourced and to provide information on the status of the trust fund;

22. *Reiterates its request* to the Secretary-General to include least developed country issues in all relevant reports in the economic, social and related fields in order to ensure follow-up to their development in the broader context of the world economy and contribute to preventing their marginalization while promoting their further integration into the world economy;

23. *Recalls* paragraph 114 of the Programme of Action on holding a fourth United Nations Conference on the Least Developed Countries towards the end of the current decade, and notes the steps being taken in this regard, in accordance with General Assembly resolution 62/203;

24. *Requests* the Secretary-General to step up appropriate measures for the implementation of the advocacy strategy on the effective and timely implementation of the Programme of Action for the Least Developed Countries for the Decade 2001–2010, in coordination with all relevant stakeholders;

25. *Also requests* the Secretary-General to submit an analytical and results-oriented annual progress report on the further implementation of the Programme of Action and to make available adequate resources, within existing resources, for the preparation of such a report.

Trade and Development Board action. The UNCTAD Trade and Development Board (TDB), at its fifty-fifth session (Geneva, 15–26 September) [A/63/15 (Part IV)], considered the seventh progress report [TD/B/55/8 & Corr.1] on UNCTAD-wide activities in the implementation of the Programme of Action for the Least Developed Countries for the Decade 2001–2010, and adopted agreed conclusions [493(LV)] on the review of progress in the implementation of the Programme of Action. The Board welcomed the recent improvement in the economic performance of many LDCs, but was concerned that growth remained fragile and LDCs were lagging behind in the achievement of the MDGs, notwithstanding some progress in primary education and gender equality. It invited Member States and UN organizations to consider the policy recommendations contained in *The Least Developed Countries Report 2008: Growth, Poverty and the Terms of Development Partnership* [Sales No. E.08.II.D.20] in designing development policies and strategies, and the terms of development partnership. TDB urged LDCs to assume greater ownership of national development strategies by designing and implementing inclusive policies suited to their particular needs, and to mobilize domestic resources and build State capacities and good governance, including by adopting transparent aid management policies, bearing in mind the Accra Agenda for Action adopted at the Third High-level Forum on Aid Effectiveness (Accra, Ghana, 2–4 September) [E/63/539]. LDC development partners should support country leadership in designing and implementing national development strategies and help strengthen LDCs' capacity to exercise such leadership. The Board invited LDCs, when designing and implementing country-owned national development strategies, to emphasize productive sectors and infrastructure and to make their aid requests support such emphasis. Development partners should fulfil their aid commitments and provide aid consistent with the development priorities identified by LDCs in their strategies.

The Board recommended that UNCTAD should promote the exchange of country experiences and best practices among LDCs in trade and development and the interrelated areas of finance, technology, investment and sustainable development. It acknowledged the importance of EIF and invited the UNCTAD secretariat to intensify cooperation with the Framework to complement its technical cooperation activities and capacity-building for LDCs. UNCTAD should provide technical assistance to LDCs, many of which were suffering from the effects of the food crisis, climate change and natural disasters, and donors and other countries in a position to do so should contribute to the UNCTAD LDC trust fund and regularly replenish it, so as to diversify the funding sources. UNCTAD should also focus on the needs of LDCs across all areas of its mandate and contribute to the upcoming Fourth United Nations Conference on the Least Developed Countries (see below). It should undertake further studies on sectors of specific interest to LDCs, especially new and non-traditional sectors; reallocate part of its regular budget to fund *The Least Developed Countries Report*; and increase its operational effectiveness so that funds for the report were provided with the least possible disturbance of its other activities.

Preparatory process for Fourth UN Conference on LDCs

Report of Secretary-General. In August, the Secretary-General, in response to General Assembly resolution 62/203 [YUN 2007, p. 866], submitted a report on the outline of modalities of the Fourth United Nations Conference on the Least Developed Countries [A/63/284]. The Conference would convene to assess the implementation of the Programme of Action for the Least Developed Countries for the Decade 2001–2010 and formulate new strategies and an action plan for the sustainable development of LDCs in the following decade. An analysis of past performance would shed light on the most critical constraints on the realization of the goals of the previous programmes of action and suggest new strategies to reverse them. The Fourth Conference should: assess the implementation of the Programme of Action during the first decade of the twenty-first century towards halving the proportion of people living in extreme poverty and suffering from hunger, and promoting sustainable and steady increases in gross domestic product growth rates in LDCs; review the implementation of international support measures, particularly in the areas of ODA, debt, investment and trade; and consider the formulation and adoption of national and international policies and measures for the sustainable development of LDCs and their progressive integration into the world economy. The Conference would provide an opportunity to share lessons learned and best practices; identify international and domestic policies in light of the outcomes of the appraisals; agree on additional international support measures in favour of LDCs; enhance partnerships between stakeholders; reaffirm the commitment to poverty eradication and sustainable development in LDCs, as well as the commitment to address their needs, made at major UN conferences and summits, including the Millennium Summit [YUN 2000, p. 47] and the 2005 World Summit [YUN 2005, p. 47]; mobilize international support and action; and identify new challenges and opportunities for LDCs and means to address them.

The preparatory process for the Conference should promote dialogue between stakeholders, establish linkages and ensure synergies at all levels. To that end, various multi-stakeholder events were encouraged. National preparations would build on country review processes to avoid duplication and ensure UN system coordination at the country level. They would also take into account the recent stocktaking exercise in preparation for the MDG-based national development strategies, undertaken by most LDCs, with the support of UN resident coordinators, as well as the national reviews held within the framework of the annual ministerial reviews during the high-level segments of the Council's substantive sessions. Regional preparations should bring the regional perspective into the review process. The global preparatory process would build on the reviews of other major UN conferences and stocktaking exercises between 2008 and 2010. To that end, the Secretariat would map out all major reviews between 2008 and 2010 and prepare a road map, consisting of a comprehensive list of preparatory events. Offers to host the Conference had been received from Turkey and Austria. The Secretary-General recommended that the Assembly should decide at its sixty-third (2008) session on the convening of the Conference, including its dates and venue. The United Nations Office of the High Representative for the Least Developed Countries, Landlocked Developing Countries and Small Island Developing States would serve as the focal point for the preparatory process. The UN Secretary-General would designate the Conference Secretary-General following the Assembly's decisions on the convening of the conference.

Communications. On 17 November, Bangladesh transmitted to the Secretary-General the Ministerial Declaration of the Least Developed Countries, issued at their meeting held in New York on 29 September [A/C.2/63/8]. The Ministers expressed their concern about the fact that two years after the midterm comprehensive global review of the implementation of the

Brussels Programme of Action [YUN 2006, p. 1014], the progress achieved in its implementation was insufficient and uneven. Economic growth in LDCs had not translated into poverty eradication and improved well-being. If the trend continued, many of their countries would not meet the MDGs and other internationally agreed development goals. They welcomed the convening of the Fourth United Nations Conference on the Least Developed Countries, which would be an opportunity for their countries and development partners to establish a new strategic framework for the following decade for development efforts in a complex and changing world.

The Foreign Ministers of the Group of 77, at their thirty-second annual meeting (New York, 26 September) [A/63/464] (see also p. 904), recognized the special challenges and needs of LDCs, particularly in the face of new and emerging challenges. They supported the convening of the Fourth United Nations Conference on the Least Developed Countries, which would represent an opportunity for LDCs and their partners to review past performance—especially in areas of failures and weak implementation—and establish a new strategic framework for the next decade for development efforts.

GENERAL ASSEMBLY ACTION

On 19 December [meeting 72], the General Assembly, on the recommendation of the Second Committee [A/63/417/Add.1], adopted **resolution 63/227** without vote [agenda item 52 *(a)*].

Implementation of the Brussels Programme of Action for the Least Developed Countries for the Decade 2001–2010

The General Assembly,

Recalling the Brussels Declaration and the Programme of Action for the Least Developed Countries for the Decade 2001–2010,

Recalling also the United Nations Millennium Declaration,

Recalling further its resolution 57/270 B of 23 June 2003 on the integrated and coordinated implementation of and follow-up to the outcomes of the major United Nations conferences and summits in the economic and social fields,

Recalling the 2005 World Summit Outcome,

Recalling also its resolution 62/203 of 19 December 2007,

Taking note of Economic and Social Council resolution 2008/37 of 25 July 2008,

Taking note also of the Ministerial Declaration adopted at the Annual Meeting of Ministers for Foreign Affairs of the Least Developed Countries on 29 September 2008 in New York,

Reaffirming that the Programme of Action constitutes a fundamental framework for a strong global partnership, whose goal is to accelerate sustained economic growth, sustainable development and poverty eradication in the least developed countries,

1. *Takes note* of the report of the Secretary-General and his note on the modalities of the Fourth United Nations Conference on the Least Developed Countries;

2. *Welcomes* the contributions made in the lead-up to the midterm comprehensive global review of the implementation of the Programme of Action for the Least Developed Countries for the Decade 2001–2010, and notes the Cotonou Strategy for the Further Implementation of the Programme of Action for the Least Developed Countries for the Decade 2001–2010 as an initiative owned and led by the least developed countries;

3. *Also welcomes* the Declaration adopted by Heads of State and Government and heads of delegations participating in the high-level meeting of the sixty-first session of the General Assembly on the midterm comprehensive global review of the implementation of the Programme of Action, in which they recommitted themselves to addressing the special needs of the least developed countries by making progress towards the goals of poverty eradication, peace and development;

4. *Decides* to convene, as called for in paragraph 114 of the Programme of Action, the Fourth United Nations Conference on the Least Developed Countries at a high level in 2011 for a duration of not more than five working days, with the following mandate:

(a) To undertake a comprehensive appraisal of the implementation of the Programme of Action by the least developed countries and their development partners, share best practices and lessons learned, and identify obstacles and constraints encountered as well as actions and initiatives needed to overcome them;

(b) To identify effective international and domestic policies in the light of the outcome of the appraisal as well as new and emerging challenges and opportunities and the means to address them;

(c) To reaffirm the global commitment to addressing the special needs of the least developed countries made at the major United Nations conferences and summits, including the Millennium Summit and the 2005 World Summit, in particular the needs related to sustainable development in its economic, social and environmental dimensions, and to support the least developed countries in eradicating poverty and integrating beneficially into the global economy;

(d) To mobilize additional international support measures and action in favour of the least developed countries, and, in this regard, to formulate and adopt a renewed partnership between the least developed countries and their development partners;

5. *Also decides* to convene, towards the end of 2010 and/or early in 2011, an intergovernmental preparatory committee, which would hold no more than two meetings;

6. *Further decides* that the meeting of the preparatory committee will be preceded by two regional-level preparatory meetings, one in collaboration with the Economic Commission for Africa and the other in collaboration with the Economic and Social Commission for Asia and the Pacific, in the context of the regular annual sessions of each Commission, those regional-level meetings to be supported by broad-based and inclusive country-level preparations;

7. *Stresses* that the Conference and the preparatory activities should be carried out within the budget level proposed by the Secretary-General for the biennium 2010–2011 and should be organized in the most effective and efficient manner possible;

8. *Decides* to take a decision on the organizational aspects, date and venue of the Conference, and on the venue, duration and dates of the preparatory committee meetings, before the end of its sixty-third session;

9. *Recognizes* the importance of the contributions of civil society actors at the Conference and in its preparatory process, and in this regard stresses the need for their active participation in accordance with the rules of procedure of the General Assembly;

10. *Decides* that the Office of the High Representative for the Least Developed Countries, Landlocked Developing Countries and Small Island Developing States will be the focal point for the preparations for the Conference, in accordance with mandates given in General Assembly resolution 56/227 of 24 December 2001, to ensure that those preparations are carried out effectively, and to mobilize and coordinate the active involvement of the organizations of the United Nations system;

11. *Requests* the organizations of the United Nations system, including the United Nations Development Programme, the United Nations Conference on Trade and Development, the regional commissions, the specialized agencies, and funds and programmes, and invites the Bretton Woods institutions, the World Trade Organization and other relevant international and regional organizations, within their respective mandates, to provide necessary support and actively contribute to the preparatory process and to the Conference itself;

12. *Requests* the Secretary-General to ensure, as appropriate, the full involvement of resident coordinators and country teams in preparations for the Conference, in particular in the country- and regional-level preparations;

13. *Also requests* the Secretary-General to ensure the active involvement of the organizations of the United Nations system in the preparatory process for the Conference in a coordinated and coherent manner, inter alia, by making use of the existing coordination mechanisms of the United Nations system;

14. *Further requests* the Secretary-General to submit to the General Assembly at its sixty-fourth session a report on the further implementation of the Programme of Action for the Least Developed Countries for the Decade 2001–2010 as well as on the implementation of the present resolution, including a report on the state of the substantive, organizational and logistic preparations for the Conference.

Small island developing States

During 2008, UN bodies continued to review progress in the implementation of the Programme of Action for the Sustainable Development of Small Island Developing States (Barbados Programme of Action), adopted at the 1994 Global Conference on the subject [YUN 1994, p. 783]. Member States also reviewed the Mauritius Strategy for the Further Implementation of the Programme of Action for the Sustainable Development of Small Island Developing States, adopted by the 2005 International Meeting to Review the Implementation of the 1994 Programme of Action [YUN 2005, p. 946].

Commission on Sustainable Development consideration. On 12 May, the Commission on Sustainable Development, at its sixteenth session (New York, 11 May 2007, 5–16 May 2008) [E/2008/29], reviewed implementation of the Mauritius Strategy, focusing on the thematic cluster for the 2008–2009 implementation cycle. It had before it a February report of the Secretary-General [E/CN.17/2008/9] on the integrated review of the thematic cluster of agriculture, rural development, land, drought, desertification and Africa in small island developing States, which described continuing challenges faced by those States in advancing implementation of the Mauritius Strategy as a basis for consideration of a way forward. The Commission expressed concern at the slow rate of implementation of the Strategy and noted that, while the small island developing States had made some progress at the national and regional levels in building institutional capacity for sustainable development, formulating strategies and action plans and carrying out policy reforms, many continued to encounter constraints which impeded their sustainable development, including limited technical, financial and human resources. It also addressed the means of implementation to advance the agenda for the sustainable development of small island developing States, inter alia, the need to reverse the downward trend in international financial flows to those States, including ODA; improve terms of trade; facilitate the transfer of technology; and strengthen capacity-building in support of their efforts to adapt to climate change. Attention was drawn to the structural disadvantages of those States in terms of their small land area and population and resource base, and high dependence on imports. Many of them had been particularly affected by the dramatic rise in food and energy prices, and most had not benefited from the expansion of global trade and investment.

An integrated review of the thematic issues under consideration by the Commission was undertaken through two panel-led discussions on sustainable land management and drought and desertification. The panel discussions also addressed land policy administration and management and the challenges and impacts of desertification, drought and invasive species in small island developing States. Also considered were the need for effective land-use strategies to address the increasing pressure on their limited land resources, as well as agriculture and rural development. Discussions focused on agro-tourism and a range of niche markets which offered scope for the development of rural industries. The sustainable management of fisheries, forestry and agriculture and freshwater resources was also highlighted as important for improving food security and access. Support was expressed for the opportunity to review the achievements and challenges faced by small island developing States in respect of the thematic cluster of issues under discussion, and commitments of continued support for their sustainable development efforts were renewed. The need was underscored for strengthening the Secretariat unit for small island developing States to support the implementation of the Barbados Programme of Action and the Mauritius Strategy.

The Commission also had before it the conclusions [E/CN.17/2008/16] of the High-level Round Table on International Cooperation for Sustainable Development in Caribbean Small Island Developing States (Bridgetown, Barbados, 25–27 March), which launched new partnerships between Iceland and Caribbean small island developing States.

On 16 May [dec. 16/2], the Commission decided to devote one day of its review sessions exclusively to the Mauritius Strategy.

Reports of Secretary-General. In the context of that review, the Secretary-General submitted an August report [A/62/945] on measures to strengthen the capacity of the Small Island Developing States Unit of the DESA Division for Sustainable Development to fulfil its mandate and to strengthen, in particular, its Technical Assistance Programme (SIDSTAP) and its Network (SIDSNet). The Secretariat had taken measures to strengthen the Unit by deploying additional established posts, and had secured extrabudgetary resources to provide for an Interregional Adviser for one year and an Associate Expert for two years. The Unit would also continue to benefit from its interaction with the Division for Sustainable Development. Consultations were ongoing with donors to secure extrabudgetary resources to revitalize SIDSNet and to restore, for two years, the technical posts lost in 2005 for lack of resources. The Secretary-General concluded that, in view of the new and emerging challenges facing the small island developing States, systematic efforts were needed to scale up the capacity to deliver the Unit's mandates. Special consideration should be given to expanding the established posts in the Unit beyond the current three Professional and two General Service posts, in particular by assigning additional established posts for the management of SIDSNet.

In another August report [A/63/296], submitted in accordance with General Assembly resolution 62/191 [YUN 2007, p. 868], the Secretary-General presented a comprehensive review of efforts by the UN system, the international community and small island developing States to operationalize the Mauritius Strategy. He also gave an account of recent initiatives to promote the mainstreaming of the Strategy in small island developing States' sustainable development plans.

The Secretary-General concluded that concerted efforts were being made at the national, regional and international levels to further implement the Mauritius Strategy. Continued support for the development and strengthening of national sustainable development strategies would enhance national capacity for more effective and coherent development administration. In that regard, support for the design and implementation of those strategies in small island developing States would continue in the Pacific region, and the possibility of pursuing similar projects in the other regions would be explored. Further work on the design of a framework for mainstreaming and monitoring the implementation of the Strategy would be pursued, while promoting its coordinated implementation with existing development strategies and plans, including the MDGs. Particular attention would be given to the challenges of capacity that small island developing States continued to face in implementing the Strategy.

Significant attention had been given in the previous year to the impact of climate change on the well-being and security of small island developing States. The Assembly's decision to review at its sixty-fifth (2010) session progress made in addressing their vulnerabilities through implementation of the Strategy was therefore both relevant and timely, and substantial attention would be given in the coming year to preparation for that review.

GENERAL ASSEMBLY ACTION

On 19 December [meeting 72], the General Assembly, on the recommendation of the Second Committee [A/63/414/Add.2], adopted **resolution 63/213** without vote [agenda item 49 *(b)*].

Follow-up to and implementation of the Mauritius Strategy for the Further Implementation of the Programme of Action for the Sustainable Development of Small Island Developing States

The General Assembly,

Reaffirming the Declaration of Barbados and the Programme of Action for the Sustainable Development of Small Island Developing States, adopted by the Global Conference on the Sustainable Development of Small Island Developing States, and recalling its resolution 49/122 of 19 December 1994 on the Global Conference,

Reaffirming also the Mauritius Declaration and the Mauritius Strategy for the Further Implementation of the Programme of Action for the Sustainable Development of Small Island Developing States ("Mauritius Strategy for Implementation"), adopted by the International Meeting to Review the Implementation of the Programme of Action for the Sustainable Development of Small Island Developing States on 14 January 2005,

Recalling its resolutions 59/311 of 14 July 2005, 60/194 of 22 December 2005, 61/196 of 20 December 2006 and 62/191 of 19 December 2007,

Recalling also the 2005 World Summit Outcome,

Reaffirming that the Commission on Sustainable Development is the primary intergovernmental forum for monitoring the implementation of the Barbados Programme of Action and the Mauritius Strategy for Implementation,

Recalling the convening of one half-day session of the Intergovernmental Preparatory Meeting for the fifteenth session of the Commission on Sustainable Development, as called for by the General Assembly in its resolution 61/196, to discuss policy options for addressing the barriers and constraints facing small island developing States in the four thematic areas of the session, taking into account the review of the implementation of the Mauritius Strategy for Implementation conducted during the fourteenth session of the Commission,

Reaffirming that the adverse effects of climate change and sea-level rise present significant risks to the sustainable development of small island developing States, that the effects of climate change may threaten the very existence of some of them and that adaptation to the adverse effects of climate change and sea-level rise therefore remains a major priority for small island developing States,

Recognizing the urgent need to increase the level of resources provided to small island developing States for the effective implementation of the Mauritius Strategy for Implementation,

Underlining the importance of developing and strengthening national sustainable development strategies in small island developing States,

Recalling its request to the Secretary-General to submit a report on actions taken to strengthen the Small Island Developing States Unit of the Department of Economic and Social Affairs of the Secretariat,

Recalling also the decision to review progress made in addressing the vulnerabilities of small island developing States through the implementation of the Mauritius Strategy for Implementation at the sixty-fifth session of the General Assembly,

1. *Takes note* of the report of the Secretary-General on the follow-up to and implementation of the Mauritius Strategy for Implementation;

2. *Also takes note* of the report of the Secretary-General on actions taken to strengthen the Small Island Developing States Unit;

3. *Welcomes* the renewed commitment of the international community to the implementation of the Programme of Action for the Sustainable Development of Small Island Developing States;

4. *Urges* Governments and all relevant international and regional organizations, United Nations funds and programmes, the specialized agencies and regional commissions, international financial institutions and the Global Environment Facility, as well as other intergovernmental organizations and major groups, to take timely action for the effective implementation of and follow-up to the Mauritius Declaration and the Mauritius Strategy for Implementation, including the further development and operationalization of concrete projects and programmes;

5. *Calls for* the full and effective implementation of the commitments, programmes and targets adopted at the International Meeting to Review the Implementation of the Programme of Action for the Sustainable Development of Small Island Developing States and, to this end, for the fulfilment of the provisions for the means of implementation, as contained in the Mauritius Strategy for Implementation, and encourages small island developing States and their development partners to continue to consult widely in order to develop further concrete projects and programmes for the implementation of the Mauritius Strategy for Implementation;

6. *Reaffirms* the decision taken by the Commission on Sustainable Development at its sixteenth session that one day of its review sessions should be devoted exclusively to the review of the Mauritius Strategy for Implementation, focusing on that year's thematic cluster, as well as on any new developments in the sustainable development efforts of small island developing States using existing modalities;

7. *Invites* the Commission to devote one half-day of its Intergovernmental Preparatory Meeting to discussing policy options for addressing the barriers and constraints facing small island developing States identified in the thematic cluster of each implementation cycle, taking into account the review conducted during the respective review session;

8. *Encourages* enhanced, closer and early consultation with small island developing States in the planning and coordination, as appropriate, of the activities of the Commission devoted to the review of the Mauritius Strategy for Implementation, and emphasizes the importance of enhanced interaction between small island developing States and the relevant agencies of the United Nations system addressing issues concerning small island developing States;

9. *Calls upon* the international community to enhance support for the efforts of small island developing States to adapt to the adverse impacts of climate change, including through the provision of dedicated sources of financing, capacity-building and the transfer of appropriate technologies to address climate change;

10. *Requests* the relevant agencies of the United Nations system, within their respective mandates, to intensify efforts aimed at mainstreaming the Mauritius Strategy for Implementation in their work programmes and to establish a focal point for matters related to small island developing States within their respective secretariats to support coordinated implementation of the Programme of Action at the national, subregional, regional and global levels;

11. *Calls upon* the international community to enhance its support for the implementation of the programme of work on island biodiversity as a set of actions to address characteristics and problems that are specific to islands, adopted by the Conference of the Parties to the Convention on Biological Diversity at its eighth meeting, in 2006;

12. *Calls for* continued support for the design and implementation of national sustainable development strategies in all small island developing States;

13. *Encourages* the implementation of partnership initiatives, within the framework of the Mauritius Strategy for Implementation, in support of the sustainable development of small island developing States;

14. *Underlines* the importance of providing the Small Island Developing States Unit with adequate, stable and predictable funding to facilitate the full and effective implementation of its mandates in accordance with the priority accorded to the Unit and in view of the demand for its services, in particular with respect to the provision of assistance and support to small island developing States;

15. *Reiterates* the importance of ensuring sufficient and sustainable staffing of the Small Island Developing States Unit so that it may undertake its broad range of mandated functions with a view to facilitating the full and effective implementation of the Mauritius Strategy for Implementation, and in this regard requests the Secretary-General to take the necessary actions;

16. *Calls for* the provision of new and additional voluntary resources to ensure the revitalization and sustainability of the Small Island Developing States Information Network;

17. *Reaffirms* its decision to review, at its sixty-fifth session, the progress made in addressing the vulnerabilities of small island developing States through the implementation of the Mauritius Strategy for Implementation, decides to convene a two-day high-level review in September 2010 as a part of that session, and requests the Secretary-General to report to the Assembly at its sixty-fourth session on possible arrangements for the review;

18. *Decides* that the two-day high-level review should be preceded, where necessary, by national, subregional, regional and substantive preparations in a most effective, well-structured and broad participatory manner and that, for this purpose, the Department of Economic and Social Affairs of the Secretariat, through its Small Island Developing States Unit, the Office of the High Representative for the Least Developed Countries, Landlocked Developing Countries and Small Island Developing States and the relevant agencies of the United Nations system, including regional commissions, within their respective mandates and existing resources, should organize, facilitate and provide necessary support to the review process at the national, regional and international levels; and stresses that the review should provide the international community with an opportunity to conduct an assessment of the progress made, lessons learned and constraints encountered in the implementation of the Mauritius Strategy for Implementation and agree on what needs to be done to further address the vulnerabilities of small island developing States;

19. *Invites* the small island developing States to consider at their relevant intergovernmental meetings assessments of and relevant contributions to the review process;

20. *Calls upon* the international community to support the efforts to review progress made in addressing the vulnerabilities of small island developing States through the implementation of the Mauritius Strategy for Implementation, including by facilitating the participation of small island developing States in review activities;

21. *Requests* the Secretary-General to submit a report to the General Assembly at its sixty-fourth session on the follow-up to and implementation of the Mauritius Strategy for Implementation;

22. *Decides* to include in the provisional agenda of its sixty-fourth session, under the item entitled "Sustainable development", the sub-item entitled "Follow-up to and implementation of the Mauritius Strategy for the Further Implementation of the Programme of Action for the Sustainable Development of Small Island Developing States".

Landlocked developing countries

Ministerial Communiqué of Landlocked Developing Countries. Trade Ministers of landlocked developing countries, meeting within the framework of UNCTAD XII (Accra, Ghana, 20–25 April) [TD/442], issued on 22 April the Ministerial Communiqué of Landlocked Developing Countries, in which they called on World Trade Organization (WTO) member States to take into account the specific needs and problems of landlocked developing countries in the process of WTO accession negotiations. UNCTAD should give special attention to those countries' needs in its analytical work and technical assistance activities that helped attract foreign direct investment (FDI), including in UNCTAD investment policy reviews, investment guides and FDI Blue Books. Ministers welcomed the forthcoming midterm review of the implementation of the Almaty Programme of Action (see below) as an opportunity to take stock and focus on the next steps. They requested the UNCTAD Secretary-General to strengthen UNCTAD institutional and operational capacity for addressing the development challenges faced by landlocked developing countries and, in cooperation with the Office of the High Representative for the Least Developed Countries, Landlocked Developing Countries and Small Island Developing States and other UN organizations and international agencies, to assist landlocked developing countries in organizing a meeting of their trade Ministers in 2009. The UN Secretary-General should strengthen the Office of the High Representative, and donors should increase financial and technical assistance to landlocked developing countries to enable them to meet their special development needs and overcome the impediments of geography, with a view to helping them participate effectively in the multilateral trading system.

Report of Secretary-General. In response to General Assembly resolution 62/204 [YUN 2007, p. 870], the Secretary-General submitted a July report [A/63/165] on the implementation of the Almaty Programme of Action: Addressing the Special Needs of Landlocked Developing Countries within a New Global Framework for Transit Transport Cooperation for Landlocked and Transit Developing Countries, adopted by the International Ministerial Conference of Landlocked and Transit Developing Countries and Donor Countries and International Financial and Development Institutions on Transit Transport Cooperation in 2003 [YUN 2003, p. 875]. The report described the overall socio-economic situation in landlocked developing countries and the four priority areas of the Programme of Action: fundamental transit policy issues; infrastructure development and maintenance; international trade and trade facilitation; and international support measures. It also detailed the preparatory process for the midterm review and monitoring of the implementation of the Programme of Action.

The Secretary-General said that the high cost of international trade was a serious constraint to the trade and economic development of landlocked developing countries. Measures to deal with their transit problems addressed inadequate infrastructure, trade imbalance, inefficient transport organization, and weak managerial, procedural, regulatory and institutional systems. Without real solutions to the disadvantages that beset the landlocked developing countries, those States would continue to be driven to the outer fringes of the global economy. While tangible progress had been registered in the implementation of the Almaty Programme of Action, its implementation should be further accelerated. Both landlocked and transit developing countries, with the support of development partners, produced notable achievements in all of the Programme of Action's priorities. Development partners were more actively engaged with respect to transport infrastructure development, trade facilitation, aid, debt relief and market access, while multilateral and development institutions and regional organizations had allocated much greater resources to the establishment of efficient transit systems. The Secretary-General proposed further strengthening of regional cooperative arrangements for transit cooperation and of the role of regional and subregional organizations. The United Nations and other international organizations should support regional initiatives in that regard, including the development of regional integrated infrastructure networks, viable multimodal transport, ways to complete missing links, trade facilitation measures and broader application of information technology. Transit transport policy reforms and trade facilitation measures that had a positive impact on transit costs should be facilitated at all levels, including the commercialization and liberalization of transport services and efforts to improve institutional, procedural, regulatory and managerial systems, and reduce excessive paperwork and red tape requirements. The international community should provide greater market access for goods originating in landlocked developing countries, and extend to them increased technical assistance to ensure their effective participation in WTO trade negotiations, particularly those related to trade facilitation. Donor countries and financial and development institutions, in particular the World Bank, the Asian Development Bank, the African Development Bank and the Inter-American Development Bank, should provide greater financial resources to transit transport infrastructure projects in landlocked and transit developing countries, and special attention should be given to them in the context of the Aid for Trade initiative.

Midterm review of Almaty Programme of Action. The General Assembly conducted its midterm review of the Almaty Programme of Action on 2 and 3 October, in accordance with its resolutions 61/212 [YUN 2006, p. 1019] and 62/204 [YUN 2007, p. 870]. As part of the preparatory process, substantive/thematic meetings were organized in 2007 on transit transport infrastructure development in Ouagadougou, Burkina Faso, and in Ulaanbaatar, Mongolia [ibid. p. 870]. Regional review meetings were held during 2008: the Regional Preparatory Expert Group Meeting of Euro-Asian Landlocked Developing and Transit Countries for the Midterm Review of the Almaty Programme of Action (Bangkok, Thailand, 22–23 April) [CSN/2008/EGM/APA/3]; the African Regional Review Meeting of the Almaty Programme of Action (Addis Ababa, Ethiopia, 18–20 June) [E/ECA/ALMATY/08]; and the Latin American Regional Review Meeting for the Midterm Review of the Almaty Programme of Action (Buenos Aires, Argentina, 30 June) [LC/L.2922]. Other events included: the Euro-Asian Transport Links Ministerial Meeting (Geneva, 19–21 February); the Meeting on Trade Facilitation and Aid for Trade: keys for unlocking the landlocked (Accra, Ghana, 19 April); the Workshop on Logistics Performance Index and New Approaches on Improving Trade and Transport Services to and from Landlocked Countries (New York, 2 June); the Briefing on the progress in the trade facilitation negotiations at WTO and on developments in the Aid for Trade initiative (New York, 27 June); the Meeting on Trade Facilitation Opportunities for Landlocked and Transit Developing Countries (Geneva, 8–9 July); and the High-Level Investment Forum "Investing in Landlocked Developing Countries: Trends, Experiences and the Way Forward" (New York, 1 October).

GENERAL ASSEMBLY ACTION

On 3 October [meeting 19], the General Assembly adopted **resolution 63/2** [draft: A/63/L.3] without vote [agenda item 52 *(b)*].

Outcome document of the midterm review of the Almaty Programme of Action: Addressing the Special Needs of Landlocked Developing Countries within a New Global Framework for Transit Transport Cooperation for Landlocked and Transit Developing Countries

The General Assembly,

Recalling its resolution 62/204 of 19 December 2007, in particular paragraph 11 thereof,

Adopts the following outcome document:

Declaration of the high-level meeting of the sixty-third session of the General Assembly on the midterm review of the Almaty Programme of Action

We, the Ministers and heads of delegations participating in the high-level plenary meeting of the General Assembly on the midterm review of the Almaty Programme of Action: Addressing the Special Needs of Landlocked Developing Countries within a New Global Framework for Transit Transport Cooperation for Landlocked and Transit Developing Countries, held in New York on 2 and 3 October 2008,

Recalling the United Nations Millennium Declaration, in which Heads of State and Government recognized the particular needs and problems of landlocked developing countries and urged both bilateral and multilateral donors to increase financial and technical assistance to that group of countries to meet their particular development needs and to help them to overcome the impediments of geography by improving their transit transport systems, and resolved to create an environment, at the national and global levels alike, that is conducive to development and to the eradication of poverty,

Reaffirming our commitment to urgently addressing the special development needs of and challenges faced by the landlocked developing countries through the full, timely and effective implementation of the Almaty Programme of Action, as called for in the 2005 World Summit Outcome,

Also reaffirming that the Almaty Programme of Action constitutes a fundamental framework for genuine partnerships between landlocked and transit developing countries and their development partners at the national, bilateral, subregional, regional and global levels,

Recognizing that the primary responsibility for establishing effective transit systems rests with the landlocked and transit developing countries, which need to seek to create conditions in which resources can be generated, attracted and effectively mobilized to address their development challenges, but that their efforts need to be given continued international support by the development partners and international and regional organizations in a spirit of shared responsibility, including South-South cooperation and triangular cooperation, and taking into account regional integration agreements,

Also recognizing that the private sector is an important stakeholder, whose contribution to the development of infrastructure and productive capacity should be increased, including through public-private partnerships,

Further recognizing that cooperation between landlocked and transit developing countries results in better transit transport systems. This cooperation must be promoted on the basis of the mutual interest of both landlocked and transit developing countries,

Reaffirming the right of access of landlocked countries to and from the sea and freedom of transit through the territory of transit countries by all means of transport, in accordance with applicable rules of international law,

Also reaffirming that transit countries, in the exercise of their full sovereignty over their territory, have the right to take all measures necessary to ensure that the rights and facilities provided for landlocked countries in no way infringe upon their legitimate interests,

Expressing support to those landlocked developing countries that are emerging from conflict, with a view to enabling them to rehabilitate and reconstruct, as appropriate, their political, social and economic infrastructure and assisting them in achieving their development priorities in accordance with the goals and targets of the Almaty Programme of Action, as well as the Millennium Development Goals,

Taking note of the outcome documents of the Thematic Meeting on Transit Transport Infrastructure Development, held in Ouagadougou from 18 to 20 June 2007, and of the Thematic Meeting on International Trade and Trade Facilitation, held in Ulaanbaatar on 30 and 31 August 2007,

Also taking note of the respective outcome documents of the regional review meeting for Asia and Europe, held in Bangkok on 22 and 23 April 2008, the regional review meeting for Africa, held in Addis Ababa from 18 to 20 June 2008, and the regional review meeting for Latin America, held in Buenos Aires on 30 June 2008,

1. *Reaffirm* the commitment made in the Almaty Programme of Action to address the special needs of the landlocked developing countries, taking into account the challenges confronted by their transit developing neighbours, through measures identified in the five priorities of the Programme of Action;

General assessment

2. *Acknowledge* that despite persisting problems, landlocked developing countries, as a group, have achieved some progress in their overall economic development and growth. They have recorded increased growth rates of gross domestic product and foreign direct investment in the past five years; and exports have surged, particularly for oil and other mineral resources;

3. *Express concern* that the economic growth and social well-being of landlocked developing countries remain very vulnerable to external shocks as well as the multiple challenges the international community faces;

4. *Acknowledge* that landlocked and transit developing countries, with the support of their development partners, have registered some progress in implementing the specific actions agreed upon in the Almaty Programme of Action. Landlocked and transit developing countries in Africa, Asia, Europe and Latin America have strengthened their policy and governance reform efforts. Donor countries, financial and development institutions and international and regional organizations have paid greater attention to the establishment of efficient transit systems;

5. *Recognize* that, although the difficulties of being landlocked permeate every aspect of the development process and poverty eradication, their negative impact on external trade is particularly severe. While some progress, even though uneven, has been made, landlocked developing countries continue to be marginalized from international trade, which prevents them from fully using trade as an instrument for achieving their development goals;

6. *Stress* that the higher cost of moving goods across borders for landlocked developing countries puts their products at a competitive disadvantage and discourages foreign investment, and that landlocked developing countries continue to face challenges in their efforts to establish

efficient transit transport systems, such as inadequate transport infrastructure, insufficient carrying capacity at ports, port and customs clearance delays, transit dependence, fees and obstacles owing to cumbersome customs procedures and other regulatory constraints, an underdeveloped logistics sector, weak legal and institutional arrangements, as well as costly bank transactions. Also, in most cases, the transit neighbours of landlocked developing countries are themselves developing countries, often of broadly similar economic structure and beset by similar scarcities of resources. These challenges need to be urgently addressed through acceleration of the implementation of the specific actions under each of the priorities laid out in the Almaty Programme of Action;

Fundamental transit policy issues

7. *Welcome* the efforts made by many landlocked and transit developing countries to reform their administrative, legal and macroeconomic policies on the basis of an integrated approach to trade and transport. Reform measures have included the liberalization of transit and transport services, accession to relevant international conventions, the establishment of regional intermodal transport corridors and the development of transparent, streamlined and common rules and standards that have strengthened private and public sector dialogue to address the bottlenecks that exist at different segments of transit services. Continued efforts need to be made to ensure the effective implementation of those positive reforms and to ensure that transport strategies and programmes, particularly where they involve the regulation of transport operations or the construction of major new infrastructure, take full account of environmental aspects and development needs to ensure sustainable development at the local and global levels. The international community, including financial and development institutions and donor countries, should provide greater assistance to landlocked and transit developing countries in this regard;

8. *Recognize* the important role of regional cooperation and integration involving landlocked developing countries and their transit neighbours for the effective and integrated solution to cross-border trade and transit transport problems. In this context, we particularly welcome regional initiatives aimed at promoting the development of regional rail and road transit transport networks, such as the agreements on the Asian Highway and Trans-Asian Railway, the New Partnership for Africa's Development Short-term Action Plan on Infrastructure, the Sub-Saharan Africa Transport Policy Programme, the Initiative for the Integration of Regional Infrastructure in South America, the Transport Corridor Europe-Caucasus-Asia, the Africa Infrastructure Country Diagnostic study for infrastructure development in Africa and the Infrastructure Consortium for Africa;

9. *Also recognize* that international conventions on transport and transit, as well as the regional, subregional and bilateral agreements ratified by landlocked and transit developing countries are the main vehicles by which the harmonization, simplification and standardization of rules and documentation can be achieved. We encourage both landlocked developing countries and transit developing countries to effectively implement the provisions of those conventions and agreements;

Transit transport infrastructure development and maintenance

10. *Acknowledge* that, in spite of some improvement in the development of the transit transport infrastructure in landlocked developing countries, inadequate and deteriorating physical infrastructure in rail transport, road transport, ports, inland waterways, pipelines, air transport, and information and communications technology in many landlocked developing countries, along with few harmonized rules and procedures, little cross-border investment and private-sector participation, are the major obstacles to developing viable and predictable transit transport systems. Physical links of landlocked developing countries to the regional transport infrastructure network fall well short of expectations. Missing links are a major problem and need to be addressed urgently;

11. *Recognize* that the construction of transit transport infrastructure, especially the missing links to complete regional networks, and the improvement and maintenance of existing facilities play a key role in the process to achieve the internationally agreed development goals, including the Millennium Development Goals;

12. *Encourage* landlocked and transit developing countries to allocate a greater share of public investment to the development and maintenance of infrastructure supported by, as appropriate, financial assistance and investment from donors, international financial institutions and development assistance agencies. We note that private sector participation should also be encouraged in this regard;

13. *Emphasize* that the development and improvement of transit transport facilities and services should be integrated into the overall development strategies of the landlocked and transit developing countries and that donor countries should consequently take into account the requirements for the long-term restructuring of the economies of the landlocked developing countries;

International trade and trade facilitation

14. *Note* that some progress, although limited and uneven, has been achieved by landlocked developing countries in the area of international trade;

15. *Express concern* that the share of world merchandise trade of landlocked developing countries has remained small. Most landlocked developing countries are still dependent on the export of a limited number of commodities. Their continued marginalization from the international trading system prevents them from fully using trade as an instrument for achieving the Millennium Development Goals;

16. *Note with concern* that approximately one third of all landlocked developing countries are still outside the rules-based multilateral trading system. Therefore, we stress that the accession of landlocked and transit developing countries to the World Trade Organization should be further accelerated. In this respect, the accession process for landlocked and transit developing countries should take into account their individual level of development, including the special needs and problems caused by geographical disadvantage. The development partners should provide assistance in this matter;

17. *Recognize* that one of the main causes of the marginalization of landlocked developing countries from the

international trading system is high trade transaction costs. Therefore, we stress the need for the current negotiations on market access for agricultural and non-agricultural goods to consider giving particular attention to products of special interest to landlocked developing countries;

18. *Reaffirm* that, in accordance with the commitments contained in the Doha Ministerial Declaration, in particular paragraphs 13 and 16 thereof, and the rules of the World Trade Organization, current trade negotiations should give full attention to the needs and interests of developing countries, including landlocked and transit developing countries;

19. *Note* that ongoing World Trade Organization negotiations on trade facilitation, particularly on the relevant articles of the General Agreement on Tariffs and Trade, such as article V on freedom of transit, article VIII on fees and formalities, and article X on transparency, as per the modalities contained in annex D to the decision of the General Council of the World Trade Organization of 1 August 2004, are particularly important for landlocked developing countries to gain a more efficient flow of goods and services as well as the improved international competitiveness that result from lower transaction costs. In this context, technical assistance should be provided to developing countries, in particular, to landlocked developing countries;

20. *Recognize* that some progress has been reached on coordination of border crossings, infrastructure investment, facilities for the storing of merchandise, normative frameworks and other facilities that benefit both landlocked and transit developing countries;

21. *Acknowledge*, however, that a large number of bottlenecks related to trade facilitation persist in many landlocked and transit developing countries. Those bottlenecks need to be urgently addressed. They include: an excessive number of documents required for export/import; the multiplication of scheduled and unscheduled roadblocks; lack of adjacent border controls; unnecessary customs convoys; complicated and non-standardized procedures for custom clearance and inspection; an insufficient application of information and communications technology; non-transparency of trade and customs laws, regulations and procedures; lack of institutional capacities and trained human resources; underdeveloped logistics services; lack of interoperability of transport systems and absence of competition in the transit transport services sector; slow progress in establishing or strengthening national trade and transport facilitation committees; and a low level of adherence to international conventions on transit transport;

International support measures

22. *Acknowledge* the increase in development assistance and debt relief measures in favour of landlocked developing countries. However, we note that much of the official development assistance goes to emergency and food aid. The allocation of development assistance to transport, storage and communications has not changed over the past five years, whereas the need for increased financial support for the construction and maintenance of infrastructure remains valid and urgent. In spite of enhanced Heavily Indebted Poor Countries and Multilateral Debt Relief Initiatives, which have provided debt relief to several landlocked and transit developing countries, the debt burden remains high for many of those countries;

23. *Stress* the need to attract private investment, including foreign direct investment. Private sector participation through co-financing can play a catalytic role in this regard. We recall that notwithstanding the increase of flows in foreign direct investment, private sector involvement in infrastructure development still has a considerable potential;

24. *Acknowledge* the increased attention and resources devoted by the United Nations system and international organizations to the challenges facing landlocked and transit developing countries. We recognize with appreciation the progress made towards developing effective monitoring mechanisms to measure the progress in implementation of the Almaty Programme of Action. We appreciate the work undertaken by the United Nations Office of the High Representative for the Least Developed Countries, Landlocked Developing Countries and Small Island Developing States on a set of macroeconomic, trade and transport indicators, by the Economic and Social Commission for Asia and the Pacific on the time/cost methodology and the World Bank with its Logistics Performance Index and the Doing Business indicators that provide quantifiable data to measure the progress, and emphasize that these efforts should be pursued further;

Future actions to accelerate the implementation of the Almaty Programme of Action

25. *Call upon* landlocked and transit developing countries to undertake the following measures to speed up the implementation of the Almaty Programme of Action:

(a) Promote the learning of lessons from existing regional infrastructure initiatives that aim to encourage integrated cross-border infrastructure investment;

(b) Further strengthen the legal framework governing transit transport operations, including through full and effective implementation of bilateral, subregional and regional agreements;

(c) Promote inter-railway cooperation with a view to facilitating the operation of through trains;

(d) Facilitate road transit operations by harmonizing road transit charges, vehicle dimensions, axle load limits and gross vehicle mass, third-party motor insurance schemes and contracts of carriage of goods by road;

(e) Effectively implement trade facilitation measures, including the implementation of regional customs transit schemes, the reduction/minimization of the number of trade and transport documents, the harmonization of working hours at national borders, the publication of transit formalities and fees and charges, inter-agency coordination of border control services and the establishment of port communities and promotion of their effective operation;

(f) Consider the possibility of negotiating and granting duty-free zones at maritime ports, where this has not been done;

(g) Make efforts towards eliminating the practice of customs convoys. For this purpose, negotiate mutually beneficial arrangements to introduce a system of approved secure vehicles for transit operations and, where escort is warranted, arrange daily customs escorts;

(*h*) Take appropriate and effective measures to monitor control agents on road transport corridors in order to reduce roadblocks. In this context, the regional commissions should assist transit developing countries in addressing the issue of diversion of transit goods to domestic markets;

(*i*) Improve border infrastructure facilities and introduce a one-window/one-stop border system along with necessary capacity-building programmes;

(*j*) Make full use of available information and communications technology in order to enhance trade facilitation and to facilitate information-sharing between and among transport and trade stakeholders;

(*k*) Widen and deepen public and private sector cooperation and collaboration and, in this context, expand platforms for public-private sector dialogue, such as trade and transport facilitation committees or corridor management committees;

(*l*) Mobilize adequate investment from all sources, including the private sector, for the development and maintenance of transport networks, as well as the construction of missing links;

(*m*) Where appropriate, use mutually beneficial public-private partnerships for securing additional financial resources and modern technological and management systems;

(*n*) Keep abreast of changing technologies and management systems which have an impact on trade and transport. In this context, the expansion of container capacity is urgent in many maritime ports;

(*o*) Consider designating a focal point who would be responsible for the implementation of the Almaty Programme of Action and its coordination at the national level;

26. *Welcome* the proposal to set up in Ulaanbaatar an international think tank to enhance the analytical capability of landlocked developing countries needed to maximize the efficiency of our coordinated efforts for the effective implementation of the internationally agreed provisions, particularly the Almaty Programme of Action and the Millennium Development Goals. For this purpose, we urge international organizations and donor countries to assist them in realizing this initiative;

27. *Call upon* donors and the multilateral, regional, financial and development institutions to provide landlocked and transit developing countries with appropriate, substantial and better coordinated technical and financial assistance, particularly in the form of grants or concessionary loans, for the implementation of the Almaty Programme of Action, in particular for the construction, maintenance and improvement of their transport, storage and other transit-related facilities, including alternative routes and improved communications, to promote subregional, regional and interregional projects and programmes;

28. *Call upon* the development partners to effectively operationalize the Aid for Trade initiative so as to support trade facilitation measures and trade-related technical assistance, as well as the diversification of export products through the development of small and medium-sized enterprises and private sector involvement in landlocked developing countries;

29. *Encourage* the international community to enhance efforts to facilitate access to and encourage the transfer of technologies related to transit transport systems, including information and communications technology;

30. *Also encourage* the further strengthening of South-South cooperation and triangular cooperation with the involvement of donors, as well as cooperation among subregional and regional organizations in support of landlocked and transit developing countries towards the full and effective implementation of the Almaty Programme of Action;

31. *Call upon* the relevant organizations of the United Nations system, the regional commissions, the United Nations Development Programme and the United Nations Conference on Trade and Development, and invite other international organizations, including the World Bank, the regional development banks, the World Customs Organization, the World Trade Organization, regional economic integration organizations and other relevant regional and subregional organizations, to further integrate the Almaty Programme of Action into their relevant programmes of work, taking into account the midterm review, and encourage them to continue, as appropriate, within their respective mandates, their support to the landlocked and transit developing countries, inter alia, through well-coordinated and coherent technical assistance programmes in transit transport and trade facilitation. In particular, we:

(*a*) Encourage the United Nations Office of the High Representative for the Least Developed Countries, Landlocked Developing Countries and Small Island Developing States to continue to ensure coordinated follow-up and effective monitoring and reporting on the implementation of the Almaty Programme of Action, in line with General Assembly resolution 57/270 B of 23 June 2003, to step up its advocacy efforts to raise international awareness of the Almaty Programme of Action as well as mobilize resources; and to further develop cooperation with the United Nations system organizations in order to ensure the timely and effective implementation of the Programme of Action;

(*b*) Encourage the regional commissions to continue to strengthen their efforts to work with landlocked and transit developing countries in order to develop integrated regional transit transport systems, harmonize regulatory requirements and procedures for import/export and transit with international conventions and standards, promote intermodal transport corridors, encourage accession to and more effective implementation of international conventions on transit transport, and assist in the establishment of national trade and transport facilitation coordination mechanisms and in improving the planning and development of the missing links in regional infrastructure networks, especially in Africa;

(*c*) Encourage the United Nations Conference on Trade and Development to continue to strengthen its technical assistance in the areas of infrastructure and services, transit transport arrangements, electronic commerce and trade facilitation, as well as trade negotiations with and accession to the World Trade Organization. The Division for Africa, Least Developed Countries and Special Programmes should, within its mandate, strengthen its analytical work and technical assistance to the landlocked developing countries. The United Nations Conference on Trade and Development should also develop pragmatic tools and investment guides, as well as identify best practices, to assist the landlocked developing countries in their efforts to attract a larger share of flows of foreign direct investment;

(d) Encourage the United Nations Development Programme to enhance its provision of trade-related technical assistance and capacity-building programmes to landlocked developing countries;

(e) Invite the World Trade Organization to continue to provide technical assistance to landlocked developing countries in order to enhance their negotiating capabilities;

(f) Invite the World Bank to continue to give priority to requests for technical assistance to supplement national and regional efforts to promote the efficient use of existing transit facilities, including the application of information technologies and the simplification of procedures and documents;

(g) Invite the World Customs Organization and other relevant international and regional organizations to continue to strengthen the provision of technical assistance and capacity-building programmes to landlocked and transit developing countries in the area of customs reform, the simplification and harmonization of procedures, and enforcement and compliance;

32. *Invite* the General Assembly to consider, at the appropriate time, undertaking the final review of the implementation of the Almaty Programme of Action, in accordance with paragraph 49 thereof.

Also on 19 December [meeting 72], the General Assembly adopted, on the recommendation of the Second Committee [A/63/417/Add.2], **resolution 63/228** without vote [agenda item 52 *(b)*].

Groups of countries in special situations: specific actions related to the particular needs and problems of landlocked developing countries: outcome of the International Ministerial Conference of Landlocked and Transit Developing Countries and Donor Countries and International Financial and Development Institutions on Transit Transport Cooperation

The General Assembly,

Recalling its resolutions 58/201 of 23 December 2003, 60/208 of 22 December 2005, 61/212 of 20 December 2006 and 62/204 of 19 December 2007,

Recalling also the United Nations Millennium Declaration, and the 2005 World Summit Outcome,

Recognizing that the lack of territorial access to the sea, aggravated by remoteness from world markets, and prohibitive transit costs and risks continue to impose serious constraints on export earnings, private capital inflow and domestic resource mobilization of landlocked developing countries and therefore adversely affect their overall growth and socio-economic development,

Expressing support to those landlocked developing countries that are emerging from conflict, with a view to enabling them to rehabilitate and reconstruct, as appropriate, political, social and economic infrastructure and to assisting them in achieving their development priorities in accordance with the goals and targets of the Almaty Programme of Action: Addressing the Special Needs of Landlocked Developing Countries within a New Global Framework for Transit Transport Cooperation for Landlocked and Transit Developing Countries,

Recalling the New Partnership for Africa's Development, an initiative for accelerating regional economic cooperation and development, as many landlocked and transit developing countries are located in Africa,

Reaffirming that the Almaty Programme of Action constitutes a fundamental framework for genuine partnerships between landlocked and transit developing countries and their development partners at the national, bilateral, subregional, regional and global levels,

Recalling its resolution 63/2 of 3 October 2008, by which it adopted the Declaration of the high-level meeting of the sixty-third session of the General Assembly on the midterm review of the Almaty Programme of Action,

1. *Takes note* of the report of the Secretary-General on the implementation of the Almaty Programme of Action;

2. *Reaffirms* the right of access of landlocked countries to and from the sea and freedom of transit through the territory of transit countries by all means of transport, in accordance with the applicable rules of international law;

3. *Also reaffirms* that transit countries, in the exercise of their full sovereignty over their territory, have the right to take all measures necessary to ensure that the rights and facilities provided for landlocked countries in no way infringe upon their legitimate interests;

4. *Further reaffirms* its full commitment to the Declaration adopted by the Ministers and heads of delegations participating in the high-level plenary meeting of the General Assembly on the midterm review of the Almaty Programme of Action, in which they recommitted themselves to urgently addressing the special development needs of and challenges faced by the landlocked developing countries through the full, timely and effective implementation of the Almaty Programme of Action;

5. *Acknowledges* that landlocked and transit developing countries in Africa, Asia, Europe and Latin America have strengthened their policy and governance reform efforts and that donor countries, financial and development institutions and international and regional organizations have paid greater attention to the establishment of efficient transit systems; notes with concern, however, that the landlocked developing countries continue to be marginalized from international trade, thus preventing them from fully using trade as an instrument for achieving their development goals, including the Millennium Development Goals, and face challenges in their efforts to establish efficient transit transport systems; and therefore notes the importance of the ongoing World Trade Organization negotiations on trade facilitation, particularly on the relevant articles of the General Agreement on Tariffs and Trade that are important to landlocked developing countries, such as those referred to in the Declaration on the midterm review of the Almaty Programme of Action;

6. *Calls upon* landlocked and transit developing countries to take all appropriate measures, as set out in the Declaration, to speed up the implementation of the Almaty Programme of Action;

7. *Calls upon* donors and multilateral, regional, financial and development institutions to provide landlocked and transit developing countries with appropriate, sub-

stantial and better-coordinated technical and financial assistance, particularly in the form of grants or concessionary loans, for the implementation of the Almaty Programme of Action, in particular for the construction, maintenance and improvement of their transport, storage and other transit-related facilities, including alternative routes, completion of missing links and improved communications, so as to promote subregional, regional and interregional projects and programmes;

8. *Calls upon* the development partners to effectively operationalize the Aid for Trade initiative so as to support trade facilitation measures and trade-related technical assistance, as well as the diversification of export products through the development of small and medium-sized enterprises and private sector involvement in landlocked developing countries;

9. *Encourages* the international community to enhance efforts to facilitate access to and encourage the transfer of technologies related to transit transport systems, including information and communications technology;

10. *Encourages* the further strengthening of South-South cooperation and triangular cooperation with the involvement of donors, as well as cooperation among subregional and regional organizations, in support of the efforts of landlocked and transit developing countries towards achieving the full and effective implementation of the Almaty Programme of Action;

11. *Calls upon* the relevant organizations of the United Nations system, the regional commissions, the United Nations Development Programme and the United Nations Conference on Trade and Development, and invites other international organizations, including the World Bank, the regional development banks, the World Customs Organization, the World Trade Organization, regional economic integration organizations, and other relevant regional and subregional organizations, to further integrate the Almaty Programme of Action into their relevant programmes of work, taking full account of the Declaration on the midterm review, and encourages them to continue, as appropriate, within their respective mandates, their support to the landlocked and transit developing countries, inter alia, through well-coordinated and coherent technical assistance programmes in transit transport and trade facilitation;

12. *Encourages* the Office of the High Representative for the Least Developed Countries, Landlocked Developing Countries and Small Island Developing States to continue to ensure coordinated follow-up to and effective monitoring and reporting on the implementation of the Almaty Programme of Action, in line with General Assembly resolution 57/270 B of 23 June 2003, and to step up its advocacy efforts directed towards raising international awareness and mobilizing resources, as well as to further develop cooperation and coordination with organizations within the United Nations system in order to ensure the timely and effective implementation of the Almaty Programme of Action and the Declaration on the midterm review;

13. *Encourages* the Economic Commission for Africa, the Economic Commission for Europe, the Economic Commission for Latin America and the Caribbean and the Economic and Social Commission for Asia and the Pacific to continue their efforts to work with landlocked and transit developing countries to develop integrated regional transit transport systems, harmonize regulatory requirements and procedures for import/export and transit with international conventions and standards, promote intermodal transport corridors, encourage access to and more effective implementation of international conventions on transit transport, and assist in the establishment of national trade and transport facilitation coordination mechanisms and in improving the planning and development of the missing links in regional infrastructure networks, especially in Africa;

14. *Encourages* the United Nations Conference on Trade and Development to continue to strengthen its technical assistance activities and analytical work related to logistics and transit transport cooperation;

15. *Encourages* the United Nations Development Programme to enhance its provision of trade-related technical assistance and capacity-building programmes to landlocked developing countries;

16. *Invites* the World Trade Organization to continue to provide technical assistance to landlocked developing countries in order to enhance their negotiating capabilities;

17. *Invites* the World Bank to continue to give priority to requests for technical assistance to supplement national and regional efforts to promote the efficient use of existing transit facilities, including the application of information technologies and the simplification of procedures and documents;

18. *Invites* the World Customs Organization and other relevant international and regional organizations to continue to strengthen the provision of technical assistance and capacity-building programmes to landlocked and transit developing countries in the area of customs reform, simplification and harmonization of procedures, and enforcement and compliance;

19. *Encourages* donors and the international financial and development institutions, as well as private entities, to make voluntary contributions to the trust fund established by the Secretary-General to support the activities related to the follow-up to the implementation of the outcome of the Almaty International Ministerial Conference;

20. *Requests* the Secretary-General to submit to the General Assembly at its sixty-fourth session an analytical report on the implementation of the Almaty Programme of Action and the Declaration on the midterm review;

21. *Decides* to include in the provisional agenda of its sixty-fourth session the item entitled "Specific actions related to the particular needs and problems of landlocked developing countries: outcome of the International Ministerial Conference of Landlocked and Transit Developing Countries and Donor Countries and International Financial and Development Institutions on Transit Transport Cooperation".

Economies in transition

In response to General Assembly resolution 61/210 [YUN 2006, p. 1021], the Secretary-General, in an August report [A/63/256], reviewed progress made in the integration of the economies in transition into the world economy during the period 2006–2007, and highlighted major policy challenges facing them. According to the report, the high prices for primary commodities and increased capital inflows had supported robust growth in South-Eastern Europe and the Commonwealth of Independent States (CIS) in recent years. However, the weakening of the global economy since mid-2007, due to the global financial turmoil and the food crisis, had affected economic performance, especially in the more vulnerable smaller economies, where economic vulnerability was linked to limited diversification of domestic production sectors and high dependence on a few export commodities of low value-added content. Therefore, a major challenge for those countries was promoting economic diversification and upgrading their production to higher value-added activities, thereby reducing their exposure to the volatility of world markets. Despite the recent significant increase in FDI inflows to those countries, more investment was required to revitalize their industrial capacity and diversify their output and export base. To attract more FDI, however, economies in transition needed to continue focusing on systemic and market-enhancing reforms, institutions able to support markets, legal and regulatory systems designed to promote competition, intellectual and property rights, the rule of law, good governance and financial services.

The countries of South-Eastern Europe, in particular, faced multiple challenges with respect to enhancing their gains from further integration into the world economy. Regional cooperation within the context of the Central European Free Trade Agreement and the Regional Cooperation Council needed to be strengthened and non-tariff barriers eliminated in order to boost intraregional trade. In addition, market access for exports should be enhanced through WTO-compatible export promotion activities and completion of WTO accession, while further export and output diversification would require attracting more FDI inflows and the upgrading of physical infrastructure. Further integration into European markets would be helped by the adoption of European and international standards and further harmonizing of those countries' legislation with that of the European Union. To improve market access for South-Eastern Europe and CIS countries, international organizations should support export and investment promotion activities in the region. Assistance could be provided in securing potential customers and business partners for exporters and in reaching the retail networks in potential markets. Adequate resources should be mobilized, including through multilateral development banks, to help those countries develop infrastructure, including the revitalization of regional road and rail networks, particularly in CIS landlocked countries. Special attention should be given to the development of telecommunications, which lagged well behind European standards, and the energy shortages in the region should be addressed. The issues of migration and protection of migrant workers should also be addressed, and the fight against human trafficking intensified. The International Labour Organization should continue to provide advice on improving labour migration policies and the protection of the rights of migrant workers, and work towards the ratification of all relevant conventions by more countries. The banking systems, as well as non-banking transfer services in the region, should be developed in order to reduce transaction costs for remittances and to divert flows of funds to official channels. It was also important to encourage policies aimed at channelling those funds into productive investment.

On 19 December, the Assembly took note of the Secretary-General's report (**decision 63/542**).

Chapter II

Operational activities for development

In 2008, the United Nations system continued to provide development assistance to developing countries and countries with economies in transition through the United Nations Development Programme (UNDP), the central United Nations funding body for technical assistance. UNDP income reached $6 billion. Total expenditure for all programme activities and support costs in 2008 increased to $5.39 billion. Total income for the United Nations Capitol Development Fund (UNCDF) reached $50.1 million in 2008, including $6 million managed by UNCDF on behalf of UNDP. At year's end, United Nations Foundation allocations to projects of the United Nations Fund for International Partnerships reached approximately $1.06 billion.

In April, the Secretary-General reported on the implementation of General Assembly resolution 62/208 on the 2007 triennial comprehensive policy review of operational activities for development of the UN system. In an August report, the Secretary-General analysed the implications of aligning the strategic planning cycles of the UN funds and programmes with the comprehensive policy review, and provided recommendations on changing the review from a three-year to a four-year cycle.

In September, the UNDP/United Nations Population Fund Executive Board approved the enhanced and integrated UNDP accountability system, which included an accountability framework and an oversight policy. It also amended the UNDP financial regulations and rules to enable the UNDP Administrator to make ex-gratia payments of up to $75,000 per year.

In 2008, the United Nations Office for Project Services (UNOPS) delivered $1.06 billion through project implementation and spent $61.9 million administering it. The contribution to the operational reserve was $4.9 million, bringing it to $30.06 million. In September, the Executive Board approved a change to the UNOPS governance structure, realigning the functions and composition of its Management Coordination Committee to allow it to perform a policy advisory function; the body was renamed the Policy Advisory Committee to reflect its new role. At its September session, the Executive Board approved the revised UNOPS accountability framework and oversight policies. It also took note of the draft fourth cooperation framework for South-South Cooperation (2009–2011) and encouraged Member States to support UNDP and the Special Unit for South-South Cooperation in implementing the framework.

In 2008, 7,753 volunteers working for the UNDP-administered United Nations Volunteer programme carried out 7,991 assignments in 132 countries.

UNCDF achieved its programmatic targets in 2008, expanding its interventions to 38 least developed countries. During the year, UNDP and UNCDF met most of their objectives with respect to elaborating the UNCDF/UNDP partnership framework.

System-wide activities

Operational activities segment of the Economic and Social Council

The Economic and Social Council, during its 2008 substantive session [A/63/3/Rev.1], considered the question of operational activities of the United Nations for international development cooperation at meetings held on 10, 11 and 18 July. On 5 February (**decision 2008/207**), the Council decided to devote the work of the operational activities segment to progress on and implementation of General Assembly resolution 62/208 [YUN 2007, p. 877] on the triennial comprehensive policy review of operational activities for development of the UN system. The Council considered follow-up to policy recommendations of the Assembly and the Council, and the reports of the Executive Boards of the United Nations Development Programme (UNDP)/United Nations Population Fund (UNFPA), the United Nations Children's Fund (UNICEF) and the World Food Programme (WFP).

Among the documents before the Council were the Secretary-General's reports on the comprehensive statistical analysis of the financing of operational activities for development [A/63/71-E/2008/46]; the management process for implementation of Assembly resolution 62/208 on the triennial comprehensive policy review [E/2008/49]; the resident coordinator system [E/2008/60]; and the summary statement of outcomes of the seminar of the programme pilot countries on "Delivering as one" [A/63/85-E/2008/83].

On 10 July, the Council held a high-level panel discussion on "The United Nations system in a changing aid environment: implications and comparative advantages", and another on "Strengthening United Nations development system's responsiveness to the different needs of programme countries". On 11 July, it held a panel discussion with heads of UN funds and programmes.

Implementation of resolution 62/208

An April report of the Secretary-General [E/2008/49] presented an overview of a management process for the full implementation of General Assembly resolution 62/208 [YUN 2007, p. 877] relating to the 2007 triennial comprehensive policy review of operational activities for development of the UN system [ibid., p. 874]. The 2007 review affirmed the overarching importance of national ownership and leadership over UN system operational activities. The management process revolved around the key concepts set out in the resolution, including that operational activities for development were carried out at the request and for the benefit of programme countries, in accordance with their own development policies and priorities. The internationally agreed development goals, including the Millennium Development Goals (MDGs), offered a framework for planning, reviewing and assessing UN operational activities for development. The UN system should focus on long-term development goals and on enhancing national capacity to pursue poverty eradication, sustained economic growth and sustainable development. Reform was aimed at making the UN system more efficient, effective and coherent in its support to developing countries.

The process placed considerable emphasis on the role of inter-agency mechanisms, including the United Nations System Chief Executives Board for Coordination (CEB) and the United Nations Development Group (UNDG) with respect to UN development cooperation. The key actions to ensure a growing trend in funding, especially core resources, rested principally with Member States that contributed resources to the UN system. The role of the Secretary-General would mainly consist of advocacy and dialogue with donors.

UN system development efforts encompassed four dimensions: capacity-building and development, South-South cooperation, gender equality and empowerment, and the transition from relief to development. UNDG had adopted the approach of making use of the common country assessment and United Nations Development Assistance Framework (UNDAF) processes as capacity-building tools. It would also encourage UN country teams to promote South-South and triangular cooperation as modalities for capacity-building in implementing UNDAF. The Interagency Network on Women and Gender Equality would complete by 2009 an action plan to implement the CEB strategy for gender mainstreaming. Regarding the transition from relief to development, the post-conflict needs assessment would continue to serve as a tool for the United Nations to work with the World Bank in designing country-tailored support.

Improved functioning of the UN development system under resolution 62/208 was guided by the principles of national ownership, strengthening national capacities, and ownership of the resident coordinator system by the UN development system as a whole. Efforts would continue to align all planning and programming documents of the UN development system, including UNDAF and the common country assessment, with national planning and programming cycles and processes. Other areas of focus included improving the functioning of the resident coordinator system and further enhancing the performance appraisal system for the resident coordinators and the UN country teams. The latest UNDAF guidelines would be updated to encourage end-of-cycle evaluations in close cooperation with the Government, and the CEB High-level Committee on Management would work to define a system-wide approach to strengthening evaluation throughout the UN system. A matrix setting out actions, targets and benchmarks of the management process for the implementation of resolution 62/208 was annexed to the Secretary-General's report.

In response to resolution 62/208, the Secretary-General submitted a May report [E/2008/60] on the functioning of the resident coordinator system, including costs and benefits. The report discussed coherence, system-wide participation and accountability mechanisms within the context of national ownership and leadership. The resident coordinator system, while managed by UNDP, was owned by the UN development system as a whole. It encompassed all the entities of the UN system that carried out operational activities for development in programme countries, regardless of their formal presence in country. Key elements of the system included the UN country team, the resident coordinator and his or her office at the country level; the regional director and regional manager teams at the regional level; and UNDG and UNDP as the manager of the system at the Headquarters level.

The General Assembly, in resolution 32/197 [YUN 1977, p. 438], established the concept of a single official—the resident coordinator—to coordinate operational activities for development within the UN system. The resident coordinator system was also the main mechanism for coordinating the UN system's emergency, recovery and transition activities in programme countries. The resident coordinator was the designated representative of the Secretary-General and led the UN country team, which comprised representatives of the UN funds and programmes, specialized agencies and other UN entities accredited to a given country. Management of the resident coordinator system remained anchored in UNDP, with management oversight the responsibility of the Administrator. The resident coordinator reported to the Secretary-General through the UNDP Administrator as UNDG Chair. Although most resident coordinators historically came from UNDP, the number of non-UNDP resident coordinators more than doubled between 2001 and April 2008, from 13 per cent to 30 per cent. Joint programmes were increasingly used for coordination in areas where agencies needed to work together in implementing UNDAF. As at March, 428 joint programmes addressed, among other themes, HIV/AIDS, gender, health, poverty reduction, governance and democracy, and measurement of—and reporting on—the MDGs.

As the organization that managed and funded the resident coordinator system, UNDP funded the basic coordination capacities of the United Nations. Between 2004 and 2007, total core UNDP resources attributed to the resident coordinator function averaged $67.7 million, with minimal increments during 2004–2006. In 2007, that amount rose to $74.1 million, an 11 per cent increase over the 2006 total.

Significant progress in the resident coordinator system had been made through measures aimed at: improving programmatic and operational coherence at the country level, system-wide participation and strengthening accountability. Major challenges to achieving effectiveness and efficiency in operational activities for development through the resident coordinator system included the need to respond adequately to demands placed on the system, mobilize the expertise of the UN system to provide support to country development processes and address divergences in business practices. The report contained recommendations to the Council regarding future reporting on the resident coordinator system. Among other measures, the Council might wish to recommend that Secretariat reports to the governing bodies of UN system organizations included quantifiable information on contributions to the resident coordinator system and measures on the decentralization and delegation of authority in the field.

Also in May [A/63/71-E/2008/46], the Secretary-General issued a report on the comprehensive statistical analysis of the financing of UN system operational activities for development, which was to be read in conjunction with his April report on the implementation of resolution 62/208 [YUN 2007, p. 877]. The report presented and analysed contributions and expenditures for 2006, expenditure trends and targeting, and the contributions of the specialized agencies. It also compared trends in UN system financing with trends in multilateral and bilateral development assistance, and described progress in building a comprehensive and sustainable financial data and reporting system on UN operational activities.

ECONOMIC AND SOCIAL COUNCIL ACTION

On 18 July [meeting 34], the Economic and Social Council adopted **resolution 2008/2** [draft: E/2008/L.12] without vote [agenda item 3 *(a)*].

Progress in the implementation of General Assembly resolution 62/208 on the triennial comprehensive policy review of operational activities for development of the United Nations system

The Economic and Social Council,

Recalling General Assembly resolution 62/208 of 19 December 2007 on the triennial comprehensive policy review of operational activities for development of the United Nations system,

Reaffirming the importance of the triennial comprehensive policy review of operational activities for development, through which the General Assembly establishes key system-wide policy orientations for the development cooperation and country-level modalities of the United Nations system,

Recalling the role of the Economic and Social Council in providing coordination and guidance to the United Nations system to ensure that policy orientations set out by the General Assembly are implemented on a system-wide basis in accordance with Assembly resolutions 57/270 B of 23 June 2003, 61/16 of 20 November 2006, 62/208 and other relevant resolutions,

Management process for the implementation of General Assembly resolution 62/208

1. *Takes note* of the report of the Secretary-General on the management process for the implementation of General Assembly resolution 62/208 on the triennial comprehensive policy review of operational activities for development of the United Nations system, and the efforts of the Secretary-General to strengthen the results-orientation of that report, in line with paragraph 141 of resolution 62/208;

2. *Notes* the response of the United Nations system in implementing resolution 62/208 at the agency and inter-agency levels, as specified in the above-mentioned report of the Secretary-General, and requests the United Nations system to pursue the management process for the implementation of resolution 62/208;

3. *Reiterates* the call of the General Assembly for the governing bodies of the funds, programmes and specialized agencies of the United Nations development system to take appropriate actions for the full implementation of resolution 62/208;

4. *Also reiterates* the requests of the General Assembly to the executive heads of those organizations to report annually to their governing bodies on measures taken and envisaged for the implementation of the resolution on the triennial comprehensive policy review;

5. *Reaffirms* that the fundamental characteristics of the operational activities for development of the United Nations system should be, inter alia, their universal, voluntary and grant nature, their neutrality and multilateralism, and their ability to respond to the development needs of programme countries in a flexible manner, and that the operational activities are carried out for the benefit of

programme countries, at the request of those countries and in accordance with their own policies and priorities for development;

6. *Requests* the Secretary-General, as called for in paragraph 142 of resolution 62/208, to submit to the Economic and Social Council, at its substantive session of 2009, a detailed report on results achieved and measures and processes implemented in follow-up to that resolution in order for the Council to evaluate the implementation of the resolution, with a view to ensuring its full implementation;

7. *Also requests* the Secretary-General, in responding to paragraph 142 of resolution 62/208, to strengthen efforts to identify results and fine-tune targets, benchmarks and time frames;

8. *Recalls* the request of the General Assembly to the Secretary-General, in paragraph 125 of resolution 62/208, to prepare a report identifying human resources challenges within the development system at the country level and formulating recommendations for improvements, and requests the Secretary-General, in consultation with the International Civil Service Commission, to submit that report to the Economic and Social Council at its substantive session of 2009 and to cover in the report the issues raised in paragraph 126 of resolution 62/208;

9. *Welcomes* the ongoing efforts of the United Nations system to achieve an upward trend and an expanding base of financial support for operational activities for development, and requests the United Nations system to pursue and consult with Member States on efforts to increase resources and achieve a better balance between core/regular funding and non-core/extrabudgetary funding;

10. *Requests* the United Nations system, in line with paragraphs 45 and 46 of resolution 62/208, to undertake concrete efforts, in consultation with Member States, to support capacity-building for development, the promotion and transfer of new and emerging technologies to programme countries, and the facilitation of access of developing countries to new and emerging technologies in support of operational activities for development;

11. *Reaffirms* paragraph 139 of resolution 62/208, and in this regard takes note of the seminar of the "programme country pilot" countries on the theme "Delivering as one: exchange of experiences and lessons learned", held in Maputo from 21 to 23 May 2008;

Functioning of the resident coordinator system, including its costs and benefits

12. *Takes note* of the report of the Secretary-General on the functioning of the resident coordinator system, including costs and benefits;

13. *Requests* the Secretary-General, in his annual report on the functioning of the resident coordinator system, to report on the participation in and support of the United Nations system, including the non-resident agencies, to the functioning of the resident coordinator system, and on progress in enhancing development impact, coherence, effectiveness and efficiency and costs and benefits of coordination through the resident coordinator system, with specific attention to the regional and country levels;

14. *Requests* the heads of the funds, programmes and specialized agencies and other United Nations organizations to include in the annual reports to their governing bodies any proposed measures to enhance participation by their respective organizations in financial, technical and organizational support to the resident coordinator system;

15. *Underscores* that the resident coordinator, supported by the United Nations country team, should report to national authorities on progress made against results agreed in the United Nations Development Assistance Framework;

16. *Encourages* the United Nations Development Group, within the United Nations System Chief Executives Board for Coordination and in close cooperation with the United Nations Development Programme, to further develop approaches to measure and report on the costs and benefits of coordination, and further encourages the Secretary-General to consolidate this information, to the extent possible, and present it to the Economic and Social Council at its substantive sessions of 2009 and 2010;

17. *Requests* the Secretary-General, in his response to paragraph 94 of resolution 62/208, to bear in mind the various coordination functions of the resident coordinators;

Comprehensive statistical analysis of the financing of operational activities for development of the United Nations system for 2006

18. *Takes note* of the report of the Secretary-General on the comprehensive statistical analysis of the financing of operational activities for development of the United Nations system for 2006, and recognizes the progress made to broaden and improve the reporting in line with paragraph 28 of resolution 62/208;

19. *Encourages* the organizations of the United Nations development system to participate fully in this exercise;

20. *Requests* the Secretary-General, making use of existing capacities within the Secretariat and, if necessary, voluntary contributions, to continue efforts:

(*a*) To continue to broaden and improve the coverage, timeliness, reliability, quality and comparability of system-wide financial data, definitions and classifications for the financial reporting of operational activities for development of the United Nations system, in a coherent way;

(*b*) To build a comprehensive, sustainable and consistent financial data and reporting system for the operational activities for development of all the relevant organizations and entities of the United Nations system;

(*c*) To invite Member States to contribute to the support of the work mentioned above;

Simplification and harmonization of the United Nations development system

21. *Takes note* of the actions taken by the executive boards and governing bodies of the United Nations funds and programmes and specialized agencies in the area of simplification and harmonization of the United Nations development system;

22. *Requests* the Secretary-General to make every effort to ensure that the information provided in response to paragraph 112 of resolution 62/208 is presented at future sessions of the Economic and Social Council in the form of a report;

23. *Requests* the executive heads of the funds, programmes and specialized agencies to report in a timely manner to the executive boards and governing bodies on progress regarding simplification and harmonization to support the assessment by the executive boards and governing bodies in this area.

Operational activities

Trends in contributions

A July report of the Secretary-General [A/63/201] provided an overview of trends in contributions to operational activities for development of the UN system and measures to promote an adequate, predictable and expanding base of UN development assistance. It noted that adequacy of funding for the UN system was linked to overall performance in achieving the target of 0.7 per cent of gross national income for official development assistance (ODA). ODA performance had generally declined from its 1995 level for the period 1996–2004, only returning to the 1995 level in 2005. Over the previous few years, the international community had made renewed efforts to scale up the volume of aid flows and improve aid effectiveness, but most donors would need to make unprecedented efforts to meet their targets. At the end of 2007, ODA from the Organisation for Economic Cooperation and Development (OECD)/Development Assistance Committee (DAC) donors stood at $103.7 billion, down 8.4 per cent in real terms since 2006. Multilateral aid continued to represent around 40 per cent of global flows and 50 per cent of flows from DAC donors, but around 50 per cent of that funding, including for the United Nations, was earmarked for specific initiatives, sectors or themes. There was an urgent need for donor countries to increase their funding to UN operational activities, notably through the provision of core resources. Broadening the donor base could help enhance long-term financial sustainability, as heavy reliance on a limited number of donors was the norm. The top 10 donors to UNDP provided close to 80 per cent of its total regular resources for 2008. Contributions of non-DAC member States to the UN system became increasingly important, totalling $451 million in 2006 (excluding self-supporting contributions), representing a 104 per cent increase over the $221 million contributed in 2004. The so-called "self-supporting" resources channelled by Governments through UN agencies for expenditure in their own countries amounted to $1.89 billion in 2006, coming from 154 countries.

Uncertainties in the world economy negatively affected further scaling-up of funding for the United Nations. The voluntary nature of the funding of UN operational activities made it vulnerable to cutbacks in times of constrained Government budgets. World economic growth registered 3.8 per cent in 2007, but was expected to decline markedly, to 1.8 and 2.1 per cent in 2008 and 2009, respectively. Humanitarian assistance represented the biggest share of overall expenditure of the UN development system. It was estimated that the humanitarian assistance expenditure increased at an average of 15.3 per cent per year during the 11-year period from 1993 to 2003, compared to the much lower and even-paced rate of increase for operational activities for development (net of the humanitarian assistance component) of 7.4 per cent per year.

In general, ODA remained unpredictable, with only 60 to 65 per cent of aid flows disbursed by donors in the fiscal year for which they were scheduled. The multi-year funding frameworks or strategic plans enabled Member States to monitor the effective use of financial resources by comparing them with the results achieved through planned activities. In some cases, thematic contributions in line with priorities set out in strategic plans resulted in increased predictability of non-core resources, which constituted a growing portion of total funding. Thematic funds also involved low administrative costs, simplified annual reporting and greater flexibility, allowing for longer-term planning and more sustainable results. The "One Fund" established as part of the "Delivering as one" pilot initiative [YUN 2006, p. 1584] allowed donors to fund a strategic plan for a coordinated UN response to development challenges, while aiming to reduce transaction costs and enhance flexibility and predictability for implementing agencies. As the implementation of the One UN funds in the pilot countries was at an early stage, however, it needed to be carefully monitored and assessed.

The General Assembly highlighted the need to enhance the core contributions to the UN development system. In 2006, non-core/extrabudgetary resources for operational activities amounted to $12.1 billion, as compared to core resources of $5.1 billion. Thus, the share of core resources represented only 29.5 per cent of total funding. In constant dollars, the increase in non-core funds from 2002 to 2006 was 9.9 per cent, compared to just 0.3 per cent per year, on average, for core funds. With the exception of the United Nations Relief and Works Agency for Palestine Refugees in the Near East (UNRWA), whose resources were consistently 100 per cent core, patterns on the balance between core and non-core resources varied among individual UN organizations.

The Assembly stressed that an increase in funding, particularly core resources, should correspond to parallel progress in efficiency, effectiveness, coherence and impact in the UN development system and its organizations. In the 2006–2007 period, UNDP, UNFPA and UNICEF took significant steps to harmonize results-based budgeting for their biennial support budgets, and an increasing number of UN organizations were introducing a results-based management approach in their internal functioning. The UN system was also working towards harmonized approaches with regard to cost recovery, in order to avoid using core resources to cover the management of extrabudgetary funds.

Aligning planning cycles with comprehensive policy review

In August [A/63/207], the Secretary-General submitted a report analysing the implications of aligning the strategic planning cycles of the UN funds and programmes with the comprehensive policy review. The analysis covered the planning activities of UNDP, UNFPA, UNICEF and WFP, which together accounted for more than 60 per cent of the expenditures on UN system operational activities for development. The report set out the advantages of changing the comprehensive policy review from a three-year to a four-year cycle. The change would allow enough time for the UN system to put in place measures to implement guidance given by the General Assembly in the comprehensive policy review. It would open the possibility of synchronizing the strategic plans of the funds and programmes with the comprehensive policy review, so that the plans could reflect the guidance from the review. A four-year cycle might allow for a midterm review, which could provide a more solid basis for guiding the preparations for the following comprehensive review. It might also generate savings for the UN Secretariat, with regard to both regular and extrabudgetary resources.

The strategic plans constituted the main instruments by which the funds and programmes implemented their mandates and the policy guidance of the Assembly and the Economic and Social Council. The budgeting processes of the four funds and programmes were aligned with their strategic plans. UNDP and UNFPA had the same Executive Board; UNICEF and WFP each had its own Executive Board, with WFP also reporting to the Food and Agriculture Organization of the United Nations (FAO). UNDP, UNFPA and WFP were operating within four-year strategic planning cycles for the 2008–2011 period; UNICEF was operating within a four-year cycle for the 2006–2009 period. UNDP, UNFPA and UNICEF used fixed planning cycles, while WFP had a rolling system whereby it reviewed and adjusted its plan every two years. In September (see p. 1286), the UNICEF Executive Board decided to extend its planning cycle by two years, to 2011. As a benefit of doing so, the following UNICEF planning cycle would cover the period 2012–2015, coinciding with the other funds and programmes. With the 2015 target date for realizing the MDGs approaching, it would be critical for the funds and programmes to enhance efforts towards reaching the Goals, which should be reflected in the strategic plans. Alignment with the comprehensive policy review would also bolster consistency among the plans concerning the review's themes and approaches.

The report examined two options for changing the comprehensive policy review from a three-year to a four-year cycle: proceeding with the triennial review as scheduled in 2010 and shifting to a quadrennial review beginning in 2011, with the first quadrennial review to be held in 2014 (option 1); or holding the first quadrennial review in 2011, thus extending the period for the implementation of the 2007 triennial review by one year (option 2). Option 1 would require the fewest adjustments to the current and subsequent planning cycles of UNDP, UNFPA and WFP, including their budget processes. Only UNICEF would need to make an adjustment to extend its current cycle by two years. If UNDP, UNFPA and UNICEF aligned their planning cycles, WFP would not be in alignment with the cycles every two years; it would therefore need to consider adopting a fixed, four-year cycle starting in 2012 to ensure full alignment. Option 2 would require that all four organizations made adjustments to adopt the 2013–2016 period as a synchronized plan period, which would also have implications for adjusting the biennial support budgets.

The Secretary-General recommended that the Assembly consider changing the comprehensive policy review from a triennial to a quadrennial cycle. The Assembly should also recommend that UNDP, UNFPA, UNICEF and WFP make the changes required to align their planning and budgetary processes with the quadrennial review.

GENERAL ASSEMBLY ACTION

On 19 December [meeting 72], the General Assembly, on the recommendation of the Second (Economic and Financial) Committee [A/63/419], adopted **resolution 63/232** without vote [agenda item 54].

Operational activities for development

The General Assembly,

Recalling its resolution 62/208 of 19 December 2007 on the triennial comprehensive policy review of operational activities for development of the United Nations system,

Reaffirming the importance of the triennial comprehensive policy review of operational activities for development, through which the General Assembly establishes key system-wide policy orientations for the development cooperation and country-level modalities of the United Nations system,

1. *Takes note* of the reports of the Secretary-General and of the note by the Secretary-General transmitting the report on the activities of the United Nations Development Fund for Women;

2. *Also takes note* of Economic and Social Council resolution 2008/2 of 18 July 2008 on the progress in the implementation of General Assembly resolution 62/208 on the triennial comprehensive policy review of operational activities for development of the United Nations system;

Funding of operational activities of the United Nations development system

3. *Reiterates* paragraphs 18 to 20 of Economic and Social Council resolution 2008/2, on the comprehensive statistical analysis of the financing of operational activities for development of the United Nations system;

4. *Requests* the United Nations Development Programme and the Department of Economic and Social Affairs of the Secretariat, making use of existing capacities within the Secretariat and, if necessary, voluntary contributions, to take the necessary steps to integrate by 2010 information from the report on United Nations system technical cooperation expenditures and its statistical addendum into the report on the comprehensive statistical analysis of the financing of operational activities for development of the United Nations system, to provide appropriate online access to this information and to report to the Economic and Social Council in 2009 on progress in this regard, and encourages the Executive Board of the United Nations Development Programme/United Nations Population Fund to take the necessary decision to make this possible;

5. *Expresses concern* at:

(a) The fact that the upward trend in contributions in real terms received by the United Nations system for operational activities since 2002 came to a halt in 2006;

(b) The continuing imbalance between core and non-core funding;

(c) The limited progress towards greater predictability and adequacy of funding;

6. *Emphasizes* that increasing financial contributions to the United Nations development system is key to achieving the internationally agreed development goals, including the Millennium Development Goals, and in this regard recognizes the mutually reinforcing links between increased effectiveness, efficiency and coherence of the United Nations development system, achieving concrete results in assisting developing countries in eradicating poverty and achieving sustained economic growth and sustainable development through operational activities for development and the overall resourcing of the United Nations development system;

7. *Stresses* that core resources, because of their untied nature, continue to be the bedrock of the operational activities for development of the United Nations system;

8. *Urges* donor countries and other countries in a position to do so to substantially increase their voluntary contributions to the core/regular budgets of the United Nations development system, in particular its funds, programmes and specialized agencies, and to contribute on a multi-year basis, in a sustained and predictable manner;

9. *Invites* countries to consider increasing their contributions to the budgets of the specialized agencies in order to enable the United Nations development system to respond in a more comprehensive and effective manner to the demands of the United Nations development agenda;

10. *Emphasizes* the importance of taking measures to broaden the donor base and increase the number of donor countries and other partners making financial contributions to the United Nations development system in order to reduce reliance of the United Nations development system on a limited number of donors;

11. *Welcomes* the growth in funding provided to the United Nations system from non-governmental sources, such as civil society, private organizations and foundations;

12. *Notes* that non-core resources represent an important supplement to the regular resource base of the United Nations development system to support operational activities for development, thus contributing to an increase in total resources, while recognizing that non-core resources are not a substitute for core resources and that unearmarked contributions are vital for the coherence and harmonization of the operational activities for development;

13. *Underscores* the importance of mobilizing more predictable levels of voluntary contributions to the core operational programmes of the United Nations development system, recognizes the establishment of thematic trust funds, multi-donor trust funds and other voluntary non-earmarked funding mechanisms linked to organization-specific funding frameworks and strategies established by the respective governing bodies as funding modalities complementary to regular budgets, and encourages the measurement of the funding received by the United Nations development system through these modalities as part of the comprehensive statistical analysis of financing of operational activities for development of the United Nations system;

14. *Recognizes* the increasing complexity of the international aid architecture, and in this regard encourages the organizations of the United Nations development system to continue to explore ways to engage with other development partners in order to strengthen their complementarity and the implementation of their mandates, taking into account the importance of national priorities of programme countries, and requests the Secretary-General, in consultation with the United Nations development system, to report on efforts in this regard in the context of his annual report on the implementation of resolution 62/208;

15. *Encourages* the organizations of the United Nations system, if they have not done so, to mobilize and allocate resources, on the basis of a strategic plan, including a multi-year resource programming framework;

16. *Reiterates its request* to the Secretary-General to take, in full consultation with Member States and observer States, measures:

(a) To promote an adequate and expanding base of development assistance from the United Nations system, taking into account, inter alia, the development priorities of programme countries;

(b) To promote an upward trend in real contributions to operational activities for development, to identify obstacles to the achievement of that goal, and to make appropriate recommendations in this regard;

(c) To promote the predictability and the multi-year pledging of funding for operational activities for development;

(d) To promote an appropriate balance between core and non-core contributions;

17. *Requests* the Secretary-General to report, in the context of his annual report on the implementation of resolution 62/208, on measures taken in response to paragraph 16 above, bearing in mind the provisions of the present resolution, and including feedback from Member States on ways to achieve the aims contained therein;

Aligning the strategic planning cycles of the United Nations funds and programmes with the comprehensive policy review of operational activities for development of the United Nations system

18. *Decides* to change the comprehensive policy review of operational activities from a triennial to a quadrennial cycle in order to better provide policy guidance to the United Nations funds and programmes and the specialized agencies;

19. *Also decides* in this regard to hold its next comprehensive policy review in 2012 and subsequent reviews on a quadrennial basis;

20. *Urges* the funds and programmes and encourages the specialized agencies to carry out any changes required to align their planning cycles with the quadrennial comprehensive policy review, including the implementation of midterm reviews as necessary, and to report to the Economic and Social Council on adjustments made to fit the new comprehensive review cycle at the substantive session of the Council.

Financing of operational activities

UN system expenditures on operational activities totalled $17.3 billion in 2007 [A/64/75-E/2009/59], the most recent year for which figures were available, compared to $15.9 billion in 2006, representing a nominal increase of 8.4 per cent over 2006 and an average annual increase of 9 per cent since 2003. Taking account of inflation and exchange rate movements, there was no change in expenditures in 2007 compared to 2006, while the real annual increase since 2003 was 3.3 per cent.

Of total expenditures for 2007, $4,679 million was distributed in development grants by UNDP and UNDP-administered funds; $2,642 million by WFP; $2,517 million by UNICEF; $1,760 million by the World Health Organization; $1,342 million by the United Nations High Commissioner for Refugees; $699 million by UNRWA; $591 million by FAO; $515 million by UNFPA; $381 million by the International Labour Organization; $308 million by the United Nations Educational, Scientific and Cultural Organization; $239 million by the Joint United Nations Programme on HIV/AIDS (UNAIDS); $219 million by the United Nations Industrial Development Organization; $185 million by the UN Office on Drugs and Crime/UN International Drug Control Programme; $137 million by the UN Office for the Coordination of Humanitarian Affairs; $130 million by the United Nations Environment Programme (UNEP); $99 million by the United Nations Human Settlements Programme; $61 million by the UN Department of Economic and Social Affairs; $60 million by the International Trade Centre of the United Nations Conference on Trade and Development (UNCTAD); $58 million by the UN regional commissions; $32 million by UNCTAD; $2 million by the Peacebuilding Support Office; and $284 million by other specialized agencies. The International Fund for Agricultural Development (IFAD) disbursed $401 million in loans.

In July [DP/2008/40 & Add.1], the UNDP Administrator reported $13 billion in technical cooperation expenditures in 2007 (excluding the World Bank Group), a 6.5 per cent increase over the $12.2 billion expended in 2006. Executing and specialized agencies reported an increase of 14 per cent in technical assistance delivery to $3.5 billion. Increases were also reported by WFP (3.3 per cent to $2.8 billion); UNICEF (18.2 per cent, to $2.4 billion), and UNFPA (21.8 per cent, to $477.8 million). UNDP experienced a 4.5 per cent decrease in delivery, to $3.9 billion.

By region, Africa received the largest amount of development assistance (28 per cent or $3.7 billion), followed by Asia and the Pacific (21 per cent or $2.8 billion), the Arab States (19 per cent or $2.5 billion), Latin America and the Caribbean (16 per cent or $2.1 billion) and Europe (5 per cent or $0.6 billion). Interregional, global and other initiatives received 11 per cent or $1.3 billion. The top three recipients of the technical cooperation delivered were the Sudan ($982.7 million), Afghanistan ($482.2 million) and Brazil ($354.4 million), totalling $1.8 billion or 14 per cent out of the total of $13 billion. The next highest recipients were the Democratic Republic of the Congo ($340.3 million) and Ethiopia ($337.9 million). Spending in the humanitarian sector amounted to $3.2 billion (25 per cent of the total expenditure). Aggregate expenditure in the humanitarian, health, education, and agriculture, forestry and fisheries sectors amounted to $9.5 billion (73 per cent of the total), with the balance of $3.5 billion (27 per cent) spread among 15 other sectors.

The UNDP/UNFPA Executive Board, at its September session [E/2008/35 (dec. 2008/38)], took note of the report on UN system technical cooperation expenditures in 2007 and its addendum.

A later report [DP/2009/29 & Add.1] provided information on technical cooperation activities funded by UN system organizations in 2008. Expenditure of technical cooperation on the MDGs across the UN system and programme countries (excluding the World Bank group) reached $15.2 billion. Executing and specialized organizations reported an overall increase of 16.8 per cent in expenditure, from $3.5 billion in 2007 to $4.1 billion in 2008. UNDP expenditure grew 11 per cent to $4.3 billion in 2008, accounting for 28 per cent of the total spent on technical cooperation. WFP reported a 28 per cent increase in expenditure to $3.5 billion (23 per cent of the total). UNICEF spending increased 11 per cent to $2.7 billion (18 per cent of the total), and UNFPA spending increased 16 per cent to $554 million (4 per cent of the total). The combined expenditures of the other specialized organizations, funds and programmes amounted to $4.1 billion (27 per cent of the total). Assistance to developing nations from the World Bank/International Development Association amounted to $138.8 million—a decrease of 38.8 per cent compared with $227.2 million spent in 2007.

Contributions to executing and specialized organizations dropped nearly 12 per cent, from $4.1 billion in 2007 to $3.6 billion in 2008. Contributions to UNDP decreased some 2 per cent to $1 billion. Those received by WFP, however, increased 77 per cent to $5 billion. UNICEF funding increased 14 per cent to $3.4 billion; and UNFPA funding increased 12 per cent to $754.8 million.

Technical cooperation was distributed among the five major regions as follows: Africa, $4.4 billion (29 per cent of the total); Asia and the Pacific, $3.2 billion (21 per cent); the Arab States, $3.1 billion (21 per cent); Latin America and the Caribbean, approximately $1.8 billion (12 per cent); and Europe, $0.6 billion (4 per cent). Interregional, global and other initiatives accounted for the remaining $1.9 billion (13 per cent). Out of the combined pool of $15.2 billion, $5.4 billion (36 per cent) was spent among 15 programme countries. The three largest recipients of technical cooperation were the Sudan, receiving $1.1 billion (7 per cent) of the total; Afghanistan, receiving $729.9 million (5 per cent), and Ethiopia, receiving $489.6 million (3 per cent).

In 2008, UNDP mapped its corporate outcomes to the sector approach of the Administrative Committee on Coordination, renamed the United Nations System Chief Executives Board for Coordination. Applying the 2008 sector classification, the humanitarian assistance sector received $3.8 billion (25 per cent) of the total expenditure; health, some $3.1 billion (20 per cent); general development, $1.8 billion (12 per cent); education, $1 billion (7 per cent); and agriculture, forestry and fisheries $843.9 million (some 6 per cent). Aggregate expenditure for the five sectors was $10.5 billion (69 per cent of the total). The balance of the funds—approximately $4.6 billion, representing 31 per cent of the total technical cooperation amount expended—was spread among 15 sectors.

At the 2008 United Nations Pledging Conference for Development Activities (New York, 10 November) [A/CONF.208/2008/3], the Conference noted that several Governments would communicate their pledges to the Secretary-General as soon as they were able to do so.

In August [A/CONF.208/2008/2 & Corr.1] and September [A/CONF.208/2008/2/Add.1], the Secretary-General provided statements of contributions pledged or paid at the 2007 Pledging Conference, as at 30 June 2008, to 23 funds and programmes, amounting to some $584.9 million.

Voluntary contributions in UN system

The Joint Inspection Unit (JIU), in its report on voluntary contributions in UN system organizations: impact on programme delivery and resource mobilization strategies, which was issued in 2007 [YUN 2007, p. 1474] and subsequently transmitted by the Secretary-General to the General Assembly [A/62/546], found that extrabudgetary/non-core funding in UN system organizations grew at a faster rate than regular/core funding during the 2000–2005 period. The trends in voluntary funding had some positive effects on programme delivery, but the lack of predictability in such funding and its impact on the sustainability of programme delivery was a major concern. Conditions attached to voluntary contributions reduced the flexibility of funding and inhibited the secretariats of organizations in delivering their mandated programmes. Faced with increasing competition for resources, some organizations sought to increase the flow of funds from the private sector, but those resources remained a small component of overall funding from contributions. Some organizations made considerable progress in developing strategies for resource mobilization. UN system organizations and donor agencies were increasingly decentralizing funding processes and activities, which might give rise to inefficiencies, including duplication and lack of uniformity.

JIU recommended, among other measures, that the legislative bodies of each UN fund and programme establish an intergovernmental working group to develop proposals for a voluntary indicative scale of contributions for core resources, based on the model adopted by UNEP. The legislative bodies of UN system organizations should request their respective executive heads to: expedite work on the harmonization of support cost recovery policies being conducted under the auspices of CEB; ensure that agreements negotiated with individual donor countries for associate/junior professional officer programmes included a funding component from underrepresented countries; and develop a corporate resource mobilization strategy for the consideration and approval of the bodies.

By a January note [A/62/546/Add.1], the Secretary-General transmitted his comments on the JIU report and those of CEB. Although CEB generally concurred with the JIU recommendations, its members did not generally support the recommendation that the legislative bodies of each UN fund and programme should establish an intergovernmental working group to develop proposals for a voluntary indicative scale of contributions for core resources.

Technical cooperation through UNDP

In response to General Assembly resolutions 56/201 [YUN 2001, p. 783], 59/250 [YUN 2004, p. 868] and 62/208 [YUN 2007, p. 877] on the triennial comprehensive policy review of operational activities for development of the UN system, the UNDP Administrator and the UNFPA Executive Director issued a joint report in December [E/2009/5] on the reform programme of the Secretary-General and implementation of the review's provisions. The report stated that capacity development was the core UNDP service in programme countries, with priority given to creating opportunities for sustainable capacity, including institutional reform; the promotion of leadership, education and learning; and enhanced accountability. UNDP hosted a capacity development network with over 1,000 participants from UN organizations, Governments, and other development partners. It supported programme countries in all regions through capacity assessments and responses in the areas of programme delivery, disaster risk management and the implementation of national growth and development strategies and plans.

UNDP and UNFPA engaged with UN country teams in the "Delivering as one" pilot countries [YUN 2007, p. 1418] to simplify and harmonize processes and procedures and reduce transaction costs. A key initiative was the harmonization of financial regulations and rules among UNDP, UNICEF, UNFPA, WFP and the United Nations; the final harmonized financial regulations and rules were to be ready for consideration by the governing bodies of those entities in 2009. UNDP, UNFPA, UNICEF and WFP continued to implement the harmonized approach to cash transfers (HACT) across country offices in order to strengthen national capacities in public financial management. In 2008, 13 countries were fully HACT compliant, and many were partially compliant.

UNDP and UNFPA worked with 25 civil society and UN organizations in the areas of global policy on gender and climate change; climate change financing mechanisms that benefited women and men equitably; and the integration of women and gender into climate-change plans and processes. Responding to its South-South cooperation evaluation findings (see p. 988), UNDP was implementing a strategy to consolidate and strengthen its support to South-South cooperation with new country-level programming initiatives in South Africa, Timor-Leste and Zambia.

UNDP and its partners jointly reviewed UN coordination arrangements in the post-crisis recovery phase to strengthen the transition from relief to development, and established modalities to provide predictable and sustainable coordination support to UN country teams and partners in transition countries.

The UN Evaluation Group (UNEG) formally entrusted UNDP with the responsibility of being its Executive Coordinator and hosting its secretariat. The UNEG programme of work focused on UN reform and evaluation, the evaluation function, and professionalizing evaluation. Internationally agreed development goals, including the MDGs, formed the cornerstone of UNDP and UNFPA work at the international, regional, national and local levels. Some 23 countries had completed MDG needs assessments, and more than 60 countries were involved in MDG-based planning.

On 24 January [dec. 2008/7], the UNDP/UNFPA Executive Board took note of the report of the Administrator and Executive Director on 2007 activities [YUN 2007, p. 887]; transmitted the report to the Economic and Social Council; and requested UNDP and UNFPA to include in future reports a more qualitative assessment and analysis of results achieved, progress made and difficulties encountered, as well as lessons learned.

The Council took note of the 2007 report on 18 July (**decision 2008/215**).

UNDP/UNFPA Executive Board

In 2008, the UNDP/UNFPA Executive Board held its first (21–28 January) and second (8–12 and 19 September) sessions in New York, and an annual session (16–27 June) in Geneva [E/2008/35].

The Board adopted 38 decisions in 2008, including those providing an overview of actions taken at its January [E/2008/35 (dec. 2008/8)], June [dec. 2008/25] and September [dec. 2008/38] sessions. Other decisions dealt with the work of UNDP, the United Nations Office for Project Services and the United Nations Capital Development Fund (see above and sections below), as well as that of UNFPA (see PART THREE, Chapter VIII) and the United Nations Development Fund for Women (UNIFEM) (see PART THREE, Chapter X).

The Economic and Social Council, by **decision 2008/215** of 18 July, took note of the Board's report on its work in 2007 [YUN 2007, p. 887].

UNDP/UNFPA reports

Human Development Report

The Executive Board, at its annual session in June, considered an April update report [DP/2008/30] on the *Human Development Report* consultations. In response to General Assembly resolution 57/264 [YUN 2002, p. 841], the report detailed actions taken to improve the quality of consultations with Member States and with the community of human development practitioners at large. It also described the content of informal consultations held in 2008, including a consultation held by the Director of the Human Development Report Office, who ceased his functions as at 31 December 2008; a consultation on the selection of the theme of the *Human Development Report 2009* and plans for the elaboration of the 2010 *Report*; and a thematic consultation on statistics. Following the usual practice, the Office, which was charged with preparing the *Report*, held a special network consultation in 2008 to choose the theme for the *Human Development Report 2009*.

The Executive Board took note of the update report in June [dec. 2008/25].

A later report [DP/2009/17] stated that the *Human Development Indices: A statistical update 2008* was released in December. For the first time, the human development index was released separately from the main report, so as to explain significant changes in the underlying data. In June 2008, the Office announced that *Human Development Report 2009* would focus on migration. The Office held an informal consultation with the UNDP/UNFPA Executive Board on 17 November to review the concept note and outline for the 2009 *Report*.

UNDP operational activities

Country and regional programmes

The UNDP/UNFPA Executive Board, at its January session [dec. 2008/8], approved country programme documents for 14 countries; multi-country programmes for 2 countries; and 3 regional programmes.

At its annual session in June [dec. 2008/25], the Board took note of draft country programme documents and the comments made thereon for four countries. It also took note of the one-year extensions of the country programmes for Afghanistan, Argentina, Ecuador, Guatemala, the Republic of Korea and the Turks and Caicos Islands, and approved the two-year extension of the country programme for Pakistan; information on the extensions was provided in an April note by the UNDP Administrator [DP/2008/31]. At the same session, the Board took note of reports on the joint field visit of the Executive Boards of UNDP/UNFPA, UNICEF and WFP to Haiti (1–9 March) [DP/FPA/2008/CRP.1-E/ICEF/2008/CRP.11] and the joint field visit of the UNDP/UNFPA Executive Board to Kazakhstan (6–12 April) [DP/2008/CRP.3-DP/FPA/2008/CRP.2].

At the same session [dec. 2008/11], the Executive Board requested UNDP and UNFPA to provide a short explanation of the reasons for the deferment of draft country programme documents from the Board's annual session to its second regular session, and urged them to increase their efforts to present such documents at the annual session, as decided by the Board in 2006 [YUN 2006, p. 1038].

At its second regular session in September [dec. 2008/38], the Board approved country programmes for four countries. It also approved a second one-year extension of the programme for Burundi and a third one-year extension of the programme for Lebanon; information on the extensions was provided in a July note by the Administrator [DP/2008/48]. It took note of the draft country programme documents and comments made thereon for nine countries. The Board also organized an oral briefing on the UNDP response to the humanitarian emergency caused by Cyclone Nargis, which struck Myanmar in May (see p. 421).

UNDP global programme

Evaluation of third global cooperation framework, 2005–2007

A July report [DP/2008/44] summarized the findings, conclusions and recommendations of the independent evaluation of the third UNDP global cooperation framework for the 2005–2007 period [YUN 2005, p. 964], the duration of which was extended by the Board in June 2007 for one year. The evaluation found that the framework had fallen short in its strategic mission to underpin and integrate the UNDP practice architecture. Its effectiveness in meeting demand was constrained by weak strategic choices regarding focus areas, implementation modalities, allocation of resources and partnerships. Although it had contributed to UNDP becoming a more globally networked knowledge organization, weak management and lack of corporate oversight had limited its effectiveness. The evaluation concluded that, although the third global framework did not fulfil its role, there was a need for a global programme in UNDP.

The evaluation recommended that UNDP design a new programme that would be based on demand from programme countries, be fully integrated within UNDP, and add value as a global programme. It should clearly set out its global role, development goals, a strategic focus and a corresponding results and accountability framework based on a clear rationale and criteria to distinguish global programme initiatives from those at the regional and country levels, as well as a programme approach, to replace the current framework approach. The global programme should also be based on a clear definition of its global contribution and its contribution to programme countries, through the UNDP regional and country programme architecture; alignment with the UNDP strategic plan; a concentration on mainstreaming approaches in the cross-cutting areas of gender equality, capacity development and HIV/AIDS; and the identification of means to reduce the dependency on the global programme to fund required posts. UNDP should develop improved corporate strategies and delivery mechanisms so the new global programme might better support the achievement of results at the country level. The programme should have an explicit strategy to partner systematically with other UN agencies and development institutions, with the aim of fostering policy debates and approaches critical to programme countries for the achievement of their development goals. UNDP should establish a system to ensure results orientation and accountability for the new global programme, and institutionalize mechanisms to ensure corporate oversight and ownership of the programme.

In its August response [DP/2008/45] to the evaluation of the third global programme (formerly known as the global cooperation framework), UNDP management expressed its agreement with the findings related to the weaknesses of the programme in monitoring and evaluation, the reporting of results, and some aspects of programme management. Subsequent actions were aimed at improving substantive focus and arrangements for policy development, service delivery, results-based management, transparency and accountability, and the relevance and quality of UNDP work.

Under the fourth global programme, resources would continue to be used to support country and regional development initiatives. Although the primary role of UNDP was to support country-level development programmes, it was also essential that it engage global processes to ensure that policies were developed on the basis of a thorough understanding of country-level needs and opportunities. Integrated teams across country, regional and global units would identify and respond to demand and emerging issues, promoting consistency and quality while ensuring that the advice and input provided were grounded in local reality.

In September [dec. 2008/32], the Executive Board took note of the conclusions of the evaluation of the third global cooperation programme framework and the related management response. It requested that UNDP continue to reflect the conclusions in the new fourth global programme, 2009–2011 (see below), and in its implementation.

Global programme, 2009–2011

The UNDP/UNFPA Executive Board, at its September session, considered the fourth UNDP global programme, 2009–2011 [DP/GP/2], which was designed to streamline UNDP policy approaches across its mandated areas and facilitate communication between local and global actors. It would play a vital role in the implementation of the UNDP strategic plan, 2008–2011 [YUN 2007, p. 897], strengthening the ability of country offices to respond quickly and effectively, and using global engagement to identify opportunities, resources and innovations that could help countries address multifaceted development challenges. The purpose of the proposed programme was to support countries in achieving internationally agreed development goals, including the MDGs. The global programme was charged with supporting both development and institutional results. It highlighted the mainstreaming of cross-cutting results in the areas of capacity development, gender equality and women's empowerment, and South-South cooperation. Through the global programme, UNDP aimed to connect country, regional and headquarters staff to share expertise and knowledge from across the UN development system.

The UNDP/UNFPA Executive Board, at its September session [dec. 2008/32], reaffirmed that all activities under the global programme 2009–2011 would be fully consistent with the provisions of General Assembly resolution 62/208 on the triennial comprehensive policy review [YUN 2007, p. 877] and the revised 2008–2011 UNDP strategic plan (see p. 975). It requested the UNDP Administrator, in the context of proposals to be presented to the Board in line with its decision on realigning the cost classification of UNDP activities (see p. 977), to include proposals on the future classification of UNDP policy advisory capacities. The Administrator was also asked to include, in his annual report to the Board, improvements and implementation of the global programme, 2009–2011. The Board noted that a midterm review of the global programme would be submitted in 2010, and a final comprehensive report on performance and results would be submitted in 2012. It approved the global programme, 2009–2011, and decided that the decision would serve as the preface to, and an integral part of, the global programme.

Implementation of Paris Declaration on Aid Effectiveness

The UNDP/UNFPA Executive Board, at its June session, considered a summary report [DP/2008/28 & Corr.1,2] on the joint evaluation of the United Nations Development Group (UNDG) contribution to the implementation of the 2005 Paris Declaration on Aid Effectiveness [YUN 2005, p. 957]. In 2006, UNDG, a Declaration signatory, agreed with partner countries and donors to conduct an evaluation of its contribution to implementing the Declaration between 2007 and 2010, using a two-phased approach. The first phase focused on inputs, the implementation process and outputs. The evaluation was conducted jointly with IFAD,

UNAIDS, the United Nations Economic Commission for Africa, UNFPA and UNIFEM. Nine countries and 11 development partner organizations conducted an evaluation of their performance under the Declaration as an input to the first phase.

The evaluation concluded that the UNDG experience in applying the principles of the Declaration varied substantially across the principles. The role of the resident coordinator and the UN country team extended beyond the Declaration's aid effectiveness objectives. The UNDG/UN country team assisted Governments in strengthening capacities to prepare and execute their country development strategies and deal with new aid modalities, including sector-wide approaches and direct budget support.

Areas of progress included aligning the planning cycles of United Nations Development Assistance Frameworks with those of national development plans. Some progress was also made in improving coordination among country team members and other development partners, mainly under the harmonized approach to cash transfers initiative. Implementation of the Declaration's principles among the crosscutting issues was uneven. UNAIDS—a UNDG entity—was helpful in implementing the principles in the critical area of HIV/AIDS, but implementation was less successful in the remaining three cross-cutting issues of gender equality, rural development and capacity development.

The report recommended that UNDG make increased use of national systems for support services, when appropriate and to the benefit of the partner countries, in order to strengthen national capacities and reduce transaction costs. UNDG should further harmonize and simplify its business practices in order to increase the accountability and transparency of operational activities and further standardize and harmonize concepts and practices. It should create specific, measurable, achievable and relevant results frameworks and strategies, and encourage partner countries to initiate and conduct joint and country-led evaluations.

UNDP management submitted its response to the evaluation in June [DP/2008/29].

At its June session [dec. 2008/19], the UNDP/UNFPA Executive Board, having considered the evaluation of the UNDG contribution to implementing the Paris Declaration and the management response thereto, encouraged UNDP to continue to make increased use of national systems to strengthen national capacities and reduce transaction costs, and conduct joint evaluations with UN organizations on development effectiveness while retaining a focus on UNDP accountability, in order to increase the value of evaluation to programme countries.

UNDP role in Arab region net contributor countries

In June, the Executive Board had before it the independent evaluation, issued in March [DP/2008/26 & Corr.1,2], of the role of UNDP in the net contributor countries (NCCs) of the Arab region. All countries were eligible to participate in UNDP programmes, but those with higher levels of income were affected by special policies that limited the resources that UNDP could provide. The five NCCs within the group of Arab States—Bahrain, Kuwait, the Libyan Arab Jamahiriya, Saudi Arabia, and the United Arab Emirates—had experienced rapidly growing economies and were moving towards greater political openness. At the same time, they had to adapt to globalization and find their role in the new external environment. Their relationship with UNDP had to change to reflect those realities.

Apart from Libya, all the Arab region NCCs were high-income countries in the "high human development" category, and all were making progress towards achieving the MDGs. Poverty existed in Libya and Saudi Arabia, but it had largely been eradicated in the other three countries. Bahrain, Kuwait, Libya and the United Arab Emirates had achieved universal primary education, and Saudi Arabia was making significant progress towards that goal. All five countries, however, faced challenges in the areas of economic diversification, employment creation, public administration and governance, gender equality, and protecting the environment.

The evaluation found a strong justification for a strengthened UNDP presence in the five Arab region NCCs. UNDP should be prepared to respond to the demands of NCCs with greater flexibility in a new relationship based on full and equal partnership at the strategic and programmatic levels. The UNDP minimum delivery threshold to justify a country office presence needed to be revisited and specific guidelines developed on the application of UNDP policies to NCCs. The evaluation recommended that the overall relationship and interaction between UNDP headquarters units and country offices in the Arab region NCCs be strengthened to align them more closely with evolving UNDP strategies and policies.

UNDP management, in its April response to the evaluation [DP/2008/27], stated that fulfilling the UNDP policy requirement of delivering a minimum of $10 million per programming cycle to justify a UNDP country presence had been a challenge for some NCCs, and UNDP would explore improving the country presence criteria, as recommended by the evaluation. UNDP welcomed the recommendation to redefine its role and strategy in the NCC context and develop a common understanding and set of approaches for technical cooperation. It would strengthen its substantive engagement in programmes and improve the quality of its technical advisory services. UNDP would also explore opportunities for joint programming with relevant UN agencies.

UNDP recognized the important role that it could play in facilitating Government, civil society and private-sector partnerships, as well as in providing capacity-building support to civil society organizations, given the nascent state of such organizations in most NCCs. In the context of national execution, UNDP needed to harmonize project management and implementation systems with national systems. It fully accepted the recommendations to strengthen the capacity of country offices to contribute to the development effectiveness of UNDP programmes and projects in the Arab States NCCs. As an interim measure, UNDP had taken action to place deputy resident representatives, using extrabudgetary funding, in all of the NCCs except Bahrain, where such representatives would be placed in the near future. In order to meet the specific needs of NCCs looking to UNDP for the delivery for high-end consultancy services and skills, UNDP would provide dedicated support to the NCCs within the structure of its Regional Service Centre for the Arab States.

During its June session [dec. 2008/18], the Executive Board took note of the evaluation and the management response. It requested UNDP to include the Board in its consultations concerning the review and development of criteria for continued UNDP presence in NCCs. The Board urged UNDP to give high priority to strengthening its support to NCCs in the area of capacity development, based on national priorities and systems, in order to strengthen the sustainability of its programming.

UNDP programme results

UNDP activities under the 2008–2011 strategic plan, endorsed by the UNDP/UNFPA Executive Board in 2007 [YUN 2007, p. 898] and updated in 2008 (see p. 975), were conducted in four focus areas: poverty reduction and achievement of the MDGs, democratic governance, crisis prevention and recovery, and environment and sustainable development. Other areas of work, as outlined in a later report on the operationalization of the UNDP strategic plan [DP/2009/11], included capacity-building and development, gender equality and women's empowerment, and South-South cooperation.

(For information on South-South cooperation, see p. 988; for all other areas of UNDP work, see sections below.)

Poverty eradication and MDG achievement

In 2008, increased food prices, turmoil in financial markets, economic downturns and climate change had a particular impact on the poor, with long-term implications for poverty reduction and human development. Working with its global partners, UNDP would: help build national capacities to manage crises and address their long-term implications through initiatives to assess the impact of crises on growth and human development; monitor vulnerability; and provide countries with policy options for combining short-term growth and poverty reduction strategies with longer-term efforts to build resilience to volatility in the world economy.

Other initiatives would aim to strengthen national capacities to attract and manage domestic and external resources, and develop and implement national development strategies based on the MDGs to address bottlenecks, scale up proven MDG interventions, and prioritize the needs of the most vulnerable.

During the year, UNDP contributed to the development of tools and analysis for monitoring MDG achievements and partnered with UN regional commissions, Governments, and civil society organizations to improve MDG monitoring and reporting.

Democratic governance

UNDP support to public administration reform sought to build capacities to address development challenges at the national and local levels, with activities in 89 programme countries. It also supported the work of national parliaments in over 50 programme countries, including through an initiative to enhance parliamentary oversight of human security in post-conflict countries. A significant development was the increased demand from programme countries for strengthening the electoral cycle. The Bangladesh Electoral Commission, supported by UNDP and donors, trained 500,000 people, who in turn registered 81 million voters, nearly 51 per cent of them female. Globally, UNDP directly supported 19 electoral processes.

Many UNDP initiatives focused on strengthening youth participation in development, in cooperation with the United Nations Volunteers programme. Access to information, which UNDP directly supported in 12 countries, was being mainstreamed into more traditional areas such as local governance and public administration reform.

Within the framework of the 2003 United Nations Convention against Corruption, adopted by the General Assembly in resolution 58/4 [YUN 2003, p. 1127], UNDP supported 12 programme countries with anti-corruption initiatives and provided technical advice on anti-corruption for programmes on strengthening institutions.

Crisis prevention and recovery

Crisis affected 45 to 60 per cent of the countries in which UNDP worked. UNDP sought to help those countries develop capacities for preventing and mitigating the effects of crisis, elaborate strategic options for addressing long-term implications and promote recovery. Disaster risk reduction was the largest area of demand, with activities in 37 countries. At the local level, activities included support to community-based disaster risk reduction programmes, strengthening local early warning systems and urban disaster risk management.

Based on demand, UNDP established early recovery coordination mechanisms in 28 programme countries, deployed early recovery advisers to 20 countries, and supported needs assessments and strategic frameworks in 10 countries. The demand for developing capacities to manage potentially violent tensions also increased in 2008. In response to demand from nine programme countries, UNDP launched a global initiative on strengthening the rule of law in conflict and post-conflict situations. Reintegration programmes highlighted the critical contribution of employment and income generation to peacebuilding, as well as the importance of providing "peace dividends" to communities affected by conflict.

Environment and sustainable development

UNDP, through its new climate change strategy, sought to focus the attention of the development community on issues related to climate change, and help countries develop public policies and partnerships to leverage resources, transform markets and drive investment towards initiatives on lower carbon emissions and climate resilience. In 2008, UNDP mobilized more than $500 million in grant resources and more than $1 billion in related co-financing through the Global Environment Facility (GEF), the Multilateral Fund of the 1987 Montreal Protocol on Substances that Deplete the Ozone Layer [YUN 1987, p. 686], and other initiatives. UNDP was assisting programme countries in removing barriers and finding new sources of environmental financing through such mechanisms as the MDG Carbon Facility, which mobilized private-sector financing for developing countries through global carbon markets. The Facility screened 160 projects in 31 countries in 2008.

With support from Japan, UNDP designed a $92 million programme to integrate climate change issues into national development processes in 21 countries in Africa. The GEF Small Grants Programme expanded its portfolio and secured additional funding for activities that supported community-based adaptation to climate change. With 300 projects in 60 countries, UNDP helped expand local access to energy services for over half a million people.

Evaluation of UNDP role in the environment and energy

In September, the UNDP/UNFPA Executive Board considered a July report [DP/2008/46] on the evaluation, conducted by the UNDP Evaluation Office, of the role and contribution of UNDP in the area of the environment and energy at the global, regional and national levels. The evaluation team visited eight countries and two regional centres. Global consultations focused on UNDP headquarters staff and management, and on organizations whose interests and goals overlapped with those of UNDP. The evaluation was hampered by a lack of reliable financial data for activities not financed by GEF and a lack of useful performance measures.

The report stated that the project design and the implementation work carried out by UNDP and its partners were generally of high quality. The availability of GEF funding, however, was the most important driving force determining where, how, and when UNDP country-level environment and energy work was undertaken. As a result, high-priority national environmental issues—including environmental health, water supply and sanitation, and energy management—were replaced by GEF priorities related to climate change mitigation, biodiversity and international waters. UNDP staff at headquarters and in the regional centres were recognized for their expertise and the results they achieved, but most were funded through extrabudgetary sources, which was not conducive to long-term capacity or career development.

The evaluation concluded that energy and the environment were central to the UNDP mission, and the UNDP role in that area within the United Nations was potentially important but not fully realized. UNDP responsiveness to national priorities was uneven, and the type and effectiveness of the Programme's environment and energy work varied significantly between partner countries. Capacity for planning and managing environment and energy work also varied considerably within UNDP, and most country offices lacked the capacity to engage in high-level policy dialogue with Governments. The mainstreaming of environmental considerations in other major UNDP practice areas was limited at all levels, and measuring progress continued to be a challenge.

The evaluation recommended that UNDP demonstrate more clearly the pursuit of its mandate with regard to the environment and energy, rather than the specific priorities of a limited number of major donors or funds. UNDP should assume a proactive role to respond to national priorities, and identify and implement institutional arrangements and incentives to promote the mainstreaming of environmental considerations throughout all major practice areas. It should also identify options for strengthening the environment and energy capacities of its country offices.

In its August response to the evaluation [DP/2008/47], UNDP management stated that many of the issues raised had received considerable attention, but much work remained to be done. UNDP took steps to augment its funding base, resulting in some successes at the global level. In that regard, Spain was channelling $62.5 million through UNDP under the Millennium Development Goals Achievement Fund for environment and climate change. The Gates Foundation committed $19 million to promote energy access for the poor in West Africa, and Japan was providing $92.7 million through UNDP to support climate change adaptation in Africa.

UNDP committed itself to promoting the visibility and prominence of environmental concerns by making environment and sustainable development one of its four main focus areas, and establishing environment and energy as a distinct practice. It was working with UNDG to enhance guidance and support on mainstreaming environmental sustainability and integrating climate change into programming. UNDP was negotiating the renewal of its three-year memorandum of understanding with UNEP, including agreements and working arrangements on the Poverty and Environment Initiative. In February, it launched an enhanced, results-based management platform that included tools for managing for results in support of national development priorities; provided UNDP with performance data for accountability purposes, organizational learning and decision-making; and provided the substantive basis for communicating UNDP results to the general public.

In September [dec. 2008/30], the Executive Board took note of the evaluation and the management response. It emphasized the need for UNDP to strengthen national capacity development in the area of the environment and energy, and urged it to improve its responsiveness to national priorities, especially the specific needs of least developed countries and small island developing States. It requested the Administrator to identify and implement institutional mechanisms and incentives to mainstream the environment and energy into all major practice areas, and to strengthen its capacities throughout the organization, especially in UNDP country offices. The Administrator was also asked to report orally to the Board at its first regular session in 2009 on the UNDP strategy on the environment and energy, based on the evaluation, and on the finalization of its memorandum of understanding with UNEP.

Capacity development

The strategic plan, 2008–2011, endorsed by the Executive Board in 2007 [YUN 2007, p. 898], positioned capacity development as the overarching service provided by UNDP to programme countries. Demand increased in 2008, particularly for mainstreaming capacity development into programmes and projects; designing thematic, sector and national capacity development plans; and the provision of collective approaches to capacity development by the UN development system. UNDP responded to requests to facilitate capacity assessments and diagnostics in 65 programme countries. It helped shape a UN approach to capacity development by designing materials to assist UN country teams in integrating capacity development into frameworks and programmes, and facilitating inter-agency learning on the issue. UNDP would improve its services and focus on helping programme countries to scale up and sustain capacity development, adapt and respond to global crises, and deliver on human development.

Gender equality and women's empowerment

UNDP embarked on a programme to integrate gender equality throughout its work and ensure that countries were supported in reducing gender inequality and improving women's lives. With UNDP support, the Governments of 22 African countries adopted and incorporated gender needs assessments as planning and costing tools. In Latin America, UNDP partnered with the private sector, civil society, mass media and Government on innovative approaches to address gender-based violence. Attention and resources were focused on integrating women's needs into UNDP crisis prevention and recovery operations through the provision of dedicated resources for women's empowerment, the deployment of experienced gender advisors and the adoption of performance incentives.

Programming arrangements

At its January session, the UNDP/UNFPA Executive Board considered a report on providing information on the "target for resources assignment from the core" (TRAC)-2 allocation methodology and criteria for establishing fixed lines in programming arrangements [DP/2008/14]; the report was submitted in response to a 2007 Board decision [YUN 2007, p. 895]. UNDP employed three primary criteria as the main determinants for allocating TRAC-2 resources: national capacities for the MDGs and human development, policy and plans; national capacities for implementing development strategies and goals; and response to emerging development priorities of programme countries. At the beginning of each programming cycle, TRAC-1 resources were computed and allocated based on the latest gross national income per capita (GNI) and population data available. For the 2008–2011 programming period, the 2005 GNI and population data would be used. TRAC-2 resources were allocated based on a thorough assessment of the effective integration by country programmes of some of the criteria. The overall quality of programmes remained a key cross-cutting element. The TRAC-2 framework was implemented through the common country assessment/UNDAF and country programme document/action plan process. Annexes to the report contained information on the total TRAC-2 allocation per country from 2004 to 2007; regional shares and distribution by income categories; and the fixed lines in the programming arrangements for the 2008–2011 period.

Monitoring and evaluation

The UNDP/UNFPA Executive Board, at its June session, considered the annual report on evaluation in UNDP, issued in April [DP/2008/25]. The report, which covered the period from March 2007 to February 2008, provided information on evaluation coverage, compliance, quality, institutional arrangements and use. It highlighted systematic constraints to effective implementation of the evaluation policy. The report also presented key findings and outlined the proposed UNDP Evaluation Office programme of work for the 2008–2009 period.

The Evaluation Office and evaluation units in the associated funds and programmes continued to support the effective implementation of the evaluation policy by all parts of the organization. The Office revised the operational guidelines for evaluation in the UNDP *Programme and Operations Policies and Procedures* to promote good evaluation practices. It was also revising the *Handbook for Monitoring and Evaluation for Results* to reflect the requirements and principles of the evaluation policy, as well as the United Nations Evaluation Group (UNEG) *Standards for Evaluation in the UN system*. UNDP and its associated funds and programmes continued to build on professional partnerships in evaluation with UNEG, the OECD/Development Assistance Committee (DAC) Network on Evaluation and other partners.

The Evaluation Office conducted nine evaluations during the reporting period. Programme units completed 186 evaluations, including two by the regional bureaux and one by the Bureau for Development Policy. At the country level, UNDP offices in 137 countries completed 183 evaluations, of which 138 were project evaluations and 28 were outcome evaluations. The evaluations found that the comparative advantages of UNDP, including its ability to bring partners together and its universal presence, enabled it to establish relationships with a wide range of national and international actors, and to play a useful role in advocacy, facilitation and coordination. The evaluations also found, however, that UNDP did not fully utilize its development knowledge. Inadequate regular resources restricted the UNDP ability to pursue core activities related to its priorities. The evaluations stressed that efforts to mobilize resources should not detract from strategic focus. UNDP should continue to build its capacity in its core areas of competence while recognizing the importance of raising resources. Capacity development continued to be central to the work of UNDP, but its contribution to strengthening local capacities was mixed. UNDP partnership and engagement with Governments was generally strong, but partnerships with the private sector and civil society were often weak or not fully used.

In June [dec. 2008/17], the Executive Board took note of the annual report on evaluation and urged the relevant evaluation units to provide additional information and analysis on the evaluation functions and activities of the United Nations Capital Development Fund (UNCDF), UNIFEM and the United Nations Volunteers programme in future annual reports. It requested the UNDP Administrator to increase oversight to improve the quality and implementation of country office evaluation plans. The Administrator was also asked to strengthen regional and country office capacities in results-based management, project design, monitoring and reporting. The Board urged UNDP to strengthen senior management supervision and support for monitoring and evaluation by programme units, and continue to improve its use of evaluation to support learning and a culture of results. UNDP was asked to continue to support national partners in developing capacities, so as to exercise their national ownership in evaluation, and report to the Board in 2009 on its follow-up to management responses. The Board approved the assessments of development results and activities to strengthen the evaluation function from the proposed 2008–2009 programme of work for the Evaluation Office. It requested additional consultation on the new independent evaluations to be conducted by the Evaluation Office, as proposed in the programme of work, for approval at the second regular Executive Board session in September 2008.

An August report [DP/2008/49] submitted in response to the Board's June decision contained additional information on the 2008–2009 Evaluation Office work programme, which included nine new evaluations. In September [dec. 2008/31], the Executive Board approved the independent evaluations contained in the work programme and the August report. It stressed the importance of clear linkages of subsequent work programmes with the UNDP strategic plan, 2008–2011 [YUN 2007, p. 897].

Evaluation of results-based management in UNDP

At its January session, the UNDP/UNFPA Executive Board considered a report containing the executive summary of the evaluation of results-based management in UNDP [DP/2008/6]. The evaluation focused on the organizational strategy, vision and expectations of the results-based management approach; the design, implementation and use of the system to operationalize the approach; and the results of those efforts. The scope of the study covered the 1999–2006 period, all geographic regions, and the adoption of results-based management at the programme, country, regional and corporate levels.

The evaluation found that the goals in the UNDP strategic framework had changed in presentation, but the underlying areas of work remained the same. Focus areas under the goals were rationalized and simplified, but it was difficult to identify substantive change in the scope of activities at the country level. Overall, UNDP established a cycle of setting and revising corporate goals, introduced improved office systems to manage project finances, institutionalized the need to report on performance, and raised awareness about results throughout the organization. It concluded that the UNDP experience with introducing results-based management was similar to that of other organizations. UNDP had a weak culture of results, however, and its corporatist approach had only a limited effect on development effectiveness at the country level. Results-based management had been misinterpreted as not supporting the decentralized way in which UNDP worked, and improved financial administration and management systems were not helping build a results-based culture. The report recommended that UNDP strengthen its leadership and direction; sharpen the role of the strategic results framework to distinguish more clearly between corporate goals and country programme outcomes; support managing for outcomes at country offices; and expand investment in, and the use of, evaluation and performance audits.

UNDP management, in its response to the evaluation [DP/2008/7], stated that many of the issues raised confirmed certain persistent limitations with respect to the implementation of results-based management that UNDP was committed to addressing. The findings might have overestimated what could be attributed to UNDP, but they provided the Programme with a number of useful inputs for organizational learning. The report outlined the main conclusions and recommendations of the evaluation report and the UNDP response, including steps that the Programme was taking to address the issues raised in the evaluation.

In January [dec. 2008/8], the Executive Board took note of the evaluation of results-based management in UNDP and the management response to the evaluation.

Multi-year funding framework, 2004–2007

At its annual session in June, the Executive Board considered an April report [DP/2008/23 & Corr.1] on UNDP performance and results for 2007, the final year of the 2004–2007 multi-year funding framework (MYFF) cycle. The report, which complemented the 2007 cumulative MYFF report [YUN 2007, p. 896], contained an overview of the global UNDP portfolio; highlighted trends in demand and performance, and described UNDP work on the ground during the year. It also provided an update on priority UNDP management activities and work in support of UN coordination efforts, and reviewed income and expenditures. The Board also had before it a statistical annex, issued in May [DP/2008/23/Add.2], and a joint UNDP/UNFPA report, issued in April [DP/2008/23/Add.1-DP/FPA/2008/5(Part II)], which provided a synopsis of management responses to key recommendations of JIU in 2007 that were of specific relevance to those organizations.

At the same session [dec. 2008/14], the Executive Board took note of the MYFF report on UNDP performance and results for 2007 and the statistical annex. It noted with concern that the poverty eradication practice area did not receive top priority in terms of the percentage of total spending during 2007, and emphasized that appropriate activities should be used to support direct poverty reduction initiatives. The Board urged UNDP to undertake relevant poverty reduction activities and give top priority to achieving the MDGs and reducing human poverty. It reaffirmed the commitment of UNDP to results-based management and programming and requested UNDP to include in future reports, starting in 2009, a comprehensive comparative analysis of spending for UN system coordination and programming. The Board took note of the report on the 2007 recommendations of JIU and urged UNDP to continue to pay particular attention to the recommendations relating to human resources management. It noted with concern that earmarked resources continued to far exceed UNDP regular resources, which affected the ability of UNDP to fulfil its mandate adequately and to effectively support the development agenda of partner countries. UNDP was urged to give enhanced priority to direct poverty reduction results in implementing the strategic plan, 2008–2011 (see p. 975). The Board asked UNDP to allocate sufficient levels of financial and staff resources across the practice areas of the strategic plan, with particular attention to least developed countries, in the context of achieving the MDGs, and to report in that regard at the Board's 2009 annual session. UNDP was also asked to submit, in 2009, a distribution of total and regular resources expenditure by practice area, and to highlight in future reports per capita programme expenditure and programme expenditure figures for the least developed countries.

Strategic plan, 2008–2011

The UNDP/UNFPA Executive Board, at its annual session in June, considered a May report [DP/2007/43/Rev.1] containing the updated UNDP strategic plan, 2008–2011. The plan was endorsed by the Board in 2007 [YUN 2007, p. 898] and was subsequently revised pursuant to the same decision. Addenda to the report discussed the development and institutional results frameworks of the strategic plan [DP/2007/43/Add.1] and the implications for the plan of General Assembly resolution 62/208 on the triennial comprehensive policy review of operational activities for development of the UN system [YUN 2007, p. 877].

At the same session [dec. 2008/15], the Executive Board took note of the revisions to the UNDP strategic plan, 2008–2011, as contained in the May report.

Financial and administrative matters

The UNDP Administrator, in his annual review of the financial situation [DP/2009/28 & Corr.1 & Add.1], reported that total income in 2008 was $6.03 billion, comprised of contributions ($5.5 billion), interest ($180 million) and other income ($360 million). Total contributions to UNDP, in nominal terms, were $5.5 billion, 6 per cent above the 2007 level of $5.19 billion. Regular resources contributions to UNDP registered $1.1 billion, amounting to 20 per cent of overall contributions, whereas other resources contributions reached $4.16 billion, representing 75.5 per cent of total contributions in 2008. Total income in nominal terms, including interest and other income, increased by 6 per cent, from $1.14 billion in 2007 to $1.21 billion in 2008. Total expenditure increased by 9 per cent, from $965 million to $1.05 billion.

Of the total other resources contributions of $4.16 billion, $1.44 billion was contributed by bilateral donor Governments; $1.35 billion came from non-bilateral/multilateral sources; $960 million from local sources; and $410 million from other sources. Contributions from the top 10 donors decreased by 5 per cent in 2008 to $859 million in nominal terms, down from $900 million in 2007. In real terms, 2008 contributions totalled $827 million, representing an 8 per cent decrease from 2007. The value of fund flows for multi-donor trust funds, joint programmes and support to other UN organizations totalled $1.5 billion in 2008, down from $1.9 billion in 2007.

Programme expenditure, including programme support to the resident coordinator system, development support services, and the UNDP economist programme, increased by 10 per cent, from $561 million in 2007 to $617 million in 2008. By category, 74 per cent of expenditure in 2008 was spent on the harmonized biennial support budget functions, 19 per cent on the UNDP-specific function of country office support to UN activities, 1 per cent on the United Nations Development Operations Coordination Office, 5 per cent on the United Nations Volunteers (UNV) programme, and 1 per cent on UNCDF. In total, 62 per cent of the 2008–2009 biennial support budget expenditure related to country offices, with the remaining 38 per cent attributed to headquarters locations, including UNV.

By region, Africa recorded the highest expenditure of regular resources, with $286 million, followed by Asia and the Pacific with $140 million, Europe and the Commonwealth of Independent States with $47 million, the Arab States with $42 million and Latin America with $34 million. The expenditure for global and other programmes was $64 million.

Overall income of other resources increased by $220 million (5 per cent), from $4.33 billion in 2007 to $4.55 billion in 2008. In real terms, income increased by $260 million or 6 per cent, from $4.11 billion in 2007 to $4.37 billion in 2008. At the end of 2008, the balance of unexpended regular resources was $499 million, an increase of 32 per cent over the 2007 figure of $377 million.

In September [dec. 2008/27], the Executive Board took note of the Administrator's annual review of the financial situation for 2007 [YUN 2007, p. 898].

Regular funding commitments to UNDP

In May [DP/2008/24], UNDP submitted a report on the status of regular funding commitments to the Programme and its associated funds and programmes for 2008 and onward. Following five consecutive years of increases in UNDP regular resources since 2001, resources remained at the 2005 level in 2006, but increased again in 2007. Provisional data showed that contributions to regular resources for 2007 reached $1.1 billion. Some donors, however, announced reductions in their contributions, while others had not yet indicated their level.

Fourteen OECD/DAC members increased their contributions to regular resources in 2007, many for the fifth consecutive year. One doubled its contribution, three increased their contribution by 20 per cent or more, and four others by 10 per cent or more. Eight donors increased their contribution annually over the full MYFF period (2004–2007), and eight programme countries contributed $1 million or more. Although a number of donors delayed payment of significant proportions of their pledges in the last quarter of 2007, the operational reserves did not have to be used.

In June [dec. 2008/16], the Executive Board took note of the report on the status of regular funding commitments to UNDP for 2008 and onward, and noted that UNDP was unable to meet the fourth and overall (2007) annual funding target of its second MYFF (2004–2007). It underscored the vital importance of maintaining the 2007 level of regular resources in 2008, so as to enable UNDP to meet the first annual funding target in the integrated resources framework of the strategic plan, 2008–2011. The Board requested that all countries that had not yet done so provide contributions to regular resources for 2008. Member States were encouraged to announce multiyear pledges and payment schedules for the 2008–2011 planning cycle and adhere to such pledges and schedules thereafter.

Biennial support budget, 2008–2009

At its first regular session in January, the UNDP/UNFPA Executive Board considered a report of the UNDP Administrator [DP/2008/3] containing UNDP results-based budget proposals and estimates for the 2008–2009 biennium. The Administrator proposed a regular resources funded budget of $778.7 million in net terms; in nominal terms, that amount was $120.8 million greater than the net budget approved by the Board for the 2006–2007 biennium [YUN 2005, p. 974]. The proposal incorporated total net volume increases of $14.7 million and net cost increases amounting to $109.8 million. The estimates also incorporated an increase of $3.7 million to projected income that offset the gross support budget, amounting to $74.9 million in 2008–2009, up from $71.2 million in 2006–2007. The total gross regular resources proposals for the 2008–2009 period amounted to $853.6 million.

The Administrator proposed that $31.2 million for United Nations-mandated security costs continue to be treated as a distinct requirement from regular resources, and at the same nominal level approved for the 2006–2007 biennium. In addition, the Administrator proposed that $9 million for International Public Sector Accounting Standards (IPSAS) be treated as a distinct requirement from regular resources, in order to meet United Nations-mandated system-wide compliance during the 2008–2009 biennium.

The Advisory Committee on Administrative and Budgetary Questions (ACABQ), in its January report [DP/2008/5] on the UNDP and UNIFEM estimates for the 2008–2009 biennial support budget, stated that UNDP efforts to implement results-based budgeting could be improved, particularly with regard to distinct information on links with specific programmes of work or activities, which should allow assessment of the cost-effectiveness and degree of achievement of expected results. ACABQ reiterated its previous request that UNDP, as well as UNFPA and UNICEF, avail themselves of lessons learned by other UN entities that had implemented results-based techniques. It emphasized the importance of timely implementation of the recommendations of the Board of Auditors, information on which should be provided by UNDP in future budget presentations. ACABQ stressed the importance of including in the support budget submission information on major objects of expenditure under post and non-post costs to ensure greater transparency. Consideration should be given to presenting a comprehensive support budget, reflecting the support requirements related to all sources of funding, in order to enable thorough intergovernmental analysis and scrutiny

The Committee noted that the establishment of a number of UNDP country director positions through the creation of 11 D-1 posts significantly expanded the number of countries in which the Programme was financing such posts. It expressed concern about the multiple layers of management, as well as at the large number of posts proposed for reclassification. The Committee recommended that those management and staffing arrangements, including their effectiveness and cost, be reviewed. It also recommended that comprehensive information on the rationale followed in the post classification exercise be provided to the Executive Board.

In January [dec. 2008/1], the Executive Board took note of the functions, management results, indicators and resource requirements in the budget estimates for the 2008–2009 biennium, and approved gross regular resources in the amount of $853.6 million, as presented in the Executive Director's report, subject to the provisions of the decision. It requested the Administrator to ensure that the biennial support budget was consistent with the UNDP strategic plan, 2008–2011, and its annexes, as augmented and amended in accordance with the Board's 2007 decision on the plan [YUN 2007, p. 898] and the 2007 triennial comprehensive policy review [ibid., p. 874]; and to report to the Board at its September session. The Board requested UNDP to exercise restraint in implementing its proposal for reclassifications, with clear justifications in line with International Civil Service Commission standards. The Administrator was also asked to include in future budget submissions an annex on budget estimates by cost category for major objects of expenditure and to report on estimates and efficiency targets in the annual financial reporting. The Board decided that future biennial support budgets should aim at progressive decrease as a proportion of resources. It urged UNDP to continue to exercise scrutiny of management costs so as to ensure a higher allocation of funds for programmes, and to increase its efforts to bring greater efficiency to its operations. The Board encouraged the Administrator to intensify consultations with other UN funds and programmes in order to harmonize, to the extent possible, the attribution of costs between the programme and support budgets. The Administrator was requested to include in the report on cost classification information on the concept and methodology determining the minimum base structure, as well as a description of that structure. The Board reaffirmed its 2007 decision on cost recovery [ibid., p. 899] and requested the Administrator to realign the funding modality of UNDP management activities to ensure that cost-recovery income bore the support cost associated with all other resources-funded activities within the next biennium. It requested the Administrator, in close cooperation with other UN funds and programmes, to continue to harmonize the methodology of results-based budgeting and improve targets and indicators.

The Board approved the maximum expenditure of $9 million from regular resources to cover the costs of introducing IPSAS by the end of 2009. It asked the Administrator to include information on support requirements related to all sources of funding in future biennial support budgets, in accordance with recommendations contained in the ACABQ report, and present the biennial support budget, 2010–2011, for approval by the Board in 2009.

The Board took note of the consolidated summary of UNDP funding requirements for security activities [DP/2008/CRP.2]. It approved the net amount of $51.2 million as a separate requirement from regular resources to cover security measures mandated by the United Nations, as proposed in the summary, and endorsed the proposal of the Administrator to grant him exceptional authority, during the 2008–2009 period, to access up to an additional 20 per cent ($10.2 million) of the approved amount.

Cost classification in UNDP

A December report [DP/2009/3], submitted in response to a 2007 Executive Board decision on programming arrangements for the 2008–2009 period [YUN 2007, p. 895] and the Board's January 2008 decision on the UNDP support budget for that period (see above), provided an initial conceptual framework and road map for realigning the cost classification of activities within the overall UNDP resource plan. A joint consultancy, commissioned by UNDP, UNICEF and UNFPA in mid-2008 to assess the degree of harmonization in cost classification among the three entities, found that their agreed harmonized cost definitions were still applicable. They defined direct costs as those incurred for, and traceable in full to, the activities, projects and programmes of an organization in fulfilment of its mandate. Fixed indirect costs were those incurred by the organization regardless of the scope and level of its activities, and which could not be traced unequivocally to specific activities, projects or programmes. Variable indirect costs were those incurred by the organization in support of its activities, projects and programmes, and which could not be traced unequivocally to specific activities, projects or programmes. The definitions facilitated the classification of costs across the three organizations as "direct" development costs, and as "fixed indirect" or "variable indirect" management costs.

Three guiding principles underlying a transparent, strategic and fully aligned cost classification system in UNDP were the transparent identification and attribution of costs; the rationalization and simplification of cost classification groupings; and the alignment of cost classifications and funding frameworks with the UNDP business model and the strategic plan. The two broad cost groupings that existed—development and management—remained relevant. A third category could deal with special-purpose activities.

In the context of the four UNDP focus areas (poverty reduction and achievement of the MDGs, democratic governance, crisis prevention and recovery, environment and sustainable development), development costs could lend themselves to further classification within three major subcategories: programmes; programme effectiveness activities; and UN development coordination activities. Management activities were the functions and activities required to ensure the delivery of development activities. They would include executive leadership and direction, corporate oversight and accountability, compliance with statutory obligations, and effective human and financial resources management. Special-purpose activities could include United Nations-mandated security costs, after-service health insurance costs and capital investment costs.

The business model and strategic plan, as well as the resource frameworks and cost classification system that underpinned them, were the key to the future relevance and sustainability of UNDP. The approach presented in the report should result in a more optimal allocation of resources to meet the myriad funding priorities of UNDP, including a longer-term view of the need for sustainability.

Direct budget support and pooled funds

An April report [DP/2008/36 & Corr.1,2] discussed UNDP engagement in direct budget support and pooled funds. The UNDP policy and approach stated in the report was aligned with that of UNFPA. Direct budget support was defined as a method of financing the budget of a partner country through a transfer of resources from an external financing agency to the national treasury of the partner Government. UNDP recognized direct budget support as a development finance instrument that promoted national ownership, transparency and harmonization in aid allocations and alignment with national budget priorities. A country's preparedness to absorb direct budget support in transparent, efficient and results-oriented ways centred on the capacities of national institutions, aid coordination mechanisms and management systems to negotiate, manage and monitor the use of such funds for their agreed purposes. Direct budget support could be classified as general budget support—a non-earmarked contribution directed at overall Government policy and expenditures that included balance-of-payments support—or as sector budget support, which was an earmarked contribution to the national budget towards programme-specific results. Unlike sector budget support funds, pooled funds were contracted out by a Government to be managed by an agreed party.

The report stated that the preferred value-added contribution of UNDP would be to support national capacities to negotiate, design and manage direct budget support for development effectiveness. If UNDP was requested by a Government to manage a pooled fund in a transition period to strengthen national capacities in a given area, it would be done under existing UNDP direct execution guidelines and cost-sharing agreements, and the standard UNDP management agent fee of 7 per cent would apply. Where UNDP provided a financial contribution to the fund, the project document would specify the implementation arrangements and the modified results framework, reporting, auditing, and monitoring and evaluation arrangements. UNDP would not transfer monies into a pooled fund not managed by a UN specialized agency, fund or programme. The report outlined requirements for direct financial contributions.

It was proposed that the UNDP/UNFPA Executive Board consider the 2008–2011 cycle as a pilot period for UNDP to assume an enhanced role in the direct budget support environment that included the ability to contribute to a Government-managed sector budget support fund, or to a UN fund, programme or specialized agency-managed pooled fund, in a given number of demonstration countries. Such action would require the addition of financial regulations specific to direct budget support and pooled funds, and would constitute amended versions of financial regulations to allow for reporting on co-mingled funds; fund-level auditing in accordance with the agreement of the fund participants; and definitions for direct budget support, sector budget support and pooled funds. Annexed to the report were proposed amendments to the UNDP Financial Regulations and Rules.

In a June report [DP/2008/42], ACABQ stated that it had no objection to the proposed amendments to the UNDP Financial Regulations, subject to the observations made in its report.

At its June session [dec. 2008/24], the Executive Board took note of the report on UNDP engagement in direct budget support and pooled funds and requested UNDP to give preference to engagement in direct budget support, in the form of sector budget support, as a signatory, without fiduciary obligation, taking into account the views of programme countries. It endorsed, in principle, a four-year pilot period, starting in September 2008, for enabling UNDP financial contributions to pooled funding and sector budget support within the limitations and provisions provided in the April report on the issue. The Board requested UNDP to prepare an additional report for approval by the Board in 2008, including an update on the common UNDG approach towards the changing aid environment, an analysis of the UNDP role in the new aid environment, and a further elaboration of the criteria of engagement in sector budget support and pooled funding, as well as indicators to measure the effectiveness of the new aid modality. It approved, for the duration of the pilot period, the proposed changes in the regulations and rules as contained in the April report, including the requirements for direct financial contributions, taking into account the ACABQ recommendations. UNDP was requested to include, during the pilot period, a progress report in the Administrator's annual report, and an overview of contributions to pooled funding and sector budget support in the annual review of the financial situation. The Board asked UNDP to prepare a report at the end of the pilot period, including an evaluation and audit of the pilot programme and an update on its efforts towards the harmonization of regulations and rules under consideration in the United Nations, including the changes needed to allow participation in pooled funding and sector budget support.

Changing aid environment

An August report [DP/2008/53], submitted in response to the Executive Board's June decision on UNDP engagement in direct budget support and pooled funds (above), outlined the UNDP response to the changing aid environment at the country level and the Programme's engagement with UNDG on a common approach in that regard. It built on the April report on UNDP engagement in direct budget support and pooled funds (see p. 977), and provided indicators for measuring effectiveness and evaluating the process by which the results for the pilot period for UNDP engagement in sector budget support and pooled funding would be evaluated. The report stated that UNDP was helping to facilitate and negotiate aid modalities, including direct budget support. While acknowledging that direct budget support was not its core business, UNDP recognized it as a development finance instrument that promoted national ownership, transparency and harmonization in aid allocations, as well as alignment with national plan and budget priorities. The rationale for UNDP engagement in sector budget support and pooled funds was to respond to growing country demands for capacity development and for expanded inclusion of UNDP in efforts towards harmonization and alignment. UNDP would only engage in pooled funding in areas or sectors in which it was already present through a separate project.

The overarching principles for UNDP engagement were that sector budget support and pooled funding had to: contribute to strengthening partner countries' ownership; enhance the performance and accountability of programme countries' public financial management systems; seek to minimize transaction costs incurred by participating countries; and be delivered in a way that enhanced the predictability of resources and reduced their volatility.

During its September session [dec. 2008/29], the Executive Board took note of the report on the role of UNDP in the changing aid environment at the country level and approved implementation of the pilot programme.

Ex-gratia payments

An August report [DP/2008/41] proposed amendments to the UNDP financial regulations and rules regarding ex-gratia payments, or payments that were justified by moral obligation in cases where there was no legal liability to UNDP. The report stated that, in the aftermath of the 2007 bombing in Algiers that affected UN personnel [YUN 2007, p. 61], it was evident that ex-gratia payments might, in certain circumstances, need to exceed the limit set in the current UNDP financial regulations and rules. UNDP therefore asked the Board to approve an amendment to its regulation 23.01 to permit ex-gratia payments in excess of $50,000. UNDP was also correcting its rule 123.01 *(a)* to reflect that an opinion on the matter of ex-gratia payments should be provided by the UNDP Legal Support Office, rather than the United Nations Office of Legal Affairs.

In June [DP/2008/42], ACABQ recommended approval of the proposed amendments.

During its September session [dec. 2008/26], the Executive Board took note of the report on the revision of the UNDP financial regulations and the corresponding ACABQ report. It decided on new wording for financial regulation 23.01, enabling the Administrator to make ex-gratia payments, not exceeding $75,000 per year, as he or she deemed necessary in the interest of UNDP. In the case of an emergency where, at the Administrator's discretion, immediate ex-gratia payments were necessary for humanitarian reasons, in instances such as injury or death suffered in connection with UNDP activities, the Administrator might make such payments without limitation as to the amount. The Administrator would immediately inform the Executive Board when any single situation resulted in payments in excess of $50,000. The Board noted the corresponding change in financial rule 123.01.

Audit reports

The UNDP/UNFPA Executive Board, at its January session, considered the Administrator's report [DP/2008/15] on the implementation of the recommendations of the Board of Auditors for the 2004–2005 biennium [YUN 2006, p. 1631]. Since the Administrator's previous update [YUN 2007, p. 900], UNDP had implemented 105 out of 115 audit recommendations, resulting in a 91 per cent implementation rate. With the exception of one recommendation, UNDP had implemented all recommendations targeted for completion by the third quarter of 2007 and was on schedule to implement the remaining 9 per cent, or 10 recommendations, by the end of 2007.

In response to a 2007 Executive Board decision [ibid.], the report reviewed progress in addressing nationally executed (NEX) projects; bank reconciliation and staff professionalization programmes; internal controls in the Atlas enterprise resource planning system; and progress in mainstreaming risk management into UNDP policies and processes. It also reviewed initiatives to strengthen accountability and organizational responsiveness to audit recommendations in UNDP, including leveraging the recommendations and feedback of the Audit Advisory Committee on key strategic initiatives and related oversight matters; formalizing the regular review of the top 15 audit priorities and accountability matrix for audit follow-up; using the web-based audit dashboard for transparent reporting and follow-up; and formalizing periodic country scans to better understand the programmatic, financial and human resource challenges and audit issues for all UNDP country offices.

In January [dec. 2008/8], the Executive Board took note of the report on the implementation of the recommendations of the Board of Auditors for the 2004–2005 biennium.

A March report on internal audit and investigations [DP/2008/20] provided information on the activities of the Office of Audit and Investigations (OAI) for the year ended 31 December 2007. The former Office of Audit and Performance Review was renamed effective 8 February to better reflect its two core functions: internal audit and investigations. During the year, OAI issued 58 internal audit reports, pertaining to five headquarters audits and 53 country office audits. During the last quarter of 2007, it conducted a new audit risk assessment for the purpose of the 2008 work plan for country office audits, which showed that three (2 per cent) of the 141 offices assessed were ranked very high risk, 50 (35 per cent) were high risk, and the remainder medium risk. Compared to the audit risk assessment results in 2006, there was no change in the risk ranking of 85 per cent of the offices.

With respect to country office audits, the areas needing the most improvement remained essentially the same as in previous years. Seventeen audit reports noted that project monitoring and evaluation required improvement. Bank reconciliation issues were raised in 14 audit reports; 14 reports described instances of non-compliance or partial compliance with procurement rules; and 16 reports described weaknesses in the recruitment of personnel, including non-transparent and non-competitive recruitment processes. As at 31 December 2007, the implementation rate for seven headquarters audits conducted between 2005 and 30 September 2007 was 76 per cent on average, ranging from 24 per cent to 96 per cent.

As to projects executed by non-governmental organizations and/or national Governments (NGO/NEX), the report stated that as at 31 December, OAI had received 1,790 (96 per cent) of the audit reports encompassing NGO/NEX expenditures totalling $2.0 billion. Of those received, OAI reviewed 1,711 audit reports (or 96 per cent), representing $1.7 billion. The audit reports for fiscal year 2006 expenditures had generated 5,364 audit issues, 70 per cent of which lay in the areas of financial management, recordkeeping systems and controls, and the management and use of equipment and inventory. The majority of the issues (80 per cent) were noted as medium- and low-risk, with most of the high-risk issues (20 per cent) related to financial management, project progress and rate of delivery.

OAI was entrusted in 2007 with conducting all formal investigations of harassment, sexual harassment and abuse of authority cases. A total of 113 complaints were received in 2007. By the end of the year, 83 per cent of the complaints carried forward to 2007 were closed. Of the 104 complaints closed, 35 per cent were found unsubstantiated and did not require further investigation, while 4 per cent were referred to the Office of Human Resources and the Legal Support Office (LSO). The balance, representing 62 per cent of the complaints, were formally investigated by OAI. After formal investigation, 25 per cent were found to be unsubstantiated and another 35 per cent were referred to LSO for review.

During its June session [dec. 2008/13], the Executive Board took note of the report on internal audit and investigations in UNDP and the report on UNFPA internal audit and oversight activities in 2007 (see p. 1193). It called on UNDP and UNFPA to further strengthen the national execution modality by addressing the operational risks and weaknesses identified in the audit reports, with particular attention given to capacity-building, and requested UNDP and UNFPA to inform the Board of the implementation of the proposed actions. The Board noted that specific audit procedures and guidelines were being developed in response to the use of the harmonized approach to cash transfers, and called on UNDP to develop such procedures and guidelines in coordination with other UN funds, programmes and agencies. UNDP and UNFPA were asked to report to the Board in 2009 on progress made and lessons learned in implementing the harmonized approach to cash transfers. The Board urged the UNDP Administrator to further strengthen risk-based audit planning and fill vacant OAI posts rapidly. It expressed concern that 13 per cent of the ratings in the internal audit reports were unsatisfactory, that some audit findings remained unresolved for 18 months, and that there were investigation findings on the misconduct of staff members. UNDP was asked to report to the Board in 2009 on progress made in those areas, as part of the annual report on internal audit and investigations.

UNDP accountability system

An August report [DP/2008/16/Rev.1] presented the enhanced and integrated UNDP accountability system, which included an accountability framework and an oversight policy. The accountability framework underscored the commitment of UNDP to results and risk-based performance management, as well as the shared values and culture of accountability and transparency. The oversight policy included the organization of independent internal and external oversight to provide assurances that functional systems of internal controls were in place, including evaluation of the policy framework, efficient utilization of resources and adherence to professional and ethical standards.

In a decision adopted during its September session [dec. 2008/37], the Executive Board took note of the report on the UNDP accountability system and approved the accountability framework and oversight policy contained therein, subject to the provisions of the decision. It decided that the UNDP Ethics Office should submit a report to the Board at its annual session. The Board also decided that the UNDP Administrator, and the UNFPA/UNOPS Executive Directors, could disclose internal audit reports to Member States, in accordance with the relevant provisions stipulated in the UNDP accountability framework and oversight policy, the UNFPA oversight policy (see p. 1193) and the UNOPS accountability and oversight policies (see p. 985), respectively. The UNPD Administrator and the UNFPA/UNOPS Executive Directors were requested to submit to the Board a report on the implementation of the decision in 2010.

Other technical cooperation

Development Account

The Secretary-General, in his February report [A/62/708] on improving the effective and efficient delivery of the mandates of development-related activities and revised estimates relating to the programme budget for the 2008–2009 biennium (see p. 1552), proposed, among other measures, the establishment of a Development Account Programme Management Unit to strengthen the Account's programme management and oversight. The proposal required additional resources in the amount of $357,600. The Secretary-General said that the additional resources dedicated to management and oversight would lead to enhanced monitoring, evaluation and impact; assessment; information-sharing and transparency, and coordination with other programmes.

In July [A/62/7/Add.40], ACABQ recommended acceptance of the proposals put forth in the Secretary-General's report under Programme support. It also recommended that the Secretary-General be requested to carry out a comprehensive assessment of programme activities of the Unit and its actual impact on the delivery of activities funded from the Development Account, and report thereon in the context of the programme performance report.

In response to section VIII of General Assembly resolution 62/238 [YUN 2007, p. 1453], the Secretary-General submitted an August report [A/63/335] on the Development Account. It included the status of implementation of projects funded from additional resources provided under Assembly resolutions 62/235 A [YUN 2007, p. 1436] ($5 million); 62/238 [ibid., p. 1451] ($2.5 million); and 62/237 A [ibid., p. 1449] on the initial appropriation of the programme budget for the biennium 2008–2009 ($18,651,300). Nine entities would implement 15 new projects in the Asia and the Pacific and the Latin America and the Caribbean regions, and in Africa and Europe. Ten of the projects would be included in the programme budget for the 2006–2007 biennium and five would be included in the 2008–2009 biennium. All of the projects would assist in achieving the internationally agreed development goals.

The report also discussed the status of implementation of the provisions of section VIII of resolution 62/238 with regard to the identification of savings through the reduction in administrative and overhead costs. The Secretary-General noted in previous reports on the Development Account that while efficiency measures helped simplify processes, procedures, rules and services, improved the quality of services and had an impact on mandated programmes in the form of increased benefits, the results of the measures could not be quantified. He stated that identifying efficiency savings in order to increase the resources base of the Account had not been feasible.

In October [A/63/479], ACABQ stated that it was not convinced by the Secretary-General's argument concerning efficiency measures and pointed out that anticipated efficiency gains were calculated and routinely reflected in the budget submissions of peacekeeping operations. It suggested that the Secretary-General explore the possibility of using a similar approach in the regular budget. ACABQ also recommended that the General Assembly request the Secretary-General to develop a proper methodology to quantify savings from possible reductions, including in administration and other overhead costs, through improvements in internal procedures and ongoing human resources, information and communications technology and other management reforms, as well as resources released from discontinued activities and outputs. It expressed disappointment that the Secretary-General's report did not provide any options for tangible, predictable and sustainable funding for the Development Account, despite the concerns expressed by the Assembly in section VIII of resolution 62/238. The Committee repeated its recommendation that the Assembly might wish to review the Account in all its aspects.

The Assembly, in **resolution 63/260** of 24 December (see p. 1553), took note of the reports of the Secretary-General on improving the effective and efficient delivery of the mandates of development-related activities and revised estimates related to the programme budget for the 2008–2009 biennium and the Development Account; and endorsed the conclusions contained in the related ACABQ reports.

UN activities

Department of Economic and Social Affairs

During 2008, the UN Department of Economic and Social Affairs (DESA) had approximately 452 technical cooperation projects under execution in a dozen substantive sectors, with total project expenditures of $68.1 million. Projects financed by UNDP represented $4.2 million, and those by trust funds, $63.9 million. On a geographical basis, the Department's technical cooperation programme included expenditures of $36.8 million for Interregional and global programmes, $23.6 million in Asia and the Pacific, $4.9 million in Africa, $2.2 million in the Middle East; and $0.6 million in the Americas.

Distribution of expenditures by substantive sectors was as follows: associate expert programme, $26.6 million; programme support, $22.4 million; socio-economic governance management, $6.7 million; governance and public administration, $6 million; water, $2.6 million; knowledge management, $2.2 million; statistics, $1 million; energy, $0.2 million; social development, $0.2 million; the United Nations Forum on Forests, $0.2 million; and advancement of women, $0.01 million. Of the total delivery of $68.1 million, the associate expert programme comprised 39 per cent; programme support, 33 per cent; and socio-economic governance management, 10 per cent.

On a component basis, the Department's delivery in 2008 included $56.7 million for project personnel, $4.3 million for sub-contracts, $3.7 million for training, $2.7 million for equipment; and $0.7 million for miscellaneous expenses.

The total expenditure for DESA against the UN regular programme of technical cooperation was $4.9 million. The total expenditure against the UN Development Account (see p. 981) was $1.7 million.

UN Office for Partnerships

The United Nations Office for Partnerships, formed in 2006 [YUN 2006, p. 1046], served as the gateway for public-private partnerships with the UN system in furtherance of the MDGs. It oversaw the United Nations Fund for International Partnerships, the United Nations Democracy Fund, and Partnership Advisory Services and Outreach.

The Secretary-General, in his report on the activities of the Office in 2008 [A/64/91], said that the Office continued to help the underprivileged by harnessing interest, competencies and resources across sectors. Working with leaders in business and civil society, it provided a platform for strategic policy dialogue and engaged financial, technical and management expertise to achieve the MDGs. In 2008, the Office focused on building networks with organizations, leveraging their membership of more than 10,000 prospective partners.

The General Assembly, by **decision 63/548** of 24 December, took note of the Secretary-General's report on the 2007 activities of the Office for Partnerships [YUN 2007, p. 903].

UN Fund for International Partnerships

The United Nations Fund for International Partnerships (UNFIP) was established in 1998 [YUN 1998, p. 1297] to serve as an interface between the UN system and the United Nations Foundation, the public charity responsible for administering Robert E. Turner's $1 billion contribution in support of UN causes. At the end of 2008, the Foundation's allocations to UNFIP projects reached approximately $1.06 billion, which comprised $438.3 million in core Turner funds and $622.1 million (nearly 58.7 per cent) generated by other partners. More than 455 projects had been implemented by 39 UN entities in 123 countries.

At the end of 2008, the children's health portfolio of projects was valued at $638.6 million for 87 projects; the women and population portfolio, $137.4 million for 101 projects; the environment portfolio, $164 million for 144 projects; and the peace, security and human rights portfolio, $53.9 million for 60 projects. Sixty-three other projects were valued at $65.5 million.

United Nations Democracy Fund

The United Nations Democracy Fund (UNDEF) was established in 2005 [YUN 2005, p. 655] to support democratization throughout the world. UNDEF focused on supporting democratic institutions, promoting human rights and ensuring the participation of all groups in democratic processes. Through UNDEF, the UN Office for Partnerships had channelled a total of $58.7 million for 204 projects around the world, including 157 projects in 94 countries, 34 regional projects covering a further 13 countries, and 13 global projects. The projects were aimed at strengthening civil society leadership skills and promoting the participation of women and youth, among other issues, and included civil society media programmes. The majority of project funds went to local NGOs from countries in the transition and consolidation phases of democratization.

In 2008, UNDEF began funding its second round of projects. It launched its third round for project proposals in November; by year's end, it had received 2,143 applications from organizations in 138 countries, representing a 14 per cent increase over the number of applications received in the second (2007) round. The majority of the applications came from local or regional NGOs, with 34.1 per cent from sub-Saharan Africa, 23.8 per cent from Asia, 21 per cent from Europe, 10.4 per cent from the Americas, 8.6 per cent from Arab States, and 2.1 per cent from global organizations. The projects would support community development (24.8 per cent); women's empowerment (19.3 per cent); the rule of law and human rights (16.8 per cent); tools for democratization (13.5 per cent); youth (11.6 per cent); strengthening the instrumentalities of Government (7.9 per cent); and media (6.0 per cent). As at 31 December, total contributions to the Fund exceeded $91 million.

Partnership Advisory Services and Outreach

Partnership Advisory Services and Outreach, established in 2006, provided advice to various entities, including academic institutions, companies, foundations, Government agencies and civil society organizations, on how best to implement public-private partnerships. Investment in high-impact initiatives was encouraged by providing advice to potential partners both within and outside the UN system.

Regarding internal services, Governments, foundations, businesses and civil society organizations announced significant new commitments estimated at $16 billion to meet the MDGs. The commitments were made mainly during the more than 60 partnership events coordinated by the Office for Partnerships from 21 to 25 September. On the external front, the Office received nearly 1,000 requests for advisory services in 2008, a nearly 45 per cent increase over 2007. The requests came from a wide range of private-sector companies, foundations, civil society organizations, academic institutions and philanthropists. The majority of requests from non-State actors concerned assistance in partnering on programmes focused on poverty reduction, education, health and disaster relief, as well as humanitarian assistance in the least developed countries.

UN Office for Project Services

The United Nations Office for Project Services (UNOPS) was established in 1995 [YUN 1995, p. 900], in accordance with General Assembly decision 48/501 [YUN 1994, p. 806], as a separate, self-financing entity of the UN system to act as a service provider to UN organizations. It offered a broad range of services, from overall project management to the provision of single inputs.

2008 activities

The UNOPS Executive Director, in his annual report on UNOPS activities [DP/2009/22], informed the UNDP/UNFPA Executive Board of progress made in 2008 towards implementing the UNOPS business strategy, 2007–2009 [YUN 2007, p. 905], which focused on financial viability, client satisfaction, world-class business practices and performance, and workforce competence and motivation. Significant advances were made in generating income, boosting productivity, standardizing and refining business processes, and recruiting and retaining staff. UNOPS delivered $1.1 billion through project implementation in 2008 and spent $61.9 million administering it. The contribution to the operational reserve was $4.9 million, bringing the reserve to $30.1 million. However, bad debt provisions and write-offs, predominantly from the pre-2006 period, including the inter-fund balance with UNDP (see p. 984), amounted to $6.5 million. UNOPS business acquisition rose to $1.5 billion, representing an increase of 3.3 per cent over the previous year and an all-time record demand for UNOPS services.

The leading sectors for project implementation expenditures in 2008 were conflict prevention and resolution, peace and security (23 per cent of expenditures); health (18 per cent); Government and civil society (13 per cent); humanitarian aid (11.4 per cent); environmental protection (10.6 per cent); and transport and storage (9.9 per cent). The major sub-sectors included post-conflict peacebuilding (12.1 per cent); road transport (8.6 per cent); Government administration (8.5 per cent); landmine clearance (7.9 per cent), medical services (7.8 per cent) and material relief assistance and services (7.6 per cent).

The main financial initiatives implemented in 2008 included a financial data tool that enabled UNOPS to provide client reports in line with internationally accepted standards; further movement towards Atlas-based transaction processing; preparation of 2009–2010 budgets using the results-based budgeting process; the submission of revised UNOPS Financial Regulations and Rules to the Executive Board for its consideration; and the establishment of a project team to lead and implement the International Public Sector Accounting Standards (IPSAS) in UNOPS.

The report provided an overview of how UNOPS contributed to the results of UN peacekeeping, humanitarian and development operations. It contained information on project outputs and partnerships in education; emergency response and humanitarian relief; the environment; gender; governance; health; justice, security and public order; local economic development; and public works.

In June [dec. 2008/20], the UNDP/UNFPA Executive Board took note of the annual report of the Executive Director on 2007 activities [YUN 2007, p. 904] and requested the UNDP Administrator and the UNOPS Executive Director to report on the UNOPS governance structure at its September session (see p. 984).

Financial, administrative and operational matters

Budget estimates

The Executive Board, at its January session, considered a report on the UNOPS budget estimates for the 2008–2009 biennium [DP/2008/13]. The UNOPS Executive Director proposed a results-based budget of $120,009,900 for the 2008–2009 biennium. The proposal was based on a gross revenue target of

$133,343,900 and a resulting contribution to the operational reserve of $13,334,000 or 10 per cent of gross revenue. The budget proposals underpinned the specific objectives of the 2007–2009 UNOPS business strategy [YUN 2007, p. 905]. Specific priorities for the biennium included continued improvement and external certification of business practices; learning and certification of staff competencies; knowledge-sharing; and the introduction of IPSAS.

Estimated actual gross revenue for the 2006–2007 period amounted to $137.4 million; expenditures totalled $118.5 million. The resulting net revenue of $18.9 million exceeded the target of $13.7 million by $5.2 million.

In a decision adopted at the same session [dec. 2008/5], the Board approved the UNOPS budget contained in the report. It requested UNOPS and UNDP to finalize the settlement of the matter related to the balance of the inter-fund with UNDP [ibid.]. The Executive Director was requested to continue efforts to harmonize the UNOPS budget format with the biennial support budgets of other UN funds and programmes and contribute to improving the methodology of results-based budgeting. He was also asked to present the biennial support budget, 2010–2011, for the approval of the Board in 2009, and submit the UNOPS accountability framework and oversight policy for consideration and approval by the Board at its annual session in June 2008.

UNOPS governance structure

An August report [DP/2008/52] on the UNOPS governance structure contained a proposal to realign the Management Coordination Committee (MCC) to more effectively define and assign accountability for UNOPS in light of its evolution and future prospects as a self-financed provider of operational services. It was proposed that the role, functions, and composition of MCC be revised to permit it to perform a policy advisory function, and that it be renamed the Policy Advisory Committee to reflect its new focus. The proposed model would entrust the UNOPS Executive Director with full and independent authority and accountability for the conduct of UNOPS business. The Policy Advisory Committee would provide policy guidance to ensure that the strategy and activities of UNOPS corresponded to the broader objectives of the United Nations, and that they were coordinated with the work of other entities to ensure a complementary approach and avoid overlap. Responsibility for the use of UNOPS financial and other resources would lie with the Executive Director. It was proposed that the Committee's membership include the UNDP Administrator; the Chair of the CEB High-level Committee on Management; and the Under-Secretaries General of the Departments of Management and Field Services, and of the Office for the Coordination of Humanitarian Affairs.

During its September session [dec. 2008/35], the Executive Board took note of the report on the UNOPS governance structure and approved the amended role and function of MCC—to be renamed the Policy Advisory Committee—as outlined in the report. It requested UNOPS to submit to the Board in 2009 a comprehensively revised set of UNOPS financial regulations and rules, taking into account the changes in the UNOPS governance structure and the specifics of the UNOPS business model. The Board recommended that the Secretary-General delegate authority to the UNOPS Executive Director to administer UN staff rules and regulations in respect of UNOPS staff.

Audit reports

In May [DP/2008/21], the Head of the Internal Audit Office provided an activity report on internal audit and related services in UNOPS for the year ended 31 December 2007. Based on mutual agreement, the Office of Audit and Performance Review (OAPR) ended its services to UNOPS with effect from 30 June 2007 [YUN 2007, p. 906]. As part of the transition arrangement, the former chief of the Project Services Audit Section was assigned as officer-in-charge of the Internal Audit Office from 1 July until 10 September 2007, when the Office began to function as the UNOPS Internal Audit Office.

The Office stated that 24 audit reports were issued in 2007. The reports contained 145 recommendations for improving internal controls and organizational efficiency and effectiveness. The status of implementation of the 2007 recommendations as at 6 April 2008 was 67 per cent.

The Office assisted UNOPS management in the initial formulation and distribution of an internal control framework. It also assisted in preparing a settlement proposal with respect to the unresolved UNOPS/UNDP inter-fund differences prior to 2006 [YUN 2007, p. 906]; the Executive Director communicated the proposal to UNDP for discussion and approval. An internal audit charter containing the mandate, authority, responsibilities and general scope of work of the Internal Audit Office was submitted to the Executive Director and approved. The Office established channels of communication with other oversight groups in the United Nations, particularly with the UN Office of Internal Oversight Services and the Board of Auditors.

During its June session [dec. 2008/13], the Executive Board took note of the report of UNOPS on internal audit and oversight in 2007. It welcomed the establishment of the Internal Audit Office and the transition from OAPR to the new office.

In June, the Board of Auditors transmitted to the General Assembly the UNOPS financial report and audited financial statements for the biennium ended 31 December 2007 [A/63/5/Add.10]. The Board issued a modified opinion on the financial statements for the period under review. The unconfirmed difference in the inter-fund debt with UNDP, amounting to $9.9 million in 2005 had increased to approximately $33.9 million as at 31 December 2007. The UNOPS inter-fund account with UNFPA showed a difference of $0.6 million, which UNOPS was investigating. The Board obtained confirmations from five other UN agencies and noted differences amounting to $1.03 million. It was not able to confirm 21 balances from other entities that amounted to a net difference of $0.6 million. The Board reported shortcomings in asset management and noted significant errors in asset registers that supported the amount of $10.3 million disclosed in the financial statements. UNOPS performed a comprehensive review of all the submissions received from its regional offices and operations centres, and made adjustments of $2.3 million to the value of non-expendable property disclosed. The report contained 48 main recommendations based on the Board's audit observations.

In a July report [DP/2008/50], UNOPS provided a status report on the implementation of the recommendations of the Board of Auditors for the 2004–2005 biennium [YUN 2007, p. 906] and a summary of the management plan addressing the recommendations, including actions yet to be fully implemented. The Board acknowledged that of the 43 main recommendations made in the audit report, 23 (54 per cent) were fully implemented and 20 (46 per cent) were partially implemented by the end of 2007. UNOPS management was confident that the remaining 20 recommendations would be substantially implemented by the end of 2008.

UNOPS took steps to fund its operational reserve to the specified level in a timely manner. The UNOPS operational reserves for the year ending 31 December 2007 amounted to some $25.1 million, or 72.1 per cent of the mandatory reserve balance, representing a significant improvement in the UNOPS financial position. Regarding the creation of an accounts payable suspense account, UNOPS initiated discussions with the information technology development team to design a customized report in the Atlas enterprise resource planning system, to be ready by the end of 2008, that would allow close monitoring of the liquidation of such account balances. As at June 2008, UNOPS had collected 75 per cent of the outstanding rental receivables balance. UNOPS was continuing its clean-up exercise and hoped to liquidate most outstanding balances by the end of 2008. The inter-fund transaction first-time acceptance rate reached 98 per cent during the 2006–2007 biennium, and UNOPS pledged to do its utmost to liquidate all the long-outstanding inter-fund items by the end of 2008. As part of its drive to enhance internal controls, UNOPS put new procedures and tools in place during 2007 for the regular monitoring of project budgets and expenditures incurred.

During its September session, the Executive Board [dec. 2008/33], took note of the status report on the implementation of the recommendations of the Board of Auditors for the 2004–2005 biennium.

In October [DP/2009/6], UNOPS submitted a report on its implementation of the recommendations of the Board of Auditors for the 2006–2007 biennium. All of the Board's main recommendations were addressed in an annex to the report.

UNOPS accountability framework and oversight policies

In response to a January decision of the Executive Board (see p. 984), the UNOPS Executive Director submitted, in May [DP/2008/22], the draft UNOPS accountability framework and oversight policy. In June [dec. 2008/13], the Board requested the Executive Director to revert to the Board with the policy at its September session, ensuring coordination and harmonization with UNDP and UNFPA.

Pursuant to the Board's June decision, the Executive Director submitted a revised draft of the UNOPS accountability framework and oversight policies in an August report [DP/2008/55]. The framework, which aimed to strengthen UNOPS accountability, risk management and assurance processes, described the roles and responsibilities of the various parties and the resulting synergies that could enhance its oversight mechanisms. The report stated that during the 2006–2007 and 2008–2009 bienniums, UNOPS made significant progress in the areas of accountability, assurance, risk management, internal controls, and fraud prevention. It established the independent Strategy and Audit Advisory Committee to provide independent, senior-level advice to the Executive Director. UNOPS developed anti-fraud initiatives and adopted the UN "whistleblower" policy against retaliation for reporting wrongdoing. It also implemented a "balanced scorecard" programme—a performance-based, strategic management tool that provided stakeholders with a comprehensive indication of how the organization was progressing towards its strategic goals.

UNOPS updated and strengthened its internal control and risk management framework, formalized and implemented its cost recovery and pricing policy, and procured various business insurance policies as an integral part of its comprehensive risk management. It completed its information and communications technology strategy for 2008–2012 and introduced an individual contractor agreement, an essential tool for its business operations. Addressing two cornerstones of accountability for UNOPS—its staff and contract performance review systems—the Office established a comprehensive performance and results assessment programme, and planned to introduce, in the 2008–2009 biennium, project acceptance and contractor performance review policies.

The Executive Board, in a decision adopted during its September session [dec. 2008/37], approved the revised UNOPS accountability framework and oversight policies set out in the August report, subject to the provisions of the decision.

Procurement

A July report [DP/2008/43 & Corr.1] of the Inter-Agency Procurement Services Office (IAPSO) provided an update on IAPSO activities for the 2006–2007 biennium. UNDP and UNOPS initiated a partial merger of certain IAPSO functions with UNOPS in 2007 [YUN 2007, p. 905], which was successfully implemented on 1 January 2008. The Office continued to be self-financing, requiring no UNDP budget support to sustain its operations. It used the revenue it generated to invest in procurement capacity development for UNDP, and to support its inter-agency functions. Overall, the IAPSO fund balance increased from $9.4 million as at 1 January 2006 to $10.1 million as at 31 December 2007.

IAPSO played a major role in supporting procurement activities of UNDP country offices, mainly by providing procurement transaction services. It fielded over 30 missions to country offices to provide hands-on training to procurement staff. IAPSO was the resource for procurement support and advice in developing electoral assistance projects, including procurement strategies and plans, budget and timeline review, and procurement training. It provided support for business seminars and published consolidated statistics on UN system procurement.

By the end of 2006, UNDP country offices represented more than half of the total IAPSO procurement volume, a trend that slowed in 2007 due to the partial merger with UNOPS. During the 2006–2007 biennium, IAPSO continued to increase the range of supply markets in which it procured repeatedly, and sought to support that activity with long-term agreements.

In response to a 2007 Executive Board decision [ibid., p. 905], the UNOPS Executive Director submitted, in August, the annual statistical report on the procurement activities of UN system in 2007 [DP/2008/51]. UNOPS assumed responsibility for collecting and compiling the UN system-wide procurement data following its partial merger with IAPSO. The report stated that total UN system procurement of good and services under all sources of funding rose to $10.08 billion in 2007 from $9.4 billion in 2006, an increase of $679.5 million (about 6.7 per cent). Procurement of goods increased by $608 million, a gain of 2.7 per cent of total procurement volume, while the procurement of services grew by $71 million but decreased its share by 2.7 per cent of total procurement volume.

Although procurement from developing countries and countries with economies in transition increased by $198 million in 2007 over 2006, their share of overall total procurement volume decreased by 1.3 per cent, to 53.5 per cent. Procurement of goods and services from the top 20 developing countries and countries with economies in transition represented 33.7 per cent of overall UN procurement volume, an increase of 1 per cent over 2006.

At its September session, the Executive Board took note of the Administrator's report on IAPSO activities for the 2006–2007 biennium [dec. 2008/28] and the annual statistical report on the procurement activities of the UN system organizations [dec. 2008/34].

UN Volunteers

In 2008, 7,753 volunteers worked for the UNDP-administered United Nations Volunteers (UNV) programme, compared to 7,521 in 2007. The volunteers, representing 159 nationalities, carried out 7,991 assignments in 132 countries. Volunteers from developing countries represented 79 per cent of the total number; women accounted for 36 per cent. By region, 48 per cent of assignments were carried out in sub-Saharan Africa, 20 per cent in Asia and the Pacific, 16 per cent in the Arab States, 11 per cent in Latin America and the Caribbean, and 5 per cent in Europe and the Commonwealth of Independent States. Total contributions to UNV in 2008 amounted to $197 million; other income totalled $10.9 million. The total expenditure for the year was $207.9 million.

During its June session [dec. 2008/22], the Executive Board took note of the annual report of the Administrator on UNV activities for the 2006–2007 period [DP/2008/34]. It encouraged countries in a position to do so to contribute to the UNV Special Voluntary Fund to enable UNV to further expand and strengthen the role of volunteerism in development. The Board called on UN system organizations to increase their efforts towards achieving gender parity in the recruitment of volunteers, and reaffirmed its support for UNV as focal point for the follow-up (see below) to the International Year of Volunteers (2001) [YUN 2001, p. 814].

Follow-up to International Year of Volunteers (2001)

In response to General Assembly resolution 60/134 [YUN 2005, p. 981] the Secretary-General issued a July report [A/63/184] on the follow-up to the implementation of the International Year of Volunteers (2001). It discussed the state of volunteerism and developments with regard to the recognition of the contribution of volunteerism to development; the facilitation and promotion of volunteerism; networking; and volunteerism in the UN system. The report also contained proposals on possible ways to mark the tenth anniversary of the International Year in 2011. Ideas on possible actions had emerged from extensive consultations with Governments, civil society and the UN system. Multi-stakeholder International Year committees could be re-established to plan and implement activities. Some committees established in 2001 still existed and had helped to "institutionalize" volunteering. Recognition of the contribution of volunteerism to development should be incorporated into Government and UN system policies to provide a solid basis for taking full advantage of the anniversary. Such recognition could be engendered in the wider population through high-profile cultural, sports and other events. International, regional and national media events could link broadcasters across the world to showcase the best of volunteering, including through performances, documentaries, and interviews with celebrities and political leaders. On International Volunteer Day for Economic and Social Development (5 December), all public sector and UN system employees could be given the opportunity to volunteer with a cause of their choice.

GENERAL ASSEMBLY ACTION

On 18 December [meeting 70], the General Assembly, on the recommendation of the Third (Social, Humanitarian and Cultural) Committee [A/63/424], adopted **resolution 63/153** without vote [agenda item 55 *(b)*].

Follow-up to the implementation of the International Year of Volunteers

The General Assembly,

Recalling its resolution 60/134 of 16 December 2005 on the follow-up to the International Year of Volunteers,

Noting that the momentum created by the International Year has contributed to the vibrancy of volunteerism globally with the involvement of more people, from a broader cross-section of societies,

Recognizing that volunteerism is an important component of any strategy aimed at, inter alia, such areas as poverty reduction, sustainable development, health, disaster prevention and management and social integration and, in particular, overcoming social exclusion and discrimination,

Recognizing also that volunteerism makes significant contributions to development and that appropriate policies are needed to ensure that this potential is realized,

Acknowledging the existing contribution of the organizations of the United Nations system to supporting volunteering, especially the work of the United Nations Volunteers programme around the world, and acknowledging also the efforts of the International Federation of Red Cross and Red Crescent Societies to promote volunteerism throughout its global network,

Bearing in mind the need for an integrated and coordinated follow-up to the International Year to be pursued in the relevant parts of the United Nations system,

1. *Welcomes* the report of the Secretary-General;

2. *Reaffirms* the need to recognize and promote all forms of volunteerism as an issue that involves and benefits all segments of society, including women, children, young persons, older persons, persons with disabilities, minorities, migrants and those who remain excluded for social or economic reasons;

3. *Recognizes* the importance of supportive legislative and fiscal frameworks for the growth and development of volunteerism, and encourages Governments to enact such measures;

4. *Welcomes* the work of Governments, the United Nations system and other stakeholders to create a supportive environment for the promotion of volunteerism;

5. *Takes note* of the actions by Governments to support volunteerism, and reiterates its call upon them to continue such action;

6. *Acknowledges* the importance of civil society organizations for the promotion of volunteerism, and in that respect recognizes that strengthening the dialogue and interaction between civil society and the United Nations contributes to the expansion of volunteerism;

7. *Encourages* Governments to establish partnerships with civil society in order to build up volunteer potential at the national level, given the important contribution that volunteerism makes to the fulfilment of the internationally agreed development goals, including those contained in the United Nations Millennium Declaration;

8. *Welcomes* the expanding involvement of the private sector in support of volunteerism, and encourages Governments to support this trend;

9. *Invites* Governments to mobilize and support the research community globally to carry out more studies on the subject of volunteerism, in partnership with civil society, in order to provide sound knowledge as a foundation for policies and programmes;

10. *Recognizes* that greater efforts are needed to ensure that climate change and the environment feature on the volunteerism agenda of Governments and the United Nations;

11. *Calls for* the relevant organizations and bodies of the United Nations system to integrate volunteerism in its various forms into their policies, programmes and reports, and encourages the recognition and inclusion of volunteer contributions in future United Nations and other relevant international conferences;

12. *Reaffirms* its recognition of the work of the United Nations Volunteers programme as the focal point for the

follow-up to the International Year of Volunteers, and requests it to continue to raise awareness of the contribution of volunteerism to peace and development, to act as a convener on the subject for the various interested stakeholders, to make available networking and reference resources and to provide technical cooperation to developing countries, upon their request;

13. *Invites* the Commission for Social Development to consider "volunteerism for development" in the context of its theme of social integration at its forty-seventh and forty-eighth sessions, in 2009 and 2010 respectively;

14. *Decides* that, on or around 5 December 2011, the International Volunteer Day for Economic and Social Development, two plenary meetings of the sixty-sixth session of the General Assembly shall be devoted to follow-up to the International Year and the commemoration of its tenth anniversary, under the item entitled "Social development";

15. *Invites* Governments, with the active support of the media, civil society and the private sector, as well as development partners and the relevant organizations and bodies of the United Nations system, to carry out activities focused on marking the tenth anniversary of the International Year, in 2011, at the regional and national levels;

16. *Requests* the Secretary-General to report to the General Assembly at its sixty-seventh session on the implementation of the present resolution under the item entitled "Social development".

Economic and technical cooperation among developing countries

South-South cooperation

The UNDP/UNFPA Executive Board, at its January session, considered the evaluation of the UNDP contribution to South-South cooperation [DP/2008/8]. The evaluation addressed the nature and extent of support provided by the Special Unit for South-South Cooperation and UNDP in promoting and expanding South-South cooperation, and their ability to learn from experience and strengthen and institutionalize support to such cooperation across all UNDP practice areas. It considered the appropriateness, relevance, effectiveness and sustainability of UNDP efforts, as well as UNDP preparedness to address emerging demands.

The evaluation found that the effectiveness of support under the third cooperation framework for South-South cooperation, endorsed by the Executive Board in 2005 [YUN 2005, p. 982], was constrained by a mismatch between the mandate, resources and implementation strategy of the Special Unit. UNDP was a responsive partner at the country level, but its effectiveness was constrained by uneven recognition, inadequate resources and incentives, and an inability to systematize learning. UNDP and the Special Unit had not fully leveraged their collective strengths and capacities. The evaluation recommended that the fourth cooperation framework be shaped around knowledge-sharing, policy development and advocacy, and innovation. In programming initiatives, the Special Unit should adopt strict criteria and leverage the capacities of UNDP and other UN organizations to enhance the contribution of South-South cooperation to development effectiveness. UNDP should develop a corporate strategy on South-South cooperation that addressed emerging issues, drew on its experience, integrated its programme frameworks and was underpinned by resources, incentives and accountability. It should also define clear collaboration arrangements between the Special Unit and UNDP.

UNDP management, in its response to the evaluation [DP/2008/9], stated that it was committed to establishing a more effective, integrated approach to South-South cooperation, based on a clearer division of responsibilities across the organization and a closer, mutually supportive collaboration with the Special Unit. It acknowledged that its extensive capacity with respect to regional service centres, thematic knowledge networks and communities of practice should be leveraged further to facilitate South-South cooperation more systematically. UNDP was reviewing and clarifying its role in middle-income countries.

In January [dec. 2008/8], the Executive Board took note of the evaluation of the UNDP contribution to South-South cooperation and the management response. It approved the one-year extension, until 31 December 2008, of the third cooperation framework for South-South cooperation, as discussed in a 2007 note by the UNDP Administrator [YUN 2007, p. 908].

In June [dec. 2008/25], the Executive Board took note of the draft fourth cooperation framework for South-South cooperation (2009–2011) [DP/CF/SSC/4].

At its September session, the Executive Board considered a later draft of the fourth cooperation framework, issued in July [DP/CF/SSC/4/Rev.1]. Under the framework, the Special Unit would work to develop and provide all interested partners with the policy tools necessary to help developing countries build capacities to achieve their development goals, as well as internationally agreed development goals, including the MDGs, through South-South and triangular cooperation. The Special Unit would continue to focus its work in three strategic areas: policy dialogue, development and advocacy; the promotion of South-South knowledge- and experience-sharing by development partners; and the piloting of mechanisms and partnerships for scaling up South-South exchanges.

At the same session [dec. 2008/36], the Executive Board took note of the fourth cooperation framework and requested that UNDP take into account the recommendations made by Member States in its implementation.

Preparations for high-level conference on South-South Cooperation

In a 5 November letter [A/C.2/63/7], the General Assembly President transmitted to the Second Committee Chairperson the October report of the President of the High-level Committee on South-South Cooperation concerning the proposed High-level United Nations Conference on South-South Cooperation. The report was prepared in response to Assembly resolution 62/209 [YUN 2007, p. 908], in which the Assembly decided to convene the Conference on the occasion of the thirtieth anniversary of the adoption of the 1978 Buenos Aires Plan of Action for Promoting and Implementing Technical Cooperation among Developing Countries [YUN 1978, p. 467], no later than the first half of 2009. The report summarized the consultations undertaken by the President of the High-level Committee with Member States to prepare for the Conference, as well as the outcomes and recommendations of those consultations.

GENERAL ASSEMBLY ACTION

On 19 December [meeting 72], the General Assembly, on the recommendation of the Second Committee [A/63/419], adopted **resolution 63/233** without vote [agenda item 54].

High-level United Nations Conference on South-South Cooperation

The General Assembly,

Reaffirming its resolution 33/134 of 19 December 1978, in which it endorsed the Buenos Aires Plan of Action for Promoting and Implementing Technical Cooperation among Developing Countries,

Recalling the 2005 World Summit Outcome,

Recalling also its resolution 62/209 of 19 December 2007, in which it decided to convene a High-level United Nations Conference on South-South Cooperation,

Taking note with appreciation of the report of the President of the High-level Committee on South-South Cooperation submitted pursuant to its resolution 62/209,

Taking note of the draft fourth cooperation framework for South-South cooperation (2009–2011) and the recommendations contained therein,

Reaffirming its previous relevant resolutions pertaining to South-South cooperation,

Requests that the President of the General Assembly entrust the President of the High-level Committee on South-South Cooperation with undertaking, while making use of the existing coordination mechanisms of the United Nations system, the necessary consultations with Member States in order to prepare for the proposed High-level United Nations Conference on South-South Cooperation, with a view to the Assembly taking a decision, during its sixty-third session, on the nature, date, budgetary implications, objectives and modalities of the Conference.

UN Capital Development Fund

The United Nations Capitol Development Fund (UNCDF) achieved its programmatic targets in 2008. The Fund expanded its interventions to 38 least developed countries (LDCs), of which 10 were post-conflict countries, from 31 in 2007. It was making progress towards expanding its programmes to 45 LDCs by 2011, as set out in the UNCDF investment plan (2008–2011). Its overall budget delivery rate stood at 70 per cent. The UNCDF performance rate in the decentralization and local development practice area was 77 per cent, and its performance rate in the inclusive finance practice area was 80 per cent.

Total income increased from $28.5 million in 2007 to $50.1 million in 2008, including $6 million managed by UNCDF on behalf of UNDP, in accordance with a 2007 Executive Board decision [YUN 2007, p. 910]. Contributions to UNCDF regular (core) resources increased by 51 per cent, from $15.6 million in 2007 to $23.5 million in 2008, including the $6 million contributed by UNDP. When other resources were factored in, there was an overall increase in contributions of 76 per cent over 2007. Total resources expenditures in 2008 amounted to $37 million, of which the local development practice area accounted for $22.1 million (72 per cent), slightly lower than the $23.8 million in expenditures recorded in 2007. The level of operational reserves remained at $22.6 million, the same level as in 2007.

During its January 2007 session, the UNDP/UNFPA Executive Board considered a report [DP/2008/12] on the UNCDF partnership framework with UNDP, proposed in 2007 [YUN 2007, p. 909], including programming and funding arrangements and the cost-recovery policy. Over the course of the previous year, UNDP and UNCDF worked to finalize the details of the strategic partnership. Most of the their objectives were achieved, and the two entities issued a joint guidance note for UNDP country offices and regional bureaux to inform them of the agreements reached. Outstanding actions were scheduled to be completed in six to 12 months. The report stated that issues related to financial alignment might require a decision by the Executive Board.

At the same session [dec. 2008/4], the Board took note of the report on the UNCDF partnership framework with UNDP. It decided that the UNCDF cost-recovery policy would entail a recovery rate of 7 per cent for recovery of indirect support costs for new third party contributions and a basic 3 per cent recovery rate of indirect support costs for all new programme country contributions. The Board requested UNCDF management to report on the implementation of the cost-recovery policy, including the impact of the applied rates on regular and other resources, as well as the use and allocation of indirect costs recovered, for consideration at the annual session in June. UNDP and UNCDF were asked to report to the Executive Board in 2009 on progress made in implementing the strategic partnership.

In April [DP/2008/33], UNCDF submitted to the Executive Board its results-oriented annual report, which outlined the programmatic, management and financial results achieved against established targets in 2007. The report reflected the Fund's efforts to monitor and improve performance in its two practice areas: decentralization and local development, and inclusive finance. In response to the Board's January decision (above), the report also included information on the implementation of the UNCDF cost-recovery policy. With an overall performance rate of 85 per cent in its decentralization and local development practice area and 76 per cent in its inclusive finance practice area, UNCDF achieved its programmatic targets. The Fund also performed well in terms of its objective of geographical expansion. By the end of 2007, it had programmes in 31 of the 49 LDCs. Contributions to regular resources increased from $13.9 million in 2006 to $15.6 million in 2007; contributions to other resources increased by 59 per cent, from $8.1 million to $12.9 million. Total income increased by almost 30 per cent, from $22 million in 2006 to approximately $28.5 million in 2007. The increase was not sufficient, however, to reach the 2007 regular resources target of $18.5 million. Regular resources expenditures increased from $16.8 million in 2006 to $19 million in 2007. Other resources expenditures increased to $9.7 million and accounted for one third of total programme expenditures. Headquarters expenditures increased from $4.6 million in 2006 to $5.4 million in 2007; the increase was largely attributable to the settlement of outstanding reimbursements to UNDP for services delivered in 2006 and a higher overall level of personnel expenditures, as vacant positions were filled.

In June [dec. 2008/21], the Executive Board took note of the UNCDF results-oriented annual report, including the section on the implementation of the UNCDF cost-recovery policy. It noted with concern that UNCDF did not reach its 2007 resource mobilization targets, despite the upward trend in regular and other resources. The Board reiterated its request that UNDP and UNCDF continue their efforts to secure stable funding for UNCDF activities, and its call on donor countries, and other countries in a position to do so, to provide and sustain additional funding support for UNCDF programmes and activities in the LDCs. UNCDF management was requested to report in 2009 on the implementation of the cost recovery policy, including the impact of the applied rates on regular and other resources, as well as the use and allocation of indirect costs recovered. The UNDP Administrator was asked to appoint, as soon as possible, a new Executive Secretary for UNCDF.

Chapter III

Humanitarian and special economic assistance

In 2008, the United Nations, through the Office for the Coordination of Humanitarian Affairs (OCHA), continued to mobilize and coordinate humanitarian assistance to respond to international emergencies. During the year, consolidated inter-agency and flash appeals were launched for Bolivia, the Central African Republic, Chad, Côte d'Ivoire, the Democratic Republic of Congo, Georgia, Haiti, Honduras, Iraq, Kenya, Kyrgyzstan, Liberia, Madagascar, Myanmar, the Occupied Palestinian Territory, Somalia, Southern Africa, the Sudan, Tajikistan, Uganda, West Africa, Yemen and Zimbabwe. OCHA received contributions for natural disaster assistance totalling $1.4 billion.

The Ad Hoc Advisory Groups on Guinea-Bissau and Haiti continued to develop long-term programmes of support for those countries. Due to progress made in Guinea-Bissau, and following the corresponding Group's recommendation, the Economic and Social Council terminated that Group's mandate in July.

In other development activities, the General Assembly held a high-level meeting on Africa's development needs in September and adopted a political declaration on the topic.

In 2008, some 354 disasters associated with natural hazards, such as earthquakes, floods, cyclones and droughts, caused 235,264 deaths and affected approximately 214 million people. The cost of natural disasters was estimated at $190 billion in economic damages. The relative economic impact of disasters was greatest in low- and middle-income countries. Efforts continued to implement the Hyogo Declaration and the Hyogo Framework for Action 2005–2015, the 10-year plan for reducing disaster risks, adopted at the World Conference on Disaster Reduction in 2005. Preparations were under way for the second session of the Global Platform for Disaster Risk Reduction scheduled for 2009.

During the year, the Economic and Social Council considered ways to strengthen United Nations humanitarian assistance coordination by implementing improved humanitarian response at all levels. Implementation of the humanitarian reform agenda advanced with the launch of the cluster approach in five new sudden-onset emergencies.

The Central Emergency Response Fund continued to allow for the rapid provision of assistance to populations affected by sudden-onset disasters and underfunded emergencies.

Humanitarian assistance

Coordination

Humanitarian affairs segment of the Economic and Social Council

The humanitarian affairs segment of the Economic and Social Council (15–17, 24 and 25 July) [A/63/3/Rev.1] considered, in accordance with Council **decision 2008/213**, the theme "Building capabilities and capacities at all levels for timely humanitarian assistance, including disaster risk reduction". It also convened panels on disaster risk reduction and preparedness: addressing the humanitarian consequences of natural disasters, including the impact of climate change; and on humanitarian challenges related to global food aid. On 29 April, the Council decided to hold an informal event on 15 July to discuss the transition from relief to development (**decision 2008/212**).

The Council considered the Secretary-General's May report [A/63/81-E/2008/71] on strengthening the coordination of UN emergency humanitarian assistance, submitted in response to General Assembly resolutions 46/182 [YUN 1991, p. 421] and 62/94 [YUN 2007, p. 915] and Council resolution 2007/3 [ibid., p. 913]. The report summarized humanitarian trends and challenges during the preceding year, including disasters associated with natural hazards and complex emergencies; examined ongoing challenges such as strengthening the coordination of humanitarian assistance, the use of foreign military assets in disaster relief and integrating a gender perspective in humanitarian assistance; and addressed the themes of the Council's humanitarian affairs segment (see above).

During the reporting period, the largest driver of disasters was the increased incidence and severity of extreme weather events, with nine out of every 10 being linked to climate change. The United Nations issued an unprecedented 15 funding appeals for sudden disasters, five more than in the previous year, of which 14 were climate-related. Some 414 disasters associated with climate change affected 234 million people and caused over 16,000 deaths. Floods or storms were responsible for 86 per cent of all natural disaster deaths and 98 per cent of populations affected by natural disasters. Since 1987, climate-related disasters had increased by almost 90 per cent, while geological hazards had increased by nearly 40 per cent, with part of the increase being attributed to better reporting. The humanitarian consequences of conflict remained high, with displacement continuing to be a major source of concern. The Office of the United Nations High Commissioner for Refugees (UNHCR) reported that by the end of 2007 there were 11.4 million refugees worldwide, and some 52 million displaced people due to violence and persecution or hazard-related disasters. Those figures included long-standing displaced populations in Colombia and Sri Lanka, as well as new population displacements in the Central African Republic, Chad, Iraq, Kenya, the Sudan and Somalia. In response to some of those needs, the 2008 humanitarian consolidated appeal reported that 25 million people would require humanitarian assistance at a cost of $3.8 billion. Meanwhile, the recent jumps in food and fuel prices, which had compounded the challenges of climate change and armed conflict and led to violent protests in some countries, posed a further threat as high food prices could sharply increase the incidence and depth of food insecurity. The World Bank predicted that in addition to the estimated 800 million people suffering from hunger, an additional 100 million people could be pushed into poverty by the food security crisis, thereby reversing progress towards the Millennium Development Goals (MDGs). The crisis had an immediate impact on the cost of humanitarian operations and could lead to significant additional demand for food, health and nutritional assistance. Consequently, global demand for humanitarian assistance was likely to increase in the coming decade. In May, the Secretary-General established a high-level task force on the global food security crisis (see p. 1343) that aimed to develop a comprehensive framework for action; humanitarian actors would play a central role, particularly in the short term.

Complex emergencies, those that were long-standing or those that arose from political unrest in countries that had previously enjoyed relative stability, remained a challenge. During six weeks of rioting in Kenya following the announced results of the disputed presidential election in December 2007 (see p. 326), more than 1,000 civilians were killed and 300,000 displaced. In more than 30 countries, violent riots and protests against the escalation of food prices could risk derailing critical development programmes. The five-year-old crisis in Darfur, which had displaced some 2.4 million people, mostly women and children, continued with no immediate end in sight. Sexual violence remained a significant problem, while two thirds of the population required some form of humanitarian assistance. Ongoing violence in Iraq and other aid delivery challenges were preventing millions from accessing essential services. The United Nations estimated that four million Iraqis were in urgent need of food assistance and only 40 per cent of the population had reliable access to safe drinking water. The situation in Somalia had deteriorated further, and it was estimated that two million people would be in need of humanitarian assistance or livelihood support in 2008, an increase of more than 50 per cent from 2007. In the Occupied Palestinian Territory, in Gaza, where 80 per cent of the population depended on humanitarian aid, the lockdown of crossing points into the Gaza Strip since June 2007 had impeded humanitarian aid from entering and being distributed. The United Nations and its humanitarian partners responded to such complex emergencies where they were able, and delivered timely assistance to people in need. However, in too many places humanitarian workers were denied access to populations in need and were attacked when trying to provide assistance. In that connection, the report provided an overview of the situation of humanitarian workers on the ground, including threats to their safety; emphasized the need for acceptance of, and respect for, the principles that underpinned humanitarian action; and noted the growing challenge to the application of humanitarian principles due to the increasingly blurred distinction between military and humanitarian civilian actors and the need for humanitarian actors to distinguish themselves from other actors in the field.

In the context of ongoing challenges, capacity and coordination in the field was bolstered by the cluster approach [YUN 2006, p. 1057], whereby thematic leads were designated for areas that had no clear, prior lead organization. The approach contributed to enhanced coordination, decision-making and partnerships among humanitarian actors. It was implemented during the reporting period in 12 out of 26 countries where resident and humanitarian coordinators were in place. That number was expected to increase throughout the rest of 2008 as more coordinators introduced the cluster approach to improve coordination in preparedness exercises and ongoing emergency response operations. The need for a common analytical framework that allowed humanitarian stakeholders to jointly determine humanitarian needs and priorities to ensure the timely, accountable and equitable provision of humanitarian assistance was stressed. In that regard, OCHA initiated a mapping of ongoing assessment initiatives in a bid to develop a global needs assessment framework for the joint collection and use of data. On financing aspects, significant success was achieved with pooled funding mechanisms. Donors had pledged $1.1 billion to the Central Emergency Response Fund since its inception, and the Fund had committed $708.9 million to 879 projects in 60 countries. A two-year evaluation of the Fund—as mandated by the General Assembly—was under way. The Secretary-General was expected to report on the evaluation findings to the Assembly at its sixty-third (2008) session. In other developments, an independent study commissioned by OCHA on the use of foreign military assets in disaster relief found that, while humanitarian relief was and should remain a predominantly civilian function, foreign military assets could play a valuable role in disaster relief operations. The effectiveness of using those assets, however, depended on the timeliness of deploying them and making them operational. Progress was achieved in integrating a gender perspective in humanitarian assistance with the update of the Inter-Agency Standing Committee (IASC) policy on gender equality, which was endorsed in May, and the launch of the coalition's "United Nations Action against Sexual Violence in Crisis" [YUN 2007, p. 1168], which harmonized the UN system's response to sexual violence in emergencies and supported field activities in several countries.

The Secretary-General observed that trends such as the increased incidence of climate-related disasters and the continued rise of food prices required a strengthened humanitarian response with enhanced coordination at all levels, as well as respect by all stakeholders of the humanitarian principles underpinning humanitarian assistance. He made a series of recommendations for consideration by States on promoting respect for the humanitarian principles of humanity, neutrality, impartiality and independence; facilitating the rapid and unimpeded passage of humanitarian personnel to populations in need; ensuring the safety and security of humanitarian personnel operating within their borders; developing risk reduction and preparedness measures against disasters in coordination with relevant actors and in accordance with the Hyogo Framework for Action [YUN 2005, p. 1015]; strengthening operational and legal frameworks for international disaster relief through implementation of internationally recognized guidelines; intensifying research to better understand the humanitarian consequences of climate change; increasing the availability of resources to meet global humanitarian challenges; and providing military assets for disaster relief based on humanitarian considerations and broadly disseminating guidelines on civil-military coordination, such as the Oslo Guidelines [YUN 1994, p. 823]. He called for support for the work of his high-level task force on the global food security crisis. He also urged the United Nations and humanitarian partners to ensure that all aspects of humanitarian response addressed equally the needs of women, girls, men and boys, including through the improved collection, analysis and reporting of sex- and age-disaggregated data.

Report of Secretary-General. The Council also had before it the report of the Secretary-General [A/63/84-E/2008/80] on strengthening emergency relief, rehabilitation, reconstruction and prevention in the aftermath of the 2004 Indian Ocean tsunami disaster (see p. 1032).

ECONOMIC AND SOCIAL COUNCIL ACTION

On 25 July [meeting 45], the Economic and Social Council adopted **resolution 2008/36** [draft: E/2008/L.28, orally revised], without vote [agenda item 5].

Strengthening of the coordination of emergency humanitarian assistance of the United Nations

The Economic and Social Council,

Reaffirming General Assembly resolution 46/182 of 19 December 1991 and the guiding principles contained in the annex thereto, and recalling other relevant Assembly and Economic and Social Council resolutions and agreed conclusions of the Council,

Welcoming the decision to consider the theme "Building capabilities and capacities at all levels for timely humanitarian assistance, including disaster risk reduction" at the humanitarian affairs segment of its substantive session of 2008,

Welcoming also the decision to hold panels on "Disaster risk reduction and preparedness: addressing the humanitarian consequences of natural disasters, including the impact of climate change" and "Humanitarian challenges related to global food aid, including enhancing international efforts and cooperation in this field" and to hold an informal event on "Coordination in the transition phase between emergency relief and sustainable recovery",

Expressing grave concern at the increase in the number of people affected by humanitarian emergencies, including those associated with natural hazards and complex emergencies, and at the increased impact of natural disasters as well as the displacement resulting from humanitarian emergencies,

Reaffirming the need for all actors engaged in the provision of humanitarian assistance in complex emergency situations and natural disasters to promote and fully respect the humanitarian principles of humanity, neutrality, impartiality and independence,

Reiterating the need to mainstream a gender perspective into humanitarian assistance in a comprehensive and consistent manner, and taking note of the updated policy of the Inter-Agency Standing Committee on gender equality in humanitarian action,

Expressing its deep concern at the increasing challenges posed to Member States and to the United Nations humanitarian response capacity by the consequences of natural disasters, including the impact of climate change, and by the humanitarian implications of the current global food crisis,

Condemning the increasing number of attacks and other acts of violence against humanitarian personnel, and expressing its deep concern about the implications for the provision of humanitarian assistance to populations in need,

Recognizing the clear relationship between emergency relief, rehabilitation and development, and reaffirming that, in order to ensure a smooth transition from relief to rehabilitation and development, emergency assistance must be provided in ways that will be supportive of recovery and long-term development, and that emergency measures should be seen as a step towards long-term development,

Welcoming the holding of the High-level Conference on World Food Security in Rome from 3 to 5 June 2008, and noting the importance of implementing its outcome, including those elements related to humanitarian assistance,

1. *Takes note* of the report of the Secretary-General on the strengthening of the coordination of emergency humanitarian assistance of the United Nations;

2. *Encourages* Member States to create and strengthen an enabling environment for the capacity-building of their national and local authorities, national societies of the Red Cross and Red Crescent, and national and local non-governmental and community-based organizations in providing timely humanitarian assistance, and also encourages the international community, the relevant entities of the United Nations system and other relevant institutions and organizations to support national authorities in their capacity-building programmes, including through technical cooperation and long-term partnerships based on recognition of their important role in providing humanitarian assistance;

3. *Stresses* that the United Nations system should make efforts to enhance existing humanitarian capacities, knowledge and institutions, including, as appropriate, through the transfer of technology and expertise to developing countries, and encourages the international community to support efforts of Member States aimed at strengthening their capacity to prepare for and respond to disasters;

4. *Urges* Member States to develop, update and strengthen disaster preparedness and risk reduction measures at all levels, in accordance with priority 5 of the Hyogo Framework for Action, taking into account their own circumstances and capacities and in coordination with relevant actors, as appropriate, and encourages the international community and relevant United Nations entities to continue to support national efforts in this regard;

5. *Encourages* Member States and, where applicable, regional organizations to strengthen operational and legal frameworks for international disaster relief, taking into account, as appropriate, the Guidelines for the Domestic Facilitation and Regulation of International Disaster Relief and Initial Recovery Assistance, adopted at the thirtieth International Conference of the Red Cross and Red Crescent, held in Geneva in November 2007;

6. *Calls upon* the relevant organizations of the United Nations system and, as appropriate, other relevant humanitarian actors to continue to strengthen the coordination of humanitarian assistance at the field level, including with national authorities of the affected State, as appropriate, and to further enhance transparency, performance and accountability;

7. *Recognizes* the benefits of engagement of and coordination with relevant humanitarian actors to the effectiveness of humanitarian response, and encourages the United Nations to continue to pursue efforts to strengthen partnerships at the global level with the International Red Cross and Red Crescent Movement, relevant humanitarian non-governmental organizations and other participants of the Inter-Agency Standing Committee;

8. *Urges* Member States to continue to take the necessary steps to ensure the safety and security of humanitarian personnel operating within their borders, recognizes the need for appropriate collaboration between humanitarian actors and relevant authorities of the affected State in matters related to their safety and security, requests the Secretary-General to continue his efforts to contribute to enhancing the safety and security of personnel involved in United Nations humanitarian operations, and urges Member States to ensure that perpetrators of crimes committed on their territory against humanitarian personnel do not operate with impunity and are brought to justice as provided for by national laws and obligations under international law;

9. *Welcomes* decisions taken during the United Nations Climate Change Conference in 2007, in particular the Bali Action Plan, encourages Member States, as well as regional organizations and relevant international organizations, in accordance with their specific mandates, to support adaptation to the effects of climate change and to strengthen disaster risk reduction and early warning systems in order to minimize the humanitarian consequences of natural disasters, including the impact of climate change, and also encourages relevant entities to continue research on these humanitarian implications;

10. *Takes note* of the recent establishment by the Secretary-General of the High-level Task Force on the Global Food Security Crisis, and encourages its continued engagement with Member States;

11. *Takes note with interest* of the section on the use of foreign military assets in disaster relief contained in the report of the Secretary-General on the strengthening of the coordination of emergency humanitarian assistance of the United Nations, emphasizes the fundamentally civilian character of humanitarian assistance, and reaffirms the need, in situations where military capacity and assets are used to support the implementation of humanitarian assistance, for their use to be undertaken with the consent of the affected State and in conformity with international law, including international humanitarian law, as well as humanitarian principles;

12. *Recalls* the Guidelines on the Use of Foreign Military and Civil Defence Assets in Disaster Relief, also known as the Oslo Guidelines, stresses the value of their use, and invites Member States to raise awareness about them;

13. *Requests* Member States, relevant United Nations organizations and other relevant actors to ensure that all aspects of humanitarian response address the specific needs of women, girls, men and boys, including through the improved collection, analysis and reporting of sex- and age-disaggregated data, taking into account, inter alia, the available information provided by States;

14. *Urges* Member States to continue to prevent, investigate and prosecute acts of gender-based violence, including sexual violence in humanitarian emergencies, calls upon Member States and relevant organizations to strengthen support services to victims of such violence, and also calls for a more effective response in this regard;

15. *Welcomes* the continued efforts to strengthen the humanitarian response capacity and the progress made in strengthening support to resident/humanitarian coordinators, including by improving their identification, selection and training, in order to provide a timely, predictable and appropriate response to humanitarian needs and to strengthen United Nations coordination activities at the field level, and requests the Secretary-General to continue efforts in this regard, in consultation with Member States;

16. *Encourages* Member States, the private sector and other relevant entities to make contributions and consider increasing their contributions to humanitarian funding mechanisms, including consolidated and flash appeals, the Central Emergency Response Fund and other funds,

based on and in proportion to assessed needs, as a means of ensuring flexible, predictable, timely, needs-based and, where possible, multi-year and additional resources, to meet global humanitarian challenges;

17. *Calls upon* United Nations humanitarian organizations, in consultation with Member States, as appropriate, to strengthen the evidence base for humanitarian assistance by further developing common mechanisms to improve the quality, transparency and reliability of humanitarian needs assessments, to assess their performance in assistance and to ensure the most effective use of humanitarian resources by these organizations;

18. *Requests* the Secretary-General to reflect the progress made in the implementation of and follow-up to the present resolution in his next report to the Economic and Social Council and to the General Assembly on the strengthening of the coordination of emergency humanitarian assistance of the United Nations.

Humanitarian reform agenda

In 2008, reform became the humanitarian norm and significant improvements were made within the international humanitarian system. Coordination leadership was strengthened through increased accountability; partnerships between the United Nations and non-UN parts of the humanitarian system were further reinforced; the cluster approach [YUN 2006, p. 1057] was rolled out in five sudden-onset emergencies that arose during the year; and pooled funding at the global and national level made a major contribution to humanitarian relief and coordination. An increasing amount of funding—a total of $859 million—was funnelled through humanitarian pooled funds managed by OCHA.

During the year, humanitarian partners focused on implementing and further integrating the various pillars of reform, thereby overhauling humanitarian coordination and ensuring a tighter, more robust delivery of humanitarian assistance. Working with IASC partners, efforts were made to ensure closer integration and coherence of the mutually reinforcing elements constituting reform—leadership, coordination, partnership and financing—to sustain a stronger framework for humanitarian action. Key improvements helped systematize humanitarian leadership, including the revision of the Terms of Reference for Resident and Humanitarian Coordinators (RC/HCs); the re-launch of the HC pool to develop a professional, transparent and participatory selection system; the signing of compacts between the Emergency Relief Coordinator and HCs; and the development of the RC/HC/Designated Official Performance Appraisal System to strengthen accountability. Progress was made on the implementation of the cluster approach, particularly at the field level, with 21 of 27 countries with HCs reaching an agreement on using the approach. Improvements were evident in the response to the surge of humanitarian needs in Gaza, Georgia, Haiti, Myanmar and Sri Lanka. In addition to strengthening partnerships on the ground, OCHA strengthened partnerships at the global level. Three new non-governmental organizations (NGOs) became members of the IASC Principals Forum. The Global Humanitarian Platform, which met for the second time in July, stepped up its efforts to broaden the inclusion of national NGOs. More predictable humanitarian financing at the country level helped strengthen the efficacy of response. OCHA established a Funding Coordination Section to better oversee country-based pooled funds and strengthen coherence among pooled funding mechanisms. OCHA also played a key role in the Secretary-General's Policy Committee (PC) decision on integration in June, which reaffirmed "integration" as the guiding principle in an integrated UN presence and stipulated that integration arrangements should take full account of humanitarian principles and safeguard humanitarian space, while facilitating coordination with all humanitarian actors. The need to operationalize the PC decision led OCHA to initiate a Policy Instruction on OCHA Structural Relationships within an Integrated UN Presence that clarified how and under what conditions decisions were made about the structural aspects of integration. The Office also increased its engagement in the Integrated Missions Planning Process, including the revision of guidelines for both headquarters and field-level planning.

Global Cluster Approach Evaluation. Following the 2005 Humanitarian Response Review [YUN 2005, p. 991], IASC established the "cluster leadership approach" as a mechanism to improve humanitarian response effectiveness and to strengthen partnerships among all humanitarian actors [YUN 2006, p. 1057], and requested an evaluation of the cluster approach after two years. The first phase of the evaluation took place in 2007, while the second phase was to be commissioned in 2008 [YUN 2007, p. 915]. The early part of the year provided an opportunity to reflect on the findings of the Phase I Cluster Evaluation and to address collectively many of its recommendations. A steering group led by OCHA and composed of donors, NGOs and UN agencies was established to develop the terms of reference for the Phase II Cluster Evaluation. Consequently, in August, OCHA issued a "Revised Note on a proposed Approach for the Cluster Evaluation phase II", which described the purpose, objectives and scope, and organizational approach of the second evaluation, as well as key issues it would address. The evaluation, which aimed to assess the main outcomes of the joint humanitarian response at country level and the overall effectiveness of the approach in facilitating and supporting the coordinated joint humanitarian response at that level through a global analysis of common country-level findings, would be launched in different phases and would take place between August 2008 and September 2009. The phases involved the following: the development of methodology, frameworks and guidance; country-level evaluations; country surveys conducted by one or more survey specialists; and synthesis of the country-level evaluations, studies and surveys.

Other developments. In other efforts, IASC continued to clarify its operational guidance on the use of the cluster approach. In July, the Operational Guidance on the Concept of "Provider of Last Resort", which set out the responsibilities of cluster leads in the field, was endorsed. Meanwhile, the Steering Group developed a framework for Phase II of the cluster evaluation, which was expected to begin in May 2009 and would be conducted in six countries. With the leadership of OCHA and the Global Cluster Leads, a cluster evaluation management response matrix was finalized and a monitoring plan was initiated.

GENERAL ASSEMBLY ACTION

On 11 December [meeting 68], the General Assembly adopted **resolution 63/139** [draft: A/63/L.49 & Add.1] without vote [agenda item 65 *(a)*].

Strengthening of the coordination of emergency humanitarian assistance of the United Nations

The General Assembly,

Reaffirming its resolution 46/182 of 19 December 1991 and the guiding principles contained in the annex thereto, other relevant General Assembly and Economic and Social Council resolutions and agreed conclusions of the Council,

Taking note of the reports of the Secretary-General on the strengthening of the coordination of emergency humanitarian assistance of the United Nations and on the Central Emergency Response Fund, and of the independent review of the Central Emergency Response Fund, a summary of which is presented in the latter report,

Reaffirming the principles of neutrality, humanity, impartiality and independence for the provision of humanitarian assistance,

Deeply concerned about the impact of the current global food crisis and the urgent humanitarian challenges related to this crisis, welcoming the establishment by the Secretary-General of the High-level Task Force on the Global Food Security Crisis, and emphasizing the importance of implementing the Comprehensive Framework for Action,

Emphasizing the need to mobilize adequate, predictable, timely and flexible resources for humanitarian assistance based on and in proportion to assessed needs, with a view to ensuring fuller coverage of the needs in all sectors and across humanitarian emergencies, and in this regard recognizing the achievements of the Central Emergency Response Fund,

Expressing its deep concern at the increasing challenges faced by Member States and the United Nations humanitarian response capacity as a result of the consequences of natural disasters, including the impact of climate change, reaffirming the importance of implementing the Hyogo Framework of Action 2005–2015: Building the Resilience of Nations and Communities to Disasters, including by providing adequate resources for disaster risk reduction, including disaster preparedness,

Emphasizing that enhancing international cooperation on emergency humanitarian assistance is essential, and reaffirming its resolution 63/141 of 11 December 2008 on international cooperation on humanitarian assistance in the field of natural disasters,

Noting with grave concern that violence, including gender-based violence, including sexual violence, and violence against children, continues to be deliberately directed against civilian populations in many emergency situations,

Condemning the increasing number of deliberate violent attacks against humanitarian personnel and facilities and the negative implications for the provision of humanitarian assistance to populations in need,

Paying tribute to all humanitarian personnel, including United Nations and associated personnel, who have worked to promote the humanitarian cause, as well as to those who have perished in the cause of duty,

Recognizing that building national and local preparedness and response capacity is critical to a more predictable and effective response,

Noting with appreciation the efforts made by the United Nations to improve humanitarian response, including by strengthening humanitarian response capacities, improving humanitarian coordination, enhancing predictable and adequate funding and strengthening accountability to all stakeholders,

Recognizing that in strengthening the coordination of humanitarian assistance in the field, United Nations organizations should continue to work in close coordination with national Governments,

1. *Takes note* of the outcome of the eleventh humanitarian affairs segment of the Economic and Social Council at its substantive session of 2008;

2. *Requests* the Emergency Relief Coordinator to continue his efforts to strengthen the coordination of humanitarian assistance, and calls upon relevant United Nations and other relevant intergovernmental organizations, as well as other humanitarian and relevant development actors, to continue to work with the Office for the Coordination of Humanitarian Affairs of the Secretariat to enhance the coordination, effectiveness and efficiency of humanitarian assistance;

3. *Calls upon* the relevant organizations of the United Nations system and, as appropriate, other relevant humanitarian actors, to continue efforts to improve the humanitarian response to natural and man-made disasters and complex emergencies by further strengthening the humanitarian response capacities at all levels, by continuing to strengthen the coordination of humanitarian assistance at the field level, including with national authorities of the affected State, as appropriate, and by further enhancing transparency, performance and accountability;

4. *Recognizes* the benefits of engagement and coordination with relevant humanitarian actors to the effectiveness of humanitarian response, and encourages the United Nations to continue to pursue efforts to strengthen partnerships at the global level with the International Red Cross and Red Crescent Movement, relevant humanitarian non-

governmental organizations and other participants in the Inter-Agency Standing Committee;

5. *Requests* the Secretary-General to strengthen the support provided to United Nations resident/humanitarian coordinators and to United Nations country teams, including through the provision of necessary training, the identification of resources and by improving the identification of and selection process for United Nations resident/humanitarian coordinators;

6. *Reaffirms* the importance of implementing the Hyogo Framework for Action 2005–2015: Building the Resilience of Nations and Communities to Disasters, and calls upon national Governments and the international community to increase resources towards disaster risk reduction measures, including for preparedness for effective response and contingency planning;

7. *Encourages* the international community, including relevant United Nations organizations and the International Federation of Red Cross and Red Crescent Societies, to support efforts of Member States aimed at strengthening their capacity to prepare for and respond to disasters and to support efforts, as appropriate, to strengthen systems for identifying and monitoring disaster risk, including vulnerability and natural hazards;

8. *Recognizes* the importance of the work of international and, as appropriate, regional organizations in supporting State efforts to improve international cooperation in disaster response, and encourages Member States and, where applicable, regional organizations to strengthen operational and legal frameworks for international disaster relief, taking into account, as appropriate, the Guidelines for the Domestic Facilitation and Regulation of International Disaster Relief and Initial Recovery Assistance, adopted at the Thirtieth International Conference of the Red Cross and Red Crescent, held in Geneva from 26 to 30 November 2007;

9. *Urges* Member States, the United Nations and other relevant organizations to take further steps to provide coordinated emergency response to food and nutrition needs of affected populations, while aiming to ensure that these measures are supportive of national strategies and programmes aimed at improving food security;

10. *Encourages* States to create an enabling environment for the capacity-building of local authorities and national and local non-governmental and community-based organizations in order to ensure better preparedness in providing humanitarian assistance;

11. *Encourages* efforts to enhance cooperation and coordination of United Nations humanitarian entities, other relevant humanitarian organizations and donor countries with the affected State, with a view to planning and delivering emergency humanitarian assistance in ways that are supportive of early recovery as well as sustainable rehabilitation and reconstruction efforts;

12. *Also encourages* efforts to provide education in emergencies, including in order to contribute to a smooth transition from relief to development;

13. *Calls upon* relevant United Nations organizations to support the improvements of the consolidated appeals process, inter alia, by engaging in the preparation of needs analysis and common humanitarian action plans, in order to further the development of the process as an instrument for United Nations strategic planning and prioritization, and by involving other relevant humanitarian organizations in the process, while reiterating that consolidated appeals are prepared in consultation with affected States;

14. *Calls upon* United Nations humanitarian organizations, in consultation with Member States, as appropriate, to strengthen the evidence base for humanitarian assistance by further developing common mechanisms to improve the quality, transparency and reliability of humanitarian needs assessments, to assess their performance in assistance and to ensure the most effective use of humanitarian resources by these organizations;

15. *Calls upon* donors to provide adequate, timely, predictable and flexible resources based on and in proportion to assessed needs, including for underfunded emergencies, and encourages efforts to adhere to the principles of Good Humanitarian Donorship;

16. *Welcomes* the important achievements made by the Central Emergency Response Fund in ensuring a more timely and predictable response to humanitarian emergencies, and stresses the importance of addressing the findings and recommendations contained in the report on the Central Emergency Response Fund, in order to ensure that the resources are used in the most efficient, effective and transparent manner possible;

17. *Calls upon* all Member States and invites the private sector and all concerned individuals and institutions to consider increasing voluntary contributions to the Central Emergency Response Fund, and emphasizes that contributions should be additional to current commitments to humanitarian programming and not to the detriment of resources made available for international cooperation for development;

18. *Requests* the Secretary-General to commission an independent comprehensive review of the activities of the Central Emergency Response Fund, including the ability to meet its objectives, its administration, the needs assessment process and criteria for resource allocations, at the end of its fifth year of operation, and to submit a report on its findings and recommendations to the General Assembly at its sixty-sixth session;

19. *Invites* Member States, the private sector and all concerned individuals and institutions to consider voluntary contributions to other humanitarian funding mechanisms;

20. *Reiterates* that the Office for the Coordination of Humanitarian Affairs should benefit from adequate and more predictable funding;

21. *Reaffirms* the obligation of all States and parties to an armed conflict to protect civilians in armed conflicts in accordance with international humanitarian law, and invites States to promote a culture of protection, taking into account the particular needs of women, children, older persons and persons with disabilities;

22. *Calls upon* States to adopt preventive measures and effective responses to acts of violence committed against civilian populations in armed conflicts and to ensure that those responsible are promptly brought to justice, as provided for by national law and obligations under international law;

23. *Urges* all Member States to address gender-based violence in humanitarian emergencies and to ensure

that their laws and institutions are adequate to prevent, promptly investigate and prosecute acts of gender-based violence, and calls upon States, the United Nations and all relevant humanitarian organizations to improve coordination, harmonize response and strengthen capacity in support services to victims of such violence;

24. *Recognizes* the Guiding Principles on Internal Displacement as an important international framework for the protection of internally displaced persons, encourages Member States and humanitarian agencies to continue to work together in endeavours to provide a more predictable response to the needs of internally displaced persons, and in this regard calls for international support, upon request, for capacity-building efforts of States;

25. *Calls upon* all States and parties in complex humanitarian emergencies, in particular in armed conflict and in post-conflict situations, in countries in which humanitarian personnel are operating, in conformity with the relevant provisions of international law and national laws, to cooperate fully with the United Nations and other humanitarian agencies and organizations and to ensure the safe and unhindered access of humanitarian personnel, as well as delivery of supplies and equipment, in order to allow them to efficiently perform their task of assisting affected civilian populations, including refugees and internally displaced persons;

26. *Decides* to designate 19 August as World Humanitarian Day in order to contribute to increasing public awareness about humanitarian assistance activities worldwide and the importance of international cooperation in this regard, as well as to honour all humanitarian and United Nations and associated personnel who have worked in the promotion of the humanitarian cause and those who have lost their lives in the cause of duty, and invites all Member States and the entities of the United Nations system, within existing resources, as well as other international organizations and non-governmental organizations, to observe it annually in an appropriate manner;

27. *Requests* the Secretary-General to report to the General Assembly at its sixty-fourth session, through the Economic and Social Council at its substantive session of 2009, on progress made in strengthening the coordination of emergency humanitarian assistance of the United Nations and to submit a report to the Assembly on the detailed use of the Central Emergency Response Fund.

UN and other humanitarian personnel

In response to General Assembly resolution 62/95 [YUN 2007, p. 1504], the Secretary-General, in an August report [A/63/305 & Corr.1], provided updates on the safety and security of humanitarian and UN personnel over the preceding year and on the efforts by the UN Department of Safety and Security to implement that resolution. He expressed concern over the wide scale of threats, the rise in deliberate targeting of humanitarian and UN personnel and their vulnerability worldwide, particularly as hostage incidents and targeted attacks in areas of humanitarian emergencies continued unabated. He also indicated that locally recruited personnel of the UN and humanitarian organizations in conflict and post-conflict areas were most vulnerable.

The Assembly, in **resolution 63/138** of 11 December, called on Governments and parties in complex humanitarian emergencies to cooperate fully with the United Nations and other humanitarian agencies and organizations and to ensure the safe and unhindered access of humanitarian personnel (see p. 1611).

Resource mobilization

Central Emergency Response Fund

In 2008, the Central Emergency Response Fund (CERF), formerly known as the Central Emergency Revolving Fund [YUN 2006, p. 1061], a cash-flow mechanism for the initial phase of humanitarian emergencies established in 1992 [YUN 1992, p. 584], continued to allow for the rapid provision of assistance to populations affected by sudden-onset disasters and underfunded emergencies. The Fund was upgraded by General Assembly resolution 60/124 [YUN 2005, p. 991] to include a grant element, targeted at $450 million, to ensure the availability of immediate resources to address humanitarian crises. The loan element of the Fund continued to operate as a distinct and separately managed revolving fund with a target of $50 million. The 16-member CERF Advisory Group established to provide the Secretary-General with policy guidance and advice on the use and impact of the Fund met in June and November. In 2008, CERF reached its annual funding target for the first time, with over $453 million in pledges and contributions from donors. As at 31 December, $428.8 million in CERF funds had been allocated to support relief operations in 54 countries and the Occupied Palestinian Territory. In addition, by early December, some $380 million had already been secured towards the $450 million grant facility target for 2009.

Report of Secretary-General. In his October report on CERF [A/63/348], the Secretary-General provided information on its activities from 1 January 2007 to 30 June 2008, and on an evaluation of the Fund that was conducted after its second year of operation. The evaluation concluded that CERF had largely achieved its objectives and had become a valuable and impartial tool for humanitarian action by helping to speed up response and increase coverage of needs, and by serving as a catalyst for improved field-level coordination and evidence-based prioritization. Conversely, several challenges were also identified. The evaluation was conducted during the first half of 2008 by a team of independent consultants who focused on assessing the grant and loan elements of the Fund; its administration; the criteria for resource allocation; actions and responses supported by the Fund; and the Fund's ability to meet its objectives. In its report, the team presented its key findings, as well as

33 operational and four strategic recommendations, which included the progressive increase in the size of the Fund; improved consistency of the quality of CERF-funded programmes; strengthened capacity of the CERF secretariat and OCHA; and clarification of the multiple lines of accountability for CERF. As there was insufficient time to discuss the evaluation's findings and recommendations with key stakeholders, a detailed response to the evaluation would be compiled and provided at the General Assembly's 2008 plenary session on humanitarian affairs. On CERF activities, the Fund's loan mechanism continued to serve as a tool for UN system entities to bridge funding gaps caused by delays in the receipt of funding, with $41.3 million advanced in 2007, all to the Sudan, and another $30 million advanced through June 2008. On the grant component of the Fund, $350.9 million was committed to humanitarian projects in 2007, while some $249.1 million was committed in the first half of 2008.

The Secretary-General stated that the areas of improvement pinpointed by the evaluation would be taken up expeditiously to ensure that the Fund continued to build on its track record. In that connection, strengthening of the CERF Secretariat and ensuring that the Emergency Relief Coordinator had sufficient resources to meet the costs associated with the functioning, management and oversight of the Fund were key. He also observed that for the Fund to remain an effective response tool, it must be adequately supported so that it continued to reach the annual target of $500 million. He urged States to contribute to the Fund, including through early and multi-year commitments, and to support agencies' individual emergency reserves, in addition to country-based humanitarian pooled funds, such as emergency response funds and common humanitarian funds. He also encouraged the General Assembly to keep the Fund's progress under review and to consider requesting the conduct of another independent review in 2011.

Advisory Group meetings. At its June meeting, the CERF Advisory Group discussed the draft report of the two-year evaluation of CERF (see above), inter alia, in the context of observations and recommendations made by the Group during the course of its mandate; debated a range of issues related to the Fund's performance; and addressed outstanding challenges since its last meeting in October 2007 [YUN 2007, p. 918]. In a note issued following the meeting, the Group made a series of observations and recommendations based on updates by the Under-Secretary-General and Manager of the Fund; consultations with UN agencies, the International Organization for Migration, non-governmental organization (NGO) partners, and the Humanitarian/Resident Coordinator of the Democratic Republic of the Congo; and, in particular, discussions surrounding the evaluation of CERF with the team leader of the evaluation. Although the Group noted that they were in broad agreement with the report's conclusions and that the evaluation covered many issues and proposed recommendations that the Group had already raised, it called for a number of clarifications in the evaluation, including on analysis and evidence.

In November [A/63/665], the Group reviewed the management response to the evaluation of the Fund, the potential impact of the global financial crisis on the Fund and its performance since the Group's June meeting. It expressed concern about the impact of the global financial crisis on future CERF funding and noted that the high-level conference on 4 December would provide an early indication as to the effect of the crisis on donor behaviour. The Group made recommendations for the Fund to develop a resource mobilization strategy that included an adequate focus on small donors; explore complementarities with other funding sources; harmonize policies and procedures in accordance with the principles of good humanitarian donorship; and support only the highest-priority humanitarian projects. It also encouraged the CERF secretariat to strictly enforce the life-saving criteria when reviewing proposals. On the two-year evaluation, the Group supported its recommendations and the matrix summarizing the response of the Emergency Relief Coordinator. It noted that many of the recommendations had been implemented or were being implemented. Nonetheless, the most difficult outstanding issues, including partnerships, needs assessments and prioritization, reflected weaknesses in the overall humanitarian system and could not be resolved by the Fund itself. The Group proposed that the major challenges highlighted by the evaluation be divided into three strategic issues: performance and accountability, partnership arrangements, and the role of humanitarian/resident coordinators. It also recommended that OCHA play a leadership role in addressing systemic issues and lead the initiative to develop a performance and accountability framework to be used at the level of the overall humanitarian response, which could feed information to the Fund as required.

On 11 December, the General Assembly, in resolution 63/139 (see p. 996), requested the Secretary-General to commission an independent review of CERF and report on its findings and recommendations at the Assembly's sixty-sixth (2011) session.

Consolidated appeals

The consolidated appeals process, an inclusive and coordinated programme cycle for analysing context, assessing needs and planning prioritized humanitarian response, was the humanitarian sector's main strategic planning and programming tool. In 2008, the United Nations and its humanitarian partners issued consolidated and flash appeals seeking $7.1 billion in assistance to Bolivia, the Central African Republic, Chad, the Democratic Republic of the Congo, Georgia, Haiti, Honduras, Iraq, Kenya, Kyrgyzstan, Madagascar, Myanmar, the Occupied Palestinian Territory, Somalia, the Southern African Region (Malawi, Mozambique, Zambia, Zimbabwe), the Sudan, Tajikistan, Uganda, the West Africa subregion (Benin, Burkina Faso, Cape Verde, Côte d'Ivoire, Gambia, Ghana, Guinea, Guinea-Bissau, Liberia, Mali, Mauritania, Niger, Nigeria, Senegal, Sierra Leone, Togo) and Yemen. Separate appeals were launched for Côte d'Ivoire, Liberia and Zimbabwe.

The latest available data indicated that 72 per cent ($5.1 billion) of requirements had been met.

New international humanitarian order

In 2008, the UN system continued efforts to promote a new international humanitarian order and strengthen its capacity, as well as that of States, to provide assistance to victims of humanitarian emergencies. OCHA, IASC and other UN agencies played a role in those efforts, and the Global Humanitarian Platform (GHP), which was established in 2006 to enhance the effectiveness of humanitarian action—based on the premise that no single humanitarian agency could cover all humanitarian needs—continued its activities in accordance with the GHP Action Plan 2007–2009.

GENERAL ASSEMBLY ACTION

On 18 December [meeting 70], the General Assembly, on the recommendation of the Third (Social, Humanitarian and Cultural) Committee [A/63/423], adopted **resolution 63/147** without vote [agenda item 39].

New international humanitarian order

The General Assembly,

Recalling its resolution 61/138 of 19 December 2006, all previous resolutions concerning the promotion of a new international humanitarian order and all relevant resolutions, in particular resolution 46/182 of 19 December 1991 on the strengthening of the coordination of humanitarian emergency assistance of the United Nations, and the annex thereto, and resolution 62/94 of 17 December 2007 on the strengthening of the coordination of emergency humanitarian assistance of the United Nations,

Noting with appreciation the continuing efforts of the Office for the Coordination of Humanitarian Affairs of the Secretariat and the Inter-Agency Standing Committee, as well as other United Nations agencies in the context of international humanitarian assistance,

Recognizing the importance of action at the national and regional levels and the role that regional organizations can play in certain cases to prevent humanitarian crises, and emphasizing the importance of continued international cooperation in support of affected States in dealing with natural disasters and complex emergencies,

Noting with appreciation the continuing efforts of the United Nations system to increase its capacity and that of its Member States to provide assistance to victims of humanitarian emergencies,

Recognizing the important role that international organizations, intergovernmental organizations, civil society, including non-governmental organizations, and the private sector can play, within their respective mandates, in the humanitarian context,

1. *Recognizes* the need for the further strengthening of national, regional and international efforts to address humanitarian emergencies;

2. *Expresses its appreciation* for the continuing efforts of the Secretary-General in the humanitarian field, and invites him to continue to promote strict adherence to refugee law, international humanitarian law and internationally agreed norms and principles in humanitarian emergency situations;

3. *Urges* Governments, intergovernmental organizations and civil society, including non-governmental organizations, to extend cooperation and support to the efforts of the Secretary-General, inter alia, through the relevant United Nations agencies and organizational mechanisms set up to address the assistance and protection needs of affected populations as well as the safety and security of United Nations and other humanitarian workers;

4. *Encourages* intergovernmental organizations and civil society, including non-governmental organizations, as well as the private sector, where appropriate, to assist and support national and international efforts to respond to humanitarian emergencies;

5. *Invites* Member States, the Office for the Coordination of Humanitarian Affairs, relevant entities of the United Nations system and intergovernmental organizations and civil society, including non-governmental organizations, to reinforce activities and cooperation so as to continue to develop an agenda for humanitarian action;

6. *Requests* the Secretary-General to report on these issues to the General Assembly at its sixty-fifth session in his annual report on the strengthening of the coordination of emergency humanitarian assistance of the United Nations.

Humanitarian activities

Africa

Central African Republic

The UN Consolidated Inter-Agency Appeal for the Central African Republic, launched for $118.7 million in 2008, received 90 per cent ($107.3 million) of its target.

The conflict in the Central African Republic between three militant groups and the Government had ended, and the Government had drawn up a long-term development plan to tackle chronic poverty and underdevelopment. Donors had started to re-engage, pledging $600 million in development aid over a three-year period. Nonetheless, many Central Africans still lived in fear and the threat to security and progress was growing more complex. The sources of conflict in the country had multiplied, with attacks and violence by bandits becoming the grimmest source of human suffering. Criminal gangs who robbed travellers, assailed, looted and burned entire villages and kidnapped children for ransom were responsible for one third of all displacement, and had forced 100,000 Central Africans to flee from their villages or remain displaced in the bush, in towns or in neighbouring Chad and Cameroon. Some 10,000 Central Africans had fled to Chad, and at least 13,000 were forced into internal displacement due to banditry. The most obvious consequences of the violence were the 197,000 displaced persons who had fled their villages. Improved information gathering enabled the Humanitarian and Development Partnership Team (HDPT) to design and coordinate its programmes more effectively. HDPT revised its strategy for humanitarian action until the end of the year. While the overall strategic priorities remained the same: providing protection and emergency assistance, and linking humanitarian assistance to recovery and development, the objectives and projects in each sector were reviewed by both clusters and the Humanitarian Coordinator.

Chad

The UN Consolidated Inter-Agency Appeal for Chad in 2008 sought $317.9 million, of which 81 per cent ($257.5 million) was received.

Humanitarian needs in Chad increased due to renewed fighting in the north of the country and developments in Darfur and the Central African Republic over the first half of the year. In February, armed opposition groups reached the capital of N'Djamena in an attempt to overthrow the Government. Given the climate of political instability, the second half of 2008 was critical for determining whether security and stability would improve or worsen in Chad. As a result of humanitarian aid, half a million people were able to survive. In preparation for potential recovery, progress had also been made in promoting livelihoods, decreasing food aid dependency, improving access to drinking water and health care, and promoting human rights for the most vulnerable people. Education was a priority not only for the well-being of children and their families, but to sustain hopes for future development. Nonetheless, humanitarian work was becoming increasingly dangerous, with access to some areas being limited. An international presence in Chad established by Security Council resolution 1778(2007) [YUN 2007, p. 153], with a military component, had yet to become operational. The appeal, which originally sought $288 million, was revised to $306 million.

Democratic Republic of Congo

The UN Consolidated Inter-Agency Appeal for the Democratic Republic of Congo, launched for $736.5 million in 2008, received 77 per cent ($564.5 million) of its request.

Developments early in the year had a positive impact on the humanitarian situation. Following the Goma peace conference in January, violence decreased in North and South Kivu, compared to the previous six months, and there were reports of people returning to both provinces. Progress was also observed in other provinces. Only a small number of displaced persons remained in Katanga, compared to over 100,000 in September 2006. The number of displaced persons in the Orientale province decreased from 152,000 in June 2007 to 63,000 in May 2008. Despite those gains, the humanitarian situation in the country remained fragile. Since the Goma conference, 188 violations of the ceasefire by armed groups were recorded in North Kivu, displacing some 91,000 people. Within the framework of the "Amani Programme" established to follow up on the conference, humanitarian actors worked to develop sustainable conditions and solutions for internally displaced persons (IDPs) after years of conflict. During the development of the 2008 Humanitarian Action Plan, the country team introduced a new approach. Humanitarian actors identified five priority areas and established multi-sectoral programmes for assistance activities to: reduce mortality and morbidity rates; combat malnutrition; reduce violence against civilians; protect and assist IDPs; and facilitate the return and reintegration of IDPs. Preliminary results indicated that 91 per cent of the 12,627 undernourished children admitted to nutritional centres were treated successfully; more than 137,000 displaced families, returnees and vulnerable people were given assistance as non-food items; over 28,466 tonnes of goods had been distributed since the beginning of the year; and mortality and morbidity rates dropped below the humanitarian threshold within several territories, such as Bomongo and Equateur. Due to the evolving humanitarian situation, the country team revised the Plan, increasing the financing requirements from $575 million to $736 million. A revised, consolidated set of indicators allowed 79 territories to be classified as humanitarian priority zones. Following an earthquake that struck South Kivu in February, humanitarian actors offered their assistance.

Kenya

The UN Consolidated Inter-Agency Appeal for Kenya, which sought $207.6 million in 2008, received 66 per cent ($136.9 million) of the requirements.

The widespread violence that followed the disputed presidential elections in December 2007 led to a growing humanitarian crisis in the country. Following claims from national and international observers that the vote had been seriously flawed, rioting and looting broke out in cities and towns particularly in the west of the country and in and around Nairobi. An estimated 500,000 people were displaced or otherwise affected by the crisis, including some 250,000 IDPs who found shelter in camps and other sites. Although a power-sharing arrangement was signed between the opposing parties on 28 February, how the agreement would be implemented was a source of anxiety for the population at large, and the displaced in particular. In addition to the political crisis, there were increasing indications that the country was facing the early stages of drought. The projected rain shortages in the arid and semi-arid lands would compound food insecurity stemming from the production shortfalls caused by the post-election violence and the consequent loss of the March planting in the country's grain-basket areas. In western Kenya, humanitarian actors began trucking water in several districts and preparedness activities were needed to preserve fragile livelihoods. In January 2008, humanitarian partners launched the Emergency Humanitarian Response Plan and sought $41.9 million for urgent, lifesaving humanitarian activities. As an increasingly comprehensive assessment of needs became available, humanitarian partners revised their response strategies in line with the evolving political situation, which added to the emerging humanitarian needs due to poor expected rainfall. The revised appeal included projects from 13 UN system entities and 37 international and national NGOs through the end of 2008 and addressed three main areas: drought; maintenance of IDPs, including host families; and resettlement, early recovery and restoring livelihoods. The largest increase was in the food sector, owing to expanding drought-related needs.

Somalia

The UN Consolidated Inter-Agency Appeal for Somalia for 2008, which sought $662.5 million, received 74 per cent ($489.8 million) of the requirements.

Somalia experienced a serious deterioration of the humanitarian situation, at a more rapid and larger scale than anticipated during the development of the appeal. Drought and severe water shortages affected wide geographical areas from the north to most of central Somalia, while displacement caused by insecurity and conflict continued in and around Mogadishu, with the IDP population reaching 300,000 in the Afgooye corridor, and 1.1 million in total. The crisis was compounded by the growing IDP population, the effects of drought, deepening insecurity and a number of economic factors. In April, the Food Security Analysis Unit (FSAU) of the Food and Agriculture Organization of the United Nations (FAO) indicated that 2.6 million or 35 per cent of the population faced the conditions of Humanitarian Emergency (HE) or Acute Food and Livelihoods Crisis (AFLC), an increase of more than 40 per cent since January. The FSAU analysis also gave an early warning that in the event the *Gu* rains failed, the Somali shilling would continue to be devalued, food prices would continue to increase and civil insecurity would worsen, with potentially 3.5 million people—nearly half the population—facing HE or AFLC conditions. The situation called for the immediate scaling-up of the humanitarian and livelihood-support programmes. The financial requirements for the appeal were revised upwards from the original $406 million to $641 million (57 per cent increase) to assist those 2.6 to 3.5 million people in need.

Sudan

The UN Consolidated Inter-Agency Appeal for the Sudan, launched for $2 billion in 2008, received 70 per cent ($1.4 billion) of the requirements.

Three years after the Sudan's warring factions signed the Comprehensive Peace Agreement [YUN 2005, p. 301] to end the war between the north and the south, there was still fighting in parts of the country, and millions continued to suffer and rely on humanitarian aid. Nonetheless, some gains had been achieved: roads were built, mines cleared, millions of children were vaccinated and dozens more were removed from armed groups. More than 85,000 displaced Sudanese received UN assistance to return home from northern Sudan and neighbouring countries, while some 3.4 million people received food. The need to manage Sudan's resources became a priority, since their depletion would not only make people more reliant on aid, but would also aggravate the fundamental causes of conflict. Continuing violence, on the other hand, increasingly complicated the delivery of vital humanitarian aid. Within the first six months of the year, conflict in Darfur deepened, displacing an additional 200,000 people, increasing the number of displaced and vulnerable to 4.3 million. Meanwhile, camps were overcrowded, water was in short supply and consecutive bad harvests and rising food and fuel prices had led to more malnutrition. The humanitarian community became the target of violence, with 12 aid workers killed; and insecurity cut off thousands of people from much-needed aid. The UN decision to raise security levels both in Darfur and the rest of the north might also impact future operations and planning. The 2008 Sudan Work Plan introduced a new category: early recovery, intended to highlight the gradual transition towards long-term sustainable solutions. The 2009 Work Plan would present only humanitarian and early recovery portfolios, while a separate UN Development Assistance Framework would plan for recovery and development.

Uganda

The UN Consolidated Inter-Agency Appeal for Uganda, which sought $374.4 million in 2008, received 71 per cent ($265.4 million) of its target.

Steady improvement was made in the humanitarian situation in northern Uganda, with the lifting of the last remaining restrictions on the freedom of movement and a gradual increase in the number of returnees across the Acholi and Teso sub-regions, which prompted the Government and aid agencies to develop coordinated strategies for consolidating the peace dividends that had accrued since August 2006. Therefore, across the districts hosting IDPs, the humanitarian priority from July 2008 to December 2009 would be to help consolidate peace by supporting the Government's lead role in stabilizing the needs of the vulnerable population, while working to ensure that IDPs achieved the durable solutions recognized under the Uganda IDP Policy, namely, voluntary return; settlement in the former IDP camp; and relocation to another part of the country. Low donor support, which had left various clusters without the means of implementing most of their transitional programming, was a concern, as was the deteriorating situation in Karamoja, where visible signs of malnutrition had been reported. In an effort to sharpen the humanitarian focus in northern Uganda, humanitarian and development partners prioritized all projects in the revised appeal on a three-tier system that indicated projects that had been classified as humanitarian, early recovery or recovery.

West Africa

The UN Consolidated Inter-Agency Appeal for the West Africa subregion, launched for $459 million in 2008 to assist beneficiaries in Benin, Burkina Faso, Cape Verde, Côte d'Ivoire, the Gambia, Ghana, Guinea, Guinea-Bissau, Liberia, Mali, Mauritania, the Niger, Nigeria, Senegal, Sierra Leone and Togo, received 67 per cent ($309.2 million) of the requirements.

At the regional level, humanitarian partners agreed to focus on five priority areas: food security and nutrition; rapid response to health emergencies; protection and population movements; natural disaster preparedness; and water, sanitation and hygiene. As reform efforts rallied humanitarian partners into cluster leadership and cross-sector coordination, the challenge would be making the transition from a culture of coordinating humanitarian actions related to conflicts to a new role of coordinating humanitarian affairs to ensure that countries, regional organizations and new actors were fully engaged in disaster risk reduction activities that spanned from conflict to natural disasters. That would require a shift from a humanitarian response system based on addressing highly visible needs to a livelihood-based approach that placed rights to food, protection and health at the centre of a search for better human security, a prerequisite for sustainable development. As a result of the mid-year review, revised requirements for the appeal totalled $416.5 million.

Côte d'Ivoire

The UN Consolidated Inter-Agency Appeal for Côte d'Ivoire, which sought $58.1 million in 2008, received 47 per cent ($27.1 million) of the requirements.

Following the signature of the Ouagadougou Agreement in March 2007 [YUN 2007, p. 174], Côte d'Ivoire entered a post-conflict phase for the first time since the socio-political crisis erupted in 2002 [YUN 2002, p. 180]. That transition led to improvements in the security situation and reinforced collaboration between humanitarian partners and the Government, which helped facilitate response efforts to meet the relief and protection needs of an estimated 120,000 IDPs in the western part of the country. Consequently, between March 2007 and September 2008, humanitarian agencies recorded the voluntary return of 70,000 IDPs in the west. Another benchmark of the transition was the closure of the IDPs transit camp in Guiglo on 31 July, marking significant progress in the returns process. The cluster approach was formalized and the terms of reference for all sector groups were revised in accordance with IASC generic guidelines for cluster/sector leads. Humanitarian efforts in the country resulted in 13,300 households assisted by FAO during the rainy season; food rations provided by the World Food Programme (WFP) to 42,151 vulnerable groups, including 17,000 IDPs in transit and IDPs in camp Guiglo; and the vaccination of some two million people in response to the yellow fever outbreak in August. Efforts to strengthen mechanisms for preventing gender-based violence also continued. Nonetheless, high rates of malnutrition were revealed in July. A joint survey carried out by UNICEF, WFP and an external partner concluded that the food security situation in the north had deteriorated following a poor maize and rice harvest in 2007, erosion of the means of production with the loss of oxen, and a loss of purchasing power as a result of high food prices. The acute malnutrition rate was 17.5 per cent in the north, well above the emergency threshold of 10 per cent. Other potential threats to long-term peace and security persisted, with little or no progress in the disarmament of former rebels and dismantling of militias, and weapons remaining prolific. The revised appeal, which modified the food security sector, sought $54.8 million.

Liberia

The UN Consolidated Inter-Agency Appeal for Liberia, launched for $43.8 million in 2008, received 62 per cent ($27.2 million) of its target.

Despite the gains achieved in previous years to consolidate peace and strengthen national authority in Liberia, which had paved the way to more sustainable recovery and development, many Liberians remained vulnerable, faced with acute humanitarian needs on a daily basis. Those included lack of access to health care, safe drinking water, shelter and education. In response to the many challenges, the Government was leading efforts to formulate a poverty reduction strategy that would prioritize development efforts. In order to ensure a more coherent response, the United Nations in Liberia formulated a United Nations Development Assistance Framework that advanced programmatic initiatives aligned with national priorities. During the crisis and immediate post-crisis period, Liberia relied on the support of international humanitarian organizations to provide basic social services, many of which closed operations or were scaling back due to reduced funding. The situation was a reminder that the international community had yet to come to grips with the humanitarian-to-development gap, and that steps were needed to ensure that vulnerabilities were not exacerbated in a nation that remained fragile. Against that background, the Government and the humanitarian community agreed on the need to highlight the most critical humanitarian gaps (CHG) and mobilized resources to respond. Nineteen high-priority projects were presented in the sectors of health, food security, and water, sanitation, and hygiene, which had been particularly underfunded in previous humanitarian appeals. The CHG projects would play a role in advancing efforts to lay the foundation for recovery and development; build upon successful work in Liberia supported by CERF in 2006–2007; and benefit from the strengthened collaboration and joint analysis fostered by the CERF prioritization process.

Zimbabwe

For Zimbabwe, the UN Consolidated Inter-Agency Appeal sought $583.4 million in 2008, of which 69 per cent ($400.5 million) was received.

In 2008, the alarming degradation of Zimbabwe's economy and the rise in social vulnerability exacerbated the humanitarian situation. A protracted election period, from March through August, put the country on hold for six months, during which election violence and Government restrictions halted most humanitarian field activities. Consequently, half a year of critical humanitarian service delivery in support of food security, clean water, health, and education services was lost. A third consecutive failed agricultural season further increased dependence on food and non-food assistance. It was estimated that 5.1 million Zimbabweans would rely on food aid by the first quarter of 2009. The infrastructure for delivering basic social services was seriously affected, resulting in unprecedented levels of disease incidence and prevalence throughout the country. Hyperinflation and a collapsing banking system also posed challenges to humanitarian operations, with most agencies affected by the lack of cash and inability to access foreign currency. As at November 2008, it was estimated that further deterioration of the humanitarian situation could be averted if a Government of national unity could be created. In support of effective response, the cluster approach was adopted in 2008 covering five priority sectors: agriculture; emergency telecommunications; health; nutrition; and water, sanitation and hygiene. Early recovery, education, and protection working groups were expected to be formalized into clusters in 2009. In addition, HIV focal points for each cluster would ensure the integration of HIV in emergency preparations and management.

Asia

Afghanistan

In 2008, the humanitarian situation in Afghanistan worsened and was characterized by food insecurity due to drought and exacerbated by high global food prices that affected as much as one sixth of the population. The impact of armed conflict on civilians also contributed to the deteriorating humanitarian situation. An increasingly dangerous operational environment for humanitarian personnel constrained their ability to access and deliver assistance, as there had been an increase in the number of attacks against humanitarian personnel and assets in recent years. The ongoing conflict also posed a threat to the protection of the Afghan population in affected areas and had a severe impact on livelihoods, coping mechanisms and access to essential services, especially in vulnerable areas inaccessible by road. As at October, approximately 40 per cent of the country, including much of the south, could not be accessed by most humanitarian organizations. More than half of Afghanistan's land area received less than 25 per cent of its normal rainfall during the year. As a consequence of the drought, an estimated 1.2 million children under five, along with 550,000 pregnant and lactating women in 22 provinces, were at high risk of severe malnutrition. An appeal to provide a safety net for the 425,000 most vulnerable households was launched in January and sought $81.3 million (Afghanistan Joint Appeal for the Humanitarian Consequences of the Rise of Food Prices). In July, a second Afghanistan joint emergency appeal for $404 million was launched to support nearly 2 million people affected by the food insecurity and drought conditions in addition to the 2.6 million assisted during the previous six months.

In September [A/63/372-S/2008/617], the Secretary-General reported that the humanitarian situation was worsening and the food insecurity situation had become serious. He said that the most pressing humanitarian problems were the drought and high global food prices that had created food shortages affecting one sixth of the population, and that the situation called for urgent action with both a short-term and a longer-term perspective.

Iraq

The UN Consolidated Inter-Agency Appeal for Iraq sought $274.3 million in 2008, of which 71 per cent ($194.4 million) of the requirements was received.

In 2008, the humanitarian situation in Iraq continued to call for a concerted and comprehensive international response. Urgent needs across key humanitarian sectors were widespread and accumulating due to acute deprivation of essential services; armed conflict; generalized violence and rights violations; long-term internal displacement and challenging return situations; and lack of access to impartial humanitarian assistance. The consolidated appeal and the Common Humanitarian Plan underpinning it were launched in mid-February. The overarching strategic priorities for humanitarian actors remained: relieve immediate suffering in communities acutely deprived by the crisis by bridging the gap in access to essential services; provide protection for the most vulnerable civilians against grave violations of their human rights; improve the capacity, coverage, coordination and impact of humanitarian action; and strengthen links between immediate action for families in crises and support for sustainable recovery.

While the overall appeal was 47 per cent funded as at July, financial contributions were unevenly allocated across the sectors, and key humanitarian sectors faced funding shortages. Moreover, funding for the emergency response had been late coming in, while other emergency programmes still needed funding to be delivered to Iraqi communities.

Nepal

In 2008, landmark political achievements took place in Nepal, with the holding of successful elections in April, the first election in the country of a President and Vice-President, the swearing-in of the first Prime Minister, and the formation of a new Government. Nonetheless, the new Government faced several challenges, such as the global food and fuel crisis, elaborating a new Federal Constitution, the integration of armies and addressing floods. The humanitarian situation, which remained a concern with high malnutrition rates exacerbated by the food crisis, was further compounded by floods and landslides in two regions of the country, affecting an estimated 250,000 persons. The Nepal IASC elaborated an appeal for transition support to improve monitoring and response to needs of the people affected by the conflict, internal disturbances and natural disasters; provide timely and effective humanitarian services for the most vulnerable population; and ensure coherence between humanitarian assistance and development and peacebuilding efforts. Total appeal requirements amounted to $121.9 million, which included the revised Transition Appeal ($106.4 million) and the supplementary flood response plan ($15.5 million).

Pakistan

In August, Pakistan suffered a series of overlapping crises that led to substantial internal displacement and left hundreds of thousands in need of humanitarian assistance when the country was reeling from the effects of the global food crisis. Unusually heavy monsoon rains and flash floods in early August affected over 300,000 people in the northern part of the country, with the Peshawar District in the North West Frontier Province (NWFP) and Rajanpur District in Punjab Province particularly adversely affected. In addition, renewed fighting between the Government and militant groups in the Federally Administered Tribal Areas and in the Swat District in NWFP caused significant internal displacement. While a significant proportion of an estimated 260,000 people displaced by operations in Bajaur Agency were reported to have returned home following the ceasefire announcement, it was likely that the conflict would escalate again and cause new displacement. Moreover, although the acute phase of the flooding appeared to have passed, the humanitarian situation remained critical.

The Humanitarian Response Plan sought a total of $55 million to cover the identified and estimated needs of approximately 400,000 people affected by floods and conflict and needing immediate assistance over a period of six months. Programming also took into account the volatile security situation and the need to respond rapidly to possible further displacement of up to 400,000 people in the ensuing months, making an overall projected caseload of 800,000.

Occupied Palestinian Territory

The UN Consolidated Inter-Agency Appeal for the Occupied Palestinian Territory, which sought $452.2

million in 2008, received 75 per cent ($337.1 million) of the requirements.

In 2008, the overall humanitarian situation in the Territory continued to deteriorate, with the exception of slight improvements in some sectors, and was characterized by a desperate environment in the Gaza Strip. Palestinians living in Gaza were confronted with interference in their normal social and political lives and daily degradations such as reduced access to water, electricity, proper sanitation and garbage collection, and adequate health care. They also faced increased violence and casualties; extended closures of crossings; severe limitations on basic supplies; shortages of spare parts, raw materials, and other commercial and agricultural supplies; and an overall economic contraction. Over 70 per cent of households continued to rely on food aid, and shortages of fuel and electricity supplies due to Israel's restrictions exacerbated the situation. There was also a significant rise in Palestinian and Israeli casualties, including a major increase in child fatalities among Palestinians. In the West Bank, the humanitarian situation was affected by a slight deterioration in internal freedom of movement, reflected by the increasing number of closure obstacles and restrictions for Palestinians using key roads. Some areas experienced improvements with restrictions/closures being lifted. Other factors affecting the situation were the previous winter's drought and frost, and the increase in housing demolitions during the first quarter of the year. In both Gaza and the West Bank, the humanitarian situation worsened due to a significant rise in food prices, with vulnerable groups being hardest hit. Although some measures were taken to improve movement restrictions and the economic situation, those efforts were unlikely to have a significant impact on short-term humanitarian needs. The midyear review of the 2008 consolidated appeal revealed that the main needs identified at the end of 2007 remained unchanged. Meanwhile, the Gaza Strip was identified as an increasing priority in terms of the delivery of humanitarian aid.

Sri Lanka

In 2008, developments in the 25-year-long conflict in Sri Lanka adversely impacted the humanitarian situation. In January, the Government withdrew from the 2002 ceasefire agreement [YUN 2002, p. 1213] and stepped up efforts to impair the operational capacities of the Liberation Tigers of Tamil Eelam. The humanitarian situation was characterized by a significant decrease in the provision of adequate shelter, water and sanitation for the growing number of displaced persons in the Kilinochchi and Mullaitivu Districts due to a ban on transporting construction materials for national security reasons. Implementing partners prioritized the provision of shelter, camp management and supply of non-food relief items, assisting some 100,000 individuals in five districts. Some 220,000 people were provided with access to safe water and essential hygiene items, while 5,700 persons benefited from better access to sanitation. Nearly 784,000 people, including 336,900 IDPs, received food assistance during the year. In September, as fighting intensified, Kilinochchi (the main base for humanitarian operations in the north) grew increasingly insecure, and the United Nations and international NGOs had to relocate to Vavuniya. Limited access, as well as the relocation of UN/NGO personnel from Kilinochchi, hampered efforts by humanitarian workers to assess, implement and monitor assistance and protection programmes. On the other hand, as fighting intensified in the north, the end of fighting in the east led to the return of 160,000 IDPs.

Syrian Arab Republic

In 2008, Syria experienced its worst drought in four decades. The Government estimated that 200,000 families—predominantly herders and subsistence farmers, who risked malnutrition and the loss of their livelihoods—had suffered from its impact. The Government approached the UN Resident Coordinator requesting the mobilization of emergency funds from UN agencies and the donor community. The UN country team conducted a UN joint rapid drought impact assessment from 11 to 25 August to verify the impact of rain shortfall on crop production and range vegetation, livestock, vulnerable groups, herders and household income. The UN Inter-Agency mission estimated that some 204,000 families (1 million people) in north-eastern Syria were food insecure; their income from crops and livestock sales had been depleted; and many of them were resorting to damaging coping mechanisms, such as decreased food intake, sale of agriculture and household assets, or migration. The availability of safe drinking water had decreased considerably in the rural areas of north-eastern Syria, and the migration of the rural population towards less water-stressed urban areas was 20 to 30 per cent higher than in previous years due to the impact of the drought, loss of livelihoods and water shortages. The situation was not expected to improve until the spring of 2009, when the crops sown in October 2008 would mature—if the rains did not fail for a second consecutive year. Through the Syria drought appeal, five UN agencies sought $20.2 million to work with governmental partners and NGOs in addressing emergency humanitarian needs and preventing further impact on approximately 1 million drought-affected persons for a period of six months.

Timor-Leste

In 2008, Timor-Leste continued to transition from relief to development. Humanitarian actors recognized that there was no short-term solution to internal displacement and that a phased and multidimensional approach was required to reach a sustainable resolution. Consequently, the Transitional Strategy and Appeal (TSA) for Timor-Leste contained a modular framework, including feasible and realistic humanitarian and recovery assistance projects, to be implemented during the year. While humanitarian assistance in the IDP camps continued to be an imperative, the Government and its partners focused on a recovery strategy and initiatives aimed at creating an enabling environment for the return or resettlement of IDPs. As natural disasters seriously impacted human and national security, strengthening the national disaster risk management capacity was also a focus to prevent future humanitarian needs. The TSA included 67 projects submitted by NGOs, UN agencies and affiliated organizations and amounted to $33.5 million.

Europe

Georgia

On 8 August, following an increase in the number of military incidents, the situation in the breakaway Georgian province of South Ossetia escalated into open hostilities. It deteriorated further with renewed fighting in the Abkhazia province, and fighting in other parts of Georgia, particularly in and around the city of Gori. Hundreds of people were reportedly killed or wounded, and the fighting led to internal and external displacement of large numbers of people. An estimated 128,700 people were displaced in Georgia, of which 30,000 were in the South Ossetia region. Another 30,000 people were believed to have sought refuge in North Ossetia, Russian Federation. Georgia was a country with some 220,000 displaced persons from previous conflicts in the South Ossetia and Abkhazia regions. Challenges to the delivery of assistance included the multiple sites of displaced persons and the presence of Russian military forces around several towns in Georgia, particularly Gori, along the main east-west transport link, which limited access to populations in the west and north-west. An initial appeal sought $59.6 million to cover the identified and estimated needs of a projected caseload of 128,700 persons for a six-month planning horizon. By October, although 68,000 of the 127,499 displaced persons from South Ossetia and Abkhazia had returned home, a significant number remained displaced, with an estimated 10,000 to 15,000 within South Ossetia.

Based on improved assessments and access, humanitarian organizations in Georgia revised the appeal, including refinements to food security, health and nutrition, protection, and shelter activities, as well as the introduction of a range of early recovery initiatives, which would cover the needs of 127,499 displaced persons and returnees until March 2009. The revised UN Flash Appeal sought $114.3 million, of which 64 per cent ($73 million) was received.

Special economic assistance

African economic recovery and development

New Partnership for Africa's Development

The General Assembly, by resolution 57/7 [YUN 2002, p. 910], endorsed the Secretary-General's recommendation [ibid., p. 909] that the New Partnership for Africa's Development (NEPAD), adopted in 2001 by the Assembly of Heads of State and Government of the Organization of African Unity [YUN 2001, p. 900], should be the framework within which the international community should concentrate its efforts for Africa's development. During 2008, efforts continued to focus on UN and international support for NEPAD, its implementation and the holding of a high-level meeting by the General Assembly, which resulted in the adoption of a political declaration on Africa's development needs.

High-level meeting on Africa's development needs

The General Assembly, in resolution 62/179 [YUN 2007, p. 935] reaffirmed its decision to hold a high-level meeting on the theme "Africa's development needs: state of implementation of various commitments, challenges and the way forward" during its sixty-third (2008) session. On 4 March, by resolution 62/242 (see p. 1008) the Assembly agreed on the date (22 September), modalities and format of the meeting, which would be held at the highest political level, with the participation of Heads of State or Government, ministers and special representatives, and decided that the meeting would result in a political declaration on Africa's development needs. It also mandated the United Nations to consult with the African Union (AU) in preparing for the meeting and requested the Secretary-General to submit to the meeting a comprehensive report, with recommendations on the theme, in cooperation with relevant development agencies of the United Nations, the Bretton Woods institutions and other regional and international financial and trade institutions.

GENERAL ASSEMBLY ACTION

On 4 March [meeting 85], the General Assembly adopted **resolution 62/242** [draft: A/62/L.29/Rev.1 & Add.1] without vote [agenda item 64 *(a)*].

Modalities, format and organization of the high-level meeting on Africa's development needs

The General Assembly,

Recalling its resolutions 61/229 of 22 December 2006 and 62/179 of 19 December 2007, in which it decided to convene, during its sixty-third session, a high-level meeting on the theme "Africa's development needs: state of implementation of various commitments, challenges and the way forward",

Recalling also the 2005 World Summit Outcome and its follow-up resolution 60/265 of 30 June 2006,

Recalling further its resolutions 57/270 B of 23 June 2003, 61/230 of 22 December 2006 and 61/296 of 17 September 2007 and the ministerial declaration of the high-level segment of the substantive session of 2001 of the Economic and Social Council of 18 July 2001, entitled "The role of the United Nations in support of the efforts of African countries to achieve sustainable development",

Reaffirming its determination to address the special needs of Africa, which is the only continent not on track to meet the Millennium Development Goals by 2015,

Noting that the implementation of commitments made to and by African countries will contribute to the continent's achievement of the Millennium Development Goals by 2015,

Convinced that the high-level meeting will constitute a significant event that will review the implementation of all commitments made to and by Africa in order to comprehensively address the special development needs of the continent,

1. *Decides* that the high-level meeting will be held on 22 September 2008, prior to the general debate of the sixty-third session of the General Assembly;

2. *Decides also* that the meeting will be held at the highest possible political level, with the participation of Heads of State or Government, ministers, special representatives and other representatives, as appropriate;

3. *Decides further* that the meeting will be composed of an opening plenary meeting, followed by two high-level round tables in the morning and two high-level round tables in the afternoon, which will address the overall theme of the meeting, and a closing plenary meeting;

4. *Requests* the President of the General Assembly to finalize the organizational arrangements for the meeting;

5. *Decides* that the meeting will result in a political declaration on Africa's development needs;

6. *Requests* the President of the General Assembly to produce a concise draft text, in consultation with Member States and based on their inputs, and convene informal consultations on the initial draft text at an appropriate date to enable sufficient discussion;

7. *Strongly urges* all Member States to actively participate in the meeting;

8. *Decides* that the preparations for the meeting will be conducted in close consultations between the United Nations and the African Union;

9. *Invites* the Holy See, in its capacity as observer State, and Palestine, in its capacity as observer, to participate in the meeting;

10. *Decides* that the President of the General Assembly will consult with representatives of non-governmental organizations in consultative status with the Economic and Social Council, civil society organizations and the private sector, and with Member States, as appropriate, on the list of representatives of non-governmental organizations, civil society organizations and the private sector that may participate in the round tables of the meeting;

11. *Decides also* that the meeting will be chaired by the President of the General Assembly;

12. *Invites* intergovernmental organizations and entities that have observer status with the General Assembly to participate in the meeting;

13. *Invites* heads of the United Nations funds, programmes and agencies to participate in the meeting, in consultation with the President of the General Assembly;

14. *Invites* the Bretton Woods institutions, the World Trade Organization, the regional development banks, the United Nations Conference on Trade and Development and development partners to participate in the meeting;

15. *Requests* the Secretary-General to submit to the meeting a comprehensive report, with recommendations, on "Africa's development needs: state of implementation of various commitments, challenges and the way forward" in cooperation with relevant development agencies of the United Nations, the Bretton Woods institutions and other relevant regional and international financial and trade institutions.

Report of Secretary-General (July). Pursuant to General Assembly resolution 62/242 (above), the Secretary-General submitted a July report [A/63/130] on Africa's development needs: state of implementation of various commitments, challenges and the way forward. The report highlighted Africa's underlying development needs and challenges, including recurrent armed conflict and the lack of human and institutional capacity to design and implement sound policies; reviewed the main commitments made by the international community to address the continent's needs; and considered the implementation of pledges made by international development partners in key areas such as international development assistance, debt relief and debt cancellation, trade liberalization and aid for trade, and peace and security. It also analysed the UN role in supporting the AU and NEPAD, and assessed progress in attaining the MDGs in Africa. In that connection, the report indicated that 2008 marked the midpoint of the global effort to achieve the goals by 2015, and on the basis of current trends, no African country was likely to achieve all of them. Fragile and post-conflict countries faced particular challenges in generating momentum to reduce poverty and improve living standards. Nonetheless, success stories on individual goals across a range of countries demonstrated that rapid progress could be made when sound domestic policies were matched with substantial technical and financial support from the international community. Consequently, the high-level meeting on Africa's development needs, as well as the high-level event on the MDGs on 25 September (see p. 926), would provide key opportunities to renew the political will to implement existing commitments to address Africa's development needs and for all stakeholders to announce commitments to tangible action in support of the achievement of the MDGs in Africa. The report also drew on the work of the MDG Africa Steering Group, which was first convened in September 2007 [YUN 2007, p. 934] to catalyse, at the midpoint, more effective and efficient action by the international community in support of the MDGs in Africa.

The report concluded that progress towards the MDGs and other internationally agreed development goals remained off track and that more needed to be done to fulfil existing African and international commitments, as most remained only partially realized. Significant progress had been made in providing debt relief, aid for trade and support for peace and security, yet more needed to be done to follow through on pledges of sectoral-level support for Africa's development. Meeting Africa's development needs was within reach provided that African States and the international community acted with determination to turn commitments into concrete action. The report made recommendations for African States to strengthen mechanisms for the participation, inclusion and empowerment of all segments of society; the AU Commission and NEPAD secretariat to intensify efforts towards the ongoing integration of NEPAD into the structures of the Commission; and African countries to take further steps to improve economic and political governance. African countries were urged to integrate climate issues into economic planning and management at both national and regional levels. International partners were encouraged to support mitigation and adaptation efforts, "climate proof" all projects and policies intended to achieve agreed development goals, and provide compensatory financing for that process. In the follow-up to the MDG Africa Steering Group assessment, the international community needed to increase external financing for African agriculture from $1–2 billion per year to some $8 billion by 2010, while $8.3 billion was required each year to meet the education MDGs, and an estimated $25–30 billion would be required per year by 2010 for health. Some $52.2 billion was required annually in public and private investment finance to resolve the critical bottlenecks in infrastructure. Other recommendations addressed shortcomings in the quality of aid and on harmonizing delivery, prioritizing quick-impact projects, development partners' fulfilling their ODA commitments, and African countries' improving their supply-side capacities and deepening their regional integration; and the donor community concentrating its efforts on conflict prevention/early warning, post-war reconstruction, peacekeeping and peace enforcement, in order to achieve a conflict-free Africa by 2010.

Political declaration on Africa's development needs. On 22 September, the General Assembly convened a high-level plenary meeting [A/63/PV.3 & 4] on the theme "Africa's development needs: state of implementation of various commitments, challenges and the way forward", which considered the Secretary-General's report on that topic (see above) and discussed the progress made towards achieving the goals set out in the Millennium Declaration [YUN 2000, p. 49]. In his address to the meeting, the Secretary-General said that current trends indicated that no African country would achieve all the MDGs by 2015. The meeting on Africa's development needs was important in itself, yet was also critical to preparations for the high-level meeting on the MDGs to be held on 25 September and the Doha Review Conference on Financing for Development in November (see p. 1076). He stated that through concerted action by African Governments and their development partners, the MDGs remained achievable in Africa. On the estimated cost of $72 billion per year in external financing to achieve the goals by 2015, he appealed to all donors to implement the 2005 Gleneagles summit pledge to more than double aid to Africa. He also urged participants to strengthen their commitment to change the course of history and bring hope and development to Africa. On the same date, the Assembly adopted a political declaration on Africa's development needs (see below), in which States reaffirmed their commitment to address the special needs of Africa and to strengthen support for the implementation of NEPAD and national and subregional development plans and strategies.

GENERAL ASSEMBLY ACTION

On 22 September [meeting 4], the General Assembly adopted **resolution 63/1** [draft: A/63/L.1] without vote [agenda item 57 *(a)*].

Political declaration on Africa's development needs

The General Assembly,

Recalling its resolution 62/242 of 4 March 2007, in particular paragraph 5,

Adopts the following political declaration:

Political declaration on Africa's development needs

1. We, Heads of State and Government, Ministers and representatives of Member States gathered at a high-level meeting at United Nations Headquarters in New York on 22 September 2008 to address "Africa's development needs: state of implementation of various commitments,

challenges and the way forward", stress that the high-level meeting represents a unique opportunity to strengthen the global partnership for development in Africa, which is pivotal to bringing Africa into the mainstream of the global economy.

2. We reaffirm the special needs of Africa as contained in the United Nations Millennium Declaration, the United Nations Declaration on the New Partnership for Africa's Development, the Monterrey Consensus of the International Conference on Financing for Development, the Plan of Implementation of the World Summit on Sustainable Development ("Johannesburg Plan of Implementation") and the 2005 World Summit Outcome.

3. We recommit ourselves to reinvigorate and strengthen a global partnership of equals based on our common values, mutual accountability, shared responsibility and the determination to collectively act for our common future and to mobilize the resources, including human, financial and technological, required to end poverty, hunger and underdevelopment in Africa, with the explicit objective of turning existing commitments into concrete actions.

4. We commit to strengthening support for the implementation of the New Partnership for Africa's Development, which is an overarching framework for socioeconomic sustainable development in Africa, as well as for the implementation of national and subregional development plans and strategies.

5. We stress that eradicating poverty, particularly in Africa, is the greatest global challenge facing the world today. We underline the importance of accelerating sustainable broad-based economic growth, including employment generation and decent work, towards a vibrant Africa.

6. We reaffirm our commitment to address the special needs of Africa, a continent where, despite recent considerable improvements, the full and timely achievement of the internationally agreed development goals, including the Millennium Development Goals, remains elusive.

7. We commit to supporting the consolidation of democracy in Africa and assisting African countries in their struggle for lasting peace, economic growth, poverty eradication and sustainable development.

8. We underline that good governance at all levels is essential for sustained economic growth, poverty eradication and sustainable development. We welcome the progress many African countries have made with respect to implementing pro-poor economic policies, deepening democracy and protecting human rights. We stress the importance of African-led initiatives to strengthen political, economic and corporate governance, such as the African Peer Review Mechanism. We recommit ourselves to actively protecting and promoting all human rights, the rule of law and democracy.

9. We welcome the efforts of African Governments to mobilize domestic resources and attract private capital to finance the investments and expenditures needed to achieve their development goals. We underscore the importance of an enabling environment at all levels, which is vital for mobilizing domestic resources, increasing productivity, generating employment, especially for youth, reducing capital flight, fighting corruption, encouraging the private sector and attracting foreign direct investment, and in this regard we underline the importance of human, professional and institutional capacity-building for development.

10. We stress the importance of strengthening domestic financial sectors as a source of capital by making them inclusive, thus expanding access to financial services.

11. We underline the importance of increasing foreign direct investment in the extractive industries value chain as well as diversification in other sectors, in order to achieve higher levels of employment and facilitate the transfer of technology and knowledge.

12. We are concerned that, at the current rate, the commitment of doubling aid to Africa by 2010 as articulated at the Summit of the Group of Eight, held at Gleneagles from 6 to 8 July 2005, will not be reached. We call for the fulfillment of all official development assistance-related commitments, including the commitments made by many developed countries to achieve the target of 0.7 per cent of gross national income for official development assistance by 2015, as well as the target of 0.15 per cent to 0.20 per cent of gross national income for least developed countries, and urge those developed countries that have not yet done so to make concrete efforts in this regard in accordance with their commitments.

13. We welcome the increased aid flows from new development actors, including some developing countries, global funds, the private sector and civil society organizations, as well as from innovative sources of finance.

14. We emphasize that debt sustainability is essential for underpinning growth, and underline the importance of debt sustainability and effective debt management to the efforts to achieve national development goals, including the Millennium Development Goals. Debtors and creditors must share the responsibility for preventing and resolving unsustainable debt situations. We note with appreciation the progress under the Heavily Indebted Poor Countries Initiative and the Multilateral Debt Relief Initiative, but remain concerned that a number of African countries are still facing difficulties in finding a durable solution to their debt problems, which could adversely affect their sustainable development. We therefore call for continued efforts to achieve long-term debt sustainability.

15. We recommit to improving the effectiveness of development assistance, including the fundamental principles of ownership, alignment, harmonization, managing for results and mutual accountability. We call for a continuing dialogue to improve the effectiveness of aid, including the full implementation of the Accra Agenda for Action by countries and organizations that commit to it.

16. We commit to promoting South-South cooperation and triangular cooperation, which have great potential to facilitate the exchange of successful strategies, practices and experiences. The impact of South-South cooperation may be further harnessed through synergies with other bilateral or multilateral development partners. We recognize South-South cooperation initiatives that are rooted in the principle of national ownership and are aimed at strengthening productive capacity as well as accelerating economic growth and sustainable development.

17. We welcome the commitments made by Africa and its development partners in the context of various important initiatives and partnerships in recent years, inter alia, the Africa Partnership Forum, the New Asian-African Strategic

Partnership, the China-Africa Partnership, the European Union-Africa Strategic Partnership, the Group of Eight-Africa Partnership, the Millennium Challenge Account, the Emergency Plan for AIDS Relief of the President of the United States of America, the Africa-Turkey Cooperation Summit, the Africa-South America Summit, the Tokyo International Conference on African Development, the comprehensive health-care initiative sponsored by the Government of Cuba, the Initiative for Africa's Development of the Republic of Korea, the special technical assistance programme for Africa of Pakistan, the Viet Nam-Africa cooperation partnership and the India-Africa Forum.

18. We urge the United Nations system, international and regional financial institutions and other multilateral development partners to continue and strengthen support for African Governments in their efforts to implement national development strategies and programmes. We stress the need to strengthen the capacities and capabilities of the United Nations system in supporting Africa's development.

19. We stress the need for well-functioning national and international financial systems, which should have the capacity to help reduce uncertainty and support economic growth. We recognize the need to enhance the voice and participation of developing countries in policymaking in the areas of trade, money and finance.

20. We are concerned that Africa's share of international trade is only 2 per cent, and underline the important role that trade plays in promoting economic growth. We stress the need to promote Africa's international trade, including through regional integration and greater integration into the global economy and fulfilment of our commitment to a well-functioning, universal, rules-based, open, non-discriminatory and equitable multilateral trading system which promotes sustainable development. We commit to redoubling our efforts towards the reinvigoration of the multilateral trade negotiations and to achieve a successful development-oriented outcome of the Doha Round of the World Trade Organization. We call for stronger national action and international support to build domestic productive competitive export supply capacities, as well as trade support, infrastructure and institutions for African countries.

21. We underline that development, peace and security and human rights are interlinked and mutually reinforcing. We stress that conflict prevention, resolution and management and post-conflict consolidation are essential for the achievement of the objectives of the special needs of Africa. We welcome the progress that the African Union and the subregional organizations have made in this regard, inter alia, through the strengthening of Africa's peace and security architecture.

22. We call for intensified efforts and a coordinated approach between national Governments, the African Union, subregional organizations, the United Nations system and partners with a view to achieving further progress towards the goal of a conflict-free Africa. We stress the importance of and pledge to support peace consolidation mechanisms and processes, including the Panel of the Wise, the African Union Post-Conflict Reconstruction and Development Framework, the early warning system and the operationalization of the African Standby Force. We also stress the importance of and pledge to support relevant United Nations bodies, inter alia, the Peacebuilding Commission. We welcome the intensification of cooperation between the United Nations and the African Union on peace and security and underline the importance of the implementation of the ten-year capacity-building programme for the African Union. We call upon the international community to assist post-conflict countries in achieving a smooth transition from relief to development.

23. We recognize that Africa faces a number of serious challenges, including poverty, hunger, climate change, land degradation and desertification, rapid urbanization, lack of adequate water supplies and energy supply and HIV/AIDS, malaria, tuberculosis and other endemic diseases. We commend African countries for their leadership in addressing those challenges and charting the way forward for the region in the context of the African Union as well as through national and subregional development plans and strategies.

24. We stress that climate change has serious implications for sustainable development. We express concern that Africa faces high risks from the negative effects of climate change, although it emits the least amount of greenhouse gases. We acknowledge that the global nature of climate change calls for the widest possible cooperation by all countries and their participation in an effective and appropriate international response, in accordance with their common but differentiated responsibilities and respective capabilities and their social and economic conditions. We reaffirm our support for the United Nations Framework Convention on Climate Change, and welcome the decisions adopted by the Conference of the Parties to the Convention at its thirteenth session, held in Bali from 3 to 15 December 2007, including the Bali Action Plan. We remain deeply concerned that all countries, in particular developing countries, including least developed countries, small island developing States and African countries, face increased risks from the negative effects of climate change, and stress the need to urgently address adaptation needs relating to such effects. In this context, we underline in particular the need for new and additional financial resources.

25. We are concerned about the consequences of the global food crisis on the achievement of the Millennium Development Goals, and in this regard we acknowledge the African Union's declaration on responding to the challenges of high fuel prices and agricultural development. We call for an integrated response by African countries and the international community, working in partnership to support integrated and sustainable agriculture and rural development approaches, and stress the importance of food security and strengthening the agricultural sector, as set out in, inter alia, the Comprehensive Africa Agriculture Development Programme of the New Partnership for Africa's Development. We call upon all donors and the United Nations system to increase their assistance to Africa, in particular to least developed countries and those that are most negatively affected by high food prices.

26. We welcome Africa's commitment to the Africa Water Vision 2025, the Sirte declaration on agriculture and water in Africa and the Sharm el-Sheikh Commitments for Accelerating the Achievement of Water and Sanitation Goals in Africa.

27. We recognize the challenges of inadequate infrastructure and industrialization in Africa and the need to substantively increase investment in all forms of infrastructure in accordance with the New Partnership for Africa's Devel-

opment. We recognize the contribution that private capital can make towards the development of infrastructure.

28. We recognize the urgent need for large-scale investments in energy infrastructure, as outlined in the New Partnership for Africa's Development, and are committed to promoting renewable sources of energy, clean energy, energy efficiency and conservation.

29. We reaffirm the universal commitment to promoting gender equality and the empowerment of women, recognizing that they are key actors in development.

30. We resolve to increase our efforts to reduce maternal and child mortality, and reaffirm the commitment to achieve universal access to reproductive health by 2015.

31. We note with concern that violence against women and children everywhere continues and often increases, and resolve to ensure the strict universal adherence to international norms regarding violence against women and girls.

32. We express our grave concern at the negative effects on development, peace, security and human rights posed by transnational crime, including the smuggling of and trafficking in human beings.

33. We commit ourselves to safeguarding the principle of refugee protection and to upholding our responsibility in resolving the plight of refugees, including through support of efforts aimed at addressing the causes of refugee movement, bringing about the safe and sustainable return of those populations.

34. We recognize the Guiding Principles on Internal Displacement as an important international framework for the protection of internally displaced persons, and welcome the fact that an increasing number of States, United Nations agencies and regional and non-governmental organizations are applying them as a standard, and encourage all relevant actors to make use of the Guiding Principles when dealing with situations of internal displacement.

35. We recognize that HIV/AIDS, malaria, tuberculosis and other infectious diseases pose severe risks for the entire world and serious challenges to the achievement of development goals. In this regard, we welcome the commitment by African Governments and regional institutions to scale up their own responses in order to curb the devastating effects of those pandemics. We reaffirm our commitment to pursuing all necessary efforts to scale up support for nationally driven, sustainable and comprehensive responses in Africa to achieve broad multisectoral coverage for prevention, treatment, care and support, with the full and active participation of people living with HIV, vulnerable groups, most affected communities, civil society and the private sector, towards the goal of universal access to comprehensive prevention programmes, treatment, care and support by 2010, in line with the 2006 Political Declaration on HIV/AIDS.

36. We renew our resolve to fulfil our commitments towards providing quality basic education and promoting literacy, using the full range of bilateral and multilateral instruments, including continued efforts to mobilize resources to meet the education needs of African countries. We emphasize the importance of expanded primary, secondary and higher education as well as vocational education and technical training, especially for girls and women.

37. We recognize that the way forward for meeting Africa's development needs requires taking coordinated, balanced and integrated actions at all levels for the full and timely achievement of the Millennium Development Goals and comprehensively addressing all challenges to Africa's development. In this regard, we welcome the Secretary-General's initiative to hold a high-level event on the Millennium Development Goals on 25 September 2008.

38. This political declaration is adopted on 22 September 2008 on the occasion of the high-level meeting on "Africa's development needs: state of implementation of various commitments, challenges and the way forward". It seeks to reaffirm the commitment of all States to addressing the development needs on the African continent. In adopting this political declaration, Member States reaffirm their belief in a prosperous future for Africa in which core human values of dignity and peace are fully enshrined. In this context, Member States further confirm their adherence to the spirit of cooperation that defines the United Nations system and that is based on a partnership among equals.

39. The high-level meeting has reviewed the implementation of all commitments made to and by Africa in order to comprehensively address the special development needs of the continent. All commitments to and by Africa should be effectively implemented and given appropriate follow-up by the international community and by Africa itself. We underscore the urgency of finding solutions to Africa's major challenges. In this regard, we request the Secretary-General to submit to the General Assembly at its sixty-fourth session a comprehensive report, with recommendations, on "Africa's development needs: state of implementation of various commitments, challenges and the way forward" with a view to the formulation, by the sixty-fifth session of the Assembly, of a mechanism to review the full and timely implementation of all commitments related to Africa's development, building on existing mechanisms, to ensure that Member States remain seized of the issue of addressing Africa's special development needs.

Implementation and support for NEPAD

Report of Secretary-General (March). The Secretary-General, responding to a request of the Committee for Programme and Coordination (CPC) [YUN 2005, p. 1004], submitted a March report [E/AC.51/2008/5] on UN system support for NEPAD, which detailed work undertaken since May 2007 and was organized around nine thematic clusters corresponding to the Partnership's priorities and strategies: infrastructure development; governance; peace and security; agriculture, food security and rural development; industry, trade and market access; environment, population and urbanization; human resources development, employment and HIV/AIDS; science and technology; and communication, advocacy and outreach. The report also examined different dimensions of individual and collective activities initiated by entities of the UN system, as well as challenges it faced in supporting NEPAD. In addition, three policy issues in the implementation of NEPAD were examined: strengthening the cluster system and enhanced UN-AU cooperation; support for the mobilization of financial resources for NEPAD implementation; and cross-cutting issues and institutional support. The report identified a number of challenges and constraints in the cluster system, such as the need for stronger commitment and leadership; increased participation of the AU Commission, the NEPAD secretariat, regional economic communities and the African Development Bank; increased resource mobilization; enhanced monitoring and evaluation of activities; and increased communication and information-sharing.

The Secretary-General concluded that the recommendations made in various meetings, including the external review of the cluster system and the latest regional consultation meeting, needed to be implemented fully and that monitoring and evaluation needed to be improved. He made recommendations for greater UN inter-agency collaboration rather than a sector-driven approach, the development by the UN system of an integrated framework for supporting the AU Commission, which incorporated support of NEPAD, and the further harmonization of the policies and support of UN system entities to create synergies across thematic clusters. He said that an expanded source of funding was needed to ensure adequate, predictable and timely core resources.

CEB report. The United Nations System Chief Executives Board for Coordination (CEB), in its annual overview report for 2007–2008 [E/2008/58], continued its consideration of UN system support for Africa's development. CEB focused on the need for clarity with respect to the various initiatives in the system and for the approach the system was taking to be clearly articulated to States and to African Governments in particular. Emerging challenges impacting UN system efforts to support African development included the rise in food prices, the slowing world economy and the need for more rapid progress in the Doha Development Round of trade negotiations to improve market access for developing countries. CEB members welcomed the Secretary-General's initiative in launching the Millennium Development Goal (MDG) Africa Steering Group and the MDG Africa Working Group to galvanize support for the implementation of the MDGs and other internationally agreed goals in Africa.

CPC action. CPC, at its forty-eighth session (9 June–3 July) [A/63/16], welcomed the Secretary-General's report on NEPAD (see above) and requested the UN system to continue to provide assistance to the AU, the NEPAD secretariat and African countries in developing projects and programmes within the scope of NEPAD priorities and in monitoring and evaluating their effectiveness. The Committee also called for greater UN inter-agency collaboration to ensure that NEPAD was integrated in the activities of the UN system to strengthen the secretariats of both the AU Commission and NEPAD through capacity-building; urged the UN system to develop an integrated framework for supporting the AU Commission and to enhance its support to the Commission in the areas of economic and social development, as well as peace and security, in a balanced and equitable manner; and called on UN system entities to further harmonize their policies to create synergies across thematic clusters. CPC also stressed that the merger of the Office of the Special Adviser on Africa and the Office of the High Representative for the Least Developed Countries, Landlocked Developing Countries and Small Island Developing States should not undermine the UN system's focus on and support for NEPAD programmes. The Committee welcomed the high priority CEB continued to attach to ensuring the effectiveness and coordination of UN system support for Africa and NEPAD and encouraged CEB member organizations to further align their priorities with those of NEPAD and to scale up their efforts to support it.

Reports of Secretary-General (August). In response to General Assembly resolution 62/179 [YUN 2007, p. 935], the Secretary-General submitted, in August, the sixth consolidated report [A/63/206] on progress achieved to implement and support NEPAD, which highlighted policy measures taken by African countries and organizations in the implementation of NEPAD; the response of the development partners; the support of the UN system; and activities undertaken by the private sector and civil society in support of NEPAD during the previous year. It also drew from the work of the MDG Africa Steering Group and the Secretary-General's July report on Africa's development needs (see p. 1008). The August report acknowledged that African countries had made progress in implementing NEPAD sectoral priorities, yet called for urgent action to mitigate the socio-economic impact of increasingly high food prices by launching the African green revolution within the context of the Africa Agriculture Development Programme. It urged countries to allocate more resources towards NEPAD priorities and to adopt reforms to further encourage private sector participation in NEPAD projects. It also encouraged development partners to scale up development aid to ensure that commitments were achieved within the set deadline.

Significant progress was made in implementing the NEPAD short-term Action Plan infrastructure projects, as well as the Medium to Long Term Strategic Framework—in all four sectors—despite human resource and funding constraints. In 2007, members of the Infrastructure Consortium for Africa committed an estimated $10 billion, an increase of 20 per cent from the $7.7 billion committed in 2006. Multilateral institutions and bilateral donors also significantly increased their financial support. On agriculture, progress was made in implementing the Comprehensive Africa Agriculture Development Programme (CAADP), including strengthened coordination by the AU Commission, the NEPAD secretariat and regional economic communities. The three institutions made progress in delineating the core responsibilities within an overall framework for joint responsibility in coordinating CAADP implementation at the country and regional levels. NEPAD supported countries in incorporating the CAADP agenda into their agriculture and rural development programmes. With the support of the TerrAfrica partnership, it mobilized $150 million under the Global Environment Facility Strategic Investment Programme for Sustainable Land Management in Sub-Saharan Africa, which resulted in an additional $1 billion to support the scaling-up of land and water management practices. In response to the rise in world food prices, through the CAADP framework, the AU and NEPAD convened a workshop in May 2008 composed of African Governments, development partners, regional economic communities, NGOs, farmer associations and research institutions.

On health and education issues, African Governments adopted the African Health Strategy 2007–2015, which articulated required health system interventions. NEPAD began to collaborate with the Global Fund to Fight AIDS, Tuberculosis and Malaria in an effort to be more responsive to African priorities and inputs. Gains were also achieved in implementing various education projects in a number of countries within the context of regional economic communities. In other efforts, the NEPAD capacity-building programme completed subregional environment action plans with the support of the United Nations Environment Programme, which would promote regional cooperation in policy development and planning for environment and natural resource management. On information and communication technology, progress was made in accelerating the implementation of components of NEPAD e-Schools, including developments in its Demonstration Project (Demo) and e-Schools Business Plan. Efforts continued in implementing the programmes of Africa's Science and Technology Plan of Action: African Biosciences Initiative; and in establishing a high-level African panel on biotechnology, the African Water Sciences and Technology Network, the African Energy Research and Innovation Network, and the African Science, Technology and Innovation Indicators Initiative.

On gender mainstreaming, the NEPAD Gender Task Force recommended a number of changes to the African Peer Review Mechanism (APRM), following gender analysis of the APRM country reports. It proposed that the reports cover four themes: implementation of the Solemn Declaration on Gender Equality in Africa; the Convention on the Elimination of All Forms of Discrimination Against Women and the Protocol to the African Charter on Human and Peoples Rights on the Rights of Women in Africa; financial support for the implementation of gender issues through enterprises; and the status of representation of women in parliament. Meanwhile, the APRM process continued to move forward. As at June, 29 countries had voluntarily acceded to the Review Mechanism, of which 14 had set up national structures and were at various stages of implementing the APRM process. In order to streamline and fast track the APRM process, a workshop was held in Algeria in November 2007 that conducted a review of the experience achieved by countries that had been peer-reviewed and by those that had reached an advanced stage in the process. The workshop also made recommendations to improve peer-review monitoring and evaluation activities.

On the response of the international community, there was evidence that African countries had, through NEPAD, created an effective leadership process for engaging international partners on a number of issues ranging from international trade arrangements to debt relief, including the Organisation for Economic Co-operation and Development (OECD)/ Development Assistance Committee (DAC). In that connection, the 2008 G-8 Summit endorsed a five-year time frame for providing $60 billion to fight infectious diseases and to strengthen health systems. In December 2007, at the second European Union (EU)-Africa Summit in Lisbon, both continents strengthened their partnership by adopting a joint Africa-EU strategy comprising a common strategic vision and road map. Nonetheless, despite renewed interest in Africa's development issues, OECD estimates indicated that official development assistance (ODA) to Africa had dropped from $44 billion in 2006 to $35 billion in 2007, a decrease of 20.5 per cent. The drop was due mainly to debt relief being phased out, which meant that ODA to Africa had fallen short of 2005 pledges to double aid by 2010 by $25 billion. On debt relief, the previous year had witnessed continued progress in multilateral and bilateral debt relief and cancellation efforts within the framework of the Heavily Indebted Poor Countries Initiative and the Multilateral Debt Relief Initiative.

In the trade sector, little progress had been made in the Doha trade talks to reach an agreement on matters affecting Africa, such as agricultural market access and further reducing trade-distorting agricultural subsidies. In late 2007, the World Trade Organization facilitated global meetings on aid for trade in order to highlight the need for improvements in aid for trade flows and the importance of improving performance indicators for donors and recipients, as well as increasing country, regional and sector focus. Limited progress was made in negotiations on economic partnership agreements between the EU and six regional clusters of African countries. On South-South cooperation, non-DAC and emerging partners were playing an increasing role in development cooperation, offering new ideas and approaches to achieve globally agreed development goals. Following the launch of the China-Africa Development Fund in 2007 [YUN 2007, p. 934], over $90 million had been contributed to the Fund. At the first India-Africa Forum Summit in April 2008, India offered $5.4 billion in financial credit for the next five years and $500 million in development grants. In June, African and South American trade ministers met to plan a new trade framework between the two continents. Turkey became a non-regional member of the African Development Bank (ADB) in early 2008, and in August would host the first Turkey-Africa Cooperation Summit to consider ways to strengthen that partnership.

The UN system continued to provide support to the AU and NEPAD. The Eighth Regional Consultations Meeting, held in November 2007, noted the increasing effectiveness of the Regional Consultation Mechanism in terms of enhancing leadership and sharpening the focus of cluster activities. The meeting called for the establishment of a steering committee to oversee the activities of the Regional Consultation Mechanism, further aligning the cluster system with AU and NEPAD priorities, and the development by the clusters of three-year business plans and for them to mainstream cross-cutting work on gender, health and culture. In response to Africa's remaining as a whole off-track with regard to achieving the MDGs, the Secretary-General launched the Africa Steering Group in 2007 [ibid., p. 934], which for the first time brought together a handful of international organizations to identify actions to attain the MDGs in Africa. In June 2008, the Steering Group published its recommendations on key sectors, including agriculture, education, health, infrastructure, climate change and aid predictability, which were endorsed by the AU Summit. Since the Millennium Project launched the Millennium Villages initiative in 2006 [YUN 2006, p. 10], 13 countries had established Villages, and early results in countries across Africa proved that rapid progress towards achieving the MDGs was possible when a holistic set of interventions was combined with local leadership, Government support and adequate donor financing.

The Secretary-General concluded that while significant progress had been achieved, persistent challenges needed to be addressed, such as the need for: modern and efficient physical infrastructure; coordination among the various key regional institutions on the continent to accelerate implementation of infrastructure projects; implementation of the agreed programmes of action and recommendations of APRM country reports; increased spending by African countries on agricultural and rural development to 10 per cent of public expenditure; improved linkages and coordination among African countries, the regional economic communities, the AU Commission, ADB and ECA; the scaling-up of aid by donor countries; the removal of obstacles to an open trading system in agricultural commodities, to the benefit of African countries in particular; and, in the context of South-South cooperation, the establishment of a facility whereby countries receiving windfall earnings from oil export would contribute to the most vulnerable African countries.

On 4 August, the Secretary-General submitted a report [A/63/212] on the implementation of his 1998 recommendations on the causes of conflict and the promotion of durable peace and sustainable development in Africa [YUN 1998, p. 66], which was to be read together with his August report on NEPAD (see above). On 11 September, in **resolution 62/275** (see p. 113), the General Assembly reaffirmed its commitment to address the special needs of Africa and to strengthen cooperation with NEPAD by providing coherent support for the programmes drawn up by African leaders within that framework.

Communication. On 6 June [A/62/859], Japan transmitted to the General Assembly the outcome documents of the Fourth Tokyo International Conference on African Development (TICAD IV), held from 28 to 30 May in Yokohama and co-organized by the Government of Japan, the United Nations, the United Nations Development Programme (UNDP) and the World Bank. The Conference reaffirmed the importance of Africa's exercising full ownership of its development agenda and the need for a genuine partnership with the international community in those efforts, and issued the Yokohama Declaration and the TICAD IV action plan and follow-up mechanism.

On 24 December, the Assembly decided that the agenda item on the "New Partnership for Africa's Development: progress in implementation and international support" would remain for consideration during its resumed sixty-third (2009) session (**decision 63/552**).

Social dimensions of NEPAD

The Commission for Social Development, at its forty-sixth session (New York, 16 February 2007, 6–15 February and 22 February 2008) [E/2008/26], recommended to the Economic and Social Council for adoption a resolution on the social dimensions of NEPAD. In resolution 2008/17 (see p. 1016), the Council requested the Commission to continue to give prominence to and raise awareness of the social dimensions of NEPAD, and the Secretary-General to submit a report on the subject to the Commission's forty-seventh (2009) session.

ECONOMIC AND SOCIAL COUNCIL ACTION

On 24 July [meeting 42], the Economic and Social Council, on the recommendation of the Commission for Social Development [E/2008/26], adopted **resolution 2008/17** without vote [agenda item 14 *(b)*].

Social dimensions of the New Partnership for Africa's Development

The Economic and Social Council,

Recalling the outcomes of the World Summit for Social Development, held in Copenhagen from 6 to 12 March 1995, and the twenty-fourth special session of the General Assembly, entitled "World Summit for Social Development and beyond: achieving social development for all in a globalizing world", held in Geneva from 26 June to 1 July 2000,

Reaffirming the United Nations Millennium Declaration of 8 September 2000, the United Nations Declaration on the New Partnership for Africa's Development of 16 September 2002, General Assembly resolution 57/7 of 4 November 2002 on the final review and appraisal of the United Nations New Agenda for the Development of Africa in the 1990s and support for the New Partnership for Africa's Development,

Noting the conclusions of the African Union Extraordinary Summit on Employment and Poverty Alleviation in Africa, held in Ouagadougou on 8 and 9 September 2004,

Recognizing the commitments made in meeting the special needs of Africa at the 2005 World Summit,

Remaining concerned that Africa is the only continent currently not on track to achieve any of the goals set out in the Millennium Declaration by 2015, and in this regard emphasizing that concerted efforts and continued support are required to fulfil the commitments to address the special needs of Africa,

Recognizing that capacity-building is essential for the successful implementation of the New Partnership for Africa's Development, and recognizing also the need for continued support from the international community,

Bearing in mind that African countries have primary responsibility for their own economic and social development, that the role of national policies and development strategies cannot be overemphasized and that their development efforts need to be supported by an enabling international economic environment, and in this regard recalling the support given by the International Conference on Financing for Development to the New Partnership,

1. *Welcomes* the progress made by the African countries in fulfilling their commitments in the implementation of the New Partnership for Africa's Development to deepen democracy, human rights, good governance and sound economic management, and encourages African countries, with the participation of stakeholders, including civil society and the private sector, to intensify their efforts in this regard by developing and strengthening institutions for governance and creating an environment conducive to attracting foreign direct investment for the development of the region;

2. *Also welcomes* the good progress that has been achieved in implementing the African Peer Review Mechanism, in particular the completion of the peer review process in some countries, the progress in implementing the recommendations of those reviews in some countries and the completion of the self-assessment process, the hosting of country support missions and the launching of the national preparatory process for the peer review in others, and urges African States that have not yet done so to join the peer review, as a matter of priority, and to strengthen the peer review process so as to ensure its efficient performance;

3. *Further welcomes* the efforts made by African countries and regional and subregional organizations, including the African Union, to mainstream a gender perspective and the empowerment of women in the implementation of the New Partnership;

4. *Emphasizes* that the African Union and the regional economic communities have a critical role to play in the implementation of the New Partnership, and in this regard encourages African countries, with the assistance of their development partners, to increase and coordinate effectively their support for enhancing the capacities of those institutions;

5. *Also emphasizes* that progress in the implementation of the New Partnership depends also on a favourable national and international environment for Africa's growth and development, including measures to promote a policy environment conducive to private sector development and entrepreneurship;

6. *Further emphasizes* that democracy, respect for all human rights and fundamental freedoms, including the right to development, transparent and accountable governance and administration in all sectors of society and effective participation by civil society, non-governmental organizations and the private sector are among the indispensable foundations for the realization of social and people-centred sustainable development;

7. *Emphasizes* that the rising poverty levels and social exclusion faced by most African countries require a comprehensive approach to the development and implementation of social and economic policies, inter alia, to reduce poverty, to promote economic activity, growth and sustainable development, to ensure employment creation and decent work for all, and to enhance social inclusion, political stability, democracy and good governance and the promotion and protection of human rights and fundamental freedoms, so as to ensure the achievement of Africa's social and economic objectives;

8. *Recognizes* that, while social development is primarily the responsibility of Governments, international cooperation and assistance are essential for the full achievement of that goal;

9. *Also recognizes* the contribution made by Member States to the implementation of the New Partnership in the context of South-South cooperation, welcomes, in that regard, the convening of the Beijing Summit of the Forum on China-Africa Cooperation on 4 and 5 November 2006 and the Africa-South America Summit, held in Abuja on 30 November and 1 December 2006, and encourages the international community, including the international financial institutions, to support the efforts of African countries, including through triangular cooperation;

10. *Welcomes* the various important initiatives of Africa's development partners in recent years, including those

of the Organisation for Economic Co-operation and Development, the Africa Action Plan of the Group of Eight, the 2007 European Union-Africa Summit, the Africa-Asia Business Forum, the report of the Commission for Africa entitled "Our common interest" and the Africa Partnership Forum, as well as the Fourth Tokyo International Conference on African Development, held in Yokohama, Japan, from 28 to 30 May 2008, on the theme "Towards a vibrant Africa: continent of hope and opportunity", and in this regard emphasizes the importance of coordination in such initiatives on Africa;

11. *Urges* continuous support of measures to address the challenges of poverty eradication and sustainable development in Africa, including, as appropriate, debt relief, improved market access, support for the private sector and entrepreneurship, enhanced official development assistance, increased foreign direct investment and the transfer of technology;

12. *Welcomes* the recent increase in official development assistance pledged by many of the development partners, including the commitments of the Group of Eight and the European Union, which will lead to an increase in official development assistance to Africa of 25 billion dollars per year by 2010, and encourages all development partners to ensure aid effectiveness through the implementation of the Paris Declaration on Aid Effectiveness: Ownership, Harmonization, Alignment, Results and Mutual Accountability, of 2005;

13. *Recognizes* the need for national Governments and the international community to make continued efforts to increase the flow of new and additional resources for financing for development from all sources, public and private, domestic and foreign, to support the development of African countries;

14. *Welcomes* the efforts by development partners to align their financial and technical support to Africa more closely with the priorities of the New Partnership, as reflected in national poverty reduction strategies or in similar strategies, and encourages development partners to increase their efforts in this regard;

15. *Acknowledges* the activities of the Bretton Woods institutions and the African Development Bank in African countries, and invites those institutions to continue their support for the implementation of the priorities and objectives of the New Partnership;

16. *Notes* the growing collaboration among the entities of the United Nations system in support of the New Partnership, and requests the Secretary-General to promote greater coherence in the work of the United Nations system in support of the New Partnership, on the basis of the agreed clusters;

17. *Requests* the United Nations system to continue to provide assistance to the African Union and the secretariat of the New Partnership and to African countries in developing projects and programmes within the scope of the priorities of the New Partnership;

18. *Invites* the Secretary-General, as a follow-up to the 2005 World Summit, to urge the organizations and bodies of the United Nations system to assist African countries in implementing quick-impact initiatives, based on their national development priorities and strategies, to enable them to achieve the Millennium Development Goals, and in this respect acknowledges recent commitments by some donor countries;

19. *Requests* the Secretary-General to continue to take measures to strengthen the Office of the Special Adviser on Africa, and requests the Office to collaborate with the Department of Economic and Social Affairs of the Secretariat and to include the social dimensions of the New Partnership in its comprehensive reports to the General Assembly at its sixty-third session;

20. *Requests* the Commission for Social Development to discuss, in its annual programme of work, regional programmes to promote social development so as to enable all regions of the United Nations system to share experiences and best practices, with the concurrence of concerned countries;

21. *Decides* that the Commission for Social Development should continue to give prominence to and raise awareness of the social dimensions of the New Partnership during its forty-seventh session;

22. *Requests* the Secretary-General, in collaboration with the Office of the Special Adviser on Africa, while also taking into consideration General Assembly resolution 62/179 of 19 December 2007 entitled "New Partnership for Africa's Development: progress in implementation and international support", to submit to the Commission for Social Development at its forty-seventh session a report on the social dimensions of the New Partnership.

Report of Secretary-General. In response to Economic and Social Council resolution 2008/17 (above), the Secretary-General submitted a November report [E/CN.5/2009/3] on the social dimensions of NEPAD that emphasized the need to address plans of action in such areas as governance, agricultural development, infrastructure development, health and education. It also highlighted the importance of social inclusion, social protection, global partnerships and the need to strengthen data in respect of the social dimensions of NEPAD. The report concluded with a set of recommendations to elevate and champion Africa's social development agenda.

Liberia

In response to General Assembly resolution 61/218 [YUN 2006, p. 1081], the Secretary-General submitted an August report [A/63/295] on humanitarian assistance and the reconstruction of Liberia that provided an analysis of the challenges to the delivery of assistance faced by the United Nations and its partners.

The Secretary-General said that the presence of peacekeeping troops of the United Nations Mission in Liberia had stabilized the security situation in all 15 counties of Liberia, creating an environment conducive to the return and reintegration of refugees and IDPs to their places of origin, supporting the re-establishment of a democratic Government and resuscitating the economy. Regarding the humanitarian situation, in 2007, there were more than 10 reported cases of flooding in five counties; strong winds damaged 44 homes and other structures in two counties; and fire destroyed 43 homes in two counties. Overall, some 21,000 people were affected. Although the destruction was not on the same scale as that caused by natural disasters in other parts of the world, limited financial support for critical humanitarian needs, poor response and inadequate absorptive capacity had an extraordinarily negative impact on affected communities. The National Disaster Relief Commission was working with partners to develop a comprehensive national disaster management policy. Despite the natural disasters, the overall humanitarian situation had continued to improve since the Secretary-General's 2006 report [YUN 2006, p. 1081]. The Government, with the assistance of the United Nations and the humanitarian community, focused on urgent humanitarian needs. A common humanitarian action plan was launched in 2007 [YUN 2007, p. 927] to address key humanitarian needs, including basic health care, water and sanitation facilities and food security. Meanwhile, funding from CERF allowed UN agencies and partners to provide urgent life-saving assistance to more than 1 million vulnerable people. Ongoing efforts to repatriate Liberian refugees in the subregion continued. In April 2008, a voluntary return exercise was launched following a tripartite agreement between Ghana, Liberia and UNHCR, primarily for the return of the 27,000 refugees remaining in Ghana at the end of 2008. An estimated 72,000 registered Liberian refugees remained in asylum countries. Although the capacity to absorb returnees had improved since 2006, many IDPs and refugees were returning home amid high unemployment and rising food and fuel prices, which had increased by 22 per cent between January 2007 and January 2008. A World Bank grant of $10 million to address urgent food needs was a welcome initiative, as were UN efforts to support the Government's food security and nutrition strategy through a $140.2 million joint UN programme. Another key development challenge remained security. Increasing waves of armed robbery in residential as well as corporate quarters were posing a challenge to the National Police. In addition, severe institutional, material and national capacity constraints were hampering the achievement of the MDGs. Other constraints to progress included inadequate technical capacity and the lack of resources to drive reforms and the development agenda of the country; the lack of basic social services and infrastructure; and the high level of formal unemployment, estimated at 80 per cent.

The Secretary-General concluded that massive poverty alleviation and economic recovery efforts were essential to making substantial progress in attaining the MDGs. Substantial donor support was required to help the new Government provide some services on a large scale and help meet the expectations of the people of Liberia. Consolidation of the hard-won peace was dependent upon it. In line with the poverty reduction strategy, he said that creating employment through the private sector was at the heart of recovery and sustainable development in Liberia, and urged development partners to focus on attracting investment into the country and stabilizing the economic environment to foster economic growth. He also made recommendations for building the capacity of national institutions and implementation of the joint Government of Liberia/UN programme to prevent and respond to sexual and gender-based violence.

GENERAL ASSEMBLY ACTION

On 11 December [meeting 68], the General Assembly adopted **resolution 63/136** [A/63/L.45 & Add.1] without vote [agenda item 65 *(b)*].

Humanitarian assistance and reconstruction of Liberia

The General Assembly,

Recalling its resolutions 45/232 of 21 December 1990, 46/147 of 17 December 1991, 47/154 of 18 December 1992, 48/197 of 21 December 1993, 49/21 E of 20 December 1994, 50/58 A of 12 December 1995, 51/30 B of 5 December 1996, 52/169 E of 16 December 1997, 55/176 of 19 December 2000, 57/151 of 16 December 2002, 59/219 of 22 December 2004 and 61/218 of 20 December 2006,

Having considered the report of the Secretary-General,

Commending the Economic Community of West African States, the African Union, the International Contact Group on the Mano River Basin, the United Nations system and its specialized agencies, donor countries and institutions and governmental and non-governmental organizations for their continued support for the peacebuilding process and development of Liberia,

Commending also the United Nations Mission in Liberia for its important role in the maintenance of peace and stability in the country,

Noting with appreciation the progress made by the Truth and Reconciliation Commission, despite many difficulties, and expressing its appreciation to the Government of Liberia and those of its partners that have so far provided assistance to the Commission,

Taking note, while conscious of further challenges, of the progress made in a number of areas, including the consolidation of governmental authority throughout the country, as evidenced by the national development agenda, which encompasses four benchmarks: security; good governance and the rule of law; economic revitalization and infrastructure; and basic services, which are also important elements for sustainable economic growth and development,

Strongly condemning all acts of gender-based violence, including sexual violence committed against civilians, in particular women and children, and underlining the need to implement the Government of Liberia/United Nations Joint Programme to Prevent and Respond to Sexual Gender-based Violence (2008–2012),

Stressing the need to protect women and children in post-conflict situations, and recalling the Security Council resolutions and presidential statements on women and peace and security, in particular Council resolution 1325(2000) of 31 October 2000,

Taking note that the situation in Liberia remains generally stable, although fragile,

1. *Expresses its gratitude* to the Economic Community of West African States, the African Union, donor countries and institutions, the United Nations system and its specialized agencies and non-governmental organizations for their valuable support in their adoption of a comprehensive approach to peacebuilding in Liberia and in the subregion;

2. *Commends* the Secretary-General for his continued efforts in mobilizing the international community, the United Nations system and other organizations to provide assistance to Liberia;

3. *Renews its invitation* to all States and intergovernmental and non-governmental organizations to provide assistance to Liberia to facilitate the continued creation of an enabling environment for the promotion of peace, socio-economic development and regional security, including by emphasizing capacity-building, institution-building and employment generation in their work and ensuring that such work complements and contributes to the development of an economy characterized by a predictable investment climate conducive to entrepreneurship, good governance and the rule of law;

4. *Welcomes* the agreement, in June 2008, on the Government of Liberia/United Nations Joint Programme to Prevent and Respond to Sexual Gender-based Violence (2008–2012), and calls upon all parties to implement it;

5. *Takes note with appreciation* of the fact that the Government of Liberia's poverty reduction strategy has been finalized and overwhelmingly endorsed by its partners at the Liberia Poverty Reduction Forum, held in Berlin on 26 and 27 June 2008;

6. *Strongly encourages* the international community to translate the tremendous goodwill expressed at the Liberia Poverty Reduction Forum into tangible resources and support for the Government's national reconstruction agenda, including its poverty reduction strategy and actions for the achievement of the Millennium Development Goals;

7. *Urges* the Government to continue to create an environment conducive to the promotion of socio-economic development, peace and security in the country, to the reintegration of refugees and internally displaced persons and to its commitment to ensure the upholding of human rights, the rule of law and national reconciliation;

8. *Appeals* to the international community and intergovernmental and non-governmental organizations to provide adequate assistance to programmes and projects identified in the report of the Secretary-General;

9. *Requests* the Secretary-General:

(a) To continue his efforts in coordinating the work of the United Nations system and mobilize financial, technical and other assistance for the rehabilitation and reconstruction of Liberia;

(b) To submit to the General Assembly at its sixty-fifth session the final and comprehensive report on the implementation of humanitarian assistance and reconstruction of Liberia, under the item entitled "Strengthening of the coordination of humanitarian and disaster relief assistance of the United Nations, including special economic assistance", taking into account the peacebuilding activities in the country financed through the Peacebuilding Fund;

10. *Decides* to consider, at its sixty-fifth session, the status of international assistance for the rehabilitation and reconstruction of Liberia.

African countries emerging from conflict

Guinea-Bissau

Pursuant to Economic and Social Council resolution 2007/15 [YUN 2007, p. 940], the mandate of the Ad Hoc Advisory Group on Guinea-Bissau was extended until the Council's 2008 substantive session. Following its two previous reports in 2007 [ibid., p. 939] and 2006 [YUN 2006, p. 1085], in which the Group recognized the limitations inherent in its structure and mandate and invited the Council to consider recommending that Guinea-Bissau be placed on the agenda of the Peacebuilding Commission, on 11 December 2007, the Security Council agreed to support the country's inclusion on the Commission's agenda [YUN 2007, p. 230].

In May 2008, the Group submitted a report [E/2008/55], which provided an overview of its work since the Group's establishment in 2002 [YUN 2002, p. 920], highlighting its main accomplishments and key recommendations, and concluded with observations about Guinea-Bissau which the Group believed might be relevant to the Peacebuilding Commission. The Group also recommended the termination of its mandate at the Council's substantive session.

(For more information on Guinea-Bissau, see p. 220).

ECONOMIC AND SOCIAL COUNCIL ACTION

On 25 July [meeting 44], the Economic and Social Council adopted **resolution 2008/30** [draft: E/2008/L.34] without vote [agenda item 7 *(f)*].

Ad Hoc Advisory Group on Guinea-Bissau

The Economic and Social Council,

Recalling its resolutions 2005/32 of 26 July 2005, 2006/11 of 26 July 2006 and 2007/15 of 26 July 2007 and its decision 2002/304 of 25 October 2002,

1. *Takes note* of the report of the Ad Hoc Advisory Group on Guinea-Bissau;

2. *Welcomes* the decision of the Peacebuilding Commission to place Guinea-Bissau in its agenda and the creation of a country-specific configuration;

3. *Takes note* of the political and economic evolution of the situation, and welcomes the support of the international community for this process;

4. *Looks forward* to continued support for Guinea-Bissau from donors, the United Nations system and the Bretton Woods institutions, and, in this regard, welcomes the decision by the Executive Board of the International Monetary Fund to renew access by Guinea-Bissau to emergency post-conflict assistance;

5. *Reaffirms* the importance of promoting sustainable development and improved governance as fundamental to consolidating peace, in addition to ongoing efforts for socio-economic recovery and reforms in the public administration, security and defence sectors;

6. *Invites* the partners of Guinea-Bissau to provide predictable and adequate resources to ensure the effective implementation of the strategic framework of the Peacebuilding Commission;

7. *Stresses* the importance of addressing the structural causes of conflict, and, in this connection, urges continued support and funding for the implementation of the country's poverty reduction strategy, its security sector reform plan and its anti-narcotics operational plan;

8. *Expresses its appreciation* for the positive and constructive role of the Advisory Group in supporting the country in its efforts to rebuild its economy and society, and invites its members to continue their support through the Peacebuilding Commission;

9. *Expresses its appreciation* to the Secretary-General for the support provided to the work of the Advisory Group;

10. *Decides* to terminate the mandate of the Ad Hoc Advisory Group on Guinea-Bissau;

11. *Invites* the Peacebuilding Commission to consider the work of the Ad Hoc Advisory Group on Guinea-Bissau of the Economic and Social Council and to draw upon the lessons learned from that experience;

12. *Also invites* the Peacebuilding Commission to continue to inform it about the economic and social aspects of peacebuilding in Guinea-Bissau;

13. *Decides* to consider this matter at its substantive session of 2009 under the item entitled "African countries emerging from conflict".

Other economic assistance

Haiti

In response to Economic and Social Council resolution 2007/13 [YUN 2007, p. 942], the Ad Hoc Advisory Group on Haiti reported in June [E/2008/90] on the follow-up to recommendations contained in its 2007 report [YUN 2007, p. 941] on key issues for the long-term development of Haiti, including development planning and aid coordination; institutional capacity-building; and the Haitian and international levers for economic and social development. It also provided information on the food crisis and ensuing demonstrations, which led to the destitution of the Government in April 2008 and an institutional and political vacuum, and on action needed to end the crisis. The Group had postponed its mission to Haiti, scheduled for 27 to 30 April, due to the uncertain context. Given the lack of progress in the political situation, it decided to cancel its visit at the end of May, as the time had become too short for it to visit the country and prepare a meaningful report to the Council for consideration at its July session.

On development planning and aid coordination, the Group reported that by the end of 2007, Haitian authorities had finalized the national growth and poverty reduction strategy paper, which presented three main areas of action: promoting vectors of growth (agriculture and rural development, tourism, infrastructure, and science and technology); strengthening human development, with a focus on improving the delivery of basic services; and improving democratic governance, including security and the justice system. Environmental protection, disaster risk reduction and HIV/AIDS were presented as cross-cutting issues. On institutional capacity-building, despite progress made to improve programme delivery, the key challenge remained the strengthening of local capacities to manage development programmes. A positive development in judicial reform was the adoption by Parliament of legislation on magistrates. The security situation remained a concern owing to the kidnappings and violence that had been on the rise since the April crisis, and the potential negative impact the deterioration of security conditions could have on the capacity of NGOs to support the country. Meanwhile, improvements in macroeconomic governance brought a more stable environment with an increase in remittances and donor flows, and debt relief by the Inter-American Development Bank. However, between August 2007 and March 2008, the price of basic food commodities had increased by up to 65 per cent, exacerbating the situation of an already vulnerable population. The Group noted that the international community had come to the country's aid swiftly, including through the UN system in Haiti, which had released resources for emergency assistance, and the provision by international donors and Governments of food aid and in-kind donations. The Inter-American Development Bank accelerated the disbursement of $27 million and the World Bank supported the Government with a $10 million grant.

The Group concluded that while there had been improvements on various fronts, the persistent instability and vulnerability in the country remained a concern. As political stability was paramount to the development work, the Group stressed the importance of the installation of a new Government. It called on international stakeholders to increase their support to Haiti; stated that it was still imperative for Haiti to remain on the international agenda; and recommended a strong UN presence on the ground. In that connection, the Group supported further renewals of the mandate of the United Nations Stabilization Mission in Haiti. It also made a series of recommendations on development planning and aid coordination, institutional capacity-building and international levers for economic and social development.

(For more information on Haiti, see p. 334.)

ECONOMIC AND SOCIAL COUNCIL ACTION

On 23 July [meeting 40], the Economic and Social Council adopted **resolution 2008/10** [draft: E/2008/L.15] without vote [agenda item 7 *(d)*].

Ad Hoc Advisory Group on Haiti

The Economic and Social Council,

Recalling its resolutions 2004/52 of 23 July 2004, 2005/46 of 27 July 2005, 2006/10 of 26 July 2006 and 2007/13 of 25 July 2007 and its decision 2004/322 of 11 November 2004,

1. *Takes note* of the report of the Ad Hoc Advisory Group on Haiti and the recommendations contained therein;

2. *Also takes note* of the political and economic evolution of the situation, and welcomes the support provided by the international community to this process;

3. *Notes* the progress made by the Government of Haiti in terms of gender equality, and also notes the importance of gender equality as a necessary dimension of any strategy for development;

4. *Commends* the finalization of the growth and poverty reduction strategy paper by the Haitian authorities, and looks forward to continued support from donors, the United Nations system and the Bretton Woods institutions in connection with the implementation of this strategy;

5. *Expresses concern* over the especially adverse effects of the global food crisis on Haiti, and encourages the international community to continue providing support for the short- and long-term needs for the recovery of Haiti, and, in this regard, welcomes the holding of meetings on this issue, such as the High-level Meeting on Food Security in Haiti, held in Rome on 2 June 2008, and the Conference on Food Sovereignty and Rural Development in Haiti, held in Madrid on 15 July 2008;

6. *Recognizes* the need for effective coordination between the Government of Haiti and donors, as well as a standing mechanism for consultation with the main non-governmental organizations active in Haiti;

7. *Decides* to extend the mandate of the Advisory Group until the substantive session of the Economic and Social Council in July 2009, with the purpose of following closely and providing advice on Haiti's long-term development strategy to promote socio-economic recovery and stability, with particular attention to the need to ensure coherence and sustainability in international support for Haiti, based on the long-term national development priorities and building upon the Interim Cooperation Framework and the growth and poverty reduction strategy paper, and stressing the need to avoid overlap and duplication with respect to existing mechanisms;

8. *Expresses its satisfaction* to the Secretary-General for the support provided to the Advisory Group, and requests him to continue to support the Group's activities adequately from within existing resources;

9. *Requests* the Advisory Group, in accomplishing its mandate, to continue to cooperate with the Secretary-General and his Special Representative in Haiti, the head of the United Nations Stabilization Mission in Haiti, the United Nations Development Group, relevant United Nations funds and programmes and the specialized agencies, the Bretton Woods institutions, regional organizations and institutions, including the Economic Commission for Latin America and the Caribbean, the Organization of American States, the Caribbean Community and the Inter-American Development Bank, and other major stakeholders;

10. *Also requests* the Advisory Group to submit a report on its work, with recommendations, as appropriate, to the Economic and Social Council at its substantive session of 2009.

Kazakhstan

In response to General Assembly resolution 60/216 [YUN 2005, p. 1013], the Secretary-General submitted a report [A/63/659] on humanitarian assistance and rehabilitation for selected countries and regions that provided information on international cooperation and coordination for the human and ecological rehabilitation and economic development of the Semipalatinsk region of Kazakhstan, a former nuclear test site, including a summary of actions undertaken in the previous three years by the Government of Kazakhstan, the UN system and the international community. Those efforts had not been sufficient to mitigate the suffering caused by years of nuclear testing.

On the economic and social conditions, although Kazakhstan was a middle-income country that enjoyed macroeconomic stability due to reforms in social, monetary and credit policy, land relations and private sector development, and had achieved the first three MDGs in their regional formulation by 2004, the 2007 national report on the MDGs indicated that nearly 40 per cent of the population lived close to the poverty line in 2006 and that significant disparities existed among provinces. The territories of the former Semipalatinsk test site belonged to three provinces: East Kazakhstan, Pavlodar and Karagandar; the share of population with income below the minimum subsistence level in those provinces was, respectively, 12.5 per cent, 12 per cent and 20.2 per cent, in comparison to the national average of 18.2 per cent. Child and maternal mortality rates in those provinces remained high. On the institutional framework for the delivery of assistance, the Government took the lead in setting priority areas and supporting the rehabilitation of the region through its 2005–2007 programme, which aimed to improve the ecological, economic, medical and social factors affecting the living standards of the population in the region. In follow-up to its 2002–2005 programme, in 2008, UNDP, along with the UN Volunteers, UNICEF and UNFPA started a three-year joint project entitled "Enhancing human security in the former nuclear test site of Semipalatinsk". The report also provided information on donor assistance to the Semipalatinsk region to address various economic and social issues, as well as on international aid and development organizations that had contributed funds to help the Semipalatinsk region implement projects in the education, environment and health sectors. On priorities for future action, the Ministry of Environment Protection and the Ministry of Energy and Mineral Resources developed a new programme for the Semipalatinsk region for 2009–2011 that aimed to optimize State control over the nuclear testing site area; create a more secure situation with regard to radiation and rehabilitate the environment in the region; safely secure objects using atomic energy located within the former nuclear testing site; and rehabilitate the population and develop the social infrastructure.

The Secretary-General recommended the organization of a conference with the participation of international and national partners to review the work that had been accomplished and to set future priorities. Based on the findings of the conference, the international community would be called upon to reinforce donor interest and assistance to the Semipalatinsk region. He also made recommendations for the Government to focus on the improvement of administration, including the training of central authorities in the more effective use of resources, and the establishment of a multi-stakeholder mechanism, which would include Government ministries, donors, local government and civil society organizations. In that regard, the Government could call on the UN Resident Coordinator and the UNDP office in Kazakhstan to assist in those efforts. The main priority areas were: radiation safety, socio-economic development, health, providing information and communicating risk to the population, and strengthening NGOs in their efforts to carry out socio-economic initiatives.

Third States affected by sanctions

In response to General Assembly resolution 62/69 [YUN 2007, p. 1381], the Secretary-General submitted an August report [A/63/224] that highlighted developments concerning General Assembly and Economic and Social Council activities in the area of assistance to third States affected by the application of sanctions; arrangements in the Secretariat related to assistance to those States; and operational changes as a result of the shift in focus towards targeted sanctions in the procedures and working methods of the Security Council and its sanctions committees.

The Assembly took action with regard to the Secretary-General's report in **resolution 63/127** (see p. 1476).

Disaster response

In 2008, disasters associated with natural hazards such as earthquakes, floods, cyclones and droughts continued to trigger humanitarian emergencies and were driven by the increased frequency and severity of extreme weather events, mostly associated with climate change. Some 354 disasters associated with natural hazards caused 235,264 deaths and affected approximately 214 million people. Although the number of disasters was below the average of 397 per year for the period 2000–2007, the number of deaths was three times higher than the average owing to Cyclone Nargis in Myanmar and the Sichuan earthquake in China, which killed 138,366 and 87,476 people, respectively. Floods were the most common type of disaster recorded, with 166 events, followed by 112 storms and 23 earthquakes. Climate-related hazards caused 91 per cent of disasters. The cost of natural disasters was estimated at $190 billion in economic damages. Despite high absolute financial losses in the United States and Europe, the relative economic impact of disasters was greatest in low- and middle-income countries. Where Governments and affected communities were adequately prepared, an effective response to natural hazards could be mounted before they happened.

In southern Africa, recurrent drought jeopardized the livelihoods of millions, with rainfall below average across the region and almost non-existent in Ethiopia, Kenya and Somalia. In other regions, torrential rains caused severe flooding and destroyed crops. More than 40,000 people were displaced by floods in southern Sudan, while flooding and landslides in Kenya affected 300,000 people. In West Africa, flooding from July to September affected more than 300,000 people and damaged crops and vital infrastructure. In Asia, heavy monsoon rains caused flooding that affected more than half a million people in India, Nepal and Pakistan, while the October earthquake in Pakistan's Balochistan Province affected 68,200 people and destroyed or damaged 7,600 houses. In the Middle East, Yemen faced the most devastating flash floods in decades, displacing an estimated 25,000 people. In Latin America and the Caribbean, Cuba was hit by four successive hurricanes and tropical storms, damaging or destroying some 500,000 homes. In Haiti, those same hazards affected more than 800,000 people and caused losses estimated at $900 million. Meanwhile, Guatemala and Panama experienced an intense rainy season affecting 203,300 persons. In Eastern Europe, heavy rains and storms in the summer led to severe flooding affecting 40,000 people in Moldova, Romania and Ukraine.

International cooperation

Report of Secretary-General. In response to General Assembly resolution 62/92 [YUN 2007, p. 945], the Secretary-General, in an August report on international cooperation on humanitarian assistance in the field of natural disasters [A/63/277], provided an overview of disasters associated with natural hazards and the humanitarian response to them and highlighted emerging trends, their implications for humanitarian action and the key challenges that needed to be addressed. The report stated that 2007 figures conformed to a longer-term trend of increasing frequency and intensity of natural hazard disasters, with some 414 disasters affecting over 211 million people and resulting in 16,800 deaths. It also indicated that while the number of recorded disasters had increased significantly over the past two decades, so had disaster resilience in some countries. Strengthened preparedness was essential to saving lives and livelihoods in disasters, as an increased capacity to predict, monitor, warn and respond to the needs of those adversely affected by an emergency was essential for effective humanitarian action.

A number of key steps were taken at the global level to strengthen early warning and preparedness for response capacity. Investment in the global cluster approach coordination system had ensured improved collaboration on preparedness in a number of countries, as well as more effective and timely global support at the outset of several disasters. Following an extensive review process in November 2007, IASC endorsed the revised Inter-Agency Contingency Planning Guidelines for Humanitarian Assistance, which outlined how the international community could organize itself to complement national action. Enhancing partnerships between humanitarian organizations to improve humanitarian action was also the focus of the second meeting of the Global Humanitarian Platform in July 2008. The UN disaster assessment and coordination system and the International Search and Rescue Advisory Group continued to work with States to enhance preparedness and response capacity. The UN disaster assessment and coordination system deployed 13 response missions: eight to the Americas and Caribbean region, two to Africa and three to Asia. Humanitarian actors also intensified efforts to share good practices in preparedness for disaster response. A review of the Central Register of Disaster Management Capacities was scheduled to commence in 2008. The Register comprised a series of standby directories to support the United Nations and the international community in delivering humanitarian emergency assistance. Meanwhile, preparations for the second session of the Global Platform for Disaster Risk Reduction [YUN 2007, p. 949], due to take place in June 2009, were under way. Other issues addressed in the report included the use of information technology for improved humanitarian action, including space-based technology; strengthening the transition from relief to development; the use of military assets for disaster response and the outcome of a study on the topic, which was completed in March 2008; and humanitarian financing for disasters associated with natural hazards. In that regard, the Emergency Relief Coordinator had committed $148 million in CERF funding to 28 countries affected by hazard events during the reporting period.

The Secretary-General made a series of recommendations. He encouraged Member States and humanitarian agencies to promote natural disaster preparedness activities, including contingency planning at all levels. The UN system and other humanitarian actors should improve dissemination of tools and services to support disaster risk reduction. Member States should increase allocation of funds for disaster risk reduction activities; enhance or develop funding mechanisms to support strengthened preparedness for response and early recovery activities; and support humanitarian organizations in meeting the increasing humanitarian burden exacerbated by climate change and high food and fuel prices.

He also recommended that States make use of the Guidelines for the Domestic Facilitation and Regulation of International Disaster Relief and Initial Recovery Assistance to strengthen their legal frameworks for international disaster assistance, and consider the applicability of the Guidelines on the Use of Foreign Military and Civil Defense Assets in Disaster Relief for the coordination of foreign military assets to their national and regional disaster structures.

UN-SPIDER programme. The Committee on the Peaceful Uses of Outer Space (see p. 684) submitted a report [A/AC.105/929] on the 2008 activities of the United Nations Platform for Space-based Information for Disaster Management and Emergency Response (UN-SPIDER). On 5 December, in **resolution 63/90**, the General Assembly noted the progress made in the implementation of the UN-SPIDER 2007–2009 programme, including inaugurating and making fully operational its office in Bonn, Germany (ibid.).

GENERAL ASSEMBLY ACTION

On 11 December [meeting 68], the General Assembly adopted **resolution 63/141** [draft: A/63/L.53 & Add.1, orally revised] without vote [agenda item 65 *(a)*].

International cooperation on humanitarian assistance in the field of natural disasters, from relief to development

The General Assembly,

Reaffirming its resolution 46/182 of 19 December 1991, the annex to which contains the guiding principles for the strengthening of the coordination of emergency humanitarian assistance of the United Nations system, as well as all its resolutions on international cooperation on humanitarian assistance in the field of natural disasters, from relief to development, and recalling the resolutions of the humanitarian segments of the substantive sessions of the Economic and Social Council,

Recognizing the importance of the principles of neutrality, humanity, impartiality and independence for the provision of humanitarian assistance,

Welcoming the Hyogo Declaration, the Hyogo Framework for Action 2005–2015: Building the Resilience of Nations and Communities to Disasters and the common statement of the special session on the Indian Ocean disaster: risk reduction for a safer future, as adopted by the World Conference on Disaster Reduction, held in Kobe, Hyogo, Japan, from 18 to 22 January 2005,

Emphasizing that the affected State has the primary responsibility in the initiation, organization, coordination and implementation of humanitarian assistance within its territory and in the facilitation of the work of humanitarian organizations in mitigating the consequences of natural disasters,

Emphasizing also the responsibility of all States to undertake disaster preparedness, response and early recovery efforts in order to minimize the impact of natural disasters, while recognizing the importance of international cooperation in support of the efforts of affected countries which may have limited capacities in this regard,

Expressing its deep concern at the increasing challenges to Member States and to the United Nations humanitarian response capacity presented by the consequences of natural disasters, including the impact of climate change, and by the humanitarian implications of the current global food crisis,

Noting that local communities are the first responders in most disasters, and underlining the critical role played by in-country capacities in disaster risk reduction, including preparedness, response and recovery,

Recognizing the importance of international cooperation in support of the efforts of the affected States in dealing with natural disasters in all their phases, in particular in preparedness, response and the early recovery phase, and of strengthening the response capacity of countries affected by disaster,

Noting with appreciation the important role played by Member States, including developing countries, that have granted necessary and continued generous assistance to countries and peoples stricken by natural disasters,

Recognizing the significant role played by national Red Cross and Red Crescent societies, as part of the International Red Cross and Red Crescent Movement, in disaster preparedness and risk reduction, disaster response, rehabilitation and development,

Emphasizing the importance of addressing vulnerability and integrating risk reduction into all phases of natural disaster management, post-natural disaster recovery and development planning,

Recognizing that efforts to achieve economic growth, sustainable development and internationally agreed development goals, including the Millennium Development Goals, can be adversely affected by natural disasters, and noting the positive contribution that those efforts can make in strengthening the resilience of populations to such disasters,

Emphasizing, in this context, the important role of development organizations in supporting national efforts to mitigate the consequences of natural disasters,

1. *Takes note* of the report of the Secretary-General;

2. *Expresses its deep concern* at the number and scale of natural disasters and their increasing impact, resulting in massive losses of life and property worldwide, in particular in vulnerable societies lacking adequate capacity to mitigate effectively the long-term negative social, economic and environmental consequences of natural disasters;

3. *Calls upon* States to fully implement the Hyogo Declaration and the Hyogo Framework for Action 2005–2015: Building the Resilience of Nations and Communities to Disasters, in particular those commitments related to assistance for developing countries that are prone to natural disasters and for disaster-stricken States in the transition phase towards sustainable physical, social and economic recovery, for risk-reduction activities in post-disaster recovery and for rehabilitation processes;

4. *Calls upon* all States to adopt, where required, and to continue to implement effectively, necessary legislative and other appropriate measures to mitigate the effects of natural disasters and integrate disaster risk reduction strategies into development planning, and in this regard requests the international community to continue to assist developing countries as well as countries with economies in transition, as appropriate;

5. *Encourages* Member States and, where applicable, regional organizations to strengthen operational and legal frameworks for international disaster relief, taking into account, as appropriate, the Guidelines for the Domestic Facilitation and Regulation of International Disaster Relief and Initial Recovery Assistance, adopted at the Thirtieth International Conference of the Red Cross and Red Crescent, held from 26 to 30 November 2007;

6. *Welcomes* the effective cooperation among the affected States, relevant bodies of the United Nations system, donor countries, regional and international financial institutions and other relevant organizations, such as the International Red Cross and Red Crescent Movement, and civil society, in the coordination and delivery of emergency relief, and stresses the need to continue such cooperation and delivery throughout relief operations and medium- and long-term rehabilitation and reconstruction efforts, in a manner that reduces vulnerability to future natural hazards;

7. *Reiterates* the commitment to support the efforts of countries, in particular developing countries, to strengthen their capacities at all levels in order to prepare for and respond rapidly to natural disasters and mitigate their impact;

8. *Urges* Member States to develop, update and strengthen disaster preparedness and risk reduction measures at all levels, in accordance with priority five of the Hyogo Framework for Action, taking into account their own circumstances and capacities and in coordination with relevant actors, as appropriate, and encourages the international community and relevant United Nations entities to continue to support national efforts in this regard;

9. *Encourages* Member States to consider elaborating and presenting to the International Strategy for Disaster Reduction secretariat their national platforms for disaster

reduction in accordance with the Hyogo Framework for Action, and also encourages States to cooperate with each other to reach this objective;

10. *Stresses* that, to increase further the effectiveness of humanitarian assistance, particular international cooperation efforts should be undertaken to enhance and broaden further the utilization of national and local capacities and, where appropriate, of regional and subregional capacities of developing countries for disaster preparedness and response, which may be made available in closer proximity to the site of a disaster, and more efficiently and at lower cost;

11. *Also stresses*, in this context, the importance of strengthening international cooperation, particularly through the effective use of multilateral mechanisms, in the timely provision of humanitarian assistance through all phases of a disaster, from relief and recovery to development, including the provision of adequate resources;

12. *Takes note* that a review of the Central Register of Disaster Management Capacities, planned for 2009, is expected to assess its value added and user satisfaction, and requests the Secretary-General to report on its findings;

13. *Reaffirms* the role of the Office for the Coordination of Humanitarian Affairs of the Secretariat as the focal point within the overall United Nations system for advocacy for and coordination of humanitarian assistance among United Nations humanitarian organizations and other humanitarian partners;

14. *Welcomes*, so as to increase further the effectiveness of humanitarian assistance, the incorporation of experts from developing countries that are prone to natural disasters into the United Nations Disaster Assessment and Coordination system, and the work of the International Search and Rescue Advisory Group in assisting such countries in strengthening urban search and rescue capacities and establishing mechanisms for improving their coordination of national and international response in the field, and recalls in this regard its resolution 57/150 of 16 December 2002 entitled "Strengthening the effectiveness and coordination of international urban search and rescue assistance";

15. *Recognizes* that information and telecommunication technology can play an important role in disaster response, encourages Member States to develop emergency response telecommunication capacities, and encourages the international community to assist the efforts of developing countries in this area, where needed, including in the recovery phase;

16. *Encourages* States that have not acceded to or ratified the Tampere Convention on the Provision of Telecommunication Resources for Disaster Mitigation and Relief Operations, to consider doing so;

17. *Encourages* the further use of space-based and ground-based remote-sensing technologies, as well as the sharing of geographical data, for the prevention, mitigation and management of natural disasters, where appropriate, and invites Member States to continue to provide their support to the consolidation of the United Nations capability in the area of satellite-derived geographical information for early warning, preparedness, response and early recovery;

18. *Encourages* Member States, relevant United Nations organizations and international financial institutions to enhance the global capacity for sustainable post-disaster recovery in areas such as coordination with traditional and non-traditional partners, identification and dissemination of lessons learned, development of common tools and mechanisms for recovery needs assessment, strategy development and programming, and incorporation of risk reduction into all recovery processes, and welcomes the ongoing efforts to this end;

19. *Encourages* Member States and relevant regional and international organizations to identify and improve the dissemination of best practices for improving disaster preparedness, response and early recovery and to scale up successful local initiatives, as appropriate;

20. *Requests* the United Nations system to improve its coordination of disaster recovery efforts, from relief to development, inter alia, by strengthening institutional, coordination and strategic planning efforts in disaster recovery, in support of national authorities;

21. *Calls upon* relevant United Nations humanitarian and development organizations, in consultation with Member States, to strengthen tools and mechanisms to ensure that early recovery needs and support are considered part of the planning and implementation of humanitarian response and development cooperation activities, as appropriate;

22. *Calls upon* the United Nations system and other humanitarian actors to improve the dissemination of tools and services to support enhanced disaster risk reduction;

23. *Calls upon* relevant United Nations humanitarian and development organizations to continue efforts to ensure continuity and predictability in their response and to further improve coordination in recovery processes in support of the efforts of national authorities;

24. *Emphasizes* the need to mobilize adequate, flexible and sustainable resources for recovery, preparedness and disaster risk reduction activities;

25. *Stresses* the importance of rapid access to funds to ensure a more predictable and timely United Nations response to humanitarian emergencies, and welcomes in this regard the achievements of the Central Emergency Response Fund and its contribution to the promotion and enhancement of early humanitarian response;

26. *Calls upon* all Member States and invites the private sector and all concerned individuals and institutions to consider increasing voluntary contributions to the Central Emergency Response Fund, and emphasizes that contributions should be additional to current commitments to humanitarian programming and not to the detriment of resources made available for international cooperation for development;

27. *Invites* Member States, the private sector and all concerned individuals and institutions to consider voluntary contributions to other humanitarian funding mechanisms;

28. *Requests* the Secretary-General to continue to improve the international response to natural disasters and to report thereon to the General Assembly at its sixty-fourth session, and to include in his report, within existing resources, an analysis of the possible gaps existing in the assistance provided in the period between emergency relief and development, taking into account information provided by Member States and relevant United Nations entities, with a view to formulating recommendations on how to address any problems identified in a systematic manner and to ensuring sustainable solutions, particularly in rehabilitation and reconstruction.

Disaster reduction

International Strategy for Disaster Reduction

In response to General Assembly resolution 62/192 [YUN 2007, p. 950], the Secretary-General, in a September report [A/63/351], provided an overview on implementation of the International Strategy for Disaster Reduction (ISDR), adopted by the programme forum of the International Decade for Natural Disaster Reduction (1990–2000) in 1999 [YUN 1999, p. 859] and endorsed by the Assembly in resolution 54/219 [ibid., p. 861]. It also detailed efforts to implement the Hyogo Framework for Action, the 10-year plan for reducing disaster risks adopted at the World Conference on Disaster Reduction in 2005 [YUN 2005, p. 1015] and endorsed by the Assembly in resolution 60/195 [ibid., p. 1018]. The report indicated that disasters related to hydro-meteorological hazards, particularly floods and storms, had continued to increase in recent years. Over the period from 2000 to 2007, their frequency rose on average by 8.4 per cent annually, with an average annual cost exceeding $80 billion, making up the largest source of disaster costs. Environmental degradation continued to be one of the main factors responsible for increased vulnerability to natural hazards. Worldwide, some 70 per cent of the 5.2 billion hectares of dry lands used for agriculture were already degraded and threatened by desertification. Climate change and the growth of unplanned urban areas, which were often located in high-risk areas for earthquakes, floods, landslides and technological hazards, were also of concern.

Regarding the Hyogo Framework for Action (2005–2015), the Secretary-General said that while progress had been made on many fronts, the world was not on track to achieve the Framework's goal of a substantial reduction in disaster losses by 2015. At the national level, increased commitment by Governments, parliamentarians, NGOs and other stakeholders had resulted in some gains in implementing disaster risk reduction, including a number of countries adopting instruments to guide policy and enact legislation for risk reduction, while others had integrated risk reduction into their national development plans or poverty reduction strategies. Some 55 States had either established multi-stakeholder national platforms for disaster risk reduction or were in advanced stages of preparation, and 120 Governments had designated official focal points for the implementation, follow-up and monitoring of progress of the Hyogo Framework. However, 147 countries had yet to establish national platforms, and 66 lacked Hyogo Framework focal points. At the international level, the ISDR secretariat facilitated and promoted the engagement of numerous partners in disaster risk reduction in a coordinated manner. UN system entities enhanced their own commitments to the Hyogo Framework, and the Global Facility for Disaster Reduction and Recovery, a partnership between the World Bank and ISDR, contributed to the scaling-up of the Bank's commitment to integrate disaster risk reduction into poverty reduction strategies and climate change adaptation. Key UN coordination mechanisms—including CEB, the United Nations Development Group and IASC—had taken action on disaster risk reduction, including climate change adaptation, in coordination with ISDR.

Following the first session of the Global Platform for Disaster Risk Reduction in 2007 [YUN 2007, p. 949], ISDR was strengthened to provide better coordinated support and guidance to regional, national and local actors. The second session of the Global Platform, in June 2009, would serve to initiate the midterm review of the implementation of the Hyogo Framework, expected by 2010. ISDR had also established a global, regional and national reporting system with the partners, releasing a global assessment report every two years that fed into Global Platform sessions. In January 2008, the United Nations Educational, Scientific and Cultural Organization (UNESCO) hosted the first meeting of the ISDR Scientific and Technical Committee, which provided specific reviews aimed at ensuring that a sound scientific base was available for ongoing ISDR system processes. In other developments, the Bali Action Plan of the Framework Convention on Climate Change, adopted in December 2007 [ibid., p. 1060], called for strategies to lessen the impact of disasters on developing countries and on risk management, including risk transfer mechanisms such as insurance. Those topics would be the subject of a workshop to be held in Poznań, Poland in December 2008. In June, at climate change negotiations in Bonn, Germany, parties recommended the inclusion of disaster risk reduction strategies and the Hyogo Framework in national policies and programmes.

On investment in disaster risk reduction, a substantial increase was urgently needed if the goals and objectives of the Hyogo Framework were to be attained by 2015, as the resources available fell short of the amount required to build the resilience of nations and communities. The expanding scope of work of the ISDR system work programme and the secretariat's 2008–2009 work plan amounted to $90.6 million. While 40 per cent of commitments were pledged for the work plan by mid-2008, commitments to the system's joint programmes were poor. States were encouraged to make multi-annual, unearmarked contributions as early in the fiscal year as possible. Moreover, if the Hyogo Framework was to be effectively implemented, increased contributions to the UN Trust Fund for Disaster Reduction would be needed to fill, by 2009, the gap of over $70 million to support the work of organizations involved in the ISDR system joint work programme. The report concluded with recommendations on accelerating implementation of the Hyogo Framework; ensuring synergy between climate change adaptation and disaster risk reduction agendas; strengthening the funding arrangements of ISDR; and investing in disaster risk reduction, including the setting of targets by States for public spending on multi-year disaster risk reduction programmes at the national and local levels, as well as increased investment in disaster risk reduction by Governments, donors and funding institutions as an integral component of all programmes for humanitarian action, economic and social development and environmental protection.

On 3 September [A/63/347], Tajikistan transmitted the Dushanbe Declaration on water-related disaster reduction, adopted at the close of the International Conference on Water-Related Disaster Reduction (Dushanbe, Tajikistan, 27–29 June) held in the framework of the International Decade for Action "Water for Life" (2005–2015) [YUN 2003, p. 1034].

Ministerial meeting on disaster reduction. The Secretary-General convened a ministerial meeting on "Reducing disaster risks in a changing climate" (New York, 29 September), which emphasized the need to promote and invest in disaster risk reduction as the first line of defense in climate change adaptation and to mobilize resources for disaster risk reduction from the national to the international level. The meeting, attended by nearly 200 high-level officials from 86 Member States, demonstrated an increased collective commitment to accelerate the implementation of disaster risk reduction and find innovative, robust solutions to the increasing disaster risks created by a rapidly changing climate.

GENERAL ASSEMBLY ACTION

On 19 December [meeting 72], the General Assembly, on the recommendation of the Second (Economic and Financial) Committee [A/63/414/Add.3], adopted **resolution 63/216** without vote [agenda item 49 *(c)*].

International Strategy for Disaster Reduction

The General Assembly,

Recalling its resolutions 44/236 of 22 December 1989, 49/22 A of 2 December 1994, 49/22 B of 20 December 1994, 53/185 of 15 December 1998, 54/219 of 22 December 1999, 56/195 of 21 December 2001, 57/256 of 20 December 2002, 58/214 of 23 December 2003, 59/231 of 22 December 2004, 60/195 of 22 December 2005, 61/198 of 20 December 2006 and 62/192 of 19 December 2007 and Economic and Social Council resolutions 1999/63 of 30 July 1999 and 2001/35 of 26 July 2001, and taking into due consideration its resolution 57/270 B of 23 June 2003 on the integrated and coordinated implementation of and follow-up to the outcomes of the major United Nations conferences and summits in the economic and social fields,

Recalling also the 2005 World Summit Outcome,

Reaffirming the Hyogo Declaration, the Hyogo Framework for Action 2005–2015: Building the Resilience of Nations and Communities to Disasters and the common statement of the special session on the Indian Ocean disaster: risk reduction for a safer future, as adopted by the World Conference on Disaster Reduction,

Reaffirming also its role in providing policy guidance on the implementation of the outcomes of the major United Nations conferences and summits,

Expressing its deep concern at the number and scale of natural disasters and their increasing impact in recent years, which have resulted in massive loss of life and long-term negative social, economic and environmental consequences for vulnerable societies throughout the world and hamper the achievement of their sustainable development, in particular in developing countries,

Emphasizing that disaster risk reduction, including reducing vulnerability to natural disasters, is an important cross-cutting element that contributes to the achievement of sustainable development,

Recognizing the clear relationship between development, disaster risk reduction, disaster response and disaster recovery and the need to continue to deploy efforts in all these areas,

Recognizing also the urgent need to further develop and make use of the existing scientific and technical knowledge to build resilience to natural disasters, and emphasizing the need for developing countries to have access to appropriate, advanced, environmentally sound, cost-effective and easy-to-use technologies so as to seek more comprehensive solutions to disaster risk reduction and to effectively and efficiently strengthen their capabilities to cope with disaster risks,

Recognizing further that certain measures for disaster risk reduction in the context of the Hyogo Framework for Action can also support adaptation to climate change, and emphasizing the importance of strengthening the resilience of nations and communities to natural disasters through disaster risk reduction programmes,

Stressing the importance of advancing the implementation of the Plan of Implementation of the World Summit on Sustainable Development and its relevant provisions on vulnerability, risk assessment and disaster management,

Taking note of the ministerial meeting on "Reducing disaster risks in a changing climate", convened by the Secretary-General on 29 September 2008,

Noting the declaration "Together for humanity" of the thirtieth International Conference of the Red Cross and Red Crescent, held in Geneva from 26 to 30 November 2007, in particular concerning the need to ensure that environmental degradation and adaptation to climate change are integrated in disaster risk reduction and disaster management policies and plans,

Recognizing the need to continue to develop an understanding of, and to address, socio-economic activities that exacerbate the vulnerability of societies to natural disasters and to build and further strengthen community capability to cope with disaster risks,

Taking note of the workshop on risk management and risk reduction strategies, including risk sharing and transfer mechanisms such as insurance, held in Poznań, Poland, in December 2008,

Having considered the recommendation of the Secretary-General regarding General Assembly resolution 54/219,

1. *Takes note* of the report of the Secretary-General on the implementation of the International Strategy for Disaster Reduction;

2. *Recalls* that the commitments of the Hyogo Declaration and the Hyogo Framework for Action 2005–2015: Building the Resilience of Nations and Communities to Disasters include the provision of assistance for developing countries that are prone to natural disasters and disaster-stricken States in the transition phase towards sustainable physical, social and economic recovery, for risk reduction activities in post-disaster recovery and for rehabilitation processes;

3. *Welcomes* the progress made in the implementation of the Hyogo Framework for Action, and stresses the need for a more effective integration of disaster risk reduction into sustainable development policies, planning and programming; for the development and strengthening of institutions, mechanisms and capacities to build resilience to hazards; and for a systematic incorporation of risk reduction approaches into the implementation of emergency preparedness, response and recovery programmes;

4. *Calls upon* the international community to increase its efforts to fully implement the commitments of the Hyogo Declaration and the Hyogo Framework for Action;

5. *Invites* Member States, the United Nations system, international financial institutions, regional bodies and other international organizations, including the International Federation of Red Cross and Red Crescent Societies, as well as civil society, including non-governmental organizations and volunteers, the private sector and the scientific community, to increase efforts to support, implement and follow up the Hyogo Framework for Action, and stresses the importance in this regard of the continued cooperation and coordination of all stakeholders with respect to addressing effectively the impact of natural disasters;

6. *Calls upon* the United Nations system, and invites international financial institutions and regional and international organizations, to integrate the goals of, and take into full account, the Hyogo Framework for Action in their strategies and programmes, making use of existing coordination mechanisms, and to assist developing countries with those mechanisms to design and implement, as appropriate, disaster risk reduction measures with a sense of urgency;

7. *Also calls upon* the United Nations system, and invites the international financial institutions and regional banks and other regional and international organizations, to support, in a timely and sustained manner, the efforts led by disaster-stricken countries for disaster risk reduction in post-disaster recovery and rehabilitation processes;

8. *Recognizes* that each State has the primary responsibility for its own sustainable development and for taking effective measures to reduce disaster risk, including for the protection of people on its territory, infrastructure and other national assets from the impact of disasters, including the implementation of and follow-up to the Hyogo Framework for Action, and stresses the importance of international cooperation and partnerships to support those national efforts;

9. *Also recognizes* the efforts made by Member States to develop national and local capacities to implement the Hyogo Framework for Action, including through the establishment of national platforms for disaster reduction, and encourages Member States that have not done so to develop such capacities;

10. *Further recognizes* the importance of coordinating adaptation to climate change with relevant disaster risk reduction measures, invites Governments and relevant international organizations to integrate these considerations in a comprehensive manner into, inter alia, development plans and poverty eradication programmes and, in least developed countries, National Adaptation Programmes of Action, and invites the international community to support the ongoing efforts of developing countries in this regard;

11. *Welcomes* the regional and subregional initiatives developed in order to achieve disaster risk reduction, and reiterates the need to further develop regional initiatives and risk reduction capacities of regional mechanisms where they exist and to strengthen them and encourage the use and sharing of all existing tools;

12. *Expresses its satisfaction* with the work carried out by the Global Facility for Disaster Reduction and Recovery, a partnership of the Strategy system managed by the World Bank on behalf of the participating donor partners and other partnering stakeholders, as a significant initiative to support the implementation of the Hyogo Framework for Action;

13. *Encourages* the secretariat of the Strategy to continue to develop improved methods for predictive multi-risk assessments, including on the economics of disaster risk reduction and socio-economic cost-benefit analysis of risk reduction actions at all levels;

14. *Calls upon* the international community to support the development and strengthening of institutions, mechanisms and capacities at all levels, in particular at the community level, that can systematically contribute to building resilience to hazards;

15. *Encourages* Member States to increase their commitment to the effective implementation of the Hyogo Framework for Action, making full use of the mechanisms of the Strategy system, such as the Global Platform for Disaster Risk Reduction;

16. *Welcomes* the upcoming second session of the Global Platform for Disaster Risk Reduction, on the theme "Disasters, poverty and vulnerability", to be held in Geneva from 16 to 19 June 2009, which will serve to initiate the midterm review of the implementation of the Hyogo Framework for Action, expected by 2010, and requests the Secretary-General to include information on the Global Platform in his next report;

17. *Recognizes* the importance of integrating a gender perspective and empowering and engaging women in the design and implementation of all phases of disaster management, as well as in risk reduction strategies and programmes, and encourages the secretariat of the Strategy to continue to increase the promotion of gender mainstreaming and empowerment of women;

18. *Acknowledges* the importance of the work of the United Nations in disaster risk reduction and the growing demands on the secretariat of the Strategy and the need for increased, timely, stable and predictable resources for the implementation of the Strategy;

19. *Expresses its appreciation* to those countries that have provided financial support for the activities of the Strategy by making voluntary contributions to the United Nations Trust Fund for Disaster Reduction;

20. *Encourages* the international community to continue providing adequate voluntary financial contributions to the Trust Fund in the effort to ensure adequate support for the follow-up activities to the Hyogo Framework for Action, and encourages Member States to make multi-annual, unearmarked contributions as early in the year as possible;

21. *Encourages* Governments, multilateral organizations, international and regional organizations, international and regional financial institutions, the private sector and civil society to systematically invest in disaster risk reduction with a view to implementing the objectives of the Strategy;

22. *Stresses* the importance of disaster risk reduction and subsequent increased responsibilities of the secretariat of the Strategy, and requests the Secretary-General to explore all means of securing additional funding to ensure predictable and stable financial resources for the operation of the secretariat and to report on this to the General Assembly at its sixty-fourth session;

23. *Encourages* Member States to integrate early warning systems into their national disaster risk reduction strategies and plans, and invites the international community to support the secretariat of the Strategy in its role in facilitating the development of early warning systems;

24. *Stresses* the need to foster better understanding and knowledge of the causes of disasters, as well as to build and strengthen coping capacities through, inter alia, the transfer and exchange of experiences and technical knowledge, educational and training programmes for disaster risk reduction, access to relevant data and information and the strengthening of institutional arrangements, including community-based organizations;

25. *Emphasizes* the need for the international community to maintain its focus beyond emergency relief and to support medium- and long-term rehabilitation, reconstruction and risk reduction, and stresses the importance of implementing programmes related to the eradication of poverty, sustainable development and disaster risk reduction management in the most vulnerable regions, particularly in developing countries prone to natural disasters;

26. *Stresses* the need to address risk reduction of and vulnerabilities to all natural hazards, including geological and hydrometeorological hazards, in a comprehensive manner;

27. *Requests* the Secretary-General to submit to the General Assembly at its sixty-fourth session a report on the implementation of the present resolution, under the item entitled "Sustainable development".

Natural disasters and vulnerability

In response to General Assembly resolution 61/200 [YUN 2006, p. 1097], the Secretary-General submitted a report [A/63/351] on ISDR implementation providing information on measures taken to reduce vulnerability to severe climate-related hazards. The ISDR secretariat engaged the Framework Convention on Climate Change, the World Bank, UNDP, regional organizations and individual Governments in several workshops and high-level policy forums to foster better understanding among policymakers of the benefits of linking frameworks for risk reduction to climate change adaptation and poverty reduction. UNDP developed a programming framework to "climate proof" the MDGs and started a pilot Climate Risk Management Technical Support Project in four countries.

GENERAL ASSEMBLY ACTION

On 19 December [meeting 72], the General Assembly, on the recommendation of the Second Committee [A/63/414/Add.3], adopted **resolution 63/217** without vote [agenda item 49 *(c)*].

Natural disasters and vulnerability

The General Assembly,

Recalling its decision 57/547 of 20 December 2002 and its resolutions 58/215 of 23 December 2003, 59/233 of 22 December 2004, 60/196 of 22 December 2005 and 61/200 of 20 December 2006,

Reaffirming the Johannesburg Declaration on Sustainable Development and the Plan of Implementation of the World Summit on Sustainable Development ("Johannesburg Plan of Implementation"),

Reaffirming also the Hyogo Declaration and the Hyogo Framework for Action 2005–2015: Building the Resilience of Nations and Communities to Disasters, adopted by the World Conference on Disaster Reduction,

Recalling the 2005 World Summit Outcome,

Recognizing the need to continue to develop an understanding of, and to address, the underlying risk factors, as identified in the Hyogo Framework for Action, including socio-economic factors, that exacerbate the vulnerability of societies to natural hazards, to build and further strengthen the capacity at all levels to cope with disaster risks and to enhance resilience against hazards associated with disasters, while also recognizing the negative impact of disasters on economic growth and sustainable development, in particular in developing countries and disaster-prone countries,

Emphasizing the importance of addressing vulnerability and integrating risk reduction into all phases of disaster management, post-disaster recovery and development planning,

Recognizing the need to integrate a gender perspective in the design and implementation of all phases of disaster risk reduction management, with a view to reducing vulnerability,

Noting that the global environment continues to suffer degradation, adding to economic and social vulnerabilities, in particular in developing countries,

Taking into account the various ways and forms in which all countries, in particular the more vulnerable countries, are affected by severe natural hazards such as earthquakes, tsunamis, landslides and volcanic eruptions and extreme weather events such as heatwaves, severe droughts, floods and storms, and the El Niño/La Niña events which have global reach,

Expressing deep concern at the recent increase in the frequency and intensity of extreme weather events and associated natural disasters in some regions of the world and their substantial economic, social and environmental impacts, in particular upon developing countries in those regions,

Taking into account that geological and hydrometeorological hazards and their associated natural disasters and their reduction must be addressed in a coherent and effective manner,

Noting the need for international and regional cooperation to increase the capacity of countries to respond to the negative impacts of all natural hazards, including earthquakes, tsunamis, landslides and volcanic eruptions and extreme weather events such as heatwaves, severe droughts and floods, and associated natural disasters, in particular in developing countries and disaster-prone countries,

Bearing in mind the importance of addressing disaster risks related to changing social, economic, environmental conditions and land use, and the impact of hazards associated with geological events, weather, water, climate variability and climate change, in sector development planning and programmes as well as in post-disaster situations,

Stressing that the impacts of natural disasters are severely hampering efforts in achieving the internationally agreed development goals, including the Millennium Development Goals, and emphasizing the importance of reducing vulnerabilities to natural disasters,

1. *Takes note* of the report of the Secretary-General on the implementation of its resolution 61/200;

2. *Urges* the international community to continue to address ways and means, including through development cooperation and technical assistance, to reduce the adverse effects of natural disasters, including those caused by extreme weather events, in particular in vulnerable developing countries, including least developed countries and in Africa, through the implementation of the International Strategy for Disaster Reduction, including the Hyogo Framework for Action 2005–2015: Building the Resilience of Nations and Communities to Disasters, and encourages the institutional arrangement for the International Strategy to continue its work in this regard;

3. *Recognizes* that each State has the primary responsibility for its own sustainable development and for taking effective measures to reduce disaster risk, including for the protection of people on its territory, infrastructure and other national assets from the impact of disaster, including the implementation and follow-up of the Hyogo Framework for Action, and stresses the importance of regional and international cooperation and partnerships to support those national efforts;

4. *Stresses* the importance of the Hyogo Declaration and the Hyogo Framework for Action and the priorities for action that States, regional and international organizations and international financial institutions as well as other concerned actors should take into consideration in their approach to disaster risk reduction and implement, as appropriate, according to their own circumstances and capacities, bearing in mind the vital importance of promoting a culture of prevention in the area of natural disasters, including through the mobilization of adequate resources for disaster risk reduction, and of addressing disaster risk reduction, including disaster preparedness at the community level, and the adverse effects of natural disasters on efforts to implement national development plans and poverty reduction strategies with a view to achieving the internationally agreed development goals, including the Millennium Development Goals;

5. *Recognizes* the importance of considering enhanced action on adaptation, including, inter alia, risk management and risk reduction strategies, including risk sharing and transfer mechanisms such as insurance, and disaster reduction strategies and means to address loss and damage associated with climate change impacts in developing countries that are particularly vulnerable to the adverse effects of climate change;

6. *Expresses its deep concern* at the number and scale of natural disasters and the increasing challenges posed by the consequences of natural disasters, as well as the impact of climate change, to all countries, in particular developing countries, especially small island developing States and least developed countries, as well as other particularly vulnerable countries;

7. *Encourages* continued and greater support by the international community for adaptation strategies, particularly in countries vulnerable to the adverse effects of climate change, in order to contribute to disaster management efforts, and encourages enhanced coordination between adaptation strategies and disaster management strategies;

8. *Encourages* Governments, through their respective International Strategy for Disaster Reduction national platforms and national focal points for disaster risk reduction, in cooperation with the United Nations system, the International Federation of Red Cross and Red Crescent Societies and other stakeholders, to strengthen capacity-building in the most vulnerable regions, to enable them to address the social, economic and environmental factors that increase vulnerability, and to develop measures that will enable them to prepare for and cope with natural disasters, including those associated with earthquakes and extreme weather events, and encourages the international community to provide effective assistance to developing countries in this regard;

9. *Emphasizes*, in order to build resilience, particularly in developing countries, especially those vulnerable among them, the importance of addressing the underlying risk factors identified in the Hyogo Framework for Action, promoting the integration of risk reduction associated with geological and hydrometeorological hazards in disaster risk reduction programmes and enhancing knowledge and public awareness of disaster risk reduction;

10. *Stresses* that, in order to reduce vulnerability to natural hazards, risk assessments should be integrated into disaster risk reduction programmes at national and local levels;

11. *Encourages* the institutional arrangement for the International Strategy for Disaster Reduction to continue, within its mandate, particularly the Hyogo Framework for Action, to enhance the coordination of activities to promote natural disaster risk reduction and to make available to Member States, the relevant United Nations entities and other relevant stakeholders information on options for natural disaster risk reduction, including severe natural hazards and extreme weather-related disasters and vulnerabilities;

12. *Stresses* the importance of close cooperation and coordination among Governments, the United Nations system, and other international and regional organizations, as

well as non-governmental organizations and other partners such as the International Federation of Red Cross and Red Crescent Societies, as appropriate, taking into account the need for the development of disaster management strategies encompassing prevention, preparedness and response, including the effective establishment of early warning systems that are, inter alia, people-centred, while taking advantage of all available resources and expertise for that purpose;

13. *Also stresses* that, to reduce vulnerability to all natural hazards, including geological and hydrometeorological events and associated natural disasters, closer and more systematic cooperation, and information-sharing on disaster preparedness among the scientific and academic communities and disaster managers at all levels, should be strengthened;

14. *Encourages* the Conference of the Parties to the United Nations Framework Convention on Climate Change and the parties to the Kyoto Protocol to the United Nations Framework Convention on Climate Change to continue to address the adverse effects of climate change, especially in developing countries that are particularly vulnerable, in accordance with the provisions of the Convention, and also encourages the Intergovernmental Panel on Climate Change to continue to assess the adverse effects of climate change on the socio-economic and natural disaster reduction systems of developing countries;

15. *Calls upon* the international community, in particular the developed countries, to provide adequate and predictable resources and access to and transfer of technology, as mutually agreed, to developing countries vulnerable to the adverse effects of natural hazards with a view to enhancing their adaptation capacity;

16. *Stresses* the need to address risk reduction of and vulnerabilities to all natural hazards, including geological and hydrometeorological hazards;

17. *Requests* the Secretary-General to report to the General Assembly at its sixty-fifth session on the implementation of the present resolution, and decides to consider the issue of natural disasters and vulnerability at that session, under the sub-item entitled "International Strategy for Disaster Reduction" of the item entitled "Sustainable development".

On 24 December, in **resolution 63/262** (see p. 1592), the General Assembly noted that the Secretariat lacked an Organization-wide approach to disaster recovery and business continuity, and requested the Secretary-General to submit a unified disaster recovery and business continuity plan, including a permanent solution for UN Headquarters.

El Niño

In response to General Assembly resolution 61/199 [YUN 2006, p. 1099], the Secretary-General submitted a report [A/63/351] on ISDR implementation, which provided information on international cooperation to reduce the impact of the El Niño phenomenon. The report indicated that over the previous five years, the Guayaquil, Ecuador-based International Research Centre on the El Niño Phenomenon [YUN 1998, p. 873], had consolidated its role in the Western South America region, particularly in identifying and monitoring the phenomenon, providing information products and tools, and establishing networks for broad dissemination. The Centre collected climate and oceanographic information from several international centres, as well as from national meteorological and hydrological services to monitor climate and related hazards. The World Meteorological Organization (WMO) continued to facilitate development of an El Niño/Southern Oscillation (ENSO) consensus report on engaging all the major climate centres worldwide and facilitated regional climate outlook forums in different regions that analysed expected impacts on ENSO and other climatic regimes. WMO was initiating those forums in South-Eastern Europe with assistance from the World Bank and held its first workshop in 2008.

GENERAL ASSEMBLY ACTION

On December 19 [meeting 72], the General Assembly, on the recommendation of the Second Committee [A/63/414/Add.3], adopted **resolution 63/215** without vote [agenda item 49 *(c)*].

International cooperation to reduce the impact of the El Niño phenomenon

The General Assembly,

Recalling its resolutions 52/200 of 18 December 1997, 53/185 of 15 December 1998, 54/220 of 22 December 1999, 55/197 of 20 December 2000, 56/194 of 21 December 2001, 57/255 of 20 December 2002, 59/232 of 22 December 2004 and 61/199 of 20 December 2006, and Economic and Social Council resolutions 1999/46 of 28 July 1999, 1999/63 of 30 July 1999 and 2000/33 of 28 July 2000,

Noting that the El Niño phenomenon has a recurring character and that it can lead to extensive natural hazards with the potential to seriously affect humankind,

Reaffirming the importance of developing strategies at the national, subregional, regional and international levels that aim to prevent, mitigate and repair the damage caused by natural disasters that result from the El Niño phenomenon,

Noting that technological developments and international cooperation have enhanced the capabilities for the prediction of the El Niño phenomenon and thereby the potential for the preventive actions that may be taken to reduce its negative impacts,

Taking into account the Johannesburg Declaration on Sustainable Development and the Plan of Implementation of the World Summit on Sustainable Development ("Johannesburg Plan of Implementation"), in particular paragraph 37 *(i)* thereof,

Reaffirming the Hyogo Declaration and the Hyogo Framework for Action 2005–2015: Building the Resilience of Nations and Communities to Disasters,

1. *Takes note* of the report of the Secretary-General on the implementation of the International Strategy for Disaster Reduction, in particular annex II of the report, entitled

"International cooperation to reduce the impact of the El Niño phenomenon", and calls upon the international community to make greater efforts to assist countries affected by this phenomenon;

2. *Recognizes* the efforts made by the Government of Ecuador, the World Meteorological Organization and the inter-agency secretariat of the International Strategy for Disaster Reduction which led to the establishment of the International Research Centre on El Niño at Guayaquil, Ecuador, and encourages them to continue their support for the advancement of the Centre;

3. *Also recognizes* the technical and scientific support of the World Meteorological Organization to producing regionally coordinated monthly and seasonal forecasts;

4. *Encourages*, in this regard, the World Meteorological Organization to strengthen collaboration and the exchange of data as well as of information with the relevant institutions;

5. *Welcomes* the activities undertaken so far to strengthen the International Research Centre on El Niño, through collaboration with international monitoring centres, including the national oceanographic institutions, and efforts to enhance regional and international recognition and support for the Centre and to develop tools for decision makers and Government authorities for reducing the impact of the El Niño phenomenon;

6. *Calls upon* the Secretary-General and the relevant United Nations organs, funds and programmes, in particular those taking part in the International Strategy for Disaster Reduction, and the international community to adopt, as appropriate, the necessary measures to strengthen the International Research Centre on El Niño, and invites the international community to provide scientific, technical and financial assistance and cooperation for this purpose, as well as to strengthen, as appropriate, other centres devoted to the study of the El Niño phenomenon;

7. *Underscores* the importance of maintaining the El Niño/Southern Oscillation observation system, continuing research into extreme weather events, improving forecasting skills and developing appropriate policies for reducing the impact of the El Niño phenomenon and other extreme weather events, and emphasizes the need to further develop and strengthen these institutional capacities in all countries, in particular developing countries;

8. *Requests* the Secretary-General to include a section on the implementation of the present resolution in his report to the General Assembly at its sixty-fifth session on the implementation of the International Strategy for Disaster Reduction.

Disaster assistance

Indian Ocean tsunami aftermath

Three and a half years after the 2004 Indian Ocean tsunami [YUN 2004, p. 952], progress was apparent across affected regions: displaced persons were residing in newly constructed homes, children were in schools and hospitals were being rebuilt and repaired. While physical reconstruction efforts had been actualized, many complex challenges remained as the region continued to recover. Each affected country faced different challenges and consequently, progress was uneven. However, what was common to all countries was that it would take many years for individual households and the wider economies on which they depended to recover. During the course of the recovery efforts, considerable strides had been taken towards rehabilitation and reconstruction. Across the five most affected countries, progress was evident throughout 2006 and 2007. Many countries had fulfilled their promise of rebuilding better and had taken important steps forward in disaster risk management and disaster risk reduction. Continuing challenges for leading agencies included the linkage of various ongoing recovery processes, provision or access to critical information and capacity-building of local governments. Moreover, while needs had changed considerably in many sectors, the planning systems of many implementing agencies continued to be based on original assessments and commitments.

During the year, the Tsunami Trust Fund established to manage contributions for recovery and reconstruction, and managed by OCHA, disbursed $527,889 to finance activities undertaken for the coordination of humanitarian action, including relief to victims and longer-term development of infrastructure or to support UNDP development activities. As the Fund was in its final stages, activities were projected to cease during 2009, with the fund closing in 2010. As at 31 December 2008, the closing balance of the Fund was $3.5 million. The Multi-Donor Voluntary Trust Fund on Tsunami Early Warning Arrangements in the Indian Ocean and Southeast Asia, established by the United Nations Economic and Social Commission for Asia and the Pacific in 2005, continued to build and enhance tsunami warning capabilities in accordance with the needs of Indian Ocean and South-East Asian countries. As at the end of 2008, the Fund had conducted five rounds of funding and received 51 proposals from regional, subregional and national organizations. A total of 11 projects were approved with a total budget of approximately $9.2 million.

Report of Secretary-General. In response to General Assembly resolution 62/91 [YUN 2007, p. 953], the Secretary-General, in June, submitted a report [A/63/84-E/2008/80] on strengthening emergency relief, rehabilitation, reconstruction, recovery and prevention in the aftermath of the Indian Ocean tsunami disaster that provided information on progress, achievements and challenges experienced by five affected countries: India, Indonesia, Maldives, Sri Lanka and Thailand. The report focused primarily on recovery efforts in key social sectors. It also addressed aid and recovery coordination, models of Government humanitarian and recovery institutions, transparency, and accountability to donors, as well as risk reduction, tsunami early warning and incorporation of prevention in development planning. The report did not purport to cover the field in terms of progress achieved, which had been substantial in all five countries, or the challenges that recovery actors would continue to face as efforts became mainstreamed.

On coordination in the humanitarian and recovery phases, a virtual knowledge management network of international and local recovery/governance professionals and decision makers would be established in 2008 to enhance coordination and manage challenges and opportunities across thematic and geographical areas. The network—an international UN best practice known as "solutions exchange"—would develop six virtual "communities of practice" supported by a coordination and research secretariat to ensure high-quality, timely and targeted solutions in all phases of recovery and governance planning, programming and implementation. To facilitate the recovery process, with regard to shelter and infrastructure in particular, community-driven approaches were implemented to ensure that skills and investments remained in communities and strengthened donorship and solidarity. Training communities and local government officials to enable that process was also essential. Partners of the Tsunami Recovery Impact Assessment and Monitoring System (TRIAMS) made recommendations on assessing damages and needs to be considered by those proposing reform in needs assessment processes. In addition, progress was made in developing and implementing several tools to increase transparency and accountability among actors involved in the tsunami response—notably the Tsunami Evaluation Coalition, the development assistance database TRIAMS, and the analytical framework for assisting Governments, aid agencies and affected populations assess and monitor the rate and direction of recovery.

Local and international organizations continued to provide comprehensive information to the development assistance database system, and the four national databases established to track recovery and reconstruction were updated regularly and provided data on projects and assistance. On TRIAMS, significant progress was made in further developing and piloting the framework. Participating countries updated and added disaster risk reduction indicators to the framework in April 2007, reflecting significant changes to the recovery situation in most countries. The Tsunami Evaluation Coalition produced five thematic evaluations and two synthesis reports in 2006. Four main findings and over 200 sub-recommendations were noted in the initial synthesis report. The work of the Coalition was expected to continue throughout 2008, with milestone events planned at UN agencies; international, bilateral and non-governmental organizations and others would discuss their approaches in adopting the Coalition's recommendations. On risk reduction, tsunami early warning and the incorporation of prevention in development planning, the report indicated that many measures to evaluate/strengthen early warning systems had focused primarily on establishing system governance structures, technical advice and implementation, public awareness and preparedness, and training. Targeted training activities involving more than 150 national officers and researchers had taken place in tsunami-affected countries. Twenty-five of 28 possible nations had established official tsunami warning focal points capable of receiving and disseminating tsunami advisories around the clock. At the national level, countries were working to establish clearer responsibilities to ensure people-centred early warning systems. However, critical elements of community preparedness, community education and outreach programmes were generally not yet in place in most countries. Only a few countries had developed tsunami emergency plans or tested response procedures for tsunamis and earthquakes. Nonetheless, there was much greater awareness among policymakers of the importance of those disaster risk reduction and environmental issues.

The report concluded that the two previous reports in 2006 [YUN 2006, p. 1100] and 2007 [YUN 2007, p. 952] on the Indian Ocean tsunami aftermath highlighted a number of issues that guided recovery and reconstruction efforts and policies and subsequently influenced significant progress, achievements and outcomes. As those efforts were being integrated into long-term development assistance projects and programmes, the Secretary-General said that continued specific reporting to the Economic and Social Council was no longer warranted.

On 25 July, the Council took note of the report of the Secretary-General on strengthening emergency relief, rehabilitation, reconstruction, recovery and prevention in the aftermath of the Indian Ocean tsunami (**decision 2008/259**).

GENERAL ASSEMBLY ACTION

On 11 December [meeting 68], the General Assembly adopted **resolution 63/137** [draft: A/63/L.47 & Add.1] without vote [agenda item 65 *(a)*].

Strengthening emergency relief, rehabilitation, reconstruction and prevention in the aftermath of the Indian Ocean tsunami disaster

The General Assembly,

Recalling its resolutions 46/182 of 19 December 1991, 57/152 of 16 December 2002, 57/256 of 20 December 2002, 58/25 of 5 December 2003, 58/214 and 58/215 of 23 December 2003, 59/212 of 20 December 2004, 59/231 and 59/233 of 22 December 2004, 59/279 of 19 January 2005, 60/15 of 14 November 2005, 61/132 of 14 December 2006 and 62/91 of 17 December 2007,

Commending the prompt response, continued support, generous assistance and contributions of the international community, Governments, civil society, the private sector and individuals, in the relief, rehabilitation and reconstruction efforts, which reflect the spirit of international solidarity and cooperation to address the disaster,

Noting the Declaration on Action to Strengthen Emergency Relief, Rehabilitation, Reconstruction and Prevention in the Aftermath of the Earthquake and Tsunami Disaster of 26 December 2004, adopted at the special meeting of leaders of the Association of Southeast Asian Nations, held in Jakarta on 6 January 2005,

Recalling the Hyogo Declaration and the Hyogo Framework for Action 2005–2015, as well as the common statement of the special session on the Indian Ocean disaster, adopted at the World Conference on Disaster Reduction, held in Kobe, Hyogo, Japan, from 18 to 22 January 2005,

Taking note of the report of the Secretary-General,

Stressing the need to continue to develop and implement disaster risk reduction strategies and to integrate them, where appropriate, into national development plans, in particular through the implementation of the International Strategy for Disaster Reduction, so as to enhance the resilience of populations in disasters and reduce the risks to them, their livelihoods, the social and economic infrastructure and environmental resources, and stressing also the need for Governments to develop and implement effective national plans for hazard warning systems with a disaster risk reduction approach,

Emphasizing that disaster reduction, including reducing vulnerability to natural disasters, is an important element that contributes to the achievement of sustainable development,

Emphasizing also the role of the Intergovernmental Oceanographic Commission of the United Nations Educational, Scientific and Cultural Organization in coordinating the establishment of the Indian Ocean Tsunami Warning and Mitigation System, given the importance of strengthening regional and subregional cooperation and coordination, which is essential for effective early warning system arrangements for tsunamis,

Commending the operationalization of the Multi-Donor Voluntary Trust Fund on Tsunami Early Warning Arrangements in the Indian Ocean and Southeast Asia, and inviting Governments, donor countries, relevant international organizations, international and regional financial institutions, the private sector and civil society to consider contributing to the Trust Fund through financial contributions and technical cooperation to support the establishment of the tsunami early warning system in accordance with the needs of the countries of the Indian Ocean and Southeast Asia so that the Trust Fund contributes to the development of an integrated early warning system based on adequate resources and comprising a network of collaborative centres connected to the global system,

Stressing the need for continued commitment to assist the affected countries and their peoples, particularly the most vulnerable groups, to fully recover from the catastrophic and traumatic effects of the disaster, including in their medium- and long-term rehabilitation and reconstruction efforts, and welcoming Government and international assistance measures in this regard,

Noting that progress has been achieved in the recovery and rehabilitation efforts of tsunami-affected countries, and noting also that efforts and assistance are still required to re-establish the basis for long-term sustainable development,

Welcoming the development or strengthening of disaster management institutions in some affected countries that provide leadership in comprehensive disaster risk reduction as well as strengthen emergency response at local and national levels,

1. *Notes with appreciation* the efforts by the Governments of affected countries to undertake the rehabilitation and reconstruction phase, as well as in enhancing financial transparency and accountability, with respect to the channelling and utilization of resources, including, as appropriate, through the involvement of international public auditors;

2. *Recognizes and encourages* ongoing efforts to promote transparency and accountability among donors and recipient countries by means of, inter alia, a unified financial and sectoral information online tracking system, and highlights the importance of timely and accurate information on assessed needs and the sources and uses of funds, and the continued support of donors, where needed, for further development of online tracking systems in the affected countries;

3. *Encourages* the sharing of lessons learned by tsunami-affected countries and other relevant stakeholders with other disaster-affected and disaster-prone countries, including on how prevention, risk reduction and humanitarian assistance measures could be improved in the future;

4. *Encourages* donor communities and international and regional financial institutions, as well as the private sector and civil society, to strengthen partnerships and to continue to support the medium- and long-term rehabilitation and reconstruction needs of the affected countries;

5. *Urges* Governments of the affected countries to identify their unmet needs in terms of financial and technical assistance in order to foster the ongoing efforts to enhance national capacity and create a reliable tsunami early warning system in the region in concert with the activities of the Intergovernmental Oceanographic Commission of the United Nations Educational, Scientific and Cultural Organization;

6. *Welcomes* the steps taken by those Governments and regional organizations to improve their legal and institutional frameworks for disaster management, and encourages them to continue to examine ways to strengthen their regulatory frameworks for international disaster assistance, including by taking into consideration, as appropriate, the Guidelines for the Domestic Facilitation and Regulation of International Disaster Relief and Initial Recovery Assistance adopted at the Thirtieth International Conference of the Red Cross and Red Crescent, held from 26 to 30 November 2007;

7. *Notes with appreciation* the efforts of international agencies, donor countries and relevant civil society organizations in supporting the Governments of affected countries to develop national capacity for tsunami warning and response so as to increase public awareness and provide community-based support for disaster risk reduction;

8. *Encourages* the continued effective coordination among the Governments of affected countries, relevant bodies of the United Nations system, international organizations, donor countries, regional and international financial institutions, civil society, the International Red

Cross and Red Crescent Movement and private sectors involved in rehabilitation and reconstruction efforts, in order to ensure the effective implementation of existing joint programmes and to prevent unnecessary duplication and reduce vulnerability to future natural hazards, as well as to adequately respond to the remaining humanitarian needs, where needed;

9. *Emphasizes* the need for the development of stronger institutions, mechanisms and capacities at the regional, national and local levels, as affirmed in the Hyogo Declaration and the Hyogo Framework for Action 2005–2015, and the promotion of public education, awareness and community participation, in order to systematically build resilience to hazards and disasters, as well as reduce the risks and the vulnerability of populations to disasters, including an effective and sustained tsunami warning system;

10. *Stresses* the need for relevant bodies of the United Nations system, international organizations, regional and international financial institutions, civil society and the private sector to implement programmes according to assessed needs and agreed priorities of the Governments of tsunami-affected countries and to ensure full transparency and accountability for their programme activities;

11. *Calls upon* States to fully implement the Hyogo Declaration and the Hyogo Framework for Action 2005–2015, in particular those commitments related to assistance for developing countries that are prone to natural disasters and for disaster-stricken States in the transition phase towards sustainable, physical, social and economic recovery, for risk-reduction activities in post-disaster recovery and for rehabilitation processes;

12. *Stresses* the importance of and the need for regular updating of recovery assessment by the Governments of affected countries, the United Nations system and international and regional financial institutions, based on the affected countries' national data and utilizing a consistent methodology, in order to reassess progress and identify gaps and priorities, with the participation of the local community during the recovery and reconstruction phase, in order to build back better;

13. *Recognizes* that the Tsunami Recovery Impact Assessment and Monitoring System is a valuable common analytical framework for assessing and monitoring the impact of tsunami recovery and for informing effective planning and programming;

14. *Acknowledges* that relevant activities in evaluating and strengthening the tsunami early warning systems have focused principally on establishing the system's governance structure, its technical implementation, increasing public awareness and preparedness, including training, and technical advice;

15. *Welcomes* the operationalization of Tsunami Warning Focal Points capable of receiving and disseminating tsunami advisories around the clock, and encourages the continuation of the efforts of the Intergovernmental Oceanographic Commission supported by Member States, United Nations agencies and donors, including for developing national action plans for all countries participating in the Indian Ocean tsunami early warning system;

16. *Also welcomes* the work of the secretariat of the International Strategy for Disaster Reduction in establishing partnership among relevant actors, and stresses the importance for countries to establish early warning systems that are people-centred;

17. *Urges* Governments and the United Nations system, in planning for disaster preparedness and responding to natural disasters, and in implementing recovery, rehabilitation and reconstruction efforts, to integrate a gender perspective and provide every opportunity for women to take a full, active and equal role in all phases of disaster management;

18. *Expresses its deep appreciation* to relevant United Nations organizations, in particular the Office for the Coordination of Humanitarian Affairs of the Secretariat, and other humanitarian and relevant development actors, including the International Red Cross and Red Crescent Movement, in the relief, rehabilitation and reconstruction efforts in the affected countries;

19. *Welcomes* significant progress, achievements and outcomes in the affected countries, and requests the United Nations system to continue to provide its support to those countries as efforts are being mainstreamed into long-term development assistance projects and programmes.

Other disaster assistance

Bolivia

In February, extreme climatic events caused by the La Niña phenomenon since November 2007 affected all nine departments of Bolivia. Heavy rainfall in the country and extreme water flows from upstream areas towards lower regions raised rivers in several departments to historic levels, creating extensive floods in many communities. Floods, landslides and mudslides caused loss of lives, injury and displacements, as well as damage to housing, infrastructure and agriculture. The most vulnerable communities lost their livelihoods and income, in many cases for the third consecutive year. As at 13 February 2008, the floods had killed 52 persons and affected 58,887 households (some 300,000 persons). Especially critical was the situation in Trinidad, the capital city of Beni department, as its population and the displaced people sheltered in urban camps were at risk of evacuation. Water levels in the north and the lowest regions were expected to keep rising in the ensuing weeks, and the situation would remain precarious for months. On 12 February, the Government declared a national emergency situation and requested support from the international community. The UN system, in coordination with the Government and other partners, prioritized in order of importance the following sectors: food security and nutrition; shelter and housing; water and sanitation; child protection; education; minimum accessibility restoration for humanitarian assistance; agriculture; health; and institutional coordination and territorial integration.

The UN Flash Appeal sought $18.2 million for international partners to support the Government in its response to the floods, of which 80 per cent ($14.6

million) was received. As at October 2008, the appeal closed and unmet requirements were reduced to zero.

China

On 12 May, a massive earthquake struck the Sichuan Province in China. State media reported that over 41,000 people had lost their lives, 32,000 were missing, 250,000 had been injured and five million were homeless. The World Health Organization rushed emergency health kits to the quake-affected areas and the International Telecommunication Union deployed satellite terminals to coordinate relief and rescue operations. UNDP allocated $100,000 for relief activities and the United Nations contributed $8 million from CERF.

Cuba

In 2008, between August and September, Cuba was hit by two tropical hurricanes and two tropical storms. More than 500,000 homes were damaged or destroyed and nearly 113,000 hectares of crops were damaged, resulting in lost harvested crops, agricultural tools, food storage facilities and approximately 53,000 tonnes of food. In order to avoid human suffering, 3 million people were evacuated, approximately 28 per cent of the country's population. While many found shelter in the houses of friends or relatives, some 500,000 were provided with temporary shelters. In support of the initial response, the UN system contributed $8.7 million. UN agencies designed the Post-Hurricane Plan of Action to alleviate the basic needs of the population and promote the recovery of livelihoods in a period of 12 months. The Plan of Action required $30 million.

Djibouti

Successive years of low rainfall and subsequent drought in Djibouti led in 2008 to massive deaths of livestock and consequently a significant reduction in milk production. The suffering caused by the drought was aggravated by sharp increases in food prices since late 2007, which severely compromised the food security, health, and livelihoods of some 24,000 families or 120,000 people, including 36,000 sub-urban people, 8,500 refugees and 20,000 asylum-seekers. In many cases, those affected migrated to urban areas seeking assistance and remittances. The Djibouti UN country team received a CERF allocation of $2.6 million in February for emergency projects submitted by UN system agencies, which allowed them to initiate a humanitarian response in food aid, water and sanitation, nutrition and health, and agriculture and livestock health. However, the prevalence of acute malnutrition continued, as did the need for intervention. The UN country team appealed for $31.7 million to help support the Government response to the food and nutrition crisis with a consolidated approach to cover the last six months of 2008. The emergency response plan was expected to continue and strengthen the CERF allocation through the critical hot season from July to December.

Haiti

In 2008, the combined impact of four successive hurricanes and tropical storms (Fay, Gustav, Hanna and Ike), which hit Haiti between August and September, affected 9 out of 10 regions in the country, causing 793 deaths and injuring 548 people. As at 19 December, some 310 people were still missing. More than 165,000 families (800,000 people) were affected due to destroyed or damaged houses (approximately 100,000) and the loss of their livelihoods. Many main roads and bridges across the country were destroyed or blocked, compounding an already difficult logistics operation. Following a request from the Government for international assistance, a flash appeal was launched in September for $107 million for humanitarian and early recovery activities for six months. In December, a post-disaster needs assessment (PDNA) was being finalized by the Government with the support of the international community, which would provide a comprehensive framework for early recovery, rehabilitation and reconstruction. Based on a better understanding of the disaster's impact, a revised appeal, which would run until the end of April 2009, was tailored to ensure consistency with the PDNA.

The revised UN Flash Appeal for Haiti, which sought $121.1 million in 2008, received 60 per cent ($73.2 million) of the requirement.

Honduras

In October, Honduras was affected by heavy rainfall due to Tropical Depression 16, which remained in the country for approximately 15 days and produced floods in 17 of the country's 18 departments. The resulting flooding and landslides caused extensive damage or loss of shelter and/or livelihoods and loss of life and injuries, affecting over 271,000 people. Some 72,085 hectares of crops were lost and extensive damage was sustained to public infrastructure. An Inter-Agency Emergency Response Plan was being implemented and sectoral groups were activated for water and sanitation, shelter, health, food security and nutrition, early recovery, and telecommunications and logistics. The UN country team, UN disaster management team and UN emergency team were activated to assist in coordinating the international response. During the first weeks, priority would be given to life-saving and life-sustaining activities to support those affected in terms of basic needs, as well as to the coordination of assistance and definition of the most immediate needs.

The UN Flash Appeal for Honduras sought $17.1 million for emergency relief projects, of which 35 per cent ($6 million) was received.

Kyrgyzstan

In 2008, low precipitation during the spring and summer, which had followed a harsh winter in 2007, depleted the country's hydroelectric resources, causing power cuts when electricity was most needed for home heating. Soaring food and fuel prices, adverse weather and declining remittances weakened the purchasing power of the most vulnerable and contributed to a precarious food security situation. An estimated 800,000 people were considered specifically vulnerable to the effects of water, energy and food insecurity, including the extremely poor, homeless people, street children, persons living in institutions or in extremely remote locations, and people who lacked proper documentation, which made them ineligible for many of the social protection schemes. Those factors prompted a flash appeal that aimed to respond to actual and imminent humanitarian needs between December 2008 and May 2009, focusing on the most vulnerable groups and social services institutions such as hospitals and orphanages. It also included support for the urgent implementation of priority interventions of the Country Development Strategy, including linkages between humanitarian assistance and early recovery actions.

The initial UN Flash Appeal for Kyrgyzstan sought $20.6 million, while the revised appeal sought $14.8 million, of which 54 per cent ($8 million) was received.

Lao People's Democratic Republic

In 2008, heavy rainfall between 12 and 18 August in the Lao People's Democratic Republic in and around the Mekong watershed caused severe flooding that affected the Northern and Central regions of Laos in particular, with flash floods causing 11 deaths. Across the country, it was estimated that 204,189 people were affected in 866 villages of 53 districts in 11 provinces. Preliminary Government estimates indicated that 74,989 hectares of agricultural land were inundated during the peak of the floods and nearly 50,000 hectares out of the total inundated area suffered damage. Thousands of households lost their assets, livelihoods and, in some cases, their dwellings. A needs assessment found that damage and contamination of water systems and wells had caused an acute shortage of safe drinking water in affected areas. The global surge in food prices had strained household coping strategies, and access to food was limited. The loss of crops, livestock, and other sources of livelihood due to the August flood, as well as damage to crops, fishponds, food stocks and livestock, had a negative impact on medium- to long-term food security. The appeal for flood recovery and rehabilitation submitted by UN agencies in partnership with the Government and other development partners, which was launched for $9.9 million, proposed 15 projects in eight sectors to address key humanitarian and early recovery needs for a one-year period.

Madagascar

By March, Madagascar had been hit by two cyclones during the year. Both cyclones brought heavy rainfall to most parts of the island and affected more than 239,000 people in the northeastern and northwestern parts of the country. The ensuing floods hit heavily populated areas, including the capital city of Antananarivo, as well as important farming areas, such as the Alaotra Mangoro region. As a result, the food security situation deteriorated dramatically and the risk of maternal and child mortality due to a lack of access to quality services, and to water- and vector-borne diseases, increased. On 22 February, the Government appealed to the United Nations and the diplomatic community for international solidarity and assistance in addressing the situation.

The UN Flash Appeal for Madagascar, which sought $36.5 million to address the immediate needs of more than 239,000 people affected by the cyclones, heavy rains and winds, received 50 per cent ($18.8 million) of its target. As at November, the appeal closed and unmet requirements were reduced to zero.

Myanmar

On 2 and 3 May, Cyclone Nargis struck Myanmar, causing widespread devastation in the Ayeyarwady and Yangon Divisions. An estimated 84,537 people were killed, another 53,836 were missing, and nearly 20,000 were injured. Some 2.4 million people—more than a third of the population of 7.3 million in the affected townships—were thought to have been severely affected in the loss of livelihoods, shelter, or similarly severe loss, and up to 800,000 were displaced from their homes. The impact on the Ayeyarwady Delta, a remote area that was heavily populated and difficult to reach, was particularly severe. In addition to the lives and livelihoods lost, the timing and extent of the natural disaster affected the critical planting season in what was Myanmar's breadbasket region, with significant quantities of seeds and harvested crops lost. The initial flash appeal for $187 million was issued on 9 May. Following a wide-ranging assessment to identify key humanitarian and recovery needs in the affected areas and the observations made by clusters and agencies after 10 weeks of operations, it was determined that those needs remained significant and required a more comprehensive and prolonged response than the appeal's six-month planning horizon.

The revised plan, which expanded the UN Flash Appeal to 103 projects in 13 key sectors to assist 2.4 million people with a planning horizon until April 2009, sought $477.1 million, of which 73 per cent ($348.8 million) was received.

Nepal

On 18 August, the Koshi River, with one of the largest river basins in Asia, breached its eastern embankment, inundating four Village Development Committees (VDCs) in the district of Sunsari in Nepal. The disaster led to extensive flooding and the displacement of several million people in Bihar, south of Nepal's border with India. The force of the water led to 80 per cent of the river changing its course, rendering parts of the flooded areas inaccessible. An estimated 70,000 to 100,000 people were affected, with up to 40,000 being displaced from the flood-affected areas into neighbouring VDCs. The Government declared a state of emergency on 4 September. In collaboration with the Government, the Nepal IASC developed a humanitarian response plan that was a supplement to the 2008 Nepal Common Appeal for Transition Support (see p. 1005). The response plan sought $15.5 million to cover the needs of at least 70,000 people for a six-month period, prioritizing immediate life-saving activities in 10 sectors.

Southern Africa

In 2008, Southern Africa faced unusually early and torrential rainfall, which by February had damaged the homes and crops of some 449,000 people in Malawi, Mozambique, Zambia and Zimbabwe; 120,000 persons were displaced—more than 80 per cent in Mozambique. Eleven tropical storms had already formed and regional forecasts indicated a likelihood of above-normal rainfall across most of Southern Africa until April; national authorities in the four affected countries predicted that it would continue with the same severity. In all four countries, Governments sought international assistance in implementing their contingency and response plans, and took immediate preparedness measures to ensure a rapid response to a deterioration of the situation. While the flooding in Malawi, Zambia and Zimbabwe had been localised, the early onset of rains and likelihood of more posed an imminent threat to populations living in the catchment areas of rising rivers, dams and lakes. The UN Flash Appeal sought $89.1 million, of which 33 per cent ($29.5 million) was received, to address the needs of more than 449,000 people already affected by the floods, as well as to undertake preparedness measures in all four countries to address the needs of an additional 805,000 persons at immediate risk of being affected, for a six-month period. Concerted efforts would be made to mobilize longer-term programmes for recovery and mitigation. In November, the appeal was closed and unmet requirements were reduced to zero.

Tajikistan

In early 2008, Tajikistan experienced the worst winter in 44 years, with heavy snowfall that isolated communities and severe weather that hampered travel between major commercial centres. The exceptionally cold weather caused breakdowns in the country's energy infrastructure and water supply systems. Heating was limited in urban areas, while heating prices increased in rural areas. Essential services were also affected, with many health facilities and schools forced to close. The rural food security status that had already begun to deteriorate markedly in 2007 due to rising fuel, transportation and food costs, as well as prolonged drought in the spring and summer, was exacerbated by a locust invasion in 2008 that taxed the capacities of households through further food insecurity. The combined effects of those conditions on vulnerable populations were particularly acute. The price of bread and cooking oil doubled during the period, while prices for most other basic commodities increased by 50 per cent. An appeal was launched in February to cover the needs of 2 million people. Response activities helped to alleviate suffering, sustain minimum essential services, mitigate further disease outbreaks and avoid further deterioration in the nutrition status. Joint food security, livelihoods, agriculture and nutrition needs assessments conducted in April and June found that some 2.2 million people were food insecure, and of those 800,000 were severely food insecure. In May, the Tajikistan UN country team launched a revised appeal to support the Government in its efforts to address the humanitarian needs arising from the compounded crisis. It sought to stimulate support and early recovery by creating an integrated early recovery plan and network to restore basic services, infrastructure and livelihood opportunities.

The revised UN Flash Appeal for Tajikistan sought $26.9 million, of which 57 per cent ($15.4 million) was received.

Yemen

In 2008, floods and heavy rains that affected eastern Yemen from 24 to 25 October resulted in one of the most serious natural disasters in the country in decades. Flash floods and surging waters killed at least 73 people and displaced an additional 20,000 to 25,000 people. Some 3,264 predominantly mud-brick houses were totally destroyed or damaged beyond repair, while hundreds of others were uninhabitable, particularly in several Wadi Hadramout villages that had been listed as UNESCO World Heritage Sites. In addition to houses, several health facilities and an estimated 166 schools were damaged or destroyed. The flooding and surging water also caused extensive damage to the local agriculture and honey production, as well as the loss of livelihoods, which impacted some 650,000 people. The United Nations estimated that food, medicine and non-food items delivered through bilateral channels would suffice for several weeks of the initial response to the emergency. The Yemen Floods Response Plan was prepared based on the findings of a UN/International Organization for Migration rapid needs assessment mission that visited Wadi Hadramout; communication with the authorities of the affected governorates; and missions by UN staff in the affected areas. It sought funding in the areas of food, water and sanitation, health, nutrition, shelter/non-food items, camp coordination and management, protection, education, and livelihoods, including agriculture.

The UN Flash Appeal for Yemen sought $11.5 million in 2008, of which 45 per cent ($5.1 million) was received.

GENERAL ASSEMBLY ACTION

On 11 November [meeting 45], the General Assembly adopted **resolution 63/20** [draft: A/63/L.21 & Add.1] without vote [agenda item 65 *(b)*].

Special economic assistance for Yemen

The General Assembly,

Concerned about the floods and heavy rain that occurred in the eastern provinces of Yemen on 24 October 2008, resulting in a natural disaster that caused damage to infrastructure and the loss of human lives, and undermined the Government's effort to achieve the Millennium Development Goals,

Acknowledging with appreciation the timely assistance extended by the regional and international donor community, as well as by United Nations agencies and other humanitarian actors,

Noting the immediate response by the Government of Yemen to this disaster,

1. *Expresses its solidarity with and support* for the Government and people of Yemen;

2. *Invites* Member States and relevant United Nations entities, as well as international financial institutions and development agencies, to provide economic and technical assistance in the post-disaster recovery and rehabilitation process;

3. *Invites* the international community and the United Nations system and other international organizations to support the disaster risk management and disaster preparedness capacity of Yemen.

Chapter IV

International trade, finance and transport

The World Trade Organization (WTO) Doha Round of trade negotiations stood at a critical juncture as negotiations entered the seventh year in 2008, when they were scheduled to conclude. The focus was on establishing full modalities for reducing commitments in agriculture and non-agricultural market access. In July, an informal WTO "mini-ministerial" meeting, convened to establish modalities on agriculture and non-agricultural market access, failed to achieve a breakthrough to set the basis for concluding the Doha Round in 2008.

From 20 to 25 April, the United Nations Conference on Trade and Development (UNCTAD) held its twelfth session (UNCTAD XII) in Accra, Ghana, under the theme "Addressing the opportunities and challenges of globalization for development". The Conference adopted the Accra Declaration, a political statement in which member States commended UNCTAD for its contribution to advancing the development agenda and supporting developing countries in addressing challenges and maximizing benefits from the globalized world economy. It also adopted the Accra Accord, which built upon the 2004 São Paulo Consensus, and provided updated policy analysis and responses, as well as guidelines for strengthening UNCTAD and enhancing its development role, impact and institutional effectiveness.

In April, the Economic and Social Council held a special high-level meeting with the Bretton Woods institutions (the World Bank Group and the International Monetary Fund), WTO and UNCTAD under the theme "Coherence, coordination and cooperation in the context of the implementation of the 2002 Monterrey Consensus, including new challenges and emerging issues". The meeting identified new initiatives on financing for development, which it viewed as important for achieving the objectives of the Consensus. The Follow-up International Conference on Financing for Development to Review Implementation of the Monterrey Consensus was held in Doha, Qatar, from 29 November to 2 December. The Conference had as its theme "Looking ahead: further cooperative actions in financing for development". It adopted the Doha Declaration on Financing for Development: outcome document of the Follow-up International Conference on Financing for Development to Review the Implementation of the Monterrey Consensus, in which States reaffirmed the Consensus. It also recognized that mobilizing financial resources for development and the effective use of those resources were central to the global partnership for sustainable development and for achieving the internationally agreed development goals, including the Millennium Development Goals (MDGs). On 24 December, the General Assembly endorsed the Doha Declaration.

The *World Economic Situation and Prospects 2009*, jointly issued by UNCTAD and the UN Department of Economic and Social Affairs, stated that the global financial crisis, coming on the heels of the food and energy security crises, would most likely set back progress towards poverty reduction and the achievement of the MDGs. Restoring confidence in financial markets in order to normalize credit flows remained of primary importance. In that regard, the General Assembly President convened, in October, an Interactive Panel on the Global Financial Crisis to secure a more stable and sustainable global economic order, and welcomed the establishment of a High-level Task Force of Experts to undertake a comprehensive review of the international financial system. In 2008, developing countries continued to make increasing substantial net outward transfers of financial resources to developed countries, reaching an all-time high of $933 billion. Net transfers from countries with economies in transition increased to $171 billion, owing mainly to the strong increase in the trade surplus of the Russian Federation. In contrast, in Latin America and the Caribbean and East and South Asia, net outward transfers declined as a consequence of the financial turmoil, leading to a reduction in private capital flows from the third quarter of the year onwards.

Total contributions to UNCTAD voluntary trust funds amounted to $36.8 million, reflecting in nominal terms a 26.4 per cent increase over the previous year. Developed countries' contributions accounted for 58 per cent of the total, an increase of 30 per cent in nominal terms, while contributions from developing countries and economies in transition declined by 17 per cent and accounted for 21 per cent. Contributions from multilateral donors increased sharply, with the European Commission providing 14.5 per cent of the total, a 127 per cent increase, and the UN system providing 5 per cent. The private and public sectors provided 1.8 per cent.

At its fifty-fifth session in September, the UNCTAD Trade and Development Board adopted agreed conclusions on review of progress in the implementation of the Programme of Action for the Least Developed Countries for the Decade 2001–2010; economic development in Africa: trade liberalization and export performance in Africa; and review of UNCTAD technical cooperation activities and their financing.

UNCTAD XII

The twelfth session of the United Nations Conference on Trade and Development (UNCTAD XII) was held in Accra, Ghana, from 20 to 25 April [TD/442 & Corr.1], in accordance with General Assembly resolutions 1995(XIX) [YUN 1964, p. 210] and 60/184 [YUN 2005, p. 1042]. Attended by 149 States, the Holy See and Palestine; 23 intergovernmental organizations; 12 UN organizations, bodies and programmes; 9 specialized agencies; and 104 non-governmental organizations, the Conference had as its theme "Addressing the opportunities and challenges of globalization for development". Discussions centred around four sub-themes: enhancing coherence for sustainable economic development and poverty reduction in global policymaking; key trade and development issues and new realities in the world economy; enhancing the enabling environment for productive capacity, trade and investment: mobilizing resources and harnessing knowledge for development; and strengthening UNCTAD's development role, impact and institutional effectiveness.

The Conference adopted the provisional agenda [TD/414], and established a Committee of the Whole to consider and report on the specific substantive item referred to it, and the draft negotiated text and annex thereto [TD/L.398 & Add.1–4], prepared and approved by the Trade and Development Board (TDB), acting as the Preparatory Committee for the Conference.

The main Conference events were: a high-level segment on trade and development for Africa's prosperity: action and direction; and nine round tables on: social and gender dimensions of globalization, development and poverty reduction; creating an institutional environment conducive to increased foreign investment and sustainable development; the changing face of commodities in the twenty-first century; emergence of a new South and South-South trade as a vehicle for integration for development; harnessing knowledge and technology for development; debt management solutions supporting trade and development; developing productive capacities in least developed countries (LDCs); and strengthening UNCTAD.

Parallel events included: meeting of the Investment Advisory Council [TD/L.403]; Global Leaders Investment Debate; capacity-building workshops on investment; Annual Conference of the World Association of Investment Promotion Agencies; Civil Society Forum (Accra, 17–25 April); meeting of the United Nations Chief Executives Board for Coordination: Inter-agency Cluster on Trade and Productive Capacity; ministerial meetings of least developed countries (LDCs) (19 April), of the Group of 77 and China (20 April) and of landlocked developing countries (22 April); meeting of senior officials of the Global System of Trade Preferences; high-level meeting on trade facilitation and Aid for Trade for the landlocked; and World Investment Forum, on prospects for global foreign direct investment (FDI) and new business opportunities, global value chains [TD/435], and Africa: a new emerging market for FDI [TD/438].

Other events focused on perspectives on a development agenda in commodities trade; UNCTAD's role in development; trade and gender: perspectives for sustainable growth and poverty reduction [TD/L.409]; making sustainability standards work for pro-poor agricultural trade and development; Aid for Trade (perspectives of regional commissions); Compal (deliverables on competition law and policy) [TD/L.407]; making trade work for biodiversity sustainable use [TD/L.410]; trade and investment between developing countries and transition economies [TD/L.411]; biofuels (small producers in developing countries); Amandla (light) project initiative with Philips, and exhibition of its corporate social responsibility products; UNCTAD Empretec Africa Forum launch; inauguration of the Dominican Republic Sugar Cane Industry Project; launch of the Creative Economy Report; exhibition of African Art; Women's Business Awards; and Creative Africa: concert and film festival.

The meeting had before it the report of the UNCTAD Secretary-General to UNCTAD XII entitled "Globalization for development: opportunities and challenges [TD/413]; the report of TDB to the Conference [TD/441]; an issues note on trade and development for Africa's prosperity [TD/433]; and notes by the UNCTAD secretariat on: the outcome of the expert meeting in preparation for UNCTAD XII: identifying issues and priorities for LDCs during and beyond UNCTAD XII [TD/415]; developing productive capacities in LDCs [TD/420]; harnessing knowledge and technology [TD/421]; the interface between trade and climate change policies and the role of UNCTAD [TD(XII)/BP/2]; debt management [TD/424]; emergence of a new South and South-South trade as a vehicle for regional and interregional integration [TD/425]; creating an institutional environment conducive to increased foreign investment and sustainable development [TD/426]; social and gender dimensions of globalization, development and poverty reduction [TD/422]; strengthening UNCTAD's development role [TD/430] and its impact and institutional effectiveness [TD/431]; and the changing face of commodities [TD/428 & Corr.1].

A list of the Conference participants was issued in May [TD/INF.41].

Accra Declaration and Accra Accord

The Conference concluded on 25 April [TD/442] with the adoption of the Accra Declaration, in which member States commended UNCTAD for its contribution to advancing the development agenda and supporting developing countries in addressing challenges and maximizing benefits from the globalized world economy. They recommitted themselves to upholding a well-functioning, universal, rules-based, open, non-discriminatory and equitable multilateral trading system that promoted development and maximized development gains for all. UNCTAD member States resolved to find integrated solutions to the challenges of rising food and energy prices, and global economic uncertainties compounded by climate change, and committed to redoubling efforts to combat poverty and hunger. They pledged to bolster the world's food security, meet urgent humanitarian needs in developing countries, particularly LDCs and Africa, and pay special attention to the food and nutritional needs of mothers and children. Those efforts should be accompanied by collective measures and an enabling environment, particularly by meaningful reform and liberalization of trade in agriculture and improved official development assistance (ODA) flows to the agricultural sector of developing countries. Participants noted that a new phase of globalization had emerged, in which developing countries played an important role as a new engine of the global economy, but recognized that many of them—especially African countries and LDCs—remained on the margins of globalization and were lagging behind in the achievement of the Millennium Development Goals (MDGs). Their development would remain a priority of the international community. States also undertook to strengthen support for integration in Africa, in particular the New Partnership for Africa's Development. They resolved to redouble efforts to conclude the Doha Round of trade negotiations (see p. 1050) and emphasized that the agreement reached at the Sixth World Trade Organization Ministerial Conference [YUN 2005, p. 1041] to provide duty-free and quota-free market access for LDCs should be implemented, as well as those made with regard to cotton. In the context of the Aid for Trade Initiative, they called for stronger national action and international support to help build domestic productive competitive export supply, especially for Africa, LDCs, landlocked developing countries, small island developing States and other structurally weak and vulnerable small economies. They called upon donors to honour their ODA commitments and improve ODA effectiveness in support of nationally owned development strategies. States recognized the need to enhance the coherence, governance and consistency of the international monetary, financial and trading systems, and urged the participation, in trade, money and finance policymaking, of developing countries and countries with economies in transition. As inclusive globalization would require fuller participation of countries in the global knowledge and information society, they encouraged the public and private sectors and civil society to put information, technology, innovation, creativity and diversity at the service of fair and equitable development for all. States also underlined the importance of sound policies and good governance, and of the effective participation and contribution of all stakeholders, including the Government, private sector and civil society. Climate change adaptation and mitigation should be urgently addressed, including its trade and development aspects.

The Accra Accord stated that UNCTAD should examine new and long-standing issues which could foster a better understanding of ways of ensuring that the positive impact of globalization and trade on development was maximized. It should enhance its work on the problems of Africa and LDCs, and the needs of small island developing States, landlocked developing countries and other structurally weak, vulnerable and small economies, and assist transit developing countries with their challenges of infrastructure and transport. UNCTAD should contribute to the implementation of and follow-up to the outcomes of relevant conferences and the achievement of internationally agreed development goals, including the MDGs, and help implement the global development agenda by 2015. It should also contribute to the implementation of specific actions requested at international summits and conferences, and of the internationally agreed goals in the Doha Ministerial Declaration and other relevant decisions.

Under the sub-theme on enhancing coherence at all levels for sustainable economic development and poverty reduction in global policymaking, including the contribution of regional approaches, UNCTAD XII stated that, in order to complement national efforts, the coherence, governance and consistency of the international monetary, financial and trading systems should be enhanced. Towards that end, it was important to improve global economic governance, strengthen the UN leadership in promoting development and enhance coordination among relevant ministries and institutions. Similarly, policy and programme coordination of international institutions and coherence at the operational and international levels should be encouraged in order to meet the MDGs of sustained economic growth, poverty eradication and sustainable development. At the national level, coherence between macroeconomic and microeconomic policies was crucial. Microeconomic and structural policies should provide incentives for investment that could bring about productivity growth and improve the international competitiveness of domestic enterprises. The impact of policies to foster industrial development and technological upgrading could be enhanced by policies to attract FDI and trade and competition policies. Regional cooperation among developing countries, as well as integration, could reinforce national development strategies and multilateral agreements and enhance developing countries' output growth, trade and influence. Such cooperation could deliver development gains if it encompassed policies in support of growth, stability, industrial development, infrastructure, employment and structural change. UNCTAD should conduct research into and analysis of macroeconomic policies, trade, investment, finance, debt and poverty, and their interdependence, to help developing countries meet their development goals, including poverty eradication, improve the welfare of their citizens and address the opportunities and challenges created by globalization. It should also continue its role in delivering policy analysis and identifying options at the global and national levels.

As to the sub-theme on key trade and development issues and the new realities in the geography of the world economy, the Accra Accord stated that, to make globalization a positive force for all, with its benefits shared equitably, a comprehensive and coherent set of development policies and initiatives was required. Ensuring the effective participation of all countries, in particular developing countries, in the international trading system was a critical challenge and opportunity. All World Trade Organization (WTO) members should promote a well-functioning, rules-based, open, equitable, predictable and non-discriminatory multilateral trading system, and demonstrate their political will to achieve the completion of the WTO Doha Round and the realization of its core agenda, within its overall development dimension. Developing countries, LDCs and countries with economies in transition acceding to WTO should be able to do so on terms reflecting their individual trade, financial and development circumstances, and countries engaging in regional trade agreements should ensure policy coherence and compatibility with WTO rules. Attention should be paid to helping countries with economies in transition and developing countries to benefit mutually from increased trade and investment flows. Aid for Trade, including technical assistance, should help developing countries implement and benefit from trade liberalization and reform so as to build productive capacities and trade-related infrastructure based on each country's needs and priorities. Increased and more effective Aid for Trade was needed to support developing countries, in particular LDCs, to benefit from the rule-based international trading system. Standards and technical regulations should be developed transparently and applied non-discriminatorily, and developing countries should be provided with technical assistance and capacity-building support to meet standards effectively. Trade liberalization would also require addressing non-tariff measures, including unilateral measures, where they might act as unnecessary trade barriers. Efforts should prevent and dismantle anti-competitive structures and practices and promote responsibility and accountability of corporate actors at both the national and international levels, thereby enabling developing countries' producers, enterprises and consumers to take advantage of trade liberalization. Further work was needed to support developing countries, in particular LDCs, and countries with economies in transition, on key issues at the interface between trade, the environment and development, such as new standards, including issues concerning eco-labelling and certification, as well as environmentally preferable products and the transfer of, and cooperation on, environmentally sound technology. UNCTAD should intensify its trade and trade-related technical cooperation and capacity-building activities, strengthen its contribution to the Enhanced Integrated Framework for Trade-related Technical Assistance to LDCs and the Joint Integrated Technical Assistance Programme, and continue to provide and strengthen technical support to, and cooperation with, developing countries, according to their level of development, prior to, during and in the follow-up to their WTO accession process.

Addressing the sub-theme on enhancing the enabling environment at all levels to strengthen productive capacity, trade and investment: mobilizing resources and harnessing knowledge for development, the Accord stated that efforts to promote a conducive environment for development and to introduce reform and eradicate poverty needed to be supported in order to achieve the internationally agreed development goals. Attracting and benefiting from FDI required appropriate national investment and development policies, and improved data and more analysis were needed on the social, economic and development impacts of FDI and transnational corporation activities to enable policymakers to make better informed decisions. Investment in basic economic and social infrastructure was vital for developing countries, whose efforts to identify and overcome obstacles to mobilizing domestic resources should be complemented by external flows, including FDI, other private flows and ODA. Governments, international institutions and the international community could help countries create an attractive investment environment by providing better information on national laws and regulations, as well as on international agreements and country opportunities and risks. Sovereign risk assessments made by the private sector should maximize the use of strict, objective and transparent parameters, which could be facilitated by high-quality data and analysis. In the areas of international trade and transportation, the development of internationally agreed rules and standards, such as international conventions and other legal instruments agreed under the auspices of the United Nations Commission on International Trade Law (UNCITRAL) and other bodies, was required to bring about benefits to traders and help reduce legal, administrative and transaction costs. Developing countries should participate in international consensus-building and negotiation processes, and their concerns and interests should be taken into account. Developing countries might also require capacity-building and technical assistance to help them in the implementation of internationally agreed rules and standards. With the increasing involvement of the private sector in transport infrastructure development, developing countries should strengthen their capacity to monitor, regulate and facilitate that sector at the national level. Policies were needed to promote competitive and effective transportation systems for both landlocked and transit developing countries. In that context, full support should be given to the implementation of the Almaty Programme of Action and Declaration [YUN 2003, p. 875], and efforts should ensure that the outcome of the Midterm Review of the Implementation of the Programme of Action (see p. 949) contributed to the establishment of efficient transit and transport systems, addressing the challenges of transit developing countries and the integration of landlocked developing countries into the international trading system. Measures to enhance the security of international supply chains and to address environmental concerns also had to be taken into account. UNCTAD work on investment should assist developing countries, in particular LDCs and countries with special needs, in designing and implementing policies to boost productive capacities and international competitiveness. Attention should be paid to the role of both North-South and South-South investment and domestic investment. UNCTAD should address the particular needs of LDCs, as well as the needs and problems of landlocked developing countries, small island developing States and other structurally weak, vulnerable and small economies.

Regarding the sub-theme on strengthening UNCTAD: enhancing its development role, impact and institutional effectiveness, the Accord stated that in the context of the changing global economy and development needs, UNCTAD's development role, impact and institutional effectiveness should be strengthened in order for it to provide guidance and support with respect to both emerging issues and long-standing problems at the interface between trade and development. That strengthening process should include the adoption of new and improved indicators of achievement and performance measures, the continued adaptation of its working methods and structures and a more focused approach to address trade and development issues that responded to the needs, concerns and priorities of its membership. UNCTAD would mainstream cross-cutting issues of gender equality and the empowerment of women, the promotion of sustainable development and full and productive employment. It should strengthen its internal coordination; align more closely the thematic focus of its research and analysis, technical assistance and intergovernmental discussions; and designate regional focal points to deepen its regional perspectives. In view of the challenges in commodities markets, the UN Secretary-General was urged to transform the Commodities Branch into an autonomous unit reporting directly to the UNCTAD Secretary-General, while retaining the Branch's mandate and taking into account, without duplicating, the work of other organizations. The unit should contribute more effectively to developing countries' efforts to formulate strategies and policies to respond to the challenges and opportunities of commodity markets. As the highest UNCTAD body between Conferences, TDB should strengthen its decision-making, policy and governance functions, and ensure overall consistency in the organization's activities. The Board's agenda should reflect the interests and concerns of the UNCTAD membership, and be policy-oriented and organized around themes agreed by member States. It would add to the agenda of its regular session an item entitled "Development strategies in a globalized world". The agenda item "Evaluation and review of UNCTAD implementation of the Accra Accord" would be added to its regular session in 2010, extended by one week, and the UNCTAD Secretary-General would present a report on UNCTAD implementation of the Accra Accord. The TDB annual regular session would take place in early September, and monthly consultations with the extended Bureau of the Board and interested States should be held to serve as a forum for dialogue between the secretariat and States on issues of interest to the organization. Welcoming the establishment of the Global Network of Development Think Tanks, involving institutions at the country level and regional networks, the Conference invited the UNCTAD Secretary-General to explore the feasibility of organizing an annual meeting of the Global Network to be held in conjunction with the TDB regular session. As to the commissions (TDB subsidiary bodies), their reports would be submitted to TDB for approval, and their role would be to conduct policy dialogue on one or two selected issues; consider reports of expert meetings and recommend for approval their work programmes; and promote and strengthen synergies among the UNCTAD three pillars of research and analysis, consensus-building and technical cooperation. There would be two commissions: the Trade and Development Commission, with the mandate of the previous Commission on Trade in Goods and Services, and Commodities, and the responsibility for transport and trade logistics issues from the previous Commission on Enterprise, Business Facilitation and Development; and the Investment, Enterprise and Development Commission, with the mandate of the previous Commission on Investment, Technology and Related Financial Issues, and the responsibility for enterprise and information and communication technology (ICT) issues from the previous Commission on Enterprise, Business Facilitation and Development. Commission sessions would be held at the same time each year back-to-back for five days in the spring, and their outcomes would be agreed conclusions from the policy dialogue and recommendations to the secretariat. TDB would decide on their substantive topics, upon the recommendation of the Bureau of the Board. Expert meetings would continue to be held under the auspices of the commissions, in single or multi-year sessions for a period of three days, and their number would remain at eight. TDB, at its fifty-fifth session, would determine the topics and terms of reference for multi-year expert meetings, which would continue for up to four years and report annually to the commissions. In that regard, TDB would establish a multi-year expert meeting on commodities. Single-session expert meetings would be convened on specific topics that required in-depth examination, to be decided on by TDB. Funding for the participation of experts from developing countries should be sustainable and predictable and come from the existing trust fund. The UNCTAD Secretary-General should attract contributions to the funds and States should contribute. The Intergovernmental Group of Experts on Competition Law and Policy and the Intergovernmental Working Group of Experts on International Standards of Accounting and Reporting would continue to meet annually.

UNCTAD technical cooperation should be fully integrated with the other two pillars and should: deliver results at the interregional, regional and national levels, to the benefit of developing countries; be demand-driven and embrace country ownership; be based on the principles of transparency, efficiency, effectiveness and accountability; address the needs of developing countries, in particular LDCs, as well as the needs of Africa; be planned and implemented in a geographically balanced manner; address the special needs and problems of landlocked developing countries, small island developing States and other structurally weak, vulnerable and small economies; and accord with TBD decisions 492(LIV) [YUN 2007, p. 1002] and 478(L) [YUN 2003, p. 996], and with the conclusions of the 2006 midterm review [YUN 2006, p. 1109]. Regional partnership-based delivery of technical assistance activities should be maximized, and local and regional expertise and material resources should enhance the institutional capacity of recipient countries and the sustainability of benefits. UNCTAD should intensify its contribution to the Enhanced Integrated Framework for Trade-related Technical Assistance to LDCs, and strengthen in-country capacities for the management, implementation and monitoring of the mainstreaming of trade into LDCs' national development plans. The Conference took note of the outcome of the 2007 Pledging Conference on the Enhanced Integrated Framework. It stated that efforts should improve the management, evaluation and reporting of technical assistance activities, with greater attention paid to: measuring the effectiveness and evaluating the impact of those activities, in accordance with TDB decision 478(L) and relevant UN rules and procedures on technical cooperation evaluation; identifying the roles and responsibilities within the secretariat; and tracking the demand for assistance and availability of funding. There should be more cross-divisional cooperation to promote a holistic, UNCTAD-wide perspective and to enhance synergies, cost-effectiveness and the sharing of best practices and lessons learned in the design and implementation of technical assistance activities. The Conference underscored TDB decision 492(LIV) and encouraged its implementation in order to increase predictability, transparency and coherence in the planning and implementation of technical assistance programmes, with a view to enhancing UNCTAD technical cooperation. Fund-raising should also be improved. Donors and potential donors should provide multi-year contributions to the newly established thematic trust funds so as to increase predictability in the planning and implementation of the relevant technical assistance programmes, and other ways and options should be explored, such as more effective outreach and presentation of UNCTAD technical cooperation capacities and programmes and of funding needs. UNCTAD should reinforce its operational links with other UN organizations, particularly those operating at country level. The Conference welcomed the establishment by the UN System Chief Executives Board for Coordination of the inter-agency thematic cluster on trade and productive sectors to enhance the role of trade in UN development assistance plans, undertake joint operations at the country level and enhance inter-agency cooperation in system-wide initiatives. The newly established training programme for UN resident coordinators on the activities and programmes of the thematic cluster should be pursued, and the regional focal points should assist coordinators in developing UNCTAD programmes for their countries and their inclusion in UN development frameworks. General Assembly resolution 62/208 on the triennial policy review of operational activities for development of the United Nations [ibid., p. 877], and subsequent resolutions on that subject, should be implemented by UNCTAD.

The Conference also encouraged the implementation of the Aid for Trade initiative and noted that

UNCTAD could contribute to its realization through its technical cooperation activities. UNCTAD should also improve its outreach towards potential recipients, including LDCs. The interaction between the secretariat, potential beneficiaries and donors on technical cooperation should be more structured and facilitated within the framework of the Working Party on the Medium-term Plan and the Programme Budget.

The activities outlined in the operational paragraphs on UNCTAD's contribution and on strengthening UNCTAD in the Accra Accord should be presented as the work programme for the following four years with defined objectives and outputs. The UNCTAD Secretary-General should present the work programme to States for discussion at the first meeting of the Working Party on the Medium-term Plan and the Programme Budget and the subsequent TDB session.

Annexed to the report of the conference were: the Ministerial Declaration of the Group of 77 and China on the occasion of UNCTAD XII [TD/436 & Corr.1]; the Declaration of the Least Developed Countries Ministerial Meeting at UNCTAD XII [TD/434] (see p. 939); the Ministerial Communiqué of Landlocked Developing Countries [TD/439] (see p. 948); and the Civil Society Forum Declaration to UNCTAD XII [TD/437]. In addition, the report contained two resolutions and statements of position on the outcome of the Conference by the United States and Iran.

Other action. On 25 April, the Conference expressed its gratitude to Ghana for hosting the Conference; welcomed the offer of Qatar to host UNCTAD XIII in 2012; endorsed the lists of States contained in the annex to resolution 1995(XIX) [TD/B/INF.211]; and took note of the TDB report to the Conference [TD/441] and of the statement by the Director of the Division of Management that TDB, at its fifty-fifth session, would carry out a review of the Accord and make related decisions. In that light, a statement of programme budget implications, if applicable, would be submitted by the secretariat.

In July, the UN Secretary-General transmitted to the Assembly the UNCTAD XII report [A/63/168].

GENERAL ASSEMBLY ACTION

On 19 December [meeting 72], the General Assembly, on the recommendation of the Second (Economic and Financial) Committee [A/63/412/Add.1], adopted **resolution 63/204** without vote [agenda item 47 *(a)*].

Report of the twelfth session of the United Nations Conference on Trade and Development

The General Assembly,

1. *Notes with satisfaction* the outcome of the twelfth session of the United Nations Conference on Trade and Development, held in Accra from 20 to 25 April 2008, specifically the Accra Declaration and the Accra Accord;

2. *Expresses its deep gratitude* to the Government and people of Ghana for the hospitality extended to participants in the twelfth session of the Conference;

3. *Welcomes* the generous offer of the Government of Qatar to host the thirteenth session of the Conference in 2012.

Preparatory process

Pre-conference events. In preparation for the convening of UNCTAD XII, the following pre-conference events were held: conference on Global Initiative on Commodities: re-launching the commodities agenda (Brasilia, Brazil, 7–11 May 2007) [TD(XII)/BP/1]; expert meeting on identifying issues and priorities for LDCs for action during and beyond UNCTAD XII (Arusha, United Republic of Tanzania, 22–24 October 2007) [TD/415]; India–Africa Hydrocarbon Conference and Exhibition (New Delhi, India, 6–7 November 2007) [TD/418]; meeting on trade and development implications of tourism services for developing countries (Geneva, 19–20 November 2007) [TD/427]; conference on biofuels: an option for a less carbon-intensive economy (Rio de Janeiro, Brazil, 4–5 December 2007) [TD/416]; meeting on science, technology, innovation and ICTs for development (Geneva, 6 December 2007) [TD/417]; meeting on globalization of port logistics: opportunities and challenges for developing countries (Geneva, 12 December 2007) [TD/419]; Secretary-General's high-level panel on the creative economy and industries for development (Geneva, 14–15 January 2008) [TD/423]; Aid for Trade and development: towards a new global solidarity initiative (Bangkok, Thailand, 24–25 January) [TD/429]; hearings with civil society and the private sector (Geneva, 28 January and 3 March) [TD(XII)/PC/2, TD(XII)/PC/3]; high-level workshop for African LDCs (Izmir, Turkey, 4–5 March) [TD/432]; South-South trade in Asia and the role of regional trade agreements (Tokyo, 25 March); Lessons learned from South-South trade in Asian regions (Geneva, 2 April); expert meeting on making sustainability work for small farmers (Arusha, 7–9 April); and workshop on development strategies in Africa (Accra, 19 April).

TDB action. On 3 March [A/63/15 (Part I)], TDB, at its forty-third executive session, was addressed by the UN Secretary-General, who stressed that UNCTAD XII could contribute to building an international economic environment that fostered development by galvanizing support for a more development-friendly global economic, trading and financial system. It should also articulate a strategy to leverage globalization, trade and investment for poverty reduction and economic growth. Zimbabwe, speaking on behalf of the Group of 77 and China, stressed that the outcome of UNCTAD XII should encompass new and emerging issues such as climate change and migration, and provide stimulus to traditional issues such as commodities and South-South trade. It should also result in a strengthening of three pillars of UNCTAD work. TDB received an overview of the proceedings of UNCTAD XII and an update of the programme and other conference information from the host country.

At its twenty-fourth special session (Geneva, 17–20 March) [A/63/15 (Part II)], the TDB President, acting also as Chairman of the UNCTAD XII Preparatory Committee, presented the Committee's report [TD/B(S-XXIV)/L.2] and reports on the two hearings with civil society [TD(XII)/PC/2, TD(XII)/PC/3]. The President said that negotiations on the text from the Preparatory Committee were not yet concluded. The Board took note of all three reports. At its plenary meeting on 7 April, the Preparatory Committee decided to transmit the draft UNCTAD XII negotiated text to the Conference [TD/L.398 & Add.1–4].

International trade

The *World Economic Situation and Prospects 2009* [Sales No. E.09.II.C.2], jointly issued by UNCTAD and the UN Department of Economic and Social Affairs (DESA), stated that growth in the volume of trade slowed to an estimated 4.4 per cent in 2008, nearly half of the average annual growth of 8.6 per cent during 2004–2007. During 2008, the signs of significantly weakening world trade were visible in the Baltic Dry Index, a leading indicator of global trade activity measuring the demand for shipping capacity to transport commodities versus the supply of dry bulk carriers, which had declined by 85 per cent between May and November. However, the value of trade flows increased significantly, due largely to extraordinary rises in the prices of oil and most commodities during the first half of the year. At an aggregate level, oil producers in North Africa, the Commonwealth of Independent States (CIS) and Western Asia doubled their rate of nominal export revenue growth to 53 per cent, 48 per cent and 38 per cent, respectively. In addition, countries in sub-Saharan Africa (excluding Nigeria and South Africa) and LDCs as a group achieved remarkable rates of growth of export revenue following the primary commodity boom, averaging about 42 per cent. Latin America, which had a somewhat more diversified trade structure, saw the doubling of its rate of export revenue growth offset by a more rapidly increasing import bill. Manufactured goods exporters in East and South Asia were affected by the rise in commodity prices. In Europe, although import growth was less dramatic, it outpaced export growth, but fortunes reversed following the dramatic fall in the prices of oil and primary commodities in the second half of 2008.

Import demand in the United States, which had weakened since 2007, fell further in 2008. Export growth fell from August, due to weakening demand worldwide and the rebound of the United States dollar. Trade growth in Western Europe was affected by the United States slowdown. Growth of the total European export volume slowed from 3.9 to 3.6 per cent, except for export performance in the United Kingdom, which recovered from the 2007 contraction in trade. Import demand in Europe slowed from 5.2 per cent in 2007 to 3.2 per cent in 2008. The softening of import demand in the United States and elsewhere was also slowing export growth in developed Asia (Japan and Australia in particular). Falling oil prices reversed the trend in preceding years of a rising import bill in Japan and helped preserve the country's trade surplus, despite the poorer export performance. Australia reduced its trade deficit, thanks to sharp increases in the negotiated price for its iron ore and coal exports, underpinning an increase in its export revenues by more than 20 per cent. Canada's external sector suffered from the weak United States economy, especially in the automobile industry, and, from mid-2008, also from the drop in oil prices and the appreciation of the Canadian dollar.

Among the new European Union (EU) member States, Estonia and Latvia saw their imports decline in real terms as a consequence of the bursting housing and credit bubbles. In other new EU members, most notably Bulgaria and Romania, strong private consumption, continued foreign direct investment inflows and strong domestic investment drove import growth by 12 per cent. Exports by new EU members continued to expand at an annualized rate of 11 per cent in real terms. South-Eastern Europe experienced strong import growth of about 8 per cent, amplified in nominal terms by higher food and energy prices. The region's exports grew at about 9 per cent. Export revenue growth of CIS countries was strong, outpacing import value growth. The surge in oil and gas prices in the first half of 2008 helped boost trade surpluses in Azerbaijan, Kazakhstan and the Russian Federation. Growth in the volume of exports from the Russian Federation remained weak, while imports increased by more than 20 per cent. However, owing to the strong rise in hydrocarbon prices in the first six months of 2008, the economy increased its trade surplus, and, in some other parts of the CIS, import growth outpaced export growth in value terms, and trade deficits widened, especially in Armenia, Kyrgyzstan, Moldova and Tajikistan. Ukraine suffered most from the rising costs of imported food, oil and gas, and its trade deficit surged as import demand was further fuelled by strong domestic demand.

Trends in trade differed strongly between the oil and the non-oil exporters in Western Asia. Despite strong import growth, trade surpluses in the major oil-exporting countries of the Gulf Cooperation Council and Iraq increased from their already high levels of 2007. Saudi Arabia's trade surplus reached an estimated 65 per cent of gross domestic product, and Kuwait's 72 per cent. In contrast, in the non-oil economies of the region, such as Jordan, Lebanon and Turkey, rising import costs outpaced increased export revenues, resulting in a further widening of trade and current-account deficits. Export volume growth for the region as a whole was estimated to have weakened from an annual average of 13.7 per cent during 2001–2007 to about 8 per cent in 2008.

China's trade balance continued to widen in dollar terms, despite the appreciation of the renminbi. The Republic of Korea, the second largest exporter in the region, sustained high rates of export growth until the third quarter of 2008, after which the economy's trade balance moved into deficit as a consequence of strongly increasing import costs for energy and materials. Singapore and the Taiwan Province of China suffered from lower demand for information technology products, consistent with the weak demand in industrial countries.

The developing countries most vulnerable to a global economic downturn and volatile commodity prices were primarily found in Africa and Latin America. The good performance of commodity exporters in Africa, owing to the rise in prices in the first part of the year, was expected to give way to a much less favourable outcome, as the demand for their exports declined. A similar reversal of trends would also affect those African countries heavily reliant on agricultural exports and tourism. Oil exporters would see lower current-account surpluses in 2008 compared with previous years, and oil importers, in contrast, were expected to experience widening current-account deficits. South Africa was an exception, as its current-account deficit narrowed substantially in 2008, following its recovery from the electricity crisis that had stalled mining exports the year before. The recession in the United States would be felt most immediately in Mexico and Central America, inasmuch as they relied on United States markets for the largest share of their exports. Countries in South America that relied on a more diverse group of trading partners would feel the consequences once demand for their exports slowed in Europe and in Asia's emerging market economies.

The *Trade and Development Report, 2008* [Sales No. E.08.II.D.21], published by UNCTAD, discussed trends and issues in the world economy, including global growth and trade and macroeconomic responses to the commodity boom, particularly the commodity price shocks and the risk of inflation. It stated that in 2007, world trade in real terms expanded less than in the preceding four years, but continued to grow unabated in developing and transition economies, where exports rose by more than 9 per cent in volume terms, with considerable regional differences. As the supply response to higher commodity prices had generally been weak, regions that had a large share of primary commodities in their exports saw lower growth in export volumes than regions with a large share of manufactures in their exports. The United States experienced a particularly sharp slowdown in import volume growth, associated with a significant improvement in its current-account balance owing to sluggish domestic demand and a sharp depreciation of the dollar. In the light of the economic turmoil, for a large number of developing countries the outlook depended primarily on future trends in the prices of their primary commodity exports. Although several structural factors supported the expectation that prices would remain higher than they had been over the previous 20 years, cyclical factors, the end of speculation on higher prices and delayed supply responses could result in a weakening of some commodity prices.

Multilateral trading system

Report of Secretary-General. In response to General Assembly resolution 62/184 [YUN 2007, p. 969], the Secretary-General submitted an August report [A/63/324] on international trade and development prepared in collaboration with UNCTAD. The report reviewed recent developments in international trade and the trading system, particularly negotiations under the World Trade Organization (WTO) Doha Round and their implications for developing countries. Attention was paid to the linkages of trade and the trading system with the achievement of internationally agreed development goals, particularly the MDGs, and to the emerging challenges of the global economy.

According to the report, robust output and export growth worldwide had marked recent years, driven by the growth in productive capacities in many parts of the developing world. However, global demand and supply shocks, on account of finance, fuel and food prices, had cast uncertainties over the world economy. Growth in 2008 was expected to be lower than in previous years, and the economic slowdown and emerging challenges could undermine the development and poverty alleviation prospects of developing countries and progress towards the MDGs. With increasing economic uncertainty, protectionist and anti-globalization sentiments had re-emerged and concerns over adjustment intensified. In 2007, world merchandise exports expanded by 14.4 per cent, to $13.8 trillion, and exports of services grew by 18.1 per cent, to $3.3 trillion. Developing countries' merchandise exports grew by 15.2 per cent and their share in merchandise exports increased from 37.3 to 37.5 per cent, while their share in exports of services remained unchanged at 25.4 per cent. Merchandise exports from LDCs grew by 21.2 per cent, increasing their world share from 0.85 to 0.91 per cent, while their share of world services trade remained constant at 0.5 per cent. The most dynamic growth in merchandise exports among developing regions was recorded in Asia (16.3 per cent), followed by Latin America (12 per cent) and Africa (10.7 per cent). China recorded the fastest export growth (25.7 per cent), while India's exports grew by 20.3 per cent and Brazil's by 16.6 per cent. South-South trade continued to accelerate, accounting for 46 per cent of total developing country exports, with Asia accounting for 85 per cent and Latin America and Africa for 10 and 5 per cent, respectively. Tariff protection continued to fall. Global most-favoured-nation tariffs averaged 9.4 per cent in 2007. From 2001 to 2007, average most-favoured-nation tariffs imposed by developed countries on low- and middle-income country exports had declined from 11.1 to 6.8 per cent for agriculture, from 4 to 3.4 per cent for industrial products and from 8.5 to 5.9 per cent for textiles and clothing. Relatively high tariffs and peaks, and tariff escalation, remained in developed countries on products exported by developing countries, including agricultural products and textiles and clothing. Globally, duty-free trade increased (34 per cent on average) in all regions over the previous decade, to about 40 per cent. The proportion of trade-related capacity-building in total official development assistance declined from 4.4 per cent in 2001 to 3.5 per cent in 2005, against the backdrop of insufficient progress towards the target of 0.7 per cent of gross national product by 2015, consistent with the Monterrey Consensus [YUN 2002, p. 953]. As to services, developing country exports remained relatively concentrated, as the top five exporters supplied half of all exports, while the top 15 exporters supplied 75 per cent. Asia accounted for three quarters of developing country exports. In 2007, the most dynamic exporter was Africa, with export growth of 19.8 per cent, followed by Asia (18.9 per cent) and Latin America (13 per cent). LDC's exports of services grew by 11.4 per cent. Labour mobility and migration contributed to fostering a trade, investment and development link between countries of origin and of destination. Over 200 million people lived and worked outside their country of origin, and global remittance flows, which reached $318 billion in 2007, were an important source of income and foreign exchange.

The Secretary-General concluded that, halfway to the 2015 target for achieving the MDGs, global economic realities; financial, food, fuel and energy crises; climate change; and migration posed challenges for developing countries. The international trading system could make an important contribution by addressing such challenges, although it alone could not solve the deep-rooted and multifaceted problems. The multilateral trading system remained the cornerstone of global trade governance; however, it should operate within a broader system of global economic governance, and greater coherence across different layers and systems of governance was needed at the national, regional and global levels. International trade continued to be a powerful engine of growth and development, but the majority of developing countries could not fully benefit from it, owing to insufficient productive supply capacities and competitiveness, lack of infrastructure, and enabling policy environment and market access and entry barriers on their exports. The UN system, including UNCTAD, continued to support developing countries, and Aid for Trade was a key component of such support. Ensuring their participation in the international trading system was a challenge that had to be addressed if globalization was to be a positive force for all with its benefits shared equitably. As underlined in the Accra Accord (see p. 1042), maximizing the benefits and minimizing the costs of international trade liberalization called for mutually supportive and coherent policies and governance at all levels. It was critical, in that regard, that the Doha Round be brought to a successful conclusion, and it was necessary to secure increased and effective market access and entry for developing country exports; implement fairer rules; strengthen the development orientation of North-South, South-South and regional trade and cooperation arrangements; mobilize the potential of the services trade and economy for development; and strengthen trade and productive capacity in developing countries.

UNCTAD XII action. In the Accra Accord [TD/442], adopted by UNCTAD XII (see p. 1042), under the sub-theme on key trade and development issues and the new realities in the geography of the world economy, UNCTAD member States stated that a challenge in the development of the multilateral trading system was to ensure that trade would be an engine of economic growth and sustainable development, as well as of poverty eradication. A well-functioning, universal, rules-based, open, non-discriminatory and equitable multilateral trading system could deliver major benefits for development. The Doha Round should contribute by facilitating the integration of developing countries, including LDCs and countries with economies in transition, into the international trading system, and its results should ensure fair, balanced, equitable and market-opening commitments among all members. If the opportunities arising from liberalization and integration were to be fully exploited, there should be an enabling environment that might include both national and regional competition policies and international cooperation to deal with anti-competitive practices, particularly those that affected trade and development of developing countries. The increased scope of anti-competitive practices, including abuse of dominance, might negate the benefits of trade and investment liberalization.

TDB action. In September [A/63/15 (Part IV)], at the high-level segment of its fifty-fifth session on trade and productive capacities for achieving internationally agreed development goals, including the MDGs, the Trade and Development Board (TDB) considered an UNCTAD secretariat report on the subject [TD/B/55/3], which reviewed progress at the midpoint of the achievement of the MDGs and specific policy mechanisms for strengthening the global partnership for development.

Participants stated that the global economic environment and development challenges gave cause for concern and, in that context, trade had an essential role to play. Enhanced market access for developing countries remained crucial, but each country needed the productive capacity to make use of it, and many developing countries would need corresponding assistance. The imbalance between assistance for social development and for the development of economic infrastructure and productive activities, including agriculture, also needed to be redressed. The development effectiveness of aid had to be improved. Policies that promoted economic growth were more likely to reach the objectives set out in the MDGs. Participants stressed that action was needed to integrate efforts within a broader economic development strategy; greater emphasis should be given to production, improvement of productivity and productive capacities in agriculture, manufacturing and services, and infrastructure development; and the global partnership for development should be strengthened. Action was also needed to reorient the role of the State to deliver development objectives; promote country ownership of national strategies; approach the food crisis as a long-term development failure and climate change and energy security problems as critical cross-cutting issues; pursue the conclusion of the Doha Round with a significant development package; implement Aid for Trade without delay, regardless of the outcome of the Doha Round; scale up ODA to meet the MDGs, in line with existing commitments; reverse the decline in ODA for the agriculture sector; introduce new policies and collaborative schemes in both home and recipient countries to harness the role of remittances, both as a potential form of productive investment and a source of income security, through cash transfer programmes or matching funds from the State; make use of the Follow-up International Conference on Financing for Development to Review the Implementation of the Monterrey Consensus (see p. 1076); encourage donor countries to ensure that their domestic policies in trade, finance and technology were supportive of productive capacity-building in developing countries; and improve coordination among international organizations.

Negotiating frameworks

Resumption of Doha Round negotiations

As noted in the Secretary-General's report on international trade and development [A/63/324], in 2008, the Doha Round entered its seventh year and stood at a critical juncture, as negotiations were scheduled to conclude that year. Focus had been given to establishing full modalities for reducing commitments in agriculture and non-agricultural market access. Achieving progress in other areas of negotiations, such as services, the Agreement on Trade-Related Aspects of Intellectual Property Rights, rules and trade facilitation, had also been given importance to achieve an overall balance within a single undertaking. Following the issuance, in July 2007 [YUN 2007, p. 968], of the first draft modalities on agriculture and non-agricultural market access, revised texts on both subjects were issued in February, May and July 2008 as the basis for discussion. An informal WTO "mini-ministerial" meeting (21–30 July), with the participation of some 40 ministers and senior officials, convened to establish modalities on agriculture and non-agricultural market access, failed to achieve a breakthrough. The meeting was held to resolve key issues through intersectoral negotiations: the extent of reduction in agricultural tariffs and in the overall trade-distorting domestic support for agriculture in developed countries; flexibilities for developing countries in agricultural tariff reduction; and the extent of tariff cuts for industrial products in developing countries. Despite the progress made on many core issues, the small-group discussion among Australia, Brazil, China, India, Japan, the United States and the EU failed on the issue of the special safeguard mechanism in agriculture, and the collapse of the negotiations meant, among other things, that a more ambitious and expeditious reduction of cotton subsidies, sought by African countries, was not addressed by ministers. There was a perceived imbalance in the level of concessions sought from developing countries, particularly in light of the principles of special and differential treatment, including on the proposed extent of industrial tariff cuts by developing countries and of farm subsidy-reductions by developed countries. The failure to set the basis for the concluding stage of the negotiations made it impossible for the Round to be concluded by the end of 2008, and more difficult to resuscitate in 2009. Another complicating factor was the lack of trade promotion authority for the United States Administration. Its renewal was regarded as essential for that country's engagement in the negotiations. There was concern that the Round might be put on hold for some time, possibly two years, while more and more calls were made to resume the negotiations at the earliest date possible. Intensive consultations were under way, including by the WTO Director-General, to determine ways forward and make possible a resumption of negotiations.

The Secretary-General stressed that the delayed conclusion of the Round could lead to greater recourse to trade litigation and the intensification of bilateral and regional trade agreements, which risked further fragmentation of the international trading system. Efforts should be made to re-engage in the negotiations and deliver the development promise of the Round. Careful reflection might be warranted on the definition of the negotiating agenda, as well as on ways in which the multilateral trading system managed a complex, broad-based agenda of negotiations under a single undertaking in an inclusive and transparent manner. The emergence of the dynamic South also called for an adaptation of mindsets, policies and approaches in the trading system. The promise of the Doha development agenda required that development objectives and aspirations would be given greater prominence and that the specific situations and concerns of a diverse membership would receive adequate systemic responses and considerations. The principle of special and differential treatment was essential in all aspects of market access and rule-making negotiations. On the other hand, it had become increasingly challenging to balance the diverse and sometimes mutually competing interests of members, including within developed and developing countries, and such augmentation of diversity added further complexity to the overall calculation of balance.

UNCTAD consideration. TDB, at its fifty-fifth session (Geneva, 15–26 September) [A/63/15 (Part IV)], considered an UNCTAD secretariat report on the evolution of the international trading system and of international trade from a development perspective [TD/B/55/4] that reviewed developments in the international trading system of particular relevance to developing countries, especially developments in the post-Doha work programme, as well as various bilateral and regional initiatives, and coherence between those trade agendas in light of recent trends in international trade. Particular attention was placed on the linkages of trade and trade negotiations with the achievement of the MDGs and with the global food crisis.

The report concluded that the world economy and the international trading system stood at a critical stage for developing countries' trade and development and for the achievement of internationally agreed development goals. Halfway to the 2015 goal of achieving the MDGs, current global economic realities, looming economic slowdown, food and financial crises, and high energy and commodity prices, climate change and migration posed challenges to development prospects of developing countries, as well as to the international trading system. The emergence of the dynamic South within the new geography of trade called for an adaptation of the international trading system to reflect the evolving realities. Bilateral free trade agreements and regional trade agreements continued to proliferate, which risked fragmenting the international trading system. While regional trade agreements could generate gains, they also entailed inherent systemic implications. Despite their contributions, trade agreements alone could not respond to deep-rooted, far-reaching global challenges, and both trade policy and the trading system should operate within a broader system of global economic governance. Greater coherence across different layers and systems of governance at all levels, encompassing development, trade, investment, finance, monetary policy and technology, was essential, and innovative national, regional and global cooperative mechanisms should be explored, particularly in energy and food security. Careful reflection might be warranted on the ways in which the multilateral trading system operated. With WTO membership reaching 153 countries, agreement should take into account their diverse interests and priorities. The widening diversity of membership added further complexity in the calculation of balance in the negotiations, and it would also be necessary to ensure greater inclusiveness and transparency in a bottom-up and member-driven approach to the negotiations.

The TDB President's summary of the deliberations stated that participants regretted the failure of the WTO meeting in July (see p. 1050) to set the basis for concluding the Doha Round in 2008. The collapse was partly attributed to disagreement over the issue of special safeguard mechanisms; however, many other issues remained unresolved. Participants agreed that the setback should not be allowed to derail the entire Doha Round or weaken the multilateral trading system, and recognized that the trading system had to adapt itself better to the structural changes occurring in economies, including the prominence of developing countries emerging as the "new South" and their growing divergence. The trading system also faced the challenge of managing an ever-enlarging diverse and complex trade agenda, while many development-related issues remained unaddressed. Complexities created by proliferating regional and bilateral agreements were a matter of concern, and the importance of improving multilateral oversight and improved transparency was stressed.

GENERAL ASSEMBLY ACTION

On 19 December [meeting 72], the General Assembly, on the recommendation of the Second Committee [A/63/412/Add.1], adopted **resolution 63/203** without vote [agenda item 47 *(a)*].

International trade and development

The General Assembly,

Recalling its resolutions 56/178 of 21 December 2001, 57/235 of 20 December 2002, 58/197 of 23 December 2003, 59/221 of 22 December 2004, 60/184 of 22 December 2005, 61/186 of 20 December 2006 and 62/184 of 19 December 2007 on international trade and development, and recalling also the provisions of the United Nations Millennium Declaration pertaining to trade and related development issues, as well as the outcomes of the International Conference on Financing for Development and the World Summit on Sustainable Development, the 2005 World Summit Outcome and General Assembly resolution 60/265 of 30 June 2006 on the follow-up to the development outcome of the Summit, and the Accra Accord adopted by the United Nations Conference on Trade and Development at its twelfth session, held from 20 to 25 April 2008,

1. *Takes note* of the report of the Secretary-General on international trade and development and the report of the Trade and Development Board on its fifty-fifth session, held from 15 to 26 September 2008;

2. *Notes* the deliberations held in the context of the preparatory process for the Follow-up International Conference on Financing for Development to Review the Implementation of the Monterrey Consensus, held in Doha from 29 November to 2 December 2008, at which the issue of international trade and development was substantively addressed;

3. *Stresses* the importance of the continued substantive consideration of the issue of international trade and development;

4. *Decides* to include in the provisional agenda of its sixty-fourth session, under the item entitled "Macroeconomic policy questions", the sub-item entitled "International trade and development";

5. *Requests* the Secretary-General, in collaboration with the secretariat of the United Nations Conference on Trade and Development, to submit to the General Assembly at its sixty-fourth session a report on international trade and development.

Trade Policy

Trade in goods and services, and commodities

The Commission on Trade in Goods and Services, and Commodities, at its twelfth session (Geneva, 7–8 February) [TD/B/COM.1/92], had before it the following documentation: a progress report on the implementation of the agreed conclusions and recommendations of the Commission since UNCTAD XI [TD/B/COM.1/91]; a secretariat background note on globalization's contribution to development: trade perspective and UNCTAD's contribution [TD/B/COM.1/90]; and reports of the expert meetings on the participation of developing countries in new and dynamic sectors of world trade: the South-South dimension [YUN 2007, p. 973], and on trade and development implications of financial services and commodity exchanges [ibid.].

The Commission's report contained the Chairman's summary on globalization's contribution to development: trade perspective and UNCTAD's contribution. Participants commended the secretariat for providing a balanced picture of the challenges and opportunities in addressing key emerging trade and development issues, with a view to promoting the achievement of internationally agreed development goals, and noted that issues regarding terms of trade and LDCs' participation in trade and investment required further treatment. It was suggested that UNCTAD research should identify policies conducive to enhancing the effects of both trade-driven and investment-driven globalization, especially in the case of LDCs; and identify the enabling policy environment, regulations and institutions that could help maximize the contribution of international trade to development. Developing countries should sensitize themselves to the importance of regional integration agreements as stepping stones to global integration, especially South-South trade partnerships, and UNCTAD should help them in analysing and identifying possible avenues for South-South trade partnership and dialogue between the dynamic and the less dynamic economies. UNCTAD should also promote and strengthen regional and interregional trade and economic cooperation and integration among developing countries. Particular attention should be given to enhancing the Global System of Trade Preferences among Developing Countries for greater South-South development cooperation, and UNCTAD should prioritize its support for implementation of the Aid for Trade initiative, strengthen its research and analysis work for monitoring economic and policy trends in international trade, and provide early warning and prognosis regarding their impact on development.

As to UNCTAD's contribution to maximizing gains and minimizing costs from trade-driven globalization, participants noted that trade-led globalization had brought about development gains, of which some developing countries were major beneficiaries, but financial instability and commodity and preference dependence had led to the exclusion of the poorest from global trade. That dual and contrasting experience with globalization remained a challenge that UNCTAD should address in building an enabling environment for trade and development. Regarding the challenges of multilateral and other trade negotiations, participants requested UNCTAD to ensure that the development gains from the Doha Round of trade negotiations and regional integration processes were maximized; strengthen its support to developing countries; conduct independent analyses to assist them in trade negotiations; and provide negotiating options for promoting their trade and wider development goals.

With regard to commodities, participants recognized that transforming the commodity sector in developing countries into a dynamic development engine, in the context of high commodity prices and revenues, was a critical challenge, and urged UNCTAD to provide new ideas in that regard. A realistic agenda for commodity trade and development was required: its elements could be found in the UNCTAD XII pre-events on the Global Initiative on Commodities (see p. 1046), the event on hydrocarbon cooperation between India and Africa, the UNCTAD Secretary-General's high-level panel discussion on commodities (ibid.) and the 2005 Arusha Declaration on Commodities adopted by the African Union. In the area of the Aid for Trade initiative, participants highlighted that the UNCTAD XII pre-event on "Aid for trade and development: towards a new global solidarity initiative" (Bangkok, Thailand, 24–25 January) had provided an important forum for discussing the UN role in contributing to its implementation. While services development was the new frontier for trade growth, many developing countries did not have the capacities to play an active role in it, and the initiative should support their national and regional strategies for exploiting the services economy. As to the challenges of emerging trade and development issues, participants recommended that UNCTAD should continue to assist developing countries in addressing them in the global development agenda; strengthen the provision of expert analysis and technical assistance focused on the challenges and opportunities presented by globalization for weak and vulnerable developing countries; and expand in-depth analysis of how the international trading system could contribute to an equitable distribution of the benefits of globalization among countries, while providing them with opportunities to diversify their economies.

The Commission discussed the reports of the two expert meetings and the progress report on the implementation of the agreed conclusions and recommendations of the Commission since UNCTAD XI, and concluded that the integration of developing countries into the global economy through trade was essential and that UNCTAD could make a difference in helping developing countries, especially LDCs and small and vulnerable economies, as well as countries with economies in transition, meet the challenges facing them and take advantage of emerging opportunities. In that connection, there was a need for cooperation in creating an enabling and complementary environment.

At its twenty-fourth special session (Geneva, 17–20 March) [A/63/15 (Part II)], TDB took note of the Commission's report.

At its forty-fourth executive session (Geneva, 10 July) [A/63/15 (Part III)], TDB approved the agenda for the first session of the Trade and Development Commission, which was to succeed the Commission on Trade in Goods and Services, and Commodities.

Interdependence and global economic issues

TDB, in September [A/63/15 (Part IV)], considered interdependence: mobilizing resources for development—commodity prices, productive capacity, supply and distribution. The Board welcomed the *Trade and Development Report, 2008* [Sales No. E.08.II.D.21] and its focus on the mobilization of resources for development. Concern was expressed about the deterioration of the global economic situation due to the financial crisis in the United States and its possible repercussions for other countries, especially developing countries, as well as the increasing risk that the slowdown in developed countries would be transmitted to developing countries. As for policies to respond to the crisis, it was agreed that public assistance should not be free of charge and regulation of financial markets should be increased to prevent the recurrence of financial crises. Market discipline was not sufficient, and the State should be more proactive in monitoring financial markets and preventing financial crises. Global macroeconomic coordination implied that surplus countries, particularly in the EU, should adopt policies to counter the recessionary trends and expand demand, and should include coordination of exchange rate policies. Delegations acknowledged the relevance of regional cooperation for development in other areas, such as trade and infrastructure development, as well as addressing the global food crisis.

They also agreed on the importance of commodities for development in developing countries and the need for a multifaceted approach. Price increases had benefited many commodity-producing developing countries, with corresponding improvements in their terms of trade and current-account balances. However, many other developing countries were facing the challenge of increasing food and energy prices, particularly in Africa. The surge in commodity prices did not translate into increased revenues in commodity-exporting developing countries, but was often absorbed by an increase in transnational corporations' profits. Delegations agreed on the pertinence of the *Trade and Development Report, 2008* recommendation regarding the improvement and creation of mechanisms to tackle commodity price volatility, as well as limiting excessive speculation in commodity markets. The solution to commodity dependence in developing countries would come through diversification and industrialization, which would require increasing investment in productive capacities. The food crisis and its social consequences were a challenge for developing countries, particularly low-income countries. The solution should be global, helping developing countries to enhance food production capacity, and the needs of small farmers should be addressed with a focus on sustainable agricultural production. Measures to restrict trade in food products should be avoided and agricultural subsidies in developed countries eliminated. ODA should be increased to address both emergency needs and long-term agricultural production constraints.

Delegations supported the call made in the *Report* to increase ODA to developing countries and target it to growth-related activities. They emphasized the relevance of the Accra Accord (see p. 1042) mandate, welcomed UNCTAD's initial steps to implement it and emphasized the need to strengthen UNCTAD's integrated and holistic approach to development. UNCTAD should continue its independent research and analysis, foster greater coherence among the multilateral trading, financial and monetary systems and continue providing policy advice to developing countries to help them address the challenges and opportunities posed by globalization and interdependence.

Development strategies in a globalized world

In September [A/63/15 (Part IV)], TDB considered development strategies in a globalized world: financial policies and productive investment related to trade and development. It had before it the *Trade and Development Report, 2008*. The discussion highlighted that since 2000, developing countries as a group had been net exporters of capital. The increase in capital exports, which was the counterpart to a substantial improvement of current-account balances, was attributed to an increase in commodity prices. That was benefiting commodity-exporting economies, and marked a reorientation of macroeconomic policies in many emerging economies to maintain competitive exchange rates and avoid real currency overvaluation. It was suggested that the reorientation was largely the result of financial crises that had struck many developing countries during the previous decade. Countries with net capital exports were also those with higher rates of investment and growth. That fact challenged orthodox economic theories, which maintained that capital should flow from rich to poor countries, where marginal returns were higher, and that poor countries depended on foreign capital to finance higher investments.

In most developing countries, stock markets accounted for a very small portion of investment financing, and the weakness of the banking sector was a major concern. Financial sector reforms had rarely delivered on their promises and had not contributed to lasting improvements in investment financing. Lending rates remained high and bank credit was extended primarily to the public sector and for private consumption. Many delegations saw a role for Governments and central banks in directing credit to private sector investment through instruments such as development banks, public ownership of commercial banks and public credit guarantees. The fact that in many developing countries the largest part of the economy lacked access to banking services was another major problem. It was suggested that, although microfinance institutions played an important role in some countries, they were no substitute for a functioning commercial banking sector as they provided credit in relatively small volumes at high interest rates and for short durations, and it was important to link informal financing schemes with formal ones.

While the increase in ODA since 2002 was welcomed, it was pointed out that most donors were not on track to meet their pledges; that a large part of that increase was due to debt relief, and not fully additional as stipulated in the Monterrey Consensus; and that many developing countries could require further debt relief. Delegations took note of two shifts in aid: measured as a share of total ODA, development-oriented aid had decreased relative to emergency-related aid, and the share of economic aid had decreased relative to social aid. While ODA for social sectors was considered important for progress towards the MDGs, additional ODA should flow into projects related to economic infrastructure and production. Meeting the MDGs still required raising the annual flows of ODA to poor nations. Additional resources were needed to finance investment in infrastructure and production, and national and international support for facilitating workers' remittances could also foster investment finance. It was also suggested that the current financial crisis should lead to a paradigm shift in economic theory and policy, as it had highlighted the inherent risks associated with liberated and unregulated financial markets, and pointed to the need for a strengthened role for the State in supervising and regulating financial activities. Governments should be more active, intervening before bailouts of financial firms became necessary. However, if such bailouts were inevitable, they should not be free of charge, and the financial institutions saved from bankruptcy should be regulated more closely to prevent the recurrence of financial crises. In order to prevent destabilizing financial speculation, prolonged exchange-rate misalignments and unsustainable economic imbalance, several delegations saw a need for international action to strengthen supervision and regulation of financial markets. A framework for timely and orderly exchange-rate adjustments and an effective mechanism for international coordination of macroeconomic policies were considered desirable. Avoiding a recession would require surplus economies to increase domestic demand to compensate for declining demand by the United States, and it was necessary to prevent a competitive devaluation of exchange rates in response to a falling dollar.

Trade promotion and facilitation

In 2008, UN bodies continued to assist developing countries and transition economies in promoting their exports and facilitating their integration into the multilateral trading system. The main originator of technical cooperation projects in that area was the International Trade Centre, under the joint sponsorship of UNCTAD and WTO.

International Trade Centre

According to its Annual Report 2008 [ITC/AG(XLIII)/226], the UNCTAD/WTO International Trade Centre (ITC) delivery of technical assistance stood at $29.4 million during the year. The largest portion of programme funds was spent in Africa (36 per cent), followed by Asia and the Pacific (24 per cent), Latin America and the Caribbean (10 per cent), Europe and the CIS (7 per cent) and the Arab States (3 per cent). The rest (20 per cent) went to global programmes. The share of assistance to LDCs rose to 43 per cent.

ITC devoted an increased share of its activities to LDCs, landlocked developing countries and small island developing States, moving closer (43 per cent) to its target of 50 per cent of technical cooperation for those groups of countries. It also devoted a larger share of its expenditure to enhancing its tools and to a significant investment for improving a selected number of those tools and its products. The research and development investment covered the enhancement of global goods, taking into account non-tariff measures, assessing trade for sustainable development, developing a benchmarking scheme for trade support institutions to improve their effectiveness, developing marketing and branding as part of enterprise competitiveness, and expanding the ITC range of business environment tools for legal, finance and facilitation services. ITC launched a Modular Learning Programme to address the main features of the international trading system as they impacted on business. Its assistance in that area was designed to respond to the specific needs of the private sector in African, Caribbean and Pacific countries to enable them to engage in negotiations on Economic Partnership Agreements with the European Commission. ITC produced a Business Guide to help identify business opportunities in specific sectors targeted for export development, and launched two regional programmes: the Programme for African Capacity Building, funded by Canada, and the Supply Chain and Logistic Programme for Selected Southern African Development Community Countries, funded by the Belgium-Flemish Government. Those programmes, aimed at enhancing regional integration through trade capacity-building assistance and, based on the premise of the commonality of needs that could be addressed at subregional or regional levels, emphasized the strengthening of regional institutions.

Throughout 2008, ITC corporate development was characterized by major change, founded on rigorous review and a focus on export impact for goods. ITC began the year with a new organizational structure and a new Strategic Framework for 2008–2009, which emphasized the context for ITC and its support for the three key client groupings through its mission and three objectives: strengthening the international competitiveness of enterprises through its training and support; increasing the capacity of trade support institutions to support businesses; and strengthening the integration of business into the global economy through enhanced support to policymakers. ITC adopted a new evaluation policy as part of its enhanced performance management and, through the creation of five business lines, refocused its approach to trade-related technical assistance. Those changes came together with the completion of the 2009–2012 Strategic Plan.

Joint Advisory Group

UNCTAD consideration. At its fifty-fifth session (Geneva, 15–26 September) [A/63/15 (Part IV)], TDB considered the report of the ITC Joint Advisory Group (JAG) on its forty-first session [YUN 2007, p. 977]. TDB felt that more consideration should be given to JAG substantive work, because the reform of ITC governance was at a standstill. In addition, there was an impression that ITC was ignoring work done at the country and regional levels, it was duplicating UNCTAD work and not paying enough attention to the ITC work. To address those problems, it was suggested that UNCTAD's coordinating role with ITC be strengthened, including measures for UNCTAD to provide input into ITC without duplicating its work, as provided for in the Accra Accord (see p. 1042). It was also noted that ITC did not have a specific division devoted to LDCs.

ITC representatives acknowledged those criticisms and expressed their commitment to more transparency and to formalize the informal consultations between ITC and member States. Acknowledging that there was no division on LDCs, they said that several cross-cutting units were working on LDC issues, and stressed their intention to spend 50 per cent of the organization's resources on LDCs. Representatives also promised to include TDB comments in the next JAG report.

On 23 September, TDB took note of the JAG report on its forty-first session.

JAG action. JAG, at its forty-second session (Geneva, 10–11 December) [ITC/AG(XLII)/225], considered the reports on ITC 2007 [YUN 2007, p 975] and 2008 (see p. 1055) activities, the 2009 consolidated programme document: trade for the MDGs, the 2009–2012 Strategic Plan and the ITC Strategic Framework, and proposals for ITC governance. Statements were made by the UNCTAD Secretary-General, the WTO Director-General and the ITC Executive Director. JAG decided that the annual reports should be more objective and analytical, contain lessons learned and show more clearly how ITC activities contributed to its programme objectives. ITC should increase its work at the regional level, both in terms of regional programmes as well as supporting increased intraregional trade. Its work should be tailored to levels of country development. With respect to middle-income countries, more efforts should be applied to the diversification of export structures and development of production with a higher value added, including innovative products. ITC should take advantage of collaborative arrangements when promoting cooperation and trade development, and develop strategies to guide its trade-related technical assistance, taking into account the financial, energy, food and economic crises in order to support beneficiary countries. Greater priority should be given to trade finance. ITC should also give priority to the MDGs and should work closely with UNCTAD on joint programming, including work on trade and the environment, and with WTO in relation to accession countries, with an emphasis on drawing the business sector into the process.

Pledges of trust fund contributions to ITC were announced by China, Denmark, Finland, Germany, the Netherlands, New Zealand, Norway, Sweden and the United Kingdom.

ITC administrative arrangements

JAG endorsed the consolidated programme document and decided that ITC should: prioritize projects therein according to the criteria set out in its Strategic Plan; provide for transparency in the development of projects and distribution of funds; invest more efforts to develop in-house expertise in some industrial and service sectors for some countries; and achieve a balance in its programming among the five regions and between the lower and middle-income countries within each region. JAG also endorsed the ITC Strategic Plan 2009–2012 and the revised Strategic Framework as a basis for the ITC 2010–2011 budget submissions. In response to the decision taken at its forty-first session [YUN 2007, p. 977] on proposals for ITC governance, it discussed two options proposed by informal meetings of interested delegations (June and September) for the composition of an ITC Advisory Board: a Board comprising the ITC Executive Director, one representative each from UNCTAD and WTO, and 20 developing country members (four representatives from each region), as well as 7–20 donor country members. No consensus was reached on a preferred option. JAG decided that the Consultative Committee remained the oversight body for voluntary contributions to the ITC Trust Fund, while JAG remained its policymaking organ.

The General Assembly, in **resolution 63/264A** of 24 December (see p. 1543), approved revised appropriations for ITC in the amount of $30,873,700.

Enterprise, business facilitation and development

The Commission on Enterprise, Business Facilitation and Development, at its twelfth session (Geneva, 4–5 February) [TD/B/COM.3/86 & Corr.1], considered trade logistics and global value chains [TD/B/COM.3/84]; reports of expert meetings on regional cooperation in transit transport: solutions for landlocked and transit developing countries, and on increasing the participation of developing countries' small and medium-sized enterprises (SMEs) in global value chains [YUN 2007, p. 978]; and a progress report on the implementation of agreed conclusions and recommendations of the Commission at its eleventh session, including assessment of the work of the Commission since UNCTAD XI [TD/B/COM.3/85]. The Commission agreed that the agenda for its next session would be examined after UNCTAD XII (see p. 1041) and that no agreed recommendations would be adopted in view of the Conference. The final report would contain the Chair's summary, as well as an account of procedural matters, and would be submitted to TDB.

The Chairman, in a summary of the deliberations, noted that the Commission's twelfth session offered an opportunity to take stock of progress made over the previous four years and to consider key issues in view of the upcoming UNCTAD XII. The statements emphasized that consideration should be given to the conditions of SMEs in developing countries, and in particular to their specific requirements in LDCs. In that respect, attention was drawn to the need to enhance private-sector participation to improve infrastructure and productive capacities; promote SME development through business linkages and skills upgrading programmes; and adopt multilateral approaches in trade facilitation.

TDB, at its twenty-fourth special session (Geneva, 17–20 March) [A/63/15 (Part II)], took note of the Commission's report.

TDB, at its forty-fourth executive session (Geneva, 10 July) [A/63/15 (Part III)], approved the agenda for the first session of the Investment, Enterprise and Development Commission, which was to succeed the Commission on Enterprise, Business Facilitation and Development (see p. 1045).

Commodities

The UNCTAD/DESA report *World Economic Situation and Prospects 2009* [Sales No. E.09.II.C.2] stated that prices of oil and non-oil primary commodities showed strong fluctuations during 2008, largely driven by financial factors as well as shifts in the balance between supply and demand. The prices of most commodities rose sharply in the first half of 2008, continuing a multi-year upward trend that began in 2003. Food prices, especially the price of rice, surged the most in early 2008, leading to a food crisis in some 40 developing countries (see p. 1343). Oil prices also soared by about 50 per cent. While some commodity-specific factors on either the supply or demand side could explain part of that surge, a common factor was the relocation of funds by investors towards commodity markets, along with the declining value of other financial assets. However, those trends reversed sharply in mid-2008. In November, oil prices plummeted by more than 60 per cent from their peak levels of July, and the UNCTAD commodity price index lost 11.5 per cent in dollar terms between June and September. That trend held for all commodity groups, although specific commodities or groups were more affected than others. The change in trends could be partially explained by high price incentives and favourable weather conditions that contributed to increased planting and harvesting of cereals. World production of wheat, maize and rice was expected to exceed demand and contribute to a partial replenishment of stocks. In addition, the appreciation of the United States dollar might also explain part of the price decline in nominal terms. While the replenishment of stocks and lower prices was a welcome turn of events for consumers, the sharp rise in price volatility during the year hurt both consumers and producers.

The tropical beverage price index, which had increased steadily until mid-2008, declined thereafter. In real terms, price levels would remain below the pre-crisis level in the immediate outlook. The vegetable oils and oilseeds price index rose by almost 174 per cent between January 2006 and June 2008, partly owing to the indirect effect of increased production of biofuels, which competed for agricultural inputs and capital utilization. However, prices fell by 30 per cent between June and September 2008, along with falling prices of fossil fuels and most basic grains. Developments in agricultural raw material prices were dominated by price increases for cotton. With a price average of $75.8 per pound over the first six months of 2008, the Cotlook 'A' index increased by 30 per cent, compared with its level in January 2006. Nominal prices surged to levels not recorded since 1997. Between June and September 2008, however, cotton prices fell by 4.5 per cent, following the trend in other commodity prices, albeit less dramatically. The price of natural rubber rose by 73 per cent from January 2006 to June 2008, mainly influenced by rising petroleum prices, which drove the price of synthetic rubber. Declining oil prices pushed down the prices of natural and synthetic rubber by 10 per cent between June and September. The prices of most minerals, ores and metals increased during the commodity price boom, although they peaked at different times. The prospect of a worldwide recession depressed prices in the second half of 2008 as projections for demand fell well short of current capacity. The situation with regard to gold was different, as prices remained at very high levels—about $800 per ounce—owing in part to its use as a safe storage of wealth in times of economic and currency turmoil. China became the largest gold-producing country in 2007, with a total production of 276 tons, outstripping South Africa's 272 tons.

Oil prices were volatile throughout 2008, until the global commodity boom came to an end in the summer. The price of Brent crude, which stood at $100 per barrel (pb) in early January, rose to an all-time high of $145 pb in July, before dropping sharply to $60 pb in November. As was the case with other commodities, the surge in oil prices during the first half of 2008 reflected both a tight balance between supply and demand and increased speculation and herding behaviour. In October, international crude oil prices registered their biggest monthly drop ever as expectations mounted that a severe global economic downturn would sharply reduce demand for oil in 2009. Prices continued to slide even when the Organization of Petroleum Exporting Countries decided to lower production considerably in late October and announced further cuts in subsequent months. Despite the steep decline in the second half of 2008, the price of Brent crude averaged $101 pb for the year as a whole, almost 40 per cent above the average annual price of $72.5 pb in 2007.

UNCTAD action. In the Accra Accord [TD/442] (see p. 1042), the role and mandate of UNCTAD on commodities issues were reconfirmed. The Accord stipulated that UNCTAD should continue to play a key role, with other international and regional actors and international commodity bodies, addressing the trade and development problems associated with the commodity economy, giving due attention to all commodity sectors such as agriculture, forestry, fisheries, metals and minerals and oil and gas; monitor developments and challenges in commodity markets and address links between international commodity trade and national development, particularly with regard to poverty reduction; and enhance efforts, under the three pillars of its work (research and analysis, technical cooperation and consensus-building), to help commodity-dependent developing countries harness development gains from the boom in commodity prices, as well as to deal with trade and development problems related to commodity dependence.

In that context, the Accord provided that UNCTAD should help commodity-dependent developing countries, particularly small commodity producers: develop national commodity strategies, including mainstream policies into their national and regional development strategies; build supply-side capacity and attain competitiveness; move up value chains and diversify commodity sectors; comply with international trade standards; access commodity information and databases; and take advantage of export opportunities for commodities in emerging markets. Futher, UNCTAD should assist developing countries in building human and institutional capacities and in promoting and improving transparency and accountability in the public, private and corporate sectors; establishing effective marketing systems and supporting frameworks for small commodity producers; and developing commodity financing and risk management schemes. It should also promote intergovernmental cooperation in commodities and consensus-building on ways to integrate commodity policies into national, regional and international development and poverty reduction strategies; promote trade-related policies and instruments for resolving commodity problems, as well as investment and financial policies for accessing financial resources for commodity-based development; and contribute to building multi-stakeholder partnerships with a view to identifying innovative approaches to commodity-related problems. The Accord also mandated TDB to establish a multi-year expert meeting on commodities to provide practical options and actionable outcomes, and provided for a strengthening of secretariat arrangements in support of the implementation of the Accra mandate on commodities.

Report of Secretary-General. In response to General Assembly resolution 61/190 [YUN 2006, p. 1122], the Secretary-General submitted, in August [A/63/267], an UNCTAD secretariat report on world commodity trends and prospects that examined commodity market developments and their impact on developing countries; continuing realities, emerging issues and long-term trade prospects of the global commodity economy; and developments contributing to the implementation of resolution 61/190. According to the report, the broad-based rise in commodity prices since 2002 had accelerated over the previous 18 months in all major commodity groups. While those increases improved the prospects for growth and development of the commodity-producing countries, soaring fuel and food prices were raising concern about the implications for global economic growth and poverty reduction. Following the steep decline from 1995–1997 to 2002, international commodity prices had been on a sustained upward trend since 2002. The UNCTAD price index for non-fuel commodities reached its highest level in current dollars since 1960, rising 110 per cent between 2002 and 2007, and 71 per cent in the first six months of 2008 compared to 2007. The broad-based rise in prices was led by the boom in metal and mineral prices, which had increased by 226 per cent since 2002. There had also been a sharp rise in the price of oil, from a 2002 average monthly level of $25 pb to an average of $108 pb in the first half of 2008. Among agricultural commodities, there had been notable price increases over the period from 2002 to 2007 for agricultural raw materials: mainly rubber, with a price rise of 199 per cent, and tropical logs and cotton, with an increase of 64 and 37 per cent, respectively.

The driving forces behind the boom in commodity prices were a combination of strong global demand, owing to brisk economic growth worldwide, particularly in Asia, led by China, and a slow supply response, together with low inventories for a number of commodities, particularly oil, minerals and metals and grains. Commodity prices were also influenced by speculation, fed by high liquidity in international financial markets and relatively low interest rates, seeking higher returns in comparison to equity and debt securities. The increase in dollar-denominated commodity prices was also partly explained by the depreciation of the dollar vis-à-vis other major currencies. Another major factor in the rise in demand for and prices of some agricultural commodities, particularly maize and oilseeds, was the expansion in the demand for biofuels. Trade in commodities was of vital importance to both exporting and importing countries. A large number of developing countries depended on primary commodity exports, which were critical to employment and income levels, and a major source of Government revenues, accounting for a large share of their resources to be used for financing development. On the other hand, importing countries needed predictable and affordable access to supplies of raw materials in order to maintain and fuel industrial growth and satisfy consumption demands. Other concerns, particularly food and energy security, were also important to both importing and exporting countries. The recent turmoil in commodity markets had underlined the shared interest of all countries in ensuring that commodity markets did not become a source of global macroeconomic instability and social and political upheaval. Despite the progress made in narrowing differences in the Doha Round over the previous 18 months, WTO members had not reached agreement to move the agricultural reform agenda forward. Meanwhile, the existence of high agricultural prices undercut the rationale for large farm subsidies and protection.

The report concluded that the commodity boom had improved the situation of primary commodities in world trade and revived the potential role of commodity trade in contributing to sustained economic growth and poverty reduction in the globalized economy. However, key realities of the commodity economy remained, including high price volatility, declining long-term trends in some commodity prices and incomes in real terms, limited development gains from the production and trade of primary commodities for many developing countries (especially low-income countries) and continued difficulties in diversification. Several emerging issues had a bearing on the extent to which stronger demand and higher prices for commodities would translate into sustainable growth and development and poverty reduction. Those included the distribution of the gains from higher prices between foreign investors and host countries in the extractive industries, the preservation of a competitive environment in commodity supply chains, and energy and food security. The comprehensive framework for action released in July by the High-level Task Force on the Global Food Security Crisis—composed of UN specialized agencies, funds and programmes, the Bretton Woods institutions (the World Bank Group and the International Monetary Fund) and relevant UN Secretariat entities, chaired by the Secretary-General—provided a plan of action for addressing the global food crisis, with a focus on immediate measures to boost global food and nutrition security. The Accra Accord provided an effective framework for dealing with the other commodity issues reviewed in the report. The General Assembly might wish to monitor progress in the implementation of actions in each of those frameworks.

Communication. On 17 September [A/C.2/63/4], the Dominican Republic transmitted to the President of the General Assembly the Declaration adopted at the First Workshop-Conference on Energy and Development (Santo Domingo, Dominican Republic, 30 August), with the theme "Oil speculation". The Conference brought together journalists, economists and energy experts from the Dominican Republic, the United States and a number of Latin American and Caribbean countries to communicate the increasing urgency and complexity of speculation and price manipulation in the international commodities markets, particularly oil and its derivatives. The Conference placed particular emphasis on their impact on increasing prices of energy and food commodities and the achievement of the MDGs.

GENERAL ASSEMBLY ACTION

On 19 December [meeting 72], the General Assembly, on the recommendation of the Second Committee [A/63/412/Add.4], adopted **resolution 63/207** without vote [agenda item 47 *(d)*].

Commodities

The General Assembly,

Recalling its resolutions 59/224 of 22 December 2004 and 61/190 of 20 December 2006 on commodities,

Recalling also the United Nations Millennium Declaration adopted by Heads of State and Government on 8 September 2000, the 2005 World Summit Outcome adopted on 16 September 2005 and its resolution 60/265 of 30 June 2006 on the follow-up to the development outcome of the 2005 World Summit, including the Millennium Development Goals, and the other internationally agreed development goals,

Recalling further the International Conference on Financing for Development and its outcome,

Recalling the Plan of Implementation of the World Summit on Sustainable Development,

Recalling also the Programme of Action for the Least Developed Countries for the Decade 2001–2010 and the outcome of the high-level meeting of the sixty-first session of the General Assembly on the midterm comprehensive global review of the implementation of the Programme of Action for the Least Developed Countries for the Decade 2001–2010, held in New York on 18 and 19 September 2006, and taking note of *The Least Developed Countries Report, 2008: Growth, Poverty and the Terms of Development Partnership*,

Taking note of the Arusha Declaration and Plan of Action on African Commodities adopted at the African Union Conference of Ministers of Trade on Commodities, held in Arusha, United Republic of Tanzania, from 21 to 23 November 2005, and endorsed by the Executive Council of the African Union at its eighth ordinary session, held in Khartoum from 16 to 21 January 2006,

Taking note also of the Accra Accord, adopted by the United Nations Conference on Trade and Development at its twelfth session, which addresses, inter alia, commodities issues,

1. *Takes note* of the note by the Secretary-General transmitting the report on world commodity trends and prospects prepared by the secretariat of the United Nations Conference on Trade and Development;

2. *Notes* the deliberations held in the context of the preparatory process for the Follow-up International Conference on Financing for Development to Review the Implementation of the Monterrey Consensus, held in Doha from 29 November to 2 December 2008;

3. *Stresses* the importance of the continuing substantive consideration of the sub-item entitled "Commodities";

4. *Requests* the Secretary-General to submit to the General Assembly at its sixty-fourth session a report on commodities;

5. *Decides* to include in the provisional agenda of its sixty-fourth session, under the item entitled "Macroeconomic policy questions", the sub-item entitled "Commodities", to be considered thereafter on a biennial basis.

Individual commodities

Timber. As at 31 December, the International Tropical Timber Agreement, 2006 [YUN 2006, p. 1124] had 42 signatories and 17 parties. During the year, Australia, Belgium, Bulgaria, the Central African Republic, China, the Congo, the Czech Republic, the Democratic Republic of the Congo, Finland, France, Gabon, Honduras, India, Italy, Liberia, Lithuania, New Zealand, Peru, the Philippines, Portugal, Romania, Slovenia, Spain and Sweden signed the agreement. Australia, Côte d'Ivoire, Ecuador, Gabon, Ghana, Guyana, India, Liberia, Mexico, New Zealand, Norway, Panama and Sweden became parties.

Sugar. As at 31 December, the International Sugar Agreement, 1992 [YUN 1992, p. 625] had 22 signatories and 59 parties. During the year, Croatia and Ghana became parties.

Common Fund for Commodities

The 1980 Agreement establishing the Common Fund for Commodities [YUN 1980, p. 621], a mechanism intended to stabilize the commodities market by helping to finance buffer stocks of specific commodities, as well as commodity development activities such as research and marketing, had entered into force in 1989, and the Fund became operational later that year. As at 31 December 2008, the Agreement had 114 parties. The Andean Community became party during the year.

Finance

Financial policy

The *World Economic and Social Survey 2008* [Sales No. E.08.II.C.1] stated that the pro-cyclical behaviour of finance and the vulnerability of countries to external shocks had resulted in economic insecurity, which was further aggravated by the absence of a social contract that provided minimum protection to citizens against unanticipated income loss. The problem was particularly serious in many developing countries, in view of their limited capacity to pursue effective counter-cyclical macroeconomic policies. Extreme poverty was the most damaging expression of economic insecurity. Economic growth in recent years had, in many cases, failed to generate greater economic security and rising incomes for the poor, and even countries that had been growing faster and showed more stability were not able to translate growth into poverty reduction. Such an outcome reflected, in part, the links among growth, investment and labour-market performance in the new economic environment. Concerns about the instability of employment, low pay and lack of protection appeared among the top preoccupations in all countries. For economic growth to be inclusive in the sense of reducing vulnerability, macroeconomic policies should place employment and economic security at the centre of the policy agenda and should be embedded in a broader development strategy, as was the case in the fast-growing East Asian economies. Fiscal policies would give priority to development spending, including investment in education, health and infrastructure. As with the East Asian experience, monetary policy would be coordinated with financial sector and industrial policies, including directed and subsidized credit schemes and managed interest rates, so as to directly influence investment and savings. The right mix of those policies could be applied deliberately so as to promote investment in specific industries at specific times, but it should be especially promoted in sectors with the greatest potential for upgrading skills, reaping economies of scale and raising productivity growth, thereby increasing the rates of return on investment. Governments could enhance the scope for counter-cyclical policies by improving the institutional framework for macroeconomic policymaking. Setting fiscal targets that were independent of short-term fluctuations in economic growth, as well as commodity stabilization funds, could be effective in forcing a counter-cyclical policy stance. In developing countries with open capital accounts, where conducting counter-cyclical monetary policies had become increasingly difficult, there was a need to consider measures to control and regulate international capital flows, as well as the operations of the domestic financial sector. Countries should avoid pro-cyclical biases in fiscal policy through the establishment of broad fiscal rules that guaranteed the long-term sustainability of fiscal balances, including targets for the budget deficit and limits to public indebtedness. The establishment of stabilization funds could also help smooth out fiscal revenues, especially in countries where commodity prices had a large impact on the economy and the fiscal balance.

The *World Economic Situation and Prospects 2009* [Sales No. E.09.II.C.2], jointly issued by UNCTAD and the UN Department of Economic and Social Affairs (DESA), stated that, coming on the heels of the food and energy security crises, the global financial crisis would most likely set back progress towards poverty reduction and the achievement of the MDGs. The tightening of access to credit and weaker growth would cut into public revenues and limit the ability of developing countries to make the necessary investments to meet education, health and other human development goals. Unless adequate social safety nets were in place, the poor would be hit the hardest. Policymakers worldwide initially underestimated the depth and breadth of the financial crisis. As a result, policy actions fell behind the curve and, in the early stages, policy stances were inadequate for handling the scale and nature of the crisis. Only after the systemic risks for the global financial system became manifest in September 2008 did six major central banks decide to move in a more coordinated fashion by agreeing to cut their respective official target rates simultaneously and increase direct liquidity injections into financial markets. Further monetary easing was expected in the world economy in 2009. However, with consumer and business confidence seriously depressed and banks reluctant to lend, further lowering of interest rates by central banks would do little to stimulate credit supplies to the non-financial sector or to encourage private spending.

Restoring confidence in financial markets in order to normalize credit flows remained of primary importance. Hence, counter-cyclical macroeconomic policies were needed to complement efforts to rescue the financial sector from widespread systemic failure. With limited space for monetary stimulus, fiscal policy options would need to be examined as ways of reactivating the global economy. The severity of the financial crisis called for policy actions that were commensurate with the scale of the problem and should go beyond any normal range of budgetary considerations. The United States fiscal stimulus package adopted in early 2008 had failed to sustain the economy, and at the end of the year, a second, more substantial package was under discussion. Similarly, European countries were easing monetary policies and preparing for significant fiscal expansion in 2009. A large number of developing countries and economies in transition were reluctant to ease monetary policy over concerns of inflationary pressures and currency depreciation. The scope for counter-cyclical policies would vary greatly across developing countries, mainly for two reasons. First, many countries had a history of pro-cyclical macroeconomic policy adjustment, partly driven by policy rules (such as inflation targeting), and providing greater monetary and fiscal stimuli in such cases would require a departure from existing policy practice and rules. Second, not all countries had sufficient foreign exchange reserves, and some were likely to suffer strong balance-of-payments shocks. There were countries with ample policy space for acting more aggressively to stave off a recession. China had already started to use its policy space, for instance, and had designed a large-scale plan of fiscal stimulus, amounting to 15 per cent of its gross domestic product, to be spent during 2009 and 2010, which was expected to contribute to reinvigorating global demand. For many of the middle- and low-income countries, the scope for providing such stimuli would be even more limited, as they might see their foreign-exchange reserves evaporate quickly, with either continued capital reversals taking place or strong reductions in the demand for their export products, or both. In order to enhance their scope for counter-cyclical responses in the short run, enhancement of compensatory financing and additional and reliable foreign aid flows would be needed to cope with the drops in export earnings and reduced access to private capital flows.

Looking to the long run, a broadening of the development policy framework was needed to conduct active investment and technology policies so as to diversify those countries' economies and reduce their dependence on a few commodity exports, thereby allowing them to meet key development goals. That would require massive resources for public investment in infrastructure, food production, education, health and renewable energy sources. The crisis also presented opportunities to align fiscal stimulus packages with long-term goals for sustainable development. To ensure sufficient stimulus at the global level, it would be desirable to coordinate fiscal stimulus packages internationally.

The financial crisis had also revealed major deficiencies in the regulatory and supervisory frameworks of financial markets. First, the new approach to the regulation of finance, including that under the New Basel Capital Accord (Basel II) rules (recommendations on banking laws and regulations issued by the Basel Committee on Banking Supervision), placed the burden of regulation on the financial institutions themselves. Second, the more complex the trade in securities and other financial instruments became, the greater was the reliance on rating agencies that proved inadequate in part due to conflicts of interest over their own sources of earnings—which were proportional to the trade volume of the instruments they rated. Consequently, risk assessments by rating agencies tended to be highly pro-cyclical as they reacted to the materialization of risks rather than to their build-up. Third, approaches to financial regulation tended to act pro-cyclically, hence exacerbating a credit crunch during a crisis. Fourth, the spread of financial networks across the world, and the character of securitization itself, had made all financial operations hinge on the confidence that each institution in isolation was capable of backing up its operations. However, as insolvencies emerged, such confidence was weakened and might vanish, causing a generalized credit freeze. The risk models applied by regulatory agencies typically disregarded such "contagion" effects and failed to account for the vulnerabilities of the financial system as a whole. The basic objectives of the reform of prudential regulation and supervision of financial sectors should thus be to introduce strong, internationally concerted counter-cyclical rules supported by counter-cyclical macroeconomic policies.

Financial flows

According to the *World Economic Situation and Prospects 2009*, amid the unfolding global financial crisis, developing countries continued to make increasing substantial net outward transfers of financial resources to developed countries, reaching an all-time high of $933 billion in 2008, after a moderation in the rate of increase in 2007. Much of the increase was concentrated in Western Asia and Africa, as the economies in those regions generated increasing trade surpluses, largely owing to the surge in oil and commodity prices in the first half of 2008. As capital inflows also remained relatively strong up until the third quarter of the year, those regions further increased international reserve positions in the aggregate. Net transfers from countries with economies in transition increased from $101 billion in 2007 to $171 billion, owing mainly to the strong increase in the trade surplus of the Russian Federation. By contrast, in Latin America and the Caribbean and East and South Asia, net outward transfers declined as a consequence of the financial turmoil, leading to a significant reduction in private capital flows from the third quarter of the year onwards.

In terms of foreign direct investment (FDI), developing countries had attracted high and growing levels of private capital flows since 2002, and that trend continued until the end of the second quarter of 2008. With the exception of net portfolio investments, all components registered significant gains. Given the change in financial conditions facing developing countries since the beginning of the third quarter of 2008, the ability of a number of them to raise capital was severely compromised. While at the onset of the financial crisis net commercial bank lending to emerging market economies was stable, despite the weakness in mature credit markets, heightened concerns about the quality of global credit affected most developing markets. The deterioration in investor confidence was mainly triggered by the impact of the United States sub-prime mortgage crisis on balance sheets of banks across the global economy, but especially on those in the United States and Europe. With the failure of major financial institutions in developed countries, global interbank funding conditions deteriorated and, as a result, emerging market sovereign bond spreads widened dramatically.

Economic development in Africa

UNCTAD activities in favour of Africa

The UNCTAD Trade and Development Board (TDB), at its forty-fourth executive session (Geneva, 10 July) [A/63/15 (Part III)], considered the UNCTAD Secretary-General's report [TD/B/EX(44)/2] on activities undertaken in favour of Africa, which provided an overview of UNCTAD research and analysis with regard to Africa's development and a summary of activities, including advisory services and technical cooperation. According to the report, increased efforts were made during the year to disseminate findings of policy analysis and research and create material usable by policymakers. In that regard, UNCTAD continued its work in connection with the United Nations Development Account project on "Developing local capacities for the identification of growth opportunities through resource mobilization", launched in February 2007, whose objective was to strengthen the capacity of African countries to identify and utilize non-debt-creating domestic and foreign resources for growth and poverty reduction within the framework of the MDGs. A policy handbook on enhancing the role of domestic resources in Africa's development was prepared. UNCTAD also continued to provide policy analysis and research in favour of small island developing States and landlocked countries in Africa. It provided advisory services to Cape Verde in the last year of its three-year transition period before its graduation from LDC status in 2007. As part of the preparatory process for the midterm review of the implementation of the Almaty Programme of Action on addressing the special needs of landlocked and transit developing countries [YUN 2003, p. 875], UNCTAD produced two publications that addressed transit transport issues of specific relevance to African landlocked developing countries.

Concerning international trade and commercial diplomacy, UNCTAD cooperated with the African Union and other partners in supporting African countries' engagement, both collectively through the WTO African Group, LDC Group and African, Caribbean and Pacific Group, and individually, in the Doha Round of trade negotiations in key negotiating areas affecting their development interests, including agriculture, non-agricultural market access, services, special and differential treatment, development issues, Aid for Trade, trade-related aspects of intellectual property, and trade facilitation. UNCTAD participated in the WTO African Group seminar on agriculture and non-agricultural market access modalities (Chavannes-de-Bogis, Switzerland, 16–17 February). In the field, it supported national and regional trade policymakers and stakeholders in managing their trade policymaking and multilateral and regional trade negotiations.

Such activities were delivered under the Joint Integrated Technical Assistance Programme, a project on trade capacity-building for Africa funded by the United Nations Development Programme (UNDP), Southern African Development Community projects, WTO accession projects and various country-specific projects. UNCTAD supported African countries in assessing the contribution of services to reform the sector, with an emphasis on development, including strengthening access to essential services, and to generate data and reference material for multilateral and regional trade negotiations. It also continued to develop the Measures Affecting Services Trade database for undertaking cross-country and cross-sectoral analysis of legal measures applied to services. It launched the Regional Standards Programme to enable African producers and exporters to meet both official and private-sector standards and assisted small producers in achieving market acceptance by supermarkets, in cooperation with the Swiss supermarket chain Migros.

UNCTAD continued to provide capacity-building and technical activities on competition law and policy to African countries in formulating, revising and enforcing competition policies and legislation, including through study tours, workshops and expert reviews. The assistance included: helping create a competition culture among Government officials, the private sector, State-owned enterprises and consumers; and providing support to regional cooperation arrangements on competition issues that were supportive of trade, investment and development. During the reporting period, it supported African and other debtor countries in preparing their negotiations on the rescheduling or restructuring of bilateral official debt in the framework of the Paris Club, and also supported a number of African countries in investment promotion to enable them to attract and benefit from FDI. The investment policy reviews for Morocco, Rwanda and Zambia were published and presented to the international community through UNCTAD intergovernmental machinery, while those for Mauritania and Nigeria were under preparation.

The report stated that the evaluation of the impact of UNCTAD activities in favour of Africa was a complex task, especially the impact of the research and policy analysis, as UNCTAD work contributed to a broader stream of national and international policy analysis, and many factors influenced the uptake of ideas. However, important steps were taken during the year to disseminate findings at the country level through regional workshops and the elaboration of a policymakers' handbook based on national and regional workshops. The immediate impact of technical cooperation activities could be gauged in terms of activities implemented during projects. Similarly, the impact of training activities was evident in increased understanding of issues, options and commitments. However, the long-term developmental impact of technical cooperation activities was more difficult to measure. UNCTAD activities had facilitated the development of competition and investment policy in a number of African countries. With regard to competition policy, there had been noticeable policy changes in Egypt, Kenya, Malawi and Mozambique, where UNCTAD had provided assistance. Nevertheless, the broader impact of the introduction of competition law and policy on development, poverty reduction and the achievement of the MDGs was more nebulous.

Despite those difficulties of evaluation, one positive indicator was the continued demand from African countries for a number of long-standing UNCTAD technical cooperation activities, such as the Automated System for Customs Data, the Debt Management and Financial Analysis System, support in the Paris Club negotiations, support for trade negotiations and commercial diplomacy, and improvement in port services, as well as interest in new initiatives such as the Virtual Institute. There was also buoyant demand for expertise in relation to policies to attract FDI and increase investment development linkages. Overall, UNCTAD support for Africa covered a large number of countries, and an important feature of its work was its cooperation with African subregional organizations and the broad alignment of its work with the New Partnership for Africa's Development priorities.

TDB took note of the UNCTAD Secretary-General's report.

African export performance following trade liberalization

TDB, at its fifty-fifth session [A/63/15 (Part IV)], considered economic development in Africa: trade liberalization and export performance, on the basis of the 2008 report by the UNCTAD secretariat entitled *Economic Development in Africa 2008—Export Performance Following Trade Liberalization: Some Patterns and Policy Perspectives* [Sales No. E.08.II.D.22]. The report discussed the history of trade policy in Africa and the rationale for trade liberalization and its timing, and provided an overview of Africa's export performance in value, volume and composition, as well as of its performance in agriculture. It also investigated the reasons for Africa's failure to diversify into the manufacturing sector in order to increase manufacturing exports, and identified the factors underlying the trends in exports of agricultural and manufacturing products. The report examined some policy options for improving Africa's export performance, revolving around the issues of productivity, competitiveness, market access and access to factors of production, both in agriculture and manufacturing. It stated that the trade liberalization efforts by African countries over the previous 25 years had removed most of the policy barriers considered to be their main impediments. However, though there had been some improvement in Africa's export performance after trade liberalization, the level and composition of its exports had not substantially changed: the performance of the export sector fell short of expectations and the improvement was small relative to the experience of other developing regions. African countries had not diversified their exports towards more dynamic primary commodities and manufacturing goods, which were less prone to the vagaries of international markets. Africa as a whole had even lost export market share, which was down from 6 per cent of world exports in 1980 to 3 per cent in 2007. Hence, it was clear that the recent substantial rises in African countries' export earnings had not allowed Africa to recover its lost market share.

In terms of policy responses and perspectives, an overview of the report [TD/B/55/6] stated that poor export performance in Africa pointed to the need to identify the constraints that continued to limit it. Trade liberalization measures had addressed macroeconomic policies such as overvalued exchange rates and restrictive trade policies that constrained export performance. The lack of a supply response to the removal of those constraints suggested the existence of deeper problems related to the production and marketing of exports in both the agricultural and manufacturing sectors, and policies were therefore needed to target those constraints. African Governments should focus on promoting horizontal and vertical diversification towards higher value-added products through a combination of incentives to promote investment in irrigation facilities or other aspects of agricultural production and exports, as well as through the provision of physical infrastructure, agricultural research, extension services and export facilitation services. In the medium to long term, they should tackle such issues as land tenure systems and the gender division of labour in rural areas in order to improve the productivity of agriculture. Steps could also be taken at the global level to improve agricultural export performance, such as liberalizing agricultural trade in developed-country markets, and revisiting previously explored options such as international commodity agreements and diversification funds in order to improve the terms on which African agricultural exporters interacted with the market. Aid for Trade and other technical assistance programmes should be directed at upgrading Africa's trade infrastructure to strengthen its capacity to trade and attain quality and consistency in exports, including by meeting the health and safety requirements for food in export markets. In manufacturing, more attention should be paid to production and marketing aspects to facilitate a substantial increase in exports. In particular, manufacturing firms' competitiveness should be addressed as a priority, at the level of both the economy and the firm. The positive effect of the size of firms on indicators of performance and exports highlighted the need to promote large firms by encouraging FDI in Africa's manufacturing sector, as firms with foreign ownership tended to be larger than domestic ones and were more export-oriented. Domestic investment in existing firms should also be increased to allow them to grow and export more. Another crucial aspect was the access of manufacturing firms to factors of production. Limited access to capital, for example, was identified in many countries as a key constraint to firms' growth. There was an urgent need, therefore, to improve the efficiency of the credit market in African countries by creating credit information bureaux to collect information on creditworthiness and share it with potential lenders. Closer relations should also be encouraged between the private sector and financial institutions. Overall, if African countries were to reap the potential benefits of trade liberalization, attention should be refocused on the productive and marketing constraints facing their agricultural and manufacturing producers.

On 26 September [agreed conclusions 494(LV)], TDB took note of the report's finding that export development required more than trade liberalization and that complementary policies were needed to address the factors constraining supply capacity. It recognized the trade liberalization efforts undertaken unilaterally, regionally and multilaterally by African countries over the previous 25 years, which would require continued and complementary efforts to be fully realized. TDB was concerned about the relatively weak export performance, notably in terms of diversification into higher value-added products in the agricultural and manufacturing sectors, and recognized the impact of the erosion of trade preferences for African countries, which had both trade and development repercussions. In that context, effective solutions had to be found, including through the outcome of multilateral trade negotiations, to address market access opportunities and diversification. TDB reaffirmed that each African country was responsible for its own development, and national strategies should include supply-side sectoral measures such as incentive packages, productivity promotion and institutional reforms, targeting all sectors of the economy, including monetary policies, in order to enhance its supply response to the export opportunities resulting from trade liberalization. TDB was also concerned about the effect of the food crisis on several countries, and recognized the importance of agricultural sector development strategies for achieving internationally agreed development goals and reducing the likelihood of future crises—for example, through measures aimed at increasing public investment in agriculture, providing financial incentives for the modernization of the sector and developing export diversification programmes. It stressed that national structural policies to promote the manufacturing sector should focus on: creating reliable infrastructure that supported efficient production and exports; encouraging firms to become more competitive by increasing labour productivity and developing technological capabilities; and promoting the creation of larger markets and firms in order to benefit from economies of scale, while taking action to support small and medium-sized enterprises (SMEs). TDB regretted the weakness of internal commercial exchanges between African countries, and recognized that regional and interregional economic cooperation and integration, including opportunities offered by South-South and North-South partnerships, had the potential to help them increase their exports, allowing them to diversify away from traditional bulk primary commodities into market-dynamic products.

The Board invited Africa's trade partners to further open up their markets to products of export interest to African countries and continue to assist them in upgrading their capacity to adjust to rising technical standards, in particular food and health standards. It also invited them to address the effects of non-tariff barriers, tariff peaks and tariff escalation, including on Africa's agricultural exports, which hampered diversification; and called on all countries to honour their commitments on duty-free and quota-free market access for LDCs, as provided for in the Ministerial Declaration of the Sixth WTO Ministerial Conference [YUN 2005, p. 1041]. TDB emphasized that donor countries and relevant multilateral organizations played a critical role in helping African countries, including through Aid for Trade, improve their productive and export capacity; and encouraged UNCTAD, as agreed in the Accra Accord, to continue to undertake insightful and critical analysis and to widen the dissemination of its research findings.

Africa's development needs

On 22 September, the General Assembly, in accordance with its **resolution 62/242** of 4 March (see p. 1008), held a high-level meeting on Africa's development needs. On the same date (**resolution 63/1**) (see p. 1009), the Assembly adopted the Political Declaration on Africa's Development Needs, in which it stated that the high-level meeting had reviewed the implementation of all commitments made to and by Africa in order to comprehensively address the special development needs of the continent. All commitments should be effectively implemented and given appropriate follow-up by the international community and by Africa itself. The Assembly underscored the urgency of finding solutions to Africa's major challenges.

International financial system

Report of Secretary-General. In response to General Assembly resolution 62/185 [YUN 2007, p. 983], the Secretary-General submitted a July report [A/63/96] on the international financial system and development that complemented his reports on the follow-up to the outcome of the International Conference on Financing for Development (see p. 1073) and on the debt crisis and development (see p. 1072). The report reviewed trends in international official and private capital flows to developing countries and international policy challenges arising from the financial crisis, which were critical in expanding the flow and sustainability of development financing. It also highlighted the critical role of multilateralism in addressing the economic challenges facing the international community. According to the report, developing countries continued to make increasing substantial net outward transfers of financial resources to developed countries, reaching $792 billion in 2007. That increase was accompanied by continued net private capital inflows to all developing country subgroupings, propelled by the abundant global liquidity. The expansion of private capital flows enabled emerging economies to sustain their growth and to stay resilient in the face of the ongoing turmoil in developed country financial markets caused by the sub-prime mortgage crisis. However, the increased exposure to those flows left developing countries vulnerable to sudden changes in investor sentiment and to a possible deterioration in global financial market conditions. In the current financial turmoil, developing countries proved to be better prepared than in previous crises. Large currency reserves, improved macroeconomic fundamentals and strong economic growth in emerging economies helped sustain high levels of private capital flows. However, against a backdrop of continuing weakness in financial markets, threats to systemic stability intensified. Strong capital inflows and rising inflationary pressures in emerging economies, due to higher food and energy prices, were leading to expectations that policymakers would increase domestic interest rates or allow for more currency appreciation.

Efforts to craft and implement policy responses to the financial crisis exposed additional challenges related to: improving the governance structure of the international financial institutions; strengthening the foundations of surveillance and policy cooperation on key systemic issues; exploring the role of official financing of emerging market and developing countries; and clarifying the modalities of engagement with low-income countries. The crisis highlighted the multilateral aspects indispensable to building and sustaining sound financial markets, and demonstrated that increased use of newly invented risk transfer instruments in globalized markets carried a number of shortcomings, both in the markets themselves and in the regulatory and supervisory systems. While a process of financial rehabilitation had begun, those actions needed to be reinforced by measures to address the underlying causes of the disruptions. To that end, the report by the Financial Stability Forum on enhancing market and institutional resilience was presented in April and endorsed by the Group of Seven most industrialized countries (G-7), Central Bank Governors and the International Monetary and Financial Committee of the Board of Governors of the International Monetary Fund (IMF). That report set out policy recommendations on prudential oversight of capital, liquidity and risk management; transparency, disclosure and valuation policies; the role and uses of credit ratings; and the authorities' responsiveness to risks and their arrangements to deal with stress in the financial system. The G-7 also identified a number of recommendations by the Financial Stability Forum considered priorities for implementation before the end of summer 2008. The Forum's report emphasized the importance of prompt implementation of the Basel II framework (see p. 1061), which might help make the capital base more reflective of the changing risk profile of banks and serve to institute incentives for better risk measurement and management. Basel II rules required that banks would disclose more information on their risk profile and their nature than called for under Basel I. However, there was also a need for revisions to Basel II to amplify the impact of changing market values on the financing activities of banks.

In terms of the governance reform of the Bretton Woods institutions (the World Bank Group and IMF), the Secretary-General noted that, by the voting deadline of 28 April, governors from 175 of the 185 IMF member countries had voted in favour of the proposed resolution on the IMF quota and voice reform package, which included a second round of ad hoc quota increases of close to 10 per cent, based on a new quota formula; the tripling of basic votes; and the appointment of a second Alternate Director for constituencies consisting of at least 19 members. Also in the resolution, the Executive Board was requested to recommend further realignments of members' quota shares in the context of future general quota reviews, beginning with the fourteenth general review of quotas in 2013, to ensure that those shares reflected their relative positions in the world economy. As to multilateral surveillance, the IMF Executive Board reached an agreement on a "Statement of surveillance priorities" in the context of the 2008 triennial surveillance review. The goal was to strengthen cooperation by reaching consensus on the role of surveillance in helping Governments deal with the challenges of the integrated economy. In addition, the International Working Group of Sovereign Wealth Funds, comprising 25 IMF member countries, was established in May to agree on a common set of voluntary practices. The World Bank launched its own process of voice and participation reform: at its 2007 meeting, the IMF/World Bank Development Committee had welcomed an options paper on voice and participation, detailing a two-stage timetable for possible actions. The Committee also acknowledged that further consultations would be necessary to reach a political consensus and, at its spring 2008 meeting, asked the Bank's Board to prepare options by the 2008 annual meeting, with a view to reaching consensus on a comprehensive package by the spring 2009 meeting.

In his conclusions, the Secretary-General noted that both national and international prudential regulatory frameworks needed to give more attention to the systemic components of risk build-up in financial markets, with particular focus on the inherent pro-cyclicality of financial markets. In the context of integrated global markets, a cooperative and multilaterally coordinated approach to regulatory reform in the financial sector was indispensable. The ongoing reform of the governance structures of the international financial institutions, critical to the integrity of the international financial system, had taken only small first steps, and efforts in that regard should be intensified. In terms of global financial stability, it was vital to reach a consensus on the role of IMF surveillance and its key responsibilities in the international financial system. The international community should strengthen instruments to support low-income countries facing sharp rises in food and energy prices and, to reduce poverty, increased financing for gender equality should be a key feature of the financing for development process.

IMF/World Bank Development Committee. The joint IMF/World Bank Development Committee, in a communiqué issued following its meeting on 13 April, endorsed the overall World Bank Group objective of contributing to an inclusive and sustainable globalization to overcome poverty and enhance growth with care for the environment. The Committee noted that while the balance of risks to the global outlook had become more negative, emerging and developing economies had been less affected by financial market developments. The impact of higher commodity prices was mixed across countries, depending on whether they were net importers or exporters. The Committee asked the World Bank Group and IMF to respond to developing countries' requests for advice on the management of natural resource revenues, and to provide timely policy and financial support to vulnerable countries dealing with shocks, including from energy and food prices. The Committee welcomed the call by the World Bank President to combat hunger and malnutrition through a "New Deal for Global Food Policy", combining immediate assistance with medium- and long-term efforts to boost agricultural productivity in developing countries. It urged donors to provide assistance to the World Food Programme to enable immediate support for countries most affected by the high food prices; encouraged the Group to strengthen its engagement in the agricultural sector; supported efforts to agree on a pro-development Doha Round that improved access to markets; and stressed the need to integrate trade and competitiveness within national development strategies, while stepping up support for Aid for Trade. The Committee acknowledged the work under way on the design, governance and financing of the new Climate Investment Funds to address the challenge of climate change. It also welcomed the Managing Director's report on the reform of IMF quota and voice, and encouraged the Bank to advance work on all aspects of voice and participation, keeping in mind the distinct nature of the Bank's development mandate and the importance of enhancing voice and participation for all developing and transition countries.

At its 12 October meeting, the Development Committee expressed concern over the impact of the financial turmoil and the continued high prices of fuel and food, and asked the World Bank Group and IMF to help address those challenges, in particular the impact on developing countries, and draw lessons from the current crises. Noting the package of reforms enhancing voice and participation of developing and transition countries in the Group's governance and work, it stated that further realignment of Bank shareholding would be taken up by the Bank's Board in a shareholding review that would develop principles, criteria and proposals for doing so, and would consider the evolving weight of all members in the world economy and other Bank-specific criteria consistent with its development mandate, moving towards equitable voting power between developed and developing members. The Board would develop proposals by 2010, with a view to reaching consensus on realignment. There was agreement on the importance of a selection process for the President of the Bank that was merit-based and transparent, with nominations open to all members and transparent Board consideration of all candidates. In addition, the Bank's management committed to continue enhancing diversity of management and staff and decentralizing decision-making. The Committee asked the Group's Boards and management to implement that agreed first step, and looked forward to periodic reports on progress and proposals for a realignment of Bank shareholding.

G-8 statement on global economy. In a 15 October statement, the leaders of the Group of Eight most industrialized countries (G-8) and the President of the European Commission said that they were united in their commitment to fulfil their shared responsibility to resolve the current crisis, strengthen financial institutions, restore confidence in the financial system and provide a sound economic footing for citizens and businesses. They welcomed and commended the decisions taken in support of implementation of the G-7 Plan of Action, which set forth a concerted framework for action and would help financial institutions gain access to needed capital; support important financial institutions and prevent their failure; unfreeze credit markets; restart secondary markets for mortgages; and protect savers and depositors. They undertook to implement those measures on an urgent, transparent and non-discriminatory basis; pledged continued cooperation and coordination; committed to mitigating the adverse impacts of the crisis on emerging economies and developing nations; and supported the critical IMF role in assisting affected countries. They also reaffirmed that open economies and well-regulated markets were essential to economic growth, employment and prosperity, and underscored the importance of continuing efforts to promote trade and investment liberalization. While their focus was on the immediate task of stabilizing markets and restoring confidence, they recognized that changes to the regulatory and institutional regimes for the world's financial sectors were needed. The discussions elaborating such changes, building on the efforts of the Financial Stability Forum and IMF, should involve both developed and developing countries.

CEB consideration. The High-level Committee on Programmes of the United Nations Chief Executives Board for Coordination (CEB), at its sixteenth session (Rome, 30 September–1 October) [CEB/2008/6], discussed, among other subjects, the current financial crisis. It noted that uncertainty existed over the economic consequence of the disruption in financial markets, whether it would have a long- or short-term impact on the rate of sustainable growth, and that the financial crisis would be the main focus of the World Bank/IMF annual meeting in mid-October. The Committee agreed that the crisis was a major market failure, the size and significance of which would lead to re-regulation or to a redefinition of the regulations that applied to the financial markets. The financial crisis also presented an opportunity for the multilateral system, given that there would be a greater demand for public action and for the global public system to evolve. It was observed that the crisis also posed a challenge to the World Bank's ability to fund activities through the international markets; that could have serious consequences not only for the role of the Bank, but also for making headway on issues such as the MDGs. The Committee explored its role in helping prepare the CEB discussion on the crisis so as to focus on system-wide efforts to safeguard critical social and development programmes and to help countries remain on course for the achievement of the MDGs. In that context, the Board should consider the social dimensions of the crisis, which would help in identifying the key contributions that the UN system organizations could make. The financial crisis presented an additional hurdle to raising required resources, and the question was how to create a conducive framework for attracting investments. Linking immediate actions with long-term needs remained a challenge, the importance of environmental protection was highlighted, and it was suggested that the food crisis should also be given increased attention. The Committee was informed that a working group on financing for development within the Development Group structure was looking at UN system preparations for the Doha review conference. At the UN Development Group meeting on 24 September, participants emphasized that the knowledge and capacity of the UN system should be drawn upon in that regard, in an effort to enhance system-wide coherence and elaborate a One United Nations approach. It was suggested that a joint UN Development Group and High-level Committee on Programmes working group be established, and that the Committee nominate organizations to represent it in that group to work alongside the two UN Development Group co-convening organizations, the United Nations Development Programme (UNDP) and the United Nations Children's Fund (UNICEF). The Committee agreed to establish the joint High-level Committee on Programmes/UN Development Group working group on financing for development, with the International Fund for Agricultural Development, the International Labour Organization and the World Bank as co-conveners.

CEB, at its second regular session (New York, 24 October) [CEB/2008/2], held a thematic discussion on the financial crisis.

Interactive Panel on Global Financial Crisis. On 30 October, the General Assembly President convened an Interactive Panel on the Global Financial Crisis to identify steps to secure a more stable and sustainable global economic order. The Panel, which included six eminent experts as well as representatives of Member States, marked the first of what was expected to be a series of intergovernmental consultations on the response to the unfolding financial crisis. It represented an important step in an effort to develop proposals regarding the UN economic and development agenda and the role the United Nations should play in the search for new policy initiatives. There was widespread concern that global economic governance arrangements needed to be radically reformed to be responsive to current economic conditions. It was agreed that the onset of the food, fuel and financial crises had thrown a spotlight on the inadequacies of global institutions in enforcing accountability for economic decisions and maintaining growth and stability, and that developing countries—which represented a much larger proportion of world economic activity than they did when the Bretton Woods institutions were founded—were not sufficiently represented in the global councils of economic governance. As a group, they were net creditors to the global economic system and had an abiding interest in a rules-based and impartial revamping of global financial policies and institutions. As the pressure for change increased, the design of the new architecture had to be inclusive and democratic. In its report on the discussion, the Office of the President stated that the exchange among the six panellists and representatives of Member States and regional groups revealed the strong conviction that an integral global response to the crisis was required, States should have a key role in rebuilding the international rules and institutions that had failed to ensure global financial stability, sustained growth and social progress, and the international community should develop the institutional instruments for improving the global system. Participants recognized the need for changes in the governance of international financial institutions, particularly by making the decision-making process more inclusive and equitable, and pointed to the importance of introducing new standards and regulatory schemes and effective compliance mechanisms. They presented recommendations for changes in the international financial architecture and views on the UN role, and called for resources to be made available to help countries mitigate the social impact of the crisis. They also called for the United Nations to play a central role in the search for solutions and implementation of decisions, and agreed that dealing with the financial crisis required consideration, not only of the financial sphere, but also of the crises surrounding food, energy and climate change, without compromising support for the MDGs. The President welcomed the establishment of the High-level Task Force of Experts to undertake a comprehensive review of the international financial system and to forward recommendations to the Assembly.

G-20 consideration. Leaders of the Group of 20 industrialized and developing country economies (G-20) (Washington, D.C., 15 November), in a declaration, expressed their determination to enhance cooperation to restore global growth and achieve needed reforms in the world's financial systems. They said that major underlying factors to the current situation were inconsistent and insufficiently coordinated macroeconomic policies and inadequate structural reforms, which led to unsustainable global macroeconomic outcomes. Noting the actions taken to address the financial crisis, they agreed that a broader policy response was needed, based on closer macroeconomic cooperation, to restore growth, avoid negative spillovers and support emerging market economies and developing countries. As immediate steps, they agreed to: take actions to stabilize the financial system; recognize the importance of monetary policy support; use fiscal measures to stimulate domestic demand to rapid effect, while maintaining a policy framework conducive to fiscal sustainability; help emerging and developing economies gain access to finance in the current difficult financial conditions, including through liquidity facilities and programme support; stress IMF's important role in crisis response, welcome its new short-term liquidity facility and urge the ongoing review of its instruments and facilities to ensure flexibility; encourage the World Bank and other multilateral development banks (MDBs) to support their development agenda, especially the recent introduction of new facilities by the World Bank in the areas of infrastructure and trade finance; and ensure that IMF, the World Bank and other MDBs had resources to continue playing their role in overcoming the crisis.

In addition, they undertook to implement reforms to strengthen financial markets and regulatory regimes and to implement policies consistent with the following common principles for reform: strengthen financial market transparency; strengthen regulatory regimes, prudential oversight, and risk management, and ensure that financial markets, products and participants were regulated or subject to oversight; exercise strong oversight over credit rating agencies, consistent with the agreed and strengthened international code of conduct; make regulatory regimes more effective over the economic cycle, while ensuring that regulation was efficient, did not stifle innovation and encouraged trade in financial products and services; protect the integrity of the financial markets by bolstering investor and consumer protection; promote information-sharing; call upon national and regional regulators to formulate regulations and other measures in a consistent manner; enhance coordination and cooperation across all segments of financial markets and strengthen cooperation on crisis prevention, management and resolution; and advance the reform of the Bretton Woods institutions, giving greater voice and representation to emerging and developing economies. The leaders committed themselves to implementing those principles and set out an initial list of measures in the Action Plan to Implement Principles of Reform, including high priority actions to be completed prior to 31 March 2009.

Doha Declaration. In the Doha Declaration on Financing for Development, adopted at the Follow-up International Conference on Financing for Development to Review the Implementation of the Monterrey Consensus (Doha, Qatar, 29 November–2 December) [A/CONF.212/7] (see p. 1076), States agreed to hold a conference at the highest level on the world financial and economic crisis and its impact on development, the modalities of which would be defined by the General Assembly President by March 2009.

On 16 December [A/C.5/63/19], the Secretary-General, in a statement on programme budget implications of the draft resolution on the Doha Declaration on Financing for Development: outcome document of the Follow-up International Conference on Financing for Development [A/63/L.57], stated that its adoption could give rise to additional resource requirements in the current biennium. However, in the absence of sufficient details at that stage regarding the conference, it was difficult for the Secretariat to determine the extent of the programme budget implications arising from it. He said that, should the Assembly adopt the draft resolution, a detailed statement of programme budget implications would be submitted to it for consideration during its current session as soon as specific information on the format and modalities of the conference was available.

On 30 December [A/63/657], the Fifth (Administrative and Budgetary) Committee, having considered the Secretary-General's statement and the related report of the Advisory Committee on Administrative and Budgetary Questions [A/63/625], decided to so inform the Assembly.

GENERAL ASSEMBLY ACTION

On 19 December [meeting 72], the General Assembly, on the recommendation of the Second Committee [A/63/412/Add.2], adopted **resolution 63/205** without vote [agenda item 47 *(b)*].

International financial system and development

The General Assembly,

Recalling its resolutions 55/186 of 20 December 2000 and 56/181 of 21 December 2001, both entitled "Towards a strengthened and stable international financial architecture responsive to the priorities of growth and development, especially in developing countries, and to the promotion of economic and social equity", as well as its resolutions 57/241 of 20 December 2002, 58/202 of 23 December 2003, 59/222 of 22 December 2004, 60/186 of 22 December 2005, 61/187 of 20 December 2006 and 62/185 of 19 December 2007,

Recalling also the United Nations Millennium Declaration and its resolution 56/210 B of 9 July 2002, in which it endorsed the Monterrey Consensus of the International Conference on Financing for Development, and the Plan of Implementation of the World Summit on Sustainable Development ("Johannesburg Plan of Implementation"),

Recalling further the 2005 World Summit Outcome,

Recalling its resolution 60/265 of 30 June 2006 on the follow-up to the development outcome of the 2005 World Summit, including the Millennium Development Goals and the other internationally agreed development goals, and its resolution 61/16 of 20 November 2006 on strengthening of the Economic and Social Council,

1. *Takes note* of the report of the Secretary-General;

2. *Expresses concern* at the impact of the current global financial crisis on development, and notes that its impact on financing for development was addressed at the Follow-up International Conference on Financing for Development to Review the Implementation of the Monterrey Consensus, held in Doha from 29 November to 2 December 2008;

3. *Stresses* the importance of the continued substantive consideration by the General Assembly of the issue of the international financial system and development, and in this regard notes the deliberations held in the context of the preparatory process for the Follow-up International Conference on Financing for Development, at which this issue was addressed;

4. *Decides* to include in the provisional agenda of its sixty-fourth session, under the item entitled "Macroeconomic policy questions", the sub-item entitled "International financial system and development";

5. *Requests* the Secretary-General to submit to the General Assembly at its sixty-fourth session a report on the international financial system and development.

Debt problems of developing countries

In response to General Assembly resolution 62/186 [YUN 2007, p. 986], the Secretary-General submitted a July report [A/63/181] entitled "Towards a durable solution to the debt problems of developing countries". It included a comprehensive analysis of the external debt situation and debt-servicing problems of developing countries and a review of debt management capacity-building efforts, in particular those of the UN system. It also elucidated new developments and key trends in external debt and related areas of development finance and provided a basis for deliberation of policy issues.

According to the report, during 2007, the total external debt of developing and transition economies increased by $373 billion, to a total of $3,357 billion. That increase was more than compensated for by accumulation of international reserves, which grew by over $1,000 billion from 2006, reaching $3,719 billion at the end of 2007. As most international reserves were held in debt instruments issued by the developed economies, by 2008 developing and transition economies as a group had no net external debt, but held net external debt assets of $350 billion. The growth rate of international reserves also outpaced that of short-term debt. At the end of 2007, all developing regions had reserves-to-short-term-debt ratios above 250 per cent (the average was 475 per cent). However, there were large differences between countries in the accumulation of international reserves: four countries (Brazil, China, India and the Russian Federation) held two thirds of all international reserves controlled by developing and transition economies, and several developing countries had reserves well below the level of their short-term external debt. As gross national product (GNP) grew faster than debt, the external debt-to-GNP ratio of developing and transition economies dropped to 24.4 per cent, two points lower than in 2006. Over the same period, the debt-to-export and debt-service-to-export ratios decreased by three percentage points. While the overall decline was similar to that of 2005–2006, the regional composition had changed. Over 2006–2007, debt ratios decreased in all regions by between one and two percentage points, and sub-Saharan Africa was the region with the smallest decrease (0.8 of a percentage point). That comparatively weak improvement contrasted with a decade of continuous debt reduction that had brought Africa's external debt from 70 per cent of GNP in the second half of the 1990s to 25 per cent by 2007.

Since the start of 2007, progress under the enhanced Highly Indebted Poor Countries (HIPC) Initiative had continued at a slower pace. As at 31 May 2008, just over half of the 41 eligible countries had reached the completion point, with 10 countries at the interim stage between decision and completion points, and 8 at the pre-decision point. From January 2007 to 31 May 2008, three countries (Afghanistan, the Central African Republic and Liberia) had reached the decision point and two (Sao Tome and Principe and the Gambia) their completion points. Since the previous report, four countries (the Gambia, Guinea, Liberia and Togo) had rescheduled their debt with Paris Club creditors, and there was some activity in prepayment and regularizing relations with those creditors.

In his conclusions, the Secretary-General stated that domestic policies aimed at ensuring external debt sustainability should complement macro-level analysis with a careful evaluation of the sustainability of each project. Before borrowing abroad on commercial terms, a country should evaluate a project by ensuring that its social return was higher than the cost of funds, that it would generate the foreign currency necessary to service the debt and that the resource flow would match the payment schedule of the debt contract. In low-income countries, some high-return projects might not satisfy the second and third requirements, so such projects should be financed with grants and concessional loans. Given that an increasing share of borrowing by emerging market countries originated within the private sector, those countries should supervise the activities of private agents and ensure that private borrowing did not generate excessive vulnerabilities in the balance sheets of domestic banks and corporations. Countries that issued sovereign debt in the international capital market and had a well-functioning domestic financial system should adopt a debt strategy incorporated into the framework of a proper asset-liability management approach. Assessing sustainability also required accurate and timely information on debt level and composition, and all developing countries would need a well-functioning mechanism for collecting and reporting data on sovereign debt. The Debt Sustainability Framework, based on the primacy of debt servicing, did not explicitly include an evaluation of the needs to be fulfilled in order to achieve the MDGs. Debt sustainability should be defined as the level of debt that allowed a country to achieve the MDGs and reach 2015 without an increase in debt ratios. Debt relief delivered over the previous few years crowded out non-debt relief aid flows, suggesting that the design and evaluation of initiatives should include an explicit measure of the additionality of debt relief. Donors should recognize that past efforts had been unfair to countries with large developmental needs but low debt levels, and should ensure that those countries were appropriately rewarded for maintaining prudent macroeconomic policies by including them in the Multilateral Debt Relief Initiative (MDRI). Policymakers in advanced economies should acknowledge that shocks that might lead to a liquidity crisis in the developing world often depended on external factors that originated in policy decisions made by the advanced economies. Those externalities called for more international coordination in policymaking. Until recently, research and policy had focused on external debt because there were no data on domestic debt, but collecting and disseminating data on the composition of total public debt was not an impossible task. Because vulnerabilities could not be identified without reliable data on the composition of both external and domestic public debt, the international community should promote efforts aimed at producing and disseminating such data. Economists and practitioners were converging towards the idea that debt crises were related to both debt levels and composition and that there were important interactions between domestic public debt and external debt. As a consequence, the distinction between external and domestic debt was becoming less relevant and the international dialogue should be refocused from external debt to external and public debt. Donors should support programmes designed to improve the debt management and data collection capacity of developing countries and ensure that all countries reported comparable data and covered domestic public debt. The international community recognized the importance of public sector debt information and management as a global public good, as well as its importance in the overall public financial management reform programmes of developing countries. A stronger global partnership framework in debt management capacity-building was nevertheless still needed and should ensure sustained financing from the international community for the continuation of the capacity-building efforts and reliable tools for the majority of developing countries. Since debt crises were bound to occur, even with improved debt management and instruments, the international community should create a mechanism for guaranteeing a speedy resolution of those crises and fair burden-sharing among creditors and debtors. In that regard, an independent international body could be mandated by both debtors and creditors to evaluate the debt situation of all countries faced with external debt problems and propose the level and form of relief to be provided.

Other actions. The UNCTAD/DESA report *World Economic Situation and Prospects 2009* [Sales No. E.09.II.C.2] stated that the success of the implementation of the HIPC Initiative required sustained efforts on behalf of the international creditor community. Important challenges were still to be met to implement the Initiative and enable the remaining 18 pre-completion-point countries to reach their completion points. Those included ensuring full participation by creditors and mobilizing additional resources to finance debt relief to all remaining HIPCs. Although most multilateral financial institutions had provided debt relief under the HIPC Initiative and MDRI, some small multilateral institutions still needed to be encouraged to participate in the Initiative. While Paris Club members made strong efforts in their debt-relief commitments, the participation of non-Paris Club official creditors had been low, delivering only about 40 per cent of their expected share in debt-relief operations for HIPCs. So far, 8 non-Paris Club creditors had delivered full debt relief, 22 creditors partial relief and 21 no relief at all. The participation of commercial creditors also remained low, providing 33 per cent of their commitments in 2008—but which was better than only 5 per cent the preceding year.

Another issue related to the implementation of the HIPC Initiative concerned litigation actions by commercial creditors against low-income countries. Even though the amounts involved were small in relation to total debt, the costs of litigation or resolution were significant in relation to debtor countries' export earnings and public budgets. Reducing debt to a sustainable level remained an issue for many HIPCs, which were far from achieving debt sustainability. Risks of debt distress remained high among them, including those that had received full debt relief. Only 10 out of the 23 post-completion-point HIPCs could be classified as being at "low risk" of debt distress, highlighting the fact that many countries continued to be vulnerable. Indeed, several middle- and low-income countries were suffering from debt distress but were not eligible for the HIPC Initiative and had no access to debt relief or to orderly sovereign debt workouts, as granting debt relief was conditional and only countries with unsustainable levels of debt were eligible.

GENERAL ASSEMBLY ACTION

On 19 December [meeting 72], the General Assembly, on the recommendation of the Second Committee [A/63/412/Add.3], adopted **resolution 63/206** without vote [agenda item 47 *(c)*].

External debt and development: towards a durable solution to the debt problems of developing countries

The General Assembly,

Recalling its resolutions 58/203 of 23 December 2003, 59/223 of 22 December 2004, 60/187 of 22 December 2005 and 61/188 of 20 December 2006, and 62/186 of 19 December 2007, entitled "External debt and development: towards a durable solution to the debt problems of developing countries",

Recalling also the International Conference on Financing for Development and its outcome, which recognizes sustainable debt financing as an important element for mobilizing resources for public and private investment,

Recalling further the United Nations Millennium Declaration adopted on 8 September 2000,

Recalling the 2005 World Summit Outcome,

Recalling also its resolution 60/265 of 30 June 2006 on follow-up to the development outcome of the 2005 World Summit, including the Millennium Development Goals and other internationally agreed development goals,

Recalling further its resolution 57/270 B of 23 June 2003,

1. *Takes note* of the report of the Secretary-General;

2. *Notes* the deliberations held in the context of the preparatory process for the Follow-up International Conference on Financing for Development to Review the Implementation of the Monterrey Consensus, held in Doha from 29 November to 2 December 2008, at which the issue of "External debt and development: towards a durable solution to the debt problems of developing countries" was substantively addressed;

3. *Stresses* the importance of the continued substantive consideration of the sub-item entitled "External debt and development: towards a durable solution to the debt problems of developing countries";

4. *Requests* the Secretary-General to submit to the General Assembly at its sixty-fourth session a comprehensive report on the issue;

5. *Decides* to include in the provisional agenda of its sixty-fourth session, under the item entitled "Macroeconomic policy questions", the sub-item entitled "External debt and development: towards a durable solution to the debt problems of developing countries".

Financing for development

Follow-up to International Conference on Financing for Development

General Assembly review session on Monterrey Consensus thematic areas. In accordance with General Assembly resolution 62/187 [YUN 2007, p. 992], the Assembly President convened, between February and May, review sessions on the six thematic areas of the Monterrey Consensus, adopted at the 2002 International Conference on Financing for Development [YUN 2002, p. 953]: mobilizing domestic financial resources for development (14 February); mobilizing international resources for development: FDI and other private flows (15 February); external debt (10–11 March); addressing systemic issues: enhancing the coherence and consistency of the international monetary, financial and trading systems in support of development (11–12 March); increasing international financial and technical cooperation for development (15–16 April); and international trade as an engine for development (19–20 May). The review sessions consisted of panel presentations and policy deliberations. The President also held interactive hearings with representatives of civil society and the business sector. The summaries of the review sessions were submitted to the Assembly in an August report [A/62/921].

High-level meeting of Economic and Social Council, Bretton Woods institutions, WTO and UNCTAD. The Economic and Social Council, in accordance with **decision 2008/203** of 5 February, held a special high-level meeting with the Bretton Woods institutions, WTO and UNCTAD in New York on 14 April, under the theme "Coherence, coordination and cooperation in the context of the implementation of the Monterrey Consensus, including new challenges and emerging issues". The Secretary-General submitted a March note on the theme to the meeting [E/2008/7] that provided background information and appended a number of points for reflection to inform discussion. Under the overall theme of the high-level meeting, five sub-themes were chosen: new initiatives on financing for development; supporting development efforts and enhancing the role of middle-income countries, including in the area of trade; supporting development efforts of LDCs, including through trade capacity-building; building and sustaining solid financial markets: challenges for international cooperation; and financing of climate change adaptation and mitigation.

The Council President, in his summary of the high-level meeting [A/63/80-E/2008/67], reported on the five sub-themes. As to the new initiatives on financing for development, which were important for achieving the objectives of the Monterrey Consensus, he stated that ODA was hovering around $100 billion. Only five Organization for Economic Cooperation and Development (OECD)/Development Assistance Committee (DAC) members (Denmark, Luxembourg, the Netherlands, Norway and Sweden) had met the UN aid target of 0.7 per cent of gross national income. It was uncertain whether the commitment of the G-8 leaders at their 2005 summit [YUN 2005, p. 1057] to reach $130 billion in 2010 would be attained. Nonetheless, donor countries should honour the aid commitments made at the International Conference on Financing for Development in 2002 and at the 2005 G-8 summit. The need for further resources was evident. The fulfilment of the internationally agreed development goal, as well as resources needed for adaptation to and mitigation of climate change, and for simultaneously facing the energy and food crisis, required vast additional flows. Support for a number of "innovative sources of finance"—a tool suggested in the Monterrey Consensus—was gathering momentum. Several initiatives were implemented and others continued to be explored or were at an initial stage. Participants welcomed those developments, particularly since the funds involved were viewed as additional and often more predictable than ODA. The innovative sources had become an effective tool in development cooperation and should be presented as such in the Doha International Conference, but were not a substitute for, nor should they be counted as, ODA. It was crucial to enhance information channels regarding existing initiatives and new efforts, since that was central to encouraging new countries and other actors to enter the field, and the United Nations should play a greater role in the information efforts. Some participants noted that the new initiatives should not be burdensome for developing countries and that their impact should be thoroughly examined. Efforts in that area should not be scattered too widely and the resources should be distributed in a transparent fashion, preferably using traditional aid distribution mechanisms.

ECONOMIC AND SOCIAL COUNCIL ACTION

On 24 July [meeting 42], the Economic and Social Council adopted **resolution 2008/14** [draft: E/2008/L.16] without vote [agenda item 6 *(a)*].

Follow-up to the International Conference on Financing for Development

The Economic and Social Council,

Recalling the International Conference on Financing for Development, held in Monterrey, Mexico, from 18 to 22 March 2002, and General Assembly resolutions 56/210 B of 9 July 2002, 57/250, 57/272 and 57/273 of 20 December 2002, 57/270 B of 23 June 2003, 58/230 of 23 December 2003, 59/225 of 22 December 2004, 60/188 of 22 December 2005, 61/191 of 20 December 2006 and 62/187 of 19 December 2007,

Recalling also its resolutions 2002/34 of 26 July 2002, 2003/47 of 24 July 2003, 2004/64 of 16 September 2004, 2006/45 of 28 July 2006 and 2007/30 of 27 July 2007,

Recalling further the 2005 World Summit Outcome and General Assembly resolution 60/265 of 30 June 2006 on the follow-up to the development outcome of the 2005 World Summit, including the Millennium Development Goals and the other internationally agreed development goals,

Recalling General Assembly resolution 61/16 of 20 November 2006,

Welcoming the decision by the General Assembly, contained in its resolution 62/187, that the Follow-up International Conference on Financing for Development to Review the Implementation of the Monterrey Consensus will be held in Doha from 29 November to 2 December 2008,

Welcoming also the ongoing preparatory process for the Review Conference, in accordance with Assembly resolution 62/187,

Noting the holding of the High-level Dialogue on Financing for Development in New York, from 23 to 25 October 2007,

Welcoming the first session of the Development Cooperation Forum, held in New York on 30 June and 1 July 2008,

1. *Takes note* of the summary by the President of the Economic and Social Council of the special high-level meeting of the Council with the Bretton Woods institutions, the World Trade Organization and the United Nations Conference on Trade and Development, held in New York on 14 April 2008, and of the note by the Secretary-General on coherence, coordination and cooperation in the context of the implementation of the Monterrey Consensus of the International Conference on Financing for Development, including new challenges and emerging issues, prepared in collaboration with the major institutional stakeholders and other relevant organizations of the United Nations system;

2. *Requests* the President of the Council, with the support of the Financing for Development Office of the Department of Economic and Social Affairs of the Secretariat, to undertake consultations, including with all major institutional stakeholders, on the role of the Council in the implementation of the Monterrey Consensus following the outcome of the Doha Review Conference, and to report thereon to the Council at its organizational session for 2009.

Report of Secretary-General. In response to General Assembly resolution 62/187 [YUN 2007, p. 992], the Secretary-General submitted a 28 July report [A/63/179] on the latest developments related to the review process on financing for development and the implementation of the Monterrey Consensus that outlined the main developments under each of the six thematic chapter headings of the Consensus (see p. 1072). The report noted the renewed interest in addressing the negative impact of illicit capital flows on domestic resource mobilization. In a special event hosted by Norway at UN Headquarters on 14 February, it was estimated that at least two thirds of illegal international transfers of funds were motivated by tax evasion and the other third by efforts to conceal the proceeds of illegal activities such as drug trade or terrorism financing. At the Technical Group meeting of the Initiative against Hunger and Poverty (Madrid, Spain, 23 May), the importance of an agreement to consider tax evasion as a corrupt practice among countries signatory to the United Nations Convention against Corruption was also highlighted. A working group led by Norway on the development impact of illicit capital flows identified the need to expand cooperation in tax evasion, and referred to the work of the UN Committee of Experts on International Cooperation in Tax Matters and to a proposal to upgrade it to a full intergovernmental body. In the long run, a sustained increase in the revenue capability of the public sector and diversification of the tax base would be critical for mobilizing resources for development and meeting the internationally agreed development goals. Attention was also drawn to the persistence of gender inequalities in labour markets, credit markets and assets distribution. The Commission on the Status of Women, at its fifty-second session (New York, 25 February–7 March) (see p. 1278), called for the strengthening of the Monterrey Consensus regarding gender equality issues, including financing for gender equality. To achieve gender equality, better understanding of the role of women in development was needed, beyond that as caregivers and labourers, and macroeconomic policies should be more coherent with other policies.

In terms of mobilizing international resources for development, the report stated that over the previous five years, buoyed by strong economic growth and improved macroeconomic fundamentals, as well as improvements in investment in many developing countries, global flows of private investment had grown significantly. During the review session on chapter II of the Monterrey Consensus (15 February), it was noted that while there had been a rising trend since 1970, private flows to developing countries were characterized by boom-bust cycles. UNCTAD data showed that FDI inflows remained the single largest component of private resource flows to developing countries and amounted to almost $500 billion in 2007, with a significant part involving South-South investment among developing countries. Through risk mitigation and capacity-building, MDB's and bilateral donors could help broaden FDI flows to a wider range of countries, including LDCs, landlocked developing countries and small island developing States, and relevant multilateral, regional and national institutions could review functions and instruments that allowed them to mitigate the risks facing foreign investors in developing country infrastructure projects. The review session acknowledged the importance of mechanisms to mitigate regulatory risk, increase the role of multilateral and regional development banks in risk mitigation by increasing leverage for their guarantees, and strengthen local currency lending. South-South flows were important in inward FDI to many LDCs, and it was acknowledged that those flows should be facilitated, especially as investors from the South possessed certain advantages when operating in other developing countries. The possibilities for supporting them should also be explored in the context of South-South-North triangular cooperation and collaboration among developing country institutions.

As to international trade as an engine for development, it was acknowledged that more open trade was, by itself, not a guarantee of development and poverty reduction, and that developing countries needed time to enhance their productive capabilities to take advantage of the opportunities from increased market access and to minimize the costs of adjustment entailed by trade reforms and losses in preferential access. In that regard, they also needed access to technology at an affordable price, infrastructure investment and human resource development, an enabling domestic environment for private investment and innovation, and appropriate social safety nets. It was also noted that developing countries needed adequate policy space to manage their trade, financial and development policies in line with their national development priorities and strategies.

With regard to increasing international financial and technical cooperation, both the Assembly review session (New York, 14–16 April) and the first Economic and Social Council Development Cooperation Forum (see p. 902) deliberated on the mixed progress in international development cooperation since 2002. While some donors were meeting, and others surpassing, their commitments in delivering aid, aggregate aid flows from OECD/DAC countries as a whole had fallen significantly short of overall targets. On the other hand, new sources of aid money had proliferated, notably from the assistance programmes of other developing countries and private foundations, although data from non-traditional donors (bilateral and private) were imprecise. It was estimated that new sources currently contributed roughly one fourth of global aid flows. The importance of providing public resources for development was also highlighted. Since ODA provided the resources that would otherwise not be forthcoming from the private sector, the fall-off in resources for development constituted both a political challenge and a developmental threat. Development-oriented assistance normally required many years of predictable funding, preferably through budget support based on strategies identified by national policymakers. The discussions in the review session and the Development Cooperation Forum noted that the Monterrey Consensus had brought together donors and recipients to form a global development cooperation partnership for the first time. The report noted that developing countries that were signatories to, or affected by, the principles of the Paris Declaration were not all members of OECD or even the DAC Working Party on Aid Effectiveness, and that there was an imbalance in development cooperation if recipients were not partners in influencing cooperation guidelines, including in international financial institutions.

In the review session on aid, there was a discussion on the establishment of a peer review process to evaluate aid programmes in order to help address that imbalance. A peer review mechanism could also play an important role in setting guidelines on the use of conditionality to ensure aid effectiveness.

The progress achieved in its many aspects provided the starting point for the Assembly review session on external debt (10–11 March). Since the adoption of the Monterrey Consensus, debt indicators had improved, aided by a confluence of factors, notably the most recent years of low international interest rates and rapid growth in developing countries underpinned by strong export growth. Most developing countries had debt management programmes in place and had built up reserves, thus reducing vulnerability. The prepayment of debt by many developing countries, as well as debt relief for many low-income countries and sizeable debt reductions in countries such as Iraq and Nigeria, contributed to a stable scenario and pointed towards the possibilities for establishing a positive developmental role for external debt. Despite those developments, the review session also examined the obstacles to ensuring debt sustainability and making progress towards the MDGs. The risk of debt distress remained for more than half of the post-completion-point HIPCs; highlighted was the importance of strengthened debt management capacity and the possibility of the joint Bank-Fund Debt Sustainability Framework as a coordination point for creditors. Commercial debt buy-backs complementary to THE debt relief operations of HIPCs and executed by their Governments had been applied to extinguish eligible commercial debt and prevent costly and unjust litigation against those countries. National laws in the major financial centres provided the bases for those lawsuits. The potential profitability of "vulture litigation" also derived from the fact that none of the existing mechanisms provided a guarantee of equivalent treatment to non-participating creditors. There was also a discussion on the non-participation of new creditors in the Paris Club and the difficulty of their inclusion in a body whose procedures had been set previously. Those procedures could be seen as constituting a de facto "court of creditors" with power to make judgements on creditor claims and debt servicing, and thus contravened commonly held principles that decisions be made by an impartial agent.

The review session on addressing systemic issues (11–12 March) discussed the challenges in supporting more effective functioning and coordination of the international financial architecture and the economic aspects of global governance. The international community's attention had been focused on the challenge of crafting policy responses to financial system weaknesses posed by the financial turmoil. Those responses were spawning additional challenges in adapting the governance structures of the international institutions and other global decision-making bodies. A process of financial rehabilitation had begun, as well as measures to address the underlying causes of the disruptions. The final report of the Financial Stability Forum, presented on 11 April and endorsed by the G-7 and the International Monetary and Financial Committee, set out policy recommendations in prudential oversight of capital, liquidity and risk management; transparency, disclosure and valuation policies; the role and uses of credit ratings; and the authorities' responsiveness to risks and their arrangements to deal with stress in the financial system. In response to the financial crisis and as a key element in sustaining efficient investment processes during the recovery, the process of strengthening domestic regulatory frameworks over financial markets was accelerating. On 31 March, the United States Treasury initiated that process, and parallel efforts were undertaken in the United Kingdom and other European economies. During the spring meeting of the Bretton Woods institutions, many participants highlighted the international impact of national financial regulatory policies and standards, which affected the access of developing countries to external finance. It was therefore important for developing countries to have a secure voice in the design of future financial regulatory frameworks. In June, credit rating agencies signed an agreement with the New York State Attorney-General setting new standards and guidelines governing how to evaluate investments backed by risky mortgage debt. In July, the United States Federal Reserve indicated that it would issue new lending rules to regulate exotic mortgages and sub-prime loans, and the Securities and Exchange Commission proposed restricting the short selling of stocks of financial companies. Those developments put a spotlight on how a process of re-regulation, heightened disclosure requirements and enhanced public sector oversight over financial markets had started in various locations, and on the potential flaws of unilateral, uncoordinated regulatory reform. In the review session on systemic issues, participants highlighted the changed economic context since the Monterrey Conference, as well as the heightened pressure to update international public oversight and governance structures to make them consistent with the global economic structure. Developing economies had become a much larger proportion of the global economy, and the size and complexity of international private markets in trade and finance had challenged the monitoring and financial capabilities of international public institutions. Many of the more successful developing economies had built up their own reserves as self-insurance against vulnerabilities stemming from private markets. In that context, members of the international community stressed that the governance regime of the international financial institutions was in need of significant reforms to increase the voice of developing countries. Renewed calls were also made to strengthen the intergovernmental follow-up mechanisms to the Monterrey and Doha Conferences and to maintain the UN partnership with the other major institutional stakeholders. In that regard, it was noted that any mechanism had to be effective, inclusive and transparent in view of the need to sustain the "Monterrey spirit" in a follow-up to the Monterrey Consensus and the agreements to be reached at the upcoming Doha Conference (see below). It was also pointed out that the follow-up of the International Conference on Financing for Development should ensure a continuing multi-stakeholder and multi-sector approach and build on the experiences and lessons learned, including strengthening of the interface with the Bretton Woods institutions, with a view to promoting a results-oriented framework for consultations and substantive dialogue, which would secure a larger opportunity for representatives of Bretton Woods institutions to voice their views.

Follow-up International Conference on Financing for Development to Review Implementation of the Monterrey Consensus

The Follow-up International Conference on Financing for Development to Review the Implementation of the Monterrey Consensus was held in Doha, Qatar, from 29 November to 2 December [A/CONF.212/7], in conformity with General Assembly resolution 62/187 [YUN 2007, p. 992] and **decision 63/509** of 18 November. The Conference was attended by 171 Member States, the European Community, the Holy See and Palestine, as well as 4 regional commissions, 12 UN bodies, funds and programmes, 9 specialized agencies and related organizations, 18 intergovernmental organizations, the Inter-Parliamentary Union and representatives of a large number of business entities and organizations and non-governmental organizations (NGOs). The work was organized around eight plenary sessions and six interactive multi-stakeholder round tables under the overall theme "Looking ahead: further cooperative actions in financing for development". The thematic areas considered by the round tables were: mobilizing domestic financial resources for development; mobilizing international resources for development: FDI and other private flows; international trade as an engine for development; increasing international financial and technical cooperation for development; external debt; and addressing systemic issues: enhancing the coherence and consistency of the international monetary, financial and trading systems in support of development.

Parallel and associated events included the Global Civil Society Forum (26–27 November) held under the theme "Investing in people-centred development"; an International Business Forum (28 November), which considered "The impact of the financial crisis and proposed road maps: mobilizing private-sector resources for development"; and a Parliamentary Hearing (28 November), at which members of parliament evaluated the implementation of the Monterrey Consensus and discussed new challenges and emerging issues.

In his address to the Conference, the Secretary-General said that the global financial crisis had brought an abrupt end to a long era of global growth, and compounded other major threats, such as climate change, food insecurity and the persistence of extreme poverty. If not handled properly, the crisis would become tomorrow's human crisis. The emergency G-20 summit in November (see p. 1068) showed that Governments were deeply concerned and trying to coordinate their actions. Fiscal measures had to be bold, decisive and strongly coordinated. To promote that coordination, a bridge should be built between the G-20 and the rest of the world—the full membership of the United Nations. That bridge should stand on the three pillars of cooperation, sustainability and inclusive governance. The Secretary-General affirmed that the Monterrey Consensus was a major achievement, opening a new era of cooperation that bridged the old North-South divide. The Monterrey vision, if faithfully implemented, could be a path out of the current predicament. The Secretary-General discussed six aspects of development financing. Concerning the first aspect, liquidity, he said that while the wealthiest nations had moved to keep credit flowing at home, efforts should be made to ensure that developing countries could do so as well. Additional emergency financing from IMF, the World Bank and other sources was needed; if not, the credit crisis would spread to emerging economies. As to the second aspect, the MDGs, an increase in grants and long-term lending should be part of the response and donors should hold to their pledges of assistance. Concerning the third aspect, climate change and green growth, he called for a rededication to fighting climate change as part of the solution to the economic downturn. Investments in green technologies would yield pay-offs in the long term for a safer environment and more sustainable growth. The fourth aspect, debt relief, called for stepped-up programmes for the poorest nations so that a greater number of them could benefit. That burden would only weigh more heavily in the current climate, impeding investment and Government spending that might otherwise contribute to growth and economic development. Concerning the fifth aspect, mobilizing local resources, he said that in the new climate, financing for development would come increasingly from within, and Governments should develop new ways to raise revenues, while encouraging domestic firms to make productive investments. Specifically, more international cooperation was needed to minimize harmful tax competition and stem the loss of tax revenues, particularly in resource-rich nations. The sixth aspect, protectionism, required renewed commitment to ensure a development outcome for the Doha round of multilateral trade negotiations and to see the Doha trade round revived and concluded as soon as possible.

Summaries of the plenary meetings and the round-table discussions were contained in a Secretariat note [A/CONF.212/6 & Add.1–7]. The Assembly President submitted the draft outcome document of the Conference [A/CONF.212/3/Rev.1], which the Conference adopted on 2 December as resolution 1, containing in its annex the Doha Declaration on Financing for Development: outcome document of the Follow-up Conference on Financing for Development (see below).

In other action, the Conference expressed its appreciation to Qatar for hosting the Conference (resolution 2) and approved the report of the Credentials Committee (resolution 3).

GENERAL ASSEMBLY ACTION

On 19 December [meeting 72], the General Assembly, on the recommendation of the Second Committee [A/63/413 (Part II)], adopted **resolution 63/208** without vote [agenda item 48].

Follow-up International Conference on Financing for Development to Review the Implementation of the Monterrey Consensus

The General Assembly,

Recalling the International Conference on Financing for Development, held in Monterrey, Mexico, from 18 to 22 March 2002, and its resolutions 56/210 B of 9 July 2002, 57/250 of 20 December 2002, 57/270 B of 23 June 2003, 57/272 and 57/273 of 20 December 2002, 58/230 of 23 December 2003, 59/225 of 22 December 2004, 60/188 of 22 December 2005, 61/191 of 20 December 2006 and 62/187 of 19 December 2007, as well as Economic and Social Council resolutions 2002/34 of 26 July 2002, 2003/47 of 24 July 2003, 2004/64 of 16 September 2004, 2006/45 of 28 July 2006, 2007/30 of 27 July 2007 and 2008/14 of 24 July 2008,

Recalling also the 2005 World Summit Outcome,

Recalling further its resolution 60/265 of 30 June 2006 on the follow-up to the development outcome of the 2005 World Summit, including the Millennium Development Goals and the other internationally agreed development goals, and its resolution 61/16 of 20 November 2006 on the strengthening of the Economic and Social Council,

Taking note of the report of the Secretary-General,

Taking note also of the summary by the President of the General Assembly of the High-level Dialogue on Financing for Development, held in New York from 23 to 25 October 2007,

Taking note further of the summary by the President of the Economic and Social Council of the special high-level meeting of the Council with the Bretton Woods institutions, the World Trade Organization and the United Nations Conference on Trade and Development, held in New York on 14 April 2008,

Welcoming with appreciation the efforts undertaken by the Government of Qatar to organize the Follow-up International Conference on Financing for Development to Review the Implementation of the Monterrey Consensus,

Welcoming the work undertaken by the President of the General Assembly during the sixty-second session of the Assembly, by means of direct intergovernmental consultations of the whole, with the participation of all Member States and the major institutional stakeholders involved in the financing for development process, on all issues related to the Review Conference, and taking note of the summaries of those consultations,

1. *Notes* the deliberations held in the context of the preparatory process for the Follow-up International Conference on Financing for Development to Review the Implementation of the Monterrey Consensus, held in Doha from 29 November to 2 December 2008;

2. *Stresses* the importance of continued discussions on the issue of financing for development;

3. *Requests* the Secretary-General to report to the General Assembly at its sixty-fourth session on the progress made in the implementation of the Monterrey Consensus of the International Conference on Financing for Development;

4. *Decides* to include in the provisional agenda of its sixty-fourth session an item entitled "Follow-up to and implementation of the outcome of the 2002 International Conference on Financing for Development and the 2008 Review Conference".

On 24 December [meeting 74], the General Assembly adopted **resolution 63/239** [draft: A/63/L.57] without vote [agenda item 48].

Doha Declaration on Financing for Development: outcome document of the Follow-up International Conference on Financing for Development to Review the Implementation of the Monterrey Consensus

The General Assembly,

Taking note of the Follow-up International Conference on Financing for Development to Review the Implementation of the Monterrey Consensus, held in Doha from 29 November to 2 December 2008, and the adoption by the Conference of the Doha Declaration on Financing for Development,

1. *Expresses its profound gratitude* to the State of Qatar for hosting the Follow-up International Conference on Financing for Development to Review the Implementation of the Monterrey Consensus and for providing all the necessary support;

2. *Decides* to endorse the Doha Declaration on Financing for Development: outcome document of the Follow-up International Conference on Financing for Development to Review the Implementation of the Monterrey Consensus, which is annexed to the present resolution.

Annex

Doha Declaration on Financing for Development: outcome document of the Follow-up International Conference on Financing for Development to Review the Implementation of the Monterrey Consensus

Introduction

Reaffirming the goals and commitments of the Monterrey Consensus

1. We, Heads of State and Government and High Representatives, gathered in Doha, Qatar, from 29 November to 2 December 2008, almost seven years after the landmark International Conference on Financing for Development, held in Monterrey, Mexico, reiterate our resolve to take concrete action to implement the Monterrey Consensus and address the challenges of financing for development in the spirit of global partnership and solidarity. We once again commit ourselves to eradicate poverty, achieve sustained economic growth and promote sustainable development as we advance to a fully inclusive and equitable global economic system.

2. We reaffirm the Monterrey Consensus in its entirety, in its integrity and holistic approach, and recognize that mobilizing financial resources for development and the effective use of all those resources are central to the global partnership for sustainable development, including in support of the achievement of the internationally agreed development goals, including the Millennium Development Goals. We also reaffirm the importance of freedom, peace and security, respect for all human rights, including the right to development, the rule of law, gender equality and an overall commitment to just and democratic societies for development, as spelled out in the Monterrey Consensus. We reiterate that each country has primary responsibility for its own economic and social development and that the role of national policies, domestic resources and development strategies cannot be overemphasized. At the same time, domestic economies are now interwoven with the global economic system and, inter alia, the effective use of trade and investment opportunities can help countries to fight poverty. National development efforts need to be supported by an enabling international economic environment.

3. We recognize that the international context has changed in profound ways since we met in Monterrey. There has been progress in some areas, but inequality has widened. We welcome the substantial increase in public and private flows since 2002, which has contributed to higher economic growth in most developing countries and a reduction in global poverty rates. Yet we express our deep concern that the international community is now challenged by the severe impact on development of multiple, interrelated global crises and challenges, such as increased food insecurity, volatile energy and commodity prices, climate change and a global financial crisis, as well as the lack of results so far in the multilateral trade negotiations and a loss of confidence in the international economic system. While acknowledging the response of the international community to these crises and challenges to date, such as the High-level Conference on World Food Security, held in Rome from 3 to 5 June 2008, and the recent Summit on Financial Markets and the World Economy, held in Washington, D.C., on 15 November 2008, we are determined to take immediate and decisive actions and initiatives to overcome all these obstacles and challenges through achievement of people-centred development and to devise important measures for the full, effective and timely implementation of the Monterrey Consensus.

4. We recall that gender equality is a basic human right, a fundamental value and an issue of social justice; it is essential for economic growth, poverty reduction, environmental sustainability and development effectiveness. We reiterate the need for gender mainstreaming into the formulation and implementation of development policies, including financing for development policies, and for dedicated resources. We commit ourselves to increasing our efforts to fulfil our commitments regarding gender equality and the empowerment of women.

5. The spectre of terrorism continues to haunt us and is on the rise. This has serious implications for economic development and social cohesion, apart from its horrific human misery. We resolve to act together stronger than ever to address terrorism in all its forms and manifestations.

6. We reaffirm the political declaration on "Africa's development needs: state of implementation of various commitments, challenges and the way forward", adopted at the high-level meeting of the General Assembly on 22 September 2008. We further reaffirm our commitment to provide and strengthen support to the special needs of Africa and stress that eradicating poverty, particularly in Africa, is the greatest global challenge facing the world today. We underline the importance of accelerating sustainable broad-based economic growth, which is pivotal to bringing Africa into the mainstream of the global economy. We reaffirm the commitment of all States to establish a monitoring mechanism to follow up on all commitments related to the development of Africa as contained in the political declaration on "Africa's development needs". All commitments to and by Africa should be effectively implemented and given appropriate follow-up by the international community and Africa itself. We underscore the urgency of addressing the special needs of Africa based on a partnership among equals.

7. We welcome the decision to convene the Fourth United Nations Conference on the Least Developed Countries at a high level in 2011.

Mobilizing domestic financial resources for development

8. In the years following the Monterrey Conference, a number of developing countries have made significant progress in the implementation of development policies in key areas of their economic frameworks, often contributing to increased mobilization of domestic resources and higher levels of economic growth. We will continue to build upon this progress by promoting inclusive and equitable growth, eradicating poverty and pursuing sustainable development in its economic, social and environmental dimensions, and by ensuring the necessary enabling environment for mobilizing public and private resources and expanding productive investments. Greater efforts are required to support the creation and sustenance of a conducive environment through appropriate national and international actions.

9. We reaffirm that national ownership and leadership of development strategies and good governance are

important for effective mobilization of domestic financial resources and fostering sustained economic growth and sustainable development. In this context, we should take into account the different characteristics and specificities of each country.

10. We recognize that a dynamic, inclusive well-functioning and socially responsible private sector is a valuable instrument for generating economic growth and reducing poverty. In order to foster private-sector development, we shall endeavour to promote an enabling environment that facilitates entrepreneurship and doing business by all, including women, the poor and the vulnerable. The international community, national Governments and regional economic groups should continue to support these efforts.

11. We will continue to pursue appropriate policy and regulatory frameworks at our respective national levels and in a manner consistent with national laws to encourage public and private initiatives, including at the local level, and to foster a dynamic and well-functioning business sector, while improving income growth and distribution, raising productivity, empowering women and protecting labour rights and the environment. We recognize that the appropriate role of Government in market-oriented economies will vary from country to country.

12. Human development remains a key priority, and human resources are the most precious and valuable asset that countries possess. The realization of full and productive employment and decent work for all is essential. We will continue to invest in human capital through inclusive social policies, inter alia, on health and education, in accordance with national strategies. The provision of, and access to, financial and credit services to all is also important. Such facilities have begun to show results, but increased efforts, where appropriate, supported by the international community, are needed. We stress the importance of fostering diverse local and supporting industries that create productive employment and strengthen local communities. We will strive to ensure social security systems that protect the vulnerable in particular.

13. To advance towards the goals of the Monterrey Consensus, policies that link economic and social considerations are required to reduce inequalities within and among countries and guarantee that the poor and vulnerable groups benefit from economic growth and development. Measures aimed at integrating the poor into productive activities, investing in the development of their labour skills and facilitating their entry into the labour market are necessary. In this regard, greater efforts are required for mobilizing more resources, as appropriate, to provide universal access to basic economic and social infrastructure and inclusive social services, as well as capacity-building, taking special care of women, children, older persons and persons with disabilities in order to enhance their social protection.

14. The increasing interdependence of national economies in a globalizing world and the emergence of rules-based regimes for international economic relations have meant that the space for national economic policy, that is, the scope for domestic policies, especially in the areas of trade, investment and international development, is now often framed by international disciplines, commitments and global market considerations. It is for each Government to evaluate the trade-off between the benefits of accepting international rules and commitments and the constraints posed by the loss of policy space.

15. We reiterate that macroeconomic policies should be aimed at sustaining high rates of economic growth, full employment, poverty eradication, and low and stable inflation, and seek to minimize domestic and external imbalances to ensure that the benefits of growth reach all people, especially the poor. They should also attach high priority to avoiding abrupt economic fluctuations that negatively affect income distribution and resource allocation. In this context, the scope for appropriate counter-cyclical policies to preserve economic and financial stability should be expanded. Public investment, consistent with medium- and long-term fiscal sustainability, may have a proactive role and encourage a virtuous cycle of investment.

16. We will continue to undertake fiscal reform, including tax reform, which is key to enhancing macroeconomic policies and mobilizing domestic public resources. We will also continue to improve budgetary processes and to enhance the transparency of public financial management and the quality of expenditures. We will step up efforts to enhance tax revenues through modernized tax systems, more efficient tax collection, broadening the tax base and effectively combating tax evasion. We will undertake these efforts with an overarching view to make tax systems more pro-poor. While each country is responsible for its tax system, it is important to support national efforts in these areas by strengthening technical assistance and enhancing international cooperation and participation in addressing international tax matters, including in the area of double taxation. In this regard, we acknowledge the need to further promote international cooperation in tax matters, and request the Economic and Social Council to examine the strengthening of institutional arrangements, including the United Nations Committee of Experts on International Cooperation in Tax Matters.

17. The development of a sound and broad-based financial sector is central to the mobilization of domestic financial resources and should be an important component of national development strategies. We will strive for diversified, well-regulated, inclusive financial systems that promote savings and channel them to sound growth-generating projects. We will further refine, as appropriate, the supervisory and regulatory mechanisms to enhance the transparency and accountability of the financial sector. We will aim to increase the domestic supply of long-term capital and promote the development of domestic capital markets, including through multilateral, regional, subregional and national development banks.

18. To achieve equitable development and foster a vibrant economy, it is vital to have a financial infrastructure that provides access to a variety of sustainable products and services for micro-, small- and medium-sized businesses, with particular emphasis on women, rural populations and the poor. We will make sure that the benefits of growth reach all people by empowering individuals and communities and by improving access to services in the fields of finance and credit. We recognize that microfinance, including microcredit, has proven to be effective in generating productive self-employment, which can contribute to the achievement of the internationally agreed development goals, including the Millennium Development Goals.

Despite some progress, there is widespread demand for microfinance. We underline the need to appropriately support, in a coordinated manner, the efforts of developing countries, including in capacity-building for their microfinance, including microcredit institutions.

19. Gender equality and women's empowerment are essential to achieve equitable and effective development and to foster a vibrant economy. We reaffirm our commitment to eliminate gender-based discrimination in all its forms, including in the labour and financial markets, as well as, inter alia, in the ownership of assets and property rights. We will promote women's rights, including their economic empowerment, and effectively mainstream gender in law reforms, business support services and economic programmes, and give women full and equal access to economic resources. We will further promote and reinforce capacity-building of State and other stakeholders in gender-responsive public management, including, but not limited to, gender budgeting.

20. Capital flight, where it occurs, is a major hindrance to the mobilization of domestic resources for development. We will strengthen national and multilateral efforts to address the various factors that contribute to it. It is vital to address the problem of illicit financial flows, especially money-laundering. Additional measures should be implemented to prevent the transfer abroad of stolen assets and to assist in the recovery and return of such assets, in particular to their countries of origin, consistent with the United Nations Convention against Corruption, as well as to prevent capital flows that have criminal intent. We note the efforts of the United Nations Office on Drugs and Crime and the World Bank Group through the Stolen Asset Recovery Initiative and other relevant initiatives. In this regard, we urge as a matter of priority all States that have not yet done so to consider becoming parties to the International Convention for the Suppression of the Financing of Terrorism, and call for increased cooperation with the same objective.

21. The ongoing fight against corruption at all levels is a priority. Progress among countries has varied since 2002. Corruption affects both developed and developing countries, and both the public and private sectors. We are thus determined to take urgent and decisive steps to continue to combat corruption in all of its manifestations in order to reduce obstacles to effective resource mobilization and allocation and avoid the diversion of resources away from activities that are vital for development. This requires strong institutions at all levels, including, in particular, effective legal and judicial systems and enhanced transparency. We welcome the increased commitment of States that have already ratified or acceded to the United Nations Convention against Corruption, and, in this regard, urge all States that have not yet done so to consider ratifying or acceding to the Convention. We call upon all States parties to fully implement the Convention without delay and to work jointly in the establishment of a mechanism for follow-up on implementation of the Convention.

22. While the pursuit of economic resilience is important for all countries, it requires constant and more concerted efforts in small and vulnerable economies. These national efforts need to be reinforced by international support for capacity-building, including through financial and technical assistance, and United Nations operational activities for development in accordance with national development strategies and priorities. In development cooperation policies, we will pay special attention to the efforts and specific needs of Africa, the least developed countries, landlocked developing countries and small island developing States. Similarly, special and sustained attention is needed to support post-conflict countries in their rebuilding and development efforts.

Mobilizing international resources for development: foreign direct investment and other private flows

23. We recognize that private international capital flows, particularly foreign direct investment, are vital complements to national and international development efforts. We appreciate the rise in private international capital flows to developing countries since the Monterrey Conference and the improvements in business climates that have helped to encourage it. However, we take note with concern that a significant number of developing countries have not experienced a rise in private international capital flows. We will seek to enhance such flows to support development. In this context, we will strengthen national, bilateral and multilateral efforts to assist developing countries in overcoming the structural or other constraints which currently limit their attractiveness as a destination for private capital and foreign direct investment. To that end, we acknowledge the need to particularly assist those countries that have been at a particular disadvantage in attracting such flows, including a number of African countries, least developed countries, landlocked developing countries, small island developing States and countries emerging from conflict or recovering from natural disasters. Such efforts could include the provision of technical, financial and other forms of assistance; the promotion and strengthening of partnerships, including public-private partnerships; and cooperation arrangements at all levels.

24. We will enhance efforts to mobilize investments from all sources in human resources, transport, energy, communications, information technology and other physical, environmental, institutional and social infrastructure that serve to strengthen the business environment, enhance competitiveness and expand trade in developing countries and economies in transition. We recognize the need for bilateral and multilateral partners to provide technical assistance and share best practices relating to these efforts. The programmes, mechanisms and instruments at the disposal of multilateral development agencies and bilateral donors can be used for encouraging business investment, including by contributing to mitigating some of the risks faced by private investors in critical sectors in developing and transition economies. Official development assistance (ODA) and other mechanisms, such as, inter alia, guarantees and public-private partnerships, can play a catalytic role in mobilizing private flows. At the same time, multilateral and regional development banks should continue to explore innovative modalities with developing countries, including low- and middle-income countries and countries with economies in transition, so as to facilitate additional private flows to such countries.

25. Experience has shown that providing an enabling domestic and international investment climate is fundamental to fostering domestic and foreign private investment. Countries need to continue their efforts to achieve a stable and predictable investment climate, with proper

contract enforcement and respect for property rights. We will continue to put in place transparent and appropriate regulations at the national and international levels. Efforts should be enhanced to upgrade the skills and technical capabilities of human resources, improve the availability of finance for enterprise, facilitate public-private consultative mechanisms and promote corporate social responsibility. Bilateral investment treaties may promote private flows by increasing legal stability and predictability to investors. It is important that bilateral investment treaties, as well as tax treaties and other tax measures to facilitate foreign investments, take into account regional and multilateral cooperation, including at the regional level. We acknowledge the importance of supporting capacity-building in developing countries aimed at improving their abilities to negotiate mutually beneficial investment agreements. It is important to promote good tax practices and avoid inappropriate ones.

26. To complement national efforts, there is a need for the relevant international and regional institutions, as well as appropriate institutions in source countries, to increase their support for private foreign investment in infrastructure development and other priority areas, including projects to bridge the digital divide in developing countries and countries with economies in transition. To this end, it is important to provide export credits, co-financing, venture capital and other lending instruments, risk guarantees, leveraging aid resources, information on investment opportunities, business development services, forums to facilitate business contacts and cooperation between enterprises of developed and developing countries, as well as funding for feasibility studies. Inter-enterprise partnership is a powerful means for the transfer and dissemination of technology. In this regard, strengthening the multilateral and regional financial and development institutions is desirable. Additional source country measures should also be devised to encourage and facilitate investment flows to developing countries.

27. We recognize that the development impact of foreign direct investment should be maximized. We further recognize that the transfer of technology and business skills is a key channel through which foreign direct investment can positively impact development. We will strengthen national and international efforts aimed at maximizing linkages with domestic production activities, enhancing the transfer of technology and creating training opportunities for the local labour force, including women and young people. It is also important to enact and uphold, as appropriate, labour and environmental protection and anti-corruption laws and regulations in accordance with obligations undertaken in relevant international conventions. We welcome efforts to promote corporate social responsibility and good corporate governance. In this regard, we encourage the work undertaken at the national level and by the United Nations, including through the United Nations Global Compact, and the promotion of internationally agreed corporate social responsibility frameworks, such as the International Labour Organization Tripartite Declaration. We reaffirm that every State has, and shall freely exercise full permanent sovereignty over, all its wealth, natural resources and economic activity. We support measures to enhance corporate transparency and accountability of all companies, taking into account the fundamental principles of domestic law. We take note of voluntary initiatives in this regard, including, inter alia, the Extractive Industries Transparency Initiative.

28. We realize that the perception of a country's current economic conditions and prospects influences the international private financial flows that it attracts. The provision of objective, high-quality information from all sources, including private and public entities, such as national statistical agencies, the International Monetary Fund (IMF), the World Bank, the United Nations system, investment advisers and credit-rating agencies, is vital for informed decisions by potential domestic and foreign investors alike. We will continue to strengthen modalities, including through the efforts of the country itself, the United Nations system and relevant multilateral agencies, to enhance and improve the level and objectivity of information regarding a country's economic situation and outlook.

29. Remittances have become significant private financial resources for households in countries of origin of migration. Remittances cannot be considered as a substitute for foreign direct investment, ODA, debt relief or other public sources of finance for development. They are typically wages transferred to families, mainly to meet part of the needs of the recipient households. The manner of their disposal or deployment is an individual choice. A large portion of migrants' incomes is spent in destination countries and constitutes an important stimulus to domestic demand in their economies. In this regard, we will strengthen existing measures to lower the transaction costs of remittances through increased cooperation between originating and receiving countries and create opportunities for development-oriented investments.

International trade as an engine for development

30. We reaffirm that international trade is an engine for development and sustained economic growth. We also reaffirm that a universal, rules-based, open, non-discriminatory and equitable multilateral trading system, as well as meaningful trade liberalization, can substantially stimulate development worldwide, benefiting all countries at all stages of development. We are encouraged that international trade, especially the trade of developing countries as a group, has expanded at a fast pace in the current decade. Trade among developing countries has now become one of the most dynamic elements in world trade. However, many developing countries, in particular the least developed countries, have remained at the margins of these developments and their trade capacity needs to be enhanced to enable them to exploit more effectively the potential of trade to support their development. We also reaffirm our commitment to meaningful trade liberalization and to ensure that trade plays its full part in promoting economic growth, employment and development for all. We recall our commitment in the Monterrey Consensus to the decisions of the World Trade Organization to place the needs and interests of developing countries at the heart of its work programme and to implement its recommendations.

31. A well-functioning multilateral trading system can bring benefits to all and can contribute to enhancing the integration of the developing countries in the system, in particular the least developed countries. We reiterate our urgent resolve to ensure that the ongoing efforts to improve the operation of the multilateral trading system to better re-

spond to the needs and interests of all developing countries, in particular the least developed countries. This is particularly important at a time when the systemic impact of the financial crisis is affecting us all. We call for the implementation of the ministerial declaration of the World Trade Organization adopted at its Sixth Ministerial Conference, held in Hong Kong, China, from 13 to 18 December 2005, on the central importance of the development dimension in every aspect of the Doha Development Agenda work programme and its commitment to making the development dimension a meaningful reality. We emphasize that maximizing the benefits and minimizing the costs of international trade liberalization calls for development-oriented and coherent policies at all levels.

32. We are very concerned that, despite significant efforts, the Doha Development Agenda round of multilateral trade negotiations has not yet been concluded. A successful result should support the expansion in the exports of developing countries, reinforce the potential for trade to play its due role as the engine of growth and development, and provide increased opportunities for developing countries to use trade to support development. It is important to make progress in key areas of the Doha Development Agenda of special interest to developing countries, such as those outlined in paragraph 28 of the Monterrey Consensus, reaffirming the importance of special and differential treatment referred to therein. To this end, flexibility and political will are essential. We welcome recent commitments concerning trade and the critical importance of rejecting protectionism and not turning inward in times of financial uncertainty, especially as this might particularly affect developing countries. On this basis, we will urgently re-engage and strive to reach agreement by the end of the year on modalities that lead to a successful and early conclusion to the World Trade Organization Doha Development Agenda with an ambitious, balanced and development-oriented outcome.

33. We acknowledge that the optimum pace and sequence of trade liberalization depends on the specific circumstances of each country, and that each country will make this decision based on its own evaluation of the costs and benefits. Trade liberalization must be complemented by appropriate action and strategies at the national level for the expansion of productive capacities, the development of human resources and basic infrastructure, the absorption of technology and the implementation of adequate social safety nets. Achieving the positive impact of trade liberalization on developing countries will also depend to a significant extent on international support for the above measures and actions against policies and practices that distort trade.

34. We recognize the particular challenges faced by least developed countries in integrating beneficially into the international trading system. We acknowledge that least developed countries require special measures and international support to benefit fully from world trade, as well as in adjusting to and integrating beneficially into the global economy. We welcome the decision at the Sixth World Trade Organization Ministerial Conference, held in Hong Kong, China, from 13 to 18 December 2005, on improved market access for least developed countries as set out in the decision and its annex, and call for its full implementation. We also welcome the actions taken by some individual countries since Monterrey towards the goal of full duty-free and quota-free market access for all least developed countries, and call upon other developed and developing countries declaring themselves in a position to do so to take steps towards this objective. We will also reinforce efforts to provide technical assistance to least developed countries that request it in order to enable them to participate more effectively in the multilateral trading system, including through the effective operation of the Enhanced Integrated Framework for Trade-related Technical Assistance to Least Developed Countries and by providing support to allow them to participate effectively in international trade negotiations.

35. We also recognize the particular challenges that may be faced by other developing countries, including small and vulnerable economies, to fully benefit from the multilateral trading system. Appropriate consideration and support should be provided to these countries to help to facilitate their effective participation in the global economy. In this regard, we encourage progress in the implementation of the World Trade Organization work programme on small economies, mandated in the Doha Ministerial Declaration.

36. Aid for Trade is an important component of the measures that will assist developing countries in taking advantage of the opportunities offered by the international trading system, the outcome of the Doha round and regional trade agreements. A critical aim of Aid for Trade should be to enhance trade capacity and international competitiveness while ensuring ownership and alignment with national development strategies of individual developing countries. Aid for Trade should aim to help developing countries, particularly least developed countries, with trade policy and regulations; trade development; building productive capacities; trade-related infrastructure; trade-related adjustment and other trade-related needs. However, Aid for Trade is a complement and not a substitute for a successful outcome of the Doha Development Agenda or any other trade negotiation. Successful programmes under the Aid for Trade Initiative require joint efforts by concerned partners. The commitments by individual donors relating to Aid for Trade should be fully implemented in a timely manner. It is also important that the Aid for Trade needs and priorities of recipient countries are fully integrated and reflected in their national development strategies. United Nations specialized agencies that have a relevant mandate in this field should continue to help developing countries to build their trade-related productive capacities.

37. Broader and effective participation of developing countries in the multilateral trading system, including in any round of multilateral trade negotiations and in the World Trade Organization Doha Development Agenda negotiations, are key objectives. We note progress in this area since Monterrey, as evidenced by the countries that have acceded to the World Trade Organization, the countries that have newly engaged in World Trade Organization accession and the countries that have made progress towards World Trade Organization accession over the past six years. We welcome additional progress in this regard. We also reaffirm our undertaking in Monterrey to facilitate the accession of all developing countries, particularly the least developed countries, as well as countries with economies in transition, that apply for membership in the World Trade Organization. In this regard, we note the decision of the

Sixth World Trade Organization Ministerial Conference to give priority to the ongoing accessions with a view to concluding them as rapidly and smoothly as possible.

38. We recognize that regional integration as well as bilateral trade and economic cooperation agreements are important instruments to expand trade and investment. We should continue to ensure that these agreements promote long-term development, advance the goals of the World Trade Organization and are complementary elements of the multilateral trading system. International support for cooperation in trade and other trade-related areas can be catalytic in strengthening and consolidating regional and subregional integration. We stress the importance of increased support to South-South trade and cooperation initiatives in trade-related areas, including through triangular cooperation, consistent with World Trade Organization rules.

39. We welcome the ongoing work of international institutions that assist developing countries in realizing the benefits of trade liberalization, in particular the United Nations, the World Trade Organization, the World Bank, IMF and the regional development banks, and encourage their continuing efforts to facilitate trade that results in economic growth and development. In this context, we welcome the outcome of the twelfth session of the United Nations Conference on Trade and Development (UNCTAD), held in Accra from 20 to 25 April 2008, and reaffirm the role of UNCTAD in trade and development.

Increasing international financial and technical cooperation for development

40. We recognize the severe impacts that the current financial and economic crises are having on the ability of developing countries to mobilize resources for development. We stress the importance that ODA plays, leveraging and sustaining financing for development in developing countries. In this regard, we recall our commitments to the internationally agreed development goals, including the Millennium Development Goals, and call for the international community to redouble its efforts to facilitate the achievement of these goals.

41. We reaffirm the essential role that ODA plays, as a complement to other sources of financing for development, in facilitating the achievement of development objectives, including the internationally agreed development goals, in particular the Millennium Development Goals. For many African countries, least developed countries, small island developing States and landlocked developing countries, ODA is still the largest source of external financing. ODA can play a catalytic role in assisting developing countries in removing constraints to sustained, inclusive and equitable growth, such as enhancing social institutional and physical infrastructure; promoting foreign direct investment, trade and technological innovation; improving health and education; fostering gender equality; preserving the environment; and eradicating poverty.

42. We are encouraged by the recovery of ODA from its declining trend before the Monterrey Conference (ODA in real terms increased by 40 per cent between 2001 and 2007), while noting that a significant part of aid flows after 2002 comprised debt relief and humanitarian assistance. However, we note with concern the overall decline in ODA in 2006 and 2007, driven in particular by the drop-off in debt relief from its peak in 2005. We are encouraged by the fact that some donor countries have met or surpassed the ODA targets referenced in the Monterrey Consensus (0.7 per cent of gross national product (GNP) for ODA to developing countries and 0.15 to 0.20 per cent of GNP for ODA to least developed countries). We are also encouraged by others that have established timetables for fulfilling their long-standing commitments, such as the European Union, which has agreed to provide, collectively, 0.56 per cent of GNP for ODA by 2010 and 0.7 per cent by 2015 and to channel at least 50 per cent of collective aid increases to Africa, while fully respecting the individual priorities of Member States in development assistance. We welcome the more than doubling of ODA by the United States. We also welcome the declaration by the leaders of the Group of Eight in Hokkaido, Japan, that they are firmly committed to working to fulfil their commitments made at Gleneagles, including increasing, compared to 2004, with other donors, ODA to Africa by 25 billion United States dollars a year by 2010. We encourage donors to work on national timetables, by the end of 2010, to increase aid levels within their respective budget allocation processes towards achieving the established ODA targets. The full implementation of these commitments will substantially boost the resources available to push forward the international development agenda.

43. The fulfilment of all ODA commitments is crucial, including the commitments by many developed countries to achieve the target of 0.7 per cent of GNP for ODA to developing countries by 2015 and to reach the level of at least 0.5 per cent of GNP for ODA by 2010, as well as a target of 0.15 to 0.20 per cent of GNP for ODA to least developed countries. To reach their agreed timetables, donor countries should take all necessary and appropriate measures to raise the rate of aid disbursements to meet their existing commitments. We urge those developed countries that have not yet done so to make additional concrete efforts towards the target of 0.7 per cent of GNP for ODA to developing countries, including the specific target of 0.15 to 0.20 per cent of GNP for ODA to least developed countries in line with the Brussels Programme of Action for the Least Developed Countries for the Decade 2001–2010, in accordance with their commitments. To build on progress achieved in ensuring that ODA is used effectively, we stress the importance of democratic governance, improved transparency and accountability, and managing for results. We strongly encourage all donors to establish, as soon as possible, rolling indicative timetables that illustrate how they aim to reach their goals, in accordance with their respective budget allocation process. We stress the importance of mobilizing greater domestic support in developed countries towards the fulfilment of their commitments, including through raising public awareness, and by providing data on aid effectiveness and demonstrating tangible results.

44. We stress the importance of addressing the development needs of low-income developing countries, including through the provision of technical, financial and other forms of assistance, the promotion and strengthening of partnerships and cooperation arrangements at all levels.

45. We recognize that middle-income countries still face significant challenges in the area of poverty eradication and that their efforts to address those challenges should be strengthened and supported by the United Nations system, the international financial institutions and all other stakeholders, in order to ensure that achievements made to

date are sustained. We also acknowledge that ODA is still essential for a number of these countries and has a role to play in targeted areas, taking into account the needs and domestic resources of these countries.

46. We welcome increasing efforts to improve the quality of ODA and to increase its development impact. The Economic and Social Council Development Cooperation Forum, along with recent initiatives, such as the High-level Forums on Aid Effectiveness, which produced the 2005 Paris Declaration on Aid Effectiveness, and the 2008 Accra Agenda for Action, make important contributions to the efforts of those countries which have committed to them, including through the adoption of the fundamental principles of national ownership, alignment, harmonization and managing for results. Continued building on these initiatives, including through more inclusive and broad-based participation, will contribute to enhancing national ownership and making aid delivery more effective and efficient and lead to improved outcomes. We also encourage all donors to improve the quality of aid, increase programme-based approaches, use country systems for activities managed by the public sector, reduce transaction costs and improve mutual accountability and transparency and, in this regard, we call upon all donors to untie aid to the maximum extent. We will make aid more predictable by providing developing countries with regular and timely, indicative information on planned support in the medium term. We recognize the importance of efforts by developing countries to strengthen leadership of their own development, national institutions, systems and capacity to ensure the best results of aid by engaging with parliaments and citizens in shaping those policies and deepening engagement with civil society organizations. We should also bear in mind that there is no one-size-fits-all formula that will guarantee effective assistance. The specific situation of each country needs to be fully considered.

47. We note that the aid architecture has significantly changed in the current decade. New aid providers and novel partnership approaches, which utilize new modalities of cooperation, have contributed to increasing the flow of resources. Further, the interplay of development assistance with private investment, trade and new development actors provides new opportunities for aid to leverage private resource flows. We re-emphasize the importance of the Development Cooperation Forum of the Economic and Social Council as the focal point within the United Nations system for holistic consideration of issues of international development cooperation, with participation by all relevant stakeholders. We shall pursue efforts, both in the United Nations and in collaboration with other relevant institutions, such as the Organization for Economic Cooperation and Development (OECD)/ Development Assistance Committee (DAC), to advance dialogue and cooperation among the increasingly diverse community of development partners. All development actors should cooperate closely to ensure that increased resources from all sources are used in a manner which ensures maximum effectiveness. We shall also pursue enhanced collaboration at the country level with the private sector, non-official donors, regional organizations and official donors.

48. There is a growing need for more systematic and universal ways to follow quantity, quality and effectiveness of aid flows, giving due regard to existing schemes and mechanisms. We invite the Secretary-General, with relevant United Nations system agencies, in close cooperation with the World Bank, the regional and subregional development banks, OECD/DAC and other relevant stakeholders, to address this issue and to provide a report for consideration by the Development Cooperation Forum.

49. We reiterate our support for South-South cooperation, as well as triangular cooperation, which provides much needed additional resources to the implementation of development programmes. We recognize the importance and different history and particularities of South-South cooperation and stress that South-South cooperation should be seen as an expression of solidarity and cooperation between countries, based on their shared experiences and objectives. Both forms of cooperation support a development agenda that addresses the particular needs and expectations of developing countries. We also recognize that South-South cooperation complements rather than substitutes for North-South cooperation. We acknowledge the role played by middle-income developing countries as providers and recipients of development cooperation. Regional cooperation could also be strengthened as an effective vehicle for mobilizing resources for development, inter alia, by strengthening regional financial institutions to better assist in upgrading critical sectors in developing countries.

50. We encourage developing countries in a position to do so to continue to make concrete efforts to increase and make more effective their South-South cooperation initiatives in accordance with the principles of aid effectiveness.

51. We recognize the considerable progress made since the Monterrey Conference in voluntary innovative sources of finance and innovative programmes linked to them. We acknowledge that a number of the initiatives of the Technical Group created by the Global Action Initiative against Hunger and Poverty and the Leading Group on Solidarity Levies to Fund Development have become a reality or are in an advanced stage towards implementation. These include, inter alia, the International Finance Facility for Immunization; the pilot advance market commitments and the airline ticket solidarity levies, which finance health programmes in several developing countries, including the International Drug Purchase Facility, UNITAID, to help to combat HIV/AIDS, tuberculosis and malaria; and instruments based on the carbon market. Other noteworthy initiatives include the United States Millennium Challenge Corporation, the President's Emergency Plan for AIDS Relief, the India-Brazil-South Africa Fund, the Egyptian Fund for Technical Cooperation with Africa, the Libya-Africa Investment Portfolio and the PetroCaribe Initiative. We encourage the scaling up and the implementation, where appropriate, of innovative sources of finance initiatives. We acknowledge that these funds should supplement and not be a substitute for traditional sources of finance, and should be disbursed in accordance with the priorities of developing countries and not unduly burden them. We call upon the international community to consider strengthening current initiatives and explore new proposals, while recognizing their voluntary and complementary nature. We request the Secretary-General of the United Nations to continue to address the issue of innovative sources of development finance, public and private, and to produce a progress report by the sixty-fourth session of the General Assembly, taking into account all existing initiatives.

52. We reiterate our resolve to operationalize the World Solidarity Fund established by the General Assembly and invite those countries in a position to do so to make voluntary contributions to the Fund. We also recall the establishment of the Digital Solidarity Fund and encourage voluntary contributions to its financing, including by considering innovative financing mechanisms.

53. We underscore the importance of capacity development and strengthening technical cooperation as important avenues for developing countries to attain their development objectives. In this regard, we reiterate the importance of human resources development, including training, exchange of expertise, knowledge transfer and technical assistance for capacity-building, which involves strengthening institutional capacity, project management and programme planning. The capacity of developing countries to absorb long-term development aid has begun to increase.

54. We underline the important role of an effective, well-managed and adequately resourced United Nations system through its operational activities in delivering capacity-building support for development with long-term sustainability. This is particularly important for least developed countries. Given that the level of core funding inevitably affects the ability of the United Nations system to fulfil this mandate, we urge donor countries and other countries in a position to do so to substantially increase voluntary contributions to the core/regular budgets of the United Nations development system, in particular its funds, programmes and specialized agencies, and to contribute on a multi-year basis, in a sustained and predictable manner. We also note that non-core resources represent an important supplement to the regular resource base of the United Nations development system to support operational activities for development, thus contributing to an increase in total resources, while recognizing that non-core resources are not a substitute for core resources and that unearmarked contributions are vital for the coherence and harmonization of operational activities for development. We welcome the efforts to improve efficiency, coherence and effectiveness of the United Nations development system.

55. The multilateral development banks, including the World Bank, regional and subregional development banks and other international institutions that promote development, can be an important source of financing for development. They provide strategic resources, including in the form of technical assistance, for such areas as governance, institution and capacity-building and the promotion of best practices. They play an important role in enhancing the integration of developing countries in the world economy and in supporting regional integration and other cooperation efforts. They also constitute a valuable forum for exchange of information on best practices between developing countries. For some countries, the net outflow of resources from some of these institutions has become negative and, therefore, we will work with these institutions to enhance their financing to developing countries as part of the measures for further implementation of the Monterrey Consensus. These institutions should continue to explore innovative ways to use their capital to leverage additional finance to foster development while preserving their capital and ensuring their activity is sustainable.

External debt

56. The debt stock of developing countries as a group continues to increase, while key debt sustainability indicators have improved significantly since Monterrey, but care needs to be taken to avoid a recurrence of unsustainable levels of debt. Debt repayment by several developing countries, debt relief under the Heavily Indebted Poor Countries Initiative (HIPC), the Multilateral Debt Relief Initiative (MDRI) and the Evian treatment in the Paris Club, together with other debtor countries' efforts and ongoing initiatives, such as the World Bank/IMF Debt Sustainability Framework, have contributed to achieving such progress. The HIPC initiative is estimated to provide a total of $71 billion to 41 eligible countries, while MDRI is expected to provide an additional $28 billion. Borrowing countries have also enhanced their debt management programmes and many have built reserves. Debt relief initiatives also helped beneficiary countries to mobilize much needed resources for poverty reduction, as part of wider efforts to mobilize financial resources for development. We recognize that the current global financial and economic crises carry the possibility of undoing years of hard work and gains made in relation to the debt of developing countries. The situation demands the implementation of existing and any future bold and encompassing initiatives and mechanisms to resolve the current debt problems of developing countries, particularly for Africa and the least developed countries, in an effective and equitable manner, including through debt cancellation.

57. We stress the importance of continued flexibility with regard to the eligibility criteria for debt relief under HIPC and MDRI. We recall our encouragement to donor countries to take steps to ensure that resources provided for debt relief do not detract from ODA resources intended to be available for developing countries.

58. We underline that heavily indebted poor countries eligible for debt relief will not be able to enjoy its full benefits unless all creditors, including public and private, contribute their fair share and become involved in the international debt resolution mechanisms to ensure the debt sustainability of low-income countries.

59. We emphasize that middle-income developing countries are mainly responsible for the achievement and maintenance of a sustainable debt situation and for addressing their external debt situation. While welcoming the Evian approach, we emphasize the importance of sustained efforts by all towards achieving sustainable debt of middle-income countries, including by improving their sustainable debt management and through debt relief based on current debt mechanisms and debt swap mechanisms on a voluntary basis.

60. We recognize that important challenges remain. Debt service accounts for a significant portion of the fiscal budget and is still unsustainable in a number of developing countries. The existing international debt resolution mechanisms are creditor-driven, while taking into account debtor country situations. More efforts are needed through international debt resolution mechanisms to guarantee equivalent treatment of all creditors, just treatment of creditors and debtors, and legal predictability. We are deeply concerned about increasing vulture fund litigation. In this respect, we welcome recent steps taken to prevent aggressive litigation against HIPC-eligible countries, including

through the enhancement of debt buy-back mechanisms and the provision of technical assistance and legal support, as appropriate, by the Bretton Woods institutions and the multilateral development banks. We call upon creditors not to sell claims on HIPC to creditors that do not participate adequately in the debt relief efforts.

61. We will intensify our efforts to prevent debt crises by enhancing international financial mechanisms for crisis prevention and resolution, in cooperation with the private sector, and by finding solutions that are transparent and agreeable to all. These mechanisms need to be underpinned by principles that have served us well in dealing effectively with many debt problems. These include the need to ensure that debt resolution is a joint responsibility of all debtors and creditors, both State and commercial; to recognize that furthering development and restoring debt sustainability are the main objectives of debt resolution; to strengthen transparency and accountability among all parties; to promote responsible borrowing and lending practices; to improve debt management and national ownership of debt management strategies; and to facilitate equivalent treatment of all creditors.

62. We recognize that a shift has occurred from official to commercial borrowing and from external to domestic public debt, although for most low-income countries external finance is still largely official. We note that the number of creditors, both official and private, has increased significantly. We stress the need to address the implications of these changes, including through improved data collection and analysis.

63. In debt renegotiations, we stress the need for full involvement of debtors as well as creditors and the importance of taking into account debtors' national policies and strategies linked to attaining the internationally agreed development goals, including the Millennium Development Goals.

64. Technical assistance to manage debt and address debt problems can be crucial for many countries, in particular the most vulnerable. We reaffirm the importance of adequate capacities of debtor countries during debt negotiations, debt renegotiations and for debt management. In this regard, we will continue to provide developing countries with the necessary assistance, including technical assistance, upon request, to enhance debt management, negotiations and renegotiation capacities, including tackling external debt litigation, in order to achieve and maintain debt sustainability. The Bretton Woods institutions and other relevant organizations should continue to play an important role in this field, as appropriate, given their respective mandates. Preserving long-term debt sustainability is a shared responsibility of lenders and borrowers. To this end, we encourage the use of the joint IMF/World Bank Debt Sustainability Framework by creditors and debtors, as appropriate. Borrowers should strive to implement sound macroeconomic policies and public resource management, which are key elements in reducing national vulnerabilities.

65. Particular attention should be paid to keeping the debt sustainability frameworks under review to enhance the effectiveness of monitoring and analysing debt sustainability and consider fundamental changes in debt scenarios, in the face of large exogenous shocks, including those caused by natural catastrophes, severe terms-of-trade shocks or conflict. We stress the need to construct debt indicators based on comprehensive, objective and reliable data. We also need to increase information-sharing, transparency and the use of objective criteria in the construction and evaluation of debt scenarios, including an assessment of domestic public and private debt in order to achieve development goals. We are convinced that enhanced market access to goods and services of export interest to debtor countries is an important factor in enhancing debt sustainability.

66. Debt sustainability frameworks should also give due weight to the development needs of debtor countries, including benefits from expenditures and investment that have long-term social and economic returns. Given the imperative of maintaining debt sustainability and the external financing requirements for meeting development goals, particularly in least developed countries and low-income countries facing increased risks of debt distress, bilateral donors and multilateral financial institutions should seek to increasingly provide grants and concessional loans as the preferred modalities of their financial support instruments to ensure debt sustainability.

67. We acknowledge the need to continue to address all relevant issues regarding external debt problems, including through the United Nations, and we will consider ways to explore enhanced approaches of sovereign debt restructuring mechanisms based on existing frameworks and principles, with broad creditors' and debtors' participation and ensuring comparable burden-sharing among creditors, with an important role for the Bretton Woods institutions.

Addressing systemic issues: enhancing the coherence and consistency of the international monetary, financial and trading systems in support of development

68. Some results have been achieved since Monterrey in addressing systemic issues, but significant additional progress is needed. This is all the more urgent given the current financial crisis. The progress expected after Monterrey with the mandated work of the multilateral financial institutions, including the role of IMF in strengthening surveillance, giving high priority to the identification and prevention of potential crises and strengthening the underpinnings of international financial stability, remains incomplete. The current financial crisis, as well as the continued weaknesses in the international financial system, further underline the need to strengthen the international financial architecture. The reform of the international financial architecture should focus on providing greater transparency and strengthening the voice and participation of developing countries and countries with economies in transition in international decision-making and norm-setting. Thus, we resolve to undertake appropriate and timely steps to improve the functioning of the international economic and financial system. It is essential to maintain the involvement of the United Nations in these undertakings. This is crucial for an integrated implementation of the Monterrey Consensus.

69. We resolve to strengthen the coordination of the United Nations system and all other multilateral financial, trade and development institutions to support economic growth, poverty eradication and sustainable development worldwide. Greater cooperation between the United Nations, the Bretton Woods institutions and the World Trade

Organization is needed, based on a clear understanding and respect for their respective mandates and governance structures.

70. We encourage better coordination and enhanced coherence among relevant ministries in all countries to assist in the formulation and effective implementation of policies at all levels. We also encourage international financial and development institutions to continue to enhance policy coherence for development, taking into account diversified needs and changing circumstances. In order to complement national development efforts, we call upon all countries whose policies have an impact on developing countries to increase their efforts to formulate policies consistent with the objectives of sustained growth, poverty eradication and sustainable development of developing countries.

71. Stable international financial markets require sound macroeconomic and financial policies. It is crucial that all countries manage their macroeconomic and financial policies in ways that contribute to global stability and sustained economic growth and sustainable development. Solid and strong financial institutions at the national and international levels are essential pillars of a well-functioning international financial system. Countries should continue to pursue sound macroeconomic policies and, as appropriate, structural reform while also strengthening their financial systems and economic institutions.

72. New and highly globalized financial instruments continue to change the nature of risks in the world economy, requiring continuing enhancement of market oversight and regulation. To strengthen the resilience of the international financial system, we will implement reforms that will strengthen the regulatory and supervisory frameworks of financial markets as needed. We will strive to improve key accounting standards to remedy weaknesses and deficiencies, including those exposed by the current financial crisis. National regulators should enhance financial information and transparency at the domestic level. We will further enhance cooperation among national regulators from all countries to strengthen international financial standards. These efforts should address timely and adequate risk disclosure standards in order to improve the foundation of decisions of investors. There is also a need for enhanced transparency by financial institutions. Enhanced disclosure practices and transparency should assist efforts to reduce illicit capital flows.

73. We reaffirm that the international financial institutions, including the Bretton Woods institutions, need to be further reformed. The reformed multilateral financial institutions should have the technical capacities, credit facilities and financial resources to deal with the management and swift resolution of financial crises in a manner that elicits and facilitates international cooperation and that is consistent with their respective mandates. The international financial institutions should continue to foster the multilateral cooperation needed to restore and safeguard international monetary and financial stability and should stand ready to quickly make available sufficient resources to help countries in overcoming crises. The International Monetary Fund, in collaboration with an expanded and representative Financial Stability Forum and other bodies, should work to better identify vulnerabilities, anticipate potential stresses and act swiftly to play a key role in crisis response. Similarly, the World Bank can also play a significant role to mitigate the difficulties countries face. The Bretton Woods institutions must continue, within their respective mandates, to help developing countries to deal with the adverse effects of exogenous shocks, such as large fluctuations in the prices of key commodities, for example, through the reformed IMF Exogenous Shocks Facility. We also recognize the need for keeping under review the allocation of special drawing rights for development purposes.

74. Regional development banks play a vital role in supporting economic development and assisting regional integration efforts. We encourage continued cooperation and coordination among the regional development banks and other international financial institutions, as appropriate. We should review the adequacy of resources required to accomplish their tasks, as necessary. Other regional cooperation frameworks, such as financial and monetary arrangements that complement the international financial system, can be instrumental in fostering development and financial stability among their members and should be in line with multilateral frameworks, as appropriate. Those arrangements can facilitate financial flows and lower transaction costs and may serve as mechanisms that assist in the prevention of financial crises and render parties to such arrangements more resilient.

75. Credit rating agencies also play a significant role in the provision of information, including assessment of corporate and sovereign risks. The information provided by credit rating agencies should be based on broadly accepted, clearly defined, objective and transparent parameters. The ongoing financial crisis has revealed weaknesses and raised concerns about accounting standards and the way credit rating agencies currently operate. We will exercise strong oversight over credit rating agencies, consistent with the agreed and strengthened international code of conduct, and take additional action to strengthen financial market transparency and enhance the convergence of global accounting standards.

76. We recognize the need to address the often expressed concern at the extent of representation of developing countries in the major standard-setting bodies. We therefore welcome the proposed expansion of the membership in the Financial Stability Forum and encourage the major standard-setting bodies to review their membership promptly while enhancing their effectiveness.

77. We underscore that the Bretton Woods institutions must be comprehensively reformed so that they can more adequately reflect changing economic weights in the world economy and be more responsive to current and future challenges. We reaffirm that the enhancement of the voice and participation of developing countries in the Bretton Woods institutions, in accordance with their respective mandates, is central to strengthening the legitimacy and effectiveness of these institutions. We recognize the governance reforms that the international financial institutions have already undertaken, including the recent agreement regarding the quota review and voice reforms at IMF and related steps in the World Bank, and encourage further reforms in that direction.

78. Welcoming the ongoing international discussions on global economic governance structures, we acknowledge the need to ensure that all countries, including low-income countries, are able to effectively participate in this process.

This debate should review the international financial and monetary architecture and global economic governance structures in order to ensure a more effective and coordinated management of global issues. Such a debate should associate the United Nations, the World Bank, IMF and the World Trade Organization, should involve regional financial institutions and other relevant bodies and should take place in the context of the current initiatives aimed at improving the inclusiveness, legitimacy and effectiveness of the global economic governance structures. Greater cooperation among the United Nations, the Bretton Woods institutions and the World Trade Organization is needed, based on a clear understanding and respect for their respective mandates and governance structures.

79. The United Nations will hold a conference at the highest level on the world financial and economic crisis and its impact on development. The conference will be organized by the President of the General Assembly and the modalities will be defined by March 2009 at the latest.

Other new challenges and emerging issues

80. We commit ourselves to reinvigorating the global partnership for development in order to effectively address the full range of financing for development challenges facing the world today. We recognize that multiple financing for development challenges and opportunities have emerged since the Monterrey Conference, including the impact of the financial crisis, additional costs of climate change mitigation and adaptation and damage to the Earth's environment, price volatility in international markets of key commodities, expanding economic cooperation and the growing needs for reconstruction and development of post-conflict countries. We reaffirm our resolve to take concerted global action to address all these areas while consistently furthering economic and human development for all.

81. We are deeply concerned by the impact of the current financial crisis and global economic slowdown on the ability of developing countries to access the necessary financing for their development objectives. Developing countries and countries with economies in transition risk suffering very serious setbacks to their development objectives, in particular the achievement of the internationally agreed development goals, including the Millennium Development Goals. It is critical to adopt further decisive and prompt actions to contain the current crisis and restore sustained economic growth. Given this global context, we call the attention of all donors to the situation and needs of the poorest and most vulnerable. We also urge all donors to maintain and deliver on their ODA commitments and call upon the international community, including the World Bank and IMF, to draw on the full range of their policy advice and resources, as appropriate, to help developing countries and countries with economies in transition to strengthen their economies, maintain growth and protect the most vulnerable groups against the severe impacts of the current crisis. In this context, it is also important for developing countries to maintain sound macroeconomic policies that support sustained economic growth and poverty eradication.

82. The concern of the international community about climate change has increased markedly since the adoption of the Monterrey Consensus. We reiterate the importance of reaching an agreed outcome at the fifteenth session of the Conference of the Parties to the United Nations Framework Convention on Climate Change, to be held in Copenhagen from 7 to 18 December 2009, and urge all parties to engage constructively in negotiations consistent with the Bali Action Plan. Ongoing and potential responses to tackle this phenomenon have major financing for development implications and will incur substantial additional costs on all countries, thus requiring additional resource mobilization, including from the private sector, particularly for developing countries to address the challenges of climate change, in order to support appropriate national adaptation and mitigation strategies and actions. We reiterate that it is critical to address the pressing needs of developing countries, especially those that are particularly vulnerable to the adverse impacts of climate change, such as the least developed countries, small island developing States, and other affected countries in Africa. In this regard, we urge all parties to engage in the ongoing process in a manner that will ensure an agreed outcome commensurate with the scope and urgency of the climate change challenge. The States parties to the Kyoto Protocol welcome the launching of the Adaptation Fund within the structure of the United Nations Framework Convention on Climate Change and look forward to its early operationalization with full support.

83. We also underscore the special challenges emerging from volatility in international commodity markets, particularly the volatility of food and energy prices. We take note of recent initiatives and will continue to mobilize resources to assist developing countries, in particular the least developed countries, in attaining food and energy security. At the same time, we recognize the necessity of a substantial sustainable expansion of food production in developing countries by enhancing investments and productivity in the agricultural sector, including in small-scale farms, promoting rural development and intensifying agricultural research. It is critical to eliminate barriers to food production, to improve processing and distribution over time and to have carefully targeted safety nets in the event of food crises. We recognize that food insecurity has multiple and complex causes and that its consequences require a comprehensive and coordinated response in the short, medium and long terms by national Governments and the international community. We thus encourage the development of an inclusive global partnership for agriculture and food. We acknowledge the work of the High-level Task Force on the Global Food Security Crisis established by the Secretary-General and encourage its continued engagement with States Members of the United Nations, relevant organizations, the private sector and, especially, farmers.

84. We acknowledge the recent volatility in energy markets and its impact on low- and middle-income countries. We will strengthen cooperation to develop energy systems that can assist in meeting development needs and are consistent with the efforts to stabilize the global climate, in accordance with the principle of common but differentiated responsibilities and respective capabilities. We will strengthen our efforts to substantially increase the share of renewable energies and to promote energy efficiency and conservation. We reaffirm that access to basic energy services and to clean and sustainable energy is important to eradicate extreme poverty and to achieve the internation-

ally agreed development goals, including the Millennium Development Goals.

85. We acknowledge the recent efforts to bring to light the particular challenges faced by middle-income countries in the area of development, poverty eradication and inequality. We note the conferences held in Madrid in March 2007, in Sonsonate, El Salvador, in October 2007 and in Windhoek in August 2008 on international development cooperation with middle-income countries. We welcome the positive impact of expanding economic relations among middle-income countries, as well as recent initiatives by the international financial institutions to enhance their facilities for them.

86. Consensus has emerged since Monterrey that countries emerging from conflict are an important part of the international agenda. Many of the poorest continue to live in post-conflict States where inadequate infrastructure and low investment prevent the delivery of basic social services and limit the productive capacity of the economy. We affirm the importance of providing seamless assistance to peacebuilding efforts, including humanitarian assistance, rehabilitation and nation building, and assistance for governance and the improvement of the social and economic infrastructure. We welcome the efforts of the international community to provide flexibility to post-conflict developing countries regarding debt relief and restructuring and stress the need to continue those efforts in order to help those countries, especially those that are heavily indebted and poor, to achieve initial reconstruction for economic and social development, particularly for the early recovery period. We will step up our efforts to assist countries in accessing financing for development in the post-conflict context. In this regard, we welcome the valuable work of the United Nations Peacebuilding Commission and the Peacebuilding Fund, as well as commitments outlined in the Accra Agenda for Action.

Staying engaged

87. We recommit ourselves to staying fully engaged, nationally, regionally and internationally, to ensuring proper and effective follow-up to the implementation of the Monterrey Consensus, taking into account the intergovernmentally agreed outcome document adopted at this Conference. We will also continue our unremitting efforts to build bridges between all relevant stakeholders within the holistic agenda of the financing for development process. We appreciate the role played by the United Nations as a focal point for the financing for development follow-up process. It will be important to maintain this role to ensure the continuity and dynamism of our process. We reaffirm the need to further intensify the engagement of all stakeholders, including the United Nations system, the World Bank, IMF and the World Trade Organization, in the follow-up and implementation of the commitments made in Monterrey and reiterated here at Doha.

88. We recognize that maintaining a comprehensive and diverse multi-stakeholder follow-up process, including with civil society and the private sector, is critical. We also recognize the core responsibility of all participants in the financing for development process to exercise ownership of it and to implement their respective commitments. It is important that the follow-up process be undertaken in an integrated fashion, including through the continued engagement of all relevant ministries, in particular ministries of development, finance, trade and foreign affairs. An integrated treatment of financing for development issues in national development plans is also important in enhancing national ownership and implementation of financing for development. The international community should continue to draw upon the expertise, data and analysis available in multiple forums, while enhancing information-sharing and dialogue between the various United Nations and non-United Nations bodies that monitor progress on financing for development issues. There is substantial room to enhance the sharing of best practices.

89. We acknowledge the need for a strengthened and more effective intergovernmental inclusive process to carry out the financing for development follow-up, which would review progress in the implementation of commitments, identify obstacles, challenges and emerging issues and propose concrete recommendations and actions, taking into account various proposals that have been put forward. We request the Economic and Social Council to consider this matter during its spring meeting and at its substantive session of 2009, in consultation with all relevant stakeholders, with a view to making appropriate and timely recommendations for final action by the General Assembly as early as possible in its sixty-fourth session.

90. We will consider the need to hold a follow-up financing for development conference by 2013.

Preparatory process

Economic and Social Council consideration. By **decision 2008/235** of 23 July, the Economic and Social Council decided to transmit to the General Assembly agreed conclusions adopted on 13 May by the Commission on the Status of Women at its fifty-second session (see p. 1278) as an input to the preparations for and outcome of the Follow-up International Conference on Financing for Development to Review the Implementation of the Monterrey Consensus. The Commission reaffirmed the Beijing Declaration and Platform for Action [YUN 1995, p. 1170], in which it was emphasized that political commitment was needed to make available resources for the empowerment of women and that funding had to be identified and mobilized from all sources and across all sectors to achieve the goals of gender equality and the empowerment of women; and the outcome of the Assembly's twenty-third special session [YUN 2000, p. 1082], in which Governments were called on to incorporate a gender perspective into the design, development, adoption and execution of all policies and budgetary processes to promote equitable, effective and appropriate resource allocation and establish adequate budgetary allocations to support gender equality and development programmes that enhanced women's empowerment.

UNCTAD consideration. At its fifty-fifth session (Geneva, 15–26 September) [A/63/15 (Part IV)], TDB requested the extended Bureau to decide on the holding of an executive session in mid-November to provide input to the Follow-up International Conference on Financing for Development.

TDB, at its forty-fifth executive session (Geneva, 13 November) [TD/B/EX(45)/3], considered an October UNCTAD secretariat note [TD/B/EX(45)/2] that reviewed the six chapters of the Monterrey Consensus, ranging from mobilization of domestic resources for development to official flows and coherence of the international monetary, financial and trading systems. It highlighted the new features that had evolved in the world economy since the adoption of the Monterrey Consensus in 2002, such as the paradox of capital flows, the speculation in commodity markets and the shortcomings in the functioning of financial markets, and suggested main issues for consideration by the Board, updated to take account of recent developments in the financial and economic environment. The note also addressed implications for developing countries of the financial market crisis and pointed to the need for strengthening global coordination on monetary and financial matters.

The President, in his summary of the meeting, stated that it was an opportunity for States to express their views on the objectives and process of a reform of global economic governance just before the G-20 summit meeting in Washington, D.C. (see p. 1068), scheduled to launch a global effort to reform the international monetary and financial system. Speakers emphasized that the financial and economic crisis called for global solutions to stabilize the system and prevent future crises, and recognized that a shift in thinking had taken place—from purely market-driven solutions towards measures involving an active role of the State. There was a general hope that the Doha Conference would prepare the ground for a comprehensive follow-up to, and strengthening of, the financing for development process, and would help put in place a new approach to development, taking account of lessons to be learned from the crisis and the need to reform the international economic system in order to overcome systemic weaknesses.

The Board agreed that the crisis showed the need, in an increasingly globalized economy, for stronger economic governance, building on the principles of multilateralism with a clear set of global financial rules and regulations. There was broad agreement on the need to examine, with the participation of all States, the international financial system and to address the issue of systemic coherence. The United Nations had the universality of membership, the political credibility and the competence to play a key role in the process of revising the global economic architecture, as well as the legitimacy and confidence of the global community to make that role viable. The debate reflected agreement that the Doha Conference should provide new impetus to the implementation of the Monterrey Consensus and contribute to ensuring that the financial turmoil did not compromise the engagement of the international community in the financing of development. Moreover, it should strengthen the gender dimension and respond to new challenges, such as climate change, the food crisis and energy security.

Participants put forward a number of recommendations to the Conference. Under the sub-theme on mobilizing domestic financial resources for development, they recommended that developing countries should give that issue heightened attention. In particular, special attention should be given to enhancing the role of the banking system in the financing of productive investment, tax collection should be made more effective through greater transparency in rules and regulations, and international cooperation in tax matters should be strengthened. As to the sub-theme on mobilizing international resources for development: FDI and other private flows, efforts should be made to avoid a drop in private capital flows to developing countries; particular support should be given to South-South flows of FDI; and the role of sovereign wealth funds from developing countries in meeting the external financing needs of other developing countries should be strengthened. Efforts to reform the international financial architecture should contain speculation in international financial and currency markets in order to reduce the instability of private capital flows to developing countries. Under the sub-theme on international trade as an engine for development, TDB stressed the importance for developing countries that the financial crisis and the economic slowdown did not lead to a new wave of protectionism. The deadlock in the Doha Round (see p. 1050) should be broken, and efforts to achieve an outcome that reflected the interests of developing countries should be reinforced. Developing countries, especially in Africa, needed to address supply-side constraints, which should be supported by further opening of developed country markets for exports of interest to developing countries. Increased attention should be given to the commodity problem; reforms of the international financial system should also reduce speculation in international commodity markets; and the international community should support national efforts to integrate local producers into international supply chains and innovative financing and risk management tools for agricultural commodity producers.

In relation to the sub-theme on increasing international financial and technical cooperation for development, priority should be given to meeting the new challenges faced by the world's poor as a result of the financial crisis and the recession in the developed countries. The Doha Conference should therefore pay attention to the continuation and increase of ODA flows, especially for countries suffering from a decline in public revenue, should urge the implementation of aid commitments already made by bilateral donors to close the MDG financing gap and, in that context, debt relief should not be considered as part of ODA. Increased official financing to assist developing countries was also necessary and aid had to be provided on a predictable and sustained basis. The development of a framework for Aid for Trade was imperative for countries to reap the potential benefits from trade, as was the Enhanced Integrated Framework and the provision of additional resources for trade financing. The international community should bring forward innovative financing mechanisms, and a new IMF facility should be created to stop the crisis spillover to middle-income countries. Under the sub-theme on external debt, bolder initiatives should be taken to solve the external debt problems of developing countries, particularly in those most affected by reduced foreign exchange incomes and higher costs of their external debt. It was important to achieve and maintain sustainable debt situations in developing countries, and debt sustainability strategies should be linked to a country's capacity to achieve its national development goals.

As to the sub-theme on addressing systemic issues: enhancing the coherence and consistency of the international monetary, financial and trading systems in support of development, in the short term, efforts should ensure a global policy response to restore financial stability and economic growth, and measures should help markets regain confidence and stimulate demand in order to combat a credit crunch and mitigate the impact of the crisis on output growth and employment. Fiscal and monetary policy instruments should be used and implemented. In the medium and long term, Governments should play a more active role in the management of the financial system by strengthening the regulation and supervision of financial intermediaries. The role of credit rating agencies should be reassessed and their activities subjected to stronger public scrutiny. To avoid future crises and reduce the risk of excessive speculation, early-warning systems should be established. The financial system should be reformed around the core principles of transparency, integrity, responsibility, sound banking practice and international governance, and globally acceptable standards of supervision should be elaborated and applied equally in all countries. The international monetary and financial system should be better equipped with instruments to prevent prolonged exchange-rate misalignments and currency speculation, and, in order to achieve coherence between the international trading and financial systems and avoid large current account imbalances, a multilateral exchange rate mechanism and macroeconomic policy should become central in a new economic governance system. Monitoring and surveillance of the financial system through an international body should be strengthened and cover all economies, especially those whose national economic policies and performances had an impact on the rest of the world. The debate on the lessons from the crisis and the process of reform of the economic governance system should take place with universal, democratic and equitable participation of all States, and developing countries should be included in the decision-making and norm-setting processes of the key financial, monetary and trading institutions.

There was a widespread view among delegations that the Doha Conference should be seized to bring developing country concerns to bear on the process of consensus-building on a better international financial architecture. Because of its broad political legitimacy, and adequate representation of different groups of developing countries, the UN system was perceived as having a particular legitimacy to play a key role in international financial reform. UNCTAD was called upon to help contain the negative effects of the crisis on developing countries, building on its proven competence in policy analysis and technical cooperation.

Communications. On 6 October [A/C.2/63/2], Chile transmitted to the Secretary-General the Declaration on Innovative Sources of Financing for Development of the initiative "Action against Hunger and Poverty", adopted on 25 September at the UN High-level Event on the MDGs (see p. 926).

On the same date [A/C.2/63/3], Namibia transmitted to the Secretary-General the Windhoek Ministerial Declaration on Development Cooperation with Middle-Income Countries, adopted at the third International Conference on Development Cooperation with Middle-Income Countries (Windhoek, 4–6 August).

On 8 July [A/63/123], Italy transmitted to the Secretary-General a resolution entitled "Parliamentary oversight of State policies on foreign aid", adopted by the one hundred and eighteenth Assembly of the Inter-Parliamentary Union (Cape Town, South Africa, 13–18 April).

General Assembly action. On 18 November, the General Assembly decided that the arrangements and organization of work of the Follow-up International Conference on Financing for Development would be as set out in the note of the Secretary-General [A/63/345] (**decision 63/509**). It also decided to recommend for adoption by the Follow-up Conference the provisional rules of procedure for the Conference [A/CONF.212/2] (**decision 63/510**) and the provisional agenda annexed to its decision (**decision 63/511**), and to accredit to the Conference three intergovernmental organizations (**decision 63/512**) and 46 NGOs (**decision 63/513**).

On 24 December, the Assembly decided that the agenda item "Follow-up to and implementation of the outcome of the 2002 International Conference on Financing for Development and the preparation of the 2008 Review Conference" would remain for consideration at its resumed sixty-third (2009) session (**decision 63/552**).

Investment, technology and related financial issues

The UNCTAD Commission on Investment, Technology and Related Financial Issues held its twelfth session in Geneva on 12 and 13 February [TD/B/COM.2/82]. It had before it a progress report [TD/B/COM.2/81] on the implementation of the recommendations adopted by the Commission at its eleventh session [YUN 2007, p. 994] and on the Commission's work since UNCTAD XI [YUN 2004, p. 954]. The report focused on UNCTAD's work on policies and measures to help developing countries attract and benefit more from FDI and build productive capacities and international competitiveness, including in-depth analysis, consensus-building and the provision of technical assistance and capacity-building. The work was carried out in cooperation and joint programmes with other related international, regional and national institutions.

On the question of FDI and financing for development, the Commission was briefed by the secretariat on issues discussed in the two panels on trends and on financing infrastructure, highlighting the policy challenges related to the maximization of benefits that countries could achieve from FDI and the need to explore the potential synergies between ODA and FDI in the context of the development of infrastructure industries. It also received the reports of expert meetings on: development implications of international investment-rule-making; and comparing best practices for creating an environment conducive to maximizing development benefits, economic growth and investment in developing countries and countries with economies in transition [YUN 2007, p. 995].

Concerning implementation of the Commission's recommendations, the Chairman's summary stated that delegates called on UNCTAD to: examine the discrepancy between investment images of developing countries and countries with economies in transition and their actual investment climate; study public-private partnerships and particularly the identification of related investment policy tools; examine member countries' legislation related to restrictions of FDI due to national security protection considerations, with a view to increasing transparency and predictability; and analyse the issue of reciprocity in investment treaties and the correlation between the bilateral and multilateral levels of FDI regulation. UNCTAD was urged to produce guidelines to raise the awareness of countries concerning that problem.

TDB, at its twenty-fourth special session (Geneva, 17–20 March) [A/63/15 (Part II)], took note of the Commission's report.

Competition law and policy

The Intergovernmental Group of Experts on Competition Law and Policy, at its ninth session (Geneva, 15–18 July) [TD/B/COM.2/CLP/72], had before it UNCTAD secretariat reports on: abuse of dominance [TD/B/COM.2/CLP/66], review of capacity-building and technical assistance in the area of competition law and policy [TD/B/COM.2/CLP/70], recent important competition cases involving more than one country [TD/B/COM.2/CLP/71], the attribution of competence to community and national competition authorities in the application of competition rules [TD/B/COM.2/CLP/69], competition policy and the exercise of intellectual property rights [TD/B/COM.2/CLP/68], and independence and accountability of competition authorities [TD/B/COM.2/CLP/67]. It also had before it the *Handbook on Competition Legislation* [TD/B/COM.2/CLP/64]. The Group focused on peer reviews on competition law and policy; review of the Model Law on Competition; studies related to the provisions of the 1980 Set of Multilaterally Agreed Equitable Principles and Rules for the Control of Restrictive Business Practices (known as the Set) [YUN 1980, p. 626]; and its work programme.

In agreed conclusions, the Group of Experts recognized the progress achieved in the elaboration and enforcement of Costa Rica's competition law, and invited States to assist UNCTAD by providing experts or other resources for future activities in connection with voluntary peer reviews. It decided that UNCTAD should undertake a further voluntary peer review on the competition law and policy of a member State or regional grouping of States, during the Group's tenth session; emphasized the importance of independence and accountability of competition authorities; and requested the UNCTAD secretariat to disseminate the summary of the Group's discussions on the topic to interested States, including through its technical cooperation activities, and to prepare a report based on contributions from States for submission to its tenth session. UNCTAD should also promote and support cooperation between competition authorities and Governments, in accordance with paragraphs 103 and 211 of the Accra Accord (see p. 1042). The tenth session of the Intergovernmental Group should consider the following issues for better implementation of the Set: public monopolies, concessions, and competition law and policy; the relationship between competition and industrial policies in promoting economic development; and voluntary peer review on the competition law and policy of Indonesia. The UNCTAD secretariat should prepare reports on those issues, with a view to facilitating the consultations at the peer review, an executive summary of the peer review report in all working languages and a full report in its original language for submission to the Group's tenth session. The secretariat should include on its website an updated review of capacity-building and technical assistance; further issues of the *Handbook on Competition Legislation* containing commentaries on national competition legislation as the base for further revision and updating of the Model Law; and an updated version of the *Directory of Competition Authorities.* The Group requested States to assist UNCTAD by providing experts, training facilities or financial resources, and urged the secretariat to focus its capacity-building and technical cooperation activities (including training) on maximizing their impact in all regions.

International standards of accounting and reporting

The Intergovernmental Working Group of Experts on International Standards of Accounting and Reporting (ISAR), at its twenty-fifth session (Geneva, 4–6 November) [TD/B/C.II/ISAR/51 & Corr.1,2], had before it UNCTAD secretariat notes on the 2008 reviews of: the implementation status of corporate governance disclosures: an examination of reporting practices among large enterprises in 10 emerging markets [TD/B/C.II/ISAR/CRP.1], the reporting status of corporate responsibility indicators [TD/B/C.II/ISAR/CRP.2], and the corporate responsibility performance of large emerging market enterprises [TD/B/C.II/ISAR/CRP.3]; as well as notes on: the review of practical implementation issues of international financial reporting standards (IFRS) [TD/B/COM.2/ISAR/28]; guidance on corporate responsibility indicators in annual reports [TD/B/COM.2/ISAR/41]; reviews of practical implementation issues relating to IFRS: case studies of Egypt [TD/B/C.II/ISAR/45], Poland [TD/B/C.II/ISAR/46], Switzerland [TD/B/C.II/ISAR/47] and the United Kingdom [TD/B/C.II/ISAR/48]; practical challenges and related considerations in implementing international standards on auditing (ISAS) [TD/B/C.II/ISAR/49]; and Accounting and Financial Reporting Guidelines for SMES (SMEGA): level 3 guidance [TD/B/C.II/ISAR/50].

In agreed conclusions, the Working Group noted the country case studies on the implementation of IFRS and the study on implementation of ISAS. It highlighted a number of technical and institutional challenges in their implementation, requested the UNCTAD secretariat to continue conducting studies on their practical implementation, and expressed appreciation to the secretariat for the publication *Practical Implementation of International Financial Reporting Standards: Lessons Learned* [UNCTAD/DIAE/ED/2008/1], requested at its twenty-fourth session [YUN 2007, p. 996]. It reviewed the revised version of SMEGA level 3 guidance and requested the secretariat to finalize its publication and disseminate it widely, as well as to compile feedback on its implementation to facilitate further revision. The Working Group deliberated on the growing demand for technical and institutional capacity-building in financial reporting, auditing, corporate governance disclosure and reporting, and agreed to communicate to the secretariat requests for technical cooperation, with a view to addressing such requests through bilateral or multilateral technical cooperation projects.

A high-level segment on financial stability and ISAR agreed on the need for further consultations and deliberations on the implications of the credit crisis for corporate financial reporting vis-à-vis financial stability challenges, and requested the secretariat to organize a special meeting to address those matters. At the Chairpersons round table, experts agreed to set up a small group to provide advisory support to the UNCTAD secretariat, and requested the secretariat to make arrangements for the group's establishment and to explore the possibilities of integrating deliberations on implementation of International Public Sector Accounting Standards (IPSAS) into UNCTAD's institutional framework and, in cooperation with the IPSAS Board, to organize technical capacity-building workshops and seminars to assist States in implementing IPSAS. Noting the 2008 review of the implementation status of corporate governance disclosures, the Working Group requested the secretariat to continue to carry out such studies, with a focus on providing information to policymakers, investors and other stakeholders. With respect to the other reviews (see above), UNCTAD should work with the investment analysis community and other experts to provide better understanding of the relationship between investment—particularly in developing countries—and the disclosure practices of enterprises on environmental, social and governance issues, and should also conduct further studies on the voluntary use of corporate responsibility reporting frameworks around the world. The Group welcomed the signing of a memorandum of understanding between UNCTAD and the Global Reporting Initiative.

Strengthening transparency in industries

On 11 September [meeting 121], the General Assembly adopted **resolution 62/274** [draft: A/62/L.41/Rev.1 & Add.1] without vote [agenda item 56].

Strengthening transparency in industries

The General Assembly,

Recalling the 2005 World Summit Outcome,

Reaffirming the Accra Accord, the outcome of the twelfth session of the United Nations Conference on Trade and Development, held in Accra from 20 to 25 April 2008,

Recalling the United Nations Convention against Corruption, which reaffirms that corruption is no longer a local matter but a transnational phenomenon that affects all societies and economies, making international cooperation to prevent and control it essential,

Also recalling its resolution 1803(XVII) of 14 December 1962, in which it declared that the right of peoples and nations to permanent sovereignty over their natural wealth and resources must be exercised in the interest of their national development and of the well-being of the people of the State concerned,

Reaffirming that every State has and shall freely exercise full permanent sovereignty over all its wealth, natural resources and economic activities,

Taking note of all relevant voluntary initiatives, including the Extractive Industries Transparency Initiative, aimed at improving transparency in the extractive industries,

Convinced that rule-based and predictable trade and financial systems are essential to promote transparency in trade and financial industries and combat corruption in commercial and financial transactions in all countries,

1. *Emphasizes* that transparency and accountability are objectives that should be embraced and promoted by all Member States, regardless of their size, level of development or resource endowment;

2. *Reaffirms*, as stated in the United Nations Convention against Corruption, the need to combat corruption and enhance transparency, in accordance with the fundamental principles of domestic law, and to take such measures as may be necessary to enhance transparency in public administration, including with regard to organization, functioning and decision-making processes, where appropriate;

3. *Encourages* the international community to strengthen, as appropriate, upon request, the capacity of States endowed with natural resources, especially those emerging from conflict situations, to negotiate mutually satisfactory, transparent and equitable contractual terms for the use, extraction and processing of their natural resources;

4. *Notes* the efforts of countries that are participating in all relevant voluntary initiatives to improve transparency and accountability in industries, including in the Extractive Industries Transparency Initiative in the extractive sector, and to share their experience with interested Member States;

5. *Reaffirms its commitment* to governance, equity and transparency in the financial, monetary and trading systems, as well as its commitment to open, equitable, rule-based, predictable and non-discriminatory multilateral trading and financial systems;

6. *Encourages* business and industry, in particular transnational corporations, to establish worldwide corporate policies on sustainable development, arrange for environmentally sound technologies to be available to affiliates owned substantially by their parent company in developing countries without extra external charges and to modify procedures in order to reflect local ecological conditions and share experiences with local authorities, national Governments and international organizations;

7. *Urges* the private sector, including corporations engaged in the extractive industries, to ensure transparency and verifiable processes, while adhering to and promoting the principles of honesty, transparency and accountability in order to maximize the contribution of the private sector to the realization of social and people-centred sustainable development.

Taxation

In March, the Secretary-General submitted to the Economic and Social Council a report on the financing of the Committee of Experts on International Cooperation in Tax Matters [E/2008/4], which addressed the funding of two key areas of the Committee's work: its working methods, specifically the work of its subcommittees and working groups; and its capacity-building activities in support of developing countries and countries with economies in transition. An amount of $324,600 had been appropriated under section 9, Economic and social affairs, of the 2008–2009 programme budget to support the participation of Committee members at its annual sessions in Geneva. However, no funds had been appropriated under the regular budget for the intersessional meetings and working groups, which had to rely on the goodwill of its members and on funding by their employers. The average cost per meeting of the subcommittees and working groups over the biennium was estimated at $27,600 for travel and per diem costs for their members, and an additional $35,000 for one staff member. For the biennium, $367,000 would be required to cover 12 intersessional meetings. In terms of funding options, the Council might wish to consider either providing additional regular budget resources for all 12 meetings, or funding from the regular budget of only a fixed number of meetings for the biennium. While funding through voluntary contributions was an option, the uncertainty of their level would make it difficult to plan the activities of the various subcommittees and working groups and would not guarantee adequate representation from developing countries. In addition, voluntary contributions might be earmarked for specific subcommittees or working groups only, thereby resulting in uneven progress.

As to the provision of capacity-building activities in support of developing countries and countries with economies in transition, as requested by the Council in resolution 2006/48 [YUN 2006, p. 1139], an amount of $450,000 in voluntary contributions would be required during 2008–2009 to conduct at least five regional training workshops and cover the cost of travel and per diem of workshop participants, expert trainers and staff members, including other logistical workshop-related costs. In addition to offers from States to host such capacity-building activities, most of those activities were to be funded through voluntary contributions to the trust fund for tax cooperation matters referred to in Council resolution 2007/39 [YUN 2007, p. 997]. Despite frequent calls for contributions, no funds had been pledged. The Council might wish to further encourage States to make contributions to the trust fund.

By **decision 2008/211** of 29 April, the Council deferred consideration of the Secretary-General's report on financing of the Committee to its 2008 substantive session.

ECONOMIC AND SOCIAL COUNCIL ACTION

On 24 July [meeting 42], the Economic and Social Council, having considered the report of the third session of the Committee of Experts on International Cooperation in Tax Matters [YUN 2007, p. 997] and the Secretary-General's report on the financing of the Committee (see above), adopted **resolution 2008/16** [draft: E/2008/L.27] without vote [agenda item 13 *(h)*].

Committee of Experts on International Cooperation in Tax Matters

The Economic and Social Council,

Recalling its resolution 2004/69 of 11 November 2004, in which the Council decided that the Ad Hoc Group of Experts on International Cooperation in Tax Matters would be renamed the Committee of Experts on International Cooperation in Tax Matters,

Recognizing the call made in the Monterrey Consensus of the International Conference on Financing for Development for the strengthening of international tax cooperation through enhanced dialogue among national tax authorities and greater coordination of the work of the concerned multilateral bodies and relevant regional organizations, giving special attention to the needs of developing countries and countries with economies in transition,

Recalling the report of the Secretary-General on the implementation of and follow-up to commitments and agreements made at the International Conference on Financing for Development and the recommendations contained therein,

Recognizing the need for an inclusive, participatory and broad-based dialogue on international cooperation in tax matters,

Noting the activities developing within the concerned multilateral bodies and relevant subregional and regional organizations,

1. *Takes note* of the report of the Committee of Experts on International Cooperation in Tax Matters on its third session and the significant progress made in the work of the Committee;

2. *Also takes note* of the report of the Secretary-General on the financing of the Committee of Experts on International Cooperation in Tax Matters, taking into account the issues raised by the Committee at its second and third sessions;

3. *Recognizes* that the Committee agreed to create, as necessary, ad hoc subcommittees composed of experts and observers who would work according to the Committee's rules of procedure to prepare and determine the supporting documentation for the agenda items, including requests for papers by independent experts, for consideration at its regular session;

4. *Notes* that five subcommittees on substantive matters, namely, the improper use of treaties, the definition of permanent establishment, the exchange of information, including a possible code of conduct on cooperation in combating international tax evasion, dispute resolution and the treatment of Islamic financial instruments, and two working groups, on the revision of the *Manual for the Negotiation of Bilateral Tax Treaties between Developed and Developing Countries* and on general issues in the revision of the commentaries on the articles of the *United Nations Model Double Taxation Convention between Developed and Developing Countries*, have been created and are currently working intersessionally;

5. *Also notes* the importance of adequate representation from developing countries in the meetings of the subcommittees and working groups, and in this regard invites the Secretary-General to intensify efforts to seek appropriate resources;

6. *Further notes* the establishment of the trust fund by the Secretary-General to supplement regular budget resources, and urges all Member States and relevant organizations to contribute generously to the fund;

7. *Invites* the Committee to work with the Secretariat on organizing training workshops, in collaboration with concerned multilateral bodies, and regional, subregional and relevant international organizations, for developing countries and countries with economies in transition as part of the work required to carry out its mandate, which includes making recommendations on capacity-building and providing technical assistance, provided that funding is available from the trust fund;

8. *Decides* that the fourth session of the Committee shall be convened in Geneva from 20 to 24 October 2008;

9. *Approves* the provisional agenda for the fourth session of the Committee as contained in its report on its third session.

Fourth meeting of Committee of Experts. In accordance with Council resolution 2008/16, the fourth session of the Committee of Experts on International Cooperation in Tax Matters was held in Geneva from 20 to 24 October [E/2008/45]. The Committee discussed general issues in the revision of the commentaries [E/C.18/2008/CRP.1 & Add.1]; taxation of development projects; definition of permanent establishment [E/C.18/2008/CRP.3]; improper use of treaties [E/C.18/2008/CRP.2 & Add.1]; exchange of information, including the proposed United Nations Code of Conduct on Cooperation in Combating International Tax Evasion and Avoidance [E/C.18/2008/3 & Corr.1 & Add.1 & Add.1/Corr.1]; revision of the United Nations Manual for the Negotiation of Bilateral Tax Treaties between Developed and Developing Countries [E/C.18/2008/CRP.5 & Add.1,2]; dispute resolution [E/C.18/2008/CRP.6 & Add.1]; and treatment of Islamic financial instruments [E/C.18/2008/4 & Corr.1]. The Secretariat also gave a briefing on the linkage of the mandate and work of the Committee to the Follow-up International Conference on Financing for Development to Review the Implementation of the Monterrey Consensus [E/C.18/2008/2] (see p. 1076).

The Committee, in respect of general issues in the revision of the commentaries, asked the Working Group on General Issues in the Review of Commentaries to continue considering the topic, with a view to a further paper available to the Committee's new membership in 2009. Concerning taxation of development projects, participants were urged to discuss the guidelines presented in 2007 [YUN 2007, p. 997] with their relevant ministries or agencies. As to the definition of permanent establishment, the Committee noted the final redrafted commentary on the text of article 5, the suggested improvements and an accompanying commentary. It also noted the proposals submitted by the Subcommittee on Permanent Establishment, including the treatment of article 14 and possible deletion; taxation of fees for technical services; treatment of services and a provision for services under article 5. Regarding the retention or deletion of article 14, the Subcommittee was asked to reconfigure the way it was addressed, so that the article was retained in the UN Model Convention; provide an alternative to its removal and apply articles 5 and 7 to situations previously dealt with under article 14; and focus on an alternative to article 14, with a view to completing consideration by June 2009. The Subcommittee was asked to commence its work with a view to achieving as much as possible before July 2009, when its new members would commence their terms of office. As to improper use of treaties, the Committee concluded that there was a need to refine the concept of beneficial ownership, including by examining developments in the OECD Model Convention, and agreed that the paper submitted by the consultant [E/C.18/2008/CRP.2 & Add.1] could contribute to improved understanding through its inclusion in the Manual for the Negotiation of Bilateral Tax Treaties between Developed and Developing Countries. The Committee agreed that practical application of the concept of beneficial ownership should be recommended to its next membership for consideration, and elaborated on in the Manual. In that respect, any cases and materials on that application in developing countries would be taken into account. It also agreed that the Subcommittee on Improper Use of Treaties should not consider the issue further, and considered proposed additions to the UN Model Convention and commentary addressing approaches for dealing with the improper use of treaties. The Committee agreed that the Subcommittee should continue its work on the proposed UN Code of Conduct on Cooperation in Combating International Tax Evasion and Avoidance, and that an updated version of the Code should be made available by the time of the Follow-up International Conference on Financing for Development. Concerning dispute resolution, it was agreed that a recommendation should be made to the following membership on the importance of improving the mutual agreement procedures and addressing the possibilities for arbitration (either in the UN Model Convention or as an alternative provision). The format of the Manual for the Negotiation of Bilateral Tax Treaties between Developed and Developing Countries was approved, and it was agreed that the Working Group should take into account the current discussions. Concerning the treatment of Islamic financial instruments, the Committee noted that the Working Group had proposed wording for new paragraphs 20.1 to 20.4 of the commentary of the UN Model Convention, which would be inserted between quoted paragraphs 21.1 and 22 of the commentary of the OECD Model Convention. It also noted that other articles might need to be amended to deal with specific Islamic financial instruments, but that it was better to wait until the part of the Manual dealing with such financing had been released and there had been an opportunity to comment thereon.

Transport

Maritime transport

The *Review of Maritime Transport, 2008* [Sales No. E.08.II.D.26], prepared by the UNCTAD secretariat, reported that world seaborne trade reached 8.02 billion tons of goods loaded in 2007, a volume increase of 4.8 per cent over the previous year. Dry cargo, including bulk, break-bulk and containerized cargo, accounted for the largest share of goods loaded (66.6 per cent), with oil making up the balance. Measured in ton-miles, world seaborne trade was estimated at 32,932 billion ton-miles in 2007. Strong consumer demand and rapid industrial expansion in emerging developing economies continued to drive growth in world seaborne trade. The world merchant fleet expanded by 7.2 per cent to 1.12 billion deadweight tons (dwt) at the beginning of 2008. The tonnage of oil tankers increased by 6.5 per cent and that of bulk carriers by 6.4 per cent, together representing 71.5 per cent of total tonnage. The fleet of general cargo ships increased by 4.5 per cent in 2007, while the fleet of container ships increased by 16.3 million dwt, or 12 per cent, representing 12.9 per cent of the total world fleet. Total tonnage on order was at its highest level, reaching 10,000 vessels, with a total tonnage of almost 500 million dwt. It consisted of 125 million dwt of oil tankers, 8 million dwt of general cargo vessels, 78 million tons of container ships and 57 million dwt of other vessel types.

As to fleet ownership, at the beginning of 2008, nationals of the 35 top ship-owning economies controlled 95.35 per cent of the world fleet. Greece, the country with the largest fleet, followed by Japan, Germany, China and Norway, together held a market share of 54.2 per cent. Among developing countries, oil exporters controlled a relatively high share of oil tankers, while large exporters of agricultural commodities and other dry bulk tended to be host to dry bulk shipping companies.

Transport of dangerous goods

The Committee of Experts on the Transport of Dangerous Goods and on the Globally Harmonized System of Classification and Labelling of Chemicals, at its fourth session (Geneva, 12 December) [ST/SG/AC.10/36 & Corr.1 & Add.1-3 & Add.1/Corr.1 & Add.2/Corr.1], took note of Economic and Social Council **decision 2008/201 C** of 29 April, approving the application of Nigeria [E/2008/9/Add.12] for membership in the Subcommittee of Experts on the Globally Harmonized System of Classification and Labelling of Chemicals. It also noted the publication of the revised Recommendations on the Transport of Dangerous Goods, Model Regulations [ST/SG/AC.10/1/Rev.15], Amendment 2 to the fourth revised edition of the Recommendations on the Transport of Dangerous Goods, Manual of Test and Criteria [ST/SG/AC.10/11/Rev.4/Amdt.2] and the second revised edition of the Globally Harmonized System of Classification and Labelling of Chemicals (GHS) [ST/SG/AC.10/30/Rev.2] in all UN official languages.

The Committee took note of the reports of the Subcommittee of Experts on the Transport of Dangerous Goods on its thirty-first and thirty-second [YUN 2007, p. 998], as well as its thirty-third (Geneva, 30 June–9 July) [ST/SG/AC.10/C.3/66 & Add.1] and thirty-fourth (Geneva, 1–9 December) [ST/SG/AC.10/C.3/68] sessions. It endorsed the reports, including the amendments to the recommendations on the transport of dangerous goods and the new recommendations made, annexed to the report. The Committee also endorsed the reports of the Subcommittee of Experts on GHS on its thirteenth, fourteenth [YUN 2007, p. 998], fifteenth (Geneva, 9–11 July) [ST/SG/AC.10/C.4/30] and sixteenth (Geneva, 10–12 December) [ST/SG/AC.10/C.4/32] sessions, including the amendments to the text of GHS and the new provisions adopted, annexed to its report. It approved the programme of work of the two Subcommittees, agreed on the schedules of their 2009 meetings and adopted a draft resolution for consideration by the Economic and Social Council in 2009.

UNCTAD institutional and organizational questions

The United Nations Conference on Trade and Development (UNCTAD) held its twelfth session (UNCTAD XII) in Accra, Ghana, from 20 to 25 April, at which it adopted the Accra Declaration and the Accra Accord, which contained a number of actions to strengthen its institutional bodies (see p. 1042). Its governing body, the Trade and Development Board (TDB), held the following sessions, all in Geneva: twenty-fourth special session (17–20 March); forty-third (3 March), forty-fourth (10 July) and forty-fifth (13 November) executive sessions; and fifty-fifth annual session (15–26 September) [A/63/15 (Parts I–IV) & TD/B/EX(45)/3].

TDB, on 3 March, received a special address by the UN Secretary-General, which stressed that UNCTAD XII could contribute to building an international economic environment that fostered development.

In March, TDB received a briefing by Ghana on the preparations for UNCTAD XII. It took note of the reports of the twelfth sessions of the Commission on Trade in Goods and Services, and Commodities, the Commission on Investment, Technology and Related Financial Issues and the Commission on Enterprise, Business Facilitation and Development. TDB approved the membership of Kazakhstan and Montenegro in the Board and the addition of Estonia, Montenegro and Kazakhstan to list D of the lists of States referred to in General Assembly resolution 1995(XIX) [YUN 1964, p. 210]. It also accepted the change requested by Group D that the approval of Kazakhstan's application would be without prejudice to the composition of the five UN regional groups for the purpose of distribution of posts within the Assembly and its bodies.

In July, TDB approved the agendas for the first sessions of the Trade and Development Commission and of the Investment, Enterprise and Development Commission. It also approved the topics for multi-year expert meetings—transport and trade facilitation; enterprise development policies and capacity-building in science, technology and innovation; services, development and trade: the regulatory and institutional dimension; commodities and development; and investment for development—as well as the terms of reference of the expert meetings for the first three topics, annexed to its report; and authorized the extended Bureau to finalize and approve the topics and terms of reference for the three others. The Board approved the calendar of meetings for the remainder of 2008 and the first half of 2009.

In September, TDB adopted agreed conclusions on: review of progress in the implementation of the Programme of Action for the Least Developed Countries (LDCs) for the Decade 2001–2010; economic development in Africa: trade liberalization and export performance in Africa; and review of technical cooperation activities of UNCTAD and their financing. It took note of the forty-first annual report on the United Nations Commission on International Trade Law [A/63/17], the report of the forty-first session of the Joint Advisory Group (JAG) on the International Trade Centre (ITC) [ITC/AG(XLI)/216], and the secretariat report on progress made in the implementation of the outcomes of the major UN conferences and summits and UNCTAD's contribution [TD/B/55/7]. It also took note of the reports of the fiftieth [TD/B/WP/200] and fifty-first [TD/B/WP/206] sessions of the Working Party on the Medium-term Plan and the Programme Budget, endorsed the conclusions contained therein and adopted the draft decision contained in the report of the fifty-first session.

TDB took note of the report by the President of the Advisory Body set up in accordance with the Bangkok Plan of Action [YUN 2000, p. 891] on the implementation of courses by the secretariat in 2007–2008 and their relevant impact; of the UNCTAD secretariat report [TD/B/55/2] on assistance to the Palestinian people; and of the summary of a hearing with civil society. It approved topics and terms of reference for multi-year and single-year expert meetings and asked the secretariat to issue a compilation as an official document [TD/B/55/9]. It requested the extended Bureau to meet to decide on the holding of an executive session in mid-November, with a view to providing input to the Follow-up International Conference on Financing for Development to Review the Implementation of the Monterrey Consensus (see p. 1076).

In November, TDB discussed the agenda item on financing for development: Follow-up International Conference on Financing for Development, and adopted a number of recommendations to the Conference.

Appointment of UNCTAD Secretary-General. By **decision 63/552** of 24 December, the General Assembly deferred consideration of the sub-item "Confirmation of the appointment of the Secretary-General of the United Nations Conference on Trade and Development" until its resumed sixty-third (2009) session.

Working Party. The Working Party on the Medium-term Plan and the Programme Budget held two sessions in Geneva: fiftieth (16–20 June) [TD/B/WP/200] and fifty-first (1–5 September) [TD/B/WP/206] sessions.

Technical cooperation

In a July report [TD/B/WP/202 & Add.1,2 & Add.1/Corr.1], the UNCTAD Secretary-General provided a review of technical cooperation activities in 2007. Contributions to UNCTAD voluntary trust funds amounted to $36.8 million, reflecting, in nominal terms, a 26.4 per cent increase over the previous year. Although the depreciation of the United States dollar in the last quarter of 2007 played a role in shaping the dollar amount and the rate at which the contribution grew in 2007, the increase was mainly attributable to a marked growth of resources provided by developed countries and multilateral donors. Developed countries' contributions accounted for 58 per cent ($21.3 million) of the total contributions, an increase of 30 per cent in nominal terms. Contributions from developing countries and economies in transition declined by 17 per cent, and accounted for 21 per cent ($7.7 million) of total contributions. Contributions from multilateral donors increased sharply, with the European Commission providing $5.3 million, a 127 per cent increase over the previous year or 14.5 per cent of total contributions, and the UN system $1.9 million, or 5.2 per cent. The private and public sectors provided $0.7 million, or 1.8 per cent of contributions. UNCTAD technical cooperation expenditures contracted by over 10 per cent to $31.5 million.

By region, $6.7 million (21.4 per cent) went to Asia and the Pacific, $6.2 million (19.8 per cent) to Africa, $3.1 million (9.7 per cent) to Latin America and the Caribbean, and $0.7 million (2.2 per cent) to Europe. LDCs accounted for 41.5 per cent of total delivery. By programme, services infrastructure for development and trade efficiency accounted for 43.2 per cent ($13.6 million) of total expenditures; international trade in goods and services, and commodities, 19.6 per cent ($6.2 million); globalization and development strategies, 16.6 per cent ($5.2 million); investment, technology and enterprise development, 12.4 per cent ($3.9 million); Africa, LDCs and special programmes, 4.3 per cent ($1.3 million); UN regular programme of technical cooperation, 3.3 per cent ($1 million); executive direction and management and support services, 0.4 per cent ($0.12 million); and technical cooperation service, 0.3 per cent ($0.8 million). Major technical assistance programmes in order of expenditure included: Automated System for Customs Data ($11.2 million); debt management and financial analysis system programme ($4.6 million); trade negotiations and commercial diplomacy ($3.1 million); policy and capacity-building ($2.7 million); human resources and information and communication technology ($1.6 million); and trade, environment and development ($1.4 million).

Technical cooperation strategy

The Working Party on the Medium-term Plan and the Programme Budget, at its fifty-first session in September [TD/B/WP/206], considered the July report on UNCTAD technical cooperation activities (see above). It adopted a draft decision for consideration by TDB on the review of the technical cooperation activities of UNCTAD and their financing.

TDB, at its fifty-fifth session in September [A/63/15 (Part IV) (dec. 495(LV))], took note of UNCTAD technical cooperation activities. It welcomed the establishment of the 17 thematic clusters—including existing and proposed multi-year, multi-donor trust funds—and invited the secretariat to continue the consolidation process. It also invited donors in a position to do so to provide multi-year contributions to the newly established thematic trust funds, and urged the secretariat to provide administrative information on the trust funds and donors to provide the secretariat with the required financial instructions for the establishment of multi-donor trust funds and the closing of completed projects. TDB encouraged more communication among the secretariat, beneficiaries and donors, so as to make progress in the clustering process, and requested the secretariat to include an agenda item in the fifty-third session of the Working Party for that interaction on UNCTAD technical cooperation in accordance with the Accra Accord. The secretariat should also explore the possibilities for increasing the number of training courses on key issues of the international economic agenda and other capacity-building activities. TDB encouraged States to include in their delegations officials from the field in beneficiary countries involved in the implementation of technical cooperation to participate in the sessions of the Working Party and to provide an assessment of the impact of technical assistance in their countries. It also encouraged UNCTAD to facilitate the use of virtual conference facilities to enable the broadest possible participation; invited donors and countries to provide funds to assist field-based beneficiary officials to take part in the Working Party's discussion; and proposed that an assessment be made by the UN Chief Executives Board for Coordination cluster, led by UNCTAD and within a year of the conduct of each training workshop for resident coordinators, of the extent to which trade and trade-related issues had been included in UN Development Assistance Frameworks.

Evaluation

In July, in response to a request of the Working Party on the Medium-term Plan and the Programme Budget [YUN 2007, p. 1003], the UNCTAD secretariat submitted a progress report [TD/B/WP/204] on the implementation of the recommendations and observations contained in the evaluation of UNCTAD advisory services on investment. Based on its review of its advisory services in light of those recommendations, UNCTAD restructured and streamlined various activities and projects. All the recommendations contained in the evaluation had been implemented, and investment had been strengthened in terms of relevance, efficiency, effectiveness and impact as a result of the exercise.

Also in response to a Working Party request [YUN 2007, p. 1003], the secretariat submitted a July progress report [TD/B/WP/205] on the implementation of the recommendations contained in the evaluation of UNCTAD trade-related technical assistance and capacity-building on accession to WTO, which addressed only those recommendations that had not been implemented.

The Working Party took note of the changes implemented to UNCTAD's advisory services on investment and encouraged the secretariat to continue efforts towards that end. It also noted the technical assistance programme on accession to WTO, and invited donors in a position to do so to make multi-year contributions to UNCTAD technical cooperation in order to increase predictability in the planning and implementation of the relevant technical assistance programmes. It encouraged the secretariat to continue to strengthen the programme.

Medium-term plan and programme budget

At its fiftieth session (Geneva, 16–20 June) [TD/B/WP/200], the Working Party on the Medium-term Plan and the Programme Budget reviewed the UNCTAD section of the proposed 2010–2011 UN strategic framework [TD/B/L.130] and emphasized that the Accra Accord was the basis for UNCTAD work for the following four years. It therefore recommended that the General Assembly and its competent bodies consider the revision to the UNCTAD section of the proposed strategic framework, which should also be considered as a revision to the strategic framework for the current biennium (2008–2009), so that UNCTAD XII outcomes could be implemented with minimum delay. The Working Party noted that the four-year work plan (2008–2011), developed on the basis of UNCTAD XII outcomes, would be discussed at its fifty-first session.

Recalling the need, set out in the Accra Accord, to establish a mechanism for UNCTAD to contribute more effectively to developing countries' efforts to formulate strategies and policies to respond to the challenges and opportunities of commodity markets, the Working Party noted that the clearly defined resources referred to in the strategic framework under paragraph 10.5 were the existing resources of the

Commodities Branch of the Division on International Trade in Goods and Services, and Commodities, which would henceforth be located in a sub-account under subprogramme 3. It welcomed the UNCTAD Secretary-General's guidance on commodities and the new arrangement, and invited him, based on his experience with that arrangement, to explore the option of locating the sub-account on commodities in another subprogramme. Regarding the development of performance indicators in the strategic framework, it called on UNCTAD to strengthen its results-oriented performance measurement and evaluation systems in order to enhance the effectiveness and relevance of the institution, and encouraged all divisions to continue their cooperative work with a view to developing a common, user-friendly reporting format for all subprogrammes. The Party requested the secretariat to report in September on institutional changes to be realized for the implementation of the Accra outcomes, based on the mandates contained in sub-theme 4 of the Accord on strengthening UNCTAD: enhancing its development role, impact and institutional effectiveness. It recommended to TDB that the Working Party be renamed the Working Party on the Strategic Framework and the Programme Budget.

At its fifty-first session (Geneva, 1–5 September) [TD/B/WP/206], the Working Party, in agreed conclusions, noted the four-year work plan for the period 2008–2011 [TD/B/WP/203/Rev.1] and advised the secretariat to implement the 2008–2009 work programme, as reflected in the revised plan, and to reflect the plan in the 2010–2011 work programme. It requested the UNCTAD secretariat to implement the Accra Accord and report regularly on its implementation; to review the progress in the implementation of the work plan against the UNCTAD indicators of achievement; and to report thereon to the Working Party. It also encouraged the secretariat to increase its interdivisional work in the implementation of the work plan, taking advantage of each division's complementary skills and synergies. The secretariat, within the framework of the preparation of the draft programme budget for the next biennium, should review the use of ad hoc expert groups, with a view to improving their cost-effectiveness, including by exploring the use of virtual meetings, and to ensure that they supported full implementation of the Accra Accord. The secretariat should also mainstream cross-cutting issues contained in paragraph 173 of the Accord into the work of all divisions, and ensure that UNCTAD work was conducted in accordance with sub-theme 4 of the Accord.

The Working Party also considered a progress report on the implementation of sub-theme 4 of the Accord [TD/B/WP/207], welcomed the measures taken in the implementation of the Accord, inter alia, through the creation of the Accra Accord Steering Group, and encouraged the secretariat to continue its efforts in that regard and to keep States informed on a regular basis, particularly during the monthly consultations of the TDB President. The Party emphasized the importance of partnership among States, relevant UN system bodies and the secretariat in strengthening the organization, stressed the importance of developing a new communication strategy and encouraged the secretariat to consult with States in that connection. Reiterating the priority UNCTAD should accord to helping countries integrate trade into their UN Development Assistance Frameworks, it requested the secretariat to periodically update States on progress in that regard. UNCTAD should also assist UN resident coordinators in identifying and developing UNCTAD programmes for their countries and their inclusion in UN development frameworks. The secretariat should inform States on the efforts made by the UNCTAD Secretary-General to attract voluntary contributions for the funding of the participation of experts from developing countries in expert meetings, including through the funding campaign to be launched in September.

TDB, at its fifty-fifth session [A/63/15 (Part IV)], took note of the reports of the Working Party on its fiftieth and fifty-first sessions and endorsed the agreed conclusions contained therein, including the change of name to the Working Party on the Strategic Framework and the Programme Budget.

Chapter V

Regional economic and social activities

The five regional commissions continued in 2008 to provide technical cooperation, including advisory services, to their member States to promote programmes and projects and provide training to enhance national capacity-building in various sectors. Four of them—the Economic Commission for Africa (ECA), the Economic and Social Commission for Asia and the Pacific (ESCAP), the Economic Commission for Latin America and the Caribbean (ECLAC) and the Economic and Social Commission for Western Asia (ESCWA)—held regular sessions during the year. The Economic Commission for Europe (ECE) did not meet in 2008, but was scheduled to do so in 2009.

The Executive Secretaries of the commissions continued to meet periodically to exchange views and coordinate activities and positions on major development issues. In July, the Economic and Social Council held a dialogue with the Executive Secretaries on the theme "The regional dimension of the themes of the high-level segment for 2008".

In 2008, ECA organized its annual session as part of the first joint meetings of the African Union (AU) Conference of Ministers of Economy and Finance and the ECA Conference of African Ministers of Finance, Planning and Economic Development. At its March–April session, ECA met on the theme "Meeting Africa's New Development Challenges in the 21st Century", and adopted a ministerial statement in which Ministers reaffirmed their commitment to the internationally agreed development goals, including the Millennium Development Goals (MDGs), and to the AU New Partnership for Africa's Development programme as the shared framework for development and global partnership.

Meeting in April on the theme "Energy security and sustainable development in Asia and the Pacific", ESCAP adopted a resolution calling upon all members and associate members to cooperate in developing renewable energy technologies through the sharing of policy and technological experiences.

During its June session, ECLAC held a regional consultation in preparation for the Follow-up International Conference on Financing for Development to Review the Implementation of the Monterrey Consensus, holding panel discussions on financing and cooperation, mobilization of domestic resources, systemic issues, and gender policies in financing for development. In addition, ECLAC approved the admission of the Cayman Islands as an associate member.

At its May session, ESCWA reviewed financing for development in the region, in preparation for the Follow-up International Conference, and strengthening regional cooperation for achieving the MDGs. It launched a portal for information gathering and issued a report on the MDGs in the Arab region as at 2007. In July, the Economic and Social Council approved the admission of the Sudan as a member of ESCWA.

The regional commissions also found themselves dealing with the effects of the financial crisis that reached significant global proportions towards the end of the year. Within the context of their mandates, the Commissions began to consider what actions they might take to mitigate the effects of that crisis in their regions.

Regional cooperation

In 2008, the United Nations continued to strengthen cooperation among its regional commissions, between them and other UN entities, and with regional and international organizations.

On 8 February (**decision 2008/209**), the Economic and Social Council decided that the theme for the regional cooperation item of its 2008 substantive session would be "The regional dimension of the themes of the high-level segment for 2008". Accordingly, the Council held a dialogue with the Executive Secretaries of the regional commissions on that subject on 7 July.

Meetings of Executive Secretaries. As noted by the Secretary-General in his annual report on regional cooperation in the economic, social and related fields [E/2008/15], the 2008 annual meeting of the regional commissions, held by the current coordinator—the Executive Secretary of the Economic Commission for Africa (ECA)—took place in Addis Ababa, Ethiopia, on 16 and 17 June. The Executive Secretaries of the regional commissions also met in New York on the margins of the Economic and Social Council session in July, and of the Second Committee of the General Assembly in October. Notable on their agenda were the regional commissions' coordinated actions and efforts to support UN system-wide coherence at the regional and global levels, as well as their substantive contributions to, and regional perspectives on, the challenges of climate change, food and energy security, and the ongoing economic and financial crisis. Those issues were also addressed as part of their dialogues with the Council and the Second Committee.

The Executive Secretaries and selected senior staff held their first retreat at the United Nations System Staff College in Turin, Italy, in September, and identified the following main areas for the regional commissions to foster their interregional cooperation and exchange of best practices: statistics, including statistical alignment with the Millennium Development Goals (MDGS) and international standards; energy security and efficiency; transport infrastructure, border crossing and facilitation; aid for trade; disaster risk reduction; and social policy. In addition, two side events were organized at the margins of the Follow-up International Conference on Financing for Development to Review the Implementation of the Monterrey Consensus [YUN 2002, p. 953], held in Doha, Qatar, from 29 November to 2 December (see p. 1072), in which the regional commissions discussed the issues of financing for development and the economics of gender, and the role of regional cooperation and global partnership in financing for development.

Addenda to the Secretary-General's report [E/2008/15/Add.1,2] contained the texts of resolutions and decisions adopted at recent meetings of the regional commissions that called for the Council's attention or action.

By **decision 2008/234** of 23 July, the Council took note of the Secretary-General's reports on: regional cooperation and the economic situation in Europe, 2007–2008 [E/2008/16]; the economic and social conditions in Africa, 2008 [E/2008/17]; the economic and social survey of Asia and the Pacific, 2008 [E/2008/18]; the economic situation and outlook of Latin America and the Caribbean, 2007–2008 [E/2008/19]; and the survey of economic and social developments in the ESCWA region, 2007–2008 [E/2008/20].

The Council also adopted resolutions on: the venue of the twenty-fifth (2008) session of ESCWA (see p. 1135); the restructuring of the conference structure of ESCAP (see p. 1114); the admission of the Sudan as a member of ESCWA (see p. 1134); and the venue of the thirty-third (2010) session of ECLAC (see p. 1129).

(For the summaries of the economic surveys and the texts of the resolutions, see the relevant sections of this chapter.)

Global economic and financial crisis

In a later report [E/2009/15], the Secretary-General drew attention to the unfolding of the worst global economic and financial crisis since the Great Depression. The crisis, which became full-blown in September, was rapidly spreading to developing countries and emerging market economies, which were affected by lower export revenues because of lower volumes and prices, less tourism, increased unemployment, and decreased capital flows, foreign direct investment and remittances, along with fiscal budgetary constraints.

Although unprecedented measures had been taken to avert the worsening of the crisis, the global recovery would be protracted and further policy action would be required to help restore confidence and to relieve the financial markets of the uncertainties that were affecting the prospects for economic recovery. While the prices of food and fuel had decreased since the peak they reached in July, the commodities markets remained highly volatile and uncertain. According to World Bank figures, higher food prices were estimated to have increased global poverty by some 130 million to 135 million people. Meanwhile, fuel prices experienced sharp swings, with oil prices peaking in July and declining by 70 per cent at the end of the year. According to the International Energy Agency, current global trends in energy supply and consumption were patently unsustainable—environmentally, economically and socially.

Each region in the world was affected differently by the multiple crises and each was responding according to its particular conditions and circumstances. However, lessons learned by some regions from previous crises had increased their resilience to the current one. Regional responses had proven to be a valuable means of buffering countries against the impact of the economic and financial crisis, but much remained to be done. Strong regional platforms and South-South cooperation could serve as a basis to address development challenges and implement innovative solutions through enhanced and strengthened coordination and collaboration. The report examined how the different regions were affected by the crises, how they were responding, how those initiatives could be further enhanced and how the five UN regional commissions were supporting Member States in those efforts.

Establishment of posts

By **resolution 63/260** of 24 December, the General Assembly established a number of posts for development-related activities, effective 1 January 2009, under the following budget sections: 17, Economic and social development in Africa; 18, Economic and social development in Asia and the Pacific; 19, Economic development in Europe; 20, Economic and social development in Latin America and the Caribbean; and 21, Economic and social development in Western Asia. It also established posts, effective 1 July 2009, for the following sections: 10, Least developed countries, landlocked developing countries and small island developing States; 11, United Nations support for the New Partnership for Africa's Development; and 12, Trade and development. The Assembly decided not to abolish the post of the Special Adviser on Africa at the Under-Secretary-General level, and not to approve the non-post resources for travel of staff, consultants and experts and contractual services, excluding the regional commissions.

Africa

The Economic Commission for Africa (ECA) organized its 2008 annual session as part of the joint meetings of the African Union (AU) Conference of Ministers of Economy and Finance and the ECA Conference of African Ministers of Finance, Planning and Economic Development, according to Economic and Social Council resolution 2007/4 [YUN 2007, p. 1014]. ECA held its forty-first session/First Joint Annual Meetings of the AU and ECA Conference of African Ministers (Addis Ababa, Ethiopia, 31 March–2 April) [E/2008/38-E/ECA/CM.41/5] under the theme "Meeting Africa's New Challenges in the Twenty-first Century". It had before it an issues paper prepared by the ECA secretariat on the theme [E/ECA/COE/27/2], and also considered the report of the twenty-seventh meeting of the Committee of Experts of the Conference of African Ministers of Finance, Planning and Economic Development [E/ECA/COE/27/5] (Addis Ababa, 26–29 March). A high-level thematic debate covered the issues of empowering the poor; growth, employment and poverty; climate change and development; and HIV/AIDS. A ministerial panel discussion was organized on the impact of the recent rise in oil and food prices on African economies; and Africa's debt situation. Resolutions were adopted on: financing for development [E/2008/38 (res. 854(XLI))]; climate change and development in Africa [res. 855(XLI)]; science with Africa: strengthening research and development, and innovation for Africa's socio-economic development [res. 856(XLI)]; the proposed strategic framework/biennial programme plan for the period 2010–2011 [res. 857(XLI)]; the special meeting of the Governing Council of the African Institute for Economic Development and Planning [res. 858(XLI)]; African Charter on Statistics [res. 859(XLI)]; the Millenium Development Goals (MDGs) [res. 860(XLI)]; and the assessment of progress on regional integration in Africa [res. 861(XLI)].

The session adopted a ministerial statement [E/ECA/CM/41/3] in which Ministers reaffirmed their commitment to the internationally agreed development goals, including the MDGs, and to the AU New Partnership for Africa's Development (NEPAD) [YUN 2001, p. 899] programme as the shared framework for development and global partnership. They also reiterated their commitment to making employment creation a central objective of their economic and social policies, and welcomed the new opportunities for accelerating economic growth and employment creation as a result of rapidly expanding South-South cooperation. Given the finite nature of gas and oil resources, they underscored the need to pursue alternative sources of energy, and committed to implementing all the pillars of the Comprehensive African Agricultural Development Programme to address the escalating food prices. The Ministers also underscored the need to prepare for participation in the global review of the Monterrey Consensus on Financing for Development, to be held in Doha, Qatar, from 29 November to 2 December (see p. 1072), and committed to efforts to mobilize domestic savings, strengthen their financial systems, stem capital flight, promote Pan-African stock exchange and reduce the transaction costs of remittances. Expressing concern about desertification and deforestation, they reaffirmed their commitment to integrate climate change adaptation and mitigation strategies into their national and regional development frameworks.

Economic trends

In 2008, a period in which world growth declined to 2.5 per cent from 3.7 per cent in 2007, Africa's gross domestic product (GDP) fell from 6 to 5.1 per cent, according to an overview of the economic and social conditions in Africa [E/2009/17]. The main driver of Africa's growth was the rise in commodity prices, especially oil, with oil-exporting countries growing at 5.9 per cent—compared to 4.4 per cent for the non-oil countries—and thus accounting for 61.4 per cent of the continent's overall growth. Other factors beneath that sustained growth momentum included good macroeconomic policies and institutional reforms. During the year, GDP growth decelerated in three of five subregions. West Africa grew from 5.2 to 5.4 per cent and Central Africa from 3.9 to 4.9 per cent. GDP growth rates decreased in North Africa (to 5.4 per cent), East Africa (to 5.7 per cent) and Southern Africa (to 4.2 per cent). Overall, East Africa maintained the highest growth rate in 2006–2008, owing to expansion in agriculture, horticulture and services, especially finance, telecommunications and construction, as well as healthy inflows of aid and strong growth in tourism and foreign direct investment.

The *Economic Report on Africa*, a joint publication of ECA and the AU aiming to disseminate key findings of ECA's research activities, devoted its 2008 edition to *Africa and the Monterrey Consensus: Tracking Performance and Progress* [Sales No. E.08.II.K.1]. The *Report* considered the main developments in the world economy; recent economic performance and growth prospects in Africa; and major global development challenges. It also discussed Africa's progress in meeting the goals of the Monterrey Consensus, adopted at the 2002 International Conference on Financing for Development [YUN 2002, p. 953] and the results of the ECA survey on African policymakers' views on its implementation.

Activities in 2008

The ECA programme of work in 2008 was organized under 10 subprogrammes: trade, finance and economic development; food security and sustainable development; governance and public administration; information, science and technology for development; economic cooperation and regional integration; gender and women in development; subregional activities for development; development planning and administration; statistics; and social development [E/2009/38].

Trade, finance and economic development

ECA continued in 2008 to strengthen the capacity of member States to design and implement appropriate policies to achieve sustained economic growth for poverty reduction, in line with the priorities of the Millennium Declaration [YUN 2000, p. 49] and NEPAD. Its work under this subprogramme aimed at promoting higher and sustained economic growth through enhanced capacity for macroeconomic and sectoral policy analysis, international trade and finance.

In 2008, ECA contributed to the preparation of the African Economic Outlook for 2008–2009, providing substantive inputs to the analyses on the short-term and medium-term outlook. In the area of trade, several policy inputs were provided to ongoing initiatives. Key among those was an audit report on the interim Economic Partnership Agreements (EPA) with the European Union and a set of draft policy recommendations on the way forward for the EPA negotiations prepared by the ECA secretariat and submitted to the AU Conference of Ministers of Trade and Finance in April. The ECA African Trade Policy Centre, a field project supported by Canada, expanded its trade-related capacity-building services in 2008, with more than 20 African countries benefiting from training. The Centre also collaborated with GAINDE 2000—a Senegalese customs computer system providing automated solutions for efficiency in trade and transport—in organizing the International Single Window Conference in Dakar in November.

Through research support and advocacy, ECA contributed to an effective participation by African countries in the Follow-up International Conference on Financing for Development to Review the Implementation of the Monterrey Consensus (see p. 1076). It also contributed to the review of commitments by African countries and made several presentations outlining Africa's views and concerns on implementation of the Monterrey Consensus. In addition, the third African Economic Conference was jointly organized with the African Development Bank (AfDB) in Tunis in November, bringing together more than 300 economists and policymakers to discuss issues related to the theme of the Conference: "Globalization, institutions and economic development of Africa". The international financial crisis was also a key focus of attention, as a special meeting of African finance ministers and central bank governors was convened on the first day of the Conference to discuss Africa's response to the crisis.

New Partnership for Africa's Development

As the coordinator of UN agencies and organizations working in Africa in support of NEPAD, a programme for the continent's development initiated by African leaders in 2001 [YUN 2001, p. 899], ECA provided strong and tangible support for the implementation of NEPAD priorities through its analytical work and technical assistance in different areas, with particular focus on socio-economic development and political governance issues. It also collaborated with UN agencies and other partners, in particular AfDB and the regional economic communities, in supporting NEPAD infrastructure development.

(For more information on NEPAD, see p. 1007).

Food security and sustainable development

The objective of the subprogramme on food security and sustainable development was to strengthen the capacity of States to implement policies, strategies and programmes that took account of the synergies between agriculture and environment. Best practices for selected commodities were assessed in West Africa, Central Africa and Southern Africa, with a focus on palm oil and banana plantain in Cameroon, maize in Malawi, cassava in Nigeria, rice and tomato in Senegal, and milk in South Africa. To promote biotechnology uptake in Africa, ECA developed a UN-Biotech/Africa website and embarked on production of a related newsletter.

ECA acted in the context of the AU/NEPAD Comprehensive Africa Agricultural Development Programme (CAADP) to strengthen the development of value chains for strategic food commodities. It also collaborated with the Food and Agriculture Organization of the United Nations to champion the development of major agricultural and food products value chains in East Africa; with the United Nations Industrial Development Organization (UNIDO) to promote development in the agribusiness sector; and with the AU/NEPAD and the AfDB to establish an African common market for agricultural products. Within the CAADP framework, it continued to promote the AU/ECA/AfDB Joint Initiative on Land Policy in Africa, aimed at improving the management of land and land resources.

Climate change

The African Ministerial Conference on the Environment, at its twelfth session (Johannesburg, South Africa, 10–12 June) [UNEP/AMCEN/12/9], approved the Climate for Development in Africa (ClimDev-Africa) programme, a joint AU/ECA/AfDB initiative developed with the Global Climate Observing System to facilitate development of policies, practices, services, observation networks and communication with stakeholders to enable effective climate change mitigation and adaptation in Africa.

In August, ECA participated in negotiations in Accra, Ghana, which advanced work on a strengthened international climate change deal under the UN Framework Convention on Climate Change, as well as on emission reduction rules and tools under the Kyoto Protocol. In November, it played an important role in organizing the Preparatory Meeting on Climate Change for African National Focal Points and Negotiators and the African Conference of Ministers in Charge of Environment on Climate Change.

Jointly with the United Nations Development Programme (UNDP) Drylands Development Centre and the International Strategy for Disaster Reduction (see p. 1026), ECA organized the Third African Drought Adaptation Forum (Addis Ababa, 17–19 September), which brought together some 80 policymakers, Government officials, UN agencies, donors, practitioners from local and international non-governmental and community-based organizations, the media and researchers from around Africa and the Arab States to exchange experience, findings and ideas on how to adapt to the increasing threat of drought and climate change in the drylands of Africa.

Governance and public administration

ECA's objective under this subprogramme was to promote good governance practices for all sectors of society, including civil service, the public sector, the private sector and civil society; and to support the African Peer Review Mechanism process by assisting member States in all stages of the process.

ECA expanded its project on "Assessing and monitoring progress towards good governance in Africa", which was designed to inform policymaking on governance-related issues and would culminate in the 2009 publication of the second edition of the African Governance Report, aimed at helping African countries develop, sustain and internalize the norms of good governance.

ECA engaged major stakeholders in the fight against corruption, including the judiciary, national anti-corruption institutions, Parliaments and the pan-African association of national anti-corruption institutions. In October, it organized in Addis Ababa, jointly with the Council for the Development of Social Science Research in Africa, an International Conference on Institutions, Culture and Corruption in Africa, to discuss the issue from an African perspective and develop policies and strategies.

Information, science and technology for development

ECA's work under this subprogramme aimed at strengthening and sustaining an African information society, as well as developing capacity for the formulation, adaptation and implementation of appropriate science and technology policies and programmes. ECA fulfilled its objective of improving States' capacities to formulate, implement, coordinate and evaluate policies and strategies for information for development.

In response to requests by African countries to initiate a programme on cyber security, ECA launched an African Cyber Security Strategy programme in Burkina Faso, Ghana, Kenya and Mozambique. As part of the recent ECA repositioning, more emphasis was placed on strengthening States' capacity to harness the potential of science, technology and innovation for their socio-economic development, mainly through eight science and technology programmes implemented in 2008.

Economic cooperation and regional integration

The objective of ECA under this subprogramme was to promote effective economic cooperation among States and strengthen the process of regional integration in Africa through enhanced intra-African trade and physical integration, with particular emphasis on the development of infrastructure and natural resources. With ECA's support, Burundi and the United Republic of Tanzania ratified a protocol to create a Central African corridor aimed at increasing intra-regional trade in the subregion. ECA's coordinating role contributed to the conclusion of an understanding to create a common free trade area among three regional economic communities: the Common Market for Eastern and Southern Africa (COMESA), the Southern African Development Community (SADC) and the East African Community (EAC).

In June, under the auspices of ECA, experts from 21 African countries and 8 African organizations involved in transport facilitation attended an African regional meeting in Addis Ababa to review the Almaty Programme of Action: Addressing the Special Needs of Landlocked Developing Countries within a New Global Framework for Transit Transport Cooperation for Landlocked and Transit Developing Countries [YUN 2003, p. 875]. In September, in collaboration with the United Nations Department of Economic and Social Affairs, ECA organized a regional forum in Addis Ababa on "Interconnections and electricity access for sustainable development", under the United Nations Development Account project on "Capacity-building for interregional electricity access and supply in Africa". The forum adopted a set of recommendations on how to expand electricity transmission lines and gas pipelines between African countries. It was attended by some 30 policymakers and energy experts representing national power utilities, subregional power pools, river basin organizations, regional economic communities and a group of 10 leading electric companies from the Group of Eight (G-8) most industrialized countries.

Gender and women in development

ECA's activities under this subprogramme aimed at contributing to the achievement of women's advancement and gender equality. In August, at the Conference of Ministers of Gender and Women's Affairs, ECA launched an African Women's Rights Observatory, to serve as a comprehensive source of data on research findings and resources, institutions, developments and events related to women's rights in Africa, and to track the progress of African countries in the area of women's human rights. In partnership with the United Nations Human Settlements Programme (UN-Habitat) and UNDP's regional gender programme for Africa, ECA embarked on a study to assess progress in implementing the MDGs in Africa, taking account of the gender dimension in all the indicators of those goals.

The Beijing Platform for Action [YUN 1995, p. 1170] was a key framework used by ECA in its efforts to enhance States' ability to implement and monitor the implementation of regional and global resolutions, conventions, instruments and protocols on women's human rights. In preparation for the review of the Beijing Platform for Action, ECA developed an evaluation process which it presented to its Committee on Women and Development in August. The Committee adopted the process and encouraged ECA to work with speed towards ensuring a successful review.

In November, the Sixth African Development Forum considered the theme "Action on gender equality, women's empowerment and ending violence against women in Africa". The Forum brought together over 800 participants and provided an opportunity for the continent to take stock of progress made towards achieving gender equality and women's empowerment, ending violence against women, identifying the challenges constraining implementation of policies and strategies, and articulating actions to hasten the translation of African countries' commitments into reality. It recommended three priority actions: launching an Africa-wide, three-year campaign to eliminate violence against women and girls, addressing the underlying economic and social causes of their vulnerability and strengthening the legal system and provision of supportive services; scaling up efforts to improve financing for gender equality; and strengthening the collection of reliable data on gender equality, women's empowerment and violence against women and girls.

Subregional development activities

ECA continued to carry out its activities at the subregional level through its five subregional offices, located in Central Africa (Yaoundé, Cameroon), East Africa (Kigali, Rwanda), North Africa (Rabat, Morocco), Southern Africa (Lusaka, Zambia) and West Africa (Niamey, Niger). Their activities aimed primarily at strengthening States' capacities for regional integration by spearheading the delivery of ECA's operational activities targeted at the specific priorities of each subregion, within the overall framework of the implementation of NEPAD and achievement of the MDGS.

The subregional offices also provided guidance to ECA's overall programme delivery, while continuing to operate as subregional nodes for knowledge management and networking to strengthen ECA's outreach. In tracking progress towards the achievement of the MDGs at the country level, they continued to collaborate with other UN agencies through such means as the Common Country Assessment, the United Nations Development Assistance Framework and Delivering as one.

All five offices developed extensive and elaborate multi-year programmes of support and collaboration with major regional economic communities in their subregions, and ECA concluded multi-year programmes of support with the Central African Monetary and Economic Community, the Economic Community of the Great Lakes Countries, COMESA,

EAC, the Economic Community of Central African States, the Economic Community of West African States (ECOWAS), the Intergovernmental Authority on Development, the Indian Ocean Commission, SADC, the Community of Sahel-Saharan States and the Maghreb Arab Union.

Development planning and administration

The objective of this subprogramme, implemented by the African Institute for Economic Development and Planning (IDEP), based in Dakar, Senegal, was to enhance national and regional capacities to formulate and implement development policies and economic management strategies. Despite its fragile financial situation, the Institute continued to design and implement programmes that supported policymakers' priorities in the area of economic policy and to spearhead efforts in capacity-building. In April, 10 trainees from eight countries graduated from its 18-month Master of Arts degree programme in economic policy and management.

Five courses plus a course in economic report writing in the areas of industrial policy, applied econometrics, debt management, regional integration and project monitoring and evaluation were delivered in 2008. A bilingual session on industrial policy analysis in Africa, sponsored by IDEP with technical assistance from UNIDO, contributed to developing a critical mass of policymakers who would be better equipped to design and manage industrial development policies in Africa. The course was attended by 25 participants from 25 countries, including 10 women. In July, IDEP organized, in collaboration with ECOWAS, a short course on economic report writing for the benefit of National Coordinating Committees operating under the ECOWAS Multilateral Surveillance Mechanism. The course, aimed at enhancing the capacity of Committee officials to produce quarterly economic reports, brought together 31 participants from eight French-speaking countries in the ECOWAS subregion.

Statistics

The objective of ECA's work under this subprogramme was to improve the production, dissemination and use of key demographic, social, economic and environmental statistics, including the MDG indicators, in accordance with internationally agreed standards and good practice, and in order to promote the implementation of the new Reference Regional Strategic Framework for Statistical Capacity-building in Africa.

ECA continued to coordinate the work of the Statistics Cluster of the MDG Africa Working Group, designing a business plan for the Cluster, making recommendations to the MDG Africa Steering Group, and monitoring progress in the implementation of the business plan. It was also involved in a study of discrepancies among national and international data arising from monitoring of work towards the MDGs in Africa. Together with AfDB, it produced a two-year programme of work aimed at reinforcing the capacity of African countries to report on the Goals.

ECA published the quarterly *African Statistical Newsletter* as a medium for the exchange of knowledge, experience and best practice in statistics and statistical development, with articles written by statisticians from different countries and organizations in and outside Africa. It also continued to work with AfDB to publish the *African Statistical Journal*, an outlet for technical and research work. ECA also followed up progress in creating awareness among statisticians about gender issues and integrating them into national statistical programmes. A high-level policy dialogue on gender statistics was held in Kampala, Uganda, in June, and a first regional workshop on gender statistics in Addis Ababa in December.

Social development

ECA's objective under this subprogramme was to strengthen the capacity of States to formulate policies and programmes for poverty reduction and for delivering equitable social services and integrating social dimensions in the development process, in line with internationally agreed development goals, including the MDGs. In May, it organized an international conference on the UN Convention on the Rights of Persons with Disabilities, in collaboration with Leonard Cheshire International. That resulted in the adoption of the Addis Ababa Call to Action, designed to help promote and protect the rights of persons with disabilities in Africa and ensure that their concerns were integrated in development policies.

The Commission produced a number of significant reports in 2008: "Youth employment opportunities" focused on promoting decent employment for young women through entrepreneurship training and microfinance; "The state of older people in Africa, 2007–2008: Regional review and appraisal of the Madrid International Plan of Action on Ageing" drew attention to the issue of ageing as a major emerging challenge for Africa; and "Placing social integration at the centre of Africa's development agenda" noted that, despite recent years of relatively high economic growth in Africa, chronic poverty persisted in many countries, partly because Governments and development partners did not pay adequate attention to socially excluded groups.

Programme and organizational questions

Strategic Framework, 2010–2011

The twenty-seventh meeting of the Committee of Experts of the First Joint Annual Meetings of the AU Conference of Ministers of Economy and Finance and ECA Conference of African Ministers of Finance, Planning and Economic Development (Addis Ababa, Ethiopia, 26–29 March) [E/2008/38] considered the proposed ECA Strategic Framework/Biennial Programme Plan for the period 2010–2011 [E/ECA/COE/27/17], to be submitted to the Committee on Programme and Coordination at its June session, and eventually recommended to the General Assembly for approval. The Framework reaffirmed the ECA mandate and scaled up its assistance to African States and their development partners to formulate and implement policies and programmes leading to sustainable economic growth and social development. It noted that ECA would continue to promote regional integration in support of the AU vision and priorities, to meet Africa's special needs and emerging global challenges and to develop a stronger subregional presence by empowering its subregional offices and strengthening its partnerships with the AU, the AfDB and other UN agencies.

The Committee noted that the Framework clearly articulated ECA's priorities for the biennium, took account of some emerging challenges to Africa's development and offered opportunities for collaboration between ECA and Member States. It observed that transport remained a major challenge to Africa's development, and underscored the need to improve air transport services and address aviation safety within the continent. The Committee also underscored the need to translate the Framework into specific and concrete activities, and urged ECA to promote South-South cooperation, including intra-African cooperation, as a strategy for achieving the Framework's objectives.

In response to the issues raised by the Committee, ECA assured the meeting that comments and suggestions made would be taken into consideration and concrete outputs derived from the Framework would be presented in the programme budget. ECA would continue to implement the results-based management framework. It further informed the Committee that transport concerns were addressed under its subprogramme 5, on economic cooperation and regional integration. The Committee recommended the Framework to the Conference of Ministers for its consideration and endorsement.

By resolution 857(XLI), the ECA Conference of Ministers at its forty-first session (Addis Ababa, 31 March–2 April) endorsed the proposed Strategic Framework, taking into account the preceding discussion and related observations.

Asia and the Pacific

The Economic and Social Commission for Asia and the Pacific (ESCAP) held its sixty-fourth session in Bangkok, Thailand, in two parts: the senior officials segment from 24 to 26 April and the ministerial segment from 28 to 30 April [E/2008/39]. The session's theme was "Energy security and sustainable development in Asia and the Pacific". Introducing the theme at the Ministerial Round Table, the ESCAP Executive Secretary stressed the need to create a virtuous cycle of sustainable energy that would place greater reliance on renewable energy and improved energy efficiency, and strengthen efforts to mitigate climate change.

On 30 April, in a resolution on promoting renewables for energy security and sustainable development in Asia and the Pacific [E/2008/39 (res. 64/3)], the Commission called upon all members and associate members to cooperate proactively in developing various renewable energy technologies through the sharing of policy and technological experiences; and to encourage and participate actively in subregional, regional and intraregional initiatives on capacity-building, renewable energy demonstration projects and public-private partnerships to improve their reliability and affordability. The Commission also called on them to closely involve developing countries in the development of new and renewable energy technologies, products and services, to make them cost-competitive; to encourage the rapid dissemination of new and renewable energy technologies to developing countries; to make their research institutions accessible to developing countries; and to facilitate, by working with intellectual property rights holders, the transfer of new and renewable energy technologies to developing countries by considering, on a voluntary basis, the reduction of technical and licensing costs.

The Executive Secretary was asked to coordinate with the multilateral funding agencies to enhance financial and technology flows for the development and deployment of new and renewable energy technologies in developing countries; to facilitate synergies with regional groupings to promote the development of renewable energy technologies; to establish an institutional cooperation mechanism with the active engagement of expert research institutions in the region on renewable energy technologies; and to increase participation in public-private partnerships and initiatives to expand the use of renewable technologies through innovative policy options and practical measures.

The Commission also discussed thematic and cross-cutting issues (poverty reduction, globalization, emerging social issues, and countries with special needs); management issues; and technical cooperation activities. In the ministerial segment, it considered the theme of the session, and such policy issues as key challenges for inclusive and sustainable economic and social development since the Commission's previous session; the *Economic and Social Survey of Asia and the Pacific 2008* [Sales No. E.08.II.F.7]; and achieving the MDGs in the region.

Economic trends

According to the summary of the economic and social survey of Asia and the Pacific, 2009 [E/2009/18], the Asia-Pacific region, for the second time in a decade, had been hit by financial crisis. Although the crisis had its roots outside the region, its magnitude left no economy untouched, and the region continued to experience significant downward pressures on growth, with social consequences that were still unfolding. The increasing spill-over of the effects of the financial crisis into the real sector, together with long-term challenges posed by climate change and huge volatilities in food and fuel prices dimmed the prospect that the MDGs would be attained by 2015.

Activities in 2008

Poverty reduction

During its sixty-fourth session (24–30 April), the Commission had before it the report of the Committee on Poverty Reduction on its fourth (2007) session [YUN 2007, p. 1017] and secretariat notes on: the summary of progress in the implementation of resolutions relating to the theme of poverty reduction [E/ESCAP/64/2]; financing for development 2008 [E/ESCAP/64/3]; and aid effectiveness [E/ESCAP/64/4].

With respect to the Committee's report, the Commission noted the socio-economic progress of countries in the region, including in the achievement of MDGs. It said that higher food and oil prices were adversely affecting poverty reduction in some countries and that increased regional cooperation would help address that issue. The Commission emphasized that the revitalization of agriculture was key to efforts to address food shortages and contain food inflation. It also noted that microfinance and microcredit were effective tools for poverty reduction.

As for its previous resolutions on poverty reduction, the Commission noted the progress made in the implementation of its resolutions 63/4 [YUN 2007, p. 1017], on achieving the MDGs in the ESCAP region; 62/9 [YUN 2006, p. 1160], on regional follow-up to the Mauritius Strategy for the Further Implementation of the Programme of Action for the Sustainable Development of Small Island Developing States [YUN 2005, p. 946]; and 62/11 [YUN 2006, p. 1159], on implementation of the Programme of Action for the Least Developed Countries for the Decade 2001–2010 [YUN 2001, p. 770].

On the subject of financing for development, the Commission observed that savings had increased while the region had attracted more foreign resources for development, particularly foreign direct investment. International trade had increased and external debt had fallen substantially. Steps had also been taken to address systemic issues at both the national and regional levels. However, challenges remained with regard to achieving progress in all of those areas. Nevertheless, some developing countries had made the transition from being recipients of development assistance to being donor countries themselves.

Addressing the question of aid effectiveness, the Commission noted that effective and sustainable assistance should be demand-driven and accompanied by efforts to build absorptive capacity to ensure that aid was used to maximum effectiveness. It also noted the importance of strengthening existing partnerships as well as exploring new ones, in particular under South-South and trilateral North-South-South cooperation frameworks.

Managing globalization

The Commission had before it the reports of the Committee on Managing Globalization on its fourth session [E/ESCAP/64/5, E/ESCAP/64/6], held in two parts in 2007 [YUN 2007, p. 1018]. It also had before it a series of documents relating to four subprogrammes in that area, namely: trade and investment; transport and tourism; environment and sustainable development; and information, communication and space technology [E/ESCAP/64/7, E/ESCAP/64/8 & Corr.1, E/ESCAP/64/9, E/ESCAP/64/10, E/ESCAP/64/11, E/ESCAP/64/12].

Trade and investment

The Commission recognized the importance of sustained trade and investment liberalization for economic and social development. It noted the progress achieved and the initiatives undertaken by developing countries and countries with economies in transition in reducing tariffs and liberalizing and facilitating trade, including through participation in the ongoing Doha round of negotiations and the conclusion of regional and bilateral trade agreements, and it took note of the assistance that some of those countries had provided for neighbouring countries in an effort to promote trade among developing countries.

The Commission noted the importance of trade facilitation, including simplification of trade and customs procedures and documents; e-commerce, including single-window systems; and the elimination of non-tariff barriers to trade. It also noted the policies of various countries in support of an improvement in the investment climate.

Transport and tourism

Noting the importance of transport for economic, social and trade development, the Commission expressed support for the work of the secretariat in the development of the Asian Highway and Trans-Asian Railway. It acknowledged that the Asian Highway and the Trans-Asian Railway networks were building blocks for the development of an international integrated intermodal transport and logistics network for the region, as envisioned in the 2006 Busan Declaration on Transport Development in Asia and the Pacific [YUN 2006, p. 1161]. It recognized the role of the Trans-Asian Railway network in connecting people and expanding trade, and noted the importance of road and transport linkages for creating opportunities for economic activities such as trade, investment and tourism, which would benefit people along the routes. The Commission noted the importance of road safety and expressed its support for the implementation of the Ministerial Declaration on Improving Road Safety in Asia and the Pacific [ibid.]. It also noted that the General Assembly, in its **resolution 62/244** of 31 March on improving global road safety (see p. 1340), had welcomed the offer of the Russian Federation to host the first high-level (ministerial) conference on road safety in Moscow in 2009, in order to exchange experiences and foster cooperation.

On 30 April [E/2008/39 (res. 64/4)], the Commission adopted a resolution on the implementation of the 2007 Seoul Declaration on Public-Private Partnerships for Infrastructure Development in Asia and the Pacific [YUN 2007, p. 1019]. It urged members and associate members to place high priority on national development agendas on infrastructure development; promote the role of public-private partnerships and recognize that they could complement Governments' efforts in developing infrastructure facilities and services; and implement policies on public-private partnerships. It encouraged members and associate members to engage in regional cooperation initiatives, and requested the Executive Secretary to work with donor countries and development partners to assist members and associate members in meeting infrastructure development challenges; assist them in their capacity-building programmes; provide technical support to help assess their public-private partnership readiness; and undertake a periodic review of the progress made.

Also on 30 April [ibid. (res. 64/5)], the Commission established the Forum of Asian Ministers of Transport as a regional mechanism within the framework of the Commission's conference structure. It requested the Executive Secretary to convene the Forum's first session in 2009 and subsequently on a regular basis, and to ensure that a regional policy-oriented agenda was placed before the Forum.

Environment and sustainable development

The Commission acknowledged the importance of environment and sustainable development as a key cross-cutting issue in dealing with globalization in Asia and the Pacific, and highlighted the importance of the consensus reached at the 2007 United Nations Climate Change Conference [YUN 2007, p. 1060]. It also noted the importance of regional cooperation in energy security for fostering sustainable development in the region.

On 30 April [res. 64/2], the Commission adopted a resolution on regional cooperation in the implementation of the Hyogo Framework for Action, 2005–2015: Building the Resilience of Nations and Communities to Disasters in Asia and the Pacific [YUN 2005, p. 1016]. The Commission encouraged the countries in the region to host the Asian Ministerial Conference on Disaster Risk Reduction once every two years on a rotational basis.

Also on 30 April [res. 64/3], the Commission, in a resolution on promoting renewables for energy security and sustainable development in Asia and the Pacific, called upon its members and associate members to cooperate in the development of renewable energy technologies through the sharing of policy and technological experiences; to encourage and participate actively in subregional, regional and intraregional initiatives in the areas of capacity-building, renewable energy demonstration projects and public-private partnerships so as to promote renewable energy technologies; to involve developing countries in the development of new and renewable energy technologies, products and services that would eventually make their deployment cost-competitive; and to encourage the rapid dissemination of new and renewable energy technologies to developing countries.

Information, communications and space technology

During its session, the Commission recognized the important role played by information, communications and space technology in economic and social development and in bridging technological gaps among countries of Asia and the Pacific.

On 30 April [res. 64/10], the Commission adopted a resolution on the review of the operational details of the feasibility study for the establishment of an Asian and Pacific centre for information, communications and space technology-enabled disaster management. It invited Iran to review the operational details of the latest proposal for the centre, to clarify the implications, if any, of such changes on the scope, functions and value-added products and services to be offered, along with timelines for scheduling the introduction of information-sharing activities, and to submit them to the Commission's 2009 session.

By a decision of the same date [dec. 64/2], the Commission deferred consideration of the draft resolution sponsored by Iran, entitled "Establishment of the Asian and Pacific Centre for Information, Communication and Space Technology-enabled Disaster Management", to its 2009 session.

Emerging social issues

The Commission had before it the report of the Committee on Emerging Social Issues on its fourth session (Bangkok, Thailand, 26–28 November 2007) [E/ESCAP/64/13] and secretariat notes on: the summary of progress in the implementation of resolutions relating to emerging social issues [E/ESCAP/64/14]; the implementation of the Declaration of Commitment on HIV/AIDS: an assessment of the progress made by ESCAP members: challenges and opportunities [E/ESCAP/64/15]; and the follow-up to the High-level Dialogue on International Migration and Development and the Global Forum on International Migration and Development [E/ESCAP/64/16].

Noting the importance of addressing the threat posed by HIV/AIDS in the light of its impact on social and economic development in the region, the Commission welcomed the technical and financial assistance provided by Japan in the fight against HIV/AIDS—with $800 million having been contributed through the Global Fund to Fight AIDS, Tuberculosis and Malaria since 2002. It also recognized the multifaceted linkages between international migration and development, in particular the impact of migration on poverty reduction, and noted the progress in the implementation of its resolution 63/7 on international migration and development for least developed countries (LDCs), landlocked developing countries and small island developing States [YUN 2007, p. 1019]. It also recognized that persons with disabilities represented one of the most marginalized and underserved group, marked by high levels of illiteracy, poor nutritional status, high unemployment rates and low occupational mobility.

On 30 April [res. 64/8], the Commission adopted a resolution on the regional implementation of the Biwako Millennium Framework for Action [YUN 2002, p. 991] and Biwako Plus Five: Further Efforts towards an Inclusive, Barrier-free and Rights-based Society for Persons with Disabilities in Asia and the Pacific [YUN 2007, p. 1021]. It called on its members and associate members to develop and implement inclusive, barrier-free and rights-based policies on disability in line with the recommendations contained in the Framework and Biwako Plus Five.

Also on 30 April [res. 64/9], the Commission addressed the midpoint review of the implementation of the Plan of Action on Population and Poverty, adopted at the Fifth Asian and Pacific Population Conference [YUN 2003, p. 1013]. The Commission requested its Executive Secretary to assist members and associate members in building their capacity to integrate population factors into development planning; to conduct analytical studies and to compile and disseminate relevant demographic and population-related information and data with a view to identifying key demographic trends and emerging issues in the region; and to convene an expert group meeting to review the implementation of the Plan of Action.

Least developed, landlocked and island developing countries

For its consideration of countries with special needs—LDCs, landlocked developing countries and small island developing States—the Commission had before it the report of the Special Body on Pacific Island Developing Countries on its tenth session (Bangkok, 22–23 April) [E/ESCAP/64/17] and a secretariat note [E/ESCAP/64/18] on "Emerging issues in the implementation of the Almaty Programme of Action" [YUN 2003, p. 875]. The note outlined the Programme's five priority areas—fundamental transit policy issues; infrastructure development and maintenance; trade and trade facilitation; international support measures; and implementation and midterm review—and provided an overview of the issues encountered in its implementation in the ESCAP region.

Citing the seriousness of the unprecedented rise in food and fuel prices, the Commission requested the secretariat to hold, on an urgent basis, a high-level consultative meeting to address, through partnerships, the challenges of the food and fuel crisis prevailing in Asian and Pacific developing countries, including LDCs. It noted that accession to the World Trade Organization (WTO) provided an important opportunity for integrating into the global economy and for sharing the benefits of increased trade. It also noted that the pace of the accession was largely in the hands of each acceding developing country, and was based on that country's implementation of WTO compliant provisions and the successful completion of its bilateral market access negotiations with WTO members.

The Commission took note of the outcome document of the Regional Preparatory Expert Meeting of Euro-Asian Landlocked and Transit Developing Countries for the Mid-term Review of the Almaty Programme of Action (Bangkok, 22–23 April) [E/ESCAP/64/INF/6].

Technical cooperation

The Commission had before it an overview of ESCAP technical cooperation activities, including extrabudgetary contributions in 2007 [E/ESCAP/64/32]. Introducing that report, the Executive Secretary said that ESCAP technical cooperation work ensured that its analytical and normative work was well grounded in national realities. During the year, partnerships with UN and other entities had been a key element of its technical cooperation strategy. The total contributions received for those activities from the regular budget and voluntary contributions amounted to some $15 million. The cost of the delivery of ESCAP programmes in 2007 was approximately $17.6 million, an increase of some 30 per cent over 2006.

A total of $5.5 million had been expended through grants to countries and agencies under the Multi-Donor Voluntary Trust Fund on Tsunami Early Warning Arrangements in the Indian Ocean and Southeast Asia. Those grants had been provided to support tsunami advisory services, the dissemination of warnings and other disaster communications at the regional and national levels, capacity-building in standard operating procedures and related tools, and community-based hazard mapping. ESCAP also worked closely with the Special Unit for South-South Cooperation of UNDP to promote South-South cooperation in such areas as Pacific connectivity through information and communications technology and disaster risk reduction.

Ministerial round table

During its ministerial segment, from 28 to 30 April, the Commission held round tables on the session's theme, "Energy security and sustainable development in Asia and the Pacific". Opening the segment, the Executive Secretary said that the region's energy security challenges were the result of rapid growth in demand for energy, skyrocketing energy prices, and uncertainties with regard to other development concerns. There were grave threats to development prospects for countries in the region on all fronts—economic, social and environmental, including climate change. Some countries, in particular the least developed and landlocked countries and small island developing States, were expected to bear the brunt of the effects of rising energy insecurity.

The Executive Secretary stressed the need for a shift towards a new sustainable energy paradigm, to create a virtuous cycle of sustainable energy that would discourage waste and high energy consumption with their far-reaching economic and environmental costs. Such a paradigm shift would emphasize the quality of economic growth, place greater reliance on renewable energy and improved energy efficiency, and strengthen efforts to mitigate climate change; and it would require regional cooperation. Promoting public-private partnerships to expand the energy infrastructure and energy trade in the region was of utmost urgency. That included the vision of the session's theme study, the creation of a trans-Asian energy system spanning the entire region and linking together the various subregions through a common energy infrastructure.

The Asia-Pacific Business Forum 2008 (Bangkok, Thailand, 27 April), a side event of the Commission's session, was held on the theme "Energy security: opportunities through regional energy cooperation and public-private partnerships" and was attended by some 250 participants from member States, the private sector, civil society, intergovernmental organizations and UN bodies. Addressing the Forum, the Co-chair stressed that the region should expand access to renewable energy sources without jeopardizing long-term prosperity and environmental sustainability, and that energy security, access and efficiency were vital components of a long-term regional strategy. A change was needed from independent to interdependent energy policies by building trust within the region, and Government policies should facilitate energy infrastructure investment, including small-scale projects that would introduce important new supplies of energy. Collective efforts were needed for climate change mitigation and adaptation, and States should have a role in reducing greenhouse gas emissions through the new energy system paradigm.

Policy issues

In a policy statement to the Commission, its Executive Secretary identified four kinds of imbalances in the Asia-Pacific region that needed to be addressed if the region was to achieve the MDGs. The first was the considerable economic imbalance across the region: while the region was the most dynamic in the world, it still had 640 million people living on less than $1 a day. The problems in the agricultural sector, which provided the main livelihood of the poor, warranted urgent attention. The second was social imbalance: in many places, social grievances and exclusion continued along the fault lines of ethnicity, religion and class, together with systemic discrimination and violence against women and girls. Social exclusion and discrimination prevented access to basic services and put many communities at risk. The third kind of imbalance pertained to ecological issues: the region was suffering from a mounting ecological burden that exceeded its ecological carrying capacity. Rapid economic growth and population expansion were exerting increasing pressure on natural resources and on economic and social progress. The challenge for the region's developing countries was to move away from the use of fossil fuels to less polluting sources of energy, while maintaining their growth and development. The fourth was "empathy imbalance": while sizeable sections of the bureaucracy were sensitive to the needs of the marginalized and the disadvantaged, there were many who did not empathize with them or understand their struggles to secure their rights.

The Executive Secretary also highlighted the steps she had taken to strengthen the Commission. First, a more strategic and focused programme direction had been established to guide the delivery of ESCAP services to member States, transforming the Commission into a key player that could support them in shaping a more balanced and integrated economic and social order. Second, strong and strategic partnerships with other regional players had been developed to create greater and more lasting impact. Third, she had revitalized the role of the Regional Coordination Mechanism, which ESCAP chaired, transforming it into a regional platform for system-wide coherence and partnerships. Fourth, she was preparing ESCAP to serve as the regional platform for South-South cooperation and meaningful discussions on the transfer of technologies within the region.

Key challenges

The Commission had before it the report of its Executive Secretary on key challenges for inclusive and sustainable economic and social development since its previous session [E/ESCAP/64/35]. It noted with concern the adverse socio-economic impact of rising food and oil prices. Against that backdrop, it recognized the importance of energy security and sustainable development. The Commission observed that disasters could have a negative impact on sustainable development, and emphasized the importance of regional cooperation for disaster management. It also noted that the transfer of technology and sharing of best practices were crucial to boosting agricultural productivity, promoting alternative energy and improving energy efficiency, and that the building of infrastructure was an important precondition for the development of the energy sector.

Economic and social survey

The Commission had before it a secretariat note [E/ESCAP/64/36] on the summary of the *Economic and Social Survey of Asia and the Pacific 2008*. The note took stock of the economic and social situation in the region, assessed the risks to its economy and provided an overview of the region's agricultural sector and possible ways to address the emerging food crisis by reviving that sector. During 2007, the developing economies in Asia and the Pacific had recorded an impressive economic performance, but the region had since entered a phase of uncertainty, with a possible slowdown in the global economy, increased risks in international financial markets and relentlessly rising food and oil prices. Observing that the region was still home to about two thirds of the world's poor, the Commission was concerned that high food and energy prices, if continued, could undermine efforts to reduce poverty and achieve the MDGs.

Achieving the MDGS

The Commission had before it a secretariat note entitled "A future within reach: progress towards achieving the Millennium Development Goals in the Asian and Pacific region" [E/ESCAP/64/37]. In addition, a High-level Panel on Millennium Development Goals in Asia and the Pacific, organized as part of the Commission's session, drew attention to the challenges and opportunities for achieving the MDGs in the region.

In her keynote speech, the Executive Secretary observed that achieving the MDGs by 2015 was the cornerstone of the region's development strategy, and that accelerating progress towards the Goals was a shared agenda. The midpoint to 2015 had been crossed and there was mixed news on achievement. Significant progress had been made in reducing income poverty, raising enrolment rates in primary and secondary schools and increasing the participation of women in the economy. Nevertheless, 641 million people in the region still lived below the poverty line, 97 million children below the age of five were underweight, and another 4 million died every year before reaching the age of five. A quarter of a million women died every year during childbirth and as a result of pregnancy-related complications, and 6 million people were living with HIV/AIDS. She noted that children, women, persons with disabilities and other vulnerable groups were the most severely affected by hunger, and women faced widespread discrimination. The development gains made during the last decade or two could be reversed and income poverty could surge if the current high prices of food and energy were not addressed.

By a 30 April resolution on achieving the MDGs in the ESCAP region [res. 64/6], the Commission requested that the Executive Secretary reinforce regional partnerships on the MDGs; assess progress towards achieving all Goals and targets in the ESCAP region and transmit a progress assessment to the Economic and Social Council; assist countries in the region in achieving the Goals, in particular LDCs, landlocked developing countries and Pacific island developing countries; and advocate for the Goals in order to focus the attention of policymakers and other stakeholders.

By a resolution of the same date [ibid. (res. 64/7)], on financing for the achievement of the MDGs by 2015 in the ESCAP region, the Commission urged the developed countries that had not done so to make efforts towards the target of 0.7 per cent of gross national product (GNP) as official development assistance (ODA) to developing countries and 0.15 to 0.20 per cent of GNP to LDCs. It encouraged developing countries to build on progress achieved in ensuring that ODA was used effectively to help achieve development goals and targets, and requested that its Executive Secretary explore the feasibility of establishing a regional MDG resource facility.

Programme and organizational questions

Programme performance, 2006–2007

During its sixty-fourth session (Bangkok, 24–30 April) [E/2008/39], the Commission took note of the ESCAP programme performance report for the biennium 2006–2007 [E/ESCAP/64/20], which included highlights of programme achievements by thematic areas, as well as results and lessons learned under each of the eight subprogrammes during the biennium.

Monitoring and evaluation

The Commission had before it a secretariat note on the biennial evaluation report for 2006–2007 [E/ESCAP/64/21], which focused on the main findings and recommendations from those evaluation exercises and provided an overview of the secretariat's monitoring and evaluation system, which was launched by the Executive Secretary in July 2007.

The Commission also had before it a secretariat note presenting the outcome of an inspection of results-based management practices at ESCAP undertaken by the Office of Internal Oversight Services [E/ESCAP/64/30]. The Commission took note of the plan of action developed by the secretariat in response to the report, and of its current status of implementation.

Draft Strategic Framework, 2010–2011

During its session, the Commission had before it the draft strategic framework for ESCAP for 2010–2011 [E/ESCAP/64/22/Rev.1]. The Executive Secretary informed the Commission that efforts had been made to ensure a more focused and results-oriented draft strategic framework, building on the comparative advantages of ESCAP. A draft had been reviewed by the Advisory Committee of Permanent Representatives and Other Representatives Designated by Members of the Commission at its special session on 19 March, and major changes, as suggested by the Advisory Committee, had been incorporated into the draft framework. The Commission generally endorsed the draft, subject to the comments and reservations set out in its annual report.

ESCAP sixty-fifth session

On 30 April, the Commission, having considered a secretariat note on the dates, venue and theme topic for its sixty-fifth (2009) session [E/ESCAP/64/33], decided that it would be held in Bangkok in April/May 2009, bearing in mind the celebration of various national holidays in countries of the region in April and early May. It decided that the theme topic for its sixty-fifth session would be: "Sustainable agriculture and food security" [dec. 64/1].

Revised conference structure

On 30 April [res. 64/1], the Commission decided to revise its conference structure, with immediate effect, to conform to the pattern outlined in annex I to the resolution, and requested the Executive Secretary to take into account the revision in the future programme of work and strategic framework. It also requested the Executive Secretary, bearing in mind the goal of maximizing the UN impact on the economic and social development of the region, to reorganize the secretariat so as to enhance its capability to service the subsidiary structure; to provide members and associate members with a preliminary assessment of the organizational and staffing implications of the revision within the next six months; and to undertake systematic monitoring and evaluation of the conference structure and its link to the ESCAP programme priorities. The Commission requested the Executive Secretary to report to the Commission at its sixty-seventh (2011) session on the implementation of the resolution, and decided to review its conference structure at its sixty-ninth (2013) session.

ECONOMIC AND SOCIAL COUNCIL ACTION

On 22 July [meeting 38], the Economic and Social Council adopted **resolution 2008/7** [draft: E/2008/15/Add.1] without vote [agenda item 10].

Restructuring of the conference structure of the Economic and Social Commission for Asia and the Pacific

The Economic and Social Council,

Noting the adoption by the Economic and Social Commission for Asia and the Pacific at its sixty-fourth session, held in Bangkok from 24 to 30 April 2008, of resolution 64/1 on the restructuring of the conference structure of the Commission,

1. *Endorses* Economic and Social Commission for Asia and the Pacific resolution 64/1, on the restructuring of the conference structure of the Commission, as set out in the annex to the present resolution;

2. *Also endorses* the annexes to resolution 64/1, on the conference structure of the Commission, on issues to be addressed by the committees subsidiary to the Commission, and on the terms of reference of the Advisory Committee of Permanent Representatives and Other Representatives Designated by Members of the Commission.

ANNEX

Resolution 64/1 on the restructuring of the conference structure of the Economic and Social Commission for Asia and the Pacific

[*For the text of resolution 64/1 and the annexes thereto, see chapter IV of the annual report of the Commission for the period 24 May 2007 to 30 April 2008.*]

Cooperation with regional bodies

The Secretary-General, in his August consolidated report [A/63/228-S/2008/531 & Corr.1] on cooperation between the United Nations and regional and other organizations, outlined UN relations with the Association of Southeast Asian Nations, the Economic Cooperation Organization and the Pacific Islands Forum.

GENERAL ASSEMBLY ACTION

On 26 November [meeting 60], the General Assembly adopted **resolution 63/35** [draft: A/63/L.40 & Add.1] without vote [agenda item 114 *(c)*].

Cooperation between the United Nations and the Association of Southeast Asian Nations

The General Assembly,

Bearing in mind the aims and purposes of the Association of Southeast Asian Nations, as enshrined in the Bangkok Declaration of 8 August 1967, in particular the maintenance of close and beneficial cooperation with existing international and regional organizations with similar aims and purposes,

Recalling all previous resolutions on cooperation between the United Nations and the Association of Southeast Asian Nations,

Noting with appreciation the report of the Secretary-General,

Noting with satisfaction that the activities of the Association of Southeast Asian Nations are consistent with the purposes and principles of the United Nations,

Welcoming efforts to strengthen partnership between the United Nations and regional organizations, and in this context welcoming also efforts to strengthen cooperation between the United Nations system and the Association of Southeast Asian Nations,

Welcoming also the participation of the Association of Southeast Asian Nations in the high-level meetings between the United Nations and regional organizations, as well as the collaboration between the Association of Southeast Asian Nations and the Economic and Social Commission for Asia and the Pacific to promote dialogue and cooperation among regional organizations in Asia and the Pacific,

Welcoming further the Association of Southeast Asian Nations as an observer in the General Assembly,

Recalling the First and Second Association of Southeast Asian Nations-United Nations Summits, held in Bangkok on 12 February 2000 and at United Nations Headquarters on 13 September 2005, respectively, and the commitment of leaders of the Association of Southeast Asian Nations and the Secretary-General of the United Nations to further broaden cooperation between the Association of Southeast Asian Nations and the United Nations,

1. *Welcomes* the signing on 20 November 2007 of the Charter of the Association of Southeast Asian Nations by leaders of the Association of Southeast Asian Nations at the Thirteenth Association of Southeast Asian Nations Summit, held in Singapore from 18 to 22 November 2007, which represents a historic milestone for the Association of Southeast Asian Nations, reflecting a common vision and commitment to the development of an Association of Southeast Asian Nations community so as to ensure lasting peace, stability, sustained economic growth, shared prosperity and social progress in the region;

2. *Continues to encourage* both the United Nations and the Association of Southeast Asian Nations to further strengthen and expand their areas of cooperation, and in this context welcomes the signing on 27 September 2007 of the Memorandum of Understanding between the Association of Southeast Asian Nations and the United Nations on Association of Southeast Asian Nations-United Nations cooperation at United Nations Headquarters, which aims at establishing a partnership between the Association of Southeast Asian Nations and the United Nations that will encompass the full range of cooperation based on mutual benefits;

3. *Commends* the President of the General Assembly, the Secretary-General of the United Nations and the Ministers for Foreign Affairs of the member States of the Association of Southeast Asian Nations for their efforts to hold regular meetings, on an annual basis, with the presence of the Secretary-General of the Association of Southeast Asian Nations, during the regular session of the Assembly, with a view to further strengthening the cooperation between the United Nations and the Association of Southeast Asian Nations;

4. *Continues to encourage* the United Nations and the Association of Southeast Asian Nations to convene Association of Southeast Asian Nations-United Nations Summits regularly, and underlines the importance of the presence thereat of the Secretary-General of the United Nations and heads of relevant United Nations departments, funds and

programmes, and specialized agencies, and in this context welcomes the decision to convene the Third Association of Southeast Asian Nations-United Nations Summit, to be held in Thailand on 17 December 2008;

5. *Recognizes* the value of partnership between the United Nations and the Association of Southeast Asian Nations in providing timely and effective responses to global issues of mutual concern, in the context of partnership between the United Nations and regional organizations, and thus encourages the United Nations and the Association of Southeast Asian Nations to explore concrete measures for closer cooperation, particularly in the areas of food and energy security and achievement of the Millennium Development Goals;

6. *Welcomes* the establishment of the Association of Southeast Asian Nations Humanitarian Task Force for the Victims of Cyclone Nargis, and acknowledges the progress achieved in assisting the post-Nargis relief work by the Tripartite Core Group comprising the Government of Myanmar, the United Nations and the Association of Southeast Asian Nations, and the assistance provided by the international community to those in need;

7. *Encourages* effective cooperation between member countries of the Association of Southeast Asian Nations and the appropriate United Nations organizations in the delivery of operational activities in the area of development at the country level;

8. *Takes note* of the efforts of the Association of Southeast Asian Nations to hold meetings with other regional organizations at the fringes of the sessions of the General Assembly to promote cooperation in support of multilateralism;

9. *Requests* the Secretary-General to submit to the General Assembly at its sixty-fifth session a report on the implementation of the present resolution;

10. *Decides* to include in the provisional agenda of its sixty-fifth session the sub-item entitled "Cooperation between the United Nations and the Association of Southeast Asian Nations".

On 15 December [meeting 69], the General Assembly adopted **resolution 63/144** [draft: A/63/L.39/Rev.1 & Add.1] without vote [agenda item 114 *(i)*].

Cooperation between the United Nations and the Economic Cooperation Organization

The General Assembly,

Recalling its resolution 48/2 of 13 October 1993, by which it granted observer status to the Economic Cooperation Organization,

Recalling also its previous resolutions on cooperation between the United Nations and the Economic Cooperation Organization, in which it invited various specialized agencies as well as other organizations and programmes of the United Nations system and relevant international financial institutions to join in the efforts towards realizing the goals and objectives of the Economic Cooperation Organization,

Recalling further the Articles of the Charter of the United Nations that encourage activities through regional cooperation for the promotion of the purposes and principles of the United Nations,

Expressing its support for the plans and programmes of the Economic Cooperation Organization aimed at achieving internationally agreed development goals, including those contained in the United Nations Millennium Declaration,

Welcoming the efforts of the Economic Cooperation Organization to consolidate ties with the United Nations system and relevant international and regional organizations,

1. *Takes note with appreciation* of the report of the Secretary-General on the implementation of resolution 61/12 of 13 November 2006, and expresses satisfaction at the enhanced cooperation between the United Nations and the Economic Cooperation Organization;

2. *Takes note* of the Herat Declaration, adopted at the seventeenth meeting of the Council of Ministers of the Economic Cooperation Organization, held in Herat, Afghanistan, on 20 October 2007, in which the Council reaffirmed its commitment to establish a free-trade area in the Economic Cooperation Organization region by 2015 as a priority task, extended the Programme of Action for the Economic Cooperation Organization Decade of Transport and Communications, and called for joint action for human resources development, poverty alleviation and disaster mitigation and management;

3. *Stresses* the importance of the continuation and expansion of areas of cooperation between the United Nations and the Economic Cooperation Organization, including the provision of financial and technical assistance for pre-feasibility and feasibility studies of projects, consultancy services, workshops and training courses and project management services by specialized agencies of the United Nations, in the ongoing as well as future activities of the Economic Cooperation Organization;

4. *Appreciates* the technical and financial assistance extended by the United Nations and its specialized agencies, as well as other international and regional organizations, to the Economic Cooperation Organization for its economic development programmes and projects, and encourages them to continue to support its activities;

5. *Calls for* a further increase in the technical assistance of the World Trade Organization, the United Nations Conference on Trade and Development and the International Trade Centre UNCTAD/WTO to the States members of the Economic Cooperation Organization, which are at various levels of development and some of which are in the process of acceding to the World Trade Organization, with a view to expanding their intra- and interregional trade, which may promote their sustainable economic development goals, including trade liberalization, leading to regional and global integration;

6. *Welcomes* the enhancement of cooperation between the United Nations Industrial Development Organization and the Economic Cooperation Organization, and recommends continuation of their joint programmes to strengthen the institutional infrastructure to overcome the technical barriers to trade and promote sanitary and phytosanitary measures to be taken by the States members of the Economic Cooperation Organization;

7. *Also welcomes* the initiative to sign a trilateral agreement between the Economic Cooperation Organization, the Islamic Development Bank and the Economic and Social Commission for Asia and the Pacific for joint projects under the Asian Highway Network and Trans-Asian Railway Network initiatives of the Commission, as well as the implementation of the Economic Cooperation Organization Transit Transport Framework Agreement and the Programme of Action for the Economic Cooperation Organization Decade of Transport and Communications, and invites the donor institutions and countries to support the projects;

8. *Takes note* of progress on the Istanbul-Almaty container and passenger train project of the Economic Cooperation Organization, and calls upon the relevant United Nations agencies to join the Organization's efforts to revitalize the China-Middle East-Europe railway corridor, providing an uninterrupted railway connection between China and Europe through the Economic Cooperation Organization region;

9. *Also takes note* of the Tashkent Declaration on the United Nations Special Programme for the Economies of Central Asia, and welcomes coordination between the Economic Cooperation Organization and the Special Programme;

10. *Takes note with appreciation* of the initiative of the Economic Cooperation Organization to launch a demonstration train on the Islamabad-Tehran-Istanbul route as well as on the route through Afghanistan, and calls upon the relevant regional and international institutions to assist the Organization in operationalizing the routes by making up the missing links;

11. *Appreciates* the efforts of the Economic Cooperation Organization to develop energy trade in the region in cooperation with international organizations, especially the Economic and Social Commission for Asia and the Pacific, the World Bank and the Islamic Development Bank, and requests their continued support for the preparation and efficient implementation of regional programmes on energy efficiency and conservation;

12. *Also appreciates* the holding of the donor conference in Turkey on 8 May 2008 in support of the regional programme of the Economic Cooperation Organization for food security, invites the relevant United Nations bodies, international organizations and donor agencies to assist in the efficient implementation of the programme, and calls for their support for the technical cooperation programme for strengthening seed supply in the region;

13. *Welcomes* the establishment of the Economic Cooperation Organization Regional Centre for Risk Management of Natural Disasters, and invites United Nations institutions and international donors and financial institutions to extend their support for the further development of the Centre and to assist member States in developing their early warning systems and their capacity for timely response and rehabilitation, with a view to reducing human casualties and the socio-economic impact of natural disasters;

14. *Notes with satisfaction* the priority given by the Economic Cooperation Organization to Millennium Development Goals related to child mortality, maternal health and combating HIV/AIDS, and recommends that United Nations agencies, especially the United Nations Development Programme, the World Health Organization, the United Nations Population Fund and the United Nations Children's Fund, assist the Economic Cooperation Organization in preparing an analytical regional report on the health-related Millennium Development Goals;

15. *Calls for* the strengthening of the technical assistance provided by the relevant United Nations bodies, in particular the United Nations Environment Programme, to the Economic Cooperation Organization plan of action for cooperation on the environment, especially in such priority areas as the transfer of technology and the implementation of strategic plans and projects;

16. *Notes with satisfaction* the adoption of the work plan on biodiversity in the Economic Cooperation Organization region aimed at achieving, with the assistance of the relevant United Nations bodies, the common objectives of the global 2010 biodiversity target and ensuring the sustainable use of biological and genetic resources as well as equitable sharing of the resulting benefits;

17. *Appreciates* the efforts of the Economic Cooperation Organization and its member States in combating the production of and trafficking in narcotic drugs and calls for increased cooperation between the Organization and relevant United Nations bodies, including the United Nations Office on Drugs and Crime, as well as the European Commission and the international community, and also calls for further exploration of the capacity of the Economic Cooperation Organization to effectively combat the production of and trafficking in narcotic and psychotropic drugs;

18. *Also appreciates* the initiatives of the Economic Cooperation Organization to combat transnational crime, and encourages closer collaboration between the Economic Cooperation Organization and the United Nations Office on Drugs and Crime for the prevention of corruption and money laundering;

19. *Welcomes* the memorandums of understanding between the Economic Cooperation Organization and the secretariat of the International Strategy for Disaster Reduction and the International Road Transport Union as well as the exchange of notes verbales between the Organization and the Office for the Coordination of Humanitarian Affairs of the Secretariat, and calls for the effective implementation of those agreements;

20. *Takes note with appreciation* of the progress made by the Economic Cooperation Organization in expanding external relations, especially strengthening relations with regional peers and other international organizations;

21. *Requests* the Secretary-General to submit to the General Assembly at its sixty-fifth session a report on the implementation of the present resolution;

22. *Decides* to include in the provisional agenda of its sixty-fifth session the sub-item entitled "Cooperation between the United Nations and the Economic Cooperation Organization".

On 19 December [meeting 72], the General Assembly adopted **resolution 63/200** [draft: A/63/L.56 & Add.1] without vote [agenda item 114 *(s)*].

Cooperation between the United Nations and the Pacific Islands Forum

The General Assembly,

Recalling its resolutions 49/1 of 17 October 1994, 59/20 of 8 November 2004 and 61/48 of 4 December 2006,

Welcoming the ongoing efforts towards closer cooperation between the United Nations and the Pacific Islands Forum and its associated institutions,

Bearing in mind that the Pacific Islands Forum was established in 1971 and that leaders of the Pacific Islands Forum endorsed in 2005 the Pacific Plan, which has the goal of enhancing and stimulating economic growth, sustainable development, good governance and security for Pacific countries through regionalism,

Affirming the need to strengthen the cooperation that already exists between entities of the United Nations system and the Pacific Islands Forum in the areas of sustainable development, environmental protection, good governance and peace and security,

Having considered the report of the Secretary-General on cooperation between the United Nations and regional and other organizations,

1. *Takes note* of the report of the Secretary-General, in particular paragraphs 90 to 97 on cooperation between the United Nations and the Pacific Islands Forum, and encourages further such cooperation;

2. *Invites* the Secretary-General of the United Nations to take the necessary measures, in consultation with the Secretary-General of the Pacific Islands Forum, to promote and expand cooperation and coordination between the two secretariats in order to increase the capacity of the organizations to attain their common objectives;

3. *Requests* the Secretary-General to submit to the General Assembly at its sixty-fifth session a report on the implementation of the present resolution;

4. *Decides* to include in the provisional agenda of its sixty-fifth session the sub-item entitled "Cooperation between the United Nations and the Pacific Islands Forum".

Europe

The Economic Commission for Europe (ECE) did not meet in 2008. Its sixty-third session was to be held in 2009. The state of the European region and the activities of ECE's subsidiary bodies during 2008 are discussed below.

Economic trends

A report on the economic situation in the ECE region: Europe, North America and the Commonwealth of Independent States [E/2009/16] stated that, in 2008, the region entered into what was forecast to be the worst economic downturn since the Second World War. The decline was accompanied by rising unemployment and by especially large declines in international trade and capital flows, while Government fiscal positions had deteriorated significantly. The global slowdown, the result of a financial crisis that began in the United States, was noteworthy not only because of its severity, but also because of its global synchronization.

Activities in 2008

Trade

The Committee on Trade did not meet in 2008. At its second session in 2007 [YUN 2007, p. 1023], it had considered a number of reports and taken various actions dealing with trade. Although its third session was to have been held from 13 to 17 October, it was postponed to 25–26 February 2009.

Timber

The Timber Committee, at its sixty-sixth session (Rome, 21–24 October) [ECE/TIM/2008/9], held jointly with the thirty-fourth session of the European Forestry Commission of the Food and Agriculture Organization of the United Nations (FAO), addressed a range of issues, including forests and climate change, forests and energy, and forests and water. On climate change, it considered how climate change mitigation and adaptation measures could be integrated into forest sector policies, how forest management strategies could contribute to reducing forests' vulnerabilities to climate change, and how coordination and communication between climate change negotiations and forest sector policies could be improved. With respect to energy, the Committee discussed the growing need for renewable energy, notably from wood, and the consequences for forest policy. It considered the role of wood energy in climate change mitigation and the implications for forest-based industries in Europe, and stressed the importance of sustainable forest management in supplying wood and safeguarding biodiversity. As to the linkages between the forest and water sectors, it presented international legal and policy frameworks and discussed areas for interaction between the forest and water sectors, and strategies which linked forest management and water risk management to deal with floods, droughts, soil erosion and landslides in the context of climate change. The Committee also discussed market developments in 2008 and the prospects for 2009. In addition, it welcomed the Strategic Review and Planning process which took place in 2007–2008, and adopted the Strategic Plan 2008–2013 [ECE/TIM/2008/7 & Add.1] of the ECE/FAO integrated programme of work on timber and forestry, agreed during the Timber Committee's Special Session on the strategic review and plan of the ECE/FAO integrated programme of work on timber and forestry (Geneva, 28–30 April) [ECE/TIM/S/2008/6].

The Joint FAO/ECE Working Party on Forest Economics and Statistics, at its thirtieth session (Geneva, 2–3 April) [ECE/TIM/EFC/WP.2/2008/11], reviewed a range of issues, including potential wood supply, markets and statistics, forest resource assessment, and forest sector outlook studies. It also reviewed its methods of work, and adopted the conclusions and recommendations of a workshop on national wood resource balances (31 March–1 April).

Transport

The seventieth session of the Inland Transport Committee (Geneva, 19–21 February) [ECE/TRANS/200] reviewed, among other topics: Euro-Asian transport links; transport and security; assistance to countries with economies in transition; transport trends and economics; road transport; road traffic safety; harmonization of vehicle regulations; rail transport infrastructure; inland water transport; intermodal transport and logistics; border crossing facilitation; transport of dangerous goods and of perishable foodstuffs; transport statistics; the status of accession to international ECE transport agreements and conventions; the transport situation in ECE member countries and emerging development trends; transport of people with reduced mobility; and the draft programme of work of the Committee 2008–2012. It also considered action taken by its Working Parties on: the Transport of Dangerous Goods; Road Transport; Transport Trends and Economics; Road Traffic Safety; Rail Transport; Inland Water Transport; the Standardization of Technical Safety Requirements in Inland Navigation; the Transport of Perishable Foodstuffs; and Transport Statistics.

On 20 February, the Inland Transport Committee adopted an Additional Protocol to the Convention on the Contract for the International Carriage of Goods by Road Concerning the Electronic Consignment Note.

Energy

The Committee on Sustainable Energy, at its seventeenth session (Geneva, 19–21 November) [ECE/ENERGY/78], focused its energy security dialogue on "Strategic Alliances for Energy Security", with particular attention to the cooperation and relationship between international and national oil companies on energy security strategies. It also reviewed cooperation and coordination with other bodies, including the Commission's other sectoral committees; the regional advisory services programme in the field of energy; the Committee's work programme for 2009–2010; and the performance of the sustainable energy subprogramme.

The Committee endorsed the requests for two-year mandate renewals by its Ad Hoc Groups of Experts on: Financing Energy Efficiency Investments for Climate Change Mitigation; Cleaner Electricity Production from Coal and Other Fossil Fuels; and Coal Mine Methane. It also endorsed the request to renew its Ad Hoc Group of Experts on the Supply and Use of Gas for one year, and endorsed the work programme of the Ad Hoc Group of Experts on Harmonization of Fossil Energy and Mineral Resources Terminology for 2008–2009.

The Committee reviewed and adopted its programme of work for 2009–2010, and approved its provisional calendar of meetings for 2009.

Environment

The Committee on Environmental Policy, at its fifteenth session (Geneva, 21–23 April) [ECE/CEP/148], reviewed the environmental performance reviews of Kazakhstan and adopted related recommendations. It also reviewed its work programme, which included: environmental monitoring; building capacity and partnerships through multilateral environment agreements; ECE's environment and security initiative, and partnerships with the private sector; and such cross-sectoral initiatives as the Transport, Health and Environment Pan-European Programme, education for sustainable development, and environment and health.

The Committee took note of the outcome of the third regional implementation meeting on sustainable development (Geneva, 28–29 January), addressing agriculture, rural development, land, drought, desertification and Africa [ECE/AC.25/2008/2]. It also considered the outcome of the Sixth Ministerial Conference "Environment for Europe" (EfE) Conference [YUN 2007, p. 1025] and discussed modalities for the reform of the EfE process, as decided by the ministers at the Conference. Ahead of the Committee's session, the ECE Steering Committee on Education for Sustainable Development held its third meeting (Geneva, 31 March–1 April) [ECE/CEP/AC.13/2008/2], at which it reviewed progress by ECE members in implementing the ECE Strategy for Education for Sustainable Development and related issues.

Housing and land management

The Committee on Housing and Land Management, at its sixty-ninth session (Geneva, 22–23 September) [ECE/HBP/149], decided that two workshops would be held in 2009, in Bulgaria and Austria, on energy efficiency in housing. It considered the relationship between housing and regional demographic changes, and reviewed a draft study on informal settlements. It welcomed the adoption of a new logo for its housing and land management activities; endorsed the new newsletter, *Vital Spaces*, recommending that it be published at least quarterly; and supported a thesis award for graduate students working on housing- and land management-related issues.

The Committee reviewed its 2008–2009 work programme [ECE/HBP/2008/1], with its focus on country profiles; improving urban environmental performance; land registration and markets; and housing modernization and management. It was informed of progress achieved in developing the country profiles of Belarus and Kyrgyzstan, and of the publication, in May, of *Spatial Planning–Key Instruments for Development and Effective Governance, with Special Reference to Countries in Transition*. The Working Party on Land Administration announced that its Real Estate Market Advisory Group planned to host, in Rome, a workshop on "Real estate market: risks and benefits" in March 2009. Preparations were also under way for a project on the multi-family housing sector [ECE/HBP/2008/5], and for a workshop on homelessness in May 2009.

Statistics

The Conference of European Statisticians, at its fifty-sixth session (Paris, 10–12 June) [ECE/CES/74], considered the implications of the meetings of one of its parent bodies—the February session of the UN Statistical Commission (see p. 1379). It also considered the coordination of international statistical work in the ECE region, particularly with respect to business statistics; statistics on income, living conditions and poverty; and statistics on gender, culture and the environment. The Conference congratulated the Joint ECE/Organisation for Economic Cooperation and Development (OECD)/Statistical Office of the European Communities (Eurostat) Working Group on Statistics for Sustainable Development for its *Report on Statistics for Sustainable Development* [ECE/CES/2008/29 & Add.1,2], which provided an overview of different approaches on measurement of sustainable development with a particular focus on the capital approach.

The Conference reviewed the work of the ECE Statistical Division in 2007 and its plans for 2008 [ECE/CES/2008/31], and considered progress made by the Joint ECE/OECD/Eurostat Working Group on the Impact of Globalisation on National Accounts [ECE/CES/2008/32]. It also reported on two seminars held during the Conference session: a Seminar on Strategic Issues Linked to the Measurement of International Transactions, organized by the International Monetary Fund and the United States Bureau of Economic Analysis, and a Seminar on Measuring Population Movement and Integration in a Globalized World, organized by Germany and Eurostat.

Economic cooperation and integration

The Committee on Economic Cooperation and Integration (CECI), at its third session (Geneva, 3–5 December) [ECE/CECI/2008/2], discussed the impact of the economic and financial crisis on issues related to its work, and reviewed the implementation of its 2006–2008 work programme, concluding that its main objectives and outputs had been achieved. The Committee organized policy segment panels on "Cooperative solutions to global challenges: eco-innovation and clean energy for higher competitiveness" and "Wider economic integration through innovative development of efficient and safe transport and trade links."

The Committee noted the establishment of an active constituency of CECI stakeholders, including business community and expert networks in ECE member States, that contributed to successful programme implementation while benefiting from CECI results and outputs. It emphasized the role of the CECI Teams of Specialists as important pillars of its activities, and encouraged use of its Information Exchange Platform as an instrument of knowledge-sharing by its Teams of Specialists and expert networks.

The Committee adopted its work programme for 2009–2010, taking account of its deliberations on that item [ECE/CECI/2008/6]. Noting that the demand for CECI capacity-building activities and other technical cooperation services from countries with economies in transition had increased considerably in 2008, it agreed on the need to match that demand with an adequate level of regular budget and extrabudgetary resources. It also recommended that the mandates of the Teams of Specialists on Innovation and Competitiveness Policies, on Intellectual Property, and on Public-Private Partnerships be renewed for the period 2009–2010.

The Committee also supported proposals to organize joint events in 2009, including: with the Economic Research Institute of the Ministry of Economy and Budget Planning (Kazakhstan), an international event on "Public-Private Partnerships Facing Global Challenges" to be held in March within the framework of the II Astana Economic Forum; with the Russian Private Equity and Venture Capital Association, an international conference on "Practical Aspects of Public-Private Partnerships in Innovation", to be held in St. Petersburg, Russian Federation, in October within the framework of the Tenth Venture Capital Fair; and with the Market Research Foundation (Russian Federation), an international conference on "World Economic Crisis: New Opportunities for Public-Private Partnerships" to be held in Kaliningrad, Russian Federation, in April.

Cooperation with regional bodies

The Secretary-General, in his August consolidated report [A/63/228-S/2008/531 & Corr.1] on cooperation between the United Nations and regional and other organizations, outlined UN relations with the Eurasian Economic Community and the Black Sea Economic Cooperation Organization.

GENERAL ASSEMBLY ACTION

On 3 November [meeting 37], the General Assembly adopted **resolution 63/15** [draft: A/63/L.13 & Add.1] without vote [agenda item 114 *(j)*].

Cooperation between the United Nations and the Eurasian Economic Community

The General Assembly,

Recalling its resolutions 58/84 of 9 December 2003, in which it granted the Eurasian Economic Community observer status in the General Assembly, and 62/79 of 6 December 2007 on cooperation between the United Nations and the Eurasian Economic Community,

Recalling also that one of the purposes of the United Nations is to achieve international cooperation in solving international problems of an economic, social, cultural and humanitarian nature,

Recalling further the Articles of the Charter of the United Nations that encourage activities through regional cooperation for the promotion of the purposes and principles of the United Nations,

Taking note of the fact that the membership of the Eurasian Economic Community includes countries with economies in transition, and recalling in this regard its resolution 61/210 of 20 December 2006, in which it invited the United Nations system to enhance dialogue with and increase support to the regional and subregional cooperation organizations whose membership includes countries with economies in transition and whose efforts include assisting their members to fully integrate into the world economy,

Noting that the Treaty on the Establishment of the Eurasian Economic Community reaffirms the commitment of the States members of the Community to the principles of the Charter and also to the generally accepted principles and norms of international law,

Convinced that the strengthening of cooperation between the United Nations and other organizations of the United Nations system and the Eurasian Economic Community contributes to the promotion of the purposes and principles of the United Nations,

Expressing concern over the persistent natural disasters in countries of the region,

Recognizing that the issues of water and energy resources management, as well as the development, dissemination and transfer of technologies, have particular importance for the sustainable development of the countries members of the Eurasian Economic Community,

Recognizing also that the Eurasian Economic Community includes some landlocked countries, and in this regard underlining the key role of regional integration institutions such as the Eurasian Economic Community in the implementation of the Almaty Programme of Action: Addressing the Special Needs of Landlocked Developing Countries within a New Global Framework for Transit Transport Cooperation for Landlocked and Transit Developing Countries,

1. *Takes note* of the report of the Secretary-General on the implementation of General Assembly resolution 62/79, and expresses satisfaction with regard to the mutually beneficial interaction between the United Nations and the Eurasian Economic Community;

2. *Also takes note* of the activities of the Eurasian Economic Community in support of United Nations goals through the strengthening of regional cooperation in such areas as trade and economic development, the establishment of a customs union, energy, transport, agriculture and agro-industry, the regulation of migration, banking and finance, communications, education, health care and pharmaceuticals, biotechnology, environmental protection and natural disaster risk reduction;

3. *Commends* the commitment of the States members of the Eurasian Economic Community to scaling up regional economic integration by establishing a customs union and free trade zone, consistent with the multilateral trading system, as well as the formation of a common energy market;

4. *Notes with appreciation* the progress achieved in cooperation between the Eurasian Economic Community and the Economic Commission for Europe, the Economic and Social Commission for Asia and the Pacific and the United Nations Development Programme, including in the fields of water and energy resources management, the development, dissemination and transfer of technologies, trade facilitation, transport and capacity-building, promoting effective interaction within the framework of the United Nations Special Programme for the Economies of Central Asia;

5. *Underlines* the importance of further strengthening dialogue, cooperation and coordination between the United Nations system and the Eurasian Economic Community, and invites the Secretary-General of the United Nations to continue conducting, to this end, regular consultations with the Secretary-General of the Eurasian Economic Community, within existing resources, using for this purpose the relevant inter-institutional forums and formats, including the annual consultations between the Secretary-General of the United Nations and heads of regional organizations;

6. *Invites* the specialized agencies and other organizations, programmes and funds of the United Nations system, as well as international financial institutions, to enhance cooperation and direct contacts with the Eurasian Economic Community for the purpose of undertaking joint implementation of programmes to achieve their goals;

7. *Invites in particular* the Economic Commission for Europe, the Economic and Social Commission for Asia and the Pacific and other related organizations of the United Nations system to further contribute to the development by the Eurasian Economic Community of a concept for the effective use of water and energy resources in States members of the Community as well as to the resolution of water-related disaster risk reduction issues in the region;

8. *Requests* the Secretary-General to submit to the General Assembly at its sixty-fifth session a report on the implementation of the present resolution;

9. *Decides* to include in the provisional agenda of its sixty-fifth session the sub-item entitled "Cooperation between the United Nations and the Eurasian Economic Community".

Also on 3 November [meeting 37], the Assembly adopted **resolution 63/11** [draft: A/63/L.9 & Add.1] without vote [agenda item 114 *(d)*].

Cooperation between the United Nations and the Black Sea Economic Cooperation Organization

The General Assembly,

Recalling its resolution 54/5 of 8 October 1999, by which it granted observer status to the Black Sea Economic Cooperation Organization, as well as its resolutions 55/211 of 20 December 2000, 57/34 of 21 November 2002, 59/259 of 23 December 2004 and 61/4 of 20 October 2006 on cooperation between the United Nations and the Black Sea Economic Cooperation Organization,

Recalling also that one of the purposes of the United Nations is to achieve international cooperation in solving international problems of an economic, social or humanitarian nature,

Recalling further the Articles of the Charter of the United Nations that encourage activities through regional cooperation for the promotion of the purposes and principles of the United Nations,

Recalling its Declaration on the Enhancement of Cooperation between the United Nations and Regional Arrangements or Agencies in the Maintenance of International Peace and Security of 9 December 1994,

Recognizing that any dispute or conflict in the region impedes cooperation, and stressing the need to solve such a dispute or conflict on the basis of the norms and principles of international law,

Convinced that the strengthening of cooperation between the United Nations and other organizations contributes to the promotion of the purposes and principles of the United Nations,

Recalling the report of the Secretary-General submitted pursuant to resolution 61/4,

1. *Takes note* of the Declaration adopted by the Heads of State and Government of the States members of the Black Sea Economic Cooperation Organization on the occasion of the Fifteenth Anniversary Summit of the Organization, held in Istanbul, Turkey, on 25 June 2007;

2. *Reiterates* the conviction that multilateral economic cooperation contributes to enhancing peace, stability and security to the benefit of the Black Sea region;

3. *Welcomes* the efforts towards the completion of the process of reforms in the Black Sea Economic Cooperation Organization envisaged in the Bucharest statement of 26 April 2006, issued by the Council of Ministers for Foreign Affairs of the States members of the Organization, thus contributing to the enhancement of the efficiency and effectiveness of the Organization, as well as its role in the economic and social development of its member States;

4. *Takes note* of the resolve of the Black Sea Economic Cooperation Organization to foster a pragmatic and project- and results-oriented approach in the spheres of common interest for its member States, where improved regional cooperation could create synergies and increase the efficiency of resources used;

5. *Welcomes* the activities of the Black Sea Economic Cooperation Organization aimed at strengthening regional cooperation in fields such as energy, transport, institutional reform and good governance, trade and economic development, banking and finance, communications, agriculture and agroindustry, health care and pharmaceuticals, environmental protection, tourism, science and technology, exchange of statistical data and economic information, collaboration among Customs services, and combating organized crime and illicit trafficking in drugs, weapons and radioactive material, acts of terrorism and illegal migration, and in other related areas;

6. *Also welcomes* the efforts of the Black Sea Economic Cooperation Organization to elaborate and realize concrete joint regional projects, particularly in the fields of energy and transport, which will contribute to the development of the Euro-Asian transport links;

7. *Takes note*, within this framework, of the signing in Belgrade on 19 April 2007 of the memorandum of understanding for the coordinated development of the Black Sea Ring Highway and the memorandum of understanding on the development of the Motorways of the Sea at the Black Sea Economic Cooperation Organization region;

8. *Welcomes* the financing of projects by the Project Development Fund of the Black Sea Economic Cooperation Organization to the benefit of the sustainable development of the Black Sea region;

9. *Appeals* for greater cooperation between the Black Sea Economic Cooperation Organization and international financial institutions in co-financing feasibility and prefeasibility studies of the projects in the wider Black Sea area;

10. *Takes note* of the positive contributions of the Parliamentary Assembly of the Black Sea Economic Cooperation Organization, the Business Council, the Black Sea Trade and Development Bank and the International Centre for Black Sea Studies to the strengthening of multifaceted regional cooperation in the wider Black Sea area;

11. *Also takes note* of the enhanced cooperation between the Black Sea Economic Cooperation Organization and the Economic Commission for Europe, the United Nations Development Programme and the United Nations Industrial Development Organization and the working contacts of the Black Sea Economic Cooperation Organization with the World Bank, the United Nations Children's Fund and the World Health Organization, aimed at promoting the sustainable development of the region of the Black Sea Economic Cooperation Organization;

12. *Welcomes* the multifaceted and fruitful cooperation between the Black Sea Economic Cooperation Organization and the Economic Commission for Europe, especially in the area of transport, within the framework of the Cooperation Agreement signed between the two organizations on 2 July 2001;

13. *Also welcomes* the launching of the Black Sea Trade and Investment Promotion Programme, the first partnership project between the Black Sea Economic Cooperation

Organization and the United Nations Development Programme, on 1 December 2006, and the signing of the cooperation agreement between the two organizations in Istanbul on 28 June 2007;

14. *Takes note* of the establishment of cooperation between the Black Sea Economic Cooperation Organization and the International Centre for Hydrogen Energy Technologies of the United Nations Industrial Development Organization, with emphasis placed on energy and environment;

15. *Also takes note* of the increased cooperation between the Black Sea Economic Cooperation Organization and the United Nations Office on Drugs and Crime and, within this framework, welcomes the launching on 1 September 2007 of the joint Black Sea Economic Cooperation Organization-United Nations Office on Drugs and Crime project on strengthening the criminal justice response to trafficking in persons in the Black Sea region;

16. *Acknowledges* the commitment of the Black Sea Economic Cooperation Organization to contributing to the attainment of the Millennium Development Goals at national, regional and global levels;

17. *Takes note* of the intensified cooperation between the Black Sea Economic Cooperation Organization and the European Union, and supports the efforts of the Organization to take concrete steps to advance this cooperation in line with the provisions of the Declaration of 14 February 2008 on a Black Sea Economic Cooperation Organization-European Union Enhanced Relationship, issued by the Council of Ministers for Foreign Affairs of the States members of the Organization;

18. *Also takes note* of the cooperation established between the Black Sea Economic Cooperation Organization and other regional organizations and initiatives;

19. *Invites* the Secretary-General to strengthen dialogue with the Black Sea Economic Cooperation Organization with a view to promoting cooperation and coordination between the two secretariats;

20. *Invites* the specialized agencies and other organizations and programmes of the United Nations system to cooperate with the Black Sea Economic Cooperation Organization in order to continue programmes with the Organization and its associated institutions for the achievement of their objectives;

21. *Requests* the Secretary-General to submit to the General Assembly at its sixty-fifth session a report on the implementation of the present resolution;

22. *Decides* to include in the provisional agenda of its sixty-fifth session the sub-item entitled "Cooperation between the United Nations and the Black Sea Economic Cooperation Organization".

Latin America and the Caribbean

During its thirty-second session, (Santo Domingo, Dominican Republic, 9–13 June) [E/2008/40], the Economic Commission for Latin America and the Caribbean (ECLAC) considered the report *Structural Change and Productivity Growth—20 Years Later. Old problems, new opportunities* [LC/G.2368(SES.32/4)], which examined the region's performance in the world economy, along with its opportunities and challenges in the new global economic environment; reviewed the region's economic and export performance in the past quarter century; and looked at the emerging opportunities associated with the new techno-economic paradigms. The Commission held a high-level seminar on that subject, which included panel discussions on Latin America and the Caribbean and structural changes in the world economy; competitiveness and learning in the natural-resources sector and in the manufacturing and services sectors; and public-private alliances for innovation and restructuring of production.

ECLAC also discussed the draft work programme of the ECLAC system for 2010–2011, and held a Regional Consultation Preparatory to the Follow-up International Conference on Financing for Development to Review the Implementation of the Monterrey Consensus [YUN 2002, p. 953], to be held in Doha, Qatar, on 29 November–2 December, where it considered the report *Trends and challenges in international cooperation and the mobilization of resources for development in Latin America and the Caribbean* [LC/G.2380(SES.32/15)]. It held panel discussions on financing and cooperation; mobilization of domestic resources; systemic issues; and financing for development: gender policies. The Commission also had before it reports of the ECLAC sessional Ad Hoc Committee on Population and Development and the Committee on South-South Cooperation, which were annexed to its report.

ECLAC adopted 13 resolutions on various regional issues, including: the Santo Domingo resolution [res. 633(XXXII)], which addressed the issues raised in the report on structural change and productivity growth; ECLAC calendar of conferences for 2008–2010 [res. 634(XXXII)]; ECLAC priorities and programme of work for the 2010–2011 biennium [res. 635(XXXII)]; support for the work of the Latin American and Caribbean Institute for Economic and Social Planning [res. 636(XXXII)]; follow-up to the Plan of Action for the Information Society in Latin America and the Caribbean [res. 637(XXXII)]; ECLAC Statistical Conference of the Americas [res. 638(XXXII)]; ECLAC activities in relation to follow-up to the MDGs and implementation of the outcomes of the major UN conferences and summits in the economic, social and related fields [res. 639(XXXII)]; admission of the Cayman Islands as an associate member of ECLAC [res. 640(XXXII)]; Caribbean Development and Cooperation Committee [res. 641(XXXII)]; South-South Cooperation [res. 642(XXXII)]; location of the Commission's next session [res. 643(XXXII)]; population and development: priority activities for the period 2008–2010 [res. 644(XXXII)]; and Regional Conference on Women in Latin America and the Caribbean [res. 645(XXXII)].

Economic trends

A report on the economic situation in and outlook for Latin America and Caribbean, 2008–2009 [E/2009/19] said that the growth of GDP in the region stood at 4.2 per cent in 2008, its sixth consecutive year of expansion. However, the mid-2007 subprime mortgage market problem in the United States had become, just over a year later, a systemic crisis that crippled the credit markets of the developed countries, with worldwide effects. In the ECLAC region, a fall in economic activity to -0.3 per cent was expected in 2009, and regional unemployment was expected to rise from 7.5 per cent in 2008 to 8.6 per cent. Trends in the world prices of foodstuffs and fuels were likely to bring about a marked fall in inflation, from 8.3 per cent in 2008 to 5.5 to 6 per cent.

Activities in 2008

An ECLAC report on the Commission's work in 2008 and 2009 [LC/G.2436(SES.33/7)] addressed activities undertaken and progress made under its 12 subprogrammes: regional integration and cooperation; production and innovation; macroeconomic policies and growth; equity and social cohesion; mainstreaming the gender perspective in regional development; population and development; public administration; sustainable development and human settlements; natural resources and infrastructrure; statistics and economic projections; subregional activities in Mexico and Central America; and subregional activities in the Caribbean.

Regional integration and cooperation

The ECLAC International Trade and Integration Division strengthened the Commission's role as a forum for policy discussion, the exchange of experiences, and as a catalyst for consensus-building. The Division played a pioneering role in helping several countries organize public-sector institutional processes, strategic national visions, and public-private partnerships. It also addressed opportunities for interregional trade and investment, publishing: *Opportunities for Trade and Investment between Latin America and the Asia-Pacific region: the link with the Asia-Pacific Economic Cooperation (APEC)*, *Economic and Trade Relations between Latin America and Asia-Pacific: the link with China*, and *The Latin American Pacific Basin Initiative and the Asia-Pacific region*, which it presented at regional and interregional meetings. It also participated in the 2008 China International Auto Parts Expo at Beijing in November.

Significant changes were introduced to the Division's website, resulting in easier access and optimized use of search engines on trade and regional integration. The flagship publication *Latin America and the Caribbean in the World Economy 2007: Trends 2008* was launched in Mexico City and received wide media coverage. A document on the international crisis and the opportunities for regional cooperation was prepared for the Summit of Latin America and the Caribbean on Integration and Development, which met at Costa do Saupe, Brazil, in December.

The Division's technical cooperation activities focused mainly on public-private partnerships; the relationship between trade and development, with special emphasis on social issues and sustainability; negotiation and administration of trade agreements; innovation and competitiveness; and trade development. Its 74 technical cooperation missions addressed competitiveness and export promotion (47 per cent); trade agreements (23 per cent); integration (16 per cent); and relations between Asia and Latin America (14 per cent). In November, a forum was held in Mexico City on attracting FDI, export promotion and export development in the framework of public-private partnerships. It was organized with the support of the Ibero-American Secretariat, ProMéxico, the Mexican Importers and Exporters Association, and the Mexican Business Council for Trade, Investment and Technology.

Production and innovation

The ECLAC Production, Productivity and Management Division devoted considerable effort to strengthening the capacity of Governments to formulate and implement policies and strategies to enhance the productivity and competitiveness of their countries' production structures. In the face of the economic crisis, its flagship publication, *Foreign Direct Investment in Latin America,* included a special section on the impacts of the crisis on capital flows to the region, as well as an analysis of investment in large coastal hotel and real estate complexes in tropical countries, which were hit hard by the crisis. The Division's research on the determinants of productivity growth in developing countries remained an important reference for policymakers and research institutions.

The Commission's post-graduate summer school hosted 50 young researchers interested in studying and analysing the Latin American and Caribbean economies. The Division continued to maintain the Observatory for the Information Society in Latin America and the Caribbean, which aimed to centralize and harmonize data monitoring the information society in the region. Technical cooperation and support for policymaking included 207 missions, addressing information and communication technologies (ICTs) and innovation (47 per cent); industrial development and small and medium-sized enterprises (35 per cent); agricultural and rural development (13 per cent); and investment and corporate strategy (5 per cent).

Macroeconomic policies and growth

In the context of the financial and economic crisis, the ECLAC Economic Development Division placed emphasis on providing rapid analytical and technical support to Latin American and Caribbean countries, in order to assist them in assessing the impacts of the crisis and formulating policy response. The Division remained a leading contributor to the dissemination of up-to-date information on current macroeconomic policy topics and to the promotion of information-sharing. Its 172 technical cooperation missions focused on financial crisis management (53 per cent); economic growth (15 per cent); employment (13 per cent); development financing (10 per cent); fiscal policy (6 per cent); and monetary and exchange-rate policy (3 per cent).

The Division enhanced the awareness of policymakers in the region about key issues relating to short-term macroeconomic policies within a long-term growth framework by undertaking a systematic assessment of the application of economic policies and reforms and of their impact on the economies of the region, and disseminated its main analyses and findings through its publications. The Division's leading publications—*Preliminary Overview of the Economies of Latin America and the Caribbean* and *Economic Survey of Latin America and the Caribbean*—were widely read, and readers' surveys, including feedback from policymakers, academics, the press, non-governmental organizations representatives and economists from the private sector, showed a 94.5 per cent satisfaction rate. The Division also continued to disseminate economic analyses on fiscal policy and labour markets, including a variety of specialized, in-depth macroeconomic analyses, through its working paper series "Macroeconomía del desarrollo". Through such publications as "Regulation, Worker Protection and Active Labour-Market Policies in Latin America", it continued to contribute to the policy debate regarding labour market institutions in the region, and to inform decision-makers and technical personnel of policy options with respect to regulation and protection.

Equity and social cohesion

The global financial crisis, which also affected the social situation, brought an end to six years of successes in reducing poverty, expanding employment, extending social protection coverage and improving income distribution in the region. During the period under review, the ECLAC Social Development Division strengthened its assessment and monitoring of social protection systems and poverty reduction policies, and of the links between families and social protection policies. Its 145 technical cooperation missions focused on social protection (26 per cent); social cohesion and vulnerable groups (25 per cent); education, health and nutrition (25 per cent); poverty eradication (15 per cent); and social indicators (9 per cent).

The 2008 edition of the flagship publication *Social Panorama of Latin America* provided up-to-date poverty figures from 18 countries, thus contributing to policy discussions regarding the new employment-related targets incorporated into MDGs, the demographic dividend as an opportunity for expanding secondary education coverage, and the issue of youth and family violence from a perspective of social inclusion. The steady increase in downloads of that edition was indicative of the demand for crucial information for assessing social conditions, advances in poverty reduction, migration and health issues, and public social expenditure, as well as of the role of ECLAC in furthering the regional social development agenda.

The Division continued to provide technical cooperation to Governments to develop methodologies for measuring social expenditure. It also devoted much of its work to social protection and conditional cash transfer programmes, as fundamental tools for achieving greater equality and reducing poverty in the region. The Division also disseminated information through the website of the Latin American and Caribbean Network of Social Institutions. Its publication, *Youth and Social Cohesion in Ibero-America: A model in the making*, which provided a comprehensive, up-to-date picture of the situation of youth in Ibero-America, was presented in October to Heads of State and Government at the eighteenth Ibero-American Summit of Heads of State and Government in El Salvador.

Mainstreaming the gender perspective

The ECLAC Division for Gender Affairs, in its transition from the Women and Development Unit [YUN 2007, p. 1030], was significantly upgraded and strengthened, enabling ECLAC to demonstrate its role in generating knowledge and enhancing capacity for gender equality and the empowerment of women and in contributing to gender mainstreaming in the region. The launching of the Gender Equality Observatory for Latin America and the Caribbean; the implementation of the Quito Consensus [ibid., p. 1031]; and the integration of a gender perspective into the main institutional documents and work priorities of ECLAC were the Division's most important achievements during the period under review.

The Division also carried out preparatory work aimed at fostering collaboration between users and producers of statistical information at the country level through the organization of two technical meetings—Aguascalientes, Mexico, October, and Port-of-

Spain, Trinidad and Tobago, December—with participation by representatives of national machineries for the advancement of women/gender affairs and national statistical offices from the region in defining the basic set of indicators necessary for the functioning of the Gender Equality Observatory. The Division's 37 technical cooperation missions focused on women's rights (49 per cent); gender statistics (38 per cent); institutions and representation of women (8 per cent); and gender and the environment (5 per cent).

ECLAC participated in consolidating efforts to support the UN Secretary-General's Campaign "UNite to End Violence against Women", launched in February, through collaborative response, participatory action and sharing of best practices. The Division contributed to work on the issue of gender-based violence through various means, including the creation of an inter-institutional regional working group to define a regional strategy. It also prepared a series of seven video clips on violence against women, which were widely distributed by the five regional commissions and the regional working group on the occasion of the 2008 International Day for the Elimination of Violence against Women.

Population and development

The ECLAC Latin American and Caribbean Demographic Centre-Population Division was guided by mandates arising from international agreements, especially the Programme of Action of the 1994 International Conference on Population and Development [YUN 1994, p. 955] and the Madrid International Plan of Action on Ageing, 2002 [YUN 2002, p. 1194]. It presented a background document on the socio-economic impact of demographic changes at the 2008 ECLAC sessional Ad Hoc Committee on Population and Development, and prepared a chapter for the 2008 edition of the ECLAC publication *Social Panorama of Latin America*, on the opportunity to improve secondary education brought about by the demographic dividend.

During 2008, a survey on the activities of national statistical offices in relation to the forthcoming 2010 round of censuses identified thematic areas in which countries of the region needed technical cooperation and support. As a result, the Division organized four workshops on such emerging issues as measurement of racial and ethnic identity; measurement of migration and other forms of mobility; the use of cartography; and the inclusion of health-related questions in censuses.

The Division's 177 technical cooperation missions focused on population censuses and statistics (24 per cent); ageing (19 per cent); indigenous peoples and Afro-descendants (19 per cent); migration (17 per cent); population growth and public policy (11 per cent); fertility and reproductive health (7 per cent); and a rights-based approach in social policy (3 per cent).

Public administration

The Latin American and Caribbean Institute for Economic and Social Planning (ILPES) underscored the need for the countries of the region to strike the necessary balance between private initiative and public action and to consolidate a fiscal and social covenant, defined as the institutional arrangements that ensured effective governance. It sought to foster a healthy, long-term balance between the State, civil society and the market economy through the art of governing for sustainable economic, social and institutional development.

ILPES/ECLAC worked in specialized areas, offering short courses which featured a combination of theory and practice, and systematized the experiences of the countries of the region, assisting government officials in the design and implementation of their development programmes and policies. ILPES was the leading voice within ECLAC for development planning, performance-informed budgeting and public management in the region, at both the national and subnational levels, through its research, technical cooperation and training activities. It catalyzed the collective discussion on those issues, contributing to efforts to improve the quality of public policies and strengthen institutional capacities.

The Division's 393 technical cooperation missions focused on local and regional development (58 per cent); results-based management (21 per cent); planning and budget (11 per cent); and socio-economic project evaluation (10 per cent).

Sustainable development and human settlements

The ECLAC Sustainable Development and Human Settlements Division continued to work on the interrelationships between economic growth, environmental protection, urban development and social equity. Its technical cooperation and studies strengthened the capacity of the countries of the region to assess their progress towards sustainable development, by generating empirical information and constructing sustainability indicators to measure the magnitude of the economic, social and environmental costs associated with their development strategies at national and subnational levels. Eight studies on climate change mitigation, including evaluation of carbon markets and economic adaptation in the region, were undertaken jointly with national Government institutions of Argentina, Bolivia, Chile, Colombia, Ecuador, Mexico, Paraguay, Peru and Uruguay.

The Division worked on the integration of public policies and the follow-up of international and regional agreements on sustainable development, including their links with environmental goods and services markets. It coordinated a multi-agency report on regional progress under MDG 7 (ensuring environmental sustainability), which included information on carbon dioxide emissions per unit of GDP and deforestation, and the potential impacts of climate change on the achievement of other MDGs, and elaborated on additional difficulties for addressing climate change. The report showed important advances in aspects of environmental sustainability, such as increased number of protected areas, reduced consumption of products that damaged the ozone layer, and increased water and sanitation services in the region.

ECLAC also raised awareness and disseminated its analyses and policy recommendations on the issue of climate change to regional policymakers at major meetings. The Division published four methodological guides aimed at facilitating decision-making in the construction of composite indices of sustainable development, economic analysis of environmental externalities and strategic environmental assessment. In addition, urban infrastructure sustainability analyses were presented at expert group meetings.

The Division's 154 technical cooperation missions focused on natural disasters (38 per cent); climate change (29 per cent); the environment (19 per cent); and development and urban planning (14 per cent). Support was provided to countries and local authorities to enable them to cope with the estimated increase of 40 million inhabitants in urban populations over the following five years, and with the repercussions that the increase would have on demand for housing and public services and in terms of the exacerbation of environmental pollution and soil degradation.

Natural resources and infrastructure

The ECLAC Natural Resources and Infrastructure Division produced analyses and research and provided technical cooperation services to Governments, civil society and academia aimed at improving public policy formulation in the management of natural resources and the provision of public utility and infrastructure services. It focused on strengthening the institutional capacity of countries in the region to formulate and implement public policies and regulatory frameworks, in order to increase efficiency in the sustainable management of natural resources and the provision of public utilities and infrastructure services, and in coordinating and sharing best practices.

In the area of infrastructure, the Division provided support and cooperation to enable countries to address three kinds of challenges threatening future social and economic development: the infrastructure gap resulting from delays in investment coupled with explosive growth in demand for transportation; the lack of sustainable criteria in planning infrastructure services; and problems in the operation of transport and logistics chains that increased costs and affected the competitiveness and productivity of national economies, among other negative externalities.

In the energy sector, the Division supported the region's Governments in the promotion of an integral and sustainable energy policy, with emphasis on renewable energies, energy efficiency and biofuels. With respect to mining, the countries that were most active in that sector—including Argentina, Bolivia, Chile, Colombia, Ecuador, Honduras, Peru and others—received technical cooperation services on environmental management of the mining industry, including aspects of management such as mining liabilities, mine closures and social responsibility.

The Division organized eight seminars and expert meetings, including a regional conference on policies for economically efficient, environmentally sustainable and socially equitable water supply and sewerage services (Santiago, Chile, September). It provided the Latin American and Caribbean energy ministers meeting at the third Regional Energy Integration Forum (Buenos Aires, Argentina, November) with an assessment of the local and regional energy situation and an evaluation of policy proposals on regional integration from the perspective of regional energy markets. The Division's 160 technical cooperation missions focused on energy (42 per cent); maritime transport and ports (19 per cent); land transport and road safety (14 per cent); water (14 per cent); and mining (11 per cent).

Statistics and economic projections

The ECLAC Statistics and Economic Projections Division continued its work in the area of systematization and dissemination of statistics. It supported at least 15 countries of the region in strengthening their national statistical systems and capacities in the areas of national accounts, development of suitable indicators for measuring progress towards the MDGs, household surveys and the production of environmental statistics. In July, together with the Central Bank of Chile, ECLAC hosted a workshop on the application of statistical methods to national accounts; in October, a regional seminar on national accounts was held in Santiago.

Technical cooperation provided by the Division facilitated the estimation of national account data in 17 countries, and five countries implemented the

1993 System of National Accounts recommendations. A set of indicators for measuring social cohesion in the region was also identified, including qualitative indicators on public perceptions on different issues. The Division also provided support to countries to improve the quality and availability of household surveys. Another effort involved improving the accessibility of data collected by ECLAC as a whole, by enabling access to all ECLAC databases through CEPALSTAT, a new statistical information portal on the Commission's website.

The Division's annual flagship publication, *Statistical Yearbook for Latin America and the Caribbean,* was a leading source of statistical information, providing social, economic and environmental data from the countries of the region. Despite improvements in the quality and completeness of the region's statistical output on economic, environmental, demographic and social matters, more was needed to cope with future challenges. With the support of the United Nations Environment Programme and the Latin American and Caribbean Initiative for Sustainable Development, environmental indicators were developed and adapted to take account of the region's statistical development. A similar process of harmonization was carried out for regional manufacturing business trend surveys.

The Division's 176 technical cooperation missions focused on economic statistics (40 per cent); social statistics (37 per cent); institution-building (17 per cent); and environmental statistics (17 per cent). The main direct beneficiaries were senior technical staff from national statistics offices in ECLAC member States. Their responsibilities included the collection, processing and analysis of economic statistics and data on such social indicators as employment and poverty. Other beneficiaries included central bank officials working on national accounts.

Subregional activities

Caribbean

The ECLAC subregional headquarters for the Caribbean in Port of Spain, Trinidad and Tobago, strengthened its contribution to policymaking in the subregion through the delivery of substantive research outputs, technical cooperation, and training and capacity-building support. Studies were prepared on public-private partnerships and on the escalation in world food and oil prices and the resulting impact on Caribbean economies. Work on analysing the economics of climate change in the Caribbean began in late 2008, focusing initially on determining the situation in terms of available data and policies, and with respect to other instruments relating to climate change impacts.

The subregional headquarters assisted government officials and public and private institutions from 24 Caribbean countries on sustainable development and integration. Efforts were made to increase access for policymakers in the subregion to the work of the subregional office, and to provide them with an opportunity to increase their knowledge on global matters relating to sustainable development and integration in the Caribbean. Expert meetings were convened in the areas of youth issues, crime and violence, gender and sustainable development, including climate change and the Mauritius Strategy for the Further Implementation of the Programme of Action for the Sustainable Development of Small Island Developing States [YUN 2005, p. 946].

In addition, the subregional headquarters continued to highlight developments in the world economy with respect to international trade, tourism, remittance flows, FDI and external financing—all of which strongly influenced the small open economies of the subregion—and to advocate prudent fiscal and policy responses. The annual *Economic Survey of the Caribbean* [LC/CAR/L.216], which included an economic overview of the subregion in 2008 and the outlook for 2009, provided policymakers with an in-depth discussion of the subregion's economic performance, and put forward recommendations for policy and fiscal change.

The subregional headquarters' 138 technical cooperation missions focused on climate change and the environment (25 per cent); natural disasters (21 per cent); censuses and statistics (21 per cent); gender (10 per cent); economic development (10 per cent); social development (8 per cent); and energy (5 per cent). The headquarters also contributed to economic policymaking in the subregion through studies conducted on public-private partnerships and the subprime mortgage crisis in the United States.

Mexico and Central America

The economies of the northern region of Central America and the Caribbean suffered soaring commodities prices and a devastating hurricane season in 2008, followed by the worldwide economic and financial crisis which erupted at year's end. In response, the ECLAC subregional headquarters in Mexico redirected its activities within its programme of work. Its document "Confronting the crisis. The Central American Isthmus and the Dominican Republic: economic evolution in 2008 and prospects for 2009" [LC/MEX/L.904] examined the causes of the crisis, the channels through which it was transmitted and its economic and social effects, and provided a set of policy recommendations.

In 2008, the subregional headquarters evaluated the impact of international food and oil price hikes on inflation and poverty in Central America. Twice during the year it published a detailed analysis of the economic evolution and outlook for each of the subregion's 10 countries. It also implemented a successful strategy for electronic distribution of information and publications via its website. In addition, ECLAC and Cuba agreed on a methodology for estimating the Cuban GDP.

In the energy field, it produced studies on the externalities and costs of electricity-generating plants using fossil fuels and of refinery complexes in Mexico—providing the technical basis for the establishment of the national standard for reducing carbon dioxide emissions. Its studies on bioethanol provided the technical basis for a Costa Rican project on introducing biofuels into the country's gasoline supply, for which a pilot stage was carried out in 2008.

The subregional headquarters conducted a feasibility study on the economics of climate change in Central America and prepared a project proposal for a comprehensive study on the subject, which was approved by the ministries of environment of the countries of the Central American Isthmus. The Presidents of the subregion, at their Summit on Climate Change and Environment (San Pedro Sula, Honduras, 23–27 May) gave their ministries of environment and finance a mandate to support the study.

The 228 technical cooperation missions of the subregional headquarters focused on economic development (21 per cent); integration and international trade (19 per cent); natural disasters (16 per cent); climate change and the environment (14 per cent); social development (11 per cent); energy and natural resources (10 per cent); and productive development (9 per cent).

Programme and organizational questions

During its thirty-second session (Santo Domingo, 9–13 June) [E/2008/40], the Commission adopted a number of resolutions on programme and organizational matters.

ECLAC calendar of conferences

By its resolution on the ECLAC calendar of conferences for the period 2008–2010 [res. 634(XXXII)], the Commission reaffirmed the decision to maintain the current intergovernmental structure and existing pattern of meetings and approved the calendar of conferences of the Commission as it appeared in the annex to that resolution. It also reaffirmed that the Commission's conference servicing system had been found to be efficient and cost-effective, and recommended that its tasks continue to be the responsibility of the Executive Secretary. It further reaffirmed the importance of continuing to entrust the Commission with the task of organizing and holding regional and subregional meetings to prepare for and follow up on world conferences of the United Nations in the economic and social fields.

ECLAC priorities and programme of work for 2010–2011

In June [res. 635(XXXII)], the Commission endorsed the proposed priorities for the work of the Commission for the 2010–2011 biennium as set forth by the Executive Secretary, which encompassed the consolidation of the advances achieved in the following areas: macroeconomic stability and the promotion of policies to reduce vulnerability; an increase in the region's production potential and a reduction in productivity gaps; an improvement in the region's position in the international economy and the promotion of long-term production development strategies involving appropriate forms of public- and private-sector cooperation and participation; the promotion of a broad social agreement to strengthen social cohesion, to reduce social risks and to strengthen gender mainstreaming in public policies; the refinement of sustainable development policies and an examination of the socio-economic implications of climate change; the strengthening of public management; and the improvement and consolidation of institutions relating to the management of global issues at the regional level.

The Commission urged the Executive Secretary to examine the challenges faced by the region in connection with the global energy and food crisis, and approved the programme of work for the system of the Commission for 2010–2011, which included the Latin American and Caribbean Institute for Economic and Social Planning, and which, with the guidance provided by the resolutions adopted at the Commission's thirty-second session, would become the legislative mandate for the execution of programmes, projects and technical cooperation activities and for the production of recurrent publications identified therein.

Admission of the Cayman Islands to ECLAC membership

At its thirty-second session in June [res. 640(XXXII)], the Commission decided to admit the Cayman Islands as an associate member of ECLAC.

Venue of ECLAC thirty-third session

At its thirty-second session in June [res. 643(XXXII)], the Commission recommended that the Economic and Social Council approve the decision to hold the thirty-third session of ECLAC in Brazil in 2010.

ECONOMIC AND SOCIAL COUNCIL ACTION

On 22 July [meeting 38], the Economic and Social Council, on the recommendation of ECLAC [E/2008/15/Add.2], adopted **resolution 2008/9** without vote [agenda item 10].

Venue of the thirty-third session of the Economic Commission for Latin America and the Caribbean

The Economic and Social Council,

Bearing in mind paragraph 15 of the terms of reference of the Economic Commission for Latin America and the Caribbean and rules 1 and 2 of the rules of procedure of the Commission,

Considering the invitation of the Government of Brazil to host the thirty-third session of the Commission,

1. *Expresses its gratitude* to the Government of Brazil for its generous invitation;

2. *Notes* the acceptance by the Economic Commission for Latin America and the Caribbean of this invitation with pleasure;

3. *Endorses* the decision of the Commission to hold its thirty-third session in Brazil in 2010.

Cooperation with regional bodies

The Secretary-General, in his August consolidated report [A/63/228-S/2008/531 & Corr.1] on cooperation between the United Nations and regional and other organizations, outlined UN relations with the Latin American and Caribbean Economic System.

GENERAL ASSEMBLY ACTION

On 3 November [meeting 37], the General Assembly adopted **resolution 63/12** [draft: A/63/L.10 & Add.1] without vote [agenda item 114 *(m)*].

Cooperation between the United Nations and the Latin American and Caribbean Economic System

The General Assembly,

Recalling its resolution 59/258 of 23 December 2004 on cooperation between the United Nations and the Latin American Economic System,

Having considered the report of the Secretary-General on cooperation between the United Nations and regional and other organizations,

Bearing in mind the Agreement between the United Nations and the Latin American Economic System, in which the parties agree to strengthen and expand their cooperation in matters that are of common concern in the fields of their respective competence pursuant to their constitutional instruments,

Noting that cooperation between the Latin American and Caribbean Economic System and the United Nations has been evolving over the last few years and diversifying with regard to areas of cooperation,

Welcoming the evolution in the treatment of topics relating to the United Nations system, in close contact with the delegations of the Member States participating in such deliberations,

1. *Takes note* of the holding of the thirty-third regular meeting of the Latin American Council of the Latin American and Caribbean Economic System from 26 to 28 November 2007;

2. *Urges* the Economic Commission for Latin America and the Caribbean to continue deepening its coordination and mutual support activities with the Latin American and Caribbean Economic System;

3. *Urges* the specialized agencies and other organizations, funds and programmes of the United Nations system, in particular, the Food and Agriculture Organization of the United Nations, the International Organization for Migration, the World Health Organization, the United Nations Industrial Development Organization, the World Food Programme, the United Nations Development Programme, the United Nations Conference on Trade and Development, the United Nations Educational, Scientific and Cultural Organization and the United Nations Children's Fund, to continue and intensify their support for and to strengthen their cooperation with activities of the Latin American and Caribbean Economic System and to contribute to joint actions to achieve the internationally agreed development objectives, including those contained in the United Nations Millennium Declaration, in Latin America and the Caribbean;

4. *Requests* the Secretary-General of the United Nations and the Permanent Secretary of the Latin American and Caribbean Economic System to assess, at the appropriate time, the implementation of the Agreement between the United Nations and the Latin American Economic System and to report thereon to the General Assembly at its sixty-fifth session;

5. *Requests* the Secretary-General to submit to the General Assembly at its sixty-fifth session a report on the implementation of the present resolution.

The Assembly, by **resolution 63/34** of 26 November (see p. 350), invited the Secretary-General to continue to promote and expand cooperation and coordination between the United Nations and the Caribbean Community in order to increase the capacity of the two organizations. It also urged the specialized agencies and other UN system organizations and programmes to step up their cooperation with the UN Secretary-General and the Secretary-General of the Caribbean Community with a view to intensifying their consultations and programmes of cooperation with the Caribbean Community and its associated institutions.

Western Asia

The Economic and Social Commission for Western Asia (ESCWA) held its twenty-fifth session in Sana'a, Yemen, from 26 to 29 May [E/2008/41]. Session meetings were held in two segments, one for senior officials and the other for ministers. The senior officials segment considered: a report of the Executive Secretary on the Commission's activities [E/ESCWA/25/5]; management issues; the draft convention on international multimodal transport of goods in the Arab Mashreq; and the request for membership in the Commission by the Sudan. The ministerial segment held two round tables: the first on financing for development in the ESCWA region, in preparation for the Follow-up International Conference on Financing for Development to Review the Implementation of the Monterrey Consensus [YUN 2002, p. 953], to be held in Doha, Qatar, from 29 November to 2 December; the second on strengthening regional cooperation for achieving the MDGs.

With regard to financing for development, delegates reviewed the progress made by countries of the region in implementing the Monterrey Consensus, and took into account the outcome of the regional preparatory meeting on the subject (Doha, 29–30 April). On the achievement of the MDGs, the situation was assessed as at 2007, which marked the mid-point towards their attainment. ESCWA encouraged the strengthening of regional cooperation to counter the main obstacles facing certain Arab countries and subregions, in particular the least developed and conflict-affected countries.

During the session, ESCWA launched the Information Society Portal for the ESCWA Region—a bilingual (English and Arabic), database-driven and open-source Web application dedicated to building an online network for partnerships on information and communication technology (ICT) initiatives. It also issued a report on the MDGs in the Arab region in 2007.

The Commission adopted 12 resolutions, including a resolution concerning the Sudan's request to become a member of ESCWA, which required action by the Economic and Social Council (see p. 1135).

Economic trends

According to the summary of the survey of economic and social developments in the ESCWA region, 2008–2009 [E/2009/20], until the last quarter of 2008, ESCWA member countries exhibited steady economic expansion, boosted by higher-than-usual oil prices, except in conflict-affected areas. However, with the onset of the global financial crisis and the steep drop in oil prices, growth prospects became increasingly uncertain. At the economic level, the impact of the crisis had a fourfold effect in 2008: a plunge in financial and real estate asset prices; a collapse in commodity prices, including energy, metal and food—although food prices remained relatively high; shortages of monetary liquidity, particularly of the United States dollar, in local and international money markets; and a rapid decline in export earnings. Against that global backdrop, ESCWA countries showed resilience in terms of economic expansion until the end of 2008. The increasing economic and social uncertainty further undermined the already precarious sense of security shared by the ESCWA population.

Activities in 2008

In 2008, ESCWA continued to strengthen the complementarity between its normative and analytical work and its technical assistance activities, and to strengthen strategic partnerships with regional and national players, in particular with UN agencies and the League of Arab States and its subsidiary bodies. ESCWA activities under its 2008–2009 work programme [E/ESCWA/26/5(Part I)] focused on seven subprogrammes: integrated management of natural resources; integrated social policies; economic development and integration; ICT for regional integration; statistics for evidence-based policymaking; advancement of women; and conflict mitigation and development.

Climate change and sustainable development

By its resolution on climate change issues in the Arab region [res. 281(XXV)], the Commission asked the secretariat to assess the economic and social vulnerability of the region to climate change, with emphasis on freshwater resources, to increase awareness of climate change and to develop an Arab framework action plan on climate change in partnership with the League of Arab States, the Regional Office for West Asia of the United Nations Environment Programme, and other regional organizations.

In response, ESCWA would continue its efforts to build member countries' capacity to address climate change and foster a deeper understanding of measures to mitigate it. It would address such issues as the vulnerability of the water sector to climate change; large-scale renewable energy applications; reducing transport emissions; and enhancing energy efficiency, while continuing to offer technical assistance. ESCWA expanded its communication and networking efforts through the Arab Integrated Water Resources Management Network. In 2008, training activities were conducted on climate change, economic and financial instruments for integrated water resource management, and gender and water.

During the year, a study and field surveys were prepared for the Qatar General Electricity and Water Corporation, in order to evaluate the situation in Qatar and identify areas for improvement. In Yemen, as part of efforts to support the Ministry of Electricity and Energy, ESCWA held a January workshop on energy efficiency and conservation that focused on integrated energy resource planning, demand-side management and energy audits. It also held an October seminar on national cleaner-fuels strategies that provided an opportunity for collecting data and information.

Social policy

The ESCWA Social Development Division focused on strengthening the capacity of member countries to formulate and promote region-specific, integrated social development policies, with a view to achieving social equity, poverty reduction and sustainable development. It also strove to increase their capacity to develop and implement intersectoral social development plans, programmes and projects focusing on youth, migrant workers, persons with disabilities, and the rural and urban poor. During the year, it produced the *Integrated Social Policy Report II: From Concept to Practice* [E/ESCWA/SDD/2008/3], and launched technical assistance projects on integrated social policy in Egypt and Palestine. It also published a report, *The Status and Prospects of the Arab City I: Urbanization and the Challenge of Urban Slums*, focusing on good urban gover-nance, social inclusion and security of tenure, presenting a framework for the dimensions of urbanization and slum areas and examining means to improve life in urban slums and prevent the emergence of new slum areas, while highlighting principles and good practices at the regional and international level.

At its May session [res. 285(XXV)], the Commission encouraged member countries to initiate consultative dialogue aimed at adopting an integrated social policy approach; encourage partnership between Government institutions, the private sector and civil society organizations in the formulation, implementation and monitoring of social policies; adopt and institutionalize integrated social policy and seek a balance between economic priorities and social outcomes; and formulate national youth policies as part of that policy and of national development plans and programmes. ESCWA also requested the secretariat to advocate and enhance the capacity of countries to formulate and adopt an integrated social policy approach.

Economic development

During 2008, the ESCWA Economic Development and Globalization Division (EDGD) enhanced the capacity of member countries to design and implement sound economic policies and strategies for sustainable economic growth, employment creation and poverty alleviation. It organized a wide range of activities on key priority issues of economic importance to the region, in order to increase its capacity to promote foreign direct investment (FDI), formulate and implement adequate trade policies and economic policies for accelerating progress towards achieving the MDGs, and strengthen the processes by which they implemented programmes for improving transport infrastructure and logistics within the framework of the Integrated Transport System in the Arab Mashreq. In line with the Monterrey Consensus of the International Conference on Financing for Development, EDGD continued to support countries in promoting finance for development, and organized a consultative preparatory meeting (Doha, Qatar, 29–30 April) for the Follow-up International Conference.

The division also prepared its *Annual Review of Developments in Globalization and Regional Integration in the Arab World, 2008* [Sales No. E.09.II.L.1], which focused on FDI and regional integration, highlighting labour movement in the region. As part of the Review's follow-up activities, an expert group meeting was organized (Beirut, Lebanon, 20 November). Throughout the year, EDGD continued to provide training services for member countries on financing for development, double taxation, FDI statistics and bilateral investment agreements and their economic implications. As to trade promotion activities, it conducted the Third Forum on Arab Business Community and World Trade Organization Agreements (Beirut, July) to enhance the capacity of countries to negotiate and implement subregional, regional and multilateral trade agreements, and to increase awareness in the Arab business community of developments in WTO negotiations and their implications for businesses in the region. It also assessed trade policy trends, trade facilitation, service liberalization measures and the WTO accession process; and provided related policy advocacy and advice through an expert group meeting on the assessment of trends in the region and their implications for trade and economic performance (Beirut, 17–18 December).

By a resolution on regional action to accelerate implementation of the Monterrey Consensus in Western Asia [res. 290(XXV)], the Commission adopted the draft final communiqué issued by the consultative preparatory meeting and affirmed the need for developing countries, including ESCWA member countries, to be more involved in the management of the global financial, monetary and trade system. It urged countries to support regional integration and small and medium-sized enterprises, and make available the financial resources to create new youth employment opportunities. It also called on countries to continue efforts to eradicate financial and administrative corruption and increase their FDI share, and to stress the importance of education and its central role in eradicating poverty and achieving wider socio-economic development goals. The Commission requested the developed donor countries to increase their ODA in order to assist in achieving the MDGs and affirmed the need for member countries to make a contribution at the highest possible level to the Follow-up International Conference. The secretariat was urged to strengthen cooperation with relevant regional and international organizations and other UN regional commissions on Monterrey Consensus-related issues; to follow up the outcome of the Conference; and to support country efforts.

Yemen

On 29 May [res. 289(XXV)], the Commission commended the comprehensive development efforts undertaken by Yemen, which were aimed at eradicating poverty and meeting economic and social needs with the involvement of civil society and the professional, academic and political social sectors. It recommended that ESCWA provide more support to Yemen with a view to achieving the activities undertaken as a part of the comprehensive development and national efforts to realize the MDGs.

ICT and related development issues

During the year, the ESCWA region experienced a widening digital divide and faced major challenges in building the information society. It needed evidence-based policymaking that relied on basic indicators to produce strategies that optimized development. Broadband represented a challenge to developing the region's ICT infrastructure, since most online applications required the transfer and display of significant amounts of data. The financing of ICT projects was another major obstacle. Digital Arabic Content (DAC) was still very limited compared with Internet content in other languages, and increased efforts were needed to promote the DAC industry in the region in order to preserve Arabic language and culture in a digital world.

At its April meeting in Bahrain, the ESCWA Consultative Committee on Scientific and Technological Development and Technological Innovation, through its Information and Communications Technology Division, reviewed progress made towards the establishment of the ESCWA technology centre, including a detailed assessment of regional needs and priorities, and proposed implementation mechanisms for the centre.

At its May session [res. 284(XXV)], the Commission requested the secretariat to set up within ESCWA a multidisciplinary team to support and monitor progress in the operationalization of the ESCWA regional technology centre, to be funded by extrabudgetary resources.

Statistics

The ESCWA Statistics Division aimed at strengthening the capacity of national institutional frameworks for official statistics in member countries, while strengthening their capacity to participate in the 2010 round of population censuses and implement household and other surveys, in order to provide evidence-based data for attainment of the MDGs by 2015.

ESCWA member countries faced major challenges in producing and disseminating reliable and up-to-date data. Their national statistics offices faced significant obstacles in incorporating appropriate data collection plans into statistical strategies; improving methodologies for basic data and metadata collection; raising the accuracy of estimates to bring them into line with international standards; and strengthening reporting mechanisms at the national and international levels.

On 29 May [res. 283(XXV)], the Commission adopted a resolution on ESCWA member country compliance with international standards for enhancing national statistical systems. It requested countries to take measures to produce high-quality official statistics that could be used in international comparisons; adopt the 1994 Fundamental Principles of Official Statistics of the UN Statistical Commission and take action to apply them; complete the implementation of national strategies for statistical development; and enhance the position of the national statistical machinery within the institutional structure. The Commission requested the secretariat to hold training workshops on international concepts, classifications and standards, and to support countries in adopting and undertaking to apply the Fundamental Principles and in designing and implementing national strategies for statistical development.

On the same date [res. 287(XXV)], the Commission adopted a resolution on strengthening statistical capacities for evidence-based policymaking, and encouraged countries to produce MDG indicators and, in particular, indicators related to poverty, education and health, using surveys and other relevant sources; exchange information for best practice in the development of statistical activities; and adopt the Common Set of Core ICT Indicators issued by the Global Partnership on Measuring ICT for Development. The Commission stressed the need to strengthen the impartiality of national statistical offices in order to produce objective data and improve coordination mechanisms within the statistical system.

Gender equality

Despite positive developments in advancing gender equality in ESCWA member countries in recent years, the region still lagged behind on a number of key indicators. With ESCWA assistance, countries addressed three main challenges: promoting and integrating gender in policies, programmes and projects; mitigating the effects of regional instability and conflict; and continuing to implement the 1995 Beijing Declaration and Platform for Action [YUN 1995, p. 1170] and the 1979 Convention on the Elimination of all Forms of Discrimination against Women (CEDAW) [YUN 1979, p. 895].

Through its Centre for Women, the Commission provided policymakers with recommendations on advancing the rights of women in the region; engaging in capacity-building activities on women's rights and the need to adhere to international instruments; engaging in activities aimed at enhancing the capacity of Government institutions in such gender issues as national machineries for women; and raising awareness on gender issues. The full implementation of CEDAW and its optional protocol in the region remained a priority for ESCWA, which organized several capacity-building workshops and advisory missions to raise awareness of its importance and the need for countries to withdraw their reservations.

On 29 May, by a resolution on gender statistics for equality and empowerment of women [res. 286(XXV)], the Commission encouraged member countries to adopt the set of indicators in the Arab Gender Issues and Indicators Framework as a common set of indicators; develop a mechanism for the collection, dissemination and analysis of gender-sensitive indicators and sex-disaggregated data by rural, urban and age information for the formulation of gender-related and gender-sensitive policies and programmes; and implement training programmes to mainstream gender issues and statistics into their statistical systems, with a view to sensitizing data producers and users to the issue of gender quality and women's empowerment.

Conflict mitigation and development

During 2007 and 2008, the ESCWA Emerging and Conflict-related Issues (ECRI) section conducted numerous capacity-building modules for over 4,500 participants from Iraq, Lebanon, Palestine and Yemen, geared towards enhancing the ability of the public sector to take the lead in attainment of development objectives, including the MDGs. Through such training, ESCWA worked to strengthen good governance practice in conflict-affected countries. As part of its technical cooperation activities, ECRI organized two training of trainers workshops on strategic planning for Palestinian and Yemeni public sector managers, in Beirut, Lebanon, and Sana'a, Yemen, respectively.

On 29 May [res. 282(XXV)], the Commission adopted a resolution on mitigating the impact on development of conflict, occupation and instability in ESCWA member countries, and called on them to enhance institutional capacities to respond to the challenges associated with conflict and occupation and to support conflict- or occupation-afflicted countries in overcoming socio-economic and political challenges. It urged the secretariat to raise awareness of the potential impact of conflict and instability on development; build on successful ESCWA interventions in conflict- or occupation-afflicted countries through the development and interchange of best practice and adaptation for use by other countries; contribute to the capacity-building of Government officials; mobilize extrabudgetary resources to finance the implementation of capacity-building and other activities; and enhance partnerships with relevant local, regional and international organizations. It also invited member countries and donors to support ESCWA.

Programme and organizational questions

Establishment of UN Arabic language centre

Pursuant to its resolution 239(XXII) [YUN 2003, p. 1028], the Executive Secretary submitted to ESCWA at its twenty-fifth session an April report on the follow-up to the establishment of a UN Arabic language centre at ESCWA [E/ESCWA/25/5(Part III)]. The report considered ESCWA activities, including carrying out consultations with relevant UN departments, academic institutions and member country experts; preparing technical studies and discussing them at an expert group meeting; and preparing a project document in accordance with the meeting's recommendations.

On 29 May [res. 288(XXV)], the Commission, cognizant of the project document presented to the senior officials segment of its session concerning the establishment of an Arabic language centre at ESCWA—to be involved in the coordination of Arabic terminology, organization of training sessions and building of cooperative relationships with translation institutes and universities, in coordination with the UN Department of General Assembly and Conference Services—encouraged continued cooperation with ESCWA by the focal points designated by member countries for the project. It also requested the Executive Secretary to fund the project from extrabudgetary resources.

Admission of the Sudan to ESCWA membership

On 29 May [res. 280(XXV)], the Commission requested the secretariat to submit to the Economic and Social Council for action the recommendation that the request for membership by the Sudan should be approved.

ECONOMIC AND SOCIAL COUNCIL ACTION

On 22 July [meeting 38], the Economic and Social Council adopted **resolution 2008/8** [draft: E/2008/15/Add.1] without vote [agenda item 10].

Admission of the Sudan as a member of the Economic and Social Commission for Western Asia

The Economic and Social Council,

Taking into consideration paragraph 2 of Economic and Social Council resolution 1818(LV) of 9 August 1973 concerning the terms of reference of the Economic and Social Commission for Western Asia, which provided that members of the Commission should consist of the States Members of the United Nations situated in Western Asia that called on the services of the then United Nations Economic and Social Office in Beirut, and that future applications for membership by Member States should be decided on by the Council upon the recommendation of the Commission,

Recalling that the terms of reference and rules of procedure of the Economic and Social Commission for Western Asia do not cover the geographical location of countries that may become members thereof nor proscribe a member of one regional commission from being at the same time a member of another regional commission,

Recalling also that most of the other regional commissions have as members countries that are not located in the region that they serve,

1. *Welcomes with satisfaction* the request by the Government of the Sudan that it be admitted to membership in the Economic and Social Commission for Western Asia;

2. *Approves* the admission of the Sudan as a member of the Commission.

Cooperation with LAS

The General Assembly, by **resolution 63/17** of 10 November (see p. 1531), commended the continued efforts of the League of Arab States (LAS) to promote multilateral cooperation among Arab States, and requested the UN system to continue to lend its support. It requested the UN Secretariat and the LAS General Secretariat, within their respective fields of competence, to intensify their cooperation, and called on the Secretary-General to strengthen cooperation and coordination between the United Nations and other UN system organizations and agencies and LAS and its specialized organizations, in order to enhance their capacity to serve the mutual interests and objectives of the two organizations in the political, economic, social, humanitarian, cultural and administrative fields.

Venue and dates of ESCWA twenty-fifth session

On 29 April [meeting 6], the Economic and Social Council adopted **resolution 2008/1** [draft: E/2008/L.3 & E/2008/SR.6] without vote [agenda item 2].

Venue and dates of the twenty-fifth session of the Economic and Social Commission for Western Asia

The Economic and Social Council,

Having considered the letter dated 27 February 2008 from the Executive Secretary of the Economic and Social Commission for Western Asia informing the Council of the offer of the Government of Yemen to host the twenty-fifth session of the Commission,

1. *Expresses its gratitude* to the Government of Yemen for its generous offer;

2. *Approves* the holding of the twenty-fifth session of the Economic and Social Commission for Western Asia in Sana'a from 26 to 29 May 2008.

Frequency of sessions of ESCWA and its subsidiary bodies

In March [E/ESCWA/25/6(Part I)/Add.1], the secretariat provided the background to its evaluation efforts on the conduct of sessions of ESCWA and its subsidiary bodies. It assessed the quality of the services provided to countries in facilitating their consultations and reported on the lessons learned from 18 sessions from 2004 to 2007. In April [E/ESCWA/25/6(Part I)/Add.2], the secretariat reported on the frequency of the sessions and considered the challenges for ESCWA in responding to the emerging needs in light of the ongoing UN reform in the field of development, and the latest intergovernmental machineries of other regional commissions and the frequency of their sessions.

On 29 May [res. 291(XXV)], the Commission called on the secretariat to carry out an in-depth evaluation of the ESCWA intergovernmental structure in light of both programme priority, as identified by countries, and UN reforms. The Commission expressed appreciation for the lessons learned from the evaluation of the intergovernmental sessions during 2004–2007.

Chapter VI

Energy, natural resources and cartography

The conservation, development and use of energy and natural resources continued to be the focus of several UN bodies in 2008, including the Commission on Sustainable Development, which commenced its first two-year implementation cycle (2008–2009) on the thematic cluster: agriculture, rural development, land, drought, desertification and Africa.

Recognizing the important role of energy in sustainable development, poverty eradication and achievement of internationally agreed development goals, the Commission, at its sixteenth session in May, discussed the need for new energy technologies, especially renewable energy; energy and industrial development; water services; demand for biofuels; and the improvement of access to energy, water and sanitation in the rural areas. The Commission also observed that despite progress being made with regard to energy for sustainable development, higher energy prices and climate change posed new challenges.

The Director General of the International Atomic Energy Agency (IAEA), in his annual address to the General Assembly in October, expressed his concern about the proliferation of nuclear weapons and the possibility of extremist groups having access to nuclear or radioactive material. He also noted that IAEA was at the nexus of development and security and had established effective partnerships with the World Health Organization and the Food and Agricultural Organization of the United Nations. Consequently, the use of radiation therapy for treating cancer had increased, higher-yielding food crops had been developed, and more people had access to clean drinking water. Some 439 nuclear power reactors were operating in 30 countries, and 36 new plants were under construction. The Director General cautioned that the primary responsibility for ensuring safety and security depended upon the countries concerned.

The issue of sanitation was the focus of World Water Day (22 March) and one of the main subjects of the *UN-Water Annual Report 2008*. The United Nations celebrated 2008 as the International Year of Sanitation, which emphasized that disease control and poverty eradication could not be achieved without sanitation, highlighting its importance for health, dignity, and sustainable social and economic development.

The Economic and Social Council recommended that the tenth Conference on the Standardization of Geographical Names be convened in 2012, and that the twenty-fifth session of the United Nations Group of Experts on Geographical Names be held in May 2009.

Energy and natural resources

The Commission on Sustainable Development, at its sixteenth session (New York, 11 May 2007 and 5–16 May 2008) [E/2008/29], focused on the thematic cluster of agriculture, rural development, land, drought, desertification, and Africa for the implementation cycle (2008–2009). In preparation for the session, the Secretary-General submitted reports on each of those areas containing information on issues related to energy and natural resources. A report on the integrated review of the thematic cluster of agriculture, rural development, land, drought, desertification, and Africa in small island developing States [E/CN.17/2008/9] was also submitted.

The Commission reviewed the implementation of the Mauritius Strategy for the Further Implementation of the Programme of Action for the Sustainable Development of Small Island Developing States [YUN 2005, p. 946], focusing on the thematic cluster for the implementation cycle (2008–2009), and adopted a decision on the issue. It also reviewed the implementation of the decisions on water and sanitation and their interlinkages made during its thirteenth session [YUN 2005, p. 1126]. With regard to meeting water and sanitation targets, the Under-Secretary-General for Economic and Social Affairs stated that the world might meet the water target, but not that for sanitation by 2015.

Documents before the Commission included the Secretary-General's report [E/CN.17/2008/2] on the review of implementation of Agenda 21 [YUN 1992, p. 672], the Programme for the Further Implementation of Agenda 21 [YUN 1997, p. 792] and the Johannesburg Plan of Implementation [YUN 2002, p. 821]. The report noted the continued need for better access to energy for the rural poor in South Asia and sub-Saharan Africa, how climate change made the development of low-carbon energy technologies a priority, and the uneven progress in slowing natural resource degradation. Despite advances with regard to energy for sustainable development, higher energy prices and climate change posed new demands. For most developing regions, accessibility and affordability of modern energy services remained challenges. Increased energy efficiency and swift development and deployment of advanced, cleaner low-carbon energy technologies were required to balance harmful effects of air pollution and climate change.

In his report on agriculture [E/CN.17/2008/3], the Secretary-General emphasized its role—as by far the largest user of global water supplies—in efforts to reduce hunger and poverty, improve rural livelihoods and achieve sustainable development. He noted that it was difficult for small shareholders to afford fertilizers due to higher energy costs and the depletion of phosphate stocks. As biofuels were gaining international attention and yielding results in many countries, he estimated that their share in global transport energy production would rise from 1 per cent in 2008 to 4–7 per cent in 2030. By 2025, 1.8 billion people would live in absolute water scarcity, exacerbated by climate change; and two thirds of the world's population would live under water-stressed conditions.

As for rural development [E/CN.17/2008/4], the Secretary-General indicated that a majority of the rural population in developing countries continued to lack access to water, sanitation and modern energy sources. He noted that low access to a safe water supply and adequate sanitation caused many diseases in Africa. According to the World Health Organization (WHO), approximately 50 per cent of Africans suffered from one of six water-related diseases.

With regard to implementation on land [E/CN.17/2008/5], the Secretary-General stated that improved soil and water management could enhance land productivity and the availability of water resources. Integrated water resources management was a means to improve interaction in land and water resources management.

In his report on the implementation of Agenda 21 and the Johannesburg Plan of Implementation [E/CN.17/2008/6], the Secretary-General considered the issue of drought and emphasized its impact on the energy sector by exemplifying the case of Ghana in 2007, where the water level of the Akosombo dam dropped below the minimum level of 240 feet, leading to a severe reduction in electricity generation from hydropower and load-shedding of electricity in the entire country. Recent events related to climate change, particularly droughts associated with El Niño, exerted pressures on affected communities and led to overexploitation of natural resources. In reviewing the implementation of Agenda 21 and the Johannesburg Plan of Implementation with regard to desertification [E/CN.17/2008/7], the Secretary-General stated thar this was a global issue, and emphasized its serious implications for worldwide eco-safety, poverty eradication, socio-economic stability and sustainable development. He noted that 90 per cent of people in developing countries lagged behind the rest of the world in accessing clean drinking water and adequate sanitation.

In his report on Africa [E/CN.17/2008/8], the Secretary-General underscored that sub-Saharan Africa lacked sufficient access to energy, and that energy production remained expensive, relying heavily on fossil fuels. Moreover, old and inefficient power stations contributed to frequent power shortages in Africa. Water infrastructure development was a priority of most African countries, and many multilateral organizations were involved in working towards the achievement of MDGS with regard to water access. The World Bank had launched the Ethiopian Water Supply and Sanitation Project as a means to improving 5,500 rural water-supply schemes serving 2 million people.

In preparation for the sixteenth session, a number of intersessional meetings were held in 2008, including the International Conference on Combating Desertification (Beijing, 22–24 January), Oslo Policy Forum on Changing the Way We Develop: Dealing with Disasters and Climate Change (Oslo, Norway, 27–29 February) and the High-level Round Table on International Cooperation for Sustainable Development in Caribbean Small Island Developing States (Bridgetown, Barbados, 25–27 March).

Energy

Transit of energy

During 2008, the General Assembly considered the issue of the stable transit of energy and its role in ensuring sustainable development and international cooperation, including the development of transportation systems and pipelines. In that connection, Turkmenistan took the initiative to convene a high-level international conference to discuss the issue in 2009.

GENERAL ASSEMBLY ACTION

On 19 December [meeting 72], the Assembly, on the recommendation of the Second Committee [A/63/414 & Corr.1], adopted **resolution 63/210** without vote [agenda item 49].

Reliable and stable transit of energy and its role in ensuring sustainable development and international cooperation

The General Assembly,

Bearing in mind the growing role of the transit of energy in global processes,

Recognizing the importance of Central Asia and all other transportation and communication hubs and their vital role in the production of energy and its transportation to international markets,

Noting that stable, efficient and reliable energy transportation, as a key factor of sustainable development, is in the interest of the entire international community,

Reiterating the principles of the Rio Declaration on Environment and Development and of Agenda 21, and recalling the recommendations and conclusions contained in the Plan of Implementation of the World Summit on Sustainable Development concerning energy for sustainable development,

1. *Welcomes* international cooperation in developing transportation systems and pipelines;

2. *Recognizes* the need for extensive international cooperation in determining ways of ensuring the reliable transportation of energy to international markets through pipelines and other transportation systems;

3. *Welcomes* the initiative of Turkmenistan to convene in 2009 a high-level international conference to discuss the issue of ensuring the reliable and stable transportation of energy to international markets.

Nuclear energy

By an August note [A/63/276], the Secretary-General transmitted to the General Assembly the 2007 report of the International Atomic Energy Agency (IAEA). Presenting the report on 27 October [A/63/PV.31], the IAEA Director General stated that concern about the proliferation of nuclear weapons, coupled with the possibility of nuclear or radioactive material falling into the hands of extremist groups, had not diminished since he last addressed the Assembly in 2007. As a development agency, IAEA had established successful partnerships, with WHO and the Food and Agricultural Organization of the United Nations (FAO). Through those partnerships, the use of radiation therapy for treating cancer had increased, higher-yielding food crops had been developed and more people had access to clean drinking water.

The Director General underscored that every aspect of development required reliable access to modern energy resources and that developing countries should view nuclear power as a source of energy that could liberate their citizens from poverty. He stated that the Agency's support had been sought by some 50 States expressing interest in the possible introduction of nuclear power. Increased demand for assistance was particularly strong from developing countries.

In 2008, some 439 nuclear power reactors were operating in 30 countries, and the number of new plants under construction stood at 36. In order to ensure newcomers' nuclear energy safety, efficiency, and minimal proliferation risk, IAEA stressed the need for planning properly, building human resources and infrastructure, establishing independent and effective regulators, and adhering to international safety, security, and non-proliferation instruments. The Director General also stressed that the primary responsibility to ensure safety and security rested with the countries concerned, and emphasized that a single nuclear accident anywhere in the world could undermine the nuclear energy future everywhere. Therefore, the highest safety standards should be maintained.

An important implication of a nuclear renaissance was the wider dissemination of nuclear material, which would increase the risk of nuclear material diversion to produce nuclear weapons. He noted that countries experienced in uranium enrichment and plutonium separation would be able to develop nuclear weapons if they withdrew from the 1968 Treaty on the Non-Proliferation of Nuclear Weapons (NPT) [YUN 1968, p. 17]. He therefore recommended a nuclear fuel bank under IAEA supervision so that new enrichment and reprocessing activities could be brought under multilateral control.

The possibility that terrorists might obtain nuclear material remained a serious concern. The Director General indicated that theft or loss of nuclear material was shockingly high, and that the number of such incidents in the year was nearly 250 as at June 2008. Effective nuclear verification required four elements: adequate legal authority, state-of-the-art technology, timely access to all relevant information, and sufficient human and financial resources. As many as 30 States party to NPT had yet to implement their required comprehensive safeguards agreements with the Agency.

The Director General reported that the Democratic People's Republic of Korea briefly suspended access to the Yongbyon nuclear facilities from the Agency's inspectors, who monitored and verified shutdown of the facilities (see p. 595). However, access was restored following an agreement between the United States and the Democratic People's Republic of Korea on a verification protocol.

The IAEA annual report 2008 provided a survey of nuclear developments around the world and of the Agency's work within the framework of the three pillars of technology, safety and security, and verification. The expansion and near- and long-term growth prospects remained centred in Asia. China was considering a significant increase in its growth targets for nuclear power; in 2008, six of the ten construction starts were in China.

GENERAL ASSEMBLY ACTION

On 27 October [meeting 32], the General Assembly adopted **resolution 63/6** [draft: A/63/L.6 & Add.1] without vote [agenda item 80].

Report of the International Atomic Energy Agency

The General Assembly,

Having received the report of the International Atomic Energy Agency for 2007,

Taking note of the statement by the Director General of the International Atomic Energy Agency, in which he provided additional information on the main developments in the activities of the Agency during 2008,

Recognizing the importance of the work of the Agency,

Recognizing also the cooperation between the United Nations and the Agency and the Agreement governing the relationship between the United Nations and the Agency as approved by the General Conference of the Agency on 23 October 1957 and by the General Assembly in the annex to its resolution 1145(XII) of 14 November 1957,

1. *Takes note with appreciation* of the report of the International Atomic Energy Agency;

2. *Takes note* of resolutions GC(52)/RES/9A on measures to strengthen international cooperation in nuclear, radiation, transport and waste safety and GC(52)/RES/9B on transport safety; GC(52)/RES/10 on progress on measures to protect against nuclear and radiological terrorism; GC(52)/RES/11 on strengthening of the Agency's technical cooperation activities; GC(52)/RES/12 on strengthening the Agency's activities related to nuclear science, technology and applications, comprising GC(52)/RES/12A on non-power nuclear applications, GC(52)/RES/12B on nuclear power applications and GC(52)RES/12C on nuclear knowledge; GC(52)/RES/13 on strengthening the effectiveness and improving the efficiency of the safeguards system and application of the Model Additional Protocol; GC(52)/RES/14 on the implementation of the Agreement between the Agency and the Democratic People's Republic of Korea for the application of safeguards in connection with the Treaty on the Non-Proliferation of Nuclear Weapons; GC(52)/RES/15 on the application of Agency safeguards in the Middle East; and decisions GC(52)/DEC/9 on the amendment to article XIV. A of the Statute and GC(52)/DEC/10 on cooperation agreements with intergovernmental organizations, adopted by the General Conference of the Agency at its fifty-second regular session, held from 29 September to 4 October 2008;

3. *Reaffirms its strong support* for the indispensable role of the Agency in encouraging and assisting the development and practical application of atomic energy for peaceful uses, in technology transfer to developing countries and in nuclear safety, verification and security;

4. *Appeals* to Member States to continue to support the activities of the Agency;

5. *Requests* the Secretary-General to transmit to the Director General of the Agency the records of the sixty-third session of the General Assembly relating to the activities of the Agency.

Natural resources

Water resources

On 22 March, World Water Day [YUN 1992, p. 654], which focused on the theme "Sanitation", was a major outreach event of the International Year of Sanitation. It was coordinated jointly by the United Nations Children's Fund (UNICEF), WHO and the Water Supply and Sanitation Collaborative Council on behalf of UN-Water. At a gathering in Geneva, a number of prominent speakers gave their perspectives on the challenges related to sanitation.

The *UN-Water Annual Report 2008* presented the activities of UN-Water and stated that communication had become increasingly important for UN-Water during the year. A major activity was the restructuring of its website, which was launched in December. A number of seminars and workshops were organized, and an increasing number of documents, reports and fact sheets were prepared by UN-Water or through task forces. Assessment reports focused on the status and trends in water management, and evaluated the progress made toward reaching international development targets related to water as well as challenges and emerging issues. UN-Water also supported coordination among UN agencies and their efforts to monitor the state and utilization of water resources. Activities during the year carried out by seven operational task forces focused on: indicators, monitoring and reporting; sanitation; transboundary waters; IWRM; climate change and water; country-level coordination; and water and gender.

The eighteenth World Water Week (Stockholm, Sweden, 17–23 August) organized workshops, seminars and side events. A specific UN-Water seminar focused on the theme "Transboundary waters—sharing benefits, sharing responsibilities". Other seminars focused on sanitation and the outcomes of regional sanitation conferences and on indicators for action on water management. A UN-Water exhibition was also organized.

The WHO/UNICEF Joint Monitoring Programme for Water Supply and Sanitation continued monitoring activities to provide global reports on water and sanitation coverage in order to facilitate sector planning and management, support countries in their efforts to improve their monitoring systems and provide information for advocacy.

The Chairman of the Commission on Sustainable Development noted the successful efforts of UN-Water and called for its increased role in monitoring the progress of water, sanitation, and IWRM commitments.

Water and sanitation

The Commission considered the Secretary-General's report [E/CN.17/2008/11] on the review of progress in implementing the decision of its thirteenth session on water and sanitation in 2005, which stated that the MDG target on safe drinking water might be achieved, but current trends did not support meeting the sanitation target. It noted that while South Asia, Latin America and the Caribbean, East Asia and the Pacific were on track for meeting water supply targets, West Asian States and sub-Saharan Africa lagged behind. Some of the world's most populous developing countries—including Brazil, Egypt, India, Mexico, Myanmar, Pakistan, Thailand, Turkey and Viet Nam—managed to exceed their targets for providing access to safe drinking water and took strides towards achieving universal access by 2015. Many countries had prioritized water and sanitation services in their national development plans. With regard to basic sanitation services, Latin America and the Caribbean made progress to meet the MGDS target, East Asia and the Pacific moved close to the targeted yearly access figures, but sub-Saharan Africa and South Asia lagged behind. Several countries implemented the Commission's recommendation by establishing an institutional home for sanitation and prioritizing sanitation in national development plans.

Commission consideration. With regard to issues related to water, the Commission warned that projected climate change was likely to intensify problems related to water quality and water shortage in many water-stressed regions. As pressure on water supplies continued to increase, more frequent and severe drought were a matter of concern in both water-short and water-surplus regions. That called for a comprehensive response in respect of climate change mitigation, adaptation, technology transfer and finance. The importance of mainstreaming adaptation to climate change in the water management process was noted. The Commission addressed different aspects of water and sanitation, including the importance of global and national monitoring of the sector; the need for reliable data supported by improved knowledge and research; transfer of technology and capacity-building; the importance of water governance; the role of partnerships; and the importance of strengthening water utilities.

The Commission highlighted the importance of access to safe drinking water and sanitation services for poverty alleviation and for meeting other MDGs, and its interlinkages with health. In addition to limited availability of financial resources, the lack of legislation and national policies on water and sanitation continued to impede progress. In some areas, the absence of water treatment facilities posed an obstacle to environmental management and the provision of safe drinking water. Greater investment in water supply and sanitation and IWRM—in particular by national Governments, the private sector and through official development assistance (ODA)—was required, as well as support to further strengthen local institutional capacities and the use of technologies suited to local conditions.

International Year of Sanitation, 2008

The General Assembly, by resolution 61/192 [YUN 2006, p. 1419], proclaimed 2008 the "International Year of Sanitation" to increase awareness of the importance of sanitation and promote action at all levels. The goals of the year were to stimulate dialogue and create a context for political leadership, leading to the allocation of greater resources to sanitation for the poor. UN-Water supported the Year, and its Task Force on sanitation produced a publication entitled *Tackling a global crisis: International Year of Sanitation 2008*, jointly undertaken by the United Nations Human Settlements Programme (UN-Habitat) and UNICEF on behalf of UN-Water. The report stated that 2.6 billion people around the world, mainly from rural areas, had no sanitation. The Year provided an opportunity to examine the needs of over one third of the world's population for the most basic of services, and to promote the message that sanitation was vital for health, contributed to social development, was a good economic investment, helped the environment and could be achieved. The report indicated that progress towards the 2015 Sanitation Goal was slow and called for political will, financial investment, popular participation, and affordable technological and hygiene education approaches towards achieving the target. It emphasized that disease control and poverty eradication could not be achieved without sanitation, and called for accelerated progress towards meeting the 2015 Sanitation Goal.

Communication. By a 28 November letter [A/63/598-E/2009/7], Spain transmitted to the Secretary-General the "2008 Zaragoza Charter", adopted at the 2008 Zaragoza International Exhibition (Zaragoza, Spain, 14 June–14 September), which focused on the theme "Water and Sustainable Development."

Cartography

Standardization of geographical names

On 23 July, the Economic and Social Council took note of the report of the ninth United Nations Conference on the Standardization of Geographical Names [YUN 2007, p. 1044], and endorsed the recommendation that the tenth Conference be convened in 2012. The Council also recommended that the twenty-fifth session of the United Nations Group of Experts on Geographical Names be convened in the first half of 2009 (**decision 2008/241**).

On 12 September, the Council decided that the twenty-fifth session of the Group of Experts would be held at the United Nations Office at Nairobi from 5 to 12 May 2009, to facilitate and prepare the work of the tenth Conference on the Standardization of Geographical Names. The Council requested the Secretary-General to take measures, as appropriate, to implement the decision (**decision 2008/260**).

On 23 July, the Council took note of the report of the UN Group of Experts on Geographical Names at its twenty-fourth session [ibid.] (**decision 2008/242**).

Chapter VII

Environment and human settlements

In 2008, the United Nations and the international community continued to work towards protecting the environment through legally binding instruments and the activities of the United Nations Environment Programme (UNEP).

The tenth special session of the UNEP Governing Council/Global Ministerial Environment Forum discussed the emerging policy themes of globalization and the environment—mobilizing finance to meet the climate challenge, and international environmental governance and UN reform. The Executive Director developed the UNEP Medium-term Strategy 2010–2013, which set out the vision and strategic direction for UNEP activities for that period. The Council authorized the Executive Director to use the Strategy in formulating the strategic frameworks and programmes of work and budgets for the 2010–2011 and 2012–2013 periods. In October, the Executive Director submitted the final review of the first UNEP long-term Tunza strategy (2003–2008) for engaging young people in environmental issues, and proposed a second long-term strategy (2009–2014).

In February, the General Assembly held a thematic debate on "Addressing Climate Change: The United Nations and the World at Work". The UNEP Governing Council invited the Economic and Social Council to consider a proposal for proclaiming an international decade for addressing climate change for the 2010–2020 period. In a decision on the sustainable development of the Arctic region, the Governing Council requested the Governments of Arctic States and other stakeholders to implement measures to facilitate adaptation to climate change, including by indigenous communities. The twenty-eighth session of the Intergovernmental Panel on Climate Change, held in April in Budapest, Hungary, decided to produce a fifth assessment report on climate change, to be finalized in 2014. A global strategy was initiated to follow up on the Millennium Ecosystem Assessment, which was completed in 2005.

In August, the Secretary-General recommended the establishment of the Eastern Mediterranean Oil Spill Restoration Trust Fund. The Fund would provide assistance and support to the States adversely affected by the oil slick that resulted from the destruction by Israel of oil storage tanks in Lebanon in 2006, following the outbreak of hostilities between Israel and the paramilitary group Hizbullah. The General Assembly established the Fund in December.

The ninth meeting of the Conference of the Parties to the Convention on Biological Diversity, which took place in May in Bonn, Germany, adopted a roadmap for negotiating an international regime for access to and sharing the benefits of genetic resources.

The United Nations Human Settlements Programme (UN-Habitat) continued to support the implementation of the 1996 Habitat Agenda and the Millennium Development Goals. A new Global Campaign for Sustainable Urbanization merged two previous campaigns on secure tenure and urban governance, and addressed the adaptation and mitigation challenges of climate change. In December, the UN-Habitat Committee of Permanent Representatives endorsed an action plan for implementing the 2008–2013 Medium-term Strategic and Institutional Plan.

Environment

UN Environment Programme

Governing Council/Ministerial Forum

The tenth special session of the United Nations Environment Programme (UNEP) Governing Council (GC)/Global Ministerial Environment Forum (GMEF) was held in Monaco from 20 to 22 February [A/63/25].

Ministerial-level consultations (20–22 February) discussed the emerging policy themes of international environmental governance and UN reform, and globalization and the environment—mobilizing finance to meet the climate challenge and international environmental governance. The Council/Forum had before it a background paper [UNEP/GCSS.X/9] including policy options emanating from the President's summary of the ministerial consultations held during the twenty-fourth (2007) GC/GMEF session [YUN 2007, p. 1045].

The Committee of the Whole [UNEP/GCSS.X/10], established by the Council/Forum on 20 February, considered policy issues, including the state of the environment; environment and development; and follow-up to and implementation of the outcomes of UN summits and major intergovernmental meetings, including Governing Council decisions. The policy statement by UNEP Executive Director Achim Steiner was also annexed to the report on the proceedings.

On 23 July (**decision 2008/242**), the Economic and Social Council took note of the Governing Council's report on its tenth special session.

The General Assembly took note of the report in resolution 63/220 of 19 December (see below).

Subsidiary body

In 2008, the Committee of Permanent Representatives, which was open to representatives of all UN Member States and members of specialized agencies, held an extraordinary meeting on 5 February [UNEP/CPR/102/3] and regular meetings on 18 June [UNEP/CPR/104/2], 17 September [UNEP/CPR/105/2] and 15 December [UNEP/CPR/106/2]. The Committee discussed, among other matters, preparations for the twenty-fifth (2009) Governing Council session.

GENERAL ASSEMBLY ACTION

On 19 December [meeting 72], the General Assembly, on the recommendation of the Second (Economic and Financial) Committee [A/63/414/Add.7], adopted **resolution 63/220** without vote [agenda item 49 *(g)*].

Report of the Governing Council of the United Nations Environment Programme on its tenth special session

The General Assembly,

Recalling its resolutions 2997(XXVII) of 15 December 1972, 53/242 of 28 July 1999, 56/193 of 21 December 2001, 57/251 of 20 December 2002, 58/209 of 23 December 2003, 59/226 of 22 December 2004, 60/189 of 22 December 2005, 61/205 of 20 December 2006 and 62/195 of 19 December 2007,

Recalling also the 2005 World Summit Outcome,

Recognizing the need for more efficient environmental activities in the United Nations system, and noting the need to consider possible options to address this need, including through the ongoing informal consultative process on the institutional framework for United Nations environmental activities,

Taking into account Agenda 21 and the Plan of Implementation of the World Summit on Sustainable Development ("Johannesburg Plan of Implementation"),

Reaffirming the role of the United Nations Environment Programme as the leading global environmental authority and principal body within the United Nations system in the field of environment, which should take into account, within its mandate, the sustainable development needs of developing countries,

Emphasizing that capacity-building and technology support to developing countries in environment-related fields are important components of the work of the United Nations Environment Programme,

Recognizing the need to accelerate implementation of the Bali Strategic Plan for Technology Support and Capacity-building, including through the provision of additional financial resources for that purpose,

1. *Takes note* of the report of the Governing Council of the United Nations Environment Programme on its tenth special session and the decisions contained therein;

2. *Welcomes* the continued efforts of the United Nations Environment Programme in shifting emphasis from delivery of outputs to achievement of results within its budget and programme of work, and also welcomes, in this regard, the United Nations Environment Programme Medium-term Strategy 2010–2013, which is results-based and elaborates six cross-cutting thematic priority areas of work and various means of implementation as a way of strengthening the work of the United Nations Environment Programme, bearing in mind all the relevant provisions of decisions of the Governing Council, and in this regard invites partner organizations to cooperate closely with the Programme;

3. *Stresses* the need to further advance and fully implement the Bali Strategic Plan for Technology Support and Capacity-building, in this regard calls upon Governments and other stakeholders in a position to do so to provide the necessary funding and technical assistance, and welcomes the particular emphasis of the Medium-term Strategy 2010–2013 on significantly enhancing the capacity of the United Nations Environment Programme to deliver on the Bali Strategic Plan;

4. *Recognizes* the progress made so far in the implementation of the Strategic Approach to International Chemicals Management, particularly through its Quick Start Programme, and invites Governments, regional economic integration organizations, intergovernmental organizations and non-governmental organizations to engage actively and cooperate closely to support the Strategic Approach implementation activities of the United Nations Environment Programme, including by providing adequate resources;

5. *Also recognizes* the global challenges posed by mercury, and, in this regard, welcomes the work of the ad hoc open-ended working group on mercury, established by the Governing Council at its twenty-fourth session, to review and assess options for enhanced voluntary measures and new or existing international legal instruments, and notes that the Governing Council will consider the outcomes of the work of the ad hoc open-ended working group at its twenty-fifth regular session;

6. *Emphasizes* the need for the United Nations Environment Programme, within its mandate, to further contribute to sustainable development programmes, the implementation of Agenda 21 and the Johannesburg Plan of Implementation, at all levels, and to the work of the Commission on Sustainable Development, bearing in mind the mandate of the Commission;

7. *Notes* that the Governing Council, at its tenth special session, emphasized the need to implement fully its decision SS.VII/1 on international environmental governance, and also notes the continued discussions scheduled for the twenty-fifth session of the Governing Council;

8. *Recognizes* that the current global crises could adversely impact sustainable development and the achievement of the internationally agreed development goals, including the Millennium Development Goals, emphasizes

the need for mobilization of adequate funding to address their environmental aspects, and takes note of the proposal of the Executive Director of the United Nations Environment Programme, following consultations with the Bureau of the Governing Council and the Committee of Permanent Representatives to the Programme, to address "Global crisis: national chaos?" as one of the themes for the ministerial consultations, to be held at the twenty-fifth session of the Governing Council;

9. *Emphasizes* the need to further enhance coordination and cooperation among the relevant United Nations organizations in the promotion of the environmental dimension of sustainable development, and to enhance the cooperation between the United Nations Environment Programme and regional and subregional organizations, and welcomes the continued active participation of the Programme in the United Nations Development Group and the Environment Management Group;

10. *Takes note* of the finding of *Global Environment Outlook: Environment for Development*, published by the United Nations Environment Programme, that current environmental degradation represents a serious challenge for human well-being and sustainable development, and expresses its deep concern over the evidence of unprecedented environmental changes at all levels, including possible irreversible changes with potentially negative implications for economic and social development, especially for the poor and vulnerable groups in society;

11. *Reaffirms* the need to strengthen the scientific base of the United Nations Environment Programme, as recommended by the intergovernmental consultation on strengthening of the scientific base of the Programme, including the reinforcement of the scientific capacity of developing countries, in the area of protection of the environment, including through the provision of adequate financial resources, and in this respect emphasizes the importance of building on the experiences gained from the preparation of different global environmental assessments as well as other relevant developments in this field;

12. *Reiterates* the need for stable, adequate and predictable financial resources for the United Nations Environment Programme, and, in accordance with General Assembly resolution 2997(XXVII), underlines the need to consider the adequate reflection of all administrative and management costs of the Programme in the context of the United Nations regular budget;

13. *Invites* Governments that are in a position to do so to increase their contributions to the Environment Fund;

14. *Emphasizes* the importance of the Nairobi headquarters location of the United Nations Environment Programme, and requests the Secretary-General to keep the resource needs of the Programme and the United Nations Office at Nairobi under review so as to permit the delivery, in an effective manner, of necessary services to the Programme and to the other United Nations organs and organizations in Nairobi;

15. *Decides* to include in the provisional agenda of its sixty-fourth session, under the item entitled "Sustainable development", a sub-item entitled "Report of the Governing Council of the United Nations Environment Programme on its twenty-fifth session".

International environmental governance

In November [UNEP/GC.25/3], the UNEP Executive Director submitted to the Governing Council a report summarizing actions taken or proposed on international environmental governance. The report discussed the follow-up to the 2005 World Summit Outcome [YUN 2005, p. 48], in which Governments agreed to explore the possibility of a more coherent institutional framework, including a more integrated structure, for UN system environmental activities, among other measures. Pursuant to the Outcome, the General Assembly established an informal consultative process on the institutional framework for UN environmental activities. Following consultations in 2007, the co-chairs of the process—Mexico and Switzerland—presented an option paper. In July 2008, the co-chairs prepared a draft resolution on international environmental governance for consideration by Member States. The report also dealt with the Bali Strategic Plan for Technology Support and Capacity-building [YUN 2004, p. 1040]; strengthening the UNEP scientific base and financing; issues related to multilateral environmental agreements; and enhanced coordination across the UN system, including the Environment Management Group.

A December note by the Executive Director [UNEP/GC.25/INF/33] contained the 2008 report of the Joint Inspection Unit on the management review of environmental governance within the UN system [JIU/REP/2008/3].

Ministerial meeting. On 30 July [A/62/922], Costa Rica transmitted to the Secretary-General the final document of the Ministerial Meeting on International Environmental Governance (New York, 13 May). The objective of the Meeting, which was chaired by the Minister of Environment and Energy of Costa Rica, was to continue the dialogue on international environmental governance that had taken place in various forums over the previous year, and to elaborate proposals to strengthen UNEP as part of UN reform.

UNEP activities

Monitoring and assessment

In a decision of 22 February [A/63/25, dec. SS.X/5], the UNEP Governing Council expressed its continued concern over the evidence presented in the *Global Environment Outlook 4* report (GEO-4), published by UNEP in 2007 [YUN 2007, p. 1056], of unprecedented environmental changes at all levels. It acknowledged that environmental degradation represented a challenge for human well-being and sustainable development, and, in some cases, peace and security. The Council requested the Executive Director to encourage and support the efforts of national bodies to conduct assessments of environmental change and its implications for development within the framework of the Bali Strategic Plan [YUN 2004, p. 1040], which was adopted by the Governing Council in 2005 [YUN 2005, p. 1135]. It also asked the Executive Director, in consultation with the Committee of Permanent Representatives, to present to the Council an overview of the international environmental assessment landscape, identifying possible gaps and duplications, as well as options for the possible development of a scientifically credible and policy-relevant global assessment of environmental change and its implications for development, including a cost analysis and an indicative benefit analysis for each option.

In response to the Council's decision, the Executive Director in November submitted a report [UNEP/GC.25/4/Add.1], which provided a synthesis of the main findings of studies of the environmental assessment landscape at the national level, detailed in a November note [UNEP/GC.25/INF/12/Add.1], and at the global and regional levels, set out in a December note by the Executive Director [UNEP/GC.25/INF/12]. In the 15 years since the 1992 United Nations Conference on Environment and Development (UNCED) [YUN 1992, p. 670], environmental reporting had become a well-established process at the national level. The national-level study found broad differences in environmental assessment and reporting approaches. Of the 196 countries and territories examined, 161 (82 per cent), were involved in state-of-the-environment reporting, producing at least one such report since 1992 or having a first report in process; 35 (18 per cent) demonstrated no evidence of such reporting; 50 (26 per cent) published reports at regular intervals; and 11 countries and territories (6 per cent) no longer prepared reports. Current integrated environmental assessments were broader and more policy-relevant than previous reports, and they sought to provide scenarios that explored the consequences of possible policy options.

As to the regional and global assessment landscape, the report stated that regional assessments were often conducted within global assessment processes, including regional chapters in GEO-4 and the reports of the Intergovernmental Panel on Climate Change. There was, however, considerable overlap concerning the issues covered in the assessments, most notably in the area of biodiversity. The main gaps in the regional and global assessment process occurred less in the coverage and more in the awareness of the importance of designing a salient, credible and legitimate process to ensure that the assessment was influential. Progress was made in linking environmental change and changes in ecosystem services to human well-being in GEO-4 and the Millennium Ecosystem Assessment, which was launched in 2001 [YUN 2001, p. 961] and completed in 2005 [YUN 2005, p. 1154]. The assessments of impacts and adaptations to climate change and GEO-4 also advanced the use of vulnerability assessment as a way to consider the impacts of multiple stresses, the differential exposure of individuals and societal groups and the importance of adaptive capacity. The science-policy interface in assessment processes varied widely, and it was often difficult to identify clearly the influence of particular assessments on policymaking. More attention to the design and documentation of assessment processes was needed to enhance their credibility, relevance and legitimacy. The goal of any assessment process was to influence policy and action, and much had been learned about the best ways to deliver the assessment results and most significant messages to target audiences. The overview study found a significant problem in gaining access to state of the environment information. While information technology provided easy access, few countries maintained a website storing a complete collection of their state of environment reports. In the case of printed reports, distribution was the limiting factor for reasons of cost, but electronic media were particularly fragile, as older information could be lost when websites were redesigned or abandoned. It was important for assessment processes to learn from the experience of others, which required the processes to be documented and stored in a central repository.

UNEP would work with countries in which environmental assessment was weak or non-existent to build their reporting capacity until it became self-sustaining. It would encourage regional cooperation in assessment and reporting and seek opportunities to join with multilateral environmental agreements and other partners to simplify reporting requirements and make them more coherent. UNEP and its partners would maintain web-based assessment databases with links to national assessment processes and review their content for significant regional and global trends. UNEP global environmental assessments had to provide an overview of the world environmental situation and an objective means to help policymakers set priorities. Future assessments should continue to be framed in the broader context of sustainable development. The report outlined guiding principles and best practices for future global assessments of environmental change. It also presented five options for the possible development of a future global assessment of environmental change, together with a cost and indicative benefit analysis for each. The options included updating global integrated environmental assessments to use information technology better (option 1); providing objective, expert outsourced assessments (option 2); providing a coherent set of integrated and thematic UNEP assessments (option 3); adopting an indicator-based approach (option 4); and undertaking targeted assessments on thematic priority areas supported by a 'UNEP-Live' enabling framework (option 5). The report stated that option 3 was the preferred option in the near term, and that the online and interactive characteristics of that option should be targeted as a model for the long term.

In November [UNEP/GC.25/4], the Executive Director submitted to the Governing Council a report on the state of the environment and the UNEP contribution to addressing substantive environmental challenges. The report summarized issues emanating from UNEP activities in the area of assessment, monitoring and early warning. It also summarized services that UNEP provided to Governments and other stakeholders to build capacity in scientific environmental assessment and information for decision-making through the implementation of the Bali Strategic Plan for Technology Support and Capacity-building, adopted by the Council in 2005 [YUN 2005, p. 1135], and the "Delivering as one" approach [YUN 2006, p. 1584] within UN development assistance frameworks. The report discussed the findings of global assessments conducted since the twenty-fourth (2007) Governing Council session [YUN 2007, p. 1045], including GEO-4 (see below); the Global Outlook for Ice and Snow; Global Glacier Changes: Facts and Figures; the International Assessment of Agricultural Knowledge, Science and Technology for Development; the report World Resources 2008: Roots of Resilience—Growing the Wealth of the Poor; the World's Protected Areas report; and the report of the United Nations Scientific Committee on the Effects of Atomic Radiation [A/63/46] (see p. 694).

A global strategy was initiated to follow up on the Millennium Ecosystem Assessment. The four components of the strategy were to: build the knowledge base; integrate the ecosystem service approach into decision-making at all levels; enhance outreach and dissemination of the Assessment; and explore the needs and options for future global ecosystem services assessments. Together with follow-up partners, UNEP was implementing the strategy through a three-year project on implementing the Assessment's findings and recommendations, focusing primarily on sub-global assessments; the first project meeting was held in April. UNEP also facilitated consultations with Governments and other stakeholders on the proposed intergovernmental science-policy platform on biodiversity and ecosystem services. At the first platform meeting (Putrajaya, Malaysia, 10–12 November), UNEP was requested to undertake a gap analysis and prepare a second meeting to explore and discuss mechanisms to improve the science-policy interface for biodiversity and ecosystem services.

A November note by the Executive Director [UNEP/GC.25/INF/11] contained a synthesis report of global environmental assessments, prepared by the Netherlands Environmental Assessment Agency at the request of UNEP. It reviewed key messages of recent global environmental assessments and examined their policy messages in terms of: trends in persistent environmental problems, including the costs and benefits of early action and costs of inaction; policy options with regard to interlinked, persistent environmental problems; and effective policy-making.

Environment Watch strategy

In response to a 2007 Governing Council decision [YUN 2007, p. 1048], the Executive Director, in a November note [UNEP/GC.25/INF/20], presented the updated Environment Watch strategy: Vision 2020, first outlined in 2006 [YUN 2006, p. 1211], as an integral component of the implementation of the UNEP medium-term strategy (see p. 1153). The revised strategy was designed to achieve enhanced institutional, scientific and technological infrastructures and capacities for cooperation in keeping the state of the environment under review and providing timely, accurate and consistent environmental data and information across the six priorities of the medium-term strategy. It was based on five components: capacity-building and technology support; assessment; early warning, monitoring and observation; environmental indicators, data support and information-sharing; and networking and partnerships. Time-bound targets for each component were outlined in the note. Implementation of the Environment Watch strategy required a collective commitment by Governments and partners. National implementation would be monitored through the annual UN development assistance framework review and evaluation processes, as well as the evaluation of UNEP subprogrammes. Monitoring and evaluation of the overall strategy would be conducted through GC/GMEF and UNEP internal programme and project monitoring procedures. Targets to be met within time frames from 2009 to 2020 were outlined in an annex to the note. The note set out the expected benefits and added value of the strategy. The strategy would be implemented by the Executive Director in close cooperation with Governments, UN partners and a consortium of international organizations and financial institutions. The total estimated cost of implementation within the 2010–2011 UNEP programme of work was $123.3 million. It was anticipated that UNEP would have to contribute 20 per cent of the estimated cost of delivery of any given service package.

Global Environment Outlook

By a December note [UNEP/GC.25/INF/13], the Executive Director transmitted a report setting out the findings of the review of the initial impact of the fourth *Global Environmental Outlook: Environment for Development* report (GEO-4), published in 2007 [YUN 2007, p. 1056]. The report, prepared by a team of independent evaluation specialists, assessed the extent to which GEO-4 and its summary for decision-makers had reached their intended target groups, and examined the use and influence of GEO-4 in the 10 months following its launch. The review team found that GEO continued to fill an important niche in the global assessment landscape by being relevant and useful, and by adding value to most of its primary environmental constituencies. It concluded that more could be done to increase the use and influence of GEO assessments among stakeholders. More attention could also be given to maximizing the potential of GEO to ensure that environmental problems and emerging issues of wide international significance received appropriate and timely consideration by key stakeholders, particularly with respect to human and ecosystem well-being and the role of the private sector in global sustainable development. The report outlined the review's findings related to the use, utility and value, salience, and targeting and reach of GEO-4, as well as lessons learned in the review and the findings of the GEO-4 self-assessment survey.

UNEP Year Book

UNEP published its fifth annual report on the changing environment, the UNEP *Year Book 2008* (formerly known as the GEO *Year Book*), which highlighted the increasing complexity and interconnections of climate change, ecosystem integrity, human well-being and economic development. The *Year Book*, produced in collaboration with world environmental experts, examined the emergence and influence of economic mechanisms and market-driven approaches for addressing environmental degradation. It described recent findings and policy decisions that affected the response to changes in the global environment.

Support to Africa

In response to a 2007 Governing Council decision [YUN 2007, p. 1048], the Executive Director in October submitted a report [UNEP/GC.25/7] on support to Africa in environmental management and protection. The report summarized UNEP activities in Africa related to climate change, minimizing threats from the environmental causes and consequences of conflict and disaster, ecosystem management, environmental governance, alleviating the environmental and health impacts of harmful substances and hazardous wastes, and sustainable consumption and production. Under the project on capacity development for the Clean Development Mechanism, UNEP worked towards building the skills and knowledge of countries and companies to design, submit and secure cleaner energy schemes. The project's second phase (2007–2009) included Algeria, Mauritius and the United Republic of Tanzania. UNEP supported and provided substantive inputs to the twelfth session of the African Ministerial Conference on the Environment (AMCEN) (Johannesburg, South Africa, 7–12 June), which adopted a decision on developing a common negotiating position on a comprehensive international climate change regime beyond 2012 and a comprehensive framework of African climate change programmes. UNEP launched activities on environmental legislation, post-conflict assessment and capacity-building for the conservation and management of environmental resources in the Democratic Republic of the Congo. The activities would provide environmental support to the UN country team and the United Nations Organization Mission in the Democratic Republic of the Congo. UNEP was working to promote an integrated approach to ecosystem management to reverse the decline in ecosystem services and improve ecosystem resilience to external impacts. In Kenya, UNEP initiated a project to reduce emissions from deforestation in developing countries. The project also aimed to alleviate poverty and maintain water supplies in rivers leading into the Masai Mara National Reserve in Kenya and the Serengeti National Park in Tanzania. An Africa-wide rainwater harvesting programme was developed and presented for peer review at the first African Water Week (Tunis, Tunisia, 26–28 March). UNEP initiated a $2.3 million project on improving water management and governance in African countries through support for developing and implementing integrated water resource management plans partially funded by the European Union; implementation began in 2008 and would continue for three years. The first interministerial conference on health and environment in Africa (Libreville, Gabon, 26–29 August), organized jointly by the World Health Organization (WHO) and UNEP, focused on health security through healthy environments. The *Atlas of Africa's Changing Environment* was launched during the twelfth AMCEN session; the *Atlas* complemented the *Africa Environment Outlook* report and provided a graphical presentation of environmental change in the 53 countries of Africa using satellite images of selected sites. UNEP was working to support the goals of the United Nations Decade of Education for Sustainable Development 2005–2014, proclaimed by the General Assembly in resolution 57/254 [YUN 2002, p. 826]; beginning in February, it was engaged in establishing the Kenya e-Learning Centre and its environmental component. The fifth African round table on sustainable consumption and production, organized as a pre-sessional event to the twelfth AMCEN session, reviewed progress made in the African Programme to facilitate Africa's participation in the Marrakech Process on sustainable consumption and production [YUN 2003, p. 840] and identified follow-up actions and future directions, which were endorsed by AMCEN. UNEP, the United Nations Human Settlements Programme (UN-Habitat) and the United Nations Economic Commission for Africa produced *The State of African Cities 2008*, a report examining trends in urban growth, productivity, governance and environmental sustainability.

The UNEP programme in Africa continued to face challenges in its delivery. The lack of funding from the UNEP Environment Fund posed a threat to achieving the expected results, and more importantly, to fulfilling the expectations of Governments and other key stakeholders. Another major challenge was fragmentation and lack of coherence in delivery—a programmatic approach was needed with sufficient resources for its implementation. Coordination and collaboration, including with multilateral environmental agreement secretariats, were critical in the delivery of the UNEP programme in the region. Integration of the work of the UNEP divisions and the regional offices had to be enhanced.

Water policy and strategy

In response to a 2007 Governing Council decision [YUN 2007, p. 1050], the Executive Director in October submitted a report [UNEP/GC.25/9 & Corr.1] on implementation in 2007 and 2008 of the UNEP water policy and strategy, adopted by the Council in 2007 [ibid.]. The report discussed progress in implementing the three components of the strategy: assessment, management and coordination. Under the assessment component, UNEP undertook water vulnerability assessments for Central Asia, North-East Asia, South Asia and South-East Asia to support decision-making, and supported Nepal in developing a comprehensive and integrated action plan for the Bagmati River. Through the Africa-Asia project on vulnerability assessment of freshwater resources to environmental change, UNEP examined integrated impacts of potential environmental changes on water resources. The Global Environment Monitoring System Water Programme network grew to more than 3,100 stations with more than 4 million data points. In follow-up to the Sudan post-conflict assessment [YUN 2007, p. 1052] on freshwater, UNEP was providing technical advice on sustainable groundwater extraction in camps for internally displaced persons, and supporting the re-establishment of the water governance framework at the state level with its integrated water resources management project. UNEP and the World Glacier Monitoring Service jointly launched the report *Global Glacier Changes: Facts and Figures* at the twenty-ninth session of the Intergovernmental Panel on Climate Change (Geneva, 1 September) (see p. 1164).

The management component of the water policy and strategy followed the three integrated water resources management pillars: strengthening the enabling environment; strengthening institutional functions; and improving access to management instruments. UNEP conducted a survey on integrated water resources management planning to support the international community in monitoring the development of the integrated water resources management plans. The results provided the basis of the *UN-Water Status Report on Integrated Water Resources Management and Water Efficiency Plans*, presented to the Commission on Sustainable Development at its sixteenth (2008) session (see p. 915). As a strategic partner of the African Union (AU) Commission and the African Ministers' Council on Water, UNEP provided technical support and policy advice in the preparatory process of the eleventh AU summit (Sharm el-Sheikh, Egypt, 24 June–1 July), which focused on accelerating progress toward the 2015 Millennium Development Goal (MDG) targets on water and sanitation. UNEP provided technical support to the African Ministers' Council on Water in the implementation of key regional initiatives, including the rural water supply and sanitation initiative; the programme on water and sanitation for African cities; the integrated water resources management initiative; and the networking of water basin organizations and transboundary water initiatives.

The UN mechanism for inter-agency coordination on water resources improved cooperation between UN agencies. During the 2007–2008 period, UNEP clarified its priorities, which were based on its 2010–2013 medium-term strategy (see p. 1153). As a result, the water policy and strategy would be implemented through the six cross-cutting thematic priority areas, which comprised the six subprogrammes in the 2010–2011 programme of work. Gender equality and equity would be integrated in all activities.

A December note by the Executive Director [UNEP/GC.25/INF/31] summarized major outputs and results from the implementation of the UNEP water policy and strategy.

Environment and sustainable development

The Commission on Sustainable Development, at its sixteenth session (New York, 5–16 May) [E/2008/29], considered, for its 2008–2009 implementation cycle, the thematic cluster issues of agriculture, rural development, land, drought, desertification and Africa (see p. 1166). The Commission had before it reports of the Secretary-General on the review of implementation of Agenda 21 [YUN 1992, p. 672] and the Johannesburg Plan of Implementation [YUN 2002,

p. 822] with regard to drought [E/CN.17/2008/6] and desertification [E/CN.17/2008/7]; the integrated review [E/CN.17/2008/9] of the thematic cluster of agriculture, rural development, land, drought, desertification and Africa in small island developing States (see below); and the review [E/CN.17/2008/11] of progress in implementing the 2005 Commission decision [YUN 2005, p. 1130] on water and sanitation (see p. 1139).

Small island developing States

In October [UNEP/GC.25/6], the Executive Director submitted a report reviewing progress made in implementing a 2007 Governing Council decision on small island developing States (SIDS) [YUN 2007, p. 1050]. UNEP undertook activities aimed mainly at supporting SIDS in the implementation of the Mauritius Strategy for the Further Implementation of the Programme of Action for the Sustainable Development of Small Island Developing States [YUN 2005, p. 946], following the tailored and regional approach called for in a 2005 Council decision [ibid., p. 1138]. UNEP was implementing a Global Environment Facility-funded project on coastal resilience to climate change for assessing vulnerability and adaptation of mangroves and associated ecosystems. It implemented projects on integrating the management of watersheds and coastal areas in Caribbean SIDS—supporting 13 such States—and on sustainable integrated water resource and wastewater management in the Pacific Island countries—supporting14 SIDS. Projects related to the recovery and recycling of ozone-depleting substances were under way in all regions, benefitting 9 Pacific, 14 Caribbean and 6 Atlantic and Indian Ocean SIDS. UNEP was supporting financially and technically the assessment of the economic, social and environmental impacts of trade-related policies in the agricultural sector, focusing on biodiversity impacts. It was implementing a regional project demonstrating and capturing best practices and technologies for the reduction of land-sourced impacts of coastal tourism. The report described UNEP activities according to the thematic areas outlined in the Mauritius Strategy, including activities related to climate change and sea-level rise; natural and environmental disasters; waste management; coastal and marine resources; freshwater, land, energy, tourism and biodiversity resources; science and technology; sustainable capacity development and education for sustainable development; sustainable production and consumption; national and regional enabling environments; knowledge management and information for decision-making; and South-South cooperation. The report also provided information on specific UNEP actions in Caribbean and Pacific SIDS. An October note by the Executive Director [UNEP/GC.25/INF/18] provided additional information on the activities covered in the report.

Reports of Secretary-General. In February, the Secretary-General issued a report [E/CN.17/2008/9] on the integrated review of the thematic cluster of agriculture, rural development, land, drought, desertification and Africa in SIDS, which described the continuing challenges faced by SIDS in their effort to advance implementation of the Mauritius Strategy.

In a report issued in August [A/63/296], the Secretary-General reviewed efforts of the UN system, the international community and SIDS to operationalize the Mauritius Strategy, and described initiatives to promote the integration of the Strategy in the sustainable development plans of SIDS.

(For further information on the sustainable development of SIDS, see p. 945).

South-South cooperation

In response to a 2007 Governing Council decision [YUN 2007, p. 1050], the Executive Director in October submitted a report [UNEP/GC.25/8] which summarized UNEP activities to promote South-South cooperation for sustainable development and outlined planned activities. The Bali Strategic Plan for Technology Support and Capacity-building, adopted by the Council in 2005 [YUN 2005, p. 1135] established South-South cooperation as a key mechanism for implementing the Plan. In response to the Council's 2007 decision, UNEP adopted a strategic approach that focused on conducting internal and external consultations to advance the integration of South-South cooperation into its work, and in developing partnerships and alliances in support of its capacity-building and technology support activities. A major component of the approach comprised promoting the application of a comprehensive set of strategic and operational guidelines, which served as the reference document for guiding the integration of South-South cooperation into existing and proposed activities. Other key components included further developing and refining the guidelines; holding consultations with UNEP divisions to promote the application of the guidelines and the integration of South-specific approaches in the capacity-building activities of the divisions; consulting with the United Nations Development Programme (UNDP) special unit for South-South cooperation, other UN agencies, multilateral environmental agreement secretariats, regional cooperation mechanisms and South-South cooperation initiatives to establish strategic partnerships and develop joint activities; coordinating the development of a clearing-house mechanism for South-South cooperation; and developing and implementing effective outreach. The report described key UNEP activities and achievements related to South-South cooperation, including technical training and capacity-building. The implementation of South-South cooperation faced challenges related to internal funding support; the lack of a systematic approach to UNEP capacity-building activities; matching expertise to expressed needs; and effective outreach and related promotional impacts.

An October note by the Executive Director [UNEP/GC.25/INF/19] detailed other South-South cooperation activities implemented by UNEP.

(For further information on South-South cooperation, see p. 988.)

Sustainable development of the Arctic region

On 22 February, the Governing Council adopted a decision on the sustainable development of the Arctic region [dec. SS.X/2]. Recalling its 2003 decision on the topic [YUN 2003, p. 1042], and expressing its concern over the impact of climate change on the polar regions, the Council urged the Governments of Arctic States and other stakeholders to continue to apply the precautionary approach as set forth in principle 15 of the Rio Declaration on Environment and Development [YUN 1992, p. 671], adopted at the 1992 United Nations Conference on Environment and Development [ibid., p. 670], in connection with their activities potentially affecting the Arctic environment, including its biodiversity; and to continue to conduct environmental impact assessments. It requested Governments, together with the International Council for Science and the World Meteorological Organization (WMO), the sponsoring agencies of the International Polar Year 2007–2008, and other bodies, including UNEP and the Arctic Council, to enhance the scientific basis for informed decision-making by promoting international scientific collaboration and coordination to better track, understand and predict Arctic change as a key International Polar Year legacy activity. It also requested the Governments of Arctic States and other stakeholders to implement measures to facilitate adaptation to climate change at all levels, including by indigenous and other communities. UNEP was encouraged to join with other organizations and programmes to seek means to sustain and enhance Arctic observing networks beyond the Year's research phase.

Coordination and cooperation

Environmental emergencies

In 2008, UNEP continued to assist vulnerable or crisis-affected countries and communities by providing environmental expertise for assessments, and integrating environmental concerns in emergency response, post-crisis reconstruction, recovery projects, and long-term sustainable development.

On 12 May, an 8.0 magnitude earthquake struck the Sichuan Province of China, affecting approximately 70 million people. As at December, the death toll had reached more than 100,000; more than 374,643 were injured and 17,923 were missing. As the primary international environmental actor on the ground, UNEP coordinated the environmental response to the earthquake. It provided rapid assessment and advisory support for the prevention and control of secondary disasters and assisted the Chinese Government in integrating environmental considerations into long-term recovery and reconstruction. UNEP strengthened its office in Beijing with technical experts in domestic, industrial and hazardous waste management, enabling UNEP to provide environmental expertise to the UN country team and Chinese authorities. At China's request, UNEP facilitated training workshops on post-disaster environmental management for Chinese civil servants, environmental experts, Government representatives and Beijing-based international organizations.

In Myanmar, UNEP supported the environmental recovery from the impact of Cyclone Nargis, which struck the country on 2 May. The cyclone affected an estimated 2.4 million people; official figures indicated that more than 77,000 people were killed and almost 56,000 were missing. From 16 to 21 May the Joint Environment Unit of UNEP and the Office for the Coordination of Humanitarian Affairs (OCHA) conducted an assessment of the immediate risks stemming from environmental damage, following which UNEP deployed an environmental expert to work on the UN disaster recovery programme as part of the country team. The Joint Unit and its partners responded to several other events, such as the environmental impact of Hurricane Ike, which affected the Turks and Caicos Islands in September; toxic pesticides carried aboard a capsized ferry in the Philippines in June; and landslides triggered by heavy rainfall in Honduras in September and October.

In cooperation with the United Nations International Strategy for Disaster Reduction, UNEP established the Partnership for Environment and Disaster Reduction to advance an integrated approach to climate change, disaster reduction and ecosystem services.

Oil slick in Lebanon

In August [A/63/225], the Secretary-General reported on progress in implementing General Assembly resolutions 61/194 [YUN 2006, p. 1215] and 62/188 [YUN 2007, p. 1053] related to the oil slick on Lebanese shores that resulted from the 2006 destruction by

Israel of oil storage tanks in Lebanon following the outbreak of hostilities between Israel and the paramilitary group Hizbullah [YUN 2006, p. 574]. The release of 15,000 tons of fuel oil into the Mediterranean Sea led to the contamination of 150 kilometre of coastline in Lebanon and the Syrian Arab Republic. The report reiterated and updated the overall assessment, presented in the Secretary-General's 2006 report on the issue [ibid., p. 1052], of the impact of the oil spill on human health, biodiversity, fisheries and tourism, and the implications for livelihoods and the economy of Lebanon. It also reviewed progress made in cleaning up and rehabilitating Lebanon's polluted shores and sea.

The Secretary-General noted that Israel had yet to assume responsibility for providing compensation to the Government of Lebanon and other countries for the costs of repairing the environmental damage caused by the destruction of the oil storage tanks, including the restoration of the marine environment, as called for in resolutions 61/194 and 62/188. A response in that regard was formally sought by the UNEP Post-Conflict and Disaster Management Branch in a letter of 16 August 2007 to the Permanent Mission of Israel to the United Nations Office at Geneva, and in a further letter of 5 June 2008 from the UNEP Executive Director to the Permanent Representative of Israel to UNEP. No response to either communication had been received.

By June 2008, approximately 500 cubic meters of liquid and 3,120 cubic meters of semi-solid and solid waste had been collected during a two-phase clean-up operation implemented by the Lebanese Ministry of the Environment in partnership with several Member States and organizations. As at June 2008, total financial assistance received by Lebanon in support of its clean-up efforts amounted to about 10 per cent of the average upper limit range of between $137 million and $205 million, as recommended by the Experts Working Group for Lebanon, and about 24 per cent of the minimum value of $77.8 million. No progress was made towards creating an eastern Mediterranean oil spill restoration fund, as called for in resolution 62/188.

The Secretary-General urged Member States, international organizations, international and regional financial institutions, non-governmental organizations (NGOs) and the private sector to continue their support for Lebanon in addressing the impact of the oil spill, in particular for rehabilitation activities on the Lebanese coast, as well as in the broader recovery effort. The international effort should be intensified, as Lebanon was still engaged in oil removal, waste treatment and recovery monitoring. The spill was not covered by any of the international oil-spill compensation funds and thus merited special consideration. In that context, the Secretary-General recommended establishing the eastern Mediterranean oil spill restoration fund.

GENERAL ASSEMBLY ACTION

On 19 December [meeting 72], the General Assembly, on the recommendation of the Second Committee [A/63/414 & Corr.1], adopted **resolution 63/211** by recorded vote (165-7-2) [agenda item 49].

Oil slick on Lebanese shores

The General Assembly,

Recalling its resolutions 61/194 of 20 December 2006 and 62/188 of 19 December 2007 on the oil slick on Lebanese shores,

Reaffirming the outcome of the United Nations Conference on the Human Environment, especially principle 7 of the Declaration of the Conference, in which States were requested to take all possible steps to prevent pollution of the seas,

Emphasizing the need to protect and preserve the marine environment in accordance with international law,

Taking into account the 1992 Rio Declaration on Environment and Development, especially principle 16, in which it was stipulated that the polluter should, in principle, bear the cost of pollution, and taking into account also chapter 17 of Agenda 21,

Noting again with great concern the environmental disaster caused by the destruction by the Israeli Air Force on 15 July 2006 of the oil storage tanks in the direct vicinity of El-Jiyeh electric power plant in Lebanon, resulting in an oil slick that covered the entirety of the Lebanese coastline and extended to the Syrian coastline,

Noting again with appreciation the assistance offered by donor countries and international organizations for the early recovery and reconstruction of Lebanon through bilateral and multilateral channels, including the Athens Coordination Meeting on the response to the marine pollution incident in the Eastern Mediterranean, held on 17 August 2006, as well as the Stockholm Conference for Lebanon's Early Recovery, held on 31 August 2006,

1. *Takes note* of the report of the Secretary-General on the implementation of General Assembly resolution 62/188 on the oil slick on Lebanese shores;

2. *Reiterates the expression of its deep concern* about the adverse implications of the destruction by the Israeli Air Force of the oil storage tanks in the direct vicinity of the Lebanese El-Jiyeh electric power plant for the achievement of sustainable development in Lebanon;

3. *Considers* that the oil slick has heavily polluted the shores of Lebanon and partially polluted Syrian shores and consequently has had serious implications for livelihoods and the economy of Lebanon, owing to the adverse implications for natural resources, biodiversity, fisheries and tourism, and for human health, in the country;

4. *Requests* the Government of Israel to assume responsibility for prompt and adequate compensation to the Government of Lebanon and other countries directly affected by the oil slick, such as the Syrian Arab Republic whose shores have been partially polluted, for the costs

of repairing the environmental damage caused by the destruction, including the restoration of the marine environment;

5. *Expresses its appreciation* for the efforts of the Government of Lebanon and those of the Member States, regional and international organizations, regional and international financial institutions, non-governmental organizations and the private sector in the initiation of clean-up and rehabilitation operations on the polluted shores, and encourages the Member States and above-mentioned entities to continue their financial and technical support to the Government of Lebanon towards achieving the completion of clean-up and rehabilitation operations, with the aim of preserving the ecosystem of Lebanon and that of the Eastern Mediterranean Basin;

6. *Decides* to establish an Eastern Mediterranean Oil Spill Restoration Trust Fund, based on voluntary contributions, to provide assistance and support to the States directly adversely affected in their integrated environmentally sound management, from clean-up to safe disposal of oily waste, of this environmental disaster resulting from the destruction of the oil storage tanks at El-Jiyeh electric power plant, and requests the Secretary-General to implement this decision before the end of the sixty-third session of the General Assembly;

7. *Invites* States, intergovernmental organizations, non-governmental organizations and the private sector to make voluntary financial contributions to the Trust Fund, and, in this regard, requests the Secretary-General to mobilize international technical and financial assistance in order to ensure that the Trust Fund has sufficient and adequate resources;

8. *Recognizes* the multidimensionality of the adverse impact of the oil slick, and requests the Secretary-General to submit to the General Assembly at its sixty-fourth session a report on the implementation of the present resolution under the item entitled "Sustainable development".

RECORDED VOTE ON RESOLUTION 63/211:

In favour: Afghanistan, Albania, Algeria, Andorra, Angola, Antigua and Barbuda, Argentina, Armenia, Austria, Azerbaijan, Bahamas, Bahrain, Bangladesh, Barbados, Belarus, Belgium, Belize, Benin, Bhutan, Bolivia, Bosnia and Herzegovina, Brazil, Brunei Darussalam, Bulgaria, Burkina Faso, Burundi, Cambodia, Cape Verde, Chad, Chile, China, Comoros, Congo, Costa Rica, Côte d'Ivoire, Croatia, Cuba, Cyprus, Czech Republic, Democratic People's Republic of Korea, Denmark, Djibouti, Dominica, Dominican Republic, Ecuador, Egypt, El Salvador, Eritrea, Estonia, Ethiopia, Fiji, Finland, France, Georgia, Germany, Ghana, Greece, Grenada, Guatemala, Guinea, Guyana, Haiti, Honduras, Hungary, Iceland, India, Indonesia, Iran, Iraq, Ireland, Italy, Jamaica, Japan, Jordan, Kazakhstan, Kenya, Kuwait, Kyrgyzstan, Lao People's Democratic Republic, Latvia, Lebanon, Liberia, Libyan Arab Jamahiriya, Liechtenstein, Lithuania, Luxembourg, Madagascar, Malawi, Malaysia, Maldives, Mali, Malta, Mauritania, Mauritius, Mexico, Moldova, Monaco, Mongolia, Montenegro, Morocco, Mozambique, Myanmar, Namibia, Nepal, Netherlands, New Zealand, Nicaragua, Niger, Nigeria, Norway, Oman, Pakistan, Panama, Papua New Guinea, Paraguay, Peru, Poland, Portugal, Qatar, Republic of Korea, Romania, Russian Federation, Rwanda, Saint Lucia, Saint Vincent and the Grenadines, Samoa, San Marino, Sao Tome and Principe, Saudi Arabia, Senegal, Serbia, Singapore, Slovakia, Slovenia, Solomon Islands, South Africa, Spain, Sri Lanka, Sudan, Swaziland, Sweden, Switzerland, Syrian Arab Republic, Timor-Leste, Togo, Trinidad and Tobago, Tunisia, Turkey, Tuvalu, Uganda, Ukraine, United Arab Emirates, United Kingdom, United Republic of Tanzania, Uruguay, Uzbekistan, Vanuatu, Venezuela, Viet Nam, Yemen, Zambia, Zimbabwe.

Against: Australia, Canada, Israel, Marshall Islands, Nauru, Palau, United States.

Abstaining: Cameroon, Colombia.

Memorandums of understanding

A December note by the Executive Director [UNEP/GC.25/INF/8] summarized the two memorandums of understanding (MOUs) concluded between UNEP and other UN bodies since his last report on the subject [YUN 2006, p. 1216]. In June, UNEP signed a corporate MOU with the United Nations Office for Project Services (UNOPS) that covered projects implemented from 1 July; it would remain in effect until 31 December 2011. In December, UNEP concluded an MOU with UNDP under which the two Programmes would cooperate in areas of common interest, including climate change, the Poverty and Environment Initiative and other environmental endeavours.

Participation of civil society

The ninth Global Civil Society Forum (Monaco, 19 February) [UNEP/GCSF/9/1] discussed civil society engagement during the tenth (2008) GC/GMEF special session; guidelines for improving the Forum cycle; globalization and the environment: mobilizing finance to meet the climate challenge; and the UNEP Medium-term Strategy 2010–2013 (see p. 1153). A dialogue was held between Forum participants and the UNEP Executive Director.

A note by the Executive Director [UNEP/GCSS.X/INF/5] contained regional civil society statements to the tenth (2008) special session of the Governing Council.

In response to a 2003 Governing Council decision [YUN 2003, p. 1046], the Executive Director in October submitted a report [UNEP/GC.25/10] presenting the final review of the first UNEP long-term Tunza strategy (2003–2008) for the engagement of and involvement of young people in environmental issues [YUN 2002, p. 1040] as well as the proposed second long-term strategy (2009–2014). Under the first Tunza strategy, UNEP established regional and subregional environmental networks and organized 13 conferences and workshops annually for young people. Through the networks, UNEP was able to reach out with environmental information to over 30,000 young people's organizations. UNEP organized six Tunza international conferences between 2003 and

2008 and published 23 issues of *Tunza* magazine. The 2008 Tunza International Children's Conference was held in Stavanger, Norway, from 17 to 21 June. UNEP also facilitated and supported the participation of young leaders in GC/GMEF and the Global Civil Society Forum, meetings of conferences of the parties to environmental conventions and other international environmental discussions. The lack of adequate financial and human resources greatly limited UNEP work with young people. Nevertheless, the Tunza programme was able to achieve most of its planned activities for the first strategy through private sector funding. UNEP received substantial funding for the Tunza programme from the Bayer company, which provided €1 million annually from 2004 to 2007 and €1.2 million in 2008 to support children and youth in environmental activities. The main challenge for UNEP in its work with young people was the lack of access to environmental information at the national level. An October note by the Executive Director [UNEP/GC.25/INF/17] reviewed the implementation of the first Tunza strategy.

The proposed 2009–2014 strategy was developed in line with the recommendations from the midterm independent evaluation of the first strategy, released in 2006 [YUN 2006, p. 1216], and received inputs from children and young people's focal points in UNEP divisions and regional offices, partner organizations, the Tunza Youth Advisory Council and Junior Board, participants in the 2008 Tunza International Conference and others. Under the overall Tunza concept, the second strategy was designed to increase the participation of young people in environmental issues. It sought to promote a global movement through which children and young people would engage in environmental activities and influence politicians, leaders and society to make environmental changes. The second strategy also sought to enhance, inspire and enable the involvement of children and young people in sustainable development, particularly in the six thematic priorities identified in the UNEP medium-term strategy for the 2010–2013 period.

Cooperation with UN-Habitat

The Governing Council considered a note by the Executive Director [UNEP/GC.25/INF/10], which contained the joint report of the Executive Directors of UNEP and UN-Habitat on progress made in the 2007–2008 period to strengthen cooperation between the Programmes. Cooperation between UNEP and UN-Habitat was expanded and institutionalized. The Partnership Framework 2008–2013 was adopted by the senior management of both Programmes. A joint implementation plan for 2008–2009 focused on: cities and climate change, with a special focus on Africa; the Global Alliance for Ecomobility, a partnership aimed at reducing people's dependency on private automobiles; integrated waste management; city biodiversity and ecosystems; and joint outreach activities. The overall goal of cooperation between UNEP and UN-Habitat was to integrate the environmental perspective into local, national and global urban policymaking; incorporate urban perspectives into environmental policymaking; and highlight the local-global linkages of environmental issues.

General Assembly issues

The Executive Director in February provided information on issues arising from resolutions adopted by the General Assembly in 2007 that called for action by, or were of relevance to, UNEP [UNEP/GCSS.X/INF/3].

Administrative and budgetary matters

Budget execution

A February note by the Executive Director [UNEP/GCSS.X/INF/4] contained information on the execution of the UNEP 2006–2007 biennial budget. Total provisional resources for the biennium, including the UN regular budget, the Environment Fund, trust funds, earmarked contributions and trust fund support, amounted to $414.4 million, including a balance as at 1 January 2006 of $90.5 million. Total claims on resources were estimated at $303 million. The estimated total year-end balance of funds as at 31 December 2007 was projected to be $111.4 million.

Board of Auditors report

A note by the Executive Director [UNEP/GC/25/INF/6] contained the report of the Board of Auditors, which included the financial report and audited financial statements of UNEP for the biennium ended 31 December 2007 [A/63/5/Add.6]. UNEP financial statements covered the major funds, including the Environment Fund, general trust funds, the Multilateral Fund for the Implementation of the Montreal Protocol on Substances that Deplete the Ozone Layer, technical cooperation trust funds and other trust funds. The Environment Fund reported a total income of $122 million in 2006–2007, $6 million for the Fund's programme reserve activities and $16 million for its biennial support budget. The total approved programme budget for the biennium was $144 million. Resources were shifted from contractual services to cover increased staffing costs in order to meet the commitments of the Environment Fund within the projected funding. On 31 December 2007, contributions represented $2.3 million for the Environment Fund and $18.5 million for all general trust funds.

At the end of the biennium, there was a net excess of income over expenditure before adjustments of $36.8 million as compared to $8.3 million in 2004–2005. Contributions to technical cooperation trust funds, earmarked contributions and Professional Officer trust funds were accounted for when received in cash. Overall, total reserves and fund balances decreased by $4 million (1.7 per cent) to $237.4 million. That was mainly due to non-budgeted expenditure in respect of the accrual of end-of-service benefits. The Multilateral Fund reported a net deficit of $37.7 million, while in 2004–2005, the deficit amounted to $44.6 million. Nevertheless, the Fund's financial statements showed a positive total reserves and fund balances of $480.5 million as at 31 December 2007.

The Board made recommendations relating to travel costs; the level of UNEP liquidity and the progress of its projects; liabilities for end-of-service and post-retirement benefits, particularly health insurance; disclosure of financial statements received from the regular budget and the related expenditure and regarding advances paid to implementing partners; the establishment of a working group for both the International Public Sector Accounting Standards and the enterprise resource planning system; the review of its service agreement with the United Nations Office at Nairobi (UNON); improvement of its internal control procedures; payment of long-outstanding contributions to multilateral environment agreements; justification of the amount of non-expendable property disclosed in the financial statements; and options for reducing the manual processing of financial statements to a minimum.

Medium-term Strategy (2010–2013)

In response to a 2007 Governing Council decision [YUN 2007, p. 1057], the Executive Director developed the proposed UNEP Medium-term Strategy for 2010–2013, which was outlined in a note by the Executive Director [UNEP/GCSS.X/8]. The Strategy set out the vision and strategic direction for UNEP activities for the 2010–2013 period, including results to be delivered through the UNEP biennial programmes of work for 2010–2011 and 2012–2013; the UNEP GEF portfolio for 2010–2014; and UNEP earmarked contributions. For the 2010–2013 period, UNEP would focus on exercising environmental leadership on six cross-cutting thematic priorities: climate change; disasters and conflicts; ecosystem management; environmental governance; harmful substances and hazardous waste; and resource efficiency, sustainable consumption and production. Each priority included an objective and expected accomplishments. In line with the priorities, UNEP objectives under the Medium-term Strategy were to: strengthen the ability of countries to integrate climate change responses into national development processes; minimize environmental threats to human well-being from the environmental causes and consequences of conflicts and disasters; ensure that countries utilized the ecosystem approach to enhance human well-being; ensure that environmental governance at the country, regional and global levels was strengthened to address agreed environmental priorities; minimize the impact of harmful substances and hazardous waste on the environment and human beings; and ensure that natural resources were produced, processed and consumed in a more environmentally sustainable way. The vision for the medium-term was for UNEP to set the global environmental agenda; promote the coherent implementation of the environmental dimension of sustainable development within the UN system; and serve as an authoritative advocate for the global environment. The Strategy was developed by UNEP in consultation with the Committee of Permanent Representatives, the secretariats of UNEP-administered multilateral environmental agreements, and representatives of civil society and the private sector. Its priorities emerged from a review of scientific evidence; the comparative advantage and mandate of UNEP; priorities emerging from global and regional forums; and an assessment of areas in which UNEP could make a transformative difference. UNEP would monitor progress against the objectives and expected accomplishments contained in the Strategy and programmes of work, and would report to the Committee of Permanent Representatives every six months.

On 22 February [dec. SS.X/3], the Governing Council authorized the Executive Director to use the Medium-term Strategy 2010–2013 in formulating the strategic frameworks and programmes of work and budgets for 2010–2011 and for 2012–2013, and as a means to encourage coordination among UNEP divisions. It noted that any budgetary issues arising from the Medium-term Strategy would be addressed through the programmes of work and budgets for 2010–2011 and 2012–2013 that would be approved by the Council. The Executive Director was encouraged to strengthen results-based management in UNEP and, working within the approved programme of work for 2008–2009, use that period to begin the transition to a fully results-based organization. The Council requested the Executive Director to inform Governments about the implementation of the Medium-term Strategy 2010–2013 at regular intervals and to submit to the Council in 2011 a progress report on implementation.

The Strategy's six thematic cross-cutting priorities constituted the six proposed subprogrammes of the proposed UN strategic framework for the period 2010–2011 for programme 11, Environment, which was submitted to the General Assembly in March [A/63/6(Prog.11)]. The forty-eighth session of the Committee for Programme and Coordination (CPC) (New York, 9 June–3 July) [A/63/16] (see p. 1527) recommended that the General Assembly approve the narrative of programme 11. The Assembly, in **resolution 63/247** of 24 December (see p. 1563), endorsed the Committee's recommendations.

Global Environment Facility

The Global Environment Facility (GEF) was established in 1991 as a joint programme of UNDP, UNEP and the World Bank [YUN 1991, p. 505] to help solve global and environmental problems. In 2008, GEF united 178 member Governments—in partnership with international institutions, NGOs and the private sector—to address global environmental issues. An independent financial organization, GEF provided grants to developing countries and countries with economies in transition for projects related to biodiversity, climate change, international waters, land degradation, the ozone layer and persistent organic pollutants (POPs). The GEF partnership included 10 agencies: UNDP, UNEP, the World Bank, the Food and Agriculture Organization of the United Nations (FAO), the United Nations Industrial Development Organization, the African Development Bank, the Asian Development Bank, the European Bank for Reconstruction and Development, the Inter-American Development Bank and the International Fund for Agricultural Development. GEF functioned as the financial mechanism for the 1992 Convention on Biological Diversity [YUN 1992, p. 683] (see p. 1158), the 1992 United Nations Framework Convention on Climate Change [ibid., p. 681] (see p. 1155), the 1994 United Nations Convention to Combat Desertification in Those Countries Experiencing Serious Drought and/or Desertification, Particularly in Africa [YUN 1994, p. 944] (see p. 1161) and the 2001 Stockholm Convention on Persistent Organic Pollutants [YUN 2001, p. 971] (see p. 1173).

From 1 July 2007 to 20 June 2008, GEF financed 185 projects worth $4.05 billion, investing $634 million in GEF resources and mobilizing $3.4 billion in co-financing. Biodiversity accounted for 59 projects, climate change for 33, POPs for 23, international waters for 22, land degradation for 10, and ozone depletion for 1, in addition to 37 multi-focal area projects.

During the reporting period, the GEF Council approved 33 new projects in the climate change focal area; total GEF allocation was approximately $154 million, supplemented by an additional $1.2 billion generated in co-financing from partners, including the GEF agencies, bilateral agencies, recipient countries, NGOs and the private sector. The Council approved 59 new projects in the area of biological diversity and biosafety, with grants totalling approximately $154 million, supplemented by an additional $734 million generated in co-financing from partners. Twenty-three new projects were approved in the POPs focal area; total GEF allocation was approximately $86.7 million, supplemented by an additional $191.8 million in co-financing. A medium-sized project in the ozone depletion focal area was approved, with an allocation of $740,000, supplemented by an additional $500,000 in co-financing. The Council approved 10 new projects in the land degradation focal area, with an allocation of approximately $15.8 million, supplemented by an additional $53.1 million in co-financing. Thirty new projects were approved in the area of sustainable forest management, with allocations of $135 million, supplemented by an additional $659 million in co-financing. In the area of sustainable land management, 19 new projects were approved, with an allocation of $55 million and an expected additional $514 million generated in co-financing. The Council approved 22 new projects in the international waters focal area, with an allocation of $93.5 million, supplemented by an additional $594.8 million in co-financing. Six multi-focal area projects with strong international waters components were also approved.

The UNDP-administered Small Grants Programme during that period provided grants of up to $50,000 to finance 1,191 projects executed by community-based organizations, indigenous people's organizations, NGOs and others. Total new GEF allocation was approximately $35.36 million, supplemented by cash and in-kind co-financing.

International conventions and mechanisms

In response to General Assembly resolutions 62/86 [YUN 2007, p. 1060], 62/193 [ibid., p. 1065] and 62/194 [ibid., p. 1063], the Secretary-General, by an August note [A/63/294], transmitted reports submitted by the secretariats of the United Nations Framework Convention on Climate Change (see p. 1155), the United Nations Convention to Combat Desertification in Those Countries Experiencing Serious Drought and/or Desertification, Particularly in Africa (see p. 1161) and the Convention on Biological Diversity (see p. 1158), respectively.

A November report by the UNEP Executive Director [UNEP/GC.25/3] discussed issues concerning multilateral environmental agreements. The UNEP multilateral environmental agreements management team met in April to enhance effective administration and communication and ensure greater cohesion in tackling substantive issues of common interest among UNEP and UNEP-administered multilateral environmental agreements. The Ad Hoc Joint Working Group on Enhancing Cooperation and Coordination

Among the 1989 Basel Convention on the Control of Transboundary Movements of Hazardous Wastes and their Disposal [YUN 1989, p. 420], the 1998 Rotterdam Convention on the Prior Informed Consent Procedure for Certain Hazardous Chemicals and Pesticides in International Trade [YUN 1998, p. 997] and the 2001 Stockholm Convention on Persistent Organic Pollutants [YUN 2001, p. 971] met three times since March 2007 and concluded its work at its third meeting (Rome, 25–28 March) [UNEP/FAO/CHW/RC/POPS/JWG.3/3]. It adopted a set of recommendations that identified the general direction and practical course of action for the three Conferences of the Parties to improve cooperation and coordination, enhance implementation of the Conventions and improve effectiveness and efficiency in administering the Conventions through joint arrangements and services. It was also recommended that simultaneous extraordinary meetings of the Conferences of the Parties to the Conventions should be held in conjunction with the eleventh (2010) special session of the Governing Council/Global Ministerial Environment Forum. The ninth meeting of the Conference of the Parties to the Basel Convention (see p. 1173) and the fourth meeting of the Conference of the Parties to the Rotterdam Convention (see p. 1170) adopted the recommendations of the Ad Hoc Joint Working Group.

A December note by the UNEP secretariat [UNEP/GC.25/INF/16] contained a preliminary compilation of internationally agreed environmental goals and objectives that were drawn from the outcome documents of relevant UN summits and conferences, General Assembly resolutions, decisions of other global intergovernmental conferences, multilateral environmental agreements and decisions of their governing bodies.

A December note by the Executive Director [UNEP/GC.25/INF/16/Add.1] on efforts to meet internationally agreed environmental goals and objectives presented highlights of a preliminary study of demands and outputs of selected multilateral environmental agreements from 1992 to 2007. The note provided information on ratification of agreements, institutional arrangements, the number of meetings held, decisions taken by governing bodies, and budgets for the agreements.

Climate change convention

As at 31 December, 191 States and the European Union (EU) were parties to the United Nations Framework Convention on Climate Change (UNFCCC), which was opened for signature in 1992 [YUN 1992, p. 681] and entered into force in 1994 [YUN 1994, p. 938].

At year's end, 183 States and the EU were parties to the Kyoto Protocol to the Convention [YUN 1997, p. 1048], which entered into force in 2005 [YUN 2005, p. 1146]. There were 11 Parties to the 2006 amendment to annex B of the Protocol [YUN 2006, p. 1220], which had not yet entered into force.

The fourteenth session of the Conference of the Parties to UNFCCC (Poznań, Poland, 1–12 December) [FCCC/CP/2008/7 & Add.1] decided to continue the pilot phase for activities implemented jointly by developed country parties and other parties included in annex I of the Convention to reduce greenhouse gases or enhance their removal. It also adopted decisions on advancing the Bali Action Plan, launched in 2007 [YUN 2007, p. 1060] to enable implementation of the Convention through long-term, cooperative action up to and beyond 2012; the development and transfer of environmentally sound technologies; the fourth review of the Convention's financial mechanism; additional guidance to GEF; further guidance for the operation of the Least Developed Countries Fund; capacity-building for developing countries under the Convention; and administrative and financial matters.

The fourth session of the Conference of the Parties serving as the meeting of the parties to the Kyoto Protocol, held concurrently with the fourteenth UNFCCC Conference session [FCCC/KP/CMP/2008/11 & Add.1], adopted decisions related to the Adaptation Fund; further guidance relating to the clean development mechanism; advancing the work of the Ad Hoc Working Group on Further Commitments for annex I parties under the Protocol; the work of the Compliance Committee; guidance on implementation of article 6 of the Protocol; capacity-building for developing countries; privileges and immunities for individuals serving on constituted bodies established under the Protocol; and administrative and financial matters.

In November, the Executive Board of the Protocol's clean development mechanism issued its annual report [FCCC/KP/CMP/2008/4], covering its work from 20 October 2007 to 24 October 2008.

In 2008, the Subsidiary Body for Scientific and Technological Advice (SBSTA) [FCCC/SBSTA/2008/6] and the Subsidiary Body for Implementation (SBI) [FCCC/SBI/2008/8 & Add.1] held their twenty-eighth sessions (Bonn, Germany, 4–13 June). SBSTA [FCCC/SBSTA/2008/13] and SBI [FCCC/SBI/2008/19] also held their twenty-ninth sessions (Poznań, 1–10 December).

GENERAL ASSEMBLY ACTION

On 26 November [meeting 60], the General Assembly, on the recommendation of the Second Committee [A/63/414/Add.4], adopted **resolution 63/32** without vote [agenda item 49 *(d)*].

Protection of global climate for present and future generations

The General Assembly,

Recalling its resolutions 43/53 of 6 December 1988, 54/222 of 22 December 1999, 61/201 of 20 December 2006 and 62/86 of 10 December 2007 and other resolutions and decisions relating to the protection of the global climate for present and future generations of mankind,

Recalling also the provisions of the United Nations Framework Convention on Climate Change, including the acknowledgement that the global nature of climate change calls for the widest possible cooperation by all countries and their participation in an effective and appropriate international response, in accordance with their common but differentiated responsibilities and respective capabilities and their social and economic conditions,

Recalling further the United Nations Millennium Declaration, in which Heads of State and Government resolved to make every effort to ensure the entry into force of the Kyoto Protocol and to embark on the required reduction in emissions of greenhouse gases,

Recalling the Johannesburg Declaration on Sustainable Development, the Plan of Implementation of the World Summit on Sustainable Development ("Johannesburg Plan of Implementation"), the outcome of the thirteenth session of the Conference of the Parties to the Convention and the third session of the Conference of the Parties serving as the Meeting of the Parties to the Kyoto Protocol, held in Bali, Indonesia, from 3 to 15 December 2007, and the outcomes of all previous sessions,

Reaffirming the Programme of Action for the Sustainable Development of Small Island Developing States, the Mauritius Declaration and the Mauritius Strategy for the Further Implementation of the Programme of Action for the Sustainable Development of Small Island Developing States,

Recalling the 2005 World Summit Outcome,

Remaining deeply concerned that all countries, in particular developing countries, including the least developed countries and small island developing States, face increased risks from the negative effects of climate change, and stressing the need to address adaptation needs relating to such effects,

Noting that, to date, there are one hundred and ninety-two parties to the Convention, including one hundred and ninety-one States and one regional economic integration organization,

Noting also that, currently, the Kyoto Protocol to the United Nations Framework Convention on Climate Change has attracted one hundred and eighty-three ratifications, accessions, acceptances or approvals, including by thirty-nine parties included in annex I to the Convention,

Noting further the amendment to annex B to the Kyoto Protocol,

Noting the work of the Intergovernmental Panel on Climate Change and the need to build and enhance scientific and technological capabilities, inter alia, through continuing support to the Panel for the exchange of scientific data and information, especially in developing countries,

Noting also the significance of the scientific findings of the fourth assessment report of the Intergovernmental Panel on Climate Change, providing an integrated scientific, technical and socio-economic perspective on relevant issues and contributing positively to the discussions under the Convention and the understanding of the phenomenon of climate change, including its impacts and risks,

Reaffirming that economic and social development and poverty eradication are global priorities,

Recognizing that deep cuts in global emissions will be required to achieve the ultimate objective of the Convention,

Reaffirming its commitment to the ultimate objective of the Convention, namely, to stabilize greenhouse gas concentrations in the atmosphere at a level that prevents dangerous anthropogenic interference with the climate system,

Noting with appreciation the efforts of the Secretary-General in raising awareness of the need to respond to the global challenge of climate change,

Taking note of the Beijing High-level Conference on Climate Change: Technology Development and Technology Transfer, held in Beijing on 7 and 8 November 2008, and the third World Climate Conference on the theme "Climate prediction and information for decision-making", to be held in Geneva from 31 August to 4 September 2009,

Acknowledging women as key actors in the efforts towards sustainable development, and recognizing that a gender perspective can contribute to efforts to address climate change,

Taking note of the note by the Secretary-General transmitting the report of the Executive Secretary of the United Nations Framework Convention on Climate Change,

1. *Stresses* the seriousness of climate change, and calls upon States to work cooperatively towards achieving the ultimate objective of the United Nations Framework Convention on Climate Change through the urgent implementation of its provisions;

2. *Urges* parties to the Convention, and invites parties to the Kyoto Protocol to the United Nations Framework Convention on Climate Change, to continue to make use of the information contained in the fourth assessment report of the Intergovernmental Panel on Climate Change in their work;

3. *Notes* that States that have ratified the Kyoto Protocol welcome the entry into force of the Protocol on 16 February 2005 and strongly urge States that have not yet done so to ratify it in a timely manner;

4. *Takes note* of the outcome of the thirteenth session of the Conference of the Parties to the Convention and the third session of the Conference of the Parties serving as the Meeting of the Parties to the Kyoto Protocol, hosted by the Government of Indonesia from 3 to 15 December 2007;

5. *Welcomes* the decisions adopted during the thirteenth session of the Conference of the Parties to the Convention, including the Bali Action Plan, by which the Conference of the Parties decided to launch a comprehensive process aimed at enabling the full, effective and sustained implementation of the Convention through long-term cooperative action, now, up to and beyond 2012, in order to reach an agreed outcome and adopt a decision at the fifteenth session of the Conference of the Parties, and takes note of the work under way in the open-ended ad hoc working group of parties to the Kyoto Protocol established under decision 1/CMP.1;

6. *Notes* that States that have ratified the Kyoto Protocol welcome the launch of the Adaptation Fund during the third session of the Conference of the Parties serving as the Meeting of the Parties to the Kyoto Protocol, and notes also that developing-country parties to the Kyoto Protocol that are particularly vulnerable to the adverse effects of climate change are eligible for funding from the Adaptation Fund to assist them in meeting the costs of adaptation and look forward to its early operationalization;

7. *Takes note with appreciation* of the offer of the Government of Poland to host the fourteenth session of the Conference of the Parties and the fourth session of the Meeting of the Parties to the Kyoto Protocol, to be held in Poznań, from 1 to 12 December 2008, and looks forward to a successful outcome, including advancement towards an agreed outcome in 2009;

8. *Also takes note with appreciation*, in this regard, of the offer of the Government of Denmark to host the fifteenth session of the Conference of the Parties and the fifth session of the Meeting of the Parties to the Kyoto Protocol, to be held in Copenhagen from 30 November to 11 December 2009;

9. *Recognizes* that climate change poses serious risks and challenges to all countries, particularly to developing countries, especially the least developed countries, landlocked developing countries, small island developing States and countries in Africa, including those that are particularly vulnerable to the adverse effects of climate change, and calls upon States to take urgent global action to address climate change in accordance with the principles identified in the Convention, including the principle of common but differentiated responsibilities and respective capabilities, and, in this regard, urges all countries to fully implement their commitments under the Convention, to take effective and concrete actions and measures at all levels, and to enhance international cooperation in the framework of the Convention;

10. *Reaffirms* that efforts to address climate change in a manner that enhances the sustainable development and sustained economic growth of the developing countries and the eradication of poverty should be carried out through promoting the integration of the three components of sustainable development, namely, economic development, social development and environmental protection, as interdependent and mutually reinforcing pillars, in an integrated, coordinated and balanced manner;

11. *Recognizes* the need to provide financial and technical resources, as well as capacity-building and access to and transfer of technology, to assist those developing countries adversely affected by climate change;

12. *Calls upon* the international community to fulfil the commitments made during the fourth replenishment of the Global Environment Facility Trust Fund;

13. *Notes* the ongoing work of the liaison group of the secretariats and offices of the relevant subsidiary bodies of the Framework Convention, the United Nations Convention to Combat Desertification in Those Countries Experiencing Serious Drought and/or Desertification, Particularly in Africa, and the Convention on Biological Diversity, and encourages cooperation to promote complementarities among the three secretariats while respecting their independent legal status;

14. *Invites* the conferences of the parties to the multilateral environmental conventions, when setting the dates of their meetings, to take into consideration the schedule of meetings of the General Assembly and the Commission on Sustainable Development so as to ensure the adequate representation of developing countries at those meetings;

15. *Invites* the secretariat of the Framework Convention to report, through the Secretary-General, to the General Assembly at its sixty-fourth session on the work of the Conference of the Parties;

16. *Decides* to include in the provisional agenda of its sixty-fourth session the sub-item entitled "Protection of global climate for present and future generations".

On 24 December (**decision 63/552**), the General Assembly decided that the agenda item on the protection of global climate for present and future generations of mankind would remain for consideration during its resumed sixty-third (2009) session.

Vienna Convention and Montreal Protocol

As at 31 December, 192 States and the EU were parties to the 1985 Vienna Convention for the Protection of the Ozone Layer [YUN 1985, p. 804], which entered into force in 1998 [YUN 1998, p. 810].

Parties to the Montreal Protocol on Substances that Deplete the Ozone Layer, which was adopted in 1987 [YUN 1987, p. 686], numbered 192 States and the EU; to the 1990 Amendment to the Protocol, 188 States and the EU; to the 1992 Amendment, 183 States and the EU; to the 1997 Amendment, 167 States and the EU; and to the 1999 Amendment, 146 States and the EU.

The combined eighth meeting of the Conference of the Parties to the Vienna Convention and the twentieth Meeting of the Parties to the Montreal Protocol was held in Doha, Qatar, from 16 to 20 November [UNEP/OzL.Conv.8/7-UNEP/OzL.Pro.20/9]. The Conference of the Parties to the Convention approved the revised budget for the Trust Fund for the Vienna Convention for 2008, 2009, 2010 and 2011. It endorsed the recommendations adopted by the Ozone Research Managers at their seventh meeting (Geneva, 18–21 May) and adopted decisions on the status of ratification of the Convention and the Montreal Protocol and its Amendments, and other administrative and budgetary matters.

The Meeting of the Parties to the Montreal Protocol adopted the Doha Declaration, which addressed the destruction of ozone-depleting substances and other issues. Other decisions related to ratification of the Convention, the Protocol, and amendments to the Protocol; essential-use nominations for parties not operating under article 5 of the Protocol for controlled substances for 2009 and 2010; essential-use exemptions for parties operating under article 5; production of chlorofluorocarbons for metered-dose inhalers; critical-use exemptions for methyl bromide for 2009 and 2010; actions by parties to reduce methyl bromide use for quarantine and pre-shipment purposes and related emissions; the environmentally sound management of banks of ozone-depleting substances; application of the Protocol's trade provisions to hydrochlorofluorocarbons; the 2009–2011 replenishment of the Multilateral Fund; information provided by the parties in accordance with article 7 of the Protocol; reports submitted by parties under article 9; the report on the establishment of licensing systems under article 4B; difficulties faced by Iraq as a new party to the Convention, the Protocol and amendments to the Protocol; a request by Saudi Arabia for a change in baseline data; compliance issues; and administrative and budgetary issues.

The Implementation Committee under the Non-compliance Procedure held its fortieth (Bangkok, Thailand, 2–4 July) [UNEP/OzL.Pro/ImpCom/40/6] and forty-first (Doha, 12–14 November) [UNEP/OzL.Pro/ImpCom/41/8] meetings.

Convention on air pollution

As at 31 December, the number of parties to the 1979 Convention on Long-Range Transboundary Air Pollution [YUN 1979, p. 710], which entered into force in 1983 [YUN 1983, p. 645] remained at 50 States and the EU. Eight protocols to the Convention dealt with the programme for monitoring and evaluation of pollutants in Europe (1984), the reduction of sulphur emissions or their transboundary fluxes by at least 30 per cent (1985), the control of emissions of nitrogen oxides or their transboundary fluxes (1988), the control of volatile organic compounds or their transboundary fluxes (1991), further reduction of sulphur emissions (1994), heavy metals (1998), persistent organic pollutants (POPs) (1998) and the abatement of acidification, eutrophication and ground-level ozone (1999).

The twenty-sixth session of the Executive Body for the Convention (Geneva, 15–18 December) [ECE/EB.AIR/96 & Add.1, 2] approved guidelines for reporting on the monitoring and modelling of air pollution effects [ECE/EB.AIR/2008/11], which were adopted by the twenty-seventh session of the Working Group on Effects (Geneva, 24–26 September) [ECE/EB.AIR/WG.1/2008/2]. Other decisions dealt with emission data reporting under the Convention and its protocols and compliance issues.

Convention on Biological Diversity

As at 31 December, 190 States and the EU were parties to the 1992 Convention on Biological Diversity [YUN 1992, p. 638], which entered into force in 1993 [YUN 1993, p. 210].

At year's end, the number of parties to the Cartagena Protocol on Biosafety, which was adopted in 2000 [YUN 2000, p. 973] and entered into force in 2003 [YUN 2003, p. 1051], stood at 152 States and the EU.

The thirteenth meeting of the Subsidiary Body on Scientific, Technical and Technological Advice (Rome, Italy, 18–22 February) [UNEP/CBD/COP/9/3] adopted seven recommendations for consideration by the ninth (2008) meeting (see below) of the Conference of the Parties to the Convention.

The ninth meeting of the Conference of the Parties (Bonn, Germany, 13–30 May) [UNEP/CBD/COP/9/29] adopted a roadmap for negotiating an international regime for access to, and sharing the benefits of, genetic resources. It also adopted scientific criteria for identifying ecologically or biologically significant marine areas in need of protection in open-ocean waters and deep-sea habitats, and the scientific guidance for designing representative networks of marine protected areas. Other Conference decisions related to agricultural biodiversity; plant conservation; alien species that threatened ecosystems; forest biodiversity; incentive measures; the ecosystem approach; the Strategic Plan of the Convention; preparation of the third edition of the *Global Biodiversity Outlook*; implementation of articles 20 and 21 of the Convention; access and benefit-sharing; article 8(j) of the Convention, on traditional knowledge; and technology transfer and cooperation. Further decisions dealt with follow-up to the Millennium Ecosystem Assessment, which was completed in 2005 [YUN 2005, p. 1154]; biodiversity and climate change; the biodiversity of dry and sub-humid lands; protected areas; inland water ecosystems; marine and coastal biodiversity; island biodiversity; the Global Taxonomy Initiative; liability and redress for damage to biological diversity; the Gender Plan of Action under the Convention; South-South cooperation; business engagement; cooperation among multilateral environmental agreements and other organizations; promoting engagement of cities and local authorities; scientific and technical cooperation; communication, education and public awareness; the International Year of Biodiversity (2010), declared by the General Assembly in resolution 61/203 [YUN 2006, p. 1225]; and administrative and budgetary matters.

Cartagena Protocol on Biosafety

The fourth meeting of the Conference of the Parties to the Convention serving as the Meeting of the Parties to the Cartagena Protocol on Biosafety (Bonn, Germany, 12–16 May) [UNEP/CBD/BS/COP-MOP/4/18] approved a revised set of indicators for monitoring the updated Action Plan for Building Capacities for the Effective Implementation of the Protocol and established an Ad Hoc Technical Expert Group on Risk

Assessment and Risk Management. Other decisions dealt with the Compliance Committee; the Biosafety Clearing-House; the roster of biosafety experts; co-operation with other organizations, conventions and initiatives; the handling, transport, packaging and identification of living modified organisms; liability and redress under the Protocol; the establishment of subsidiary bodies under the Protocol; monitoring and reporting under the Protocol; assessment and review; socio-economic considerations; public awareness, education and participation in the implementation of the Protocol; notification requirements under the Protocol; and financial and budgetary matters.

Intergovernmental meeting. In November [UNEP/GC.25/15], the UNEP Executive Director reported on the ad hoc intergovernmental and multi-stakeholder meeting on an intergovernmental science-policy platform on biodiversity and ecosystem services (Putrajaya, Malaysia, 10–12 November) that was convened by the Executive Director and hosted by Malaysia. Participants agreed that there was a need to strengthen the science-policy interface and identified the main areas of work for the proposed platform, including early warning and horizon scanning, multi-scale assessments, policy information and capacity-building. UNEP was requested to undertake a preliminary gap analysis for facilitating discussions on strengthening the science-policy interface. The report on the gap analysis would be submitted to GC/GMEF in 2009. The meeting recommended that, subject to a Governing Council decision, the Executive Director convene a second intergovernmental multi-stakeholder meeting on the issue. The summary of the Chair of the meeting was annexed to the report.

In a December note [UNEP/GC.25/INF/32] the Executive Director set out documents submitted to the November meeting, including a revised concept note on the proposed platform; a programme of work and budget for the platform for an initial four-year period; and outlines for a governance structure, secretariat functions and rules and procedures.

GENERAL ASSEMBLY ACTION

On 19 December [meeting 72], the General Assembly, on the recommendation of the Second Committee [A/63/414/Add.6], adopted **resolution 63/219** without vote [agenda item 49 *(f)*].

Convention on Biological Diversity

The General Assembly,

Recalling its resolutions 55/201 of 20 December 2000, 61/204 of 20 December 2006 and 62/194 of 19 December 2007 and other previous resolutions relating to the Convention on Biological Diversity,

Recalling also its resolution 61/203 of 20 December 2006 on the International Year of Biodiversity, 2010,

Reiterating that the Convention on Biological Diversity is the key international instrument for the conservation and sustainable use of biological resources and the fair and equitable sharing of benefits arising from the use of genetic resources,

Noting that one hundred and ninety States and one regional economic integration organization have ratified the Convention and that one hundred and forty-seven States and one regional economic integration organization have ratified the Cartagena Protocol on Biosafety to the Convention on Biological Diversity,

Recalling the commitments of the World Summit on Sustainable Development to pursue a more efficient and coherent implementation of the three objectives of the Convention and the achievement by 2010 of a significant reduction in the current rate of loss of biological diversity, which will require action at all levels, including the implementation of national biodiversity strategies and action plans and the provision of new and additional financial and technical resources to developing countries,

Deeply concerned by the continued loss of biological diversity and the associated decline in the ecosystem services of our planet and their far-reaching environmental, social, economic and cultural impacts, and acknowledging that an unprecedented effort is needed to achieve by 2010 a significant reduction in the rate of loss of biological diversity,

Noting the need for enhanced cooperation among the Convention on Biological Diversity, the United Nations Convention to Combat Desertification in Those Countries Experiencing Serious Drought and/or Desertification, Particularly in Africa, and the United Nations Framework Convention on Climate Change ("the Rio Conventions"), while respecting their individual mandates, concerned by the negative impacts that loss of biodiversity, desertification, land degradation and climate change have on each other, and recognizing the potential benefits of complementarities in addressing these problems in a mutually supportive manner with a view to achieving the objectives of the Convention on Biological Diversity,

Acknowledging the contribution that the ongoing work of the Intergovernmental Committee on Intellectual Property and Genetic Resources, Traditional Knowledge and Folklore, of the World Intellectual Property Organization, can make in enhancing the effective implementation of the provisions of the Convention on Biological Diversity,

Noting the contribution that South-South cooperation can make in the area of biological diversity,

Expressing deep appreciation to the Government of Germany for hosting the ninth meeting of the Conference of the Parties to the Convention on Biological Diversity and its fourth meeting serving as the Meeting of the Parties to the Cartagena Protocol on Biosafety, and welcoming the offer of the Government of Japan to hold the tenth meeting of the Conference of the Parties and its fifth meeting serving as the Meeting of the Parties to the Cartagena Protocol on Biosafety, in 2010,

Taking note of the reports of the Millennium Ecosystem Assessment,

Noting the efforts of the Life Web initiative promoted by the Government of Germany and other countries,

Noting also the holding in Putrajaya, Malaysia, from 10 to 12 November 2008, of an ad hoc intergovernmental and multi-stakeholder meeting on an intergovernmental science-policy platform on biodiversity and ecosystem services, convened by the Executive Director of the United Nations Environment Programme,

Noting further the initiative launched at the meeting of the environmental ministers of the Group of Eight in Potsdam, Germany, in March 2007, to develop a study on the economic cost of the global loss of biodiversity,

1. *Takes note* of the report of the Executive Secretary of the Convention on Biological Diversity on the work of the Conference of the Parties to the Convention;

2. *Encourages* developed countries parties to the Convention on Biological Diversity to contribute to the relevant trust funds of the Convention, in particular so as to enhance the full participation of the developing countries parties in all of its activities;

3. *Urges* all Member States to fulfil their commitments to significantly reduce the rate of loss of biodiversity by 2010, and emphasizes that this will require an appropriate focus on the loss of biodiversity in their relevant policies and programmes and the continued provision of new and additional financial and technical resources to developing countries, including through the Global Environment Facility;

4. *Takes note* of the outcomes of the ninth meeting of the Conference of the Parties to the Convention and its fourth meeting serving as the Meeting of the Parties to the Cartagena Protocol on Biosafety;

5. *Urges* the parties to the Convention to facilitate the transfer of technology for the effective implementation of the Convention in accordance with its provisions, and in this regard takes note of the strategy for the practical implementation of the programme of work on technology transfer and scientific and technological cooperation developed by the Ad Hoc Technical Expert Group on Technology Transfer and Scientific and Technological Cooperation, as a preliminary basis for concrete activities by parties and international organizations;

6. *Notes* the ongoing work of the Heads of Agencies Task Force on the 2010 Biodiversity Target, of the chairpersons of the scientific advisory bodies of the biodiversity-related conventions and of the Joint Liaison Group of the secretariats and offices of the relevant subsidiary bodies of the United Nations Framework Convention on Climate Change, the United Nations Convention to Combat Desertification in Those Countries Experiencing Serious Drought and/or Desertification, Particularly in Africa, and the Convention on Biological Diversity, aimed at enhancing scientific and technical collaboration for achieving the 2010 biodiversity target;

7. *Notes also* the adoption by the Conference of the Parties to the Convention on Biological Diversity at its ninth meeting of a strategy for resource mobilization in support of the achievement of the three objectives of the Convention, and, in accordance with Conference of the Parties decision IX/11 and the annexes thereto, invites parties to submit, to the secretariat of the Convention, views on concrete activities and initiatives, including measurable targets and/or indicators to achieve the strategic goals contained in the strategy, and on indicators to monitor its implementation;

8. *Takes note* of decision IX/12 of the Conference of the Parties to the Convention, on access and benefit-sharing, and the annexes thereto, by which the Conference established a road map for the negotiations contained in that decision and, inter alia:

(a) Reiterated its instruction to the Ad Hoc Open-ended Working Group on Access and Benefit-sharing to complete the elaboration and negotiation of the international access and benefit-sharing regime at the earliest possible time before the tenth meeting of the Conference of the Parties to the Convention, in accordance with decisions VII/19 D and VIII/4 A; and

(b) Further instructed the Working Group to finalize the international regime and to submit for consideration and adoption by the Conference of the Parties to the Convention at its tenth meeting an instrument or instruments to effectively implement the provisions of articles 15 and 8 (*j*) of the Convention and its three objectives, without in any way prejudging or precluding any outcome regarding the nature of such instrument/instruments;

9. *Takes note also* of decision IX/20 of the Conference of the Parties to the Convention, on marine and coastal biodiversity, and the annexes thereto, by which the Conference, inter alia, adopted a set of scientific criteria for identifying ecologically or biologically significant marine areas in need of protection, contained in annex I to the decision, and scientific guidance for designing representative networks of marine protected areas, contained in annex II;

10. *Takes note further* of decision IX/5 of the Conference of the Parties to the Convention, on forest biodiversity;

11. *Encourages* the efforts being made to implement the seven thematic programmes of work, as established by the Conference of the Parties to the Convention, as well as the ongoing work on cross-cutting issues;

12. *Reaffirms* the commitment, subject to national legislation, to respect, preserve and maintain the knowledge, innovations and practices of indigenous and local communities embodying traditional lifestyles relevant to the conservation and sustainable use of biological diversity, promote their wider application with the approval and involvement of the holders of such knowledge, innovations and practices and encourage the equitable sharing of the benefits arising from their utilization;

13. *Takes note* of decision IX/33 of the Conference of the Parties to the Convention, and the annex thereto, and invites parties to the Convention, other Member States, relevant international organizations and other relevant stakeholders to make preparations to celebrate in 2010 the International Year of Biodiversity, and in that regard:

(a) Invites all Member States to create national committees, with the participation of representatives of indigenous and local communities, to celebrate the International Year of Biodiversity, and invites all international organizations to mark the event;

(b) Invites the Secretary-General to consider appointing before 2010, within existing resources, an honorary ambassador for the International Year of Biodiversity, who would have a mandate to call for practical actions and solutions towards meeting the objectives of the Convention;

(*c*) Decides, as a contribution to the International Year of Biodiversity, to convene at its sixty-fifth session, in 2010, a one-day high-level meeting of the General Assembly, with participation of heads of State, Governments and delegations, taking into consideration the schedule of meetings of the Convention;

(*d*) Encourages United Nations departments, funds and programmes, the specialized agencies and regional commissions to fully support and participate, as appropriate, in the activities being envisaged for the observance of 2010 as the International Year of Biodiversity, under the auspices of the secretariat of the Convention;

14. *Stresses* the importance of private-sector engagement for the implementation of the objectives of the Convention and the achievement of the 2010 target, and invites businesses to align their policies and practices more explicitly with the objectives of the Convention, including, inter alia, through partnerships;

15. *Notes* the adoption by the Conference of the Parties to the Convention of decision IX/25, on South-South cooperation on biodiversity for development, and the ongoing efforts of the Executive Secretary in that regard;

16. *Notes also* the development of the gender plan of action under the Convention, and invites parties to support the implementation of the plan by the Convention secretariat;

17. *Takes note* of decision IX/16 of the Conference of the Parties to the Convention, on biodiversity and climate change, and the annexes thereto, by which the Conference, inter alia, established an Ad Hoc Technical Expert Group on Biodiversity and Climate Change with a mandate to develop scientific and technical advice on biodiversity in so far as it relates to climate change;

18. *Also takes note* of the ongoing work of the Joint Liaison Group of the secretariats and offices of the relevant subsidiary bodies of the United Nations Framework Convention on Climate Change, the United Nations Convention to Combat Desertification in Those Countries Experiencing Serious Drought and/or Desertification, Particularly in Africa, and the Convention on Biological Diversity, and further encourages continuing cooperation in order to promote complementarities among the secretariats, while respecting their independent legal status;

19. *Encourages* all parties to the Convention on Biological Diversity to contribute to the discussions leading to an updated strategic plan for the Convention to be adopted at the tenth meeting of the Conference of the Parties, bearing in mind that this strategic plan should cover all three objectives of the Convention;

20. *Invites* the countries that have not yet done so to ratify or to accede to the Convention;

21. *Invites* countries to consider ratifying or acceding to the International Treaty on Plant Genetic Resources for Food and Agriculture;

22. *Invites* the parties to the Convention that have not yet ratified or acceded to the Cartagena Protocol on Biosafety to consider doing so, reiterates the commitment of States parties to the Protocol to support its implementation, and stresses that this will require the full support of parties and of relevant international organizations, in particular with regard to the provision of assistance to developing countries in capacity-building for biosafety;

23. *Invites* the secretariat of the Convention to report, through the Secretary-General, to the General Assembly at its sixty-fourth session on the work of the Conference of the Parties and to include in the report information on the preparation of the high-level meeting of the General Assembly referred to above;

24. *Decides* to include in the provisional agenda of its sixty-fourth session, under the item entitled "Sustainable development", the sub-item entitled "Convention on Biological Diversity".

Convention to Combat Desertification

As at 31 December, the total number of parties to the 1994 United Nations Convention to Combat Desertification in Those Countries Experiencing Serious Drought and/or Desertification, Particularly in Africa (UNCCD) [YUN 1994, p. 944], which entered into force in 1996 [YUN 1996, p. 958], stood at 193 States and the EU.

The seventh session of the Committee for the Review of the Implementation of the Convention (CRIC) (Istanbul, Turkey, 3–14 November) [ICCD/CRIC(7)/5], a subsidiary body of the Conference of the Parties to the Convention, discussed, among other issues, the 10-year strategic plan and framework to enhance the implementation of the Convention 2008–2018 (the Strategy). The report of the session contained conclusions and recommendations to further the implementation of the Strategy, which was adopted by the eighth (2007) session of the Conference of the Parties [YUN 2007, p. 1064]. The Committee on Science and Technology, another subsidiary body of the Conference, held its first special session in Istanbul concurrently with CRIC [ICCD/CST(S-1)/5].

GENERAL ASSEMBLY ACTION

On 19 December [meeting 72], the General Assembly, on the recommendation of the Second Committee [A/63/414/Add.5], adopted **resolution 63/218** without vote [agenda item 49 (*e*)].

Implementation of the United Nations Convention to Combat Desertification in Those Countries Experiencing Serious Drought and/or Desertification, Particularly in Africa

The General Assembly,

Recalling its resolutions 58/211 of 23 December 2003, 61/202 of 20 December 2006, 62/193 of 19 December 2007 and other resolutions relating to the implementation of the United Nations Convention to Combat Desertification in Those Countries Experiencing Serious Drought and/or Desertification, Particularly in Africa,

Recalling also the 2005 World Summit Outcome,

Reasserting its commitment to combating and reversing desertification and land degradation in arid, semi-arid and dry sub-humid areas, consistent with articles 1, 2 and 3 of the Convention, and to mitigating the effect of drought, eradicating extreme poverty, promoting sustainable development and improving the livelihoods of people affected by drought and/or desertification, taking into account the ten-year strategic plan and framework to enhance the implementation of the Convention (2008–2018),

Determined to build upon the momentum and to boost the spirit of international solidarity generated by the designation of 2006 as the International Year of Deserts and Desertification, and welcoming the adoption of the ten-year strategic plan and framework,

Reaffirming the universal membership of the Convention, and acknowledging that desertification, land degradation and drought are problems of a global dimension in that they affect all regions of the world,

Emphasizing that desertification, land degradation and drought seriously threaten the ability of developing countries to achieve the internationally agreed development goals, including the Millennium Development Goals, and recognizing that the timely and effective implementation of the Convention would help to achieve these goals,

Noting the need for enhanced cooperation among the United Nations Convention to Combat Desertification in Those Countries Experiencing Serious Drought and/or Desertification, Particularly in Africa, the United Nations Framework Convention on Climate Change and the Convention on Biological Diversity (the "Rio Conventions"), while respecting their individual mandates, concerned by the negative impacts that desertification, land degradation, loss of biodiversity and climate change have on each other, and recognizing the potential benefits of complementarities in addressing these problems in a mutually supportive manner,

Reaffirming the Plan of Implementation of the World Summit on Sustainable Development ("Johannesburg Plan of Implementation"), which recognizes the Convention to Combat Desertification as one of the tools for poverty eradication,

Recognizing the need to provide the secretariat of the Convention with stable, adequate and predictable resources in order to enable it to continue to discharge its responsibilities in an efficient and timely manner,

Welcoming the decision of the Commission on Sustainable Development at its eleventh session to consider, inter alia, the issue of desertification and drought during its sixteenth and seventeenth sessions,

Welcoming also the fact that the Commission on Sustainable Development at its sixteenth session convened an intergovernmental forum to review some topics that are relevant to the Convention in preparation for policy decisions on those topics by the Commission at its seventeenth session,

Expressing its deep appreciation to the Government of Germany for hosting the High-level Policy Dialogue in Bonn on 27 May 2008,

Expressing its deep appreciation also to the Government of Turkey for hosting the seventh session of the Committee for the Review of the Implementation of the Convention and the first special session of the Committee on Science and Technology in Istanbul from 3 to 14 November 2008,

1. *Takes note* of the report of the Secretary-General on the implementation of the United Nations Convention to Combat Desertification in Those Countries Experiencing Serious Drought and/or Desertification, Particularly in Africa;

2. *Reaffirms its resolve* to support and strengthen the implementation of the Convention with a view to addressing causes of desertification and land degradation, as well as poverty resulting from land degradation, through, inter alia, the mobilization of adequate and predictable financial resources, the transfer of technology and capacity-building at all levels;

3. *Reaffirms its decision* to declare the decade 2010–2020 as the United Nations Decade for Deserts and the Fight against Desertification;

4. *Continues to support* the efforts of the Executive Secretary of the Convention to continue the administrative renewal and reform of the secretariat and to realign its functions in order to fully implement the recommendations of the Joint Inspection Unit and bring them into line with the ten-year strategic plan and framework to enhance the implementation of the Convention (2008–2018);

5. *Notes* the request made for an assessment of the Global Mechanism by the Joint Inspection Unit, and looks forward to its findings, which are to be submitted to the Conference of the Parties at its ninth session;

6. *Reiterates its call upon* Governments, where appropriate, in collaboration with relevant multilateral organizations, including the Global Environment Facility implementation agencies, to integrate desertification and land degradation into their plans and strategies for sustainable development;

7. *Invites* the affected countries to prepare national strategies for the effective implementation of sustainable land management, and invites donors to support such efforts, on request, and in accordance with all agreed commitments on aid effectiveness;

8. *Notes* the ongoing work of the Joint Liaison Group of the secretariats and offices of the relevant subsidiary bodies of the United Nations Framework Convention on Climate Change, the Convention on Biological Diversity and the United Nations Convention to Combat Desertification in Those Countries Experiencing Serious Drought and/or Desertification, Particularly in Africa, and encourages continuing cooperation in order to promote complementarities in the work of the secretariats, while respecting their independent legal status;

9. *Recognizes* the potential of the Convention to Combat Desertification to contribute to addressing global food security, including by protecting land from becoming degraded and mitigating the effects of drought in arid, semi-arid and dry sub-humid areas, in order to offer new economic opportunities for enhancing rural development, agricultural productivity and food security for impoverished populations living in those areas;

10. *Invites* developed countries that are parties to the Convention and other Governments, multilateral organizations, the private sector and other relevant organizations to make resources available to affected developing countries for the implementation of the ten-year strategic plan and framework;

11. *Invites* the Executive Secretary of the Convention, in coordination with the Department of Economic and Social Affairs of the Secretariat, to actively prepare for and participate in the seventeenth session of the Commission

on Sustainable Development with a view to ensuring that the core issues of the Convention, in particular those relating to land degradation, drought and desertification, are duly considered in the context of sustainable development during the deliberations of the policy session, with a view to ensuring a successful outcome from the entire cycle of the Commission;

12. *Encourages* developed countries that are parties to the Convention to consider, in accordance with their different obligations under the Convention, prioritizing the need for supporting the implementation of the ten-year strategic plan and framework in their respective policies and programmes for cooperation, and further encourages affected developing countries to consider making this a priority in their cooperation assistance arrangements;

13. *Invites* donors to the Global Environment Facility to ensure that the Facility is adequately resourced during the next replenishment period in order to allow it to allocate sufficient and adequate resources to its six focal areas, in particular its land degradation focal area;

14. *Recognizes* the cross-sectoral nature of desertification, land degradation and drought mitigation, and in this regard invites all relevant United Nations organizations to cooperate with the Convention secretariat in supporting an effective response to desertification and drought;

15. *Urges* the Committee on Science and Technology to accelerate its efforts to establish links with scientific communities in order to make full use of relevant initiatives in areas relating to sustainable land and water management;

16. *Requests* all States parties to the Convention to promote awareness among local populations, particularly women, youth and civil society organizations, of, and to include them in, the implementation of the ten-year strategic plan and framework, and encourages affected States parties and donors to take into account the issue of participation of civil society in Convention processes when setting priorities in national development strategies;

17. *Stresses* the need to accelerate the ongoing process of adopting the euro as the budgetary and accounting currency of the Convention secretariat, and in this regard requests the Secretary-General, taking into account the institutional linkage and related administrative arrangements between the Convention secretariat and the United Nations Secretariat, to facilitate the implementation of decisions of the Conference of the Parties related to the protection of the Convention budget against the negative effects of currency fluctuations;

18. *Invites* the Conference of the Parties to the Convention, when setting the dates of its meetings, to take into consideration the schedule of meetings of the General Assembly and the Commission on Sustainable Development so as to help to ensure the adequate representation of developing countries at those meetings;

19. *Decides* to include in the provisional agenda of its sixty-fourth session the sub-item entitled "Implementation of the United Nations Convention to Combat Desertification in Those Countries Experiencing Serious Drought and/or Desertification, Particularly in Africa";

20. *Requests* the Secretary-General to submit to the General Assembly at its sixty-fourth session a report on the implementation of the present resolution, including a report on the implementation of the Convention.

International Conference on Combating Desertification

In a letter of 14 March [E/CN.17/2008/15], China transmitted to the Secretary-General the report of the International Conference on Combating Desertification (Beijing, China, 22–24 January). The Conference was jointly organized by the State Forestry Administration of China and the UN Department of Economic and Social Affairs (DESA), with support from the Beijing Municipal Bureau of Parks and Forestry and the UNCCD secretariat. It brought together some 240 participants from 55 countries and 40 UN organizations and international and regional institutions. Thematic discussions were held on the barriers and constraints faced by countries in combating desertification and land degradation, and on lessons learned and best practices in addressing those challenges. The Conference adopted the Beijing Statement on Combating Desertification and Promoting Sustainable Development, which set out the key points highlighted during the Conference.

Environmental activities

The atmosphere

Report of Secretary-General. In response to General Assembly resolution 62/8 [YUN 2007, p. 1067], the Secretary-General in January submitted a report [A/62/644] which reviewed UN system activities related to climate change. The report was based on written submissions from members of the United Nations Chief Executives Board for Coordination (CEB) and consultations in the framework of the CEB High-level Committee on Programmes. It described activities related to science, assessment, monitoring and early warning, and support of global, regional and national action on climate change. It outlined UN activities in the sectors of adaptation to, and mitigation of climate change, as well as technology and financing for climate change responses. Cross-cutting sectors included education, advocacy and awareness-raising.

The report contained a paper prepared by CEB on coordinated UN system action on climate change. Under the Secretary-General's leadership, CEB was aligning its strengths to achieve a coordinated approach to climate change. The objective was to support the process for an international agreement within the 1992 United Nations Framework Convention on Climate Change (UNFCCC) [YUN 1992, p. 681] (see p. 1155), as well as the efforts of Member States to tackle the challenges presented by climate change. The paper defined key areas of action and an effective coordination structure for the UN system. It highlighted the critical role of the UN system in the areas of science, assessment, monitoring and early warning as a basis for informed action, and articulated its contribution in supporting global, regional and national action on climate change. The paper also outlined the means by which the UN system could coordinate its substantive work in the key sectors of energy, agriculture and fisheries, water, oceans, forestry, health, transport, disaster risk reduction, population and human settlements, education, and raising public awareness.

It also discussed the UN system's efforts for establishing climate-neutrality in its own work. The Secretary-General tasked the Environment Management Group, under the leadership of the UNEP Executive Director, to develop approaches on how to best make the United Nations climate-neutral. The Group proposed to CEB a framework for guiding efforts on climate-neutrality, a strategic approach on achieving a climate-neutral United Nations and a commitment from all agencies to implement the initiative. The UN system would seek to reduce energy consumption at UN Headquarters, conduct an environmental audit of procurement and renovations at Headquarters, calculate emissions from air travel, and lead by example in individual institutions. The report also listed areas of potential UN system support to the implementation of climate change negotiation results.

General Assembly thematic debate. The resumed sixty-second (2008) session of the General Assembly held a thematic debate entitled "Addressing Climate Change: The United Nations and the World at Work" from 11 to 13 February, with plenary meetings on 12 and 13 February [A/62/PV.80–84]. The Assembly President, in his opening statement, said that the Assembly had a unique role to play on climate change, but in order to contribute most effectively, it needed to create more effective partnerships with a common vision and a global alliance for action. It also needed to help define a global strategy for the UN system to respond to climate change. The President emphasized that climate change was a sustainable development issue as well as an environmental one.

The Secretary-General, in a statement made at the opening session, said that the international community was armed with a combination of authoritative and compelling science on climate change, a rising tide of public concern and declarations of political will voiced at the 2007 Bali Climate Change Conference [YUN 2007, p. 1060]. The UN system was committed to supporting Member States as an effective, inclusive and credible partner in mitigating and adapting to climate change. Success was only possible if all countries acted, but developed countries needed to take the lead. Representatives of 101 countries and seven international organizations spoke in the ensuing debate.

Governing Council action. On 22 February [dec. SS.X/4], the UNEP Governing Council reaffirmed its commitment to support efforts to mitigate and adapt to climate change, which were interlinked with efforts to reduce the loss of biodiversity, control desertification, eradicate extreme poverty and famine, promote sustainable development and improve the lives of affected or vulnerable populations. It invited the Economic and Social Council to consider a proposal for the proclamation of an International Decade for addressing Climate Change for the period 2010–2020 and inform the General Assembly prior to its sixty-third (2008) session.

Communication. A letter of 14 March [A/63/66] from the Sudan to the Assembly President contained the Arab Ministerial Declaration on Climate Change, adopted by the Council of Arab Ministers Responsible for the Environment at its nineteenth session (Cairo, Egypt, 5–6 December 2007). The Declaration reflected the Arab position on addressing climate change and constituted a basis for future action.

High-Level Conference. The Beijing High-Level Conference on Climate Change: Technology Development and Technology Transfer (Beijing, 7–8 November) issued a statement in which the ministers and Government representatives participating in the Conference reaffirmed their commitment to UNFCCC and the 2007 Bali Action Plan for implementing the Convention [YUN 2007, p. 1060].

Intergovernmental Panel on Climate Change

The twenty-eighth session of the Intergovernmental Panel on Climate Change (IPCC) (Budapest, Hungary, 9–10 April) decided to produce a fifth assessment report, to be finalized in 2014, with a target date of early 2013 for the release of the Working Group I report. The current structure of IPCC Working Groups would be retained, with Groups dealing with the physical science basis; impacts, adaptation and vulnerability; and climate change mitigation. The Panel agreed to organize the new assessment work around a revised set of scenarios of socio-economic, climate and environmental conditions. It decided to prepare a special report on renewable energy sources and climate change mitigation, to be delivered in 2010.

IPCC also discussed the review of the principles governing its work; the use of funds from the Nobel Peace Prize 2007, won jointly with former United States Vice President Albert Arnold Gore, Jr. [YUN 2007, p. 1067]; admission of observer organizations; outreach activities; and progress reports of IPCC Working Groups and Task Forces.

The twenty-ninth IPCC session (Geneva, 31 August–4 September) commemorated the Panel's twentieth anniversary. It adopted its 2009 budget and took note of the indicative budgets for 2010 and 2011, and for the three following years up to the end of the Fifth Assessment cycle. The Panel, having considered proposals for the use of the funds from the Nobel Peace Prize 2007, decided to set up a scholarship fund for young post-graduate or post-doctoral students in climate change sciences from developing countries, especially least developed countries, as described in a report to the session [IPCC-XXIX/Doc.8, Rev.1]. IPCC elected its Bureau and the Task Force Bureau, and discussed procedural matters, future activities and other issues.

Terrestrial ecosystems

Deforestation and forest degradation

The United Nations Forum on Forests (UNFF) did not meet in 2008. In accordance with Economic and Social Council decision 2007/274 [YUN 2007, p. 1068], the eighth session of UNFF would be held in 2009.

In September [E/CN.18/2008/2], the Secretariat issued a note on financing for sustainable forest management: mobilizing financial resources to support the implementation of the non-legally binding instrument on all types of forests [YUN 2007, p. 1069], adopted by the General Assembly in resolution 62/98 [ibid., p. 1072], and to promote sustainable forest management. The note was prepared to facilitate discussions at the meeting of the Open-ended Ad Hoc Expert Group to Develop Proposals for the Development of a Voluntary Global Financial Mechanism/ Portfolio Approach/Forest Financing Framework (Vienna, 10–14 November) [E/CN.18/2009/11]. The meeting reviewed the instrument and major forest and finance issues; discussed the role of the private sector; reviewed recent international financial cooperation; described emerging issues; and presented conclusions for consideration by the Ad Hoc Expert Group.

Illicit trafficking in forest products

The seventeenth session of the Commission on Crime Prevention and Criminal Justice (Vienna, 14–18 April) [E/2008/30] (see p. 1222) considered the report of the meeting of the Open-ended Expert Group on International Cooperation in Preventing and Combating Illicit International Trafficking in Forest Products, including Timber, Wildlife and Other Forest Biological Resources (Jakarta, Indonesia, 26–28 March) [E/CN.15/2008/20]. The report, prepared pursuant to Commission resolution 16/1 [YUN 2007, p. 1148], reflected the views of the experts on ways and means of fostering international cooperation to combat illicit international trafficking in forest products through the use of the 2000 United Nations Convention against Transnational Organized Crime [YUN 2000, p. 1048] and the 2003 United Nations Convention against Corruption [YUN 2003, p. 1127], and of enhancing the capacity of law enforcement and forestry authorities to enforce the rule of law in the forest sector. The Expert Group noted the serious economic, social and environmental consequences of illicit international trafficking in forest products. Such trafficking exacerbated unsustainable forest practices; increased the cost of forest management and distorted the marketplace; and had an adverse environmental impact on forest ecosystems and on the conservation of forest resources and biodiversity. The Group emphasized the social consequences of forest crime for local communities and vulnerable groups that were heavily dependent upon forests for their livelihoods and security.

The Expert Group stressed the need to expand knowledge of the scope and scale of the problems created by illicit international trafficking in forest products, including the severe economic, environmental and social impact of such crime. Gaining a common understanding of such problems was a prerequisite for more coherent and consistent action at the national level and to enhancing bilateral, regional and interregional cooperation. It was also important to ensure that countries had common perceptions of the definition of legality and the conceptualization of legal and illegal acts in the forest sector. Rationalizing and streamlining national laws and regulations was essential for effective forest law enforcement and governance. Forest law enforcement responses could best be enhanced by improving detection methods, establishing specialized enforcement units, allowing direct channels of communication and creating networks for information-sharing. Preventive policies in the field of forest crime should include educational campaigns and the development of public information material to raise awareness among the public and ensure their support for forest law enforcement action. Implementation of national strategies and policies should foster inter-agency coordination and promote synergies and partnerships with NGOs and the private sector.

ECONOMIC AND SOCIAL COUNCIL ACTION

On 24 July [meeting 42], the Economic and Social Council, on the recommendation of the Commission on Crime Prevention and Criminal Justice [E/2008/30], adopted **resolution 2008/25** without vote [agenda item 14 *(c)*].

International cooperation in preventing and combating illicit international trafficking in forest products, including timber, wildlife and other forest biological resources

The Economic and Social Council,

Recalling its resolutions 2001/12 of 24 July 2001 and 2003/27 of 22 July 2003 on illicit trafficking in protected species of wild flora and fauna, and its resolutions 2000/35 of 18 October 2000 and 2006/49 of 28 July 2006 concerning the international arrangements on forests,

Bearing in mind the relevance of international instruments such as the Convention on Biological Diversity and the Convention on International Trade in Endangered Species of Wild Fauna and Flora,

Recalling General Assembly resolution 62/98 of 17 December 2007, by which the Assembly adopted the non-legally binding instrument on all types of forests, contained in the annex to that resolution,

Recalling also resolution 16/1 adopted by the Commission on Crime Prevention and Criminal Justice at its sixteenth session,

Noting with concern that illicit international trafficking in forest products, including timber, wildlife and other forest biological resources, constitutes a major source of concern because such activities have an adverse environmental, social and economic impact on many countries,

1. *Takes note with appreciation* of the report of the meeting of the Open-ended Expert Group on International Cooperation in Preventing and Combating Illicit International Trafficking in Forest Products, including Timber, Wildlife and Other Forest Biological Resources, held in Jakarta from 26 to 28 March 2008;

2. *Encourages* Member States to continue to provide the United Nations Office on Drugs and Crime with information on measures taken pursuant to Commission on Crime Prevention and Criminal Justice resolution 16/1, taking into consideration the emphasis that the Open-ended Expert Group, in its report, placed on, inter alia, the need for holistic and comprehensive national multisectoral approaches to preventing and combating illicit international trafficking in forest products, including timber, wildlife and other forest biological resources, as well as for international coordination and cooperation in support of such approaches, including through technical assistance activities to build the capacity of relevant national officials and institutions;

3. *Requests* the Executive Director of the United Nations Office on Drugs and Crime to make the text of the present resolution and the report of the Open-ended Expert Group available to the Conference of the Parties to the United Nations Convention against Transnational Organized Crime at its fourth session;

4. *Also requests* the Executive Director to report on the implementation of the present resolution and to provide a brief summary of the mandates and the work of other relevant organizations in this area to the Commission at its eighteenth session.

Drought and desertification

The Commission on Sustainable Development, at its sixteenth session (New York, 5–16 May) [E/2008/29] (see p. 915), considered a February report of the Secretary-General [E/CN.17/2008/6] reviewing the implementation of the goals related to the thematic area of drought, as contained in Agenda 21 [YUN 1992, p. 672]; the Programme for the Further Implementation of Agenda 21, adopted by the nineteenth special session of the General Assembly in resolution S/19-2 [YUN 1997, p. 792]; and the Johannesburg Plan of Implementation [YUN 2002, p. 822]. The report discussed facts and figures on drought, issues related to drought management and early warning and climate and weather information. It stated that projected climatic changes were likely to further exacerbate the frequency and severity of droughts, with adverse impacts on food production and food security, in particular in Africa. The challenge was to reduce the vulnerability of the agricultural sector to climate variability and the projected changes in extreme weather events. Improved access to appropriate and affordable technologies and related field training and capacity-building to grow resilient crops proved to be important in maintaining soil productivity and increasing food production in drought-affected drylands. The projected persistence and severity of droughts underscored the urgency of gradually shifting priority in drought management of affected countries and regions from essentially sector-specific strategies and policies to those that integrated management of natural resources and ecosystems with social and economic development strategies and action plans. A proactive, risk-based approach to drought management proved to be effective in preventing or reducing the physical and economic losses associated with drought. Inadequate financial resources and technical capacities often hampered the implementation of programmes and projects on drought risk management. The lack of systematic collection and analysis of drought-relevant data in many affected countries also hampered effective drought impact assessment.

The Commission also had before it the February report of the Secretary-General [E/CN.17/2008/7] reviewing the implementation of Agenda 21, the Programme for the Further Implementation of Agenda 21, and the Johannesburg Plan of Implementation with regard to desertification. The report discussed facts and figures on desertification and the correlation between land use, land productivity and livelihoods in drylands. It addressed issues related to the conservation of dryland vegetation; maintaining freshwater bodies and groundwater resources; and various means of combating desertification. The level of rural poverty in many developing countries affected by desertification and drought, which was particularly high in Africa, continued to be the overarching challenge in the fight against desertification. The projected intensification of freshwater scarcity would cause greater stresses in drylands and, if left unmitigated, would further exacerbate desertification. Weak institutional and legal structures and capacities, poor coordination and collaboration among stakeholders involved in combating desertification and poor enforcement of legislation to guarantee clear legal ownership and access rights to land, water and other natural resources hampered the implementation of effective interventions. Providing economic and non-economic incentives to national stakeholders to encourage investments in the sustainable management of land, forests and other ecosystems could play a critical role in mobilizing financial resources. Dissemination of new and emerging technologies to field application in affected developing countries also remained a challenge. The 10-year strategic plan and framework adopted by the Conference of the Parties to the United Nations Convention to Combat Desertification at its eighth (2007) session [YUN 2007, p. 1064] had strengthened the international commitment to combat desertification, mitigate the effects of drought and combat climate change. The Convention offered a platform for adaptation, mitigation and resilience.

Marine ecosystems

Oceans and seas

In response to General Assembly resolutions 61/222 [YUN 2006, p. 1557] and 62/215 [YUN 2007, p. 1402], the ninth meeting of the United Nations Open-ended Informal Consultative Process on Oceans and Law of the Sea (New York, 23–27 June) [A/63/174 & Corr.1] focused on maritime security and safety. The meeting reached agreement on elements relating to that issue, which were proposed by the Co-Chairpersons of the Consultative Process for consideration by the Assembly. The Assembly took action with regard to maritime safety and security and the Consultative Process in sections VIII and XIV of **resolution 63/111** of 5 December (see pp. 1503 & 1510).

Assessment of assessments

The Group of Experts for the start-up phase of the "assessment of assessments" [YUN 2004, p. 1332] of the regular process for the global reporting and assessment of the state of the marine environment, including socio-economic aspects, held its third meeting (Copenhagen, Denmark, 15–17 April) [GRAME/GOE/3/2]. The meeting agreed on the outlines for the "assessment of assessments" report, and agreed that the first draft of the Introduction and Part II, along with the outlines for Parts I and III, would be submitted for peer review by the end of May.

UNEP and the Intergovernmental Oceanographic Commission of the United Nations Educational, Scientific and Cultural Organization (UNESCO), the lead agencies for the "assessment of assessments", prepared a progress report on the "assessment of assessments" that was issued in June.

The third meeting of the Ad Hoc Steering Group for the "assessment of assessments" (New York, 19–20 June) [GRAME/AHSG/3/2] discussed the approach for presenting the final "assessment of assessments" report to the General Assembly's sixty-fourth (2009) session, as well as a new resource mobilization strategy to ensure adequate financial resources for completing scheduled activities.

The fourth meeting of the Group of Experts (London, 4–6 November) focused on finalizing the chapters of the "assessment of assessments" report so that they could be submitted for Government and expert peer review, which was scheduled to take place from 1 December 2008 to 31 January 2009. The Group of experts also discussed the procedures of the peer review process and proposed a list of reviewers to be invited to participate in that process. The Group agreed on the production schedule of the report and the summary for decision makers.

The General Assembly, in section XII of **resolution 63/111** of 5 December (see p. 1509) took note of the report of the third meeting of the Ad Hoc Steering Group and the "assessment of assessments" progress report, endorsed by the Steering Group. It urged all members of the Steering Group to participate in the review of the completed "assessment of assessments" report and the summary for decision makers at the Group's meeting in 2009.

Regional Seas Programme

The tenth Global Meeting of the Regional Seas Conventions and Action Plans (Guayaquil, Ecuador, 25–27 November) discussed climate change and the regional seas programme; ecosystem management and the regional seas programmes; cooperation with multilateral environmental agreements; sustainable financing and legal instruments to further the implementation of the Regional Seas Work Programme; and enhancing communication.

Caribbean Sea management

In response to General Assembly resolution 61/197 [YUN 2006, p. 1243], the Secretary-General submitted an August report [A/63/297] that described regional and national activities undertaken in the Caribbean region to ensure the protection of the Caribbean Sea from degradation, pollution and loss of marine biodiversity. It also provided an update on regional and international support extended to the promotion of the sustainable development of the resources of the Caribbean Sea for present and future generations. The Association of Caribbean States (ACS) remained engaged in supporting the ongoing initiative of the region to have the Caribbean Sea declared a special area in the context of sustainable development.

To that end, the Caribbean Sea Commission was established in September 2006 to provide a structure for political oversight, technical resources and research support for the Caribbean Sea initiative, and promote regional efforts for achieving the preservation and sustainable use of the Caribbean Sea. Regional experts working through a technical advisory group created by ACS provided technical support for the Commission's work.

Annexed to the Secretary-General's report was the report on the work of ACS, submitted in response to resolution 61/197. ACS provided details on its activities related to sustainable tourism and disaster reduction. The outcome of the High-level Conference on Disaster Reduction of the Association of Caribbean States (Saint-Marc, Haiti, 14–16 November 2007), known as the Saint-Marc Plan of Action, was endorsed by the ACS Ministerial Council as a 27-point document that would inform the ACS work programme in the area of disaster risk reduction. The report also outlined the Commission's Plan of Action, which, along with its programme of activities, was finalized at the Commission's July 2008 meeting.

GENERAL ASSEMBLY ACTION

On 19 December [meeting 72], the General Assembly, on the recommendation of the Second Committee [A/63/414/Add.2], adopted **resolution 63/214** without vote [agenda item 49 (*b*)].

Towards the sustainable development of the Caribbean Sea for present and future generations

The General Assembly,

Reaffirming the principles and commitments enshrined in the Rio Declaration on Environment and Development, the principles embodied in the Declaration of Barbados, the Programme of Action for the Sustainable Development of Small Island Developing States, the Johannesburg Declaration on Sustainable Development and the Plan of Implementation of the World Summit on Sustainable Development ("Johannesburg Plan of Implementation"), as well as other relevant declarations and international instruments,

Recalling the Declaration and review document adopted by the General Assembly at its twenty-second special session,

Taking into account all other relevant General Assembly resolutions, including resolutions 54/225 of 22 December 1999, 55/203 of 20 December 2000, 57/261 of 20 December 2002, 59/230 of 22 December 2004 and 61/197 of 20 December 2006,

Taking into account also the Mauritius Strategy for the Further Implementation of the Programme of Action for the Sustainable Development of Small Island Developing States,

Recalling the 2005 World Summit Outcome,

Recalling also the Convention for the Protection and Development of the Marine Environment of the Wider Caribbean Region, signed at Cartagena de Indias, Colombia, on 24 March 1983, and the protocols thereto, which contain the definition of the wider Caribbean region of which the Caribbean Sea is part,

Reaffirming the United Nations Convention on the Law of the Sea, which provides the overall legal framework for ocean activities, and emphasizing its fundamental character, conscious that the problems of ocean space are closely interrelated and need to be considered as a whole through an integrated, interdisciplinary and intersectoral approach,

Emphasizing the importance of national, regional and global action and cooperation in the marine sector as recognized by the United Nations Conference on Environment and Development in chapter 17 of Agenda 21,

Recalling the relevant work done by the International Maritime Organization,

Considering that the Caribbean Sea area includes a large number of States, countries and territories, most of which are developing countries and small island developing States that are ecologically fragile and socially and economically vulnerable and are also affected, inter alia, by their limited capacity, narrow resource base, need for financial resources, high levels of poverty and the resulting social problems and the challenges and opportunities of globalization and trade liberalization,

Recognizing that the Caribbean Sea has unique biodiversity and highly fragile ecosystems,

Recognizing also that the Caribbean has been shown to be the most tourism-dependent region in the world relative to its size,

Noting that the Caribbean Sea, when compared to all other large marine ecosystems, is surrounded by the largest number of countries in the world,

Emphasizing that the Caribbean countries have a high degree of vulnerability occasioned by climate change, climate variability and associated phenomena, such as the rise in sea level, the El Niño phenomenon and the increase in the frequency and intensity of natural disasters caused by hurricanes, floods and droughts, and that they are also subject to natural disasters, such as those caused by volcanoes, tsunamis and earthquakes,

Bearing in mind the heavy reliance of most of the Caribbean economies on their coastal areas, as well as on the marine environment in general, to achieve their sustainable development needs and goals,

Acknowledging that the intensive use of the Caribbean Sea for maritime transport, as well as the considerable number and interlocking character of the maritime areas under national jurisdiction where Caribbean countries exercise their rights and duties under international law, present a challenge for the effective management of the resources,

Noting the problem of marine pollution caused, inter alia, by land-based sources and the continuing threat of pollution from ship-generated waste and sewage, as well as from the accidental release of hazardous and noxious substances in the Caribbean Sea area,

Taking note of the relevant resolutions of the General Conference of the International Atomic Energy Agency on safety of transport of radioactive materials,

Mindful of the diversity and dynamic interaction and competition among socio-economic activities for the use of the coastal areas and the marine environment and their resources,

Mindful also of the efforts of the Caribbean countries to address in a more holistic manner the sectoral issues relating to the management of the wider Caribbean Sea region and, in so doing, to promote integrated management of the wider Caribbean Sea region in the context of sustainable development, through a regional cooperative effort among Caribbean countries,

Welcoming the continued efforts of the States members of the Association of Caribbean States to develop and implement regional initiatives to promote the sustainable conservation and management of coastal and marine resources, and recognizing in this regard the firm commitment by Heads of State and Government of the Association to take the steps necessary to ensure the recognition of the Caribbean Sea as a special area within the context of sustainable development, without prejudice to relevant international law,

Taking note of the creation by the Association of Caribbean States of the Caribbean Sea Commission, and welcoming its ongoing work,

Cognizant of the importance of the Caribbean Sea to present and future generations and to the heritage and the continuing economic well-being and sustenance of people living in the area, and the urgent need for the countries of the region to take appropriate steps for its preservation and protection, with the support of the international community,

1. *Recognizes* that the Caribbean Sea is an area of unique biodiversity and a highly fragile ecosystem that requires relevant regional and international development partners to work together to develop and implement regional initiatives to promote the sustainable conservation and management of coastal and marine resources, including, inter alia, the consideration of the concept of the Caribbean Sea as a special area in the context of sustainable development, including its designation as such without prejudice to relevant international law;

2. *Takes note* of the efforts of the Caribbean States and the work undertaken by the Caribbean Sea Commission of the Association of Caribbean States, including, inter alia, the development of their concept of the designation of the Caribbean Sea as a special area within the context of sustainable development, and invites the international community to support such efforts;

3. *Welcomes* the plan of action adopted by the Caribbean Sea Commission, including its scientific and technical components and governance and outreach components, and invites the international community and the United Nations system to support, as appropriate, Caribbean countries and their regional organizations in their efforts to implement the plan of action;

4. *Recognizes* the efforts of Caribbean countries to create conditions leading to sustainable development aimed at combating poverty and inequality, and in this regard notes with interest the initiatives of the Association of Caribbean States in the focal areas of sustainable tourism, trade, transport and natural disasters;

5. *Calls upon* the United Nations system and the international community to assist, as appropriate, Caribbean countries and their regional organizations in their efforts to ensure the protection of the Caribbean Sea from degradation as a result of pollution from ships, in particular through the illegal release of oil and other harmful substances, and from illegal dumping or accidental release of hazardous waste, including radioactive materials, nuclear waste and dangerous chemicals, in violation of relevant international rules and standards, as well as pollution from land-based activities;

6. *Invites* the Association of Caribbean States to submit a report to the Secretary-General on the progress made in the implementation of the present resolution, for consideration during the sixty-fifth session of the General Assembly;

7. *Calls upon* all States to become contracting parties to relevant international agreements to enhance maritime safety and promote the protection of the marine environment of the Caribbean Sea from pollution, damage and degradation from ships and ship-generated waste;

8. *Supports* the efforts of Caribbean countries to implement sustainable fisheries management programmes and to meet the principles of the Code of Conduct for Responsible Fisheries of the Food and Agriculture Organization of the United Nations;

9. *Calls upon* States, taking into consideration the Convention on Biological Diversity, to develop national, regional and international programmes to halt the loss of marine biodiversity in the Caribbean Sea, in particular fragile ecosystems such as coral reefs and mangroves;

10. *Invites* Member States and intergovernmental organizations within the United Nations system to continue their efforts to assist Caribbean countries in becoming parties to the relevant conventions and protocols concerning the management, protection and sustainable utilization of Caribbean Sea resources and in implementing them effectively;

11. *Calls upon* the international community, the United Nations system and the multilateral financial institutions, and invites the Global Environment Facility, within its mandate, to support actively the national and regional activities of the Caribbean States towards the promotion of the sustainable management of coastal and marine resources;

12. *Expresses deep concern* about the severe destruction and devastation caused to several countries by heightened hurricane activity in the wider Caribbean region in recent years;

13. *Urges* the United Nations system and the international community to continue to provide aid and assistance to the countries of the Caribbean region in the implementation of their long-term programmes of disaster prevention, preparedness, mitigation, management, relief and recovery, based on their development priorities, through the integration of relief, rehabilitation and reconstruction into a comprehensive approach to sustainable development;

14. *Acknowledges* the pivotal role of the Association of Caribbean States in regional dialogue and in the consolidation of a wider Caribbean cooperation zone in the field of disaster risk reduction, as well as the importance of the international community in deepening existing cooperation and consolidating new initiatives with that regional mechanism within the context of the outcomes of the High-level Conference on Disaster Reduction of the Association of Caribbean States, held in Saint-Marc, Haiti, from 14 to 16 November 2007, and the plan of action approved by the

Ministerial Council of the Association upon the recommendation of the Conference;

15. *Invites* Member States, international and regional organizations and other relevant stakeholders to consider training programmes for the development of a human resource capacity at different levels and to developing research aimed at enhancing the food security of Caribbean countries, as well as the sustainable management of renewable marine and coastal resources;

16. *Calls upon* Member States to improve as a matter of priority their emergency response capabilities and the containment of environmental damage, particularly in the Caribbean Sea, in the event of natural disasters or of an accident or incident relating to maritime navigation;

17. *Requests* the Secretary-General to report to it at its sixty-fifth session, under the sub-item entitled "Follow-up to and implementation of the Mauritius Strategy for the Further Implementation of the Programme of Action for the Sustainable Development of Small Island Developing States" of the item entitled "Sustainable development", on the implementation of the present resolution, including a section on the possible legal and financial implications of the concept of the Caribbean Sea as a special area within the context of sustainable development, including its designation as such without prejudice to relevant international law, taking into account the views expressed by Member States and relevant regional organizations.

Protection against harmful products and waste

Chemical safety

As at 31 December, 126 States and the EU were parties to the 1998 Rotterdam Convention on the Prior Informed Consent Procedure for Certain Hazardous Chemicals and Pesticides in International Trade [YUN 1998, p. 997], which entered into force in 2004 [YUN 2004, p. 1063].

The Chemical Review Committee, a subsidiary body of the Conference of the Parties to the Rotterdam Convention, at its fourth meeting (Geneva, 10–13 March) [UNEP/FAO/RC/CRC.4/11], agreed to consider the notifications of final regulatory action scheduled for review by the Committee in line with the priorities suggested in a secretariat note [UNEP/FAO/RC/CRC.4/3]; and reviewed notifications of final regulatory action to ban or severely restrict six chemicals. The Committee also discussed its role and mandate, which were described in a secretariat note [UNEP/FAO/RC/CRC.4/4], as well as its intersessional work, working papers and policy guidance.

The fourth meeting of the Conference of the Parties to the Rotterdam Convention (Rome, 27–31 October) [UNEP/FAO/RC/COP.4/24] adopted a decision on enhancing cooperation and coordination among the Rotterdam Convention, the 1989 Basel Convention on the Control of Transboundary Movements of Hazardous Wastes and their Disposal [YUN 1989, p. 420] and the 2001 Stockholm Convention on Persistent Organic Pollutants [YUN 2001, p. 971]. In accordance with that decision, the Conference of the Parties adopted—as an extraordinary, one-time measure—a three-year budget cycle for the 2009–2011 period to facilitate synchronization with the budget cycles of the Basel and Stockholm Conventions, UNEP and FAO; and approved the programme activities and operational programme budget for the triennium. The Conference of the Parties amended annex III of the Convention to list all tributylin compounds and decided that the amendment would enter into force on 1 February 2009. Other decisions dealt with the inclusion of chrysotile asbestos and endosulfan in annex III; progress in implementing the Convention; confirmation of the appointments of Government-designated experts as members of the Chemical Review Committee; nomination of Governments to designate experts for the Committee; compliance procedures and mechanisms; options for lasting and sustainable financial mechanisms; national and regional delivery of technical assistance; and cooperation with the World Trade Organization.

IFCS session. The sixth session of the Intergovernmental Forum on Chemical Safety (IFCS) (Dakar, Senegal, 15–19 September) [IFCS/FORUM-VI/07w] focused on the role of partnerships for chemical safety in achieving the goal of the 2002 World Summit on Sustainable Development [YUN 2002, p. 821] that, by 2020, chemicals had to be used and produced in ways that minimized significant adverse effects on human health and the environment [ibid., p. 822]. IFCS adopted the Dakar Resolution on the future of the Forum, in which it invited the International Conference on Chemicals Management (ICCM) to integrate IFCS into the Conference by establishing the Forum as an ICCM advisory body. IFCS also adopted a resolution for eliminating lead in paints; a statement on manufactured nanomaterials; and recommendations on the substitution and alternatives to hazardous substances in products and processes, and on key elements of pesticide risk reduction strategies.

International chemicals management

On 22 February [dec. SS.X/1], the UNEP Governing Council decided to consider at its twenty-fifth (2009) session the programme-related matters raised in the reports of the Executive Director on waste management (see p. 1174); progress of the ad hoc open-ended working group on mercury (see p. 1171); and efforts of the secretariat of the Strategic Approach to International Chemicals Management (SAICM) [YUN 2006, p. 1247] to explore more effective use of funding provisions of the Approach and the implementation of SAICM by the Inter-Organization Programme for the Sound Management of Chemicals (IOMC) [YUN 2007, p. 1077]. It requested the Executive Director to continue to implement its 2007 multi-part decision on chemicals management [YUN 2007, p. 1077] and its 2007 decision on waste management [ibid., p. 1080].

In response to the Council's decision, the Executive Director in November submitted a report [UNEP/GC.25/5], which described UNEP activities to support SAICM implementation; IOMC efforts to implement SAICM; the second (2009) session of the International Conference on Chemicals Management; and UNEP activities related to lead, cadmium and mercury (see below). UNEP activities on chemicals contributed to the SAICM policy framework for efforts to attain the 2020 goal of the Plan of Implementation of the 2002 World Summit on Sustainable Development [YUN 2002, p. 821] related to chemicals [ibid., p. 822]. UNDP and UNEP developed a partnership to facilitate the integration of the sound management of chemicals into development planning to support sustainable development in developing countries and countries with economies in transition. With funding support secured through the Quick Start Programme Trust Fund under SAICM, the partnership initiative was launched in the former Yugoslav Republic of Macedonia and Uganda; activities in Belarus, Belize, Ecuador, Honduras, Liberia and Mauritania would begin in 2009.

Lead and cadmium

In response to a 2007 Governing Council decision [YUN 2007, p. 1078], the Executive Director, in his November report on chemicals management [UNEP/GC.25/5], provided information on UNEP activities related to lead and cadmium. The Partnership for Clean Fuels and Vehicles continued to support countries in eliminating the use of leaded gasoline and reducing sulphur levels in fuels. At the beginning of 2008, 19 countries were still using leaded gasoline. During the year, three countries—Jordan, the Lao People's Democratic Republic and Mongolia—and the Occupied Palestinian Territory ceased using leaded gasoline. Afghanistan and Morocco were expected to phase out its use at the end of 2008. Tunisia committed itself to phasing out leaded gasoline in the near future. Leaded gasoline phase-out was a major component of three subregional events coordinated by the Partnership in the Eastern Europe, Caucasus and Central Asia region in January; the Gulf region in March; and North Africa in August. Through the events, countries were assisted in setting timelines and strategies to end the use of such gasoline. Sweden contributed approximately $180,000 to support the development of a study on the effects of trade in products containing lead, cadmium and mercury in Africa. The study [UNEP/GC.25/INF/23/Add.1] was presented at an intergovernmental workshop in December.

Notes by the Executive Director [UNEP/GC.25/INF/23 & UNEP/GC.25/INF/24] contained reviews of scientific information on lead and cadmium, an overview of legislation and an inventory of risk management measures.

Mercury

The ad hoc open-ended working group on mercury held its second meeting (Nairobi, Kenya, 6–10 October) [UNEP(DTIE)/Hg/OEWG.2/13] to finalize the report on how to respond to the challenges presented by mercury. In response to the Governing Council's 2007 decision on mercury [YUN 2007, p. 1078], the report was to be submitted to the Council in 2009. In reviewing and assessing options for enhanced voluntary measures and new or existing international legal instruments dealing with mercury, the meeting considered possible elements of a mercury framework [UNEP(DTIE)/Hg/OEWG.2/8] and discussed capacity-building and financial mechanisms for the framework and modalities for the Working Group's report to the Governing Council. It also discussed progress in developing a study on atmospheric emissions of mercury and strengthening the UNEP Global Mercury Partnership (see below).

A November note by the Executive Director [UNEP/GC.25/5/Add.1] contained the Working Group's final report, in which the Group recommended that the Governing Council adopt a policy framework for addressing the global challenges posed by mercury at its twenty-fifth (2009) session. Possible elements of such a framework, which were outlined in an annex to the report, included priorities identified by the Council in its 2007 decision on mercury; the range of possible response measures identified by the Working Group; and other actions related to the implementation and administration of the framework. The elements reflected the special needs and situations of developing countries and countries with economies in transition. The Working Group identified two options for implementing the elements of the mercury policy framework: adoption by Governments of a new, legally binding mercury convention, and enhanced voluntary measures. Possible components of such measures would build on existing activities, including the UNEP mercury programme and Global Mercury Partnership; existing legal instruments; SAICM; and a proposed new voluntary instrument, the Programmatic and Organizational Structure on Mercury.

In response to a 2007 Governing Council decision on mercury [YUN 2007, p. 1078], the December report of the Executive Director on chemicals management [UNEP/GC.25/5] contained information on UNEP activities related to mercury. Switzerland and the United States provided funding for a project to investigate the possibility of closing the last exporting primary mercury mine, located in Kyrgyzstan. The UNEP Chemicals Branch, together with the United Nations Institute for Training and Research and the UNEP Global Resource Information Database office, located in Arendal, Norway, assisted in preparing a technical report on the mine. Information on the market and social and economic effects of the control of mercury pollution was collected and analysed by a project conducted by the Nordic Council of Ministers. The project report [UNEP(DTIE)/Hg/OEWG.2/INF/7] was considered by the second meeting of the Ad Hoc Open-ended Working Group on Mercury (see below). Norway supported a pilot project to investigate suitable sites for the sound storage of mercury in Asia and Latin America. The export of mercury and mercury compounds from the European Union would be prohibited from 15 March 2011. In the United States, the federal sale and export of elemental mercury was banned with immediate effect, and all exports of elemental mercury would be banned as at 1 January 2013.

The UNEP secretariat prepared a report on the supply of and demand for mercury. The report analysed the projected demand for mercury until 2020 and potential limitations on supply over that period. UNEP, with the support of Sweden and the United States, undertook a number of country-level projects to develop inventories of mercury uses and emissions. The inventories enabled countries to develop national action plans to tackle issues related to mercury. The Executive Director's report also described progress in strengthening the UNEP Global Mercury Partnership.

A December note by the Executive Director [UNEP/GC.25/INF/27] provided additional information on activities undertaken to strengthen the Global Mercury Partnership. UNEP, in consultation with Governments and stakeholders, developed an overarching framework for the Partnership, which was finalized at a Partnership meeting (Geneva, 1–3 April). The meeting report and the overarching framework were annexed to the note. The framework established an overall goal for the Partnership: to protect human health and the global environment from the release of mercury and its compounds by minimizing and, where feasible, ultimately eliminating global anthropogenic mercury releases to air, water and land. It also established a partnership advisory group to encourage the work of the partnership areas; review the partnership area business plans; report to the Executive Director on progress; communicate overarching issues and lessons learned while promoting synergy and collaboration; and report on Partnership activities. Business plans were drafted for six partnership areas: artisanal and small-scale gold mining; mercury cell chlor-alkali production; mercury air transport and fate research; mercury-containing products; mercury releases from coal combustion; and mercury waste management. The note highlighted activities in each of the areas.

Harmful products

In response to Economic and Social Council decision 2007/264 [YUN 2007, p. 1079], the Secretary-General in May submitted a report [A/63/76-E/2008/54] on products harmful to health and the environment. The report presented the views of Member States and intergovernmental entities on the continued usefulness for Member States of the Consolidated List of Products Whose Consumption and/or Sale have been Banned, Withdrawn, Severely Restricted or Not Approved by Governments [YUN 1982, p. 1010]. The Secretary-General concluded that the lack of response from any intergovernmental entity dealing with the issue, except FAO, and the few responses received from Member States pointed towards the diminishing value of the List. He recommended that the Council consider recommending the elimination of the mandate of regularly updating the List, as contained in General Assembly resolution 37/137 [ibid., p. 1011].

ECONOMIC AND SOCIAL COUNCIL ACTION

On 23 July [meeting 41], the Economic and Social Council adopted **resolution 2008/13** [draft: E/2008/L.21] without vote [agenda item 13 *(e)*].

Protection against products harmful to health and the environment

The Economic and Social Council,

Recalling its decision 2007/264 of 27 July 2007, in which it requested the Secretary-General, in consultation with Member States and relevant intergovernmental entities, to evaluate the continued usefulness for the Member States of the Consolidated List of Products Whose Consumption and/or Sale Have Been Banned, Withdrawn, Severely Restricted or Not Approved by Governments and to report to the Council at its substantive session of 2008, and taking note of the report of the Secretary-General on products harmful to health and the environment,

1. *Invites* the United Nations Environment Programme to continue updating the chemicals volume of the Consolidated List of Products Whose Consumption and/or Sale Have Been Banned, Withdrawn, Severely Restricted or Not Approved by Governments and to report to the Economic and Social Council at its substantive session in 2010;

2. *Invites* the World Health Organization to continue updating the pharmaceuticals volume of the Consolidated List and to report to the Council at its substantive session of 2010.

Persistent organic pollutants

As at 31 December, 161 States and the EU were parties to the 2001 Stockholm Convention on Persistent Organic Pollutants (POPs) [YUN 2001, p. 971], which entered into force in 2004 [YUN 2004, p. 1066].

The Conference of the Parties to the Convention did not meet in 2008.

The fourth meeting of the Persistent Organic Pollutants Review Committee (Geneva, 13–17 October) [UNEP/POPS/POPRC.4/15] adopted risk management evaluations for commercial octabromodiphenyl ether; pentachlorobenzene; and alpha and beta hexachlorocyclohexane. Other decisions related to endosulfan; conflicts of interest on the part of members of the Committee; the Committee's terms of reference; and the effective participation of the parties to the Stockholm Convention in the Committee's work. The Committee made recommendations to the Conference of the Parties pertaining to commercial pentabromodiphenyl ether; chlordecone; hexabromobiphenyl; lindane, alpha hexachlorocyclohexane and beta hexachlorocyclohexane; perfluorooctane sulfonate; commercial octabromodiphenyl ether; and pentachlorobenzene.

Hazardous wastes

As at 31 December, 171 States and the EU were parties to the 1989 Basel Convention on the Control of Transboundary Movements of Hazardous Wastes and their Disposal [YUN 1989, p. 420], which entered into force in 1992 [YUN 1992, p. 685]. The 1995 amendment to the Convention [YUN 1995, p. 1333], not yet in force, had been ratified, accepted or approved by 64 parties. The number of parties to the 1999 Basel Protocol on Liability and Compensation for Damage Resulting from Transboundary Movements of Hazardous Wastes and their Disposal [YUN 1999, p. 998] rose to nine.

The second meeting of the Expanded Bureau of the eighth (2006) meeting [YUN 2006, p. 1248] of the Conference of the Parties to the Convention (Geneva, 26–27 February) [UNEP/SBC/BUREAU/8/2/5] discussed the draft 2009–2010 programme budget and financial matters; the status of preparations for the ninth (2008) Conference of the Parties; commemoration of the twentieth anniversary of the adoption of the Convention in 2009; implementation of decisions adopted at the eighth meeting of the Conference of the Parties; and administrative and other matters.

The ninth meeting of the Conference of the Parties to the Convention (Bali, Indonesia, 23–27 June) [UNEP/CHW.9/39] adopted the Bali Declaration on Waste Management for Human Health and Livelihood, in which ministers and other heads of delegations from the parties to the Convention and other States reaffirmed their commitment to the principles and purposes of the Convention and to sustainable development, including the principles set out in Agenda 21 [YUN 1992, p. 672], adopted by the 1992 United Nations Conference on Environment and Development [ibid., p. 670]. They also called on international and regional partners to support and enhance the implementation of the Basel Convention at the bilateral, regional and global levels.

The Secretary-General, in his message to the ninth meeting of the Conference of the Parties at its high-level segment (26–27 June), said that the Convention, by establishing the principle of environmentally sound management of hazardous and other wastes, was a key to pursuing environmental sustainability and the MDGs. In order to reach those targets, all States should provide the necessary political commitment and resources to the Convention, and integrate efforts to carry out its provisions into the broader campaign for sustainable development. The United Nations would continue to take an active role in meeting the global waste challenge.

The Conference of the Parties invited the parties to take into consideration the statement of the President of the ninth meeting of the Conference. It adopted—as an extraordinary, one-time measure—a three-year budget cycle for the 2009–2011 period in order to facilitate synchronization of the budget cycle of the Basel Convention with those of the 1998 Rotterdam Convention [YUN 1998, p. 997] and the 2001 Stockholm Convention [YUN 2001, p. 971]; and approved programme activities and the programme budget for the Basel Convention Trust Fund for 2009, 2010 and 2011. It also approved the membership and work programme for 2009–2011 of the Committee for Administering the Mechanism for Promoting Implementation and Compliance of the Basel Convention. The Conference adopted the Convention's workplan for the environmentally sound management of electrical and electronic waste (e-waste); the Convention Partnership Programme workplan for 2009–2011; and the work programme of the Open-ended Working Group for 2009–2011. The Conference also adopted decisions on the Strategic Plan and new strategic framework for the implementation of the Convention; the review of the operation of the Convention's regional and coordinating centres; a proposal for establishing a regional centre for South Asia in the South Asia Cooperative Environment Programme; the Mobile Phone Partnership Initiative; the Partnership for Action on Computing Equipment; cooperation and coordination among the Basel, Rotterdam and Stockholm Conventions; international cooperation and coordination; cooperation between the Basel Convention and the International Maritime Organization; national reporting of data on transboundary movements of hazardous wastes and other wastes; the environmentally sound management of used tyres; technical guidelines on the environmentally sound management of mercury wastes; POPs; the review of technical guidelines on the environmentally sound management of hazardous wastes; and the review of work on the guidance papers on hazard characteristics H10 and H11. Further decisions dealt with cooperation with the World Customs Organization and its Harmonized System Committee; harmonization and coordination; national classification and control procedures for the import of wastes contained in annex IX to the Convention; the Trust Fund to Assist Developing and Other Countries in Need of Assistance in the Implementation of the Convention; national legislation and other measures to implement the Convention and combat illegal traffic; the Protocol on Liability and Compensation; interpretation of article 17 of the Convention; national definitions of hazardous wastes; agreements and arrangements under article 11 of the Convention; the designation of competent authorities and focal points for the Convention; the dismantling of ships; and administrative matters.

Waste management

The UNEP Governing Council, at its tenth special session in February, had before it a report of the Executive Director on waste management [UNEP/GCSS.X/7], submitted in response to a 2007 Council decision [YUN 2007, p. 1080]. The report stated that the rapid increase in the volume and types of solid waste and hazardous waste generation, due mainly to economic growth, urbanization and industrialization, represented a growing problem for national and local governments, as well as municipal authorities. UNEP, in collaboration with its partners, intended to intensify and strengthen its waste management activities. In support of the Bali Strategic Plan for Technology Support and Capacity-building [YUN 2004, p. 1040], adopted by the Council in 2005 [YUN 2005, p. 1135], UNEP activities would focus on capacity-building and support for technology identification, assessment and implementation. The report reviewed work being carried out or planned by relevant organizations, institutions, forums and processes in the field of waste management, and aimed to identify needs and gaps. The activities and programmes of international organizations were assessed to identify areas requiring further work to assist countries in improving their waste management systems. The analysis addressed needs at the policy and regulatory, technical, financial, social and institutional levels, and generally referred to situations in developing countries. Nuclear and space wastes and wastes linked to chemical weapons were not covered in the analysis, as special management systems for such wastes were set up and strictly controlled by Governments. The report provided recommendations on how to bridge gaps in waste management and outlined the outcomes of the process of cooperation between UNEP and other organizations.

An addendum [UNEP/GC.25/5/Add.2] to the November report of the Executive Director on chemicals management (see p. 1171) contained a report on waste management, submitted in response to the Governing Council's February decision on chemicals management (see p. 1170). The report reviewed work by organizations that carried out or were planning waste management activities, set out recommendations and provided information on cooperation between UNEP and other organizations.

Notes by the Executive Director [UNEP/GCSS.X/INF/6, UNEP/GC.25/INF/29] contained information on the waste management activities and programmes of the Asian Development Bank (ADB), the European Bank for Reconstruction and Development (EBRD), OECD, the secretariat for the Basel Convention, UNDP, UNEP, UN-Habitat, the United Nations Industrial Development Organization (UNIDO) and the World Bank.

Other matters

Environmental Law

The meeting of senior government officials expert in environmental law to prepare a fourth Programme for the Development and Periodic Review of Environmental Law (Montevideo Programme IV) (Nairobi, 29 September–3 October) [UNEP/Env.Law/MTV4/IG/2/2] adopted the draft fourth Programme [UNEP/GC.25/INF/15], which was annexed to the meeting's report. The draft fourth Programme contained 27 programme areas. It proposed objectives, strategies and actions to increase the effectiveness of environmental law, including in the areas of implementation, compliance and enforcement; capacity-building; prevention and mitigation of and compensation for environmental damage; avoidance and settlement of international disputes; the strengthening and development of international environmental law; harmonization, coordination and synergies of relevant institutions; public participation and access to information; information technology; governance; and other means. The draft programme also addressed issues related to conservation, management and sustainable use of natural resources; challenges for environmental law; and relationships between the environment and other fields, including human rights, trade, security and military activities. The draft programme was developed by UNEP in conjunction with senior advisers and reviewed by the consultative meeting of Government officials and experts on the Programme

(Nairobi, 26–30 November 2007) [UNEP/Env.Law/MTV4/IG/1/4].

In an October report [UNEP/GC.25/11], the Executive Director submitted to the Governing Council information for its consideration in 2009 and suggested action on the draft fourth Programme.

An October note by the Executive Director [UNEP/GC.25/INF/15/Add.2] contained the report of the consultative meeting of Government officials and experts to review and further develop the draft guidelines for developing national legislation on access to information, public participation and access to justice in environmental matters (Nairobi, 20–21 June), and the draft guidelines on the topic. An addendum [UNEP/GC.25/11/Add.1] contained information and suggested action on the draft guidelines.

A November note by the Executive Director [UNEP/GC.25/INF/15/Add.3] contained the report of the consultative meeting of Government officials and experts to review and further develop draft guidelines for developing national legislation on liability, response action and compensation for damage caused by activities dangerous to the environment (Nairobi, 18–19 June), and the draft guidelines on the topic. An addendum [UNEP/GC.25/11/Add.2] contained information and suggested action on the draft guidelines.

Human settlements

Follow-up on the 1996 UN Conference on Human Settlements (Habitat II)

In August [A/63/291], the Secretary-General, in response to General Assembly resolution 62/198 [YUN 2007, p. 1083], reported on the implementation the Habitat Agenda [YUN 1996, p. 994], adopted by the 1996 United Nations Conference on Human Settlements (Habitat II) [ibid., p. 992], and on the strengthening of the United Nations Human Settlements Programme (UN-Habitat). In 2008, the increasing importance of the human settlements dimension of sustainable development was underscored by a rapid rise in food and energy prices; growing awareness of the consequences of climate change; the financial crisis associated with the collapse of the sub-prime mortgage market; and devastating natural disasters in a number of countries. UN-Habitat studies showed that levels of inequality in cities were rising across the globe. Levels of urbanization and city size were not the key determinants of the quantity of greenhouse gas emissions; rather, consumption patterns and lifestyles with regard to land-use and urban sprawl played a more critical role.

In December, the Committee of Permanent Representatives—the subsidiary body of the UN-Habitat Governing Council—endorsed an action plan for implementing the 2008–2013 UN-Habitat Medium-term Strategic and Institutional Plan, which was approved by the Governing Council in 2007 [YUN 2007, p. 1086]. The anticipated outcomes of the Plan's start-up phase included: a revised and updated set of substantive policies and strategies spearheaded by a global campaign on sustainable development; an enhanced normative and operational framework to provide policy and operational support services to Member States in attaining the human settlements-related MDGs; and a series of institutional reforms for the progressive realization of excellence in management. The new Global Campaign for Sustainable Urbanization merged two previous campaigns on secure tenure and urban governance, and addressed the adaptation and mitigation challenges of climate change. It was conceived as an advocacy tool to help UN-Habitat raise awareness of the need to include the urbanization and urban poverty agendas in national development plans and priorities, and disseminate a set of policy recommendations to Member States in support of socially inclusive and environmentally sound human settlements development. The Campaign was accompanied by a normative and operational framework that combined policy recommendations and tools emanating from the Campaign for Sustainable Urbanization with services to support the efforts of Member States, UN country teams and the United Nations Development Assistance Framework in attaining the human settlements-related MDGs.

UN-Habitat developed a methodology and proposed integrated approaches to slum upgrading and water and sanitation, including working with international and regional financial institutions, the private sector and domestic financial institutions. Collaboration with the African Development Bank (AfDB) was instrumental in facilitating investment flows into African cities for basic infrastructure and services; joint activities generated over $250 million in pipeline investments. A partnership with AfDB and the East African Community provided a framework of collaboration to expand the Lake Victoria Region Water and Sanitation Initiative in an additional 15 towns in five countries. In India, four cities of Madhya Pradesh state benefited from a $181 million loan from the Asian Development Bank (ADB) based on the role of UN-Habitat in supporting reforms in the water and sanitation sector. In Asia, UN-Habitat was engaged in 47 towns and cities in five countries and was expanding its activities to Indonesia and Cambodia. In China, UN-Habitat forged a partnership with the city of Nanjing for a diagnostic study that became the basis for follow-up investment by ABD to improve the city's water and sanitation sector. In Iraq, it partnered with the International Finance Corporation to study and address local housing supply constraints. In Latin America and the Caribbean, UN-Habitat formed a strategic partnership with the Inter-American Development Bank to support the Water for Cities programme.

The UN-Habitat Slum Upgrading Facility continued to field-test innovative financing mechanisms in four pilot countries: Ghana, Indonesia, Sri Lanka and the United Republic of Tanzania. UN-Habitat and the Committee of Permanent Representatives approved a set of operational procedures for engaging in the experimental reimbursable seeding operations activities approved by the Governing Council in 2007 [YUN 2007, p. 1088]. The procedures would be used by a steering and monitoring committee to select pilot projects for leveraging seed capital with domestic capital to finance pro-poor housing and urban development. A micro-mortgage financing initiative for low-income housing in developing countries, starting in Latin American cities, was launched in partnership with the Global Housing Foundation and the Merrill Lynch firm. The partnership's objective was to offer the working poor segment of the world's 1 billion slum dwellers an opportunity to own a home financed through micro-mortgage instruments and, in the process, help develop the local economy.

Following the Governing Council's approval in 2007 of the guidelines on decentralization [YUN 2007, p. 1087], UN-Habitat worked closely with Habitat Agenda partners to support interested Member States in undertaking policy and institutional reform. Two meetings of the Advisory Group of Experts on Decentralization were convened in India and Norway in 2008 to develop a strategic framework for launching support services for the implementation of the guidelines. The resulting implementation strategy consisted of four major components: advocacy and norm-setting; capacity-building and institutional development; networking and synergy building with key stakeholders; and monitoring and assessment.

The UN-Habitat Executive Director was appointed to the WHO Commission on the Social Determinants of Health. UN-Habitat and WHO developed a framework for collaboration, focusing on generating evidence on urban health inequities; setting up urban thematic groups at the national level; establishing a city-to-city learning facility on urban health; and working jointly towards a global forum on urban health in 2010. In 2008, the Province of Gangwon, Republic of Korea, and UN-Habitat launched the International Urban Training Centre. The Centre was established to build the capacity of cities and towns nationally and in the Asian and Pacific region in support of sustainable urbanization. UN-Habitat was implementing an approach whereby populations affected by disasters were placed at the centre of the recovery and reconstruction process. In the Asia and Pacific region, a seamless process between disaster relief and recovery was implemented in a number of countries, including Afghanistan, Indonesia, Maldives, Sri Lanka and Pakistan. In Somalia, interventions by UN-Habitat and an inter-agency group helped more than 50,000 internally displaced persons regain a permanent home, access basic services and begin to restore their livelihoods.

Contributions to the United Nations Habitat and Human Settlements Foundation reached an all-time high of $153.3 million in 2007 as compared to $126.0 million in 2006. Non-earmarked contributions increased by over 70 per cent, from $10.2 million in 2006 to $17.6 million received from 36 Governments in 2007. Earmarked contributions—funding intended for a theme, a region, a country or a project—amounted to $135.7 million. The imbalance between earmarked and non-earmarked contributions remained a challenge. In April 2008, an initial contribution of $2.9 million was received for experimental reimbursable seeding operations as at 31 December 2007.

The Secretary-General stated that the Habitat Agenda was important for addressing some of the underlying causes of global trends such as climate change and the rise in food and fuel prices and for mitigating their social, economic and environmental consequences. The experimental reimbursable seeding operations would take place simultaneously with the 2008–2013 Medium-term Strategic and Institutional Plan and over a similar period of time. The Human Settlements Foundation offered a unique opportunity for Member States to reduce urban poverty. Voluntary contributions to the Foundation would enable local partners to combine grants for technical assistance with reimbursable seeding operations. In that regard, the adoption of the principle of assessed voluntary indicative scale of contributions would facilitate the mobilization of resources and the broadening of the donor base. Governments and other entities were encouraged to contribute to the capitalization of UN-Habitat and the Human Settlements Foundation as an effective means of providing financial and seed capital to slum upgrading, slum prevention and pro-poor water and sanitation in urban areas.

A progress report of the Executive Director [HSP/GC/22/2/Add.2] reviewed progress made in implementing the Medium-Term Strategic and Institutional Plan for 2008–2013.

Coordinated implementation of Habitat Agenda

In response to a 2007 Economic and Social Council decision [YUN 2006, p. 1251], the Secretary-General submitted a May report [E/2008/64] on the coordinated implementation of the Habitat Agenda. The report highlighted major new developments and milestones in the implementation of the Agenda and underscored the increasing awareness on the part of the international community of the issues and challenges associated with rapid urbanization, including the consequences for attaining the MDGs. It discussed the decisions of the twenty-first (2007) session of the UN-Habitat Governing Council, including the approval of the 2008–2013 Medium-term Strategic and Institutional Plan [YUN 2007, p. 1086]; emerging responses to the challenges of rapid urbanization; human settlements and crises; and the participation and contribution of UN-Habitat to "Delivering as one" at the country level, in response to the recommendations contained in the 2006 report of the High-level Panel on United Nations System-wide Coherence in the Areas of Development, Humanitarian Assistance and the Environment [YUN 2006, p. 1584].

The Secretary-General concluded that the robust response to the coordinated implementation of the Habitat Agenda and related MDGs was a strong indication of the coming of age of the urban agenda. The unprecedented increase in collaboration, coordination, partnerships and networking covered all aspects of the Agenda at all levels, including advocacy and knowledge generation, capacity-building and resource mobilization to expand pilot initiatives and prepare for follow-up investment. The key contributing factors to the growing awareness and recognition were rooted in the realization that the urbanization of poverty and social exclusion was becoming a major challenge to the attainment of internationally agreed development goals and to sustainable development itself. Major global challenges underscored the importance of addressing the social, economic and environmental consequences of urbanization. Trends in rapid urbanization would place further pressure on the demand for energy, including biofuels, thus affecting the pricing of both energy and food. A concerted and integrated approach to the social, economic and environmental challenges of rapid urbanization was required. For such an approach to become effective, it was proposed that the Council include sustainable urbanization, with a major focus on urban poverty, as a cross-cutting issue to complement and reinforce follow-up within the social, economic and environmental pillars of sustainable development.

On 23 July, the Economic and Social Council, by **decision 2008/239**, took note of Secretary-General's report; decided to transmit it to the General Assembly for consideration at its sixty-third (2008) session; and requested the Secretary-General to submit a report on the coordinated implementation of the Habitat Agenda to the Council in 2009.

In response to the Council's decision, the Secretary-General, by a September note [A/63/353], transmitted his May report to the Assembly.

GENERAL ASSEMBLY ACTION

On 19 December [meeting 72], the General Assembly, on the recommendation of the Second Committee [A/63/415], adopted **resolution 63/221** without vote [agenda item 50].

Implementation of the outcome of the United Nations Conference on Human Settlements (Habitat II) and strengthening of the United Nations Human Settlements Programme (UN-Habitat)

The General Assembly,

Recalling its resolutions 3327(XXIX) of 16 December 1974, 32/162 of 19 December 1977, 34/115 of 14 December 1979, 56/205 and 56/206 of 21 December 2001, 57/275 of 20 December 2002, 58/226 and 58/227 of 23 December 2003, 59/239 of 22 December 2004, 60/203 of 22 December 2005, 61/206 of 20 December 2006 and 62/198 of 19 December 2007,

Taking note of Economic and Social Council resolutions 2002/38 of 26 July 2002 and 2003/62 of 25 July 2003 and Council decisions 2004/300 of 23 July 2004, 2005/298 of 26 July 2005, 2006/247 of 27 July 2006, 2007/249 of 26 July 2007 and 2008/239 of 23 July 2008,

Recalling the goal contained in the United Nations Millennium Declaration of achieving a significant improvement in the lives of at least 100 million slum-dwellers by 2020 and the goal contained in the Plan of Implementation of the World Summit on Sustainable Development ("Johannesburg Plan of Implementation") to halve, by 2015, the proportion of people who lack access to safe drinking water and sanitation,

Recalling also the Habitat Agenda, the Declaration on Cities and Other Human Settlements in the New Millennium, the Johannesburg Plan of Implementation and the Monterrey Consensus of the International Conference on Financing for Development,

Recalling further the 2005 World Summit Outcome, which calls upon the States Members of the United Nations to achieve significant improvement in the lives of at least 100 million slum-dwellers by 2020, recognizing the urgent need for the provision of increased resources for affordable housing and housing-related infrastructure, prioritizing slum prevention and slum upgrading, and to encourage support for the United Nations Habitat and Human Settlements Foundation and its Slum Upgrading Facility,

Recognizing the negative impact of environmental degradation, including climate change, desertification and loss of biodiversity, on human settlements,

Recognizing also that the current financial crisis could negatively affect the ability of the United Nations Human Settlements Programme (UN-Habitat) to mobilize resources and promote the use of incentives and market measures as well as the mobilization of domestic and international financial resources for supporting private sector investment in affordable housing,

Noting the important contribution of UN-Habitat, within its mandate, to more cost-effective transitions between emergency relief, recovery and reconstruction, and also welcoming the decision to admit UN-Habitat to the Inter-Agency Standing Committee,

Recognizing the significance of the urban dimension of poverty eradication and the need to integrate water and sanitation and other issues within a comprehensive framework for sustainable development,

Recognizing also the importance of decentralization policies for achieving sustainable human settlements development in line with the Habitat Agenda and the internationally agreed development goals, including the Millennium Development Goals,

Noting the progress so far made by UN-Habitat in the implementation of its Medium-term Strategic and Institutional Plan for the period 2008–2013,

Welcoming the efforts of UN-Habitat, as a non-resident agency and through its national Habitat programme managers, in helping programme countries to mainstream the Habitat Agenda in their development frameworks,

Expressing its appreciation to the Government of China and the city of Nanjing for hosting the fourth session of the World Urban Forum from 3 to 6 November 2008 and to the Government of Brazil for its offer to host the fifth session of the World Urban Forum in 2010,

Noting the efforts of UN-Habitat in strengthening its collaboration with the World Bank, the regional development banks and domestic financial institutions, ensuring that its policy advisory and capacity-building activities leverage investment finance to improve water and sanitation as entry point to the attainment of internationally agreed development goals, including the Millennium Development Goals,

Recognizing the need for UN-Habitat to sharpen its focus on all areas within its mandate,

Recognizing also the continued need for increased and predictable financial contributions to the United Nations Habitat and Human Settlements Foundation to ensure timely, effective and concrete global implementation of the Habitat Agenda, the Declaration on Cities and Other Human Settlements in the New Millennium and the relevant internationally agreed development goals, including those contained in the Millennium Declaration and the Johannesburg Declaration on Sustainable Development and Johannesburg Plan of Implementation,

Recognizing further the progress being made by UN-Habitat in the development of the Experimental Reimbursable Seeding Operations Trust Fund of the United Nations Habitat and Human Settlements Foundation, established by the Governing Council of UN-Habitat in its resolution 21/10,

1. *Takes note* of the report of the Secretary-General on the coordinated implementation of the Habitat Agenda and the report of the Secretary-General on the implementation of the outcome of the United Nations Conference on Human Settlements (Habitat II) and strengthening of the United Nations Human Settlements Programme (UN-Habitat);

2. *Welcomes* the efforts of UN-Habitat in the implementation of its Medium-term Strategic and Institutional Plan for the period 2008–2013, and encourages Governments in a position to do so, and other stakeholders, to contribute to UN-Habitat so as to further strengthen its efforts in institutional reform and the pursuit of management excellence, including results-based management;

3. *Encourages* Governments to promote the principles and practice of sustainable urbanization and strengthen the role and contribution of their respective local authorities in applying those principles and practice, in order to improve the living conditions of vulnerable urban populations, including slum-dwellers and the urban poor, and as a major contribution to mitigating the causes of climate change, adapting to the effects of climate change and reducing risks and vulnerabilities in a rapidly urbanizing world, including human settlements in fragile ecosystems, and invites the international donor community to support the efforts of developing countries in this regard;

4. *Reiterates its call* for continued financial support to UN-Habitat through increased voluntary contributions, and invites Governments in a position to do so, and other stakeholders, to provide predictable multi-year funding and increased non-earmarked contributions to support the strategic and institutional objectives of the Medium-term Strategic and Institutional Plan for the period 2008–2013 and its Global Campaign on Sustainable Urbanization;

5. *Invites* the international donor community and financial institutions to contribute generously to the Water and Sanitation Trust Fund, the Slum Upgrading Facility and the technical cooperation trust funds to enable UN-Habitat to assist developing countries in mobilizing public investment and private capital for slum upgrading, shelter and basic services;

6. *Also invites* the international donor community and financial institutions to contribute to the Experimental Reimbursable Seeding Operations Trust Fund of the United Nations Habitat and Human Settlements Foundation;

7. *Requests* the Secretary-General to keep the resource needs of UN-Habitat under review so as to enhance its effectiveness in supporting national policies, strategies and plans in attaining the poverty eradication, gender equality, water and sanitation and slum upgrading targets of the United Nations Millennium Declaration, the Johannesburg Plan of Implementation and the 2005 World Summit Outcome;

8. *Calls upon* UN-Habitat to strengthen efforts to coordinate and implement its normative and operational activities through the enhanced normative and operational framework elaborated in the Medium-term Strategic and Institutional Plan, reinforcing its normative activities, and invites all countries in a position to do so to support the activities of UN-Habitat in this regard;

9. *Invites* UN-Habitat to enhance cooperation with regional and subregional organizations and to consider strengthening the strategic presence of its programmes in the regions in contributing to sustainable development programmes;

10. *Requests* UN-Habitat, within the framework of its experimental reimbursable seeding operations for housing finance, and in close collaboration with international and regional financial institutions, to document and disseminate lessons learned, bearing in mind the provisions of resolution 21/10 of the Governing Council of UN-Habitat, and

fully taking into account the recent housing finance crisis, as well as other relevant factors;

11. *Invites* the Governing Council of UN-Habitat to keep under review developments in the housing finance systems in view of the current financial crisis, and decides to explore the possibility of convening a high-level event of the General Assembly on this subject;

12. *Encourages* Member States to strengthen or establish, as appropriate, broad-based national Habitat committees with a view to mainstreaming sustainable urbanization and urban poverty reduction in their respective national development strategies;

13. *Encourages* the Economic and Social Council to include sustainable urbanization, urban poverty reduction and slum upgrading as a cross-cutting issue in the follow-up to the outcome of relevant summits and major international conferences;

14. *Emphasizes* the importance of the Nairobi headquarters location of UN-Habitat, and requests the Secretary-General to keep the resource needs of UN-Habitat and the United Nations Office at Nairobi under review so as to permit the delivery, in an effective manner, of necessary services to UN-Habitat and the other United Nations organs and organizations in Nairobi;

15. *Requests* the Secretary-General to submit to the General Assembly at its sixty-fourth session a report on the implementation of the present resolution;

16. *Decides* to include in the provisional agenda of its sixty-fourth session the item entitled "Implementation of the outcome of the United Nations Conference on Human Settlements (Habitat II) and strengthening of the United Nations Human Settlements Programme (UN-Habitat)".

UN Human Settlements Programme

Governing Council

In accordance with General Assembly resolution 56/206 [YUN 2001, p. 987], the Governing Council of the United Nations Human Settlements Programme (UN-Habitat), which met biennially, did not meet in 2008. The twenty-second session of the Governing Council would take place in 2009.

Committee of Permanent Representatives

The Committee of Permanent Representatives, the intersessional body of the UN-Habitat Governing Council, met four times in 2008 (3 April, 11 June, 24 September and 3 December). The Committee discussed the implementation of the Medium-term Strategic and Institutional Plan for the period 2008–2013, adopted by the Council in 2007 [YUN 2007, p. 1086], including the experimental reimbursable seeding operations [YUN 2007, p. 1088]; preparations for and the outcome of the fourth session of the World Urban Forum (see p. 1181) and the sixty-third (2008) session of the General Assembly; preparations for the twenty-second (2009) session of the Governing Council; the efficiency and effectiveness of the UN-Habitat governance structure; and the UN-Habitat financial situation.

Board of Auditors report

In June, the Board of Auditors transmitted to the General Assembly its report on the UN-Habitat financial statements for the biennium ended 31 December 2007 [A/63/5/Add.8]. Total income amounted to $289.9 million, compared with $228.4 million for the previous biennium, representing a 27 per cent increase. Total expenditure increased by 48 per cent to $250.4 million, compared with $169.2 million for the previous biennium; the increase resulted in an excess of income over expenditure of $39.5 million, compared with an excess of $59.2 million in the previous biennium. Taking into consideration non-budgeted accrued expenses of $8 million acknowledged for end-of-service liabilities, the funding of which had not yet been provided, and after the prior-period adjustment, the adjusted net result as at 31 December 2007 represented an excess of $32 million; reserves and funds totalled $116.7 million at the end of the period, compared to $85.1 million for the previous biennium.

The Board recommended, among other measures, that UN-Habitat: conduct an inventory of expendable items as at the end of the biennium and account for and disclose them pursuant to the UN system accounting standards; monitor regularly its level of liquidity, in order to eliminate any potential for unnecessary delay in the implementation of projects; set up specific funding for end-of-service and after-service health insurance liabilities; disclose in its financial statements its resources from the UN regular budget and the related expenditure; establish a working group for implementing the International Public Sector Accounting Standards and the enterprise resource planning system; justify amounts relating to non-expendable property and reconcile them with values provided by physical inventories; and consider options for minimizing the manual processing done in the course of preparing financial statements.

UN-Habitat activities

In 2008, UN-Habitat continued to implement the key components of its work programme in line with Governing Council resolutions and the goals of the UN system and the international community. Under the Medium-term Strategic and Institutional Plan, approved by the Council in 2007 [YUN 2007, p. 1086], UN-Habitat focused on six key areas: effective advocacy, monitoring and partnerships; the promotion of participatory planning, management and governance; the promotion of pro-poor land and housing; environmentally sound basic infrastructure and services; strengthened human settlements finance systems; and excellence in management. Cooperation programmes and projects were being conducted in 50 countries, most of which were least developed countries. More than 20 other countries were benefitting from UN-Habitat global programmes.

During the year, the Advisory Group of Experts on decentralization met to develop a strategy for the implementation and follow-up to the guidelines on decentralization and the strengthening of local authorities, which were approved by the Governing Council in 2007 [YUN 2007, p. 1087]. UN-Habitat held regional consultative meetings with ministers for local government from Africa (Yaoundé, Cameroon, June) and Latin America and the Caribbean (Quito, Ecuador, July). With the support of France, and through close collaboration with the organization United Cities and Local Governments (UCLG), UN-Habitat continued to work with the UCLG Global Observatory of Local Democracy and Decentralization, focusing on the compilation of country profiles, which would enable countries to exchange information on their respective laws and local government. In response to a 2007 Council decision [YUN 2007, p. 1087], UN-Habitat established a group comprising experts and stakeholders to solicit inputs to the draft guidelines on access to basic services for all. A series of regional consultations culminated in a global meeting held on the occasion of the fourth session of the World Urban Forum (Nanjing, China, 3–6 November) (see p. 1181). The Opportunities Fund for Urban Youth-led Development was launched at the Forum. Under the UN-Habitat Youth Empowerment Programme, work continued in the Kibera slum and the Mavoko informal settlement in Nairobi to provide on-the-job training for youth through the construction of their own youth training centre. The centre would serve as a regional hub in Eastern Africa for innovative and appropriate technologies for building affordable housing.

Working relationships with the private sector marked a shift in 2008 as a result of the 2008–2013 Medium-term Strategic and Institutional Plan. UN-Habitat initiated new forms of global and national partnerships and cooperation with, among others, water utility companies and the real estate sector to develop new concepts for products and service delivery. Work intensified on the Human Settlements Financing Tools and Best Practices initiative, which documented and disseminated financing tools such as social investment funds, community-based housing finance and community mortgage programmes. UN-Habitat's joint activities with private sector companies sought to make use of the core competencies and comparative advantages of those companies. The objectives of such activities were to improve the living conditions of the urban poor and harness private sector capacity, knowledge and technology in support of actions aimed at mitigating and adapting to climate change.

The Slum Upgrading Facility pilot programme made progress in the selected pilot countries: Ghana, Indonesia, Sri Lanka and the United Republic of Tanzania. Innovative approaches in mobilizing formal commercial credit were being implemented to finance slum upgrading and low-income housing projects. UN-Habitat provided technical and substantive support for the second African Ministerial Conference on Housing and Urban Development (Abuja, Nigeria, 28–30 July); the Conference adopted the Abuja Resolution and an action plan that provided guidelines on financing housing, slum upgrading and urban development. UN-Habitat continued to provide technical assistance and advisory services to women's land access trusts in Ghana, Kenya, Uganda and Tanzania, and supported the formation of new land access trusts in Burundi, Ethiopia, Mozambique and Rwanda. Through its Global Land Tool Network, UN-Habitat worked with the International Federation of Surveyors to advocate the development of pro-poor and gender responsive land tools.

UN-Habitat continued to facilitate cooperation between domestic banks, municipal authorities and urban poor organizations to mobilize domestic capital, public investment and community savings for slum upgrading. Those efforts were supported by the establishment of the experimental reimbursable seeding operations facility in 2007 [YUN 2007, p. 1088]. UN-Habitat further expanded its partnerships with financial institutions, leveraging investment in basic urban infrastructure and services by aligning its pre-investment capacity-building services with the lending portfolios of international and regional development banks. In 2008, it concluded an arrangement with the Inter-American Development Bank to promote water quality, sanitation and hygiene education; the arrangement called for leveraging $10 million in technical assistance and institutional reform to yield up to $1 billion in annual investments.

The *State of the World's Cities 2008/2009* report, published by UN-Habitat in 2008, adopted the concept of "harmonious cities" as a theoretical framework for understanding the urban world and as an operational tool for confronting the most important challenges facing urban areas and their development. It focused on the key areas of spatial or regional harmony, social harmony and environmental harmony. The report stated, among other findings, that Governments played a critical role in determining the prosperity and growth of cities; high levels of urban inequality could be socially destabilizing and economically unsustainable; focused and targeted investments could significantly improve the lives of slum dwellers;

and cities provided opportunities to mitigate or even reverse the effects of global climate change, as they provided the economies of scale needed to reduce per capita costs and demand for resources.

Report to Permanent Forum on Indigenous Issues. In response to recommendations made by the Permanent Forum on Indigenous Issues at its fourth [YUN 2005, p. 881], fifth [YUN 2006, p. 935] and sixth [YUN 2007, p. 798] sessions, UN-Habitat issued a February report [E/C.19/2008/4/Add.7] on its activities related to the rights and needs of indigenous peoples. In response to an invitation made by the 2007 International Expert Group Meeting on Urban Indigenous People and Migration [ibid., p. 1090], UN-Habitat began to coordinate the elaboration of policy guidelines for Governments and local authorities to assist in developing public policies related to the challenges faced by indigenous peoples in urban areas, as agreed by the Permanent Forum and the Inter-Agency Support Group on Indigenous Issues in 2007. The policy guidelines would be developed for the following thematic areas: employment and local economic development; education; health; transition/settlement services; cultural and linguistic continuity/identities/ethnic mobility; human security, particularly for indigenous women and youth; and housing. The first of the planned series of policy guides—on housing—was expected to contribute to the realization of indigenous peoples' housing rights and secure tenure in the urban setting. Several UN-Habitat policy instruments and programme activities were relevant to the area of indigenous peoples, climate change challenges and mitigation. Those included the Global Campaign for Sustainable Urbanization and the advocacy work of the Sustainable Urban Development Network. In response to the 2007 decision of the UN-Habitat Governing Council on the sustainable development of Arctic cities [YUN 2007, p. 1087], UN-Habitat was exploring partnerships with the Arctic Council and other stakeholders on climate change issues and impacts on Arctic communities, which were largely made up of indigenous peoples.

World Urban Forum. UN-Habitat convened the fourth session of the World Urban Forum (Nanjing, China, 3–6 November) [HSP/GC/22/INF/2] on the theme "harmonious urbanization". Attended by approximately 8,000 participants from 155 countries, the Forum underscored the need for policies and interventions to ensure that the growing numbers of urban poor were not left behind, and stressed the link between overcoming urban poverty and addressing climate change. There was wide agreement that attaining the MDGs would greatly contribute to improvements in the area of affordable housing and that Governments had to provide better support for cities and local authorities in the quest for safer, cleaner, greener and inclusive cities with affordable housing for all. The private sector needed to be encouraged to do more for the urban communities in which it operated. The Forum reinforced and firmly established several of the main pillars of the UN-Habitat 2008–2013 Medium-term Institutional and Strategic Plan, including the centrality of partnerships, governance, affordable housing and services, and strengthening housing finance systems for sustainable urbanization. Accordingly, the Forum's recommendations were to be used to guide UN-Habitat activities under the Plan. The fifth session of the Forum would be held in Rio de Janeiro, Brazil, in 2010.

Cooperation with UNEP

A report of the Executive Director [HSP/GC/22/2/Add.4] contained the joint report of the Executive Directors of UN-Habitat and UNEP on progress made in the 2007–2008 period to strengthen cooperation between the Programmes.

Other matters

OIOS report

In response to a decision of the twenty-second (1982) session of the Committee for Programme and Coordination (CPC) [YUN 1982, p. 1441], the Office of Internal Oversight Services (OIOS) in March submitted a report [E/AC.51/2008/3] on the triennial review of the implementation of recommendations made in its 2005 report on the in-depth evaluation of UN-Habitat [YUN 2005, p. 1172], as endorsed by CPC [ibid.] and by the General Assembly in resolution 60/257 [YUN 2006, p. 1639]. OIOS found that UN-Habitat had implemented all 12 endorsed recommendations. Many of the recommendations were addressed, either entirely or in part, through the UN-Habitat comprehensive strategic planning process and the development of the 2008–2013 Medium-term Strategic and Institutional Plan, approved by the Governing Council in 2007 [YUN 2007, p. 1086].

Chapter VIII

Population

In 2008, world population stood at 6.8 billion, and was projected to reach 9 billion in 2045 if fertility levels continued to decline in developing countries. While 53 developed countries had fertility below that needed to ensure the replacement of generations, 42 developing countries—many of them least developed—had total fertility above 4.0 children per woman. In addition, population was shifting. For the first time in history, there were more urban dwellers than rural inhabitants, and urban dwellers were likely to compose 70 per cent of the world population by 2050.

UN population activities continued to be guided by the Programme of Action adopted at the 1994 International Conference on Population and Development (ICPD) and the key actions for its implementation adopted at the twenty-first special session of the General Assembly in 1999. The Commission on Population and Development—the body responsible for monitoring, reviewing and assessing implementation of the Programme of Action—considered as its special theme "Population distribution, urbanization, internal migration and development". The Population Division continued to analyse and report on world demographic trends and policies and to make its findings available in publications and on the Internet.

The United Nations Population Fund (UNFPA) assisted countries in implementing the ICPD agenda and the Millennium Development Goals through their use of population data to formulate sound policies and programmes. In 2008, UNFPA provided assistance to 158 countries, areas and territories, with emphasis on increasing the availability and quality of reproductive health services, fighting gender discrimination and gender-based violence, formulating effective population policies and intensifying HIV prevention.

Follow-up to 1994 Conference on Population and Development

Implementation of Programme of Action

Commission on Population and Development

At its forty-first session (New York, 13 April 2007 and 7–11 April 2008) [E/2008/25], the Commission on Population and Development considered as its special theme "Population, distribution, urbanization, internal migration and development." It discussed follow-up actions to the recommendations of the 1994 International Conference on Population and Development (ICPD) [YUN 1994, p. 955], and adopted a resolution [E/2008/25 (res. 2008/1)] on national, regional and international action relating to its special theme.

Documents before the Commission included the report of its Bureau on its intersessional meetings (New York, 16 October and 11 December 2007 and Sofia, Bulgaria, 14–15 January 2008) [E/CN.9/2008/2], and reports by the Secretary-General on: world population monitoring [E/CN.9/2008/3 & Corr.1] (see p. 1183); monitoring of population programmes [E/CN.9/2008/4] (see p. 1189); and flow of financial resources for assisting in the implementation of the ICPD Programme of Action, [E/CN.9/2008/5] (see p. 1184). It also had before it statements by three non-governmental organizations (NGOs) in consultative status with the Economic and Social Council: International Planned Parenthood Federation [E/CN.9/2008/NGO/1]; World Youth Alliance [E/CN.9/2008/NGO/2]; and Population Action International [E/CN.9/2008/NGO/3].

The Commission adopted and brought to the Economic and Social Council's attention a resolution on population distribution, urbanization, internal migration and development [E/2008/25 (res. 2008/1)] (see p. 1184). The Commission decided that the special theme for its forty-third (2010) session would be "Health, morbidity, mortality and development" [dec. 2008/101].

The Commission took note [dec. 2008/102] of the Secretary General's report on programme implementation and progress of work in the field of population in 2007: Population Division of the Department of Economic and Social Affairs [E/CN.9/2008/6], and of his note on the proposed strategic framework for the period 2010–2011 with respect to population [E/CN.9/2008/7]. It also recommended to the Council the draft provisional agenda for its forty-second (2009) session.

By **decision 2008/240** of 23 July, the Economic and Social Council took note of the report of the Commission on Population and Development on its forty-first (2008) session and approved the provisional agenda for the Commission's forty-second (2009) session.

In preparation for its forty-second session, the Commission's Bureau held two meetings in 2008 (New York, 21 October and 15 December) [E/CN.9/2009/2].

Population distribution, urbanization, internal migration and development

The Secretary-General's report on world population monitoring, focusing on population distribution, urbanization, internal migration and development [E/CN.9/2008/3 & Corr.1] reviewed trends in and prospects for urban and rural population growth and changes in the population of cities. It found that between 1920 and 2007, the world's urban population increased from about 270 million to 3.3 billion, with 1.5 billion urban dwellers added to Asia, 750 million to the more developed regions, just under 450 million to Latin America and the Caribbean, and just over 350 million to Africa. Between 2007 and 2050, the urban population was expected to increase almost as much as it did from 1920 to 2007: up to 3.1 billion additional urban dwellers by 2050, including 1.8 billion in Asia and 900 billion in Africa.

By one estimate, 80 per cent of the world's gross domestic product (GDP) was generated by urban areas. As cities attracted businesses and jobs, they became magnets for migrants seeking better opportunities, bringing together both the human and the entrepreneurial resources to generate new ideas, innovations and increasingly productive uses of technology. At the macro level, there was a positive correlation between per capita income and level of urbanization, and all the evidence indicated that people benefited from living in urban areas. Average urban incomes were generally higher than those in rural areas. However, despite its many positive facets, urbanization was not without its ills. Large cities, in particular, were prone to suffer from environmental contamination stemming from traffic congestion, the concentration of industry and inadequate waste disposal systems. In addition, income inequality in the cities of developing countries was stark, and it was increasing. According to the United Nations Human Settlements Programme (UN-Habitat), 840 million people lived in slums in 2005. In 2004, more than 600 million urban dwellers lacked access to improved sanitation and 180 million lacked access to an improved water source.

In 2007, 19 urban agglomerations qualified as megacities, having at least 10 million inhabitants. The most populous, Tokyo, had nearly 36 million inhabitants. Asia had 10 other megacities, while Latin America had four, North America two and Africa and Europe one each. The next tier of large cities, with populations ranging from 5 million to just under 10 million, numbered 31 in 2005 and was expected to number 48 in 2025, while accounting for just 7 per cent of the urban population. Cities with fewer than 5 million inhabitants but more than a million were considerably more numerous (361 in 2005, increasing to 526 in 2025) and accounted for 22 per cent of the urban population in 2005. All those categories together accounted for 48 per cent of the urban population, implying that smaller cities comprised over half of that population.

At the world level, poverty remained concentrated in rural areas, with 75 per cent of the poor living in rural areas in 2002. Although there were important regional differences, overall, the percentage of poor living at under $1 a day in urban areas declined from 14 per cent in 1993 to 13 per cent in 2002, whereas it declined from 37 to 30 per cent in rural areas. In general, the prevalence of poverty tended to be lower at higher levels of urbanization, and the difference between urban and rural poverty tended to decline with rising urbanization. Thus, by contributing to aggregate economic growth, urbanization played a positive role in overall poverty reduction.

Infant and child mortality were on average higher in rural than in urban areas, owing in large part to better urban public infrastructure, higher levels of maternal education and better access to health care in cities. Urban children overall were healthier on average than rural children. However, those in poor urban families were generally worse off than other urban children and, in some cases, even worse off than rural children.

A subsequent report of the Secretary-General [E/CN.9/2009/6] reviewed world demographic trends and prospects. It noted that as at 2008, world population was 6.8 billion, and was projected to reach 9 billion by 2045 if fertility levels continued to decline in developing countries. As a consequence of varying levels, high population growth was expected in several developing countries, while the population of developed countries would grow little, if at all. In 2008, 86 countries, including 53 developed countries, had fertility below that needed to ensure the replacement of generations, while 42 developing countries, many of which were least developed countries (LDCs), had total fertility above 4.0 children per woman. Because of the prevailing low fertility in the more developed regions, international migration accounted for 75 per cent of population growth in those regions in 2000–2005. If current trends continued, net migration would account for virtually all their growth from 2010 to 2030.

In most of the world, longevity continued to increase, and life expectancy was estimated at 67.2 years globally—averaging 76.5 years in the more developed regions and 65.4 in the less developed regions. In LDCs, two thirds of which were severely affected by the HIV/AIDS epidemic, life expectancy averaged a low 54.6 years. In the future, the population would be older and more urban, and, globally, the number of persons aged 60 or over would almost triple, reaching 2 billion in 2050.

Another later report of the Secretary-General [E/CN.9/2009/3] monitored world population, focusing on the contribution of the ICPD Programme of Action to the internationally agreed development goals, including the Millennium Development Goals (MDGs). It reviewed the goals related to population and health (in particular to reducing child and maternal mortality, ensuring reproductive health, combating malaria, and controlling the HIV/AIDS epidemic) and also considered the other main development goals—eradicating extreme poverty and hunger; achieving universal education; ensuring reproductive health; promoting gender equality and empowering women; and ensuring environmental sustainability. The report noted that the Programme of Action could make a significant contribution to the achievement of the Goals. However, gaps in its implementation were particularly common in LDCs, especially in sub-Saharan Africa, and population growth remained high in many low-income countries, imposing increasing demands on resources and reducing the capacity of Governments to respond to new challenges.

Commission action. The Commission brought its resolution on national, regional and international action on the subject of population, distribution, urbanization, internal migration and development [E/2008/25 (res. 2008/1)] to the attention of the Economic and Social Council. It recognized that the world population was undergoing an unprecedented transformation from being mostly rural to predominantly urban, with major disparities in the level of urbanization remaining among regions and countries; and that the rapid urbanization required integrated and participatory approaches to spatial management, including coordinated action between national Governments and local authorities with the support of the international community.

The Commission urged Governments to promote linkages between urban and rural areas in recognition of their economic, social and environmental interdependence and to take prompt, forward-looking and sustained action to ensure that urban growth and internal migration had a positive impact on economic growth, poverty eradication and environmental sustainability. It urged Governments to improve the plight of the urban poor and promote the integration of internal migrants form rural to urban areas, and called upon the international community to support the efforts of developing countries to build their capacities to respond to the challenges and opportunities of migration and urban growth.

Financial resources

In accordance with General Assembly resolutions 49/128 [YUN 1994, p. 963] and 50/124 [YUN 1995, p. 1094], the Secretary-General submitted to the Commission a report [E/CN.9/2009/5] on the flow of financial resources for assisting in the implementation of the ICPD Programme of Action. The report examined expected levels of donor and domestic expenditures for population activities in developing countries for 2007, and provided estimates for population expenditures in 2008 and projections for 2009. It stated that donor assistance had been increasing steadily over the past few years, reaching $7.4 billion in 2006, and that it was expected to surpass $8 billion in 2007 and further increase to $11 billion over the following two years.

A rough estimate of resources mobilized by developing countries, as a group, was projected at $18.5 billion for 2007. However, given the global financial crisis, it was uncertain whether countries would continue to increase funding levels for population. Overall funding was still significantly less than necessary to meet the ICPD targets agreed upon in 1994, when no one had foreseen the escalation of the AIDS pandemic. The challenge before the international community was to continue to mobilize sufficient resources to meet needs with respect to family planning services; reproductive health services; sexually transmitted diseases, including HIV/AIDS; and basic research, data and population and development policy analysis.

Fifteenth anniversary of ICPD

GENERAL ASSEMBLY ACTION

On 3 November [meeting 36], the General Assembly adopted **resolution 63/9** [draft: A/63/L.15 & Add.1] without vote [agenda item 44].

Commemoration of the fifteenth anniversary of the International Conference on Population and Development

The General Assembly,

Considering that 2009 will mark the fifteenth anniversary of the International Conference on Population and Development, held in Cairo from 5 to 13 September 1994,

Decides to devote one day, during its sixty-fourth session, to the commemoration of the fifteenth anniversary of the International Conference on Population and Development.

International migration and development

In response to General Assembly resolution 61/208 [YUN 2006, p. 1262], the Secretary-General submitted an August report on international migration and development [A/63/265 & Corr.1] to provide a basis for the consideration of possible options for the follow-up to the 2006 High-level Dialogue on International Migration and Development [YUN 2006, p. 1261]. The report, prepared by the Population Division, assessed the activities of all relevant bodies, agencies, funds and programmes of the UN system and other international and regional organizations in addressing international migration and development, and included an evaluation of cooperation mechanisms among Governments with respect to including development considerations in their regional and interregional mechanisms.

Global Forum meeting. The second Global Forum on Migration and Development (Manila, Philippines, 27–30 October) was held on the theme "Protecting and Empowering Migrants for Development". It included a meeting of civil society (27–28 October), followed by an intergovernmental meeting (29–30 October). At the former, 220 representatives of civil society—including NGOs, trade unions, faith-based organizations and academics—adopted recommendations to the latter. Those included considering the benefits of migration and resisting the temptation to cut migrant numbers in the current economic circumstances; recognizing the need to develop a global architecture, ensuring a rights-based approach to migration; and reaffirming the commitment to development through realizing the MDGs and giving priority to full employment and decent work.

The intergovernmental meeting gathered 1,130 delegates representing 163 Member States and UN observers. Round tables considered migration, development and human rights; secure, regular migration to achieve a stronger development impact; and policy and institutional coherence and partnerships. The ensuing deliberations yielded 33 practical recommendations and possible follow-up actions.

Seventh Meeting on International Migration and Development. The UN Population Division, in response to Assembly resolution 58/208 [YUN 2003, p. 1087], held the Seventh Coordination Meeting on International Migration and Development on 20–21 November in New York. Its main objectives included discussing the follow-up to the High-level Dialogue on International Migration and Development, assessing the consequences of the financial and economic crisis, and exchanging information on current and planned activities. Other conferences, meetings and forums on the subject included an Expert Group Meeting on Emerging Issues on International Migration and Development in Asia and the Pacific (Bangkok, Thailand, 20–21 September), and an Asia-Pacific High-level Meeting on International Migration and Development (Bangkok, 22–23 September).

GENERAL ASSEMBLY ACTION

On 20 June [meeting 109], the General Assembly adopted **resolution 62/270** [draft: A/62/L.25/Rev.2 & Add.1] by recorded vote (86-2-55) [agenda item 116].

Global Forum on Migration and Development

The General Assembly,

Recalling that the 2005 World Summit Outcome acknowledged the important nexus between international migration and development and the need to deal with the challenges and opportunities that migration presents and reaffirmed the resolve to take measures to ensure respect for and protection of the human rights of migrants, migrant workers and members of their families,

Considering that the summary of the High-level Dialogue on International Migration and Development, held in New York on 14 and 15 September 2006, as contained in a note by the President of the General Assembly, underlined the close link between migration, development and human rights, as well as the fact that respect for the human rights and fundamental freedoms of all migrants was essential for taking advantage of the positive aspects of international migration,

Recalling its resolutions 61/208 of 20 December 2006 on international migration and development and 62/156 of 18 December 2007 on the protection of migrants,

Stressing the need to promote a comprehensive and coherent discussion on all aspects of the phenomenon of migration, taking into account its importance on the global agenda,

Recognizing the need for Member States to consider the multidimensional aspects of international migration and development, in order to identify appropriate ways and means of dealing with the challenges and opportunities that international migration presents,

Recalling the important contribution provided by migrants and migration to development, as well as the interrelationship between migration and development, and the importance of including the perspective of the human rights of migrants as a priority matter in relevant debates and discussions that are held in the United Nations system,

Considering that the report of the Secretary-General of 18 May 2006 on international migration and development, prepared pursuant to General Assembly resolutions 59/241 of 22 December 2004 and 60/227 of 23 December 2005, highlighted the fact that, within the United Nations system, there is no entity mandated to systematically address all matters related to international migration,

Recalling that Member States participating in the High-level Dialogue on International Migration and Development expressed interest in continuing the dialogue on migration and development, and that there was widespread support for the proposal of the Secretary-General to create a global forum to address, in depth and in a systematic manner, all topics related to international migration and development,

Taking note of the summary report of the first meeting of the Global Forum on Migration and Development, held in Brussels from 9 to 11 July 2007 under the auspices of the Government of Belgium, and the generous offer of the Government of the Philippines to host the second meeting, from 27 to 30 October 2008, in Manila,

Noting with appreciation that the convening of the first meeting of the Global Forum on Migration and Development has already resulted in the establishment of official focal points on migration and development at the national level,

Recognizing that the Global Forum on Migration and Development currently functions under the Guiding Principles of the Forum of 2007 and as a State-led initiative, and that it should be strengthened with the aim of addressing the multidimensional aspects of international migration and development with a comprehensive approach,

1. *Recognizes* that exchanges of information and expertise, consultation and closer cooperation between the Global Forum on Migration and Development and the United Nations could have a positive impact, and in this regard:

(a) Welcomes the transmission to the Secretary-General by the Government of Belgium of the summary report of the first meeting of the Global Forum on Migration and Development, circulated as a document of the General Assembly, and invites organizers of subsequent meetings of the Forum to continue this practice;

(b) Requests the Secretary-General to include in his report called for in resolution 61/208 an evaluation of the existing cooperation mechanisms on migration and development and to make it available to the Global Forum on Migration and Development, at its second meeting, in 2008;

(c) Encourages Member States to participate actively in, and the organizations that are members of the Global Migration Group, within their respective areas of expertise, to contribute and to provide technical support to, the Global Forum on Migration and Development;

(d) Notes that the Global Forum on Migration and Development, through its Steering Group, maintains links with the Secretary-General, notably through his Special Representative on International Migration and Development;

2. *Takes note with interest* of the agenda prepared for the discussions of the Global Forum on Migration and Development, and the title of the second meeting of the Global Forum, "Protecting and empowering migrants for development", and particularly welcomes the inclusion of the topic of the human rights of migrants;

3. *Requests* the Secretary-General to submit to the General Assembly at its sixty-third session a report on the implementation of the present resolution.

RECORDED VOTE ON RESOLUTION 62/270:

In favour: Afghanistan, Albania, Algeria, Angola, Antigua and Barbuda, Argentina, Armenia, Azerbaijan, Bahrain, Bangladesh, Barbados, Belarus, Bolivia, Brazil, Burkina Faso, Cameroon, Chile, China, Colombia, Comoros, Congo, Costa Rica, Côte d'Ivoire, Cuba, Democratic People's Republic of Korea, Dominican Republic, Ecuador, Egypt, El Salvador, Ethiopia, Fiji, Ghana, Guatemala, Guinea-Bissau, Guyana, Haiti, Honduras, India, Iraq, Israel, Jamaica, Jordan, Kazakhstan, Kenya, Kuwait, Kyrgyzstan, Lebanon, Lesotho, Libyan Arab Jamahiriya, Madagascar, Malawi, Maldives, Mali, Mauritania, Mauritius, Mexico, Mongolia, Morocco, Mozambique, Nepal, Nicaragua, Niger, Nigeria, Oman, Pakistan, Panama, Paraguay, Peru, Qatar, Rwanda, Saudi Arabia, Senegal, South Africa, Sri Lanka, Sudan, Suriname, Syrian Arab Republic, Tajikistan, Togo, Tunisia, United Arab Emirates, Uruguay, Venezuela, Yemen, Zambia, Zimbabwe.

Against: Canada, United States.

Abstaining: Andorra, Australia, Austria, Bahamas, Belgium, Bosnia and Herzegovina, Brunei Darussalam, Bulgaria, Croatia, Cyprus, Czech Republic, Denmark, Estonia, Finland, France, Germany, Greece, Hungary, Iceland, Indonesia, Ireland, Italy, Japan, Latvia, Liechtenstein, Lithuania, Luxembourg, Malaysia, Malta, Moldova, Monaco, Myanmar, Namibia, Netherlands, New Zealand, Norway, Philippines, Poland, Portugal, Republic of Korea, Romania, Russian Federation, San Marino, Serbia, Singapore, Slovakia, Slovenia, Spain, Sweden, Switzerland, Thailand, The former Yugoslav Republic of Macedonia, Turkey, Ukraine, United Kingdom.

On 19 December [meeting 72], the Assembly, on the recommendation of the Second (Economic and Financial) Committee [A/63/416/Add.2], adopted **resolution 63/225** without vote [agenda item 51 *(b)*].

International migration and development

The General Assembly,

Recalling its resolutions 58/208 of 23 December 2003, 59/241 of 22 December 2004, 60/227 of 23 December 2005, 60/206 of 22 December 2005 on the facilitation and reduction of the cost of transfer of migrant remittances, 62/156 of 18 December 2007 on the protection of migrants, 62/270 of 20 June 2008 on the Global Forum on Migration and Development and 61/208 of 20 December 2006 on international migration and development,

Recalling also the 2005 World Summit Outcome and its resolution 60/265 of 30 June 2006 on the follow-up to the development outcome of the 2005 World Summit, including the Millennium Development Goals and the other internationally agreed development goals, and taking note of the Doha Declaration on Financing for Development, adopted on 2 December 2008,

Recalling further its resolution 57/270 B of 23 June 2003 on the integrated and coordinated implementation of and follow-up to the outcomes of the major United Nations conferences and summits in the economic and social fields,

Reaffirming the Universal Declaration of Human Rights, and recalling the International Covenant on Civil and Political Rights, the International Covenant on Economic, Social and Cultural Rights, the International Convention on the Elimination of All Forms of Racial Discrimination, the Convention on the Elimination of All Forms of Discrimination against Women, and the Convention on the Rights of the Child,

Recalling the International Convention on the Protection of the Rights of All Migrant Workers and Members of Their Families, and the invitation to Member States that have not yet done so to consider signing and ratifying or acceding to the Convention,

Recalling also the importance of the decent work agenda of the International Labour Organization, including for migrant workers, and the eight fundamental Conventions of the International Labour Organization,

Recalling further Commission on Population and Development resolution 2006/2 of 10 May 2006,

Bearing in mind the summary by the President of the General Assembly of the 2006 High-level Dialogue on International Migration and Development,

Acknowledging that the High-level Dialogue on International Migration and Development provided a useful opportunity to address constructively the issue of international migration and development and heightened awareness of the issue,

Acknowledging also the important nexus between international migration and development and the need to deal with the challenges and opportunities that migration presents to countries of origin, transit and destination, and recognizing that migration brings benefits as well as challenges to the global community,

Acknowledging further the important contribution provided by migrants and migration to development, as well as the complex interrelationship between migration and development,

Recognizing that remittance flows constitute sources of private capital and that remittances have increased over time, complement domestic savings and are instrumental in improving the well-being of recipients,

1. *Takes note* of the report of the Secretary-General;

2. *Encourages* efforts by Member States and the international community to promote a balanced, coherent and comprehensive approach to international migration and development, particularly by building partnerships and ensuring coordinated action to develop capacities, including for the management of migration;

3. *Emphasizes* that respect for the human rights and fundamental freedoms of all migrants is essential for reaping the benefits of international migration;

4. *Recognizes with appreciation* the important contribution made by migrants and migration to development in countries of origin and destination;

5. *Takes note* of the Global Forum on Migration and Development, which held its first meeting in Brussels from 9 to 11 July 2007, and its second meeting in Manila from 27 to 30 October 2008, as an informal, voluntary, open, State-led initiative, and also takes note of the generous offer of the Government of Greece to host the third meeting of the Global Forum, to be held in Athens on 4 and 5 November 2009, as well as the offers of other Governments to hold subsequent meetings of the Forum;

6. *Invites* the countries of origin and destination, in accordance with domestic legislation, to undertake appropriate measures to facilitate the contribution of migrants and migrant communities to the development of their countries of origin;

7. *Recognizes* the need for Member States to continue considering the multidimensional aspects of international migration and development in order to identify appropriate ways and means of maximizing the development benefits and minimizing the negative impacts;

8. *Reaffirms* that there is a need to address and promote conditions for cheaper, faster and safer transfers of remittances in both source and recipient countries and, as appropriate, to encourage opportunities for development-oriented investment in recipient countries by beneficiaries that are willing and able to undertake such action, bearing in mind that remittances cannot be considered a substitute for foreign direct investment, official development assistance, debt relief or other public sources of financing for development;

9. *Reiterates* the need to consider how the migration of highly skilled persons and those with advanced education affects the development efforts of developing countries;

10. *Acknowledges* the need to analyse the impact of certain forms of temporary migration, circular migration and return migration on the development of countries of origin, transit and destination, as well as on migrants themselves;

11. *Urges* Member States and relevant international organizations to incorporate a gender perspective in all policies and programmes on international migration in order to, inter alia, reinforce the positive contributions that migrant women can make to the economic, social and human development of their countries of origin and their host countries, and to strengthen the protection of women migrants from all forms of violence, discrimination, trafficking, exploitation and abuse by promoting their rights and welfare, while recognizing in this regard the importance of joint and collaborative approaches and strategies at the bilateral, regional, interregional and international levels;

12. *Requests* all Member States, in accordance with their relevant international obligations and commitments, to promote cooperation at all levels in addressing the challenge of undocumented or irregular migration so as to foster a secure, regular and orderly process of migration;

13. *Calls upon* all relevant bodies, agencies, funds and programmes of the United Nations system, and other relevant intergovernmental, regional and subregional organizations, including the Global Migration Group, within their respective mandates, to continue to address the issue of international migration and development, with a view to integrating migration issues, including a gender perspective and cultural diversity, in a more coherent way, within the context of the implementation of the internationally agreed development goals, including the Millennium Development Goals, and with respect for human rights;

14. *Calls upon* the United Nations system and other relevant international organizations and multilateral institutions to enhance their cooperation in the development of methodologies for the collection and processing of statistical data on international migration and the situation of migrants in countries of origin, transit and destination and to assist Member States in their capacity-building efforts in this regard;

15. *Encourages* the United Nations system and other relevant international organizations to support developing countries in their efforts to address migration issues within their respective development strategies in the context of the implementation of the internationally agreed development goals, including the Millennium Development Goals;

16. *Decides* to hold, within existing resources, a High-level Dialogue on International Migration and Development during its sixty-eighth session, in 2013, the focus and modalities of which will be decided upon at its sixty-seventh session;

17. *Also decides* to convene, within existing resources, at its sixty-fifth session, in 2011, a one-day informal thematic debate on international migration and development;

18. *Further decides* to include in the provisional agenda of its sixty-fifth session the sub-item entitled "International migration and development";

19. *Invites* the regional commissions to examine regional aspects of international migration and development and to provide inputs, in accordance with the respective mandates and within existing resources, to the report of the Secretary-General on this item;

20. *Requests* the Secretary-General to submit to the General Assembly at its sixty-fifth session a report on the implementation of the present resolution.

United Nations Population Fund

2008 activities

Reports of Executive Director. A report by the Executive Director of the United Nations Population Fund (UNFPA) [DP/FPA/2009/2 (Part I)] reviewed major initiatives undertaken by UNFPA in 2008 in implementing its strategic plan for 2008–2011. In analysing progress made and challenges encountered in helping countries implement the Programme of Action of the International Conference on Population and Development (ICPD), the report used both a development results framework and a management results framework. It focused on the Fund's efforts to help countries achieve their nationally owned development objectives in the interrelated areas of population and development, reproductive health and rights, and gender equality.

The year 2008 was marked by an extraordinary outbreak of food, fuel and financial crises that disproportionately affected the most vulnerable groups, particularly women and girls. The financial crisis resulted in a significant economic downturn worldwide. It was estimated that one third of all developing countries, mostly in Africa and Asia, were highly exposed to its effects on poverty. In this context, UNFPA continued to contribute to a better understanding of the links between population, poverty, environment and climate change. Climate change and poverty, in particular, had increased the potential for both in-country and cross-border migration, since affected populations were often forced to move to less disaster-prone and more productive areas to seek new opportunities.

The year also marked the transition of UNFPA to its new organizational structure in support of more effective country operations, including the establishment of subregional and regional offices in Africa, Asia and the Pacific, and Latin America and the Caribbean. The Arab States regional office and the office for Eastern Europe and Central Asia were temporarily operating out of UNFPA headquarters while their premises were made ready to open in 2009.

As to management, 88 per cent of UNFPA country offices reported that at least 75 per cent of the year's work plan outputs were achieved. Country offices reported numerous knowledge-sharing initiatives, as well as 189 South-South initiatives. All 121 country reports cited strategic partnerships and collaboration with a broad range of partners, including women's and human rights institutions, parliamentarians and the private sector, as well as youth, faith-based and community organizations. The Fund participated in 224 joint programmes with UN agencies covering all the UNFPA strategic plan outcome areas. The top three areas of those programmes were HIV/AIDS, gender-based violence and maternal health.

Significant measures were adopted to improve accountability, including the establishment of an Ethics Office and the introduction of mandatory ethics training for all staff. At the global level, UNFPA exceeded its resource mobilization target by $13 million for regular resources raised and $122 million for co-financing. Overall, the Fund's reorganization helped UNFPA become a stronger field-focused organization.

An addendum to the Executive Director's report [DP/FPA/2009/2 (Part I)/Add.1] provided a statistical and financial review for the year. It stated that from 2007 to 2008, total UNFPA income increased by $93.1 million, or 12.4 per cent, to $845.3 million. UNFPA resources surpassed the $500 million level for the fifth sequential year, including $469.5 million in regular resources—the highest total ever in the Fund's history. Regular resource contribution income increased by $9.8 million, or 2.3 per cent, and total expenditures by $72.9 million, or 11.6 per cent, to $701.9 million. Of that increase, $51.4 million (70.5 per cent) was attributable to increased programme activities. UNFPA closed the year in robust financial health.

UNDP/UNFPA Executive Board. The UNFPA Executive Director reported, jointly with the Administrator of the United Nations Development Programme (UNDP), to the Economic and Social Council on the Organization's triennial comprehensive policy review of operational activities for development [E/2009/5]. They said that an unprecedented UN system-wide collaboration at the country and regional levels was used to respond to the knowledge-sharing and management endeavours envisaged in the triennial comprehensive policy review, 2007.

By encouraging eight pilot country teams to implement agreed reforms, and allowing broad latitude to innovate "as one United Nations team" [YUN 2006, p. 1584], the pilot countries accelerated the pace of change and demonstrated the potential for a more coherent UN system. UNDP and UNFPA supported the design of a local area network and a wide area network for a "Delivering as one" pilot initiative in Mozambique, and the same design was proposed for Tanzania. The result was a decrease in fragmentation, duplication and internal UN competition for resources, and strengthened Government leadership, ownership and alignment with national priorities. The programmes also ensured that Governments had full access to the experience and expertise of the wider UN system.

A key initiative of 2008 was the harmonization of financial regulations and rules among UNDP, the United Nations Children's Fund (UNICEF), UNFPA, the World Food Programme (WFP) and the United Nations. Drafts had been considered, and the final harmonized regulations and rules were to be reviewed by the governing bodies in 2009. UNDP, UNFPA and UNICEF also worked to increase harmonization in the areas of cost classification and results-based budgeting, and agreed on classifying costs as either programme (development) or support (management). UNDP, UNFPA, UNICEF and WFP continued implementing their harmonized approach to cash transfers across country offices, to the extent that 13 countries were fully compliant with that approach and many others were partially compliant.

UNFPA strengthened its South-South cooperation initiatives in census and population surveys, the delivery of reproductive health services, development of training modules, and research in population and development. The Fund took the lead, with the Joint United Nations Programme on HIV/AIDS (UNAIDS) and the UN Department of Peacekeeping Operations, drafting guidelines on HIV/AIDS with respect to disarmament, demobilization and reintegration. It also led efforts to ensure that reproductive health and gender issues were incorporated in all disarmament, demobilization and reintegration guidelines.

On 20 June [E/2008/35 (dec. 2008/9)], the UNDP/UNFPA Executive Board, at its annual session (Geneva, 16–27 June), took note of the reports of the UNFPA Executive Director for 2007 [DP/FPA/2008/5 (Part I & Add.1, Part II)]. It urged UNFPA to continue to improve results-based management indicators and baselines.

By **decision 2008/215** of 18 July, the Economic and Social Council took note of the annual report of the UNDP/UNFPA Executive Board [E/2007/35] and of the joint report of the UNDP Administrator and the UNFPA Executive Director to the Economic and Social Council [E/2008/5].

Report of Secretary-General. The Secretary-General in January submitted to the Commission on Population and Development a report on monitoring population programmes, focusing on population distribution, urbanization, internal migration and development [E/CN.9/2008/4]. The report covered the unprecedented transformation of world population from rural to urban, its economic, social, demographic and environmental implications, and UNFPA activities to assist countries in responding to the challenges of rapid urbanization.

The Fund's aim was to influence public policy in order to respond to these challenges, and to meet the needs of all persons, especially the poor and most vulnerable. To that end, it encouraged the inclusion of the urban poor in decision-making in matters that concerned them; advocated for the empowerment of women and their participation in sustainable urban development; and supported activities promoting access to basic social services, including health care, education, nutrition, water, sanitation and shelter for all.

UNFPA offered assistance in policy formulation—for example, in Benin, Ethiopia, Nigeria and Rwanda, where it supported the formulation of national population policies; in Sierra Leone, where it provided support for the review of its national policy, and in the Lao People's Democratic Republic, where it supported the revision of its national policy; in Cambodia, where it participated as an observer on a recently established inter-ministerial task force on migration; and in Burkina Faso, where it provided technical and financial support for convening a national symposium on migration.

UNFPA supported the collection of data and research for evidence-based policy formulation and programme implementation. Those included a League of Arab States project aimed at providing health ministries with an up-to-date databank on population, health and development, and technical and financial support for a study on internal migration in Bolivia. It supported Eritrea in conducting an urban census in 19 areas of the country, and Honduras in research on internal migration and its effects on labour market participation and poverty.

The Fund also promoted capacity-building by supporting training institutions and by providing technical assistance, which included training courses in Brazil for Government officials, academia and civil society relating to internal migration; scholarships in Mozambique for the Centre for Population Studies to build capacity in the area of migration and urbanization; and training for National Statistical Office staff and university researchers in Mauritania.

In its advocacy role, UNFPA promoted in the Caribbean the inclusion of population issues, including urbanization and internal migration, in development plans, strategies and frameworks. In Brazil, Eritrea, Honduras, Mauritania, the Russian Federation and Rwanda, it launched its *State of World Population 2007* to raise awareness about urbanization and migration. In Viet Nam, it supported the Parliament in conducting policy advocacy workshops for senior Government officials on the effect of current policies on migrants' rights and the linkages between migration and poverty reduction.

Population, development and poverty reduction

In 2008, UNFPA programme assistance in population and development totalled $68.9 million from regular resources and $55.1 million from other resources. The goal of UNFPA work in population and development was to improve quality of life and reduce poverty through the systematic use of population dynamics analyses to guide increased investments in the areas of gender equality, youth development, reproductive health and HIV/AIDS.

Among its activities, in Cameroon, Chad, the Congo and Côte d'Ivoire, UNFPA provided support to review their poverty reduction strategy papers. It also supported review of Armenia's poverty reduction strategy, and contributed to the development of socio-demographic information and analysis for Mexico's national population policy. In Honduras, UNFPA cooperated with other agencies in providing technical support for the national youth policy and for the strengthening of youth institutions. It provided technical and financial support for psychosocial services to young people in the Occupied Palestinian Territory, and supported implementation of an integrated sexual and reproductive health programme in a refugee camp in Namibia. In Myanmar, the Fund mobilized youth volunteers to help assemble and distribute hygiene kits to women and girls in the areas affected by Cyclone Nargis.

Support to 2010 census operations was a key priority area during 2008, including that for post-crisis census work in Botswana, the Congo, the Democratic Republic of the Congo, Kenya and Tajikistan. In Asia, support was provided in key areas such as census maps in Bangladesh, training of national statistics programmers in Indonesia, capacity-building for data analysis in the Lao People's Democratic Republic, and information technology and mapping software in Mongolia. In Latin America, UNFPA supported the presentation of population estimates and projections based on census data in Brazil, and the updating of rural digital cartography in the Dominican Republic.

The Fund provided technical support for the development and establishment of integrated national databases. In collaboration with the United Nations Programme on Ageing, regional training workshops were organized to strengthen the capacity of national focal points on ageing. In Albania and Ukraine, UNFPA collaborated with NGOs and private sector partners in developing an action plan in line with the 2002 Madrid International Plan of Action on Ageing [YUN 2002, p. 1194]. In Mongolia, it provided technical assistance in establishing a regional institute on ageing.

UNFPA chaired the Global Migration Group and coordinated its contribution to the Global Forum on Migration and Development. It also prepared the Secretary-General's report on the monitoring of population programmes. Together with the International Organization for Migration (IOM), it convened an Economic and Social Council ministerial roundtable meeting on migration, environment and climate change: the gender perspective. In several countries, it supported policy round tables and policy dialogues on climate change and population ageing.

Reproductive health and rights

In 2008, UNFPA programme assistance in the area of reproductive health totalled $165 million from regular resources and $135.5 million from other resources. Its efforts to address unmet need for family planning included policy dialogue and advocacy; communications; programming support, particularly for repositioning family planning; procurement and logistics management and information systems for contraceptives; training; and capacity development. Among its activities, UNFPA supported demand generation for family planning through a national campaign in Angola, and an initiative for working with religious communities to reach people at the grassroot levels in Kyrgyzstan.

During the year, global and regional initiatives contributed to strengthening capacity for the integration of demographic, gender and reproductive health issues into emergency preparedness, humanitarian response and transition. To that end, the ICPD Programme of Action was integrated into humanitarian assistance funding frameworks, including the Central Emergency Response Fund. In Albania, UNFPA supported the Government in developing antenatal standards and protocols; in Bangladesh, it supported the training of community-level skilled birth attendants with midwifery skills; and in Ethiopia, a country with one of the lowest rates of skilled birth attendance, it supported midwifery schools.

UNFPA collaborated with Columbia University to form an alliance to build capacity in national and regional institutions, focusing on emergency obstetric and newborn care. In the Sudan, it supported the creation of core teams of trainers to accelerate capacity-building; and in Azerbaijan, specialized centres for neonatal care were established at the community level through a UNFPA-brokered partnership between civil society, the Government and the private sector. With respect to modern contraceptive methods, the Fund, together with its partners, supported contraceptive procurement in several countries, including Madagascar, Panama and Turkmenistan. It also supported guidelines development and staff training for the provision of various contraceptive methods in Lesotho, Mongolia, Namibia, Nepal, Nigeria, Rwanda, Senegal, South Africa, Uganda and Zambia.

With respect to HIV prevention among young women and men, the Fund continued to strengthen support for youth participation and most-at-risk adolescents through various strategies. It supported data collection in Brazil, Iran, Pakistan, Syria and Ukraine, and youth-friendly service centres for young people on sexual and reproductive health in Nigeria, Tanzania and ten island countries in the Pacific region. In Ghana and Haiti, support continued for in- and out-of-school youth programmes. With gender inequality and unequal power relations between women and men continuing to be major drivers of HIV transmission, global and regional efforts did not sufficiently catalyse expanded country action. UNFPA supported work to reduce the overall vulnerability of women to HIV in more than 45 countries.

In Azerbaijan, Bangladesh, Burundi, Haiti, Kenya, Lesotho, Mali, Mozambique, Nigeria, Thailand, Uganda and Zambia, UNFPA and its partners provided support to the prevention of mother-to-child HIV transmission. The Fund supported family life education at secondary schools in the Niger, and adolescent sexual and reproductive health education programmes in all schools under the central board of secondary education in India. In the Russian Federation, it collaborated with UNAIDS and the Government on developing and piloting a curriculum on HIV prevention in secondary schools.

Gender equality and women's empowerment

In 2008, UNFPA continued to develop and implement policies and support programming for women's empowerment and gender equality by integrating human rights, gender mainstreaming and cultural sensitivity throughout its work. That three-pronged approach allowed for a more comprehensive strategy that was better able to take account of the socio-cultural realities that populations faced. UNFPA programme assistance in the area of gender totalled $35.6 million from regular resources and $23.5 million from other resources.

The Fund continued to follow up on Security Council resolution 1325 [YUN 2000, p. 1113] on women, peace and security in conflict and post-conflict situations. In Côte d'Ivoire, it supported an action plan to improve the health condition of women in post-conflict situations. In the Occupied Palestinian Territory, it formed women's coalitions and networks to improve the protection of women and girls. With other UN agencies, it supported Government efforts to implement the recommendations of the 1979 Convention on the Elimination of All Forms of Discrimination against Women [YUN 1979, p. 895], particularly those on reproductive rights and gender-based violence. In Nepal and Pakistan, it supported sensitization and advocacy efforts with members of the Constituent Assembly/Parliament.

Given the demonstrated value of encouraging men's positive roles in building gender equality and improving men's and women's health, UNFPA was active in promoting such involvement. It was a member of the steering committee of the Men Engage Alliance—a global alliance of NGOs and UN agencies that sought to engage boys and men to achieve gender equality—and was engaged in mobilizing faith-based organizations to that end. In Bangladesh, Ethiopia and Guatemala there were several instances where the capacity-building of faith-based organizations and advocacy with religious leaders led to noticeable changes in discourse around sexual and reproductive health issues, and in efforts to enhance related legislation.

In collaboration with UNICEF and other partners, UNFPA supported Governments in creating national mechanisms for accelerated abandonment of female genital mutilation/cutting. Those included the development of a national strategy and action plan in the Sudan, and the strengthening of legislation against the practice in Egypt. The Fund co-chaired the inter-agency task force on violence against women, and supported training and capacity development initiatives on gender-based violence in several countries, including Cambodia, Sudan, Swaziland and Turkey.

The Fund also supported efforts to strengthen the health sector's response to gender-based violence. Working with a number of partners, its initiatives included the development of manuals, protocols, guidelines and curricula on the issue in Albania, Botswana, China, Rwanda and Uganda; training service providers in Côte d'Ivoire, Mongolia, Nepal, South Africa and Zambia; advocacy and policy dialogue on integrating gender-based violence issues in health plans and programmes in Jordan; and medical kits to treat survivors in Guatemala. In Honduras, a model of integrated care for victims of gender-based violence was developed and implemented in 26 centres.

Country and intercountry programmes

UNFPA project expenditures for country, global and regional activities in 2008 totalled $340.5 million, compared to $273.6 million in 2007, according to the Executive Director's statistical and financial review [DP/FPA/2009/2 (Part I)/Add.1)]. The 2008 figure included $197.7 million for country programmes and $48 million for global and regional programmes. In accordance with the Executive Board's procedure for allocating resources [YUN 1996, p. 989], total expenditures in 2008 for countries most in need of assistance to realize ICPD goals amounted to $197.2 million, compared to $150.1 million in 2007.

Africa. Provisional data for UNFPA expenditures for programmes in sub-Saharan Africa gave a total of $141.3 million in 2008, compared to $95.3 million in 2007. Most of that amount went to reproductive health and family planning (64.7 per cent), followed by population and development (34.1 per cent), programme coordination and assistance (29 per cent) and gender equality and women's empowerment (13.5 per cent).

On 24 January [E/2008/35 (dec. 2008/8)], the UNDP/UNFPA Executive Board, at its first regular session of

2008 (New York, 21–28 January), approved UNFPA country programmes for the Democratic Republic of the Congo, Equatorial Guinea, Lesotho, Liberia, Madagascar, Rwanda and Togo. On 27 June [dec. 2008/25], it took note of the draft country programme documents for Benin, the Congo, the Niger and Nigeria, and approved the second one-year extension of the country programme for Burundi. On 19 September [dec. 2008/38], the Executive Board, at its second regular session of 2008 (New York, 8–12 and 19 September), approved the country programmes for Benin, the Congo, the Niger and Nigeria on a no-objection basis, and took note of the draft country programme documents for Angola, Côte d'Ivoire, Kenya and Mauritania.

Arab States. Provisional expenditures for UNFPA programmes in the Arab States totalled $26.2 million in 2008. Most of that amount was spent on reproductive health (47.7 per cent), followed by programme coordination and assistance (18.3 per cent), population and development (20.3 per cent), and gender equality and women's empowerment (13.7 per cent). In 2007, the combined expenditures for Arab States, Europe and Central Asia was $34.3 million. On 27 June [dec. 2008/25], the Executive Board approved the UNFPA country programme for Somalia and took note of the draft country programme document for the Sudan. On 19 September [dec. 2008/38], it approved the country programme for the Sudan on a no-objection basis and the third one-year extension of the country programme for Lebanon.

Eastern Europe and Central Asia. Provisional expenditures for UNFPA programmes in Eastern Europe and Central Asia totalled $15.1 million. Most of that amount was spent on reproductive health (47.7 per cent), followed by programme coordination and assistance (24.5 per cent), population and development (19.2 per cent), and gender equality and women's empowerment (8.6 per cent). On 27 June [dec. 2008/25], the Executive Board approved the two-year extension of the country programme for Pakistan and took note of the one-year extensions of the country programmes for Afghanistan, Ecuador and Guatemala.

Asia and the Pacific. Provisional expenditures for UNFPA programmes in Asia and the Pacific amounted to $85 million, compared to $79.5 million in 2007. Most of them went to reproductive health (66.7 per cent), followed by population and development (13.9 per cent), programme coordination and assistance (11.4 per cent), and gender equality and women's empowerment (8 per cent). On 24 January [dec. 2008/8], the Executive Board approved UNFPA country programmes for Nepal and the Pacific Island countries. On 19 September [dec. 2008/38], it took note of the draft country programme document for Timor-Leste.

Latin America and the Caribbean. Provisional expenditures for UNFPA programmes in Latin America and the Caribbean totalled $34.3 million, compared to $25.4 million in 2007. Most of the total went to reproductive health (43.4 per cent), followed by programme coordination and assistance (21.6 per cent), population and development (21.3 per cent), and gender equality and women's empowerment (13.7 per cent). On 24 January [dec. 2008/8], the Executive Board approved UNFPA country programmes for Colombia, Costa Rica, Mexico and Nicaragua. On 19 September [dec. 2008/38], it took note of the draft country programme documents for Haiti and Venezuela.

Global programme. Provisional expenditures for the UNFPA global programme totalled $40.9 million in 2008, compared to $42.3 million in 2007. Most of the total went to reproductive health (90.5 per cent), followed by gender equality and women's empowerment (5.4 per cent), and population and development (4.1 per cent).

Financial and management questions

Financing

UNFPA income from all sources totalled $845.3 million in 2008, compared to $752.2 million in 2007 [DP/FPA/2009/2 (Part I)/Add.1)], comprising $428.8 million from regular resources, $366.1 million from other contributions, interest income of $23.6 million and other income of $26.8 million. Expenditures totalled $701.9 million, up from $629 million in 2007, comprising $452.4 million related to regular resources and $249.5 million related to other resources, resulting in a net excess of $141.3 million after adjustments were made for prior periods.

On 24 January [E/2008/35 (dec. 2008/6)], the Executive Board approved gross resources in the amount of $259.8 million, representing the total UNFPA biennial support budget for 2008–2009 [DP/FPA/2008/1]. It also noted that, after offsetting an indirect cost recovery amount of $24 million, the estimated net resources totalled $235.8 million. Comments on the budget were made by the Advisory Committee on Administrative and Budgetary Questions (ACABQ) [DP/FPA/2008/2].

Internal audit and oversight

The Executive Director submitted to the UNDP/UNFPA Executive Board a report [DP/FPA/2008/3] on UNFPA follow-up to recommendations by the UN Board of Auditors for the 2004–2005 biennium [A/61/5/Add.7]. UNFPA reported that it had completed action on 33 recommendations and expected to complete implementation of all 42 recommendations by

January 2010. On 24 January [E/2008/35 (dec. 2008/8)], the Executive Board took note of the report.

The Executive Director reported on the internal audit and oversight activities carried out by UNFPA in 2007 [DP/FPA/2008/11]. Those included: management audits of 17 offices (nine in Africa, four in Latin America and the Caribbean, two in the Arab States, Europe and Central Asia, and two in the Asia and Pacific region). Based on the analysis of risks and the recurring types of audit recommendations, the main areas needing attention were business processes, national execution and human resource management. In other respects, the conclusions of the previous year's report [YUN 2007, p. 1100] remained valid.

On 26 June [E/2008/35 (dec. 2008/13)], the Executive Board, taking note of that report, welcomed the focus on key and recurrent management issues, the clarity and format of the recommendations, and the risk-based audit planning in the report, and requested that future such reports provide additional explanations of the significant audit results and their causes, identify the systemic issues of concern, and provide more information on quality improvements in the oversight systems of UNFPA.

The Executive Director reported to the Board on the Fund's oversight policy on 28 November 2007 [DP/FPA/2008/4] and 7 August 2008 [DP/FPA/2008/14]. On 24 January [E/2008/35 (dec. 2008/8)], the Board requested that the Executive Director revert to it on that matter at its second regular session in September, after consultations with the Board and taking into account the concerns of Member States. On 19 September [dec. 2008/37], the Board took note of the August 2008 report and approved the oversight policy contained therein, subject to the provisions of its decision.

Evaluation

In his biennial report on evaluation activities undertaken within UNFPA in 2006–2007 [DP/FPA/2008/10], the Executive Director stated that during that biennium, the Fund conducted 170 evaluations—159 at the country level, five at the regional level and six at the global level. Forty-five per cent of the evaluations were in the area of reproductive health, including adolescent reproductive health; 21 per cent were multisectoral, including country programme evaluations; and 13 per cent concerned gender themes.

Several evaluations reported successful interventions on improving the coverage and quality of reproductive health services and resulting increases in condom use and contraceptive prevalence rates (for example, in Kyrgyzstan, Mongolia, Thailand and Senegal). A pilot literacy project targeting the poorest of Bolivia's indigenous population—mostly women—succeeded in making 16 per cent of the illiterates in the country literate. Initiatives on adolescent reproductive health services in Asia (Bangladesh, Cambodia, the Lao People's Democratic Republic, Nepal, Pakistan, Sri Lanka and Viet Nam) and Africa (Botswana, Ghana, Uganda and the United Republic of Tanzania) resulted in marked improvement in young people's reproductive health knowledge, attitudes and behaviours. Evaluation of the humanitarian programme for internally displaced adolescents in seven countries/territories (Burundi, Colombia, Democratic Republic of the Congo, Liberia, the Occupied Palestinian Territory, Rwanda and Sierra Leone) found that the interventions had multiple positive impacts on the adolescents, their parents and communities. Some 40 per cent of the evaluations conducted in the area of gender dealt with gender-based violence. With regard to specific vulnerable groups, an example of success was found in Ethiopia, which introduced the use of female condoms among commercial sex workers, allowing them to negotiate safe sex.

In early 2007, an external assessment of the effectiveness of the UNFPA multi-year funding framework (MYFF), 2004–2007, as a strategic planning tool concluded that it had provided an overview of the mission and strategic direction of UNFPA which had hitherto been missing, while being flexible enough to allow country-level interventions to be tailored to national priorities. A review of the UNFPA intercountry programme, 2004–2007, comprising 348 regional and interregional projects with funding of $255 million, was completed in 2007. It found a number of successful projects and initiatives, including the obstetric fistula campaign, global advocacy with parliamentarians, the reproductive health commodity security programme, adolescent reproductive health initiatives in Africa and Asia, and the publication of the report *State of World Population 2008* [Sales No. E.08.III.H.1].

Three fourths of UNFPA country offices reported that they had implemented most of the recommendations made by project, country programme and thematic evaluations from 2006. In response to the evaluations of adolescent and youth reproductive health interventions, UNFPA developed an assessment tool to identify gaps in programming for young people, and was developing a conceptual framework on sexual and reproductive health programming for adolescents and youth. Following up on the recommendations on the effectiveness of the MYFF, 2004–2007, UNFPA took several actions, including implementation of a planning system that provided real time financial and substantive data to all managers in the Fund.

On 20 June [E/2008/35 (dec. 2008/12)], the UNDP/UNFPA Executive Board took note of the biennial report on evaluation activities and welcomed the steps taken and planned by UNFPA to strengthen evaluation at all levels.

Joint UN Programme on HIV/AIDS

A July report presented by UNFPA and UNDP [DP/2008/54-DP/FPA/2008/13] focused on actions taken by those organizations in support of UNAIDS, as at April 2008. It noted that UNFPA led the UNAIDS response in the provision of information and education, condom programming, prevention efforts for young people outside schools, and prevention efforts targeting vulnerable groups, including sex workers.

Over the preceding year, UNFPA had chaired inter-agency task teams on young people and on comprehensive condom programming. It had co-convened two key areas of work within the Global Coalition on Women and AIDS: preventing HIV in young women and girls, and female-controlled prevention methods. At the 2006 high-level meeting on HIV/AIDS [YUN 2006, p. 1410], it had led support for the panel focusing on "Making the Response to AIDS Work for Women and Girls", together with the United Nations Development Fund for Women (UNIFEM), the UNAIDS secretariat and UNDP.

UNFPA country-level report cards on women and AIDS were available for 23 countries, and advocacy guidance for HIV prevention among women and girls was slated for completion in 2008. At the end of 2007, 47 country offices cited major efforts to expand partnership and build the capacities of networks involving women, young people, sex workers and people living with HIV. The Fund was also in the process of commissioning an evaluation of the effectiveness of strengthening its country offices in the area of HIV over the past 18–24 months.

In the Dominican Republic, UNFPA provided support to Ministries, NGOs and groups of people living with HIV for developing a national strategy to address linkages between HIV and gender-based violence. It strengthened efforts to assist migrant women crossing the border between the Dominican Republic and Haiti, including through a strategy to provide women with education on HIV prevention, gender-based violence prevention and human rights, and to improve health service delivery and coordination between border hospitals in both countries.

Other financial issues

In a report on funding commitments to UNFPA [DP/FPA/2008/9], the Executive Director analysed contributions by States for 2008 and future years. General Assembly resolution 62/208 [YUN 2007, p. 877] on operational activities for development had stressed that core resources, due to their untied nature, remained the bedrock of those UN system activities. UNFPA considered a stable base of regular resources as critical to enabling it to support countries in implementing the ICPD Programme of Action and achieving the MDGS.

The approved requirements for all resources under the UNFPA strategic plan for 2008–2011 amounted to $2.6 billion. The 2008–2011 framework increased the proportion and amount of resources directed to country programmes over the previous framework. If UNFPA was to succeed in implementing its country programmes and supporting countries in achieving the MDGS and the ICPD goals, its regular resources would need to exceed the $450 million level annually, and its other resources the $200 million level. All countries were encouraged to translate their commitments to achieving those goals into increased contributions to the Fund, through regular and other resources, including thematic funding and multi-year pledges.

On 20 June [E/2008/35 (dec. 2008/10)], the UNDP/UNFPA Executive Board took note of the report on funding commitments to UNFPA, and encouraged all countries in a position to do so to make contributions early in the year and to make multi-year pledges.

On 11 September [dec. 2008/26], the Board, recognizing the substantial increase in the number and gravity of attacks and threats against UN personnel, decided to revise the UNFPA Financial Regulations with respect to cases in which, at the discretion of the Executive Director, immediate ex gratia payments were necessary for humanitarian reasons (in instances such as injury or death suffered in connection with UNFPA activities). That followed a report on the matter by the Executive Director [DP/FPA/2008/15 & Corr.1] and comments by ACABQ [DP/FPA/2008/16].

United Nations Population Award

The 2008 United Nations Population Award was presented to Dame Billie Miller of Barbados in the individual category, and to Family Care International of the United States in the institutional category.

The Award was established by General Assembly resolution 36/201 [YUN 1981, p. 792], to be presented annually to individuals or institutions for outstanding contributions to increasing awareness of population problems and to their solutions. In August, the Secretary-General transmitted to the Assembly the report of the UNFPA Executive Director on the Population Award [A/63/255].

Other population activities

UN Population Division

In a report on programme implementation and progress of the UN Population Division in 2008

[E/CN.9/2009/7], the Secretary-General described the Division's activities dealing with the analysis of fertility, mortality and international migration, world population estimates and projections, the monitoring of population policies, the interrelations between population and development, the monitoring and dissemination of population information, and technical cooperation.

The Division's work in fertility and family planning included compiling and revising two databases, *World Fertility Data 2008* and *World Marriage Data 2008*, which contained indicators on fertility and marriage for 224 countries or areas, including all 192 Member States. Addressing the MDGs target of universal access to reproductive health, the Division produced indicators on contraceptive prevalence rate, adolescent birth rate and unmet need for family planning—the latter in collaboration with the United Nations Population Fund.

A wall chart and an Excel data set issued on CD-ROM provided the most recent national data available on contraceptive use and unmet need for family planning for 169 countries or areas, accounting for 99.7 per cent of women aged 15–49 who were married or in union worldwide. They showed that contraceptive prevalence among married women of reproductive age had reached 63 per cent at the world level, although it remained low—usually below 20 per cent—in the majority of the least developed countries (LDCs) for which data were available.

On mortality and health, the Division convened the second Coordination Meeting on the Estimation of Adult Mortality (New York, 31 July), which reviewed progress in methodological developments for estimating mortality in countries with deficient data, and identified future directions for research and collaboration. The Division also collaborated in organizing and servicing a high-level event on the MDGs (New York, 25 September), which reaffirmed both the political and financial commitments to MDGs, particularly those relating to health and education.

The Division continued to participate in the Inter-agency Group for Child Mortality Estimation, and it also undertook an analysis of sex differentials in child mortality, producing estimates by sex of infant mortality, child mortality, and under-five mortality for as many countries as possible. Preliminary results revealed that due to biological factors, boys in most countries were subject to higher risks of dying in childhood than girls, with considerable variations worldwide. The analysis was expected to yield information for guiding policy development towards attainment of MDG 4 concerning the reduction of infant and under-five mortality.

The Division also prepared the Secretary-General's report on international migration and development [A/63/265 & Corr.1] (see p. 1184), which presented options for follow-up to the 2006 High-level Dialogue on International Migration and Development [YUN 2006, p. 1261]. With the Economic and Social Commission for Asia and the Pacific, the Division organized a High-level Meeting on International Migration and Development in Asia and the Pacific (Bangkok, Thailand, 22–23 September), which comprised round tables on remittances in development; migration and development in countries with special needs; the social dimensions of migration; and data and research. In November, it organized the seventh Coordination Meeting on International Migration (see p. 1185).

To meet the growing demand for data on international migrants, the Division developed the United Nations Global Migration Database. It included the most complete set of data on the stock of international migrants and allowed users to download information by country of origin or destination. The Division also issued the *2008 Revision of Trends in Total Migrant Stock* on CD-ROM.

The preparation of biennial population estimates and projections for all countries and areas remained a key part of the Division's mandate. Analytical reports prepared using that information included *World Population Ageing*, the *World Fertility Report*, the *World Mortality Report* and the *World Migration Report*. In 2008, the Division issued the publication *Highlights of World Urbanization Prospects: the 2007 Revision*. The data was also made available via an online database, as well as in two wall charts: *Urban and Rural Areas 2007* and *Urban Agglomerations 2007*. According to the 2007 *Revision*, world urban population would likely increase by 3.1 billion between 2007 and 2050, to 6.4 billion, surpassing the 2.5 billion increase in total world population over that period. Rural population would begin decreasing in about a decade, resulting in 0.6 billion fewer rural inhabitants by 2050—a drop from 3.4 billion in 2007 to 2.8 billion in 2050. Urban areas would absorb all the population growth expected over the next four decades, as well as some of the rural population through rural-urban migration or the transformation of rural settlements into urban centres.

On population policies, the Division developed a framework for describing the potential interactions between Government entities and international migrants, including the issuance of visas and permits; granting of asylum and citizenship; preparation of migrants for emigration; and managing the social and economic aspects of migration. It compiled and would analyse information on Government entities involved in managing migration in over 100 countries, to improve coherence in that process for the benefit of development.

The Division organized an expert panel on "The contribution of population policy to the achievement of the internationally agreed development goals, including the MDGs" (New York, 15 December), which documented global population trends. It noted that high population growth was prevalent in most LDCs, and that if such were to continue, it would remain an obstacle for the attainment of key development goals, especially the reduction of poverty and hunger.

On population and development, a United Nations Expert Group Meeting on Population Distribution, Urbanization, Internal Migration and Development (New York, 21–23 January) discussed the unprecedented scale of urbanization, including the policy implications of the fact that in most developing countries, urban population growth was driven mostly by natural increase and not, as usually thought, by rural-urban migration. It also produced estimates of urban and rural populations in the 175 countries with more than 300,000 inhabitants in 2005, for the beginning of each five-year period from 1950 to 2005. The estimates were issued as a CD-ROM entitled "Urban and Rural Population by Age and Sex, 1950–2005".

The Population Division also issued a CD-ROM entitled "World Population Ageing 2007" that included a digital version of the printed volume of the same title published in 2007 and contained files with all the data from the regional and country profiles in the published report. In order to provide information on the impact of urbanization and the challenges faced by rural populations, the Division published two wall charts in 2008: *Urban Population, Development and the Environment 2007* and *Rural Population, Development and the Environment 2007*.

The Division's work on monitoring population trends and policies included the production of the annual world population monitoring report, devoted to population distribution, urbanization, internal migration and development. With respect to dissemination, the Division's website provided access to most of its publications and included highlights, key findings, papers presented at meetings, proceedings of meetings, population reports, wall charts, data sets and interactive databases. The Division also maintained a website focusing exclusively on international migration.

The Population Division's regular programme of technical cooperation focused on building and strengthening capacity in developing countries to analyse demographic information needed to guide the formulation and implementation of population policy. During 2008, the Division conducted a survey among Governmental units engaged in demographic analysis which indicated that many developing countries lacked the human resources to conduct in-depth demographic analysis. The results of the survey were being used to develop a cost-effective strategy for supporting the building of analytical capacity in developing countries.

Chapter IX

Social policy, crime prevention and human resources development

In 2008, the United Nations continued to promote social, cultural and human resources development, and to strengthen its crime prevention and criminal justice programme.

The Commission for Social Development, in February, again considered as its priority theme "Promoting full employment and decent work for all". It also reviewed UN plans and programmes of action pertaining to the situation of social groups and discussed the issue of incorporating disability in the development agenda.

In December, the General Assembly—having considered the implementation of the Copenhagen Declaration on Social Development and the Programme of Action, adopted at the 1995 World Summit for Social Development, and further initiatives for social development adopted at its twenty-fourth (2000) special session—recognized the relevance of the Declaration on Social Justice for a Fair Globalization, adopted by the International Labour Organization in June to promote an integrated approach to the decent work agenda and respond to the growing challenges of globalization. In July, the Economic and Social Council, following discussions on the promotion of full employment and decent work for all, reaffirmed the issue's central importance to poverty eradication and social integration and requested members of the UN system and financial institutions to integrate the goals of full and productive employment and decent work for all in their policies, programmes and activities.

With regard to persons with disabilities, UN bodies continued to monitor the implementation of the 1982 World Programme of Action concerning Disabled Persons and the 1993 Standard Rules on the Equalization of Opportunities for Persons with Disabilities. The 2006 Convention on the Rights of Persons with Disabilities entered into force on 3 May. In July, the Council renewed the mandate of the Special Rapporteur on Disability of the Commission for Social Development until 31 December 2011.

In the area of cultural development, the Assembly, in December, invited Member States to promote a culture of peace and non-violence, and, following a two-day high-level meeting on a culture of peace, affirmed that mutual understanding and interreligious dialogue constituted important dimensions of the dialogue among civilizations and of the culture of peace. In other action, the Assembly urged States and the UN system to foster peace and accelerate the attainment of the Millennium Development Goals through sport-based initiatives, and to promote the integration of sport for development and peace in the development agenda.

In April, the Commission on Crime Prevention and Criminal Justice considered, among other things, the preparations for the Twelfth (2010) United Nations Congress on Crime Prevention and Criminal Justice; protection against trafficking in cultural property; strengthening prevention of urban crime; and international cooperation in preventing and combating illicit international trafficking in forest products, including timber, wildlife and other forest biological resources. It also held a thematic discussion on aspects of violence against women.

The Assembly, in December, urged Governments to criminalize trafficking in persons in all its forms, and encouraged Member States that had not yet done so to ratify or accede to the United Nations Convention against Transnational Organized Crime and its Protocol to Prevent, Suppress and Punish Trafficking in Persons, Especially Women and Children. The Assembly also condemned corruption in all its forms and urged Governments to combat and penalize corruption and to enhance international cooperation.

As to human resources development, the Assembly recognized that a renewed collective commitment would be needed to meet the objectives of the International Plan of Action for the United Nations Literacy Decade (2003–2012). It called on Member States to give literacy higher priority within their educational planning and budgeting, and to devise strategies for reaching groups disproportionately affected by illiteracy.

The Assembly proclaimed 2011 the International Year of Chemistry.

Social policy and cultural issues

Social development

Follow-up to 1995 World Summit and to General Assembly special session

In response to General Assembly resolution 62/131 [YUN 2007, p. 1107], the Secretary-General submitted a July report [A/63/133] on the implementation of the Copenhagen Declaration on Social Development and the Programme of Action, adopted at the 1995 World Summit for Social Development [YUN 1995, p. 1113], and of the further initiatives for social development adopted by the Assembly's twenty-fourth (2000) special session [YUN 2000, p. 1012]. The report provided an overview of the discussions during the forty-sixth session of the Commission for Social Development (see p. 1204) on the priority theme "Promoting full employment and decent work for all" and on issues pertaining to social groups. It also addressed extending social protection; promoting youth employment; and mainstreaming disability in the development agenda.

With regard to the policy framework for employment and decent work, the report stated that the 2008 International Labour Conference (Geneva, 28 May–13 June) had adopted the Declaration on Social Justice for a Fair Globalization, designed to strengthen the capacity of the International Labour Organization (ILO) to promote its Decent Work Agenda and forge a response to the growing challenges of globalization (see p. 1203). The report stated that achieving full employment and decent work would require a major policy commitment; the failure of globalization to create quality jobs deserved priority attention. At the international level, policies should focus on the challenges posed by trade and financial market liberalization, foreign direct investment, fiscal policy and labour market reforms, and international migration. At the national level, policy efforts should address economic growth, employment generation and productivity growth while maintaining focus on the promotion of the decent work agenda. Strategies for employment creation should address income inequality, social exclusion and discrimination, and extending labour standards and social protection programmes. Stronger systems for guaranteeing a minimum wage were also needed. As to the role of the UN system, it noted that advancing full employment and decent work as part of the development agenda required a coherent approach and collaboration between UN entities. It highlighted the importance of ILO's decent work country programmes to support national development efforts and urged UN system entities to implement the ILO toolkit for mainstreaming employment and decent work; provide support in developing projects aimed at generating employment opportunities and capacity-building; and strengthen the employment content of poverty reduction strategies.

With reference to issues pertaining to social groups, the report noted that women, youth, older persons, persons with disabilities, indigenous peoples, migrants and other disadvantaged groups were often subjected to social and economic exclusion in the labour market, education and health care. Policies to achieve full employment and decent work for all should include measures to promote gender equality and foster social integration, including by providing disadvantaged groups with equal access to employment opportunities and social protection and ensuring their full participation in the workforce. With regard to violence against women in the work environment, the report stressed the need to ensure the coherence of existing laws from a gender perspective and to design policy interventions targeting all types of discrimination. As to ageing and development, it urged Governments to include the concerns of older persons in their policy agenda and to consult with older persons and their organizations in planning, implementing and evaluating policies on ageing, poverty eradication and social protection.

The Secretary-General observed that three emerging issues—extending social protection and establishing universal, basic social protection in all countries; promoting youth employment; and mainstreaming disability in the development agenda—had gained increasing attention in the context of social development. ILO estimated that 80 per cent of the world population had no adequate social protection, while 50 per cent had no coverage at all. Under its decent work agenda, ILO was exploring ways to operationalize basic universal social protection programmes worldwide as part of global efforts to eradicate poverty and achieve internationally agreed development goals, including the Millennium Development Goals (MDGs). Extending social security at the national level required a multipronged approach, including expanding and reforming statutory social insurance programmes, promoting community-based social insurance schemes and improving cost-effective tax-financed social benefits. At the international level, advocacy efforts were necessary to place social protection at the top of the development agenda and to strengthen technical assistance and knowledge development.

With regard to youth, the report noted that unemployment of that population group stood at 85 million in 2005; a quarter of all youth in sub-Saharan Africa, a third in Central and Eastern Europe, and one in seven in developed countries were neither in education nor in employment. The challenge in the volatile global economic environment was to create opportunities for young people to participate in the world of work in ways that promoted economic and social development. The Secretary-General urged States to give priority to promoting youth employment through national action plans, and to join the Youth Employment Network, a 2001 initiative [YUN 2001, p. 1100] of the United Nations, ILO and the World Bank to support the commitment contained in the United Nations Millennium Declaration [YUN 2000, p. 49] to develop strategies to promote youth employment.

Concerning incorporating disability in the development agenda, the Secretary-General stressed that it was a strategy for achieving equality of opportunities for persons with disabilities, which required improved awareness and involvement of relevant stakeholders, broadened participation of persons with disabilities at all levels of decision-making, and their involvement in formulating and monitoring the implementation of policies aimed at benefiting them directly. Policies and programme design was crucial and should: identify barriers, including societal attitudes, that hindered persons with disabilities from participating in and benefiting from public policies and programmes; assess the costs and benefits of specific actions to remove those barriers; and review national legal and regulatory frameworks and ensure that laws and regulations were non-discriminatory and complied with the Convention on the Rights of Persons with Disabilities, adopted by the General Assembly in resolution 61/106 [YUN 2006, p. 785].

The report concluded that in order to reduce poverty and promote social integration, it was critical to expand employment and decent work opportunities for all. That goal should be placed at the centre of economic and social policymaking at both national and international levels; it was important to integrate economic and social policies to ensure that social objectives were part of macroeconomic policies. In promoting employment and decent work, priority had to be placed on: encouraging agricultural development and small and medium-sized enterprises, and entrepreneurship; investing in education, training and skills development; strengthening social protections systems; and extending labour standards. Programmes aimed at integrating women, young people, persons with disabilities, older persons, indigenous peoples and other groups into the labour market and overcoming discrimination in employment had to be developed. The report recommended that social protection systems be more effective and responsive to economic changes. Governments should provide workers in the informal economy with basic social protection; and, in developing countries, expanding basic social protection programmes should become an integral part of national development and poverty reduction strategies.

By **decision 2008/257** of 25 July, the Economic and Social Council adopted the theme "Current global and national trends and their impact on social development, including public health" for its 2009 thematic discussion.

GENERAL ASSEMBLY ACTION

On 18 December [meeting 70], the General Assembly, on the recommendation of the Third (Social, Humanitarian and Cultural) Committee [A/63/424], adopted **resolution 63/152** without vote [agenda item 55 *(a)*].

Implementation of the outcome of the World Summit for Social Development and of the twenty-fourth special session of the General Assembly

The General Assembly,

Recalling the World Summit for Social Development, held at Copenhagen from 6 to 12 March 1995, and the twenty-fourth special session of the General Assembly entitled "World Summit for Social Development and beyond: achieving social development for all in a globalizing world", held at Geneva from 26 June to 1 July 2000,

Reaffirming that the Copenhagen Declaration on Social Development and the Programme of Action and the further initiatives for social development adopted by the General Assembly at its twenty-fourth special session, as well as a continued global dialogue on social development issues, constitute the basic framework for the promotion of social development for all at the national and international levels,

Recalling the United Nations Millennium Declaration and the development goals contained therein, as well as the commitments made at major United Nations summits, conferences and special sessions, including the commitments made at the 2005 World Summit,

Recalling also its resolution 57/270 B of 23 June 2003 on the integrated and coordinated implementation of and follow-up to the outcomes of the major United Nations conferences and summits in the economic and social fields,

Recalling further its resolution 60/209 of 22 December 2005 on the implementation of the first United Nations Decade for the Eradication of Poverty (1997–2006),

Noting with appreciation the ministerial declaration adopted at the high-level segment of the substantive session of 2006 of the Economic and Social Council, on "Creating an environment at the national and international levels conducive to generating full and productive employment and decent work for all, and its impact on sustainable development",

Noting that the decent work agenda of the International Labour Organization, with its four strategic objectives, has an important role to play, as reaffirmed in the International Labour Organization Declaration on Social Justice for a Fair Globalization, in achieving the objective of full and productive employment and decent work for all,

Emphasizing the need to enhance the role of the Commission for Social Development in the follow-up and review of the World Summit for Social Development and the outcome of the twenty-fourth special session of the General Assembly,

Recognizing that a people-centred approach must be at the centre of economic and social development,

Expressing deep concern that attainment of the social development objectives can be hindered by instability in global and national financial markets as well as challenges brought about by the ongoing food and energy crises,

Affirming its strong support for fair globalization and the need to translate growth into eradication of poverty and commitment to strategies and policies that aim to promote full, freely chosen and productive employment and decent work for all and that these should constitute a fundamental component of relevant national and international policies as well as national development strategies, including poverty reduction strategies, and reaffirming that employment creation and decent work should be incorporated into macroeconomic policies, taking fully into account the impact and social dimension of globalization, the benefits and costs of which are often unevenly shared and distributed,

1. *Takes note* of the report of the Secretary-General;

2. *Welcomes* the reaffirmation by Governments of their will and commitment to continue implementing the Copenhagen Declaration on Social Development and the Programme of Action, in particular to eradicate poverty, promote full and productive employment and foster social integration to achieve stable, safe and just societies for all;

3. *Recognizes* that the implementation of the Copenhagen commitments and the attainment of the internationally agreed development goals, including the Millennium Development Goals, are mutually reinforcing and that the Copenhagen commitments are crucial to a coherent people-centred approach to development;

4. *Reaffirms* that the Commission for Social Development continues to have the primary responsibility for the follow-up and review of the World Summit for Social Development and the outcome of the twenty-fourth special session of the General Assembly and that it serves as the main United Nations forum for an intensified global dialogue on social development issues, and calls upon Member States, the relevant specialized agencies, funds and programmes of the United Nations system and civil society to enhance their support for its work;

5. *Recognizes* that the broad concept of social development affirmed by the World Summit for Social Development and the twenty-fourth special session of the General Assembly has been weakened in national and international policymaking and that, while poverty eradication is a central part of development policy and discourse, further attention should be given to the other commitments agreed to at the Summit, in particular those concerning employment and social integration, which have also suffered from a general disconnect between economic and social policymaking;

6. *Acknowledges* that the first United Nations Decade for the Eradication of Poverty (1997–2006), launched after the World Summit for Social Development, has provided the long-term vision for sustained and concerted efforts at the national and international levels to eradicate poverty;

7. *Recognizes* that the implementation of the commitments made by Governments during the first Decade has fallen short of expectations, and welcomes the proclamation of the Second United Nations Decade for the Eradication of Poverty (2008–2017) by the General Assembly in its resolution 62/205 of 19 December 2007 in order to support, in an efficient and coordinated manner, the internationally agreed development goals related to poverty eradication, including the Millennium Development Goals;

8. *Emphasizes* that the major United Nations conferences and summits, including the Millennium Summit and the 2005 World Summit, as well as the International Conference on Financing for Development, in its Monterrey Consensus, have reinforced the priority and urgency of poverty eradication within the United Nations development agenda;

9. *Also emphasizes* that poverty eradication policies should attack poverty by addressing its root and structural causes and manifestations, and that equity and the reduction of inequalities need to be incorporated in those policies;

10. *Stresses* that an enabling environment is a critical precondition for achieving equity and social development and that, while economic growth is essential, entrenched inequality and marginalization are an obstacle to the broad-based and sustained growth required for sustainable, inclusive, people-centred development, and recognizes the need to balance and ensure complementarity between measures to achieve growth and measures to achieve economic and social equity in order for there to be an impact on overall poverty levels;

11. *Also stresses* that stability in global financial systems and corporate social responsibility and accountability, as well as national economic policies that have an impact on other stakeholders, are essential in creating an enabling international environment to promote economic growth and social development;

12. *Recognizes* the need to promote respect for all human rights and fundamental freedoms in order to address the most pressing social needs of people living in poverty, including through the design and development of appropriate mechanisms to strengthen and consolidate democratic institutions and governance;

13. *Reaffirms* the commitment to the empowerment of women and gender equality, as well as to the mainstreaming of a gender perspective into all development efforts, recognizing that these are critical for achieving sustainable development and for efforts to combat hunger, poverty and disease and to strengthen policies and programmes that improve, ensure and broaden the full participation of women in all spheres of political, economic, social and cultural life, as equal partners, and to improve their access to all resources needed for the full exercise of all their human rights and fundamental freedoms by removing persistent barriers, including ensuring equal access to full and productive employment and decent work, as well as strengthening their economic independence;

14. *Also reaffirms* the commitment to promote opportunities for full, freely chosen and productive employment, including for the most disadvantaged, as well as decent work for all, in order to deliver social justice combined with economic efficiency, with full respect for fundamental principles and rights at work under conditions of equity, equality, security and dignity, and further reaffirms that macroeconomic policies should, inter alia, support employment creation, taking fully into account the social impact and dimension of globalization;

15. *Takes note with interest* of the adoption by the International Labour Conference on 10 June 2008 of the International Labour Organization Declaration on Social Justice for a Fair Globalization, which acknowledges the particular role of the Organization in promoting a fair globalization and its responsibility to assist its members in their efforts;

16. *Reaffirms* that there is an urgent need to create an environment at the national and international levels that is conducive to the attainment of full and productive employment and decent work for all as a foundation for sustainable development and that an environment that supports investment, growth and entrepreneurship is essential to the creation of new job opportunities, and also reaffirms that

opportunities for men and women to obtain productive work in conditions of freedom, equity, security and human dignity are essential to ensuring the eradication of hunger and poverty, the improvement of economic and social well-being for all, the achievement of sustained economic growth and sustainable development of all nations and a fully inclusive and equitable globalization;

17. *Stresses* the importance of removing obstacles to the realization of the right of peoples to self-determination, in particular of peoples living under colonial or other forms of alien domination or foreign occupation, which adversely affect their social and economic development, including their exclusion from labour markets;

18. *Reaffirms* that violence, in its many manifestations, including domestic violence, especially against women, children, older persons and persons with disabilities, is a growing threat to the security of individuals, families and communities everywhere; total social breakdown is an all too real contemporary experience; organized crime, illegal drugs, the illicit arms trade, trafficking in women and children, ethnic and religious conflict, civil war, terrorism, all forms of extremist violence, xenophobia, and politically motivated killing and even genocide present fundamental threats to societies and the global social order; they also present compelling and urgent reasons for action by Governments individually and, as appropriate, jointly to foster social cohesion while recognizing, protecting and valuing diversity;

19. *Calls upon* the organizations of the United Nations system to commit to mainstreaming the goal of full and productive employment and decent work for all in their policies, programmes and activities;

20. *Requests* the United Nations funds, programmes and agencies and invites financial institutions to support efforts to mainstream the goals of full and productive employment and decent work for all in their policies, programmes and activities;

21. *Recognizes* that promoting full employment and decent work also requires investing in education, training and skills development for women and men, and girls and boys, strengthening social protection and health systems and applying labour standards;

22. *Also recognizes* that full and productive employment and decent work for all, which encompass social protection, fundamental principles and rights at work and social dialogue, are key elements of sustainable development for all countries and are therefore a priority objective of international cooperation;

23. *Stresses* that policies and strategies to achieve full employment and decent work for all should include specific measures to promote gender equality and foster social integration for social groups such as youth, persons with disabilities, and older persons, as well as migrants and indigenous peoples;

24. *Also stresses* the need to allocate adequate resources for the elimination of all forms of discrimination against women in the workplace, including unequal access to labour market participation and wage inequalities, as well as reconciliation of work and private life for both women and men;

25. *Encourages* States to promote youth employment by, inter alia, developing and implementing action plans in collaboration with all relevant stakeholders;

26. *Also encourages* States to pursue efforts to promote the concerns of older persons and persons with disabilities and their organizations in the planning, implementing and evaluating of all development programmes and policies;

27. *Stresses* that policies and programmes designed to achieve poverty eradication, full employment and decent work for all should include specific measures to foster social integration, including by providing marginalized socio-economic sectors and groups with equal access to opportunities and social protection;

28. *Acknowledges* the important nexus between international migration and social development, and stresses the importance of enforcing labour law effectively with regard to migrant workers' labour relations and working conditions, inter alia, those related to their remuneration and conditions of health, safety at work and the right to freedom of association;

29. *Reaffirms* that social integration policies should seek to reduce inequalities, promote access to basic social services, education for all and health care, increase the participation and integration of social groups, particularly youth, older persons and persons with disabilities, and address the challenges posed by globalization and market-driven reforms to social development in order for all people in all countries to benefit from globalization;

30. *Urges* Governments, with the cooperation of relevant entities, to develop systems of social protection and to extend or broaden, as appropriate, their effectiveness and coverage, including for workers in the informal economy, recognizing the need for social protection systems to provide social security and support labour-market participation, and invites the International Labour Organization to strengthen its social protection strategies, and policies on extending social security coverage, and also urges Governments, while taking account of national circumstances, to focus on the needs of those living in, or vulnerable to, poverty and give particular consideration to universal access to basic social security systems;

31. *Reaffirms* the commitment to promote the rights of indigenous peoples in the areas of education, employment, housing, sanitation, health and social security, and also notes the attention paid to those areas in the United Nations Declaration on the Rights of Indigenous Peoples;

32. *Recognizes* the need to formulate social development policies in an integral, articulated and participative manner, recognizing poverty as a multidimensional phenomenon, calls for interlinked public policies on this matter, and underlines the need for public policies to be included in a comprehensive development and well-being strategy;

33. *Acknowledges* the important role that the public sector can play as an employer and in developing an environment that enables the effective generation of full and productive employment and decent work for all;

34. *Also acknowledges* the vital role that the private sector can play in generating new investments, employment and financing for development and in advancing efforts towards full employment and decent work;

35. *Recognizes* that the majority of poor people live and work in rural areas, that priority should be given to agricultural and non-farm sectors and that steps should be taken to anticipate and offset the negative social and economic

consequences of globalization and to maximize its benefits for poor people living and working in rural areas;

36. *Also recognizes* the need to give priority to investing in and further contributing to sustainable agricultural development and microenterprises, small and medium-sized enterprises and entrepreneurship cooperatives and other forms of social enterprises and the participation and entrepreneurship of women as means to promote full productive employment and decent work for all;

37. *Reaffirms* the commitments made in respect of "Meeting the special needs of Africa" at the 2005 World Summit, underlines the call of the Economic and Social Council for enhanced coordination within the United Nations system and the ongoing efforts to harmonize the current initiatives on Africa, and requests the Commission for Social Development to continue to give due prominence in its work to the social dimensions of the New Partnership for Africa's Development;

38. *Also reaffirms* that each country has the primary responsibility for its own economic and social development and that the role of national policies and development strategies cannot be overemphasized, and underlines the importance of adopting effective measures, including new financial mechanisms, as appropriate, to support the efforts of developing countries to achieve sustained economic growth, sustainable development, poverty eradication and the strengthening of their democratic systems;

39. *Further reaffirms*, in this context, that international cooperation has an essential role in assisting developing countries, including the least developed countries, in strengthening their human, institutional and technological capacity;

40. *Stresses* that the international community shall enhance its efforts to create an enabling environment for social development and poverty eradication through increasing market access for developing countries, technology transfer on mutually agreed terms, financial aid and a comprehensive solution to the external debt problem;

41. *Also stresses* that international trade and stable financial systems can be effective tools to create favourable conditions for the development of all countries and that trade barriers and some trading practices continue to have negative effects on employment growth, particularly in developing countries;

42. *Acknowledges* that good governance and the rule of law at the national and international levels are essential for sustained economic growth, sustainable development and the eradication of poverty and hunger;

43. *Urges* developed countries that have not yet done so in accordance with their commitments, to make concrete efforts towards meeting the targets of 0.7 per cent of their gross national product for official development assistance to developing countries and 0.15 to 0.2 per cent of their gross national product to least developed countries, and encourages developing countries to build on the progress achieved in ensuring that official development assistance is used effectively to help to meet development goals and targets;

44. *Welcomes* the contribution to the mobilization of resources for social development by the initiatives taken on a voluntary basis by groups of Member States based on innovative financing mechanisms, including those that aim to provide further drug access at affordable prices to developing countries on a sustainable and predictable basis, such as the International Drug Purchase Facility, UNITAID, as well as other initiatives, such as the International Finance Facility for Immunization and the Advance Market Commitments for Vaccines, and notes the New York Declaration of 20 September 2004, which launched the Action against Hunger and Poverty initiative and called for further attention to raise funds urgently needed to help meet the Millennium Development Goals and to complement and ensure the long-term stability and predictability of foreign aid;

45. *Reaffirms* that social development requires the active involvement of all actors in the development process, including civil society organizations, corporations and small businesses, and that partnerships among all relevant actors are increasingly becoming part of national and international cooperation for social development, and also reaffirms that, within countries, partnerships among the Government, civil society and the private sector can contribute effectively to the achievement of social development goals;

46. *Underlines* the responsibility of the private sector, at both the national and the international levels, including small and large companies and transnational corporations, regarding not only the economic and financial but also the development, social, gender and environmental implications of their activities, their obligations towards their workers and their contributions to achieving sustainable development, including social development, and emphasizes the need to take concrete actions on corporate responsibility and accountability, including through the participation of all relevant stakeholders, inter alia, for the prevention or prosecution of corruption;

47. *Stresses* the importance of promoting corporate social responsibility and accountability, encourages responsible business practices, such as those promoted by the Global Compact, and invites the private sector to take into account not only the economic and financial but also the development, social, human rights, gender and environmental implications of its undertakings, and underlines the importance of the International Labour Organization Tripartite Declaration of Principles concerning Multinational Enterprises and Social Policy;

48. *Invites* the Secretary-General, the Economic and Social Council, the regional commissions, the relevant specialized agencies, funds and programmes of the United Nations system and other intergovernmental forums, within their respective mandates, to continue to integrate into their work programmes and give priority attention to the Copenhagen commitments and the Declaration on the tenth anniversary of the World Summit for Social Development, to continue to be actively involved in their follow-up and to monitor the achievement of those commitments and undertakings;

49. *Invites* the Commission for Social Development to emphasize in its review of the implementation of the Copenhagen Declaration on Social Development and the Programme of Action the increased exchange of national, regional and international experiences, the focused and interactive dialogues among experts and practitioners and the sharing of best practices and lessons learned, and to ad-

dress, inter alia, the potential impact of the ongoing food, financial and energy crises on social development goals;

50. *Decides* to include in the provisional agenda of its sixty-fourth session the sub-item entitled "Implementation of the outcome of the World Summit for Social Development and of the twenty-fourth special session of the General Assembly", and requests the Secretary-General to submit a report on the question to the Assembly at that session.

Social Justice for a Fair Globalization

Communication. By a 21 October letter to the Secretary-General [A/63/538-E/2009/4], Norway and the United Republic of Tanzania transmitted the ILO Declaration on Social Justice for a Fair Globalization, unanimously adopted on 10 June by the ILO General Conference at its ninety-seventh session (Geneva, 28 May–13 June). The Declaration reflected a wide consensus on the need for a strong social dimension to globalization in achieving improved and fair outcomes for all. It also provided a clear direction to accelerate progress in implementing the decent work agenda, as called for in various UN resolutions, including the 2005 World Summit Outcome, contained in General Assembly resolution 60/1 [YUN 2005, p. 48], and other regional agreements.

GENERAL ASSEMBLY ACTION

On 19 December [meeting 72], the General Assembly adopted **resolution 63/199** [draft: A/63/L.29/Rev.1 & Add.1] without vote [agenda item 44].

International Labour Organization Declaration on Social Justice for a Fair Globalization

The General Assembly,

Recalling the outcomes of the major United Nations conferences and summits in the economic, social and related fields, including the development goals and objectives contained therein, and recognizing the vital role played by these conferences and summits in shaping a broad development vision and in identifying commonly agreed objectives, which have contributed to the improvement of human life in different parts of the world,

Reaffirming the commitment made in the 2005 World Summit Outcome to full and productive employment and decent work for all, including for women and young people, as a central objective of relevant national and international policies as well as national development strategies, including poverty reduction strategies, as part of the efforts to achieve the Millennium Development Goals,

Recalling its resolution 59/57 of 2 December 2004 on the report of the World Commission on the Social Dimension of Globalization entitled *A Fair Globalization: Creating Opportunities for All*,

Recalling also its resolution 62/208 of 19 December 2007 on the triennial comprehensive policy review of operational activities for development of the United Nations system,

Reaffirming the resolve expressed in the United Nations Millennium Declaration to ensure that globalization becomes a positive force for the people of the entire world and the commitment to ensuring greater policy coherence and better cooperation between the United Nations, its agencies, the Bretton Woods institutions and other multilateral bodies, with a view to achieving the internationally agreed development goals, including the Millennium Development Goals,

Recognizing that full and productive employment and decent work for all is one of the key elements of poverty reduction strategies that facilitate the achievement of the internationally agreed development goals, including the Millennium Development Goals, and that it requires a multidimensional focus that incorporates Governments, the private sector, civil society, non-governmental organizations, representatives of employers and workers, international organizations and, in particular, the agencies of the United Nations system and the international financial institutions,

Reaffirming that development is a central goal in and of itself and that sustainable development in its economic, social and environmental aspects constitutes a key element of the overarching framework of United Nations activities,

1. *Takes note with interest* of the adoption of the Declaration on Social Justice for a Fair Globalization and its accompanying resolution at the ninety-seventh session of the International Labour Conference, and calls for their implementation;

2. *Recognizes* that in the present context of globalization, achieving an improved and fair outcome for all has become even more necessary in order to meet the universal aspiration for social justice, reach full employment, ensure the sustainability of open societies and the global economy, achieve social cohesion and combat poverty and rising inequalities;

3. *Also recognizes* that the social impact of the current economic crisis may disproportionately affect the weakest and most vulnerable segments of society, through increased poverty, underemployment, growth in inequality and difficult social conditions;

4. *Reiterates its support* for a fair globalization, and resolves to make the goals of full and productive employment and decent work for all, including for women and young people, a central objective of relevant national and international policies, including poverty reduction strategies, as well as other measures which may be developed in response to the current economic crisis, as appropriate, with the aim of achieving the internationally agreed development goals, including the Millennium Development Goals;

5. *Supports* the call of the Declaration to promote and contribute to the implementation of an integrated approach to the decent work agenda, based on the four inseparable, interrelated and mutually supportive strategic objectives of employment creation, fundamental principles and rights at work, social dialogue and social protection;

6. *Reiterates* that the Toolkit for Mainstreaming Employment and Decent Work, as adopted by the United Nations System Chief Executives Board for Coordination and endorsed by the Economic and Social Council, provides a practical method for advancing coherence in policy-

making and implementation on these issues within the United Nations system;

7. *Requests* the United Nations funds, programmes, specialized agencies and financial institutions to continue to mainstream the goals of full and productive employment and decent work for all in their policies, programmes and activities through promotion of an integrated approach, including the application of the Toolkit;

8. *Encourages* Member States to consider applying the principles set out in the Toolkit at the national level in an effort to promote policy coherence around the promotion of full and productive employment and decent work for all;

9. *Recognizes* the particular relevance of the International Labour Organization Declaration on Social Justice for a Fair Globalization in the light of the World Day of Social Justice, and encourages active dialogue and collaboration among the various funds, programmes and specialized agencies of the United Nations system, as well as at the national level, including civil society and non-governmental organizations;

10. *Requests* the Secretary-General to duly take into account the International Labour Organization Declaration on Social Justice for a Fair Globalization when considering related reports in the economic and social fields.

Commission for Social Development

The Commission for Social Development, at its forty-sixth session (New York, 16 February 2007, 6–15 February and 22 February 2008) [E/2008/26], considered its priority theme "Promoting full employment and decent work for all". A panel discussion was held on the theme and the Commission recommended to the Economic and Social Council for adoption a policy-oriented resolution by which the Council would decide to keep full and productive employment and decent work for all under review and would request the Secretary-General to submit a report on implementation of the resolution to the Commission in 2009 and to the General Assembly later that year as part of the report on the implementation of the 1995 World Summit for Social Development and of the Assembly's twenty-fourth (2000) special session. The Commission also held a discussion on the theme "Full employment and decent work: intensification of efforts to eliminate all forms of discrimination against women"; a summary of the discussion was transmitted to the Secretary-General for his annual report to the Assembly, as requested in Assembly resolution 61/143 [YUN 2006, p. 1334]. The Commission recommended to the Council for adoption a resolution on the social dimensions of the New Partnership for Africa's Development (NEPAD) [YUN 2001, p. 900], in which the Commission would be asked to continue to give prominence to and raise awareness of the social dimensions of NEPAD and the Secretary-General would be asked to submit a report on the subject to the Commission in 2009 (see p. 1007). In connection with its review of plans and programmes of action pertaining to the situation of social groups, the Commission held a panel discussion on the regional review and appraisal of the Madrid International Plan of Action on Ageing, 2002 [YUN 2002, p. 1194] and adopted a resolution on the Plan of Action's first review and appraisal (see p. 1300). The Commission also adopted a resolution on further promotion of equalization of opportunities by, for and with persons with disabilities and protection of their human rights, in which the Council would renew the mandate of the Commission's Special Rapporteur on Disability until 31 December 2011. It also held a panel discussion on the theme "Mainstreaming disability in the development agenda" as an emerging issue and adopted a resolution in which the Council would encourage Member States, the UN system and other international entities to ensure that issues affecting persons with disabilities were incorporated into the formulation of policies aiming at their full and effective participation in development. In addressing its future organization and methods of work, the Commission recommended to the Council that "Social integration" be the priority theme for the 2009–2010 review and policy cycle, taking into account the relation with poverty eradication and full employment and decent work for all.

For its consideration of its priority theme, the Commission had before it a November 2007 report of the Secretary-General [E/CN.5/2008/4] prepared in response to Council resolution 2006/18 [YUN 2006, p. 1277]. The report examined labour market trends and challenges and addressed a policy framework for achieving full employment and decent work, focusing on macroeconomic policies, enterprise and rural development, education, training and skills, and social protection, as well as standards and regulatory policies. It stressed that achieving the goals of full and productive employment and decent work was an integral part of the efforts to meet the internationally agreed development goals, including the MDGs, and the broader UN development agenda. Those goals should be made a central objective of economic and social policies and incorporated into national development strategies, including poverty reduction strategies. Governments should promote enterprise development, and measures should be directed at increasing investment, improving access to market and infrastructure and facilitating diversification from agriculture to other economic activities. Training and skills enhancement should be provided to increase the employability of the workforce and its adaptability to changing labour markets. Social protection systems should adapt to labour-market conditions in order to provide economic security. Greater attention should be given to developing appropriate institutions and regulation for the effective and fair functioning of labour markets. National regulatory frameworks should be reviewed and strengthened in order to ensure that core labour standards were fully enforced in both the formal and informal sectors. The UN system should incorporate more effectively the goals of full employment and decent work into its policies and programmes in support of national development efforts.

Also before the Commission were Secretariat notes on: the future organization and methods of work of the Commission [E/CN.5/2008/5] (see p. 1208); mainstreaming disability in the development agenda [E/CN.5/2008/6] (see p. 1213); and the intensification of efforts to eliminate all forms of violence against women [E/CN.5/2008/8] [YUN 2007, p. 1158]. The Commission also considered a report by the Secretary-General on the first review and appraisal of the Madrid International Plan of Action on Ageing, 2002: preliminary assessment [E/CN.5/2008/7 & Corr.1], and a note transmitting the report of the regional commissions on the regional implementation of the Madrid Plan of Action [E/CN.5/2008/2] (see p. 1300). It also had before it notes by the Secretary-General on: monitoring the implementation of the Standard Rules on the Equalization of Opportunities for Persons with Disabilities [E/CN.5/2008/3] (see p. 1211); and the proposed strategic framework for the biennium 2010–2011: subprogramme 3, social policy and development [E/CN.5/2008/9].

On 24 July, the Council took note of the Commission's report on its forty-sixth session and approved the provisional agenda and documentation for its forty-seventh (2009) session (**decision 2008/244**).

ECONOMIC AND SOCIAL COUNCIL ACTION

On 24 July [meeting 42], the Economic and Social Council, on the recommendation of the Commission for Social Development [E/2008/26], adopted **resolution 2008/18** without vote [agenda item 14 *(b)*].

Promoting full employment and decent work for all

The Economic and Social Council,

Recalling the outcomes of the World Summit for Social Development and the twenty-fourth special session of the General Assembly,

Reaffirming that the Copenhagen Declaration on Social Development and the Programme of Action of the World Summit for Social Development and the further initiatives for social development adopted by the General Assembly at its twenty-fourth special session, and a continued global dialogue on social issues, constitute the basic framework for the promotion of social development for all at the national and international levels,

Recognizing that a people-centred approach must be at the centre of economic and social development,

Recalling the United Nations Millennium Declaration and the 2005 World Summit Outcome,

Recalling also the ministerial declaration adopted by the Economic and Social Council at the high-level segment of its substantive session of 2006,

Recalling further its resolution 2007/2 of 17 July 2007 and the theme of the coordination segment of its 2007 substantive session, "The role of the United Nations system in promoting full and productive employment and decent work for all",

Recognizing that approximately 1.5 billion people, or one third of the working-age population worldwide, were either unemployed or underemployed in 2006, that of this number about 200 million were unemployed, and that the remaining 1.3 billion constituted the working poor who are unable to earn enough to lift themselves and their family members out of poverty, and hence emphasizing the dual challenge of creating new productive jobs and improving the quality of existing ones,

Recognizing also that the decent-work agenda of the International Labour Organization is an important instrument for achieving the objective of full and productive employment and decent work for all through the promotion and realization of the fundamental principles and rights at work, creation of greater and equal opportunities for women and men to secure decent employment and income, and enhancement of the coverage and effectiveness of social protection for all and the strengthening of social dialogue,

1. *Reaffirms* the central importance of full and productive employment and decent work to poverty eradication and social integration;

2. *Also reaffirms* that the goals of full and productive employment and decent work are crucial to poverty eradication and should be made a central objective of relevant national and international policies as well as national development strategies, including poverty reduction strategies, as part of the efforts to achieve the internationally agreed development goals, including the Millennium Development Goals;

3. *Calls upon* Governments as a matter of priority to continue efforts towards ratifying, where Member States have not done so, and fully implementing the International Labour Organization conventions concerning respect for fundamental principles and rights at work, namely, freedom of association and the effective recognition of the right to organize and bargain collectively, and the elimination of all forms of forced or compulsory labour, as well as the effective elimination of child labour and discrimination in respect of employment and occupation, and to consider also the ratification and full implementation of other International Labour Organization conventions concerning the employment rights of women, youth, persons with disabilities, migrants and indigenous peoples;

4. *Affirms* its strong support for fair globalization and the need to translate growth into eradication of poverty and commitment to strategies and policies that aim to promote full, freely chosen and productive employment and decent work for all and that these should constitute a fundamental component of relevant national and international policies as well as national development strategies, including poverty reduction strategies, and reaffirms that employment creation and decent work should be incorporated into macroeconomic policies, taking fully into account the impact and social dimension of globalization,

the benefits and costs of which are often unevenly shared and distributed;

5. *Reaffirms* that there is an urgent need to create an environment at the national and international levels that is conducive to the attainment of full and productive employment and decent work for all as a foundation for sustainable development and that an environment that supports investment, growth and entrepreneurship is essential to the creation of new job opportunities, and also reaffirms that opportunities for men and women to obtain productive work in conditions of freedom, equity, security and human dignity are essential to ensuring the eradication of hunger and poverty, the improvement of economic and social well-being for all, the achievement of sustained economic growth and sustainable development of all nations and a fully inclusive and equitable globalization;

6. *Stresses* the importance of removing obstacles to the realization of the right of peoples to self-determination, in particular people living under colonial or other forms of alien domination or foreign occupation, which adversely affect their social and economic development, including their exclusion from labour markets;

7. *Reaffirms* that violence, in its many manifestations, including domestic violence, especially against women, children, older persons and persons with disabilities, is a growing threat to the security of individuals, families and communities everywhere; that total social breakdown is an all-too-real contemporary experience; that organized crime, illegal drugs, the illicit arms trade, trafficking in women and children, ethnic and religious conflict, civil war, terrorism, all forms of extremist violence, xenophobia, and politically motivated killing and even genocide present fundamental threats to societies and the global social order; and that they also present compelling and urgent reasons for action by Governments individually and, as appropriate, jointly to foster social cohesion while recognizing, protecting and valuing diversity;

8. *Also reaffirms* that each country has the primary responsibility for its own economic and social development and that the role of national policies and development strategies cannot be overemphasized, and underlines the importance of adopting effective measures, including new financial mechanisms, as appropriate, to support the efforts of developing countries to achieve sustained economic growth, sustainable development, poverty eradication and the strengthening of their democratic systems;

9. *Calls upon* the international community to enhance its efforts to create an enabling environment for social development and poverty eradication through increasing market access for developing countries, technology transfer on mutually agreed terms, financial aid and a comprehensive solution to the external debt problem;

10. *Welcomes* the increased resources that are becoming available as a result of the establishment of timetables by many developed countries for achieving the target of 0.7 per cent of gross national product for official development assistance to developing countries, as well as the target of 0.15 to 0.20 per cent of gross national product of developed countries for official development assistance to least developed countries, and urges those developed countries that have not yet done so to make concrete efforts in this regard in accordance with their commitments;

11. *Acknowledges* that good governance and the rule of law at the national and international levels are essential for sustained economic growth, sustainable development and the eradication of poverty and hunger;

12. *Stresses* that full and productive employment and decent work for all are key elements of sustainable development of all countries, and should therefore be a priority objective of national policies and international cooperation;

13. *Also stresses* that policies should be devised through which to pursue both economic efficiency and equity;

14. *Urges* Governments, with the cooperation of relevant entities, to develop systems of social protection and to extend or broaden, as appropriate, their effectiveness and coverage, including for workers in the informal economy, recognizing the need for social protection systems to provide social security and support labour-market participation; invites the International Labour Organization to strengthen its social protection strategies and policies on extending social security coverage; and also urges Governments, while taking account of national circumstances, to focus on the needs of those living in, or vulnerable to, poverty and give particular consideration to universal access to basic social security systems;

15. *Invites* the International Labour Organization to continue to assist States, as appropriate and upon request, in the strengthening of their social protection strategies and policies on extending social security coverage;

16. *Calls upon* the public sector to continue to play its important role in developing an environment that enables the effective generation of full and productive employment and decent work for all, while acknowledging its role as an employer;

17. *Calls upon* the private sector to continue to exercise its vital role in generating new investments, employment and financing for development and in advancing efforts towards full employment and decent work;

18. *Encourages* Governments to continue to pursue the creation of a conducive environment for enterprise development in both rural and urban areas, including by giving particular attention to policies that promote microenterprises, small and medium-sized enterprises, cooperatives and other forms of social enterprises and the participation and entrepreneurship of women, including rural women, through, inter alia, improved administrative regimes for the registration of small businesses, access to microcredit, social security systems and information on markets and new technology, as well as improved regulations;

19. *Stresses* that policies and strategies for achieving full employment and decent work for all should include specific measures to promote gender equality and foster social integration of social groups, such as youth, persons with disabilities, and older persons, as well as migrants and indigenous peoples;

20. *Also stresses* that these policies and strategies should promote gender equality, empowerment of women and better possibilities for all to reconcile work and private and family life;

21. *Encourages* Governments, the private sector, non-governmental organizations and other actors of civil society to promote and protect the rights of women workers, to take action to remove structural and legal barriers as well as stereotypic attitudes towards gender equality at work,

and to initiate positive steps to promote equal pay for equal work or work of equal value;

22. *Reaffirms* that social integration policies should seek to reduce inequalities, promote access to basic social services, education for all and health care, and increase the participation and integration of social groups;

23. *Also reaffirms* the commitment to develop and implement strategies that give persons with disabilities everywhere equal opportunities to secure full access to productive employment and decent work on an equal basis with others and without any kind of discrimination, including by promoting a labour market and a work environment that are open, inclusive and accessible to all and by ensuring just and favourable conditions of work;

24. *Urges* the development and implementation of integrated policies and strategies that promote opportunities for youth, including those living in rural areas, to prepare for, access and retain full and productive employment and decent work, and for mainstreaming youth employment into national development strategies, as well as encourage young people's entrepreneurship, inter alia, through entrepreneurship education; at the same time, also urges that Governments should promote access to work through integrated policies that enable the creation of new and quality jobs for young people and facilitate access to those jobs; and stresses the importance of the Youth Employment Network as a peer exchange mechanism at the national, regional and international levels;

25. *Stresses* the importance of creating an enabling environment for social dialogue by ensuring effective representation and participation of workers' organizations in order to contribute to the development of policies for achieving broad-based social progress, in particular for promoting full and productive employment and decent work for all;

26. *Also stresses* that non-discrimination against older persons, especially in the labour market, is crucial;

27. *Acknowledges* the important nexus between international migration and social development, and stresses the importance of effectively enforcing labour laws applicable to migrant workers and members of their families, including any related to remuneration, conditions of health, safety at work and the right of freedom of association, and reaffirms that migrants, regardless of their immigration status, should be accorded the protection of all human rights;

28. *Recognizes* the importance of the International Labour Organization Declaration on Fundamental Principles and Rights at Work;

29. *Reaffirms* the critical role of both formal and nonformal education in the achievement of full employment and decent work for all, in particular basic education and training for eradicating illiteracy; and in this regard also reaffirms the need to intensify efforts to implement effectively the International Plan of Action for the United Nations Literacy Decade and to integrate substantially those efforts in the Education for All process and other activities of the United Nations Educational, Scientific and Cultural Organization, as well as other literacy initiatives within the framework of the internationally agreed development goals, including the Millennium Development Goals;

30. *Also reaffirms* that priority needs to be given to providing training and skills enhancement to increase the employability of the workforce and its adaptability to changing labour markets and that comprehensive policies need to be designed to provide access to education, vocational education and technical training, capacity-building, upgrading skills and acquisition of new knowledge and lifelong learning, and to raise the quality of education with the help of the international community, as appropriate;

31. *Emphasizes* that promoting decent work aims at the overall improvement of living and working conditions for all and encourages efforts, as appropriate to the country context, to address the challenge to gradually formalizing economic activities in the informal sector and improving working conditions and achieving increased social protection coverage for all therein;

32. *Stresses* the importance of promoting corporate social responsibility and accountability, encourages responsible business practices such as those promoted by the Global Compact, and invites the private sector to take into account not only the economic and financial but also the development, social, human rights, gender and environmental implications of its undertakings; and underlines the importance of the International Labour Organization Tripartite Declaration of Principles concerning Multinational Enterprises and Social Policy;

33. *Invites*, being mindful of General Assembly resolution 62/131 of 18 December 2007, the Commission for Social Development and other relevant entities of the United Nations system to continue to integrate into their work programmes and give priority attention to the Copenhagen commitments and the Declaration on the tenth anniversary of the World Summit for Social Development, to continue to be actively involved in their follow-up and to monitor the achievement of those commitments and undertakings; and to emphasize in its review of the implementation of the Copenhagen Declaration on Social Development and the Programme of Action of the World Summit for Social Development, the increased exchange of national, regional and international experiences, the focused and interactive dialogues among experts and practitioners and the sharing of best practices and lessons learned;

34. *Calls for* increased national investment in and international development funding and investment flows to developing countries and countries with economies in transition that are targeted to sectors of the economy with greater potential in order to generate productive employment and decent work for all, and strongly encourages multilateral and bilateral donor and inter-agency cooperation in the pursuit of these goals and full and productive employment and decent work for all, in accordance with national development strategies;

35. *Encourages* all relevant organizations of the United Nations system to collaborate in using, adapting and evaluating the application of the Toolkit for Mainstreaming Employment and Decent Work developed by the International Labour Organization and endorsed by the United Nations System Chief Executives Board for Coordination;

36. *Calls upon* the United Nations funds, programmes and specialized agencies to assess and adopt in their action plans, as appropriate within their respective mandates, the three-phased approach proposed by the International

Labour Organization to promote the goals of full employment and decent work for all as presented in the report of the Secretary-General entitled "The role of the United Nations system in promoting full and productive employment and decent work for all";

37. *Requests* the funds, programmes and agencies of the United Nations system and invites financial institutions to support efforts to mainstream the goals of full and productive employment and decent work for all in their policies, programmes and activities, and in this regard invites stakeholders to duly take account of the International Labour Organization decent-work country programmes in order to achieve a more coherent and pragmatic United Nations approach to development at the national level on a voluntary basis;

38. *Decides* to keep full and productive employment and decent work for all under review, and requests the Secretary-General to submit a report on the implementation of the present resolution to the Commission for Social Development at its forty-seventh session and to the General Assembly at its sixty-fourth session as part of the report on the outcome of the implementation of the World Summit for Social Development and of the twenty-fourth special session of the Assembly.

Future organization and methods of work of the Commission for Social Development

In response to Economic and Social Council resolutions 2005/11 [YUN 2005, p. 1192] and 2006/18 [YUN 2006, p. 1277], the Secretariat submitted a November 2007 note on future organization and methods of work of the Commission on Social Development [E/CN.5/2008/5]. The note provided background on the review of the Commission's methods of work and stated that since the Commission had taken up the issue of poverty eradication at its 2006 session and full employment and decent work at its 2007 and 2008 sessions, the Secretariat, in consultation with the Bureau of the Commission, proposed "Social integration" as the priority theme for its 2009–2010 review and policy cycle.

ECONOMIC AND SOCIAL COUNCIL ACTION

On 24 July [meeting 42], the Economic and Social Council, on the recommendation of the Commission for Social Development [E/2008/26], adopted **resolution 2008/19** without vote [agenda item 14 *(b)*].

Future organization and methods of work of the Commission for Social Development

The Economic and Social Council,

Recalling its resolution 2005/11 of 21 July 2005 on the future organization and methods of work of the Commission for Social Development, in which the Economic and Social Council decided that the Commission should review the functioning of the two-year review and policy cycle in order to ensure that that approach enhanced its effectiveness and functioning,

Recalling also its resolution 2006/18 of 26 July 2006, in which the Council noted the usefulness of identifying the themes for the 2009–2010 review and policy cycle during the forty-sixth session of the Commission,

Noting that the Commission discussed the priority theme of "Promoting full employment and decent work for all" at its forty-fifth and forty-sixth sessions, as the first of the core themes of the World Summit for Social Development addressed under the two-year review and policy cycle,

1. *Reaffirms* that discussing one core issue as presented in the outcome document of the World Summit for Social Development over a two-year period allows the Commission for Social Development to go into greater depth by also addressing related cross-cutting issues, emerging issues and linkages with other issues relevant to the theme under discussion;

2. *Decides* that the priority theme for the 2009–2010 review and policy cycle should be "Social integration", taking into account its relationship with poverty eradication and full employment and decent work for all;

3. *Takes note* of its decision in resolution 2005/11, as recalled in resolution 2006/18, that the Commission should discuss each of the core themes of the World Summit for Social Development, namely, poverty eradication, full employment and social integration, under the two-year review and policy cycle;

4. *Notes* the usefulness of identifying the theme for the 2011–2012 review and policy cycle during the forty-eighth session of the Commission;

5. *Decides* that the Commission should maintain the two-year review and policy cycle until its fiftieth session and that it should continue to keep its methods of work under review.

Follow-up to International Year of Volunteers (2001)

In General Assembly **resolution 63/153** (see p. 987) of 18 December, the Assembly invited the Commission for Social Development to consider "volunteerism for development" in the context of its theme of social integration at its forty-seventh (2009) and forty-eighth (2010) sessions. It also decided that, on or around 5 December 2011—the International Volunteer Day for Economic and Social Development—two plenary meetings of the Assembly's sixty-sixth session should be devoted to follow-up to the International Year and the commemoration of its tenth anniversary, under the item entitled "Social development".

United Nations Research Institute for Social Development

During 2008, the United Nations Research Institute for Social Development (UNRISD) continued to conduct research into social and economic development, promoting a multidisciplinary approach that emphasized the social effects of development policies and the factors and contexts that shape decision-making processes.

A November report by the UNRISD Board [E/CN.5/2009/8] described the Institute's activities in 2007 and 2008, carried out under the programme designed for 2005–2009, which focused on social policy, poverty reduction and equity. Research was carried out on the flagship project, Poverty Reduction and Policy Regimes, and on 15 other projects under five programme areas: social policy and development; gender and development; markets, business and regulation; civil society and social movements; and identities, conflict and cohesion. During the reporting period, UNRISD issued 55 publications and two CD-ROM libraries of publications issued from the mid-1980s through 2007; it also tracked nearly 80 references to its work in the official documents and publications of UN bodies and the specialized agencies. The Institute's core funding came from voluntary contributions from seven Governments in 2007 and 2008. It also received project-specific contributions from Governments, international agencies and foundations.

Persons with disabilities

World Programme of Action concerning Disabled Persons

In response to General Assembly resolution 62/127 [YUN 2007, p. 1116], the Secretary-General submitted a July report [A/63/183] on the fifth quinquennial review and appraisal of the World Programme of Action concerning Disabled Persons, adopted by Assembly resolution 37/52 [YUN 1982, p. 981]. The report, based on the contributions of 36 Governments, 17 UN system entities and other data available to the Secretariat, noted that major developments since the fourth review and appraisal [YUN 2003, p. 1105] included the 2006 adoption by the Assembly, in resolution 61/106 [YUN 2006, p. 785], of the Convention on the Rights of Persons with Disabilities and its Optional Protocol, and their entry into force on 3 May (see p. 749), and the emergence of a new international architecture concerning the advancement of persons with disabilities. The report considered the international disability architecture; international norms and standards concerning the advancement of persons with disabilities; and progress and challenges in implementing the World Programme of Action in the context of development. The Secretary-General stressed the need to address the absence of more than 10 per cent of the world's population in the implementation, review and evaluation of the MDGs, and noted that the lack of a disability perspective undermined the objective of the Goals, which was to measure human development benchmarks on the way to more inclusive and equitable global development. He concluded that while the outcomes of major UN conferences and summits addressed advancement of persons with disabilities in their policy recommendations, such persons were yet to obtain recognition as agents and beneficiaries in furthering the development goals of the Millennium Declaration, in particular in progress on achieving on a sustainable and equitable basis: reduction of poverty and extreme hunger; access to universal primary education; gender equality; reduction of child mortality and improvements in maternal health; and action on HIV/AIDS, malaria and other diseases.

Recommendations to the General Assembly included: linking the international disability architecture with the MDG processes; developing and evaluating policies, plans and programmes based on the international disability architecture; disability-inclusive development cooperation; promoting capacity-building of all stakeholders, Governments, organizations of persons with disabilities and other civil society organizations; encouraging national collection of data and statistics on persons with disabilities; and making UN services more accessible to persons with disabilities. Annexed to the report were proposed updates of the World Programme of Action and examples of and guidelines for incorporating disability in monitoring and evaluating the MDGs.

Communication. In a 7 July note verbale to the Secretary-General [A/63/142], the Philippines proposed the inclusion in the provisional agenda of the Assembly's sixty-third (2008) session, under the item entitled "Social development", of a sub-item entitled "Review and appraisal of the World Programme of Action concerning Disabled Persons".

GENERAL ASSEMBLY ACTION

On 18 December [meeting 70], the General Assembly, on the recommendation of the Third Committee [A/63/424], adopted **resolution 63/150** without vote [agenda item 55 *(e)*].

Realizing the Millennium Development Goals for persons with disabilities through the implementation of the World Programme of Action concerning Disabled Persons and the Convention on the Rights of Persons with Disabilities

The General Assembly,

Recalling its previous resolutions concerning persons with disabilities, in particular resolutions 62/127 and 62/170 of 18 December 2007,

Recognizing the important role of the World Programme of Action concerning Disabled Persons as a policy instrument and of the Standard Rules on the Equalization of Opportunities for Persons with Disabilities as an instrument in support of efforts for persons with disabilities, and the need to update those instruments in the light of the provisions of the Convention on the Rights of Persons with Disabilities,

Welcoming the entry into force, on 3 May 2008, of the Convention and the Optional Protocol thereto, the purpose of which is to promote, protect and ensure the full and equal enjoyment of all human rights and fundamental freedoms by all persons with disabilities and to promote respect for their inherent dignity, and recognizing that the adoption of the Convention represents a crucial opportunity to consolidate disability-related activities within the United Nations system,

Aware that there are at least 650 million persons with disabilities worldwide, of whom 80 per cent live in developing countries, and that the majority of persons with disabilities live in conditions of poverty, and in this regard recognizing the critical need to address the negative impact of poverty on persons with disabilities,

Bearing in mind that conditions of peace and security based on full respect for the purposes and principles contained in the Charter of the United Nations and observance of applicable human rights instruments are indispensable for the full protection of persons with disabilities, in particular during armed conflicts and foreign occupation,

Underlining the importance of mobilizing resources at all levels for the successful implementation of the World Programme of Action and the Convention, and recognizing the importance of international cooperation and its promotion in support of national efforts, in particular in developing countries,

Reaffirming the need to include and integrate the rights, well-being and perspective of persons with disabilities in development efforts at the national, regional and international levels, without which the internationally agreed development goals, in particular the Millennium Development Goals, will not be genuinely achieved, and in this regard stressing the need to build or strengthen the effectiveness of national and regional legislation, the domestic policy environment and development programmes affecting persons with disabilities,

1. *Welcomes* the report of the Secretary-General on the fifth quinquennial review and appraisal of the World Programme of Action concerning Disabled Persons and his report on the status of the Convention on the Rights of Persons with Disabilities and the Optional Protocol thereto;

2. *Expresses concern* about the persistent gap between policy and practice regarding mainstreaming the perspective of persons with disabilities, including their rights and well-being, in the work of the United Nations in realizing the Millennium Development Goals;

3. *Urges* States to involve persons with disabilities on an equal basis with other persons in the formulation of strategies and plans, in particular those of most relevance to them;

4. *Encourages* States, in cooperation with, inter alia, intergovernmental and non-governmental organizations, as well as regional and international financial institutions and the private sector, as appropriate, to be guided in their work by the objectives of the United Nations instruments related to disability by, inter alia:

(a) Examining development strategies, policies and programmes aimed at implementing internationally agreed development goals, including the Millennium Development Goals, and ensuring that they are inclusive of issues concerning persons with disabilities and that they promote the equalization of opportunities for all;

(b) Ensuring accessibility and reasonable accommodation to enable persons with disabilities to realize their right to live independently and participate fully in all aspects of life, as well as to be agents and beneficiaries of development;

(c) Providing appropriate resources and accessible services and safety nets for persons with disabilities to ensure improved well-being for all;

(d) Ensuring an adequate standard of living and social protection for persons with disabilities, including through equal access to poverty and hunger eradication programmes, inclusive quality education, in particular free and compulsory primary education and the progressive introduction of free secondary education, as well as the same range, quality and standard of free or affordable health care in order to ensure the highest attainable standard of health for persons with disabilities, without discrimination on the basis of disability, and access to full and productive employment and decent work for all;

(e) Promoting and strengthening national capacities for participatory, democratic and accountable processes and mechanisms that further the equalization of opportunities for the full and effective participation of persons with disabilities in civil, political, economic, social and cultural life;

5. *Encourages* States to collect and analyse appropriate information, including statistical and research data that are disaggregated by age and sex, on the situation of persons with disabilities, bearing in mind appropriate protection of personal data, for purposes of policy planning, analysis and evaluation that include the perspective of persons with disabilities, and in this regard invites States to avail themselves of the technical services of the Statistics Division of the Department of Economic and Social Affairs of the Secretariat;

6. *Reaffirms* the role of the United Nations Voluntary Fund on Disability, and encourages States, intergovernmental organizations, concerned non-governmental organizations and the private sector to continue to support the Fund, with a view to strengthening its capacity to support catalytic and innovative activities to implement fully the development goals and objectives of the World Programme of Action concerning Disabled Persons, the Standard Rules on the Equalization of Opportunities for Persons with Disabilities and the Convention on the Rights of Persons with Disabilities, including the work of the Special Rapporteur on disability of the Commission for Social Development, and to facilitate international cooperation, including building national capacities, with emphasis on priorities for action identified in the present resolution;

7. *Calls upon* States to consider including in country reports in connection with the forthcoming periodic reviews of progress in achieving the Millennium Development Goals, a review and evaluation of the impact of development efforts on the rights, well-being and livelihood of persons with disabilities;

8. *Urges* States to pay special attention to the gender- and age-specific needs of persons with disabilities, including by taking measures to ensure their full and effective enjoyment of all human rights and fundamental freedoms;

9. *Also urges* States to take, in accordance with their obligations under international law, including international humanitarian law and international human rights law, all necessary measures to ensure the protection and safety of

persons with disabilities in situations of risk, including situations of armed conflict, humanitarian emergencies and the occurrence of natural disasters;

10. *Recognizes* the evolution of thought and discourse surrounding disability issues and the importance of aligning terminologies, definitions and models with the Convention, and requests the Secretary-General to update the World Programme of Action in this regard, while maintaining its thrust and objective of addressing disability issues in the context of economic and social development;

11. *Requests* the Secretary-General to give higher priority to the concerns of and issues related to persons with disabilities and their inclusion within the work programme of the United Nations system, and, within existing resources, to strengthen the role of the United Nations and its development programmes and agencies in mainstreaming disability issues, in promoting the rights and well-being of persons with disabilities and in taking into account the perspective and inclusion of persons with disabilities in the work of the United Nations system by:

(a) Promoting the inclusion of the perspective of persons with disabilities into the policies, programmes and projects of the Secretariat and the other United Nations bodies and agencies on a broader scale and with higher priority, based on a holistic approach in the work done in the fields of social development, human rights and non-discrimination, and in this regard ensuring that the 2010 World Programme on Population and Housing Censuses is inclusive of the perspective of persons with disabilities;

(b) Further strengthening action in all countries and providing assistance to developing countries, in particular to least developed countries, with special attention to persons with disabilities in vulnerable circumstances;

(c) Assisting Member States in formulating comprehensive and coherent policies and action plans, as well as projects, including pilot projects that promote, inter alia, international cooperation and technical assistance, in particular to enhance the capacities of government agencies, as well as civil society, including organizations of persons with disabilities, to implement programmes on disability;

12. *Encourages* States, in their efforts to realize the Millennium Development Goals, to recognize the importance of international cooperation and its promotion in support of national efforts for the realization of the purpose and objectives of the World Programme of Action and the Convention, and to undertake appropriate and effective measures in this regard between and among States and, as appropriate, in partnership with relevant international and regional organizations and civil society, in particular organizations of persons with disabilities;

13. *Requests* the Secretary-General:

(a) To submit to the General Assembly at its sixty-fourth session a report on the situation of persons with disabilities with respect to the realization of all the Millennium Development Goals and on lessons learned and synergies and complementarities achieved, based on the implementation of the World Programme of Action, the Standard Rules and the Convention, in order to provide a framework for Member States in their efforts to achieve the internationally agreed development goals for persons with disabilities;

(b) To submit to the General Assembly at its sixty-fifth session a comprehensive biennial report on the implementation of the World Programme of Action, and progress and challenges concerning the advancement of persons with disabilities in the context of development and the realization of the Millennium Development Goals;

(c) To request the Inter-Agency Support Group on the Convention on the Rights of Persons with Disabilities to integrate the rights of persons with disabilities into United Nations development activities and to provide guidelines for United Nations country teams.

Standard Rules on the Equalization of Opportunities for Persons with Disabilities

In response to Economic and Social Council resolution 2005/9 [YUN 2005, p. 1196], the Secretary-General submitted to the Commission for Social Development the annual report [E/CN.5/2008/3] of its Special Rapporteur on Disability on the monitoring of the implementation of the Standard Rules on the Equalization of Opportunities for Persons with Disabilities, adopted by General Assembly resolution 48/96 [YUN 1993, p. 977]. The Special Rapporteur stated that her activities over the previous 12 months had focused on: urging the proper and more intensive implementation of the Standard Rules; advocating for the issues of persons with disabilities and deepening awareness of their rights; developing strong national disability legislation; increasing interregional cooperation; supporting the activities of international disability organizations and federations; ensuring that the work of international development agencies was targeted to persons with disabilities; and urging Governments to sign and ratify the Convention on the Rights of Persons with Disabilities and sustaining the spirit of cooperation and collaboration that prevailed during its negotiation and drafting. Work also continued on the second phase of the Global Survey on government action in implementing the Standard Rules. The second phase looked at the discrepancies and similarities in implementation across the globe and the extent and coverage of the implementation of each of the rules. It also included a comparative analysis between the responses obtained from organizations of persons with disabilities and Governments from a sample of 28 countries or areas in which Governments and organizations responded to the Survey. The results revealed a great discrepancy in implementation between regions as well as between Governments and organizations. However, the results were consistent with the social, economic and developmental realities of each region.

The Special Rapporteur emphasized that the legally binding nature of the Convention and the procedural and methodological nature of the Standard Rules were essential elements in the struggle for rights and recognition of persons with disabilities, and recommended that the Standard Rules co-exist alongside the Convention in all activities relating to the enjoyment and exercise of their rights. All States parties to the Convention should begin setting up systems and mechanisms to monitor implementation and remedy violations, while at the same time raising awareness of the Convention and its articles; the monitoring systems and structures should include persons with disabilities who themselves were the best experts on what constituted violations of their rights. The importance of accurate disaggregated information on the size, scope, types, causes, geographical distribution and concentration of disability and division by age, gender and socio-economic conditions was emphasized. National censuses should include detailed information on disability and persons with disabilities, and Governments should make efforts to obtain the information upon which they could base policy decisions, make financial allocations, and deliver services. The Special Rapporteur stressed the importance of international cooperation in implementing and universalizing a new international culture based on non-discrimination and respect for all human beings, regardless of ability. She recommended that countries commit to the exchange of ideas, practices and expertise, and to international financial aid. Cooperation should also take place at the interregional level where countries should include Governments and organizations of persons with disabilities.

ECONOMIC AND SOCIAL COUNCIL ACTION

On 24 July [meeting 42], the Economic and Social Council, on the recommendation of the Commission for Social Development [E/2008/26], adopted **resolution 2008/20** without vote [agenda item 14 *(b)*].

Further promotion of equalization of opportunities by, for and with persons with disabilities and protection of their human rights

The Economic and Social Council,

Recalling General Assembly resolution 37/52 of 3 December 1982, by which the Assembly adopted the World Programme of Action concerning Disabled Persons, resolution 48/96 of 20 December 1993, by which it adopted the Standard Rules on the Equalization of Opportunities for Persons with Disabilities, and resolution 61/106 of 13 December 2006, by which it adopted the Convention on the Rights of Persons with Disabilities,

Recalling its resolution 2005/9 of 21 July 2005 on the further promotion of equalization of opportunities by, for and with persons with disabilities and protection of their human rights, as well as General Assembly resolutions 60/131 of 16 December 2005 and 62/127 and 62/170 of 18 December 2007,

Welcoming the fact that since the opening for signature of the Convention on the Rights of Persons with Disabilities and the Optional Protocol thereto on 30 March 2007, one hundred and twenty-five States have signed and thirty States have ratified the Convention and seventy-one States have signed and eighteen States have ratified the Optional Protocol, and looking forward to their entering into force,

Mindful of the need to design, adopt and implement effective strategies, policies and programmes to promote and protect the rights and well-being of persons with disabilities as well as to promote their full and effective participation in the civil, political, economic, social and cultural spheres on an equal basis with others in order to achieve a society for all,

Stressing the need to enhance complementarity and synergy in the implementation of the United Nations disability agenda through the World Programme of Action concerning Disabled Persons, the Standard Rules on the Equalization of Opportunities for Persons with Disabilities and the Convention on the Rights of Persons with Disabilities,

Encouraging States to continue to formulate comprehensive and coherent policies and action plans, as well as projects, that promote international cooperation and technical assistance, particularly to enhance the capacities of Government agencies and institutions, as well as civil society, including organizations of persons with disabilities, to implement programmes on disability for the equalization of opportunities for, the full enjoyment of all human rights by, and the well-being of persons with disabilities,

Noting with grave concern that persons with disabilities are subject to multiple or aggravated forms of discrimination, and recognizing the critical need to address the negative impact of poverty affecting the majority of persons with disabilities, who continue to be excluded from the benefits of development, such as education and access to gainful and productive employment and decent work as well as appropriate health care and accessible social services,

1. *Welcomes* the work of the Special Rapporteur on Disability of the Commission for Social Development, and takes note of her report on the monitoring of the implementation of the Standard Rules on the Equalization of Opportunities for Persons with Disabilities;

2. *Decides* to renew the mandate of the Special Rapporteur until 31 December 2011 to further the promotion and monitoring of the Standard Rules on the Equalization of Opportunities for Persons with Disabilities in accordance with the provisions set down in section IV of the Standard Rules, including the human rights dimensions of disability, and with the provisions of the present resolution;

3. *Requests* the Special Rapporteur to further:

(a) Advocate the equalization of opportunities for, the full enjoyment of all human rights by, and the well-being of persons with disabilities in all respects, in line with the Standard Rules on the Equalization of Opportunities for Persons with Disabilities, the World Programme of Action concerning Disabled Persons and the Convention on the Rights of Persons with Disabilities;

(b) Create awareness of the Convention on the Rights of Persons with Disabilities, including for the purpose of ensuring its wider signature and ratification by Member States;

(c) Act as a catalyst to promote international and technical cooperation on disability issues, including by identifying strategic areas for the exchange and sharing of expertise, best practices, knowledge, information and relevant technologies, in order to enhance the capacity-building of Member States;

(d) Collaborate, in the fulfilment of the above tasks, with all relevant stakeholders, including organizations of persons with disabilities;

4. *Calls upon* all Governments to continue to cooperate and engage in direct dialogue with the Special Rapporteur and to provide him or her with all the relevant information needed to fulfil the mandate effectively;

5. *Calls upon* those States and regional integration organizations that have not yet signed or ratified the Convention on the Rights of Persons with Disabilities and the Optional Protocol thereto to consider doing so as a matter of priority;

6. *Urges* Governments, the Secretary-General, intergovernmental organizations and non-governmental organizations, and invites relevant human rights treaty bodies, relevant bodies and organizations of the United Nations system, including the Bretton Woods institutions, multilateral development agencies and regional commissions, in accordance with their mandates, to create greater awareness and support for the further implementation of the World Programme of Action concerning Disabled Persons, the Standard Rules on the Equalization of Opportunities for Persons with Disabilities and the Convention on the Rights of Persons with Disabilities, and to promote the enjoyment of all human rights and fundamental freedoms as well as the equalization of opportunities and the well-being of persons with disabilities, and to improve consultation, exchange of information and coordination;

7. *Encourages* Governments, intergovernmental organizations, non-governmental organizations and the private sector to continue to contribute to the United Nations Voluntary Fund on Disability in order to support the activities of the Special Rapporteur as well as new and expanded initiatives to strengthen national capacities for the equalization of opportunities by, for and with persons with disabilities;

8. *Expresses concern* at the insufficiency of resources for the Special Rapporteur, and recognizes the importance of providing adequate resources for the implementation of his or her mandate by the Special Rapporteur;

9. *Requests* the Special Rapporteur to submit to the Commission for Social Development an annual report on his or her activities in implementing the present resolution.

Convention on the Rights of Persons with Disabilities

The Convention on the Rights of Persons with Disabilities and its Optional Protocol, adopted by General Assembly resolution 61/106 [YUN 2006, p. 785], entered into force on 3 May (see p. 749).

By **resolution 63/192** of 18 December (see p. 750), the Assembly welcomed the entry into force, the holding of the first session of the Conference of States Parties to the Convention on 31 October and 3 November, and the establishment of the Committee on the Rights of Persons with Disabilities. The Assembly invited the Secretary-General to assist States in becoming parties to the Convention and the Optional Protocol, to continue the progressive implementation of standards and guidelines for the accessibility of facilities and services of the UN system, and to promote the rights of persons with disabilities in the UN system.

By **resolution 63/263** of 24 December (see p. 1545), the Assembly took note of the report of the Secretary-General on revised estimates resulting from the Convention's entry into force.

Mainstreaming disability in the development agenda

In response to Economic and Social Council resolution 2006/18 [YUN 2006, p. 1277], the Secretariat submitted to the Commission for Social Development a November 2007 note [E/CN.5/2008/6] that reviewed the background, practicalities and resources related to mainstreaming disability in the development agenda in the context of the 2006 adoption of the Convention on the Rights of Persons with Disabilities [YUN 2006, p. 785]. The Secretariat noted that there were some 650 million persons with disabilities in the world, or 10 per cent of the global population. It stated that the Convention offered an opportunity to consolidate disability-related activities and to develop policies and structures that ensured that persons with disabilities were mainstreamed within the UN system. Lessons learned from gender and HIV/AIDS mainstreaming could provide guidance in that regard. The adoption of the Convention was also an opportunity for human rights and development actors to combine and integrate those two areas. As a human rights and development instrument, the Convention identified practical measures to create development programmes that were inclusive of, and accessible to, persons with disabilities. The note stated that halfway to the MDG target date of 2015, persons with disabilities remained absent from programming and discourse on achievement of the Goals. An estimated 80 per cent of those persons were living in developing countries, and the failure to integrate them in development activities would mean failure to achieve the MDGs. Ensuring that persons with disabilities could access decent work was of critical importance in order for them to be represented in the development agenda on an equal basis with others, and the involvement of civil society, including organizations of persons with disabilities, in national and international mechanisms would guide the development agenda towards integrating and including persons with disabilities.

ECONOMIC AND SOCIAL COUNCIL ACTION

On 24 July [meeting 42], the Economic and Social Council, on the recommendation of the Commission for Social Development [E/2008/26], adopted **resolution 2008/21** without vote [agenda item 14 (b)].

Mainstreaming disability in the development agenda

The Economic and Social Council,

Reaffirming that the Copenhagen Declaration on Social Development and the Programme of Action of the World Summit for Social Development and the further initiatives for social development adopted by the General Assembly at its twenty-fourth special session, as well as a continued global dialogue on social development issues, constitute the basic framework for the promotion of social development for all at the national and international levels,

Recalling its previous resolutions concerning persons with disabilities and the relevant resolutions adopted by the General Assembly,

Acknowledging that the majority of the 650 million persons with disabilities in the world live in conditions of poverty, and in this regard recognizing the critical need to address the negative impact of poverty on persons with disabilities,

Acknowledging also that persons with disabilities, in particular women and children with disabilities, are subject to aggravated and multiple forms of discrimination,

Convinced that addressing the profound social, cultural and economic disadvantage experienced by many persons with disabilities and that promoting the progressive removal of barriers to their full and effective participation in all aspects of development will further the equalization of opportunities and contribute to the realization of a "society for all" in the twenty-first century,

Welcoming the adoption of the Convention on the Rights of Persons with Disabilities and the Optional Protocol thereto on 13 December 2006 and the fact that since their opening for signature on 30 March 2007, one hundred and twenty-five States have signed and thirty States have ratified the Convention and seventy-one States have signed and eighteen States have ratified the Optional Protocol,

Recognizing the importance of the forthcoming fifth review and appraisal of the World Programme of Action concerning Disabled Persons, including its updating, to be conducted by the General Assembly in 2008,

Concerned that halfway to the target date of 2015, the situation of persons with disabilities has not been adequately considered, including in the discussions and reports on the internationally agreed development goals, including the Millennium Development Goals,

1. *Calls upon* those States that have not yet done so to consider signing and ratifying the Convention on the Rights of Persons with Disabilities and the Optional Protocol thereto as a matter of priority;

2. *Expresses concern* about the persistent gap between policy and practice regarding mainstreaming the perspective of persons with disabilities, including their rights and well-being, into the work of the United Nations in realizing the Millennium Development Goals;

3. *Encourages* States, entities of the United Nations system and other members of the international community to take advantage of the range of international normative and policy instruments on disability, including the World Programme of Action concerning Disabled Persons, the Standard Rules on the Equalization of Opportunities for Persons with Disabilities, and the Convention on the Rights of Persons with Disabilities, in guiding their efforts to ensure that the issues related to persons with disabilities, including the perspective of persons with disabilities, are incorporated into the formulation of policies, the conduct of their mandate and missions and their budget allocations, aiming at the full and effective participation and inclusion of persons with disabilities in development, both as beneficiaries and as agents;

4. *Invites* States, relevant entities of the United Nations system, including the agencies, funds and programmes, as well as regional and international financial and development institutions, civil society and the private sector, to take into account and include mainstreaming of the issues related to persons with disabilities, including the perspective of persons with disabilities, when developing their work strategies and action plans to promote the education and training of personnel so as to foster increased sensitivity, knowledge and skills in respect of understanding how to address issues related to persons with disabilities in their respective mandates and work;

5. *Requests* relevant entities of the United Nations system, including the agencies, funds and programmes, as well as regional and international financial institutions, to include issues related to persons with disabilities, including the perspective of persons with disabilities, when planning country offices in accordance with their mandates;

6. *Urges* States, relevant entities of the United Nations system, including the agencies, funds and programmes, regional and international financial and development institutions, civil society and the private sector, to give priority to the promotion of full and productive employment and decent work for persons with disabilities, as a key factor in ensuring that persons with disabilities benefit from development on an equal basis with others, and fully enjoy all human rights, including the right to work, and the opportunity to gain a living by work freely chosen or accepted, including by providing access to education and training, access to microcredit schemes and entrepreneurial opportunities, fostering a labour market and work environment that is open, inclusive and accessible to persons with disabilities, and promoting inclusive employment and human resources policies and reasonable accommodation in the workplace;

7. *Also urges* States, relevant entities of the United Nations system, including the agencies, funds and programmes, as well as regional and international financial and development institutions, civil society and the private sector, to promote the participation of persons with disabilities on an equal basis with others in decision-making and their involvement in the formulation, implementation and evaluation of strategies, plans and programmes pertaining to them;

8. *Stresses* the need to enhance the accountability of all actors, including at the highest levels of decision-making, in the work of mainstreaming disability in the development agenda, including in the assessment of the impact of development efforts on the situation of persons with disabilities;

9. *Recognizes* the strategic importance of complementing efforts towards the mainstreaming of the issues related to persons with disabilities, including the perspective of persons with disabilities, inter alia, while considering the allocation of resources;

10. *Encourages* all States, concerned intergovernmental organizations and international organizations, civil society, in particular organizations of persons with disabilities, and the private sector to engage in cooperative arrangements that aim at providing the necessary technical and expert assistance to enhance capacities in mainstreaming issues related to persons with disabilities, including the perspective of persons with disabilities, in development efforts, and in this regard encourages the Secretariat and other relevant bodies to find improved ways to enhance international technical cooperation;

11. *Encourages* States to mainstream disability in poverty eradication policies and strategies to ensure their accessibility, and in this regard encourages the international community to provide support and assistance;

12. *Urges* all States, international and regional organizations and civil society, in particular organizations of persons with disabilities, to ensure that international cooperation, including international development programmes, is inclusive of and accessible to persons with disabilities;

13. *Urges* States, relevant entities of the United Nations system, including the agencies, funds and programmes, and invites international and regional development organizations and financial institutions, to take concrete measures to incorporate issues related to persons with disabilities, including the perspective of persons with disabilities, and accessibility requirements into development cooperation and development finance activities;

14. *Requests* the Secretary-General to prepare a report on the implementation of the present resolution for submission to the Commission for Social Development at its forty-eighth session.

Cultural development

Culture of peace

Report of UNESCO Director-General. In response to General Assembly resolution 62/89 [YUN 2007, p. 1119], the Secretary-General transmitted a July report [A/63/127] of the Director-General of the United Nations Educational, Scientific and Cultural Organization (UNESCO) on the International Decade for a Culture of Peace and Non-Violence for the Children of the World, 2001–2010, proclaimed in Assembly resolution 53/25 [YUN 1998, p. 639]. The report, which followed on from the UNESCO 2007 annual progress report on the Decade [YUN 2007, p. 1119], provided an overview of the activities carried out by UNESCO and other UN entities to promote and implement the Programme of Action on a Culture of Peace [YUN 1999, p. 594]. Eight actions were defined in the Programme of Action: fostering a culture of peace through education; promoting sustainable economic and social development; promoting respect for all human rights; ensuring equality between women and men; fostering democratic participation; advancing understanding, tolerance and solidarity; supporting participatory communication and the free flow of information; and promoting international peace and security. Also addressed were the role of civil society, and communication and networking arrangements.

The Director-General encouraged UN agencies, funds and programmes to continue focusing their programmes on the various dimensions of the culture of peace, especially at the country level. States were encouraged to: increase educational efforts to remove hate messages, distortions, prejudice, and negative bias from textbooks and other educational media, and ensure a basic knowledge and understanding of the world's main cultures, civilizations and religions; update and revise education and cultural policies to reflect a human rights-based approach, cultural diversity, intercultural dialogue and sustainable development; revise national laws and policies that were discriminatory against women, and adopt legislation that addressed domestic violence, the trafficking of women and girls and gender-based violence; eliminate the practice of female genital mutilation, including through legal and policy reforms, national capacity-building and work at the community level; ensure that the gender dimension was integrated into all national development plans; and expand access to information and communications technologies to bring the benefits of all levels and means of education to girls and women, the excluded, the poor, the marginalized and those with special needs.

The Director-General's report was considered at the Assembly's high-level meeting on the culture of peace (12–13 November) (see p. 1217).

GENERAL ASSEMBLY ACTION

On 5 December [meeting 64], the General Assembly adopted **resolution 63/113** [draft: A/63/L.23 & Add.1] without vote [agenda item 45].

International Decade for a Culture of Peace and Non-Violence for the Children of the World, 2001–2010

The General Assembly,

Bearing in mind the Charter of the United Nations, including the purposes and principles contained therein, and especially the dedication to saving succeeding generations from the scourge of war,

Recalling the Constitution of the United Nations Educational, Scientific and Cultural Organization, which states that, "since wars begin in the minds of men, it is in the minds of men that the defences of peace must be constructed",

Recalling also its previous resolutions on a culture of peace, in particular resolution 52/15 of 20 November 1997 proclaiming 2000 the International Year for the Culture of Peace, resolution 53/25 of 10 November 1998 proclaiming the period 2001–2010 the International Decade for a Culture of Peace and Non-Violence for the Children of the World, and resolutions 56/5 of 5 November 2001, 57/6 of 4 November 2002, 58/11 of 10 November 2003, 59/143 of 15 December 2004, 60/3 of 20 October 2005, 61/45 of 4 December 2006 and 62/89 of 17 December 2007,

Reaffirming the Declaration and Programme of Action on a Culture of Peace, recognizing that they serve, inter alia, as the basis for the observance of the Decade, and convinced that the effective and successful observance of the Decade throughout the world will promote a culture of peace and non-violence that benefits humanity, in particular future generations,

Recalling the United Nations Millennium Declaration, which calls for the active promotion of a culture of peace,

Taking note of Commission on Human Rights resolution 2000/66 of 26 April 2000, entitled "Towards a culture of peace",

Taking note also of the report of the Secretary-General on the International Decade for a Culture of Peace and Non-Violence for the Children of the World, including paragraph 28 thereof, which indicates that each of the ten years of the Decade will be marked with a different priority theme related to the Programme of Action,

Noting the relevance of the World Summit on Sustainable Development, held in Johannesburg, South Africa, from 26 August to 4 September 2002, the International Conference on Financing for Development, held in Monterrey, Mexico, from 18 to 22 March 2002, the special session of the General Assembly on children, held in New York from 8 to 10 May 2002, the World Conference against Racism, Racial Discrimination, Xenophobia and Related Intolerance, held in Durban, South Africa, from 31 August to 8 September 2001, and the United Nations Decade for Human Rights Education, 1995–2004, for the International Decade for a Culture of Peace and Non-Violence for the Children of the World, 2001–2010, as well as the need to implement, as appropriate, the relevant decisions agreed upon therein,

Recognizing that all efforts made by the United Nations system in general and the international community at large for peacekeeping, peacebuilding, the prevention of conflicts, disarmament, sustainable development, the promotion of human dignity and human rights, democracy, the rule of law, good governance and gender equality at the national and international levels contribute greatly to the culture of peace,

Noting that its resolution 57/337 of 3 July 2003 on the prevention of armed conflict could contribute to the further promotion of a culture of peace,

Taking into account the "Manifesto 2000" initiative of the United Nations Educational, Scientific and Cultural Organization promoting a culture of peace, which has so far received over seventy-five million signatures of endorsement throughout the world,

Taking note with appreciation of the report of the Director-General of the United Nations Educational, Scientific and Cultural Organization on the implementation of resolution 62/89,

Taking note of the 2005 World Summit Outcome adopted at the High-level Plenary Meeting of the General Assembly,

Welcoming the designation of 2 October as the International Day of Non-Violence,

Recalling the proclamation by the United Nations Educational, Scientific and Cultural Organization of 21 February as the International Mother Language Day, which aims at promoting and preserving linguistic and cultural diversity, and multilingualism, in order to foster a culture of peace, harmony, cross-cultural dialogue and mutual understanding,

Appreciating the ongoing efforts of the Alliance of Civilizations and the Tripartite Forum on Interfaith Cooperation for Peace in promoting a culture of peace,

1. *Reiterates* that the objective of the International Decade for a Culture of Peace and Non-Violence for the Children of the World, 2001–2010, is to strengthen further the global movement for a culture of peace following the observance of the International Year for the Culture of Peace in 2000;

2. *Invites* Member States to continue to place greater emphasis on and expand their activities promoting a culture of peace and non-violence, in particular during the Decade, at the national, regional and international levels and to ensure that peace and non-violence are fostered at all levels;

3. *Commends* the United Nations Educational, Scientific and Cultural Organization for recognizing the promotion of a culture of peace as the expression of its fundamental mandate, and encourages it, as the lead agency for the Decade, to strengthen further the activities it has undertaken for promoting a culture of peace, including the dissemination of the Declaration and Programme of Action on a Culture of Peace and related materials in various languages across the world;

4. *Commends* the relevant United Nations bodies, in particular the United Nations Children's Fund, the United Nations Development Fund for Women and the University for Peace, for their activities in further promoting a culture of peace and non-violence, including the promotion of peace education and activities related to specific areas identified in the Programme of Action, and encourages them to continue and further strengthen and expand their efforts;

5. *Encourages* the Peacebuilding Commission to promote a culture of peace and non-violence for children in its activities;

6. *Encourages* the appropriate authorities to provide education, in children's schools, that includes lessons in mutual understanding, tolerance, active citizenship, human rights and the promotion of a culture of peace;

7. *Commends* civil society, including non-governmental organizations and young people, for their activities in further promoting a culture of peace and non-violence, including through their campaign to raise awareness on a culture of peace, and takes note of the progress achieved by more than seven hundred organizations in more than one hundred countries;

8. *Encourages* civil society, including non-governmental organizations, to further strengthen its efforts in furtherance of the objectives of the Decade, inter alia, by adopting its own programme of activities to complement the initiatives of Member States, the organizations of the United Nations system and other international and regional organizations;

9. *Encourages* the involvement of the mass media in education for a culture of peace and non-violence, with particular regard to children and young people, including through the planned expansion of the Culture of Peace News Network as a global network of Internet sites in many languages;

10. *Welcomes* the efforts made by the United Nations Educational, Scientific and Cultural Organization to continue the communication and networking arrangements established during the International Year for providing an instant update of developments related to the observance of the Decade;

11. *Invites* Member States to observe 21 September each year as the International Day of Peace, as a day of global ceasefire and non-violence, in accordance with resolution 55/282 of 7 September 2001;

12. *Invites* Member States, as well as civil society, including non-governmental organizations, to continue providing information to the Secretary-General on the observance of the Decade and the activities undertaken to promote a culture of peace and non-violence;

13. *Appreciates* the participation of Member States in the day of plenary meetings to review progress made in the implementation of the Declaration and Programme of Action and the observance of the Decade at its midpoint;

14. *Requests* the Secretary-General to explore enhancing mechanisms for the implementation of the Declaration and Programme of Action;

15. *Also requests* the Secretary-General to submit to the General Assembly at its sixty-fourth session a report on the implementation of the present resolution;

16. *Decides* to include in the provisional agenda of its sixty-fourth session the item entitled "Culture of peace".

On 24 December (**decision 63/552**), the Assembly decided that the item entitled "Culture of peace" would remain for consideration during its resumed sixty-third (2009) session.

Interreligious and intercultural understanding

In response to General Assembly resolution 62/90 [YUN 2007, p. 1122], the Secretary-General submitted an August report [A/63/262] in which he highlighted the activities carried out by key UN entities involved in interreligious and intercultural dialogue and provided information on the observance of the International Day of Non-violence (2 October) and the International Day of Peace (21 September). The report, which complemented that of the UNESCO Director-General on the International Decade for a Culture of Peace and Non-Violence for the Children of the World, 2001–2010 (see p. 1215), focused on activities carried out by UNESCO, the Alliance of Civilizations—launched by the Secretary-General in 2005 [YUN 2005, p. 1201]—the United Nations Population Fund, the Office of the United Nations High Commissioner for Human Rights, the UN Department of Public Information and the UN Department of Economic and Social Affairs. The Secretary-General also provided an overview of other regional and international activities aimed at promoting and deepening intercultural and interreligious dialogue. In conclusion, he suggested that given the growing number of actors involved, the Assembly should focus its future requests for reporting on preparations by the UN system and other major international actors for the International Year for the Rapprochement of Cultures (2010).

Communications. On 26 August [A/62/949], Cambodia informed the Secretary-General that it had hosted a regional conference on "Dialogue on Interfaith Cooperation for Peace and Harmony" (Phnom Penh, Cambodia, 3–6 April), with the participation of countries of South-East Asia and the Pacific.

On 21 October [A/63/510], the Netherlands and Thailand transmitted to the General Assembly President a document entitled "Amsterdam Statement on Interfaith Dialogue", issued by the Asia-Europe Meeting (ASEM) partners at the Fourth ASEM Interfaith Dialogue (Amsterdam, Netherlands, 3–5 June).

On 22 October [A/63/499], Saudi Arabia forwarded to the Secretary-General the revised text of the Madrid Declaration, issued by the World Conference on Dialogue (Madrid, Spain, 16–18 July).

Alliance of Civilizations

In a May letter [A/63/336], the Secretary-General transmitted to the President of the General Assembly the annual report of the High Representative for the Alliance of Civilizations, which covered the main activities carried out by the Alliance between May 2007 and April 2008 and highlighted the importance of the First Alliance of Civilizations Forum (Madrid, 15–16 January).

High-level meeting

The General Assembly President convened a high-level meeting on the culture of peace on 12 and 13 November [A/63/PV.46–50]. The high-level meeting had before it the report of the UNESCO Director-General on the International Decade for a Culture of Peace and Non-Violence for the Children of the World, 2001–2010 (see p. 1215) and the Secretary-General's report on interreligious and intercultural dialogue, understanding and cooperation for peace (see above).

GENERAL ASSEMBLY ACTION

On 13 November [meeting 50], the General Assembly adopted **resolution 63/22** [draft: A/63/L.24/Rev.1 & Add.1] without vote [agenda item 45].

Promotion of interreligious and intercultural dialogue, understanding and cooperation for peace

The General Assembly,

Reaffirming the purposes and principles enshrined in the Charter of the United Nations and the Universal Declaration of Human Rights, in particular the right to freedom of thought, conscience and religion,

Recalling its resolutions 56/6 of 9 November 2001, on the Global Agenda for Dialogue among Civilizations, 57/6 of 4 November 2002, concerning the promotion of a culture of peace and non-violence, 57/337 of 3 July 2003, on the prevention of armed conflict, 58/128 of 19 December 2003, on the promotion of religious and cultural understanding, harmony and cooperation, 59/23 of 11 November 2004, on the promotion of interreligious dialogue, 59/143 of 15 December 2004, on the International Decade for a Culture of Peace and Non-Violence for the Children of the World, 2001–2010, 60/167 of 16 December 2005, on human rights and cultural diversity, and 62/157 of 18 December 2007, on the elimination of all forms of intolerance and of discrimination based on religion or belief,

Recalling also its resolution 62/90 of 17 December 2007 on the promotion of interreligious and intercultural dialogue, understanding and cooperation for peace, and the declaration of 2010 as the International Year for the Rapprochement of Cultures,

Recognizing that cultural diversity and the pursuit of cultural development by all peoples and nations are a source of mutual enrichment for the cultural life of humankind,

Taking note of the various initiatives at the national, regional and international levels to enhancing dialogue, understanding and cooperation among religions, cultures and civilizations, which are mutually reinforcing and interrelated, inter alia, the fourth Asia-Pacific Dialogue on Interfaith Cooperation for Peace and Harmony, held in Phnom Penh from 3 to 6 April 2008, the Third Global Inter-Media Dialogue, held in Bali, Indonesia, on 7 and 8 May 2008, the Fourth Asia-Europe Meeting Interfaith Dialogue, held in Amsterdam from 3 to 5 June 2008, the World Conference on Dialogue, held in Madrid from 16 to 18 July 2008, the Sixth General Meeting of the World Public Forum "Dialogue of Civilizations", held in Rhodes, Greece, from 9 to 13 October 2008, the Second Alliance of Civilizations Forum, to be held in Istanbul, Turkey, on 2 and 3 April 2009, the Special Non-Aligned Movement Ministerial Meeting on Interfaith Dialogue and Cooperation for Peace and Development, to be held in Manila from 26 to 28 May 2009, the fifth Asia-Pacific Regional Interfaith Dialogue, to be held in Australia in 2009, the Parliament of the World's Religions, to be held in Melbourne, Australia, from 3 to 9 December 2009, and the Third Congress of Leaders of World and Traditional Religions, to be held in Astana on 1 and 2 July 2009, with the participation and technical assistance of the United Nations system,

Affirming the importance of sustaining the process of engaging all stakeholders in the interreligious, intercultural and intercivilizational dialogue within the appropriate initiatives at the various levels,

Recognizing the commitment of all religions to peace,

1. *Affirms* that mutual understanding and interreligious dialogue constitute important dimensions of the dialogue among civilizations and of the culture of peace;

2. *Takes note* of the report of the Secretary-General on interreligious and intercultural dialogue, understanding and cooperation for peace;

3. *Also takes note* of the work of the United Nations Educational, Scientific and Cultural Organization on interreligious dialogue in the context of its efforts to promote dialogue among civilizations, cultures and peoples, as well as activities related to a culture of peace, and welcomes its focus on concrete action at the global, regional and subregional levels and its flagship project on the promotion of interfaith dialogue;

4. *Reaffirms* the solemn commitment of all States to fulfil their obligations to promote universal respect for, and observance and protection of, all human rights and fundamental freedoms for all in accordance with the Charter of the United Nations, the Universal Declaration of Human Rights and other instruments relating to human rights and international law, the universal nature of these rights and freedoms being beyond question;

5. *Encourages* the promotion of dialogue among the media from all cultures and civilizations, emphasizes that everyone has the right to freedom of expression, and reaffirms that the exercise of this right carries with it special duties and responsibilities and may therefore be subject to certain restrictions, but these shall be only such as are provided by law and necessary for respect of the rights or reputations of others, protection of national security or of public order, or of public health or morals;

6. *Encourages* Member States to consider, as and where appropriate, initiatives that identify areas for practical action in all sectors and levels of society for the promotion of interreligious and intercultural dialogue, tolerance, understanding and cooperation, inter alia, the ideas suggested during the High-level Dialogue on Interreligious and Intercultural Understanding and Cooperation for Peace, held on 4 and 5 October 2007, including the idea of an enhanced process of dialogue among world religions;

7. *Takes note* of the plenary meeting of the General Assembly on the culture of peace, held on 12 and 13 November 2008, during the sixty-third session of the Assembly, in which the President of the Assembly had invited participation at the highest possible level;

8. *Requests* the Office for Economic and Social Council Support and Coordination in the Department of Economic and Social Affairs of the Secretariat, as the focal point for interreligious, intercultural and intercivilizational matters, to coordinate with the United Nations Educational, Scientific and Cultural Organization in facilitating consideration of the possibility of proclaiming a United Nations decade for interreligious and intercultural dialogue, understanding and cooperation for peace;

9. *Takes note* of the Third Ministerial Meeting on Interfaith Dialogue and Cooperation for Peace, held on 25 September 2008 in New York;

10. *Invites* the United Nations Educational, Scientific and Cultural Organization, in consultation with Member States, and through extrabudgetary resources, to play a leading role in the preparations for the celebration of the International Year for the Rapprochement of Cultures, in 2010, taking into account General Assembly resolution 61/185 of 20 December 2006 and the relevant provisions of Assembly resolution 62/90;

11. *Requests* the Secretary-General to report to the General Assembly at its sixty-fourth session on the implementation of the present resolution.

Sport for development and peace

At its resumed sixty-second session in July, the General Assembly considered the Secretary-General's 2007 report [A/62/325 & Corr.1] on sport for development and peace [YUN 2007, p. 1123].

GENERAL ASSEMBLY ACTION

On 23 July [meeting 115], the General Assembly adopted **resolution 62/271** [draft: A/62/L.46 & Add.1] without vote [agenda item 45 *(a)*].

Sport as a means to promote education, health, development and peace

The General Assembly,

Recalling its resolutions 60/9 of 3 November 2005 and 61/10 of 3 November 2006, in which it underlines the importance of sport as a means to encourage, enhance and promote peace, dialogue and understanding between peoples and civilizations,

Recalling also its resolution 62/4 of 31 October 2007, in which it urges Member States to observe, within the framework of the Charter of the United Nations, the Olympic Truce, individually or collectively, during the Games of the XXIX Olympiad in Beijing,

Taking note with appreciation of the report of the Secretary-General which details the actions carried out by States Members of the United Nations, United Nations funds, programmes and specialized agencies and other partners, using sport as a tool for development and peace,

Welcoming the decision of the Secretary-General to renew the mandate of the Special Adviser to the Secretary-General on Sport for Development and Peace,

Also welcoming the decision of the Secretariat to make the necessary arrangements for the effective functioning of the Office of Sport for Development and Peace,

Further welcoming the decision of the Secretary-General to establish a Trust Fund for Sport for Development and Peace,

1. *Requests* the Secretary-General to report to the General Assembly at its sixty-third session on progress at the national, regional and international levels to encourage policies and best practices on sport for development and peace;

2. *Decides* to include in the provisional agenda of its sixty-third session the item entitled "Sport for peace and development".

Report of Secretary-General. In accordance with the above resolution, the Secretary-General submitted an October report on sport for development and peace: building on the foundations [A/63/466].

The report reviewed initiatives by both Member States and UN funds, programmes and specialized agencies during the second year of the three-year United Nations Action Plan on Sport for Development and Peace [YUN 2006, p. 1283], particularly measures implemented within the framework of the Games of the XXIX Olympiad and the XIII Paralympic Games in Beijing, China, in August and September. It also addressed the Olympic Truce (see p. 1221) and the work of the Sport for Development and Peace International Working Group, and focused on the contribution of sport to achieving the MDGs.

The report stated that, during the reporting period, Member States and the UN system, while recognizing that sport alone could not resolve complex economic and social challenges, had continued to draw on its power to promote education, health, development and peace. Renewed efforts to coordinate activities throughout the world had been undertaken following the appointment by the Secretary-General of a new Special Adviser on Sport for Development and Peace in April. The Beijing Olympic and Paralympic Games brought together the UN system and China to create improvements for the Chinese people, particularly in the areas of environment, HIV/AIDS awareness, the benefits of volunteer work and labour rights. While the global framework referred to in the Action Plan required greater investment and conceptualizing, numerous measures had been undertaken to ensure coordinated and coherent international responses. The second year of the Action Plan showed that support was required from the Sport for Development and Peace International Working Group to assist Governments in implementing the Working Group's policy recommendations in order to consolidate sport in cross-cutting development strategies and incorporate sport and physical education in international, regional and national development policies and programmes. Greater resources were needed to enhance the implementation of the Action Plan. A diverse funding base was required for the United Nations Office of Sport for Development and Peace that would make use of multi-stakeholder arrangements and creative partnership arrangements, on a voluntary basis, to ensure its position within the UN system. Efforts were also required to encourage aid agencies to refer to sport and physical education in their policy documents as a tool that could attract funding from Government aid budgets. In addition, a more comprehensive monitoring and evaluation framework should be developed and reinforced with systematic and scientific monitoring tools; sports celebrities should be encouraged to serve as spokespersons and goodwill ambassadors; and Member States should be urged to ratify the International Convention against Doping in Sport, adopted by UNESCO in 2005 and welcomed by the Assembly in resolution 60/9 [YUN 2005, p. 1207], and to increase international coordination for a more effective fight against doping.

GENERAL ASSEMBLY ACTION

On 11 December [meeting 68], the General Assembly adopted **resolution 63/135** [draft: A/63/L.51 & Add.1] without vote [agenda item 42].

Sport as a means to promote education, health, development and peace

The General Assembly,

Recalling its resolutions 58/5 of 3 November 2003, 59/10 of 27 October 2004, its decision to proclaim 2005 the International Year for Sport and Physical Education, to strengthen sport as a means to promote education, health, development and peace, and its resolutions 60/1 of 16 September 2005, 60/9 of 3 November 2005, 61/10 of 3 November 2006, and 62/271 of 23 July 2008,

Taking note with appreciation of the report of the Secretary-General entitled "Sport for development and peace: building on the foundations", which reviews the programmes and initiatives implemented by States Members of the United Nations, United Nations funds, programmes and specialized agencies and other partners, using sport as a tool for development and peace,

Recognizing the need to strengthen and further coordinate efforts at the international level to maximize the potential of sport for contributing to the achievement of the United Nations Millennium Development Goals,

Acknowledging the major role of Member States and the United Nations system in promoting human development through sport and physical education, through its country programmes,

Acknowledging also the opportunities provided by the Games of the XXIX Olympiad and the XIII Paralympic Games in Beijing for education, understanding, peace, harmony and tolerance among and between peoples and civilizations, as reflected in General Assembly resolution 62/4 of 31 October 2007 on the Olympic Truce,

Recalling article 31 of the Convention on the Rights of the Child, outlining a child's right to play and leisure, and the outcome document of the twenty-seventh special session of the General Assembly on children, entitled "A world fit for children", stressing the promotion of physical, mental and emotional health through play and sports,

Recalling also article 30 of the Convention on the Rights of Persons with Disabilities, outlining the right of persons with disabilities to take part on an equal basis with others in cultural life, recreation, leisure and sport,

Recognizing the important role played by the International Convention against Doping in Sport in harmonizing the actions taken by Governments in the fight against doping in sport, which are complementary to those undertaken by the sporting movement under the World Anti-Doping Code,

Acknowledging the recommendations contained in the final report of the Sport for Development and Peace International Working Group entitled "Harnessing the power of sport for development and peace: recommendations to Governments", and encouraging Member States to implement the recommendations,

Recognizing the Beijing Declaration on Sport for Development and Peace, calling for a renewed mandate of the Sport for Development and Peace International Working Group under the leadership of the United Nations,

Recognizing also the need for indicators and benchmarks based on commonly agreed standards to assist Governments to enable the consolidation of sport in cross-cutting development strategies and the incorporation of sport and physical education in international, regional and national development policies and programmes,

Recognizing further the imperative need to engage women and girls in the practice of sport for development and peace, and in this regard welcomes activities that aim to foster and encourage such initiatives at the global level, such as the 2008 International Federation of Association Football U-20 Women's World Cup, held in Chile,

1. *Welcomes* the Secretary-General's decision to renew the mandate of a Special Adviser to the Secretary-General on Sport for Development and Peace and to incorporate the Sport for Development and Peace International Working Group into the United Nations system under the leadership of the Special Adviser;

2. *Also welcomes* the establishment of a United Nations Office of Sport for Development and Peace, which constitutes a policy and communications platform that will facilitate partnerships, coordinate common strategies, policy and programmes and increase coherence and synergies, while simultaneously raising awareness within the United Nations system and among external partners;

3. *Invites* Member States, the organizations of the United Nations system, including their governing bodies, international peacekeeping missions, sport-related organizations, athletes, the media, civil society and the private sector to collaborate with the United Nations Office of Sport for Development and Peace to promote greater awareness and action to foster peace and accelerate the attainment of the Millennium Development Goals through sport-based initiatives and promote the integration of sport for development and peace in the development agenda, by working along the following principles, adapted from the United Nations Action Plan on Sport for Development and Peace contained in the report of the Secretary-General to the General Assembly at its sixty-first session:

(a) Global framework for sport for development and peace: further develop a framework to strengthen a common vision, define priorities and further raise awareness to promote and mainstream policies on sport for development and peace that are easily replicable;

(b) Policy development: promote and support the integration and mainstreaming of sport for development and peace in development programmes and policies;

(c) Resource mobilization: promote innovative funding mechanisms and multi-stakeholder arrangements at all levels, on a voluntary basis, including the engagement of sport organizations, civil society, athletes and the private sector;

(d) Evidence of impact: promote and facilitate common evaluation and monitoring tools, indicators and benchmarks based on commonly agreed standards;

4. *Encourages* Member States to designate focal points for sport for development and peace within their governments;

5. *Also encourages* Member States to provide institutional structures, appropriate quality standards and competencies and promote academic research and expertise in the field to enable ongoing training, capacity-building and education of physical education teachers, coaches and community leaders in sport for development and peace programmes;

6. *Encourages* the use of sport as a vehicle to foster development and strengthen education for children and young persons; prevent disease and promote health; empower girls and women; foster the inclusion and well-being of persons with disabilities; and facilitate social inclusion, conflict prevention and peacebuilding;

7. *Also encourages* the use of mass sport events to promote and support sport for development and peace initiatives;

8. *Invites* Member States and international sport organizations to assist developing countries, in particular the least developed countries, in their capacity-building efforts in sport and physical education, by providing national experiences and best practices, as well as financial, technical and logistic resources for the development of sport programmes;

9. *Urges* Member States that have not yet done so to consider signing, ratifying and acceding to the Convention on the Rights of the Child, the Convention on the Rights of Persons with Disabilities and the International Convention against Doping in Sport;

10. *Invites* the international community to provide voluntary contributions to and to enter into innovative partnerships with the United Nations Office of Sport for Development and Peace and the Sport for Development and Peace International Working Group;

11. *Requests* the Secretary-General to report to the General Assembly at its sixty-fifth session on the implementation of the present resolution, including progress made by Member States towards implementation of the Sport for Development and Peace International Working Group policy recommendations and on the functioning of the United Nations Office of Sport for Development and Peace and the Trust Fund for Sport for Development and Peace, and to present an action plan on sport for development and peace.

Olympic Truce

On 28 July [A/62/912], the President of the General Assembly made a solemn appeal in connection with the observance of the Olympic Truce. He called on all Member States to demonstrate their commitment to the Olympic Truce for the 2008 Beijing Olympic Games, and to undertake concrete actions at the local, national, regional and world levels to promote and strengthen a culture of peace and harmony based on the spirit of the Truce.

By **decision 62/550** of 28 July, the Assembly took note of the President's appeal.

Culture and development

On 19 September, the General Assembly decided to include the item entitled "Culture and development" in the agenda of its sixty-third (2008) session. However, no documents were submitted and, in a Second (Economic and Financial) Committee report [A/63/416/Add.3], it was stated that no action had been taken on the item. On 19 December, the Assembly took note of the report of the Second Committee (**decision 63/541**).

Cultural property

Trafficking in cultural property

The Economic and Social Council had before it a report of the Secretary-General on protection against trafficking in cultural property [E/CN.15/2006/14] that had been considered by the Commission on Crime Prevention and Criminal Justice at its 2006 session [YUN 2006, p. 1287].

ECONOMIC AND SOCIAL COUNCIL ACTION

On 24 July [meeting 42], the Economic and Social Council, on the recommendation of the Commission on Crime Prevention and Criminal Justice [E/2008/30], adopted **resolution 2008/23** without vote [agenda item 14 *(c)*].

Protection against trafficking in cultural property

The Economic and Social Council,

Recalling General Assembly resolution 56/8 of 21 November 2001, in which the Assembly proclaimed 2002 the United Nations Year for Cultural Heritage, and resolutions 58/17 of 3 December 2003 and 61/52 of 4 December 2006 on the return or restitution of cultural property to the countries of origin,

Recalling also the model treaty for the prevention of crimes that infringe on the cultural heritage of peoples in the form of movable property, adopted by the Eighth United Nations Congress on the Prevention of Crime and the Treatment of Offenders and welcomed by the General Assembly in its resolution 45/121 of 14 December 1990,

Emphasizing the importance for States of protecting and preserving their cultural heritage in accordance with relevant international instruments such as the Convention on the Means of Prohibiting and Preventing the Illicit Import, Export and Transfer of Ownership of Cultural Property, adopted by the United Nations Educational, Scientific and Cultural Organization on 14 November 1970, the Convention on Stolen or Illegally Exported Cultural Objects, adopted in Rome on 24 June 1995 by the International Institute for the Unification of Private Law, and the Convention for the Protection of Cultural Property in the Event of Armed Conflict, adopted at The Hague on 14 May 1954, and the two Protocols thereto of 14 May 1954 and 26 March 1999,

Reiterating the significance of cultural property as part of the common heritage of humankind and as unique and important testimony of the culture and identity of peoples and the necessity of protecting it,

Reaffirming the necessity of international cooperation in preventing and combating all aspects of trafficking in cultural property, and noting that such cultural property is especially transferred through licit markets, such as auctions, including through the Internet,

Reaffirming also its resolution 2004/34 of 21 July 2004 entitled "Protection against trafficking in cultural property", and resolution 2003/29 of 22 July 2003 entitled "Prevention of crimes that infringe on the cultural heritage of peoples in the form of movable property",

Recalling the deliberations of the Eleventh United Nations Congress on Crime Prevention and Criminal Justice, and the Bangkok Declaration on Synergies and Responses: Strategic Alliances in Crime Prevention and Criminal Justice, in which the Congress took note of the increased involvement of organized criminal groups in the theft of and trafficking in cultural property and reaffirmed the fundamental importance of the implementation of existing instruments and the further development of national measures and international cooperation in criminal matters, calling upon Member States to take effective action to that end,

Expressing concern about the demand for cultural property, which leads to its loss, destruction, removal, theft and trafficking,

Alarmed at the growing involvement of organized criminal groups in all aspects of trafficking in cultural property,

Expressing regret that the United Nations Office on Drugs and Crime could not convene the expert group meeting envisaged in Economic and Social Council resolution 2004/34, mainly because of the lack of extrabudgetary resources,

Stressing the importance of fostering international law enforcement cooperation to combat trafficking in cultural property and, in particular, the need to increase the exchange of information and experiences in order for competent authorities to operate in a more effective manner,

Stressing also that the entry into force of the United Nations Convention against Transnational Organized Crime has created a new impetus to international cooperation in countering and curbing transnational organized crime, which will in turn lead to innovative and broader approaches to dealing with the various manifestations of such crime, including trafficking in cultural property,

Expressing the need, where appropriate, to strengthen and fully implement mechanisms for the return or restitution of cultural property after it has been stolen or trafficked and for its protection and preservation,

1. *Takes note with appreciation* of the report of the Secretary-General on protection against trafficking in cultural property;

2. *Welcomes* national, regional and international initiatives for the protection of cultural property, in particular the work of the United Nations Educational, Scientific and Cultural Organization and its Intergovernmental Committee for Promoting the Return of Cultural Property to its Countries of Origin or its Restitution in Case of Illicit Appropriation;

3. *Reiterates its request* that the United Nations Office on Drugs and Crime, in close cooperation with the United Nations Educational, Scientific and Cultural Organization, convene an open-ended intergovernmental expert group meeting, with interpretation in all the official languages of the United Nations, to submit to the Commission on Crime Prevention and Criminal Justice at its eighteenth session relevant recommendations on protection against trafficking in cultural property, including ways of making more effective the model treaty for the prevention of crimes that infringe on the cultural heritage of peoples in the form of movable property, and invites Member States and other donors to provide extrabudgetary contributions for these purposes in accordance with the rules and procedures of the United Nations;

4. *Encourages* Member States asserting State ownership of cultural property to consider means of issuing statements of such ownership with a view to facilitating the enforcement of property claims in other States;

5. *Urges* Member States and relevant institutions, as appropriate, to strengthen and fully implement mechanisms to strengthen international cooperation, including mutual legal assistance, in order to combat trafficking in cultural property, including trafficking committed through the use of the Internet, and to facilitate the recovery, return or restitution of cultural property;

6. *Urges* Member States to protect cultural property and prevent trafficking in such property by introducing appropriate legislation, including, in particular, procedures for the seizure, return or restitution of cultural property, promoting education, launching awareness-raising campaigns, mapping and carrying out inventories of cultural property, providing adequate security measures, developing the capacities and human resources of monitoring institutions such as the police, customs services and the tourism sector, involving the media and disseminating information on the theft and pillaging of cultural property;

7. *Also urges* Member States to take effective measures to prevent the transfer of illicitly acquired or illegally obtained cultural property, especially through auctions, including through the Internet, and to effect its return or restitution to its rightful owners;

8. *Further urges* Member States to continue to strengthen international cooperation and mutual assistance for the prevention and prosecution of crime against cultural property that forms part of the cultural heritage of peoples, and to ratify and implement the Convention on the Means of Prohibiting and Preventing the Illicit Import, Export and Transfer of Ownership of Cultural Property and other relevant international instruments;

9. *Requests* the United Nations Office on Drugs and Crime to develop its relations with the cooperative network established among the United Nations Educational, Scientific and Cultural Organization, the International Council of Museums, the International Criminal Police Organization (INTERPOL), the International Institute for the Unification of Private Law and the World Customs Organization in the areas of trafficking in cultural property and its return or restitution;

10. *Requests* the Secretary-General to report to the Commission on Crime Prevention and Criminal Justice at its nineteenth session on the implementation of the present resolution.

Crime prevention and criminal justice

Preparations for Twelfth (2010) United Nations Crime Congress

The Commission on Crime Prevention and Criminal Justice, at its seventeenth session [E/2008/30], considered a February report by the Secretary-General [E/CN.15/2008/14] on the follow-up to the Eleventh United Nations Congress on Crime Prevention and

Criminal Justice [YUN 2005, p. 1208] and preparations for the Twelfth Congress, scheduled for 2010 in Brazil. The report, prepared in response to General Assembly resolution 62/173 [YUN 2007, p. 1125], stated that the Secretariat had initiated consultations with the Government of Brazil to discuss a possible venue and dates for the Twelfth Congress. The informal open-ended working group on Congress preparations had agreed that the theme would be "Comprehensive strategies for global challenges: crime prevention and criminal justice systems and their development in a changing world". It had also identified a number of topics for possible inclusion in the draft provisional agenda of the Congress and several issues that could be considered by the workshops to be held within the Congress framework. The Twelfth Congress would adopt a single declaration for consideration by the Commission at its twentieth (2011) session, in accordance with Assembly resolution 56/119 [YUN 2001, p. 1030]. Within the programme budget for the 2008–2009 biennium, resources had been allocated for the holding of four regional preparatory meetings (in Africa, Asia and the Pacific, Latin America and the Caribbean, and Western Asia), including necessary resources for the participation of the least developed countries. Following the finalization of the programme for the Twelfth Congress, including the selection of the theme, agenda items and workshop topics, the discussion guide would be prepared for consideration and approval by the Commission at its eighteenth (2009) session.

The report requested the Commission to take action in 2009 on: a decision on possible amendment of the rules of procedure for UN crime congresses, if required; recommendations on the documentation for the Twelfth Congress; and a recommendation on public information activities that should be undertaken in a timely manner in order to ensure that Governments and civil society were fully aware of and participated in the Congress and its preparations. It also recommended that the Commission, at its seventeenth session, take into consideration the action that would be required in 2009 regarding the rules of procedure, documentation and public information activities; and make its final recommendations, through the Economic and Social Council to the Assembly, on the theme of the Twelfth Congress and on the organization of round tables and workshops to be held by panels of experts.

ECONOMIC AND SOCIAL COUNCIL ACTION

On 24 July [meeting 42], the Economic and Social Council, on the recommendation of the Commission on Crime Prevention and Criminal Justice [E/2008/30], adopted **resolution 2008/22** without vote [agenda item 14 *(c)*].

Preparations for the Twelfth United Nations Congress on Crime Prevention and Criminal Justice

The Economic and Social Council,

Recommends to the General Assembly the adoption of the following draft resolution:

[For text, see General Assembly **resolution 63/193** below.]

GENERAL ASSEMBLY ACTION

On 18 December [meeting 71], the General Assembly, on the recommendation of the Third Committee [A/63/431], adopted **resolution 63/193** without vote [agenda item 97].

Preparations for the Twelfth United Nations Congress on Crime Prevention and Criminal Justice

The General Assembly,

Recalling its resolution 56/119 of 19 December 2001 on the role, function, periodicity and duration of the United Nations congresses on the prevention of crime and the treatment of offenders, and its resolution 62/173 of 18 December 2007 on the follow-up to the Eleventh United Nations Congress on Crime Prevention and Criminal Justice and preparations for the Twelfth United Nations Congress on Crime Prevention and Criminal Justice, in which it, inter alia, accepted with gratitude the offer of the Government of Brazil to act as host to the Twelfth Congress,

Considering that, pursuant to its resolutions 415(V) of 1 December 1950 and 46/152 of 18 December 1991, the Twelfth Congress is to be held in 2010,

Bearing in mind the guidelines for and the format of United Nations congresses, as stipulated in paragraph 2 of its resolution 56/119, as well as paragraphs 29 and 30 of the statement of principles and programme of action of the United Nations Crime Prevention and Criminal Justice Programme, annexed to its resolution 46/152,

Bearing in mind also the conclusions and recommendations contained in the report of the meeting of the Intergovernmental Group of Experts on Lessons Learned from United Nations Congresses on Crime Prevention and Criminal Justice, held in Bangkok from 15 to 18 August 2006, which the General Assembly endorsed in its resolution 62/173,

Recognizing the significant contributions of the United Nations congresses on crime prevention and criminal justice in promoting the exchange of experience in research, law and policy development and the identification of emerging trends and issues in crime prevention and criminal justice among States, intergovernmental organizations and individual experts representing various professions and disciplines,

Recalling that, in its resolution 62/173, it requested the Commission on Crime Prevention and Criminal Justice, at its seventeenth session, to finalize the programme for the Twelfth Congress and to make its final recommendations on the theme and on the organization of round tables and workshops to be held by panels of experts, through the Economic and Social Council, to the General Assembly,

Recalling also that, in its resolution 62/173, it requested the Secretary-General to prepare a discussion guide for the regional preparatory meetings for the Twelfth Congress,

Recalling further its resolution 60/177 of 16 December 2005, in which it endorsed the Bangkok Declaration on Synergies and Responses: Strategic Alliances in Crime Prevention and Criminal Justice adopted by the Eleventh Congress, as contained in the annex to that resolution, and Economic and Social Council resolution 2005/15 of 22 July 2005, in which the Council endorsed the Bangkok Declaration,

Stressing the importance of undertaking all preparatory activities for the Twelfth Congress in a timely and concerted manner,

Having considered the report of the Secretary-General on the follow-up to the Eleventh Congress and preparations for the Twelfth Congress,

1. *Notes* the progress made thus far in the preparations for the Twelfth United Nations Congress on Crime Prevention and Criminal Justice;

2. *Decides* to hold the Twelfth Congress in Salvador, Brazil, from 12 to 19 April 2010, with pre-Congress consultations to be held on 11 April 2010;

3. *Also decides* that the high-level segment of the Twelfth Congress shall be held during the last two days of the Congress in order to allow Heads of State or Government and Government ministers to focus on the main substantive agenda items of the Congress;

4. *Further decides* that the main theme of the Twelfth Congress shall be "Comprehensive strategies for global challenges: crime prevention and criminal justice systems and their development in a changing world";

5. *Approves* the following provisional agenda for the Twelfth Congress, finalized by the Commission on Crime Prevention and Criminal Justice at its seventeenth session:

   1. Opening of the Congress.
   2. Organizational matters.
   3. Children, youth and crime.
   4. Provision of technical assistance to facilitate the ratification and implementation of the international instruments related to the prevention and suppression of terrorism.
   5. Making the United Nations guidelines on crime prevention work.
   6. Criminal justice responses to the smuggling of migrants and trafficking in persons: links to transnational organized crime.
   7. International cooperation to address money-laundering based on existing and relevant United Nations and other instruments.
   8. Recent developments in the use of science and technology by offenders and by competent authorities in fighting crime, including the case of cybercrime.
   9. Strengthening international cooperation in fighting crime-related problems: practical approaches.
   10. Crime prevention and criminal justice responses to violence against migrants, migrant workers and their families.
   11. Adoption of the report of the Congress;

6. *Decides* that the following issues shall be considered in workshops within the framework of the Twelfth Congress:

(*a*) International criminal justice education for the rule of law;

(*b*) Survey of United Nations and other best practices in the treatment of prisoners in the criminal justice system;

(*c*) Practical approaches to preventing urban crime;

(*d*) Links between drug trafficking and other forms of organized crime: international coordinated response;

(*e*) Strategies and best practices against overcrowding in correctional facilities;

7. *Requests* the Secretary-General, in cooperation with the institutes of the United Nations Crime Prevention and Criminal Justice Programme network, to prepare a discussion guide for the regional preparatory meetings for the Twelfth Congress in a timely manner in order to enable the regional preparatory meetings to commence early in 2009, and invites Member States to be actively involved in that process;

8. *Urges* participants in the regional preparatory meetings to examine the substantive items on the agenda and the topics of the workshops of the Twelfth Congress and to make action-oriented recommendations to serve as a basis for the draft recommendations and conclusions for consideration by the Twelfth Congress and the Commission at its nineteenth session;

9. *Emphasizes* the importance of the workshops to be held within the framework of the Twelfth Congress, and invites Member States, intergovernmental and non-governmental organizations and other relevant entities to provide financial, organizational and technical support to the United Nations Office on Drugs and Crime and the institutes of the United Nations Crime Prevention and Criminal Justice Programme network for the preparations for the workshops, including the preparation and circulation of relevant background material;

10. *Invites* donor countries to cooperate with developing countries to ensure their full participation, in particular in the workshops;

11. *Requests* the Secretary-General to prepare a plan for the documentation for the Twelfth Congress, in consultation with the extended Bureau of the Commission;

12. *Reiterates its request* to the Secretary-General to facilitate the organization of regional preparatory meetings for the Twelfth Congress and to make available the necessary resources for the participation of the least developed countries in those meetings and in the Congress itself, in accordance with past practice;

13. *Encourages* Governments to undertake preparations for the Twelfth Congress at an early stage by all appropriate means, including, where appropriate, the establishment of national preparatory committees, with a view to contributing to focused and productive discussion on the topics to be discussed in the workshops and to participating actively in the organization of and follow-up to the workshops;

14. *Reiterates its invitation* to Member States to be represented at the Twelfth Congress at the highest possible level, for example, by Heads of State or Government or Government ministers and attorneys general, to make statements on the theme and topics of the Congress and to participate in thematic interactive round tables;

15. *Requests* the Secretary-General to facilitate the organization of ancillary meetings of non-governmental and professional organizations participating in the Twelfth Congress, in accordance with past practice, as well as meetings of professional and geographical interest groups, and to take appropriate measures to encourage the participation of the academic and research community in the Congress;

16. *Again encourages* the relevant specialized agencies, United Nations programmes and intergovernmental and non-governmental organizations, as well as other professional organizations, to cooperate with the United Nations Office on Drugs and Crime in the preparations for the Twelfth Congress;

17. *Requests* the Secretary-General to appoint a Secretary-General and an Executive Secretary of the Twelfth Congress, in accordance with past practice, to perform their functions under the rules of procedure for United Nations congresses on crime prevention and criminal justice;

18. *Requests* the Commission to accord sufficient time at its eighteenth session to reviewing the progress made in the preparations for the Twelfth Congress, to finalize in good time all the necessary organizational and substantive arrangements and to make its recommendations to the General Assembly through the Economic and Social Council;

19. *Requests* the Secretary-General to ensure the proper follow-up to the present resolution and to report thereon to the General Assembly through the Commission at its eighteenth session.

Commission on Crime Prevention and Criminal Justice

The Commission on Crime Prevention and Criminal Justice, at its seventeenth session (Vienna, 30 November 2007 and 14–18 April 2008) [E/2008/30], recommended to the Economic and Social Council one draft resolution on preparations for the Twelfth (2010) United Nations Congress on Crime Prevention and Criminal Justice (see above), for adoption by the General Assembly, and three draft resolutions and two draft decisions for adoption by the Council. The three draft resolutions for adoption by the Council related to: protection against trafficking in cultural property (see p. 1221); strengthening prevention of urban crime: an integrated approach (see p. 1227); and international cooperation in preventing and combating illicit international trafficking in forest products, including timber, wildlife and other forest biological resources (see p. 1244). It also adopted two resolutions and two decisions, which it brought to the attention of the Council.

In addition to a thematic discussion on aspects of violence against women that pertained directly to the Commission, the following matters were considered: world crime trends and responses: integration and coordination of efforts by the United Nations Office on Drugs and Crime (UNODC) and by Member States in the field of crime prevention and criminal justice; UN congresses on crime prevention and criminal justice; use and application of UN standards and norms in crime prevention and criminal justice; policy directives for UNODC's crime programme and the role of the Commission as its governing body, including administrative, strategic management and budgetary questions; and the provisional agenda for its eighteenth (2009) session. A workshop on the theme "Eliminating violence against women: forms, strategies and tools" also took place.

On 24 July (**decision 2008/245**), the Council took note of the Commission's report on its seventeenth session and decided that the topics for the thematic discussion at its eighteenth (2009) session would be: "Economic fraud and identity-related crime" and "Penal reform and reduction of prison overcrowding, including the provision of legal aid in criminal justice systems". It decided that the discussion on each of the themes would last one day and approved the provisional agenda and documentation for the eighteenth session.

Administrative and budgetary questions

In response to Commission on Narcotic Drugs resolution 50/14 [YUN 2007, p. 1300] and Commission on Crime Prevention and Criminal Justice resolution 16/6 [ibid., p. 1128], the UNODC Executive Director submitted to the two Commissions a 7 February report [E/CN.7/2008/12-E/CN.15/2008/16] on the programmes and initiatives to be implemented by UNODC in the bienniums 2008–2009 and 2010–2011 and on how they conformed with the UNODC strategy for the period 2008–2011, approved by Economic and Social Council resolution 2007/12 [YUN 2007, p. 1301], as reflected in the proposed strategic framework of the United Nations for 2010–2011. The report reviewed the programmes and initiatives to be pursued in 2008 and supplemented the information provided in the 2008–2009 consolidated budget [ibid., p. 1128].

Also in response to the 2007 resolutions of the two Commissions, the Executive Director submitted the first annual report on financial issues and difficulties faced by UNODC in implementing its mandates and an initial assessment of ways and means of improving the financial situation [E/CN.7/2008/11-E/CN.15/2008/15]. The report provided an overview of the programmes and initiatives to be pursued in 2008, in addition to the information provided in the 2008–2009 consolidated budget. It described some of the financial difficulties faced by UNODC in implementing its mandates, outlined measures taken to cope with them and presented proposals to address those problems. The Executive Director concluded that, in order to meet UNODC's financial challenges, Member States should: acknowledge and maintain the increasingly strong support provided to UNODC from many countries and institutions; stress the importance of stable and predictable multilateral core resources; and establish an informal open-ended working group to explore ways and means to address the Office's financial challenges. The working group could be co-chaired by the chairmen of the two Commissions, along the lines of the process that led to the 2008–2011 strategy for UNODC. He also recommended that UNODC continue to align, under the UN strategic framework, the consolidated budget with the 2008–2011 strategy, thereby ensuring integrated planning and budgeting as a basis for better result-based reporting to States and compliance with their policy directives.

In accordance with the same 2007 resolutions of the Commissions, the Executive Director submitted a 14 March report on deviations from the standard programme support charge of 13 per cent during the 2005–2007 period [E/CN.7/2008/14-E/CN.15/2008/19]. The report described exemptions and reductions provided to donors in respect of the 13 per cent charge and the basis for them. It provided information on the UN policy on programme support costs and on the application and evolution of that policy, on the definition and purpose of the programme support charge and on UNODC experience in that regard. It stated that, in 2008 and 2009, UNODC would continue to apply the UN policies and procedures with respect to the programme support charge and to ensure the application of clear and consistent criteria in the granting of exceptions to the standard 13 per cent rate. UNODC would also ensure the application of the programme support charge policies developed under the One United Nations initiative [YUN 2006, p. 1584].

A 20 March note by the Secretariat [E/CN.7/2008/18], prepared in response to Commission on Crime Prevention and Criminal Justice resolution 16/6 [YUN 2007, p. 1128], provided information on the implementation status and resource requirements of resolutions and decisions relating to the crime prevention and criminal justice programme adopted by the General Assembly, the Economic and Social Council and the Commission on Crime Prevention and Criminal Justice in the period 2003–2007 in which action by UNODC was requested.

On 18 April [E/2008/30 (dec. 17/2)], the Commission on Crime Prevention and Criminal Justice took note of the three reports cited above. It decided to establish an open-ended intergovernmental working group to discuss and prepare recommendations, to be submitted to the Commission's eighteenth (2009) session, on how to ensure political ownership by Member States and on how to improve the UNODC governance structure and financial situation. The Office was requested to assist the working group.

Crime prevention programme

At its seventeenth session, the Commission on Crime Prevention and Criminal Justice considered the UNODC Executive Director's report on the Office's 2007 activities [E/CN.7/2008/3-E/CN.15/2008/3], which focused on how drug control, crime prevention, terrorism prevention and criminal justice interacted with peace, security, development and the rule of law. During the period under review, UNODC supported Member States in their efforts to achieve a world safe from crime, drugs and terrorism through the three pillars of its work programme: research to increase knowledge and understanding of drug and crime issues and to expand the evidence base for policy and operational decisions; normative work to assist States in the ratification and implementation of international treaties, the development of domestic legislation on drugs, crime and terrorism and the provision of substantive and secretariat services to treaty-based and governing bodies; and field-based technical cooperation projects. The report also contained the information requested by Economic and Social Council resolution 2006/21 [YUN 2006, p. 1315] concerning implementation of the Programme of Action, 2006–2010, on strengthening the rule of law and criminal justice systems in Africa.

With regard to transnational organized crime, the report noted that a UNODC priority was to promote the ratification and implementation of the United Nations Convention against Transnational Organized Crime [YUN 2000, p. 1048] (see p. 1233) and its three supplementary Protocols (Protocol to Prevent, Suppress and Punish Trafficking in Persons, Especially Women and Children [ibid., p. 1063]; Protocol against the Smuggling of Migrants by Land, Sea and Air [ibid., p. 1067]; Protocol against the Illicit Manufacturing of and Trafficking in Firearms, Their Parts and Components and Ammunition [YUN 2001, p. 1036]). UNODC helped States implement the provisions of the Protocol to Prevent, Suppress and Punish Trafficking in Persons in order to prevent human trafficking, protect the victims and bring the traffickers to justice. It identified shortcomings in the implementation of the Protocol against the Smuggling of Migrants, and stressed that policies to reduce smuggling of migrants should be regional in scope and comprehensive, consistent and anticipatory, while upholding human rights and protecting the safety and lives of migrants should be central elements. UNODC also emphasized the development of ways to prevent trafficking, protect victims and prosecute offenders. In March, the United Nations Global Initiative to Fight Human Trafficking (UN.GIFT) was launched, with support from the United Arab Emirates, to increase awareness of human trafficking, promote rights-based responses, build the capacity of state and non-state actors, and foster partnerships for joint action. During the year, the Office prepared a draft model law against trafficking in persons and developed a draft legislative checklist of complementary measures, including legal measures to facilitate an effective response to trafficking in persons. UNODC continued to be the custodian of the 2003 United Nations Convention against Corruption [YUN 2003, p. 1127].

In the area of international cooperation against terrorism, the Office reinforced its technical assistance work on the legal and related aspects of counter-terrorism, pursuant to the United Nations Global Counter-Terrorism Strategy, adopted by General Assembly resolution 60/288 [YUN 2006, p. 66]. It also helped countries ratify and implement the international instruments related to terrorism, worked closely with the Counter-Terrorism Committee of the Security Council and its Executive Directorate, and contributed to the work of the multi-agency Counter-Terrorism Implementation Task Force. As to emerging policy issues, the report highlighted the increase in the transnational occurrence and range of offences of economic fraud and identity-related crime; cybercrime, including the use of the Internet for child exploitation, Internet pharmacies and money-laundering; and environmental crime, noting that international trafficking in forest products had a particularly adverse environmental, social and economic impact in many countries. UNODC carried out research and analysis on laws, resolutions and recommendations on the prevention of trafficking in protected species in connection with organized criminal groups. With regard to justice reform, the report noted that strengthening criminal justice institutions was central to UNODC work and that the Office had led more than 12 justice reform missions in transitional, post-conflict and developing countries in 2007, including 5 large judicial programmes, mainly in Africa.

During the year, the Office published an updated edition of the *Compendium of United Nations Standards and Norms in Crime Prevention and Criminal Justice* in the six official languages of the Organization; the report *Crime and Development in Central America: Caught in the Crossfire*; and a joint study with the World Bank entitled *Crime, Violence and Development: Trends, Costs and Policy Options in the Caribbean*.

The report recommended that the Commission on Crime Prevention and Criminal Justice: provide financial resources for the establishment and maintenance of an online information-sharing system concerning technical assistance activities for both donor and beneficiary States and international organizations; strengthen UNODC work on counter-terrorism; give higher priority to the development of sustainable forensic science services and of networks of laboratories and scientists with a view to ensuring a more effective exchange of expertise; strengthen drug and crime data collection activities; encourage Member States to use manuals and handbooks showing how the standards and norms could be applied and assist developing countries, countries with economies in transition and those in post-conflict situations in applying standards and norms and introducing criminal justice reform; keep apprised of emerging policy issues and possible responses in the areas of cybercrime, child sexual exploitation, fraud and identity theft, and environmental crime; and emphasize the importance of providing regular and adequate financial resources to UNODC.

In **resolution 63/197** (see p. 1348), the General Assembly urged States that had not yet done so to ratify or accede to, and States parties to implement, as a matter of priority, the provisions of the United Nations Convention against Transnational Organized Crime and the Protocols thereto and the United Nations Convention against Corruption.

Strengthening urban crime prevention

ECONOMIC AND SOCIAL COUNCIL ACTION

On 24 July [meeting 42], the Economic and Social Council, on the recommendation of the Commission on Crime Prevention and Criminal Justice [E/2008/30], adopted **resolution 2008/24** without vote [agenda item 14 *(c)*].

Strengthening prevention of urban crime: an integrated approach

The Economic and Social Council,

Recalling General Assembly resolution 62/175 of 18 December 2007 on strengthening the United Nations Crime Prevention and Criminal Justice Programme, in particular its technical cooperation capacity, in which the Assembly reaffirmed the importance of the Programme in promoting effective action to strengthen international cooperation in crime prevention and criminal justice, as well as of the work of the United Nations Office on Drugs and Crime in the fulfilment of its mandate in crime prevention and criminal justice, including providing to Member States, upon request and as a matter of high priority, technical cooperation, advisory services and other forms of assistance, and coordinating with and complementing the work of all relevant and competent United Nations bodies and offices, and recalling also that, in that resolution, the Assembly drew attention to urban crime as an emerging policy issue,

Recalling also its resolution 2007/12 of 25 July 2007 on the strategy for the period 2008–2011 for the United Nations Office on Drugs and Crime, in which community-centred crime prevention was designated a result area,

Mindful of its resolution 1995/9 of 24 July 1995, in which it adopted guidelines for cooperation and technical assistance in the field of urban crime prevention, as contained in the annex to that resolution, and its resolution 2002/13 of 24 July 2002, in which it accepted the Guidelines for the Prevention of Crime, contained in the annex to that resolution,

Recalling its resolution 2005/22 of 22 July 2005 on action to promote effective crime prevention and resolution 2006/20 of 27 July 2006 on United Nations standards and norms in crime prevention, in which it acknowledged the need to achieve a balanced approach between crime prevention and criminal justice responses,

Considering that the fight against crime can effectively reach its objectives through a combination of national policies on criminal justice and crime prevention to address the causes of crime and violence, bearing in mind that allocating resources to crime prevention can greatly reduce the financial and social costs of crime,

Recognizing the importance of the engagement between civil society and law enforcement authorities in the planning and implementation of crime prevention activities,

Recalling the commitments made by the international community in the United Nations Millennium Declaration, in particular regarding the fight against crime and the objective of making the right to development a reality for everyone,

1. *Encourages* Member States to adopt and strengthen, as appropriate, effective urban crime prevention responses, with a view to achieving an appropriate balance with criminal justice actions;

2. *Also encourages* Member States to integrate crime prevention considerations into all relevant social and economic policies and programmes in order to effectively address the conditions in which crime and violence can emerge;

3. *Requests* the United Nations Office on Drugs and Crime to explicitly address the crime prevention component in its programme of work and reporting, where relevant, including good practices that integrate crime prevention and criminal justice;

4. *Invites* Member States and other donors to provide extrabudgetary contributions to the United Nations Office on Drugs and Crime to support technical assistance activities in this area, in accordance with the rules and procedures of the United Nations.

Strengthening technical cooperation

In response to General Assembly resolution 62/175 [YUN 2007, p. 1130], the Secretary-General submitted a July report on strengthening the United Nations Crime Prevention and Criminal Justice Programme, in particular its technical cooperation capacity [A/63/99], which summarized UNODC work in supporting Member States in countering transnational organized crime, corruption and terrorism, and in preventing crime and strengthening criminal justice systems. It also provided information on efforts to strengthen the United Nations Crime Prevention and Criminal Justice Programme, with a focus on the role of the Commission on Crime Prevention and Criminal Justice as its governing body, and on the financial situation of the Office and the funding structure of the United Nations Crime Prevention and Criminal Justice Fund. In addition, it highlighted emerging policy issues and possible responses and, as requested in Assembly resolution 62/173 [ibid., p. 1125], described preparations for the Twelfth United Nations Congress on Crime Prevention and Criminal Justice. The report also contained recommendations aimed at further enhancing the Programme on: organized crime; fighting human trafficking; countering the smuggling of migrants; curbing corruption; countering terrorism; UN standards and norms in crime prevention and criminal justice; violence against women; data collection, research and analysis; emerging policy issues; and financial support.

GENERAL ASSEMBLY ACTION

On 18 December [meeting 71], the General Assembly, on the recommendation of the Third Committee [A/63/431], adopted **resolution 63/195** without vote [agenda item 97].

Strengthening the United Nations Crime Prevention and Criminal Justice Programme, in particular its technical cooperation capacity

The General Assembly,

Recalling its resolution 46/152 of 18 December 1991 on the creation of an effective United Nations crime prevention and criminal justice programme, and its resolution 62/175 of 18 December 2007 on strengthening the United Nations Crime Prevention and Criminal Justice Programme, in particular its technical cooperation capacity,

Recalling also its resolution 60/1 of 16 September 2005 on the 2005 World Summit Outcome, in particular the sections on transnational crime and terrorism,

Taking note with appreciation of the adoption by the Economic and Social Council of the strategy for the period 2008–2011 for the United Nations Office on Drugs and Crime, which aims, inter alia, to enhance its effectiveness and flexibility in providing technical assistance and policy services,

Recalling section XI of its resolution 61/252 of 22 December 2006, entitled "Strengthening the United Nations Crime Prevention and Criminal Justice Programme and the role of the Commission on Crime Prevention and Criminal Justice as its governing body", in which the Commission, as the principal United Nations policymaking body on crime prevention and criminal justice issues, was given the authority to approve the budget of the United Nations Crime Prevention and Criminal Justice Fund, and welcoming the outcome of the reconvened sixteenth session of the Commission, held on 29 and 30 November 2007,

Recalling also its resolution 62/173 of 18 December 2007 entitled "Follow-up to the Eleventh United Nations Congress on Crime Prevention and Criminal Justice and preparations for the Twelfth United Nations Congress on Crime Prevention and Criminal Justice",

Recalling further its resolution 62/202 of 19 December 2007 entitled "Preventing and combating corrupt practices and transfer of assets of illicit origin and returning such assets, in particular to the countries of origin, consistent with the United Nations Convention against Corruption",

Reaffirming its resolutions relating to the urgent need to strengthen international cooperation and technical assistance in promoting and facilitating the ratification and implementation of the United Nations Convention against Transnational Organized Crime and the Protocols thereto, the United Nations Convention against Corruption and all the international conventions and protocols against terrorism, including those that recently entered into force,

Reaffirming also the commitments undertaken by Member States in the United Nations Global Counter-Terrorism Strategy adopted on 8 September 2006,

Recalling its resolution 61/180 of 20 December 2006 on improving the coordination of efforts against trafficking in persons and the coordinating role of the United Nations Office on Drugs and Crime in this respect,

Recalling also its resolution 62/172 of 18 December 2007 entitled "Technical assistance for implementing the international conventions and protocols related to terrorism",

Taking note with appreciation of the holding of the Vienna Forum to Fight Human Trafficking, from 13 to 15 February 2008, in accordance with decision 16/1 of 27 April 2007 of the Commission on Crime Prevention and Criminal Justice,

Taking into consideration all relevant Economic and Social Council resolutions, in particular resolutions 2008/23, 2008/24 and 2008/25 of 24 July 2008, and all those relating to the strengthening of international cooperation as well as the technical assistance and advisory services of the United Nations Crime Prevention and Criminal Justice Programme of the United Nations Office on Drugs and Crime in the field of crime prevention and criminal justice, promotion and reinforcement of the rule of law and reform of criminal justice institutions, including with regard to the implementation of technical assistance,

Emphasizing that its resolution 61/143 of 19 December 2006 on the intensification of efforts to eliminate all forms of violence against women has considerable implications for the United Nations Crime Prevention and Criminal Justice Programme and its activities,

Welcoming the outcome of the thematic discussion on aspects of violence against women that pertain directly to the Commission on Crime Prevention and Criminal Justice held by the Commission at its seventeenth session, in 2008, pursuant to Economic and Social Council decision 2007/253 of 26 July 2007,

Recalling the Bangkok Declaration on Synergies and Responses: Strategic Alliances in Crime Prevention and Criminal Justice,

Recognizing that actions against transnational organized crime and terrorism are a common and shared responsibility, and stressing the need to work collectively to prevent and combat transnational organized crime, corruption and terrorism in all its forms and manifestations,

Recognizing also the need to maintain a balance in the technical cooperation capacity of the United Nations Office on Drugs and Crime between all relevant priorities identified by the General Assembly and the Economic and Social Council,

Concerned by the serious challenges and threats posed by the illicit trafficking in firearms, their parts and components and ammunition, and about its links with other forms of transnational organized crime, including drug trafficking and other criminal activities, in particular terrorism, and reaffirming that, in order to better understand and combat these problems, it is necessary to adopt comprehensive strategies and facilitate close and effective cooperation among States,

1. *Takes note with appreciation* of the report of the Secretary-General on the progress made in the implementation of General Assembly resolution 62/175;

2. *Reaffirms* the importance of the United Nations Crime Prevention and Criminal Justice Programme in promoting effective action to strengthen international cooperation in crime prevention and criminal justice, as well as of the work of the United Nations Office on Drugs and Crime in the fulfilment of its mandate in crime prevention and criminal justice, including providing to Member States, upon request and as a matter of high priority, technical cooperation, advisory services and other forms of assistance, and coordinating with and complementing the work of all relevant and competent United Nations bodies and offices;

3. *Recognizes* the general progress made by the United Nations Office on Drugs and Crime in the delivery of advisory services and assistance to requesting Member States in the areas of corruption, organized crime, money-laundering, terrorism, kidnapping and trafficking in persons, including the support and protection of victims, as well as drug trafficking and international cooperation, with special emphasis on extradition and mutual legal assistance;

4. *Urges* the United Nations Office on Drugs and Crime to continue providing technical assistance to Member States to combat money-laundering and the financing of terrorism through the Global Programme against Money-Laundering, in accordance with United Nations related instruments and internationally accepted standards, including, where applicable and appropriate, recommendations from relevant intergovernmental bodies, inter alia, the Financial Action Task Force on Money Laundering, and relevant initiatives of regional, interregional and multilateral organizations against money-laundering;

5. *Recognizes* the efforts made by the United Nations Office on Drugs and Crime to assist Member States in developing abilities and strengthening their capacity to prevent and combat kidnapping, and requests the Office to continue developing tools for providing technical assistance and cooperation to effectively counter this growing serious crime;

6. *Urges* the United Nations Office on Drugs and Crime to increase collaboration with intergovernmental, international and regional organizations that have transnational organized crime mandates, as appropriate, in order to share best practices and to take advantage of their unique and comparative advantage;

7. *Draws attention* to the emerging policy issues identified in the report of the Secretary-General, inter alia, urban crime, the sexual exploitation of children, economic fraud and identity theft, illicit international trafficking in forest products, including timber, wildlife and other forest biological resources, and, in the context of advisory services and technical assistance, the issue of cybercrime, and invites

the United Nations Office on Drugs and Crime to explore, within its mandate, ways and means of addressing these issues, bearing in mind Economic and Social Council resolutions 2007/12 of 25 July 2007 and 2007/19 of 26 July 2007 on the strategy for the period 2008–2011 for the Office;

8. *Urges* Member States and relevant international organizations to develop national and regional strategies, as appropriate, and other necessary measures, in cooperation with the United Nations Crime Prevention and Criminal Justice Programme, to address effectively transnational organized crime, including trafficking in persons, the smuggling of migrants and illicit manufacturing of and transnational trafficking in firearms, as well as corruption and terrorism;

9. *Urges* the United Nations Office on Drugs and Crime to continue to assist Member States, upon request, in combating the illicit trafficking in firearms, their parts and components and ammunition, and to support them in their efforts to address its links with other forms of transnational organized crime, through, inter alia, technical assistance;

10. *Reaffirms* the importance of the United Nations Office on Drugs and Crime and its regional offices in building capacity at the local level in the fight against transnational organized crime and drug trafficking, and urges the Office to consider regional vulnerabilities, projects and impact in the fight against transnational organized crime, in particular in developing countries, when deciding to close and allocate offices, with a view to maintaining an effective level of support to national and regional efforts in those areas;

11. *Urges* all Member States that have not yet done so to consider ratifying or acceding to the United Nations Convention against Transnational Organized Crime (Palermo Convention) and the Protocols thereto, the United Nations Convention against Corruption (Merida Convention) and the international conventions and protocols related to terrorism, and encourages States parties to continue to provide full support to the Conference of the Parties to the United Nations Convention against Transnational Organized Crime and the Conference of the States Parties to the United Nations Convention against Corruption, including providing information to the conferences regarding compliance with the treaties;

12. *Welcomes* the progress achieved by the Conference of the Parties to the United Nations Convention against Transnational Organized Crime and the Conference of the States Parties to the United Nations Convention against Corruption in the implementation of their respective mandates, and requests the Secretary-General to continue to provide the United Nations Office on Drugs and Crime with adequate resources to promote, in an effective manner, the implementation of the United Nations Convention against Transnational Organized Crime and the United Nations Convention against Corruption and to discharge its functions as the secretariat of the conferences of the parties to the conventions, in accordance with its mandate;

13. *Requests* the United Nations Office on Drugs and Crime to enhance its technical assistance to Member States, upon request, to strengthen international cooperation in preventing and combating terrorism through the facilitation of the ratification and implementation of the universal conventions and protocols related to terrorism, in close consultation with the Counter-Terrorism Committee and its Executive Directorate, as well as to contribute to the work of the Counter-Terrorism Implementation Task Force, and invites Member States to provide the Office with appropriate resources for its mandate;

14. *Takes note with appreciation* of decision 17/1 of 18 April 2008 of the Commission on Crime Prevention and Criminal Justice entitled "Strengthening crime prevention and criminal justice responses to violence against women and girls", in which the Commission requested the United Nations Office on Drugs and Crime to convene an intergovernmental group of experts to review and update, as appropriate, the Model Strategies and Practical Measures on the Elimination of Violence against Women in the Field of Crime Prevention and Criminal Justice and to make recommendations on addressing violence against women and girls, to be considered by the Commission at its nineteenth session, and requests the Commission to report through the Economic and Social Council to the General Assembly on the outcome of this work;

15. *Encourages* Member States to take relevant measures, as appropriate to their national contexts, to ensure the use and application of the United Nations standards and norms in crime prevention and criminal justice, including the consideration and, where they deem it necessary, dissemination of existing manuals and handbooks developed and published by the United Nations Office on Drugs and Crime;

16. *Reiterates* the importance of providing the United Nations Crime Prevention and Criminal Justice Programme with sufficient, stable and predictable funding for the full implementation of its mandates, in conformity with the high priority accorded to it and in accordance with the increasing demand for its services, in particular with regard to the provision of increased assistance to developing countries, countries with economies in transition and those emerging from conflict, in the area of crime prevention and criminal justice reform;

17. *Welcomes* Commission decision 17/2 of 18 April 2008 entitled "Improving the governance and financial situation of the United Nations Office on Drugs and Crime", in which the Commission decided to establish an open-ended intergovernmental working group to discuss how to ensure political ownership by the Member States and how to improve the governance structure and financial situation of the Office and to make recommendations thereon, to be submitted to the Commission at its eighteenth session, and requests the Commission to report through the Economic and Social Council to the General Assembly to enable further consideration of and potential action on those recommendations;

18. *Reiterates its request* to the Secretary-General to provide the United Nations Crime Prevention and Criminal Justice Programme with sufficient resources for the full implementation of its mandates, in conformity with its high priorities, and to provide adequate support to the Commission;

19. *Requests* the Secretary-General to submit a report to the General Assembly at its sixty-fourth session on the implementation of the mandates of the United Nations Crime Prevention and Criminal Justice Programme, reflecting also emerging policy issues and possible responses.

Crime Prevention and Criminal Justice Programme network

In a January report [E/CN.15/2008/8] to the Commission on Crime Prevention and Criminal Justice, the Secretary-General summarized the activities carried out in 2007 by the institutions comprising the United Nations Crime Prevention and Criminal Justice Programme network, which included the United Nations Interregional Crime and Justice Research Institute (UNICRI); 13 regional and affiliated institutes; and the International Scientific and Professional Advisory Council.

United Nations Interregional Crime and Justice Research Institute

In a January note [E/CN.15/2008/13], the Secretary-General submitted to the Commission on Crime Prevention and Criminal Justice the report of the Board of Trustees of UNICRI on its sixteenth session (Turin, Italy, 4–5 October 2007), in accordance with the statute of the Institute, annexed to Economic and Social Council resolution 1989/56 [YUN 1989, p. 637]. The report considered the work programme and related budget proposals for 2008–2009 and reviewed and evaluated the Institute's activities in 2006–2007.

In a February note [E/CN.15/2008/17], the Secretary-General drew the Commission's attention to the expiry, on 30 November, of the five-year terms of office of two members of the UNICRI Board of Trustees and provided background information on candidates nominated to fill those positions.

The Commission [E/2008/30] recommended to the Council the adoption of a draft decision by which it would endorse the appointment of two members to the UNICRI Board of Trustees.

By **decision 2008/246** of 24 July, the Council endorsed those appointments.

United Nations African crime prevention institute

In response to General Assembly resolution 62/174 [YUN 2007, p. 1132], the Secretary-General submitted a July report on the United Nations African Institute for the Prevention of Crime and the Treatment of Offenders (UNAFRI) [A/63/87]. He described UNAFRI's substantive programme and the activities developed to support African States in crime prevention and criminal justice. He also examined the governance and management of UNAFRI and measures taken to initiate and maintain international cooperation and partnerships with other agencies, and identified further opportunities for funding and support. He also addressed the future of the Institute as a unique regional promoter of socio-economic development through crime prevention initiatives and suggested measures to ensure its sustainability. Information available to UNAFRI showed the difficulties faced by African countries in managing their criminal justice systems; in most African States, the rule of law and good governance were compromised by conflict or its aftermath. Because of limited human resources, insufficient infrastructure and inappropriate equipment, viable investments in effective crime prevention and criminal justice systems, in particular in the fight against organized criminal groups, remained a challenge in Africa. Nonetheless, efforts were increasingly being made to build capacity in crime prevention and criminal justice administration.

UNAFRI continued to: promote crime prevention through the incorporation into the action plans of States of the provisions of relevant international instruments and good practices; consolidate information-sharing capacity through awareness-raising programmes and collaboration with partner agencies; and encourage the upgrading of skills through research, knowledge-sharing, the encouragement of professionalism and the exchange of expertise. Efforts were made to incorporate international instruments in national legislation, while taking into consideration the needs and realities of each country and exposing officials to selected traditions relating to crime prevention and criminal justice administration.

Thanks to the pivotal role of UNODC, UNAFRI continued to cooperate with other members of the United Nations Crime Prevention and Criminal Justice Programme Network. It also established contacts with organizations in countries that promoted crime prevention programmes, and maintained close links with regional and subregional political entities, such as the Commission of the African Union, the East African Community, the Economic Commission of West African States, the Intergovernmental Authority on Development and the Southern African Development Community.

UNAFRI's income for 2007 totalled $344,422, a drastic drop from the $826,106 received in 2006. The decline was attributed to the low level of contributions received from States. The sources of the funds were: assessed contributions from States (13 per cent); a UN grant (67 per cent); and other income received from rental of the Institute's premises and facilities, as well as interest on deposits (20 per cent). For the period January–May 2008, resources amounted to $356,935, consisting of the 2008 portion of the UN grant for 2008–2009, and income received from the rental of UNAFRI premises.

The report concluded that the impact of crime was imposing an escalating cost on social development in Africa, and the complex nature of transnational organized crime posed unprecedented challenges to the existing competences, weak facilities and scarce resources available for combating crime. Those challenges increased vulnerability and the need for concerted strategies, specialized technical support for capacity-building, the sharing of good practices based on regional and international initiatives and research to facilitate the development of policies and the implementation of remedial measures. As a mechanism for harnessing the available potential at local, regional and international levels, UNAFRI continued to design programmes that were mindful of the needs of African countries for the development of effective crime prevention measures and the establishment of suitable criminal justice administrations.

GENERAL ASSEMBLY ACTION

On 18 December [meeting 71], the General Assembly, on the recommendation of the Third Committee [A/63/431], adopted **resolution 63/196** without vote [agenda item 97].

United Nations African Institute for the Prevention of Crime and the Treatment of Offenders

The General Assembly,

Recalling its resolution 62/174 of 18 December 2007 and all other relevant resolutions,

Taking note of the report of the Secretary-General,

Bearing in mind the urgent need to establish effective crime prevention strategies for Africa, as well as the importance of law enforcement agencies and the judiciary at the regional and subregional levels,

Bearing in mind also the Programme of Action, 2006–2010, endorsed by the Round Table for Africa, held in Abuja on 5 and 6 September 2005,

Aware of the devastating impact of crime on the national economies of African States and of the fact that crime is a major obstacle to harmonious and sustainable development in Africa,

Noting that the financial situation of the United Nations African Institute for the Prevention of Crime and the Treatment of Offenders has greatly affected its capacity to deliver its services to African Member States in an effective and comprehensive manner,

1. *Commends* the United Nations African Institute for the Prevention of Crime and the Treatment of Offenders for its efforts to promote and coordinate regional technical cooperation activities related to crime prevention and criminal justice systems in Africa;

2. *Also commends* the initiative of the United Nations Office on Drugs and Crime in strengthening its working relationship with the Institute by supporting and involving the Institute in the implementation of a number of activities, including those contained in the Programme of Action, 2006–2010, on strengthening the rule of law and criminal justice systems in Africa;

3. *Further commends* the Secretary-General for his efforts to mobilize the financial resources necessary to provide the Institute with the core professional staff required to enable it to function effectively in the fulfilment of its mandated obligations;

4. *Reiterates* the need to strengthen further the capacity of the Institute to support national mechanisms for crime prevention and criminal justice in African countries;

5. *Notes* the efforts of the Institute to establish contacts with organizations in those countries which are promoting crime prevention programmes and its maintenance of close links with regional and subregional political entities, such as the African Union Commission, the East African Community, the Commission of the Economic Community of West African States, the Intergovernmental Authority on Development and the Southern African Development Community;

6. *Urges* the States members of the Institute to continue to make every possible effort to meet their obligations to the Institute;

7. *Welcomes* the decision of the Governing Board of the Institute, at its tenth annual meeting, held in Khartoum on 19 and 20 May 2008, to convene a conference of African ministers to discuss measures for improving the flow of resources to the Institute;

8. *Urges* all Member States and non-governmental organizations and the international community to continue adopting concrete practical measures to support the Institute in the development of the requisite capacity and to implement its programmes and activities aimed at strengthening crime prevention and criminal justice systems in Africa;

9. *Urges* all States that have not already done so to consider ratifying or acceding to the United Nations Convention against Transnational Organized Crime and the Protocols thereto, as well as the United Nations Convention against Corruption;

10. *Requests* the Secretary-General to intensify efforts to mobilize all relevant entities of the United Nations system to provide the necessary financial and technical support to the Institute to enable it to fulfil its mandate;

11. *Also requests* the Secretary-General to continue his efforts to mobilize the financial resources necessary to maintain the Institute with the core professional staff required to enable it to function effectively in the fulfilment of its mandated obligations;

12. *Calls upon* the United Nations Office on Drugs and Crime to continue to work closely with the Institute;

13. *Requests* the Secretary-General to enhance the promotion of regional cooperation, coordination and collaboration in the fight against crime, especially in its transnational dimension, which cannot be dealt with adequately by national action alone;

14. *Also requests* the Secretary-General to continue making concrete proposals, including for the provision of additional core professional staff, to strengthen the programmes and activities of the Institute and to report to the General Assembly at its sixty-fourth session on the implementation of the present resolution.

Crime data collection

In a January note on world crime trends and responses [E/CN.15/2008/7], the Secretariat submitted to the Commission on Crime Prevention and Criminal Justice a summary of UNODC's work in the area of crime data collection, through the analysis of the Ninth and Tenth United Nations Surveys of Crime Trends and Operations of Criminal Justice Systems, and a number of international data sources. It also provided an overview of studies and activities carried out in 2007 in crime and development, trafficking in persons and corruption. The United Nations survey on crime trends and operations of criminal justice systems was the Organization's main data-collection instrument, collecting police and judicial statistics from all Member States. Nine surveys had been concluded, representing data for the period 1976–2004; the questionnaires for the tenth survey were disseminated in 2007. In accordance with the recommendations of the 2006 expert group on ways of improving crime data collection, research and analysis [YUN 2006, p. 1296], UNODC developed a plan to increase and facilitate country responses to the survey, including an analysis of response patterns and a survey of users of the results. The questionnaire for the tenth survey was revised, with most changes relating to crime definitions and the establishment of a system aimed at eliminating ambiguities of interpretation and solving problems of data consistency. New crime categories were added and the definitions of others slightly changed to align them with international instruments or other international data collections.

UNODC contributed to building capacity for crime data collection and reporting, including by promoting crime and victimization surveys. During 2007, preparations for several surveys in African countries were carried out and activities within UNODC's Data for Africa initiative were closely coordinated with UNAFRI. UNODC worked on the identification of core indicators of conventional crime and on developing indicators of transnational organized crime. It also cooperated with UN entities and non-governmental organizations (NGOs) on initiatives to improve crime data and national capacities to collect data. In particular, it engaged in the UN system-wide process of developing indicators to measure violence against women and emphasized the importance of developing indicators on such violence that related well to existing work in the assessment and monitoring of crime trends. Following the publication of the *Manual for the Measurement of Juvenile Justice Indicators*, UNODC continued to explore with the United Nations Children's Fund ways to support Member States in gathering systematic data on children in conflict with the law.

The Secretariat recommended that the Commission urge Member States to engage in regular reporting of data on crime trends at the national, regional and international levels, including through systematic participation in the United Nations survey on crime trends and operations of criminal justice systems and crime victim surveys. In particular, it should encourage States to participate in the tenth and subsequent surveys. The Commission might also support and encourage States in developing national capacity for the generation and collection of criminal justice statistics, including by the police, prosecutors, courts and penal systems, and the development of population-based surveys. It might also wish to explore ways to enhance statistical and research capacity for the collection of data on the issues of trafficking in persons, corruption, children in conflict with the law, violence against women and transnational organized crime.

Transnational organized crime

United Nations Convention against Transnational Organized Crime

In response to Economic and Social Council resolution 2005/17 [YUN 2005, p. 1224] and General Assembly resolution 61/181 [YUN 2006, p. 1293], the Secretary-General submitted to the Commission on Crime Prevention and Criminal Justice a February report on international cooperation in combating transnational organized crime and corruption [E/CN.15/2008/4] (see also below, under "Corruption"). The report reviewed UNODC activities and complemented the report of the Conference of the Parties to the United Nations Convention against Transnational Organized Crime on its third session [YUN 2007, p. 1134] and of the Conference of the States Parties to the United Nations Convention against Corruption at its second session (see p. 1239). The United Nations Convention against Transnational Organized Crime, adopted by Assembly resolution 55/25 [YUN 2000, p. 1048], and its three supplementary Protocols (Protocol to Prevent, Suppress and Punish Trafficking in Persons, Especially Women and Children [ibid., p. 1063]; Protocol against the Smuggling of Migrants by Land, Sea and Air [ibid., p. 1067]; Protocol against the Illicit Manufacturing of and Trafficking in Firearms, Their Parts and Components and Ammunition, adopted by the Assembly in resolution 55/255 [YUN 2001, p. 1036]) continued to attract adherence. As at 31 December, 147 States were parties to the Convention, 124 were parties to the trafficking-in-persons Protocol, 117 were parties to the migrants Protocol and 77 were parties to the firearms Protocol. UNODC made it a priority to promote universal ratification of those instruments and provide assistance to States seeking to ratify and implement them.

The report recommended that the Commission support the work of the Conference of the Parties to the Convention. In particular, it might urge States to make financial contributions in support of technical assistance activities and explore ways to maintain and strengthen the political momentum necessary for the Conference to perform its mandated functions. The

Commission might also urge States that had not yet done so to ratify or accede to the Convention and the Protocols, invite them to pursue efforts for implementation and take advantage of the wide array of tools and assistance that UNODC continued to offer in the fight against transnational organized crime.

Conference of Parties to the Convention

The Conference of the Parties to the United Nations Convention against Transnational Organized Crime, at its fourth session (Vienna, 8–17 October) [CTOC/COP/2008/19], adopted eight decisions on: possible mechanisms to review implementation of the Convention and the Protocols thereto; implementation of the provisions on international cooperation of the Convention; implementation of the provisions on technical assistance of the Convention; trafficking in human beings; implementation of the Protocol against the Smuggling of Migrants by Land, Sea and Air, supplementing the Convention; implementation of the Protocol against the Illicit Manufacturing of and Trafficking in Firearms, Their Parts and Components and Ammunition, supplementing the Convention; amendment of rule 18 of the rules of procedure for the Conference of the Parties to the Convention; and reorganization of the work of the fifth (2010) session of the Conference of the Parties to the Convention.

Trafficking in persons

Commission action. In response to Economic and Social Council resolution 2006/27 [YUN 2006, p. 1297], the Secretary-General submitted to the Commission on Crime Prevention and Criminal Justice a January report on strengthening international cooperation in preventing and combating trafficking in persons and protecting victims of such trafficking [E/CN.15/2008/6]. The report contained an analysis of replies received by UNODC, as at 24 January, from 23 States and one regional organization on their efforts to implement that resolution in the areas of: ratification of the Protocol to Prevent, Suppress and Punish Trafficking in Persons, Especially Women and Children and legal provisions; enforcement; training and seminars; prevention and awareness-raising; assistance to and protection of victims; national coordination mechanisms; and international cooperation. It provided an account of UNODC technical assistance in 2007, in particular through its Inter-Agency Cooperation Group against Trafficking in Persons (ICAT), which fostered coordination and cooperation among UN agencies and other international organizations to assist States in preventing and combating human trafficking. ICAT also promoted the effective use of resources and shared information, experiences and good practices on anti-trafficking activities of the partner agencies with Governments, international and regional organizations, NGOs and other relevant bodies. The report concluded that national coordination mechanisms and plans were valuable in developing a multi-agency response to prevent and counter human trafficking, and well-planned, comprehensive and effectively delivered awareness-raising and information campaigns were important components of national strategies. It encouraged States to consider providing training programmes and courses for law enforcement officers and other professionals and to consider introducing measures to ensure the protection of victims of trafficking. Continued efforts were also needed to promote cooperation between law enforcement agencies and legal authorities at the bilateral, regional and international levels. In light of the lack of information available with respect to trafficking in persons in post-conflict situations and regions of natural disaster, States might wish to consider that issue further.

In a February report to the Commission on Crime Prevention and Criminal Justice [E/CN.15/2008/10], the UNODC Executive Director provided an overview of the activities of the United Nations Global Initiative to Fight Human Trafficking (UN.GIFT), launched by UNODC in 2007 [YUN 2007, p. 1141], with the financial support of the United Arab Emirates, to raise awareness, stimulate international action and implement the Protocol to Prevent, Suppress and Punish Trafficking in Persons, Especially Women and Children, supplementing the UN Convention against Transnational Organized Crime. The report, based on information available as at 31 January, noted that, in accordance with the Commission's 2007 decisions 16/1 [ibid.] and 16/2 [ibid.], UNODC had held consultative meetings at which Member States provided guidance for the Global Initiative and for the Vienna Forum to Fight Human Trafficking, to be held from 13 to 15 February 2008. In addition, a Steering Committee met regularly to coordinate UN.GIFT's activities. The Executive Director recommended that UNODC should prepare a report on the Vienna Forum and on progress of the Global Initiative for submission to the Conference of the Parties to the UN Convention against Transnational Organized Crime at its fourth session (see above), with further reporting to the Commission on Crime Prevention and Criminal Justice. The Steering Committee was urged to review the results of the Vienna Forum and coordinate any further action. Member States were encouraged to ratify and implement the trafficking-in-persons Protocol and to promote the use of the wide array of tools and assistance offered by UNODC to prevent and counter trafficking.

The Commission on Crime Prevention and Criminal Justice, in April [E/2008/30 (res.17/1)], welcomed the holding of the Vienna Forum (see p. 1235) as a part of the awareness-raising efforts to fight human trafficking, and requested UNODC to continue consultations with Member States, to ensure that the Global Initiative was carried out as a technical assistance project and to brief States on the UN.GIFT workplan, to be executed before the end of the project in 2009. It also requested UNODC to use the Conference of the Parties to the UN Convention against Transnational Organized Crime and other relevant intergovernmental mechanisms to raise public awareness, increase knowledge, facilitate cooperation and partnerships and implement actions to combat human trafficking. States that had not yet done so were urged to ratify or accede to the Convention, particularly the trafficking in persons Protocol, and all States were encouraged to strengthen their national policies and cooperation with the UN system and to discourage the demand that fostered exploitation, in accordance with the trafficking-in-persons Protocol. UNODC, in its capacity as ICAT coordinator, was requested to report to the Commission's eighteenth (2009) session, and States were invited to provide voluntary contributions to UNODC for technical assistance activities and to participate in the General Assembly's 2008 thematic debate on human trafficking (see below).

Vienna Forum to Fight Human Trafficking

The Vienna Forum to Fight Human Trafficking (Vienna, 13–15 February) [CTOC/COP/2008/CRP.1], convened by UN.GIFT, aimed to raise awareness about human trafficking, forge new partnerships and facilitate cooperation. Three main themes were discussed in panels and workshops: vulnerability to trafficking in persons; its impact on individuals and society; and action against it. The various dimensions of human trafficking were considered in relation to security, development and human rights, and the Forum set the path for future anti-trafficking efforts. The Chairperson emphasized the need to address aggressively all forms of exploitation, including forced labour, and underscored UN.GIFT's critical role.

The Forum emphasized the need for adequate national legislation to cover all aspects of trafficking and for a victim-centred, human rights approach to preventing and combating trafficking in persons, with an understanding that supporting victims could positively impact criminal justice actions. It also highlighted the importance of increased research and awareness-raising and of increased cooperation among agencies, civil society and the private sector within countries and on an international level. The Forum called for a greater effort to confront all aspects of trafficking, including sexual exploitation and forced labour, and recommended that monitoring and evaluation mechanisms should be developed and implemented, and the nature of appropriate monitoring mechanisms should be addressed. It was agreed that the root causes of human trafficking should be confronted using a balanced approach, but that increased attention should be placed on how to reduce demand for trafficked persons in destination countries.

General Assembly thematic debate. On 3 June, the General Assembly held a thematic debate on human trafficking. Two panels considered the issues of: enhancing multilateral cooperation to prevent trafficking in persons; and protecting victims of trafficking and cross-border cooperation in prosecuting traffickers in persons.

ECONOMIC AND SOCIAL COUNCIL ACTION

On 25 July [meeting 44], the Economic and Social Council adopted **resolution 2008/33** [draft: E/2008/L.31] without vote [agenda item 14].

Strengthening coordination of the United Nations and other efforts in fighting trafficking in persons

The Economic and Social Council,

Recalling its role in providing overall coordination and guidance for the United Nations operational development programmes and funds on a system-wide basis,

Recalling also the United Nations Convention against Transnational Organized Crime and the Protocol to Prevent, Suppress and Punish Trafficking in Persons, Especially Women and Children, supplementing the United Nations Convention against Transnational Organized Crime,

Reaffirming all previous resolutions of United Nations bodies on the problem of trafficking in persons,

Recalling resolution 17/1 of the Commission on Crime Prevention and Criminal Justice on efforts in the fight against trafficking in persons, which underlined the need to continue to work towards a comprehensive and coordinated approach to the problem of human trafficking through the appropriate national, regional and international mechanisms,

Recognizing that the provision of effective support to the work of the Conference of the Parties to the United Nations Convention against Transnational Organized Crime and the Protocols thereto should be an important part of the coordination efforts of the United Nations system on the issue of trafficking in persons,

Noting the Vienna Forum to Fight Human Trafficking, held from 13 to 15 February 2008, the thematic debate of the General Assembly on human trafficking, held in New York on 3 June 2008, and the observations made at the thematic debate and the Vienna Forum,

Bearing in mind General Assembly resolution 61/180 of 20 December 2006 entitled "Improving the coordination of efforts against trafficking in persons", and Economic and Social Council resolution 2006/27 of 27 July 2006 entitled "Strengthening international cooperation in preventing and combating trafficking in persons and protecting victims of such trafficking",

Recognizing the importance of bilateral, subregional and regional and international cooperation mechanisms and initiatives, including information exchanges on best practices, of Governments and intergovernmental and non-governmental organizations in respect of addressing the problem of trafficking in persons, especially women and children,

Highlighting that strengthened international cooperation and coordination are needed to combat the activities of transnational criminal organizations and others that profit from trafficking in persons, to protect and assist all victims, with full respect for their human rights, and to ensure the exercise of due diligence with respect to prevention and investigation and punishment of perpetrators,

Underlining the need to continue to work towards a comprehensive and coordinated approach to the problem of trafficking in persons through the appropriate national, regional and international mechanisms,

Recognizing that addressing the problem of trafficking in persons requires a comprehensive approach, including addressing social and economic factors that make persons more vulnerable to trafficking, such as poverty, lack of opportunity, discrimination and marginalization, as well as strengthening the rule of law, combating corruption and discouraging and reducing demand that fosters all forms of exploitation of persons, especially women and children, and that thus promotes trafficking,

1. *Urges* all States, individually and through international cooperation, as well as the United Nations system, to increase, in a coherent, comprehensive and coordinated manner, efforts to counter trafficking in persons;

2. *Urges* all States that have not yet done so to consider ratifying or acceding to the United Nations Convention against Transnational Organized Crime and the Protocol to Prevent, Suppress and Punish Trafficking in Persons, Especially Women and Children, supplementing the United Nations Convention against Transnational Organized Crime, as well as the Convention for the Suppression of the Traffic in Persons and of the Exploitation of the Prostitution of Others;

3. *Invites* all States Members of the United Nations to make full use of existing instruments against trafficking in persons;

4. *Invites* Governments, regional and international organizations, and civil society to address, inter alia, the economic and social factors that breed and encourage trafficking in persons as well as to provide for the physical, psychological and social recovery of victims of trafficking in persons through:

(a) Appropriate housing;

(b) Counselling and information, in particular as regards their legal rights, in a language that the victims of trafficking in persons can understand;

(c) Medical, psychological and material assistance;

(d) Employment, educational and training opportunities;

5. *Calls upon* Governments and relevant actors from the international community to take into account the age, gender and special needs of victims of trafficking in persons;

6. *Calls upon* all States to fully implement the provisions of Council resolution 2006/27, entitled "Strengthening international cooperation in preventing and combating trafficking in persons and protecting victims of such trafficking";

7. *Calls for* full implementation of relevant instruments for the prevention and combating of trafficking in persons, and protection of victims of trafficking;

8. *Reiterates* the invitation to Member States to consider the advisability of establishing a United Nations strategy or plan of action on preventing trafficking in persons, prosecuting traffickers and protecting and assisting victims of trafficking;

9. *Welcomes* the work carried out under the United Nations Global Initiative to Fight Human Trafficking (UN.GIFT), and encourages the United Nations Office on Drugs and Crime to continue to cooperate with relevant international organizations outside of the United Nations system, utilizing extrabudgetary resources, and to invite such organizations to participate, when appropriate, in the meetings of the Inter-Agency Cooperation Group against Trafficking in Persons and to keep Member States informed of the schedule of and the progress made by the Cooperation Group;

10. *Invites* Member States to provide voluntary contributions to the United Nations Office on Drugs and Crime in order to facilitate optimum implementation of coordination functions;

11. *Highlights* the role of the Conference of the Parties to the United Nations Convention against Transnational Organized Crime and the Protocols thereto in ensuring the full and effective implementation of the Protocol to Prevent, Suppress and Punish Trafficking in Persons, Especially Women and Children;

12. *Reiterates its request* to the Secretary-General to provide the United Nations Crime Prevention and Criminal Justice Programme with sufficient resources for the full implementation of its mandates, in conformity with its high priorities, and to provide adequate support to the Commission on Crime Prevention and Criminal Justice.

Report of Secretary-General. In response to General Assembly resolution 61/180 [YUN 2006, p. 1299], the Secretary-General transmitted a July report on improving the coordination of efforts against trafficking in persons [A/63/90] that contained information on mechanisms utilized and activities carried out by UNODC to implement its coordination functions, through its own research, technical assistance and legal advisory services, as well as its inter-agency coordination and cooperation activities. It described data collection; collaboration between UNODC and other international bodies; and UN.GIFT activities. The Secretary-General noted that during the thematic debate on human trafficking held by the Assembly on 3 June (see p. 1235), several States had called for the elaboration of a global action plan in support of the implementation of the trafficking in persons Protocol. Such an action plan could spell out concrete measures for Member States to take in addressing the conditions that made people vulnerable to trafficking, to prevent and combat trafficking, to protect victims and to assist all partners. The framework could be based on the three "Ps" of efforts against human trafficking:

prevention, prosecution and protection; and a fourth "P", on partnership, could also be considered. The Assembly played an important role in coordinating international action against trafficking in persons and facilitating the implementation of the trafficking-in-persons Protocol and the Protocol against the Smuggling of Migrants by Land, Sea and Air.

GENERAL ASSEMBLY ACTION

On 18 December [meeting 71], the General Assembly, on the recommendation of the Third Committee [A/63/431], adopted **resolution 63/194** without vote [agenda item 97].

Improving the coordination of efforts against trafficking in persons

The General Assembly,

Recalling its resolution 61/180 of 20 December 2006 on improving the coordination of efforts against trafficking in persons and other relevant General Assembly resolutions on trafficking in persons and other contemporary forms of slavery,

Recalling also Economic and Social Council resolution 2008/33 of 25 July 2008 on strengthening coordination of the United Nations and other efforts in fighting trafficking in persons and previous Council resolutions on trafficking in persons,

Recalling further the United Nations Convention against Transnational Organized Crime and the Protocol to Prevent, Suppress and Punish Trafficking in Persons, Especially Women and Children, supplementing the United Nations Convention against Transnational Organized Crime, the Optional Protocol to the Convention on the Rights of the Child on the sale of children, child prostitution and child pornography and the Supplementary Convention on the Abolition of Slavery, the Slave Trade, and Institutions and Practices Similar to Slavery,

Welcoming the progress made at the fourth session of the Conference of the Parties to the United Nations Convention against Transnational Organized Crime, and taking note of the decisions of the Conference on the issue of trafficking in persons,

Recognizing that trafficking in persons impairs the enjoyment of human rights, continues to pose a serious challenge to humanity and requires a concerted international response,

Welcoming the decisions of the Human Rights Council to establish the mandate of the Special Rapporteur on contemporary forms of slavery, including its causes and consequences, and to extend the mandates of the Special Rapporteur on trafficking in persons, especially women and children and the Special Rapporteur on the sale of children, child prostitution and child pornography,

Recognizing that broad international cooperation between Member States and relevant intergovernmental and non-governmental organizations is essential for effectively countering the threat of trafficking in persons and other contemporary forms of slavery,

Recognizing also the need to continue fostering a global partnership against trafficking in persons and other contemporary forms of slavery,

Recognizing further that the provision of effective support to the work of the Conference of the Parties to the Convention should be an important part of the coordination efforts of the United Nations system on the issue of trafficking in persons,

Recognizing the importance of bilateral, subregional, regional and international cooperation mechanisms and initiatives, including information exchanges on good practices, of Governments and intergovernmental and non-governmental organizations to address the problem of trafficking in persons, especially women and children,

Reaffirming the commitment made by world leaders at the Millennium Summit and the 2005 World Summit to devise, enforce and strengthen effective measures to combat and eliminate all forms of trafficking in persons to counter the demand for trafficked victims and to protect the victims,

1. *Urges* Member States that have not yet done so to consider taking measures to ratify or accede to the United Nations Convention against Transnational Organized Crime and the Protocol to Prevent, Suppress and Punish Trafficking in Persons, Especially Women and Children, supplementing the United Nations Convention against Transnational Organized Crime, and to implement fully all aspects of those instruments;

2. *Also urges* Member States that have not yet done so to consider taking measures to ratify or accede to the Optional Protocol to the Convention on the Rights of the Child on the sale of children, child prostitution and child pornography, the Convention on the Elimination of All Forms of Discrimination against Women and the Supplementary Convention on the Abolition of Slavery, the Slave Trade, and Institutions and Practices Similar to Slavery, and to implement fully all aspects of those instruments;

3. *Recognizes* that broad international cooperation between Member States and relevant intergovernmental and non-governmental organizations is essential for effectively countering the threat of trafficking in persons and other contemporary forms of slavery;

4. *Welcomes* the steps taken by human rights treaty bodies and the Special Rapporteur on trafficking in persons, especially women and children, United Nations agencies and other concerned intergovernmental and governmental organizations, within their mandates, as well as civil society, to address the problem of trafficking in persons, and encourages them to continue doing so and to share their knowledge and best practices as widely as possible;

5. *Calls upon* Governments to continue their efforts to criminalize trafficking in persons in all its forms, including for the sexual exploitation of children, to take measures to criminalize child sex tourism, to condemn the practice of trafficking in persons, and to investigate, prosecute, condemn and penalize traffickers and intermediaries, while providing protection and assistance to the victims of trafficking with full respect for their human rights, and invites Member States to continue to support those United Nations agencies and international organizations that are actively involved in victim protection;

6. *Encourages* all stakeholders, including the private sector, to strengthen the coordination of efforts, including through the Inter-Agency Coordination Group against Trafficking in Persons and regional as well as bilateral initiatives that promote cooperation and collaboration;

7. *Welcomes* the holding of the Vienna Forum to Fight Human Trafficking, from 13 to 15 February 2008, as a part of the awareness-raising efforts to fight human trafficking, and requests the United Nations Office on Drugs and Crime to continue consultations with Member States, to ensure that the Global Initiative to Fight Human Trafficking is carried out as a technical assistance project within the mandates agreed to by the relevant governing bodies and to brief Member States on the workplan of the Global Initiative, to be executed before the end of the project in 2009;

8. *Recognizes* the importance of comparable data disaggregated by types of trafficking in persons, sex and age, as well as of strengthening national capacity for the gathering, analysing and reporting of such data, and welcomes the efforts of the Inter-Agency Coordination Group against Trafficking in Persons, drawing on the comparative advantages of the respective agencies, to share information, experiences and good practices on anti-trafficking activities of the partner agencies with Governments, other international and regional organizations, non-governmental organizations and other relevant bodies;

9. *Acknowledges* the important work on data collection and analysis conducted by the United Nations Office on Drugs and Crime under its Global Programme against Trafficking in Human Beings, as well as by the International Organization for Migration through its global Counter-Trafficking Module database;

10. *Takes note* of the discussions at the thematic debate of the General Assembly on human trafficking, held in New York on 3 June 2008, which included a discussion on the advisability of a United Nations strategy or plan of action on preventing trafficking in persons and protecting and assisting victims of trafficking;

11. *Calls upon* the Secretary-General to collect the views of all stakeholders, including Member States and regional and international organizations, on how to achieve the full and effective coordination of efforts against trafficking in persons of all Member States, organizations, machineries, treaty bodies and all other partners within and outside the United Nations system, including civil society, and to ensure the full and effective implementation of all legal instruments relevant to trafficking in persons, particularly the United Nations Convention against Transnational Organized Crime and the Protocol to Prevent, Suppress and Punish Trafficking in Persons, Especially Women and Children, without prejudice to the mandate of the working group established by the Conference of the Parties to the Convention, and submit, no later than 1 June 2009, a background paper to the General Assembly at its sixty-third session;

12. *Invites* all Member States to accelerate the consideration of the advisability of a global plan of action on preventing trafficking in persons, prosecuting traffickers and protecting and assisting victims of trafficking, which would achieve the full and effective coordination of efforts against trafficking in persons of all Member States, organizations, machineries, treaty bodies and all other partners within and outside the United Nations system, including civil society, and ensure the full and effective implementation of all legal instruments relevant to trafficking in persons, particularly the United Nations Convention against Transnational Organized Crime and the Protocol to Prevent, Suppress and Punish Trafficking in Persons, Especially Women and Children;

13. *Reiterates its request* to the Secretary-General to provide the United Nations Crime Prevention and Criminal Justice Programme with sufficient resources for the full implementation of its mandates on combating trafficking in persons, in conformity with its high priorities, and to provide adequate support to the Commission on Crime Prevention and Criminal Justice, and invites Member States to provide voluntary contributions to the United Nations Office on Drugs and Crime for the purpose of providing assistance to Member States upon request;

14. *Requests* the Secretary-General to submit to the Conference of the Parties to the Convention and the General Assembly at its sixty-fourth session a report on the implementation of the present resolution and on possible approaches to strengthen the coordination efforts against trafficking in persons of the Inter-Agency Coordination Group against Trafficking in Persons.

Also on 18 December, the Assembly took note of the Secretary-General's report on improving the coordination of efforts against trafficking in persons (**decision 63/536**).

Strategies for crime prevention

Corruption

United Nations Convention against Corruption

In response to Economic and Social Council resolution 2006/24 [YUN 2006, p. 1301] and General Assembly resolution 61/181 [ibid., p. 1293], the Secretary-General submitted to the Commission on Crime Prevention and Criminal Justice a February report on international cooperation in combating transnational organized crime and corruption [E/CN.15/2008/4] (see also above, under "Transnational organized crime"). The report described UNODC activities to promote ratification and implementation of the UN Convention against Corruption, adopted by Assembly resolution 58/4 [YUN 2003, p. 1127], and complemented the report of the Conference of the Parties to the Convention on its second session (see below).

The report suggested that the Commission urge States that had not yet done so to ratify or accede to the Convention and to ensure its implementation. In particular, States might be urged to provide financial and material contributions for the convening of working groups and workshops for the Convention's implementation.

As at 31 December, 129 States were parties to the Convention.

Conference of States Parties to the Convention

In response to General Assembly resolution 62/202 [YUN 2007, p. 1135], the Secretary-General, by a June note [A/63/86], transmitted to the Assembly the report of the Conference of the States Parties to the United Nations Convention against Corruption on its second session (Nusa Dua, Indonesia, 28 January–1 February) [CAC/COSP/2008/15].

The Conference adopted five resolutions on: review of implementation; appeal to States parties and invitation to signatories to the Convention to continue to adapt their legislation and regulations; asset recovery; strengthening coordination and enhancing technical assistance for the Convention's implementation; and consideration of the issue of bribery of officials of public international organizations. It also adopted one decision on the venue for its third (2009) session.

Assets of illicit origin

In response to General Assembly resolution 62/202 [YUN 2007, p. 1135], the Secretary-General submitted a June report on preventing and combating corrupt practices and transfer of assets of illicit origin and returning such assets, in particular to the countries of origin, consistent with the UN Convention against Corruption [A/63/88]. The report provided information on the outcome of the second session of the Conference of the States Parties to the Convention (see above) and on preparations for its third session, and described measures taken by States to prevent and combat corruption and to work for the prompt return of assets of illicit origin. It also provided an overview of international action being taken against corruption and for asset recovery, reviewed UNODC work carried out individually and in partnership with other entities, and presented information on matters related to resources.

The report recommended that the Assembly encourage Member States to ratify or accede to the Convention and support its implementation. It also stressed the need to consolidate the achievements made at the first and second sessions of the Conference of the States Parties and to ensure appropriate preparations for the third (2009) session, noting that an important challenge facing the third session would be to reach agreement on the terms of reference of the mechanism for reviewing the Convention's implementation. To that end, the working groups of the Conference needed to engage in dialogue on the possible terms of reference for such a mechanism and discuss steps for the implementation of chapter V of the Convention, on asset recovery, and the technical assistance to be provided. Success in the priority area of asset recovery would depend on the ability of the Conference to focus on substantive issues and the implementation of the relevant provisions of the Convention. The report concluded that more financial and human resources would be required to enable UNODC to promote the implementation of the Convention and discharge its functions as the secretariat of the Conference. It suggested that the Assembly might wish to give early consideration to the needs of UNODC and explore ways of addressing them in the 2010–2011 biennium.

GENERAL ASSEMBLY ACTION

On 19 December [meeting 72], the General Assembly, on the recommendation of the Second Committee [A/63/416/Add.4], adopted **resolution 63/226** without vote [agenda item 51 *(d)*].

Preventing and combating corrupt practices and transfer of assets of illicit origin and returning such assets, in particular to the countries of origin, consistent with the United Nations Convention against Corruption

The General Assembly,

Recalling its resolutions 54/205 of 22 December 1999, 55/188 of 20 December 2000, 56/186 of 21 December 2001 and 57/244 of 20 December 2002, 58/205 of 23 December 2003, 59/242 of 22 December 2004, 60/207 of 22 December 2005, 61/209 of 20 December 2006 and 62/202 of 19 December 2007,

Welcoming the entry into force on 14 December 2005 of the United Nations Convention against Corruption,

Welcoming also the convening of the second session of the Conference of the States Parties to the United Nations Convention against Corruption, in Nusa Dua, Indonesia, from 28 January to 1 February 2008, and stressing the need for States parties to take steps to implement the outcome of that Conference,

Recalling the Monterrey Consensus of the International Conference on Financing for Development, which underlined that fighting corruption at all levels is a priority, and the Plan of Implementation of the World Summit on Sustainable Development ("Johannesburg Plan of Implementation"),

Recognizing that fighting corruption at all levels is a priority and that corruption is a serious barrier to effective resource mobilization and allocation and diverts resources away from activities that are vital for poverty eradication, the fight against hunger, and economic and sustainable development,

Emphasizing the need for solid democratic institutions responsive to the needs of the people and the need to improve the efficiency, transparency and accountability of domestic administration and public spending and the rule of law, to ensure full respect for human rights, including the right to development, and to eradicate corruption and build sound economic and social institutions,

Recalling that the fight against all forms of corruption requires strong institutions at all levels, including at the local level, able to undertake efficient preventive and law enforcement measures consistent with the United Nations Convention against Corruption, in particular chapters II and III,

Determined to prevent, detect and deter in a more effective manner international transfers of illicitly acquired assets and to strengthen international cooperation on asset recovery, consistent with the Convention,

Reiterating its concern about the seriousness of problems and threats posed by corruption to the stability and security of societies, undermining the institutions and the values of democracy, ethical values and justice and jeopardizing sustainable development and the rule of law, in particular when an inadequate national and international response leads to impunity,

Convinced that corruption is no longer a local matter but a transnational phenomenon that affects all societies and economies, making international cooperation to prevent and control it essential,

Convinced also that a stable and transparent environment for national and international commercial transactions in all countries is essential for the mobilization of investment, finance, technology, skills and other important resources, and recognizing that effective efforts at all levels to prevent and combat corruption in all its forms in all countries are essential elements of an improved national and international business environment,

Mindful of the very important role that the private sector can play in fostering economic growth and development and of the active involvement of the United Nations system in facilitating the constructive participation and orderly interaction of the private sector in the development process by embracing universal principles and norms, such as honesty, transparency and accountability,

Recognizing the concern about the laundering and the transfer of assets of illicit origin derived from corruption, and stressing the need to address this concern consistent with the Convention,

Concerned about the links between corruption in all its forms, including bribery, corruption-related money-laundering and the transfer of assets of illicit origin, and other forms of crime, in particular organized crime and economic crime,

Noting the particular concern of developing countries and countries with economies in transition regarding the return of assets of illicit origin derived from corruption, in particular to countries from which they originated, consistent with the principles of the Convention, in particular chapter V, so as to enable countries to design and fund development projects in accordance with their national priorities, in view of the importance that such assets can have to their sustainable development,

Noting also that corrupt practices include public funds being illegally acquired, transferred, invested abroad or laundered,

1. *Takes note* of the report of the Secretary-General;

2. *Expresses concern* about the magnitude of corruption at all levels, including the scale of the transfer of assets of illicit origin derived from corruption, and in this regard reiterates its commitment to preventing and combating corrupt practices at all levels, consistent with the United Nations Convention against Corruption;

3. *Condemns* corruption in all its forms, including bribery, as well as the laundering of proceeds of corruption and other forms of economic crime;

4. *Urges* all Governments to combat and penalize corruption in all its forms as well as the laundering of proceeds of corruption, to prevent the transfer of illicitly acquired assets, and to work for the prompt return of such assets through asset recovery consistent with the principles of the Convention, particularly chapter V;

5. *Stresses* the need for transparency in financial institutions, invites Member States to work on the identification and tracing of financial flows linked to corruption, the freezing or seizing of assets derived from corruption and the return of such assets, consistent with the Convention, and encourages the promotion of human and institutional capacity-building in this regard;

6. *Affirms* the need for Member States, consistent with the Convention, to take measures to prevent the transfer abroad and laundering of assets derived from corruption, including to prevent the financial institutions in both countries of origin and destination from being used to transfer or receive illicit funds, as well as to assist in their recovery and to return such assets to the requesting State, consistent with the Convention;

7. *Stresses* the importance of mutual legal assistance, and encourages Member States to enhance international cooperation, consistent with the Convention;

8. *Welcomes* the high number of Member States that have already ratified or acceded to the Convention, and in this regard urges all Member States and competent regional economic integration organizations, within the limits of their competence, that have not yet done so to consider ratifying or acceding to the Convention as a matter of priority, and calls upon all States parties to fully implement the Convention as soon as possible;

9. *Calls upon* States parties to continue to support the work carried out by the Open-ended Intergovernmental Expert Working Groups on Asset Recovery, Technical Assistance and Review of Implementation in order to facilitate the full implementation of the Convention, and the review thereof, and in this regard encourages the Conference of the States Parties to the Convention at its third session to consider the recommendations prepared by the three working groups, including the terms of reference for a review mechanism;

10. *Welcomes* the responses already received to the self-assessment checklist on the implementation of the Convention, and encourages all States parties that have not yet done so to submit the self-assessment checklist to the United Nations Office on Drugs and Crime;

11. *Also welcomes* the efforts of Member States that have enacted laws and taken other positive measures in the fight against corruption in all its forms, including in accordance with the Convention, and in this regard encourages Member States that have not yet done so to enact such laws and to implement effective measures at the national level and, in accordance with domestic law and policies, at the local level, to prevent and combat corruption;

12. *Takes note with appreciation* of the Stolen Asset Recovery Initiative of the United Nations Office on Drugs and Crime and the World Bank, takes note of its cooperation with relevant partners, including the International Centre for Asset Recovery, and encourages coordination among existing initiatives;

13. *Calls for* further international cooperation, inter alia, through the United Nations system, in support of national, subregional and regional efforts to prevent and combat corrupt practices and the transfer of assets of illicit origin, consistent with the principles of the Convention, and in this regard encourages close cooperation between anti-corruption agencies, law enforcement agencies and financial intelligence units;

14. *Urges* all Member States, consistent with the Convention, to abide by the principles of proper management of public affairs and public property, fairness, responsibility and equality before the law and the need to safeguard integrity and to foster a culture of transparency, accountability and rejection of corruption;

15. *Encourages* Member States to provide adequate financial and human resources to the United Nations Office on Drugs and Crime, including for the effective implementation of the Convention, and also encourages the Office to give high priority to technical cooperation, upon request, inter alia, to promote and facilitate the ratification, acceptance, approval of or accession to, and the implementation of, the Convention;

16. *Requests* the international community to provide, inter alia, technical assistance to support national efforts to strengthen human and institutional capacity aimed at preventing and combating corrupt practices and the transfer of assets of illicit origin as well as for asset recovery consistent with the principles of the Convention, particularly chapter V, and to support national efforts in formulating strategies for mainstreaming and promoting transparency and integrity in both the public and the private sectors;

17. *Encourages* Member States that have not yet done so to require financial institutions to properly implement comprehensive due diligence and vigilance programmes, consistent with the principles of the Convention and those of other relevant applicable instruments;

18. *Reiterates its call upon* the private sector, at both the international and the national levels, including small and large companies and transnational corporations, to remain fully engaged in the fight against corruption, notes in this context the role that the Global Compact can play in fighting corruption and promoting transparency, and emphasizes the need for all relevant stakeholders, including within the United Nations system, as appropriate, to continue to promote corporate responsibility and accountability;

19. *Requests* the Secretary-General to continue to provide the United Nations Office on Drugs and Crime with the resources necessary to enable it to promote, in an effective manner, the implementation of the Convention and to discharge its functions as the secretariat of the Conference of the States Parties to the Convention, in accordance with its mandate;

20. *Takes note* of the offer of the Government of Qatar to host the third session of the Conference of the States Parties to the Convention in 2009, and invites all States parties and signatories to take measures aimed at promoting the full and effective implementation of the Convention;

21. *Requests* the Secretary-General to submit to the General Assembly, at its sixty-fourth session, a report on the implementation of the present resolution and also to transmit to the Assembly a report on the third session of the Conference of the States Parties to the Convention;

22. *Decides* to include in the provisional agenda of its sixty-fourth session, under the item entitled "Globalization and interdependence", the sub-item entitled "Preventing and combating corrupt practices and transfer of assets of illicit origin and returning such assets, in particular to the countries of origin, consistent with the United Nations Convention against Corruption".

Terrorism

In a January report to the Commission on Crime Prevention and Criminal Justice on assistance in implementing the universal conventions and protocols related to terrorism [E/CN.15/2008/5], the Secretary-General reviewed progress made by UNODC in delivering technical assistance on legal and related capacity-building in the area of counter-terrorism, in particular by its Terrorism Prevention Branch. The report also addressed the challenges ahead, especially in the implementation of the United Nations Global Counter-Terrorism Strategy, adopted by the General Assembly in resolution 60/288 [YUN 2006, p. 66], and emphasized the need for enhanced governmental support in that regard.

The scope of specialized technical assistance in the legal and related capacity-building areas provided by UNODC had grown consistently since 2003 in terms of geographical reach, the number of countries receiving assistance and its substantive content, and partnerships had been developed with international, regional and subregional organizations. The increased number of requests for assistance had to be met expeditiously to sustain and increase the momentum for action at the national level and to ensure effective long-term follow-up. As more States ratified the relevant international legal instruments, enhanced implementation assistance was needed, especially to strengthen the capacity of national criminal justice systems to apply the provisions of the legal regime against terrorism in conformity with the principles of the rule of law and human rights. In that regard, sustained services and follow-up needed to be ensured, new specialized tools developed and existing tools refined. Moreover, in response to the United Nations Global Counter-Terrorism Strategy, UNODC had to promote legal cooperation at the regional and subregional levels, good practices, legal research and academic training in the area of counter-terrorism. It should also strengthen its network of field-level experts and integrate counter-terrorism aspects into all substantive areas of its mandates and work, such as money-laundering, transnational organized crime, drug trafficking, corruption and criminal justice reform. The Commission could provide guidance with regard to the reinforcement of UNODC's technical assistance work on counter-terrorism and on the strengthening of its network of field-level experts. UNODC would contribute to the work of the Counter-Terrorism Implementation Task Force to assist States in their implementation of the Global Counter-Terrorism Strategy, and would continue to establish and reinforce partnerships with other organizations, both within and outside the UN system, to enhance the impact of its technical assistance. It was suggested that the Commission might wish to invite international, regional and subregional organizations to enhance their cooperation with UNODC on counter-terrorism. While acknowledging that donor countries had provided invaluable voluntary contributions towards UNODC work in counter-terrorism, it was noted that the resource level was inadequate to meet the increasing number of requests for technical assistance and the corresponding expansion in operational activities and initiatives. Increased and multi-year voluntary contributions by donors and cost-sharing arrangements with assisted countries were essential. It was also necessary to provide from the regular budget the minimum core capacity required in terms of the specialized expertise and secretariat functions needed to deliver the expanded programme.

In accordance with General Assembly resolution 62/172 [YUN 2007, p. 1138], the Secretary-General submitted a June report on assistance in implementing the universal conventions and protocols related to terrorism [A/63/89], in which he focused on activities carried out by UNODC, in particular by its Terrorism Prevention Branch, with regard to delivery of technical assistance between 1 June 2007 and 31 May 2008. He updated the information contained in his January report to the Commission on Crime Prevention and Criminal Justice (see above). The Secretary-General suggested that the Assembly might wish to provide further guidance with regard to the reinforcement of the technical assistance delivered by UNODC on counter-terrorism issues, covering both the specialized services for strengthening the legal regime against terrorism and the services for addressing the cross-cutting issues of drug control and crime and terrorism prevention. The Assembly might also reiterate its call with regard to UNODC involvement in the work of the Counter-Terrorism Implementation Task Force, urge relevant organizations to enhance their cooperation with the Office on counter-terrorism issues, and invite States to increase the level of extrabudgetary and regular budget resources for UNODC activities in the area of terrorism prevention. Given the ongoing potential threat posed by terrorism, it was imperative to continue to provide support to efforts to strengthen the legal regime against terrorism and enhance related national capacities.

Communications. By a 16 April letter [E/CN.15/2008/21], the Russian Federation and the United States transmitted to the UNODC Executive Director the United States-Russian Strategic Framework Declaration, adopted in Sochi, Russian Federation, on 6 April. A significant part of the Declaration concerned the rule of law and combating global terrorism.

On 17 June [A/62/884], Uzbekistan conveyed to the Secretary-General information about the existing system in that country on opposing the legalization of income derived from criminal activity and countering the financing of terrorism.

By a 15 August letter [A/62/947-S/2008/585], Panama transmitted to the Secretary-General the Panama Declaration, adopted by Colombia, Costa Rica, the Dominican Republic, El Salvador, Guatemala, Honduras, Mexico, Nicaragua, Panama and Peru at the Second Ministerial Conference on International Cooperation against Terrorism and Transnational Organized Crime (Panama City, Panama, 26–29 May).

On 11 December, the Assembly, in **resolution 63/129** (see p. 1441), requested the UNODC Terrorism Prevention Branch to continue its efforts to enhance UN capabilities in preventing terrorism and recognized UNODC's role in assisting States in becoming parties to and implementing the relevant international conventions and protocols relating to terrorism and in strengthening internal cooperation mechanisms in criminal matters related to terrorism, including through national capacity-building.

The Assembly, on 18 December, took note of the Secretary-General's report on assistance in implementing the universal conventions and protocols related to terrorism (above) (**decision 63/536**).

Violence against women and girls

In response to Economic and Social Council resolution 2006/29 [YUN 2006, p. 1338], the Secretary-General submitted to the Commission on Crime Prevention and Criminal Justice a February report on crime prevention and criminal justice responses to violence against women and girls [E/CN.15/2008/2] (see also p. 1263). The report provided an overview of the development of UNODC's technical assistance programme and contained information received from Member States on their response to the problem of violence against women and girls. All of those countries that had provided information reported that efforts were being made to ensure that national strategies, action plans and legislative frameworks included provision and/or guidelines for ensuring effective criminal justice responses to violence against women. They recognized that efforts should be made in the areas of: national action plans; legislation and judicial procedures; the police; victim support and assistance; training; awareness-raising/information campaigns; research and data collection; ensuring effective criminal justice responses to violence against women and girls;

and special considerations on children. UNODC continued to expand its technical assistance programme for strengthening criminal justice system responses to gender-based violence, and had made efforts to build partnerships with other UN entities, regional organizations and NGOs and to include the criminal justice system as part of a holistic response. However, there was a need to expand its work in the context of overall UN efforts in that regard.

The Secretary-General recommended that the Commission might wish to encourage Member States to provide extrabudgetary resources for continuing the development and implementation of field-based projects and programmes, with a focus on victims and witnesses; encourage UNODC to continue to assist States in the area of criminal justice system responses to violence against women and girls; and urge States to support the use of UN indicators on violence against women and girls through population-based surveys and the collection of administrative information. The Commission might also wish to enhance national statistical and research capacity for data collection; emphasize the importance of UNODC incorporating the issue of gender more broadly into its programmes and projects in the justice sector; and urge UNODC to provide assistance to States, with a particular focus on: access to justice for women victims of violence; access to health and other services for female victims of violence; strengthening data collection on all forms of violence against women and girls; and the situation of women in detention, as well as children residing in prison with their mothers.

The Commission on Crime Prevention and Criminal Justice, in April [E/2008/30 (dec. 17/1)], condemned all acts of violence against women and girls, including violence against women migrants and women migrant workers, whether those acts were perpetrated by the State, by private persons or by non-State actors, and called for the elimination of all forms of gender-based violence in the family, in the community and where perpetrated or condoned by the State. It stressed that violence against women meant any act of gender-based violence that resulted in, or was likely to result in, physical, sexual or psychological harm or suffering to women, including the threat of such acts, coercion or arbitrary deprivation of liberty, whether occurring in public or private life. The Commission requested UNODC to convene an intergovernmental group of experts, in cooperation with the institutes of the United Nations Crime Prevention and Criminal Justice Programme Network, the Commission on the Status of Women and the Special Rapporteur on violence against women, its causes and consequences, to review and update the Model Strategies and Practical Measures on the Elimination of Violence against Women in the Field of Crime Prevention and Criminal Justice, taking into account developments, research, tools and the outcome of the Commission's deliberations at its seventeenth session, and to make recommendations on addressing violence against women and girls, to be considered by the Commission at its nineteenth (2010) session. Member States and other donors were invited to provide extrabudgetary contributions for those purposes, and the offer of Thailand to act as host to the meeting of the intergovernmental group of experts, to be held in 2008, was welcomed. The Commission requested UNODC's Executive Director to submit a report to its nineteenth (2010) session.

UN standards and norms

Guidelines on justice for child victims and witnesses

In response to Economic and Social Council resolution 2005/20 [YUN 2005, p. 1236], the Secretary-General submitted to the Commission on Crime Prevention and Criminal Justice a January report on implementation of the Guidelines on Justice in Matters involving Child Victims and Witnesses of Crime [E/CN.15/2008/11], which were annexed to the resolution. The report, based on information received from 27 Member States on legislation procedures, policies and practices relating to child victims and witnesses of crime, provided a summary of measures taken by States in relation to the rights established in the Guidelines: to be treated with dignity and compassion; to be protected from discrimination; to be informed; to be heard and to express views and concerns; to effective assistance; to privacy; to be protected from hardship during the justice process; to safety; to reparation; and to special preventive measures. It also contained an overview of UNODC activities to assist countries in the use and application of the Guidelines.

The replies indicated that most of the respondent countries had taken measures to implement, at least to a certain extent, the rights contained in the Guidelines. Most respondent States provided information on existing legislative measures in line with the Guidelines' provisions; however, only very few submitted information on court decisions and judgements that could provide a more comprehensive overview of effective implementation of the rights. Moreover, the right to receive reintegration and rehabilitation assistance was one of the least established in national legal frameworks. The Secretary-General noted that the information received highlighted the different degree of implementation from country to country. While some countries had developed comprehensive measures dealing with child victims and witnesses, others had adopted only basic or general provisions. The report suggested that the Commission might wish to encourage States to draw on the Guidelines in developing legislation, procedures, policies and practices for child victims and witnesses. In particular, it might draw the attention of countries to the need to develop rehabilitation and reintegration programmes. It might also invite States to draw on some of the legislation, policies and practices cited by some States, including the preparation of child witnesses and the use of audio-visual means for children to provide their testimony in order to avoid the stress and possible trauma associated with their appearance in the courtroom. Further, the Commission might invite States to make voluntary contributions to the United Nations Crime Prevention and Criminal Justice Fund to support UNODC in providing technical assistance and advisory services to requesting countries, in order to strengthen and improve their national capacities to protect and assist child victims and witnesses of crime.

Strengthening the rule of law

The Secretary-General submitted to the Commission on Crime Prevention and Criminal Justice a February report [E/CN.15/2008/12] on strengthening justice, integrity and the rule of law through technical assistance in developing, transitional and post-conflict societies, with a focus on Africa. The report reviewed activities and programmes carried out in accordance with Economic and Social Council resolutions 2006/22 [YUN 2006, p. 1316], 2006/25 [ibid., p. 1291] and 2007/22 [YUN 2007, p. 1146], and provided a framework for an integrated UNODC programme for the period 2008–2011 in the area of justice and integrity in accordance with the UNODC strategy. The reporting period saw a strong emphasis in the UN system on assistance to developing countries, in particular post-conflict States, in rule of law and justice reform, as well as increased attention to UN system-wide coordination and cooperation.

In his conclusions, the Secretary-General noted the strong increase in UNODC technical assistance in the area of judicial integrity and criminal justice reform. The implementation of projects and programmes provided evidence that: technical assistance in the areas of justice and integrity reform depended on national ownership through long-term interventions; it was not sufficient to strengthen only one aspect of the system or one of its institutions, and reform initiatives aimed only at one aspect had shown not to be sustainable; in the area of integrity and accountability, it was also necessary to address law enforcement and prosecution services in support of efforts to strengthen the integrity of the judiciary; interventions relating to technical or administrative aspects such as case management could have a significant impact on the efficiency of justice systems and human rights of prisoners; assessments and data collection were essential components of such programmes; and UNODC technical expertise and mandates were in greater demand both by Member States and other agencies, including in post-conflict settings. He suggested that the Commission might wish to recommend that UNODC continue designing and implementing technical assistance projects in the areas of access to justice and penal reform, the integrity of the justice sector, and urban security and youth crime prevention; and continue its efforts towards integration in peacekeeping missions and other joint UN missions. The Commission might also recommend that Member States provide support to such integrated programmes on justice and integrity, in particular those in post-conflict and transitional States.

The Commission on Crime Prevention and Criminal Justice, in April [E/2008/30 (res.17/2)], requested UNODC to circulate the Standards of Professional Responsibility and Statement of the Essential Duties and Rights of Prosecutors—annexed to its resolution—to Member States for their consideration and comments. It also requested UNODC to prepare, by the third quarter of 2008, a structured, verbatim compilation of the comments received from States, as an addendum to the Standards and Statement, and to provide technical assistance to allow States to strengthen the integrity and capacity of their prosecution services. The Commission invited States to encourage their prosecution services to take into consideration the Standards and Statement and the above-mentioned addendum when reviewing or developing rules with respect to the professional and ethical conduct of members of prosecution services, and also invited States and other donors to provide extrabudgetary contributions. The Secretary-General was requested to report to the Commission at its twentieth (2011) session.

Other crime prevention and criminal justice issues

Trafficking in forest products

The Commission on Crime Prevention and Criminal Justice, in April [E/2008/30], had before it a February report by the UNODC Executive Director on international cooperation in preventing and combating illicit international trafficking in forest products, including timber, wildlife and other forest biological resources [E/CN.15/2008/9]. The report, submitted in response to Commission resolution 16/1 of 2007 [YUN 2007, p. 1148], provided an overview and brief analysis of replies received from Member States on their efforts to implement that resolution and to combat illicit trafficking in forest products, harvested in contravention of national laws. It also contained information on matters related to forest law enforcement and governance, as provided by the secretariat of the United Nations Forum on Forests.

The information received from States confirmed the importance that they attached to the fight against the illicit international trade in forest products. In order to better target that crime, national laws and regulations should be adopted, regional instruments and mechanisms set up and international law enforcement cooperation strengthened. The information received also mentioned efforts to counter money-laundering and corruption, strengthen border controls and address organized crime in general as contributions to combating illicit trade in forest products. Input from the Forum on Forests secretariat echoed the Commission's call to increase synergies on matters related to forest law enforcement and for action to address illegal trade and, in particular, to prosecute significant offenders, leaders of organized criminal groups and financiers of forest-related crime. In accordance with Commission resolution 16/1, UNODC would organize an open-ended expert group meeting, explore the possibility of obtaining extrabudgetary resources for that purpose, and invite States, UN bodies and other intergovernmental bodies to increase synergies between the work of those involved in combating illicit trade in forest products and the criminal justice work of UNODC.

The Commission also considered the report of the meeting of the Open-ended Expert Group on International Cooperation in Preventing and Combating Illicit International Trafficking in Forest Products, including Timber, Wildlife and Other Forest Biological Resources (Jakarta, Indonesia, 26–28 March) [E/CN.15/2008/20], prepared in response to Commission resolution 16/1. The report described the Expert Group's discussions on the economic, social and environmental impact of the crimes under consideration and on appropriate legal and law enforcement responses. It reflected the views of the experts on ways and means of fostering international cooperation, through the use, where applicable, of the UN Convention against Transnational Organized Crime [YUN 2000, p. 1048] and the UN Convention against Corruption [YUN 2003, p. 1127], and of enhancing the institutional capacity of law enforcement and forestry authorities to enforce the rule of law in the forest sector. The report contained the conclusions of the Expert Group for further consideration by the Commission.

The Commission recommended to the Economic and Social Council for adoption a draft resolution on international cooperation in preventing and combating illicit international trafficking in forest products, including timber, wildlife and other forest biological resources.

By **resolution 2008/25** of 24 July (see p. 1165), the Council encouraged Member States to continue to provide UNODC with information on measures taken pursuant to Commission resolution 16/1, taking into consideration the emphasis placed by the Expert Group on the need for holistic and comprehensive national multisectoral approaches to preventing and combating illicit international trafficking in forest products, as well as for international coordination and cooperation in support of such approaches. It requested the UNODC Executive Director to make available the resolution and the report of the Expert Group to the Conference of the Parties to the UN Convention against Transnational Organized Crime at its fourth session in October, and to report in 2009.

Human resources development

United Nations Institute for Training and Research

In response to General Assembly resolution 62/210 [YUN 2007, p. 1150], the Secretary-General submitted a June report [E/2008/72] on the United Nations Institute for Training and Research (UNITAR), which focused on the financial aspects of the UNITAR core training activities—diplomatic training—in distinction to its training and capacity-development activities in other fields. The report described the particularities of core diplomatic training and provided information on the increasing demand for it, the complexities of funding such a service and what the impact would be if the service were no longer offered to diplomats. It examined its implementation costs and financial implications involved in maintaining the service, outlined the comprehensive financial situation of UNITAR, including the levels of voluntary contributions, and provided details of how core diplomatic training had been supported in the past, the actual expenditures incurred in the previous biennium and forecasted expenditures for the current and future bienniums. It also presented a cost/benefit analysis of the service, the costs per beneficiary and a market survey of comparable services offered outside the UN context. It further reviewed the positive and negative aspects of options other than recourse to the UN regular budget, most notably that of a fee-based system.

The Secretary-General recommended that multilateral training on diplomacy should continue to be offered in a multilateral setting. The burden of covering its costs should fall on the collective membership of the United Nations, and support from the UN regular budget would be a show of solidarity for continuous learning and for reform efforts to make the United Nations a venue for effective and efficient decision-making. He recommended that the Assembly's Fifth

(Administrative and Budgetary) Committee reconsider financing UNITAR core training activities from the regular budget, and that Member States increase or resume their contributions to UNITAR. Specifically, the Secretary-General recommended that an annual subvention of $600,000, or half the costs of core diplomatic training, be granted from the regular budget.

ECONOMIC AND SOCIAL COUNCIL ACTION

On 25 July [meeting 44], the Economic and Social Council adopted **resolution 2008/35** [draft: E/2008/L.37] without vote [agenda item 15].

United Nations Institute for Training and Research

The Economic and Social Council,

Recalling General Assembly resolutions 51/188 of 16 December 1996, 52/206 of 18 December 1997, 53/195 of 15 December 1998, 54/229 of 22 December 1999, 55/208 of 20 December 2000, 56/208 of 21 December 2001, 57/268 of 20 December 2002, 58/223 of 23 December 2003, 59/252 of 22 December 2004, 60/213 of 22 December 2005 and 62/210 of 19 December 2007 and Assembly decision 61/542 of 20 December 2006,

Welcoming the decision to streamline the reporting arrangements of the United Nations Institute for Training and Research in accordance with Assembly resolution 62/210,

Recalling in particular paragraph 9 of Assembly resolution 62/210,

Taking note of the report of the Secretary-General,

Noting that the Institute is self-funded to date, not receiving any kind of subsidies from the United Nations regular budget, and delivers, free of charge, training courses to diplomats and delegates accredited to United Nations Headquarters in New York and to the United Nations Offices at Geneva, Vienna and Nairobi,

Stressing that core diplomatic training offered by the Institute is a service accessible to diplomats of the entire membership of the United Nations and strengthens capacities of diplomats to perform their multilateral duties,

Noting the solid overall financial situation of the Institute, with a projected increase in funding of at least 26 per cent between the previous and current bienniums, and expressing its appreciation to the Governments and private institutions that have made or pledged financial and other contributions to the Institute,

Noting also that, despite the growing need for training and capacity development, voluntary contributions remain at a low level, putting at risk the training courses that the Institute delivers to diplomats and delegates accredited to United Nations Headquarters in New York and to the United Nations Offices at Geneva, Vienna and Nairobi,

Reiterating that training and capacity-development activities should be accorded a more visible and larger role in support of the management of international affairs, and in the execution of the economic and social development programmes of the United Nations system,

1. *Acknowledges* the progress made by the United Nations Institute for Training and Research, in the light of the strategic reforms introduced by its Executive Director and endorsed by its Board of Trustees, for the Institute to be a centre of excellence;

2. *Also acknowledges* the work of the Board of Trustees, and welcomes the contributions of its newly reconstituted membership with respect to guiding the Institute through its reforms;

3. *Considers* that the core diplomatic training offered by the Institute is unique in its beneficiary base and its reliance on United Nations expertise;

4. *Notes with concern* that a lack of voluntary contributions could lead to a cessation of this service, which is particularly important for the training of delegates from developing and least developed countries;

5. *Appeals*, in this regard, to the Institute to continue its fund-raising strategy and to all Governments, in particular those of developed countries, and to private institutions that have not yet contributed financially or otherwise to the Institute, to give it their generous financial and other support, and urges the States that have interrupted their voluntary contributions to consider resuming them in view of the Institute's strategic reforms;

6. *Requests*, in this regard, the Secretary-General to submit a report to the General Assembly at its sixty-third session on the issue of financing the core diplomatic training activities of the Institute.

In response to Council resolution 2008/35 (above), the Secretary-General submitted to the General Assembly a December report on financing of the core diplomatic training activities of UNITAR [A/63/592]. The Secretary-General provided information on UNITAR's financial situation in respect of core diplomatic training, its cost-effectiveness, the demand for it by Member States and the potential impact of its reduction or cessation on the overall performance of diplomats, in particular those from developing and least developed countries, in carrying out their duties. The Secretary-General recommended that in order to maintain the current level of core diplomatic training activities, the Assembly might wish to provide UNITAR with an annual subvention of $600,000, or half of the $1,200,000 annual cost of core diplomatic training, in the context of the proposed programme budget for the 2010-2011 biennium, taking into account the concern expressed by the Council in resolution 2008/35 that a lack of voluntary contributions could lead to a cessation of that service. He also suggested that the Assembly might request the Secretary-General to amend, after consultation with the UNITAR Board of Trustees, the statute of UNITAR in order to include a subvention from the regular budget.

On 24 December, the Assembly decided that the agenda items on the report of the Economic and Social Council and on the programme budget for the 2008–2009 biennium would remain for consideration at its resumed sixty-third (2009) session (**decision 63/552**).

University for Peace

By **resolution 63/132** of 11 December (see p. 1538), the General Assembly decided to invite the University for Peace to participate in its sessions and work in the capacity of observer.

Education for all

In response to General Assembly resolution 61/140 [YUN 2006, p. 1326], the Secretary-General transmitted a July report by the UNESCO Director-General on the implementation of the International Plan of Action for the United Nations Literacy Decade (2003–2012) [A/63/172], proclaimed by the Assembly in resolution 56/116 [YUN 2001, p. 1052]. The report reviewed the status, trends and challenges of literacy at the mid-point of the Decade, focusing on non-literate youth and adults (those having no or low literacy skills), and provided a framework for the second half of the Decade. It recognized that the right to education included to that literacy—an essential condition of learning and human development. It remained a grave concern that one in five adults in the world (774 million in total) had no literate access to written communication, that 75 million children were not attending school, and that millions more young people left school without a level of literacy adequate for productive and active participation in their societies.

The Director-General observed that at the global level, the challenge of literacy inequalities remained undiminished since the beginning of the Decade; progress on adult literacy was halting and funding insufficient. In addition, provision for women, young people and rural populations was often inadequate. Ensuring adequate provision to diverse population groups would require that improvements in mass literacy not be accompanied by decreasing linguistic and cultural diversity of minority and indigenous groups. The delivery and management of literacy programmes included three main challenges: to improve national-level literacy development strategies and coordination to ensure adequate coverage and targeting; to ensure quality programmes based on the needs of the learner; and to improve monitoring and financial planning mechanisms. He recommended that: Member States give literacy higher priority within their educational planning and budgeting; UNESCO strengthen its coordinating role and develop a strategic framework for renewed action in literacy, in cooperation with international partners, including the UN system agencies; the international community deepen its commitment to literacy, with greater integration into international development targets, such as the Millennium Development Goals, and intensify efforts to implement the International Plan of Action of the Decade. The remaining five years of the Decade had to focus on: stronger commitment, with particular concern to issues of gender, young people and marginalization; more effective programme design and delivery on the ground, with a determination to orient national and international support to the needs and characteristics of communities; and new resources—in particular, increased allocation of funds and strengthened institutional mechanisms for financing adult literacy and the development of new models and databases on literacy programme costs.

On 25 July, by **decision 2008/258**, the Economic and Social Council adopted the theme "Implementing the internationally agreed goals and commitments in regard to education" for its 2011 annual ministerial-level substantive review.

GENERAL ASSEMBLY ACTION

On 18 December [meeting 70], the General Assembly, on the recommendation of the Third Committee [A/63/424], adopted **resolution 63/154** without vote [agenda item 55 *(d)*].

United Nations Literacy Decade: education for all

The General Assembly,

Recalling its resolution 56/116 of 19 December 2001, by which it proclaimed the ten-year period beginning on 1 January 2003 the United Nations Literacy Decade, its resolution 57/166 of 18 December 2002, in which it welcomed the International Plan of Action for the United Nations Literacy Decade, and its resolutions 59/149 of 20 December 2004 and 61/140 of 19 December 2006,

Recalling also the United Nations Millennium Declaration, in which Member States resolved to ensure that, by 2015, children everywhere, boys and girls alike, will be able to complete a full course of primary schooling and that girls and boys will have equal access to all levels of education, which requires a renewed commitment to promote literacy for all,

Reaffirming the emphasis placed by the 2005 World Summit on the critical role of both formal and non-formal education in the achievement of poverty eradication and other development goals as envisaged in the Millennium Declaration, in particular basic education and training for achieving universal literacy, and the need to strive for expanded secondary and higher education as well as vocational education and technical training, especially for girls and women, the creation of human resources and infrastructure capabilities and the empowerment of those living in poverty,

Reaffirming also that quality basic education is crucial to nation-building, that literacy for all is at the heart of basic education for all and that creating literate environments and societies is essential for achieving the goals of eradicating poverty, reducing child mortality, curbing population growth, achieving gender equality and ensuring sustainable development, peace and democracy,

Convinced that literacy is crucial to the acquisition by every child, youth and adult of the essential life skills that will enable them to address the challenges that they can face in life and represents an essential condition of lifelong learning, which is an indispensable means for effective participation in the knowledge societies and economies of the twenty-first century,

Affirming that the realization of the right to education, especially for girls, contributes to the promotion of gender equality and the eradication of poverty,

Welcoming the considerable efforts that have been made so far by Member States and the international community to address the objectives of the Decade and to implement the International Plan of Action,

Reaffirming the right of indigenous peoples, in particular children, to have non-discriminatory access to all levels and forms of education provided by States,

Noting with deep concern that 774 million adults do not have basic literacy skills, 75 million children remain out of school, and millions more young people leave school without a level of literacy adequate for productive and active participation in their societies, that the issue of literacy may not be sufficiently high on national agendas to generate the kind of political and economic support required to address global literacy challenges and that the world is unlikely to meet those challenges if the present trends continue,

Deeply concerned about the persistence of the gender gap in education, which is reflected by the fact that nearly two thirds of the world's adult illiterates are women,

1. *Takes note* of the report of the Director-General of the United Nations Educational, Scientific and Cultural Organization on the implementation of the International Plan of Action for the United Nations Literacy Decade;

2. *Takes note also* of the summary outcomes of the Regional Conferences in Support of Global Literacy, held in Azerbaijan, China, India, Mali, Mexico and Qatar in 2007 and 2008, which indicate that the second half of the Decade should develop appropriate networks for greater regional collaboration;

3. *Recognizes* that a renewed collective commitment will be needed if the objectives of the Decade are to be met;

4. *Calls upon* Member States to further reinforce political will, giving literacy higher priority within their educational planning and budgeting;

5. *Appeals* to all Governments to develop reliable literacy data and information and more inclusive policymaking environments and to devise innovative strategies for reaching the groups disproportionately affected by illiteracy, in particular the poorest and most marginalized groups, and for seeking alternative formal and non-formal approaches to learning with a view to achieving the goals of the Decade;

6. *Appeals* to Governments to take full account of the use of languages in different contexts by promoting multilingual approaches to literacy, through which learners may acquire initial literacy in the language they know best and in additional languages as needed;

7. *Urges* all Governments to take the lead in coordinating the activities of the Decade at the national level, bringing all relevant national actors together in a sustained dialogue and collaborative action on policy formulation, implementation and evaluation of literacy efforts;

8. *Appeals* to all Governments to strengthen national and subnational professional institutions in their countries and to foster greater collaboration among all literacy partners with a view to developing greater capacity to design and deliver high-quality literacy programmes for youth and adults;

9. *Appeals* to all Governments and to economic and financial organizations and institutions, both national and international, to lend greater financial and material support to the efforts to increase literacy and achieve the goals of Education for All and those of the Decade;

10. *Takes note* of the three priority areas for the remaining years of the Decade identified through the mid-Decade review, namely, mobilizing stronger commitment to literacy, reinforcing more effective literacy programme delivery and harnessing new resources for literacy;

11. *Requests* the United Nations Educational, Scientific and Cultural Organization to reinforce its coordinating and catalysing role in the fight against illiteracy and to develop, in cooperation with other international partners, in particular the specialized agencies and organizations of the United Nations system, a strategic framework for renewed cooperation and action, on the basis of the mid-Decade review and the outcomes of the Regional Conferences in Support of Global Literacy, including the above-mentioned three priorities;

12. *Invites* Member States, the specialized agencies and other organizations of the United Nations system, as well as relevant intergovernmental and non-governmental organizations, to support the implementation of the above priorities within the framework of the internationally agreed development goals, including those contained in the United Nations Millennium Declaration;

13. *Calls upon* Member States, in the implementation of the International Plan of Action in the second half of the Decade, to give adequate attention to the cultural diversity of minorities and indigenous peoples;

14. *Requests* all relevant entities of the United Nations system, in particular the United Nations Educational, Scientific and Cultural Organization, in cooperation with national Governments, to take immediate, concrete steps to address the needs of countries with high illiteracy rates and/or with large populations of illiterate adults, with particular regard to women, including through programmes that promote low-cost and effective literacy provisions;

15. *Requests* the Secretary-General, in cooperation with the Director-General of the United Nations Educational, Scientific and Cultural Organization, to seek the views of Member States on the progress achieved in implementing their national programmes and plans of action for the Decade and to submit the next progress report on the implementation of the International Plan of Action to the General Assembly in 2010;

16. *Decides* to include in the provisional agenda of its sixty-fifth session, under the item entitled "Social development", the sub-item entitled "United Nations Literacy Decade: education for all".

International years

International Year of Chemistry (2011)

On 17 April, in follow-up to General Assembly resolution 61/185 [YUN 2006, p. 1608] on the proclamation of international years, and a 2007 resolution of the International Union of Pure and Applied Chemistry, the UNESCO Executive Board endorsed the proposal for proclamation by the United Nations of 2011 as the International Year of Chemistry.

GENERAL ASSEMBLY ACTION

On 19 December [meeting 72], the General Assembly, on the recommendation of the Second Committee [A/63/414 & Corr.1], adopted **resolution 63/209** without vote [agenda item 49].

International Year of Chemistry

The General Assembly,

Recalling its resolution 61/185 of 20 December 2006 on the proclamation of international years,

Recognizing that humankind's understanding of the material nature of our world is grounded, in particular, in our knowledge of chemistry,

Stressing that education in and about chemistry is critical in addressing challenges such as global climate change, in providing sustainable sources of clean water, food and energy and in maintaining a wholesome environment for the well-being of all people,

Considering that the science of chemistry and its applications produce medicines, fuels, metals and virtually all other manufactured products,

Being aware that the year 2011 provides the opportunity to celebrate the contributions of women to science on the one-hundredth anniversary of the awarding of the Nobel Prize in Chemistry to Maria Sklodowska-Curie,

Being aware also that the year 2011 provides the opportunity to highlight the need for international scientific collaboration on the one-hundredth anniversary of the founding of the International Association of Chemical Societies,

Noting the adoption by the Executive Board of the United Nations Educational, Scientific and Cultural Organization at its one hundred and seventy-ninth session of a proposal for the proclamation by the United Nations of 2011 as the International Year of Chemistry, and noting also the unanimous resolution of the International Union of Pure and Applied Chemistry, at its 2007 Council meeting, to have 2011 proclaimed the International Year of Chemistry,

Recognizing the leading role of the International Union of Pure and Applied Chemistry in coordinating and promoting chemistry activities at the national and regional levels around the world,

1. *Decides* to proclaim 2011 the International Year of Chemistry;

2. *Designates* the United Nations Educational, Scientific and Cultural Organization as the lead agency and focal point for the Year and invites it to organize activities to be realized during the Year, in collaboration with other relevant entities of the United Nations system, the International Union of Pure and Applied Chemistry and its associated organizations and federations across the world, and, in this regard, notes that the activities of the Year will be funded from voluntary contributions, including from the private sector;

3. *Encourages* all Member States, the United Nations system and all other actors to take advantage of the Year to promote actions at all levels aimed at increasing awareness among the public of the importance of chemistry and promoting widespread access to new knowledge and to chemistry activities.

International Year of Languages

In response to General Assembly resolution 61/266 [YUN 2007, p. 1515], the Secretary-General transmitted, in September, the interim report [A/63/349] by the UNESCO Director-General on the impact of activities carried out by UNESCO during the International Year of Languages, which was launched on 21 February. The report stated that the International Year had raised awareness of and contributed to a shift in practices and policies towards languages and multilingualism. Languages should be considered as an interdisciplinary domain and a factor for analysis and action in different policy areas. Many multilateral projects in international cooperation, peace and development could be better planned, implemented and achieved if linguistic factors were taken into account and if such projects were delivered in the languages of their beneficiaries. To overcome the difficulties encountered in the field for the effective development of multilingual society, UNESCO called upon Member States, the UN Secretariat and UN specialized agencies to develop common initiatives. A further report would be transmitted following the conclusion of the Year on 21 February 2009.

Chapter X

Women

In 2008, United Nations efforts to advance the status of women worldwide continued to be directed by the principles and guidelines of the Beijing Declaration and Platform for Action, adopted at the Fourth (1995) World Conference on Women, and the outcome of the General Assembly's twenty-third (2000) special session (Beijing+5), which reviewed progress in their implementation.

The Commission on the Status of Women, at its fifty-second session in March, adopted conclusions on financing for gender equality and the empowerment of women, which the Economic and Social Council transmitted to the Assembly as input to the preparations for the follow-up international conference on financing for development. The Commission recommended to the Council for adoption a draft resolution on the situation of and assistance to Palestinian women, which the Council adopted in July. The Council also took action on mainstreaming a gender perspective into all UN system policies and programmes. The Commission adopted and brought to the attention of the Council resolutions on women and children taken hostage in armed conflict; women, the girl child and HIV/AIDS; ending female genital mutilation; and strengthening of the International Research and Training Institute for the Advancement of Women (INSTRAW).

The General Assembly adopted resolutions on eliminating violence against women; trafficking in women and girls; supporting efforts to end obstetric fistula; and the future operation of INSTRAW. The United Nations Development Fund for Women continued to focus on women's economic security and rights, ending violence against women, reducing the prevalence of HIV/AIDS, and advancing gender justice in democratic governance. The United Nations continued efforts to strengthen and revitalize INSTRAW. The Executive Board approved the Institute's strategic framework for 2008–2011.

Follow-up to the Fourth World Conference on Women and Beijing+5

During 2008, the Commission on the Status of Women, the Economic and Social Council and the General Assembly considered follow-up to the 1995 Fourth World Conference on Women, particularly the implementation of the Beijing Declaration and Platform for Action [YUN 1995, p. 1170] and the political declaration, and further actions and initiatives to implement both instruments, adopted at the twenty-third (2000) special session of the Assembly (Beijing+5) by resolution S/23-2 [YUN 2000, p. 1084]. The Declaration had reaffirmed the commitment of Governments to the goals and objectives of the Fourth World Conference and to the implementation of the 12 critical areas of concern outlined in the Platform for Action: women and poverty; education and training of women; women and health; violence against women; women and armed conflict; women and the economy; women in power and decision-making; institutional mechanisms for the advancement of women; human rights of women; women and the media; women and the environment; and the girl child. The issue of mainstreaming a gender perspective into UN policies and programmes continued to be addressed.

Report of Secretary-General. In response to General Assembly resolution 62/137 [YUN 2007, p. 1153], the Secretary-General, in an August report [A/63/217], provided information on the follow-up to the Fourth World Conference on Women, which examined the extent to which intergovernmental bodies had paid attention to gender perspectives in their work, focusing on the advances made during the sixty-second (2007) session of the Assembly; the 2007 substantive session of the Economic and Social Council; and the work of its functional commissions, including the fifty-first (2007) session of the Commission on the Status of Women. It also assessed, pursuant to Economic and Social Council resolution 2006/9 [YUN 2006, p. 1356], the impact of the Commission's input in deliberations within the UN system.

The Secretary-General concluded that while the Assembly had advanced global policy on gender equality in a number of areas, attention to gender perspectives was not systematically included in all outcomes of the Assembly or documentation before it. However, the Assembly paid some attention to gender perspectives in the preparation of and follow-up to major international conferences and summits, and high-level dialogues and events. A noticeable gap in the area of climate change was identified. Overall, more than a quarter of the resolutions analysed in preparation for the report (as at 25 May 2008) included gender equality issues. As in previous years, resolutions submitted by the Second (Economic and Social) and Third (Social, Humanitarian and Cultural) Committees, as well as those adopted without reference to a Main Committee, paid greater attention to gender perspectives than other Assembly Committees. The Economic and Social Council paid explicit attention to gender equality in some of its segments and during high-level meetings. Gender perspectives were also reflected in some of the Secretary-General's reports before the Council and in Council outcomes, including the Ministerial Declaration of the Council's high-level segment, "Strengthening efforts to eradicate poverty and hunger, including through the global partnership for development" [YUN 2007, p. 833], which reaffirmed that gender equality and promotion and protection of human rights for all were essential to eradicate poverty and hunger. Most of the functional commissions took gender perspectives into account, to some extent, in their deliberations. However, apart from the Commission on the Status of Women, only three functional commissions of the Council paid attention to gender perspectives in their outcomes across a range of policy areas, including population ageing, crime prevention, social development and population.

The Secretary-General recommended to the Assembly that efforts to mainstream gender perspectives in preparation for and follow-up to major UN conferences and summits should be strengthened, including, for example, the incorporation of gender perspectives in documentation, interactive activities and outcomes of the Follow-up International Conference on Financing for Development to Review Implementation of Monterrey Consensus in 2008 (see p. 1076) and the Durban Review Conference in 2009, as well as in other high-level dialogue events of the Assembly. He said that greater efforts were needed to facilitate more systematic attention to gender perspectives in the work of all the Council's functional commissions, including through increased consultation with the Commission on the Status of Women. In order to enhance the Commission's role in promoting and monitoring the implementation of the gender mainstreaming strategy, its outcomes should be systematically transmitted through the Council to the Assembly, the functional commissions of the Council and other relevant intergovernmental bodies. The outcomes should also be disseminated to UN entities to ensure effective support to States. In addition, regular reporting on intergovernmental outcomes on gender equality and their impact on the work of intergovernmental bodies and UN entities could help advance the global policy agenda on gender equality and women's empowerment and ensure follow-up and implementation at the national level.

GENERAL ASSEMBLY ACTION

On 18 December [meeting 70], the General Assembly, on the recommendation of the Third Committee [A/63/425], adopted **resolution 63/159** without vote [agenda item 56].

Follow-up to the Fourth World Conference on Women and full implementation of the Beijing Declaration and Platform for Action and the outcome of the twenty-third special session of the General Assembly

The General Assembly,

Recalling its previous resolutions on the question, including resolution 62/137 of 18 December 2007,

Deeply convinced that the Beijing Declaration and Platform for Action and the outcome of the twenty-third special session of the General Assembly entitled "Women 2000: gender equality, development and peace for the twenty-first century" are important contributions to the achievement of gender equality and the empowerment of women, and must be translated into effective action by all States, the United Nations system and other organizations concerned,

Reaffirming the commitments to gender equality and the advancement of women made at the Millennium Summit, the 2005 World Summit and other major United Nations summits, conferences and special sessions, and reaffirming also that their full, effective and accelerated implementation are integral to achieving the internationally agreed development goals, including the Millennium Development Goals,

Welcoming progress made towards achieving gender equality, but stressing that challenges and obstacles remain in the implementation of the Beijing Declaration and Platform for Action and the outcome of the twenty-third special session,

Recognizing that the responsibility for the implementation of the Beijing Declaration and Platform for Action and the outcome of the twenty-third special session rests primarily at the national level and that strengthened efforts are necessary in this respect, and reiterating that enhanced international cooperation is essential for full, effective and accelerated implementation,

Welcoming the work of the Commission on the Status of Women in reviewing the implementation of the Beijing Declaration and Platform for Action, and noting with appreciation the agreed conclusions on financing for gender equality and the empowerment of women, adopted by the Commission at its fifty-second session,

Reaffirming that gender mainstreaming is a globally accepted strategy for promoting the empowerment of women and achieving gender equality by transforming structures of inequality, and reaffirming also the commitment to actively promote the mainstreaming of a gender perspective in the design, implementation, monitoring and evaluation of policies and programmes in all political, economic and social spheres, as well as the commitment to strengthen the capabilities of the United Nations system in the area of gender equality,

Bearing in mind the challenges and obstacles to changing discriminatory attitudes and gender stereotypes, and stressing that challenges and obstacles remain in the implementation of international standards and norms to address the inequality between men and women,

Expressing serious concern that the urgent goal of 50/50 gender balance in the United Nations system, especially at senior and policymaking levels, with full respect for the principle of equitable geographical distribution, in conformity with Article 101, paragraph 3, of the Charter of the United Nations, remains unmet, and that the representation of women in the United Nations system has remained almost static, with negligible improvement in some parts of the system, and in some cases has even decreased, as reflected in the report of the Secretary-General on the improvement of the status of women in the United Nations system,

Acknowledging its resolution 62/277 of 15 September 2008, in particular its gender-specific provisions, and in this context encouraging the ongoing work on gender equality and the empowerment of women,

Reaffirming the important role of women in the prevention and resolution of conflicts and in peacebuilding,

Reaffirming also the Declaration of Commitment on HIV/AIDS and the Political Declaration on HIV/AIDS adopted at the High-level Meeting on HIV/AIDS, held from 31 May to 2 June 2006, which, inter alia, acknowledged the feminization of the pandemic,

Noting with appreciation the report of the Secretary-General on mainstreaming a gender perspective into all policies and programmes of the United Nations system,

1. *Takes note with appreciation* of the report of the Secretary-General on the measures taken and progress achieved in follow-up to the implementation of the Beijing Declaration and Platform for Action and the outcome of the twenty-third special session of the General Assembly;

2. *Reaffirms* the Beijing Declaration and Platform for Action adopted at the Fourth World Conference on Women, the outcome of the twenty-third special session of the General Assembly, and the declaration adopted on the occasion of the ten-year review and appraisal of the implementation of the Beijing Declaration and Platform for Action at the forty-ninth session of the Commission on the Status of Women, and also reaffirms its commitment to their full, effective and accelerated implementation;

3. *Recognizes* that the implementation of the Beijing Declaration and Platform for Action and the fulfilment of the obligations of States parties under the Convention on the Elimination of All Forms of Discrimination against Women are mutually reinforcing in achieving gender equality and the empowerment of women, and in this regard welcomes the contributions of the Committee on the Elimination of Discrimination against Women to promoting the implementation of the Platform for Action and the outcome of the twenty-third special session, and invites States parties to the Convention to include information on measures taken to enhance implementation at the national level in their reports to the Committee under article 18 of the Convention;

4. *Calls upon* Governments, the United Nations system and other international and regional organizations, and all sectors of civil society, including non-governmental organizations, as well as all women and men, to fully commit themselves and to intensify their contributions to the implementation of the Beijing Declaration and Platform for Action and the outcome of the twenty-third special session;

5. *Calls upon* States parties to comply fully with their obligations under the Convention on the Elimination of All Forms of Discrimination against Women and the Optional Protocol thereto and to take into consideration the concluding comments as well as the general recommendations of the Committee, urges States parties to consider limiting the extent of any reservations that they lodge to the Convention, to formulate any reservations as precisely and narrowly as possible, and to regularly review such reservations with a view to withdrawing them so as to ensure that no reservation is incompatible with the object and purpose of the Convention, also urges all Member States that have not yet ratified or acceded to the Convention to consider doing so, and calls upon those Member States that have not yet done so to consider signing, ratifying or acceding to the Optional Protocol;

6. *Encourages* all actors, inter alia, Governments, the United Nations system, other international organizations and civil society, to continue to support the work of the Commission on the Status of Women in fulfilling its central role in the follow-up to and review of the implementation of the Beijing Declaration and Platform for Action and the outcome of the twenty-third special session, and, as applicable, to carry out its recommendations, and welcomes in this regard the revised programme and methods of work of the Commission adopted at its fiftieth session, which give particular attention to the sharing of experiences, lessons learned and good practices in overcoming challenges to full implementation at the national and international levels as well as to the evaluation of progress in the implementation of priority themes;

7. *Calls upon* Governments, and the relevant funds and programmes, organs and specialized agencies of the United Nations system, within their respective mandates, and invites the international financial institutions and all relevant actors of civil society, including non-governmental organizations, to intensify action to achieve the full and effective implementation of the Beijing Declaration and Platform for Action and the outcome of the twenty-third special session, through, inter alia:

(a) Sustained political will and commitment at the national, regional and international levels to take further action, inter alia, through the mainstreaming of gender perspectives, including through the development and use of gender equality indicators, as applicable, in all policies and programmes and the promotion of full and equal participation and empowerment of women, and enhanced international cooperation;

(b) Promotion and protection of, and respect for, the full enjoyment of human rights and fundamental freedoms by women and girls, including through the full implementation by States of their obligations under all human rights instruments, especially the Convention on the Elimination of All Forms of Discrimination against Women;

(c) Ensuring full representation and full and equal participation of women in political, social and economic decision-making as an essential condition for gender equal-

ity, and the empowerment of women and girls as a critical factor in the eradication of poverty;

(d) Involving women actively in environmental decision-making at all levels, integrating gender concerns and perspectives in policies and programmes for sustainable development, and strengthening or establishing mechanisms at the national, regional and international levels to assess the impact on women of development and environmental policies and strategies, including those related to climate change, deforestation and desertification;

(e) Integrating a gender perspective into the design, implementation, monitoring, evaluation and reporting of national environmental policies, strengthening mechanisms and providing adequate resources to ensure full and equal participation of women in decision-making at all levels on environmental issues, in particular on strategies related to the impact of climate change on the lives of women and girls;

(f) Enhancing the role of women at all levels and in all aspects of rural development, agriculture, nutrition and food security, including by ensuring legislation and administrative reforms, including access to ownership and control over land and other forms of property, credit, inheritance, natural resources and new technology;

(g) Providing technical assistance to women, particularly in developing countries, to ensure the continuing promotion of human resources development and the development of environmentally sound technologies and of women's entrepreneurship;

(h) Respect for the rule of law, including legislation, and continued efforts to repeal laws and eradicate policies and practices that discriminate against women and girls, and to adopt laws and promote practices that protect their rights;

(i) Strengthening the role of national institutional mechanisms for gender equality and the advancement of women, including through financial and other appropriate assistance, to increase their direct impact on women;

(j) Undertaking socio-economic policies that promote sustainable development and ensure poverty eradication programmes, especially for women and girls, and strengthening the provision of and ensuring equal access to adequate, affordable and accessible public and social services, including education and training at all levels, as well as to all types of permanent and sustainable social protection/social security systems for women throughout their life cycle, and supporting national efforts in this regard;

(k) Promoting and supporting increased access for all women and girls to information and communication technology, particularly women and girls living in poverty, and women and girls living in rural and remote areas and in disadvantaged situations, and enhancing international support to overcome the digital divide among countries and regions, and between women and men and girls and boys;

(l) Taking further steps to ensure that the education system and the media, to the extent consistent with freedom of expression, support the use of non-stereotypic, balanced and diverse images of women presenting them as key actors of the process of development as well as promoting non-discriminatory roles of women and men in their private and public life;

(m) Ensuring women's and girls' full and equal access to all levels of quality education and training, while ensuring progressively and on the basis of equal opportunities that primary education is compulsory, accessible and available free to all;

(n) Incorporating gender perspectives and human rights in health-sector policies, programmes and research activities, paying attention to women's and girls' specific needs and priorities, ensuring women's right to the highest attainable standards of health and their access to affordable and adequate health-care services, including sexual, reproductive and maternal health care and lifesaving obstetric care, in accordance with the Programme of Action of the International Conference on Population and Development, and recognizing that the lack of economic empowerment and independence has increased women's vulnerability to a range of negative consequences, involving the risk of contracting HIV/AIDS, malaria, tuberculosis and other poverty-related diseases;

(o) Eliminating gender inequalities, gender-based abuse and violence; increasing the capacity of women and adolescent girls to protect themselves from the risk of HIV infection, principally through the provision of health care and services, including sexual and reproductive health, and the provision of full access to comprehensive information and education; ensuring that women can exercise their right to have control over, and decide freely and responsibly on, matters related to their sexuality in order to increase their ability to protect themselves from HIV/AIDS infection, including their sexual and reproductive health, free of coercion, discrimination and violence; and taking all necessary measures to create an enabling environment for the empowerment of women and to strengthen their economic independence, while, in this context, reiterating the importance of the role of men and boys in achieving gender equality;

(p) Strengthening national health and social infrastructures to reinforce measures to promote women's access to public health and taking action at the national level to address shortages of human resources for health by, inter alia, developing, financing and implementing policies, within national development strategies, to improve training and management and effectively govern the recruitment, retention and deployment of health workers, including through international cooperation in this area;

(q) Adequate mobilization of resources at the national and international levels, as well as new and additional resources for the developing countries, including the least developed countries and countries with economies in transition, from all available funding mechanisms, including multilateral, bilateral and private sources;

(r) Increased partnerships among Governments, civil society and the private sector;

(s) Encouraging joint responsibility of men and boys with women and girls in the promotion of gender equality and the empowerment of women, based on the conviction that this is essential to the achievement of the goals of gender equality and the empowerment of women, development and peace;

(t) Removing structural and legal barriers, as well as eliminating stereotypic attitudes, to gender equality at work, promoting equal pay for equal work or work of

equal value and promoting the recognition of the value of women's unremunerated work, as well as developing and promoting policies that facilitate the reconciliation of employment and family responsibilities;

8. *Reaffirms* that States have an obligation to exercise due diligence to prevent violence against women and girls, provide protection to the victims and investigate, prosecute and punish the perpetrators of violence against women and girls, and that failure to do so violates and impairs or nullifies the enjoyment of their human rights and fundamental freedoms, and calls upon Governments to elaborate and implement laws and strategies to eliminate violence against women and girls;

9. *Welcomes* the adoption of Security Council resolution 1820(2008) on 19 June 2008;

10. *Calls upon* Governments, in this regard, to promote awareness and information campaigns on women's rights and the responsibility to respect them, including in rural areas, and to encourage men and boys to speak out strongly against violence against women;

11. *Strongly encourages* Governments to continue to support the role and contribution of civil society, in particular non-governmental organizations and women's organizations, in the implementation of the Beijing Declaration and Platform for Action and the outcome of the twenty-third special session;

12. *Resolves* to intensify the efforts of its Main Committees and subsidiary bodies to fully mainstream a gender perspective in their work, including by paying more attention to issues related to the status of women under their consideration and within their mandates, as well as in all United Nations summits, conferences and special sessions and in their follow-up processes;

13. *Requests* that reports of the Secretary-General submitted to the General Assembly and its subsidiary bodies systematically address gender perspectives through qualitative gender analysis and, where available, quantitative data, in particular through concrete conclusions and recommendations for further action on gender equality and the advancement of women, in order to facilitate gender-sensitive policy development;

14. *Urges* Governments and all entities of the United Nations system, including United Nations agencies, funds and programmes, and all relevant actors of civil society, to ensure the integration of gender perspectives in the implementation of and follow-up to all United Nations summits, conferences and special sessions and to give attention to gender perspectives in preparation for such events, including the Follow-up International Conference on Financing for Development to Review the Implementation of the Monterrey Consensus in Doha in 2008;

15. *Reaffirms its call* to include a gender perspective in the consideration of all issues in the agenda and activities of the Peacebuilding Commission and the Human Rights Council;

16. *Encourages* the Economic and Social Council to continue its efforts to ensure that gender mainstreaming is an integral part of its work and that of its subsidiary bodies, through, inter alia, implementation of its agreed conclusions 1997/2 of 18 July 1997 and its resolution 2004/4 of 7 July 2004;

17. *Welcomes* the ministerial declaration of the high-level segment of the substantive session of 2008 of the Economic and Social Council, which, inter alia, reaffirmed the commitment to promoting gender equality and the empowerment of women, recognizing that they are key actors in development, and to identifying and accelerating concrete actions towards that end;

18. *Requests* all bodies that deal with programme and budgetary matters, including the Committee for Programme and Coordination, to ensure that programmes, plans and budgets visibly mainstream gender perspectives;

19. *Reaffirms* the primary and essential role of the General Assembly and the Economic and Social Council, as well as the central role of the Commission on the Status of Women, in promoting the advancement of women and gender equality;

20. *Requests* the Economic and Social Council to continue to encourage its functional commissions to mainstream a gender perspective in their respective follow-up actions to major United Nations conferences and summits and to develop more effective means to ensure the implementation of outcomes on gender equality at the national level, including through increased consultation with the Commission on the Status of Women;

21. *Underlines* the catalytic role played by the Commission on the Status of Women, as well as the important role played by the Economic and Social Council and the General Assembly, in promoting and monitoring gender mainstreaming within the United Nations system;

22. *Requests* that the entities of the United Nations system systematically incorporate the outcomes of the Commission on the Status of Women into their work within their mandates, inter alia, to ensure effective support for the efforts of Member States towards the achievement of gender equality and the empowerment of women;

23. *Reaffirms* the commitment made at the 2005 World Summit to the full and effective implementation of Security Council resolution 1325(2000) of 31 October 2000, while noting the eighth anniversary of its adoption and the open debates in the Council on women and peace and security, and encourages Governments to ensure systematic attention to, recognition of and support for the role of women in the prevention and resolution of conflicts and in peacebuilding efforts;

24. *Urges* Governments and the United Nations system to take further steps to ensure the integration of a gender perspective and the full and equal participation of women in all efforts to promote peace and security, including in peace negotiations, peacekeeping, peacebuilding and post-conflict situations, as well as to increase their role in decision-making at all levels, including through the development of national action plans and strategies;

25. *Calls upon* all parts of the United Nations system to continue to play an active role in ensuring the full, effective and accelerated implementation of the Beijing Platform for Action and the outcome of the twenty-third special session, through, inter alia, the work of the Office of the Special Adviser on Gender Issues and Advancement of Women and the Division for the Advancement of Women and the maintenance of gender specialists in all entities of the United Nations system, as well as by ensuring that all personnel, especially in the field, receive training and ap-

propriate follow-up, including tools, guidance and support, for accelerated gender mainstreaming, and reaffirms the need to strengthen the capabilities of the United Nations system in the area of gender;

26. *Requests* the Secretary-General to review and redouble his efforts to make progress towards achieving the goal of 50/50 gender balance at all levels in the Secretariat and throughout the United Nations system, with full respect for the principle of equitable geographical distribution, in conformity with Article 101, paragraph 3, of the Charter of the United Nations, considering, in particular, women from developing and least developed countries, from countries with economies in transition and from unrepresented or largely underrepresented Member States, and to ensure managerial and departmental accountability with respect to gender balance targets, and strongly encourages Member States to identify and regularly submit more women candidates for appointment to positions in the United Nations system, especially at more senior and policymaking levels;

27. *Encourages* the subsidiary bodies of the General Assembly to incorporate gender-equality perspectives systematically in their discussions and outcomes, including through effective use of the analysis, data and recommendations contained in reports of the Secretary-General, and to follow up on the outcomes;

28. *Requests* that reports of the Secretary-General submitted to the General Assembly facilitate gender-sensitive policy development by more systematically including qualitative gender analysis, data and recommendations for further action;

29. *Calls upon* the United Nations system to continue its efforts towards achieving the goal of gender balance, including with the active support of gender focal points, and requests the Secretary-General to provide an oral report to the Commission on the Status of Women at its fifty-third and fifty-fourth sessions, to report to the General Assembly on a biennial basis, beginning at its sixty-fifth session, under the item entitled "Advancement of women", and to include in his report on human resources management information on the status of women in the United Nations system, including on progress made and obstacles encountered in achieving gender balance, recommendations for accelerating progress, and up-to-date statistics, including the number and percentage of women and their functions and nationalities throughout the United Nations system, and information on the responsibility and accountability of the Office of Human Resources Management of the Secretariat and the secretariat of the United Nations System Chief Executives Board for Coordination for promoting gender balance;

30. *Requests* the Secretary-General to continue to report annually to the General Assembly under the item entitled "Advancement of women", as well as to the Commission on the Status of Women and the Economic and Social Council, on the follow-up to and progress made in the implementation of the Beijing Declaration and Platform for Action and the outcome of the twenty-third special session, with an assessment of progress in gender mainstreaming, including information on key achievements, lessons learned and good practices, and recommendations on further measures to enhance implementation.

Critical areas of concern

Women and health

Women, the girl child and HIV/AIDS

In a March resolution on women, the girl child and HIV/AIDS [E/2008/27 (res.52/4)], the Commission on the Status of Women, expressing concern that the HIV/AIDS pandemic reinforced gender inequalities and disproportionately affected women and girls as they bore the burden to support and care for those affected by the disease, stressed that the crisis required urgent action in all fields and at all levels. It called on Governments and the international donor community to integrate a gender perspective in all international assistance matters and ensure that resources concomitant with the effect of HIV/AIDS on women and girls were made available, especially funding for national HIV/AIDS programmes to promote and protect the human rights of women and girls in the context of the epidemic. The Commission requested the Secretariat, the Joint United Nations Programme on HIV/AIDS (UNAIDS), and other UN entities responding to the pandemic, including the Global Fund to Fight AIDS, Tuberculosis and Malaria [YUN 2002, p. 1217], to mainstream a gender and human rights perspective throughout their HIV/AIDS-related operations. It requested the Secretary-General to invite States to work with the Global Coalition on Women and HIV/AIDS [YUN 2004, p. 1219] to mobilize and support a wide range of national actors, including women's groups and networks of women living with HIV/AIDS, in order to ensure that national HIV/AIDS programmes were better able to respond to the specific needs of women, girls and adolescents. The Commission also requested the Secretary-General to consider the gender dimensions of the HIV/AIDS epidemic when preparing the report requested in General Assembly resolution 62/178 [YUN 2007, p. 1262] and in the preparations for the 2008 High-level meeting on HIV/AIDS (see p. 1329).

Elimination of obstetric fistula

In response to General Assembly resolution 62/138 [YUN 2007, p. 1169], the Secretary-General in August submitted a report [A/63/222] on supporting efforts to end obstetric fistula, a devastating childbirth injury that made women incontinent and often isolated from their communities, and one that could also result in maternal death. The condition was an example of poor maternal and reproductive health and an indication of unacceptably high levels of maternal death and disability. Obstetric fistula disproportionately affected impoverished women and girls living in rural communities in developing countries and was almost entirely preventable through access to quality maternal health care. The report outlined efforts to end obstetric fistula at international, regional and national levels, including by the UN system.

The Secretary-General observed that significant progress had been achieved over the last two decades in focusing attention on maternal death and disability, and more recently on obstetric fistula in particular, due to increased evidence on effective interventions, enhanced data collection and analysis, advocacy programmes, partnerships, and stronger political and financial commitments. Awareness of the problem had grown exponentially and countries were increasingly investing in and promoting the prevention, treatment and reintegration of affected women as part of efforts to advance maternal health. Despite those positive developments, serious challenges remained. There was a need to intensify interventions to prevent the more than 500,000 deaths and 9 million morbidities that occurred annually due to the complications of pregnancy and childbirth. Recommendations for action included: greater investment in health systems; focused attention on areas with the highest maternal mortality and morbidity, particularly sub-Saharan Africa and South Asia; investments supporting national health plans and addressing health-care coverage inequities among socio-economic and age groups; mobilization and empowerment of communities to facilitate their involvement in supporting women and addressing maternal health needs; strengthened interventions to keep adolescent girls in school, stop child marriages and promote positive health-seeking behaviours; strengthened research, monitoring and evaluation to guide implementation of maternal health programmes; and the maintenance of partnerships and coordination among various stakeholders at local, national, regional and global levels to address the multifaceted determinants of maternal mortality and morbidity. The Secretary-General, estimating that support for priority countries would require $1.2 billion for family planning and $6 billion for maternal health care annually, recommended that continued support be provided to countries' national plans, UN entities—including the global Campaign to End Fistula [YUN 2002, p. 1078] and the Thematic Fund for Maternal Health [YUN 2007, p. 1169]—and other global initiatives.

GENERAL ASSEMBLY ACTION

On 18 December [meeting 70], the General Assembly, on the recommendation of the Third Committee [A/63/425], adopted **resolution 63/158** without vote [agenda item 56 *(a)*].

Supporting efforts to end obstetric fistula

The General Assembly,

Recalling its resolution 62/138 of 18 December 2007 on supporting efforts to end obstetric fistula,

Reaffirming the Beijing Declaration and Platform for Action, the outcome of the twenty-third special session of the General Assembly entitled "Women 2000: gender equality, development and peace for the twenty-first century", and the declaration adopted at the forty-ninth session of the Commission on the Status of Women,

Reaffirming also the international commitments in the field of social development and to gender equality and the advancement of women made at the World Conference on Human Rights, the International Conference on Population and Development, the World Summit for Social Development and the World Conference against Racism, Racial Discrimination, Xenophobia and Related Intolerance, as well as those made in the United Nations Millennium Declaration and at the 2005 World Summit,

Reaffirming further the Convention on the Elimination of All Forms of Discrimination against Women and the Convention on the Rights of the Child, and urging States that have not done so to consider, as a matter of priority, signing, ratifying or acceding to those Conventions and the Optional Protocols thereto,

Taking note with appreciation of the report of the Secretary-General on supporting efforts to end obstetric fistula, and welcoming the conclusions and recommendations contained therein,

Stressing the interlinkages between poverty, malnutrition, lack of or inadequate or inaccessible health services, early childbearing, early marriage of the girl child, violence against young women and girls and gender discrimination as root causes of obstetric fistula, and that poverty remains the main social risk factor,

Recognizing that the difficult socio-economic conditions that exist in many developing countries, in particular the least developed countries, have resulted in the acceleration of the feminization of poverty,

Recognizing also that early pregnancy and early childbearing entail complications during pregnancy and delivery and a much higher risk of maternal mortality and morbidity, and deeply concerned that early childbearing and limited access to the highest attainable standard of health, including sexual and reproductive health, including in the area of emergency obstetric care, cause high levels of obstetric fistula and other maternal morbidities as well as maternal mortality,

Recognizing further the serious immediate and long-term implications for health, including sexual and reproductive health, as well as increased vulnerability to HIV/AIDS, and the negative impact on psychological, social and economic development, that violence against the girl child and adolescent girls represents for individuals, families, communities and States,

Deeply concerned about discrimination against the girl child and the violation of the rights of the girl child, which often result in less access by girls to education, nutrition and physical and mental health and in enjoyment by girls of fewer of the rights, opportunities and benefits of childhood and adolescence compared with boys and their often being subjected to various forms of cultural, social, sexual and economic exploitation and to violence and harmful practices,

Welcoming the contribution by Member States, the international community and civil society to the global

Campaign to End Fistula, bearing in mind that a people-centred approach to social and economic development is fundamental for protecting and empowering individuals and communities,

Welcoming also ongoing partnerships between stakeholders at all levels to address the multifaceted determinants of maternal mortality and the commitments announced at the 2008 high-level event on the Millennium Development Goals to accelerate progress on millennium development goal 5,

1. *Recognizes* the interlinkages between poverty, malnutrition, lack of or inadequate or inaccessible health services, early childbearing, early marriage of the girl child and gender discrimination as root causes of obstetric fistula, that poverty remains the main social risk factor, that the eradication of poverty is critical to meeting the needs and protecting and promoting the rights of women and girls and that continued urgent national and international action is required to eliminate it;

2. *Stresses* the need to address the social issues that contribute to the problem of obstetric fistula, such as early marriage of the girl child, early pregnancy, lack of access to sexual and reproductive health, lack of or inadequate education of women and girls, poverty and low status of women and girls;

3. *Also stresses* that States have the obligation to promote and protect all human rights and fundamental freedoms of women and girls, that they must exercise due diligence in order to prevent, investigate and punish the perpetrators of violence against women and girls and to provide protection to the victims, and that failure to do so violates and impairs or nullifies the enjoyment of their human rights and fundamental freedoms;

4. *Calls upon* States to take all necessary measures to ensure the right of women and girls to the enjoyment of the highest attainable standard of health, including sexual and reproductive health, and develop sustainable health systems and social services, with a view to ensuring access to such systems and services without discrimination, while paying special attention to adequate food and nutrition, water and sanitation, family planning information, increasing knowledge and awareness and securing appropriate prenatal and post-natal care for the prevention of obstetric fistula;

5. *Also calls upon* States to ensure that women and girls have equal access to free and compulsory primary education of good quality and that they complete their education at that level, and to renew their efforts to improve and expand girls' and women's education at all levels, including at the secondary and higher levels, as well as vocational education and technical training, in order to, inter alia, achieve gender equality, the empowerment of women and poverty eradication;

6. *Urges* States to enact and strictly enforce laws to ensure that marriage is entered into only with the free and full consent of the intending spouses and, in addition, to enact and strictly enforce laws concerning the minimum legal age of consent and the minimum age for marriage, and to raise the minimum age for marriage where necessary;

7. *Calls upon* the international community to support the activities of the United Nations Population Fund and other partners in the global Campaign to End Fistula, including the World Health Organization, in establishing and financing regional fistula treatment and training centres by identifying and supporting health facilities that have the potential to serve as centres for treatment, training and convalescent care;

8. *Calls upon* States and/or the relevant funds and programmes, organs and specialized agencies of the United Nations system, within their respective mandates, and invites the international financial institutions and all relevant actors of civil society, including non-governmental organizations, and the private sector:

(*a*) To redouble their efforts to meet the internationally agreed goal of improving maternal health by making maternal health services and obstetric fistula treatment geographically and financially accessible, including by increasing access to skilled attendance at birth and emergency obstetric care, and appropriate prenatal and post-natal care;

(*b*) To develop, implement and support national and international prevention, care and treatment and reintegration and support strategies, as appropriate, to address effectively the condition of obstetric fistula and to develop further a multisectoral, multidisciplinary, comprehensive and integrated approach in order to bring about lasting solutions and put an end to obstetric fistula, maternal mortality and related morbidities, including through ensuring access to affordable, comprehensive, quality maternal health-care services, including skilled birth attendance and emergency obstetric care;

(*c*) To strengthen the capacity of health systems, in particular public health systems, to provide the essential services needed to prevent obstetric fistula and to treat those cases that do occur by providing the continuum of services, including family planning, prenatal care, skilled birth attendance, emergency obstetric care and post-partum care, to young women and girls, including those living in poverty and in underserved rural areas where obstetric fistula is most common;

(*d*) To strengthen research, monitoring and evaluation systems, including community-based notification of obstetric fistula cases and maternal and newborn deaths, to guide the implementation of maternal health programmes;

(*e*) To provide essential health services, equipment and supplies and skills training and income-generating projects to women and girls so that they can break out of a cycle of poverty;

(*f*) To mobilize funding to provide free or subsidized fistula repairs, including through encouraging more networking among providers and the sharing of new treatment techniques and protocols;

(*g*) To provide health education, rehabilitation and reintegration counselling, including medical counselling, as key components of post-operative care;

(*h*) To bring obstetric fistula to the attention of policymakers and communities, thereby reducing the stigma and discrimination associated with it and helping women and girls suffering from obstetric fistula so that they can overcome abandonment and social exclusion together with the psychosocial implications thereof, inter alia, through the support of social reintegration projects;

(*i*) To educate individual women and men, girls and boys, communities, policymakers and health professionals about how obstetric fistula can be prevented and treated and increase awareness of the needs of pregnant women and girls, including their right to the highest attainable standard of health, through working with community and religious leaders, traditional birth attendants, media, radio stations, influential public figures and policymakers, support the training of doctors, midwives, nurses and other health workers in lifesaving obstetric care, and include training on fistula repair, treatment and care as a standard element of health professionals' training curricula;

(j) To develop means of transportation and financing that enable women and girls to access obstetric care and treatment, and provide incentives and other means to secure the presence in rural areas of qualified health professionals who are able to perform interventions to prevent obstetric fistula;

9. *Encourages* communication and networking among existing fistula centres to facilitate training, research, advocacy and fund-raising and the development and application of relevant standards, including *Obstetric Fistula: Guiding Principles for Clinical Management and Programme Development*, published in 2006 by the World Health Organization, which provides background information along with principles for developing fistula prevention and treatment strategies and programmes;

10. *Urges* the international community to address the shortages of doctors, midwives, nurses and other health workers trained in lifesaving obstetric care, and of space and supplies, which limit the capacity of most of the fistula centres;

11. *Urges* multilateral donors, and invites international financial institutions, within their respective mandates, and regional development banks to review and implement policies to support national efforts to ensure that a higher proportion of resources reaches young women and girls, in particular in rural and remote areas;

12. *Invites* Member States to contribute to efforts to end obstetric fistula, including, in particular, the United Nations Population Fund global Campaign to End Fistula, with the goal of eliminating obstetric fistula by 2015, in line with the targets of the millennium development goal of improving maternal health;

13. *Requests* the Secretary-General to report to the General Assembly at its sixty-fifth session on the implementation of the present resolution under the item entitled "Advancement of women".

Traditional practices affecting the health of women and girls

Female genital mutilation

In response to Commission on the Status of Women resolution 51/2 [YUN 2007, p. 1171], the Secretary-General submitted a report [E/CN.6/2008/3] on ending female genital mutilation, a practice with harmful health consequences. Each year, approximately 3 million girls and women were subjected to female genital mutilation, and the World Health Organization (WHO) estimated that between 100 and 140 million girls and women had undergone some form of female genital mutilation in more than 28 countries in Africa and in some countries in Asia and the Middle East. Since the prevalence of female genital mutilation remained high after nearly three decades of efforts by countries to eradicate the practice, new approaches continued to be developed that were both culturally sensitive and addressed the practice as a human rights violation. The report outlined key issues on female genital mutilation addressed by intergovernmental and human rights treaty bodies, and activities undertaken by 27 States and 13 UN entities to end the practice. It indicated that partnerships between Governments, UN entities, civil society, and other stakeholders had enhanced awareness and strengthened efforts towards ending female genital mutilation. There was greater understanding of the practice as a violation of human rights and of its harmful consequences. Many actions had been taken to end female genital mutilation, including legal reforms; the development of policies, strategies and action plans; the training of health-care professionals, law enforcement agents, and other relevant professional groups; and advocacy and awareness-raising campaigns at the national and local levels. However, challenges were also identified, such as the lack of enforcement of policies and legislation; insufficient awareness and commitment; persistence of norms that encouraged continuation of the practice; lack of data to facilitate monitoring of progress; and limited resources for sustained programmes.

The Secretary-General made recommendations for, among others, policies and programmes to be guided by a human rights-based approach; the establishment and enforcement of laws to prohibit and criminalize female genital mutilation; the development of strategies to enhance awareness among communities, families and the general public on the human rights of girls; improved access for women and girls to education and health care; the establishment of safe houses to protect girls from the practice; the involvement of religious leaders and young people in awareness-raising campaigns; and action-oriented research on the socio-cultural dimensions of female genital mutilation, including why women as well as men continued to support the practice despite its harmful consequences.

Commission action. In a March resolution [E/2008/27 (res. 52/2)], the Commission called on States to develop and implement integrated strategies for the prevention of female genital mutilation; strengthen advocacy and awareness-raising programmes; mobilize girls and boys to take part in developing preventive and elimination programmes to address harmful traditional practices, especially female genital mutilation; engage communities and religious leaders, educational institutions, the media and families; and increase financial support to end those practices. It called on the international community, UN system entities and civil society to support innovative programmes and to disseminate best practices that addressed the needs and priorities of girls in vulnerable situations. In that connection, it welcomed the 27 February commitment of 10 UN agencies to continue working towards the elimination of female genital mutilation. The Commission also requested the Secretary-General to ensure that all relevant UN entities took into account the protection and promotion of the rights of girls against female genital mutilation in their country programmes.

Violence against women

In response to General Assembly resolution 61/143 [YUN 2006, p. 1334], the Secretary-General in August submitted a report [A/63/214 & Corr.1] on intensification of efforts to eliminate all forms of violence against women that reviewed measures taken by States, as well as intergovernmental bodies, to address violence against women. Based on the inputs of 44 States, the report summarized measures taken to strengthen gender equality frameworks; develop policy frameworks and provide resources to address violence against women; end impunity for perpetrators and protect women against violence; prevent violence against women; provide services and support for victims and survivors; build the capacity of stakeholders; and enhance data collection. It also provided information on measures taken by UN bodies to implement resolution 61/143, including setting priorities for future work programmes to address the issue, and efforts towards the development of indicators on violence against women. In that regard, the Commission on the Status of Women and the Statistical Commission convened a joint dialogue that discussed the proposal for a set of global indicators to measure the scope, prevalence and incidence of violence against women. The Statistical Commission subsequently approved the formation of a "friends of the chair" group to conduct an in-depth technical review of the proposed indicators.

The report concluded that States had taken measures to promote gender equality and the elimination of discrimination against women, including a growing number of States that had established new or strengthened legislation on violence against women. Other efforts by States included the establishment of national action plans on violence against women; the increased availability of integrated services—medical, psychological, social and legal—for victims and survivors of violence; and increased attention paid to the protection of women in situations of increased risk. However, data and information on all forms of violence against women, from different sources, remained inadequate, which constituted a challenge to effective prevention and response. The Secretary-General made recommendations for States to intensify efforts to evaluate and assess the impact of legislation, rules and procedures; ensure that national action plans incorporated measurable goals and timetables, as well monitoring measures; take concrete steps to strengthen women's awareness of their rights and legal remedies; provide leadership at the highest levels to enhance prevention of violence against women; intensify data-collection efforts and fully integrate data into national data-collection systems; and evaluate the impact of all initiatives on violence against women.

The Special Rapporteur on violence against women submitted the second thematic report on violence against women, its causes and consequences [A/HRC/7/6] to the Human Rights Council (see p. 846).

UNIFEM activities. In compliance with General Assembly resolution 50/166 [YUN 1995, p. 1188], the Secretary-General transmitted a report [A/HRC/10/43-E/CN.6/2009/10] of the United Nations Development Fund for Women (UNIFEM) on its 2008 activities to eliminate violence against women, including management of the UN Trust Fund in Support of Actions to Eliminate Violence against Women. Implementation of the 2005–2008 Trust Fund continued in accordance with its five pillars: enhancing impact, deepening involvement, ensuring efficiency, generating knowledge and developing capacities, and mobilizing resources. With the involvement of more than 20 UN entities, UNIFEM convened 16 inter-agency programme appraisal committees, at the regional level, on eliminating violence against women. Although the Trust Fund had $22 million to offer for grant-making during the year, annual contributions fell short of demand, with the Fund only meeting 4 per cent of the $525 million in requests that were received in 2008. Grant-making during the year focused on supporting the implementation of laws, policies and action plans on ending violence against women under two categories: "Meeting the implementation and upscaling challenge" and "Catalytic, innovative and learning initiatives". Under the thirteenth grant-making cycle, the Trust Fund provided $22 million to 28 initiatives in 38 countries and territories, which meant that since its inception in 1997 the Trust Fund had awarded more than $44 million in grants to 291 initiatives in 119 countries.

Moving forward, UNIFEM would continue efforts to bridge the implementation and accountability gap by supporting intensified country-level action through technical assistance; intensified capacity-development; broadened advocacy and awareness-raising endeavours; strengthened partnerships within and outside the UN system; intensified mobilization of resources; and provision of new and innovative learning and knowledge-sharing opportunities and products.

GENERAL ASSEMBLY ACTION

On 18 December [meeting 70], the General Assembly, on the recommendation of the Third Committee [A/63/425], adopted **resolution 63/155** without vote [agenda item 56 *(a)*].

Intensification of efforts to eliminate all forms of violence against women

The General Assembly,

Recalling its resolutions 61/143 of 19 December 2006 and 62/133 of 18 December 2007, and all its previous resolutions on the elimination of violence against women,

Reaffirming the obligation of all States to promote and protect all human rights and fundamental freedoms, and reaffirming also that discrimination on the basis of sex is contrary to the Charter of the United Nations, the Convention on the Elimination of All Forms of Discrimination against Women and other international human rights instruments, and that its elimination is an integral part of efforts towards the elimination of all forms of violence against women,

Reaffirming also the Declaration on the Elimination of Violence against Women, the Beijing Declaration and Platform for Action, the outcome of the twenty-third special session of the General Assembly entitled "Women 2000: gender equality, development and peace for the twenty-first century", and the declaration adopted at the forty-ninth session of the Commission on the Status of Women,

Reaffirming further the international commitments in the field of social development and to gender equality and the advancement of women made at the World Conference on Human Rights, the International Conference on Population and Development, the World Summit for Social Development and the World Conference against Racism, Racial Discrimination, Xenophobia and Related Intolerance, as well as those made in the United Nations Millennium Declaration and at the 2005 World Summit, and noting the attention paid to the elimination of all forms of violence against indigenous women in the United Nations Declaration on the Rights of Indigenous Peoples adopted by the General Assembly in its resolution 61/295 of 13 September 2007,

Recalling the inclusion of gender-related crimes and crimes of sexual violence in the Rome Statute of the International Criminal Court, as well as the recognition by the ad hoc international criminal tribunals that rape can constitute a war crime, a crime against humanity or a constitutive act with respect to genocide or torture,

Recalling also Security Council resolution 1325(2000) of 31 October 2000, and welcoming the adoption of Council resolution 1820(2008) of 19 June 2008 on women and peace and security,

Deeply concerned about the pervasiveness of violence against women and girls in all its different forms and manifestations worldwide, and reiterating the need to intensify efforts to prevent and eliminate all forms of violence against women and girls throughout the world,

Recognizing that violence against women is rooted in historically unequal power relations between men and women and that all forms of violence against women seriously violate and impair or nullify the enjoyment by women of all human rights and fundamental freedoms and constitute a major impediment to the ability of women to make use of their capabilities,

Recognizing also that women's poverty and lack of empowerment, as well as their marginalization resulting from their exclusion from social policies and from the benefits of sustainable development, can place them at increased risk of violence, and that violence against women impedes the social and economic development of communities and States, as well as the achievement of the internationally agreed development goals, including the Millennium Development Goals,

Recognizing further that the empowerment of women, by ensuring their full representation and full and equal participation at all levels of decision-making, is important in eliminating violence against women and girls,

Acknowledging the need to address violence against women holistically, including through the recognition of linkages between violence against women and other issues such as HIV/AIDS, poverty eradication, food security, peace and security, humanitarian assistance, health and crime prevention,

Expressing its appreciation for the high number of activities undertaken by States to eliminate all forms of violence against women, such as enacting or amending legislation relating to acts of violence against women and adopting comprehensive national action plans to combat such violence,

Recognizing the important role of civil society, in particular women's organizations, in the efforts to eliminate all forms of violence against women,

1. *Stresses* that "violence against women" means any act of gender-based violence that results in, or is likely to result in, physical, sexual or psychological harm or suffering to women, including threats of such acts, coercion or arbitrary deprivation of liberty, whether occurring in public or in private life;

2. *Recognizes* that violence against women and girls persists in every country in the world as a pervasive violation of the enjoyment of human rights and a major impediment to achieving gender equality, development, peace and the internationally agreed development goals, in particular the Millennium Development Goals;

3. *Expresses its concern* about the continuing level of impunity for acts of violence against women worldwide;

4. *Welcomes* the report of the Secretary-General on the intensification of efforts to eliminate all forms of violence against women, and takes note of the report of the Secretary-General on eliminating rape and other forms of sexual violence in all their manifestations, including in conflict and related situations;

5. *Welcomes also* the efforts and important contributions at the local, national, regional and international levels to eliminate all forms of violence against women, including by the Committee on the Elimination of Discrimination against Women and the Special Rapporteur on violence against women, its causes and consequences, in particular the second thematic report on violence against women, its causes and consequences submitted by the Special Rapporteur to the Human Rights Council in 2008;

6. *Recognizes* the important role of the family in preventing and combating violence against women and girls and the need to support its capacity to prevent and combat violence against women;

7. *Welcomes* the launch of the Secretary-General's campaign to end violence against women "UNiTE to End Violence against Women", supported, inter alia, by the United Nations Development Fund for Women advocacy campaign "Say NO to violence against women" and the United Nations inter-agency initiative "Stop Rape Now: United Nations Action against Sexual Violence in Conflict", stresses the need to ensure that concrete follow-up activities will be undertaken by the United Nations system to intensify action to end violence against women, in close consultation with existing system-wide activities on violence against women, and requests the Secretary-General to identify, announce and report on the basis of the expected results of his campaign;

8. *Strongly condemns* all acts of violence against women and girls, whether these acts are perpetrated by the State, by private persons or by non-State actors, and calls for the elimination of all forms of gender-based violence in the family, within the general community and where perpetrated or condoned by the State;

9. *Stresses* that it is important that States strongly condemn all forms of violence against women and refrain from invoking any custom, tradition or religious consideration to avoid their obligations with respect to its elimination as set out in the Declaration on the Elimination of Violence against Women;

10. *Stresses also* that States have the obligation to promote and protect all human rights and fundamental freedoms of women and girls and must exercise due diligence to prevent, investigate, prosecute and punish the perpetrators of violence against women and girls and to provide protection to the victims, and that failure to do so violates and impairs or nullifies the enjoyment of their human rights and fundamental freedoms;

11. *Urges* States to end impunity for violence against women by investigating, prosecuting with due process and punishing all perpetrators, by ensuring that women have equal protection of the law and equal access to justice and by holding up to public scrutiny and eliminating those attitudes that foster, justify or tolerate all forms of violence against women and girls;

12. *Reaffirms* that the persistence of armed conflicts in various parts of the world is a major impediment to the elimination of all forms of violence against women, and, bearing in mind that armed and other types of conflicts and terrorism and hostage-taking still persist in many parts of the world and that aggression, foreign occupation and ethnic and other types of conflicts are an ongoing reality affecting women and men in nearly every region, calls upon all States and the international community to place particular focus on and give priority attention and increased assistance to the plight and suffering of women and girls living in such situations and to ensure that, where violence is committed against them, all perpetrators of such violence are duly investigated and, as appropriate, prosecuted and punished in order to end impunity, while stressing the need to respect international humanitarian law and human rights law;

13. *Stresses* the need for the exclusion of the killing and maiming of women and girls, as prohibited under international law, and sexual violence crimes from amnesty provisions in the context of conflict resolution processes;

14. *Stresses also* that States should take measures to ensure that all officials responsible for implementing policies and programmes aimed at preventing violence against women, protecting and assisting the victims, and investigating and punishing violence against women, receive proper training to sensitize them to the different and specific needs of women, in particular women who have been subjected to violence, so that women are not revictimized when seeking justice and redress;

15. *Stresses further* that States should take all possible measures to empower women and inform them of their rights in seeking redress through mechanisms of justice, inform everyone of women's rights and of the existing penalties for violating those rights, and engage men and boys, as well as families, as agents of change in preventing and condemning violence against women;

16. *Urges* States to continue to develop their national strategy and a more systematic, comprehensive, multisectoral and sustained approach aimed at eliminating all forms of violence against women, including by achieving gender equality and the empowerment of women, and by using best practices to end impunity and a culture of tolerance towards violence against women, inter alia, in the fields of legislation, prevention, law enforcement, victim assistance and rehabilitation, such as:

(a) Establishing, in partnership with all relevant stakeholders, a comprehensive integrated national plan dedicated to combating violence against women in all its aspects, which includes data collection and analysis, prevention and protection measures, as well as national information campaigns using resources to eliminate in the media gender stereotypes that lead to violence against women and girls;

(b) Reviewing and, where appropriate, revising, amending or abolishing all laws, regulations, policies, practices and customs that discriminate against women or have a discriminatory impact on women, and ensuring that the provisions of multiple legal systems, where they exist, comply with international human rights obligations, commitments and principles, including the principle of non-discrimination;

(c) Evaluating and assessing the impact of current legislation, rules and procedures regarding violence against women, including the reasons for low reporting, and, where necessary, reinforcing criminal law and procedure relating to all forms of violence against women and, where necessary, incorporating into law measures aimed at preventing violence against women;

(d) Ensuring that there is sufficient knowledge, including expertise in effective legal approaches to eliminating violence against women, awareness and coordination in the legal system and, to that end, where appropriate, appointing a focal point in the legal system for cases of violence against women;

(e) Ensuring the systematic collection and analysis of data to monitor all forms of violence against women, while ensuring and maintaining the privacy and confidentiality of the victims, including with the involvement of national statistical offices and, where appropriate, in partnership with other actors;

(f) Establishing appropriate national mechanisms for monitoring and evaluating the implementation of national measures, including national action plans, taken to eliminate violence against women and girls, including through the use of national indicators;

(g) Providing adequate financial support for the implementation of national action plans to end violence against women and other relevant activities;

(h) Allocating adequate resources to promote the empowerment of women and gender equality and to prevent and redress all forms and manifestations of violence against women;

(i) Adopting all appropriate measures, especially in the field of education, to modify the social and cultural patterns of conduct of men and women and to eliminate prejudices, customary practices and all other practices based on the idea of the inferiority or superiority of either of the sexes and on stereotyped roles for men and women;

(j) Empowering women, in particular women living in poverty, through, inter alia, social and economic policies that guarantee them full and equal access to all levels of quality education and training and to affordable and adequate public and social services, as well as equal access to financial resources and full and equal rights to own land and other property, and taking further appropriate measures to address the increasing rate of homelessness or inadequate housing for women in order to reduce their vulnerability to violence;

(k) Treating all forms of violence against women and girls as a criminal offence, punishable by law, and ensuring penalties commensurate with the severity of the crimes and sanctions in domestic legislation to punish and redress, as appropriate, the wrongs caused to women who are subjected to violence;

(l) Taking effective measures to prevent the victim's consent from becoming an impediment to bringing perpetrators of violence against women to justice, while ensuring that appropriate safeguards to protect the victim are in place;

(m) Ensuring that effective legal assistance is available to all female victims of violence so that they can make informed decisions regarding, inter alia, legal proceedings and issues relating to family law, and also ensuring that victims have access to just and effective remedies for the harm that they have suffered, including through the adoption of national legislation where necessary;

(n) Ensuring that all relevant public officials coordinate effectively in the prevention, investigation, prosecution and punishment of all forms of violence against women, and provide protection and support to victims;

(o) Developing or improving and disseminating specialized training programmes, including practical tools and good practices guidelines on how to identify, prevent and deal with cases of violence against women and on how to assist victims, for police officers, the judiciary, health workers, law enforcement personnel and other relevant public authorities;

(p) Strengthening national health and social infrastructure to reinforce measures to promote women's equal access to public health and address the health consequences of all forms of violence against women, including by providing support to victims;

(q) Establishing or supporting integrated centres through which shelter, legal, health, psychological, counselling and other services are provided to victims of all forms of violence against women and, where such centres are not yet feasible, promoting collaboration and coordination among agencies, in order to make remedies more accessible and to facilitate the physical, psychological and social recovery of victims, and ensuring that victims have access to such services;

(r) Ensuring adequate and comprehensive rehabilitation and reintegration of victims of violence into society;

(s) Ensuring that the prison system and probation services provide appropriate rehabilitation programmes for perpetrators, as a preventive tool to avoid recidivism;

(t) Supporting and engaging in partnerships with non-governmental organizations, in particular women's organizations, and other relevant actors and the private sector to end violence against women;

17. *Calls upon* the international community, including the United Nations system and, as appropriate, regional and subregional organizations, to support national efforts to promote the empowerment of women and gender equality in order to enhance national efforts to eliminate violence against women and girls, including, upon request, in the development and implementation of national action plans on the elimination of violence against women and girls, through, inter alia, and taking into account national priorities, official development assistance and other appropriate assistance, such as facilitating the sharing of guidelines, methodologies and best practices;

18. *Stresses* the contribution of the ad hoc international criminal tribunals in ending impunity through ensuring accountability and punishing perpetrators of violence against women, as well as the contribution the International Criminal Court can make, and urges States to consider ratifying or acceding as a matter of priority to the Rome Statute, which entered into force on 1 July 2002;

19. *Welcomes* the steps taken by several United Nations bodies to discuss, within their respective mandates, the question of violence against women in all its forms and manifestations, and encourages all relevant bodies to continue to address this issue in their future efforts and work programmes;

20. *Reiterates its request* to the Inter-Agency Network on Women and Gender Equality to consider ways and means to enhance the effectiveness of the United Nations Trust Fund in Support of Actions to Eliminate Violence against Women as a system-wide funding mechanism for preventing and redressing all forms of violence against women and girls, and in this regard stresses the importance of new and increased contributions from all States to the Fund in order to achieve the target set by the United Nations Development Fund for Women;

21. *Calls upon* all United Nations bodies, entities, funds and programmes and the specialized agencies and invites the Bretton Woods institutions to intensify their efforts at all levels to eliminate all forms of violence against women and girls and to better coordinate their work, inter alia, through the Task Force on Violence against Women of the Inter-Agency Network on Women and Gender Equality;

22. *Requests* the Secretary-General to submit:

(a) To the General Assembly at its sixty-fourth session a report with information provided by the United Nations bodies, funds and programmes and the specialized agencies on their follow-up activities to implement Assembly resolutions 61/143 and 62/133 and the present resolution, including on their assistance to States in their efforts to eliminate all forms of violence against women;

(b) To the General Assembly at its sixty-fifth session a report with information provided by States on their follow-up activities to implement the present resolution;

23. *Also requests* the Secretary-General to present an oral report to the Commission on the Status of Women at its fifty-third session with information provided by the United Nations bodies, funds and programmes and the specialized agencies on recent follow-up activities to implement resolutions 61/143 and 62/133, including on the progress made in enhancing the effectiveness of the United Nations Trust Fund in Support of Actions to Eliminate Violence against Women as a system-wide United Nations mechanism and on the progress of the Secretary-General's campaign to end violence against women, and urges United Nations bodies, entities, funds and programmes and the specialized agencies to contribute promptly to that report;

24. *Decides* to continue the consideration of the question at its sixty-fourth session under the item entitled "Advancement of women".

Elimination of rape and other forms of sexual violence

In response to General Assembly resolution 62/134 [YUN 2007, p. 1159], the Secretary-General in August submitted a report [A/63/216 & Corr.1] on eliminating rape and other forms of sexual violence in all their manifestations, including in conflict situations, which provided information on the measures taken by States and other stakeholders to address those issues. The report, which was based on input from 29 States and 16 UN system entities, summarized initiatives undertaken by States with regard to: human rights instruments, constitutional frameworks and follow-up to resolution 1325(2000) [YUN 2000, p. 1113]; protection measures; measures pertaining to the justice system; services and support to victims; strategies for prevention, prosecution and monitoring; and resources to prevent and respond to rape and sexual violence. Measures taken by UN system entities were related to support for efforts to eliminate rape; integrating the needs of victims into UN humanitarian assistance programmes; and resources for the elimination of violence against women. The report also complemented the Secretary-General's 2007 report on the intensification of efforts to eliminate all forms of violence against women [YUN 2007, p. 1157].

In his conclusions, the Secretary-General indicated that the Security Council had taken action on the question of sexual violence and would continue to consider the issue in the context of situations on its agenda, including resolution 1820(2008) (see p. 1265). He also made recommendations for States to establish or strengthen and effectively implement legal and policy frameworks to protect women and girls from rape, including marital rape, and sexual violence, and to end impunity for perpetrators. Since only a small percentage of such crimes were reported to the police, and a smaller number resulted in convictions, it was critical for States to create an environment that encouraged victims of rape and sexual violence to seek and obtain justice and redress; to ensure that criminal justice systems responded effectively to sexual offences and achieved higher reporting and conviction rates; and to establish protocols in all relevant services to ensure consistent professionalism and standards of treatment of victims. Specialized training for all professionals who came into contact with victims was critical. States should also consider adopting plans that specifically targeted the prevention of and response to sexual violence, expanded monitoring and evaluation of their efforts, and disseminated lessons learned and good practices in order to facilitate the sharing of experiences.

Crime prevention and criminal justice responses to violence against women and girls

In response to Economic and Social Council resolution 2006/29 [YUN 2006, p. 1338], the Secretary-General in February submitted to the Commission on Crime Prevention and Criminal Justice a report [E/CN.15/2008/2] on crime prevention and criminal justice responses to violence against women and girls, which reviewed Secretariat efforts to implement the resolution, including the work of the United Nations Office on Drugs and Crime (UNODC). The report also presented information received from 26 States on efforts to address the problem of violence against women and girls, outlining initiatives undertaken to ensure that national strategies, action plans and legislative frameworks were established, and discussed other issues, such as the role of the police, victim support and assistance, training, awareness-raising and information campaigns, research and data collection, ensuring effective criminal justice responses, and special measures concerning child victims of violence. During the reporting period, UNODC expanded its programmes of technical assistance for strengthening criminal justice system responses to gender-based violence and made efforts to build effective partnerships with other UN entities and regional and non-governmental organizations (NGOs) active in the field. The Secretary-General made a series of recommendations for consideration by the Commission (see p. 1243).

On 15 April [E/2008/30], the Commission held a thematic discussion on aspects of violence against women pertaining directly to the Commission and considered the Secretary-General's report. By its decision 17/1 of 18 April, the Commission requested UNODC to convene an intergovernmental group of experts to review and update the Model Strategies and Practical Measures on the Elimination of Violence against Women in the Field of Crime Prevention and Criminal Justice.

Women and armed conflict

Women, peace and security

Report of Secretary-General. In response to the request by the Security Council in presidential statement S/PRST/2007/40 [YUN 2007, p. 1167] for a follow-up report on the implementation of resolution 1325(2000) [YUN 2000, p. 1113], the Secretary-General in September submitted a report [S/2008/622] on women, peace and security which covered critical areas and concerns related to the impact of armed conflict on women. The report also reviewed progress and challenges in the implementation of that resolution by States, UN entities and civil society, including best practices to improve the capacities of States. The report was based on information and data provided by 30 States and 28 UN system entities, as well as civil society and NGO partners. Initiatives had been taken by a broad range of actors, whose efforts included: developing policies, action plans, guidelines and indicators, increasing access to gender expertise, providing training, promoting consultation with, and the participation of women, increasing attention to human rights, and supporting the initiatives of women's groups. Although slower than desired, a culture of gender equality and women's empowerment in the area of peace and security was increasingly taking hold.

The Secretary-General observed that important progress had been made towards developing and pursuing more comprehensive approaches towards full implementation of resolution 1325(2000), including through a more well-defined role of the Security Council. The cumulative effect of those efforts was particularly visible in peacekeeping and humanitarian assistance and, increasingly, in peacebuilding. However, a noticeable gap between policies and their effective implementation needed to be closed. More needed to be done at the country level to integrate gender perspectives into every stage of conflict prevention, resolution and management, as well as in peacebuilding, which would include security sector reform; preventing and ending sexual and gender-based violence; increasing women's representation in decision-making bodies and security institutions; increasing resources and technical support for women's organizations; and ensuring stronger UN capacity to support States in implementing resolution 1325(2000). The Secretary-General also proposed recommendations for future action to accelerate implementation of the resolution.

Security Council debate. On 29 October [meeting 6005], the Security Council held a discussion on the implementation of resolution 1325(2000) and had before it a concept paper [S/2008/655] submitted by China. The Under-Secretary-General for Peacekeeping Operations presented an update on progress regarding the contribution of women to the prevention and resolution of conflicts and peacebuilding. The Council was also briefed by the Special Adviser on Gender Issues and Advancement of Women (OSAGI) on the Secretary-General's report. On the same date, the Council called upon the Secretary-General to appoint more women to pursue good offices on his behalf.

SECURITY COUNCIL ACTION

On 29 October [meeting 6005], following consultation among Security Council members, the President made statement **S/PRST/2008/39** on behalf of the Council:

The Security Council reaffirms its commitment to the full and effective implementation of its resolutions 1325(2000) and 1820(2008) on women and peace and security and recalls the relevant statements by its President.

The Council takes note of the report of the Secretary-General on women and peace and security.

The Council remains concerned about the underrepresentation of women at all stages of peace processes and in peacebuilding, and recognizes the need to facilitate the full and effective participation of women in these areas, given the vital role of women in the prevention and resolution of conflicts and in peacebuilding.

The Council urges Member States and international, regional and subregional organizations to take measures to increase the participation of women in conflict prevention, conflict resolution and peacebuilding and to strengthen the role of women as decision-makers in these areas. The Council calls upon the Secretary-General to appoint more women to pursue good offices on his behalf, particularly as Special Representatives and Special Envoys.

The Council strongly condemns all violations of international law committed against women and girls during and after armed conflicts, urges the complete cessation by all parties of such acts with immediate effect, and also urges Member States to bring to justice those responsible for crimes of this nature.

The Council requests the Secretary-General to provide a report on the implementation of resolution 1325(2000) over the coming year, including information on the impact of armed conflict on women and girls in situations of which the Council is seized; and on the obstacles and challenges to strengthening the participation of women in conflict prevention, conflict resolution and peacebuilding, and recommendations to address those issues, to be submitted to the Council by October 2009.

Sexual violence and armed conflict

On 19 June [meeting 5916], the Security Council held a high-level debate on "Women and peace and security: sexual violence in situations of armed conflict". In its consideration of the topic, the Council had before it a concept paper [S/2008/364] submitted by the United States, and a summary report [S/2008/402] of the conference "Women targeted or affected by armed conflict: what role for military peacekeepers?" (Sussex, United Kingdom, 27–29 May) submitted by the United Kingdom. The Secretary-General and Deputy Secretary-General briefed the Council on efforts made by UN system entities to address all forms of violence against women and girls, including sexual violence in armed conflict. The Secretary-General indicated that he was eager to deploy more women as police, military and civilian personnel, including at the highest levels of mission leadership, and reaffirmed the UN zero-tolerance policy against sexual exploitation or abuse by UN personnel.

On the same date, the Council requested that the Secretary-General develop guidelines and strategies to enhance the ability of UN peacekeeping operations to protect civilians and prevent sexual violence against women and girls in conflict and post-conflict situations. It also affirmed its intention, when establishing and renewing State-specific sanctions regimes, to consider the appropriateness of targeted and graduated measures against parties to situations of armed conflict committing rape and other forms of sexual violence against women and girls.

SECURITY COUNCIL ACTION

On 19 June [meeting 5916], the Security Council unanimously adopted **resolution 1820(2008)**. The draft [S/2008/403] was submitted by Armenia, Australia, Austria, Belgium, Bulgaria, Burkina Faso, Canada, Chile, Costa Rica, Croatia, Cyprus, Czech Republic, Democratic Republic of the Congo, Denmark, Estonia, Finland, France, Germany, Greece, Hungary, Iceland, Ireland, Israel, Italy, Jamaica, Japan, Latvia, Lichtenstein, Lithuania, Luxembourg, Malta, Netherlands, New Zealand, Nigeria, Norway, Panama, Poland, Portugal, Republic of Korea, Romania, San Marino, Slovakia, Slovenia, South Africa, Spain, Sweden, Switzerland, United Republic of Tanzania, United Kingdom and United States.

The Security Council,

Reaffirming its commitment to the continuing and full implementation of its resolutions 1325(2000) of 31 October 2000, 1612(2005) of 26 July 2005 and 1674(2006) of 28 April 2006, and recalling the statements by its President of 31 October 2001, 31 October 2002, 28 October 2004, 27 October 2005, 26 October 2006, 7 March 2007 and 23 October 2007,

Guided by the purposes and principles of the Charter of the United Nations,

Reaffirming the resolve expressed in the 2005 World Summit Outcome to eliminate all forms of violence against women and girls, including by ending impunity and by ensuring the protection of civilians, in particular women and girls, during and after armed conflicts, in accordance with the obligations that States have undertaken under international humanitarian law and international human rights law,

Recalling the commitments contained in the Beijing Declaration and Platform for Action as well as those contained in the outcome documents of the twenty-third special session of the General Assembly entitled "Women 2000: gender equality, development and peace for the twenty-first century", in particular those concerning sexual violence and women in situations of armed conflict,

Reaffirming the obligations of States parties to the Convention on the Elimination of All Forms of Discrimination against Women, the Optional Protocol thereto, the Convention on the Rights of the Child and the Optional Protocols thereto, and urging States that have not yet done so to consider ratifying or acceding to them,

Noting that civilians account for the vast majority of those adversely affected by armed conflict; that women and girls are particularly targeted by the use of sexual violence, including as a tactic of war to humiliate, dominate, instill fear in, disperse and/or forcibly relocate civilian members of a community or ethnic group; and that sexual violence perpetrated in this manner may in some instances persist after the cessation of hostilities,

Recalling its condemnation in the strongest terms of all sexual and other forms of violence committed against civilians in armed conflict, in particular women and children,

Reiterating its deep concern that, despite its repeated condemnation of violence against women and children in situations of armed conflict, including sexual violence in situations of armed conflict, and despite its calls addressed to all parties to armed conflict for the cessation of such acts with immediate effect, such acts continue to occur, and in some situations have become systematic and widespread, reaching appalling levels of brutality,

Recalling the inclusion of a range of sexual violence offences in the Rome Statute of the International Criminal Court and the statutes of the ad hoc international criminal tribunals,

Reaffirming the important role of women in the prevention and resolution of conflicts and in peacebuilding, and stressing the importance of their equal participation and full involvement in all efforts for the maintenance and promotion of peace and security, and the need to increase their role in decision-making with regard to conflict prevention and resolution,

Deeply concerned about the persistent obstacles and challenges to the participation and full involvement of women in the prevention and resolution of conflict as a result of violence, intimidation and discrimination, which erode women's capacity and legitimacy to participate in post-conflict public life, and acknowledging the negative impact this has on durable peace, security and reconciliation, including post-conflict peacebuilding,

Recognizing that States bear the primary responsibility to respect and ensure the human rights of their citizens, as well as all individuals within their territory, as provided for by relevant international law,

Reaffirming that parties to armed conflict bear the primary responsibility to take all feasible steps to ensure the protection of affected civilians,

Welcoming the ongoing coordination of efforts within the United Nations system, marked by the inter-agency initiative "United Nations Action against Sexual Violence in Conflict," to create awareness about sexual violence in armed conflicts and post-conflict situations and, ultimately, to put an end to it,

1. *Stresses* that sexual violence, when used or commissioned as a tactic of war in order to deliberately target civilians or as a part of a widespread or systematic attack against civilian populations, can significantly exacerbate situations of armed conflict and may impede the restoration of international peace and security, affirms in this regard that effective steps to prevent and respond to such acts of sexual violence can significantly contribute to the maintenance of international peace and security, and expresses its readiness, when considering situations on the agenda of the Security Council, to, where necessary, adopt appropriate steps to address widespread or systematic sexual violence;

2. *Demands* the immediate and complete cessation by all parties to armed conflict of all acts of sexual violence against civilians with immediate effect;

3. *Demands also* that all parties to armed conflict immediately take appropriate measures to protect civilians, including women and girls, from all forms of sexual violence, which could include enforcing appropriate military disciplinary measures and upholding the principle of command responsibility, training troops on the categorical prohibition of all forms of sexual violence against civilians, debunking myths that fuel sexual violence, vetting armed and security forces to take into account past actions of rape and other forms of sexual violence, and evacuation of women and children under imminent threat of sexual violence to safety; and requests the Secretary-General, where appropriate, to encourage dialogue to address this issue in the context of broader discussions of conflict resolution between appropriate United Nations officials and the parties to the conflict, taking into account, inter alia, the views expressed by women of affected local communities;

4. *Notes* that rape and other forms of sexual violence can constitute a war crime, a crime against humanity, or a constitutive act with respect to genocide, stresses the need for the exclusion of sexual violence crimes from amnesty provisions in the context of conflict resolution processes, and calls upon Member States to comply with their obligations for prosecuting persons responsible for such acts and to ensure that all victims of sexual violence, particularly women and girls, have equal protection under the law and equal access to justice, and stresses the importance of ending impunity for such acts as part of a comprehensive approach to seeking sustainable peace, justice, truth and national reconciliation;

5. *Affirms its intention*, when establishing and renewing State-specific sanctions regimes, to take into consideration the appropriateness of targeted and graduated measures against parties to situations of armed conflict who commit rape and other forms of sexual violence against women and girls in situations of armed conflict;

6. *Requests* the Secretary-General, in consultation with the Council, the Special Committee on Peacekeeping Operations and its Working Group and relevant States, as appropriate, to develop and implement appropriate training programmes for all peacekeeping and humanitarian personnel deployed by the United Nations in the context of missions as mandated by the Council to help them to better prevent, recognize and respond to sexual violence and other forms of violence against civilians;

7. *Also requests* the Secretary-General to continue and strengthen efforts to implement the policy of zero tolerance of sexual exploitation and abuse in United Nations peacekeeping operations, and urges troop- and police-contributing countries to take appropriate preventative action, including predeployment and in-theatre awareness training, and other action to ensure full accountability in cases of such conduct involving their personnel;

8. *Encourages* troop- and police-contributing countries, in consultation with the Secretary-General, to consider steps they could take to heighten awareness and the responsiveness of their personnel participating in United Nations peacekeeping operations to protect civilians, including women and children, and prevent sexual violence against women and girls in conflict and post-conflict situations, including, wherever possible, the deployment of a higher percentage of women peacekeepers or police;

9. *Requests* the Secretary-General to develop effective guidelines and strategies to enhance the ability of relevant United Nations peacekeeping operations, consistent with their mandates, to protect civilians, including women and girls, from all forms of sexual violence and to systematically include in his written reports to the Council on conflict situations his observations concerning the protection of women and girls and recommendations in this regard;

10. *Requests* the Secretary-General and relevant United Nations agencies, inter alia, through consultation with women and women-led organizations, as appropriate, to develop effective mechanisms for providing protection from violence, including, in particular, sexual violence, to women and girls in and around United Nations-managed refugee and internally displaced persons camps, as well as in all disarmament, demobilization and reintegration processes, and in justice and security sector reform efforts assisted by the United Nations;

11. *Stresses* the important role that the Peacebuilding Commission can play by including in its advice and recommendations for post-conflict peacebuilding strategies, where appropriate, ways to address sexual violence committed during and in the aftermath of armed conflict, and ensuring consultation and effective representation of women's civil society in its country-specific configurations, as part of its wider approach to gender issues;

12. *Urges* the Secretary-General and his Special Envoys to invite women to participate in discussions pertinent to the prevention and resolution of conflict, the maintenance of peace and security, and post-conflict peacebuilding, and encourages all parties to such talks to facilitate the equal and full participation of women at decision-making levels;

13. *Urges* all parties concerned, including Member States, United Nations entities and financial institutions,

to support the development and strengthening of the capacities of national institutions, in particular of judicial and health systems, and of local civil society networks in order to provide sustainable assistance to victims of sexual violence in armed conflict and post-conflict situations;

14. *Urges* appropriate regional and subregional bodies, in particular, to consider developing and implementing policies, activities and advocacy for the benefit of women and girls affected by sexual violence in armed conflict;

15. *Requests* the Secretary-General to submit a report to the Council by 30 June 2009 on the implementation of the present resolution in the context of situations which are on the agenda of the Council, utilizing information from available United Nations sources, including country teams, peacekeeping operations and other United Nations personnel, which would include information on situations of armed conflict in which sexual violence has been widely or systematically employed against civilians; analysis of the prevalence and trends of sexual violence in situations of armed conflict; proposals for strategies to minimize the susceptibility of women and girls to such violence; benchmarks for measuring progress in preventing and addressing sexual violence; appropriate input from United Nations implementing partners in the field; information on his plans for facilitating the collection of timely, objective, accurate and reliable information on the use of sexual violence in situations of armed conflict, including through improved coordination of United Nations activities on the ground and at Headquarters; and information on actions taken by parties to armed conflict to implement their responsibilities as described in the present resolution, in particular by immediately and completely ceasing all acts of sexual violence and taking appropriate measures to protect women and girls from all forms of sexual violence;

16. *Decides* to remain actively seized of the matter.

Women and children taken hostage

Report of Secretary-General. In response to Commission on the Status of Women resolution 50/1 [YUN 2006, p. 1341], the Secretary-General submitted a report [E/CN.6/2008/7] on the release of women and children taken hostage, including those subsequently imprisoned, in armed conflicts, which included information provided by six Member States, 12 UN system entities and one international organization. Only one State provided information on women taken hostage or imprisoned in armed conflict and little information was provided on the release of women taken hostage or imprisoned. Most of the input drew attention to support provided to children demobilized from situations of forced recruitment into armed forces. Much of the information from UN entities focused on the follow-up to Security Council resolution 1325(2000). The Secretary-General proposed that the Special Representative for children and armed conflict take into account the release of children taken hostage, including those subsequently imprisoned, in armed conflicts, and provide sex-disaggregated data, where available, when preparing the reports requested by the General Assembly.

Commission action. In a March resolution [E/2008/27 (res. 52/1)], the Commission requested the Secretary-General to facilitate the immediate release of civilian women and children who had been taken hostage, to ensure the widest possible dissemination of relevant material, in particular material related to Security Council resolution 1325(2000), and to submit to the Commission, at its fifty-fourth (2010) session, a report on the implementation of resolution 52/1.

Women in power and decision-making

Financing for gender equality and the empowerment of women

In response to Economic and Social Council resolution 2006/9 [YUN 2006, p. 1356], the Secretary-General submitted a report [E/CN.6/2008/2] on financing for gender equality and the empowerment of women, which analysed progress achieved and remaining gaps and challenges in financing for gender equality and the empowerment of women, including information on the Monterrey Consensus [YUN 2002, p. 953], innovative sources of funding, financing critical stakeholders, and measurement challenges. On implementation of global commitments, there had been limited assessment of resource allocations to translate global commitments into national action, and it was estimated that the financing gap for achieving Goal 3 of the MDGs—promote gender equality and empower women—in low-income countries ranged from $8.6 billion in 2006 to what would be $23.8 billion in 2015. In addition, the 10-year review of the implementation of the Platform for Action [YUN 2005, p. 1247] indicated that there was a significant gap between policy and practice in many countries and that a lack of resources was a key obstacle to effective implementation at the national level.

In follow-up to the Monterrey Consensus, the Secretary-General observed that the most significant achievements had been made in the area of gender-responsive budgets. However, further efforts were needed to ensure a shift from analysis to implementation, as well as to broaden the focus to include both revenue and expenditures and ensure the full involvement of all stakeholders. Insufficient budgetary resources continued to undermine the effectiveness and sustainability of both national mechanisms for the advancement of women and women's organizations in their efforts towards supporting and monitoring implementation of the Platform for Action. Although some progress had been made in reporting on resource allocations, monitoring and reporting remained insufficient. Further development of sex-disaggregated data and indicators was required in order to measure progress more systematically and effectively. The

Secretary-General proposed a series of recommendations that the Commission might wish Governments, the UN system and other actors to undertake, which included ensuring that gender perspectives were fully incorporated in the preparations for and the outcome of the Follow-up International Conference on Financing for Development to Review the Implementation of the Monterrey Consensus (see p. 1076), to be held in Doha, Qatar, from 29 November to 2 December.

Report of Secretary-General. In response to Economic and Social Council resolution 2006/9 and General Assembly resolution 61/145 [YUN 2006, p. 1330], the Secretary-General submitted a report [E/CN.6/2008/5] on progress in mainstreaming a gender perspective in the development, implementation and evaluation of national policies and programmes, with a particular focus on financing for gender equality and the empowerment of women, which was to be read in conjunction with his report on the same topic. The report summarized national initiatives undertaken on financing for gender equality and the empowerment of women in the areas of public finance management, including gender-responsive budgeting; national economic policies, plans and programmes; mechanisms and instruments on gender equality; financing for national mechanisms for the advancement of women; financing for women's organizations; development cooperation; and new aid modalities and strengthened delivery mechanisms.

The Secretary-General observed that although gender-responsive budget initiatives had been implemented by a large number of States, many initiatives had not been adequately linked to overall public finance management or moved beyond the analysis of expenditures. Other obstacles to progress included the failure to assess the cost of, and secure resources for, the implementation of gender equality policies, strategies and plans, including the gender mainstreaming strategy, and the fact that gender equality was not seen as a central goal in all national economic policies, plans and programmes. The report concluded with recommendations for consideration by the Commission.

Commission action. In February [E/2008/27], the Commission held parallel high-level round tables on the theme "Financing for gender equality and the empowerment of women", as well as panel discussions on key policy initiatives and on capacity-building on mainstreaming a gender perspective in the development, implementation and evaluation of national policies and programmes. On 13 March, the Commission adopted its agreed conclusions on financing gender equality and the empowerment of women, which made recommendations for actions to be taken by Governments, UN system entities, international financial institutions, civil society, NGOs and the private sector.

On 23 July, the Economic and Social Council transmitted the agreed conclusions to the General Assembly as an input to the preparations for the follow-up international conference (**decision 2008/235**). On 25 July, the Council adopted "Implementing the internationally agreed goals and commitments in regard to gender equality and the empowerment of women" as the theme for its 2010 annual ministerial-level substantive review (**decision 2008/258**).

Institutional mechanisms for the advancement of women

Inter-Agency Network. The United Nations Inter-Agency Network on Women and Gender Equality (IANWGE), at its seventh annual session (New York, 19–21 February) [IANWGE/2008/Report], reviewed progress in the implementation of the Economic and Social Council agreed conclusions 1997/2 on mainstreaming a gender perspective into all UN system policies and programmes [YUN 1997, p. 1186] and followed up on various inter-sessional activities. It focused on matters for consideration by the High-level Committees on Management (HLCM) and on Programmes (HLCP) of the United Nations System Chief Executives Board for Coordination (CEB), discussing issues related to UN reform; integration of a gender perspective into the ongoing intergovernmental processes, including financing for development, development and trade, and mid-term review of the MDGs; emerging trends and challenges, including climate change and rape; and the Secretary-General's campaign to end violence against women and girls [YUN 2007, p. 1157].

The report also summarized the oral reports provided by task force managers. On gender and the MDGs, the World Bank's Global Monitoring Report 2007 found that data on all the official indicators of the MDG on gender equality and empowering women were available for only 59 out of 154 countries, and even fewer countries had time series data that would allow tracking over time. On gender mainstreaming, a concept note of evaluation guidance was prepared by the Office of Internal Oversight Services (OIOS), and the International Labour Organization (ILO) developed its gender equality action plan for the 2008–2009 biennium in a results-based format, comprising outcomes, indicators, targets and activities, as well as roles and responsibilities in the areas of staffing, programmes and institutional arrangements. The Network decided to intensify its work on the operationalization of the system-wide action plan on gender mainstreaming by tasking its Ad Hoc Working Group on the action plan to prepare a concept paper and a road map on the draft action plan by July. IANWGE also decided to establish five new task forces to address the following issues: capacity-building for gender mainstreaming; the development of a programme of action for the Secretary-General's campaign to end violence against women and girls; climate change; the tracking of gender-related resources within the UN system; and the implementation of General Assembly resolution 62/134 [ibid., p. 1159] on eliminating rape and other forms of sexual violence in all their manifestations, including in conflict and related situations. The Network expressed concern regarding the funding of its activities, and agreed that system-wide fundraising must be undertaken and that greater interagency financial support at the level of CEB activities carried out by IANWGE should be explored.

Report of Secretary-General. In response to Economic and Social Council resolution 2007/33 [YUN 2007, p. 1186], the Secretary-General in May submitted a report [E/2008/53] on mainstreaming a gender perspective into all UN system policies and programmes. The report—based on the responses from 32 UN system entities to a questionnaire designed by OSAGI and approved by IANWGE —indicated that many entities had developed or strengthened entity-specific policies, strategies and action plans on gender equality and had undertaken a range of activities to incorporate gender perspectives into country programming. Most entities reported using results-based management frameworks as one of the key actions in improving gender mainstreaming and reducing the gap between policy and practice. Entities were increasingly setting concrete targets and indicators, at country programme levels, to be monitored on a systematic basis. However, as indicated in the agreed conclusions adopted by the Commission at its 2008 session (see p. 1268), under-resourcing of gender equality activities persisted throughout the UN system, and in particular in the gender-specific entities, namely OSAGI, UNIFEM, the Division for the Advancement of Women (DAW) and the International Research and Training Institute for the Advancement of Women (INSTRAW). On implementation of resolution 2006/36 [YUN 2006, p. 1350], most entities had developed generic gender-mainstreaming training, as well as training and resource materials for various categories of staff. There had also been some promising initiatives and increased attention to capacity-building, but no entity had yet established an effective systematic capacity-building programme on gender equality. Stronger efforts were needed to address identified constraints, including lack of conceptual clarity, inadequate resources, lack of leadership and accountability, the ad hoc nature of many training programmes, and weak follow-up.

The Secretary-General concluded that UN entities needed to strengthen their efforts to implement the gender-mainstreaming strategy in support of States' efforts at the national level for gender equality and the empowerment of women. In most entities, gender-equality policies, strategies and action plans included concrete actions to develop capacity and improve accountability and monitoring and reporting on the implementation of gender mainstreaming. A wide range of effective methodologies, tools and resources had been developed and applied across the UN system. Nonetheless, in many entities, lack of responsibility for gender mainstreaming among staff and managers remained a challenge. The overall low number of gender specialists at all levels and the continued problems with gender focal point systems at the country level were significant constraints to the systematic and effective implementation of gender mainstreaming. The Secretary-General made recommendations for the Council to encourage UN entities to strengthen leadership on gender mainstreaming by requiring more explicit attention to the strategy at the highest levels; establishing the responsibilities of resident coordinators vis-à-vis gender mainstreaming at the country level; requiring senior management to report regularly on gender equality results; and substantially increasing resources for gender mainstreaming activities, including capacity-building and inter-agency collaboration.

UNDP consideration. In January [E/2008/35], during the first regular session of the United Nations Development Programme/United Nations Population Fund (UNDP/UNFPA) Executive Board, the Director (Gender Team, Bureau for Development Policy) presented an oral report on the 2007 gender action plan and the gender equality strategy for 2008–2011. She noted that UNDP had enhanced its role as a knowledge broker in the field, while acknowledging ongoing challenges in developing capacity, increasing accountability, monitoring progress and building partnerships. Delegations commended UNDP on the progress made with respect to women's empowerment, supported the gender equality strategy and encouraged UNDP to implement relevant elements of the triennial comprehensive policy review.

ECONOMIC AND SOCIAL COUNCIL ACTION

On 25 July [meeting 44], the Economic and Social Council adopted **resolution 2008/34** [draft: E/2008/L.32] without vote [agenda item 14 *(a)*].

Mainstreaming a gender perspective into all policies and programmes in the United Nations system

The Economic and Social Council,

Reaffirming its agreed conclusions 1997/2 of 18 July 1997 on mainstreaming a gender perspective into all policies and programmes in the United Nations system, and recalling its resolutions 2001/41 of 26 July 2001, 2002/23 of 24 July 2002, 2003/49 of 24 July 2003, 2004/4 of 7 July 2004, 2005/31 of 26 July 2005, 2006/36 of 27 July 2006 and 2007/33 of 27 July 2007,

Reaffirming also the commitment made at the 2005 World Summit to actively promote the mainstreaming of a gender perspective in the design, implementation, monitoring and evaluation of policies and programmes in all political, economic and social spheres and to further undertake to strengthen the capabilities of the United Nations system in the area of gender,

Acknowledging that enhancing the opportunities, potential and activities of women requires a dual focus, namely, programmes aimed at meeting the basic and specific needs of women for capacity-building, organizational development and empowerment, together with gender mainstreaming in all programme formulation and implementation activities,

Recognizing that gender equality and the empowerment of women make an essential contribution to the work of the United Nations,

Noting the ongoing discussions in the General Assembly on the report of the Secretary-General on the recommendations contained in the report of the High-level Panel on United Nations System-wide Coherence in the areas of development, humanitarian assistance and the environment,

Reaffirming that gender mainstreaming is a globally accepted strategy for achieving gender equality and constitutes a critical strategy in the implementation of the Beijing Platform for Action and the outcome of the twenty-third special session of the General Assembly,

Recognizing that training is critical for increasing the awareness, knowledge, commitment and capacity of staff to mainstream a gender perspective into United Nations policies and programmes and that the provision of effective gender training requires adequate financial and human resources,

Underlining the catalytic role played by the Commission on the Status of Women, as well as the important role played by the Economic and Social Council and the General Assembly, in promoting and monitoring gender mainstreaming within the United Nations system,

Expressing serious concern that the urgent goal of achieving 50/50 gender balance in the United Nations system, especially at senior and policymaking levels, with full respect for the principle of equitable geographical distribution, in conformity with Article 101, paragraph 3, of the Charter of the United Nations, remains unmet and that the representation of women in the United Nations system has remained almost static, with negligible improvement in some parts of the system, and in some cases has even decreased, as reflected in the report of the Secretary-General on the improvement of the status of women in the United Nations system,

1. *Takes note with appreciation* of the report of the Secretary-General and the recommendations contained therein;

2. *Recognizes* that the Inter-Agency Network on Women and Gender Equality remains an important forum for the exchange and cross-fertilization of ideas on gender mainstreaming within the United Nations system, and takes note of the ongoing discussions on the implementation of the policy and strategy for gender mainstreaming within the United Nations system;

3. *Encourages* all United Nations entities to continue investing in capacity development, including through mandatory training for all staff and personnel and training for senior managers, as a critical means of increasing the awareness, knowledge, commitment and competencies of staff with regard to mainstreaming a gender perspective in all United Nations policies and programmes;

4. *Recognizes* that a large gap remains between policy and practice and that building United Nations staff capacities alone is not sufficient for the Organization to meet its commitments and obligations with respect to gender mainstreaming, and requests the United Nations system, including the agencies, funds and programmes of the United Nations system within their organizational mandates:

(*a*) To strengthen institutional accountability mechanisms, including through a more effective monitoring and evaluation framework for gender mainstreaming based on common United Nations evaluation standards;

(*b*) To strengthen accountability systems for both management and staff, through, inter alia, the inclusion of objectives and results related to gender mainstreaming in personnel workplans and appraisals;

(*c*) To continue efforts to achieve gender balance in appointments within the United Nations system at the Headquarters and country levels in positions that affect operational activities, including resident coordinator appointments and other high-level posts, with due regard to representation of women from developing countries and keeping in mind the principle of equitable geographical representation, in conformity with Article 101, paragraph 3, of the Charter of the United Nations;

(*d*) To ensure that programmes, plans and budgets visibly mainstream gender perspectives and allocate adequate financial and human resources for gender mainstreaming commensurate with the organizational gender equality goals, including for mandatory training on gender mainstreaming, especially gender analysis, for all staff and for the implementation of strategies, policies and action plans;

(*e*) To share and disseminate good practices, tools and methodologies electronically and through regular meetings on gender mainstreaming, including through the Inter-Agency Network on Women and Gender Equality and its task forces, as well as the United Nations country teams;

(*f*) To address gaps by strengthening coordination and synergy between policy and practice in mainstreaming a gender perspective in their respective fields of work;

(*g*) To enhance collaboration and coordination in the work of gender specialists and gender focal points working, inter alia, in the areas of peace and security, humanitarian affairs and economic and social development;

(*h*) To provide specific ongoing capacity-building, inter alia, through training for gender specialists and gender focal points, including in the field;

(*i*) To promote a United Nations system-wide common understanding of a results-based management framework with benchmarks and indicators for measuring progress in the application of the gender mainstreaming strategy to achieve gender equality;

(*j*) To include clear gender equality results and gender-sensitive indicators in their strategic frameworks;

(*k*) To assess the gaps in gender mainstreaming and unify methodologies for evaluation after the implementation of gender mainstreaming policies and programmes within the United Nations system;

(l) To strengthen collaboration between United Nations country teams on gender equality programmes, including through joint activities and the strengthening of the capacity of gender theme groups to support such activities;

(m) To mainstream a gender perspective and pursue gender equality in their country programmes, planning instruments and sector-wide programmes and articulate specific country-level goals and targets in this field in accordance with national development strategies;

(n) To collaborate with the resident coordinator system to provide gender specialist resources in support of gender mainstreaming in country-level activities in all sectors in which they operate, working closely with relevant national counterparts;

(o) To promote inter-agency cooperation through the Inter-Agency Network on Women and Gender Equality and the United Nations System Chief Executives Board for Coordination, through its High-level Committee on Programmes, the United Nations Development Group and its High-level Committee on Management, in order to ensure consistency and synergy in the implementation of the United Nations system-wide policy and strategy on gender mainstreaming;

(p) To promote the collection, analysis and use of data disaggregated by sex during programme development and evaluation of gender mainstreaming to assess progress towards achieving gender equality and the empowerment of women;

5. *Requests* all relevant United Nations entities to maintain their efforts to raise awareness of gender issues within their organizations and across the United Nations system;

6. *Stresses* the important role that senior management plays in creating an environment that actively supports gender mainstreaming, and calls upon it to perform that role;

7. *Requests* the Inter-Agency Network on Women and Gender Equality to continue to provide practical support to its members in gender mainstreaming, explore possibilities for developing an accessible and consolidated database of trained facilitators at the country and regional levels, in consultation with Member States, and report regularly to the United Nations System Chief Executives Board for Coordination in order to facilitate the incorporation of gender mainstreaming perspectives into their work;

8. *Requests* the Secretary-General to submit to the Economic and Social Council at its substantive session of 2009 a detailed report on progress made in the implementation of the present resolution, including updated information on the implementation of paragraph 4 of Council resolution 2006/36.

Strengthening of UN gender equality architecture

During 2008, United Nations efforts towards strengthening the gender architecture of the Organization continued. Informal consultations of the General Assembly were convened on 16 May, 16 June and 8 September by the Co-Chairs for system-wide coherence. The second meeting had before it a 5 June note submitted by the Deputy Secretary-General, which guided the deliberations. The note outlined achievements, gaps and challenges, and highlighted the increasing demand on the UN system to support countries in advancing implementation of their commitments on gender equality and women's empowerment. During the consultations, there was a broad-based momentum to address the manifest weaknesses of the UN system. There was also an agreement that the Secretary-General should be requested to provide a paper by mid-July presenting a range of institutional options on how to reorganize the gender-related bodies of the Organization with a view to improving performance in the area of gender equality and the empowerment of women.

Report of Co-Chairs. On 21 July, the Co-Chairs on system-wide coherence released a report [A/63/362] which summarized the extensive process of consultations conducted with the UN membership in New York and in the pilot countries visited, and set out a direction for moving forward. On gender equality and empowerment, the report indicated that critical gaps had been identified in the way the UN system assisted States in implementing globally agreed mandates and their own internationally made commitments. The Co-Chairs recommended that the Assembly be invited to address the matter in early September and pointed out that the report, taken together with the forthcoming institutional options paper from the Secretary-General, would complete the substantive picture for Member States and equip them for decision-making.

Institutional options paper. In a letter dated 23 July, the Deputy Secretary-General transmitted a document entitled, "Institutional Options to Strengthen United Nations Work on Gender Equality and the Empowerment of Women", which provided information on the existing intergovernmental and institutional arrangements and presented three non-prescriptive options in order to facilitate the consultations of Member States. Two approaches were presented. The first involved maintaining the status quo, which would not require any structural change, with institutional arrangements being strengthened through consolidation of the four existing gender-related entities: OSAGI, DAW, UNIFEM and INSTRAW. The second approach entailed establishing an entity following three possible organizational options: an autonomous fund/programme consolidating the four existing entities into a single entity; a department of the Secretariat; or a composite entity that would combine normative and operational work. The Deputy Secretary-General invited Member States to consider the options and stated that decisive action was critical to achieving progress in gender equality and women's empowerment.

Following informal consultations convened by the Co-Chairs on 8 September, by **resolution 62/277** of 15 September (see p. 1516) the General Assembly welcomed the Deputy Secretary-General's paper and requested that the Secretary-General provide a further, detailed modalities paper in respect of the institutional options set out in the Deputy Secretary-General's paper. As specified, the Secretary-General's paper would cover funding, governance structure, staffing, specific functions, and the relationship with the Commission on the Status of Women and other relevant bodies. Particular focus would be given to the "composite entity" option.

Status of women in the United Nations

In response to General Assembly resolution 62/137 [YUN 2007, p. 1153], the Secretary-General submitted a report [A/63/364] on progress made in the representation of women in the organizations and agencies of the UN system from 1 January 2005 to 31 December 2007, and in the UN Secretariat from 1 July 2006 to 30 June 2008.

In resolution 63/159 of 18 December (see p. 1251), the Assembly requested the Secretary-General to review and redouble his efforts to make progress towards the goal of achieving a 50/50 gender balance at all levels in the Secretariat and throughout the UN system.

Women and human rights

Division for the Advancement of Women and OHCHR activities

During the year, cooperation continued between the UN Division for the Advancement of Women and the Office of the United Nations High Commissioner for Human Rights (OHCHR) with the aim of achieving equality between women and men and promoting and protecting women's human rights. In December, the Secretary-General transmitted a report [A/HRC/10/42-E/CN.6/2009/7] on implementation of the 2008 joint work plan of the Division and OHCHR, which summarized the major activities that were carried out and contained the joint workplan for 2009.

Special Rapporteur on laws discriminating against women

In response to the ongoing review of the question on the advisability of appointing a special rapporteur on laws discriminating against women [YUN 2007, p. 1177] OHCHR released in March an analytical study on such laws and the usefulness of creating a new mechanism to address the issue. The study, entitled "Project on a mechanism to address laws that discriminate against women", aimed to obtain national data on such laws and review UN mechanisms to ascertain the extent to which they addressed the issue of discriminatory laws. The report also presented arguments for and against the appointment of a special rapporteur, as well as a possible mandate for the rapporteur.

Trafficking in women and girls

In response to General Assembly resolution 61/144 [YUN 2006, p. 1342], the Secretary-General in August submitted a report [A63/215] on trafficking in women and girls, which provided information on measures taken by 40 States and 10 UN system entities to combat the practice. The report described initiatives taken by States with regard to international instruments; legislation and the justice system; national action plans, strategies and national coordination mechanisms; bilateral, regional and international agreements and cooperation; prevention measures, including awareness-raising and capacity-building; the role of the business sector and media providers; services and support for victims; and data collection and research. Efforts by States included strengthening legal frameworks, establishing strategies for better coordination and cooperation with different stakeholders, and reinforcing prevention action and efforts to prosecute perpetrators and protect and support victims.

UN system activities focused on analysis, studies and initiatives in support of national and regional efforts. Emphasis was placed on improving cooperation and collaboration and on strengthening a multi-stakeholder, holistic approach to combating trafficking, in particular by providing support for the development of strategic partnerships among government actors, civil society organizations, the private sector and other stakeholders. In March, the Human Rights Council adopted resolution 7/29 on the rights of the child (see p. 738), which addressed the issue of trafficking in children. UNODC organized the first global forum to fight human trafficking (Vienna, 13–15 February) [E/CN.15/2008/CRP.2], which brought together over 1,500 government officials, business leaders, NGOs, academics, UN system representatives and victims of trafficking. In addition, the General Assembly convened a thematic debate on human trafficking (New York, 3 June) that focused on the way forward in the global fight against trafficking.

The Secretary-General said that many actions had been taken at the national, regional and international levels to prevent and combat trafficking in persons, especially women and girls, and the number of States parties to relevant international instruments had increased considerably. Many States had introduced a specific criminal offence of human trafficking in their laws; in others, a number of related offences were applicable to trafficking. Despite those developments, trafficking in persons persisted, as it was a crime that was often transboundary, took place in multiple settings, and involved perpetrators at different levels. A comprehensive, coordinated and gender-sensitive approach was required to address the root causes and risk factors that made women and girls vulnerable to being trafficked and ensured prosecution of the perpetrators and protection and support for victims. He observed that reliable data on the scope and nature of trafficking in women and girls was lacking and that there was a need for more and better-quality data to guide the development of national policies and programmes, monitor their impact and assess progress. He recommended that data collection and analysis be accelerated and qualitative research be intensified to facilitate improved understanding and more efficient and effective responses. The report concluded with a series of recommendations for consideration by States.

GENERAL ASSEMBLY RESOLUTION

On 18 December [meeting 70], the General Assembly, on the recommendation of the Third Committee [A/63/425] adopted **resolution 63/156** without vote [agenda item 56 *(a)*]

Trafficking in women and girls

The General Assembly,

Recalling all international conventions that deal specifically with the problem of trafficking in women and girls, such as the Convention on the Elimination of All Forms of Discrimination against Women and the Optional Protocol thereto, the Convention on the Rights of the Child and the Optional Protocol thereto on the sale of children, child prostitution and child pornography, the Convention for the Suppression of the Traffic in Persons and of the Exploitation of the Prostitution of Others and the United Nations Convention against Transnational Organized Crime and the Protocols thereto, in particular the Protocol to Prevent, Suppress and Punish Trafficking in Persons, Especially Women and Children, supplementing the United Nations Convention against Transnational Organized Crime and the Protocol against the Smuggling of Migrants by Land, Sea and Air, supplementing the United Nations Convention against Transnational Organized Crime, as well as previous resolutions of the General Assembly and its subsidiary body the Human Rights Council, and the Economic and Social Council and its functional commissions on the issue,

Reaffirming the provisions pertaining to trafficking in women and girls contained in the outcome documents of relevant international conferences and summits, in particular the strategic objective on the issue of trafficking contained in the Beijing Declaration and Platform for Action adopted by the Fourth World Conference on Women,

Reaffirming also the commitment made by world leaders at the Millennium Summit and the 2005 World Summit to devise, enforce and strengthen effective measures to combat and eliminate all forms of trafficking in persons to counter the demand for trafficked victims and to protect the victims,

Recalling the reports of the Special Rapporteur on the sale of children, child prostitution and child pornography, the Special Rapporteur on trafficking in persons, especially women and children, and the Special Rapporteur on violence against women, its causes and consequences, as well as the information that deals with trafficking in women and girls contained in the report of the Secretary-General on the in-depth study on all forms of violence against women,

Recalling also the report of the United Nations Office on Drugs and Crime entitled "Trafficking in Persons: Global Patterns" of April 2006 and the attention paid in it to the situation of trafficked women and girls,

Taking note of the Vienna Forum to Fight Human Trafficking, held from 13 to 15 February 2008, within the framework of the Global Initiative to Fight Human Trafficking, and of the thematic debate on the issue of trafficking in persons, held on 3 June 2008, within the framework of the General Assembly,

Taking note also of the renewal of the mandate of the Special Rapporteur on trafficking in persons, especially women and children, and of the fact that part of her task is to integrate a gender- and age-specific perspective throughout the work of her mandate, inter alia, through the identification of gender- and age-specific vulnerabilities in relation to the issue of trafficking in persons,

Acknowledging the inclusion of gender-related crimes in the Rome Statute of the International Criminal Court, which entered into force on 1 July 2002,

Bearing in mind that all States have an obligation to exercise due diligence to prevent, investigate and punish perpetrators of trafficking in persons, and to rescue victims as well as provide for their protection, and that not doing so violates and impairs or nullifies the enjoyment of the human rights and fundamental freedoms of the victims,

Seriously concerned that an increasing number of women and girls from some developing countries and countries with economies in transition are being trafficked to developed countries, as well as within and between regions and States, and that men and boys are also victims of trafficking, including for sexual exploitation,

Recognizing that certain efforts against trafficking in persons lack the gender and age sensitivity needed to address effectively the situation of women and girls, who are particularly vulnerable to trafficking for the purposes of sexual exploitation, forced labour, services and other forms of exploitation, thus highlighting the need to incorporate a gender- and age-sensitive approach in all anti-trafficking efforts,

Recognizing also the need to address the impact of globalization on the particular problem of trafficking in women and children, in particular girls,

Recognizing further the challenges to combating trafficking in women and girls owing to the lack of adequate legislation and implementation of existing legislation, the lack of availability of reliable sex-disaggregated data and statistics, and the lack of resources,

Concerned about the use of new information technologies, including the Internet, for purposes of exploitation of the prostitution of others, for trafficking in women as brides, for sex tourism exploiting women and children and for child pornography, paedophilia and any other forms of sexual exploitation of children,

Concerned also about the increasing activities of transnational criminal organizations and others that profit from international trafficking in persons, especially women and children, without regard to dangerous and inhuman conditions and in flagrant violation of domestic laws and international standards,

Recognizing that victims of trafficking are particularly exposed to racism, racial discrimination, xenophobia and related intolerance and that women and girl victims are often subject to multiple forms of discrimination and violence, including on the grounds of their gender, age, ethnicity, culture and religion, as well as their origins, and that these forms of discrimination themselves may fuel trafficking in persons,

Noting that some of the demand for prostitution and forced labour is met by trafficking in persons in some parts of the world,

Acknowledging that women and girl victims of trafficking, on account of their gender, are further disadvantaged and marginalized by a general lack of information or awareness and recognition of their human rights and by the stigmatization often associated with trafficking, as well as by the obstacles they meet in gaining access to information and recourse mechanisms in cases of violation of their rights, and that special measures are required for their protection and to increase their awareness,

Reaffirming the importance of bilateral, subregional, regional and international cooperation mechanisms and initiatives, including information exchanges on best practices, of Governments and intergovernmental and non-governmental organizations to address the problem of trafficking in persons, especially women and children,

Reaffirming also that global efforts, including international cooperation and technical assistance programmes, to eradicate trafficking in persons, especially women and children, demand the strong political commitment, shared responsibility and active cooperation of all Governments of countries of origin, transit and destination,

Recognizing that policies and programmes for prevention, rehabilitation, repatriation and reintegration should be developed through a gender- and age-sensitive, comprehensive and multidisciplinary approach, with concern for the security of the victims and respect for the full enjoyment of their human rights and with the involvement of all actors in countries of origin, transit and destination,

Convinced of the need to protect and assist all victims of trafficking, with full respect for the human rights of the victims,

1. *Welcomes* the efforts of Governments, United Nations bodies and agencies and intergovernmental and non-governmental organizations to address the particular problem of trafficking in women and girls, and encourages them to enhance their efforts and cooperation, including by sharing their knowledge, technical expertise and best practices as widely as possible;

2. *Calls upon* Governments to discourage, with a view to eliminating, the demand that fosters the trafficking of women and girls for all forms of exploitation, and in this regard to enhance preventive measures, including legislative measures, to deter exploiters of trafficked persons, as well as ensure their accountability;

3. *Also calls upon* Governments to take appropriate measures to address the factors that increase vulnerability to being trafficked, including poverty and gender inequality, as well as other factors that encourage the particular problem of trafficking in women and girls for prostitution and other forms of commercialized sex, forced marriage and forced labour, in order to prevent and eliminate such trafficking, including by strengthening existing legislation with a view to providing better protection of the rights of women and girls and to punishing perpetrators, through both criminal and civil measures;

4. *Calls upon* Governments, the international community and all other organizations and entities that deal with conflict and post-conflict, disaster and other emergency situations to address the heightened vulnerability of women and girls to trafficking and exploitation, and associated gender-based violence;

5. *Urges* Governments to devise, enforce and strengthen effective gender- and age-sensitive measures to combat and eliminate all forms of trafficking in women and girls, including for sexual and economic exploitation, as part of a comprehensive anti-trafficking strategy that integrates a human rights perspective, and to draw up, as appropriate, national action plans in this regard;

6. *Urges* Governments, in cooperation with intergovernmental and non-governmental organizations, to support and allocate resources to strengthen preventive action, in particular education for women and men, as well as for girls and boys, on gender equality, self-respect and mutual respect, and campaigns, carried out in collaboration with civil society, to increase public awareness of the issue at the national and grass-roots levels;

7. *Encourages* Governments to take appropriate measures to eliminate sex tourism demand, especially of children, through all possible preventive actions;

8. *Urges* Governments to develop educational and training programmes and policies and consider, as appropriate, enacting legislation aimed at preventing sex tourism and trafficking, giving special emphasis to the protection of young women and children;

9. *Also urges* Governments to consider signing and ratifying and States parties to implement relevant United Nations legal instruments, such as the United Nations Convention against Transnational Organized Crime and the Protocols thereto, in particular the Protocol to Prevent, Suppress and Punish Trafficking in Persons, Especially Women and Children, supplementing the United Nations Convention against Transnational Organized Crime, the Convention on the Elimination of All Forms of Discrimination against Women and the Optional Protocol thereto and the Convention on the Rights of the Child and the Optional Protocol thereto on the sale of children, child prostitution and child pornography, as well as the Convention concerning Forced or Compulsory Labour, 1930 (Convention No. 29), the Convention concerning Discrimination in respect of Employment and Occupation, 1958 (Convention No. 111) and the Convention concerning the Prohibition and Immediate Action for the Elimination of the Worst

Forms of Child Labour, 1999 (Convention No. 182), of the International Labour Organization;

10. *Encourages* Member States to strengthen national programmes and to engage in bilateral, subregional, regional and international cooperation, including by forging regional initiatives or plans of action, to address the problem of trafficking in persons through, inter alia, the enhancement of information-sharing, gender- and age-specific data collection and other technical capacities, and mutual legal assistance, as well as the combating of corruption and laundering of proceeds derived from trafficking, including for purposes of commercial sexual exploitation, and to ensure that such agreements and initiatives are particularly responsive to the problem of trafficking as it affects women and girls;

11. *Calls upon* all Governments to criminalize all forms of trafficking in persons, recognizing its increasing occurrence for purposes of sexual exploitation, commercial sexual exploitation and abuse, sex tourism and forced labour, and to bring to justice and punish the offenders and intermediaries involved, whether local or foreign, through the competent national authorities, either in the country of origin of the offender or in the country in which the abuse occurs, in accordance with due process of law, as well as to penalize persons in authority found guilty of sexually assaulting victims of trafficking in their custody;

12. *Urges* Governments to take all appropriate measures to ensure that victims of trafficking are not penalized for being trafficked and that they do not suffer from revictimization as a result of actions taken by government authorities, and encourages Governments to prevent, within their legal framework and in accordance with national policies, victims of trafficking in persons from being prosecuted for their illegal entry or residence;

13. *Invites* Governments to consider setting up or strengthening a national coordinating mechanism, for example, a national rapporteur or an inter-agency body, with the participation of civil society, including non-governmental organizations, to encourage the exchange of information and to report on data, root causes, factors and trends in violence against women, in particular trafficking, and to include data disaggregated by sex and age;

14. *Encourages* Governments and relevant United Nations bodies, within existing resources, to take appropriate measures to raise public awareness of the issue of trafficking in persons, particularly women and girls; to discourage, with a view to eliminating, the demand that fosters all forms of exploitation, including sexual exploitation and forced labour; to publicize the laws, regulations and penalties relating to this issue; and to emphasize that trafficking is a serious crime;

15. *Calls upon* concerned Governments to allocate resources, as appropriate, to provide comprehensive programmes for the physical, psychological and social recovery of victims of trafficking, including through job training, legal assistance in a language that they can understand and health care, including for HIV/AIDS, and by taking measures to cooperate with intergovernmental and non-governmental organizations to provide for the social, medical and psychological care of the victims;

16. *Encourages* Governments, in cooperation with intergovernmental and non-governmental organizations, to undertake or strengthen campaigns aimed at clarifying opportunities, limitations and rights in the event of migration, as well as information on the risks of irregular migration and the ways and means used by traffickers, so as to enable women to make informed decisions and to prevent them from becoming victims of trafficking;

17. *Encourages* Governments to intensify collaboration with non-governmental organizations to develop and implement gender- and age-sensitive programmes for effective counselling, training and reintegration into society of victims of trafficking and programmes that provide shelter and helplines to victims or potential victims;

18. *Urges* Governments to provide or strengthen training for law enforcement, judicial, immigration and other relevant officials in the prevention and combating of trafficking in persons, including the sexual exploitation of women and girls, and in this regard calls upon Governments to ensure that the treatment of victims of trafficking, especially by law enforcers, immigration officers, consular officials, social workers and other first-response officials, is conducted with full respect for the human rights of those victims and with gender and age sensitivity, and observes the principles of non-discrimination, including the prohibition of racial discrimination;

19. *Invites* Governments to take steps to ensure that criminal justice procedures and witness protection programmes are sensitive to the particular situation of trafficked women and girls and that they are supported and assisted, as appropriate, in making complaints to the police or other authorities without fear and being available when required by the criminal justice system, and to ensure that during this time they have access to gender- and age-sensitive protection and, as appropriate, social, medical, financial and legal assistance, including the possibility of obtaining compensation for damages suffered;

20. *Also invites* Governments to encourage media providers, including Internet service providers, to adopt or strengthen self-regulatory measures to promote the responsible use of media, particularly the Internet, with a view to eliminating the exploitation of women and children, in particular girls, which could foster trafficking;

21. *Invites* the business sector, in particular the tourism and telecommunications industries, including mass media organizations, to cooperate with Governments in eliminating trafficking in women and children, in particular girls, including through the dissemination by the media of information regarding the dangers of trafficking, the rights of trafficked persons and the services available to victims of trafficking;

22. *Stresses* the need for the systematic collection of sex- and age-disaggregated data and comprehensive studies at both the national and the international levels and the development of common methodologies and internationally defined indicators to make it possible to develop relevant and comparable figures, and encourages Governments to enhance information-sharing and data-collection capacity as a way of promoting cooperation to combat the trafficking problem;

23. *Invites* Governments, United Nations bodies, agencies and special mechanisms, intergovernmental and non-governmental organizations and the private sector to undertake collaborative and joint research and studies on

trafficking in women and girls that can serve as a basis for policy formulation or change;

24. *Invites* Governments, with the support of the United Nations, when necessary, and other intergovernmental organizations, taking into account best practices, to formulate training manuals and other informational materials and provide training for law enforcement, judicial and other relevant officers, and medical and support personnel, with a view to sensitizing them to the special needs of women and girl victims;

25. *Encourages* Governments, relevant intergovernmental bodies and international organizations to ensure that military, peacekeeping and humanitarian personnel deployed in conflict, post-conflict and other emergency situations are provided training on conduct that does not promote, facilitate or exploit trafficking in women and girls, including for sexual exploitation, and to raise the awareness of such personnel of the potential risks to victims of conflict and other emergency situations, including natural disasters, of being trafficked;

26. *Invites* States parties to the Convention on the Elimination of All Forms of Discrimination against Women, the Convention on the Rights of the Child and the International Covenants on Human Rights to include information and statistics on trafficking in women and girls as part of their national reports to their respective committees and to work towards developing a common methodology and statistics to obtain comparable data;

27. *Requests* the Secretary-General to submit to the General Assembly at its sixty-fifth session a report that compiles successful interventions and strategies, as well as the gaps, in addressing the gender dimensions of the problem of trafficking in persons, and provides recommendations on the strengthening of gender- and age-sensitive approaches within the various aspects of efforts to address trafficking in persons.

Women in Afghanistan

In response to Economic and Social Council resolution 2006/7 [YUN 2006, p. 1346], the Secretary-General incorporated a gender perspective into his reports on the situation in Afghanistan (see p. 354). In his March report [A/62/722-S/2008/159], the Secretary-General said that tangible improvement in the status of women remained a challenge, despite numerous Government policies and programmes addressing gender issues. Implementation of the National Action Plan for the Women of Afghanistan had begun through pilot projects; progress on women's economic advancement was achieved, with women constituting 66 per cent of microfinance borrowers and 38 per cent of the participants in the National Skills Development Programme; and the Independent Administrative Reform and Civil Service Commission adopted a gender equity policy to strengthen women's participation in the civil service. Nonetheless, violence and harmful practices against women and girls remained a concern. In 2007, the United Nations Assistance Mission in Afghanistan received over 2,000 complaints of gender-based violence. A special fund for the protection of women at risk was established by UNIFEM with support from the Office of the United Nations High Commissioner for Refugees.

Progress reported in September [A/63/372-S/2008/617] included the adoption of the National Action Plan by the Cabinet in May and the commitment of both the Government and the international community to support its implementation. With the aim of capacity-building in the area of gender integration, the UNDP Gender Equality Project was active in seven ministries. Still, sexual and gender-based violence against women and children was common. In the justice system, the criminalization of women who had been victims of gender-based violence and gender discrimination in the application of customary law continued to be a concern. Two convicted perpetrators of a 2005 gang rape in Sar-i-Pul were released in May, allegedly as a result of corruption in the justice system. The high incidence of sexual assault was denounced by the President and the Ministry of the Interior in August, and initiatives by UN agencies and programmes along with the corresponding ministries and civil society groups had increased the visibility of serious violations of women's rights.

Palestinian women

In response to Economic and Social Council resolution 2007/7 [YUN 2007, p. 460], the Secretary-General reported [E/CN.6/2008/6] to the Commission on the Status of Women on the situation of and assistance to Palestinian women during the period from October 2006 to September 2007 (see p. 514).

On 23 July, the Council took action on the situation of and assistance to Palestinian women in **resolution 2008/11** (see p. 514).

The girl child

Forced marriage of the girl child

In response to Commission on the Status of Women resolution 51/3 [YUN 2007, p. 1171], the Secretary-General submitted a report [E/CN.6/2008/4] on forced marriage of the girl child, which reviewed consideration of the issue at the international level and the evolving approach for addressing it, as well as information on legal and policy measures implemented by 32 States and activities undertaken by nine UN system entities. Legislative action taken by States included establishing: a minimum legal age for marriage; laws requiring the free and full consent of the intending spouses; and procedures pertaining to birth and marriage registration, which facilitated monitoring of the age of marriage and supported implementation of laws protecting the girl child from forced marriage. A number of UN entities focused on the promotion and protection of the rights of girls. Efforts from the United Nations Children's Fund (UNICEF), the World Bank and the United Nations Educational, Scientific and Cultural Organization (UNESCO) in the field of education contributed to delaying the marriage of girls and young women, thereby enhancing their capacity to claim their rights. UNICEF issued a publication entitled *Early Marriage: A Harmful Traditional Practice: A Statistical Exploration*, which analysed the effects of and life-cycle characteristics of child marriage.

The Secretary-General observed that while many States had established policies and legislation to address the issue, forced marriage of the girl child persisted. Challenges included limited compliance with the legislation, insufficient resources for monitoring and enforcing laws and procedures, and lack of knowledge about the scope and prevalence of the practice. He made recommendations for States to establish strategies aimed at changing discriminatory social and cultural patterns of conduct and creating a supportive environment for girls and young women to exercise their rights, and to ensure that there was awareness among the general public, especially girls and young women, of their marriage rights. He urged States to strengthen training and capacity-building measures for government officials, community leaders and other professionals likely to come into contact with victims of forced marriage; establish measures of protection and support for victims of forced marriage, including access to safe shelters, counselling and legal aid; implement legislation placing a minimum age on marriage for boys and girls; consider enacting a specific provision in the penal code on forced marriage with adequate penalties; and ratify international instruments protecting the rights of women and girls. Attention should also be given to ensuring reintegration, after armed conflicts, of the girl child, particularly those who had been subjected to forced marriage and sexual exploitation, as well as to enhancing the knowledge base on forced marriage and on practices for preventing such marriages.

In March [E/2008/27 (dec. 52/102)], the Commission took note of the Secretary-General's report.

UN machinery

Convention on the elimination of discrimination against women

As at 31 December, 185 States were parties to the 1979 Convention on the Elimination of All Forms of Discrimination against Women, adopted by the General Assembly in resolution 34/180 [YUN 1979, p. 895]. During the year, Azerbaijan and Cuba acceded to the Convention. At year's end, 53 States had accepted the amendment to article 20, paragraph 1, of the Convention in respect of the meeting time of the Committee on the Elimination of Discrimination against Women, which was adopted by States parties in 1995 [YUN 1995, p. 1178]. The amendment would enter into force when accepted by a two-thirds majority of States parties.

The Optional Protocol to the Convention, adopted by the Assembly in resolution 54/4 [YUN 1999, p. 1100] and which entered into force in 2000 [YUN 2000, p. 1123], had 96 States parties as at 31 December.

CEDAW

In 2008, the Committee on the Elimination of Discrimination against Women (CEDAW), established in 1982 [YUN 1982, p. 1149] to monitor compliance with the 1979 Convention, held three regular sessions in New York [A/63/38 & A/64/38].

At its fortieth session (14 January–1 February), CEDAW reviewed the initial or periodic reports of Bolivia, Burundi, France, Lebanon, Luxembourg, Morocco, Saudi Arabia and Sweden on measures taken to implement the Convention. CEDAW considered a Secretariat report on ways and means of expediting its work [CEDAW/C/2008/I/4 & Add.1] and a report on the status of submission of reports by States parties under article 18 of the Convention [CEDAW/C/2008/I/2]. Two specialized agencies—the Food and Agriculture Organization of the United Nations (FAO) and UNESCO—had submitted reports in accordance with article 21 of the Convention [CEDAW/C/2008/I/3 & Add.1,3]. The Committee adopted Convention-specific reporting guidelines to be applied in conjunction with the harmonized guidelines on a common core document. Consequently, reports of States parties on implementation of the Convention constituted two parts: a common core document containing information of a general and factual nature, and a document that specifically related to implementation of the Convention [A/63/38 (dec. 40/I)]. As the Committee and independent national human rights institutions shared the common goals of protecting, promoting and fulfilling the human rights of women and girls, the Committee was exploring ways to create further interaction and links with those institutions. It adopted a statement on its relationship with national human rights institutions [A/63/38 (dec. 40/II)], and in line with efforts to harmonize the working methods of the human rights treaty bodies, the Committee decided to change the title of its "Concluding comments" to "Concluding observations" [A/63/38 (dec. 40/III)]. It also decided to request States parties that reported at the fortieth session to present their subsequent two reports as combined reports [A/63/38 (dec. 40/IV)].

At its forty-first session (30 June–18 July), CEDAW reviewed the initial or periodic reports of Finland, Iceland, Lithuania, Nigeria, Slovakia, the United Kingdom, the United Republic of Tanzania and Yemen. The Committee considered a report on the status of submission of reports by States parties under article 18 of the Convention [CEDAW/C/2008/II/2]. It also considered the report on ways and means of expediting its work [CEDAW/C/2008/II/4] and the reports of specialized agencies [CEDAW/C/2008/II/3 & Add.1,2], including the International Labour Organization [CEDAW/C/2008/II/3/Add.4], on the implementation of the Convention in areas that fell within the scope of their activities. On the issue of the compatibility of reservations with the object and purpose of the Convention, the Committee decided that the determination of that issue, and therefore the permissibility of reservations, not only fell within its function in relation to the reporting procedure under article 18 of the Convention, but also in relation to the individual communications and inquiry procedures under the Optional Protocol [A/63/38 (dec. 41/I)]. In other action, the Committee decided to adopt the practice of including titles (subject headings) in its concluding observations [A/63/38 (dec. 41/II)], and to introduce a follow-up procedure whereby it would request, in the concluding observations of its reports, information from individual States parties on steps taken to implement specific recommendations contained in those observations [A/63/38 (dec. 41/III)]. The Committee further decided that requests by States parties to utilize technology, such as video-links, during the presentation of reports and constructive dialogue with the Committee must be submitted well in advance [A/63/38 (dec. 41/IV)].

At its forty-second session (20 October–7 November), CEDAW reviewed the initial or periodic reports of Bahrain, Belgium, Cameroon, Canada, Ecuador, El Salvador, Kyrgyzstan, Madagascar, Mongolia, Myanmar, Portugal, Slovenia and Uruguay. It also considered reports on ways and means of expediting the Committee's work [CEDAW/C/2008/III/4]; the status of submission of reports by States parties under article 18 of the Convention [CEDAW/C/2008/III/2]; and on implementation of article 21 of the Convention by specialized agencies [CEDAW/C/2008/III/3 & Add.1,2]. On the issue of migrant women, the Committee decided to adopt general recommendation No. 26, on some categories of women migrant workers who might be at risk of abuse and discrimination [A/64/38 (dec. 42/I)]. That recommendation intended to contribute to the fulfilment of the obligations of States parties to respect, protect and fulfil the human rights of women migrant workers, alongside the legal obligations contained in other treaties, the commitments assumed under plans of action of world conferences and the work of migration-focused treaty bodies. The Committee also adopted a statement on the commemoration of the sixtieth anniversary of the adoption of the Universal Declaration of Human Rights [A/64/38 (dec. 42/II)] (see p. 726).

In other action, the Committee, in respect of issues arising under article 2 of the Optional Protocol, decided to discontinue the examination of communications 9/2005, 14/2007 and 16/2007; endorsed the reports of the Working Group on Communications under the Optional Protocol on its eleventh, twelfth and thirteenth sessions (annexed to the reports); and adopted a note on the formulation and format of individual opinions on Committee decisions. The Committee took action on communication 15/2007, deciding that it was inadmissible under article 4, paragraph 1, of the Optional Protocol on the basis that all available domestic remedies had not yet been exhausted; a dissenting opinion was included with that decision. CEDAW also adopted a report on the follow-up to its views on individual communications.

On 25 July, by **decision 2008/256**, the Economic and Social Council took note of the Secretariat's note [E/2008/91] on the results of the fortieth session of CEDAW.

Commission on the Status of Women

The Commission on the Status of Women, at its fifty-second session (New York, 25 February–7 March and 13 March) [E/2008/27] recommended to the Economic and Social Council the adoption of a draft resolution on the situation of and assistance to Palestinian women (see p. 514), as well as a draft decision on the report of the Commission's fifty-second session and the provisional agenda and documentation for its fifty-third (2009) session (see below). The Commission also adopted and brought to the Council's attention resolutions on the release of women and children taken hostage, including those subsequently imprisoned, in armed conflicts; women, the girl child and HIV/AIDS; ending female genital mutilation; strengthening of the International Research and Training Institute for the Advancement of Women; and its agreed conclusions on financing gender equality and the empowerment of women, which was also the priority theme of the session. It further adopted and brought to the Council's attention decisions on the future work of the Working Group on Communications [dec. 52/101] and on documents before the Commission, of which it took note [dec. 52/102]. Among those documents were the UNIFEM report on its activities to eliminate violence against women [A/HRC/7/53-E/CN.6/2008/9] and the joint work plan of the Division for the Advancement of Women and OHCHR [A/HRC/7/52-E/CN.6/2008/8]. By **decision 2008/236** of 23 July, the Economic and

Social Council took note of the Commission's report on its fifty-second session and approved the provisional agenda for its fifty-third (2009) session.

Communication. In a letter to the Commission dated 3 December [E/CN.6/2009/9], the Council detailed the outcome of its 2008 substantive session and attached a list of resolutions adopted by the Council calling for action by the functional commissions.

Communications on the status of women

Working Group. At a closed meeting in March [E/2008/27], the Commission considered the report of the Working Group on Communications on the Status of Women, established in 1993 [YUN 1993, p. 1050], which considered 21 confidential communications received by the Division for the Advancement of Women. No non-confidential communications were received. The Group noted that Governments had replied to five of the 21 communications received by the Division. One Government had sent a reply to a communication on the previous year's list of confidential communications and replies by Governments. The Group discerned that communications were most frequently submitted on sexual violence against women, including rape and gang rape against women and girls, committed by private individuals, law enforcement personnel, military personnel and paramilitaries, including in armed conflict and related situations, as well as on the failure by the State to prevent such violations, provide adequate protection and medical and psychological care to victims, bring perpetrators to justice and provide adequate compensation; other forms of violence against women and girls, with a lack of due diligence by States to adequately investigate, prosecute and punish the perpetrators; abuse of power, impunity, bribery and corruption, lack of due process, arbitrary detention, and failure to grant a fair trial; trafficking in women, inhumane treatment in detention and inadequate conditions of imprisonment for women; the impact of armed conflict and situations of insecurity, in particular on women and girls belonging to vulnerable groups, such as elderly women, indigenous women, rural women and women with disabilities and the failure of States to abide by international humanitarian law as well as international human rights law and to protect and assist them; serious violations of the human rights of women and girls, including torture, killings and extrajudicial executions; physical and psychological threats and pressuring of victims of violence, their families and witnesses by Government officials in order to force retraction of complaints or testimony; differential application of punishments in law based on sex, including cruel, inhuman or degrading forms of punishment; and impact of legislation and practices discriminating against women in the areas of civil and political rights, procedural guarantees and personal status, including religious and minority status, as well as equal recognition before the law.

The Working Group expressed its concern about rape and other forms of sexual violence against women and girls; the mistreatment of women human rights defenders; the climate of impunity, the abuse of power and corruption in many cases where violence against women, especially sexual violence, was perpetrated or condoned by law enforcement personnel and military personnel; the failure by States to exercise due diligence to prevent acts of violence against women, in particular girls, and adequately investigate such crimes and punish perpetrators; and the continued existence of legislation or practices intended to discriminate, or with the effect of discriminating against women, despite States' international obligations and commitments and constitutional provisions to outlaw such discrimination.

From the replies received, the Working Group noted that some Governments had improved services provided to women, carried out awareness-raising activities, enacted new legislation and taken other steps to promote gender equality and the advancement of women.

UN Development Fund for Women (UNIFEM)

During 2008 [A/64/164], the activities of the United Nations Development Fund for Women (UNIFEM) continued to focus on four key goals: enhancing women's economic security and rights; ending violence against women; reducing the prevalence of HIV/AIDS among women and girls; and advancing gender justice in democratic governance, which were guided by its 2008–2011 strategic plan, approved by the UNDP/UNFPA Executive board in 2007 [YUN 2007, p. 1195]. The strategic plan was comprised of elements of the UNIFEM accountability framework, against which UNIFEM measured its contributions to progress on gender equality at the national, regional and global levels; performance, on the basis of the outputs and corresponding indicators in its development results framework; and progress towards mobilizing, allocating and expending the financial resources required to implement its programme, as laid out in its integrated resources framework.

Over the 2008–2011 period, UNIFEM contributed to enhancing women's economic and security rights in 71 countries; ending violence against women by giving support in aligning national and local laws, policies and programmes in 56 countries; and supporting gender-responsive budgeting in 45 countries. UNIFEM worked with national AIDS councils to advocate for gender-sensitive responses to the HIV/AIDS pandemic in 13 countries. It also aided the advancement of gender justice in democratic governance in 70 countries, including by supporting the passage of 15 laws and 13 policies to strengthen women's participation in democratic governance. Despite progress achieved, gaps and challenges were also identified, such as the absence of agreed standards on what constituted a national development strategy or plan that was fully aligned with gender equality, which made it difficult to assess the extent of results generated. Programme guidance was needed to strengthen public-sector reform efforts, and UNIFEM needed to invest in a rigorous, systematic evaluation of successful strategies to prevent, respond to and end impunity for violence against women. Two events that would help address the deficit in women's participation in peace processes over the next year were the Secretary-General's report on implementation of resolution 1820(2008) (see p. 1265) and the forthcoming tenth anniversary of resolution 1325(2000) [YUN 2000, p. 1113]. UNIFEM was building partnerships and capacities to make the most of those opportunities.

On the management results framework, while demand exceeded its ability to respond, UNIFEM was able to respond to requests for programming and technical support in 82 countries. UNIFEM support aligned with national development priorities and the overall programme framework of the UN country teams, yet the range of support UNIFEM provided varied. In 42 of those countries, UNIFEM supported a relatively small programme, while in 40 countries it supported multidimensional strategies with a broad range of partners and focused on contributing to a range of interlinked outcomes related to national development priorities. There was a need for enhanced systems and knowledge for improving performance in a number of areas.

In 2008, UNIFEM increased its total contributions by 18 per cent, with total resources received amounting to $121 million, including regular (core) resources of $51 million and $5 million in contributions to UNIFEM trust funds. During the year, UNIFEM instituted the practice of reporting separately on the UNIFEM-administered UN Trust Fund in Support of Actions to Eliminate Violence Against Women, which received $18.3 million (compared with $15.9 million the previous year). The number of countries that contributed to regular and other UNIFEM resources increased from 49 in 2007 to 80 in 2008. Contributions from UNIFEM national committees increased in 2008 by 191 per cent over 2007. Expenditure of regular resources in 2008 amounted to $42.3 million, representing an increase of $20.9 million—almost double the expenditure and delivery of the previous year.

In August [A/63/205], the Secretary-General transmitted to the General Assembly a report on UNIFEM activities in 2007 [YUN 2007, p. 1193], of which the Assembly took note on 19 December in **resolution 63/232** (see p. 962).

UNDP/UNFPA Board action. In January, the UNDP/UNFPA Executive Board [E/2008/35 (dec. 2008/2)] took note of the functions, management results, indicators and resource requirements in the estimated budget for the 2008–2009 biennium [DP/2008/4]; approved gross appropriations in the amount of $23,044,000; decided that future biennial support budgets should aim at progressive decrease as a proportion of overall resources; and requested that the UNIFEM Executive Director continue to harmonize and improve the methodology of results-based budgeting. The Board also took note of the Administrator's report on the UNIFEM cost-recovery policy [DP/2008/11] and requested the UNIFEM management to report, at the annual session, on the implementation of the cost-recovery policy [E/2008/35 (dec. 2008/3)].

In June [E/2008/35 (dec. 2008/23)], the Board took note of the annual report of the UNIFEM Executive Director [DP/2008/35]; requested UNIFEM to avoid using core resources to cover costs related to the management of extrabudgetary resources; and decided that a recovery rate of 7 per cent be adopted for the recovery of indirect support costs and for new third-party contributions and a rate of 5 per cent on programme country cost-sharing contributions. The Board also urged UNIFEM to continue harmonizing its cost classification and cost-recovery policy with other UN funds and programmes.

International Research and Training Institute (INSTRAW)

The Executive Board of INSTRAW, at its fifth session (New York, 21 February–22 May) [E/2008/73], considered the implementation of the programme of work during the period October 2007–April 2008; the implementation of the INSTRAW networking strategy for the period October 2007–February 2008; activities undertaken in the implementation of the Institute's action plan—fund-raising strategy, advocacy and image enhancement 2008–2009 during the period February–April 2008; the Institute's staffing situation; the proposed workplan and operational budget for 2009; and the directorship of the Institute.

The Executive Board adopted a decision that requested the Secretary-General to continue providing administrative assistance and support to the Institute through several measures; ensure continuity in the Institute's directorship; and seek the possibility of upgrading the position of Social Affairs Officer. It also requested the Director to intensify coordination with stakeholders and continue with fund-raising efforts. The Board instructed the Institute to implement its work programme in accordance with the Institute's Strategic Framework for the period 2008–2011; approved the workplan and operational budget for 2009 on the understanding that sufficient funds would be available to finance the activities; and compiled a shortlist of candidates for the post of Director, to be submitted to the Secretary-General as stipulated in the statute of the Institute. It took note of the Institute's networking strategy for 2008–2009, the work undertaken by the Institute in implementing its programme of work during the period October 2007–April 2008, and the progress made in the implementation of the action plan. The Board made several recommendations, which included expanding the Institution's outreach to other gender mechanisms at the regional and international levels, expanding collaborations with other UN entities and international organizations, increasing its partnerships and networking activities, proceeding with implementation of the Institute's new accounting and financial system, and pursuing fund-raising activities and undertaking capacity-building activities.

On 25 July, the Economic and Social Council took note of the report of the INSTRAW Executive Board (**decision 2008/256**).

Future of INSTRAW

In response to Economic and Social Council resolution 2007/37 [YUN 2007, p. 1198], the Secretary-General submitted a report [E/2008/62] on future work to strengthen INSTRAW, which summarized the Institute's efforts to strengthen and expand its training and research activities in the following areas: gender, migration and development; governance and women's political participation at the local level; and gender, peace and security, in accordance with its strategic frameworks for 2004–2007 and 2008–2011. The report also described INSTRAW efforts to mobilize resources for its core budget from donors, which resulted in the raising of sufficient funds to finance its activities and reimburse the subvention allocated from the UN budget earlier in the year.

The report concluded that the successful completion of the 2004–2007 strategic framework positioned the Institute to contribute to the goals set out in the three pillars of the United Nations: development, peace and security, and human rights. The strategic framework for 2008–2011 would carry forward the priorities established in 2004—to consolidate the Institute's research and training programmes and enhance its knowledge management capacity to ensure that research results had a concrete impact on policy and programme development and implementation.

GENERAL ASSEMBLY ACTION

On 18 December [meeting 70], the General Assembly, on the recommendation of the Third Committee [A/63/425], adopted **resolution 63/157** without vote [agenda item 56].

Future operation of the International Research and Training Institute for the Advancement of Women

The General Assembly,

Recalling all of its previous resolutions on the situation of the International Research and Training Institute for the Advancement of Women, in particular resolution 60/229 of 23 December 2005,

Recalling also its resolution 62/208 of 19 December 2007 on the triennial comprehensive policy review of operational activities for development of the United Nations system,

Acknowledging its resolution 62/277 of 15 September 2008, in particular its gender-specific provisions, and in this context encouraging the ongoing work on gender equality and the empowerment of women,

Recalling Economic and Social Council resolution 2007/37 of 27 July 2007, in which the Council reaffirmed the specific mandate of the Institute to conduct research and training for gender equality and the empowerment of women as a central focal point for research and training on gender issues within the United Nations system,

Taking into account Commission on the Status of Women resolution 52/3 of 7 March 2008 entitled "Strengthening of the International Research and Training Institute for the Advancement of Women",

Welcoming the contributions of the Institute to the achievement of the Millennium Development Goals, the implementation of the Convention on the Elimination of All Forms of Discrimination against Women and the implementation of the Beijing Declaration and Platform for Action and the outcome document of the twenty-third special session of the General Assembly,

Taking note with appreciation of the progress report on the Institute by its Director with respect to the implementation of the programme of work for the period from 15 May to 30 September 2008, which measures progress through the utilization of indicators of achievement as established in the revised workplan for 2008,

Welcoming the approval by the Executive Board of the Institute of the revised workplan for 2008 and its endorsement of the operational budget for 2008,

Acknowledging the contributions of the Institute in promoting gender equality and the empowerment of women in the areas of security, international migration, in particular remittances and development, and governance and political participation,

Recognizing the contribution of the Institute to the ongoing efforts in gender mainstreaming through its research and training outputs involving national gender machineries, academic institutes, regional intergovernmental organizations, non-governmental organizations and the private sector,

Reaffirming the importance of seeking medium-term sustainable financial resources for the Institute,

Welcoming the activities undertaken by the Director of the Institute to actively promote a fund-raising strategy for the Institute,

Expressing its satisfaction with the progress of the Institute in the area of resource mobilization, which has enabled the Institute to fully reimburse the amount committed by the Secretary-General on an exceptional basis from the United Nations regular budget, and recognizing the improved financial standing of the Institute,

Recognizing that the implementation of the programme of work and strategic plan of the Institute will contribute to a comprehensive discussion on international migration and development from a gender perspective,

1. *Requests* the International Research and Training Institute for the Advancement of Women, in accordance with its mandate, to coordinate further its activities and to develop its programme of work in collaboration with other relevant United Nations entities, such as the United Nations Development Fund for Women, the Office of the Special Adviser on Gender Issues and Advancement of Women, the Division for the Advancement of Women of the Department of Economic and Social Affairs of the Secretariat, the Commission on the Status of Women, the Women's Human Rights and Gender Unit in the Office of the United Nations High Commissioner for Human Rights and the Committee on the Elimination of Discrimination against Women, and calls upon those entities to continue their collaborative efforts;

2. *Also requests* the Institute, in accordance with its mandate, to collaborate with the United Nations system, national machinery, non-governmental organizations and the private sector in promoting international cooperation to foster the empowerment of women and gender equality, including through the promotion of better access to education for women and girls and the mainstreaming of a gender perspective in all policies and programmes;

3. *Further requests* the Institute, in accordance with its mandate and in close coordination with the United Nations Population Fund, the United Nations Children's Fund and other relevant United Nations programmes and funds, to actively participate in and contribute to discussions on issues related to international migration and development;

4. *Invites* the Institute to continue, in close cooperation with other relevant United Nations bodies, to promote and undertake research and training programmes on gender mainstreaming, in the context of the Millennium Development Goals, the implementation of the Convention on the Elimination of All Forms of Discrimination against Women and the Beijing Declaration and Platform for Action, as well as the commitments made at the twenty-third special session of the General Assembly;

5. *Requests* the Institute, within its mandate, to continue to assist countries in promoting and supporting the political participation and economic and social advancement of women through training programmes;

6. *Stresses* the critical importance of voluntary financial contributions by Member States to the United Nations Trust Fund for the International Research and Training Institute for the Advancement of Women to enable it to carry out its mandate, and invites Member States to make voluntary contributions to the Trust Fund;

7. *Calls for* the diversification of funding resources, and in this regard invites Member States to continue to provide assistance and support to the Institute through voluntary contributions and substantive involvement in its projects and activities;

8. *Looks forward* to the enhanced implementation of the strategic plan of the Institute under the leadership of the new Director, to be appointed shortly by the Secretary-General;

9. *Requests* the Secretary-General to continue to provide, within existing resources, appropriate administrative assistance and support to the Institute, in accordance with the provisions of the statute of the Institute, including by enhancing coordination among the Institute and the Department of Economic and Social Affairs and the Department of Management of the Secretariat, in order to ensure that the objectives of the strategic plan, including resource mobilization efforts, are effectively and efficiently carried out;

10. *Also requests* the Secretary-General to include information on the implementation of the present resolution in his report to be submitted to the Economic and Social Council at its substantive session of 2009 through the Commission on the Status of Women at its fifty-third session, and to submit his report to the General Assembly at its sixty-fourth session.

Chapter XI

Children, youth and ageing persons

In 2008, the United Nations Children's Fund (UNICEF) continued its work to ensure that every child received the best possible start in life; was fully immunized and protected from disease, including HIV/AIDS, and disability; had access to a quality primary school education; and was protected from violence, abuse, exploitation and discrimination.

Progress was achieved in realizing the commitments set out in "A world fit for children", the final document of the twenty-seventh special session of the General Assembly on children, held in 2002. Many countries had incorporated the commitments into their planning by developing plans of action for children's issues.

UNICEF continued its focus on five areas for 2006–2009: young child survival and development; basic education and gender equality; HIV/AIDS and children; child protection from violence, exploitation and abuse; and policy advocacy and partnerships for children's rights. In 2008, UNICEF cooperated with 155 countries and responded to emergencies in 78 countries.

Progress and constraints with respect to the well-being of youth and their role in society were recorded in implementing the 1995 World Programme of Action for Youth to the Year 2000 and Beyond.

The United Nations continued its action to implement the 2002 Madrid International Plan Action on Ageing. In February, the Commission for Social Development completed the first review and appraisal of the International Plan. In July, the Secretary-General provided the outline of a strategic implementation framework for the Plan. In December, the Assembly encouraged Governments to build capacity to eradicate poverty among older persons by integrating ageing issues into poverty eradication strategies and national development plans. The Assembly also stressed the need for additional national capacity-building.

Children

Follow-up to 2002 General Assembly special session on children

In his sixth report [A/63/308] on the follow-up to the General Assembly's twenty-seventh (2002) special session on children [YUN 2002, p. 1168], submitted in response to Assembly resolution 58/282 [YUN 2004, p. 1175], the Secretary-General reviewed progress achieved in realizing the commitments relating to children and young people set out in the Declaration and Plan of Action contained in the session's final document entitled "A world fit for children", adopted in resolution S-27/2 [YUN 2002, p. 1169]. Those commitments focused on promoting healthy lives; providing quality education; protecting against abuse, exploitation and violence; and combating HIV/AIDS.

Progress had been achieved in promoting healthy lives and in other health-related goals, but not at the required pace, said the Secretary-General. Child mortality was declining globally, but the proportion of fully immunized children was far from the 2010 target of 90 per cent set at the 2002 special session. There were concerns about several other child health issues such as diarrhoeal diseases and undernutrition. The number of deaths due to measles had continued to fall, and sub-Saharan Africa had achieved the UN goal of cutting measles deaths by 90 per cent well before the target date of 2010. Advances had been made in eliminating maternal and neonatal tetanus. Vaccination coverage through at least two doses of tetanus toxoid vaccine or tetanus-diphtheria toxoid vaccine was estimated at 69 per cent in 2006, while an estimated 81 per cent of newborns were protected against neonatal tetanus through immunization—up from 79 per cent in 2005. Coverage rates increased in a number of countries through routine immunization systems and campaigns.

About half of all countries had early childhood care and education programmes for children under three. Sub-Saharan Africa had made significant progress in expanding primary school enrolment. Some 91 developing countries had achieved gender parity in primary enrolment. Yet some 50 million girls were still not attending primary school, of whom nearly three quarters belonged to excluded groups. Girls continued to be excluded from education more often than boys. In most developing countries, girls continued to face discrimination with regard to access to school. As a result, they comprised about 57 per cent of all out-of-school children. As many countries had limited capacity for the provision of education beyond the primary level, it was estimated that 185 million children of secondary school age were missing out on secondary education, and that 127 million of them were still attending primary school.

As for improvements in child protection since the special session, nearly 60 countries had produced national child labour statistics, and special efforts were being made to collect data on children engaged in hazardous work. A total of 29 countries had collected data on child discipline, and 27 on female genital mutilation/cutting, by the end of 2007. Many countries were strengthening their overall child protection capacities, including legislative and enforcement systems. There was a growing understanding of the significance of systematic approaches to protection, primarily through legal and social welfare systems and through addressing social norms. Progress had been considerable in data gathering, birth registration and reduction of child labour, and many countries were implementing plans to address violence against children. However, despite those successes, challenges persisted in protecting children against abuse, exploitation and violence. Sub-Saharan Africa had the highest proportion of children under five who were not registered at birth—two out of three. The largest number of unregistered children was in South Asia—nearly 23 million. National child protection capacities remained weak overall, and funding was inconsistent and unpredictable.

Progress continued to be made towards the goals of the special session relating to HIV and children, albeit at a pace slower than desired. Globally, children under the age of 15 accounted for 2.1 million of the estimated 33.2 million people living with HIV in 2007. Some 420,000 children were newly infected with HIV, and 290,000 had died of AIDS in 2007 alone. Sub-Saharan Africa was home to nearly 90 per cent of all children living with HIV. There had been progress in combating the HIV pandemic since the special session. By the end of 2006, 21 low- and middle-income countries were on track to meet the 80 per cent antiretroviral coverage target for prevention of mother-to-child transmission of HIV by 2010. There was also progress in many countries in the protection and care of children affected by AIDS and in access for those children to social services.

Many challenges remained, including inadequate attention to the rights of children in the most vulnerable and marginalized sections of society. Emergencies resulting from both man-made and natural causes posed huge constraints on the achievement of international development goals. Measures to ensure and coordinate disaster prevention as well as rapid humanitarian response and reconstruction needed to be expedited.

Measures suggested by the Secretary-General included the implementation of high-impact interventions, as well as sustained efforts for developing education and health care systems. Filling funding gaps required attention by Governments and the international community. Recent advancements in resource mobilization, such as for combating HIV, indicated the importance of the timely provision of resources for achieving the goals of the special session. At the same time, a renewed focus on communication for development should be pursued. The journey to 2010 and 2015, the years in which most targets for children converged, would be demanding. Achieving the goals would require a greater sense of urgency to address surmountable obstacles.

The Secretary-General noted that failure to achieve the goals adopted at the special session on children would undermine efforts towards realizing the aspirations of the Millennium Declaration. He called for scaled-up responses by Governments, increased commitments from the international community and broader and more focused partnerships to achieve the goals of the special session.

General Assembly action. Taking note of the Secretary-General's report, the General Assembly, in **resolution 63/241** (see p. 739), called upon States to create an environment in which the well-being of the child was ensured, including by strengthening international cooperation. By **resolution 63/113** (see p. 1215), the Assembly invited States to expand their activities in the framework of the International Decade for a Culture of Peace and Non-violence for the Children of the World, 2001–2010 [YUN 2001, p. 609].

United Nations Children's Fund

In 2008, UNICEF remained committed to achieving the Millennium Development Goals (MDGs) [YUN 2000, p. 51] and the goals contained in the document "A world fit for children", adopted by the General Assembly in resolution S-27/2 [YUN 2002, p. 1169], at its twenty-seventh (2002) special session on children (see above). UNICEF's work was also guided by the 1989 Convention on the Rights of the Child, adopted by the Assembly in resolution 44/25 [YUN 1989, p. 560], and its Optional Protocols (see p. 737). Its mission was to defend children's rights, help meet their basic needs, ensure their survival and increase their opportunities to flourish. It was also mandated to rally political will and resources to invest in children's well-being; respond to emergencies to protect children; work with partners to provide a rapid response for those in need; and ensure special protection for the most disadvantaged children, such as victims of war, disasters, extreme poverty, violence and exploitation and those with disabilities. The Fund further aimed to promote equal rights for women and girls and encourage their full participation in developing their communities, and work towards the human development goals adopted by the world community.

In line with its 2006–2009 medium-term strategic plan (MTSP) [YUN 2005, p. 1284], UNICEF continued to focus its work on five priorities—young child survival and development; basic education and gender equality; HIV/AIDS and children; child protection from violence, exploitation and abuse; and policy advocacy and partnerships for children's rights.

The annual UNICEF flagship publication, *The State of the World's Children 2008* [Sales No. E.08.XX.1], focused on child survival, observing that child mortality was a sensitive indicator of a country's development. Investing in the health of children and their mothers was not only a human rights imperative: it was a sound economic decision and one of the surest ways for a country to set its course towards a better future. Thus, it was central in achieving MDG 4, which sought to reduce the global under-five mortality rate by two thirds between 1990 and 2015. Examining the survival rates and health of children, the report outlined what needed to be done to reduce the number of child death from 9.7 million in 2006 to around 4 million by 2015. That would require accelerated action on multiple fronts: reducing poverty and hunger; improving maternal health; combating HIV/AIDS, malaria and other major diseases; increasing the usage of improved water and sanitation; and providing affordable essential drugs on a sustainable basis. It would also require a re-examination of strategies to reach the poorest, most marginalized communities.

In 2008, UNICEF cooperated with 155 countries, areas and territories: 44 in sub-Saharan Africa, 35 in America and the Caribbean, 35 in Asia, 20 in the Middle East and 21 in Central and Eastern Europe and the Commonwealth of Independent States.

Total expenditures were $3,081 million in 2008, an 11 per cent increase from $2,782 million in 2007. Expenditures on programme assistance rose from $2,517 million in 2007 to $2,808 million in 2008, an increase of 12 per cent. Combined expenditures on programme support at $167 million, management and administration at $74 million, and centrally shared cost at $10 million, amounted to $251 million, an increase of $1 million or 0.4 per cent compared to 2007. UNICEF operations in 2008 were described in the *UNICEF Annual Report 2008*, the UNICEF annual report to the Economic and Social Council [E/2009/6] and the annual report of the Executive Director on progress and achievements against the Fund's extended 2006–2013 MTSP [E/ICEF/2009/9 & Corr.1].

In 2008, the UNICEF Executive Board held its first regular session (29 January–1 February), its annual session (3–5 June) and its second regular session (15–18 September), all in New York [E/2008/34/Rev.1], during which it adopted 23 decisions.

By **decision 2008/215** of 18 July, the Economic and Social Council took note of the annual report of UNICEF to the Council covering the year 2007 [E/2008/6 & Corr.1]; the Board's report on the work of its first regular session of 2008 and on the joint meeting of the Executive Boards of UNICEF, United Nations Development Programme (UNDP)/United Nations Population Fund (UNFPA) and World Food Programme (WFP) [E/2008/34/Rev.1]; and the extract from the Board's report on its 2008 annual session [E/2008/L.8].

On 18 September, the Executive Board adopted the programme of work for its 2009 sessions [E/2008/34/Rev.1 (dec. 2008/13)].

Programme policies

In her annual report to the Economic and Social Council covering 2008 [E/2009/6], the Executive Director described action taken by UNICEF to promote child rights and ensure that sustainable results for children were achieved in close partnership with Governments, the UN system and non-governmental organization (NGOs). The report provided information on funding for operational activities for development of the UN system; contribution to national capacity development and development effectiveness; and improved functioning of the UN development system. It addressed policies and initiatives to foster South-South cooperation, gender equality and the transition from relief to development. The UNICEF action plan in response to the triennial comprehensive policy review (TCPR) of operational activities for development of the UN system [YUN 2007, p. 874] would be periodically reviewed. A senior-level steering committee was overseeing progress in implementing the TCPR recommendations and reported regularly to the Executive Director.

Medium-term strategic plan (2006–2009)

A report of the Executive Director [E/ICEF/2008/18] provided information on the midterm review of the medium-term strategic plan (MTSP) 2006–2009. The review, carried out during the first half of 2008, drew on a wide range of sources, including the latest available data on child-related indicators for the MDGs, information on progress towards MTSP targets, as well as major evaluations undertaken during the reporting period.

Extensive consultations were undertaken on the validity, use and relevance of the MTSP. A questionnaire generated responses from 32 Member States, including 9 Executive Board members and 16 programme countries. A vast majority (90 per cent) of respondents indicated that the MTSP significantly contributed to improving their understanding of UNICEF's work. Most respondents agreed that the MTSP assisted in monitoring the work of the organization and enhanced their understanding of the strategic objectives of UNICEF. A majority (58 per cent) of the 12 national committees that provided feedback indicated that the design of the MTSP helped them communicate UNICEF's work to supporters, partners and the general public. A survey of all UNICEF country offices confirmed the usefulness of the MTSP for working with partners to design, focus and review planned results for children. UNICEF assumed significant responsibilities as the global lead for the nutrition and water, sanitation and hygiene (WASH) clusters and as co-lead for the education and the emergency telecommunications clusters. Water safety plans had been introduced by key countries in Asia, while home drinking water treatment helped contain the spread of cholera in Africa. The *Unite for Children, Unite against AIDS* campaign [YUN 2005, p. 1290] had provided a platform for UNICEF to put children at the centre of the global fight against AIDS. Major areas of progress in basic education and gender equality included standard-setting and policy development for early learning, parent education programmes and the launch of a global child-to-child approach, aimed at providing cost-effective school-readiness interventions for young children. As for collecting and analysing information on the situation of children and women, UNICEF provided data dissemination through the database system DevInfo, used by 103 countries as their national platform for MDG monitoring. The Fund also piloted in several countries EmergencyInfo, a decision-support system for emergency response.

Yet a range of new challenges had become apparent. Capacity for sanitation and hygiene remained weak and sustainability remained a concern. Much remained to be done for vulnerable children and families in building national justice systems, laws and policies; strengthening social norms and values to prevent violence, abuse and exploitation; promoting school readiness; integrating prevention of mother-to-child transmission of HIV and paediatric AIDS treatment into health systems; strengthening HIV/AIDS services in emergencies; and improving the contribution of UNICEF to gender equality.

The report suggested extending the MTSP by two years, to the end of 2011. As explained in a UNICEF background note [E/ICEF/2008/25], such extension would allow the MTSP cycle to be harmonized with the cycles of the strategic plans of UNDP and UNFPA, and would bring the following MTSP (2012–2015) in line with the 2015 deadline for achieving the MDGs.

On 18 September [dec. 2008/14], the Executive Board endorsed the general conclusions of the mid-term review, including the adjustments envisaged for the remaining period and the implications identified for preparing the next plan. Recognizing the benefits of extending the period of the MTSP in order to align it with the strategic planning cycles of UNDP and UNFPA, and align the subsequent UNICEF strategic planning cycle, covering the 2012–2015 period, with the target date for the MDGs, the Board extended the period of the current MTSP by two years, until the end of 2011. The Executive Director was requested to report at the Board's 2010 session on the MTSP performance and results. A discussion on the end-of-cycle review of the extended MTSP would be held at the first regular session of 2011.

On 5 June [dec. 2008/11], the Board took note of the Executive Director's report on progress and achievements against the MTSP, covering 2007 [YUN 2007, p. 1206]. It requested UNICEF to give high priority in the annual report to information and analysis on key challenges in achieving results in each focus area to support progress towards critical goals and targets for children.

MTSP support strategies

At its February session, the Executive Board had before it the UNICEF child protection strategy [E/ICEF/2008/5] for endorsement as the official strategy documents for programmes of protection and for achieving the MDGs within the context of the MTSP. The strategy addressed issues such as building national protection systems, supporting social change, strengthening child protection in conflict and natural disasters and leveraging results through the strategic use of resources.

On 1 February [dec. 2008/1], the Board took note of the draft and acknowledged the need for further consultations.

On 5 June [dec. 2008/12], the Board endorsed the UNICEF child protection strategy [E/ICEF/2008/5/Rev.1] as the support strategy document for programmes and actions in support of child protection, developed for the implementation of the MTSP.

Medium-term financial plan (2008–2011)

In September, the Executive Board considered the planned financial estimates for the period 2008–2011 [E/ICEF/AB/L.5]. The UNICEF secretariat recommended that the Board approve the framework of planned financial estimates for 2008–2011 and the preparation of programme expenditures submitted to the Board of up to $915 million from regular resources in 2009, subject to the availability of resources and the continued validity of those planned financial estimates. The Board was also requested to approve the annual transfer of $30 million to the reserve for after-service health insurance for the period 2010–2011.

The Board approved those recommendations on 18 September [dec. 2008/20].

Global strategy for collaborative relationships and partnerships

In response to a 2007 request [YUN 2007, p. 1208] of the Executive Board, the UNICEF secretariat submitted in June a preliminary concept note [E/ICEF/2008/12 & Corr.1] on a global strategy for collaborative relationships and partnerships. The note outlined the rationale, proposed content and process for developing such a strategy. It noted that UNICEF had been working with partners to improve the lives of children since its inception. Those partnerships were of various kinds: programmatic partnerships to achieve better outcomes for children in programme countries; partnerships in global policy development; partnerships in resource mobilization; and partnerships in advocacy for promoting child rights. UNICEF country programmes of cooperation were implemented with national and local partners. Also important were partnerships and collaborative relationships for resource mobilization at all levels, many of which were forged and maintained at country level. From IKEA in India to the Nakumatt supermarket chain in Kenya, the private sector was making significant social investments to support child survival, protection, education and other areas critical for children. In Latin America and the Caribbean, UNICEF was working with Nickelodeon to use a charismatic cartoon character to inspire positive change in the lives of children. UNICEF also engaged in a wide range of partnerships with humanitarian NGOs to provide critical assistance to children in times of emergencies.

The strategy would help to guide the organization's engagement with others. It would help to address the rapidly evolving external landscape to position UNICEF as a partner of choice to deliver results for children. The guiding principles in developing the strategy would be: ensuring that collaborations and partnerships, individually and collectively, were making the maximum possible contribution to achieving outcomes for children; ensuring that children were consistently at the centre of the national and international socio-economic policy and development agendas; and supporting UNICEF efforts to expand interventions and leverage resources for children.

The report concluded that a consultative process for developing the strategy would be pursued, for discussion at the annual session of the Executive Board in 2009. The strategy would build on the global mandate of UNICEF as well as on the diversity of experience that covered different regional and country levels, and on the range of stakeholders and partners for children.

The Executive Board in June requested UNICEF to hold consultations with the Board in autumn 2008 and spring 2009 to provide updates on progress in developing the strategy and to consult on outstanding issues.

Evaluation system

In response to a 2006 Executive Board decision [YUN 2006, p. 1366], the UNICEF secretariat submitted a report on its evaluation policy [E/ICEF/2008/4] to ensure that UNICEF had timely, strategically focused and objective information on the performance of its policies, programmes and initiatives. The report noted that UNICEF conducted evaluations at five institutional levels, reflecting the organizational accountability framework: local or project, country programme of cooperation, regional, global strategic, and institutional performance. At the global level, evaluation served to assess UNICEF performance against the objectives and targets set in the MTSP. Evaluation was also conducted to analyse the contribution of UNICEF to global strategies in collaboration with key partners, particularly the achievement of the objectives of the Millennium Declaration and MDGs. Regarding the evaluation with partners, UNICEF would need to seize the growing opportunities to participate in multi-partite evaluations, thereby drawing attention to results and impact for children on the evaluation agendas of other organizations. The implementation of the evaluation policy and the evaluation function would be reviewed periodically to draw lessons and make improvements. The first such review would take place in 2010.

On 1 February [dec. 2008/4], the Executive Board approved the evaluation policy as outlined in the report and called upon UNICEF to conduct evaluations of operations at the country level in close consultation with Governments, also assisting them in developing national evaluation capacities. UNICEF should also submit a biennial work plan to the Board and report annually on the evaluation function and evaluation findings and recommendations. The Executive Director was requested to safeguard the integrity and independence of the evaluation function and to submit a review of the evaluation policy at the second regular session in 2009.

In accordance with that decision, the UNICEF secretariat in July submitted a report on its evaluation function and major evaluations in UNICEF [E/ICEF/2008/21], which provided information on the state of evaluation functions in UNICEF at country, regional and global levels and strategic orientations for its strengthening. The report noted that, in 2006–2007, 495 evaluations had been conducted in the five focus areas of MTSP, as well as in other areas.

The UNICEF Evaluation Office provided leadership and management of the evaluation system. The Office, in cooperation with the UNICEF Office of Internal Audit, was developing a new tool—the Programme Performance Assessment—to measure the contribution of country offices to national development and humanitarian efforts. The approach was being developed in a number of pilot countries and would be reviewed after 18 months.

In the context of the 2006–2009 MTSP, UNICEF would strengthen its evaluation function in six main areas: national capacity-building and strengthened national leadership in country-level evaluations; strengthened evaluation within the UN system and with other partners; evaluation in humanitarian crises; evaluations related to MTSP focus areas, strategies and operational effectiveness; strengthened organizational capacity in evaluation; and heightened management attention to the evaluation function.

On 18 September [dec. 2008/22], the Executive Board took note of the report on the evaluation function and major evaluations in UNICEF; noted the steps taken and planned by UNICEF to strengthen evaluation; expressed concern that a key recurrent finding of the internal audit report was UNICEF's weakness in prioritizing evaluation and research activities at field level; and requested UNICEF to report back to the Board in its review of the evaluation policy at the second regular session in 2009 on measures taken to address that finding as well as on additional steps to improve the evaluation function. The UNICEF Evaluation Office was urged to submit to the Board a biennial work plan at its second regular session in 2009.

Concerning the evaluation of gender policy implementation in UNICEF, the Executive Board in June had before it a paper on the topic [E/ICEF/2008/CRP.12]. On 5 June [dec. 2008/10], the Board requested UNICEF to present to the Board at its first regular session of 2009 a management response to all recommendations of the evaluation of gender policy implementation in UNICEF, including actions and timeframes for completion. It also requested UNICEF to ensure and track timely implementation of the evaluation recommendations in accordance with the management response, develop a tracking and monitoring framework to measure progress in implementation, and track and monitor allocations and expenditures for gender equality results. The Board further requested that the annual report of the Executive Director include reporting on progress in achieving gender equality results as an integral element, particularly at the outcome and impact levels.

Emergency assistance

In 2008, UNICEF responded to emergencies in 78 countries. Interventions covered complex emergencies and natural disasters, with continued assistance in chronic crises, from the global rise in food prices to natural disasters in Myanmar and China. The revolving internal Emergency Programme Fund (EPF) loan facility continued to be the fastest, most reliable and flexible funding mechanism available to UNICEF and served as a bridge to other mechanisms. In 2008, $83.3 million in EPF loans was released to help 38 country responses. Emergency preparedness and response planning remained a central strategy to ensure that staff members were ready to implement a UNICEF response in all humanitarian crises. Eighty-seven per cent of country offices and four regional offices updated their plans in 2008. To address the global rise in food prices, UNICEF allocated $55 million in additional funds to 60 countries with high levels of nutrition insecurity to address some of the immediate response.

UNICEF served as global cluster lead in nutrition and in water, sanitation and hygiene, as co-lead in education with the International Save the Children Alliance, and as co-lead in emergency telecommunications with WFP and the United Nations Office for the Coordination of Humanitarian Affairs (OCHA). UNICEF continued to support the provision of clean water, especially in underserved rural areas and among indigenous communities. The sustainability of services was a high priority. UNICEF focused on strengthening local capacities for operation and maintenance, while also emphasizing the protection of water resources, especially in areas facing water stress. UNICEF also supported the expansion of household water treatment and safe storage, particularly in countries where cholera was endemic. Support continued for national efforts to detect arsenic in drinking water and mitigate its impact on children and families in affected parts of Asia, Africa and the Americas. More than 50,000 water sources were tested in 2008.

In north Sudan, Sri Lanka and the Philippines, UNICEF contributed to new agreements on child soldier disarmament, demobilization and reintegration. In countries in transition, it contributed to the social reintegration of demobilized child soldiers. UNICEF continued to collaborate with partners to provide trauma counselling and psychosocial support to help children and their families cope with the long-term impact of armed conflict and natural disasters. Common activities included recreation and play, parent discussion groups, training of community workers and the provision of psychosocial support to specific groups of children. Child-friendly spaces were also commonly used, and a challenge was to ensure that they provided integrated services for children beyond psychosocial support.

UNICEF continued to respond to the humanitarian needs of conflict-affected people in the Democratic Republic of the Congo (DRC) and Sierra Leone, which were among the countries in which UNICEF had supported gender-based violence prevention and response programmes in the areas of medical, psychosocial, legal and socio-economic assistance. It also led the development of an inter-agency training package called "Caring for survivors" and the development of a research study in the DRC on children born of sexual violence in conflict. UNICEF was the co-chair of United Nations Action against Sexual Violence in Conflict [YUN 2007, p. 1157], and co-led with the NGO V-Day an advocacy campaign against rape in the DRC, "Stop raping our greatest resource".

Ending Child Hunger and Undernutrition Initiative

In response to a 2007 request [YUN 2007, p. 1208] of the Executive Board, the UNICEF secretariat submitted in June a report [E/ICEF/2008/11] on the implementation of the Ending Child Hunger and Undernutrition Initiative (ECHUI), an effort to promote sustained actions to address that challenge, based on interventions of proven effectiveness. The report pointed out that 143 million children under the age of five years continued to suffer from undernutrition. Some 51 developing countries, representing nearly half of the countries for which data was available, were not making sufficient progress towards the 'hunger target' of MDG 1 as measured by the prevalence of underweight in children under five years of age. Some 18 of those countries were making no progress at all or were retrogressing in terms of that indicator.

The report noted that maternal and child undernutrition was a contributing cause of more than a third of child deaths and some 10 per cent of global disease burden. While nutrition interventions of proven effectiveness needed to be more widely available to children and families, long-term investments in empowering women, in education and in reducing inequities needed to work in tandem with technical solutions. Nutrition interventions were most effective in the period from pregnancy to two years of age. Although undernutrition occurred widely, four fifths of all undernourished children lived in just 20 countries, with the largest number living in South Asia. Intensified nutrition action in those countries would help to accelerate the achievement of health-related MDGs and greatly contribute to the Goals relating to poverty and hunger reduction, education and gender equality.

The report also noted that ECHUI partners should focus their country support and country-level and global advocacy efforts on four critical areas: increasing coverage of early initiation and continued exclusive breastfeeding; improving micronutrient intakes of mothers and children as well as dietary intake, especially during pregnancy and the first two years of life; preventing and treating severe acute malnutrition through the expanded use of ready-to-use therapeutic foods, such as Plumpy'nut; and reducing rates of diarrhoea by improving hygiene and parasite control.

Regarding monitoring and evaluation, UNICEF would continue to be one of the lead partners in the initiative, while WFP, as part of its partnership contribution, was expected to continue to host the inter-agency team. Given the food price increases, the focus of the initiative would be adjusted to provide more proactive support to national monitoring of and responses to the impact of the food crisis in vulnerable countries and communities.

UNICEF programmes by region

In 2008 [E/ICEF/2009/9 & Corr.1], UNICEF programme assistance expenditure totalled $2,808 million, of which $1,557.9 million (55.5 per cent) went to sub-Saharan Africa; $775.4 million (27.6 per cent) to Asia; $135.0 million (4.8 per cent) to the Middle East and North Africa; $148.5 million (5.3 per cent) to the Americas and the Caribbean; and $105.0 million (3.7 per cent) to interregional programmes.

Programme expenditures were highest in countries with low income and high under-five mortality rates. The 51 low-income countries—defined as those with a per capita gross national income of $935 or less—which had a total child population in 2007 of 595 million, or 30 per cent of all children worldwide, received 57 per cent of programme expenditures. Countries with high under-five mortality rates accounted for 64 per cent of total assistance.

In September [E/2008/34/Rev.1], the Executive Board had before it the summaries of the mid-term reviews and major evaluations of country programmes in Eastern and Southern Africa [E/ICEF/2008/P/L.14], Latin America and the Caribbean [E/ICEF/2008/P/L.15 & Corr.1], East Asia and the Pacific [E/ICEF/2008/P/L.16], and Central and Eastern Europe and the Commonwealth of Independent States [E/ICEF/2008/P/L.17]. The reports reviewed progress made, resources used and constraints faced in country programmes.

Field visits

The visit of members of the Bureau of the Executive Board to the Lao People's Democratic Republic (9–16 February) [E/ICEF/2008/13] sought to gain a first-hand understanding of UNICEF work at the country level and demonstrate concrete examples of UNICEF cooperation with the Government and other partners, including the UN country team. The UNICEF programme of cooperation in the country had five main elements: young child survival and development, water, sanitation and hygiene, basic education, child protection and HIV/AIDS and children. Challenges included limited investment in the social sector, limited human resources capacity, the relatively small number of implementing partners and dependency on official development assistance. Noting the Government policy on resettlement, the delegation highlighted the need to ensure the protection of children's rights in such moves, and recommended that the UN country team and UNICEF monitor how the relocation of communities from remote areas to resettled villages affected children. The delegation noted the sense of rapid change in the country, as well as the growing regionalization, and underlined the importance of giving adequate attention to the possible negative side effects of the increased cross-border movement of persons and goods and services. The delegation invited UNICEF to monitor the situation to determine the possible impact on children, and to continue its advocacy and information work about the possible risks and threats to children and youth and their families.

In a joint visit to Haiti (1–9 March) [DP-FPA/2008/CRP.1-E/ICEF/2008/CRP.11], 20 members of the Executive Boards of UNDP/UNFPA, UNICEF and WFP sought to witness first-hand the operations of the four organizations, including inter-agency collaboration and cooperation. They also sought to gain insight into the contributions the organizations were making to assist Haiti in attaining its national development goals. The delegation found that after four years of crisis, the country was slowly but increasingly gaining in stability and confidence with the help of the United Nations Stabilization Mission in Haiti (MINUSTAH), the UN development system and the international donor community. Given the challenges the country faced, predictable funding was crucial for humanitarian and recovery programmes. Core funding and funding with low levels of earmarking, such as thematic trust funds, remained the most effective and preferred means for delivering UN programmes. The delegation recommended greater international engagement in supporting the Government in promoting decentralization efforts. The UN country team was encouraged to support South-South cooperation initiatives to meet Haiti's development needs.

During a visit to Niger (29 March–4 April) [E/ICEF/2008/15], members of the UNICEF Executive Board observed the UNICEF field operations and the work of the UN country team in order to understand the relationship of the Niger-UNICEF country programme of cooperation to national development priorities, the United Nations Development Assistance Framework (UNDAF) and bilateral development assistance. They observed that like many other least developed countries, Niger faced a critical time as the MDGs target date of 2015 drew closer. The Government recognized the challenges and obstacles facing the country, as well the measures needed to overcome them, but that recognition was not uniformly present at all levels of government. The delegation observed that resource constraints and low level of capacity experienced by Niger amplified the importance of promoting greater coherence, cooperation and collaboration among the members of the UN country team. A full scaling-up of UNICEF programmes would benefit the children of Niger. For resource reasons, the UNICEF-supported multi-sectoral programmatic interventions were carried out only in a handful of communes. It was therefore intended that similar interventions in other communes would be supported by other development partners, while ensuring that the same standards were applied.

UNICEF programmes by sector

In 2008, UNICEF programme expenditures, which were linked to the five organizational priorities established in 2005 under the 2006–2009 MTSP [YUN 2005, p. 1284], totalled $2,808 million [E/ICEF/2009/9 & Corr.1], a 12 per cent increase over 2007. The largest share of expenditure, $1,418.5 million (50.5 per cent), went to young child survival and development, followed by basic education and gender equality ($597.8 million, or 21.3 per cent), child protection from violence, exploitation and abuse ($307.6 million, or 11.0 per cent), policy advocacy and partnerships for children's rights ($267.6 million, or 9.5 per cent) and HIV/AIDS and children ($187.2 million, or 6.7 per cent). Some $29.7 million (1.1 per cent) was expended in other areas. Programme support costs amounted to an additional $167 million.

Programme expenditures increased substantially in 2008 in all five MTSP focus areas compared to 2007. Overall shares in total expenditure remained stable except for a 2 percentage point fall in the share of young child survival and development, due mainly to trends in other resources. The share of HIV/AIDS and children continued to be well below the amount projected when the MTSP was adopted in 2005. Despite the crisis that occurred in world financial markets, UNICEF was able to protect its investment portfolio and produce a healthy return.

Young child survival and development

In 2008, UNICEF continued to work with partners to scale up a package of low-cost, high-impact child survival interventions through support for integrated child health events and routine health services. The number of countries supporting Child Health Days, integrating the delivery of immunization with other interventions, increased to more than 50. Furthermore, 138 countries had introduced the *Haemophilus influenzae* type B vaccine into their infant immunization schedules by the end of 2008. The number of measles deaths worldwide fell from an estimated

750,000 to 197,000 (74 per cent) from 2000 to 2007. The number of deaths from measles in sub-Saharan Africa also declined dramatically, from an estimated 395,000 in 2000 to 45,000 in 2007. Maternal and neonatal tetanus were eliminated in Bangladesh and in two additional states in India in 2008. As a core partner of the Polio Eradication Initiative, UNICEF provided leadership in vaccine procurement in all polio-affected countries. In 2008, more than 2 billion doses of oral polio vaccines were delivered through UNICEF. Wild polio virus transmission continued in the four endemic countries: Afghanistan, India, Nigeria and Pakistan. UNICEF support to polio eradication also included intensified communication designed to increase community demand for vaccination.

Full coverage (two doses) of vitamin A supplementation in the least developed countries had increased to an average of over 80 per cent. That progress was largely due to integrated delivery strategies and improved coverage in hard-to-reach areas. Thirty-two countries, almost half of them in sub-Saharan Africa, had reached the goal of at least 80 per cent coverage. In 2008, UNICEF supplied over 800 million capsules, representing an increase of nearly 31 per cent over 2007.

In its efforts to combat malaria, UNICEF procured about 4 million diagnostic test kits and over 19 million insecticide-treated mosquito nets for 48 countries in 2008. All sub-Saharan African countries with available data had shown good progress in increasing the use of those nets among children under five. With regard to malaria case management, 45 countries in sub-Saharan Africa had changed their treatment policies, with 38 of them implementing the more effective artemisinin-based combination therapies. UNICEF procured 31 million combination therapy treatments; globally, procurement of such treatments increased to around 130 million.

Although progress had been made in preventing mother-to-child transmission of HIV and in paediatric treatment for HIV and AIDS, only 4 per cent of HIV-exposed children began cotrimoxazole prophylaxis within two months of birth. Child Health Days had emerged as the common platform to deliver those interventions and services.

With regard to child survival and development, UNICEF supported targeted complementary feeding programmes for young children, either in selected communities or through integrated campaigns, which resulted in significant increases in local practice of appropriate complementary feeding. It also supported the scaling-up of community-based child nutrition initiatives in several countries. Multiple indicator cluster survey data were used to advocate for increased resources and heightened priority for young child feeding initiatives, including through new national nutrition policies and protocols. Significant progress was achieved in increasing the rate of exclusive breastfeeding. Thirteen countries, including several in sub-Saharan Africa, achieved gains of more than 20 percentage points between 1996 and 2007, using a comprehensive approach to improving infant feeding practices. Worldwide, 71 countries had national legislation or regulatory provisions in force to protect breastfeeding based on the International Code of Marketing of Breastmilk Substitutes. Increased use was being made, with UNICEF support, of evidence-based communication campaigns that featured exclusive breastfeeding along with other key messages. Those were being integrated with programmes addressing HIV in high-prevalence settings.

The number of countries with national programmes that promoted good parenting rose slightly in 2008. The health extension programme of Ethiopia, rolled out with UNICEF support in 2008, included community-based therapeutic feeding centres in over 100 districts. Similar centres and referral systems were established or strengthened in other parts of Africa and Asia.

UNICEF supported WASH activities in 101 countries, including 57 of the 60 countries with both low water and sanitation coverage and high under-five mortality rates. Its cooperation increasingly focused on policies and community efforts for expanding high-impact, cost-effective interventions: hand-washing with soap, sanitation promotion and home drinking-water treatment. Those areas—an essential part of child survival and development strategies—were increasingly integrated with health, nutrition and early childhood interventions. The percentage of programme countries that incorporated into their national development plans measures for achieving the MDGs target on sustainable access to safe drinking water and basic sanitation increased from 58 per cent in 2005 to 73 per cent in 2008.

Under the Core Commitments for Children in Emergencies, revised in 2003 [YUN 2003, p. 1205], UNICEF was a strong contributor to humanitarian reforms, serving as the global cluster lead in nutrition and in water, sanitation and hygiene. Emergencies in Ethiopia and Zimbabwe and large-scale natural disasters, such as the China earthquake and the Myanmar cyclone, received significant funding.

Basic education and gender equality

Progress continued in many countries towards achieving the education- and gender-related MDGs. The progress made in increasing primary school enrolment rates in Africa and Asia was undermined by low retention and completion rates. Too many children started school at a later age than that prescribed for the first grade. Many of them repeated grades. That resulted in a high proportion of over-aged children in primary school and the crowding out of other children. Social exclusion often was a major barrier to education access. Children from disadvantaged and minority populations, as well as working children and children living in remote areas, added to the numbers of those excluded. Girls within those groups often faced a double disadvantage. In 2008, UNICEF supported capacity development of national partners in major areas: improving quality through child-friendly schools; education policy and reform; and education in emergencies, post-conflict and transition.

UNICEF assisted programmes in all regions to reduce disparities in relation to access to, participation in, and completion of quality basic education. The number of countries with national education plans that included measures to reduce gender disparities had increased rapidly, from 58 in 2005 to 87 in 2008. The number of countries with national education plans that included measures to reduce disparities due to poverty, ethnicity and disability also increased significantly, to 110 in 2008 from 74 in 2005. Measures implemented by countries included free public elementary education, provision of free school supplies, and incentives for girls who performed well. UNICEF support to national sector plans included advocacy for human rights-based planning criteria using information on gender and other disparities, and the coordination of funding proposals. UNICEF direct support and contributions to national capacity-building helped to increase girls' enrolment rates significantly in parts of Afghanistan, Burkina Faso, Mozambique and other countries. A study of the UNICEF-supported integrated districts programme in India, reaching 4.6 million households, showed an increase in girls' completion rates from 53 per cent in 2005 to 72 per cent in 2008.

There was strong evidence that investment in early childhood development (ECD) prepared children for school, helped to sustain their performance well into the primary cycle and reduced inequalities. Since 2005, the number of programme countries that had national standards for monitoring school or developmental readiness had increased, from 37 to 69. Some 45 programme countries used assessment tools for monitoring school readiness, which in some cases had been developed with UNICEF support. Fifty programme countries had a national policy on universal school readiness. The child-to-child approach for school readiness, which offered new possibilities for improving quality in education, was implemented on a pilot basis in six countries. However, widespread problems persisted, including low investment in ECD and weak links between health and early learning initiatives. In some countries, a narrow view that upheld kindergartens as the only means of ECD continued to impede progress.

To improve education and address problems of retention and achievement, 78 countries had incorporated life skills-based education in the primary national curriculum, compared to 49 in 2005. Some 47 programme countries had included environmental education or climate change into their primary school curriculum, and 51 had done so at the secondary level. Some 79 programme countries had a national policy against corporal punishment in schools. Governments were also increasingly recognizing the importance of WASH for education quality and achievement. The number of programme countries that developed national plans to provide WASH education to all primary schools increased to 75 in 2008 from 50 in 2005, in many cases with long-term support from UNICEF. The Fund also continued to support the construction of water and sanitation facilities in schools through pilot projects or in emergency situations, benefiting an estimated 3.6 million children in 2008.

An estimated 3.1 million children in emergencies were reached in 2008 through interventions in education, with UNICEF assistance. Those included back-to-school programmes involving large-scale mobilization, which resulted, for example, in a 20.4 per cent increase in primary enrolment in the DCR, as well as continued enrolment gains in Afghanistan and the Sudan.

HIV/AIDS

HIV/AIDS had caused an estimated 25 million deaths since HIV was first identified, severely affecting child survival and development, school attendance and livelihoods. It continued to strain health and welfare systems as well as communities and families who were supporting people affected by the epidemic. The call of the *Unite for Children, Unite against AIDS* initiative [YUN 2005, p. 1290] to place children "more front and centre" in the global response had produced tangible results and strengthened partnerships for action. Evidence for advocacy, policy and action at country level had been strengthened by improved knowledge management tools; leadership at the Implementers Meeting of the Joint United Nations Programme on HIV/AIDS (UNAIDS), held in Uganda; the focus on children at the international AIDS conferences in Mexico and Senegal; and expansion of academic partnerships in the Inter-Agency Task Teams on Preventing mother-to-child transmission (PMTCT), Paediatrics, Orphans and Vulnerable Children, and HIV and Young People.

UNICEF continued to expand its support to paediatric HIV reduction programmes, working in 102 countries in 2008. The proportion of HIV-positive pregnant women requiring antiretrovirals who actually received them increased from 10 per cent in 2004 to 33 per cent in 2007. Children also benefited, as indicated by an increase in the number of HIV-positive children on antiretroviral therapy from 75,000 in 2005 to nearly 200,000 in 2007. PMTCT service coverage, however, remained far below the medium-term strategic plan target of 80 per cent access to antiretrovirals for PMTCT. UNICEF procurement for HIV/AIDS commodities totalled $68.7 million in 2008. Antiretrovirals represented 81 per cent by value of the total commodities procured, followed by HIV rapid diagnostic test kits (16 per cent, or 12 million) and tests for sexually transmitted infections (3 per cent). Paediatric treatments still accounted for less than 5 per cent of antiretrovirals; some 95 per cent of antiretrovirals procured in 2008 were for PMTCT.

Regarding the proportion of children orphaned or made vulnerable by HIV/AIDS, worldwide in 2007 there were an estimated 15 million children who had lost one or both parents to AIDS, including nearly 12 million in sub-Saharan Africa. Many millions more were orphaned due to other causes: household survey data in 47 countries showed that orphanhood from all causes exceeded 5 per cent in many countries, and was over 20 per cent in Lesotho, Rwanda, Swaziland and Zimbabwe. Weaknesses persisted in monitoring the situation of orphans and other vulnerable children and in evaluating the response. Fragmented efforts and weak coordination were common. Some countries, such as Uganda, had developed quality standards for the care and support of orphans and vulnerable children.

The number of programme countries that integrated HIV/AIDS education into the national secondary curriculum rose to 79 in 2008. UNICEF continued to work with partners to improve awareness among schoolchildren on HIV prevention, with encouraging progress in countries such as Ghana and Mozambique. However, reaching marginalized children, including displaced children and refugees, continued to pose significant challenges for outreach programmes and information campaigns. Studies in several countries highlighted the need to better tailor education and outreach campaigns towards women and girls.

UNAIDS programme coordination

At its second regular session in September, the Executive Board considered a report [E/ICEF/2008/24] on recommendations and decisions of relevance to UNICEF adopted at recent meetings of the UNAIDS Programme Coordinating Board. Issues addressed in the report included the status of implementation of the Global Task Team (GTT) recommendations and follow-up to the GTT independent assessment; collaboration with the Global Fund to Fight AIDS, Tuberculosis and Malaria; gender sensitivity of AIDS responses; the cycle of UNAIDS unified budget and workplan; the Second Independent Evaluation of UNAIDS; and the process for nominating the UNAIDS Executive Director.

Child protection from violence, exploitation and abuse

Improved protection of children in 2008 resulted from greater political commitment and the strengthening of national policies, international standards and guidance. Continued efforts were made throughout the year to enhance the evidence base of child protection through gender analysis of key child protection issues; inclusion of disaggregated data on child protection in national reports to the Committee on the Rights of the Child; support to multiple indicator cluster surveys, demographic and health surveys and other household surveys; community-based child protection networks; specialized databases on child protection violations; and the expansion of the Monitoring and Reporting Mechanism in accordance with Security Council resolution 1612(2005) [YUN 2005, p. 863].

The Fund promoted devoting greater attention to issues such as gender-based violence and the recruitment of children, and played a leadership role in the expansion of inter-agency initiatives under the cluster system for emergencies. Through participation in major international forums, UNICEF also ensured that children's issues were highlighted in relation to landmines and other indiscriminate or illicit weapons. Psychosocial support was more systematically included in UNICEF emergency response. However, the poor availability of sex-disaggregated data continued to constrain child protection advocacy and programme development. Only 14 programme countries had sex-disaggregated data on child protection indicators for all age groups.

UNICEF supported programmes to end female genital mutilation/cutting (FGM/C) in 14 countries. UNICEF and UNDP started a Joint Programme and Trust Fund for the accelerated abandonment of FGM/C within a generation in 17 countries in Africa, with initial implementation in eight countries. Several African countries demonstrated progress following efforts to mobilize influential leaders as partners for change.

Over one third of programme countries (46 countries) had incorporated child protection related to emergency preparedness and response into national planning mechanisms by 2008, and 30 other countries had made partial progress. UNICEF support helped to strengthen national capacity for monitoring child rights violations and for protecting children in emergencies. In countries with declared emergencies in 2008, 62 per cent of UNICEF offices supported training for government and non-government partners on child protection in emergencies, and 59 per cent supported national systems for monitoring and reporting violations in accordance with Security Council resolution 1612(2005).

Important progress was made in all regions in establishing legal and policy frameworks in line with international standards promoting deprivation of liberty as a measure of last resort. In many countries, UNICEF facilitated broad consultative processes, including with children. In cooperation with the United Nations Office on Drugs and Crime (UNODC), UNICEF developed guidance for juvenile justice legislative reform and a model law for justice in matters involving child victims and witnesses of crimes. The Fund also promoted due process and protection of the rights of former child soldiers who had come in contact with the law.

UNICEF offices in some 50 countries reported progress on alternative care in 2008, including the development of comprehensive reintegration plans and the piloting of "small group homes"— family-like environments for children without suitable parental care. Efforts to improve national social work capacity increased, with over 35 countries reporting significant progress. UNICEF, particularly in Central and Eastern Europe and the Commonwealth of Independent States, worked with ministries of labour and universities to recognize social work as a profession and to create capacity to train personnel. The Fund also supported the establishment of community-based networks for child protection in several African countries. In India, UNICEF facilitated the creation of an Internet-based tracking system for separated children in 36 cities, working with over 55 national NGOs.

Policy advocacy and partnerships for children's rights

UNICEF continued to work with partners to strengthen capacities to design and implement social and economic policies, child-focused legislative measures and budgetary allocations that enabled countries to meet their obligations under the 1989 Convention on the Rights of the Child [YUN 1989, p. 560] and the 1979 Convention on the Elimination of All Forms of Discrimination against Women [YUN 1979, p. 895]. To that end, the Fund supported the collection of data and information on children and women to inform strategic decision-making; supported participation by children and young people; promoted research and policy analysis on children and women; and engaged in advocacy and policy dialogue with decision-makers.

The UNICEF-supported DevInfo, a database system for compiling and disseminating data on human development, had been critical in making key data available to Governments, UN and bilateral partners, and international NGOs to help them make informed decisions on policy and programmes for children. During 2008, UNICEF supported 63 countries in consolidating DevInfo implementation in the field. That resulted in more than 2,000 national and UN professionals being trained in the use of the system. Some 121 countries were using DevInfo, and 221 databases had been published by countries and organizations. In addition, UNICEF launched a child mortality database that informed users on how estimates were calculated and the data underlying the adjusted annual inter-agency estimates of under-five mortality.

The Fund supported programme countries in conducting participatory Situation Analyses of the rights of children and women. In addition to Situation Analysis reports, the UNICEF website hosted an increasing number of staff working papers. In 2008, seven working papers were added on migration and remittances, four on legislative reforms for child rights, and two on food prices and the financial crisis. Overall, UNICEF sponsored 76 major thematic studies related to children and women in 2008, in addition to comprehensive Situation Analyses. Over two thirds of those used a human rights framework, and over half used a gender analysis framework.

UNICEF also supported national sector-wide approaches in 44 countries, compared to 38 in 2005, and in an increasing number of countries (13) contributed directly to basket funding mechanisms. The continuing strategic engagement with the World Bank helped to leverage significant levels of new funding for programmes for children in countries around the world, notably through the Education for All Fast Track Initiative, and also for early childhood development, nutrition and HIV prevention.

The Fund worked with other UN agencies and partners in coordinating advocacy and programme support for achieving global commitments for adolescents. That included a Joint Programming Framework on Adolescent Girls and 'most-at-risk adolescents' tools developed as part of a UNAIDS prevention toolkit.

Operational and administrative matters

UNICEF finances

In 2008, UNICEF income totalled \$3,390 million, an increase of \$377 million (13 per cent) over 2007 and 10 per cent higher than forecast in the financial plan. Income to regular resources decreased by 2 per cent to \$1,085 million, and fell behind the 2008 financial plan by $51 million (5 per cent). UNICEF derived its incomes mainly from Governments, which contributed $2,040 million (60.2 per cent), and from private sector sources, which contributed $986 million (29.1 per cent). The balance came from inter-organizational arrangements, with contributions of $256 million (7.6 per cent), and other sources, with contributions of $108 million (3.2 per cent).

Budget appropriations

On 1 February [dec. 2008/7], the Executive Board approved a regular resources programme budget for the 2008–2009 biennium [E/ICEF/2008/P/L.1 & Corr.1] in the amount of $28,750,000 (other than the Emergency Programme Fund). It authorized UNICEF to transfer, if necessary, between programme fields an amount not exceeding 10 per cent of the approved budget of the fund to which the transfer was made. The Board also approved a programme budget ceiling of $456,826,000 for other resources for the 2008–2009 biennium, subject to the availability of specific-purpose contributions. Funds in excess of indicated amounts for specific programme areas and regions could be received, provided that the total amount of funds received was within the approved limit.

The Executive Board also considered the biennial support budget for 2008–2009 [E/ICEF/2008/AB/L.1] and the related report of the Advisory Committee on Administrative and Budgetary Questions (ACABQ) [E/ICEF/2008/AB/L.2]. On 1 February [dec. 2008/2], it approved a gross appropriation of $912.8 million for the biennial support budget, to be offset by estimated income of $223 million, resulting in an estimated net appropriation of $689.8 million. It requested the Executive Director to include in future budget submissions an annex on budget estimates by cost category for major objects of expenditure, with information on cost efficiencies achieved against targets and indicators therein, and to report on the estimates and efficiency targets in the annual financial reporting. The Board approved the amount of $26.2 million from regular resources for covering the UN mandated central-shared security cost. It also requested the Executive Director to present the 2010–2011 biennial support budget for Executive Board approval at the second regular session of 2009.

On the same day, on the basis on a UNICEF report [E/ICEF/2008/P/L.2], the Executive Board approved [dec. 2008/5] additional regular resources for 14 country programmes totalling $42.7 million. It also approved [dec. 2008/6], on the basis of a UNICEF report [E/ICEF/2008/P/L.3], $246,100,000 in additional resources for 13 country programmes.

On 5 June [dec. 2008/8], the Executive Board approved the aggregate indicative budget for 9 country programmes, amounting to the following totals for regular and other resources, respectively, by region: Africa, $266,373,900 and $444,590,000; Americas and the Caribbean, $1,492,200 and $9,619,500; South Asia, $58,851,900 and $147,584,000; Middle East and North Africa, $30,427,000 and $240,000,000.

According to a July report [E/ICEF/2008/AB/L.4], an amount of $5,891,211 from regular resources would be used to cover those overexpenditures for completed projects financed from other resources for which no additional support had been forthcoming. The report noted that the allocation of regular resources would allow UNICEF to finalize the accounting for other resources for the period to 31 December 2005.

On 18 September [dec. 2008/16], the Executive Board approved the aggregate indicative budget for 10 country programmes, amounting to the following totals of regular and other resources, respectively, by region: East and Southern Africa, $83,577,500 and $298,282,000; West and Central Africa, $34,387,200 and $124,500,000; the Americas and the Caribbean, $10,864,800 and $59,640,000; Central and Eastern Europe and Commonwealth of Independent States, $600,000 and $3,500,000; East Asia and the Pacific, $5,063,000 and 55,000,000; the Middle East and North Africa, $600,000 and $2,000,000. Additionally, the Board on the same date [dec. 2008/17], having considered the draft country programme documents presented to the Board at its second regular session of 2008, requested the UNICEF Executive Director to ensure that country programme results and performance data consolidated over the programme duration were made available on the UNICEF website at the end of the country programme cycle. It urged UNICEF to increase its efforts to present draft country programme documents for discussion at the annual session of the Executive Board and requested UNICEF to provide at the annual session a short explanation of the reasons for deferring draft country programme documents to the second regular session.

In response to a 2003 Executive Board decision [YUN 2003, p. 1212], the UNICEF secretariat in September submitted a report [E/ICEF/2008/20] on implementation of the modified system for allocation for regular resources for programmes. The report informed the Board on lessons learned since 2003, and proposed modifications to the system. In line with Board decisions, UNICEF continued to review the situation of the countries near or at the established graduation level, where regular resource assistance would cease, as well as the level and types of engagement required for children in those countries. Concerns regarding the extent of disparities in development indicators and their implications for children had increased in both least developed countries and middle-income countries. It was also increasingly evident that many of the most common factors that threatened children's rights and created vulnerabilities among children, such as violence, marginalization and effects of migration, were not confined to low-income countries alone. In 2008, allocations for cooperation in upper middle-income countries amounted to 2 per cent of total regular resources allocations, or $13.9 million. The secretariat would pursue innovative and effective options for cooperation modalities to further benefit the children of such countries. The secretariat would also monitor and review the implications for children of implementing the regular resource allocation system, including those modifications, and to advise the Executive Board of any issues arising from the review.

On 18 September [dec. 2008/15], the Executive Board endorsed the report on the implementation of the modified system, decided to maintain the system with a number of modifications, and requested a report on the topic at its second regular session in 2012.

On the same date [dec. 2008/21], the Executive Board, on the basis of a UNICEF secretariat report [E/ICEF/2008/AB/L.8], approved $21.4 million as an additional requirement from regular resources to cover security measures mandated by the UN. The Board also authorized the UNICEF Executive Director, on an exceptional basis, to access up to an additional 20 per cent ($4.3 million) of that amount during 2008–2009. UNICEF would limit the use of those funds to new and emerging security mandates, as defined in the UN Department of Safety and Security directives, and would report to the Board on the use of those funds in its annual report of the Executive Director on progress and achievements against the medium-term strategic plan.

Audits

In the annual report to the Executive Board on internal audit activities in 2007 [E/ICEF/2008/AB/L.7 & Corr.1], the Director of the Office of the Internal Audit (OIA) stated that OIA had completed 23 country office audits, one zone office audit and one audit of a joint UN office. Two of the audits were related to the response to the 2004 Indian Ocean tsunami. All completed audits met OIA's performance standards for planning, implementation and reporting. Each of the audits included a risk statement that described why the finding were important and should be addressed, a statement of the facts found in the audit, and one or more recommendations to establish adequate control over the identified risk. In 2007, OIA issued 444 risk observations and 75 positive practice observations. A positive observation was made when all aspects of a particular work process step in an audited area were found to function as expected. OIA issued 51 high-risk observations to field offices, in the areas of programme management (31 per cent), supply management (22 per cent), financial controls (18 per cent), cash transfers to implementing partners (16 per cent) and implementation of prior audit recommendations (10 per cent).

On 18 September [dec. 2008/23], the Executive Board took note of that report and requested that UNICEF closely consult with the Board in preparing the accountability framework foreseen for the first regular session of 2009, including by presenting a draft of the framework prior to the session. The Board expressed concern about the high percentage of unsatisfactory ratings by audited field offices, especially in the areas of programme management, cash assistance and supply assistance. It called upon the UNICEF management to address those issues by following up closely with country offices that had unsatisfactory ratings and by implementing measures to strengthen the performance of all country offices and to report back in 2009. The Board requested the UNICEF management to report on progress made and lessons learned in implementing the harmonized approach to cash transfers, including in connection with the development of procedures and reporting mechanisms, in conjunction with the annual report on internal audit at the second regular session in 2009.

In a July report [E/ICEF/2008/AB/L.9], the UNICEF secretariat described steps taken to implement the recommendation of the Board of Auditors on the Fund accounts for the 2004–2005 biennium. The report focused on those recommendations that either were not implemented or only partially implemented at the time of the previous report [YUN 2007, p. 1218].

Report of Secretary-General. In response to General Assembly resolution 48/216 B [YUN 1993, p. 1207], the Secretary-General in September transmitted to the Assembly a report [A/63/327/Add.1] on the implementation of the recommendations of the Board of Auditors contained in the Board's report on UNICEF [A/63/5/Add.2 & Corr.1] for the biennium ended 31 December 2007. The Secretary-General provided information on the status of implementation, the office responsible, the estimated completion date and the priority for each recommendation.

Resource mobilization

UNICEF continued to collaborate with Governments to mobilize regular and other resources. By the ninth pledging event in January, 48 countries had committed $383.8 million for 2008 regular resources. By year's end, 109 Governments had contributed to UNICEF resources. Total income from public sector donors (Governments, intergovernmental organizations and inter-organizational arrangements) amounted to $2,295 million—an increase of 17 per cent over 2007. Out of that amount, $616 million was received from public sector donors for regular resources, $1,057 million for other resources-regular, and $623 million for other resources-emergency. While regular resource contributions from the private sector and NGOs declined by 8 per cent, from $392 million to $361 million, contributions to other resources in those categories increased by 32 per cent, from $476 million to $626 million. The lower level of regular resources income classified as "other income" was largely caused by unfavourable exchange rate movements that affected the valuation of outstanding payments and income from investments.

The United States remained the largest donor to UNICEF ($301 million), followed by the United Kingdom ($213 million), Norway ($197 million), the Netherlands ($196 million) and Sweden ($170 million). Overall thematic funding in 2008 increased by 17 per cent, due to the increase in the humanitarian category, from $294 million to $343 million. In addition to contributions from 18 Governments and 32 national committees, thematic funding was also provided by the European Commission for the first time. The public sector contributed 68 per cent of all thematic funds in 2008. The top 10 donors to thematic funds contributed $178,881,000.

UNICEF overall income for humanitarian assistance was $735 million. Funding included 75 appeals and requests for humanitarian assistance. Consolidated appeals were relatively well funded, receiving 63 per cent of requirements. Flash appeals attracted 68 per cent of the requirements. The other crises were the least funded, with 43 per cent of their financial needs met.

International Public Sector Accounting Standards

In September, the Executive Board had before it a note [E/ICEF/2008/AB/L.10] on developments in implementation by UNICEF of the International Public Sector Accounting Standards (IPSAS), as called for in General Assembly resolution 60/283 [YUN 2006, p. 1580]. The note proposed that UNICEF report periodically to the Executive Board on progress towards IPSAS adoption.

Private Fundraising and Partnerships

The Executive Board in January had before it a report on the 2008 Private Fundraising and Partnerships (PFP) workplan and budget [E/ICEF/2008/AB/L.3], according to which PFP in 2008 would generate a projected sum of $746.4 million in net consolidated income, of which $395.3 million would be for regular resources and $351.1 million for other resources. That would be achieved with expenditures of $124.3 million. PFP incorporated the functions of the previous Private Sector Division, elements of fund-raising and national committee for UNICEF support of the Regional Office for Europe, the entire Office of Public Partnerships, and management of the UNICEF International Goodwill Ambassador programme. Core work regarding partnership and advocacy remained financed through the UNICEF biennial support budget [E/ICEF/2008/1]. For 2007, the total net consolidated income was estimated at $694.9 million. The actual result for 2006 was $734.9 million, which included the 2004 Indian Ocean tsunami emergency funds of about $50.0 million.

On 1 February [dec. 2008/3], the Executive Board approved budgeted expenditures of $124.3 million for the 2008 PFP work plan. It authorized UNICEF to redeploy resources between the various budget lines up to a maximum of 10 per cent of the amounts approved and to spend an additional amount between Executive Board sessions, when necessary, up to the amount caused by currency fluctuations, to implement the 2008 approved work plan. The Board also renewed investment funds with $21.4 million established for 2008. It authorized UNICEF to incur expenditures in the 2008 fiscal period related to cost of goods delivered (production and purchase of raw materials, cards and other products) for the 2009 fiscal year up to $34.1 million, as indicated in the PFP medium-term fundraising plan. It approved an interim one-month allocation of $11.0 million for January 2009, to be absorbed in the annual PFP budget for 2009, and also approved the PFP medium-term fundraising plan for 2009–2012.

Country programme approval process

The Executive Board had before it an April report [E/ICEF/2008/P/L.13] containing recommendations to increase the other resources ceiling for country programmes previously approved by the Board, as the contributions to other resources for country programmes had exceeded, or were expected to exceed, the planning levels originally approved by the Board. The Fund recommended that the Board approve $251,230,050 in other resources for approved country programmes for 27 countries. On 5 June [dec. 2008/9], the Executive Board approved additional other resources in that amount for the remaining periods of those programmes, subject to the availability of other resources contributions.

At the September session, UNICEF requested [E/ICEF/2008/P/L.28] that the Executive Board approve $98,064,270 in additional regular resources to allow uninterrupted implementation of 24 country programmes previously approved.

On 18 September [dec. 2008/18], the Executive Board approved additional regular resources in that amount to fund the approved country programmes of the 24 countries for 2009, whose regular resources planning levels, based on the modified allocation system and estimated global levels of programmable regular resources, were higher than the levels originally approved by the Board.

Joint programming

The joint meeting of the Executive Boards of UNICEF, UNDP/UNFPA and WFP (New York, 29 January–1 February) discussed progress towards achieving the MDGs. Introducing the background paper and discussion on behalf of the four participating organizations, the UNICEF Deputy Executive Director highlighted the uneven picture of progress given by recent data and said that a collective sense of urgency was needed if the MDGs were to be met. Various delegations noted progress made but expressed concern that several countries, particularly in sub-Saharan Africa, were not on track.

Recommendations made by delegations to accelerate progress, included: emphasizing Government leadership and national ownership as well as increased support from multilateral organizations in scaling up efforts; taking more "bottom-up" approaches so that marginalized groups benefited from scaling-up; ensuring the availability of UN staff to support country efforts; reaching out to the private sector and NGOs; and encouraging South-South cooperation in sharing and implementing good practices. More attention should be given to addressing debt relief for poor countries, the fulfilment of aid promises by donor countries, unequal trade relations, gender inequality and the degradation of the environment.

The joint meeting also discussed feedback from "Delivering as one" pilots. The UNFPA Executive Director noted that feedback from the pilots showed that the UNDAF formed the foundation of the "One United Nations" approach and was derived from national development priorities. Joint programming and programmes had received positive reviews. The strategic alignment of UN support to national development would reduce duplication and transaction costs, and the initiative's overall direction was positive.

On disaster risk reduction, the WFP Deputy Executive Director emphasized adaptation and the need to mitigate the risks of natural disasters and build resilience among those most likely to be hardest hit. There was an urgent need to engage fully in disaster risk reduction, and UN organizations could do more to mitigate risks and build resilience. A stronger link between humanitarian and development efforts was needed to reduce the impact of disasters on vulnerable communities.

JIU reports

In January, the Executive Board considered a secretariat note [E/ICEF/2008/6] on reports of the Joint Inspector Unit (JIU) of relevance to UNICEF. The note provided information on reports prepared between October 2006 and October 2007, action taken by UNICEF and views held on the issues raised by the inspectors. During that period, JIU issued five reports of interest to UNICEF on age structure of human resources in UN system [JIU/REP/2007/4]; Goodwill Ambassadors in the UN system [JIU/NOTE/2006/1]; lessons learned from the Indian Ocean tsunami disaster [JIU/REP/2006/5]; voluntary contributions in UN system organizations [JIU/REP/2007/1]; and UN system staff medical coverage [JIU/REP/2007/2]. The Board took note of the report at its January session.

Innocenti Research Centre

In July, UNICEF submitted to the Executive Board a progress report [E/ICEF/2008/23] on the work of the Innocenti Research Centre (IRC) (Florence, Italy) in strengthening the capacity of UNICEF, partner Governments and institutions to respond to the needs of children and to promote a strong global ethic for children. The report reviewed implementation by IRC of its 2006–2008 programme of work and proposed a one-year extension of the programme. The 2006–2008 work programme had enhanced the role of IRC in the generation and brokering of knowledge, and strengthened its partnerships with organizations and research institutions in the various regions, with an emphasis on developing countries.

In September [dec. 2008/19], the Executive Board, following the recommendation of the report, authorized the extension of the Centre's programme until the end of 2009 to ensure its alignment with the UNICEF strategic planning process, with the programme of work for the Office of Research 2010–2011, and with the UNICEF biennial support budget for 2010–2011. It also authorized an increase in the other resources ceiling of $7 million, for a total other resources ceiling of $24 million for the period 2006–2009. The Board invited all donors to contribute to the Centre's programme activities. The UNICEF Executive Director was requested to inform the Executive Board, through informal consultations in the first half of 2009, on the future direction, focus and details of the organizational arrangements for the research function, in view of the discussions on that function for the preparation of the biennial support budget for 2010–2011.

Youth

World Programme of Action for Youth

In 2008, United Nations policies and programmes on youth continued to focus on efforts to implement the 1995 World Programme of Action for Youth to the Year 2000 and Beyond, adopted by the General Assembly in resolution 50/81 [YUN 1995, p. 1211]. The Programme of Action addressed problems faced by youth worldwide and identified ways to enhance youth participation in national and international policy- and decision-making.

The Programme of Action identified 10 priority issues for youth: education, employment, hunger and poverty, health, environment, drug abuse, juvenile delinquency, leisure-time activities, girls and young women, and participation in society and decision-making. In resolution 60/2 [YUN 2005, p. 1296], the General Assembly added five additional issues of concern to young people: globalization, the increased use of information and communication technology, HIV/AIDS, the increased participation of young people in armed conflict as both victims and perpetrators, and the growing importance of intergenerational relations in an ageing global society. The World Youth Report 2005 [YUN 2005, p. 1295] and a related report of the Secretary-General [ibid.] suggested that the 15 priority areas of the Programme of Action be grouped into three clusters—youth in the global economy, youth in civil society and youth and their well-being. By resolution 60/2, the Assembly took note of those three clusters and requested their use in future analyses of the implementation programme.

Youth and their well-being

Expert group meeting. A report of the Secretary-General [A/64/61-E/2009/3] summarized the conclusions of the expert group meeting on goals and targets for the World Programme of Action for Youth (New York, 19–21 May), which suggested numerous goals and targets for the cluster "Youth and their well-being", one of the three clusters of the World Programme of Action. The meeting was attended by representatives from Member States, youth-led organizations and other NGOs, as well as UN programmes, regional commissions and specialized agencies. The goals and targets were chosen for their global relevance, scope and measurability.

The goals and targets for health highlighted the need to have access to affordable and comprehensive health information and services, including on diseases related to lifestyle choices. They aimed at minimizing the prevalence of reproductive health morbidities and mortality, promoting training for health professionals in identifying and treating common sexually transmitted infections, and ensuring that health facilities had adequate resources for providing youth-friendly care and counselling.

Halting and reversing the spread of HIV/AIDS could not be achieved without a specific focus on youth, and that would require that all young people were knowledgeable about HIV and how to prevent it. Thus, the recommended goals and targets sought to ensure that those most vulnerable to infection were reached, and that their social and economic vulnerability was given attention. The availability of opportunities for testing was also important in stemming the spread of HIV/AIDS.

Proposed goals and targets on reducing substance abuse by young people focused on both supply and demand reduction. Attention was given to youth access to substance abuse treatment and rehabilitation programmes, as well as the need to include in those programmes alternative income-earning strategies and skills training.

In the area of juvenile justice, the goals and targets recognized that the first key step was to reduce the involvement of youth in crime. Access to education and training, as well as increased employment opportunities, were seen as key in achieving that end. Protection of youth offenders in the justice system was emphasized, in particular by ensuring the separation of juvenile from adult judicial and penal systems and by reducing the number of juveniles committed to locked institutions.

Regarding gender, the goals and targets highlighted the need to ensure the availability of facilities and services required for the full engagement of girls and young women in society, and the need to engage boys and young men in promoting gender equality. The goals and targets also sought to eliminate violence against women and girls, including by addressing gender-based violence in all basic education curricula, and by ensuring that every case of violence against girls and young women was investigated and prosecuted.

Interventions to address the engagement of youth in armed conflict should, above all, focus on building a culture of peace. That required the involvement of education systems, as well as reducing the prevalence of light weapons. Also addressed was the need to engage youth in conflict prevention and reconstruction.

Youth employment

Commission for Social Development action. The Commission for Social Development, at its February session [E/2008/26] (see p. 1204), discussed trends in youth employment under its priority theme "Promoting full employment and decent work for all".

Economic and Social Council action. As recommended by the Commission, the Economic and Social Council, by **resolution 2008/18** (see p. 1205), urged the development and implementation of integrated policies and strategies that promoted full employment and decent work opportunities for youth, including those living in rural areas; integrating youth employment into national development strategies; and encouraging young people's entrepreneurship, including through entrepreneurship education. The Council called on Governments to promote access to work through policies that enabled the creation of new quality jobs for young people and facilitated access to those jobs; and stressed the importance of the Youth Employment Network [YUN 2001, p. 1100] as a national, regional and international peer exchange mechanism.

Ageing persons

Follow-up to Second World Assembly on Ageing (2002)

Commission for Social Development. The Commission for Social Development, at its forty-sixth session (6–15 and 22 February) [E/2008/26], completed the first review and appraisal of the Madrid International Plan of Action on Ageing, 2002 [YUN 2002, p. 1194], which was adopted by the Second World Assembly on Ageing [ibid., p. 1193]. In 2004 [YUN 2004, p. 1192], the Commission, decided to review and appraise the Plan of Action every five years; in 2006 [YUN 2006, p. 1382], the Commission decided to start the first global cycle of review and appraisal in 2007 and to conclude it in 2008. The global theme for the first review and appraisal was "Addressing the challenges and opportunities of ageing".

In response to a 2007 request of the Commission [YUN 2007, p. 1231], the Secretary-General submitted a report [E/CN.5/2008/7 & Corr.1] on the preliminary assessment of the first review and appraisal of the Plan of Action. The report addressed a range of socio-economic issues, such as income security, intergenerational solidarity and care provision, human resources development in health care, research on ageing and policy action, and age-friendly cities. It noted that since the Second World Assembly, Governments had introduced a wide range of policies and programmes aimed at addressing challenges stemming from population ageing.

The Secretary-General recommended that the Commission invite Governments and other major stakeholders to continue their cooperation with the UN Department of Economic and Social Affairs (DESA), as the UN global focal point on ageing, in implementing the Madrid Plan of Action, including by contributing to the development of the strategic framework for implementing the Plan. The Commission might request the Secretary-General, in preparing that framework, to consult Governments, intergovernmental organizations, UN bodies, academia and NGOs on its substantive and practical content. The Secretary-General might also be requested to improve the institutional capacity of the UN system, including maintaining and strengthening the focal points on ageing, so that they might further the implementation of the Plan of Action and the elaboration of its framework. Finally, The Commission might emphasize that the framework should include proposals for improving international cooperation on ageing to support implementation of the Plan of Action.

The Commission had before it the report [E/CN.5/2008/2] of the regional commissions on the regional implementation of the Madrid Plan of Action, which provided regional perspectives on the activities related to the implementation of the Plan, underlined challenges in the regions and offered recommendations for consideration by the Commission. On 8 February, the Commission held a panel discussion, with the participation of the executive secretaries of the regional commissions, on the regional review and appraisal of the Plan of Action.

On 22 February, the Commission adopted a resolution [E/2008/26 (res. 46/1)] on the first review and appraisal of the Plan of Action, in which it recognized the successful conclusion of the first review and appraisal of the Plan of Action and its results at the international, regional and national levels. The Commission encouraged Governments to integrate the concerns of older persons into their policy agendas and to participate in the implementation of the Madrid Plan of Action, including by improving data collection and sharing ideas, information and good practices. Member States were invited to develop their national capacity to address the national implementation priorities identified during the review and appraisal exercise. The Secretary-General was requested to submit to the Commission's 2009 session a report on the analysis of the conclusions of the first review and appraisal exercise, including a strategic implementation framework based on the analysis of national activities since 2002. The framework was to identify future policy priorities, including measures for international cooperation to support national implementation activities.

Report of Secretary-General. In response to General Assembly resolution 62/130 [YUN 2007, p. 1232], the Secretary-General in July submitted a report [A/63/95] on follow-up to the Second World

Assembly on Ageing, which summarized the results of the first review and appraisal of the Madrid Plan of Action and outlined a strategic implementation framework, requested by the Assembly.

Member States had made considerable strides in implementing policies that benefited older persons, said the report. Policy efforts made by Governments were often wide-ranging and innovative, and focused on: establishing new social protection mechanisms, such as social pensions in some developing countries or reforms to stabilize retirement and pension schemes in the more developed regions; extending health-care benefits to older persons; adjusting labour markets and care systems to correspond to accelerated population ageing; increasing the participation of older persons in various areas of society, including promoting the employment of older persons; giving attention to training in geriatrics and gerontology; preventing discrimination against and abuse of older persons; establishing intergenerational solidarity programmes; and enhancing the awareness of ageing-related issues.

Several UN entities carried out capacity development in the follow-up to the Second World Assembly, such as data collection and analysis (Population Division of DESA, United Nations Statistics Division, UNFPA); formulation of national population policies and programmes on issues related to demographic ageing and training of personnel (UNFPA); provision of recommendations to individual Member States on how to strengthen their employment and labour-market policies (International Labour Organization) and how to promote the participation of older persons in rural development and food security strategies (Food and Agriculture Organization of the United Nations). The World Health Organization focused on capacity-building for primary health-care services for older persons, support for active ageing in urban areas and integration of health and social care policies. The World Bank provided support for countries undertaking reforms of their pension systems.

Since the adoption of the Madrid Plan of Action, DESA assisted several Member States in their implementation of the Plan. As a result of a joint DESA-UNFPA advisory mission to Armenia in 2007, the Government decided to develop a national strategy on ageing based on evidence obtained from a national survey, which was completed in June 2008. DESA needs assessment missions to Moldova in April and to Kazakhstan in June helped those Governments to identify priorities for further action on ageing. A stakeholder workshop in June assisted the Government of Saint Kitts and Nevis to revise and finalize a draft policy on ageing.

Turning to the proposed strategic framework, the report said that it would focus on two major dimensions of the implementation process: determining key priority areas to focus on in the second half of its first decade; and building national capacity on ageing issues. Although the focus would be on national implementation activities, another objective of the framework was to improve international cooperation on ageing, including the institutional capacity of the UN system to support national policy efforts on ageing.

The Secretary-General proposed that the General Assembly recommend that Member States devise strategies for overcoming obstacles to the implementation of the Madrid Plan of Action based on life-course and intergenerational solidarity approaches in order to increase the likelihood of success in the years ahead. Member States were encouraged to choose national priorities that were realistic, feasible and achievable; to develop targets and indicators to measure progress in implementation; and to present their views on the outline of the strategic implementation framework so that they could be reflected in the final draft, to be presented to the Commission for Social Development in February 2009. The Assembly might also recommend that Member States raise greater awareness of the Plan of Action; reaffirm the role of UN focal points on ageing; increase technical cooperation efforts; expand the role of the regional commissions on ageing issues; facilitate the coordination of national and international NGOs on ageing; and enhance cooperation with academia on a research agenda on ageing.

GENERAL ASSEMBLY ACTION

On 18 December [meeting 70], the General Assembly, on the recommendation of the Third (Social, Humanitarian and Cultural) Committee [A/63/424] adopted **resolution 63/151** without vote [agenda item 55 *(c)*].

Follow-up to the Second World Assembly on Ageing

The General Assembly,

Recalling its resolution 57/167 of 18 December 2002, in which it endorsed the Political Declaration and the Madrid International Plan of Action on Ageing, 2002, its resolution 58/134 of 22 December 2003, in which it took note, inter alia, of the road map for the implementation of the Madrid Plan of Action, and its resolutions 60/135 of 16 December 2005, 61/142 of 19 December 2006 and 62/130 of 18 December 2007,

Taking note of the report of the Secretary-General,

1. *Recognizes* the successful conclusion of the first review and appraisal of the Madrid International Plan of Action on Ageing, 2002, and its results at the international, regional and national levels;

2. *Encourages* Governments to pay greater attention to building capacity to eradicate poverty among older persons, in particular older women, by mainstreaming ageing issues into poverty eradication strategies and national development plans, and to include both ageing-specific policies and ageing-mainstreaming efforts in their national strategies;

3. *Encourages* Member States to strengthen their efforts to develop national capacity to address their national implementation priorities identified during the review and appraisal exercise, and invites Member States that have not done so to consider a step-by-step approach to developing capacity that includes the setting of national priorities, the strengthening of institutional mechanisms, research, data collection and analysis and the training of necessary personnel in the field of ageing;

4. *Also encourages* Member States to overcome obstacles to the implementation of the Madrid Plan of Action by devising strategies that take into account the entirety of the human life-course and foster intergenerational solidarity in order to increase the likelihood of greater success in the years ahead;

5. *Further encourages* Member States to place particular emphasis on choosing national priorities that are realistic, feasible and have the greatest likelihood of being achieved in the years ahead, to develop targets and indicators to measure progress in the implementation process and to present their views on the outline of the strategic implementation framework contained in the report of the Secretary-General so that they can be reflected in the final draft of the framework to be presented to the Commission for Social Development at its forty-seventh session, in February 2009;

6. *Recommends* that Member States increase awareness-raising of the Madrid Plan of Action, including by strengthening networks of national focal points on ageing, working with the regional commissions and enlisting the help of the Department of Public Information of the Secretariat to expand media coverage on ageing issues;

7. *Invites* Governments that have not done so to designate focal points for handling follow-up of national plans of action on ageing;

8. *Invites* Governments to conduct their ageing-related policies through inclusive and participatory consultations with relevant stakeholders and social development partners, in the interest of developing effective policies creating national policy ownership and consensus-building;

9. *Stresses* that, in order to complement national development efforts, enhanced international cooperation is essential to support developing countries in implementing the Madrid Plan of Action, while recognizing the importance of assistance and the provision of financial assistance;

10. *Encourages* the international community to support national efforts to forge stronger partnerships with civil society, including organizations of older persons, academia, research foundations, community-based organizations, including caregivers, and the private sector, in an effort to help to build capacity on ageing issues;

11. *Calls upon* Governments to ensure, as appropriate, conditions that enable families and communities to provide care and protection to persons as they age and to evaluate improvement in the health status of older persons, including on a gender-specific basis, and to reduce disability and mortality;

12. *Encourages* Governments to continue their efforts to implement the Madrid Plan of Action and to mainstream the concerns of older persons into their policy agendas, bearing in mind the crucial importance of family intergenerational interdependence, solidarity and reciprocity for social development and the realization of all human rights for older persons, and to prevent age discrimination and provide social integration;

13. *Encourages* the international community to enhance international cooperation to support national efforts to eradicate poverty, in keeping with internationally agreed goals, in order to achieve sustainable social and economic support for older persons;

14. *Encourages* the international community and the relevant agencies of the United Nations system, within their respective mandates, to support national efforts to provide funding for research and data-collection initiatives on ageing in order to better understand the challenges and opportunities presented by population ageing and to provide policymakers with more accurate and more specific information on gender and ageing;

15. *Recommends* that Member States reaffirm the role of United Nations focal points on ageing, increase technical cooperation efforts, expand the role of the regional commissions on ageing issues and provide added resources for those efforts, facilitate the coordination of national and international non-governmental organizations on ageing and enhance cooperation with academia on a research agenda on ageing;

16. *Reiterates* the need for additional capacity-building at the national level in order to promote and facilitate further implementation of the Madrid Plan of Action, as well as the result of its first review and appraisal cycle, and in that connection encourages Governments to support the United Nations Trust Fund for Ageing to enable the Department of Economic and Social Affairs of the Secretariat to provide expanded assistance to countries, upon their request;

17. *Recommends* that ongoing efforts to achieve the internationally agreed development goals, including those contained in the United Nations Millennium Declaration, take into account the situation of older persons;

18. *Requests* the Secretary-General to translate the *Guide to the National Implementation of the Madrid International Plan of Action on Ageing* into all official languages of the United Nations so that it can be used more effectively by Member States, and encourages Member States to translate the *Guide* into their respective languages when appropriate;

19. *Also requests* the Secretary-General to submit to the General Assembly at its sixty-fourth session a report on the implementation of the present resolution, including information on the promotion and protection of human rights as they pertain to older persons.

Chapter XII

Refugees and displaced persons

In 2008, there were 34.4 million people of concern to the Office of the United Nations High Commissioner for Refugees (UNHCR), including 10.5 million refugees. The number of identified stateless persons stood at 6.6 million and the number of stateless persons worldwide was estimated at 12 million. The number of people displaced remained high, at an estimated 26 million, with 14.4 million benefiting from UNHCR protection assistance. The latter figure constituted an increase of more than 600,000 compared to the previous year. More than 1.3 million internally displaced persons (IDPs) were able to go back to their places of origin, and more than 600,000 refugees were able to return to their homes.

During the year, UNHCR exercised its protection mandate more effectively in relation to statelessness, and progress was made in that area, with encouraging developments taking place in countries as diverse as Bangladesh, Ukraine and the United Arab Emirates. UNHCR helped more than 150,000 refugees in Central Africa and the Great Lake region find a durable solution through voluntary repatriation and reintegration in their home countries, including 40,000 refugees who repatriated to the Democratic Republic of the Congo (DRC), 95,000 to Burundi and some 8,600 to Rwanda. UNHCR provided international protection and material assistance to some 676,000 refugees, of whom 68,300 were Congolese in camps in Burundi, Rwanda and the United Republic of Tanzania.

The Office also protected and assisted 2,700 Burundians in Rwanda, 112,000 Angolans in the DRC, more than 8,500 refugees from Chad, the Sudan and the DRC in the Central African Republic (CAR) and some 81,000 refugees in Cameroon, of whom almost 63,000 were from the CAR. UNHCR led the efforts of the protection cluster to improve the safety and security of IDPs in the CAR and the DRC.

The volatile situations in Afghanistan and Pakistan, ongoing conflicts in the Darfur region of the Sudan and Colombia, and violence in Georgia, the DRC and Somalia continued to generate forced movements within and across borders. The continued conflict in Somalia caused massive displacement of populations, and the IDP population rose from 450,000 to approximately 1.1 million people. Clashes in Ethiopia's Ogaden region triggered the internal displacement of thousands of Ethiopians; there were some 200,000 conflict-induced IDPs, living mainly in Somali, Oromiya, Gambella and Tigray regional states. In Kenya, post-election violence that erupted in late 2007 led to the displacement of between 350,000 and 500,000 people to camps and host communities, especially in the Rift Valley.

Fighting between Government forces and irregular armed groups severely affected civilians in the north of the CAR, and the number of IDPs rose to 197,000. The total number of Central African refugees stood at 104,000. The situation in eastern Chad worsened markedly along the volatile border with Darfur. Cross-border movements of armed groups, militia clashes, acts of banditry and general impunity affected the safety and security of 250,000 refugees from Darfur, 186,000 Chadian IDPs and the host communities. South Africa was hit by a wave of unprecedented xenophobic violence targeting Zimbabweans and other foreign nationals, which displaced up to 100,000 people.

Despite States' obligations to extend cooperation under the 1951 Convention relating to the Status of Refugees [YUN 1951, p. 520], the Office was often denied access to detention centres to determine international protection needs. UNHCR also continued to face challenges in all aspects of beneficiary and staff safety.

In October, the Executive Committee adopted general conclusions on international protection, which called upon States to scrupulously respect the principle of non-refoulement. It also called on States to take steps to prevent acts of violence against refugees and other persons of concern.

In January, the African Union (AU) Executive Council adopted two decisions on the situation of refugees, returnees and IDPs in Africa. The Council called upon the international community to redouble its assistance to victims of forced displacement in Africa.

In December, the General Assembly adopted resolution 63/149 on assistance to refugees, returnees and displaced persons in Africa. The Assembly emphasized that States had the primary responsibility for the protection of, and assistance to, refugees on their territory. The Assembly also emphasized the need to redouble efforts to develop and implement comprehensive durable solution strategies, in cooperation with the international community.

Office of the United Nations High Commissioner for Refugees

Programme policy

Executive Committee action. At its fifty-ninth session (Geneva, 6–10 October) [A/63/12/Add.1], the Executive Committee of the UNHCR Programme, in a conclusion on international protection, called upon States to scrupulously respect the principle of non-refoulement; to take steps to prevent acts of violence against refugees and other persons of concern; to facilitate their access without discrimination to effective legal remedies; to safeguard their physical safety; to strengthen justice systems; and to bring perpetrators of such violence to justice. The Committee commended UNHCR for pursuing its age, gender and diversity mainstreaming approach aimed at ensuring gender equality and equal enjoyment of rights, regardless of age, gender or background.

In other actions, the Committee adopted a conclusion on international protection, as well as decisions on programme budgets and funding, on the UNHCR programme in the UN proposed strategic framework for the 2010–2011 biennium and on administrative, financial and programme matters.

In his opening statement to the Committee [A/AC.96/SR.618], the High Commissioner said that adverse economic trends, financial turmoil and the unforeseen consequences of globalization and climate change had increased the number of people on the move in search of security and opportunities. Likewise, rapid population growth, urbanization, lack of employment and rising prices had created tensions, which were compounded by conflicts that increasingly involved competition over scarce resources. The result was that the number of refugees and IDPs worldwide was rising, especially in urban areas. Those trends, which generated an increasing number of emergency deployments, had important implications for UNHCR and its capacity and resources. He noted that spending from the operational reserve in 2008 would be almost double what it was in 2007 and global expenditure in 2008 was set to increase by around 50 per cent over 2006. In a drive to base its planning process on beneficiaries' rights and needs, and mainstream that approach in all its operations, UNHCR launched the Global Needs Assessment process in eight countries. Efficiency savings released additional resources for field operations, which made a real difference to beneficiaries. In 2008, savings of $7 million were freed up for new projects to address critical water and sanitation problems and high levels of anaemia among women and children in refugee camps. UNHCR approved an additional $13.25 million for a water and sanitation project covering 16 countries, and the Budget Committee was deciding on an anaemia reduction programme. The Office had also taken further steps to strengthen field operations. The High Commissioner noted that the new budget structure and resource allocation framework demonstrated the commitment of UNHCR to achieving results. In that regard, the Global Needs Assessment and the Global Accountability Framework would lay the foundations for a results-based management system. The field review had made good progress, and new policies would be introduced on expanding the use of national officers, improving work with implementing partners and attracting more senior staff to deep field locations. Moreover, comprehensive and much-needed reforms in human resources were under way, in close consultation with the Staff Council, with a new emphasis on training that would be supported by the establishment of a learning centre in Budapest.

Regarding protection, UNHCR had drawn up a list of five priority issues, including refugee protection in the context of international migration and mixed population movements. It continued to work with the International Organization for Migration (IOM) to implement the 10-Point Plan of Action on Refugee Protection and International Migration [YUN 2006, p. 1386], while promoting improvements in asylum legislation and procedures. The High Commissioner noted that UNHCR had just completed a global evaluation of its work to prevent and respond to sexual and gender-based violence, and that it intended to establish a concerted strategy for the protection of women and girls. Some progress had been made in protecting stateless persons, and UNHCR had strengthened its commitment to protecting IDPs in the framework of the Guiding Principles on Internal Displacement [YUN 1998, p. 675]. The preparation of an African Union convention on IDPs was viewed as an encouraging development in that regard.

The High Commissioner said that in 2007, with support from UNHCR, some 700,000 refugees and 2 million IDPs had voluntarily returned home in safety. Local initiatives in the United Republic of Tanzania, Latin America and the Economic Community of West African States (ECOWAS) region had provided refugees with access to the labour market and education and fostered positive relationships with host communities, thus contributing to their successful reintegration upon return.

UNHCR was also engaged in advocacy to promote sustainable reintegration with States, institutional partners and UN agencies through the Delivering as one initiative [YUN 2006, p. 1060]. He noted UNHCR's strong commitment to the initiative, which it saw as a key opportunity to engage the entire UN system in finding durable solutions for the challenges included in its mandate. However, while good results had been achieved in the past year, UNHCR did not have the resources or capacity to provide all the essential elements of successful reintegration. The Office had recently evaluated its reintegration operations in Angola and Southern Sudan and had adopted a new reintegration policy, emphasizing the strategic role of UNHCR, the importance of partnerships and the need to build on the capacities of returnees and to support Governments in reassuming their responsibilities towards their citizens. The policy also stressed the need for return and reintegration to be built into national recovery strategies, development frameworks and peacebuilding processes.

The High Commissioner was encouraged by the progress made in strengthening humanitarian financing. The Central Emergency Response Fund had already provided valuable support to a number of UNHCR operations, although the experience with country-level pooled funds had been more mixed. UNHCR and other humanitarian organizations encountered complex dilemmas when engaging with integrated UN missions. While UNHCR recognized the important role of those missions and continued to work closely with them, particularly in the context of return and reintegration, it was also aware of the importance of preserving the autonomy of the humanitarian space and safeguarding the humanitarian principles of neutrality, impartiality and independence, particularly in countries where a durable peace settlement had yet to be reached. UNHCR was determined to establish a full strategic partnership with its sister UN agencies, the International Red Cross and Red Crescent Movement and the NGO community. The Office's cooperation with the World Food Programme (WFP) had helped avert disaster for many of its beneficiaries during recent food crises, and UNHCR had some 650 NGO partners through which it was channelling increasingly significant levels of expenditure.

The High Commissioner highlighted concerns, including about 2009 funding, which was insufficient to meet the global needs of beneficiaries and cope with growing demands. He also called for a systematic debate on the international response to the growing scale of forced displacement, in which the following questions would be addressed: what impact would climate change and other adverse trends have on forced displacement; and could the international community address those challenges with the current legal and normative framework, or would it be necessary to develop new standards and instruments. He concluded by saying that those questions formed the basis of an important and necessary debate, and called on Member States to assume leadership. Only by thinking and acting together, said the High Commissioner, would it be possible to preserve the rights of the people who fell under the UNHCR mandate.

GENERAL ASSEMBLY ACTION

On 18 December [meeting 70], the General Assembly, on the recommendation of the Third (Social, Humanitarian and Cultural) Committee [A/63/423], adopted **resolution 63/148** without vote [agenda item 39].

Office of the United Nations High Commissioner for Refugees

The General Assembly,

Having considered the report of the United Nations High Commissioner for Refugees on the activities of his Office and the report of the Executive Committee of the Programme of the United Nations High Commissioner for Refugees on the work of its fifty-ninth session and the conclusions and decisions contained therein,

Recalling its previous annual resolutions on the work of the Office of the United Nations High Commissioner for Refugees since its establishment by the General Assembly,

Expressing its appreciation for the leadership shown by the High Commissioner, commending the staff and implementing partners of the Office of the High Commissioner for the competent, courageous and dedicated manner in which they discharge their responsibilities, and underlining its strong condemnation of all forms of violence to which humanitarian personnel and United Nations and associated personnel are increasingly exposed,

1. *Endorses* the report of the Executive Committee of the Programme of the United Nations High Commissioner for Refugees on the work of its fifty-ninth session;

2. *Welcomes* the important work undertaken by the Office of the United Nations High Commissioner for Refugees and its Executive Committee in the course of the year, which is aimed at strengthening the international protection regime and at assisting Governments in meeting their protection responsibilities;

3. *Notes with appreciation* the important guidance provided in the Executive Committee general conclusion on international protection;

4. *Reaffirms* the 1951 Convention relating to the Status of Refugees and the 1967 Protocol thereto as the foundation of the international refugee protection regime, recognizes the importance of their full and effective application by States parties and the values they embody, notes with satisfaction that one hundred and forty-seven States are now parties to one instrument or to both, encourages States not parties to consider acceding to those instruments, underlines, in particular, the importance of full respect for the principle of non-refoulement, and recognizes that a number of States not parties to the international refugee instruments have shown a generous approach to hosting refugees;

5. *Notes* that sixty-three States are now parties to the 1954 Convention relating to the Status of Stateless Persons and that thirty-five States are parties to the 1961 Convention on the Reduction of Statelessness, encourages States that have not done so to give consideration to acceding to those instruments, notes the work of the High Commissioner in regard to identifying stateless persons, preventing and reducing statelessness and protecting stateless persons, and urges the Office of the High Commissioner to continue

to work in this area in accordance with relevant General Assembly resolutions and Executive Committee conclusions;

6. *Re-emphasizes* that the protection of refugees is primarily the responsibility of States, whose full and effective cooperation, action and political resolve are required to enable the Office of the High Commissioner to fulfil its mandated functions, and strongly emphasizes, in this context, the importance of active international solidarity and burden- and responsibility-sharing;

7. *Also re-emphasizes* that prevention and reduction of statelessness are primarily the responsibility of States, in appropriate cooperation with the international community;

8. *Further re-emphasizes* that protection of and assistance to internally displaced persons are primarily the responsibility of States, in appropriate cooperation with the international community;

9. *Takes note* of the current activities of the Office of the High Commissioner related to protection of and assistance to internally displaced persons, including in the context of inter-agency arrangements in this field, emphasizes that such activities should be consistent with relevant General Assembly resolutions and should not undermine the mandate of the Office for refugees and the institution of asylum, and encourages the High Commissioner to continue his dialogue with States on the role of his Office in this regard;

10. *Notes with appreciation* the process of structural and management change being undertaken by the Office of the High Commissioner, and encourages the Office to continue its pursuit of reforms, including the implementation of a results-based management framework and strategy, that would enable it to respond adequately and in a more efficient manner to the needs of its beneficiaries and ensure effective and transparent use of its resources;

11. *Encourages* the Office of the High Commissioner to pursue its efforts to strengthen its capacity to respond adequately to emergencies and thereby ensure a more predictable response to inter-agency commitments in case of emergency;

12. *Strongly condemns* attacks on refugees, asylum-seekers and internally displaced persons as well as acts that pose a threat to their personal security and well-being, and calls upon all concerned States and, where applicable, parties involved in an armed conflict to take all necessary measures to ensure respect for human rights and international humanitarian law;

13. *Deplores* the refoulement and unlawful expulsion of refugees and asylum-seekers, and calls upon all concerned States to ensure respect for the relevant principles of refugee protection and human rights;

14. *Emphasizes* that international protection of refugees is a dynamic and action-oriented function that is at the core of the mandate of the Office of the High Commissioner and that it includes, in cooperation with States and other partners, the promotion and facilitation of, inter alia, the admission, reception and treatment of refugees in accordance with internationally agreed standards and the ensuring of durable, protection-oriented solutions, bearing in mind the particular needs of vulnerable groups and paying special attention to those with specific needs, and notes in this context that the delivery of international protection is a staff-intensive service that requires adequate staff with the appropriate expertise, especially at the field level;

15. *Affirms* the importance of age, gender and diversity mainstreaming in analysing protection needs and in ensuring the participation of refugees and other persons of concern to the Office of the High Commissioner, as appropriate, in the planning and implementation of programmes of the Office and State policies, and also affirms the importance of according priority to addressing discrimination, gender inequality and the problem of sexual and gender-based violence, recognizing the importance of addressing the protection needs of women and children in particular;

16. *Strongly reaffirms* the fundamental importance and the purely humanitarian and non-political character of the function of the Office of the High Commissioner of providing international protection to refugees and seeking permanent solutions to refugee problems, and recalls that those solutions include voluntary repatriation and, where appropriate and feasible, local integration and resettlement in a third country, while reaffirming that voluntary repatriation, supported, as necessary, by rehabilitation and development assistance to facilitate sustainable reintegration, remains the preferred solution;

17. *Expresses concern* about the particular difficulties faced by the millions of refugees in protracted situations, and emphasizes the need to redouble international efforts and cooperation to find practical and comprehensive approaches to resolving their plight and to realize durable solutions for them, consistent with international law and relevant General Assembly resolutions;

18. *Recognizes* the importance of achieving durable solutions to refugee problems and, in particular, the need to address in this process the root causes of refugee movements in order to avert new flows of refugees;

19. *Recalls* the important role of effective partnerships and coordination in meeting the needs of refugees and in finding durable solutions to their situations, welcomes the efforts under way, in cooperation with countries hosting refugees and countries of origin, including their respective local communities, relevant United Nations agencies, international and intergovernmental organizations, regional organizations, as appropriate, non-governmental organizations and development actors, to promote a framework for durable solutions, particularly in protracted refugee situations, which includes an approach to sustainable and timely return which encompasses repatriation, reintegration, rehabilitation and reconstruction activities, and encourages States, in cooperation with relevant United Nations agencies, international and intergovernmental organizations, regional organizations, non-governmental organizations and development actors, to support, inter alia, through the allocation of funds, the implementation of such a framework to facilitate an effective transition from relief to development;

20. *Recognizes* that no solution to displacement can be durable unless it is sustainable, and therefore encourages the Office of the High Commissioner to support the sustainability of return and reintegration;

21. *Welcomes* the progress that has been achieved in increasing the number of refugees resettled and the number of States offering opportunities for resettlement, and the contribution that those States make to durable solutions to refugees, and invites interested States, the Office of the High Commissioner and other relevant partners to make

use of the Multilateral Framework of Understandings on Resettlement, where appropriate and feasible;

22. *Notes* the progress that is being made by interested States and the Office of the High Commissioner to take forward elements outlined in the Mexico Plan of Action to Strengthen International Protection of Refugees in Latin America, adopted on 16 November 2004, and expresses its support for the efforts to promote its implementation with the cooperation and assistance of the international community, as appropriate, as well as by supporting host communities that receive large numbers of persons who require international protection;

23. *Also notes* that some progress is being made by interested States and the Office of the High Commissioner within the context of the European-Asian Programme on Forced Displacement and Migration on issues related to asylum and forced displacement, consistent with the mandate of the Office;

24. *Further notes* the importance of States and the Office of the High Commissioner discussing and clarifying the role of the Office in mixed migratory flows, in order to better address protection needs in the context of mixed migratory flows, including by safeguarding access to asylum for those in need of international protection, and notes the readiness of the High Commissioner, consistent with his mandate, to assist States in fulfilling their protection responsibilities in this regard;

25. *Emphasizes* the obligation of all States to accept the return of their nationals, calls upon States to facilitate the return of their nationals who have been determined not to be in need of international protection, and affirms the need for the return of persons to be undertaken in a safe and humane manner and with full respect for their human rights and dignity, irrespective of the status of the persons concerned;

26. *Notes* the important number of displaced in and from Iraq and its serious impact on the social and economic situation of countries in the region, and calls upon the international community to act in a targeted and coordinated manner to provide protection and increased assistance to the persons displaced to enable the countries in the region to strengthen their capacity to respond to the needs in partnership with the Office of the High Commissioner, other United Nations agencies, the International Red Cross and Red Crescent Movement and non-governmental organizations;

27. *Urges* all States and relevant non-governmental and other organizations, in conjunction with the Office of the High Commissioner, in a spirit of international solidarity and burden- and responsibility-sharing, to cooperate and to mobilize resources with a view to enhancing the capacity of and reducing the heavy burden borne by host countries, in particular those that have received large numbers of refugees and asylum-seekers, and calls upon the Office to continue to play its catalytic role in mobilizing assistance from the international community to address the root causes as well as the economic, environmental and social impact of large-scale refugee populations in developing countries, in particular the least developed countries, and countries with economies in transition;

28. *Calls upon* the Office of the High Commissioner to further explore ways and means to broaden its donor base, so as to achieve greater burden-sharing by reinforcing cooperation with governmental donors, non-governmental donors and the private sector;

29. *Recognizes* that adequate and timely resources are essential for the Office of the High Commissioner to continue to fulfil the mandate conferred upon it through its statute and by subsequent General Assembly resolutions on refugees and other persons of concern, recalls its resolutions 58/153 of 22 December 2003, 58/270 of 23 December 2003, 59/170 of 20 December 2004, 60/129 of 16 December 2005, 61/137 of 19 December 2006 and 62/124 of 18 December 2007 concerning, inter alia, the implementation of paragraph 20 of the statute of the Office, and urges Governments and other donors to respond promptly to annual and supplementary appeals issued by the Office for requirements under its programmes;

30. *Requests* the High Commissioner to report on his activities to the General Assembly at its sixty-fourth session.

Strengthening UNHCR

Oral report of UNHCR. In response to General Assembly resolution 58/153 [YUN 2003, p. 1226] on strengthening UNHCR capacity to carry out its mandate, a UNHCR representative on 24 July provided an oral report to the Economic and Social Council [E/2008/SR.42]. In the framework of the "Delivering as one" initiative [YUN 2006, p. 1060], UNHCR was involved in five pilot countries—Albania, Mozambique, Pakistan, Rwanda and the United Republic of Tanzania—and supported the goal of coherence in country-level policy development and implementation.

The representative said that under its revised policy framework and implementation strategy for reintegration, UNHCR was committed to establishing early, strategic cooperation with key partners and to situating its reintegration interventions in the context of mid- and longer-term development frameworks developed under national leadership. It was also working with other UN entities to address the humanitarian consequences of climate change. It supported the work of the Inter-Agency Standing Committee (IASC) and the High Level Committees on Management and Programmes (HLCP) within the mechanisms established by the Secretary-General and was considering the impact of climate change on human displacement and UNHCR operations. In support of the campaign for the sixtieth anniversary of the Universal Declaration of Human Rights, its June 2008 annual consultations with NGOs had taken place under the theme of human rights.

Non-United Nations organizations with which UNHCR worked included the International Organization for Migration (IOM), the International Committee of the Red Cross (ICRC) and the International Federation of Red Cross and Red Crescent Societies (IFRC).

On 25 July, the Economic and Social Council took note of the UNHCR oral report (**decision 2008/256**).

Coordination of emergency humanitarian assistance

In 2008 [A/64/12], UNHCR continued to participate in initiatives to reform the UN system and improve the global humanitarian response capacity, particularly in the area of inter-agency cooperation. It strengthened its strategic partnerships with a wide variety of actors, including governments, the European Commission, UN agencies, international and regional organizations, and the International Red Cross and Red Crescent movement. The Office also bolstered collaboration with NGOs, academic institutions, financial institutions, bilateral donor agencies, corporations, and individuals from the private sector. In the Inter-Agency Standing Committee, UNHCR contributed to formulating policies on humanitarian reform, managing the Central Emergency Response Fund (CERF), and redefining and improving the humanitarian coordinator system. UNHCR was fully engaged in the cluster approach—a humanitarian coordination structure aimed at enhancing the predictability and accountability of humanitarian response—and prioritized its cluster-led responsibilities both at the global and field levels, in the areas of protection, emergency shelter, and camp coordination and management. Significant emphasis was placed on the issue of humanitarian space, and access to beneficiaries in particular.

As bilateral relations with a large number of agencies remained a key feature of implementation of the UNHCR mandate, the Office continued to work closely with WFP to include people of concern in food assistance programmes. In 2008, some 30 countries received WFP food assistance. Other UN system entities that UNHCR collaborated with included the United Nations Children's Fund (UNICEF), the United Nations Development Programme (UNDP), the Joint United Nations Programme on HIV/AIDS (UNAIDS), and the United Nations Educational, Scientific and Cultural Organization (UNESCO). In 2008, one fourth of UNHCR's budget was channelled through 635 NGOs—163 international and 472 national—which remained the Office's largest group of partners.

Evaluation activities

In a July report [A/AC.96/1058], UNHCR described the activities of its Policy Development and Evaluation Service (PDES), which focused on issues and operations that were of particular interest to UNHCR and the Executive Committee. At the same time, the Service made continued efforts to strengthen and integrate the policy development and evaluation functions; ensured the effective dissemination and utilization of evaluation findings and recommendations; and promoted the principles of transparency and accountability within the Office. In that context, the High Commission requested PDES to lead UNHCR's involvement in a peer review on accountability to disaster-affected populations.

The other components of the PDES work programme focused on: refugee protection and international migration; the return and reintegration of displaced populations; protection and solutions for persons of concern to UNHCR; humanitarian and United Nations reform; and strengthening the UNHCR policy development and evaluation function.

On refugee protection and international migration, PDES published a study on international protection for trafficked persons and those who feared being trafficked and initiated an evaluation of UNHCR's role in relation to human trafficking. The Service completed a review of State practice in relation to the treatment of unaccompanied and separated children in mixed movements and also planned to evaluate UNHCR's operational role in a number of those movements, focusing initially on the Mediterranean region. Regarding the return and reintegration of displaced populations, PDES continued to work on the reformulation and articulation of UNHCR policy on the issue, in consultation with the Executive Committee. In order to ensure that the policymaking process was empirically well-founded, the Service initiated a series of evaluations of UNHCR return and reintegration programmes, beginning with those in Angola and Southern Sudan. In association with the Division of Operational Support, PDES convened an inter-agency workshop on the use of cash grants in voluntary repatriation programmes. On the protection and solutions for persons of concern to UNHCR, PDES managed an independent evaluation of UNHCR's role in preventing and responding to sexual and gender-based violence in situations of human displacement. PDES also published an analysis of UNHCR's role in the refugee protection regime, focusing on the means and methods that the Office could employ in encouraging States to respect the founding principles of that regime; another PDES study examined the protection of forced migrants in Islamic law. PDES completed an initial study on IDPs in urban areas and was assisting the Division of Protection Services in the finalization of a new UNHCR policy on refugees in urban areas. It also played a central role in the formulation of the High Commissioner's Initiative on Protracted Refugee Situations, and prepared a Standing Committee paper on the issue. On humanitarian and UN reform, PDES completed a stocktaking of UNHCR's engagement with the Delivering as one initiative and was reviewing the role and experience of the Office in integrated UN missions. On strengthening the UNHCR policy development and evaluation function, it continued to represent UNHCR in relation to the United Nations Evaluation Group (UNEG) and the Active Learning Network on Accountability and Performance in Humanitarian Action (ALNAP). The Service also acted as UNHCR's focal point for a number of external or inter-agency evaluation initiatives—an Office of Internal Oversight Services (OIOS) review on strengthening the role of evaluation and the application of evaluation findings to programme design, delivery and policy directives; an OIOS thematic evaluation of lessons-learned protocols and practices in the UN system; and a Swiss Agency for Development and Cooperation (SDC) evaluation of the UNHCR programme for internally displaced persons in Georgia.

Inspections

During 2008 [A/64/12], the UNHCR Inspector General's Office (IGO) carried out 10 standard inspections, two compliance missions, and two ad hoc inquiries. Three scheduled standard inspections had to be postponed to 2009 due to resource limitations. IGO received 274 complaints and opened 113 investigations into alleged misconduct. The number of investigations represented a 3.5 per cent reduction compared with 2007. In the context of UNHCR's own reform process, the High Commissioner requested the Anti-Fraud Office of the European Commission (OLAF) to undertake a periodic independent review of IGO during 2008. The OLAF panel presented its findings and recommendations in November, and a Working Group was established to prepare a road map for implementing the report's recommendations. That implementation had already resulted in improvements in the procedures used by IGO for conducting inspections, investigations and ad hoc inquiries. A report [A/AC.96/1057] on the activities of the Inspector General's Office was transmitted to the UNHCR Executive Committee in July.

OIOS activities. The UN Office of Internal Oversight Services (OIOS), which provided the internal audit function for UNHCR, conducted 16 audits in 2008. In August, OIOS submitted to the UNHCR Executive Committee a report [A/AC.96/1056] on its internal audit of UNHCR for the period from 1 July 2007 to 30 June 2008, which focused on areas such as internal control; programme management, including implementing partners; procurement and asset management; human resources management; travel and transportation; and safety and security. OIOS issued 13 audit reports during the period, including 201 recommendations to improve internal controls, governance processes and organizational efficiency and effectiveness.

Enlargement of Executive Committee

On 25 July, the Economic and Social Council, by **decision 2008/255**, took note of requests from Djibouti [E/2008/63] and Moldova [E/2008/84] for membership in the UNHCR Executive Committee and recommended that the General Assembly take a decision at its sixty-third (2008) session on the question of enlarging the Committee's membership from 76 to 78 States.

GENERAL ASSEMBLY ACTION

On 18 December [meeting 70], the General Assembly, on the recommendation of the Third Committee [A/63/423], adopted **resolution 63/146** without vote [agenda item 39].

Enlargement of the Executive Committee of the Programme of the United Nations High Commissioner for Refugees

The General Assembly,

Taking note of Economic and Social Council decision 2008/255 of 25 July 2008 concerning the enlargement of the Executive Committee of the Programme of the United Nations High Commissioner for Refugees,

Taking note also of the requests regarding the enlargement of the Executive Committee contained in the letter dated 29 February 2008 from the Permanent Representative of Djibouti to the United Nations addressed to the Secretary-General and the letter dated 30 May 2008 from the Chargé d'affaires a.i. of the Permanent Mission of the Republic of Moldova to the United Nations addressed to the Secretary-General,

1. *Decides* to increase the number of members of the Executive Committee of the Programme of the United Nations High Commissioner for Refugees from seventy-six to seventy-eight States;

2. *Requests* the Economic and Social Council to elect the additional members at its resumed organizational session for 2009.

Financial and administrative questions

The Executive Committee set the UNHCR initial annual programme budget for 2008 at $919.2 million [A/AC/.96/1055]. Total income for 2008 amounted to $1,755 million, comprising $1,070.8 million in contributions, transfers and miscellaneous income (including currency exchange gains) towards the annual programme budget and $565.6 million towards supplementary programmes, $19.6 million for the Junior Professional Officer (JPO) programme and $33.9 million from the regular UN budget. Expenditures totalled $1,628 million, of which Africa accounted for $650.0 million; the Middle East and North Africa $268.7 million; Europe $124.4 million; Asia and the

Pacific $221.8 million; and the Americas $47.5 million.

In an October decision [A/63/12/Add.1], the Executive Committee approved the revised annual programme budget for 2008, amounting to $1,163.2 million, which, with the provisions for JPOs of $10 million and $577.2 million for supplementary programmes, brought total requirements in 2008 to $1,750.4 million. The Committee authorized the High Commissioner, within those total appropriations, to effect adjustments in regional programmes, global programmes and headquarters budgets.

The Committee approved $1,265.5 million for the 2009 annual programme budget, which included the UN regular budget contribution, an operational reserve of $108.2 million, or 10 per cent of programme activities, $75 million for new or additional mandate-related activities, and $63.5 million for the global needs assessment identified by UNHCR in eight pilot countries. Those provisions, together with $10 million for JPOs, brought total requirements in 2009 to $1,275.5 million. The Committee authorized the High Commissioner, within those total appropriations, to effect adjustments in regional programmes, global programmes and headquarters budgets. The Committee requested the High Commissioner, within the resources available, to respond flexibly and efficiently to the needs indicated for the 2008–2009 biennial programme budget. The Committee authorized the High Commissioner, in case of additional new emergency needs that could not be fully met from the operational reserve, to create supplementary programmes and issue special appeals.

Accounts (2007)

The audited financial statements of voluntary funds administered by UNHCR for the year ending 31 December 2007 [A/63/5/Add.5] showed a total expenditure of $1,345.8 million and total available funds of $300.8 million, with a reserve balance of $178.1 million.

The UN Board of Auditors coordinated with the Office of Internal Oversight Services in the planning of the UNHCR audit in order to avoid duplication of efforts. It also reviewed the internal audit coverage of the operations of UNHCR so as to assess the extent to which reliance could be placed on its work. With regard to the follow-up on previous recommendations, as requested by the Advisory Committee on Administrative and Budgetary Questions (ACABQ) and in accordance with General Assembly resolution 59/264 [YUN 2004, p. 1398], the Board evaluated previous recommendations that had not yet been fully implemented and indicated the financial periods in which such recommendations were first made. It reported on the overall financial overview for the year ended 31 December 2007, in which the total income amounted to $1,333 million, compared with $1,151 million for the previous year, which represented a 15.8 per cent increase. Total expenditure amounted to $1,352 million, which, compared with $1,104 million for the previous year, was a 22.4 per cent increase. The result was a $19 million shortfall of income over expenditure, compared with a $47 million surplus of income over expenditure in 2006. After prior-period adjustments were taken into account, the gross deficit of $19 million increased to a net deficit of $382 million. The deficit did not result from a sudden deterioration in the financial situation of UNHCR, but rather from the disclosure for the first time of accrued end-of-service and post-retirement liabilities, notably those for after-service health insurance benefits. Previously, those liabilities were only indicated in notes to the financial statements. Funding for the liabilities had not yet been decided upon by the General Assembly. The current expenditure reduction trend observed in 2006 did not continue in 2007. UNHCR expenditures increased by 22.4 per cent, while income rose by 15.8 per cent. On the other hand, the deficit resulting from the provision for end-of-service and post-retirement liabilities without appropriate funding resulted in a negative balance of $178 million in funds and reserves as at 31 December 2007.

There was progress towards implementation of the International Public Sector Accounting Standards (IPSAS) in a plan which UNHCR had prepared. The plan was adopted in June and the key players in charge were appointed. The total cost for the implementation of IPSAS was estimated at $3.2 million for the period 2007–2009, but that amount needed to be reviewed. The Board found that certain current accounts remained inactive without being closed, and discovered accounting errors in the petty cash accounts. The Board also discovered that the total amount of accrued liabilities for after-service health insurance benefits, estimated by actuarial valuation, amounted to $308 million as at 31 December 2007, out of a total $374.1 million in liabilities for all the end-of-service benefits. It had validated the after-service health insurance liabilities reported in the financial statements.

UNHCR pursued its efforts to clean up its non-expendable property database, as recommended by the Board in previous reports. However, the total value of non-expendable property as at 31 December 2007, as calculated by the Board, was different from the value disclosed in note 15 to the financial statements, illustrating that the clean-up of the database had not been completed. UNHCR made progress compared with previous years in receiving monitoring subproject reports from its implementing partners, as well as audit certificates. As at 25 June 2008, 352 audit certificates were received, representing $150.5 million, or 49 per cent of the total due. In June 2007, only 22 audit certificates were received from project independent auditors, totalling $9.9 million, or 3.3 per cent of 2006 expenditure. The Board made several recommendations based on its audit.

UNHCR, in a September report [A/AC.96/1054 & Add.1] described measures taken or proposed in response to the Board's recommendations.

ACABQ, in October [A/63/474], concurred with the Board that any outstanding inter-fund balances should be resolved expeditiously. It noted that while the Board's comments indicated an overall improvement in the United Nations Office for Project Services (UNOPS) operations, further measures were required. ACABQ stressed the importance of continued review by the Board, particularly in respect of the recent partial merger of UNOPS with the Inter-Agency Procurement Services Office. It further noted that it was essential for all organizations to develop comprehensive funding strategies and principles to guide their fundraising policies in order to support the objectives set by their governing bodies, and that it shared the Board's views that UN system organizations should develop effective funding strategies and diversify funding sources. On the implementation of IPSAS, it recommended that the General Assembly keep the matter of consolidation of the UN financial statements under review as the Organizations moved towards migration to IPSAS.

The Executive Committee, in an October decision [A/63/12/Add.1], requested that it be kept regularly informed on the measures taken to address the recommendations and the observations raised by the Board of Auditors and ACABQ.

Management and administrative change

Lump-sum arrangement

Report of Secretary-General. Under paragraph 23.20, Sect. 23, of the proposed programme budget for the 2002–2003 biennium [YUN 2001, p. 1296], UNHCR was to review, after three bienniums, the lump-sum arrangement which began in the biennium 2002–2003 to fund a portion of the Office's management- and administration-related costs under the UN regular budget. In compliance with that provision, the Secretary-General in November submitted a report [A/63/537] on the review of the UNHCR lump-sum arrangement. The report reviewed the budgetary process prior to the lump-sum arrangement, lump-sum grant arrangement, and the proposed retention of the lump-sum grant arrangement. The Secretary-General concluded that the arrangement to provide a lump sum from the UN regular budget to UNHCR had streamlined the budgetary presentation and simplified the work of the Office by eliminating the need for separate administrative procedures in respect of the management and administration posts funded under the UN regular budget. Recommending that the arrangement be maintained, the Secretary-General requested that the General Assembly take note of the report and endorse the maintenance of the arrangement in future budget presentation of the proposed programme budget.

In December [A/63/616], ACABQ endorsed the Secretary-General's recommendations.

General Assembly action. On 24 December, by section VII of **resolution 63/263** (see p. 1547), the General Assembly took note of the Secretary-General's report and endorsed the recommendations of ACABQ.

Standing Committee

The UNHCR Standing Committee held three meetings in 2008 (4–6 March [A/AC.96/1052 & Corr.1]; 24–26 June [A/AC.96/1060]; and 23–24 September [A/AC.96/1061]). It considered issues relating to UNHCR programme budgets and funding; international protection; regional activities and global programmes; programme/protection policy; coordination; management, financial control, administrative oversight and human resources; governance; and consultations.

In October [A/63/12/Add.1], the Executive Committee called upon its members to ensure that debate at the Executive Committee and its Standing Committee be of a substantive and interactive nature, yielding practical guidance and clear advice to the High Commissioner, in keeping with the Committee's statutory functions; and called on UNHCR to be explicit and analytical in its reports and presentations to the Committee and to submit documentation in a timely manner. It also called on UNHCR to consult with the Committee with regard to ongoing reform measures and the consequent structural and management changes within the organization, including the proposed new budget structure, through informal consultative meetings as well as at Standing Committee meetings. It requested the Standing Committee to report on its work in 2009. The Executive Committee approved applications by six Government delegations to participate as observers in Standing Committee meetings, as well as a list of intergovernmental and international organizations to be invited to participate as observers in relevant meetings of its Standing Committee from October 2008 to October 2009. It adopted the provisional agenda for its sixtieth session.

Staff safety

At the June meeting of the Standing Committee [A/AC.96/1060], the Deputy Director of the UNHCR Division of Operational Services presented an update on staff safety and security issues [EC/59/SC/CRP.17], which described efforts to implement the recommendations of the UNHCR Security Policy and Policy Implementation Review, as well as new initiatives in support of the security of beneficiaries and other security-related activities. He noted that over 40 per cent of UNHCR staff worked in high-risk security environments and that since 2004 additional resources had been allocated to security-related activities. UNHCR was working closely with other UN departments and agencies to ensure adequate coordination of security management. The Office welcomed a stronger inter-agency security mechanism, but cautioned that the UN security management system needed to give more consideration to the specific organizational and mandate-related concerns of UNHCR, notably the physical protection of people of concern. The Deputy Director also informed the meeting of the global assessment on vulnerability to explosions that had been carried out following the bombing of the UN premises in Algiers in December 2007 [YUN 2007, p. 61]. Delegations welcomed UNHCR's efforts to increase security for staff and people of concern, notably in respect of Minimum Operating Security Standards compliance and the inclusion of partners in security training. They also took note of the corresponding increase in costs and the need for additional support. UNHCR confirmed that great importance was placed on working on security with non-UN partners through information-sharing and joint training. Although it was often difficult to quantify requirements to mitigate constantly evolving risks and manage security standards, the Office was in the process of calculating current and additional costs, which would be shared with the Committee. In that context, a renewed focus on local risk assessments was needed.

Refugee protection and assistance

Protection issues

In his annual report covering 2008 [A/64/12], the High Commissioner said that the provision of protection and humanitarian assistance to refugees, stateless persons and IDPs had become increasingly challenging. He noted that forced population displacement had grown in size and complexity. Major challenges included the reduction of humanitarian space, restrictions on access for humanitarian workers, more emphasis by States on sovereignty, increasing urbanization, extreme poverty and poor governance. In addition, environmental factors such as climate change, drought, and declining resources and inequitable access to them, were having a greater impact on displacement than ever before. Finding durable solutions for assisting the estimated 5.7 million refugees who had been living in exile for more than five years remained a serious concern for the Office. At the end of 2008, there were 34.4 million people of concern to UNHCR, including some 10.5 million refugees. The numbers of people displaced in their own country as a result of conflicts remained high at an estimated 26 million, with 14.4 million of them benefiting from UNHCR protection and assistance activities. The latter constituted an increase of more than 600,000 compared to the previous year (13.7 million) and that was the highest figure ever recorded by UNHCR. By the end of the year, developing countries were hosting 8.4 million refugees, or 80 per cent of the global refugee population. Pakistan again topped the list, hosting nearly 1.8 million, most of whom were refugees from Afghanistan. Afghan and Iraqi refugees accounted for almost half of the refugee population under UNHCR's responsibility. During 2008, at least 839,000 applications for asylum or refugee status were submitted to Governments or UNHCR offices in 154 countries. UNHCR made operational the concept of an evacuation transit facility to provide a temporary safe haven for refugees, pending final resettlement to a third country. The first evacuation facility opened in Romania in 2008 and further initiatives in other regions of the world were being explored.

With regard to refugee protection in the context of international migration, UNHCR received credible accounts of hundreds of Eritreans being detained and deported, despite repeated appeals to the authorities to refrain from forcible return. The Office was often denied access to detention centres to determine international protection needs, despite States' obligations to extend cooperation under the 1951 Convention relating to the Status of Refugees [YUN 1951, p. 520]. On a positive note, the hospitality extended by major refugee-hosting countries in the Middle East, notably Jordan and the Syrian Arab Republic, to large numbers of Iraqi refugees in addition to hundreds of thousands of Palestinian refugees, was noteworthy. Yemen had also been a positive example, generously granting prima facie refugee recognition to Somalis fleeing hostilities in their country.

The second meeting of the High Commissioner's Dialogue on Protection Challenges (Geneva, 10–11 December), attended by 135 delegations representing some 90 States and more than 50 national, international, intergovernmental and non-governmental organizations, focused on protracted refugee situations and the need for durable solutions. Participants examined various approaches aimed at finding solutions for the 6 million refugees in some 30 different situations worldwide who had been in exile for at least five years—many of them for decades—and examined the challenges and opportunities for refugees and other stakeholders in camps, rural and urban contexts. In particular, the Dialogue examined instruments that could unlock protracted refugee situations: those included providing resettlement places; ensuring that voluntary repatriation and reintegration were sustainable; supporting self-reliance activities; and fostering local integration. Participants emphasized the importance of providing education and training as ways of building self-reliance. However, repatriation remained the preferred solution whenever feasible.

In October [A/63/12/Add.1], the Executive Committee encouraged States to prevent and reduce statelessness by adopting and implementing safeguards in nationality laws and policies, consistent with fundamental principles of international law, and by facilitating birth registration as a means of providing an identity. The Committee stressed the importance of safeguarding the right of every child to acquire a nationality, particularly where the child might otherwise be stateless. States should consider facilitating the naturalization of habitually and lawfully residing stateless persons in accordance with national legislation. It also requested UNHCR to continue to provide technical advice and operational support to States.

In March [A/AC.96/1052], the Director of the International Protection Services briefed the Standing Committee on the first meeting of the High Commissioner's Dialogue on Protection Challenges [YUN 2007, p. 1243], which focused on refugee protection, durable solutions and international migration.

In a June note on international protection [A/AC.96/1053], the High Commissioner examined developments from mid-2007 to mid-2008 and outlined protection measures taken to address them, including the right to seek asylum; the legal framework established by the 1951 Convention relating to the Status of Refugees [YUN 1951, p. 520] and its 1967 Protocol [YUN 1967, p 477]; the right to enjoy asylum; the right to a nationality; the rights of internally displaced persons; and durable solutions. The note showed how the Universal Declaration of Human Rights provided the underlying framework supporting persons of concern to secure non-discriminatory enjoyment of their rights, including the rights to seek and enjoy asylum, to a nationality, and to return to one's country. It also highlighted examples of how UNHCR and its partners used international human rights and refugee law in complementary ways to support States in securing the rights of persons of concern, including by using a rights-based approach; by drawing on international human rights law standards in legal interventions; and by using the human rights machinery to reinforce initiatives. In bringing out the linkages between international refugee law and international human rights law, the note pointed towards the value of developing that interface in mutually reinforcing ways. Mainstreaming human rights throughout the UN system, including UNHCR, and strengthening cooperation among UN bodies, including the Office of the High Commissioner for Human Rights, could only reinforce the protection of persons of concern. Likewise, the integration of issues relevant to persons of concern into the work of the human rights mechanisms, including the Universal Periodic Review, affirmed the applicability of that framework to the subject of protection.

In October [A/63/12/Add.1], the UNHCR Executive Committee adopted conclusions on: general international protection; age, gender and diversity mainstreaming approach; refugees and others of concern with disabilities; protracted refugee situations; resettlement; internal displacement; and statelessness. It welcomed UNHCR's initiative to commence a review of achievements under the Agenda for Protection, to identify outstanding challenges and assist States to devise national plans of action in consultation with relevant stakeholders and actors so as to enhance the international protection of refugees and others of concern.

International instruments

In 2008, the numbers of parties to the 1951 Convention relating to the Status of Refugees [YUN 1951, p. 520] and its 1967 Protocol [YUN 1967, p. 477] remained at 144, while the number of State parties to one or both instruments increased to 149. The number of States parties to the 1954 Convention relating to the Status of Stateless Persons [YUN 1954, p. 416] increased to 63. With the accession of Finland, the number of States parties to the 1961 Convention on the Reduction of Statelessness [YUN 1961, p. 533] increased to 35.

In October, the UNHCR Executive Committee welcomed the entry into force of the Convention on the Rights of Persons with Disabilities and its Optional Protocol [YUN 2006, p. 785]; and, for State parties, the Committee underlined that refugees and others of concern to UNHCR with disabilities were entitled on the same basis as others to the full enjoyment of the rights and standards set forth in those instruments.

Assistance measures

The global population of concern to UNHCR increased to 34.4 million in 2008 from 31.7 million in 2007. The number of IDPs receiving UNHCR assistance rose from 13.7 million in 2007 to 14.4 million in 2008 due to the outbreak, renewal and prolongation of armed conflicts in many regions of the world such as Afghanistan and Pakistan, ongoing conflict in the Darfur region of the Sudan and in Colombia, and violence in Georgia, Somalia and the DRC, which continued to generate forced movements within and across borders. Improvements in the security situation in Iraq brought tempered optimism, but conditions were not yet sufficiently stable to envisage voluntary return and the sustainable reintegration of the displaced. The number of identified stateless people stood at almost 6.6 million; however, the actual number of stateless people worldwide was estimated to be closer to 12 million. During 2008, over 839,000 individual applications for asylum or refugee status were submitted to Governments or UNHCR offices in 154 countries, which constituted a 28 per cent increase compared to the previous year (635,800).

Situations of concern included the escalating conflict and the deliberate targeting of aid workers in Afghanistan, which limited access by humanitarian organizations to approximately half of the country, as well as the plight of some 2.7 million Afghans who remained in exile in Iran and Pakistan, deterred from returning by the ongoing violence. While the overall security situation improved in Iraq at the beginning of the year, some 1.6 million Iraqis remained in exile in Jordan and the Syrian Arab Republic and some 2.6 million Iraqis remained displaced within the country. In the Sudan's Darfur region, some 2.7 million people remained internally displaced. In the Central African Republic, some 25,000 refugees were forced to flee to Chad and Cameroon during 2008, bringing the total number of refugees from the Central African Republic in those two countries to almost 124,000. Hostilities in the DRC, particularly in the eastern provinces, aggravated the humanitarian situation there and provoked renewed displacement. The estimated 1.4 million IDPs in the country were often subject to armed attacks, sexual and gender-based violence (SGBV), and the recruitment, including of children, by armed groups. In Somalia, where UNHCR coordinated protection and shelter activities for 1.3 million displaced people, the security situation remained volatile. In Colombia, an estimated 3 million people were internally displaced, with nearly 300,000 in a refugee-like situation in neighbouring countries. In Georgia, out of the more than 130,000 people who fled the South Ossetia conflict in August, some 14,000 were still displaced.

The main countries which saw voluntary repatriation in 2008 included Afghanistan (278,500), Angola (13,100), Burundi (95,400), the DRC (54,000), Iraq (25,600) and the Sudan (90,100). An estimated 1.3 million IDPs protected/assisted by UNHCR returned to their places of origin, including some 700,000 within Uganda and 350,000 inside Kenya. More than 600,000 refugees were also able to return to their homes. UNHCR provided cash and transport assistance for Sierra Leonean refugees who wished to be repatriated. Furthermore, UNHCR's repatriation operation for Burundian refugees living in the United Republic of Tanzania, which began in 2002, reached the 300,000 mark in March. More than 30,000 refugees from old settlements established after the 1972 influx were included in the return figures for 2008. The repatriation movements included 14,000 Mauritanian refugees who repatriated with UNHCR's assistance, and nearly 11,000 Liberian refugees, mainly from Ghana. More than 121,000 resettlement submissions and 65,800 departures in 2008 represented a 22 per cent and 32 per cent increase, respectively, compared to 2007. In Asia, the naturalization of around 3,000 former Cambodian refugees in Viet Nam also represented progress. In Latin America, the "Cities of Solidarity" and "Borders of Solidarity" programmes through the Mexico Plan of Action [YUN 2004, p. 1210] aimed to facilitate self-sufficiency and local integration. In Asia, more than 16,000 refugees from Myanmar left Thailand and over 13,000 Bhutanese left Nepal in major resettlement efforts.

Refugees and the environment

During the year, UNHCR continued to implement its environmental policy and activities, based on the four principles outlined in the 2005 revision [YUN 2005, p. 1310] of its *Environmental Guidelines*: prevention, integrated approach, cost-effectiveness and local participation. That was in line with the Office's broader objective to defend the institution of asylum, as widespread damage to the environment or depletion of natural resources could be a source of conflict and affect States' willingness to provide asylum. The Office continued to work together with other agencies concerned with environmental management, particularly in the context of cluster arrangements, Delivering as one [YUN 2006, p. 1060], and other coordination mechanisms to promote the sustainable conservation and rehabilitation of areas affected by the presence of displaced populations.

Refugees and HIV/AIDS

During 2008, in accordance with its HIV/AIDS Strategic Plan 2008–2009, UNHCR continued to combat HIV/AIDS among refugees and other persons of concern and ensure that the basic rights of those affected by HIV/AIDS were respected. Close collaboration with the World Health Organization (WHO) Department for Mental Health and Substance Abuse enabled the Office to undertake rapid assessments and programmatic interventions on alcohol and substance abuse and their linkages to HIV transmission and prevention, as well as other health and social issues, among refugees and IDPs in selected countries in Africa and Asia. In the Asian region, UNHCR worked closely with the United Nations Office on Drugs and Crime (UNODC) on HIV transmission among injection drug users, refugees and returnees. In partnership with the United Nations Population Fund (UNFPA), UNHCR worked more comprehensively on HIV and sex work in eastern Africa and eastern Europe. That was carried out through a series of capacity-building workshops and programmatic reviews of the extent of access for sex workers and their families and clients to HIV protection, prevention, care and treatment. UNHCR continued to work closely with the UNAIDS co-sponsors and secretariat, as well as with other UN agencies, on all HIV policies and programmes related to HIV and conflict and displacement. Under the UNAIDS Inter-Agency Task Team for Young People, UNHCR helped develop a global guidance brief on HIV and young people in humanitarian emergency settings.

Significant improvements were made to the quality of public health programmes by involving local authorities and people of concern. To make those programmes sustainable, the Office focused on capacity development at the national level and among the populations concerned. UNHCR and its operational partners carried out training programmes in primary health care, including reproductive and child health. UNHCR strove to ensure universal access to HIV prevention, care, treatment and support programmes. By the end of 2008, more than 90 per cent of UNHCR's refugee operations had access to culturally and linguistically appropriate education and information on HIV/AIDS. The Office focused on developing prevention materials targeting young people and reducing discrimination against those with the disease. It continued to advocate for the inclusion of refugees and IDPs in national HIV plans and policies. At the end of 2008, refugees had equal access to antiretroviral treatment where it was available to surrounding host communities in 85 per cent of UNHCR operations. The Office also expanded its programmes in Africa to prevent mother-to-child transmission.

Refugee women

In 2008, UNHCR completed the introduction of the age, gender and diversity mainstreaming (AGDM) strategy to all operations and developed the AGDM Action Plan. The Plan established responsibility for supporting field operations in implementing the AGDM strategy across the organization in a corporate manner.

During the year, the Office undertook an analysis of the AGDM Accountability Framework, which provided field operations with a mechanism to measure progress in implementing policies specifically related to the protection of women and children, as well as a community-based approach to operations management. The Framework placed accountability on senior management and aimed to identify gaps in compliance with relevant policies and standards. The analysis revealed that progress in compliance varied by region. Operations in Africa reported the highest rates of compliance with SGBV prevention, response actions, and AGDM activities. Operations in Asia reported the highest levels of compliance on activities targeting the enhanced protection of children, women and girls. The analysis also revealed constraints related to staffing, socio-cultural obstacles and the engagement of partners. In 2008, the Framework was expanded to countries in Europe, North America and Asia, where the main focus of UNHCR's work was advocacy. Gender equality was addressed from the perspectives of both leadership and livelihoods. Women were encouraged to participate in camp committees and food and non-food item distribution. They were also assisted in organizing women's groups and in communicating with UNHCR, as well as other organizations and relevant authorities. In some operations, displaced women's groups established contacts with local women's organizations that supported their work and, at times, their local integration. In all operations, UNHCR continued to strive to reach the targets for the participation of refugee women in refugee management and leadership committees. UNHCR was committed to women's economic self-reliance and promoted livelihood strategies that included gender analysis and design. That also included targeting training and vocational capacity-building to the specific needs of women and men. To that end, an important initiative was the Women Leading for Livelihoods project, aimed at the economic self-sufficiency of displaced women through a range of activities focusing on computer literacy, language and vocational training, innovative farming and market access, micro-credit and small business centres. At the beginning of 2008, the UNHCR *Handbook for the Protection of Women and Girls* was published and distributed widely within and outside the Office.

Refugee children

In 2008, UNHCR continued to emphasize education, nutrition and protection from violence in addressing the needs of refugee children. It started drafting guidelines on effective child protection systems in accordance with the 2007 Executive Committee conclusion on children at risk [YUN 2007, p. 1234], which called for children's non-discriminatory access to such systems. It also recommended improvements in identifying children at risk and the mechanisms for monitoring, reporting and referral; strengthening strategic partnerships; and giving greater attention to prevention, family support and early intervention. Testing of the approach began in five operations in late 2008.

In May, UNHCR finalized its Guidelines on Determining the Best Interests of the Child, which recommended that a best interest determination (BID) be conducted under strict procedural safeguards for particularly important decisions affecting a child, such as durable solutions for unaccompanied and separated children; temporary care arrangements for unaccompanied or separated children in exceptional situations; and the involuntary separation of a child from his or her parents.

In 2008, UNHCR also reviewed minimum standards for education in emergencies, chronic crises and early recovery, and aligned its Education Field Guidelines with other policies and standards. A comprehensive report analysing UNHCR's progress in education highlighted that 67 per cent of refugee children aged 6–17 were enrolled in primary and secondary schooling.

Regional activities

Africa

In 2008, persons of concern to UNHCR in Africa, excluding North Africa, decreased from 10.5 million in 2007 to 10.2 million. The total comprised some 2.1 million refugees, 6.3 million IDPs, 305,620 asylum-seekers, and 1.3 million returned refugees and IDPs and others of concern.

Report of Secretary-General. In response to General Assembly resolution 62/125 [YUN 2007 p. 1250], the Secretary-General submitted an August report [A/63/321] on assistance to refugees, returnees and displaced persons in Africa, covering 2007 and the first half of 2008. He stated that displacement by armed conflict and other situations of violence in Africa increased during 2007, with the total number of uprooted people growing by approximately 1 million. At the end of 2007, the total population of concern to the Office stood at 15.2 million, with IDPs outnumbering refugees by a wide margin. The estimated 12.7 million IDPs in Africa made up almost half the worldwide total. African nations hosted 2.3 million refugees in 2007, continuing the trend of decreasing numbers observed since 2001. Underlying those broad trends were both the significant progress made in achieving durable solutions and the impact of several new population movements across the continent. More than 2 million displaced people found solutions to their plight. In 2007, an estimated 300,000 refugees and 1.7 million IDPs made the decisive step of returning home, often after years of exile. Significant progress was made in the local integration of residual refugee groups in Central, Southern and West Africa. For some 19,000 refugees across the continent, third-country resettlement provided the most appropriate long-term solution. At the same time, conflict in the north of the Central African Republic, Chad, North Kivu Province of the DRC, Somalia and the Darfur region of the Sudan caused new displacement within and across international borders and exacerbated already dire humanitarian situations. Providing assistance and protection was challenging and frequently dangerous, yet vital for millions of people fleeing insecurity, political unrest and persecution. African countries continued to require the bulk of international funding for humanitarian emergencies and operations. Between January 2007 and July 2008, humanitarian activities in Africa identified in 36 inter-agency appeals of the United Nations and its partners received over $5.5 billion. The Central Emergency Response Fund (CERF) contributed to ensuring a more predictable response to emergencies, including grants for Africa of over $398 million against global disbursements of $613 million. In addition, several donors continued to pool humanitarian resources for the Sudan and the DRC, giving the humanitarian coordinators in those countries a strategic funding mechanism to ensure early support for critical activities. UN entities and NGOs received significant funding through emergency response funds in the Central African Republic, the DRC, Somalia, the Sudan and Zimbabwe. The report also described humanitarian response and inter-agency cooperation in the context of UN reform, promotion of international protection principles, ending forced displacement, delivery of assistance and special needs and partnerships with non-UN entities.

East Africa and the Horn of Africa were hit hard by conflict and natural disasters, particularly Ethiopia, Kenya, Somalia and the Sudan, which resulted in additional population displacements. Overall, the number of refugees in that region increased by 15 per cent in 2007 despite improvements in Southern Sudan that allowed a significant number of refugees and IDPs to return to their places of origin. The Sudan was the site of the largest humanitarian operation in Africa. That situation included handling the biggest IDP crisis, with 5.8 million persons affected, as well as the largest refugee repatriation operations. The Sudan was also the largest refugee-producing country on the continent in 2007, with its refugees numbering some 523,000. Darfur remained in a state of humanitarian emergency as a result of unabated violence and deteriorating security. New displacement occurred within Darfur and into neighbouring Chad and the Central

African Republic. In Somalia, the continued conflict in south and central Somalia caused the massive displacement of populations. During the reporting period, the IDP population rose from 450,000 to approximately 1.1 million people. Clashes in the Ogaden region, coupled with drought, floods and food insecurity in southern Ethiopia, triggered the internal displacement of thousands of Ethiopians. There were some 200,000 conflict-induced IDPs, living mainly in Somali, Oromiya, Gambella and Tigray regional states. In Kenya, post-election violence that erupted in late 2007 led to the displacement of between 350,000 and 500,000 people to camps and host communities, especially in the Rift Valley. In addition, some 12,000 Kenyans sought refuge in Uganda. In Uganda, Southern Sudanese refugees showed strong interest in returning home, and between January and June 2008, some 41,000 Sudanese were assisted to repatriate. The consolidation of security, the lifting of restrictions on freedom of movement and ongoing development efforts in northern Uganda allowed over 1.1 million IDPs to begin returning and re-establishing their livelihoods.

In Central Africa and the Great Lakes region, deteriorating security in parts of the Central African Republic, Chad and the DRC caused more suffering and displacements. On a positive note, progress in achieving durable solutions for refugees in the camps in the north-west of the United Republic of Tanzania had led to a decrease in the refugee population from 285,000 to 160,000 in the previous 18 months, as well as to the closure of seven camps. In Burundi, while clashes between Government forces and rebel groups continued in the north-west, at times limiting humanitarian access, the recent return of the leader of the Forces nationales de libération (FNL) and the start of the cantonment process of FNL troops gave hope for further stabilization of the country. Refugees continued to repatriate to Burundi, almost exclusively from the United Republic of Tanzania. Since January 2007, almost 80,000 refugees had returned home. In the Central African Republic, fighting between Government forces and irregular armed groups, combined with widespread banditry, severely affected civilians in the north of the country and the number of IDPs rose to 197,000. Tens of thousands of civilians also sought asylum in neighbouring Chad, Cameroon and the Sudan. The total number of refugees from the Central African Republic stood at 104,000. The situation in eastern Chad worsened markedly along the volatile border with Darfur, where cross-border movements of armed groups, militia clashes, acts of banditry and general impunity affected the safety and security of 250,000 refugees from Darfur, 186,000 Chadian IDPs and the host communities. In the DRC, fighting continued in eastern parts of the country, particularly in North Kivu and certain parts of South Kivu. Insecurity caused the internal displacement of about half a million people in 2007. Congolese IDPs totalled 1.3 million. In total, some 158,700 Congolese refugees had returned home since the repatriation operation started in 2004.

In Southern Africa, repatriation efforts were completed for Angolan refugees and launched for Congolese refugees in Zambia, contributing to the achievement of durable solutions and reducing the number of refugees in the subregion. Another encouraging trend was the growing willingness of Governments to consider the possibility of local integration for remaining refugee groups. Zimbabwe slipped deeper into turmoil as the human rights situation worsened in the aftermath of the March 2008 presidential and parliamentary elections. Politically motivated violence resulted in significant new internal displacement, adding to the victims of forced evictions and displacing farm workers—who constituted the majority of those previously displaced. In May, South Africa was hit by a wave of unprecedented xenophobic violence targeting Zimbabweans and other foreign nationals, resulting in some 60 deaths and displacing up to 100,000 people. About 25,000 displaced foreign nationals were accommodated at temporary sites where they received physical protection and assistance. By the end of June, the number of people in those sites had decreased by almost half.

West Africa remained relatively stable in 2007, with the consolidation of peace and strengthening of constitutional order in previously war-ravaged countries such as Liberia and Sierra Leone. In 2007, West Africa had 175,000 refugees—30 per cent fewer compared to 2006—owing to successful voluntary repatriation operations and positive achievements in terms of resettlement to third countries. By the end of the assisted repatriation operation in June 2007, over 158,000 refugees had returned to Liberia. In 2008, repatriation continued on a case-by-case basis. In Côte d'Ivoire, the signing of the Ouagadougou Peace Agreement in March 2007 between the Government and the Forces nouvelles improved prospects for stability and the return of refugees and an estimated 700,000 IDPs. By the end of May 2008, some 61,000 IDPs had returned to their areas of origin, mainly in western and central Côte d'Ivoire.

The Secretary-General said that while certain post-conflict situations had stabilized, millions more Africans were still forcibly displaced. He concluded that African States, which remained the primary bearers of the responsibility to protect and assist victims of forced displacement, should redouble their efforts to develop and implement strategies for durable solutions, including by expanding opportunities for local integration for refugees. In addition, States, the AU, subregional organizations and the international community should enhance their collaboration and interventions to ensure that peace would be sustainable in countries emerging from conflict. The recovery process and bridging the gap between humanitarian relief and longer-term development continued to be real and problematic challenges to that goal. He noted that, in particular, the international donor community must abide by its commitment to increase its post-conflict and development aid to Africa. It was recommended that the AU conclude the draft convention for the protection and assistance of internally displaced persons in Africa. Once adopted, that convention would be a groundbreaking achievement as the first international treaty focusing on IDPs. The Secretary-General said that humanitarian workers were at times faced with grave security problems and limited access to displaced populations. States and other parties to conflicts must ensure safe, timely and unhindered access to displaced populations. Troop-contributing countries and donors must provide the necessary resources and capacities to peacekeeping operations that were mandated to protect civilians, including displaced people.

Subregional developments

UNHCR report. According to the UNHCR Global Report 2008, UNHCR helped more than 150,000 refugees in Central Africa and the Great Lakes region find a durable solution through voluntary repatriation and reintegration in their home countries, including 40,000 refugees who repatriated to the DRC, 95,000 to Burundi and some 8,600 to Rwanda. The Office strengthened its resettlement capacity and almost 2,400 refugees departed for third countries. UNHCR provided international protection and material assistance to some 676,000 refugees, of whom 68,300 Congolese were in camps in Burundi, Rwanda and the United Republic of Tanzania. UNHCR also protected and assisted 2,700 Burundians in Rwanda, 112,000 Angolans in the DRC, more than 8,500 refugees from Chad, Sudan and the DRC in the Central African Republic and some 81,000 refugees in Cameroon, of whom almost 63,000 were from the Central African Republic. The Office led the efforts of the protection cluster to improve the safety and security of IDPs in the Central African Republic and the DRC. Among other challenges, refugees in the Central African Republic did not live in camps but were scattered across more than 70 settlements along the border. Their mobility and dispersion over a vast swathe of territory, in addition to bad road conditions, hindered humanitarian access. Access to IDPs in the country remained a challenge given the lack of security in some areas.

In East Africa and the Horn of Africa, continuing conflicts in Somalia in 2008 prompted large-scale displacements. More than 70,000 Somali refugees sought asylum in neighbouring countries, with more than 60,000 entering Kenya. In Somalia, the deteriorating security situation and the shrinking humanitarian space compelled most aid agencies, including UNHCR, to withdraw staff from the central and southern parts of the country. The Head of UNHCR's Mogadishu office was abducted in June and was released in late August. UNHCR could not implement planned activities in Somalia due to insecurity in the country. In December, Ethiopian forces ended their two-year intervention in Somalia. The decommissioning of the United Nations Mission in Ethiopia and Eritrea and the termination of the mandate of the Boundary Commission heightened tensions between Ethiopia and Eritrea. Nevertheless, UNHCR carried out participatory assessments in all refugee and IDP sites. The absence of a peace accord between the Lord's Resistance Army and the Government of Uganda had a negative impact on UNHCR activities. The protracted nature of the refugee situation in Uganda was exacerbated by the lack of a comprehensive policy on local integration. UNHCR advocated that acceptable standards of treatment for all refugees be maintained and that newly enacted refugee legislation be implemented in Kenya. The Office registered all newly arrived refugees in Kenya in three camps in Dadaab, including some 20,000 who arrived before 2008. The successful repatriation to Southern Sudan from Ethiopia led to the closure of two camps hosting Sudanese refugees from Bonga and Dimma in the Gambella region of Ethiopia, and to the dramatic downsizing of the Sherkole camp in Benshangul-Gumuz. However, the ongoing influx from Eritrea and Somalia required the opening of two new camps in Mayani and Shedar, respectively. In Eritrea, UNHCR continued to face restrictions in movement which affected its ability to monitor the condition of deportees. The protection environment in Djibouti continued to be challenging throughout 2008. More than 19,000 refugees, about half of them from Ethiopia, were referred for resettlement from the region.

In West Africa, UNHCR's Regional Office in Dakar protected and assisted some 65,500 refugees and nearly 5,000 asylum-seekers in the Gambia, Guinea-Bissau, Mali and Senegal. The agreement reached between Senegal and Mauritania in 2007 allowed the repatriation of some 7,000 Mauritanian refugees from Senegal in 2008. A re-profiling exercise boosted the number of candidates for return among refugees in Senegal and Mali from some 25,000 to 35,000. The Dakar Office conducted a verification exercise for Sierra Leonean refugees in preparation for invocation of the cessation clause. Some 1,900 refugees applied for local integration and would be assisted in 2009 with documentation and livelihood support. The Office in Benin coordinated activities for Benin, Burkina Faso, Niger and Togo until the end of 2008. Some 4,650

Togolese refugees were repatriated, more than 4,250 of them from Ghana. In Nigeria, the UNHCR Office assisted more than 10,100 refugees and some 1,200 asylum-seekers. Some 300 Liberian refugees and 70 Sierra Leonean refugees were repatriated in 2008. However, the challenging socio-economic situation in the region was restricting progress in the areas of local integration and livelihood. High expectations of resettlement led some 800 Sierra Leonean refugees in the Gambia, Guinea-Bissau and Nigeria to apply for exemptions to the cessation clause. Resettlement from Benin and Nigeria also affected the voluntary repatriation of Togolese and Liberian refugees. Difficulties rose in mobilizing development agencies to support durable solutions and in promoting the local integration of smaller and dispersed groups in urban areas.

In Southern Africa, UNHCR assisted 350 Congolese refugees from Mozambique in returning home in 2008. The UNHCR Office in the subregion referred more than 1,340 people for resettlement, and some 560 refugees departed for various third countries during the year. UNHCR in Southern Africa provided support and guidance to Governments in the region to enable them to properly conduct refugee status determination and handle registration and data management for refugees and asylum-seekers. That support aided Government authorities in clearing backlogs of pending refugee status applications and gradually assuming responsibility for registration. UNHCR also encouraged the Governments of Botswana, Mozambique, Namibia and Zambia to adopt the legal frameworks needed to facilitate access to local integration. Following the outbreak of xenophobic violence against foreigners in South Africa, as well as the mixed outflow of Zimbabweans to the country, UNHCR's Regional Office in Pretoria devoted much of its attention and resources towards meeting the needs of displaced populations. By the end of 2008, the majority had returned to local communities, although many continued to experience problems with reintegration and a few hundred persons remained in temporary sites established for the displaced. The huge challenges in South Africa taxed the capacity of the Pretoria Office, hampered its regional support functions and slowed progress in meeting some of its objectives. Despite those constraints, UNHCR trained more than 100 employees of Governments and implementing partners in Botswana, Mozambique, South Africa and Zambia to conduct registration in both emergencies and continuous asylum environments. While the organized repatriation of Angolan refugees ended in 2007, new opportunities emerged to bring home some of the remaining Angolan refugees in the region, particularly from Zambia, Namibia and Botswana. The Angolan Government affirmed its readiness to welcome the remaining Angolan refugees home and a series of tripartite meetings with neighbouring countries and UNHCR were scheduled to take place in order to prepare for their return.

By subregion, UNHCR assisted 3.2 million persons in Central Africa and the Great Lakes region, which received $273 million in agency expenditures. In East Africa and the Horn of Africa, $260 million was spent on 5.7 million persons of concern, while some $75 million was spent on programmes assisting 910,000 persons in need in West Africa. In Southern Africa, $42 million was spent on 418,000 persons of concern.

Other developments. The African Union (AU) Executive Council, at its twelfth ordinary session (Addis Ababa, Ethiopia, 25–29 January), adopted two decisions (EX.CL/Dec.381(XII) and EX.CL/Dec.382(XII)) on the situation of refugees, returnees and internally displaced persons in Africa. In decision EX.CL/Dec.381(XII), the Council called upon the international community to redouble its assistance to victims of forced displacement in Africa. It requested the AU Commission, together with the Permanent Representatives Committee's Sub-Committee on Refugees and the AU partners, in particular UNHCR, ICRC, WFP and IOM, to continue monitoring the problem of forced displacement in Africa. It further requested the AU Commission to develop a mechanism for verifying the statistics provided on victims of forced displacement. The Council, in decision EX.CL/Dec.382(XII), adopted the revised Rules of Procedure of the Revitalized African Union Coordinating Committee on Assistance and Protection to Refugees, Returnees and IDPs in Africa and the Terms of Reference of its Working Group, as amended by the Permanent Representatives Committee. It requested the Commission to reactivate the Coordinating Committee as soon as possible so as to enable it to address the challenges of forced displacement in Africa.

GENERAL ASSEMBLY ACTION

On 18 December [meeting 70], the General Assembly, on the recommendation of the Third Committee [A/63/423], adopted **resolution 63/149** without vote [agenda item 39].

Assistance to refugees, returnees and displaced persons in Africa

The General Assembly,

Recalling the Organization of African Unity Convention governing the specific aspects of refugee problems in Africa of 1969 and the African Charter on Human and Peoples' Rights,

Reaffirming that the 1951 Convention relating to the Status of Refugees, together with the 1967 Protocol thereto, as complemented by the Organization of African Unity Convention of 1969, remains the foundation of the international refugee protection regime in Africa,

Recognizing the particular vulnerability of women and children among refugees and other persons of concern, including exposure to discrimination and sexual and physical abuse,

Recognizing also that refugees, internally displaced persons and, in particular, women and children are at an increased risk of exposure to HIV/AIDS, malaria and other infectious diseases,

Expressing its appreciation for the decision of the African Union to convene the Special Summit of Heads of State and Government of the African Union on Refugees, Returnees and Internally Displaced Persons in Africa, and welcoming the ongoing process to elaborate a draft African Union convention for the protection and assistance of internally displaced persons in Africa,

Noting with appreciation the Pact on Security, Stability and Development in the Great Lakes Region and its instruments, in particular two of the Protocols to the Pact which are relevant to the protection of displaced persons, namely, the Protocol on Protection and Assistance to Internally Displaced Persons and the Protocol on the Property Rights of Returning Persons,

Recognizing that host States have the primary responsibility for the protection of and assistance to refugees on their territory, and the need to redouble efforts to develop and implement comprehensive durable solution strategies, in appropriate cooperation with the international community, and burden- and responsibility-sharing,

Emphasizing that States have the primary responsibility to provide protection and assistance to internally displaced persons within their jurisdiction, as well as to address the root causes of the displacement problem in appropriate cooperation with the international community,

1. *Takes note* of the reports of the Secretary-General and the United Nations High Commissioner for Refugees;

2. *Notes* the need for African States to address resolutely root causes of all forms of forced displacement in Africa and to foster peace, stability and prosperity throughout the African continent so as to forestall refugee flows;

3. *Notes with great concern* that, despite all of the efforts made so far by the United Nations, the African Union and others, the situation of refugees and displaced persons in Africa remains precarious, and calls upon States and other parties to armed conflict to observe scrupulously the letter and spirit of international humanitarian law, bearing in mind that armed conflict is one of the principal causes of forced displacement in Africa;

4. *Welcomes* decision EX.CL/Dec.423(XIII) on the situation of refugees, returnees and displaced persons in Africa adopted by the Executive Council of the African Union at its thirteenth ordinary session, held in Sharm el-Sheikh, Egypt, on 27 and 28 June 2008;

5. *Expresses its appreciation* for the leadership shown by the Office of the United Nations High Commissioner for Refugees, and commends the Office for its ongoing efforts, with the support of the international community, to assist African countries of asylum and to respond to the protection and assistance needs of refugees, returnees and displaced persons in Africa;

6. *Notes* the initiatives taken by the African Union and the African Commission on Human and Peoples' Rights, in particular the role of its Special Rapporteur on Refugees, Asylum Seekers, Migrants and Internally Displaced Persons in Africa;

7. *Notes with appreciation* the general conclusion on international protection adopted by the Executive Committee of the Programme of the United Nations High Commissioner for Refugees at its fifty-ninth session, held in Geneva from 6 to 10 October 2008;

8. *Acknowledges* the important contribution of the age, gender and diversity mainstreaming strategy in identifying, through a participatory approach, the protection risks faced by the different members of the refugee community, in particular the non-discriminatory treatment and protection of refugee women and refugee children and minority groups of refugees;

9. *Affirms* that children, because of their age, social status and physical and mental development, are often more vulnerable than adults in situations of forced displacement, recognizes that forced displacement, return to post-conflict situations, integration in new societies, protracted situations of displacement and statelessness can increase child-protection risks, taking into account the particular vulnerability of refugee children to forcible exposure to the risks of physical and psychological injury, exploitation and death in connection with armed conflict, and acknowledges that wider environmental factors and individual risk factors, particularly when combined, may generate different protection needs;

10. *Recognizes* that no solution to displacement can be durable unless it is sustainable, and therefore encourages the Office of the High Commissioner to support the sustainability of return and reintegration;

11. *Also recognizes* the importance of early registration and effective registration systems and censuses as a tool of protection and as a means to the quantification and assessment of needs for the provision and distribution of humanitarian assistance and to implement appropriate durable solutions;

12. *Recalls* the conclusion on registration of refugees and asylum-seekers adopted by the Executive Committee at its fifty-second session, notes the many forms of harassment faced by refugees and asylum-seekers who remain without any form of documentation attesting to their status, recalls the responsibility of States to register refugees on their territories and, as appropriate, the responsibility of the Office of the High Commissioner or mandated international bodies to do so, reiterates in this context the central role that early and effective registration and documentation can play, guided by protection considerations, in enhancing protection and supporting efforts to find durable solutions, and calls upon the Office, as appropriate, to help States to conduct this procedure should they be unable to register refugees on their territory;

13. *Calls upon* the international community, including States and the Office of the High Commissioner and other relevant United Nations organizations, within their respective mandates, to take concrete action to meet the protection and assistance needs of refugees, returnees and displaced persons and to contribute generously to projects and programmes aimed at alleviating their plight and facilitating durable solutions for refugees and displaced persons;

14. *Reaffirms* the importance of timely and adequate assistance and protection for refugees, returnees and displaced persons, also reaffirms that assistance and protection are mutually reinforcing and that inadequate material assistance and food shortages undermine protection, notes the importance of a rights- and community-based approach in engaging constructively with individual refugees, returnees and displaced persons and their communities so as to achieve fair and equitable access to food and other forms of material assistance, and expresses concern in regard to situations in which minimum standards of assistance are not met, including those in which adequate needs assessments have yet to be undertaken;

15. *Also reaffirms* that respect by States for their protection responsibilities towards refugees is strengthened by international solidarity involving all members of the international community and that the refugee protection regime is enhanced through committed international cooperation in a spirit of solidarity and burden- and responsibility-sharing among all States;

16. *Further reaffirms* that host States have the primary responsibility to ensure the civilian and humanitarian character of asylum, calls upon States, in cooperation with international organizations, within their mandates, to take all necessary measures to ensure respect for the principles of refugee protection and, in particular, to ensure that the civilian and humanitarian nature of refugee camps is not compromised by the presence or the activities of armed elements or used for purposes that are incompatible with their civilian character, and encourages the High Commissioner to continue efforts, in consultation with States and other relevant actors, to ensure the civilian and humanitarian character of camps;

17. *Condemns* all acts that pose a threat to the personal security and well-being of refugees and asylum-seekers, such as refoulement, unlawful expulsion and physical attacks, calls upon States of refuge, in cooperation with international organizations, where appropriate, to take all necessary measures to ensure respect for the principles of refugee protection, including the humane treatment of asylum-seekers, notes with interest that the High Commissioner has continued to take steps to encourage the development of measures to better ensure the civilian and humanitarian character of asylum, and encourages the High Commissioner to continue those efforts, in consultation with States and other relevant actors;

18. *Deplores* the continuing violence and insecurity which constitute an ongoing threat to the safety and security of staff members of the Office of the High Commissioner and other humanitarian organizations and an obstacle to the effective fulfilment of the mandate of the Office and the ability of its implementing partners and other humanitarian personnel to discharge their respective humanitarian functions, urges States, parties to conflict and all other relevant actors to take all measures necessary to protect activities related to humanitarian assistance, prevent attacks on and kidnapping of national and international humanitarian workers and ensure the safety and security of the personnel and property of the Office and that of all humanitarian organizations discharging functions mandated by the Office, and calls upon States to investigate fully any crime committed against humanitarian personnel and bring to justice the persons responsible for such crimes;

19. *Calls upon* the Office of the High Commissioner, the African Union, subregional organizations and all African States, in conjunction with agencies of the United Nations system, intergovernmental and non-governmental organizations and the international community, to strengthen and revitalize existing partnerships and forge new ones in support of the protection system for refugees, asylum-seekers and internally displaced persons;

20. *Calls upon* the Office of the High Commissioner, the international community and other entities concerned to intensify their support to African Governments through appropriate capacity-building activities, including training of relevant officers, disseminating information about refugee instruments and principles, providing financial, technical and advisory services to accelerate the enactment or amendment and implementation of legislation relating to refugees, strengthening emergency response and enhancing capacities for the coordination of humanitarian activities, in particular those Governments that have received large numbers of refugees and asylum-seekers;

21. *Reaffirms* the right of return and the principle of voluntary repatriation, appeals to countries of origin and countries of asylum to create conditions that are conducive to voluntary repatriation, and recognizes that, while voluntary repatriation remains the pre-eminent solution, local integration and third-country resettlement, where appropriate and feasible, are also viable options for dealing with the situation of African refugees who, owing to prevailing circumstances in their respective countries of origin, are unable to return home;

22. *Also reaffirms* that voluntary repatriation should not necessarily be conditioned on the accomplishment of political solutions in the country of origin in order not to impede the exercise of the refugees' right to return, recognizes that the voluntary repatriation and reintegration process is normally guided by the conditions in the country of origin, in particular that voluntary repatriation can be accomplished in conditions of safety and dignity, and urges the High Commissioner to promote sustainable return through the development of durable and lasting solutions, particularly in protracted refugee situations;

23. *Calls upon* the international donor community to provide financial and material assistance that allows for the implementation of community-based development programmes that benefit both refugees and host communities, as appropriate, in agreement with host countries and consistent with humanitarian objectives;

24. *Appeals* to the international community to respond positively, in the spirit of solidarity and burden- and responsibility-sharing, to the third-country resettlement needs of African refugees, notes in this regard the importance of using resettlement strategically, as part of situation-specific comprehensive responses to refugee situations, and to this end encourages States, the Office of the High Commissioner and other relevant partners to make full use of the Multilateral Framework of Understandings on Resettlement, where appropriate;

25. *Calls upon* the international donor community to provide material and financial assistance for the implementation of programmes intended for the rehabilitation

of the environment and infrastructure affected by refugees in countries of asylum;

26. *Urges* the international community, in the spirit of international solidarity and burden-sharing, to continue to fund generously the refugee programmes of the Office of the High Commissioner and, taking into account the substantially increased needs of programmes in Africa, inter alia, as a result of repatriation possibilities, to ensure that Africa receives a fair and equitable share of the resources designated for refugees;

27. *Encourages* the Office of the High Commissioner and interested States to identify protracted refugee situations which might lend themselves to resolution through the development of specific, multilateral, comprehensive and practical approaches to resolving such refugee situations, including improvement of international burden- and responsibility-sharing and realization of durable solutions, within a multilateral context;

28. *Expresses grave concern* about the plight of internally displaced persons in Africa, notes the efforts of African States in strengthening the regional mechanisms for protection of and assistance to internally displaced persons, calls upon States to take concrete action to pre-empt internal displacement and to meet the protection and assistance needs of internally displaced persons, recalls in that regard the Guiding Principles on Internal Displacement, takes note of the current activities of the Office of the High Commissioner related to protection of and assistance to internally displaced persons, including in the context of inter-agency arrangements in this field, emphasizes that such activities should be consistent with relevant General Assembly resolutions and should not undermine the refugee mandate of the Office and the institution of asylum, and encourages the High Commissioner to continue his dialogue with States on the role of his Office in this regard;

29. *Invites* the Representative of the Secretary-General on the human rights of internally displaced persons to continue his ongoing dialogue with Member States and the intergovernmental and non-governmental organizations concerned, in accordance with his mandate, and to include information thereon in his reports to the Human Rights Council and the General Assembly;

30. *Requests* the Secretary-General to submit a comprehensive report on assistance to refugees, returnees and displaced persons in Africa to the General Assembly at its sixty-fourth session, taking fully into account the efforts expended by countries of asylum, under the item entitled "Report of the United Nations High Commissioner for Refugees, questions relating to refugees, returnees and displaced persons and humanitarian questions".

The Americas

In North America and the Caribbean, UNHCR advocated for the political and financial support of the Governments of the United States and Canada and sought their backing for protection and durable solutions programmes for refugees. The United States resettled some 65,000 refugees in 2008. Of those, some 49,000 (or 75 per cent) were referred by UNHCR. That represented the highest number and proportion of UNHCR referrals in that country for the past 20 years. With national security concerns affecting domestic asylum policies in the United States, the Department of Homeland Security continued to emphasize enforcement, including more use of detention and stricter border controls. In 2008, Canada resettled over 10,000 refugees, some 7,300 through its Government assisted programme and more than 3,500 through its Private Sponsorship of Refugees scheme. Since 2006, UNHCR had been urging the Canadian Government to fill vacant posts in the Immigration and Refugee Board (IRB) to avoid the re-emergence of a backlog. The number of asylum-seekers awaiting a decision at IRB had increased from a low of 20,000 in mid-2006 to more than 54,000 in 2008. The IRB did not have the resources to address the caseload. In the Caribbean, where systematic interception, detention and return policies were widely implemented, returns were often carried out through bilateral agreements which lacked specific asylum safeguards. Most of the Caribbean States and territories did not have adequate procedures to address existing gaps. UNHCR also faced resource constraints, including limited programme funding and human resources and an insufficient travel budget, which made it difficult to achieve its objectives.

In Latin America, UNHCR witnessed a rise in the number of regional and extra-regional asylum-seekers and refugees travelling within broader migratory movements. Mexico appointed child protection officers within its National Migration Institute to protect unaccompanied minors trapped in massive mixed migratory flows in Central America. The Regional Solidarity Resettlement Programme of the Mexico Plan of Action was revamped and confirmed as a key strategy in providing durable solutions to Colombian refugees in the southern cone. A resettlement programme for women at risk began in Argentina and Chile. After receiving 225 Palestinian refugees for resettlement, Brazil and Chile began taking steps to assist in their local integration. Nevertheless, the global economic crisis caused a decline in remittances to the region, especially to the Central American countries whose economies were highly dependent on them. In Mexico and Central America, north-bound migratory movements faced tightened border security, influenced by the fight against terrorism and human and narcotics trafficking. Interception, detention and deportation practices intensified, and there was an increase in human rights violations against undocumented immigrants. The mixed migration flow included asylum-seekers from elsewhere in the region, principally from Central America and the Caribbean, as well as migrants and asylum-seekers from Africa, the Middle East and Asia. They also included thousands of unaccompanied children who were particularly vulnerable to human rights violations and were often the victims of smugglers or traffickers.

The crisis in Colombia, which also involved or affected Costa Rica, Ecuador, Panama, Peru and Venezuela, remained UNHCR's major concern and largest operation in Latin America. Nevertheless, the Mexico Plan of Action (MPA) [YUN, 2004, p. 1210] confirmed its value as a strategic framework for protection and durable solutions. In line with the Plan, UNHCR offices in the region sought to influence legislation affecting refugees and promoted differentiated asylum procedures. In Chile, UNHCR continued to advocate for the adoption of comprehensive refugee legislation. In Brazil, despite the positive attitudes expressed by central and local governments, a vast majority of the 3,800 refugees and 427 asylum-seekers in the country still depended on some kind of UNHCR assistance. Refugees and asylum-seekers in the southern cone received UNHCR's help with local integration and the promotion of self-sufficiency. At the end of 2008, the population of concern in the region stood at some 7,100. In the course of 2008, some 1,900 people filed asylum applications. Approximately 140 individuals were resettled in the region under the Regional Solidarity Resettlement Programme of the MPA: 78 in Argentina, 19 in Brazil and 45 in Chile. The majority were Colombian refugees from urban and rural backgrounds in Costa Rica and Ecuador. In Nicaragua, the National Assembly in July passed one of the most advanced asylum laws in the region. The right to asylum was also incorporated into the new Constitution of Bolivia.

Total UNHCR expenditure in the Americas and the Caribbean for the year was $47.5 million for a population of concern of 4.0 million.

Asia and the Pacific, the Middle East and North Africa

In 2008, UNHCR spent $221.8 million on activities in Asia and the Pacific for a population of concern of 10.1 million. Expenditures for operations in the Middle East and North Africa amounted to $268.7 million for a population of concern of 6.1 million.

South Asia

In 2008, UNHCR led the collective humanitarian response in a difficult security environment in Sri Lanka, which saw considerable displacement in the north of the country as military operations there were intensified. By the end of the year, the progress of the Sri Lankan Army and the retreat of the Liberation Tigers of Tamil Eelam (LTTE) to a smaller geographical area aggravated the situation. An estimated 150,000 civilians were trapped by the hostilities, with limited access to humanitarian aid and no chance to move to safer locations. At the same time, in the east UNHCR monitored the protection of 20,000 IDPs and assisted them in returning to their homes. Throughout the year, the total number of IDPs in Sri Lanka stood at more than 500,000. In Nepal, the cooperation of the Government and the support of a core group of countries committed to finding durable solution for refugees allowed for the start of a large-scale resettlement of camp-based refugees. Some 8,000 refugees left for third countries in 2008. The Government's proactive engagement allowed for a secure environment in the camps. That enabled refugees to access information on settlement and other durable solutions provided by UNHCR and its partners, and to make free and informed decisions. In India, the rise in the number of arrivals of asylum-seekers stretched UNHCR's capacity to address their concerns in a timely and efficient manner, compelling the Office to initiate a review of its procedures. At the end of 2008 there were almost 3,800 pending applications. In Bangladesh, the living conditions started to improve for 28,300 refugees from Myanmar living in two camps, particularly in the areas of shelter, health, skills training, education and community mobilization. UNHCR and its partners completed projects to improve water supply and sanitation in both camps. They also ensured better access to primary and secondary health care. The construction of new shelters for refugees in Kutupalong camp was completed and, subject to continued funding, rehabilitation in Nayapara, which started in 2008, was expected to be finished by the end of 2009.

East Asia and the Pacific

During 2008, UNHCR focused on the search for durable solutions. In Malaysia, the Office submitted a landmark 9,000 resettlement submissions during the year, and saw 6,000 refugees departing for third countries. Approximately 17,000 persons of concern were registered by UNHCR in 2008, bringing the total number of those registered in Malaysia to over 45,400. In addition, in Malaysia UNHCR was able to enhance awareness of refugees' issues through dialogue with the national authorities and by strengthening ties with civil societies. In Thailand, the large-scale resettlement process reduced the number of registered refugees in the border camps to some 111,100 by the end of 2008, down from some 124,000 in the previous year. However, the arrival in Thailand of people from Myanmar and their informal settlement in refugee camps resulted in an unregistered population of some 30,000 to 40,000. To address that concern, the Office and the Government agreed at the end of 2008 to take steps to ensure screening of the unregistered population. UNHCR's continued cooperation with the authorities to prepare for Indonesia's accession to the international refugees instruments helped promote asylum issues. The Office's enhanced capacity in Indonesia contributed to more efficient protection and helped develop the capacity of stakeholders. In China, the Government revived discussions on the development of national refugee legislation during the second half of the year. In Hong Kong, the Government and UNHCR finalized a Memorandum of Understanding (MOU) on enhanced cooperation, through which the training of immigration officers on screening procedures would be improved. In December, the Government of Japan announced its decision to pilot a three-year resettlement programme for 90 refugees from Myanmar, starting in 2010, which made Japan the first country on the Asian continent to adopt a resettlement programme. Asylum applications increased multi-fold, from 384 in 2005 to an estimated 1,600 by the end of 2008. In the Republic of Korea, UNHCR and the Korea Immigration Service signed an Exchange of Letters aimed at enhancing the quality and sustainability of refugee status determination (RSD) in the country. Australia's resettlement programme continued in 2008 and provided durable solutions for approximately 6,000 UNHCR-referred refugees. In Cambodia, following the Government's decision to assume responsibility for RSD, a Refugee Office was established under the Ministry of the Interior in October. There was significant progress in the search for solutions for Montagnard refugees in Cambodia following implementation of the MOU signed by UNHCR, Cambodia and Viet Nam in 2005 [YUN 2005, p. 1317]. At the end of 2008, only 236 Montagnards remained at UNHCR-assisted sites awaiting a durable solution. In Viet Nam, UNHCR was able to travel to the Central Highlands to observe the situation of Montagnards who had returned from Cambodia. Further strides were made in the prevention and reduction of statelessness as the naturalization process for some 9,500 former Cambodian refugees began to take effect in September.

Central Asia, South-West Asia, North Africa and the Middle East

In 2008, South-West Asia saw more than 278,000 registered Afghans return to their country with UNHCR assistance. All benefited from a $100 per person return and reintegration cash grant to meet their basic needs during the first months after return. The Government of Afghanistan and the international community endorsed the incorporation of returnee reintegration needs in the Afghanistan National Development Strategy at the Kabul Conference in November. That was expected to lead to increased support for returnees in national development programmes. In Iran, the authorities completed the online Amayesh III re-registration project, which provided some level of continued protection for the approximately 936,000 Afghan refugees who were included in the process. The issuance of work permits to registered Afghan refugees in Iran had commenced. Towards the end of the year, the Government of Pakistan indicated that the Three-Year Plan, which foresaw all registered Afghans returning to their home country in advance of the 2009 expiration of their proof of residence cards, would be reviewed.

In Central Asia, the number of new Afghan asylum-seekers in Tajikistan increased by 80 per cent. All new arrivals, with UNHCR's support, were registered. However, the recognition rate fell significantly in 2008. The majority of those arrivals were in great need of care, straining the UNHCR and the Government assistance programmes. The Office revised its social assistance policy and programmes to target refugees with specific needs. UNHCR also advocated for refugees and asylum issues to be included in training activities for Border Security and Ministry of the Interior officials. With UNHCR support and advocacy, the Government of Kazakhstan developed a draft national refugee legislation and presented it to Parliament at the end of the year. In line with its regionalization priorities, UNHCR established a Regional Office for Central Asia in the capital, Almaty. In Turkmenistan, an inter-ministerial working group was established to review the refugee and citizenship laws. The Government also agreed to take over RSD from UNHCR in accordance with its international and national obligations. The Kyrgyz Government provided citizenship to the remaining Tajik refugees in the country. Uzbekistan was not a signatory to either the 1951 Refugee Convention or the 1967 Protocol, nor had it adopted refugee legislation. Under those circumstances, resettlement remained the most viable solution for refugees and in 2008 UNHCR resettled 238 people to third countries. The Office was committed to finding solutions for the approximately 750 refugees remaining in the country, primary through resettlement. UNHCR operations in Central Asia focused on improving the quality of asylum in accordance with international standards, preventing refoulement, providing access to appropriate durable solutions, reducing and preventing statelessness, and strengthening emergency preparedness and contingency planning. Sustained advocacy efforts by UNHCR and its NGO partners led to an improved draft of the refugee law in Kazakhstan. However, in some Central Asian countries, access to asylum procedures was selective and based on political and economic issues and perceived national security concerns. That resulted in a decline in the recognition of certain groups of refugees and asylum-seekers. UNHCR was obliged to establish or maintain parallel systems to ensure RSD and provide the necessary protection and assistance to people of concern.

In 2008, UNHCR worked to protect and assist large numbers of refugees and others of concern throughout North Africa. The large mixed migration movements in North Africa were straining the capacities of national migration management structures and challenging UNHCR's ability to protect and assist refugees and other people of concern in the region. The Office provided monthly subsidies and education and housing allowances to the most vulnerable among the urban refugees. UNHCR's advocacy and capacity-building efforts had generated support for its 10-Point Plan of Action on Refugee Protection and International Migration and forged partnerships aimed at protecting people of concern moving to and through North Africa. The establishment of a national asylum procedure or process in Mauritania, and the Moroccan Government's interest in creating a national asylum system resulted from those efforts. In the Libyan Arab Jamahiriya, UNHCR's partnership with the authorities resulted in the drafting of a national refugee law and the conclusion of a partnership agreement with the National Association of Youth Voluntary Work, as well as improved access to refugees and asylum-seekers in detention. In collaboration with WFP and other partners, UNHCR provided the Sahrawi refugees in the Tindouf camps in Algeria with food, shelter, water, sanitation, health care and education. In order to improve the refugees' nutritional status and address rampant anaemia among women and children, UNHCR widened the range of foodstuffs provided to the refugees by including more fresh meat, fruits and vegetables. In Tunisia, UNHCR conducted RSD under its mandate and ensured respects for the rights of refugees and asylum-seekers. The Office also promoted refugees' self reliance through vocational training. Tunisia expressed readiness to prepare asylum legislation as part of a comprehensive asylum system.

In the Middle East, UNHCR faced a complicated picture of displacement. That included millions of Iraqis who had fled their homes to seek safety in other parts of their country and hundred of thousands more who found refuge in Jordan, the Syrian Arab Republic and other countries in the region and beyond. Both Syria and Jordan remained particularly generous in their treatment of Iraqis despite already bearing the burden of large numbers of Palestinians and other refugees. There was some improvement in the situation in Iraq, however, with many parts of the country seeing a notable reduction in the number of security incidents. Furthermore, there was a rise in the numbers of people returning to their home areas, especially among IDPs. In anticipation of such returns, UNHCR developed an individual case management mechanism to respond to the returnees' protection and assistance needs. However, the security situation in Iraq remained fragile and was not conducive to large-scale returns. The humanitarian crisis in Gaza dominated events in the region in late 2008. Although hostilities between Israel and the Hamas Government in Gaza did not lead to significant external displacements, UNHCR provided non-food items and logistical support to the United Nations Relief and Works Agency for Palestine Refugees in the Near East (UNRWA). The High Commissioner issued a public statement reiterating the need to protect civilians fleeing the violence. In Israel, a strengthened UNHCR presence helped to build the Government's capacity to protect and assist refugees. The Office supported the Government's efforts to establish responsive national asylum systems consistent with international standards. It also intervened in detention and other protection cases. In 2008, UNHCR recorded a 70 per cent increase in the number of asylum-seekers and immigrants arriving in Yemen from the Horn of Africa, with more than 50,000 people making the dangerous journey across the Gulf of Aden on smugglers' boats. Some 950 individuals were reported to have drowned or gone missing during the voyage. The traditionally positive protection climate in Egypt was negatively affected by an increase in the number of asylum-seekers and migrants attempting to cross the Sinai desert to Israel. Several asylum-seekers and migrants were returned by the Israeli authorities, without prior assessments of their protection needs. Also, hundreds of Eritreans were detained and deported from Egypt, despite UNHCR's appeals to the authorities of both countries to refrain from forcible return and grant the Office access to detention centres. With the exception of a group detained in the Aswan prison in Egypt, UNHCR was not permitted access to detained Eritrean asylum-seekers, nor did it receive any verifiable information about them.

Europe

In 2008, UNHCR expenditures for activities in Europe totalled $124.4 million, for a population of concern of 4.1 million. More than one third of that amount ($47.9 million) was for the 1.2 million persons of concern in Eastern Europe, while $39.5 million was for the 598,620 persons of concern in South-Eastern Europe.

West, Central and Eastern Europe

In 2008, the number of asylum applications in Western Europe increased by some 6 per cent over the previous year. Some western European States like Italy, Norway, the Netherlands and Switzerland had to deal with massive increases in the number of asylum applications. Cyprus, Greece and Sweden, which had been major recipients of new asylum-seekers in 2007, saw a considerable decline. The change in asylum policy in Sweden, especially towards Iraqis in 2008, had immediate repercussions in the Nordic countries, with the number of asylum-seekers sharply rising in Finland and Norway. While the number of individuals requesting refugee status continued to decrease in most of the industrialized countries in 2008, the Nordic countries recorded an increase of about 2 per cent. Mixed migration flows at the southern borders of Europe continued to grow during the year. Greece reported 146,000 arrivals of irregular migrants, while Spain saw a decrease in arrivals over the same period, with some 13,000 individuals reaching its shores. In Ireland, the Office supported the revision of the new refugee bill. In Portugal, the newly adopted law on asylum incorporated most of UNHCR's recommendations. In the United Kingdom, the Government endorsed recommendations made by UNHCR on improving the asylum system, as part of the European Quality Initiative project aimed at promoting a fair and efficient asylum system. The Office advocated in several multilateral and national forums for the creation of a Common European Asylum System that adhered to the spirit of the 1951 Refugee Convention. UNHCR followed the transposition of the European Union (EU) Qualification and Procedures Directives in a number of EU member States. It signed an exchange of letters with Frontex, the EU External Border Agency, including on protection training in the context of border management. The Office collaborated closely with the European Commission, the European Council and the European Parliament, the Council of Europe, the European Court of Justice and the Organization for Security and Cooperation in Europe (OSCE), as well as national counterparts. It continued its effective partnerships with competent national authorities in Spain, Italy and to some degree in Greece and Malta to identify people in need of international protection or with special needs. In the Nordic countries, working relationships with civil society were strengthened through NGOs. France, Switzerland and Germany responded to UNHCR's call to resettle vulnerable refugees for whom no other solution could be found. They joined the traditional (Sweden, Norway, Finland, Denmark, the Netherlands and the United Kingdom), new (Ireland and Portugal) and ad hoc (Italy, Spain) resettlement countries. Malta continued to be the only western European country from where resettlement took place. The Office advocated with European States for the eventual naturalization of refugees who had no perspective of return.

In Central Europe and the Baltic States, the number of asylum applications decreased in 2008 compared to 2007. The only exception was Romania, where the number of applications surged by some 70 per cent over the same period. The Office's main goals in Central Europe and the Baltic States included: access to territory and RSD procedures; advocacy for better reception conditions in line with international standards; promotion of durable solutions for refugees and stateless persons; advocacy for fair and efficient asylum procedures; and promotion of external relations and partnership. The Office had redoubled its efforts to promote resettlement as a tool. In that respect, a recent innovation in Europe was the establishment of an Emergency Transit Centre in Romania. The Centre provided a temporary safe location for refugees who were at risk or could not remain in their host country while their resettlement was finalized. In September the Office formally launched the Asylum System Quality Assurance and Evaluation Mechanism, also known as the Quality Initiative project. The project covered Austria, Bulgaria, Germany, Hungary, Poland, Romania, Slovakia and Slovenia. Based on UNHCR's mandated responsibilities, the project would also play a key role in the development of fair and efficient asylum procedures. While UNHCR continued to advocate that Europe remain a continent of asylum, a number of States had security concerns about asylum-seekers. In Bulgaria, cases of refoulement were observed in 2008. The detention of asylum-seekers, including those with specific needs, was reported. In the Czech Republic, an increase in the detention of those applying for international protection was of concern to the Office. The prospects for durable solutions in Central Europe and the Baltic States remained a challenge. Meanwhile, States in the region had shown increasing interest in establishing national resettlement programmes. In the Baltic States (Estonia, Latvia and Lithuania), the year ended without a clear indication that they would consider adhering to the 1954 and 1961 Statelessness Conventions.

In Eastern Europe, the conflicts over South Ossetia in August displaced 134,000 people. Some 102,800 returned by the end of 2008, leaving some 21,000 IDPs in need of humanitarian assistance. In response to the August crisis, UNHCR provided some 65,000 new IDPs in Georgia with basic non-food items and winterization packages, including stoves and firewood. The adoption by the Government in July of a National IDP Action Plan, which provided UNHCR with a legal basis for its interventions for durable solutions, was a major step towards resolving the situation of long-term IDPs. Although the Plan was suspended due to the August events, the Government adapted it to the new circumstances and expressed a strong commitment to finding durable solutions for people in protracted displacement. With UNHCR's support, national legislation in the region was brought closer to international standards. Under the 10-point Plan of Action, border monitoring was discussed within the Söderköping/Cross-Border Cooperation Process and improved in Belarus, Moldova, and Ukraine, with particular focus on protection-sensitive entry systems. In addition, Belarus, Moldova and Ukraine strove to align their policies, legislation and governance within EU standards. Belarus made substantial progress in the areas of border management, immigration and asylum. Moldova finalized the implementation of the Moldova-EU Action Plan under the European Neighbourhood Policy. For Ukraine, the signature on 9 September of the Association Agreement with the EU was an important step towards its closer cooperation with the latter. The Government of the Russian Federation took steps to improve migration legislation. Several legal acts became effective, among them amendments to the federal law, *On Registration of Foreign Nations and Stateless Persons Temporarily Residing in the Russian Federation*, which streamlined registration procedures and allowed UNHCR to focus on building national capacity to deal with refugee matters. In 2008, the UNHCR shelter programme in the Russian Federation completed 37 houses in Ingushetia and 29 in the Chechen Republic, allowing IDPs to return to their places of origin. UNHCR accorded priority to IDPs in temporary collective shelters who did not have alternative shelter, met the vulnerability criteria and were from rural areas where the Government's shelter programme had not begun. Hostile attitudes by the local population towards foreigners in Ukraine and the Russian Federation posed a risk to people of concern to UNHCR. The Office worked with international partners, Government authorities and civil society to promote tolerance, acceptance of diversity and law enforcement action to combat racially motivated crimes. In Azerbaijan, UNHCR promoted a fair and efficient asylum regime that complied with minimum international standards in the provision of protection and assistance to asylum-seekers and recognized refugees. In December, the Parliament of Moldova adopted a new law on asylum that was drawn up with the participation of UNHCR, NGOs and other experts.

South-Eastern Europe

In 2008, UNHCR protected and assisted some 133,000 refugees and some 354,000 IDPs in South-Eastern Europe. Some countries, such as Serbia and Croatia, saw internal divisions linked to the elections. In February, the unilateral declaration of independence by Kosovo (see p. 435) affected regional relations. UNHCR's efforts to find durable solution for persons of concern resulted in a decline in the total number of refugees and IDPs in the region to some 486,000 by the end of the year. Political developments in Serbia and Kosovo cut IDP returns to Kosovo drastically in 2008. The Office sought durable solutions by facilitating returns to Kosovo. During the year, some 122 individuals were repatriated to Serbia and Kosovo, either with UNHCR's assistance or spontaneously. In Croatia, the Office sought sustainable solutions for the returnees and helped the authorities establish a fair and efficient asylum and immigration system. It monitored the implementation of the Housing Care programme, which aimed to provide accommodation to returnees and foster developments in private property repossession. It also cooperated with the Government and NGOs in setting up a border monitoring project. Some refugees in Serbia hesitated to opt for local integration and linked their eventual decision to a resolution of the occupancy/tenancy rights issue still pending in Croatia. That issue also affected the naturalization process in Serbia. Certain minority IDP groups faced additional difficulties upon returning to their places of origin. In some areas of potential return, security remained a concern. The Roma, Ashkali and so-called Egyptian communities were the most disadvantaged in that respect. In Montenegro, four new laws were passed that had a direct bearing on populations of concern to UNHCR. Additionally, UNHCR continued to pursue durable solutions, facilitating returns to Serbia and Kosovo. In the Former Yugoslav Republic of Macedonia, there were 1,772 persons of concern to UNHCR, mostly Roma from Kosovo. In December, UNHCR's advocacy activities translated into the adoption by the Government of a strategy for the integration of refugees and foreigners in the country, which provided a policy framework for integration. Refugee repatriation and IDP returns stagnated in the region in 2008, and the Sarajevo Declaration [YUN 2005, p. 1320] had yet to be fully implemented. In December, the High Commissioner's Dialogue on Protracted Refugee Situations brought the issue of durable solutions to the fore. It gave new momentum to efforts to resolve long-standing issues affecting repatriation to Croatia and local integration of refugees in Serbia.

Chapter XIII

Health, food and nutrition

In 2008, the United Nations continued to promote human health and food security, coordinate food aid and support research in nutrition.

At the end of the year, about 33.4 million people were living with HIV/AIDS, and an estimated 2.7 million people had become infected with the virus. Deaths due to AIDS-related illnesses were estimated at 2 million. The Joint United Nations Programme on HIV/AIDS (UNAIDS) issued the 2008 *Report on the global AIDS epidemic*—the most comprehensive global assessment of the HIV/AIDS response ever assembled. The report confirmed that out of the 147 countries which had documented their progress in implementing the 2001 Declaration of Commitment on HIV/AIDS, many had made considerable gains in addressing their national epidemics. Increases in financing for HIV programmes in low- and middle-income countries resulted in progress in reducing AIDS deaths and preventing new infections. In June, the General Assembly held a high-level meeting to review the progress achieved in realizing the Declaration of Commitment and the Political Declaration on HIV/AIDS.

In 2008, the United Nations focused on sickle-cell anaemia as a public health issue. According to World Health Organization (WHO) estimates, some 100 million people carried the sickle-cell trait, and at least 500,000 children were born each year with the most severe form of the disease. Major disparities persisted between countries of the North and countries of the South with respect to management of the disease. In a December resolution, the General Assembly urged Member States and the UN system to promote health-care services, training and technology-transfer programmes to improve the lives of those affected, and to raise awareness of the disease on 19 June of each year.

The Conference of the Parties to the WHO Framework Convention on Tobacco Control, at its third session in November, established a working group to develop guidelines for implementation of article 14, dealing with demand reduction. The Intergovernmental Negotiating Body on a Protocol on Illicit Trade in Tobacco Products held its first and second sessions, at which it negotiated the objectives, scope and outline of a draft protocol. In May, the Secretary-General advised the United Nations to take a strong stance on the issue of second-hand smoke, and in a November resolution the General Assembly banned smoking and tobacco sales at UN Headquarters.

A WHO report to the General Assembly on the Decade to Roll Back Malaria in Developing Countries, Particularly in Africa (2001–2010) noted that at least 29 out of 109 countries around the world were on course to meet targets for reducing the burden caused by malaria by 2010. In February, the Secretary-General appointed Ray Chambers (United States) as his first Special Envoy for Malaria. The Assembly in a December resolution expressed concern about the continued morbidity and mortality attributed to malaria. It noted that more efforts were needed if the malaria and MDG targets for 2010 and 2015 were to be reached.

In May, the World Health Assembly adopted a resolution urging Member States, international organizations and stakeholders to prioritize the implementation of a global strategy and plan of action on public health, innovation and intellectual property. Also adopted were resolutions on monitoring the achievement of the health-related MDGs and implementation of the International Health Regulations.

The General Assembly debated the issue of global road safety in March. During the deliberations, the Russian Federation presented an initiative to host the first global high-level conference on road safety in 2009 in Moscow. In a related resolution, the Assembly commended WHO for working with the UN regional commissions to coordinate road safety issues in the UN system and the World Bank for establishing the Global Road Safety Facility—the first funding mechanism to support capacity-building for road safety.

In 2008, the World Food Programme (WFP) distributed 3.9 million metric tons of food aid, assisting 102.1 million hungry people in 78 countries. During the year, WFP faced challenges such as turmoil in international financial systems, extreme weather, political upheaval and complex emergencies in Afghanistan, Somalia and the Sudan. WFP succeeded in scaling up assistance to vulnerable populations hit by soaring food and fuel prices. The complexity of WFP emergency operations was exemplified by its response to Cyclone Nargis in Myanmar, for which WFP provided $154 million of relief for 1.1 million victims. Donor contributions in 2008 reached a record $5 billion.

In 2008, the Food and Agriculture Organization of the United Nations (FAO) continued to address the world food crisis. In June, FAO held a high-level conference on "World Food Security: the Challenges of Climate Change and Bioenergy". The conference adopted a Declaration that called on the international community to increase assistance for developing countries, in particular the least developed countries and those most negatively affected by high food prices. In April, the Secretary-General established the High-level Task Force on the Global Food Security Crisis, which brought together relevant parts of the UN system and Bretton Woods institutions to produce a unified response to the food price crisis.

Health

AIDS prevention and control

Comprehensive review of implementation of the Declaration of Commitment on HIV/AIDS

General Assembly 2008 high-level meeting on HIV/AIDS. In accordance with resolution 60/262 [YUN 2006, p. 1410], the General Assembly, during its high-level meeting on HIV/AIDS (10–12 June) [A/62/895], undertook a comprehensive review of progress achieved in realizing the 2001 Declaration of Commitment on HIV/AIDS, adopted at its twenty-sixth special session by resolution S-26/2 [YUN 2001, p. 1126]. In addition to discussing progress and challenges in the global AIDS response, the review focused on universal access to HIV prevention, treatment, care and support by considering key findings and recommendations. Among other outcomes, the meeting determined that successes must be built upon to ensure sustained progress towards full achievement of the international HIV/AIDS goals.

The meeting consisted of plenary sessions in the General Assembly with statements from 158 delegates, including 152 Member States and six observers. In addition to five panel discussions, there was an interactive hearing with civil society on the theme "Action for universal access: myths and realities".

The meeting had before it the report of the Secretary-General entitled "Declaration of Commitment on HIV/AIDS and Political Declaration on HIV/AIDS: Midway to the Millennium Development Goals" (see below), which provided the basis for deliberations.

The Secretary-General, in his statement at the opening session, emphasized the need to build on recent successes to bridge gaps in the global AIDS response. Observing that 2008 marked the sixtieth anniversary of the Universal Declaration of Human Rights [YUN 1948–49, p. 543], he said that continued discrimination against people living with HIV and groups at high risk represented an unacceptable reality. He expressed particular gratitude to Dr. Peter Piot, who would leave UNAIDS as its Executive Director at the end of 2008.

The UNAIDS Executive Director noted in his address that progress had been made in almost every region, but the pace of change was not enough to achieve universal access in most low- and middle-income countries by 2010. AIDS remained the leading cause of death in Africa and the seventh highest cause of mortality worldwide. He said that unless efforts to prevent new HIV infections were strengthened, treatment queues would lengthen, dooming efforts to achieve universal access to antiretroviral therapy. He also stressed that long-term success in the AIDS response required improved HIV prevention for young people, effective action to address gender inequality and other human rights violations, and substantial increases in funding.

Report of Secretary-General. As requested in General Assembly resolution 60/262 [YUN 2006, p. 1410], the Secretary-General submitted to the high-level meeting a report [A/62/780] entitled "Declaration of Commitment on HIV/AIDS and Political Declaration on HIV/AIDS: Midway to the Millennium Development Goals", which reviewed progress in implementing the 2001 Declaration of Commitment on HIV/AIDS [YUN 2001, p. 1126] and the 2006 Political Declaration on HIV/AIDS [YUN 2006, p. 1411].

The Secretary-General observed that, as at 10 March, 147 Member States had reported national information against 25 core indicators that were developed to track implementation of the 2001 Declaration of Commitment. The core indicators covered a broad array of variables, such as HIV prevalence among young people aged 15–24; coverage of antiretroviral therapy and key HIV prevention interventions; services to support children orphaned or made vulnerable by HIV; and national adoption of recommended HIV policies. He also noted that in nearly all countries, civil society groups were involved in monitoring and reporting progress on the core indicators for the Declaration of Commitment. In addition to having provided data to supplement national reports, those groups had engaged in national reporting workshops and produced shadow reports. More than 80 per cent of countries, including 85 per cent of those in sub-Saharan Africa, had policies in place to ensure equal access for women to HIV prevention, treatment, care and support. Women in sub-Saharan Africa had equal or greater access to antiretrovirals, but the reverse was true for women in concentrated epidemics. Although most countries had strategic frameworks that addressed the epidemic's burden on women, only 53 per cent provided budgeted support for women-focused programmes. Funding for HIV-related activities in low-income and middle-income countries reached $10 billion in 2007, a 12 per cent increase over 2006 and a tenfold increase in less than a decade. In low-income and lower middle-income countries, per capita domestic spending on HIV more than doubled between 2005 and 2007.

Worldwide, reported the Secretary-General, gender parity seemed to exist in terms of coverage with antiretrovirals. In a number of countries with generalized epidemics, however, coverage was significantly higher among females. By contrast, women in need were significantly less likely to be on antiretrovirals in several countries with concentrated epidemics. Notwithstanding the considerable achievements in expanding access to life-preserving HIV treatments, substantial progress would be required to achieve universal access to HIV treatment and care. In that regard, the Secretary-General noted that if the current trajectory of treatment scale-up continued, 4.6 million people in need would be on antiretrovirals in 2010 and 8 million in 2015. Those figures fell short of projected need: in 2007, an estimated 9.8 million people living with HIV were medically eligible to be put on antiretrovirals, and that number was certain to rise as the disease progressed among the more than 33 million people who were living with HIV.

The Secretary-General recommended that senior political leaders, with the assistance of donors, technical agencies and civil society, lead the implementation of HIV policies. He also recommended that national leaders and Governments, donors, researchers, non-governmental organizations (NGOs) and other stakeholders engaged in the HIV response begin planning for the long-term, building into their efforts strategies to ensure the sustainability of the robust, adaptable and enduring collective effort that would be required over generations.

On 24 December, the General Assembly decided that the item on the implementation of the Declaration of Commitment on HIV/AIDS and the Political Declaration on HIV/AIDS would remain for consideration during its resumed sixty-third (2009) session (**decision 63/552**).

Civil society participation. On 29 April, prior to the high-level meeting, the General Assembly approved for participation in that meeting the list of civil society representatives drawn up by the Assembly President [A/62/CRP.1], pursuant to resolution 62/178 [YUN 2007, p. 1262] (**decision 62/548**).

JIU review

The Secretary-General in July transmitted to the General Assembly the report [A/63/152] of the Joint Inspection Unit (JIU) entitled "Review of the progress made by the UN system organizations in achieving Millennium Development Goal 6, Target 7, to combat HIV/AIDS". The review focused on the role and involvement of the UNAIDS secretariat and the co-sponsors and other stakeholders in the achievement of Goal 6, Target 7: to have halted by 2015 and begun to reverse the spread of HIV/AIDS. The review also assessed the effectiveness of coordination and cooperation among the various UN entities and other stakeholders involved in combating HIV/AIDS.

JIU recommended that the Economic and Social Council review and strengthen the mandate of UNAIDS, including by enhancing the authority of the secretariat so that it may effectively lead, coordinate and monitor the fight against HIV/AIDS and ensure proper accountability of the co-sponsors to the joint programme. As part of the review, the number of co-sponsors should be restricted to the six original organizations/cosponsors, namely, the United Nations Development Programme (UNDP), the World Health Organization (WHO), the United Nations Population Fund (UNFPA), the United Nations Children's Fund (UNICEF), the United Nations Educational, Scientific and Cultural Organization (UNESCO) and the World Bank. Other organizations could participate through the co-sponsors on the basis of a memorandum of understanding. The Economic and Social Council should also review and revise the authority, role and responsibility of the UNAIDS Programme Coordinating Board to enable it to have supervisory responsibility over the UNAIDS secretariat and the co-sponsors in relation to the joint programme on HIV/AIDS.

Joint UN Programme on HIV/AIDS

UNAIDS, which became fully operational in 1996 [YUN 1996, p. 1121] continued to serve as the main advocate for global action on HIV/AIDS. In 2008, UNAIDS had ten co-sponsors: the International Labour Organization (ILO); UNDP; UNESCO; UNICEF; the Office of the United Nations High Commissioner for Refugees (UNHCR); the United Nations Office on Drugs and Crime (UNODC); WHO; the World Food Programme (WFP); UNFPA; and the World Bank.

Reports on the global AIDS epidemic

UNAIDS issued the 2008 *Report on the global AIDS epidemic* at the halfway mark between the 2001 Declaration of Commitment on HIV/AIDS [YUN 2001, p. 1126] and the 2015 target of MDG Goal 6: to have halted by 2015 and begun to reverse the spread of HIV/AIDS. Based on information from 147 countries, which documented their progress in implementing the 2001 Declaration of Commitment, the report provided the most comprehensive global assessment of the response to HIV/AIDS ever assembled. By joining with their government counterparts, unprecedented numbers of civil society groups participated in the reporting process.

The HIV response was critical to fostering progress across the breadth of the global development agenda, said the report. A six-fold increase in financing for HIV programmes in low- and middle-income countries was beginning to achieve results, with many countries making major progress in lowering AIDS deaths and preventing new infections. However, progress remained uneven and the epidemic's future was still uncertain, which underscored the need for intensified action to move towards universal access to HIV prevention, treatment, care and support.

Monitoring and evaluation systems were being improved, largely with external funding, as countries began to take advantage of the standard provision that up to 10 per cent of programme funds could be directed to strengthening such systems.

Subsequently, UNAIDS and WHO issued the 2009 *AIDS epidemic update*, which contained key data on the global epidemiology of HIV/AIDS as at December 2008. That report estimated that the number of persons living with HIV worldwide in 2008 totalled 33.4 million, representing a slight increase over the 2007 estimate of 33.2 million. The estimated number of people newly infected with HIV in 2008 was 2.7 million.

The rise in the number of people living with HIV reflected the combined effects of continued high rates of new HIV infections and the beneficial impact of antiretroviral therapy. As at December 2008, the number of people in low- and middle-income countries receiving antiretroviral therapy was approximately 4 million, indicating a ten-fold increase in access to such treatment over five years.

The epidemic appeared to have stabilized in most regions, although prevalence continued to increase in Eastern Europe and Central Asia and in other parts of Asia due to a high rate of new HIV infections. Sub-Saharan Africa remained the most heavily affected region, accounting for 71 per cent of all new HIV infections in 2008. The resurgence of the epidemic among men who had sex with men in high-income countries was increasingly well-documented. Differences were apparent in all regions, with some national epidemics continuing to expand even as the overall regional HIV incidence stabilized.

The estimated number of AIDS-related deaths in 2008 was 2 million worldwide. Seventy-two per cent of those deaths occurred in sub-Saharan Africa, where the epidemic continued to have an enormous impact on households, communities, businesses, public services and national economies, with women and girls continuing to be disproportionately affected. In 2008, sub-Saharan Africa accounted for 67 per cent of HIV infections worldwide, 68 per cent of new HIV infections among adults and 91 per cent of new HIV infections among children.

UNAIDS activities

In 2008, UNAIDS continued to promote universal access to comprehensive programmes of prevention, treatment, care and support, and advocate on behalf of people living with HIV, their families, their loved ones and the communities in which they lived. Working with Governments and civil society, and engaging with parliamentarians, UNAIDS sought to address stigma and discrimination and champion a global AIDS response that was evidence-informed and grounded in human rights.

UNAIDS and the Global Fund to Fight HIV/AIDS, Tuberculosis and Malaria entered into a comprehensive framework to improve the coordination of their efforts to aid countries in moving towards universal access to HIV prevention, treatment, care and support. Under the agreed division of responsibilities, UNAIDS would help countries develop evidence-informed funding proposals, support the Global Fund's technical review process, and provide countries with focused technical assistance to accelerate the implementation of programmes approved by the Global Fund. The Global Implementation Support Team (GIST)—a collaboration between the Global Fund, UNAIDS, UNFPA, UNICEF, WHO, the World Bank, UNDP, the German Agency for Technical Cooperation (GTZ), the United States Government, the AIDS Alliance, the International Council of AIDS Service Organizations (ICASO), the Interagency Coalition on AIDS and Development (ICAD) of Canada, and the International Centre for Technical Cooperation (ICTC) of Brazil—worked together to reduce barriers inhibiting the provision of universal access to HIV prevention, treatment, care and support services.

Programme Coordinating Board. The UNAIDS Programme Coordinating Board (PCB), at its twenty-second meeting (Chiang Mai, Thailand, 23–25 April), requested that the UNAIDS secretariat and WHO establish mechanisms for accountability of HIV programmes to prevent, diagnose and treat tuberculosis (TB) in people living with HIV, through the incorporation of relevant indicators in national AIDS action frameworks, which included the goal of reducing TB mortality in people living with HIV. PCB also requested that the UNAIDS secretariat work with WHO and other co-sponsoring organizations, as well as Governments, to expand the coverage of voluntary counselling and testing to achieve early diagnosis and treatment of HIV so that opportunistic infection, including TB, could be prevented. UNAIDS approved the new memorandum of understanding between UNAIDS and the Global Fund to Fight AIDS, Tuberculosis and Malaria, taking into account the comments from the floor. It endorsed, based on a review, the development of the next unified budget and workplan, as well as the extension to 2011 of the UNAIDS 2007–2010 strategic framework. It confirmed a four-year planning framework and a two-year budget cycle for the unified budget and workplan. It also endorsed the Executive Director's proposal for the utilization of $16 million of the available fund balance to cover priorities and investments that were not included in the 2008–2009 unified budget and workplan.

A July report [DP/2008/54], presented jointly by the Executive Boards of UNDP and UNFPA, provided an update on the implementation of decisions of PCB from its twenty-first and twenty-second meetings, held in December 2007 and April 2008, respectively. Key issues from those meetings that were of relevance to UNDP and UNFPA included: advancing implementation of the recommendations of the Global Task Team on Improving HIV/AIDS Coordination among Multilateral Institutions and International Donors; intensifying action on gender and HIV/AIDS; strengthening partnerships with the Global Fund to Fight AIDS, Tuberculosis and Malaria; extending the UNAIDS unified budget and workplan to a four-year planning cycle; and preparations for the second five-year independent evaluation of UNAIDS. UN country teams had established joint UN teams on HIV/AIDS in 89 countries, as recommended by the Global Task Team and as directed by the Secretary General in December 2005 [YUN 2005, p. 1327]. Fifty-six of those teams reported having developed a joint programme for more effective support to countries.

PCB in 2007 had requested UNAIDS to assist countries in planning, programming and implementing interventions in contexts that addressed diverse sexualities and women, girls and gender inequality, including through country pilots and other activities. In follow-up to the PCB decision, UNDP, along with the United Nations Development Fund for Women (UNIFEM), UNESCO, UNFPA, WHO and the UNAIDS secretariat, was establishing an expert group to assist in the design and oversight of a gender and HIV/AIDS pilot process in four countries. The pilot process would focus on assisting countries in planning, programming and implementing interventions that addressed women, girls and gender inequality, while a parallel process would be initiated to address male sexuality.

In April, PCB endorsed the extension of the unified budget work (UBW) planning period from a two-year cycle to four years, while maintaining a two-year budget cycle. In addition to reducing transaction costs, the four-year framework was expected to facilitate longer-term planning and a more effective monitoring of results. As a result, the 2008–2009 UBW would be extended to 2011.

PCB held an extraordinary meeting on 2 October and its twenty-third meeting from 15 to 17 December, both in Geneva.

Sickle-cell anaemia

In 2008, the United Nations focused on sickle-cell anaemia as a public health issue. By a 6 October letter [A/63/233] to the Secretary-General, the Congo requested that an item on the recognition of sickle-cell anaemia as a public health priority be included in the agenda of the General Assembly's sixty-third session. An explanatory memorandum annexed to the letter described sickle-cell anaemia as the most widespread genetic blood disorder in the world. According to WHO estimates, some 100 million people carried the sickle-cell trait and at least 500,000 children were born each year with the most severe form of the disease (HB SS), mostly in Africa, the Caribbean and the Americas. Major disparities persisted between countries of the North and countries of the South with respect to management of the disease, including lack of access to appropriate health-care services for children in areas where it was most prevalent. Despite the seriousness of the issue, sickle-cell anaemia continued to receive little attention and remained unknown among the general public. Its pathology, however, had been the focus at various meetings of international organizations between 2000 and 2007. Those meetings concluded that there was need for a framework to promote care, research and training of health personnel to benefit those affected; greater recognition by the United Nations of sickle-cell anaemia as a public health priority; more public education aimed at increasing the life expectancy of affected persons; and that 19 June of each year be proclaimed the international day to combat sickle-cell anaemia.

In December, by resolution 63/237 (see below), the General Assembly recognized sick-cell anaemia as a public health problem and encouraged support for efforts to combat the disease.

GENERAL ASSEMBLY ACTION

On 22 December [meeting 73], the General Assembly adopted **resolution 63/237** [draft: A/63/L.63 & Add.1] without vote [agenda item 155].

Recognition of sickle-cell anaemia as a public health problem

The General Assembly,

Recognizing the need to promote better physical and mental health, bearing in mind the Universal Declaration of Human Rights and other relevant human rights instruments,

Welcoming World Health Assembly resolution 59.20 of 27 May 2006 and resolution 22 of the General Conference of the United Nations Educational, Scientific and Cultural Organization of 19 October 2005, and taking note of decision Assembly/AU/Dec.81(V) adopted by the Assembly of the African Union at its fifth ordinary session, held in Sirte, Libyan Arab Jamahiriya, on 4 and 5 July 2005,

Recognizing that sickle-cell anaemia is one of the world's foremost genetic diseases, that it has severe physical, psychological and social consequences for those affected and their families, and that in its homozygote form it is one of the most lethal genetic diseases,

Aware of the need for greater international cooperation, including through partnerships, to facilitate access to education, management, surveillance and treatment for sickle-cell anaemia,

Recognizing that proper management of sickle-cell anaemia will contribute to an appreciable decrease in mortality from malaria and in the risk of HIV infection,

Recalling the Abuja Declaration on Roll Back Malaria in Africa of 25 April 2000 and the global "Roll Back Malaria" initiative,

Taking note of the reports of the first, second and third international congresses of the Sickle Cell Disease International Organization, held in Paris on 25 and 26 January 2002, in Cotonou from 20 to 23 January 2004 and in Dakar from 22 to 24 November 2006, respectively, and the report of the first global consultations on sickle-cell anaemia, held in Brazzaville from 14 to 17 June 2005,

Recognizing that education, information and communication technologies should play a crucial role in preventing sickle-cell anaemia and that there is an urgent need to create effective research and training programmes in the countries most affected by this disease,

1. *Recognizes* that sickle-cell anaemia is a public health problem;

2. *Underlines* the need to raise public awareness about sickle-cell anaemia and to eliminate harmful prejudices associated with the disease;

3. *Urges* Member States and the organizations of the United Nations system to raise awareness of sickle-cell anaemia on 19 June each year at the national and international levels;

4. *Encourages* Member States, as well as United Nations agencies, funds and programmes, international institutions and development partners, to support health systems and primary health-care delivery, including efforts to improve the management of sickle-cell anaemia;

5. *Invites* Member States, international organizations and civil society to support the efforts being made to combat sickle-cell anaemia, including as part of health-system strengthening efforts, in the various development programmes, and to encourage basic and applied research on the disease;

6. *Urges* the Member States in which sickle-cell anaemia is a public health problem to establish national programmes and specialized centres for the treatment of sickle-cell anaemia and to facilitate access to treatment;

7. *Requests* the Secretary-General to bring the present resolution to the attention of all Member States and organizations of the United Nations system.

Tobacco

The WHO Framework Convention on Tobacco Control (FCTC), adopted by the World Health Assembly in 2003 [YUN 2003, p. 1251], entered into force in 2005. At the end of 2008, 162 States and the European Union were parties to the Convention.

The third session of the Conference of the Parties to the Convention (Durban, South Africa, 17–22 November) [FCTC/COP/3/REC/1] took note of the recommendations of the working group on tobacco advertising on measures that would contribute to the elimination of cross-border advertising, promotion and sponsorship (article 13) [YUN 2007, p. 1267] and decided to further consider those recommendations at its fourth (2010) session. It also requested that the Convention secretariat assess the recommendations, propose options for further work, and report on its findings at the fourth session.

The session established a working group to elaborate guidelines for implementation of article 14 (demand reduction measures concerning tobacco dependence and cessation) of the Convention. The working group should prepare a report or, if possible, draft guidelines for consideration by the Conference of the Parties at its fourth session. In so doing, the working group should take into account the 2008 Convention secretariat report in relation to article 14 [FCTC/COP/3/10], which was presented to the third session for consideration. The session also requested the Convention secretariat to invite relevant intergovernmental and non-governmental organizations to participate in the working group.

It decided further that the third session of the Intergovernmental Negotiating Body on a Protocol on Illicit Trade in Tobacco Products (see below) would be held from 28 June to 5 July 2009 in Geneva. In that regard, it requested the Convention secretariat to facilitate the participation of low-income and lower-middle-income parties in the work of that body.

Intergovernmental Negotiating Body on a Protocol on Illicit Trade in Tobacco Products. The second (2007) session of the Conference of the Parties to the FCTC established the Intergovernmental Negotiating Body on a Protocol on Illicit Trade in Tobacco Products [YUN 2007, p. 1267], which held its first (11–15 February) and second (20–25 October) sessions in Geneva [FCTC/COP/INB-IT/2/4 Rev.1]. The first session, which was attended by representatives of 132 parties, 20 States non-parties, three intergovernmental organizations and nine NGOs, discussed the objectives, scope and outline for a protocol. The Chairperson of the Body subsequently drafted a preliminary text, using as a basis the discussions from the first session, as well as existing international agreements, the provisions of the FCTC, and support from the Convention secretariat and other experts. The second session, which was attended by representatives of 133 parties, 16 States non-parties, two intergovernmental organizations and nine NGOs, accepted that text as a basis for negotiations and examined it through plenary, committee and working group deliberations. The third session of the Negotiating Body, to be held in Geneva from 28 June to 5 July 2009, would consider a revised text to be prepared by the Chairperson.

Ad Hoc Inter-Agency Task Force

In May, the Secretary-General submitted to the Economic and Social Council, in accordance with its decision 2006/248 [YUN 2006, p. 1421], a report on progress made by the Ad Hoc Inter-Agency Task Force on Tobacco Control [E/2008/59] in implementing multisectoral collaboration on tobacco or health. Using data from the WHO Report on the Global Tobacco Epidemic, 2008, the report described the burden of tobacco consumption and focused on areas of concern where inter-agency collaboration could be important. Those included issues related to tobacco growing and alternatives to tobacco; the link between tobacco and development; gender and tobacco; tobacco industry activities and corporate social responsibility; and exposure to second-hand smoke, particularly the issue of smoking on UN premises. The report also provided an update on the WHO Framework Convention on Tobacco Control and its implementation.

The Secretary-General recommended that exposure to second-hand smoke be strictly regulated in order to protect the health of workers. He also advised the United Nations to take a strong stance on the issue and adopt a resolution on smoke-free premises in accordance with Economic and Social Council resolution 2006/42 [YUN 2006, p. 1421].

On 22 July, the Council requested the Secretary-General to submit a report on the work of the Ad Hoc Inter-Agency Task Force on Tobacco Control to the Council at its substantive session of 2010 (**decision 2008/232**). Also on 22 July, the Council, recalling its resolution 2006/42 of July 2006 on smoke-free UN premises, recommended that the General Assembly, at its sixty-third session, consider the recommendations set out in that resolution (**decision 2008/231**).

On 3 November, by resolution 63/8 (see below), the General Assembly decided to implement a complete ban on smoking and the sale of tobacco products at UN Headquarters indoor premises. It also recommended that the same ban be implemented at all UN indoor premises, including regional and country offices.

GENERAL ASSEMBLY ACTION

On 3 November [meeting 36], the General Assembly adopted **resolution 63/8** [draft: A/63/L.14 & Add.1,] without vote [agenda item 40].

Smoke-free United Nations premises

The General Assembly,

Recalling Economic and Social Council resolution 2006/42 of 27 July 2006 and Council decision 2008/231 of 22 July 2008,

Noting with concern the serious harmful impact of second-hand smoke on the health of non-smokers, which can lead to disease, disability and death,

Acknowledging that second-hand smoke at the workplace is a fully preventable occupational health hazard,

Emphasizing the importance of protecting the well-being of individuals in their working environments,

1. *Decides* to implement a complete ban on smoking at United Nations Headquarters indoor premises and on sales of tobacco products at United Nations Headquarters premises;

2. *Recommends* the implementation of a complete ban on smoking at all United Nations indoor premises, including regional and country offices throughout the United Nations system, and the implementation of a complete ban on sales of tobacco products at all United Nations premises;

3. *Requests* the Secretary-General to submit to the General Assembly at its sixty-fourth session a report on the measures for the implementation of the present resolution.

Malaria

In August, the Secretary-General transmitted to the General Assembly a report [A/63/219] on the Decade to Roll Back Malaria in Developing Countries, Particularly in Africa (2001–2010), prepared by WHO pursuant to General Assembly resolution 62/180 [YUN 2007, p. 1268]. The Decade was proclaimed by the General Assembly in resolution 55/284 [YUN 2001, p. 1139]. The report was based on data collected for the World Malaria Report 2008, which would be published in September. It highlighted progress made in meeting the goals concerning malaria to be achieved by 2010.

Funding and availability of key products for malaria prevention and treatment had started to increase in Africa starting in 2005, and by 2006, 26 African countries had spent $688 million on malaria. The targets for use of insecticide-treated nets, prompt and appropriate use of antimalarial treatments, and use of intermittent preventive therapy in pregnant women in Africa were 80 per cent or more. Average usage of treated nets across 18 countries where surveys were conducted in 2006 was well below that target: 34 per cent of houses owned an insecticide-treated net, and 23 per cent of children under 5 years of age and 27 per cent of pregnant women slept under a treated net. Although that was much below the 2010 target, it was much higher than in previous years and represented a significant achievement. Among 18 national household surveys carried out in Africa in 2006, relatively high ownership and usage of insecticide-treated nets was found in Ethiopia, the Niger, Sao Tome and Principe and Zambia.

Between 2001 and 2006, national malaria control programmes in Africa reported large increases in the number of courses of antimalarial medicines supplied through public health services. In particular, dispensing of artemisinin-based combination therapy treatments increased from 6 million doses in 2005 to 45 million doses in 2006. Those figures probably underestimated usage, and the exact consumption of artemisinin-based treatments was not known. In 2006, the average percentage of children under 5 years of age receiving any type of antimalarial treatment for fever in the past two weeks was 38 per cent. The use of artemisinin-based combination therapy was much lower: just 3 per cent of children, on average. Therefore, access to that therapy remained inadequate. Coverage of pregnant women with two doses of intermittent preventive treatment was also low (18 per cent) compared to the target of above 80 per cent.

From an Africa-wide perspective, there was no evidence that malaria had declined from 2000 to 2006. However, there were two reasons for optimism. First, data available to WHO included data only until 2006; rapid increases in use of insecticide-treated nets and artemisinin-based combination therapy in 2006 and 2007 would not be expected to show their full impact by 2006. Secondly, four low-income countries (or parts of countries) with high coverage of insecticide-treated nets and antimalarial medicines—and indoor residual spraying of insecticide in some cases—showed dramatic declines in malaria. In Eritrea, Rwanda, Sao Tome and Principe and Zanzibar, United Republic of Tanzania, the burden caused by malaria appeared to be reduced by 50 per cent or more between 2000 and 2006–2007, thus achieving the morbidity reduction targets. Three other higher-income African countries (Namibia, South Africa and Swaziland) also had significant declines in reported malaria cases. Within Africa, the large increase in availability of products to prevent and treat malaria in 2006 and 2007 had a reasonable probability of yielding an impact in 2007 and 2008.

In regions outside of Africa, malaria cases fell by 50 per cent over the period 2000–2006 in at least 22 out of 64 countries. Thus, routine surveillance data indicated that at least 29 out of 109 countries were on course to meet targets for reducing the burden caused by malaria by 2010.

Plasmodium falciparum malaria parasites that had a reduced susceptibility to artemisinins, possibly heralding resistance, had been detected at the Cambodia/Thailand border, and malaria vectors in several countries had displayed some degree of resistance to pyrethroids. Therefore, the continuous monitoring of their efficacy and adoption of measures to mitigate the risk of resistance were considered priorities for malaria control.

The report made a number of recommendations. Member States should increase funding for financing long-lasting insecticide-treated nets, artemisinin-based combination therapy and indoor residual spraying. Countries and partners needed to ensure that drug- and insecticide-resistance testing was fully operational in order to protect insecticides and artemisinin-based combination therapy, and needed to strengthen health information systems so that data were monitored continuously at national, district and health-facility levels. Malaria partners needed to resolve financial and delivery bottlenecks that were responsible for stock-outs of long-lasting insecticide-treated nets, artemisinin-based combination therapy treatments, and rapid diagnostic tests. Malaria programme management at the country level needed to be strengthened to address low use of insecticide-treated nets, as well as stock-outs of long-lasting insecticide-treated nets, artemisinin-based combination therapy treatments and rapid diagnostic tests at health facilities.

Special Envoy for Malaria. On 14 February, the Secretary-General announced the appointment of Ray Chambers (United States) as his first Special Envoy for Malaria [SG/A/1118], charged with raising the issue of malaria on the international political and developmental agendas and doing all in his power to reduce child deaths from the disease. In December, by resolution 63/234 (see below), the General Assembly welcomed the designation of a Special Envoy for Malaria.

GENERAL ASSEMBLY ACTION

On 22 December [meeting 73], the General Assembly adopted **resolution 63/234** [draft: A/63/L.62 & Add.1] without vote [agenda item 43].

2001–2010: Decade to Roll Back Malaria in Developing Countries, Particularly in Africa

The General Assembly,

Recalling that the period 2001–2010 has been proclaimed the Decade to Roll Back Malaria in Developing Countries, Particularly in Africa, by the General Assembly, and that combating HIV/AIDS, malaria, tuberculosis and other diseases is included in the internationally agreed development goals, including those contained in the United Nations Millennium Declaration,

Recalling also its resolution 62/180 of 19 December 2007 and all previous resolutions concerning the struggle against malaria in developing countries, particularly in Africa,

Recalling further resolution 60.18, adopted by the World Health Assembly on 23 May 2007, urging a broad range of national and international actions to scale up malaria control programmes,

Bearing in mind the relevant resolutions of the Economic and Social Council relating to the struggle against malaria and diarrhoeal diseases, in particular resolution 1998/36 of 30 July 1998,

Taking note of the declarations and decisions on health issues adopted by the Organization of African Unity, in particular the declaration and plan of action on the "Roll Back Malaria" initiative adopted at the Extraordinary Summit of Heads of State and Government of the Organization of African Unity, held in Abuja on 24 and 25 April 2000, as well as decision AHG/Dec.155(XXXVI) concerning the implementation of that declaration and plan of action, adopted by the Assembly of Heads of State and Government of the Organization of African Unity at its thirty-sixth ordinary session, held in Lomé from 10 to 12 July 2000,

Also taking note of the Maputo Declaration on Malaria, HIV/AIDS, Tuberculosis and Other Related Infectious Diseases, adopted by the Assembly of the African Union at its second ordinary session, held in Maputo from 10 to 12 July 2003, and the Abuja call for accelerated action towards universal access to HIV and AIDS, tuberculosis and malaria services in Africa, issued by the Heads of State and Government of the African Union at the special summit of the African Union on HIV and AIDS, tuberculosis and malaria, held in Abuja, from 2 to 4 May 2006,

Recognizing the linkages in efforts being made to reach the targets set at the Abuja Summit in 2000 as necessary and important for the attainment of the "Roll Back Malaria" goal and the targets of the Millennium Declaration by 2010 and 2015, respectively, and welcomes in this regard the commitment of Member States to respond to the specific needs of Africa,

Also recognizing that malaria-related ill health and deaths throughout the world can be substantially reduced with political commitment and commensurate resources if the public is educated and sensitized about malaria and appropriate health services are made available, particularly in countries where the disease is endemic,

Expressing concern about the continued morbidity, mortality and debility attributed to malaria, and recalling that more efforts are needed if the malaria targets for 2010 and the malaria and Millennium Development Goal targets for 2015 are to be reached on time,

Commending the efforts of the World Health Organization, the United Nations Children's Fund, the Roll Back Malaria Partnership, the Global Fund to Fight AIDS, Tuberculosis and Malaria, the World Bank and other partners to fight malaria over the years,

Taking note of the Roll Back Malaria Global Strategic Plan 2005–2015 and the Global Malaria Action Plan developed by the Roll Back Malaria Partnership,

1. *Welcomes* the report prepared by the World Health Organization, and calls for support for the recommendations contained therein;

2. *Also welcomes* the Global Malaria Action Plan, which provides for the first time a comprehensive plan for combating malaria in the short, medium and long term, including by giving further impetus to internationally agreed targets of universal coverage of malaria interventions for all at-risk populations by 2010, of continuing the scale-up to achieve nearly zero preventable deaths from malaria by 2015 and of eliminating and, with additional research and development, ultimately eradicating the disease;

3. *Further welcomes* the theme "Malaria—a disease without borders" that was chosen for the first World Malaria Day, as well as activities undertaken by the Member States, relevant organizations of the United Nations system, international institutions, non-governmental organizations, the private sector and civil society to commemorate this day, and encourages them to continue to observe World Malaria Day and to collaborate in the observance of the final two years of the Decade to Roll Back Malaria in Developing Countries, Particularly in Africa, in order to raise public awareness of and knowledge about the prevention, control and treatment of malaria as well as the importance of meeting the Millennium Development Goals;

4. *Welcomes* the designation by the Secretary-General of a Special Envoy for Malaria to raise the issue in collaboration with other United Nations organizations already working on those issues on the international political and development agendas and to work with national and global leaders to help to secure the political will, the partnerships and the funds to drastically reduce malaria deaths by 2010 through increased access to protection and treatment, especially in Africa;

5. *Also welcomes* the adoption by the sixty-first World Health Assembly of resolution 61.21 of 24 May 2008, in which it adopted the global strategy and the agreed parts of the plan of action on public health, innovation and intellectual property;

6. *Further welcomes* the increased funding for malaria interventions and for research and development of preventive and control tools from the international community, through funding from multilateral and bilateral sources and from the private sector, as well as by making predictable financing available through appropriate and effective aid modalities and in-country health financing mechanisms aligned with national priorities, which are key to strengthening health systems and promoting universal and equitable access to high-quality malaria prevention and treatment services;

7. *Welcomes* recent commitments and initiatives to promote overall malaria prevention, control and treatment, including those announced at the high-level event on the Millennium Development Goals, held in New York on 25 September 2008;

8. *Also welcomes* World Health Assembly resolution 61.18 of 24 May 2008, in which the Assembly initiated annual monitoring of the achievement of the health-related Millennium Development Goals;

9. *Urges* the international community to deliver on programmes and activities at the country level in order to achieve internationally agreed targets on malaria;

10. *Calls upon* the international community to continue to support the secretariat of the Roll Back Malaria Partnership and partner organizations, including the World Health Organization, the World Bank and the United Nations Children's Fund, as vital complementary sources of support for the efforts of malaria-endemic countries to combat the disease;

11. *Appeals* to the international community to work in a spirit of cooperation towards effective, increased, harmonized and sustained bilateral and multilateral assistance to combat malaria, including support for the Global Fund to Fight AIDS, Tuberculosis and Malaria, in order to assist States, in particular malaria-endemic countries, to implement sound national plans, in particular health plans and sanitation plans, including malaria control strategies and integrated management of childhood illnesses, in a sustained and equitable way that, inter alia, contributes to health system development;

12. *Appeals* to the malaria partners to resolve the financial and delivery bottlenecks that are responsible for stockouts of long-lasting insecticide-treated nets, artemisinin-based combination therapies and rapid diagnostic tests at the national level, whenever they occur, including through

the strengthening of malaria programme management at the country level;

13. *Welcomes* the contribution to the mobilization of additional and predictable resources for development by voluntary innovative financing initiatives taken by groups of Member States, and in this regard notes the International Drug Purchase Facility, UNITAID, the International Finance Facility for Immunization, the Affordable Medicines Facility for Malaria, the Global Alliance for Vaccines and Immunization and the advance market commitment initiatives;

14. *Urges* malaria-endemic countries to work towards financial sustainability, to increase, to the extent possible, domestic resource allocation to malaria control and to create favourable conditions for working with the private sector in order to improve access to good-quality malaria services;

15. *Urges* Member States to assess and respond to the needs for integrated human resources at all levels of the health system, in order to achieve the targets of the Abuja Declaration on Roll Back Malaria in Africa and the internationally agreed development goals of the United Nations Millennium Declaration, to take actions, as appropriate, to effectively govern the recruitment, training and retention of skilled health personnel, and to give particular focus to the availability of skilled personnel at all levels to meet technical and operational needs as increased funding for malaria control programmes becomes available;

16. *Calls upon* the international community, inter alia, by helping to meet the financial needs of the Global Fund to Fight AIDS, Tuberculosis and Malaria and through country-led initiatives with adequate international support, to intensify access to affordable, safe and effective antimalarial combination treatments, intermittent preventive treatment in pregnancies, long-lasting insecticide-treated mosquito nets, including, where appropriate, through the free distribution of such nets and, where appropriate, to insecticides for indoor residual spraying for malaria control, taking into account relevant international rules, including the Stockholm Convention on Persistent Organic Pollutants standards and guidelines;

17. *Requests* relevant international organizations, in particular the World Health Organization and the United Nations Children's Fund, to assist efforts of national Governments to provide universal access to malaria control interventions to at-risk young children and pregnant women in malaria-endemic countries, particularly in Africa, as rapidly as possible, with due regard to ensuring proper use of those interventions, including long-lasting insecticide nets, and sustainability through full community participation and implementation through the health system;

18. *Calls upon* Member States, in particular malaria-endemic countries, to establish and/or strengthen national policies and operational plans, with a view to ensuring the achievement of the targets for 2010 and 2015, in accordance with the technical recommendations of the World Health Organization, so as to ensure the achievement of targets set out in the Global Malaria Action Plan and to promote the achievement of the malaria-related Millennium Development Goals;

19. *Encourages* all African countries that have not yet done so to implement the recommendations of the Abuja Summit in 2000 to reduce or waive taxes and tariffs for nets and other products needed for malaria control, both to reduce the price of the products to consumers and to stimulate free trade in those products;

20. *Invites* all malaria-endemic countries, with the support of the international community, to scale up their efforts to meet the internationally agreed targets on malaria for 2010 and 2015;

21. *Calls upon* United Nations agencies and their partners to continue to provide the technical support necessary to build and enhance the planning and implementation capacity of Member States to meet the internationally agreed goals;

22. *Expresses its concern* about the increase in resistant strains of malaria in several regions of the world, and calls upon Member States, with support from the World Health Organization and other partners, to strengthen surveillance systems for drug and insecticide resistance and upon the World Health Organization to coordinate a global network for the monitoring of drug and insecticide resistance and to ensure that drug and insecticide testing is fully operational in order to enhance the use of current insecticide- and artemisinin-based combination therapies;

23. *Urges* all Member States experiencing resistance to conventional monotherapies to replace them with combination therapies, as recommended by the World Health Organization, and to develop the necessary financial, legislative and regulatory mechanisms in order to introduce artemisinin combination therapies at affordable prices and to prohibit the marketing of oral artemisinin monotherapies, in a timely manner;

24. *Recognizes* the importance of the development of safe and cost-effective vaccines and new medicines to prevent and treat malaria and the need for further and accelerated research, including into safe, effective and high-quality traditional therapies, using rigorous standards, including by providing support to the Special Programme for Research and Training in Tropical Diseases and through effective global partnerships, such as the various malaria vaccine initiatives and the Medicines for Malaria Venture, where necessary stimulated by new incentives to secure their development and through effective and timely support towards pre-qualification of new antimalarials and their combinations;

25. *Calls upon* the international community, including through existing partnerships, to increase investment in and efforts towards the research and development of new, safe and affordable malaria-related medicines, products and technologies, such as vaccines, rapid diagnostic tests, insecticides and delivery modes, to prevent and treat malaria, especially for at-risk children and pregnant women, in order to enhance effectiveness and delay the onset of resistance;

26. *Calls upon* malaria-endemic countries to assure favourable conditions for research institutions, including allocation of adequate resources and development of national policies and legal frameworks, where appropriate, with a view to, inter alia, informing policy formulation and strategic interventions on malaria;

27. *Reaffirms* the right to use, to the fullest extent, the provisions contained in the World Trade Organization Agreement on Trade-Related Aspects of Intellectual Property Rights (TRIPS Agreement), the Doha Declara-

tion on the TRIPS Agreement and Public Health, the decision of the World Trade Organization's General Council of 30 August 2003 and amendments to article 31 of the Agreement, which provide flexibilities for the protection of public health, and in particular to promote access to medicines for all, including the production, under compulsory licensing, of generic drugs in the prevention and treatment of malaria, and resolves to assist developing countries in this regard;

28. *Calls upon* the international community to support ways to expand access to and the affordability of key products, such as vector control measures, including indoor residual spraying, long-lasting insecticide-treated nets and artemisinin-based combination therapy for populations at risk of exposure to resistant strains of falciparum malaria in malaria-endemic countries, particularly in Africa, including through additional funds and innovative mechanisms, inter alia, for the financing and scaling up of artemisinin production and procurement, as appropriate, to meet the increased need;

29. *Welcomes* the increased level of public-private partnerships for malaria control and prevention, including the financial and in-kind contributions of private sector partners and companies operating in Africa, as well as the increased engagement of non-governmental service providers;

30. *Encourages* the producers of long-lasting insecticide-treated nets to accelerate technology transfer to developing countries, and the World Bank and regional development funds to consider supporting malaria-endemic countries in establishing factories to scale up production of long-lasting insecticide-treated nets;

31. *Calls upon* the international community and malaria-endemic countries, in accordance with existing guidelines and recommendations of the World Health Organization and the requirements of the Stockholm Convention to increase capacity for the safe, effective and judicious use of indoor residual spraying and other forms of vector control;

32. *Urges* the international community to become fully knowledgeable about World Health Organization technical policies and strategies and the provisions in the Stockholm Convention related to the use of DDT, including for indoor residual spraying, long-lasting insecticide-treated nets and case management, intermittent preventive treatment for pregnant women and monitoring of in vivo resistance studies to artemisinin-based combination therapy treatment, so that projects support those policies, strategies and provisions;

33. *Requests* the World Health Organization, the United Nations Children's Fund and donor agencies to provide support to those countries which choose to use DDT for indoor residual spraying so as to ensure that it is implemented in accordance with international rules, standards and guidelines, and to provide all possible support to malaria-endemic countries to manage the intervention effectively and prevent the contamination, in particular, of agricultural products with DDT and other insecticides used for indoor residual spraying;

34. *Encourages* the World Health Organization and its member States, with the support of the parties to the Stockholm Convention, to continue to explore possible alternatives to DDT as a vector control agent;

35. *Calls upon* malaria-endemic countries to encourage regional and intersectoral collaboration, both public and private, at all levels, especially in education, health, agriculture, economic development and the environment, to advance malaria control objectives;

36. *Calls upon* the international community to support increased interventions, in line with the Global Malaria Action Plan and the recommendations of the World Health Organization and the Roll Back Malaria Partnership, in order to ensure their rapid, efficient and effective implementation, to strengthen health systems and national pharmaceutical policies, to monitor and fight against the trade in counterfeit antimalarial medicines and prevent the distribution and use of them, and to support coordinated efforts, inter alia, by providing technical assistance to improve surveillance, monitoring and evaluation systems and their alignment with national plans and systems so as to better track and report changes in coverage, the need for scaling up recommended interventions and the subsequent reductions in the burden of malaria;

37. *Urges* Member States, the international community and all relevant actors, including the private sector, to promote the coordinated implementation and enhance the quality of malaria-related activities, including via the Roll Back Malaria Partnership, in accordance with national policies and operational plans that are consistent with the technical recommendations of the World Health Organization and recent efforts and initiatives, including, where appropriate, the Paris Declaration on Aid Effectiveness and the Accra Agenda for Action, adopted during the Third High-level Forum on Aid Effectiveness, held in Accra from 2 to 4 September 2008;

38. *Requests* the Secretary-General, in close collaboration with the Director-General of the World Health Organization and in consultation with Member States, to submit to the General Assembly at its sixty-fourth session an evaluation report on progress achieved towards the internationally agreed targets for 2010, including funding and implementation of activities necessary to reach those targets.

Global public health

Global health and foreign policy

On 24 May, the World Health Assembly (WHA), at its sixty-first session (Geneva, 19–24 May) [WHA61/2008/REC/1], adopted a resolution [WHA61.21] on a global strategy and plan of action on public health, innovation and intellectual property. The Assembly adopted the strategy, which was annexed to the resolution, and urged members States, international organizations and stakeholders to prioritize and consider providing resources towards implementation of the strategy and plan of action. It also requested the Director-General to finalize outstanding components of the plan concerning timeframes, progress indicators and funding needs, and submit the final plan of action for consideration by the sixty-second WHA; to prepare a quick-start programme and begin to implement those elements of the strategy and plan which fell under the responsibility of WHO; to establish a working group to examine financing and coordination of research and development and submit a progress report to the sixty-second WHA and a final report to the sixty-third WHA; and to monitor progress in implementation of the strategy and plan and report progress to the sixty-third WHA.

The Assembly also adopted a resolution [WHA61.18] on monitoring the achievement of the health-related MDGs. It urged States to continue sustaining their high-level political commitments and to work with development partners towards strengthening national health systems, including health information systems for monitoring progress towards achievement of the MDGs. It requested the Director-General to submit annually a report on the status of progress made in the achievement of the health-related MDGs according to the new monitoring framework.

Another WHA resolution [WHA61.2] concerned the implementation of the 2005 International Health Regulations (IHR) [YUN 2005, p. 1331]. It urged States to ensure that the contact details of the IHR Focal Points were up to date; to ensure that the core national capacity requirements specified in Annex 1 (surveillance and response) to the Regulations were developed, strengthened and maintained; and to designate an expert for the IHR Roster of Experts. It requested the Director-General to support States with vulnerable health systems in strengthening core capacity requirements, and to submit, on an annual basis, a report including information provided by States parties and about the secretariat's activities, to enhance communication between national IHR Focal Points and to encourage information-sharing on actual outbreaks.

Further resolutions addressed the subjects of climate change and health; global immunization strategy; infant and young child nutrition; prevention and control of non-communicable diseases; and strategies to reduce the harmful use of alcohol.

Economic and Social Council action. On 25 July, the Economic and Social Council adopted the following theme for its 2009 thematic discussion: "Current global and national trends and their impact on social development, including public health" (**decision 2008/257**).

Oslo Ministerial Declaration. By a 4 December letter [A/63/591] to the Secretary-General, Brazil transmitted the text of the Oslo Ministerial Declaration: "Global health—a pressing foreign policy issue of our time", and the Oslo Agenda for Action: "Foreign policy taking up the challenges of global health", adopted by the Ministers of Foreign Affairs of Brazil, France, Indonesia, Norway, Senegal, South Africa and Thailand in Oslo on 20 March 2007.

GENERAL ASSEMBLY ACTION

On 26 November [meeting 60], the General Assembly adopted **resolution 63/33** [draft: A/63/L.28 & Add.1] without vote [agenda item 44].

Global health and foreign policy

The General Assembly,

Recalling the outcomes of the major United Nations conferences and summits in the economic, social and related fields, especially those related to global health,

Recalling also its resolutions 58/3 of 27 October 2003, 59/27 of 23 November 2004 and 60/35 of 30 November 2005, all entitled "Enhancing capacity-building in global public health", and other health-related resolutions, as well as resolutions of the World Health Assembly,

Welcoming the theme of the annual ministerial review to be held by the Economic and Social Council in 2009, "Implementing the internationally agreed goals and commitments in regard to global public health",

Recalling that achieving the health-related Millennium Development Goals is essential to socio-economic development, concerned by the relatively slow progress in achieving them, and mindful that special consideration should be given to the situation in sub-Saharan Africa,

Recognizing the leading role of the World Health Organization as the primary specialized agency for health, including its roles and functions with regard to health policy in accordance with its mandate,

Welcoming the adoption on 24 May 2008 of World Health Assembly resolution 61.18, which initiated the annual monitoring by the World Health Assembly of the achievement of the health-related Millennium Development Goals,

Recognizing the contribution of initiatives in the field of global health such as, among others, the GAVI Alliance, the Global Fund to Fight AIDS, Tuberculosis and Malaria, the International Finance Facility for Immunization, and the International Drug Purchase Facility, UNITAID, as well as other national and regional initiatives,

Noting the role and contribution of the Foreign Policy and Global Health Initiative in promoting synergy between foreign policy and global health, as well as the contribution of the Oslo Ministerial Declaration entitled "Global health—a pressing foreign policy issue of our time" to placing health as a foreign policy issue on the international agenda,

Noting also the outcome of the Thirty-fourth Summit of the Group of Eight, held in Toyako, Hokkaido, Japan, from 7 to 9 July 2008, which highlighted the principles for action on global health to achieve all the health-related Millennium Development Goals,

Emphasizing that the United Nations system has an important responsibility to assist Governments in the follow-up to and full implementation of agreements and commitments reached at the major United Nations conferences and summits, especially those focusing on health-related areas,

Underscoring the fact that global health is also a long-term objective which is national, regional and international in scope and requires sustained attention, commitment and closer international cooperation beyond emergency,

Appreciating the contribution made by civil society, including non-governmental organizations and the private sector, on issues related to foreign policy and global health,

Welcoming ongoing partnerships between a variety of stakeholders at the local, national, regional and global levels aimed at addressing the multifaceted determinants of global health and the commitments and initiatives to accelerate progress on the health-related Millennium Development Goals, including those announced at the high-level event on the Millennium Development Goals, held at United Nations Headquarters on 25 September 2008,

1. *Recognizes* the close relationship between foreign policy and global health and their interdependence, and in that regard also recognizes that global challenges require concerted and sustained efforts by the international community;

2. *Urges* Member States to consider health issues in the formulation of foreign policy;

3. *Stresses* the importance of achieving the health-related Millennium Development Goals;

4. *Recognizes* that the annual ministerial review to be held by the Economic and Social Council in 2009 will focus on the theme "Implementing the internationally agreed goals and commitments in regard to global public health", and in that regard calls for enhanced coordination within the United Nations system;

5. *Requests* the Secretary-General, in close collaboration with the Director-General of the World Health Organization, and in consultation with Member States, to submit to the General Assembly at its sixty-fourth session, in 2009, a comprehensive report, with recommendations, on challenges, activities and initiatives related to foreign policy and global health, taking into account the outcome of the annual ministerial review to be held by the Economic and Social Council in 2009;

6. *Decides* to include in the provisional agenda of its sixty-fourth session an item entitled "Global health and foreign policy", taking into account the cross-cutting nature of issues related to foreign policy and global health.

Road safety

On 31 March, the General Assembly considered the issue of global road safety, including the report on improving global road safety prepared in 2007 by WHO, in consultation with the regional commissions and other partners of the UN Road Safety Collaboration [YUN 2007, p. 1271]. During the Assembly's deliberations, the Russian Federation presented an initiative to host the first global high-level (ministerial) conference on road safety in 2009 in Moscow, together with other actors interested in international cooperation in the area of road safety. That conference, in addition to providing a forum for information-sharing, would be an opportunity to discuss progress in implementing the recommendations of the *World Report on Road Traffic Injury Prevention* [YUN 2004, p. 1223] and General Assembly resolutions on improving global road safety.

GENERAL ASSEMBLY ACTION

On 31 March [meeting 87], the General Assembly adopted **resolution 62/244** [draft: A/62/L.43 & Add.1] without vote [agenda item 46].

Improving global road safety

The General Assembly,

Recalling its resolutions 57/309 of 22 May 2003, 58/9 of 5 November 2003, 58/289 of 14 April 2004 and 60/5 of 26 October 2005 on improving global road safety,

Having considered the note by the Secretary-General transmitting the report on improving global road safety,

Noting with appreciation the adoption on 23 May 2007 of World Health Assembly resolution 60.22 on emergency care systems,

Underlining the importance for Member States to continue using the *World Report on Road Traffic Injury Prevention* as a framework for road safety efforts and implementing its recommendations by paying particular attention to five of the main risk factors identified, namely, the non-use of safety belts and child restraints, the non-use of helmets, drinking and driving, inappropriate and excessive speed and the lack of appropriate infrastructure, and by paying particular attention also to the needs of vulnerable road users such as pedestrians, cyclists and motorcyclists, and users of public transport, and improving post-crash care for victims of road crashes,

Commending the World Health Organization for its role in implementing the mandate conferred upon it by the General Assembly to work with the United Nations regional commissions to coordinate road safety issues within the United Nations system, and the progress of the United Nations Road Safety Collaboration as a coordination mechanism whose members are providing Governments and civil society with good-practice guidelines to support action to tackle the major road safety risk factors,

Recognizing the work of the United Nations regional commissions and their subsidiary bodies in increasing their road safety activities and advocating for increased political commitment to road safety, and in this context also recognizing the continuing commitment of the Economic Commission for Europe to global action in the elaboration of safety-related global technical vehicle regulations and amendments to the Convention on Road Traffic and the Convention on Road Signs and Signals, resolution 63/9 of 23 May 2007 of the Economic and Social Commission for Asia and the Pacific, in which the Commission encouraged members to continue to act upon recommendations contained in the Ministerial Declaration on Improving Road Safety in Asia and the Pacific, the Accra Declaration of African Ministers responsible for transport and health of 8 February 2007, the Declaration of San José on road safety of 14 September 2006 and resolution 279(XXIV) of 11 May 2006 of the Economic and Social Commission for Western Asia on follow-up to implementation of components of the Integrated Transport System in the Arab Mashreq, including follow-up on road safety,

Commending the World Bank for its initiative in establishing the Global Road Safety Facility, the first funding mechanism designed to support capacity-building and provide technical support for road safety at the global, regional and country levels, welcoming the financial assistance given to the Facility by the Governments of Australia, the Netherlands and Sweden, and by the FIA Foundation for the Automobile and Society, and encouraging more financial contributions to the Facility,

Commending also the World Health Organization and the United Nations regional commissions for organizing, in collaboration with the other members of the United Nations Road Safety Collaboration, the first United Nations Global Road Safety Week in April 2007, during which hundreds of events were held all over the world, including the World Youth Assembly for Road Safety and the second Stakeholders' Forum for Global Road Safety, in Geneva, which helped to draw attention to the fact that road traffic crashes have become the leading cause of death among young people aged between 10 and 24,

Taking note of all national and regional initiatives to improve awareness of road safety issues, including the second European Road Safety Day, to be observed on 13 October 2008,

Taking note also of the report of the Commission for Global Road Safety, *Make Roads Safe: A New Priority for Sustainable Development*, which links road safety with sustainable development and which calls for increased resources for road safety, a new commitment for road infrastructure assessment and a global ministerial conference on road safety under the auspices of the United Nations,

Expressing its concern at the continued increase in road traffic fatalities and injuries worldwide, in particular in developing countries,

Reaffirming the need for the further strengthening of international cooperation and knowledge-sharing in road safety, taking into account the needs of developing countries,

1. *Invites* Member States to actively participate in the development of the global road safety status report being prepared by the World Health Organization;

2. *Invites* all Member States to participate in the projects to be implemented by the United Nations regional commissions to assist low- and middle-income countries in setting their own national road traffic casualty reduction targets, as well as regional targets;

3. *Reaffirms* the importance of addressing global road safety issues and the need for the further strengthening of international cooperation, taking into account the needs of developing countries by building capacities in the field of road safety and providing financial and technical support for their efforts;

4. *Encourages* Member States to continue to strengthen their commitment to road safety, including by observing the World Day of Remembrance for Road Traffic Victims on the third Sunday of November every year;

5. *Invites* the World Health Organization and the United Nations regional commissions, in cooperation with other partners in the United Nations Road Safety Collaboration, to promote multisectoral collaboration by organizing, when appropriate, United Nations Global Road Safety Weeks, including Stakeholders' Forums for Global Road Safety;

6. *Encourages* organizations in both the private and the public sector with vehicle fleets, including agencies of the United Nations system, to develop and implement policies and practices that will reduce crash risks for vehicle occupants and other road users;

7. *Welcomes* the offer by the Government of the Russian Federation to host and provide the necessary financial support for the first global high-level (ministerial) conference on road safety, to be held in 2009, to bring together delegations of ministers and representatives dealing with transport, health, education, safety and related traffic law enforcement issues, to discuss progress in implementing the recommendations of the *World Report on Road Traffic Injury Prevention* and the General Assembly resolutions on improving global road safety, and provide an opportunity for Member States to exchange information and best practices;

8. *Decides* to include in the provisional agenda of its sixty-fourth session the item entitled "Global road safety crisis", and requests the Secretary-General to report to the General Assembly at that session on the progress made in improving global road safety.

Food and agriculture

Food aid

World Food Programme

At its 2008 substantive session in July, the Economic and Social Council had before it two reports pertaining to the World Food Programme (WFP): the annual report of the Executive Director for 2007 [E/2008/14], and the report of the WFP Executive Board [E/2008/36] containing the decisions and recommendations of its 2007 sessions. By **decision 2008/215** of 18 July, the Council took note of those reports.

The WFP Executive Board, at its 2008 sessions—first regular session (4–6 February); annual session (9–12 June); and second regular session (27–30 October)—all of which were held in Rome, decided on organizational and programme matters and approved a number of projects. In October, the Board approved the Biennial Programme of Work of the Executive Board for 2009–2010 [WFP/EB.2/2008/11].

WFP activities

According to the Annual Performance Report for 2008 [WFP/EB.A/2009/4], WFP distributed 3.9 million metric tons (MT) of food aid in 2008, compared with 3.3 million MT in 2007. A total of 102.1 million hungry people were assisted in 78 countries during the year, compared with 86.1 million in 80 countries in 2007. Of the total number of people assisted in 2008, 17.6 million (23.8 million in 2007) were helped through development projects; 25 million (15.3 million in 2007) through emergency operations; and 59.4 million (47 million in 2007) through protracted relief and recovery operations.

During the year, WFP faced particular challenges stemming from dramatically rising food and fuel prices and turmoil in international financial systems. Progress towards achieving the MDGs was suddenly reversed. In March, WFP launched an extraordinary appeal for $755 million to cover estimated additional food and fuel costs. By May, new contributions had passed that target and eventually totalled $1 billion, including a historic contribution of $500 million from Saudi Arabia. Donor contributions for all of 2008 totalled $5 billion, more resources per annum than in any other year.

For the first time in a number of years, contributions for development projects increased substantially, reaching $406 million, the highest amount since 2000. Nevertheless, due to the elevated cost of the WFP food basket caused by high food prices, the actual number of beneficiaries of development assistance decreased to 17.6 million in 2008. The proportion of multilateral contributions also increased, from less than 10 per cent in recent years to 18 per cent in 2008.

Extreme weather continued to affect the work of WFP, which launched 23 relief operations for victims of floods, earthquakes and windstorms. The targeting of humanitarian and UN staff was a growing concern, with four WFP staff killed and 17 injured as a result of malicious acts. An increase in incidents targeting WFP contractors and partners led to an additional 13 fatalities.

Administrative and financial matters

In 2008, with the help of donor contributions and staff in the field and at headquarters, WFP scaled up assistance for hungry people affected by extreme weather, political turmoil, and complex emergencies such as those found in Afghanistan, Somalia and the Sudan, but also for vulnerable populations hit by soaring global food and fuel prices. Throughout the food price crisis, WFP increased food purchases for developing countries to $1.1 billion, thereby helping to break the cycle of hunger.

High food prices in 2008 affected WFP food procurement. WFP spent a record $1.4 billion on procurement in 2008, 30 per cent more than the previous record in 2004. Greater demand for assistance meant that WFP purchased 2.8 million MT of food, the second highest tonnage on record, but the high price of food in local markets meant that it procured a smaller proportion of food from low-income countries—26 per cent, compared with 55 per cent in 2007—and a greater proportion from middle-income countries—50 per cent, compared with 24 per cent in 2007.

WFP began to deploy new hunger solutions, informed by analysis of the causes of hunger and shaped by market conditions and people's needs. The WFP strategic plan (2008–2011), approved in June, aimed to support nations in meeting emergency needs and identifying longer-term solutions to hunger. The Plan's strategic objectives repositioned WFP from a food aid agency to a food assistance agency. More flexible approaches were set out, including cash and voucher programmes and Purchase for Progress (P4P) proposals to enable small-scale farmers to access new markets and to encourage increased production.

Vulnerability analysis and mapping, one of WFP's core strengths, was particularly important in the response to natural disasters and the food crisis in 2008, when the number of those assessments increased by 80 per cent. WFP widened the net of its assessment data, factoring in economic impact, food security issues, nutrition analyses and urban populations.

Building staff capacity was a focus in 2008, as WFP repositioning would have implications for staff capacity and adaptability in view of its changing needs. In that regard, the Executive Board adopted the policy paper "Preparing for Tomorrow Today: WFP Strategy for Managing and Developing Human Resources (2008–2011)" [WFP/EB.2/2008/4-C]. WFP also established an Ethics Office in 2008, as well as a Division of Performance and Accountability Management.

In 2008, the WFP financial statements were prepared for the first time in accordance with International Public Sector Accounting Standards, which introduced the presentation of revenues and expenses on a full accrual basis.

Private-sector partnerships were strong. The year ended with companies and foundations contributing $145.5 million in cash and $48.8 million in kind, double the value of private donations in 2007. The Bill and Melinda Gates Foundation provided a significant donation to help alleviate the effects of high food prices in West Africa. In conjunction with the Howard G. Buffett Foundation, it contributed a $66 million grant to the P4P initiative, designed to ensure that WFP procurements benefited small farmers.

In 2008, partnership with the World Bank increased as it rolled out its $1.2 billion Global Food Crisis Response Programme. Some funds from that programme were directly channelled to WFP, such as in the Central African Republic, Guinea Bissau and Liberia, and through Governments in Burundi and Nepal.

Resources and financing

In 2008, WFP operational expenditures exceeded $3.5 billion, an increase over the 2007 figure of approximately $2.8 billion. Confirmed contributions reached $5 billion, an increase from the 2007 figure of $2.7 billion. Of the total contributions, $2.3 billion went to protracted relief and recovery operations, $406.2 million to development activities, $172.0 million to special operations, $1.4 billion to emergency operations, including $60 million to the Immediate Response Account, and $131.8 million to other activities.

Food security

Food and Agriculture Organization

In 2008, the Food and Agriculture Organization of the United Nations (FAO) continued to address the world food crisis. FAO held a high-level conference on "World Food Security: the Challenges of Climate Change and Bioenergy" (Rome, 3–5 June), in which 181 member countries participated. Forty-two Heads of State attended the event, as well as 100 ministers and 60 non-governmental and civil society organizations. Issues addressed by the conference forums included the causes, consequences and solutions to high food prices; and the challenges that climate change, bioenergy, and transboundary pests and diseases posed to world food security.

The conference discussed the issue of high food prices in the context of an information paper entitled "Soaring food prices: facts, perspectives, impacts and actions required" [HLC/08/INF/1]. As noted in that document, agricultural commodity prices rose sharply in 2006 and 2007 and continued to rise even more sharply in the first three months of 2008. While the FAO food price index rose, on average, by 8 per cent in 2006 compared with the previous year, it increased by 24 per cent in 2007 compared to 2006. The increase in the average of the index for the first three months of 2008 compared to the same three months in 2007 stood at 53 per cent. The continuing surge in prices was led by vegetable oils, which on average increased by more than 97 per cent during the same period, followed by grains with 87 per cent, dairy products with 58 per cent and rice with 46 per cent. The prices of sugar and meat products also rose, but not to the same extent. Large increases in some commodity prices pointed to increased volatility and uncertainty in the market environment.

The conference concluded with the adoption of the Declaration of the High-Level Conference on World Food Security: the Challenges of Climate Change and Bioenergy, which reaffirmed the conclusions of the 1996 World Food Summit, including the Rome Declaration on World Food Security and the World Food Summit Plan of Action [YUN 1996, p. 1129]. The Declaration called on the international community to increase assistance for developing countries, in particular the least developed countries and those that were most negatively affected by high food prices. The Declaration underscored the need to help developing countries and countries in transition to expand agriculture and food production, and increase investment in agriculture, agribusiness and rural development, from both public and private sources. It noted that, in view of the challenges posed by climate change, the question of how to increase the resilience of food production systems was all the more essential.

Committee on World Food Security. At its one hundred and thirty-fifth session (Rome, 17–18 November), the FAO Council considered the report [CL 135/10] of the thirty-fourth session of the Committee on World Food Security (CFS) (Rome, 14–17 October), as well as several other CFS-issued reports, including the "Follow-Up to the World Food Summit: Report on Progress in the Implementation of the Plan of Action" [CFS:2008/3]; the report on "Proposals to Strengthen the Committee on World Food Security to Meet New Challenges" [CFS:2008/6]; and the report on the "Assessment of the World Food Security and Nutrition Situation" [CFS:2008/2].

High-level Task Force on Food Security Crisis. In April, the Secretary-General established a High-level Task Force (HLTF) on the Global Food Security Crisis under his chairmanship. The HLTF brought together relevant parts of the UN Secretariat, UN agencies, funds and programmes, and the Bretton Woods institutions (the World Bank Group and the International Monetary Fund) to produce a unified response to the food price crisis. To that end, it developed a strategy and action plan—the Comprehensive Framework for Action (CFA). The CFA comprised a twin-track approach: one set of actions aimed to meet the immediate needs of food-insecure populations; the second set aimed to build resilience and contribute to longer-term global food and nutrition security. In December, by resolution 63/235 (see below), the General Assembly acknowledged the establishment of the HLTF by the Secretary-General.

GENERAL ASSEMBLY ACTION

On 22 December [meeting 73], the General Assembly adopted **resolution 63/235** [draft: A/63/L.64 & Add.1] without vote [agenda item 107].

Agriculture development and food security

The General Assembly,

Recalling the Rio Declaration on Environment and Development, Agenda 21, the Programme for the Further Implementation of Agenda 21, the Johannesburg Declaration on Sustainable Development and the Plan of Implementation of the World Summit on Sustainable Development ("Johannesburg Plan of Implementation"), the Monterrey Consensus of the International Conference on Financing for Development, the 2005 World Summit Outcome and the Doha Declaration on Financing for Development: outcome document of the Follow-up International Conference on Financing for Development to Review the Implementation of the Monterrey Consensus,

Reaffirming the goal set out in paragraph 19 of the United Nations Millennium Declaration, to halve, by 2015, the proportion of the world's people whose income is less than one dollar a day and the proportion of people who suffer from hunger,

Recalling the Rome Declaration on World Food Security and the World Food Summit Plan of Action, the Declaration of the World Food Summit: five years later, including the goal of achieving food security for all through an ongoing effort to eradicate hunger in all countries, with an immediate view to reducing by half the number of undernourished people by no later than 2015, as well as the commitment to achieving the Millennium Development Goals,

Recognizing that agriculture plays a crucial role in addressing the needs of a growing global population and is inextricably linked to poverty eradication, especially in developing countries, and stressing that integrated and sustainable agriculture and rural development approaches are therefore essential to achieving enhanced food security and food safety in an environmentally sustainable way,

Emphasizing the urgent need to increase efforts at the national, regional and international level to address food security and agriculture development as part of the international development agenda,

Remaining concerned that high and volatile food prices and the global food crisis pose a serious challenge to the fight against poverty and hunger, as well as to the efforts of developing countries to attain food security and achieve the objective of reducing by half the number of undernourished people by no later than 2015 as well as other internationally agreed development goals, including the Millennium Development Goals, and reiterating that the global food crisis has multiple and complex causes and that its consequences require a comprehensive and coordinated response in the short, medium and long term by national Governments and the international community,

Welcoming the holding of the High-level Conference on World Food Security: the Challenges of Climate Change and Bioenergy, from 3 to 5 June 2008 in Rome, and acknowledging the initiative of the Secretary-General in establishing the High-level Task Force on the Global Food Security Crisis, which has produced the Comprehensive Framework for Action, as well as other multilateral, regional and national initiatives,

Taking note with appreciation of the work undertaken by relevant international bodies and organizations, including the Food and Agriculture Organization of the United Nations, the International Fund for Agricultural Development and the World Food Programme, on agriculture development and enhancing food security and by the Commission on Sustainable Development on the thematic cluster of issues on agriculture, rural development, land, drought, desertification and Africa,

Emphasizing that the United Nations can play an effective role in building a global consensus in addressing agriculture development and food security,

1. *Reiterates* the need to adequately and urgently address agriculture development and food security in the context of national and international development policies;

2. *Decides* to include in the provisional agenda of its sixty-fourth session an item entitled "Agriculture development and food security", to be taken up by the Second Committee;

3. *Requests* the Secretary-General to submit to the General Assembly at its sixty-fourth session a report on national, regional and international efforts within the context of the present resolution, under the item entitled "Agriculture development and food security", in close cooperation and coordination with United Nations relevant bodies and organizations.

Nutrition

Standing Committee on Nutrition

The thirty-fifth session of the United Nations System Standing Committee on Nutrition (SCN) (Hanoi, Viet Nam, 3–6 March) conducted a symposium on "Accelerating the Reduction of Maternal and Child Undernutrition". The Committee considered reports from its working groups on nutrition in emergencies; nutrition and HIV/AIDS; nutrition, ethics and human rights; breastfeeding and complementary feeding; household food security; nutrition of school age children; capacity development in food and nutrition; micronutrients; and nutrition throughout the life cycle.

Among other actions, SCN participants agreed that the Lancet Nutrition Series, launched in January, brought an important new body of evidence to address the enormous burden and consequences of maternal and child undernutrition that inhibited global development. That Series also provided important new evidence for the benefit of a set of specific nutrition interventions which, in addition to other poverty reduction efforts, could help accelerate the reduction of maternal and child undernutrition and, in doing so, contribute to achieving the MDGs. Participants, including the SCN constituencies (UN agencies, bilateral partners and non-governmental and civil society organizations) and thematic working groups, discussed how the Series would help move the agenda forward in their respective working areas and the role of SCN in making that happen. They also agreed to draw together the conclusions from those discussions and prepare a set of recommendations.

UNU activities

The United Nations University, through its Food and Nutrition Programme for Human and Social Development (UNU-FNP), assisted developing regions in enhancing individual, organizational and institutional capacities, carried out coordinated global research activities and served as an academic arm for the UN system in areas of food and nutrition that were best addressed in a non-regulatory, non-normative environment.

UNU-FNP, together with Cornell University—a UNU-associated institution—and the UNU Office at the United Nations in New York, held a series of four public symposia aiming to identify the gaps in knowledge and policy which limited sub-Saharan Africa in achieving the MDGs for the alleviation of hunger, malnutrition and poor health. Since more Africans were suffering from those conditions in 2008 than in 1990—the beginning of the MDG period—the problem was severe and the trends continued to worsen. Knowledge about food systems and health and nutrition in Africa was abundant, but understanding of the interaction between food systems and health and nutrition was deficient, and the potential health gains from changes in the food system were frequently overlooked in policy design and implementation. The series began in 2007, but the latter two symposia, entitled "The Governance Dimension of the MDGs in Africa" (New York, 21 May) and "HIV/AIDS and Public Health" (New York, 19 September), took place in 2008. Results informed the General Assembly's high-level meeting on "Africa's Development Needs" (see p. 1007).

Further UNU activities, as indicated by its annual report for 2008, included an Africa Day Symposium at the UNU Centre, Tokyo (Tokyo, 9 September), held in conjunction with the African Diplomatic Corps, entitled "Africa's Food Situation: Crisis to Opportunities; New Perspectives for Africa". UNU-FNP conducted two training courses (Potchefstroom, South Africa, 11–21 March and Ouarzazate, Morocco, 23–30 June) as part of its African Nutrition Leadership Programme. The UNU World Institute for Development Economics Research (UNU-WIDER), located in Helsinki, Finland, conducted a project on health inequalities and development that aimed to provide a better understanding of the factors that underpin health status in developing and transitional countries, particularly for children. UNU-WIDER also published a policy brief entitled "Can We Eradicate Hunger?" that addressed the topic of hunger from economic, social and political perspectives, drawing upon academic research of the experiences of international organizations and civil society.

Chapter XIV

International drug control

In 2008, the United Nations, through the Commission on Narcotic Drugs, the International Narcotics Control Board (INCB) and the United Nations Office on Drugs and Crime (UNODC), continued to strengthen international cooperation in countering the world drug problem. Activities focused on carrying out the 1998 Action Plan against Illicit Manufacture, Trafficking and Abuse of Amphetamine-type Stimulants and Their Precursors; the 1998 Action Plan on International Cooperation on the Eradication of Illicit Drug Crops and on Alternative Development; and the 1999 Action Plan for the Implementation of the Declaration on the Guiding Principles of Drug Demand Reduction.

UNODC provided technical assistance, legal advice and research to the main UN policymaking bodies in the field of drug control and assisted Member States in developing domestic legislation on drugs and in ratifying and implementing the international drug control conventions. It developed and promoted field-based technical cooperation projects with a view to enhancing the capacity of States to counteract illicit drugs, and supported States in illicit crop monitoring and alternative development programmes in the framework of poverty reduction and sustainable development strategies. It also expanded its initiatives to promote drug supply and demand reduction, and to prevent and treat drug abuse and dependence. States were assisted in improving border control practices and promoting the integration of drug control approaches and strategies into a broader development agenda.

The Commission on Narcotic Drugs—the main UN policymaking body dealing with drug control—recommended two draft resolutions to the Economic and Social Council for adoption and adopted resolutions on the follow-up to the General Assembly's twentieth (1998) special session on: countering the world drug problem; demand reduction and the prevention of drug abuse; HIV/AIDS and other blood-borne diseases; illicit cultivation, manufacture and trafficking; West Africa; and Afghanistan.

INCB reviewed the origins of international drug control and how it had evolved in the twentieth century. It discussed the challenges facing the international community in applying the drug conventions, how Governments were responding to them and what action they might wish to take. It continued to oversee the implementation of the three major international drug control conventions, analyse the global drug situation and draw the attention of Governments to weaknesses in national control and treaty compliance, making suggestions and recommendations for improvements at the national and international levels.

In July, the Council emphasized that illicit production of narcotic drugs was often related to development problems—in particular poverty, poor health conditions and illiteracy—and should be tackled in a larger development context through a holistic and integrated approach. It agreed on the relevance of enhancing alternative development, focusing on improving people's livelihoods, and recognized the role played by developing countries with extensive expertise in those areas and the importance of outreach activities aimed at promoting best practices and lessons learned. In another July resolution, the Council noted that the illicit cultivation of opium poppy and production of opiates in Afghanistan had increased and that the bulk of the illicit drugs originating in Afghanistan were smuggled through Iran, Pakistan and other neighbouring countries before reaching their countries of destination. The Council therefore encouraged cross-border cooperation, enhanced coordination and information exchange among Afghanistan, Iran and Pakistan, and called on States and UNODC to provide technical assistance and support for strengthening their initiatives and efforts to fight drug trafficking. In December, the General Assembly adopted a resolution on international cooperation against the world drug problem that addressed the follow-up to the twentieth special session and action by the UN system. It recognized that countering the world drug problem was a common and shared responsibility that should be dealt with through sustained and collective efforts, and reaffirmed the importance of a balanced approach between demand and supply reduction.

Follow-up to twentieth special session

Report of Secretary-General. In response to General Assembly resolutions 55/65 [YUN 2000, p. 1175], 56/124 [YUN 2001, p. 1144] and 62/176 [YUN 2007, p. 1277], the Secretary-General submitted a July report [A/63/111] on international cooperation against the world drug problem: progress achieved in meeting the goals and targets set out in the Political Declaration adopted by the Assembly at its twentieth special session in resolution S-20/2 [YUN 1998, p. 1136]. The report described action taken by the Commission on Narcotic Drugs and the UN system to counter the world drug problem, including demand reduction; supply reduction and law enforcement; alternative livelihoods; data collection, research and monitoring of drug trends; and strengthening of the drug programme of UNODC.

The Secretary-General stated that Member States had an obligation to reaffirm the commitments that they had assumed by adopting the Political Declaration, noting that progress continued to be made in all areas addressed therein; despite an apparent increase in the absolute numbers of cannabis, cocaine and opiate users, the annual prevalence levels remained stable in all drug markets. He observed that, even if a country had developed a national drug control strategy and established a national authority to coordinate its implementation, there might still be a need to strengthen that strategy or authority politically or in terms of its technical, institutional or human resource capacity. The impact of the world drug problem on the social, economic, health, political and governance aspects of societies remained significant and States had an obligation to consider their commitments, review achievements and develop new actions. He recommended that States call for UNODC to be provided with adequate regular budget resources, and encouraged them to continue and increase their financial and political support for its work. The Secretary-General also made recommendations in the areas of demand reduction; amphetamine-type stimulants (ATS) and their precursors; judicial cooperation; money-laundering; and illicit crop eradication and alternative development.

Commission on Narcotic Drugs. In response to Commission on Narcotic Drugs resolutions 49/1 [YUN 2006, p. 1431] and 50/12 [YUN 2007, p. 1277], the UNODC Executive Director submitted a report on the collection and use of complementary drug-related data and expertise to support the global assessment by Member States of the implementation of the declarations and measures adopted at the twentieth special session [E/CN.7/2008/8]. He summarized work undertaken by UNODC to engage with experts from all geographical regions and from relevant international organizations on the collection and use of data and expertise, and to obtain supplementary information.

The report also reflected the outcome of informal expert consultations (Vienna, 6–8 February and 18–20 September 2007) organized by UNODC, with the financial support of the European Commission. The experts made observations and recommendations relevant to the 10-year assessment of the outcome of the Assembly's twentieth special session and to the period beyond the assessment. With regard to possible action beyond 2008, the experts made suggestions on such areas as: demand reduction; eradicating illicit crop cultivation and alternative development; judicial cooperation; ATS and their precursors; control of precursors; and money-laundering.

In February, the UNODC Executive Director submitted to the Commission his fifth report on the world drug problem [E/CN.7/2008/2 & Add.1–6], prepared pursuant to Commission resolutions 42/11 [YUN 1999, p. 1191] and 50/12 [YUN 2007, p. 1277]. The report reviewed progress achieved by Member States in implementing the goals and targets set at the twentieth special session, based on responses received from Governments to the questionnaire for each of the five reporting periods, from 1998 to 2007. The information covered the subjects addressed in the action plans: national drug control strategies; demand reduction; eradication of illicit crops and alternative development; judicial cooperation; ATS and their precursors; control of precursors; and countering money-laundering. By 6 November 2007, 108 States had returned their responses for the reporting period 2006–2007.

The report showed that States had made significant progress over the preceding 10 years in implementing the goals and targets set at the twentieth special session. Most responding States had adopted balanced and comprehensive national drug control strategies and established central coordination bodies to guide national drug control policies. In relation to the drug abuse situation, consumption pointed towards stabilization at the global level, and a decline was generally occurring in countries that had implemented long-term and sustained demand reduction strategies. Most States had made progress in establishing national demand reduction strategies, assessing the abuse problem and providing prevention, treatment and rehabilitation services. Progress achieved in reducing opium poppy cultivation in South-East Asia was offset by an increase in cultivation and illicit opium production in Afghanistan. In Bolivia, Colombia and Peru, the area under coca bush cultivation had declined between 1998 and 2006; however, higher crop yields had resulted in an increase in cocaine manufacture during that period. Since 1998, States had developed and improved national plans and strategies to address illicit crop cultivation, including alternative development and eradication measures. Nevertheless, financial constraints continued to pose difficulties for the sustainability of alternative development programmes. Progress had been made in judicial cooperation, and adherence to the international drug control treaties was virtually universal. Measures relating to extradition, mutual legal assistance, controlled delivery and law enforcement cooperation had registered a high rate of implementation. Progress had also been achieved in implementing the Action Plan against Illicit Manufacture, Trafficking and Abuse of ATS and Their Precursors, contained in resolution S-20/4 A [YUN 1998,

p. 1139], adopted at the Assembly's special session. The percentage of countries that had carried out precursor control measures increased substantially. Most States had placed under control the substances listed in the 1988 United Nations Convention against Illicit Traffic in Narcotic Drugs and Psychotropic Substances [ibid., p. 690], and major successes were noted in the area of international cooperation. Compliance with measures to combat money-laundering had increased since 1998, with most Member States having put in place legislation and measures to counter drug-related money-laundering.

On 14 March [E/2008/28 (res. 51/4)], the Commission on Narcotic Drugs established open-ended, intergovernmental expert working groups to work in a coordinated manner on the topics corresponding to the subjects of the action plans, declarations and measures adopted at the Assembly's twentieth special session. Each of the groups would assess both the achievement of the goals and targets set at the special session and areas requiring further action, and draw conclusions for further intersessional discussions. UNODC was asked to organize the meetings of the working groups back-to-back with each other, and States were urged to ensure the participation of experts and practitioners and invited to provide resources for the attendance of experts from developing countries. The Commission decided that intersessional meetings should be held during the second half of 2008 to prepare recommendations for the decisions to be adopted at its fifty-second (2009) session. The Commission resolved that a political declaration and other declarations and measures to enhance international cooperation should be considered and adopted at the high-level segment, identifying future priorities and areas requiring further action, as well as goals and targets to be set in countering the world drug problem beyond 2009. It also resolved that the outcome of the high-level segment should be submitted to the Assembly, and called on States and observers to ensure representation at the highest possible level.

International Narcotics Control Board. In its report covering 2008 [Sales No. E.09.XI.1], INCB considered follow-up to the Assembly's twentieth special session. In accordance with Commission resolution 51/4 (above), the Board had been involved in the preparations for the high-level segment of the Commission's fifty-second session. It participated in and contributed to the five open-ended intergovernmental expert working groups, providing papers on: demand reduction; supply reduction; countering money-laundering and promoting judicial cooperation; international cooperation on illicit drug crop eradication and on alternative development; and control of precursors and ATS. The Board underlined that the goals set for 2008 by the Assembly's twentieth special session continued to be relevant and that new challenges to international drug control had emerged. It called on Governments and the international community to achieve further progress in addressing the world drug problem. INCB would continue to work with Governments and international organizations towards the adoption, at the Commission's 2009 high-level segment, of a political declaration and action plans.

The Report of INCB on Follow-up to the Twentieth Special Session of the General Assembly [Sales No. E.09.XI.7] outlined the activities undertaken by the Board and progress made. It also identified remaining challenges and presented recommendations on further action to be taken by Governments and international organizations.

GENERAL ASSEMBLY ACTION

On 18 December [meeting 71], the General Assembly, on the recommendation of the Third (Social, Humanitarian and Cultural) Committee [A/63/432], adopted **resolution 63/197** without vote [agenda item 98].

International cooperation against the world drug problem

The General Assembly,

Recalling the United Nations Millennium Declaration, the provisions of the 2005 World Summit Outcome addressing the world drug problem, its resolution 62/176 of 18 December 2007 and its other previous relevant resolutions,

Reaffirming the Political Declaration adopted by the General Assembly at its twentieth special session and the importance of meeting the objectives targeted for 2008,

Reaffirming also the joint ministerial statement adopted at the ministerial segment of the forty-sixth session of the Commission on Narcotic Drugs, the Action Plan for the Implementation of the Declaration on the Guiding Principles of Drug Demand Reduction and the Action Plan on International Cooperation on the Eradication of Illicit Drug Crops and on Alternative Development adopted by the General Assembly at its twentieth special session,

Recalling that, in its resolution 62/176, it welcomed the decision by the Commission on Narcotic Drugs to convene a high-level segment, during its fifty-second session, in order to allow time to assess the implementation of the declarations and measures adopted by the General Assembly at its twentieth special session,

Gravely concerned that, despite continued increased efforts by States, relevant organizations, civil society and non-governmental organizations, the world drug problem continues to constitute a serious threat to public health and safety and the well-being of humanity, in particular children and young people and their families, and to the national security and sovereignty of States, and that it undermines socio-economic and political stability and sustainable development,

Concerned by the serious challenges and threats posed by the continuing links between illicit drug trafficking and terrorism and other national and transnational criminal activities and transnational criminal networks, inter alia, trafficking in human beings, especially women and children, money-laundering, financing of terrorism, corruption, trafficking in arms and trafficking in chemical precursors, and reaffirming that strong and effective international cooperation is needed to counter these threats,

Recalling Commission on Narcotic Drugs resolution 51/10 of 14 March 2008, in which the Commission emphasized the importance of further national and international measures to counter trafficking in substances used as precursors in the illicit manufacture of narcotic drugs and psychotropic substances, including synthetic drugs,

Recalling also Commission on Narcotic Drugs resolution 51/11 of 14 March 2008, in which the Commission recognized the increasing links between illicit drug trafficking and illicit manufacturing of and trafficking in firearms,

Underlining the value of objective, scientific, balanced and transparent assessment by Member States of the global progress achieved and of the difficulties encountered in meeting the goals and targets set by the General Assembly at its twentieth special session,

Reaffirming that countering the world drug problem in all its aspects requires a political commitment to reducing supply, as an integral component of a balanced and comprehensive drug control strategy under the principles enshrined in the Political Declaration adopted by the General Assembly at its twentieth special session and in the measures to enhance international cooperation to counter the drug problem, including the Action Plan on International Cooperation on the Eradication of Illicit Drug Crops and on Alternative Development, adopted at that session,

Reaffirming equally that reducing illicit drug use and its consequences requires a political commitment to efforts to reduce demand, which must be demonstrated by sustained widespread demand reduction initiatives that integrate a comprehensive public health approach spanning the spectrum of prevention, education, early intervention, treatment, recovery support, rehabilitation and reintegration efforts in accordance with the Declaration on the Guiding Principles of Drug Demand Reduction adopted by the General Assembly at its twentieth special session,

Recognizing the importance of the effective evaluation of comprehensive strategies, including alternative development programmes, at the national and international levels to combat the world drug problem,

Recognizing also that international cooperation in countering drug abuse and illicit production and trafficking has shown that positive results can be achieved through sustained and collective efforts, and expressing its appreciation for the initiatives in this regard,

Bearing in mind the important role that civil society, including non-governmental organizations, plays in combating the world drug problem, and noting that there are various initiatives at all levels undertaken in this regard, in particular the "Beyond 2008" process, which provided an opportunity for non-governmental organizations to contribute to the review of the twentieth special session of the General Assembly,

I

International cooperation to counter the world drug problem and follow-up to the twentieth special session

1. *Reaffirms* that countering the world drug problem is a common and shared responsibility that must be addressed in a multilateral setting, requires an integrated and balanced approach and must be carried out in full conformity with the purposes and principles of the Charter of the United Nations and other provisions of international law, and in particular with full respect for the sovereignty and territorial integrity of States, for the principle of non-intervention in the internal affairs of States and for all human rights and fundamental freedoms, and on the basis of the principles of equal rights and mutual respect;

2. *Also reaffirms* that there shall be a balanced approach between demand reduction and supply reduction, each to reinforce the other in an integrated approach to solving the world drug problem;

3. *Welcomes* the adoption, by the Commission on Narcotic Drugs on 14 March 2008, of resolution 51/4, by which the Commission decided to establish five open-ended intergovernmental expert working groups, which were convened from June to September 2008, to work in a coordinated manner on the topics of drug demand reduction, supply reduction, countering money-laundering and promoting judicial cooperation, international cooperation on the eradication of illicit drug crops and on alternative development, and control of precursors and of amphetamine-type stimulants, topics which correspond to the subjects of the Action Plan on International Cooperation on the Eradication of Illicit Drug Crops and on Alternative Development, the Declaration on the Guiding Principles of Drug Demand Reduction and the measures to enhance international cooperation to counter the drug problem, adopted by the General Assembly at its twentieth special session;

4. *Notes* that 2009 marks the centennial of the convening of the International Opium Commission, which was the first multilateral initiative on drug control, and in this regard looks forward to the commemorative event to be held on 26 February 2009 in Shanghai, China;

5. *Calls upon* States and other relevant actors to evaluate progress made since 1998 towards meeting the goals and targets set at the twentieth special session of the General Assembly;

6. *Urges* all States to continue to promote and implement, including by allocating adequate resources and developing clear and consistent national policies, the outcomes of the twentieth special session of the General Assembly, as well as the outcome of the ministerial segment of the forty-sixth session of the Commission on Narcotic Drugs, to implement the Action Plan for the Implementation of the Declaration on the Guiding Principles of Drug Demand Reduction and to strengthen their national efforts to counter the abuse of illicit drugs in their populations, taking into account, inter alia, the results of the assessment of the implementation of the declarations and measures adopted by the Assembly at its twentieth special session;

7. *Urges* States that have not done so to consider ratifying or acceding to, and States parties to implement, as a matter of priority, all the provisions of the Single Convention on Narcotic Drugs of 1961 as amended by the 1972 Protocol, the Convention on Psychotropic Substances of 1971, the United Nations Convention against Illicit Traffic in Narcotic Drugs and Psychotropic Substances of 1988, the United Nations Convention against Transnational Organized Crime and the Protocols thereto and the United Nations Convention against Corruption;

8. *Urges* all States to strengthen their efforts to achieve the goals set for 2003 and 2008 at the twentieth special session of the General Assembly by:

(*a*) Promoting national and international initiatives to eliminate or reduce significantly the illicit manufacture, trafficking and marketing of drugs and other psychotropic substances, including synthetic drugs, and the diversion of precursors, other transnational criminal activities, including money-laundering and trafficking in arms, and corruption;

(*b*) Achieving significant and measurable results in the field of demand reduction, including through prevention and treatment strategies and programmes to reduce drug use, with particular focus on children and young people, and recognizing the role that the family plays in this regard;

9. *Encourages* States to consider prevention, treatment and rehabilitation of drug use disorders and to take measures to reduce the social and health consequences of drug abuse as governmental health and social priorities, consulting and working with civil society, including non-governmental organizations, and recognizing the role played by the family, in developing, implementing and evaluating policies and programmes, in particular those related to demand reduction and prevention of drug abuse, with particular focus on children and young people, and also to consider cooperating with civil society, including non-governmental organizations, in alternative development programmes;

10. *Calls upon* States and organizations with expertise in community capacity-building to provide, as needed, access to treatment, health care and social services for drug users, in particular those living with HIV/AIDS and other blood-borne diseases, and to extend support to States requiring such expertise, consistent with the international drug control treaties;

11. *Urges* all Member States to implement the Action Plan for the Implementation of the Declaration of the Guiding Principles of Drug Demand Reduction and to strengthen their national efforts to counter the abuse of illicit drugs in their populations, in particular among children and young people;

12. *Encourages* Member States to identify drug control priorities to be set for future concerted action and to consider making voluntary public commitments to tackle present challenges in drug trafficking;

13. *Calls upon* States to expand demand reduction measures, including prevention, treatment and rehabilitation, while fully respecting the dignity of drug-addicted persons, and to take further action to improve data collection and evaluation capacity on the demand for illicit drugs, including the demand for synthetic drugs, and, where appropriate, abuse of and addiction to prescription drugs;

14. *Urges* States to continue working towards achieving a significant and measurable reduction of drug abuse and to share the results obtained on this subject during the high-level segment of the fifty-second session of the Commission on Narcotic Drugs that will be held in March 2009;

15. *Encourages* Member States to take effective measures at the national, regional and international levels and to promote close international cooperation to prevent criminal organizations, in particular those involved in drug trafficking, from acquiring and using firearms, their parts and components and ammunition, in order to enhance public security;

16. *Reaffirms* the need for a comprehensive approach to the elimination of illicit narcotic crops in line with the Action Plan on International Cooperation on the Eradication of Illicit Drug Crops and on Alternative Development adopted by the General Assembly at its twentieth special session;

17. *Calls for* a comprehensive approach integrating alternative development programmes, including, where appropriate, preventive and innovative alternative development, into wider economic and social development programmes, with the support of a deeper international cooperation and the participation of civil society, including non-governmental organizations, and the private sector, as appropriate;

18. *Invites* States to sustain and increase international cooperation and, where needed, technical assistance to countries implementing policies and programmes against drug production, including illicit crop eradication and alternative development programmes;

19. *Recognizes* the significant role played by developing countries with extensive expertise in alternative development and the importance of outreach activities aimed at promoting a set of best practices and lessons learned in that area and sharing those best practices and lessons learned with States affected by illicit crop cultivation, including those emerging from conflict, with a view to using them, where appropriate, in accordance with the national specificities of each State;

20. *Invites* Member States, where alternative development programmes are implemented, to share their best practices and lessons learned, as well as the qualitative and quantitative impacts of those programmes, during the high-level segment of the fifty-second session of the Commission on Narcotic Drugs, in March 2009;

21. *Stresses* the importance of the contribution of the United Nations system and the international community to the economic and social development of the communities that benefit from innovative alternative programmes to eradicate illicit drug production, inter alia, in reforestation, agriculture and small and medium-sized enterprises;

22. *Encourages* States to establish comprehensive national monitoring systems and to enhance regional, international and multisectoral cooperation, including with industry, to prevent the diversion, manufacture, trafficking and abuse of amphetamine-type stimulants and their precursors;

23. *Calls upon* States to consider ways to strengthen mechanisms for the collection and sharing of information on trafficking in precursors, in particular for making seizures, preventing diversions, detaining consignments, dismantling laboratories and assessing emerging trafficking and diversion trends, new manufacturing methods and the use of non-controlled substances, with a view to enhancing the effectiveness of the international control framework;

24. *Emphasizes* the need to ensure that adequate mechanisms are in place, where necessary and to the extent possible, to prevent the diversion of preparations containing

substances listed in tables I and II of the United Nations Convention against Illicit Traffic in Narcotic Drugs and Psychotropic Substances of 1988, pertaining to illicit drug manufacture, which could easily be used or recovered by readily applicable means, in particular those containing ephedrine and pseudoephedrine;

25. *Urges* all States and relevant international organizations to cooperate closely with the International Narcotics Control Board, in particular in Project Cohesion and Project Prism, in order to enhance the success of those international initiatives, and to initiate, where appropriate, investigations by their law enforcement authorities into seizures and cases involving the diversion or smuggling of precursors and essential equipment, with a view to tracking them back to the source of diversion in order to prevent continuing illicit activity;

26. *Stresses* that international cooperation on domestic precursor policies and practices would assist in complementing existing law enforcement cooperative initiatives, and encourages States to cooperate at the regional level on measures to prevent and control the domestic diversion of precursors, drawing on best practices and sharing experiences;

27. *Recognizes* that the illegal distribution of pharmaceutical products containing substances under international control via the Internet is a serious problem, and encourages Member States to notify the International Narcotics Control Board of seizures of pharmaceutical products or counterfeit drugs containing substances under international control that are ordered via the Internet and received by mail so that it may conduct a detailed analysis of trafficking trends, and encourages the Board to continue its work with a view to raising awareness of and preventing the misuse of the Internet for the illegal supply, sale and distribution of internationally controlled licit substances;

28. *Calls upon* States to implement and strengthen, as appropriate, the measures to promote judicial cooperation adopted at the twentieth special session of the General Assembly, in particular with regard to mutual legal assistance, exchange of information and joint operations, as appropriate, including with technical assistance from the United Nations Office on Drugs and Crime;

29. *Calls upon* Member States to strengthen international cooperation among judicial and law enforcement authorities at all levels in order to prevent and combat illicit drug trafficking and to share and promote best operational practices in order to interdict illicit drug trafficking, including by establishing and strengthening regional mechanisms, providing technical assistance and establishing effective methods for cooperation, in particular in the areas of air, maritime, port and border control and in the implementation of extradition treaties, while respecting international human rights obligations;

30. *Urges* States to strengthen action, in particular international cooperation and technical assistance aimed at preventing and combating the laundering of proceeds derived from drug trafficking and related criminal activities, with the support of the United Nations system, international institutions such as the World Bank and the International Monetary Fund, as well as regional development banks and, where appropriate, the Financial Action Task Force on Money Laundering and similarly styled regional bodies, to develop and strengthen comprehensive international regimes to combat money-laundering and its possible links with organized crime and the financing of terrorism, and to improve information-sharing among financial institutions and agencies in charge of preventing and detecting the laundering of those proceeds;

31. *Encourages* Member States that have not done so to consider updating their legal and regulatory frameworks and establishing financial investigation units and, to that end, to seek technical assistance, including from the United Nations Office on Drugs and Crime, in particular regarding the identification, freezing, seizing and confiscation of the proceeds of crime, in order to effectively prevent and combat money-laundering;

32. *Considers* that the outcomes of the open-ended intergovernmental expert working groups established by the Commission on Narcotic Drugs in its resolution 51/4, and their conclusions, to be taken into account by the Commission at its intersessional meetings, may contribute to the preparation of a political declaration and, as appropriate, other declarations and measures to enhance international cooperation for consideration and adoption at the high-level segment of the fifty-second session of the Commission, in 2009;

33. *Urges* Member States to be represented at the highest possible level at the high-level segment of the fifty-second session of the Commission on Narcotic Drugs, and to reaffirm their commitment to combating the world drug problem and to endorse the principles and goals set by the General Assembly at its twentieth special session, with a view to enhancing cooperative efforts in this regard;

34. *Also urges* Member States to identify, on the basis of the results of the process to review the declarations and measures adopted by the General Assembly at its twentieth special session, future priorities and areas requiring further action, as well as goals and targets to be set in countering the world drug problem beyond 2009;

35. *Requests* the Commission on Narcotic Drugs to forward to the General Assembly, through the Economic and Social Council, the results of the high-level segment of the fifty-second session of the Commission on the progress achieved in meeting the goals and targets set in the Political Declaration adopted by the General Assembly at its twentieth special session;

36. *Decides* to consider the results of the high-level segment of the fifty-second session of the Commission on Narcotic Drugs at a plenary meeting of the General Assembly at its sixty-fourth session;

II

Action by the United Nations system

37. *Reaffirms* the importance of the United Nations Office on Drugs and Crime and its regional offices in building capacity at the local level in the fight against transnational organized crime and drug trafficking, and urges the Office to consider regional vulnerabilities, projects and impact in the fight against drug trafficking, in particular in developing countries, when deciding to close and allocate offices, with a view to maintaining an effective level of support to national and regional efforts in combating the world drug problem;

38. *Welcomes* the work carried out by the United Nations Office on Drugs and Crime, and requests the Office

to continue to carry out its mandate in accordance with previous relevant resolutions of the General Assembly, the Economic and Social Council and the Commission on Narcotic Drugs, in close cooperation with other relevant United Nations organizations and programmes, such as the World Health Organization, the United Nations Development Programme and the Joint United Nations Programme on HIV/AIDS;

39. *Welcomes also* the decision of the United Nations Office on Drugs and Crime to share relevant decisions of the Programme Coordinating Board of the Joint United Nations Programme on HIV/AIDS with Member States at the session of the Commission on Narcotic Drugs held in the first half of each year, starting with the fifty-second session, in order to promote better coordination and alignment of the response to HIV and to scale up efforts towards the goal of universal access to comprehensive prevention, care, treatment and support services for drug users;

40. *Notes* that the International Narcotics Control Board needs sufficient resources to carry out all its mandates, reaffirms the importance of its work, encourages it to continue to carry out its work in accordance with its mandate, urges Member States to commit themselves in a common effort to assigning adequate and sufficient budgetary resources to the Board, in accordance with Economic and Social Council resolution 1996/20 of 23 July 1996, emphasizes the need to maintain its capacity, inter alia, through the provision of appropriate means by the Secretary-General and adequate technical support from the United Nations Office on Drugs and Crime, and calls for enhanced cooperation and understanding between Member States and the Board to enable it to implement all its mandates under the international drug control conventions;

41. *Urges* the United Nations Office on Drugs and Crime to increase collaboration with intergovernmental, international and regional organizations that have drug control mandates, as appropriate, in order to share best practices and to take advantage of their unique comparative advantage;

42. *Requests* the United Nations Office on Drugs and Crime to carry out, at the request of Member States, training programmes to support the adoption of sound methods and to harmonize indicators used for statistics on drug use, which have already been considered by the Statistical Commission, in order to collect and analyse comparable data on drug abuse;

43. *Urges* all Governments to provide the fullest possible financial and political support to the United Nations Office on Drugs and Crime by widening its donor base and increasing voluntary contributions, in particular general-purpose contributions, so as to enable it to continue, expand and strengthen its operational and technical cooperation activities, within its mandates, and recommends that a sufficient share of the regular budget of the United Nations be allocated to the Office to enable it to carry out its mandates and to work towards securing assured and predictable funding;

44. *Takes note* of the outcomes of the fifty-first session of the Commission on Narcotic Drugs, the *World Drug Report 2008* of the United Nations Office on Drugs and Crime and the most recent report of the International Narcotics Control Board, and calls upon States to strengthen international and regional cooperation to counter the threat to the international community caused by the illicit production of and trafficking in drugs and to continue to take concerted measures such as the framework of the Paris Pact and other relevant international initiatives;

45. *Encourages* the meetings of Heads of National Drug Law Enforcement Agencies and of the Subcommission on Illicit Drug Traffic and Related Matters in the Near and Middle East of the Commission on Narcotic Drugs to continue to contribute to the strengthening of regional and international cooperation, taking into account the outcomes of the twentieth special session of the General Assembly and the joint ministerial statement adopted at the ministerial segment of the forty-sixth session of the Commission;

46. *Encourages* the Commission on Narcotic Drugs, as the global coordinating body in international drug control and as the governing body of the drug programme of the United Nations Office on Drugs and Crime, and the International Narcotics Control Board to continue their useful work on the control of precursors and other chemicals used in the illicit manufacture of narcotic drugs and psychotropic substances;

47. *Calls upon* the relevant United Nations agencies and entities, and other international organizations, and invites international financial institutions, including regional development banks, to mainstream drug control issues into their programmes, and calls upon the United Nations Office on Drugs and Crime to maintain its leading role by providing relevant information and technical assistance;

48. *Takes note* of the report of the Secretary-General, and requests the Secretary-General to submit to the General Assembly at its sixty-fourth session a report on the implementation of the present resolution.

Conventions

International efforts to control narcotic drugs were governed by three global conventions: the 1961 Single Convention on Narcotic Drugs [YUN 1961, p. 382], which, with some exceptions of detail, replaced earlier narcotics treaties and was amended by the 1972 Protocol [YUN 1972, p. 397] to strengthen the role of INCB; the 1971 Convention on Psychotropic Substances [YUN 1971, p. 380]; and the 1988 United Nations Convention against Illicit Traffic in Narcotic Drugs and Psychotropic Substances [YUN 1988, p. 690].

As at 31 December, 183 States were parties to the 1961 Convention, as amended by the 1972 Protocol. Afghanistan, Chad and the Lao People's Democratic Republic continued to be parties to the 1961 Convention in its unamended form only.

The number of parties to the 1971 Convention remained at 183 as at 31 December.

At year's end, 182 States and the European Union (EU) were parties to the 1988 Convention.

Commission action. In March [E/2008/28], the Commission on Narcotic Drugs reviewed implementation of the international drug control treaties. It had before it the INCB report covering its 2007 activities [YUN 2007, p. 1283] and the 2007 INCB technical report on the implementation of Article 12 of the 1988 Convention, dealing with precursors and chemicals frequently used in the illicit manufacture of narcotic drugs and psychotropic substances [E/INCB/2007/4].

On 14 March [E/2008/28 (res. 51/9)], the Commission urged Governments to contribute to maintaining a balance between the licit supply of and demand for opiate raw materials used for medical and scientific purposes, supporting traditional and established supplier countries, and to prevent the proliferation of production sources. It also urged producer countries to adhere strictly to the provisions of the 1961 Convention, as amended by the 1972 Protocol, and to prevent the illicit production or diversion of opiate raw materials to illicit channels, and encouraged improvements in opium poppy cultivation and the production of opiate raw materials. Consumer countries were urged to assess their licit requirements for opiate raw materials realistically on the basis of actual consumption and utilization of those raw materials and the opiates derived from them, and to communicate those requirements to INCB in order to ensure effective supply; countries cultivating opium poppy should limit its cultivation to the estimates confirmed by the Board, in accordance with the 1961 Convention; and producer countries, in providing estimates of such cultivation, should consider the actual demand requirements of importing countries. The Commission endorsed the concern expressed by the Board in 2005 regarding the advocacy by a non-governmental organization of legalization of opium poppy cultivation in Afghanistan and urged Governments to oppose such proposals and strengthen control in compliance with their treaty obligations. It urged countries where opium poppy had not been cultivated for the licit production of opiate raw materials to refrain from engaging in the commercial cultivation of opium poppy, in order to avoid the proliferation of supply sites, and to enact legislation to prevent and prohibit the proliferation of sites used for the production of opiate raw materials. It also urged countries where opium poppy was cultivated for the extraction of alkaloids to implement and maintain control mechanisms in accordance with the 1961 Convention, as amended by the 1972 Protocol. INCB was commended for its efforts in monitoring the implementation of the relevant Economic and Social Council resolutions and was requested to continue its efforts.

Also on 14 March [res. 51/17], the Commission called on States to ensure national restrictions on narcotic drugs and psychotropic substances in relation to cannabis, and to comply fully with the provisions of the international conventions with regard to cannabis.

On the same date [res. 51/12], the Commission adopted a resolution on strengthening cooperation between UNODC and other UN entities for the promotion of human rights in the implementation of the international drug control treaties. It reaffirmed that countering the world drug problem was a common and shared responsibility that should be addressed in a multilateral setting. This required an integrated and balanced approach to be carried out in conformity with the UN Charter and other provisions of international law and, in particular, with respect for the sovereignty and territorial integrity of States, the principle of non-intervention in their internal affairs and all human rights and fundamental freedoms, and on the basis of the principles of equal rights and mutual respect. It requested that UNODC continue to work closely with the competent UN entities, including the UN human rights agencies, and requested the UNODC Executive Director to report to the Commission at its fifty-third (2010) session.

INCB action. In its report covering 2008 [Sales No. E.09.XI.1], INCB reiterated its request to those States that were not parties to one or more of the international drug control treaties to accede to them without delay and called on Governments to furnish in a timely manner all statistical reports required under the conventions and to allocate adequate resources to their competent authorities for reporting purposes. Governments were asked to identify the causes for deficiencies in reporting statistics and/or estimates. The Board encouraged Governments to review and update on a regular basis the assessments of their actual medical and scientific requirements for psychotropic substances and to introduce the requirement of import and export authorizations for substances in Schedules III and IV of the 1971 Convention. It further encouraged Governments to revise the annual estimates of their legitimate requirements for four precursor chemicals used in the manufacture of synthetic drugs and to provide accurate information. States that had not done so were urged to provide information on substances used in the illicit manufacture of narcotic drugs and psychotropic substances, pursuant to article 12 of the 1988 Convention.

Distribution of internationally controlled drugs on the unregulated market

On 14 March [E/2008/28 (res. 51/13)], the Commission, responding to the threat posed by the distribution of internationally controlled drugs on the unregulated market, a problem addressed by INCB in 2006 [YUN 2006, p. 1438], requested that Member States offer cooperation and support to affected States through the provision of human and material resources and urged States that were parties to the international conventions to fully implement their mandatory provisions, including by adopting laws prohibiting the illicit distribution of internationally controlled substances on the unregulated market and by enforcing those laws. The Commission encouraged affected States to adopt measures to enable the swift detection of new forms of illicit distribution of internationally controlled drugs, requested States to implement the applicable 2006 INCB recommendations, and encouraged concerned States to increase the availability of drugs through legitimate channels, particularly in areas where there was little or no access. It invited UNODC to explore ways to cooperate with the World Health Organization (WHO), the World Customs Organization (WCO), the International Criminal Police Organization (INTERPOL) and other international bodies in assisting States in implementing INCB's recommendations.

INCB shared the Commission's concern over the fact that the distribution of internationally controlled substances in the unregulated market was increasingly characterized by the involvement of organized criminal networks and by the expansion of the range of products containing narcotic drugs or psychotropic substances on the market. It emphasized the need for all parties to strictly enforce the applicable control requirements and the need for States to enforce legislation. The Board stated that the elimination of the unregulated market should be done through a concerted effort involving Governments and relevant parties such as the pharmaceutical industry, professional associations and international organizations.

Centennial of the convening of the International Opium Commission

On 14 March [E/2008/28 (res. 51/8)], the Commission decided to commemorate on 26 February 2009 the centennial of the convening of the International Opium Commission. It noted with appreciation that China would host an event to celebrate the centennial and encouraged other Governments, organizations and civil society to hold celebrations to mark it. China was invited to report on the event and the Secretary-General was requested to transmit the Commission's resolution to Governments and relevant international organizations.

International Narcotics Control Board

The 13-member International Narcotics Control Board held its ninety-first (4–8 February), ninety-second (19–30 May) and ninety-third (28 October–14 November) sessions, all in Vienna.

In accordance with the tasks assigned to it under the international conventions, the Board monitored the implementation of the international drug control treaties and maintained a permanent dialogue with Governments. The information received from Governments was used to identify the enforcement of treaty provisions requiring them to limit to medical and scientific purposes the licit manufacture of, trade in and distribution and use of narcotic drugs and psychotropic substances. The Board, which was requested by the treaties to report annually on the drug control situation worldwide, noted weaknesses in national control and treaty compliance and made recommendations for improvements at the national and international levels.

The Board's 2008 report [Sales No. E.09.XI.1] reviewed the historical development of international drug control, describing its origins and outlining how it had evolved over the course of the twentieth century. It discussed the challenges facing the international community in applying the conventions, how Governments were responding and what action they should take. Some of those challenges, which were not envisaged at the time the conventions were drawn up and yet affected the capacity of Governments to implement them, included: health-related challenges; legal challenges; the challenge of prevention; and the challenge of globalization. The Board stated that the international control system for narcotic drugs and psychotropic substances could be considered one of the twentieth century's most important achievements in international cooperation: over 95 per cent of the UN membership (representing 99 per cent of the world's population) were States parties to the three conventions, and the number of substances controlled under the 1961 and 1971 Conventions had risen steadily over the years. At the same time, demand for narcotic drugs and psychotropic substances had soared: global consumption of morphine had grown from less than 5 tons in 1987 to 39.2 tons in 2007. In the period 1998–2007, the number of countries affected by illicit drug crop cultivation was reduced; however, where such cultivation continued to occur, the problems had become more acute for the population as a whole. To ensure more effective implementation of the three international drug treaties, the Board invited Governments: to consider how best to ensure their efficient functioning; to make greater investments in prevention, especially with regard to youth and vulnerable groups; and to study the discrepancies between international and domestic law with a view to fulfilling their obligations under the conventions. The Board encouraged Governments of countries where the consumption of opioid analgesics was low to stimulate their rational use through measures promoted by the Access to Controlled Medications Programme, a WHO initiative in which the Board was an active participant, and to ensure that such incentives were accompanied by measures to prevent the diversion of such drugs. Governments might work with the pharmaceutical industry with a view to making high-quality opioid analgesics more affordable in the poorest countries, and international aid programmes might donate essential drugs as part of their aid programmes. The Board recommended that Governments study the Fairtrade model with a view to improving the trading position and market access for products from alternative development projects in areas affected by illicit cultivation, taking into consideration the appropriateness and feasibility in each case. Governments were also encouraged to support multilateral initiatives against cybercrime and to use the Guidelines for Governments on Preventing the Illegal Sale of Internationally Controlled Substances through the Internet. The Guidelines were developed by INCB and included recommendations promoting measures to facilitate national and multilateral cooperation on legal steps such as the registration and licensing of Internet pharmacies, and on campaigns to raise awareness of the risks involved in online purchases.

INCB stated that the diversion from licit distribution channels and abuse of pharmaceutical preparations containing narcotic drugs were taking place in an increasing number of countries. In some countries, the extent of their abuse surpassed that of illicit drugs. The narcotic drugs most often diverted and abused included codeine, dextropropoxyphene, dihydrocodeine, fentanyl, hydrocodone, methadone, morphine, oxycodone, pethidine and trimeperidine. The Board invited Governments to remain vigilant with regard to the abuse of pharmaceutical preparations containing narcotic drugs and of preparations containing substances not internationally controlled.

The Board called on countries that produced and/or utilized opiate raw materials to ensure that their estimates and statistics were of a high quality and to keep INCB informed of any new developments. Global stocks of opiate raw materials should cover global demand for about one year to ensure the availability of opiates for medical and scientific purposes. The Board called on Governments to contribute to the maintenance of a balance between the licit supply of and demand for opiate raw materials and to prevent the proliferation of sources of their production. It appealed to them to comply with Commission resolution 51/9 (see p. 1353). Global consumption of opioid analgesics for the treatment of moderate to severe pain had increased during the preceding decade, mainly in Europe and North America. However, consumption remained low in many developing countries. INCB urged Governments concerned to identify the impediments to their adequate use and to improve their availability for medical purposes.

The diversion of psychotropic substances—mainly stimulants, benzodiazepines and the analgesic buprenorphine—from licit domestic distribution channels continued, and the non-medical use of prescription drugs containing psychotropic substances remained a serious and growing problem in many countries. The diversion and abuse of preparations containing buprenorphine remained a cause for concern; abuse had increased in countries where it was used for the treatment of opioid addicts. The Board requested countries and territories that authorized its licit consumption to inform it of the control measures applicable to it.

The Board called on Governments to increase their vigilance regarding trafficking in and abuse of preparations containing buprenorphine and to enhance control measures applied to the domestic distribution of such preparations and their use for the treatment of addicts. It also requested Governments to monitor the consumption levels of prescription drugs containing psychotropic substances, with a view to identifying possible diversions, and to raise awareness about the consequences of their abuse. It noted that the diversion of preparations containing controlled psychotropic substances through illegally operating Internet sites continued. Mail was used for trafficking to a considerable extent in many countries. Improved cooperation between postal, customs and police authorities at the national and international levels was therefore required.

As to precursors, the Board noted that, as at 1 November, 98 countries and territories had registered to use the Pre-Export Notification Online (PEN Online) system, the automated electronic system for exchanging pre-export notifications, introduced in 2006 [YUN 2006, p. 1439]. INCB encouraged Governments that had not done so to register with and utilize the system, which was instrumental in identifying suspicious transactions and preventing diversion.

INCB continued to support Project Cohesion and Project Prism, initiatives that yielded results in identifying trafficking in non-scheduled substances, weaknesses in control mechanisms, and diversion methods and routes. While mechanisms, for controlling and monitoring trade in ephedrine and pseudoephedrine were strengthened in some countries, traffickers were exploring new means of supplying illicit laboratories; new substances were being used as precursors and new distribution routes utilized. In addition, traffickers were placing orders through licit pharmaceutical companies and using them to divert preparations containing those precursors, particularly in Africa and West Asia. Measures introduced by Mexico to prohibit the import of ephedrine and pseudoephedrine continued to have an impact on the movement of precursors in Central America, where their imports had increased significantly. Trafficking networks in Central and

South America were obtaining precursors and establishing illicit laboratories. INCB therefore encouraged countries to strengthen their mechanisms for monitoring precursor chemicals and to provide information to help identify all the stages of ATS' illicit manufacture. The diversion and smuggling of chemicals for the illicit manufacture of heroin in Afghanistan continued to pose problems. INCB was concerned that the existing control mechanisms were not sufficient and urged Afghanistan to take additional measures, such as strengthening precursor control measures and investigating and reporting all seizures of chemicals. The Board also continued to be concerned about the origins of diverted potassium permanganate in South America, as well as the methods used to divert it. It urged Governments to strengthen their controls over domestic distribution channels and invited countries in the Americas to take advantage of the experience acquired during Project Cohesion, focusing on acetic anhydride, and to design similar strategies to combat the diversion of chemicals used in the illicit manufacture of cocaine.

To address the illegal sale and purchase through the Internet of pharmaceutical preparations containing internationally controlled substances, the Board developed the Guidelines for Governments on Preventing the Illegal Sale of Internationally Controlled Substances through the Internet, whose aim was to assist Governments in formulating national legislation and policies and in identifying the control measures most appropriate for their countries. The Guidelines included recommendations for international and national action and were divided into three parts: legislative and regulatory provisions; general measures; and national and international cooperation. The Board invited Governments to use the Guidelines and to provide information on their experience in implementing them. A format had also been developed to be used by countries to report in a standardized manner on seizures of narcotic drugs and psychotropic substances illegally sold through the Internet and delivered through the mail. Governments were invited to use the format, which would be brought to their attention in 2009, in reporting information to INCB and to continue to inform the Board of legislation regarding the sale of internationally controlled substances through the Internet, national cooperative mechanisms and practical experience in the control of such sales, as well as details of national focal points for activities related to illegal Internet pharmacies.

The misuse of courier services for drug trafficking occurred in all regions. The drugs smuggled included illicitly manufactured drugs as well as pharmaceutical preparations containing narcotic drugs and psychotropic substances that had been diverted from licit distribution channels. The Board encouraged Governments that had not done so to establish legislative and administrative measures to ensure adequate safeguards against the misuse of postal and courier services for trafficking, and invited them to take similar measures against the shipment of cannabis seeds and drug paraphernalia.

The INCB report was supplemented by: the Report of INCB on Follow-up to the Twentieth Special Session of the General Assembly [E/INCB/2008/1/Supp.1]; Narcotic Drugs: Estimated World Requirements for 2009; Statistics for 2007 [E/INCB/2008/2]; Psychotropic Substances: Statistics for 2007; Assessments of Annual Medical and Scientific Requirements for Substances in Schedules II, III and IV of the Convention on Psychotropic Substances of 1971 [E/INCB/2008/3]; and Precursors and Chemicals Frequently Used in the Illicit Manufacture of Narcotic Drugs and Psychotropic Substances: Report of INCB for 2008 on the Implementation of Article 12 of the United Nations Convention against Illicit Traffic in Narcotic Drugs and Psychotropic Substances of 1988 [E/INCB/2008/4].

By **decision 2008/248** of 24 July, the Economic and Social Council took note of the INCB report for 2007 [YUN 2007, p. 1283].

World drug situation

In its 2008 report [Sales No.E.09.XI.1], INCB presented a regional analysis of world drug abuse trends and control efforts, to keep Governments aware of situations that might endanger the objectives of international drug control treaties.

Africa

Cannabis production, trafficking and abuse continued in Africa, which remained the world's second largest producer of cannabis herb after the Americas, accounting for an estimated 26 per cent of global production. Most of the illicitly produced cannabis was abused locally. However, in a limited number of countries—mainly Ghana, Morocco, Nigeria and South Africa—it was also smuggled to destinations outside Africa, notably in Europe and, to a lesser extent, East Asia. Morocco remained the world's largest producer of cannabis resin, supplying the illicit markets in Western Europe and North Africa. In 2007, owing to intensified interdiction efforts, seizures of both cannabis resin and herb increased, with cannabis resin seizures increasing to 118 tons in 2007 from 89 tons in 2006. Seizures continued to increase during the first half of 2008. Most of the cannabis resin from Morocco destined for Europe was trafficked through Spain, France and Italy. Resin destined for Europe or West Asia passed through Mauritania, Mali, the Niger, the Libyan Arab Jamahiriya and Chad to Egypt. In 2006, large seizures were reported in Libya (14.8 tons), Algeria (10 tons), Senegal (8.4 tons) and Egypt (5.1 tons). About 42 million people in Africa were abusers of cannabis; the highest prevalence rates were found in West and Central Africa (12.6 per cent), where States reported large increases, followed by Southern Africa (8.4 per cent).

Although cocaine was not manufactured in Africa, consignments destined mainly for illicit markets in Europe were increasingly being smuggled through the region, which had become an important transit and stockpiling area for consignments from South America. Between 2005 and 2007, at least 33 tons were seized en route to Europe from West Africa, especially off the coast of the Canary Islands, Cape Verde and Guinea-Bissau, as well as in countries along the Gulf of Guinea, including Benin, Côte d'Ivoire, Ghana, Nigeria, Togo and, farther west, Guinea, Liberia, Mauritania, Senegal and Sierra Leone. About 27 per cent of the cocaine abused in Europe passed through West Africa. The drug was mostly transported by sea in large quantities to West Africa, where it was stockpiled, repackaged into smaller consignments and transported to Europe and the United States, usually by air couriers or, also in large quantities, through checked-in luggage. Consignments transiting West Africa also originated in East Africa and were also transported by both land and air from West Africa to North Africa before being smuggled into Europe. In addition, some cocaine continued to be smuggled into Southern Africa, mainly through Angola into South Africa, the only country reporting a relatively high level of seizures. The increase in its trafficking resulted in increased abuse in the region and was particularly noticeable in West and Southern Africa and along the Atlantic coast of North Africa. About 1.1 million people in Africa abused cocaine, and its increasing abuse and that of crack cocaine was reported in some Southern African countries, such as Namibia and South Africa.

East Africa was the major conduit for smuggling heroin from South-West Asia, mainly through the major airports of Addis Ababa (Ethiopia) and Nairobi (Kenya). From East Africa, large quantities were transported across the continent to countries in West Africa, especially Côte d'Ivoire, Ghana and Nigeria, and from there to Europe and the United States. Seizures continued in Côte d'Ivoire, Kenya, Mauritius, Nigeria and the United Republic of Tanzania. About 1.4 million people in the region abused opiates, mostly heroin, and increased abuse was reported in East and Southern Africa. Egypt constituted the largest market for opiates, and illicit opium poppy cultivation continued on the Sinai peninsula. However, the opium derived from that cultivation was consumed locally and not used for the illicit manufacture of heroin.

Illicitly manufactured pharmaceutical preparations or prescription drugs containing narcotic drugs and psychotropic substances that had been diverted from licit distribution channels continued to be available on the unregulated markets in many countries in West and Central Africa. The situation remained unresolved because of inadequate legislative frameworks, ineffective administrative mechanisms and insufficient resources for enforcement of controls. Illicit manufacture of amphetamines occurred in South Africa and, on a small scale, in Egypt. Methcathinone ("cat") was manufactured clandestinely and was widely available in South Africa. The growing abuse of crystal methamphetamine (locally dubbed "tik") in the Cape Town area became a cause for concern. Methaqualone (Mandrax) illicitly manufactured in China or India continued to enter South Africa, mainly through Mozambique, Swaziland and Zimbabwe; it was also manufactured in clandestine laboratories in Southern Africa. From South Africa, regarded as the largest market for methaqualone in the world, some of the drug was smuggled into countries in the subregion, where it was also abused. Africa continued to be a major area for the diversion of ephedrine and pseudoephedrine to be used in the illicit manufacture of methamphetamine in the Americas and elsewhere. Traffickers took advantage of weaknesses in precursor control mechanisms in many African countries. In view of the increasing abuse of khat in Madagascar, the Government prohibited its cultivation, sale and consumption as at January 2008. Khat was grown mainly in East Africa and on the Arabian peninsula and was abused locally. The total amount seized globally had increased significantly and the largest seizures in 2007 were made by Canada (13 tons), Germany (7 tons), Sweden (6 tons), Denmark (1.6 tons) and Switzerland (1.4 tons), where it was abused by expatriates with origins in East Africa and the Arabian peninsula.

In the area of regional cooperation, the third session of the African Union (AU) Conference of Ministers for Drug Control and Crime Prevention (Addis Ababa, 3–7 December 2007) endorsed the Revised Plan of Action on Drug Control and Crime Prevention (2007–2012), subsequently adopted at the meeting of the AU Heads of State (Addis Ababa, 30 January–2 February). Within the framework of the Economic Community of West African States (ECOWAS), West African countries were involved in joint efforts to combat the increasing transit traffic in drugs, particularly cocaine from Latin America passing through West Africa to Europe. The ECOWAS Conference on Drug Trafficking as a Security Threat to West Africa (Praia, Cape Verde, 26–29 October) adopted a political declaration on the prevention of abuse, trafficking and organized crime in West Africa and a regional action plan listing regional initiatives to be undertaken by the ECOWAS Commission.

At the national level, in response to the urgent problems confronting Guinea-Bissau in combating cocaine trafficking through its territory, UNODC and the Ministry of Justice of Guinea-Bissau prepared an integrated multidisciplinary programme aimed at combating drug trafficking and organized crime, which began in April. Ghana took legislative and administrative measures to address the increase in drug trafficking and developed a national control strategy for the period 2008–2010. Ethiopia took steps to address trafficking through the international airport at Addis Ababa, and Nigeria strengthened control measures at several airports. Nigeria's National Agency for Food and Drug Administration and Control strengthened the regulatory framework, improved drug registration and closed down many companies importing counterfeit medicines destined for unregulated markets in Nigeria and beyond. In April, South Africa strengthened its precursor control legislation by including ephedrine and pseudoephedrine in its Medicines and Related Substances Act of 1965.

In March, an INCB mission to Ethiopia examined steps taken against cannabis cultivation and abuse. It encouraged the Government to carry out periodic studies on the prevalence of drug abuse and to strengthen its capacity for the treatment of drug addicts. INCB invited the Government to promote the rational use of opioid analgesics. In October, an INCB mission to Mauritius—where drug abuse by injection, particularly heroin, was a problem—encouraged the Government to set up a mechanism for sharing information, as well as coordinating machinery involving all bodies, services and agencies involved in drug control activities. INCB commended the Government for offering a large variety of demand reduction services to abusers and recommended that more psychosocial support be provided to abusers.

West Africa

On 14 March [E/2008/28 (res. 51/18)], the Commission on Narcotic Drugs reaffirmed its commitment to confronting the world drug problem in all its manifestations, including in the area of new emerging trends such as the increasing use of West Africa as a transit area for cocaine consignments destined for international markets, mainly in Europe. It called on Member States and international organizations, in coordination with ECOWAS, to strengthen initiatives and programmes, in particular those designed and developed by West African States and ECOWAS. It also called on Member States to facilitate the development of other programmes considered appropriate by the States concerned, in order to combat trafficking through West Africa by providing technical and financial assistance, including strengthening support for subregional law enforcement initiatives—such as the West African Joint Operations initiative and the interregional initiative financed by the EU for the sharing of intelligence among States in the Caribbean, Latin America and West Africa. The Commission invited Member States and international organizations to support those West African States most affected by the problem of trafficking, particularly Guinea-Bissau, and to strengthen their coordination in support of the efforts of West African States, in collaboration with ECOWAS and other stakeholders. The ECOWAS Commission was invited to finalize and implement its subregional action plan against trafficking. The Commission called on States, especially the main countries of destination of illicit drug consignments—particularly cocaine—smuggled through West Africa, to reduce demand in line with the provisions of the international drug control treaties. It urged West African States to combat trafficking and adopt demand reduction measures, including the provision of treatment and rehabilitation for abusers, and to address the drug problem in a balanced and integrated manner within their development priorities. Member States and international organizations were called on to provide assistance to West African States with regard to both supply and demand reduction measures. The Commission requested the UNODC Executive Director to facilitate the coordination of efforts, in consultation with West African States and international partners, to address cocaine smuggling through West Africa, within the framework of the drug control component of the Programme of Action, 2006–2010, which emanated from the Round Table for Africa held in 2005, pursuant to Council decision 2005/248 [YUN 2005, p. 1220]. He was also requested to report to the Commission in 2010.

Americas

Central America and the Caribbean

Corruption, poorly funded judiciary systems, lack of public trust and weak law enforcement undermined efforts to strengthen drug control policy in Central America and the Caribbean. Its geographical location made it an important transit and storage area for South American consignments en route to Mexico and destined for North America and Europe. Drug trafficking had an impact on both abuse and drug-related crime and led to increased money-laundering activities, especially in the Caribbean. About 18 per cent of the cocaine smuggled into Mexico entered through Belize and Guatemala; trafficking along that route increased and Belize was used as a transshipment area for cocaine consignments entering Europe via the West Africa route. Mexican criminal organizations were increasingly making use of Belizean territory for stockpiling illicit drugs and coordinating trafficking operations. Since maritime routes were increasingly monitored, traffickers were using low-flying light aircraft, in addition to other aircraft, and speedboats continued to be used to smuggle drugs across the Caribbean. Illicit consignments were usually concealed in personal luggage, canned food or industrial containers; however, the use of "mules" (people who smuggled drugs by ingesting them) continued.

Jamaica remained the main producer and exporter of cannabis in the region. Despite eradication efforts and significant seizures and arrests, it was illicitly cultivated in most parts of the country and consignments from Jamaica were sent through the Bahamas, the Dominican Republic and Haiti to North America or Europe. Cannabis was produced for domestic consumption in other countries in the Caribbean, such as Barbados, Saint Vincent and the Grenadines, and Trinidad and Tobago. Guatemala was the only country in the region with a significant illicit opium poppy cultivation, which increased in 2008. Guatemalan authorities reported that the amount of cocaine seized in the first quarter of 2008 was more than the amount seized in 2006 and 2007 combined. In Costa Rica, seizures of cocaine and heroin increased, mainly on maritime routes. Colombian traffickers continued to hire fishermen from Costa Rica and use their vessels in their operations. The majority of the seizures that originated in Costa Rica were reported by Spain, followed by the Netherlands, Germany and Belgium; most of them involved mail shipments. In Honduras, drug trafficking increased in the north and along its border with Nicaragua, while Haiti was used as a major trans-shipment area for consignments of South American cocaine bound for the United States, and trafficking increased along its border with the Dominican Republic. The availability of drugs in the streets of the Dominican Republic was rising, with concomitant increased drug abuse. Instead of receiving money, traffickers were paid in drugs, thus expanding local networks and increasing local demand. The growing market mainly affected the poorest segment of the population and was reflected in increasing violence and criminal activity. In Trinidad and Tobago, cannabis was the most abused drug and cannabis plants were mainly cultivated locally, although more potent varieties were brought into the country from Saint Vincent and the Grenadines.

The abuse of methylenedioxymethamphetamine (MDMA), commonly known as ecstasy, increased, particularly in El Salvador and Guatemala. Abuse was also rising in Jamaica, especially in the tourist areas of Montego Bay and Negril. MDMA found in the region continued to be smuggled from Europe or, more recently, from Canada. The Dominican Republic was the Caribbean country with the highest annual prevalence of abuse of amphetamines (excluding MDMA).

Reports indicated that methamphetamine laboratories were being established in Central America. In Mexico, measures adopted to limit the availability of pseudoephedrine had an impact on trafficking in precursors in Central America. Honduras and El Salvador reported an increase in demand for pharmaceutical preparations containing pseudoephedrine. In Central America, measures were taken to address the increasing diversion of precursors used in illicit manufacture. Some Caribbean countries, such as Antigua and Barbuda, Barbados and Grenada, had mechanisms for regulating the use and distribution of controlled chemicals. In the region as a whole, however, their movement was poorly monitored and regulated due to weak infrastructure and insufficient funding.

With regard to regional cooperation, the demand reduction programme of the Inter-American Drug Abuse Control Commission (CICAD) started in 2008 a professional certificate programme in Haiti. Antigua and Barbuda, Dominica, the Dominican Republic and Panama received technical assistance from CICAD for the drafting of their national drug control plans and strategies. The first interregional forum of CICAD and the EU twin-city initiative (Santo Domingo, Dominican Republic, April) aimed to improve strategies for drug abuse treatment. As part of the Merida Initiative, an initiative of Mexico and the United States that was incorporated into law in June 2008, the United States would provide $65 million in 2008 to the Dominican Republic, Haiti and countries in Central America, to be used for equipment and training in drug control. Member States of the Caribbean Community (CARICOM) strengthened cooperation mechanisms for security and recognized drug trafficking as a major threat.

North America

The major challenge in North America was the domination of illicit drug production and trafficking by organized crime and the growing violence in fighting among drug cartels and between traffickers and law enforcement officers, particularly in Mexico. The strong presence of Mexican drug syndicates was being felt in Mexico and the United States and the increasing influence of Asian organizations was noticeable in Canada and the United States. Colombian organizations continued to focus their operations on cocaine and heroin trafficking, but Mexican syndicates had taken over their smuggling and distribution from South America to the United States. In addition, Mexican organizations were heavily involved in the distribution of methamphetamine from Mexican-operated illicit drug manufacture and cannabis cultivation and trafficking within and into the United States. Asian trafficking organizations operating from Canada were involved in the illicit cultivation of high-potency cannabis and illicit methamphetamine manufacturing in Canada and the United States.

North America remained one of the main areas of illicit cannabis production and abuse, with Mexico, the United States and Canada producing 7,400, 4,700 and 3,500 tons, respectively. Despite eradication efforts, the area under illicit cultivation increased in Mexico, while in Canada illicit cultivation continued to thrive and growers utilized advanced cultivation methods to meet the high demand in Canada and the United States. One cause for concern in both countries was the very high tetrahydrocannabinol content of cannabis grown indoors under hydroponic conditions. In the United States, cannabis remained the most commonly abused drug and its illicit market was supplied by an increasing number of domestic indoor and outdoor cultivation sites. It was also smuggled out of Canada, Colombia, Jamaica and Mexico.

Cocaine continued to be easy to obtain in Canada, where the total amount seized increased slightly. It was mostly smuggled over land routes, leading through Central America, Mexico and the United States, and on direct flights from South America, as well as through various transit countries in the Caribbean. Cocaine was also smuggled through Canada into other countries such as Australia. Crack cocaine continued to be abused throughout Canada, where cocaine laced with methamphetamine was also identified as an emerging trend. In 2007, domestic and international efforts resulted in large cocaine seizures in the Eastern Pacific, which contributed to a cocaine shortage in the United States and to the decline in its annual prevalence rate. In addition, cocaine deliveries across the border to the United States declined due to intensive efforts by the Mexican authorities. However, the estimated amount of cocaine smuggled from South America into the United States remained significant, with about 90 per cent of it passing through the Central America corridor.

In Canada, heroin abuse remained low and was partly replaced by the abuse of prescription opiates. Most of the heroin in Canada was smuggled by air passengers or through postal or courier services and was mostly supplied by countries in South-West Asia, with India continuing to be the primary source or transit country. India was also the primary source of the opium seized, which increased considerably from 16 kg in 2005 to about 124 kg in 2006. In Canada, opium was mainly abused by older members of some ethnic groups. In the United States, heroin abuse was stable at a relatively low level, despite the fact that it was easily available in most large urban areas and some suburban and rural areas, mostly in the north-eastern part of the country, where its abuse increased among young adults (persons aged 25–34). The concentration of its abuse in the north-east was partly the result of abusers of prescription opiates switching to heroin because of its lower cost and higher purity. In the United States, a combination of Mexican "black tar" heroin and over-the-counter medication containing diphenhydramine hydrochloride was sold under the street name "cheese heroin". Most of the heroin abused in the United States was illicitly manufactured in Colombia or Mexico. Mexico experienced a continuous decline in opium poppy eradication levels, the total area eradicated dropping from 21,609 hectares in 2005 to 7,784 hectares in 2007, partly as the result of unfavourable climate conditions and the realignment of responsibilities for aerial eradication.

In the United States, the abuse of prescription drugs was higher than the abuse of cocaine, heroin, hallucinogens, MDMA and/or inhalants, and second only to cannabis. In 2007, about 16.3 million people reported having abused prescription drugs (6.6 per cent of the population aged 12 and above), compared with 14.8 million in 2002. One matter of concern was the high rate of their abuse among youth. While legislation allowing prescription drug monitoring programmes was adopted in 38 of the 50 states in the United States, Florida had still not adopted such legislation due to privacy concerns. In the United States, the number of Internet pharmacies selling controlled prescription drugs without the required prescription increased by 70 per cent between 2006 and 2007. In Canada, diverted prescription drugs were mostly obtained from domestic sources, and the abuse of oxycodone remained a cause for concern. It continued to be smuggled out of Canada and into the United States.

Methamphetamine abuse remained a problem in Canada and traffickers continued to adulterate MDMA and cannabis with methamphetamine in order to increase methamphetamine demand. In the United States, the abuse of methamphetamine in 2007 was slightly less than in previous years, with Mexico remaining the primary source. Canada, traditionally an MDMA importer and consumer, became a major manufacturer and exporter, as reflected in the unprecedented quantities seized in other countries, such as Australia and the United States. As the smuggling of MDMA from Canada into the United States increased, the importance of European sources decreased. In the United States, the illicit manufacture of MDMA remained limited. *Gamma*-hydroxybutyric acid (GHB) continued to be abused in Canada, mostly supplied by clandestine laboratories, while lysergic acid diethylamide (LSD) and psilocybin continued to be abused in the United States, where LSD abuse among youth was low and psilocybin was the most widely abused hallucinogen. Organized criminal groups in Canada smuggled ephedrine from China and India, while traffickers in Mexico responded to the restrictions on the import and sale of precursors of methamphetamine by smuggling them using new routes leading from China and India, importing non-restricted chemical derivatives instead of those precursors and using alternative manufacturing methods, which ensured a stable level of illicitly manufactured and smuggled methamphetamine in the United States.

As to substances not under international control, while the main transit countries used for smuggling khat into Canada remained the Netherlands and the United Kingdom, seizures of khat smuggled into Canada from France, Germany, Italy and the United States increased slightly. In Canada, it was mainly used by members of ethnic communities. Ketamine continued to be abused in Canada, where it had gained popularity as a new "club drug". In the United States, the over-the-counter cough and cold medicines that were abused mostly contained dextromethorphan, and the abuse of inhalants by youth had risen since 2003.

A new major step in regional cooperation in 2008 was the Merida initiative, an example of security cooperation involving Mexico and the United States, as well as the countries in Central America, to combat drug trafficking, transnational crime and terrorism. The United States law enforcement agencies supported their Mexican counterparts by providing training in precursor detection, investigative techniques and methamphetamine investigations in the main areas of illicit methamphetamine manufacturing in Mexico. Cooperation between Canada and the United States progressed and bilateral forums, such as the Cross-Border Crime Forum and Project North Star, increased information-sharing and joint training among law enforcement officers. United States law enforcement agencies and the Royal Canadian Mounted Police stepped up their intelligence-sharing and coordinated law enforcement operations to fight criminal organizations manufacturing MDMA.

South America

The annual illicit production of cannabis in South America was estimated at about 10,000 tons, almost 25 per cent of global production in 2006; Paraguay was the main producer. Most illicit cultivation occurred in remote and inaccessible areas. Brazil continued to report the largest seizures in the region.

In 2007, the total area of coca bush cultivation increased in all three of the main countries in which it was illicitly grown (Bolivia, Colombia, Peru) to 181,600 hectares, 16 per cent more than in 2006. Colombia accounted for 55 per cent of the area under cultivation, Peru 29 per cent and Bolivia 16 per cent. That overall increase in coca cultivation was offset by decreased yields in some areas; thus potential global manufacture of cocaine increased by only 10 tons over 2006. In 2007, potential cocaine manufacture in Colombia decreased by 10 tons compared to 2006. Some 67,000 hectares of illicitly cultivated coca bush were eradicated manually in Colombia in 2007 and a further 153,000 hectares were subjected to aerial spraying. In Peru, coca bush cultivation increased by 4 per cent in 2007 and estimated cocaine manufacture totalled 290 tons. In 2007, eradication in Peru decreased by 5 per cent to 12,072 hectares. In Bolivia, coca bush cultivation increased slightly in 2007 for the second consecutive year, amounting to 28,900 hectares. In September 2008, the Bolivian Government signed an agreement with coca growers of the Yungas region allowing them to cultivate coca bush in that area. In Bolivia, potential cocaine manufacture in 2007 increased by 9 per cent, to 104 tons. The world's main cocaine trafficking routes continued to run from countries in the Andean subregion, notably Colombia, to the United States. In recent years, the amount of cocaine from South America smuggled via West Africa into Europe had increased dramatically.

In 2006, the region accounted for 45 per cent of cocaine seizures worldwide; large seizures continued to be concentrated in a few countries. In 2007, seizures increased in Bolivia, Brazil and Colombia and decreased in Ecuador and Peru. In Bolivia, seizures of cocaine hydrochloride doubled in 2007 over the previous year and seizures of cocaine base tripled compared with 2002. Cocaine seizures increased by one third in the first half of 2008 compared with the same period in 2007. In Colombia, seizures of cocaine hydrochloride and cocaine base increased slightly in 2007; about 80 per cent of the illicit drugs leaving the country were smuggled by sea through the Mexico–Central American corridor, the Euro-African corridor and the Caribbean corridor, in that order. Most of the drugs were trafficked by sea and the use of submersible vessels was reported. More illicit drugs were trafficked by sea than by air, and were smuggled across borders by air rather than by land. Ecuador was affected not only by drug trafficking, but also by stockpiling, the diversion of precursor chemicals and, to some extent, illicit production. Venezuela continued to be used as a major departure area for drugs destined for Europe; between 2002 and 2007, an average of 35 tons of cocaine was seized each year. In Colombia, traditional use of coca leaf was marginal and statistically insignificant; virtually the entire coca leaf production was destined for illicit cocaine manufacture. Colombian farmers processed half of their coca leaf production into cocaine base to gain a higher income per hectare, and the last step in the process of manufacturing cocaine hydrochloride was usually carried out by traffickers in clandestine laboratories. In recent years, most South American countries had reported increasing abuse of cocaine, probably a spillover effect of its trafficking throughout the region. Several countries in the southern part of South America previously used as transit areas had been used more and more for drug processing, resulting in the increased availability of inexpensive semi-refined cocaine derivatives, such as cocaine base and coca paste, in the local markets. Changes in drug abuse patterns, including increased abuse of *paco* (coca paste), were reported by Argentina, Brazil, Chile and Uruguay. The average past-year prevalence of cocaine abuse in South America was 1.4 per cent, 0.3 per cent higher than the global average. It was highest in Argentina, followed by Uruguay, Chile, Bolivia, Peru and Ecuador.

Illicit opium poppy cultivation in South America accounted for less than 1 per cent of cultivation worldwide. The highest annual prevalence of abuse of opiates was found in Brazil, the lowest in Bolivia and Suriname. Most of the abuse in the region involved opioids diverted from licit sources. Contrary to the situation in other South American countries, in Uruguay the relative number of females who abused drugs by injection was high.

Several countries in South America reported an increase in the non-medical use of psychotropic substances, in particular sedatives and tranquillizers, and expressed their concern at the increased abuse of so-called "date rape drugs", mainly GHB, flunitrazepam and ketamine (a substance not under international control). Although some countries in the region, including Argentina, Chile and Peru, reported increased abuse of MDMA in 2006, seizures continued to be low. Large-scale diversion of precursor chemicals continued, with over 90 per cent of potassium permanganate seizures being made in Colombia. Imports of ephedrine and pseudoephedrine in some South American countries, including Argentina, increased significantly.

With regard to regional cooperation, CICAD remained the main forum for coordinating drug control issues in the Americas. In a 2007 report, it summarized progress made by each country and in the region as a whole regarding the development of policies and programmes to combat illicit drugs between 1997 and 2007. The report highlighted the importance of established national drug control authorities and drug observatories to assist Governments in implementing their national drug control strategies. South American countries participated in the Drug Treatment City Partnership initiative, focusing on the establishment of a network between cities in Latin America and the Caribbean and in Europe to facilitate the exchange of information and best practices regarding drug control policies, in order to improve treatment and rehabilitation programmes for abusers and demand reduction programmes. At the Tenth High-Level Specialized Dialogue on Drugs between the Andean Community and the EU (Bogota, Colombia, 1–2 November 2007), Bolivia, Colombia and Peru presented their national strategies for alternative development and illicit crop eradication, while Ecuador reported on preventive alternative development programmes implemented in the northern areas along its borders with Colombia. In July 2008, Bolivia, Colombia, Ecuador and Peru, in cooperation with the EU, launched a project to provide support to the Andean Community in the area of synthetic drugs. At the Regional Summit on the World Drug Problem, Security and Cooperation (Cartagena de Indias, Colombia, 30 July–1 August), representatives of 25 countries of Central America, the Caribbean and South America adopted the Cartagena Declaration, which emphasized the importance of a balanced approach to implementing drug supply and demand strategies.

Asia

East and South-East Asia

The illicit cultivation of cannabis continued in East and South-East Asia, including in Indonesia and Thailand; Viet Nam reported an increase in cannabis cultivation in some provinces in 2007 and 2008. States in the region continued to report significant seizures. Cambodia, Malaysia and the Philippines reported the highest annual prevalence of abuse of cannabis. Cannabis was the second most commonly abused substance (after solvents) among persons aged 15 and older in Japan.

Preliminary data on the total area under illicit opium poppy cultivation in Myanmar indicated a slight increase between 2007 and 2008. In 2007, Myanmar eradicated 3,598 of the 27,700 hectares under illicit cultivation, while in the Lao People's Democratic Republic, which reported a decrease in opium abuse, 779 of 1,500 hectares were eradicated. Illicitly cultivated opium poppy was also eradicated in Thailand and Viet Nam. In Thailand, the total area under cultivation stood at 231 hectares, mainly in remote northern areas. In China, the decreasing trend in heroin seizures continued; the decrease in its availability in the illicit market was largely attributed to efforts by drug control authorities. However, in China, Malaysia and Viet Nam, heroin continued to be the most commonly abused drug.

An increase in the illicit manufacture of ATS was reported, particularly in China and Indonesia, and the illicit manufacture of methamphetamine continued in China, Indonesia, Myanmar and the Philippines. China (including the Hong Kong Special Administrative Region (SAR)), Japan, the Republic of Korea, Thailand and Viet Nam continued to report significant seizures of methamphetamine. During 2007, there was an increase in ATS seizures, mainly methamphetamine originating in China (including the Hong Kong SAR) and destined for Indonesia, while China (including the Hong Kong SAR), Japan and the Republic of Korea continued to report seizures of MDMA. The Philippines had the highest annual prevalence of abuse of amphetamines in the world (6 per cent), and other countries in the region, including Cambodia, the Lao People's Democratic Republic, Malaysia and Thailand, also had a high abuse rate. Countries in East and South-East Asia continued to report seizures of significant amounts of precursor chemicals.

Ketamine was the most commonly abused psychotropic substance in China, including in the Hong Kong SAR, where it was the drug of choice for 73 per cent of abusers under the age of 21. Its abuse was also reported in Cambodia and its illicit manufacture was a growing problem in China. The Hong Kong SAR, Myanmar, the Philippines, Singapore and Taiwan Province of China continued to report significant seizures, and trafficking and seizures were also reported in Viet Nam.

Regionally, the countries in East and South-East Asia continued to cooperate in the field of drug control through bilateral, multilateral and regional organizations. The fifth meeting of the Association of Southeast Asian Nations (ASEAN) Inter-Parliamentary Assembly Fact-Finding Committee to Combat the Drug Menace (Singapore, 22–25 June) agreed to continue cooperation to address common threats related to drug control. The eighth ministerial meeting of signatory countries of the 1993 Memorandum of Understanding on Drug Control was held in Vientiane, Lao People's Democratic Republic, in June. The fifteenth ASEAN Regional Forum (Singapore, 24 July) adopted the Statement Promoting Collaboration on the Prevention of Diversion of Precursors into Illicit Drug Manufacture.

In October, an INCB mission to Japan invited the Government to share with the international community the measures carried out to prevent drug abuse, to monitor all types of substance abuse, including the abuse of pharmaceutical preparations containing controlled substances, and to expand services for treatment of abusers to cover all segments of the population, with a view to facilitating rehabilitation and social reintegration.

South Asia

India was one of the largest illicit producers of cannabis herb and resin in South Asia. Although law enforcement authorities regularly eradicated large areas of illicitly cultivated plants, a significant amount of cannabis found its way onto the illicit market in that country. Nepal was the most important producer of cannabis resin in the region, and the increase in seizures in the country accounted for the fact that the amount seized in the entire region in 2006 was twice the amount in 2003. In addition to being abused locally, cannabis resin in Nepal was smuggled into other countries in Asia and the Pacific—mainly to India, where 40–50 per cent of the resin seized in recent years had originated in Nepal. Seizures of cannabis resin from Nepal were also regularly reported in China, including in the Hong Kong SAR, Japan and Thailand. Cannabis remained the most abused drug in Sri Lanka, where it was cultivated in the eastern and southern provinces.

Every year, Indian counter-narcotics forces eradicated areas in which opium poppy grew wild or was illicitly cultivated. On average, about 2,000 kg of opium derived from illicit cultivations were seized annually. However, the proportion of the seized opium of Indian origin was unclear, since opium was still smuggled out of neighbouring countries where opium poppy was illicitly cultivated. Heroin and morphine continued to be among the substances most commonly abused in India. A significant portion of the heroin seized in India originated in neighbouring countries. The amount of heroin smuggled into Maldives had increased in recent years. The increase indicated that the country was becoming an important transit area for smuggling operations. Heroin continued to be widely abused in Sri Lanka; it was not produced locally but brought into the country from India and Pakistan. Small quantities were smuggled by airline passengers and on fishing boats coming from the west coast of India.

Small quantities of cocaine had begun to be smuggled into India, and investigations into seizures made in 2008 suggested that it was being smuggled out of West Africa.

Pharmaceutical preparations diverted from licit manufacture in India continued to feed their widespread abuse in South Asia. Drugs smuggled into neighbouring countries included pethidine and codeine-based cough syrups. A popular form of methamphetamine abused in Asia was a tablet known as "yaba", containing a mixture of caffeine and about 30 per cent methamphetamine. Increasingly large seizures of "yaba" tablets were reported in Bangladesh, where the drug—most of which was smuggled out of neighbouring countries such as Myanmar—had gained popularity among young people. Several seizures of LSD were reported in India in 2007. Trafficking in ATS and their precursor chemicals increased throughout the region. Since the start of 2008, several seizures of ATS had been made in India, where they were illicitly manufactured and also smuggled into the country from South-East Asia. In spite of efforts to curb the clandestine manufacture of methaqualone in India, seizures were reported every year. Nepal was used as a new transit area for ATS consignments destined for the increasingly lucrative illicit markets on the Arabian peninsula. Nepal remained a common destination for consignments of pharmaceutical preparations smuggled out of India. Some of the acetic anhydride licitly produced on an industrial scale in India was subject to diversion for the illicit manufacture of methaqualone and heroin. The diversion of ephedrine, pseudoephedrine and norephedrine, precursor chemicals used in ATS manufacture, was also a matter of concern in India.

With regard to regional cooperation, the First Asian Consultation on the Prevention of HIV Related to Drug Use (Goa, India, 23–31 January) focused on various issues related to drug abuse in Asia. The fifteenth summit meeting of the South Asian Association for Regional Cooperation (Colombo, Sri Lanka, August) recognized the interlinkages between terrorism and trafficking in narcotic drugs and psychotropic substances and reiterated the commitment to fostering regional cooperation to combat those problems.

West Asia

Illicit opium poppy cultivation in Afghanistan dropped from its record level of 193,000 hectares in 2007 to 157,000 in 2008. The number of provinces free of opium poppy increased from 13 to 18, and about 98 per cent of the illicit cultivation in the country took place in just seven provinces. However, Afghanistan continued to account for by far the largest share of the world's illicit cultivation and, due to the higher crop yield, actual opium production dropped by only 6 per cent, from 8,200 tons in 2007 to 7,700 in 2008. The link between security conditions and illicit opium poppy cultivation was strong; in the southern provinces of Afghanistan, security was weak and the overwhelming majority of villages were involved in illicit cultivation. Moreover, eradication efforts in Afghanistan were hampered by lack of security, poor planning and inadequate equipment and funding. Inadequate security, ineffective Government control and problems in ensuring the rule of law were major factors contributing to illicit cultivation in other countries in the region as well; it increased in the Bekaa valley in Lebanon, and took place in Pakistan, though on a much smaller scale than in Afghanistan and mainly in remote areas near the Afghan border, where the Government had difficulties in enforcing laws. The large-scale smuggling of Afghan opiates resulted in a wide range of social ills, including organized crime, corruption and a high demand for opiates. Afghan opiates were smuggled mainly through Iran, Pakistan and Central Asian countries into Eastern and Western Europe. In Afghanistan, significant seizures were made, though small in comparison with the amount of illicit production in the country. More opiates were seized in Iran than in any other country in the world; in 2007, seizures increased by 51 per cent compared with 2006. Pakistan continued to be used as a major transit area for Afghan opiates, though to a lesser extent than Iran; about 35 per cent of Afghan opiates were smuggled through Pakistan. In Central Asia, heroin seizures in 2007 fell slightly (by 9 per cent) compared with 2006, mainly because of the significant decrease in Tajikistan and Uzbekistan. In contrast, in Kyrgyzstan and Turkmenistan, heroin seizures increased by over 60 per cent. Seizures of opium increased significantly in many countries in Central Asia, indicating a possible shift in trafficking patterns. Trafficking organizations increasingly exploited the situation in Iraq to smuggle drugs, including heroin, from countries outside of West Asia, mainly into the Arabian peninsula. New routes led through Jordan, the Syrian Arab Republic and the United Arab Emirates. Jordan and Syria were increasingly used as trans-shipment points for trafficking: cannabis from Lebanon was smuggled into Jordan; heroin was smuggled through Syria and then Jordan on its way to Israel; and counterfeit Captagon tablets were smuggled through Syria and then Jordan on their way to the Arabian peninsula. Trafficking in Yemen also increased, as evidenced by more drug-related offences and drug seizures, mainly of cannabis.

The large amount of opiates from Afghanistan continued to cause major abuse problems in the region. Nearly all the countries neighbouring Afghanistan had high rates of abuse: Iran had the world's highest rate of abuse of opiates (estimated prevalence at 2.8 per cent), and Pakistan and many countries in Central Asia also had high rates. Heroin was the main opiate abused in Central Asian countries and injection was the main method used; HIV/AIDS transmission through the sharing of needles continued. Cannabis was the most commonly seized type of drug in Central Asia, partly because the plants grew wild in Kazakhstan and Kyrgyzstan. A worrying development was the increase in illicit cannabis cultivation in Afghanistan, which became an important producer: 70,000 hectares were cultivated in 2007, compared with 50,000 in 2006. Cannabis was also illicitly cultivated in the Occupied Palestinian Territory, in the Bekaa valley in Lebanon and in many countries in Central Asia.

Although cocaine trafficking was spreading in West Asia, it was still abused in small quantities. In May, Israel seized 104 kg of cocaine in Haifa. In 2007, seizures totalled 114 kg in Turkey, compared with 3 kg in 2003. Kazakhstan seized a consignment of 555 grams in 2007, the largest seizure ever made there. It had apparently been brought into the country from Germany, Lithuania and Poland via the Russian Federation.

The Arabian peninsula continued to be faced with a long-standing problem of ATS abuse, in particular of counterfeit Captagon tablets, which continued to be smuggled in large amounts into many countries on the peninsula. The world's largest seizures of counterfeit Captagon took place in Saudi Arabia, increasing to 13.9 tons in 2007. Seizures of amphetamines also rose sharply in Saudi Arabia, suggesting a surge in the abuse of illicit stimulants. The amount of Captagon seized in Turkey rose significantly in 2007. Precursor chemicals, acetic anhydride in particular, continued to be available for heroin manufacture in Afghanistan, where more than 3 tons of precursor chemicals, including ammonium chloride and sodium carbonate, were seized in July. In Turkey, the total amount of acetic anhydride seized increased nearly threefold in 2007 compared with 2006.

With regard to regional cooperation, the international community continued to provide support and assistance to Afghanistan under the umbrella of the Afghanistan Compact, adopted in 2006 [YUN 2006, p. 363]. In April, the Afghanistan National Development Strategy for 2008–2013 was finalized; it outlined the steps to be taken to achieve the Afghanistan Compact benchmarks regarding security, governance and development. Countries in West Asia continued to take joint measures against trafficking. In particular, they increased their bilateral and multilateral cooperation in reducing illicit drug supply and demand, precursor control, border management, countering the spread of HIV/AIDS, and fighting organized crime and money-laundering. They also participated in regional projects and international operations. Cooperation among Central Asian countries improved. In February, Kazakhstan, the Russian Federation, Tajikistan and Uzbekistan launched Operation Typhoon, which targeted one of the largest trafficking groups in Central Asia. Operation Channel, conducted under the auspices of the Collective Security Treaty Organization (CSTO), also contributed to countering trafficking in the region. Azerbaijan, Kazakhstan, Kyrgyzstan, the Russian Federation, Tajikistan, Turkmenistan and Uzbekistan continued to cooperate towards the establishment of the Central Asia Regional Information and Coordination Centre (CARICC). Countries in West Asia worked to establish the Gulf Centre for Criminal Intelligence in Doha, Qatar, which would serve as a focal point for international cooperation in information collection and intelligence development to counter trafficking and other forms of organized crime. In a meeting held in Dubai, United Arab Emirates, drug control agencies from countries on the Arabian peninsula, as well as the Council of Arab Ministers of the Interior, adopted the Dubai statement on strategic planning and cooperation in drug control. Afghanistan, Iran and Pakistan held a meeting in Tehran in May to appoint border liaison officers on each of their countries' borders to plan joint operations targeting the smuggling of opiates out of Afghanistan. Countries on the Arabian peninsula and in other subregions adopted the Tripoli Action Plan on Combating Trafficking and Money-Laundering through the Mail, while Israeli and Palestinian officials continued to explore methods of improving cooperation. A meeting hosted by Turkmenistan led to the initiation of two international projects against trafficking in West Asia: the Caspian Sea initiative and the Turkmen border initiative.

In January, INCB sent a mission to the United Arab Emirates, where the implementation of controls over drugs and precursor chemicals in the free trade zones continued to face difficulties. The Board urged the Government to take measures against trafficking in all areas under its jurisdiction, including the free trade zones. It noted that there were no comprehensive activities aimed at identifying the drug abuse situation in the country and recommended that the Government take measures to collect data on the extent and nature of the drug problem.

Afghanistan

In response to Commission on Narcotic Drugs resolution 50/1 [YUN 2007, p. 1295], the UNODC Executive Director submitted a report on follow-up to the Second Ministerial Conference on Drug Trafficking Routes from Afghanistan [E/CN.7/2008/10]; that Conference was held in 2006 [YUN 2006, p. 1450]. The Executive Director reviewed key achievements and measures taken during the first operational year of the second phase of the Paris Pact initiative [YUN 2003, p. 1263], stating that the second three-year phase of the project, launched in January 2007, included six new elements: improving the operational focus of the expert round tables; following up the Paris Pact recommendations more effectively; ensuring the wider use and sustainability of the Automated Donor Assistance Mechanism (ADAM); strengthening counter-narcotic analytical capacities; advocating a balanced approach to drug issues; and fostering partnerships with subregional, regional and international players. In 2007, in order to make the Paris Pact more action-oriented, UNODC grouped the outcomes and recommendations of the Paris Pact expert round tables into seven action plans known as the "Rainbow Strategy". Since the inception of the second phase of the initiative, three round-table meetings of senior experts in counter-narcotic enforcement and drug demand reduction had been organized, each with a separate geographical or thematic focus. An important element of the second phase was the explicit inclusion of demand reduction issues.

To improve inter-agency cooperation between law enforcement agencies at the national, regional and international levels, the five Central Asian States (Kazakhstan, Kyrgyzstan, Tajikistan, Turkmenistan and

Uzbekistan), the Russian Federation and Azerbaijan participated in a UNODC project to establish CARICC. The purpose of CARICC was to facilitate information exchange, analyse and develop information, provide support and assist in the coordination of the operational activities of law enforcement agencies in the region. A six-month pilot phase of CARICC started on 1 November 2007. The report noted that ADAM, an Internet-based tool for coordinating counter-narcotics technical assistance in countries along the main trafficking routes from Afghanistan, underwent a number of improvements in 2007.

On 14 March [E/2008/28 (res. 51/1)], the Commission called on Paris Pact partners to promote initiatives against trafficking in opiates from Afghanistan and to strengthen cooperation with ongoing operations in the region. It commended the input provided by training centres and institutions in enhancing the capacities of drug law enforcement agencies, and underscored the importance of exploring additional possibilities and modalities for organizing training courses for officers from Afghanistan, neighbouring States and States in Central Asia and other subregions. The Commission welcomed the launch, under the guidance of UNODC and the Project Cohesion Task Force, of the Targeted Anti-trafficking Regional Communication, Expertise and Training initiative, targeting precursors used in heroin manufacture in Afghanistan, and urged Paris Pact partners to cooperate with it. It encouraged time-bound operations focusing on trafficking in precursors, in particular acetic anhydride. Paris Pact partners were invited to strengthen control over the transnational movement of monetary proceeds of trafficking in illicit crops cultivated or drugs produced in Afghanistan, money-laundering and other transnational criminal activities related to such proceeds, as well as the financing of terrorist activities. The Commission called on the partners to implement prevention, treatment and rehabilitation initiatives and exchange best practices in demand reduction. It expressed its satisfaction with the beginning of the pilot phase in the implementation of the initiative to establish CARICC and noted the importance of ADAM in coordinating counter-narcotics technical assistance in countries along the main trafficking routes from Afghanistan. The UNODC Executive Director was requested to report on the issue in 2009.

Security Council action. On 11 June, the Security Council adopted **resolution 1817(2008)** (see p. 359), in which it called on States to increase international and regional cooperation in order to counter illicit drug production and trafficking in Afghanistan, including by strengthening the monitoring of the international trade in precursor chemicals, notably but not limited to acetic anhydride. It also invited States, in particular those producing precursor chemicals, Afghanistan, its neighbouring countries and all countries on the trafficking routes, to increase their cooperation with INCB.

ECONOMIC AND SOCIAL COUNCIL ACTION

On 24 July [meeting 42], the Economic and Social Council, on the recommendation of the Commission on Narcotic Drugs [E/2008/28], adopted **resolution 2008/27** without vote [agenda item 14 *(d)*].

Provision of international assistance to the most affected States neighbouring Afghanistan

The Economic and Social Council,

Recalling its resolutions 2001/16 of 24 July 2001, 2002/21 of 24 July 2002, 2003/34 and 2003/35 of 22 July 2003 and 2005/27 of 22 July 2005 and other relevant resolutions on international assistance to States affected by the transit of illicit drugs,

Taking note with concern of the report of the United Nations Office on Drugs and Crime entitled "Afghanistan Opium Survey 2007", in which the Office emphasized that, in 2007, Afghanistan had produced 8,200 tons of opium, representing 93 per cent of global production,

Noting the progress that Afghanistan has made in implementing the National Drug Control Strategy of the Government of Afghanistan, including the fact that the number of its provinces free of opium poppy more than doubled, from six to thirteen, in 2007,

Reaffirming the commitments assumed by Member States in the Political Declaration adopted by the General Assembly at its twentieth special session and the measures to enhance international cooperation to counter the world drug problem,

Welcoming the Paris Pact initiative on assistance to States affected by the transit of illicit drugs,

Acknowledging the ongoing efforts of the Government of Afghanistan and the international community, including States neighbouring Afghanistan, to counter the scourge of illicit drugs, despite the continuing increase in the illicit cultivation of opium poppy and the illicit production of opiates in Afghanistan,

Emphasizing that international drug traffickers are constantly changing their modus operandi, rapidly reorganizing and gaining access to modern technology,

Acknowledging that transit States are faced with multifaceted challenges related to the increasing amount of illicit drugs transiting through their territory as a result of the increasing supply and demand on illicit drug markets,

Keeping in mind that the bulk of the illicit drugs originating in Afghanistan is smuggled through the Islamic Republic of Iran, Pakistan and other countries neighbouring Afghanistan before reaching countries of destination,

Considering that a large number of transit States, in particular the States neighbouring Afghanistan, are developing countries or countries with economies in transition and are faced with multifaceted challenges, including rising levels of drug-related crime and increased prevalence of drug abuse,

Bearing in mind that the constantly changing tactics of drug traffickers and the introduction of new varieties of illicit drugs increase the challenges and harm that they cause in Afghanistan, in the States neighbouring Afghanistan and in other parts of the world,

1. *Reaffirms its commitment*, in accordance with the principle of shared responsibility, to counter the world drug problem in all its manifestations, in a coordinated manner, in particular by providing technical assistance and support to the transit States most affected by drug trafficking;

2. *Calls upon* the Government of Afghanistan to intensify, with the support of the international community, its efforts to continue implementing, in particular, the eight pillars of the National Drug Control Strategy, to identify and dismantle laboratories illicitly manufacturing heroin and morphine and to trace and curb the illicit supply of precursors;

3. *Commends* regional initiatives to strengthen international and regional cooperation aimed at countering the threat posed by the illicit production of drugs in Afghanistan and trafficking in drugs originating in that country;

4. *Encourages* cross-border cooperation among Afghanistan, the Islamic Republic of Iran and Pakistan;

5. *Calls upon* all Member States and the United Nations Office on Drugs and Crime to provide the technical assistance and support needed for strengthening the initiatives and efforts of Afghanistan, the Islamic Republic of Iran and Pakistan to fight drug trafficking, thereby also reducing the deleterious impact of illicit drugs in all parts of the world, and invites Member States and other donors to provide extrabudgetary contributions for those purposes in accordance with the rules and procedures of the United Nations;

6. *Encourages* the States neighbouring Afghanistan to enhance coordination through existing regional mechanisms for strengthening border cooperation and information exchange;

7. *Encourages* Member States and the United Nations Office on Drugs and Crime to provide technical assistance and support needed for strengthening the efforts of States neighbouring Afghanistan to fight drug trafficking, and invites Member States and other donors to provide extrabudgetary contributions for those purposes in accordance with the rules and procedures of the United Nations;

8. *Welcomes* the trilateral ministerial meeting held in Vienna in June 2007, with the assistance of the United Nations Office on Drugs and Crime, which brought together high-level officials from Afghanistan, the Islamic Republic of Iran and Pakistan, and supports the decision to hold another trilateral meeting in the Islamic Republic of Iran in 2008;

9. *Emphasizes* the importance of taking measures to reduce demand and the adverse consequences of drug abuse in conjunction with measures to reduce supply in order to effectively counter the menace posed by illicit drugs to the entire international community;

10. *Calls upon* Afghanistan to mainstream, with the assistance of the international community, the counternarcotics programme in the forthcoming Afghan national development strategy;

11. *Emphasizes* the need to strengthen the law enforcement capacity of the main transit States and the importance of inter-agency coordination in developing effective drug control strategies;

12. *Urges* the international partners, all relevant organizations of the United Nations and, in particular, the United Nations Office on Drugs and Crime and invites international financial and development institutions to assist transit States, in particular the States neighbouring Afghanistan that are most affected by the transit of illicit drugs, by providing them with adequate technical assistance to effectively address the drug trafficking problem through a comprehensive and integrated shared plan, and invites Member States and other donors to provide extrabudgetary contributions for those purposes in accordance with the rules and procedures of the United Nations;

13. *Requests* the Executive Director of the United Nations Office on Drugs and Crime to report to the Commission on Narcotic Drugs at its fifty-second session on the implementation of the present resolution.

Europe

Cannabis remained the most widely abused drug in Europe, but there were indications that its abuse was stabilizing or declining at a fairly high level. Illicit cultivation continued to be reported in many countries in Western Europe; in Central and Eastern Europe most of the cannabis herb originated in Albania, Moldova, Montenegro, Serbia, the former Yugoslav Republic of Macedonia and Ukraine. In Albania, cannabis plants were cultivated on public land. Europe was the region with the largest illicit market for cannabis resin. The amount of cannabis resin seized in the region increased in 2007, with more cannabis resin seized in Spain than in any other country in the world. A large amount was also seized in Belgium, France and Portugal. In European countries, lifetime prevalence of cannabis abuse ranged from 2 to 37 per cent, the lowest rates being in Bulgaria, Malta and Romania and the highest in Denmark, France, Italy and the United Kingdom.

Europe continued to be the second largest market for cocaine in the world. Large consignments from South America were smuggled into Europe by sea, often through West African countries. However, cocaine smuggling through Eastern Europe had significantly increased in recent years. The total amount of cocaine seized in Europe remained high and increased dramatically in Eastern European countries in 2007. The increased number of cocaine shipments from South America to countries in Eastern Europe was part of a new development; cocaine arriving in Western Europe was increasingly smuggled into Eastern Europe and then transported back into Western Europe via the Balkan route, the route traditionally used for trafficking in opiates. Cocaine abuse became more prevalent in some parts of Western Europe; in

France, lifetime prevalence was 2.6 per cent among the adult population and had more than doubled over the preceding 10 years.

Europe also remained the region with the second largest illicit market for opiates, which continued to expand in Eastern Europe. Their abuse remained stable or declined in Central and Western Europe, but increased in the Russian Federation and other countries in Eastern Europe, particularly in member States of the Commonwealth of Independent States and in countries in South-Eastern Europe along the Balkan route. Most of the laboratories illicitly producing opiates continued to be located in Eastern Europe. The Russian Federation was the largest illicit market for opiates in Europe, while the second largest illicit market in Eastern Europe was Ukraine. Almost all the heroin available on illicit markets in Europe originated in Afghanistan. The traditional (northern) Balkan route, passing through Turkey, Bulgaria, Romania, Hungary and then Austria, was used for smuggling heroin more frequently in 2007, as evidenced by the more than 2.5 tons of heroin seized on that route. The alternative (southern) Balkan route through Greece, Albania and then the former Yugoslav Republic of Macedonia to Italy, was used less often in 2007 than in previous years. With opium production shifting towards the southern provinces of Afghanistan, it became less convenient for traffickers to ship opiates via the so-called silk route, via Central Asia into the Russian Federation and from there to countries in Europe; therefore, trafficking along that route declined in 2007. Train connections between the Russian Federation and its western neighbouring countries (Belarus, Poland, Ukraine) were increasingly used for heroin smuggling into Western Europe. Heroin was also increasingly trafficked by air from Eastern and Central Europe to Western Europe. Major heroin seizures were reported in Bulgaria, the Russian Federation and Serbia, and seizures increased in some Western European countries, such as Germany and Spain.

The illicit manufacture of synthetic drugs continued to rise in Central and Eastern Europe, while Western Europe remained a major source of ATS, particularly MDMA. However, as MDMA was increasingly manufactured in other parts of the world, seizures in Western Europe declined. Belgium and the Netherlands were the main exporters of amphetamine and substances in the MDMA group. Most MDMA seizures were reported in France, Germany, the Netherlands and the United Kingdom. The main source of methamphetamine was the Czech Republic, which also reported the largest number of dismantled laboratories. Annual prevalence of amphetamine abuse among the general population in the United Kingdom, the largest market for amphetamine in Europe, decreased significantly in 2007. Seizures of precursors of amphetamine increased in Eastern European countries, which also continued to be used as a transit area for consignments of acetic anhydride destined for Afghanistan; almost 80 per cent of the precursor chemicals required for illicit drug laboratories in Afghanistan was smuggled through South-Eastern and Eastern Europe.

With regard to regional cooperation, the Paris Pact expert round table for the Black Sea area (Bucharest, Romania, 9–11 July) discussed ways to support and utilize existing communication and information networks to achieve maximum law enforcement coverage of the routes used for trafficking in opiates from Afghanistan. In September, the European Commission proposed a new European Union Drugs Action Plan for 2009–2012. CSTO and the Federal Drug Control Service of the Russian Federation carried out the second stage of operation Channel 2007 in November and December 2007, with the participation of Armenia, Belarus, Kazakhstan, Kyrgyzstan, the Russian Federation, Tajikistan and Uzbekistan. The goal of the operation was to build a system of enhanced collective security to prevent trafficking from Afghanistan.

In October, an INCB mission to Romania noted that the mechanism for the monitoring and control of internationally controlled substances was neither sufficient nor functioning adequately; it requested the Government to put in place legislation and provide resources and personnel to enable drug regulatory authorities to perform their control functions. It also urged the Government to strengthen customs and border control activities, determine the national medical and/or scientific requirements for narcotic drugs and psychotropic substances and ensure that those substances were available for medical purposes. In May, a Board mission visited Ukraine, where the transit traffic in heroin and cocaine posed serious drug control problems. Although a mechanism had been established to coordinate efforts to fight trafficking, problems continued to exist, largely because of lack of cooperation among authorities involved in drug control; the Board recommended that the Government should define clearly the lines of responsibility between the law enforcement agencies and improve the coordination of their activities.

Oceania

Drug smuggling from Canada to Australia increased. While comprehensive seizure data for Australia and New Zealand were available, limited data were available for other countries in the region. However, illicit substances including cannabis, cocaine, heroin and precursor chemicals were seized in Fiji, Papua New Guinea and Vanuatu during 2007, confirming concerns that countries in Oceania other than Australia and New Zealand were also vulnerable to drug trafficking. States in Oceania continued to report cocaine seizures. Australia reported the seizure of 634 kg of cocaine in the period 2006–2007, compared with 46 kg in 2005–2006. An additional 610 kg were seized at the Australian border in 2006–2007, more than seven times the amount seized in 2005–2006. Although parcel post continued to be the preferred method of smuggling cocaine into Australia, an increase in smuggling by sea was noted.

Cannabis continued to be illicitly cultivated throughout the region, with Australia being the largest producer. Fiji reported a significant decrease in the number of cannabis plants eradicated during 2007. Cannabis continued to be the most abused drug in the region. A particularly high incidence of abuse was reported in Australia, Micronesia, New Zealand and Papua New Guinea. Nonetheless, the annual prevalence of its abuse among the Australian population aged 14 and above gradually decreased from its high level of 17.9 per cent in 1998 to 9.1 per cent in 2007. In contrast, the annual prevalence of cocaine abuse in Australia for the same age group increased from 0.5 per cent in 1993 to 1.6 per cent in 2007, the highest prevalence recorded in all surveyed years.

In Australia and New Zealand, ATS continued to be supplied predominantly by clandestine manufacturers operating there. However, the fact that methamphetamine and tablets made of a combination of MDMA and methamphetamine were also regularly seized at those countries' borders indicated that ATS were also smuggled into Oceania. While the incidence of abuse of amphetamines among the Australian population aged 14 and above declined from 3.7 per cent in 1998 to 2.3 per cent in 2007, MDMA abuse surpassed that of other ATS, making it the second most abused substance in Australia and New Zealand. Oceania continued to report seizures of ephedrine and pseudoephedrine. Traffickers smuggled large amounts of the substances in air and sea cargo and smaller amounts through the postal system. Seizures of substances not under international control continued to be reported in the region. In 2007, Australian customs authorities seized 45 consignments of *gamma*-butyrolactone, a precursor of GHB, totalling approximately 68 litres. The primary method of transportation continued to be through the postal system. Sixty per cent of the seized consignments originated in the United Kingdom.

The Pacific Islands Forum continued to bring countries in Oceania together to address drug control issues. Australia and New Zealand remained active in supporting capacity-building initiatives in drug control in the region.

UN action to combat drug abuse

UN Office on Drugs and Crime

The United Nations Office on Drugs and Crime implemented the Organization's drug and crime programmes in an integrated manner, addressing the interrelated issues of drug control, crime prevention and international terrorism in the context of sustainable development and human security (see also Economic and Social Questions, Chapter IX). The drug programme continued to be implemented in accordance with General Assembly resolution 45/179 [YUN 1990, p. 874]. The Office was responsible for coordinating all UN drug control activities and was the repository of technical expertise in international drug control for the UN Secretariat. It acted on behalf of the Secretary-General in fulfilling his responsibilities under the terms of international treaties and resolutions relating to drug control, and provided services to the General Assembly, the Economic and Social Council, and committees and conferences dealing with drug control matters.

The UNODC Executive Director described the Office's 2008 activities in a report to the Commission on Narcotic Drugs and to the Commission on Crime Prevention and Criminal Justice [E/CN.7/2009/3-E/CN.15/2009/3]. With regard to sustainable livelihoods, the Office assisted States by supporting illicit crop monitoring and alternative development programmes within the framework of poverty eradication and sustainable development. It conducted monitoring surveys in Afghanistan, Bolivia, Colombia, the Lao People's Democratic Republic, Myanmar and Peru, and was developing a monitoring system in Ecuador. In Afghanistan, the Office strengthened the capacity of the Ministry of Counter Narcotics and supported the Government in building institutions and capacity for alternative livelihoods, criminal justice, cross-border operations and illicit crop monitoring. In Bolivia, Colombia and Peru, UNODC supported alternative development programmes that focused on poverty alleviation. In Peru, it supported conservation efforts and provided assistance to enable farmers to engage in commercially viable and sustainable licit activities. It supported Colombia's alternative development programme, which expanded the family forest warden initiative and assisted farmers to engage in commercially viable and sustainable licit activities. In Myanmar, in the framework of its project "Global partnership on alternative development", UNODC addressed poverty reduction issues related to opium poppy cultivation.

As to supply reduction, the Office strengthened the rule of law and helped States to improve border control practices, introduce witness protection programmes and address issues relating to the proceeds of crime, corruption and the countering of money-laundering. In Haiti, it provided advice in support of legislative reform, ratification of the UN conventions on drugs, crime and terrorism, institution-building and the preparation of a new statute on judicial officers. It prepared a regional programme for promoting the rule of law and human security in the Caribbean for 2009–2011. With a view to strengthening regional cooperation among law enforcement authorities, a number of meetings of subsidiary bodies of the Commission on Narcotic Drugs were held. In addition, UNODC assisted States in Central Asia and in the Persian Gulf area in the establishment of agencies to counter cross-border trafficking.

UNODC expanded its initiatives in drug abuse prevention, treatment and rehabilitation. In partnership with the Vienna Non-Governmental Organization (NGO) Committee on Narcotic Drugs, it facilitated a series of regional and online consultations with NGOs that culminated in a global forum entitled "Beyond 2008" (Vienna, 7–9 July). With regard to synthetic drugs, the global Synthetics Monitoring: Analyses, Reporting and Trends (SMART) programme was launched, along with a report to address the scarcity of data and enhance the capacity of States and authorities in priority regions to generate, manage, analyse and report synthetic drug information and apply the knowledge to policy design and operational programme interventions.

As to law enforcement, UNODC supported the Central Asian Regional Information and Coordination Centre (CARICC), a subregional drug control initiative implemented in cooperation with Azerbaijan, Kazakhstan, Kyrgyzstan, the Russian Federation, Tajikistan, Turkmenistan and Uzbekistan. During the pilot stage, CARICC established operational cooperation among the States of the subregion, and law enforcement agencies achieved results in the area of drug control. Under the UNODC Container Control Programme and the World Customs Organization (WCO), special operational units to profile containers for inspection were established in Ghana, Pakistan and Senegal. The Programme was expanded to include other seaports and dry ports in Central Asia, and regional concept notes were developed for the Caribbean, the Caspian Sea, Central America and South America.

During the year, the Office analysed the situation in West Africa in the report *Drug Trafficking as a Security Threat in West Africa*; launched a study on the threat of transnational trafficking in Afghan opiates; and published *Amphetamines and Ecstasy: 2008 Global ATS Assessment* [Sales No. E.08.XI.12]. It also published the *World Drug Report 2008* [Sales No. E.08.XI.1], which, in addition to providing an in-depth trend analysis of world drug markets, traced the history of international drug control since its inception a century earlier in response to the Chinese opium epidemic. Illicit opium survey reports were published for South-East Asia (Lao People's Democratic Republic, Myanmar and Thailand) and new data on coca bush cultivation in the Andean countries in 2007 were issued. In response to Commission resolution 50/4 on improving the quality and performance of drug analysis laboratories [YUN 2007, p. 1299], UNODC supported institutions and individuals from over 85 States in the form of quality assurance support, guidelines and best practice manuals, reference samples and field identification test kits. It also completed a manual on the implementation of quality management systems in drug testing laboratories.

Administrative and budgetary matters

In response to Commission on Narcotic Drugs resolution 50/14 [YUN 2007, p. 1300] and Commission on Crime Prevention and Criminal Justice resolution 16/6 [ibid., p. 1128], the Executive Director submitted a February report on programmes and initiatives to be implemented by UNODC in the bienniums 2008–2009 and 2010–2011 [E/CN.7/2008/12-E/CN.15/2008/16]. The report also addressed how the programmes and initiatives conformed with the strategy for the period 2008–2011 for UNODC, approved by the Economic and Social Council in resolution 2007/12 [YUN 2007, p. 1301]. The report provided an overview of the programmes and initiatives to be pursued in 2008 and supplemented the information provided in the 2008–2009 consolidated budget.

In accordance with the same resolutions, the Executive Director submitted a February report on financial issues and difficulties faced by UNODC in implementing its mandates and an initial assessment of ways and means of improving its financial situation [E/CN.7/2008/11-E/CN.15/2008/15]. The report provided an overview of the programmes and initiatives to be pursued in 2008, in addition to the information provided in the 2008–2009 consolidated budget; outlined measures taken to cope with the financial difficulties faced by the Office; and presented a number of proposals to address those problems. The Executive Director suggested that States should acknowledge and maintain the increasingly strong support provided to UNODC from many countries and institutions, stress the importance of stable and predictable multilateral core resources, and consider establishing an informal open-ended working group to explore ways and means to address UNODC's financial challenges. The working group could be co-chaired by the chairmen of the two Commissions, in line with the process that led to the 2008–2011 strategy for the Office. He also suggested that UNODC continue to align the consolidated budget with the 2008–2011 strategy, thereby ensuring integrated planning and budgeting as a basis for better result-based reporting to States and compliance with their policy directives.

Further in response to the same resolutions, the Executive Director submitted to the Commissions a March report on deviations from the standard programme support charge of 13 per cent during the period 2005–2007 [E/CN.7/2008/14-E/CN.15/2008/19]. He gave an account of the exemptions and reductions provided to donors in respect of that charge and the basis for them. The Executive Director stated that UNODC would continue to apply UN policies and procedures with respect to the programme support charge in 2008 and 2009 and would ensure the application of clear and consistent criteria in the granting of exceptions to the standard 13 per cent rate.

A March Secretariat note [E/CN.7/2008/13], prepared in response to Commission on Narcotic Drugs resolution 50/14 [YUN 2007, p. 1300], provided information on the implementation status and resource requirements of resolutions and decisions relating to the UNODC drug programme adopted by the General Assembly, the Economic and Social Council and the Commission on Narcotic Drugs in the period 2003–2007 in which action by the Office was requested.

On 14 March [E/2008/28 (dec. 51/1)], the Commission established an open-ended intergovernmental working group to discuss and prepare recommendations—taking into account the above reports of the Executive Director and the Secretariat note—to be presented to the Commission's fifty-second (2009) session on how to ensure political ownership by Member States and on how to improve the governance structure and the financial situation of UNODC.

Commission on Narcotic Drugs

The Commission on Narcotic Drugs held its fifty-first session in Vienna from 10 to 14 March, during which it recommended two resolutions and two decisions for adoption by the Economic and Social Council. It also adopted 18 resolutions and one decision, which it brought to the attention of the Council.

Following the closure of its fifty-first session on 14 March, the Commission opened its fifty-second session to elect the new chairperson and other bureau members.

By **decision 2008/247** of 24 July, the Council took note of the Commission's report on its fifty-first session [E/2008/28] and approved the provisional agenda and documentation for the fifty-second (2009) session.

Drug demand reduction and drug abuse

The Commission on Narcotic Drugs had before it a January report by the Secretariat [E/CN.7/2008/4] that reviewed trends in the abuse of the main types of illicit drugs over the period 1998–2006, based on a review of key indicator data and the informed opinion of national experts in each region. Although national experts reported largely increasing trends in illicit drug abuse for 1998–2004, some positive developments were reported more recently regarding global trends. Overall, abuse of two main types of drug (opioids and cocaine) stabilized or decreased, in particular in countries where consumption was high (cocaine in North America and heroin in Central and Western Europe). The prevalence of heroin injection remained high in Central Asia and Eastern Europe, where increased efforts in treatment and rehabilitation were needed. Increases in the use of amphetamine-type stimulants (ATS) were tapering off, with trends in their consumption showing a decrease or stabilization in Central and Western Europe, East and South-East Asia, North America and Oceania. Cannabis consumption remained globally widespread and increasing experimentation by youth underlined the need for more investment in preventive action, using evidence-based approaches.

The report noted that, despite marked improvements in the quality and reliability of drug abuse data since 1998, up-to-date information regarding the most vulnerable population groups—in particular youth, women and injecting drug users—was not available. Large differences in data collection capacity among regions and the lack of periodically collected data remained a cause for concern in many countries, where only partial progress had been made in establishing the principles, structures and indicators necessary for effective drug information systems. It was necessary, said the report, to enhance the information base for a comprehensive and harmonized assessment. As part of the work undertaken by the Global Assessment Programme on Drug Abuse, UNODC helped lay the foundation for evidence-based responses in partnership with national counterparts and in coordination with other agencies. It was suggested that the Commission might wish to encourage the international community and relevant regional and national entities to work together to enhance drug abuse monitoring mechanisms so as to facilitate the exchange of information and expertise in order to strengthen responses, in particular in regions where activities for demand reduction could not affect abuse prevalence due to lack of resources or expertise.

On 14 March [E/2008/28 (res. 51/2)], the Commission appealed to Member States and relevant international organizations to raise awareness of the health risks of cannabis use among youth and adults and invited States to share effective, evidence-based strategies and best practices for preventing cannabis use by children and youth. States were encouraged to: implement programmes preventing the onset of cannabis use, targeting youth, especially children under the age of 12, to maximize the impact of such programmes; urge the health and social research community to continue to study both prevention and treatment practices addressing the health risks and other related risks of cannabis use; and implement comprehensive prevention and treatment approaches focusing on individuals and their relationships with their peers, families, schools and communities. The Commission requested States to raise awareness among pregnant women of the risks involved in smoking cannabis, to carry out studies on cannabis use by youth, and to examine the scientific and medical data available on the health consequences of its use.

Also on 14 March [res. 51/3], the Commission—noting the relationship between substance abuse and health, social and economic consequences—acknowledged the value of using the techniques of early detection, brief intervention and linking people to treatment by integrating substance abuse prevention and intervention into general health- and social-care settings. It supported the use of those techniques as a means of reducing any stigma associated with substance abuse in the field of health, and encouraged their implementation as a set of preventive measures to be applied in health- and social-care settings. The Commission invited States to: educate health- and social-care providers; raise awareness and build capacity by training health- and social-care providers in the use of those techniques as tools for identifying at-risk populations and urge providers to encourage early intervention; share with each other and with relevant international organizations their research findings and best practices; and adopt legislation to safeguard the voluntary participation of patients and to protect privacy and confidentiality in communications between providers and patients. The World Health Organization was invited to promote worldwide the practices of early detection, brief intervention and linking people to treatment and to work closely with UNODC.

HIV/AIDS and other blood-borne viruses

A January report by the UNODC Executive Director [E/CN.7/2008/7], submitted in response to Commission resolution 49/4 [YUN 2006, p. 1456], provided an update on progress in responding to the prevalence of HIV/AIDS and other blood-borne diseases among drug users. It discussed action by States and coordination among multilateral institutions and international donors—including follow-up on the recommendations of the Global Task Team on Improving AIDS Coordination among Multilateral Institutions and International Donors—and described technical assistance provided by UNODC as a co-sponsor of the Joint United Nations Programme on HIV/AIDS (UNAIDS) and as the lead UN agency for HIV prevention and care associated with injecting drug use and in prison settings. During 2006–2007, many States had demonstrated increased awareness and interest in addressing HIV/AIDS among drug users, in particular injecting drug users (IDUs). They established legal, policy and institutional frameworks and adapted policies specifically addressing HIV/AIDS prevention, treatment and care for IDUs. Projects and programmes providing services to IDUs commenced for the first time in many countries, and States expanded components of the comprehensive package of HIV/AIDS prevention, treatment and care services for IDUs recommended by UNAIDS. However, service provision was still inadequate as just 13 per cent of reporting States provided all the measures recommended in the package.

The report concluded that, despite marked increases in financing for the global HIV response, the gap between the resources available and the amounts needed to achieve universal access to HIV services by 2010 had widened. Changes in the legal and policy fields had not been rapid enough and many States had yet to develop a strategic vision. In some countries the development of effective programmes continued to be inhibited by policy choices and legislation that did not facilitate the implementation of all components of the UNAIDS package. Structural issues continued to limit the effectiveness of the response. Even in countries where the national legal and policy framework facilitated the provision of all measures of the package, regulations and guidelines for implementation were often lacking. A more sustained effort was needed to prevent the transition from non-injecting to injecting use, to address the needs of female IDUs and to deal with HIV in prison settings. Management challenges were especially difficult in resource-limited countries, such as many in sub-Saharan Africa, and the continuing lack of reliable data presented a particular problem. The challenge for UNODC was to engage Governments, local programmes and policymakers to develop favourable legislation and policies that would support implementation of effective responses to the HIV epidemic among drug users. The Office continued to address the issues of ignorance, stigma and discrimination, which were often the only identifiable reasons for limited or non-response. Overcoming those challenges required sustained political and financial support (including for UNODC), increased national capacity and upgrading of proven, evidence-informed strategies.

On 14 March [E/2008/28 (res. 51/14)], the Commission called for collaboration among States represented both in the Commission and on the UNAIDS Programme Coordinating Board in promoting better coordination and alignment of the HIV/AIDS response in order to scale up towards the goal of universal access to comprehensive prevention, care, treatment and support services for drug users. It requested the UNODC Executive Director to share relevant decisions of the UNAIDS Programme Coordinating Board with States at each session of the Commission held in the first half of the year, starting with the fifty-second (2009) session, and to transmit relevant resolutions of the Commission each year to the Chairman of the Programme Coordinating Board. The UNODC Executive Director was requested to report to the Commission in that regard.

Illicit cultivation, manufacture and trafficking

On 14 March [E/2008/28 (res. 51/5)], the Commission on Narcotic Drugs emphasized the importance of taking measures to facilitate cross-border cooperation in the area of drug control, in accordance with bilateral and multilateral agreements, and recommended that States that shared common borders enter into bilateral agreements so that cross-border cooperation could take place within an established legal framework consistent with their respective legal and administrative systems. It requested States to ensure that channels of communication among them were effective and efficient for exchanging information and urged them to conduct joint investigations of transnational criminal groups involved in illicit drug production and trafficking.

Also on 14 March [res. 51/7], the Commission called on transit States, countries of destination and countries of origin to enhance bilateral, regional and international cooperation in the areas of border control, mutual legal assistance, law enforcement, information exchange and demand reduction, and called on all States to support and promote such cooperation. It urged States and UNODC to strengthen initiatives to provide assistance and technical support to States affected by the transit of illicit drugs, especially developing countries and countries with economies in transition, and invited States and other donors to provide extrabudgetary contributions. It also urged international financial institutions to provide financial support. The UNODC Executive Director was requested to report to the Commission in 2010.

On the same date [res. 51/10], the Commission adopted a resolution on strengthening international cooperation for the control of precursor chemicals used in the manufacture of synthetic drugs, in which it recognized the important work of INCB as the principal body and global focal point for the international control of precursors. It invited Governments to contribute to the Board's efforts, particularly with regard to the Pre-Export Notification (PEN) Online system, Project Prism, Project Cohesion and related operations such as Operation Crystal Flow. It called on INCB to reinforce communication with States and work with them in identifying opportunities for more effective precursor control, and urged States to strengthen, update or establish national legislation and mechanisms relating to the control of precursors used in the illicit manufacture of drugs, pursuant to the 1988 Convention. Member States were invited to: consider applying measures to control substances used as precursors; strengthen the control of preparations containing substances that could be easily used or recovered for the illicit manufacture of drugs; further strengthen controls on the importation of precursors to ensure their legal use; and provide INCB with information on any new substances replacing precursors. The Commission also invited States to continue to notify INCB and Member States concerned of any new routes and methods being used in the diversion of precursors, such as the Internet and other delivery systems. It encouraged States to consider precursor control as one of the central questions to be discussed at the high-level segment of the Commission's fifty-second (2009) session.

Also on the same date [res. 51/16], the Commission called on INCB to request States to provide to the Board available information on alternate precursors and on methods of illicit manufacture of narcotic drugs and psychotropic substances, and to collate and share such information through special alerts. It invited States to continue to exchange, on a bilateral and regional basis, information relating to the use of alternate precursors and new methods of manufacture of illicit drugs.

Secretariat report. A report by the Secretariat [E/CN.7/2009/4] provided an overview of trends in illicit drug production and trafficking worldwide, focusing on seizure statistics for 2006–2007 and on cultivation and production for 2006–2008. Information on cultivation and production of plant-based drugs was drawn from UNODC's illicit crop-monitoring surveys; information on trafficking was based on replies by Governments to the annual questionnaire relating to illicit supply, submitted for 2007 and previous years. Other sources included reports on significant seizures, the *World Drug Report 2008* [Sales No. E.08.XI.11] and other reports received by UNODC or submitted to the Commission and its subsidiary bodies.

Cannabis continued to be the most widely produced, trafficked and consumed plant-based drug worldwide. Global seizures of cannabis resin increased significantly in 2007, in particular in Western and Central Europe; preliminary data also suggested a moderate increase in seizures of cannabis herb. The total area under cannabis cultivation in 2007 in Afghanistan was estimated to be comparable to that in Morocco. The total area under opium poppy cultivation in Afghanistan decreased by almost one fifth in 2008. Nonetheless, Afghanistan continued to account for the vast majority of the world's production of opium. Opium seizures continued to rise in 2007, driven mainly by seizures in Iran, which also contributed significantly to a moderate increase in global heroin seizures. Cultivation of coca bush and manufacture of cocaine continued to be concentrated in Colombia, Peru and Bolivia (in that order). While the total area under coca bush cultivation increased, the stable trend in manufacture of recent years was sustained into 2007. Data for 2007, while incomplete, suggested that such stability was reflected in global seizures of cocaine. Information on individual drug seizures confirmed the growing role of Africa as a transit area for cocaine trafficking. Seizures of ATS worldwide stabilized in 2006, but in 2007 increased quantities of MDMA were seized at the global level and increases in amphetamine seizures were recorded in Central and Western Europe. Estimated global manufacture of ATS remained largely unchanged in 2006.

The report noted that most of the global illicit opium production occurred in Afghanistan, where illicit opium poppy cultivation and opium production continued to be matters of concern, and recommended that international efforts to assist the country be strengthened. In Afghanistan, the area under cannabis cultivation in 2007 was more than one third of the area under opium poppy cultivation, and the country accounted for almost one third of global production of cannabis resin in 2006. As the cultivation of cannabis plant was becoming as lucrative as that of opium poppy, the report stressed that the scale of opium trade in Afghanistan should not detract attention from the growing problem of cannabis. The volume of cocaine trafficked via the African continent, in particular to Western Europe, had increased. As many law enforcement agencies in Africa lacked the necessary technical equipment, trained personnel and access to forensic services, further international support was required. Trafficking in ATS remained a matter of concern, in particular in Central and Western Europe and in the Near and Middle East/South-West Asia. Governments in the latter subregion in particular needed to address Captagon and counterfeit captagon trafficking in a coordinated manner with the assistance of international organizations such as INTERPOL, INCB and WCO.

Statistical analysis could be useful in developing a global strategy against drug trafficking. However, such an analysis was subject to the availability of quality data from States; serious gaps in seizure data had arisen in those subregions that were at the forefront of the latest developments, such as the Near and Middle East and West Africa. The report recommended that States submit their comprehensive responses to the annual reports questionnaire in a regular and timely fashion.

Control of international trade in poppy seeds

On 14 March [E/2008/28 (res. 51/15)], the Commission urged States: to endeavour, consistent with their domestic laws and regulations and applicable international regulations, to import poppy seeds derived from licitly grown opium poppy crops; to be vigilant and to ensure that poppy seeds traded for food purposes were not derived from illicitly cultivated opium poppy plants; and to strengthen their resolve to implement Economic and Social Council resolution 1999/32 [YUN 1999, p. 1166]. INCB was requested to gather information regarding implementation of that resolution by States, with a view to strengthening the control of international movement of poppy seeds obtained from illicitly grown plants and to share that information with States. The Commission asked INCB and UNODC to ensure the full implementation of article 22 of the 1961 Convention by the States concerned.

Illicit drug and firearms trafficking

On 14 March [E/2008/28 (res. 51/11)], the Commission on Narcotic Drugs recognized the increasing links between drug trafficking and the illicit manufacturing of and trafficking in firearms in some regions, and the need to prevent the spread of that problem to other regions. It noted that reducing illicit firearms manufacturing and trafficking was a major component of the efforts to reduce the illicit drug supply in some regions and encouraged States to take adequate measures to prevent the acquisition and use of firearms and ammunition by criminal organizations involved in drug trafficking. It emphasized the need for cooperation among States in reinforcing border control and urged States to allocate resources and provide training and capacity-enhancing measures for intelligence, law enforcement, customs and related authorities responsible for fighting drug trafficking in order to assist in the prevention, detection and investigation of cases involving firearms manufacturing and trafficking, and to identify and dismantle networks and links between those illicit activities.

Noting that efforts to combat drug trafficking could be complemented by providing training in fighting firearms trafficking for law enforcement personnel responsible for investigating such activities, the Commission urged States to promote and increase bilateral and multilateral cooperation, including through programmes administered by UNODC, focused on capacity-building and training and to exchange experiences and best practices.

The Commission also encouraged States to exchange information and provide judicial cooperation in order to identify and investigate links between drug trafficking and firearms and ammunition manufacturing and trafficking, and to provide information to UNODC linking patterns in firearms trafficking and drug-related trafficking. The Executive Director was asked to report to the Commission at its fifty-third (2010) session on information received from States, and UNODC was requested to take into consideration the information provided by States on the relation between drug trafficking and firearms and ammunition trafficking when preparing the *World Drug Report* and other reports on the world drug problem.

Alternative development

In a report on using alternative development programmes to reduce the cultivation of cannabis plants [E/CN.7/2008/9], prepared in response to Economic and Social Council resolution 2006/31 [YUN 2006, p. 1459], the Executive Director presented a summary of the work undertaken by Member States in implementing both that resolution and General Assembly resolution 59/160 [YUN 2004, p. 1252]. Topics covered included: international cooperation and the sharing of experience and expertise on illicit crop eradication and alternative development; large-scale cannabis cultivation; and integration of alternative development into other drug control measures. It also outlined activities carried out by UNODC in the implementation of Assembly resolution 59/160; knowledge-sharing and feasibility studies; and the global strategy for alternative development.

The report concluded that only a few States had provided information on efforts made to implement Council resolution 2006/31 and only four African countries had responded to a note verbale sent in 2007, in which States were invited to provide such information. The efforts reported by responding States with respect to the implementation of the resolution were commendable. In particular, the efforts of Morocco, a country affected by large-scale cannabis plant cultivation, deserved the support of the international community. It was noted that, prior to formulating or designing alternative development interventions in any geographical area, a thorough analysis of the situation and a technical assessment of the extent of cannabis plant cultivation were required.

The international community was urged to provide technical and financial support to those States engaged in alternative development for areas affected by cannabis plant cultivation; and donor States were encouraged to enable UNODC to assist the affected States. States should review ambiguous drug laws and recognize that they impeded efforts by other States to address the elimination of illicit cannabis plant cultivation and fuelled crime and violence in countries where cannabis plants were cultivated. States affected by large-scale cannabis plant cultivation should incorporate development-oriented illicit crop reduction programmes within a wider framework of traditional development programmes and include them in poverty reduction strategy papers, as well as country assistance strategies, in their negotiations with international financial institutions. The report stressed that progress in alternative development should be measured through development indicators and not solely in terms of illicit crop production figures. Any future international action plans should include baseline indicators and well-targeted questionnaires related to development.

On 14 March [E/2008/28 (res. 51/6)], the Commission on Narcotic Drugs requested UNODC to support the establishment or strengthening of national strategies and action plans to eliminate illicit cannabis cultivation, and invited States and other donors to provide extrabudgetary contributions for those purposes. It urged Member States to provide affected States with support in the area of alternative development, including by funding research on crops that were alternatives to cannabis, and in the areas of environmental protection and technical assistance. It also encouraged States that had technical experience in eliminating the illicit cultivation of drug crops and in implementing alternative development programmes to share that experience with affected States.

ECONOMIC AND SOCIAL COUNCIL ACTION

On 24 July [meeting 42], the Economic and Social Council, on the recommendation of the Commission on Narcotic Drugs [E/2008/28], adopted **resolution 2008/26** without vote [agenda item 14 *(d)*].

Promoting sustainability and integrality in alternative development as an important part of drug control strategy in States where illicit crops are grown to produce drugs

The Economic and Social Council,

Bearing in mind the provisions of the Single Convention on Narcotic Drugs of 1961, that Convention as amended by the 1972 Protocol, the Convention on Psychotropic Substances of 1971 and the United Nations Convention against Illicit Traffic in Narcotic Drugs and Psychotropic Substances of 1988,

Recalling the Political Declaration adopted by the General Assembly at its twentieth special session, in which Member States recognized that action against the world drug problem was a common and shared responsibility,

Reaffirming the United Nations Millennium Declaration, in particular the Millennium Development Goals of eradicating extreme poverty and hunger and ensuring environmental sustainability,

Reaffirming also its resolutions 2003/37 of 22 July 2003 and 2006/33 of 27 July 2006 and Commission on Narcotic Drugs resolutions 45/14 of 15 March 2002 and 48/9 of 11 March 2005,

Taking into consideration the report of the International Narcotics Control Board for 2005 and the report entitled *Alternative Development: A Global Thematic Evaluation*, prepared by the United Nations Office on Drugs and Crime,

Convinced that, in the review of the progress achieved in meeting the goals and targets set in the Political Declaration adopted by the General Assembly at its twentieth special session, there is a genuine need for the international community to assess the way alternative development has been practised in the past and ensure that, overall, the approaches to alternative development are fully implemented,

Recognizing the significant achievements and efforts of countries in South-East Asia in recent decades towards eliminating the illicit cultivation of opium poppy and cannabis, and recognizing also the commitment of the Association of Southeast Asian Nations to making South-East Asia free of illicit drugs by 2015,

Recognizing also the significant achievements of the Andean countries in the implementation of alternative development and preventive alternative development programmes, as presented in the fifth report of the Executive Director of the United Nations Office on Drugs and Crime on the world drug problem, and noting that those achievements were attained in accordance with national specificities, with significant national resources and with the support of international cooperation,

Recognizing further the success of the long-term, holistic and integrated approach to solving the problem of opium poppy cultivation, including its correlation with poverty, that has been applied for forty years in national and international programmes in Thailand, which led the United Nations Development Programme in May 2006 to present the first Human Development Lifetime Achievement Award to King Bhumibol Adulyadej of Thailand as the initiator of that approach,

Acknowledging that the success of alternative development and preventive alternative development, as appropriate, may be dependent upon, inter alia, the following essential elements:

(*a*) Long-term investments by Governments and international donors,

(*b*) The efficiency of national institutions responsible for drug control policies and of institutions related to the promotion of alternative development,

(*c*) Synergy and trust among the Government, local administrations and communities in building local ownership,

(*d*) An adequate response to human needs and dignity in the context of sustainable rural development and community self-reliance,

(*e*) The creation of a value chain by utilizing local wisdom, capacity-building, marketing and entrepreneurship,

(*f*) Broader market access for alternative development products consistent with national and international obligations and consideration of measures to facilitate access and positioning in markets for alternative development products, taking into account applicable multilateral trade rules,

1. *Recalls* the Action Plan on International Cooperation on the Eradication of Illicit Drug Crops and on Alternative Development, which continues to have practical relevance and in which it is stated that alternative development is an important component of a balanced and comprehensive illicit crop eradication strategy and is intended to promote lawful and sustainable socio-economic options for those communities and population groups that have resorted to illicit cultivation as their only viable means of obtaining a livelihood, contributing in an integrated way to the eradication of poverty;

2. *Emphasizes* that the problem of illicit production of narcotic drugs is often related to development problems, in particular poverty, poor health conditions and illiteracy, and that it must be tackled in a larger development context through a holistic and integrated approach;

3. *Agrees* on the relevance of enhancing alternative development and preventive alternative development, as appropriate, in a manner focusing on the sustainability and integrality of uplifting people's livelihood, and recommends that such elements be considered by relevant bodies in the United Nations system;

4. *Recognizes* the significant role played by developing countries with extensive expertise in alternative development and preventive alternative development and the importance of outreach activities aimed at promoting a set of best practices and lessons learned in that area and sharing those best practices and lessons learned with States affected by illicit crop cultivation, including those emerging from conflict, with a view to using them, where appropriate, in accordance with the national specificities of each State;

5. *Urges* donor Governments, as well as multilateral, international and regional financial institutions, in conformity with the principle of shared responsibility and as a sign of their commitment to fighting illicit drugs in a comprehensive and balanced manner, to redouble their efforts to enhance international cooperation, especially trilateral cooperation aimed at utilizing the expertise of developing countries and the financial support of developed countries in assisting other developing countries in reducing illicit drug crops through alternative development and preventive alternative development, as appropriate, and to consider increasing their financial and material support and technical assistance and providing a flexible and sufficiently long-term commitment to States affected by illicit crop cultivation;

6. *Commends* the United Nations Office on Drugs and Crime for its continued and progressive work on alternative development, described in its report entitled *Alternative Development: A Global Thematic Evaluation*, especially the lessons learned and the recommendations contained therein, and acknowledges the need to consider providing the Office with additional funding in that area;

7. *Calls upon* Member States, consistent with their national and international obligations, and relevant international organizations to consider measures to enable products of alternative development to have easier access to

markets, taking into account applicable multilateral trade rules;

8. *Encourages* Member States, in the context of the review of the progress achieved in meeting the goals and targets set in the Political Declaration adopted by the General Assembly at its twentieth special session, to consider developing a set of international guiding principles on alternative development, based on the sharing of best practices and lessons learned in different countries and regions, and acknowledging the best practices and lessons learned in sustainable alternative livelihood development of Thailand, annexed to the present resolution;

9. *Requests* the Secretary-General to transmit the text of the present resolution to multilateral, international and regional financial institutions and to all Governments for consideration and implementation;

10. *Requests* the Executive Director of the United Nations Office on Drugs and Crime to report to the Commission on Narcotic Drugs at its fifty-second session on the implementation of the present resolution.

Annex

Best practices and lessons learned in sustainable alternative livelihood development of Thailand

1. First and foremost, alternative development, which in the context of the Thai experience is referred to as "sustainable alternative livelihood development", must be people-centred. The Doi Tung development project in Thailand served as the model for the present set of best practices and lessons learned. The outlook, design and implementation were developed taking into account a fundamental question: how will people benefit from this project? That became the key performance indicator for the project.

2. The main objective of sustainable alternative livelihood development is to transform poor and vulnerable communities, especially in rural areas, from social and economic dependency or sub-sufficiency to full socio-economic sufficiency, in a participatory manner and at a pace appropriate to each stage, to allow the changes to be accepted and introduced by the communities. Keeping in mind the goal of sustainability, development practitioners should see their role as facilitators of progress and should plan their exit strategy to enable the communities to continue the activities without external intervention.

3. Sustainability in this context means that the communities have sufficient economic capacity in their factors of production and marketing and are able to maintain equitable social and cultural integrity and live in harmony with their natural environment (coexist with nature). With this definition in mind, sufficient health care must be made available because sick people cannot be economically productive. Ideally, an income-generating mechanism should be employed that allows people and a healthy natural environment to benefit greatly from one another. Continuous education will ensure that future generations will be able to pursue legitimate livelihoods, cope with the pressures of globalization and create for themselves opportunities for growth.

4. When applying sustainable alternative livelihood development in the context of drug control, the eradication of illicit crops should not be the only immediate goal. The progressive introduction of viable alternative livelihoods in the broader context of rural development is needed to tackle the root cause of illicit crop cultivation—poverty—without severely curtailing the only available means of survival of the people involved.

5. Activities that provide people with alternative cash income and/or produce immediate health or social benefits within the first few months or days (so-called quick hits) are vital to building trust and enabling an immediate transition from illegitimate to legitimate sources of income, which can begin to transform the economic prospects of a community. Successful quick hits build confidence and strengthen cooperation among stakeholders at all levels, from people at the grassroots level and local authorities to leaders at the national level.

6. Medium-term and long-term activities are introduced simultaneously in order to ensure that the economic and social benefits are long-lasting and that the areas concerned remain free of illicit drug cultivation for a long time. Development activities must be based on continuity: each activity should lead into another, build on the success of previous initiatives and, over time, increase the hope and capabilities of the persons involved.

7. It is necessary to achieve a balance between a bottom-up and a top-down approach. Strong and committed leadership is required to ensure that development policies and activities are based on a true understanding of the needs and concerns of the target communities at the grass-roots level. Clear and constant communication is critical, especially at the beginning, for knowledge and experiences to be transferred not only from development practitioners but also to them.

8. Viable livelihoods should be available to all members of the community: the young and the elderly; the fit and the infirm; and men and women alike. Having a variety of income-generating activities may serve as a safeguard against weakened interests in an individual product or activity. Livelihood diversification is in fact a major success factor in sustainable alternative livelihood development (single-crop solutions are rarely sustainable).

9. Combining local wisdom and available resources with a market-driven product development approach and effective management will lead to the creation of a viable value chain at the local level. Revenue from value-added goods locally manufactured by such an enterprise must contribute to the social benefits of the target communities and society in general. Such social entrepreneurship—the practice of using business profits to generate social goods—can lead to real socio-economic sustainability.

10. To ensure that development objectives are realized as expected, mechanisms must be in place to allow frequent assessments and necessary adjustments, starting with comprehensive census baseline data captured through both qualitative and quantitative development indicators. Project monitoring and evaluation hold development practitioners accountable for their action, and that is crucial, as people's lives depend on the performance of those practitioners and imprudent and uncaring development often has adverse effects.

11. Ultimately, the key to sustainable alternative livelihood development is community ownership, where capacities and economic activities have been developed to such an extent that the communities can become owners in their

ventures instead of serving only as contract farmers or employees. Community ownership means not only physical ownership of the enterprises but also emotional ownership, on the part of the community, of its own development and future, from the very start.

12. Since the issue of sustainability envisages the long-term commitment of all parties involved, it also calls for longer-term and sufficiently flexible funding from a variety of sources, including Governments, international organizations, multilateral financial institutions and other donors and development partners.

Regional cooperation

A Secretariat report [E/CN.7/2009/5] described action taken by regional subsidiary bodies of the Commission on Narcotic Drugs in 2008. Following a review of drug trafficking trends and regional and subregional cooperation, each subsidiary body addressed drug law enforcement issues of priority in its region and made recommendations. The eighteenth meeting of Heads of National Drug Law Enforcement Agencies (HONLEA), Africa (Yamoussoukro, Côte d'Ivoire, 8–12 September) [UNODC/HONLAF/2008/5] considered managing the investigation of major drug cases and the professional handling of exhibits; developing successful strategies to address trafficking in cannabis; and the issue of trafficking in ATS and associated problems of precursor control. The eighteenth meeting of HONLEA, Latin America and the Caribbean (Tegucigalpa, Honduras, 13–17 October) [UNODC/HONLAC/2008/5] examined the region's response to trafficking in cocaine; strengthening information exchange and operational cooperation at the inter-agency, cross-border and regional levels; and law enforcement's role in supporting demand-reduction policies. The forty-third session of the Subcommission on Illicit Drug Traffic and Related Matters in the Near and Middle East (Tehran, Iran, 16–20 November) [UNODC/SUBCOM/2008/5] considered the use and effectiveness of special investigative techniques, including controlled delivery as an operational response to dismantle drug trafficking groups; ensuring the efficient exchange of information and extending operational cooperation against drug trafficking groups at the inter-agency, cross-border and regional levels; and controlling the manufacture of and addressing trafficking in synthetic drugs and associated problems in the area of precursor control.

Chapter XV

Statistics

In 2008, the United Nations statistical work programme was conducted mainly through the activities of the Statistical Commission and the United Nations Statistics Division. In February, the Commission adopted the *International Recommendations for Tourism Statistics 2008*, the *International Recommendations for Distributive Trade Statistics 2008* and part I of the *International Recommendations for Industrial Statistics 2008*. It also adopted, in principle, volume 1 of the updated System of National Accounts as the international standard for national accounts statistics. The Commission welcomed the completion of the 2005 round of the International Comparison Programme and endorsed the Programme's continuation, with a target year of 2011 for the next round. The Commission also approved its multi-year programme of work for 2008–2011.

The Commission reviewed the work of groups of countries and international organizations in various areas of economic, social, demographic and environmental statistics and made specific recommendations and suggestions.

Work of Statistical Commission

The Statistical Commission held its thirty-ninth session in New York from 26 to 29 February [E/2008/24] and brought to the attention of the Council 17 decisions adopted during the session. It commended the high-quality programme review report on labour statistics prepared by the United Kingdom. It also took note of the recommendations and welcomed the commitments made by the International Labour Organization (ILO), as well as the work done by the ILO Conference of Labour Statisticians. The Commission reinforced the importance of the Task Force on Education Statistics as a forum for discussion to elaborate on a general framework for international education statistics and to provide recommendations on mechanisms for improved coordination among international agencies mandated to work in education statistics. The Commission welcomed the completion of the 2005 round of the International Comparison Programme (ICP) [YUN 2005, p. 1369] and endorsed the continuation of ICP with a target year of 2011 for the next round in order to sustain the momentum of the 2005 round in terms of accumulated experience and enhanced capacity at the country level and to link ICP more effectively with the Organisation for Economic Cooperation and Development (OECD)/Eurostat Programme. It requested the World Bank to continue hosting the ICP Global Office and endorsed the establishment of an interim executive board.

The Commission adopted, in principle, volume 1 of the updated System of National Accounts (SNA) as the international standard for national accounts statistics, and recognizing that the time required to evaluate volume 1 of SNA as a whole was insufficient, endorsed the proposal of the Intersecretariat Working Group on National Accounts to extend the review period by two months. The Commission agreed with the finding and recommendations of the Friends of the Chair report on integrated economic statistics and agreed that there might be a need to develop a framework for establishing guidelines for countries in the process of implementing an integrated approach in their national statistical systems. It adopted the International Recommendations for Tourism Statistics 2008 and requested the World Tourism Organization (UNWTO) and the Statistics Division to develop an implementation programme in collaboration with supranational and regional organizations.

The Commission adopted the *International Recommendations for Distributive Trade Statistics 2008* and agreed on the implementation programme. It also adopted part I and endorsed part II of the *International Recommendations for Industrial Statistics 2008*; endorsed the initiative and strategy to revise the recommendations for international merchandise trade statistics; underscored the importance of the *Human Development Report* (see p. 935) as a source of information on development issues and emphasized the need for the Human Development Report Office to further improve transparency in the process of preparing the *Report*. On data collection, dissemination and exchange, the Commission encouraged the Statistics Division to make data available free of charge to facilitate their dissemination and use; continue its initiatives to reduce the reporting burden on countries, including through joint data-collection agreements; and facilitate the exchange of experiences among countries with respect to dissemination policies and practices. It welcomed the report on the Statistical Data and Metadata Exchange initiative. The Commission expressed satisfaction with the establishment of the African Centre for Statistics and the proposed recommendations aimed at addressing the challenges facing African national statistical systems. It considered the Secretary-General's report on the indicators for monitoring the Millennium Development Goals (MDGs), commended the efforts of the Inter-Agency and Expert Group on Millennium Development Goal Indicators in implementing some of the recommendations contained in Economic and Social Council resolution 2006/6 [YUN 2006, p. 1472] on statistical capacity-building and requested that the Group and all bodies involved increase efforts to further improve the indicators of all MDGs through methodological and technical refinements. It also expressed its support for the ongoing work of the Intersecretariat Working Group on Health Statistics to improve the coordination of health statistics and the proposed development of a framework; and in compliance with General Assembly resolution 62/133 [YUN 2007, p. 1158J] approved the formation of a Friends of the Chair group on indicators to measure violence against women.

On 23 July, the Economic and Social Council took note of the Commission's report, decided that the fortieth session would be held in New York from 24 to 27 February 2009 and approved the provisional agenda and documentation for the session (**decision 2008/238**).

Economic statistics

National accounts

The Secretary-General submitted the report of the Intersecretariat Working Group on National Accounts (ISWGNA) [E/CN.3/2008/5], which provided an overview of the preparation of the updated System of National Accounts (SNA) [YUN 1993, p. 1112], including the drafting and review of volume 1 and the next steps in preparation of volume 2. The report also presented a strategy for implementing the updated SNA, described actions taken to establish a high-level group on development of the SNA and provided points for discussion by the Commission. On the drafting and review of volume 1 of the SNA, the 10 chapters drafted in 2007 and posted on the project website, with invitations to countries (national statistical offices and interested central banks) to comment received, on average, 17 sets of comments on each chapter [YUN 2007, p. 1314]. Some 31 statistical offices, central banks and individual experts submitted comments in addition to the Intersecretariat Working Group Organizations. The drafting and review of volume 2 would proceed following the Commission's 2008 session; the list of chapters planned for that volume were annexed to the report. The latest assessments indicated that the level of implementation of the 1993 SNA by developing countries had risen sharply in recent years with 90 per cent of countries in regions other than Africa reporting national accounts statistics to the Statistics Division. In Africa, the response rate was somewhat lower; 33 out of 53 countries reported national accounts statistics. The report also identified impediments to SNA implementation that needed to be addressed when developing the SNA implementation strategy. On the high-level group on national accounts, a final proposal about its composition and work programme would be submitted at the Commission's fortieth (2009) session.

In February [E/2008/24], the Commission adopted, in principle, volume 1 of the updated SNA as the international standard for national accounts statistics, and encouraged member States and regional and international organizations to implement the standard and support all aspects of their implementation, including the national and international reporting of national accounts statistics based on the updated SNA. The Commission recognized that the time required to evaluate volume 1 of the updated SNA was insufficient, and endorsed the ISWGNA proposal to introduce an additional two-month period, until the end of April 2008, for completing its review. That would allow all stakeholders to examine the conceptual coherence and consistency of the System with the recommendations on the 44 issues adopted by the Commission in 2007 [YUN 2007, p. 1314]. During the review period, countries and international organizations would be invited to submit their observations to ISWGNA. The Commission requested the Working Group to take appropriate measures to ensure that volume 2 of the updated SNA was completed and submitted for adoption to the Commission at its fortieth (2009) sessions and to submit at that session a strategy for implementation of the updated SNA that would take into account the inputs of the Conference on international outreach and coordination in national accounts for sustainable growth and development, to be held in May 2008.

Service statistics

The Secretary-General transmitted to the Statistical Commission the report of the Inter-agency Task Force on Statistics of International Trade in Services [E/CN.3/2008/19], which outlined activities undertaken since its previous report in 2005 [YUN 2005, p. 1369], including the planning and management of the revision of the *Manual on Statistics of International Trade in Services*; the contribution to the revision of related frameworks, such as the *Balance of Payment Manual* of the International Monetary Fund (IMF); and the completion of the work of the Task Force's technical subgroup on movement of natural persons. The report also provided information on other areas, such as technical cooperation and expert meetings; the Task Force website and other communication media utilized in its work; and cross-cutting issues between trade in goods and trade in services. In that connection, a joint meeting of the Task Force and the Task Force on International Merchandise Trade Statistics to discuss common issues would be held in March, leading to new outputs.

In February [E/2008/24], the Commission took note of the report.

International Comparison Programme

The Statistical Commission had before it the Secretary-General's note [E/CN.3/2008/33] transmitting the World Bank report on the International Comparison Programme (ICP), which reviewed the Programme's achievements and outlined remaining steps to complete the ICP 2005 round [YUN 2005, p. 1370]. Significant achievements had been made since the round started in 2003 [YUN 2003, p. 1291]. The statistical system, which included a network of expertise in place for gathering data and establishing regional and global purchasing power parities (PPPs), provided a sound basis for the future rounds of ICP. The launch of the global data results on 17 December 2007 brought together the data of two separate PPP programmes. The first was the global ICP programme conducted by the ICP Global Office within the World Bank, which had provided overall coordination for the collection of data and calculation of PPPs in more than 100 (mostly developing) economies. In parallel, the Statistical Office of the European Communities (Eurostat) and OECD had conducted their own 2005 PPP programme, which covered 46 countries. The ICP Global Office combined the results into an overall global comparison so that the results for all participating countries could be compared directly.

Other achievements included the release of regional data throughout 2007; the participation of 18 "ring comparison" countries in conducting special price collections using a global product list; the use of data validation and handling of special data issues; approval of a data revision policy by the ICP Executive Board; the sharing of knowledge gained from the ICP round through various media; and the introduction of innovative software tools. On steps remaining to complete the 2005 round since the preliminary data release in December 2007, the Global Office maintained its focus on releasing the final data in the first quarter of 2008. The *ICP Handbook* would be published in final form at the same time. The report concluded that the round was near completion, with a number of regional reports and the preliminary global report released in December 2007, marking the successful outcome of one of the largest international statistical programmes. The Statistical Commission was requested to comment on areas that still needed to be addressed by the ICP 2005 round.

The Commission also had before it the report of the Friends of the Chair on the review of the ICP 2005 round [E/CN.3/2008/4], which presented the results of its evaluation and assessment of the scope, activities and lessons learned from the current round of ICP; provided recommendations where improvements could be made; and proposed the continuation of the programme, drawing on the main elements of the current governance structure and the experiences obtained during the 2005 round.

In February [E/2008/24], the Commission took note of the Friends of the Chair report; supported its conclusions and recommendations; and endorsed the continuation of ICP with a target year of 2011 for the next round and the establishment of an interim executive board. Concerned that 2011, the proposed benchmark year for the next round, might present difficulties in several countries since the year overlapped with the conduct of population censuses, the Commission requested that the ICP organizers consider a suitable strategy to deal with the matter and encouraged ICP partners to continue their capacity-building efforts in developing countries to increase the quality of the data available for the next round.

Other economic statistics

Price indexes and statistics

The Secretary-General transmitted to the Statistical Commission the report of the Ottawa Group on Price Indexes [E/CN.3/2008/20], which indicated that, since its 2005 report to the Commission [YUN 2005, p. 1370], it had met twice—in London (14–16 May 2006) and in Ottawa (10–12 October 2007). Fundamental problems of price measurement, particularly at the micro level, had been recurring themes of recent meetings, as were discussions on the price index manuals. At its 2007 meeting, the Ottawa Group discussed a progress report on the development of a supplementary handbook entitled "Practical guide to compiling consumer price indexes". In other activities, the Ottawa Group steering committee concurred with the descriptions developed by the Intersecretariat Working Group on Price Statistics of the respective roles of the Working Group, the Ottawa Group and the joint United Nations Economic Commission for Europe (ECE)/ILO consumer price index meetings, which were annexed to the report. The next meeting of the Group was scheduled to be held in Neuchâtel, Switzerland, in 2009.

In February [E/2008/24], the Commission took note of the report.

Tourism statistics

The Statistical Commission had before it a joint report of the Secretary-General and the World Tourism Organization (UNWTO) [E/CN.3/2008/7] on tourism statistics, which described activities undertaken to revise the international recommendations for tourism statistics, including progress on the six components of the revision process: the creation and work of the Inter-Agency Coordination Group on Tourism Statistics; the holding of the UNWTO electronic forum; the conduct of the International Workshop on Tourism Statistics; the organization of the dedicated meetings of the UNWTO Committee on Statistics and Macroeconomic Analysis of Tourism; a meeting of the UN Expert Group on Tourism Statistics to review and endorse the provisional draft of the *International Recommendations on Tourism Statistics 2008*; and the conduct of a worldwide consultation with national statistical offices and national tourism administrations.

In February [E/2008/24], the Commission adopted the *International Recommendations for Tourism Statistics 2008* and requested that the final text be edited to reflect the Commission's suggestions. It also requested UNWTO and the Statistics Division to develop an implementation programme, including preparation of a compilation guide and organization of training workshops, in collaboration with supranational and regional organizations. The Commission took note of the updated version of the Tourism Satellite Account: Recommended Methodological Framework 2008 and requested that the *Recommendations* and the Tourism Satellite Account be made available in all of the six UN official languages.

Statistics of science and technology

The Secretary-General transmitted to the Statistical Commission the report of the Directorate for Science, Technology and Industry of OECD and the Institute for Statistics of the United Nations Educational, Scientific and Cultural Organization (UNESCO) [E/CN.3/2008/21], which elaborated on current and future plans in the area of science and technology statistics. The report indicated that statistics on science and technology were fundamental to an understanding of the processes by which development had an impact on societies and their economies—an impact which was uneven across the world. It discussed science and technology statistics on research and development, innovation, human resources for science and technology, patents and general-purpose technologies such as biotechnology and nanotechnology. It recommended that concepts, classifications and methodologies employed in science and technology statistics be regularly updated to capture emerging scientific fields and technologies which might not easily fit into existing frameworks and might be multidisciplinary. In its conclusion, the report noted that in many countries, increased resources were needed for collecting timely and relevant science and technology statistics of high quality, based on international methodologies. In that connection, the community of statisticians needed to work together to make a better case for the importance and relevance of such data.

In February [E/2008/24], the Commission took note of the report.

Business surveys and informal sector statistics

The Statistical Commission had before it the report of the Round Table on Business Survey Frames [E/CN.3/2008/17], which focused on the Round Table's most recent meetings and their outcomes. At the twentieth International Round Table on Business Survey Frames (Wiesbaden, Germany, 21–26 October 2007), some 70 experts from 40 countries and international organizations exchanged their experiences in the methodological developments of business registers and discussed the possibilities of register-based business statistics. Participating countries presented their progress reports, with each country describing its problems and highlighting its key activities. In the concluding session, the future of the Group was discussed and participants reached an agreement on changing the name of the forum to "Wiesbaden Group on Business Registers", in accordance with the practice of similar expert groups. Participants also agreed that beginning in 2008, the meetings would be held biannually, alternating with the joint meeting of ECE, OECD and Eurostat, scheduled for 2009. OECD offered to host the 2008 meeting and several potential hosts had shown interest in holding the 2010 meeting. Following the conference, a special workshop for developing countries brought together experts from 18 developing and developed countries to discuss the prospects of supporting other countries in their developments in the field of business registers and register-based business statistics. In the future, a session within the official agenda of the conference would deal with the needs of the countries starting up business registers and register-based business statistics.

Also before the Commission was the report of the Delhi Group on informal sector statistics [E/CN.3/2008/22], which summarized the ninth (New Delhi, India, 11–12 May 2006) and tenth (Geneva, 8–10 October 2007) meetings held by the Group. At the 2006 meeting, the Group discussed the informal sector in the updated System of National Accounts, 1993 [YUN 1993, p. 1112]; measuring the contribution of the informal sector to gross domestic product and informal employment; measuring the links between poverty and informal employment; and the data quality of surveys on the informal sector and informal employment. The meeting also brought the Delhi Group and the Advisory Expert Group on National Accounts together to discuss issues related to the updating of 1993 SNA in respect to the informal sector. Another important achievement was the drawing up of the road map for the release of the manual on surveys of the informal sector and informal employment. The Group looked forward to the identification of good practices in the prospective manual and in the chapter on the informal sector in the updated 1993 SNA. At the 2007 meeting, the Group considered the progress report on the manual, draft chapters 1–5 and 10 of the manual, and the draft chapter of the updated 1993 SNA on the informal sector. The other four chapters would be drafted by June 2008 and the complete manual would be placed before the Delhi Group at its eleventh meeting in 2010.

In February [E/2008/24], the Commission took note of both reports.

Environment statistics

The Statistical Commission had before it a report of the Intersecretariat Working Group on Environment Statistics [E/CN.3/2008/24], which reviewed the Group's activities and work accomplished in 2006–2007 and presented the planned outputs and programme of work for 2008 and 2009. The focus of methodological work in 2006 and 2007 remained on water statistics, which was carried out by the Subgroup on Water Statistics, established in 2005. The Subgroup reviewed the questionnaires used by international organizations engaged in the collection of water statistics, such as the Statistical Division of the United Nations Environment Programme (UNEP), Eurostat, OECD and the Food and Agriculture Organization of the United Nations (FAO), and worked out a comparison and concordance of the terms, definitions and classifications applied. The System of Environmental Economic Accounts for Water (SEEAW) was used in the review as the reference framework. Meanwhile, the questionnaires of the UNEP Statistical Division and OECD/Eurostat were being revised as part of the preparations for the 2008 data-collection cycle; the revision would improve consistency between the questionnaires, as well as with SEEAW standard tables. The activities of the Subgroup also contributed to ongoing work by the Statistics Division in developing international recommendations for the compilation of water statistics and accounts. On data collection activities, the 2006 cycle was implemented by the UNEP Statistical Division, OECD and Eurostat in a coordinated manner and the Working Group agreed in June 2007 on coordination mechanisms for data collection in 2008. The revision of questionnaires for the 2008 data-collection cycle was under way, with the circulation of UNEP questionnaires scheduled for the end of March and OECD/Eurostat questionnaires for May. With regard to training and capacity-building, the UNEP Statistical Division and the Economic Commission for Africa (ECA) co-organized a training workshop on environment statistics in July 2007 in Ethiopia, with FAO providing a resource person to the workshop. In addition, resource persons from the Statistical Division contributed to workshops organized within the environmental component of the Euro-Mediterranean Statistical Co-operation Programme (MEDSTAT) in 2006 and 2007.

The 2008–2009 work programme of the Working Group would focus on: continuing methodological and harmonization work in the subject area of water; finalizing work on the joint glossary of environment statistics; working on a proposal for harmonized metadata guidelines for environment statistics; and establishing the subgroup on land use and land cover statistics. Other activities would include the organization of a joint international work session on land-use and land-cover statistics; implementation of the 2008 data collection and dissemination programme; and the pooling of resources by joint training and capacity-building actions.

Report of Secretary-General. The Commission also had before it the report of the Secretary-General on the Committee of Experts on Environmental-Economic Accounting [E/CN.3/2008/25], which described its work progress, including the status of the project management framework for the revision of the *Handbook of National Accounting: Integrated Environmental-Economic Accounting 2003*; presented the implementation strategy for SEEAW; and reported on the progress of phase II of the Global Assessment of Environment Statistics and Environmental-Economic Accounting.

In February [E/2008/24], the Commission took note of both reports.

Industrial statistics

The Statistical Commission considered the report of the Secretary-General [E/CN.3/2008/9] on industrial statistics, which described activities undertaken in response to Commission requests and outlined future work. The Expert Group on Industrial Statistics, which was established to provide guidance in reviewing the work programme on industrial statistics and in revising of the *International Recommendations for Industrial Statistics*, the manual on *Index Numbers of Industrial Production* and the UN list of industrial products, held a meeting (New York, 16–19 July) in which it reviewed the revised draft of the *International*

Recommendations for Industrial Statistics 2008; provided guidance on issues that had emerged during its drafting between 2005 and 2007; and amended the document for submission to the Commission in 2008. A major goal of the meeting was to ensure consistency between the revised *International Recommendations for Industrial Statistics 2008* and the *International Recommendations for Distributive Trade Statistics 2008*, which were discussed at a parallel meeting of the Expert Group on Distributive Trade Statistics. The Expert Group on Industrial Statistics also reviewed progress on the revision of the manual on *Index Numbers of Industrial Production* and endorsed the outline of the manual and the timetable of work. The Statistics Division continued to carry out a number of activities in the area of industrial statistics. Future work included the organization of training workshops on industrial statistics and the development of a knowledge-based platform on country practices for basic economic statistics.

In February [E/2008/24], the Commission, adopted part I of the *International Recommendation for Industrial Statistics 2008*, containing the recommendations for statistical units, characteristics of statistical units, data items and their definitions and the data items for international reporting as the international recommendations for industrial statistics. It endorsed part II of the document, containing guidance on performance indicators, data sources and data compilation methods, data collection strategies, data quality and metadata and dissemination of industrial statistics, as supplementary guidance for implementing the *Recommendations*. It agreed to the proposal for implementing the *Recommendations* through regional capacity-building workshops in cooperation with the United Nations Industrial Development Organization (UNIDO) and the development of a knowledge-based platform on basic economic statistics. The Commission took note of the proposed future work of the Statistics Division on industrial statistics and requested that implementation concerns expressed by the Commission be taken into account.

International trade statistics

The Secretary-General transmitted to the Statistical Commission a report on international merchandise trade statistics [E/CN.3/2008/10], which stressed the need for a revision of the Commission's recommendations for international merchandise trade statistics, outlined the Statistics Division strategy on the organization of the revision process, described actions undertaken, and provided a summary of the Division's 2008–2011 action plan. The Secretary-General made recommendations for the Commission to endorse the Division's initiative to revise the recommendations and request that the draft revised recommendations be submitted to the Commission for adoption at its forty-first (2010) session. He added that the draft revised recommendations should provide an updated conceptual framework of international merchandise trade statistics and guidance on data compilation and dissemination in the context of an integrated approach to economic statistics. In February [E/2008/24], the Commission welcomed the report.

Report of Secretary-General. The Commission also had before it the report of the Inter-Agency Task Force on International Merchandise Trade Statistics [E/CN.3/2008/18], which discussed follow-up actions related to the development of a manual on international trade indices and the fourth revision of the Standard International Trade Classification; summarized the Task Force's activities since the Commission's 2006 session; and presented new issues and related activities, as well as the updated terms of reference of the Task Force.

In February [E/2008/24], the Commission took note of the report, endorsed the Statistics Division's initiative and strategy to revise the recommendations and requested submission of the draft for adoption at its forty-first (2010) session. It requested that the revised recommendations provide an updated conceptual framework, as well as guidance on data compilation and dissemination, and be harmonized with the updated recommendations for statistics of international trade in services, the system of national accounts and the balance of payments statistics.

Distributive trade statistics

The Statistics Commission had before it the Secretary-General's report on distributive trade statistics [E/CN.3/2008/8], which summarized activities undertaken by the Statistics Division in response to decisions taken by the Commission at its 2006 session [YUN 2006, p. 1470] in the area of distributive statistics, including the revision of the *International Recommendations on Statistics of the Distributive Trades and Services*. Regarding progress in the revision of the *Recommendations*, the report provided information on activities related to the initial assessment of country practices in the compilation of distributive trade statistics; the work of the Expert Group on Distributive Trade Statistics; the creation of an electronic discussion forum/password-protected website; and global country consultations on the recommendations for distributive trade statistics.

A background document, entitled draft *International Recommendations for Distributive Trade Statistics 2008*, contained the full text of the revised recommendations, endorsed by the Expert Group on Distributive Trade Statistics.

In February [E/2008/24], the Commission adopted the *International Recommendations for Distributive Trade Statistics 2008*, as contained in the background document, and agreed to the implementation programme of the *Recommendations* as outlined in the report.

Integrated economic statistics

The Statistical Commission considered the report of the Friends of the Chair on integrated economic statistics [E/CN.3/2008/6], which presented a concept paper on modalities of an integrated approach to economic statistics and discussed three components of work for the integration of economic statistics programmes: the use of a common conceptual framework; the statistical production issues; and legal, institutional, organizational and statistical conditions across countries. It also addressed aspects related to the production of integrated economic statistics and institutional arrangements for managing integrated economic statistics.

The Friends of the Chair group concluded that the integration of economic statistics was mainly driven by demand for data consistency and coherence; that institutional arrangements at both national and international levels were important for the management of integrated economic statistics and should be part of the corresponding reform programmes; and that it was neither possible nor desirable to propagate one single and detailed implementing approach towards integrated economic statistics because national statistics systems were different. It also made recommendations for strengthening coordination among international institutions working in the field of economic statistics and on the role of the 1993 SNA as a coordinating framework for economic statistics, as well as for developing more extensive and practical guidelines that would include case studies on practices of integrated economic statistics.

In February [E/2008/24], the Commission agreed with the findings and recommendations of the Friends of the Chair report on integrated economic statistics, including the need to collect and disseminate case studies and develop other practical knowledge material to share experiences and guide countries in implementing an integrated approach in their national statistical systems. The Commission made recommendations for guidance on practical aspects of integration to focus on the need for cooperation with users and data suppliers; the development of central business registers and use of administrative data; conceptual harmonization of data content across surveys; strong and centralized coordination of survey operations within the national statistical institution; the need for an entity—within a national statistical institution—specialized in preparing administrative data to be matched to survey data; and a sampling strategy that took into account the burden of the reporting entities.

Agricultural statistics

The Secretary-General transmitted the report of the Wye Group on statistics on rural development and agriculture household income [E/CN.3/2008/23], which provided information on the Group's first meeting to be held in York, England, in April. The Group was formed as the successor to the Intersecretariat Working Group on Agriculture Statistics (IWG.AGRI) task force, which held its final meeting in June 2006. The Wye Group would include 20 to 30 statistics and economics experts from national statistics offices, ministries of agriculture, universities and research institutes, who had a shared interest in improving methods for collecting data on rural environment, communities and farm and non-farm households. Its first meeting would discuss the Group's objectives and intended outputs and would consist of three half-day sessions with a focus on rural statistics, agriculture household income and developing nations.

In February [E/2008/24], the Commission took note of the report.

Regional statistical development

The Secretary-General transmitted to the Statistical Commission a report of the Economic Commission for Africa (ECA) on regional statistical development in Africa [E/CN.3/2008/14], which highlighted issues and challenges facing African countries in enhancing their statistical capacity; reviewed ongoing initiatives by African stakeholders to overcome those challenges, including the establishment of a statistical commission for Africa (Statcom-Africa) and the African Statistical Coordination Committee; and elaborated on a way forward and on the role ECA could play in addressing the challenges.

In February [E/2008/24], the Commission expressed satisfaction with the re-establishment of an ECA focal point on statistics activities and endorsed the report's recommendations to address the challenges facing African national statistical systems. It called upon African countries to intensify efforts to develop their national capacities to produce timely and reliable statistics in support of their development efforts; noted the provision of technical and financial support for statistical capacity-building in the African region by various agencies and development partners; and urged international agencies and the donor community to strengthen their support for statistical development in Africa.

Demographic and social statistics

Population and housing censuses

The Statistical Commission had before it the Secretary-General's report on population and housing censuses [E/CN.3/2008/16], which presented activities completed in respect of the implementation of the 2010 World Programme on Population and Housing Censuses, including the conduct of expert group meetings and training workshops; finalization of the *Principles and Recommendations for Population and Housing Censuses, Rev.2*; and the development of a website to serve as a census knowledge base. It also contained future activities related to the 2010 World Programme.

The Commission took note of the report in February [E/2008/24].

Human Development Report

The Secretary-General transmitted to the Statistical Commission the report of the Human Development Report Office of the United Nations Development Programme (UNDP) [E/CN.3/2008/11], which discussed issues such as data quality assurance, country coverage and data gaps, and the use of international data, as they pertained to the *Human Development Report*. It also indicated that the *Report*, which explored in depth a different topic each year relevant to the field of human development, contained an extensive statistical annex of the latest human development indicators, some of which were summarized in four composite indices of which the Human Development Index was the most widely known and quoted.

In February [E/2008/24], the Commission supported the steps being taken to enhance data quality assurance and actions taken to ensure the quality of data and indicators published in the *Human Development Report*, including the creation of a statistical advisory panel, the institution of a statistical peer review process and the initiative on holding regular consultations with member States. It emphasized the need for the Human Development Report Office to further improve transparency in the process of preparing the *Report*; took note of the initiative by the Committee for the Coordination of Statistical Activities to compile information on regional training institutions that would help to assess statistical training needs and capacities across regions; and invited the Statistics Division and the World Bank to explore the feasibility of developing an electronic platform that could house information on demand for training, potential training providers and funding options.

Health statistics

The Statistics Commission considered the report of the Intersecretariat Working Group on Health Statistics [E/CN.3/2008/15], which described projects in the area of health statistics that were of interest to national statistical offices, illustrated work under development by the Health Metric Network on health surveys, and indicated that a detailed report of the meeting of the Working Group, to be held in December 2007, would be circulated at the Commission's 2008 session.

In February [E/2008/24], the Commission took note of the Working Group's report on health statistics and the report of the Group's December 2007 meeting. It expressed support for the ongoing work to improve coordination of health statistics and the proposed development of a framework.

Labour statistics

The Statistical Commission considered a report prepared by the Office for National Statistics of the United Kingdom [E/CN.3/2008/2] on labour statistics, which focused on areas where improvements could be made in the future. The report outlined the mandate and approach of the programme review of employment statistics, which was completed in November 2007; identified the successes and gaps in the work of different organizations involved in labour statistics; presented the findings of an August 2007 international survey of UN Member States on labour statistics; and discussed the challenges of obtaining a complete picture of the labour market despite the large amount of labour market data available. Problems encountered were related to incomplete coverage, contradictory results between data sources, difficulties and limitations in describing labour market dynamics, and the absence of links between labour market statistics and other social and economic statistics. The Commission was requested to recommend that ILO: prioritize the activities required to improve the harmonization of concepts and methods that supported the production, transmission and dissemination of comparable labour statistics, as well as produce an action plan and coordinate its implementation; develop a coordinated system for providing technical assistance to help countries provide high-quality labour statistics; establish working groups to discuss each of the five topics identified for development work in the review; develop an updated version of the labour statistics framework; and work with the Statistics Division, OECD and Eurostat to improve the process of setting international standards.

In February [E/2008/24], the Commission emphasized the need for better coordination to improve the quality and coherence of national and global labour statistics, which should be done in consultation with the Committee for the Coordination of Statistical Activities. It welcomed the work done by the ILO Conference of Labour Statisticians and recommended that the Conference review its methods of operation, in particular the frequency and duration of its sessions. It also requested ILO to report to the Commission in 2009 on the Conference outcomes and other actions taken in implementing the recommendations of the review report.

At the eighteenth International Conference of Labour Statisticians (Geneva, 24 November–5 December) [ICLS/18/2008/1], participants discussed, among other proposals, the future work of ILO in labour statistics (2009–2013) and options for the organization, frequency and duration of the Conference.

Education statistics

The Statistical Commission had before it the report of the UNESCO Institute for Statistics on the work of the Task Force on Education Statistics [E/CN.3/2008/3], which reviewed the main measurement frameworks in the field of education being used for data collection at the international, regional or national levels and how those frameworks affected the production and use of statistics. The review discussed coordination mechanisms among relevant agencies with respect to different stages of the statistical production and dissemination cycle. The report proposed ways to improve coordination with regard to data collection and production and dissemination; presented a timeline for the preparation of the Task Force's final report; and requested the Commission to advise on the future direction of the Task Force's work.

In February [E/2008/24], the Commission took note of the proposed method of work in producing the final report of the Task Force, requested the Task Force to broaden its regional representation in terms of national statistical offices to better reflect the diverse realities in different parts of the world, and requested the Institute, on behalf of the Task Force, to report to the Commission's 2009 session.

Other statistical activities

International economic and social classifications

The Statistical Commission had before it an ILO report on updating the International Standard Classification of Occupations (ISCO-88) [E/CN.3/2008/28]. The work was scheduled for completion to allow sufficient time for the updated classification, or national adaptations of it, to be available for use in the 2010 round of national population censuses. ILO convened in December 2007 a meeting of experts [MELS/2007/2], which evaluated an updated classification structure, made a small number of amendments to it and adopted a draft resolution endorsing the structure, which was annexed to the draft resolution. The updated classification, known as the International Standard Classification of Occupations 2008 (ISCO-08), would be available at the Commission's 2008 session as a background document. ILO would provide support for implementing the updated ISCO from 2008 to ensure that ISCO-08 could be used in the round of national population censuses to be conducted beginning in 2010.

In February [E/2008/24], the Commission took note of the ILO report.

Standards for data dissemination and exchange

The Commission considered the Secretary-General's report on collection and dissemination of statistics by the Statistics Division [E/CN.3/2008/12], which described ongoing activities and recent developments in the work programme of the Division with respect to data collection and dissemination. It discussed the Division's initiatives to better coordinate data-collection activities by international agencies for easy access to the UN system data and to facilitate the exchange of experience among developing countries with respect to data dissemination policies and practices.

In February [E/2008/24], the Commission encouraged the Division to make data available free of charge so as to facilitate their dissemination and use, continue initiatives for reducing the reporting burden on countries, including joint data-collection agreements, and facilitate the exchange of experiences among countries with respect to dissemination policies and practices. The Commission congratulated the Division for the development of the data portal UNdata and urged it to accelerate implementation of the portal to develop its full potential by bringing together sectoral global, regional and national databases.

Statistical data and metadata exchange

The Secretary-General transmitted to the Statistical Commission a report on common open standards for the exchange and sharing of data and metadata [E/CN.3/2008/13], which reviewed activities related to the Statistical Data and Metadata Exchange (SDMX) initiative and included a proposal for its recognition as the international standard for data and metadata exchange. The goal of the SDMX initiative was to foster standards and guidelines that allowed national and international organizations to gain efficiencies and avoid duplication of work in the area of data and metadata exchange through the use of modern technology. The report concluded that SDMX technical standards and content-oriented guidelines had demonstrated their potential for improving the exchange and sharing of statistical data and metadata using modern technology. A number of implementations were in progress and a widening range of international and national statistical agencies was endorsing SDMX.

In February [E/2008/24], the Commission recognized and supported SDMX as the preferred standard for the exchange and sharing of data and metadata, requested the sponsors to continue their work on the initiative, and encouraged its further implementation by national and international statistical organizations. It also emphasized the need to further involve national and international agencies in the initiative by enabling opportunities for collaboration with the sponsoring organizations and underlined the importance of capacity-building and outreach. The Commission requested the sponsors of the initiative to continue fostering the development of freely available tools and software to benefit statistical systems in interchanges of data and metadata and took note of the list of applications and projects at the national and international levels, which were making use of SDMX as a standard.

Statistical capacity-building

The Secretary-General transmitted to the Statistical Commission the report of the Partnership in Statistics for Development in the Twenty-first Century (PARIS21) on statistical capacity-building [E/CN.3/2008/27], which outlined PARIS21 efforts to promote the use of better statistics as a central part of the enabling environment for development progress, as well as PARIS21 activities in 2007 in the following areas: advocacy and the development of statistical advocacy tools; regional programmes; the promotion of donor collaboration; the development of national strategies methodology; and satellite programmes. The report also discussed future plans, including PARIS21 partnering with international institutions, regional organizations and bilateral donors in a scaling-up of investment in national statistical systems.

In February [E/2008/24], the Commission took note of the report.

Follow-up to UN conferences and summits

The Statistics Commission had before it the report of the Secretary-General [E/CN.3/2008/29 & Corr.1] on the indicators for monitoring the Millennium Development Goals (MDGs) [YUN 2000, p. 51], which described the work of the Inter-Agency and Expert Group on MDGs Indicators in 2007 and the Statistics Division, in its capacity as coordinator of the Group, in the areas of improvement of the coverage, transparency and reporting on all indicators as presented in the database on all MDGs; implementation of the recommendations contained in Economic and Social Council resolution 2006/6 [YUN 2006, p. 1472] on strengthening statistical capacity; coordination of data collection at the global level; and preparation of the yearly analysis and reports on progress towards the MDGs. Annexed to the report were the revised MDGs monitoring framework, including new targets and indicators, an assessment of country data availability in the MDGs indicators database, and the summary of the recommendations by the Inter-Agency and Expert Group at its twelfth meeting in November 2007. The report concluded with proposals on the way forward.

In February [E/2008/24], the Commission commended the efforts by the Inter-Agency and Expert Group on MDGs Indicators to implement resolution 2006/6 and include an increasing number of States in its deliberations. It took note of the Group's deliberations and recommendations on the way forward and the concerns expressed by States about the quality of the measurement of indicators, and requested the submission of an updated report to the Commission at its 2009 session. It further requested the Group to give greater consideration to the need for improving the capacity of countries to produce the indicators, develop recommendations on ways to improve statistical capacity-building in countries for submission to the Commission's 2009 session, and increase efforts to further improve the indicators of all MDGs through methodological and technical refinements.

Coordination and integration of statistical programmes

The Secretary-General transmitted to the Statistical Commission a report on the work of the Committee for the Coordination of Statistical Activities (CCSA) [E/CN.3/2008/26], which summarized the main conclusions of the ninth and tenth sessions of CCSA, held in New York on 26 February 2007, and in Madrid on 10 and 11 September 2007, respectively. It also provided information on the work of the Committee in areas such as statistical training for staff of international agencies; an assessment of the costs and benefits of adopting SDMX; the work of the Inter-Agency and Expert Group on MDGs Indicators on implementing Economic and Social Council resolution 2006/6; data imputations by international agencies; the use of population estimates; the modalities of data-sharing among international organizations; the CCSA special session on the implementation of quality assurance frameworks; coordination of technical cooperation activities; and the review of CCSA functions.

The Commission also had before it a CCSA information note on implementation of principles governing international statistical activities [E/CN.3/2008/31], which summarized the main findings and highlighted examples of action taken to implement the ten principles governing international statistical activities: relevance, impartiality and equal access to high-quality international statistics; professional standards and ethics; accountability and transparency; prevention of misuse of concepts; sources of official statistics; confidentiality in individual data collection; regulation of erroneous interpretation and misuse of statistics; regional coordination of standards for national and international statistics; the use of international standards in statistics; and international cooperation. The report also mentioned the areas where, in the view of some agencies, further work was needed.

In February [E/2008/24], the Commission took note of the report and the information note.

Follow-up to Economic and Social Council policy decisions

The Statistical Commission had before it a note by the Secretary-General on policy decisions of the Economic and Social Council adopted in 2007 that were relevant to the Commission's work [E/CN.3/2008/30]. The note covered actions related to the follow-up to major UN conferences and summits, the reform of the Economic and Social Council, mainstreaming gender perspectives, strengthening national capacity in statistics, and the 2010 World Programme on Population and Housing Censuses.

In February [E/2008/24], the Commission took note of the Secretary-General's note.

Programme and institutional questions

The Commission approved its 2008–2011 multi-year programme of work [E/CN.3/2008/32], as orally amended, and approved the provisional agenda and documentation for its fortieth session, to be held in New York from 24 to 27 February 2009.

PART FOUR

Legal questions

Chapter I

International Court of Justice

In 2008, the International Court of Justice (ICJ) delivered three Judgments, made nine Orders, and had 17 contentious cases and one request for an advisory opinion pending before it. In a 30 October address to the General Assembly, the ICJ President, Judge Rosalyn Higgins, noted that the period from 1 August 2007 to 31 July 2008 marked the Court's most productive year in its history and that the cases decided during the previous year had involved States from every UN regional group. The universal character of the Court was also reflected in the wide range of subjects addressed in those cases, which included human rights, territorial sovereignty, mutual legal assistance, maritime delimitation, and the interpretation of an earlier Judgment.

Judicial work of the Court

During 2008, the Court delivered its Judgment on the merits in the cases concerning *Sovereignty over Pedra Branca/Pulau Batu Puteh, Middle Rocks and South Ledge (Malaysia/Singapore)* and *Certain Questions of Mutual Assistance in Criminal Matters (Djibouti v. France)*; and a Judgment on the preliminary objections raised by Serbia in the case concerning *Application of the Convention on the Prevention and Punishment of the Crime of Genocide (Croatia v. Serbia).*

During the year, the Court was seized of six new cases: *Maritime Dispute (Peru v. Chile)*; *Aerial Herbicide Spraying (Ecuador v. Colombia)*; *Request for Interpretation of the Judgment of 31 March 2004 in the Case concerning* Avena and Other Mexican Nationals (Mexico v. United States) *(Mexico v. United States)*; *Application of the International Convention on the Elimination of All Forms of Racial Discrimination (Georgia v. Russian Federation)*; *Application of the Interim Accord of 13 September 1995 (The former Yugoslav Republic of Macedonia v. Greece)*; and *Jurisdictional Immunities of the State (Germany v. Italy).*

It held public hearings in the cases concerning *Certain Questions of Mutual Assistance in Criminal Matters (Djibouti v. France)*; *Application of the Convention on the Prevention and Punishment of the Crime of Genocide (Croatia v. Serbia)*; *Request for Interpretation of the Judgment of 31 March 2004 in the Case concerning* Avena and Other Mexican Nationals (Mexico v. United States) *(Mexico v. United States)*; *Maritime Delimitation in the Black Sea (Romania v. Ukraine)*; and *Application of the International Convention on the Elimination of All Forms of Racial Discrimination (Georgia v. Russian Federation).*

The Court or its President made Orders on the conduct of the proceedings in the cases concerning *Ahmadou Sadio Diallo (Guinea v. Democratic Republic of the Congo)*; *Territorial and Maritime Dispute (Nicaragua v. Colombia)*; *Maritime Dispute (Peru v. Chile)*; *Aerial Herbicide Spraying (Ecuador v. Colombia)*; and *Application of the International Convention on the Elimination of All Forms of Racial Discrimination (Georgia v. Russian Federation)*; and Orders indicating provisional measures in the cases concerning *Request for Interpretation of the Judgment of 31 March 2004 in the Case concerning* Avena and Other Mexican Nationals (Mexico v. United States) *(Mexico v. United States)* and *Application of the International Convention on the Elimination of All Forms of Racial Discrimination (Georgia v. Russian Federation).* It also made an Order in relation to the request for an advisory opinion on the question of the *Accordance with International Law of the Unilateral Declaration of Independence by the Provisional Institutions of Self-Government of Kosovo.*

During the year, there were no new developments in the cases concerning *Gabcikovo-Nagymaros Project (Hungary/Slovakia)* [YUN 1998, p. 1186]; *Armed Activities on the Territory of the Congo (Democratic Republic of the Congo v. Uganda)* [YUN 1999, p. 1209]; *Certain Criminal Proceedings in France (Republic of the Congo v. France)* [YUN 2002, p. 1263]; *Dispute regarding Navigational and Related Rights (Costa Rica v. Nicaragua)* [YUN 2005, p. 1385]; and *Pulp Mills on the River Uruguay (Argentina v. Uruguay)* [YUN 2006, p. 1481].

ICJ activities in 2008 were covered in two reports to the General Assembly, for the periods 1 August 2007 to 31 July 2008 [A/63/4] and 1 August 2008 to 31 July 2009 [A/64/4]. On 30 October, the Assembly took note of the 2007/2008 report (**decision 63/508**).

Contentious proceedings

Ahmadou Sadio Diallo (Guinea v. Democratic Republic of the Congo)

In 1998 [YUN 1998, p. 1190], Guinea instituted proceedings against the Democratic Republic of the Congo (DRC) by an "Application with a view to diplomatic protection", in which it requested the Court to condemn the DRC for the grave breaches of international law perpetrated upon the person of a Guinean national, Ahmadou Sadio Diallo.

According to Guinea, Mr. Diallo, a businessman who had been a resident of the DRC for 32 years, was "unlawfully imprisoned by the authorities of that State" for two and a half months, "divested from his important investments, companies, bank accounts, movable and immovable properties, then expelled". The expulsion took place on 2 February 1996, as a result of his attempts to recover sums owed to him by the DRC (especially by Gécamines, a State enterprise and mining monopoly) and by oil companies operating in that country (Zaire Shell, Zaire Mobil and Zaire Fina), by virtue of contracts concluded with businesses owned by him, namely Africom-Zaïre and Africontainers-Zaïre.

As a basis of the Court's jurisdiction, Guinea invoked its own declaration of acceptance of the compulsory jurisdiction of the Court of 11 November 1998 and a declaration of the DRC of 8 February 1989. Guinea filed its Memorial within the time limit as extended by the Court by an Order of 8 September 2000 [YUN 2000, p. 1213]. On 3 October 2002, within the time limit for the deposit of its Counter-Memorial, the DRC filed preliminary objections to the Court's jurisdiction and the admissibility of Guinea's Application; the proceedings on the merits were accordingly suspended [YUN 2002, p. 1266].

By an Order of 7 November 2002 [ibid.], the Court fixed 7 July 2003 as the time limit within which Guinea might present a written statement of its observations and submissions on the preliminary objections raised by the DRC; the written statement was filed within the time limit [YUN 2003, p. 1303].

Public hearings on the preliminary objections were held from 27 November to 1 December 2006 [YUN 2006, p. 1479], during which the Parties presented final submissions to the Court. The DRC requested the Court to adjudge and declare that the Application of Guinea was inadmissible on the grounds that Guinea had no status to exercise diplomatic protection in the proceedings, since its Application sought essentially to secure reparation for injury suffered on account of the violation of rights of companies which did not possess its nationality, and, in any event, neither the companies in question nor Mr. Diallo had exhausted the effective local remedies available in the DRC. Guinea requested the Court to reject the preliminary objections raised by the DRC; declare its Application admissible; and fix time limits for further proceedings.

On 24 May 2007 [YUN 2007, p. 1327], the Court rendered its Judgment on the preliminary objections. The Court unanimously rejected the preliminary objection to admissibility raised by the DRC for lack of standing by Guinea to exercise diplomatic protection in the case, insofar as it concerned protection of Mr. Diallo's direct rights as *associé* in Africom-Zaïre and Africontainers-Zaïre. By 14 votes to 1, it upheld the objection insofar as it concerned protection of Mr. Diallo in respect of alleged violations of rights of Africom-Zaïre and Africontainers-Zaïre. On the preliminary objection to admissibility raised by the DRC on account of non-exhaustion by Mr. Diallo of local remedies, the Court unanimously rejected the objection insofar as it concerned protection of Mr. Diallo's rights as an individual. By 14 votes to 1, the Court rejected the objection insofar as it concerned protection of Mr. Diallo's direct rights as *associé* in Africom-Zaïre and Africontainers-Zaïre. Consequently, it unanimously declared the Application of Guinea to be admissible insofar as it concerned protection of Mr. Diallo's rights as an individual. By two separate votes of 14 to 1, the Court declared the Application of Guinea to be admissible insofar as it concerned protection of Mr. Diallo's direct rights as *associé* in Africom-Zaïre and Africontainers-Zaïre; and declared it to be inadmissible insofar as it concerned protection of Mr. Diallo in respect of alleged violations of rights of Africom-Zaïre and Africontainers-Zaïre.

By an Order of 27 June 2007 [ibid., p. 1328], the Court fixed 27 March 2008 as the time limit for the filing of a Counter-Memorial by the DRC, which was filed within the time limit.

By an Order of 5 May 2008, the Court authorized the submission of a reply by Guinea and a rejoinder by the DRC. It fixed 19 November 2008 and 5 June 2009 as the respective time limits for the filing of those written pleadings. Guinea filed the reply on 19 November.

Application of the Convention on the Prevention and Punishment of the Crime of Genocide (Croatia v. Serbia)

Croatia instituted proceedings against Serbia and Montenegro, then known as the Federal Republic of Yugoslavia (FRY), on 2 July 1999 [YUN 1999, p. 1210] for alleged violations of the 1948 Convention on the Prevention and Punishment of the Crime of Genocide, adopted by the General Assembly in resolution 260 A(III) [YUN 1948–49, p. 959], said to have been committed between 1991 and 1995. In its Application, Croatia contended that by "directly controlling the activity of its armed forces, intelligence agents, and various paramilitary detachments, on the territory of … Croatia, in the Knin region, eastern and western Slovenia, and Dalmatia, [Serbia and Montenegro] is liable [for] the 'ethnic cleansing' of Croatian citizens from these areas … and is required to provide reparation for the resulting damage". It further alleged that, "by directing, encouraging, and urging Croatian citizens of Serb ethnicity in the Knin region to evacuate the area in 1995, as … Croatia reasserted its legitimate governmental authority ... [Serbia and Montenegro] engaged in conduct amounting to a second round of 'ethnic cleansing'". Croatia invoked the jurisdiction of the Court based on Article 36, paragraph 1, of the Statute and on article IX of the Convention. Croatia reserved the right to introduce to the Court at a future date a precise evaluation of the damages.

By an Order of 14 September 1999, the Court took account of an agreement of the Parties expressed on 13 September and fixed 14 March 2000 as the time limit for the filing of the Memorial of Croatia and 14 September 2000 for the filing of the Counter-Memorial of Serbia and Montenegro.

In 2000 [YUN 2000, p. 1219], at Croatia's request, the President of the Court twice extended the time limits, which finally were set at 14 March 2001 for the Memorial of Croatia and at 16 September 2002 for the Counter-Memorial of Serbia and Montenegro. The Memorial of Croatia was filed within the time limit thus extended. On 11 September 2002 [YUN 2002, p. 1268], within the extended time limit for filing its Counter-Memorial, Serbia and Montenegro filed certain preliminary objections to jurisdiction and admissibility. The proceedings on the merits were suspended, in accordance with Article 79 of the Rules of the Court.

On 25 April 2003, within the time limit fixed by an Order of the Court of 14 November 2002 [ibid.], Croatia filed a written statement of its observations and submissions on the preliminary objections raised by Serbia and Montenegro [YUN 2003, p. 1304].

Public hearings on the preliminary objections on jurisdiction and admissibility were held from 26 to 30 May 2008. At the conclusion of those hearings, the Parties presented final submissions to the Court. Serbia requested the Court to adjudge and declare that the Court lacked jurisdiction, or, in the alternative, that claims based on acts or omissions which took place prior to 27 April 1992 were beyond the jurisdiction of the Court and inadmissible; and that claims referring to submission to trial of certain persons within the jurisdiction of Serbia, providing information regarding the whereabouts of missing Croatian citizens, and the return of cultural property were beyond the jurisdiction of the Court and were inadmissible.

Croatia requested the Court to reject the first, second and third preliminary objection of Serbia, with the exception of that part of the second preliminary objection which related to the claim concerning the submission to trial of Slobodan Milošević; and accordingly to adjudge and declare that it had jurisdiction to adjudicate upon the Application filed by Croatia.

In its Judgment of 18 November 2008, the Court, by 10 votes to 7, rejected the first preliminary objection submitted by Serbia insofar as it related to its capacity to participate in the proceedings instituted by the Application of Croatia. By 12 votes to 5, it rejected the first preliminary objection submitted by Serbia insofar as it related to the jurisdiction *ratione materiae* of the Court under article IX of the Convention on the Prevention and Punishment of the Crime of Genocide to entertain the Application of Croatia. By 10 votes to 7, the Court found that subject to paragraph 4 of the present operative clause, it had jurisdiction to entertain the Application of Croatia. By 11 votes to 6, it found that the second preliminary objection submitted by Serbia did not, in the circumstances of the case, possess an exclusively preliminary character. By 12 votes to 5, the Court rejected the third preliminary objection submitted by Serbia.

Appended to the Judgment was a declaration by Judge Bennouna; a joint declaration by Judges Ranjeva, Shi, Koroma, and Parra-Aranguren; separate opinions by Vice-President Al-Khasawneh, Judges Tomka and Abraham, and Judge ad hoc Vukas; and dissenting opinions by Judges Ranjeva, Owada, Skotnikov and Judge ad hoc Kreća.

Territorial and Maritime Dispute (Nicaragua v. Colombia)

In 2001 [YUN 2001, p. 1195], Nicaragua instituted proceedings against Colombia in respect of a dispute concerning "a group of related legal issues subsisting" between the two States "concerning title to territory and maritime delimitation". In its Application, Nicaragua requested the Court to adjudge and declare, first, that Nicaragua had sovereignty over the islands of Providencia, San Andrés and Santa Catalina and all the appurtenant islands and keys, and also over the Roncador, Serrana, Serranilla and Quitasueño keys (insofar as they were capable of appropriation); and, second, in the light of the determinations concerning the title requested above, asked the Court to determine the course of the single maritime boundary between the areas of the continental shelf and the exclusive economic zone appertaining respectively to Nicaragua and Colombia, in accordance with equitable principles and relevant circumstances recognized by general international law as applicable to such a delimitation of a single maritime boundary. Nicaragua reserved the right to claim compensation for elements of unjust enrichment consequent upon Colombian possession of the islands of San Andrés and Providencia, as well as the keys and maritime spaces up to the 82nd meridian, in the absence of lawful title. It also reserved the right to claim compensation for interference with fishing vessels of Nicaraguan nationality or vessels licensed by Nicaragua.

By an Order of 26 February 2002 [YUN 2002, p. 1271], the Court fixed 28 April 2003 and 28 June 2004, respectively, as the time limits for the filing of a Memorial by Nicaragua and of a Counter-Memorial by Colombia. The Memorial of Nicaragua was filed within the time limit [YUN 2003, p. 1305].

On 21 July 2003 [ibid.], Colombia filed preliminary objections to the jurisdiction of the Court; under Article 79 of the Rules of Court, proceedings on the merits were suspended accordingly. Nicaragua filed a written statement of its observations and submissions on the preliminary objections raised by Colombia within the time limit of 26 January 2004 [YUN 2004, p. 1268], fixed by the Court by an Order of 24 September 2003.

Public hearings were held on the preliminary objections from 4 to 8 June 2007 [YUN 2007, p. 1329]. At the conclusion of those hearings, the Parties presented their final submissions to the Court. Colombia requested the Court to adjudge and declare that under the 1948 American Treaty on Pacific Settlement (Pact of Bogotá), and in particular in pursuance of articles VI and XXXIV, the Court was without jurisdiction to hear the controversy submitted to it by Nicaragua under article XXXI, and to declare the controversy ended; that under Article 36, paragraph 2, of the Statute of the Court, the Court had no jurisdiction to entertain Nicaragua's Application; and that its Application was dismissed. Nicaragua asked the Court to adjudge and declare that the preliminary objections submitted by Colombia were invalid both in respect of the jurisdiction based upon the Pact of Bogotá, and upon Article 36, paragraph 2, of the Statute of the Court. In the alternative, Nicaragua asked the Court to adjudge and declare, in accordance with the provisions of Article 79, paragraph 7, of the Rules of Court, that the objections submitted by Colombia did not have an exclusively preliminary character, and to reject the request of Colombia to declare the controversy submitted to it by Nicaragua under article XXXI of the Pact of Bogotá 'ended', in accordance with articles VI and XXXIV of the same instrument.

On 13 December 2007 [ibid., p. 1330], the Court rendered its Judgment on the preliminary objections. By 13 votes to 4, the Court upheld the objection to its jurisdiction raised by Colombia on the basis of articles VI and XXXIV of the Pact of Bogotá, insofar as it concerned sovereignty over the islands of San Andrés, Providencia and Santa Catalina. It unanimously rejected the objection to its jurisdiction insofar as it concerned sovereignty over the other maritime features in dispute between the Parties and the maritime delimitation between the Parties. By 14 votes to 3, the Court upheld the second preliminary objection to jurisdiction raised by Colombia relating to the declarations made by the Parties recognizing the compulsory jurisdiction of the Court insofar as it concerned sovereignty over the islands of San Andrés, Providencia and Santa Catalina. By 16 votes to 1, it found that it was not necessary to examine the objection to its jurisdiction insofar as it concerned sovereignty over the other maritime features in dispute between the Parties and the maritime delimitation between the Parties. With regard to its own jurisdiction, the Court unanimously found that it had jurisdiction, on the basis of article XXXI of the Pact of Bogotá, to adjudicate upon the dispute concerning sovereignty over the maritime features claimed by the Parties other than the islands of San Andrés, Providencia and Santa Catalina, and upon the dispute concerning the maritime delimitation between the Parties.

Appended to the Judgment were declarations by Judges Parra-Aranguren, Simma, Keith and Tomka and Judge ad hoc Gaja; separate opinions by Judges Ranjeva and Abraham; and dissenting opinions by Vice-President Al-Khasawneh and Judge Bennouna.

By an Order of 11 February 2008, the President of the Court fixed 11 November 2008 as the time limit for the filing of the Counter-Memorial of Colombia, which was filed within that time limit.

By an Order of 18 December, the Court directed Nicaragua to submit a Reply and Colombia to submit a Rejoinder, and fixed 18 September 2009 and 18 June 2010 as the respective time limits for the filing of those written pleadings.

Communication. On 29 February [A/62/733], Colombia transmitted to the Secretary-General the text of a note sent to the President of Nicaragua on 25 February 2008 in reference to the judgment on preliminary objections handed down by the Court on 13 December 2007.

Sovereignty over Pedra Branca/Pulau Batu Puteh, Middle Rocks and South Ledge (Malaysia/Singapore)

On 24 July 2003 [YUN 2003, p. 1308], Malaysia and Singapore jointly notified the Court of a Special Agreement, which was signed between them on 6 February 2003 at Putrajaya, Malaysia, and entered into force on 9 May 2003. In article 2 of the Special Agreement, the Parties requested the Court to determine whether sovereignty over Pedra Branca/Pulau Batu Puteh, Middle Rocks and South Ledge belonged to Malaysia or Singapore. In article 6, the Parties agreed to accept the judgment of the Court as final and binding upon them. The Parties further set out their views on the procedure to be followed.

By an Order of 1 September 2003 [ibid., p. 1309], the Court, taking into account the provisions of article 4 of the Special Agreement, fixed 25 March 2004 and 25 January 2005 as the respective time limits for the filing, by each of the Parties, of a Memorial and of a Counter-Memorial. The Memorial [YUN 2004, p. 1271] and Counter-Memorial [YUN 2005, p. 1385] were filed within the time limit.

By an Order of 1 February 2005, the Court fixed 25 November 2005 as the time limit for the filing of a Reply by each of the Parties, which were filed within the time limit [ibid.].

By a joint letter of 23 January 2006, the Parties informed the Court that they had agreed there was no need for an exchange of Rejoinders in the case. The Court itself subsequently decided that no further pleadings were necessary, and that the written proceedings were accordingly closed [YUN 2006, p. 1480].

Public hearings were held from 6 to 23 November 2007 [YUN 2007, p. 1330]. At the conclusion of those hearings, the Parties presented their final submissions to the Court. Singapore requested the Court to adjudge and declare that Singapore had sovereignty over Pedra Branca/Pulau Batu Puteh, Middle Rocks and South Ledge. Malaysia asked the Court to adjudge and declare that Malaysia had sovereignty over the disputed islands.

In its Judgment delivered on 23 May 2008, the Court, by 12 votes to 4, found that sovereignty over Pedra Branca/Pulau Batu Puteh belonged to Singapore. By 15 votes to 1, it found that sovereignty over Middle Rocks belonged to Malaysia. By 15 votes to 1, it found that sovereignty over South Ledge belonged to the State in the territorial waters of which it was located.

Appended to the Judgment were declarations by Judges Ranjeva and Bennouna; separate opinions by Judge Parra-Aranguren and Judge ad hoc Sreenivasa Rao; a joint dissenting opinion by Judges Simma and Abraham; and a dissenting opinion by ad hoc Judge Dugard.

Maritime Delimitation in the Black Sea (Romania v. Ukraine)

On 16 September 2004 [YUN 2004, p. 1271], Romania filed an Application instituting proceedings against Ukraine in respect of a dispute concerning the establishment of a single maritime boundary between the two States in the Black Sea, thereby delimiting the continental shelf and the exclusive economic zones appertaining to them. Romania requested the Court to draw, in accordance with international law, and specifically the criteria laid down in article 4 of the Additional Agreement to the June 1997 Treaty on Relations of Co-operation and Good Neighbourliness between Romania and Ukraine, a single maritime boundary between the continental shelf and the exclusive economic zone of the two States in the Black Sea.

As a basis for the Court's jurisdiction, Romania invoked article 4 *(h)* of the Additional Agreement, which provided that, if the negotiations should not determine the conclusion of an agreement on the delimitation of the continental shelf and the exclusive economic zones in the Black Sea in a reasonable period of time, no later than two years after their initiation, Romania and Ukraine would agree that the delimitation problem would be solved by ICJ, at their request, provided that the treaty on the regime of the State border between Romania and Ukraine had entered into force. However, should ICJ consider that the delay of the entry into force of the treaty on the border regime was the result of the other Party's fault, it might examine the request concerning the delimitation before the entry into force of the treaty.

Romania contended that the two conditions set out in article 4 *(h)* of the Additional Agreement had been fulfilled, since the negotiations had by far exceeded two years and the Treaty on the Romanian-Ukrainian State Border Régime had entered into force on 27 May 2004.

In its Application, Romania further provided an overview of the applicable law for solving the dispute, citing a number of provisions of the Additional Agreement of 1997, as well as the 1982 United Nations Convention on the Law of the Sea [YUN 1982, p. 181], to which both Ukraine and Romania were parties, together with other relevant instruments binding the two countries.

On 19 November 2004 [YUN 2004, p. 1272], the Court fixed 19 August 2005 and 19 May 2006, respectively, as the time limits for the filing of a Memorial by Romania and a Counter-Memorial by Ukraine, which were filed within the time limit.

By an Order of 30 June 2006 [YUN 2006, p. 1480], the Court authorized the filing of a Reply by Romania and a Rejoinder by Ukraine, and fixed 22 December 2006 and 15 June 2007 as the respective time limits for the filing of those pleadings. Romania filed its Reply within the time limit. On 8 June 2007 [YUN 2007, p. 1331], the Court extended the time limit for the filing of the Rejoinder by Ukraine to 6 July 2007, which was filed within the extended time limit.

Public hearings were held from 2 to 19 September 2008.

Certain Questions of Mutual Assistance in Criminal Matters (Djibouti v. France)

On 9 January 2006 [YUN 2006, p. 1480], Djibouti filed an Application instituting proceedings against France regarding the alleged violation by the latter of its international obligations in respect of mutual assistance in criminal matters in the context of the investigation into the death of the French Judge Bernard Borrel in Djibouti in 1995. Djibouti explained that the dispute concerned the refusal by the French governmental and judicial authorities to execute an international letter rogatory regarding the transmission to the Djiboutian judicial authorities of the record relating to the investigation in the case against X for the murder of Judge Borrel. Djibouti maintained that the refusal constituted a violation of France's international obligations under the 1977 Treaty of Friendship and Co-operation signed by the two States and the 1986 Convention on Mutual Assistance in Criminal Matters between France and Djibouti. Djibouti further asserted that, in summoning certain internationally protected nationals of Djibouti, including the Head of State, as *témoins assistés* (legally assisted witnesses) in connection with a criminal complaint for subornation of perjury against X in the Borrel case, France had violated its obligation to prevent attacks on the person and on the freedom or dignity of persons enjoying such protection. Djibouti sought to found the jurisdiction of the Court on Article 38, paragraph 5, of the Rules of Court. In accordance with that Article, the Application by Djibouti was transmitted to the French Government.

In a 25 July 2006 letter [ibid., p. 1481], France informed the Court that it consented to the jurisdiction of the Court to entertain the Application filed by Djibouti, pursuant to Article 38, paragraph 5, of its Rules. That consent made it possible to enter the case in the Court's General List on 9 August 2006 and to open the proceedings.

By an Order of 15 November 2006 [ibid.], the Court fixed 15 March 2007 as the time limit for the filing of a Memorial by Djibouti and 13 July 2007 as the time limit for the filing of a Counter-Memorial by France, which were filed within the prescribed time limits [YUN 2007, p. 1332].

Public hearings were held from 21 to 29 January 2008. At the conclusion of the hearings, the Parties presented final submissions to the Court. Djibouti requested the Court to adjudge and declare that France had violated its obligations under the 1986 Convention by not acting upon its undertaking of 27 January 2005 to execute the letter rogatory addressed to it by Djibouti dated 3 November 2004; in the alternative, by not performing its obligation pursuant to article 1 of the aforementioned Convention following its wrongful refusal given in the letter of 6 June 2005; in the further alternative, by not performing its obligation pursuant to Article 1 of the aforementioned Convention following its wrongful refusal given in the letter of 31 May 2005. Djibouti further requested the Court to adjudge and declare that France should immediately, after the delivery of the judgment by the Court, transmit the 'Borrel file' in its entirety to Djibouti, or, in the alternative, transmit the 'Borrel file' to Djibouti within the terms and conditions determined by the Court; that France had violated its obligation pursuant to the principles of customary and general international law not to attack the immunity, honour and dignity of the President of Djibouti by issuing a witness summons to the President on 17 May 2005; by repeating such attack or by attempting to repeat such attack on 14 February 2007; by making both summonses public by immediately circulating the information to the French media; and by not responding appropriately to the two letters of protest from the Ambassador of Djibouti in Paris dated 18 May 2005 and 14 February 2007, respectively; that France had violated its obligation pursuant to the principles of customary and general international law to prevent attacks on the immunity, honour and dignity of the President of Djibouti; that France should immediately after the delivery of the judgment by the Court, withdraw the witness summons dated 17 May 2005 and declare it null and void; that France had violated its obligation pursuant to the principles of customary and general international law not to attack the person, freedom and honour of the Procureur général of Djibouti and the Head of National Security of Djibouti; that France had violated its obligation pursuant to the principles of customary and general international law to prevent attacks on the person, freedom and honour of the Procureur général of Djibouti and the Head of National Security of Djibouti; that France should immediately after the delivery of the judgment by the Court, withdraw the summonses to attend as *témoins assistés* and the arrest warrants issued against the Procureur général of Djibouti and the Head of National Security of Djibouti and declare them null and void; that France, by acting contrary to or by failing to act in accordance with articles 1, 3, 4, 6 and 7 of the Treaty of Friendship and Cooperation of 1977 individually or collectively, had violated the spirit and purpose of that Treaty, as well as the obligations deriving therefrom; that France should cease its wrongful conduct and abide strictly by the obligations incumbent on it in the future; and that France should provide Djibouti with specific assurances and guarantees of non-repetition of the wrongful acts as complained by Djibouti.

France requested the Court to declare that it lacked jurisdiction to rule on those claims presented by Djibouti upon completion of its oral argument, which went beyond the subject of the dispute as set out in its Application, or to declare them inadmissible, or, in the alternative, to declare those claims to be unfounded; and to reject all the other claims made by Djibouti.

In its Judgment of 4 June, the Court, unanimously found that it had jurisdiction to adjudicate upon the dispute concerning the execution of the letter rogatory addressed by Djibouti to France on 3 November 2004. By 15 votes to 1, it found that it had jurisdiction to adjudicate upon the dispute concerning the summons as witness addressed to the President of Djibouti on

17 May 2005, and the summonses as *témoins assistés* addressed to two senior Djiboutian officials on 3 and 4 November 2004 and 17 June 2005. By 12 votes to 4, it found that it had jurisdiction to adjudicate upon the dispute concerning the summons as witness addressed to the President of Djibouti on 14 February 2007. By 13 votes to 3, it found that it had no jurisdiction to adjudicate upon the dispute concerning the arrest warrants issued against two senior Djiboutian officials on 27 September 2006. On the final submissions of Djibouti on the merits, the Court unanimously found that France, by not giving Djibouti the reasons for its refusal to execute the letter rogatory presented by the latter on 3 November 2004, failed to comply with its international obligation under article 17 of the 1986 Convention on Mutual Assistance in Criminal Matters between the two Parties and that its finding of that violation constituted appropriate satisfaction. By 15 votes to 1, the Court rejected all other final submissions by Djibouti.

Appended to the Judgment were declarations by Judges Owada, Keith, Skotnikov and Judge ad hoc Guillaume; and separate opinions by Judges Ranjeva, Koroma, Parra-Aranguren, Tomka, and Judge ad hoc Yusuf.

Maritime Dispute (Peru v. Chile)

On 16 January 2008, Peru filed an Application instituting proceedings against Chile concerning a dispute in relation to "the delimitation of the boundary between the maritime zones of the two States in the Pacific Ocean, beginning at a point on the coast called Concordia, ... the terminal point of the land boundary established pursuant to the Treaty ... of 3 June 1929", and also to recognition in favour of Peru of a "maritime zone lying within 200 nautical miles of the Coast of Peru, and thus appertaining to Peru, but which Chile considered to be part of the high seas".

In its Application, Peru claimed that the "maritime zones between Chile and Peru have never been delimited by agreement or otherwise" and that, accordingly, "the delimitation is to be determined by the Court in accordance with customary international law". Peru stated that, since the 1980s, it had consistently endeavoured to negotiate the various issues in dispute, but had "constantly met a refusal from Chile to enter into negotiations". It asserted that a note of 10 September 2004 from the Minister for Foreign Affairs of Chile to the Minister for Foreign Affairs of Peru made further attempts at negotiation impossible.

Peru consequently requested the Court to determine the course of the boundary between the maritime zones of the two States in accordance with international law, and to adjudge and declare that Peru possessed exclusive sovereign rights in the maritime area situated within the limit of 200 nautical miles from its coast, but outside Chile's exclusive economic zone or continental shelf.

As basis for the Court's jurisdiction, Peru invoked article XXXI of the Pact of Bogotá of 30 April 1948, to which both States were parties without reservation.

By an Order of 31 March, the Court fixed 20 March 2009 and 9 March 2010 as the respective time limits for the filing of a Memorial by Peru and a Counter-Memorial by Chile.

Aerial Herbicide Spraying (Ecuador v. Colombia)

On 31 March 2008, Ecuador filed an Application instituting proceedings against Colombia with respect of a dispute concerning the alleged "aerial spraying by Colombia of toxic herbicides at locations near, at and across its border with Ecuador". Ecuador maintained that the spraying had already caused serious damage to people, crops, animals and the environment on the Ecuadorian side of the frontier, and posed a grave risk of further damage over time. It further contended that it had made "repeated and sustained efforts to negotiate an end to the fumigations" but that "those negotiations had proved unsuccessful".

Ecuador requested the Court to adjudge and declare that Colombia had violated its obligations under international law by causing or allowing the deposit of toxic herbicides on the territory of Ecuador that had caused damage to human health, property and the environment; that Colombia should indemnify Ecuador for any loss or damage caused by its internationally unlawful acts, namely the use of herbicides, including by aerial dispersion, and in particular the death or injury to the health of any person or persons arising from the use of such herbicides, any loss of or damage to the property or livelihood or human rights of such persons, environmental damage or the depletion of natural resources, the costs of monitoring to identify and assess future risks to public health, human rights and the environment resulting from Colombia's use of herbicides, and any other loss or damage. It further requested the Court to adjudge and declare that Colombia should respect the sovereignty and territorial integrity of Ecuador; and forthwith take all steps necessary to prevent, on any part of its territory, the use of any toxic herbicides in such a way that they could be deposited onto the territory of Ecuador, and to prohibit the use, by means of aerial dispersion, of such herbicides in Ecuador, or on or near any part of its border with Ecuador.

As basis for the Court's jurisdiction, Ecuador invoked article XXXI of the 1948 Pact of Bogotá, to which both States were parties. Ecuador also relied on article 32 of the United Nations Convention against Illicit Traffic in Narcotic Drugs and Psychotropic

Substances [YUN 1988, p. 688], to which both countries were parties.

In its Application, Ecuador reaffirmed its opposition to the export and consumption of illegal narcotics, but stressed that the issues it presented to the Court related exclusively to the methods and locations of Colombian operations to eradicate illicit coca and poppy plantations—and the harmful effects in Ecuador of such operations.

By an Order of 30 May, the Court fixed 29 April 2009 and 29 March 2010 as the respective time limits for the filing of a Memorial by Ecuador and a Counter-Memorial by Colombia.

Interpretation of the Judgment of 31 March 2004 in the Case concerning Avena and Other Mexican Nationals (Mexico v. United States)

On 5 June 2008, Mexico filed a request for interpretation of the Judgment delivered on 31 March 2004 [YUN 2004, p. 1270] by the Court in the case concerning *Avena and Other Mexican Nationals (Mexico v. United States)* [YUN 2003, p. 1306].

Mexico invoked Article 60 of the Statute of the Court, which provided that "in the event of dispute as to the meaning or scope of the judgment, the Court shall construe it upon the request of any party". A request for interpretation opened a new case.

Mexico noted that the Court had ruled in previous cases that its jurisdiction to provide an interpretation of one of its own judgments "[was] a special jurisdiction deriving directly from Article 60 of the Statute".

In its request, Mexico recalled that in the *Avena* Judgment, the Court, inter alia, had found "that the United States had breached article 36 of the Vienna Convention on Consular Relations in the cases of 51 of the Mexican nationals by failing to inform them … of their rights to consular access and assistance" and that the Court had determined, in paragraph 153(9) of the Judgment, the remedial obligations incumbent upon the United States. Mexico contended that a fundamental dispute had arisen between the parties as to the scope and meaning of paragraph 153(9) and that the Court needed to provide guidance to the parties. It therefore sought the interpretation of said paragraph, which indicated that by 14 votes to 1, the Court found that the appropriate reparation in the case consisted in the obligation of the United States to provide, by means of its own choosing, review and reconsideration of the convictions and sentences of the Mexican nationals referred to in subparagraphs (4), (5), (6) and (7), by taking account both of the violation of the rights set forth in article 36 of the Vienna Convention on Consular Relations and of paragraphs 138 to 141 of the Judgment.

The Request of Mexico for interpretation was accompanied by a request for the indication of provisional measures on the ground that such measures "are clearly justified in order both to protect Mexico's paramount interest in the life of its nationals and to ensure the Court's ability to order the relief Mexico seeks". Public hearings were held on 19 and 20 June 2008 in order to hear the oral arguments of the Parties regarding the request for the indication of provisional measures.

By an Order of 16 July, the Court, by 7 votes to 5, found that the submission by the United States seeking the dismissal of the application filed by Mexico could not be upheld. With regard to provisional measures, by 7 votes to 5, it indicated that the United States should take all measures necessary to ensure that José Ernesto Medellín Rojas, César Roberto Fierro Reyna, Rubén Ramírez Cárdenas, Humberto Leal García and Roberto Moreno Ramos were not executed pending judgment on the request for interpretation submitted by Mexico, unless and until those five Mexican nationals received review and reconsideration consistent with paragraphs 138 to 141 of the Court's Judgment delivered on 31 March 2004 in the case concerning *Avena and Other Mexican Nationals (Mexico v. United States)*. By 11 votes to 1, it indicated that the Government of the United States should inform the Court of the measures taken to implement the Order. By 11 votes to 1, it decided that until the Court had rendered its judgment on the Request for interpretation, it would remain seized of the matters which formed the subject of the Order.

After ascertaining the views of the Parties, the Court, pursuant to Article 98, paragraph 3, of the Rules of Court, fixed 29 August 2008 as the time limit for the filing by the United States of written observations on Mexico's Request for interpretation, which was filed within the prescribed time limit.

On 28 August, Mexico, informing the Court of the execution on 5 August 2008 of José Ernesto Medellín Rojas in the state of Texas, United States, and referring to Article 98, paragraph 4 of the Rules of Court, requested the Court to afford Mexico the opportunity of furnishing further written explanations for the purpose, on the one hand, of elaborating on the merits of the Request for interpretation in the light of the written observations which the United States was due to file, and on the other, of amending its pleading to state a claim based on the violation of the Order of 16 July 2008.

On 2 September, the Court authorized Mexico and the United States to furnish further written explanations, pursuant to Article 98, paragraph 4, of the Rules of Court and fixed 17 September and 6 October 2008, respectively, as the time limits by which they were to be filed. Those written explanations were filed within the fixed time limits.

Application of the International Convention on the Elimination of All Forms of Racial Discrimination (Georgia v. Russian Federation)

On 12 August 2008, Georgia instituted proceedings against the Russian Federation on the grounds of "its actions on and around the territory of Georgia" in breach of the International Convention on the Elimination of All Forms of Racial Discrimination (CERD) [YUN 1965, p. 433]. In its Application, Georgia also sought to ensure that the individual rights under the Convention of all persons on the territory of Georgia were fully respected and protected.

Georgia claimed that the "Russian Federation, through its State organs, State agents, and other persons and entities exercising governmental authority, and through the South Ossetian and Abkhaz separatist forces and other agents acting on the instructions of, and under the direction and control of the Russian Federation, is responsible for serious violations of its fundamental obligations under [the] Convention, including articles 2, 3, 4, 5 and 6", and that the Russian Federation had "violated its obligations under [the] Convention during three distinct phases of its interventions in South Ossetia and Abkhazia" in the period from 1990 to August 2008.

Georgia requested the Court to order the Russian Federation to take all steps necessary to comply with its obligations under the Convention. As a basis for the jurisdiction of the Court, Georgia relied on article 22 of the Convention. It also reserved its right to invoke, as an additional basis of jurisdiction, article IX of the Convention on the Prevention and Punishment of the Crime of Genocide, to which Georgia and the Russian Federation were parties.

Georgia's Application was accompanied by a request for the indication of provisional measures, in order to preserve its rights under the Convention, "to protect its citizens against violent discriminatory acts by Russian armed forces, acting in concert with separatist militia and foreign mercenaries".

In its request, Georgia reiterated its contention that "beginning in the early 1990s and acting in concert with separatist forces and mercenaries in the Georgian regions of South Ossetia and Abkhazia, the Russian Federation had engaged in a systematic policy of ethnic discrimination directed against the ethnic Georgian population and other groups in those regions". It further stated that "on 8 August 2008, the Russian Federation launched a full-scale military invasion against Georgia in support of ethnic separatists in South Ossetia and Abkhazia", and that the "military aggression had resulted in hundreds of civilian deaths, extensive destruction of civilian property, and the displacement of virtually the entire ethnic Georgian population in South Ossetia". Georgia claimed that "despite the withdrawal of Georgian armed forces and the unilateral declaration of a ceasefire, Russian military operations continued beyond South Ossetia into territories under Georgian government control" and that "the continuation of those violent discriminatory acts constituted an extremely urgent threat of irreparable harm to Georgia's rights under the Convention in dispute in this case".

Georgia requested the Court, as a matter of utmost urgency, to order the following measures to protect its rights pending the determination of the case: that the Russian Federation should give full effect to its obligations under the Convention; the Russian Federation should immediately cease and desist from any and all conduct that could result, directly or indirectly, in any form of ethnic discrimination by its armed forces, or other organs, agents, and persons and entities exercising elements of governmental authority, or through separatist forces in South Ossetia and Abkhazia under its direction and control, or in territories under the occupation or effective control of Russian forces; and that the Russian Federation should, in particular, immediately cease and desist from discriminatory violations of the human rights of ethnic Georgians, including attacks against civilians and civilian objects, murder, forced displacement, denial of humanitarian assistance, extensive pillage and destruction of towns and villages, and any measures that would render permanent the denial of the right to return of internally displaced persons, in South Ossetia and adjoining regions of Georgia, and in Abkhazia and adjoining regions of Georgia, and any other territories under Russian occupation or effective control.

On 15 August, having considered the gravity of the situation, the President of the Court, acting under Article 74, paragraph 4, of the Rules of the Court, urgently called upon the Parties "to act in such a way as will enable any order the Court may take on the request for provisional measures to have its appropriate effects".

Public hearings were held from 8 to 10 October to hear the oral observations of the Parties on the request for the indication of provisional measures.

By an Order of 15 October, the Court, reminding the Parties of their duty to comply with their obligations under the Convention, indicated, by 8 votes to 7, the provisional measures that both Parties, within South Ossetia and Abkhazia and adjacent areas in Georgia, should refrain from any act of racial discrimination against persons, groups of persons or institutions; abstain from sponsoring, defending or supporting racial discrimination by any persons or organizations; do all in their power, whenever and wherever possible, to ensure, without distinction as to national or ethnic origin: security of persons, the right of persons to freedom of movement and residence within the border of the State, and the protection of the property of displaced persons and of refugees; and do all in their power to ensure that public authorities and public institutions under their control or influence did not engage in acts of racial discrimination against persons, groups of persons or institutions.

By 8 votes to 7, the Court indicated that both Parties should facilitate and refrain from placing any impediment to humanitarian assistance in support of the rights to which, under the Convention, the local populations were entitled. By 8 votes to 7, it indicated that each Party should refrain from any action which might prejudice the rights of the other Party in respect of whatever judgment the Court might render in the case, or which might aggravate or extend the dispute before the Court or make it more difficult to resolve. By 8 votes to 7, it indicated that each Party should inform the Court as to its compliance with the provisional measures.

Appended to the Order was a declaration by Judge ad hoc Gaja and a joint dissenting opinion by Vice-President Al-Khasawneh and Judges Ranjeva, Shi, Koroma, Tomka, Bennouna and Skotnikov.

By an Order of 2 December, the President fixed 2 September 2009 as the time limit for the filing of a Memorial by Georgia and 2 July 2010 as the time limit for the filing of a Counter-Memorial by the Russian Federation.

Application of the Interim Accord of 13 September 1995 (The former Yugoslav Republic of Macedonia v. Greece)

On 17 November 2008, the former Yugoslav Republic of Macedonia (FYROM) instituted proceedings against Greece for what it described as "a flagrant violation of its obligations under article 11" of the Interim Accord signed by the Parties on 13 September 1995.

In its Application, FYROM requested the Court to protect its rights under the Interim Accord and to ensure that it was allowed to exercise its rights as an independent State acting in accordance with international law, including the right to pursue membership of international organizations. It contended that in accordance with article 11, paragraph 1, of the Interim Accord, Greece had undertaken a binding obligation under international law not to object to the application by, or the membership of, FYROM in international, multilateral and regional organizations and institutions of which Greece was a member. However, Greece reserved the right to object to any membership referred to above, if and to the extent FYROM was to be referred to in such organization or institution differently than in paragraph 2 of UN Security Council resolution 817(1993) [YUN 1993, p. 208], i.e. as "the former Yugoslav Republic of Macedonia".

FYROM contended in its Application that Greece violated its rights under the Interim Accord by objecting, in April 2008, to its application to join the North Atlantic Treaty Organization (NATO). It contended, in particular, that Greece vetoed its application to join NATO because Greece desired "to resolve the difference between the Parties concerning the constitutional name of the Applicant as an essential precondition" for such membership.

FYROM argued that it had met its obligations under the Interim Accord not to be designated as a member of NATO with any designation other than "the former Yugoslav Republic of Macedonia" and affirmed that "the subject of this dispute did not concern—either directly or indirectly—the difference that had arisen between Greece and itself over its name".

FYROM requested the Court to order Greece to immediately take all necessary steps to comply with its obligations under article 11, paragraph 1 of the Interim Accord and "to cease and desist from objecting in any way, whether directly or indirectly, to its membership in NATO and/or of any other 'international, multilateral and regional organizations and institutions' of which [Greece] was a member".

As a basis for the jurisdiction of the Court, FYROM invoked article 21, paragraph 2, of the Interim Accord, which provided that "any difference or dispute that arises between the Parties concerning the interpretation or implementation of the Accord may be submitted by either of them to ICJ, except for the differences referred to in article 5, paragraph 1".

Jurisdictional Immunities of the State (Germany v. Italy)

On 23 December 2008, Germany instituted proceedings against Italy, alleging that "through its judicial practice ... Italy has infringed and continues to infringe its obligations towards Germany under international law".

In its Application, Germany contended that "in recent years, Italian judicial bodies have repeatedly disregarded the jurisdictional immunity of Germany as a sovereign State. The critical stage of that development was reached by the judgment of the Corte di Cassazione of 11 March 2004 in the *Ferrini* case, where that court declared that Italy held jurisdiction with regard to a claim ... brought by a person who during World War II had been deported to Germany to perform forced labour in the armaments industry". After that judgment had been rendered, numerous other proceedings were instituted against Germany before Italian courts by persons who had also suffered injury as a consequence of the armed conflict. The *Ferrini* judgment having been recently confirmed "in a series of decisions delivered on 29 May 2008 and in a further judgment of 21 October 2008", Germany was concerned "that hundreds of additional cases may be brought against it".

Germany recalled that enforcement measures had already been taken against German assets in Italy: a "judicial mortgage" on Villa Vigoni, the German-Italian centre for cultural exchange, had been recorded in the land register. In addition to the claims brought against it by Italian nationals, Germany also cited "attempts by Greek nationals to enforce in Italy a judgment obtained in Greece on account of a ... massacre committed by German military units during their withdrawal in 1944". Germany concluded its Application by requesting the Court to adjudge and declare that Italy, by allowing civil claims based on violations of international humanitarian law by the German Reich during World War II from September 1943 to May 1945 to be brought against Germany, committed violations of obligations under international law in that it had failed to respect the jurisdictional immunity which Germany enjoyed under international law; by taking measures of constraint against Villa Vigoni, German State property used for government non-commercial purposes, also committed violations of Germany's jurisdictional immunity; and by declaring Greek judgments based on occurrences similar to those defined above enforceable in Italy, committed a further breach of Germany's jurisdictional immunity. Accordingly, Germany requested the Court to adjudge and declare that Italy's international responsibility was engaged; that Italy must, by means of its own choosing, take any and all steps to ensure that all the decisions of its courts and other judicial authorities infringing Germany's sovereign immunity became unenforceable; and that Italy must take any and all steps to ensure that in the future Italian courts would not entertain legal actions against Germany founded on the occurrences described in the request above. Germany reserved the right to request the Court to indicate provisional measures in accordance with Article 41 of the Statute of the Court, "should measures of constraint be taken by Italian authorities against German State assets, in particular, diplomatic and other premises that enjoy protection against such measures pursuant to general rules of international law".

As the basis for the jurisdiction of the Court, Germany invoked article 1 of the European Convention for the Peaceful Settlement of Disputes of 29 April 1957, ratified by Italy on 29 January 1960 and by Germany on 18 April 1961. That article stated that "The High Contracting Parties shall submit to the judgment of ICJ all international legal disputes which may arise between them including, in particular, those concerning the interpretation of a treaty; any question of international law; the existence of any fact which, if established, would constitute a breach of an international obligation; and the nature or extent of the reparation to be made for the breach of an international obligation". Germany asserted that, although the present case was between two Member States of the European Union, the Court of Justice of the European Communities in Luxembourg had no jurisdiction to entertain it, since the dispute was not governed by any of the jurisdictional clauses in the treaties on European integration. It added that outside of that "specific framework" the Member States "continue to live with one another under the regime of general international law".

The Application by Germany was accompanied by a Joint Declaration adopted on the occasion of German-Italian Governmental Consultations in Trieste on 18 November 2008, whereby both Governments declared that they "share the ideals of reconciliation, solidarity and integration, which form the basis of the European construction". In the declaration, Germany "fully acknowledges the untold suffering inflicted on Italian men and women" during World War II. Italy, for its part, "respects Germany's decision to apply to ICJ for a ruling on the principle of state immunity [and] is of the view that the ICJ's ruling on State immunity will help to clarify this complex issue".

Advisory proceedings

Accordance with International Law of the Unilateral Declaration of Independence by the Provisional Institutions of Self-Government of Kosovo

In response to General Assembly resolution 63/3 of 8 October 2008 (see p. 1404), which referred to Article 65 of the ICJ Statute and requested the Court to render an advisory opinion on the question of whether the unilateral declaration of independence by the Provisional Institutions of Self-Government of Kosovo was in accordance with international law, the Court, by an Order of 17 October 2008, decided that the United Nations and its Member States were considered likely to be able to furnish information on the question submitted to the Court for an advisory opinion. It fixed 17 April 2009 as the time limit within which written statements on the question could be presented to the Court, and 17 July 2009 as the time limit within which States and organizations having presented written statements could submit written comments on the other statements. The Court further decided that since the unilateral declaration of independence by the Provisional Institutions of Self-Government of Kosovo of 17 February 2008 was the subject of the question submitted to the Court for an advisory opinion, the authors of the declaration were considered likely to be able to furnish information on the question and were invited to make written contributions to the Court within the time limits.

Communication. On 15 August [A/63/195], Serbia transmitted to the Secretary-General a letter requesting the inclusion of a supplementary item entitled, "Request for an advisory opinion of the International Court of Justice on whether the unilateral declaration of independence of Kosovo is in accordance with international law" in the agenda of the sixty-third (2008) session of the General Assembly, with subsequent consideration of the item directly at a plenary meeting of the Assembly.

GENERAL ASSMEBLY ACTION

On 8 October [meeting 22], the General Assembly adopted **resolution 63/3** [draft: A/63/L.2] by recorded vote (77-6-74) [agenda item 71].

Request for an advisory opinion of the International Court of Justice on whether the unilateral declaration of independence of Kosovo is in accordance with international law

The General Assembly,

Mindful of the purposes and principles of the United Nations,

Bearing in mind its functions and powers under the Charter of the United Nations,

Recalling that on 17 February 2008 the Provisional Institutions of Self-Government of Kosovo declared independence from Serbia,

Aware that this act has been received with varied reactions by the Members of the United Nations as to its compatibility with the existing international legal order,

Decides, in accordance with Article 96 of the Charter of the United Nations, to request the International Court of Justice, pursuant to Article 65 of the Statute of the Court, to render an advisory opinion on the following question:

"Is the unilateral declaration of independence by the Provisional Institutions of Self-Government of Kosovo in accordance with international law?"

RECORDED VOTE ON RESOLUTION 63/3:

In favour: Algeria, Angola, Antigua and Barbuda, Argentina, Azerbaijan, Belarus, Bolivia, Botswana, Brazil, Brunei Darussalam, Cambodia, Chile, China, Congo, Costa Rica, Cuba, Cyprus, Democratic People's Republic of Korea, Democratic Republic of the Congo, Djibouti, Dominica, Dominican Republic, Egypt, El Salvador, Equatorial Guinea, Eritrea, Fiji, Greece, Guatemala, Guinea, Guyana, Honduras, Iceland, India, Indonesia, Iran, Jamaica, Kazakhstan, Kenya, Kyrgyzstan, Lesotho, Liechtenstein, Madagascar, Mauritius, Mexico, Montenegro, Myanmar, Namibia, Nicaragua, Niger, Nigeria, Norway, Panama, Papua New Guinea, Paraguay, Philippines, Romania, Russian Federation, Saint Vincent and the Grenadines, Serbia, Singapore, Slovakia, Solomon Islands, South Africa, Spain, Sri Lanka, Sudan, Suriname, Swaziland, Syrian Arab Republic, Timor-Leste, United Republic of Tanzania, Uruguay, Uzbekistan, Viet Nam, Zambia, Zimbabwe.

Against: Albania, Marshall Islands, Micronesia, Nauru, Palau, United States.

Abstaining: Afghanistan, Andorra, Armenia, Australia, Austria, Bahamas, Bahrain, Bangladesh, Barbados, Belgium, Belize, Benin, Bhutan, Bulgaria, Burkina Faso, Cameroon, Canada, Colombia, Croatia, Czech Republic, Denmark, Estonia, Finland, France, Georgia, Germany, Ghana, Grenada, Haiti, Hungary, Ireland, Israel, Italy, Japan, Jordan, Latvia, Lebanon, Lithuania, Luxembourg, Malaysia, Malta, Moldova, Monaco, Mongolia, Morocco, Nepal, Netherlands, New Zealand, Oman, Pakistan, Peru, Poland, Portugal, Qatar, Republic of Korea, Saint Lucia, Samoa, San Marino, Saudi Arabia, Senegal, Sierra Leone, Slovenia, Sweden, Switzerland, Thailand, The former Yugoslav Republic of Macedonia, Togo, Trinidad and Tobago, Uganda, Ukraine, United Arab Emirates, United Kingdom, Vanuatu, Yemen.

By **decision 63/551** of 24 December, the Assembly took note of the report of the Fifth (Administrative and Budgetary) Committee [A/63/654] on the programme budget implications of resolution 63/3. On the same date, it decided that the agenda item on the "Request for an advisory opinion of ICJ on whether the unilateral declaration of independence of Kosovo is in accordance with international law" would remain for consideration during its resumed sixty-third (2009) session (**decision 63/552**).

Other questions

Functioning and organization of the Court

Conditions of service and compensation

In a 12 March report [A/62/7/Add.36] on the conditions of service and compensation for officials other than Secretariat officials, the Advisory Committee on Administrative and Budgetary Questions (ACABQ), with regard to standards of travel and the assignment grant, recommended that no changes be made in the provisions of articles 1 and 2, and article 3, paragraph 1 *(a)*(ii) of the travel and subsistence regulations of ICJ. ACABQ noted the concern expressed by the ICJ President in April 2007 [YUN 2007, p. 1333] regarding members' emoluments and the inequalities among judges that would be created by the General Assembly's proposed action, which took effect with the adoption of resolution 61/262 [ibid., p. 1499], as well as a letter dated 29 May 2007. Therein, the ICJ President notified the Secretary-General that an ad hoc judge appointed to sit in the case concerning the territorial and maritime dispute between Nicaragua and Colombia following the adoption of resolution 61/262 would receive the same emolument as the ad hoc judge appointed prior to the adoption of the resolution. The Committee noted that such action was incompatible with the decision of the Assembly in resolution 61/262 and upon inquiry, was informed that a similar situation could arise in a limited number of other cases pending before the Court. ACABQ stated that the Assembly might wish to examine the impact of the implementation of resolution 61/262 on the position of ad hoc judges sitting in those cases. As the UN Legal Counsel largely concurred with the arguments pertaining to resolution 61/262 presented by the ICJ President, the Committee noted that the interpretation could affect the exercise of the Assembly's mandate under Article 32 of the Statute of the Court. The Committee further noted the financial implications of two options proposed by the Secretary-General to address the issue and, on retirement benefits for members of the Court, recommended that the Assembly defer consideration of that issue pending receipt of the pension study.

On 3 April, by **decision 62/547**, the Assembly endorsed ACABQ's conclusions and recommendations; decided to set, effective 1 April 2008, the annual net base salary of ICJ members at $158,000, with the corresponding post adjustment per multiplier point equal to 1 per cent of the net base salary, to which would be applied the post adjustment multiplier, as appropriate, taking into account the adjustment mechanism proposed by the Secretary-General; and decided to revert to the issue of the pension scheme during the second part of its resumed sixty-second (2008) session.

In her 30 October address to the Assembly, ICJ President Judge Rosalyn Higgins noted her appreciation of the Assembly's action to meet the concerns expressed by the Court and for having resolved that matter. She added that the principle of equality among judges was central to the Court's function as the principal judicial organ of the United Nations.

Composition of the Court

Election of judges

In a 30 July memorandum [A/63/186-S/2008/502], the Secretary-General notified the General Assembly and the Security Council that the terms of office of five members of the Court would expire on 5 February 2009, and therefore the Assembly and the Council would elect five judges for a term of office of nine years, beginning on 6 February 2009. He provided information on ICJ's composition and described the procedure in the Assembly and the Council for the election of a new member of the Court. By notes of 30 July [A/63/187-S/2008/503] and 31 July [A/63/188-S/2008/504], the Secretary-General submitted, respectively, the list of candidates nominated by national groups and their curricula vitae.

In a 23 September letter [A/63/373-S/2008/619], Spain informed the Secretary-General that the list of candidates nominated by national groups to fill ICJ vacancies did not include the nomination by the Spanish national group of Antônio Augusto Cançado Trindade (Brazil), although it transmitted the nomination to the Secretariat in a timely manner. In notes of 31 October [A/63/187/Add.1-S/2008/503/Add.1] and 3 November [A/63/187/Add.2-S/2008/503/Add.2], the Secretary-General provided information on additional nominations by national groups and on the withdrawal of a candidate.

On 6 November, the Assembly and the Council elected five members of the Court to fill the vacancies occurring on 6 February 2009 (**decision 63/406**).

Modernization of the Court

In her 30 October address to the General Assembly, the ICJ President stated that the Court would seek funds for the replacement and modernization of the conference systems and audio-visual equipment in its historic courtroom, the Great Hall of Justice. She noted that updating the technology was essential to enhancing communication among the judges and the parties during the oral hearings. The upgrading would also facilitate the immediate sharing of data and documents and the clear display of maps and images relevant to a given case. She said that no modern court could operate without those electronic facilities and that the modernization would enable the Court to achieve greater efficiency.

Trust Fund to Assist States in the Settlement of Disputes

In August [A/63/229], the Secretary-General reported on the activities and status of the Trust Fund to Assist States in the Settlement of Disputes through ICJ since the submission of his 2007 report [YUN 2007, p. 1333]. The Fund, established in 1989 [YUN 1989, p. 818], provided financial assistance to States for expenses incurred in connection with a dispute submitted to ICJ by way of a special agreement or an application, or the execution of a Judgment of ICJ.

During the period under review (1 July 2007–30 June 2008), the Fund did not receive any applications for financial assistance from States. Five States contributed to the Fund, which as at 30 June had a balance of some $2.6 million.

Noting that in the period under review the amount of financial assistance awarded exceeded the amount of contributions by more than double, and the overall number of contributions remained low, the Secretary-General urged States and other entities to consider making substantial contributions to the Fund and to contribute on a regular basis.

Chapter II

International tribunals and court

In 2008 the international tribunals for the former Yugoslavia and Rwanda, as well as the International Criminal Court (ICC), worked towards the completion of their mandates.

The International Tribunal for the Prosecution of Persons Responsible for Serious Violations of International Humanitarian Law Committed in the Territory of the Former Yugoslavia since 1991 (ICTY) took steps towards implementing its completion strategy, focusing on the most senior-level individuals accused of the most serious crimes. Only five cases remained to be started, four of which involved late arrests. The Tribunal was running seven trials simultaneously in its three courtrooms, involving 27 accused.

The International Criminal Tribunal for the Prosecution of Persons Responsible for Genocide and Other Serious Violations of International Humanitarian Law Committed in the Territory of Rwanda and Rwandan Citizens Responsible for Genocide and Other Such Violations Committed in the Territory of Neighbouring States between 1 January and 31 December 1994 (ICTR) remained committed to meeting its completion strategy targets while respecting due process. By the end of the year, it had apprehended and detained 66 persons out of some 81 persons indicted, including the Prime Minister of the Interim Government of Rwanda during the genocide, 11 Ministers of that Government in 1994, senior military officials and members of the clergy. The Tribunal concluded all its multiple-accused cases, with one exception, involving some 14 accused persons. No new arrests could be reported for the 13 fugitives still at large as the end of the Tribunal's mandate drew near.

In July, during its fifth year of functioning, the ICC marked the tenth anniversary of the adoption of the Rome Statute, which established the Court. It continued its proceedings with respect to situations of concern in four countries. At the end of July, there were seven warrants of arrest outstanding.

International Tribunal for the Former Yugoslavia

In 2008, the International Tribunal for the Former Yugoslavia (ICTY), established by Security Council resolution 827(1993) [YUN 1993, p. 440] and based in The Hague, took steps towards implementing its completion strategy [YUN 2002, p. 1275] endorsed by Council resolution 1503(2003) [YUN 2003, p. 1330]. Proceedings before the Tribunal focused on the most senior-level individuals accused of the most serious crimes. The Office of the Prosecutor strengthened its relations with prosecutors and courts in the region through training sessions, conferences and seminars. Meanwhile, the Registry continued negotiations for the relocation of witnesses and enforcement of sentence agreements, concluding three new agreements.

On 1 January, Serge Brammertz (Belgium) began his four-year term as ICTY Prosecutor, replacing Carla Del Ponte (Switzerland) [YUN 2007, p. 1339]. On 4 November, Judge Patrick Robinson (Jamaica) was elected as the new ICTY president, with effect from 17 November, when the term of office of Fausto Pocar (Italy) expired.

During the year, the Security Council adopted three resolutions—1800(2008), 1837(2008) and 1849(2008)—on the appointment of judges and extension of their terms (see pp. 1410, 1411 & 1412). In December, acting on the recommendation of the Fifth (Administrative and Budgetary) Committee, the General Assembly adopted resolution 63/255 on the financing of the Tribunal (see p. 1414).

The ICTY President informed the Security Council on 12 December [S/PV.6041] that the Tribunal's achievements, to date, far surpassed those of any other international or hybrid court, both in respect of the number of accused tried and in its contribution to the development of international criminal law. Of the 161 persons indicted by the Tribunal, proceedings had been fully concluded against 116 of them.

Only five cases remained to be started, four of which involved late arrests—those of Zdravko Tolimir, Vlastimir Đorđević, Stojan Župljanin and Radovan Karadžić. The fifth case, that of Jovica Stanišić and Franko Simatović, had been delayed owing to the ill health of one of the accused. The Tribunal was running seven trials simultaneously in its three courtrooms, with its eighth trial, that of Mr. Đorđević, scheduled to begin in January 2009. Those trials involved a total of 27 accused.

The activities of ICTY were covered in two reports to the Security Council and the General Assembly, for the periods 1 August 2007 to 31 July 2008 [A/63/210-S/2008/515] and 1 August 2008 to 31 July 2009 [A/64/205-S/2009/394]. On 13 October, the Assembly took note of the 2007/2008 report (**decision 63/506**).

The Chambers

During the reporting period of 1 August 2007 to 31 July 2008 [A/63/210], the Tribunal's three Trial Chambers operated at full capacity, running eight trials simultaneously. The Trial Chambers rendered 213 decisions on pretrial matters in eight cases, heard one case of contempt and rendered five judgements. The Appeals Chamber issued 123 decisions comprising six appeals from judgement, 32 interlocutory appeals, 79 pre-appeal decisions and 6 review, reconsideration or other decisions. ICTY had 30 judges from 27 countries. The Chambers were composed of 14 permanent judges; two permanent judges from the International Criminal Tribunal for Rwanda serving in the Appeals Chamber; and 14 ad litem (short-term) judges.

New arrests

On 11 June, Stojan Župljanin, charged with crimes against humanity and violations of the laws or customs of war allegedly committed in Bosnia and Herzegovina in 1992, was arrested by Serbian authorities. He was transferred to The Hague on 21 June 2008. The Office of the Prosecutor filed a motion for joinder (consolidation) of the Župljanin case with the case of Mićo Stanišić, who was facing the same charges.

On 21 July, Radovan Karadžić, a fugitive for over a decade, was arrested by Serbian authorities and transferred to The Hague on 30 July. The Trial Chamber had previously established the existence of a joint criminal enterprise, involving Mr. Karadžić and other Bosnian Serb leaders, intended to "ethnically recompose the territories targeted by the Bosnian-Serb leadership by drastically reducing the proportion of Bosnian Muslims and Bosnian Croats through expulsion" [YUN 2006, p. 1489].

Serbia's National Security Council, the Action Team in charge of tracking ICTY fugitives, and the Office of the War Crimes Prosecutor had a central role in the arrests. The failure to arrest the remaining two fugitives, Ratko Mladić and Goran Hadžić, remained a matter of concern to the Tribunal.

Ongoing cases and trials

Radovan Karadžić, former President of Republika Srpska and Supreme Commander of its armed forces, was charged under 11 counts with genocide, crimes against humanity, and violations of the laws or customs of war allegedly committed in Bosnia and Herzegovina between 1992 and 1995. Following his arrest and transfer to the Tribunal on 30 July 2008, pleas of not guilty were entered on his behalf to all charges. The pretrial conference was expected to be held in September 2009. Mr. Karadžić was President of the three-member Presidency of the Republika Srpska from its creation on 12 May 1992 until 17 December 1992, and thereafter sole President of Republika Srpska and Supreme Commander of its armed forces. The Serbian authorities announced his arrest on 21 July 2008.

In the case against Ante Gotovina, Ivan Čermak and Mladen Markač, who were charged with crimes against humanity and violations of the laws or customs of war allegedly committed in Croatia in 1995, the trial commenced on 10 March 2008. The indictment against Mr. Gotovina, a former high-ranking Croatian military official, was unsealed in 2001 [YUN 2001, p. 1199]. After evading arrest for almost four years, Mr. Gotovina was arrested in 2005 in the Canary Islands by the Spanish authorities and transferred to The Hague [YUN 2005, p. 1388]. He was charged with crimes against humanity and violations of the laws or customs of war, allegedly committed during and after a Croatian offensive in the Krajina region of Croatia in 1995 [YUN 1995, p. 580]. On 14 July 2006 [YUN 2006, p. 1489], the Trial Chamber decided to join two cases involving Mr. Gotovina and Messrs. Čermak and Markač [YUN 2004, p. 1276] in one indictment and accepted proposed amendments to the indictment. The three were charged with persecutions, deportation, inhumane acts, plunder of public or private property, wanton destruction of cities, towns or villages, murder, and cruel treatment; all allegedly committed against Serbs in 1995, during, and in the aftermath of a Croatian military offensive. At that time, Mr. Gotovina and Mr. Čermak were senior military commanders on the ground, while Mr. Markač was the commander of the Croatian Special Police. On 5 December 2006, the accused made further appearances to enter pleas to the new counts in the joinder (consolidated) indictment. All three pleaded not guilty [YUN 2007, p. 1335].

The trial of Ramush Haradinaj, Idriz Balaj and Lahi Brahimaj, who were charged with crimes against humanity and violations of the laws or customs of war allegedly committed in Kosovo in 1998, began on 5 March 2008. Judgement was delivered on 3 April. Mr. Brahimaj was sentenced to six years of imprisonment. The accused Haradinaj and Balaj were acquitted. Mr. Haradinaj and Mr. Brahimaj, who belonged to the Kosovo Liberation Army, had surrendered to the Tribunal on 9 March 2005 [YUN 2005, p. 1388]. Mr. Balaj, who was serving a sentence pursuant to a conviction in 2002, had been transferred to the Tribunal on the same day [YUN 2007, p. 1335].

The trial of Rasim Delić, who was charged with violations of the laws or customs of war allegedly committed in Bosnia and Herzegovina between July 1993 and December 1995, commenced on 9 July 2007, and the evidence closed on 11 June 2008. Judgement was rendered on 15 September, when he was sentenced to three years of imprisonment. Mr. Delić, commander of the main staff of the Army of Bosnia-Herzegovina, was indicted on 15 February 2005 and charged, on the basis of his superior command responsibility, with four counts of violations of the laws or customs of war [YUN 2005, p. 1388].

Milan Martić, a former political leader of Croatian Serbs, was sentenced to 35 years of imprisonment on 12 June 2007 for crimes against humanity and violations of the laws or customs of war committed in Croatia between 1991 and 1995. Mr. Martić was found to have participated in a joint criminal enterprise that included former Serbian President Slobodan Milošević, whose aim was to create a unified Serbian State through a systematic campaign of crimes against non-Serbs inhabiting areas in Croatia and Bosnia and Herzegovina envisaged to become parts of such a State. He was also convicted of ordering rocket attacks on downtown Zagreb on 2 and 3 May 1995 in which seven people died and more than 200 were wounded [YUN 2007, p. 1336]. On 8 October 2008, the Appeals Chamber rendered final judgement on the case, dismissing nine of the 10 grounds of Mr. Martić's appeal and affirming the 35-year sentence of imprisonment handed down at the trial.

Mile Mrkšić, Miroslav Radić and Veselin Šljivančanin were indicted in 1997 [YUN 1997, p. 1322] for alleged involvement in the execution of some 200 Croatians and non-Serbs removed from Vukovar hospital in 1991 [YUN 2006, p. 1490]. On 27 September 2007, the Tribunal sentenced Messrs. Mrkšić and Šljivančanin, former senior officers of the Yugoslav People's Army (JNA), to 20 years' imprisonment and five years' imprisonment, respectively, for their role in the crimes at Ovčara. Mr. Radić, a former JNA captain, was acquitted of all charges [YUN 2007, p. 1336]. Appeals for Messrs. Mrkšić and Šljivančanin were pending.

With regard to the Popović et al. case [YUN 2005, p. 1390], the trial commenced on 14 July 2006 [YUN 2006, p. 1488]. The prosecution case closed on 7 February 2008 and the defence case began on 2 June. The indictment jointly charged Vujadin Popović, Ljubiša Beara, Drago Nikolić, Ljubomir Borovčanin and Vinko Pandurević with genocide, conspiracy to commit genocide, extermination, murder, persecutions, forcible transfer and deportation, committed in 1995. It also charged Radivoje Miletić and Milan Gvero with crimes against humanity and a violation of the laws or customs of war. All the charges related to the mass murder and ethnic cleansing of Bosnian Muslims in Srebrenica after the fall of the former UN safe haven to Bosnian Serb forces in July 1995 [YUN 2007, p. 1336].

The trial of Ljube Boškoski and Johan Tarčulovski, who were charged with violations of the laws or customs of war allegedly committed against ethnic Albanians in the former Yugoslav Republic of Macedonia (FYROM) in August 2001, commenced on 16 April 2007. Mr. Boškoski was the Minister of Interior of FYROM between May 2001 and November 2002, and Mr. Tarčulovski was a police officer acting as an escort inspector to the President's security unit in 2001 [YUN 2007, p. 1336]. The trial concluded on 8 May 2008, and judgement was delivered on 10 July. Mr. Boškoski was acquitted on all counts and Mr. Tarčulovski was sentenced to 12 years of imprisonment.

The trial of Vojislav Šešelj, who was charged with 14 counts of crimes against humanity and violations of the laws or customs of war in Croatia, Bosnia and Herzegovina and Vojvodina (Serbia) from 1991 until 1993 [YUN 2003, p. 1311; YUN 2004, p. 1277], commenced on 27 November 2006 in his absence [YUN 2006, p. 1490]. His trial began anew on 7 November 2007 and the presentation of evidence began on 11 December. Mr. Šešelj was the founder and president of the Serbian Radical Party and was elected as a member of the Assembly of the Republic of Serbia in June 1991. The indictment alleged that he was a leader of a movement whose purpose was the permanent forcible removal of a majority of the non-Serb populations from approximately one third of the territory of Croatia, from large parts of Bosnia and Herzegovina and from parts of Vojvodina, in order to make those areas part of a Serb-dominated state [YUN 2007, p. 1337].

In May 2006, the Trial Chamber charged Jovica Stanišić, former head of the State Security Service (DB) of the Ministry of Internal Affairs of the Republic of Serbia, and Franko Simatović, Commander of the DB Special Operations Unit, with four counts of crimes against humanity and one count of violation of the laws or customs of war [YUN 2007, p. 1337]. Owing to the health condition of Mr. Stanišić, the Appeals Chamber on 16 May 2008 adjourned the proceedings for a minimum of three months and directed the Trial Chamber to reassess his state of health before deciding when the trial should commence.

In the case against Milan Lukić, the leader of a paramilitary group called the "White Eagles" or "Avengers," and his cousin Sredoje Lukić, the trial commenced on 9 July 2008 and the prosecution completed its case-in-chief on 11 November. Sredoje Lukić's defence case commenced on 1 December and concluded on 2 December. Milan Lukić's defence case commenced on 17 December. The two were charged with murdering approximately 70 Bosnian Muslim women, children and elderly in a house in Višegrad, by forcing the victims into the house, barricading all the exits and throwing in several explosive devices.

They were also charged with beating Bosnian Muslim men who were detained in the detention camp at the Uzamnica military barracks in Višegrad [YUN 2007, p. 1337].

Momčilo Perišić was charged with crimes against humanity and violations of the laws or customs of war allegedly committed in Bosnia and Herzegovina and Croatia between October 1992 and December 1995. According to the indictment, between August 1993 and November 1995, Mr. Perišić, Chief of the General Staff of the Yugoslav Army, aided and abetted the planning, preparation, or execution of a military campaign of artillery and mortar shelling and sniping onto civilian areas of Sarajevo, killing and wounding thousands of civilians [ibid.]. His trial commenced on 2 October 2008.

Milan Milutinović, Nikola Šainović, Dragoljub Ojdanić, Nebojša Pavković, Vladimir Lazarević and Sreten Lukić [YUN 2006, p. 1487], in the Milutinović et al. case, were charged with crimes against humanity and violations of the laws or customs of war allegedly committed in Kosovo in 1999. Their trial commenced on 10 July 2006. The Chamber recessed on 21 May 2008, and the President reported to the Security Council regarding Serbia's failure to serve a summons on a potential Chamber witness. Following that report, Serbia served a subpoena on the witness, and in July the Chamber heard the witness' testimony. Closing arguments were made from 19 to 27 August.

Vlastimir Đorđević, a former senior Serbian police official, was arrested on 17 June 2007 in Montenegro and transferred to the Tribunal the next day. Indicted in October 2003 [YUN 2003, p. 1312], he managed to evade arrest for almost four years. At his initial appearance on 16 July 2007, he pleaded not guilty to all counts. Mr. Đorđević was charged with deportation, inhumane acts (forcible transfer), murder and persecutions in Kosovo. Originally his case was part of the Milutinović et al. case [YUN 2005, p. 1390], but when that case began with Mr. Đorđević still at large, his case was severed from that of the others [YUN 2007, p. 1337]. As at year's end 2008, his case had not yet come to trial.

Jadranko Prlić, Bruno Stojić, Slobodan Praljak, Milivoj Petković, Valentin Ćorić and Berislav Pušić, in the Prlić et al. case, were charged with grave breaches of the 1949 Geneva Conventions, crimes against humanity and violations of the laws or customs of war allegedly committed against Serbs and Muslims in the Croatian-held part of Bosnia and Herzegovina between November 1991 and April 1994. [YUN 2006, p. 1487]. Their trial commenced on 26 April 2006. The six surrendered in April 2004 [YUN 2004, p. 1276] and pleaded not guilty. The prosecution case ended on 24 January 2008, and the Chamber began hearing defence evidence on 5 May.

On 21 December 2007, Dragomir Milošević, a former Bosnian Serb Army General, who was found guilty of a range of crimes committed against civilians during the final months of the 1992–1995 siege of Sarajevo, was sentenced to 33 years' imprisonment. Mr. Milošević was convicted on five counts of terror, murder and inhumane acts conducted during a campaign of sniping and shelling which resulted in the injury and death of a great number of civilians in the besieged Bosnian capital [YUN 2007, p. 1338]. The case was in the appellate process.

Mićo Stanišić, former Minister of Internal Affairs of Bosnia and Herzegovina in charge of the police of the Republika Srpska, was charged with crimes against humanity and violations of the laws or customs of war allegedly committed in Bosnia and Herzegovina in 1992 [ibid.]. On 16 July 2008, the Prosecution filed a motion requesting that the cases of Stanišić and Župljanin be joined. On 23 September, the Trial Chamber granted the motion and ordered the Prosecution to file an amended consolidated indictment. The joinder indictment was filed on 29 September. According to the indictment, Messrs. Stanišić and Župljanin participated in a joint criminal enterprise as co-perpetrators. They were charged with persecutions, extermination, murder, torture, inhumane acts (including forcible transfer) and deportation; and murder, torture, and cruel treatment. Mr. Stanišić was transferred to The Hague on 11 March 2005, Mr. Župljanin on 21 June 2008.

Zdravko Tolimir was charged with genocide, conspiracy to commit genocide, crimes against humanity and a violation of the laws or customs of war allegedly committed in Bosnia and Herzegovina in 1995. Mr. Tolimir was Assistant Commander for Intelligence and Security of the Bosnian Serb Army, Main Staff, reporting directly to the Commander of the Main Staff, General Ratko Mladić. He was arrested on 31 May 2007 in Bosnia and Herzegovina and transferred to The Hague on 1 June [YUN 2007, p. 1335]. His trial was expected to commence in December 2009.

On 17 July, the Appeals Chamber rendered a final judgement in the case of Pavle Strugar. Dismissing all grounds of appeal by Mr. Strugar and taking his post-trial health into account as a mitigating circumstance, it entered a new sentence of seven and a half years of imprisonment. Mr. Strugar, a former commander in the Yugoslav People's Army, had been sentenced by the Trial Chamber in 2005 to eight years' imprisonment [YUN 2005, p. 1389] for having failed to prevent attacks against civilians and the destruction of property in Dubrovnik in 1991 [YUN 2003, p. 1314; YUN 2004, p. 1279].

On 22 April, the Appeals Chamber allowed Enver Hadžihasanović's appeal in part and reduced his sentence of five years of imprisonment [YUN 2006, p. 1486] to three years and six months of imprisonment. Amir Kubura's appeal was also allowed in part, and the Appeals Chamber reduced his sentence of two years and six months of imprisonment [ibid.] to two years of imprisonment.

Naser Orić, a former senior commander of Bosnian Muslim forces in and around Srebrenica, was sentenced in 2006 to two years in prison, was credited for time spent in custody since 2003 [YUN 2003, p. 1311] and was released. Both the defence and the prosecution filed notices of appeal [YUN 2006, p. 1489]. On 3 July 2008, the Appeals Chamber reversed his conviction, finding him not guilty.

Judges of the Court

Ad litem judges

In letters forwarded by the Secretary-General to the Security Council on 31 December 2007 [YUN 2007, p. 1339], 22 January 2008 [S/2008/44] and 8 February 2008 [S/2008/99], the ICTY President, Judge Fausto Pocar, outlined the Tribunal's need for additional ad litem judges, beyond the Tribunal's statutory maximum of 12, and requested that the Council make provisions to meet that need.

SECURITY COUNCIL ACTION

On 20 February [meeting 5841], the Security Council unanimously adopted **resolution 1800(2008)**. The draft [S/2008/107] was prepared in consultations among Council members.

The Security Council,

Recalling its resolutions 1581(2005) of 18 January 2005, 1597(2005) of 20 April 2005, 1613(2005) of 26 July 2005, 1629(2005) of 30 September 2005, 1660(2006) of 28 February 2006 and 1668(2006) of 10 April 2006,

Taking note of the letters dated 31 December 2007 and 22 January and 8 February 2008 from the Secretary-General to the President of the Security Council,

Having considered the proposal made by the President of the International Tribunal for the Prosecution of Persons Responsible for Serious Violations of International Humanitarian Law Committed in the Territory of the Former Yugoslavia since 1991 (the International Tribunal) that the Secretary-General be authorized, within existing resources, to appoint additional ad litem judges upon request of the President of the International Tribunal, notwithstanding the fact that their number will from time to time temporarily exceed the maximum of twelve provided for under article 12, paragraph 1, of the statute of the International Tribunal, to a maximum of sixteen at any one time, returning to a maximum of twelve by 31 December 2008, to enable the International Tribunal to conduct additional trials once one or more of the permanent judges of the International Tribunal become available,

Recalling that in its resolution 1503(2003) of 28 August 2003, it called upon the International Tribunal to take all possible measures to complete all trial activities at first instance by the end of 2008 and to complete all work in 2010 (the International Tribunal's completion strategy), and that in its resolution 1534(2004) of 26 March 2004, it emphasized the importance of fully implementing the International Tribunal's completion strategy,

Convinced of the advisability of allowing the Secretary-General to appoint ad litem judges additional to the twelve ad litem judges authorized by the statute, as a temporary measure to enable the International Tribunal to conduct additional trials as soon as possible in order to meet completion strategy objectives,

Acting under Chapter VII of the Charter of the United Nations,

1. *Decides*, therefore, that the Secretary-General may appoint, within existing resources, additional ad litem judges upon request of the President of the International Tribunal, in order to conduct additional trials, notwithstanding the fact that the total number of ad litem judges appointed to the Chambers will from time to time temporarily exceed the maximum of twelve provided for in article 12, paragraph 1, of the statute of the International Tribunal, to a maximum of sixteen at any one time, returning to a maximum of twelve by 31 December 2008;
2. *Decides also* to remain seized of the matter.

Appointment of new judge

By a letter of 25 July [S/2008/507], the Secretary-General informed the Security Council President that Judge Wolfgang Schomburg (Germany) had resigned as a permanent judge of the Tribunal, effective 18 November, and that Germany had presented the candidacy of Christoph Flügge, a person who met the qualifications prescribed for the Tribunal and whom he wished to appoint for the remainder of Judge Schomburg's term. On 30 July [S/2008/508], the Council President supported the Secretary-General's intention. On 17 November [A/63/548], the Secretary-General informed the General Assembly President of Judge Flügge's appointment, of which the Assembly took note on 20 November [meeting 56].

Extension of terms of office

On 24 September [A/63/458-S/2008/621], the Secretary-General transmitted to the General Assembly and the Security Council two letters from the ICTY President seeking the extension of the terms of office of the permanent and ad litem judges elected to serve with the Tribunal in 2005, whose terms of office would expire on 16 November 2009 and 23 August 2009, respectively. In addition, the President requested an extension of the terms of the remaining ad litem judges who were not currently appointed to serve at the Tribunal due to the need to ensure that the judges could complete the cases to which they were assigned. The statute of the Tribunal did not provide for the extension of the terms of office of the judges. In the absence of such a provision, the approval of the Council, as the parent organ of the Tribunal, and of the Assembly, as the organ that elected its judges, was needed.

SECURITY COUNCIL ACTION

On 29 September [meeting 5986], the Security Council unanimously adopted **resolution 1837(2008)**. The draft [S/2008/618] was prepared in consultations among Council members.

The Security Council,

Taking note of the letter dated 24 September 2008 from the Secretary-General to the President of the Security Council attaching two letters dated 5 June and 1 September 2008 from the President of the International Tribunal for the Prosecution of Persons Responsible for Serious Violations of International Humanitarian Law Committed in the Territory of the Former Yugoslavia since 1991 ("the International Tribunal") to the Secretary-General,

Recalling its resolutions 1581(2005) of 18 January 2005, 1597(2005) of 20 April 2005, 1613(2005) of 26 July 2005, 1629(2005) of 30 September 2005, 1660(2006) of 28 February 2006, 1668(2006) of 10 April 2006 and 1800(2008) of 20 February 2008,

Recalling in particular its resolutions 1503(2003) of 28 August 2003 and 1534(2004) of 26 March 2004, in which the Council calls upon the International Tribunal to take all possible measures to complete investigations by the end of 2004, to complete all trial activities at first instance by the end of 2008 and to complete all work in 2010,

Expressing its determination to support the efforts made by the International Tribunal towards the completion of its trial work at the earliest date,

Expressing its expectation that the extension of the terms of office of the judges concerned will enhance the effectiveness of trial proceedings and contribute towards the implementation of the completion strategy,

Acting under Chapter VII of the Charter of the United Nations,

1. *Decides* to extend the term of office of the following permanent judges at the International Tribunal who are members of the Appeals Chamber until 31 December 2010, or until the completion of the cases before the Appeals Chamber if sooner:

—Mr. Liu Daqun (China)
—Mr. Theodor Meron (United States of America)
—Mr. Fausto Pocar (Italy)
—Mr. Mohamed Shahabuddeen (Guyana)

2. *Decides also* to extend the term of office of the following permanent judges at the International Tribunal who are members of the Trial Chambers until 31 December 2009, or until the completion of the cases to which they are assigned if sooner:

—Mr. Carmel A. Agius (Malta)
—Mr. Jean-Claude Antonetti (France)
—Mr. Iain Bonomy (United Kingdom of Great Britain and Northern Ireland)
—Mr. Christoph Flügge (Germany)
—Mr. O-gon Kwon (Republic of Korea)
—Mr. Bakone Melema Moloto (South Africa)
—Mr. Alphonsus Martinus Maria Orie (Netherlands)
—Mr. Kevin Horace Parker (Australia)
—Mr. Patrick Lipton Robinson (Jamaica)
—Ms. Christine Van Den Wyngaert (Belgium)

3. *Decides further* to extend the term of office of the following ad litem judges, currently serving at the International Tribunal, until 31 December 2009, or until the completion of the cases to which they are assigned if sooner:

—Mr. Ali Nawaz Chowhan (Pakistan)
—Mr. Pedro David (Argentina)
—Ms. Elizabeth Gwaunza (Zimbabwe)
—Mr. Frederik Harhoff (Denmark)
—Ms. Tsvetana Kamenova (Bulgaria)
—Mr. Uldis Kinis (Latvia)
—Ms. Flavia Lattanzi (Italy)
—Mr. Antoine Mindua (Democratic Republic of the Congo)
—Ms. Janet Nosworthy (Jamaica)
—Ms. Michèle Picard (France)
—Mr. Árpád Prandler (Hungary)
—Ms. Kimberly Prost (Canada)
—Mr. Ole Bjørn Støle (Norway)
—Mr. Stefan Trechsel (Switzerland)

4. *Decides* to extend the term of office of the following ad litem judges, who are not currently appointed to serve at the International Tribunal, until 31 December 2009, or until the completion of any cases to which they may be assigned if sooner:

—Mr. Melville Baird (Trinidad and Tobago)
—Mr. Frans Bauduin (Netherlands)
—Sir Burton Hall (Bahamas)
—Mr. Frank Höpfel (Austria)
—Mr. Raimo Lahti (Finland)
—Mr. Jawdat Naboty (Syrian Arab Republic)
—Ms. Chioma Egondu Nwosu-Iheme (Nigeria)
—Ms. Prisca Matimba Nyambe (Zambia)
—Mr. Brynmor Pollard (Guyana)
—Ms. Vonimbolana Rasoazanany (Madagascar)
—Mr. Krister Thelin (Sweden)
—Mr. Klaus Tolksdorf (Germany)
—Tan Sri Dato' Lamin bin Haji Mohd Yunus (Malaysia)

5. *Decides also*, without prejudice to the provisions of resolution 1800(2008), to amend article 12, paragraphs 1 and 2, of the statute of the International Tribunal and to replace those paragraphs with the provisions set out in the annex to the present resolution;

6. *Decides further* to remain seized of the matter.

ANNEX

Article 12

Composition of the Chambers

1. The Chambers shall be composed of a maximum of sixteen permanent independent judges, no two of whom

may be nationals of the same State, and a maximum at any one time of twelve ad litem independent judges appointed in accordance with article 13 ter, paragraph 2, of the Statute, no two of whom may be nationals of the same State.

2. A maximum at any one time of three permanent judges and nine ad litem judges shall be members of each Trial Chamber. Each Trial Chamber to which ad litem judges are assigned may be divided into sections of three judges each, composed of both permanent and ad litem judges, except in the circumstances specified in paragraph 5 below. A section of a Trial Chamber shall have the same powers and responsibilities as a Trial Chamber under the Statute and shall render judgement in accordance with the same rules.

On 9 October, the General Assembly, by **decision 63/402**, endorsed the Secretary-General's recommendation on the extension of ICTY judges' terms of office (see p. 1410).

Further authorization to appoint ad litem judges

In a letter [S/2008/767] transmitted by the Secretary-General to the Security Council on 5 December, the ICTY President sought an extension of the terms of Council resolution 1800(2008), so that the Tribunal could be authorized to have more than the statutory maximum of 12 ad litem judges beyond 31 December.

SECURITY COUNCIL ACTION

On 12 December [meeting 6040], the Security Council, unanimously adopted **resolution 1849(2008)**. The draft [S/2008/780] was prepared in consultations among Council members.

The Security Council,

Taking note of the letter dated 5 December 2008 from the Secretary-General to the President of the Security Council attaching the letter dated 26 November 2008 from the President of the International Tribunal for the Prosecution of Persons Responsible for Serious Violations of International Humanitarian Law Committed in the Territory of the Former Yugoslavia since 1991 to the Secretary-General,

Recalling its resolution 1800(2008) of 20 February 2008, by which it permitted the total number of ad litem judges appointed at any one time to the Chambers of the International Tribunal for the Former Yugoslavia ("the International Tribunal") to be increased to sixteen until 31 December 2008,

Noting that the International Tribunal currently has a total of fourteen ad litem judges assigned to cases, that three of them are assigned to a case where the judgement delivery is expected by 12 February 2009, and that the appointment of a further ad litem judge to another case expected to commence on 15 December 2008 would take the total number of ad litem judges to fifteen until 12 February 2009,

Recalling that in its resolution 1503(2003) of 28 August 2003, it called upon the International Tribunal to take all possible measures to complete investigations by the end of 2004, to complete all trial activities at first instance by the end of 2008 and to complete all work in 2010, and that in its resolution 1534(2004) of 26 March 2004, it emphasized the importance of fully implementing the completion strategy of the International Tribunal,

Convinced of the advisability of extending this exceptional authorization granted to the Secretary-General in resolution 1800(2008) as a temporary measure to enable the International Tribunal to complete trials and conduct additional trials as soon as possible in order to meet its completion strategy,

Acting under Chapter VII of the Charter of the United Nations,

1. *Decides* that the Secretary-General may appoint, within existing resources, additional ad litem judges upon request of the President of the International Tribunal in order to complete existing trials or conduct additional trials, notwithstanding the fact that the total number of ad litem judges appointed to the Chambers will from time to time temporarily exceed the maximum of twelve provided for in article 12, paragraph 1, of the statute of the International Tribunal, to a maximum of sixteen at any one time, returning to a maximum of twelve by 28 February 2009,
2. *Decides also* to remain seized of the matter.

On 24 December, the General Assembly, by **decision 63/552**, decided that the agenda item on judges of the ICTY would remain for consideration during its resumed sixty-third (2009) session.

Office of the Prosecutor

In 2008, the Office of the Prosecutor focused on completing trials and appeals in accordance with the Tribunal's completion strategy, as well as on international cooperation and the arrest of fugitives, the transfer of cases and material, and capacity-building. Radovan Karadžić and Stojan Župljanin were arrested, but Ratko Mladić and Goran Hadžić remained at large. The new Prosecutor, Serge Brammertz, took office on 1 January. Norman Farrell was appointed as Deputy Prosecutor, taking up his duties on 1 July.

Compared with the previous year, the number of trials had increased. By the end of July, the Office was prosecuting 26 persons in seven simultaneous trials, two of which were awaiting judgement. The cases of seven accused were at the pretrial stage, one of which had commenced earlier, but was adjourned because of the health of an accused. One contempt case had been completed, and a further contempt case, involving two accused, was awaiting trial. Two accused remained at large. The Office was also involved in appellate proceedings on the merits in 11 cases.

The Office continued to develop interaction with the States of the former Yugoslavia to encourage cooperation with the Tribunal and support domestic war crimes prosecutions. In terms of cooperation with the Office, Serbia had provided adequate responses to a number of requests for assistance and had facilitated the appearance of certain important witnesses. Continued cooperation in providing documents and access to archives sought by the Office would be paramount during the remaining senior leadership trials, including the Karadžić case. The most critical aspect of Serbia's cooperation remained the apprehension of fugitives Ratko Mladić and Goran Hadžić.

Although Croatia made available certain archival materials, requests for key documents were still pending. The authorities of Bosnia and Herzegovina had granted access to Government archives, provided documents requested, and provided adequate responses to requests for assistance and in facilitating the appearance of witnesses before the Tribunal. Nevertheless, the fact that Radovan Stanković had not yet been apprehended remained a concern. The cooperation of the authorities of the former Yugoslav Republic of Macedonia was generally satisfactory. The Office continued to seek cooperation from Montenegro to take the necessary action against the networks supporting fugitives.

The Registry

The Registry continued to provide operational support to the Chambers and the Office of the Prosecutor and to manage the administration of the Tribunal. It also managed the Detention Unit, the Victims and Witnesses Section, the legal aid office, and the interpretation and translation service. The Registry facilitated the implementation of the completion strategy [YUN 2002, p. 1275], and worked closely with the UN Secretariat in New York and with the International Criminal Tribunal for Rwanda. Its Registry Advisory Section for Legal and Policy Matters diversified its services to include advice on contracts, legal procurement and human resources matters, claims against ICTY, the negotiation of international agreements on privileges and immunities, liaison with the UN Office of Legal Affairs and Member States, and host State relations.

Between August 2007 and July 2008, the Court Management and Support Services Section supported 12 trials involving 35 accused, as well as several contempt and appeals hearings, while the Administrative Support Services Division was responsible for coordinating the preparation of the second performance report for the 2006–2007 biennium. As the departure of key personnel in advance of the completion dates would have a negative impact on the Tribunal's ability to meet its mandate, the Human Resources Section implemented measures to retain staff, including extended training activities, in which some 950 staff took part. Subsequently, the Division coordinated the preparation of the revised estimates for the 2008–2009 biennium and the proposed programme budget for the 2010–2011 biennium.

The Tribunal's Communications Service in December launched a new website to provide greater information about the Tribunal's history, achievements and ongoing work. It included such research tools as the Tribunal's Court Records Database, which provided access to the Tribunal's court records, comprising nearly 160,000 court filings, and was an important vehicle for the transfer of the Tribunal's knowledge and expertise to the region of the former Yugoslavia and beyond. The Tribunal's outreach programme continued to set the standard for international courts, while its media office remained active with such major media events as the transfer of Radovan Karadžić.

Financing

2008–2009 biennium

Ad litem judges. A report [A/62/809] issued in April estimated that the requirements for appointing up to four additional ad litem judges at any one time (to a total of 16) and returning to a maximum of 12 by 31 December, as provided for in Security Council resolution 1800(2008) (see p. 1410), would amount to $374,500. Every effort would be made to meet the related costs within the appropriation for the 2008–2009 biennium, with the actual expenditures being reported in the second performance report for 2008–2009.

ACABQ report. In June [A/62/7/Add.38], the Advisory Committee on Administrative and Budgetary Questions (ACABQ) noted that the appointment of additional ad litem judges was a way to reduce the time frame for completing the Tribunal's work. To assess progress made, the Committee requested that information on the appointment of additional ad litem judges be submitted in the first performance report for the 2008–2009 biennium. It also expected that their appointment would be implemented within existing resources, in accordance with resolution 1800(2008). On that basis, the Committee recommended that the General Assembly take note of the Secretary-General's report.

Reports of Secretary-General. In October, the Secretary-General transmitted a report on revised estimates for the 2008–2009 biennium [A/63/513] reflecting additional resource requirements in the amount of $14,979,500, net of staff assessment, over the initial appropriation for 2008–2009 as approved by General Assembly resolution 62/230 [YUN 2006, p. 1341]. The resources related primarily to the revised trial schedule for 2009 as a result of the apprehension of certain high-level accused, and the continuation into 2009 of trials that had been planned for completion by the end of 2008. The Assembly was requested to approve an additional appropriation of $16,043,500 gross ($14,979,500 net) to the ICTY Special Account.

The first performance report of ICTY for the 2008–2009 biennium [A/63/559], submitted in November in response to resolution 62/230, reflected a requirement for additional appropriations of $11.4 million, net of staff assessment, over the initial appropriation for that biennium. The Assembly was requested to approve an additional appropriation of $13,117,900 gross ($11,404,700 net) to the ICTY Special Account.

ACABQ report. In December [A/63/595], ACABQ recommended that the Assembly approve additional appropriations for the 2008–2009 biennium in the amount of $15,548,100 gross to the ICTY Special Account.

GENERAL ASSEMBLY ACTION

On 24 December [meeting 74], the General Assembly, on the recommendation of the Fifth (Administrative and Budgetary) Committee [A/63/644], adopted **resolution 63/255** without vote [agenda item 131].

Financing of the International Tribunal for the Prosecution of Persons Responsible for Serious Violations of International Humanitarian Law Committed in the Territory of the Former Yugoslavia since 1991

The General Assembly,

Having considered the report of the Secretary-General on the revised estimates under the budget, for the biennium 2008–2009, of the International Tribunal for the Prosecution of Persons Responsible for Serious Violations of International Humanitarian Law Committed in the Territory of the Former Yugoslavia since 1991, his first performance report on the International Tribunal for the Former Yugoslavia for the biennium, and his report on the revised estimates arising in respect of Security Council resolution 1800(2008) on the appointment of additional ad litem judges at the International Tribunal for the Former Yugoslavia,

Having also considered the report of the Board of Auditors on the International Tribunal for the Former Yugoslavia and the recommendations contained therein,

Having further considered the related reports of the Advisory Committee on Administrative and Budgetary Questions,

Stressing the need fully to respect and maintain the balance between the principal organs of the United Nations within their respective purviews and mandates in accordance with the Charter,

Reaffirming its authority in the consideration of all budgetary issues, as stipulated in the Charter,

Recalling its resolution 47/235 of 14 September 1993 on the financing of the International Tribunal for the Former Yugoslavia and its subsequent resolutions thereon, the latest of which was resolution 62/230 of 22 December 2007,

1. *Takes note* of the report of the Secretary-General on the revised estimates under the budget, for the biennium 2008–2009, of the International Tribunal for the Prosecution of Persons Responsible for Serious Violations of International Humanitarian Law Committed in the Territory of the Former Yugoslavia since 1991, his first performance report of the International Tribunal for the Former Yugoslavia for the biennium, and his report on the revised estimates arising in respect of Security Council resolution 1800(2008) on the appointment of additional ad litem judges at the International Tribunal for the Former Yugoslavia;

2. *Endorses* the conclusions and recommendations contained in the reports of the Advisory Committee on Administrative and Budgetary Questions;

3. *Reaffirms*, in the context of all Security Council decisions on the International Tribunals, the prerogatives of the General Assembly in the issues related to administrative and budgetary matters;

4. *Reiterates* that, in accordance with the Financial Regulations and Rules of the United Nations, the submission of the budget proposals is a prerogative of the Secretary-General;

5. *Invites* the Secretary-General to provide all intergovernmental bodies with the required information regarding procedures for administrative and budgetary matters;

6. *Requests* the President of the General Assembly to bring to the attention of the President of the Security Council the contents of the present resolution;

7. *Decides* on a revised appropriation to the Special Account for the International Tribunal for the Prosecution of Persons Responsible for Serious Violations of International Humanitarian Law Committed in the Territory of the Former Yugoslavia since 1991 of a total amount of 376,232,900 United States dollars gross (342,332,300 dollars net) for the biennium 2008–2009, as detailed in the annex to the present resolution;

8. *Also decides*, for 2009, to apportion among Member States, in accordance with the scale of assessments applicable to the regular budget of the United Nations for the year, the amount of 101,158,400 dollars gross (91,981,800 dollars net), including 14,333,000 dollars gross (12,930,100 dollars net), being the increase in assessments;

9. *Further decides*, for 2009, to apportion among Member States, in accordance with the rates of assessment applicable to peacekeeping operations for the year, the amount of 101,158,400 dollars gross (91,981,800 dollars net), including 14,333,000 dollars gross (12,930,100 dollars net), being the increase in assessments;

10. *Decides* that, in accordance with the provisions of its resolution 973(X) of 15 December 1955, there shall be set off against the apportionment among Member States, as provided for in paragraphs 8 and 9 above, their respective share in the Tax Equalization Fund in the amount of 18,353,200 dollars, including 2,805,800 dollars, being the increase in the estimated staff assessment income approved for the International Tribunal for the Former Yugoslavia for the biennium 2008–2009.

ANNEX

Financing for the biennium 2008–2009 of the International Tribunal for the Prosecution of Persons Responsible for Serious Violations of International Humanitarian Law Committed in the Territory of the Former Yugoslavia since 1991

	Gross	Net
	(United States dollars)	
1. Initial appropriation for the biennium 2008–2009 (resolution 62/230)	347,566,900	316,472,100
Add:		
2. Revised estimates for the biennium 2008–2009 after recosting (A/63/513 and A/63/595)	15,548,100	14,455,500
3. First performance report for the biennium 2008–2009 (A/63/559)	13,117,900	11,404,700
4. **Estimated revised appropriation for the biennium 2008–2009**	**376,232,900**	**342,332,300**
Less:		
5. Estimated income for the biennium 2008–2009	(265,300)	(265,300)
6. Assessment for 2008	173,650,800	158,103,400
7. **Balance to be assessed for 2009**	**202,316,800**	**183,963,600**
Including:		
8. Contributions assessed on Member States in accordance with the scale of assessments applicable to the regular budget of the United Nations for 2009	101,158,400	91,981,800
9. Contributions assessed on Member States in accordance with the rates of assessment applicable to peacekeeping operations of the United Nations for 2009	101,158,400	91,981,800

On 24 December, the Assembly decided that the agenda item on the financing of ICTY would remain for consideration during its resumed sixty-third (2009) session (**decision 63/552**).

International Tribunal for Rwanda

In 2008, the International Criminal Tribunal for Rwanda (ICTR), established by Security Council resolution 955(1994) [YUN 1994, p. 299] and based in Arusha, United Republic of Tanzania, delivered four Trial Chamber judgements and two Appeals Chamber judgements. In total, by the end of 2008, it had apprehended and detained 66 persons out of some 81 persons indicted. Those detainees had been apprehended in some 23 countries outside of Rwanda. Arrested persons included the Prime Minister of the Interim Government of Rwanda during the genocide, 11 Ministers of that Government in 1994, senior military officials and members of the clergy.

Addressing the Security Council on 12 December [S/PV.6041], ICTR Prosecutor Hassan Bubacar Jallow said that much progress had been achieved during the year in implementing the Tribunal's completion strategy. A significant development in the trial programme had been the conclusion of all the multiple-accused cases with one exception, involving some 14 accused persons. The Office of the Prosecutor was preparing the cases of all detainees awaiting trial, in order to ensure that their cases would proceed in 2009 in accordance with the trial schedule submitted by the Tribunal President.

Also addressing the Council, ICTR President Judge Dennis Byron said that new cases facing the Tribunal in 2009 would include the trials of three accused arrested in 2007 and 2008, a retrial ordered by the Appeals Chamber, and a contempt of court case. However, the denial of the Prosecutor's requests to refer one case to Norway and four cases to Rwanda for trial put a strain on the Tribunal's capacity, as those referrals had formed an integral part of its completion strategy. The Prosecutor explained that the Appeals Chamber, while acknowledging the independence and impartiality of the Rwandan judiciary, had upheld the rejection of the request by the Trial Chambers essentially out of concern that the work of the defence could be impeded by the possible reluctance of defence witnesses to travel to Rwanda to testify, as well as the potential security risks those witnesses might face. That setback had not closed the door on the referral strategy. The Office of the ICTR Prosecutor, together with the Office of the Prosecutor General in Rwanda, had identified measures that Rwanda could take to meet the concerns of the Chambers. They had agreed that, once those measures were implemented by the Rwandan Government, the ICTR Prosecutor would consider submitting new requests to the judges early in 2009 for the referral of cases to Rwanda.

The ICTR President stated that unfortunately no new arrests could be reported for the 13 fugitives still at large. As the end of the Tribunal's mandate drew near, he reiterated his call upon Member States to cooperate fully with the Tribunal to ensure their arrest and transfer as soon as possible.

The activities of ICTR were covered in two reports to the Security Council and the General Assembly, for the periods of 1 July 2007 to 30 June 2008 [A/63/209-S/2008/514] and 1 July 2008 to 30 June 2009 [A/64/206-S/2009/396].

On 13 October, the Assembly took note of the 2007/2008 report (**decision 63/505**).

The Chambers

ICTR Chambers were composed of 16 permanent judges and nine ad litem judges at the end of June. Nine permanent judges sat in the three Trial Chambers, while seven permanent judges sat in the Appeals Chamber. Each Trial Chamber to which ad litem judges were assigned could be divided into sections of three judges each, composed of both permanent and ad litem judges. The Appeals Chamber was common with the International Criminal Tribunal for the Former Yugoslavia, and for each appeal, the Appeals Chamber was composed of five judges.

New arrests

Augustin Ngirabatware, former Minister of Planning, was arrested in Frankfurt, Germany, on 17 September 2007 and was transferred to the UN Detention Facility in Arusha on 8 October 2008. He was charged with genocide, complicity to genocide, direct and public incitement to commit genocide, crimes against humanity and war crimes. Callixte Nzabonimana, the former Minister of Youth and Sports, was arrested in Tanzania in February 2008 and transferred to Arusha. He was charged with six counts of genocide, conspiracy to commit genocide, complicity to genocide, direct and public incitement to commit genocide, as well as crimes against humanity and war crimes. Dominique Ntawukuriryayo, a former sub-prefect in the Butare prefecture, was arrested in France in October 2007 and transferred to Arusha on 5 June 2008. He was charged with three counts of genocide, complicity in genocide and direct and public incitement to commit genocide.

Ongoing trials

In the trial of Tharcisse Renzaho, closing arguments were heard on 14 and 15 February, and judgement was expected in July 2009. Colonel Renzaho, a former prefect of Kigali-ville, was arrested on 29 September 2002 in Kinshasa, Democratic Republic of the Congo (DRC), and transferred to the Tribunal on the following day [YUN 2002, p. 1285]. In 2005, he pleaded not guilty to six counts of genocide, complicity in genocide, crimes against humanity (murder, rape) and violations of the Geneva Conventions and Additional Protocol II.

In the trial of Emmanuel Rukundo, former military chaplain in the armed forces, closing arguments were heard on 20 February. Mr. Rukundo was charged with three counts of genocide and crimes against humanity [YUN 2006, p. 1497].

Athanase Seromba, a Roman Catholic priest of Nyange Parish in Kivumu commune, was convicted in 2006 of genocide and extermination as a crime against humanity and sentenced to 15 years' imprisonment [YUN 2006, p. 1497]. The Appeals Chamber, on 12 March, quashed the finding that he aided and abetted genocide by certain acts and held that he committed genocide and extermination as a crime against humanity by virtue of his role in the destruction of a church and the consequent death of the approximately 1,500 Tutsi refugees sheltering inside. It also affirmed that he aided and abetted genocide in relation to the killings of two people. Consequently, the Appeals Chamber quashed the sentence imposed by the Trial Chamber and entered a new sentence of life imprisonment.

The trial in the case of Callixte Kalimanzira, the former acting Minister of the Interior [YUN 2005, p. 1397], began on 5 May and concluded on 30 June. He was charged with genocide, complicity in genocide and direct and public incitement to commit genocide. The defence case was expected to be completed in 2008, with judgement to be delivered in the first half of 2009.

The defence case in the trial of Hormisdas Nsengimana—a former priest and Rector of Christ-Rio college in Nyanza (Butare prefecture) charged with three counts of crimes against humanity, including genocide, murder and extermination—began on 2 June. Following his arrest in Yaoundé, Cameroon, on 21 March 2002 [YUN 2002, p. 1285], Mr. Nsengimana was transferred to the Tribunal on 10 April. He was alleged to have been at the centre of a group of Hutu extremists that planned and carried out targeted attacks in Nyanza in 1994. Moreover, he purportedly participated directly and indirectly in killings. His trial began on 22 June 2007 [YUN 2007, p. 1343].

In the trial of Karemera et al.—against Edouard Karemera, Mathieu Ngirumpatse and Joseph Nzirorera—the defence case for Edouard Karemera, former Minister of the Interior, began on 7 April. The trial was stayed from August 2008 to March 2009 due to the ill-health of the second accused, Matthieu Ngirumpatse, former President of the Mouvement républicain national pour la démocratie et le développement, save for the testimony of four witnesses in November 2008.

In the trial of Siméon Nchamihigo, a former Deputy Prosecutor in Cyangugu prefecture [YUN 2006, p. 1497], the parties made closing arguments on 23 January. On 24 September, he was convicted of genocide and extermination, murder and other inhumane acts as crimes against humanity based on his participation in the killing of Tutsi in April 1994 at various places in Cyangugu. Considering in particular his prominent public position as an aggravating circumstance, the Chamber sentenced him to life imprisonment.

The trial of Lieutenant-Colonel Ephrem Setako, former Director of the Judicial Affairs Division of the Ministry of Defence [YUN 2004, p. 1286], began on 25 August.

Augustin Ngirabatware, the former Minister of Planning, made his initial appearance before the Court on 10 October, following his arrest and transfer from Germany; he pleaded not guilty to all counts in the indictment.

In the case of Casimir Bizimungu et al. [YUN 1999, pp. 1222 & 1223]—against former Health Minister Casimir Bizimungu, former Trade and Industry Minister Justin Mugenzi, former Civil Service Minister Prosper Mugiraneza and former Foreign Affairs and Cooperation Minister Jérôme Bicamumpaka—the evidentiary phase of the case had concluded and the Chamber conducted a site visit in Rwanda from 5 to 10 October. The parties filed their closing briefs between 1 October and 21 November, and oral arguments were heard between 1 and 5 December.

The Pauline Nyiramasuhuko et al. ("Butare") case closed on 2 December and the filing of closing briefs was expected. The case, involving six persons charged with genocide, crimes against humanity and serious violations of the Geneva Conventions, opened in 2001 [YUN 2001, p. 1208]. The accused were Pauline Nyiramasuhuko, former Rwandan Minister for Family and Women Affairs (the first woman to be indicted by an international criminal tribunal and the only woman to be indicted by the ICTR so far); her son and former leader of the Interahamwe militia, Arsène Shalom Ntahobali; Sylvain Nsabimana, former prefect of Butare; Alphonse Nteziryayo, former Commanding Officer of the Military Police and former prefect of Butare; Joseph Kanyabashi, former Mayor of Ngoma; and Elie Ndayambaje, former Mayor of Muganza. They were accused of committing killings in a calculated, cold-blooded and methodical manner and playing a prominent role in the commission of the crimes in Butare, a religious and academic centre in Rwanda [YUN 2007, p. 1343].

In the trial of Simon Bikindi, composer and singer of popular music [YUN 2002, p. 1285], the Chamber conducted a site visit in Rwanda from 14 to 18 April and the parties presented closing arguments on 26 May. On 2 December, the Chamber convicted Mr. Bikindi of direct and public incitement to commit genocide and sentenced him to 15 years of imprisonment; he was acquitted of conspiracy to commit genocide, genocide, complicity in genocide and crimes against humanity. The Prosecution had charged that Mr. Bikindi participated in the anti-Tutsi campaign in 1994 through his musical compositions and speeches he made at public gatherings, inciting and promoting hatred and violence against Tutsi [YUN 2007, p. 1343].

In the Ndindiliyimana et al. ("Military II") case [YUN 2006, p. 1497]—against Augustin Ndindiliyimana, former Chief of Staff of the Gendarmerie, Augustin Bizimungu, former Chief of Staff of the Army, François-Xavier Nzuwonemeye, former Commander of the Reconnaissance Battalion, and Innocent Sagahutu, former Second-in-Command of the Reconnaissance Battalion—Mr. Ndindiliyimana commenced his case on 16 January and closed it on 23 June. Mr. Nzuwonemeye commenced his defence on 23 June and completed his case on 8 October. The Chamber commenced hearing the case of the final accused, Mr. Sagahutu, on 20 October. On 4 December, the proceedings were adjourned until 2009.

In the trial of businessman Protais Zigiranyirazo [YUN 2001, p. 1207], the parties delivered closing arguments on 28 and 29 May. On 18 December, he was found guilty of having participated in a joint criminal enterprise with the common purpose of committing genocide and extermination of Tutsi, as well as aiding and abetting genocide, and was sentenced to 20 years' imprisonment. Mr. Zigiranyirazo had been a member of the Akazu, the inner circle of the late President of Rwanda, Juvénal Habyarimana [YUN 2007, p. 1344].

On 18 December, the Chamber rendered a judgement in the Bagosora et al. ("Military I") case involving four senior army officers [YUN 2007, p. 1345]. Colonel Théoneste Bagosora, former Director of Cabinet in the Ministry of Defence, Major Aloys Ntabakuze, former Commander of the Para Commando Battalion, and Colonel Anatole Nsengiyumva, former commander of the Gisenyi operational sector, were convicted of genocide, crimes against humanity and war crimes and sentenced to life imprisonment. The Chamber acquitted General Gratien Kabiligi, head of the operations bureau of the Army General Staff, of all charges and ordered his release.

On 28 May, the Chamber denied the Prosecutor's request to transfer the case of one detainee, former Interahamwe leader Yusuf Munyakazi [YUN 2004, p. 1286], to Rwanda. The Chamber found that the applicable sentence to the crimes alleged against Mr. Munyakazi, life imprisonment in isolation, precluded the referral of his case. It was also not satisfied that, upon referral, the accused's rights to an independent tribunal and to obtain the attendance and examination of witnesses would be guaranteed.

On 17 November, the Chamber denied the Prosecutor's request to refer the case of Jean-Baptiste Gatete [YUN 2002, p. 1285], a businessman, to Rwanda. The decision, which the Prosecution did not appeal, followed the Chamber's previous denial of transfer to Rwanda in the case of Gaspard Kanyarukiga in June 2008. That decision, which raised concerns about possible problems in obtaining witnesses and the risk of solitary confinement in Rwanda, was upheld by the Appeals Chamber in October.

On 4 December, the Trial and the Appeals Chambers rejected the requested referral of the case of Ildephonse Hategekimana, commander of the Ngoma Military Camp, to Rwanda for trial.

On 14 January, François Karera, former prefect of Kigali-Rural, filed his notice of appeal against his conviction on 7 December 2007 [YUN 2007, p. 1344], of genocide and extermination and murder as crimes against humanity, based on his participation in the killing of Tutsi in April and May 1994, for which he was sentenced to life imprisonment. The hearing of the appeal took place on 28 August.

On 13 March, the Appeals Chamber heard an appeal on the conviction of Tharcisse Muvunyi, a Lieutenant-Colonel stationed at the École des sous-officiers in Butare, for genocide, direct and public incitement to commit genocide, and other inhumane acts as a crime against humanity; he had been sentenced to 25 years' imprisonment [YUN 2006, p. 1495]. On 29 August, the Chamber dismissed the Prosecutor's appeal and granted Mr. Muvunyi's appeal in part. It reversed his convictions for genocide and other inhumane acts as a crime against humanity; reversed one conviction for direct and public incitement to commit genocide; quashed a second such conviction along with the sentence; and ordered a retrial of an allegation under one count of the indictment.

Judges of the Court

Extension of terms of office

The President of ICTR, Judge Dennis Byron, in letters transmitted by the Secretary-General to the General Assembly and the Security Council on 13 June [A/62/896-S/2008/436], sought authorization for extending the terms of office of nine permanent judges and eight ad litem judges (whose terms were to expire on 31 December 2008) to 31 December 2009, or until the completion of the cases to which they were assigned if sooner. He also sought an extension to 31 December 2009 of the terms of the remaining nine ad litem judges who were not yet appointed to serve at the Tribunal.

SECURITY COUNCIL ACTION

On 18 July [meeting 5937], the Security Council unanimously adopted **resolution 1824(2008)**. The draft [S/2008/467] was prepared in consultations among Council members.

The Security Council,

Taking note of the letter dated 13 June 2008 from the Secretary-General to the President of the Security Council attaching the letter dated 6 June 2008 from the President of the International Criminal Tribunal for Rwanda ("the Tribunal") to the Secretary-General,

Recalling its resolutions 955(1994) of 8 November 1994, 1165(1998) of 30 April 1998, 1329(2000) of 30 November 2000, 1411(2002) of 17 May 2002, 1431(2002) of 14 August 2002 and 1449(2002) of 13 December 2002,

Recalling in particular its resolutions 1503(2003) of 28 August 2003 and 1534(2004) of 26 March 2004, in which it called upon the Tribunal to take all possible measures to complete investigations by the end of 2004, to complete all trial activities at first instance by the end of 2008, and to complete all work in 2010,

Recalling that on 13 June 2006, the Council decided, in its resolution 1684(2006), to extend the term of office of eleven permanent judges of the Tribunal until 31 December 2008, and that on 13 October 2006, the Council decided in its resolution 1717(2006) to extend the term of office of the eighteen ad litem judges of the Tribunal until 31 December 2008,

Noting that two of the permanent judges and one of the ad litem judges currently serving at the Tribunal have indicated their intention to resign in 2008 upon the completion of their respective cases, and that at this stage it is not expected that their replacement will be necessary,

Noting also the progress made by the Tribunal towards the completion of its trial work at the earliest date,

Noting further the projections provided by the Tribunal as to the completion of all the remaining cases at trial stage before the end of December 2009,

Expressing its expectation that the extension of the terms of office of the judges concerned will enhance the effectiveness of trial proceedings and contribute towards ensuring the implementation of the completion strategy,

Acting under Chapter VII of the Charter of the United Nations,

1. *Decides* to extend the term of office of the following permanent judges of the Tribunal who are members of the Appeals Chamber until 31 December 2010, or until the completion of the cases before the Appeals Chamber if sooner:
   —Mr. Mehmet Güney (Turkey)
   —Ms. Andrésia Vaz (Senegal)
2. *Decides also* to extend the term of office of the following permanent judges of the Tribunal who are members of the Trial Chambers until 31 December 2009, or until the completion of the cases to which they are assigned if sooner:
   —Sir Charles Michael Dennis Byron (Saint Kitts and Nevis)
   —Mr. Asoka de Silva (Sri Lanka)
   —Mr. Sergei Alekseevich Egorov (Russian Federation)
   —Ms. Khalida Rachid Khan (Pakistan)
   —Mr. Erik Møse (Norway)
   —Ms. Arlette Ramaroson (Madagascar)
   —Mr. William Hussein Sekule (United Republic of Tanzania)
3. *Decides further* to extend the term of office of the following ad litem judges, currently serving at the Tribunal, until 31 December 2009, or until the completion of the cases to which they are assigned if sooner:
   —Ms. Florence Rita Arrey (Cameroon)
   —Ms. Solomy Balungi Bossa (Uganda)
   —Ms. Taghreed Hikmat (Jordan)
   —Mr. Vagn Joensen (Denmark)
   —Mr. Gberdao Gustave Kam (Burkina Faso)
   —Mr. Lee Gacuiga Muthoga (Kenya)
   —Mr. Seon Ki Park (Republic of Korea)
   —Mr. Emile Francis Short (Ghana)
4. *Decides* to extend the term of office of the following ad litem judges, who have not yet been appointed to serve at the Tribunal, until 31 December 2009, or until the

completion of any cases to which they may be assigned if sooner:

—Mr. Aydin Sefa Akay (Turkey)
—Ms. Karin Hökborg (Sweden)
—Ms. Flavia Lattanzi (Italy)
—Mr. Kenneth Machin (United Kingdom of Great Britain and Northern Ireland)
—Mr. Joseph Edward Chiondo Masanche (United Republic of Tanzania)
—Tan Sri Dato' Hj. Mohd. Azmi Dato' Hj. Kamaruddin (Malaysia)
—Mr. Mparany Mamy Richard Rajohnson (Madagascar)
—Mr. Albertus Henricus Joannes Swart (Netherlands)
—Ms. Aura E. Guerra de Villalaz (Panama)

5. *Decides also* to amend article 11, paragraphs 1 and 2, of the statute of the Tribunal and to replace those paragraphs with the provisions set out in the annex to the present resolution;

6. *Decides further* to remain seized of the matter.

ANNEX

Article 11

Composition of the Chambers

1. The Chambers shall be composed of a maximum of sixteen permanent independent judges, no two of whom may be nationals of the same State, and a maximum at any one time of nine ad litem independent judges appointed in accordance with article 12 ter, paragraph 2, of the present Statute, no two of whom may be nationals of the same State.

2. A maximum at any one time of three permanent judges and six ad litem judges shall be members of each Trial Chamber. Each Trial Chamber to which ad litem judges are assigned may be divided into sections of three judges each, composed of both permanent and ad litem judges. A section of a Trial Chamber shall have the same powers and responsibilities as a Trial Chamber under the present Statute and shall render judgement in accordance with the same rules.

The General Assembly, by **decision 62/421** of 28 July, endorsed the recommendation of the Secretary-General (see p. 1418) on the extension of ICTR judges' terms of office and decided that it would take effect as at 1 January 2009.

Letter from ICTR President. In a letter [S/2008/799] transmitted by the Secretary-General to the Security Council on 18 December, the ICTR President requested consideration of three issues: increasing, from 1 January to 31 December 2009, the maximum number of ad litem judges to serve at the Tribunal at any one time from 9 to 12; the possibility for the section of a Trial Chamber to sit in any particular case to be composed of ad litem judges only; and permission for judges whose term was coming to an end to take on another judicial or quasi-judicial position while they finalized the judgement-writing phase of their remaining cases. Those measures would allow the Tribunal to downsize and at the same time complete both ongoing and new trials.

SECURITY COUNCIL ACTION

On 19 December [meeting 6052], the Security Council unanimously adopted **resolution 1855(2008)**. The draft [S/2008/798] was prepared in consultations among Council members.

The Security Council,

Recalling its resolutions 955(1994) of 8 November 1994, 1165(1998) of 30 April 1998, 1329(2000) of 30 November 2000, 1411(2002) of 17 May 2002 and 1431(2002) of 14 August 2002,

Recalling in particular that in its resolution 1503(2003) of 28 August 2003, it called upon the International Criminal Tribunal for Rwanda ("the International Tribunal") to take all possible measures to complete all trial activities at first instance by the end of 2008 and to complete all work in 2010, and that in its resolution 1534(2004) of 26 March 2004, it emphasized the importance of fully implementing the completion strategy of the International Tribunal,

Taking note of the letter dated 18 December 2008 from the Secretary-General to the President of the Security Council attaching the letter dated 10 December 2008 from the President of the International Tribunal to the Secretary-General, and having considered the proposals made by the President of the International Tribunal,

Noting that two permanent judges currently serving at the International Tribunal will resign by the end of 2008, and that three other permanent judges have indicated their intention to resign upon the completion of their respective cases, and that their replacement will not be necessary if the International Tribunal is authorized to assign more ad litem judges to cases,

Convinced of the advisability of allowing the Secretary-General to appoint ad litem judges additional to the nine ad litem judges authorized by the statute of the International Tribunal, as a temporary measure to enable the International Tribunal to complete trials and conduct additional trials as soon as possible in order to meet its completion strategy,

Acting under Chapter VII of the Charter of the United Nations,

1. *Decides* that the Secretary-General may appoint, within existing resources, additional ad litem judges upon request of the President of the International Tribunal in order to complete existing trials or conduct additional trials, notwithstanding the fact that the total number of ad litem judges appointed to the Chambers will from time to time temporarily exceed the maximum of nine provided for in article 11, paragraph 1, of the statute of the International Tribunal, to a maximum of twelve at any one time, returning to a maximum of nine by 31 December 2009;

2. *Decides also* to amend article 11, paragraph 2, of the statute of the International Tribunal as set out in the annex to the present resolution;

3. *Decides further* to remain seized of the matter.

ANNEX

Article 11

Composition of the Chambers

2. Each Trial Chamber may be divided into sections of three judges each. A section of a Trial Chamber shall have the same powers and responsibilities as a Trial Chamber under the present Statute and shall render judgement in accordance with the same rules.

Office of the Prosecutor

The Office of the Prosecutor continued to receive and to respond to requests for mutual legal assistance from national jurisdictions investigating for prosecution or extradition of Rwandan fugitives appearing on the International Criminal Police Organization (ICPO-INTERPOL) wanted list. It also continued the hunt for the remaining 13 fugitives and particularly four high-level accused, including Félicien Kabuga.

There was no indication of any steps taken by the Government of Kenya—other than the earlier seizure of one property—to implement the recommendations of the ICTR-Kenya Police Joint Task Force or the requests of ICTR in respect of the person and property of Félicien Kabuga, accused of committing crimes against humanity and participating in the 1994 genocide, principally through financial support.

In September, the Prosecutor held consultations with the United Nations Organization Mission in the Democratic Republic of the Congo (MONUC) and Government officials in Kinshasa regarding the arrest and transfer to Arusha of some half a dozen indictees who had taken shelter in the DRC. The discussions with the Government had been positive and encouraging. However, conflict in the eastern part of the DRC, where most of the fugitives were located, had set back the tracking and arrest programme.

In November, the Office hosted a conference of all the Prosecutors of the Tribunals, as well as prosecutors from countries involved in the investigation and prosecution of international crimes. The meeting was convened in the context of the increasingly important role of national systems in combating impunity, with a view to sharing information and experiences and creating a forum through which such an exchange could continue beyond the lifetime of the ad hoc tribunals. There was much concern amongst the tribunals and national prosecuting authorities that the latter should continue to have access to the tribunals' information and databases in order to facilitate national investigation and prosecution.

With completion in sight, ICTR continued to lose critical staff at a difficult time. Since January, the Office of the Prosecutor had lost 20 per cent of its staff. The adoption of measures to provide incentives to staff whose services were critical was all the more urgent.

The Registry

The Registry continued to support the judicial process by servicing the Tribunal's other organs and the defence, as well as by seeking support from States, international organizations and other stakeholders in the conduct of proceedings. It maintained high-level diplomatic contacts with States and international organizations, and saw a significant increase in judicial cooperation with Member States. Through formal and informal agreements, it secured their cooperation with the Tribunal in support of the smooth running of trials. Rwanda continued to cooperate with the Tribunal in facilitating the flow of witnesses from Kigali to Arusha and providing documents to trial proceedings. In addition, on 4 March, the Registrar signed an agreement on enforcement of sentences between Rwanda and the United Nations.

Through its Outreach Programme, the Tribunal conducted workshops aimed at strengthening the Rwandan judicial capacity in areas such as international criminal law, advocacy skills, online legal research, rights of the accused and court information management.

Financing

2008–2009 biennium

Reports of Secretary-General. In October [A/63/506], the Secretary-General submitted additional requirements of $28,851,100 gross ($26,959,100 net) over the initial appropriation for ICTR for the 2008–2009 biennium, as approved by the General Assembly in resolution 62/229 [YUN 2007, p. 1347]. The increased requirements related primarily to the revision of the trial schedule for 2009 as a result of the apprehension of certain high-level accused, as well as the continuation into 2009 of some of the trials that were originally planned for completion by the end of 2008.

In the first performance report of ICTR for the 2008–2009 biennium [A/63/558], submitted in November pursuant to Assembly resolution 62/229, the Secretary-General requested an additional appropriation in the amount of $7,831,700 gross ($6,948,000 net) over the initial appropriation for the biennium, reflecting changes with respect to exchange rates, inflation and standard salary costs.

ACABQ report. In December [A/63/595], ACABQ, recommended that the Assembly approve additional appropriations for the 2008–2009 biennium in the amount of $30,190,700 gross.

GENERAL ASSEMBLY ACTION

On 24 December [meeting 74], the General Assembly, on the recommendation of the Fifth Committee [A/63/643], adopted **resolution 63/254** without vote [agenda item 130].

Financing of the International Criminal Tribunal for the Prosecution of Persons Responsible for Genocide and Other Serious Violations of International Humanitarian Law Committed In the Territory of Rwanda and Rwandan Citizens Responsible for Genocide and Other Such Violations Committed in the Territory of Neighbouring States between 1 January and 31 December 1994

The General Assembly,

Having considered the report of the Secretary-General on the revised estimates under the budget, for the biennium 2008–2009, of the International Criminal Tribunal for the Prosecution of Persons Responsible for Genocide and Other Serious Violations of International Humanitarian Law Committed in the Territory of Rwanda and Rwandan Citizens Responsible for Genocide and Other Such Violations Committed in the Territory of Neighbouring States between 1 January and 31 December 1994, and his first performance report on the International Criminal Tribunal for Rwanda for the biennium 2008–2009,

Having also considered the report of the Board of Auditors on the International Criminal Tribunal for Rwanda and the recommendations contained therein,

Having further considered the related report of the Advisory Committee on Administrative and Budgetary Questions,

Recalling its resolution 49/251 of 20 July 1995 on the financing of the International Criminal Tribunal for Rwanda and its subsequent resolutions thereon, the latest of which was resolution 62/229 of 22 December 2007,

1. *Takes note* of the report of the Secretary-General on the revised estimates under the budget, for the biennium 2008–2009, of the International Criminal Tribunal for the Prosecution of Persons Responsible for Genocide and Other Serious Violations of International Humanitarian Law Committed in the Territory of Rwanda and Rwandan Citizens Responsible for Genocide and Other Such Violations Committed in the Territory of Neighbouring States between 1 January and 31 December 1994, and his first performance report on the International Criminal Tribunal for Rwanda for the biennium 2008–2009;

2. *Endorses* the conclusions and recommendations contained in the report of the Advisory Committee on Administrative and Budgetary Questions;

3. *Decides* on a revised appropriation to the Special Account for the International Criminal Tribunal for the Prosecution of Persons Responsible for Genocide and Other Serious Violations of International Humanitarian Law Committed in the Territory of Rwanda and Rwandan Citizens Responsible for Genocide and Other Such Violations Committed in the Territory of Neighbouring States between 1 January and 31 December 1994, of a total amount of 305,378,600 United States dollars gross (282,597,100 dollars net) for the biennium 2008–2009, as detailed in the annex to the present resolution;

4. *Also decides*, for the year 2009, to apportion among Member States, in accordance with the scale of assessments applicable to the regular budget of the United Nations for the year, the amount of 84,657,900 dollars gross (78,253,300 dollars net), including 19,011,200 dollars gross (17,565,250 dollars net), being the increase in assessments;

5. *Further decides*, for the year 2009, to apportion among Member States, in accordance with the rates of assessment applicable to peacekeeping operations for the year, the amount of 84,657,900 dollars gross (78,253,300 dollars net), including 19,011,200 dollars gross (17,565,250 dollars net), being the increase in assessments;

6. *Decides* that, in accordance with the provisions of its resolution 973(X) of 15 December 1955, there shall be set off against the apportionment among Member States, as provided for in paragraphs 4 and 5 above, their respective share in the Tax Equalization Fund in the amount of 12,809,200 dollars, including 2,891,900 dollars, being the increase in the estimated staff assessment income approved for the International Criminal Tribunal for Rwanda for the biennium 2008–2009.

ANNEX

Financing for the biennium 2008–2009 of the International Criminal Tribunal for the Prosecution of Persons Responsible for Genocide and Other Serious Violations of International Humanitarian Law Committed in the Territory of Rwanda and Rwandan Citizens Responsible for Genocide and Other Such Violations Committed in the Territory of Neighbouring States between 1 January and 31 December 1994

	Gross	*Net*
	(United States dollars)	
Initial appropriation for the biennium 2008–2009 (resolution 62/229)	267,356,200	247,466,600
Add:		
Revised estimates for the biennium 2008–2009 after recosting (A/63/506 and A/63/595)	30,190,700	28,182,500
First performance report for the biennium 2008–2009 (A/63/558)	7,831,700	6,948,000
Proposed revised appropriation for the biennium 2008–2009	**305,378,600**	**282,597,100**
Assessment for 2008	136,062,800	126,090,500
Balance to be assessed for 2009	169,315,800	156,506,600
Including:		
Contributions assessed on Member States in accordance with the scale of assessments applicable to the regular budget of the United Nations for 2009	84,657,900	78,253,300
Contributions assessed on Member States in accordance with the rates of assessment applicable to peacekeeping operations of the United Nations for 2009	84,657,900	78,253,300

On 24 December, the Assembly decided that the agenda item on the financing of ICTR would remain for consideration during its resumed sixty-third (2009) session (**decision 63/552**).

Functioning of the Tribunals

Staff retention

In its resolution 61/274 [YUN 2007, p. 1349], the General Assembly noted that there might be difficulties in retaining and recruiting key staff as the Tribunals completed their mandates, and asked the

Secretary-General to report on related cost implications and updated human resources data, including current and projected staff turnover. In response to that resolution, the International Civil Service Committee (ICSC) [A/62/30 & Corr.1] advised that special financial retention incentives for the Tribunals were not considered appropriate, because they were not provided for in the common system and thus would set a precedent, which should be avoided. ICSC also stated that the existing contractual framework should be used to grant contracts that would remove the uncertainty with regard to future employment; that other non-monetary incentives should be made available; and that staff from the Tribunals who were offered appointments in another common system organization should have their reporting date for the new assignment set to coincide with completion of their work with the Tribunal.

Report of Secretary-General. Pursuant to resolution 61/274, the Secretary-General, on 8 February, submitted a comprehensive proposal on appropriate incentives to retain ICTR and ICTY staff [A/62/681]. He recommended that a financial incentive be approved for qualifying staff who remained in their posts until their functions were no longer needed. Considering that the designation of only limited groups of staff as "key" would have a detrimental impact on staff morale, likely resulting in a perception of unequal treatment and a negative impact on staff retention, he recommended that the incentive be applied on as wide a post coverage basis as possible. The financial implications of the incentive would be more than offset by the savings associated with reduced turnover rates, in terms of lower rotation costs and higher productivity and efficiency.

Bearing in mind the views expressed by ACABQ, ICSC and the Assembly, the Secretary-General recommended the introduction of a financial retention incentive scheme. By its terms, staff members would not be considered for an incentive payment unless they had worked for one of the Tribunals for a minimum of five years at the time of their separation. The scheme would target staff having greater seniority and hence the specialized knowledge that the Tribunals wished to retain. The financial implications would amount to $6.9 million for ICTR and $7.2 million for ICTY.

ACABQ report. In March, the Committee noted [A/62/734] that the Tribunals had initiated a number of non-monetary incentives to retain staff until their posts were no longer required—incentives aimed at broadening career options for staff when they left the Tribunals, improving working conditions, and assisting staff in dealing with host country residency and administrative issues. Contracts for all regular posts had been extended until August or October 2009, and the Tribunals were exploring possibilities for the secondment of staff from Member States, the United Nations and other common system organizations on temporary assignment during the final stages of the Tribunals' operations.

ACABQ recognized the importance of retaining highly skilled and specialized staff in order to complete all trial proceedings and meet the targets set out in the completion strategies of the Tribunals. The Committee was of the view that the Tribunals should employ a variety of tools to retain the services of personnel as long as they were needed. It therefore recommended that the Assembly authorize, on an exceptional basis, the payment of a retention incentive to staff required to remain with the Tribunals until their services and posts were no longer needed, as set out in the drawdown plans of each Tribunal, targeting staff with a minimum of five years of service. The Committee recommended that the incentive be capped at five months' salary for all staff members, irrespective of the number of years of service at the Tribunals beyond five years. Payment of the retention incentive would become effective with the 2008–2009 biennium, from a date to be fixed by the Assembly.

Responding to the ICSC view that payment of such an incentive would create an inappropriate precedent, ACABQ recommended that, should the Assembly authorize it, the related administrative arrangements should be based only on an ad hoc decision of the Assembly and not on an amendment to the Staff Rules, emphasizing that the exceptional nature of such arrangements for the Tribunals would preclude their application elsewhere in the UN system.

GENERAL ASSEMBLY ACTION

On 24 December [meeting 74], the General Assembly, on the recommendation of the Fifth Committee [A/63/645], adopted **resolution 63/256** without vote [agenda items 130 & 131].

Comprehensive proposal on appropriate incentives to retain staff of the International Criminal Tribunal for Rwanda and the international Tribunal for the Former Yugoslavia

The General Assembly,

Having considered the report of the Secretary-General on the comprehensive proposal on appropriate incentives to retain staff of the International Criminal Tribunal for Rwanda and the International Tribunal for the Former Yugoslavia,

Having also considered the related chapter of the report of the International Civil Service Commission for the year 2007,

Having further considered the related report of the Advisory Committee on Administrative and Budgetary Questions,

Recalling its resolution 61/274 of 29 June 2007 on the comprehensive proposal on appropriate incentives to retain staff of the International Criminal Tribunal for Rwanda and the International Tribunal for the Former Yugoslavia,

1. *Takes note* of the report of the Secretary-General on the comprehensive proposal on appropriate incentives to retain staff of the International Criminal Tribunal for Rwanda and the International Tribunal for the Former Yugoslavia;

2. *Endorses* the conclusions and recommendations contained in the report of the Advisory Committee on Administrative and Budgetary Questions, subject to the provisions contained in the present resolution;

3. *Takes note* of paragraphs 14 and 15 of the report of the Advisory Committee;

4. *Recognizes* the critical importance of retaining highly-skilled and specialized staff in order to successfully complete all trial proceedings and to meet the targets set out in the respective completion strategies of the Tribunals in a timely manner;

5. *Requests* the Secretary-General to use the existing contractual frameworks to offer contracts to staff, in line with dates of planned post reductions in accordance with the relevant prevailing trial schedules, in order to remove uncertainty with regard to future employment with the aim of ensuring that the Tribunals have the necessary capacity to complete their respective mandates effectively, as recommended by the International Civil Service Commission in paragraph 21 *(b)* of its report.

Implementation of completion strategies

ICTY

In response to Security Council resolution 1534(2004) [YUN 2004, p. 1292], the ICTY President reported in May [S/2008/326] and November [S/2008/729 & Add.1] on progress made in implementing the ICTY completion strategy. Most of the measures adopted to ensure the timely implementation of that strategy stemmed from a thorough examination of trial and appeal practices carried out by the Working Groups on Speeding up Appeals and Trials. Both Working Groups were reconstituted in April—not only to confirm the success of those measures, but also to examine whether further improvements could be made. By November, both Working Groups had submitted their reports, and fresh recommendations were being implemented.

Out of the 161 accused indicted by the Tribunal, only five remained in the pretrial stage as at late November. With the arrest of Župljanin and Karadžić during the reporting period, only two accused, Mladić and Hadžić, were still at large. Twenty-six accused were being tried and another 10 had appeals pending. All other cases had been completed. It was estimated that all but five of the pending trials would be completed by the end of 2009. The trials of the four most recently accused were estimated to finish during 2010, and the Prlić et al. multi-accused case might also run into 2010. It also appeared likely that a small number of trials would spill over to 2012.

Eight trials had been heard simultaneously, with two separate sittings in each of the Tribunal's three courtrooms. To expedite the conduct of trials, one of the Trial Chambers hearing a multi-accused case held additional hearings during the three-week summer recess, so as to make use of the extended availability of the Tribunal's courtrooms at that time. The Trial Chamber Judges also managed seven cases in the pretrial stage, issuing written and oral decisions on such matters as form of the indictment, challenges to jurisdiction, disclosure of evidence, protective measures for victims and witnesses, provisional release, adjudicated facts, and the admissibility of witness statements.

The Appeals Chamber continued to work at maximum productivity on appeals from both ICTY and ICTR. It delivered judgements on four appeals, leaving only seven appeals pending. As at November, only five accused in four cases were awaiting the start of their trial.

The Office of the Prosecutor continued to work closely with other organs of the Tribunal to expedite proceedings while respecting the rights of the accused. Considerable progress had been made by advancing the multi-leadership cases, narrowing the scope of prosecutions and presenting evidence more efficiently. State cooperation had improved, but there remained a number of outstanding issues, notably concerning the production of documents and the arrest of fugitives—factors which had an important bearing on the dates by which the Tribunal would be able to complete its programme of trials and appeals.

The Prosecutor worked closely with the Offices of the State Prosecutors in Bosnia and Herzegovina and Croatia and the Office of the War Crimes Prosecutor in Serbia. As trial and appeals work progressed, the Office remained committed to strengthening judicial systems in the States of the former Yugoslavia. Cooperation with national prosecution authorities was a cornerstone of its strategy and would remain a priority. Although the Prosecutor's principal obligation was to maintain the quality and progress of prosecution cases before the Tribunal, the Office was managing its resources with a view to the eventual downsizing of its staff and the design of a future residual international mechanism.

ICTR

In response to Security Council resolution 1534(2004) [YUN 2004, p. 1292], the ICTR President submitted reports in May [S/2008/322] and November [S/2008/726] that assessed progress made in implementing the ICTR completion strategy. That strategy called for completing investigations by the end of 2004, all trial activities at first instance by the end of 2008, and all of its work in 2010.

Between May and November 2008, one judgement concerning one accused had been delivered. Five cases concerning eight accused were in the judgement drafting phase, with three judgements to be delivered in December. Evidence in two cases concerning five accused had been completed, with closing arguments yet to be heard. Five trials involving 15 accused were ongoing. Six single-accused trials were scheduled to commence within the next months. On 29 August, the Appeals Chamber delivered its judgement in the case of Tharcisse Muvunyi, bringing to 26 the number of persons whose appeals had been completed.

Tools and elements used by the Tribunal to fulfil its completion strategy included use of the judicial calendar to optimize the use of courtrooms and to make the most efficient use of time and resources. For example, between May and November, seven different sections of the Trial Chambers used the Tribunal's four courtrooms in nine different cases. Measures had been developed to improve trial-readiness of cases by pre-prosecution and pre-defence status conferences. In October and November, two external consultants had assisted efforts to improve the management of proceedings. The Tribunal President continued to explore mechanisms to enable the Appeals Chamber to deal with the substantially increased workload expected in 2009 and 2010 in light of the increased number of first-instance judgements to be issued.

The Office of the Prosecutor's tracking team intensified its efforts in locating the 13 remaining fugitives. The Prosecutor intended to request the referral of nine of these cases to national jurisdictions for trial. However, four were earmarked for trial at the Tribunal because of the leadership roles played by the accused—Félicien Kabuga, Protais Mpiranya, Augustin Bizimana and Idelphonse Nizeyimana—during the 1994 genocide. Their possible arrest and transfer to the Tribunal would require a reassessment of the Tribunal's judicial calendar. The Tribunal remained committed to the goal of completing first-instance trials by the end of 2009. Whether that goal could be achieved would depend on the final number of new cases tried before the Tribunal in 2009.

Establishment of ad hoc mechanism

A Working Group on the International Tribunals was established in 2000 on an informal basis to consider matters relating to the United Nations and UN-assisted Tribunals, consisting of legal advisers to permanent missions of States that were members of the Security Council. It was assisted by the Office of Legal Affairs, which acted as the secretariat and provided advice on legal issues.

In a letter of 19 December [S/2008/849], its Chairman informed the Council that the Group made significant progress during the year regarding the establishment of a residual mechanism or mechanisms to carry out certain essential functions of the Tribunals for the former Yugoslavia and Rwanda following their closure. Working closely with both Tribunals on a draft resolution to be submitted to the Council, early agreement had emerged on a number of issues: fugitives must face trial; impunity was unacceptable; the most senior fugitives, those most responsible, must face international trial by the mechanism(s); transfer to national jurisdictions was an important part of the completion strategies of the Tribunals; continuing witness protection was of critical importance; and the archives of the Tribunals were the property of the United Nations and must be kept under its control.

Although important differences remained with respect to the structure of the residual mechanism(s), the following basic structure had emerged: the residual mechanism(s) would have a trial capacity, based on a roster of judges that could be activated to compose a Trial or Appeals Chamber; the staff of the residual mechanism(s) would be small in number; it would inherit the rights and obligations of the Tribunals and have jurisdiction to try the most senior and most responsible indictees; it would also continue certain essential residual functions of the Tribunals, including the protection of witnesses; the residual mechanism(s) would be established at a date to be determined by a Council resolution, setting out its statutes based on amended statutes of the Tribunals; and the Rules of Procedure and Evidence of the Tribunals would also require amendment, in ways yet to be determined.

SECURITY COUNCIL ACTION

On 19 December [meeting 6053], following consultations among Security Council members, the President made statement **S/PRST/2008/47** on behalf of the Council:

> The Security Council recalls its resolution 827(1993) of 25 May 1993, in which it established the International Tribunal for the Former Yugoslavia, and its resolution 955(1994) of 8 November 1994, in which it established the International Criminal Tribunal for Rwanda ("the Tribunals") and further recalls that in its resolution 1503(2003) of 28 August 2003, it called upon the Tribunals to take all possible measures to complete all trial activities at first instance by the end of 2008 and to complete all work in 2010 (the completion strategies) and that in its resolution 1534(2004) of 26 March 2004, it emphasized the importance of fully implementing the completion strategies.

The Council recalls that the Tribunals were established in particular circumstances of the former Yugoslavia and Rwanda as an ad hoc measure contributing to the restoration and maintenance of peace.

The Council takes note of the presentations made on 12 December 2008 by the Presidents and Prosecutors of the Tribunals to the Council on the implementation of the completion strategies.

Noting with concern that the deadline for the completion of trial activities at first instance has not been met and that the Tribunals have indicated that their work is not likely to end in 2010, the Council emphasizes that trials must be conducted by the Tribunals as quickly and efficiently as possible and expresses its determination to support their efforts toward the completion of their work at the earliest date.

The Council reaffirms the necessity of persons indicted by the International Tribunal for the Former Yugoslavia and the International Criminal Tribunal for Rwanda being brought to justice.

The Council calls upon all States, especially States where fugitives are suspected to be at large, to further intensify cooperation with and render all necessary assistance to the International Tribunal for the Former Yugoslavia and the International Criminal Tribunal for Rwanda, as appropriate, in particular to achieve the arrest and surrender of all remaining fugitive indictees.

The Council also reaffirms in this context that the referral of cases to competent national jurisdictions is an essential part of the completion strategies and in this regard underlines again the need for the Tribunals to concentrate their work on the prosecution and trial of the most senior leaders suspected of being most responsible for crimes within their jurisdiction, and urges the Tribunals to work with relevant national authorities to secure the transfer of cases which do not involve this level of responsibility for prosecution by competent national jurisdictions.

The Council acknowledges the need to establish an ad hoc mechanism to carry out a number of essential functions of the Tribunals, including the trial of high-level fugitives, after the closure of the Tribunals. In view of the substantially reduced nature of these residual functions, this mechanism should be a small, temporary and efficient structure. Its functions and size will diminish over time. Its expenses will be expenses of the Organization in accordance with Article 17 of the Charter of the United Nations.

The Council emphasizes that any such mechanism will derive its authority from a resolution of the Council and from statutes and rules of procedure and evidence based on those existing for the International Tribunal for the Former Yugoslavia and the International Criminal Tribunal for Rwanda, modified as appropriate, and that accommodations may be needed to address the differing needs and circumstances of the International Tribunal for the Former Yugoslavia and the International Criminal Tribunal for Rwanda.

The Council expresses its appreciation to its Informal Working Group on International Tribunals for its work to date on the establishment of this mechanism, including through a thorough examination of which functions of the Tribunals are necessary for the administration of justice after their closure. The Council requests the Informal Working Group to continue its efforts in that regard and to concentrate on the main outstanding issues with a view to drafting as soon as possible appropriate instruments necessary for the performance of residual functions of the Tribunals.

In order to facilitate the further work of the Informal Working Group, the Council requests the Secretary-General to present a report within 90 days on the administrative and budgetary aspects of the options for possible locations for the archives of the Tribunals and the seat of the residual mechanism, including the availability of suitable premises for the conduct of judicial proceedings by the residual mechanism, with particular emphasis on locations where the United Nations has an existing presence.

The Council requests the Secretariat to provide the Informal Working Group with all necessary assistance, including interpretation in the six working languages of the Council.

International Criminal Court

In 2008, the International Criminal Court (ICC), established by the Rome Statute [YUN 1998, p. 1209] as a permanent institution with jurisdiction over persons accused of the most serious crimes of international concern (genocide, crimes against humanity, war crimes and the crime of aggression), carried out investigations in the Central African Republic, the Democratic Republic of the Congo (DRC), Darfur (the Sudan) and Uganda.

The activities of ICC were reported to the General Assembly in two annual reports [A/63/323; A/64/356], covering the period from August 2007 through July 2009. As at 31 December, 108 countries had ratified the Rome Statute.

At the end of July, there were seven arrest warrants outstanding. All had been outstanding for over a year; four had been outstanding for over three years. The Court did not have the power to make arrests: that responsibility belonged to States and, by extension, international organizations.

On 13 February, Bruno Cathala, the Court's first Registrar, submitted his resignation to take up a position as President of the Tribunal de grande instance d'Evry (France); on 28 February, the judges of the Court elected Silvana Arbia to succeed him. On 29 July, Judge Navanethem Pillay submitted her resignation, effective 31 August, following approval of her appointment as the United Nations High Commissioner for Human Rights. On 9 September, the judges of the Court elected Didier Daniel Preira as its first Deputy Registrar, for a five-year term beginning on 17 October. On 26 November, the Office of the Prosecutor announced the appointment of Professor

Catharine MacKinnon as Special Gender Adviser to the Prosecutor.

The tenth anniversary of the Statute's adoption on 17 July 1998 was marked by States parties to the Statute and by civil society organizations. An obser-vance was held at The Hague on 3 July. The Secretary-General addressed an informal meeting of the Assembly of States Parties on 17 July in New York. Other events included a subregional conference in Benin, attended by the Registrar of the Court, and a celebration in South Africa, attended by Judge Navanethem Pillay on behalf of the Presidency of the Court.

GENERAL ASSEMBLY ACTION

On 11 November [meeting 45], the General Assembly adopted **resolution 63/21** [draft: A/63/L.19 & Add.1], without vote [agenda item 69].

Report of the International Criminal Court

The General Assembly,

Recalling its resolution 62/12 of 26 November 2007, and all its previous relevant resolutions,

Recalling also that the Rome Statute of the International Criminal Court reaffirms the purposes and principles of the Charter of the United Nations,

Reiterating the historic significance of the adoption of the Rome Statute and its tenth anniversary, which was celebrated on 17 July 2008,

Emphasizing that justice, especially transitional justice in conflict and post-conflict societies, is a fundamental building block of sustainable peace,

Convinced that ending impunity is essential if a society in conflict or recovering from conflict is to come to terms with past abuses committed against civilians affected by armed conflict and to prevent future such abuses,

Noting with satisfaction the fact that the International Criminal Court has achieved considerable progress in its analyses, investigations and judicial proceedings in various situations and cases which were referred to it by States parties to the Rome Statute and by the Security Council, in accordance with the Rome Statute,

Recalling that effective and comprehensive cooperation and assistance in all aspects of its mandate by States, the United Nations and other international and regional organizations remains essential for the International Criminal Court to carry out its activities,

Expressing its appreciation to the Secretary-General for providing effective and efficient assistance to the International Criminal Court in accordance with the Relationship Agreement between the United Nations and the International Criminal Court ("Relationship Agreement"),

Acknowledging the Relationship Agreement as approved by the General Assembly in its resolution 58/318 of 13 September 2004, including paragraph 3 of the resolution with respect to the payment in full of expenses accruing to the United Nations as a result of the implementation of the Relationship Agreement, which provides a framework for continued cooperation between the International Criminal Court and the United Nations, which could include the facilitation by the United Nations of the Court's field activities, and encouraging the conclusion of supplementary arrangements and agreements, as necessary,

Welcoming the continuous support given by civil society to the International Criminal Court,

Recognizing the role of the International Criminal Court in a multilateral system that aims to end impunity, establish the rule of law, promote and encourage respect for human rights and achieve sustainable peace, in accordance with international law and the purposes and principles of the Charter,

Expressing its appreciation to the International Criminal Court for providing assistance to the Special Court for Sierra Leone,

1. *Welcomes* the report of the International Criminal Court for 2007/08;

2. *Welcomes* the States that have become parties to the Rome Statute of the International Criminal Court in the past year, and calls upon all States in all regions of the world that are not yet parties to the Rome Statute to consider ratifying or acceding to it without delay;

3. *Welcomes* the States parties as well as States not parties to the Rome Statute that have become parties to the Agreement on the Privileges and Immunities of the International Criminal Court, and calls upon all States that have not yet done so to consider becoming parties to that Agreement;

4. *Calls upon* States parties to the Rome Statute that have not yet done so to adopt national legislation to implement obligations emanating from the Statute and to cooperate with the International Criminal Court in the exercise of its functions, and recalls the provision of technical assistance by States parties in this respect;

5. *Welcomes* the cooperation and assistance provided thus far to the International Criminal Court by States parties as well as States not parties, the United Nations and other international and regional organizations, and calls upon those States that are under an obligation to cooperate to provide such cooperation and assistance in the future, in particular with regard to arrest and surrender, the provision of evidence, the protection and relocation of victims and witnesses and the enforcement of sentences;

6. *Emphasizes* the importance of cooperation with States that are not parties to the Rome Statute;

7. *Invites* regional organizations to consider concluding cooperation agreements with the International Criminal Court;

8. *Recalls* that, by virtue of article 12, paragraph 3, of the Rome Statute, a State which is not a party to the Statute may, by declaration lodged with the Registrar of the International Criminal Court, accept the exercise of jurisdiction by the Court with respect to specific crimes that are mentioned in paragraph 2 of that article;

9. *Encourages* all States parties to take the interests, needs for assistance and mandate of the International Criminal Court into account when relevant matters are being discussed in the United Nations;

10. *Emphasizes* the importance of the full implementation of the Relationship Agreement, which forms a framework for close cooperation between the two organizations and for consultation on matters of mutual interest pursuant to the provisions of that Agreement and in conformity with the respective provisions of the Charter of the United Nations and the Rome Statute, as well as the need for the Secretary-General to inform the General Assembly at its

sixty-fourth session on the expenses incurred and reimbursements received by the United Nations in connection with assistance provided to the International Criminal Court;

11. *Notes* the fact that the International Criminal Court liaison office to United Nations Headquarters is now fully operational, and encourages the Secretary-General to continue to work closely with that office;

12. *Encourages* States to contribute to the Trust Fund established for the benefit of victims of crimes within the jurisdiction of the International Criminal Court and the families of such victims, and acknowledges with appreciation contributions made to the Trust Fund thus far;

13. *Notes* the work of the Special Working Group on the Crime of Aggression, which is open to all States on an equal footing, and encourages all States to consider participating actively in the Working Group with a view to elaborating proposals for a provision on the crime of aggression, in accordance with article 123 of the Rome Statute;

14. *Also notes* that the Review Conference to be held in 2010 may provide an opportunity to address issues, in addition to those relating to the possible definition of the crime of aggression, that have been identified by States, including States that are not parties to the Rome Statute;

15. *Takes note* of the decision of the Assembly of States Parties to the Rome Statute at its sixth session, while recalling that, according to article 112, paragraph 6, of the Rome Statute, the Assembly of States Parties shall meet at the seat of the International Criminal Court or at United Nations Headquarters, to hold its seventh session at The Hague, looks forward to the seventh session of the Assembly of States Parties, which is to be held at The Hague from 14 to 22 November 2008, as well as to the resumed seventh session, which is to be held in New York from 19 to 23 January 2009 and from 9 to 13 February 2009, and requests the Secretary-General to provide the necessary services and facilities in accordance with the Relationship Agreement and resolution 58/318;

16. *Encourages* the widest possible participation of States in the Assemblies of States Parties, invites States to contribute to the Trust Fund for the participation of the least developed countries, and acknowledges with appreciation contributions made to the Trust Fund thus far;

17. *Invites* the International Criminal Court to submit, in accordance with article 6 of the Relationship Agreement, a report on its activities for 2008/09, for consideration by the General Assembly at its sixty-fourth session.

Assembly of States Parties

The Assembly of States Parties to the Rome Statute of the International Criminal Court adopted two resolutions at its resumed sixth session (New York, 2–6 June) [ICC-ASP/6/20/Add.1] and seven resolutions at its seventh session (The Hague, 14–22 November) [ICC-ASP/7/20].

On 6 June, the Assembly adopted resolutions on funding the disability pension of a former judge of the Court [ICC-ASP/6/Res.7] and on a venue for its next Review Conference [ICC-ASP/6/Res.8].

On 21 November, in its resolution on permanent premises for the Court [ICC-ASP/7/Res.1], the Assembly adopted various measures relating to its financing and construction. By other resolutions adopted on that date, it decided that the Court's Review Conference would be held in Kampala, Uganda, during the first semester of 2010 [ICC-ASP/7/Res.2].

In its resolution on strengthening the Court and the Assembly [ICC-ASP/7/Res.3], it welcomed the entry into force of the Headquarters Agreement between ICC and the host country on 1 March; commended the work of the Court's Liaison Office in New York; stressed the importance of dialogue between the Court and the Bureau of the Assembly; and encouraged States, international and regional organizations and civil society to intensify their support to the Court in its efforts with respect to preserving and providing evidence, sharing information, securing the arrest and surrender to the Court of persons for whom arrest warrants had been issued, and protecting victims and witnesses. It also decided to hold its eighth session from 18 to 26 November 2009 in The Hague.

Also on 21 November, the Assembly adopted resolutions on the role of its Committee of Budget and Finance [ICC-ASP/7/Res.5]; on the languages in which its decisions and other official documents should be published [ICC-ASP/7/Res.6]; and the languages in which the recommendations and other documents of its Committee on Budget and Finance should be published [ICC-ASP/7/Res.7].

As to financing, the Assembly approved the Court's programme budget for 2009 [ICC-ASP/7/Res.4] with appropriations totalling €101,229,900. It resolved that the Working Capital Fund for 2009 would be established in the amount of €7,405,983, and authorized the Registrar to make advances from the Fund.

The Chambers

The judicial activities of the Court were conducted by the Chambers, which consisted of 18 judges, organized in three divisions: the Appeals Division, the Trial Division and the Pre-Trial Division. The Presidency constituted three Pre-Trial Chambers: Pre-Trial Chamber I—the DRC and Darfur (the Sudan); Pre-Trial Chamber II—Uganda; and Pre-Trial Chamber III—Central African Republic.

On 13 June, Trial Chamber I issued a stay of proceedings in the case of Thomas Lubanga Dyilo, alleged leader of the Union des Patriotes Congolais pour la Réconciliation et la Paix and Commander-in-Chief of its military wing, the Forces Patriotiques pour la Libération du Congo. Finding that a fair trial was not possible owing to the prosecution's failure to disclose a significant body of potentially exculpatory evidence to the defence or to make it available to the judges, the Chamber ordered his unconditional release. On 2 July, the prosecution appealed the release. Over a period of five months, the prosecution, having obtained the consent of the relevant information providers, disclosed those materials or made them available to the judges. On 18 November, the Chamber found that the prosecution had met its obligations and that the trial could proceed.

On 29 April, Pre-Trial Chamber I unsealed a warrant of arrest issued on 22 August 2006 against Bosco Ntaganda, alleged Deputy Chief of General Staff for Military Operations of the Forces Patriotiques pour la Libération du Congo. It found that there were reasonable grounds to believe he had committed such war crimes as enlisting and conscripting children under 15 year of age and using them to participate in hostilities. At the end of the year, his arrest warrant remained outstanding.

During the year, Pre-Trial Chamber II continued to monitor the status of execution of the arrest warrants, and to address issues relating to the participation of victims in proceedings.

New arrests, warrants and surrenders

During the year ending 31 July, the Court issued or unsealed four new arrest warrants—three in the situation in the DRC and one in the situation in the Central African Republic. Seven arrest warrants were outstanding: four pertaining to the situation in Uganda, two in Darfur and one in the DRC. All had been outstanding for over a year, and four had been outstanding for over three years.

Mathieu Ngudjolo Chui was surrendered to the Court on 7 February. He and Germain Katanga, who was surrendered to the Court in 2007, were each charged with nine counts of war crimes and four counts of crimes against humanity in the DRC. A hearing was held from 27 June to 16 July, and on 26 September, Pre-Trial Chamber I confirmed seven charges of war crimes and three charges of crimes against humanity. Their joint trial was scheduled to begin in 2009.

In the situation in the Central African Republic, Jean-Pierre Bemba Gombo was arrested in Belgium on 24 May and surrendered to the Court on 3 July. He was suspected of having committed three counts of crimes against humanity and five counts of war crimes.

On 14 July, the Prosecutor submitted an application for a warrant of arrest against Omar Hassan Ahmad Al-Bashir, President of the Sudan, on counts of genocide, crimes against humanity and war crimes. The application was being considered by the judges of Pre-Trial Chamber I.

Office of the Prosecutor

In 2008, the Prosecutor continued to investigate the situations in the Central African Republic, the DRC, Darfur (the Sudan) and Uganda. In the DRC, the Office of the Prosecutor was looking into the numerous reports of crimes committed by a multiplicity of perpetrators and groups in North and South Kivu. In September, the Prosecutor announced the opening of a third case in the DRC, focusing on alleged crimes committed in the Kivu province by perpetrators and groups including the Forces démocratiques de libération du Rwanda, the Congrès national pour la défense du peuple, the regular forces and the Mai-Mai, as well as numerous reports of sexual crimes. Eight missions were conducted inside or outside the DRC to collect information in the context of that new case.

The Office sent an investigation mission to Uganda in May and June to collect additional evidence of supply and support to the Lord's Resistance Army (LRA). The Office had also collected a range of information on the crimes allegedly being committed by LRA in the DRC, including abduction of civilians for the purpose of recruitment, forced labour and sexual enslavement. The incidence of alleged crimes rose sharply from September, as LRA, operating increasingly freely across a wide area between Garamba National Park in the DRC and border areas of southern Sudan close to the Central African Republic, put into operation plans to expand their numbers by several hundred through the abduction of civilians, primarily children. The Office received reports of particularly savage attacks taking place in December.

In Darfur, the Office was investigating the mobilization of the State apparatus to plan, commit and cover up crimes against civilians, in particular the Fur, Massaleit and Zaghawa tribes. It was also investigating allegations of rebel crimes, focusing among others on the Haskanita attack against peacekeepers.

In the Central African Republic, the Office continued to gather evidence and establish responsibility for the crimes allegedly committed against the civilian population in 2002/2003, including rape, torture and pillaging. The Office alleged that hundreds of rapes were committed, and that sexual crimes would feature in the case against Mr. Bemba. In parallel, the Office was closely monitoring allegations of crimes committed since the end of 2005 and whether any investigation and prosecution had been conducted. A letter was sent to President François Bozizé to receive information about possible relevant national proceedings.

The Registry

The ICC Registry provided judicial and administrative support to all organs of the Court and carried out its specific responsibilities concerning victims, witnesses, defence and outreach. The Registry sought to develop understanding and awareness of ICC and its activities by strengthening the Court's public information capacity for outreach services in countries where the Court was active. It provided security, administrative and logistical support to the Court's investigations.

Among the Registry's activities, 17 victims participating in the proceedings relating to the DRC were declared indigent and were granted legal aid by the Registrar. Regarding the case against Jean-Pierre Bemba Gombo, relating to rape and sexual crimes committed in the Central African Republic between October 2002 and March 2003, the Registrar travelled there to increase awareness about the Court's activities.

International cooperation

The Rome Statute obliged its States parties to cooperate fully with the Court in its investigations and prosecutions and provided the basis for the cooperation of States, international organizations and civil society with the Court. Cooperation with the United Nations continued to be essential to the Court institutionally and in the different situations and cases. The Court received public and diplomatic support by the United Nations and operational support from UN missions in the field. The first phase of the digitization of the entire legislative history of the Rome process was concluded with cooperation from the Secretariat of the Assembly of States Parties and the UN Office of Legal Affairs.

The Headquarters Agreement between ICC and the host State entered into force on 3 March, providing clarity and certainty on issues that were not adequately covered by the interim arrangements. In executing decisions of the Court, the DRC surrendered two individuals to the Court and Belgium surrendered a third. As at 31 July, the Court had concluded 10 agreements with States on the protection and relocation of witnesses and two ad hoc arrangements. Efforts to finalize a memorandum of understanding between the African Union and the Court continued. On 2 September, the Prosecutor met with the Secretary-General of INTERPOL to pursue a cooperation agreement.

Report of Secretary-General. The General Assembly, in resolution 62/12 [YUN 2007, p. 1351], requested the Secretary-General to inform it on the expenses incurred and reimbursements received by the United Nations for assistance provided to ICC. In October [A/63/471], he informed the Assembly that from October 2004 to August 2008, the United Nations had provided facilities and services in the amount of $989,785, including reimbursements for conference and related services, field security costs, library services and document digitization. In addition, MONUC provided transportation and other services to ICC amounting to $102,253. The Court had regularly reimbursed the United Nations upon receipt of invoices. Two annexes to the report provided information on facilities and services provided to ICC by the United Nations and by MONUC since October 2004.

Chapter III

International legal questions

In 2008, the International Law Commission continued to examine topics relating to the progressive development and codification of international law. It adopted draft articles on the law of transboundary aquifers, and provisionally adopted draft articles on the effects of armed conflicts on treaties. It adopted draft guidelines on reservations to treaties, and provisionally adopted eight draft articles on invocation of the international responsibility of an international organization. It established a Working Group to consider issues relating to the expulsion of aliens, and held debates on the protection of persons in the event of disasters, issues relating to the immunity of State officials from foreign criminal jurisdiction, and aspects of the obligation to extradite or prosecute.

The Ad Hoc Committee established by the General Assembly continued to elaborate a draft comprehensive convention on international terrorism. In July, the Secretary-General reported on measures taken by States, UN system entities and intergovernmental organizations to implement the 1994 General Assembly Declaration on Measures to Eliminate International Terrorism. In December, the Assembly condemned all acts, methods and practices of terrorism as criminal and unjustifiable and called on States to adopt further measures to prevent terrorism.

The United Nations Commission on International Trade Law finalized and approved a draft text, which was adopted in December by the Assembly as the United Nations Convention on Contracts for the International Carriage of Goods Wholly or Partly by Sea. It continued work on public procurement, arbitration and conciliation, insolvency law, and security interests, and considered future work in the areas of electronic commerce and commercial fraud. The Commission also welcomed initiatives undertaken to commemorate the fiftieth anniversary of the 1958 New York Convention on Foreign Arbitral Awards.

The Special Committee on the Charter of the United Nations and on the Strengthening of the Role of the Organization continued to consider, among other items, proposals relating to the maintenance of international peace and security in order to strengthen the Organization and the implementation of Charter provisions on assistance to third States affected by the application of sanctions under Chapter VII.

The Committee on Relations with the Host Country addressed a number of issues raised by permanent missions to the United Nations, including transportation and parking matters, the security of missions and their personnel, delays in issuing visas and accelerating immigration and customs procedures.

Legal aspects of international political relations

International Law Commission

The 34-member International Law Commission (ILC) held its sixtieth session in Geneva in two parts (5 May–6 June; 7 July–8 August) [A/63/10]. During the second part, the International Law Seminar held its forty-fourth session, which was attended by 27 participants, mostly from developing countries. They observed ILC meetings, attended specially arranged lectures and participated in working groups on specific topics. The Commission also convened a two-day commemorative meeting on the occasion of its sixtieth anniversary session.

ILC carried out its work with the assistance of various working groups and a Drafting Committee. On the topic of shared natural resources, the Commission considered the fifth report of the Special Rapporteur, containing a set of 20 draft articles on the law of transboundary aquifers, together with comments from Governments on the draft articles adopted on first reading, completed the second reading, and adopted a preamble and a set of 19 draft articles, together with commentaries. On the effects of armed conflicts on treaties, ILC had before it the fourth report of the Special Rapporteur dealing with the procedure for the suspension or termination of treaties as a consequence of an armed conflict. It provisionally adopted, on first reading, a set of 18 draft articles and an annex, together with commentaries, and transmitted them to Governments for comments and observations. On reservations to treaties, ILC considered the thirteenth report of the Special Rapporteur dealing with reactions to interpretative declarations, referred 10 draft guidelines to the Drafting Committee on reactions to interpretative declarations, and adopted 23 draft guidelines dealing with formulation and withdrawal of acceptances and objections, as well as the procedure for acceptance of reservations, together with commentaries thereto. The Commission provisionally adopted eight draft articles, together with commentaries, on invocation of the international responsibility of an international organization and took note of seven draft articles provisionally adopted by the Drafting Committee on countermeasures.

On the expulsion of aliens, the Commission considered the fourth report of the Special Rapporteur dealing with questions relating to the expulsion of dual or multiple nationals, as well as loss of nationality or denationalization in relation to expulsion, and established a Working Group to consider the issues in the report. ILC held debates based on the preliminary report of the Special Rapporteur on the protection of persons in the event of disasters and on the preliminary report of the Special Rapporteur on the immunity of State officials from foreign criminal jurisdiction, which considered such issues as the officials and acts to be covered, as well as possible exceptions. With respect to the obligation to extradite or prosecute (*aut dedere aut judicare*), the Commission held a debate based on the third report of the Special Rapporteur, addressing such issues as the customary nature of the obligation, the relation with universal jurisdiction and international courts, and procedural aspects to be dealt with in future.

ILC established a Planning Group to consider its programme, procedures and working methods, which decided to reconstitute the Working Group on the Long-term programme of Work. The Commission decided that its sixty-first session would be held in Geneva from 4 May to 5 June and 6 July to 7 August 2009.

GENERAL ASSEMBLY ACTION

On 11 December [meeting 67], the General Assembly, on the recommendation of the Sixth (Legal) Committee [A/63/439], adopted **resolution 63/123** without vote [agenda item 75].

Report of the International Law Commission on the work of its sixtieth session

The General Assembly,

Having considered the report of the International Law Commission on the work of its sixtieth session,

Emphasizing the importance of furthering the progressive development of international law and its codification as a means of implementing the purposes and principles set forth in the Charter of the United Nations and in the Declaration on Principles of International Law concerning Friendly Relations and Cooperation among States in accordance with the Charter of the United Nations,

Recognizing the desirability of referring legal and drafting questions to the Sixth Committee, including topics that might be submitted to the International Law Commission for closer examination, and of enabling the Sixth Committee and the Commission to enhance further their contribution to the progressive development of international law and its codification,

Recalling the need to keep under review those topics of international law which, given their new or renewed interest for the international community, may be suitable for the progressive development and codification of international law and therefore may be included in the future programme of work of the International Law Commission,

Reaffirming the importance to the successful work of the International Law Commission of the information provided by Member States concerning their views and practice,

Recognizing the importance of the work of the special rapporteurs of the International Law Commission,

Recalling the role of Member States in submitting proposals for the consideration of the International Law Commission,

Welcoming the holding of the International Law Seminar, and noting with appreciation the voluntary contributions made to the United Nations Trust Fund for the International Law Seminar,

Acknowledging the importance of facilitating the timely publication of the *Yearbook of the International Law Commission* and eliminating the backlog,

Stressing the usefulness of focusing and structuring the debate on the report of the International Law Commission in the Sixth Committee in such a manner that conditions are provided for concentrated attention to each of the main topics dealt with in the report and for discussions on specific topics,

Wishing to enhance further, in the context of the revitalization of the debate on the report of the International Law Commission, the interaction between the Sixth Committee as a body of governmental representatives and the Commission as a body of independent legal experts, with a view to improving the dialogue between the two bodies,

Welcoming initiatives to hold interactive debates, panel discussions and question time in the Sixth Committee, as envisaged in resolution 58/316 of 1 July 2004 on further measures for the revitalization of the work of the General Assembly,

1. *Takes note* of the report of the International Law Commission on the work of its sixtieth session, and recommends that the Commission continue its work on the topics in its current programme, taking into account the comments and observations of Governments, whether submitted in writing or expressed orally in debates in the Sixth Committee;

2. *Expresses its appreciation* to the International Law Commission for the work accomplished at its sixtieth session, in particular for the following accomplishments:

(*a*) The completion of the second reading of the draft articles on the law of transboundary aquifers under the topic "Shared natural resources";

(*b*) The completion of the first reading of the draft articles on the topic "Effects of armed conflicts on treaties";

3. *Draws the attention* of Governments to the importance for the International Law Commission of having their views on the various aspects involved in the topics on the agenda of the Commission, in particular on all the specific issues identified in chapter III of its report, regarding:

(*a*) Reservations to treaties;

(*b*) Responsibility of international organizations;

(*c*) Protection of persons in the event of disasters;

4. *Invites* Governments, within the context of paragraph 3 above, to provide information to the International Law Commission regarding practice with regard to the topics "Reservations to treaties" and "Protection of persons in the event of disasters";

5. *Draws the attention* of Governments to the importance for the International Law Commission of having their comments and observations by 1 January 2010 on the draft articles and commentaries on the topic "Effects of armed conflicts on treaties" adopted on first reading by the Commission at its sixtieth session;

6. *Takes note* of the decision of the International Law Commission to include the topics "Treaties in time" and "The Most-Favoured-Nation clause" in its programme of work;

7. *Invites* the International Law Commission to continue taking measures to enhance its efficiency and productivity and to consider making proposals to that end;

8. *Encourages* the International Law Commission to continue taking cost-saving measures at its future sessions without prejudice to the efficiency of its work;

9. *Requests* the Secretary-General to submit to the General Assembly, in accordance with the established procedures, and bearing in mind its resolution 56/272 of 27 March 2002, a report on the assistance currently provided to special rapporteurs and options regarding additional support of the work of special rapporteurs;

10. *Takes note* of paragraph 363 of the report of the International Law Commission, and decides that the next session of the Commission shall be held at the United Nations Office at Geneva from 4 May to 5 June and from 6 July to 7 August 2009;

11. *Welcomes* the enhanced dialogue between the International Law Commission and the Sixth Committee at the sixty-third session of the General Assembly, stresses the desirability of further enhancing the dialogue between the two bodies, and in this context encourages, inter alia, the continued practice of informal consultations in the form of discussions between the members of the Sixth Committee and the members of the Commission attending the sixty-fourth session of the Assembly;

12. *Encourages* delegations, during the debate on the report of the International Law Commission, to adhere as far as possible to the structured work programme agreed to by the Sixth Committee and to consider presenting concise and focused statements;

13. *Encourages* Member States to consider being represented at the level of legal adviser during the first week in which the report of the International Law Commission is discussed in the Sixth Committee (International Law Week) to enable high-level discussions on issues of international law;

14. *Requests* the International Law Commission to continue to pay special attention to indicating in its annual report, for each topic, any specific issues on which expressions of views by Governments, either in the Sixth Committee or in written form, would be of particular interest in providing effective guidance for the Commission in its further work;

15. *Takes note* of paragraphs 336 to 340 of the report of the International Law Commission and commends the convening of the sixtieth anniversary commemorative meeting in Geneva on 19 and 20 May 2008, and also commends Member States, in association with existing regional organizations, professional associations, academic institutions and members of the Commission, that convened national or regional meetings dedicated to the work of the Commission;

16. *Also takes note* of paragraphs 355 and 356 of the report of the International Law Commission with regard to cooperation with other bodies, and encourages the Commission to continue the implementation of article 16, paragraph *(e)*, and article 26, paragraphs 1 and 2, of its statute in order to further strengthen cooperation between the Commission and other bodies concerned with international law, having in mind the usefulness of such cooperation;

17. *Encourages* the International Law Commission to undertake consultations, if it finds it appropriate, with key humanitarian actors, including the United Nations and the International Federation of Red Cross and Red Crescent Societies, in connection with work on the topic "Protection of persons in the event of disasters";

18. *Notes* that the International Law Commission, in accordance with article 26, paragraph 1, of its statute, envisages a meeting during its sixty-first session with legal advisers of international organizations within the United Nations system, in order to hold a discussion on matters of mutual interest;

19. *Also notes* that consulting with national organizations and individual experts concerned with international law may assist Governments in considering whether to make comments and observations on drafts submitted by the International Law Commission and in formulating their comments and observations;

20. *Reaffirms* its previous decisions concerning the indispensable role of the Codification Division of the Office of Legal Affairs of the Secretariat in providing assistance to the International Law Commission, including in the preparation of memorandums and studies on topics on the agenda of the Commission;

21. *Approves* the conclusions reached by the International Law Commission in paragraph 359 of its report, and reaffirms its previous decisions concerning the documentation and summary records of the Commission;

22. *Takes note* of paragraph 360 of the report of the International Law Commission and, without prejudice to the importance of ensuring necessary allocations in the regular budget, acknowledges the establishment by the Secretary-General of a trust fund to accept voluntary contributions so as to address the backlog relating to the *Yearbook of the International Law Commission*, and invites voluntary contributions to that end;

23. *Welcomes* the continuous efforts of the Codification Division to maintain and improve the website relating to the work of the International Law Commission;

24. *Expresses the hope* that the International Law Seminar will continue to be held in connection with the sessions of the International Law Commission and that an increasing number of participants, in particular from developing countries, will be given the opportunity to attend the Seminar, and appeals to States to continue to make urgently needed voluntary contributions to the United Nations Trust Fund for the International Law Seminar;

25. *Requests* the Secretary-General to provide the International Law Seminar with adequate services, including interpretation, as required, and encourages him to continue considering ways to improve the structure and content of the Seminar;

26. *Also requests* the Secretary-General to forward to the International Law Commission, for its attention, the records of the debate on the report of the Commission at the sixty-third session of the General Assembly, together with such written statements as delegations may circulate in conjunction with their oral statements, and to prepare and distribute a topical summary of the debate, following established practice;

27. *Requests* the Secretariat to circulate to States, as soon as possible after the conclusion of the session of the International Law Commission, chapter II of its report containing a summary of the work of that session, chapter III containing the specific issues on which the views of Governments would be of particular interest to the Commission and the draft articles adopted on either first or second reading by the Commission;

28. *Encourages* the International Law Commission to continue considering ways in which specific issues on which the views of Governments would be of particular interest to the Commission could be framed so as to help Governments to have a better appreciation of the issues on which responses are required;

29. *Recommends* that the debate on the report of the International Law Commission at the sixty-fourth session of the General Assembly commence on 26 October 2009.

Shared natural resources

The Commission had before it the fifth report [A/CN.4/591] on shared natural resources by Special Rapporteur Chusei Yamada (Japan), which contained a set of 20 draft articles on the law of transboundary aquifers for its consideration on second reading, as well as the comments and observations received from Governments on the draft articles adopted on first reading [A/CN.4/595 & Add.1]. ILC referred those draft articles to its Drafting Committee on 7 and 8 May, while a draft preamble was referred on 21 May. The Committee decided to omit draft article 20, considering it premature to address issues concerning the relationship with other instruments, which were best left to negotiating parties to resolve.

ILC [A/63/10] adopted a preamble and a set of 19 draft articles on the law of transboundary aquifers on 4 June and the commentaries to those articles on 4 and 5 August. The Commission recommended that the General Assembly take note of the draft articles on the law of transboundary aquifers in a resolution; annex them to the resolution; and consider at a later stage the elaboration of a convention based upon them. It further recommended that States concerned make appropriate bilateral or regional arrangements for the proper management of their transboundary aquifers on the basis of those draft articles.

GENERAL ASSEMBLY ACTION

On 11 December [meeting 67], the General Assembly, on the recommendation of the Sixth Committee [A/63/439], adopted **resolution 63/124** without vote [agenda item 75].

The law of transboundary aquifers

The General Assembly,

Having considered chapter IV of the report of the International Law Commission on the work of its sixtieth session, which contains the draft articles on the law of transboundary aquifers,

Noting that the Commission decided to recommend to the General Assembly *(a)* to take note of the draft articles on the law of transboundary aquifers in a resolution, and to annex the articles to the resolution; *(b)* to recommend to States concerned to make appropriate bilateral or regional arrangements for the proper management of their transboundary aquifers on the basis of the principles enunciated in the articles; and *(c)* to also consider, at a later stage, and in view of the importance of the topic, the elaboration of a convention on the basis of the draft articles,

Emphasizing the continuing importance of the codification and progressive development of international law, as referred to in Article 13, paragraph 1 *(a)*, of the Charter of the United Nations,

Noting that the subject of the law of transboundary aquifers is of major importance in the relations of States,

Taking note of the comments of Governments and the discussion in the Sixth Committee at the sixty-third session of the General Assembly on this topic,

1. *Welcomes* the conclusion of the work of the International Law Commission on the law of transboundary aquifers and its adoption of the draft articles and a detailed commentary on the subject;

2. *Expresses its appreciation* to the Commission for its continuing contribution to the codification and progressive development of international law;

3. *Also expresses its appreciation* to the International Hydrological Programme of the United Nations Educational, Scientific and Cultural Organization and to other relevant organizations for the valuable scientific and technical assistance rendered to the International Law Commission;

4. *Takes note* of the draft articles on the law of transboundary aquifers, presented by the Commission, the text of which is annexed to the present resolution, and commends them to the attention of Governments without prejudice to the question of their future adoption or other appropriate action;

5. *Encourages* the States concerned to make appropriate bilateral or regional arrangements for the proper management of their transboundary aquifers, taking into account the provisions of these draft articles;

6. *Decides* to include in the provisional agenda of its sixty-sixth session an item entitled "The law of transboundary aquifers" with a view to examining, inter alia, the question of the form that might be given to the draft articles.

ANNEX

The law of transboundary aquifers

Conscious of the importance for humankind of life-supporting groundwater resources in all regions of the world,

Bearing in mind Article 13, paragraph 1 *(a)*, of the Charter of the United Nations, which provides that the General Assembly shall initiate studies and make recommendations for the purpose of encouraging the progressive development of international law and its codification,

Recalling General Assembly resolution 1803(XVII) of 14 December 1962 on permanent sovereignty over natural resources,

Reaffirming the principles and recommendations adopted by the United Nations Conference on Environment and Development of 1992 in the Rio Declaration on Environment and Development and Agenda 21,

Taking into account increasing demands for freshwater and the need to protect groundwater resources,

Mindful of the particular problems posed by the vulnerability of aquifers to pollution,

Convinced of the need to ensure the development, utilization, conservation, management and protection of groundwater resources in the context of the promotion of the optimal and sustainable development of water resources for present and future generations,

Affirming the importance of international cooperation and good-neighbourliness in this field,

Emphasizing the need to take into account the special situation of developing countries,

Recognizing the necessity to promote international cooperation,

Part one
Introduction

Article 1

Scope

The present articles apply to:

(a) Utilization of transboundary aquifers or aquifer systems;

(b) Other activities that have or are likely to have an impact upon such aquifers or aquifer systems; and

(c) Measures for the protection, preservation and management of such aquifers or aquifer systems.

Article 2

Use of terms

For the purposes of the present articles:

(a) "aquifer" means a permeable water bearing geological formation underlain by a less permeable layer and the water contained in the saturated zone of the formation;

(b) "aquifer system" means a series of two or more aquifers that are hydraulically connected;

(c) "transboundary aquifer" or "transboundary aquifer system" means, respectively, an aquifer or aquifer system, parts of which are situated in different States;

(d) "aquifer State" means a State in whose territory any part of a transboundary aquifer or aquifer system is situated;

(e) "utilization of transboundary aquifers or aquifer systems" includes extraction of water, heat and minerals, and storage and disposal of any substance;

(f) "recharging aquifer" means an aquifer that receives a non-negligible amount of contemporary water recharge;

(g) "recharge zone" means the zone which contributes water to an aquifer, consisting of the catchment area of rainfall water and the area where such water flows to an aquifer by run-off on the ground and infiltration through soil;

(h) "discharge zone" means the zone where water originating from an aquifer flows to its outlets, such as a watercourse, a lake, an oasis, a wetland or an ocean.

Part two
General principles

Article 3

Sovereignty of aquifer States

Each aquifer State has sovereignty over the portion of a transboundary aquifer or aquifer system located within its territory. It shall exercise its sovereignty in accordance with international law and the present articles.

Article 4

Equitable and reasonable utilization

Aquifer States shall utilize transboundary aquifers or aquifer systems according to the principle of equitable and reasonable utilization, as follows:

(a) They shall utilize transboundary aquifers or aquifer systems in a manner that is consistent with the equitable and reasonable accrual of benefits therefrom to the aquifer States concerned;

(b) They shall aim at maximizing the long-term benefits derived from the use of water contained therein;

(c) They shall establish individually or jointly a comprehensive utilization plan, taking into account present and future needs of, and alternative water sources for, the aquifer States; and

(d) They shall not utilize a recharging transboundary aquifer or aquifer system at a level that would prevent continuance of its effective functioning.

Article 5

Factors relevant to equitable and reasonable utilization

1. Utilization of a transboundary aquifer or aquifer system in an equitable and reasonable manner within the meaning of article 4 requires taking into account all relevant factors, including:

(a) The population dependent on the aquifer or aquifer system in each aquifer State;

(b) The social, economic and other needs, present and future, of the aquifer States concerned;

(c) The natural characteristics of the aquifer or aquifer system;

(d) The contribution to the formation and recharge of the aquifer or aquifer system;

(e) The existing and potential utilization of the aquifer or aquifer system;

(f) The actual and potential effects of the utilization of the aquifer or aquifer system in one aquifer State on other aquifer States concerned;

(*g*) The availability of alternatives to a particular existing and planned utilization of the aquifer or aquifer system;

(*h*) The development, protection and conservation of the aquifer or aquifer system and the costs of measures to be taken to that effect;

(*i*) The role of the aquifer or aquifer system in the related ecosystem.

2. The weight to be given to each factor is to be determined by its importance with regard to a specific transboundary aquifer or aquifer system in comparison with that of other relevant factors. In determining what is equitable and reasonable utilization, all relevant factors are to be considered together and a conclusion reached on the basis of all the factors. However, in weighing different kinds of utilization of a transboundary aquifer or aquifer system, special regard shall be given to vital human needs.

Article 6

Obligation not to cause significant harm

1. Aquifer States shall, in utilizing transboundary aquifers or aquifer systems in their territories, take all appropriate measures to prevent the causing of significant harm to other aquifer States or other States in whose territory a discharge zone is located.

2. Aquifer States shall, in undertaking activities other than utilization of a transboundary aquifer or aquifer system that have, or are likely to have, an impact upon that transboundary aquifer or aquifer system, take all appropriate measures to prevent the causing of significant harm through that aquifer or aquifer system to other aquifer States or other States in whose territory a discharge zone is located.

3. Where significant harm nevertheless is caused to another aquifer State or a State in whose territory a discharge zone is located, the aquifer State whose activities cause such harm shall take, in consultation with the affected State, all appropriate response measures to eliminate or mitigate such harm, having due regard for the provisions of articles 4 and 5.

Article 7

General obligation to cooperate

1. Aquifer States shall cooperate on the basis of sovereign equality, territorial integrity, sustainable development, mutual benefit and good faith in order to attain equitable and reasonable utilization and appropriate protection of their transboundary aquifers or aquifer systems.

2. For the purpose of paragraph 1, aquifer States should establish joint mechanisms of cooperation.

Article 8

Regular exchange of data and information

1. Pursuant to article 7, aquifer States shall, on a regular basis, exchange readily available data and information on the condition of their transboundary aquifers or aquifer systems, in particular of a geological, hydrogeological, hydrological, meteorological and ecological nature and related to the hydrochemistry of the aquifers or aquifer systems, as well as related forecasts.

2. Where knowledge about the nature and extent of a transboundary aquifer or aquifer system is inadequate, aquifer States concerned shall employ their best efforts to collect and generate more complete data and information relating to such aquifer or aquifer system, taking into account current practices and standards. They shall take such action individually or jointly and, where appropriate, together with or through international organizations.

3. If an aquifer State is requested by another aquifer State to provide data and information relating to an aquifer or aquifer system that is not readily available, it shall employ its best efforts to comply with the request. The requested State may condition its compliance upon payment by the requesting State of the reasonable costs of collecting and, where appropriate, processing such data or information.

4. Aquifer States shall, where appropriate, employ their best efforts to collect and process data and information in a manner that facilitates their utilization by the other aquifer States to which such data and information are communicated.

Article 9

Bilateral and regional agreements and arrangements

For the purpose of managing a particular transboundary aquifer or aquifer system, aquifer States are encouraged to enter into bilateral or regional agreements or arrangements among themselves. Such agreements or arrangements may be entered into with respect to an entire aquifer or aquifer system or any part thereof or a particular project, programme or utilization except insofar as an agreement or arrangement adversely affects, to a significant extent, the utilization by one or more other aquifer States of the water in that aquifer or aquifer system, without their express consent.

Part three

Protection, preservation and management

Article 10

Protection and preservation of ecosystems

Aquifer States shall take all appropriate measures to protect and preserve ecosystems within, or dependent upon, their transboundary aquifers or aquifer systems, including measures to ensure that the quality and quantity of water retained in an aquifer or aquifer system, as well as that released through its discharge zones, are sufficient to protect and preserve such ecosystems.

Article 11

Recharge and discharge zones

1. Aquifer States shall identify the recharge and discharge zones of transboundary aquifers or aquifer systems that exist within their territory. They shall take appropriate measures to prevent and minimize detrimental impacts on the recharge and discharge processes.

2. All States in whose territory a recharge or discharge zone is located, in whole or in part, and which are not aquifer States with regard to that aquifer or aquifer system, shall cooperate with the aquifer States to protect the aquifer or aquifer system and related ecosystems.

Article 12

Prevention, reduction and control of pollution

Aquifer States shall, individually and, where appropriate, jointly, prevent, reduce and control pollution of their transboundary aquifers or aquifer systems, including through the recharge process, that may cause significant harm to other aquifer States. Aquifer States shall take a precautionary approach in view of uncertainty about the nature and extent of a transboundary aquifer or aquifer system and of its vulnerability to pollution.

Article 13

Monitoring

1. Aquifer States shall monitor their transboundary aquifers or aquifer systems. They shall, wherever possible, carry out these monitoring activities jointly with other aquifer States concerned and, where appropriate, in collaboration with competent international organizations. Where monitoring activities cannot be carried out jointly, the aquifer States shall exchange the monitored data among themselves.

2. Aquifer States shall use agreed or harmonized standards and methodology for monitoring their transboundary aquifers or aquifer systems. They should identify key parameters that they will monitor based on an agreed conceptual model of the aquifers or aquifer systems. These parameters should include parameters on the condition of the aquifer or aquifer system as listed in article 8, paragraph 1, and also on the utilization of the aquifers or aquifer systems.

Article 14

Management

Aquifer States shall establish and implement plans for the proper management of their transboundary aquifers or aquifer systems. They shall, at the request of any of them, enter into consultations concerning the management of a transboundary aquifer or aquifer system. A joint management mechanism shall be established, wherever appropriate.

Article 15

Planned activities

1. When a State has reasonable grounds for believing that a particular planned activity in its territory may affect a transboundary aquifer or aquifer system and thereby may have a significant adverse effect upon another State, it shall, as far as practicable, assess the possible effects of such activity.

2. Before a State implements or permits the implementation of planned activities which may affect a transboundary aquifer or aquifer system and thereby may have a significant adverse effect upon another State, it shall provide that State with timely notification thereof. Such notification shall be accompanied by available technical data and information, including any environmental impact assessment, in order to enable the notified State to evaluate the possible effects of the planned activities.

3. If the notifying and the notified States disagree on the possible effect of the planned activities, they shall enter into consultations and, if necessary, negotiations with a view to arriving at an equitable resolution of the situation. They may utilize an independent fact-finding body to make an impartial assessment of the effect of the planned activities.

Part four

Miscellaneous provisions

Article 16

Technical cooperation with developing States

States shall, directly or through competent international organizations, promote scientific, educational, technical, legal and other cooperation with developing States for the protection and management of transboundary aquifers or aquifer systems, including, inter alia:

(a) Strengthening their capacity-building in scientific, technical and legal fields;

(b) Facilitating their participation in relevant international programmes;

(c) Supplying them with necessary equipment and facilities;

(d) Enhancing their capacity to manufacture such equipment;

(e) Providing advice on and developing facilities for research, monitoring, educational and other programmes;

(f) Providing advice on and developing facilities for minimizing the detrimental effects of major activities affecting their transboundary aquifer or aquifer system;

(g) Providing advice in the preparation of environmental impact assessments;

(h) Supporting the exchange of technical knowledge and experience among developing States with a view to strengthening cooperation among them in managing the transboundary aquifer or aquifer system.

Article 17

Emergency situations

1. For the purpose of the present article, "emergency" means a situation, resulting suddenly from natural causes or from human conduct, that affects a transboundary aquifer or aquifer system and poses an imminent threat of causing serious harm to aquifer States or other States.

2. The State within whose territory the emergency originates shall:

(a) Without delay and by the most expeditious means available, notify other potentially affected States and competent international organizations of the emergency;

(b) In cooperation with potentially affected States and, where appropriate, competent international organizations, immediately take all practicable measures necessitated by the circumstances to prevent, mitigate and eliminate any harmful effect of the emergency.

3. Where an emergency poses a threat to vital human needs, aquifer States, notwithstanding articles 4 and 6, may take measures that are strictly necessary to meet such needs.

4. States shall provide scientific, technical, logistical and other cooperation to other States experiencing an emergency. Cooperation may include coordination of international emergency actions and communications, making available emergency response personnel, emergency response equipment and supplies, scientific and technical expertise and humanitarian assistance.

Article 18

Protection in time of armed conflict

Transboundary aquifers or aquifer systems and related installations, facilities and other works shall enjoy the protection accorded by the principles and rules of international law applicable in international and non-international armed conflict and shall not be used in violation of those principles and rules.

Article 19

Data and information vital to national defence or security

Nothing in the present articles obliges a State to provide data or information vital to its national defence or security. Nevertheless, that State shall cooperate in good faith with other States with a view to providing as much information as possible under the circumstances.

Responsibility of international organizations

ILC considered the sixth report on responsibility of international organizations [A/CN.4/597] by Special Rapporteur Giorgio Gaja (Italy), as well as written comments received from international organizations [A/CN.4/593]. The report contained 12 draft articles corresponding to Part Three of the articles on State responsibility. Draft articles 46 to 51 dealt with invocation of the responsibility of an international organization, while draft articles 52 to 57 addressed the issue of countermeasures.

The Commission [A/63/10] considered the Special Rapporteur's report from 9 to 16 May and established a Working Group to consider the issue of countermeasures, as well as the advisability of including a provision relating to the admissibility of claims. On 4 June, ILC adopted the Drafting Committee's report on draft articles 46 to 53. In August, the Commission took note of draft articles 54 to 60 on countermeasures as provisionally adopted by the Drafting Committee and adopted the title of Chapter I of Part Three of the draft articles, "Invocation of the responsibility of an international organization", in addition to the commentaries to draft articles 46 to 53.

Expulsion of aliens

ILC had before it the fourth report on the expulsion of aliens [A/CN.4/594] by Special Rapporteur Maurice Kamto (Cameroon), which analysed the issue of expulsion of dual nationals and the question of deprivation of nationality as a prelude to expulsion. The Commission [A/63/10] considered the report on 30 May and 5 and 6 June. It also established a Working Group to consider the issues raised by the expulsion of persons having dual or multiple nationality and by denationalization in relation to expulsion, which determined that there was no need to have separate draft articles on the matter, as the necessary clarifications would be made in the commentaries. On 14 July, the Working Group concluded that the commentary to the draft articles should: indicate that, for the purposes of the draft articles, the principle of the non-expulsion of nationals applied also to persons who had legally acquired one or several other nationalities, and include wording to make it clear that States should not use denationalization as a means of circumventing their obligations under the principle of the non-expulsion of nationals.

During its discussions, some Commission members were of the view that ILC could not ignore the question of dual or multiple nationality—a phenomenon increasingly common in the modern age. Contrary to the view of the Special Rapporteur, a number of members believed that, with regard to expulsion, international law did not allow a State to consider its nationals having one or several other nationalities as aliens. It was proposed that a draft article be prepared stating that persons having dual or multiple nationality had the same rights as those holding only the nationality of the expelling State. It was also observed that the existence of a receiving State, for example one of the States of nationality of the person expelled, was not a decisive factor in determining the legality of an expulsion.

The Commission approved the Working Group's conclusions on 24 July; requested the Drafting Committee to take them into consideration in its work; and received an oral progress report by the Committee Chairman on 4 August. The draft articles referred to the Committee would remain with it until work on all draft articles was completed.

Extradition

ILC considered the third report by Special Rapporteur Zdzislaw Galicki (Poland) on the obligation to extradite or prosecute (*aut dedere aut judicare*) [A/CN.4/603], as well as comments and information received from Governments [A/CN.4/599]. The report formulated questions addressed both to States and ILC members on the most essential aspects of the topic, to enable the Special Rapporteur to draw final conclusions on the main question of whether the obligation to extradite or prosecute existed under customary international law. It also elaborated on draft articles 1, 2 and 3, regarding, respectively, the scope of application of the draft articles, the use of terms, and the recognition of treaties as a source of the obligation to extradite or prosecute.

The Commission [A/63/10] considered the report in July, and established a Working Group on the topic. The Special Rapporteur suggested that ILC renew its request for Governments to provide their comments and information on the issue and find a compromise solution on how to address the problem of the mutual relationship between the obligation *aut dedere aut judicare* and the principle of universal jurisdiction. On the "triple alternative"—the surrender of the alleged offender to a competent international criminal tribunal—he stated that total rejection of the question was premature and recommended that consideration be given to recent domestic laws of implementation of the Rome Statute of the International Criminal Court (ICC). During the Commission's discussions, the Special Rapporteur was requested to continue to address general substantive issues and propose articles relating to the obligation to extradite or prosecute, such as the question of its source (customary law, general principle of law), its relationship with universal jurisdiction, crimes that would be subject to the obligation (in particular, serious crimes under international law), and the "triple alternative". He could then undertake an examination of procedural questions, such as the possible grounds for denying extradition, the guarantees in case of extradition, how to deal with simultaneous requests for extradition, and other pending matters under discussion. The Special Rapporteur's fourth report would focus on the main substantive issues arising from the topic, such as the sources of the obligation to extradite or prosecute, and its content and scope, making reference to the previous work of the Commission on the draft Code of Crimes against the Peace and Security of Mankind.

Effects of armed conflicts on treaties

ILC considered the fourth report on the effects of armed conflicts on treaties [A/CN.4/589 & Corr.1] by Special Rapporteur Ian Brownlie (United Kingdom), which dealt with the question of the procedure for suspension or termination, with particular reference to article 65 of the Vienna Convention on the Law of Treaties. The Commission also had before it a note prepared by the Chairperson of the Working Group [A/CN.4/L.721] on draft article 8 and the applicability of articles 42 to 45 of the Convention, as well as a compilation of comments and observations received from international organizations [A/CN.4/592 & Add.1].

On 16 May, the Commission [A/63/10] decided to re-establish the Working Group on the Effects of Armed Conflicts on Treaties, which subsequently considered, with respect to draft article 8, the applicability of the procedure in article 65 of the Vienna Convention for the termination or suspension of treaties, as well as the applicability of articles 42 to 45 of the Convention and, in particular, article 44 on the separability of treaty provisions. It also considered draft article 9, on the resumption of suspended treaties; and draft articles 12, 13 and 14, relating to third States as neutrals, the termination or suspension of treaties by operation of the Vienna Convention, and the competence of parties to negotiate a specific agreement regulating the maintenance in force or revival of treaties, respectively. On 29 May, ILC adopted the Working Group's report [A/CN.4/L.726].

In July, the Commission considered the reports of the Drafting Committee, and adopted on first reading a set of 18 draft articles on the effects of armed conflicts on treaties, together with an annex. It also adopted, in August, a set of commentaries to those draft articles and transmitted the draft articles to Governments for comments and observations.

Protection of persons in the event of disasters

The Commission had before it a preliminary report on the protection of persons in the event of disasters [A/CN.4/598] by Special Rapporteur Eduardo Valencia-Ospina (Colombia), which aimed to identify the basic assumptions that would inform the work of codification and progressive development of the topic, and presented the evolution of the protection of persons in the event of disasters; references to the sources and international efforts to codify and develop the law on the topic; a broad outline of various aspects of the general scope with a view to identifying the main legal questions to be covered; and a tentative conclusion without prejudice to the outcome of the discussion it aimed to generate in the Commission. It also had before it a Secretariat memorandum [A/CN.4/590 & Add.1–3], which focused primarily on natural disasters.

In July, the Commission [A/63/10] held a debate based on the Special Rapporteur's preliminary report. Among the many issues discussed were the main legal questions to be covered by the topic, including questions concerning the approach to the topic, as well as its scope in terms of the subject matter, personal scope, space and time. While several members agreed with a rights-based approach in the consideration of the topic as suggested by the Special Rapporteur, other members were of the view that a general understanding of what was meant by a rights-based approach was necessary. According to one perspective, a human rights approach should not only be perceived from the angle of according the protection of the individual, but also take into account community interests, in particular of the vulnerable groups, while bearing in mind the obligations and limitations of States affected by disaster. It was also essential to determine what consequences would flow from a rights-based approach and whether such an approach would require addressing questions on how such rights would be enforced. Several members agreed to exclude armed conflict from the scope of the topic, suggesting that the primary focus should be on natural disasters.

On the future programme of work and final form, some members noted that it would be desirable to decide on the form at an early stage in the consideration of the topic and expressed a preference for a framework convention setting out general principles, which could form a point of reference in the elaboration of special or regional agreements. Others favoured non-binding guidelines or said that it was premature to take a decision on the final form. A suggestion for the Special Rapporteur to provide a provisional plan of future work for discussion by a working group was also considered premature by some members with regard to the establishment of a working group. In his final remarks, the Special Rapporteur said that he was convinced that the Commission would steer the topic towards a successful conclusion, notwithstanding its complexity and challenges. He also noted that it would be the task of the Commission to elaborate draft articles, without prejudice to the final form.

Immunity of State officials

The Commission had before it a preliminary report on the immunity of State officials from foreign criminal jurisdiction [A/CN.4/601] by Special Rapporteur Roman Anatolevich Kolodkin (Russian Federation), which aimed to describe the history of the consideration by ILC and the Institute of International Law of the question of immunity of State officials from foreign jurisdiction; outline the range of issues proposed for consideration by ILC in the preliminary phase of work on the topic; and provide a rough outline of two types of issues: those to be analysed by the Commission as part of its consideration of the topic, and those to be addressed by the Commission in a possible formulation of any instrument resulting from consideration of the topic—for example, draft guiding principles or draft articles. It also had before it a Secretariat memorandum [A/CN.4/596] on the topic.

In July, the Commission [A/63/10] held a debate based on the Special Rapporteur's preliminary report. Among the many issues discussed were the main legal questions to be considered when defining the scope of the topic, including the officials to be covered, the nature of the acts to be covered, as well as whether there were possible exceptions. There was agreement that the Commission should not consider, within the topic, the questions of immunity before international criminal tribunals and before the courts of the State of nationality of the official. Some members emphasized that the immunities of diplomatic agents, consular officials, members of special missions and representatives of States to international organizations had already been codified and did not need to be addressed in the context of that topic.

In his closing remarks, the Special Rapporteur observed that there was general agreement that the basic source of the immunity of State officials from foreign criminal jurisdiction was to be found in international law, particularly customary international law, and noted that some members had highlighted the importance of national practice and judicial decisions in this regard. As divergent views were expressed on the question of whether ILC should study the issue of jurisdiction, the Special Rapporteur explained his intention to consider analytically the issue in his future work without, however, proposing draft articles on the subject. The debates had also clarified the scope of the topic, with the general perception that the immunities of diplomatic agents, consular officials, members of special missions and representatives of States in and to international organizations were outside of the topic. In light of the different opinions on the issue of recognition, the Special Rapporteur suggested that ILC could examine the possible effects of *non-recognition* of an entity as a State on whether immunity was granted to its officials. On the scope of the topic with respect to the persons covered, the majority of members favoured consideration of the status of all "State officials" and had supported the use of such term, which was to be defined in the future work of the Commission. As to immunity *ratione personae*, there was broad agreement that it was enjoyed by Heads of State, Heads of Government and ministers for foreign affairs, yet divergent views had been expressed as to its extension to other high-ranking officials. The Special Rapporteur noted that further consideration should be given, in that regard, *inter alia* to the ICJ Judgment in the case concerning *Certain Questions of Mutual Assistance in Criminal Matters* (see p. 1397).

International State relations and international law

State succession

The Sixth Committee, on 21 October and 5 and 14 November, considered the item on nationality of natural persons in relation to the succession of States. For its consideration of the item, the Committee had before it a note [A/63/113] by the Secretariat containing the comments of 15 Governments concerning the advisability of elaborating a legal instrument on the question of nationality of natural persons in relation to the succession of States, submitted in response to General Assembly resolution 59/34 [YUN 2004, p. 1302]. ILC, at its fifty-first session in 1999 [YUN 1999, p. 1230], had adopted draft articles on the item and recommended that they be adopted by the Assembly in the form of a declaration. Subsequently, the Assembly, in resolutions 54/112 [ibid.], 55/153 [YUN 2000, p. 1242] and 59/34, invited Governments to submit comments and observations, with a view to considering the elaboration of such a convention at a future session.

GENERAL ASSEMBLY ACTION

On 11 December [meeting 67], the General Assembly, on the recommendation of the Sixth Committee [A/63/436], adopted **resolution 63/118** without vote [agenda item 72].

Nationality of natural persons in relation to the succession of States

The General Assembly,

Having examined the item entitled "Nationality of natural persons in relation to the succession of States",

Recalling its resolution 54/112 of 9 December 1999, in which it decided to consider at its fifty-fifth session the draft articles on nationality of natural persons in relation to the succession of States prepared by the International Law Commission,

Recalling also its resolution 55/153 of 12 December 2000, the annex to which contains the articles on nationality of natural persons in relation to the succession of States,

Recalling further its resolution 59/34 of 2 December 2004,

Taking into consideration the comments and observations of Governments and the discussion held in the Sixth Committee at the fifty-ninth and sixty-third sessions of the General Assembly on the question of nationality of natural persons in relation to the succession of States, with a view, in particular, to preventing the occurrence of statelessness as a result of a succession of States, as well as on the advisability of elaborating a legal instrument on this question,

Taking note, in this regard, of the efforts made at the regional level towards the elaboration of a legal instrument on the avoidance of statelessness in relation to State succession,

1. *Reiterates its invitation* to Governments to take into account, as appropriate, the provisions of the articles contained in the annex to resolution 55/153, in dealing with issues of nationality of natural persons in relation to the succession of States;

2. *Encourages* States to consider, as appropriate, at the regional or subregional levels, the elaboration of legal instruments regulating questions of nationality of natural persons in relation to the succession of States, with a view, in particular, to preventing the occurrence of statelessness as a result of a succession of States;

3. *Invites* Governments to submit comments concerning the advisability of elaborating a legal instrument on the question of nationality of natural persons in relation to the succession of States, including the avoidance of statelessness as a result of a succession of States;

4. *Decides* to include in the provisional agenda of its sixty-sixth session the item entitled "Nationality of natural persons in relation to the succession of States", with the aim of examining the subject, including the question of the form that might be given to the draft articles.

Jurisdictional immunities of States and their properties

The General Assembly, by resolution 59/38 [YUN 2004, p. 1304], adopted the Convention on Jurisdictional Immunities of States and Their Property. The Convention was opened for signature from 17 January 2005 until 17 January 2007 at UN Headquarters. As at 31 December 2008, the Convention had 28 signatories and six States parties. The Convention would enter into force when ratified by 30 parties.

International terrorism

Convention on international terrorism

Ad Hoc Committee. In accordance with General Assembly resolution 62/71 [YUN 2007, p. 1366], the Ad Hoc Committee established by Assembly resolution 51/210 [YUN 1996, p. 1208] held its twelfth session (New York, 25–26 February and 6 March) to continue the elaboration of a draft comprehensive convention on international terrorism within the framework of a working group of the Sixth Committee, including consideration of outstanding issues.

The Ad Hoc Committee held informal consultations and contacts on the draft comprehensive convention on international terrorism as well as informal consultations on the question of convening a high-level conference under UN auspices to formulate a joint organized response of the international community to terrorism in all its forms and manifestations. Delegations stressed the importance of finalizing the draft comprehensive convention and reaffirmed their commitment to the negotiating process and the early adoption of the convention. Discussions on various aspects of the convention focused on the need for the convention to provide for a clear legal definition of terrorism and include provisions relating to military activities not covered by international law. On draft article 18, some delegations stated that the latest draft proposed by the Coordinator could be a sound basis for negotiating and reaching a consensus on the text, while others recalled that they had already accepted the previous draft of the former Coordinator. Meanwhile, some other delegations, while remaining committed to finding a solution to all outstanding issues, reconfirmed their previously preferred position relating to the draft article. On the work format of the Committee, some delegations that viewed the conduct of bilateral consultations as useful reiterated the necessity of conducting negotiations multilaterally in a transparent and representative format. Support was also expressed for the convening of a working group during the Sixth Committee to continue the work of the Ad Hoc Committee with a view to concluding the draft convention.

Egypt, as sponsor delegation, reiterated the importance of convening of a high-level conference [YUN 2006, p. 1515], recalled that the proposal had been endorsed by the Movement of Non-Aligned Countries, the Organization of the Islamic Conference, the African Union and the League of Arab States, and stressed that its convening should not be tied to completion of the work on the draft convention. Some delegations reiterated their support for convening the conference, yet emphasized that the question should be considered after the finalization of the draft convention, which should remain the focus of the Committee. The view was also expressed that discussions on both the draft convention and the convening of a high-level conference could continue in parallel.

On 26 February, the Ad Hoc Committee adopted its report [A/63/37], to which were annexed the Chairman's informal summaries on the exchange of views in the plenary meeting and on the results of the informal consultations and contacts in connection with the draft convention, and on the convening of a high-level conference.

Measures to eliminate international terrorism

In accordance with General Assembly resolution 50/53 [YUN 1995, p. 1330], the Secretary-General, in July [A/63/173], issued his annual report on measures taken by 25 States, five UN system entities and three intergovernmental organizations to implement the 1994 Declaration on Measures to Eliminate International Terrorism, approved by Assembly resolution 49/60 [YUN 1994, p. 1293] and Security Council resolution 1269(1999) [YUN 1999, p. 1240]. It listed 30 international instruments pertaining to terrorism, indicating the status of State participation in each, and provided information on workshops and training courses on combating terrorism by two UN bodies and two international organizations. It also announced the publication of the third edition of *International Instruments related to the Prevention and Suppression of International Terrorism* prepared by the UN Office of Legal Affairs in collaboration with the Office on Drugs and Crime (UNODC). A September addendum to the report [A/63/173/Add.1] summarized information submitted by seven other States and one UN system entity.

On 18 December, the General Assembly, by **resolution 63/193** (see p. 1223), approved the provisional agenda for the Twelfth United Nations Congress on Crime Prevention and Criminal Justice in 2010, which included the item on the "provision of technical assistance to facilitate the ratification and implementation of the international instruments related to the prevention and suppression of terrorism".

GENERAL ASSEMBLY ACTION

On 11 December [meeting 67], the General Assembly, on the recommendation of the Sixth Committee [A/63/444], adopted **resolution 63/129** without vote [agenda item 99].

Measures to eliminate international terrorism

The General Assembly,

Guided by the purposes and principles of the Charter of the United Nations,

Reaffirming the United Nations Global Counter-Terrorism Strategy in all its aspects adopted on 8 September 2006, enhancing the overall framework for the efforts of the international community to effectively counter the scourge of terrorism in all its forms and manifestations, and recalling the first biennial review of the Strategy, on 4 and 5 September 2008, and the debates that were held on that occasion,

Recalling the Declaration on the Occasion of the Fiftieth Anniversary of the United Nations,

Recalling also the United Nations Millennium Declaration,

Recalling further the 2005 World Summit Outcome, and reaffirming in particular the section on terrorism,

Recalling the Declaration on Measures to Eliminate International Terrorism, contained in the annex to General Assembly resolution 49/60 of 9 December 1994, and the Declaration to Supplement the 1994 Declaration on Measures to Eliminate International Terrorism, contained in the annex to resolution 51/210 of 17 December 1996,

Recalling also all General Assembly resolutions on measures to eliminate international terrorism, and Security Council resolutions on threats to international peace and security caused by terrorist acts,

Convinced of the importance of the consideration of measures to eliminate international terrorism by the General Assembly as the universal organ having competence to do so,

Deeply disturbed by the persistence of terrorist acts, which have been carried out worldwide,

Reaffirming its strong condemnation of the heinous acts of terrorism that have caused enormous loss of human life, destruction and damage, including those which prompted the adoption of General Assembly resolution 56/1 of 12 September 2001, as well as Security Council resolutions 1368(2001) of 12 September 2001, 1373(2001) of 28 September 2001 and 1377(2001) of 12 November 2001, and those that have occurred since the adoption of the latter resolution,

Recalling the strong condemnation of the atrocious and deliberate attack against the headquarters of the United Nations Assistance Mission for Iraq in Baghdad on 19 August 2003 in General Assembly resolution 57/338 of 15 September 2003 and Security Council resolution 1502(2003) of 26 August 2003,

Affirming that States must ensure that any measure taken to combat terrorism complies with all their obligations under international law and adopt such measures in accordance with international law, in particular international human rights, refugee and humanitarian law,

Stressing the need to strengthen further international cooperation among States and among international organizations and agencies, regional organizations and arrangements and the United Nations in order to prevent, combat and eliminate terrorism in all its forms and manifestations, wherever and by whomsoever committed, in accordance with the principles of the Charter, international law and the relevant international conventions,

Noting the role of the Security Council Committee established pursuant to resolution 1373(2001) concerning counter-terrorism in monitoring the implementation of that resolution, including the taking of the necessary financial, legal and technical measures by States and the ratification or acceptance of the relevant international conventions and protocols,

Mindful of the need to enhance the role of the United Nations and the relevant specialized agencies in combating international terrorism, and of the proposals of the Secretary-General to enhance the role of the Organization in this respect,

Mindful also of the essential need to strengthen international, regional and subregional cooperation aimed at enhancing the national capacity of States to prevent and suppress effectively international terrorism in all its forms and manifestations,

Reiterating its call upon States to review urgently the scope of the existing international legal provisions on the prevention, repression and elimination of terrorism in all its forms and manifestations, with the aim of ensuring that there is a comprehensive legal framework covering all aspects of the matter,

Emphasizing that tolerance and dialogue among civilizations, and enhancing interfaith and intercultural understanding, are among the most important elements in promoting cooperation and success in combating terrorism, and welcoming the various initiatives to this end,

Reaffirming that no terrorist act can be justified in any circumstances,

Recalling Security Council resolution 1624(2005) of 14 September 2005, and bearing in mind that States must ensure that any measure taken to combat terrorism complies with their obligations under international law, in particular international human rights, refugee and humanitarian law,

Taking note of the recent developments and initiatives at the international, regional and subregional levels to prevent and suppress international terrorism, including those of, inter alia, the African Union, the ASEAN Regional Forum, the Asia-Pacific Economic Cooperation, the Association of Southeast Asian Nations, the Bali Counter-Terrorism Process, the Central American Integration System, the Collective Security Treaty Organization, the Common Market for Eastern and Southern Africa, the Cooperation Council for the Arab States of the Gulf, the Council of Europe, the East African Community, the Economic Community of West African States, the Euro-Mediterranean Partnership, the European Free Trade Association, the European Union, the Group of Eight, the Intergovernmental Authority on Development, the International Maritime Organization, the International Civil Aviation Organization, the League of Arab States, the Movement of Non-Aligned Countries, the North Atlantic Treaty Organization, the Organization for Economic Cooperation and Development, the Organization for Security and Co-operation in Europe, the Organization of American States, the Organization of the Islamic Conference, the Pacific Islands Forum, the Shanghai Cooperation Organization, the Southern African Development Community and the World Customs Organization,

Noting regional efforts to prevent, combat and eliminate terrorism in all its forms and manifestations, wherever and by whomsoever committed, including through the elaboration of and adherence to regional conventions,

Recalling its decision in resolutions 54/110 of 9 December 1999, 55/158 of 12 December 2000, 56/88 of 12 December 2001, 57/27 of 19 November 2002, 58/81 of 9 December 2003, 59/46 of 2 December 2004, 60/43 of 8 December 2005, 61/40 of 4 December 2006 and 62/71 of 6 December 2007 that the Ad Hoc Committee established by General Assembly resolution 51/210 should address, and keep on its agenda, the question of convening a high-level conference under the auspices of the United Nations to formulate a joint organized response of the international community to terrorism in all its forms and manifestations,

Recalling also the Final Document of the Fourteenth Conference of Heads of State or Government of Non-Aligned Countries, adopted in Havana on 16 September 2006, which reiterated the collective position of the Movement of Non-Aligned Countries on terrorism and reaffirmed its previous initiative calling for an international summit conference under the auspices of the United Nations to formulate a joint organized response of the international community to terrorism in all its forms and manifestations, as well as other relevant initiatives,

Aware of its resolutions 57/219 of 18 December 2002, 58/187 of 22 December 2003, 59/191 of 20 December 2004, 60/158 of 16 December 2005, 61/171 of 19 December 2006 and 62/159 of 18 December 2007,

Having examined the report of the Secretary-General, the report of the Ad Hoc Committee established by resolution 51/210 and the oral report of the Chairperson on the work of the Working Group established by the Sixth Committee during the sixty-third session of the General Assembly,

1. *Strongly condemns* all acts, methods and practices of terrorism in all its forms and manifestations as criminal and unjustifiable, wherever and by whomsoever committed;

2. *Calls upon* all Member States, the United Nations and other appropriate international, regional and subregional organizations to implement the United Nations Global Counter-Terrorism Strategy, as well as the resolution on the first biennial review of the Strategy, in all its aspects at the international, regional, subregional and national levels without delay, including through mobilizing resources and expertise;

3. *Recalls* the pivotal role of the General Assembly in following up the implementation and updating of the Strategy, and in this regard also recalls its invitation to the Secretary-General to contribute to the future deliberations of the General Assembly, and requests the Secretary-General when doing so to provide information on relevant activities within the Secretariat to ensure overall coordination and coherence in the counterterrorism efforts of the United Nations system;

4. *Reiterates* that criminal acts intended or calculated to provoke a state of terror in the general public, a group of persons or particular persons for political purposes are in any circumstances unjustifiable, whatever the considerations of a political, philosophical, ideological, racial, ethnic, religious or other nature that may be invoked to justify them;

5. *Reiterates its call upon* all States to adopt further measures in accordance with the Charter of the United Nations and the relevant provisions of international law, including international standards of human rights, to prevent terrorism and to strengthen international cooperation in combating terrorism and, to that end, to consider in particular the implementation of the measures set out in paragraphs 3 *(a)* to *(f)* of resolution 51/210;

6. *Also reiterates its call upon* all States, with the aim of enhancing the efficient implementation of relevant legal instruments, to intensify, as and where appropriate, the exchange of information on facts related to terrorism and, in so doing, to avoid the dissemination of inaccurate or unverified information;

7. *Reiterates its call upon* States to refrain from financing, encouraging, providing training for or otherwise supporting terrorist activities;

8. *Urges* States to ensure that their nationals or other persons and entities within their territory that wilfully provide or collect funds for the benefit of persons or entities who commit, or attempt to commit, facilitate or participate in the commission of terrorist acts are punished by penalties consistent with the grave nature of such acts;

9. *Reminds* States of their obligations under relevant international conventions and protocols and Security Council resolutions, including Security Council resolution 1373(2001), to ensure that perpetrators of terrorist acts are brought to justice;

10. *Reaffirms* that international cooperation as well as actions by States to combat terrorism should be conducted in conformity with the principles of the Charter, international law and relevant international conventions;

11. *Recalls* the adoption of the International Convention for the Suppression of Acts of Nuclear Terrorism, the Amendment to the Convention on the Physical Protection of Nuclear Material, the Protocol of 2005 to the Convention for the Suppression of Unlawful Acts against the Safety of Maritime Navigation and the Protocol of 2005 to the Protocol for the Suppression of Unlawful Acts against the Safety of Fixed Platforms Located on the Continental Shelf, and urges all States to consider, as a matter of priority, becoming parties to these instruments;

12. *Urges* all States that have not yet done so to consider as a matter of priority, and in accordance with Security Council resolution 1373(2001), and Council resolution 1566(2004) of 8 October 2004, becoming parties to the relevant conventions and protocols as referred to in paragraph 6 of General Assembly resolution 51/210, as well as the International Convention for the Suppression of Terrorist Bombings, the International Convention for the Suppression of the Financing of Terrorism, the International Convention for the Suppression of Acts of Nuclear Terrorism, and the Amendment to the Convention on the Physical Protection of Nuclear Material, and calls upon all States to enact, as appropriate, the domestic legislation necessary to implement the provisions of those conventions and protocols, to ensure that the jurisdiction of their courts enables them to bring to trial the perpetrators of terrorist acts, and to cooperate with and provide support and assistance to other States and relevant international and regional organizations to that end;

13. *Urges* States to cooperate with the Secretary-General and with one another, as well as with interested intergovernmental organizations, with a view to ensuring, where appropriate within existing mandates, that technical and other expert advice is provided to those States requiring and requesting assistance in becoming parties to and implementing the conventions and protocols referred to in paragraph 12 above;

14. *Notes with appreciation and satisfaction* that, consistent with the call contained in paragraphs 11 and 12 of resolution 62/71, a number of States became parties to the relevant conventions and protocols referred to therein, thereby realizing the objective of wider acceptance and implementation of those conventions;

15. *Reaffirms* the Declaration on Measures to Eliminate International Terrorism and the Declaration to Supplement the 1994 Declaration on Measures to Eliminate International Terrorism, and calls upon all States to implement them;

16. *Calls upon* all States to cooperate to prevent and suppress terrorist acts;

17. *Urges* all States and the Secretary-General, in their efforts to prevent international terrorism, to make the best use of the existing institutions of the United Nations;

18. *Requests* the Terrorism Prevention Branch of the United Nations Office on Drugs and Crime in Vienna to continue its efforts to enhance, through its mandate, the capabilities of the United Nations in the prevention of terrorism, and recognizes, in the context of the United Nations Global Counter-Terrorism Strategy and Security Council resolution 1373(2001), its role in assisting States in becoming parties to and implementing the relevant international conventions and protocols relating to terrorism, including the most recent among them, and in strengthening international cooperation mechanisms in criminal matters related to terrorism, including through national capacity-building;

19. *Welcomes* the current efforts by the Secretariat to prepare the third edition of the publication *International Instruments related to the Prevention and Suppression of International Terrorism* in all official languages;

20. *Invites* regional intergovernmental organizations to submit to the Secretary-General information on the measures they have adopted at the regional level to eliminate international terrorism, as well as on intergovernmental meetings held by those organizations;

21. *Notes* the progress attained in the elaboration of the draft comprehensive convention on international terrorism during the meetings of the Ad Hoc Committee established by General Assembly resolution 51/210 and the Working Group established by the Sixth Committee during the sixty-third session of the General Assembly, and welcomes continuing efforts to that end;

22. *Decides* that the Ad Hoc Committee shall, on an expedited basis, continue to elaborate the draft comprehensive convention on international terrorism, and shall continue to discuss the item included in its agenda by Gen-

eral Assembly resolution 54/110 concerning the question of convening a high-level conference under the auspices of the United Nations;

23. *Also decides* that the Ad Hoc Committee shall meet from 29 June to 2 July 2009 in order to fulfil the mandate referred to in paragraph 22 above;

24. *Requests* the Secretary-General to continue to provide the Ad Hoc Committee with the necessary facilities for the performance of its work;

25. *Requests* the Ad Hoc Committee to report to the General Assembly at its sixty-third session in the event of the completion of the draft comprehensive convention on international terrorism;

26. *Also requests* the Ad Hoc Committee to report to the General Assembly at its sixty-fourth session on progress made in the implementation of its mandate;

27. *Decides* to include in the provisional agenda of its sixty-fourth session the item entitled "Measures to eliminate international terrorism".

On 24 December, the Assembly decided that the item on measures to eliminate international terrorism would remain for consideration during its resumed sixty-third (2009) session (**decision 63/552**).

Additional Protocols I and II to the 1949 Geneva Conventions

In response to General Assembly resolution 61/30 [YUN 2006, p. 1519], the Secretary-General submitted a July report [A/63/118 & Corr.1] on the status of the two 1977 Protocols Additional to the Geneva Conventions of 12 August 1949 relating to the protection of victims of armed conflicts [YUN 1977, p. 706], as well as on measures taken to strengthen the existing body of international humanitarian law with respect to, among other things, its dissemination and implementation at the national level, based on information received from 19 States and the International Committee of the Red Cross (ICRC). Annexed to the report was a list of 167 States parties to one or both of the Protocols as at 11 July 2008. A subsequent addendum [A/63/118/Add.1] summarizes additional information received from 12 States and ICRC.

GENERAL ASSEMBLY ACTION

On 11 December [meeting 67], the General Assembly, on the recommendation of the Sixth Committee [A/63/440] adopted **resolution 63/125**, without vote [agenda item 76].

Status of the Protocols Additional to the Geneva Conventions of 1949 and relating to the protection of victims of armed conflicts

The General Assembly,

Recalling its resolutions 32/44 of 8 December 1977, 34/51 of 23 November 1979, 37/116 of 16 December 1982, 39/77 of 13 December 1984, 41/72 of 3 December 1986, 43/161 of 9 December 1988, 45/38 of 28 November 1990, 47/30 of 25 November 1992, 49/48 of 9 December 1994, 51/155 of 16 December 1996, 53/96 of 8 December 1998, 55/148 of 12 December 2000, 57/14 of 19 November 2002, 59/36 of 2 December 2004 and 61/30 of 4 December 2006,

Having considered the report of the Secretary-General,

Thanking Member States and the International Committee of the Red Cross for their contribution to the report of the Secretary-General,

Reaffirming the continuing value of established humanitarian rules relating to armed conflicts and the need to respect and ensure respect for those rules in all circumstances within the scope of the relevant international instruments, pending the earliest possible termination of such conflicts,

Stressing the possibility of making use of the International Humanitarian Fact-Finding Commission in relation to an armed conflict, pursuant to article 90 of Protocol I to the Geneva Conventions of 1949,

Stressing also the possibility for the International Humanitarian Fact-Finding Commission to facilitate, through its good offices, the restoration of an attitude of respect for the Geneva Conventions and Protocol I,

Stressing further the need to consolidate the existing body of international humanitarian law through its universal acceptance and the need for wide dissemination and full implementation of such law at the national level, and expressing concern about all violations of the Geneva Conventions and the Additional Protocols,

Noting with satisfaction the increasing number of national commissions and other bodies involved in advising authorities at the national level on the implementation, dissemination and development of international humanitarian law,

Noting with appreciation the meetings of representatives of those bodies organized by the International Committee of the Red Cross to facilitate the sharing of concrete experience and the exchange of views on their roles and on the challenges they face,

Mindful of the role of the International Committee of the Red Cross in offering protection to the victims of armed conflicts,

Noting with appreciation the continuing efforts of the International Committee of the Red Cross to promote and disseminate knowledge of international humanitarian law, in particular the Geneva Conventions and the Additional Protocols,

Recalling the undertakings at the Thirtieth International Conference of the Red Cross and Red Crescent, held in Geneva from 26 to 30 November 2007, which reaffirmed the need to reinforce the implementation of and respect for international humanitarian law,

Noting the serious concern expressed by States regarding the humanitarian impact caused by cluster munitions, and taking note of the adoption of the Convention on Cluster Munitions in Dublin on 30 May 2008 and the ongoing negotiation of a proposal on this subject within the context of the Convention on Prohibitions or Restrictions on the Use of Certain Conventional Weapons Which May Be Deemed to Be Excessively Injurious or to Have Indiscriminate Effects,

Noting also the entry into force, on 14 January 2007, of the Protocol additional to the Geneva Conventions of 12

August 1949, and relating to the Adoption of an Additional Distinctive Emblem (Protocol III) of 8 December 2005,

Welcoming the significant debate generated by the publication in 2005 of the study by the International Committee of the Red Cross on Customary International Humanitarian Law and current initiatives by the Committee to update volume II of the study, on practice, as well as the growing number of translations into other languages of parts of the study, and looking forward to further constructive discussion on the subject,

Calling upon Member States to disseminate knowledge of international humanitarian law as widely as possible, and calling upon all parties to armed conflict to apply international humanitarian law,

Noting the special responsibilities of national Red Cross and Red Crescent societies, as auxiliaries to the public authorities of their respective States in the humanitarian field, to cooperate with and assist their Governments in the promotion, dissemination and implementation of international humanitarian law,

Acknowledging the fact that the Rome Statute of the International Criminal Court, which entered into force on 1 July 2002, includes the most serious crimes of international concern under international humanitarian law, and that the Statute, while recalling that it is the duty of every State to exercise its criminal jurisdiction over those responsible for such crimes, shows the determination of the international community to put an end to impunity for the perpetrators of such crimes and thus to contribute to their prevention,

Acknowledging also the usefulness of discussing in the General Assembly the status of instruments of international humanitarian law relevant to the protection of victims of armed conflicts,

1. *Welcomes* the universal acceptance of the Geneva Conventions of 1949, and notes the trend towards a similarly wide acceptance of the two Additional Protocols of 1977;

2. *Calls upon* all States parties to the Geneva Conventions that have not yet done so to consider becoming parties to the Additional Protocols at the earliest possible date;

3. *Calls upon* all States that are already parties to Protocol I, or those States not parties, on becoming parties to Protocol I, to make the declaration provided for under article 90 of that Protocol and to consider making use, where appropriate, of the services of the International Humanitarian Fact-Finding Commission in accordance with the provisions of article 90 of Protocol I;

4. *Calls upon* all States that have not yet done so to consider becoming parties to the Convention for the Protection of Cultural Property in the Event of Armed Conflict and the two Protocols thereto, and to other relevant treaties on international humanitarian law relating to the protection of victims of armed conflict;

5. *Calls upon* all States parties to the Protocols Additional to the Geneva Conventions to ensure their wide dissemination and full implementation;

6. *Notes with appreciation* the adoption by the Thirtieth International Conference of the Red Cross and Red Crescent of resolution 3, on the reaffirmation and implementation of international humanitarian law, entitled "Preserving human life and dignity in armed conflict", which, inter alia, reiterates the obligation of States to take national measures to implement international humanitarian law, including training of the armed forces and making this law known among the general public, as well as the adoption of legislation to punish war crimes in accordance with their international obligations;

7. *Affirms* the necessity of making the implementation of international humanitarian law more effective;

8. *Welcomes* the advisory service activities of the International Committee of the Red Cross in supporting efforts made by Member States to take legislative and administrative action to implement international humanitarian law and in promoting the exchange of information on those efforts between Governments;

9. *Also welcomes* the increasing number of national commissions or committees for the implementation of international humanitarian law and for promoting the incorporation of treaties on international humanitarian law into national law and disseminating the rules of international humanitarian law;

10. *Calls upon* States to consider becoming parties to the Optional Protocol to the Convention on the Rights of the Child on the involvement of children in armed conflict;

11. *Requests* the Secretary-General to submit to the General Assembly at its sixty-fifth session a report on the status of the Additional Protocols relating to the protection of victims of armed conflicts, as well as on measures taken to strengthen the existing body of international humanitarian law, inter alia, with respect to its dissemination and full implementation at the national level, based on information received from Member States and the International Committee of the Red Cross;

12. *Decides* to include in the provisional agenda of its sixty-fifth session the item entitled "Status of the Protocols Additional to the Geneva Conventions of 1949 and relating to the protection of victims of armed conflicts".

Montreux Document. In a 2 October letter [A/63/467-S/2008/636] to the Secretary-General, Switzerland transmitted the "Montreux Document", a text containing rules and good practices relating to private military and security companies operating in armed conflict, as a result of an international process launched in 2006 by the Swiss Government and ICRC. On 17 September, 17 participating States came to an understanding on the Document, which included references to the Geneva Conventions and aimed to promote respect for international humanitarian and human rights law. States were invited to consider adopting its measures and communicate their support for the Document to the Swiss Department of Foreign Affairs.

Privileges and immunities

In accordance with articles 35 and 36 of the 1947 Convention on the Privileges and Immunities of the Specialized Agencies of the United Nations, adopted by General Assembly resolution 179(II) [YUN 1947–48, p. 190], in a March note [E/2008/8], the Secretary-

General transmitted the request of the World Tourism Organization (UNWTO) that the Economic and Social Council take note of resolution 545(XVII) of the UNWTO General Assembly accepting that the Convention be applied to itself and recommend the revised draft annex outlining the privileges and immunities of UNWTO for final approval by the Organization.

On 29 April, the Council took note of UNWTO General Assembly resolution 545(XVII) and recommended the revised draft annex to UNWTO for final approval (**decision 2008/210**).

Diplomatic relations

Protection of diplomatic and consular missions and representatives

As at 31 December, the States parties to the following conventions relating to the protection of diplomatic and consular relations numbered: 186 States parties to the 1961 Vienna Convention on Diplomatic Relations [YUN 1961, p. 512], 51 parties to the Optional Protocol concerning the acquisition of nationality [ibid., p. 516] and 66 parties to the Optional Protocol concerning the compulsory settlement of disputes [ibid.].

The 1963 Vienna Convention on Consular Relations [YUN 1963, p. 510] had 172 parties, the Optional Protocol concerning acquisition of nationality [ibid., p. 512] had 39, and the Optional Protocol concerning the compulsory settlement of disputes [ibid.] had 48.

Parties to the 1973 Convention on the Prevention and Punishment of Crimes against Internationally Protected Persons, including Diplomatic Agents [YUN 1973, p. 775] numbered 171.

Report of Secretary-General. In a July report [A/63/121], with a later addendum [A/63/121/Add.1 & Corr.1], the Secretary-General summarized information received from 29 Member States and the Holy See, pursuant to General Assembly resolution 61/31 [YUN 2006, p. 1521], on instances of serious violations of the protection, security and safety of diplomatic and consular missions and representatives.

GENERAL ASSEMBLY ACTION

On 11 December [meeting 67], the General Assembly, on the recommendation of the Sixth Committee [A/63/441], adopted **resolution 63/126** without vote [agenda item 77].

Consideration of effective measures to enhance the protection, security and safety of diplomatic and consular missions and representatives

The General Assembly,

Having considered the report of the Secretary-General,

Conscious of the need to develop and strengthen friendly relations and cooperation among States,

Convinced that respect for the principles and rules of international law governing diplomatic and consular relations is a basic prerequisite for the normal conduct of relations among States and for the fulfilment of the purposes and principles of the Charter of the United Nations,

Alarmed by the recent acts of violence against diplomatic and consular representatives, as well as against representatives of international intergovernmental organizations and officials of such organizations, which have endangered or taken innocent lives and seriously impeded the normal work of such representatives and officials,

Expressing sympathy for the victims of such illegal acts,

Concerned at the failure to respect the inviolability of diplomatic and consular missions and representatives,

Recalling that, without prejudice to their privileges and immunities, it is the duty of all persons enjoying such privileges and immunities to respect the laws and regulations of the receiving State,

Recalling also that diplomatic and consular premises must not be used in any manner incompatible with the functions of diplomatic and consular missions,

Emphasizing the duty of States to take all appropriate measures as required by international law, including measures of a preventive nature, and to bring offenders to justice,

Welcoming measures already taken by States to this end in conformity with their international obligations,

Convinced that the role of the United Nations, which includes the reporting procedures established pursuant to General Assembly resolution 35/168 of 15 December 1980 and further elaborated in subsequent Assembly resolutions, is important in promoting efforts to enhance the protection, security and safety of diplomatic and consular missions and representatives,

1. *Takes note* of the report of the Secretary-General;

2. *Strongly condemns* acts of violence against diplomatic and consular missions and representatives, as well as against missions and representatives of international intergovernmental organizations and officials of such organizations, and emphasizes that such acts can never be justified;

3. *Urges* States to strictly observe, implement and enforce the applicable principles and rules of international law governing diplomatic and consular relations, including during a period of armed conflict, and, in particular, to ensure, in conformity with their international obligations, the protection, security and safety of the missions, representatives and officials mentioned in paragraph 2 above officially present in territories under their jurisdiction, including practical measures to prohibit in their territories illegal activities of persons, groups and organizations that encourage, instigate, organize or engage in the perpetration of acts against the security and safety of such missions, representatives and officials;

4. *Also urges* States to take all appropriate measures at the national and international levels to prevent any acts of violence against the missions, representatives and officials mentioned in paragraph 2 above, including during a period of armed conflict, and to ensure, with the participation of the United Nations where appropriate, that such acts are fully investigated with a view to bringing offenders to justice;

5. *Recommends* that States cooperate closely through, inter alia, contacts between the diplomatic and consular missions and the receiving State with regard to practical measures designed to enhance the protection, security and safety of diplomatic and consular missions and representatives and with regard to the exchange of information on the circumstances of all serious violations thereof;

6. *Urges* States to take all appropriate measures, in accordance with international law, at the national and international levels, to prevent any abuse of diplomatic or consular privileges and immunities, in particular serious abuses, including those involving acts of violence;

7. *Recommends* that States cooperate closely with the State in whose territory abuses of diplomatic and consular privileges and immunities may have occurred, including by exchanging information and providing assistance to its juridical authorities in order to bring offenders to justice;

8. *Calls upon* States that have not yet done so to consider becoming parties to the instruments relevant to the protection, security and safety of diplomatic and consular missions and representatives;

9. *Calls upon* States, in cases where a dispute arises in connection with a violation of their international obligations concerning the protection of the missions or the security of the representatives and officials mentioned in paragraph 2 above, to make use of the means available for peaceful settlement of disputes, including the good offices of the Secretary-General, and requests the Secretary-General, when he deems it appropriate, to offer his good offices to the States directly concerned;

10. *Requests*:

(a) All States to report to the Secretary-General as promptly as possible serious violations of the protection, security and safety of diplomatic and consular missions and representatives as well as missions and representatives with diplomatic status to international intergovernmental organizations;

(b) The State in which the violation took place—and, to the extent possible, the State where the alleged offender is present—to report to the Secretary-General as promptly as possible on measures taken to bring the offender to justice and eventually to communicate, in accordance with its laws, the final outcome of the proceedings against the offender, and to report on measures adopted with a view to preventing a repetition of such violations;

(c) The States so reporting to consider using or taking into account the guidelines prepared by the Secretary-General;

11. *Requests* the Secretary-General:

(a) To send, without delay, a circular note to all States reminding them of the request contained in paragraph 10 above;

(b) To circulate to all States, upon receipt, the reports received by him pursuant to paragraph 10 above, unless the reporting State requests otherwise;

(c) To draw the attention, when appropriate, of the States directly concerned to the reporting procedures provided for in paragraph 10 above, when a serious violation has been reported pursuant to subparagraph 10 *(a)* above;

(d) To address reminders to States where such violations have occurred if reports pursuant to subparagraph 10 *(a)* above or follow-up reports pursuant to subparagraph 10 *(b)* above have not been made within a reasonable period of time;

12. *Also requests* the Secretary-General to invite States, in the circular note referred to in paragraph 11 *(a)* above, to inform him of their views with respect to any measures needed or already taken to enhance the protection, security and safety of diplomatic and consular missions and representatives as well as missions and representatives with diplomatic status to international intergovernmental organizations;

13. *Further requests* the Secretary-General to submit to the General Assembly at its sixty-fifth session a report containing:

(a) Information on the state of ratification of, and accessions to, the instruments referred to in paragraph 8 above;

(b) A summary of the reports received and views expressed pursuant to paragraphs 10 and 12 above;

14. *Invites* the Secretary-General to include in his report to the General Assembly any views he may wish to express on the matters referred to in paragraph 13 above;

15. *Decides* to include in the provisional agenda of its sixty-fifth session the item entitled "Consideration of effective measures to enhance the protection, security and safety of diplomatic and consular missions and representatives".

Treaties and agreements

Reservations to treaties

At its sixtieth session [A/63/10], ILC considered the thirteenth report of Special Rapporteur Alain Pellet (France) on reactions to interpretative declarations [A/CN.4/600], a note relating to draft guideline 2.1.9 on the statement of reasons of reservations [A/CN.4/586], and the draft guidelines contained in the Special Rapporteur's eleventh [YUN 2006, p. 1523] and twelfth [YUN 2007, p. 1371] reports. The Commission adopted 23 draft guidelines dealing with formulation and withdrawal of acceptances and objections, as well as the procedure for acceptance of reservations, together with commentaries, and referred 10 draft guidelines on reactions to interpretative declarations to its Drafting Committee.

The Commission provisionally adopted draft guidelines 2.1.6 (Procedure for communication of reservations), 2.1.9 (Statement of reasons for reservations), 2.6.6 (Joint formulation), 2.6.7 (Written form), 2.6.8 (Expression of intention to preclude the entry into force of the treaty), 2.6.9 (Procedure for the formulation of objections), 2.6.10 (Statement of reasons), 2.6.13 (Time period for formulating an objection), 2.6.14 (Conditional objections), 2.6.15 (Late objections), 2.7.1 (Withdrawal of objections to reservations), 2.7.2 (Form of withdrawal), 2.7.3 (Formulation and communication of the withdrawal of objections to reservations), 2.7.4 (Effect on reservation of withdrawal of an objection), 2.7.5 (Effective date of withdrawal of an objection), 2.7.6 (Cases in which an objecting State or international organization may unilaterally set the effective date of withdrawal of an objection to a reservation), 2.7.7 (Partial withdrawal of an objection), 2.7.8 (Effect of a partial withdrawal of an objection), 2.7.9 (Widening of the scope of an objection to a reservation), 2.6.5 (Author of an objection), 2.6.11 (Non-requirement of confirmation of an objection made prior to formal confirmation of a reservation), 2.6.12 (Requirement of confirmation of an objection made prior to the expression of consent to be bound by a treaty) and 2.8 (Forms of acceptance of reservations).

In July, the Commission took note of draft guidelines 2.8.1 to 2.8.12 as provisionally adopted by the Drafting Committee.

Treaties involving international organizations

The 1986 Vienna Convention on the Law of Treaties between States and International Organizations or between International Organizations [YUN 1986, p. 1006], which had not yet entered into force, had 40 parties as at 31 December 2008.

UN registration and publication of treaties

During 2008, 1,233 treaties were received and 1,058 subsequent actions were registered or filed and recorded with the Secretariat. In addition, 1,096 treaty actions (signatures, ratifications, acceptances, approvals, accessions and other formalities) were received in the UN Treaty Section for deposit with the Secretary-General in his capacity as depositary of multilateral treaties. Twelve issues of the *Monthly Statement of Treaties and International Agreements* were published.

Thirty-three volumes of the *United Nations Treaty Series* (UNTS) were published, incorporating the texts of treaties registered or filed and recorded and related subsequent actions in the original languages, with translations into English and French where necessary. The United Nations Treaty Collection (UNTC) on the Internet, which contained published UNTS volumes up to 2005, the *League of Nations Treaty Series*, the *Treaty Handbook*, *Multilateral Treaties Deposited with the Secretary-General*, the *Summary of Practice of the Secretary-General as Depositary of Multilateral Treaties*, the Treaty Event Booklets, information on capacity-building trainings and a range of materials on treaty law and practice, generated over 200,000 page views and had over 1,400 subscribers to its automated treaty information services.

The UN Treaty Section completed a major upgrade to its Treaty Information and Publishing System, with a fully operational redesigned treaty registration and publishing platform for UNTS and related publications being made fully operational. On 8 September, the Treaty Section launched its new and enhanced website http://treaties.un.org, featuring online automated subscription services, varied search and retrieval options, daily updates posted for all major databases, in particular for the multilateral treaties deposited with the Secretary-General, and other improvements.

The "2008 Treaty Event: Towards Universal Participation and Implementation—Dignity and Justice for All of Us" (New York, 23–26 and 29 September and 1 October) resulted in 84 treaty actions undertaken by 44 States with respect to 37 treaties deposited with the Secretary-General. Those treaties related to human rights; the environment, sustainable development, water, sanitation and the polar regions; disarmament and penal matters; privileges and immunities and the safety of UN and associated personnel; and transit customs and trade agreements of concern to landlocked and transit developing countries.

Advice and capacity-building in treaty law and practice

Advice and assistance on treaty law and practice were provided to Member States, specialized agencies, regional commissions, other UN bodies and other entities. Two seminars on treaty law and practice were conducted at UN Headquarters for legal advisors from Member States and other officials. Two regional capacity-building workshops on treaty law and practice and the implementation of treaty obligations were also held: one in Bangkok, Thailand, attended by 43 participants from landlocked developing countries, transit developing countries, UN system entities, and relevant international and regional organizations; and the other in Accra, Ghana, attended by 36 participants from 14 countries. A presentation on treaty law and practice was also given at the UN Conference Centre in Addis Ababa, Ethiopia.

Multilateral treaties

The UN Treaty Series and the regularly updated status of multilateral treaties deposited with the Secretary-General were available on the Internet at the UN Treaty Collection website.

New multilateral treaties concluded under UN auspices

The following new treaties, concluded under UN auspices, were deposited with the Secretary-General during 2008:

Additional Protocol to the Convention on the Contract for the International Carriage of Goods by Road (CMR) concerning the Electronic Consignment Note, adopted in Geneva on 20 February

Convention on Cluster Munitions, adopted in Dublin on 30 May

Protocol to the Statutes of the International Centre for Genetic Engineering and Biotechnology on the Seat of the Centre, adopted in Trieste, Italy, on 24 October 2007 and received on 29 May 2008

Optional Protocol to the International Covenant on Economic, Social and Cultural Rights, adopted in New York on 10 December

United Nations Convention on Contracts for the International Carriage of Goods Wholly or Partly by Sea, adopted in New York on 11 December

Annex XVIII (World Tourism Organization) to the Convention on Privileges and Immunities of the Specialized Agencies, 1947, adopted in Jeju, Republic of Korea, on 30 July

Multilateral treaties deposited with the Secretary-General

At the end of 2008, the Secretary-General performed depositary functions for 544 multilateral treaties.

The following multilateral treaties deposited with the Secretary-General came into force in 2008:

Optional Protocol to the Convention on the Rights of Persons with Disabilities, adopted on 13 December 2006

Convention on the Rights of Persons with Disabilities, adopted on 13 December 2006

European Agreement concerning the International Carriage of Dangerous Goods by Inland Waterways (ADN), adopted on 26 May 2000

Protocol to the Statutes of the International Centre for Genetic Engineering and Biotechnology on the Seat of the Centre, adopted on 24 October 2007

Other international legal questions

Rule of law at the national and international levels

Pursuant to General Assembly resolution 61/39 [YUN 2006, p. 1525], the Secretary-General submitted a March report [A/63/64] on the rule of law at the national and international levels, containing an inventory of UN rule-of-law activities, based on information provided by 40 UN entities. Those activities were first divided into two main categories, depending on whether they were intended to promote the rule of law at the international or national level, and further divided into subcategories based on the particular aspect of the rule of law they were intended to promote in response to the specific needs of Member States. There was a separate entry for each activity or series of related activities performed by a UN entity. Under each entry, the inventory provided the title and brief description of the activity and also indicated the field of law concerned, such as administration of justice, crime prevention and criminal justice, human rights law, international terrorism; the beneficiaries of the activity (government officials, judges, parliamentarians, non-governmental institutions, the general public); and, if appropriate, the specific circumstances under which the activity was performed, such as in a conflict or post-conflict situation. Entries also included, when available, information on the mandate providing the legal basis or authorization for the activity concerned; the person or entity authorized to initiate or request performance of the activity; the entities involved in its implementation and/or monitoring and those with which the entity performing the activity cooperated for that purpose; and financing of the activity.

In an August report [A/63/226], submitted pursuant to General Assembly resolution 62/70 [YUN 2007, p. 1373], the Secretary-General highlighted ways and means to strengthen and coordinate UN rule-of-law activities, which focused on areas such as enhancing and harmonizing UN engagement; ensuring strategic coordination and coherence in UN collective efforts; measuring the effectiveness and evaluating the impact of UN rule-of-law assistance; and establishing meaningful partnerships. He also made a series of recommendations to States and other rule-of-law stakeholders on working as one rule-of-law community.

Rule of Law Unit. In a July report [A/63/154], pursuant to resolution 62/70 [YUN 2007, p. 1373], the Secretary-General submitted revised estimates to the 2008–2009 programme budget related to the Rule of Law Unit [YUN 2006, p. 47], which described the establishment of the Rule of Law Coordination and Resource Group and the Rule of Law Unit in the Executive Office of the Secretary-General; the rationale for the Unit; its functions; and the staffing and other resource requirements. Estimated additional resources totalled $953,800. In December, the Advisory Committee on Administrative and Budgetary Questions recommended that the staff required for 2009 continue to be provided through secondment (preferably of existing personnel) and that any additional staff required could be requested in the 2010–2011 proposed programme budget [A/63/594].

On 24 December, by section II of **resolution 63/263** (see p. 1547), the Assembly established four professional posts for the Rule of Law Unit, effective 1 January 2009; requested that the Unit Director continue to be provided, for 2009, through secondment; and decided to revert to the issue in the context of the 2010–2011 proposed programme budget.

GENERAL ASSEMBLY ACTION

On 11 December [meeting 67], the General Assembly, on the recommendation of the Sixth Committee [A/63/443], adopted **resolution 63/128** without vote [agenda item 79].

The rule of law at the national and international levels

The General Assembly,

Recalling its resolution 62/70 of 6 December 2007,

Reaffirming its commitment to the purposes and principles of the Charter of the United Nations and international law, which are indispensable foundations of a more peaceful, prosperous and just world, and reiterating its determination to foster strict respect for them and to establish a just and lasting peace all over the world,

Reaffirming also that human rights, the rule of law and democracy are interlinked and mutually reinforcing and that they belong to the universal and indivisible core values and principles of the United Nations,

Reaffirming further the need for universal adherence to and implementation of the rule of law at both the national and international levels and its solemn commitment to an international order based on the rule of law and international law, which, together with the principles of justice, is essential for peaceful coexistence and cooperation among States,

Convinced that the advancement of the rule of law at the national and international levels is essential for the realization of sustained economic growth, sustainable development, the eradication of poverty and hunger and the protection of all human rights and fundamental freedoms, and acknowledging that collective security depends on effective cooperation, in accordance with the Charter and international law, against transnational threats,

Reaffirming the duty of all States to refrain in their international relations from the threat or use of force in any manner inconsistent with the purposes and principles of the United Nations and to settle their international disputes by peaceful means in such a manner that international peace and security, and justice, are not endangered, in accordance with Chapter VI of the Charter, and calling upon States that have not yet done so to consider accepting the jurisdiction of the International Court of Justice in accordance with its Statute,

Convinced that the promotion of and respect for the rule of law at the national and international levels, as well as justice and good governance, should guide the activities of the United Nations and of its Member States,

Recalling paragraph 134 *(e)* of the 2005 World Summit Outcome,

1. *Notes with appreciation* the inventory of current rule of law activities of the United Nations submitted by the Secretary-General and the report of the Secretary-General on strengthening and coordinating United Nations rule of law activities;

2. *Reaffirms* the role of the General Assembly in encouraging the progressive development of international law and its codification, and reaffirms further that States shall abide by all their obligations under international law;

3. *Stresses* the importance of adherence to the rule of law at the national level, and the need to strengthen support to Member States, upon their request, in the domestic implementation of their respective international obligations through enhanced technical assistance and capacity-building, based on greater coordination and coherence within the United Nations system and among donors, and calls for greater evaluation of the effectiveness of such activities;

4. *Calls upon* the United Nations system to systematically address, as appropriate, aspects of the rule of law in relevant activities, recognizing the importance of the rule of law to virtually all areas of United Nations engagement;

5. *Expresses full support* for the overall coordination and coherence role of the Rule of Law Coordination and Resource Group within the United Nations system within existing mandates, supported by the Rule of Law Unit in the Executive Office of the Secretary-General, under the leadership of the Deputy Secretary-General, and requests the Secretary-General to submit an annual report on United Nations rule of law activities, in particular the work of the Group and the Unit, with special regard to the improvement of the coordination, coherence and effectiveness of rule of law activities, taking note of the elements set out in paragraphs 77 and 78 of the report of the Secretary-General;

6. *Encourages* the Secretary-General and the United Nations system to accord high priority to rule of law activities;

7. *Invites* the International Court of Justice, the United Nations Commission on International Trade Law and the International Law Commission to continue to comment, in their respective reports to the General Assembly, on their current roles in promoting the rule of law;

8. *Invites* the Rule of Law Coordination and Resource Group and the Rule of Law Unit to interact with Member States, in particular in informal briefings;

9. *Stresses* the need to consider without delay the report of the Secretary-General on the resource requirements of the Unit, and urges the Secretary-General and Member States to continue to support the functioning of the Unit during the interim phase;

10. *Decides* to include in the provisional agenda of its sixty-fourth session the item entitled "The rule of law at the national and international levels", and invites Member States to focus their comments in future Sixth Committee debates on the sub-topics "Promoting the rule of law at the international level" (sixty-fourth session), "Laws and practices of Member States in implementing international law" (sixty-fifth session), and "Rule of law and transitional justice in conflict and post-conflict situations" (sixty-sixth session), without prejudice to the consideration of the item as a whole.

International economic law

In 2008, legal aspects of international economic law continued to be considered by the United Nations Commission on International Trade Law (UNCITRAL) and by the Sixth Committee of the General Assembly.

International trade law

At its forty-first session (New York, 16 June–3 July), UNCITRAL finalized and approved the draft Convention on Contracts for the International Carriage of Goods Wholly or Partly by Sea and submitted the text to the General Assembly for adoption as the basis of a UN Convention. It continued work on public procurement, arbitration and conciliation, electronic commerce, insolvency law, commercial fraud and security interests. It also monitored implementation of the 1958 New York Convention on the Recognition and Enforcement of Foreign Arbitral Awards (the New York Convention) [YUN 1958, p. 390], the work on the collection and dissemination of case law on UNCITRAL texts (CLOUT), and training and technical assistance activities.

The report of the session [A/63/17 & Corr.1] described actions taken on those topics (for details, see below).

GENERAL ASSEMBLY ACTION

On 11 December [meeting 67], the General Assembly, on the recommendation of the Sixth Committee [A/63/438], adopted **resolution 63/120** without vote [agenda item 74].

Reports of the United Nations Commission on International Trade Law on the work of its resumed fortieth and its forty-first sessions

The General Assembly,

Recalling its resolution 2205(XXI) of 17 December 1966, by which it established the United Nations Commission on International Trade Law with a mandate to further the progressive harmonization and unification of the law of international trade and in that respect to bear in mind the interests of all peoples, in particular those of developing countries, in the extensive development of international trade,

Reaffirming its belief that the progressive modernization and harmonization of international trade law, in reducing or removing legal obstacles to the flow of international trade, especially those affecting the developing countries, would contribute significantly to universal economic cooperation among all States on a basis of equality, equity, common interest and respect for the rule of law, to the elimination of discrimination in international trade and, thereby, to peace, stability and the well-being of all peoples,

Having considered the reports of the Commission on the work of its resumed fortieth and its forty-first sessions,

Reiterating its concern that activities undertaken by other bodies in the field of international trade law without adequate coordination with the Commission might lead to undesirable duplication of efforts and would not be in keeping with the aim of promoting efficiency, consistency and coherence in the unification and harmonization of international trade law,

Reaffirming the mandate of the Commission, as the core legal body within the United Nations system in the field of international trade law, to coordinate legal activities in this field, in particular to avoid duplication of efforts, including among organizations formulating rules of international trade, and to promote efficiency, consistency and coherence in the modernization and harmonization of international trade law, and to continue, through its secretariat, to maintain close cooperation with other international organs and organizations, including regional organizations, active in the field of international trade law,

1. *Takes note with appreciation* of the reports of the United Nations Commission on International Trade Law on the work of its resumed fortieth and its forty-first sessions;

2. *Commends* the Commission for the completion and adoption of the Legislative Guide on Secured Transactions;

3. *Also commends* the Commission for the completion and approval of the draft Convention on Contracts for the International Carriage of Goods Wholly or Partly by Sea;

4. *Welcomes* the progress made by the Commission in its work on a revision of its Model Law on Procurement of Goods, Construction and Services, on the preparation of a draft legislative guide on the treatment of enterprise groups in insolvency, on the compilation of practical experience with negotiating and using cross-border insolvency agreements to facilitate cross-border insolvency proceedings and on the preparation of an annex to its Legislative Guide on Secured Transactions dealing with security rights in intellectual property, and endorses the decision of the Commission to undertake further work in the area of electronic commerce and commercial fraud;

5. *Also welcomes* the progress made by the Commission in its work on a revision of its Arbitration Rules, and encourages the Commission to complete this work as soon as possible so that the revised Rules may be considered by the Commission at its forty-second session, in 2009;

6. *Endorses* the efforts and initiatives of the Commission, as the core legal body within the United Nations system in the field of international trade law, aimed at increasing coordination of and cooperation on legal activities of international and regional organizations active in the field of international trade law, as well as promoting the rule of law at the national and international levels in this field, and in this regard appeals to relevant international and regional organizations to coordinate their legal activities with those of the Commission, to avoid duplication of efforts and to promote efficiency, consistency and coherence in the modernization and harmonization of international trade law;

7. *Reaffirms* the importance, in particular for developing countries, of the work of the Commission concerned with technical assistance and cooperation in the field of international trade law reform and development, and in this connection:

(a) Welcomes the initiatives of the Commission towards expanding, through its secretariat, its technical assistance and cooperation programme and, in that respect, encourages the Secretary-General to seek partnerships with State and non-State actors to increase awareness about the work of the Commission and facilitate the effective implementation of legal standards resulting from its work;

(b) Expresses its appreciation to the Commission for carrying out technical assistance and cooperation activities,

including at the country, subregional and regional levels, and for providing assistance with legislative drafting in the field of international trade law, and draws the attention of the Secretary-General to the limited resources that are made available in this field;

(c) Expresses its appreciation to the Governments whose contributions enabled the technical assistance and cooperation activities to take place, and appeals to Governments, the relevant bodies of the United Nations system, organizations, institutions and individuals to make voluntary contributions to the United Nations Commission on International Trade Law Trust Fund for Symposia and, where appropriate, to the financing of special projects, and otherwise to assist the secretariat of the Commission in carrying out technical assistance activities, in particular in developing countries;

(d) Reiterates its appeal to the United Nations Development Programme and other bodies responsible for development assistance, such as the World Bank and regional development banks, as well as to Governments in their bilateral aid programmes, to support the technical assistance programme of the Commission and to cooperate and coordinate their activities with those of the Commission, in the light of the relevance and importance of the work and programmes of the Commission for promotion of the rule of law at the national and international levels and for the implementation of the United Nations development agenda, including the achievement of the Millennium Development Goals;

8. *Expresses its appreciation* to the Government whose contribution to the trust fund established to provide travel assistance to developing countries that are members of the Commission, at their request and in consultation with the Secretary-General, enabled renewal of the provision of that assistance, and appeals to Governments, the relevant bodies of the United Nations system, organizations, institutions and individuals to make voluntary contributions to the trust fund in order to increase expert representation from developing countries at sessions of the Commission and its working groups, necessary to build local expertise and capacities in the field of international trade law in those countries to facilitate the development of international trade and the promotion of foreign investment;

9. *Decides*, in order to ensure full participation by all Member States in the sessions of the Commission and its working groups, to continue, in the competent Main Committee during the sixty-third session of the General Assembly, its consideration of granting travel assistance to the least developed countries that are members of the Commission, at their request and in consultation with the Secretary-General;

10. *Welcomes*, in the light of the recent increase in membership of the Commission and the number of topics being dealt with by the Commission, the comprehensive review undertaken by the Commission of its working methods, which was started at its last session, with the aim of continuing consideration of the matter during its next sessions and with a view to ensuring the high quality of the work of the Commission and international acceptability of its instruments, and in this regard recalls its previous resolutions related to this matter;

11. *Also welcomes* the discussion by the Commission of its role in promoting the rule of law at the national and international levels, in particular the conviction of the Commission that the implementation and effective use of modern private law standards on international trade are essential for advancing good governance, sustained economic development and the eradication of poverty and hunger and that promotion of the rule of law in commercial relations should be an integral part of the broader agenda of the United Nations to promote the rule of law at the national and international levels, including through the Rule of Law Coordination and Resource Group, supported by the Rule of Law Unit in the Executive Office of the Secretary-General, and the fact that that the Commission is looking forward to being part of strengthened and coordinated activities of the Organization and sees its role in particular as providing assistance to States that seek to promote the rule of law in the area of international and domestic trade and investment;

12. *Further welcomes* the consideration by the Commission of the proposed strategic framework for the period 2010–2011 and its review of the proposed biennial programme plan for the progressive harmonization, modernization and unification of the law of international trade (subprogramme 5), and takes note that, while the Commission noted with satisfaction that the objectives and expected accomplishments of the Secretariat and the overall strategy for subprogramme 5 were in line with its general policy, the Commission also expressed concern that the resources allotted to the Secretariat under subprogramme 5 were insufficient for it to meet, in particular, the increased demand for technical assistance from developing countries and countries with economies in transition to meet their urgent need for law reform in the field of commercial law, and urged the Secretary-General to take steps to ensure that the comparatively small amount of additional resources necessary to meet a demand so crucial to development are made available promptly;

13. *Recalls* its resolutions on partnerships between the United Nations and non-State actors, in particular the private sector, and its resolutions in which it encouraged the Commission to further explore different approaches to the use of partnerships with non-State actors in the implementation of its mandate, in particular in the area of technical assistance, in accordance with the applicable principles and guidelines and in cooperation and coordination with other relevant offices of the Secretariat, including the Global Compact Office;

14. *Reiterates its request* to the Secretary-General, in conformity with the General Assembly resolutions on documentation-related matters, which, in particular, emphasize that any reduction in the length of documents should not adversely affect either the quality of the presentation or the substance of the documents, to bear in mind the particular characteristics of the mandate and work of the Commission in implementing page limits with respect to the documentation of the Commission;

15. *Requests* the Secretary-General to continue providing summary records of the meetings of the Commission relating to the formulation of normative texts;

16. *Recalls* its resolution approving the establishment of the *Yearbook of the United Nations Commission on International Trade Law*, with the aim of making the work of the Commission more widely known and readily available,

expresses its concern regarding the timeliness of the publication of the *Yearbook*, and requests the Secretary-General to explore options to facilitate the timely publication of the *Yearbook*;

17. *Stresses* the importance of bringing into effect the conventions emanating from the work of the Commission for the global unification and harmonization of international trade law, and to this end urges States that have not yet done so to consider signing, ratifying or acceding to those conventions;

18. *Welcomes* the preparation of digests of case law relating to the texts of the Commission, such as a digest of case law relating to the United Nations Convention on Contracts for the International Sale of Goods and a digest of case law relating to the Model Law on International Commercial Arbitration of the United Nations Commission on International Trade Law, with the aim of assisting in the dissemination of information on those texts and promoting their use, enactment and uniform interpretation;

19. *Takes note with appreciation* of conferences celebrating the fiftieth anniversary of the Convention on the Recognition and Enforcement of Foreign Arbitral Awards done in New York on 10 June 1958 ("the New York Convention"), the progress made in the ongoing project of the Commission on monitoring the implementation of the New York Convention, the decision of the Commission to develop a guide to enactment of the New York Convention to promote a uniform interpretation and application of the Convention and its decision that, resources permitting, the activities of the secretariat in the context of its technical assistance programme could usefully include dissemination of information on the judicial interpretation of the New York Convention, to complement other activities in support of the Convention;

20. *Recalls* its resolutions affirming the importance of high-quality, user-friendly and cost-effective United Nations websites and the need for their multilingual development, maintenance and enrichment, commends the website of the Commission in the six official languages of the United Nations, and welcomes the continuous efforts of the Commission to maintain and improve its website in accordance with the applicable guidelines;

21. *Expresses its appreciation* to Jernej Sekolec, Secretary of the United Nations Commission on International Trade Law since 2001, who retired on 31 July 2008, for his outstanding and devoted contribution to the process of unification and harmonization of international trade law in general and to the Commission in particular.

Procurement

UNCITRAL [A/63/17] took note of the reports of Working Group I (Procurement) on its twelfth (Vienna, 3–7 September 2007) [A/CN.9/640] and thirteenth (New York, 7–11 April 2008) [A/CN.9/648] sessions relating to the revision of the UNCITRAL Model Law on Procurement of Goods, Constructions and Services, in response to the Commission's 2004 request [YUN 2004, p. 1356]. At those sessions, the Working Group adopted the timeline for its deliberations, considered the issue of framework agreements, and decided that the issue of suppliers' lists would not be addressed in the Model Law, for reasons that would be set out in the Guide to Enactment. UNCITRAL also approved a fourteenth session of the Working Group, which was held in Vienna from 8 to 12 September.

Commending the Working Group for the progress made, UNCITRAL invited the Group to proceed expeditiously with the completion of the project, with a view to permitting the finalization and adoption of the revised Model Law, together with its Guide to Enactment, within a reasonable time.

International commercial arbitration

UNCITRAL [A/63/17] considered the reports of Working Group II (Arbitration and Conciliation) on its forty-seventh (Vienna, 10–14 September 2007) [A/CN.9/641] and forty-eighth (New York, 4–8 February 2008) [A/CN.9/646] sessions relating to revision of the UNCITRAL Arbitration Rules and commended the Group on progress made. It also approved a forty-ninth session of the Working Group, which was held in Vienna from 15 to 19 September.

The Commission noted that the Working Group had decided to proceed with its work on the revision of the Rules in their generic form and to seek guidance from UNCITRAL on whether the Group should consider in further depth the specificity of treaty-based arbitration, and agreed that it was not desirable to include specific provisions on such arbitration in the Rules. UNCITRAL also agreed that the topic of transparency in treaty-based investor-State arbitration should be dealt with as a matter of priority immediately after revision of the Rules, yet should not delay revision of the Rules in their generic form, which UNCITRAL hoped the Group would complete so their final review and adoption would take place at the Commission's 2009 session. To facilitate consideration of the topic of transparency at a future session, the Commission requested the Secretariat to undertake preliminary research and compile information on current practices. It urged States to contribute broad information on their practices with respect to transparency in investor-State arbitration.

Implementation of the 1958 New York Convention

Under the ongoing project approved by UNCITRAL in 1995 [YUN 1995, p. 1364], aimed at monitoring the legislative implementation of the New York Convention on the Recognition and Enforcement of Foreign Arbitral Awards [YUN 1958, p. 390], UNCITRAL, at its forty-first session [A/63/17 & Corr.1], considered a written report covering implementation of the Convention by States, its interpretation and application, and the requirements and procedures established by States for enforcing an award, based on replies sent by 108 States parties to the Convention [A/CN.9/656 & Add.1]. UNCITRAL noted that the report's recommendations and conclusions highlighted areas where additional work might be needed to enhance uniform interpretation and effective implementation of the Convention.

The Commission agreed that work should be undertaken to eliminate or limit the effect of legal disharmony with respect to the application of national rules of procedure to matters on which the Convention was silent, which had given rise to diverging solutions to the many different procedural requirements that governed the recognition and enforcement of awards under the Convention. The Commission envisaged that the outcome of the project should consist in the development of a guide to enactment of the Convention. It requested that the Secretariat study the feasibility of such a guide and publish on the UNCITRAL website the information collected during the project implementation, in the language in which it was received. The Commission also urged States to provide the Secretariat with accurate information to ensure that the data published on the website remained up to date.

In other developments, on the occasion of the fiftieth anniversary of the Convention, the Commission was informed that a one-day conference, organized jointly by the United Nations and the International Bar Association, was held in New York on 1 February 2008, with more than 600 people from 50 countries participating in the event. A conference celebrating the anniversary had also been organized (Vienna, 13–14 March) under the auspices of UNCITRAL and the International Arbitral Centre of the Austrian Federal Economic Chamber.

Transport Law

UNCITRAL [A/63/17 & Corr.1] considered the reports of Working Group III (Transport Law) on its twentieth (Vienna, 15–25 October 2007) [A/CN.9/642] and twenty-first (New York, 14–25 January 2008) [A/CN.9/645] sessions, with the latter report containing in an annex the text of the draft Convention on Contracts for the International Carriage of Goods Wholly or Partly by Sea, approved by the Working Group. The Commission also had before it a compilation of comments submitted by Governments and intergovernmental organizations regarding the draft Convention as approved by the Working Group [A/CN.9/658 & Add.1–14]. The Commission approved the draft Convention and on 3 July decided to submit the draft Convention, as set forth in annex I of the report, to the General Assembly for adoption.

On 11 December, by resolution 63/122, the Assembly adopted the United Nations Convention on Contracts for the International Carriage of Goods Wholly or Partly by Sea, authorized a ceremony for the opening for signature to be held on 23 September 2009 in Rotterdam, the Netherlands and recommended that the rules embodied in the Convention be known as "the Rotterdam Rules".

GENERAL ASSEMBLY ACTION

On 11 December [meeting 67], the General Assembly, on the recommendation of the Sixth Committee [A/63/438], adopted **resolution 63/122** without vote [agenda item 74].

United Nations Convention on Contracts for the International Carriage of Goods Wholly or Partly by Sea

The General Assembly,

Recalling its resolution 2205(XXI) of 17 December 1966, by which it established the United Nations Commission on International Trade Law with a mandate to further the progressive harmonization and unification of the law of international trade and in that respect to bear in mind the interests of all peoples, in particular those of developing countries, in the extensive development of international trade,

Concerned that the current legal regime governing the international carriage of goods by sea lacks uniformity and fails to adequately take into account modern transport practices, including containerization, door-to-door transport contracts and the use of electronic transport documents,

Noting that the development of international trade on the basis of equality and mutual benefit is an important element in promoting friendly relations among States,

Convinced that the adoption of uniform rules to modernize and harmonize the rules that govern the international carriage of goods involving a sea leg would enhance legal certainty, improve efficiency and commercial predictability in the international carriage of goods and reduce legal obstacles to the flow of international trade among all States,

Believing that the adoption of uniform rules to govern international contracts of carriage wholly or partly by sea will promote legal certainty, improve the efficiency of international carriage of goods and facilitate new access opportunities for previously remote parties and markets, thus playing a fundamental role in promoting trade and economic development, both domestically and internationally,

Noting that shippers and carriers do not have the benefit of a binding and balanced universal regime to support the operation of contracts of carriage involving various modes of transport,

Recalling that, at its thirty-fourth and thirty-fifth sessions, in 2001 and 2002, the Commission decided to prepare an international legislative instrument governing door-to-door transport operations that involve a sea leg,

Recognizing that all States and interested international organizations were invited to participate in the preparation of the draft Convention on Contracts for the International Carriage of Goods Wholly or Partly by Sea and in the forty-first session of the Commission, either as members or as observers, with a full opportunity to speak and make proposals,

Noting with satisfaction that the text of the draft Convention was circulated for comment to all States Members of the United Nations and intergovernmental organizations invited to attend the meetings of the Commission as observers, and that the comments received were before the Commission at its forty-first session,

Taking note with satisfaction of the decision of the Commission at its forty-first session to submit the draft Convention to the General Assembly for its consideration,

Taking note of the draft Convention approved by the Commission,

Expressing its appreciation to the Government of the Netherlands for its offer to host a signing ceremony for the Convention in Rotterdam,

1. *Commends* the United Nations Commission on International Trade Law for preparing the draft Convention on Contracts for the International Carriage of Goods Wholly or Partly by Sea;

2. *Adopts* the United Nations Convention on Contracts for the International Carriage of Goods Wholly or Partly by Sea, contained in the annex to the present resolution;

3. *Authorizes* a ceremony for the opening for signature to be held on 23 September 2009 in Rotterdam, the Netherlands, and recommends that the rules embodied in the Convention be known as "the Rotterdam Rules";

4. *Calls upon* all Governments to consider becoming party to the Convention.

ANNEX

United Nations Convention on Contracts for the International Carriage of Goods Wholly or Partly by Sea

The States Parties to this Convention,

Reaffirming their belief that international trade on the basis of equality and mutual benefit is an important element in promoting friendly relations among States,

Convinced that the progressive harmonization and unification of international trade law, in reducing or removing legal obstacles to the flow of international trade, significantly contributes to universal economic cooperation among all States on a basis of equality, equity and common interest, and to the well-being of all peoples,

Recognizing the significant contribution of the International Convention for the Unification of Certain Rules of Law relating to Bills of Lading, signed in Brussels on 25 August 1924, and its Protocols, and of the United Nations Convention on the Carriage of Goods by Sea, signed in Hamburg on 31 March 1978, to the harmonization of the law governing the carriage of goods by sea,

Mindful of the technological and commercial developments that have taken place since the adoption of those conventions and of the need to consolidate and modernize them,

Noting that shippers and carriers do not have the benefit of a binding universal regime to support the operation of contracts of maritime carriage involving other modes of transport,

Believing that the adoption of uniform rules to govern international contracts of carriage wholly or partly by sea will promote legal certainty, improve the efficiency of international carriage of goods and facilitate new access opportunities for previously remote parties and markets, thus playing a fundamental role in promoting trade and economic development, both domestically and internationally,

Have agreed as follows:

Chapter 1
General provisions

Article 1

Definitions

For the purposes of this Convention:

1. "Contract of carriage" means a contract in which a carrier, against the payment of freight, undertakes to carry goods from one place to another. The contract shall provide for carriage by sea and may provide for carriage by other modes of transport in addition to the sea carriage.

2. "Volume contract" means a contract of carriage that provides for the carriage of a specified quantity of goods in a series of shipments during an agreed period of time. The specification of the quantity may include a minimum, a maximum or a certain range.

3. "Liner transportation" means a transportation service that is offered to the public through publication or similar means and includes transportation by ships operating on a regular schedule between specified ports in accordance with publicly available timetables of sailing dates.

4. "Non-liner transportation" means any transportation that is not liner transportation.

5. "Carrier" means a person that enters into a contract of carriage with a shipper.

6. *(a)* "Performing party" means a person other than the carrier that performs or undertakes to perform any of the carrier's obligations under a contract of carriage with respect to the receipt, loading, handling, stowage, carriage, care, unloading or delivery of the goods, to the extent that such person acts, either directly or indirectly, at the carrier's request or under the carrier's supervision or control.

(b) "Performing party" does not include any person that is retained, directly or indirectly, by a shipper, by a documentary shipper, by the controlling party or by the consignee instead of by the carrier.

7. "Maritime performing party" means a performing party to the extent that it performs or undertakes to perform any of the carrier's obligations during the period between the arrival of the goods at the port of loading of a ship and their departure from the port of discharge of a ship. An inland carrier is a maritime performing party only if it performs or undertakes to perform its services exclusively within a port area.

8. "Shipper" means a person that enters into a contract of carriage with a carrier.

9. "Documentary shipper" means a person, other than the shipper, that accepts to be named as "shipper" in the transport document or electronic transport record.

10. "Holder" means:

(a) A person that is in possession of a negotiable transport document; and (i) if the document is an order document, is identified in it as the shipper or the consignee, or is the person to which the document is duly endorsed; or (ii) if the document is a blank endorsed order document or bearer document, is the bearer thereof; or

(b) The person to which a negotiable electronic transport record has been issued or transferred in accordance with the procedures referred to in article 9, paragraph 1.

11. "Consignee" means a person entitled to delivery of the goods under a contract of carriage or a transport document or electronic transport record.

12. "Right of control" of the goods means the right under the contract of carriage to give the carrier instructions in respect of the goods in accordance with chapter 10.

13. "Controlling party" means the person that pursuant to article 51 is entitled to exercise the right of control.

14. "Transport document" means a document issued under a contract of carriage by the carrier that:

(a) Evidences the carrier's or a performing party's receipt of goods under a contract of carriage; and

(b) Evidences or contains a contract of carriage.

15. "Negotiable transport document" means a transport document that indicates, by wording such as "to order" or "negotiable" or other appropriate wording recognized as having the same effect by the law applicable to the document, that the goods have been consigned to the order of the shipper, to the order of the consignee, or to bearer, and is not explicitly stated as being "non-negotiable" or "not negotiable".

16. "Non-negotiable transport document" means a transport document that is not a negotiable transport document.

17. "Electronic communication" means information generated, sent, received or stored by electronic, optical, digital or similar means with the result that the information communicated is accessible so as to be usable for subsequent reference.

18. "Electronic transport record" means information in one or more messages issued by electronic communication under a contract of carriage by a carrier, including information logically associated with the electronic transport record by attachments or otherwise linked to the electronic transport record contemporaneously with or subsequent to its issue by the carrier, so as to become part of the electronic transport record, that:

(a) Evidences the carrier's or a performing party's receipt of goods under a contract of carriage; and

(b) Evidences or contains a contract of carriage.

19. "Negotiable electronic transport record" means an electronic transport record:

(a) That indicates, by wording such as "to order", or "negotiable", or other appropriate wording recognized as having the same effect by the law applicable to the record, that the goods have been consigned to the order of the shipper or to the order of the consignee, and is not explicitly stated as being "non-negotiable" or "not negotiable"; and

(b) The use of which meets the requirements of article 9, paragraph 1.

20. "Non-negotiable electronic transport record" means an electronic transport record that is not a negotiable electronic transport record.

21. The "issuance" of a negotiable electronic transport record means the issuance of the record in accordance with procedures that ensure that the record is subject to exclusive control from its creation until it ceases to have any effect or validity.

22. The "transfer" of a negotiable electronic transport record means the transfer of exclusive control over the record.

23. "Contract particulars" means any information relating to the contract of carriage or to the goods (including terms, notations, signatures and endorsements) that is in a transport document or an electronic transport record.

24. "Goods" means the wares, merchandise, and articles of every kind whatsoever that a carrier undertakes to carry under a contract of carriage and includes the packing and any equipment and container not supplied by or on behalf of the carrier.

25. "Ship" means any vessel used to carry goods by sea.

26. "Container" means any type of container, transportable tank or flat, swapbody, or any similar unit load used to consolidate goods, and any equipment ancillary to such unit load.

27. "Vehicle" means a road or railroad cargo vehicle.

28. "Freight" means the remuneration payable to the carrier for the carriage of goods under a contract of carriage.

29. "Domicile" means *(a)* a place where a company or other legal person or association of natural or legal persons has its (i) statutory seat or place of incorporation or central registered office, whichever is applicable, (ii) central administration or (iii) principal place of business, and *(b)* the habitual residence of a natural person.

30. "Competent court" means a court in a Contracting State that, according to the rules on the internal allocation of jurisdiction among the courts of that State, may exercise jurisdiction over the dispute.

Article 2

Interpretation of this Convention

In the interpretation of this Convention, regard is to be had to its international character and to the need to promote uniformity in its application and the observance of good faith in international trade.

Article 3

Form requirements

The notices, confirmation, consent, agreement, declaration and other communications referred to in articles 19, paragraph 2; 23, paragraphs 1 to 4; 36, subparagraphs 1 *(b)*, *(c)* and *(d)*; 40, subparagraph 4 *(b)*; 44; 48, paragraph 3; 51, subparagraph 1 *(b)*; 59, paragraph 1; 63; 66; 67, paragraph 2; 75, paragraph 4; and 80, paragraphs 2 and 5, shall be in writing. Electronic communications may be used for these purposes, provided that the use of such means is with the consent of the person by which it is communicated and of the person to which it is communicated.

Article 4

Applicability of defences and limits of liability

1. Any provision of this Convention that may provide a defence for, or limit the liability of, the carrier applies in any judicial or arbitral proceeding, whether founded in contract, in tort, or otherwise, that is instituted in respect of loss of, damage to, or delay in delivery of goods covered by a contract of carriage or for the breach of any other obligation under this Convention against:

(a) The carrier or a maritime performing party;

(b) The master, crew or any other person that performs services on board the ship; or

(c) Employees of the carrier or a maritime performing party.

2. Any provision of this Convention that may provide a defence for the shipper or the documentary shipper applies in any judicial or arbitral proceeding, whether founded in contract, in tort, or otherwise, that is instituted against the shipper, the documentary shipper, or their subcontractors, agents or employees.

Chapter 2
Scope of application

Article 5

General scope of application

1. Subject to article 6, this Convention applies to contracts of carriage in which the place of receipt and the place of delivery are in different States, and the port of loading of a sea carriage and the port of discharge of the same sea carriage are in different States, if, according to the contract of carriage, any one of the following places is located in a Contracting State:

(a) The place of receipt;

(b) The port of loading;

(c) The place of delivery; or

(d) The port of discharge.

2. This Convention applies without regard to the nationality of the vessel, the carrier, the performing parties, the shipper, the consignee, or any other interested parties.

Article 6

Specific exclusions

1. This Convention does not apply to the following contracts in liner transportation:

(a) Charter parties; and

(b) Other contracts for the use of a ship or of any space thereon.

2. This Convention does not apply to contracts of carriage in non-liner transportation except when:

(a) There is no charter party or other contract between the parties for the use of a ship or of any space thereon; and

(b) A transport document or an electronic transport record is issued.

Article 7

Application to certain parties

Notwithstanding article 6, this Convention applies as between the carrier and the consignee, controlling party or holder that is not an original party to the charter party or other contract of carriage excluded from the application of this Convention. However, this Convention does not apply as between the original parties to a contract of carriage excluded pursuant to article 6.

Chapter 3
Electronic transport records

Article 8

Use and effect of electronic transport records

Subject to the requirements set out in this Convention:

(a) Anything that is to be in or on a transport document under this Convention may be recorded in an electronic transport record, provided the issuance and subsequent use of an electronic transport record is with the consent of the carrier and the shipper; and

(b) The issuance, exclusive control, or transfer of an electronic transport record has the same effect as the issuance, possession, or transfer of a transport document.

Article 9

Procedures for use of negotiable electronic transport records

1. The use of a negotiable electronic transport record shall be subject to procedures that provide for:

(a) The method for the issuance and the transfer of that record to an intended holder;

(b) An assurance that the negotiable electronic transport record retains its integrity;

(c) The manner in which the holder is able to demonstrate that it is the holder; and

(d) The manner of providing confirmation that delivery to the holder has been effected, or that, pursuant to articles 10, paragraph 2, or 47, subparagraphs 1 *(a)*(ii) and *(c)*, the electronic transport record has ceased to have any effect or validity.

2. The procedures in paragraph 1 of this article shall be referred to in the contract particulars and be readily ascertainable.

Article 10

Replacement of negotiable transport document or negotiable electronic transport record

1. If a negotiable transport document has been issued and the carrier and the holder agree to replace that document by a negotiable electronic transport record:

(a) The holder shall surrender the negotiable transport document, or all of them if more than one has been issued, to the carrier;

(b) The carrier shall issue to the holder a negotiable electronic transport record that includes a statement that it replaces the negotiable transport document; and

(c) The negotiable transport document ceases thereafter to have any effect or validity.

2. If a negotiable electronic transport record has been issued and the carrier and the holder agree to replace that electronic transport record by a negotiable transport document:

(a) The carrier shall issue to the holder, in place of the electronic transport record, a negotiable transport document that includes a statement that it replaces the negotiable electronic transport record; and

(b) The electronic transport record ceases thereafter to have any effect or validity.

Chapter 4
Obligations of the carrier

Article 11

Carriage and delivery of the goods

The carrier shall, subject to this Convention and in accordance with the terms of the contract of carriage, carry the goods to the place of destination and deliver them to the consignee.

Article 12

Period of responsibility of the carrier

1. The period of responsibility of the carrier for the goods under this Convention begins when the carrier or a performing party receives the goods for carriage and ends when the goods are delivered.

2. *(a)* If the law or regulations of the place of receipt require the goods to be handed over to an authority or other third party from which the carrier may collect them, the period of responsibility of the carrier begins when the carrier collects the goods from the authority or other third party.

(b) If the law or regulations of the place of delivery require the carrier to hand over the goods to an authority or other third party from which the consignee may collect them, the period of responsibility of the carrier ends when the carrier hands the goods over to the authority or other third party.

3. For the purpose of determining the carrier's period of responsibility, the parties may agree on the time and location of receipt and delivery of the goods, but a provision in a contract of carriage is void to the extent that it provides that:

(a) The time of receipt of the goods is subsequent to the beginning of their initial loading under the contract of carriage; or

(b) The time of delivery of the goods is prior to the completion of their final unloading under the contract of carriage.

Article 13

Specific obligations

1. The carrier shall during the period of its responsibility as defined in article 12, and subject to article 26, properly and carefully receive, load, handle, stow, carry, keep, care for, unload and deliver the goods.

2. Notwithstanding paragraph 1 of this article, and without prejudice to the other provisions in chapter 4 and to chapters 5 to 7, the carrier and the shipper may agree that the loading, handling, stowing or unloading of the goods is to be performed by the shipper, the documentary shipper or the consignee. Such an agreement shall be referred to in the contract particulars.

Article 14

Specific obligations applicable to the voyage by sea

The carrier is bound before, at the beginning of, and during the voyage by sea to exercise due diligence to:

(a) Make and keep the ship seaworthy;

(b) Properly crew, equip and supply the ship and keep the ship so crewed, equipped and supplied throughout the voyage; and

(c) Make and keep the holds and all other parts of the ship in which the goods are carried, and any containers supplied by the carrier in or upon which the goods are carried, fit and safe for their reception, carriage and preservation.

Article 15

Goods that may become a danger

Notwithstanding articles 11 and 13, the carrier or a performing party may decline to receive or to load, and may take such other measures as are reasonable, including unloading, destroying, or rendering goods harmless, if the goods are, or reasonably appear likely to become during the carrier's period of responsibility, an actual danger to persons, property or the environment.

Article 16

Sacrifice of the goods during the voyage by sea

Notwithstanding articles 11, 13, and 14, the carrier or a performing party may sacrifice goods at sea when the sacrifice is reasonably made for the common safety or for the purpose of preserving from peril human life or other property involved in the common adventure.

Chapter 5
Liability of the carrier for loss, damage or delay

Article 17

Basis of liability

1. The carrier is liable for loss of or damage to the goods, as well as for delay in delivery, if the claimant proves that the loss, damage, or delay, or the event or circumstance that caused or contributed to it took place during the period of the carrier's responsibility as defined in chapter 4.

2. The carrier is relieved of all or part of its liability pursuant to paragraph 1 of this article if it proves that the cause or one of the causes of the loss, damage, or delay is not attributable to its fault or to the fault of any person referred to in article 18.

3. The carrier is also relieved of all or part of its liability pursuant to paragraph 1 of this article if, alternatively to proving the absence of fault as provided in paragraph 2 of this article, it proves that one or more of the following events or circumstances caused or contributed to the loss, damage, or delay:

(a) Act of God;

(b) Perils, dangers, and accidents of the sea or other navigable waters;

(c) War, hostilities, armed conflict, piracy, terrorism, riots, and civil commotions;

(d) Quarantine restrictions; interference by or impediments created by governments, public authorities, rulers, or people including detention, arrest, or seizure not attributable to the carrier or any person referred to in article 18;

(e) Strikes, lockouts, stoppages, or restraints of labour;

(f) Fire on the ship;

(g) Latent defects not discoverable by due diligence;

(h) Act or omission of the shipper, the documentary shipper, the controlling party, or any other person for whose acts the shipper or the documentary shipper is liable pursuant to article 33 or 34;

(i) Loading, handling, stowing, or unloading of the goods performed pursuant to an agreement in accordance with article 13, paragraph 2, unless the carrier or a performing party performs such activity on behalf of the shipper, the documentary shipper or the consignee;

(j) Wastage in bulk or weight or any other loss or damage arising from inherent defect, quality, or vice of the goods;

(k) Insufficiency or defective condition of packing or marking not performed by or on behalf of the carrier;

(l) Saving or attempting to save life at sea;

(m) Reasonable measures to save or attempt to save property at sea;

(n) Reasonable measures to avoid or attempt to avoid damage to the environment; or

(o) Acts of the carrier in pursuance of the powers conferred by articles 15 and 16.

4. Notwithstanding paragraph 3 of this article, the carrier is liable for all or part of the loss, damage, or delay:

(a) If the claimant proves that the fault of the carrier or of a person referred to in article 18 caused or contributed to the event or circumstance on which the carrier relies; or

(b) If the claimant proves that an event or circumstance not listed in paragraph 3 of this article contributed to the loss, damage, or delay, and the carrier cannot prove that this event or circumstance is not attributable to its fault or to the fault of any person referred to in article 18.

5. The carrier is also liable, notwithstanding paragraph 3 of this article, for all or part of the loss, damage, or delay if:

(a) The claimant proves that the loss, damage, or delay was or was probably caused by or contributed to by (i) the unseaworthiness of the ship; (ii) the improper crewing, equipping, and supplying of the ship; or (iii) the fact that the holds or other parts of the ship in which the goods are carried, or any containers supplied by the carrier in or upon which the goods are carried, were not fit and safe for reception, carriage, and preservation of the goods; and

(b) The carrier is unable to prove either that: (i) none of the events or circumstances referred to in subparagraph 5 *(a)* of this article caused the loss, damage, or delay; or (ii) it complied with its obligation to exercise due diligence pursuant to article 14.

6. When the carrier is relieved of part of its liability pursuant to this article, the carrier is liable only for that part of the loss, damage or delay that is attributable to the event or circumstance for which it is liable pursuant to this article.

Article 18

Liability of the carrier for other persons

The carrier is liable for the breach of its obligations under this Convention caused by the acts or omissions of:

(a) Any performing party;

(b) The master or crew of the ship;

(c) Employees of the carrier or a performing party; or

(d) Any other person that performs or undertakes to perform any of the carrier's obligations under the contract of carriage, to the extent that the person acts, either directly or indirectly, at the carrier's request or under the carrier's supervision or control.

Article 19

Liability of maritime performing parties

1. A maritime performing party is subject to the obligations and liabilities imposed on the carrier under this Convention and is entitled to the carrier's defences and limits of liability as provided for in this Convention if:

(a) The maritime performing party received the goods for carriage in a Contracting State, or delivered them in a Contracting State, or performed its activities with respect to the goods in a port in a Contracting State; and

(b) The occurrence that caused the loss, damage or delay took place: (i) during the period between the arrival of the goods at the port of loading of the ship and their departure from the port of discharge from the ship; (ii) while the maritime performing party had custody of the goods; or (iii) at any other time to the extent that it was participating in the performance of any of the activities contemplated by the contract of carriage.

2. If the carrier agrees to assume obligations other than those imposed on the carrier under this Convention, or agrees that the limits of its liability are higher than the limits specified under this Convention, a maritime performing party is not bound by this agreement unless it expressly agrees to accept such obligations or such higher limits.

3. A maritime performing party is liable for the breach of its obligations under this Convention caused by the acts or omissions of any person to which it has entrusted the performance of any of the carrier's obligations under the contract of carriage under the conditions set out in paragraph 1 of this article.

4. Nothing in this Convention imposes liability on the master or crew of the ship or on an employee of the carrier or of a maritime performing party.

Article 20

Joint and several liability

1. If the carrier and one or more maritime performing parties are liable for the loss of, damage to, or delay in delivery of the goods, their liability is joint and several but only up to the limits provided for under this Convention.

2. Without prejudice to article 61, the aggregate liability of all such persons shall not exceed the overall limits of liability under this Convention.

Article 21

Delay

Delay in delivery occurs when the goods are not delivered at the place of destination provided for in the contract of carriage within the time agreed.

Article 22

Calculation of compensation

1. Subject to article 59, the compensation payable by the carrier for loss of or damage to the goods is calculated by reference to the value of such goods at the place and time of delivery established in accordance with article 43.

2. The value of the goods is fixed according to the commodity exchange price or, if there is no such price, according to their market price or, if there is no commodity exchange price or market price, by reference to the normal value of the goods of the same kind and quality at the place of delivery.

3. In case of loss of or damage to the goods, the carrier is not liable for payment of any compensation beyond what is provided for in paragraphs 1 and 2 of this article except when the carrier and the shipper have agreed to calculate compensation in a different manner within the limits of chapter 16.

Article 23

Notice in case of loss, damage or delay

1. The carrier is presumed, in absence of proof to the contrary, to have delivered the goods according to their description in the contract particulars unless notice of loss of or damage to the goods, indicating the general nature of such loss or damage, was given to the carrier or the performing party that delivered the goods before or at the time of the delivery, or, if the loss or damage is not apparent, within seven working days at the place of delivery after the delivery of the goods.

2. Failure to provide the notice referred to in this article to the carrier or the performing party shall not affect the right to claim compensation for loss of or damage to the goods under this Convention, nor shall it affect the allocation of the burden of proof set out in article 17.

3. The notice referred to in this article is not required in respect of loss or damage that is ascertained in a joint inspection of the goods by the person to which they have been delivered and the carrier or the maritime performing party against which liability is being asserted.

4. No compensation in respect of delay is payable unless notice of loss due to delay was given to the carrier within twenty-one consecutive days of delivery of the goods.

5. When the notice referred to in this article is given to the performing party that delivered the goods, it has the same effect as if that notice was given to the carrier, and notice given to the carrier has the same effect as a notice given to a maritime performing party.

6. In the case of any actual or apprehended loss or damage, the parties to the dispute shall give all reasonable facilities to each other for inspecting and tallying the goods and shall provide access to records and documents relevant to the carriage of the goods.

Chapter 6

Additional provisions relating to particular stages of carriage

Article 24

Deviation

When pursuant to applicable law a deviation constitutes a breach of the carrier's obligations, such deviation of itself shall not deprive the carrier or a maritime performing party of any defence or limitation of this Convention, except to the extent provided in article 61.

Article 25

Deck cargo on ships

1. Goods may be carried on the deck of a ship only if:

(a) Such carriage is required by law;

(b) They are carried in or on containers or vehicles that are fit for deck carriage, and the decks are specially fitted to carry such containers or vehicles; or

(c) The carriage on deck is in accordance with the contract of carriage, or the customs, usages or practices of the trade in question.

2. The provisions of this Convention relating to the liability of the carrier apply to the loss of, damage to or delay in the delivery of goods carried on deck pursuant to paragraph 1 of this article, but the carrier is not liable for loss of or damage to such goods, or delay in their delivery, caused by the special risks involved in their carriage on deck when the goods are carried in accordance with subparagraphs 1 *(a)* or *(c)* of this article.

3. If the goods have been carried on deck in cases other than those permitted pursuant to paragraph 1 of this article, the carrier is liable for loss of or damage to the goods or delay in their delivery that is exclusively caused by their carriage on deck, and is not entitled to the defences provided for in article 17.

4. The carrier is not entitled to invoke subparagraph 1 *(c)* of this article against a third party that has acquired a negotiable transport document or a negotiable electronic transport record in good faith, unless the contract particulars state that the goods may be carried on deck.

5. If the carrier and shipper expressly agreed that the goods would be carried under deck, the carrier is not entitled to the benefit of the limitation of liability for any loss of, damage to or delay in the delivery of the goods to the extent that such loss, damage, or delay resulted from their carriage on deck.

Article 26

Carriage preceding or subsequent to sea carriage

When loss of or damage to goods, or an event or circumstance causing a delay in their delivery, occurs during the carrier's period of responsibility but solely before their loading onto the ship or solely after their discharge from the ship, the provisions of this Convention do not prevail over those provisions of another international instrument that, at the time of such loss, damage or event or circumstance causing delay:

(a) Pursuant to the provisions of such international instrument would have applied to all or any of the carrier's activities if the shipper had made a separate and direct contract with the carrier in respect of the particular stage of carriage where the loss of, or damage to goods, or an event or circumstance causing delay in their delivery occurred;

(b) Specifically provide for the carrier's liability, limitation of liability, or time for suit; and

(c) Cannot be departed from by contract either at all or to the detriment of the shipper under that instrument.

Chapter 7

Obligations of the shipper to the carrier

Article 27

Delivery for carriage

1. Unless otherwise agreed in the contract of carriage, the shipper shall deliver the goods ready for carriage. In any event, the shipper shall deliver the goods in such condition that they will withstand the intended carriage, including their loading, handling, stowing, lashing and securing, and unloading, and that they will not cause harm to persons or property.

2. The shipper shall properly and carefully perform any obligation assumed under an agreement made pursuant to article 13, paragraph 2.

3. When a container is packed or a vehicle is loaded by the shipper, the shipper shall properly and carefully stow, lash and secure the contents in or on the container or vehicle, and in such a way that they will not cause harm to persons or property.

Article 28

Cooperation of the shipper and the carrier in providing information and instructions

The carrier and the shipper shall respond to requests from each other to provide information and instructions required for the proper handling and carriage of the goods if the information is in the requested party's possession or the instructions are within the requested party's reasonable ability to provide and they are not otherwise reasonably available to the requesting party.

Article 29

Shipper's obligation to provide information, instructions and documents

1. The shipper shall provide to the carrier in a timely manner such information, instructions and documents relating to the goods that are not otherwise reasonably available to the carrier, and that are reasonably necessary:

(a) For the proper handling and carriage of the goods, including precautions to be taken by the carrier or a performing party; and

(b) For the carrier to comply with law, regulations or other requirements of public authorities in connection with the intended carriage, provided that the carrier notifies the shipper in a timely manner of the information, instructions and documents it requires.

2. Nothing in this article affects any specific obligation to provide certain information, instructions and documents related to the goods pursuant to law, regulations or other requirements of public authorities in connection with the intended carriage.

Article 30

Basis of shipper's liability to the carrier

1. The shipper is liable for loss or damage sustained by the carrier if the carrier proves that such loss or damage was caused by a breach of the shipper's obligations under this Convention.

2. Except in respect of loss or damage caused by a breach by the shipper of its obligations pursuant to articles 31, paragraph 2, and 32, the shipper is relieved of all or part of its liability if the cause or one of the causes of the loss or damage is not attributable to its fault or to the fault of any person referred to in article 34.

3. When the shipper is relieved of part of its liability pursuant to this article, the shipper is liable only for that part of the loss or damage that is attributable to its fault or to the fault of any person referred to in article 34.

Article 31

Information for compilation of contract particulars

1. The shipper shall provide to the carrier, in a timely manner, accurate information required for the compilation of the contract particulars and the issuance of the transport documents or electronic transport records, including the particulars referred to in article 36, paragraph 1; the name of the party to be identified as the shipper in the contract particulars; the name of the consignee, if any; and the name of the person to whose order the transport document or electronic transport record is to be issued, if any.

2. The shipper is deemed to have guaranteed the accuracy at the time of receipt by the carrier of the information that is provided according to paragraph 1 of this article. The shipper shall indemnify the carrier against loss or damage resulting from the inaccuracy of such information.

Article 32

Special rules on dangerous goods

When goods by their nature or character are, or reasonably appear likely to become, a danger to persons, property or the environment:

(a) The shipper shall inform the carrier of the dangerous nature or character of the goods in a timely manner before they are delivered to the carrier or a performing party. If the shipper fails to do so and the carrier or performing party does not otherwise have knowledge of their dangerous nature or character, the shipper is liable to the carrier for loss or damage resulting from such failure to inform; and

(b) The shipper shall mark or label dangerous goods in accordance with any law, regulations or other requirements of public authorities that apply during any stage of the intended carriage of the goods. If the shipper fails to do so, it is liable to the carrier for loss or damage resulting from such failure.

Article 33

Assumption of shipper's rights and obligations by the documentary shipper

1. A documentary shipper is subject to the obligations and liabilities imposed on the shipper pursuant to this chapter and pursuant to article 55, and is entitled to the shipper's rights and defences provided by this chapter and by chapter 13.

2. Paragraph 1 of this article does not affect the obligations, liabilities, rights or defences of the shipper.

Article 34

Liability of the shipper for other persons

The shipper is liable for the breach of its obligations under this Convention caused by the acts or omissions of any person, including employees, agents and subcontractors, to which it has entrusted the performance of any of its obligations, but the shipper is not liable for acts or omissions of the carrier or a performing party acting on behalf of the carrier, to which the shipper has entrusted the performance of its obligations.

Chapter 8

Transport documents and electronic transport records

Article 35

Issuance of the transport document or the electronic transport record

Unless the shipper and the carrier have agreed not to use a transport document or an electronic transport record, or it is the custom, usage or practice of the trade not to use one, upon delivery of the goods for carriage to the carrier or performing party, the shipper or, if the shipper consents, the documentary shipper, is entitled to obtain from the carrier, at the shipper's option:

(a) A non-negotiable transport document or, subject to article 8, subparagraph *(a)*, a non-negotiable electronic transport record; or

(b) An appropriate negotiable transport document or, subject to article 8, subparagraph *(a)*, a negotiable electronic transport record, unless the shipper and the carrier have agreed not to use a negotiable transport document or negotiable electronic transport record, or it is the custom, usage or practice of the trade not to use one.

Article 36

Contract particulars

1. The contract particulars in the transport document or electronic transport record referred to in article 35 shall include the following information, as furnished by the shipper:

(a) A description of the goods as appropriate for the transport;

(b) The leading marks necessary for identification of the goods;

(c) The number of packages or pieces, or the quantity of goods; and

(d) The weight of the goods, if furnished by the shipper.

2. The contract particulars in the transport document or electronic transport record referred to in article 35 shall also include:

(a) A statement of the apparent order and condition of the goods at the time the carrier or a performing party receives them for carriage;

(b) The name and address of the carrier;

(c) The date on which the carrier or a performing party received the goods, or on which the goods were loaded on board the ship, or on which the transport document or electronic transport record was issued; and

(d) If the transport document is negotiable, the number of originals of the negotiable transport document, when more than one original is issued.

3. The contract particulars in the transport document or electronic transport record referred to in article 35 shall further include:

(a) The name and address of the consignee, if named by the shipper;

(b) The name of a ship, if specified in the contract of carriage;

(c) The place of receipt and, if known to the carrier, the place of delivery; and

(d) The port of loading and the port of discharge, if specified in the contract of carriage.

4. For the purposes of this article, the phrase "apparent order and condition of the goods" in subparagraph 2 *(a)* of this article refers to the order and condition of the goods based on:

(a) A reasonable external inspection of the goods as packaged at the time the shipper delivers them to the carrier or a performing party; and

(b) Any additional inspection that the carrier or a performing party actually performs before issuing the transport document or electronic transport record.

Article 37

Identity of the carrier

1. If a carrier is identified by name in the contract particulars, any other information in the transport document or electronic transport record relating to the identity of the carrier shall have no effect to the extent that it is inconsistent with that identification.

2. If no person is identified in the contract particulars as the carrier as required pursuant to article 36, subparagraph 2 *(b)*, but the contract particulars indicate that the goods have been loaded on board a named ship, the registered owner of that ship is presumed to be the carrier, unless it proves that the ship was under a bareboat charter at the time of the carriage and it identifies this bareboat charterer and indicates its address, in which case this bareboat charterer is presumed to be the carrier. Alternatively, the registered owner may rebut the presumption of being the carrier by identifying the carrier and indicating its address. The bareboat charterer may rebut any presumption of being the carrier in the same manner.

3. Nothing in this article prevents the claimant from proving that any person other than a person identified in the contract particulars or pursuant to paragraph 2 of this article is the carrier.

Article 38

Signature

1. A transport document shall be signed by the carrier or a person acting on its behalf.

2. An electronic transport record shall include the electronic signature of the carrier or a person acting on its behalf. Such electronic signature shall identify the signatory in relation to the electronic transport record and indicate the carrier's authorization of the electronic transport record.

Article 39

Deficiencies in the contract particulars

1. The absence or inaccuracy of one or more of the contract particulars referred to in article 36, paragraphs 1, 2 or 3, does not of itself affect the legal character or validity of the transport document or of the electronic transport record.

2. If the contract particulars include the date but fail to indicate its significance, the date is deemed to be:

(a) The date on which all of the goods indicated in the transport document or electronic transport record were loaded on board the ship, if the contract particulars indicate that the goods have been loaded on board a ship; or

(b) The date on which the carrier or a performing party received the goods, if the contract particulars do not indicate that the goods have been loaded on board a ship.

3. If the contract particulars fail to state the apparent order and condition of the goods at the time the carrier or a performing party receives them, the contract particulars are deemed to have stated that the goods were in apparent good order and condition at the time the carrier or a performing party received them.

Article 40

Qualifying the information relating to the goods in the contract particulars

1. The carrier shall qualify the information referred to in article 36, paragraph 1, to indicate that the carrier does not assume responsibility for the accuracy of the information furnished by the shipper if:

(a) The carrier has actual knowledge that any material statement in the transport document or electronic transport record is false or misleading; or

(b) The carrier has reasonable grounds to believe that a material statement in the transport document or electronic transport record is false or misleading.

2. Without prejudice to paragraph 1 of this article, the carrier may qualify the information referred to in article 36, paragraph 1, in the circumstances and in the manner set out in paragraphs 3 and 4 of this article to indicate that the carrier does not assume responsibility for the accuracy of the information furnished by the shipper.

3. When the goods are not delivered for carriage to the carrier or a performing party in a closed container or vehicle, or when they are delivered in a closed container or vehicle and the carrier or a performing party actually inspects them, the carrier may qualify the information referred to in article 36, paragraph 1, if:

(a) The carrier had no physically practicable or commercially reasonable means of checking the information furnished by the shipper, in which case it may indicate which information it was unable to check; or

(b) The carrier has reasonable grounds to believe the information furnished by the shipper to be inaccurate, in which case it may include a clause providing what it reasonably considers accurate information.

4. When the goods are delivered for carriage to the carrier or a performing party in a closed container or vehicle, the carrier may qualify the information referred to in:

(a) Article 36, subparagraphs 1 *(a)*, *(b)*, or *(c)*, if:

(i) The goods inside the container or vehicle have not actually been inspected by the carrier or a performing party; and

(ii) Neither the carrier nor a performing party otherwise has actual knowledge of its contents before issuing the transport document or the electronic transport record; and

(b) Article 36, subparagraph 1 *(d)*, if:

(i) Neither the carrier nor a performing party weighed the container or vehicle, and the shipper and the carrier had not agreed prior to the shipment that the container or vehicle would be weighed and the weight would be included in the contract particulars; or

(ii) There was no physically practicable or commercially reasonable means of checking the weight of the container or vehicle.

Article 41

Evidentiary effect of the contract particulars

Except to the extent that the contract particulars have been qualified in the circumstances and in the manner set out in article 40:

(a) A transport document or an electronic transport record is prima facie evidence of the carrier's receipt of the goods as stated in the contract particulars;

(b) Proof to the contrary by the carrier in respect of any contract particulars shall not be admissible, when such contract particulars are included in:

(i) A negotiable transport document or a negotiable electronic transport record that is transferred to a third party acting in good faith; or

(ii) A non-negotiable transport document that indicates that it must be surrendered in order to obtain delivery of the goods and is transferred to the consignee acting in good faith;

(c) Proof to the contrary by the carrier shall not be admissible against a consignee that in good faith has acted in reliance on any of the following contract particulars included in a non-negotiable transport document or a non-negotiable electronic transport record:

(i) The contract particulars referred to in article 36, paragraph 1, when such contract particulars are furnished by the carrier;

(ii) The number, type and identifying numbers of the containers, but not the identifying numbers of the container seals; and

(iii) The contract particulars referred to in article 36, paragraph 2.

Article 42

"Freight prepaid"

If the contract particulars contain the statement "freight prepaid" or a statement of a similar nature, the carrier cannot assert against the holder or the consignee the fact that the freight has not been paid. This article does not apply if the holder or the consignee is also the shipper.

Chapter 9

Delivery of the goods

Article 43

Obligation to accept delivery

When the goods have arrived at their destination, the consignee that demands delivery of the goods under the contract of carriage shall accept delivery of the goods at the time or within the time period and at the location agreed in the contract of carriage or, failing such agreement, at the time and location at which, having regard to the terms of the contract, the customs, usages or practices of the trade and the circumstances of the carriage, delivery could reasonably be expected.

Article 44

Obligation to acknowledge receipt

On request of the carrier or the performing party that delivers the goods, the consignee shall acknowledge receipt of the goods from the carrier or the performing party in the manner that is customary at the place of delivery. The carrier may refuse delivery if the consignee refuses to acknowledge such receipt.

Article 45

Delivery when no negotiable transport document or negotiable electronic transport record is issued

When neither a negotiable transport document nor a negotiable electronic transport record has been issued:

(a) The carrier shall deliver the goods to the consignee at the time and location referred to in article 43. The carrier may refuse delivery if the person claiming to be the consignee does not properly identify itself as the consignee on the request of the carrier;

(b) If the name and address of the consignee are not referred to in the contract particulars, the controlling party shall prior to or upon the arrival of the goods at the place of destination advise the carrier of such name and address;

(c) Without prejudice to article 48, paragraph 1, if the goods are not deliverable because (i) the consignee, after having received a notice of arrival, does not, at the time or within the time period referred to in article 43, claim delivery of the goods from the carrier after their arrival at the place of destination, (ii) the carrier refuses delivery because the person claiming to be the consignee does not properly identify itself as the consignee, or (iii) the carrier is, after reasonable effort, unable to locate the consignee in order to request delivery instructions, the carrier may so advise the controlling party and request instructions in respect of the delivery of the goods. If, after reasonable effort, the carrier is unable to locate the controlling party, the carrier may so advise the shipper and request instructions in respect of the delivery of the goods. If, after reasonable effort, the carrier is unable to locate the shipper, the carrier may so advise the documentary shipper and request instructions in respect of the delivery of the goods;

(d) The carrier that delivers the goods upon instruction of the controlling party, the shipper or the documentary shipper pursuant to subparagraph *(c)* of this article is discharged from its obligations to deliver the goods under the contract of carriage.

Article 46

Delivery when a non-negotiable transport document that requires surrender is issued

When a non-negotiable transport document has been issued that indicates that it shall be surrendered in order to obtain delivery of the goods:

(a) The carrier shall deliver the goods at the time and location referred to in article 43 to the consignee upon the consignee properly identifying itself on the request of the carrier and surrender of the non-negotiable document. The carrier may refuse delivery if the person claiming to be the consignee fails to properly identify itself on the request of the carrier, and shall refuse delivery if the non-negotiable document is not surrendered. If more than one original of the non-negotiable document has been issued, the surrender of one original will suffice and the other originals cease to have any effect or validity;

(b) Without prejudice to article 48, paragraph 1, if the goods are not deliverable because (i) the consignee, after having received a notice of arrival, does not, at the time or within the time period referred to in article 43, claim delivery of the goods from the carrier after their arrival at the place of destination, (ii) the carrier refuses delivery because the person claiming to be the consignee does not properly identify itself as the consignee or does not surrender the document, or (iii) the carrier is, after reasonable effort, unable to locate the consignee in order to request delivery instructions, the carrier may so advise the shipper and request instructions in respect of the delivery of the goods. If, after reasonable effort, the carrier is unable to locate the shipper, the carrier may so advise the documentary shipper and request instructions in respect of the delivery of the goods;

(c) The carrier that delivers the goods upon instruction of the shipper or the documentary shipper pursuant to subparagraph *(b)* of this article is discharged from its obligation to deliver the goods under the contract of carriage, irrespective of whether the non-negotiable transport document has been surrendered to it.

Article 47

Delivery when a negotiable transport document or negotiable electronic transport record is issued

1. When a negotiable transport document or a negotiable electronic transport record has been issued:

(a) The holder of the negotiable transport document or negotiable electronic transport record is entitled to claim delivery of the goods from the carrier after they have arrived at the place of destination, in which event the carrier shall deliver the goods at the time and location referred to in article 43 to the holder:

(i) Upon surrender of the negotiable transport document and, if the holder is one of the persons referred to in article 1, subparagraph 10 *(a)*(i), upon the holder properly identifying itself; or

(ii) Upon demonstration by the holder, in accordance with the procedures referred to in article 9, paragraph 1, that it is the holder of the negotiable electronic transport record;

(b) The carrier shall refuse delivery if the requirements of subparagraph *(a)*(i) or *(a)*(ii) of this paragraph are not met;

(c) If more than one original of the negotiable transport document has been issued, and the number of originals is stated in that document, the surrender of one original will suffice and the other originals cease to have any effect or validity. When a negotiable electronic transport record has been used, such electronic transport record ceases to have any effect or validity upon delivery to the holder in accordance with the procedures required by article 9, paragraph 1.

2. Without prejudice to article 48, paragraph 1, if the negotiable transport document or the negotiable electronic transport record expressly states that the goods may be delivered without the surrender of the transport document or the electronic transport record, the following rules apply:

(a) If the goods are not deliverable because (i) the holder, after having received a notice of arrival, does not, at the time or within the time period referred to in article 43, claim delivery of the goods from the carrier after their arrival at the place of destination, (ii) the carrier refuses delivery because the person claiming to be a holder does not properly identify itself as one of the persons referred to in article 1, subparagraph 10 *(a)*(i), or (iii) the carrier is, after reasonable effort, unable to locate the holder in order to request delivery instructions, the carrier may so advise the shipper and request instructions in respect of the delivery of the goods. If, after reasonable effort, the carrier is unable to locate the shipper, the carrier may so advise the documentary shipper and request instructions in respect of the delivery of the goods;

(b) The carrier that delivers the goods upon instruction of the shipper or the documentary shipper in accordance with subparagraph 2 *(a)* of this article is discharged from its obligation to deliver the goods under the contract of carriage to the holder, irrespective of whether the negotiable transport document has been surrendered to it, or the person claiming delivery under a negotiable electronic transport record has demonstrated, in accordance with the procedures referred to in article 9, paragraph 1, that it is the holder;

(c) The person giving instructions under subparagraph 2 *(a)* of this article shall indemnify the carrier against loss arising from its being held liable to the holder under subparagraph 2 *(e)* of this article. The carrier may refuse to follow those instructions if the person fails to provide adequate security as the carrier may reasonably request;

(d) A person that becomes a holder of the negotiable transport document or the negotiable electronic transport record after the carrier has delivered the goods pursuant to subparagraph 2 *(b)* of this article, but pursuant to contractual or other arrangements made before such delivery acquires rights against the carrier under the contract of carriage, other than the right to claim delivery of the goods;

(e) Notwithstanding subparagraphs 2 *(b)* and 2 *(d)* of this article, a holder that becomes a holder after such delivery, and that did not have and could not reasonably have had knowledge of such delivery at the time it became a holder, acquires the rights incorporated in the negotiable transport document or negotiable electronic transport record. When the contract particulars state the expected time of arrival of the goods, or indicate how to obtain information as to whether the goods have been delivered, it is presumed that the holder at the time that it became a holder had or could reasonably have had knowledge of the delivery of the goods.

Article 48

Goods remaining undelivered

1. For the purposes of this article, goods shall be deemed to have remained undelivered only if, after their arrival at the place of destination:

(a) The consignee does not accept delivery of the goods pursuant to this chapter at the time and location referred to in article 43;

(b) The controlling party, the holder, the shipper or the documentary shipper cannot be found or does not give the carrier adequate instructions pursuant to articles 45, 46 and 47;

(c) The carrier is entitled or required to refuse delivery pursuant to articles 44, 45, 46 and 47;

(d) The carrier is not allowed to deliver the goods to the consignee pursuant to the law or regulations of the place at which delivery is requested; or

(e) The goods are otherwise undeliverable by the carrier.

2. Without prejudice to any other rights that the carrier may have against the shipper, controlling party or consignee, if the goods have remained undelivered, the carrier may, at the risk and expense of the person entitled to the goods, take such action in respect of the goods as circumstances may reasonably require, including:

(a) To store the goods at any suitable place;

(b) To unpack the goods if they are packed in containers or vehicles, or to act otherwise in respect of the goods, including by moving them; and

(c) To cause the goods to be sold or destroyed in accordance with the practices or pursuant to the law or regulations of the place where the goods are located at the time.

3. The carrier may exercise the rights under paragraph 2 of this article only after it has given reasonable notice of the intended action under paragraph 2 of this article to the person stated in the contract particulars as the person, if any, to be notified of the arrival of the goods at the place of destination, and to one of the following persons in the order indicated, if known to the carrier: the consignee, the controlling party or the shipper.

4. If the goods are sold pursuant to subparagraph 2 *(c)* of this article, the carrier shall hold the proceeds of the sale for the benefit of the person entitled to the goods, subject to the deduction of any costs incurred by the carrier and any other amounts that are due to the carrier in connection with the carriage of those goods.

5. The carrier shall not be liable for loss of or damage to goods that occurs during the time that they remain undelivered pursuant to this article unless the claimant proves that such loss or damage resulted from the failure by the carrier to take steps that would have been reasonable in the circumstances to preserve the goods and that the carrier knew or ought to have known that the loss or damage to the goods would result from its failure to take such steps.

Article 49

Retention of goods

Nothing in this Convention affects a right of the carrier or a performing party that may exist pursuant to the contract of carriage or the applicable law to retain the goods to secure the payment of sums due.

Chapter 10
Rights of the controlling party

Article 50

Exercise and extent of right of control

1. The right of control may be exercised only by the controlling party and is limited to:

(a) The right to give or modify instructions in respect of the goods that do not constitute a variation of the contract of carriage;

(b) The right to obtain delivery of the goods at a scheduled port of call or, in respect of inland carriage, any place en route; and

(c) The right to replace the consignee by any other person including the controlling party.

2. The right of control exists during the entire period of responsibility of the carrier, as provided in article 12, and ceases when that period expires.

Article 51

Identity of the controlling party and transfer of the right of control

1. Except in the cases referred to in paragraphs 2, 3 and 4 of this article:

(a) The shipper is the controlling party unless the shipper, when the contract of carriage is concluded, designates

the consignee, the documentary shipper or another person as the controlling party;

(b) The controlling party is entitled to transfer the right of control to another person. The transfer becomes effective with respect to the carrier upon its notification of the transfer by the transferor, and the transferee becomes the controlling party; and

(c) The controlling party shall properly identify itself when it exercises the right of control.

2. When a non-negotiable transport document has been issued that indicates that it shall be surrendered in order to obtain delivery of the goods:

(a) The shipper is the controlling party and may transfer the right of control to the consignee named in the transport document by transferring the document to that person without endorsement. If more than one original of the document was issued, all originals shall be transferred in order to effect a transfer of the right of control; and

(b) In order to exercise its right of control, the controlling party shall produce the document and properly identify itself. If more than one original of the document was issued, all originals shall be produced, failing which the right of control cannot be exercised.

3. When a negotiable transport document is issued:

(a) The holder or, if more than one original of the negotiable transport document is issued, the holder of all originals is the controlling party;

(b) The holder may transfer the right of control by transferring the negotiable transport document to another person in accordance with article 57. If more than one original of that document was issued, all originals shall be transferred to that person in order to effect a transfer of the right of control; and

(c) In order to exercise the right of control, the holder shall produce the negotiable transport document to the carrier, and if the holder is one of the persons referred to in article 1, subparagraph 10 *(a)*(i), the holder shall properly identify itself. If more than one original of the document was issued, all originals shall be produced, failing which the right of control cannot be exercised.

4. When a negotiable electronic transport record is issued:

(a) The holder is the controlling party;

(b) The holder may transfer the right of control to another person by transferring the negotiable electronic transport record in accordance with the procedures referred to in article 9, paragraph 1; and

(c) In order to exercise the right of control, the holder shall demonstrate, in accordance with the procedures referred to in article 9, paragraph 1, that it is the holder.

Article 52

Carrier's execution of instructions

1. Subject to paragraphs 2 and 3 of this article, the carrier shall execute the instructions referred to in article 50 if:

(a) The person giving such instructions is entitled to exercise the right of control;

(b) The instructions can reasonably be executed according to their terms at the moment that they reach the carrier; and

(c) The instructions will not interfere with the normal operations of the carrier, including its delivery practices.

2. In any event, the controlling party shall reimburse the carrier for any reasonable additional expense that the carrier may incur and shall indemnify the carrier against loss or damage that the carrier may suffer as a result of diligently executing any instruction pursuant to this article, including compensation that the carrier may become liable to pay for loss of or damage to other goods being carried.

3. The carrier is entitled to obtain security from the controlling party for the amount of additional expense, loss or damage that the carrier reasonably expects will arise in connection with the execution of an instruction pursuant to this article. The carrier may refuse to carry out the instructions if no such security is provided.

4. The carrier's liability for loss of or damage to the goods or for delay in delivery resulting from its failure to comply with the instructions of the controlling party in breach of its obligation pursuant to paragraph 1 of this article shall be subject to articles 17 to 23, and the amount of the compensation payable by the carrier shall be subject to articles 59 to 61.

Article 53

Deemed delivery

Goods that are delivered pursuant to an instruction in accordance with article 52, paragraph 1, are deemed to be delivered at the place of destination, and the provisions of chapter 9 relating to such delivery apply to such goods.

Article 54

Variations to the contract of carriage

1. The controlling party is the only person that may agree with the carrier to variations to the contract of carriage other than those referred to in article 50, subparagraphs 1 *(b)* and *(c)*.

2. Variations to the contract of carriage, including those referred to in article 50, subparagraphs 1 *(b)* and *(c)*, shall be stated in a negotiable transport document or in a non-negotiable transport document that requires surrender, or incorporated in a negotiable electronic transport record, or, upon the request of the controlling party, shall be stated in a non-negotiable transport document or incorporated in a non-negotiable electronic transport record. If so stated or incorporated, such variations shall be signed in accordance with article 38.

Article 55

Providing additional information, instructions or documents to carrier

1. The controlling party, on request of the carrier or a performing party, shall provide in a timely manner information, instructions or documents relating to the goods not yet provided by the shipper and not otherwise reasonably available to the carrier that the carrier may reasonably need to perform its obligations under the contract of carriage.

2. If the carrier, after reasonable effort, is unable to locate the controlling party or the controlling party is unable to provide adequate information, instructions or documents to the carrier, the shipper shall provide them. If the carrier, after reasonable effort, is unable to locate the shipper, the documentary shipper shall provide such information, instructions or documents.

Article 56

Variation by agreement

The parties to the contract of carriage may vary the effect of articles 50, subparagraphs 1 *(b)* and *(c)*, 50, paragraph 2, and 52. The parties may also restrict or exclude the transferability of the right of control referred to in article 51, subparagraph 1 *(b)*.

Chapter 11
Transfer of rights

Article 57

When a negotiable transport document or negotiable electronic transport record is issued

1. When a negotiable transport document is issued, the holder may transfer the rights incorporated in the document by transferring it to another person:

(a) Duly endorsed either to such other person or in blank, if an order document; or

(b) Without endorsement, if: (i) a bearer document or a blank endorsed document; or (ii) a document made out to the order of a named person and the transfer is between the first holder and the named person.

2. When a negotiable electronic transport record is issued, its holder may transfer the rights incorporated in it, whether it be made out to order or to the order of a named person, by transferring the electronic transport record in accordance with the procedures referred to in article 9, paragraph 1.

Article 58

Liability of holder

1. Without prejudice to article 55, a holder that is not the shipper and that does not exercise any right under the contract of carriage does not assume any liability under the contract of carriage solely by reason of being a holder.

2. A holder that is not the shipper and that exercises any right under the contract of carriage assumes any liabilities imposed on it under the contract of carriage to the extent that such liabilities are incorporated in or ascertainable from the negotiable transport document or the negotiable electronic transport record.

3. For the purposes of paragraphs 1 and 2 of this article, a holder that is not the shipper does not exercise any right under the contract of carriage solely because:

(a) It agrees with the carrier, pursuant to article 10, to replace a negotiable transport document by a negotiable electronic transport record or to replace a negotiable electronic transport record by a negotiable transport document; or

(b) It transfers its rights pursuant to article 57.

Chapter 12
Limits of liability

Article 59

Limits of liability

1. Subject to articles 60 and 61, paragraph 1, the carrier's liability for breaches of its obligations under this Convention is limited to 875 units of account per package or other shipping unit, or 3 units of account per kilogram of the gross weight of the goods that are the subject of the claim or dispute, whichever amount is the higher, except when the value of the goods has been declared by the shipper and included in the contract particulars, or when a higher amount than the amount of limitation of liability set out in this article has been agreed upon between the carrier and the shipper.

2. When goods are carried in or on a container, pallet or similar article of transport used to consolidate goods, or in or on a vehicle, the packages or shipping units enumerated in the contract particulars as packed in or on such article of transport or vehicle are deemed packages or shipping units. If not so enumerated, the goods in or on such article of transport or vehicle are deemed one shipping unit.

3. The unit of account referred to in this article is the Special Drawing Right as defined by the International Monetary Fund. The amounts referred to in this article are to be converted into the national currency of a State according to the value of such currency at the date of judgement or award or the date agreed upon by the parties. The value of a national currency, in terms of the Special Drawing Right, of a Contracting State that is a member of the International Monetary Fund is to be calculated in accordance with the method of valuation applied by the International Monetary Fund in effect at the date in question for its operations and transactions. The value of a national currency, in terms of the Special Drawing Right, of a Contracting State that is not a member of the International Monetary Fund is to be calculated in a manner to be determined by that State.

Article 60

Limits of liability for loss caused by delay

Subject to article 61, paragraph 2, compensation for loss of or damage to the goods due to delay shall be calculated in accordance with article 22 and liability for economic loss due to delay is limited to an amount equivalent to two and one-half times the freight payable on the goods delayed. The total amount payable pursuant to this article and article 59, paragraph 1, may not exceed the limit that would be established pursuant to article 59, paragraph 1, in respect of the total loss of the goods concerned.

Article 61

Loss of the benefit of limitation of liability

1. Neither the carrier nor any of the persons referred to in article 18 is entitled to the benefit of the limitation of liability as provided in article 59, or as provided in the contract of carriage, if the claimant proves that the loss resulting from the breach of the carrier's obligation under this Convention was attributable to a personal act or omission of the person claiming a right to limit done with the intent to cause such loss or recklessly and with knowledge that such loss would probably result.

2. Neither the carrier nor any of the persons mentioned in article 18 is entitled to the benefit of the limitation of liability as provided in article 60 if the claimant proves that the delay in delivery resulted from a personal act or omission of the person claiming a right to limit done with the intent to cause the loss due to delay or recklessly and with knowledge that such loss would probably result.

Chapter 13
Time for suit

Article 62

Period of time for suit

1. No judicial or arbitral proceedings in respect of claims or disputes arising from a breach of an obligation under this Convention may be instituted after the expiration of a period of two years.

2. The period referred to in paragraph 1 of this article commences on the day on which the carrier has delivered the goods or, in cases in which no goods have been delivered or only part of the goods have been delivered, on the last day on which the goods should have been delivered. The day on which the period commences is not included in the period.

3. Notwithstanding the expiration of the period set out in paragraph 1 of this article, one party may rely on its claim as a defence or for the purpose of set-off against a claim asserted by the other party.

Article 63

Extension of time for suit

The period provided in article 62 shall not be subject to suspension or interruption, but the person against which a claim is made may at any time during the running of the period extend that period by a declaration to the claimant. This period may be further extended by another declaration or declarations.

Article 64

Action for indemnity

An action for indemnity by a person held liable may be instituted after the expiration of the period provided in article 62 if the indemnity action is instituted within the later of:

(a) The time allowed by the applicable law in the jurisdiction where proceedings are instituted; or

(b) Ninety days commencing from the day when the person instituting the action for indemnity has either settled the claim or been served with process in the action against itself, whichever is earlier.

Article 65

Actions against the person identified as the carrier

An action against the bareboat charterer or the person identified as the carrier pursuant to article 37, paragraph 2, may be instituted after the expiration of the period provided in article 62 if the action is instituted within the later of:

(a) The time allowed by the applicable law in the jurisdiction where proceedings are instituted; or

(b) Ninety days commencing from the day when the carrier has been identified, or the registered owner or bareboat charterer has rebutted the presumption that it is the carrier, pursuant to article 37, paragraph 2.

Chapter 14
Jurisdiction

Article 66

Actions against the carrier

Unless the contract of carriage contains an exclusive choice of court agreement that complies with article 67 or 72, the plaintiff has the right to institute judicial proceedings under this Convention against the carrier:

(a) In a competent court within the jurisdiction of which is situated one of the following places:

(i) The domicile of the carrier;

(ii) The place of receipt agreed in the contract of carriage;

(iii) The place of delivery agreed in the contract of carriage; or

(iv) The port where the goods are initially loaded on a ship or the port where the goods are finally discharged from a ship; or

(b) In a competent court or courts designated by an agreement between the shipper and the carrier for the purpose of deciding claims against the carrier that may arise under this Convention.

Article 67

Choice of court agreements

1. The jurisdiction of a court chosen in accordance with article 66, subparagraph *(b)*, is exclusive for disputes between the parties to the contract only if the parties so agree and the agreement conferring jurisdiction:

(a) Is contained in a volume contract that clearly states the names and addresses of the parties and either (i) is individually negotiated or (ii) contains a prominent statement that there is an exclusive choice of court agreement and specifies the sections of the volume contract containing that agreement; and

(b) Clearly designates the courts of one Contracting State or one or more specific courts of one Contracting State.

2. A person that is not a party to the volume contract is bound by an exclusive choice of court agreement concluded in accordance with paragraph 1 of this article only if:

(a) The court is in one of the places designated in article 66, subparagraph *(a)*;

(b) That agreement is contained in the transport document or electronic transport record;

(c) That person is given timely and adequate notice of the court where the action shall be brought and that the jurisdiction of that court is exclusive; and

(d) The law of the court seized recognizes that that person may be bound by the exclusive choice of court agreement.

Article 68

Actions against the maritime performing party

The plaintiff has the right to institute judicial proceedings under this Convention against the maritime performing party in a competent court within the jurisdiction of which is situated one of the following places:

(a) The domicile of the maritime performing party; or

(b) The port where the goods are received by the maritime performing party, the port where the goods are delivered by the maritime performing party or the port in which the maritime performing party performs its activities with respect to the goods.

Article 69

No additional bases of jurisdiction

Subject to articles 71 and 72, no judicial proceedings under this Convention against the carrier or a maritime performing party may be instituted in a court not designated pursuant to article 66 or 68.

Article 70

Arrest and provisional or protective measures

Nothing in this Convention affects jurisdiction with regard to provisional or protective measures, including arrest. A court in a State in which a provisional or protective measure was taken does not have jurisdiction to determine the case upon its merits unless:

(a) The requirements of this chapter are fulfilled; or

(b) An international convention that applies in that State so provides.

Article 71

Consolidation and removal of actions

1. Except when there is an exclusive choice of court agreement that is binding pursuant to article 67 or 72, if a single action is brought against both the carrier and the maritime performing party arising out of a single occurrence, the action may be instituted only in a court designated pursuant to both article 66 and article 68. If there is no such court, such action may be instituted in a court designated pursuant to article 68, subparagraph *(b)*, if there is such a court.

2. Except when there is an exclusive choice of court agreement that is binding pursuant to article 67 or 72, a carrier or a maritime performing party that institutes an action seeking a declaration of non-liability or any other action that would deprive a person of its right to select the forum pursuant to article 66 or 68 shall, at the request of the defendant, withdraw that action once the defendant has chosen a court designated pursuant to article 66 or 68, whichever is applicable, where the action may be recommenced.

Article 72

Agreement after a dispute has arisen and jurisdiction when the defendant has entered an appearance

1. After a dispute has arisen, the parties to the dispute may agree to resolve it in any competent court.

2. A competent court before which a defendant appears, without contesting jurisdiction in accordance with the rules of that court, has jurisdiction.

Article 73

Recognition and enforcement

1. A decision made in one Contracting State by a court having jurisdiction under this Convention shall be recognized and enforced in another Contracting State in accordance with the law of such latter Contracting State when both States have made a declaration in accordance with article 74.

2. A court may refuse recognition and enforcement based on the grounds for the refusal of recognition and enforcement available pursuant to its law.

3. This chapter shall not affect the application of the rules of a regional economic integration organization that is a party to this Convention, as concerns the recognition or enforcement of judgements as between member States of the regional economic integration organization, whether adopted before or after this Convention.

Article 74

Application of chapter 14

The provisions of this chapter shall bind only Contracting States that declare in accordance with article 91 that they will be bound by them.

Chapter 15

Arbitration

Article 75

Arbitration agreements

1. Subject to this chapter, parties may agree that any dispute that may arise relating to the carriage of goods under this Convention shall be referred to arbitration.

2. The arbitration proceedings shall, at the option of the person asserting a claim against the carrier, take place at:

(a) Any place designated for that purpose in the arbitration agreement; or

(b) Any other place situated in a State where any of the following places is located:

(i) The domicile of the carrier;

(ii) The place of receipt agreed in the contract of carriage;

(iii) The place of delivery agreed in the contract of carriage; or

(iv) The port where the goods are initially loaded on a ship or the port where the goods are finally discharged from a ship.

3. The designation of the place of arbitration in the agreement is binding for disputes between the parties to the agreement if the agreement is contained in a volume contract that clearly states the names and addresses of the parties and either:

(a) Is individually negotiated; or

(b) Contains a prominent statement that there is an arbitration agreement and specifies the sections of the volume contract containing the arbitration agreement.

4. When an arbitration agreement has been concluded in accordance with paragraph 3 of this article, a person that is not a party to the volume contract is bound by the designation of the place of arbitration in that agreement only if:

(a) The place of arbitration designated in the agreement is situated in one of the places referred to in subparagraph 2 *(b)* of this article;

(b) The agreement is contained in the transport document or electronic transport record;

(c) The person to be bound is given timely and adequate notice of the place of arbitration; and

(d) Applicable law permits that person to be bound by the arbitration agreement.

5. The provisions of paragraphs 1, 2, 3 and 4 of this article are deemed to be part of every arbitration clause or agreement, and any term of such clause or agreement to the extent that it is inconsistent therewith is void.

Article 76

Arbitration agreement in non-liner transportation

1. Nothing in this Convention affects the enforceability of an arbitration agreement in a contract of carriage in non-liner transportation to which this Convention or the provisions of this Convention apply by reason of:

(a) The application of article 7; or

(b) The parties' voluntary incorporation of this Convention in a contract of carriage that would not otherwise be subject to this Convention.

2. Notwithstanding paragraph 1 of this article, an arbitration agreement in a transport document or electronic transport record to which this Convention applies by reason of the application of article 7 is subject to this chapter unless such a transport document or electronic transport record:

(a) Identifies the parties to and the date of the charter party or other contract excluded from the application of this Convention by reason of the application of article 6; and

(b) Incorporates by specific reference the clause in the charter party or other contract that contains the terms of the arbitration agreement.

Article 77

Agreement to arbitrate after a dispute has arisen

Notwithstanding the provisions of this chapter and chapter 14, after a dispute has arisen the parties to the dispute may agree to resolve it by arbitration in any place.

Article 78

Application of chapter 15

The provisions of this chapter shall bind only Contracting States that declare in accordance with article 91 that they will be bound by them.

Chapter 16
Validity of contractual terms

Article 79

General provisions

1. Unless otherwise provided in this Convention, any term in a contract of carriage is void to the extent that it:

(a) Directly or indirectly excludes or limits the obligations of the carrier or a maritime performing party under this Convention;

(b) Directly or indirectly excludes or limits the liability of the carrier or a maritime performing party for breach of an obligation under this Convention; or

(c) Assigns a benefit of insurance of the goods in favour of the carrier or a person referred to in article 18.

2. Unless otherwise provided in this Convention, any term in a contract of carriage is void to the extent that it:

(a) Directly or indirectly excludes, limits or increases the obligations under this Convention of the shipper, consignee, controlling party, holder or documentary shipper; or

(b) Directly or indirectly excludes, limits or increases the liability of the shipper, consignee, controlling party, holder or documentary shipper for breach of any of its obligations under this Convention.

Article 80

Special rules for volume contracts

1. Notwithstanding article 79, as between the carrier and the shipper, a volume contract to which this Convention applies may provide for greater or lesser rights, obligations and liabilities than those imposed by this Convention.

2. A derogation pursuant to paragraph 1 of this article is binding only when:

(a) The volume contract contains a prominent statement that it derogates from this Convention;

(b) The volume contract is (i) individually negotiated or (ii) prominently specifies the sections of the volume contract containing the derogations;

(c) The shipper is given an opportunity and notice of the opportunity to conclude a contract of carriage on terms and conditions that comply with this Convention without any derogation under this article; and

(d) The derogation is neither (i) incorporated by reference from another document nor (ii) included in a contract of adhesion that is not subject to negotiation.

3. A carrier's public schedule of prices and services, transport document, electronic transport record or similar document is not a volume contract pursuant to paragraph 1 of this article, but a volume contract may incorporate such documents by reference as terms of the contract.

4. Paragraph 1 of this article does not apply to rights and obligations provided in articles 14, subparagraphs *(a)* and *(b)*, 29 and 32 or to liability arising from the breach thereof, nor does it apply to any liability arising from an act or omission referred to in article 61.

5. The terms of the volume contract that derogate from this Convention, if the volume contract satisfies the requirements of paragraph 2 of this article, apply between the carrier and any person other than the shipper provided that:

(a) Such person received information that prominently states that the volume contract derogates from this Convention and gave its express consent to be bound by such derogations; and

(b) Such consent is not solely set forth in a carrier's public schedule of prices and services, transport document or electronic transport record.

6. The party claiming the benefit of the derogation bears the burden of proof that the conditions for derogation have been fulfilled.

Article 81

Special rules for live animals and certain other goods

Notwithstanding article 79 and without prejudice to article 80, the contract of carriage may exclude or limit the obligations or the liability of both the carrier and a maritime performing party if:

(a) The goods are live animals, but any such exclusion or limitation will not be effective if the claimant proves that the loss of or damage to the goods, or delay in delivery, resulted from an act or omission of the carrier or of a person referred to in article 18, done with the intent to cause such loss of or damage to the goods or such loss due to delay or done recklessly and with knowledge that such loss or damage or such loss due to delay would probably result; or

(b) The character or condition of the goods or the circumstances and terms and conditions under which the carriage is to be performed are such as reasonably to justify a special agreement, provided that such contract of carriage is not related to ordinary commercial shipments made in the ordinary course of trade and that no negotiable transport document or negotiable electronic transport record is issued for the carriage of the goods.

Chapter 17
Matters not governed by this convention

Article 82

International conventions governing the carriage of goods by other modes of transport

Nothing in this Convention affects the application of any of the following international conventions in force at the time this Convention enters into force, including any future amendment to such conventions, that regulate the liability of the carrier for loss of or damage to the goods:

(a) Any convention governing the carriage of goods by air to the extent that such convention according to its provisions applies to any part of the contract of carriage;

(b) Any convention governing the carriage of goods by road to the extent that such convention according to its provisions applies to the carriage of goods that remain loaded on a road cargo vehicle carried on board a ship;

(c) Any convention governing the carriage of goods by rail to the extent that such convention according to its provisions applies to carriage of goods by sea as a supplement to the carriage by rail; or

(d) Any convention governing the carriage of goods by inland waterways to the extent that such convention according to its provisions applies to a carriage of goods without trans-shipment both by inland waterways and sea.

Article 83

Global limitation of liability

Nothing in this Convention affects the application of any international convention or national law regulating the global limitation of liability of vessel owners.

Article 84

General average

Nothing in this Convention affects the application of terms in the contract of carriage or provisions of national law regarding the adjustment of general average.

Article 85

Passengers and luggage

This Convention does not apply to a contract of carriage for passengers and their luggage.

Article 86

Damage caused by nuclear incident

No liability arises under this Convention for damage caused by a nuclear incident if the operator of a nuclear installation is liable for such damage:

(a) Under the Paris Convention on Third Party Liability in the Field of Nuclear Energy of 29 July 1960 as amended by the Additional Protocol of 28 January 1964 and by the Protocols of 16 November 1982 and 12 February 2004, the Vienna Convention on Civil Liability for Nuclear Damage of 21 May 1963 as amended by the Joint Protocol Relating to the Application of the Vienna Convention and the Paris Convention of 21 September 1988 and as amended by the Protocol to Amend the 1963 Vienna Convention on Civil Liability for Nuclear Damage of 12 September 1997, or the Convention on Supplementary Compensation for Nuclear Damage of 12 September 1997, including any amendment to these conventions and any future convention in respect of the liability of the operator of a nuclear installation for damage caused by a nuclear incident; or

(b) Under national law applicable to the liability for such damage, provided that such law is in all respects as favourable to persons that may suffer damage as either the Paris or Vienna Conventions or the Convention on Supplementary Compensation for Nuclear Damage.

Chapter 18
Final clauses

Article 87

Depositary

The Secretary-General of the United Nations is hereby designated as the depositary of this Convention.

Article 88

Signature, ratification, acceptance, approval or accession

1. This Convention is open for signature by all States at Rotterdam, the Netherlands, on 23 September 2009, and thereafter at the Headquarters of the United Nations in New York.

2. This Convention is subject to ratification, acceptance or approval by the signatory States.

3. This Convention is open for accession by all States that are not signatory States as from the date it is open for signature.

4. Instruments of ratification, acceptance, approval and accession are to be deposited with the Secretary-General of the United Nations.

Article 89

Denunciation of other conventions

1. A State that ratifies, accepts, approves or accedes to this Convention and is a party to the International Convention for the Unification of certain Rules of Law relating to Bills of Lading signed at Brussels on 25 August 1924, to the Protocol to amend the International Convention for the Unification of certain Rules of Law relating to Bills of Lading, signed at Brussels on 23 February 1968, or to the Protocol to amend the International Convention for the Unification of certain Rules of Law relating to Bills of Lading as Modified by the Amending Protocol of 23 February 1968, signed at Brussels on 21 December 1979, shall at the same time denounce that Convention and the protocol or protocols thereto to which it is a party by notifying the Government of Belgium to that effect, with a declaration that the denunciation is to take effect as from the date when this Convention enters into force in respect of that State.

2. A State that ratifies, accepts, approves or accedes to this Convention and is a party to the United Nations Convention on the Carriage of Goods by Sea concluded at Hamburg on 31 March 1978 shall at the same time denounce that Convention by notifying the Secretary-General of the United Nations to that effect, with a declaration that the denunciation is to take effect as from the date when this Convention enters into force in respect of that State.

3. For the purposes of this article, ratifications, acceptances, approvals and accessions in respect of this Convention by States parties to the instruments listed in paragraphs 1 and 2 of this article that are notified to the

depositary after this Convention has entered into force are not effective until such denunciations as may be required on the part of those States in respect of these instruments have become effective. The depositary of this Convention shall consult with the Government of Belgium, as the depositary of the instruments referred to in paragraph 1 of this article, so as to ensure necessary coordination in this respect.

Article 90

Reservations

No reservation is permitted to this Convention.

Article 91

Procedure and effect of declarations

1. The declarations permitted by articles 74 and 78 may be made at any time. The initial declarations permitted by article 92, paragraph 1, and article 93, paragraph 2, shall be made at the time of signature, ratification, acceptance, approval or accession. No other declaration is permitted under this Convention.

2. Declarations made at the time of signature are subject to confirmation upon ratification, acceptance or approval.

3. Declarations and their confirmations are to be in writing and to be formally notified to the depositary.

4. A declaration takes effect simultaneously with the entry into force of this Convention in respect of the State concerned. However, a declaration of which the depositary receives formal notification after such entry into force takes effect on the first day of the month following the expiration of six months after the date of its receipt by the depositary.

5. Any State that makes a declaration under this Convention may withdraw it at any time by a formal notification in writing addressed to the depositary. The withdrawal of a declaration, or its modification where permitted by this Convention, takes effect on the first day of the month following the expiration of six months after the date of the receipt of the notification by the depositary.

Article 92

Effect in domestic territorial units

1. If a Contracting State has two or more territorial units in which different systems of law are applicable in relation to the matters dealt with in this Convention, it may, at the time of signature, ratification, acceptance, approval or accession, declare that this Convention is to extend to all its territorial units or only to one or more of them, and may amend its declaration by submitting another declaration at any time.

2. These declarations are to be notified to the depositary and are to state expressly the territorial units to which the Convention extends.

3. When a Contracting State has declared pursuant to this article that this Convention extends to one or more but not all of its territorial units, a place located in a territorial unit to which this Convention does not extend is not considered to be in a Contracting State for the purposes of this Convention.

4. If a Contracting State makes no declaration pursuant to paragraph 1 of this article, the Convention is to extend to all territorial units of that State.

Article 93

Participation by regional economic integration organizations

1. A regional economic integration organization that is constituted by sovereign States and has competence over certain matters governed by this Convention may similarly sign, ratify, accept, approve or accede to this Convention. The regional economic integration organization shall in that case have the rights and obligations of a Contracting State, to the extent that that organization has competence over matters governed by this Convention. When the number of Contracting States is relevant in this Convention, the regional economic integration organization does not count as a Contracting State in addition to its member States which are Contracting States.

2. The regional economic integration organization shall, at the time of signature, ratification, acceptance, approval or accession, make a declaration to the depositary specifying the matters governed by this Convention in respect of which competence has been transferred to that organization by its member States. The regional economic integration organization shall promptly notify the depositary of any changes to the distribution of competence, including new transfers of competence, specified in the declaration pursuant to this paragraph.

3. Any reference to a "Contracting State" or "Contracting States" in this Convention applies equally to a regional economic integration organization when the context so requires.

Article 94

Entry into force

1. This Convention enters into force on the first day of the month following the expiration of one year after the date of deposit of the twentieth instrument of ratification, acceptance, approval or accession.

2. For each State that becomes a Contracting State to this Convention after the date of the deposit of the twentieth instrument of ratification, acceptance, approval or accession, this Convention enters into force on the first day of the month following the expiration of one year after the deposit of the appropriate instrument on behalf of that State.

3. Each Contracting State shall apply this Convention to contracts of carriage concluded on or after the date of the entry into force of this Convention in respect of that State.

Article 95

Revision and amendment

1. At the request of not less than one third of the Contracting States to this Convention, the Secretary-General of the United Nations shall convene a conference of the Contracting States for revising or amending it.

2. Any instrument of ratification, acceptance, approval or accession deposited after the entry into force of an amendment to this Convention is deemed to apply to the Convention as amended.

Article 96

Denunciation of this Convention

1. A Contracting State may denounce this Convention at any time by means of a notification in writing addressed to the depositary.

2. The denunciation takes effect on the first day of the month following the expiration of one year after the notification is received by the depositary. If a longer period is specified in the notification, the denunciation takes effect upon the expiration of such longer period after the notification is received by the depositary.

DONE at New York, this eleventh day of December two thousand and eight, in a single original, of which the Arabic, Chinese, English, French, Russian and Spanish texts are equally authentic.

IN WITNESS WHEREOF the undersigned plenipotentiaries, being duly authorized by their respective Governments, have signed this Convention.

Insolvency law

UNCITRAL [A/63/17] noted the progress of Working Group V (Insolvency Law) regarding consideration of the treatment of corporate groups in insolvency, including post-commencement finance, as reflected in the reports of its thirty-third (Vienna, 5–9 November 2007) [A/CN.9/643] and thirty-fourth (New York, 3–7 March 2008) [A/CN.9/647] sessions. The Commission also considered a Secretariat note on facilitation of cooperation, direct communication and coordination in cross-border insolvency proceedings [A/CN.9/654]. It expressed satisfaction with the progress made on compiling practical experience with negotiating and using cross-border insolvency agreements, and decided that the compilation should be presented as a working paper to the Working Group at its next session for an initial discussion. The Group could then decide to continue discussing the compilation and make its recommendations to the Commission's 2009 session. UNCITRAL also approved a thirty-fifth session of the Working Group, which was held in Vienna from 17 to 21 November.

Electronic commerce

UNCITRAL [A/63/17] had before it a note by the Secretariat [A/CN.9/655] on possible future work in electronic commerce: legal issues arising from implementation and operation of single windows in international trade, which set out policy considerations and legal issues for implementing and operating single windows. Submitting proposals for future work in cooperation with other international organizations, UNCITRAL defined a "single window" as a facility that allowed parties involved in trade and transport to lodge standardized information and documents with a single entry point to fulfil all-important export and transit-related regulatory requirements. If information was electronic, individual data elements would only be submitted once.

UNCITRAL noted that the use of single windows could result in improved efficiency and effectiveness of official controls and reduce costs for Governments and traders. However, it also gave rise to several legal issues, including the legislative authority to operate single windows; identification, authentication and authorization to exchange documents and messages through single windows; data protection; liability of operators of single windows; and legal validity of documents exchanged in electronic form. UNCITRAL agreed it would be worthwhile to study the legal aspects involved in implementing a cross-border single window facility, with a view to formulating a comprehensive international reference document to which legislators, Government policymakers, single window operators and other stakeholders could refer for advice on legal aspects of creating and managing a single window designed to handle cross-border transactions. It also agreed it would be worthwhile to keep under examination legal issues related to electronic equivalents to negotiable documents and other electronic systems for negotiating and transferring of rights in goods, securities and other rights in electronic form.

Commercial fraud

UNCITRAL [A/63/17] considered the comments of States and organizations on indicators of commercial fraud submitted to the Secretariat [A/CN.9/659 & Add.1,2] and the text of the indicators circulated in 2007 [YUN 2007, p. 1378]. The Commission reiterated its support for the preparation and dissemination of those indicators. On completing work on the indicators of commercial fraud, given the technical nature of the comments received and bearing in mind that such treatment should keep separate any criminal law aspects of commercial fraud, UNCITRAL requested the Secretariat to make such adjustments and additions as were advisable to improve the materials and then publish them as an informational note for educational purposes and fraud prevention.

The Commission was advised that the United Nations Office on Drugs and Crime (UNODC) had continued its work in pursuing various aspects of fraud, including work on identity fraud. The UNCITRAL secretariat, which had cooperated with UNODC in order to provide appropriate private sector and commercial expertise, was requested to continue to cooperate with and to assist UNODC in its work with respect to commercial and economic fraud, and report to the Commission on any developments.

Security interests

UNCITRAL [A/63/17] considered the report of Working Group VI (Security Interests) on its thirteenth session (New York, 19–23 May) [A/CN.9/649] and noted the progress made during the initial discussions, which had enabled the Group to request that the Secretariat prepare a first draft of the annex to the *UNCITRAL Legislative Guide on Secured Transactions* [YUN 2007, p. 1378] dealing with security rights in intellectual property. UNCITRAL also noted that the Working Group was unable to reach agreement as to whether certain matters related to the impact of insolvency on a security right in intellectual property were sufficiently linked with secured transactions law in order to justify their discussion in the annex to the *Guide*. The Group had decided to revisit those matters at a future meeting and to recommend that Working Group V (Insolvency Law) be requested to consider them. In that connection, the Commission decided that Working Group V should be invited to express any preliminary opinion at its next session and if any remaining issue required joint consideration by the two Working Groups, the UNCITRAL Secretariat should have the discretion to organize a joint discussion of the impact of insolvency on a security right in intellectual property when the two Groups were to meet back to back in the spring of 2009. The Commission also approved a fourteenth session of Working Group VI, which was held in Vienna, from 20 to 24 October.

GENERAL ASSEMBLY ACTION

On 11 December [meeting 67], the General Assembly, on the recommendation of the Sixth Committee [A/63/438], adopted **resolution 63/121** without vote [agenda item 74].

Legislative Guide on Secured Transactions of the United Nations Commission on International Trade Law

The General Assembly,

Recognizing the importance to all countries of efficient secured transactions regimes promoting access to secured credit,

Recognizing also that access to secured credit is likely to assist all countries, in particular developing countries and countries with economies in transition, in their economic development and in fighting poverty,

Emphasizing the expectation that modern and harmonized secured transactions regimes which balance the interests of all stakeholders (including grantors of security rights, secured and unsecured creditors, retention-of-title sellers and financial lessors, privileged creditors and the insolvency representative in the grantor's insolvency) will demonstrably facilitate access to secured credit, thereby promoting the movement of goods and services across national borders,

Noting that the development of international trade on the basis of equality and mutual benefit is an important element in promoting friendly relations among States,

Taking into account the need for reform in the field of secured transactions laws at both the national and international levels as demonstrated by the numerous current national law reform efforts and the work of international organizations, such as the Hague Conference on Private International Law, the International Institute for the Unification of Private Law and the Organization of American States, and of international financial institutions, such as the Asian Development Bank, the European Bank for Reconstruction and Development, the Inter-American Development Bank, the International Monetary Fund and the World Bank,

Expressing its appreciation to intergovernmental and international non-governmental organizations active in the field of secured transactions law reform for their participation in and support for the development of the Legislative Guide on Secured Transactions of the United Nations Commission on International Trade Law,

1. *Expresses its appreciation* to the United Nations Commission on International Trade Law for the completion and adoption of the Legislative Guide on Secured Transactions;

2. *Requests* the Secretary-General to disseminate broadly the text of the Legislative Guide, transmitting it to Governments and other interested bodies, such as national and international financial institutions and chambers of commerce;

3. *Recommends* that all States give favourable consideration to the Legislative Guide when revising or adopting legislation relevant to secured transactions, and invites States that have used the Legislative Guide to advise the Commission accordingly;

4. *Recommends also* that all States continue to consider becoming party to the United Nations Convention on the Assignment of Receivables in International Trade, the principles of which are also reflected in the Legislative Guide.

Case law on UNCITRAL texts

UNCITRAL [A/63/17] noted the continuing work under the system established for the collection and dissemination of case law on UNCITRAL texts (CLOUT), consisting of the preparation of case-law abstracts. A total of 72 issues of CLOUT had been prepared for publication dealing with 761 cases.

It was widely agreed that CLOUT continued to be an important aspect of UNCITRAL technical assistance, and its broad dissemination promoted the uniform interpretation and application of UNCITRAL texts. The Commission expressed appreciation to national correspondents and other contributors for their work in developing the CLOUT system. It noted that the digest of case law on the United Nations Sales Convention, published in 2004 [YUN 2004, p. 1355], had been revised and was being published, that a quarterly bulletin and an information brochure on the CLOUT system had been developed to facilitate dissemination of information on the system, and that the UNCITRAL website had received over one million visits since the Commission's fortieth (2008) session. UNCITRAL also took note of developments related to the UNCITRAL Law Library and UNCITRAL publications, including the Secretariat note containing a bibliography of recent writings concerning UNCITRAL work [A/CN.9/650].

Training and technical assistance

UNCITRAL [A/63/17] had before it a note by the Secretariat [A/CN.9/652] describing technical cooperation and assistance activities undertaken since 2007. UNCITRAL noted that its ability to participate in technical cooperation and assistance activities, in response to specific requests of States, was dependent upon the availability of funds to meet associated costs. Despite efforts by the Secretariat to solicit new donations, funds remaining in the UNCITRAL Trust Fund for Symposia were very limited. Beyond the end of 2008, requests for technical cooperation and assistance involving the expenditure of funds for travel or other associated costs would have to be declined unless new donations to the Trust Fund were received or other alternative sources of funds could be found.

The Commission reiterated its appeal [YUN 2007, p. 1379] to States, international organizations and other entities to contribute to its Trust Fund for Symposia to meet the increasing requests for technical assistance and cooperation activities, and to the trust fund established to provide travel assistance to developing countries that were members of UNCITRAL.

Future work

UNCITRAL considered [A/63/17] a note by the Secretariat describing practices of the Commission as regards decision-making, the status of observers in UNCITRAL and the preparatory work undertaken by the Secretariat, and outlining observations by the Secretariat on working methods [A/CN.9/653]. The note had been circulated for comments on 6 May. The Commission also had before it a note by the Secretariat compiling the comments received prior to the 2008 session [A/CN.9/660 & Add.1–4]. On decision-making, the Commission agreed that consensus should remain the preferred method, yet supported clarifying the manner in which consensus operated in practice. On the role of observers, the Commission agreed that its approach should continue to be based on flexibility and inclusiveness. It also agreed, with regard to working methods, that it was important for the Secretariat to preserve the flexibility necessary to organize its work efficiently, including through recourse to external expertise. On the question of further work, a proposal was made to establish a working group, while there was also support for holding informal consultations instead. It was agreed that a meeting of such an informal group would take place in connection with the next session of the Commission.

UNCITRAL requested the Secretariat to prepare a first draft of a reference document, based on the Secretariat note for use by chairpersons, delegates and observers and the Secretariat; circulate the draft reference document for comments by States and international organizations; and prepare a compilation of those comments for consideration by the Commission at its 2009 session.

UNCITRAL approved the holding of its forty-second session in Vienna from 29 June to 17 July 2009. It was noted that the duration of the session might be modified, should a shorter session become advisable in light of the progress of work in Working Group II (Arbitration and Conciliation) and Working Group V (Insolvency Law).

International organizations and international law

Strengthening the role of the United Nations

Special Committee on United Nations Charter

In accordance with General Assembly resolution 62/69 [YUN 2007, p. 1381], the Special Committee on the Charter of the United Nations and on the Strengthening of the Role of the Organization, at its sixty-third session (New York, 27–29 February, 3–5 and 7 March) [A/63/33], continued to consider proposals relating to: the maintenance of international peace and security; the peaceful settlement of disputes between States; the improvement of the Committee's working methods; and the status of the publications *Repertory of Practice of United Nations Organs* and *Repertoire of the Practice of the Security Council.*

With regard to the first item, the Russian Federation introduced the revised working paper entitled, "Basic conditions and standard criteria for the introduction and implementation of sanctions imposed by the United Nations" [A/C.6/62/L.6], which was submitted to the Committee in 2004 [YUN 2004, p. 1342] and revised in 2005 [YUN 2005, p. 1445]. Although diverging views were expressed in informal consultations, general support was expressed for continued consideration of the proposal and the Committee decided to continue to consider the working document, which was annexed to the report, with a view to focusing on the outstanding issues.

The Committee also discussed the revised working paper submitted by Belarus and the Russian Federation in 2005 [ibid., p. 1446], which recommended that an advisory opinion be requested from the International Court of Justice (ICJ) as to the legal consequences of the resort to the use of force by States without prior authorization by the Security Council, except in the exercise of the right to self-defence. Some delegations reiterated their support for the proposal, holding that it would strengthen the principle of the non-use of force or threat of force. Concern was expressed over attempts to justify the unilateral use of force without Council authorization under a false pretext of self-defence, which was considered a violation of the Charter. Delegations against the proposal said that the use of force was adequately and clearly addressed in the Charter, and consequently, the proposed Assembly request for an ICJ advisory opinion on the matter could not be supported. Although some held it was time to reconsider or discontinue further discussion on those issues, which had been on the Committee's agenda for many years without any immediate chance of reaching consensus, the Committee decided to keep the proposal on its agenda.

The Committee concluded its consideration of a Russian Federation working paper on fundamentals of the legal basis for UN peacekeeping operations in the context of Chapter VI of the Charter [YUN 1998, p. 1233], which was then removed from its agenda. The Committee also discussed the revised proposal by the Libyan Arab Jamahiriya on strengthening the UN role in the maintenance of international peace and security [ibid.]; the revised working paper submitted by Libya on the strengthening of certain principles concerning the application of sanctions [YUN 2002, p. 1329]; and the working papers on strengthening the role of the Organization and enhancing its effectiveness, submitted by Cuba at its 1997 and 1998 sessions [YUN 1998, p. 1233].

During the exchange of views on the peaceful settlement of disputes, delegations recalled the obligation of States to settle disputes by peaceful means, as well as the principle of free choice of means. Reference was also made to the important role and record of ICJ in the judicial settlement of disputes.

Delegations commended ongoing Secretariat efforts to reduce the backlog in preparation of the *Repertory of Practice of United Nations Organs* and the *Repertoire of the Practice of the Security Council*, including the enhanced cooperation with academic institutions and progress made towards making both publications available on the Internet. The *Repertory* website continued to be updated regularly and the eleventh supplement to the *Repertoire* had recently been published. Meanwhile, supplement 12 was being edited with an advance version available in its entirety on the Internet, and progress had been made on supplements 13, 14 and 15, with advance versions of several chapters of those supplements accessible online. The Committee made recommendations for the General Assembly, among other things, to commend the Secretary-General for progress made on both publications and call on him to continue efforts to update the two publications and make them available in all language versions, as well as to reiterate its call for voluntary contributions to the trust funds for updating the *Repertoire* and eliminating the backlog of the *Repertory*.

Concerning the identification of new subjects, the Dominican Republic, on behalf of the Rio Group, introduced a proposal entitled "Consideration of the legal aspects of the reform of the United Nations" [A/AC.182/L.126]. Following preliminary discussions, the Committee decided to keep the proposal on its agenda.

Report of Secretary-General. In response to General Assembly resolution 62/69 [YUN 2007, p. 1381], the Secretary-General submitted a July report [A/63/98] outlining the progress made in updating the *Repertory of Practice of United Nations Organs* and *Repertoire of the Practice of the Security Council*. With respect to the *Repertory*, the Secretary-General concluded that the Assembly might wish to note the progress made in the preparation of *Repertory* studies and their posting on the Internet in English, French and Spanish; express appreciation for the contribution received to the trust fund for the elimination of the backlog of the *Repertory*; and consider the recommendations of the Special Committee, including the increased use of the UN internship programme and expanded cooperation with academic institutions for the preparation of the studies and the sponsoring, on a voluntary basis, and with no cost to the United Nations, of associate experts to assist in updating the publication. With regard to the *Repertoire*, the Secretary-General concluded that the Assembly might wish to note the progress made towards its updating and its posting in electronic form in all language versions on the UN website; call for voluntary contributions to the trust fund for updating the *Repertoire*; and note the support of Germany, Italy and Norway for sponsoring associate experts and encourage other States to consider providing such assistance.

GENERAL ASSEMBLY ACTION

On 11 December [meeting 67], the General Assembly, on the recommendation of the Sixth Committee [A/63/442], adopted **resolution 63/127** without vote [agenda item 78].

Report of the Special Committee on the Charter of the United Nations and on the Strengthening of the Role of the Organization

The General Assembly,

Recalling its resolution 3499(XXX) of 15 December 1975, by which it established the Special Committee on the Charter of the United Nations and on the Strengthening of the Role of the Organization, and its relevant resolutions adopted at subsequent sessions,

Recalling also its resolution 47/233 of 17 August 1993 on the revitalization of the work of the General Assembly,

Recalling further its resolution 47/62 of 11 December 1992 on the question of equitable representation on and increase in the membership of the Security Council,

Taking note of the report of the Open-ended Working Group on the Question of Equitable Representation on and

Increase in the Membership of the Security Council and Other Matters related to the Security Council,

Recalling the elements relevant to the work of the Special Committee contained in its resolution 47/120 B of 20 September 1993,

Recalling also its resolution 51/241 of 31 July 1997 on the strengthening of the United Nations system and its resolution 51/242 of 15 September 1997, entitled "Supplement to an Agenda for Peace", by which it adopted the texts on coordination and the question of sanctions imposed by the United Nations, which are annexed to that resolution,

Concerned about the special economic problems confronting certain States arising from the carrying out of preventive or enforcement measures taken by the Security Council against other States, and taking into account the obligation of Members of the United Nations under Article 49 of the Charter of the United Nations to join in affording mutual assistance in carrying out the measures decided upon by the Council,

Recalling the right of third States confronted with special economic problems of that nature to consult the Security Council with regard to a solution of those problems, in accordance with Article 50 of the Charter,

Recalling also that the International Court of Justice is the principal judicial organ of the United Nations, and reaffirming its authority and independence,

Mindful of the adoption of the revised working papers on the working methods of the Special Committee,

Taking note of the report of the Secretary-General on the *Repertory of Practice of United Nations Organs* and the *Repertoire of the Practice of the Security Council*,

Taking note also of paragraphs 106 to 110, 176 and 177 of the 2005 World Summit Outcome,

Mindful of the decision of the Special Committee in which it expressed its readiness to engage, as appropriate, in the implementation of any decisions that might be taken at the High-level Plenary Meeting of the sixtieth session of the General Assembly in September 2005 that concerned the Charter and any amendments thereto,

Recalling the provisions of its resolutions 50/51 of 11 December 1995, 51/208 of 17 December 1996, 52/162 of 15 December 1997, 53/107 of 8 December 1998, 54/107 of 9 December 1999, 55/157 of 12 December 2000, 56/87 of 12 December 2001, 57/25 of 19 November 2002, 58/80 of 9 December 2003 and 59/45 of 2 December 2004,

Recalling also its resolution 62/69 of 6 December 2007,

Having considered the report of the Special Committee on the work of its session held in 2008,

Noting with appreciation the work done by the Special Committee to encourage States to focus on the need to prevent and to settle peacefully their disputes which are likely to endanger the maintenance of international peace and security,

1. *Takes note* of the report of the Special Committee on the Charter of the United Nations and on the Strengthening of the Role of the Organization;

2. *Decides* that the Special Committee shall hold its next session from 17 to 25 February 2009;

3. *Requests* the Special Committee, at its session in 2009, in accordance with paragraph 5 of General Assembly resolution 50/52 of 11 December 1995:

(*a*) To continue its consideration of all proposals concerning the question of the maintenance of international peace and security in all its aspects in order to strengthen the role of the United Nations, and, in this context, to consider other proposals relating to the maintenance of international peace and security already submitted or which may be submitted to the Special Committee at its session in 2009;

(*b*) To continue its consideration, on a priority basis, of the working document submitted by the Russian Federation, entitled "Basic conditions and standard criteria for introduction and implementation of sanctions", with a view to focusing on the outstanding issues;

(*c*) To continue to consider, on a priority basis and in an appropriate substantive manner and framework, the question of the implementation of the provisions of the Charter of the United Nations related to assistance to third States affected by the application of sanctions under Chapter VII of the Charter based on all of the related reports of the Secretary-General and the proposals submitted on the question;

(*d*) To keep on its agenda the question of the peaceful settlement of disputes between States;

(*e*) To consider, as appropriate, any proposal referred to it by the General Assembly in the implementation of the decisions of the High-level Plenary Meeting of the sixtieth session of the Assembly in September 2005 that concern the Charter and any amendments thereto;

(*f*) To continue to consider, on a priority basis, ways and means of improving its working methods and enhancing its efficiency with a view to identifying widely acceptable measures for future implementation;

4. *Notes* that the Special Committee decided not to keep on its agenda the topic relating to the consideration of the working paper submitted by the Russian Federation, entitled "Fundamentals of the legal basis for United Nations peacekeeping operations in the context of Chapter VI of the Charter of the United Nations";

5. *Invites* the Special Committee at its session in 2009 to continue to identify new subjects for consideration in its future work with a view to contributing to the revitalization of the work of the United Nations;

6. *Notes* the readiness of the Special Committee to provide, within its mandate, such assistance as may be sought at the request of other subsidiary bodies of the General Assembly in relation to any issues before them;

7. *Requests* the Special Committee to submit a report on its work to the General Assembly at its sixty-fourth session;

8. *Recognizes* the important role of the International Court of Justice, the principal judicial organ of the United Nations, in adjudicating disputes among States and the value of its work, as well as the importance of having recourse to the Court in the peaceful settlement of disputes, takes note, consistent with Article 96 of the Charter, of the Court's advisory jurisdiction that may be requested by the General Assembly, the Security Council or other authorized organs of the United Nations and the specialized agencies, and requests the Secretary-General to distribute, in due course, the advisory opinions requested by the principal organs of the United Nations as official documents of the United Nations;

9. *Commends* the Secretary-General for the progress made in the preparation of studies of the *Repertory of Practice of United Nations Organs*, including the increased use of the internship programme of the United Nations and further expanded cooperation with academic institutions for this purpose, as well as the progress made towards updating the *Repertoire of the Practice of the Security Council*;

10. *Notes with appreciation* the contributions made by Member States to the trust fund for the updating of the *Repertoire*, as well as the trust fund for the elimination of the backlog in the *Repertory*;

11. *Reiterates its call* for voluntary contributions to the trust fund for the updating of the *Repertoire*, as well as the trust fund for the elimination of the backlog in the *Repertory*, and the sponsoring, on a voluntary basis, and with no cost to the United Nations, of associate experts to assist in the updating of the two publications;

12. *Calls upon* the Secretary-General to continue his efforts towards updating the two publications and making them available electronically in all their respective language versions;

13. *Reiterates* the responsibility of the Secretary-General for the quality of the *Repertory* and the *Repertoire* and, in particular, with regard to the *Repertoire*, calls upon the Secretary-General to continue to follow the modalities outlined in paragraphs 102 to 106 of his report of 18 September 1952;

14. *Requests* the Secretary-General to submit a report on both the *Repertory* and the *Repertoire* to the General Assembly at its sixty-fourth session;

15. *Also requests* the Secretary-General to brief the Special Committee at its next session on the information referred to in paragraph 11 of his report on the implementation of the provisions of the Charter of the United Nations related to assistance to third States affected by the application of sanctions;

16. *Further requests* the Secretary-General to submit a report on the implementation of the provisions of the Charter of the United Nations related to assistance to third States affected by the application of sanctions to the General Assembly at its sixty-fourth session, under the item entitled "Report of the Special Committee on the Charter of the United Nations and on the Strengthening of the Role of the Organization";

17. *Decides* to include in the provisional agenda of its sixty-fourth session the item entitled "Report of the Special Committee on the Charter of the United Nations and on the Strengthening of the Role of the Organization".

Charter provisions relating to sanctions

Special Committee consideration. During the Special Committee's [A/63/33] consideration of the implementation of the Charter provisions related to assistance to third States affected by sanctions, delegations emphasized that sanctions should be implemented and monitored effectively, in accordance with specific terms and goals, subsequent to an objective assessment of unintended consequences that they could generate. Recognizing that the targeted nature of recently imposed sanctions was minimizing unintended consequences for civilian populations and third States, they commended the progress made by the Security Council, which included new procedures for the listing and delisting of individuals and entities on sanctions lists and the adoption of a focal point. Other delegations held that even targeted sanctions could entail unintended negative effects for third States and, therefore, the Special Committee should remain seized of the matter with the aim of establishing a comprehensive and objective framework that would allow for broad-based adaptation of sanctions and mitigate their adverse effects on third States and civilian populations. Some called for the establishment of a mechanism to assist third States at the time of the introduction of sanctions which would not depend on a specific request from such States. It was also suggested that any reform of the UN Charter should include a mandate for the Economic and Social Council to undertake studies relating to the socio-economic and humanitarian effects of sanctions, prior to their application.

Report of Secretary-General. In response to General Assembly resolution 62/69 [YUN 2007, p. 1381], the Secretary-General submitted an August report [A/63/224] highlighting Secretariat arrangements concerning assistance to third States affected by the application of sanctions; operational changes that had occurred following the shift in focus in the Security Council and its sanctions committees towards targeted sanctions; and recent developments concerning the activities of the Assembly and the Economic and Social Council regarding assistance to such States.

Cooperation with Asian-African Legal Consultative Organization

In response to General Assembly resolution 58/316 [YUN 2004, p. 1374] and Security Council **resolution 1809(2008)** (see p. 109), the Secretary-General in August submitted a consolidated report [A/63/228-S/2008/531 & Corr.1] on cooperation between the United Nations and regional and other organizations, providing information on cooperation between the United Nations and the Asian-African Legal Consultative Organization (AALCO). He reported that cooperation between the two organizations had included mutual representation at each other's meetings and the exchange of information and documentation. Consultations were regularly conducted on matters of common interest, including between the UN Legal Counsel and the AALCO Secretary-General. Cooperation in the area of international law included matters relating to the law of the sea, international trade law, international environmental law, criminal law, human rights law, refugee law, humanitarian law, terrorism, human trafficking, and the peaceful settlement of disputes.

The report provided details on AALCO representation at UN meetings and conferences, including two General Assembly sessions and the fifty-ninth session of ILC. AALCO and ICC concluded a memorandum of understanding on 5 February to promote awareness of international criminal law, and the AALCO Centre for Research and Training was engaged in capacity-building by carrying out research projects on international law. AALCO also established regional centres for arbitration in Cairo, Kuala Lumpur, Lagos and Tehran, and agreement was reached with Kenya on a fifth centre in Nairobi.

GENERAL ASSEMBLY ACTION

On 3 November [meeting 37], the General Assembly, adopted **resolution 63/10** [draft: A/63/L.7 & Add.1] without vote [agenda item 114 *(b)*].

Cooperation between the United Nations and the Asian-African Legal Consultative Organization

The General Assembly,

Recalling its resolutions 36/38 of 18 November 1981, 37/8 of 29 October 1982, 38/37 of 5 December 1983, 39/47 of 10 December 1984, 40/60 of 9 December 1985, 41/5 of 17 October 1986, 43/1 of 17 October 1988, 45/4 of 16 October 1990, 47/6 of 21 October 1992, 49/8 of 25 October 1994, 51/11 of 4 November 1996, 53/14 of 29 October 1998, 55/4 of 25 October 2000, 57/36 of 21 November 2002, 59/3 of 22 October 2004 and 61/5 of 20 October 2006,

Having considered the report of the Secretary-General,

Having heard the statement made by the representative of the Asian-African Legal Consultative Organization on the steps taken by the Consultative Organization to ensure continuing, close and effective cooperation between the two organizations,

Acknowledging in particular the close interaction between the Consultative Organization and the Sixth Committee,

1. *Takes note with appreciation* of the report of the Secretary-General;

2. *Recognizes* the continuing efforts of the Asian-African Legal Consultative Organization towards strengthening the role and function of the United Nations and its various organs in enhancing the rule of law and wider adherence to related international instruments;

3. *Notes with satisfaction* the commendable progress achieved towards enhancing cooperation between the United Nations, its agencies, other international organizations and the Consultative Organization;

4. *Notes with appreciation* the work of the Consultative Organization aimed at strengthening the efforts of the United Nations in respect of issues such as combating corruption, international terrorism and trafficking in women and children, as well as human rights issues;

5. *Also notes with appreciation* the initiative and efforts the Consultative Organization has undertaken to promote the objectives and principles set out in the United Nations Millennium Declaration, including wider acceptance of treaties deposited with the Secretary-General;

6. *Recommends* that, with a view to promoting close interaction between the Consultative Organization and the Sixth Committee, the consideration of the sub-item entitled "Cooperation between the United Nations and the Asian-African Legal Consultative Organization" should be scheduled to coincide with the deliberations of the Committee on the work of the International Law Commission;

7. *Requests* the Secretary-General to submit to the General Assembly at its sixty-fifth session a report on cooperation between the United Nations and the Consultative Organization;

8. *Decides* to include in the provisional agenda of its sixty-fifth session the sub-item entitled "Cooperation between the United Nations and the Asian-African Legal Consultative Organization".

Host country relations

At five meetings held in New York (22 January, 22 April, 23 July, and 2 and 31 October), the Committee on Relations with the Host Country considered the following aspects of relations between the UN diplomatic community and the United States, the host country: the security of missions and the safety of their personnel; entry visas issued by the host country; acceleration of immigration and customs procedures; and transportation, including the use of motor vehicles, parking and related matters.

The recommendations and conclusions on those items, approved by the Committee at its 31 October meeting, were incorporated in its report [A/63/26]. The Committee expressed appreciation for the host country's efforts to maintain appropriate conditions for delegations and missions accredited to the United Nations and anticipated that all issues raised at its meetings would be duly settled in a spirit of cooperation and in accordance with international law. Noting the importance of the observance of privileges and immunities, the Committee emphasized the need to solve, through negotiations, problems that might arise in that regard for the normal functioning of accredited delegations and missions. It urged the host country to continue to take appropriate action, such as the training of police, security, customs and border control officers, with a view to maintaining respect for diplomatic privileges and immunities. In case of violations, the Committee urged the host country to ensure that such cases were properly investigated and remedied, in accordance with applicable law. Considering that the security of missions and the safety of their personnel were indispensable for their effective functioning, the Committee appreciated the host country's efforts to that end and anticipated that all measures to prevent any interference with the missions' functioning would continue to be taken.

Noting the problems experienced by some missions in connection with the implementation of the Parking Programme for Diplomatic Vehicles, in force since 2002 [YUN 2002, p. 1338], the Committee decided to remain seized of the matter, with a view to continuously ensuring its proper implementation in a manner that was fair, non-discriminatory, effective and therefore consistent with international law.

The Committee requested the host country to continue to bring to the attention of New York City officials reports about other problems experienced by permanent missions or their staff, in order to improve the conditions for their functioning and to promote compliance with international norms concerning diplomatic privileges and immunities. It anticipated that the host country would enhance its efforts to ensure the issuance, in a timely manner, of entry visas to representatives of Member States, pursuant to the Headquarters Agreement, to travel to New York on official UN business, and noted that a number of delegations had requested shortening the time frame applied by the host country for issuance of entry visas since the current time frame posed difficulties for the full-fledged participation of Member States in UN meetings. Concerning travel regulations issued by the host country with regard to personnel of certain missions and staff members of the Secretariat of certain nationalities, the Committee urged the host country to remove the remaining restrictions.

The Committee stressed the importance of permanent missions, their personnel and Secretariat personnel meeting their financial obligations. Finally, the Committee reiterated its appreciation to the representative of the United States Mission in charge of host country affairs and to the Host Country Affairs Section of the United States Mission to the United Nations, as well as to those local entities, in particular the New York City Commission for the United Nations, Consular Corps and Protocol, that contributed to its efforts to help accommodate the needs, interests and requirements of the diplomatic community and to promote mutual understanding between the diplomatic community and the people of the City of New York.

Communications. Letters were submitted to the Committee by Cuba on the delay in processing of a visa application by the host country [A/AC.154/385], and by the United States as host country, transmitting its response to Cuba's letter [A/AC.154/386].

GENERAL ASSEMBLY ACTION

On 11 December [meeting 67], the General Assembly, on the recommendation of the Sixth Committee [A/63/452], adopted **resolution 63/130** without vote [agenda item 150].

Report of the Committee on Relations with the Host Country

The General Assembly,

Having considered the report of the Committee on Relations with the Host Country,

Recalling Article 105 of the Charter of the United Nations, the Convention on the Privileges and Immunities of the United Nations, the Agreement between the United Nations and the United States of America regarding the Headquarters of the United Nations and the responsibilities of the host country,

Recalling also that, in accordance with paragraph 7 of General Assembly resolution 2819(XXVI) of 15 December 1971, the Committee should consider, and advise the host country on, issues arising in connection with the implementation of the Agreement between the United Nations and the United States of America regarding the Headquarters of the United Nations,

Recognizing that effective measures should continue to be taken by the competent authorities of the host country, in particular to prevent any acts violating the security of missions and the safety of their personnel,

1. *Endorses* the recommendations and conclusions of the Committee on Relations with the Host Country contained in paragraph 51 of its report;

2. *Considers* that the maintenance of appropriate conditions for the normal work of the delegations and the missions accredited to the United Nations and the observance of their privileges and immunities, which is an issue of great importance, are in the interest of the United Nations and all Member States, and requests the host country to continue to solve, through negotiations, problems that might arise and to take all measures necessary to prevent any interference with the functioning of missions; and urges the host country to continue to take appropriate action, such as training of police, security, customs and border control officers, with a view to maintaining respect for diplomatic privileges and immunities and if violations occur to ensure that such cases are properly investigated and remedied, in accordance with applicable law;

3. *Notes* the problems experienced by some permanent missions in connection with the implementation of the Parking Programme for Diplomatic Vehicles and shall remain seized of the matter, with a view to continuing to maintain the proper implementation of the Parking Programme in a manner that is fair, non-discriminatory, effective and therefore consistent with international law;

4. *Requests* the host country to consider removing the remaining travel restrictions imposed by it on staff of certain missions and staff members of the Secretariat of certain nationalities, and, in this regard, notes the positions of affected States as reflected in the report of the Committee, of the Secretary-General and of the host country;

5. *Notes* that the Committee anticipates that the host country will enhance its efforts to ensure the issuance, in a timely manner, of entry visas to representatives of Member States, pursuant to article IV, section 11, of the Agreement between the United Nations and the United States of America regarding the Headquarters of the United Nations to travel to New York on United Nations business; and

notes that the Committee anticipates that the host country will enhance efforts to facilitate participation, including visa issuance, of representatives of Member States in other United Nations meetings as appropriate;

6. *Notes also* that a number of delegations have requested shortening the time frame applied by the host country for issuance of entry visas to representatives of Member States, since this time frame poses difficulties for the full-fledged participation of Member States in United Nations meetings;

7. *Expresses its appreciation* for the efforts made by the host country, and hopes that the issues raised at the meetings of the Committee will continue to be resolved in a spirit of cooperation and in accordance with international law;

8. *Affirms* the importance of the Committee being in a position to fulfil its mandate and meet on short notice to deal with urgent and important matters concerning the relations between the United Nations and the host country, and in that connection requests the Secretariat and the Committee on Conferences to accord priority to requests from the Committee on Relations with the Host Country for conference-servicing facilities for meetings of that Committee that must be held while the General Assembly and its Main Committees are meeting, without prejudice to the requirements of those bodies and on an "as available" basis;

9. *Requests* the Secretary-General to remain actively engaged in all aspects of the relations of the United Nations with the host country;

10. *Requests* the Committee to continue its work in conformity with General Assembly resolution 2819(XXVI);

11. *Decides* to include in the provisional agenda of its sixty-fourth session the item entitled "Report of the Committee on Relations with the Host Country".

Chapter IV

Law of the sea

In 2008, the United Nations continued to promote universal acceptance of the 1982 United Nations Convention on the Law of the Sea and its two implementing Agreements, on the implementation of Part XI of the Convention and on the conservation and management of straddling fish stocks and highly migratory fish stocks.

The three institutions created by the Convention—the International Seabed Authority, the International Tribunal for the Law of the Sea and the Commission on the Limits of the Continental Shelf—held sessions during the year. In December, the General Assembly designated 8 June as World Oceans Day.

UN Convention on the Law of the Sea

Signatures and ratifications

In 2008, Congo and Liberia ratified or acceded to the United Nations Convention on the Law of the Sea (UNCLOS), bringing the number of parties to 157. The Convention, which was adopted by the Third United Nations Conference on the Law of the Sea in 1982 [YUN 1982, p. 178], entered into force on 16 November 1994 [YUN 1994, p. 1301].

Meeting of States Parties

The eighteenth Meeting of States Parties to the Convention (New York, 13–20 June) [SPLOS/184] discussed the 2007 activities of the International Tribunal for the Law of the Sea [YUN 2007, p. 1400] and took action on a number of Tribunal-related financial and administrative issues, including the appointment of the Tribunal auditor for 2009–2012, and the election of seven members of the Tribunal. Also discussed were the 2007 activities of the International Seabed Authority (see p. 1494), the Commission on the Limits of the Continental Shelf (see p. 1495), the allocation of seats on the Commission and the Tribunal, as well as the Secretary-General's report under article 319 of the Convention (see p. 1496).

Agreement relating to the Implementation of Part XI of the Convention

During 2008, the number of parties to the 1994 Agreement relating to the Implementation of Part XI of the Convention (governing exploitation of seabed resources beyond national jurisdiction), adopted by the General Assembly in resolution 48/263 [YUN 1994, p. 1301], reached 135, with Cape Verde, the Congo, Guyana and Liberia becoming parties. The Agreement, which entered into force on 28 July 1996 [YUN 1996, p. 1215], sought to address certain difficulties with the seabed mining provisions contained in Part XI of the Convention, which had been raised primarily by the industrialized countries. The Agreement was to be interpreted and applied together with the Convention as a single instrument, and, in the event of any inconsistency between the Agreement and Part XI of the Convention, the provisions of the Agreement would prevail. Any ratification of or accession to the Convention after 28 July 1994 represented consent to be bound by the Agreement also. Parties to the Convention prior to the Agreement's adoption had to deposit a separate instrument of ratification of or accession to the Agreement.

Agreement relating to conservation and management of straddling fish stocks and highly migratory fish stocks

As at 31 December, the number of parties to the 1995 Agreement for the Implementation of the Provisions of the United Nations Convention on the Law of the Sea of 10 December 1982 relating to the Conservation and Management of Straddling Fish Stocks and Highly Migratory Fish Stocks [YUN 1995, p. 1334] reached 74, with Hungary, Mozambique, Oman, Palau, Panama, the Republic of Korea and Slovakia becoming parties. Referred to as the Fish Stocks Agreement, it entered into force on 11 December 2001 [YUN 2001, p. 1232].

Report of Secretary-General. In response to General Assembly resolution 62/177 [YUN 2007, p. 1389], the Secretary-General submitted a July report [A/63/128] on the status of implementation of the Fish Stocks Agreement. The report contained information on initiatives taken or recommended to improve the conservation and management of fishery and other marine living resources, with a view to achieving sustainable fisheries and protecting vulnerable marine ecosystems and biodiversity.

The report emphasized the importance of the full implementation by States of all international fishery instruments, whether legally binding or voluntary. It also stressed the importance of cooperation among

States, directly or through subregional and regional fisheries management organizations or arrangements, to address unsustainable fishing practices and promote sustainable fisheries in areas beyond natural jurisdiction, including through implementing their responsibilities as flag States; improving governance of those organizations or arrangements; and cooperating in the establishment of new ones where none existed. A report on the status and activities of the UN Fish Stocks Agreement Assistance Fund was included.

The report dealt with achieving sustainable fisheries, implementation of international instruments for the long-term conservation, management and sustainable use of fishery resources, promotion of responsible fisheries in the marine ecosystem, impediments to sustainable fisheries, and international cooperation to promote sustainable fisheries. It underscored the need for increased efforts towards responsible fisheries if the commitments set out in the Johannesburg Plan of Implementation to achieve sustainable fisheries by 2015 [YUN 2002, p. 822] were to be met. It stressed that States needed to pursue new initiatives to promote sustainable fisheries that targeted economic incentives behind unsustainable fishing practices.

GENERAL ASSEMBLY ACTION

On 5 December [meeting 64], the General Assembly adopted **resolution 63/112** [draft: A/63/L.43 & Add.1] without vote [agenda item 70 *(b)*].

Sustainable Fisheries, including through the 1995 Agreement for the Implementation of the Provisions of the United Nations Convention on the Law of the Sea of 10 December 1982 relating to the Conservation and Management of Straddling Fish Stocks and Highly Migratory Fish Stocks, and related instruments

The General Assembly,

Reaffirming its resolutions 46/215 of 20 December 1991, 49/116 of 19 December 1994, and 50/24 and 50/25 of 5 December 1995, as well as its resolutions 56/13 of 28 November 2001, 58/14 of 24 November 2003, 59/25 of 17 November 2004, 60/31 of 29 November 2005, 61/105 of 8 December 2006 and 62/177 of 18 December 2007, and other relevant resolutions,

Recalling the relevant provisions of the United Nations Convention on the Law of the Sea ("the Convention"), and bearing in mind the relationship between the Convention and the 1995 Agreement for the Implementation of the Provisions of the United Nations Convention on the Law of the Sea of 10 December 1982 relating to the Conservation and Management of Straddling Fish Stocks and Highly Migratory Fish Stocks ("the Agreement"),

Recognizing that, in accordance with the Convention, the Agreement sets forth provisions concerning the conservation and management of straddling fish stocks and highly migratory fish stocks, including provisions on compliance and enforcement by the flag State and subregional and regional cooperation in enforcement, binding dispute settlement and the rights and obligations of States in authorizing the use of vessels flying their flags for fishing on the high seas, and specific provisions to address the requirements of developing States in relation to the conservation and management of straddling fish stocks and highly migratory fish stocks and the development of fisheries for such stocks,

Welcoming the fact that a growing number of States, and entities referred to in the Convention and in article 1, paragraph 2 *(b)*, of the Agreement, as well as subregional and regional fisheries management organizations and arrangements, have taken measures, as appropriate, towards the implementation of the provisions of the Agreement,

Welcoming also the recent ratifications of and accessions to the Agreement,

Welcoming further the work of the Food and Agriculture Organization of the United Nations and its Committee on Fisheries and the 2005 Rome Declaration on Illegal, Unreported and Unregulated Fishing, adopted by the Ministerial Meeting on Fisheries of the Food and Agriculture Organization of the United Nations on 12 March 2005, which calls for effective implementation of the various instruments already developed to ensure responsible fisheries, and recognizing that the Code of Conduct for Responsible Fisheries of the Food and Agriculture Organization of the United Nations ("the Code") and its associated international plans of action set out principles and global standards of behaviour for responsible practices for conservation of fisheries resources and the management and development of fisheries,

Noting with concern that effective management of marine capture fisheries has been made difficult in some areas by unreliable information and data caused by unreported and misreported fish catch and fishing effort and that this lack of accurate data contributes to overfishing in some areas,

Recognizing the significant contribution of sustainable fisheries to food security, income, wealth and poverty alleviation for present and future generations,

Recognizing also the urgent need for action at all levels to ensure the long-term sustainable use and management of fisheries resources through the wide application of the precautionary approach,

Expressing concern over the current and projected adverse effects of climate change on food security and the sustainability of fisheries, and noting in that regard the work of the Intergovernmental Panel on Climate Change, the Food and Agriculture Organization of the United Nations and the United Nations Environment Programme, including the findings that climate change is likely to have substantial impacts on commercial and artisanal fisheries and food security,

Noting the convening by the Food and Agriculture Organization of the United Nations of the Expert Workshop on Climate Change Implications for Fisheries and Aquaculture, in Rome from 7 to 9 April 2008,

Deploring the fact that fish stocks, including straddling fish stocks and highly migratory fish stocks, in many parts of the world are overfished or subject to sparsely regulated and heavy fishing efforts, as a result of, inter alia, illegal, unreported and unregulated fishing, inadequate flag State control and enforcement, including monitoring, control and surveillance measures, inadequate regulatory measures, harmful fisheries subsidies and overcapacity, and noting the report of the Food and Agriculture Organization of the United Nations, *The State of World Fisheries and Aquaculture 2006*,

Noting the joint study by the World Bank and the Food and Agriculture Organization of the United Nations, *The Sunken Billions: The Economic Justification for Fisheries Reform*, and taking note of its conclusions, including that sustainable fisheries and reform of the global fisheries sector could generate additional economic growth and alternative livelihoods, and that reforms would need to include a reduction in fishing effort and fishing capacity,

Noting also the limited information available on measures taken by States to implement, individually and through regional fisheries management organizations and arrangements, the International Plan of Action for the Management of Fishing Capacity adopted by the Food and Agriculture Organization of the United Nations,

Particularly concerned that illegal, unreported and unregulated fishing constitutes a serious threat to fish stocks and marine habitats and ecosystems, to the detriment of sustainable fisheries as well as the food security and the economies of many States, particularly developing States,

Concerned that some operators increasingly take advantage of the globalization of fishery markets to trade fishery products stemming from illegal, unreported and unregulated fishing and make economic profits from those operations, which constitutes an incentive for them to pursue their activities,

Recognizing that effective deterrence and combating of illegal, unreported and unregulated fishing has significant financial and other resource implications,

Recognizing also that illegal, unreported and unregulated fishing may give rise to safety and security concerns for individuals on vessels engaged in such activities,

Welcoming cooperation between the Food and Agriculture Organization of the United Nations and the International Maritime Organization, in particular in assisting States and regional fisheries management organizations and arrangements to combat illegal, unreported and unregulated fishing activities,

Recognizing the duty provided in the Convention, the Agreement to Promote Compliance with International Conservation and Management Measures by Fishing Vessels on the High Seas ("the Compliance Agreement"), the Agreement and the Code for flag States to exercise effective control over fishing vessels flying their flag, and vessels flying their flag which provide support to fishing vessels, to ensure that the activities of such fishing and support vessels do not undermine the effectiveness of conservation and management measures taken in accordance with international law and adopted at the national, subregional, regional or global levels,

Recalling paragraphs 65 and 66 of its resolution 62/177, and noting in this regard the convening by the Food and Agriculture Organization of the United Nations of the Expert Consultation on the Development of a Comprehensive Global Record of Fishing Vessels, in Rome from 25 to 28 February 2008, and the findings of the Expert Consultation regarding the development of a comprehensive global record,

Noting the obligation of all States, in accordance with international law, as reflected in the relevant provisions of the Convention, to cooperate in the conservation and management of living marine resources, and recognizing the importance of coordination and cooperation at the global, regional, subregional as well as national levels in the areas, inter alia, of data collection, information-sharing, capacity-building and training for the conservation, management and sustainable development of marine living resources,

Welcoming recent developments regarding recommended best practices for regional fisheries management organizations and arrangements that may help to strengthen their governance and promote their improved performance,

Calling attention to the need for States, individually and through regional fisheries management organizations and arrangements, to continue to develop and implement effective port State measures and schemes to combat overfishing and illegal, unreported and unregulated fishing, and the critical need for cooperation with developing States to build their capacity in this regard, taking note of the work of the Food and Agriculture Organization of the United Nations to develop a legally binding instrument on minimum standards for port State measures,

Noting that the Commission for the Conservation of Antarctic Marine Living Resources, the General Fisheries Commission for the Mediterranean, the North East Atlantic Fisheries Commission and the Northwest Atlantic Fisheries Organization have adopted port State measures, to be applied by their members, which include prohibition of entry and use of port services, including landing and trans-shipment, to vessels identified by those regional fisheries management organizations as engaged in illegal, unreported and unregulated fishing activities, and that those measures prevent and deter such activities,

Concerned that marine pollution from all sources, including vessels and, in particular, land-based sources, constitutes a serious threat to human health and safety, endangers fish stocks, marine biodiversity and marine and coastal habitats and has significant costs to local and national economies,

Recognizing that marine debris is a global transboundary pollution problem and that, due to the many different types and sources of marine debris, different approaches to their prevention and removal are necessary,

Noting that the contribution of sustainable aquaculture to global fish supplies continues to respond to opportunities in developing countries to enhance local food security and poverty alleviation and, together with the efforts of other aquaculture producing countries, will make a significant contribution to meeting future demands in fish consumption, bearing in mind article 9 of the Code, and therefore welcoming the adoption in 2007 of the Strategy and Outline Plan for Improving Information on Status and Trends of Aquaculture by the Food and Agriculture Organization of the United Nations to improve knowledge and understanding of the status and trends of aquaculture,

Calling attention to the circumstances affecting fisheries in many developing States, in particular African States and small island developing States, and recognizing the urgent need for capacity-building, including the transfer of marine technology and in particular fisheries-related technology, to enhance the ability of such States to meet their obligations and exercise their rights under international instruments, in order to realize the benefits from fisheries resources,

Recognizing the need for appropriate measures to minimize by-catch, waste, discards, including high-grading, loss of fishing gear and other factors, which adversely affect fish stocks and may also have undesirable effects on the economies and food security of small island developing States, other developing coastal States, and subsistence fishing communities,

Recognizing also the need to further integrate ecosystem approaches into fisheries conservation and management and, more generally, the importance of applying ecosystem approaches to the management of human activities in the ocean, and noting in this regard the Reykjavik Declaration on Responsible Fisheries in the Marine Ecosystem, the work of the Food and Agriculture Organization of the United Nations related to guidelines for the implementation of the ecosystem approach to fisheries management and the importance of this approach to relevant provisions of the Agreement and the Code, as well as decision VII/11 and other relevant decisions of the Conference of the Parties to the Convention on Biological Diversity,

Recognizing further the economic and cultural importance of sharks in many countries, the biological importance of sharks in the marine ecosystem as key predatory species, the vulnerability of certain shark species to overexploitation, the fact that some are threatened with extinction, the need for measures to promote the long-term conservation, management and sustainable use of shark populations and fisheries, and the relevance of the International Plan of Action for the Conservation and Management of Sharks, adopted by the Food and Agriculture Organization of the United Nations in 1999, in providing guidance on the development of such measures,

Reaffirming its support for the initiative of the Food and Agriculture Organization of the United Nations and relevant subregional and regional fisheries management organizations and arrangements on the conservation and management of sharks, while noting with concern that basic data on shark stocks and harvests continue to be lacking, that only a small number of countries have implemented the International Plan of Action for the Conservation and Management of Sharks, and that not all regional fisheries management organizations and arrangements have adopted conservation and management measures for directed shark fisheries,

Expressing concern that the practice of large-scale pelagic drift-net fishing remains a threat to marine living resources, and emphasizing that efforts should be made to ensure that the implementation of resolution 46/215 in some parts of the world does not result in the transfer to other parts of the world of drift nets that contravene the resolution,

Expressing concern also over reports of continued losses of seabirds, particularly albatrosses and petrels, as well as other marine species, including sharks, fin-fish species and marine turtles, as a result of incidental mortality in fishing operations, particularly longline fishing, and other activities, while recognizing considerable efforts to reduce by-catch in longline fishing by States and through various regional fisheries management organizations and arrangements,

Taking note with appreciation of the report of the Secretary-General, in particular its useful role in gathering and disseminating information on practices relating to the sustainable development of the world's living marine resources,

I

Achieving sustainable fisheries

1. *Reaffirms* the importance it attaches to the long-term conservation, management and sustainable use of the marine living resources of the world's oceans and seas and the obligations of States to cooperate to this end, in accordance with international law, as reflected in the relevant provisions of the Convention, in particular the provisions on cooperation set out in Part V and Part VII, section 2, of the Convention, and where applicable, the Agreement;

2. *Encourages* States to give due priority to the implementation of the Plan of Implementation of the World Summit on Sustainable Development ("Johannesburg Plan of Implementation"), in relation to achieving sustainable fisheries;

3. *Urges* States, either directly or through appropriate subregional, regional or global organizations or arrangements, to intensify efforts to assess and address, as appropriate, the impacts of global climate change on the sustainability of fish stocks and the habitats that support them;

4. *Emphasizes* the obligations of flag States to discharge their responsibilities, in accordance with the Convention and the Agreement, to ensure compliance by vessels flying their flag with the conservation and management measures adopted and in force with respect to fisheries resources on the high seas;

5. *Calls upon* all States that have not done so, in order to achieve the goal of universal participation, to become parties to the Convention, which sets out the legal framework within which all activities in the oceans and seas must be carried out, taking into account the relationship between the Convention and the Agreement;

6. *Calls upon* all States, directly or through regional fisheries management organizations and arrangements, to apply widely, in accordance with international law and the Code, the precautionary approach and an ecosystem approach to the conservation, management and exploitation of fish stocks, including straddling fish stocks, highly migratory fish stocks and discrete high seas fish stocks, and also calls upon States parties to the Agreement to implement fully the provisions of article 6 of the Agreement as a matter of priority;

7. *Encourages* States to increase their reliance on scientific advice in developing, adopting and implementing conservation and management measures, and to increase their efforts to promote science for conservation and management measures that apply, in accordance with international law, the precautionary approach and an ecosystem approach to fisheries management, enhancing understanding of ecosystem approaches, in order to ensure the long-term conservation and sustainable use of marine living resources, and in this regard encourages the implementation of the Strategy for Improving Information on Status and Trends of Capture Fisheries of the Food and Agriculture Organization of the United Nations as a framework for the improvement and understanding of fishery status and trends;

8. *Calls upon* all States, directly or through regional fisheries management organizations and arrangements, to apply stock-specific precautionary reference points, as de-

scribed in Annex II to the Agreement and in the Code, to ensure that populations of harvested stocks, in particular straddling fish stocks, highly migratory fish stocks and discrete high seas fish stocks, and, where necessary, associated or dependent species, are maintained at, or restored to, sustainable levels, and to use these reference points for triggering conservation and management action;

9. *Encourages* States to apply the precautionary approach and an ecosystem approach in adopting and implementing conservation and management measures addressing, inter alia, by-catch, pollution, overfishing, and protecting habitats of specific concern, taking into account existing guidelines developed by the Food and Agriculture Organization of the United Nations;

10. *Also encourages* the ongoing development of observer programmes by regional fisheries management organizations and arrangements to improve data collection on, inter alia, target and by-catch species, which could also assist monitoring, control and surveillance tools, and encourages States, both individually and collectively, where appropriate, to develop, fully implement, and, where necessary, continue to improve robust observer programmes, taking into account standards for such programmes developed by some regional fisheries management organizations and arrangements and the forms of cooperation with developing States as set out in article 25 of the Agreement and article 5 of the Code;

11. *Calls upon* States and regional fisheries management organizations and arrangements to collect and, where appropriate, report to the Food and Agriculture Organization of the United Nations required catch and effort data, and fishery-related information, in a complete, accurate and timely way, including for straddling fish stocks and highly migratory fish stocks within and beyond areas under national jurisdiction, discrete high seas fish stocks, and by-catch and discards; and, where they do not exist, to establish processes to strengthen data collection and reporting by members of regional fisheries management organizations and arrangements, including through regular reviews of member compliance with such obligations, and, when such obligations are not met, require the member concerned to rectify the problem, including through the preparation of plans of action with timelines;

12. *Invites* States and regional fisheries management organizations and arrangements to cooperate with the Food and Agriculture Organization of the United Nations in the implementation and further development of the Fisheries Resources Monitoring System initiative;

13. *Reaffirms* paragraph 10 of resolution 61/105, and calls upon States, including through regional fisheries management organizations or arrangements, to urgently adopt measures to fully implement the International Plan of Action for the Conservation and Management of Sharks for directed and non-directed shark fisheries, based on the best available scientific information, through, inter alia, limits on catch or fishing effort, by requiring that vessels flying their flag collect and regularly report data on shark catches, including species-specific data, discards and landings, undertaking, including through international cooperation, comprehensive stock assessments of sharks, reducing shark by-catch and by-catch mortality, and, where scientific information is uncertain or inadequate, not increasing fishing effort in directed shark fisheries until measures have been established to ensure the long-term conservation, management and sustainable use of shark stocks and to prevent further declines of vulnerable or threatened shark stocks;

14. *Calls upon* States to take immediate and concerted action to improve the implementation of and compliance with existing regional fisheries management organization or arrangement and national measures that regulate shark fisheries, in particular those measures which prohibit or restrict fisheries conducted solely for the purpose of harvesting shark fins, and, where necessary, to consider taking other measures, as appropriate, such as requiring that all sharks be landed with each fin naturally attached;

15. *Requests* the Food and Agriculture Organization of the United Nations to prepare a report containing a comprehensive analysis of the implementation of the International Plan of Action for the Conservation and Management of Sharks, as well as progress in implementing paragraph 11 of General Assembly resolution 62/177, for presentation to the Committee on Fisheries at its twenty-eighth session, in 2009;

16. *Urges* States to eliminate barriers to trade in fish and fisheries products which are not consistent with their rights and obligations under the World Trade Organization agreements, taking into account the importance of the trade in fish and fisheries products, particularly for developing countries;

17. *Urges* States and relevant international and national organizations to provide for the participation of small-scale fishery stakeholders in related policy development and fisheries management strategies in order to achieve long-term sustainability for such fisheries, consistent with the duty to ensure the proper conservation and management of fisheries resources;

II

Implementation of the 1995 Agreement for the Implementation of the Provisions of the United Nations Convention on the Law of the Sea of 10 December 1982 relating to the Conservation and Management of Straddling Fish Stocks and Highly Migratory Fish Stocks

18. *Calls upon* all States, and entities referred to in the Convention and in article 1, paragraph 2 *(b)*, of the Agreement, that have not done so to ratify or accede to the Agreement and in the interim to consider applying it provisionally;

19. *Calls upon* States parties to the Agreement to harmonize, as a matter of priority, their national legislation with the provisions of the Agreement, and to ensure that the provisions of the Agreement are effectively implemented into regional fisheries management organizations and arrangements of which they are a member;

20. *Emphasizes* the importance of those provisions of the Agreement relating to bilateral, subregional and regional cooperation in enforcement, and urges continued efforts in this regard;

21. *Calls upon* all States to ensure that their vessels comply with the conservation and management measures that have been adopted by subregional and regional fisheries management organizations and arrangements in accordance with relevant provisions of the Convention and of the Agreement;

22. *Urges* States parties to the Agreement, in accordance with article 21, paragraph 4, thereof to inform, either directly or through the relevant subregional or regional fisheries management organization or arrangement, all States whose vessels fish on the high seas in the same subregion or region of the form of identification issued by those States parties to officials duly authorized to carry out boarding and inspection functions in accordance with articles 21 and 22 of the Agreement;

23. *Also urges* States parties to the Agreement, in accordance with article 21, paragraph 4 thereof, to designate an appropriate authority to receive notifications pursuant to article 21 and to give due publicity to such designation through the relevant subregional or regional fisheries management organization or arrangement;

24. *Invites* regional fisheries management organizations and arrangements which have not yet done so to adopt procedures for high seas boarding and inspection that are consistent with articles 21 and 22 of the Agreement;

25. *Calls upon* States, individually and, as appropriate, through subregional and regional fisheries management organizations and arrangements with competence over discrete high seas fish stocks, to adopt the necessary measures to ensure the long-term conservation, management and sustainable use of such stocks in accordance with the Convention and consistent with the Code and the general principles set forth in the Agreement;

26. *Invites* States to assist developing States in enhancing their participation in regional fisheries management organizations or arrangements, including by facilitating access to fisheries for straddling fish stocks and highly migratory fish stocks, in accordance with article 25, paragraph 1, of the Agreement, taking into account the need to ensure that such access benefits the developing States concerned and their nationals;

27. *Invites* States and international financial institutions and organizations of the United Nations system to provide assistance according to Part VII of the Agreement, including, if appropriate, the development of special financial mechanisms or instruments to assist developing States, in particular the least developed among them and small island developing States, to enable them to develop their national capacity to exploit fishery resources, including developing their domestically flagged fishing fleet, value-added processing and the expansion of their economic base in the fishing industry, consistent with the duty to ensure the proper conservation and management of fisheries resources;

28. *Encourages* States, intergovernmental organizations, international financial institutions, national institutions and non-governmental organizations, as well as natural and juridical persons, to make voluntary financial contributions to the Assistance Fund established under Part VII of the Agreement;

29. *Notes with satisfaction* that the Food and Agriculture Organization of the United Nations and the Division for Ocean Affairs and the Law of the Sea of the Office of Legal Affairs of the Secretariat have taken measures to publicize the availability of assistance through the Assistance Fund;

30. *Encourages* accelerated progress by States, individually and, as appropriate, through subregional and regional fisheries management organizations and arrangements, in the implementation of the recommendations of the Review Conference on the Agreement, held in New York from 22 to 26 May 2006, and the identification of emerging priorities;

31. *Recalls* paragraph 16 of resolution 59/25, and requests the Secretary- General to resume the Review Conference, convened pursuant to article 36 of the Agreement, in New York for one week in the first part of 2010, with a view to assessing the effectiveness of the Agreement in securing the conservation and management of straddling fish stocks and highly migratory fish stocks, and to render the necessary assistance and provide such services as may be required for the resumption of the Review Conference;

32. *Requests* the Secretary-General to submit to the resumed Review Conference an updated comprehensive report, prepared in cooperation with the Food and Agriculture Organization of the United Nations, to assist the Conference in discharging its mandate under article 36, paragraph 2, of the Agreement;

33. *Recalls* paragraph 6 of resolution 56/13, and requests the Secretary-General to convene in 2009, in accordance with past practice, an eighth round of informal consultations of States parties to the Agreement for a duration of at least four days, to consider, inter alia, promoting a wider participation in the Agreement through a continuing dialogue, in particular with developing States, and initial preparatory work for the resumption of the Review Conference, and to make any appropriate recommendations to the General Assembly;

34. *Requests* the Secretary-General to invite States, and entities referred to in the Convention and in article 1, paragraph 2 *(b)*, of the Agreement, not parties to the Agreement, as well as the United Nations Development Programme, the Food and Agriculture Organization of the United Nations and other specialized agencies, the Commission on Sustainable Development, the World Bank, the Global Environment Facility and other relevant international financial institutions, subregional and regional fisheries management organizations and arrangements, other fisheries bodies, other relevant intergovernmental bodies and relevant non-governmental organizations, in accordance with past practice, to attend the eighth round of informal consultations of States parties to the Agreement as observers;

35. *Reaffirms its request* that the Food and Agriculture Organization of the United Nations initiate arrangements with States for the collection and dissemination of data on fishing in the high seas by vessels flying their flag at the subregional and regional levels where no such arrangements exist;

36. *Also reaffirms its request* that the Food and Agriculture Organization of the United Nations revise its global fisheries statistics database to provide information on straddling fish stocks, highly migratory fish stocks and discrete high seas fish stocks on the basis of where the catch is taken;

III

Related fisheries instruments

37. *Emphasizes* the importance of the effective implementation of the provisions of the Compliance Agreement, and urges continued efforts in this regard;

38. *Calls upon* all States and other entities referred to in article X, paragraph 1, of the Compliance Agreement that have not yet become parties to that Agreement to do so as a matter of priority and, in the interim, to consider applying it provisionally;

39. *Urges* States and subregional and regional fisheries management organizations and arrangements to implement and promote the application of the Code within their areas of competence;

40. *Urges* States to develop and implement, as a matter of priority, national and, as appropriate, regional plans of action to put into effect the international plans of action of the Food and Agriculture Organization of the United Nations;

41. *Welcomes* the adoption by the Technical Consultation, convened by the Food and Agriculture Organization of the United Nations, in Rome from 25 to 29 August 2008, of the International Guidelines for the Management of Deep-sea Fisheries in the High Seas, as requested in paragraph 89 of resolution 61/105, which include standards and criteria for use by States and regional fisheries management organizations or arrangements in identifying vulnerable marine ecosystems in areas beyond national jurisdiction and the impacts of fishing on such ecosystems and in establishing standards for the management of deep sea fisheries in order to facilitate the adoption and the implementation of conservation and management measures pursuant to paragraphs 83 and 86 of resolution 61/105, and calls upon States and regional fisheries management organizations or arrangements, as appropriate, to implement those Guidelines;

IV

Illegal, unreported and unregulated fishing

42. *Emphasizes once again its serious concern* that illegal, unreported and unregulated fishing remains one of the greatest threats to marine ecosystems and continues to have serious and major implications for the conservation and management of ocean resources, and renews its call upon States to comply fully with all existing obligations and to combat such fishing and urgently to take all necessary steps to implement the International Plan of Action to Prevent, Deter and Eliminate Illegal, Unreported and Unregulated Fishing of the Food and Agriculture Organization of the United Nations;

43. *Urges* States to exercise effective control over their nationals, including beneficial owners, and vessels flying their flag, in order to prevent and deter them from engaging in illegal, unreported and unregulated fishing activities or supporting vessels engaging in illegal, unreported and unregulated fishing activities, including those vessels listed by regional fisheries management organizations or arrangements as engaged in those activities, and to facilitate mutual assistance to ensure that such actions can be investigated and proper sanctions imposed;

44. *Also urges* States to take effective measures, at the national, regional and global levels, to deter the activities, including illegal, unreported and unregulated fishing, of any vessel which undermines conservation and management measures that have been adopted by subregional and regional fisheries management organizations and arrangements in accordance with international law;

45. *Calls upon* States not to permit vessels flying their flag to engage in fishing on the high seas or in areas under the national jurisdiction of other States, unless duly authorized by the authorities of the States concerned and in accordance with the conditions set out in the authorization, and to take specific measures, including deterring the reflagging of vessels by their nationals, in accordance with the relevant provisions of the Convention, the Agreement and the Compliance Agreement, to control fishing operations by vessels flying their flag;

46. *Recalls* its resolution 62/177, in which it invited the Food and Agriculture Organization of the United Nations, as requested by the Committee on Fisheries at its twenty-seventh session, to further consider the possibility of convening an expert consultation to develop criteria for assessing the performance of flag States, encourages the Food and Agriculture Organization of the United Nations to convene such an expert consultation as early as possible in 2009 and also to consider the possibility of further work on this issue, and calls upon States to support this important initiative, noting the preparatory work conducted by an expert workshop on flag State responsibilities, held in Vancouver, Canada, from 25 to 28 March 2008;

47. *Urges* States, individually and collectively through regional fisheries management organizations and arrangements, to develop appropriate processes to assess the performance of States with respect to implementing the obligations regarding fishing vessels flying their flag set out in relevant international instruments;

48. *Reaffirms* the need to strengthen, where necessary, the international legal framework for intergovernmental cooperation, in particular at the subregional and regional levels, in the management of fish stocks and in combating illegal, unreported and unregulated fishing, in a manner consistent with international law, and for States and entities referred to in the Convention and in article 1, paragraph 2 *(b)*, of the Agreement to collaborate in efforts to address these types of fishing activities;

49. *Encourages* regional fisheries management organizations and arrangements to further coordinate measures for combating illegal, unreported and unregulated fishing activities, such as through the development of a common list of vessels identified as engaged in illegal, unreported and unregulated fishing or the mutual recognition of the illegal, unreported and unregulated vessel lists established by each organization or arrangement;

50. *Reaffirms its call upon* States to take all necessary measures consistent with international law, without prejudice to a State's sovereignty over ports in its territory and to reasons of force majeure or distress, including the prohibition of vessels from accessing their ports followed by a report to the flag State concerned, when there is clear evidence that they are or have been engaged in or have supported illegal, unreported and unregulated fishing, or when they refuse to give information either on the origin of the catch or on the authorization under which the catch has been made;

51. *Urges* enhanced action consistent with international law, including cooperation and coordination, to eliminate illegal, unreported and unregulated fishing by vessels flying "flags of convenience", to require that a "genuine link" be established between States and fishing vessels flying their

flags, and to clarify the role of the "genuine link" in relation to the duty of States to exercise effective control over such vessels, and calls upon States to implement the 2005 Rome Declaration on Illegal, Unreported and Unregulated Fishing as a matter of priority;

52. *Recognizes* the need for enhanced port State measures to combat illegal, unreported and unregulated fishing, and urges States to cooperate, in particular at the regional level and through subregional and regional fisheries management organizations and arrangements, to adopt all necessary port measures, consistent with international law taking into account article 23 of the Agreement, particularly those identified in the Model Scheme on Port State Measures to Combat Illegal, Unreported and Unregulated Fishing, adopted by the Food and Agriculture Organization of the United Nations in 2005, and to promote the development and application of minimum standards at the regional level;

53. *Welcomes* the intergovernmental Technical Consultation, held by the Food and Agriculture Organization of the United Nations in Rome from 23 to 27 June 2008 to develop a legally binding instrument on minimum standards for port State measures, based on the Model Scheme on Port State Measures to Combat Illegal, Unreported and Unregulated Fishing and the International Plan of Action to Prevent, Deter and Eliminate Illegal, Unreported and Unregulated Fishing, and encourages all relevant States to participate in the resumed session of the Technical Consultation, to be held in Rome from 26 to 30 January 2009, with a view to presenting the finalized text of the instrument to the Committee on Fisheries at its twenty-eighth session, in 2009;

54. *Encourages* strengthened collaboration between the Food and Agriculture Organization of the United Nations and the International Maritime Organization, taking into account the respective competencies, mandates and experience of the two organizations, to combat illegal, unreported and unregulated fishing, particularly in improving the implementation of flag State responsibilities and port State measures;

55. *Encourages* States, with respect to vessels flying their flag, and port States, to make every effort to share data on landings and catch quotas, and in this regard encourages regional fisheries management organizations or arrangements to consider developing open databases containing such data for the purpose of enhancing the effectiveness of fisheries management;

56. *Calls upon* States to take all necessary measures to ensure that vessels flying their flag do not engage in transshipment of fish caught by fishing vessels engaged in illegal, unreported and unregulated fishing;

57. *Urges* States, individually and through regional fisheries management organizations and arrangements, to adopt and implement internationally agreed market-related measures in accordance with international law, including principles, rights and obligations established in World Trade Organization agreements, as called for in the International Plan of Action to Prevent, Deter and Eliminate Illegal, Unreported and Unregulated Fishing;

58. *Welcomes* the adoption of the Technical Guidelines for Responsible Fish Trade by the Sub-Committee on Fish Trade of the Committee on Fisheries of the Food and Agriculture Organization of the United Nations at its eleventh session, held in Bremen, Germany, from 2 to 6 June 2008, notes the discussion in the Sub-Committee on Fish Trade regarding emerging market- and trade-related measures, and encourages information-sharing by States and other relevant actors in this regard with appropriate international and regional forums, consistent with the established plan of work of the Committee on Fisheries and given the potential implications of these measures for all States;

59. *Notes* the concerns about possible connections between international organized crime and illegal fishing in certain regions of the world, and encourages States, including through the appropriate international forums and organizations, to study the causes and methods of and contributing factors to illegal fishing to increase knowledge and understanding of those possible connections, and to make the findings publicly available, bearing in mind the distinct legal regimes and remedies under international law applicable to illegal fishing and international organized crime;

V

Monitoring, control and surveillance and compliance and enforcement

60. *Calls upon* States, in accordance with international law, to strengthen implementation of or, where they do not exist, adopt comprehensive monitoring, control and surveillance measures and compliance and enforcement schemes individually and within those regional fisheries management organizations or arrangements in which they participate, in order to provide an appropriate framework for promoting compliance with agreed conservation and management measures, and further urges enhanced coordination among all relevant States and regional fisheries management organizations and arrangements in these efforts;

61. *Encourages* further work by competent international organizations, including the Food and Agriculture Organization of the United Nations and subregional and regional fisheries management organizations and arrangements, to develop guidelines on flag State control of fishing vessels;

62. *Urges* States, individually and through relevant regional fisheries management organizations and arrangements, to establish mandatory vessel monitoring, control and surveillance systems, in particular to require that vessel monitoring systems be carried by all vessels fishing on the high seas as soon as practicable, and in the case of large-scale fishing vessels no later than December 2008, and to share information on fisheries enforcement matters;

63. *Calls upon* States, individually and through regional fisheries management organizations or arrangements, to strengthen or establish, consistent with national and international law, positive or negative lists of vessels fishing within the areas covered by relevant regional fisheries management organizations and arrangements in order to verify compliance with conservation and management measures and identify products from illegal, unreported and unregulated catches, and encourages improved coordination among all parties and regional fisheries management organizations and arrangements in sharing and using this information, taking into account the forms of cooperation with developing States as set out in article 25 of the Agreement;

64. *Requests* States and relevant international bodies to develop, in accordance with international law, more effective measures to trace fish and fishery products to enable importing States to identify fish or fishery products caught in a manner that undermines international conservation and management measures agreed in accordance with international law, taking into account the special requirements of developing States and the forms of cooperation with developing States as set out in article 25 of the Agreement, and at the same time to recognize the importance of market access, in accordance with provisions 11.2.4, 11.2.5 and 11.2.6 of the Code, for fish and fishery products caught in a manner that is in conformity with such international measures;

65. *Requests* States to take the necessary measures, consistent with international law, to help to prevent fish and fishery products caught in a manner that undermines applicable conservation and management measures adopted in accordance with international law from entering international trade;

66. *Encourages* States to establish and undertake cooperative surveillance and enforcement activities in accordance with international law to strengthen and enhance efforts to ensure compliance with conservation and management measures, and prevent and deter illegal, unreported and unregulated fishing;

67. *Urges* States, individually and through regional fisheries management organizations or arrangements, to develop and adopt effective monitoring, control and surveillance measures for trans-shipment, as appropriate, in particular at-sea trans-shipment, in order to, inter alia, monitor compliance, collect and verify fisheries data, and to prevent and suppress illegal, unreported and unregulated fishing activities, in accordance with international law; and, in parallel, to encourage and support the Food and Agriculture Organization of the United Nations in studying the current practices of trans-shipment as it relates to fishing operations for straddling fish stocks and highly migratory fish stocks and produce a set of guidelines for this purpose;

68. *Expresses its appreciation* for financial contributions from States to improve the capacity of the existing voluntary International Monitoring, Control and Surveillance Network for Fisheries-Related Activities, and encourages States to join and actively participate in the Network and to consider supporting, when appropriate, its transformation in accordance with international law into an international unit with dedicated resources to further assist Network members, taking into account the forms of cooperation with developing States as set out in article 25 of the Agreement;

VI

Fishing overcapacity

69. *Calls upon* States to commit themselves to urgently reducing the capacity of the world's fishing fleets to levels commensurate with the sustainability of fish stocks, through the establishment of target levels and plans or other appropriate mechanisms for ongoing capacity assessment, while avoiding the transfer of fishing capacity to other fisheries or areas in a manner that undermines the sustainable management of fish stocks, including, inter alia, those areas where fish stocks are overexploited or in a depleted condition, and recognizing in this context the legitimate rights of developing States to develop their fisheries for straddling fish stocks and highly migratory fish stocks consistent with article 25 of the Agreement, article 5 of the Code, and paragraph 10 of the International Plan of Action for the Management of Fishing Capacity;

70. *Also calls upon* States, individually and through regional fisheries management organizations and arrangements, to ensure that the urgent actions required in the International Plan of Action for the Management of Fishing Capacity are undertaken expeditiously and that its implementation is facilitated without delay;

71. *Requests* the Food and Agriculture Organization of the United Nations to report on the state of progress in the implementation of the International Plan of Action for the Management of Fishing Capacity, as provided for in paragraph 48 of the Plan of Action;

72. *Encourages* those States which are cooperating to establish subregional and regional fisheries management organizations and arrangements, taking into account the best scientific information available as well as the precautionary approach, to exercise voluntary restraint of fishing effort levels in those areas that will come under the regulation of the future organizations and arrangements until adequate regional conservation and management measures are adopted and implemented, taking into account the need to ensure the long-term conservation, management and sustainable use of the relevant fish stocks and to prevent significant adverse impacts on vulnerable marine ecosystems;

73. *Urges* States to eliminate subsidies that contribute to illegal, unreported and unregulated fishing and to overfishing and overcapacity, while completing the efforts undertaken at the World Trade Organization in accordance with the Doha Declaration to clarify and improve its disciplines on fisheries subsidies, taking into account the importance of this sector, including small-scale and artisanal fisheries and aquaculture, to developing countries;

VII

Large-scale pelagic drift-net fishing

74. *Reaffirms* the importance it attaches to continued compliance with its resolution 46/215 and other subsequent resolutions on large-scale pelagic drift-net fishing, and urges States and entities referred to in the Convention and in article 1, paragraph 2 *(b)*, of the Agreement to enforce fully the measures recommended in those resolutions in order to eliminate the use of large-scale pelagic drift nets;

VIII

Fisheries by-catch and discards

75. *Urges* States, subregional and regional fisheries management organizations and arrangements and other relevant international organizations that have not done so to take action, including with consideration of the interests of developing coastal States and, as appropriate, subsistence fishing communities, to reduce or eliminate by-catch, catch by lost or abandoned gear, fish discards and post-harvest losses, including juvenile fish, consistent with international law and relevant international instruments, including the Code, and in particular to consider measures including, as appropriate, technical measures related to fish size, mesh size or gear, discards, closed seasons and areas and zones reserved for selected fisheries, particularly artisanal fisheries, the establishment of mechanisms for communicating

information on areas of high concentration of juvenile fish, taking into account the importance of ensuring the confidentiality of such information, and support for studies and research that will reduce or eliminate by-catch of juvenile fish, and to ensure that these measures are implemented so as to optimize their effectiveness;

76. *Encourages* States to consider the development of standards for reducing or eliminating discards, such as through the development of an international plan of action, at the twenty-eighth session of the Committee on Fisheries of the Food and Agriculture Organization of the United Nations;

77. *Encourages* States and entities referred to in the Convention and in article 1, paragraph 2 *(b)*, of the Agreement to give due consideration to participation, as appropriate, in subregional and regional instruments and organizations with mandates to conserve non-target species taken incidentally in fishing operations;

78. *Encourages* States to strengthen, if necessary, the capacity of those subregional and regional fisheries management organizations and arrangements in which they participate to ensure the adequate conservation of non-target species taken incidentally in fishing operations, taking into consideration best practices for non-target species management, and to expedite their ongoing efforts in this regard;

79. *Requests* States and regional fisheries management organizations and arrangements to urgently implement, as appropriate, the measures recommended in the Guidelines to Reduce Sea Turtle Mortality in Fishing Operations and the International Plan of Action for Reducing Incidental Catch of Seabirds in Longline Fisheries of the Food and Agriculture Organization of the United Nations in order to prevent the decline of sea turtles and seabird populations by minimizing by-catch and increasing post-release survival in their fisheries, including through research and development of gear and bait alternatives, promoting the use of available by-catch mitigation technology, and establishing and strengthening data-collection programmes to obtain standardized information to develop reliable estimates of the by-catch of these species;

IX

Subregional and regional cooperation

80. *Urges* coastal States and States fishing on the high seas, in accordance with the Convention, the Agreement and other relevant instruments, to pursue cooperation in relation to straddling fish stocks and highly migratory fish stocks, either directly or through appropriate subregional or regional fisheries management organizations or arrangements, to ensure the effective conservation and management of such stocks;

81. *Urges* States fishing for straddling fish stocks and highly migratory fish stocks on the high seas, and relevant coastal States, where a subregional or regional fisheries management organization or arrangement has the competence to establish conservation and management measures for such stocks, to give effect to their duty to cooperate by becoming members of such an organization or participants in such an arrangement, or by agreeing to apply the conservation and management measures established by such an organization or arrangement, or to otherwise ensure that no vessel flying their flag is authorized to access the fisheries resources to which regional fisheries management organizations and arrangements or conservation and management measures established by such organizations or arrangements apply;

82. *Invites*, in this regard, subregional and regional fisheries management organizations and arrangements to ensure that all States having a real interest in the fisheries concerned may become members of such organizations or participants in such arrangements, in accordance with the Convention, the Agreement and the Code;

83. *Encourages* relevant coastal States and States fishing on the high seas for a straddling fish stock or a highly migratory fish stock, where there is no subregional or regional fisheries management organization or arrangement to establish conservation and management measures for such stocks, to cooperate to establish such an organization or enter into another appropriate arrangement to ensure the conservation and management of such stocks, and to participate in the work of the organization or arrangement;

84. *Urges* all signatory States and other States whose vessels fish within the area of the Convention on the Conservation and Management of Fishery Resources in the South-East Atlantic Ocean for fishery resources covered by that Convention to become parties to that Convention as a matter of priority and, in the interim, to ensure that vessels flying their flags fully comply with the measures adopted;

85. *Encourages* signatory States and States having a real interest to become parties to the South Indian Ocean Fisheries Agreement, and urges those States to agree on and implement interim measures, including measures in accordance with resolution 61/105, to ensure the conservation and management of the fisheries resources and their marine ecosystems and habitats in the area to which that Agreement applies until such time as that Agreement enters into force;

86. *Takes note* of recent efforts at the regional level to promote responsible fishing practices, including combating illegal, unreported and unregulated fishing;

87. *Notes with satisfaction* the progress of negotiations to establish subregional and regional fisheries management organizations or arrangements in several fisheries, in particular in the North-West Pacific and the South Pacific, encourages States having a real interest to participate in such negotiations, urges participants to expedite those negotiations and to apply provisions of the Convention and the Agreement to their work, and encourages those participants to implement fully the voluntary interim conservation and management measures adopted in accordance with resolution 61/105;

88. *Takes note* of the ongoing efforts of the members of the Indian Ocean Tuna Commission to strengthen the functioning of the Commission so that it can more effectively discharge its mandate, and requests the Food and Agriculture Organization of the United Nations to continue to provide members of the Commission with the necessary assistance to this end;

89. *Urges* further efforts by regional fisheries management organizations and arrangements, as a matter of priority, in accordance with international law, to strengthen and modernize their mandates and the measures adopted by such organizations or arrangements, and to implement modern approaches to fisheries management, as reflected

in the Agreement and other relevant international instruments, relying on the best scientific information available and application of the precautionary approach and incorporating an ecosystem approach to fisheries management and biodiversity considerations, where these aspects are lacking, to ensure that they effectively contribute to long-term conservation and management and sustainable use of marine living resources;

90. *Calls upon* regional fisheries management organizations with the competence to conserve and manage highly migratory fish stocks that have not yet adopted effective conservation and management measures in line with the best scientific information available to conserve and manage stocks falling under their mandate to do so urgently;

91. *Urges* States to strengthen and enhance cooperation among existing and developing regional fisheries management organizations and arrangements in which they participate, including increased communication and further coordination of measures, such as through the holding of joint consultations, and to strengthen integration, coordination and cooperation by such regional fisheries management organizations and arrangements with other relevant fisheries organizations, regional seas arrangements and other relevant international organizations;

92. *Welcomes* the meeting to be held in 2009 of the members, cooperating members and non-members of the five tuna regional fisheries management organizations to review progress and discuss ways to expedite the implementation of, and build upon, the agreed Course of Actions adopted in Kobe, Japan, in January 2007;

93. *Urges* regional fisheries management organizations and arrangements to improve transparency and to ensure that their decision-making processes are fair and transparent, rely on the best scientific information available, incorporate the precautionary approach and ecosystem approaches, address participatory rights, including through, inter alia, the development of transparent criteria for allocating fishing opportunities which reflects, where appropriate, the relevant provisions of the Agreement, taking due account, inter alia, of the status of the relevant stocks and the respective interests in the fishery;

94. *Welcomes* the progress made by some regional fisheries management organizations and arrangements to initiate performance reviews, and the fact that the Commission for the Conservation of Southern Bluefin Tuna, the International Commission for the Conservation of Atlantic Tunas and the North East Atlantic Fisheries Commission, as well as the Commission for the Conservation of Antarctic Marine Living Resources, have completed performance reviews, and urges States, through their participation in regional fisheries management organizations and arrangements that have not done so, to undertake, on an urgent basis, performance reviews of those regional fisheries management organizations and arrangements, initiated either by the organization or arrangement itself or with external partners, including in cooperation with the Food and Agriculture Organization of the United Nations, using transparent criteria based on the provisions of the Agreement and other relevant instruments, and taking into account the best practices of regional fisheries management organizations or arrangements and, as appropriate, any set of criteria developed by States or other regional fisheries management organizations or arrangements, and encourages that such performance reviews include some element of independent evaluation and propose means for improving the functioning of the regional fisheries management organization or arrangement, as appropriate;

95. *Encourages* regional fisheries management organizations and arrangements to make the results of those performance reviews publicly available and to discuss the results jointly;

96. *Urges* States to cooperate, taking into account those performance reviews, to develop best practice guidelines for regional fisheries management organizations and arrangements and to apply, to the extent possible, those guidelines to organizations and arrangements in which they participate;

97. *Encourages* the development of regional guidelines for States to use in establishing sanctions for non-compliance by vessels flying their flag and by their nationals, to be applied in accordance with national law, that are adequate in severity for effectively securing compliance, deterring further violations and depriving offenders of the benefits deriving from their illegal activities, as well as in evaluating their systems of sanctions to ensure that they are effective in securing compliance and deterring violations;

X

Responsible fisheries in the marine ecosystem

98. *Encourages* States to apply by 2010 the ecosystem approach, in accordance with paragraph 30 *(d)* of the Johannesburg Plan of Implementation;

99. *Also encourages* States, individually or through regional fisheries management organizations and arrangements and other relevant international organizations, to work to ensure that fisheries and other ecosystem data collection is performed in a coordinated and integrated manner, facilitating incorporation into global observation initiatives, where appropriate;

100. *Further encourages* States to increase scientific research in accordance with international law on the marine ecosystem;

101. *Calls upon* States, the Food and Agriculture Organization of the United Nations and other specialized agencies, subregional and regional fisheries management organizations and arrangements, where appropriate, and other appropriate intergovernmental bodies, to cooperate in achieving sustainable aquaculture, including through information exchange, developing equivalent standards on such issues as aquatic animal health and human health and safety concerns, assessing the potential positive and negative impacts of aquaculture, including socio-economics, on the marine and coastal environment, including biodiversity, and adopting relevant methods and techniques to minimize and mitigate adverse effects, and in this regard encourages the implementation of the Strategy and Outline Plan for Improving Information on Status and Trends of Aquaculture of the Food and Agriculture Organization of the United Nations, as a framework for the improvement and understanding of aquaculture status and trends;

102. *Calls upon* States to take action immediately, individually and through regional fisheries management organizations and arrangements, and consistent with the precautionary approach and ecosystem approaches, and

urges the implementation of the International Guidelines for the Management of Deep-sea Fisheries in the High Seas of the Food and Agriculture Organization of the United Nations in order to sustainably manage fish stocks and protect vulnerable marine ecosystems, including seamounts, hydrothermal vents and cold water corals, from destructive fishing practices, recognizing the immense importance and value of deep sea ecosystems and the biodiversity they contain;

103. *Reaffirms* the importance it attaches to paragraphs 83 to 91 of resolution 61/105 addressing the impacts of bottom fishing on vulnerable marine ecosystems and the urgent actions called for in that resolution;

104. *Recalls* that nothing in paragraphs 83 to 86 of resolution 61/105 is to prejudice the sovereign rights of coastal States over their continental shelf or the exercise of the jurisdiction of coastal States with regard to that shelf under international law as reflected in the Convention;

105. *Welcomes* the further progress in regulating bottom fisheries in accordance with resolution 61/105 by the Commission for the Conservation of Antarctic Marine Living Resources, the General Fisheries Commission for the Mediterranean, the North East Atlantic Fisheries Commission, the Northwest Atlantic Fisheries Organization and the South-East Atlantic Fisheries Organization, and by the participants in negotiations to establish subregional and regional fisheries management organizations or arrangements in the North-West Pacific and the South Pacific, as well as by States in respect of vessels flying their flag conducting bottom fisheries in areas beyond national jurisdiction where there is no regional fisheries management organization or arrangement competent to regulate such fisheries or for which no multilateral interim measures to this end have been adopted;

106. *Urges* States, including States participating in negotiations to establish new regional fisheries management organizations or arrangements with the competence to regulate bottom fisheries, and regional fisheries management organizations or arrangements with the competence to regulate bottom fisheries, to continue, and expedite where necessary, their efforts to fully and effectively implement measures in accordance with paragraphs 80 and 83 to 87 of resolution 61/105;

107. *Requests* the Secretary-General, in cooperation with the Food and Agriculture Organization of the United Nations, to report to the General Assembly at its sixty-fourth session on the actions taken by States and regional fisheries management organizations and arrangements to give effect to paragraphs 83 to 90 of resolution 61/105, in order to facilitate the further review of progress on actions taken, referred to in paragraph 91 of that resolution, with a view to further recommendations, where necessary;

108. *Requests* States and regional fisheries management organizations and arrangements to submit detailed information to the Secretary-General in a timely manner on actions taken pursuant to paragraphs 83 to 90 of resolution 61/105 to facilitate a further review of such actions;

109. *Encourages* accelerated progress to establish criteria on the objectives and management of marine protected areas for fisheries purposes, and in this regard welcomes the proposed work of the Food and Agriculture Organization of the United Nations to develop technical guidelines in accordance with the Convention and the Code on the design, implementation and testing of marine protected areas for such purposes, and urges coordination and cooperation among all relevant international organizations and bodies;

110. *Urges* all States to implement the Global Programme of Action for the Protection of the Marine Environment from Land-based Activities and to accelerate activity to safeguard the marine ecosystem, including fish stocks, against pollution and physical degradation;

111. *Reaffirms* the importance it attaches to paragraphs 77 to 81 of resolution 60/31 concerning the issue of lost, abandoned, or discarded fishing gear and related marine debris and the adverse impacts such debris and derelict fishing gear have on, inter alia, fish stocks, habitats and other marine species, and urges accelerated progress by States and regional fisheries management organizations and arrangements in implementing those paragraphs of the resolution;

XI

Capacity-building

112. *Reiterates* the crucial importance of cooperation by States directly or, as appropriate, through the relevant subregional and regional organizations, and by other international organizations, including the Food and Agriculture Organization of the United Nations through its FishCode programme, including through financial and/or technical assistance, in accordance with the Agreement, the Compliance Agreement, the Code and its associated international plans of action, to increase the capacity of developing States to achieve the goals and implement the actions called for in the present resolution;

113. *Welcomes* the work of the Food and Agriculture Organization of the United Nations in developing guidance on the strategies and measures required for the creation of an enabling environment for small-scale fisheries, including the development of a code of conduct and guidelines for enhancing the contribution of small-scale fisheries to poverty alleviation and food security that include adequate provisions with regard to financial measures and capacity-building, including transfer of technology, and encourages studies for creating possible alternative livelihoods for coastal communities;

114. *Encourages* increased capacity-building and technical assistance by States, international financial institutions and relevant intergovernmental organizations and bodies for fishers, in particular small-scale fishers, in developing countries, and in particular small island developing States, consistent with environmental sustainability;

115. *Encourages* the international community to enhance the opportunities for sustainable development in developing countries, in particular the least developed countries, small island developing States and coastal African States, by encouraging greater participation of those States in authorized fisheries activities being undertaken within areas under their national jurisdiction, in accordance with the Convention, by distant-water fishing nations in order to achieve better economic returns for developing countries from their fisheries resources within areas under their national jurisdiction and an enhanced role in regional fisheries management, as well as by enhancing the ability of developing countries to develop their own fisher-

ies, as well as to participate in high seas fisheries, including access to such fisheries, in conformity with international law, in particular the Convention and the Agreement, and taking into account article 5 of the Code;

116. *Requests* distant-water fishing nations, when negotiating access agreements and arrangements with developing coastal States, to do so on an equitable and sustainable basis, including by giving greater attention to fish processing and fish-processing facilities within the national jurisdiction of the developing coastal State to assist the realization of the benefits from the development of fisheries resources, and also the transfer of technology and assistance for monitoring, control and surveillance and compliance and enforcement within areas under the national jurisdiction of the developing coastal State providing fisheries access, taking into account the forms of cooperation set out in article 25 of the Agreement and article 5 of the Code;

117. *Encourages* States, individually and through regional fisheries management organizations and arrangements, to provide greater assistance and to promote coherence in such assistance for developing States in designing, establishing and implementing relevant agreements, instruments and tools for the conservation and sustainable management of fish stocks, including in designing and strengthening their domestic regulatory fisheries policies and those of regional fisheries management organizations or arrangements in their regions, and the enhancement of research and scientific capabilities through existing funds, such as the Assistance Fund under Part VII of the Agreement, bilateral assistance, regional fisheries management organizations and arrangements assistance funds, the FishCode programme, the World Bank's global programme on fisheries and the Global Environment Facility;

118. *Calls upon* States to promote, through continuing dialogue and the assistance and cooperation provided in accordance with articles 24 to 26 of the Agreement, further ratification of or accession to the Agreement by seeking to address, inter alia, the issue of lack of capacity and resources that might stand in the way of developing States becoming parties;

119. *Notes with satisfaction* the efforts undertaken by the Secretary-General to gather information on assistance and resources available for developing States to assist them in becoming parties to the Agreement and in implementing the Agreement, and looks forward to the compilation and publication of this information for the use of States;

120. *Encourages* States, regional fisheries management organizations and arrangements and other relevant bodies to assist developing States in the implementation of the actions called for in paragraphs 83 to 91 of resolution 61/105;

XII

Cooperation within the United Nations system

121. *Requests* the relevant parts of the United Nations system, international financial institutions and donor agencies to support increased enforcement and compliance capabilities for regional fisheries management organizations and their member States;

122. *Invites* the Food and Agriculture Organization of the United Nations to continue its cooperative arrangements with United Nations agencies on the implementation of the international plans of action and to report to the Secretary-General, for inclusion in his annual report on sustainable fisheries, on priorities for cooperation and coordination in this work;

XIII

Sixty-fourth session of the General Assembly

123. *Requests* the Secretary-General to bring the present resolution to the attention of all members of the international community, relevant intergovernmental organizations, the organizations and bodies of the United Nations system, subregional and regional fisheries management organizations and relevant non-governmental organizations, and to invite them to provide the Secretary-General with information relevant to the implementation of the present resolution;

124. *Also requests* the Secretary-General to submit to the General Assembly at its sixty-fifth session a report on "Sustainable fisheries, including through the 1995 Agreement for the Implementation of the Provisions of the United Nations Convention on the Law of the Sea of 10 December 1982 relating to the Conservation and Management of Straddling Fish Stocks and Highly Migratory Fish Stocks, and related instruments", taking into account information provided by States, relevant specialized agencies, in particular the Food and Agriculture Organization of the United Nations, and other appropriate organs, organizations and programmes of the United Nations system, subregional and regional organizations and arrangements for the conservation and management of straddling fish stocks and highly migratory fish stocks, as well as other relevant intergovernmental bodies and non-governmental organizations, and consisting, inter alia, of elements provided in relevant paragraphs in the present resolution;

125. *Decides* to include in the provisional agenda of its sixty-fourth session, under the item entitled "Oceans and the law of the sea", the sub-item entitled "Sustainable fisheries, including through the 1995 Agreement for the Implementation of the Provisions of the United Nations Convention on the Law of the Sea of 10 December 1982 relating to the Conservation and Management of Straddling Fish Stocks and Highly Migratory Fish Stocks, and related instruments".

Institutions created by the Convention

International Seabed Authority

Through the International Seabed Authority, established by UNCLOS and the 1994 Implementation Agreement [YUN 1994, p. 1301], States organized and conducted exploration of the resources of the seabed and ocean floor and subsoil beyond the limits of national jurisdiction. In 2008, the Authority, which had 157 members as at 31 December, held its fourteenth session (Kingston, Jamaica, 26 May–6 June) [ISBA/14/A/1]. Its subsidiary bodies, namely, the Assembly, the Council, the Legal and Technical Commission and the Finance Committee, also met during the session.

The Assembly considered the annual report of the Authority's Secretary-General [ISBA/14/A/2], which reviewed the Authority's work since the thirteenth session and outlined the future work programme of the secretariat. The Authority continued to develop a geological model of polymetallic nodule deposits in the Clarion-Clipperton fracture zone (East Pacific Ocean), and planned to start work on a geological model of polymetallic nodule deposits in the Central Indian Ocean basin during 2009. The Authority remained the only international body with the responsibility of administering a global commons for the benefit of humankind, and its purpose was to encourage the orderly development of the resources of the deep seabed so that the international community as a whole might benefit from them.

The Authority had made significant progress in implementing the substantive tasks it identified in 1997 [YUN 1997, p. 1357]. The regulatory framework for prospecting and exploration for polymetallic nodules was completed in 2000 and significant progress was made in elaborating a similar regulatory framework for polymetallic sulphides and cobalt-rich ferromanganese crusts. The Authority had also developed preliminary environmental guidelines for mineral exploration in the Area (the seabed and ocean floor and subsoil beyond the limits of national jurisdiction) and completed a resource assessment of the areas reserved for the Authority. One of the milestones for the Authority was to provide formal recognition of the claims of former registered pioneer investors, bringing them within the single regime created by the Convention and the 1994 Agreement.

As the incumbent Secretary-General, Satya N. Nandan, would end his term of office on 31 December, the Council proposed candidate Nii Allotey Odunton (Ghana) for election as Secretary-General. The Assembly elected Mr. Odunton on 5 June [ISBA/14/A/9], for a four-year term beginning on 1 January 2009.

The Legal and Technical Commission reported to the Council on its work during the fourteenth session [ISBA/14/C/8]. It requested the secretariat to prepare a more detailed report and analysis of actual and proposed financial expenditures reported by the eight contractors exploring for polymetallic nodules in the Area. The Commission noted that there was still a lack of raw data being provided by contractors despite repeated requests from both the Commission and the Secretary-General. With regard to the classification into nodule types, the Commission noted that there was no uniformity in classifications used by different contractors and suggested that it might be useful for contractors to collaborate on standardizing such classifications. It took note of the oral report on the progress on the geological model for the Clarion-Clipperton Zone, and noted that the project was in the completion phase.

The Finance Committee held five meetings during the session [ISBA/14/A/7-ISBA/14/C/6] and recommended the approval of the proposed budget of the International Seabed Authority for the 2009–2010 financial period, amounting to $12,516,500, which the Assembly approved on 5 June.

Joint project. A report of the Secretary-General of the International Seabed Authority [A/AC.276/1] summarized the results of a joint project of the Authority with the J.M. Kaplan Fund to study biodiversity, species range and gene flow in the abyssal Pacific nodule province. The summary was prepared for the benefit of members of the Authority during the fourteenth session.

International Tribunal for the Law of the Sea

The International Tribunal for the Law of the Sea held its twenty-fifth (3–14 March) and twenty-sixth (24 September–7 October) sessions, both in Hamburg, Germany [SPLOS/191].

In the *Case concerning the Conservation and Sustainable Exploitation of Swordfish Stocks in the South-Eastern Pacific Ocean (Chile/European Community)*, by letters dated 20 and 23 October, respectively, the European Community and Chile informed the Registrar that they had agreed on a draft text of a new "Understanding concerning the conservation of swordfish stocks in the South-Eastern Pacific Ocean." The purpose of the "Understanding" was to concur on a bilateral fisheries cooperation framework for swordfish that should enable both parties to agree on discontinuing the proceedings before the Special Chamber. The Special Chamber considered the request of the parties on 10 and 11 December, and on 11 December it extended the time limit for making preliminary objections until 1 January 2010, maintaining the rights of the parties to revive the proceedings at any time.

Devoting a substantial part of its two sessions to the consideration of legal and judicial matters, the Tribunal examined various legal issues of relevance to its jurisdiction, rules and judicial procedures, and exchanged views on recent developments concerning law of the sea issues.

Commission on the Limits of the Continental Shelf

In 2008, the Commission on the Limits of the Continental Shelf, established in 1997 [YUN 1997, p. 1362], held its twenty-first (17 March–18 April) [CLCS/58] and twenty-second (11 August–12 September) [CLCS/60] sessions, both in New York. Among other things, it examined submissions by States regarding the establishment of the outer limits of the continental shelf beyond 200 nautical miles.

At the twenty-first session, the Commission adopted recommendations on the limits of the continental shelf in regard to the submission made by Australia in 2004 [YUN 2005, p. 1434] on the proposed outer limits of its continental shelf beyond 200 nautical miles. The Commission considered the submission made by New Zealand in 2006 [YUN 2006, p. 1555]; the joint submission, as well as a presentation, by France, Ireland, Spain and the United Kingdom; and submissions made by France, Mexico, and Norway. On 11 April, the Commission adopted its amended rules of procedure [CLCS/40/Rev.1].

At its twenty-second session, the Commission adopted recommendations on the limits of the continental shelf in regard to the submission made by New Zealand. The Commission continued to consider the joint submission made by France, Ireland, Spain and the United Kingdom, as well as submissions made by France, Mexico and Norway. It also examined submissions made by Barbados and the United Kingdom, but decided against establishing sub-commissions during the session.

Other developments related to the Convention

In response to General Assembly resolution 62/215 [YUN 2007, p. 1402], the Secretary-General submitted a March report, with a later addendum, on oceans and the law of the sea [A/63/63 & Add.1], detailing the status of UNCLOS and its implementing agreements, and reviewing developments regarding maritime space, security and safety, bodies established by UNCLOS, marine science and technology, conservation and management of marine fishery resources, marine biological diversity, and protection of the marine environment. The report also discussed matters relating to climate change, the settlement of disputes, international cooperation and coordination, and capacity-building activities.

Highlighting the importance of the oceans and seas for transportation, livelihood, food and a range of other ecosystem goods and services, the Secretary-General stated that all States shared in the benefits of safer and more secure oceans. The report also addressed major threats and challenges to maritime security and safety. While sustainable development of oceans and seas would ensure long-term human prosperity, the unsustainable use of the oceans, as well as the impact of human-induced climate change, would lead to the altering of oceans and seas, thereby affecting the environment, human well-being and economic development. The oceans played an essential role in the climate system, as ocean-climate coupling regulated and mitigated the exchange of heat, carbon and water within the Earth's systems. He stressed the need for international cooperation to enhance maritime security and safety. The sustainable use of marine resources and rational utilization of the oceans also required sustained international cooperation, including in the area of capacity-building. Priority needed to be given to the management of human activities that had an adverse impact on marine ecosystems, including their cumulative affect. Marine science programmes and technology played a vital role in that regard and required support.

In response to General Assembly resolution 61/222 [YUN 2006, p. 1557], the Secretary-General in September submitted a study [A/63/342] on the available assistance to and measures that could be taken by developing States, in particular the least developed States and small island developing States, as well as coastal African States, to realize the benefits of sustainable and effective development of marine resources and uses of the oceans within the limits of national jurisdiction. The study, which primarily focused on national measures, presented a list of proposed measures to be adopted by developing States. It also underscored that the benefits from the marine sector were substantially enhanced when bilateral, subregional and regional cooperation arrangements were in place.

Communications. By a February letter to the Secretary-General [A/62/697], Nicaragua highlighted the differences between Nicaragua and Colombia with respect to sovereignty over certain maritime spaces, islands and emerging areas located in the Caribbean Sea. Nicaragua had submitted that dispute to the International Court of Justice (ICJ) in 2001 [YUN 2001, p. 1195]. ICJ in 2007 had rendered its judgment on the preliminary objections by Colombia [YUN 2007, p. 1330]. In view of the Colombian authorities preventing Nicaraguan vessels from going to the east of the 82nd meridian, and a Colombian war frigate threatening the Nicaraguan fishing vessel "El Lady Dee III" in Nicaraguan waters, Nicaragua noted that the decisions of the ICJ should be treated as final and with utmost respect. Stating that Colombia's actions posed a threat to peace, Nicaragua stated that it would continue to exercise its rights in those maritime spaces for the benefit of its fishermen and other workers.

By a May letter [A/63/79 & Corr.1], the Co-Chairpersons of the Ad Hoc Open-ended Informal Working Group to study issues relating to the conservation and sustainable use of marine biological diversity beyond areas of national jurisdiction, established by General Assembly resolution 59/24 [YUN 2004, p. 1333], reported to the Assembly on its meeting (New York, 28 April–2 May), which recognized the need to ensure that all human activities in areas beyond national jurisdiction were conducted in a sustainable manner, based upon the best available science and the precautionary and ecosystem approaches. A number of proposals at the meeting addressed the conservation and sustainable use of marine biological diversity in areas beyond national jurisdiction in the short, medium and longer term.

By a May note addressed to the Secretary-General and the Presidents of the General Assembly and the Security Council [A/62/841-S/2008/310], Canada, Denmark, Greece, Japan, the Netherlands, Norway, the Republic of Korea and Spain stressed that piracy and armed robbery against commercial and humanitarian ships in the waters off Somalia posed a threat to the safety of international maritime traffic and international peace and security, and welcomed the ongoing initiative to protect the World Food Programme humanitarian convoys through the waters off Somalia, in effect since 2007. The Transitional Federal Government of Somalia, in a letter of 27 February addressed to the President of the Council, had requested immediate assistance in securing the international and territorial waters off the coast of Somalia for the safe conduct of shipping and navigation. The note stated that the Council initiatives under way to address the threat posed by piracy and armed robbery should be fully supported by Member States.

The International Convention on the Control of Harmful Anti-Fouling Systems on Ships of the International Maritime Organization (IMO) entered into force on 17 September. The treaty, adopted on 5 October 2001 [YUN 2001, p. 1426], banned the use of organotins and other harmful substances in antifouling paints used on ships' hulls.

On 2 June, by **resolution 1816(2008)**, the Security Council unanimously condemned acts of piracy and armed robbery off Somalia's coast and authorized for six months "all necessary means" to repress such acts (see p. 286).

Marine environment: Global Marine Assessment

The third meeting [GRAME/GOE/3/2] of the Group of Experts for the start-up phase, "assessment of assessments", of the regular process for the global reporting and assessment of the state of the marine environment, including socio-economic aspects, was held at the European Environment Agency headquarters (Copenhagen, 15–17 April). A preparatory meeting (4–5 March) was held at the same venue. The third meeting focused on preparing the first draft of the "assessment of assessments"; it agreed on the outlines for the report and assigned responsibilities to the members of the Group (see also p. 1167).

The fourth meeting [GRAME/GOE/4/1] of the Group of Experts for the "assessment of assessments" start-up phase was held at IMO headquarters (London, 4–6 November). A preparatory meeting (29 September–2 October) was held in Rome. The fourth meeting focused on finalizing the chapters of the report to be sent for government and expert peer-review.

The process was launched by General Assembly resolution 60/30 [YUN 2005, p. 1436], by which the Assembly established an Ad Hoc Steering Group and invited the United Nations Environment Programme and the Intergovernmental Oceanographic Commission of the United Nations Educational, Scientific and Cultural Organization to jointly lead the process of, among other things, producing a report for the Assembly on the results of the "assessment of assessments". The initial phase of the process came to be known that way because the Group of Experts, set up in 2006 [YUN 2006, p. 1557], was asked to examine various existing marine assessments. The start-up phase represented the first step of an international initiative to improve understanding of the oceans and to develop a global mechanism for delivering science-based information to decision-makers and the public.

United Nations Open-ended Informal Consultative Process

In response to General Assembly resolution 62/215 [YUN 2007, p. 1402], the ninth meeting of the United Nations Open-ended Informal Consultative Process on Oceans and the Law of the Sea (New York, 23–27 June) [A/63/174 & Corr.1] focused on maritime security and safety. At the meeting, various aspects of maritime security and safety were addressed at the plenary and in five panels. Participants also addressed inter-agency cooperation and coordination and recommended topics for further consideration, including oceans and sustainable development; integration of environmental, social and economic concerns; contribution of oceans to the achievement of internationally agreed sustainable development goals, including the Millennium Development Goals; and cooperation and coordination among flag, coastal and port States.

In a report on the treatment of persons rescued at sea [A/AC.259/17], the Office of the United Nations High Commissioner for Refugees stressed that human rights and refugee law principles provided an important point of reference in handling rescue at sea situations involving irregular maritime migrants.

GENERAL ASSEMBLY ACTION

On 5 December [meeting 64], the General Assembly adopted **resolution 63/111** [draft: A/63/L.42 & Add.1] by recorded vote (155-1-4) [agenda item 70 *(a)*].

Oceans and the law of the sea

The General Assembly,

Recalling its annual resolutions on the law of the sea and on oceans and the law of the sea, including resolution 62/215 of 22 December 2007, and other relevant resolutions concerning the United Nations Convention on the Law of the Sea ("the Convention"),

Having considered the report of the Secretary-General, the joint statement of the Co-Chairpersons of the Ad Hoc Open-ended Informal Working Group to study issues relating to the conservation and sustainable use of marine biological diversity beyond areas of national jurisdiction ("the Ad Hoc Open-ended Informal Working Group") and also the reports on the work of the United Nations Open-ended Informal Consultative Process on Oceans and the Law of the Sea ("the Consultative Process") at its ninth meeting and on the eighteenth Meeting of States Parties to the Convention,

Emphasizing the pre-eminent contribution provided by the Convention to the strengthening of peace, security, cooperation and friendly relations among all nations in conformity with the principles of justice and equal rights and to the promotion of the economic and social advancement of all peoples of the world, in accordance with the purposes and principles of the United Nations as set forth in the Charter of the United Nations, as well as to the sustainable development of the oceans and seas,

Emphasizing also the universal and unified character of the Convention, and reaffirming that the Convention sets out the legal framework within which all activities in the oceans and seas must be carried out and is of strategic importance as the basis for national, regional and global action and cooperation in the marine sector, and that its integrity needs to be maintained, as recognized also by the United Nations Conference on Environment and Development in chapter 17 of Agenda 21,

Recognizing the important contribution of sustainable development and management of the resources and uses of the oceans and seas to the achievement of international development goals, including those contained in the United Nations Millennium Declaration,

Conscious that the problems of ocean space are closely interrelated and need to be considered as a whole through an integrated, interdisciplinary and intersectoral approach, and reaffirming the need to improve cooperation and coordination at the national, regional and global levels, in accordance with the Convention, to support and supplement the efforts of each State in promoting the implementation and observance of the Convention, and the integrated management and sustainable development of the oceans and seas,

Reiterating the essential need for cooperation, including through capacity-building and transfer of marine technology, to ensure that all States, especially developing countries, in particular the least developed countries and small island developing States, as well as coastal African States, are able both to implement the Convention and to benefit from the sustainable development of the oceans and seas, as well as to participate fully in global and regional forums and processes dealing with oceans and law of the sea issues,

Emphasizing the need to strengthen the ability of competent international organizations to contribute, at the global, regional, subregional and bilateral levels, through cooperation programmes with Governments, to the development of national capacity in marine science and the sustainable management of the oceans and their resources,

Recalling that marine science is important for eradicating poverty, contributing to food security, conserving the world's marine environment and resources, helping to understand, predict and respond to natural events and promoting the sustainable development of the oceans and seas, by improving knowledge, through sustained research efforts and the evaluation of monitoring results, and applying such knowledge to management and decision-making,

Recalling also its decision, in resolutions 57/141 of 12 December 2002 and 58/240 of 23 December 2003, to establish a regular process under the United Nations for global reporting and assessment of the state of the marine environment, including socio-economic aspects, both current and foreseeable, building on existing regional assessments, as recommended by the World Summit on Sustainable Development, and noting the need for cooperation among all States to this end,

Reiterating its concern at the adverse impacts on the marine environment and biodiversity, in particular on vulnerable marine ecosystems, including corals, of human activities, such as overutilization of living marine resources, the use of destructive practices, physical impacts by ships, the introduction of invasive alien species and marine pollution from all sources, including from land-based sources and vessels, in particular through the illegal and accidental discharge of oil and other harmful substances, the loss or release of fishing gear and the illegal or accidental release of hazardous waste such as radioactive materials, nuclear waste and dangerous chemicals,

Expressing deep concern over the adverse economic, social and environmental impacts of the physical alteration and destruction of marine habitats that may result from land-based and coastal development activities, in particular those land reclamation activities that are carried out in a manner that has a detrimental impact on the marine environment,

Reiterating its serious concern over the current and projected adverse effects of climate change on the marine environment and marine biodiversity, and emphasizing the urgency of addressing this issue,

Expressing concern that climate change has increased the severity and incidence of coral bleaching throughout tropical seas over the past two decades and has weakened the ability of reefs to withstand ocean acidification, which could have serious and irreversible negative effects on marine organisms, particularly corals, as well as to withstand other pressures, including overfishing and pollution,

Reiterating its deep concern over the vulnerability of the environment and the fragile ecosystems of the polar regions, including the Arctic Ocean and the Arctic ice cap, particularly affected by the projected adverse effects of climate change,

Encouraging States to continue to contribute to the specific efforts deployed within the framework of the International Polar Year with the goal of enhancing the knowledge of the polar regions by strengthening scientific cooperation,

Recognizing that there is a need for a more integrated approach and to further study and promote measures for enhanced cooperation, coordination and collaboration relating to the conservation and sustainable use of marine biodiversity beyond areas of national jurisdiction,

Recognizing also that the realization of the benefits of the Convention could be enhanced by international cooperation, technical assistance and advanced scientific knowledge, as well as by funding and capacity-building,

Recognizing further that hydrographic surveys and nautical charting are critical to the safety of navigation and life at sea, environmental protection, including the protection of vulnerable marine ecosystems, and the economics of the global shipping industry, and recognizing in this regard that the move towards electronic charting not only provides significantly increased benefits for safe navigation and management of ship movement, but also provides data and information that can be used for sustainable fisheries activities and other sectoral uses of the marine environment, the delimitation of maritime boundaries and environmental protection,

Noting with concern the continuing problem of transnational organized crime committed at sea, including illicit traffic in narcotic drugs and psychotropic substances, the smuggling of migrants and trafficking in persons, and threats to maritime safety and security, including piracy, armed robbery at sea, smuggling and terrorist acts against shipping, offshore installations and other maritime interests, and noting the deplorable loss of life and adverse impact on international trade, energy security and the global economy resulting from such activities,

Noting the importance of the delineation of the outer limits of the continental shelf beyond 200 nautical miles and that it is in the broader interest of the international community that coastal States with a continental shelf beyond 200 nautical miles submit information on the outer limits of the continental shelf beyond 200 nautical miles to the Commission on the Limits of the Continental Shelf ("the Commission"), noting also in this regard that several States have already made submissions to the Commission and that the Commission has made recommendations for a number of those States, and welcoming the fact that summaries of recommendations have been made publicly available,

Noting also that some States may face particular challenges in relation to preparing submissions to the Commission,

Noting further that financial and technical assistance may be sought by developing countries for activities in relation to preparing submissions to the Commission, including through the voluntary trust fund established by resolution 55/7 of 30 October 2000 for the purpose of facilitating the preparation of submissions to the Commission for developing States, in particular the least developed countries and small island developing States, and compliance with article 76 of the Convention, as well as other accessible international assistance,

Recognizing the important role for developing countries of the trust funds established by resolution 55/7 for the activities of the Commission, and noting with appreciation the recent contributions made to them,

Reaffirming the importance of the work of the Commission for coastal States and the international community as a whole,

Noting the important role of the Commission in assisting States parties in the implementation of Part VI of the Convention, through the examination of information submitted by coastal States regarding the outer limits of the continental shelf beyond 200 nautical miles, and acknowledging in this regard the anticipated workload of the Commission owing to an increasing number of submissions, placing additional demands on its members and on the Division for Ocean Affairs and the Law of the Sea of the Office of Legal Affairs of the Secretariat ("the Division"), and the need to ensure that the Commission can perform its functions under the Convention effectively and maintain its high level of quality and expertise,

Welcoming the decision of the eighteenth Meeting of States Parties to the Convention regarding the workload of the Commission and the ability of States, particularly developing States, to fulfil the requirements of article 4 of annex II to the Convention, as well as the decision contained in SPLOS/72, paragraph *(a)*,

Recognizing the importance and the contribution of the work over the past nine years of the Consultative Process established by resolution 54/33 of 24 November 1999 and extended by resolutions 57/141 and 60/30 of 29 November 2005 to facilitate the annual review of developments in ocean affairs by the General Assembly,

Noting the responsibilities of the Secretary-General under the Convention and related resolutions of the General Assembly, in particular resolutions 49/28 of 6 December 1994, 52/26 of 26 November 1997 and 54/33, and in this context the increase in activities of the Division, in particular in view of the growing number of requests to the Division for additional outputs and servicing of meetings, its increasing capacity-building activities, the need for enhanced support and assistance to the Commission and the role of the Division in inter-agency coordination and cooperation,

Emphasizing that underwater archaeological, cultural and historical heritage, including shipwrecks and watercrafts, holds essential information on the history of humankind and that such heritage is a resource that needs to be protected and preserved,

Reaffirming the importance of the work of the International Seabed Authority ("the Authority") in accordance with the Convention and the Agreement relating to the Implementation of Part XI of the United Nations Convention on the Law of the Sea of 10 December 1982 ("the Part XI Agreement"),

Reaffirming also the importance of the work of the International Tribunal for the Law of the Sea ("the Tribunal") in accordance with the Convention,

I

Implementation of the Convention and related agreements and instruments

1. *Reaffirms* its annual resolutions on the law of the sea and on oceans and the law of the sea, including resolution 62/215, and other relevant resolutions concerning the Convention;

2. *Also reaffirms* the unified character of the Convention and the vital importance of preserving its integrity;

3. *Calls upon* all States that have not done so, in order to achieve the goal of universal participation, to become parties to the Convention and the Part XI Agreement;

4. *Calls upon* States that have not done so, in order to achieve the goal of universal participation, to become parties to the Agreement for the Implementation of the Provisions of the United Nations Convention on the Law of the Sea of 10 December 1982 relating to the Conservation and Management of Straddling Fish Stocks and Highly Migratory Fish Stocks ("the Fish Stocks Agreement");

5. *Calls upon* States to harmonize their national legislation with the provisions of the Convention and, where applicable, relevant agreements and instruments, to ensure the consistent application of those provisions and to ensure also that any declarations or statements that they have made or make when signing, ratifying or acceding to the Convention do not purport to exclude or to modify the legal effect of the provisions of the Convention in their application to the State concerned and to withdraw any such declarations or statements;

6. *Calls upon* States parties to the Convention to deposit with the Secretary-General charts or lists of geographical coordinates, as provided for in the Convention;

7. *Urges* all States to cooperate, directly or through competent international bodies, in taking measures to protect and preserve objects of an archaeological and historical nature found at sea, in conformity with the Convention, and calls upon States to work together on such diverse challenges and opportunities as the appropriate relationship between salvage law and scientific management and conservation of underwater cultural heritage, increasing technological abilities to discover and reach underwater sites, looting and growing underwater tourism;

8. *Notes* the forthcoming entry into force of the 2001 Convention on the Protection of the Underwater Cultural Heritage, and notes in particular the rules annexed thereto, which address the relationship between salvage law and scientific principles of management, conservation and protection of underwater cultural heritage among parties, their nationals and vessels flying their flag;

II

Capacity-building

9. *Calls upon* donor agencies and international financial institutions to keep their programmes systematically under review to ensure the availability in all States, particularly in developing States, of the economic, legal, navigational, scientific and technical skills necessary for the full implementation of the Convention and the objectives of the present resolution, as well as the sustainable development of the oceans and seas nationally, regionally and globally, and in so doing to bear in mind the interests and needs of landlocked developing States;

10. *Encourages* intensified efforts to build capacity for developing countries, in particular for the least developed countries and small island developing States, as well as coastal African States, to improve hydrographic services and the production of nautical charts, including electronic charts, as well as the mobilization of resources and building of capacity with support from international financial institutions and the donor community;

11. *Calls upon* States and international financial institutions, including through bilateral, regional and global cooperation programmes and technical partnerships, to continue to strengthen capacity-building activities, in particular in developing countries, in the field of marine scientific research by, inter alia, training personnel to develop and enhance relevant expertise, providing the necessary equipment, facilities and vessels and transferring environmentally sound technologies;

12. *Also calls upon* States and international financial institutions, including through bilateral, regional and global cooperation programmes and technical partnerships, to strengthen capacity-building activities in developing countries, in particular least developed countries and small island developing States, to develop their maritime administration and appropriate legal frameworks to establish or enhance the necessary infrastructure, legislative and enforcement capabilities to promote effective compliance with, and implementation and enforcement of, their responsibilities under international law;

13. *Recognizes* the importance of the work of the International Maritime Law Institute of the International Maritime Organization as a centre of education and training of Government legal advisers, mainly from developing States, notes that the number of its graduates in more than 102 States confirms its effective capacity-building role in the field of international law, and urges States, intergovernmental organizations and financial institutions to make voluntary financial contributions to the budget of the Institute;

14. *Welcomes* ongoing activities for capacity-building so as to address maritime security and safety needs and the protection of the marine environment of developing States, and encourages States and international financial institutions to provide additional funding for capacity-building programmes, including for transfer of technology, including through the International Maritime Organization and other competent international organizations;

15. *Recognizes* the considerable need to provide sustained capacity-building assistance, including on financial and technical aspects, by relevant international organizations and donors to developing States, with a view to further strengthening their capacity to take effective measures against the multiple facets of international criminal activities at sea, in line with the relevant international instruments, including the United Nations Convention against Transnational Organized Crime and the Protocols thereto;

16. *Also recognizes* the need to build the capacity of developing States to raise awareness of, and support the implementation of, improved waste management practices, noting the particular vulnerability of small island developing States to the impact of marine pollution from land-based sources and marine debris;

17. *Further recognizes* the importance of assisting developing States, in particular the least developed countries and small island developing States, as well as coastal African States, in implementing the Convention, and urges States, intergovernmental organizations and agencies, national institutions, non-governmental organizations and international financial institutions, as well as natural and

juridical persons, to make voluntary financial or other contributions to the trust funds, as referred to in resolution 57/141, established for this purpose;

18. *Encourages* States to use the Criteria and Guidelines on the Transfer of Marine Technology adopted by the Assembly of the Intergovernmental Oceanographic Commission of the United Nations Educational, Scientific and Cultural Organization, and recalls the important role of the secretariat of that Commission in the implementation and promotion of the Criteria and Guidelines;

19. *Calls upon* States to assist developing States, and especially the least developed countries and small island developing States, as well as coastal African States, at the bilateral and, where appropriate, multilateral levels, in the preparation of submissions to the Commission regarding the establishment of the outer limits of the continental shelf beyond 200 nautical miles, including the assessment of the nature and extent of the continental shelf of a coastal State through a desktop study, and the delineation of the outer limits of its continental shelf, as well as in the preparation of preliminary information to be submitted to the Secretary-General in accordance with the decision of the eighteenth Meeting of States Parties to the Convention;

20. *Calls upon* the Division to continue to disseminate information on relevant procedures related to the trust fund established for the purpose of facilitating the preparation of submissions to the Commission and to continue its dialogue with potential beneficiaries with a view to providing financial support to developing countries for activities to facilitate timely submissions to the Commission;

21. *Notes with appreciation* the successful conduct by the Division, in cooperation with States and relevant international organizations and institutions, of further subregional training courses in Trinidad and Tobago from 14 to 18 January 2008 and in Namibia from 15 September to 3 October 2008, the purpose of which was to train technical staff of coastal developing States in the delineation of the outer limits of the continental shelf beyond 200 nautical miles and in the preparation of submissions to the Commission, and requests the Secretary-General, in cooperation with States and relevant international organizations and institutions, to continue to support training activities to assist developing States in the preparation of their submissions to the Commission;

22. *Also notes with appreciation* the development by the Division of a training manual on developing and implementing ecosystem approaches to the management of ocean-related activities and the successful delivery, in cooperation with the United Nations Environment Programme under the TRAIN-SEA-COAST Programme, of the first regional training workshop on "Ecosystem approaches to coastal and ocean management: focus on ecosystem-based management in Eastern Africa", in Mombasa, Kenya, from 27 October to 1 November 2008;

23. *Further notes with appreciation* the regional workshop of the Tribunal, held in Buenos Aires from 26 to 28 May 2008, on the role of the Tribunal in the settlement of disputes relating to the law of the sea;

24. *Invites* Member States and others in a position to do so to support the capacity-building activities of the Division, including, in particular, the training activities to assist developing States in the preparation of their submissions to the Commission, and invites Member States and others in a position to do so to contribute to the trust fund established by the Secretary-General for the Office of Legal Affairs of the Secretariat to support the promotion of international law;

25. *Recognizes* the importance of the Hamilton Shirley Amerasinghe Memorial Fellowship on the Law of the Sea, expresses its serious concern regarding the lack of resources, which is preventing the implementation of the twenty-second and future awards, advises the Secretary-General to continue to finance the Fellowship from resources made available through an appropriate Office of Legal Affairs trust fund, and urges Member States and others in a position to do so to contribute to the further development of the Fellowship;

26. *Takes note with satisfaction* of the ongoing implementation of the United Nations and the Nippon Foundation Fellowship Programme, focusing on human resources development for developing coastal States parties and non-parties to the Convention in the field of ocean affairs and the law of the sea or related disciplines;

III

Meeting of States Parties

27. *Welcomes* the report of the eighteenth Meeting of States Parties to the Convention;

28. *Requests* the Secretary-General to convene the nineteenth Meeting of States Parties in New York, from 22 to 26 June 2009, and to provide the services required;

IV

Peaceful settlement of disputes

29. *Notes with satisfaction* the continued and significant contribution of the Tribunal to the settlement of disputes by peaceful means in accordance with Part XV of the Convention, and underlines the important role and authority of the Tribunal concerning the interpretation or application of the Convention and the Part XI Agreement;

30. *Equally pays tribute* to the important and long-standing role of the International Court of Justice with regard to the peaceful settlement of disputes concerning the law of the sea;

31. *Notes* that States parties to an international agreement related to the purposes of the Convention may submit to, inter alia, the Tribunal or the International Court of Justice any dispute concerning the interpretation or application of that agreement submitted in accordance with that agreement, and notes also the possibility, provided for in the statutes of the Tribunal and the Court, to submit disputes to a chamber;

32. *Encourages* States parties to the Convention that have not yet done so to consider making a written declaration choosing from the means set out in article 287 of the Convention for the settlement of disputes concerning the interpretation or application of the Convention and the Part XI Agreement, bearing in mind the comprehensive character of the dispute settlement mechanism provided for in Part XV of the Convention;

V

The Area

33. *Notes* the progress made by the Authority in its deliberations, encourages the finalization of the regulations

for prospecting and exploration for polymetallic sulphides as soon as possible and progress on the regulations for prospecting and exploration for cobalt-rich ferromanganese crusts in the Area, and reiterates the importance of the ongoing elaboration by the Authority, pursuant to article 145 of the Convention, of rules, regulations and procedures to ensure the effective protection of the marine environment, for, inter alia, the protection and conservation of the natural resources of the Area, and for the prevention of damage to the flora and fauna of the marine environment from harmful effects that may arise from activities in the Area;

34. *Also notes* the importance of the responsibilities entrusted to the Authority by articles 143 and 145 of the Convention, which refer to marine scientific research and protection of the marine environment, respectively;

VI

Effective functioning of the Authority and the Tribunal

35. *Appeals* to all States parties to the Convention to pay their assessed contributions to the Authority and to the Tribunal in full and on time, and also appeals to States parties in arrears with their contributions to fulfil their obligations without delay;

36. *Urges* all States parties to the Convention to attend the sessions of the Authority, and calls upon the Authority to continue to pursue all options, including making concrete recommendations on the issue of dates, in order to improve attendance in Kingston and to ensure global participation;

37. *Calls upon* States that have not done so to consider ratifying or acceding to the Agreement on the Privileges and Immunities of the Tribunal and to the Protocol on the Privileges and Immunities of the Authority;

38. *Emphasizes* the importance of the Tribunal's rules and staff regulations promoting the recruitment of a geographically representative staff in the Professional and higher categories, and welcomes the actions taken by the Tribunal in observance of those rules and regulations;

VII

The continental shelf and the work of the Commission

39. *Encourages* States parties to the Convention to make every effort to submit information to the Commission regarding the establishment of the outer limits of the continental shelf beyond 200 nautical miles, in conformity with article 76 of the Convention and article 4 of annex II to the Convention, taking into account the decision of the eleventh Meeting of States Parties to the Convention contained in SPLOS/72, paragraph *(a)*;

40. *Recognizes* the decision of the eighteenth Meeting of States Parties to the Convention that it is understood that the time period referred to in article 4 of annex II to the Convention and the decision contained in SPLOS/72, paragraph *(a)*, may be satisfied by submitting to the Secretary-General preliminary information indicative of the outer limits of the continental shelf beyond 200 nautical miles and a description of the status of preparation and intended date of submission in accordance with the requirements of article 76 of the Convention and with the rules of procedure and the Scientific and Technical Guidelines of the Commission;

41. *Notes with satisfaction* the progress in the work of the Commission, that it is giving current consideration to a number of submissions that have been made regarding the establishment of the outer limits of the continental shelf beyond 200 nautical miles and that a number of States have advised of their intention to make submissions in the near future;

42. *Takes note* of the recommendations made by the Commission on the submissions of a number of States, and welcomes the fact that summaries of recommendations have been made publicly available;

43. *Notes* that the anticipated heavy workload of the Commission, owing to an increasing number of submissions, places additional demands on its members and the Division, and in that regard emphasizes the need to ensure that the Commission can perform its functions efficiently and effectively and maintain its high level of quality and expertise;

44. *Takes note* of the decision of the seventeenth Meeting of States Parties to the Convention to continue to address, as a matter of priority, issues related to the workload of the Commission, including funding for its members attending the sessions of the Commission and the meetings of the subcommissions;

45. *Calls upon* States whose experts are serving on the Commission to do their utmost to ensure the full participation of those experts in the work of the Commission, including the meetings of subcommissions, in accordance with the Convention;

46. *Requests* the Secretary-General to take appropriate measures, including in the context of the proposed programme budget for the biennium 2010–2011, to further strengthen the capacity of the Division, serving as the secretariat of the Commission, in order to adequately increase the Division's support and assistance to the Commission and its subcommissions, in their consideration of a growing number of submissions, as required by paragraph 9 of annex III to the rules of procedure of the Commission, and taking into account the need for simultaneous work on several submissions;

47. *Urges* the Secretary-General to continue to provide all necessary secretariat services to the Commission in accordance with article 2, paragraph 5, of annex II to the Convention;

48. *Encourages* States to make additional contributions to the voluntary trust fund established by resolution 55/7 for the purpose of facilitating the preparation of submissions to the Commission and to the voluntary trust fund also established by that resolution for the purpose of defraying the cost of participation of the members of the Commission from developing States in the meetings of the Commission;

49. *Approves* the convening by the Secretary-General of the twenty-third and twenty-fourth sessions of the Commission, in New York, from 2 March to 9 April 2009 and from 10 August to 11 September 2009, respectively, on the understanding that the following periods will be used for the technical examination of submissions at the Geographic Information System laboratories and other technical facili-

ties of the Division: 2 to 20 March 2009; 6 to 9 April 2009; 10 to 21 August 2009; and 8 to 11 September 2009;

50. *Expresses its firm conviction* about the importance of the work of the Commission, carried out in accordance with the Convention, including with respect to the participation of coastal States in relevant proceedings concerning their submissions, and recognizes the continued need for active interaction between coastal States and the Commission;

51. *Encourages* States to continue exchanging views in order to increase understanding of issues, including expenditures involved, arising from the application of article 76 of the Convention, thus facilitating the preparation of submissions by States, in particular developing States, to the Commission;

52. *Requests* the Secretary-General, in cooperation with Member States, to continue supporting workshops or symposiums on scientific and technical aspects of the establishment of the outer limits of the continental shelf beyond 200 nautical miles, taking into account the need to strengthen capacity-building for developing countries in preparing their submissions;

VIII

Maritime safety and security and flag State implementation

53. *Encourages* States to ratify or accede to international agreements addressing the safety and security of navigation, as well as maritime labour, and to adopt the necessary measures consistent with the Convention and other relevant international instruments aimed at implementing and enforcing the rules contained in those agreements, and emphasizes the need for capacity-building for and assistance to developing States;

54. *Recognizes* that the legal regimes governing maritime security and maritime safety may have common and mutually reinforcing objectives that may be interrelated and could benefit from synergies, and encourages States to take this into account in their implementation;

55. *Emphasizes* that security and safety measures should be implemented with minimal negative effects on seafarers and fishers, especially in relation to their working conditions;

56. *Invites* all States to ratify or accede to the Maritime Labour Convention, 2006, the Work in Fishing Convention, 2007 (No. 188) and the Seafarers' Identity Documents Convention (Revised), 2003 (No. 185) of the International Labour Organization and to effectively implement those Conventions, and emphasizes the need to provide technical cooperation and assistance in that regard;

57. *Emphasizes* the need for further efforts to promote a culture of safety and security in the shipping industry and to address the shortage of adequately trained personnel, notes the importance of the process in the International Maritime Organization to review the International Convention on Standards of Training, Certification and Watchkeeping for Seafarers, 1973, and urges the establishment of more centres to provide the required education and training;

58. *Welcomes* ongoing cooperation among the Food and Agriculture Organization of the United Nations, the International Maritime Organization and the International Labour Organization relating to the safety of fishers and fishing vessels, underlines the urgent need for continued work in that area, and takes note of discussions in the Food and Agriculture Organization of the United Nations on the merit of an international plan of action in this area;

59. *Notes* the holding of the ninth meeting of the Conference of the Parties to the Basel Convention on the Control of Transboundary Movements of Hazardous Wastes and their Disposal, and welcomes further cooperation with the International Maritime Organization on regulations on the prevention of pollution from ships;

60. *Recalls* that all actions taken to combat threats to maritime security must be in accordance with international law, including the principles embodied in the Charter and the Convention;

61. *Recognizes* the crucial role of international cooperation at the global, regional, subregional and bilateral levels in combating, in accordance with international law, threats to maritime security, including piracy, armed robbery at sea, terrorist acts against shipping, offshore installations and other maritime interests, through bilateral and multilateral instruments and mechanisms aimed at monitoring, preventing and responding to such threats, the enhanced sharing of information among States relevant to the detection, prevention and suppression of such threats, and the prosecution of offenders with due regard to national legislation, and the need for sustained capacity-building to support such objectives;

62. *Emphasizes* the importance of prompt reporting of incidents to enable accurate information on the scope of the problem of piracy and armed robbery against ships and, in the case of armed robbery against ships, by affected vessels to the coastal State, underlines the importance of effective information-sharing with States potentially affected by incidents of piracy and armed robbery against ships, and takes note of the important role of the International Maritime Organization;

63. *Calls upon* States to take appropriate steps under their national law to facilitate the apprehension and prosecution of those who are alleged to have committed acts of piracy;

64. *Urges* all States, in cooperation with the International Maritime Organization, to actively combat piracy and armed robbery at sea by adopting measures, including those relating to assistance with capacity-building through training of seafarers, port staff and enforcement personnel in the prevention, reporting and investigation of incidents, bringing the alleged perpetrators to justice, in accordance with international law, and by adopting national legislation, as well as providing enforcement vessels and equipment and guarding against fraudulent ship registration;

65. *Welcomes* the significant decrease in the number of attacks by pirates and armed robbers in the Asian region through increased national, bilateral and trilateral initiatives as well as regional cooperative mechanisms, and calls upon other States to give immediate attention to adopting, concluding and implementing cooperation agreements at the regional level on combating piracy and armed robbery against ships;

66. *Expresses serious concern* regarding the problem of increased instances of piracy and armed robbery at sea off the coast of Somalia, expresses alarm in particular at the recent hijacking of vessels, supports the recent efforts

to address this problem at the global and regional levels, notes the adoption by the Security Council of resolutions 1816(2008) of 2 June 2008 and 1838(2008) of 7 October 2008 and also notes that the authorization in resolution 1816(2008) and the provisions in resolution 1838(2008) apply only to the situation in Somalia and do not affect the rights, obligations or responsibilities of Member States under international law, including any rights or obligations under the Convention, with respect to any other situation, and underscores in particular the fact that they are not to be considered as establishing customary international law;

67. *Notes* the initiatives of the Secretary-General of the International Maritime Organization, following up on resolution A.1002(25) adopted by the Assembly of the International Maritime Organization on 29 November 2007, to engage the international community in efforts to combat acts of piracy and armed robbery against ships sailing the waters off the coast of Somalia;

68. *Urges* States to ensure the full implementation of resolution A.1002(25) on acts of piracy and armed robbery against ships in waters off the coast of Somalia;

69. *Calls upon* States to become parties to the Convention for the Suppression of Unlawful Acts against the Safety of Maritime Navigation and the Protocol for the Suppression of Unlawful Acts against the Safety of Fixed Platforms Located on the Continental Shelf, invites States to consider becoming parties to the 2005 Protocols amending those instruments, and urges States parties to take appropriate measures to ensure the effective implementation of those instruments through the adoption of legislation, where appropriate;

70. *Also calls upon* States to effectively implement the International Ship and Port Facility Security Code and the amendments to the International Convention for the Safety of Life at Sea, and to work with the International Maritime Organization to promote safe and secure shipping while ensuring freedom of navigation;

71. *Urges* all States, in cooperation with the International Maritime Organization, to improve the protection of offshore installations by adopting measures related to the prevention, reporting and investigation of acts of violence against installations, in accordance with international law, and by implementing such measures through national legislation to ensure proper and adequate enforcement;

72. *Welcomes* the progress in regional cooperation, including the Jakarta, Kuala Lumpur and Singapore Statements on Enhancement of Safety, Security and Environmental Protection in the Straits of Malacca and Singapore, adopted on 8 September 2005, 20 September 2006 and 6 September 2007, respectively, especially the formal establishment of the Cooperative Mechanism on safety of navigation and environmental protection to promote dialogue and facilitate close cooperation between the littoral States, user States, shipping industry and other stakeholders in line with article 43 of the Convention, and in implementing the Marine Electronic Highway Demonstration Project for the Straits of Malacca and Singapore, notes with appreciation the important role of the Information Sharing Centre of the Regional Cooperation Agreement on Combating Piracy and Armed Robbery against Ships in Asia, based in Singapore, and calls upon States to give immediate attention to adopting, concluding and implementing cooperation agreements at the regional level;

73. *Recognizes* that some transnational organized criminal activities threaten legitimate uses of the oceans and endanger the lives of people at sea;

74. *Notes* that transnational organized criminal activities are diverse and may be interrelated in some cases and that criminal organizations are adaptive and take advantage of the vulnerabilities of States, in particular coastal and small island developing States in transit areas, and calls upon States and relevant intergovernmental organizations to increase cooperation and coordination at all levels to detect and suppress the smuggling of migrants and trafficking in persons, in accordance with international law;

75. *Recognizes* the importance of enhancing international cooperation at all levels to fight transnational organized criminal activities, including illicit traffic in narcotic drugs and psychotropic substances, within the scope of the United Nations instruments against illicit drug trafficking, as well as the smuggling of migrants and trafficking in persons and criminal activities at sea falling within the scope of the United Nations Convention against Transnational Organized Crime;

76. *Calls upon* States that have not yet done so to become parties to the Protocol against the Smuggling of Migrants by Land, Sea and Air, supplementing the United Nations Convention against Transnational Organized Crime, and the Protocol to Prevent, Suppress and Punish Trafficking in Persons, Especially Women and Children, supplementing the United Nations Convention against Transnational Organized Crime, and to take appropriate measures to ensure their effective implementation;

77. *Calls upon* States to ensure freedom of navigation, the safety of navigation and the rights of transit passage, archipelagic sea lanes passage and innocent passage in accordance with international law, in particular the Convention;

78. *Welcomes* the work of the International Maritime Organization relating to the protection of shipping lanes of strategic importance and significance, and in particular in enhancing safety, security and environmental protection in straits used for international navigation, and calls upon the International Maritime Organization, States bordering straits and user States to continue their cooperation to keep such straits safe, secure and environmentally protected and open to international navigation at all times, consistent with international law, in particular the Convention;

79. *Calls upon* user States and States bordering straits used for international navigation to continue to cooperate by agreement on matters relating to navigational safety, including safety aids for navigation, and the prevention, reduction and control of pollution from ships, and welcomes developments in this regard;

80. *Takes note* of the adoption of the Code of International Standards and Recommended Practices for a Safety Investigation into a Marine Casualty or Marine Incident, which will take effect on 1 January 2010 upon the entry into force of the amendments to regulation XI-1/6 of the International Convention for the Safety of Life at Sea, 1974;

81. *Calls upon* States to consider becoming members of the International Hydrographic Organization, and urges all States to work with that Organization to increase the coverage of hydrographic information on a global basis to

enhance capacity-building and technical assistance and to promote safe navigation, especially in areas used for international navigation, in ports and where there are vulnerable or protected marine areas;

82. *Notes* the progress in the implementation of the Action Plan for the Safety of Transport of Radioactive Material, approved by the Board of Governors of the International Atomic Energy Agency in March 2004, and encourages States concerned to continue their efforts in the implementation of all areas of the Action Plan;

83. *Also notes* that cessation of the transport of radioactive materials through the regions of small island developing States is an ultimate desired goal of small island developing States and some other countries, and recognizes the right of freedom of navigation in accordance with international law; that States should maintain dialogue and consultation, in particular under the auspices of the International Atomic Energy Agency and the International Maritime Organization, with the aim of improved mutual understanding, confidence-building and enhanced communication in relation to the safe maritime transport of radioactive materials; that States involved in the transport of such materials are urged to continue to engage in dialogue with small island developing States and other States to address their concerns; and that these concerns include the further development and strengthening, within the appropriate forums, of international regulatory regimes to enhance safety, disclosure, liability, security and compensation in relation to such transport;

84. *Acknowledges*, in the context of paragraph 83 above, the potential environmental and economic impacts of maritime incidents and accidents on coastal States, in particular those related to the transport of radioactive materials, and emphasizes the importance of effective liability regimes in that regard;

85. *Encourages* States to draw up plans and to establish procedures to implement the Guidelines on Places of Refuge for Ships in Need of Assistance;

86. *Invites* States to consider becoming parties to the Nairobi International Convention on the Removal of Wrecks, 2007;

87. *Requests* States to take appropriate measures with regard to ships flying their flag or of their registry to address hazards that may be caused by wrecks and drifting or sunken cargo to navigation or the marine environment;

88. *Calls upon* States to ensure that masters on ships flying their flag take the steps required by relevant instruments to provide assistance to persons in distress at sea, and urges States to cooperate and to take all necessary measures to ensure the effective implementation of the amendments to the International Convention on Maritime Search and Rescue and to the International Convention for the Safety of Life at Sea relating to the delivery of persons rescued at sea to a place of safety, as well as of the associated Guidelines on the Treatment of Persons Rescued at Sea;

89. *Recognizes* that all States must fulfil their search and rescue responsibilities and the ongoing need for the International Maritime Organization and other relevant organizations to assist, in particular, developing States both to increase their search and rescue capabilities, including through the establishment of additional rescue coordination centres and regional subcentres, and to take effective action to address, to the extent feasible, the issue of unseaworthy ships and small craft within their national jurisdiction;

90. *Welcomes* the ongoing work of the International Maritime Organization in relation to disembarkation of persons rescued at sea, and notes in this regard the need to implement all relevant international instruments;

91. *Also welcomes* the ongoing cooperation and coordination among members of the inter-agency group on the treatment of persons rescued at sea;

92. *Calls upon* States to continue to cooperate in developing comprehensive approaches to international migration and development, including through dialogue on all their aspects;

93. *Reaffirms* that flag, port and coastal States all bear responsibility for ensuring the effective implementation and enforcement of international instruments relating to maritime security and safety, in accordance with international law, in particular the Convention, and that flag States have primary responsibility that requires further strengthening, including through increased transparency of ownership of vessels;

94. *Urges* flag States without an effective maritime administration and appropriate legal frameworks to establish or enhance the necessary infrastructure, legislative and enforcement capabilities to ensure effective compliance with, and implementation and enforcement of, their responsibilities under international law and, until such action is taken, to consider declining the granting of the right to fly their flag to new vessels, suspending their registry or not opening a registry, and calls upon flag and port States to take all measures consistent with international law necessary to prevent the operation of substandard vessels;

95. *Recognizes* that international shipping rules and standards adopted by the International Maritime Organization in respect of maritime safety, efficiency of navigation and the prevention and control of marine pollution, complemented by best practices of the shipping industry, have led to a significant reduction in maritime accidents and pollution incidents, and encourages all States to participate in the Voluntary International Maritime Organization Member State Audit Scheme;

96. *Also recognizes* that maritime safety can also be improved through effective port State control, the strengthening of regional arrangements and increased coordination and cooperation among them, and increased information-sharing, including among safety and security sectors;

97. *Encourages* flag States to take appropriate measures sufficient to achieve or maintain recognition by intergovernmental arrangements that recognize satisfactory flag State performance, including, as appropriate, satisfactory port State control examination results on a sustained basis, with a view to improving quality shipping and furthering flag State implementation of relevant instruments under the International Maritime Organization as well as relevant goals and objectives of the present resolution;

IX

Marine environment and marine resources

98. *Emphasizes once again* the importance of the implementation of Part XII of the Convention in order to protect and preserve the marine environment and its living marine resources against pollution and physical degradation, and calls upon all States to cooperate and take measures consistent with the Convention, directly or through competent

international organizations, for the protection and preservation of the marine environment;

99. *Notes* the work of the Intergovernmental Panel on Climate Change, including its findings on the acidification of oceans, and in this regard encourages States and competent international organizations and other relevant institutions, individually and in cooperation, to urgently pursue further research on ocean acidification, especially programmes of observation and measurement, noting in particular paragraph 4 of decision IX/20 adopted at the ninth meeting of the Conference of the Parties to the Convention on Biological Diversity, held in Bonn, Germany, from 19 to 30 May 2008, and to increase national, regional and international efforts to address levels of ocean acidity and the projected negative impact of such acidity on vulnerable marine ecosystems, particularly coral reefs;

100. *Encourages* States, individually or in collaboration with relevant international organizations and bodies, to enhance their scientific activity to better understand the effects of climate change on the marine environment and marine biodiversity and develop ways and means of adaptation;

101. *Also encourages* States to ratify or accede to international agreements addressing the protection and preservation of the marine environment and its living marine resources against the introduction of harmful aquatic organisms and pathogens and marine pollution from all sources, including the dumping of wastes and other matter, and other forms of physical degradation, as well as agreements that provide for preparedness for, response to and cooperation on pollution incidents and that include provisions on liability and compensation for damage resulting from marine pollution, and to adopt the necessary measures consistent with the Convention aimed at implementing and enforcing the rules contained in those agreements;

102. *Further encourages* States, directly or through competent international organizations, to consider the further development, as appropriate and consistent with the Convention, of environmental impact assessment processes covering planned activities under their jurisdiction or control that may cause substantial pollution of or significant and harmful changes to the marine environment;

103. *Encourages* States to become parties to regional seas conventions addressing the protection and preservation of the marine environment;

104. *Also encourages* States, in accordance with the Convention and other relevant instruments, either bilaterally or regionally, to jointly develop and promote contingency plans for responding to pollution incidents, as well as other incidents that are likely to have significant adverse effects on the marine environment and biodiversity;

105. *Welcomes* the World Ocean Conference, to be held in Manado, Indonesia, from 11 to 15 May 2009, as an opportunity to enhance understanding of the link between oceans and climate change and the impact of climate change on marine ecosystems and coastal communities, thus promoting the urgency of mainstreaming climate change-sensitive policies and enhancing adaptation capacity at all levels, especially among developing countries and small island developing States;

106. *Welcomes* the activities of the United Nations Environment Programme relating to marine debris carried out in cooperation with relevant United Nations bodies and organizations, and encourages States to further develop partnerships with industry and civil society to raise awareness of the extent of the impact of marine debris on the health and productivity of the marine environment and consequent economic loss;

107. *Urges* States to integrate the issue of marine debris into national strategies dealing with waste management in the coastal zone, ports and maritime industries, including recycling, reuse, reduction and disposal, and to encourage the development of appropriate economic incentives to address this issue, including the development of cost recovery systems that provide an incentive to use port reception facilities and discourage ships from discharging marine debris at sea, and encourages States to cooperate regionally and subregionally to develop and implement joint prevention and recovery programmes for marine debris;

108. *Encourages* States that have not done so to become parties to the Protocol of 1997 (Annex VI-Regulations for the Prevention of Air Pollution from Ships) to the International Convention for the Prevention of Pollution from Ships, 1973, as modified by the Protocol of 1978 relating thereto, and furthermore to ratify or accede to the International Convention for the Control and Management of Ships' Ballast Water and Sediments, 2004, thereby facilitating its early entry into force;

109. *Notes* the ongoing work of the International Maritime Organization in accordance with its resolution on International Maritime Organization policies and practices related to the reduction of greenhouse gas emissions from ships and the workplan to identify and develop the mechanism or mechanisms needed to achieve the limitation or reduction of greenhouse gas emissions from international shipping, and welcomes ongoing efforts of the Organization in that regard;

110. *Urges* States to cooperate in correcting the shortfall in port waste reception facilities in accordance with the action plan to address the inadequacy of port waste reception facilities developed by the International Maritime Organization;

111. *Recognizes* that most of the pollution load of the oceans emanates from land-based activities and affects the most productive areas of the marine environment, and calls upon States as a matter of priority to implement the Global Programme of Action for the Protection of the Marine Environment from Land-based Activities and to take all appropriate measures to fulfil the commitments of the international community embodied in the Beijing Declaration on furthering the implementation of the Global Programme of Action;

112. *Expresses its concern* regarding the spreading of hypoxic dead zones in oceans as a result of eutrophication fuelled by riverine run-off of fertilizers, sewage outfall and reactive nitrogen resulting from the burning of fossil fuels and resulting in serious consequences for ecosystem functioning, and calls upon States to enhance their efforts to reduce eutrophication and, to this effect, to continue to cooperate within the framework of relevant international organizations, in particular the Global Programme of Action;

113. *Calls upon* all States to ensure that urban and coastal development projects and related land-reclamation activities are carried out in a responsible manner that

protects the marine habitat and environment and mitigates the negative consequences of such activities;

114. *Welcomes* the continued work of States, the United Nations Environment Programme and regional organizations in the implementation of the Global Programme of Action, and encourages increased emphasis on the link between freshwater, the coastal zone and marine resources in the implementation of international development goals, including those contained in the United Nations Millennium Declaration, and of the time-bound targets in the Plan of Implementation of the World Summit on Sustainable Development ("Johannesburg Plan of Implementation"), in particular the target on sanitation, and the Monterrey Consensus of the International Conference on Financing for Development;

115. *Also welcomes* the resolution of the thirtieth Consultative Meeting of Contracting Parties to the Convention on the Prevention of Marine Pollution by Dumping of Wastes and Other Matter, 1972 ("the London Convention") and the third Meeting of Contracting Parties to the London Protocol, held from 27 to 31 October 2008, on the regulation of ocean fertilization, in which the Contracting Parties agreed, inter alia, that the scope of the London Convention and Protocol includes ocean fertilization activities and that, given the present state of knowledge, ocean fertilization activities other than for legitimate scientific research should not be allowed, and that scientific research proposals should be assessed on a case-by-case basis using an assessment framework to be developed by the scientific groups under the London Convention and Protocol, and also agreed that, to this end, such other activities should be considered as contrary to the aims of the London Convention and Protocol and should not currently qualify for any exemption from the definition of dumping in article III, paragraph 1 *(b)*, of the London Convention and article 1, paragraph 4.2, of the London Protocol;

116. *Further welcomes* decision IX/16 C adopted at the ninth meeting of the Conference of the Parties to the Convention on Biological Diversity, in which the Conference of the Parties, inter alia, bearing in mind the ongoing scientific and legal analysis occurring under the auspices of the London Convention and Protocol, requested parties and urged other Governments, in accordance with the precautionary approach, to ensure that ocean fertilization activities were not carried out until there was an adequate scientific basis on which to justify such activities, including an assessment of associated risks, and that a global, transparent and effective control and regulatory mechanism was in place for those activities, with the exception of small-scale scientific research studies within coastal waters, and stated that such studies should be authorized only if justified by the need to gather specific scientific data, should be subject to a thorough prior assessment of the potential impacts of the research studies on the marine environment, should be strictly controlled and should not be used for generating and selling carbon offsets or for any other commercial purposes;

117. *Reaffirms* paragraph 119 of resolution 61/222 of 20 December 2006 regarding ecosystem approaches and oceans, including the proposed elements of an ecosystem approach, means to achieve implementation of an ecosystem approach and requirements for improved application of an ecosystem approach, and in this regard:

(a) Notes that continued environmental degradation in many parts of the world and increasing competing demands require an urgent response and the setting of priorities for management actions aimed at conserving ecosystem integrity;

(b) Notes that ecosystem approaches to ocean management should be focused on managing human activities in order to maintain and, where needed, restore ecosystem health to sustain goods and environmental services, provide social and economic benefits for food security, sustain livelihoods in support of international development goals, including those contained in the Millennium Declaration, and conserve marine biodiversity;

(c) Recalls that States should be guided in the application of ecosystem approaches by a number of existing instruments, in particular the Convention, which sets out the legal framework for all activities in the oceans and seas, and its implementing Agreements, as well as other commitments, such as those contained in the Convention on Biological Diversity and the World Summit on Sustainable Development call for the application of an ecosystem approach by 2010;

(d) Encourages States to cooperate and coordinate their efforts and take, individually or jointly, as appropriate, all measures, in conformity with international law, including the Convention and other applicable instruments, to address impacts on marine ecosystems within and beyond areas of national jurisdiction, taking into account the integrity of the ecosystems concerned;

118. *Invites* States, in particular those States with advanced technology and marine capabilities, to explore prospects for improving cooperation with, and assistance to, developing States, in particular least developed countries and small island developing States, as well as coastal African States, with a view to better integrating into national policies and programmes sustainable and effective development in the marine sector;

119. *Encourages* the competent international organizations, the United Nations Development Programme, the World Bank and other funding agencies to consider expanding their programmes within their respective fields of competence for assistance to developing countries and to coordinate their efforts, including in the allocation and application of Global Environment Facility funding;

120. *Welcomes* the study prepared by the Secretariat pursuant to paragraph 88 of resolution 61/222 and the information provided in relation to the assistance available to and measures that may be taken by developing States, in particular the least developed countries and small island developing States, as well as coastal African States, to realize the benefits of sustainable and effective development of marine resources and uses of the oceans within the limits of national jurisdiction, takes note of the information provided by States and competent international organizations and global and regional funding agencies, and urges them to provide further information for the annual report of the Secretary-General and for incorporation on the website of the Division;

X

Marine biodiversity

121. *Reaffirms* its role relating to the conservation and sustainable use of marine biological diversity beyond areas

of national jurisdiction, notes the work of States and relevant complementary intergovernmental organizations and bodies on those issues, including the Convention on Biological Diversity and the Food and Agriculture Organization of the United Nations, and invites them to contribute to its consideration of these issues within the areas of their respective competence;

122. *Notes* the discussion on the relevant legal regime on marine genetic resources in areas beyond national jurisdiction in accordance with the Convention, and calls upon States to further consider this issue in the context of the mandate of the Ad Hoc Open-ended Informal Working Group, with a view to making further progress on this issue;

123. *Recognizes* the abundance and diversity of marine genetic resources and their value in terms of the benefits, goods and services they can provide;

124. *Also recognizes* the importance of research on marine genetic resources for the purpose of enhancing the scientific understanding, potential use and application, and enhanced management of marine ecosystems;

125. *Encourages* States and international organizations, including through bilateral, regional and global cooperation programmes and partnerships, to continue in a sustainable and comprehensive way to support, promote and strengthen capacity-building activities, in particular in developing countries, in the field of marine scientific research, taking into account, in particular, the need to create greater taxonomic capabilities;

126. *Welcomes* the meeting of the Ad Hoc Open-ended Informal Working Group, established by the General Assembly in paragraph 73 of resolution 59/24 of 17 November 2004 to study issues relating to the conservation and sustainable use of marine biological diversity beyond areas of national jurisdiction, convened in accordance with paragraph 91 of resolution 61/222 and paragraph 105 of resolution 62/215, in New York from 28 April to 2 May 2008;

127. *Takes note* of the joint statement of the Co-Chairpersons of the Ad Hoc Open-ended Informal Working Group, and requests the Secretary-General to convene, in accordance with paragraph 73 of resolution 59/24 and paragraphs 79 and 80 of resolution 60/30, with full conference services, a meeting of the Working Group in 2010 to provide recommendations to the General Assembly;

128. *Requests* the Secretary-General to submit a report to the General Assembly at its sixty-fourth session to assist the Ad Hoc Open-ended Informal Working Group in preparing its agenda, in consultation with all relevant international bodies, and to arrange for the provision of support for the performance of its work by the Division;

129. *Encourages* States to include relevant experts in their delegations attending the meeting of the Ad Hoc Open-ended Informal Working Group;

130. *Recognizes* the importance of making the outcomes of the Ad Hoc Open-ended Informal Working Group widely available;

131. *Notes* the work under the Jakarta Mandate on Marine and Coastal Biological Diversity and the Convention on Biological Diversity elaborated programme of work on marine and coastal biological diversity, as well as the relevant decisions adopted at the ninth meeting of the Conference of the Parties to the Convention on Biological Diversity;

132. *Reaffirms* the need for States, individually or through competent international organizations, to urgently consider ways to integrate and improve, based on the best available scientific information and the precautionary approach and in accordance with the Convention and related agreements and instruments, the management of risks to the marine biodiversity of seamounts, cold water corals, hydrothermal vents and certain other underwater features;

133. *Calls upon* States and international organizations to urgently take further action to address, in accordance with international law, destructive practices that have adverse impacts on marine biodiversity and ecosystems, including seamounts, hydrothermal vents and cold water corals;

134. *Reaffirms* the need for States to continue and intensify their efforts, directly and through competent international organizations, to develop and facilitate the use of diverse approaches and tools for conserving and managing vulnerable marine ecosystems, including the possible establishment of marine protected areas, consistent with international law, as reflected in the Convention, and based on the best scientific information available, and the development of representative networks of any such marine protected areas by 2012;

135. *Notes* the work of States, relevant intergovernmental organizations and bodies, including the Convention on Biological Diversity, in the assessment of scientific information on, and compilation of ecological criteria for the identification of, marine areas that require protection, in light of the objective of the World Summit on Sustainable Development to develop and facilitate the use of diverse approaches and tools, such as the establishment of marine protected areas consistent with international law as reflected in the Convention and based on scientific information, including representative networks by 2012, and notes with satisfaction that the Conference of the Parties to the Convention on Biological Diversity at its ninth meeting adopted scientific criteria for identifying ecologically or biologically significant marine areas in need of protection in open-ocean waters and deep-sea habitats and the scientific guidance for selecting areas to establish representative networks of marine protected areas, including in open-ocean waters and deep-sea habitats, and took note of the four initial steps to be considered in the development of representative networks of marine protected areas;

136. *Acknowledges* the Micronesia Challenge, the Eastern Tropical Pacific Seascape project, the Caribbean Challenge and the Coral Triangle Initiative, which in particular seek to create and link domestic marine protected areas to better facilitate ecosystem approaches, and reaffirms the need for further international cooperation in support of such initiatives;

137. *Reiterates its support* for the International Coral Reef Initiative, takes note of the eleventh International Coral Reef Symposium and the International Coral Reef Initiative General Meeting, held respectively from 7 to 11 July and on 12 and 13 July 2008 in Fort Lauderdale, United States of America, supports the work under the Jakarta Mandate on Marine and Coastal Biological Diver-

sity and the elaborated programme of work on marine and coastal biological diversity related to coral reefs, and notes that the International Coral Reef Initiative is sponsoring the International Year of the Reef 2008;

138. *Encourages* States and relevant international institutions to improve efforts to address coral bleaching by, inter alia, improving monitoring to predict and identify bleaching events, supporting and strengthening action taken during such events and improving strategies to manage reefs to support their natural resilience and enhance their ability to withstand other pressures, including projected ocean acidification;

139. *Encourages* States to cooperate, directly or through competent international bodies, in exchanging information in the event of accidents involving vessels on coral reefs and in promoting the development of economic assessment techniques for both restoration and non-use values of coral reef systems;

140. *Emphasizes* the need to mainstream sustainable coral reef management and integrated watershed management into national development strategies, as well as into the activities of relevant United Nations agencies and programmes, international financial institutions and the donor community;

141. *Encourages* further studies and consideration of the impacts of ocean noise on marine living resources, and requests the Division to continue to compile the peer-reviewed scientific studies it receives from Member States pursuant to paragraph 107 of resolution 61/222 and, as appropriate, to make them, or references and links to them, available on its website;

XI

Marine science

142. *Calls upon* States, individually or in collaboration with each other or with relevant international organizations and bodies, to improve understanding and knowledge of the oceans and the deep sea, including, in particular, the extent and vulnerability of deep sea biodiversity and ecosystems, by increasing their marine scientific research activities in accordance with the Convention;

143. *Notes* the contribution of the Census of Marine Life to marine biodiversity research, and encourages participation in the initiative;

144. *Welcomes* the adoption by the Intergovernmental Oceanographic Commission of the United Nations Educational, Scientific and Cultural Organization of the guidelines for the implementation of resolution XX-6 of the Assembly of the Oceanographic Commission regarding the deployment of profiling floats in the high seas in the framework of the Argo Programme, and encourages the Advisory Body of Experts on the Law of the Sea of the Oceanographic Commission to continue its work on the legal framework, within the context of the Convention, which is applicable to the collection of oceanographic data by other specific means;

145. *Notes* the preparation by the Division of a revision of *Marine Scientific Research: A guide to the implementation of the relevant provisions of the United Nations Convention on the Law of the Sea,* with the assistance of a group of experts to be convened in early 2009, and encourages States to support this endeavour;

146. *Stresses* the importance of increasing the scientific understanding of the oceans/atmosphere interface, including through participation in ocean observing programmes and geographic information systems, such as the Global Ocean Observing System, a programme of the Intergovernmental Oceanographic Commission, particularly considering their role in monitoring and forecasting climate change and variability and in the establishment and operation of tsunami warning systems;

147. *Takes note with appreciation* of the progress made by the Intergovernmental Oceanographic Commission and Member States towards the establishment of regional and national tsunami warning and mitigation systems, welcomes the continued collaboration of the United Nations and other intergovernmental organizations in this effort, and encourages Member States to establish and sustain their national warning and mitigation systems, within a global, ocean-related multi-hazard approach, as necessary, to reduce loss of life and damage to national economies and strengthen the resilience of coastal communities to natural disasters;

148. *Notes* the outcome of the ad hoc intergovernmental and multi-stakeholder meeting on an intergovernmental science-policy platform on biodiversity and ecosystem services, held under the auspices of the United Nations Environment Programme in Putrajaya, Malaysia, from 10 to 12 November 2008;

XII

Regular process for global reporting and assessment of the state of the marine environment, including socio-economic aspects

149. *Reiterates* the need to strengthen the regular scientific assessment of the state of the marine environment in order to enhance the scientific basis for policymaking;

150. *Recalls* that the Ad Hoc Steering Group was established by resolution 60/30 to oversee the execution of the "assessment of assessments" launched as a preparatory stage towards the establishment of the regular process for global reporting and assessment of the state of the marine environment, including socio-economic aspects;

151. *Notes with appreciation* the work carried out so far and progress made in the "assessment of assessments" by the Group of Experts established pursuant to resolution 60/30 and the support of the United Nations Environment Programme and the Intergovernmental Oceanographic Commission, the lead agencies of the "assessment of assessments", in providing secretariat services to the Ad Hoc Steering Group and the Group of Experts;

152. *Takes note* of the report of the third meeting of the Ad Hoc Steering Group for the "assessment of assessments", held in New York on 19 and 20 June 2008;

153. *Also takes note* of the "assessment of assessments" progress report, endorsed by the Ad Hoc Steering Group and submitted by the United Nations Environment Programme and the Intergovernmental Oceanographic Commission to Member States, which provided the basis for an open-ended midterm review of the work and progress made so far in order to give all States Members of the United Nations an opportunity to comment on and contribute to the development of the ongoing work carried out under

the "assessment of assessments" in accordance with paragraph 93 *(c)* of resolution 60/30;

154. *Urges* Member States and other interested parties to contribute financially to the "assessment of assessments" in order to enable its completion within the specified period, as indicated in the revised budget endorsed by the Ad Hoc Steering Group;

155. *Urges* all members of the Ad Hoc Steering Group to participate in the review of the completed "assessment of assessments" report and the summary for decision makers at the meeting of the Steering Group in 2009 and to interact, as appropriate, with the Group of Experts in its deliberations, bearing in mind their respective mandates;

156. *Recalls* that the report on the results of the "assessment of assessments" to be transmitted by the United Nations Environment Programme and the Intergovernmental Oceanographic Commission on behalf of the Ad Hoc Steering Group in accordance with paragraph 94 *(d)* of resolution 60/30 should be focused on the aims and expected outcomes identified in the conclusions of the second International Workshop on the regular process for global reporting and assessment of the state of the marine environment, including socio-economic aspects, and paragraph 6 of the decision adopted by the Ad Hoc Steering Group at its first meeting in order to facilitate the successful completion of the "assessment of assessments" phase;

157. *Decides* to establish an ad hoc working group of the whole to recommend a course of action to the General Assembly at its sixty-fourth session based on the outcomes of the fourth meeting of the Ad Hoc Steering Group, and requests the Secretary-General to convene its informal meeting for one week not later than September 2009;

XIII

Regional cooperation

158. *Notes* that there have been a number of initiatives at the regional level, in various regions, to further the implementation of the Convention, takes note in that context of the Caribbean-focused Assistance Fund, which is intended to facilitate, mainly through technical assistance, the voluntary undertaking of maritime delimitation negotiations between Caribbean States, takes note once again of the Fund for Peace: Peaceful Settlement of Territorial Disputes, established by the General Assembly of the Organization of American States in 2000 as a primary mechanism, given its broader regional scope, for the prevention and resolution of pending territorial, land border and maritime boundary disputes, and calls upon States and others in a position to do so to contribute to these funds;

XIV

Open-ended informal consultative process on oceans and the law of the sea

159. *Welcomes* the report on the work of the Consultative Process at its ninth meeting, focused on the topic of maritime security and safety;

160. *Also welcomes* the work of the Consultative Process over the past nine years and the contribution of the Consultative Process to improving coordination and cooperation between States and strengthening the annual debate of the General Assembly on oceans and the law of the sea, further welcomes the attempts to improve and focus the work of the Consultative Process, and decides to continue the Consultative Process for the next two years, in accordance with resolution 54/33, with a further review of its effectiveness and utility by the Assembly at its sixty-fifth session;

161. *Recalls* the need to strengthen and improve the efficiency of the Consultative Process, and encourages States, intergovernmental organizations and programmes to provide guidance to the co-chairpersons to this effect, particularly before and during the preparatory meeting for the Consultative Process, and decides in this regard that the eleventh meeting of the Consultative Process shall be based on the decisions taken by the General Assembly at its sixty-fourth session, following the review of the Consultative Process at its tenth meeting;

162. *Requests* the Secretary-General to convene, in accordance with paragraphs 2 and 3 of resolution 54/33, the tenth meeting of the Consultative Process in New York from 17 to 19 June 2009, to provide it with the necessary facilities for the performance of its work and to arrange for support to be provided by the Division, in cooperation with other relevant parts of the Secretariat, as appropriate;

163. *Expresses its serious concern* regarding the lack of resources available in the voluntary trust fund established by resolution 55/7 for the purpose of assisting developing countries, in particular least developed countries, small island developing States and landlocked developing States, in attending the meetings of the Consultative Process, and urges States to make additional contributions to the trust fund;

164. *Decides* that those representatives from developing countries who are invited by the co-chairpersons, in consultation with Governments, to make presentations during the meetings of the Consultative Process shall receive priority consideration in the disbursement of funds from the voluntary trust fund established by resolution 55/7 in order to cover the costs of their travel, and shall also be eligible to receive daily subsistence allowance subject to the availability of funds after the travel costs of all other eligible representatives from those countries mentioned in paragraph 163 above have been covered;

165. *Also decides* that, in its deliberations on the report of the Secretary-General on oceans and the law of the sea, the Consultative Process at its tenth meeting will focus its discussions on the implementation of the outcomes of the Consultative Process, including a review of its achievements and shortcomings in its first nine meetings, and the topic for its eleventh meeting will be decided at the sixty-fourth session of the General Assembly;

XV

Coordination and cooperation

166. *Encourages* States to work closely with and through international organizations, funds and programmes, as well as the specialized agencies of the United Nations system and relevant international conventions, to identify emerging areas of focus for improved coordination and cooperation and how best to address these issues;

167. *Requests* the Secretary-General to bring the present resolution to the attention of heads of intergov-

ernmental organizations, the specialized agencies, funds and programmes of the United Nations engaged in activities relating to ocean affairs and the law of the sea, as well as funding institutions, and underlines the importance of their constructive and timely input for the report of the Secretary-General on oceans and the law of the sea and of their participation in relevant meetings and processes;

168. *Welcomes* the work done by the secretariats of relevant United Nations specialized agencies, programmes, funds and bodies and the secretariats of related organizations and conventions to enhance inter-agency coordination and cooperation on ocean issues, including through UN-Oceans, the inter-agency coordination mechanism on ocean and coastal issues within the United Nations system;

169. *Encourages* continued updates to Member States by UN-Oceans regarding its priorities and initiatives, in particular with respect to the proposed participation in UN-Oceans;

XVI

Activities of the Division for Ocean Affairs and the Law of the Sea

170. *Expresses its appreciation* to the Secretary-General for the annual comprehensive report on oceans and the law of the sea, prepared by the Division, as well as for the other activities of the Division, which reflect the high standard of assistance provided to Member States by the Division;

171. *Resolves* that, as from 2009, the United Nations will designate 8 June as World Oceans Day;

172. *Requests* the Secretary-General to continue to carry out the responsibilities and functions entrusted to him in the Convention and by the related resolutions of the General Assembly, including resolutions 49/28 and 52/26, and to ensure the allocation of appropriate resources to the Division for the performance of its activities under the approved budget for the Organization;

XVII

Sixty-fourth session of the General Assembly

173. *Requests* the Secretary-General to prepare a comprehensive report, in its current extensive format and in accordance with established practice, for the consideration of the General Assembly at its sixty-fourth session, on developments and issues relating to ocean affairs and the law of the sea, including the implementation of the present resolution, in accordance with resolutions 49/28, 52/26 and 54/33, and to make the section of the report related to the topic that is the focus of the tenth meeting of the Consultative Process available at least six weeks in advance of the meeting of the Consultative Process;

174. *Emphasizes* the critical role of the annual comprehensive report of the Secretary-General, which integrates information on developments relating to the implementation of the Convention and the work of the Organization, its specialized agencies and other institutions in the field of ocean affairs and the law of the sea at the global and regional levels, and as a result constitutes the basis for the annual consideration and review of developments relating to ocean affairs and the law of the sea by the General Assembly as the global institution having the competence to undertake such a review;

175. *Notes* that the report referred to in paragraph 173 above will also be submitted to States parties pursuant to article 319 of the Convention regarding issues of a general nature that have arisen with respect to the Convention;

176. *Also notes* the desire to further improve the efficiency of, and effective participation of delegations in, the informal consultations concerning the annual General Assembly resolution on oceans and the law of the sea and the resolution on sustainable fisheries, and decides to limit the period of the informal consultations on both resolutions to a maximum of four weeks in total and to ensure that the consultations are scheduled in such a way as to avoid overlap with the period during which the Sixth Committee is meeting and that the Division has sufficient time to produce the report referred to in paragraph 173 above, and invites States to submit text proposals for inclusion in the resolutions to the coordinators of the informal consultations at the earliest possible date;

177. *Decides* to include in the provisional agenda of its sixty-fourth session the item entitled "Oceans and the law of the sea".

RECORDED VOTE ON RESOLUTION 63/111:

In favour: Albania, Algeria, Andorra, Angola, Antigua and Barbuda, Argentina, Armenia, Australia, Austria, Azerbaijan, Bahamas, Bahrain, Bangladesh, Barbados, Belarus, Belgium, Benin, Bhutan, Bosnia and Herzegovina, Botswana, Brazil, Brunei Darussalam, Bulgaria, Burkina Faso, Cambodia, Cameroon, Canada, Cape Verde, Chile, China, Comoros, Congo, Costa Rica, Côte d'Ivoire, Croatia, Cuba, Cyprus, Czech Republic, Democratic People's Republic of Korea, Denmark, Djibouti, Dominica, Dominican Republic, Ecuador, Egypt, Eritrea, Estonia, Ethiopia, Fiji, Finland, France, Germany, Ghana, Greece, Guatemala, Guinea-Bissau, Guyana, Haiti, Honduras, Hungary, Iceland, India, Indonesia, Iran, Ireland, Israel, Italy, Jamaica, Japan, Jordan, Kazakhstan, Kuwait, Kyrgyzstan, Lao People's Democratic Republic, Latvia, Lebanon, Lesotho, Liberia, Liechtenstein, Lithuania, Luxembourg, Madagascar, Malawi, Malaysia, Maldives, Mali, Malta, Marshall Islands, Mauritania, Mauritius, Mexico, Micronesia, Moldova, Monaco, Mongolia, Montenegro, Morocco, Mozambique, Myanmar, Nauru, Nepal, Netherlands, New Zealand, Nicaragua, Norway, Oman, Pakistan, Palau, Panama, Papua New Guinea, Paraguay, Peru, Philippines, Poland, Portugal, Qatar, Republic of Korea, Romania, Russian Federation, Saint Lucia, Saint Vincent and the Grenadines, Samoa, San Marino, Sao Tome and Principe, Saudi Arabia, Senegal, Serbia, Singapore, Slovakia, Slovenia, Solomon Islands, South Africa, Spain, Sri Lanka, Sudan, Suriname, Sweden, Thailand, The former Yugoslav Republic of Macedonia, Timor-Leste, Togo, Tonga, Trinidad and Tobago, Tunisia, Uganda, Ukraine, United Arab Emirates, United Kingdom, United States, Uruguay, Vanuatu, Viet Nam, Yemen, Zambia, Zimbabwe.

Against: Turkey.

Abstaining: Colombia, El Salvador, Libyan Arab Jamahiriya, Venezuela.

Division for Ocean Affairs and the Law of the Sea

During 2008, the Division for Ocean Affairs and the Law of the Sea of the Office of Legal Affairs continued to fulfil its role as the substantive unit of the UN Secretariat responsible for reviewing and monitoring all developments related to the law of the sea and ocean affairs, as well as for the implementation of UNCLOS and related General Assembly resolutions.

The Division, in cooperation with intergovernmental bodies and host Governments, continued its capacity-building efforts through the organization of training courses. It held a training course in Port of Spain, Trinidad and Tobago, from 14–18 January.

The Hamilton Shirley Amerasinghe Fellowship on the Law of the Sea, established in 1981 [YUN 1981, pp. 130 & 139], was not awarded to any candidate in 2008, owing to insufficient funds.

The United Nations-Nippon Foundation of Japan Fellowship Programme awarded 10 fellowships for 2007–2008 and 10 for 2008–2009 to government officials and other mid-level professionals to undertake advanced academic research on ocean affairs and the law of the sea.

PART FIVE

Institutional, administrative and budgetary questions

Chapter I

United Nations restructuring and institutional matters

In 2008, the Secretary-General continued to work with the UN system and Member States to further enhance system-wide coherence in the areas of development, humanitarian assistance and the environment, and to support progress toward reaching internationally agreed development goals, including the Millennium Development Goals. A review of the lessons learned from the first year of experience of the eight "Delivering as one" pilot countries resulted in the issuance of a summary statement on the way forward. Despite remaining challenges, indicators showed that the process had yielded positive results, which was also reflected in the report of the Co-Chairs on system-wide coherence. The Co-Chairs recommended continued consultations in four priority areas: harmonization of business practices, funding, governance, and gender equality and the empowerment of women, which the General Assembly endorsed in September.

The General Assembly's informal working group on mandate review continued to review mandates older than five years, which included the examination of some 331 mandates of the humanitarian assistance and the Africa development clusters. The Working Group submitted its final report in August. The Ad Hoc Working Group on the Revitalization of the General Assembly continued to identify ways to further enhance the Assembly's role, authority, effectiveness and efficiency. The Open-ended Working Group on the Question of Equitable Representation on and Increase in the Membership of the Security Council and Other Matters related to the Security Council considered ways to advance progress on Council reforms.

The Assembly continued to focus on administrative and institutional matters. One high-level plenary meeting was convened on the midterm review of the Almaty Programme of Action on landlocked developing countries. A commemorative plenary meeting devoted to the sixtieth anniversary of the Universal Declaration of Human Rights was also held.

The Security Council held 244 formal meetings to deal with regional conflicts, peacekeeping operations and other issues related to the maintenance of international peace and security.

In addition to its organizational and substantive sessions, the Economic and Social Council held a special high-level meeting with the Bretton Woods institutions (the World Bank Group and the International Monetary Fund), the World Trade Organizations and the United Nations Conference on Trade and Development.

Restructuring issues

Programme of reform

Recommendations of High-level Panel on UN System-wide Coherence

In a letter dated 11 June [A/63/85-E/2008/83], Mozambique transmitted to the Secretary-General the "Maputo Declaration", the outcome of the seminar it hosted (Maputo, Mozambique, 21–23 May) for the representatives of the eight Governments of the "Delivering as one" pilot countries (Albania, Cape Verde, Mozambique, Pakistan, Rwanda, United Republic of Tanzania, Uruguay and Viet Nam), together with the representatives of Malawi. Launched in 2007 [YUN 2007, p. 1417], the Delivering as one pilot initiative resulted from the recommendations on development, humanitarian assistance and the environment contained in the 2006 report of the High-level Panel on United Nations System-wide Coherence [YUN 2006, p. 1584]. The seminar reviewed lessons learned from the first year of experience of the programme pilot countries and participants exchanged views on how to move the process forward and advance the recommendations of General Assembly resolution 62/208 [YUN 2007, p. 877] on the triennial policy review of operational activities for development.

In the summary statement, participants stressed that the pilot countries became pilots with the hope that a more coherent UN system would better support the Governments in achieving internationally agreed development goals, including the Millennium Development Goals (MDGs) [YUN 2000, p. 51]. They indicated that national ownership in their development partnerships with the UN system had been enhanced through the Delivering as one process. They also noted the diversity of their national circumstances and agreed that in their experience in Delivering as one, the "no one size fits all" principle was being upheld. The seminar reaffirmed the gains made by the pilot countries with respect to enhancing Government leadership of UN system operational activities for development. Initial indicators also revealed that the pilot process was yielding positive results in ensuring that the UN development system was a more effective and coherent counterpart of its national partners. Both the Governments and the UN country teams reported that there was increased availability of the UN system's mandates and expertise for meeting national plans and priorities. Major constraints to the implementation and acceleration of Delivering as one included the lack of predictability and timeliness of funding; lack of harmonization and simplification of business practices; generally high transaction costs of the United Nations; poor alignment of UN capacities with the priorities of programme countries; and a low level of use of national operational capacities. The seminar provided recommendations for accelerating implementation of Assembly resolution 62/208 in the areas of national ownership and leadership; alignment of UN capacity to the needs of programme countries; integration of planning and programme instruments; coherence of budgetary and funding processes; leadership and coordination of UN country teams; and joint offices and simplified business practices.

Report of General Assembly Co-Chairs. In a 15 September letter to the Secretary-General [A/63/362], Ireland and the United Republic of Tanzania, in their capacity as the Co-Chairs for the General Assembly consultations on System-wide Coherence, transmitted a 21 July report, which noted that the Delivering as one approach, despite remaining challenges, was making significant progress at the country level—as reported by the developing countries concerned—and that a large number of other developing countries were coming forward to embrace the approach even if there were no plans for formal designation of new pilot countries. It further noted the main reforms instituted by the approach, such as the agreement on "One Programmes" jointly prepared by the individual Governments concerned and the UN country teams, and the establishment of "One Funding" mechanisms and of "One Leader" for the UN family at the country level in the form of the Resident Coordinator, who was authorized to negotiate the One Programme with the host Government and shape the allocation of funding, while being subject to an accountability framework and oversight mechanisms. During the year, the Co-Chairs focused their efforts on four priority areas on system-wide coherence: UN Delivering as one at country level and the related area of harmonization of business practices; funding; governance; and gender equality and the empowerment of women. They recommended that the Assembly select and act upon those priority matters, which needed to be addressed in continuing discussions on system-wide coherence, and set aside other issues raised by the High-level Panel that were being pursued elsewhere. Other areas discussed in the report included the environment, humanitarian assistance and human rights.

The Co-Chairs concluded that the experience of Delivering as one at the country level (half-way through its second year) was positive, even if challenges remained with regard to the "four ones" (one programme, one budgetary framework, one leader and one office). They noted that the large and growing number of developing countries applying the approach and moving towards implementing resolution 62/208 shared that view. Important principles were being observed, including national ownership and leadership and "no one size fits all". UN country team activities were being aligned to an unprecedented degree with the national development strategies and policies of the developing countries concerned. Moreover, assistance was being delivered with greater effectiveness, savings were being realized and greater reductions in transaction costs were in prospect. The Co-Chairs recommended that the Assembly facilitate a positive political impetus to Delivering as one, thereby encouraging the developing countries which had voluntarily embraced the approach, and enjoin the UN development system to pursue it.

On funding in the context of system-wide coherence, the Co-Chairs observed that there was a need for greater flows of and greater predictability in funding. They commended the development partners which had made concrete contributions to advancing the approach at the country level in response to the strategies, priorities, policies and plans of the developing countries concerned, yet cautioned that support for Delivering as one at the country level must not be at the expense of core funding to agencies through their Headquarters. Overall, there needed to be a significantly improved balance between core and non-core funding. On gender issues, the Co-Chairs recommended that their report be considered together with the institutional options paper subsequently provided by the Deputy Secretary-General to the Assembly in July (see p. 1271).

GENERAL ASSEMBLY ACTION

On 15 September [meeting 122], the General Assembly adopted **resolution 62/277** [draft: A/62/L.51] without vote [agenda item 116].

System-wide coherence

The General Assembly,

Recalling the consensus 2005 World Summit Outcome,

Recalling also its consensus resolution 62/208 of 19 December 2007 on the triennial comprehensive policy review,

Commending the pragmatic, transparent, balanced and inclusive approach taken by the Co-Chairs of the consultative follow-up process by the General Assembly on system-wide coherence, the Permanent Representatives of Ireland and the United Republic of Tanzania to the United Nations, to their work on behalf of the Assembly, which built upon the efforts of their distinguished predecessors, the Permanent Representatives of Barbados and Luxembourg to the United Nations, at the sixty-first session of the General Assembly,

Having considered the paper on "Institutional options to strengthen United Nations work on gender equality and the empowerment of women", which the Deputy Secretary-General provided to the President of the General Assembly on 23 July 2008 in response to a consensus request from Member States,

Looking forward to the independent evaluation foreseen in its resolution 62/208, which will help it to form a comprehensive view of the "Delivering as one" approach to the provision of development assistance through the United Nations system and, in the meantime, acknowledging the interim assessment of progress made and challenges remaining in this regard, as contained in the "Maputo Declaration", issued in May 2008 by a number of least developed and middle income countries which have voluntarily embraced this approach,

1. *Takes note* of the report of the High-level Panel on United Nations System-wide Coherence and the report of the Secretary-General containing his comments thereon;

2. *Welcomes* the report presented by the Co-Chairs of the consultative follow-up process by the General Assembly on system-wide coherence, the Permanent Representatives of Ireland and the United Republic of Tanzania to the United Nations, to the President of the General Assembly on 21 July 2008, the conclusions and recommendations of which are contained in the annex to the present resolution;

3. *Decides*, accordingly, that the continuing and deepening intergovernmental work of the General Assembly on system-wide coherence will focus exclusively and in an integrated manner on "Delivering as one" at country and regional levels, harmonization of business practices, funding, governance, and gender equality and the empowerment of women;

4. *Requests* the Secretary-General, drawing on the resources and expertise of the United Nations system and building on the outcome of its triennial comprehensive policy review, to provide to Member States substantive papers on the issues of funding and governance, as those issues arise in the context of system-wide coherence, with a view to facilitating substantive action by the General Assembly during the sixty-third session;

5. *Welcomes*, in this overall context, the paper on "Institutional options to strengthen United Nations work on gender equality and the empowerment of women", which the Deputy Secretary-General provided to the President of the General Assembly on 23 July 2008, and requests the Secretary-General to provide a further, detailed modalities paper in respect of the options set out in the Deputy Secretary-General's paper, covering funding, governance structure, staffing, specific functions, relationship with the Commission on the Status of Women and other relevant bodies and, having regard to the totality of views expressed by Member States in informal plenary consultations on 8 September 2008, focusing in particular on the "composite entity" option with a view to facilitating substantive action by the General Assembly during the sixty-third session;

6. *Resolves*, at the conclusion of its entire process on system-wide coherence, to review and take stock of all of its prior actions and deliberations in a single resolution or decision.

ANNEX

Conclusions and recommendations of the Co-Chairs of the consultative follow-up process by the General Assembly on system-wide coherence, the Permanent Representatives of Ireland and the United Republic of Tanzania to the United Nations

1. As the Co-Chairs for system-wide coherence at the sixty-second session of the General Assembly we have sought to conduct an open, transparent, balanced and inclusive process of consultations among the entire membership. Our aim has been to present a report that, by and large, will sit well with all parts of the Assembly in that all groupings of States should be able to feel that the report addresses seriously many of their principal priorities and concerns. In this way we have sought to facilitate a balanced and fair compromise outcome to the deliberations of the Assembly during the sixty-second session.

2. The following conclusions and recommendations flow from the present report overall, but are perhaps best seen in tandem with the introductory section. The landmark 2006 report of the High-level Panel on United Nations System-wide Coherence, while a very important contribution to the work of the General Assembly to increase coherence across the United Nations system, did not launch that work. The Millennium Summit and the 2005 World Summit as well as consensus positions of the Assembly, not least the triennial comprehensive policy reviews, constitute much of the bedrock for building further progress in this area.

3. Since the outset of the sixty-second session, the broad membership has signalled that the continuing efforts on system-wide coherence should focus on four priority areas, namely *(a)* the United Nations delivering as one at the country level with the related aspect of harmonization of business practices; *(b)* funding; *(c)* governance; and *(d)* gender equality and the empowerment of women.

4. The present report should be taken together with the paper on gender (in its institutional dimension) which is being provided by the Secretary-General to Member States in response to their request of 16 June 2008.

5. As for "Delivering as one", we have sought to provide the Member States with an accurate and up-to-date picture of the process as it is actually developing on the ground in upwards of thirty developing countries and not simply as it is perceived from afar. We have been helped in this by our on-the-ground consultations with Heads of State and Government, Cabinet ministers, parliamentarians, United Nations country teams, development partners and others in some eight developing countries. We have also conferred at length with United Nations agency heads in New York, Geneva, Rome, Paris and Vienna. We have taken careful note of the "Maputo Declaration" issued in May 2008 by pilot and other developing countries, in which they formally request the Assembly to encourage them in the "Delivering as one" approach that they have voluntarily embraced in partnership with the United Nations system.

6. Our conclusion is that the experience of "Delivering as one" to date (that is to say, halfway through its second year) at the country level is clearly and preponderantly positive, even if a number of challenges remain to be fully addressed in regard to each of the "four ones". We note that this view is shared by the large and growing number of developing countries which are applying the "Delivering as one" approach and proactively moving towards implementing the consensus resolution on the triennial comprehensive policy review. They state that important principles are in fact being observed in practice, including national ownership and leadership and "no one size fits all". Through the "Delivering as one" approach United Nations country team activities are being aligned to an unprecedented degree with the national development strategies and policies of the developing countries concerned. Assistance is being delivered with greater effectiveness, savings are being realized and greater reductions in transaction costs are clearly in prospect.

7. At the same time the picture that emerges at present is interim in nature since the independent evaluation of "Delivering as one", as foreseen by the 2007 triennial comprehensive policy review, will come only towards the end of 2009 and, in any event, concrete development outputs arising from a new way of doing business take longer than eighteen months to emerge definitively.

8. It seems to us clear that the Assembly ought to be in a position during the sixty-second session to give a positive political impetus to "Delivering as one", thereby giving encouragement to those many developing countries which have voluntarily embraced this approach, and to enjoin the United Nations development system to continue to pursue it. Moving forward, it will be essential to safeguard the principles underlying "Delivering as one", in particular that of enhancing national ownership and leadership in the design and implementation of United Nations development system support programmes at the country level. The international community should by the same token be encouraged to continue to respond positively through additional commitments where the combination of strong national leadership and an empowered United Nations country team, delivering as one, together generate a better-aligned and more effective United Nations programme of support.

9. For the most part, the funds, programmes and specialized agencies of the system, at the leadership level, have gradually become increasingly engaged with and supportive of the "Delivering as one" approach. The atmosphere in which they collaborate within the United Nations System Chief Executives Board for Coordination under the chairmanship of the Secretary-General has been transformed for the better as they and their collaborators continue consideration of the implications of the "four ones" (one programme, one budgetary framework and fund, one leader and one office) at the country level. At the same time, it is to be recommended that headquarters levels across the system empower the respective country-level agency representatives with much greater latitude, flexibility and encouragement to advance a more coherent and therefore more effective delivery of United Nations system assistance on the ground in line with the "Delivering as one" approach.

10. In all of this, the particular situations affecting middle-income countries should receive adequate attention.

11. Turning to the issue of funding in the context of system-wide coherence, there clearly need to be greater flows of and greater predictability in funding. In general, overall commitments made solemnly and repeatedly need to be implemented more faithfully. Commendation is due to those development partners which have made concrete contributions to advancing the "Delivering as one" approach at the country level in response to the strategies, priorities, policies and plans of the developing countries concerned. At the same time, support for "Delivering as one" at the country level must not be at the expense of core funding to agencies through their headquarters. Overall, there needs to be a significantly improved balance between core and non-core funding. Funds, programmes and specialized agencies should be invited, if necessary through changes in statute, rules and/or regulations, to give effect to the consensus view in the General Assembly that savings realized at the country level ought to be ploughed back into programmatic development work in the countries where the savings are realized. In this and in other ways, "Delivering as one" must deliver more.

12. As for intergovernmental governance at the central level, we have detected no palpable appetite in the General Assembly for establishing new intergovernmental bodies, including the putative Sustainable Development Board which was recommended by the High-level Panel. At the same time the new realities emerging from a growing number of developing countries applying the "Delivering as one" approach at the country level will need to be accommodated and addressed more effectively by the existing boards and not least by the Economic and Social Council. In the light of the ongoing and emerging nature of the "Delivering as one" approach, it may be necessary to continue and to deepen discussion of these issues during the sixty-third session.

13. If, in that context, the Assembly focuses first on the functions that need to be discharged centrally and intergovernmentally in the "Delivering as one" approach, it will perhaps then be easier to address the question of which institutions, as these continue to adapt, are best placed to discharge the functions in question.

14. We also believe that the United Nations system and the Bretton Woods institutions ought to be consistently encouraged to develop, in a pragmatic manner, a far greater degree of cooperation and collaboration in the context described in the present report. Some progress is already being made. This needs to be developed and enlarged.

15. As for gender equality and the empowerment of women, we recommend that the Assembly be invited to address the matter, including in the light of the Secretary-General's paper on the institutional dimension, in open, informal plenary consultations at an early opportunity, perhaps early in September. During the sixty-second session the Member States have advanced together, by agreement, in their consideration of the issue of gender equality and women's empowerment. With assistance from the Secretary-General, they have identified critical gaps in the way the system assists Member States in implementing globally agreed mandates and their own internationally made commitments in this area. With further open and genuine

discussion the Assembly may be in a position, before the conclusion of its sixty-second session, to signal in general terms, but nevertheless clearly, which institutional option or combination of options, perhaps with adjustments, it wishes to pursue. Detailed working through of such an agreed approach could then be taken up and completed at the sixty-third session. We have the very strong impression that no Government, whether for substantive or "tactical" reasons, would wish to stand in the way of a consensus to advance the issue of gender equality and the empowerment of women through a measured but significant step forward.

16. We believe that in the light of the present report and the Secretary-General's options paper on gender equality and the empowerment of women (in its institutional aspect) Member States ought to be equipped for decision-making during the sixty-second session. With these substantive elements in hand, Member States are also better placed to weigh the format of the decision-making of the Assembly.

17. In the first instance, and on the basis of the foregoing report and these conclusions, Member States may, during the sixty-second session, wish to address, perhaps in a package decision, the four core priority areas listed in paragraph 3 above, which they have highlighted throughout.

18. The same decision could signal that henceforth, in the context of intergovernmental discussion on system-wide coherence, the Assembly will focus exclusively on these priority areas and will exclude from this context the issues of environment/environmental governance, humanitarian assistance and human rights, in line with the considerations set out in the present report.

Comprehensive accountability architecture

The General Assembly, in the 2005 World Summit Outcome [YUN 2005, p. 48], had requested the Secretary-General to take a number of actions for strengthening the United Nations in the context of the Secretariat's management reform, including establishing effective and efficient mechanisms for accountability. In that regard and pursuant to Assembly resolutions 59/272 [ibid., p. 1370] and 61/245 [YUN 2006, p. 1573], the Secretary-General submitted a report [A/62/701 & Corr.1] on the accountability framework, the enterprise risk management and internal control framework, and the results-based management framework, which included measures taken to strengthen accountability in the Secretariat. It proposed a comprehensive accountability architecture that encompassed three key elements of institutional and personal accountability: performance, compliance and integrity that reflected the Organization's commitment to achieving results while respecting its regulations, rules and ethical standards. The proposed architecture would build on the existing accountability framework, which was the chain of responsibility, authority and accountability that flowed institutionally from the intergovernmental organs to the Secretary-General, and personally to managers and staff. The architecture would include a new dimension for enterprise risk management and internal control, enabling the Secretariat to take a systematic approach to identify, assess, evaluate, prioritize, manage and control risk across the Organization. It would also reflect a fully developed results-based management framework, including improved and more frequent monitoring and evaluation.

The report illustrated synergies among the Secretariat's accountability framework, the enterprise risk management and internal control framework, and the results-based management framework, and explained how those tools complemented ongoing management reform and would collectively lead to the integrated and comprehensive accountability architecture. Under that architecture, the Assembly could more readily hold the Secretariat accountable for its activities and results, including the management of financial and human resources and programmatic activities. The Organization would focus on results rather than inputs and outputs of efforts and processes, with emphasis on ethical conduct and compliance with regulations and rules. As part of a review of the Secretariat's accountability framework, a survey was conducted to gauge staff perceptions of accountability. Results of the survey, which were annexed to the report, indicated that 88 per cent of respondents were generally in support of change. The report included proposals on how the Secretariat should respond to the support for change through the comprehensive accountability architecture.

The Secretary-General concluded that the proposed accountability architecture responded to calls for change and answered the concerns of Secretariat staff and Member States. In that regard, managerial tools had been and would continue to be developed to help in the mechanics of assessing risk, monitoring staff and performance, evaluating activities for lessons learned and educating for the achievement of results. He planned to establish a working group of the Management Performance Board [YUN 2005, p. 1468]—the Accountability for Results Working Group—that would be responsible for regularly monitoring and actively guiding senior managers to reach expected results and comprised of three or four members from Secretariat departments or offices. The findings of the Working Group would be reported to the Board with recommendations for concrete action to be taken. On enterprise risk management, the Secretary-General proposed further consultation to incorporate feedback and commentary from the multiple parties that would be involved in the process to implement and maintain the enterprise risk management and internal control framework, including the launch of a pilot project to establish and communicate standards and guidelines for risk management for staff at all levels and to integrate the concepts into areas of highest risk. On results-based management, he proposed to establish a dedicated capacity responsible for advising, supporting and monitoring departments to ensure its complete implementation. The Secretary-General recommended that the Assembly endorse the proposed comprehensive accountability architecture; the concept of an integrated framework for enterprise risk management and internal control; and the results-based management framework, including the proposal for a dedicated capacity responsible for its implementation.

In a 26 February report [A/62/701/Add.1], the Secretary-General presented the additional resource requirements ($3 million) and organizational changes that would be necessitated if the Assembly endorsed the proposals contained in his report.

ACABQ report. In September [A/63/457], the Advisory Committee on Administrative and Budgetary Questions (ACABQ) noted that the Secretary-General's report did not concretely explain how the proposed accountability frameworks would lead to a strengthened, better managed and more accountable Organization; specific timelines or benchmarks were not consistently provided; and the relationships between the various proposals or their linkage to existing structures were not clearly demonstrated. Other areas of concern included the lack of recourse to the expertise available within the UN system; the overlap of the consultants' findings with a previous report of the Joint Inspection Unit (JIU) (see below); the lack of clarity in the definition of accountability, which was one of the fundamental weaknesses in the Secretary-General's accountability architecture; the need for establishing a concrete set of measures to ensure implementation of recommendations from oversight bodies by senior management; and the lack of specific measures identified for improving personal and institutional accountability. In addition, the report responded only partially to key aspects of what was requested by the Assembly, focusing primarily on only one of the six points set out in the Secretary-General's 2006 governance report [YUN 2006, p. 1572], namely, assessment of current policies with respect to accountability and identification of omissions of weaknesses that needed to be addressed.

While noting the Secretary-General's efforts to address accountability, internal control and management practices, ACABQ recommended that those issues be further discussed with other UN system organizations through the High-level Committee on Management of the Chief Executives Board for Coordination (CEB) and the oversight bodies, and that use should be made of expertise within the UN system. It also recommended that the Assembly endorse the proposals on the concept of an integrated framework for enterprise risk management and internal control, and on the results-based management framework. ACABQ recommended against the proposed establishment of a dedicated capacity for implementation of results-based management, the proposed changes to the organizational structure of the Secretariat and the approval of the resources requested.

On 24 December, the Assembly deferred consideration of the Secretary-General's reports until its resumed sixty-third (2009) session (**decision 63/550**).

Results-based management

In February, the Secretary-General transmitted a note [A/62/704] to the General Assembly containing his comments on the 2006 JIU report on results-based management in the United Nations in the context of the reform process [YUN 2006, p. 1652], which was circulated to the Assembly in March 2007 [A/61/805]. The report, which aimed to assess UN capability to apply that management strategy with a view to highlighting best practices and identifying challenges and constraints for successfully applying a results-based approach, summarized the evolution of results-based management in the United Nations and the status of its implementation, and provided an analysis of that status versus the JIU results-based management benchmarking framework. The report examined 37 benchmarks relating to planning, evaluation and reporting cycles; delegation of authority; accountability; performance management; and contractual arrangements. It resulted in 18 recommendations for consideration by the Assembly and the Secretary-General.

In his note, the Secretary-General indicated that he was committed to the full implementation of a Secretariat-wide results-based management strategy in accordance with Assembly mandates and within the limitations of available resources. He added that the recommendations in the JIU report were taken into consideration for the development of the proposed results-based management framework presented in his report on the subject (see p. 1519), which aimed at improving the governance and oversight of the Organization and the effectiveness and accountability of management.

OIOS report. In its review of results-based management at the United Nations [A/63/268], the Office of Internal Oversight Services (OIOS) reported that the introduction of results-based management in the Secretariat had been dealt with as an addition to the myriad rules and procedural requirements that governed inputs, activities, monitoring and reporting. It had not been accompanied by any relaxation of the volume, scope or detail of regulatory frameworks pertaining to financial, programmatic and human resource management. OIOS highlighted the shortcomings of results-based management in its original design, as reflected in Assembly resolution 55/231 [YUN 2000, p. 1295] on results-based budgeting, which was inadequate because it barred the use of indicators of achievement for adjustment of resources and reiterated limitations on the Secretary-General's authority to shift resources between post and non-post budget lines. The Office observed that the introduction of results-based management had brought a superficial orientation to outcomes and that the culture of the Organization remained focused on compliance. Progress in implementing results-based management needed to begin with renewed reform of the budget system. While results-based management had been an administrative chore of little value to accountability and decision-making, OIOS recognized that it would, at some level, remain an aspiration for the Organization and provided six recommendations: establish a policy framework to outline the eventual extent and limitations of results-based management at the UN Secretariat; initiate a review and revision to the rules and regulations pertaining to programme planning, budgeting, monitoring and evaluation; consolidate the Secretary-General's reporting obligations to the General Assembly; integrate programmatic results frameworks within the first phase of the Organization's enterprise resource planning strategy; update and revise the range of output categories subject to planning and monitoring; and strengthen the technical and methodological capacities of the Organization.

By **decision 63/550** of 24 December, the Assembly deferred consideration of the JIU report, the Secretary-General's related comments and the OIOS report until its resumed sixty-third (2009) session.

Mandate review

In response to a letter prepared by the General Assembly President in November 2007 [YUN 2007, p. 1419] setting out the parameters and principles for continuing the mandate review process initiated in 2006 [YUN 2006, p. 1574], the Co-Chairs of the process developed a methodology for carrying out the work, which was based on the existing nine clusters of mandates and included the review of 279 mandates of the humanitarian assistance cluster and 52 mandates of the Africa development cluster. In a letter dated 8 August 2008, the Assembly President transmitted to Member States the final report of the Co-Chairs, which classified 43 mandates for discontinuation, presented an evaluation of the mandate review process, and made recommendations on options for future work.

On the analysis of the two clusters, 35 of the 279 humanitarian assistance mandates and 8 of the 52 Africa development mandates were classified for discontinuation. The Co-Chairs identified benefits of the review process such as Member States' increased awareness of the range of existing mandates and their sharpened interest in wider mandate and budget cycle issues of implementation and accountability. However, the benefits derived from the process were insufficient to justify the continuation of the review in its current format as it was not possible within the existing UN mandate and budget cycle to identify resources that could be reallocated. The Co-Chairs also reported that the analysis of the two clusters had revealed the extent to which the mandate registry was flawed—it had not been updated or maintained since mid-2006. Since the registry, which listed some 9,046 mandates (5,594 older than five years), would remain an essential source of information and foundation for analysis, the Co-Chairs recommended that the Secretariat be requested to establish a permanent capacity to update and maintain the registry. On future work, the Co-Chairs observed that there was a need to improve the management of mandates, yet noted obstacles to an effective mandate review process, namely the ambiguity over ownership and primary responsibility for mandates among implementing agencies and the disconnect between the mandate cycle and the budget cycle, which meant that resources implications of mandates were not transparent or fully traceable. Other concerns included the lack of clarity around mandate interpretation, accountability and follow-up, both from a Member State perspective and the Secretariat viewpoint. The Co-Chairs recommended that Member States consider making a comprehensive analysis of the mandate cycle.

GENERAL ASSEMBLY ACTION

On 15 September [meeting 122], the General Assembly adopted **resolution 62/278** [draft: A/62/L.52] without vote [agenda item 116].

Mandate review

The General Assembly,

Recalling paragraph 163 *(b)* of the 2005 World Summit Outcome, regarding mandate review,

Welcoming the last review process, initiated in 2007 by the President of the General Assembly at its sixty-second session, in a letter dated 6 November 2007, as well as the previous processes conducted during the sixtieth and sixty-first sessions,

Having considered the final report of the Co-Chairs of the mandate review process during the sixty-second session, dated 8 August 2008,

1. *Takes note* of the final report of the Co-Chairs of the mandate review process during the sixty-second session, including on the review of the thematic clusters relating to the effective coordination of humanitarian assistance and the development of Africa;

2. *Recognizes* the usefulness of the existing online mandate registry, and decides to maintain it as an accessible working tool for Member States and to revert to the issue in

the context of its consideration of the proposed programme budget for the biennium 2010–2011;

3. *Notes* that one of the important findings of the process is the difficulty of identifying resources associated with one particular mandate, which limited the potential of the review process to fulfil its objective of strengthening and updating the programme of work of the Organization and improving the allocation of resources for the effective implementation of mandates;

4. *Calls upon* its relevant bodies and subsidiary organs, within their respective mandates and in accordance with the established regulations and rules governing programme planning, to continue improving the implementation of mandates and addressing the continuing validity of legislative decisions and the effective coordination among units of the Secretariat and other structures of the United Nations system.

Strengthening of UN system

In follow-up to General Assembly resolution 60/283 [YUN 2006, p. 1580] on investing in the United Nations for a stronger Organization worldwide, the Secretary General submitted reports on investing in information and communications technology (ICT): information and communications strategy for the United Nations Secretariat [A/62/793 & Corr.1] (see p. 1589), including the related addendum [A/62/793/Add.1] (see p. 1590); and on ICT: enterprise systems for the United Nations Secretariat worldwide [A/62/510/Rev.1]. Also before the Assembly was the report of the activities of the Independent Audit Advisory Committee [A/63/328] (see p. 1562).

By **resolution 63/261** of 24 December (see p. 49), the Assembly took action on strengthening the Department of Political Affairs. On the same date, the Assembly decided that the item on strengthening the UN system would remain for consideration during its resumed sixty-third (2009) session (**decision 63/552**).

Institutional matters

Intergovernmental machinery

Revitalization of General Assembly work

In accordance with resolution 58/316 [YUN 2004, p. 1374], the Secretary-General submitted a July report [A/62/915] on the revitalization of the work of the General Assembly, which outlined the draft programme of work of the plenary and five of the six Main Committees of the Assembly for its sixty-third (2008) session. An addendum to the report [A/62/915/Add.1] contained the status of documentation for that session as at 11 August 2008.

Working Group report. Pursuant to resolution 61/292 [YUN 2007, p. 1421], the Ad Hoc Working Group on the Revitalization of the General Assembly submitted a September report [A/62/952], which summarized its activities and presented recommendations for further progress. The Working Group held seven meetings during the year and conducted its work programme in three stages: a general discussion and exchange of views on all issues related to revitalization; a general discussion on the status of implementation of relevant Assembly resolutions on revitalization; and a detailed analysis of the status of implementation, based on an inventory/chart of all relevant provisions contained in resolutions on revitalization since the fifty-first session (2000) of the Assembly. The Working Group conducted a cluster-by-cluster examination of the chart as follows: Cluster I (working methods, documentation, agenda), Cluster II (selection of the Secretary-General) and Cluster III (role and authority of the General Assembly), which were subdivided into different thematic areas. The Working Group identified a set of elements that appeared to be common areas requiring additional attention from Member States. It recommended that the process of implementation of relevant provisions on revitalization be continued and carefully monitored and, in that connection, presented practical proposals toward that effort. The Working Group also observed that further consideration was needed on the question of modern technologies, including the Assembly voting system. In that regard, the Secretariat could update previous documents on the subject, or present other proposals corresponding with arrangements made in the context of the capital master plan.

In an addendum to the report [A/62/952/Add.1], the Working Group transmitted to the Assembly three annexes that formed an integral part of its report, including the inventory/chart of Assembly resolutions on revitalization.

GENERAL ASSEMBLY ACTION

On 15 September [meeting 122], the General Assembly adopted **resolution 62/276** [A/62/952] without a vote [agenda item 121].

Revitalization of the work of the General Assembly

The General Assembly,

Reaffirming its previous resolutions relating to the revitalization of its work, including resolutions 46/77 of 12 December 1991, 47/233 of 17 August 1993, 48/264 of 29 July 1994, 51/241 of 31 July 1997, 52/163 of 15 December 1997, 55/14 of 3 November 2000, 55/285 of 7 September 2001, 56/509 of 8 July 2002, 57/300 of 20 December 2002, 57/301 of 13 March 2003, 58/126 of 19 December 2003, 58/316 of 1 July 2004, 59/313 of 12 September 2005, 60/286 of 8 September 2006 and 61/292 of 2 August 2007,

Stressing the importance of implementing resolutions on the revitalization of its work,

Recognizing the need to further enhance the role, authority, effectiveness and efficiency of the General Assembly,

1. *Takes note with appreciation* of the report of the Ad Hoc Working Group on the Revitalization of the General Assembly established by resolution 61/292;

2. *Decides* to establish, at its sixty-third session, an ad hoc working group on the revitalization of the General Assembly, open to all Member States:

(*a*) To identify further ways to enhance the role, authority, effectiveness and efficiency of the Assembly, inter alia, by building on previous resolutions;

(*b*) To submit a report thereon to the Assembly at its sixty-third session.

On 24 December, the Assembly decided that the item on the revitalization of the work of the General Assembly would remain for consideration during its resumed sixty-third (2009) session (**decision 63/552**).

Review of Security Council membership and related matters

The Open-ended Working Group on the Question of Equitable Representation on and Increase in the Membership of the Security Council and Other Matters related to the Security Council submitted a report of its work during 13 formal meetings held between December 2007 and September 2008 [A/62/47]. At its first and second meetings (14 December 2007), the Chairperson of the Working Group announced the appointment of a task force to interact with Member States, who were invited to identify negotiables that could serve as a basis for intergovernmental negotiations. In April 2008, the Chairperson forwarded to Member States the replies he had received in writing from delegations, as well as from several regional and interest groups. At the third and fourth meetings (10 April), Member States discussed various elements contained in the written contributions and the Chairperson announced that under his leadership, the task force would engage in extensive consultations with Member States to assess the situation and identify options for moving forward with Security Council reform. Following those consultations, on 9 June, the task force submitted a report entitled, "Report of the Vice-Chairpersons to the President of the General Assembly on the question of equitable representation on and increase in the membership of the Security Council", which was forwarded to Member States. At the Working Group's fifth and sixth meetings (17 June), Member States discussed the report. On 2 September, at its seventh and eighth meetings, the Working Group considered its draft report to the Assembly. The Chairperson invited Member States to put forward amendments and to conduct intensive and constructive consultations in order to reach an agreement on the recommendations. At its ninth to twelfth meetings (10, 12 and 15 September), the Working Group further considered its draft report to the Assembly, which was adopted at the final meeting on 15 September.

By **decision 62/557** of 15 September, the Assembly took note of the Working Group's report and decided to continue to address, within the Group, the framework and modalities in order to prepare and facilitate intergovernmental negotiations on the question of equitable representation on and increase in the membership of the Security Council and other matters related to the Council. It decided to commence such negotiations in an informal Assembly plenary, based on proposals by Member States, during its sixty-third session, no later than 28 February 2009. The Assembly urged the Working Group to exert efforts during that session to achieve general agreement among Member States on all issues relevant to the aforementioned question and other Council-related matters. It requested the Group's Chairperson to present the results of the consultations to an informal Assembly plenary session, no later than 1 February 2009, and requested the Working Group to submit a report to the Assembly before the end of its sixty-third session, including any agreed recommendations.

On 24 December, the Assembly decided that the item on equitable representation on and increase in the membership of the Security Council and related matters would remain for consideration during its resumed sixty-third (2009) session (**decision 63/552**).

Institutional machinery

General Assembly

The General Assembly met throughout 2008; it resumed and concluded its sixty-second session and held the major part of its sixty-third session. The sixty-second session resumed in plenary meetings on 12 and 13 February; 4 and 31 March; 2–4, 18 and 29 April; 15 and 21 May; 4, 6, 10–12 and 20 June; 8, 11, 18, 21, 23 and 28 July; and 4–5, 11 and 15 September. The sixty-third session opened on 16 September and continued until its suspension on 24 December.

The Assembly held a High-level debate on climate change (11–12 February) (see p. 1164); a High-level event on the Millennium Development Goals (MDGs) (1–2 April); and a High-level debate on management reform (8–9 April). High-level meetings also took place on HIV/AIDS (10–12 June) (see p. 1329); implementation of the new partnership for Africa's development (22 September) (see p. 1009); Africa's development needs (22 September) (ibid.); meeting the MDGs

(25 September) (see p. 926); the midterm review of the Almaty Programme of Action on landlocked developing countries (2–3 October) (see p. 949); and a High-level meeting on the culture of peace (12–13 November) (see p. 1217). It also held an interactive panel on the global financial crisis (30 October) (see p. 1068). On 10 December, the General Assembly held a commemorative meeting to mark the sixtieth anniversary of the adoption of the Universal Declaration of Human Rights (see p. 727).

Organization of Assembly sessions

2008 sessions

By **decision 63/501** of 16 September, the General Assembly authorized a number of subsidiary bodies to meet in New York during the main part of its sixty-third session. By **decision 63/502** of 19 September, the Assembly adopted a number of provisions concerning the organization of the sixty-third session [A/63/250 & Corr.1].

Credentials

The Credentials Committee, at its meeting on 19 December [A/63/633], had before it a memorandum by the Secretary-General, which indicated that 124 Member States had submitted the formal credentials of their representatives. Information concerning the representatives of 67 other Member States had also been communicated. One Member State (Guinea) had not made any communication to the Secretary-General.

The Committee adopted a resolution accepting the credentials received and recommended a draft resolution to the General Assembly for adoption. On 23 December, the Assembly, by **resolution 63/238**, approved the Committee's report.

Agenda

During its resumed sixty-second (2008) session, the General Assembly, by **decision 62/503 B**, decided to include an additional item on the agenda of the session and decided on those items to be considered directly in plenary and those on which consideration would be reopened. The Assembly, by decisions on 3 April (**decision 62/545 B**), 20 June (**decision 62/545 C**), and 15 September (**decisions 62/554, 62/555** and **62/556**), decided on those items to be deferred to its sixty-third (2008) session.

At its sixty-third session, the Assembly, by **decision 63/503** of 19 September, adopted, on the recommendation of the General Committee [A/63/250 & Corr.1 & Add.1], the agenda [A/63/251] and the allocation of items [A/63/252], including those to be deferred and included in the provisional agenda of its sixty-fourth (2009) session. By the same decision, it decided to consider in the Third (Social, Humanitarian and Cultural) Committee agenda item 58 on the report of the Human Rights Council. The Assembly also decided to include in the agenda of its sixty-third (2008) session additional items entitled "Judges of the International Tribunal for the Prosecution of Persons Responsible for Serious Violations of International Humanitarian Law Committed in the Territory of the Former Yugoslavia since 1991", "Recognition of sickle-cell anaemia as a public health priority", "Granting of observer status for the International Fund for Saving the Aral Sea in the General Assembly", and "Follow-up to and implementation of the outcome of the 2002 International Conference on Financing for Development and the preparation of the 2008 Review Conference".

On 2 December (**decision 63/520**), the Assembly, by a recorded vote of 130 to 3, with 46 abstentions, included in the provisional agenda of its sixty-fourth (2009) session the item "United Nations conference to identify appropriate ways of eliminating nuclear dangers in the context of nuclear disarmament" (see p. 566). On the same date, by **decisions 63/518** and **63/519** respectively, the Assembly decided to include in the provisional agenda of its sixty-fourth session the items entitled "Role of science and technology in the context of international security and disarmament" and "Convening of the fourth special session of the General Assembly devoted to disarmament".

By its **decision 63/552** of 24 December, the Assembly decided to retain 74 items on the agenda of its resumed sixty-third (2009) session. On the same date (**decision 63/550**), the Assembly deferred until its resumed sixty-third session its consideration of items and related documents concerning the review of the efficiency of the administrative and financial functioning of the United Nations; the programme budget for the biennium 2008–2009; and the scale of assessments for the apportionment of the expenses of the United Nations.

On 2 December, the Assembly decided to include in the provisional agenda of its sixty-fifth (2010) session the item entitled "Maintenance of international security—good neighbourliness, stability and development in South-Eastern Europe" (**decision 63/517**).

Resolutions and decisions of the General Assembly

By **decision 63/507** of 27 October, the General Assembly deferred consideration of the agenda item entitled "Implementation of the resolutions of the United Nations" and included it in the provisional agenda of its sixty-fourth (2009) session.

First, Second, Third, Fourth and Sixth Committees

The General Assembly, on 2 December, approved the proposed programme of work and timetable of the First (Disarmament and International Security) Committee for the sixty-fourth (2009) session (**decision 63/521**). On 5 December, the Assembly approved the programme of work and timetable of the Fourth (Special Political and Decolonization) Committee for the sixty-fourth session (**decision 63/527**). On 11 December, the Assembly noted that the Sixth (Legal) Committee had adopted its provisional programme of work (**decision 63/529**) for 2009. On 18 and 19 December, the Assembly approved, respectively, the programme of work for the Third Committee (**decision 63/537**) and the Second (Economic and Financial) Committee (**decision 63/545**) for the sixty-fourth session.

Security Council

The Security Council held 244 formal meetings in 2008, adopted 65 resolutions and issued 48 presidential statements. It considered 60 agenda items (see APPENDIX IV). The President also made 47 statements to the press on behalf of Council members. Monthly assessments on the work of the Council in 2008 were issued by the successive Council Presidents [S/2008/158, S/2008/499, S/2008/355, S/2008/579, S/2008/572, S/2008/580, S/2008/581, S/2008/596, S/2008/108, S/2008/696, S/2009/96, S/2009/328]. In a 22 September note [A/63/300], the Secretary-General, in accordance with Article 12, paragraph 2 of the Charter of the United Nations, and with the consent of the Security Council, notified the General Assembly of 105 matters relative to the maintenance of peace and security that the Council had discussed since his previous annual notification [YUN 2007, p. 1424]. The Assembly, on 18 November, took note of the Secretary-General's note (**decision 63/514**). On 20 November, the Assembly took note of the Council's report for the period of 1 August 2007 to 31 July 2008 [A/63/2] (**decision 63/515**).

Membership

The General Assembly continued to examine the question of expanding the Security Council membership. In that regard, it considered the report of the Open-ended Working Group on the Question of Equitable Representation on and Increase in the Membership of the Security Council and Other Matters related to the Security Council [A/62/47]. The Assembly took action with regard to the report in **decision 62/557** of 15 September (see p. 1523).

Working methods

In a 20 June letter [S/2008/418] to the Security Council President, Switzerland on behalf of the S-5 Group (Costa Rica, Jordan, Liechtenstein, Singapore and Switzerland) requested the Council to convene a meeting on improving the working methods of the Council. In a 4 August letter [S/2008/528] to the Secretary-General, Belgium transmitted a concept paper for the open debate of the Council on implementation of the measures set out in the 19 July 2006 note by the Council President [YUN 2007, p. 1424], which aimed to enhance the efficiency and transparency of the Council's work, as well as its interaction and dialogue with non-Council members. The concept paper proposed that the debate could focus on the implementation of concrete measures in three specific and interrelated fields: transparency, interaction with non-Council members and efficiency. It also provided an overview on the implementation status of measures in each of those areas.

The Security Council debate [meeting 5968] was held on 27 August and some 45 speakers participated in the discussion, including the Secretary-General. In closing, the Council President observed that the debate provided an opportunity for all—in particular non-members of the Council—to state their views on the functioning of the Council. He noted that most delegations highlighted the key role of the Council's Informal Working Group on Documentation and Other Procedural Questions and urged the Group to benefit from the debate in order to return to the Council as soon as possible with a specific outcome.

In a 31 December note [S/2008/847], the Security Council President outlined the working methods for matters of which the Security Council was seized (seizure statement). The note contained consolidated and revised provisions of paragraph 49 of the 2006 note by the Council President and of paragraphs 5 to 7 of the 2007 note of the Council President [YUN 2007, p. 1424]. The 2008 note reiterated the desirability, when possible, of the use of descriptive formulations of agenda items at the time of their adoption. At the end of each year, the Council would review the seizure statement to determine if the Council had concluded consideration of any of the listed items or if any items should be deleted from the statement. Items not considered by the Council during the preceding three calendar years would also be deleted. The preliminary annual summary statement issued each January by the Secretary-General would identify those items to be deleted from the list, and the first seizure statement issued in March of each year would reflect the deletion of those items—unless a Member State notified the Council President by the end of February that it requested that an item remain on the seizure statement. The item would then remain on the statement for one year, unless the Council decided otherwise. The deletion of an item did not imply that the item in question could not be taken up by the Council in the future. The first seizure statement of each month would contain a full and updated list of items of which the Council was seized; yet for intervening weeks, a weekly addendum would be issued, listing only those items on which the Council took further action during the previous week, or indicated there was no change during that period.

Economic and Social Council

The Economic and Social Council held its organizational session for 2008 on 14 January and 5 and 8 February; a resumed organizational session on 29 April and 12 and 20 June; a special high-level meeting with the Bretton Woods institutions (the World Bank Group and the International Monetary Fund), the World Trade Organization (WTO) and the United Nations Conference on Trade and Development (UNCTAD) on 14 April; and a special meeting on the global food crisis from 20 to 22 May, all in New York. It held its substantive session from 30 June to 25 July and its resumed substantive session on 12 September and 19 December, in New York. The work of the Council in 2008 was covered in its report to the General Assembly [A/63/3/Rev.1].

On 14 and 17 January, the Council elected its Bureau (a President and four Vice-Presidents) for 2008 and adopted the agenda of the organizational session [E/2008/2 & Add.1 & Add.1/Corr.1].

On 5 February, the Council decided on the working arrangements for its 2008 substantive session (**decision 2008/206**) and approved the provisional agenda and documentation for that session (**decision 2008/204**). On 30 June it adopted the agenda [E/2008/100] and approved the programme of work of that session [E/2008/L.5] (**decision 2008/214**).

On 8 February, the Council decided that the theme for the 2008 thematic discussion for the high-level segment would be "Promoting an integrated approach to rural development in developing countries for poverty eradication and sustainable development, taking into account current challenges" (**decision 2008/208**).

The General Assembly, by **decision 63/552** of 24 December, decided that the Council's report would remain for consideration during its resumed sixty-third (2009) session.

Sessions and segments

During 2008, the Economic and Social Council adopted 38 resolutions and 67 decisions. By **decision 2008/206**, the Council decided that the high-level segment would be held from 30 June to 3 July; the coordination segment from 7 to 9 July; the operational activities segment from 10 to 14 July; the humanitarian affairs segment from 15 to 17 July; and the general segment from 18 to 24 July. It also decided to conclude its work on 25 July. On 5 February, the Council decided that the special high-level meeting with the Bretton Woods institutions, WTO and UNCTAD would be held in New York on 14 April (**decision 2008/203**).

2008, 2009, 2010 and 2011 sessions

On 5 February, the Council decided that the work of the operational activities segment of its 2008 substantive session would be devoted to the progress on and implementation of General Assembly resolution 62/208 [YUN 2007, p. 877] on the triennial comprehensive policy review of operational activities for development of the UN system (**decision 2008/207**). On 8 February (**decision 2008/209**), it decided that the theme for the regional cooperation item would be "The regional dimension of the themes of the high-level segment for 2008". On 29 April (**decision 2008/213**), the Council decided that the theme for the humanitarian affairs segment would be "Building capabilities and capacities at all levels for timely humanitarian assistance, including disaster risk reduction" and that it would convene two panels, one on "Disaster risk reduction and preparedness: addressing the humanitarian consequences of natural disasters, including the impact of climate change" and the other on "Humanitarian challenges related to global food aid, including enhancing international efforts and cooperation in this field".

On 25 July, by **decision 2008/256**, the Council took note of the report of the Secretary-General on the role of the Economic and Social Council in the integrated and coordinated implementation of and follow-up to the outcomes of the major UN conferences and summits (see p. 1527). On the same date, the Council decided that the theme for its 2009 thematic discussion would be "Current global and national trends and their impact on social development, including public health" (**decision 2008/257**), and adopted the themes for its annual ministerial-level substantive reviews for the 2010 and 2011 sessions, respectively: implementing the internationally agreed goals and commitments in regard to gender equality and empowerment of women; and implementing the internationally agreed goals and commitments in regard to education (**decision 2008/258**).

Work programme

On 5 February, the Council took note of the list of questions for inclusion in its programme of work for 2009 [E/2008/1] (**decision 2008/205**).

Coordination, monitoring and cooperation

Institutional mechanisms

CEB activities

According to its annual overview report for 2008/09 [E/2009/67], the United Nations System Chief Executives Board for Coordination (CEB) addressed a number of emerging and important programme issues, particularly the global financial and economic crisis, climate change, and the UN development and resident coordinator system. In response to the unfolding global economic crisis, CEB agreed on nine key areas in a joint initiative that encompassed: additional financing for the most vulnerable; food security; trade; a green economy initiative; a global jobs pact; a social protection floor; humanitarian action, security and social stability; technology and innovation; and monitoring and analysis. On climate change, CEB reported that steps were taken to identify focus and cross-cutting areas for coordination and action. CEB was developing a system-wide approach to support the Secretary-General in his efforts to prepare for intergovernmental discussions at the UN Climate Change Conference in Copenhagen, Denmark, in December 2009. The Board also endorsed the management and accountability framework for the UN development and resident coordinator system, including a functional firewall for the resident coordinator system. The agreement established a vision to guide the creation of a more efficient UN development system. Other areas of focus included working together in crisis and post-crisis countries; the need to strengthen the UN security framework to protect staff and allow operations to continue in insecure and unstable environments; and the development of a plan of action for the harmonization of UN system business practices.

CEB held two regular sessions in 2008: the first in Bern, Switzerland (28 April) [CEB/2008/1] and the second in New York (24 October) [CEB/2008/2]. Its principal subsidiary bodies met as follows: the High-level Committee on Management (HLCM), fifteenth (Rome, 17–18 March) [CEB/2008/3] and sixteenth (New York, 18–19 September) [CEB/2008/5] sessions; and the High-level Committee on Programmes (HLCP), fifteenth (Rome, 13–14 March) [CEB/2008/4] and sixteenth (Rome, 30 September and 1 October) [CEB/2008/6] sessions.

CEB report

CPC consideration. The Committee for Programme and Coordination (CPC) [A/63/16] considered the CEB annual overview report for 2007/2008 [YUN 2007, p. 1426]. CPC recommended that the Secretary-General ensure that the CEB annual overview report included information on measures taken by the Board to improve its transparency and accountability and that future reports provided specific information on the main difficulties encountered in the implementation of coordination activities in different sectors, as well as on the relevant solutions adopted and the impact of CEB activities on the UN system. The Committee also recommended that the General Assembly request CEB to continue to monitor the effective collaboration of system-wide efforts against hunger and poverty and to report on the progress achieved regarding the difficulties encountered by UN system entities in addressing malnutrition and hunger. Noting the CEB endorsement of the recommendation for an evaluation of the eight "Delivering as one" pilot projects [YUN 2006, p. 1584], the Committee stressed the importance of an independent, objective and impartial evaluation process and that any criteria and methodology to assess the impact of those projects should first be considered and approved by Member States.

On 21 July, the Economic and Social Council took note of the CEB annual overview report for 2007/08 (**decision 2008/221**).

Programme coordination

The Committee for Programme and Coordination (CPC) held an organizational meeting on 30 April and its forty-eighth session from 9 June to 3 July, all in New York [A/63/16].

CPC considered questions related to programme performance of the United Nations for the 2006-2007 biennium and the proposed 2010–2011 strategic framework. It considered the in-depth evaluation of political affairs, and two triennial reviews, one on the in-depth evaluation of the United Nations Human Settlements Programme, and the other on the evaluation of linkages between Headquarters and field activities. In addition, CPC considered the Secretary-General's report on UN system support for the New Partnership for Africa's Development (see p. 1012), as well as improving its working methods and procedures.

On 21 July, the Economic and Social Council took note of the CPC report (**decision 2008/221**).

Other coordination matters

Follow-up to international conferences

Report of Secretary-General. In response to Economic and Social Council resolution 2007/29 [YUN 2007, p. 1427], the Secretary-General submitted a June report [A/63/83-E/2008/77] on the Council's role in the integrated and coordinated implementation of the outcomes of and follow-up to major UN conferences and summits, which highlighted the central role of the annual ministerial review as a forum for all stakeholders to assess progress in overall implementation of the internationally agreed development goals. The annual ministerial review, launched in 2007 [YUN 2007, p. 1427], examined cross-cutting themes common to the outcomes of the major UN conferences and was considered the most effective way for the Council to make progress in the integrated conference follow-up. The report also discussed the progress made on the conference follow-up as it related to the theme of the 2008 annual ministerial review, "Implementing the internationally agreed goals and commitments in regard to sustainable development". In other developments, several procedural improvements in the follow-up of conferences had facilitated progress in advancing an integrated approach in the substantive work of Council machinery; the Council and its subsidiary bodies had increased their interaction; and the functional commissions had completed examining their methods of work.

The Secretary-General proposed the adoption of a multi-year programme of work for the annual ministerial review to facilitate engagement by the Council system. The report also suggested that the Council consider making the report triennial to provide a reasonable time period before the next overall review of the integrated conference follow-up. Other recommendations pertained to promoting policy coherence at the intergovernmental level; reporting on the integrated and coordinated follow-up to conferences; linking normative and operational work; strengthening the relationship with the Bretton Woods institutions and WTO; and creating partnerships and alliances with all stakeholders.

ECONOMIC AND SOCIAL COUNCIL ACTION

On 24 July [meeting 43], the Economic and Social Council adopted **resolution 2008/29** [draft: E/2008/L.29] without vote [agenda item 4].

Role of the Economic and Social Council in the integrated and coordinated implementation of and follow-up to the outcomes of the major United Nations conferences and summits, in the light of relevant General Assembly resolutions, including resolution 61/16

The Economic and Social Council,

Recalling its agreed conclusions 1995/1 of 28 July 1995 and 2002/1 of 26 July 2002 and its relevant resolutions on the integrated and coordinated implementation of and follow-up to the outcomes of the major United Nations conferences and summits, including its resolutions 2006/44 of 28 July 2006, 2007/8 of 25 July 2007 and 2007/29 of 27 July 2007, its decisions 2006/206 of 10 February 2006 and 2006/274 of 15 December 2006 and General Assembly resolutions 50/227 of 24 May 1996, 52/12 B of 19 December 1997, 57/270 B of 23 June 2003, 60/265 of 30 June 2006 and 61/16 of 20 November 2006,

Recalling also the internationally agreed development goals, including the Millennium Development Goals, and the outcomes of the major United Nations conferences and summits and the review of their implementation in the economic, social and related fields,

Reaffirming the need to fully implement the internationally agreed development goals, including the Millennium Development Goals, and in this regard expressing its determination to enhance the momentum generated by the 2005 World Summit, in particular for strengthening the role of the Economic and Social Council through its new functions,

Recalling that the Council should increase its role in overseeing system-wide coordination and the balanced integration of economic, social and environmental aspects of United Nations policies and programmes aimed at promoting sustainable development, and reaffirming that the Commission on Sustainable Development should continue to be the high-level commission on sustainable development within the United Nations system and to serve as a forum for consideration of issues related to integration of the three dimensions of sustainable development, as called for in Assembly resolution 61/16,

Recognizing the important role of a strengthened Council, in accordance with Assembly resolution 61/16, in promoting integrated and coordinated follow-up to conferences and summits,

Taking note of the report of the Secretary-General on the role of the Council in the integrated and coordinated implementation of the outcomes of and follow-up to the major United Nations conferences and summits, in the light of Assembly resolutions, including resolution 61/16,

1. *Reaffirms* the need to continue to strengthen the Economic and Social Council as the central mechanism for system-wide coordination and thus promote the integrated and coordinated implementation of and follow-up to the outcomes of the major United Nations conferences in the economic, social and related fields, in accordance with the Charter of the United Nations and relevant General Assembly resolutions, in particular resolutions 50/227, 57/270 B and 61/16;

2. *Welcomes* the holding of the first Development Cooperation Forum and the second annual ministerial review as steps forward in the strengthening of the Council;

3. *Recognizes* the need to further enhance coordination and cooperation between the Council and its functional commissions, the regional commissions and other subsidiary bodies so as to allow the Council to carry out more effectively its crucial role as the central mechanism for system-wide coordination;

4. *Encourages* the functional commissions to continue to explore ways to engage agencies, funds and programmes of the United Nations system more systematically in their work within their respective mandates;

5. *Invites* the organizations of the United Nations system, including the Bretton Woods institutions and the World Trade Organization, to contribute, within their respective mandates, to the work of the Council, as appropri-

ate, including to the integrated and coordinated implementation of and follow-up to the outcomes of the major United Nations conferences and summits, in accordance with relevant Assembly resolutions, including resolution 61/16;

6. *Welcomes* the strengthened cooperation between the Council and the Bretton Woods institutions, the World Trade Organization and the United Nations Conference on Trade and Development, and emphasizes that the interaction should be further improved;

7. *Stresses* that the preparation of the annual ministerial review should be fully supported by the United Nations system, especially the funds, programmes and specialized agencies, in accordance with the respective mandates, as appropriate, in coordination with national Governments;

8. *Requests* the functional commissions, the regional commissions and other relevant subsidiary bodies of the Council, in accordance with their mandates, as appropriate, to contribute to the annual ministerial review and to the Development Cooperation Forum, in the context of their respective annual work plans, taking into account their specificities;

9. *Stresses* the important contribution of civil society in the implementation of conference outcomes, and emphasizes that the contribution of non-governmental organizations and the private sector to the work of the Council should be further encouraged and improved, in accordance with the rules and procedures of the Council;

10. *Requests* the Secretary-General to submit a report on measures taken to implement the Ministerial Declaration of the high-level segment of the Council for consideration by the Council at the coordination segment of its substantive session of the following year;

11. *Decides* to review the periodicity of the report of the Secretary-General on the role of the Council in the integrated and coordinated implementation of and follow-up to the outcomes of the major United Nations conferences and summits, in the light of relevant Assembly resolutions, at its substantive session of 2009, with a view towards further enhancing the effectiveness of the report;

12. *Requests* the Secretary-General to submit a report on the above-mentioned subject for consideration by the Council at its substantive session of 2009.

On 24 December, the General Assembly decided that the item on integrated and coordinated implementation of and follow-up to the outcomes of the major UN conferences and summits in the economic, social and related fields would remain for consideration during its resumed sixty-third (2009) session (**decision 63/552**).

UN and other organizations

Cooperation with organizations

In response to General Assembly resolution 58/316 [YUN 2004, p. 1374], the Secretary-General submitted an August consolidated report [A/63/228-S/2008/531 & Corr.1] on cooperation between the United Nations and regional and other organizations, including the African Union (see p. 108); the Asian-African Legal Consultative Organization (see p. 1478); the Association of Southeast Asian Nations (see p. 1115); the Black Sea Economic Cooperation Organization (see p. 1121); the Caribbean Community (see p. 350); the Community of Portuguese-speaking countries (see below); the Council of Europe (see p. 472); the Economic Cooperation Organization (see p. 1116); the Eurasian Economic Community (see p. 1120); the International Organization of la Francophonie (see p. 1534); the Inter-Parliamentary Union (see p. 1536); the League of Arab States (see p. 1531); the Organization of the Islamic Conference (see p. 1532); the Organization for the Prohibition of Chemical Weapons (see p. 609); the Pacific Islands Forum (see p. 1117); the Preparatory Commission for the Comprehensive Nuclear-Test-Ban Treaty Organization (see p. 581); and the Southern African Development Community (see p. 328).

On 24 December, by **decision 63/552**, the Assembly decided that the item on cooperation between the United Nations and regional and other organizations would remain for consideration during its resumed sixty-third (2009) session.

Community of Portuguese-speaking countries

In response to General Assembly resolution 61/223 [YUN 2006, p. 1598], the Secretary-General reported [A/63/228-S/2008/531 & Corr.1] on cooperation between the United Nations and the Community of Portuguese-speaking Countries (CPLP). Since 2006, Brazil and the World Food Programme (WFP) had spearheaded efforts to provide capacity development assistance for school feeding programmes in lusophone African countries. Senior officials from the Brazilian Ministry of Education and WFP met several times with high-level government officials in Angola, Cape Verde and Mozambique to identify needs for such technical assistance. The Portuguese Language Unit of Radio and Television Service of the UN Department of Public Information, in a cooperative arrangement with CPLP, continued to broadcast daily news bulletins and weekly magazine programmes reaching a worldwide audience of more than 230 million Portuguese-speaking people, via some 1,500 radio stations.

In a 20 August letter to the Assembly, Portugal, on behalf of the Presidency of CPLP, submitted its report [A/63/343], which discussed progress achieved in the cooperation between CPLP and 9 UN system entities, including the finalization of a protocol between CPLP and the secretariat of the United Nations Convention to Combat Desertification. In partnership with the Economic Community of West African States (ECOWAS), CPLP deployed efforts to introduce the issue of Guinea-Bissau onto the agenda of the Peacebuilding Commission. Subsequently, CPLP, ECOWAS, Portugal and the United Nations Peacebuilding Support Office in Guinea-Bissau (UNOGBIS) initiated the International Contact Group on Guinea-Bissau to support peacebuilding efforts in the country. CPLP and the International Fund for Agricultural Development signed a cooperation agreement to combat rural poverty in Portuguese-speaking developing countries. CPLP activities also included a March conference on international security challenges and cooperation within the Community, organized by the CPLP executive secretariat in partnership with the Defence Commission of the Portuguese Parliament. On 25 April, CPLP and the Portuguese Unit of UN Radio signed an agreement, which called for the exchange of information on the signatories' activities and news content; and cooperation for the joint production of journalistic initiatives to promote cultural diversity within CPLP member States. The report covered activities conducted within the Community under the theme of the MDGs.

On 20 August, [A/63/344] Portugal submitted to the Assembly the final declaration of the seventh Conference of Heads of State and Government of CPLP (Lisbon, Portugal, 24–25 July).

GENERAL ASSEMBLY ACTION

On 11 December [meeting 68], the General Assembly adopted **resolution 63/143** [draft: A/63/L.41 & Add.1] without vote [agenda item 114 *(f)*].

Cooperation between the United Nations and the Community of Portuguese-speaking Countries

The General Assembly,

Recalling its resolution 54/10 of 26 October 1999, by which it granted observer status to the Community of Portuguese-speaking Countries and considered it mutually advantageous to provide for cooperation between the United Nations and the Community of Portuguese-speaking Countries, as well as its resolutions 59/21 of 8 November 2004 and 61/223 of 20 December 2006,

Recalling also the Articles of the Charter of the United Nations, in particular of Chapter VIII, that encourage activities through regional cooperation for the promotion of the purposes and principles of the United Nations, and Security Council resolution 1809(2008) of 16 April 2008 on peace and security in Africa,

Considering that the activities of the Community of Portuguese-speaking Countries complement and support the work of the United Nations,

Welcoming the celebration by the United Nations Educational, Scientific and Cultural Organization, for the third consecutive year, of Portuguese Language Day, on 23 June 2008,

1. *Notes with appreciation* the outcome of the seventh Conference of Heads of State and Government of the Community of Portuguese-speaking Countries, held in Lisbon on 24 and 25 July 2008, which recognizes the economic value of the Portuguese language and the political commitment to promote it in the international and regional organizations and United Nations agencies and programmes;

2. *Expresses satisfaction* with the strengthening of cooperation between the Community of Portuguese-speaking Countries and the specialized agencies and other bodies and programmes of the United Nations, in particular the Office of the United Nations High Commissioner for Human Rights, the United Nations Educational, Scientific and Cultural Organization, the Food and Agriculture Organization of the United Nations, the International Labour Organization and the Joint United Nations Programme on HIV/AIDS;

3. *Welcomes* the signature of a cooperation agreement between the Executive Secretariat of the Community of Portuguese-speaking Countries and the Portuguese Language Unit of the Radio and Television Service of the Department of Public Information of the Secretariat, in New York on 25 April 2008, regarding the exchange of information and cooperation to organize initiatives to promote cultural diversity within the Portuguese-speaking countries;

4. *Also welcomes* the signature of a cooperation agreement between the International Fund for Agricultural Development and the Community of Portuguese-speaking Countries on 8 November 2007, on combating rural poverty in Portuguese-speaking developing countries, as well as the work done by the Executive Secretariat of the Community of Portuguese-speaking Countries, within the framework of the technical cooperation project signed in May 2008 with the Food and Agriculture Organization of the United Nations, which aims at the formulation of a South-South and North-South cooperation programme for the implementation of the United Nations Convention to Combat Desertification in Those Countries Experiencing Serious Drought and/or Desertification, Particularly in Africa;

5. *Further welcomes* the establishment of the partnership between the Community of Portuguese-speaking countries and the International Labour Organization Office in Lisbon, which aims at the creation of an interactive platform for the Governments of the Portuguese-speaking countries to exchange information and experiences within the scope of social protection, decent work, monitoring of labour standards and working conditions, and the fight against child labour;

6. *Recognizes* the importance of the signature, in Istanbul, Turkey, on 5 November 2008, of a cooperation agreement between the Community of Portuguese-speaking Countries and the secretariat of the Convention, with a view to developing joint actions in the fields of combating desertification, land degradation, drought mitigation, water scarcity and poverty;

7. *Encourages* the Secretary-General and the Executive Secretary of the Community of Portuguese-speaking Countries to initiate consultations with a view to considering the establishment of a formal cooperation agreement;

8. *Requests* the Secretary-General to submit to the General Assembly at its sixty-fifth session a report on the implementation of the present resolution;

9. *Decides* to include in the provisional agenda of its sixty-fifth session the sub-item entitled "Cooperation between the United Nations and the Community of Portuguese-speaking Countries".

League of Arab States

In response to General Assembly resolution 61/14 [YUN 2006, p, 1599], the Secretary-General, in his consolidated report [A/63/228-S/2008/531 & Corr.1] issued in August, provided information on cooperation between the United Nations and the League of Arab States (LAS).

GENERAL ASSEMBLY ACTION

On 10 November [meeting 42], the General Assembly adopted **resolution 63/17** [draft: A/63/L.20 & Add.1] without vote [agenda item 114 *(n)*].

Cooperation between the United Nations and the League of Arab States

The General Assembly,

Recalling its previous resolutions on cooperation between the United Nations and the League of Arab States,

Having considered the report of the Secretary-General on cooperation between the United Nations and regional and other organizations,

Recalling article 3 of the Pact of the League of Arab States, which entrusts the Council of the League with the function of determining the means whereby the League will collaborate with the international organizations which may be created in the future to guarantee peace and security and organize economic and social relations,

Noting the desire of both organizations to consolidate, develop and enhance further the ties existing between them in the political, economic, social, humanitarian, cultural, technical and administrative fields,

Taking into account the report of the Secretary-General entitled "An Agenda for Peace", in particular section VII concerning cooperation with regional arrangements and organizations, and the "Supplement to an Agenda for Peace",

Convinced of the need for more efficient and coordinated utilization of available economic and financial resources in order to promote the common objectives of the two organizations,

Recognizing the need for the further strengthening of cooperation between the United Nations system and the League of Arab States and its specialized organizations for the realization of the common goals and objectives of the two organizations,

1. *Takes note with satisfaction* of the report of the Secretary-General;

2. *Commends* the continued efforts of the League of Arab States to promote multilateral cooperation among Arab States, and requests the United Nations system to continue to lend its support;

3. *Expresses its appreciation* to the Secretary-General for the follow-up action taken by him to implement the proposals adopted at the meetings between representatives of the Secretariat of the United Nations and other organizations of the United Nations system and the General Secretariat of the League of Arab States and its specialized organizations, including the sectoral meeting in 2005 on the theme "Achieving and financing the Millennium Development Goals and sustainable development in the Arab region" and the general meeting on cooperation held in 2006;

4. *Requests* the Secretariat of the United Nations and the General Secretariat of the League of Arab States, within their respective fields of competence, to intensify further their cooperation for the realization of the purposes and principles embodied in the Charter of the United Nations, the strengthening of international peace and security, economic and social development, disarmament, decolonization, self-determination and the eradication of all forms of racism and racial discrimination;

5. *Requests* the Secretary-General to continue his efforts to strengthen cooperation and coordination between the United Nations and other organizations and agencies of the United Nations system and the League of Arab States and its specialized organizations in order to enhance their capacity to serve the mutual interests and objectives of the two organizations in the political, economic, social, humanitarian, cultural and administrative fields;

6. *Calls upon* the specialized agencies and other organizations and programmes of the United Nations system:

(a) To continue to cooperate with the Secretary-General and among themselves, as well as with the League of Arab States and its specialized organizations, in the follow-up of multilateral proposals aimed at strengthening and expanding cooperation in all fields between the United Nations system and the League of Arab States and its specialized organizations;

(b) To strengthen the capacity of the League of Arab States and of its institutions and specialized organizations to benefit from globalization and information technology and to meet the development challenges of the new millennium;

(c) To step up cooperation and coordination with the specialized organizations of the League of Arab States in the organization of seminars and training courses and in the preparation of studies;

(d) To maintain and increase contacts and improve the mechanism of consultation with the counterpart programmes, organizations and agencies concerned regarding projects and programmes in order to facilitate their implementation;

(e) To participate whenever possible with organizations and institutions of the League of Arab States in the execution and implementation of development projects in the Arab region;

(f) To inform the Secretary-General of the progress made in their cooperation with the League of Arab States and its specialized organizations and, in particular, of the follow-up action taken on the multilateral and bilateral proposals adopted at the previous meetings between the two organizations;

7. *Also calls upon* the specialized agencies and other organizations and programmes of the United Nations system to increase their cooperation with the League of Arab States and its specialized organizations in the priority sectors of energy, rural development, desertification and green belts, training and vocational education, technology, environment, information and documentation, trade and finance, water resources, development of the agricultural sector,

empowerment of women, transport, communications and information, promotion of the role of the private sector and capacity-building;

8. *Requests* the Secretary-General of the United Nations, in cooperation with the Secretary-General of the League of Arab States, to encourage periodic consultation between representatives of the Secretariat of the United Nations and of the General Secretariat of the League of Arab States in order to review and strengthen coordination mechanisms with a view to accelerating implementation of, and follow-up action on, the multilateral projects, proposals and recommendations adopted at the meetings between the two organizations;

9. *Recommends* that the United Nations and all organizations of the United Nations system make the greatest possible use of Arab institutions and technical expertise in projects undertaken in the Arab region;

10. *Reaffirms* that, in order to enhance cooperation and for the purpose of the review and appraisal of progress, a general meeting between representatives of the United Nations system and the League of Arab States should be held once every two years and that joint inter-agency sectoral meetings should also be convened on a biennial basis to address priority areas of major importance to the development of Arab States, on the basis of agreement between the United Nations system and the League of Arab States and its specialized organizations;

11. *Also reaffirms* the importance of holding the sectoral meeting between the United Nations and the League of Arab States and its specialized organizations during 2009 and also of holding the general meeting on cooperation between representatives of the secretariats of the organizations of the United Nations system and the General Secretariat of the League of Arab States and its specialized organizations during 2010;

12. *Requests* the Secretary-General to submit to the General Assembly at its sixty-fifth session a report on the implementation of the present resolution;

13. *Decides* to include in the provisional agenda of its sixty-fifth session the sub-item entitled "Cooperation between the United Nations and the League of Arab States".

Organization of the Islamic Conference

In response to General Assembly resolution 61/49 [YUN 2006, p. 1600], the Secretary-General, in his August consolidated report [A/63/228-S/2008/531 & Corr.1], provided information on cooperation between the United Nations and the Organization of the Islamic Conference (OIC). The Secretaries-General of both Organizations met regularly, and consultations with the Special Adviser for the International Compact with Iraq and Other Political Issues, in March 2007, and the High-level Coordinator for missing Kuwaitis and third-country citizens and missing Kuwaiti property, in June 2008, further enhanced cooperation. Representatives of the UN system and OIC met in Geneva from 8 to 10 July where they reviewed and appraised levels of cooperation in the fields of science and technology; trade and development; implementation of the MDGs; protection of and assistance to refugees; human resource development; food security and agriculture; environment; health and population; arts and crafts; and the promotion of heritage. A workshop on human rights education in the primary and secondary school system—jointly organized by the Office of the High Commissioner for Human Rights and the Islamic Educational, Scientific and Cultural Organization (ISESCO), a specialized institution of the OIC—was held in Yaoundé, Cameroon in May.

GENERAL ASSEMBLY ACTION

On 5 December [meeting 64], the General Assembly adopted **resolution 63/114** [draft: A/63/L.44 & Add.1] without vote [agenda item 114 *(r)*].

Cooperation between the United Nations and the Organization of the Islamic Conference

The General Assembly,

Recalling its resolutions 37/4 of 22 October 1982, 38/4 of 28 October 1983, 39/7 of 8 November 1984, 40/4 of 25 October 1985, 41/3 of 16 October 1986, 42/4 of 15 October 1987, 43/2 of 17 October 1988, 44/8 of 18 October 1989, 45/9 of 25 October 1990, 46/13 of 28 October 1991, 47/18 of 23 November 1992, 48/24 of 24 November 1993, 49/15 of 15 November 1994, 50/17 of 20 November 1995, 51/18 of 14 November 1996, 52/4 of 22 October 1997, 53/16 of 29 October 1998, 54/7 of 25 October 1999, 55/9 of 30 October 2000, 56/47 of 7 December 2001, 57/42 of 21 November 2002, 59/8 of 22 October 2004 and 61/49 of 4 December 2006,

Recalling also its resolution 3369(XXX) of 10 October 1975, by which it decided to invite the Organization of the Islamic Conference to participate in the sessions and the work of the General Assembly and of its subsidiary organs in the capacity of observer,

Welcoming the efforts of the Secretary-General of the Organization of the Islamic Conference in strengthening the role of the Organization in conflict prevention, confidence-building, peacekeeping, conflict resolution and post-conflict rehabilitation in member States as well as in conflict situations involving Muslim communities,

Noting the adoption by the third extraordinary session of the Islamic Summit Conference, held in Mecca, Saudi Arabia, on 7 and 8 December 2005, of the Ten-year Programme of Action, and the adoption on 14 March 2008 by the eleventh session of the Islamic Summit Conference, held in Dakar on 13 and 14 March 2008, of the amended Charter of the Organization of the Islamic Conference,

Having considered the report of the Secretary-General on cooperation between the United Nations and regional and other organizations,

Taking into account the desire of the two organizations to continue to cooperate closely in the political, economic, social, humanitarian, cultural and scientific fields and in their common search for solutions to global problems, such as questions relating to international peace and security, disarmament, self-determination, the promotion of a culture of peace through dialogue and cooperation, decolonization, fundamental human rights and economic and social development,

Recalling the Articles of the Charter of the United Nations that encourage activities through regional cooperation for the promotion of the purposes and principles of the United Nations,

Recalling also the decision of the Annual Coordination Meeting of Ministers for Foreign Affairs of the States members of the Organization of the Islamic Conference, held in New York on 26 September 2008, to recognize the merit of celebrating the fortieth anniversary of the Organization of the Islamic Conference in 2009 through national and international programmes on different aspects of the Organization of the Islamic Conference, highlighting its activities, evolution and reform through the four decades of its existence,

Noting that the report of the Secretary-General recognizes the strengthening of practical cooperation and the building of complementarity between the United Nations, its funds and programmes and the specialized agencies and the Organization of the Islamic Conference, its subsidiary organs and its specialized and affiliated institutions,

Noting also the encouraging progress made in the ten priority areas of cooperation between the two organizations and their respective agencies and institutions, as well as in the identification of other areas of cooperation between them,

Noting further that the Secretaries-General of the two organizations have met regularly, and consultations involving the Special Adviser for the International Compact with Iraq and Other Political Issues, in March 2007, and the High-level Coordinator for missing Kuwaitis and third-country citizens and missing Kuwaiti property, in June 2008, and the visit of the Executive Director of the Counter-Terrorism Committee Executive Directorate to the headquarters of the Organization of the Islamic Conference, in March 2008, have enhanced cooperation,

Convinced that the strengthening of cooperation between the United Nations and other organizations of the United Nations system and the Organization of the Islamic Conference and its organs and institutions contributes to the promotion of the purposes and principles of the United Nations,

Taking note of the results of the general meeting of the organizations and agencies of the United Nations system and the Organization of the Islamic Conference and its subsidiary organs and specialized and affiliated institutions, held in Geneva from 8 to 10 July 2008, to review and appraise the level of cooperation in the fields of science and technology, trade and development, implementation of the Millennium Development Goals, protection of and assistance to refugees, human rights, human resource development, food security and agriculture, environment, health and population, arts and crafts, and the promotion of heritage, and of the fact that these meetings are now being held every two years, with the next one scheduled for 2010,

Recalling that the Organization of the Islamic Conference remains an important partner of the United Nations in peace, security and the fostering of a culture of peace at the global level, and noting various decisions reached by the two sides, including the agreement to continue cooperation in conflict prevention, peacekeeping and peacebuilding and the agreement to improve the follow-up mechanism,

Taking note of the contribution of the Organization of the Islamic Conference in promoting intercultural dialogue and understanding within the framework of the Alliance of Civilizations and other initiatives in this regard,

Welcoming the close and multifaceted cooperation between the specialized institutions of the United Nations and the Organization of the Islamic Conference with a view to strengthening the capacities of the two organizations in addressing challenges to development and social progress, including ongoing discussions between the United Nations Children's Fund and the Organization of the Islamic Conference on formalizing their partnership through specific initiatives linked to the Millennium Development Goals, as part of the Organization of the Islamic Conference Ten-year Programme of Action to Meet the Challenges Facing the Muslim Ummah in the Twenty-first Century,

Welcoming also the existing cooperation between the Organization of the Islamic Conference and the Office for the Coordination of Humanitarian Affairs of the Secretariat, including dialogue between the two entities on reaching out to non-governmental organizations and other humanitarian actors in member States of the Organization of the Islamic Conference as well as participation in joint activities and events and information-sharing, with a view to furthering proactive engagement and implementing concrete programmes in capacity-building, emergency assistance and strategic partnerships,

Noting the request of the Organization of the Islamic Conference for greater interaction between the United Nations and the Organization of the Islamic Conference Secretariat extending beyond the current biennial arrangement so as to include a periodic review of cooperation, in light of the expanding areas of cooperation between the two organizations,

Noting with appreciation the determination of the two organizations to strengthen further the existing cooperation by developing specific proposals in the designated priority areas of cooperation, as well as in the political field,

1. *Takes note with satisfaction* of the report of the Secretary-General;

2. *Urges* the United Nations system to cooperate with the Organization of the Islamic Conference in areas of mutual interest, as appropriate;

3. *Notes with satisfaction* the active participation of the Organization of the Islamic Conference in the work of the United Nations towards the realization of the purposes and principles embodied in the Charter of the United Nations;

4. *Affirms* that the United Nations and the Organization of the Islamic Conference share a common goal of promoting and facilitating the Middle East peace process so that it can reach its objective of establishing a just and comprehensive peace in the Middle East;

5. *Requests* the United Nations and the Organization of the Islamic Conference to continue to cooperate in their common search for solutions to global problems, such as questions relating to international peace and security, disarmament, self-determination, promotion of a culture of peace through dialogue and cooperation, decolonization, human rights and fundamental freedoms, terrorism, capacity-building, health-related issues such as combating

pandemic and endemic diseases, emergency relief and rehabilitation and technical cooperation;

6. *Requests* the secretariats of the two organizations to strengthen cooperation in addressing the social and economic issues that affect the efforts of Member States to eradicate poverty and achieve sustainable development and the Millennium Development Goals;

7. *Welcomes* the efforts of the United Nations and the Organization of the Islamic Conference to continue to strengthen cooperation between the two organizations in areas of common concern and to review and explore innovative ways and means of enhancing the mechanisms of such cooperation;

8. *Also welcomes* the cooperation between the United Nations Development Programme and the Organization of the Islamic Conference and its specialized and affiliated institutions in promoting South-South cooperation in areas of common interest;

9. *Welcomes with appreciation* the continuing cooperation between the United Nations and the Organization of the Islamic Conference in the fields of peacemaking, preventive diplomacy, peacekeeping and peacebuilding, and notes the close cooperation between the two organizations in reconstruction and development in Afghanistan, Bosnia and Herzegovina and Sierra Leone;

10. *Welcomes* the efforts of the secretariats of the two organizations to strengthen information exchange, coordination and cooperation between them in areas of mutual interest in the political field and to develop practical modalities of such cooperation;

11. *Also welcomes* the periodic high-level meetings between the Secretary-General of the United Nations and the Secretary-General of the Organization of the Islamic Conference, as well as between senior secretariat officials of the two organizations, and encourages their participation in important meetings of the two organizations;

12. *Encourages* the specialized agencies and other organizations of the United Nations system to continue to expand their cooperation with the subsidiary organs and specialized and affiliated institutions of the Organization of the Islamic Conference, particularly in the domains of science and technology, higher education, health and environment, by negotiating cooperation agreements, and through necessary contacts and meetings of the respective focal points for cooperation in priority areas of interest to the United Nations and the Organization of the Islamic Conference;

13. *Urges* the United Nations and other organizations of the United Nations system, especially the lead agencies, to provide increased technical and other forms of assistance to the Organization of the Islamic Conference and its subsidiary organs and specialized and affiliated institutions in order to enhance cooperation;

14. *Expresses its appreciation* to the Secretary-General for his continued efforts to strengthen cooperation and coordination between the United Nations and other organizations of the United Nations system and the Organization of the Islamic Conference and its subsidiary organs and specialized and affiliated institutions to serve the mutual interests of the two organizations in the political, economic, social, cultural, humanitarian and scientific fields;

15. *Requests* the Secretary-General to report to the General Assembly at its sixty-fifth session on the state of cooperation between the United Nations and the Organization of the Islamic Conference;

16. *Decides* to include in the provisional agenda of its sixty-fifth session the sub-item entitled "Cooperation between the United Nations and the Organization of the Islamic Conference".

International Organization of la Francophonie

In response to General Assembly resolution 61/7 [YUN 2006, p. 1602], the Secretary-General, in his August consolidated report [A/63/228-S/2008/531 & Corr.1], detailed cooperation between the United Nations and the International Organization of la Francophonie (OIF). Following a March meeting between the Secretaries-General of the United Nations and OIF in New York, both Organizations held a series of working-level consultations in April in Paris. Participants reviewed progress achieved and explored ways to strengthen international partnerships in early warning and conflict prevention. United Nations–OIF cooperation had improved significantly in the area of peacekeeping, particularly in the implementation of Security Council resolution 1778 [YUN 2007, p. 153] on Chad. Cooperation between the organizations also contributed to the signing of a comprehensive peace agreement between the Government of the Central African Republic and two of the country's major political-military groups in June, and the Electoral Assistance Division of the UN Department of Political Affairs (DPA) engaged in consultations with OIF on the modalities of a possible collaboration related to the electoral process in Côte d'Ivoire. In September 2007, OIF and OHCHR signed a joint three-year programme of cooperation, focusing on the implementation of major international human rights instruments, conflict prevention and settlement, the fight against discrimination and the promotion of diversity. OHCHR also organized several workshops and activities with financial support and expertise from OIF. The UN Department of Economic and Social Affairs (DESA) and OIF continued to promote the development and implementation of national sustainable development strategies among French-speaking developing countries.

GENERAL ASSEMBLY ACTION

On 22 December [meeting 73], the General Assembly adopted **resolution 63/236** [draft: A/63/L.59 & Add.1] without vote [agenda item 114 *(k)*].

Cooperation between the United Nations and the International Organization of la Francophonie

The General Assembly,

Recalling its resolutions 33/18 of 10 November 1978, 50/3 of 16 October 1995, 52/2 of 17 October 1997, 54/25 of 15 November 1999, 56/45 of 7 December 2001, 57/43 of 21 November 2002, 59/22 of 8 November 2004 and 61/7 of 20 October 2006, as well as its decision 53/453 of 18 December 1998,

Recalling also its resolution 61/266 of 16 May 2007 on multilingualism,

Considering that the International Organization of la Francophonie brings together a considerable number of States Members of the United Nations, among which it promotes multilateral cooperation in areas of interest to the United Nations,

Bearing in mind the Articles of the Charter of the United Nations which encourage the promotion of the purposes and principles of the United Nations through regional cooperation,

Bearing in mind also that, according to the Charter of la Francophonie adopted on 23 November 2005 at the Ministerial Conference of la Francophonie, held in Antananarivo, the objectives of the International Organization of la Francophonie are to assist in the establishment and development of democracy, the prevention, management and settlement of conflicts and support for the rule of law and for human rights, the intensification of dialogue between cultures and civilizations, the establishment of closer ties among peoples through mutual knowledge and strengthening of their solidarity through multilateral cooperation activities with a view to promoting the growth of their economies, and the promotion of education and training,

Welcoming the steps taken by the International Organization of la Francophonie to strengthen its ties with the organizations of the United Nations system and with international and regional organizations with a view to attaining its objectives,

Noting with satisfaction the commitment to multilateral cooperation for peace, good governance and the rule of law, economic governance and solidarity, the environment, sustainable development, and climate change, undertaken by Heads of State and Government of countries using French as a common language, at their twelfth summit, held in Quebec City, Canada, from 17 to 19 October 2008, and their determination to work together to bring about, through targeted action, added value in these areas,

Having considered the report of the Secretary-General on the implementation of resolution 61/7,

Noting with satisfaction the substantial progress achieved in cooperation between the United Nations, the specialized agencies and other United Nations bodies and programmes and the International Organization of la Francophonie,

Convinced that strengthening cooperation between the United Nations and the International Organization of la Francophonie serves the purposes and principles of the United Nations,

Noting the desire of the two organizations to consolidate, develop and strengthen the ties that exist between them in the political, economic, social and cultural fields,

1. *Takes note with satisfaction* of the report of the Secretary-General, and welcomes the increasingly close and productive cooperation between the United Nations and the International Organization of la Francophonie;

2. *Notes with satisfaction* that the International Organization of la Francophonie participates actively in the work of the United Nations, to which it makes a valuable contribution;

3. *Notes with great satisfaction* the initiatives taken by the International Organization of la Francophonie in the areas of conflict prevention, the promotion of peace and support for democracy, the rule of law and human rights, in accordance with the commitments reaffirmed at the Ministerial Conference of la Francophonie on Conflict Prevention and Human Security, held on 13 and 14 May 2006 in Saint Boniface, Canada, and commends it on the genuine contribution it makes, in cooperation with the United Nations, in Haiti, the Comoros, Côte d'Ivoire, Burundi, the Democratic Republic of the Congo, the Central African Republic and Chad;

4. *Welcomes* the initiation of cooperation between the United Nations and the International Organization of la Francophonie, with the participation of other regional and subregional organizations, as well as non-governmental organizations, in the fields of early warning and conflict prevention, and encourages the pursuit of this initiative with a view to formulating practical recommendations to facilitate the establishment of relevant operational mechanisms, where necessary;

5. *Expresses its gratitude* to the International Organization of la Francophonie for the steps it has taken in recent years to promote cultural and linguistic diversity and dialogue between cultures and civilizations;

6. *Expresses its appreciation* to the Secretary-General of the United Nations and the Secretary-General of the International Organization of la Francophonie for their sustained efforts to strengthen cooperation and coordination between the two organizations, thereby serving their mutual interests in the political, economic, social and cultural fields;

7. *Welcomes* the strengthened cooperation between the International Organization of la Francophonie and the Department of Peacekeeping Operations of the Secretariat with a view to increasing the number of French-speaking personnel in United Nations peacekeeping operations;

8. *Also welcomes* the fact that the twelfth summit of la Francophonie led to concrete commitments to address the food and energy crisis, to strengthen the capacity of francophone States in the area of peacekeeping, to support efforts by international financial institutions to develop norms and codes that could be readily adopted by member States, and to mobilize all efforts and all the political will of member States to ratify the international instruments relating to the environment, and invites the United Nations to actively collaborate with the International Organization of la Francophonie and its members to meet these commitments;

9. *Further welcomes* the involvement of the countries that use French as a common language, particularly through the International Organization of la Francophonie, in the preparation for, conduct of and follow-up to international conferences organized under United Nations auspices;

10. *Welcomes* the high-level meetings held periodically between the United Nations Secretariat and the Secretariat of the International Organization of la Francophonie, and advocates the participation of the secretariats in major meetings of the two organizations;

11. *Expresses its appreciation* to the Secretary-General for including the International Organization of la Francophonie in the periodic meetings he holds with heads of regional organizations, and invites him to continue doing

so, taking into account the role played by the International Organization of la Francophonie in conflict prevention and support for democracy and the rule of law;

12. *Notes with satisfaction* the continued collaboration between the United Nations and the International Organization of la Francophonie in the area of electoral monitoring and assistance, and advocates the strengthening of cooperation between the two organizations in that area;

13. *Requests* the Secretary-General of the United Nations, acting in cooperation with the Secretary-General of the International Organization of la Francophonie, to encourage the holding of periodic meetings between representatives of the United Nations Secretariat and representatives of the Secretariat of the International Organization of la Francophonie in order to promote the exchange of information, coordination of activities and identification of new areas of cooperation;

14. *Welcomes* the participation of the International Organization of la Francophonie in the Peacebuilding Commission's work on Burundi, Guinea-Bissau and the Central African Republic, and strongly encourages the International Organization of la Francophonie and the Peacebuilding Commission to continue to cooperate actively;

15. *Invites* the Secretary-General of the United Nations to take the necessary steps, in consultation with the Secretary-General of the International Organization of la Francophonie, to continue to promote cooperation between the two organizations;

16. *Invites* the specialized agencies and the funds and programmes of the United Nations system, as well as the regional commissions, including the Economic Commission for Africa, to collaborate to this end with the Secretary-General of the International Organization of la Francophonie by identifying new synergies in favour of development, in particular in the areas of poverty elimination, energy, sustainable development, education, training and the development of new information technologies;

17. *Requests* the Secretary-General to submit to the General Assembly at its sixty-fifth session a report on the implementation of the present resolution;

18. *Decides* to include in the provisional agenda of its sixty-fifth session the sub-item entitled "Cooperation between the United Nations and the International Organization of la Francophonie".

Inter-Parliamentary Union

Pursuant to General Assembly resolution 61/6 [YUN 2006, p. 1604], the Secretary-General, in his August consolidated report [A/63/228-S/2008/531 & Corr.1], detailed the cooperation between the United Nations and the Inter-Parliamentary Union (IPU). During the IPU Statutory Assemblies in 2007 and 2008, member Parliaments adopted resolutions on global issues that were also high on the UN agenda, including climate change, poverty eradication, human trafficking and migration, employment, official development assistance, terrorism, and the peaceful coexistence of religions and cultures. IPU established a new plenary Committee on UN Affairs, which met for the first time in October 2007, and would formulate and monitor proposals for developing the IPU–UN relationship and examine major UN issues, such as funding and accountability and reform efforts. IPU was also involved in shaping the agenda of the new Development Cooperation Forum of the Economic and Social Council and participated in the preparatory events for the Forum's 2008 meeting. In November 2007, IPU and the United Nations Development Programme (UNDP) signed a memorandum of understanding providing a framework for joint activities in areas such as democratic governance, poverty reduction, development cooperation and women's empowerment. IPU established an Advisory Group on HIV/AIDS to enlist the world's legislatures in the fight against the epidemic. In collaboration with UNAIDS and UNDP, it launched a reference handbook for parliamentarians entitled *Taking action against HIV*.

GENERAL ASSEMBLY ACTION

On 18 November [meeting 53], the General Assembly adopted **resolution 63/24** [draft: A/63/L.26 & Add.1] without vote [agenda item 114 *(l)*].

Cooperation between the United Nations and the Inter-Parliamentary Union

The General Assembly,

Having considered the report of the Secretary-General of 8 August 2008 which attests to the broad and substantive cooperation between the United Nations and the Inter-Parliamentary Union over the past two years,

Taking note of the resolutions adopted by the Inter-Parliamentary Union and circulated in the General Assembly and the many activities undertaken by the organization in support of the United Nations,

Welcoming the annual parliamentary hearings at the United Nations as joint United Nations–Inter-Parliamentary Union events during the sessions of the General Assembly, as well as other specialized parliamentary meetings organized by the Inter-Parliamentary Union in cooperation with the United Nations in the context of major United Nations conferences and events,

Taking into consideration the Cooperation Agreement between the United Nations and the Inter-Parliamentary Union of 1996, which laid the foundation for cooperation between the two organizations,

Recalling the United Nations Millennium Declaration, as well as the 2005 World Summit Outcome, in which Heads of State and Government resolved to strengthen further cooperation between the United Nations and national parliaments through their world organization, the Inter-Parliamentary Union, in all fields of the work of the United Nations, including the effective implementation of United Nations reform,

Recalling also its resolution 57/32 of 19 November 2002, in which the Inter-Parliamentary Union was invited to participate in the work of the General Assembly in the capacity of observer, as well as resolutions 57/47 of 21 November 2002, 59/19 of 8 November 2004 and 61/6 of 20 October 2006,

Welcoming the close cooperation between the Inter-Parliamentary Union and the Peacebuilding Commission in fostering political dialogue and building national capacities for good governance,

Welcoming also the contribution of the Inter-Parliamentary Union in shaping the agenda and work of the new Development Cooperation Forum held by the Economic and Social Council,

Recognizing the importance of the provision of continued parliamentary support to the work of the Human Rights Council,

1. *Welcomes* the efforts made by the Inter-Parliamentary Union to provide for a greater parliamentary contribution and enhanced support to the United Nations;

2. *Encourages* the United Nations and the Inter-Parliamentary Union to continue to cooperate closely in various fields, in particular peace and security, economic and social development, international law, human rights, and democracy and gender issues, bearing in mind the significant benefits of cooperation between the two organizations, to which the report of the Secretary-General attests;

3. *Encourages* the Inter-Parliamentary Union to strengthen further its contribution to the work of the General Assembly, including its revitalization, and in relation to the process of United Nations reform and system-wide coherence;

4. *Invites* the Peacebuilding Commission to continue to work closely with the Inter-Parliamentary Union in engaging national parliaments in the countries under consideration by the Commission in efforts to promote democratic governance, national dialogue and reconciliation;

5. *Encourages* the Inter-Parliamentary Union to continue to work closely with the Development Cooperation Forum and bring a robust parliamentary contribution to the Forum process and the broader development cooperation agenda;

6. *Also encourages* the Inter-Parliamentary Union to strengthen its contribution to the Human Rights Council, particularly as it relates to the universal periodic review of the fulfilment of human rights obligations and commitments by Member States;

7. *Welcomes* the growing practice of including legislators as members of national delegations to major United Nations meetings and events, as appropriate, and invites Member States to continue this practice in a more regular and systematic manner;

8. *Calls for* the further development of the annual parliamentary hearings at the United Nations as a joint United Nations-Inter-Parliamentary Union event and for the circulation of the hearings summary report as a document of the General Assembly;

9. *Welcomes* the proposal for a regular annual exchange between the United Nations System Chief Executives Board for Coordination and the senior leadership of the Inter-Parliamentary Union, with a view to building greater coherence in the work of the two organizations and maximizing parliamentary support for the United Nations;

10. *Decides*, in recognition of the unique role of national parliaments in support of the work of the United Nations, to include in the provisional agenda of its sixty-fifth session an item entitled "Cooperation between the United Nations, national parliaments and the Inter-Parliamentary Union".

Participation in UN work

Observer status

Agency for International Trade Information and Cooperation

On 17 July [A/63/143], Paraguay requested the inclusion in the provisional agenda of the General Assembly's sixty-third session of an item on observer status for the Agency for International Trade Information and Cooperation (AITIC) in the Assembly. An explanatory memorandum stated that the Agency was established in 2004 to facilitate the participation of resource-constrained countries in international trade. AITIC provided its members trade-related technical assistance and capacity-building, as well as free, personalized assistance, tailored to the particular needs for information and analysis concerning trade and development issues. Observer status would boost the Agency's capacity to cooperate with UN agencies involved in poverty reduction.

On 24 December, by **decision 63/552**, the Assembly decided that the item on "Observer status for AITIC in the General Assembly" would remain for consideration during its resumed sixty-third (2009) session.

Global Fund to Fight AIDS, Tuberculosis and Malaria

On 15 August [A/63/196], France, on behalf of the European Union, requested the inclusion in the agenda of the General Assembly's sixty-third session of an item on observer status in the Assembly for the Global Fund to Fight AIDS, Tuberculosis and Malaria [YUN 2002, p. 1217]. An explanatory memorandum stated that the Fund was established in 2002 to provide financial support to the global fight against the epidemics of HIV/AIDS, tuberculosis and malaria in low- and middle-income countries highly affected by the diseases. Observer status would boost the Fund's capacity to collaborate with other UN agencies involved with global health and development and would allow the Fund to bring to the Assembly's attention the progress recorded by the Fund in contributing to the MDGs.

On 19 September [A/63/PV.2], pursuant to the first report of the General Committee [A/63/250], the Assembly deferred consideration of the question of the inclusion in the agenda of an item on observer status for the Fund.

International Fund for Saving the Aral Sea

In a 6 October letter to the Secretary-General [A/63/234], Kazakhstan, Kyrgyzstan, Tajikistan, Turkmenistan and Uzbekistan requested the inclusion in the agenda of the General Assembly's sixty-third session of an item on observer status for the International Fund for Saving the Aral Sea (IFAS) in the Assembly. An explanatory memorandum contained details on the founding of IFAS in 1999, the background on the environmental crisis that had led to the shrinking of the Aral Sea, and the continuing deterioration of the environmental situation, which was affecting the living conditions and health of over 35 million Aral Sea Basin inhabitants, preventing normal economic activities and causing an increase in migratory movements in the region. There was a need for more effective and targeted measures and more specific and direct cooperation between the States of the region and the United Nations and other international organizations and donors through IFAS. Observer status would allow IFAS to initiate various measures designed to improve the environmental, social and economic situation in the Aral Sea Basin.

GENERAL ASSEMBLY ACTION

On 11 December [meeting 67], the General Assembly adopted **resolution 63/133** [A/63/454] without vote [agenda item 156].

Observer status for the International Fund for Saving the Aral Sea in the General Assembly

The General Assembly,

Wishing to promote cooperation between the United Nations and the International Fund for Saving the Aral Sea,

1. *Decides* to invite the International Fund for Saving the Aral Sea to participate in the sessions and the work of the General Assembly in the capacity of observer;

2. *Requests* the Secretary-General to take the necessary action to implement the present resolution.

South Centre

In a 19 June letter to the Secretary-General [A/63/141], Tanzania requested the inclusion in the agenda of the General Assembly's sixty-third session of an item on observer status for the South Centre. An explanatory memorandum stated that the Centre, an intergovernmental organization of developing countries established in 1994, assisted in developing the points of view of the South on major policy issues relating to trade, innovation and access to knowledge, global governance, financing for development, labour and employment, and environment. It also sought to foster improved North-South dialogue and interaction on an equitable basis on key global issues, and responded to requests for policy advice and technical support from developing countries in the context of international negotiations and discussions in various international forums. The Centre considered the United Nations to be one of its major partners and that the work and agenda of the Assembly were of great relevance to the South, and consequently, of prime importance to the Centre.

GENERAL ASSEMBLY ACTION

On 11 December [meeting 67], the General Assembly adopted **resolution 63/131** [A/63/453] without vote [agenda item 151].

Observer status for the South Centre in the General Assembly

The General Assembly,

Wishing to promote cooperation between the United Nations and the South Centre,

1. *Decides* to invite the South Centre to participate in the sessions and the work of the General Assembly in the capacity of observer;

2. *Requests* the Secretary-General to take the necessary action to implement the present resolution.

University for Peace

On 11 September [A/63/231], Costa Rica requested the inclusion in the agenda of the General Assembly's sixty-third session of an item on observer status for the University for Peace. An explanatory memorandum stated that the University, established in 1980 [YUN 1980, p. 1004], was a specialized international institution for post-graduate studies, research, and dissemination of knowledge, aimed at training for peace within the United Nations University (UNU) system. The Charter of the University envisaged the creation of close links between UNU and the United Nations Educational, Scientific and Cultural Organization (UNESCO) in view of its responsibilities in the field of education. Observer status would enable the University to participate in discussions on peacebuilding and peacekeeping issues, which, in turn, would allow it to strengthen the content of its academic and training programmes.

GENERAL ASSEMBLY ACTION

On 11 December [meeting 67], the General Assembly adopted **resolution 63/132** [A/63/455] without vote [agenda item 153].

Observer status for the University for Peace in the General Assembly

The General Assembly,

Wishing to promote cooperation between the United Nations and the University for Peace,

1. *Decides* to invite the University for Peace to participate in the sessions and the work of the General Assembly in the capacity of observer;

2. *Requests* the Secretary-General to take the necessary action to implement the present resolution.

Non-governmental organizations

Committee on NGOs

The Committee on Non-Governmental Organizations (NGOs) held its regular 2008 session (21–30 January) [E/2008/32 (Part I)] and its resumed session (29 May–6 June & 25 June) [E/2008/32 (Part II) & Corr.1], both in New York. In January, the Committee considered 145 applications for consultative status with the Economic and Social Council, including applications deferred from its 1999–2007 sessions and five requests for reclassification, of which it recommended two. It recommended 70 applications for consultative status, deferred consideration of 68, took note that three NGOs had withdrawn their applications and closed consideration of two applications. It did not recommend 30 requests deferred from previous sessions. The Committee reviewed 59 quadrennial reports and heard 15 NGO representatives.

The Committee recommended one draft resolution on measures to improve quadrennial reporting procedures and four draft decisions for action by the Council. It reviewed its working methods relating to the implementation of Economic and Social Council resolution 1996/31 [YUN 1996, p. 1360], including the process of accreditation of representatives of NGOs, and Council decision 1995/304 [YUN 1995, p. 1445]. The Committee considered the general voluntary trust fund in support of the United Nations Non-Governmental Organizations Informal Regional Network (UN-NGO-IRENE). During the session, no requests for consultative status were received from NGOs pursuant to Council resolution 2006/46 [YUN 2006, p. 1001], and there were no special reports or complaints by Member States before the Committee.

On 25 and 30 January, the Committee considered the application of the American Sports Committee, an application deferred from previous sessions. On 30 January, the Committee recommended that consultative status not be granted to that organization. On 21 July, the Council decided not to grant consultative status to the NGO American Sports Committee (**decision 2008/223**).

Regarding the application of the Federación Estatal de Lesbianas, Gays, Transexuales y Bisexuales, an application deferred from a previous session, a motion to adjourn the debate until the 2008 resumed session was rejected by a roll-call vote of 8 to 8, with 2 abstentions. Subsequently, the Committee decided by a roll-call vote of 7 to 7, with 4 abstentions, that consultative status not be granted to the organization. Nonetheless, on 22 July the Council rejected the draft decision and granted special consultative status to the NGO Federación Estatal de Lesbianas, Gays, Transexuales y Bisexuales (**decision 2008/230**).

On 21 July, the Economic and Social Council granted special consultative status to 70 organizations and placed eight others on its roster; reclassified two organizations from the roster to special consultative status; and noted that the Committee had taken note of 53 quadrennial reports, closed consideration of the request for consultative status made by two NGOs, and taken note of the withdrawal by three NGOs of their applications for consultative status (**decision 2008/222**). Also on the same date, the Council took note of the Committee's report on its 2008 regular session (**decision 2008/224**).

At its resumed session, in May, the Committee considered 126 applications for consultative status, including applications deferred from its 1999–2008 sessions; recommended 64 applications for consultative status; deferred consideration of 55 applications and closed consideration of two applications. It did not recommend consultative status for one organization, whose application was deferred from previous sessions. It recommended one of three requests for reclassification of consultative status, reviewed 139 quadrennial reports, 13 of which had been deferred from previous sessions, and heard six NGO representatives.

The Committee recommended one draft resolution on strengthening the NGO Section of DESA and five draft decisions for action by the Council. It reviewed its working methods relating to the implementation of Council resolution 1996/31, including the process of accreditation of representatives of NGOs, and Council decision 1995/304. During the session, no requests for consultative status were received from NGOs pursuant to Council resolution 2006/46. With regard to Liberal International, an NGO based in the United Kingdom, which had its consultative status suspended for one year [YUN 2007, p 1433], the Committee took note and acknowledged that the organization's one year suspension would end on 20 July. It also considered the general voluntary trust fund in support of UN-NGO-IRENE.

On 6 June, the Committee considered the application of the Human Rights Foundation, a United States-based organization. A motion to adjourn debate on the application was rejected by a roll-call vote of 12 to 6, with 1 abstention. Subsequently, by a roll-call vote of 13 to 3, with 2 abstentions, the Committee decided to not grant consultative status to the organization. On 21 July, the Council adopted the draft decision of the Committee and decided not to grant consultative status to the Human Rights Foundation (**decision 2008/226**).

On 21 July, the Council granted consultative status to 64 organizations and placed 11 others on the roster; reclassified one from the roster to special consultative status; and noted that the Committee had taken note of 126 quadrennial reports, closed consideration of two applications, and taken note of the withdrawal of applications by two organizations (**decision 2008/225**). On the same date, the Council decided to dispose of the complaint against the NGO World Union for Progressive Judaism (**decision 2008/227**); decided that the 2009 regular session of the Committee would be held from 19 to 28 January 2009 and the resumed session from 18 to 27 May 2009, and approved the provisional agenda for that session (**decision 2008/228**). It also deferred until its resumed substantive session consideration of the report of the Committee on its resumed 2008 session (**decision 2008/229**).

On 19 December, the Council took note of the Committee's report on its resumed 2008 session (**decision 2008/261**).

ECONOMIC AND SOCIAL COUNCIL ACTION

On 21 July [meeting 37], the Economic and Social Council adopted **resolution 2008/4** [E/2008/32 (Part I) & E/2008/99/Corr.1] without vote [agenda item 12].

Measures to improve the quadrennial reporting procedures

The Economic and Social Council,

Recalling its resolution 1996/31 of 25 July 1996 on the consultative relationship between the United Nations and non-governmental organizations,

Reaffirming its resolution 1996/31, in which it established that one of the primary purposes of the consultative arrangement is to secure expert information or advice from organizations whose special competence and/or activities in areas of direct relevance to the aims and purposes of the United Nations qualified them to make a significant contribution to the work of the Economic and Social Council,

Mindful of the importance of an efficient and effective quadrennial reporting and review system to ensure the smooth functioning of a dynamic and productive consultative arrangement as set out in its resolution 1996/31,

Emphasizing that the quadrennial reporting exercise mandated under resolution 1996/31 constitutes the only formal monitoring mechanism established to enable the Committee on Non-Governmental Organizations to confirm the continued existence and activity of a non-governmental organization and to determine that the organization conforms at all times to the principles governing the establishment and nature of its consultative relationship,

Recalling, in particular, paragraphs 55, 57 *(c)* and 61 *(c)* of its resolution 1996/31, which set out the responsibility of non-governmental organizations in general or special consultative status to submit quadrennial reports and the basis for the suspension or withdrawal of such consultative status for those organizations that fail to make any positive or effective contribution to the work of the United Nations,

Expressing serious concern at the unsatisfactory submission of quadrennial reports,

1. *Decides* that the procedure for the submission of quadrennial reports for a non-governmental organization in general or special consultative status shall be as follows:

(a) Six months prior to the due date for the report, the Non-Governmental Organizations Section of the Department of Economic and Social Affairs of the Secretariat shall write to the non-governmental organization concerned to remind it of the reporting requirement, the expected date of the submission of the report and the penalties for non-reporting, as stipulated in the present resolution in accordance with Economic and Social Council resolution 1996/31;

(b) One month after the due date for the report, the Non-Governmental Organizations Section shall send a notice to the non-governmental organization concerned reminding it of the reporting requirement and of the penalties for non-reporting, and requesting that the report be submitted by the first day of the following January;

(c) If the outstanding report is not received by the first day of the following January, the Non-Governmental Organizations Section shall send a final letter to the non-governmental organization concerned, requesting that the report be submitted by the first day of the following May and warning that non-receipt of the report by that date shall result in the suspension of consultative status, and shall copy the letter to the permanent mission to the United Nations of the country where the non-governmental organization has its headquarters;

(d) If no report is received by the first day of the following May, the Committee on Non-Governmental Organizations shall, at its resumed session, compile a list of all non-governmental organizations with outstanding reports and recommend to the Economic and Social Council the immediate suspension of their consultative status for a period of one year;

(e) Following a decision by the Economic and Social Council to suspend the consultative status of any non-governmental organization with an outstanding report, the Non-Governmental Organizations Section shall write to the non-governmental organization concerned advising it of the suspension, requesting the submission of the outstanding report by the first day of May of the following year and warning that failure to submit the report by such time shall result in the withdrawal of consultative status, and shall copy the letter to the permanent mission to the United Nations of the country where the non-governmental organization has its headquarters;

(f) At its resumed session to be held the following May, the Committee on Non-Governmental Organizations shall review the status of reporting of the non-governmental organizations whose consultative status has been suspended and shall recommend to the Economic and Social Council either the reinstatement of consultative status for any non-governmental organization that has hitherto submitted its report or the withdrawal of consultative status for any non-governmental organization with a report still outstanding;

2. *Reiterates* that, in accordance with paragraph 56 of its resolution 1996/31, in cases where the Committee on Non-Governmental Organizations has decided to recommend that the general or special consultative status of a non-governmental organization or its listing on the Roster be suspended or withdrawn, the non-governmental organization concerned shall have an opportunity to present its response for appropriate consideration by the Committee as expeditiously as possible;

3. *Also reiterates* that, in accordance with paragraph 59 of its resolution 1996/31, a non-governmental organization whose consultative status or whose listing on the Roster is withdrawn may be entitled to reapply for consultative status or for inclusion on the Roster no sooner than three years after the effective date of such withdrawal;

4. *Requests* the Non-Governmental Organizations Section to ensure that the revised guidelines are clearly posted on the Section's website and included in the initial letter sent to each non-governmental organization that has been granted general or special consultative status.

Strengthening of NGO Section of DESA

On 5 June [E/2008/32 (Part II) & Corr.1], the Committee on NGOs was briefed by the Chief of the NGO Section of the Department of Economic and Social Affairs (DESA) on the activities and staffing of the Section. She invited the Committee to consider the Section's staffing problems and growing workload as an opportunity to review, overhaul and modernize the system and the methods used in processing applications and in the quadrennial reports review, and to consider a greater use of new information technology.

ECONOMIC AND SOCIAL COUNCIL ACTION

On 21 July [meeting 37], the Economic and Social Council adopted **resolution 2008/5** [draft: E/2008/L.9], without vote [agenda item 12].

Strengthening of the Non-Governmental Organizations Section of the Department of Economic and Social Affairs of the Secretariat

The Economic and Social Council,

Recalling the provisions of its resolution 1996/31 of 25 July 1996 on the consultative relationship between the Economic and Social Council and non-governmental organizations,

Aware of the evolving relationship between the United Nations and the non-governmental organizations community, reflecting the broader and more substantive involvement of non-governmental organizations with the Economic and Social Council and the United Nations at large,

Mindful of the significantly large increase in the number of non-governmental organizations in consultative status with the Economic and Social Council that has occurred in recent years, and conscious that the number will continue to increase in the foreseeable future,

Mindful also of the demands that the participation of the expansion of non-governmental organizations places on the workload and resources of the Non-Governmental Organizations Section of the Department of Economic and Social Affairs of the Secretariat,

Recalling paragraph 68 of its resolution 1996/31 regarding the requirement for adequate Secretariat support to fulfil the mandate defined for the Committee on Non-Governmental Organizations with respect to carrying out the wider range of activities in which the enhanced involvement of non-governmental organizations was envisaged,

Recalling also the regular programme of technical cooperation under section 22 of the programme budget of the United Nations,

Emphasizing the need to ensure that the Non-Governmental Organizations Section is able to operate efficiently in carrying out its mandate at the optimum level of performance,

Emphasizing also the need to strengthen partnership with civil society as emphasized by the Secretary-General within the context of the reform of the United Nations by integrating analytical capacity with technical cooperation activities for greater effectiveness and efficiency,

1. *Regrets* the weak capacity of the Non-Governmental Organizations Section of the Department of Economic and Social Affairs of the Secretariat, and requests the Secretary-General to ensure the full utilization of the resources allocated to it as well as the filling of all vacant posts and to report on proposals to further strengthen the capacity of the Non-Governmental Organizations Section within the context of the proposed programme budget for the biennium 2010–2011 and the maintenance of the institutional memory of the Non-Governmental Organizations Section, thereby making full use of lessons learned and best practices within the Section so as to enable it to carry out its responsibilities efficiently and effectively;

2. *Recommends* that a technical cooperation programme be established for the Non-Governmental Organizations Section aimed at providing advisory services, the conduct of capacity-building workshops designed to launch the United Nations Non-Governmental Organizations Informal Regional Network (UN-NGO-IRENE), at the regional, subregional and national levels, and the development of training materials and the promotion of pilot joint partnership initiatives, projects and programmes involving the United Nations, civil society and Governments worldwide, especially for the countries most in need.

Chapter II

United Nations financing and programming

The financial situation of the United Nations showed some improvement in 2008, although it remained fragile. Cash availability under the regular budget was lower than in 2007 and stood at $19 million by year's end. Assessments stood at $1.8 billion—a decrease of some $174 million—and unpaid assessments totalled $417 million, compared to $428 million in 2007. Cash balances were higher for peacekeeping operations, the international tribunals and the capital master plan, while debt owed to Member States stood at $431 million. The number of Member States paying their regular budget assessments in full and on time increased to 146.

In December, the General Assembly adopted revised budget appropriations for the 2008–2009 biennium of $4,865,080,200 representing an increase of $657,471,800 over the revised appropriation of $4,207,608,400 approved in April. It invited the Secretary-General to prepare his proposed 2010–2011 programme budget on the basis of a preliminary estimate of $4,871,048,700.

The Committee on Contributions continued to review the methodology for preparing the scale of assessments of Member States' contributions to the budget and to encourage the payment of arrears through the multi-year payment plan process. The General Assembly continued to review the efficiency of United Nations administrative and financial functioning.

The General Assembly also examined the proposed strategic framework for 2010–2011 and endorsed the proposed biennial programme plan for that period.

Financial situation

Although the overall United Nations financial situation showed some improvement in 2008, it remained fragile. In October [A/63/514], the Secretary-General reported that unpaid assessed contributions were concentrated among a few Member States and that the final outcome for 2008 would largely depend on payments made by those States in the last months of the year. As at 24 October, aggregate assessments were $9.1 billion (compared to $9.2 billion in 2007). That amount included increased assessments of $310 million for the international tribunals, compared to $296 million in 2007. He also said that it might be necessary to borrow $148 million from reserve accounts by the end of December. However, if the aforementioned States paid their 2008 assessments in full, there could be a positive cash balance at year's end.

As at 24 October, unpaid assessments for the regular budget, peacekeeping and the two international tribunals totalled $3.7 billion, which included: $2.9 billion for peacekeeping (compared to $3.5 billion at 31 October 2007); $756 million for the regular budget ($80 million less than in 2007); and $53 million for the international tribunals ($11 million less than in 2007). It was forecast that the Organization would owe Member States $645 million for troop and equipment costs as at 31 December 2008. That amount was significantly lower than the $779 million outstanding at 31 December 2007. Member States that had paid their regular budget assessments in full as at 24 October numbered 133, seven more than at 31 October 2007.

In his end-of-year review of the financial situation [A/63/514/Add.1], the Secretary-General noted that the performance of the four main indicators of the Organization's financial health reflected improvement as compared to 31 December 2007: regular assessments issued during 2008 had decreased by some $174 million; unpaid assessments to the regular budget had also decreased to $417 million from $428 million at 31 December 2007; cash balances were higher for peacekeeping operations, the international tribunals and the capital master plan (CMP), but lower for the regular budget; and the debt owed to Member States was $431 million. Some $19 million in cash was available for the regular budget at year's end.

The position of the international tribunals improved, as amounts outstanding decreased to $26 million, from $34 million in 2007. However, the amounts outstanding for peacekeeping operations increased to $2.9 billion, compared to $2.7 billion in 2007. The number of Member States paying their regular budget assessments in full was 146, six more than in 2007.

On 24 December, the General Assembly decided that the item on improving the financial situation of the United Nations would remain for consideration at its resumed sixty-third (2009) session **(decision 63/552)**.

UN budget

Budget for 2008–2009

Revised appropriations

In the first performance report on the 2008–2009 programme budget [A/63/573], the Secretary-General identified adjustments to the level of appropriations as a result of variations in the rates of inflation and exchange, adjustments to standard costs, unforeseen and extraordinary items, vacancies, as well as additional mandates approved by the General Assembly and the Security Council.

The adjustments yielded revised requirements of $4,388.4 million, an increase of $180.8 million more than the revised appropriation of $4,207.6 million approved by resolutions 62/237 A and B [YUN 2007, p. 1449] and 62/245 (see p. 1550), and an increase in income by $6.8 million, resulting in a revised income estimate of $526.9 million. Consequently, the revised net requirements for the 2008–2009 biennium amounted to $3,861.5 million, an increase of $174.0 million.

In December [A/63/620], the Advisory Committee on Administrative and Budgetary Questions (ACABQ) recommended that the Assembly approve the revised estimates submitted by the Secretary-General, subject to such adjustments resulting from its consideration of matters currently before it, including the consolidated statement of revised estimates and programme budget implications.

GENERAL ASSEMBLY ACTION

On 24 December [meeting 74], the General Assembly, on the recommendation of the Fifth (Administrative and Budgetary) Committee [A/63/648/Add.4], adopted **resolution 63/264 A–C** without vote [agenda item 118].

Programme budget for the biennium 2008–2009

A

REVISED BUDGET APPROPRIATIONS FOR THE BIENNIUM 2008–2009

The General Assembly,

Resolves that, for the biennium 2008–2009, the amount of 4,207,608,400 United States dollars appropriated by it in its resolutions 62/237 A of 22 December 2007 and 62/245 of 3 April 2008 shall be adjusted by 657,471,800 dollars, as follows:

Section	Amount approved in resolutions 62/237 A and 62/245	Increase/ (decrease)	Revised appropriations
	(United States dollars)		
Part I. Overall policymaking, direction and coordination			
1. Overall policymaking, direction and coordination	89,215,800	5,346,300	94,562,100
2. General Assembly and Economic and Social Council affairs and conference management	629,339,800	32,921,300	662,261,100
Total, part I	**718,555,600**	**38,267,600**	**756,823,200**
Part II. Political affairs			
3. Political affairs	527,240,800	435,341,900	962,582,700
4. Disarmament	21,607,900	851,800	22,459,700
5. Peacekeeping operations	101,412,700	4,375,800	105,788,500
6. Peaceful uses of outer space	7,439,800	202,500	7,642,300
Total, part II	**657,701,200**	**440,772,000**	**1,098,473,200**
Part III. International justice and law			
7. International Court of Justice	41,200,400	3,927,300	45,127,700
8. Legal affairs	46,069,000	1,639,200	47,708,200
Total, part III	**87,269,400**	**5,566,500**	**92,835,900**
Part IV. International cooperation for development			
9. Economic and social affairs	158,384,800	7,149,600	165,534,400
10. Least developed countries, landlocked developing countries and small island developing States	5,440,400	422,500	5,862,900
11. United Nations support for the New Partnership for Africa's Development	11,641,900	566,200	12,208,100
12. Trade and development	123,746,100	9,348,500	133,094,600
13. International Trade Centre UNCTAD/WTO	28,099,800	2,773,900	30,873,700
14. Environment	13,796,600	263,200	14,059,800
15. Human settlements	20,520,800	280,800	20,801,600
16. International drug control, crime and terrorism prevention and criminal justice	36,819,000	756,900	37,575,900
Total, part IV	**398,449,400**	**21,561,600**	**420,011,000**

Section		Amount approved in resolutions 62/237 A and 62/245	Increase/ (decrease)	Revised appropriations
		(United States dollars)		
Part V. Regional cooperation for development				
17. Economic and social development in Africa		119,798,200	8,843,900	128,642,100
18. Economic and social development in Asia and the Pacific		83,926,400	8,489,400	92,415,800
19. Economic development in Europe		59,917,100	4,809,200	64,726,300
20. Economic and social development in Latin America and the Caribbean		104,445,000	(1,285,700)	103,159,300
21. Economic and social development in Western Asia		58,107,500	6,611,200	64,718,700
22. Regular programme of technical cooperation		50,951,400	3,881,100	54,832,500
	Total, part V	**477,145,600**	**31,349,100**	**508,494,700**
Part VI. Human rights and humanitarian affairs				
23. Human rights		116,938,400	10,414,800	127,353,200
24. International protection, durable solutions and assistance to refugees		73,069,300	6,936,200	80,005,500
25. Palestine refugees		40,727,500	4,342,600	45,070,100
26. Humanitarian assistance		28,492,300	1,369,500	29,861,800
	Total, part VI	**259,227,500**	**23,063,100**	**282,290,600**
Part VII. Public information				
27. Public information		184,000,500	5,374,100	189,374,600
	Total, part VII	**184,000,500**	**5,374,100**	**189,374,600**
Part VIII. Common support services				
28A. Office of the Under-Secretary-General for Management		15,002,500	591,400	15,593,900
28B. Office of Programme Planning, Budget and Accounts		39,169 900	1,475,800	40,645,700
28C. Office of Human Resources Management		70,688,100	2,360,600	73,048,700
28D. Office of Central Support Services		236,300,100	(25,211,700)	211,088,400
28E. Administration, Geneva		112,185,000	9,862,100	122,047,100
28F. Administration, Vienna		39,019,800	632,600	39,652,400
28G. Administration, Nairobi		27,838,900	(196,700)	27,642,200
36. Office of Information and Communications Technology		—	37,031,600	37,031,600
	Total, part VIII	**540,204,300**	**26,545,700**	**566,750,000**
Part IX. Internal oversight				
29. Internal oversight		35,997,700	1,485,000	37,482,700
	Total, part IX	**35,997,700**	**1,485,000**	**37,482,700**
Part X. Jointly financed administrative activities and special expenses				
30. Jointly financed administrative activities		11,459,300	996,100	12,455,400
31. Special expenses		97,011,600	3,361,100	100,372,700
	Total, part X	**108,470,900**	**5,346,300**	**112,828,100**
Part XI. Capital expenditures				
32. Construction, alteration, improvement and major maintenance		58,782,600	3,416,800	62,199,400
	Total, part XI	**58,782,600**	**3,416,800**	**62,199,400**
Part XII. Safety and security				
33. Safety and security		197,169,300	10,756,600	207,925,900
	Total, part XII	**197,169,300**	**10,756,600**	**207,925,900**
Part XIII. Development Account				
34. Development Account		18,651,300	—	18,651,300
	Total, part XIII	**18,651,300**	—	**18,651,300**
Part XIV. Staff assessment				
35. Staff assessment		465,983,100	44,956,500	510,939,600
	Total, part XIV	**465,983,100**	**44,956,500**	**510,939,600**
	GRAND TOTAL	**4,207,608,400**	**657,471,800**	**4,865,080,200**

B

REVISED INCOME ESTIMATES
FOR THE BIENNIUM 2008–2009

The General Assembly

Resolves that, for the biennium 2008–2009, the estimates of income of 520,077,700 United States dollars approved by it in its resolutions 62/237 B of 22 December 2007 and 62/245 of 3 April 2008 shall be increased by 35,198,700 dollars, as follows:

Income section	Amount approved in resolutions 62/237 B and 62/245	Increase/ (decrease)	Revised estimates
	(United States dollars)		
1. Income from staff assessment	470,397,500	45,148,000	515,545,500
Total, income section 1	**470,397,500**	**45,148,000**	**515,545,500**
2. General income	47,946,900	(10,195,900)	37,751,000
3. Services to the public	1,733,300	246,600	1,979,900
Total, income sections 2 and 3	**49,680,200**	**(9,949,300)**	**39,730,900**
GRAND TOTAL	**520,077,700**	**35,198,700**	**555,276,400**

C

FINANCING OF THE APPROPRIATIONS
FOR THE YEAR 2009

The General Assembly,

Resolves that, for the year 2009:

1. Budget appropriations totalling 2,779,400,350 United States dollars and consisting of 2,085,679,850 dollars, being half of the appropriation initially approved for the biennium 2008–2009 in its resolution 62/237 A of 22 December 2007, 36,248,700 dollars, being the additional appropriation approved for the biennium in its resolution 62/245 of 3 April 2008, and 657,471,800 dollars, being the increase approved in resolution A above, shall be financed in accordance with regulations 3.1 and 3.2 of the Financial Regulations and Rules of the United Nations, as follows:

(a) 14,890,800 dollars, consisting of:

(i) 24,840,100 dollars, being half of the estimated income other than staff assessment income approved for the biennium in its resolution 62/237 B of 22 December 2007;

(ii) 9,949,300 dollars, being the decrease in income other than staff assessment income approved for the biennium in resolution B above;

(b) 2,764,509,550 dollars, being the assessment on Member States in accordance with its resolution 61/237 of 22 December 2006, of which 45 million dollars is subject to assessment in accordance with paragraph 8 of section XII of resolution 63/263 of 24 December 2008;

2. There shall be set off against the assessment on Member States, in accordance with the provisions of General Assembly resolution 973(X) of 15 December 1955, their respective share in the Tax Equalization Fund in the total amount of 283,193,400 dollars, consisting of:

(a) 232,890,200 dollars, being half of the estimated staff assessment income approved by the Assembly in its resolution 62/237 B;

(b) 4,617,100 dollars, being the estimated increase in income from staff assessment approved by the Assembly in its resolution 62/245;

(c) 45,148,000 dollars, being the estimated increase in income from staff assessment approved by the Assembly in resolution B above;

(d) 538,100 dollars, being the increase in income from staff assessment for the biennium 2006–2007 compared with the revised estimates approved by the Assembly in its resolution 62/235 B of 22 December 2007.

On the same date, the Assembly decided that the item on the 2008–2009 programme budget would remain for consideration during its resumed sixty-third (2009) session (**decision 63/552**).

Questions relating to the 2008–2009 programme budget

The Fifth Committee considered a number of questions related to the 2008–2009 programme budget, including the revised estimates resulting from resolutions and decisions by the Economic and Social Council and by the Human Rights Council, estimates in respect of special political missions, good offices and other political initiatives authorized by the General Assembly and/or the Security Council, the first performance report on the 2008–2009 programme budget, and the contingency fund.

Other subjects covered included the construction of additional conference facilities at the Vienna International Centre (see p. 1546) and additional office facilities at the Economic Commission for Africa in Addis Ababa (ibid.), and the improvement and modernization of conference facilities and construction of additional office facilities at the United Nations Office at Nairobi (ibid.); the construction, alteration, improvement and major maintenance related to the provision of an integrated headquarters facility in Baghdad for the United Nations Assistance Mission for Iraq (see p. 1548); the establishment of the Rule of Law Unit in the Executive Office of the Secretary-General (see p. 1547); the review of the lump-sum arrangement of the Office of the United Nations High Commissioner for Refugees (ibid.); the International Civil Service Commission (ibid.); estimates resulting from the entry into force of the Convention on the Rights of Persons with Disabilities and the Optional Protocol thereto (ibid.); human resources management (ibid.); and the United Nations Joint Staff Pension Board (see p. 1548).

GENERAL ASSEMBLY ACTION

On 24 December [meeting 74], the General Assembly, on the recommendation of the Fifth Committee [A/63/648/Add.4], adopted **resolution 63/263** without vote [agenda item 118].

Questions relating to the programme budget for the biennium 2008–2009

The General Assembly,

I

Construction of additional conference facilities at the Vienna International Centre and additional office facilities at the Economic Commission for Africa in Addis Ababa, and improvement and modernization of the conference facilities and construction of additional office facilities at the United Nations Office at Nairobi

Recalling its resolution 56/270 of 27 March 2002, section IV of its resolution 58/272 of 23 December 2003 and sections IX and X of its resolution 62/238 of 22 December 2007,

Having considered the reports of the Secretary-General on improving and modernizing the conference facilities and the construction of additional office facilities at the United Nations Office at Nairobi and on the construction of additional conference facilities at the Vienna International Centre, and the construction of additional office facilities at the Economic Commission for Africa in Addis Ababa, as well as the related report of the Advisory Committee on Administrative and Budgetary Questions,

Mindful of the fact that it is essential to construct, improve and modernize facilities at the Economic Commission for Africa in Addis Ababa, the United Nations Office at Nairobi and the Vienna International Centre to ensure the efficient work of the Organization,

1. *Takes note with appreciation* of the efforts of the Governments of Ethiopia and Kenya, as host countries, in facilitating the construction of additional office facilities at the Economic Commission for Africa in Addis Ababa and the improvement and modernization of the conference facilities and the construction of additional office facilities at the United Nations Office at Nairobi, and of the efforts of the Government of Austria, as host country, in completing the construction of new conference facilities at the Vienna International Centre, as well as in achieving good progress in the asbestos removal project;

2. *Takes note* of the reports of the Secretary-General;

3. *Endorses* the conclusions and recommendations contained in the report of the Advisory Committee on Administrative and Budgetary Questions, subject to the provisions of the present resolution;

4. *Underlines* the risks inherent in the execution of construction projects, and stresses the importance of adequate planning, coordination and project supervision to avoid going over budget;

5. *Expresses* concern about the delays and procedural difficulties in the execution of the projects at the Economic Commission for Africa in Addis Ababa and the United Nations Office at Nairobi, which are contributing to project cost escalation;

6. *Requests* the Secretary-General to undertake management reviews of the projects at the Economic Commission for Africa in Addis Ababa and the United Nations Office at Nairobi with a view to expediting implementation, to ensure that a dedicated project management capacity is in place at the Economic Commission for Africa in Addis Ababa and the United Nations Office at Nairobi and to report to the General Assembly thereon in the context of his next annual progress reports;

7. *Emphasizes* the importance of guidance, interaction and coordination between the Secretariat in New York, on the one hand, and the Economic Commission for Africa in Addis Ababa and the United Nations Office at Nairobi, on the other hand, with clear reporting lines;

8. *Requests* the Secretary-General to ensure full accountability for the delays, lack of responsiveness of management to the needs of the construction projects in Addis Ababa and Nairobi and other factors that have contributed to delays in the implementation of the projects and project cost escalation and to include that information in his next annual progress reports;

9. *Stresses* the importance of the leadership and guidance of the Secretary-General and senior management as well as a commitment to the construction projects at the Economic Commission for Africa in Addis Ababa and the United Nations Office at Nairobi by all parties concerned during the execution and completion of the projects;

10. *Requests* the Secretary-General to update the Member States through regular informal briefings on the construction projects at the Economic Commission for Africa in Addis Ababa and the United Nations Office at Nairobi;

11. *Also requests* the Secretary-General to complete the construction projects at the Economic Commission for Africa in Addis Ababa and the United Nations Office at Nairobi as planned, without any further delays or additional requirements from the regular budget, and to ensure that progress is monitored by the Under-Secretary-General for Management, and to report thereon to the General Assembly at its sixty-fourth session;

12. *Further requests* the Secretary-General to ensure that the construction regulations and rules of the Organization, including the provisions of the Convention on the Rights of Persons with Disabilities, are abided by and fully upheld in all phases of the construction projects at the Economic Commission for Africa in Addis Ababa and the United Nations Office at Nairobi;

13. *Approves* the revised estimated cost of 25,252,200 United States dollars for the construction of additional office facilities at the United Nations Office at Nairobi;

14. *Also approves* the use of interest income of 798,200 dollars as at 31 December 2007, and further approves the use of future interest income generated by accumulated rental income for the construction of additional office facilities at the United Nations Office at Nairobi;

15. *Further approves* the revised estimated cost of 3,479,000 dollars for improving and modernizing the conference facilities at the United Nations Office at Nairobi;

16. *Requests* the Secretary-General to entrust the Office of Internal Oversight Services with ensuring continuing effective audit coverage as well as regular, thorough management reviews of the construction of additional office facilities at the Economic Commission for Africa in Addis Ababa and the United Nations Office at Nairobi, to be reported on in the annual report of the Office of Internal Oversight Services to the General Assembly;

17. *Recalls* paragraphs 24, 25, 35 and 44 of the report of the Advisory Committee on Administrative and Budgetary Questions, and requests the Secretary-General to submit, in the context of the proposed programme budget for the biennium 2010–2011, information that outlines clearly the interaction between the Secretariat in New York and other duty stations for construction and long-term renovation projects, and that specifies all aspects of the division of responsibility and accountability;

II

Revised estimates relating to the Rule of Law Unit

Having considered the report of the Secretary-General on the revised estimates under the programme budget for the biennium 2008–2009 for the Rule of Law Unit and the related report of the Advisory Committee on Administrative and Budgetary Questions,

1. *Takes note* of the report of the Secretary-General;

2. *Endorses* the conclusions and recommendations contained in the report of the Advisory Committee on Administrative and Budgetary Questions, subject to the provisions of the present resolution;

3. *Decides* to establish one P-5, two P-4 and one P-3 posts for the Rule of Law Unit, effective 1 January 2009;

4. *Requests* the Secretary-General to ensure that the Director of the Unit continues to be provided, for 2009, through secondment;

5. *Decides* to revert to this issue in the context of the proposed programme budget for the biennium 2010–2011;

III

Administrative and financial implications of the decisions and recommendations contained in the report of the International Civil Service Commission for 2008

Recalling its resolution 63/251 of 24 December 2008, entitled "United Nations common system: report of the International Civil Service Commission",

Takes note of the statement submitted by the Secretary-General in accordance with rule 153 of the rules of procedure of the General Assembly on the administrative and financial implications of the decisions and recommendations contained in the report of the International Civil Service Commission for 2008 and the related report of the Advisory Committee on Administrative and Budgetary Questions;

IV

Revised estimates resulting from resolutions and decisions adopted by the Economic and Social Council at its substantive session of 2008

Takes note of the report of the Secretary-General on the revised estimates resulting from resolutions and decisions adopted by the Economic and Social Council at its substantive session of 2008, and endorses the related report of the Advisory Committee on Administrative and Budgetary Questions;

V

Revised estimates resulting from resolutions and decisions adopted by the Human Rights Council at its seventh, eighth and ninth sessions, proposals to improve the procedure for presenting to the General Assembly the financial requirements arising from the resolutions and decisions of the Council, and a consolidated statement on resolutions and decisions adopted by the Council arising from its continuing review of its subsidiary machinery and related programme budget implications

Having considered the reports of the Secretary-General and the related report of the Advisory Committee on Administrative and Budgetary Questions,

1. *Takes note* of the reports of the Secretary-General;

2. *Endorses* the conclusions and recommendations contained in the report of the Advisory Committee on Administrative and Budgetary Questions;

VI

Revised estimates resulting from the entry into force of the Convention on the Rights of Persons with Disabilities and the Optional Protocol thereto

Having considered the report of the Secretary-General and the related report of the Advisory Committee on Administrative and Budgetary Questions,

1. *Takes note* of the report of the Secretary-General;

2. *Endorses* the conclusions and recommendations contained in the report of the Advisory Committee on Administrative and Budgetary Questions;

VII

Review of the lump-sum arrangement of the Office of the United Nations High Commissioner for Refugees

Having considered the report of the Secretary-General and the related report of the Advisory Committee on Administrative and Budgetary Questions,

1. *Takes note* of the report of the Secretary-General;

2. *Endorses* the conclusions and recommendations contained in the report of the Advisory Committee on Administrative and Budgetary Questions;

VIII

Human resources management

Recalling section II of its resolution 63/250 of 24 December 2008,

1. *Decides* to approve, in connection with the harmonization of contractual arrangements, an additional appropriation in the amount of 13,165,400 dollars under section 3, Political affairs, of the programme budget for the biennium 2008–2009;

2. *Requests* the Secretary-General to include a total amount of 80,900,900 dollars in the respective budgets of the affected peacekeeping missions for the period from 1 July 2009 to 30 June 2010;

IX

Administrative and financial implications arising from the report of the United Nations Joint Staff Pension Board

Having considered the report of the Secretary-General and the related report of the Advisory Committee on Administrative and Budgetary Questions,

1. *Takes note* of the report of the Secretary-General;

2. *Requests* the Secretary-General to report on any additional requirements arising from the recommendations of the United Nations Joint Staff Pension Board in the context of the second performance report on the programme budget for the biennium 2008–2009;

X

Revised estimates under section 32, Construction, alteration, improvement and major maintenance, of the programme budget for the biennium 2008–2009, relating to the provision of an integrated headquarters facility for the United Nations Assistance Mission for Iraq, in Baghdad

Recalling its resolutions 62/237 A and 62/238 of 22 December 2007,

Having considered the report of the Secretary-General on the revised estimates under section 3, Political affairs, and section 32, Construction, alteration, improvement and major maintenance, of the programme budget for the biennium 2008–2009, relating to the provision of an integrated headquarters facility for the United Nations Assistance Mission for Iraq, in Baghdad, the relevant parts of the report of the Secretary-General on the estimates in respect of the United Nations Assistance Mission for Iraq and the related report of the Advisory Committee on Administrative and Budgetary Questions,

1. *Takes note* of the report of the Secretary-General on the revised estimates under section 3, Political affairs, and section 32, Construction, alteration, improvement and major maintenance, of the programme budget for the biennium 2008–2009, relating to the provision of an integrated headquarters facility for the United Nations Assistance Mission for Iraq, in Baghdad;

2. *Endorses* the conclusions and recommendations of the Advisory Committee on Administrative and Budgetary Questions, subject to the provisions of the present resolution;

3. *Welcomes* the contribution of the Government of Iraq, and recognizes the importance of the proposal for the construction of a purpose-built integrated headquarters for the United Nations Assistance Mission for Iraq;

4. *Approves* commitment authority for 2009 for the United Nations Assistance Mission for Iraq in the amount of 5 million dollars under section 32 of the programme budget for the biennium 2008–2009 to undertake design work in connection with the construction of the United Nations integrated compound in Baghdad;

5. *Emphasizes* the importance of ensuring that the project is based on accurate assumptions and that its planning phase takes into account the experience of the execution of other construction projects in the United Nations and also of ensuring proper accountability with regard to the implementation of the project;

6. *Requests* the Secretary-General to submit a new, complete and detailed proposal for the construction of the United Nations integrated compound in Baghdad, under section 32 of the programme budget, for its consideration early in the second part of its resumed sixty-third session, with detailed comprehensive financial requirements and clear timelines for the different phases of its implementation;

XI

Estimates in respect of special political missions, good offices and other political initiatives authorized by the General Assembly and/or the Security Council

Recalling its resolutions 62/237 A and 62/238 of 22 December 2007 and 62/245 of 3 April 2008,

Having considered the reports of the Secretary-General on estimates in respect of special political missions, good offices and other political initiatives authorized by the General Assembly and/or the Security Council and the related report of the Advisory Committee on Administrative and Budgetary Questions,

1. *Takes note* of the reports of the Secretary-General;

2. *Endorses* the conclusions and recommendations of the Advisory Committee on Administrative and Budgetary Questions, subject to the provisions of the present resolution;

3. *Regrets* that the timing of the presentation of the report of the Secretary-General to the Fifth Committee was delayed until the last week of the main part of the sixty-third session of the General Assembly, and requests the Secretary-General to present future budget proposals for the special political missions no later than the last week of October;

4. *Requests* the Secretary-General to revise the narrative and the logical framework of the budget for the Special Envoy of the Secretary-General for the implementation of Security Council resolution 1559(2004), taking into account recent developments and the concerns raised by Member States, and to submit a report thereon to the General Assembly before the first part of its resumed sixty-third session;

5. *Takes note* of paragraph 94 of the report of the Advisory Committee on Administrative and Budgetary Questions, and decides to establish one Political Affairs Officer position at the P-3 level and five Local level positions;

6. *Also takes note* of paragraph 158 of the report of the Advisory Committee on Administrative and Budgetary Questions, and decides to reclassify the Chief Technical Adviser position from the D-1 to the D-2 level;

7. *Decides* to establish a position at the P-5 level, instead of one at the P-4 level, in the Office of the Special Adviser to the Secretary-General on Cyprus;

8. *Approves* budgets totalling 429,497,600 dollars for the twenty-seven special political missions authorized by the General Assembly and/or the Security Council presented in table 1 of the report of the Secretary-General;

9. *Takes note* of the estimated unencumbered balance of 15,850,800 dollars;

10. *Decides* to appropriate, after taking into account the estimated unencumbered balance of 15,850,800 dollars,

under the procedures provided for in paragraph 11 of annex I to resolution 41/213 of 19 December 1986, an amount of 413,646,800 dollars under section 3, Political affairs, of the programme budget for the biennium 2008–2009;

11. *Also decides* to appropriate an amount of 26,432,000 dollars under section 35, Staff assessment, to be offset by a corresponding amount under income section 1, Income from staff assessment, of the programme budget for the biennium 2008–2009;

XII

First performance report on the programme budget for the biennium 2008–2009

Having considered the first performance report of the Secretary-General on the programme budget for the biennium 2008–2009 and the related report of the Advisory Committee on Administrative and Budgetary Questions,

Recalling its resolutions 62/237 A and B of 22 December 2007 and 62/245 of 3 April 2008,

Taking note of the current challenges caused by the global financial crisis,

1. *Reaffirms* the budgetary process as approved in its resolution 41/213 and reaffirmed in subsequent resolutions;

2. *Takes note* of the first performance report of the Secretary-General on the programme budget for the biennium 2008–2009, and endorses the observations and recommendations of the Advisory Committee on Administrative and Budgetary Questions contained in its report, subject to the provisions of the present resolution;

3. *Also takes note* of paragraph 5 of the report of the Advisory Committee on Administrative and Budgetary Questions, and emphasizes that the content of the first performance report should be limited, in principle, to a description of parameter changes endorsed by the General Assembly;

4. *Endorses* paragraph 11 of the report of the Advisory Committee on Administrative and Budgetary Questions, and requests the Secretary-General to explore the recosting methodologies used by other international organizations with that used by the Secretariat, taking into account the unique nature of the United Nations, and to report thereon to the General Assembly in the context of the second performance report on the programme budget for the biennium 2008–2009;

5. *Recalls* section III, paragraph 6, of its resolution 60/283 of 7 July 2006, and requests the Secretary-General to implement the provisions of that paragraph and to report to the General Assembly thereon in the context of the second performance report on the programme budget for the biennium 2008–2009;

6. *Approves* a net increase of 174 million dollars in the appropriation approved for the biennium 2008–2009 and a net increase of 6.8 million dollars in the estimates of income for the biennium, to be apportioned among expenditure and income sections as indicated in the report of the Secretary-General;

7. *Decides* to apportion among Member States 129 million dollars for expenses related to the first performance report on the programme budget for the biennium 2008–2009;

8. *Approves* up to 45 million dollars for expenses relating to the first performance report on the programme budget for the biennium 2008–2009, upon the receipt by the President of the General Assembly of a letter from the Secretary-General, to be apportioned among Member States, as an exception to regulation 3.3 of the Financial Regulations and Rules of the United Nations;

9. *Stresses*, bearing in mind the third preambular paragraph of the present section, that the provisions of paragraph 8 constitute an exceptional measure;

XIII

Contingency fund

Notes that a balance of 5,122,000 dollars remains in the contingency fund.

Contingency fund

The contingency fund, established by General Assembly resolution 41/213 [YUN 1986, p. 1024], accommodated additional expenditures relating to each biennium that derived from legislative mandates not provided for in the proposed programme budget or from revised estimates. Guidelines for its use were annexed to Assembly resolution 42/211 [YUN 1987, p. 1098].

In a 29 December report [A/C.5/63/20] on the contingency fund, the Secretary-General submitted the consolidated statement of programme budget implications and revised estimates for the fund, which included potential new charges amounting to $7,069,000 and would result in a remaining fund balance of $5,122,000.

Revised estimates in respect of matters of which the Security Council was seized

In February [A/62/512/Add.6], the Secretary-General submitted proposed additional net requirements for the period from 1 January to 31 December 2008 in the amount of $51,850,900 for the Special Envoy of the Secretary-General for the Lord's Resistance Army-affected areas, the United Nations Representative to the International Advisory and Monitoring Board, the Office of the Special Envoy of the Secretary-General for the future status process for Kosovo, the United Nations Mission in Nepal and the United Nations Political Office for Somalia.

In March [A/62/7/Add.37], ACABQ recommended that the General Assembly approve the requested resources subject to its recommendations and noted that part of the additional requirements would be met from the balance of $17,322,800 in the provision for special political missions under section 3, Political affairs, of the 2008–2009 programme budget. By resolution 62/245 of 3 April (see p. 1550), the Assembly approved net requirements of $48,954,400.

In a 27 October report [A/63/346 & Corr.1], the Secretary-General submitted proposed requirements for the period from 1 January to 31 December 2009 for 27 special political missions, which were estimated at $466,844,500 net ($495,435,000 gross).

In December [A/63/593], ACABQ recommended that the Assembly approve the requested resources subject to the Committee's recommendations.

The Assembly, in section XI of resolution 63/263 of 24 December (see p. 1548), approved budgets totalling $429,497,600 for the 27 special political missions.

Revised estimates resulting from Human Rights Council action

In a 1 February report [A/62/671], the Secretary-General submitted revised estimated requirements totalling $2,916,000 for the 2008–2009 biennium, resulting from resolutions adopted by the Human Rights Council at its sixth session and fifth special session, both held in 2007. A total of $2,449,300 had been included in the programme budget, and the balance of $466,700 would be accommodated from within existing appropriations. A consolidated statement of requirements arising from the continuing review by the Council of its subsidiary machinery and the potential absorptive capacity of the 2008–2009 programme budget under the amended programme of work would be reported to the Assembly during the biennium.

In February [A/62/7/Add.34], ACABQ noted that although the procedure used to report to the Assembly the requirements arising from resolutions and decisions adopted by the Council represented an effort at transparency on the part of the Secretariat, it nevertheless contributed to a piecemeal approach to budgeting for those requirements. The Committee therefore called for the improvement of the procedure and recommended that the Secretary-General make proposals in that regard, in time for the Committee to consider them in the context of its review of the consolidated statement, which would be submitted to the Assembly in late 2008 or early 2009. ACABQ also recommended that the Assembly note the estimated requirements of $2,916,000, which would be requested by the Secretary-General in the context of a consolidated statement of requirements arising from the continuing review by the Council of its subsidiary machinery.

In a November report [A/63/541], the Secretary-General submitted revised estimated requirements resulting from resolutions adopted by the Council at its seventh and eighth sessions held in 2008, totalling $6,889,800, of which $5,623,400 would be accommodated from within existing appropriations under the 2008–2009 programme budget. The Secretary-General also intended to submit a consolidated statement of requirements on the remaining balance of $1,266,400.

In a 4 December report [A/63/587], the Secretary-General submitted a consolidated statement of requirements arising from the continuing review by the Council of its subsidiary machinery, for which provisions had not been made in the 2008–2009 programme budgets, in the amount of $1,733,100.

In a 10 December report [A/63/541/Add.1], the Secretary-General submitted revised estimated requirements arising from resolutions and decisions adopted by the Human Rights Council at its ninth session totalling $2,149,300, of which $1,681,700 had already been included in the programme budget and $467,600 would be accommodated from within existing appropriations. In response to Human Rights Council decision 9/103 (see p. 712), the Secretary-General informed the Assembly that while requirements arising from that decision were estimated at $6,137,700 (gross) or $5,898,300 net of staff assessment, those requirements were presented in the statement of programme budget implications [A/C.3/63/L.77], which was later withdrawn.

In an 18 December report [A/63/629], ACABQ stated that the three aforementioned reports of the Secretary-General did not provide a clear and concise presentation of requirements and their background. In that regard, the Committee called for subsequent annual reports to be more clear. It also recommended that the Assembly approve the additional requirements of $1,733,100, with the understanding that any appropriations which might be necessary would be requested in the context of the consolidated statement of programme budget implications and revised estimates for 2008–2009 relating to the use of the contingency fund.

GENERAL ASSEMBLY ACTION

On 3 April [meeting 91], the General Assembly, on the recommendation of the Fifth Committee [A/62/563/Add.3], adopted **resolution 62/245** without vote [agenda item 128].

Special subjects relating to the programme budget for the biennium 2008–2009

The General Assembly,

I

Revised estimates resulting from resolutions adopted by the Human Rights Council

Having considered the report of the Secretary-General on revised estimates resulting from resolutions adopted by the Human Rights Council at its sixth session and its fifth special session in 2007 and the related report of the Advisory Committee on Administrative and Budgetary Questions,

1. *Takes note* of the report of the Secretary-General;

2. *Also takes* note of the preliminary estimated requirements of 2,916,000 United States dollars for the biennium 2008–2009;

3. *Further takes* note that the estimated requirements of 2,449,300 dollars have been included in the programme budget for the biennium 2008–2009 and that the balance of 466,700 dollars is to be considered in the context of a consolidated statement of requirements arising from the continuing review by the Human Rights Council of its subsidiary machinery;

4. *Endorses* the conclusions and recommendations contained in the report of the Advisory Committee on Administrative and Budgetary Questions;

5. *Requests* the Secretary-General to submit proposals to improve the procedure for presenting the financial requirements arising from resolutions and decisions of the Human Rights Council for consideration at its sixty-third session;

II

Financing of field missions of the Peacebuilding Commission

Having considered the note by the Secretary-General on the financing of field missions of the Peacebuilding Commission and the related report of the Advisory Committee on Administrative and Budgetary Questions,

1. *Takes note* of the note by the Secretary-General;

2. *Also takes* note of the preliminary estimate of 676,300 dollars for field missions of the Peacebuilding Commission under the programme budget for the biennium 2008–2009;

3. *Endorses* the conclusions and recommendations contained in the report of the Advisory Committee on Administrative and Budgetary Questions;

III

Estimates in respect of special political missions, good offices and other political initiatives authorized by the General Assembly and/or the Security Council: additional requirements for special political missions for the period from 1 January to 31 December 2008

Recalling section V of its resolution 62/238 of 22 December 2007,

Having considered the report of the Secretary-General on estimates in respect of special political missions, good offices and other political initiatives authorized by the General Assembly and/or the Security Council and the related report of the Advisory Committee on Administrative and Budgetary Questions,

1. *Takes note* of the report of the Secretary-General;

2. *Endorses* the conclusions and recommendations contained in the report of the Advisory Committee on Administrative and Budgetary Questions, subject to the provisions of the present resolution;

3. *Decides* to maintain the staffing for the Office of the Special Envoy of the Secretary-General for Lord's Resistance Army-affected areas at the level currently funded under the provisions of its resolution 62/239 of 22 December 2007 on unforeseen and extraordinary expenses for the biennium 2008–2009;

4. *Also decides* to review the staffing and resource allocation for the Special Envoy of the Secretary-General for Lord's Resistance Army-affected areas at the main part of its sixty-third session in the context of the 2009 budget proposal for special political missions;

5. *Further decides* to redeploy twenty-two positions (Local level) from the Electoral Assistance Office of the United Nations Mission in Nepal according to the needs of the Mission;

6. *Approves* additional budgets for special political missions for 2008 totalling 48,954,400 dollars net (53,571,500 dollars gross);

7. *Takes note* of the balance of 17,322,800 dollars in the overall provision for special political missions under section 3, Political affairs, of the programme budget for the biennium 2008–2009;

8. *Decides* to appropriate, under the procedure provided for in paragraph 11 of annex I to its resolution 41/213 of 19 December 1986, an additional amount of 31,631,600 dollars under section 3, Political affairs, of the programme budget for the biennium 2008–2009;

9. *Also decides* to appropriate an amount of 4,617,100 dollars under section 35, Staff assessment, to be offset by a corresponding amount under income section 1, Income from staff assessment, of the programme budget for the biennium 2008–2009.

Revised estimates resulting from Economic and Social Council action

In a September report [A/63/371], the Secretary-General submitted additional requirements resulting from resolutions and decisions adopted by the Economic and Social Council at its 2008 substantive sessions, relating to activities of the Ad Hoc Advisory Group on Haiti and preparations for the high-level segment of the fifty-second session of the Commission on Narcotic Drugs. Those requirements were estimated at $420,500, which could be absorbed within the resources provided for the 2008–2009 biennium.

In November [A/63/567], ACABQ stated that it had no objection to the Secretary-General's proposed expenditure requirements.

Revised estimates for business continuity management

In September [A/63/359 & Corr.1], the Secretary-General submitted additional requirements to the 2008–2009 programme budget in the amount of $4,692,400, which related to the implementation of business continuity management throughout the UN secretariat, including offices away from Headquarters and regional commissions. It was anticipated that $973,200 would be accommodated from within existing appropriations and that net additional requirements would amount to $3,719,200.

In December [A/63/584], ACABQ recommended that the Secretariat draw upon the experience of other UN entities in formulating its business continuity strategy, and that economies of scale should be possible to achieve, given that business continuity management was a matter of system-wide concern. In addition, the approach set out in the Secretary-General's report required further development and justification, including clarifying the relationship among business continuity management processes, the risk management framework, and proposals on information and communications technology. The Committee also recommended that the Secretary-General submit a fully justified request for post and non-post resources in the context of the proposed programme budget for 2008–2009. It further recommended approval of commitment authority for the net additional resource requirements for the biennium 2008–2009 in the amount of $1,236,700.

Reserve for United Nations Postal Administration

In response to General Assembly resolution 62/238 [YUN 2007, p. 1451], the Secretary-General transmitted an August report [A/63/320] on the contingent liability reserve for the United Nations Postal Administration (UNPA), which provided an update on measures that were taken as an alternative to the establishment of a contingent liability reserve to eliminate risks posed to UNPA by mass mailing. In New York, effective 1 September 2007, UNPA implemented a new stringent policy restricting large consignments of mail, specialized mail services and mass mail, which eliminated bulk mail charges while maintaining mail services for philatelic services as outlined in the UN agreement with the United States Postal Service. Since that date, no bulk mail had been presented to UNPA for posting. The elimination of bulk mail had positive effects on UNPA operations, which reported a net profit of $1.5 million for the 2006–2007 biennium.

With the implementation of the new policy and the related decrease in postal charges and liability, the Secretary-General recommended that a reserve not be established and that the existing practice be continued, which involved drawing from current income to meet any additional postage expenditures incurred from sales recorded in prior periods. He added that once a trend emerged from the implementation of the new policy, allowing the appropriate level of contingent liability to be determined with accuracy, UNPA, in coordination with the Office for Programme Planning, Budget and Accounts, would estimate the new level, which would then be brought to the attention of the Assembly.

In November [A/63/568], ACABQ noted the Secretary-General's recommendation against the establishment of a reserve. It also requested that the next report on the UNPA contingent liability reserve indicate how the value of the UNPA contingent liability for stamps that had not been sold and were to be presented for mailing in the future would be disclosed once International Public Sector Accounting Standards were implemented. The Committee reiterated the merits of creating a reserve for contingent liabilities for postal services for previously issued UNPA stamps and recommended that the feasibility of issuing value-added stamps (the sale of premium stamps at a price above their face value) be explored for the purpose of establishing such a reserve.

Working capital fund

The Working Capital Fund for the 2008–2009 biennium was established at $150 million by the General Assembly in December 2007 [YUN 2007, p. 1458]. As in the past, the Fund was to be used to finance appropriations, pending the receipt of assessed contributions, to pay for unforeseen and extraordinary expenses, as well as for miscellaneous self-liquidating purchases and advance insurance premiums, and to enable the Tax Equalization Fund to meet current commitments pending the accumulation of credits.

In December [ST/ADM/SER.B/761], the Secretariat issued an assessment of Member States' advances to the Fund and contributions to the UN regular budget as at 31 December 2008.

Unforeseen and extraordinary expenses

Under the terms of General Assembly resolution 62/239 [YUN 2007, p. 1459], the Secretary-General was authorized, with the prior concurrence of ACABQ, to enter into commitments to meet unforeseen and extraordinary expenses arising either during or subsequent to the 2008–2009 biennium, without reverting to the Assembly for approval.

In his first performance report on the 2008–2009 programme budget [A/63/573], the Secretary-General informed the Assembly that he had entered into commitments in the amount of $1,359,200, of which $1,159,200 was for activities relating to the maintenance of peace and security and $200,000 was for commitments certified by the President of the International Court of Justice.

Revised estimates in respect of development-related activities

In response to General Assembly resolution 62/236 [YUN 2007, p. 1441], the Secretary-General transmitted a February report [A/62/708], which provided a comprehensive proposal on improving the delivery of the mandates of the development-related activities of the UN Secretariat, including the Department of Economic and Social Affairs (DESA), the United Nations Conference on Trade and Development (UNCTAD), the regional commissions and the Development Account. The revised estimated requirements resulting from the proposal totalled $25,571,000, and included the establishment of 152 new posts.

In July [A/62/7/Add.40], ACABQ found that the Secretary-General's report was lacking in analysis and in the presentation of detailed information. It recommended that the Assembly request the Secretary-General to provide information on coordination issues in the context of the budget proposals for the 2010–2011 biennium. The Committee also recommended reductions totalling $9,327,700; the approval of total staffing and non-staffing requirements of $16,243,300 for the period from 1 January to 31 December 2009; and the approval of 135 new posts and one position to be funded from general temporary assistance.

GENERAL ASSEMBLY ACTION

On 24 December [meeting 74], the General Assembly, on the recommendation of the Fifth Committee [A/63/648/Add.1], adopted **resolution 63/260** without vote [agenda item 118].

Development-related activities

The General Assembly,

Having considered the reports of the Secretary-General on improving the effective and efficient delivery of the mandates of development-related activities and revised estimates relating to the programme budget for the biennium 2008–2009 and the Development Account, and the related reports of the Advisory Committee on Administrative and Budgetary Questions,

1. *Takes note* of the reports of the Secretary-General on improving the effective and efficient delivery of the mandates of development-related activities and revised estimates relating to the programme budget for the biennium 2008–2009 and the Development Account;

2. *Endorses* the conclusions and recommendations contained in the reports of the Advisory Committee on Administrative and Budgetary Questions, subject to the provisions of the present resolution;

3. *Acknowledges* that peace and security, development and human rights are the pillars of the United Nations system and the foundations for collective security and well-being, and recognizes that development, peace and security and human rights are interlinked and mutually reinforcing;

4. *Stresses* the importance of a coherent vision of the Secretariat's role in the global development architecture;

5. *Encourages* the Secretary-General, in his capacity as Chairman of the United Nations System Chief Executives Board for Coordination, to enhance the coordination of the United Nations development system with a view to ensuring greater synergies, effectiveness, efficiencies and coherence of efforts in the delivery of its social, economic and development mandates;

6. *Decides* to establish the posts as contained in the annex to the present resolution;

7. *Also decides* that the posts for section 17, Economic and social development in Africa, section 18, Economic and social development in Asia and the Pacific, section 19, Economic development in Europe, section 20, Economic and social development in Latin America and the Caribbean, and section 21, Economic and social development in Western Asia, shall be established effective 1 January 2009, and the posts for section 9, Economic and social affairs, section 10, Least developed countries, landlocked developing countries and small island developing States, section 11, United Nations support for the New Partnership for Africa's Development, and section 12, Trade and development, shall be established effective 1 July 2009;

8. *Further decides* not to abolish the post of the Special Adviser on Africa at the level of Under-Secretary-General;

9. *Decides* not to approve the non-post resources for travel of staff, consultants and experts and contractual services, excluding the regional commissions;

10. *Requests* the Secretary-General to report on the implementation of the present resolution within the context of the proposed programme budget for the biennium 2012–2013.

ANNEX

Development-related activities: posts to be established under the programme budget for the biennium 2008–2009

Section and subprogramme	*Number of posts*	*Level*
9. Economic and social affairs		
Executive direction and management	1	1 P-5
1. Economic and Social Council support and coordination	1	1 P-4
2. Gender issues and advancement of women	5	1 P-5, 2 P-4, 2 P-3
3. Social policy and development	1	1 P-4
4. Sustainable development	1	1 P-4
5. Statistics	1	1 P-3
6. Population	1	1 P-4
9. Sustainable forest management	1	1 P-5
10. Financing for development	1	1 P-4
Subtotal	**13**	**3 P-5, 7 P-4, 3 P-3**

Section and subprogramme	Number of posts	Level
10. Least developed countries, landlocked developing countries and small island developing States		
1. Least developed countries	1	1 P-4
2. Landlocked developing countries	1	1 P-4
3. Small island developing States	1	1 P-4
Subtotal	**3**	**3 P-4**
11. United Nations support for the New Partnership for Africa's Development		
1. Coordination of global advocacy of and support for the New Partnership for Africa's Development	3	1 P-4, 2 P-3
Subtotal	**3**	**1 P-4, 2 P-3**
12. Trade and development		
1. Globalization, interdependence and development	6	1 D-1, 1 P-5, 2 P-4, 2 P-3
2. Investment, enterprise and technology	2	1 P-5, 1 P-4
3. International trade	2	1 D-1, 1 P-4
5. Africa, least developed countries and special programmes	2	1 D-1, 1 P-4
Subtotal	**12**	**3 D-1, 2 P-5, 5 P-4, 2 P-3**
17. Economic and social development in Africa		
Executive direction and management	1	1 National Officer
7. Subregional activities for development	11	11 National Officer
9. Statistics	6	2 P-5, 2 P-4, 2 P-3
Programme support	1	1 National Officer
Subtotal	**19**	**2 P-5, 2 P-4, 2 P-3, 13 National Officer**
18. Economic and social development in Asia and the Pacific		
3. Subregional activities for development	11	2 D-1, 4 P-5, 1 P-4, 2 P-3, 1 Local level, 1 National Office
Subtotal	**11**	**2 D-1, 4 P-5, 1 P-4, 2 P-3, 1 Local level, 1 National Officer**
19. Economic development in Europe		
Executive direction and management	1	1 P-4
3. Statistics	1	1 P-3
5. Sustainable energy	1	1 P-4
Programme support	1	1 P-3
Subtotal	**4**	**2 P-4, 2 P-3**
20. Economic and social development in Latin America and the Caribbean		
1. Linkages with the global economy, regional integration and cooperation	2	1 P-4, 1 P-3
2. Production and innovation	1	1 P-3
4. Social development and equity	1	1 P-3
5. Mainstreaming the gender perspective in regional development	2	1 P-5, 1 P-3
6. Population and development	1	1 P-3
8. Sustainable development and human settlements	3	1 P-5, 1 P-3, 1 P-2
9. Natural resources and infrastructure	4	1 P-4, 2 P-2, 1 Local level
10. Statistics and economic projections	1	1 P-3
11. Subregional activities in Mexico and Central America	3	1 P-4, 1 P-3, 1 Local level
12. Subregional activities in the Caribbean	2	2 P-3
Subtotal	**20**	**2 P-5, 3 P-4, 10 P-3, 3 P-2, 2 Local level**
21. Economic and social development in Western Asia		
1. Integrated management of natural resources for sustainable development	1	1 P-4
2. Integrated social policies	1	1 P-4
3. Economic development and integration	1	1 P-4
4. Information and communication technology for regional integration		
5. Statistics for evidence-based policymaking	1	1 P-3
Subtotal	**6**	**1 P-5, 3 P-4, 1 P-3, 1 National Officer**
TOTAL	91	

Programme budget outline for 2010–2011

Report of Secretary-General. In December [A/63/600], the Secretary-General presented the proposed programme budget outline for the 2010–2011 biennium, describing the preliminary estimate of resources, priorities, real growth compared with the previous budget, and the size of the contingency fund as a percentage of the overall level of resources. The preliminary estimate for the 2010–2011 biennium, expressed in 2008–2009 prices, amounted to $4,617.9 million.

The preliminary estimate ($3,792.2 million), before the inclusion of special political missions, represented an increase of $20.1 million, or 0.5 per cent, compared with the 2008–2009 biennium. Taking account of the full inclusion of provisions for those missions, the total preliminary estimate of $4,617.9 million represented an increase of $410.3 million, or 9.8 per cent, compared with the 2008–2009 biennium.

Noting that the size of the contingency fund was set at 0.75 per cent of the overall resource level, the Secretary-General recommended that the fund again be set at the same rate, or $34.6 million, for the 2010–2011 biennium.

ACABQ report. In December [A/63/622], ACABQ noted that in order for the budget outline to be a practical tool in the budget preparation process, it must be submitted by the Secretary-General sufficiently early during off-budget years, instead of at the very end of off-budget years, as had been the case for several bienniums. It also drew attention to an additional amount of $44.3 million included in the outline for posts that were already being partially funded in the current biennium. With regard to the provisions for special political missions, the Committee noted that the estimated amount of $825.7 million was included in the budget outline at the level that was equivalent to the revised provision proposed for the biennium 2008–2009. In view of the magnitude of the provision for special political missions and the variability in requirements for those missions, the Committee recommended that the Secretary-General continue to present his overall estimates for the proposed budget outline in such a way as to readily identify those resources attributable to special political missions, and to use the same approach for presenting special political missions in the proposed programme budget.

With regard to the preliminary estimate of $4,617.9 million for the 2010–2011 budget outline and the items still under consideration by the Assembly, the Committee said that the proposed programme budget outline should have presented the fullest possible picture of the Organization's estimates of resources for the 2010–2011 biennium. It noted that the budget outline under consideration fell short of those requirements and was likely to increase to $5,187.1 million if it were to include the estimates of all the items before the Assembly and the foreseeable items in reports yet to be issued. The Committee recommended that the Assembly take into account the updated information contained in the report's annex in its consideration of the proposed 2010–2011 programme budget outline. It also recommended that the level of the contingency fund remain at 0.75 per cent, or $38.9 million.

GENERAL ASSEMBLY ACTION

On 24 December [meeting 74], the General Assembly, on the recommendation of the Fifth Committee [A/63/649], adopted **resolution 63/266** without vote [agenda item 117].

Proposed programme budget outline for the biennium 2010–2011

The General Assembly,

Reaffirming its resolution 41/213 of 19 December 1986, in which it requested the Secretary-General to submit in off-budget years an outline of the proposed programme budget for the following biennium,

Reaffirming also section VI of its resolution 45/248 B of 21 December 1990,

Reaffirming further rule 153 of its rules of procedure,

Recalling its resolution 58/269 of 23 December 2003,

Having considered the report of the Secretary-General on the proposed programme budget outline for the biennium 2010–2011 and the recommendations contained in the related report of the Advisory Committee on Administrative and Budgetary Questions,

1. *Reaffirms* that the Fifth Committee is the appropriate Main Committee of the General Assembly entrusted with responsibilities for administrative and budgetary matters;

2. *Endorses* the observations and recommendations contained in the report of the Advisory Committee on Administrative and Budgetary Questions, subject to the provisions of the present resolution;

3. *Reaffirms* that the proposed programme budget outline shall contain an indication of the following:

(a) A preliminary estimate of resources needed to accommodate the proposed programme of activities during the biennium;

(b) Priorities, reflecting general trends of a broad sectoral nature;

(c) Real growth, positive or negative, compared with the previous budget;

(d) Size of the contingency fund expressed as a percentage of the overall level of resources;

4. *Also reaffirms* that the budget outline should provide a greater level of predictability of resources required for the following biennium and promote greater involvement of Member States in the budgetary process, thereby facilitating the broadest possible agreement on the programme budget;

5. *Further reaffirms* that the budget proposals of the Secretary-General should reflect resource levels commen-

surate with mandates for their full, efficient and effective implementation;

6. *Requests* the Secretary-General to continue to include in the proposed budget outline and in the proposed programme budget, provisions for expenditures for special political missions related to peace and security that are expected to be extended or approved in the course of the biennium;

7. *Stresses* that the budget outline is a preliminary estimate of resources;

8. *Invites* the Secretary-General to prepare his proposed programme budget for the biennium 2010–2011 on the basis of a preliminary estimate of 4,871,048,700 United States dollars at revised 2008–2009 rates;

9. *Notes* that the preliminary estimates provided by the Secretary-General for the proposed programme budget for the biennium 2010–2011 do not include provisions for the implementation of those requirements that are under discussion by the General Assembly and that the requirements pertinent to the regular budget should be reflected in the programme budget for the biennium 2010–2011, subject to approval by the Assembly and in accordance with its resolutions 41/213 of 19 December 1986 and 42/211 of 21 December 1987;

10. *Welcomes* the information contained in paragraph 8 of the report of the Advisory Committee on Administrative and Budgetary Questions and in the annex thereto;

11. *Notes* the additional information provided in the annex to the report of the Advisory Committee on Administrative and Budgetary Questions, and requests the Secretary-General to provide similar information in an annex to future budget outlines;

12. *Requests* the Secretary-General to include in the report on special political missions an annex containing an updated estimate of the total budget for special political missions for the biennium 2010–2011 for consideration by the General Assembly at the beginning of its sixty-fourth session based on updated projected needs and without prejudging the decisions of the relevant legislative organs of the United Nations;

13. *Reiterates its request* to the Secretary-General to include, in the proposed programme budget for the biennium 2010–2011, the total amount of resources that he should have at his disposal, from all sources of financing, in order to implement fully all mandated programmes and activities;

14. *Emphasizes* that the proposed programme budget outline should be submitted sufficiently early in order to be able to serve as a practical tool in the budget preparation process, and, in this regard, requests the Secretary-General to issue future budget outlines at least thirty days prior to their scheduled introduction, but no later than 15 November of the off-budget year;

15. *Decides* that the proposed programme budget for the biennium 2010–2011 shall contain provisions for recosting on the basis of the existing methodology;

16. *Reaffirms* that the budget outline should be submitted in accordance with the priorities set by the General Assembly;

17. *Decides* that the priorities for the biennium 2010–2011 shall be the following:

(*a*) Promotion of sustained economic growth and sustainable development, in accordance with the relevant resolutions of the General Assembly and recent United Nations conferences;

(*b*) Maintenance of international peace and security;

(*c*) Development of Africa;

(*d*) Promotion of human rights;

(*e*) Effective coordination of humanitarian assistance efforts;

(*f*) Promotion of justice and international law;

(*g*) Disarmament;

(*h*) Drug control, crime prevention and combating international terrorism in all its forms and manifestations;

18. *Notes* that the preliminary indicative estimates contained in the present budget outline do not track precisely the priorities of the General Assembly in certain areas, including in the areas of development;

19. *Requests* the Secretary-General to reflect the priorities outlined in paragraph 17 above when presenting the proposed programme budget for the biennium 2010–2011;

20. *Notes* that the budget proposal will reflect the benefit of further reviews of possible obsolete activities, additional cost-effective measures and simplified procedures and, in this regard, requests the Secretary-General to rigorously pursue this in accordance with regulation 5.6 of the Regulations and Rules Governing Programme Planning, the Programme Aspects of the Budget, the Monitoring of Implementation and the Methods of Evaluation, and established practices;

21. *Decides* that the contingency fund shall be set at the level of 0.75 per cent of the preliminary estimate, namely, at 36,532,900 dollars, that this amount shall be in addition to the overall level of the preliminary estimate, and that it shall be used in accordance with the procedures for the use and operation of the contingency fund.

Contributions

According to the Secretary-General's report on improving the financial situation of the United Nations [A/63/514/Add.1], unpaid assessed contributions to the UN budget at the end of 2008 totalled $417 million (compared to $428 million in 2007); outstanding peacekeeping arrears totalled $2,900 million (compared to $2,700 million in 2007); and total unpaid assessments to the international tribunals were reduced to $26 million (compared to $34 million in 2007).

The number of Member States paying their regular budget assessment in full increased to 146 (compared to 140 at the end of 2007).

Assessments

The Committee on Contributions, at its sixty-eighth session (New York, 9–27 June) [A/63/11], considered issues related to the payment of assessments, including the methodology for preparing the scale of assessments, multi-year payment plans and the application of Article 19 of the Charter. On its working methods, following the Committee's 2007 agreement to set up a website to assist its intersessional work and to facilitate the dissemination of reports and other publicly available documents [YUN 2007, p. 1459], a public website for the Committee was launched in June 2008. With regard to intersessional work, discussions were ongoing with the Office of Central Support Services for the establishment of a restricted website, to be made accessible to the members of the Committee. The Committee decided to hold its sixty-ninth (2009) session from 1 to 26 June 2009.

The General Assembly took action on the Committee's recommendations in October and December (see below). On 24 December, the Assembly deferred consideration of the Committee's report until its resumed sixty-third (2009) session **(decision 63/550)**.

Application of Article 19

Committee on Contributions. The Committee on Contributions [A/63/11] reviewed requests from seven Member States for exemption under Article 19, whereby a Member would lose its vote in the General Assembly if the amount of its arrears should equal or exceed the amount of contributions due from it for the preceding two full years. The Committee duly noted the Members' written and oral representations and evaluated them against their payment records and economic and political circumstances.

Determining that the failure of the Central African Republic, the Comoros, Guinea-Bissau, Liberia, Sao Tome and Principe, Somalia and Tajikistan to pay the full minimum amount of their arrears necessary to avoid the application of Article 19 was due to conditions beyond their control, and recalling the Article's provision that a Member might be permitted to vote if the Assembly was satisfied that its failure to pay was due to such conditions, the Committee recommended that they be allowed to vote until the end of the sixty-third session of the Assembly. The Committee urged the Central African Republic, which had made no payments in the previous decade, to make some payments to reduce, or at least to avoid a further increase in, its unpaid assessed contributions and agreed that future considerations of requests for exemption might not be favourable in the light of the country's lack of commitment to addressing its arrears. The Committee noted that unless some minimum payments were made by Sao Tome and Principe, the debt burden would continue to increase, and urged its Government to at least pay amounts equivalent to current annual assessments to demonstrate its commitment to addressing its arrears. It also noted that the continuing payments made by Tajikistan under its multi-year payment plan had significantly exceeded the total payments foreseen in its schedule for the 2000–2008 period.

At the end of the Committee's session on 27 June, seven Member States—Central African Republic, the Comoros, Guinea-Bissau, Liberia, Sao Tome and Principe, Somalia and Tajikistan—were in arrears in the payment of their assessed contributions under the terms of Article 19, yet had been permitted to vote in the Assembly until the end of the sixty-second session, pursuant to Assembly resolution 62/1 [YUN 2007, p. 1460].

Reports of Secretary-General. During the year, the Secretary-General reported to the Assembly on payments made by certain Member States to reduce their level of arrears below that specified in Article 19, so that they could vote in the Assembly. As at 18 January [A/62/657], 15 Member States were below the gross amount assessed for the preceding two full years (2006–2007). By a series of letters from January to May [A/62/657/Add.1–8], that number was reduced to seven and remained at that number through 9 September [A/63/350].

GENERAL ASSEMBLY ACTION

On 13 October [meeting 24], the General Assembly, on the recommendation of the Fifth Committee [A/63/472], adopted **resolution 63/4** without vote [agenda item 122].

Scale of assessments for the apportionment of the expenses of the United Nations: requests under Article 19 of the Charter

The General Assembly,

Having considered chapter V of the report of the Committee on Contributions on its sixty-eighth session,

Reaffirming the obligation of Member States under Article 17 of the Charter of the United Nations to bear the expenses of the Organization as apportioned by the General Assembly,

1. *Reaffirms* its role in accordance with the provisions of Article 19 of the Charter of the United Nations and the advisory role of the Committee on Contributions in accordance with rule 160 of the rules of procedure of the General Assembly;

2. *Also reaffirms* its resolution 54/237 C of 23 December 1999;

3. *Requests* the Secretary-General to continue to bring to the attention of Member States the deadline specified in resolution 54/237 C, including through an early announcement in the Journal of the United Nations and through direct communication;

4. *Urges* all Member States requesting exemption under Article 19 of the Charter to submit as much information as possible in support of their requests and to consider submitting such information in advance of the deadline specified in resolution 54/237 C so as to enable the collation of any additional detailed information that may be necessary;

5. *Agrees* that the failure of the Central African Republic, the Comoros, Guinea-Bissau, Liberia, Sao Tome and Principe, Somalia and Tajikistan to pay the full minimum amount necessary to avoid the application of Article 19 of the Charter was due to conditions beyond their control;

6. *Decides* that the Central African Republic, the Comoros, Guinea-Bissau, Liberia, Sao Tome and Principe, Somalia and Tajikistan shall be permitted to vote in the General Assembly until the end of its sixty-third session.

On 24 December, the Assembly decided that the item on the scale of assessments for the apportionment of the expenses of the United Nations would remain for consideration during its resumed sixty-third (2009) session **(decision 63/552)**.

Multi-year payment plans

Pursuant to General Assembly resolutions 57/4 B [YUN 2002, p. 1385] and 61/237 [YUN 2006, p. 1626], the Secretary-General submitted a March report [A/63/68] on multi-year payment plans, which provided information on the payment plans/schedules submitted by Liberia, Sao Tome and Principe and Tajikistan, and on the status of their implementation as at 31 December 2007. Under the plans, each year a Member State would pay for the current year's assessments and a part of its arrears, so as to eliminate the arrears within six years. However, some of the plans had durations of between 8 and 11 years. In 2007, payments for Liberia and Sao Tome and Principe fell short of the amount foreseen in their respective plans for the year, while Tajikistan had significantly exceeded the payments foreseen in its schedule for the period 2000–2007. The Secretary-General recommended that the Assembly encourage Member States with significant arrears to consider submitting a multi-year payment plan.

The Committee on Contributions [A/63/11] concluded that the system of multi-year payment plans continued to be a viable means for Member States to reduce their unpaid assessed contributions and demonstrate their commitment to meeting their financial obligations to the United Nations. The Committee also noted that no new multi-year payment plans had been submitted.

On 24 December, the Assembly deferred consideration of the reports of the Secretary-General on multi-year payment plans until its resumed sixty-third (2009) session **(decision 63/550)**.

Other matters related to payment of assessed contributions

The General Assembly also considered the recommendations of the Committee on Contributions on the methodology for future scales of assessments, as well as the issue of the outstanding assessed contributions of the former Yugoslavia [YUN 2003, p. 1428].

Scale methodology

Committee on Contributions. Pursuant to General Assembly resolution 58/1 B [YUN 2003, p. 1424], the Committee on Contributions [A/63/11] continued to review the different elements of the methodology for preparing future scales of assessments, focusing on elements relating to income measure; conversion rates; base period; debt-burden adjustment; low per capita income adjustment; minimum (floor) and maximum (ceiling) assessment rates; annual recalculation; and large scale-to-scale increases in rates of assessment. In the absence of guidance from the Assembly, the Committee reviewed further the methodology utilized in preparing the scale of assessments for the period 2007–2009; an outline of the methodology was annexed to the report.

With regard to income measure, the Committee recommended that the scale of assessments for the next assessment period continue to be based on the most current, comprehensive and comparable gross national income (GNI) data, and encouraged Member States that had not done so to adopt the 1993 System of National Accounts [YUN 1993, p. 1112]. It also reaffirmed its recommendation for the use of conversion rates based on market exchange rates, except where it would cause excessive fluctuations and distortions in the GNI of some Member States, in which case price-adjusted rates of exchange or other appropriate conversion rates should be employed. The Committee decided to consider the questions of the debt-burden adjustment and low per capita income adjustment at its next session and to study annual recalculation at future sessions. It also decided to keep the issue of the base period under review and to consider the feasibility of applying systematic measures of transitional relief for Member States facing large scale-to-scale increases in their assessment rates.

Outstanding assessed contributions

In 2008, the General Assembly considered the Secretary-General's note on outstanding assessed contributions of the former Yugoslavia [YUN 2003, p. 1428], his letter dated 27 December 2001 to the Assembly President [YUN 2001, p. 1325], the Secretary-General's report on unpaid assessed contributions of the former Yugoslavia [YUN 2005, p. 1502] and the 2 November 2006 letter from Slovenia [YUN 2006, p. 1630].

On 24 December, by resolution 63/249 (see p. 1559), the Assembly decided that the issue of the unpaid assessed contributions of the former Yugoslavia was resolved and that the unpaid assessed contributions of the former Yugoslavia up to 27 April 1992, in the amount of $1,254,230, would be apportioned among the successor States of the Socialist Federal Republic of Yugoslavia.

GENERAL ASSEMBLY ACTION

On 24 December [meeting 74], the General Assembly, on the recommendation of the Fifth Committee [A/63/472/Add.1], adopted **resolution 63/249** without vote [agenda item 122].

Unpaid assessed contributions of the former Yugoslavia

The General Assembly,

Having considered the report of the Secretary-General on the unpaid assessed contributions of the former Yugoslavia, the letter dated 27 December 2001 from the Secretary-General addressed to the President of the General Assembly, the note by the Secretary-General on the outstanding assessed contributions of the former Yugoslavia and the letter dated 2 November 2006 from the Permanent Representative of Slovenia to the United Nations addressed to the Secretary-General,

1. *Decides* that the unpaid assessed contributions to the account of the former Yugoslavia up to 27 April 1992, in the amount of 1,254,230 United States dollars, shall be apportioned among the successor States of the Socialist Federal Republic of Yugoslavia, taking into account the respective dates on which each successor State informed the Secretary-General that it had ceased to exist as part of the Socialist Federal Republic of Yugoslavia, and the proportions set forth in article 5(2) of annex C to the Agreement on Succession Issues of 29 June 2001, as well as relevant decisions of the General Assembly concerning the United Nations Emergency Force and the United Nations Operation in the Congo;

2. *Also decides* that, after taking into account the remaining advance of 26,000 dollars to the Working Capital Fund, the net balance of the unpaid assessed contributions to the account of the former Yugoslavia in the amount of 14,817,896 dollars shall be charged against the respective fund balances;

3. *Urges,* in this regard, the successor States of the Socialist Federal Republic of Yugoslavia to inform the Secretary-General as soon as possible of their respective shares of the outstanding amounts and credits, in accordance with paragraph 1 above;

4. *Decides* that the issue of the unpaid assessed contributions to the account of the former Yugoslavia shall be considered to be finally resolved upon receipt by the Secretary-General of the information requested in paragraph 3 above, and that the resolution of the issue of the unpaid assessed contributions of the former Yugoslavia to the United Nations shall be applicable only to that issue, without prejudice to any other related decisions and issues.

Accounts and auditing

The General Assembly, at its resumed sixty-second (2008) session, considered the report of the Board of Auditors on UN peacekeeping operations for the period 1 July 2006 to 30 June 2007 [A/62/5 (Vol. II)], together with the Secretary-General's report on the implementation of the Board's recommendations [A/62/784] and related ACABQ comments and recommendations [A/62/823].

On 20 June, the Assembly, in **resolution 62/223 B**, endorsed the Board's report (see p. 92).

Board of Auditors report. The Chairman of the Board of Auditors transmitted to the Secretary-General the financial reports and audited financial statements for the biennium ended 31 December 2007 on the United Nations [A/63/5 (Vol. I)] and on the following 14 entities: the International Trade Centre UNCTAD/WTO [A/63/5 (Vol. III) & Corr.1], the United Nations University [A/63/5 (Vol. IV)], the United Nations Development Programme (UNDP) [A/63/5/Add.1 & Corr.1], the United Nations Children's Fund [A/63/5/Add.2 & Corr.1], the United Nations Relief and Works Agency for Palestine Refugees in the Near East [A/63/5/Add.3], the United Nations Institute for Training and Research [A/63/5/Add.4], the voluntary funds administered by the United Nations High Commissioner for Refugees [A/63/5/Add.5], the Fund of the United Nations Environment Programme [A/63/5/Add.6], the United Nations Population Fund [A/63/5/Add.7], the United Nations Human Settlements Programme [A/63/5/Add.8], the United Nations Office on Drugs and Crime [A/63/5/Add.9], the United Nations Office for Project Services [A/63/5/Add.10], the International Criminal Tribunal for the Prosecution of Persons Responsible for Genocide and Other Serious Violations of International Humanitarian Law Committed in the Territory of Rwanda and Rwandan Citizens Responsible for Genocide and Other Such Violations Committed in the Territory of Neighbouring States between 1 January and 31 December 1994 [A/63/5/Add.11] and the International Tribunal for the Prosecution of Persons Responsible for Serious Violations of International Humanitarian Law Committed in the Territory of the Former Yugoslavia since 1991 [A/63/5/Add.12]. The Board submitted its report on the financial statements of the United Nations Joint Staff Pension Fund for the biennium ended 31 December 2007, which was incorporated into the report of the United Nations Joint Staff Pension Board [A/63/9]. The Board also submitted, through the Secretary-General, its report on the financial statements of the United Nations Compensation Commission for the biennium ended 31 December 2007 [S/2008/509].

Introducing the reports in the Fifth Committee [A/C.5/63/SR.7], the Chairman of the Board noted that for the first time, the Board had conducted all its audits and presented its reports in accordance with the International Standards on Auditing, rather than the Common Auditing Standards of the United Nations Panel of External Auditors which had previously guided its work. It had also introduced a consistent layout to its reports. He also stated that the Board's annual report on the capital master plan [A/63/5 (Vol. V)] and a report on the activities of the Procurement Task Force (see p. 1570) would be introduced to the Committee at a later date.

According to the Chairman, the Board had issued unqualified opinions for seven entities and modified audit reports with various emphases of matter for nine entities, which related to issues including negative reserves and fund balances, unconfirmed inter-fund balances, inadequate accounting for expendable and non-expendable property and inaccurate monitoring of nationally executed expenditure. The Board also noted the efforts of all United Nations Finance and Budget Network entities to adopt the International Public Sector Accounting Standards (IPSAS), yet was concerned by the delay in the funding of the enterprise resource planning (ERP) system in the UN Secretariat and the consequent risk of delay in IPSAS implementation. In that connection, the Board also raised the question of inconsistencies in the format of the financial statements of the United Nations and its funds and programmes. With regard to action on its recommendations, the Board found that of the 788 recommendations made in previous bienniums, 505 (64 per cent) had been fully implemented, 250 (32 per cent) had been partially implemented, 19 (2 per cent) had not been implemented and 14 (2 per cent) had been overtaken by events.

By a July note [A/63/169], the Secretary-General transmitted to the Assembly a concise summary of the principal findings and conclusions contained in the Board's reports. According to the note, 10 of the 16 audited UN organizations had reported cases of fraud and presumptive fraud for the financial period that ended 31 December 2007. The administration had informed the Board that they had taken action against the staff and perpetrators involved, in addition to strengthening controls to prevent recurrences. The Board noted that some country offices had not submitted information on fraud and presumptive fraud to their headquarters, and that the statistics might not be complete in respect of matters still under investigation. Although the ethics office had been established and financial disclosure statements introduced, fraud prevention was still in the process of being enhanced, notably through the strengthening of the investigative function of the Organization.

In August, the Secretary-General submitted reports on implementation of the Board of Auditor's recommendations as contained in its reports on the United Nations for the biennium ended 31 December 2007 [A/63/327], and on UN funds and programmes for the financial period ended 31 December 2007 [A/63/327/Add.1]. The related comments and observations of ACABQ were contained in an October report [A/63/474].

GENERAL ASSEMBLY ACTION

On 24 December [meeting 74], the General Assembly, on the recommendation of the Fifth Committee [A/63/637], adopted **resolution 63/246 A** without vote [agenda item 116].

Financial reports and audited financial statements, and reports of the Board of Auditors

The General Assembly,

Recalling its resolutions 50/222 of 11 April 1996, 51/218 E of 17 June 1997, 52/212 B of 31 March 1998, 53/204 of 18 December 1998, 53/221, section VIII, of 7 April 1999, 54/13 B of 23 December 1999, 55/220 A, B and C of 23 December 2000 and 12 April and 14 June 2001, 57/278 A of 20 December 2002, 60/234 A and B of 23 December 2005 and 30 June 2006, 61/233 A and B of 22 December 2006 and 29 June 2007 and 62/223 A and B of 22 December 2007 and 20 June 2008,

Recalling also all its resolutions related to the languages of the United Nations as well as those on human resources management,

Emphasizing the need to ensure the full implementation of the Staff Regulations and Rules of the United Nations,

Having considered the financial reports and audited financial statements and the reports and audit opinions of the Board of Auditors for the period ended 31 December 2007 on the United Nations, the International Trade Centre UNCTAD/WTO, the United Nations University, the United Nations Development Programme, the United Nations Children's Fund, the United Nations Relief and Works Agency for Palestine Refugees in the Near East, the United Nations Institute for Training and Research, the voluntary funds administered by the United Nations High Commissioner for Refugees, the Fund of the United Nations Environment Programme, the United Nations Population Fund, the United Nations Human Settlements Programme, the United Nations Office on Drugs and Crime, the United Nations Office for Project Services, the International Criminal Tribunal for the Prosecution of Persons Responsible for Genocide and Other Serious Violations of International Humanitarian Law Committed in the Territory of Rwanda and Rwandan Citizens Responsible for Genocide and Other Such Violations Committed in the Territory of Neighbouring States between 1 January and 31 December 1994 and the International Tribunal for the Prosecution of Persons Responsible for Serious Violations of International Humanitarian Law Committed in the Territory of the Former Yugoslavia since 1991, the concise summary of principal findings and conclusions contained in the reports prepared by the Board of Auditors, the reports of the Secretary-General on the implementation of the recommendations of the Board of Auditors on the accounts of the United Nations for the biennium ended 31 December 2007, on the capital master plan for the year ended 31 December 2007 and on the financial statements of the funds and programmes of the United Nations for the financial period ended 31 December 2007 and the report of the Advisory Committee on Administrative and Budgetary Questions,

1. *Accepts* the financial reports and audited financial statements and the reports and audit opinions of the Board of Auditors for the above-mentioned organizations;

2. *Approves* the recommendations and conclusions contained in the reports of the Board of Auditors;

3. *Endorses* the observations and recommendations contained in the report of the Advisory Committee on Administrative and Budgetary Questions;

4. *Emphasizes* that the Board of Auditors shall be completely independent and solely responsible for the conduct of audit;

5. *Decides* to consider further the reports of the Board of Auditors on the International Criminal Tribunal for Rwanda and the International Tribunal for the Former Yugoslavia under the respective agenda items relating to the Tribunals;

6. *Commends* the Board of Auditors for the superior quality of its reports, in particular with respect to its comments on the management of resources and improving the presentation of financial statements;

7. *Recalls* the statute of the International Civil Service Commission and the central role of the Commission and the General Assembly in the regulation and coordination of the conditions of service of the United Nations common system;

8. *Also recalls* its resolution 61/233 B, in which it reiterated that the issue of outstanding assessed contributions is a policy matter of the General Assembly, and urges all Member States to make every possible effort to ensure the payment of their assessed contributions in full and on time;

9. *Stresses* that the employment of staff shall continue to be carried out in strict accordance with Article 101 of the Charter of the United Nations and in line with the relevant provisions of its resolutions;

10. *Takes note* of the reports of the Secretary-General on the implementation of the recommendations of the Board of Auditors on the accounts of the United Nations for the biennium ended 31 December 2007, on the capital master plan for the year ended 31 December 2007 and on the financial statements of the funds and programmes of the United Nations for the financial period ended 31 December 2007, and also takes note of the improvements made on the implementation rate;

11. *Reiterates its request* to the Secretary-General and the executive heads of the funds and programmes of the United Nations to ensure full implementation of the recommendations of the Board of Auditors and the related recommendations of the Advisory Committee on Administrative and Budgetary Questions in a prompt and timely manner and to hold programme managers accountable for non-implementation of the recommendations;

12. *Requests* the Secretary-General to provide in his reports on the implementation of the recommendations of the Board of Auditors on the accounts of the United Nations as well as on the financial statements of its funds and programmes a full explanation for the delays in the implementation of the recommendations of the Board, in particular those recommendations not yet fully implemented which are two or more years old;

13. *Also requests* the Secretary-General to indicate in future reports an expected time frame for the implementation of the recommendations of the Board of Auditors, the priorities for their implementation and the office holders to be held accountable.

On the same date, the Assembly deferred consideration of the item on financial reports and audited financial statements and reports of the Board of Auditors to its resumed sixty-third (2009) session (**decision 63/552**).

Financial management practices

International Public Sector Accounting Standards

In compliance with resolution 60/283 [YUN 2006, p. 1580], the Secretary-General, submitted in April, the first progress report [A/62/806] on the adoption of the International Public Sector Accounting Standards (IPSAS) by the United Nations. The report provided an update on progress made in the implementation of IPSAS through 31 March 2008. The strategy of the system-wide IPSAS adoption project included a two-level approach and phased implementation. The two-level approach involved providing resources both at the system-wide level and the individual organization level. The implementation strategy targeted UN system organizations that were at a more advanced stage of readiness (early adopters) for implementation in 2008, while the majority of organizations (fast followers) would benefit from the lessons learned and were targeted for IPSAS adoption in 2010 or as soon as possible thereafter. Since the approval of the system-wide adoption of IPSAS, progress had been most evident in the areas of project governance and organization, the development of IPSAS-compliant harmonized accounting principles and guidance, and communication and training. The report provided information on progress achieved in IPSAS adoption at the system-wide level, followed by progress at the United Nations.

On annual auditing, while IPSAS was silent on whether financial statements should be audited, it was recognized that if annual financial statements were to have greater credibility, they should be audited. Further advantages of the annual audit included increased transparency and accountability. As such, audited statements would better reflect the benefits to be gained from IPSAS adoption. After consideration of the issue of an annual audit, the CEB Finance and Budget Network recommended that annual audits be undertaken. However, it also acknowledged that the audit frequency was determined by the governing body of each organization. For the United Nations, the proposed approach on the audit of IPSAS-compliant financial statements of the Organization and the related changes to the Financial Regulations and Rules arising from IPSAS adoption and harmonization with the United Nations Development Group Executive Committee agencies would be submitted to the Assembly at a later date for approval as a whole.

In an October report [A/63/496], ACABQ recognized the considerable task involved in the preparation and implementation of IPSAS, noted the significant efforts under way, and recommended that the Assembly take note of the Secretary-General's report.

Cost accounting

In response to General Assembly resolution 59/275 [YUN 2004, p. 1401], the Secretary-General submitted a March 2007 report [A/61/826] on the feasibility of the application of cost-accounting principles in the UN Secretariat, which explored ways to apply cost-accounting techniques to the Secretariat, and considered the broader financial management framework with respect to cost-accounting, including mechanisms for regulating cost recovery and the financial frameworks for income received through cost-recovery mechanisms. The Secretary-General recommended that the application of cost-accounting principles across the Secretariat be considered further in the context of the implementation of the new enterprise resource planning (ERP) system (see p. 1591). The Secretary-General further recommended that such cost-accounting principles—if the General Assembly considered it important for the Organization to apply them—should be applied initially to all support services, following an examination of the basis for costing support services and the adoption of a standard approach for such costing. He added that the option of extending cost-accounting and, in particular, time recording to peacekeeping activities and other programme areas, should be examined at a later date following a review of the success of the implementation of cost-accounting systems for support services within the new ERP system.

ACABQ, in a November 2007 report [A/62/537], stated that the Secretary-General had not adequately responded to the Assembly's mandate, as he did not report on progress made in the development of improved tools for identifying the cost of activities or elaborate options concerning cost accounting. The Committee said that better knowledge of the costs of activities would provide a better basis for assessing the efficiency of administrative functions, the cost-effectiveness of work processes and the impact of a new administration systems. ACABQ made recommendations for the Secretary-General to ensure that cost-accounting requirements were incorporated into the review on management-accounting information and to launch the pilot projects suggested in the report of the consultants as a practical step forward, including the project for improving cost reporting on conference services and the project for a time-recording and costing system in the Office of Internal Oversight Services.

On 24 December, the General Assembly endorsed the ACABQ report and requested the Secretary-General to continue to improve the methods for calculating the costs of support services, including through a framework for cost-accounting to standardize current costing practices, and to report to the Assembly at its sixty-fifth (2010) session, including an analysis of other areas within the Organization's support services in which cost-accounting could be applied (**resolution 63/262**) (see p. 1592).

Review of UN administrative and financial functioning

In 2008, the General Assembly continued its consideration of the efficiency of the administrative and financial functioning of the United Nations. To that end, the Secretary-General issued reports on the accountability framework, enterprise management and internal control framework and results-based management (see p. 1519); Procurement Task Force activities (see p. 1570); results-based management at the United Nations (see p. 1520); information requested in **resolution 62/247** on strengthening investigations (see p. 1577); information-sharing practices between the United Nations and national law enforcement authorities (see p. 1648); and the Independent Audit Advisory Committee (see below).

Administrative and budgetary coordination

CEB report. By a July note [A/63/185], the Secretary-General transmitted to the General Assembly the United Nations System Chief Executives Board (CEB) for Coordination statistical report on the budgetary and financial situation of UN system organizations, which included information on regular resources, extrabudgetary resources, total expenditure, assessed contributions and working capital funds.

The General Assembly took note of the report on 24 December (**decision 63/547**). On the same date, the Assembly decided that both the item on the administrative and budgetary coordination of the United Nations with the specialized agencies and the International Atomic Energy Agency and the item on the review of the efficiency of the administrative and financial functioning of the United Nations, would remain for consideration during its resumed sixty-third (2009) session (**decision 63/552**).

Independent Audit Advisory Committee

Pursuant to General Assembly resolution 61/275 [YUN 2007, p. 1471], the Secretary-General submitted an August report [A/63/328] on the activities of the Independent Audit Advisory Committee, established in 2007 to serve in an expert advisory capacity and assist the Assembly in fulfilling its oversight responsibilities. The report covered the period from 1 January to 31 July 2008, in which the Committee held three sessions.

On the Office of Internal Oversight Services (OIOS) proposal for a "hub and spoke" structure for its Investigations Division, the Committee determined that it had strong conceptual merit, but nevertheless recommended that the structure be implemented in a phased manner to ensure that the transfer of investigators out of the peacekeeping missions to regional hubs would not leave any operational gaps. Other recommendations for improvements made by the Committee related to the OIOS work-planning process to improve the effectiveness of cooperation between OIOS and other oversight bodies, namely, the Joint Inspection Unit and the Board of Auditors. In regard to the Secretary-General's report on the accountability framework, the enterprise risk-management and internal control framework and the results-based management framework (see p. 1519), the Committee supported the implementation of an enterprise risk management and internal control framework; recommended the establishment of a Chief Risk Officer position to provide advice and support to senior managers and coordinate risk management strategies at the enterprise level; and suggested that the implementation project be structured in stages. Other issues highlighted included the implications of recognizing end-of-service liabilities on the face of the financial statements, the lack of controls relating to non-expendable property and the challenges and considerations related to implementation of IPSAS. Due to the timing of the sessions, there was no discussion of the Committee's report by the ACABQ or the Fifth Committee. However, since the recommendations were still relevant for OIOS operations, the Independent Audit Advisory Committee believed that they should remain open for consideration by those two bodies.

On 24 December, the Assembly, in **resolution 63/265** (see p. 1574), took note of the recommendations in the report of the Independent Audit Advisory Committee and requested the Secretary-General to ensure the full implementation of those recommendations.

Programme planning

Strategic framework for 2010–2011

In May, the Secretary-General submitted the proposed strategic framework for 2010–2011 [A/63/6 (Part one)] as a translation of legislative mandates into programmes and subprogrammes, which constituted the principal policy directive of the United Nations and served as the basis for programme planning, budgeting, monitoring and evaluation. The framework comprised two parts: the plan outline (Part one) and the biennial programme plan (Part two), covering 27 programmes. In accordance with General Assembly resolution 62/224 [YUN 2007, p. 1464], the format of Part one was improved and reflected the longer-term objectives therein by elaborating on the UN priorities agreed to by Member States. The priorities for the 2010–2011 biennium, proposed for reaffirmation by the Assembly, included: promotion of sustained economic growth and sustainable development; maintenance of international peace and security; development of Africa; promotion of human rights; coordination of humanitarian assistance; promotion of justice and international law; disarmament; and drug control, crime prevention and combating international terrorism.

The Committee for Programme and Coordination (CPC) [A/63/16], having examined the Secretary-General's proposed 2010–2011 strategic framework, noted the changes in its format and narrative and recommended that the Assembly approve the priorities for the 2010–2011 biennium contained in the plan outline in Part one and the programme narrative of the 27 programmes in Part two, with certain modifications. It also recommended that the Assembly undertake an additional review of the plan outline (Part one) so that it more accurately reflected the Organization's longer-term objectives, based on mandates approved by Member States. CPC recommended further that the Assembly allocate, for review and action, programme 19, Human rights, to the Third (Social, Humanitarian and Cultural) Committee. The Committee stressed that the provision of UN support to delivering "One United Nations" pilot projects should not prejudice the outcome of the intergovernmental deliberations on the recommendations of the High-level panel on system-wide coherence in the Assembly.

On 2, 5, 11 and 19 December, the General Assembly took note, respectively, of the reports of the First (Disarmament and International Security) Committee [A/63/446] **(decision 63/522)**, Fourth (Special Political and Decolonization) Committee [A/63/449] **(decision 63/528)**, Sixth (Legal) Committee [A/63/450] **(decision 63/530)** and Second (Economic and Financial) Committee [A/63/447] **(decision 63/546)**.

On 18 December, the Assembly, on the recommendation of the Third Committee [A/63/434], approved programme 19, Human rights **(decision 63/538)**.

GENERAL ASSEMBLY ACTION

On 24 December [meeting 74], the General Assembly, on the recommendation of the Fifth Committee [A/63/611], adopted **resolution 63/247** without vote [agenda item 119].

Programme planning

The General Assembly,

Recalling its resolutions 37/234 of 21 December 1982, 38/227 A of 20 December 1983, 41/213 of 19 December 1986, 55/234 of 23 December 2000, 56/253 of 24 December 2001, 57/282 of 20 December 2002, 58/268 and 58/269 of 23 December 2003, 59/275 of 23 December 2004, 60/257 of 8 May 2006, 61/235 of 22 December 2006 and 62/224 of 22 December 2007,

Recalling also the terms of reference of the Committee for Programme and Coordination, as outlined in the annex to Economic and Social Council resolution 2008(LX) of 14 May 1976,

Having considered the report of the Committee for Programme and Coordination on the work of its forty-eighth session, the proposed strategic framework for the period 2010–2011: part one: plan outline and part two: biennial programme plan, and the report of the Secretary-General on the programme performance of the United Nations for the biennium 2006–2007,

1. *Endorses* the conclusions and recommendations of the Committee for Programme and Coordination on the programme performance of the United Nations for the biennium 2006–2007, contained in chapter II, section A, of its report on the work of its forty-eighth session, and on the proposed biennial programme plan for the period 2010–2011, contained in chapter II, section B;

2. *Decides* that the priorities for the period 2010–2011 shall be the following:

(*a*) Promotion of sustained economic growth and sustainable development in accordance with the relevant resolutions of the General Assembly and recent United Nations conferences;

(*b*) Maintenance of international peace and security;

(*c*) Development of Africa;

(*d*) Promotion of human rights;

(*e*) Effective coordination of humanitarian assistance efforts;

(*f*) Promotion of justice and international law;

(*g*) Disarmament;

(*h*) Drug control, crime prevention and combating international terrorism in all its forms and manifestations;

3. *Stresses* that setting the priorities of the United Nations is the prerogative of the Member States, as reflected in legislative mandates;

4. *Also stresses* the need for Member States to participate fully in the budget preparation process, from its early stages and throughout the process;

5. *Requests* the Secretary-General to prepare the proposed programme budget for the biennium 2010–2011 on the basis of the above priorities and the biennial programme plan as adopted in the present resolution;

6. *Endorses* the conclusions and recommendations of the Committee for Programme and Coordination on evaluation, contained in chapter II, section C, of its report; on the annual overview report of the United Nations System Chief Executives Board for Coordination, contained in chapter III, section A; on the New Partnership for Africa's Development, contained in chapter III, section B; and on improving the working methods and procedures of the Committee within the framework of its mandate, contained in chapter IV;

7. *Reaffirms* the role of the Committee for Programme and Coordination in monitoring and evaluation, and recalls paragraph 11 of its resolution 62/224;

8. *Recognizes* the importance of continuing to improve the logical framework, and in this regard encourages programme managers to further improve the qualitative aspects of indicators of achievement in order to enable better evaluation of results, bearing in mind the importance of defining the indicators in a way that ensures their clear measurability;

9. *Reaffirms* the role of the Committee for Programme and Coordination as the main subsidiary organ of the General Assembly and the Economic and Social Council for planning, programming and coordination, recalls regulation 5.6 of the Regulations and Rules Governing Programme Planning, the Programme Aspects of the Budget, the Monitoring of Implementation and the Methods of Evaluation, and emphasizes that the Committee for Programme and Coordination should enhance its coordination role in order to increase planning efficiency and effectiveness so as to continue to ensure the timeliness of the implementation of, and prevent duplication and redundancy in, the actions of the Organization;

10. *Welcomes* the progress made by the Committee for Programme and Coordination in improving its working methods and procedures within the framework of its mandate, as well as the decision of the Committee to remain seized of the matter.

On 24 December, the Assembly decided that the item on programme planning would remain for consideration during its resumed sixty-third (2009) session **(decision 63/552)**.

Programme performance

In an April report [A/63/70] on the programme performance of the United Nations for the 2006–2007 biennium, the Secretary-General provided an overview of the key results achieved, information on the delivery of outputs and resource utilization, and a statement of appropriations of the United Nations General Fund for that biennium as at 31 December 2007. Although a major achievement of 2006–2007 was the fact that almost no dissatisfaction was expressed with the conference services provided to intergovernmental bodies, the proportion of documents at all headquarters duty stations issued in all languages in accordance with the six-week rule was not satisfactory. Other areas identified for improvement included programme performance reporting, which needed to become increasingly qualitative, and its use to inform decision-making. Under the 2006–2007 biennium, implementation rates remained high, with 24 budget sections at 90 per cent and above. Similarly, the Secretariat-wide average implementation remained at the rate of 106 per cent, reflecting a greater degree of resourcefulness and ability of programme managers and offices to cope with unforeseen circumstances. During the biennium programme, 4,420 outputs added to the programme of work by intergovernmental bodies or the Secretariat were also implemented. In addition, out of 31,964 total quantifiable outputs, 660 (2 per cent) were postponed and 2,610 (8 per cent) were terminated. With regard to the 527 outputs carried forward for implementation in 2006–2007, some 309 (59 per cent) were implemented, 96 (18 per cent) were postponed and 122 (23 per cent) were terminated. Overall, including technical cooperation outputs, the Organization delivered 44,278 outputs, some of which included capacity-building training for 195,186 government officials and representatives. Implementation utilized a total of 110,393 work months.

The Secretary-General made recommendations for CPC to take note of the report, endorse its methodological conclusions and use the detailed performance information from 2006–2007 in its review of the proposed 2010–2011 strategic framework.

CPC consideration. CPC [A/63/16] indicated that the 2006–2007 programme performance report had not been issued in accordance with the six-week rule, reiterated the need to improve the responsiveness and accountability of procedures within the Secretariat and called for the timely issuance of all relevant documents in accordance with the rule to ensure their proper consideration by the Committee. In other recommendations, the Committee called for programme managers to be held accountable for the achievement of results and documenting progress; implementation of methodological changes to improve the quality of the formulation of expected accomplishments and performance indicators in the 2010–2011 proposed programme budget; modifications to the Regulations and Rules Governing Programme Planning, the Programme Aspects of the Budget, the Monitoring of Implementation and the Methods of Evaluation; the provision of comprehensive information on all relevant cross-cutting issues in future programme performance reports; and the provision of detailed information on the outcome of monitoring and evaluation at the departmental and executive levels, including how lessons learned were shared and applied in planning activities.

Evaluation

OIOS reports to CPC. The Secretary-General transmitted to CPC the OIOS evaluation reports on the in-depth evaluation of political affairs [E/AC.51/2008/2]; the triennial review of the implementation of the recommendations made at its forty-fifth (2005) session on the United Nations Human Settlements Programme [E/AC.51/2008/3]; and the triennial review of the thematic evaluation of the linkages between Headquarters and field activities: a review of best practices for poverty eradication in the framework of the United Nations Nations Millennium Declaration [E/AC.51/2008/4 & Add.1].

CPC comments and recommendations on those reports were contained in the report on its 2008 session [A/63/16].

By **decision 2008/221** of 21 July, the Economic and Social Council took note of the CPC report.

Chapter III

Administrative and staff matters

During 2008, the General Assembly continued to review the administrative functioning of the Organization and matters related to United Nations staff, including new reform proposals.

The Organization strengthened its oversight of UN activities through the Office of Internal Oversight Services (OIOS), particularly the OIOS Procurement Task Force and its Independent Audit Advisory Committee, as well as through the Joint Inspection Unit (JIU). As a result of the work of the Procurement Task Force, established to address fraud and corruption, some 22 vendors were sanctioned by the Administration. Since its formation, the Task Force had completed 222 investigations and identified more than 20 significant fraud and corruption schemes.

The Independent Audit Advisory Committee, established in 2006 to serve in an expert advisory capacity and to assist the General Assembly in fulfilling its oversight responsibilities, became operational on 1 January and issued its first annual report.

In April, the Secretary-General presented his information and communications technology strategy for the UN Secretariat over the next three to five years. In December, the General Assembly established the Office of Information and Communications Technology.

The General Assembly approved the governance framework for the implementation of an enterprise resource planning system for the UN Secretariat and its worldwide offices. The Assembly also adopted resolutions on: the report of OIOS on its activities; strengthening investigations; the report on the work of JIU for 2007 and programme of work for 2008; the pattern of conferences; security, disaster recovery and business continuity; and the need to harmonize and improve UN informatics systems for optimal utilization and accessibility by all States.

Regarding security issues, the Assembly reaffirmed the importance of a system-wide policy on the safety and security of UN staff and requested the Secretary-General to ensure that UN and other personnel carrying out activities in fulfilment of UN mandated operations were properly informed about, and operated in conformity with, relevant codes of conduct. It also emphasized the need to pay special attention to the safety and security of UN and associated personnel engaged in peacekeeping and peacebuilding operations, and in particular to locally recruited humanitarian personnel.

During the year, the Assembly, through the International Civil Service Commission, continued to review the conditions of service of staff of the UN common system, and adopted the Commission's recommendations relating to the mobility and hardship allowance; post adjustment; education grant; conditions of service of staff in the Professional and higher categories; base/floor salary scale; and methodology and level of children's and secondary dependant's allowance.

The General Assembly approved the Secretary-General's proposals for streamlining UN contractual arrangements and harmonizing conditions of service, effective 1 July 2009. Under the proposed system, a single series of staff rules would provide for one UN staff contract, encompassing three types of appointments: temporary, fixed-term, and continuing.

The Secretary-General also reported on: the conditions of service and compensation of members of the International Court of Justice and judges and ad litem judges of the International Tribunals; safety and security of humanitarian and UN personnel; contractual arrangements and harmonization of conditions of service; civilian career peacekeepers; recruitment and staffing; activities of the Ethics Office; amendments to the Staff Regulations; multilingualism; staff mobility; and staff composition of the Secretariat.

In addition, the Secretary-General reported on: gratis personnel; employment of retirees; consultants and individual contractors; measures to improve the balance in the geographical distribution of the Office of the United Nations High Commissioner for Human Rights; reform of human resources management; national competitive recruitment examinations; protection from sexual exploitation and abuse; travel and related matters; and the United Nations Joint Staff Pension Fund.

As part of the implementation of the new system of administration of justice in the Secretariat, the Assembly adopted the statutes of the United Nations Dispute Tribunal and the United Nations Appeals Tribunal, to be operational as at 1 July 2009. It also examined and took action on the Secretary-General's reports on the activities of the Office of the Ombudsman; criminal behaviour and disciplinary action; and criminal accountability of UN officials and experts on mission.

Administrative matters

Managerial reform and oversight

Procurement

ACABQ report. The Advisory Committee on Administrative and Budgetary Questions (ACABQ), in a March comprehensive report on UN procurement activities [A/62/721], considered the Secretary-General's 2007 report on UN procurement and the report of the Office of Internal Oversight Services (OIOS) on the audit of the application of the best value for money principle relating to UN procurement [YUN 2007, p. 1467].

ACABQ encouraged the Secretary-General to broaden the scope of the annual report on procurement to include more evidence and analysis to facilitate the General Assembly's assessment of the progress being reported and the impact of the activities accomplished. That should include: data and other evidence to substantiate the statements on the progress achieved; information on the mechanisms put into place to monitor progress and ensure that the new procedures were producing the intended effects; information on problems encountered and measures planned to redress them; and fuller explanations of inordinate or repeated delays in the implementation of key reform measures.

On measures for strengthening the internal control mechanism of the procurement function, ACABQ expressed concern about the delay in issuing key guidelines for staff. It reiterated that every effort should be made to resolve outstanding issues, and to issue the ethics guidelines for procurement staff in the UN working languages. It encouraged the Secretary-General to launch the pilot project for the independent bid protest system—a key measure for enhancing transparency in the procurement decision-making process—and to report thereon to the Assembly, including the experience gained, along with proposals for implementing the system across the Secretariat in the next report on procurement activities. The Secretary-General should also accelerate implementation of the simplified vendor registration process across the Secretariat; pursue discussions within the High-level Committee on Management Procurement Network in order to reach an agreement on the proposals regarding suspect vendors and to implement them expeditiously; report on the implementation of measures to increase the delegation of authority in his next report on procurement activities; and specify how managers would be held personally accountable for the application of such procedures, as well as the performance of their duties and ethical conduct.

On the optimization of the acquisition and procurement management processes, ACABQ highlighted the best value for money principle as one of the general principles that should be given due consideration when exercising the UN procurement functions. Since policies and guidelines for the application of that principle in procurement were still evolving, ACABQ recommended that a clear definition of the principle be established, and unambiguous and transparent guidelines for its application in procurement activities be developed to ensure fairness, integrity and transparency, as well as effective international competition and protection of UN interests when awarding contracts. In developing the definition, policy and guidelines related to the best value for money principle, attention should be paid to ensuring that its application enabled the full participation of vendors from all countries, and did not restrict procurement opportunities for developing countries and countries with economies in transition. Regarding the information system challenges faced by the Procurement Division—including the lack of integrated, real-time systems, which hindered the Division's ability to optimize its operations and implement parts of its reform agenda—ACABQ expected that the Chief Information Technology Officer would examine the Division's requirements comprehensively in the forthcoming report on the enterprise resource planning system.

On the strategic management of UN procurement, ACABQ was concerned about the slow rate of progress in exploiting the potential for achieving significant savings and efficiencies and reducing duplication and waste through strengthened inter-agency coordination. It recommended that the Secretary-General intensify efforts to strengthen coordination and cooperation among UN system organizations. The lead agency concept should be explored further, given its potential for achieving economies of scale and eliminating duplication. The Secretary-General should continue discussions within the High-level Committee on Management Procurement Network and report thereon in his next report on procurement activities. With regard to promoting procurement from developing countries and countries with economies in transition, ACABQ, while recognizing the merit of continuing the organization of business seminars in those countries, requested the Secretary-General to pursue efforts to implement the other initiatives outlined in his report and to intensify the exploration of additional innovative approaches.

With the increase in both the value and complexity of procurement in support of peacekeeping operations, ACABQ said that, while the Secretary-General had made proposals for improving the procurement process, no attempt was made to review the policies and procedures for meeting the specific needs of field operations. It recommended that he be requested to address that gap.

On 3 April, by **decision 62/545 B**, the Assembly deferred until its resumed sixty-second (2008) session consideration of the Secretary-General's comprehensive report on UN procurement activities [YUN 2007, p. 1467], the ACABQ report thereon (see above), the report of OIOS on the audit of the application of the best value for money principle in UN procurement, and the Secretary-General's note transmitting his comments thereon [ibid., pp. 1467 & 1468].

GENERAL ASSEMBLY ACTION

On 20 June [meeting 109], the General Assembly, on the recommendation of the Fifth (Administrative and Budgetary) Committee [A/62/604/Add.2], adopted **resolution 62/269** without vote [agenda item 126].

Procurement reform

The General Assembly,

Recalling its resolutions 54/14 of 29 October 1999, 55/247 of 12 April 2001, 57/279 of 20 December 2002, 58/276 and 58/277 of 23 December 2003, 59/288 of 13 April 2005, 60/1 of 16 September 2005, 60/260 of 8 May 2006, 60/266 of 30 June 2006, 60/283 of 7 July 2006, 61/246 of 22 December 2006 and 61/276 and 61/279 of 29 June 2007,

Reaffirming the Financial Regulations and Rules of the United Nations, in particular those regarding the procurement process,

Having considered the comprehensive report of the Secretary-General on United Nations procurement activities, the related report of the Advisory Committee on Administrative and Budgetary Questions, the report of the Office of Internal Oversight Services on the audit of the application of the best value for money principle in United Nations procurement and the comments of the Secretary-General thereon,

1. *Endorses* the conclusions and recommendations contained in the report of the Advisory Committee on Administrative and Budgetary Questions subject to the provisions of the present resolution;

2. *Reaffirms* the need for the procurement system to be transparent, open, impartial and cost-effective, based on competitive bidding and fully reflecting the international character of the United Nations;

3. *Notes* the ongoing improvements made by the Secretary-General in procurement reform at Headquarters and in the field missions, including those set out in paragraph 8 of the report of the Advisory Committee;

4. *Recalls* its resolutions 52/226 A of 31 March 1998, 54/14, 55/247, and 62/232 of 22 December 2007, regarding the need for the Secretary-General to take steps to ensure that specifications are not deliberately tailored to predetermine the choice of supplier and that the principle of separation of responsibilities of the requisitioning and approving officers is maintained;

5. *Requests* the Secretary-General to implement all of the requests included in its previous procurement reform resolutions, in particular resolution 61/246;

Governance

6. *Reiterates its regret* for the delay in the response of the Secretary-General to its outstanding requests in its resolutions 59/288, 61/246 and 61/276, and urges him as a matter of priority to submit a report on procurement governance and other issues as requested in resolutions 61/246 and 61/276, with full justification of the reasons for the delay;

Internal controls

7. *Notes with concern* the possible weaknesses in the internal control environment with regard to procurement activities owing, inter alia, to the splitting of responsibilities between the Department of Management, the Department of Peacekeeping Operations and the Department of Field Support of the Secretariat, and requests the Secretary-General to take concrete steps to avoid any such weaknesses and to report thereon in the context of the report on the governance of United Nations procurement activities;

8. *Encourages* the Secretary-General to strengthen further the internal control framework within the Procurement Division of the Department of Management by developing a more robust regime for the oversight of vendors, including subcontractors, at the Secretariat, as well as effectively addressing vendor misconduct and suspension;

Accountability

9. *Reaffirms* paragraph 3 of its resolution 61/246, and in this regard requests the Secretary-General to continue to ensure proper accountability and training of all those involved in the procurement process at Headquarters and in the field;

Ethics

10. *Requests* the Secretary-General to continue to consider a proper mechanism for monitoring compliance of United Nations staff and vendors with ethical behaviour norms;

11. *Also requests* the Secretary-General to ensure that ethics guidelines for procurement staff are issued as a matter of priority;

12. *Notes* that conflict of interest is not officially defined under current United Nations regulations and rules, and reiterates its request contained in its resolutions 52/226 A, 54/14, 60/266, 61/246 and 61/276 that the Secretary-General submit proposals on possible amendments to the Financial Regulations and Rules of the United Nations and the Staff Regulations and Rules of the United Nations to address issues of potential conflict of interest, such as the employment of former United Nations procurement officers by United Nations suppliers and vice versa;

Vendors

13. *Endorses* paragraph 14 of the report of the Advisory Committee, and requests the Secretary-General to report to the General Assembly at its sixty-fourth session, in the context of the next comprehensive report on United Nations procurement activities, on the implementation of the simplified vendor registration process;

14. *Requests* the Secretary-General to continue to simplify and streamline the vendor registration process, to share responsibilities among the various United Nations organizations, to take into account the different circumstances and varying levels of Internet access in countries and to report to the General Assembly at its sixty-fourth session, in the context of the next comprehensive report on United Nations procurement activities, on the results achieved;

15. *Also requests* the Secretary-General to restore on the website of the Procurement Division without delay information on the Division's focal points providing advice on the vendor registration process in the six official languages of the United Nations and the Division's brochure in the six official languages on a cost-neutral basis;

Independent bid protest system

16. *Regrets* the lack of information in the report of the Secretary-General in response to paragraph 13 of its resolution 61/246, and in this context requests the Secretary-General to launch the pilot project for the independent bid protest system and to report to the General Assembly at its sixty-fourth session, in the context of the next comprehensive report on United Nations procurement activities, on the experience gained, as part of the comprehensive proposal concerning the implementation of the system, which shall be subject to the prior consideration and approval of the Assembly;

Procurement opportunities for vendors from developing countries and countries with economies in transition

17. *Reaffirms* paragraphs 6 and 20 to 24 of its resolution 61/246;

18. *Notes* the efforts made by the Secretary-General to promote procurement opportunities for vendors from developing countries and countries with economies in transition, including business seminars, and also notes the increased participation of those countries in United Nations procurement activities, reaching 53 per cent in 2006 as compared to an average of 45 per cent over the preceding four years;

19. *Encourages* the Secretary-General to continue to promote and to conduct business seminars and to follow up on their outcome as a means of sensitizing the business community in developing countries to procurement opportunities in the United Nations;

20. *Endorses* paragraph 32 of the report of the Advisory Committee, and requests the Secretary-General to continue and intensify the exploration of additional innovative ways to promote procurement from developing countries and countries with economies in transition and to report thereon to the General Assembly at its sixty-fourth session in the context of the next comprehensive report on United Nations procurement activities;

21. *Recalls* section XIX, paragraph 4, of its resolution 61/276, in which it requested the Secretary-General to identify obstacles preventing the participation of developing countries and countries with economies in transition in United Nations procurement contracts, including through seeking and analysing feedback from vendors who had attended United Nations business seminars in recent years, and requests the Secretary-General to report fully on those obstacles to the General Assembly at its sixty-fourth session in the context of the next comprehensive report on United Nations procurement activities, including on proposals to obviate such obstacles;

22. *Requests* the Secretary-General to increase the number of business seminars in developing countries and countries with economies in transition in order to increase procurement opportunities in those countries;

23. *Stresses* the need for business seminars to be more results-oriented and tailored to include adequate information on how to access business opportunities in the field of procurement with the United Nations;

Best value for money

24. *Takes note* of the recommendations of the Office of Internal Oversight Services and the comments of the Secretary-General thereon, and requests the Secretary-General to ensure the full implementation of the recommendations and to report thereon to the General Assembly at its sixty-fourth session in the context of the next comprehensive report on United Nations procurement activities;

25. *Reiterates its request* to the Secretary-General contained in paragraph 33 of its resolution 61/246, and requests the Secretary-General to report to the General Assembly at its sixty-fourth session on clear guidelines for the implementation of the best value for money methodology in United Nations procurement, including all specifics of the weighted evaluation techniques;

Awarding of contracts and competitive bidding process

26. *Requests* the Secretary-General to entrust the Office of Internal Oversight Services to include in its annual reports all cases of application of exigency it considered, as well as the high-risk cases referred to the Headquarters Committee on Contracts on which it decided to provide comments;

27. *Also requests* the Secretary-General to continue to ensure that the utilization of systems contracts is subject to prior full analysis of all costs, in accordance with current practice;

28. *Further requests* the Secretary-General to prepare a report on his proposal contained in paragraph 129 of his report relating to bidding by joint ventures, inter alia, on its justification, its legal regulation, the registration of joint ventures in the United Nations vendor roster and safeguards against possible limitations of competition in United Nations procurement for consideration by the General Assembly at its sixty-fourth session;

29. *Decides* that contract bundling shall not be used as a tool to restrict international competition in United Nations procurement;

30. *Requests* the Secretary-General to ensure that requirements with regard to goods and services being procured as set forth in the solicitation documents are formulated subject to established limitations on the number of United Nations commodity codes per vendor;

31. *Also requests* the Secretary-General to ensure that in scheduling bidders' conferences and defining their venues, visa-processing timelines are taken fully into account and such alternatives as videoconferences are fully explored to avoid any impact of visa-related policies of dif-

ferent countries on the results of United Nations competitive bidding;

Performance and bid bonds

32. *Further requests* the Secretary-General to further enhance transparency in the procurement decision-making process and, in this regard, to report to the General Assembly at its sixty-fourth session, in the context of the next comprehensive report on United Nations procurement activities, on clear guidelines and criteria for the request of bid bonds and performance bonds by procurement officers in the United Nations, as well as on exploring alternative means of ensuring the protection of the interests of the Organization throughout the term of the contractual obligation without restricting access to United Nations procurement of small and medium-sized enterprises, including those from developing countries and countries with economies in transition;

Sustainable procurement

33. *Recalls* paragraphs 137 to 140 of the report of the Secretary-General, and also recalls that the General Assembly has not considered for approval the concept of environmentally friendly and sustainable procurement, and requests the Secretary-General to prepare a comprehensive report on the content of and criteria for such a concept, including detailed information on its possible impact on the diversification of the origin of vendors and on international competition, including for developing countries and countries with economies in transition, for consideration and decision by the Assembly at its sixty-fourth session;

Delegation of authority

34. *Reiterates its request* in paragraph 20 of its resolution 59/288, and requests the Secretary-General to report on all the issues related to the levels of delegation of procurement authority, including mechanisms used to strengthen effective monitoring, oversight and accountability, in the context of his report on the governance of United Nations procurement activities;

Outsourcing practices

35. *Recalls* its resolutions 55/232 of 23 December 2000 and 59/289 of 13 April 2005 on outsourcing practices, and stresses that the procurement staff certification programme should be in line with the provisions of those resolutions;

Subcontracting

36. *Notes with concern* the risks that may be presented by the lack of disclosure regarding the issue of subcontracting;

37. *Also notes with concern* that subcontractors have not been required to comply with the relevant rules of the Organization, and requests the Secretary-General to address this lacuna in internal control associated with subcontractors as a matter of priority and to report thereon to the General Assembly at its sixty-fourth session;

Human resources management

38. *Reaffirms* sections X and XI of its resolution 61/244 of 22 December 2006;

39. *Also reaffirms* paragraph 100 of its resolution 52/220 of 22 December 1997 and paragraph 21 of resolution 52/226 A;

Training

40. *Stresses* the need for all procurement staff to receive the mandatory training in United Nations procurement techniques and ethics, and requests the Secretary-General to continue his efforts in this regard;

Enterprise resource planning

41. *Requests* the Secretary-General to develop requirements for procurement management as a part of the new enterprise resource planning system, taking into account the need to allay concern that the use of different procurement-related information technology support systems in different departments is having a negative impact on the Organization's ability to exercise comprehensive procurement oversight;

42. *Also requests* the Secretary-General to ensure that the enterprise resource planning requirements related to procurement reflect its decisions on procurement governance and to provide a comprehensive and concrete explanation as to how the new enterprise resource planning system will improve procurement-related internal control and oversight;

Other issues

43. *Stresses* the importance of efficiency in the acquisition process in the United Nations, and requests the Secretary-General to continue to improve the efficiency of the procurement process;

44. *Recalls its request* in its resolution 59/288 to review without delay options to better safeguard the independence of the Headquarters Committee on Contracts, and encourages the Secretary-General to develop further measures to mitigate higher exposure to financial risk;

45. *Requests* the Secretary-General to ensure that, on matters relating to procurement in the field, the Department of Peacekeeping Operations and the Department of Field Support follow the principles of objectivity and impartiality in advising the Procurement Division.

Procurement Task Force

Board of Auditors report. In response to General Assembly resolution 62/234 [YUN 2007, p. 1470], the Board of Auditors submitted a July report [A/63/167] on the activities of the Procurement Task Force, established in 2006 [YUN 2006, p. 1644] to address fraud and corruption in the United Nations, including its peacekeeping missions, for the period from 1 January 2006 to 30 June 2007, which contained an audit of the Task Force's activities, including its compliance with established UN transparency and accountability measures and those of OIOS. The Board found that the Task Force had initially focused on the handling of the case of eight officials placed on special leave [YUN 2007, p. 1468]. Its investigations led to three of the officials being cleared of wrongdoing and brought to light one serious case, which resulted in a lengthy prison sentence. As at 15 March 2008, the Task Force had published 25 reports dealing with more than 40 contracts and completed 142 of the 432 cases in its portfolio, with 290 remaining to be examined. Although those efforts did not expose widespread corruption at the United Nations, the Task Force had helped to eliminate undesirable suppliers from the UN list of vendors and its existence might have served as a deterrent. While the actual value of the losses incurred was difficult to calculate, the Administration had identified clear losses of $25 million, of which $20 million related to the same person. Of the 13 cases the Task Force had recommended for legal action, only five had taken place at the time of the audit. The Board was unable to ascertain whether that was due to a difference of opinion between the Administration and the Task Force, or to delays in the launching of such actions. In some instances, the Office of Legal Affairs estimated that the cost of the procedures proposed by the Task Force was in excess of the sums expected to be recovered. While it detected some instances of criminal conduct, the Task Force uncovered many more examples of mismanagement, some of which did not constitute violations of UN regulations. That result, together with the large number of cases, reinforced the need for the Administration to clearly and strictly define the conditions under which an investigation should be launched.

As to compliance of the Task Force investigations with OIOS rules of procedure, in particular those concerning due process, the Board did not uncover any violation of the investigation rules in the cases the Task Force had examined. However, the investigations were hampered by the circumstances under which the Task Force was created and operated, especially the willingness of the Secretariat to adopt emergency measures on the one hand, and the media coverage given to certain cases on the other, which were not conducive to a smooth investigative process for either the investigators or the staff under investigation. Other constraints identified in the report included the rapid turnover of staff; difficulties with access to certain countries; the need to conduct a synthesis of all new Task Force rules; and the need to clarify the boundaries between an investigation, an audit and a disciplinary procedure to staff under investigation.

The Board recommended that the Administration: incorporate into the permanent UN investigations system the skills and competencies of the Task Force, as well as the lessons learned from its operations; review the UN investigative function as a whole; use the investigation procedure cautiously, and only when there were well-founded suspicions that rules had been broken and after all other reasonable actions had been duly envisaged; standardize and consolidate the rules and procedures applicable to all UN investigations under an instruction of the Secretary-General, which should be systematically given to the staff interviewed; and ensure a proper handing over of pending investigations when the Task Force ceased to operate.

Report of Secretary-General. In his August report [A/63/167/Add.1] on the implementation of the Board of Auditor's recommendations (see above), which the Administration endorsed, the Secretary-General provided information on the status of each of the five recommendations, including the Department responsible and target date for its completion. He reported that arrangements were being made to ensure that the institutional knowledge of the Task Force would be transferred to the Investigations Division by the first quarter of 2009; the remaining caseload of the Task Force was properly transferred to the Division; and lessons learned were incorporated into the Division's operations. On the review of the UN investigative function, the Secretary-General indicated his intention to report to the Assembly after conducting a comprehensive review of UN investigations. The Investigations Division and the Task Force had established procedures to evaluate whether the matters brought to the attention of OIOS should be formally investigated. The Division had also established an intake committee to review information reported to or identified by the Division that might lead to an investigation. On the standardization and consolidation of the rules and procedures applicable to all UN investigations, OIOS was in the process of updating its investigation manual, revising and expanding its standard operating procedures and developing a learning programme to build the capacity of managers and staff with a role in the investigation process.

The Secretary-General also provided details of information-sharing practices between the United Nations and national law enforcement authorities, as well as referrals of possible criminal cases related to UN staff, UN officials and experts on mission [A/63/331] (see p. 1648).

OIOS report. In August [A/63/329], OIOS reported on the activities of its Procurement Task Force for the period from 1 July 2007 to 31 July 2008. During that period, the Task Force received 64 procurement-related cases; reported on five significant fraud or corruption schemes in cases with an aggregate contract value in excess of $20 million; and issued 68 recommendations and seven final reports. As a result of the Task Force's work, 22 vendors were sanctioned by the Administration. Consequently, since its formation, the Task Force had completed 222 investigations and identified more than 20 significant fraud and corruption schemes in cases with an aggregate contract value in excess of $630 million.

The Task Force continued to investigate allegations of corruption and fraud in procurement in peacekeeping missions and overseas offices, as well as cases at

Headquarters. It identified improprieties, corruption and malfeasance in: the General Assembly–mandated review of the pay and benefits system; a steered contract for air charter services in the United Nations Organization Mission in the Democratic Republic of the Congo (MONUC); a scheme to steer multiple contracts to preferred vendors in offices in the United Nations Office for Project Services (UNOPS) in Nairobi, Kenya; the improper use of consultants in the Department of Economic and Social Affairs; and significant cases in UNOPS Afghanistan and the Economic Commission for Africa. The Task Force referred a number of cases to national authorities for criminal prosecution or for consideration of subsequent legal action and, in a number of other cases, recommended that the Organization seek civil recovery of monetary damages.

The Task Force also concentrated on cases involving allegations of vendor misconduct, including corruption in UN contracts, bid rigging, favouritism and collusion, and conducted numerous investigations of vendors. Through its investigations, the Task Force assisted the Vendor Review Committee, the Procurement Division, the Headquarters Committee on Contracts, and the Controller in numerous vendor cases and issues. The majority of the investigations involving staff members and vendors were based in North America and Europe.

OIOS made recommendations and proposed amendments to the system of vendor sanction, rehabilitation and reinstatement. In other developments, the General Conditions of Contract were amended in January to include a revised cooperation provision requiring all vendors to cooperate with the Organization's investigations on UN-related commercial activities and extending beyond the termination of the contract. The Procurement Manual and vendor registration forms were also updated to include the requirement of vendor cooperation with investigations, as well as a requirement that vendors assert, as a condition of registration, that they and their agents would cooperate with investigations.

Despite the progress achieved, the Task Force faced both funding and staffing constraints. Due to the short-term nature of its mandate, the Task Force experienced rapid staff turnover, and late funding decisions for 2008 resulted in the departure of investigators and interference with ongoing operations. Moreover, since it was funded only until 31 December, the Task Force would be unable to complete its caseload and ongoing investigations by year's end; more than 150 cases would remain. The Task Force would be unable to examine cases and allegations in the overseas offices and peacekeeping missions; and several significant matters would remain in those locations, as well as at Headquarters. Meanwhile, additional cases requiring attention would continue to be referred. OIOS intended to transfer the Task Force's remaining caseload to its Investigations Division at the beginning of 2009 and to ensure availability of the required skill and capacity in that Division.

Note of Secretary-General. In a September note [A/63/329/Add.1], the Secretary-General provided his comments and clarifications on the OIOS report on the activities of the Procurement Task Force. He emphasized that the amount of $630 million referred to in the report did not reflect financial losses to the Organization, but the total contract value that had been tainted by corruption or fraud. On the findings of the investigations, although OIOS had completed its investigations and finalized the related report, the final determination of whether any rules had been breached was made by the Secretary-General and his programme managers, followed by internal justice proceedings where applicable. With regard to cases still under review by the Administration, the Secretary-General reiterated that each of the staff members concerned was presumed innocent pending the conclusion of his or her case and that the findings of the Task Force were not a final determination by the Organization.

In his comments on vendor investigations, the Secretary-General summarized measures the Organization had introduced to facilitate cooperation by vendors, including the introduction of new registration criteria to be applied to potential UN vendors; the adoption of the new UN General Conditions for Contract as revised in January; and the application of the UN Supplier Code of Conduct. Of the 68 recommendations issued by the Task Force during the reporting period, 34 remained unaddressed. All Task Force reports and recommendations, including those still unaddressed, were being actively considered and, where accepted by the Secretary-General, appropriate action was being taken. He added that during the first quarter of the year, the Management Committee conducted a review of the implementation of all Task Force recommendations and would conduct another by year's end.

ACABQ report. ACABQ, in an October report [A/63/490] on the activities of the Procurement Task Force, welcomed the Board of Auditors report and recommended that the General Assembly endorse the Board's recommendations. ACABQ urged the Secretary-General to pay particular attention to addressing the underlying reasons for the violations uncovered in the Task Force reports and the nature of resulting proceedings, by improving awareness of staff rules and regulations, as well as improving and updating the procurement and investigation manuals. The Secretary-General should draw on the issues raised by the Board and the Task Force's experience to ensure that the Organization had the internal capacity to deal with those matters relating to procedures in the future and avoid the need to resort to ad hoc measures. In other recommendations, the Committee stressed the need to standardize and consolidate the rules of procedure applicable to all UN investigations and to complete the integration of a comprehensive investigation learning programme in the new investigative manual. The Secretary-General's Bulletin would be the appropriate means for conveying those rules of procedure to the staff. ACABQ concurred with the Board that the Administration should become more vigilant to prevent the breaching of confidentiality of its work. ACABQ recommended that the Secretary-General proceed with the review of the procedures of other institutions relating to the vendor sanctions regime, with a view to making recommendations on the legislative framework for establishing such a regime.

The Assembly took action on those reports in section II of resolution 63/265 of 24 December (see p. 1575).

Oversight

Internal oversight

OIOS activities. In August, the Under-Secretary-General for Internal Oversight Services, Inga-Britt Ahlenius, transmitted to the General Assembly the OIOS annual report [A/63/302 (Part I)] covering its activities from 1 July 2007 to 30 June 2008, except for the results of OIOS peacekeeping oversight activities, which would be reported separately. The report covered initiatives aimed at improving OIOS operations and quality of work, including impediments to the Office's activities; oversight findings by risk category; and mandated reporting on oversight activities concerning the United Nations Compensation Commission and the capital master plan. During the reporting period, OIOS issued 305 oversight reports, including 7 reports to the General Assembly, and 28 closure reports. The reports included 1,755 recommendations to improve internal controls, accountability mechanisms and organizational efficiency and effectiveness. Of those recommendations, 804 were classified as critical to the Organization. The financial implications of OIOS recommendations issued during the period amounted to more than $12 million. Those recommendations were aimed at cost savings, overpayment recoveries, efficiency gains and other improvements. The financial implications of similar recommendations that were satisfactorily implemented totalled $4.2 million.

The report highlighted internal initiatives undertaken by OIOS, the most notable of which were the Office's 2008 risk-based work plans for audit, inspections and evaluation assignments. The Under-Secretary-General stressed the need for the Organization to develop a formal internal control framework to ensure that risks were managed consistently and systematically through focused control processes across the Organization. Without a proactive and systematic approach to managing risk as a core part of an internal control framework, the Organization would remain reactive in responding to deficiencies and vulnerable to mismanagement and misuse of resources.

An addendum to the report [A/63/302 (Part I)/Add.1] provided an analysis of the implementation of the recommendations and highlighted those of particular concern.

In a September note [A/63/302 (Part I)/Add.2], the Secretary-General submitted his comments on Part I of the OIOS annual report and the related addendum.

In addition to the above report on its activities, OIOS issued, in 2008, reports on its activities in 2007 [A/62/281(Part II)]; the triennial review of the implementation of the recommendations made by the Committee for Programme and Coordination at its forty-fifth session on the in-depth evaluation of the United Nations Human Settlements Programme [E/AC.51/2008/3]; the triennial review of the thematic evaluation of the linkages between Headquarters and field activities: a review of best practices for poverty eradication in the framework of the United Nations Millennium Declaration [E/AC.51/2008/4 & Add.1]; the in-depth evaluation of political affairs: field special political missions led by the Department of Political Affairs but supported by the Department of Field Support [E/AC.51/2008/2]; the audit of the United Nations Interim Administration Mission in Kosovo mandate implementation [A/62/807]; the audit of the special arrangements governing the recruitment of temporary assistance staff in the language services across the four main duty stations [A/63/94]; the comprehensive audit of the capital master plan [A/63/266]; the activities of the Procurement Task Force for the period 1 July 2007 to 31 July 2008 [A/63/329 & Add.1]; the review of results-based management (RBM) at the UN Secretariat [A/63/268]; the in-depth evaluation of the Office of Human Resources Management (OHRM) [A/63/221]; and the comprehensive management audit of the Department of Safety and Security [A/63/379].

Independent Audit Advisory Committee. In its first annual report [A/63/328] under its new terms of reference approved by the General Assembly in resolution 61/275 [YUN 2007, p. 1471], the Independent Audit Advisory Committee provided detailed comments on coordination and cooperation among UN oversight bodies, the status of recommendations of those bodies, OIOS 2008 workplans and budget, the risk management and internal control framework, issues and trends in the financial statements and reports of the Board of Auditors, adoption of the International Public Sector Accounting Standards and cooperation and access.

The Committee found the OIOS proposal for a "hub and spoke" structure for its Investigations Division to have strong conceptual merit, but recommended that it be implemented in a phased manner to ensure that the transfer of investigators out of the peacekeeping missions to regional hubs would not leave any operational gaps.

Other recommendations for improvements made by the Committee related to the OIOS work-planning process to improve the effectiveness of cooperation between OIOS and the other oversight bodies, namely, the Joint Inspection Unit and the Board of Auditors.

The Committee commented on the Secretary-General's report on the accountability framework, the enterprise risk management and internal control framework, and the RBM framework [A/62/701 & Corr.1 & Add.1] (see p. 1519). Overall, the Committee supported the implementation of an enterprise risk management and internal control framework, and recommended the establishment of a Chief Risk Officer position reporting to the Secretary-General or Deputy Secretary-General to provide advice and support to senior managers and coordinate risk management strategies at the enterprise level.

The Committee suggested that the implementation project should be structured in stages and the proposed pilot project planned as the first phase of a multiphase project. It highlighted two issues of significance in the report of the Board of Auditors on the UN financial statements (see p. 1559), namely, the implications of recognizing end-of-service liabilities in the financial statements and the lack of controls relating to non-expendable property. The Committee also drew attention to the challenges and considerations to be taken into account in the implementation of the International Public Sector Accounting Standards.

GENERAL ASSEMBLY ACTION

On 24 December [meeting 74], the General Assembly, on the recommendation of the Fifth Committee [A/63/658], adopted **resolution 63/265** without vote [agenda items 128 and 117].

Report of the Office of Internal Oversight Services on its activities

The General Assembly,

I

Activities of the Office of Internal Oversight Services

Recalling its resolutions 48/218 B of 29 July 1994, 54/244 of 23 December 1999, 59/272 of 23 December 2004 and 60/259 of 8 May 2006,

Having considered the report of the Office of Internal Oversight Services on its activities and the related note by the Secretary-General, as well as sections III.A to C of the annual report of the Independent Audit Advisory Committee,

1. *Reaffirms* its primary role in the consideration of and action taken on reports submitted to it;

2. *Also reaffirms* its oversight role and the role of the Fifth Committee in administrative and budgetary matters;

3. *Further reaffirms* the independence and the separate and distinct roles of the internal and external oversight mechanisms;

4. *Notes with appreciation* the work of the Independent Audit Advisory Committee;

5. *Recalls* its resolution 61/275 of 29 June 2007, in which it approved the terms of reference of the Independent Audit Advisory Committee;

6. *Takes note* of the report of the Office of Internal Oversight Services on its activities and the related note by the Secretary-General;

7. *Stresses* the importance of full implementation of accepted recommendations of the Office of Internal Oversight Services, and requests the Secretary-General to ensure that complete information is provided on the implementation of those recommendations and, where applicable, in cases where full implementation has not been achieved, detailed reasons therefor;

8. *Requests* the Secretary-General to ensure that all relevant resolutions, such as resolutions on peacekeeping operations relating to cross-cutting issues, are brought to the attention of relevant managers, and that the Office of Internal Oversight Services also takes those resolutions into account in the conduct of its activities;

9. *Also requests*, in this regard, the Secretary-General to ensure that all relevant resolutions pertaining to the work of the Office of Internal Oversight Services are brought to the attention of the relevant managers;

10. *Takes note* of the recommendations contained in sections III.A to C of the annual report of the Independent Audit Advisory Committee in respect of the Office of Internal Oversight Services, and requests the Secretary-General to ensure the full implementation of those recommendations, taking into account the provisions of its resolutions 48/218 B, 54/244 and 59/272;

11. *Encourages* United Nations internal and external oversight bodies to enhance the level of their cooperation with one another, such as joint work-planning sessions, without prejudice to the independence of each;

12. *Notes* paragraph 17 of the annual report of the Independent Audit Advisory Committee, and recalls that one of the responsibilities of the Independent Audit Advisory Committee, according to its terms of reference, is to advise the General Assembly on the effectiveness, efficiency and impact of the audit activities and other oversight functions of the Office of Internal Oversight Services;

13. *Also notes* that the five-year non-renewable term of the Under-Secretary-General for Internal Oversight Services will expire in July 2010, and in this respect urges the Secretary-General to ensure that timely arrangements are made to find a successor in full conformity with the provisions of paragraph 5 *(b)* of its resolution 48/218 B;

II

Investigations and the Procurement Task Force of the Office of Internal Oversight Services

Recalling its resolutions 48/218 B of 29 July 1994, 54/244 of 23 December 1999, 57/282, section IV, of 20 December 2002, 59/272 of 23 December 2004, 59/287 of 13 April 2005, 61/245 of 22 December 2006, 61/275 and 61/279 of 29 June 2007, 62/234 of 22 December 2007 and 62/247 of 3 April 2008,

Having considered the reports of the Secretary-General on the information requested in paragraph 17 of its resolution 62/247 and on the information-sharing practices between the United Nations and national law enforcement authorities, as well as referrals of possible criminal cases related to United Nations staff, United Nations officials and experts on mission, and the report of the Office of Internal Oversight Services on the activities of the Procurement Task Force for the period from 1 July 2007 to 31 July 2008 and the report of the Board of Auditors on the activities of the Procurement Task Force, the related notes by the Secretary-General transmitting his comments thereon and the related reports of the Advisory Committee on Administrative and Budgetary Questions,

1. *Takes note* of the report of the Secretary-General on the information requested in paragraph 17 of General Assembly resolution 62/247;

2. *Also takes note* of the report of the Secretary-General on the information-sharing practices between the United Nations and national law enforcement authorities, as well as referrals of possible criminal cases related to United Nations staff, United Nations officials and experts on mission;

3. *Further takes note* of the report of the Office of Internal Oversight Services on the activities of the Procurement Task Force for the period from 1 July 2007 to 31 July 2008, and the report of the Board of Auditors on the activities of the Procurement Task Force and the related notes by the Secretary-General transmitting his comments thereon;

4. *Endorses* the conclusions and recommendations contained in the reports of the Advisory Committee on Administrative and Budgetary Questions, subject to provisions of the present resolution;

5. *Takes note* of the work of the Procurement Task Force;

6. *Emphasizes* its commitment to preventing and deterring fraud and malfeasance within the Organization, and recognizes that such efforts cannot be sustained in the long term by an ad hoc body;

7. *Recalls* the ad hoc nature of the Procurement Task Force;

8. *Notes* the intention of the Secretary-General to transfer the remaining caseload of the Procurement Task Force of the Office of Internal Oversight Services to the Investigations Division of the Office at the beginning of 2009;

9. *Requests* the Secretary-General to ensure that the Office of Internal Oversight Services has the expertise and capacity within its approved structure to effectively investigate allegations of fraud, corruption and misconduct in procurement;

10. *Takes note* of paragraph 12 of the report of the Advisory Committee on Administrative and Budgetary Questions with regard to the specific element of human resources;

11. *Emphasizes* Article 101 of the Charter of the United Nations, reiterates section II of its resolution 61/244 of 22 December 2006, and requests the Secretary-General to ensure the full implementation of the relevant provisions of the Staff Regulations and Rules of the United Nations governing the recruitment of United Nations staff;

12. *Reiterates* that deliberate management decisions to keep a certain number of posts vacant should not be taken, as such action makes the budget process less transparent and the management of human and financial resources less efficient;

13. *Expresses concern* over a number of vacancies in the Investigations Division of the Office of Internal Oversight Services since the beginning of 2008, and requests the Secretary-General to make every effort to fill those vacancies as a matter of priority, in accordance with the existing relevant provisions governing recruitment in the United Nations;

14. *Stresses* that any changes involving administrative and financial implications shall be subject to the review and approval of the General Assembly in accordance with established procedures, including regulation 2.9 of the Financial Regulations and Rules of the United Nations;

15. *Recognizes* that investigations of fraud, corruption and misconduct in procurement are often time-sensitive;

16. *Recalls* paragraph 18 of its resolution 62/247, in which it requested the Secretary-General to prepare for its consideration and approval, in close cooperation with the Office of Internal Oversight Services, a report providing detailed information on terms of reference with regard to the proposed comprehensive review of investigations in the United Nations before the General Assembly decides on the necessity of such a review, taking into account the role and mandate of the Office of Internal Oversight Services as established in its resolution 48/218 B, the framework for investigation adopted in section IV of its resolution 57/282 and in its resolution 59/287, the reform of the system of administration of justice, the decisions of the Assembly to strengthen the investigation function of the Office of Internal Oversight Services and its decisions on the accountability framework, results-based management, enterprise risk management and the internal control framework;

17. *Stresses* that the Office of Internal Oversight Services, in the conduct of its investigations, should fully address and respect the due process rights of staff concerned;

18. *Notes* the work by the Office of Internal Oversight Services to develop a comprehensive investigation manual, revise and expand the key standard operating procedures for investigations and develop a comprehensive investigation learning programme for managers and staff on the investigative process, and stresses the importance of that work being completed and made available to all United Nations personnel as soon as possible;

19. *Requests* the Secretary-General to prepare as soon as possible standardized and consolidated rules and procedures applicable to all investigations in the United Nations other than the investigations conducted by the Office of Internal Oversight Services, and to ensure that such rules and procedures are made available to all United Nations

personnel and to provide information thereon to the General Assembly at its sixty-fourth session, without prejudice to paragraph 18 of its resolution 62/247;

20. *Stresses* the importance of effective implementation, including referrals to national authorities and recovery actions where appropriate, of the accepted recommendations of the Office of Internal Oversight Services, as well as of effective coordination between that Office and other parts of the Secretariat in this regard.

The Assembly, by **decision 63/552** of 24 December, decided that the item on the report on the activities of OIOS would remain for consideration during its resumed sixty-third (2009) session.

Strengthening investigations

ACABQ report. In a March report [A/62/7/Add.35], ACABQ considered the Secretary-General's 2007 report on strengthening investigations [YUN 2007, p. 1473]. It expressed concern that his comments did not build on the framework for investigations adopted in General Assembly resolutions 57/282 [YUN 2002, p 1393] and 59/287 [YUN 2005, p. 1474]. It also regretted the lack of information on the entities other than OIOS that carried out investigations and on the number of cases handled. In that connection, it recommended that, before a decision was made on the need for a comprehensive review of investigations, the Secretary-General should provide information on all the entities other than OIOS carrying out inquiries and investigations, including their legislative basis, precise role, the number and types of cases handled, related resources, reporting mechanisms, standards and guidelines involved, training imparted, and information on the implementation of resolution 59/287.

On the OIOS approach for improving the functioning of the Investigations Division, the Committee said that the envisaged restructuring of the Division was not solely within the purview of the Under-Secretary-General for Internal Oversight Services. It noted that the Secretary-General's 2007 report on the restructuring would have been strengthened by a more complete analysis and specific reference to the experience with resident investigators. Therefore, the submission of proposals to the Assembly should be accompanied by such an analysis. Regarding the impact on staff of the team/unit concept and the relocation of investigators, the Committee stated that it would benefit from being addressed in advance and not at the time of implementation. On the question of whether OIOS, on behalf of the United Nations, could become a party to mutual legal assistance instruments in order to expedite investigations, the Committee explained that, as the internal oversight body within the UN Secretariat, OIOS could not become party to international agreements. The Committee also cautioned against any confusion between administrative and judicial investigations. In clarifying roles and responsibilities, the Committee stressed the need to take account of Assembly resolution 61/267 B [YUN 2007, p. 69] and noted the OIOS intention to do so.

In summary, ACABQ held that fuller justification was required for the restructuring of the Investigations Division and recommended that any changes proposed be supported by a detailed analysis. It further recommended that any changes that had administrative and financial implications should be subject to Assembly review and approval.

GENERAL ASSEMBLY ACTION

On 3 April [meeting 91], the General Assembly, on the recommendation of the Fifth Committee [A/62/773], adopted **resolution 62/247** without vote [agenda items 126, 128, 136 and 140].

Strengthening investigations

The General Assembly,

Recalling its resolutions 48/218 B of 29 July 1994, 54/244 of 23 December 1999, 57/282, section IV, of 20 December 2002, 59/272 of 23 December 2004, 59/287 of 13 April 2005, 61/245 of 22 December 2006, 61/267 B of 24 July 2007, 61/275 and 61/279 of 29 June 2007 and 62/234 of 22 December 2007,

Recalling also paragraph 10 of its resolution 59/287,

Having considered the report of the Secretary-General on strengthening investigations, the report of the Office of Internal Oversight Services on the activities of the Procurement Task Force for the eighteen-month period ended 30 June 2007, the note by the Secretary-General transmitting his comments thereon and the related report of the Advisory Committee on Administrative and Budgetary Questions,

1. *Takes note* of the report of the Office of Internal Oversight Services and the related note by the Secretary-General;

2. *Endorses* the conclusions and recommendations contained in the report of the Advisory Committee on Administrative and Budgetary Questions, subject to the provisions of the present resolution;

3. *Notes in particular* the concern of the Advisory Committee stated in paragraph 5 of its report;

4. *Stresses* that the lack of explicitly written rules and regulations for procedures relating to investigations negatively affects fairness and due process rights;

5. *Expresses concern* that the current investigations manual of the Office of Internal Oversight Services of the Secretariat appears to lack useful and practical information for investigators compared with similar manuals used in other international organizations and that it also appears not to contain sufficient working instructions for conducting investigations;

6. *Notes with appreciation* the efforts being made by the Office of Internal Oversight Services to improve the conduct of its investigations by applying international best practices and ensuring respect for the due process rights of all United Nations staff;

7. *Affirms* that transparent, predictable, accountable and objective operational strategies and investigation procedures contribute to the effective functioning of the system of administration of justice;

8. *Notes with concern* that concerns have been raised regarding due process rights in investigations, stresses that the due process rights afforded to staff in investigations carried out by the Office of Internal Oversight Services have to withstand review by the system of administration of justice, and reiterates its request to the Secretary-General to develop a comprehensive approach to fully undertake the Organization's responsibility in ensuring the due process rights of its staff under investigation;

9. *Re-emphasizes* the principle of separation, impartiality and fairness on the part of those with responsibility for investigation functions;

10. *Stresses* that the purpose of the Office of Internal Oversight Services is to assist the Secretary-General in fulfilling his internal oversight responsibilities;

11. *Reaffirms* that the Office of Internal Oversight Services is the internal body entrusted with investigation in the United Nations;

12. *Also reaffirms* that trained heads of offices, programme managers and boards of inquiry, as well as the Department of Safety and Security and the Ethics Office, may carry out administrative inquiries and investigations, except in cases of serious misconduct and/or criminal behaviour, in accordance with resolution 59/287;

13. *Takes note* of the development of a comprehensive training module designed to build the capacity of United Nations staff to support administrative inquiries or investigations, as well as of a special training programme for investigating allegations of sexual harassment, by the Office of Internal Oversight Services;

14. *Recalls* paragraphs 3, 8 and 10 of its resolution 59/287, and requests the Secretary-General to continue to increase basic investigation training, as appropriate, for the handling of minor forms of misconduct;

15. *Reaffirms* its decision that in cases of serious misconduct and/or criminal behaviour, investigations should be conducted by professional investigators;

16. *Also reaffirms* that any changes that have administrative and financial implications will be submitted by the Secretary-General and will be subject to the review and approval of the General Assembly in accordance with established procedures;

17. *Requests* the Secretary-General to prepare, in close cooperation with the Office of Internal Oversight Services, for its consideration at its sixty-third session, a report providing detailed information regarding, inter alia:

(a) The status of implementation of its resolution 59/287;

(b) Updated and detailed information on all the entities other than the Office of Internal Oversight Services carrying out administrative inquiries and investigations, their legislative basis and precise role, the number and types of cases handled, related resources, reporting mechanisms, standards and guidelines involved and training imparted;

(c) The status of work done under general temporary assistance resources equivalent to six positions to establish a training capacity for the Investigations Division to enable programme managers to handle category II cases of misconduct and the assessment of such work and any other related work carried out for the same purpose, as well as the future workplan thereof;

18. *Also requests* the Secretary-General to prepare for its consideration and approval, in close cooperation with the Office of Internal Oversight Services, a report providing detailed information on terms of reference with regard to the proposed comprehensive review of investigations in the United Nations before the General Assembly decides on the necessity of such a review, taking into account the role and mandate of the Office of Internal Oversight Services as established in its resolution 48/218 B, the framework for investigation adopted in section IV of its resolution 57/282 and in its resolution 59/287, the reform of the system of administration of justice, the decisions of the Assembly to strengthen the investigation function of the Office of Internal Oversight Services and its decisions on the accountability framework, results-based management, enterprise risk management and the internal control framework;

19. *Further requests* the Secretary-General to report to the General Assembly on practices related to the sharing of information between the Organization and law enforcement authorities of Member States as well as to referrals to such authorities of possible criminal cases related to United Nations staff, United Nations officials and experts on mission, taking into account its resolution 62/63 of 6 December 2007 and other relevant legal instruments.

Report of Secretary-General. In response to resolution 62/247 (see above), the Secretary-General submitted a September report [A/63/369] containing information on the status of implementation of General Assembly resolution 59/287 [YUN 2005, p. 1474], updated and detailed information on all the entities other than OIOS carrying out administrative inquiries and investigations; and the status of work to establish a training capacity for the Investigations Division to enable programme managers to handle category II cases of possible misconduct (cases investigated by a head of office, the Department of Safety and Security or OHRM).

OIOS was designing an investigation learning programme aimed at equipping programme managers with basic investigations training for handling category II cases, consisting of three modules, which ranged from a basic introductory course on investigations to specialized modules designed to cover sexual harassment, financial misconduct, information technology and advanced interviewing techniques, as well as policy and normative aspects of investigations. The full complement of the programme modules would be developed by the end of the third quarter of 2008, with training of programme managers expected to commence by the end of 2008 or early 2009. At least one module, sexual harassment, would be ready for delivery to programme managers by September 2008. OIOS would also hold workshops to raise awareness in high-risk areas, such as procurement. In addition, OIOS had initiated regular discussions within the UN system to ensure consistency through acceptance of minimum standards for investigation.

ACABQ, in its October report [A/63/492], recommended that the Assembly take note of the information provided in the Secretary-General's report.

External oversight

Joint Inspection Unit

At its resumed sixty-second (2008) session, the General Assembly had before it the annual report of the Joint Inspection Unit (JIU) for 2007 and its programme of work for 2008 [YUN 2007, p. 1474].

GENERAL ASSEMBLY ACTION

On 3 April [meeting 91], the General Assembly, on the recommendation of the Fifth Committee [A/62/536/Add.1], adopted **resolution 62/246** without vote [agenda item 134].

Report of the work of the Joint Inspection Unit for 2007 and programme of work for 2008

The General Assembly,

Reaffirming its previous resolutions on the Joint Inspection Unit, in particular resolutions 31/192 of 22 December 1976, 50/233 of 7 June 1996, 54/16 of 29 October 1999, 55/230 of 23 December 2000, 56/245 of 24 December 2001, 57/284 A and B of 20 December 2002, 58/286 of 8 April 2004, 59/267 of 23 December 2004, 60/258 of 8 May 2006, 61/238 of 22 December 2006, 61/260 of 4 April 2007 and 62/226 of 22 December 2007,

Reiterating that the impact of the Unit on the cost-effectiveness of activities within the United Nations system is a shared responsibility of the Member States, the Unit and the secretariats of the participating organizations,

Reaffirming the commitment by the Unit, the legislative organs and the secretariats of the participating organizations to implement a system of follow-up to the recommendations of the Unit, as set out in resolution 54/16,

Reaffirming also the unique role of the Unit as the only system-wide external oversight body,

Having considered the report of the Joint Inspection Unit for 2007 and programme of work for 2008,

1. *Recalls* its resolutions 61/260 and 62/226;

2. *Takes note with appreciation* of the report of the Joint Inspection Unit for 2007 and programme of work for 2008;

3. *Welcomes* the joint presentation of the annual report and the programme of work of the Unit for consideration at the first part of its resumed session;

4. *Also welcomes* progress in the reform process of the Unit, and encourages further efforts on the part of the participating organizations to consider the recommendations of the Unit;

5. *Commends* the Unit for its internal reform process aimed at improving its efficiency and effectiveness, and invites the Unit to report to the General Assembly at its sixty-third session on measures the Unit deems necessary to continue to improve its functioning;

6. *Requests* the Unit, in line with its mandate, to continue to focus its work and reports on system-wide issues of interest and relevance to the participating organizations and the States Members of the United Nations and to provide advice on ways to ensure more efficient and effective use of resources in implementing the mandates of the Organization;

7. *Reiterates its request* to the executive heads of the participating organizations to fully comply with the statutory procedures for consideration of the reports of the Unit, in particular to submit their comments and to distribute reports in time for their consideration by legislative organs;

8. *Requests* the Secretary-General, in his capacity as Chairman of the United Nations System Chief Executives Board for Coordination, to expedite the implementation of the present resolution, including through the expected provision of support to the Unit by the secretariats of the participating organizations for the preparation of its reports, notes and confidential letters, and the consideration of and action on the Unit's recommendations in the light of pertinent resolutions of the General Assembly, and to report to the Assembly on an annual basis on the results achieved;

9. *Reiterates its request* to the Secretary-General and the other executive heads of the participating organizations to fully assist the Unit, with the timely provision of all information requested by it;

10. *Reiterates its invitation* to the legislative organs of the participating organizations to take concrete action on the recommendations of the Unit;

11. *Notes with appreciation* the ongoing efforts of the Unit to report on the impact of its recommendations, as illustrated in paragraph 49 of its annual report, and in this context requests the Unit to work in coordination with participating organizations to provide in future annual reports the financial implications that have resulted from its recommendations, wherever possible;

12. *Invites* the Unit to report in the context of its annual reports on experience in the implementation of the follow-up system by the participating organizations;

13. *Notes with appreciation* the introduction of a table for system-wide reports entitled "Overview of action to be taken by participating organizations on Joint Inspection Unit recommendations" which identifies those recommendations that are relevant to each organization and which specifies those recommendations that require legislative decisions and those that can be implemented by the executive head of the organization;

14. *Notes with concern* paragraph 39 of the annual report, in which the Unit describes the difficulty it has had in obtaining from some organizations updated information on the status of its recommendations, and in this regard requests the Unit to study the feasibility of using a web-based system to monitor the status of recommendations and receive updates from individual organizations;

15. *Expresses its readiness* to apply the follow-up system to review recommendations of the Unit requiring action by the General Assembly;

16. *Affirms* that oversight is a shared responsibility of Member States, the organizations and the internal and external oversight bodies;

17. *Recalls* paragraph 9 of its resolution 62/224 of 22 December 2007, and encourages the Secretary-General, in

his capacity as Chairman of the Chief Executives Board, to enhance the dialogue of the Board with the Joint Inspection Unit on coordination issues;

18. *Welcomes* the coordination of the Unit with the Board of Auditors and the Office of Internal Oversight Services of the Secretariat, and encourages those bodies to continue sharing experiences, knowledge, best practices and lessons learned with other United Nations audit and oversight bodies as well as with the Independent Audit Advisory Committee;

19. *Takes note with appreciation* of the information contained in paragraph 63 of the annual report, and encourages the Unit to keep the General Assembly informed, if necessary, about any difficulty or delay in obtaining visas for the official travel of the inspectors, as well as members of its secretariat;

20. *Requests* the Unit to provide at its earliest convenience a detailed explanation of the nature and scope of the investigations the Unit envisions conducting.

JIU activities. In its annual report to the Assembly [A/63/34 & Corr.1], JIU provided an overview of its activities in 2008, during which it issued reports on review of management and administration in the Universal Postal Union [JIU/REP/2008/1]; junior professional officer/associate expert/associate professional officer programmes in UN system organization [JIU/REP/2008/2]; management review of environmental governance within the UN system [JIU/REP/2008/3]; national execution of technical cooperation projects [JIU/REP/2008/4]; information and communications technology hosting services in UN system organizations [JIU/REP/2008/5]; and management of Internet websites in UN system organizations [JIU/REP/2008/6]. It also issued notes on the common services at Nairobi [JIU/NOTE/2008/1]; common services at the locations of UN regional commissions [JIU/NOTE/2008/2]; review of the United Nations Humanitarian Air Service [JIU/NOTE/2008/3]; and corporate consultancies in UN system organizations: overview of the use of corporate consultancy and procurement and contract management issues [JIU/NOTE/2008/4]. In addition, it issued a management letter on the review of management and administration in the World Meteorological Organization (WMO): additional issues [JIU/ML/2008/01], as well as a confidential letter regarding the follow-up on the JIU confidential management letter on the adequacy of internal controls at WMO [JIU/CL/2008/01].

JIU continued to streamline its internal working processes, procedures, tools and human resources. It implemented RBM for planning purposes, revised the strategic framework and prepared a new document outlining its long- and medium-term goals and objectives for 2010–2019. It also developed a comprehensive workplan for 2008 with actions to improve follow-up systems and enhance interaction with participating organizations and oversight and coordinating bodies, in particular with the United Nations System Chief Executives Board for Coordination (CEB). The job descriptions of Professional and assistant research staff were updated, principles and policies for investigation adopted in line with those adopted by the Conference of International Investigators, and a skill inventory and training needs assessment undertaken in order to design a comprehensive training and learning plan for 2008–2009. In addition, an Information Technology Committee was constituted and its terms of reference approved. The Access database was further improved to track delays in the issuance of comments and in the consideration of and action taken on JIU reports; and the time-tracking system evolved from a reporting tool into an instrument to better monitor and improve report preparation and increase accountability. In addition, JIU initiated a self-evaluation of its functions to assess its independence, credibility and utility in fulfilling its mission statement. During the reporting period, JIU continued working on 23 projects, 11 of which were completed.

JIU continued to enhance its dialogue with participating organizations. The policy and guidelines for interaction with those organizations were revised, and focal-point inspectors, by organization, were designated and given concrete responsibilities. It received information from all but four participating organizations to its request for information on recommendations issued in 2005, 2006 and 2007. JIU embarked on an assessment of the follow-up system, endorsed by the Assembly in resolution 54/16 [YUN 1999, p. 1277], and subsequently by most UN specialized agencies, including best practices and shortcomings, and reactivated efforts to conclude agreements with those organizations with which agreements were pending. The review of the follow-up system would be completed in 2009.

At the end of the year, single-organization reports issued in 2005, 2006 and 2007 showed an acceptance rate of 64 per cent, while 6 per cent of the 205 recommendations issued were rejected and 8 per cent were under consideration; system-wide reports issued in the same time period showed an acceptance rate of 51 per cent, with 4 per cent of the 144 recommendations rejected and 7 per cent under consideration. As to implementation of accepted/approved recommendations in single-organization reports, 33 per cent were implemented and 40 per cent were in progress. In 4 per cent of cases, implementation had not started, and no information was received for the remaining 24 per cent. As to implementation of accepted/approved recommendations in system-wide reports, 43 per cent of recommendations were implemented and 36 per cent were in progress. Implementation had not begun in only 5 per cent of the cases and no information was received for the remaining 17 per cent. The annual report also contained the JIU work programme for 2009.

The Assembly, by **decision 63/552** of 24 December, decided that the item on the JIU would remain for consideration during its resumed sixty-third (2009) session.

Oil-for-food programme

The oil-for-food programme, established by Security Council resolution 986(1995) [YUN 1995, p. 475] authorizing the sale of Iraqi petroleum and petroleum products as a temporary measure to finance humanitarian assistance, thereby alleviating the adverse consequences of the sanctions regime imposed by the Council, was phased out on 21 November 2003 [YUN 2003, p. 362]. In April 2004, the Secretary-General established the Independent Inquiry Committee (IIC) to investigate the administration and management of the programme, including allegations of fraud and corruption [YUN 2004, p. 364]. IIC, headed by Paul A. Volcker (United States), issued its reports and recommendations in 2005 [YUN 2005, p. 1476]. In December 2005, the Secretary-General decided to maintain the Committee's operation until the end of March 2006 [ibid., p. 436] through a follow-up entity known as the Office of the Independent Inquiry Committee. On 24 March 2006, the Secretary-General extended the Office until 31 December of that year [YUN 2006, p. 409]. From 1 January 2007, the Office was to be administered by the UN Department of Management for a two-year interim period, which could be extended by the Secretary-General. In December 2006 [ibid., p. 1654], the Secretary-General promulgated a procedure for the management of the IIC documents, which, at the conclusion of the interim period, would be transferred under the custody of the UN Archives and Records Management Section.

By **decision 62/555** of 15 September, the Assembly deferred consideration of the item entitled "Follow-up to the recommendations on administrative management and internal oversight of the Independent Inquiry Committee into the UN Oil-for-Food Programme" to its sixty-third (2008) session.

On 24 December (**decision 63/552**), the Assembly decided that the item would remain for consideration during its resumed sixty-third (2009) session.

Other administrative matters

Conference management

Committee on Conferences

The Committee on Conferences held an organizational meeting on 7 April and its substantive session from 8 to 12 September [A/63/32]. It examined requests for changes to the approved calendar of conferences and meetings for the 2008–2009 biennium [A/AC.172/2008/2 & Corr.1] and reviewed the draft revised calendar of conferences and meetings for 2009 [A/63/119/Add.1], reflecting the changes for the second year of the biennium since the adoption of the biennial calendar. The Committee also considered meetings management and improved utilization of conference-serving resources and facilities; the impact of the capital master plan accelerated strategy IV on meetings held at Headquarters; progress in integrated global management; and matters related to documentation, publication, translation and interpretation. (The Committee's deliberations and recommendations on those matters are detailed in the sections below.)

The Committee recommended that the General Assembly authorize its subsidiary bodies, listed in letters of 8 [A/63/352] and 15 September [A/63/352/Add.1] from the Committee Chairman, to meet in New York during the main part of the Assembly's sixty-third session. It also approved requests for changes to the approved calendar for 2008.

The Assembly, by **decision 63/501** of 16 September, authorized those organs to meet as recommended. On 24 December, it decided that the item "Pattern of conferences" would remain for consideration during its resumed sixty-third (2009) session (**decision 63/552**).

GENERAL ASSEMBLY ACTION

On 24 December [meeting 74], the General Assembly, on the recommendation of the Fifth Committee [A/63/638], adopted **resolution 63/248** without vote [agenda item 121].

Pattern of conferences

The General Assembly,

Recalling its relevant resolutions, including resolutions 40/243 of 18 December 1985, 41/213 of 19 December 1986, 43/222 A to E of 21 December 1988, 51/211 A to E of 18 December 1996, 52/214 of 22 December 1997, 53/208 A to E of 18 December 1998, 54/248 of 23 December 1999, 55/222 of 23 December 2000, 56/242 of 24 December 2001, 56/254 D of 27 March 2002, 56/262 of 15 February 2002, 56/287 of 27 June 2002, 57/283 A of 20 December 2002, 57/283 B of 15 April 2003, 58/250 of 23 December 2003, 59/265 of 23 December 2004, 60/236 A of 23 December 2005, 60/236 B of 8 May 2006, 61/236 of 22 December 2006 and 62/225 of 22 December 2007,

Reaffirming its resolution 42/207 C of 11 December 1987, in which it requested the Secretary-General to ensure the equal treatment of the official languages of the United Nations,

Having considered the report of the Committee on Conferences for 2008, the relevant report of the Secretary-General and the report of the Office of Internal Oversight Services on the audit of the existing special arrangements governing the recruitment of temporary assistance staff in the language services across the four main duty stations,

Having also considered the report of the Advisory Committee on Administrative and Budgetary Questions,

Reaffirming the pertinent provisions relating to conference services in its resolutions on multilingualism, in particular resolution 61/266 of 16 May 2007,

I

Calendar of conferences and meetings

1. *Welcomes* the report of the Committee on Conferences for 2008;

2. *Approves* the draft revised calendar of conferences and meetings of the United Nations for 2009, as submitted by the Committee on Conferences, taking into account the observations of the Committee and subject to the provisions of the present resolution;

3. *Authorizes* the Committee on Conferences to make any adjustments to the calendar of conferences and meetings for 2009 that may become necessary as a result of actions and decisions taken by the General Assembly at its sixty-third session;

4. *Notes with satisfaction* that the Secretariat has taken into account the arrangements referred to in General Assembly resolutions 53/208 A, 54/248, 55/222, 56/242, 57/283 B, 58/250, 59/265, 60/236 A, 61/236 and 62/225 concerning Orthodox Good Friday and the official holidays of Eid al-Fitr and Eid al-Adha, and requests all intergovernmental bodies to observe those decisions when planning their meetings;

5. *Requests* the Secretary-General to ensure that any modification to the calendar of conferences and meetings is implemented strictly in accordance with the mandate of the Committee on Conferences and other relevant resolutions of the General Assembly;

6. *Notes* that accurate, timely and consistent information provided to the Fifth Committee during its informal consultations facilitates the decision-making process in the Committee;

II

A. Utilization of conference-servicing resources

1. *Reaffirms* the practice that, in the use of conference rooms, priority must be given to the meetings of Member States;

2. *Notes* that the overall utilization factor at the four main duty stations remained at 83 per cent in 2007, the same as in 2006, which is above the established benchmark of 80 per cent;

3. *Welcomes* the steps taken by those bodies that have adjusted their programmes of work in order to achieve the optimum utilization of conference-servicing resources, and requests the Committee on Conferences to continue consultations with the secretariats and bureaux of bodies that underutilize their conference-servicing resources;

4. *Recognizes* that late starts and unplanned early endings seriously affect the bodies' utilization factor owing to the amount of time lost, and invites the secretariats and bureaux of bodies to pay adequate attention to avoiding late starts and unplanned early endings;

5. *Notes* that the percentage of meetings held by the bodies entitled to meet "as required" that were provided with interpretation services in New York in 2007 was 88 per cent, and requests the Secretary-General to continue to report on the provision of conference services to these bodies through the Committee on Conferences;

6. *Recognizes* the importance of meetings of regional and other major groupings of Member States for the smooth functioning of the sessions of intergovernmental bodies, and requests the Secretary-General to ensure that, as far as possible, all requests for conference services for the meetings of regional and other major groupings of Member States are met;

7. *Acknowledges with appreciation* the improvement in the percentage of meetings held by regional and other major groupings of Member States that were provided with interpretation services at the four main duty stations, which increased to 84 per cent in 2007 from 76 per cent in 2006, and requests the Secretary-General to continue to employ innovative means to address the difficulties experienced by Member States owing to the lack of conference services for some meetings of regional and other major groupings of Member States and to report thereon to the General Assembly through the Committee on Conferences;

8. *Once again urges* intergovernmental bodies to spare no effort at the planning stage to take into account the meetings of regional and other major groupings of Member States, to make provision for such meetings in their programmes of work and to notify conference services, well in advance, of any cancellations so that unutilized conference-servicing resources may, to the extent possible, be reassigned to meetings of regional and other major groupings of Member States;

9. *Notes with satisfaction* that, in accordance with several General Assembly resolutions, including resolution 61/236, section II.A, paragraph 9, in conformity with the headquarters rule, all meetings of Nairobi-based United Nations bodies were held in Nairobi in 2007, and requests the Secretary-General to report thereon to the Assembly at its sixty-fourth session through the Committee on Conferences;

10. *Notes with appreciation* ongoing promotional efforts and initiatives undertaken by the management of the conference centre of the Economic Commission for Africa, which led to a continued upward trend in utilization of the premises in 2007;

11. *Requests* the Secretary-General to continue to explore means to increase the utilization of the conference centre of the Economic Commission for Africa, bearing in mind the headquarters minimum operating security standards, and to report thereon to the General Assembly at its sixty-fourth session;

12. *Calls upon* the Secretary-General and Member States to adhere to the guidelines and procedures contained in the administrative instruction for the authorization of the use of United Nations premises for meetings, conferences, special events and exhibits;

13. *Emphasizes* that such meetings, conferences, special events and exhibits must be consistent with the purposes and principles of the United Nations;

14. *Regrets* the voting incident in the seventh meeting of the Fourth Committee, and requests the Secretary-

General to ensure prompt and effective communication between the Secretariat and members of the General Committee;

15. *Requests* the Secretary-General to report on the measures taken to avoid the recurrence of the above-mentioned situation in his next annual report on the pattern of conferences;

B. Impact of the capital master plan, strategy IV (phased approach), on meetings held at Headquarters during its implementation

1. *Requests* the Secretary-General to ensure that implementation of the capital master plan, including the temporary relocation of conference-servicing staff to a swing space, will not compromise the quality of conference services provided to Member States in the six official languages and the equal treatment of the language services, which should be provided with equally favourable working conditions and resources, with a view to receiving the maximum quality of services;

2. *Requests* all meeting requesters and organizers to liaise closely with the Department for General Assembly and Conference Management of the Secretariat on all matters related to the scheduling of meetings to allow maximum predictability in coordinating activities at Headquarters during the construction period;

3. *Requests* the Committee on Conferences to keep the matter under constant review, and requests the Secretary-General to report regularly to the Committee on matters pertaining to the calendar of conferences and meetings of the United Nations during the construction period;

4. *Requests* the Secretary-General to continue to provide adequate information technology support for conference services, within the existing resources of the Department for General Assembly and Conference Management, in order to ensure their seamless operation throughout the implementation of the capital master plan;

5. *Notes* that during the implementation of the capital master plan, a part of the conference-servicing staff and information technology resources of the Department for General Assembly and Conference Management will be temporarily relocated to a swing space, and requests the Secretary-General to continue to provide adequate support, within the existing resources of the Department, to ensure continued maintenance of the information technology facilities of the Department, implementation of the global information technology initiative and delivery of quality conference services;

6. *Requests* the Secretary-General to consult Member States on initiatives that affect the utilization of conference services and conference facilities;

III

Integrated global management

1. *Notes with appreciation* the progress achieved in the implementation of the global information technology project, aimed at integrating, across duty stations, information technology into meetings management and documentation-processing systems, and the global approach to harmonizing standards and information technology and sharing good practices and technological achievements among conference services at the four main duty stations;

2. *Also notes with appreciation* the initiatives undertaken in the context of integrated global management aimed at streamlining procedures, achieving economies of scale and improving the quality of conference services, and in this regard stresses the importance of ensuring equal treatment of conference-servicing staff as well as the principle of equal grade for equal work at the four main duty stations;

3. *Emphasizes* that the major goals of the Department for General Assembly and Conference Management are to provide high-quality documents in a timely manner in all official languages in accordance with established regulations, as well as high-quality conference services to Member States at all duty stations, and to achieve those aims as efficiently and cost-effectively as possible, in accordance with the relevant resolutions of the General Assembly;

4. *Requests* the Secretary-General to include in his next report on the pattern of conferences information about the financial savings achieved through implementation of the integrated global management projects;

5. *Also requests* the Secretary-General to ensure that all language services are given equal treatment and are provided with equally favourable working conditions and resources, with a view to achieving maximum quality of services, with full respect for the specificities of the six official languages and taking into account their respective workloads;

6. *Reiterates* the need for the Secretary-General to ensure the compatibility of technologies used in all duty stations and to ensure that they are user-friendly in all official languages;

7. *Requests* the Secretary-General to complete the task of uploading all important older United Nations documents onto the United Nations website in all six official languages on a priority basis, so that these archives are also available to Member States through that medium;

8. *Reiterates* that the satisfaction of Member States is a key performance indicator in conference management and conference services;

9. *Requests* the Secretary-General to continue to ensure that measures taken by the Department for General Assembly and Conference Management to seek the evaluation by Member States of the quality of the conference services provided to them, as a key performance indicator of the Department, provide equal opportunities to Member States to present their evaluations in the six official languages of the United Nations and are in full compliance with relevant resolutions of the General Assembly, and requests the Secretary-General to report to the Assembly, through the Committee on Conferences, on progress made in this regard;

10. *Also requests* the Secretary-General to continue to explore best practices and techniques in client satisfaction evaluations and to report on a regular basis to the General Assembly on the results achieved;

11. *Welcomes* the efforts made by the Department for General Assembly and Conference Management to seek the evaluation by Member States of the quality of the conference services provided to them, and requests the Secretary-General to continue to explore innovative ways to systematically capture and analyse feedback from Member States and committee chairpersons and secretaries on the quality

of conference services and to report thereon to the General Assembly through the Committee on Conferences;

12. *Requests* the Secretary-General to keep the General Assembly apprised of progress made in integrated global management;

13. *Also requests* the Secretary-General to ensure that the administrative policies, practices and procedures of conference services developed on the basis of recommendations of the task forces are in full compliance with relevant General Assembly resolutions;

IV

Documentation and publication-related matters

1. *Emphasizes* the paramount importance of the equality of the six official languages of the United Nations;

2. *Reaffirms* that the Fifth Committee is the appropriate Main Committee of the General Assembly entrusted with responsibilities for administrative and budgetary matters;

3. *Stresses* that matters related to conference management, including documentation, fall within the purview of the Fifth Committee;

4. *Reiterates with concern its request* to the Secretary-General to ensure that the rules concerning the simultaneous distribution of documents in all six official languages are strictly respected as regards both the distribution of printed copies and the posting of parliamentary documentation on the Official Document System and the United Nations website, in keeping with section III, paragraph 5, of its resolution 55/222;

5. *Reaffirms its decision* in section III, paragraph 9, of its resolution 59/265 that the issuance of documents in all six official languages on planning, budgetary and administrative matters requiring urgent consideration by the General Assembly shall be accorded priority;

6. *Requests* the Secretary-General to improve the documents planning process to ensure that the Fifth Committee receives, in the six official languages, all documents necessary for its consideration of a particular item, including reports of the Advisory Committee on Administrative and Budgetary Questions, within the established time limits;

7. *Reiterates its request* to the Secretary-General to direct all departments of the Secretariat to include the following elements in their reports:

(a) Summary of the report;

(b) Consolidated conclusions, recommendations and other proposed actions;

(c) Relevant background information;

8. *Reiterates its request* that all documents submitted to legislative organs by the Secretariat and intergovernmental and expert bodies for consideration and action have conclusions and recommendations in bold print;

9. *Requests* the Secretary-General to continue to take steps to improve the quality and accuracy of meeting records in all six official languages through full reliance in the preparation and translation of those records on sound recordings and written texts of statements as they were delivered in the original languages;

10. *Expresses its deep concern* at the unprecedented, high level of late submission of documentation by author departments, which, in turn, has a negative impact on the functioning of intergovernmental bodies, and requests the Secretary-General to report to the General Assembly at its sixty-fourth session, through the Committee on Conferences, on urgent measures taken to improve overall timely submission, in particular by those submitting entities with submission compliance below 90 per cent for three years in a row;

11. *Notes with concern* the unprecedented delays in the issuance of documents in 2008, which heavily impacted on the work of the General Assembly, and requests the Secretary-General to elaborate more effective accountability measures to ensure that both authors and their senior managers provide for the timely issuance of documents in all six official languages and to report to the General Assembly at its sixty-fourth session through the Committee on Conferences;

12. *Requests* the Secretary-General to enhance his efforts to address the problem cited in paragraph 10 above, particularly as experienced with documentation considered at the second resumed session of the Fifth Committee during the sixty-second session of the General Assembly, including convening the task force formed to study this matter, to provide an interim report on documentation concerning peacekeeping financing, to report on the results of these consultations and actions taken to solve this problem to the General Assembly, through the Committee on Conferences at its organizational session in 2009, in order for the Fifth Committee to consider the report at its second resumed session, and to provide a comprehensive report to the General Assembly at its sixty-fourth session through the Committee on Conferences;

13. *Recognizes* the increase in the workload of the Advisory Committee on Administrative and Budgetary Questions and the growing volume of reports and other documents before it, decides to authorize the Advisory Committee to meet for two additional weeks in 2009, on an exceptional basis, invites the Advisory Committee to continue considering how to better address its workload, and decides to discuss the number of weeks in a session of the Advisory Committee in the context of the proposed programme budget for the biennium 2010–2011;

14. *Requests* the Secretary-General to report on the associated expenditures in the second performance report on the programme budget for the biennium 2008–2009;

15. *Stresses* the importance of the concordance principle in order to ensure equally valid texts of resolutions in all six official languages;

16. *Recalls* section C, paragraph 12, of its resolution 54/248 and section III, paragraph 13, of its resolution 55/222, and reiterates its request to the Secretary-General to publish, prior to its sixty-fourth session, an updated version of the Financial Regulations and Rules of the United Nations in the six official languages of the Organization;

V

Translation and interpretation-related matters

1. *Recalls* rule 153 of the rules of procedure of the General Assembly;

2. *Requests* the Secretary-General to redouble his efforts to ensure the highest quality of interpretation and translation services in all six official languages;

3. *Reiterates its request* that the Secretary-General make sure that the terminology used in the translation and interpretation services reflects the latest linguistic norms and terminology of the official languages in order to ensure the highest quality;

4. *Takes note* of the recommendations provided by the Office of Internal Oversight Services of the Secretariat in its report, and requests the Secretary-General to ensure their full implementation and to report thereon to the General Assembly at its sixty-fourth session through the Committee on Conferences;

5. *Reaffirms* section IV, paragraph 3, of its resolution 59/265, section IV, paragraph 4, of its resolution 60/236 B, section V, paragraph 3, of its resolution 61/236 and section V, paragraph 3, of its resolution 62/225, and reiterates its request that the Secretary-General, when recruiting temporary assistance in the language services, ensure that all language services are given equal treatment and are provided with equally favourable working conditions and resources, with a view to achieving maximum quality of their services, with full respect for the specificities of each of the six official languages and taking into account their respective workloads;

6. *Expresses continued concern* at the high vacancy rate in the interpretation and translation services at the United Nations Office at Nairobi, and requests the Secretary-General to address this as a matter of priority through, inter alia, assistance from Member States in advertising and facilitating the conduct of competitive examinations to fill these language vacancies;

7. *Notes with appreciation* the measures taken by the Secretariat to fill current and future vacancies at the United Nations Office at Nairobi and the information contained in paragraph 107 of the report of the Secretary-General on the pattern of conferences, and requests the Secretary-General to consider further measures aimed at decreasing the vacancy rates in Nairobi and to report thereon to the General Assembly at its sixty-fourth session;

8. *Also notes with appreciation* the initiative to seek a long-term solution to the high vacancy rates in language services in the United Nations Office at Nairobi by engaging the services of a consultant to explore the possibilities of providing enhanced training programmes to potential professional translators and interpreters on the African continent, and requests the Secretary-General to report to the General Assembly at its sixty-fourth session on efforts in this regard;

9. *Requests* the Secretary-General to examine all aspects concerning recruitment and retention of language staff at the United Nations Office at Nairobi, to make recommendations in this regard and to report to the General Assembly at its sixty-fourth session through the Committee on Conferences;

10. *Recognizes* the acute problems faced by the United Nations Office at Geneva in providing conference services as required, as described by the Secretary-General in paragraph 103 of his report on the pattern of conferences, and in this connection requests the Secretary-General to address these problems and to make all efforts to meet requirements in the context of the latest surge of meetings;

11. *Requests* the Secretary-General to seek a more effective strategy to fill current and future language post vacancies at all duty stations in a timely manner, takes note of paragraph 92 of the report of the Secretary-General on the pattern of conferences, and also requests the Secretary-General to hold the competitive examinations for the recruitment of language staff referred to in that paragraph, as well as other examinations beyond 2009, well in advance so as to fill current and future language post vacancies at all duty stations in a timely manner, and to inform the General Assembly at its sixty-fourth session of efforts in this regard;

12. *Welcomes* the measures taken by the Secretary-General to address more effectively the demographic situation and the issue of succession planning, in particular by resorting to temporary assistance in dealing with acute needs, as well as enhancing internal and external training programmes, developing staff exchange programmes among organizations and participating in outreach to institutions that train language staff for international organizations, and requests him to continue to take such measures;

13. *Requests* the Secretary-General to continue exploring the possibility of introducing a traineeship programme in order to attract and train young professionals for a career in the language services of the United Nations;

14. *Notes with concern* the challenges presented by the demographic situation in the language services, as described in paragraphs 91 to 95 of the report of the Secretary-General;

15. *Notes* that the intention of the General Assembly, in adopting section VI, paragraph 1, of its resolution 57/305 of 15 April 2003, was to increase the availability of retired language staff for employment with the language services, and requests the Secretary-General to clarify and in turn implement the provisions of that paragraph concerning the ceiling on United Nations earnings of United Nations language staff retirees;

16. *Requests* the Secretary-General to continue to seek evaluation by Member States of the quality of the conference services provided to them, including through the language-specific informational meetings held twice a year, and to ensure that such measures provide equal opportunities to Member States to present their evaluations in the six official languages of the United Nations and are in full compliance with the relevant resolutions of the General Assembly;

17. *Also requests* the Secretary-General to continue to improve the accuracy of translation of documents into the six official languages, giving particular significance to the quality of translation;

18. *Further requests* the Secretary-General to take the steps necessary to enhance translation quality in all six official languages, in particular for contractual translation, and to report thereon to the General Assembly at its sixty-fourth session;

19. *Requests* the Secretary-General to provide, at all duty stations, adequate staff at the appropriate level, with a view to ensuring appropriate quality control for external translation, with due consideration of the principle of equal grade for equal work;

20. *Takes note* of the information on the impact of freelance recruitment on the quality of interpretation at all duty stations contained in paragraphs 101 to 105 of the report of the Secretary-General, and requests the Secretary-General

to report on the issue to the General Assembly at its sixty-fourth session through the Committee on Conferences;

21. *Requests* the Secretary-General to report to the General Assembly at its sixty-fourth session on the experience, lessons learned and best practices of the main duty stations in performing quality control of contractual translations, including on requirements relating to the number and appropriate level of the staff needed to carry out this function.

Use of conference services

In July [A/63/119 & Corr.1], the Secretary-General submitted a comprehensive report on issues related to the pattern of conferences, including the integrated global management of conference services, evaluation by Member States of the quality of conference services, meetings management, documents management and matters related to translation and interpretation (see sections below).

The report also provided information on the utilization of conference-servicing resources and facilities. The overall utilization factor in 2007 at the four duty stations—Geneva, Nairobi, New York and Vienna—remained at 83 per cent, the same as in 2006.

The Committee on Conferences, in September [A/63/32], noted that the overall utilization factor remained above the established benchmark of 80 per cent. The Chairperson reported on consultations held with five intergovernmental bodies that had underutilized their allocated conference resources, and made suggestions for improvement, including by providing advance notice of cancellations; beginning meetings on time, even without a quorum; scheduling shorter meetings if it was anticipated that less time would be required; using any time remaining at the end of the meeting to discuss additional agenda items; releasing unused interpretation services to meetings of regional and other major groupings of Member States; and reducing the number of meetings initially requested to accurately reflect the actual expected demand for conference services without changing the actual entitlements to such services.

Use of regional conference facilities

Nairobi and Addis Ababa

The United Nations Office at Nairobi (UNON) [A/63/119 & Corr.1] confirmed that, in 2007, all the meetings of the Nairobi-based bodies were held in Nairobi. In 2007–2008, the utilization rate at the Economic Commission for Africa (ECA) in Addis Ababa, Ethiopia, increased to 69.34 per cent, compared with 64.13 per cent in 2006 and 42.23 per cent in 2005. That improvement was to a large extent the result of promotional efforts, partnerships and marketing initiatives. As part of that effort, the Conference Centre management took an active part in selected high-profile international conventions and exhibitions to disseminate information packages and market the Centre so as to attract meeting organizers at the global level. As a result, the ECA Conference Centre was listed as a conference venue in the annual publications and the websites of IMEX (Worldwide Exhibition for Incentive Travel, Meetings and Events) and the International Congress and Convention Association. Those activities were planned and implemented in partnership with the Addis Ababa Tourism Commission, major tour/travel operators, and airlines and hotels with a stake in promoting Addis Ababa as a conference destination. The Conference Centre was also advertised in specialized magazines and the Centre's website was updated and made more attractive.

In September [A/63/32], the Committee on Conferences expressed satisfaction at the significant improvement in the utilization rate at UNON and ECA. It suggested that a more aggressive marketing strategy should be adopted to encourage additional clients to use the Nairobi conference facilities.

Integrated global management

In his July report on the pattern of conferences [A/63/119 & Corr.1], the Secretary-General stated that the integrated global management introduced in 2006 [YUN 2006, p. 1658] was not a limited time project, but a continuing collaborative process. Only through cooperation, dialogue and a strong orientation towards action could the dual requisites of increased integration and acknowledgement of the specificities of the various duty stations result in the positive synergy that could yield concrete and visible results.

Part of the integrated global management effort concentrated on the further fine-tuning and implementation of the compendium of administrative policies, practices and procedures adopted by all duty stations in 2006. Progress was achieved in management of lateral transfers of language staff between duty stations, exchanges of staff, the consolidated roster for contractual translation, harmonization of slotting procedures and advance waiver management, as well as workload forecasting and capacity planning. The progress of the integrated global management initiative was under constant review and would be the subject of a more comprehensive evaluation in 2009. In addition, the Working Group on Publishing issued an initial inventory of publishing technologies across the duty stations. A task force was set up to extend workload forecasting and capacity planning systems to such other areas of conference management as text processing and copy preparation. The integrated global management process resulted in enhanced cooperation between the Department for General Assembly and Conference Management (DGACM) and the regional commissions and more intensive exchanges of lessons learned and good practices among the duty stations in all areas of work, allowing the experience gained to be easily and seamlessly transferred from one duty station to another.

The integrated conference management system, a component of the global information technology initiative, was actively pursued. Information technology solutions were being developed to maximize the use of common processes in reporting, meetings management and documentation planning and processing. The development of the integrated conference management system was taking on added significance given the ongoing development of systems for enterprise resource planning, customer relationship management, and enterprise content management, and took into account future interface and data exchange with and among other enterprise systems.

The Committee on Conferences [A/63/32] stated that the purpose of integrated global management was to ensure a balanced division of labour between Headquarters and other duty stations, so as to increase the quality of interpretation and translation in all official languages and at all duty stations. In harmonizing methods of work, care should be taken to respect the unique aspects of each duty station and language group and to observe the principle of equal grade for equal work. All integrated global management initiatives should comply with General Assembly resolutions and other applicable mandates. The Committee expected to receive information on the savings realized from the streamlining and harmonization of processes.

In October [A/63/509], ACABQ noted the progress achieved in the implementation of the integrated global conference management system and DGACM efforts to develop it. The Advisory Committee requested the Secretary-General to include in his next report on the pattern of conferences information about the financial savings achieved through implementation of the integrated global conference management system. It stressed that the efforts to optimize efficiency gains through those initiatives should continue and be fully reported to the Assembly.

Interpretation for regional and other groupings

In July [A/63/119 & Corr.1], the Secretary-General reported that for the period from 1 January to 31 May 2007, 81 per cent of requests for meetings with interpretation for regional and other major groupings of Member States were granted, compared with 73 per cent in the same period in 2006. The upward trend continued throughout the year, with 87 per cent of requests being granted for the whole of 2007, compared with 79 per cent in 2006. In the first five months of 2008, a further improvement of 90 per cent was made. It was clear that the increased weekly strategic reserve put in place for "as required" bodies [YUN 2006, p. 1659] was having a positive effect on DGACM ability to provide interpretation services to regional and other major groupings. The Secretary-General stressed that a further increase in the strategic reserve remained the only way for the Department to address the problem of providing services to regional and other major groupings of Member States within existing resources.

The Committee on Conferences [A/63/32] noted the Secretariat's explanation that the recent increase in the percentage of meetings held by such groups with interpretation services was attributable to a combination of effective planning and ongoing consultations with the groups.

Documentation

In his July report [A/63/119 & Corr.1], the Secretary-General reported that, as at 30 June 2008, 71 per cent of documents had been submitted on time, up from 64 per cent in 2007. However, the average delay was 25 days, up from 20 days in 2007. While the past few years had witnessed some improvement in the timely submission and issuance of documents, the overall compliance in New York with the guidelines for submission was only 65 per cent in 2007, and overall compliance with guidelines for issuance only 61 per cent. An increasing number of author departments had formulated internal timelines for the preparation and approval of documents and had been requested by DGACM to provide more realistic slot dates. The Secretary-General reiterated that that any further improvement in the timely issuance of documents to intergovernmental organizations depended on author departments improving timely submission. Highlighting the 14 UN entities that achieved 100 per cent of timely submission over the past two years and a number of others that had improved noticeably, the Secretary-General stated that, with proper measures and determination, it was possible to make progress. He outlined measures DGACM had taken and made further suggestions to deal with late submission, late slotting and reslotting, unexpected submissions, and changes in the programmes of work of intergovernmental bodies. The Secretary-General stressed that proactive document management had a ripple and a multiplier effect. Rush processing came at a cost: financially, because of the overtime that might be required; in terms of the quality of processing (translation) and of consideration of reports, owing to the limited time delegates would have to read them; and in terms of the resources spent by the author departments in preparing the reports, not to mention the negative implications for the DGACM processing compliance. The impact was multiplied several times, given the multilingual nature of official documents. Strengthening proactive documents management therefore was not just vital to the timely issuance of documents, but also to the achievement of the other goals of the Secretariat, namely, quality, productivity and cost-effectiveness.

DGACM continued to enhance its publishing services, making clients more aware of the advantages of in-house printing and distribution services, leading to, among other results, the establishment at Headquarters of printing workload standards and the holding of several workshops to educate clients about the services and the processes involved in publishing. DGACM was about to launch a website, and similar efforts were being made at other duty stations to allow clients to learn about its services.

While acknowledging the challenges facing DGACM in documents management, the Committee on Conferences [A/63/32] expressed concern about the persistently late submission, processing and issuance of documents in all six official languages, especially during the second part of the resumed session of the Fifth Committee. There was general agreement on the need to take steps to prevent the recurrence of that situation. The Committee requested more detailed information and statistics on the reasons for author departments' failure to comply with submission deadlines, as well as further clarification of the slotting system and the criteria used to prioritize the various types of document. It suggested that sanctions should be imposed on managers responsible for the late submission of documents.

In October [A/63/509], ACABQ shared the concern of the Committee on Conferences about late submission of documentation by author departments. At the same time, it welcomed the fact that a number of entities had improved their rate of timely submission of documents and encouraged those entities to share best practices with others. It also encouraged the Secretary-General to continue efforts at capacity utilization and sharing, as well as increasing the use of internal printing capacity.

Translation and interpretation

In July [A/63/119 & Corr.1], the Secretary-General highlighted a number of factors that continued to affect the DGACM language service: demographic transition owing to the retirement of language staff; the depletion of language resources; and the imperative to replenish language rosters through more frequent competitive examinations. In attempting to deal with the demographic transition, DGACM developed a programme of outreach to universities and other training institutions for language staff, as well as to professional associations of language specialists, and stepped up training for serving staff to prepare them for increased responsibilities resulting from the retirement of large numbers of language staff. In addition, retired senior language staff were engaged on short-term appointments to assist in the training and monitoring of junior staff and provide substantive language services, so as to avoid any adverse impact of the demographic transition on the quality of services. DGACM also proposed to the Office of Human Resources Management (OHRM) measures for ensuring a more orderly succession in the language services, including raising, or waiving, the mandatory age of separation for language staff until such time as the staffing situation in the language services stabilized, as well as raising the ceiling on the UN earnings of retirees. Since the capacity of the OHRM Examinations and Tests Section could not cover all the examinations needed by DGACM, the Secretary-General suggested providing additional temporary resources to the Section and the OHRM units responsible for the recruitment of language staff. Otherwise, DGACM might not be able to guarantee the delivery of its mission-critical services to intergovernmental bodies. Special measures were taken to step up quality control checks of contractual translation.

As UNON, the vacancy rate for the interpretation section was 35 per cent, complicated in part by recent developments in Kenya, which led to a great number of language staff seeking opportunities elsewhere. The possibility of retaining and attracting good language staff was complicated by the low level of staff posts and the funding of a number of translator/reviser posts from extrabudgetary resources. In seeking a long-term solution to the problem of high vacancy rates in Nairobi, UNON engaged the services of a consultant to explore the possibilities of providing enhanced training programmes to potential professional translators and interpreters in Africa. In Geneva, the UN Office faced difficulty in freelance recruitment as its recruitment window made it uncompetitive with other international organizations.

In September [A/63/32], the Committee on Conferences reaffirmed its support for efforts to maintain the highest standards of quality in translation and interpretation. It also supported outreach to universities and schools of translation in all regions, especially in Latin America and Arabic-speaking countries. It welcomed efforts to work with the OHRM Examinations and Tests Section to hold more frequent competitive examinations in all official languages to replenish rosters for language posts. The proposal to waive or raise the ceiling on UN earnings for retirees in translation and interpretation as a way to ease the staffing shortage during the demographic transition was a cause for concern as it could potentially set a precedent and be viewed as giving special treatment to certain occupational groups. Furthermore, the demographic transition had long been foreseen, and other methods, such as a more frequent schedule of competitive examinations, should have been taken earlier. Raising the earnings ceiling was seen as a stop-gap measure, while long-term solutions were needed and could be found through outreach and increased contacts with educational institutions.

In October [A/63/509], ACABQ recommended that the Secretary-General engage all relevant departments with a view to holding competitive examinations for the recruitment of language staff as much in advance as possible to fill vacancies in the language services. ACABQ stressed the importance of the envisaged revamping of the examination process, as well as the outreach activities, and requested the Secretary-General to keep the Assembly apprised of progress made. With regard to the ceiling on the UN earnings of retired language staff, ACABQ indicated that the General Assembly was very clear that the ceiling was to be set in terms of workdays, not compensation days. Therefore, only those days on which the employee worked should be counted towards the ceiling of 125 days. Accordingly, there was no need to lift the ceiling of 125 days for the hiring of retired language staff. ACABQ also noted with concern that the overall vacancy rate for the interpretation section at UNON was 35 per cent.

OIOS report. In response to General Assembly resolution 62/225 [YUN 2007, p. 1476], OIOS conducted an audit of the special arrangements governing the recruitment of temporary assistance staff in the language services across the four main duty stations [A/63/94], namely, UN Headquarters and the UN Offices at Geneva, Vienna and Nairobi. The audit was to determine whether procedures were in place for identifying the requirements for temporary assistance for meetings in the language services and ensuring the recruitment of the most qualified individuals in an economical, efficient and transparent manner. The audit also sought to determine whether the recruitment of temporary assistance staff was unnecessarily skewed in favour of appointments for local, as opposed to non-local staff of the country where the services were required.

OIOS found that there was no global approach to managing the recruitment of temporary assistance staff in the language services, and no clear criteria, guidelines or standard operating procedures. Owing to that situation, and the consequent lack of transparency and consistency in selecting candidates, OIOS was unable to establish whether the recruitment of temporary assistance staff ensured that all language services were given equal treatment and provided with equally favourable working conditions and resources. The pattern of recruitment of temporary assistance staff for the language services in New York, Geneva and Vienna showed that some of the language services preferred to recruit candidates under local conditions of service, mainly because of concerns of managers of the language services about cost-effectiveness and efficiency. All four duty stations implemented capacity-planning exercises to determine their requirements for temporary assistance staff. However, there was no global planning process in place and the approach used differed from one duty station to another in terms of the frequency of planning, the relevance of the data used in the planning and the evaluation of capacity plans. OIOS recommended that DGACM review and update the agreements with the International Association of Conference Translators and the International Association of Conference Interpreters to ensure their alignment with relevant Assembly resolutions and UN Staff Regulations and Rules; ensure the implementation of standard operating procedures by all duty stations in determining the professional domicile and hence the conditions of service of temporary assistance staff in the language services; establish centrally managed rosters of candidates and related standard operating procedures to be used by all language services across the duty stations; implement centralized guidelines for capacity-planning and evaluation of capacity plans; address the issue of integrating computer-assisted tools to ensure greater interoperability of software used by the language services across the duty stations; and implement mechanisms to ensure that the approved workday limits for retirees were not exceeded. DGACM accepted all of the recommendations and was in the process of implementing them.

Workload standards

The Secretary-General included in his July report [A/63/119 & Corr.1] the performance matrix for 2007, including indicators for all duty stations as requested by the General Assembly in resolution 62/225 [YUN 2007, p. 1476], as part of a comprehensive methodology for performance measurement and management from a full-system perspective. It provided indicators for human resources, finance, meetings management and timeliness of documentation, as well as productivity measures for the language services.

In October [A/63/509], ACABQ, with the understanding that that the various measures included in the performance matrix were intended to enable Member States to draw their own conclusions about the full-system benefits of the reforms instituted, recommended that future reports of the Secretary-General contain a better analysis to demonstrate how efficiently and cost-effectively the work of DGACM was conducted, as well as a clear explanation of the units of measure and how they were calculated. It also recommended that DGACM continue to refine the cost estimates shown in the performance matrix, as well as to report on the progress of reform efforts.

Impact of CMP on conference services

In July [A/63/119 & Corr.1], the Secretary-General, reporting on the impact of the implementation of the capital master plan (CMP), (see p. 1597) on meetings held at Headquarters, stated that, since his previous report [YUN 2007, p. 1483], there had been new developments in the plan. The accelerated strategy IV (to supersede strategy IV (phased approach)), would shorten the renovation time by reducing the total number of phases required for the renovation of the Secretariat and conference buildings, and compress the total renovation period of the Headquarters complex from seven to five years, thus reducing the disruption to the operations of the Organization by two years. The Conference and General Assembly buildings would be renovated in two phases as opposed to the three phases previously proposed. The renovation of the Conference building was scheduled for late 2009 to late 2011, and when completed, the temporary North Lawn Conference building would be rearranged for meetings that normally took place in the General Assembly building. The renovation of the latter would start in late 2011 and was expected to be completed in 2013.

While sufficient conference facilities would be available to accommodate all core activities of the intergovernmental bodies normally meeting at Headquarters, facilities to accommodate activities in excess of the core meetings of the Charter organs and their subsidiary bodies, such as parallel meetings, side events and meetings of regional groups, would be limited. The off-site swing spaces for Secretariat staff had been identified and were being designed and fitted out for occupancy. Leases were concluded on a number of buildings. A related issue was the additional staffing needs for information technology support services, which would be expected to ensure that over a dozen mission-critical systems in multiple locations performed as required throughout the renovation process.

In September [A/63/32], the Committee on Conferences stressed that the implementation of the accelerated CMP should not have any negative impact on the quality and availability of conference services, or the equal treatment and working conditions of language services in all six official languages. Concern was expressed regarding the fire doors and barriers which had been installed in the General Assembly building and the Secretariat building without consulting Member States. Concern was also expressed that the "Cool UN" initiative, aimed at contributing to global efforts to combat climate change by reducing the carbon footprint of UN Headquarters, appeared to affect the working conditions not only of the Secretariat, but of Member States as well. In that connection, measures relating to the utilization of conference facilities, regardless of their essence and potential benefits, should be duly discussed and decided upon in the Committee on Conferences and the Fifth Committee.

In October [A/63/509], ACABQ was informed that dependency on temporary assistance to staff of the Information and Communications Technology (ICT) Section posed a risk during the implementation of CMP in relation to the ability of DGACM to provide and maintain high-quality ICT services, especially in the critical area of computer operations support, given the physical separation of the documentation chain, interpretation services, verbatim services and meeting planning and servicing, with the ICT systems for documents and meetings management relocated separately. ACABQ stressed the importance of ensuring that proper support was provided throughout CMP to ensure uninterrupted service and the involvement of the Chief Information Technology Officer to ensure that established information technology standards, policies and procedures were followed.

UN information systems

Information and communications technology

In April [A/62/793 & Corr.1], the Secretary-General, in his report on investing in information and communications technology, submitted in response to General Assembly resolution 60/283 [YUN 2006, p. 1581], presented the ICT strategy for the UN Secretariat over the next three to five years. The strategy encompassed five cross-cutting priority areas: the ICT management structure; strategic programme delivery; service and performance management; global architecture and standards; and financial control and reporting. The ICT strategy would be carried out through three Organization-wide programmes that built on one another: knowledge management; resource management; and infrastructure management. It would be carried out through a management framework comprising management oversight committees, advisory bodies, the Chief Information Technology Officer, the Office of Information and Communications Technology and other Secretariat ICT units.

During the first phase of implementation, the ICT Office would conduct structural reviews of Secretariat-wide ICT units with a view to rationalizing and harmonizing ICT operations and structures and defining coordination and reporting relationships between the Office and other ICT units. During the second phase, the results of the structural reviews would be implemented in all ICT units, and structures within the Office optimized to support more effectively ICT strategic programmes and services.

When fully implemented, the Secretary-General stated, the new ICT strategy would enhance the Secretariat's effectiveness, including improvements in institutional memory, agility, accessibility, transparency and accountability. It would also contribute to organizational efficiency by increasing staff productivity and helping the Secretariat reduce or avoid costs. To ensure its success, conditions had to exist or be provided, including senior management support, budgetary resources for strategic investments, streamlined policies, processes and support structures, and an organizational culture that was supportive of change. The proposed ICT strategy established the core building blocks for creating a strong ICT capable of meeting the operational and strategic needs of the global Secretariat well into the future. The Secretary-General requested the Assembly to endorse the overall approach relating to the strategy.

A September addendum [A/62/793/Add.1] provided additional information on the proposed ICT organizational structure and the reallocation of resources to establish the ICT Office. The Office would be an independent organizational unit reporting directly to the Executive Office of the Secretary-General, but would not be part of the Executive Office. That arrangement provided the necessary authority and visibility needed for the Chief Information Technology Officer to carry out a Secretariat-wide mandate and to address the current fragmentation among ICT programmes and services. The Office would be established by integrating the Information Technology Services Division of the Department of Management and the Information and Communications Technology Division of the Department of Field Support, based on a budget and staff-neutral approach through the redeployment of resources within the approved staff posts and budgets. It would be headed by a small Office of the Chief Information Technology Officer, which would be supported by two organizational units: staff-functions and line-functions. Other offices would include the Strategic Management Service, the Infrastructure Management Service and the Applications Management Division. Set out in the report was the Office's organizational structure.

As the Information Technology Services Division of the Office of Central Support Services would be consolidated under the Office of Information and Communications Technology, there were no changes to the programme aspects of the programme budget for the 2008–2009 biennium. It was proposed that the Office be treated as a separate section of the budget under the 2008–2009 programme budget. Effective 1 January 2009, all regular budget posts and financial resources appropriated for that year for the Information Technology Services Division, all extrabudgetary resources under that Division, as well as a part of the resources approved for the Information and Communications Technology Division of the Department of Field Support under the peacekeeping support account, would be redeployed and consolidated under the Office of Information and Communications Technology. The post of the Chief Information Technology Officer would be similarly redeployed and consolidated. Resources requirements for the 2008–2009 biennium were estimated at $325.5 million.

In October [A/63/487 & Corr. 2], commenting on the Secretary-General's proposal to conduct structural reviews of Secretariat-wide ICT units, ACABQ stated that such an inventory should include not only personnel dedicated to ICT functions, but also part-time staff. The exercise should lead to enhanced efficiency, which should be reported to the Assembly in the proposed 2010–2011 programme budget. ACABQ broadly agreed with the management plan proposed by the Secretary-General. The ICT governance mechanisms should involve staff and managers across all departments and duty stations affected by ICT systems and services provided by the Organization. The Secretary-General should keep the ICT governance structure under review and propose adjustments to make it simpler and operationally effective as a policy-setting and management instrument. The Assembly should be kept informed of changes to the ICT management framework in the context of its consideration of the proposed programme budget. ACABQ pointed out that the implementation of a governance structure and the establishment of the Office of Information and Communications Technology alone would not be sufficient to achieve those goals; it would be necessary to put measures into effect to support coherence and coordination. The Committee believed that there was a need to identify and quantify more precisely the efficiency gains and/or benefits expected from the implementation of the ICT strategy. It recommended that the Secretary-General define specific objectives in that regard, and explain the methodology and benchmarks used to identify and measure those benefits, and report thereon in the proposed 2010–2011 programme budget.

The Advisory Committee recommended that the Assembly endorse the overall approach relating to the comprehensive ICT strategy for the Secretariat, subject to the Committee's comments on the proposals; and note the Secretary-General's intention to proceed with structural reviews and the rationalization and harmonization of all ICT units. The Secretary-General should report to the Assembly on the results of such reviews in the context of the proposed 2010–2011 programme budget and other relevant budget proposals, including the impact on and changes proposed to the approved programme of work, changes in organizational structures and the realignment of resources that would be required.

Information and communication technology security, business continuity and disaster recovery

In response to section XI of General Assembly resolution 59/276 [YUN 2004, p. 1387] and section XV of resolution 60/266 [YUN 2006, p. 92], the Secretary-General submitted a 2007 report on ICT security, disaster recovery and business continuity [A/62/477], which updated his 2007 proposals [YUN 2007, p. 1495] for a global operational framework for ICT infrastructure, as well as for a separate initiative, related to the CMP transitioning phase in New York, to move the UN Headquarters complex data centre to a site in the new North Lawn facility and to Long Island City [YUN 2007, p.1495]. The total resource requirements under the 2008–2009 proposed programme budget was $47,292,900.

In October [A/63/487], as the proposed Long Island City site was no longer being pursued as a data centre, ACABQ recommended that the Assembly request the Secretary-General to submit a new proposal for a secondary data centre for UN Headquarters in New York, including a detailed justification of the reasons for the change and information on the costs already incurred in connection with the Long Island City site. With respect to the proposals concerning the global operational framework for ICT infrastructure, ACABQ noted that there had been no Organization-wide approach to disaster recovery and business continuity and stressed the need for a central authority under the Chief Information Technology Officer to set common standards, provide an Organization-wide perspective, optimize use of resources and improve ICT services. Recognizing the risks of relying solely on the communications facilities at the UN Logistics Base at Brindisi, Italy, as well as the need for further data storage facilities, ACABQ recommended approval of the Secretary-General's proposal to host the secondary active communications facility at Valencia, Spain, and that he be authorized to proceed with its implementation.

Enterprise resource planning system

In an April report on enterprise systems for the UN Secretariat worldwide [A/62/510/Rev.1], the Secretary-General proposed an approach for implementing an enterprise resource planning (ERP) system, set out in his previous report on the subject [YUN 2007, p. 1485], and measures for approval by the General Assembly. The implementation plan called for implementation in two waves: Wave 1 (2008–2010) and Wave 2 (2011–2012). Wave 1 would commence in the third quarter of 2008, following the completion of preparatory activities, and would focus on key management priorities. Based on the current project progress, it would be substantially completed by the end of 2010. Specific timings and technical arrangements for acceptance testing and data conversions would be determined by the integration services once they were engaged. Wave 2 would focus on the implementation of remaining functionalities of the ERP software solution. The implementation plan foresaw the first quarter of 2011 as the earliest start date for Wave 2, with substantial completion by the end of 2012. Each wave would be evaluated and annual progress reports submitted to the Assembly. The functionalities assigned to each wave would be designed and built based on configuring the ERP software solution to meet the Secretariat's requirements.

Design and build activities would be supported by associated business process re-engineering, legacy data preparation, data cleansing and change management, and would be undertaken by experts from Headquarters, offices away from Headquarters, regional commissions and field missions, coordinated by the ERP project team. Configuration would include meeting International Public Sector Accounting Standards process and data requirements. On completion of design and build, ERP functionalities would be deployed globally to all relevant Secretariat locations. The deployment would be supported by data migration, software training and technology hosting activities.

Complementary systems to be implemented included a customer relationship management (CRM) system to deal with processes connected with providing day-to-day services for end users, not dealt with under an ERP system. Its primary objective would be to improve the quality and cost-effectiveness of services provided to end-users. An enterprise content management (ECM) system would be introduced to address information assets of a substantive nature.

The ERP system would be financed from the regular and peacekeeping budgets and extrabudgetary resources. Total requirements for implementing ERP were estimated at $308.8 million ($285.6 million, including a contingency provision of $37.3 million), CRM ($8.2 million) and ECM ($15 million). The amount for the 2008–2009 biennium was estimated at $140.8 million to implement ERP ($119.6 million, including a contingency provision of $37.3 million), CRM ($7.4 million) and ECM ($13.8 million). It was proposed to fund the regular budget portion of the project under section 28A, Office of the Under-Secretary-General for Management, of the 2008–2009 programme budget, with the remaining requirements for 2008-2009 funded from the peacekeeping support account ($89.6 million) and extrabudgetary resources ($27.5 million).

The Assembly was asked to endorse the proposals and approach submitted by the Secretary-General.

In October [A/63/487 & Corr. 2], ACABQ considered that those revisions represented a significant change in the strategy for implementing ERP, and recommended that the Secretary-General submit a revised ERP project implementation plan and updated budget for the Assembly's consideration in the context of its consideration of the proposed 2010–2011 programme budget. In the meantime, the Secretary-General should be provided with sufficient resources to staff the core project team and proceed with the tasks and project activities of the detailed design phase, as well as any other tasks to be performed so as not to further delay the project. Accordingly, ACABQ recommended that the Assembly approve the revised resources for the current biennium in the amount of $37,258,700, comprising $5,588,800 to be funded under the regular budget; $23,100,400 from the support account for peacekeeping operations for the period from 1 July 2008 to 30 June 2009; and $8,569,800 to be provided from extrabudgetary resources. Remaining requirements would be included in subsequent peacekeeping support account budgets.

GENERAL ASSEMBLY ACTION

On 24 December [meeting 74], the General Assembly, on the recommendation of the Fifth Committee [A/63/648/Add.3], adopted **resolution 63/262** without vote [agenda item 118].

Information and communications technology, enterprise resource planning, and security, disaster recovery and business continuity

The General Assembly,

Recalling its resolutions 57/304 of 15 April 2003, 59/275 of 23 December 2004, 60/283, section II, of 7 July 2006 and 62/250 of 20 June 2008,

Having considered the report of the Secretary-General entitled "Investing in information and communications technology: information and communications strategy for the United Nations Secretariat" and the addendum thereto, the report of the Secretary-General entitled "Information and communications technology: enterprise systems for the United Nations Secretariat worldwide", the report of the Secretary-General on information and communications technology security, disaster recovery and business continuity for the United Nations and the related report of the Advisory Committee on Administrative and Budgetary Questions, the first progress report of the Secretary-General on the adoption of International Public Sector Accounting Standards by the United Nations and the related report of the Advisory Committee on Administrative and Budgetary Questions, the report of the Secretary-General entitled "Investing in information and communications technology: status report" and the related report of the Advisory Committee on Administrative and Budgetary Questions, the note by the Secretary-General on information and communication technology security, business continuity and disaster recovery and the related report of the Advisory Committee on Administrative and Budgetary Questions, the report of the Secretary-General entitled "Investing in the United Nations for a stronger Organization worldwide: interim report: investing in information and communications technology" and the related report of the Advisory Committee on Administrative and Budgetary Questions, the notes by the Secretary-General transmitting the report of the Joint Inspection Unit on policies of the United Nations system organizations towards the use of open source software in the secretariats and the comments of the Secretary-General and those of the United Nations System Chief Executives Board for Coordination thereon, the notes by the Secretary-General transmitting the report of the Joint Inspection Unit on knowledge management in the United Nations system and the comments of the Secretary-General and those of the United Nations System Chief Executives Board for Coordination thereon, and the report of the Secretary-General on the feasibility of the application of cost-accounting principles in the United Nations Secretariat and the related report of the Advisory Committee on Administrative and Budgetary Questions,

Underlining the importance of information and communications technology in meeting the growing demands of the Organization as it becomes increasingly reliant on its information technology and communications infrastructure,

Also underlining the importance of information and communications technology in strengthening oversight and accountability and in increasing the availability of accurate and timely information to support decision-making,

1. *Reaffirms* that the Fifth Committee is the appropriate Main Committee of the General Assembly entrusted with responsibilities for administrative and budgetary matters;

2. *Recalls* the role of the Secretary-General as the Chief Administrative Officer of the Organization, in accordance with the provisions of Article 97 of the Charter of the United Nations;

3. *Recognizes* the need for central authority to set common standards, provide an Organization-wide perspective, optimize use of resources and improve information and communications technology services;

4. *Also recognizes* the need for an integrated, global information system that makes possible the effective management of human, financial and physical resources and that is based on streamlined business processes and best practices;

5. *Further recognizes* the need for a global operational framework to enable the United Nations to respond effectively to emergency situations that may impair the operations of critical elements of its information and communications technology infrastructure and facilities;

6. *Endorses* the conclusions and recommendations contained in the reports of the Advisory Committee on Administrative and Budgetary Questions, subject to the provisions of the present resolution;

I

Information and communications technology strategy and governance

Recognizing the importance of the Secretary-General's knowledge management proposals, particularly in facilitating more informed decision-making and improving the effectiveness of the Organization,

Emphasizing the importance of strong, central leadership for the establishment and implementation of Organization-wide information and communications technology standards and activities in order to ensure efficient utilization of resources, modernization of information systems and improvement in the information and communications technology services available to the United Nations,

1. *Recognizes* that the successful integration of central information and communications technology functions across the Secretariat is essential to achieving coherence and coordination in the work of the Organization and between the Secretariat and the funds, programmes and specialized agencies;

2. *Notes* the intention of the Secretary-General to establish the Office of Information and Communications Technology in a budget-and-staff-neutral manner;

3. *Stresses* the need for a simple and operationally effective information and communications technology governance structure with clear lines of authority and accountability;

4. *Decides* to establish the Office of Information and Communications Technology as an independent organizational unit under a separate budget section, to be headed by the Chief Information Technology Officer at the level of Assistant Secretary-General;

5. *Emphasizes* that there is no single governance model for information and communications technology that can be assumed to be solely appropriate for the United Nations;

6. *Notes* the considerable level of expertise in the International Computing Centre, and requests the Secretary-General to continue to utilize the services of the Centre in supporting the information and communications technology activities of the United Nations;

7. *Requests* the Secretary-General to ensure that the centralization and integration of the information and communications technology functions in the Office of Information and Communications Technology do not have any negative impact on the support provided to field operations worldwide;

8. *Encourages* the Secretary-General, as Chairman of the United Nations System Chief Executives Board for Coordination, to foster deeper coordination and collaboration among United Nations organizations in all matters related to information and communications technology;

9. *Requests* the Secretary-General, in accordance with its resolution 58/269 of 23 December 2003, to submit a revised strategic framework to the Committee for Programme and Coordination at its forty-ninth session in the light of the programmatic aspects of the revision arising from the creation of the Office of Information and Communications Technology;

10. *Also requests* the Secretary-General to report to the General Assembly at the main part of its sixty-fifth session on his information and communications technology strategy, including on:

(*a*) Any necessary adjustments to the governance structure to make it simpler and operationally effective as a policy setting and management instrument;

(*b*) An update on such management and reporting arrangements;

(*c*) An in-depth assessment of the organizational arrangement, including the possibility of changing the placement of the Office of Information and Communications Technology in the structure of the Organization;

(*d*) A comprehensive inventory of information and communications technology capacities across the Secretariat, including dedicated and part-time personnel;

(*e*) More precisely identified and quantified efficiency gains or benefits expected from the implementation of the information and communications technology strategy;

(*f*) The methodology and benchmarks used to identify and measure those benefits;

(*g*) The roles and responsibilities of the Office of the Chief Information Technology Officer and the Department of Field Support of the Secretariat regarding information and communications technology activities, including on lines of authority, accountability and the division of labour set out in the new organizational structure;

II

Enterprise resource planning project

1. *Recalls* section II, paragraph 4, of its resolution 60/283, in which it decided to replace the Integrated Management Information System with a next-generation enterprise resource planning system or other comparable system;

2. *Stresses* that the implementation of the enterprise resource planning system should aim at consolidating the management of all financial, human and physical resources under a single integrated information system for the entire Organization, including for peacekeeping and field missions;

3. *Recognizes* the considerable operational and financial risks involved in the implementation of the enterprise resource planning system, and stresses the need for the Secretary-General to ensure full accountability and clear lines of responsibility for the project;

4. *Notes* the intention of the Secretary-General to implement the functionalities of the United Nations enterprise resource planning system in ways that would mitigate organizational and managerial risks;

5. *Stresses* the need to implement the various functions of the enterprise resource planning system across the global range of United Nations offices in a well-planned, step-by-step manner that ensures adequate preparation and training for each location and that minimizes the burden of change on the Organization and its resources, in order to further mitigate organizational and managerial risks;

6. *Notes* that the enterprise resource planning system provides for an integrated suite of information technology applications, as outlined by the Secretary-General in paragraph 20 of his report, and requests the Secretary-General to report on those applications to the General Assembly at its sixty-fourth session;

7. *Approves* the proposed governance framework of the enterprise resource planning project;

8. *Notes* that the enterprise resource planning governance structure proposed by the Secretary-General is distinct from the information and communications technology governance structure;

9. *Recognizes* that the successful implementation of the enterprise resource planning project requires the full support and commitment of senior management, as well as close and continuous engagement with key stakeholders;

10. *Emphasizes* that the enterprise resource planning project should be viewed primarily as a business project driven by business process demands and delivered through complex information technology systems requiring a high level of technical expertise;

11. *Recalls* that the objective of the enterprise resource planning project is to enhance the effective and transparent use of the resources of the Organization and, in that regard, emphasizes the need to identify tangible and measurable efficiency and productivity gains arising from the project;

12. *Requests* the Secretary-General to limit customization of the enterprise resource planning software to the extent feasible in order to ensure cost-effectiveness as well as flexibility in upgrading to new versions of the software and to report on any necessary customization with full justification of rationale and cost;

13. *Also requests* the Secretary-General, where customization for a particular function is unavoidable, to consider enhancing existing systems or using specialized software that can integrate with the enterprise resource planning system where it is more cost-effective in the long-term;

14. *Stresses* that changes to the working practices and business processes of the Secretariat should always be considered before undertaking customization;

15. *Expresses its readiness* to consider any duly justified proposal aimed at reducing customization, stressing that any proposed changes to the United Nations regulations must have prior approval of the General Assembly;

16. *Stresses* that, as a later adopter of the enterprise resource planning system, the United Nations can benefit from the lessons learned by other entities of the United Nations system that have implemented such systems;

17. *Takes note* of the overall resource requirements for the implementation of the enterprise resource planning systems for the United Nations as contained in the relevant report of the Secretary-General;

18. *Approves* the amount of 20 million United States dollars, comprising 5,110,000 dollars to be funded from the regular budget for the biennium 2008–2009, 7,050,000 dollars from the support account for peacekeeping operations for the period from 1 July 2008 to 30 June 2009 and 7,840,000 dollars from extrabudgetary resources for the biennium 2008–2009 for the implementation of the enterprise resource planning system;

19. *Decides* to approve the utilization of the amount of 2,346,000 dollars of interest accrued under the Integrated Management Information System Fund available as at 31 December 2007 to offset the regular budget requirements for the enterprise resource planning project approved in paragraph 18 of the present section;

20. *Requests* the Secretary-General to meet the regular budget share of requirements for the enterprise resource planning system in the amount of 2,764,000 dollars from the overall resources appropriated for the biennium 2008–2009 for the regular budget and to report the related expenditure as necessary in the second performance report for the biennium 2008–2009;

21. *Authorizes* the Secretary-General to enter into commitments in a total amount not to exceed 7,050,000 dollars for the support account for peacekeeping operations for the period from 1 July 2008 to 30 June 2009 in respect of the support account share for the enterprise resource planning project;

22. *Takes note* that an estimated amount of 7,840,000 dollars will be financed from extrabudgetary resources for the biennium 2008–2009;

23. *Endorses* the cost-sharing arrangement for the financing of the enterprise resource planning project proposed by the Secretary-General in paragraph 79 of his report;

24. *Decides* not to suspend the provisions for the application of credits under regulations 3.2 *(d)*, 5.3 and 5.4 of the Financial Regulations and Rules of the United Nations, regarding the use of available balances in the surplus account of the General Fund and the unencumbered balance of active peacekeeping operations;

25. *Authorizes* the Secretary-General to establish a multi-year special account to record income and expenditures for this project;

26. *Requests* the Secretary-General to keep the enterprise resource planning governance structure under review and to report to the General Assembly at the main part of its sixty-fourth session on the enterprise resource planning project, including:

(a) An assessment of the organizational arrangements;

(b) A revised enterprise resource planning project implementation and updated budget, taking stock of the design phase, with a full and detailed justification of the resources needed;

(c) An updated business case, including details on tangible and measurable efficiency and productivity gains in the areas of operation and administration to be achieved through the implementation of the enterprise resource planning system, as well as benchmarks for measuring progress and the anticipated return on investment;

(d) Highlighting those modules that are essential for the implementation of the International Public Sector Accounting Standards;

(e) An update on the implementation of the customer relationship management and enterprise content management systems, including further resources required, as well as the cost-sharing arrangement for their continued implementation;

(f) Justification of the need, and options for, contingency resources, including a possible budgetary alternative;

(g) Options for a reduced enterprise resource planning package at lower cost;

III

Customer relationship management and enterprise content management systems

1. *Recognizes* the benefits of the implementation of the customer relationship management and enterprise content

management systems, and requests the Secretary-General to continue to implement those applications throughout the Organization, as appropriate;

2. *Stresses* that the customer relationship management and enterprise content management systems shall be developed and implemented under the authority of the Chief Information Technology Officer in order to ensure a coordinated approach to the development of enterprise systems;

3. *Emphasizes* the need to ensure complementarity between the customer relationship management and enterprise content management systems with the forthcoming enterprise resource planning system;

4. *Decides* to approve additional resource requirements for the enterprise content management project in the amount of 2 million dollars, and requests the Secretary-General to meet the requirements from within the overall resources appropriated under the programme budget for the biennium 2008–2009 and to report on the related expenditure, as necessary, in the second performance report on the programme budget for the biennium;

5. *Notes* that implementation of the customer relationship management and enterprise content management systems is already in progress, and that at the time of the inception of those projects, the Secretary-General had not made a full proposal to the General Assembly;

IV

Security, disaster recovery and business continuity

1. *Emphasizes* the need for appropriate information and communications technology security, disaster recovery and business continuity plans;

2. *Requests* the Secretary-General to consolidate systems in central data centres in order to strengthen disaster recovery and business continuity and to minimize the size of local primary and secondary data centres;

3. *Also requests* the Secretary-General to prioritize systems in order to minimize the cost of disaster recovery and business continuity;

4. *Recalls* section XV of its resolution 60/266 of 30 June 2006, and stresses the need to ensure timely and secure communications and information exchange within and between duty stations, as well as to ensure that a robust and fault-tolerant infrastructure is in place to continue or restart operations in the event of a natural or a man-made disaster or disruption;

5. *Notes* that the Secretariat lacks an Organization-wide approach to disaster recovery and business continuity, thereby exposing the Organization to considerable risks, and, in this regard, welcomes the development of a unified approach to disaster recovery and business continuity activities throughout the Secretariat;

6. *Encourages* the Secretary-General to take a unified approach to disaster recovery and business continuity, utilizing all available infrastructure, in order to achieve economies of scale and cost efficiencies;

7. *Deeply regrets* that the Secretary-General entered into a long-term lease for the proposed Long Island City data centre before the viability of the site as a secondary data centre for United Nations Headquarters had been fully established, and urges the Secretary-General to explore alternative uses for the leased space as a matter of urgency;

8. *Notes with concern* that the delay this caused may lead to further cost escalation, including to the capital master plan, and risk to data;

9. *Notes* the particular challenge of providing disaster recovery and business continuity to customized departmental information and communications technology systems, and encourages the Secretary-General to pursue an enterprise information and communications technology approach wherever possible;

10. *Requests* the Secretary-General to ensure that the United Nations uses enterprise data centres rather than local data centres as far as possible;

11. *Decides* not to approve the proposal of the Secretary-General for a new secondary data centre at this stage, and requests him to report to the General Assembly at the first part of its resumed sixty-third session on the risk mitigation measures to be taken during the relocation of the primary data centre to the North Lawn;

12. *Requests* the Secretary-General to submit a unified disaster recovery and business continuity plan, including a permanent solution for Headquarters;

13. *Also requests* the Secretary-General to fully explore the possibilities for consolidating and using the most reliable and cost-effective solution for data storage, business continuity services and hosting of enterprise systems, drawing on the experience of other United Nations entities and global developments in information and communications technology, and to report thereon to the General Assembly at the main part of its sixty-fourth session;

14. *Encourages* application and data re-engineering where it supports the long-term goal of managing data recovery and business continuity in system-wide enterprise data centres and where, from a long-term perspective, it is more cost-effective than hosting them at a local data centre;

15. *Notes with appreciation* the commitment of the Government of Spain, and approves the related proposal to host a secondary active telecommunications facility at Valencia, Spain, to support peacekeeping activities;

16. *Decides* not to proceed at this stage with plans to host computing and data storage equipment relating to Secretariat business continuity operations and enterprise solutions at the secondary active communications facility at Valencia;

17. *Requests* the Secretary-General to include, in the report requested in paragraph 13 of the present section, plans to reduce the number of local data centres at Headquarters, offices away from Headquarters and peacekeeping missions;

18. *Endorses* the cost-sharing arrangement proposed by the Secretary-General for the new primary data centre of the United Nations Headquarters;

19. *Requests* the Secretary-General to submit a proposal on cost-sharing arrangements in the context of the report requested in paragraph 11 of the present section on the new secondary data centre;

20. *Takes note* of the intention to meet the estimated requirements in the amount of 149,400 dollars for the establishment of the secondary active telecommunications facility at Valencia for the period from 1 July 2008 to 30 June 2009 from within resources approved for the same period for the United Nations Logistics Base at Brindisi, Italy;

21. *Approves* the amount of 7,145,500 dollars for the establishment of a new primary data centre on the North Lawn at Headquarters, of which 5,716,400 dollars is to be funded from resources appropriated under the programme budget for the biennium 2008–2009, and authorizes the Secretary-General to report the related expenditure, as necessary, in the context of the second performance report on the programme budget for the biennium;

22. *Authorizes* the Secretary-General to enter into commitments in a total amount not to exceed 1,429,100 dollars for the support account for peacekeeping operations for the period from 1 July 2008 to 30 June 2009 in respect of support account share for the establishment of a new primary data centre on the North Lawn;

23. *Takes note* of paragraphs 89 and 96 of the report of the Advisory Committee on Administrative and Budgetary Questions, and decides to approve the amount of 2.5 million dollars, to be funded from the regular budget for the current biennium, for the provision of disaster recovery and business continuity services to Headquarters, offices away from Headquarters and field missions, and requests the Secretary-General to meet the above requirements from within the overall resources appropriated for the biennium for the regular budget and to report the related expenditures, as necessary, in the second performance report for the biennium;

V

International Public Sector Accounting Standards

1. *Takes note* of the first progress report of the Secretary-General on the adoption of the International Public Sector Accounting Standards;

2. *Endorses* the conclusions and recommendations contained in the report of the Advisory Committee on Administrative and Budgetary Questions;

3. *Recalls* that the General Assembly, in its resolution 60/283, approved the adoption of the International Public Sector Accounting Standards by the United Nations;

4. *Underlines* that the adoption of the International Public Sector Accounting Standards will improve governance, accountability and transparency in the United Nations system;

5. *Recognizes* that the enterprise resource planning system will serve as the backbone for implementation by the United Nations of the International Public Sector Accounting Standards;

6. *Encourages* the Secretary-General, as Chairman of the United Nations System Chief Executives Board for Coordination, to work within the Board to monitor the application of the International Public Sector Accounting Standards to ensure consistency within the United Nations system as a whole;

VI

Cost accounting

1. *Endorses* the report of the Advisory Committee on Administrative and Budgetary Questions, subject to the provisions of the present resolution;

2. *Takes note* of paragraphs 12, 17 and 18 of the report of the Advisory Committee on Administrative and Budgetary Questions;

3. *Notes* that cost accounting is more suitably applied to the support services of the Organization and may not be suitable for use in the substantive work of the Organization;

4. *Requests* the Secretary-General to continue to improve the methods for calculating costs of support services, including through a framework for cost accounting in order to standardize current costing practices, and to report thereon to the General Assembly at its sixty-fifth session;

5. *Also requests* the Secretary-General to include, in the report requested in paragraph 4 of the present section, an analysis of other areas within the support services of the Organization in which cost accounting could be applied.

International cooperation in informatics

In response to Economic and Social Council resolution 2007/14 [YUN 2007, p. 1486], the Secretary-General submitted a May report [E/2008/65] on international cooperation in the field of informatics, which addressed cooperation between the Ad Hoc Open-ended Working Group on Informatics and the Secretariat; connectivity and access; information technology services; and training, support and awareness. Cooperation between the Working Group and the Secretariat resulted in practical enhancements in technology that facilitated the work of Member States and observers and non-governmental organizations (NGOs) accredited to the United Nations.

The Secretariat and the Working Group continued to share responsibility for creating and maintaining web pages and document updates. With the guidance of the Working Group, the Secretariat expanded efforts to more fully utilize CandiWeb, a website built in support of elections at UN Headquarters. The Secretariat developed websites for all General Assembly Main Committees and maintained wi-fi connectivity and dedicated Internet access points for delegates throughout public areas and conference rooms of the New York campus. It was developing an ICT solution for the Protocol and Liaison Service to facilitate the accreditation of delegates of permanent missions. The Secretariat provided website services for many permanent missions and was involved in moving a number of websites over to a standard web content management system. The system would streamline permanent mission websites and provide an easy-to-use interface for missions to use in updating and maintaining their content while providing enhanced information security. In 2007, more than 270 mission staff participated in the Dag Hammarskjöld Library's training or coaching programmes. The Secretariat identified cost-neutral measures to enable relevant information posted on iSeek—the UN Secretariat intranet—to be made available to Member States. The United Nations Institute for Training and Research offered courses to some 50,000 beneficiaries who participated in its e-learning courses, and enhanced efforts to broaden the use of instructional technology to reach an additional 40,000 beneficiaries from Member States annually.

ECONOMIC AND SOCIAL COUNCIL ACTION

On 22 July [meeting 38], the Economic and Social Council adopted **resolution 2008/6** [draft: E/2008/L.18] without vote [agenda item 7 *(c)*].

The need to harmonize and improve United Nations informatics systems for optimal utilization and accessibility by all States

The Economic and Social Council,

Welcoming the report of the Secretary-General on international cooperation in the field of informatics and the initiatives of the Ad Hoc Open-ended Working Group on Informatics,

Recognizing the interest of Member States in taking full advantage of information and communications technologies for the acceleration of economic and social development,

Recalling its previous resolutions on the need to harmonize and improve United Nations information systems for optimal utilization and access by all States, with due regard to all the official languages,

Welcoming the intensification of efforts by the Information Technology Services Division of the Department of Management of the Secretariat to provide interconnectivity and unhindered Internet access to all permanent and observer missions at the United Nations,

1. *Reiterates once again* the high priority that it attaches to easy, economical, uncomplicated and unhindered access for States Members of the United Nations and Observers, as well as non-governmental organizations accredited to the United Nations, to the computerized databases and information systems and services of the United Nations, provided that the unhindered access of non-governmental organizations to such databases, systems and services will not prejudice the access of Member States nor impose an additional financial burden for their use;

2. *Requests* the President of the Economic and Social Council to convene the Ad Hoc Open-ended Working Group on Informatics for one more year to enable it to carry out, from within existing resources, the due fulfilment of the provisions of the Council resolutions on this item, to facilitate the successful implementation of the initiatives being taken by the Secretary-General with regard to the use of information technology and to continue the implementation of measures required to achieve its objectives, and, in that regard, requests the Working Group to continue its efforts to act as a bridge between the evolving needs of Member States and the actions of the Secretariat, and also requests the Working Group to consider its future role, status and mandate and develop findings in that regard;

3. *Expresses its appreciation* to the Secretariat for the continuing cooperation that it is extending to the Working Group in the endeavour to further improve the information technology services available to all permanent and observer missions at the United Nations and, in particular, for upgrading and stabilizing the e-mail services for delegates and for upgrading web-based services, such as the CandiWeb elections and candidatures site, as well as many mission websites implementing the CandiWeb elections and candidatures website, a cooperative effort of the Secretariat and the diplomatic community coordinated by the Working Group;

4. *Requests* the Secretary-General to extend full cooperation to the Working Group and to give priority to implementing its recommendations and guidance, particularly with regard to the establishment of a Member State web portal to consolidate and simplify the secure access by authorized representatives of Member States to relevant information;

5. *Also requests* the Secretary-General to report to the Economic and Social Council at its substantive session of 2009 on action taken in follow-up to the present resolution, including the findings of the Working Group and an assessment of its work and mandate.

UN premises and property

Capital master plan

Report of Secretary-General. In response to General Assembly resolution 57/292 [YUN 2002, p. 1375], the Secretary-General, in October [A/63/477], submitted his sixth annual progress report on the capital master plan (CMP), which outlined activities undertaken since his previous report [YUN 2007, p. 1486]. The Secretary-General reported that, following the approval of the accelerated strategy by the Assembly in resolution 62/87 [ibid., p. 1488], most testing requirements had been completed. A groundbreaking ceremony was held on 5 May and the construction of the temporary North Lawn Building was initiated. All remaining swing space leases were signed and preparations finalized for the temporary relocation of staff to those spaces in late 2008 and early 2009. In addition, significant progress was achieved in the design of the project, taking into account the changes required by the adoption of the accelerated strategy, the changes agreed upon as a result of the value engineering exercise, the incorporation of substantial greening measures and the incorporation of changes related to blast protection. As at September 2008, the projected cost was estimated at $1,974 million, a decrease of $122.1 million from the projected cost at August 2007. Total appropriations to date were $1,186.8 million, including $992.8 million for the 2008–2009 biennium. Actual expenditure as at 30 September was $239.5 million. Associated costs related to CMP implementation, including staffing and operational costs to support construction activities, would be reported in separate reports (see below). The Assembly was requested to take note of the progress made, and request the Secretary-General to continue to report on the status of the project, the schedule, the projected completion cost, the status of contributions, the working capital reserve, the status of the advisory board and the letter of credit in the next progress report.

Associated costs

Report of Secretary-General (April). In April [A/62/799], the Secretary-General reported on the associated costs, staffing and operational costs related to the CMP, in response to General Assembly resolution 62/87 [YUN 2007, p. 1488]. He stated that many associated costs would be incurred from mid-2008, and delays in CMP could result if the associated activities did not proceed on the same timeline. However, those costs could not be absorbed within the approved CMP budget without exceeding that budget. Associated costs estimated at $193,751,700 were identified for 2008–2013 for departments providing support during construction.

Communication. In a 5 June letter [A/C.5/62/29], the Assembly President informed the Chairman of the Fifth Committee of the Secretary-General's request for the Secretariat to enter into commitments in an amount not exceeding $22.7 million through 31 December, in respect of CMP associated costs ($9.5 million) and the UN enterprise systems ($13.2 million). The Secretary-General recommended that the Assembly take note of those costs, with the understanding that the detailed requirements should be subjected to the fullest scrutiny at its sixty-third (2008) session.

Report of Secretary-General (December). The Secretary-General, in December [A/63/582], updated his April estimated requirements for associated costs, which amounted to $185,997,400 gross ($176,569,000 net), or $7,754,300 gross ($6,569,500 net) less. For the 2008–2009 biennium, those costs amounted to $35,816,700, and $147,806,200 for 2010–2013. The Assembly was requested to approve the proposals.

Review of CMP

Report of Board of Auditors. The June report of the Board of Auditors on CMP for the year ended 31 December 2007 [A/63/5 (Vol. V)] reviewed the financial transactions and programme management for the period from 1 January to 31 December 2007, and the 11 recommendations it had made in its previous report [YUN 2007, p. 1487], five of which had been implemented, while four were under implementation and two had not been implemented. Since the design documents related to the accelerated strategy were not advanced enough, the Board was unable to give a well-informed opinion on the schedule and the global cost estimate for the project.

As at 31 December 2007, total expenditures committed or incurred since the beginning of the project amounted to $115.5 million. For 2007, expenses amounted to $46.4 million, of which $26.8 million and $19.6 million were in respect of disbursements and commitments, respectively, representing an increase of 27 per cent compared to 2006. The most noteworthy change since 2006 was the surge in deferred charges, which increased from $2.8 million to $124.1 million, due to the pre-encumbrance made for the lease of the swing spaces ($89.2 million) and for contractual services, notably those pertaining to the construction manager and the programme manager ($34.8 million).

The increase in the cash balance and deferred charges contributed to the surge in total assets, which amounted to $730.1 million as at 31 December 2007, compared to $202.3 million as at 31 December 2006. Liabilities increased less in absolute terms than the assets (from $39.3 million in 2006 to $198.3 million in 2007), which caused the reserves and fund balances amounting to $532.5 million to rise threefold from the previous financial year.

On internal control and oversight, the Board found that the CMP Office had monitoring tools, but did not have a summary scoreboard to permanently monitor progress made on the project. The Board also noted that the expenditures recorded in the Secretariat's accounting system and the expense forecasts prepared by the CMP Office were presented in different ways. Reconciling those two sources of information proved difficult, which affected the ability to manage the CMP budget.

Report of Secretary-General. In August [A/63/327], the Secretary-General provided additional information on implementation status, in response to the Board of Auditors' recommendations (see above), in accordance with Assembly resolution 48/216 B [YUN 1993, p. 1207]. As at August, three of the five main recommendations were targeted for implementation by the end of 2008 and two by the third quarter of 2009, while seven were in progress. No target date had been set for one recommendation. The report also contained detailed information on the implementation of the recommendations contained in the reports of the Board of Auditors on CMP for prior years.

OIOS report. In August [A/63/266], OIOS submitted a comprehensive audit of CMP, conducted pursuant to Assembly resolution 62/87 [YUN 2007, p. 1488]. The audit focused on the structure of the CMP Office, compliance with UN regulations and rules on procurement and contracting, adherence to the terms of contracts, the internal controls and processes in place to properly manage the project, and other high-risk areas. The audit identified the main risks to CMP as: possible delays resulting from procedural inflexibilities; cost increases due to changes to strategy and scope; and inadequate budgetary provision for associated costs.

While the overall activities of the CMP Office were adequately controlled, OIOS identified some areas in which controls could be improved and made recommendations to strengthen procedures and contribute to efficiencies. The most important of the recommendations related to avoiding delays by streamlining procurement procedures for contractual amendments so as to give the Executive Director the authority to spend up to a pre-approved contingency sum for each guaranteed maximum price contract. Recognizing the need to establish adequate controls for such a procedure, OIOS recommended that a committee be established to carry out an ex post facto review of contractual amendments and change orders over $200,000.

Associated costs (costs not budgeted or managed by the CMP Office) for the period 2008–2013 were estimated at about $194 million. OIOS stressed the need to identify and monitor all associated costs to ensure that adequate funding continued to be available, as well as to determine which of those costs should be attributed to the CMP project, as opposed to those costs which should be funded from regular departmental budgets. Recommendations were made with regard to succession planning, management coordination, delegation of procurement authority, associated costs, performance targets and stakeholder management. The CMP Office accepted the majority of OIOS recommendations.

Additional office/conference facilities

Addis Ababa. In accordance with General Assembly resolution 60/248 [YUN 2005, p. 1495], the Secretary-General submitted, in August [A/63/303], his annual report on construction of additional office facilities at the headquarters of the Economic Commission for Africa (ECA) in Addis Ababa, Ethiopia. ECA continued to negotiate with the local authorities to waive the requirement for the upfront payment of customs duties and related value added tax, to be reimbursed on the processing of applicable customs declarations and clearances. It continued to collaborate with them on the construction of an alternate public access road. Construction documents were received in January and the final tender was issued on 20 May. A bidders' conference was held in Addis Ababa on 6 June. The contract was expected to be awarded in December, with construction work commencing immediately thereafter. Owing to delays in the final negotiations with the international architect in November and December 2007, the issuance of the revised construction documents, the required in-depth coordination of the tender documents and the extension of the bid submission date, the building was expected to be completed in November 2010, with interior set-up approximately six months later.

In October [A/63/465], ACABQ expressed concern that little real progress had been made in the six and a half years since the project was initiated. The project appeared to be not well managed locally or adequately supported by Headquarters. Inadequate technical expertise had resulted in numerous technical design flaws. The Committee was also disappointed by the lack of accountability in overseeing and managing the project. There was a need to improve the entire arrangement to deal comprehensively with leadership, responsibility and accountability issues. ACABQ recommended that the management arrangements for the ECA project be clarified and improved so as to ensure that the new timeline proposed in the Secretary-General's report was implemented without further delay and that the new ECA office building became available for occupancy by mid-2011 as planned. The Secretary-General should address any unresolved issues, including the host country addendum for duty-free and tax-free status and site works, and report on actions taken in his next progress report.

The Assembly, in section I of **resolution 63/263** of 24 December (see p. 1546), expressed concern about the delays and procedural difficulties in the execution of the ECA projects. It requested the Secretary-General to undertake management reviews of the projects to ensure that a dedicated project management capacity was in place; ensure full accountability for all factors that had contributed to delays and cost escalation; update Member States through regular informal briefings on the construction project; complete the construction project as planned, without any further delays or additional requirements from the regular budget; ensure that progress was monitored by the Under-Secretary-General for Management; and report thereon to the Assembly at its sixty-fourth (2009) session.

Nairobi. In accordance with Assembly resolution 58/272 [YUN 2003, p. 1417], the Secretary-General, in April [A/62/794], submitted his annual report on improving and modernizing the conference facilities and construction of additional office facilities at the United Nations Office at Nairobi (UNON). Implementation of the modernization of the conference facilities was initially delayed by design considerations, vacancies in the Office's Facilities Management Service and the full commitment of existing resources to, inter alia, the implementation of projects to strengthen security and safety. However, UNON was taking all necessary measures to ensure that the modernization project for conference rooms 1 to 8 would start at the beginning of July 2008 and be completed by the beginning of February 2009. The project cost was revised to approximately $5,378,000, an increase of $1,899,000 over the original 2003 estimate of $3,479,000 approved by the Assembly.

The project of construction of additional office facilities at UNON moved into the detailed design and construction documentation phases in January, and UNON was expected to proceed to tender for the construction by May. The detailed design and construction documentation phases would be completed by the second quarter of the year, followed by a tender for construction. Construction was expected to begin in September, with a completion date of end-2010 and occupancy in January 2011.

The delays in the design phase, additional requirements relating, inter alia, to ensuring safety and security, and unforeseen construction components that had become necessary, had increased the cost of both projects. The total cost of the conference facilities project would amount to $5,378,000, and $25,252,200 for the additional office facilities project. The Assembly was requested to approve those amounts, the use of interest income of $1,088,000 for both projects and a commitment authority in the amount of $987,000.

In October [A/63/465], ACABQ recommended approval of the Secretary-General's proposals, but noted that the bidding process scheduled for October might affect requirements. It also recommended that updated estimates be submitted and a progress report on the construction project be submitted annually.

The Assembly, in section I of **resolution 63/263** of 24 December (see p. 1546), expressed concern about the delays and procedural difficulties in the execution of the project. It requested the Secretary-General to undertake a management review of the project; ensure full accountability for all factors that had contributed to delays in the implementation of the project and project cost escalation; and report to the Assembly in his next annual progress reports.

Vienna. In accordance with section X of Assembly resolution 62/238 [YUN 2007, p. 1454], the Secretary-General, in August [A/63/303], provided information on progress made in the construction of additional conference facilities at the Vienna International Centre. Completion of construction of the new conference facility (M building) was scheduled for the second half of 2008. The inauguration ceremony for the new building was held on 25 April and was attended by the Secretary-General. The implementation of certain installations included in the original design would take place after the M building was handed over to the organizations based at the Vienna International Centre by the host Government.

The four organizations based at the Vienna International Centre—the United Nations Office at Vienna, the International Atomic Energy Agency (IAEA), the United Nations Industrial Development Organization (UNIDO) and the Preparatory Commission of the Comprehensive Nuclear-Test-Ban Treaty Organization—would begin using the new M building in September and October. Full use was tentatively planned for 1 January 2009.

The four would collectively contribute €2.5 million for the construction of additional conference facilities. The United Nations share, set at 4 per cent, was included in the 2008–2009 programme budget under section 32, Construction, alteration, improvement and major maintenance. No additional operational and maintenance costs were anticipated while the new facility was used as swing space during the removal of asbestos from and refurbishment of the existing conference building (C building). The asbestos removal work, which began in 2004, would continue during 2008–2009 and beyond. All direct costs related to the asbestos removal were to be borne by Austria. The total project plan was expected to be completed by mid-2011.

In October [A/63/465], ACABQ welcomed the progress made towards the completion of the new conference facilities and the support of the host country for the project, and recommended that the Assembly take note of the Secretary-General's report.

Rental of office space

By **decision 63/549** of 24 December, the General Assembly decided to establish, effective 1 January 2009, a rental charge in the amount of $6 dollars per square foot per annum for the office space occupied by the Office of the Group of 77 and China at UN Headquarters, which included the provision of furniture and photocopying machine. It recognized the receivables associated with the rental obligations of the Group of 77 and China for the office space occupied by the Group at UN Headquarters, and decided that, as an exceptional measure, the outstanding receivables as at 31 December 2008 should be written off. It emphasized the need for all UN tenants to pay their rents on time, in full and without conditions; and that in the future, the Secretary-General should handle rental issues with individual tenants in accordance with existing procedures, without recourse to the Assembly.

Integrated headquarters facility for UNAMI

In response to resolution 62/238 [YUN 2007, p. 1451], the Secretary-General submitted, in May [A/62/828], a proposal for the construction of the UN integrated compound in Baghdad, Iraq. The Secretary-General said that following the adoption of Security Council resolution 1770(2007) [YUN 2007, p. 346], the mandate of the United Nations Assistance Mission in Iraq (UNAMI) was expanded and consequently would result in the long-term involvement of the Organization in Iraq. UNAMI, through the Special Representative of the Secretary-General for Iraq and in consultation with Iraqi Government representatives and United States authorities, had identified Al-Sijud Palace, located in the south-western corner of the international zone, for the development of UNAMI long-term facilities in Baghdad. That property was central to the proposed international district under the future redevelopment plan. The project, with an estimated cost of $98.6 million, was expected to be completed by October 2010. The new integrated compound would facilitate the return of the UN country team for Iraq from Amman, Jordan, and the re-establishment of UN agencies in the country, as well as increase administrative efficiency and promote cohesive and coordinated action. The new compound would have safer and more secure facilities, including the necessary security, logistics and communications infrastructure, which would provide accommodation for all UNAMI personnel and staff of UN agencies, funds and programmes. It would also provide space for the UN Guard Unit and other security personnel, as well as office space for all staff, including civilian personnel, visiting experts and delegations. The Secretary-General requested the General Assembly to approve in principle the proposal for the construction of the integrated headquarters for UNAMI at the Al-Sijud site.

In October [A/63/346/Add.5], the Secretary-General reported that the Government of Iraq was unable to allocate the Al-Sijud site to the United Nations but offered an alternative site adjacent to the original location in the international zone for a period of 25 years. The new site would enjoy the same security arrangements and other benefits of the future diplomatic areas as the Al-Sijud site, and there would be no cost increases. Meanwhile, discussions with the Government regarding the co-funding arrangement for the new UN compound were ongoing. Commitment authority was sought for 2009 to undertake design work, upon the completion of which a more comprehensive proposal would be submitted for the Assembly's consideration.

ACABQ, in a December related report [A/63/601], recommended a commitment authority for 2009 of up to $5 million for the design work, and that the Assembly request the Secretary-General to submit a new, detailed proposal for consideration at its sixty-third (2009) resumed session.

By section X of **resolution 63/263** of 24 December (see p. 1548), the Assembly approved commitment authority for 2009 for UNAMI in the amount of $5 million to undertake design work for the construction of the integrated compound and requested the Secretary-General to submit a new, complete and detailed proposal during its resumed sixty-third (2009) session.

Staff matters

Conditions of service

International Civil Service Commission

The International Civil Service Commission (ICSC), a 15-member body established in 1974 by General Assembly resolution 3357(XXIX) [YUN 1974, p. 875], continued in 2008 to regulate and coordinate the conditions of service and the salaries and allowances of the UN common system.

ICSC held its sixty-sixth (Addis Ababa, 31 March–1 April) and sixty-seventh (New York, 14–25 July) sessions, at which it considered, in addition to organizational matters, the conditions of service applicable to Professional, General Service and locally recruited categories of staff. The deliberations, recommendations and decisions of ICSC on those matters were detailed in its annual report to the General Assembly [A/63/30] (see sections below on specific issues).

By **decision 62/545 B** of 3 April, the General Assembly deferred until the second part of its resumed sixty-second (2008) session consideration of the addendum to the ICSC report for 2006 [YUN 2006, p. 1677] and the ICSC report for 2007 [YUN 2007, p. 1496]. In a 17 September statement [A/63/360], the Secretary-General estimated the administrative and financial implications of ICSC decisions and recommendations for the 2008–2009 proposed programme budget at $3,614,200, which would be taken into consideration in the first performance report for the 2008–2009 biennium.

On 23 October [A/63/501], ACABQ stated that it had no objection to the Secretary-General's approach.

In section III of **resolution 63/263** of 24 December (see p. 1547), the Assembly took note of the Secretary-General's statement and the related ACABQ report.

On the same date, the Assembly decided that the agenda item on the United Nations common system would remain for consideration during its resumed sixty-third (2009) session (**decision 63/552**).

(The Assembly's action on ICSC recommendations and decisions are contained in resolution 63/251 below.)

GENERAL ASSEMBLY ACTION

On 24 December [meeting 74], the General Assembly, on the recommendation of the Fifth Committee [A/63/640], adopted **resolution 63/251** without vote [agenda item 125].

United Nations common system: report of the International Civil Service Commission

The General Assembly,

Recalling its resolutions 44/198 of 21 December 1989, 51/216 of 18 December 1996, 52/216 of 22 December 1997, 53/209 of 18 December 1998, 55/223 of 23 December 2000, 56/244 of 24 December 2001, 57/285 of 20 December 2002, 58/251 of 23 December 2003, 59/268 of 23 December 2004, 61/239 of 22 December 2006 and 62/227 and 62/238 of 22 December 2007,

Having considered the report of the International Civil Service Commission for the year 2008,

Reaffirming its commitment to a single, unified United Nations common system as the cornerstone for the regulation and coordination of the conditions of service of the United Nations common system,

Reaffirming the statute of the Commission and the central role of the Commission and the General Assembly in the regulation and coordination of the conditions of service of the United Nations common system,

1. *Takes note with appreciation* of the work of the International Civil Service Commission;

2. *Takes note* of the report of the Commission for the year 2008;

3. *Reiterates its invitation* to the Secretary-General, in his capacity as Chairman of the United Nations System Chief Executives Board for Coordination, to urge the heads of the organizations of the United Nations common system to fully support the work of the Commission, in conformity with its statute, by providing it with relevant information in a timely manner for studies that it conducts under its statutory responsibilities for the common system, as well as by other possible means;

4. *Encourages* the Commission to continue to coordinate and regulate the conditions of service of staff of the organizations of the common system, bearing in mind the limitations imposed by Member States on their national civil services;

5. *Recalls* article 28 of the statute of the Commission;

A. Conditions of service for both categories of staff

1. Education grant

1. *Approves*, with effect from the school year in progress on 1 January 2009, the recommendations of the Commission in paragraph 62 of its report and annex II thereto;

2. *Requests* the Commission to report on the methodological review of the education grant to the General Assembly at its sixty-fifth session;

2. Performance management

1. *Reiterates* the importance of developing mechanisms for better differentiating levels of performance;

2. *Requests* the Commission to work closely with organizations to identify workable means of rewarding performance;

3. *Welcomes* the work of the Commission in benchmarking innovative practices in the area of performance management, and encourages the Commission to keep performance management under review;

4. *Requests* the Commission to submit an updated performance management framework to the General Assembly;

B. Conditions of service of staff in the Professional and higher categories

1. Evolution of the margin

Recalling section I.B of its resolution 51/216 and the standing mandate from the General Assembly, in which the Commission is requested to continue its review of the relationship between the net remuneration of United Nations staff in the Professional and higher categories in New York and that of the comparator civil service (the United States federal civil service) employees in comparable positions in Washington, D.C. (referred to as "the margin"),

1. *Notes* that the margin between net remuneration of United Nations staff in grades P-1 to D-2 in New York and that of officials in comparable positions in the United States federal civil service in Washington, D.C., for the period from 1 January to 31 December 2008 is estimated at 114.7 and that the average margin level for the past five years (2004–2008) stands at 112.9;

2. *Reaffirms* that the range of 110 to 120 for the margin between the net remuneration of officials in the Professional and higher categories of the United Nations in New York and officials in comparable positions in the comparator civil service should continue to apply, on the understanding that the margin would be maintained at a level around the desirable midpoint of 115 over a period of time;

2. Base/floor salary scale

Recalling its resolution 44/198, by which it established a floor net salary level for staff in the Professional and higher categories by reference to the corresponding base net salary levels of officials in comparable positions serving at the base city of the comparator civil service,

Approves, with effect from 1 January 2009, as recommended by the Commission in paragraph 79 of its report, the revised base/floor scale of gross and net salaries for staff in the Professional and higher categories contained in annex IV to the report;

3. Children's and secondary dependant's allowances

Approves, with effect from 1 January 2009, as recommended by the Commission in paragraph 129 of its report, the revised flat-rate allowance and the transitional measure thereto;

4. Mobility/hardship

1. *Recognizes* the hardship conditions under which staff members are often required to perform their official duties, and the personal disruption that operationally required mobility may impose on staff;

2. *Approves*, with effect from 1 January 2009, as recommended by the Commission in paragraph 94 of its report, the revised level of the hardship, mobility and non-removal allowances;

3. *Welcomes* the intent of the Commission to review whether the mobility/hardship continues to fulfil the purposes for which it was established;

4. *Encourages* the Commission to further refine the mobility/hardship scheme in order to foster, in particular, the achievement of organizational objectives;

5. *Requests* the Commission to report on the outcome of its planned review of the mobility/hardship scheme to the General Assembly at its sixty-fifth session;

5. Gender balance/geographical balance

1. *Notes with disappointment* the insufficient progress made with regard to the representation of women in the organizations of the United Nations common system, and in particular their significant underrepresentation at senior levels;

2. *Notes* the decisions of the Commission contained in paragraph 109 of its report;

3. *Invites* the Commission to continue to monitor future progress in achieving gender balance, including the aspect of regional representation if it deems it appropriate, and to make recommendations on practical steps that should be taken to improve the representation of women in the organizations of the United Nations common system;

C. Conditions of service of staff in the General Service and other locally recruited categories

Review of the methodology for surveys of best prevailing conditions of employment at headquarters and non-headquarters duty stations

Notes paragraph 148 of the report of the Commission, and requests the Commission to report on the methodological review to the General Assembly at its sixty-fourth session;

D. Conditions of service in the field

1. Effectiveness and impact of recruitment and retention measures at difficult duty stations

1. *Welcomes* the decision of the Commission to undertake a global staff survey to complement the findings of its studies;

2. *Invites* the Commission to conduct similar staff surveys periodically in support of its work, as well as any follow-up surveys;

3. *Requests* the Commission to continue its consideration of issues related to recruitment and retention and to report thereon as appropriate;

2. Hazard pay for internationally recruited staff

Expresses its appreciation for staff who live and work under hazardous conditions in the service of the United Nations;

E. Strengthening of the international civil service

Reaffirming that the staff is an invaluable asset of the Organization, and commending its contribution to furthering the purposes and principles of the United Nations,

1. *Emphasizes* that the capacity of the Commission as a source of technical expertise and policy advice should be further strengthened;

2. *Stresses* that the work of the Commission shall be given the importance and attention it deserves by the governing bodies of the organizations of the common system;

3. *Requests* the Commission to closely monitor the developments in the organizations of the United Nations common system in order to ensure the effective regulation and coordination of the conditions of service in the common system;

4. *Notes* the decision of the Commission to keep the Senior Management Network programme under review, and, bearing in mind paragraph 178 of its report, requests the Commission to monitor the envisaged redesigning of the programme and to report thereon to the General Assembly at its sixty-fourth session.

Functioning of ICSC

Strengthening ICSC

In 2008, the General Assembly requested ICSC to closely monitor the developments in the UN common system organizations to ensure the effective regulation and coordination of the conditions of service in the common system. The Assembly noted the ICSC decision to keep the Senior Management Network programme under review and requested it to monitor the redesigning of the programme and report to the Assembly at its sixty-fourth (2009) session.

Remuneration issues

In keeping with General Assembly resolutions 47/216 [YUN 1992, p. 1055] and 55/223 [YUN 2000, p. 1331], ICSC reviewed the relationship between the net remuneration of UN staff in the Professional and higher categories (grades P-1 to D-2) in New York, and that of the current comparator, the United States federal civil service employees in comparable positions in Washington, D.C. (referred to as the "margin"). In its 2008 report to the Assembly [A/63/30], ICSC reported that the net remuneration margin, for the period from 1 January to 31 December 2008, was estimated at 114.1. It drew the Assembly's attention to the fact that the average margin level for the past five years (2004–2008) had been below the desirable midpoint of 115, and currently stood at 112.8.

ICSC noted that for 2008, no duty station was expected to have a post adjustment below the new base/floor salary scale. It recommended to the Assembly, with effect from 1 January 2009, that the base/floor salary scale for the Professional and higher categories, as shown in annex IV to its report, be increased by 2.33 per cent through the standard consolidation method of increasing base salary and commensurately reducing post adjustment multiplier points.

Post adjustment

ICSC [A/63/30 & Corr.1] reviewed the operation of the post adjustment system, designed to measure cost-of-living movements through periodic place-to-place surveys at all duty stations. In that regard, it considered the report of the Advisory Committee on Post Adjustment Questions (ACPAQ), which at its thirtieth session (New York, 28 January–4 February) undertook a number of methodological studies pertaining to the 2010 round of place-to-place surveys; reviewed the results of an out-of-area survey, conducted by the Commission secretariat, aimed at a possible revision of the list of countries used in the calculation of the out-of-area index; and conducted an assessment of the extent to which the Internet could be used as a source of price data in cost-of-living surveys.

ICSC endorsed ACPAQ recommendations: to simplify the post adjustment index structure, reducing the number of basic headings from 104 to 84; for the 2010 round of surveys, the secretariat should not use hedonic regression techniques to adjust the prices of electronic and other high-technology products but keep abreast of developments in that area; increase use of the Internet as a source of price data at group I duty stations where local outlets had websites, and request the secretariat to continue its research on use of the Internet as a source of price data; base the proposed methodology for calculating the out-of-area index on a new list of 26 countries using survey weights, as well as the proposed procedure for revising the survey weights and the list of countries over time; revise the template of the biennial report of the data provider's report on its study of the cost-of-living differential between Washington, D.C., and New York, and request ACPAQ to review the structure of the 2008 report at its next session; and expand the list of organic/biological products to be priced in the next round of surveys to include all foods and beverages.

ICSC approved the ACPAQ recommendation to use the cost estimation models developed by the secretariat to estimate the financial implications of possible changes to the education grant. It authorized the secretariat to conduct the proposed housing surveys at headquarters duty stations in 2008, for the purpose of updating rental subsidy thresholds at those duty stations. It also authorized its secretariat to apply the new cost-of-living measurement methodology based on real-time comparisons with New York for the affected products, starting with the 2010 round of cost-of-living surveys.

Other remuneration issues

Conditions of service and compensation for non-Secretariat officials

Staff of international tribunals

Report of Secretary-General. Pursuant to General Assembly resolution 61/274 [YUN 2007, p. 1349], the Secretary-General submitted, in February [A/62/681] (see p. 1422), a comprehensive proposal on appropriate incentives to retain staff in the International Criminal Tribunal for Rwanda (ICTR) and the International Tribunal for the Former Yugoslavia (ICTY), including cost implications; updated human resources data; drawdown plans for each Tribunal, which would clearly show the anticipated post reductions for each year until the Tribunals completed their mandates; non-monetary incentives and measures; clear justification for the possible payment of a retention incentive; legal aspects related to the implementation of a staff retention scheme; and alternative approaches to the calculation of the amount of a retention incentive.

The Secretary-General recommended that staff members be considered for an incentive payment if they had worked for one of the Tribunals for a minimum of five years at the time of their separation. Although that option restricted the amount of the payments by increasing the qualifying years of service threshold to five years, it had the advantage of targeting those staff that had greater seniority and hence the specialized knowledge that the Tribunals wished to retain. The financial implications of that proposal were $6.9 million and $7.2 million for ICTR and ICTY, respectively.

The Secretary-General recommended that the retention incentive be applicable on an as wide a post coverage basis as possible. The Secretary-General said that the cost/benefit analysis conducted by the Tribunals clearly showed that the financial implications of the retention incentive were more than offset by the savings associated with reduced turnover rates in terms of lower rotation costs and higher productivity and efficiency.

In March [A/62/734] (see p. 1422), ACABQ presented its comments and observations on the Secretary-General's proposals, and recommended that the Assembly authorize, on an exceptional basis, the payment of a retention incentive to staff required to remain with ICTR and ICTY.

By **resolution 63/256** of 24 December (see p. 1422), the Assembly endorsed the ACABQ conclusions and recommendations and requested the Secretary-General to use the existing contractual frameworks to offer contracts to staff, in line with dates of planned post reductions in accordance with the relevant prevailing trial schedules, in order to remove uncertainty with regard to future employment, with the aim of ensuring that the Tribunals would have the necessary capacity to complete their respective mandates effectively.

Members of ICSC and Chairman of ACABQ

In accordance with the revised schedule for reviewing the compensation and other conditions of service of the full-time members of ICSC and of the Chairman of ACABQ, approved by the General Assembly in resolution 58/266 [YUN 2003, p. 1435], the Secretary-General submitted a September report [A/63/354], which examined the compensation and conditions of service of the three officials concerned. The report examined their compensation, other conditions of service and post-retirement benefits. The Secretary-General stated that, based on a projected increase in the consumer price index for New York by some 4.7 per cent, compared to November 2007, and on the adjustment procedure in effect, the annual net compensation of the three officials would be increased by 4 per cent beginning on 1 January 2009, from $197,564 to $205,467. No change was proposed with regard to the level of the special allowance payable to the Chairmen of ICSC and ACABQ, established at $10,000, nor the manner of application of the other conditions of service. However, it was noted that ICSC recommendations concerning the education grant were currently before the Assembly (see p. 1607). Based on the estimated movement of 4 per cent in the consumer price index, the pensionable remuneration of the ICSC Chairman and the ACABQ Chairman should be revised to $267,105 and that of the ICSC Vice-Chairman to $252,795.

The financial implications of those proposals would require an additional $33,194 for the 2008–2009 programme budget, to be reported in the second budget performance report for that period at the Assembly's sixty-fourth (2009) session. In accordance with resolution 58/266, the next review would be undertaken when the level of the annual compensation of the two Chairmen fell below the level of the compensation of Assistant Secretaries-General.

Members of ICJ and judges of international tribunals

At its resumed sixty-second session, the General Assembly considered the Secretary-General's 2007 report [YUN 2007, p. 1500] on the conditions of service and compensation for non-Secretariat officials, which reviewed the travel and subsistence regulations of the International Court of Justice (ICJ), as well as the remuneration and retirement benefits of ICJ members and of ICTR and ICTY judges and ad litem judges and their financial implications.

Communication. On 28 January [A/62/538/Add.1], the Secretary-General transmitted to the General Assembly President a 4 October 2007 request by the ICTY Registrar by which the Tribunal invited the Assembly to take into consideration additional information pertaining to the financial and operational benefits derived from the renewal of the term of office of judges during its consideration of their pensions. According to the Tribunal, the replacement costs for the permanent judges could be estimated at approximately €79,000 per judge. Since its inception, the Tribunal had seen the renewal of 16 permanent judges, rather than their replacement. Significant savings were achieved in the past and could be further realized if judges' terms of office were renewed in the future. The savings associated with reduced levels of rotation of judges—both economic and in terms of efficiency—warranted the implementation of measures aimed at motivating judges to seek further renewal of their terms of office rather than returning to their national jurisdictions.

ACABQ report. In a March report [A/62/7/Add.36], ACABQ noted that having an ad hoc judge appointed to sit in the ICJ case concerning the territorial and maritime dispute between Nicaragua and Colombia, following the adoption of resolution 61/262 [YUN 2007, p. 1499] and who would receive the same emolument as an ad hoc judge appointed prior to the adoption of the resolution, was incompatible with the resolution. Upon enquiry, ACABQ was informed that a similar situation could arise in a limited number of other cases pending before ICJ. Therefore, the Assembly was asked to examine the impact of the resolution's implementation on the position of ad hoc judges sitting in those cases. ACABQ also noted that establishing salaries in a currency other than the United States dollar for ICJ members and judges of the Tribunals would be a departure from current practice, the implications of which the Assembly would need to analyse, irrespective of the seats of the Court and the Tribunals and the currencies used in the countries concerned. It recommended that the Assembly defer consideration of the retirement benefits for ICJ members pending receipt of the pension study.

By **decision 62/547** of 3 April, the General Assembly endorsed the ACABQ conclusions and recommendations. It decided to set, effective 1 April 2008, the annual net base salary of ICJ members and judges and ad litem judges of the Tribunals at $158,000, with the corresponding post adjustment per multiplier point equal to 1 per cent of the net base salary, to which the post adjustment multiplier for the Netherlands or the United Republic of Tanzania, as appropriate, would be applied, taking into account the adjustment mechanism proposed by the Secretary-General. It decided to revert to the issue of the pension scheme during the second part of its resumed sixty-second (2008) session.

Report of Secretary-General. In response to General Assembly resolution 61/262 [YUN 2007, p. 1499], the Secretary-General submitted an April report [A/62/538/Add.2 & Corr.1] on the conditions of service and compensation for non-Secretariat officials, which reviewed the current pension scheme, based on the advice of a consulting firm (Mercer Human Resource Consulting) commissioned to study the options for designing pension schemes, including defined-benefit and defined-contribution schemes, taking into account the possibility of calculating pensions on the basis of the number of years served rather than the term of office. The report analysed the findings of the consulting firm.

The Secretary-General reported that the study conducted by the consulting firm corroborated most of the provisions provided for in the current respective pension schemes approved by the Assembly for ICJ members and judges of the Tribunals. He identified some principles to be considered in arriving at a revised system for calculating the pensions for both groups and stated that the system adopted had to ensure that the current level of pension for ICJ sitting members and judges of the Tribunals, and for those judges and their dependants who were currently receiving pensions, was not diminished.

The Secretary-General recommended that the pension scheme for ICJ members should remain a defined-benefit, non-contributory scheme; the retirement benefit should continue to be correlated to salaries and defined as being equal to 55 per cent of the annual net base salary (excluding post adjustment) by reference to nine years of service. The level of pension should be determined by reference to years of service rather than a term of office. An ICJ member who was re-elected should receive one three-hundredth of his or her retirement benefit for each further month of service, up to a maximum pension of three fourths of annual net base salary (excluding post adjustment). An ICTY or ICTR judge re-elected or extended for any subsequent term would receive a retirement benefit for each further month of service, by reference to the proportion of annual pension which the number of months of his or her service bore to 108 months. A judge re-elected should receive one three-hundredth of his or her retirement benefit for each further month of service, up to a maximum pension of three fourths of annual net base salary (excluding post adjustment). The retirement age should remain at 60, and the actuarial reduction factor, at a rate of 0.5 per cent per month, should continue to be applied in the case of early retirement prior to age 60. The level of the retirement benefit should be adjusted on the occasion of increases in the annual net base salary. Pensions in payment should also be adjusted on the occasion of increases in the annual net base salary of ICJ members and Tribunal judges. The programme budget implications were estimated at $8,800 for ICJ, $1,054,200 for ICTY and $476,100 for ICTR for the 2008–2009 biennium.

In a November report [A/63/570], ACABQ recommended approval of most of the Secretary-General's proposals. However, it did not agree that it was necessary to increase the base on which pensions were calculated from 50 to 55 per cent. It therefore recommended that the retirement benefit of ICJ members and Tribunal judges should continue to be based on salaries and should be 50 per cent of the annual net base salary (excluding post adjustment), or $85,040, whichever amount was higher, by reference to nine years of service, and that a re-elected ICJ member would receive one three-hundredth of his or her retirement benefit for each further month of service beyond nine years, up to a maximum pension of two thirds of annual net base salary (excluding post adjustment). With regard to the Tribunals, ACABQ recommended that a judge who had been or would be re-elected would be the recipient of the same pension plan of an ICJ judge if the Assembly approved the Committee's recommendations. As there would be consequential reductions in the financial implications, ACABQ recommended that the Secretary-General provide revised estimates for the 2008–2009 programme budget resulting from the changes in the pension scheme for ICJ members, to be reflected in the relevant 2008–2009 performance report.

GENERAL ASSEMBLY ACTION

On 24 December [meeting 74], the General Assembly, on the recommendation of the Fifth Committee [A/64/648], adopted **resolution 63/259** without vote [agenda item 118].

Conditions of service and compensation for officials other than Secretariat officials: members of the International Court of Justice and judges and ad litem judges of the International Tribunal for the Former Yugoslavia and the International Criminal Tribunal for Rwanda

The General Assembly,

Recalling section VIII of its resolution 53/214 of 18 December 1998, its resolutions 55/249 of 12 April 2001, 56/285 of 27 June 2002 and 57/289 of 20 December 2002, section III of its resolution 59/282 of 13 April 2005, paragraph 11 of its resolution 61/262 of 4 April 2007 and its decision 62/547 of 3 April 2008,

Recalling also Article 32 of the Statute of the International Court of Justice, as well as relevant resolutions of the General Assembly that govern the conditions of service and compensation for the members of the International Court of Justice and the judges of the International Tribunal for the Prosecution of Persons Responsible for Serious Violations of International Humanitarian Law Committed in the Territory of the Former Yugoslavia since 1991 and the International Criminal Tribunal for the Prosecution of Persons Responsible for Genocide and Other Serious Violations of International Humanitarian Law Committed in the Territory of Rwanda and Rwandan Citizens Responsible for Genocide and Other Such Violations Committed in the Territory of Neighbouring States between 1 January and 31 December 1994,

Having considered the report of the Secretary-General and the related report of the Advisory Committee on Administrative and Budgetary Questions,

I

1. *Takes note* of the report of the Secretary-General;

2. *Reaffirms* the principle that the conditions of service and compensation for non-Secretariat United Nations officials shall be separate and distinct from those for officials of the Secretariat;

3. *Endorses* the conclusions and recommendations of the Advisory Committee on Administrative and Budgetary Questions contained in its report;

4. *Decides* that any decisions with regard to the pension scheme shall apply only to the members of the International Court of Justice and the judges and ad litem judges of the International Tribunal for the Former Yugoslavia and the International Criminal Tribunal for Rwanda and shall not constitute a precedent for any other category of judges working within the United Nations system and that any decision regarding the service of any other category of judges shall be taken on a case-by-case basis;

5. *Requests* the Secretary-General to make the necessary revisions to article 1, paragraph 2, of the Pension Scheme Regulations for the members of the International Court of Justice and for the judges of the International Tribunal for the Former Yugoslavia and the International Criminal Tribunal for Rwanda, accordingly;

6. *Also requests* the Secretary-General to report to the General Assembly on any additional expenditures resulting from the above decision in the context of the second performance report on the programme budget for the biennium 2008–2009 and the second performance reports of the International Tribunal for the Former Yugoslavia and the International Criminal Tribunal for Rwanda for the biennium;

7. *Recalls* paragraph 11 of its resolution 61/262, in which it requested the Secretary-General to report on options for designing pension schemes, and notes that the Secretary-General has proposed essentially only one option and that, rather than seek the expertise available within the Organization, he has relied on the services of a consultant;

8. *Decides* that the emoluments, pensions, and other conditions of service for the members of the International Court of Justice and the judges of the International Tribunal for the Former Yugoslavia and the International Criminal Tribunal for Rwanda shall next be reviewed at its sixty-fifth session, including options for defined benefit and defined contribution pension schemes, and in this regard, requests the Secretary-General to ensure that, in that review, the expertise available within the United Nations is taken full advantage of;

II

Having considered the letter dated 6 March 2007 from the Secretary-General to the President of the General Assembly,

1. *Takes note* of the letter dated 6 March 2007 from the Secretary-General to the President of the General Assembly;

2. *Notes* that the International Criminal Court is not a United Nations entity;

3. *Decides* to amend article 1, paragraph 7, of the Pension Scheme Regulations for members of the International Court of Justice and article 1, paragraph 5, of the Pension Scheme Regulations for judges of the International Tribunal for the Former Yugoslavia and the International Criminal Tribunal for Rwanda to include a specific reference to the International Criminal Court so as to ensure that no former judge of any of these Courts receives a pension while also serving as a judge of the International Criminal Court;

4. *Notes*, in this regard, the issues of fairness and equality of treatment in respect of the above decision;

5. *Reaffirms* the provisions contained in its resolution 58/318 of 13 September 2004, and emphasizes that the decision contained in paragraph 3 of the present section shall not create a precedent for other organizations outside of the United Nations in respect of the application of pension benefits of judges of the International Court of Justice, the International Tribunal for the Former Yugoslavia and the International Criminal Tribunal for Rwanda.

Education grant

In July [A/63/30], ICSC informed the General Assembly that it would keep under review the education grant methodology. In the meantime, the current methodology would be maintained; the issue of designated duty stations for the purposes of the education grant would be examined before the next review of the mobility and hardship scheme in 2010; and the issue of representative schools would be examined before the next review of the levels of the education grant in 2010.

ICSC also reviewed the level of the grant, based on a related study by the Human Resources Network, which analysed 13,696 claims for the academic year 2006–2007. ICSC recommended that, as from 1 January 2009, maximum admissible expenses and the maximum education grant for 10 zones (Austria, Belgium, Italy, the Netherlands, Spain, Sweden, Switzerland, the United Kingdom, the United States, and the United States dollar area) should be adjusted, as indicated in table 1 of annex II to the ICSC 2008 report. The maximum amount of admissible expenses and the maximum grant should remain at the current level for Denmark, France, Germany, Ireland and Japan. The separate zone of Finland should be discontinued and the education grant for that country included in the United States dollar area outside the United States. Also, a separate maximum admissible expense level equal to that applicable to the United States should be established for the eight English curriculum schools in France. The amount of the special education grant for each disabled child should be equal to 100 per cent of the revised amounts of the maximum allowable expenses for the regular grant, while special measures would be maintained for China, Indonesia and the Russian Federation. Special measures would also be introduced for Bulgaria and Hungary, which would allow organizations to reimburse 75 per cent of actual expenses up to and not exceeding the maximum expenditure level in force for the United States dollar inside the United States. ICSC also recommended that flat rates for boarding, taken into account within the maximum admissible educational expenses, and the additional amounts for reimbursement of boarding costs over and above the maximum grant payable to staff members at designated duty stations, be revised as indicated in table 3 of annex II to the 2008 report.

In September [A/63/360], the Secretary-General estimated the annual financial implications of ICSC recommendations regarding the education grant at $2,850,000 and $514,300 for the 2008–2009 programme budget.

Performance recognition reward

Broad banding/reward for contribution pilot study

In July [A/63/30], ICSC reported that the comprehensive evaluation of the pilot study of broad banding/reward for contribution in five volunteer organizations it had requested in 2007 [YUN 2007, p. 1502] concluded that the pilot project had not met ICSC success criteria and had lost direction in all of the pilot organizations. The reasons for lack of progress included an apparent gap between expectations and reality, lack of involvement by all stakeholders, lack of consistency in management focus, competing priorities and lack of promised support. None of the piloting organizations had progressed to the point where performance payments were actually made. In all cases the pilot organizations were still at various stages of developing what ICSC had already defined at the launch of the pilot in 2004 as the absolute prerequisite for introducing performance pay—a credible performance evaluation system that enjoyed the confidence of both staff and management. Above all, the lack of a credible basis for distinguishing among the performances of individuals was the main reason that the project had lost its direction. Other obstacles included lack of sustained support and resources for the pilot; the fact that none of the piloting organizations had reached the level of preparedness for organizational transformation which broad banding/pay-for-performance implied; the lack of sustained commitment on the part of management in all but one of the pilot organizations, due mainly to changes in the management cadre; and the fact that a number of competing performance-improving initiatives were launched simultaneously in the majority of the piloting organizations. ICSC also considered a proposal by the United Nations Development Programme (UNDP) relating to conditions of service applicable to resident coordinators of the UN system.

ICSC decided to: discontinue the broad-banding/pay-for-performance pilot as it was originally conceived; request its secretariat to issue updated guidelines on the granting of steps based on merit; and provide for consideration at its sixty-seventh session an updated performance management framework, taking into account previous work of ICSC that could serve as a guide to organizations.

In response to that request, a concept paper outlining the approach to be taken in developing the framework was prepared for the Commission's approval and guidance. ICSC decided to keep performance management under continuing review; request its secretariat to upgrade the performance management guidelines set out by ICSC in 1997, with emphasis on the culture and environment and the leadership that should come from the top level of each organization; emphasize the role of the leadership at the top level in sustaining such a culture and environment; and request its secretariat to monitor developments in the organizations in that regard and provide assistance to the organizations.

Review of methodologies for surveys of best prevailing conditions of employment

In 2008, on the basis of the 1997 revised methodology for surveys of best prevailing conditions of employment at Headquarters and non-Headquarters duty stations [YUN 1997, p. 1453], ICSC conducted a survey of best prevailing conditions of service for General Service staff in Geneva, with a reference date of March 2007. It also undertook a similar survey for the General Service and other locally recruited categories in Vienna, with a reference date of November 2007. With regard to the Geneva survey, ICSC decided that the percentage resulting from the General Service survey would also be applied to adjust the salary scale of the other locally recruited category at Geneva—the Language Teachers. The salary scales for the General Service and the Language Teachers categories, as well as the revised levels of dependency allowances recommended to the executive heads of the Geneva-based organizations as at the date of its promulgation, were reproduced in annex V to the ICSC report [A/63/30]. The Vienna survey resulted in a new salary scale, reproduced in annex VI to its report, which was recommended to the Vienna-based common system organizations. ICSC also recommended revised rates for dependency allowances. It envisaged that financial implications of the new dependency allowances would amount to $509,990 per annum for the common system.

Dependency allowances

During its biennial review of dependency allowances for the Professional and higher categories [A/63/30], ICSC had before it a secretariat document reviewing the methodology for the children's and secondary dependant's allowances. The document described the evolution and current arrangements of the allowances, identified issues for review by ICSC and made proposals for simplifying and improving the fairness of the system. It also contained proposals for modifying some elements of the scheme with a view to making the system more reflective of national trends in social protection for children. The secretariat also developed a revised local currency denomination to replace the current system should protection against exchange-rate fluctuations be found necessary. It also proposed to establish a uniform percentage relationship between children's and secondary dependant's allowances. ICSC also reviewed the level of those allowances.

Regarding the review of the methodology, ICSC decided to inform the General Assembly that: the children's allowance should be established as a global flat-rate amount calculated as the average of United States dollar amounts of child benefits at the eight headquarters duty stations weighted by the number of staff at those locations; at the time of its implementation, the United States dollar amount of the allowance would be converted to local currency using the official UN exchange rate and would remain unchanged until the next biennial review; the flat amount would be recalculated on the same basis at the time of every subsequent review; the secondary dependant's allowance should be established at 35 per cent of the proposed children's allowance; and, as a transitional measure, where, at the time of implementation, the revised flat-rate allowance was lower than the one in effect, the allowance payable to eligible staff would be equal to the higher rate reduced by 25 per cent of the difference between the two rates; and if, during the next review of the allowance, that rate remained above the newly revised flat rate, a further reduction equal to 50 per cent of the difference would be applied. The transitional measures would come into effect as at 1 January 2009 and would be discontinued as at 1 January 2013.

Regarding the review of the level of the allowance, ICSC recommended that, as at 1 January 2009: the children's allowance be set as a global flat-rate amount of $2,686 per annum and the disabled children's allowance be double that amount i.e., $5,372 per annum; the secondary dependant's allowance be set at $940 per annum; at hard currency locations, the United States dollar amount of the allowance be converted to local currency using the official UN rate of exchange, as at the date of promulgation, and remain unchanged until the next biennial review; and, as a transitional measure, where, at the time of implementation, the revised flat-rate allowance was lower than the one in effect, the allowance payable to eligible staff would be equal to the higher rate reduced by 25 per cent of the difference between the two rates. If that transitional rate were to remain above the one set as at 1 January 2011, a further reduction equal to 50 per cent of the difference between the transitional rates set on 1 January 2009 and the rate of the allowance set for 1 January 2011 would be applied. Such transitional measures would be discontinued as at 1 January 2013. The dependency allowances should be reduced by the amount of any direct payments received by staff from a Government in respect of dependants.

In September [A/63/360], the Secretary-General estimated that the annual financial implications of the ICSC recommendations regarding the introduction of the new scheme would amount to $9 million per annum for common system organizations and $1,122,500 for the 2008–2009 programme budget.

Mobility and hardship allowance

ICSC continued its review of the mobility and hardship scheme approved in 1989 [YUN 1989, p. 886] to compensate staff for service at difficult duty stations and to encourage operational mobility. In accordance with ICSC decisions, as approved by the General Assembly in resolution 61/239 [YUN 2006, p. 1677], the amounts payable under the new mobility and hardship scheme that came into effect on 1 January 2007 were to be reviewed every three years. Since the new mobility and hardship scheme was approved late in December 2006, many organizations had reported difficulty in implementing the scheme on 1 January 2007 because of the need to make changes to their payroll systems and to inform staff of the changes. Most organizations were therefore obliged to implement the new scheme retroactively, but all organizations reported that they had implemented the new scheme during 2007.

ICSC recommended a 5 per cent increase for the hardship allowance, the mobility allowance and the non-removal allowance for implementation on 1 January 2009; requested its secretariat to suggest options for alternative adjustment factors or weightings for establishing the level of future amounts, for consideration before the 2010 methodological review; and recommended that, with effect from 1 January 2009, the amounts of the mobility, hardship and non-removal elements continue to be adjusted according to changes in the personal status of the staff member or in the hardship classification of the duty station, as under the previous scheme. It also listed factors to be considered during the 2010 review of the scheme.

In September [A/63/360], the Secretary-General estimated the annual financial implications of ICSC recommendations regarding the mobility and hardship allowance for the 2008–2009 programme budget at $959,400.

Hazard pay

Pursuant to General Assembly resolution 61/239 [YUN 2006, p. 1677], ICSC submitted a report by its secretariat which contained a proposal to increase the hazard pay for internationally recruited staff by 5 per cent effective 1 January 2009, from $1,300 to $1,365 per month.

In July [A/63/30], ICSC decided to establish the level of hazard pay for such staff at $1,365 per month as at 1 January 2009. It also requested the Chief Executives Board for Coordination, Human Resources (CEB/HR) Network to submit a report on the results of its review of the harmonization of hazard pay.

In September [A/63/360], the Secretary-General estimated the annual financial implications of the ICSC recommendations regarding hazard pay for the 2008–2009 programme budget at $783,900.

Staff safety and security

Report of Secretary-General. In response to General Assembly resolution 62/95 [YUN 2007, p. 1504], the Secretary-General, in August [A/63/305 & Corr.1], provided information on threats against the safety and security of humanitarian and UN personnel from 1 July 2007 to 30 June 2008. He noted that staff security remained precarious and personnel continued to be subjected to such threats as crimes, armed conflict, terrorism, harassment, banditry and detention. Abduction and hostage-taking, politically, economically or criminally motivated, remained the most disturbing feature, particularly in conflict and post-conflict areas. Key factors contributing to challenges for UN security worldwide included expanded and sustained operations; rising criminality owing to deteriorating public security and limited capacity of local authority; the spread of terrorist tactics; sharp increases in food and fuel prices leading to violent protests; rising public expectations and local dissatisfaction with UN operations or presence; and the climate of impunity for violent acts against UN and humanitarian personnel. During the reporting period, 25 UN civilian staff members lost their lives, 20 in Africa, one in Asia and the Pacific and four in the Middle East. In addition, 10 UN staff members died in a helicopter crash in Nepal. Locally recruited personnel remained most vulnerable to attacks and accounted for the majority of casualties and arrests, detentions or harassments. Serious violent incidents also continued unabated: overall, there were 490 recorded cases of violent attacks, 546 incidents of harassment and intimidation, 578 robberies, 263 physical assaults, 119 cases of hijacking and 199 reported cases of arrest and detention by State and non-State actors. In addition, there were 84 cases of forced entry and/or occupation of UN offices and 583 residential break-ins. The greatest number of security incidents and threats occurred in Africa and Asia and the Pacific.

In conflict and post-conflict areas, violent acts continued unabated. In the Darfur region of the Sudan, the number of vehicle hijackings involving UN and humanitarian personnel sharply increased to a monthly average of 12 incidents. In the Democratic Republic of the Congo, persistent attacks by armed groups targeting humanitarian convoys and personnel led to the suspension of humanitarian activities in certain areas in the east. In Haiti, there were 28 vehicle hijackings and seven kidnappings during the reporting period. In Afghanistan, 21 cases of intimidation and harassment were reported, as UN and humanitarian organizations continued to face direct targeted attacks. In Somalia, the deteriorating security situation led to a growing number of incidents in which perpetrators targeted, killed and abducted humanitarian and UN personnel: 81 incidents were reported, compared to 54 in 2007. The number of UN personnel arrested, under detention or missing, and regarding whom the Organization had been unable to exercise its right to protection, slightly decreased to 19 cases, from 22 the previous year. As at 30 June, 12 UN staff members remained under detention in Israel, 3 in Eritrea and 2 in Somalia.

The Secretary-General described measures taken by the Department of Safety and Security to enhance security consciousness and awareness of security procedures and policies, including comprehensive staff training, critical incident stress management, security information management, threat and risk analyses and crisis management and security mainstreaming.

The Secretary-General said that he would continue to encourage the Organization's efforts in drawing from lessons learned and taking steps to strengthen the UN security management system by improving accountability, leadership and internal management. His priorities would include addressing key policy, operational and strategic weakness, improving the safety and security of locally recruited staff, providing adequate resources, improving the framework for accountability, enhancing cooperation with host Governments and Member States, and restoring public trust in the UN at the global and local levels. As part of the efforts to promote closer cooperation with Member States and host Governments, the Secretary-General said that he would continue to include staff security issues in his regular conversations with senior officials of Member States. He called for the proactive participation and support of all Member States and host Governments, and emphasized the need for Member States to include the security of humanitarian and UN personnel as an integral part of their considerations and deliberations in UN intergovernmental bodies. With regard to the responsibilities and roles of host Governments, he urged Member States to address three topical issues: unlawful arrests, detention and harassment of UN staff; obstruction of freedom of movement of UN and humanitarian workers; and impunity for crimes committed against humanitarian and UN personnel. Moreover, as public attitudes and sentiments had a direct effect on the safety and security of humanitarian and UN personnel, the Secretary-General called on host Government authorities to refrain from public statements that could jeopardize the safety and security of humanitarian workers. Highlighting that locally recruited UN staff members continued to face increased security threats and had become victims of targeted abuse, harassment and unlawful detention in areas where their services were most critical for UN activities, he called for the Organization and the international community to review the policies and arrangements necessary to provide those personnel with adequate safety and security. The Secretary-General remained concerned by the difficulties encountered in some countries over the import of communication equipment and appealed to States that had imposed such restrictions to lift them.

Following the attack on the UN offices in Algiers on 11 December 2007 [YUN 2007, p. 61], the Secretary-General appointed the Independent Panel on Safety and Security of UN Personnel and Premises Worldwide, chaired by Lakhdar Brahimi, which in June 2008 submitted its report, "Towards a Culture of Security and Accountability". In December, the Secretary-General submitted a report [A/63/605] on a strengthened and unified security management system for the United Nations.

GENERAL ASSEMBLY ACTION

On 11 December [meeting 68], the General Assembly adopted **resolution 63/138** [draft: A/63/L.48 & Add.1] without vote [agenda item 65].

Safety and security of humanitarian personnel and protection of United Nations personnel

The General Assembly,

Reaffirming its resolution 46/182 of 19 December 1991 on strengthening of the coordination of humanitarian emergency assistance of the United Nations,

Recalling all relevant resolutions on safety and security of humanitarian personnel and protection of United Nations personnel, including its resolution 62/95 of 17 December 2007, as well as Security Council resolution 1502(2003) of 26 August 2003 and relevant statements by the President of the Council,

Recalling also all Security Council resolutions and presidential statements and reports of the Secretary-General to the Council on the protection of civilians in armed conflict,

Recalling further all relevant provisions of international law, including international humanitarian law and human rights law, as well as all relevant treaties,

Reaffirming the need to promote and ensure respect for the principles and rules of international law, including international humanitarian law,

Reaffirming also the principles of neutrality, humanity, impartiality and independence for the provision of humanitarian assistance,

Recalling that primary responsibility under international law for the security and protection of humanitarian personnel and United Nations and associated personnel lies with the Government hosting a United Nations operation conducted under the Charter of the United Nations or its agreements with relevant organizations,

Expressing its appreciation to those Governments which respect the internationally agreed principles on the protection of humanitarian and United Nations personnel, while expressing concern over the lack of respect for these principles in some areas,

Urging all parties involved in armed conflicts, in compliance with international humanitarian law, in particular their obligations under the Geneva Conventions of 12 August 1949 and the obligations applicable to them under the Additional Protocols thereto, of 8 June 1977, to ensure the security and protection of all humanitarian personnel and United Nations and associated personnel,

Welcoming the fact that the number of States parties to the Convention on the Safety of United Nations and Associated Personnel, which entered into force on 15 January 1999, has continued to rise, the number now having reached eighty-six, mindful of the need to promote universality of the Convention, and recalling with appreciation the adoption of the Optional Protocol to the Convention on the Safety of United Nations and Associated Personnel, which expands the scope of legal protection under the Convention,

Deeply concerned by the dangers and security risks faced by humanitarian personnel and United Nations and associated personnel at the field level, as they operate in increasingly complex contexts, as well as the continuous erosion, in many cases, of respect for the principles and rules of international law, in particular international humanitarian law,

Stressing the importance of fully respecting the obligations relating to the use of vehicles and premises of humanitarian personnel and United Nations and associated personnel as defined by relevant international instruments, as well as the obligations relating to distinctive emblems recognized in the Geneva Conventions,

Commending the courage and commitment of those who take part in humanitarian operations, often at great personal risk, especially locally recruited staff,

Expressing profound regret at the deaths of and violent acts against international and national humanitarian personnel and United Nations and associated personnel involved in the provision of humanitarian assistance, and strongly deploring the rising toll of casualties among such personnel in complex humanitarian emergencies, in particular in armed conflicts and in post-conflict situations,

Strongly condemning acts of murder and other forms of violence, rape and sexual assault and all forms of violence committed in particular against women and children, and intimidation, armed robbery, abduction, hostage-taking, kidnapping, harassment and illegal arrest and detention to which those participating in humanitarian operations are increasingly exposed, as well as attacks on humanitarian convoys and acts of destruction and looting of property,

Expressing deep concern that the occurrence of attacks and threats against humanitarian personnel and United Nations and associated personnel is a factor that increasingly restricts the provision of assistance and protection to populations in need,

Noting the establishment by the Secretary-General of the Independent Panel on Safety and Security of United Nations Personnel and Premises Worldwide, and looking forward to the report of the Secretary-General on all its aspects and recommendations, including on accountability, to be submitted for the consideration of the General Assembly at its sixty-third session,

Affirming the need for States to ensure that perpetrators of attacks committed on their territory against humanitarian personnel and United Nations and associated personnel do not operate with impunity, and that the perpetrators of such acts are brought to justice as provided for by national laws and obligations under international law,

Recalling the inclusion of attacks intentionally directed against personnel involved in a humanitarian assistance or peacekeeping mission in accordance with the Charter as a war crime in the Rome Statute of the International Criminal Court, and noting the role that the Court can play in appropriate cases in bringing to justice those responsible for serious violations of international humanitarian law,

Reaffirming the need to ensure adequate levels of safety and security for United Nations personnel and associated humanitarian personnel, including locally recruited staff, which constitutes an underlying duty of the Organization, and mindful of the need to promote and enhance the security consciousness within the organizational culture of the United Nations and a culture of accountability at all levels, as well as to continue to promote awareness of and sensitivity to national and local cultures and laws,

Noting the importance of reinforcing the close collaboration between the United Nations and the host country on contingency planning, information exchange and risk assessment in the context of good mutual cooperation on issues relating to the security of United Nations and associated personnel,

1. *Welcomes* the report of the Secretary-General;

2. *Urges* all States to make every effort to ensure the full and effective implementation of the relevant principles and rules of international law, including international humanitarian law, human rights law and refugee law related to the safety and security of humanitarian personnel and United Nations personnel;

3. *Strongly urges* all States to take the necessary measures to ensure the safety and security of humanitarian personnel and United Nations and associated personnel and to respect and ensure respect for the inviolability of United Nations premises, which are essential to the continuation and successful implementation of United Nations operations;

4. *Calls upon* all Governments and parties in complex humanitarian emergencies, in particular in armed conflicts and in post-conflict situations, in countries in which humanitarian personnel are operating, in conformity with the relevant provisions of international law and national laws, to cooperate fully with the United Nations and other humanitarian agencies and organizations and to ensure the safe and unhindered access of humanitarian personnel and delivery of supplies and equipment, in order to allow those personnel to perform efficiently their task of assisting the affected civilian population, including refugees and internally displaced persons;

5. *Calls upon* all States to consider becoming parties to and to respect fully their obligations under the relevant international instruments;

6. *Also calls upon* all States to consider becoming parties to the Rome Statute of the International Criminal Court;

7. *Further calls upon* all States to consider becoming parties to the Optional Protocol to the Convention on the Safety of United Nations and Associated Personnel as soon as possible so as to ensure its rapid entry into force, and urges States parties to put in place appropriate national legislation, as necessary, to enable its effective implementation;

8. *Calls upon* all States, all parties involved in armed conflict and all humanitarian actors to respect the principles of neutrality, humanity, impartiality and independence for the provision of humanitarian assistance;

9. *Expresses deep concern* that, over the past decade, threats and attacks against the safety and security of humanitarian personnel and United Nations and associated personnel have escalated dramatically and that perpetrators of acts of violence seemingly operate with impunity;

10. *Strongly condemns* all threats and acts of violence against humanitarian personnel and United Nations and associated personnel, reaffirms the need to hold accountable those responsible for such acts, strongly urges all States to take stronger action to ensure that any such acts committed on their territory are investigated fully and to ensure that the perpetrators of such acts are brought to justice in accordance with national laws and obligations under international law, and urges States to end impunity for such acts;

11. *Calls upon* all States to comply fully with their obligations under international humanitarian law, including as provided by the Geneva Convention relative to the Protection of Civilian Persons in Time of War, of 12 August 1949, in order to respect and protect all humanitarian personnel in territories subject to their jurisdiction;

12. *Also calls upon* all States to provide adequate and prompt information in the event of the arrest or detention of humanitarian personnel or United Nations and associated personnel, so as to afford them the necessary medical assistance and to allow independent medical teams to visit and examine the health of those detained, and urges them to take the necessary measures to ensure the speedy release of those who have been arrested or detained in violation of the relevant conventions referred to in the present resolution and applicable international humanitarian law;

13. *Calls upon* all other parties involved in armed conflicts to refrain from abducting humanitarian personnel or United Nations and associated personnel or detaining them in violation of the relevant conventions referred to in the present resolution and applicable international humanitarian law, and speedily to release, without harm or requirement of concession, any abductee or detainee;

14. *Requests* the Secretary-General to take the necessary measures to ensure full respect for the human rights,

privileges and immunities of United Nations and other personnel carrying out activities in fulfilment of the mandate of a United Nations operation, and also requests the Secretary-General to seek the inclusion, in negotiations of headquarters and other mission agreements concerning United Nations and associated personnel, of the applicable conditions contained in the Convention on the Privileges and Immunities of the United Nations, the Convention on the Privileges and Immunities of the Specialized Agencies and the Convention on the Safety of United Nations and Associated Personnel;

15. *Recommends* that the Secretary-General continue to seek the inclusion of, and that host countries include, key provisions of the Convention on the Safety of United Nations and Associated Personnel, among others, those regarding the prevention of attacks against members of the operation, the establishment of such attacks as crimes punishable by law and the prosecution or extradition of offenders, in future as well as, if necessary, in existing status-of-forces, status-of-mission, host country and other related agreements negotiated between the United Nations and those countries, mindful of the importance of the timely conclusion of such agreements, and encourages further efforts in this regard;

16. *Reaffirms* the obligation of all humanitarian personnel and United Nations and associated personnel to respect and, where required, observe the national laws of the country in which they are operating, in accordance with international law and the Charter of the United Nations;

17. *Stresses* the importance of ensuring that humanitarian personnel and United Nations and associated personnel remain sensitive to national and local customs and traditions in their countries of assignment and communicate clearly their purpose and objectives to local populations;

18. *Welcomes* ongoing efforts to promote and enhance security consciousness within the organizational culture of the United Nations system, and urges the Secretary-General to continue to intensify such efforts at all levels of leadership and staff, including by reviewing and further improving, in accordance with established procedures, the unified security management system, as well as by disseminating and ensuring the implementation of security procedures and regulations and ensuring accountability at all levels, and in this regard recognizes the important work of the Department of Safety and Security of the Secretariat;

19. *Takes note* of the report entitled "Towards a Culture of Security and Accountability" of the Independent Panel on Safety and Security of United Nations Personnel and Premises Worldwide, and looks forward to the report of the Secretary-General on measures to follow up on the Panel's recommendations and on the independent process on the issue of accountability, to be submitted for the consideration of the relevant Main Committee of the General Assembly during the sixty-third session;

20. *Emphasizes* the importance of paying special attention to the safety and security of United Nations and associated personnel engaged in United Nations peacekeeping and peacebuilding operations;

21. *Also emphasizes* the need to pay particular attention to the safety and security of locally recruited humanitarian personnel, who are particularly vulnerable to attacks and who account for the majority of casualties and cases of harassment and unlawful detention, requests the Secretary-General to keep under review the relevant internal United Nations policy, operational and administrative arrangements that can contribute to providing locally recruited personnel with adequate safety and security, and calls upon humanitarian organizations to ensure that their staff are adequately informed about and trained in their respective organization's relevant security measures, plans and initiatives, which should be in line with applicable national laws and international law;

22. *Requests* the Secretary-General to continue to take the necessary measures to ensure that United Nations and other personnel carrying out activities in fulfilment of the mandate of a United Nations operation are properly informed about and operate in conformity with the minimum operating security standards and relevant codes of conduct and are properly informed about the conditions under which they are called upon to operate and the standards that they are required to meet, including those contained in relevant national laws and international law, and that adequate training in security, human rights law and international humanitarian law is provided so as to enhance their security and effectiveness in accomplishing their functions, and reaffirms the necessity for all other humanitarian organizations to provide their personnel with similar support;

23. *Welcomes* the ongoing efforts of the Secretary-General and stresses the need to ensure that all United Nations staff members receive adequate security training, including training to enhance cultural awareness, prior to their deployment to the field, as well as the need to attach a high priority to stress management training and related counselling services for United Nations staff throughout the system, and reaffirms the necessity for all other humanitarian organizations to provide their personnel with similar support;

24. *Emphasizes* the importance of information on the range and scope of security incidents involving humanitarian personnel and United Nations and associated personnel, including attacks against them, to clarify their operating environment;

25. *Welcomes* the ongoing efforts of the Secretary-General to further enhance the security management system of the United Nations, and in this regard invites the United Nations and, as appropriate, other humanitarian organizations, working closely with host States, to further strengthen the analysis of threats to their safety and security in order to manage security risks by facilitating informed decisions on the maintenance of an effective presence in the field, inter alia, to fulfil their humanitarian mandate;

26. *Also welcomes* the work of the Secretary-General in enhancing security collaboration with host Governments for the purpose of contributing to staff safety and security, including efforts to support United Nations designated officials with regard to collaboration with host Government authorities;

27. *Calls upon* all relevant actors to make every effort in their public statements to support a favourable environment for the safety and security of humanitarian personnel;

28. *Stresses* that the effective functioning at the country level of security operations requires a unified capacity for policy, standards, coordination, communication, com-

pliance and threat and risk assessment, and notes the benefits thereof to United Nations and associated personnel, including those achieved by the Department of Safety and Security since its establishment;

29. *Requests* the Secretary-General, inter alia, through the Inter-Agency Security Management Network, to continue to promote increased cooperation and collaboration among United Nations departments, organizations, funds and programmes and affiliated international organizations, including between their headquarters and field offices, in the planning and implementation of measures aimed at improving staff security, training and awareness, and calls upon all relevant United Nations departments, organizations, funds and programmes and affiliated international organizations to support those efforts;

30. *Recognizes* the steps taken by the Secretary-General thus far, as well as the need for continued efforts to enhance coordination and cooperation, both at the headquarters and the field levels, between the United Nations and other humanitarian and non-governmental organizations on matters relating to the safety and security of humanitarian personnel and United Nations and associated personnel, with a view to addressing mutual security concerns in the field, taking into account relevant national and local initiatives in this regard, inter alia, those derived from the "Saving Lives Together" framework, encourages collaborative initiatives to address security training needs, invites Member States to consider increasing support to those initiatives, and requests the Secretary-General to report on steps taken in this regard;

31. *Underlines* the need to allocate adequate and predictable resources to the safety and security of United Nations personnel, including through the consolidated appeals process, and encourages all States to contribute to the Trust Fund for Security of Staff Members of the United Nations System, inter alia, with a view to reinforcing the efforts of the Department of Safety and Security for the safety and security of personnel working in emergency and humanitarian operations;

32. *Also underlines* the need for better coordination between the United Nations and host Governments, in accordance with the relevant provisions of international law and national laws, on the use and deployment of essential equipment required to provide for the safety and security of United Nations personnel and associated personnel working in the delivery of humanitarian assistance by United Nations organizations;

33. *Recalls* the essential role of telecommunication resources in facilitating the safety of humanitarian personnel and United Nations and associated personnel, calls upon States to consider acceding to or ratifying the Tampere Convention on the Provision of Telecommunication Resources for Disaster Mitigation and Relief Operations of 18 June 1998, which entered into force on 8 January 2005, and urges them to facilitate and expedite, consistent with their national laws and international obligations applicable to them, the use of communications equipment in such operations, inter alia, by limiting and, whenever possible, expeditiously lifting the restrictions placed on the use of communications equipment by United Nations and associated personnel;

34. *Requests* the Secretary-General to submit to the General Assembly at its sixty-fourth session a comprehensive and updated report on the safety and security of humanitarian personnel and protection of United Nations personnel and on the implementation of the present resolution.

Other staff matters

Managerial efficiency and accountability

Senior Management Network

In accordance with General Assembly resolution 59/268 [YUN 2004, p. 1408], ICSC, in July [A/63/30], considered the development of a Senior Management Network (SMN) (formerly Senior Management Service), the Organization's instrument for building managerial capacity throughout the common system in order to improve performance. ICSC noted that there had been little progress on SMN development, particularly on its establishment, as it was subject to the provision of funds and resources by Member States. However, the first senior management leadership programme, requested by the United Nations System Staff College and prepared by the Rotterdam School of Management on behalf of a consortium of eight universities/business schools, was attended by 47 participants from 30 organizations. In a comprehensive assessment, a steering group confirmed the need for a cross-agency and system-wide leadership development programme, which should be redesigned to focus on change within the UN system and on its leadership competencies. The United Nations Staff College would redesign the programme, and a steering group would oversee its delivery.

ICSC consideration. ICSC reiterated its view on the importance of a system-wide leadership development programme, and inquired why the pilot programme had been conducted only once rather than being tested on a greater variety of participants. ICSC decided to keep the matter under review, and requested the CEB/HR Network to keep it apprised of developments.

Personnel policies

Human resources management

The General Assembly, at its resumed sixty-second session in 2008, had before it reports of the Secretary-General on the staffing of field missions, including the use of 300- and 100-series appointments [YUN, 2007, p. 1509], on detailed proposals for streamlining UN contractual arrangements [ibid., p. 1508] and on the harmonization of conditions of service [ibid., p. 1510], the addendum to the ICSC report for the year 2006 [ibid., p. 1507] and section II of the report of the ACABQ [ibid., p. 1511].

GENERAL ASSEMBLY ACTION

On 3 April [meeting 91], the General Assembly, on the recommendation of the Fifth Committee [A/62/772], adopted **resolution 62/248** without vote [agenda item 133].

Human resources management

The General Assembly,

Recalling its resolutions 59/266 of 23 December 2004, 61/244 of 22 December 2006, section VIII of its resolution 61/276 of 29 June 2007 and section XXI of its resolution 62/238 of 22 December 2007, as well as its other relevant resolutions and decisions,

Having considered the reports of the Secretary-General on the staffing of field missions, including the use of 300- and 100-series appointments, on detailed proposals for streamlining United Nations contractual arrangements and on the harmonization of conditions of service, the addendum to the report of the International Civil Service Commission for the year 2006 and section II of the report of the Advisory Committee on Administrative and Budgetary Questions,

1. *Takes note* of the reports of the Secretary-General on the staffing of field missions, including the use of 300- and 100-series appointments, on detailed proposals for streamlining United Nations contractual arrangements and on the harmonization of conditions of service;

2. *Decides* to continue consideration of the issue of contractual arrangements and conditions of service, including in United Nations field operations, as a matter of priority at the main part of its sixty-third session, taking into account the conclusions and recommendations contained in section II of the report of the Advisory Committee on Administrative and Budgetary Questions, with a view to the implementation of new arrangements and conditions on 1 July 2009.

By **decision 62/545 B** of the same date, the Assembly deferred, until its sixty-third (2008) session, consideration of the reports of the Secretary-General, the ACABQ and ICSC.

Reform of human resources management

In response to General Assembly resolution 61/244 [YUN 2006, p. 1691] the Secretary-General submitted an August report [A/63/282] providing an overview of achievements in implementing the human resources management reform programme and planned future activities. The report was based on the areas addressed in the new human resources framework in the Secretary-General's report on "Investing in people" [YUN 2006, p. 1689], including: recruitment and staffing, mobility, career development and support, contractual arrangements and harmonization of conditions of service, and strengthening leadership and management capacity. It discussed human resources planning and monitoring, national competitive examinations, performance management, administration of justice, human resources information technology, strengthening accountability, and UN health-care services. The Secretary-General invited the Assembly to take note of the achievements and the planned activities.

ACABQ report. In a November report [A/63/526 & Corr.1], ACABQ stated that the Secretary-General's report did not provide sufficient statistical data to substantiate the progress reported, benchmarks against which progress could be measured, and the financial implications of the proposed initiatives, and did not analyse the interrelationship between the various human resources reform proposals, nor convey a sense of the relative priority accorded to each proposal. It emphasized the importance of a phased approach to implementing reform measures to allow sufficient time for improvements to take effect, as well as the need to prioritize such measures. The Advisory Committee expressed concern about the tendency of the Office of Human Resources Management (OHRM) to embark on new reform initiatives without first evaluating the effects of those implemented previously.

ACABQ recommended that the Secretary-General ensure that future reform proposals were accompanied by a comprehensive results and impact assessment of earlier reforms and existing arrangements, as well as a cost-benefit analysis of new initiatives. ACABQ noted the planned introduction of systematic and strategic workforce planning, particularly given the challenges faced by the Organization as a result of the demographic transition in the Secretariat. It urged the Secretary-General to pursue efforts in that area as a matter of priority.

ACABQ stated that, although departmental human resources planning exercises were currently in their fifth cycle, the Secretary-General's report did not contain an analysis of the results achieved to date. Furthermore, there was no indication of how compliance with the goals and targets set out in the action plans and compacts were measured, nor was there any information on measures to deal with the inability or failure to achieve those goals and targets. It recommended that the Assembly request the Secretary-General to carry out such analyses and to report on the results. OHRM should continue to strengthen its monitoring of delegated authority for human resources management, including compliance with geographic and gender targets and the prompt filling of vacancies. The Secretary-General should develop a comprehensive training strategy applicable to staff serving both at Headquarters and in the field based on sound workforce planning techniques and organizational needs. The impact of such programmes on enhancing staff members' ability to discharge their duties should be evaluated and their efficiency and effectiveness reviewed. The Secretary-General should also provide more detailed information on the proposed programme, including on its objectives and relationship with relevant Assembly resolutions and the Staff Regulations and Rules. ACABQ noted the Secretary-General's intention to develop a system for recognizing the contributions of staff during the 2008–2009 biennium, and recommended that it include incentives such as accelerated promotion as a way to motivate and reward staff for excellent performance, as well as sanctions for underperformance. The Secretary-General should indicate the financial and other administrative implications of the proposals and, in future reports on human resources management, respond more specifically to the provisions of resolution 61/244 and subsequent resolutions.

OIOS in-depth evaluation of the Office of Human Resources Management

In August [A/63/221], the Office of Internal Oversight Services (OIOS) submitted a report on the in-depth evaluation of OHRM, in response to the requests of the Committee for Programme and Coordination (CPC), endorsed by the General Assembly in resolution 61/235 [YUN 2006, p. 1636], and of the Assembly in resolution 62/236 [YUN 2007, p. 1441] that OIOS include in that evaluation a review of the recruitment, promotion and mobility policies of the past five years. The objective of the evaluation was to assess the relevance, efficiency, effectiveness and impact of OHRM activities in relation to its objectives. OIOS focused specifically on recruitment, promotion and mobility data, except for peacekeeping missions.

OIOS found that OHRM faced significant challenges as the central authority responsible for simultaneously performing strategic human resources planning and policy development, delegating human resources authority throughout the Secretariat and directly providing many human resources services. In addition, the human resources challenges faced by both OHRM and the Organization defied simple solutions. In each functional human resources area, there was a different set of multifaceted challenges, including complex interrelationships. The enormity of the Organization's human resources demands had hampered the effective capacity of OHRM to meet them fully. To be more effective and to achieve the desired human resources results, OHRM and the United Nations needed to prioritize and identify which human resources initiatives needed to be emphasized. The current level of resources, lack of prioritization and clear policies had resulted in a work overload for both OHRM staff and others performing human resources management functions. Improvements along those lines were needed to enable the United Nations to recruit, retain and develop a worldwide staff that was capable of meeting the many challenges facing the Organization.

OIOS recommended that OHRM develop an integrated framework and strategy to enhance the staff selection process, provide better support for career development and promote staff mobility. A task force or other appropriate body should be set up to propose improvements to current policies and procedures and to the services offered by OHRM. OIOS also recommended that OHRM strengthen its policy development function and corresponding interpretative guidance function; prioritize the implementation of human resources reform initiatives; clarify and streamline the delegation of authority structure; establish a systematic and comprehensive compendium of responsibilities; and strengthen the monitoring function.

GENERAL ASSEMBLY ACTION

On 24 December [meeting 74], the General Assembly, on the recommendation of the Fifth Committee [A/63/639], adopted **resolution 63/250** without vote [agenda item 123].

Human resources management

The General Assembly,

Recalling Articles 8, 97, 100 and 101 of the Charter of the United Nations,

Recalling also its resolutions 49/222 A and B of 23 December 1994 and 20 July 1995, 51/226 of 3 April 1997, 52/219 of 22 December 1997, 52/252 of 8 September 1998, 53/221 of 7 April 1999, 55/258 of 14 June 2001, 57/305 of 15 April 2003, 58/296 of 18 June 2004, 59/266 of 23 December 2004, 60/1 of 16 September 2005, 60/260 of 8 May 2006, 61/244 of 22 December 2006, 61/276, section VIII, of 29 June 2007, 62/238, section XXI, of 22 December 2007 and 62/248 of 3 April 2008, as well as its other relevant resolutions and decisions,

Reaffirming that the staff of the United Nations is an invaluable asset of the Organization, and commending its contribution to furthering the purposes and principles of the United Nations,

Paying tribute to the memory of all staff members who have lost their lives in the service of the Organization,

Having considered the relevant reports on human resources management submitted to the General Assembly,

Having also considered the report of the Office of Internal Oversight Services on an in-depth evaluation of the Office of Human Resources Management and the addendum to the report of the International Civil Service Commission for 2006,

Having further considered the related reports of the Advisory Committee on Administrative and Budgetary Questions,

Endorses the conclusions and recommendations contained in the reports of the Advisory Committee on Administrative and Budgetary Questions, subject to the provisions of the present resolution;

I

Human resources management reform

1. *Emphasizes* the fundamental importance of human resources management reform in the United Nations as a contribution to the strengthening of the international civil service, recalls, in this context, the reports of the International Civil Service Commission, and reaffirms its commitment to the implementation of these reforms;

2. *Stresses* the importance of a meaningful and constructive dialogue between staff and management, in particular on human resources-related issues, and calls upon both parties to intensify efforts to overcome differences and to resume the consultative process;

3. *Expresses concern* over the fact that staff representatives from New York and Geneva have withdrawn from participation in the Staff-Management Coordination Committee, and reiterates its call to the staff representatives from New York and Geneva and management to intensify efforts to overcome differences and to engage in a consultative process;

4. *Requests* the Secretary-General to take advantage of the existing mechanisms for conflict resolution and mediation as deemed useful and appropriate in order to facilitate renewed dialogue between staff and management;

5. *Recalls* section I, paragraphs 1 and 3, of its resolution 61/244, bearing in mind article VIII of the Staff Regulations, and requests the Secretary-General to submit proposals to the General Assembly at its sixty-fifth session to review the staff-management mechanism for addressing human resources management issues, in consultation with relevant bodies;

6. *Takes note* of the report of the Office of Internal Oversight Services on an in-depth evaluation of the Office of Human Resources Management, in particular the recommendations set out in section VI thereof;

7. *Requests* the Secretary-General, taking into account paragraph 22 of the report of the Advisory Committee on Administrative and Budgetary Questions, to ensure that measures to identify and promote future leaders have clear criteria and mechanisms for selection, and that they are implemented within the framework of the staff selection system, and to provide information on their precise financial implications;

II

Contractual arrangements and harmonization of conditions of service

1. *Stresses* the need for rationalization of the current United Nations system of contractual arrangements, which lacks transparency and is complex to administer;

2. *Approves* the new contractual arrangements which would comprise three types of appointments (temporary, fixed-term and continuing), under one set of Staff Rules, effective 1 July 2009, as set out in its resolution 62/248 and subject to the provisions of the present resolution;

3. *Requests* the Secretary-General not to appoint any staff to continuing contracts before 1 January 2010 pending consideration by the General Assembly of the additional information concerning the implementation of continuing contracts;

4. *Also requests* the Secretary-General to report to the General Assembly at its sixty-fourth session on the following issues with a view to the implementation of a system for the continuing appointment regime by 1 January 2010:

(a) Rigorous and transparent procedures for granting continuing appointments to staff, including the criteria for eligibility, the relationship with disciplinary measures and the central management of conversions;

(b) The role of the performance appraisal system and options for strengthening it to ensure that staff members considered for continuing appointments have demonstrated the highest standards of efficiency, competence and integrity, taking into account any deliberations of the International Civil Service Commission on this issue;

(c) The financial and management implications of converting appointments from fixed-term to continuing appointments, and the possible establishment of a ceiling on the number of conversions;

(d) Analysis of the implications of the proposed continuing appointments for the system of geographical ranges;

(e) Rigorous and transparent procedures to review the performance of staff and the continuing need for functions when determining the granting and termination of an appointment of a staff member, as well as clear and firm lines of accountability, to fully ensure that the granting and termination of continuing contracts is undertaken in a fair and transparent manner, with full regard to due process and the rights of staff;

(f) Options for ensuring that successful candidates from national competitive examinations and language staff are not disadvantaged by proposed changes;

(g) Analysis of the implications for Junior Professional Officers;

(h) The potential ramifications of the proposed amendment to staff regulation 9.1;

5. *Decides* to continue to suspend until 30 June 2009 the application of the four-year limit for appointments of limited duration under the 300 series of the Staff Rules in peacekeeping operations;

6. *Authorizes* the Secretary-General, bearing in mind paragraph 5 of the present section, to reappoint under the 100 series of the Staff Rules those mission staff whose service under 300-series contracts has reached the four-year limit by 30 June 2009, provided that their functions have been reviewed and found necessary and that their performance has been confirmed as fully satisfactory;

7. *Decides* that temporary appointments are to be used to appoint staff for seasonal or peak workloads and specific short-term requirements for less than one year but could be renewed for up to one additional year when warranted by surge requirements and operational needs related to field operations and special projects with finite mandates;

8. *Also decides* that staff on temporary contracts would be eligible to receive only the following benefits and allowances: post adjustment; rental subsidy; hazard pay; hardship allowance; the daily subsistence allowance portion of the assignment grant; leave (depending on the length of contract); home leave (per classification of duty station); and limited shipment allowance;

9. *Requests*, in this regard, the Secretary-General to provide information on the circumstances in which the re-

newal of a temporary appointment for up to one additional year could be granted;

10. *Decides* that the field staff serving on 300-series appointments of less than four years who are not performing temporary functions are to be given mission-specific fixed-term contracts until such time as they have gone through a competitive process subject to the review of a central review body;

11. *Also decides* that staff on 100-, 200- and 300-series contracts serving in locations other than peacekeeping operations and special political missions for a cumulative period of more than one year who are not performing temporary functions are to be given fixed-term contracts until such time as they have gone through a competitive process subject to the review of a central review body;

12. *Requests* the Secretary-General to submit to the General Assembly for consideration at the first part of its resumed sixty-third session draft regulations by which the streamlined system of contracts could be implemented;

13. *Also requests* the Secretary-General to evaluate the impact of the implementation of the new system of contracts, including its financial implications, and to report to the General Assembly on this matter no earlier than at its sixty-seventh session;

14. *Further requests* the Secretary-General to discontinue the practice of assigning staff from Headquarters to missions on a travel status basis for a period of more than three months;

15. *Recalls* section V, paragraph 2, of its resolution 51/226, in which it requested the Secretary-General to make efforts to achieve the level of 70 per cent of permanent appointments in posts subject to geographical distribution;

16. *Encourages* the Secretary-General, in accordance with legislative mandates, to ensure a judicious mix of career and fixed-term appointments, so as to have an appropriate balance between institutional memory, long-term commitment and independence and the ability to bring in fresh insight and expertise, and to dismiss non-performing staff;

17. *Recognizes* that an effective and credible performance appraisal system is an important element in the implementation of the new contractual arrangements;

18. *Acknowledges* the need to centrally manage the conversion from fixed-term to continuing appointments on a competitive and transparent basis;

19. *Decides* to revert at its sixty-fifth session to the proposal of the Secretary-General to create a cadre of civilian career peacekeepers in the light of the lessons learned from the implementation of the new arrangements for contracts and conditions of service;

20. *Stresses* that the fair and equitable implementation of new contractual arrangements will be directly linked to the effective functioning of the new system of administration of justice;

21. *Decides* that there shall be no expectations, legal or otherwise, of renewal or conversion of a fixed-term contract, irrespective of the length of service, and requests the Secretary-General to reflect this provision in the rules and regulations as well as offers and letters of appointment;

22. *Also decides* that, in the context of the Secretary-General's proposal, "in the interest of the good administration of the Organization" is to be interpreted principally as a change or termination of a mandate;

23. *Reaffirms* that, while continuing appointments are not implemented, successful candidates from national competitive recruitment examinations and staff from language services after two years of probationary service will continue to be granted open-ended appointments according to the current practice;

24. *Decides* that the period of service of Junior Professional Officers shall not be taken into account as part of the requisite period of service for a continuing appointment;

25. *Notes* that the International Civil Service Commission will be reviewing all separation payments, including the possibility of an end-of-service bonus;

26. *Decides* to designate existing established missions as family missions and existing special missions as non-family missions, effective 1 July 2009;

27. *Also decides* that all staff appointed or assigned to non-family missions shall be installed in accordance with conditions of the United Nations common system, without the special-operations approach;

28. *Requests* the International Civil Service Commission to keep the issue of United Nations common system conditions of service in the field under review;

29. *Decides* to keep the issue of United Nations common system conditions of service in the field under review;

30. *Approves* the introduction of a rest and recuperation scheme to include travel time, appropriate to the location, but no payment of travel to the staff member, for internationally recruited staff members in United Nations field operations to replace the occasional recuperation break, effective 1 January 2009;

III

Recruitment and staffing

1. *Reiterates* that the Secretary-General has to ensure that the highest standards of efficiency, competence and integrity serve as the paramount consideration in the employment of staff, with due regard to the principle of equitable geographical distribution, in accordance with Article 101, paragraph 3, of the Charter of the United Nations;

2. *Reaffirms* that measures on meeting organizational mandates, accountability targets and indicators of achievement, including with respect to geographical distribution of staff and gender balance, contained in human resources action plans and recruitment procedures, including selection decisions, shall fully correspond to the provisions contained in Article 101, paragraph 3, of the Charter as well as in relevant General Assembly mandates;

3. *Notes* that the upcoming demographic transition of United Nations staff will present organizational challenges in terms of staff continuity and possible loss of institutional knowledge as well as opportunities to rejuvenate the Organization;

4. *Emphasizes* the need for strategic workforce planning to proactively support the human resources needs of the United Nations, and in this regard urges the Secretary-General to pursue efforts in this area as a matter of priority;

5. *Urges* the Secretary-General to ensure that outreach activities cover positions both at Headquarters and in the field;

6. *Recognizes* the importance of speeding up the recruitment and staffing process, in accordance with Article 101, paragraph 3, of the Charter, which will ensure that staff are diverse, multi-skilled and versatile;

7. *Acknowledges* the need to simplify the current reference check for speeding up the recruitment process, and requests the Secretary-General to review the procedure and take necessary actions as soon as possible;

8. *Decides* that, in order to ensure the transparency of the recruitment process, all specific vacancy announcements shall continue to be advertised;

9. *Requests* the Secretary-General to continue to ensure equal treatment of candidates with equivalent educational backgrounds during the recruitment process, taking fully into account that Member States have different educational systems and that no education system shall be considered the standard to be applied to the Organization;

10. *Invites* the Secretary-General, when appointing officials at the D-1 and D-2 levels in departments of the Secretariat that provide backstopping and/or policy guidance to field missions, to fully consider the relevant field experience of the candidates, as one of the highly desirable appointment criteria;

11. *Underlines* that the upgraded electronic staff selection system of the United Nations must be clear, simplified, user-friendly and accessible to potential candidates and that regular monitoring must be in place to ensure transparency and non-discrimination, and requests the Secretary-General to report thereon to the General Assembly at its sixty-fifth session;

12. *Recognizes* that pre-screened rosters can considerably expedite the recruitment process in the United Nations;

13. *Notes* that the existing rosters for Headquarters and established duty stations under the current staff selection system have design flaws and have not been utilized widely to fill vacancies;

14. *Acknowledges* the necessity of ensuring transparency and accountability with respect to recruitment of general temporary assistance and consultants;

15. *Reaffirms* section II, paragraph 6, of its resolution 61/244, in which it decided to retain the criterion of geographical status in the staff selection system as one of the key elements to ensure geographical balance at each level for posts subject to geographical distribution;

16. *Requests* the Secretary-General to ensure that all anticipated and immediate vacancies are properly advertised and filled quickly, and to report on the success of this endeavour to the General Assembly at its sixty-fifth session;

17. *Emphasizes* the importance of the participation of staff representatives in the work of the central review bodies, and requests the Secretary-General and invites staff representatives to engage in a consultative process with a view to resuming the participation of staff representatives in the work of the central review bodies;

18. *Requests* the Secretary-General to include analysis of the implementation of the human resources action plans in the context of the report on the composition of the Secretariat;

19. *Recognizes* the added value that a redesign panel could bring to the reform of the recruitment and staffing processes;

20. *Decides* to revert to the issue of establishing a redesign panel for this purpose at its sixty-fifth session;

IV

National competitive examinations

1. *Reaffirms* that national competitive examinations are the source of recruitment for P-2 posts subject to geographical distribution in order to reduce non-representation and underrepresentation of Member States in the Secretariat;

2. *Requests* the Secretary-General to submit to the General Assembly, for consideration at its sixty-fifth session, a feasibility study, building on audit reports, to determine whether the broadening of the scope of the national competitive examination would serve to further strengthen the capacity of the Organization for programme delivery, as recommended by the Advisory Committee on Administrative and Budgetary Questions in its report;

3. *Notes with concern* that a large number of candidates who have passed national competitive examinations remain on the roster for years;

4. *Requests* the Secretary-General to ensure the expeditious placement of successful candidates from national competitive examinations;

5. *Welcomes* the enhanced efforts of the Secretary-General to centrally manage the placement of successful candidates from national competitive examinations, and requests him to intensify these efforts and to report thereon to the General Assembly at its sixty-fifth session;

6. *Requests* the Secretary-General to report to the General Assembly at its sixty-fifth session on the implementation of the recommendations of the Joint Inspection Unit aimed at reducing the length of the national competitive recruitment examination process and improving the national competitive recruitment examination roster management, as well as setting time frames for completion of the process;

7. *Also requests* the Secretary-General, in his capacity as Chairman of the United Nations System Chief Executives Board for Coordination, to further cooperate within the framework of the Human Resources Network, making better use of national competitive recruitment examinations and existing rosters, and improving inter-agency mobility;

8. *Recognizes* the importance of the Secretary-General providing career development opportunities and support, including enhancing mobility for all staff, including those recruited from national competitive examinations;

V

Accountability

1. *Recalls* its resolution 61/244 and all other relevant resolutions on human resources management, including geographical distribution and gender representation in posts, and stresses the accountability of the Secretary-General for implementation and the concrete results obtained for these important principles and mandates;

2. *Emphasizes* that robust and proactive monitoring is essential at all levels, and requests the Secretary-General to ensure that the Office of Human Resources Management continues to strengthen its monitoring of delegated authority for human resources management, including compliance with geographical and gender targets and the prompt filling of vacancies;

3. *Notes* that the senior managers' compacts are meant to improve the management of the Organization, inter alia, by increasing accountability and transparency at the senior level, and in this regard urges the Secretary-General to implement measures that adequately address the performance of senior managers, especially with regard to achieving goals and targets;

VI

Performance appraisal system

1. *Emphasizes* that a credible, fair and fully functioning performance appraisal system is critical to effective human resources management policies;

2. *Expresses concern* over the lack of credibility and effectiveness of the current performance appraisal system, and stresses the need for it to accurately reflect the full range of performance, in order to be able to reward staff for excellent performance and impose sanctions for underperformance and to strengthen the link between performance and career progression, in particular for those staff members in managerial positions;

3. *Notes* the intention of the Secretary-General to begin utilizing 360-degree performance appraisals, and requests the Secretary-General to report to the General Assembly at its sixty-fifth session on how this can be further implemented;

4. *Requests* the Secretary-General to review the current performance appraisal system in consultation with staff through the appropriate channels, and to report thereon to the General Assembly at its sixty-fifth session;

VII

Mobility

1. *Reaffirms* section VIII of its resolution 59/266;

2. *Stresses* that the purpose of enhancing mobility is to improve the effectiveness of the Organization and to foster the skills and capacity of staff;

3. *Decides* to review the regulations and rules of the Organization relating to the exercise by the Secretary-General of his authority to assign and deploy staff according to the operational needs of the Organization, and requests him to submit proposals in this regard to the General Assembly at its sixty-fifth session;

4. *Regrets* that the Secretary-General's mobility policies failed to achieve their intended purposes;

5. *Notes* the intention of the Secretary-General as set out in his report to suspend the managed mobility programmes upon completion of the D-1/D-2 exercise, in order for a review to be undertaken, including on the maximum period of occupancy of post and lessons learned, with a view to developing proposals on the mobility policy, taking into account recommendations of the Task Force on Human Resources Management, in consultation with all relevant stakeholders, including staff associations, and requests him to report thereon to the General Assembly at its sixty-fifth session in the context of his report on human resources management, with an analysis of cost and benefits, bearing in mind paragraph 46 of the report of the Advisory Committee on Administrative and Budgetary Questions;

6. *Requests* the Secretary-General to submit proposals aimed at encouraging voluntary mobility of staff in the context of the review of the mobility policy, without prejudice to the different needs of duty stations and the field;

7. *Emphasizes* that the scope of the mobility policy should be well defined;

VIII

Career development and support

1. *Requests* the Secretary-General, in complying with paragraph 17 of the report of the Advisory Committee on Administrative and Budgetary Questions, to make all possible efforts within existing resources;

2. *Reaffirms* the importance of defining the target and strategy of training and career development;

3. *Requests* the Secretary-General to make full use of the grade structure and to submit a concrete proposal to the General Assembly at the sixty-fifth session on how and where P-1 positions might be used more effectively;

4. *Also requests* the Secretary-General to submit proposals on a strategy to implement an efficient and effective training and professional development programme in the context of the budget submission for the biennium 2010–2011;

5. *Further requests* the Secretary-General to ensure that each vacancy announcement identifies accurately the skills, education and experience required for the position;

6. *Recognizes* the core role played by programme managers in career development and support, and requests the Secretary-General to strengthen the evaluation of their managerial skills and their performance in fostering staff career development;

IX

Measures to improve equitable geographical representation/composition of the Secretariat

1. *Recalls* its resolution 42/220 A of 21 December 1987, by which it introduced the current system of desirable ranges;

2. *Requests* the Secretary-General to continue his ongoing efforts to attain equitable geographical distribution in the Secretariat and to ensure as wide a geographical distribution of staff as possible in all departments, offices and levels, including the Director level and higher levels, of the Secretariat;

3. *Recalls* section X, paragraph 12, of its resolution 61/244, and expresses concern over the increase that has taken place in the number of unrepresented and underrepresented Member States since 2006;

4. *Regrets* the current insufficient accountability of heads of departments in achieving equitable geographical distribution in the Secretariat;

5. *Welcomes* the continuing efforts of the Secretary-General to improve the situation of unrepresented and underrepresented Member States and of those which might

become underrepresented under the system of desirable ranges;

6. *Notes* the analysis of the level of underrepresentation in the reports of the Secretary-General on the composition of the Secretariat;

7. *Reiterates its request* to the Secretary-General to take all necessary measures to ensure, at the senior and policymaking levels of the Secretariat, equitable representation of Member States, especially those with inadequate representation at those levels, and to continue to include relevant information thereon in all future reports on the composition of the Secretariat;

8. *Reiterates its requests* to the Secretary-General to present proposals to effectively increase the representation of developing countries in the Secretariat, and to report thereon to the General Assembly at its sixty-fifth session;

9. *Welcomes* the efforts of the Secretary-General to set specific targets throughout the Organization in order to increase recruitment from unrepresented and underrepresented Member States;

10. *Considers* that encouragement of recruitment from unrepresented and underrepresented Member States as well as gender balance targets shall not disallow other qualified candidates from competing;

11. *Reiterates its request* to the Secretary-General to ensure, through the Management Performance Board, the monitoring of the implementation of human resources action plans, including the principle of equitable geographical distribution in the Secretariat at all levels, as set out in relevant General Assembly resolutions, and the verification of the effective application of measures of transparency and accountability, including in the selection, recruitment and placement processes;

12. *Reiterates its request* as contained in section X, paragraph 8, of its resolution 61/244;

13. *Recalls* paragraph 22 of its resolution 62/250 of 20 June 2008, and requests the Secretary-General to ensure the proper representation of troop-contributing countries in the Department of Peacekeeping Operations and the Department of Field Support, of the Secretariat, taking into account their contribution to United Nations peacekeeping;

14. *Re-emphasizes* that the system of geographical ranges was designed to apply to countries rather than to regions or groups;

15. *Recalls its request* to the Secretary-General to reduce, to the extent possible, the number of unrepresented and underrepresented Member States in the Secretariat by 30 per cent by 2010, compared to the level in 2006, and requests him to report to the General Assembly thereon, as appropriate, in the context of his report on human resources management;

16. *Reaffirms* that the system of desirable ranges is the mechanism for recruitment of staff to posts subject to geographical distribution, in accordance with Article 101, paragraph 3, of the Charter;

17. *Recognizes* that considerable change has taken place in the composition and the number of staff of the global United Nations Secretariat in the past two decades, recalls the reports of the Secretary-General, and requests him to submit to the General-Assembly, at its sixty-fifth session, proposals for a comprehensive review of the system of desirable ranges, with a view to establishing a more effective tool to ensure equitable geographical distribution in relation to the total number of staff of the global United Nations Secretariat;

18. *Requests* the Secretary-General to gradually incorporate within his report on the composition of the Secretariat the overall number of staff, regardless of sources of funding, on contracts of one year or more;

19. *Reiterates its request* as contained in section X, paragraph 15, of its resolution 61/244, and recalls section II, paragraph 2, of its resolution 42/220 A;

X

Gender representation

1. *Reaffirms* the goal of 50/50 gender distribution in all categories of posts within the United Nations system, especially at senior and policymaking levels, with full respect for the principle of equitable geographical distribution, in conformity with Article 101 of the Charter, and regrets that progress towards attaining this goal has been slow;

2. *Expresses concern* at the continuing low proportion of women in the Secretariat, in particular the low proportion of women from developing countries, especially at the senior levels, and stresses that, in the recruitment process, the continuing lack of representation or underrepresentation of women from certain countries, in particular from developing countries, should be taken into account and that those women should be accorded equal opportunities, in full conformity with relevant resolutions;

3. *Notes with concern* that, in posts subject to the system of desirable ranges, only 33 women from developing countries were recruited between 1 July 2007 and 30 June 2008 among the 96 women appointed during that period;

4. *Requests* the Secretary-General to increase his efforts to attain and monitor the goal of gender parity in the Secretariat, in particular at senior levels, and in this context to ensure that women, especially those from developing countries and countries with economies in transition, are appropriately represented within the Secretariat, and to report thereon to the General Assembly at its sixty-fifth session;

5. *Notes* the renewed effort the Secretary-General has made towards attaining this goal, particularly the decision to design and implement a forward-looking strategy under the leadership of the Deputy Secretary-General, and encourages him to further strengthen these efforts;

6. *Requests* the Secretary-General, in the context of attaining this goal, to develop and implement recruitment targets, time frames for meeting those targets and accountability measures;

7. *Encourages* Member States to support the efforts of the Secretary-General by identifying more women candidates and encouraging them to apply for appointment to positions in the Secretariat and by creating awareness among their nationals, in particular women, of vacancies in the Secretariat;

XI

Consultants, individual contractors, gratis personnel and employment of retired staff

1. *Requests* the Secretary-General to adhere to existing guidelines on the selection and recruitment of consultants and individual contractors;

2. *Expresses concern* over the increase in the use of consultants, especially in the core activities of the Organization, stresses that the use of consultants should be governed by the relevant resolutions of the General Assembly, in particular resolution 53/221, section VIII, and that they should be drawn from the widest possible geographical basis, and requests the Secretary-General to make the greatest possible use of in-house capacity and to report to the Assembly at its sixty-fifth session on the measures taken to that effect;

3. *Reiterates its concern* that the continuous trend of hiring staff retirees for extended periods of time increased in the last biennium;

4. *Reiterates* that employment of retirees in decision-making positions should occur only in exceptional circumstances;

5. *Requests* the Secretary-General to include, in future reports on the employment of retirees, analysis on reasons for patterns and trends that emerge from data presented;

XII

Report of the Ethics Office

1. *Notes with appreciation* the contributions of the Ethics Office to promoting integrity within the Organization;

2. *Welcomes* the establishment of the United Nations Ethics Committee;

3. *Requests* the Secretary-General to clarify the roles of the Ethics Office, the Office of the Ombudsman, the Office of Internal Oversight Services and other related offices, and to report the findings, as well as the measures taken to avoid overlapping of mandates, to the General Assembly at its sixty-fifth session;

4. *Also requests* the Secretary-General to discuss with the executive heads of the specialized agencies, funds and programmes, within the framework of the United Nations System Chief Executives Board for Coordination, areas of possible cooperation and cost savings on ethics-related matters;

5. *Further requests* the Secretary-General to include in his report on the activities of the Ethics Office, information on the activities of the Ethics Committee, including a review of any complex ethics issues dealt with by the Committee, if deemed relevant;

XIII

Other matters

1. *Notes with concern* that many disciplinary cases have not been completed in a reasonable time, and requests the Secretary-General to include in his annual report information on measures taken to increase the number of cases closed;

2. *Invites* the Sixth Committee to consider the legal aspects of the report of the Secretary-General entitled "Implementation of the Regulations Governing the Status, Basic Rights and Duties of Officials other than Secretariat Officials and Experts on Mission" without prejudice to the role of the Fifth Committee as the Main Committee of the General Assembly responsible for administrative and budgetary matters;

3. *Requests* the Secretary-General to report to the General Assembly at its sixty-fifth session on the implementation of the human resources management information technology system;

4. *Also requests* the Secretary-General to strengthen programmes to promote health in hardship posts, including through psychological support and disease awareness, with a view to promoting productivity and a better work environment;

5. *Takes note* of the report of the Secretary-General on measures to address the imbalance in the geographical distribution of the staff in the Office of the United Nations High Commissioner for Human Rights;

6. *Also takes note* of the amendments to the Staff Rules as contained in the annex to the above-mentioned report.

Also on 24 December, the Assembly decided that the agenda item on human resources management would remain for consideration during its resumed sixty-third (2009) session (**decision 63/552**).

Contractual arrangements and harmonization of conditions of service

Reports of Secretary-General. Pursuant to General Assembly resolution 60/1 [YUN 2005, p. 48], the Secretary-General submitted an August report [A/63/298], which summarized his proposals for streamlining UN contractual arrangements and harmonizing conditions of service, including for UN field operations [YUN 2007, pp. 103, 1508 & 1510]. Under the proposed system, a single series of staff rules would provide for one UN staff contract, encompassing three types of appointments: a temporary appointment, which would cover up to a maximum period of one year (or up to two years to meet surge needs in the field), for staff appointed to meet seasonal or peak workloads and specific short-term requirements; a fixed-term appointment, which could cover up to a period of five years; and a continuing appointment, which would be open-ended. The Secretary-General added that should the Assembly approve his proposals, permanent appointments would be discontinued as from 1 July 2009. Any change of contractual framework would not, however, affect staff holding permanent appointments or staff who would have acquired rights under existing rules to be considered for permanent appointments by the time the change became effective. The simplified contractual framework would address the issues raised by the Assembly by providing clarity, transparency and fairness for all concerned and help to better attract and retain skilled, experienced and qualified civilian staff for all parts of the Secretariat, including in the field. The new single set of rules would be more user-friendly, facilitate mobility and be more efficient to administer, in particular in the context of the development and implementation of the upcoming enterprise resource planning system.

He recommended that the Assembly approve the new contractual arrangements and conditions of service contained in the report and the amendments to the Staff Regulations contained in a July report [A/63/189]; the establishment of 2,500 civilian career peacekeepers; and the proposals to designate missions as family or non-family in harmony with the practice of UN agencies, funds and programmes, effective 1 July 2009, to introduce the special operations approach in non-family duty stations, effective 1 July 2009 with implementation in April 2010, and to replace the occasional recuperation break with paid rest and recuperation travel, effective 1 July 2009. He also requested that an additional $9,469,000 be appropriated for special political missions for the period from 1 July to 31 December 2009, and that the Assembly note that resource requirements for those missions for future periods beginning 1 January 2010, and for peacekeeping missions for the period beginning 1 July 2009, would be incorporated in the budgets for the respective missions.

ACABQ report. In November [A/63/526 & Corr.1], ACABQ noted that the Secretary-General had merely presented an outline of the procedures as to the cases of staff members eligible for consideration for a continuing appointment, which would be reviewed by an advisory body. Further details, in particular the modalities for determining whether there was a continuing need for an individual staff member's services, should be elaborated and presented to the Assembly, together with information about the composition of the advisory body and its rules of procedure. Given the significant role played by the performance appraisal system in the proposed conversion procedure, ACABQ stated that it was all the more important to strengthen that system. It concurred with the Secretary-General that it was important to avoid creating different categories of staff with different thresholds for consideration for a continuing appointment and recommended that all staff, regardless of the mode of recruitment, be eligible for consideration for a continuing appointment after five years of continuous service on fixed-term appointments.

While reiterating that a prudent approach to conversions would be required, ACABQ recommended against the establishment of a ceiling on the number of yearly conversions to continuing appointments at the current stage. It noted that conversion would, in any case, be an inherently phased process. On the issue of procedures for the termination of continuing contracts, ACABQ noted the Secretary-General's effort to respond to its request in its previous report on human resources management [YUN 2007, p. 1509]. However, the proposed internal procedure for termination continued to lack clarity. As to the issue of an end-of-service grant for staff holding fixed-term appointments, ACABQ recommended deferring a decision until ICSC had concluded its deliberations on the matter. Concerning staff in the Field Service category, ACABQ noted that the impact of the Secretary-General's proposals on that category of staff should have been presented earlier, given that they accounted for a large portion of the international staff population. Furthermore, harmonization should not reduce the overall compensation of staff already serving.

By section VIII of **resolution 63/263** of 24 December (see p. 1547), the General Assembly approved, in connection with the harmonization of contractual arrangements, an additional appropriation of $13,165,400 under the 2008–2009 programme budget, and requested the Secretary-General to include $80,900,900 in the respective budgets of affected peacekeeping missions from 1 July 2009 to 30 June 2010.

Staffing of field missions

By **decision 62/549** of 20 June, the General Assembly, having considered the Secretary-General's 2007 report [YUN 2007, p. 1509] on the reappointment of mission staff who had reached the four-year limit under 300-series appointments of limited duration by 31 December 2006 and 30 June 2007, respectively, submitted in response to resolution 61/244 [YUN 2006, p. 1691], decided to continue to suspend the application of the four-year maximum limit for appointments of limited duration until 31 December 2008. It authorized the Secretary-General to reappoint, under the 100-series of the Staff Rules, those mission staff whose service under 300-series contracts reached the four-year limit by 31 December 2008, provided that their functions were reviewed and found necessary and their performance was confirmed as fully satisfactory. It also requested the Secretary-General to continue the practice of using 300-series contracts as the primary instrument for the appointment of new staff.

Mobility

In response to General Assembly resolution 61/244 [YUN 2006, p. 1691], the Secretary-General submitted an August report [A/63/208] on the implementation of the mobility policy, which was a follow-up to his 2007 report on the subject [YUN 2007, p. 1514]. The Secretary-General stated that, under the managed reassignment programme, the percentage of staff who had reached maximum post occupancy was minimal. Owing to the extensive informational campaign undertaken by OHRM, from the inception of the mobility policy in 2002, to raise awareness about the advantages of movement, it was expected that many, if not most, would have already taken steps to move to other positions. According to data derived from human resources action plans, the staff mobility index had increased significantly, from 10.8 per cent in 2002 to 27.6 per cent in 2007. That increase confirmed that greater awareness and a proactive approach, coupled with expanded learning and career development programmes, would lead to increased mobility outside of managed reassignment.

In 2008, a working group comprising staff and management representatives to monitor the implementation of the mobility policy presented its observations and recommendations to the Staff Management Coordination Committee (SMCC). The working group concluded that there was no contention between staff and management on the broad concept of mobility, and that there was general agreement that mobility would strengthen the Organization and the skill sets of staff members. However, there were diverging views on the success of the managed mobility programme, the mechanisms used to implement the programme and the need to treat all categories of staff equally. The working group identified many areas that required clarification and/or review in determining the way forward, including the outcome of the Assembly's deliberations on related human resources matters, such as the harmonization of contracts and conditions of service.

The Secretary-General concluded that the United Nations would continue to refine the mobility policy in the light of experience. As endorsed by SMCC, the managed reassignment programmes would be suspended in their current format after the final exercise was concluded for staff at the D-1 and D-2 levels. A comprehensive review of the mobility policy would be undertaken in consultation with all stakeholders, including staff, managers and Member States. The policy would need to be further refined and take into account recommendations from the Task Force on Human Resources Management. The Secretary-General recommended that the following mobility policy elements be reviewed: functional and occupational mobility for staff at the Professional and higher levels with a view to increasing geographical mobility; enforcement of post occupancy limits; incentives for staff members to move to duty stations with high vacancy rates; ways to address challenges faced by families and non-traditional arrangements; exchange programmes with international organizations outside the UN system; ways to enhance career development of locally recruited staff in lieu of managed reassignment programmes; and mapping of rotational/non-rotational posts. He also recommended instituting a programme to publicly recognize and reward service in the field; incorporating a mobility requirement in new offers of appointment, reappointments and contracts for Professional staff with appointments of one year or longer; undertaking additional efforts to address work and life issues; and establishing occupational networks.

ACABQ report. In November [A/63/526 & Corr.1], ACABQ expressed support for the Secretary-General's intention to suspend the managed reassignment programmes and to undertake a comprehensive review of the mobility policy. It also concurred with the Secretary-General that the recommendations of the Task Force on Human Resources Management be taken into account during the review. It noted, however, that the issue of career development for local staff was an ongoing management function that should not be addressed in the context of mobility. It considered that the possible inclusion of a mobility requirement in new offers of appointment required further discussion in the context of the review of the mobility policy. It requested the Secretary-General, within the framework of the review, to respond fully to the Assembly's requests contained in resolution 61/244 and other resolutions.

Recruitment and staffing

In response to General Assembly resolution 61/244 [YUN 2006, p. 1691], which called upon him to further elaborate the use of pre-screened rosters, the Secretary-General, in an August report [A/63/285], provided information on progress made in advancing the reform proposals on recruitment and staffing presented in his reports "Investing in people" [YUN 2006, p. 1689] and "Human resources management reform: recruitment and staffing" [YUN 2007, p. 1511]. The Secretary-General proposed the introduction of a talent management framework, of which rosters were an important element, as a crucial step in speeding up recruitment and ensuring that the Organization was better equipped to meet current challenges and future staffing needs, while increasing opportunities for career development. The target was to reduce staff recruitment from the current average of 162 days (previously 174) to 100 days. The framework would consist of four elements: workforce planning, which would enable the Organization to undertake proactive efforts to meet its current and future needs; staffing through recruitment and targeted outreach and roster management; performance management; and staff development.

The use of prescreened rosters would ensure that the quality of candidates remained high, and would be used for all types of staff and personnel, including consultants and individual contractors. The roster-based process would be supported by workforce planning, generic vacancy announcements, panels of experts in relevant fields, central review bodies, and centralized background checking and help desk support. Rosters would be managed to ensure that candidates were available and interested in specific vacancies and that there were sufficient numbers of candidates for selection for current and anticipated vacancies. Candidates would remain on the roster for three years, with the possibility of extension for a further two years. At the end of five years, candidates would be removed from the roster. The framework would be implemented through an e-staffing support tool, which would replace the current Galaxy recruitment system. Preparatory work on the roster-based system would commence in early 2009. The rosters would be phased in for certain types of functions, in addition to existing rosters, starting in mid-2009, as a transitional measure before full-scale application by the end of 2009. In that way, the new work processes involved in the application of the roster system could be tested and refined. To handle the anticipated large increase in workload for the clearance of candidates (three times the current volume) and in support provided to users, associated resource requirements would be considered in the context of the 2010–2011 budgetary framework. The Secretary-General requested the Assembly to approve the establishment of a roster-based approach for selection of staff for an initial period of one year, as well as the reduction in the period for the circulation of vacancy announcements from 60 days to 30 days.

ACABQ report. In November [A/63/526 & Corr.1], ACABQ noted the emphasis on outreach and urged the Secretary-General to ensure that outreach activities focused on positions both at Headquarters and in the field. It stressed that the preparation and maintenance of rosters could involve considerable human and financial resources and cautioned that experience had shown that rosters were not a panacea for the difficulties affecting the recruitment and staffing system. It welcomed the reduction in the average time taken to fill vacancies (162 days in 2007, as compared to 174 days previously) and hoped that, once all the elements of the talent management framework were in place, the target of 100 days set by the Secretary-General would be reached.

ACABQ recommended that the Secretary-General further clarify the envisaged role of the central review bodies. In its view, the report would have benefited from the inclusion of more detailed information about the composition and functioning of the panels of experts in particular occupational groups, which would determine the suitability of internal and external candidates for the types of occupations and levels for which they had expressed interest. ACABQ shared the concerns expressed by Member States that reducing the period of advertising vacancies from 60 days to a shorter period would be a disadvantage to potential candidates from some States which had limited access to the UN website due to technology gaps, and recommended against reducing the period for advertising individual vacancies from 60 to 30 days.

ACABQ was of the opinion that the proposed roster-based approach had not been sufficiently elaborated and asked the Secretary-General to present more detailed proposals to the Assembly, prepared on the basis of an in-depth evaluation of the current roster system for Headquarters and the field.

National competitive recruitment examination

JIU report. In February [A/62/707], the Secretary-General transmitted to the General Assembly the Joint Inspection Unit (JIU) report entitled "Review of the national competitive recruitment examination as a recruitment tool".

JIU found that since the establishment of the national competitive recruitment examination (NCRE) in 1980 by Assembly resolution 35/210 [YUN 1980, p. 1164] for hiring staff at the P-l and P-2 levels, it had been used as a recruitment tool by the Secretariat to select highly qualified young professionals at entry level (P-2), through competitive examinations offered to countries that were not represented or adequately represented in the Secretariat. It consisted of a written examination and an interview, and roster management and placement. Successful candidates were put on the roster, and programme managers could select and recruit from the roster for a vacant P-2 post. In general, the examination served well the objectives set by the Assembly and provided the Organization with highly qualified entry-level Professional staff. It was a useful, objective and competitive tool and programme managers were generally satisfied with the performance of staff so recruited. JIU noted that the examination, offered only to nationals from unrepresented or under-represented countries in the Secretariat, served the purpose of improving the geographical composition of the Secretariat and contributed to the equitable geographical representation set by the Assembly. However, since it was only one of the recruitment channels used by the Organization, it alone could not secure the required geographical distribution of staff.

OHRM statistics for 2002 to 2006 showed that the examination did help to improve the gender balance in the composition of the Secretariat. The proportion of female staff among the NCRE-recruited staff was 56.8 per cent. The average cost of putting a successful candidate onto the roster over the past several years varied between $5,700 and $17,400, depending on the number of applicants in a given year. The Inspectors were of the opinion that the system was a cost-effective recruitment tool, compared with the normal fees of specialized headhunting companies, as well as the costs of recruitment in some international organizations outside the United Nations. However, the excessively long duration of the NCRE cycle, two years, with final placement taking a further six months to three years, made the exercise too slow to meet the Organization's demands and the legitimate expectations of the candidates on the roster. To ensure the stability, consistency, accountability and transparency of the process, administrative regulations governing NCRE were needed. The planning process was unreliable and was not part of the Organization's overall strategic labour force planning. The roster management phase of the process faced problems and operational difficulties, such as the high number of candidates and long waiting period on the roster, the significant level of vacancies in P-2 posts, the lack of online access and search tools in the roster database for use by programme managers, the inadequate update of the roster database, the recruitment freeze from the roster in some months to implement other recruitment exercises, and the lack of effective information technology to support communication between candidates, OHRM and programme managers. Comprehensive operational measures were needed to address those difficulties.

On the strategic level, there was a need for increased "corporate responsibility" at the operational managers and senior management levels, and a long-term strategy for the future operation of NCRE in the overall UN recruitment process. JIU also called for closer cooperation on the competitive examination among UN organizations. Mutual recognition of test results or interactions on a better utilization of rosters could be beneficial for the recruitment process of other UN organizations, and would also improve and facilitate future inter-agency mobility. JIU recommended that the Assembly request the Secretary-General to report to its sixty-third session on the implementation of the recommendations, in particular those aimed at reducing the length of the NCRE process and improving the roster management. He should regulate, through an administrative issuance, the entire NCRE process, including the announcement, convocation and organization, with clear delegation of authority on the different elements in the decision-making and operational processes, and elaborate and implement measures to reduce the length of the process, in particular the examination process, by investing commensurate financial resources, and with the exact dates of the beginning and end of the examination phase made public. The Secretary-General should elaborate and implement an action plan for reorganizing the NCRE roster management system to address the identified weaknesses.

In his comments on the JIU report [A/62/707/Add.1], the Secretary-General concurred with a number of the recommendations, since the Organization was actively addressing them, but said that others would require policy decisions by the Assembly.

Report of Board of Auditors. The United Nations Board of Auditors, in its 2008 report [A/63/5 (Vol. 1)], stated that the theoretical duration of NCRE was 22 months, with the examination itself taking 11 months. That period did not take into account the process of selecting the successful candidates accepted into the pool. That time frame appeared excessive. The real time was actually much longer for certain tests owing to a lack of available examiners. The time could be reduced through continuous needs planning. OHRM could carry out the meetings with the Member States concurrently and reduce the time for marking the written exam and convocations for the oral exams. The current marking times were also excessive. In addition, the Board deemed it necessary for the dates for publishing the results to be posted and respected.

The Board recommended that the Administration ensure that OHRM implemented measures to reduce the actual duration of NCRE.

ACABQ report. In November [A/63/526 & Corr.1], ACABQ agreed with the JIU assessment and drew attention to the Ombudsman's comment that many of the candidates recruited had difficulty moving from the P-2 to the P-3 level. It recommended that the shortcomings identified by the Board of Auditors, JIU and the Ombudsman be addressed, and urged the Secretary-General to accelerate the recruitment of candidates who had passed NCRE. It also recommended that the Assembly consider requesting, for consideration at its sixty-fifth (2010) session, a feasibility study, which would build on reports of oversight bodies, to determine whether broadening the scope of NCRE would serve to further strengthen the Organization's capacity for programme delivery.

National Professional Officers

In March [A/62/762], the Secretary-General submitted a report on National Professional Officers, as requested by the General Assembly in resolution 61/276 [YUN 2007, p. 79], which described the experience in the use of those officers in UN peace operations and made recommendations for addressing challenges in attracting, recruiting and retaining them.

In 1980, ICSC decided to permit the use of National Professional Officers for functions in non-headquarters offices which, by their nature, required national knowledge and experience and could not be carried out effectively by international Professionals. ICSC established the criteria for recruiting them, which were adopted by the Assembly in resolution 49/223 [YUN 1994, p. 1374]. The number of such officer posts in UN peace operations had increased by 234 per cent, from 306 in January 2004 to 1,023 as at 31 December 2007. While missions recognized the value of their role in implementing the mission mandate, recruiting them in post-conflict environments within the ICSC framework posed significant challenges. The average vacancy rate for those posts was 38 per cent as at 31 December 2007, compared with an average vacancy rate of 13 per cent for national staff in the General Service category in field missions. Despite intensive recruitment efforts, UN peace operations invariably encountered difficulties in attracting, recruiting and retaining National Professional Officers in post-conflict environments. While missions' recruitment experiences varied in response to the unique conditions prevailing in the mission area, the difficulties could generally be attributed to a lack of required academic qualifications, a lack of professional work experience, inability to verify credentials, competition in the local marketplace for professional skills, limitations on the use of National Professional Officers and a lack of qualified candidates for positions in remote locations. Addressing those challenges required a degree of flexibility in applying recruitment standards, which would enable individual missions to respond to their unique requirements while respecting the integrity of the National Professional Officer programme and the established ICSC criteria.

The Secretary-General sought the Assembly's endorsement for his proposed flexibility measures to address those challenges. Those were: in situations where educational institutions had not been functioning for prolonged periods and difficulty had been encountered in recruiting National Professional Officers owing to a lack of candidates with a first-level university degree, missions should be given the flexibility to address the problem on a temporary basis, taking into account the unique challenges at the duty station; in situations where National Professional Officer candidates were unable to produce a university degree that was reported lost or destroyed during hostilities or where it had not been possible to verify prior professional experience, missions should be given the flexibility to recruit candidates based on the information provided in the personal history profile, while continuing to make their best efforts to obtain verification of academic qualifications and/or prior professional experience; where it was difficult to identify National Professional Officer candidates with the required prior professional experience, missions should be given the flexibility to recruit National Professional Officers who possessed a university degree at the entry level without the requirement for any previous professional experience, on a probationary basis; and National Professional Officers should be employed in UN peace operations in non-field locations, such as the United Nations Logistics Base in Brindisi, Italy, and the United Nations Peacekeeping Force in Cyprus, where the functions required knowledge of the local language or institutions.

Ethics Office

In response to General Assembly resolution 60/254 [YUN 2006, p. 1633], the Secretary-General submitted an August report [A/63/301] on the activities of the Ethics Office from 1 August 2007 to 31 July 2008. During that period, the Office continued to develop ethical standards; ensure annual training on ethics issues to enhance awareness of ethics, integrity and accountability, in collaboration with OHRM; provide confidential advice and guidance to individual staff, staff groups and departments and offices; administer the financial disclosure programme in order to maintain and enhance public trust in the integrity of the Organization; and implement procedures and methodology associated with the policy on protection against retaliation for reporting misconduct and for cooperating with audits or investigations, in collaboration with OIOS.

The Office responded to 446 staff requests for its services: 77 per cent involved ethics advice; 10 per cent were related to protection against retaliation for reporting misconduct; 6 per cent to standard-setting; 4 per cent to general information; and 3 per cent to training. New York accounted for 58 per cent of the requests; peacekeeping operations and tribunals, 12 per cent; Offices in Geneva, Vienna and Nairobi together, 11 per cent; UN bodies and agencies, 9 per cent; others, 5 per cent; regional commissions, 4 per cent; and Member States, 1 per cent. Requests were received from staff at different levels across the Secretariat, with the Professional levels accounting for 60 per cent, and the General Service and related categories, 11 per cent. Concerning financial disclosure, of the 2,528 staff members required to file a financial disclosure or declaration of interest statement in the filing period from 1 January to 31 December 2006, 2,329 or 92 per cent of staff complied with their obligation. The remaining 8 per cent consisted of 1 per cent who were not required to file as a consequence of retirement or separation from service and 7 per cent (172 staff members) who were referred to OHRM for disciplinary action. The Ethics Office received 45 complaints of retaliation, 18 of which warranted a preliminary review. Of the 27 remaining complaints, 9 were determined to fall outside the scope of the mandate, and 13 were provided with advice and guidance on recourse to more appropriate mechanisms.

The Secretary-General noted the increased demand for the service of the Office and the growing complexity of the requests. The broad diversity of the sources of the requests reaffirmed the Office's relevance and contribution to building a culture of ethics and integrity in the United Nations. A challenge for the Office was increasing the awareness and compliance of staff members with the financial disclosure programme and ensuring that conflicts of interest were prevented and managed at the outset. The programme represented a significant contribution to enhancing accountability efforts and the ethical mindset of the Organization. The Secretary-General concluded that the Ethics Office should continue to be a leading player in advocating adherence to shared organizational values and principles, with the goal of preserving its independence and impartiality and meeting the expectations of the Organization and staff alike. He recommended that the Assembly encourage UN specialized agencies and other entities to participate in the Ethics Committee through a memorandum of understanding or other arrangements.

ACABQ report. In November [A/63/526 & Corr.1], ACABQ noted that the Secretary-General's report did not include a clear description of the Office's workplan or an assessment of the impact of its activities. Furthermore, the information on the financial disclosure programme was unclear and lacked analysis. Accordingly, ACABQ recommended that in future reports, the Secretary-General should provide clear and precise data by duty station on the number of individuals covered by the programme, those who had complied with their filing obligations, and those who had failed to do so and the reasons for their failure to comply. To avoid confusion among staff members in terms of the appropriate mechanism or office to address their grievances, ACABQ stressed that staff should be provided with information on the role of the Ethics Office, the Office of the Ombudsman, the OHRM Administrative Law Unit, OIOS and other relevant offices and their interrelationship. In the next report on the question, the Secretary-General should further clarify the issue of the overlapping mandates of those offices. ACABQ encouraged the Ethics Office and OHRM to continue to work on integrating ethics training into the curriculum of regular training offered at the Secretariat. Care should be taken, however, to ensure that the Ethics Office did not duplicate the work of other departments and entities and, in particular, that ethics training modules were incorporated into training activities in substantive areas to the extent possible. ACABQ noted that it was within the purview of the Secretary-General to bring issues relating to system-wide coordination to the attention of CEB members. In that connection, the Assembly should request him to discuss with the executive heads of the UN specialized agencies, funds and programmes, within the CEB framework, areas of possible cooperation on ethics-related matters.

Staff composition

In a September annual report on the UN Secretariat's staff composition [A/63/310], the Secretary-General provided information on the demographic characteristics of the staff and on the system of desirable ranges for geographical distribution. The report, covering the period from 1 July 2007 to 30 June 2008, reviewed the global population of Secretariat staff, staff with contracts of one year or more, staff appointed under the 100 series of the Staff Rules with contracts of one year or more and those in posts subject to geographical distribution. The report also included information on all staff with valid contracts irrespective of the funding source, type of engagement, duration of contract, level or duty station, including locally recruited consultants and contractors working in field operations.

The report noted that the global number of Secretariat staff as at 30 June 2008 totalled 39,503, including 2,076 in the Tribunals. Of that number, 29,274 held contracts of one year or more. The increase in the global workforce of 8 per cent (2,924 staff), compared with 30 June 2007, was due mainly to the growth of peacekeeping missions. The number of staff in the Professional and higher categories was 11,142 (28.2 per cent), and 28,361 (71.8 per cent) in the General Service and related categories. Staff in field missions administered by the Department of Field Support (DFS) numbered 21,790 (55.2 per cent of the global Secretariat workforce). Of the global Secretariat staff, 25,928 (65.6 per cent) were men, while women accounted for 13,575 (34.4 per cent). Of the local staff in field missions administered by DFS, 82.9 per cent were men. Nationals of 187 Member States were represented in the Secretariat: 176 States were represented by staff in posts subject to geographical distribution, while 5 had no nationals among staff. In the Secretariat, 16 Member States were unrepresented, two fewer than in June 2007, while 24 were under-represented and 21 over-represented, as against 19 and 22, respectively, the previous year. The remaining 131 States were within range. Appointments to posts subject to geographical distribution totalled 176.

The report also provided information on the demographic profile of Secretariat staff, including the breakdown of staff by department or office, gender, age and length of service, and movements of staff, covering recruitment, promotion, transfer, separation, turnover and forecasts of anticipated retirements between 2008 and 2012. In addition, the report analysed the implementation status of geographical representation of staff at the senior and policymaking levels, the human resources action planning system and the level of under-representation in the composition of the Secretariat.

Measures to improve the balance in the geographical distribution of OHCHR staff

In response to General Assembly resolution 62/236 [YUN 2007, p. 1441], the Secretary-General submitted a July report [A/63/204] on the measures taken in the Office of the United Nations High Commissioner for Human Rights (OHCHR) to improve the geographical distribution of staff (see p. 719).

ACABQ report. In November [A/63/526 & Corr.1], ACABQ suggested that the Secretary-General report on how progress in geographical representation was measured and achieved, including through the use of senior managers' compacts, human resources action plans and outreach activities, and include statistical information on geographical distribution by country in future reports.

Gratis personnel

Responding to General Assembly resolutions 51/243 [YUN 1997, p. 1469] and 57/281 B [YUN 2003, p 1448], the Secretary-General submitted his biennial report [A/63/310/Add.1] on the use of gratis personnel between 1 January 2006 and 31 December 2007. The number of type I gratis personnel (associate experts, technical cooperation experts and interns) increased from 1,767 in 2006 to 1,952 in 2007. A total of 125 nationalities were represented, compared to 120 in 2006. Women constituted 60 per cent and 64 per cent in 2006 and 2007, respectively, while interns continued to constitute the majority of type I personnel for both years. The number of associate experts increased to 252 in 2007, compared to 233 in 2006, while the number of technical cooperation experts increased from 18 in 2006 to 25 in 2007.

A total of 54 type II gratis personnel (provided by Governments or other entities) representing 10 nationalities were employed in 2007, which was a significant rise from 2006 figures. The average duration of service for type II gratis personnel decreased from 4.3 months per year in 2006 to 3.9 months per year in 2007. Female representation in that category rose from 30 per cent in 2006 to 41 per cent in 2007.

ACABQ report. In November [A/63/526 & Corr.1], ACABQ, noting that the eight separate tables providing data, separately and by year, on nationality, gender, departmental assignment and functions performed by each type of gratis personnel, made it difficult to compare trends for each year of the biennium, reiterated its request that the format of the tables be streamlined so as to consolidate the information for the two years of the biennium into a single table.

Employment of retirees

In response to General Assembly resolutions 57/305 [YUN 2003, p. 1440], 59/266 [YUN 2004, p. 1418] and 61/244 [YUN 2006, p. 1691], the Secretary-General submitted an August report [A/63/310/Add.2] on the employment of retired staff in the UN Secretariat during the 2006–2007 biennium. Some 979 UN retirees, representing 98 nationalities, were employed, an increase of 99.4 and 32.4 per cent in the number hired and in national representation, respectively. The six departments/offices accounting for most of the retirees engaged (63.2 per cent) included the Department for General Assembly and Conference Management, which hired 24.3 per cent of the total; the United Nations Office at Geneva (12.8 per cent); the Department of Economic and Social Affairs (DESA) (7.4 per cent); the Economic Commission for Latin America and the Caribbean (ECLAC) (6.9 per cent); field missions administered by the Department of Peacekeeping Operations (6.5 per cent); and the Department of Management (5.4 per cent). Retired staff were used mainly in three groups of functions: language services, particularly revisers and interpreters (32 per cent of all engagements); administrative functions (23.4 per cent); and political, economic, social, environmental, humanitarian, advisory and technical assistance functions (9.4 per cent). Other functions accounted for 35 per cent. The total expenditure on retirees in the 2006–2007 biennium amounted to $50 million, of which language services and administrative functions accounted for $24.3 million and $12.8 million, respectively. The report also provided information regarding the employment of former staff 60 years or older who had opted for a withdrawal settlement and were re-employed for six months or more, those rehired in decision-making positions and for an accrued service period exceeding two years, and staff extensions beyond the mandatory age of separation.

The report concluded that retired staff provided a readily available pool of specialists with in-house expertise to meet organizational needs. Moreover, the expanding and evolving needs of field operations (peacekeeping and humanitarian activities) continued to require the immediate deployment of experienced staff. Additionally, field operations often experienced a high turnover rate (up to 30 per cent per year), and currently some 50 per cent of the staff at missions had two years or less experience in the Organization. In those circumstances, retirees were an available pool from which to draw candidates with the required institutional knowledge, skills and experience, without prejudice to the career development and redeployment opportunities of other staff.

ACABQ report. In November [A/63/526 & Corr.1], ACABQ stated that while the Secretary-General's annual report on the employment of retirees contributed to enhancing the transparency of human resources management practices, the sizeable amount of data contained therein required further analysis. Future reports should focus on identifying the possible reasons for patterns and trends, whether such trends were positive or negative, and possible approaches to remedying negative developments. It expressed concern that the trend of using retirees was becoming more widespread in many departments and offices. Upon enquiry, it was informed that staff members were often extended beyond the mandatory age of separation pending recruitment of a replacement. ACABQ was of the view that the situation could and should be avoided through rigorous succession planning and the issuance of vacancy announcements six months before the anticipated retirement. It pointed out that the employment of retirees in decision-making positions had been strongly discouraged by the Assembly and should be contemplated only in exceptional circumstances. The Secretary-General and ICSC should explore the possibility of changing the mandatory age of separation, taking into account such issues as the rejuvenation of the Secretariat, vacancy rates and the actuarial implications of that course of action for the United Nations Joint Staff Pension Fund.

Consultants and individual contractors

In response to General Assembly resolutions 57/305 [YUN 2003, p. 1440], 59/266 [YUN 2004, p. 1418] and 61/244 [YUN 2006, p. 1691], the Secretary-General, in August, submitted a biennial report [A/63/310/Add.3] on the use of consultants and individual contractors within the Secretariat and the regional commissions during the 2006–2007 biennium. The report indicated that in 2006, 3,244 consultants and 1,701 individual contractors were engaged for 4,294 and 3,137 contracts, respectively, while in 2007, the number rose to 4,275 consultants and 1,808 individual contractors for 5,713 and 3,101 contracts, respectively. Those figures represented an increase of 108 per cent compared to the numbers registered for the 2004–2005 biennium. The total expenditure for consultants for the 2006–2007 biennium increased by $59.1 million (138.9 per cent) as compared to 2004–2005. For individual contractors, the total expenditure of $13.8 million in 2006 and $16 million in 2007 corresponded to an increase of $19.8 million (197.2 per cent) compared with the previous biennium. The main UN entities hiring consultants and individual contractors included DESA, the Economic Commission for Africa, ECLAC, the United Nations Conference on Trade and Development and the United Nations Environment Programme.

The report concluded that among factors which contributed to the use of consultants and individual contractors was a worldwide growth in the demand for conference, interpretation and translation services during peak activity periods which exceeded departmental capacity. Likewise, there was a significant increase in disaster relief operations, as well as in field operations in peacekeeping. For some departments, the increase in the use of consultants and individual contractors was a result of new projects, such as the enterprise resource planning system and the capital master plan. Those projects required considerable business analysis and specific expertise not readily available in the Organization.

ACABQ report. In November [A/63/526 & Corr.1], ACABQ regretted that the Secretary-General had not reported on factors contributing to the use of consultants and individual contractors, as requested by the General Assembly in resolution 57/305. Accordingly, it reiterated its request that the data contained in the report be supplemented by an analysis of those factors. Future reports should also contain definitions of the terms "consultant", "individual contractor" and "institutional contractor" used by the Secretary-General. It also noted the increase in the number of consultants and individual contractors. It stressed that the use of consultants should be governed by the relevant Assembly resolutions. Although it understood that in some instances the skills and expertise for a particular project could not be found within the Secretariat, it was of the view that greater use should be made of in-house capacity in some areas for which consultants were routinely hired. ACABQ further noted that the report provided very little information about institutional contractors and the circumstances in which they were used. In that connection, it reiterated that, in future reports, the Secretary-General should provide that information, including institution, duration and expenditure. The Secretary-General should adhere to existing guidelines on the selection and recruitment of consultants and individual contractors Secretariat-wide, and make every effort to select consultants from the widest possible geographical base.

Common payroll

By **decision 63/550** of 24 December, the General Assembly deferred to its resumed sixty-third (2009) session consideration of the Secretary-General's note transmitting the JIU report [YUN 2005, p. 1520] on a common payroll for UN system organizations, as well as the Secretary-General's note [YUN 2006, p. 1701] containing his comments and those of the United Nations System Chief Executives Board for Coordination (CEB) on the JIU report.

Multilingualism

As requested in General Assembly resolution 61/266 [YUN 2007, p. 1515], the Secretary-General submitted an August report [A/63/338] on activities undertaken to promote multilingualism. The review showed that progress had been achieved in the promotion of multilingualism in conference management, internal communications, public information and outreach, as well as in human resources management. The Secretariat continued its commitment to provide the best possible support to Member States, particularly in their deliberative bodies. The principle of equal treatment for the six official languages, as mandated by the Assembly, was respected.

The Secretary-General noted that the launch of the International Year of Languages in 2008 presented an additional opportunity to focus on multilingualism. The extensive programme of activities undertaken to mark the Year [A/63/349] (see p. 1249) was expected to have a lasting effect and would foster the integration of language issues in UN programmes and internationally. The Assembly had also invited the Director-General of the United Nations Educational, Scientific and Cultural Organization (UNESCO) to report on the impact of the activities carried out during the Year.

On 24 December, the Assembly decided that the agenda item on multilingualism would remain for consideration during its resumed sixty-third (2009) session (**decision 63/552**).

Protection from sexual exploitation and abuse

Report of Secretary-General. Pursuant to General Assembly resolution 57/306 [YUN 2003, p. 1237], the Secretary-General submitted a June report on special measures for protection from sexual exploitation and abuse [A/62/890] that presented data on allegations of sexual exploitation and abuse in the UN system in 2007 and described progress in enforcing UN standards of conduct. Information on allegations was received from all but 4 of the 43 UN entities from which information was sought. Nine entities reported receiving new allegations in 2007, whereas 35 entities received no allegations. The number of new alleged cases totalled 159, compared with 371 in 2006. Thirty-two involved personnel of UN entities other than the Department of Peacekeeping Operations (DPKO): the Office of the United Nations High Commissioner for Refugees reported 19 cases, the United Nations Relief and Works Agency for Palestine Refugees in the Near East five, the United Nations University five and the United Nations Integrated Office in Burundi two. The majority of the allegations, 127, were from DPKO, with the highest number (59) reported in the United Nations Organization Mission in the Democratic Republic of the Congo (MONUC). Reports from other organizations suggested chronic underreporting of allegations of sexual exploitation and abuse, in particular of minors, against UN personnel, as well as personnel of the international aid community. The joint Task Force on Protection from Sexual Exploitation and Abuse produced several significant outputs, including convening a high-level conference on eliminating sexual exploitation and abuse by UN and NGO personnel; a strategy on assistance to victims; and an awareness-raising video. Five working groups were formed in September 2007 to advance the work of the Task Force in the areas of: support to field-based networks; enforcement; managerial compliance; victim assistance; and implementation guidance for the Secretary-General's bulletin on sexual exploitation and abuse [YUN 2004, p. 107].

The amendments on sexual exploitation and abuse to the model memorandum of understanding between the United Nations and troop-contributing countries, endorsed by the Assembly in resolution 61/267 B [YUN 2007, p. 69], were used by the Department of Field Support (DFS) in negotiations with potential troop-contributing countries for all new military contingents to peace operations. It was envisaged that the revisions to the model memorandum of understanding would be incorporated into existing memorandums.

The Secretary-General concluded that the United Nations continued to make progress in establishing a sustainable framework for addressing the issue. The creation of conduct and discipline teams within DPKO and DFS had led to focused and coordinated responses to prevention of sexual exploitation and abuse and enforcement of the related standards of conduct. The high-level conference on sexual exploitation and abuse [YUN 2007, p. 1518] and the work of the Task Force on Protection from Sexual Exploitation and Abuse were important steps towards institutionalizing a comprehensive, Organization-wide implementation of measures to prevent abuse, the enforcement of standards of conduct and strategic collaboration with non-governmental partners. Recently approved policies, such as the revised memorandum of understanding, the strategy on assistance to victims and the Assembly resolution on criminal accountability [YUN 2006, p. 109] were significant milestones in advancing a comprehensive strategy to address the issue, in conjunction with the UN policy of zero tolerance. He noted that the number of allegations reported in 2007 declined, particularly by DPKO and DFS. The increase in the number of cases in entities other than peacekeeping was of concern and would be monitored closely. At the same time, the increase in reporting of allegations could also be attributed to greater awareness by staff and management, as well as within the communities in which the UN operated. The Secretary-General remained committed to changing the organizational culture to deter acts of sexual exploitation and abuse. Member States were urged to continue to assist the Organization and adopt policies to ensure that the zero-tolerance policy was equally applied to all troop contingents.

ACABQ report. ACABQ, in November [A/63/526 & Corr.1], noted the substantial decline in the number of allegations, as well as the strengthening of measures for protection from sexual exploitation and sexual abuse, and recommended that the Assembly note the Secretary-General's report.

(For information on protection from sexual exploitation and abuse in UN peace operations, see PART ONE, Chapter I.)

UN International School

In 2008, the United Nations International School, first established on the premises of the United Nations at Lake Success in 1947 [YUN 1947-48, p. 137], celebrated its sixtieth anniversary. The General Assembly, in resolution 63/198 (see below), congratulated the School on its anniversary and urged Member States and others to contribute generously to the School's Capital Development Fund for the renovation programme, with a view to further enhancing international education and promoting multicultural interaction.

GENERAL ASSEMBLY ACTION

On 18 December [meeting 71], the General Assembly, [draft: A/63/L.55 & Add.1], adopted **resolution 63/198** without vote [agenda item 45].

Supporting the United Nations International School in enhancing international education and promoting multicultural interaction

The General Assembly,

Recalling its resolutions 1102(XI) of 27 February 1957, 1228(XII) of 14 December 1957, 2003(XIX) of 10 February 1965 and 2612(XXIV) of 16 December 1969, relating to the location, construction and funding of the permanent accommodation of the United Nations International School,

Noting that the School, which was first established on the premises of the United Nations at Lake Success in 1947, is now celebrating its sixtieth anniversary,

Noting also, as stated in its by-laws, that the "purposes of the School shall be to establish, operate and maintain, under the auspices of the United Nations, a school to promote and provide an international education conforming to the spirit and principles contained in the Charter of the United Nations for the children of persons officially connected with the United Nations, as well as for the children of other persons desirous of obtaining a similar education for their children and to promote educational activities of international character",

Noting further the role of the School as a factor in the recruitment and retention of international staff of the United Nations,

Recognizing that the School continues to make an indispensable contribution to the United Nations community by providing a suitable international education to successive generations of children from that community and others,

Recognizing also the high academic standards that the School has established as a premier international school recognized for its leadership in multicultural and multilingual education, and that it is a crucible of multi-ethnicity and multiculturalism which promotes the appreciation of diverse cultural capacities,

Noting that the School has embarked on much-needed renovation and improvement of its buildings and grounds that will update the facilities and add to the classroom space, which will greatly improve its educational capacities,

1. *Congratulates* the United Nations International School on its sixtieth anniversary;

2. *Expresses its appreciation* for the outstanding achievements of the School and for the valuable contribution it continues to make to the education and development of successive generations of children from the United Nations community;

3. *Notes* that the School is implementing a renovation programme to update and improve the facilities of the School;

4. *Urges* Member States and others in a position to do so to contribute generously to the Capital Development Fund of the School for the renovation programme, with a view to further enhancing international education and promoting multicultural interaction;

5. *Requests* the Secretary-General to continue to provide to the School such assistance as appropriate in furtherance of its object and purposes.

UN Joint Staff Pension Fund

As at 31 December 2008, the United Nations Joint Staff Pension Fund (UNJSPF) had 112,804 active participants, compared to 106,566 at the end of 2007 [YUN 2007, p. 1521]. The number of periodic payments in awards increased from 58,084 to 59,945: 20,550 retirement benefits; 13,653 early retirement benefits; 6,932 deferred retirement benefits; 9,538 widows' and widowers' benefits; 1,161 disability benefits; 8,072 child benefits; and 39 secondary dependants' benefits. The payroll for benefits in payment for the year ending 31 December 2008 increased by 11.8 per cent over the prior year to $1.6 billion. The total expenditure for benefits, administration and investment costs of $1.9 billion exceeded by $114 million contribution income, which increased from $1.7 billion to $1.8 billion (approximately 5.9 per cent). As at 31 December, the market value of UNJSPF amounted to $31 billion, as against $41.7 billion in 2007, representing a decrease of 25 per cent.

The Fund was administered by the 33-member United Nations Joint Staff Pension Board (UNJSPB), which held its fifty-fifth session (Rome, Italy, 10–18 July) [A/63/9] to consider actuarial matters, including the twenty-ninth actuarial valuation of the Fund as at 31 December 2007; the management of the Fund's investments and reports on the investment strategy, policies, practices and performance for the biennium ending on 31 March 2008; the enterprise resource planning project: results of the study on the Integrated Pension Administration System project; overall review of the Fund's staffing and organizational structure: medium-term human resources plan; third management charter of the Fund (2008–2011); study on the impact of currency fluctuations on UNJSPF pension benefits; revised budget estimates for the 2008–2009 biennium; and the Board's 2002 recommendations relating to the benefit provisions of the Fund. The

Board examined and noted the financial statements and schedules for the 2006–2007 biennium and considered the report of the Board of Auditors on the accounts and operations of the Fund, and a report from the Audit Committee of the Board.

Administrative and financial matters

UNJSPB, at its fifty-fifth session [A/63/9], recommended that the General Assembly approve the inclusion of contractual settlement provisions in the agreement with the Global Custodian of the Fund. In circumstances where a trade failed to settle owing to delays in transferring funds, the Global Custodian would lend the funds to the Fund at the standard bank interest rate in order to be in a position to effect the trade on the contracted settlement date.

UNJSPB also recommended an appropriation for the 2008–2009 biennium in the amount of $75,899,200 for revised administrative costs, $74,637,500 for revised investment costs and $72,700 for revised Pension Board expenses. The total budget for the biennium would increase by $2,204,000 to $153,199,100, or 1.5 per cent of the initially approved appropriation. Of that amount, $134,351,100 was chargeable to the principal of the Fund and $18,848,000 was the share borne by the United Nations under the cost-sharing arrangement.

The Board recommended approval of an amendment to the Fund's Regulations that would allow for the purchase of additional years of contributory service by part-time staff. The proposed amendment would contain strict limitations and would be monitored in the light of an experience review. The relevant amendment to the Regulations of the Fund was contained in annex XIV.

UNJSPB recommended the admission of the Special Tribunal for Lebanon to membership in the Fund, effective 1 January 2009.

In September [A/63/363], the Secretary-General presented the administrative and financial implications for the UN regular budget for the 2008–2009 biennium arising from the UNJSPF report (see above). In reviewing the revised budget estimates for the 2008–2009 biennium, UNJSPB had noted that no additional resources were requested for posts owing to the offsetting effect of recosting and adjustments related to the actual and projected vacancies for the biennium. In addition, it took note of the downward revision in the overall requirements under rental of premises, which resulted in a reduction of $150,600 in the amount apportioned to the United Nations under the cost-sharing arrangements. In the light of the Board's recommendation that $18,848,000 be the revised United Nations share under the cost-sharing arrangements, and the additional requirements for the administrative costs of the Fund for 2008–2009 as a result of implementation of the post adjustment multiplier for New York and the General Service salary scale effective 1 August, no revisions were being proposed to the United Nations share of $18,998,600 attributable to it. As a result, the current appropriation under section 1, Overall policymaking, direction and coordination, of the 2008–2009 programme budget would be maintained and the actual expenses reported in the context of the second performance report for the biennium.

ACABQ, in a November report [A/63/556], recommended approval of the Board's recommendation on the Fund's total budget for the biennium in the amount of $153.2 million. It encouraged the Fund to consult with the Chief Information Technology Officer on technical requirements of the integrated pension administration system.

In section IX of **resolution 63/263** (see p. 1548) of 24 December, the Assembly requested the Secretary-General to report on any additional requirements arising from the UNJSPB recommendations in the second performance report for the 2008–2009 biennium.

Pension fund investment

Report of Secretary-General. In September [A/C.5/63/2], the Secretary-General submitted a report on UNJSPF investments and steps and efforts undertaken to increase diversification. The report provided information on the management of the investments of the Fund during the period from 1 April 2006 to 31 March 2008 and on investment returns, diversification of investments and development-related investments. The market value of the Fund's assets increased to $40,588 million as at 31 March 2008, from $33,331 million the previous year, an increase of $7,256 million, or 21.8 per cent. The total investment return was 13.4 per cent for the year to 31 March 2007 and 8.1 per cent for the year to 31 March 2008. After adjustment by the United States consumer price index, those returns represented real rates of return of 10.3 per cent and 4 per cent, respectively. The total annualized rate of return for the biennium was, therefore, 10.7 per cent. After adjustment by the consumer price index, the real annualized rate of return for the biennium was 7.1 per cent. For the year ended 31 March 2008, the Fund outperformed the benchmarks with the return of 8.1 per cent versus the returns of 5.2 and 6.2 per cent of the new 60/31 and old 60/40 benchmarks, respectively. In terms of diversification, the fixed-income portfolio was invested in 16 different currencies; 11 per cent in United States dollars and 89 per cent in non-dollar currencies. In terms of geographical diversification, the portfolio was invested in 34 countries and seven supranational and regional institutions. As to geographical diversification, the proportion of the Fund invested in North America decreased to 36.3 per cent in March 2008, from 44.8 per cent in March 2006. Investments in Europe increased to 36 per cent from 32.4 per cent, while in Asia and the Pacific the proportion of investments increased to 20.4 per cent from 14.1 per cent during the same period. Direct and indirect investments in developing countries amounted to $3.9 billion, a 110 per cent increase from the previous year. Development-related investments accounted for some 12.6 per cent of the Fund's assets at book value.

During the turbulent markets of 2007, active management produced outperformance that added $1.033 billion to the portfolio, in excess of the benchmarks established by the Fund. With declining markets, active management continued through 31 March 2008 to provide outperformance that resulted in smaller losses than would have been experienced had indexation been implemented.

The Secretary-General concluded that the Pension Fund had performed steadily, in excess of its benchmarks. Given the economic strains in the world economy, the goal would be to focus on profitability and capital preservation through strengthened systems.

ACABQ report. ACABQ, in November [A/63/556], having considered the UNJSPB report (see p. 1633), acknowledged the positive developments in the management of the UNJSPF secretariat and recommended Assembly approval of the Board's proposals. It recommended that the Board continue to explore opportunities for investing in developing countries and countries with economies in transition. The Committee did not support the Board's recommendation that the Investment Management Service be given borrowing authority for "contractual" versus "actual" settlement of securities, given the absence of clear and compelling information on the conditions and terms of such authority. It recommended that the Board include such information in its next report to the Assembly. ACABQ shared the Board's concerns over asset allocations, and was of the view that investing in alternative asset classes (including real estate) in the current volatile market should be done cautiously.

GENERAL ASSEMBLY ACTION

On 24 December [meeting 74], the General Assembly, on the recommendation of the Fifth Committee [A/63/641], adopted **resolution 63/252** without vote [agenda item 126].

United Nations pension system

The General Assembly,

Recalling its resolutions 55/224 of 23 December 2000, 57/286 of 20 December 2002, 59/269 of 23 December 2004, 61/240 of 22 December 2006 and 62/241 of 22 December 2007,

Having considered the report of the United Nations Joint Staff Pension Board for 2008 to the General Assembly and to the member organizations of the United Nations Joint Staff Pension Fund, including the financial statements of the Fund for the biennium ended 31 December 2007, the audit opinion and report of the Board of Auditors thereon, the information provided on the internal audits of the Fund and the observations of the Pension Board, the reports of the Secretary-General on the investments of the Fund and steps and efforts undertaken to increase the diversification and on the administrative and financial implications arising from the report of the Pension Board and the related report of the Advisory Committee on Administrative and Budgetary Questions,

1. *Takes note* of the report of the United Nations Joint Staff Pension Board, and in particular the action taken by the Board as set out in chapter II.B of the report;

2. *Notes* that the report of the Board of Auditors on the accounts of the United Nations Joint Staff Pension Fund for the biennium ended 31 December 2007 indicated that the financial statements presented fairly, in all material respects, the financial position of the Fund and that the transactions tested as part of the audit were, in all significant respects, in accordance with the Regulations and Rules of the Fund and legislative authority;

3. *Endorses* the recommendations of the Advisory Committee on Administrative and Budgetary Questions, subject to the provisions of the present resolution;

I

Administrative arrangements, revised budget and longer-term objectives of the United Nations Joint Staff Pension Fund

4. *Takes note* of the information set out in paragraphs 180 to 197 of the report of the United Nations Joint Staff Pension Board on the revised budget estimates for the biennium 2008–2009;

5. *Approves* the increase of 2,204,000 United States dollars in total additional resources for the biennium 2008–2009, noting that the revised estimates for the biennium would amount to a total appropriation of 153,199,100 dollars;

II

Benefit provisions

6. *Endorses* the decision taken by the United Nations Joint Staff Pension Board in 2007, in which it reaffirmed its earlier decision maintaining that the United Nations Joint Staff Pension Fund should determine entitlements to pension benefits, in particular under articles 34 and 35 of the Regulations of the Fund, which cover spousal benefits, in accordance with the personal status of a participant as recognized and reported to the Fund by the participant's employing organization, on the understanding that the final verification that the personal status has remained the same will be done by the Fund at the time of granting such pension benefits;

7. *Approves* the changes in the benefit provisions that would streamline the application of the relevant provisions governing family members or former family members un-

der articles 35 bis, 35 ter and 36, as set out in annex XIV to the report of the Board;

8. *Also approves* the amendment to article 24 (*b*) of the Regulations of the Fund, as set out in annex XIV to the report of the Board, which would allow participants who return to active contributory service after a period of disability to count such periods of disability as contributory service without requiring the participant to pay contributions for that period;

9. *Further approves* the agreement of the Board to clarify that the scope of the revision in 2006 of article 24, concerning the elimination of the limitation on the right to restoration based on years of prior service, did not cover only those participants who had received a withdrawal settlement, but also those who had elected a deferred retirement benefit (full or partial) as long as no periodic benefit payments of their deferred benefit had been made, as set out in paragraphs 329 and 330 of the report of the Board, and as clarified in the technical amendments to the Regulations of the Fund, set out in annex XIV to the report of the Board;

III

Other matters

10. *Welcomes* the information that all the committees of the United Nations Joint Staff Pension Fund had been presented and the United Nations Joint Staff Pension Board had approved a declaration of conflict of interest, which referred to the mandate and the focus of each committee and covered the status, conduct and accountability of the members of the Investments Committee, the Committee of Actuaries and the Audit Committee;

11. *Decides*, upon the affirmative recommendation of the Board, that the Special Tribunal for Lebanon shall be admitted as a new member organization of the Fund, effective 1 January 2009;

12. *Emphasizes* that the United Nations and other member organizations of the Fund should ensure the timely and accurate processing of documentation, including, inter alia, a certification that all suitable arrangements are in place to ensure that all debts to such organizations are paid in full, as required by the Fund for the payment of benefits;

13. *Takes note* of the information provided by the Fund on the status of the ongoing implementation of resolution 62/241 regarding the one-time, ex gratia, exceptional payment to retirees residing in Ecuador;

IV

Investments of the United Nations Joint Staff Pension Fund

14. *Takes note* of the report of the Secretary-General on the investments of the United Nations Joint Staff Pension Fund and steps and efforts undertaken to increase the diversification and the observations of the United Nations Joint Staff Pension Board, as set out in its report;

15. *Approves* the inclusion of contractual settlement provisions in the agreement with the Global Custodian of the Fund, under the strict terms and conditions and for the purposes recommended by the Representative of the Secretary-General and the Board, and upon legal terms and conditions in such agreement that maximize the protection of the legal interests of the Fund;

16. *Welcomes* the continued effort of the Secretary-General, as fiduciary for the investment of the assets of the Fund, to diversify its investments between developed markets and emerging markets, and requests the Secretary-General to ensure that, under the current volatile market conditions, decisions concerning the investments of the Fund in any country should be implemented very cautiously, fully taking into account the four main criteria for investment, namely, safety, profitability, liquidity and convertibility.

By section IX of **resolution 63/263** of 24 December (see p. 1548), the General Assembly took note of the Secretary-General's report and requested him to report on any additional requirements arising from the Board's recommendations in the context of the second performance report on the programme budget for the 2008–2009 biennium.

On the same date, the Assembly decided that the item on the United Nations pension system would remain for consideration during its resumed sixty-third (2009) session (**decision 63/552**).

Travel-related matters

Report of Secretary-General. In November, the Secretary-General submitted his biennial report on standards of accommodation for air travel [A/63/524], listing exceptions to those standards from 1 July 2006 to 30 June 2008 and comparative statistics for the two-year period ended 30 June 2006.

ACABQ report. In its report [A/63/715], ACABQ noted that the purely statistical presentation in the Secretary-General's report was of limited usefulness and recommended that future biennial reports on the issue contain an analysis of the reasons for the increases and/or decreases in the number of exceptions, taking into account such issues as industry trends and security requirements, as well as other matters. ACABQ also recommended that the comprehensive report requested for harmonizing standards of travel, on the basis of a review by CEB and specific proposals, should take into account the recommendations of the OIOS audit review under way. The Secretary-General's report should also contain an update on the status of the CEB review.

Administration of justice

New system of administration of justice

Report of Secretary-General (April). In response to General Assembly resolution 62/228 [YUN 2007, p. 1528], the Secretary-General submitted an April report [A/62/782] on the administration of justice. The report included additional information on categories of non-staff personnel, and provided further details on the functioning of the formal part of the system, encompassing the United Nations Dispute Tribunal and the United Nations Appeals Tribunal. It also discussed transitional measures, including resource implications, which would be required to shift smoothly from the current internal justice system to the new system, established by Assembly resolution 61/261 [YUN 2007, p. 1525], which was expected to be in place by 1 January 2009.

The Secretary-General concluded that the approval by the Assembly of a new system for the administration of justice in the United Nations was a landmark decision and should not be viewed in isolation, but as an integral part of his quest for greater accountability. The statutes of the Dispute Tribunal and the Appeals Tribunal should be approved by the Assembly at the second part of its resumed sixty-second (2008) session to ensure that judges of both Tribunals could be elected and appointed sufficiently in advance of 1 January 2009. He urged the Assembly to decide on the transitional measures. Owing to the surge in new cases and a large backlog, extraordinary temporary measures would be necessary to ensure that the new system was allowed to function unadulterated by remnants of the old system. Decisions on transitional measures were also required so that arrangements could be made to issue relevant administrative instructions. He requested the Assembly to adopt the statutes of the Tribunals annexed to his report; approve the transitional measures of three ad litem judges, their travel and their related support staff for 2009, and the payment of remuneration to judges for the United Nations Administrative Tribunal for judgements made during the remainder of 2008; and appropriate $1,729,100 under the programme budget for the 2008–2009 biennium.

ACABQ report. In June [A/62/7/Add.39], ACABQ recommended approval of the Secretary-General's proposal to transfer all pending cases to the United Nations Dispute Tribunal once the new system was in place; and the strengthening of the Dispute Tribunal through the addition of three ad litem judges for 12 months following the establishment of the Tribunal, with a view to clearing the backlog. While it understood that the Secretary-General's intention was to divide the caseload so that the burden of the backlog would not fall on one body, it recommended that, in allocating additional capacity, he should take into account the anticipated distribution of pending cases. With regard to the payment of an honorarium for judgements of the United Nations Administrative Tribunal, the Assembly would have to decide if it wished to approve the payment of an honorarium in the event that the current system continued beyond 1 January 2009. ACABQ recommended appropriation of the resources requested by the Secretary-General for the proposed transitional measures, subject to the adoption by the Assembly of the statutes of the two Tribunals, the election and appointment of the judges and the Assembly's decision concerning the payment of an honorarium to the United Nations Administrative Tribunal judges. Should the introduction of the new system be delayed beyond 1 January 2009, resources required to continue the current system and to clear the backlog should be absorbed from within the provision for the administration of justice for the 2008–2009 biennium.

Communications. In a 29 April letter [A/C.5/62/27] to the Chairman of the Fifth Committee, the General Assembly President transmitted a 24 April letter from the Chairman of the Ad Hoc Committee on the Administration of Justice at the United Nations summarizing the preliminary observations made in the informal consultation on the draft statutes of the Tribunals.

The President of the United Nations Administrative Tribunal, in an 18 July letter [A/63/253] to the General Assembly President, expressed concern about the absence of appropriate transitional measures in the draft statutes of the Tribunals. The Assembly was requested to give urgent consideration to transitional matters before it approved the draft statutes.

Report of Secretary-General (August). In response to General Assembly resolution 62/228 (YUN 2007, p. 1528), the Secretary-General submitted an August report [A/63/314] on the administration of justice at the United Nations. The report addressed other requests made by the Assembly, including those concerning the delegation of authority on disciplinary matters; the conditions of service of judges in the new system of internal justice; mechanisms for the formal removal of judges; a staff-funded scheme for legal assistance for staff; and possible uses of ICT in the administration of justice system. He requested the Assembly's approval for the proposed course of action relating to the limited delegation of authority for disciplinary matters, and the proposed revisions to the Staff Regulations related to the introduction of the new system of administration of justice and the conditions of service of judges of the Dispute and Appeals Tribunals judges.

The Secretary-General concluded that the introduction of the new system of administration of justice was an important step in unifying the systems between the Secretariat and the separately administered UN funds and programmes. He stressed the importance of having the statutes of the Tribunals adopted, the judges appointed and amendments to the Staff Regulations approved, and to have a decision by Member States on his proposal for transitional measures as soon as possible, emphasizing that it was critical to put the basic elements of a functioning system in place by 1 January 2009. He called for the Assembly to take note of the proposal to grant limited delegation of authority for disciplinary measures in a phased manner, beginning with a select number of peacekeeping missions, and to approve the proposed conditions of service of the Dispute and Appeals Tribunals judges.

ACABQ report. In November [A/63/545], ACABQ noted that in view of delays, the new system of administration of justice would not be ready for implementation in January 2009. It emphasized that every effort should be made to complete the preparatory work required to implement the new system and recommended that the Assembly request the Secretary-General to update the timeline for its implementation. The timely appointment of an Executive Director of the Office of Administration of Justice was particularly important for providing the leadership to direct preparatory work. The Secretary-General should monitor and analyse the increasing trend in the number of disciplinary cases and keep the Assembly informed of any exceptional developments. The absence of explanation as to the underlying causes of the higher number of new disciplinary cases, as well as the variations in the time required to complete them, was of particular concern. ACABQ emphasized the need to address the backlog of disciplinary cases as a matter of urgency, using available resources as efficiently as possible. It emphasized the need to draw upon lessons learned and experiences gained in the exercise of delegation of authority and decentralization of activities and structures. It requested the Secretary-General to submit a new proposal to the Assembly, including a variety of options, with full costing. He should also discuss with the funds and programmes cost-sharing arrangements based on headcount, as originally envisaged, and conclude negotiations on that matter expeditiously. It further recommended approval of the Secretary-General's proposals regarding the compensation of judges and that consideration of the proposed revisions to staff regulations 10.1 and 11.1 be deferred.

Communication. In a 27 October letter [A/C.5/63/9] to the Chairman of the Fifth Committee, the Assembly President transmitted a 24 October letter from the Chairman of the Sixth (Legal) Committee drawing attention to specific issues related to the text of the draft statutes, including possible options relating to the draft statute of the Dispute Tribunal.

GENERAL ASSEMBLY ACTION

On 24 December [meeting 74], the General Assembly, on the recommendation of the Fifth Committee [A/63/642], adopted **resolution 63/253** without vote [agenda item 129].

Administration of justice at the United Nations

The General Assembly,

Recalling its resolutions 57/307 of 15 April 2003, 59/266 of 23 December 2004, 59/283 of 13 April 2005, 61/261 of 4 April 2007 and 62/228 of 22 December 2007, and its decisions 62/519 of 6 December 2007 and 63/531 of 11 December 2008,

Reaffirming the decision in paragraph 4 of its resolution 61/261 to establish a new, independent, transparent, professionalized, adequately resourced and decentralized system of administration of justice consistent with the relevant rules of international law and the principles of the rule of law and due process to ensure respect for the rights and obligations of staff members and the accountability of managers and staff members alike,

Having considered the reports of the Secretary-General on the administration of justice at the United Nations, on the activities of the Office of the Ombudsman and on the administration of justice in the Secretariat, including the outcome of the work of the Joint Appeals Board during 2006 and 2007 and statistics on the disposition of cases and work of the Panel of Counsel, the note by the Secretary-General on the administration of justice, including further information requested by the General Assembly, the letter dated 29 April 2008 from the President of the General Assembly addressed to the Chairman of the Fifth Committee, the letter dated 27 October 2008 from the President of the General Assembly addressed to the Chairman of the Fifth Committee and the related reports of the Advisory Committee on Administrative and Budgetary Questions,

1. *Takes note* of the reports of the Secretary-General on the administration of justice at the United Nations, on the activities of the Office of the Ombudsman and on the administration of justice in the Secretariat, including the outcome of the work of the Joint Appeals Board during 2006 and 2007 and statistics on the disposition of cases and work of the Panel of Counsel, the note by the Secretary-General on the administration of justice, including further information requested by the General Assembly, the letter dated 29 April 2008 from the President of the General Assembly addressed to the Chairman of the Fifth Committee, and the letter dated 27 October 2008 from the President of the General Assembly addressed to the Chairman of the Fifth Committee;

2. *Reaffirms* its resolutions 61/261 and 62/228 on the establishment of the new system of administration of justice;

3. *Expresses its appreciation* to staff members of the United Nations system who have participated in the system of administration of justice, including the joint disciplinary committees and the joint appeals boards;

4. *Also expresses its appreciation* to the former and present members and staff of the United Nations Administrative Tribunal for their work;

5. *Endorses* the conclusions and recommendations contained in the reports of the Advisory Committee on Administrative and Budgetary Questions, subject to the provisions of the present resolution;

I

New system of administration of justice

6. *Regrets* the delays in the filling of posts established by the General Assembly in its resolution 62/228, and requests the Secretary-General to fill the posts as a matter of priority, in particular the post of the Executive Director of the Office of Administration of Justice;

7. *Decides* that interns, type II gratis personnel and volunteers (other than United Nations Volunteers) shall have the possibility of requesting an appropriate management evaluation but shall not have access to the United Nations Dispute Tribunal or to the United Nations Appeals Tribunal;

8. *Recalls* paragraphs 7 and 9 of its resolution 62/228, and its decision 63/531, by which the Ad Hoc Committee on the Administration of Justice at the United Nations would continue its work, and decides to revert to the issue of the scope of the system of administration of justice at its sixty-fifth session, with a view to ensuring that effective remedies are available to all categories of United Nations personnel, with due consideration given to the types of recourse that are the most appropriate to that end;

9. *Commends* the role that volunteers have traditionally played in representing employees in the dispute resolution process under the existing system;

10. *Notes* that some current and former United Nations staff have been reluctant to represent their fellow staff members in the dispute resolution process because of the burden that such service would place on them;

11. *Requests* the Secretary-General to provide incentives to encourage current and former staff to assist staff members in the dispute resolution process;

12. *Decides* that the role of professional legal staff in the Office of Staff Legal Assistance shall be to assist staff members and their volunteer representatives in processing claims through the formal system of administration of justice;

13. *Recalls* paragraph 13 of its resolution 62/228, in which it decided to establish the Office of Staff Legal Assistance to succeed the Panel of Counsel, and decides to revert to the mandate and functioning of that Office, including the participation of current and former staff as volunteers, at its sixty-fifth session;

14. *Reiterates* paragraph 24 of its resolution 61/261, and requests the Secretary-General to report to the General Assembly at its sixty-fifth session on proposals for a staff-funded scheme in the Organization that would provide legal assistance and support to staff;

15. *Decides* to revert to the issue of the possibility of staff associations filing applications before the Dispute Tribunal at its sixty-fifth session;

16. *Recalls* paragraph 55 of the report of the Secretary-General, and requests the Secretary-General to work with staff associations to develop incentives to enable and encourage staff to continue to participate in the work of the Office of Staff Legal Assistance, including by providing volunteer professional legal counsel;

II

Informal system

17. *Welcomes* the steps taken by the Office of the Ombudsman towards the implementation of the new informal system as set out in resolution 62/228;

18. *Reaffirms* that the informal resolution of conflict is a crucial element of the system of administration of justice, and emphasizes that all possible use should be made of the informal system in order to avoid unnecessary litigation;

19. *Decides* that all persons who have access to the Office of the Ombudsman under the current system shall also have access to the new informal system;

20. *Requests* the Secretary-General to consider and make proposals at its sixty-fifth session for providing incentives for employees seeking dispute resolution to submit disputes to mediation under the auspices of the Office of the Ombudsman;

21. *Recalls its request* to the Secretary-General, contained in paragraph 67 *(a)* of its resolution 62/228, to report to it on the revised terms of reference for the Office of the Ombudsman, and requests the Secretary-General to ensure that the terms of reference and guidelines for the Mediation Division are promulgated as soon as possible;

22. *Requests* the Secretary-General to take advantage of existing mechanisms for conflict resolution and mediation, as deemed useful and appropriate, in order to facilitate a renewed dialogue between staff and management;

23. *Welcomes* the intention of the Secretary-General to issue a joint report in 2009 for the entities covered by the integrated Office of the Ombudsman, taking into consideration the different legislative bodies that will receive the report;

24. *Notes* section V, on systemic issues, of the report of the Secretary-General on the activities of the Office of the Ombudsman, and emphasizes that the role of the Ombudsman is to report on broad systemic issues that he or she identifies, as well as issues that are brought to his or her attention, in order to promote greater harmony in the workplace;

25. *Requests* the Secretary-General to report to the General Assembly at its sixty-fifth session on specific measures taken to address systemic issues in the context of human resources management;

III

Formal system

26. *Decides* to adopt the statutes of the United Nations Dispute Tribunal and of the United Nations Appeals Tribunal, as set out in annexes I and II to the present resolution;

27. *Also decides* that the United Nations Dispute Tribunal and the United Nations Appeals Tribunal shall be operational as of 1 July 2009;

28. *Affirms* that the United Nations Dispute Tribunal and the United Nations Appeals Tribunal shall not have any powers beyond those conferred under their respective statutes;

29. *Notes* article 7, paragraph 1, of the statute of the United Nations Dispute Tribunal and article 6, paragraph 1 of the statute of the United Nations Appeals Tribunal, requests the Secretary-General to submit, for approval, the rules of procedure of the Tribunals as soon as possible but no later than at its sixty-fourth session, and decides that until then the Tribunals may apply the rules of procedure on a provisional basis;

30. *Approves* the proposed conditions of service of the judges of the United Nations Dispute Tribunal and United Nations Appeals Tribunal, as set out in the report of the Secretary-General;

31. *Decides* that the conditions of service referred to in paragraph 30 above shall be treated separately from the

conditions of service of other judicial appointments in the United Nations system;

32. *Also decides* to carry out, at its sixty-fifth session, a review of the statutes of the Tribunals, in the light of experience gained, including on the efficiency of the overall functioning of the Tribunals, in particular regarding the number of judges and the panels of the United Nations Dispute Tribunal;

33. *Recalls* paragraph 49 of its resolution 62/228, and requests the Secretary-General to submit to the General Assembly at its sixty-fifth session a new detailed proposal, including a variety of options for delegation of authority for disciplinary measures, with full costing and a cost-benefit analysis, taking into account the recommendations contained in the report of the Advisory Committee on Administrative and Budgetary Questions;

34. *Also recalls* paragraph 23 of the report of the Advisory Committee on Administrative and Budgetary Questions, and requests the Secretary-General to further clarify the role of the Department of Management of the Secretariat in the evaluation process, in order to ensure the appropriate independence of the Management Evaluation Unit, and to report thereon to the General Assembly at its sixty-fifth session;

IV

Transitional measures

35. *Requests* the Secretary-General to ensure that the current formal system of administration of justice continues to function, as appropriate, until the completion of the transition to the new system;

36. *Recalls* paragraph 57 of its resolution 62/228, and in that context urges the Secretary-General to take the measures necessary to reduce the existing backlog;

37. *Notes* the refusal of some staff associations to participate in the joint appeals boards and the joint disciplinary committees, and authorizes the Secretary-General to obtain the assistance of other staff associations, including staff associations of the funds and programmes and at the various duty stations, in identifying staff members willing to serve on the joint appeals boards and/or joint disciplinary committees, in order to ensure that the current system continues to operate in an effective and timely manner;

38. *Decides* to abolish, as of 1 July 2009, the joint appeals boards, the joint disciplinary committees and the disciplinary committees of the separately administered funds and programmes;

39. *Also decides* that the terms of the members of the United Nations Administrative Tribunal that expire on 31 December 2008 shall be extended to 31 December 2009;

40. *Authorizes* honorariums for the members of the United Nations Administrative Tribunal as of 1 January 2009, in the amount of 1,500 United States dollars per case (1,000 dollars for the drafter and 250 dollars each for the other two signatories);

41. *Acknowledges* the need to clear the existing backlog of cases as soon as possible, requests the Secretary-General to coordinate with the United Nations Administrative Tribunal in order to hold Administrative Tribunal sessions in 2009 earlier than scheduled, and authorizes extension of the sessions by up to four weeks;

42. *Decides* that the United Nations Administrative Tribunal shall cease to accept new cases as of 1 July 2009;

43. *Also decides* to abolish the United Nations Administrative Tribunal as of 31 December 2009;

44. *Further decides* that all cases pending before the joint appeals boards, the joint disciplinary committees and the disciplinary committees shall be transferred, as from the abolishment of those bodies, to the United Nations Dispute Tribunal;

45. *Decides* that all cases from the United Nations and the separately administered funds and programmes pending before the United Nations Administrative Tribunal shall be transferred to the United Nations Dispute Tribunal, as from the abolishment of the United Nations Administrative Tribunal;

46. *Also decides* that pending cases from the United Nations Joint Staff Pension Fund and from organizations that have concluded a special agreement with the Secretary-General, according to article 2, paragraph 10, of the statute of the United Nations Appeals Tribunal, or article 2, paragraph 5, of the statute of the United Nations Dispute Tribunal, shall be transferred to the Appeals Tribunal or the Dispute Tribunal, as appropriate, as from the abolishment of the United Nations Administrative Tribunal;

47. *Invites* the United Nations Administrative Tribunal to consider cases from organizations that have concluded a special agreement under article 14 of the its statute as a matter of priority, with a view to concluding those cases before its abolishment;

48. *Decides* that three ad litem judges shall be appointed by the General Assembly to the United Nations Dispute Tribunal;

49. *Stresses* that the three ad litem judges appointed to the United Nations Dispute Tribunal shall have all the powers conferred on the permanent judges of the Dispute Tribunal and shall be appointed only for a period of one year as of 1 July 2009;

50. *Requests* the Secretary-General to ensure that all entities that utilize the United Nations Administrative Tribunal pursuant to article 14 of its statute are notified that it will cease to accept new cases as of 1 July 2009, and that if those entities (with the exception of the United Nations Joint Staff Pension Fund) wish to continue to participate in the internal justice system of the Organization they will need to negotiate new special agreements;

51. *Invites* the United Nations Joint Staff Pension Board to consider the new system of administration of justice as approved by the General Assembly;

V

Financial implications and cost-sharing arrangements

52. *Recalls* paragraphs 62 and 63 of its resolution 62/228, and requests the Secretary-General to conclude cost-sharing arrangements, based on headcount, with the relevant funds and programmes by 30 June 2009 and to report thereon;

53. *Requests* the Secretary-General to make every effort to meet any additional requirements relating to the decisions in section IV above within the existing appropriation and to report on the actual costs in the context of the

second performance report on the programme budget for the biennium 2008–2009;

VI

Other issues

54. *Recalls* paragraph 14 of its resolution 59/283, and requests the Secretary-General, in accordance with existing rules and regulations, to pursue the financial liability of managers when the situation justifies such action;

55. *Also recalls* paragraph 69 of its resolution 62/228, reiterates its request to the Secretary-General to ensure that information concerning the details of the new system of administration of justice, in particular options for recourse, is readily accessible by all persons covered under the new system, and stresses that the information should clearly explain the roles of the various elements in the new system, as well as the process for bringing complaints;

56. *Reiterates its request* to the Secretary-General to provide the terms of reference of the Registries of the United Nations Dispute Tribunal and of the United Nations Appeals Tribunal as soon as possible;

57. *Decides* that for future appointments the Internal Justice Council shall not recommend more than one candidate from any one Member State for a judgeship on the United Nations Dispute Tribunal, or more than one candidate from any one Member State for a judgeship on the United Nations Appeals Tribunal;

58. *Invites* Member States, when electing judges to the United Nations Dispute Tribunal and the United Nations Appeals Tribunal, to take due consideration of geographical distribution and gender balance;

59. *Requests* the Secretary-General to conduct a review of the new system of administration of justice and to report thereon to the General Assembly at its sixty-fifth session;

60. *Decides* that the sub-item entitled "Appointment of members of the United Nations Administrative Tribunal" of the item entitled "Appointments to fill vacancies in subsidiary organs and other appointments" shall be deleted from its agenda;

61. *Approves* revision of staff regulations 10.1 and 11.1, as proposed in paragraph 80 of the report of the Secretary-General, and decides to abolish staff regulations 10.2 and 11.2, with effect from the implementation of the new system of administration of justice on 1 July 2009.

ANNEX I

Statute of the United Nations Dispute Tribunal

Article 1

A tribunal is established by the present statute as the first instance of the two-tier formal system of administration of justice, to be known as the United Nations Dispute Tribunal.

Article 2

1. The Dispute Tribunal shall be competent to hear and pass judgement on an application filed by an individual, as provided for in article 3, paragraph 1, of the present statute, against the Secretary-General as the Chief Administrative Officer of the United Nations:

(a) To appeal an administrative decision that is alleged to be in non-compliance with the terms of appointment or the contract of employment. The terms "contract" and "terms of appointment" include all pertinent regulations and rules and all relevant administrative issuances in force at the time of alleged non-compliance;

(b) To appeal an administrative decision imposing a disciplinary measure;

(c) To enforce the implementation of an agreement reached through mediation pursuant to article 8, paragraph 2, of the present statute.

2. The Dispute Tribunal shall be competent to hear and pass judgement on an application filed by an individual requesting the Dispute Tribunal to suspend, during the pendency of the management evaluation, the implementation of a contested administrative decision that is the subject of an ongoing management evaluation, where the decision appears prima facie to be unlawful, in cases of particular urgency, and where its implementation would cause irreparable damage. The decision of the Dispute Tribunal on such an application shall not be subject to appeal.

3. The Dispute Tribunal shall be competent to permit or deny leave to an application to file a friend-of-the-court brief by a staff association.

4. The Dispute Tribunal shall be competent to permit an individual who is entitled to appeal the same administrative decision under paragraph 1 *(a)* of the present article to intervene in a matter brought by another staff member under the same paragraph.

5. The Dispute Tribunal shall be competent to hear and pass judgement on an application filed against a specialized agency brought into relationship with the United Nations in accordance with the provisions of Articles 57 and 63 of the Charter of the United Nations or other international organization or entity established by a treaty and participating in the common system of conditions of service, where a special agreement has been concluded between the agency, organization or entity concerned and the Secretary-General of the United Nations to accept the terms of the jurisdiction of the Dispute Tribunal, consonant with the present statute. Such special agreement shall provide that the agency, organization or entity concerned shall be bound by the judgements of the Dispute Tribunal and be responsible for the payment of any compensation awarded by the Dispute Tribunal in respect of its own staff members and shall include, inter alia, provisions concerning its participation in the administrative arrangements for the functioning of the Dispute Tribunal and concerning its sharing of the expenses of the Dispute Tribunal. Such special agreement shall also contain other provisions required for the Dispute Tribunal to carry out its functions vis-à-vis the agency, organization or entity.

6. In the event of a dispute as to whether the Dispute Tribunal has competence under the present statute, the Dispute Tribunal shall decide on the matter.

7. As a transitional measure, the Dispute Tribunal shall be competent to hear and pass judgement on:

(a) A case transferred to it from a joint appeals board or a joint disciplinary committee established by the United Nations, or from another similar body established by a separately administered fund or programme;

(b) A case transferred to it from the United Nations Administrative Tribunal;

as decided by the General Assembly.

Article 3

1. An application under article 2, paragraph 1, of the present statute may be filed by:

(a) Any staff member of the United Nations, including the United Nations Secretariat or separately administered United Nations funds and programmes;

(b) Any former staff member of the United Nations, including the United Nations Secretariat or separately administered United Nations funds and programmes;

(c) Any person making claims in the name of an incapacitated or deceased staff member of the United Nations, including the United Nations Secretariat or separately administered United Nations funds and programmes.

2. A request for a suspension of action under article 2, paragraph 2, of the present statute may be filed by an individual, as provided for in paragraph 1 of the present article.

Article 4

1. The Dispute Tribunal shall be composed of three full-time judges and two half-time judges.

2. The judges shall be appointed by the General Assembly on the recommendation of the Internal Justice Council in accordance with Assembly resolution 62/228. No two judges shall be of the same nationality. Due regard shall be given to geographical distribution and gender balance.

3. To be eligible for appointment as a judge, a person shall:

(a) Be of high moral character; and

(b) Possess at least 10 years of judicial experience in the field of administrative law, or the equivalent within one or more national jurisdictions.

4. A judge of the Dispute Tribunal shall be appointed for one non-renewable term of seven years. As a transitional measure, two of the judges (one full-time judge and one half-time judge) initially appointed, to be determined by drawing of lots, shall serve three years and may be reappointed to the same Dispute Tribunal for a further non-renewable term of seven years. A current or former judge of the United Nations Appeals Tribunal shall not be eligible to serve in the Dispute Tribunal.

5. A judge of the Dispute Tribunal appointed to replace a judge whose term of office has not expired shall hold office for the remainder of his or her predecessor's term, and may be reappointed for one non-renewable term of seven years, provided that the unexpired term is less than three years.

6. A judge of the Dispute Tribunal shall not be eligible for any appointment within the United Nations, except another judicial post, for a period of five years following his or her term of office.

7. The Dispute Tribunal shall elect a President.

8. A judge of the Dispute Tribunal shall serve in his or her personal capacity and enjoy full independence.

9. A judge of the Dispute Tribunal who has, or appears to have, a conflict of interest shall recuse himself or herself from the case. Where a party requests such recusal, the decision shall be taken by the President of the Dispute Tribunal.

10. A judge of the Dispute Tribunal may only be removed by the General Assembly in case of misconduct or incapacity.

11. A judge of the Dispute Tribunal may resign, by notifying the General Assembly through the Secretary-General of the United Nations. The resignation shall take effect from the date of notification, unless the notice of resignation specifies a later date.

Article 5

The three full-time judges of the Dispute Tribunal shall exercise their functions in New York, Geneva and Nairobi, respectively. However, the Dispute Tribunal may decide to hold sessions at other duty stations, as required by its caseload.

Article 6

1. The Secretary-General of the United Nations shall make the administrative arrangements necessary for the functioning of the Dispute Tribunal, including provisions for the travel and related costs of staff whose physical presence before the Dispute Tribunal is deemed necessary by the Dispute Tribunal and for judges to travel as necessary to hold sessions at other duty stations.

2. The Registries of the Dispute Tribunal shall be established in New York, Geneva and Nairobi, each consisting of a Registrar and such other staff as necessary.

3. The expenses of the Dispute Tribunal shall be borne by the United Nations.

4. Compensation ordered by the Dispute Tribunal shall be paid by the United Nations Secretariat or separately administered United Nations funds and programmes, as applicable and appropriate, or by the specialized agency, organization or entity that has accepted the jurisdiction of the Dispute Tribunal.

Article 7

1. Subject to the provisions of the present statute, the Dispute Tribunal shall establish its own rules of procedure, which shall be subject to approval by the General Assembly.

2. The rules of procedure of the Dispute Tribunal shall include provisions concerning:

(a) Organization of work;

(b) Presentation of submissions and the procedure to be followed in respect thereto;

(c) Procedures for maintaining the confidentiality and inadmissibility of verbal or written statements made during the mediation process;

(d) Intervention by persons not party to the case whose rights may be affected by the judgement;

(e) Oral hearings;

(f) Publication of judgements;

(g) Functions of the Registries;

(h) Procedure for summary dismissal;

(i) Evidentiary procedure;

(j) Suspension of implementation of contested administrative decisions;

(k) Procedure for the recusal of judges;

(l) Other matters relating to the functioning of the Dispute Tribunal.

Article 8

1. An application shall be receivable if:

(a) The Dispute Tribunal is competent to hear and pass judgement on the application, pursuant to article 2 of the present statute;

(b) An applicant is eligible to file an application, pursuant to article 3 of the present statute;

(c) An applicant has previously submitted the contested administrative decision for management evaluation, where required; and

(d) The application is filed within the following deadlines:

(i) In cases where a management evaluation of the contested decision is required:

a. Within 90 calendar days of the applicant's receipt of the response by management to his or her submission; or

b. Within 90 calendar days of the expiry of the relevant response period for the management evaluation if no response to the request was provided. The response period shall be 30 calendar days after the submission of the decision to management evaluation for disputes arising at Headquarters and 45 calendar days for other offices;

(ii) In cases where a management evaluation of the contested decision is not required, within 90 calendar days of the applicant's receipt of the administrative decision;

(iii) The deadlines provided for in subparagraphs (*d*) (i) and (ii) of the present paragraph shall be extended to one year if the application is filed by any person making claims in the name of an incapacitated or deceased staff member of the United Nations, including the United Nations Secretariat or separately administered United Nations funds and programmes;

(iv) Where the parties have sought mediation of their dispute within the deadlines for the filing of an application under subparagraph (*d*) of the present paragraph, but did not reach an agreement, the application is filed within 90 calendar days after the mediation has broken down in accordance with the procedures laid down in the terms of reference of the Mediation Division.

2. An application shall not be receivable if the dispute arising from the contested administrative decision had been resolved by an agreement reached through mediation. However, an applicant may file an application to enforce the implementation of an agreement reached through mediation, which shall be receivable if the agreement has not been implemented and the application is filed within 90 calendar days after the last day for the implementation as specified in the mediation agreement or, when the mediation agreement is silent on the matter, after the thirtieth day from the date of the signing of the agreement.

3. The Dispute Tribunal may decide in writing, upon written request by the applicant, to suspend or waive the deadlines for a limited period of time and only in exceptional cases. The Dispute Tribunal shall not suspend or waive the deadlines for management evaluation.

4. Notwithstanding paragraph 3 of the present article, an application shall not be receivable if it is filed more than three years after the applicant's receipt of the contested administrative decision.

5. The filing of an application shall not have the effect of suspending the implementation of the contested administrative decision.

6. An application and other submissions shall be filed in any of the official languages of the United Nations.

Article 9

1. The Dispute Tribunal may order production of documents or such other evidence as it deems necessary.

2. The Dispute Tribunal shall decide whether the personal appearance of the applicant or any other person is required at oral proceedings and the appropriate means for satisfying the requirement of personal appearance.

3. The oral proceedings of the Dispute Tribunal shall be held in public unless the Dispute Tribunal decides, at its own initiative or at the request of either party, that exceptional circumstances require the proceedings to be closed.

Article 10

1. The Dispute Tribunal may suspend proceedings in a case at the request of the parties for a time to be specified by it in writing.

2. At any time during the proceedings, the Dispute Tribunal may order an interim measure, which is without appeal, to provide temporary relief to either party, where the contested administrative decision appears prima facie to be unlawful, in cases of particular urgency, and where its implementation would cause irreparable damage. This temporary relief may include an order to suspend the implementation of the contested administrative decision, except in cases of appointment, promotion or termination.

3. At any time during the deliberations, the Dispute Tribunal may propose to refer the case to mediation. With the consent of the parties, it shall suspend the proceedings for a time to be specified by it. If a mediation agreement is not reached within this period of time, the Dispute Tribunal shall continue with its proceedings unless the parties request otherwise.

4. Prior to a determination of the merits of a case, should the Dispute Tribunal find that a relevant procedure prescribed in the Staff Regulations and Rules or applicable administrative issuances has not been observed, the Dispute Tribunal may, with the concurrence of the Secretary-General of the United Nations, remand the case for institution or correction of the required procedure, which, in any case, should not exceed three months. In such cases, the Dispute Tribunal may order the payment of compensation for procedural delay to the applicant for such loss as may have been caused by such procedural delay, which is not to exceed the equivalent of three months' net base salary.

5. As part of its judgement, the Dispute Tribunal may order one or both of the following:

(a) Rescission of the contested administrative decision or specific performance, provided that, where the contested administrative decision concerns appointment, promotion or termination, the Dispute Tribunal shall also set an amount of compensation that the respondent may elect to pay as an alternative to the rescission of the contested ad-

ministrative decision or specific performance ordered, subject to subparagraph *(b)* of the present paragraph;

(b) Compensation, which shall normally not exceed the equivalent of two years' net base salary of the applicant. The Dispute Tribunal may, however, in exceptional cases order the payment of a higher compensation and shall provide the reasons for that decision.

6. Where the Dispute Tribunal determines that a party has manifestly abused the proceedings before it, it may award costs against that party.

7. The Dispute Tribunal shall not award exemplary or punitive damages.

8. The Dispute Tribunal may refer appropriate cases to the Secretary-General of the United Nations or the executive heads of separately administered United Nations funds and programmes for possible action to enforce accountability.

9. Cases before the Dispute Tribunal shall normally be considered by a single judge. However, the President of the United Nations Appeals Tribunal may, within seven calendar days of a written request by the President of the Dispute Tribunal, authorize the referral of a case to a panel of three judges of the Dispute Tribunal, when necessary, by reason of the particular complexity or importance of the case. Cases referred to a panel of three judges shall be decided by a majority vote.

Article 11

1. The judgements of the Dispute Tribunal shall be issued in writing and shall state the reasons, facts and law on which they are based.

2. The deliberations of the Dispute Tribunal shall be confidential.

3. The judgements of the Dispute Tribunal shall be binding upon the parties, but are subject to appeal in accordance with the statute of the United Nations Appeals Tribunal. In the absence of such appeal, they shall be executable following the expiry of the time provided for appeal in the statute of the Appeals Tribunal.

4. The judgements of the Dispute Tribunal shall be drawn up in any of the official languages of the United Nations, in two originals, which shall be deposited in the archives of the United Nations.

5. A copy of the judgement shall be communicated to each party in the case. The applicant shall receive a copy in the language in which the application was submitted unless he or she requests a copy in another official language of the United Nations.

6. The judgements of the Dispute Tribunal shall be published, while protecting personal data, and made generally available by the Registry of the Tribunal.

Article 12

1. Either party may apply to the Dispute Tribunal for a revision of an executable judgement on the basis of the discovery of a decisive fact which was, at the time the judgement was rendered, unknown to the Dispute Tribunal and to the party applying for revision, always provided that such ignorance was not due to negligence. The application must be made within 30 calendar days of the discovery of the fact and within one year of the date of the judgement.

2. Clerical or arithmetical mistakes, or errors arising therein from any accidental slip or omission, may at any time be corrected by the Dispute Tribunal, either on its own motion or on the application of any of the parties.

3. Either party may apply to the Dispute Tribunal for an interpretation of the meaning or the scope of the final judgement, provided that it is not under consideration by the Appeals Tribunal.

4. Once a judgement is executable under article 11, paragraph 3, of the present statute, either party may apply to the Dispute Tribunal for an order for execution of the judgement if the judgement requires execution within a certain period of time and such execution has not been carried out.

Article 13

The present statute may be amended by decision of the General Assembly.

ANNEX II

Statute of the United Nations Appeals Tribunal

Article 1

A tribunal is established by the present statute as the second instance of the two-tier formal system of administration of justice, to be known as the United Nations Appeals Tribunal.

Article 2

1. The Appeals Tribunal shall be competent to hear and pass judgement on an appeal filed against a judgement rendered by the United Nations Dispute Tribunal in which it is asserted that the Dispute Tribunal has:

(a) Exceeded its jurisdiction or competence;

(b) Failed to exercise jurisdiction vested in it;

(c) Erred on a question of law;

(d) Committed an error in procedure, such as to affect the decision of the case; or

(e) Erred on a question of fact, resulting in a manifestly unreasonable decision.

2. An appeal may be filed by either party (i.e., the applicant, a person making claims in the name of an incapacitated or deceased applicant, or the respondent) to a judgement of the Dispute Tribunal.

3. The Appeals Tribunal may affirm, reverse, modify or remand the judgement of the Dispute Tribunal. It may also issue all orders necessary or appropriate in aid of its jurisdiction and consonant with the present statute.

4. In cases of appeal under paragraph 1 *(e)* of the present article, the Appeals Tribunal shall be competent:

(a) To affirm, reverse or modify findings of fact of the Dispute Tribunal on the basis of substantial evidence in the written record; or

(b) To remand the case to the Dispute Tribunal for additional findings of fact, subject to paragraph 5 of the present article, if it determines that further findings of fact are necessary.

5. In exceptional circumstances, and where the Appeals Tribunal determines that the facts are likely to be established with documentary evidence, including written testimony, it may receive such additional evidence if that is in the interest of justice and the efficient and expeditious

resolution of the proceedings. Where this is not the case, or where the Appeals Tribunal determines that a decision cannot be taken without oral testimony or other forms of non-written evidence, it shall remand the case to the Dispute Tribunal. The evidence under this paragraph shall not include evidence that was known to either party and should have been presented at the level of the Dispute Tribunal.

6. Where the Appeals Tribunal remands a case to the Dispute Tribunal, it may order that the case be considered by a different judge of the Dispute Tribunal.

7. For the purposes of the present article, "written record" means anything that has been entered in the formal record of the Dispute Tribunal, including submissions, evidence, testimony, motions, objections, rulings and the judgement, and any evidence received in accordance with paragraph 5 of the present article.

8. In the event of a dispute as to whether the Appeals Tribunal has competence under the present statute, the Appeals Tribunal shall decide on the matter.

9. The Appeals Tribunal shall be competent to hear and pass judgement on an appeal of a decision of the Standing Committee acting on behalf of the United Nations Joint Staff Pension Board, alleging non-observance of the regulations of the United Nations Joint Staff Pension Fund, submitted by:

(a) Any staff member of a member organization of the Pension Fund which has accepted the jurisdiction of the Appeals Tribunal in Pension Fund cases who is eligible under article 21 of the regulations of the Fund as a participant in the Fund, even if his or her employment has ceased, and any person who has acceded to such staff member's rights upon his or her death;

(b) Any other person who can show that he or she is entitled to rights under the regulations of the Pension Fund by virtue of the participation in the Fund of a staff member of such member organization. In such cases, remands, if any, shall be to the Standing Committee acting on behalf of the United Nations Joint Staff Pension Board.

10. The Appeals Tribunal shall be competent to hear and pass judgement on an application filed against a specialized agency brought into relationship with the United Nations in accordance with the provisions of Articles 57 and 63 of the Charter of the United Nations or other international organization or entity established by a treaty and participating in the common system of conditions of service, where a special agreement has been concluded between the agency, organization or entity concerned and the Secretary-General of the United Nations to accept the terms of the jurisdiction of the Appeals Tribunal, consonant with the present statute. Such special agreement shall provide that the agency, organization or entity concerned shall be bound by the judgements of the Appeals Tribunal and be responsible for the payment of any compensation awarded by the Appeals Tribunal in respect of its own staff members and shall include, inter alia, provisions concerning its participation in the administrative arrangements for the functioning of the Appeals Tribunal and concerning its sharing of the expenses of the Appeals Tribunal. Such special agreement shall also contain other provisions required for the Appeals Tribunal to carry out its functions vis-a-vis the agency, organization or entity. Such special agreement may only be concluded if the agency, organization or entity utilizes a neutral first instance process that includes a written record and a written decision providing reasons, fact and law. In such cases remands, if any, shall be to the first instance process of the agency, organization or entity.

Article 3

1. The Appeals Tribunal shall be composed of seven judges.

2. The judges shall be appointed by the General Assembly on the recommendation of the Internal Justice Council in accordance with General Assembly resolution 62/228. No two judges shall be of the same nationality. Due regard shall be given to geographical distribution and gender balance.

3. To be eligible for appointment as a judge, a person shall:

(a) Be of high moral character; and

(b) Possess at least 15 years of judicial experience in the field of administrative law, or the equivalent within one or more national jurisdictions.

4. A judge of the Appeals Tribunal shall be appointed for one non-renewable term of seven years. As a transitional measure, three of the judges initially appointed, to be determined by drawing of lots, shall serve three years and may be reappointed to the same Appeals Tribunal for a further non-renewable term of seven years. A current or former judge of the Dispute Tribunal shall not be eligible to serve in the Appeals Tribunal.

5. A judge of the Appeals Tribunal appointed to replace a judge whose term of office has not expired shall hold office for the remainder of his or her predecessor's term and may be reappointed for one non-renewable term of seven years, provided that the unexpired term is less than three years.

6. A judge of the Appeals Tribunal shall not be eligible for any appointment within the United Nations, except another judicial post, for a period of five years following his or her term of office.

7. The Appeals Tribunal shall elect a President and two Vice-Presidents.

8. A judge of the Appeals Tribunal shall serve in his or her personal capacity and enjoy full independence.

9. A judge of the Appeals Tribunal who has, or appears to have, a conflict of interest shall recuse himself or herself from the case. Where a party requests such recusal, the decision shall be taken by the President of the Appeals Tribunal.

10. A judge of the Appeals Tribunal may only be removed by the General Assembly in case of misconduct or incapacity.

11. A judge of the Appeals Tribunal may resign, by notifying the General Assembly through the Secretary-General of the United Nations. The resignation shall take effect from the date of notification, unless the notice of resignation specifies a later date.

Article 4

1. The Appeals Tribunal shall exercise its functions in New York. However, it may decide to hold sessions in Geneva or Nairobi, as required by its caseload.

2. The Appeals Tribunal shall hold ordinary sessions at dates to be fixed by its rules of procedure, subject to

the determination of its President that there is a sufficient number of cases to justify holding the session.

3. Extraordinary sessions may be convoked by the President, as required by the caseload.

Article 5

1. The Secretary-General of the United Nations shall make the administrative arrangements necessary for the functioning of the Appeals Tribunal, including provisions for the travel and related costs of staff whose physical presence before the Appeals Tribunal is deemed necessary by the Appeals Tribunal and for judges to travel as necessary to hold sessions in Geneva and Nairobi.

2. The Registry of the Appeals Tribunal shall be established in New York. It shall consist of a Registrar and such other staff as necessary.

3. The expenses of the Appeals Tribunal shall be borne by the United Nations.

4. Compensation ordered by the Appeals Tribunal shall be paid by the United Nations Secretariat or separately administered United Nations funds and programmes, as applicable and appropriate, or by the specialized agency, organization or entity that has accepted the jurisdiction of the Appeals Tribunal.

Article 6

1. Subject to the provisions of the present statute, the Appeals Tribunal shall establish its own rules of procedure, which shall be subject to approval by the General Assembly.

2. The rules of procedure of the Appeals Tribunal shall include provisions concerning:

(a) Election of the President and Vice-Presidents;

(b) Composition of the Appeals Tribunal for its sessions;

(c) Organization of work;

(d) Presentation of submissions and the procedure to be followed in respect thereto;

(e) Procedures for maintaining the confidentiality and inadmissibility of verbal or written statements made during the mediation process;

(f) Intervention by persons not party to the case whose rights may have been affected by the judgement of the Dispute Tribunal and whose rights might therefore also be affected by the judgement of the Appeals Tribunal;

(g) The filing of friend-of-court briefs, upon motion and with the permission of the Appeals Tribunal;

(h) Oral proceedings;

(i) Publication of judgements;

(j) Functions of the Registry;

(k) Procedure for the recusal of judges;

(l) Other matters relating to the functioning of the Appeals Tribunal.

Article 7

1. An appeal shall be receivable if:

(a) The Appeals Tribunal is competent to hear and pass judgement on the appeal, pursuant to article 2, paragraph 1, of the present statute;

(b) The appellant is eligible to file the appeal, pursuant to article 2, paragraph 2, of the present statute; and

(c) The appeal is filed within 45 calendar days of the receipt of the judgement of the Dispute Tribunal or, where the Appeals Tribunal has decided to waive or suspend that deadline in accordance with paragraph 3 of the present article, within the period specified by the Appeals Tribunal.

2. For purposes of applications alleging non-observance of the regulations of the United Nations Joint Staff Pension Fund arising out of a decision of the United Nations Joint Staff Pension Board, an application shall be receivable if filed within 90 calendar days of receipt of the Board's decision.

3. The Appeals Tribunal may decide in writing, upon written request by the applicant, to suspend or waive the deadlines for a limited period of time and only in exceptional cases. The Appeals Tribunal shall not suspend or waive the deadlines for management evaluation.

4. Notwithstanding paragraph 3 of the present article, an application shall not be receivable if it is filed more than one year after the judgement of the Dispute Tribunal.

5. The filing of appeals shall have the effect of suspending the execution of the judgement contested.

6. An appeal and other submissions shall be filed in any of the official languages of the United Nations.

Article 8

1. The Appeals Tribunal may order production of documents or such other evidence as it deems necessary, subject to article 2 of the present statute.

2. The Appeals Tribunal shall decide whether the personal appearance of the appellant or any other person is required at oral proceedings and the appropriate means to achieve that purpose.

3. The judges assigned to a case will determine whether to hold oral proceedings.

4. The oral proceedings of the Appeals Tribunal shall be held in public unless the Appeals Tribunal decides, at its own initiative or at the request of either party, that exceptional circumstances require the proceedings to be closed.

Article 9

1. The Appeals Tribunal may order one or both of the following:

(a) Rescission of the contested administrative decision or specific performance, provided that, where the contested administrative decision concerns appointment, promotion or termination, the Appeals Tribunal shall also set an amount of compensation that the respondent may elect to pay as an alternative to the rescission of the contested administrative decision or specific performance ordered, subject to subparagraph *(b)* of the present paragraph;

(b) Compensation, which shall normally not exceed the equivalent of two years' net base salary of the applicant. The Appeals Tribunal may, however, in exceptional cases order the payment of a higher compensation and shall provide the reasons for that decision.

2. Where the Appeals Tribunal determines that a party has manifestly abused the appeals process, it may award costs against that party.

3. The Appeals Tribunal shall not award exemplary or punitive damages.

4. At any time during the proceedings, the Appeals Tribunal may order an interim measure to provide temporary relief to either party to prevent irreparable harm and to maintain consistency with the judgement of the Dispute Tribunal.

5. The Appeals Tribunal may refer appropriate cases to the Secretary-General of the United Nations or executive heads of separately administered United Nations funds and programmes for possible action to enforce accountability.

Article 10

1. Cases before the Appeals Tribunal shall normally be reviewed by a panel of three judges and shall be decided by a majority vote.

2. Where the President or any two judges sitting on a particular case consider that the case raises a significant question of law, at any time before judgement is rendered, the case may be referred for consideration by the whole Appeals Tribunal. A quorum in such cases shall be five judges.

3. The judgements of the Appeals Tribunal shall be issued in writing and shall state the reasons, facts and law on which they are based.

4. The deliberations of the Appeals Tribunal shall be confidential.

5. The judgements of the Appeals Tribunal shall be binding upon the parties.

6. The judgements of the Appeals Tribunal shall be final and without appeal, subject to the provisions of article 11 of the present statute.

7. The judgements of the Appeals Tribunal shall be drawn up in any of the official languages of the United Nations, in two originals, which shall be deposited in the archives of the United Nations.

8. A copy of the judgement shall be communicated to each party in the case. The applicant shall receive a copy in the language in which the appeal was submitted unless he or she requests a copy in another official language of the United Nations.

9. The judgements of the Appeals Tribunal shall be published, while protecting personal data, and made generally available by the Registry of the Tribunal.

Article 11

1. Subject to article 2 of the present statute, either party may apply to the Appeals Tribunal for a revision of a judgement on the basis of the discovery of a decisive fact which was, at the time the judgement was rendered, unknown to the Appeals Tribunal and to the party applying for revision, always provided that such ignorance was not due to negligence. The application must be made within 30 calendar days of the discovery of the fact and within one year of the date of the judgement.

2. Clerical or arithmetical mistakes, or errors arising therein from any accidental slip or omission, may at any time be corrected by the Appeals Tribunal, either on its own motion or on the application of any of the parties.

3. Either party may apply to the Appeals Tribunal for an interpretation of the meaning or scope of the judgement.

4. Where the judgement requires execution within a certain period of time and such execution has not been carried out, either party may apply to the Appeals Tribunal for an order for execution of the judgement.

Article 12

The present statute may be amended by decision of the General Assembly.

Also on 24 December, the Assembly decided that the agenda item on the administration of justice at the United Nations would remain for consideration during its resumed sixty-third (2009) session (**decision 63/552**).

Ad Hoc Committee

In preparation for the meeting of the Ad Hoc Committee on the Administration of Justice at the United Nations scheduled for April (see below), the Secretary-General, in a March note [A/62/748 & Corr.1], in response to General Assembly decision 62/519 [YUN 2007, p. 1528], set out his responses to the Sixth Committee's requests for information, as well as the discussion on the draft statutes of the Dispute and the Appeals Tribunals, which incorporated the input provided by staff representatives through the contact group on the administration of justice in annexes I and II, respectively, to the note.

The first session of the Ad Hoc Committee (New York, 10-18, and 21 and 24 April) [A/63/55], discussed the two draft statutes, including scope *ratione personae* of the new system of the administration of justice, appointment, composition, jurisdiction and powers of the tribunals, and legal assistance.

The Ad Hoc Committee recommend that, at the Assembly's sixty-third (2008) session, its Sixth Committee should establish a working group to finalize the draft statutes of the Tribunals as a priority, bearing in mind the Assembly's decision to establish a two-tier formal system of administration of justice as from 1 January 2009, and continue the discussion of the other legal aspects of the administration of justice at the United Nations.

Communications. On 29 April [A/C.5/62/27], the General Assembly President drew to the attention of the Chairman of the Fifth Committee a 24 April letter from the Chairman of the Ad Hoc Committee on the informal consultations held during the Committee's session on the basis of the Secretary-General's March note (above), and the coordinator's summary of the preliminary observations made during those consultations on the draft statutes.

On 9 July [A/62/914], Germany, in a letter to the General Assembly President, said that informal discussions on the two draft statutes were held in May and June, coordinated by Germany, the results of which were contained in a paper by the coordinator, which updated the earlier paper annexed to the Ad Hoc Committee's April report (see above). Germany requested the re-establishment of the Committee for one meeting to take note of the coordinator's oral report on the informal inter-sessional consultations and to request the Secretary-General to issue the coordinator's summary as an addendum to the Ad Hoc Committee's report.

By **decision 62/551** of 28 July, the Assembly re-established the Ad Hoc Committee and requested the Secretary-General to issue the coordinator's summary as an addendum to the Ad Hoc Committee's report.

By **decision 63/531** of 11 December, the Assembly decided that the Ad Hoc Committee would continue its work on the outstanding legal aspects of the administration of justice at the United Nations. It would meet from 20 to 24 April 2009 and report on its work to the Assembly at its sixty-fourth (2009) session.

Joint Appeals Board

In response to General Assembly resolution 55/258 [YUN 2001, p. 1337], the Secretary-General submitted an August report [A/63/211] on the outcome of the work of the Joint Appeals Board (JAB) in New York, Geneva, Vienna and Nairobi for 2007. The report also compared 2007 and 2006 data and, in response to Assembly resolution 57/307 [YUN 2003, p. 1459], provided statistics on the disposition of cases and information on the work of the Panel of Counsel.

The Secretary-General observed that 177 appeals and suspension-of-action cases were filed with JAB in those duty stations in 2007, as compared to 152 in the previous year; JAB disposed of 181 cases, compared to 140 in 2006. Regarding disciplinary cases, which were accorded priority, 32 such cases were referred to the New York Joint Disciplinary Committee, which disposed of 21 of those cases; the Geneva Committee received seven new cases and disposed of 17; the Nairobi Committee considered one case; and no cases were submitted to the Vienna Committee. In 2007, the Secretary-General accepted fully or partially 143 (or 88 per cent) of unanimous JAB decisions, compared to 83 in 2006, and rejected 20 (12 per cent), compared to 16 (16 per cent) in 2006. In 2007, 339 cases were brought to the Panel of Counsel in New York, compared with 294 in 2006, an increase of 15.31 per cent. Of those cases, 240 (70.8 per cent) went through the formal appeals process and 99 (29.2 per cent) were dealt with informally.

Office of Ombudsman

Pursuant to General Assembly resolution 59/283 [YUN 2005, p. 1529], the Secretary-General submitted an August report [A/63/283] on the activities of the United Nations Ombudsman covering the period from 1 August 2007 to 31 July 2008, which reviewed transitional measures being developed regarding the establishment of a single integrated and decentralized office.

During the reporting period, 670 new cases were opened—almost 56 each month. Men initiating cases outnumbered women 52 per cent to 47 per cent, while groups constituted 1 per cent. The most important issues raised by staff related to promotion or career considerations (23 per cent of all cases), followed by interpersonal conflicts, conditions of service, entitlements, separation and termination, and standards of conduct. In over half of the cases, the assistance provided by the Office involved coaching and helping staff to explore options and solutions to work-related problems. Direct action by the Ombudsman to resolve problems was undertaken in 28 per cent of cases, while referral to other offices and direct mediation was provided in 9 and 2 per cent of cases, respectively.

ACABQ report. In a November report [A/63/545], ACABQ said that the Secretary-General should report regularly to the General Assembly on actions taken to address the findings of the Ombudsman on systemic issues. It noted with concern the comments of the Ombudsman about the lack of clarity and overlap in the role of the Office of the Ombudsman and that of other offices, such as the Ethics Office. It urged the Secretary-General to clarify the roles and responsibilities of both Offices, and recommended that he ensure the expeditious issuance of the updated information circular on conflict resolution in the Secretariat [ST/IC/2004/4]. It urged the Ombudsman to complete the revision of the terms of reference of that Office and to issue those terms as rapidly as possible. ACABQ said that it would be helpful if future reports on the activities of the Ombudsman included monthly data and analysis for the current period, as well as statistical information on cases and analysis of data and trends over a five-year period or longer. Consideration should be given to ways of measuring the effectiveness of the Ombudsman interventions. The report should also provide indicators that would allow an assessment of progress towards such goals. ACABQ encouraged the Ombudsman to elaborate on statistics and data in the report by providing descriptive material based on actual work performed, without prejudicing staff confidentiality.

Systemic human resources issues

In response to General Assembly resolution 62/228 [YUN 2007, p. 1528], the Secretary-General submitted a July report [A/63/132] on specific measures taken by the administration to address seven systemic human resources issues raised in the context of the reform of the internal system of the administration of justice in his 2007 report of the activities of the Ombudsman [YUN 2007, p. 1533]. Those issues included: the staff selection system; mobility; locally recruited staff; contractual practices; special entities established by the United Nations; staff welfare; and coverage for psychological care.

The Secretary-General recognized that many of the issues included in the report on the activities of the Ombudsman were under review internally and would result in proposals to the Assembly; others were already before the Assembly or were in need of further consideration. Furthermore, he intended to ask the Office of the Ombudsman, the Office of Human Resources Management and the Departments of Political Affairs, Peacekeeping Operations and Field Support to intensify their communication strategies with the staff of the entire Organization.

Criminal behaviour and disciplinary action

Reports of Secretary-General. In response to General Assembly resolution 59/287 [YUN 2005, p. 1474], the Secretary-General transmitted a July report [A/63/202] on disciplinary matters and possible criminal behaviour, covering the period from 1 July 2007 to 30 June 2008. The report provided information on the disciplinary and/or legal action taken in cases of established misconduct and/or criminal behaviour. It reviewed the administrative machinery in disciplinary matters and summarized cases for which a disciplinary measure was imposed by the Secretary-General, most of which related to abuse of authority/harassment; gross negligence; fraud/misrepresentation; theft/misappropriation; sexual exploitation and abuse; computer-related misconduct; and conflict of interest.

In response to resolution 62/63 [YUN 2007, p. 102], the Secretary-General transmitted an August report [A/63/260 & Add.1] on criminal accountability of UN officials and experts on mission, which the General Assembly acted on in **resolution 63/119** of 11 December (see p. 98).

As requested in Assembly resolution 62/247 (see p. 1576), the Secretary-General transmitted an August report [A/63/331] on the practices relating to the sharing of information between the UN and law enforcement authorities, as well as referrals of possible criminal cases related to UN staff and officials and experts on mission. The two principal situations in which information was passed between the Organization and law enforcement authorities were: when the Organization, through its own investigations, had uncovered prima facie evidence of potential criminal conduct within the jurisdiction of a Member State and decided to refer that evidence to the Member State for appropriate action; and when the Organization had been approached by a Member State for access to information or material and/or witnesses in the context of an external investigation by law enforcement authorities and/or criminal proceedings being conducted by the Member State.

The Secretary-General stated that overall the United Nations had not experienced any problems in its cooperation with the law enforcement authorities of Member States in sharing information or material for criminal investigations. There had been a significant increase in the number of requests made to the Organization from law enforcement authorities of Member States for information or material. The United Nations was currently cooperating with law enforcement authorities in 65 jurisdictions of 28 Member States.

ACABQ report. In an October report [A/63/492], ACABQ stated that the information-sharing practices between the UN and national law enforcement authorities, as well as referrals of possible criminal cases related to UN staff and officials and experts on mission, were extremely important issues that went to the heart of the independence of the international civil service and the ability of other UN officials to carry out their duties effectively, including accountability for personal conduct. Noting that the issues dealt with in the Secretary-General's report had administrative and legal implications, affecting UN officials in duty stations all over the world, ACABQ said that the procedures for such cooperation with host countries, in particular in situations involving requests for waivers of immunity, should be consistent and transparent.

UN Administrative Tribunal

In its annual note to the General Assembly [A/INF/63/5], the seven-member United Nations Administrative Tribunal reported, through the Secretary-General, that it had delivered 62 judgements in 2008, relating to cases brought by staff against the Secretary-General or the executive heads of other UN bodies concerning disputes involving terms of appointment and other issues. It also drew the Assembly's attention to cases that merited special attention. The Tribunal met in plenary in New York on 21 November and held three panel sessions (New York, 21 April–2 May; Geneva, 23 June–25 July; and New York, 27 October–26 November).

Appendices

Appendix I

Roster of the United Nations

(There were 192 Member States as at 31 December 2008.)

Member State	*Date of admission*
Afghanistan	19 Nov. 1946
Albania	14 Dec. 1955
Algeria	8 Oct. 1962
Andorra	28 July 1993
Angola	1 Dec. 1976
Antigua and Barbuda	11 Nov. 1981
Argentina	24 Oct. 1945
Armenia	2 Mar. 1992
Australia	1 Nov. 1945
Austria	14 Dec. 1955
Azerbaijan	2 Mar. 1992
Bahamas	18 Sep. 1973
Bahrain	21 Sep. 1971
Bangladesh	17 Sep. 1974
Barbados	9 Dec. 1966
Belarus[1]	24 Oct. 1945
Belgium	27 Dec. 1945
Belize	25 Sep. 1981
Benin	20 Sep. 1960
Bhutan	21 Sep. 1971
Bolivia	14 Nov. 1945
Bosnia and Herzegovina[2]	22 May 1992
Botswana	17 Oct. 1966
Brazil	24 Oct. 1945
Brunei Darussalam	21 Sep. 1984
Bulgaria	14 Dec. 1955
Burkina Faso	20 Sep. 1960
Burundi	18 Sep. 1962
Cambodia	14 Dec. 1955
Cameroon	20 Sep. 1960
Canada	9 Nov. 1945
Cape Verde	16 Sep. 1975
Central African Republic	20 Sep. 1960
Chad	20 Sep. 1960
Chile	24 Oct. 1945
China	24 Oct. 1945
Colombia	5 Nov. 1945
Comoros	12 Nov. 1975
Congo	20 Sep. 1960
Costa Rica	2 Nov. 1945
Côte d'Ivoire	20 Sep. 1960
Croatia[2]	22 May 1992
Cuba	24 Oct. 1945
Cyprus	20 Sep. 1960
Czech Republic[3]	19 Jan. 1993
Democratic People's Republic of Korea	17 Sep. 1991
Democratic Republic of the Congo[4]	20 Sep. 1960
Denmark	24 Oct. 1945
Djibouti	20 Sep. 1977
Dominica	18 Dec. 1978
Dominican Republic	24 Oct. 1945
Ecuador	21 Dec. 1945
Egypt[5]	24 Oct. 1945
El Salvador	24 Oct. 1945
Equatorial Guinea	12 Nov. 1968
Eritrea	28 May 1993
Estonia	17 Sep. 1991
Ethiopia	13 Nov. 1945
Fiji	13 Oct. 1970
Finland	14 Dec. 1955
France	24 Oct. 1945
Gabon	20 Sep. 1960
Gambia	21 Sep. 1965
Georgia	31 July 1992
Germany[6]	18 Sep. 1973
Ghana	8 Mar. 1957
Greece	25 Oct. 1945
Grenada	17 Sep. 1974
Guatemala	21 Nov. 1945
Guinea	12 Dec. 1958
Guinea-Bissau	17 Sep. 1974
Guyana	20 Sep. 1966
Haiti	24 Oct. 1945
Honduras	17 Dec. 1945
Hungary	14 Dec. 1955
Iceland	19 Nov. 1946
India	30 Oct. 1945
Indonesia[7]	28 Sep. 1950
Iran (Islamic Republic of)	24 Oct. 1945
Iraq	21 Dec. 1945
Ireland	14 Dec. 1955
Israel	11 May 1949
Italy	14 Dec. 1955
Jamaica	18 Sep. 1962
Japan	18 Dec. 1956
Jordan	14 Dec. 1955
Kazakhstan	2 Mar. 1992
Kenya	16 Dec. 1963
Kiribati	14 Sep. 1999
Kuwait	14 May 1963
Kyrgyzstan	2 Mar. 1992
Lao People's Democratic Republic	14 Dec. 1955
Latvia	17 Sep. 1991
Lebanon	24 Oct. 1945
Lesotho	17 Oct. 1966
Liberia	2 Nov. 1945
Libyan Arab Jamahiriya	14 Dec. 1955
Liechtenstein	18 Sep. 1990
Lithuania	17 Sep. 1991
Luxembourg	24 Oct. 1945
Madagascar	20 Sep. 1960
Malawi	1 Dec. 1964
Malaysia[8]	17 Sep. 1957
Maldives	21 Sep. 1965
Mali	28 Sep. 1960
Malta	1 Dec. 1964
Marshall Islands	17 Sep. 1991
Mauritania	27 Oct. 1961
Mauritius	24 Apr. 1968
Mexico	7 Nov. 1945
Micronesia (Federated States of)	17 Sep. 1991
Monaco	28 May 1993
Mongolia	27 Oct. 1961
Montenegro[2]	28 June 2006
Morocco	12 Nov. 1956
Mozambique	16 Sep. 1975
Myanmar	19 Apr. 1948
Namibia	23 Apr. 1990
Nauru	14 Sep. 1999
Nepal	14 Dec. 1955
Netherlands	10 Dec. 1945
New Zealand	24 Oct. 1945
Nicaragua	24 Oct. 1945
Niger	20 Sep. 1960
Nigeria	7 Oct. 1960
Norway	27 Nov. 1945
Oman	7 Oct. 1971
Pakistan	30 Sep. 1947
Palau	15 Dec. 1994
Panama	13 Nov. 1945
Papua New Guinea	10 Oct. 1975
Paraguay	24 Oct. 1945
Peru	31 Oct. 1945
Philippines	24 Oct. 1945
Poland	24 Oct. 1945
Portugal	14 Dec. 1955
Qatar	21 Sep. 1971
Republic of Korea	17 Sep. 1991

Member State	*Date of admission*
Republic of Moldova	2 Mar. 1992
Romania	14 Dec. 1955
Russian Federation[9]	24 Oct. 1945
Rwanda	18 Sep. 1962
Saint Kitts and Nevis	23 Sep. 1983
Saint Lucia	18 Sep. 1979
Saint Vincent and the Grenadines	16 Sep. 1980
Samoa	15 Dec. 1976
San Marino	2 Mar. 1992
Sao Tome and Principe	16 Sep. 1975
Saudi Arabia	24 Oct. 1945
Senegal	28 Sep. 1960
Serbia[2]	1 Nov. 2000
Seychelles	21 Sep. 1976
Sierra Leone	27 Sep. 1961
Singapore[8]	21 Sep. 1965
Slovakia[3]	19 Jan. 1993
Slovenia[2]	22 May 1992
Solomon Islands	19 Sep. 1978
Somalia	20 Sep. 1960
South Africa	7 Nov. 1945
Spain	14 Dec. 1955
Sri Lanka	14 Dec. 1955
Sudan	12 Nov. 1956
Suriname	4 Dec. 1975
Swaziland	24 Sep. 1968
Sweden	19 Nov. 1946
Switzerland	10 Sep. 2002
Syrian Arab Republic[5]	24 Oct. 1945
Tajikistan	2 Mar. 1992
Thailand	16 Dec. 1946
The former Yugoslav Republic of Macedonia[2]	8 Apr. 1993
Timor-Leste	27 Sep. 2002
Togo	20 Sep. 1960
Tonga	14 Sep. 1999
Trinidad and Tobago	18 Sep. 1962
Tunisia	12 Nov. 1956
Turkey	24 Oct. 1945
Turkmenistan	2 Mar. 1992
Tuvalu	5 Sep. 2000
Uganda	25 Oct. 1962
Ukraine	24 Oct. 1945
United Arab Emirates	9 Dec. 1971
United Kingdom of Great Britain and Northern Ireland	24 Oct. 1945
United Republic of Tanzania[10]	14 Dec. 1961
United States of America	24 Oct. 1945
Uruguay	18 Dec. 1945
Uzbekistan	2 Mar. 1992
Vanuatu	15 Sep. 1981
Venezuela (Bolivarian Republic of)	15 Nov. 1945
Viet Nam	20 Sep. 1977
Yemen[11]	30 Sep. 1947
Zambia	1 Dec. 1964
Zimbabwe	25 Aug. 1980

Notes

[1] On 19 September 1991, the Byelorussian Soviet Socialist Republic informed the United Nations that it had changed its name to Belarus.

[2] The Socialist Federal Republic of Yugoslavia was an original Member of the United Nations, the Charter having been signed on its behalf on 26 June 1945 and ratified 19 October 1945, until its dissolution following the establishment and subsequent admission, as new Members, of Bosnia and Herzegovina, the Republic of Croatia, the Republic of Slovenia, The former Yugoslav Republic of Macedonia, and the Federal Republic of Yugoslavia. The Republic of Bosnia and Herzegovina, the Republic of Croatia and the Republic of Slovenia were admitted as Members of the United Nations on 22 May 1992. On 8 April 1993, the General Assembly decided to admit as a Member of the United Nations the state provisionally referred to for all purposes within the United Nations as "The former Yugoslav Republic of Macedonia", pending settlement of the difference that had arisen over its name. The Federal Republic of Yugoslavia was admitted as a Member of the United Nations on 1 November 2000. On 12 February 2003, it informed the United Nations that it had changed its name to Serbia and Montenegro, effective 4 February 2003. In a letter dated 3 June 2006, the President of the Republic of Serbia informed the Secretary-General that the membership of Serbia and Montenegro was being continued by the Republic of Serbia following Montenegro's declaration of independence from Serbia on 3 June 2006. On 28 June 2006, Montenegro was accepted as a United Nations Member State by the General Assembly.

[3] Czechoslovakia, an original Member of the United Nations from 24 October 1945, changed its name to the Czech and Slovak Federal Republic on 20 April 1990. It was dissolved on 1 January 1993 and succeeded by the Czech Republic and Slovakia, both of which became Members of the United Nations on 19 January 1993.

[4] The Republic of Zaire informed the United Nations that, effective 17 May 1997, it had changed its name to the Democratic Republic of the Congo.

[5] Egypt and Syria, both of which became Members of the United Nations on 24 October 1945, joined together—following a plebiscite held in those countries on 21 February 1958—to form the United Arab Republic. On 13 October 1961, Syria, having resumed its status as an independent State, also resumed its separate membership in the United Nations; it changed its name to the Syrian Arab Republic on 14 September 1971. The United Arab Republic continued as a Member of the United Nations and reverted to the name Egypt on 2 September 1971.

[6] Through accession of the German Democratic Republic to the Federal Republic of Germany on 3 October 1990, the two German States (both of which had become Members of the United Nations on 18 September 1973) united to form one sovereign State. As from that date, the Federal Republic of Germany has acted in the United Nations under the designation Germany.

[7] On 20 January 1965, Indonesia informed the Secretary-General that it had decided to withdraw from the United Nations. On 19 September 1966, it notified the Secretary-General of its decision to resume participation in the activities of the United Nations. On 28 September 1966, the General Assembly took note of that decision, and the President invited the representatives of Indonesia to take their seats in the Assembly.

[8] On 16 September 1963, Sabah (North Borneo), Sarawak and Singapore joined with the Federation of Malaya (which became a Member of the United Nations on 17 September 1957) to form Malaysia. On 9 August 1965, Singapore became an independent State; on 21 September 1965, it became a Member of the United Nations.

[9] The Union of Soviet Socialist Republics was an original Member of the United Nations from 24 October 1945. On 24 December 1991, the President of the Russian Federation informed the Secretary-General that the membership of the USSR in all United Nations organs was being continued by the Russian Federation.

[10] Tanganyika was admitted to the United Nations on 14 December 1961, Zanzibar on 16 December 1963. Following ratification, on 26 April 1964, of the Articles of Union between Tanganyika and Zanzibar, the two States became represented as a single Member: the United Republic of Tanganyika and Zanzibar; it changed its name to the United Republic of Tanzania on 1 November 1964.

[11] Yemen was admitted to the United Nations on 30 September 1947, Democratic Yemen on 14 December 1967. On 22 May 1990, the two countries merged and were thereafter represented as one Member of the United Nations under the designation Yemen.

Appendix II

Charter of the United Nations and Statute of the International Court of Justice

Charter of the United Nations

NOTE: The Charter of the United Nations was signed on 26 June 1945, in San Francisco, at the conclusion of the United Nations Conference on International Organization, and came into force on 24 October 1945. The Statute of the International Court of Justice is an integral part of the Charter.

Amendments to Articles 23, 27 and 61 of the Charter were adopted by the General Assembly on 17 December 1963 and came into force on 31 August 1965. A further amendment to Article 61 was adopted by the General Assembly on 20 December 1971 and came into force on 24 September 1973. An amendment to Article 109, adopted by the General Assembly on 20 December 1965, came into force on 12 June 1968.

The amendment to Article 23 enlarges the membership of the Security Council from 11 to 15. The amended Article 27 provides that decisions of the Security Council on procedural matters shall be made by an affirmative vote of nine members (formerly seven) and on all other matters by an affirmative vote of nine members (formerly seven), including the concurring votes of the five permanent members of the Security Council.

The amendment to Article 61, which entered into force on 31 August 1965, enlarges the membership of the Economic and Social Council from 18 to 27. The subsequent amendment to that Article, which entered into force on 24 September 1973, further increases the membership of the Council from 27 to 54.

The amendment to Article 109, which relates to the first paragraph of that Article, provides that a General Conference of Member States for the purpose of reviewing the Charter may be held at a date and place to be fixed by a two-thirds vote of the members of the General Assembly and by a vote of any nine members (formerly seven) of the Security Council. Paragraph 3 of Article 109, which deals with the consideration of a possible review conference during the tenth regular session of the General Assembly, has been retained in its original form in its reference to a "vote of any seven members of the Security Council", the paragraph having been acted upon in 1955 by the General Assembly, at its tenth regular session, and by the Security Council.

WE THE PEOPLES OF THE UNITED NATIONS DETERMINED

to save succeeding generations from the scourge of war, which twice in our lifetime has brought untold sorrow to mankind, and

to reaffirm faith in fundamental human rights, in the dignity and worth of the human person, in the equal rights of men and women and of nations large and small, and

to establish conditions under which justice and respect for the obligations arising from treaties and other sources of international law can be maintained, and

to promote social progress and better standards of life in larger freedom,

AND FOR THESE ENDS

to practice tolerance and live together in peace with one another as good neighbours, and

to unite our strength to maintain international peace and security, and

to ensure, by the acceptance of principles and the institution of methods, that armed force shall not be used, save in the common interest, and

to employ international machinery for the promotion of the economic and social advancement of all peoples,

HAVE RESOLVED TO COMBINE OUR EFFORTS TO ACCOMPLISH THESE AIMS

Accordingly, our respective Governments, through representatives assembled in the city of San Francisco, who have exhibited their full powers found to be in good and due form, have agreed to the present Charter of the United Nations and do hereby establish an international organization to be known as the United Nations.

Chapter I

PURPOSES AND PRINCIPLES

Article 1

The Purposes of the United Nations are:

1. To maintain international peace and security, and to that end: to take effective collective measures for the prevention and removal of threats to the peace, and for the suppression of acts of aggression or other breaches of the peace, and to bring about by peaceful means, and in conformity with the principles of justice and international law, adjustment or settlement of international disputes or situations which might lead to a breach of the peace;

2. To develop friendly relations among nations based on respect for the principle of equal rights and self-determination of peoples, and to take other appropriate measures to strengthen universal peace;

3. To achieve international co-operation in solving international problems of an economic, social, cultural or humanitarian character, and in promoting and encouraging respect for human rights and for fundamental freedoms for all without distinction as to race, sex, language or religion; and

4. To be a centre for harmonizing the actions of nations in the attainment of these common ends.

Article 2

The Organization and its Members, in pursuit of the Purposes stated in Article 1, shall act in accordance with the following Principles:

1. The Organization is based on the principle of the sovereign equality of all its Members.
2. All Members, in order to ensure to all of them the rights and benefits resulting from membership, shall fulfil in good faith the obligations assumed by them in accordance with the present Charter.
3. All Members shall settle their international disputes by peaceful means in such a manner that international peace and security, and justice, are not endangered.
4. All Members shall refrain in their international relations from the threat or use of force against the territorial integrity or political independence of any state, or in any other manner inconsistent with the Purposes of the United Nations.
5. All Members shall give the United Nations every assistance in any action it takes in accordance with the present Charter, and shall refrain from giving assistance to any state against which the United Nations is taking preventive or enforcement action.
6. The Organization shall ensure that states which are not Members of the United Nations act in accordance with these Principles so far as may be necessary for the maintenance of international peace and security.
7. Nothing contained in the present Charter shall authorize the United Nations to intervene in matters which are essentially within the domestic jurisdiction of any state or shall require the Members to submit such matters to settlement under the present Charter; but this principle shall not prejudice the application of enforcement measures under Chapter VII.

Chapter II

MEMBERSHIP

Article 3

The original Members of the United Nations shall be the states which, having participated in the United Nations Conference on International Organization at San Francisco or having previously signed the Declaration by United Nations of 1 January 1942, sign the present Charter and ratify it in accordance with Article 110.

Article 4

1. Membership in the United Nations is open to all other peace-loving states which accept the obligations contained in the present Charter and, in the judgment of the Organization, are able and willing to carry out these obligations.
2. The admission of any such state to membership in the United Nations will be effected by a decision of the General Assembly upon the recommendation of the Security Council.

Article 5

A Member of the United Nations against which preventive or enforcement action has been taken by the Security Council may be suspended from the exercise of the rights and privileges of membership by the General Assembly upon the recommendation of the Security Council. The exercise of these rights and privileges may be restored by the Security Council.

Article 6

A Member of the United Nations which has persistently violated the Principles contained in the present Charter may be expelled from the Organization by the General Assembly upon the recommendation of the Security Council.

Chapter III

ORGANS

Article 7

1. There are established as the principal organs of the United Nations: a General Assembly, a Security Council, an Economic and Social Council, a Trusteeship Council, an International Court of Justice, and a Secretariat.
2. Such subsidiary organs as may be found necessary may be established in accordance with the present Charter.

Article 8

The United Nations shall place no restrictions on the eligibility of men and women to participate in any capacity and under conditions of equality in its principal and subsidiary organs.

Chapter IV

THE GENERAL ASSEMBLY

Composition

Article 9

1. The General Assembly shall consist of all the Members of the United Nations.
2. Each Member shall have not more than five representatives in the General Assembly.

Functions and Powers

Article 10

The General Assembly may discuss any questions or any matters within the scope of the present Charter or relating to the powers and functions of any organs provided for in the present Charter, and, except as provided in Article 12, may make recommendations to the Members of the United Nations or to the Security Council or both on any such questions or matters.

Article 11

1. The General Assembly may consider the general principles of co-operation in the maintenance of international peace and security, including the principles governing disarmament and the regulation of armaments, and may make recommendations with regard to such principles to the Members or to the Security Council or to both.
2. The General Assembly may discuss any questions relating to the maintenance of international peace and security brought before it by any Member of the United Nations, or by the Security Council, or by a state which is not a Member of the United Nations in accordance with Article 35, paragraph 2, and, except as provided in Article 12, may make recommendations with regard to any such questions to the state or states concerned or to the Security Council or to both. Any such question on which action is necessary shall be referred to the Security Council by the General Assembly either before or after discussion.
3. The General Assembly may call the attention of the Security Council to situations which are likely to endanger international peace and security.
4. The powers of the General Assembly set forth in this Article shall not limit the general scope of Article 10.

Article 12

1. While the Security Council is exercising in respect of any dispute or situation the functions assigned to it in the present Charter, the General Assembly shall not make any recommendation with regard to that dispute or situation unless the Security Council so requests.

2. The Secretary-General, with the consent of the Security Council, shall notify the General Assembly at each session of any matters relative to the maintenance of international peace and security which are being dealt with by the Security Council and shall similarly notify the General Assembly, or the Members of the United Nations if the General Assembly is not in session, immediately the Security Council ceases to deal with such matters.

Article 13

1. The General Assembly shall initiate studies and make recommendations for the purpose of:

a. promoting international co-operation in the political field and encouraging the progressive development of international law and its codification;

b. promoting international co-operation in the economic, social, cultural, educational and health fields, and assisting in the realization of human rights and fundamental freedoms for all without distinction as to race, sex, language or religion.

2. The further responsibilities, functions and powers of the General Assembly with respect to matters mentioned in paragraph 1 (b) above are set forth in Chapters IX and X.

Article 14

Subject to the provisions of Article 12, the General Assembly may recommend measures for the peaceful adjustment of any situation, regardless of origin, which it deems likely to impair the general welfare or friendly relations among nations, including situations resulting from a violation of the provisions of the present Charter setting forth the Purposes and Principles of the United Nations.

Article 15

1. The General Assembly shall receive and consider annual and special reports from the Security Council; these reports shall include an account of the measures that the Security Council has decided upon or taken to maintain international peace and security.

2. The General Assembly shall receive and consider reports from the other organs of the United Nations.

Article 16

The General Assembly shall perform such functions with respect to the international trusteeship system as are assigned to it under Chapters XII and XIII, including the approval of the trusteeship agreements for areas not designated as strategic.

Article 17

1. The General Assembly shall consider and approve the budget of the Organization.

2. The expenses of the Organization shall be borne by the Members as apportioned by the General Assembly.

3. The General Assembly shall consider and approve any financial and budgetary arrangements with specialized agencies referred to in Article 57 and shall examine the administrative budgets of such specialized agencies with a view to making recommendations to the agencies concerned.

Voting

Article 18

1. Each member of the General Assembly shall have one vote.

2. Decisions of the General Assembly on important questions shall be made by a two-thirds majority of the members present and voting. These questions shall include: recommendations with respect to the maintenance of international peace and security, the election of the non-permanent members of the Security Council, the election of the members of the Economic and Social Council, the election of members of the Trusteeship Council in accordance with paragraph 1 (c) of Article 86, the admission of new Members to the United Nations, the suspension of the rights and privileges of membership, the expulsion of Members, questions relating to the operation of the trusteeship system, and budgetary questions.

3. Decisions on other questions, including the determination of additional categories of questions to be decided by a two thirds majority, shall be made by a majority of the members present and voting.

Article 19

A Member of the United Nations which is in arrears in the payment of its financial contributions to the Organization shall have no vote in the General Assembly if the amount of its arrears equals or exceeds the amount of the contributions due from it for the preceding two full years. The General Assembly may, nevertheless, permit such a Member to vote if it is satisfied that the failure to pay is due to conditions beyond the control of the Member.

Procedure

Article 20

The General Assembly shall meet in regular annual sessions and in such special sessions as occasion may require. Special sessions shall be convoked by the Secretary-General at the request of the Security Council or of a majority of the Members of the United Nations.

Article 21

The General Assembly shall adopt its own rules of procedure. It shall elect its President for each session.

Article 22

The General Assembly may establish such subsidiary organs as it deems necessary for the performance of its functions.

Chapter V

THE SECURITY COUNCIL

Composition

Article 23[1]

1. The Security Council shall consist of fifteen Members of the United Nations. The Republic of China, France, the Union of Soviet Socialist Republics, the United Kingdom of Great Britain and Northern Ireland and the United States of America shall be permanent members of the Security Council. The General Assembly shall elect ten other Members of the United Nations to be non-permanent members of the Security Council, due regard being specially paid, in the first instance to the contribution of Members of the United Nations to the maintenance of international peace and security and to the other purposes of the Organization, and also to equitable geographical distribution.

2. The non-permanent members of the Security Council shall be elected for a term of two years. In the first election of the non-permanent members after the increase of the membership of the Security Council from eleven to fifteen, two of the four additional members shall be chosen for a term of one year. A retiring member shall not be eligible for immediate re-election.

3. Each member of the Security Council shall have one representative.

Functions and Powers

Article 24

1. In order to ensure prompt and effective action by the United Nations, its Members confer on the Security Council primary responsibility for the maintenance of international peace and security, and agree that in carrying out its duties under this responsibility the Security Council acts on their behalf.

2. In discharging these duties the Security Council shall act in accordance with the Purposes and Principles of the United Nations. The specific powers granted to the Security Council for the discharge of these duties are laid down in Chapters VI, VII, VIII and XII.

3. The Security Council shall submit annual and, when necessary, special reports to the General Assembly for its consideration.

Article 25

The Members of the United Nations agree to accept and carry out the decisions of the Security Council in accordance with the present Charter.

Article 26

In order to promote the establishment and maintenance of international peace and security with the least diversion for armaments of the world's human and economic resources, the Security Council shall be responsible for formulating, with the assistance of the Military Staff Committee referred to in Article 47, plans to be submitted to the Members of the United Nations for the establishment of a system for the regulation of armaments.

Voting

Article 27[2]

1. Each member of the Security Council shall have one vote.

2. Decisions of the Security Council on procedural matters shall be made by an affirmative vote of nine members.

3. Decisions of the Security Council on all other matters shall be made by an affirmative vote of nine members including the concurring votes of the permanent members; provided that, in decisions under Chapter VI, and under paragraph 3 of Article 52, a party to a dispute shall abstain from voting.

Procedure

Article 28

1. The Security Council shall be so organized as to be able to function continuously. Each member of the Security Council shall for this purpose be represented at all times at the seat of the Organization.

2. The Security Council shall hold periodic meetings at which each of its members may, if it so desires, be represented by a member of the government or by some other specially designated representative.

3. The Security Council may hold meetings at such places other than the seat of the Organization as in its judgment will best facilitate its work.

Article 29

The Security Council may establish such subsidiary organs as it deems necessary for the performance of its functions.

Article 30

The Security Council shall adopt its own rules of procedure, including the method of selecting its President.

Article 31

Any Member of the United Nations which is not a member of the Security Council may participate, without vote, in the discussion of any question brought before the Security Council whenever the latter considers that the interests of that Member are specially affected.

Article 32

Any Member of the United Nations which is not a member of the Security Council or any state which is not a Member of the United Nations, if it is a party to a dispute under consideration by the Security Council, shall be invited to participate, without vote, in the discussion relating to the dispute. The Security Council shall lay down such conditions as it deems just for the participation of a state which is not a Member of the United Nations.

Chapter VI
PACIFIC SETTLEMENT OF DISPUTES

Article 33

1. The parties to any dispute, the continuance of which is likely to endanger the maintenance of international peace and security, shall, first of all, seek a solution by negotiation, enquiry, mediation, conciliation, arbitration, judicial settlement, resort to regional agencies or arrangements, or other peaceful means of their own choice.

2. The Security Council shall, when it deems necessary, call upon the parties to settle their dispute by such means.

Article 34

The Security Council may investigate any dispute, or any situation which might lead to international friction or give rise to a dispute, in order to determine whether the continuance of the dispute or situation is likely to endanger the maintenance of international peace and security.

Article 35

1. Any Member of the United Nations may bring any dispute, or any situation of the nature referred to in Article 34, to the attention of the Security Council or of the General Assembly.

2. A state which is not a Member of the United Nations may bring to the attention of the Security Council or of the General Assembly any dispute to which it is a party if it accepts in advance, for the purposes of the dispute, the obligations of pacific settlement provided in the present Charter.

3. The proceedings of the General Assembly in respect of matters brought to its attention under this Article will be subject to the provisions of Articles 11 and 12.

Article 36

1. The Security Council may, at any stage of a dispute of the nature referred to in Article 33 or of a situation of like nature, recommend appropriate procedures or methods of adjustment.

2. The Security Council should take into consideration any procedures for the settlement of the dispute which have already been adopted by the parties.

3. In making recommendations under this Article the Security Council should also take into consideration that legal disputes should as a general rule be referred by the parties to the International Court of Justice in accordance with the provisions of the Statute of the Court.

Article 37

1. Should the parties to a dispute of the nature referred to in Article 33 fail to settle it by the means indicated in that Article, they shall refer it to the Security Council.

2. If the Security Council deems that the continuance of the dispute is in fact likely to endanger the maintenance of international peace and security, it shall decide whether to take action under Article 36 or to recommend such terms of settlement as it may consider appropriate.

Article 38

Without prejudice to the provisions of Articles 33 to 37, the Security Council may, if all the parties to any dispute so request, make recommendations to the parties with a view to a pacific settlement of the dispute.

Chapter VII

ACTION WITH RESPECT TO THREATS TO THE PEACE, BREACHES OF THE PEACE, AND ACTS OF AGGRESSION

Article 39

The Security Council shall determine the existence of any threat to the peace, breach of the peace, or act of aggression and shall make recommendations, or decide what measures shall be taken in accordance with Articles 41 and 42, to maintain or restore international peace and security.

Article 40

In order to prevent an aggravation of the situation, the Security Council may, before making the recommendations or deciding upon the measures provided for in Article 39, call upon the parties concerned to comply with such provisional measures as it deems necessary or desirable. Such provisional measures shall be without prejudice to the rights, claims or position of the parties concerned. The Security Council shall duly take account of failure to comply with such provisional measures.

Article 41

The Security Council may decide what measures not involving the use of armed force are to be employed to give effect to its decisions, and it may call upon the Members of the United Nations to apply such measures. These may include complete or partial interruption of economic relations and of rail, sea, air, postal, telegraphic, radio and other means of communication, and the severance of diplomatic relations.

Article 42

Should the Security Council consider that measures provided for in Article 41 would be inadequate or have proved to be inadequate, it may take such action by air, sea or land forces as may be necessary to maintain or restore international peace and security. Such action may include demonstrations, blockade, and other operations by air, sea, or land forces of Members of the United Nations.

Article 43

1. All Members of the United Nations, in order to contribute to the maintenance of international peace and security, undertake to make available to the Security Council, on its call and in accordance with a special agreement or agreements, armed forces, assistance and facilities, including rights of passage, necessary for the purpose of maintaining international peace and security.

2. Such agreement or agreements shall govern the numbers and types of forces, their degree of readiness and general location, and the nature of the facilities and assistance to be provided.

3. The agreement or agreements shall be negotiated as soon as possible on the initiative of the Security Council. They shall be concluded between the Security Council and Members or between the Security Council and groups of Members and shall be subject to ratification by the signatory states in accordance with their respective constitutional processes.

Article 44

When the Security Council has decided to use force it shall, before calling upon a Member not represented on it to provide armed forces in fulfilment of the obligations assumed under Article 43, invite that Member, if the Member so desires, to participate in the decisions of the Security Council concerning the employment of contingents of that Member's armed forces.

Article 45

In order to enable the United Nations to take urgent military measures, Members shall hold immediately available national airforce contingents for combined international enforcement action. The strength and degree of readiness of these contingents and plans for their combined action shall be determined, within the limits laid down in the special agreement or agreements referred to in Article 43, by the Security Council with the assistance of the Military Staff Committee.

Article 46

Plans for the application of armed force shall be made by the Security Council with the assistance of the Military Staff Committee.

Article 47

1. There shall be established a Military Staff Committee to advise and assist the Security Council on all questions relating to the Security Council's military requirements for the maintenance of international peace and security, the employment and command of forces placed at its disposal, the regulation of armaments, and possible disarmament.

2. The Military Staff Committee shall consist of the Chiefs of Staff of the permanent members of the Security Council or their representatives. Any Member of the United Nations not permanently represented on the Committee shall be invited by the Committee to be associated with it when the efficient discharge of the Committee's responsibilities requires the participation of that Member in its work.

3. The Military Staff Committee shall be responsible under the Security Council for the strategic direction of any armed forces placed at the disposal of the Security Council. Questions relating to the command of such forces shall be worked out subsequently.

4. The Military Staff Committee, with the authorization of the Security Council and after consultation with appropriate regional agencies, may establish regional sub-committees.

Article 48

1. The action required to carry out the decisions of the Security Council for the maintenance of international peace and security shall be taken by all the Members of the United Nations or by some of them, as the Security Council may determine.

2. Such decisions shall be carried out by the Members of the United Nations directly and through their action in the appropriate international agencies of which they are members.

Article 49

The Members of the United Nations shall join in affording mutual assistance in carrying out the measures decided upon by the Security Council.

Article 50

If preventive or enforcement measures against any state are taken by the Security Council, any other state, whether a Member of the United Nations or not, which finds itself confronted with special economic problems arising from the carrying out of those measures shall have the right to consult the Security Council with regard to a solution of those problems.

Article 51

Nothing in the present Charter shall impair the inherent right of individual or collective self-defence if an armed attack occurs against a Member of the United Nations, until the Security Council has taken measures necessary to maintain international peace and security. Measures taken by Members in the exercise of this right of self-defence shall be immediately reported to the Security Council and shall not in any way affect the authority and responsibility of the Security Council under the present Charter to take at any time such action as it deems necessary in order to maintain or restore international peace and security.

Chapter VIII

REGIONAL ARRANGEMENTS

Article 52

1. Nothing in the present Charter precludes the existence of regional arrangements or agencies for dealing with such matters relating to the maintenance of international peace and security as are appropriate for regional action, provided that such arrangements or agencies and their activities are consistent with the Purposes and Principles of the United Nations.

2. The Members of the United Nations entering into such arrangements or constituting such agencies shall make every effort to achieve pacific settlement of local disputes through such regional arrangements or by such regional agencies before referring them to the Security Council.

3. The Security Council shall encourage the development of pacific settlement of local disputes through such regional arrangements or by such regional agencies either on the initiative of the states concerned or by reference from the Security Council.

4. This Article in no way impairs the application of Articles 34 and 35.

Article 53

1. The Security Council shall, where appropriate, utilize such regional arrangements or agencies for enforcement action under its authority. But no enforcement action shall be taken under regional arrangements or by regional agencies without the authorization of the Security Council, with the exception of measures against any enemy state, as defined in paragraph 2 of this Article, provided for pursuant to Article 107 or in regional arrangements directed against renewal of aggressive policy on the part of any such state, until such time as the Organization may, on request of the Governments concerned, be charged with the responsibility for preventing further aggression by such a state.

2. The term enemy state as used in paragraph 1 of this Article applies to any state which during the Second World War has been an enemy of any signatory of the present Charter.

Article 54

The Security Council shall at all times be kept fully informed of activities undertaken or in contemplation under regional arrangements or by regional agencies for the maintenance of international peace and security.

Chapter IX

INTERNATIONAL ECONOMIC AND SOCIAL CO-OPERATION

Article 55

With a view to the creation of conditions of stability and well-being which are necessary for peaceful and friendly relations among nations based on respect for the principle of equal rights and self-determination of peoples, the United Nations shall promote:

a. higher standards of living, full employment, and conditions of economic and social progress and development;
b. solutions of international economic, social, health, and related problems; and international cultural and educational co-operation; and
c. universal respect for, and observance of, human rights and fundamental freedoms for all without distinction as to race, sex, language, or religion.

Article 56

All Members pledge themselves to take joint and separate action in co-operation with the Organization for the achievement of the purposes set forth in Article 55.

Article 57

1. The various specialized agencies, established by intergovernmental agreement and having wide international responsibilities, as defined in their basic instruments, in economic, social, cultural, educational, health, and related fields, shall be brought into relationship with the United Nations in accordance with the provisions of Article 63.

2. Such agencies thus brought into relationship with the United Nations are hereinafter referred to as specialized agencies.

Article 58

The Organization shall make recommendations for the coordination of the policies and activities of the specialized agencies.

Article 59

The Organization shall, where appropriate, initiate negotiations among the states concerned for the creation of any new specialized agencies required for the accomplishment of the purposes set forth in Article 55.

Article 60

Responsibility for the discharge of the functions of the Organization set forth in this Chapter shall be vested in the General Assembly and, under the authority of the General Assembly, in the Economic and Social Council, which shall have for this purpose the powers set forth in Chapter X.

Chapter X

THE ECONOMIC AND SOCIAL COUNCIL

Composition

Article 61[3]

1. The Economic and Social Council shall consist of fifty-four Members of the United Nations elected by the General Assembly.

2. Subject to the provisions of paragraph 3, eighteen members of the Economic and Social Council shall be elected each year for a term of three years. A retiring member shall be eligible for immediate re-election.

3. At the first election after the increase in the membership of the Economic and Social Council from twenty-seven to fifty-four members, in addition to the members elected in place of the nine members whose term of office expires at the end of that year, twenty-seven additional members shall be elected. Of these twenty-seven additional members, the term of office of nine members so elected shall expire at the end of one year, and of nine other members at the end of two years, in accordance with arrangements made by the General Assembly.

4. Each member of the Economic and Social Council shall have one representative.

Functions and Powers

Article 62

1. The Economic and Social Council may make or initiate studies and reports with respect to international economic, social, cultural, educational, health, and related matters and may make recommendations with respect to any such matters to the General Assembly, to the Members of the United Nations, and to the specialized agencies concerned.

2. It may make recommendations for the purpose of promoting respect for, and observance of, human rights and fundamental freedoms for all.

3. It may prepare draft conventions for submission to the General Assembly, with respect to matters falling within its competence.

4. It may call, in accordance with the rules prescribed by the United Nations, international conferences on matters falling within its competence.

Article 63

1. The Economic and Social Council may enter into agreements with any of the agencies referred to in Article 57, defining the terms on which the agency concerned shall be brought into relationship with the United Nations. Such agreements shall be subject to approval by the General Assembly.

2. It may co-ordinate the activities of the specialized agencies through consultation with and recommendations to such agencies and through recommendations to the General Assembly and to the Members of the United Nations.

Article 64

1. The Economic and Social Council may take appropriate steps to obtain regular reports from the specialized agencies. It may make arrangements with the Members of the United Nations and with the specialized agencies to obtain reports on the steps taken to give effect to its own recommendations and to recommendations on matters falling within its competence made by the General Assembly.

2. It may communicate its observations on these reports to the General Assembly.

Article 65

The Economic and Social Council may furnish information to the Security Council and shall assist the Security Council upon its request.

Article 66

1. The Economic and Social Council shall perform such functions as fall within its competence in connection with the carrying out of the recommendations of the General Assembly.

2. It may, with the approval of the General Assembly, perform services at the request of Members of the United Nations and at the request of specialized agencies.

3. It shall perform such other functions as are specified elsewhere in the present Charter or as may be assigned to it by the General Assembly.

Voting

Article 67

1. Each member of the Economic and Social Council shall have one vote.

2. Decisions of the Economic and Social Council shall be made by a majority of the members present and voting.

Procedure

Article 68

The Economic and Social Council shall set up commissions in economic and social fields and for the promotion of human rights, and such other commissions as may be required for the performance of its functions.

Article 69

The Economic and Social Council shall invite any Member of the United Nations to participate, without vote, in its deliberations on any matter of particular concern to that Member.

Article 70

The Economic and Social Council may make arrangements for representatives of the specialized agencies to participate, without vote, in its deliberations and in those of the commissions established by it, and for its representatives to participate in the deliberations of the specialized agencies.

Article 71

The Economic and Social Council may make suitable arrangements for consultation with non-governmental organizations which are concerned with matters within its competence. Such arrangements may be made with international organizations and, where appropriate, with national organizations after consultation with the Member of the United Nations concerned.

Article 72

1. The Economic and Social Council shall adopt its own rules of procedure, including the method of selecting its President.

2. The Economic and Social Council shall meet as required in accordance with its rules, which shall include provision for the convening of meetings on the request of a majority of its members.

Chapter XI

DECLARATION REGARDING NON-SELF-GOVERNING TERRITORIES

Article 73

Members of the United Nations which have or assume responsibilities for the administration of territories whose peoples have not yet attained a full measure of self-government recognize the principle that the interests of the inhabitants of these territories are paramount, and accept as a sacred trust the obligation to promote to the utmost, within the system of international peace and security established by the present Charter, the well-being of the inhabitants of these territories and, to this end:

a. to ensure, with due respect for the culture of the peoples concerned, their political, economic, social, and educational advancement, their just treatment, and their protection against abuses;
b. to develop self-government, to take due account of the political aspirations of the peoples, and to assist them in the progressive development of their free political institutions, according to the particular circumstances of each territory and its peoples and their varying stages of advancement;
c. to further international peace and security;
d. to promote constructive measures of development, to encourage research, and to co-operate with one another and, when and where appropriate, with specialized international bodies with a view to the practical achievement of the social, economic, and scientific purposes set forth in this Article; and
e. to transmit regularly to the Secretary-General for information purposes, subject to such limitation as security and constitutional considerations may require, statistical and other information of a technical nature relating to economic, social, and educational conditions in the territories for which they are respectively responsible other than those territories to which Chapters XII and XIII apply.

Article 74

Members of the United Nations also agree that their policy in respect of the territories to which this Chapter applies, no less than in respect of their metropolitan areas, must be based on the general principle of good-neighbourliness, due account being taken of the interests and well-being of the rest of the world, in social, economic, and commercial matters.

Chapter XII

INTERNATIONAL TRUSTEESHIP SYSTEM

Article 75

The United Nations shall establish under its authority an international trusteeship system for the administration and supervision of such territories as may be placed thereunder by subsequent individual agreements. These territories are hereinafter referred to as trust territories.

Article 76

The basic objectives of the trusteeship system, in accordance with the Purposes of the United Nations laid down in Article 1 of the present Charter, shall be:

a. to further international peace and security;
b. to promote the political, economic, social, and educational advancement of the inhabitants of the trust territories, and their progressive development towards self-government or independence as may be appropriate to the particular circumstances of each territory and its peoples and the freely expressed wishes of the peoples concerned, and as may be provided by the terms of each trusteeship agreement;
c. to encourage respect for human rights and for fundamental freedoms for all without distinction as to race, sex, language, or religion, and to encourage recognition of the interdependence of the peoples of the world; and
d. to ensure equal treatment in social, economic, and commercial matters for all Members of the United Nations and their nationals, and also equal treatment for the latter in the administration of justice, without prejudice to the attainment of the foregoing objectives and subject to the provisions of Article 80.

Article 77

1. The trusteeship system shall apply to such territories in the following categories as may be placed thereunder by means of trusteeship agreements:

a. territories now held under mandate;
b. territories which may be detached from enemy states as a result of the Second World War; and
c. territories voluntarily placed under the system by states responsible for their administration.

2. It will be a matter for subsequent agreement as to which territories in the foregoing categories will be brought under the trusteeship system and upon what terms.

Article 78

The trusteeship system shall not apply to territories which have become Members of the United Nations, relationship among which shall be based on respect for the principle of sovereign equality.

Article 79

The terms of trusteeship for each territory to be placed under the trusteeship system, including any alteration or amendment, shall be agreed upon by the states directly concerned, including the mandatory power in the case of territories held under mandate by a Member of the United Nations, and shall be approved as provided for in Articles 83 and 85.

Article 80

1. Except as may be agreed upon in individual trusteeship agreements, made under Articles 77, 79 and 81, placing each territory under the trusteeship system, and until such agreements have been concluded, nothing in this Chapter shall be construed in or of itself to alter in any manner the rights whatsoever of any states or any peoples or the terms of existing international instruments to which Members of the United Nations may respectively be parties.

2. Paragraph 1 of this Article shall not be interpreted as giving grounds for delay or postponement of the negotiation and conclusion of agreements for placing mandated and other territories under the trusteeship system as provided for in Article 77.

Article 81

The trusteeship agreement shall in each case include the terms under which the trust territory will be administered and designate the authority which will exercise the administration of the trust territory. Such authority, hereinafter called the administering authority, may be one or more states or the Organization itself.

Article 82

There may be designated, in any trusteeship agreement, a strategic area or areas which may include part or all of the trust territory to which the agreement applies, without prejudice to any special agreement or agreements made under Article 43.

Article 83

1. All functions of the United Nations relating to strategic areas, including the approval of the terms of the trusteeship agreements and of their alteration or amendment, shall be exercised by the Security Council.

2. The basic objectives set forth in Article 76 shall be applicable to the people of each strategic area.

3. The Security Council shall, subject to the provisions of the trusteeship agreements and without prejudice to security considerations, avail itself of the assistance of the Trusteeship Council to perform those functions of the United Nations under the trusteeship system relating to political, economic, social, and educational matters in the strategic areas.

Article 84

It shall be the duty of the administering authority to ensure that the trust territory shall play its part in the maintenance of international peace and security. To this end the administering authority may make use of volunteer forces, facilities, and assistance from the trust territory in carrying out the obligations towards the Security Council undertaken in this regard by the administering authority, as well as for local defence and the maintenance of law and order within the trust territory.

Article 85

1. The functions of the United Nations with regard to trusteeship agreements for all areas not designated as strategic, including the approval of the terms of the trusteeship agreements and of their alteration or amendment, shall be exercised by the General Assembly.

2. The Trusteeship Council, operating under the authority of the General Assembly, shall assist the General Assembly in carrying out these functions.

Chapter XIII
THE TRUSTEESHIP COUNCIL

Composition

Article 86

1. The Trusteeship Council shall consist of the following Members of the United Nations:

a. those Members administering trust territories;
b. such of those Members mentioned by name in Article 23 as are not administering trust territories; and
c. as many other Members elected for three-year terms by the General Assembly as may be necessary to ensure that the total number of members of the Trusteeship Council is equally divided between those Members of the United Nations which administer trust territories and those which do not.

2. Each member of the Trusteeship Council shall designate one specially qualified person to represent it therein.

Functions and Powers

Article 87

The General Assembly and, under its authority, the Trusteeship Council, in carrying out their functions, may:

a. consider reports submitted by the administering authority;
b. accept petitions and examine them in consultation with the administering authority;
c. provide for periodic visits to the respective trust territories at times agreed upon with the administering authority; and
d. take these and other actions in conformity with the terms of the trusteeship agreements.

Article 88

The Trusteeship Council shall formulate a questionnaire on the political, economic, social, and educational advancement of the inhabitants of each trust territory, and the administering authority for each trust territory within the competence of the General Assembly shall make an annual report to the General Assembly upon the basis of such questionnaire.

Voting

Article 89

1. Each member of the Trusteeship Council shall have one vote.

2. Decisions of the Trusteeship Council shall be made by a majority of the members present and voting.

Procedure

Article 90

1. The Trusteeship Council shall adopt its own rules of procedure, including the method of selecting its President.

2. The Trusteeship Council shall meet as required in accordance with its rules, which shall include provision for the convening of meetings on the request of a majority of its members.

Article 91

The Trusteeship Council shall, when appropriate, avail itself of the assistance of the Economic and Social Council and of the specialized agencies in regard to matters with which they are respectively concerned.

Chapter XIV
THE INTERNATIONAL COURT OF JUSTICE

Article 92

The International Court of Justice shall be the principal judicial organ of the United Nations. It shall function in accordance with the annexed Statute, which is based upon the Statute of the Permanent Court of International Justice and forms an integral part of the present Charter.

Article 93

1. All Members of the United Nations are *ipso facto* parties to the Statute of the International Court of Justice.

2. A state which is not a Member of the United Nations may become a party to the Statute of the International Court of Justice on conditions to be determined in each case by the General Assembly upon the recommendation of the Security Council.

Article 94

1. Each Member of the United Nations undertakes to comply with the decision of the International Court of Justice in any case to which it is a party.

2. If any party to a case fails to perform the obligations incumbent upon it under a judgment rendered by the Court, the other party may have recourse to the Security Council, which may, if it deems necessary, make recommendations or decide upon measures to be taken to give effect to the judgment.

Article 95

Nothing in the present Charter shall prevent Members of the United Nations from entrusting the solution of their differences to other tribunals by virtue of agreements already in existence or which may be concluded in the future.

Article 96

1. The General Assembly or the Security Council may request the International Court of Justice to give an advisory opinion on any legal question.

2. Other organs of the United Nations and specialized agencies, which may at any time be so authorized by the General Assembly, may also request advisory opinions of the Court on legal questions arising within the scope of their activities.

Chapter XV

THE SECRETARIAT

Article 97

The Secretariat shall comprise a Secretary-General and such staff as the Organization may require. The Secretary-General shall be appointed by the General Assembly upon the recommendation of the Security Council. He shall be the chief administrative officer of the Organization.

Article 98

The Secretary-General shall act in that capacity in all meetings of the General Assembly, of the Security Council, of the Economic and Social Council, and of the Trusteeship Council, and shall perform such other functions as are entrusted to him by these organs. The Secretary-General shall make an annual report to the General Assembly on the work of the Organization.

Article 99

The Secretary-General may bring to the attention of the Security Council any matter which in his opinion may threaten the maintenance of international peace and security.

Article 100

1. In the performance of their duties the Secretary-General and the staff shall not seek or receive instructions from any government or from any other authority external to the Organization. They shall refrain from any action which might reflect on their position as international officials responsible only to the Organization.

2. Each Member of the United Nations undertakes to respect the exclusively international character of the responsibilities of the Secretary-General and the staff and not to seek to influence them in the discharge of their responsibilities.

Article 101

1. The staff shall be appointed by the Secretary-General under regulations established by the General Assembly.

2. Appropriate staffs shall be permanently assigned to the Economic and Social Council, the Trusteeship Council, and, as required, to other organs of the United Nations. These staffs shall form a part of the Secretariat.

3. The paramount consideration in the employment of the staff and in the determination of the conditions of service shall be the necessity of securing the highest standards of efficiency, competence, and integrity. Due regard shall be paid to the importance of recruiting the staff on as wide a geographical basis as possible.

Chapter XVI

MISCELLANEOUS PROVISIONS

Article 102

1. Every treaty and every international agreement entered into by any Member of the United Nations after the present Charter comes into force shall as soon as possible be registered with the Secretariat and published by it.

2. No party to any such treaty or international agreement which has not been registered in accordance with the provisions of paragraph 1 of this Article may invoke that treaty or agreement before any organ of the United Nations.

Article 103

In the event of a conflict between the obligations of the Members of the United Nations under the present Charter and their obligations under any other international agreement, their obligations under the present Charter shall prevail.

Article 104

The Organization shall enjoy in the territory of each of its Members such legal capacity as may be necessary for the exercise of its functions and the fulfilment of its purposes.

Article 105

1. The Organization shall enjoy in the territory of each of its Members such privileges and immunities as are necessary for the fulfilment of its purposes.

2. Representatives of the Members of the United Nations and officials of the Organization shall similarly enjoy such privileges and immunities as are necessary for the independent exercise of their functions in connection with the Organization.

3. The General Assembly may make recommendations with a view to determining the details of the application of paragraphs 1 and 2 of this Article or may propose conventions to the Members of the United Nations for this purpose.

Chapter XVII

TRANSITIONAL SECURITY ARRANGEMENTS

Article 106

Pending the coming into force of such special agreements referred to in Article 43 as in the opinion of the Security Council enable it to begin the exercise of its responsibilities under Article 42, the parties to the Four-Nation Declaration, signed at Moscow, 30 October 1943, and France, shall, in accordance with the provisions of paragraph 5 of that Declaration, consult with one another and as occasion requires with other Members of the United Nations with a view to such joint action on behalf of the Organization as may be necessary for the purpose of maintaining international peace and security.

Article 107

Nothing in the present Charter shall invalidate or preclude action, in relation to any state which during the Second World War has been an enemy of any signatory to the present Charter, taken or authorized as a result of that war by the Governments having responsibility for such action.

Chapter XVIII
AMENDMENTS

Article 108

Amendments to the present Charter shall come into force for all Members of the United Nations when they have been adopted by a vote of two thirds of the members of the General Assembly and ratified in accordance with their respective constitutional processes by two thirds of the Members of the United Nations, including all the permanent members of the Security Council.

Article 109[4]

1. A General Conference of the Members of the United Nations for the purpose of reviewing the present Charter may be held at a date and place to be fixed by a two-thirds vote of the members of the General Assembly and by a vote of any nine members of the Security Council. Each Member of the United Nations shall have one vote in the conference.

2. Any alteration of the present Charter recommended by a two-thirds vote of the conference shall take effect when ratified in accordance with their respective constitutional processes by two thirds of the Members of the United Nations including all the permanent members of the Security Council.

3. If such a conference has not been held before the tenth annual session of the General Assembly following the coming into force of the present Charter, the proposal to call such a conference shall be placed on the agenda of that session of the General Assembly, and the conference shall be held if so decided by a majority vote of the members of the General Assembly and by a vote of any seven members of the Security Council.

Chapter XIX
RATIFICATION AND SIGNATURE

Article 110

1. The present Charter shall be ratified by the signatory states in accordance with their respective constitutional processes.

2. The ratifications shall be deposited with the Government of the United States of America, which shall notify all the signatory states of each deposit as well as the Secretary-General of the Organization when he has been appointed.

3. The present Charter shall come into force upon the deposit of ratifications by the Republic of China, France, the Union of Soviet Socialist Republics, the United Kingdom of Great Britain and Northern Ireland and the United States of America, and by a majority of the other signatory states. A protocol of the ratifications deposited shall thereupon be drawn up by the Government of the United States of America which shall communicate copies thereof to all the signatory states.

4. The states signatory to the present Charter which ratify it after it has come into force will become original Members of the United Nations on the date of the deposit of their respective ratifications.

Article 111

The present Charter, of which the Chinese, French, Russian, English, and Spanish texts are equally authentic, shall remain deposited in the archives of the Government of the United States of America. Duly certified copies thereof shall be transmitted by that Government to the Governments of the other signatory states.

In faith whereof the representatives of the Governments of the United Nations have signed the present Charter.

Done at the city of San Francisco the twenty-sixth day of June, one thousand nine hundred and forty-five.

Notes

[1]Amended text of Article 23, which came into force on 31 August 1965. The text of Article 23 before it was amended read as follows:

1. The Security Council shall consist of eleven Members of the United Nations. The Republic of China, France, the Union of Soviet Socialist Republics, the United Kingdom of Great Britain and Northern Ireland and the United States of America shall be permanent members of the Security Council. The General Assembly shall elect six other Members of the United Nations to be non-permanent members of the Security Council, due regard being specially paid in the first instance to the contributions of Members of the United Nations to the maintenance of international peace and security and to the other purposes of the Organization, and also to equitable geographical distribution.
2. The non-permanent members of the Security Council shall be elected for a term of two years. In the first election of the non-permanent members, however, three shall be chosen for a term of one year. A retiring member shall not be eligible for immediate re-election.
3. Each member of the Security Council shall have one representative.

[2]Amended text of Article 27, which came into force on 31 August 1965. The text of Article 27 before it was amended read as follows:

1. Each member of the Security Council shall have one vote.
2. Decisions of the Security Council on procedural matters shall be made by an affirmative vote of seven members.

3. Decisions of the Security Council on all other matters shall be made by an affirmative vote of seven members including the concurring votes of the permanent members; provided that, in decisions under Chapter VI, and under paragraph 3 of Article 52, a party to a dispute shall abstain from voting.

[3]Amended text of Article 61, which came into force on 24 September 1973. The text of Article 61 as previously amended on 31 August 1965 read as follows:

1. The Economic and Social Council shall consist of twenty-seven Members of the United Nations elected by the General Assembly.
2. Subject to the provisions of paragraph 3, nine members of the Economic and Social Council shall be elected each year for a term of three years. A retiring member shall be eligible for immediate re-election.
3. At the first election after the increase in the membership of the Economic and Social Council from eighteen to twenty-seven members, in addition to the members elected in place of the six members whose term of office expires at the end of that year, nine additional members shall be elected. Of these nine additional members, the term of office of three members so elected shall expire at the end of one year, and of three other members at the end of two years, in accordance with arrangements made by the General Assembly.
4. Each member of the Economic and Social Council shall have one representative.

[4]Amended text of Article 109, which came into force on 12 June 1968. The text of Article 109 before it was amended read as follows:

1. A General Conference of the Members of the United Nations for the purpose of reviewing the present Charter may be held at a date and place to be fixed by a two-thirds vote of the members of the General Assembly and by a vote of any seven members of the Security Council. Each Member of the United Nations shall have one vote in the conference.
2. Any alteration of the present Charter recommended by a two-thirds vote of the conference shall take effect when ratified in accordance with their respective constitutional processes by two thirds of the Members of the United Nations including all the permanent members of the Security Council.
3. If such a conference has not been held before the tenth annual session of the General Assembly following the coming into force of the present Charter, the proposal to call such a conference shall be placed on the agenda of that session of the General Assembly, and the conference shall be held if so decided by a majority vote of the members of the General Assembly and by a vote of any seven members of the Security Council.

Statute of the International Court of Justice

Article 1

The International Court of Justice established by the Charter of the United Nations as the principal judicial organ of the United Nations shall be constituted and shall function in accordance with the provisions of the present Statute.

Chapter I

ORGANIZATION OF THE COURT

Article 2

The Court shall be composed of a body of independent judges, elected regardless of their nationality from among persons of high moral character, who possess the qualifications required in their respective countries for appointment to the highest judicial offices, or are jurisconsults of recognized competence in international law.

Article 3

1. The Court shall consist of fifteen members, no two of whom may be nationals of the same state.
2. A person who for the purposes of membership in the Court could be regarded as a national of more than one state shall be deemed to be a national of the one in which he ordinarily exercises civil and political rights.

Article 4

1. The members of the Court shall be elected by the General Assembly and by the Security Council from a list of persons nominated by the national groups in the Permanent Court of Arbitration, in accordance with the following provisions.
2. In the case of Members of the United Nations not represented in the Permanent Court of Arbitration, candidates shall be nominated by national groups appointed for this purpose by their governments under the same conditions as those prescribed for members of the Permanent Court of Arbitration by Article 44 of the Convention of The Hague of 1907 for the pacific settlement of international disputes.
3. The conditions under which a state which is a party to the present Statute but is not a Member of the United Nations may participate in electing the members of the Court shall, in the absence of a special agreement, be laid down by the General Assembly upon recommendation of the Security Council.

Article 5

1. At least three months before the date of the election, the Secretary-General of the United Nations shall address a written request to the members of the Permanent Court of Arbitration belonging to the states which are parties to the present Statute, and to the members of the national groups appointed under Article 4, paragraph 2, inviting them to undertake, within a given time, by national groups, the nomination of persons in a position to accept the duties of a member of the Court.
2. No group may nominate more than four persons, not more than two of whom shall be of their own nationality. In no case may the number of candidates nominated by a group be more than double the number of seats to be filled.

Article 6

Before making these nominations, each national group is recommended to consult its highest court of justice, its legal faculties and schools of law, and its national academies and national sections of international academies devoted to the study of law.

Article 7

1. The Secretary-General shall prepare a list in alphabetical order of all the persons thus nominated. Save as provided in Article 12, paragraph 2, these shall be the only persons eligible.
2. The Secretary-General shall submit this list to the General Assembly and to the Security Council.

Article 8

The General Assembly and the Security Council shall proceed independently of one another to elect the members of the Court.

Article 9

At every election, the electors shall bear in mind not only that the persons to be elected should individually possess the qualifications required, but also that in the body as a whole the representation of the main forms of civilization and of the principal legal systems of the world should be assured.

Article 10

1. Those candidates who obtain an absolute majority of votes in the General Assembly and in the Security Council shall be considered as elected.
2. Any vote of the Security Council, whether for the election of judges or for the appointment of members of the conference envisaged in Article 12, shall be taken without any distinction between permanent and non-permanent members of the Security Council.
3. In the event of more than one national of the same state obtaining an absolute majority of the votes both of the General Assembly and of the Security Council, the eldest of these only shall be considered as elected.

Article 11

If, after the first meeting held for the purpose of the election, one or more seats remain to be filled, a second and, if necessary, a third meeting shall take place.

Article 12

1. If, after the third meeting, one or more seats still remain unfilled, a joint conference consisting of six members, three appointed by the General Assembly and three by the Security Council, may be formed at any time at the request of either the General Assembly or the Security Council, for the purpose of choosing by the vote of an absolute majority one name for each seat still vacant, to submit to the General Assembly and the Security Council for their respective acceptance.
2. If the joint conference is unanimously agreed upon any person who fulfils the required conditions, he may be included in its list, even though he was not included in the list of nominations referred to in Article 7.
3. If the joint conference is satisfied that it will not be successful in procuring an election, those members of the Court who have already been elected shall, within a period to be fixed by the Security Council, proceed to fill the vacant seats by selection from among those candidates who have obtained votes either in the General Assembly or in the Security Council.
4. In the event of an equality of votes among the judges, the eldest judge shall have a casting vote.

Article 13

1. The members of the Court shall be elected for nine years and may be re-elected; provided, however, that of the judges elected at the first election, the terms of five judges shall expire at the end of three years and the terms of five more judges shall expire at the end of six years.

2. The judges whose terms are to expire at the end of the above-mentioned initial periods of three and six years shall be chosen by lot to be drawn by the Secretary-General immediately after the first election has been completed.

3. The members of the Court shall continue to discharge their duties until their places have been filled. Though replaced, they shall finish any cases which they may have begun.

4. In the case of the resignation of a member of the Court, the resignation shall be addressed to the President of the Court for transmission to the Secretary-General. This last notification makes the place vacant.

Article 14

Vacancies shall be filled by the same method as that laid down for the first election, subject to the following provision: the Secretary-General shall, within one month of the occurrence of the vacancy, proceed to issue the invitations provided for in Article 5, and the date of the election shall be fixed by the Security Council.

Article 15

A member of the Court elected to replace a member whose term of office has not expired shall hold office for the remainder of his predecessor's term.

Article 16

1. No member of the Court may exercise any political or administrative function, or engage in any other occupation of a professional nature.

2. Any doubt on this point shall be settled by the decision of the Court.

Article 17

1. No member of the Court may act as agent, counsel, or advocate in any case.

2. No member may participate in the decision of any case in which he has previously taken part as agent, counsel, or advocate for one of the parties, or as a member of a national or international court, or of a commission of enquiry, or in any other capacity.

3. Any doubt on this point shall be settled by the decision of the Court.

Article 18

1. No member of the Court can be dismissed unless, in the unanimous opinion of the other members, he has ceased to fulfil the required conditions.

2. Formal notification thereof shall be made to the Secretary-General by the Registrar.

3. This notification makes the place vacant.

Article 19

The members of the Court, when engaged on the business of the Court, shall enjoy diplomatic privileges and immunities.

Article 20

Every member of the Court shall, before taking up his duties, make a solemn declaration in open court that he will exercise his powers impartially and conscientiously.

Article 21

1. The Court shall elect its President and Vice-President for three years; they may be re-elected.

2. The Court shall appoint its Registrar and may provide for the appointment of such other officers as may be necessary.

Article 22

1. The seat of the Court shall be established at The Hague. This, however, shall not prevent the Court from sitting and exercising its functions elsewhere whenever the Court considers it desirable.

2. The President and the Registrar shall reside at the seat of the Court.

Article 23

1. The Court shall remain permanently in session, except during the judicial vacations, the dates and duration of which shall be fixed by the Court.

2. Members of the Court are entitled to periodic leave, the dates and duration of which shall be fixed by the Court, having in mind the distance between The Hague and the home of each judge.

3. Members of the Court shall be bound, unless they are on leave or prevented from attending by illness or other serious reasons duly explained to the President, to hold themselves permanently at the disposal of the Court.

Article 24

1. If, for some special reason, a member of the Court considers that he should not take part in the decision of a particular case, he shall so inform the President.

2. If the President considers that for some special reason one of the members of the Court should not sit in a particular case, he shall give him notice accordingly.

3. If in any such case the member of the Court and the President disagree, the matter shall be settled by the decision of the Court.

Article 25

1. The full Court shall sit except when it is expressly provided otherwise in the present Statute.

2. Subject to the condition that the number of judges available to constitute the Court is not thereby reduced below eleven, the Rules of the Court may provide for allowing one or more judges, according to circumstances and in rotation, to be dispensed from sitting.

3. A quorum of nine judges shall suffice to constitute the Court.

Article 26

1. The Court may from time to time form one or more chambers, composed of three or more judges as the Court may determine, for dealing with particular categories of cases; for example, labour cases and cases relating to transit and communications.

2. The Court may at any time form a chamber for dealing with a particular case. The number of judges to constitute such a chamber shall be determined by the Court with the approval of the parties.

3. Cases shall be heard and determined by the chambers provided for in this Article if the parties so request.

Article 27

A judgment given by any of the chambers provided for in Articles 26 and 29 shall be considered as rendered by the Court.

Article 28

The chambers provided for in Articles 26 and 29 may, with the consent of the parties, sit and exercise their functions elsewhere than at The Hague.

Article 29

With a view to the speedy dispatch of business, the Court shall form annually a chamber composed of five judges which, at the request of the parties, may hear and determine cases by summary procedure. In addition, two judges shall be selected for the purpose of replacing judges who find it impossible to sit.

Article 30

1. The Court shall frame rules for carrying out its functions. In particular, it shall lay down rules of procedure.
2. The Rules of the Court may provide for assessors to sit with the Court or with any of its chambers, without the right to vote.

Article 31

1. Judges of the nationality of each of the parties shall retain their right to sit in the case before the Court.
2. If the Court includes upon the Bench a judge of the nationality of one of the parties, any other party may choose a person to sit as judge. Such person shall be chosen preferably from among those persons who have been nominated as candidates as provided in Articles 4 and 5.
3. If the Court includes upon the Bench no judge of the nationality of the parties, each of these parties may proceed to choose a judge as provided in paragraph 2 of this Article.
4. The provisions of this Article shall apply to the case of Articles 26 and 29. In such cases, the President shall request one or, if necessary, two of the members of the Court forming the chamber to give place to the members of the Court of the nationality of the parties concerned, and, failing such, or if they are unable to be present, to the judges specially chosen by the parties.
5. Should there be several parties in the same interest, they shall, for the purpose of the preceding provisions, be reckoned as one party only. Any doubt upon this point shall be settled by the decision of the Court.
6. Judges chosen as laid down in paragraphs 2, 3 and 4 of this Article shall fulfil the conditions required by Articles 2, 17 (paragraph 2), 20, and 24 of the present Statute. They shall take part in the decision on terms of complete equality with their colleagues.

Article 32

1. Each member of the Court shall receive an annual salary.
2. The President shall receive a special annual allowance.
3. The Vice-President shall receive a special allowance for every day on which he acts as President.
4. The judges chosen under Article 31, other than members of the Court, shall receive compensation for each day on which they exercise their functions.
5. These salaries, allowances, and compensation shall be fixed by the General Assembly. They may not be decreased during the term of office.
6. The salary of the Registrar shall be fixed by the General Assembly on the proposal of the Court.
7. Regulations made by the General Assembly shall fix the conditions under which retirement pensions may be given to members of the Court and to the Registrar, and the conditions under which members of the Court and the Registrar shall have their travelling expenses refunded.
8. The above salaries, allowances, and compensation shall be free of all taxation.

Article 33

The expenses of the Court shall be borne by the United Nations in such a manner as shall be decided by the General Assembly.

Chapter II

COMPETENCE OF THE COURT

Article 34

1. Only states may be parties in cases before the Court.
2. The Court, subject to and in conformity with its Rules, may request of public international organizations information relevant to cases before it, and shall receive such information presented by such organizations on their own initiative.
3. Whenever the construction of the constituent instrument of a public international organization or of an international convention adopted thereunder is in question in a case before the Court, the Registrar shall so notify the public international organization concerned and shall communicate to it copies of all the written proceedings.

Article 35

1. The Court shall be open to the states parties to the present Statute.
2. The conditions under which the Court shall be open to other states shall, subject to the special provisions contained in treaties in force, be laid down by the Security Council, but in no case shall such conditions place the parties in a position of inequality before the Court.
3. When a state which is not a Member of the United Nations is a party to a case, the Court shall fix the amount which that party is to contribute towards the expenses of the Court. This provision shall not apply if such state is bearing a share of the expenses of the Court.

Article 36

1. The jurisdiction of the Court comprises all cases which the parties refer to it and all matters specially provided for in the Charter of the United Nations or in treaties and conventions in force.
2. The states parties to the present Statute may at any time declare that they recognize as compulsory *ipso facto* and without special agreement, in relation to any other state accepting the same obligation, the jurisdiction of the Court in all legal disputes concerning:
   a. the interpretation of a treaty;
   b. any question of international law;
   c. the existence of any fact which, if established, would constitute a breach of an international obligation;
   d. the nature or extent of the reparation to be made for the breach of an international obligation.
3. The declarations referred to above may be made unconditionally or on condition of reciprocity on the part of several or certain states, or for a certain time.
4. Such declarations shall be deposited with the Secretary-General of the United Nations, who shall transmit copies thereof to the parties to the Statute and to the Registrar of the Court.
5. Declarations made under Article 36 of the Statute of the Permanent Court of International Justice and which are still in force shall be deemed, as between the parties to the present Statute, to be acceptances of the compulsory jurisdiction of the Inter-

national Court of Justice for the period which they still have to run and in accordance with their terms.

6. In the event of a dispute as to whether the Court has jurisdiction, the matter shall be settled by the decision of the Court.

Article 37

Whenever a treaty or convention in force provides for reference of a matter to a tribunal to have been instituted by the League of Nations, or to the Permanent Court of International Justice, the matter shall, as between the parties to the present Statute, be referred to the International Court of Justice.

Article 38

1. The Court, whose function is to decide in accordance with international law such disputes as are submitted to it, shall apply:

a. international conventions, whether general or particular, establishing rules expressly recognized by the contesting states;
b. international custom, as evidence of a general practice accepted as law;
c. the general principles of law recognized by civilized nations;
d. subject to the provisions of Article 59, judicial decisions and the teachings of the most highly qualified publicists of the various nations, as subsidiary means for the determination of rules of law.

2. This provision shall not prejudice the power of the Court to decide a case *ex aequo et bono*, if the parties agree thereto.

Chapter III
PROCEDURE

Article 39

1. The official languages of the Court shall be French and English. If the parties agree that the case shall be conducted in French, the judgment shall be delivered in French. If the parties agree that the case shall be conducted in English, the judgment shall be delivered in English.

2. In the absence of an agreement as to which language shall be employed, each party may, in the pleadings, use the language which it prefers; the decision of the Court shall be given in French and English. In this case the Court shall at the same time determine which of the two texts shall be considered as authoritative.

3. The Court shall, at the request of any party, authorize a language other than French or English to be used by that party.

Article 40

1. Cases are brought before the Court, as the case may be, either by the notification of the special agreement or by a written application addressed to the Registrar. In either case the subject of the dispute and the parties shall be indicated.

2. The Registrar shall forthwith communicate the application to all concerned.

3. He shall also notify the Members of the United Nations through the Secretary-General, and also any other states entitled to appear before the Court.

Article 41

1. The Court shall have the power to indicate, if it considers that circumstances so require, any provisional measures which ought to be taken to preserve the respective rights of either party.

2. Pending the final decision, notice of the measures suggested shall forthwith be given to the parties and to the Security Council.

Article 42

1. The parties shall be represented by agents.

2. They may have the assistance of counsel or advocates before the Court.

3. The agents, counsel, and advocates of parties before the Court shall enjoy the privileges and immunities necessary to the independent exercise of their duties.

Article 43

1. The procedure shall consist of two parts: written and oral.

2. The written proceedings shall consist of the communication to the Court and to the parties of memorials, counter-memorials and, if necessary, replies; also all papers and documents in support.

3. These communications shall be made through the Registrar, in the order and within the time fixed by the Court.

4. A certified copy of every document produced by one party shall be communicated to the other party.

5. The oral proceedings shall consist of the hearing by the Court of witnesses, experts, agents, counsel, and advocates.

Article 44

1. For the service of all notices upon persons other than the agents, counsel, and advocates, the Court shall apply direct to the government of the state upon whose territory the notice has to be served.

2. The same provision shall apply whenever steps are to be taken to procure evidence on the spot.

Article 45

The hearing shall be under the control of the President or, if he is unable to preside, of the Vice-President; if neither is able to preside, the senior judge present shall preside.

Article 46

The hearing in Court shall be public, unless the Court shall decide otherwise, or unless the parties demand that the public be not admitted.

Article 47

1. Minutes shall be made at each hearing and signed by the Registrar and the President.

2. These minutes alone shall be authentic.

Article 48

The Court shall make orders for the conduct of the case, shall decide the form and time in which each party must conclude its arguments, and make all arrangements connected with the taking of evidence.

Article 49

The Court may, even before the hearing begins, call upon the agents to produce any document or to supply any explanations. Formal note shall be taken of any refusal.

Article 50

The Court may, at any time, entrust any individual, body, bureau, commission, or other organization that it may select, with the task of carrying out an enquiry or giving an expert opinion.

Article 51

During the hearing any relevant questions are to be put to the witnesses and experts under the conditions laid down by the Court in the rules of procedure referred to in Article 30.

Article 52

After the Court has received the proofs and evidence within the time specified for the purpose, it may refuse to accept any further oral or written evidence that one party may desire to present unless the other side consents.

Article 53

1. Whenever one of the parties does not appear before the Court, or fails to defend its case, the other party may call upon the Court to decide in favour of its claim.

2. The Court must, before doing so, satisfy itself, not only that it has jurisdiction in accordance with Articles 36 and 37, but also that the claim is well founded in fact and law.

Article 54

1. When, subject to the control of the Court, the agents, counsel, and advocates have completed their presentation of the case, the President shall declare the hearing closed.

2. The Court shall withdraw to consider the judgment.

3. The deliberations of the Court shall take place in private and remain secret.

Article 55

1. All questions shall be decided by a majority of the judges present.

2. In the event of an equality of votes, the President or the judge who acts in his place shall have a casting vote.

Article 56

1. The judgment shall state the reasons on which it is based.

2. It shall contain the names of the judges who have taken part in the decision.

Article 57

If the judgment does not represent in whole or in part the unanimous opinion of the judges, any judge shall be entitled to deliver a separate opinion.

Article 58

The judgment shall be signed by the President and by the Registrar. It shall be read in open court, due notice having been given to the agents.

Article 59

The decision of the Court has no binding force except between the parties and in respect of that particular case.

Article 60

The judgment is final and without appeal. In the event of dispute as to the meaning or scope of the judgment, the Court shall construe it upon the request of any party.

Article 61

1. An application for revision of a judgment may be made only when it is based upon the discovery of some fact of such a nature as to be a decisive factor, which fact was, when the judgment was given, unknown to the Court and also the party claiming revision, always provided that such ignorance was not due to negligence.

2. The proceedings for revision shall be opened by a judgment of the Court expressly recording the existence of the new fact, recognizing that it has such a character as to lay the case open to revision, and declaring the application admissible on this ground.

3. The Court may require previous compliance with the terms of the judgment before it admits proceedings in revision.

4. The application for revision must be made at latest within six months of the discovery of the new fact.

5. No application for revision may be made after the lapse of ten years from the date of the judgment.

Article 62

1. Should a state consider that it has an interest of a legal nature which may be affected by the decision in the case, it may submit a request to the Court to be permitted to intervene.

2. It shall be for the Court to decide upon this request.

Article 63

1. Whenever the construction of a convention to which states other than those concerned in the case are parties is in question, the Registrar shall notify all such states forthwith.

2. Every state so notified has the right to intervene in the proceedings; but if it uses this right, the construction given by the judgment will be equally binding upon it.

Article 64

Unless otherwise decided by the Court, each party shall bear its own costs.

Chapter IV

ADVISORY OPINIONS

Article 65

1. The Court may give an advisory opinion on any legal question at the request of whatever body may be authorized by or in accordance with the Charter of the United Nations to make such a request.

2. Questions upon which the advisory opinion of the Court is asked shall be laid before the Court by means of a written request containing an exact statement of the question upon which an opinion is required, and accompanied by all documents likely to throw light upon the question.

Article 66

1. The Registrar shall forthwith give notice of the request for an advisory opinion to all states entitled to appear before the Court.

2. The Registrar shall also, by means of a special and direct communication, notify any state entitled to appear before the Court or international organization considered by the Court, or, should it not be sitting, by the President, as likely to be able to furnish information on the question, that the Court will be prepared to receive, within a time limit to be fixed by the President, written statements, or to hear, at a public sitting to be held for the purpose, oral statements relating to the question.

3. Should any such state entitled to appear before the Court have failed to receive the special communication referred to in paragraph 2 of this Article, such state may express a desire to submit a written statement or to be heard; and the Court will decide.

4. States and organizations having presented written or oral statements or both shall be permitted to comment on the statements made by other states or organizations in the form, to the

extent, and within the time limits which the Court, or, should it not be sitting, the President, shall decide in each particular case. Accordingly, the Registrar shall in due time communicate any such written statements to states and organizations having submitted similar statements.

Article 67

The Court shall deliver its advisory opinions in open court, notice having been given to the Secretary-General and to the representatives of Members of the United Nations, of other states and of international organizations immediately concerned.

Article 68

In the exercise of its advisory functions the Court shall further be guided by the provisions of the present Statute which apply in contentious cases to the extent to which it recognizes them to be applicable.

Chapter V
AMENDMENT

Article 69

Amendments to the present Statute shall be effected by the same procedure as is provided by the Charter of the United Nations for amendments to that Charter, subject however to any provisions which the General Assembly upon recommendation of the Security Council may adopt concerning the participation of states which are parties to the present Statute but are not Members of the United Nations.

Article 70

The Court shall have power to propose such amendments to the present Statute as it may deem necessary, through written communications to the Secretary-General, for consideration in conformity with the provisions of Article 69.

Appendix III

Structure of the United Nations

General Assembly

The General Assembly is composed of all the Members of the United Nations.

SESSIONS

Resumed sixty-second session: 12 February–15 September 2008
Sixty-third session: 16 September–23 December 2008 (suspended)

OFFICERS

Resumed sixty-second session
President: Srgjan Kerim (former Yugoslav Republic of Macedonia)
Vice-Presidents: Bahamas, Benin, Botswana, China, Cyprus, Democratic Republic of the Congo, Egypt, France, Gambia, Honduras, Iceland, Iraq, Mauritius, Palau, Russian Federation, Sri Lanka, Turkey, Turkmenistan, United Kingdom, United States, Uruguay

Sixty-third session
President: Miguel d'Escoto Brockmann (Nicaragua)[1]
Vice-Presidents:[2] Afghanistan, Bolivia, Cameroon, China, Egypt, France, Jamaica, Kyrgyzstan, Moldova, Mongolia, Myanmar, Namibia, Niger, Portugal, Russian Federation, Rwanda, Solomon Islands, Spain, Togo, United Kingdom, United States

The Assembly has four types of committees: (1) Main Committees; (2) procedural committees; (3) standing committees; (4) subsidiary and ad hoc bodies. In addition, it convenes conferences to deal with specific subjects.

Main Committees

By resolution 47/233, the General Assembly rationalized its Committee structure as follows:

Disarmament and International Security Committee (First Committee);
Special Political and Decolonization Committee (Fourth Committee);
Economic and Financial Committee (Second Committee);
Social, Humanitarian and Cultural Committee (Third Committee);
Administrative and Budgetary Committee (Fifth Committee);
Legal Committee (Sixth Committee).

The General Assembly may constitute other committees, on which all Members of the United Nations have the right to be represented.

OFFICERS OF THE MAIN COMMITTEES

Resumed sixty-second session

Fourth Committee[3]

Chairperson: Abdalmahmood Abdalhaleem Mohamad (Sudan)
Vice-Chairpersons: Hossein Maleki (Iran), Viktoriia Kuvshynnykova (Ukraine), Alexandrous Vidouris (Greece)
Rapporteur: Renier Valladares Gómez (Honduras)

Second Committee[3]

Chairperson: Kirsti Lintonen (Finland)
Vice-Chairpersons: Melanie Santizo-Sandoval (Guatemala), Hassan Ali Saleh (Lebanon), Peter Le Roux (South Africa)
Rapporteur: Tamar Tchitanava (Georgia)

Fifth Committee[3]

Chairperson: Hamidon Ali (Malaysia)
Vice-Chairpersons: Alejandro Torres Lepori (Argentina), Tomáš Micánek (Czech Republic), Klaus de Rijk (Netherlands)
Rapporteur: Steven Ssenabulya Nkayivu (Uganda)

Sixty-third session

First Committee

Chairperson: Marco Antonio Suazo (Honduras)[4]
Vice-Chairpersons: Martin Zvachula (Micronesia), Ivan Mutavdzic (Croatia), Miguel Graca (Portugal)
Rapporteur: Coly Seck (Senegal)

Fourth Committee

Chairperson: Jorge Arguello (Argentina)[4]
Vice-Chairpersons: Emr Elsherbini (Egypt), Alexandru Cujba (Moldova), Elmer Cato (Philippines)
Rapporteur: Paula Parviainen (Finland)

Second Committee

Chairperson: Uche Joy Ogwu (Nigeria)[4]
Vice-Chairpersons: Andrei Metelitsa (Belarus), Troy Torrington (Guyana), Martin Hoppe (Germany)
Rapporteur: Awsan Al-Aud (Yemen)

Third Committee

Chairperson: Frank Majoor (Netherlands)[4]
Vice-Chairpersons: Divina Adjoa Seanedzu (Ghana), Ara Margarian (Armenia), Julio Peralta (Paraguay)
Rapporteur: Khalid Alwafi (Saudi Arabia)

Fifth Committee

Chairperson: Gabor Brodi (Hungary)[4]
Vice-Chairpersons: Olivio Fermin (Dominican Republic), Mohamed Yousif Ibrahim Abdelmannan (Sudan), Henric Rasbrant (Sweden)
Rapporteur: Patrick Chuasoto (Philippines)

Sixth Committee

Chairperson: Hamid Al Bayati (Iraq)[4]
Vice-Chairpersons: El-Hadj Lamine (Algeria), Ana Cristina Rodríguez-Pineda (Guatemala), Scott Sheeran (New Zealand)
Rapporteur: Marko Rakovec (Slovenia)

Procedural committees

General Committee

The General Committee consists of the President of the General Assembly, as Chairperson, the 21 Vice-Presidents and the Chairpersons of the six Main Committees.

Credentials Committee

The Credentials Committee consists of nine members appointed by the General Assembly on the proposal of the President.

Resumed sixty-second session
Angola, Chile, China, Namibia, Russian Federation, Singapore, Suriname, Switzerland, United States

Sixty-third session[5]
Botswana, China, Cyprus, Luxembourg, Mexico, Mozambique, Russian Federation, Saint Kitts and Nevis, United States

Standing committees

The two standing committees consist of experts appointed in their individual capacity for three-year terms.

Advisory Committee on Administrative and Budgetary Questions (ACABQ)

To serve until 31 December 2008: Guillermo Kendall (Argentina), Igor V. Khalevinsky (Russian Federation), Susan M. McLurg (United States), Tommo Monthe (Cameroon), Christina Vasak (France)
To serve until 31 December 2009: Andrzej T. Abraszewski (Poland), Collen V. Kelapile (Botswana), Stafford Neil (Jamaica), Mohammad Mustafa Tal (Jordan), Nonye Udo (Nigeria)
To serve until 31 December 2010: Jorge Flores Callejas (Honduras), Imtiaz Hussain (Pakistan), Misako Kaji (Japan), Jerry Kramer (Canada), Peter Maddens (Belgium), Nagesh Singh (India)

On 20 November 2008 (dec. 63/407), the General Assembly appointed the following for a three-year term beginning on 1 January 2009 to fill vacancies occurring on 31 December 2008: Aïcha Afifi (Morocco), Renata Archini (Italy), Vladimir A. Iosifov (Russian Federation), Susan M. McLurg (United States), and Alejandro Torres Lépori (Argentina).

Committee on Contributions

To serve until 31 December 2008: Sujata Ghorai (Germany), Vyacheslav A. Logutov (Russian Federation), Richard Moon (United Kingdom), Hae-yun Park (Republic of Korea), Henrique da Silveira Sardinha Pinto (Brazil), Wu Gang (China)
To serve until 31 December 2009: Kenshiro Akimoto (Japan), Meshal Al-Mansour (Kuwait), Petru Dumitriu (Romania), Ihor V. Humenny (Ukraine), Gobona Susan Mapitse (Botswana), Lisa P. Spratt (United States)
To serve until 31 December 2010: Joseph Acakpo-Satchivi (Benin), Abdelmalek Bouheddou (Algeria), Gordon Eckersley (Australia), Bernardo Greiver del Hoyo (Uruguay), Luis Mariano Hermosillo Sosa (Mexico), Eduardo Manuel da Fonseca Fernandes Ramos (Portugal)

On 20 November 2008 (dec. 63/408), the General Assembly appointed the following for a three-year term beginning on 1 January 2009 to fill the vacancies occurring on 31 December 2008: Vyacheslav A. Logutov (Russian Federation), Richard Moon (United Kingdom), Hae-yun Park (Republic of Korea), Thomas Thomma (Germany), Courtney H. Williams (Jamaica), and Wu Gang (China).

Subsidiary and ad hoc bodies

The following is a list of subsidiary and ad hoc bodies functioning in 2008, including the number of members, dates of meetings/sessions in 2008, document numbers of reports (which generally provide specific information on membership), and relevant decision numbers pertaining to elections.

Ad Hoc Committee on the Administration of Justice at the United Nations

Session: First, New York, 10–18, 21 and 24 April
Chairperson: Ganeson Sivagurunathan (Malaysia)
Membership: Open to all States Members of the United Nations or members of the specialized agencies or of IAEA
Report: A/63/55

Ad Hoc Committee on Criminal Accountability of United Nations Officials and Experts on Mission

Session: Second, New York, 7–9, 11 April
Chairperson: Maria Telalian (Greece)
Membership: Open to all States Members of the United Nations or members of the specialized agencies or of IAEA
Report: A/63/54

Ad Hoc Committee established by General Assembly resolution 51/210 of 17 December 1996

Session: Twelfth, New York, 25–26 February and 6 March
Chairperson: Rohan Perera (Sri Lanka)
Membership: Open to all States Members of the United Nations or members of the specialized agencies or of IAEA
Report: A/63/37

Ad Hoc Committee on the Indian Ocean

Meeting: Did not meet in 2008
Membership: 43

Advisory Board on Disarmament Matters

Sessions: Forty-ninth, New York, 20–22 February; fiftieth, Geneva, 9–11 July
Chairperson: Adam Daniel Rotfeld (Poland)
Membership: 18 (plus 1 ex-officio member)
Report: A/63/279

Advisory Committee on the United Nations Programme of Assistance in the Teaching, Study, Dissemination and Wider Appreciation of International Law

Session: Forty-third, New York, 6 November
Chairperson: Leslie K. Christian (Ghana)
Membership: 25
Report: A/64/495

Board of Auditors

Session: Sixty-second, New York, 16–18 July; special session, Paris, 3 December
Chairperson: Philip Seguin (France)
Membership: 3

Committee on Conferences

Session: New York, 7 April (organizational); 8–12 September (substantive)
Chairperson: Patrick A. Chuasoto (Philippines)
Membership: 21
Report: A/63/32
Decision: GA 63/405

Committee on the Exercise of the Inalienable Rights of the Palestinian People

Meetings: Throughout the year
Chairperson: Paul Badji (Senegal)
Membership: 23
Report: A/63/35
Decision: GA 62/553

Committee on Information

Session: Thirtieth, New York, 28 April–9 May
Chairperson: Andreas Baum (Switzerland)
Membership: 112
Report: A/63/21
Decisions: GA 63/412, GA 63/524

Committee on the Peaceful Uses of Outer Space

Session: Fifty-first, Vienna, 11–20 June
Chairperson: Ciro Arévalo Yepes (Colombia)
Membership: 69
Report: A/63/20

Committee for Programme and Coordination (CPC)

Session: Forty-eighth, New York, 30 April (organizational); 9 June–3 July (substantive)
Chairperson: Ren Yisheng (China)
Membership: 34
Report: A/63/16
Decisions: ESC 2008/201 C, E & G; GA 63/414

Committee on Relations with the Host Country

Meetings: New York, 22 January, 22 April, 23 July, 2 October and 31 October
Chairpersons: Andreas D. Mavroyiannis (Cyprus) (through July), Minas Hadjimichael (Cyprus) (from October)
Membership: 19 (including the United States as host country)
Report: A/63/26

Committee for the United Nations Population Award

Meeting: New York, 18 January
Chairperson: Anders Lidén (Sweden)
Membership: 10 (plus 5 honorary members, the Secretary-General and the UNFPA Executive Director)
Report: A/63/255

Disarmament Commission

Session: New York, 18 March (organizational); 7–24 April (substantive)
Chairperson: Piet de Klerk (Netherlands)
Membership: All UN Members
Report: A/63/42

High-level Committee on South-South Cooperation[6]

Session: Did not meet in 2008
Membership: All States participating in UNDP

Human Rights Council

Sessions: Sixth special, 23–24 January; seventh special, 22 May; eighth special, 28 November and 1 December; seventh regular, 3–28 March and 1 April; eighth regular, 2–18 June; ninth regular, 8–24 September, all in Geneva
President: Doru Romulus Costea (Romania)
Membership: 47
Reports: A/63/53 & Add.1, A/64/53
Decision: GA 62/415

Independent Audit Advisory Committee

Sessions: First–fourth, New York, 20–22 February, 29 April–1 May, 16–18 July and 1–3 December
Chairperson: David M. Walker (United States)
Membership: 5
Reports: A/63/328, A/64/288

International Civil Service Commission (ICSC)

Sessions: Sixty-sixth, Addis Ababa, 31 March–11 April; sixty-seventh, New York, 14–25 July
Chairperson: Kingston Papie Rhodes (Sierra Leone)
Membership: 15
Report: A/63/30
Decision: GA 63/410

Advisory Committee on Post Adjustment Questions

Session: Thirtieth, New York, 28 January–4 February
Chairperson: Wolfgang Stöckl (Germany)
Membership: 6

International Law Commission

Session: Sixtieth, Geneva, 5 May–6 June, 7 July–8 August
Chairperson: Edmundo Vargas Carreño (Chile)
Membership: 34
Report: A/63/10

Investments Committee

Chairperson: William J. McDonough (United States)
Membership: 9
Decision: GA 63/409

Joint Advisory Group on the International Trade Centre UNCTAD/WTO

Session: Forty-second, Geneva, 10–11 December
Chairperson: Arsene Balihuta (Uganda)
Membership: Open to all States members of UNCTAD and all members of WTO
Report: ITC/AG(XLII)/225

Joint Inspection Unit (JIU)

Chairperson: Even Fontaine Ortiz (Cuba)
Membership: 11
Report: A/63/34

Office of the United Nations High Commissioner for Refugees (UNHCR)

Executive Committee of the High Commissioner's Programme

Session: Fifty-ninth, Geneva, 6–10 October
Chairperson: Boudewijn J. van Eenennaam (Netherlands)
Membership: 76
Report: A/63/12/Add.1
Decisions: ESC 2008/255, 2008/201 C
High Commissioner: António Manuel de Oliveira Guterres

Panel of External Auditors

Session: Forty-ninth, Paris, 1–2 December
Membership: Members of the UN Board of Auditors and the appointed external auditors of the specialized agencies and IAEA

Special Committee on the Charter of the United Nations and on the Strengthening of the Role of the Organization

Meetings: New York, 27–29 February, 3–5 and 7 March
Chairperson: Karim Medrek (Morocco)
Membership: Open to all States Members of the United Nations
Report: A/63/33

Special Committee to Investigate Israeli Practices Affecting the Human Rights of the Palestinian People and Other Arabs of the Occupied Territories

Meetings: Cairo, Egypt, 23–27 June; Amman, Jordan, 27 June–1 July; Damascus, Syrian Arab Republic, 1–5 July
Chairperson: Prasad Kariyawasam (Sri Lanka)
Membership: 3
Report: A/63/273

Special Committee on Peacekeeping Operations

Meetings: New York, 10 March–4 April, 3 July
Chairperson: Felix Ani Aniokoye (Nigeria)
Membership: 139
Report: A/62/19

Special Committee on the Situation with regard to the Implementation of the Declaration on the Granting of Independence to Colonial Countries and Peoples

Session: New York, 28 February and 15 April (first part); 27 May, 9, 11–12, 18–19 and 23 June (second part)
Chairperson: R. M. Marty M. Natalegawa (Indonesia)
Membership: 27
Report: A/63/23
Decisions: GA 63/413, 63/526

United Nations Administrative Tribunal

Sessions: New York, 21 April–2 May and 27 October–26 November; Geneva, 23 June–25 July
President: Spyridon Flogaitis (Greece)
Membership: 7
Report: A/INF/63/5

United Nations Capital Development Fund (UNCDF)

Executive Board

The UNDP/UNFPA Executive Board acts as the Executive Board of the Fund.
Managing Director: Kemal Dervis (UNDP Administrator)

United Nations Commission on International Trade Law (UNCITRAL)

Session: Fortieth, New York, 16 June–3 July
Chairperson: Rafael Illescas Ortiz (Spain)
Membership: 60
Report: A/63/17

United Nations Conciliation Commission for Palestine

Membership: 3
Report: A/63/317

United Nations Conference on Trade and Development (UNCTAD)

Session: Twelfth, Accra, Ghana, 20–25 April
Membership: Open to all States Members of the United Nations or members of the specialized agencies or of IAEA
Report: TD/442
Secretary-General of UNCTAD: Supachai Panitchpakdi (Thailand)

Trade and Development Board

Sessions: Fifty-fifth (annual), 15–26 September; forty-third, forty-fourth and forty-fifth (executive), 3 March, 10 July and 13 November; twenty-fourth (special), 17–20 March, all in Geneva
President: Petko Draganov (Bulgaria) (forty-third, forty-fourth executive and twenty-fourth special sessions); Debapriya

Bhattacharya (Bangladesh) (forty-fifth executive and fifty-fifth annual sessions)
Membership: Open to all States members of UNCTAD
Report: TD/B/55/10

SUBSIDIARY ORGANS OF THE TRADE AND DEVELOPMENT BOARD

COMMISSION ON ENTERPRISE, BUSINESS FACILITATION AND DEVELOPMENT
Session: Twelfth, Geneva, 4–5 February
Chairperson: El Mostapha Ait Amor (Morocco)
Membership: Open to all States members of UNCTAD
Report: TD/B/COM.3/86

COMMISSION ON INVESTMENT, TECHNOLOGY AND RELATED FINANCIAL ISSUES
Session: Twelfth, Geneva, 12–13 February
President: Fredrik Arthur (Norway)
Membership: Open to all States members of UNCTAD
Report: TD/B/COM.2/82

Intergovernmental Group of Experts on Competition Law and Policy
Session: Ninth, Geneva, 15–18 July
Chairperson: Taisiya Tkacheva (Russian Federation)
Membership: Open to all States members of UNCTAD
Report: TD/B/COM.2/CLP/72

Intergovernmental Working Group of Experts on International Standards of Accounting and Reporting
Session: Twenty-fifth, Geneva, 4–6 November
Chairperson: L. Nelson Carvalho (Brazil)
Membership: 34
Report: TD/B/C.II/ISAR/51 & Corr.1,2
Decision: ESC 2008/201 C

COMMISSION ON TRADE IN GOODS AND SERVICES, AND COMMODITIES
Session: Twelfth, Geneva, 7–8 February
Chairperson: Gusti Agung Wesaka Puja (Indonesia)
Membership: Open to all States members of UNCTAD
Report: TD/B/COM.1/92

WORKING PARTY ON THE MEDIUM-TERM PLAN AND THE PROGRAMME BUDGET
Sessions: Fiftieth and fifty-first, Geneva, 16–18 June and 1–5 September
Chairpersons: Dmitry Godunov (Russian Federation) (fiftieth session), Carmen Elena Castillo-Gallandat (El Salvador) (fifty-first session)
Membership: Open to all States members of UNCTAD
Reports: TD/B/WP/200, TD/B/WP/206

United Nations Development Fund for Women (UNIFEM)

CONSULTATIVE COMMITTEE
Session: Forty-eighth, New York, 13–14 February
Chairperson: Tiina Intelmann (Estonia)
Membership: 5
Executive Director of UNIFEM: Inés Alberdi (Spain)

United Nations Environment Programme (UNEP)

GOVERNING COUNCIL
Session: Tenth special, Monaco, 20–22 February
President: Roberto Dobles (Costa Rica)
Membership: 56
Report: A/63/25
Decision: GA 62/406 B
Executive Director of UNEP: Achim Steiner

United Nations Human Settlements Programme (UN-Habitat)

GOVERNING COUNCIL
Session: Did not meet in 2008
Membership: 58
Decision: ESC 2008/201 C
Executive Director of UN-Habitat: Anna Kajumulo Tibaijuka

United Nations Institute for Disarmament Research (UNIDIR)

BOARD OF TRUSTEES
Sessions: Forty-ninth, New York, 20–22 February; fiftieth, Geneva, 9–11 July
Chairperson: Adam Daniel Rotfeld (Poland)
Membership: 18 (plus 1 ex-officio member)
Reports: A/63/177, A/63/279
Director of UNIDIR: Patricia Lewis

United Nations Institute for Training and Research (UNITAR)

BOARD OF TRUSTEES
Session: Forty-sixth, Geneva, 15–16 May
Chairperson: Martin Lään (Estonia)
Membership: 15 (plus 2 ex-officio members)
Report: E/2008/72
Executive Director of UNITAR: Carlos Lopes

United Nations Joint Staff Pension Board

Session: Fifty-fifth, Rome, 10–18 July
Chairperson: Valeria Maria Gonzalez Posse (Argentina)
Membership: 33
Report: A/63/9
Decision: GA 63/411
Executive Director: Bernard Cochemé

United Nations Relief and Works Agency for Palestine Refugees in the Near East (UNRWA)

ADVISORY COMMISSION OF UNRWA
Meeting: Damascus, Syria, 10–11 June
Chairperson: Ali Mustafa (Syria)
Membership: 24
Report: A/63/13

WORKING GROUP ON THE FINANCING OF UNRWA
Meetings: New York, 12 and 19 September
Chairperson: Baki İlkin (Turkey)
Membership: 9
Report: A/63/375
Commissioner-General of UNRWA: Karen Koning AbuZayd

United Nations Scientific Committee on the Effects of Atomic Radiation

Session: Fifty-sixth, Vienna, 10–18 July
Chairperson: Norman Gentner (Canada)
Membership: 21
Report: A/63/46

United Nations Staff Pension Committee

Membership: 12 (plus 8 alternates)
Decision: GA 63/411

United Nations University (UNU)

COUNCIL OF THE UNITED NATIONS UNIVERSITY
Session: Fifty-fifth, Bonn, Germany, 1–5 December
Chairperson: Juan Ramón de la Fuente (Mexico)
Membership: 24 (plus 3 ex-officio members and the UNU Rector)
Rector of the University: Konrad Osterwalder

United Nations Voluntary Fund for Indigenous Populations

BOARD OF TRUSTEES
Session: Twenty-first, Geneva, 4–8 February
Chairperson: Nadir Bekirov (Ukraine)
Membership: 5
Report: A/63/166

United Nations Voluntary Fund for Victims of Torture

BOARD OF TRUSTEES
Session: Twenty-eighth, Geneva, 6–8 February
Chairperson: Krassimir Kanev (Bulgaria)
Membership: 5
Report: A/63/220

United Nations Voluntary Trust Fund on Contemporary Forms of Slavery

BOARD OF TRUSTEES
Session: Thirteenth, Geneva, 8–12 September
Chairperson: David Weissbrodt (United States)
Membership: 5
Reports: A/63/137, A/64/306

Security Council

The Security Council consists of 15 Member States of the United Nations (5 permanent members and 10 non-permanent members), in accordance with the provisions of Article 23 of the United Nations Charter as amended in 1965.

MEMBERS

Permanent members: China, France, Russian Federation, United Kingdom, United States

Non-permanent members: Belgium, Burkina Faso, Costa Rica, Croatia, Indonesia, Italy, Libya, Panama, South Africa, Viet Nam

On 17 October 2008 (dec. 63/403), the General Assembly elected Austria, Japan, Mexico, Turkey and Uganda for a two-year term beginning on 1 January 2009, to replace Belgium, Indonesia, Italy, Panama and South Africa, whose terms of office were to expire on 31 December 2008.

PRESIDENT

The presidency of the Council rotates monthly, according to the English alphabetical listing of its Member States. The following served as President during 2008:

Month	*Member*	*Representative*
January	Libya	Giadallah A. Ettalhi
February	Panama	Ricardo Alberto Arias
March	Russian Federation	Vitaly Churkin
April	South Africa	Dumisani Shadrack Kumalo
May	United Kingdom	John Sawers
June	United States	Zalmay Khalilzad
July	Vietnam	Le Luong Minh
August	Belgium	Jan Grauls
September	Burkina Faso	Michel Kafando
October	China	Zhang Yesui
November	Costa Rica	Jorge Urbina
December	Croatia	Neven Jurica

Military Staff Committee

The Military Staff Committee consists of the chiefs of staff of the permanent members of the Security Council or their representatives. It meets fortnightly.

Standing committees

Each of the three standing committees of the Security Council is composed of representatives of all Council members:

Committee of Experts (to examine the provisional rules of procedure of the Council and any other matters entrusted to it by the Council);

Committee on the Admission of New Members;

Committee on Council Meetings Away from Headquarters.

Subsidiary bodies

Counter-Terrorism Committee (CTC)

Chairperson: Neven Jurica

Membership: 15

United Nations Compensation Commission

GOVERNING COUNCIL

Sessions: Sixty-fifth and sixty-sixth, Geneva, 8–9 April and 21–22 October

President: Alex Van Meeuwen (Belgium)

Membership: 15

Reports: S/2008/265, S/2008/658

1540 Committee

Chairperson: Jorge Urbina (Costa Rica)

Membership: 15

Report: S/2008/493

International Criminal Tribunal for the former Yugoslavia (ICTY)

President: Judge Fausto Pocar (Italy)

International Criminal Tribunal for Rwanda (ICTR)

President: Judge Dennis Byron (Saint Kitts and Nevis)

Advisory Subsidiary body

United Nations Peacebuilding Commission[7]

ORGANIZATIONAL COMMITTEE

Session: Second, New York, 12, 19 and 23 June

Chairperson: Yukio Takasu (Japan)

Membership: 31

Report: A/63/92

Decisions: GA 62/419 A & B, 63/415; ESC 2008/38, 2008/201 A, D, E & G

Peacekeeping operations

United Nations Truce Supervision Organization (UNTSO)

Chief of Staff: Major General Ian Campbell Gordon

United Nations Military Observer Group in India and Pakistan (UNMOGIP)

Chief Military Observer: Major General Dragutin Repinc (until October), Major General Kim Moon Hwa (from October)

United Nations Peacekeeping Force in Cyprus (UNFICYP)

Special Representative of the Secretary-General and Head of Mission: Michael Møller (until March), Tayé-Brook Zerihoun (from April)

Force Commander: Major-General Rafael Barni (until March), Rear Admiral Mario Sánchez Debernardi (from April)

United Nations Disengagement Observer Force (UNDOF)

Head of Mission and Force Commander: Major General Wolfgang Jilke

United Nations Interim Force in Lebanon (UNIFIL)

Force Commander: Major General Claudio Graziano

United Nations Mission for the Referendum in Western Sahara (MINURSO)

Special Representative of the Secretary-General and Head of Mission: Julian Harston

Force Commander: Major General Zhao Jingmin

United Nations Observer Mission in Georgia (UNOMIG)

Special Representative of the Secretary-General and Head of Mission: Jean Arnault (until August), Johan Verbeke (from August)

Deputy Special Representative of the Secretary-General: Ivo Petrov

Chief Military Observer: Major General Niaz Muhammad Khan Khattak (until August), Major General Anwar Hussain (from August)

United Nations Interim Administration Mission in Kosovo (UNMIK)

Special Representative of the Secretary-General and Head of Mission: Joachim Rücker (until June), Lamberto Zannier (from June)

Principal Deputy Special Representative: Lawrence Rossin

Deputy Special Representative for Reconstruction: Paul Acda

Deputy Special Representative for Institution Building: Werner Wnendt

United Nations Organization Mission in the Democratic Republic of the Congo (MONUC)

Special Representative of the Secretary-General and Head of Mission: Alan Doss
Deputy Special Representative: Ross Mountain
Force Commander: Lieutenant-General Babacar Gaye (until October; reappointed from November)

United Nations Mission in Ethiopia and Eritrea (UNMEE)[8]

Acting Special Representative of the Secretary-General and Head of Mission: Azouz Ennifar (Acting)
Deputy Special Representative: Lebohang K. Moleko
Force Commander: Major-General Mohammed Taisir Masadeh

United Nations Mission in Liberia (UNMIL)

Special Representative of the Secretary-General and Head of Mission: Margrethe Løj
Deputy Special Representative: Jordan Ryan
Force Commander: Lieutenant-General Chikadibia Obiakor (until July), Lieutenant General A. T. M. Zahirul Alam (from October)

United Nations Operation in Côte d'Ivoire (UNOCI)

Special Representative of the Secretary-General and Head of Mission: Choi Young-jin
Principal Deputy Special Representative: Abou Moussa
Force Commander: Major-General Fernand Marcel Amoussou

United Nations Stabilization Mission in Haiti (MINUSTAH)

Special Representative of the Secretary-General and Head of Mission: Hédi Annabi
Principal Deputy Special Representative: Luiz Carlos da Costa
Force Commander: Major-General Carlos Alberto Dos Santos Cruz

United Nations Mission in the Sudan (UNMIS)

Special Representative of the Secretary-General and Head of Mission: Ashraf Jehangir Qazi
Deputy Special Representative: Ameerah Haq
Force Commander: Lieutenant General Jasbir Singh Lidder (until May), Major General Paban Jung Thapa (from May)

United Nations Integrated Mission in Timor-Leste (UNMIT)

Special Representative of the Secretary-General and Head of Mission: Atul Khare
Deputy Special Representative for Governance Support, Development and Humanitarian Coordination: Finn Reske-Nielsen
Deputy Special Representative for Security Sector Support and Rule of Law: Takahisa Kawakami (from September)
Police Commissioner: Rodolfo Aser Tor

African Union-United Nations Hybrid Operation in Darfur (UNAMID)

AU-UN Joint Special Representative for Darfur and Head of Mission: Rodolphe Adada
Deputy Joint Special Representative for Operations and Management: Hocine Medili
Force Commander: General Martin Agwai

United Nations Mission in the Central African Republic and Chad (MINURCAT)

Special Representative of the Secretary-General and Head of Mission: Victor da Silva Angelo
Deputy Special Representative of the Secretary-General: Rima Salah
Police Commissioner: Major-General Gerardo Christian Chaumont (from August)

Political, peacebuilding and other missions

United Nations Political Office for Somalia (UNPOS)

Representative of the Secretary-General and Head of UNPOS: Ahmedou Ould-Abdallah

United Nations Peacebuilding Support Office in Guinea-Bissau (UNOGBIS)

Representative of the Secretary-General and Head of UNOGBIS: Shola Omoregie

Office of the United Nations Special Coordinator for the Middle East (UNSCO)

Special Coordinator for the Middle East Peace Process and Personal Representative of the Secretary-General to the Palestine Liberation Organization and the Palestinian Authority: Robert H. Serry

United Nations Peacebuilding Office in the Central African Republic (BONUCA)

Representative of the Secretary-General and Head of BONUCA: François Lonseny Fall

Office of the United Nations Special Coordinator of the Secretary-General for Lebanon (UNSCOL) (formerly known as Office of the Personal Representative of the Secretary-General for Southern Lebanon)

Special Coordinator of the Secretary-General for Lebanon: Geir O. Pedersen (until February), Johan Verbeke (April–July), Michael C. Williams (from August)

Office of the Special Representative of the Secretary-General for West Africa (UNOWA)

Special Representative of the Secretary-General: Said Djinnit

United Nations Assistance Mission in Afghanistan (UNAMA)

Special Representative of the Secretary-General and Head of Mission: Kai Eide

United Nations Assistance Mission for Iraq (UNAMI)

Special Representative of the Secretary-General for Iraq: Staffan de Mistura

United Nations Integrated Office in Sierra Leone (UNIOSIL)[9]

Executive Representative for the United Nations Integrated Office in Sierra Leone: Victor da Silva Angelo

United Nations Integrated Peacebuilding Office in Sierra Leone (UNIPSIL)[10]

Executive Representative of the Secretary-General: Michael von der Schulenburg (Acting)

United Nations Integrated Office in Burundi (BINUB)

Executive Representative of the Secretary-General: Youssef Mahmoud

United Nations Mission in Nepal (UNMIN)

Special Representative of the Secretary-General in Nepal and Head of Mission: Ian Martin

United Nations Regional Centre for Preventive Diplomacy for Central Asia (UNRCCA)

Special Representative of the Secretary-General: Miroslav Jenča

Economic and Social Council

The Economic and Social Council consists of 54 Member States of the United Nations, elected by the General Assembly, each for a three-year term, in accordance with the provisions of Article 61 of the United Nations Charter as amended in 1965 and 1973.

MEMBERS

To serve until 31 December 2008: Angola, Austria, Benin, Cuba, Czech Republic, France, Greece, Guinea-Bissau, Guyana, Haiti, Japan, Liechtenstein, Madagascar, Mauritania, Paraguay, Portugal, Saudi Arabia, Sri Lanka

To serve until 31 December 2009: Algeria, Barbados, Belarus, Bolivia, Canada, Cape Verde, El Salvador, Indonesia, Iraq, Kazakhstan, Luxembourg, Malawi, Netherlands, Philippines, Romania, Somalia, Sudan, United States

To serve until 31 December 2010: Brazil, Cameroon, China, Congo, Iceland, Malaysia, Moldova, Mozambique, New Zealand, Niger, Pakistan, Poland, Republic of Korea, Russian Federation, Saint Lucia, Sweden, United Kingdom, Uruguay

On 22 October 2008 (dec. 63/404), the General Assembly elected Norway for the remaining term of office of Iceland, beginning on 1 January 2009. At the same meeting, the General Assembly elected the following for a three-year term of office beginning on 1 January 2009 to fill vacancies occurring on 31 December 2008: Côte d'Ivoire, Estonia, France, Germany, Greece, Guatemala, Guinea-Bissau, India, Japan, Liechtenstein, Mauritius, Morocco, Namibia, Peru, Portugal, Saint Kitts and Nevis, Saudi Arabia, and Venezuela.

SESSIONS

Organizational session: New York, 14 January, 5 and 8 February, 14 April

Resumed organizational session: New York, 29 April, 20–22 May, 12 and 20 June

Special high-level meeting with the Bretton Woods institutions and the World Trade Organization: New York, 14 April

Special meeting on the global food crisis: New York, 20–22 May

Substantive session of 2008: New York, 30 June–25 July

Resumed substantive session: New York, 12 September, 19 December

OFFICERS

President: Léo Mérorès (Haiti)

Vice-Presidents: Antonio Pedro Monteiro Lima (Cape Verde), Kim Hyun Chong (Republic of Korea), Andrei Dapkiunas (Belarus), Jean-Marc Hoscheit (Luxembourg)

Subsidiary and other related organs

SUBSIDIARY ORGANS

The Economic and Social Council may, at each session, set up committees or working groups, of the whole or of limited membership, and refer to them any item on the agenda for study and report.

Other subsidiary organs reporting to the Council consist of functional commissions, regional commissions, standing committees, expert bodies and ad hoc bodies.

The inter-agency United Nations System Chief Executives Board for Coordination also reports to the Council.

Functional commissions

Commission on Crime Prevention and Criminal Justice

Session: Sixteenth, Vienna, 14–18 April
Chairperson: Kenjika Linus Ekedede (Nigeria)
Membership: 40
Report: E/2008/30
Decision: ESC 2008/201 C & E

Commission on Narcotic Drugs

Session: Fifty-first, Vienna, 10–14 March
Chairperson: Eugenio María Curia (Argentina)
Membership: 53
Report: E/2008/28

Commission on Population and Development

Session: Forty-first, New York, 7–11 April
Chairperson: Ivan Piperkov (Bulgaria)
Membership: 47
Report: E/2008/25
Decision: ESC 2008/201 C

Commission on Science and Technology for Development

Session: Eleventh, Geneva, 26–30 May
Chairperson: Maximus J. Ongkili (Malaysia)
Membership: 43
Report: E/2008/31
Decision: ESC 2008/201 C, E & F

Commission for Social Development

Session: Forty-sixth, New York, 6–15 and 22 February
Chairperson: Alexei Tulbure (Moldova)
Membership: 46
Report: E/2008/26
Decision: ESC 2008/201 B, C & E

Commission on the Status of Women

Session: Fifty-second, New York, 25 February–7 and 13 March
Chairperson: Olivier Belle (Belgium)
Membership: 45
Report: E/2008/27
Decision: ESC 2008/201 C

Commission on Sustainable Development

Session: Sixteenth, New York, 5–16 May
Chairperson: Francis D. Nhema (Zimbabwe)
Membership: 53
Report: E/2008/29
Decision: ESC 2008/201 C & F

Statistical Commission

Session: Thirty-ninth, New York, 26–29 February
Chairperson: Pali Lehohla (South Africa)
Membership: 24
Report: E/2008/24
Decision: ESC 2008/201 C

United Nations Forum on Forests

Session: Did not meet in 2008
Membership: Open to all States Members of the United Nations and members of the specialized agencies

Regional commissions

Economic Commission for Africa (ECA)

Session: Forty-first session of the Commission/Conference of African Ministers of Finance, Planning and Economic Development, Addis Ababa, Ethiopia, 31 March–2 April
Chairperson: Meles Zanawi (Ethiopia)
Membership: 53
Report: E/2008/38

Economic Commission for Europe (ECE)

Session: Did not meet in 2008
Membership: 56

Economic Commission for Latin America and the Caribbean (ECLAC)

Session: Thirty-second, Santo Domingo, Dominican Republic, 9–13 June
Chair: Dominican Republic
Membership: 44 members, 8 associate members
Report: LC/G.2395

Economic and Social Commission for Asia and the Pacific (ESCAP)

Session: Sixty-fourth, Bangkok, 24–30 April
Chairperson: Kim Jonghoon (Republic of Korea)
Membership: 53 members, 9 associate members
Report: E/2008/39

Economic and Social Commission for Western Asia (ESCWA)

Session: Twenty-fifth, Sana'a, Yemen, 26–29 May
Chairpersons: Mohammad Ahmed Al-Hawri (Yemen) for the Senior Officials' segment; Abdul Kareem Alarhabi (Yemen) for the ministerial segment
Membership: 13
Report: E/2008/41

Standing committees

Committee on Non-Governmental Organizations

Session: New York, 21–30 January (regular); 29 May–6 June, 25 June (resumed)
Chairperson: Hassan Hamid Hassan (Sudan)
Membership: 19
Reports: E/2008/32 (Part I), E/2008/32 (Part II)

Committee for Programme and Coordination (CPC)

Session: Forty-eighth, New York, 30 April (organizational); 9 June–3 July 2008 (substantive)
Chairperson: Ren Yisheng (China)
Membership: 34
Report: A/63/16
Decision: ESC 2008/201 C, E & G

Expert bodies

Committee of Experts on International Cooperation in Tax Matters

Session: Fourth, Geneva, 20–24 October
Chaiperson: Noureddine Bensouda (Morocco)
Membership: 25
Report: E/2008/45
Decision: ESC 2008/201 B

Committee for Development Policy

Session: Tenth, New York, 17–20 March
Chairperson: Ricardo Ffrench-Davis (Chile)
Membership: 24
Report: E/2008/33
Decision: ESC 2008/201 F

Committee on Economic, Social and Cultural Rights

Session: Fortieth and forty-first, Geneva, 28 April–16 May and 3–21 November
Chairperson: Philippe Texier (France)
Membership: 18
Report: E/2009/22
Decision: ESC 2008/201 C

Committee of Experts on Public Administration

Session: Seventh, New York, 14–18 April
Chairperson: Jocelyne Bourgon (Canada)
Membership: 24
Report: E/2008/44
Decision: ESC 2008/201 B

Committee of Experts on the Transport of Dangerous Goods and on the Globally Harmonized System of Classification and Labelling of Chemicals

Session: Fourth, Geneva, 12 December
Chairperson: Kim Headrick (Canada)
Membership: 37
Report: ST/SG/AC.10/36
Decision: ESC 2008/201 C

Permanent Forum on Indigenous Issues

Session: Seventh, New York, 21 April–2 May
Chairperson: Victoria Tauli-Corpuz (Philippines)
Membership: 16
Report: E/2008/43
Decision: ESC 2008/201 E

United Nations Group of Experts on Geographical Names

Session: Did not meet in 2008
Membership: Representatives of the 23 geographical/linguistic divisions of the Group of Experts

Ad hoc body

United Nations System Chief Executives Board for Coordination (CEB)

Sessions: First, Bern, Switzerland, 28 April; second, New York, 24 October
Chairperson: Secretary-General Ban Ki-moon
Membership: Organizations of the UN system
Reports: CEB/2008/1, CEB/2008/2

Other related bodies

International Research and Training Institute for the Advancement of Women (INSTRAW)

Executive Board

Session: Fifth, New York, 21 February, 22 May
President: Marie Yvette L. Banzon-Abalos (Philippines) (Acting)
Membership: 10 (plus 5 ex-officio members)
Report: E/2008/73
Director of INSTRAW: Carmen Moreno

Joint United Nations Programme on Human Immunodeficiency Virus/Acquired Immunodeficiency Syndrome (UNAIDS)

Programme Coordination Board

Meetings: Twenty-second, Chiang Mai, Thailand, 23–25 April; extraordinary, Geneva, 2 October; twenty-third, Geneva, 15–17 December
Chairpersons: Chavarat Charnvirakul (Thailand) (twenty-second); Mark Dybul (United States) (twenty-third and extraordinary)
Membership: 22
Reports: UNAIDS/PCB(22)/08.22, UNAIDS/PCB(23)/08.34, UNAIDS/PCB/Extraordinary Meeting/EM1.3
Decision: ESC 2008/201 B, C, E & G
Executive Director of UNAIDS: Peter Piot

United Nations Children's Fund (UNICEF)

Executive Board

Sessions: First and second regular, 29 January–1 February and 15–18 September; annual, 3–5 June, all in New York
President: Andres Lidén (Sweden)
Membership: 36
Report: E/2008/34/Rev.1
Decision: ESC 2008/201 C
Executive Director of UNICEF: Ann M. Veneman

United Nations Development Programme (UNDP)/ United Nations Population Fund (UNFPA)

EXECUTIVE BOARD

Sessions: First and second regular, New York, 21–28 January and 8–12 September; annual, Geneva, 16–27 June
President: Jean-Marie Ehouzou (Benin)
Membership: 36
Report: E/2008/35
Decision: ESC 2008/201 C
Administrator of UNDP: Kemal Dervis
Executive Director of UNFPA: Thoraya Ahmed Obaid

UNITED NATIONS VOLUNTEERS (UNV)
Report: DP/2008/34

United Nations Research Institute for Social Development (UNRISD)

BOARD

Session: Forty-sixth, Geneva, 28 March
Chairperson: Lourdes Arizpe (Mexico)
Membership: 11
Report: Board/08/3
Director of UNRISD: Thandika Mkandawire

United Nations Interregional Crime and Justice Research Institute (UNICRI)

BOARD OF TRUSTEES

Membership: 7 (plus 4 ex-officio members)
Decision: ESC 2008/246
Director of UNICRI: Sandro Calvani (Italy)

World Food Programme (WFP)

EXECUTIVE BOARD

Sessions: First and second regular, Rome, 4–6 February and 27–30 October; annual, Rome, 9–12 June
President: José Eduardo Dantas Ferreira Barbosa (Cape Verde)
Membership: 36
Report: E/2009/36
Decision: ESC 2008/201 C
Executive Director of WFP: Josette Sheeran

Trusteeship Council

The Trusteeship Council suspended operation on 1 November 1994 following the independence of Palau, the last remaining United Nations trust territory, on 1 October 1994. The General Assembly, in resolution 60/1 of 16 September 2005, considering that the Council no longer met and had no remaining functions, decided that Chapter XIII of the United Nations Charter and references to the Council in Chapter XII should be deleted.

International Court of Justice

JUDGES OF THE COURT

The International Court of Justice consists of 15 Judges elected for nine-year terms by the General Assembly and the Security Council.

The following were the Judges of the Court serving in 2008, listed in the order of precedence:

Judge	*Country of nationality*	*End of term*
Rosalyn Higgins, *President*	United Kingdom	2009
Awn Shawkat Al-Khasawneh, *Vice-President*	Jordan	2009
Raymond Ranjeva	Madagascar	2009
Shi Jiuyong	China	2012
Abdul G. Koroma	Sierra Leone	2012
Gonzalo Parra-Aranguren	Venezuela	2009
Thomas Buergenthal	United States	2015
Hisashi Owada	Japan	2012
Bruno Simma	Germany	2012
Peter Tomka	Slovakia	2012
Ronny Abraham	France	2009
Kenneth Keith	New Zealand	2015
Bernardo Sepúlveda Amor	Mexico	2015
Mohamed Bennouna	Morocco	2015
Leonid Skotnikov	Russian Federation	2015

Registrar: Philippe Couvreur
Deputy Registrar: Thérèse de Saint Phalle
Decision: GA 63/406

CHAMBER OF SUMMARY PROCEDURE
Members: Rosalyn Higgins (ex officio), Awn Shawkat Al-Khasawneh (ex officio), Gonzalo Parra-Aranguren, Thomas Buergenthal, Leonid Skotnikov
Substitute members: Abdul G. Koroma, Ronny Abraham

PARTIES TO THE COURT'S STATUTE

All Members of the United Nations are ipso facto parties to the Statute of the International Court of Justice.

STATES ACCEPTING THE COMPULSORY JURISDICTION OF THE COURT

Declarations made by the following States, a number with reservations, accepting the Court's compulsory jurisdiction (or made under the Statute of the Permanent Court of International Justice and deemed to be an acceptance of the jurisdiction of the International Court) were in force at the end of 2008:

Australia, Austria, Barbados, Belgium, Botswana, Bulgaria, Cambodia, Cameroon, Canada, Costa Rica, Côte d'Ivoire, Cyprus, Democratic Republic of the Congo, Denmark, Djibouti, Dominica, Dominican Republic, Egypt, Estonia, Finland, Gambia, Georgia, Germany, Greece, Guinea, Guinea-Bissau, Haiti, Honduras, Hungary, India, Japan, Kenya, Lesotho, Liberia, Liechtenstein, Luxembourg, Madagascar, Malawi, Malta, Mauritius, Mexico, Netherlands, New Zealand, Nicaragua, Nigeria, Norway, Pakistan, Panama, Paraguay, Peru, Philippines, Poland, Portugal, Senegal, Slovakia, Somalia, Spain, Sudan, Suriname, Swaziland, Sweden, Switzerland, Togo, Uganda, United Kingdom, and Uruguay.

UNITED NATIONS ORGANS AND SPECIALIZED AND RELATED AGENCIES AUTHORIZED TO REQUEST ADVISORY OPINIONS FROM THE COURT

Authorized by the United Nations Charter to request opinions on any legal question: General Assembly, Security Council

Authorized by the General Assembly in accordance with the Charter to request opinions on legal questions arising within the scope of their activities: Economic and Social Council, Trusteeship Council, Interim Committee of the General Assembly, ILO, FAO, UNESCO, ICAO, WHO, World Bank, IFC, IDA, IMF, ITU, WMO, IMO, WIPO, IFAD, UNIDO, IAEA

COMMITTEES OF THE COURT

Budgetary and Administrative Committee

Members: Rosalyn Higgins (ex officio), Awn Shawkat Al-Khasawneh (ex officio), Raymond Ranjeva, Thomas Buergenthal, Hisashi Owada, Peter Tomka

Library Committee

Members: Thomas Buergenthal (Chairperson), Bruno Simma, Peter Tomka, Kenneth Keith, Mohamed Bennouna

Rules Committee

Members: Hisashi Owada (Chairperson), Bruno Simma, Ronny Abraham, Kenneth Keith, Bernardo Sepúlveda Amor, Mohamed Bennouna
Report: A/63/4

Other United Nations-related bodies

The following bodies are not subsidiary to any principal organ of the United Nations but were established by an international treaty instrument or arrangement sponsored by the United Nations and are thus related to the Organization and its work. These bodies, often referred to as "treaty organs", are serviced by the United Nations Secretariat and may be financed in part or wholly from the Organization's regular budget, as authorized by the General Assembly, to which most of them report annually.

Committee on the Elimination of Discrimination against Women (CEDAW)

Sessions: Fortieth, Geneva, 14 January–1 February; forty-first, New York, 30 June–18 July
Chairperson: Dubravka Šimonović (Croatia)
Membership: 22
Report: A/63/38

Committee on the Elimination of Racial Discrimination (CERD)

Sessions: Seventy-second and seventy-third, Geneva, 18 February–7 March and 28 July–15 August
Chairperson: Fatimata-Binta Victoire Dah (Burkina Faso)
Membership: 18
Report: A/63/18

Committee on the Protection of the Rights of All Migrant Workers and Members of Their Families

Sessions: Eighth and ninth, Geneva, 14–25 April and 24–28 November
Chairperson: Abdelhamid El Jamri (Morocco)
Membership: 10
Reports: A/63/48, A/64/48

Committee on the Rights of the Child

Sessions: Forty-seventh and forty-eighth, Geneva, 14 January–1 February and 19 May–6 June
Chairperson: Yanghee Lee (Republic of Korea)
Membership: 18
Report: A/63/41

Committee against Torture

Sessions: Fortieth and forty-first, Geneva, 28 April–16 May and 3–21 November
Chairperson: Claudio Grossman (Chile)
Membership: 10
Reports: A/63/44, A/64/44

Conference on Disarmament

Meetings: Geneva, 23 January–28 March, 12 May–27 June, 28 July–12 September
President: Tunisia, Turkey, Ukraine, United Kingdom, United States and Venezuela (successively)
Membership: 65
Report: A/63/27

Human Rights Committee

Sessions: Ninety-second, New York, 17 March–4 April; ninety-third and ninety-fourth, Geneva, 7–25 July and 13–31 October
Chairperson: Rafael Rivas-Posada (Colombia)
Membership: 18
Reports: A/63/40 (Vol. I), A/64/40 (Vol. I)

International Narcotics Control Board (INCB)

Sessions: Ninety-first, ninety-second and ninety-third, Vienna, 4–8 February, 19–30 May and 28 October–14 November
President: Hamid Ghodse (Iran)
Membership: 13
Report: E/INCB/2008/1

Principal members of the United Nations Secretariat[11]

Secretariat

The Secretary-General: Ban Ki-moon
Deputy Secretary-General: Asha-Rose Migiro

Executive Office of the Secretary-General

Under-Secretary-General, Chef de Cabinet: Vijay Nambiar
Assistant Secretary-General, Deputy Chef de Cabinet: Kim Won-soo
Assistant Secretary-General for Policy Planning: Robert Orr

Office of Internal Oversight Services

Under-Secretary-General: Inga-Britt Ahlenius

Office of Legal Affairs

Under-Secretary-General, Legal Counsel: Nicolas Michel (until July); Patricia O'Brien (from August)
Assistant Secretary-General: Larry D. Johnson (until August); Peter Taksøe-Jensen (from August)

Department of Political Affairs

Under-Secretary-General: B. Lynn Pascoe
Assistant Secretary-General, Executive Director, Counter-Terrorism Committee: Mike Smith
Assistant Secretaries-General: Haile Menkerios, Angela Kane (until May)

Office of the Special Adviser of the Secretary-General on the Prevention of Genocide

Under-Secretary-General, Special Adviser: Francis Deng

Office for Disarmament Affairs

High Representative: Sergio de Queiroz Duarte

Department of Peacekeeping Operations

Under-Secretary-General: Jean-Marie Guéhenno (until July), Alain Le Roy (from July)
Assistant Secretaries-General: Edmond Mulet, Jane Holl Lute (until May)

Department of Field Support

Officer-in-Charge: Jane Holl Lute (until May)
Under-Secretary-General: Susana Malcorra (from May)

Office for the Coordination of Humanitarian Affairs

Under-Secretary-General for Humanitarian Affairs, Emergency Relief Coordinator: John Holmes

Assistant Secretary-General, Deputy Emergency Relief Coordinator: Catherine Bragg

Department of Economic and Social Affairs

Under-Secretary-General: Sha Zukang

Assistant Secretary-General, Special Adviser on Gender Issues and Advancement of Women: Rachel Mayanja

Assistant Secretaries-General: Jomo Kwame Sundaram, Patrizio M. Civili (until March), Thomas Stelzer (from March)

Department for General Assembly and Conference Management

Under-Secretary-General: Muhammad Shaaban

Assistant Secretary-General: Yohannes Mengesha

Department of Public Information

Under-Secretary-General for Communications and Public Information: Kiyotaka Akasaka

Department of Safety and Security

Under-Secretary-General: David Veness

Department of Management

Under-Secretary-General: Alicia Bárcena Ibarra (until May), Angela Kane (from May)

OFFICE OF PROGRAMME PLANNING, BUDGET AND ACCOUNTS

Assistant Secretary-General, Controller: Warren Sach (until August), Jun Yamazaki (from August)

OFFICE OF HUMAN RESOURCES MANAGEMENT

Assistant Secretary-General: Jan Beagle (until April), Catherine Pollard (from April)

OFFICE OF CENTRAL SUPPORT SERVICES

Assistant Secretary-General: Warren Sach (from August)

CAPITAL MASTER PLAN PROJECT

Assistant Secretary-General, Executive Director: Michael Adlerstein

Office of Information and Communications Technology

Assistant Secretary-General, Chief Information Technology Officer: Choi Soon-Hong

Office of the United Nations Ombudsman

Assistant Secretary-General, Ombudsman: Nora Galer (Officer-in-Charge until April), Johnston Barkat (from April)

Peacebuilding Support Office

Assistant Secretary-General: Carolyn McAskie (until August), Jane Holl Lute (from August)

United Nations Joint Staff Pension Fund

Assistant Secretary-General, Chief Executive Officer: Bernard G. Cochemé

Economic Commission for Africa

Under-Secretary-General, Executive Secretary: Abdoulie Janneh

Economic Commission for Europe

Under-Secretary-General, Executive Secretary: Marek Belka

Economic Commission for Latin America and the Caribbean

Under-Secretary-General, Executive Secretary: José Luis Machinea (until June), Alicia Bárcena Ibarra (from July)

Economic and Social Commission for Asia and the Pacific

Under-Secretary-General, Executive Secretary: Noeleen Heyzer

Economic and Social Commission for Western Asia

Under-Secretary-General, Executive Secretary: Bader Al-Dafa

United Nations Office at Geneva

Under-Secretary-General, Director-General of the United Nations Office at Geneva: Sergei Ordzhonikidze

Office of the United Nations High Commissioner for Human Rights

Under-Secretary-General, High Commissioner: Louise Arbour (until August), Navanethem Pillay (From September)

Assistant Secretary-General, Deputy High Commissioner: Kyung-wha Kang

United Nations Office at Vienna

Under-Secretary-General, Director-General of the United Nations Office at Vienna and Executive Director of the United Nations Office on Drugs and Crime: Antonio Maria Costa

United Nations Office at Nairobi

Under-Secretary-General and Director-General of the United Nations Office at Nairobi: Anna Kajumulo Tibaijuka

International Court of Justice Registry

Assistant Secretary-General, Registrar: Philippe Couvreur

Secretariats of subsidiary organs, special representatives and other related bodies

International Trade Centre UNCTAD/WTO

Executive Director: Patricia Francis

Office of the High Representative for the Least Developed Countries, Landlocked Developing Countries and Small Island Developing States

Under-Secretary-General, High Representative: Cheick Sidi Diarra

Office of the Special Adviser to the Secretary-General on Africa

Under-Secretary-General, Special Adviser: Cheick Sidi Diarra

Office of the Special Adviser to the Secretary-General on the International Compact with Iraq and Other Issues

Under-Secretary-General, Special Adviser: Ibrahim Gambari

Office of the Special Adviser of the Secretary-General for Myanmar

Under-Secretary-General, Special Adviser: Ibrahim Gambari

Office of the Special Representative of the Secretary-General for Children and Armed Conflict

Under-Secretary-General, Special Representative: Radhika Coomaraswamy

Office of the Special Representative of the Secretary-General for West Africa

Under-Secretary-General, Special Representative: Said Djinnit

Office of the United Nations High Commissioner for Refugees

Under-Secretary-General, High Commissioner: António Manuel de Oliveira Guterres

Office of the United Nations Special Coordinator for the Middle East

Under-Secretary-General, Special Coordinator for the Middle East Peace Process and Personal Representative of the Secretary-General to the Palestine Liberation Organization and the Palestinian Authority: Robert H. Serry

Special Adviser to the Secretary-General on Latin American Issues

Under-Secretary-General, Special Adviser: Diego Cordovez

Special Representative of the Secretary-General for the Sudan

Under-Secretary-General, Special Representative: Ashraf Jehangir Qazi
Assistant Secretary-General, Principal Deputy Special Representative: Tayé-Brook Zerihoun (until April)

United Nations Children's Fund

Under-Secretary-General, Executive Director: Ann M. Veneman
Assistant Secretaries-General, Deputy Executive Directors: Hilde Johnson, Omar Abdi, Saad Houry

United Nations Compensation Commission

Assistant Secretary-General, Executive Secretary: Mojtaba Kazazi

United Nations Conference on Trade and Development

Under-Secretary-General: Supachai Panitchpakdi

United Nations Development Programme

Administrator: Kemal Dervis
Under-Secretary-General, Associate Administrator: Ad Melkert
Assistant Administrator and Director, Bureau for Crisis Prevention and Recovery: Kathleen Cravero
Assistant Administrator and Director, Bureau for Resources and Strategic Partnerships: Bruce Jenks
Assistant Administrator and Director, Bureau of Management: Akiko Yuge
Assistant Administrator and Director, Bureau for Development Policy: Olav Kjørven
Assistant Administrator and Regional Director, UNDP Africa: Gilbert Fossoun Houngbo (until September)
Assistant Administrator and Regional Director, UNDP Arab States: Amat Al Aleem Ali Alsoswa
Assistant Administrator and Regional Director, UNDP Asia and the Pacific: Ajay Chhibber (from April)
Assistant Administrator and Regional Director, UNDP Europe and the Commonwealth of Independent States: Kori Udovicki
Assistant Administrator and Regional Director, UNDP Latin America and the Caribbean: Rebeca Grynspan

United Nations Environment Programme

Under-Secretary-General, Executive Director: Achim Steiner
Assistant Secretary-General, Deputy Executive Director: Angela Cropper
Assistant Secretary-General, Executive Secretary: Yvo de Boer

United Nations Human Settlements Programme

Under-Secretary-General, Executive Director: Anna Kajumulo Tibaijuka

United Nations Institute for Training and Research

Assistant Secretary-General, Executive Director: Carlos Lopes

United Nations Population Fund

Under-Secretary-General, Executive Director: Thoraya Ahmed Obaid

United Nations Office for Project Services

Assistant Secretary-General, Executive Director: Jan Mattsson

United Nations Relief and Works Agency for Palestine Refugees in the Near East

Under-Secretary-General, Commissioner-General: Karen Koning AbuZayd
Assistant Secretary-General, Deputy Commissioner-General: Filippo Grandi

United Nations University

Under-Secretary-General, Rector: Konrad Osterwalder

NOTES

[1] Elected on 4 June 2008 (dec. 62/416).

[2] Elected on 4 June 2008 (dec. 62/418).

[3] One of the Main Committees that met during the resumed session.

[4] Elected by the Committees; announced by the Assembly President on 4 June 2008 (dec. 62/417).

[5] Appointed on 16 September 2008 (dec. 63/401).

[6] Formerly known as the "High-level Committee on the Review of Technical Cooperation among Developing Countries" and renamed by the Assembly in December 2003 (res. 58/220).

[7] Also an advisory subsidiary body of the General Assembly.

[8] Mandate terminated on 31 June 2008 (res. 1827(2008)).

[9] Mandate ended on 30 September 2008 and the mission was succeeded by UNIPSIL on 1 October 2008 (res. 1829(2008)).

[10] Established on 1 October 2008 (res. 1829(2008)).

[11] As at 30 June 2008, the total number of staff of the United Nations Secretariat with continuous service or expected service of a year or more was 39,503. Of these, 9,892 were in the Professional and higher categories, 1,250 were experts (200-series Project Personnel staff) and 28,361 were in the General Service and related categories.

Appendix IV

Agendas of the United Nations principal organs in 2008

This appendix lists the items on the agendas of the General Assembly, the Security Council and the Economic and Social Council during 2008. For the Assembly, the column headed *"Allocation"* indicates the assignment of each item to plenary meetings or committees.

General Assembly

Agenda items remaining for consideration at the resumed sixty-second session (23 December 2007–15 September 2008) [decision 62/546, A/62/49 (Vol. II)]

Item No.	*Title*	*Allocation*
10.	Report of the Peacebuilding Commission.	Plenary
11.	Elimination of unilateral extraterritorial coercive economic measures as a means of political and economic compulsion.	Plenary
14.	Prevention of armed conflict.	Plenary
15.	The situation in Central America: progress in fashioning a region of peace, freedom, democracy and development.	Plenary
16.	Protracted conflicts in the GUAM area and their implications for international peace, security and development.	Plenary
17.	The situation in the Middle East.	Plenary
18.	Question of Palestine.	Plenary
20.	The situation in the occupied territories of Azerbaijan.	Plenary
22.	Question of Cyprus.	Plenary
23.	Armed aggression against the Democratic Republic of the Congo.	Plenary
24.	Question of the Falkland Islands (Malvinas).	Plenary
25.	The situation of democracy and human rights in Haiti.	Plenary
26.	Armed Israeli aggression against the Iraqi nuclear installations and its grave consequences for the established international system concerning the peaceful uses of nuclear energy, the non-proliferation of nuclear weapons and international peace and security.	Plenary
27.	Consequences of the Iraqi occupation of and aggression against Kuwait.	Plenary
28.	Declaration of the Assembly of Heads of State and Government of the Organization of African Unity on the aerial and naval military attack against the Socialist People's Libyan Arab Jamahiriya by the present United States Administration in April 1986.	Plenary
34.	Comprehensive review of the whole question of peacekeeping operations in all their aspects.	4th
43.	Report of the Economic and Social Council.	Plenary
44.	Implementation of the Declaration of Commitment on HIV/AIDS and the Political Declaration on HIV/AIDS.	Plenary
45.	Sport for peace and development:	Plenary
	(a) Sport for peace and development;	
	(b) Building a peaceful and better world through sport and the Olympic ideal.	
46.	Global road safety crisis.	Plenary
48.	Integrated and coordinated implementation of and follow-up to the outcomes of the major United Nations conferences and summits in the economic, social and related fields.	Plenary
53.	Follow-up to and implementation of the outcome of the International Conference on Financing for Development:	Plenary
	(a) Follow-up to and implementation of the outcome of the International Conference on Financing for Development.	
54.	Sustainable development:	2nd
	(d) Protection of global climate for present and future generations of mankind.	
57.	Groups of countries in special situations:	2nd
	(b) Specific actions related to the particular needs and problems of landlocked developing countries: outcome of the International Ministerial Conference of Landlocked and Transit Developing Countries; and Donor Countries and International Financial and Development Institutions on Transit Transport Cooperation.	
64.	New Partnership for Africa's Development: progress in implementation and international support:	Plenary
	(a) New Partnership for Africa's Development: progress in implementation and international support;	
	(b) Causes of conflict and the promotion of durable peace and sustainable development in Africa.	

Item No.	*Title*	*Allocation*
86.	The rule of law at the national and international levels.	6th
98.	General and complete disarmament: (g) Convening of the fourth special session of the General Assembly devoted to disarmament.	1st
108.	Measures to eliminate international terrorism.	6th
109.	Report of the Secretary-General on the work of the Organization.	Plenary
110.	Report of the Secretary-General on the Peacebuilding Fund.	Plenary
113.	Elections to fill vacancies in subsidiary organs and other elections: (a) Election of seven members of the Committee for Programme and Coordination; (c) Election of five members of the Organizational Committee of the Peacebuilding Commission; (d) Election of fifteen members of the Human Rights Council.	Plenary
114.	Appointments to fill vacancies in subsidiary organs and other appointments: (i) Approval of the appointment of the United Nations High Commissioner for Human Rights.	Plenary
115.	Admission of new members to the United Nations.	Plenary
116.	Follow-up to the outcome of the Millennium Summit.	Plenary
117.	United Nations reform: measures and proposals.	Plenary
118.	The United Nations Global Counter-Terrorism Strategy.	Plenary
121.	Revitalization of the work of the General Assembly.	Plenary
122.	Question of equitable representation on and increase in the membership of the Security Council and related matters.	Plenary
123.	Strengthening of the United Nations system.	Plenary
124.	Follow-up to the recommendations on administrative management and internal oversight of the Independent Inquiry Committee into the United Nations Oil-for-Food Programme.	Plenary
125.	Financial reports and audited financial statements, and reports of the Board of Auditors: (a) United Nations peacekeeping operations; (b) Capital master plan; (c) Voluntary funds administered by the United Nations High Commissioner for Refugees; (d) United Nations Office for Project Services.	5th
126.	Review of the efficiency of the administrative and financial functioning of the United Nations.	5th
127.	Programme budget for the biennium 2006–2007.	5th
128.	Proposed programme budget for the biennium 2008–2009.	5th
129.	Programme planning.	Plenary and all Committees
130.	Improving the financial situation of the United Nations.	5th
131.	Pattern of conferences.	5th
132.	Scale of assessments for the apportionment of the expenses of the United Nations.	5th
133.	Human resources management.	5th
134.	Joint Inspection Unit.	5th
135.	United Nations common system.	5th
136.	Report on the activities of the Office of Internal Oversight Services.	5th
137.	Administration of justice at the United Nations.	5th
138.	Financing of the International Criminal Tribunal for the Prosecution of Persons Responsible for Genocide and Other Serious Violations of International Humanitarian Law Committed in the Territory of Rwanda and Rwandan Citizens Responsible for Genocide and Other Such Violations Committed in the Territory of Neighbouring States between 1 January and 31 December 1994.	5th
139.	Financing of the International Tribunal for the Prosecution of Persons Responsible for Serious Violations of International Humanitarian Law Committed in the Territory of the Former Yugoslavia since 1991.	5th
140.	Administrative and budgetary aspects of the financing of the United Nations peacekeeping operations.	5th
141.	Financing of the United Nations Operation in Burundi.	5th
142.	Financing of the United Nations Operation in Côte d'Ivoire.	5th
143.	Financing of the United Nations Peacekeeping Force in Cyprus.	5th
144.	Financing of the United Nations Organization Mission in the Democratic Republic of the Congo.	5th
145.	Financing of the United Nations Mission in East Timor.	5th
146.	Financing of the United Nations Mission of Support in East Timor.	5th
147.	Financing of the United Nations Integrated Mission in Timor-Leste.	5th
148.	Financing of the United Nations Mission in Ethiopia and Eritrea.	5th
149.	Financing of the United Nations Observer Mission in Georgia.	5th
150.	Financing of the United Nations Stabilization Mission in Haiti.	5th
151.	Financing of the United Nations Interim Administration Mission in Kosovo.	5th
152.	Financing of the United Nations Mission in Liberia.	5th
153.	Financing of the United Nations peacekeeping forces in the Middle East: (a) United Nations Disengagement Observer Force; (b) United Nations Interim Force in Lebanon.	5th

Item No.	Title	Allocation
154.	Financing of the United Nations Mission in Sierra Leone.	5th
155.	Financing of the United Nations Mission in the Sudan.	5th
156.	Financing of the United Nations Mission for the Referendum in Western Sahara.	5th
161.	Financing of the African Union-United Nations Hybrid Operation in Darfur.	5th
164.	Financing of the United Nations Mission in the Central African Republic and Chad.	5th

Agenda of the sixty-third session, first part (16 September–24 December 2008) [A/63/49 (Vol. I), Annex I]

Item No.	Title	Allocation
1.	Opening of the session by the President of the General Assembly.	Plenary
2.	Minute of silent prayer or meditation.	Plenary
3.	Credentials of representatives to the sixty-third session of the General Assembly: (a) Appointment of the members of the Credentials Committee; (b) Report of the Credentials Committee.	Plenary
4.	Election of the President of the General Assembly.	Plenary
5.	Election of officers of the Main Committees.	1st, 4th, 2nd, 3rd, 5th, 6th
6.	Election of the Vice-Presidents of the General Assembly.	Plenary
7.	Organization of work, adoption of the agenda and allocation of items: reports of the General Committee.	Plenary
8.	General debate.	Plenary

A. Maintenance of international peace and security

Item No.	Title	Allocation
9.	Report of the Security Council.	Plenary
10.	Report of the Peacebuilding Commission.	Plenary
11.	The role of diamonds in fuelling conflict.	Plenary
12.	Prevention of armed conflict.	Plenary
13.	Protracted conflicts in the GUAM area and their implications for international peace, security and development.	Plenary
14.	Zone of peace and cooperation of the South Atlantic.	Plenary
15.	The situation in the Middle East.	Plenary
16.	Question of Palestine.	Plenary
17.	The situation in Afghanistan.	Plenary
18.	The situation in the occupied territories of Azerbaijan.	Plenary
19.	Necessity of ending the economic, commercial and financial embargo imposed by the United States of America against Cuba.	Plenary
20.	The situation in Central America: progress in fashioning a region of peace, freedom, democracy and development.	Plenary
21.	Question of Cyprus.	Plenary
22.	Armed aggression against the Democratic Republic of the Congo.	Plenary
23.	Question of the Falkland Islands (Malvinas).	Plenary
24.	The situation of democracy and human rights in Haiti.	Plenary
25.	Armed Israeli aggression against the Iraqi nuclear installations and its grave consequences for the established international system concerning the peaceful uses of nuclear energy, the non-proliferation of nuclear weapons and international peace and security.	Plenary
26.	Consequences of the Iraqi occupation of and aggression against Kuwait.	Plenary
27.	Effects of atomic radiation.	4th
28.	International cooperation in the peaceful uses of outer space.	4th
29.	United Nations Relief and Works Agency for Palestine Refugees in the Near East.	4th
30.	Report of the Special Committee to Investigate Israeli Practices Affecting the Human Rights of the Palestinian People and Other Arabs of the Occupied Territories.	4th
31.	Comprehensive review of the whole question of peacekeeping operations in all their aspects.	Plenary, 4th
32.	Questions relating to information.	4th
33.	Information from Non-Self-Governing Territories transmitted under Article 73 e of the Charter of the United Nations.	4th
34.	Economic and other activities which affect the interests of the peoples of the Non-Self-Governing Territories.	4th
35.	Implementation of the Declaration on the Granting of Independence to Colonial Countries and Peoples by the specialized agencies and the international institutions associated with the United Nations.	4th
36.	Offers by Member States of study and training facilities for inhabitants of Non-Self-Governing Territories.	4th
37.	Implementation of the Declaration on the Granting of Independence to Colonial Countries and Peoples.	4th
38.	Permanent sovereignty of the Palestinian people in the Occupied Palestinian Territory, including East Jerusalem, and of the Arab population in the occupied Syrian Golan over their natural resources.	2nd
39.	Report of the United Nations High Commissioner for Refugees, questions relating to refugees, returnees and displaced persons and humanitarian questions.	3rd

Item No.	*Title*	*Allocation*
B.	**Promotion of sustained economic growth and sustainable development in accordance with the relevant resolutions of the General Assembly and recent United Nations conferences**	
40.	Report of the Economic and Social Council.	Plenary
41.	Implementation of the Declaration of Commitment on HIV/AIDS and the Political Declaration on HIV/AIDS.	Plenary
42.	Sport for peace and development.	Plenary
43.	2001–2010: Decade to Roll Back Malaria in Developing Countries, Particularly in Africa.	Plenary
44.	Integrated and coordinated implementation of and follow-up to the outcomes of the major United Nations conferences and summits in the economic, social and related fields.	Plenary
45.	Culture of peace.	Plenary
46.	Information and communication technologies for development.	2nd
47.	Macroeconomic policy questions: (a) International trade and development; (b) International financial system and development; (c) External debt and development: towards a durable solution to the debt problems of developing countries; (d) Commodities.	2nd
48.	Follow-up to and implementation of the outcome of the 2002 International Conference on Financing for Development and the preparation of the 2008 Review Conference.	2nd
49.	Sustainable development: (a) Implementation of Agenda 21, the Programme for the Further Implementation of Agenda 21 and the outcomes of the World Summit on Sustainable Development; (b) Follow-up to and implementation of the Mauritius Strategy for the Further Implementation of the Programme of Action for the Sustainable Development of Small Island Developing States; (c) International Strategy for Disaster Reduction; (d) Protection of global climate for present and future generations of mankind; (e) Implementation of the United Nations Convention to Combat Desertification in Those Countries Experiencing Serious Drought and/or Desertification, Particularly in Africa; (f) Convention on Biological Diversity; (g) Report of the Governing Council of the United Nations Environment Programme on its tenth special session.	2nd
50.	Implementation of the outcome of the United Nations Conference on Human Settlements (Habitat II) and strengthening of the United Nations Human Settlements Programme (UN-Habitat).	2nd
51.	Globalization and interdependence: (a) Role of the United Nations in promoting development in the context of globalization and interdependence; (b) International migration and development; (c) Culture and development; (d) Preventing and combating corrupt practices and transfer of assets of illicit origin and returning such assets, in particular to the countries of origin, consistent with the United Nations Convention against Corruption; (e) Integration of the economies in transition into the world economy.	2nd
52.	Groups of countries in special situations: (a) Third United Nations Conference on the Least Developed Countries; (b) Specific actions related to the particular needs and problems of landlocked developing countries: outcome of the International Ministerial Conference of Landlocked and Transit Developing Countries and Donor Countries and International Financial and Development Institutions on Transit Transport Cooperation.	Plenary, 2nd
53.	Eradication of poverty and other development issues: (a) Implementation of the second United Nations Decade for the Eradication of Poverty (2008–2017); (b) Industrial development cooperation.	2nd
54.	Operational activities for development.	2nd
55.	Social development: (a) Implementation of the outcome of the World Summit for Social Development and of the twenty-fourth special session of the General Assembly; (b) Social development, including questions relating to the world social situation and to youth, ageing, disabled persons and the family; (c) Follow-up to the International Year of Older Persons: Second World Assembly on Ageing; (d) United Nations Literacy Decade: education for all; (e) Review and appraisal of the World Programme of Action concerning Disabled Persons.	3rd
56.	Advancement of women: (a) Advancement of women; (b) Implementation of the outcome of the Fourth World Conference on Women and of the twenty-third special session of the General Assembly.	3rd
155.	Recognition of sickle-cell anaemia as a public health priority.	Plenary

Item No.	Title	Allocation
C.	**Development of Africa**	
57.	New Partnership for Africa's Development: progress in implementation and international support:	Plenary
	(a) New Partnership for Africa's Development: progress in implementation and international support;	
	(b) Causes of conflict and the promotion of durable peace and sustainable development in Africa.	
D.	**Promotion of human rights**	
58.	Report of the Human Rights Council.	Plenary, 3rd
59.	Holocaust remembrance.	Plenary
60.	Promotion and protection of the rights of children:	3rd
	(a) Promotion and protection of the rights of children;	
	(b) Follow-up to the outcome of the special session on children.	
61.	Indigenous issues:	3rd
	(a) Indigenous issues;	
	(b) Second International Decade of the World's Indigenous People.	
62.	Elimination of racism, racial discrimination, xenophobia and related intolerance:	3rd
	(a) Elimination of racism, racial discrimination, xenophobia and related intolerance;	
	(b) Comprehensive implementation of and follow-up to the Durban Declaration and Programme of Action.	
63.	Right of peoples to self-determination.	3rd
64.	Promotion and protection of human rights:	Plenary, 3rd
	(a) Implementation of human rights instruments;	
	(b) Human rights questions, including alternative approaches for improving the effective enjoyment of human rights and fundamental freedoms;	
	(c) Human rights situations and reports of special rapporteurs and representatives;	
	(d) Comprehensive implementation of and follow-up to the Vienna Declaration and Programme of Action;	
	(e) Convention on the Rights of Persons with Disabilities.	
E.	**Effective coordination of humanitarian assistance efforts**	
65.	Strengthening of the coordination of humanitarian and disaster relief assistance of the United Nations, including special economic assistance:	Plenary
	(a) Strengthening of the coordination of emergency humanitarian assistance of the United Nations;	
	(b) Special economic assistance to individual countries or regions;	
	(c) Assistance to the Palestinian people.	
F.	**Promotion of justice and international law**	
66.	Report of the International Court of Justice.	Plenary
67.	Report of the International Criminal Tribunal for the Prosecution of Persons Responsible for Genocide and Other Serious Violations of International Humanitarian Law Committed in the Territory of Rwanda and Rwandan Citizens Responsible for Genocide and Other Such Violations Committed in the Territory of Neighbouring States between 1 January and 31 December 1994.	Plenary
68.	Report of the International Tribunal for the Prosecution of Persons Responsible for Serious Violations of International Humanitarian Law Committed in the Territory of the Former Yugoslavia since 1991.	Plenary
69.	Report of the International Criminal Court.	Plenary
70.	Oceans and the law of the sea:	Plenary
	(a) Oceans and the law of the sea;	
	(b) Sustainable fisheries, including through the 1995 Agreement for the Implementation of the Provisions of the United Nations Convention on the Law of the Sea of 10 December 1982 relating to the Conservation and Management of Straddling Fish Stocks and Highly Migratory Fish Stocks, and related instruments.	
71.	Request for an advisory opinion of the International Court of Justice on whether the unilateral declaration of independence of Kosovo is in accordance with international law.	Plenary
72.	Nationality of natural persons in relation to the succession of States.	6th
73.	Criminal accountability of United Nations officials and experts on mission.	6th
74.	Report of the United Nations Commission on International Trade Law on the work of its forty-first session.	6th
75.	Report of the International Law Commission on the work of its sixtieth session.	6th
76.	Status of the Protocols Additional to the Geneva Conventions of 1949 and relating to the protection of victims of armed conflicts.	6th
77.	Consideration of effective measures to enhance the protection, security and safety of diplomatic and consular missions and representatives.	6th
78.	Report of the Special Committee on the Charter of the United Nations and on the Strengthening of the Role of the Organization.	6th
79.	The rule of law at the national and international levels.	6th

Item No.	*Title*	*Allocation*
G.	**Disarmament**	
80.	Report of the International Atomic Energy Agency.	Plenary
81.	Reduction of military budgets.	1st
82.	Prohibition of the development and manufacture of new types of weapons of mass destruction and new systems of such weapons: report of the Conference on Disarmament.	1st
83.	Maintenance of international security—good-neighbourliness, stability and development in South-Eastern Europe.	1st
84.	Role of science and technology in the context of international security and disarmament.	1st
85.	Developments in the field of information and telecommunications in the context of international security.	1st
86.	Establishment of a nuclear-weapon-free zone in the region of the Middle East.	1st
87.	Conclusion of effective international arrangements to assure non-nuclear-weapon States against the use or threat of use of nuclear weapons.	1st
88.	Prevention of an arms race in outer space.	1st
89.	General and complete disarmament:	1st
	(a) Notification of nuclear tests;	
	(b) Missiles;	
	(c) Problems arising from the accumulation of conventional ammunition stockpiles in surplus;	
	(d) Disarmament and non-proliferation education;	
	(e) Consolidation of peace through practical disarmament measures;	
	(f) Transparency in armaments;	
	(g) Information on confidence-building measures in the field of conventional arms;	
	(h) Mongolia's international security and nuclear-weapon-free status;	
	(i) Establishment of a nuclear-weapon-free zone in Central Asia;	
	(j) Assistance to States for curbing the illicit traffic in small arms and light weapons and collecting them;	
	(k) Implementation of the Convention on the Prohibition of the Development, Production, Stockpiling and Use of Chemical Weapons and on Their Destruction;	
	(l) Towards a nuclear-weapon-free world: accelerating the implementation of nuclear disarmament commitments;	
	(m) Promotion of multilateralism in the area of disarmament and non-proliferation;	
	(n) Observance of environmental norms in the drafting and implementation of agreements on disarmament and arms control;	
	(o) Convening of the fourth special session of the General Assembly devoted to disarmament;	
	(p) Effects of the use of armaments and ammunitions containing depleted uranium;	
	(q) Reducing nuclear danger;	
	(r) Measures to prevent terrorists from acquiring weapons of mass destruction;	
	(s) Nuclear-weapon-free southern hemisphere and adjacent areas;	
	(t) Regional disarmament;	
	(u) Follow-up to the advisory opinion of the International Court of Justice on the Legality of the Threat or Use of Nuclear Weapons;	
	(v) Nuclear disarmament;	
	(w) Transparency and confidence-building measures in outer space activities;	
	(x) Conventional arms control at the regional and subregional levels;	
	(y) Confidence-building measures in the regional and subregional context;	
	(z) The illicit trade in small arms and light weapons in all its aspects;	
	(aa) Relationship between disarmament and development;	
	(bb) United Nations conference to identify appropriate ways of eliminating nuclear dangers in the context of nuclear disarmament.	
90.	Review and implementation of the Concluding Document of the Twelfth Special Session of the General Assembly:	1st
	(a) United Nations disarmament fellowship, training and advisory services;	
	(b) United Nations Disarmament Information Programme;	
	(c) United Nations Regional Centre for Peace, Disarmament and Development in Latin America and the Caribbean;	
	(d) United Nations regional centres for peace and disarmament;	
	(e) Convention on the Prohibition of the Use of Nuclear Weapons;	
	(f) United Nations Regional Centre for Peace and Disarmament in Asia and the Pacific;	
	(g) Regional confidence-building measures: activities of the United Nations Standing Advisory Committee on Security Questions in Central Africa;	
	(h) United Nations Regional Centre for Peace and Disarmament in Africa.	

Item No.	Title	Allocation
91.	Review of the implementation of the recommendations and decisions adopted by the General Assembly at its tenth special session: (a) Report of the Disarmament Commission; (b) Report of the Conference on Disarmament.	1st
92.	The risk of nuclear proliferation in the Middle East.	1st
93.	Convention on Prohibitions or Restrictions on the Use of Certain Conventional Weapons Which May Be Deemed to Be Excessively Injurious or to Have Indiscriminate Effects.	1st
94.	Strengthening of security and cooperation in the Mediterranean region.	1st
95.	Comprehensive Nuclear-Test-Ban Treaty.	1st
96.	Convention on the Prohibition of the Development, Production and Stockpiling of Bacteriological (Biological) and Toxin Weapons and on Their Destruction.	1st

H. Drug control, crime prevention and combating international terrorism in all its forms and manifestations

Item No.	Title	Allocation
97.	Crime prevention and criminal justice.	3rd
98.	International drug control.	3rd
99.	Measures to eliminate international terrorism.	6th

I. Organizational, administrative and other matters

Item No.	Title	Allocation
100.	Report of the Secretary-General on the work of the Organization.	Plenary
101.	Report of the Secretary-General on the Peacebuilding Fund.	Plenary
102.	Notification by the Secretary-General under Article 12, paragraph 2, of the Charter of the United Nations.	Plenary
103.	Elections to fill vacancies in principal organs: (a) Election of five non-permanent members of the Security Council; (b) Election of eighteen members of the Economic and Social Council; (c) Election of five members of the International Court of Justice.	Plenary
104.	Elections to fill vacancies in subsidiary organs and other elections: (a) Election of twenty members of the Committee for Programme and Coordination; (b) Election of seven members of the Organizational Committee of the Peacebuilding Commission; (c) Election of eighteen members of the Human Rights Council.	Plenary
105.	Appointments to fill vacancies in subsidiary organs and other appointments: (a) Appointment of members of the Advisory Committee on Administrative and Budgetary Questions; (b) Appointment of members of the Committee on Contributions; (c) Confirmation of the appointment of members of the Investments Committee; (d) Appointment of members of the United Nations Administrative Tribunal; (e) Appointment of members of the International Civil Service Commission; (f) Appointment of members and alternate members of the United Nations Staff Pension Committee. (g) Appointment of members of the Committee on Conferences; (h) Appointment of a member of the Joint Inspection Unit; (i) Confirmation of the appointment of the Administrator of the United Nations Development Programme; (j) Confirmation of the appointment of the Secretary-General of the United Nations Conference on Trade and Development; (k) Appointment of the judges of the United Nations Dispute Tribunal; (l) Appointment of the judges of the United Nations Appeals Tribunal.	Plenary, 5th
106.	Admission of new Members to the United Nations.	Plenary
107.	Follow-up to the outcome of the Millennium Summit.	Plenary
108.	Follow-up to the commemoration of the two-hundredth anniversary of the abolition of the transatlantic slave trade.	Plenary
109.	Implementation of the resolutions of the United Nations.	Plenary
110.	Revitalization of the work of the General Assembly.	Plenary and all Committees
111.	Question of equitable representation on and increase in the membership of the Security Council and related matters.	Plenary
112.	Strengthening of the United Nations system.	Plenary
113.	Multilingualism.	Plenary
114.	Cooperation between the United Nations and regional and other organizations: (a) Cooperation between the United Nations and the African Union; (b) Cooperation between the United Nations and the Asian-African Legal Consultative Organization; (c) Cooperation between the United Nations and the Association of Southeast Asian Nations; (d) Cooperation between the United Nations and the Black Sea Economic Cooperation Organization; (e) Cooperation between the United Nations and the Caribbean Community; (f) Cooperation between the United Nations and the Community of Portuguese-speaking Countries; (g) Cooperation between the United Nations and the Council of Europe;	Plenary

Item No.	Title	Allocation
	(h) Cooperation between the United Nations and the Economic Community of Central African States;	
	(i) Cooperation between the United Nations and the Economic Cooperation Organization;	
	(j) Cooperation between the United Nations and the Eurasian Economic Community;	
	(k) Cooperation between the United Nations and the International Organization of la Francophonie;	
	(l) Cooperation between the United Nations and the Inter-Parliamentary Union;	
	(m) Cooperation between the United Nations and the Latin American Economic System;	
	(n) Cooperation between the United Nations and the League of Arab States;	
	(o) Cooperation between the United Nations and the Organization for the Prohibition of Chemical Weapons;	
	(p) Cooperation between the United Nations and the Organization for Security and Cooperation in Europe;	
	(q) Cooperation between the United Nations and the Organization of American States;	
	(r) Cooperation between the United Nations and the Organization of the Islamic Conference;	
	(s) Cooperation between the United Nations and the Pacific Islands Forum;	
	(t) Cooperation between the United Nations and the Preparatory Commission for the Comprehensive Nuclear-Test-Ban Treaty Organization;	
	(u) Cooperation between the United Nations and the Southern African Development Community.	
115.	Follow-up to the recommendations on administrative management and internal oversight of the Independent Inquiry Committee into the United Nations Oil-for-Food Programme.	Plenary
116.	Financial reports and audited financial statements, and reports of the Board of Auditors:	5th
	(a) United Nations;	
	(b) United Nations peacekeeping operations;	
	(c) International Trade Centre UNCTAD/WTO;	
	(d) United Nations University;	
	(e) Capital master plan;	
	(f) United Nations Development Programme;	
	(g) United Nations Children's Fund;	
	(h) United Nations Relief and Works Agency for Palestine Refugees in the Near East;	
	(i) United Nations Institute for Training and Research;	
	(j) Voluntary funds administered by the United Nations High Commissioner for Refugees;	
	(k) Fund of the United Nations Environment Programme;	
	(l) United Nations Population Fund;	
	(m) United Nations Human Settlements Programme;	
	(n) Fund of the United Nations International Drug Control Programme;	
	(o) United Nations Office for Project Services;	
	(p) International Criminal Tribunal for the Prosecution of Persons Responsible for Genocide and Other Serious Violations of International Humanitarian Law Committed in the Territory of Rwanda and Rwandan Citizens Responsible for Genocide and Other Such Violations Committed in the Territory of Neighbouring States between 1 January and 31 December 1994;	
	(q) International Tribunal for the Prosecution of Persons Responsible for Serious Violations of International Humanitarian Law Committed in the Territory of the Former Yugoslavia since 1991.	
117.	Review of the efficiency of the administrative and financial functioning of the United Nations.	5th
118.	Programme budget for the biennium 2008–2009.	5th
119.	Programme planning.	Plenary and all Committees
120.	Improving the financial situation of the United Nations.	5th
121.	Pattern of conferences.	5th
122.	Scale of assessments for the apportionment of the expenses of the United Nations.	5th
123.	Human resources management.	5th
124.	Joint Inspection Unit.	5th
125.	United Nations common system.	5th
126.	United Nations pension system.	5th
127.	Administrative and budgetary coordination of the United Nations with the specialized agencies and the International Atomic Energy Agency.	5th
128.	Report on the activities of the Office of Internal Oversight Services.	5th
129.	Administration of justice at the United Nations.	5th, 6th
130.	Financing of the International Criminal Tribunal for the Prosecution of Persons Responsible for Genocide and Other Serious Violations of International Humanitarian Law Committed in the Territory of Rwanda and Rwandan Citizens Responsible for Genocide and Other Such Violations Committed in the Territory of Neighbouring States between 1 January and 31 December 1994.	5th
131.	Financing of the International Tribunal for the Prosecution of Persons Responsible for Serious Violations of International Humanitarian Law Committed in the Territory of the Former Yugoslavia since 1991.	5th

Item No.	Title	Allocation
132.	Administrative and budgetary aspects of the financing of the United Nations peacekeeping operations.	5th
133.	Financing of the United Nations Operation in Burundi.	5th
134.	Financing of the United Nations Operation in Côte d'Ivoire.	5th
135.	Financing of the United Nations Peacekeeping Force in Cyprus.	5th
136.	Financing of the United Nations Organization Mission in the Democratic Republic of the Congo.	5th
137.	Financing of the United Nations Mission in East Timor.	5th
138.	Financing of the United Nations Integrated Mission in Timor-Leste.	5th
139.	Financing of the United Nations Mission in Ethiopia and Eritrea.	5th
140.	Financing of the United Nations Observer Mission in Georgia.	5th
141.	Financing of the United Nations Stabilization Mission in Haiti.	5th
142.	Financing of the United Nations Interim Administration Mission in Kosovo.	5th
143.	Financing of the United Nations Mission in Liberia.	5th
144.	Financing of the United Nations peacekeeping forces in the Middle East: (a) United Nations Disengagement Observer Force; (b) United Nations Interim Force in Lebanon.	5th
145.	Financing of the United Nations Mission in Sierra Leone.	5th
146.	Financing of the United Nations Mission in the Sudan.	5th
147.	Financing of the United Nations Mission for the Referendum in Western Sahara.	5th
148.	Financing of the African Union-United Nations Hybrid Operation in Darfur.	5th
149.	Financing of the United Nations Mission in the Central African Republic and Chad.	5th
150.	Report of the Committee on Relations with the Host Country.	6th
151.	Observer status for the South Centre in the General Assembly.	6th
152.	Observer status for the Agency for International Trade Information and Cooperation in the General Assembly.	6th
153.	Observer status for the University for Peace in the General Assembly.	6th
154.	Judges of the International Tribunal for the Prosecution of Persons Responsible for Serious Violations of International Humanitarian Law Committed in the Territory of the Former Yugoslavia since 1991.	Plenary
156.	Observer status for the International Fund for Saving the Aral Sea in the General Assembly.	6th

Security Council

Questions considered during 2008

The situation in the Middle East, including the Palestinian question.
The situation in the Middle East.
The situation in Cyprus.
The situation concerning Western Sahara.
The situation in Timor-Leste.
The situation between Iraq and Kuwait.
The situation in Liberia.
The situation in Somalia.
The situation in Bosnia and Herzegovina.
Security Council resolutions 1160(1998), 1199(1998), 1203(1998), 1239(1999) and 1244(1999) [Kosovo].
International Tribunal for the Prosecution of Persons Responsible for Serious Violations of International Humanitarian Law Committed in the Territory of the Former Yugoslavia since 1991.
The situation concerning Rwanda.
International Criminal Tribunal for the Prosecution of Persons Responsible for Genocide and Other Serious Violations of International Humanitarian Law Committed in the Territory of Rwanda and Rwandan Citizens Responsible for Genocide and Other Such Violations Committed in the Territory of Neighbouring States between 1 January and 31 December 1994.
The situation in Georgia.
The question concerning Haiti.
The situation in Burundi.
The situation in Afghanistan.
The situation in Sierra Leone.
Relations between Cameroon and Nigeria.
The situation in the Great Lakes region.
The situation concerning the Democratic Republic of the Congo.
The situation in the Central African Republic.
The situation between Eritrea and Ethiopia.
Children and armed conflict.
The situation in Guinea-Bissau.

Protection of civilians in armed conflict.
Small arms.
Women and peace and security.
Briefing by the President of the International Court of Justice.
Meeting of the Security Council with the troop-contributing countries [UNFYCIP, UNDOF, UNIFIL, MINURSO, UNOMIG, MONUSCO, UNMEE, UNMIL, MINUCI, MINUSTAH, UNMIS, UNAMID, MINURCAT].
Briefing by the Chairperson-in-Office of the Organization for Security and Cooperation in Europe.
Threats to international peace and security caused by terrorist acts.
The situation in Côte d'Ivoire.
Security Council mission [Africa].
Briefings by Chairpersons of subsidiary bodies of the Security Council.
Cross-border issues in West Africa.
Non-proliferation of nuclear weapons.
Reports of the Secretary-General on the Sudan.
Post-conflict peacebuilding.
The situation concerning Iraq.
Non-proliferation.
The situation in Myanmar.
Request of Nepal for United Nations assistance in support of its peace process [Report of the Secretary-General].
Maintenance of international peace and security: role of the Security Council in supporting security sector reform.
United Nations Regional Centre for Preventive Diplomacy for Central Asia.
Maintenance of international peace and security, including mediation and settlement of disputes; and strengthening collective security through general regulation and reduction of armaments.
The situation in Chad, the Central African Republic and the subregion.
Peace and security in Africa [general issues, as well as Kenya, Zimbabwe, Mauritania, and Djibouti and Eritrea].
Briefing by the Under-Secretary-General for Humanitarian Affairs and Emergency Relief Coordinator.
Communications concerning the India-Pakistan question.
Security Council mission [Afghanistan].
The situation in Chad and the Sudan.

Other matters considered during 2008

Security Council documentation and working methods and procedure.
Consideration of the draft report of the Security Council to the General Assembly.
International Court of Justice [election of members].

Economic and Social Council

Agenda of the organizational and resumed organizational session for 2008 (14 January, 5 and 8 February, 14 and 29 April, 20–22 May and 20 June 2008)

Item No. *Title*

1. Election of the Bureau.
2. Adoption of the agenda and other organizational matters.
3. Basic programme of work of the Council.
4. Elections, nominations, confirmations and appointments.

Agenda of the substantive and resumed substantive sessions of 2008 (30 June–25 July, 12 September and 19 December 2008)

Item No. *Title*

1. Adoption of the agenda and other organizational matters.

High-level segment

2. High-level segment:
   (a) High-level policy dialogue with international financial and trade institutions on current developments in the world economy;
   (b) Development Cooperation Forum;
   (c) Annual ministerial review: Implementing the internationally agreed goals and commitments in regard to sustainable development;
   (d) Thematic discussion: Promoting an integrated approach to rural development in developing countries for poverty eradication and sustainable development, taking into account current challenges.

Item No.	Title
	Operational activities segment
3.	Operational activities of the United Nations for international development cooperation:
	(a) Follow-up to policy recommendations of the General Assembly and the Council;
	(b) Reports of the Executive Boards of the United Nations Development Programme/United Nations Population Fund, the United Nations Children's Fund and the World Food Programme.
	Coordination segment
4.	The role of the United Nations system in implementing the Ministerial Declaration of the high-level segment of the substantive session of 2007 of the Council.
	Humanitarian affairs segment
5.	Special economic, humanitarian and disaster relief assistance.
	General segment
6.	Implementation of and follow-up to major United Nations conferences and summits:
	(a) Follow-up to the International Conference on Financing for Development;
	(b) Review and coordination of the implementation of the Programme of Action for the Least Developed Countries for the Decade 2001–2010.
7.	Coordination, programme and other questions:
	(a) Reports of coordination bodies;
	(b) Proposed strategic framework for the period 2010–2011;
	(c) International cooperation in the field of informatics;
	(d) Long-term programme of support for Haiti;
	(e) Mainstreaming a gender perspective into all policies and programmes in the United Nations system;
	(f) Ad hoc advisory groups on African countries emerging from conflict;
	(g) Tobacco or health.
8.	Implementation of General Assembly resolutions 50/227, 52/12 B, 57/270 B and 60/265, including 61/16.
9.	Implementation of the Declaration on the Granting of Independence to Colonial Countries and Peoples by the specialized agencies and the international institutions associated with the United Nations.
10.	Regional cooperation.
11.	Economic and social repercussions of the Israeli occupation on the living conditions of the Palestinian people in the Occupied Palestinian Territory, including Jerusalem, and of the Arab population in the occupied Syrian Golan.
12.	Non-governmental organizations.
13.	Economic and environmental questions:
	(a) Sustainable development;
	(b) Science and technology for development;
	(c) Statistics;
	(d) Human settlements;
	(e) Environment;
	(f) Population and development;
	(g) Public administration and development;
	(h) International cooperation in tax matters;
	(i) Assistance to third States affected by the application of sanctions;
	(j) Cartography;
	(k) Women and development.
14.	Social and human rights questions:
	(a) Advancement of women;
	(b) Social development;
	(c) Crime prevention and criminal justice;
	(d) Narcotic drugs;
	(e) United Nations High Commissioner for Refugees;
	(f) Comprehensive implementation of the Durban Declaration and Programme of Action;
	(g) Human rights;
	(h) Permanent Forum on Indigenous Issues;
	(i) Genetic privacy and non-discrimination.
15.	United Nations research and training institutes.

Appendix V

United Nations information centres and services

(as at December 2011)

ACCRA. United Nations Information Centre

Gamal Abdel Nasser/Liberia Roads
(P.O. Box GP 2339)
Accra, Ghana

Serving: Ghana, Sierra Leone

ALGIERS. United Nations Information Centre

41 Rue Mohamed Khoudi, El Biar
El Biar, 16030 El Biar, Alger
(Boîte postale 444, Hydra-Alger)
Algiers, Algeria

Serving: Algeria

ANKARA. United Nations Information Centre

Birlik Mahallesi, 415. Cadde No. 11
06610 Cankaya
Ankara, Turkey

Serving: Turkey

ANTANANARIVO. United Nations Information Centre

22 rue Rainitovo, Antasahavola
(Boîte postale 1348)
Antananarivo, Madagascar

Serving: Madagascar

ASUNCION. United Nations Information Centre

Avda. Mariscal López esq. Guillermo Saraví
Edificio Naciones Unidas
(Casilla de Correo 1107)
Asunción, Paraguay

Serving: Paraguay

BANGKOK. United Nations Information Service, Economic and Social Commission for Asia and the Pacific

United Nations Building
Rajdamnern Nok Avenue
Bangkok 10200, Thailand

Serving: Cambodia, Lao People's Democratic Republic, Malaysia, Singapore, Thailand, Viet Nam, ESCAP

BEIRUT. United Nations Information Centre/ United Nations Information Service, Economic and Social Commission for Western Asia

UN House, Riad El-Solh Square
(P.O. Box 11-8575-4656)
Beirut, Lebanon

Serving: Jordan, Kuwait, Lebanon, Syrian Arab Republic, ESCWA

BOGOTA. United Nations Information Centre

Calle 100 No. 8A-55, Piso 10
Edificio World Trade Center—Torre "C"
(Apartado Aéreo 058964)
Bogotá 2, Colombia

Serving: Colombia, Ecuador, Venezuela

BRAZZAVILLE. United Nations Information Centre

Avenue Foch, Case ortf 15
(Boîte postale 13210)
Brazzaville, Congo

Serving: Congo

BRUSSELS. Regional United Nations Information Centre

Résidence Palace
Rue de la Loi/Wetstraat 155
Quartier Rubens, Block C2
1040 Brussels, Belgium

Serving: Andorra, Belgium, Cyprus, Denmark, Finland, France, Germany, Greece, Holy See, Iceland, Ireland, Italy, Luxembourg, Malta, Monaco, Netherlands, Norway, Portugal, San Marino, Spain, Sweden, United Kingdom, European Union

BUCHAREST. United Nations Information Centre

48 A Primaverii Blvd.
011975 Bucharest 1, Romania

Serving: Romania

BUENOS AIRES. United Nations Information Centre

Junín 1940, 1er piso
1113 Buenos Aires, Argentina

Serving: Argentina, Uruguay

BUJUMBURA. United Nations Information Centre

117 Avenue de la Révolution
(Boîte postale 2160)
Bujumbura, Burundi

Serving: Burundi

CAIRO. United Nations Information Centre

1 Osiris Street, Garden City
(P.O. Box 262)
Cairo, Egypt

Serving: Egypt, Saudi Arabia

CANBERRA. United Nations Information Centre

Level 1 Barton, 7 National Circuit
(P.O. Box 5366, Kingston, ACT 2604)
Canberra ACT 2600, Australia

Serving: Australia, Fiji, Kiribati, Nauru, New Zealand, Samoa, Tonga, Tuvalu, Vanuatu

COLOMBO. United Nations Information Centre

202/204 Bauddhaloka Mawatha
(P.O. Box 1505, Colombo)
Colombo 7, Sri Lanka

Serving: Sri Lanka

DAKAR. United Nations Information Centre

Immeuble Soumex, Mamelles-Almadies
(Boîte postale 154)
Dakar, Senegal

Serving: Cape Verde, Côte d'Ivoire, Gambia, Guinea-Bissau, Mauritania, Senegal

DAR ES SALAAM. United Nations Information Centre

Kings Way/Mafinga Street
Plot 134-140, Kinondoni
(P.O. Box 9224)
Dar es Salaam, United Republic of Tanzania

Serving: United Republic of Tanzania

DHAKA. United Nations Information Centre

IDB Bhaban (8th floor)
Sher-e-Banglanagar
(G.P.O. Box 3658, Dhaka-1000)
Dhaka-1207, Bangladesh

Serving: Bangladesh

GENEVA. United Nations Information Service, United Nations Office at Geneva

Palais des Nations
1211 Geneva 10, Switzerland

Serving: Switzerland

HARARE. United Nations Information Centre

Sanders House (2nd floor)
Cnr. First Street/Jason Moyo Avenue
(P.O. Box 4408)
Harare, Zimbabwe

Serving: Zimbabwe

ISLAMABAD. United Nations Information Centre

Level 2, Serena Business Complex
Khayaban-e-Suhrawardy
(P.O. Box 1107)
Islamabad, Pakistan

Serving: Pakistan

JAKARTA. United Nations Information Centre

Menara Thamrin Building (floor 3A)
Jalan MH Thamrin, Kav. 3
Jakarta 10250, Indonesia

Serving: Indonesia

KATHMANDU. United Nations Information Centre

Harihar Bhavan
(P.O. Box 107, UN House)
Kathmandu, Nepal

Serving: Nepal

KHARTOUM. United Nations Information Centre

United Nations Compound House #7, Blk 5
Gamma'a Avenue
(P.O. Box 1992)
Khartoum, Sudan

Serving: Somalia, Sudan

LAGOS. United Nations Information Centre

17 Alfred Rewane (ex Kingsway) Road, Ikoyi
(P.O. Box 1068)
Lagos, Nigeria

Serving: Nigeria

LA PAZ. United Nations Information Centre

Calle 14 esq. S. Bustamante
Edificio Metrobol II, Calacoto
(Apartado Postal 9072)
La Paz, Bolivia

Serving: Bolivia

LIMA. United Nations Information Centre

Lord Cochrane 130
San Isidro (L-27)
(P.O. Box 14-0199)
Lima, Peru

Serving: Peru

LOME. United Nations Information Centre

468, Angle rue Atime
Avenue de la Libération
(Boîte postale 911)
Lomé, Togo

Serving: Benin, Togo

LUSAKA. United Nations Information Centre

Revenue House (Ground floor)
Cairo Road (Northend)
(P.O. Box 32905, Lusaka 10101)
Lusaka, Zambia

Serving: Botswana, Malawi, Swaziland, Zambia

MANAMA. United Nations Information Centre

United Nations House
Bldg. 69, Road 1901, Block 319
(P.O. Box 26004, Manama)
Manama, Bahrain

Serving: Bahrain, Qatar, United Arab Emirates

MANILA. United Nations Information Centre

GC Corporate Plaza (ex Jaka II Building) (5th floor)
150 Legaspi Street, Legaspi Village
(P.O. Box 7285 ADC (DAPO), Pasay City)
Makati City,
1229 Metro Manila, Philippines

Serving: Papua New Guinea, Philippines, Solomon Islands

MASERU. United Nations Information Centre

United Nations Road
UN House
(P.O. Box 301, Maseru 100)
Maseru, Lesotho

Serving: Lesotho

MEXICO CITY. United Nations Information Centre

Montes Urales 440 (3rd floor)
Colonia Lomas de Chapultepec
Mexico City, D.F. 11000, Mexico

Serving: Cuba, Dominican Republic, Mexico

MOSCOW. United Nations Information Centre

4/16 Glazovsky Pereulok
Moscow 119002, Russian Federation

Serving: Russian Federation

NAIROBI. United Nations Information Centre

United Nations Office, Gigiri
(P.O. Box 30552-00200)
Nairobi, Kenya

Serving: Kenya, Seychelles, Uganda

NEW DELHI. United Nations Information Centre

55 Lodi Estate
New Delhi 110 003, India

Serving: Bhutan, India

OUAGADOUGOU. United Nations Information Centre

14 Avenue de la Grande Chancellerie
Secteur no. 4
(Boîte postale 135)
Ouagadougou 01, Burkina Faso

Serving: Burkina Faso, Chad, Mali, Niger

PANAMA CITY. United Nations Information Centre

UN House Bldg 128 (1st floor)
Ciudad del Saber, Clayton
(P.O. Box 0819-01082)
Panama City, Panama

Serving: Panama

PORT OF SPAIN. United Nations Information Centre

Bretton Hall (2nd floor)
16 Victoria Avenue
(P.O. Box 130)
Port of Spain, Trinidad and Tobago, W.I.

Serving: Antigua and Barbuda, Aruba, Bahamas, Barbados, Belize, Dominica, Grenada, Guyana, Jamaica, Netherlands Antilles, Saint Kitts and Nevis, Saint Lucia, Saint Vincent and the Grenadines, Suriname, Trinidad and Tobago

PRAGUE. United Nations Information Centre

nam. Kinskych 6
15000 Prague 5, Czech Republic

Serving: Czech Republic

PRETORIA. United Nations Information Centre

Metro Park Building
351 Schoeman Street
(P.O. Box 12677), Tramshed
Pretoria, South Africa 0126

Serving: South Africa

RABAT. United Nations Information Centre

6 Angle Avenue Tarik Ibn Ziyad et rue Roudana
(Boîte postale 601, Casier ONU, Rabat-Chellah)
Rabat, Morocco

Serving: Morocco

RIO DE JANEIRO. United Nations Information Centre

Palácio Itamaraty
Av. Marechal Floriano 196
20080-002 Rio de Janeiro RJ, Brazil

Serving: Brazil

SANA'A. United Nations Information Centre

Street 5, Off Albawnya Area
Handhel Zone, beside Handhal Mosque
(P.O. Box 237)
Sana'a, Yemen

Serving: Yemen

SANTIAGO. United Nations Information Service, Economic Commission for Latin America and the Caribbean

Edificio Naciones Unidas
Avenida Dag Hammarskjöld 3477
Vitacura
(Casilla 179-D), Santiago, Chile

Serving: Chile, ECLAC

TEHRAN. United Nations Information Centre

No. 8, Shahrzad Blvd. Darrous
(P.O. Box 15875-4557, Tehran)
Tehran, Iran

Serving: Iran

TOKYO. United Nations Information Centre

UNU Building (8th floor)
53-70 Jingumae 5-Chome, Shibuya-Ku
Tokyo 150-0001, Japan

Serving: Japan

TRIPOLI. United Nations Information Centre

Khair Aldeen Baybers Street
Hay El-Andalous
(P.O. Box 286, Hay El-Andalous)
Tripoli, Libyan Arab Jamahiriya

Serving: Libyan Arab Jamahiriya

TUNIS. United Nations Information Centre

41 Bis, Av. Louis Braille, Cité El Khadra
(Boîte postale 863)
1003 Tunis, Tunisia

Serving: Tunisia

VIENNA. United Nations Information Service, United Nations Office at Vienna

Vienna International Centre
Wagramer Strasse 5
(P.O. Box 500, 1400 Vienna)
1220 Vienna, Austria

Serving: Austria, Hungary, Slovakia, Slovenia

WARSAW. United Nations Information Centre

Al. Niepodleglosci 186
(UN Centre P.O. Box 1, 02-514 Warsaw 12)
00-608 Warszawa, Poland

Serving: Poland

WASHINGTON, D.C. United Nations Information Centre

1775 K Street, N.W., Suite 400
Washington, D.C. 20006
United States

Serving: United States

WINDHOEK. United Nations Information Centre

United Nations House
38-44 Stein Street, Klein
(Private Bag 13351)
Windhoek, Namibia

Serving: Namibia

YANGON. United Nations Information Centre

6 Natmauk Road,
Tamwe Township
(P.O. Box 230)
Yangon, Myanmar

Serving: Myanmar

YAOUNDE. United Nations Information Centre

Immeuble Tchinda,
Rue 2044,
Derrière camp SIC TSINGA
(Boîte postale 836)
Yaoundé, Cameroon

Serving: Cameroon, Central African Republic, Gabon

NOTE: For more information on UNICS, please visit the website: **unic.un.org**.

Appendix VI

Intergovernmental organizations related to the United Nations

(Direction as at December 2008)

International Atomic Energy Agency (IAEA)
Vienna International Centre
Wagramer Strasse, 5
P.O. Box 100
1400 Vienna, Austria
Telephone: (43) (1) 2600-0
Fax: (43) (1) 2600-7
E-mail: official.mail@iaea.org
Internet: www.iaea.org
Director General: Mohamed El Baradei (Egypt)

IAEA Office at the United Nations
1 United Nations Plaza, Room 1155
New York, NY 10017, U.S.A.
Telephone: (1) (212) 963-6010/6011
Fax: (1) (917) 367-4046
E-mail: iaeany@un.org

International Labour Organization (ILO)
Route des Morillons, 4
1211 Geneva 22, Switzerland
Telephone: (41) (22) 799-6111
Fax: (41) (22) 798-8685
E-mail: ilo@ilo.org
Internet: www.ilo.org
Director General: Juan Somavía (Chile)

ILO Office at the United Nations
220 East 42nd Street, Suite 3101
New York, NY 10017, U.S.A.
Telephone: (1) (212) 697-5218
Fax: (1) (212) 697-0150
E-mail: newyork@ilo.org

Food and Agriculture Organization of the United Nations (FAO)
Viale delle Terme di Caracalla
00153 Rome, Italy
Telephone: (39) (06) 57051
Fax: (39) (06) 5705-3152
E-mail: fao-hq@fao.org
Internet: www.fao.org
Director General: Jacques Diouf (Senegal)

FAO Office at the United Nations
1 United Nations Plaza, Room 1125
New York, NY 10017, U.S.A.
Telephone: (1) (212) 963-6036
Fax: (1) (212) 963-5425
E-mail: lon-registry@un.org

FAO maintains liaison offices in Brussels, Geneva, Washington, D.C., and Yokohama, Japan; regional offices in Accra, Ghana; Bangkok, Thailand; Cairo, Egypt; and Santiago, Chile; and subregional offices in Apia, Samoa; Bridgetown, Barbados; Budapest, Hungary; Harare, Zimbabwe; and Tunis, Tunisia.

United Nations Educational, Scientific and Cultural Organization (UNESCO)
UNESCO House
Place de Fontenoy, 7
75352 Paris 07-SP, France
Telephone: (33) (0) (1) 45-68-10-00
Fax: (33) (0) (1) 45-67-16-90
E-mail: info@unesco.org
Internet: www.unesco.org
Director General: Koïchiro Matsuura (Japan)

UNESCO Office at the United Nations
2 United Nations Plaza, Room 900
New York, NY 10017, U.S.A.
Telephone: (1) (212) 963-5995
Fax: (1) (212) 963-8014
E-mail: newyork@unesco.org

World Health Organization (WHO)
Avenue Appia, 20
1211 Geneva 27, Switzerland
Telephone: (41) (22) 791-2111
Fax: (41) (22) 791-3111
E-mail: info@who.int
Internet: www.who.int
Director General: Dr. Margaret Chan (China)

WHO Office at the United Nations
1 Dag Hammarskjöld Plaza,
885 Second Avenue, 26th floor
New York, NY 10017, U.S.A.
Telephone: (1) (646) 626-6060
Fax: (1) (646) 626-6080

WHO is a decentralized organization, with regional offices in Brazzaville, Congo; Cairo, Egypt; Copenhagen, Denmark; Manila, Philippines; New Delhi, India; and Washington, D.C.

World Bank (IBRD and IDA)
1818 H Street, NW
Washington, D.C. 20433, U.S.A.
Telephone: (1) (202) 473-1000
Fax: (1) (202) 477-6391
E-mail: feedback@worldbank.org
Internet: www.worldbank.org
Director General: Robert B. Zoellick (United States)

The World Bank Mission to the United Nations
1 Dag Hammarskjöld Plaza
885 Second Avenue, 26th floor
New York, NY 10017, U.S.A.
Telephone: (1) (212) 355-5112
Fax: (1) (212) 355-4523

The World Bank maintains offices in Brussels, Belgium; Frankfurt, Germany; Geneva; London; Paris; Sydney, Australia; and Tokyo.

International Finance Corporation (IFC)
2121 Pennsylvania Avenue, NW
Washington, D.C. 20433, U.S.A.
Telephone: (1) (202) 473-3800
Fax: (1) (202) 974-4384
E-mail: webmaster@ifc.org
Internet: www.ifc.org
Executive Vice President & CEO: Lars H. Thunell (Sweden)

IFC c/o the World Bank, Office of the Special Representative to the United Nations
1 Dag Hammarskjöld Plaza
885 Second Avenue, 26th floor
New York, NY 10017, U.S.A.
Telephone: (1) (212) 355-5112
Fax: (1) (212) 355-5523

International Monetary Fund (IMF)
700 19th Street, NW
Washington, D.C. 20431, U.S.A.
Telephone: (1) (202) 623-7000
Fax: (1) (202) 623-4661
E-mail: publicaffairs@imf.org
Internet: www.imf.org
Managing Director: Dominique Strauss-Kahn (France)

IMF
Office at the United Nations
1 Dag Hammarskjöld Plaza
885 Second Avenue, 26th floor
New York, NY 10017, U.S.A.
Telephone: (1) (212) 317-4720
Fax: (1) (212) 317-4733

IMF maintains offices in Geneva, Paris and Tokyo.

International Civil Aviation Organization (ICAO)
999 University Street
Montréal, Quebec H3C 5H7, Canada
Telephone: (1) (514) 954-8219
Fax: (1) (514) 954-6077
E-mail: icaohq@icao.int
Internet: www.icao.int
Secretary-General: Taïeb Chérif (Algeria)

ICAO maintains regional offices in Bangkok, Thailand; Cairo, Egypt; Dakar, Senegal; Lima, Peru; Mexico City; Nairobi; and Paris.

Universal Postal Union (UPU)
Weltpost Strasse, 4
Case Postale 3000
3000 Berne 15, Switzerland
Telephone: (41) (31) 350-3111
Fax: (41) (31) 350-3110
E-mail: info@upu.int
Internet: www.upu.int
Director General: Edouard Dayan (France)

International Telecommunication Union (ITU)
Place des Nations
1211, Geneva 20, Switzerland
Telephone: (41) (22) 730-5111
Fax: (41) (22) 733-7256
E-mail: itumail@itu.int
Internet: www.itu.int
Secretary-General: Hamadoun Touré (Mali)

ITU maintains regional offices in Addis Ababa, Ethiopia; Brasilia, Brazil; Cairo, Egypt; Bangkok, Thailand; and Geneva.

World Meteorological Organization (WMO)
7 bis, avenue de la Paix
Case postale 2300
1211 Geneva 2, Switzerland
Telephone: (41) (22) 730-8111
Fax: (41) (22) 730-8181
E-mail: wmo@wmo.int
Internet: www.wmo.ch
President: Alexander Bedritsky (Russia)
Secretary-General: Michel Jarraud (France)

WMO
Office at the United Nations
866 United Nations Plaza, Room A-302
New York, NY 10017, U.S.A.
Telephone: (1) (917) 367-9867
Fax: (1) (917) 367-9868
E-mail: zbatjargal@wmo.int

International Maritime Organization (IMO)
4, Albert Embankment
London SE1 7SR
United Kingdom
Telephone: (44) (207) 735-7611
Fax: (44) (207) 587-3210
E-mail: info@imo.org
Internet: www.imo.org
Director General: Efthimios E. Mitropoulos (Greece)

World Intellectual Property Organization (WIPO)
Chemin des Colombettes, 34
P.O. Box 18
1211 Geneva 20, Switzerland
Telephone: (41) (22) 338-9111
Fax: (41) (22) 733-5428
E-mail: wipo.mail@wipo.int
Internet: www.wipo.int
Director General: Kamil Idris (Sudan) (until October 2008)
Francis Gurry (Australia)

WIPO
Office at the United Nations
2 United Nations Plaza, Room 2525
New York, NY 10017, U.S.A.
Telephone: (1) (212) 963-6813
Fax: (1) (212) 963-4801
E-mail: wipo@un.org

International Fund for Agricultural Development (IFAD)
Via Paolo di Dono, 44
00142 Rome, Italy
Telephone: (39) (06) 54591
Fax: (39) (06) 504-3463
E-mail: ifad@ifad.org
Internet: www.ifad.org
President: Lennart Båge (Sweden)

IFAD
Office at the United Nations
2 United Nations Plaza, Rooms 1128-29
New York, NY 10017, U.S.A.
Telephone: (1) (212) 963-0546
Fax: (1) (212) 963-2787

IFAD maintains offices in Eschbom, Germany, and Washington, D.C.

United Nations Industrial Development Organization (UNIDO)
Vienna International Centre
Wagramer Strasse, 5
P.O. Box 300
1400 Vienna, Austria
Telephone: (43) (1) 26026-0
Fax: (43) (1) 269-2669
E-mail: unido@unido.org
Internet: www.unido.org
Director General: Kandeh K. Yumkella (Sierra Leone)

UNIDO
Office at Geneva
Palais des Nations
Le Bocage, Rooms 77-82
Avenue de la Paix 8-14
1211 Geneva 10, Switzerland
Telephone: (41) (22) 917-1434
Fax: (41) (22) 917-0059
E-mail: office.geneva@unido.org

UNIDO
Office in New York
1 United Nations Plaza, Room 1118
New York, NY 10017, U.S.A.
Telephone: (1) (212) 963-6890
Fax: (1) (212) 963-7904
E-mail: office.newyork@unido.org

World Trade Organization (WTO)
Centre William Rappard
Rue de Lausanne, 154
1211 Geneva 21, Switzerland
Telephone: (41) (22) 739-5111
Fax: (41) (22) 731-4206
E-mail: enquiries@wto.org
Internet: www.wto.org
Director General: Pascal Lamy (France)

World Tourism Organization (UNWTO)
Capitán Haya, 42
28020 Madrid, Spain
Telephone: (34) (91) 567-8100
Fax: (34) (91) 571-3733
E-mail: omt@unwto.org
Internet: www.unwto.org
Secretary-General: Francesco Frangialli (France)

UNWTO maintains a regional support office for Asia and the Pacific in Osaka, Japan.

Indices

Subject index

BOLD CAPITAL LETTERS are used for main subject entries (e.g. **DEVELOPMENT**) and chapter topics (e.g. **DISARMAMENT**), as well as country names (e.g. **TAJIKISTAN**), region names (e.g. **AFRICA**) and principal UN organs (e.g. **GENERAL ASSEMBLY**).

CAPITAL LETTERS are used to highlight major issues (e.g. POVERTY), as well as the names of territories (e.g. MONTSERRAT), subregions (e.g. CENTRAL AMERICA), specialized agencies (e.g. WORLD HEALTH ORGANIZATION) and regional commissions (e.g. ECONOMIC COMMISSION FOR EUROPE).

Regular text is used for single and cross-reference entries (e.g. arms embargo, mercenaries, terrorism).

An asterisk (*) preceding a page number or range of page numbers indicates the presence of a text, reproduced in full, of a General Assembly, Security Council or Economic and Social Council resolution or decision, or a Security Council presidential statement.

United Nations bodies are listed alphabetically and may also appear under related entries.

A

B

D

E

H

I

M

N

R

S

W

Y

Z

Index of resolutions and decisions

(For dates of sessions please refer to Appendix III.)

General Assembly

Sixty-second session

Sixty-third session

General Assembly

Sixty-third session (cont.)

Security Council

Index of Security Council presidential statements

How to obtain volumes of the *Yearbook*

Recent volumes of the *Yearbook of the United Nations* may be obtained through bookstores worldwide, as well as ordered from:

United Nations Publications
Room 927A
300 East 42nd Street
New York, New York 10017
United States of America

e-mail: **publications@un.org**

The *Yearbook* is also available on the United Nations Publications website: **unp.un.org**.

Yearbook of the United Nations, 2008, Vol. 62
ISBN 978-92-1-101227-9
$175
eISBN 978-92-1-054459-7
$27.99

Yearbook of the United Nations, 2007, Vol. 61
ISBN 978-92-1-101226-2
$175
eISBN 978-92-1-054327-9
$27.99

Yearbook of the United Nations, 2006, Vol. 60
ISBN 978-92-1-101168-5
$175

Yearbook of the United Nations, 2005, Vol. 59
ISBN 978-92-1-100967-5
$175

Yearbook of the United Nations, 2004, Vol. 58
ISBN 978-92-1-100966-8
$175

Yearbook of the United Nations, 2003, Vol. 57
ISBN 978-92-1-100905-7
$150

Yearbook of the United Nations, 2002, Vol. 56
ISBN 978-92-1-100904-0
$150
(available in PDF only)

Yearbook of the United Nations, 2001, Vol. 55
ISBN 978-92-1-100897-5
$150

Yearbook of the United Nations, 2000, Vol. 54
ISBN 978-92-1-100857-9
$150
(available in PDF only)

Yearbook of the United Nations, 1999, Vol. 53
ISBN 978-92-1-100856-2
$150
(available in PDF only)

All volumes of the *Yearbook of the United Nations* from the 1946–47 edition (Vol. 1) to the 2007 edition (Vol. 61) can be accessed in full online on the *Yearbook* website: **unyearbook.un.org**.